Short forms used in the dictionary

abbrev.	abbreviation
adj	adjective
adv	adverb
AfrE	African English
AmE	American English
&	and
apprec	appreciative
attrib.	attributive
AustrE	Australian English
bibl	biblical
BrE	British English
CanE	Canadian English
cap.	capital
CarE	Caribbean English
comb.	combination
compar.	comparative
conj	conjunction
contr.	contraction
def.	definition(s)
derog	derogatory
dial	dialect
E	East
Eng	England
esp.	especially
etc.	et cetera; and so on
euph	euphemistic
fem.	feminine
fig.	figurative
fml	formal
Fr	French
Ger	German
Gk	Greek
humor	humorous
imper.	imperative
IndE	Indian English
infin.	infinitive
infml	informal
interj	interjection
IrE	Irish English
It	Italian
Lat	Latin
lit	literary
masc.	masculine
med	medical
n	noun
N	North
naut	nautical
neg.	negative
NZE	New Zealand English
obs	obsolete
p.	participle
PakE	Pakistani English
pass.	passive
pers.	person
phr.	phrase
phrs.	phrases
pl.	plural
poet	poetical
pomp	pompous
poss.	possessive
prep	preposition
pres.	present
pron	pronoun
refl.	reflexive
S	South
SAfrE	South African English
ScotE	Scottish English
SEU S.	Survey of English Usage (spoken)
SEU W.	Survey of English Usage (written)
sing.	singular
sl	slang
Sp	Spanish
superl.	superlative
t.	tense
tdmk	trademark
tech	technical
US	United States
usu.	usually
v	verb
W	West

Signs used in the dictionary

[ ]

| see page xxv

~

See also page xxviii for the meaning of A, B, C, etc., when shown in [ ]

Pronunciation table

CONSONANTS

SYMBOL	KEY WORD
b	back
d	day
ð	then
dʒ	jump
f	few
g	gay
h	hot
j	yet
k	key
l	led
m	sum
n	sun
ŋ	sung
p	pen
r	red
s	soon
ʃ	fishing
t	tea
tʃ	cheer
θ	thing
v	view
w	wet
z	zero
ʒ	pleasure

VOWELS

SYMBOL	KEY WORD
æ	bad
ɑ	*AmE* farm
ɑː	calm
ɒ	*BrE* pot
aɪ	bite
aʊ	now
aɪə	tire
aʊə	tower
ɔ	*AmE* form
ɔː	caught
ɔɪ	boy
ɔɪə	employer
e	bed
eə	there
eɪ	make
eɪə	player
ə	about
əʊ	note
əʊə	lower
ɜ	*AmE* bird
ɜː	bird
i	pretty
iː	sheep
ɪ	ship
ɪə	here
o	*AmE* port
uː	boot
ʊ	put
ʊə	poor
ʌ	cut

Special signs

‖	separates British and American pronunciations: British on the left, American on the right
/ˈ/	shows main STRESS
/ˌ/	shows SECONDARY STRESS
/◂/	shows STRESS SHIFT
/ʳ/	at the end of a word means that /r/ is usually pronounced in American English and is pronounced in British English when the next word begins with a vowel sound
/ɨ/	means that some speakers use /ɪ/ and others use /ə/
/i/	means many American speakers use /iː/ but many British speakers use /ɪ/
/*ə*/	means that /ə/ may or may not be used
/o/	means that American speakers use either /ɔ/ or /əʊ/
/ɑ/ /ɔ/ /ɜ/	/ɑ, ɔ, ɜ/ are used for American English to represent /ɑː, ɔː, ɜː/

These signs are fully explained pp. xvii–xxii

LONGMAN DICTIONARY OF CONTEMPORARY ENGLISH

Longman

Longman Group Limited
Burnt Mill
Harlow
Essex
England

Cased Edition: First published by Longman Group Ltd. 1978
ISBN 0 582 55608 2

Paper Edition: First published by Longman Group Ltd. 1978
ISBN 0 582 55608 2

I.S. Edition: First published by Longman Group Ltd. 1980, for sale in certain countries only
ISBN 0 582 55634 1

African Edition: First published by Longman Group Ltd. 1981, for sale in certain African countries only
ISBN 0 582 55543 4

Reprinted with corrections 1981
Reprinted 1982 (twice)
Reprinted April 1983
Reprinted 1984
Reprinted 1985 (twice)

Printed in Great Britain at The Bath Press, Avon

Editor-in-Chief
Paul Procter

Managing Editor
Robert F. Ilson

Senior Editor
John Ayto

Lexicographers
James Coakley
David Fairlamb
Jean Robinson
Janet Whitcut

Pronunciation Editor
Gordon Walsh

Assistant Lexicographers
Hope Liebersohn
John Huggins
Rosemary Courtney

Illustrations
Richard Bonson
Julia Rout
Tony Gibbons
John Fraser
Malcolm Booker
Clive Spong

Computer systems
Ken Moore
Robert Cleary
Andrew McMenemy

Clerical
Joyce Nairn
Elaine Roberts
Hazel Lilley
Lynn Kiddie

Publishing administration
Charles McGregor
Della Summers
Robert Scriven

Editorial assistance—Evelyn Attwood, René Quinault, Vincent Petti, Horace Cartledge, Peter Adams, Gillian Beaumont, Tom McArthur

Pronunciation assistance—Susan Ramsaran, Vera Grant, Kate Taylor, Judith Scott, Susan Peppé

Acknowledgments

The publishers and the editorial team of this dictionary wish to express their thanks to the many people who have contributed advice and suggestions, particularly Professor Randolph Quirk and all those at the Survey of English Usage, University College London, R. A. Close, Professor David Crystal, Denis Girard, Professor Geoffrey Leech, Louis Alexander, D. K. Swan and Roger Kingdon. Thanks are also due to the pronunciation advisers, Professor A. C. Gimson for British English and Professor Arthur Bronstein for American English.

Contents

Preface

Editing a dictionary today—above all, a dictionary of the world language, English—is a highly skilled and highly professional task. Central to it is the sensitive anticipation of the users' needs: and then, of course, devising the best way of satisfying them. When the users are envisaged as predominantly (yet not exclusively) those for whom English is a foreign language, the task becomes still more demanding, since the range of the users' proficiency, age, national background, and other variables must inevitably set up formidable problems.

It is precisely such problems that the editors of this *Longman Dictionary of Contemporary English* have kept realistically before them as they selected a "core" lexicon, the predominant meanings, the terms in which these meanings should be defined, and the supplementary information that is considered desirable. Untrammelled by a previous edition that might prescribe form or content and inhibit innovation, they have energetically engaged themselves in fundamental principles. They have evolved a lucid defining vocabulary which will help the user in two respects: first, his knowing this small set of words (about 2,000) is the only prerequisite for understanding the definitions of every word in the dictionary; second, the strict use of the defining vocabulary has in many cases resulted in a fresh and revealing semantic analysis.

The editors have been encouraged to consult widely with experts in many fields, both in Britain and abroad, and they have had frequent recourse to the Survey of English Usage at University College London. The fact that they combine among themselves expertise in linguistic research, in modern linguistic theory, and in English language teaching has indeed resulted in a further striking feature of this dictionary: a delicate system of grammatical coding. By this means, the user is offered, unobtrusively and economically, a great deal of information on the normal syntactic use of words, so that the typical dictionary entry valuably exhibits the interface of grammar and meaning.

Elegantly compact yet admirably comprehensive, the *Dictionary* represents a distinct achievement on which the publisher and editorial team alike merit warm congratulation.

Randolph Quirk
March 1978

General Introduction

0. The *Longman Dictionary of Contemporary English* combines the best principles of British and of American lexicography to present to the student a broad description of English as used throughout the world. In many respects it is a revolutionary work because it has used the findings of modern linguistics to give a fuller and more precise description of language than that found in traditional dictionaries. It is however in no way a difficult work. Most of the efforts of the compilers have gone into giving as complete a description as possible of the English language in the clearest ways that can be devised. It is the belief of the editors and publisher that simplicity of description is not at all incompatible with presentation of the complex and intricate patterns of language.

Although the dictionary is intended primarily for the foreign student, its design and the new features it contains make it particularly suitable as a small reference dictionary for any person—whether teacher, student, linguist, or writer—who requires as much information about the central "core" of the language as can be conveniently presented in an alphabetic list. For example, as described below, the definitions are presented with controlled simplicity of structure and vocabulary: this requires the greatest lexicographic skill, but also provides the greatest possible benefit to the user, whether native speaker or foreign learner. The grammatical information, which gives a comprehensive description of the syntactic behaviour of the individual items of vocabulary, is intended primarily for teachers and students of English as a foreign or second language, although others concerned with language will also find such a complete description of interest.

0.1 Treatment of structure

Although dictionaries have in general failed to describe adequately the syntactic behaviour of words, they have not hesitated to apply parts of speech (such as noun, adjective, and verb) to them. These labels are convenient and as such have been retained in this book. We have however provided a description of the finer distinctions in grammatical behaviour in the form of codes shown within square brackets [ ]: this refers the user to full tables (page xxviii) where sentences and phrases are given showing other English words which behave in the same way. The codes consist of a capital letter (which usually stands for an easily remembered term, such as L for *linking verb*) followed by a number, and one of the great advantages of the system is that the numbers always mean the same thing whatever letter they follow (thus 3 always means *to* + infinitive). *The result is a system which is easily remembered and which requires no knowledge of grammatical theory to be fully understood* but which nevertheless provides a thorough analysis that is fully acceptable to modern linguists and grammarians.

0.2 Idioms, special phrases, phrasal verbs, compounds, and associated words

It is unlikely that any general dictionary has ever before provided so thorough a description of the many important ways in which English words are used together, whether loosely bound or occurring in fixed phrases. The main emphasis has been to record current use among native speakers, although literary and old-fashioned usages, so important in reading, have not been neglected. The main types described are:

0.2.1 *Idioms, proverbs*, and other groups of words with a special meaning—see page xxvi.

0.2.2 *Special phrases* in which a word is usually (or always) found—see page xxvii.

0.2.3.1 *Phrasal verbs* (consisting of a verb together with an adverb, a preposition, or both an adverb and a preposition)—these are all treated as separate main entries in the dictionary, with the addition of a cross-reference from the entry for the verb from which they come, unless they appear close to this verb in the alphabetical list. One of the main advantages of this placement is to make it possible for a full grammatical description to be given, as for verbs consisting of only one word, so that the verbs in the two sentences

1. They *discovered* that she was mad
2. They *found out* that she was mad

can both be described with same code, [T5], although the part of speech of the first is *v*, whereas that of the second is *v adv*.

Another advantage of the placement at main entry is that the student will find phrasal verbs (such as **make up** and **get away**) next to the compounds derived from them (as in *a box of* **makeup** and *a* **getaway** *car*).

0.2.3.2 *Compounds and derived words*—these, whether spelt as one word, hyphenated, or as more than one word (with spaces), are all treated as separate main entries. Among the advantages of placing phrasal verbs and compounds as main entries are that the student will soon learn where to look for a particular item whether he finds it with or without a hyphen (if it is a compound) or spelt as one word and that the student will not be expected to know that one word (such as **madden**) is derived from another (**mad**), but will find it at its exact alphabetic position.

0.2.4 *Associated words*—another extremely important area of word grouping is that of association between nouns, adjectives, and verbs, with other words which have little meaning such as prepositions, adverbs, the articles *the* and *a/an*, and the pronoun *it*. These words are included within the square brackets which contain the grammatical codes. Since they are often not found with every grammatical structure available to a particular meaning, they are placed next to the codes to which they apply. Thus [T1 (*as*)] will tell the user that when **serve** means "to do a useful job for" the word *as* is very often found with it, as in the example sentence *He served the committee as its chairman.* Similarly, [*the* +R] will tell the student that **lash** meaning "the punishment of whipping" is used with the definite article *the*, as in *They gave him the lash.*

0.3 Controlled vocabulary

This very important feature marks this dictionary out from any but the smallest of its predecessors as a tool for the learner and student of language. All the definitions and examples in the dictionary are written in a controlled vocabulary of approximately 2,000 words which were selected by a thorough study of a number of frequency and pedagogic lists of English, particular reference having been made to *A General Service List of English Words* (Longman, 1953, reprinted 1977) by Michael West. Furthermore, a rigorous set of principles was established to ensure that only the most "central" meanings of these 2,000 words, and only easily understood derivatives, were used. The development and application of the vocabulary has benefited from Longman experience in publishing English-language teaching material for the foreign learner of English. The vocabulary can be found at the back of the dictionary.

The result of using the vocabulary is the fulfilment of one of the most basic lexicographic principles—*that is that the definitions are always written using simpler terms than the words they describe*, something that cannot be achieved without a definite policy of this kind. The vocabulary is however applied flexibly; by an extensive *cross-referencing system* the user is encouraged to look elsewhere in the text for synonyms and related words which will be useful to him.

Small capitals are used for cross-references, for example in the definition of **spaghetti**, which reads:

> an Italian food made of flour paste (PASTA) in long strips, usu. sold in dry form, for making soft again in boiling water—compare MACARONI, VERMICELLI

Further, the compilers of the dictionary have used an absolute minimum of abbreviations or specialized grammatical or linguistic terms in the text, so that the student may (with a relatively small vocabulary) understand the whole of each entry.

0.4 Treatment of structural words

This very important section of the vocabulary has been treated in great detail and with extreme care.

We are very fortunate in having been able to use the files of *The Survey of English Usage* at University College London, and to benefit from the advice and experience of Professor Randolph Quirk, the Director of the Survey (and our chief linguistic adviser on the dictionary), and his colleagues. In addition, Dr Robert Ilson and Mrs Janet Whitcut worked on the Survey before joining us. Much of the detailed work on structural words was done by Janet Whitcut, who has devoted many hours to them and presented a very detailed treatment of the prepositions, conjunctions, pronouns, and other parts of speech which the student must learn to use correctly in order to construct acceptable English sentences. Where we quote actual examples of structural words in use from the Survey files, the examples are marked (SEU W.) for quotations from written texts, and (SEU S.) for quotations from recordings of English speech.

0.5 Guidance to the user on the context in which he may expect to find or should use a word

A system of labelling has been adopted which gives the student, wherever possible, an indication of the situation in which he is likely to find a particular word or meaning. Those items that are not labelled may be assumed to be normal in writing and in relatively formal speech. For further details, see page xxiv.

0.6 Coverage of different national varieties of English (especially British and American)

In pronunciation, spelling, and vocabulary, the book presents the user with all the most important and distinctive differences between British and American usage. All items that are not labelled *BrE* (British English) or *AmE* (American English) and carry no other national or regional label may be assumed to be acceptable throughout the world.

Care has also been taken to ensure that there is some coverage of words selected from English spoken in other parts of the world. The main areas covered where English is the native language are Australia and New Zealand, Canada, South Africa, and the Caribbean. See the front inside cover for the labels used.

0.7 Choice of main spellings

Wherever possible, the spellings for the main entry are those that are equally acceptable in Britain and the United States, although common variants are shown as well. Examples of such spellings are **criticize** (with **criticise** shown as an alternative) and **judgment** (with **judgement** as alternative).

0.8 The spelling of compound words

The way in which compound words are spelt in English has not developed according to any neat system. Different words which are made up of the same type of parts are written as one word, separate words, or hyphenated. Even the same word may often be seen written in any of these three ways. In this dictionary we provide systematic guidelines to enable the user to choose the most appropriate form, taking the following factors into account: (a) the part of speech of the whole compound (b) the parts of speech of its various elements (c) the stress pattern of the compound (d) the number of syllables in each element, and (e) the nature of the letters at the boundary between elements.

Nearly all the compound words in the dictionary are spelt according to this system except for a few well-established exceptions. You will sometimes see such compounds spelt differently elsewhere, but the spellings given in the entries of the dictionary are suggested for your use, and will always be found acceptable.

0.9 Use of the computer

The dictionary has been compiled with the help of computer-checking programs, an aid which enables some lexicographic principles to be carried out with complete thoroughness. For example, every single word in the dictionary in an example or definition has been machine-checked to ensure that it is part of the controlled vocabulary.

0.10 Acknowledgments

A very large number of people have been involved in constructing this dictionary and many of them are listed in the special section dealing with acknowledgments. The main work of course has been done by the dedicated team of Longman lexicographers, supported in matters of detail and of broad policy by the group of linguistic advisers headed by Randolph Quirk.

Particular mention should be made of the original author of a manuscript which helped to form something of the basis of the current text. This was A. W. Frisby, author of two small dictionaries for the foreign learner of English, who died early in 1973.

Mention should also be made of the dedicated clerical and secretarial staff involved in the project and of the computer personnel who have been involved in devising systems and in programming.

Paul Procter
Editor-in-Chief

Guide to the Dictionary

1 Explanatory chart

main entry (page xiv)

au·tumn /'ɔːtəm/ *AmE* also **fall**— *n* [R;C;(U)] the season between summer and winter when leaves turn gold and fruits become ripe

a different word that may be used, in American English, instead of this one (page xv)

fast·ness/'fɑːstnǰs || 'fæst-/ *n* **1** [C] a safe place which is hard to reach (esp. in the phr. **a mountain fastness**) **2** [U] the quality of being firm or fixed: *the fastness of a colour|of his hold on the handle*

USAGE There is no noun formed from **fast** when it means **quick**. Use instead **speed** or **quickness**.

grammatical information about a noun; not the same for all meanings (page xxviii)

the phrase in which this word nearly always appears when it has this meaning, with more explanation if necessary (page xxvii)

note giving more information about grammar or meaning (page xxviii)

fat[1] /fæt/ *adj* [Wa1] **1** (of creatures and their bodies) having (too) much fat: *fat cattle | a fat baby | You'll get even fatter if you eat all those potatoes* **2** (of meat) containing a lot of fat **3** thick and well-filled: *a fat book* | (fig.) *a fat bank account* **4** (esp. of land) producing plentiful crops: *the fat farms in the valley* **5 a fat lot of** *sl* no; not any: *A fat lot of good|of use that is*!

many clear examples of the use of the word, with a line between each example

example showing how the same meaning can be understood when used of things not seen or touched (page xxvi)

special expression (IDIOM) (page xxvi)

fit·ting[1] /'fɪtɪŋ/ *adj fml* right for the purpose or occasion; suitable: *It is fitting that we should remember him on his birthday*— opposite **unfitting**

word with the opposite meaning (page xxvi)

part of speech (page xiv)

fox[1] /fɒks || fɑks/ *n* **1** [C] (*fem.* **vixen**) — **a** any of several types of small doglike flesh-eating wild animal with a bushy tail, esp. **b** a type of European animal with reddish fur, preserved in Britain to be hunted and often said to have a clever and deceiving nature

word for person or animal when female (page xvi)

shortened form (ABBREVIATION) shown at its own place in the dictionary (page xiv)

GCE *abbrev. for:* (in Britain) General Certificate of Education; an examination in one of many subjects set by various universities and taken by pupils aged 15 or over

verb that is always used with another word such as *with*, *on*, or *into* (a PREPOSITION), or with an adverb. These are always shown as a separate entry (page xiv)

go on[2] *v prep* [T1 *no pass.*] to use as a reason, proof, or base for further action: *We were just going on what you yourself had said*

if[1] /ɪf/ *conj* **1** (*not usu. followed by the future tense*) supposing that; on condition that: "*We can send you a map if you wish*" (SEU S.)

information about the use of a grammatical word, given either before the meaning, as here, or instead of a meaning (page xxv)

example taken from a collection of real speech and writing (page xxvi)

-i·ty /ɪ̈ti/ *suffix* [*adj*→*n* [U;(C)]] the quality or an example of being: REGULARITY | *another of his stupidities* (STUPIDITY)

information about how words are built up by adding an ending (SUFFIX); in this case, that when it is added to an adjective it forms a noun of the stated kind (page xxvii)

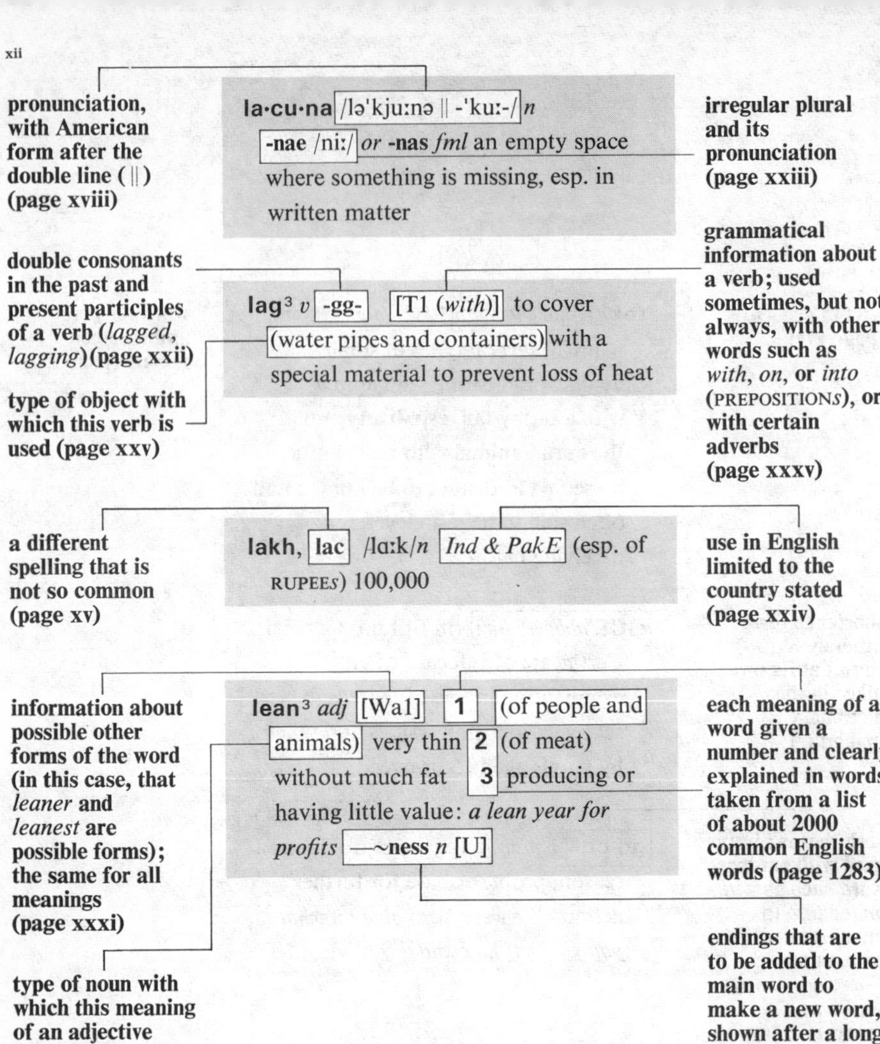
pronunciation, with American form after the double line (||) (page xviii)
la·cu·na /lə'kjuːnə || -'kuː-/ n -nae /niː/ or -nas fml an empty space where something is missing, esp. in written matter
irregular plural and its pronunciation (page xxiii)
double consonants in the past and present participles of a verb (lagged, lagging) (page xxii)
lag³ v -gg- [T1 (with)] to cover (water pipes and containers) with a special material to prevent loss of heat
grammatical information about a verb; used sometimes, but not always, with other words such as with, on, or into (PREPOSITIONS), or with certain adverbs (page xxxv)
type of object with which this verb is used (page xxv)
a different spelling that is not so common (page xv)
lakh, lac /lɑːk/ n Ind & PakE (esp. of RUPEES) 100,000
use in English limited to the country stated (page xxiv)
information about possible other forms of the word (in this case, that leaner and leanest are possible forms); the same for all meanings (page xxxi)
lean³ adj [Wa1] 1 (of people and animals) very thin 2 (of meat) without much fat 3 producing or having little value: a lean year for profits —~ness n [U]
each meaning of a word given a number and clearly explained in words taken from a list of about 2000 common English words (page 1283)
type of noun with which this meaning of an adjective is used (page xxv)

le·gal·ize, -ise /'liːgəlaɪz/ *v* [T1] to make lawful —**-ization** /ˌliːgəlaɪ'zeɪʃən || -gələ-/ *n* [U]

endings that are to be added to the main word to make a new word, shown after a long straight line. A bent line (~) before the ending means that the ending is added to the whole word; a shorter straight line (-) before the ending means that the ending is added to part of the word. The part of speech and other grammatical information are then given, and the pronunciation if it is not regular. An example of the use of the new word is often shown (page xxvii)

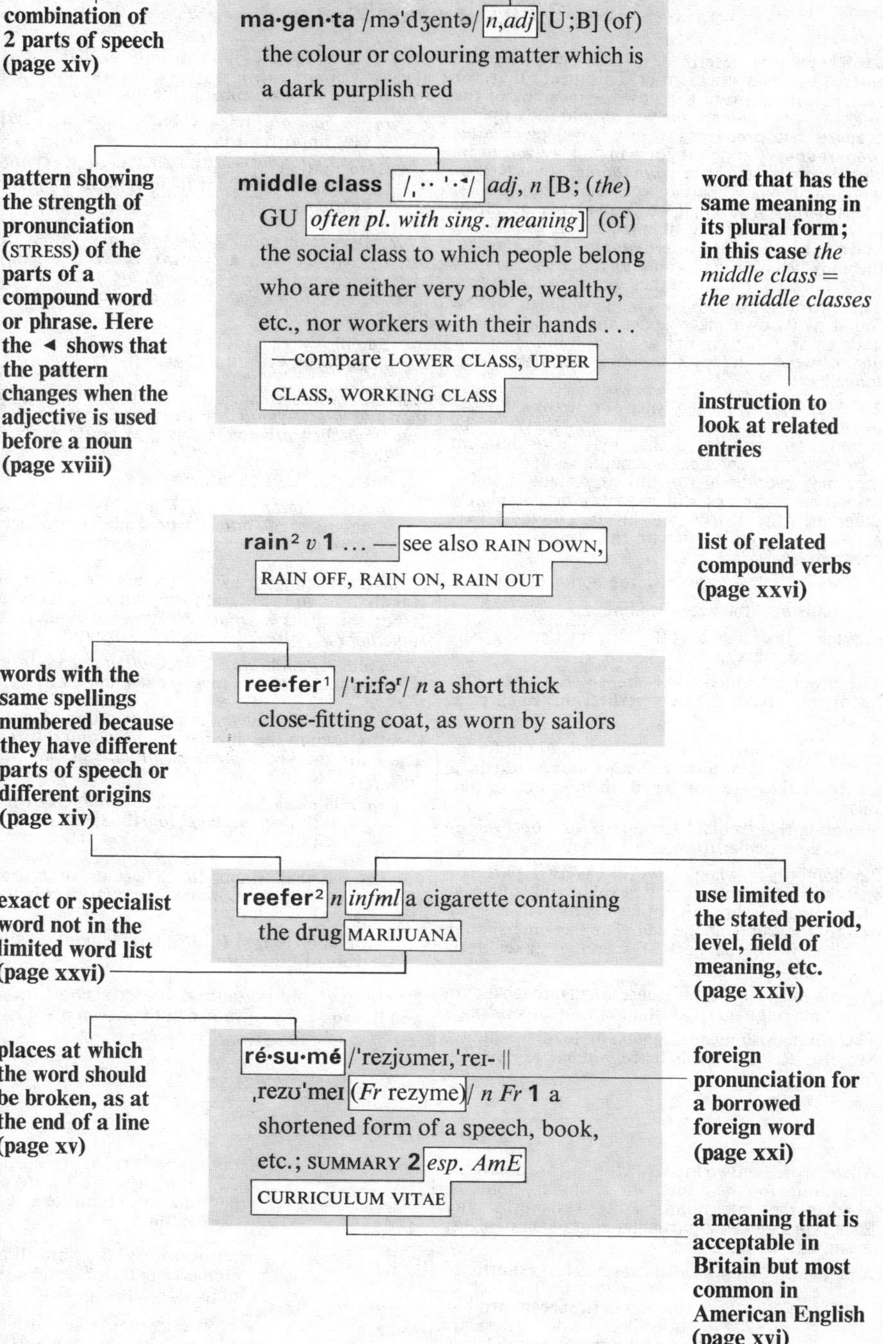

combination of 2 parts of speech (page xiv)
ma·gen·ta /mə'dʒentə/ n,adj [U;B] (of) the colour or colouring matter which is a dark purplish red
pattern showing the strength of pronunciation (STRESS) of the parts of a compound word or phrase. Here the ◂ shows that the pattern changes when the adjective is used before a noun (page xviii)
middle class /ˌ·· '·◂/ adj, n [B; (the) GU often pl. with sing. meaning] (of) the social class to which people belong who are neither very noble, wealthy, etc., nor workers with their hands . . . —compare LOWER CLASS, UPPER CLASS, WORKING CLASS
word that has the same meaning in its plural form; in this case the middle class = the middle classes
instruction to look at related entries
rain² v 1 ... —see also RAIN DOWN, RAIN OFF, RAIN ON, RAIN OUT
list of related compound verbs (page xxvi)
words with the same spellings numbered because they have different parts of speech or different origins (page xiv)
ree·fer¹ /'riːfəʳ/ n a short thick close-fitting coat, as worn by sailors
exact or specialist word not in the limited word list (page xxvi)
reefer² n infml a cigarette containing the drug MARIJUANA
use limited to the stated period, level, field of meaning, etc. (page xxiv)
places at which the word should be broken, as at the end of a line (page xv)
ré·su·mé /'rezjʊmeɪ,'reɪ- || ˌrezʊ'meɪ (Fr rezyme)/ n Fr 1 a shortened form of a speech, book, etc.; SUMMARY 2 esp. AmE CURRICULUM VITAE
foreign pronunciation for a borrowed foreign word (page xxi)
a meaning that is acceptable in Britain but most common in American English (page xvi)

2 Order of entries

2.0 The words described in this dictionary are entered in alphabetical order. This means that, for example, if you want to know the meaning of the PHRASAL VERB *prepare for* you should look up not **prepare** but **prepare for** in its own place after **preparedness**; and that you will find **lawsuit** in its alphabetical place after **lawn tennis**, not as part of the entry for **law**. This is true of all main entries, whether they are a single word, an entry made up of more than one word, or HYPHENATEd. If you cannot find a fixed group of words in its alphabetical place, this may be because it is an IDIOM; in this case look for it under one of the other words in the group. Thus, **racehorse**, which is a type of horse, will be found at its own place under the letter "r", but **dark horse**, which is not a horse at all, is shown under **horse** as a special meaning. See also **Idioms** (page xxvi).

2.1 Many words in English are spelt alike, but are in other ways completely different—they may be pronounced differently, they may have different jobs to do in a sentence (as a noun, verb, etc.), and they may even be historically unrelated, in which case their meanings will probably be completely different. Most words like this are entered separately in this dictionary, with raised numbers after them, like this:

> **lead**[1] /liːd/ *v* ... to show somebody the way; ...
>
> **lead**[2] *n* ... the act of leading ...
>
> **lead**[3] /led/ *n* ... a soft easily melted greyish-blue metal ...

The order in which these are entered is usually historical; the one used earliest in English is entered first.

2.2 In some cases, when such words are different only in that they have different jobs to do in a sentence, they are combined in one entry, like this:

> **ab·la·tive** /'æblətɪv/ *adj, n* (of or concerning) a particular form of a Latin noun ...

2.3 Sometimes when a word has two parts of speech, like **swish** below, we explain only one part of speech and show the other one, which is spelt exactly the same, at the end. The meaning should be clear when the part of speech is taken into account. Thus:

> **swish** /swɪʃ/ *v*. . . to (cause to) cut through the air making a sharp whistling noise . . .—**swish** *n*

The noun **swish** means "an example of swishing". See also **Related words listed without explanation** (page xxvii).

2.4.1 If 2 words are different only in that one is always written with a CAPITAL LETTER, they are treated as 2 separate entries, like this:

> **ref·or·ma·tion** /ˌrefə'meɪʃən ‖ ˌrefər-/ *n* [C;U] (an) improvement...
>
> **Reformation** *n* [*the* + R] (the period of) the religious movement in Europe in the 16th century ...

2.4.2 If a meaning of a word is sometimes, often, or usually written with a CAPITAL LETTER, but not always, it is not shown as a separate entry, but is marked *sometimes cap.*, *often cap.*, or *usu. cap.*, like this:

> **dev·il**[1] /devəl/ *n* **1** [*the* + R] (*usu. cap.*) the most powerful evil spirit; Satan ...

2.5.1 If 2 words are spelt the same but differ only in that one is always used in the plural form in one meaning, they are treated as 2 separate entries, like this:

> **bitter**[3] *n* [U] *BrE* bitter beer ...
>
> **bit·ters** /'bɪtəz ‖ -ərz/ *n* [U;P] a usu. alcoholic mixture of bitter-tasting plant products used ...

2.5.2 If a meaning of a word is sometimes, often, or usually used in the plural form, but not always, it is not shown as a separate entry, but is marked *sometimes pl.*, *often pl.*, or *usu. pl.*, like this:

> **stud·y**[1] /'stʌdi/ *n* ... **2** [U;C *often pl.*] a subject studied: *to give time to one's studies* ...

2.5.3 A few words have the same meaning whether they are used in the singular or in the plural form. These are marked *sometimes/ often/ usu. pl. with sing. meaning*, like this:

> **middle class** /ˌ.. '.◂/ *adj, n* [B; (*the*) GU *often pl. with sing. meaning*] (of) the social class to which ...

2.6 Letters that stand for a group of words (ABBREVIATIONs) are shown at their own place in the dictionary:

> **GCE** *abbrev. for*: (in Britain) General Certificate of Education ...

2.7 AFFIXes and COMBINING FORMs, such as **-ness** and **Russo-**, are also shown at their own place.

3 Types of word

All the words shown in this dictionary are described according to their use in grammar—that is, whether they are nouns, adjectives, verbs, etc. Each type is given a particular sign or set of signs, as shown below.

abbrev. for	=	ABBREVIATION for (a shortened form of (a word), which is often used in speech, just like an ordinary word. These are usually spoken simply as a set of letters, but for those which do not follow this rule we give the pronunciation): **PhD**
adj	=	adjective: **tall**
adv	=	adverb: **partly**
comb. form	=	COMBINING FORM (a form that combines with a word or part of a word to make a new word): **Sino-**
conj	=	CONJUNCTION (a word that connects parts of sentences, phrases, etc.): **and, but**
contr. of	=	CONTRACTION of (the shortened form of (a word or words)): **shan't**
determiner	=	DETERMINER (a word that limits the meaning of a noun and comes before adjectives that describe the same noun): **many, our**

interj = INTERJECTION (a phrase, word, or set of sounds used as a sudden remark): **ouch**

n = noun: **dog, wine**

predeterminer = PREDETERMINER (a word that can be used before *a* or *the*): **all, such**

prefix = PREFIX (an AFFIX that is placed at the beginning of a word or base): **un-, re-**

prep = PREPOSITION (a word used with a noun, PRONOUN, or *-ing* form to show its connection with another word): **in, of**

pron = PRONOUN (a word that is used in place of a noun or noun phrase): **it, me, them**

suffix = SUFFIX (an AFFIX that is placed at the end of a word): **-ity, -phile**

v = verb: **make, run, sew**

v adv = verb + adverb (a PHRASAL VERB made up of a verb and an adverb): **throw away, work out**

v adv prep = verb + adverb + PREPOSITION (a PHRASAL VERB made up of a verb, an adverb, and a PREPOSITION): **put up with, do away with**

v adv; prep = verb + adverb *or* verb + PREPOSITION (a PHRASAL VERB in which the second part (such as *through*) can be used either as an adverb or as a PREPOSITION): **lay off**

v prep = verb + PREPOSITION (a PHRASAL VERB made up of a verb and a PREPOSITION): **come into, fall for**

written abbrev. for = written ABBREVIATION for (a shortened form of (a word), which is used only in writing, never in speech): **s.a.e.** *written abbrev. for:* stamped addressed envelope

Note that many of these signs can be used in combination. This is shown by means of a COMMA (,). Thus, for example, if a word is described as *adj*, *n*, it means that it can be used both as an adjective and as a noun.

4 Syllable division

4.1 Words are made up of one or more separately-pronounced parts, called SYLLABLE*s*. If you know what the separate parts of any particular word are, you will more easily be able to read the word and to understand how it is pronounced. In this dictionary, therefore, all the SYLLABLE*s* of every word are shown. This is done by dividing each word up by means of dots, like this:

syl·la·ble

Thus, the word "syllable" has 3 SYLLABLE*s*: *syl*, *la*, and *ble*.

4.2 If you find any long word hard to read, you will find it helpful to look at what its separate parts are; and if you are in doubt about the exact meaning of the pronunciation we have given to the word, you will find that by pronouncing each SYLLABLE separately, you will arrive at the correct way of saying it.

4.3 The SYLLABLE dots have one further use. They show where a word can be broken up (HYPHENATED) if you do not have enough room at the end of a line. Thus, **syl·la·ble** may be ended on one line with

syl-
or sylla-

and continued on the next with

-lable
or -ble

But there are 2 very important points to remember when using the dots for this purpose:

4.3.1 It is not considered correct to separate only one letter from the beginning or end of a word. Thus, for example, although the words **a·lone** and **pris·m** have 2 SYLLABLE*s*, they should never be broken up at the end of a line.

4.3.2 The possible end-of-line divisions we show are not the only acceptable ones. You will often find words broken up differently. But it is not practical, in the limited space we have, to show all the possibilities. If you follow the ones we show, you will not go wrong.

4.4 When a word appears more than once as a HEADWORD we do not repeat the SYLLABLE dots after the first one, unless one of the later ones has a different pronunciation. Thus **lim·it**[1] /ˈlɪmɨt/ *n* and **limit**[2] *v* have the same SYLLABLE*s*. But **present**[1] & [2] have different pronunciations: thus

pres·ent[1] /ˈprezənt/ *n* **1** a gift ...
and
pre·sent[2] /prɪˈzent/ *v* **1** ... to give (something) away ...

5 Variants

5.0 Many words have more than one spelling, or share their meaning with one or more other words (have SYNONYM*s*). It is useful to know about such words, and therefore in this dictionary we give information about them all together in one place: the main form of any particular set of forms.

5.1.1 Information about different spellings of a particular word is given immediately after that word, like this:

caf·tan, kaftan /ˈkæftæn/ *n* a long loose garment ...

This means that the usual spelling is *caftan*, but that *kaftan* can also be used.

5.1.2 In the case of long words, only that part of the word which is spelt differently is shown:

gen·e·ral·ize, -ise /ˈdʒenərəlaɪz/ *v* ...

This means that the usual spelling is *generalize*, but that *generalise* can also be used.

5.2.1 Information about words that share the meaning of another word is given after the word "also", like this:

lap·wing /ˈlæpˌwɪŋ/ also **pewit, peewit**— *n* a type of small bird ...

This means that *lapwing* is the usual word, but that both *pewit* and *peewit* have the same meaning, and can be used instead.

5.2.2 In the case of a pair of adjectives, one ending in *-ic* and the other in *-ical*, the less common form is shown like this:

i·ron·ic /aɪ'rɒnɪk ‖ aɪ'rɑ-/also **i·ron·i·cal** /-ɪkəl/ —*adj* ...

This means that *ironic* and *ironical* have the same meaning, but that the former is the more commonly used.

5.2.3 Often a word introduced by "also" may not have the same meaning as all the meanings of the main form. In this case it is shown after the number for the particular meaning to which it belongs, like this:

la·dy /'leɪdi/ *n* **1** ... *polite* a woman, esp. a woman of good social position ... **2** also **woman**— female: *a lady doctor*

This means that for the first meaning you can use only *lady*, but for the second you may use *woman* as well: *a woman doctor*.

5.3 Many of the words differently spelt or introduced by "also" are slightly different from their main form in other ways: they may be *fml*, while the main form is not, or they may be *AmE*, while the main form is *BrE*. In 5.6 you will find an explanation of the styles we use to show you the exact differences between a main form and a differently spelt form or one introduced by "also".

5.4 For many types of animal and person there is a general word that is used for both sexes and a more particular word that is used for only one sex. In such cases, we show the general word as the main form, followed by the particular word, whether this is used for the female, as is common with words for people and animals:

fox[1] /fɒks ‖ fɑks/ *n* **1** [C] (*fem.* **vixen**)— **a** any of several types of small doglike flesh-eating wild animal ...

or for the male, as is more usual for birds:

duck[1] /dʌk/ *n* **1** [Wn1;C] (*masc.* **drake**)— any of various common swimming birds ...

5.5.1 If a differently spelt form, a form introduced by "also", or a masc. or fem. form would have come less than 10 places away from the main form in the dictionary, it is not given a separate place of its own; all the information about it, such as its pronunciation, STRESS, and SYLLABLE division, is therefore given under the main form, like this:

freez·er /'friːzə^r/ *n* ... **2** also **freezing com·part·ment** /'·· ·,··/— ...

5.5.2 But when such a form would be entered 10 or more places away from the main form, it is given a separate place of its own, where such information as its pronunciation is given, and where you are told what the main form is so that you can go to it to find out the meaning, like this:

lap·wing /'læp,wɪŋ/ also **pewit, peewit**— *n* ...
pe·wit, pee- /'piːwɪt/ *n* LAPWING

5.6.0 The following styles are used, where necessary, to explain the exact differences between a main form and a second form that is differently spelt or is a completely different word:

5.6.1 Levels of formality
When a word shares the meaning of another word, but is more *fml* or *infml*, it is shown like this:

tel·e·vi·sion /'telɪ̇'vɪʒən, ,telɪ̇'vɪʒən/ also (*infml*) **telly**— *n* ...
tel·ly ... /'teli/ *n infml* TELEVISION

5.6.2 British and American differences
The main form shown in the dictionary is always one that is used in British English. We show the relationship of other *BrE* and *AmE* forms in the following ways:

5.6.2.1 Spelling differences

1. *AmE* uses only the differently spelt form: **col·our,** *AmE* **color** /'kʌlə^r/ *n* ...
2. The differently spelt form is commoner in *AmE*: **axe,** *AmE* usu. **ax** /æks/ ...
3. Both forms are used fairly equally in *AmE*: **a·moe·ba,** *AmE* also **ameba** /ə'miːbə/ *n* ...
4. Both forms are used fairly equally in *BrE*: **jail,** *BrE* also **gaol** /dʒeɪl/ ...

5.6.2.2 Word differences

1. The main form is only *BrE*; the second form is only *AmE*: **lad·der**[1] /'lædə^r/ *n* ... **2** (*AmE* **run**)— *BrE* a ladder-shaped fault in a stocking ...
   run[2] *n* ... **15** *AmE* LADDER[1] (2)
2. The main form is used generally in world English, except in *AmE*, which uses the second form: **pave·ment** /'peɪvmənt/ *n* **1** *AmE* **sidewalk**— a PAVED surface or path
   side·walk /'saɪdwɔːk/ *n AmE* PAVEMENT (1)
3. The main form is used generally in world English, but the second form is commoner in *BrE*: **egg·plant** /'egplɑːnt ‖ 'egplænt/ *BrE* usu. **aubergine**— *n* **1** a type of plant...
4. The main form is used generally in world English, but the second form is commoner in *AmE*: **gear le·ver** /'· ,··/ ... *AmE* usu. **gear shift**— *n*
5. The main form is used generally in world English, but *AmE* also uses the second form: **au·tumn** /'ɔːtəm/ *AmE* also **fall**— *n* the season between summer and winter ...
   fall[2] *n* ... **8** *AmE* AUTUMN
6. The main form is used generally in world English; the second form is also used generally, but it is commoner in the stated area than elsewhere: **las·so**[1] /lə'suː, 'læsəʊ/also (*esp. AmE*) **lariat**— *n* ...
   la·ri·at /'lærɪət/ *n esp. AmE* LASSO[1]

For British and American pronunciation differences, see **Pronunciation,** page xviii.

6 Pronunciation

6.1 Main Symbols

The International PHONETIC Alphabet is used to represent the pronunciation of every main word in the dictionary, for both British and American varieties of English. The main signs (SYMBOL*s*) that we use are:

CONSONANTS

Symbol	Key Word
p	pen
b	back
t	tea
d	day
k	key
g	gay
tʃ	cheer
dʒ	jump
f	few
v	view
θ	thing
ð	then
s	soon
z	zero
ʃ	fishing
ʒ	pleasure
h	hot
m	sum
n	sun
ŋ	sung
l	led
r	red
j	yet
w	wet

VOWELS

Number	This Dictionary	*Concise Pronouncing Dictionary*	*English Pronouncing Dictionary* (13th ed.)	Key Word
1	iː	i	iː	sheep
2	ɪ	ɪ	i	ship
3	e	e	e	bed
4	æ	æ	æ	bad
5	ɑː	ɑ	ɑː	calm
6	ɒ	o	ɔ	pot
7	ɔː	ɔ	ɔː	caught
8	ʊ	ʊ	u	put
9	uː	u	uː	boot
10	ʌ	ʌ	ʌ	cut
11	ɜː	ɜ	əː	bird
12	ə	ə	ə	cupboard
13	eɪ	eɪ	ei	make
14	əʊ	əʊ	əu	note
15	aɪ	ɑɪ	ai	bite
16	aʊ	ɑʊ	au	now
17	ɔɪ	ɔɪ	ɔi	boy
18	ɪə	ɪə	iə	here
19	eə	eə	ɛə	there
20	ʊə	ʊə	uə	poor
—	eɪə	eɪə	eiə	player
—	əʊə	əʊə	əuə	lower
—	aɪə	ɑɪə	aiə	tire
—	aʊə	ɑʊə	auə	tower
—	ɔɪə	ɔɪə	ɔiə	employer

6.2.1 British pronunciations

The form of British speech (ACCENT) that we represent is called *Received Pronunciation*, or "RP". This is the kind of English recorded by Daniel Jones in his *English Pronouncing Dictionary* (EPD). It is common among educated speakers in England, although not in most other parts of the British Isles. Indeed, the general speech of both Scotland and Ireland is nearer to the pronunciation of American English given here than to Received Pronunciation. We use the same form of the International PHONETIC Alphabet to represent this ACCENT as Professor A.C. Gimson (our pronunciation adviser) uses in the 14th EDITION of the EPD (Dent, 1977).

The above table shows the SYMBOL*s* that we use. It also gives the vowel SYMBOLS used in *A Concise Pronouncing Dictionary of British and American English* (OUP, 1972) by J. Windsor Lewis, and those used in earlier EDITION*s* of the EPD.

The consonant SYMBOL*s* are the same in all 3 systems, and the same consonant SYMBOL*s* are used for American pronunciations too. In most cases we also use the same vowel

SYMBOL*s* for American and British pronunciations, except for a few special cases. These will be explained later.

6.2.2 American pronunciations

Unlike British English, there is no single standard of pronunciation for American English. We have therefore chosen to represent simply one of the more common forms of American pronunciation.

In many cases, the same pronunciation can be used for both British and American. Where there is a difference, the British form is given first, in full, and the American form follows after the *double bar* / ‖/. This bar therefore means that the pronunciation on the *left* is British, and that on the *right* is American (although sometimes one form can be used by speakers of the other ACCENT).

Unless the word is short, we do not repeat for American English those parts of the word that are the same as in British. For example:

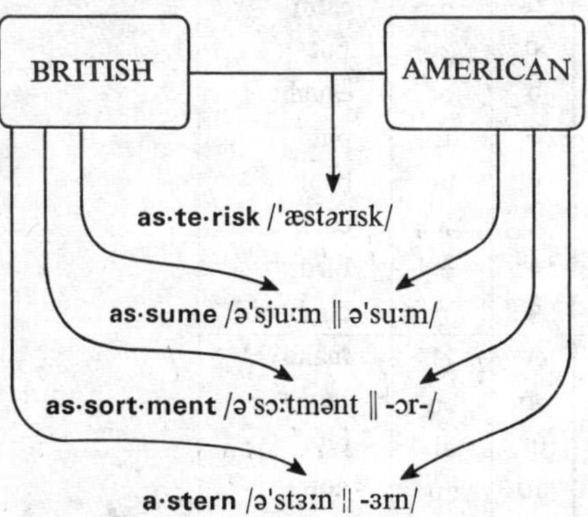

For American pronunciations, we have often used *Webster's New Collegiate Dictionary* (8th EDITION). We thank John Bollard, the Merriam-Webster pronunciation EDITOR, and also Professor Arthur J. Bronstein, of Lehman College, The City University of New York, for their help with certain difficulties; though, as reasons of space have forced us to describe American pronunciation without showing every word in the dictionary twice, we may not always have done justice to the excellent advice we have received.

6.3.1 Stress

In English words of 2 or more SYLLABLE*s*, at least one SYLLABLE stands out from the rest. We say it has greater STRESS. The mark /'/ is placed before the SYLLABLE that carries the *main* STRESS of the word. For example:

let·ter /'letəʳ/ **as·te·risk**/'æstərɪsk/

Some words also have SECONDARY STRESS (a weaker STRESS) on another SYLLABLE. The mark /ˌ/ is placed before such a SYLLABLE. For example:

arch·bish·op /ˌɑːtʃ'bɪʃəp ‖ ˌɑr-/
an·ti·mat·ter /'æntiˌmætəʳ/

Even in very long words only one SECONDARY STRESS is usually shown:

com·pre·hen·si·bil·i·ty /ˌkɒmprɪhensə'bɪlə̇ti ‖ ˌkɑm-/
in·com·pat·i·bil·i·ty /ˌɪnkəmpætə'bɪlə̇ti/

The third SYLLABLE*s* of those words do have a little more STRESS than the other unmarked ones, but it is not necessary to show this because they contain "strong" vowels, which always have a certain amount of stress.

But sometimes 2 SECONDARY STRESSes are shown, as in:

con·tra·in·di·ca·tion /ˌkɒntrəˌɪndɪ'keɪʃən/

This is because /ɪ/ may be "strong" or "weak". In that word, the first /ɪ/ is "strong", not "weak". (/ɪ/ may be strong or weak, and /ə/ is always weak. All the other vowels are always strong.) When 2 SECONDARY STRESSes are shown, the first always has more STRESS than the second.

6.3.2 Compounds with space or hyphen

Many compounds are written with either a space or a HYPHEN (-) between the parts. When all parts of such a compound also appear in the dictionary as separate main words (in their proper alphabetical place), the full pronunciation of the compound is not shown. Only its STRESS *pattern* is given. Each SYLLABLE is represented by a dot /·/, and the main STRESS mark /'/ is placed before the dot that represents the SYLLABLE with main STRESS (in the compound). Where necessary, a SECONDARY STRESS mark is also used. For example:

bus stop /'· ·/ **town hall** /ˌ· '·/
Association Foot·ball /·ˌ···· '··/

Sometimes a compound contains a main word with an ending. If the main word is in the dictionary and the ending is a common one, still only a STRESS pattern is shown. For example:

lending li·bra·ry /'·· ˌ···/

Lending is not a main word in the dictionary, but **lend** is; so only a STRESS pattern is shown, because *-ing* is a common ending. But if any part is not a main word, the full pronunciation is given:

jig·ge·ry-po·ke·ry /ˌdʒɪgəri 'pəʊkəri/

The stress patterns of PHRASAL VERB*s* are not shown, because their STRESS varies in accordance with, for example, their place in the sentence.

6.3.3 Stress Shift

A number of compounds may have a SHIFT (= "movement") in STRESS when they are used before nouns. For example, *plate glass* would have the pattern /ˌ· '·/ when spoken by itself, or in a sentence like *The window was made of plate glass*. But the phrase *plate glass window* would usually have the pattern /ˌ· · '··/ —that is, with the main STRESS of the whole phrase on *window*; *glass* loses its STRESS completely. The syllable with most STRESS in *plate glass* is now *plate*—but it has only SECONDARY STRESS in the phrase as a whole. The mark /◂/ is used after words where this happens. For example:

plate glass /ˌ· '·◂/

There is no STRESS SHIFT when the main STRESS of the whole phrase is not on the following noun. For example, *plate glass window* has the pattern /ˌ· · ˈ· ·/, but *plate glass manufacturer* would be /ˌ· ˈ· · ·ˌ· · ·/, because the main stress of the whole phrase is on *plate glass*. So it keeps its UNSHIFTED pattern.

The STRESS pattern that is shown is always the one that would be used when the word is said by itself. For example, even though *left-hand* is nearly always used before a noun in a sentence (with the STRESS-SHIFTED pattern /ˈ· ·/), it is shown in the dictionary as:

left-hand /ˌ· ˈ·◂/

This is because it has the pattern /ˌ· ˈ·/ when said by itself, not in a phrase or sentence.

STRESS SHIFT can also happen with some single words, such as:

dif·fe·ren·tial /ˌdɪfəˈrenʃəl◂/
in·de·pen·dent /ˌɪndəˈpendənt◂/

6.4.0 Use of symbols and special symbols

There are important differences between the American and British ACCENT*s* that we represent. There are also important regular differences that are made by different speakers with the same ACCENT. To cover this, we use some SYMBOL*s* in a special way, and we use some special SYMBOL*s*.

6.4.1 /r/
In the kind of American speech we represent, *r* in the spelling is usually pronounced. In RP it is pronounced only when a vowel follows. So:

6.4.1.1 at the end of a word, we use the special SYMBOL /ʳ/, above the ordinary line. For example:

far /fɑːʳ/

This means that in RP a phrase like *far down* is pronounced /ˌfɑː ˈdaʊn/, while *far away* would be /ˌfɑːr əˈweɪ/. In American *far* is /fɑr/ in both cases, but to save space the form /fɑːʳ/ represents this.

6.4.1.2 In the middle of a word, when a consonant follows, American usually uses /r/ and RP never does. This is always clearly shown. For example:

part·ner·ship /ˈpɑːtnəʃɪp ‖ ˈpɑrtnər-/
harm·less /ˈhɑːmləs ‖ ˈhɑrm-/

We do not repeat those parts of the words that are the same in both ACCENT*s*, unless the word is short. For example:

farm /fɑːm ‖ fɑrm/

6.4.2 /ə̇/
In both ACCENT*s*, there are many words where some speakers use /ɪ/ and others use /ə/. The special SYMBOL /ə̇/ therefore represents both pronunciations.
For example:

busi·ness /ˈbɪznə̇s/
de·fi·ni·tion /ˌdefə̇ˈnɪʃən/
hel·met /ˈhelmə̇t/

6.4.3 /i/
At the end of many words, a lot of RP speakers use /ɪ/ but many Americans use /iː/. We use the special SYMBOL /i/ to represent this. Remember that if you are learning RP you should try to pronounce this SYMBOL as /ɪ/, but if you are learning American English you should pronounce it as /iː/. For example:

hap·py /ˈhæpi/: usually pronounced /ˈhæpɪ/ in RP but /ˈhæpiː/ in American

The same thing is true when many endings are added:

hap·pi·ness /ˈhæpinə̇s/
fai·ry·land /ˈfeərilænd/

But when *-ly* is added, the /i/ changes to /ə̇/. To save space we do not show this, but *happily*, for example, is pronounced /ˈhæpə̇li/.

There is one exception. /ɪə/ is pronounced like that in RP, but in American it is pronounced /iːə/ quite often. We do not show this.

6.4.4 /ə/
This special SYMBOL is used in two ways. In both, the meaning is that /ə/ may be either used or missed out.

6.4.4.1 After a consonant: The sounds /m, n, l, r/ can be SYLLABIC: that is, they can themselves form a SYLLABLE. For example, it is possible to pronounce *travel* with the vowel /ə/ in the second SYLLABLE: /ˈtrævəl/. But this word is usually pronounced /ˈtrævl/. This pronunciation also has two SYLLABLE*s*, but only the first contains a vowel sound; the second SYLLABLE is simply /-vl/. We show both of these possibilities by using /ə/ in such SYLLABLE*s*. So:

1. **trav·el** /ˈtrævəl/ can represent:
   (i) /ˈtrævəl/ (*2* SYLLABLE*s*: *2 vowels*)
   (ii) /ˈtrævl/ (*2* SYLLABLE*s*: *1 vowel and 1* SYLLABIC *consonant*)

When a vowel sound follows such a consonant, there is a third possibility. It is also represented by /ə/, and means that the consonant may simply begin the following SYLLABLE. For example:

2. **mem·o·ry** /ˈmeməri/ can represent:
   (i) /ˈmeməri/ (*3* SYLLABLE*s*: *3 vowels*)
   (ii) /ˈmemr̩i/ (*3* SYLLABLE*s*: *2 vowels and 1* SYLLABIC *consonant, here shown as* /r̩/)
   (iii) /ˈmemri/ (*2* SYLLABLE*s*: *2 vowels*)

Where a pronunciation with /ə/ is shown in the dictionary, we suggest the use of a SYLLABIC consonant if possible (that is, without /ə/). So *travel* should be pronounced /ˈtrævl/ if possible.

6.4.4.2 After a vowel: Some speakers, especially in America, pronounce *vary* as /ˈveri/; others say /ˈveəri/. Again, the use of /ə/ means that /ə/ may or may not be used. For example:

fir·ing /ˈfaɪərɪŋ/
ap·pear·ance /əˈpɪərəns/
hair·y /ˈheəri/

This happens only after a vowel, and before /r/ except in a few words like **real·ly** /ˈrɪəli/.

6.4.5 /ɪ/ and /j/
In a lot of words, either /ɪ/ or /j/ may be used. In most cases we show only the /ɪ/ pronunciation. For example:

pe·cu·ni·a·ry /pɪ'kju:nɪəri/
u·ni·on /'ju:nɪən/

(In the first word we are talking about the second-from-last SYLLABLE, and in the second word we mean the last SYLLABLE.) But note:

million/'mɪljən/

6.4.6 /ɑ/, /ɔ/, and /з/
The RP vowels /ɑ:/, /ɔ:/, and /з:/ are best shown for American ACCENT*s* simply as /ɑ/, /ɔ/, and /з/ without the length mark. But where this is the only difference, we do not repeat the pronunciation. For example:

fa·ther /'fɑ:ðə^r/ in fact is /'fɑðər/ in American
claw /klɔ:/ in fact is /klɔ/ in American

But when the word has to be repeated for other reasons, we show the American vowels as /ɑ/, /ɔ/, and /з/, without the length mark. For example:

barn /bɑ:n ‖ bɑrn/ **horse** /hɔ:s ‖ hɔrs/
both·er /'bɒðə^r ‖ 'bɑ-/ **long** /lɒŋ ‖ lɔŋ/

RP /з:/ in fact is always /зr/ in American:

bird /bз:d ‖ bзrd/

6.4.7 /o/
The American pronunciation of the sound we show as /əʊ/ is really more like the pronunciation of *o* (= [o]) in other languages. Again, to save space we do not show this.

But we do use the special SYMBOL /o/ for certain words. They are words that have the RP vowel /ɔ:/, but that some Americans pronounce with /ɔ/ and others with /əʊ/. For example:

hoarse /hɔ:s ‖ hors/ is /hɔ:s/ in RP but either /hɔrs/ or /həʊrs/ in American (compare **horse** /hɔ:s ‖ hɔrs/, which is always just /hɔrs/ in American)

court /kɔ:t ‖ kort/ is /kɔ:t/ in RP but either /kɔrt/ or /kəʊrt/ in American (compare **caught** /kɔ:t/, which is always just /kɔ:t/ in both accents)

6.4.8 /n/ and /ŋ/
When /k/ or /g/ follows *n* in the spelling, the *n* is often pronounced as either /n/ or /ŋ/. We usually show only /n/, but /ŋ/ is often a possible pronunciation. For example:

in·come /'ɪnkʌm/ may also be pronounced /'ɪŋkʌm/
en·gross /en'grəʊs/ may also be pronounced /eŋ'grəʊs/

But this is so only when *n* ends a PREFIX. In other cases, only /ŋ/ is usually possible, and we show that:

ink /ɪŋk/, **fin·ger** /'fɪŋgə^r/

6.4.9 /-/
A HYPHEN in the ordinary spelling of a word is not shown in the pronunciations; a space is usually used instead (see the example under 6.3.2). In the pronunciation, a HYPHEN is usually used to represent parts of a word that are not repeated; but it is also used to avoid possible confusion. For example:

pros·o·dy /'prɒsədi ‖ 'prɑ-/ (/-sədi/ is not repeated)
ar·cha·ic /ɑ:'keɪ-ɪk ‖ ɑr-/ (to separate 2 /ɪ/s, and show the end is not repeated)
whol·ly /'həʊl-li/ (to show 2 /l/s—compare **ho·ly** /'həʊli/)
night·shirt /'naɪt-ʃз:t ‖ -ʃзrt/ (to show that the middle of the word is not /tʃ/)
fi·nal·i·za·tion /ˌfaɪnəl-aɪ'zeɪʃən/ (to show that /ˌfaɪn-laɪ'zeɪʃən/ is not possible)

A hyphen is also used when a pronunciation is broken at the end of a line.

6.5 Abbreviations

6.5.1 Usually, no pronunciation is shown for ABBREVIATION*s*, because their pronunciation is quite regular. Each letter has its usual pronunciation. The last letter always has main STRESS, and the first letter always has SECONDARY stress. With 5 letters or more, the third letter also has some STRESS. For example:

o /əʊ/
BA /ˌbi: 'eɪ/
LSD /ˌel es 'di:/
BOAC /ˌbi: əʊ eɪ 'si:/
RSPCA /ˌɑ:r es ˌpi: si: 'eɪ/

6.5.2 But a pronunciation is shown for certain ABBREVIATION*s*:

1. where the ABBREVIATION is spoken like an ordinary word:

   NATO /'neɪtəʊ/

2. where the ABBREVIATION may be spoken either like an ordinary word or like an ABBREVIATION:
   VAT /ˌvi: eɪ 'ti:, væt/
3. where the ABBREVIATION looks like an ordinary word but is not spoken that way:
   PAYE /ˌpi: eɪ waɪ 'i:/
   PRO /ˌpi: ɑ:r 'əʊ/
4. a mixture of letters and words:
   U-boat /'ju: bəʊt/

6.5.3 ABBREVIATION*s* that are marked *written abbrev.*, such as **cm** or **oz**, are never spoken. The full form is always used, so no pronunciation can be shown for the abbreviation.

6.6 Inflections

The pronunciation of INFLECTED forms (that is, irregular plurals, verb forms, etc.) is usually given when the spelling of the form is shown. For example:

gave /geɪv/ (from **give**)
houses /'haʊzɨz/ (from **house**)

6.7 Foreign words and phrases

6.7.1 English often uses foreign words and phrases, pronounced with English sounds and STRESS. In these cases, the most common English pronunciation is given. But for some words, especially from French and German, some speakers use a pronunciation that is closer to the original foreign pronunciation. Where such pronunciations are common, they are shown in round BRACKETs ( ) after the English pronunciations. For example:

> **lais·sez-faire** /ˌleɪseɪ ˈfeəʳ (*Fr* lesefɛr)/
> **lar·gesse** /lɑːˈʒes ‖ lɑrˈdʒes (*Fr* larʒɛs)/

6.7.2 Different SYMBOL*s* are often needed for these words, to represent sounds that do not exist in English. The SYMBOL*s* that can be used for foreign pronunciations are shown below.

6.7.3 The "English" pronunciations also sometimes need extra SYMBOL*s*. Those that may be used are /x, ɑ̃, ɔ̃, ɛ̃, œ̃/.

6.7.4 Note that all the consonant SYMBOL*s* shown in the English consonant table may also be used for foreign pronunciations, but they sometimes have a different sound. For example, a French or a German /r/ is quite different to the English one.

Foreign Sound					Nearest English Equivalent	
Symbol	as in					
	French	German	Spanish	Italian	Symbol	as in
i	si		si	finito	iː (i, iː)	bead
iː		die				
ɪ		bitte			ɪ	bid
e	pré	schwer	el	venti "20"	eɪ	bay
ɛ	bel	fest		venti "winds"	e	bed
a	la	Mann	la	parlare	æ	bad
aː		Vater			ɑː (aː, ɑ)	calm
ɑ	bas					
ɔ	mauvais	fort		troppo	ɒ / ɔː	cot / caught
o	pauvre	so	no	ora	əʊ	coat
ʊ		Luft			ʊ	put
u	trouver		uno	cura	uː (u, uː)	boot
uː		du				
ʏ		Hütte			—	
y	sur				— (y, yː)	
yː		für				
ø	peu	schön			ɜː (ø, œ)	bird
œ	œuf	zwölf				
ə	le	Tasse			ə	about
ɛ̃	vin				—	
ɑ̃	blanc				—	
ɔ̃	bon				—	
œ̃	un				—	
ɥ	lui				w	we
ç		ich			x (ç, x)	loch (*ScotE*)
x		ach	Juan			
ɲ	gagner		niño	gnocchi	nj (ɲ, ɲɲ)	onion
ɲɲ				ogni		
ʎ			llevar	gli	lj (ʎ, ʎʎ)	million
ʎʎ				figlia		
ddʒ				oggi	dʒ	badge
ddz				mezzo	dz	beds
ttʃ				faccia	tʃ	batch
tts				ragazzo	ts	bats

6.8 Related words listed without explanation

6.8.1 Sometimes a form of the main word comes at the end of the entry for that word (see page xxvii). It is always formed with a word-ending whose meaning is clear and known. For this reason, no pronunciation is given unless there is a change to the pronunciation of the main word. For example:

di·gest /daɪ'dʒest, də̇-/

No pronunciation is needed for the related form **~ible**; but for **~ibility**, since that ending makes a change to the pronunciation of the main word, the pronunciation is shown:

~ibility /daɪˌdʒestə'bɪlə̇ti, də̇-/

6.8.2 There are some regular exceptions to this rule:

6.8.2.1 The ending /-bəl/ always becomes /-bli/ when *-ly* is added to the main word. For example:

a·ble /'eɪbəl/ becomes **a·bly** /'eɪbli/ (See the explanation of [Wa3] on page xxxi.)

6.8.2.2 In the same way, when *-ly* is added to words ending in /-kəl/ the pronunciation becomes /-kli/:

mu·si·cal /'mjuːzɪkəl/ becomes **mu·si·cally** /'mjuːzɪkli/ (See the explanation of [Wa4] on page xxxii.)

6.8.2.3 When *-r* or *-er* is added to words ending in /-kəl/ the pronunciation becomes /-kləʳ/:

heck·le /'hekəl/ becomes **heck·ler** /'hekləʳ/ (See the explanation of [Wv3] on page xxxii.)

6.8.2.4 When certain SUFFIXes, such as *-ly* (as we have seen) or *-ity*, are added to a word ending in /-i/, the /i/ becomes /ə̇/:

hap·py /'hæpi/ becomes **hap·pi·ly** /'hæpə̇li/
jol·ly /'dʒɒli ‖ 'dʒɒli/ becomes **jol·li·ty** /'dʒɒlə̇ti ‖ 'dʒɑlə̇ti/

Since these forms are regular, they are not shown. (In all cases, the /ə̇/ is dropped.)

6.9 Strong and weak forms

Many common words have both a *strong form* and at least one *weak form*. The strong form is used when the word is STRESSed, or sometimes when it comes at the end of a sentence. Weak forms are used otherwise. As the weak forms are more common, they are shown first; the strong form follows the word *strong*. For example:

am /m, əm; *strong* æm/
are /əʳ; *strong* ɑːʳ/

6.10 Specialist or technical words

Some specialist words have 2 pronunciations: one that is used by people who are familiar with the subject, and one that is more general. For such words, the general pronunciation is given first, followed by the specialist one. For example:

lee·ward /'liːwəd, *tech* 'luːəd ‖ -ərd/

Note that the ending /-ərd/ is used for both American pronunciations.

6.11 Variant pronunciations

Generally, only one pronunciation is shown for each ACCENT. It is usually the most common pronunciation of the word. But it is sometimes necessary to show 2 pronunciations for the same ACCENT—for example, with specialist words as above. It is sometimes also necessary to do this for words where it is difficult to choose the most suitable single form. In such cases, VARIANT pronunciations are given. (That means that either form is possible.) As usual, unless the word is short, we do not repeat parts that are the same as the first pronunciation. For example:

ar·is·to·crat /'ærɪstəkræt, ə'rɪ- ‖ ə'rɪ-/

This shows that the word has 2 common pronunciations in RP, although only one, /ə'rɪstəkræt/, in American.

Gordon Walsh
Pronunciation Editor

7 Inflections

7.0 An INFLECTION is a change made in the form of a word according to its particular use in a sentence. For example, *he* changes to *him* when it is the object of a verb, *fox* to *foxes* when it is plural, and *do* to *did* when it is past tense.

7.1 In this dictionary INFLECTION*s* are shown only when their written forms or their pronunciations are irregular or when there is a possibility of confusion. They follow the part of speech and are shown in heavy black print or by special signs (CODE*s*) in SQUARE BRACKET*s* [ ].

7.1.1 When a word has more than one SYLLABLE only the part that changes is written out:

the·sis /'θiːsə̇s/ *n* **-ses** /siːz/ **1** an opinion or statement put forward ...

7.1.2 Pronunciation is shown where necessary between slanting lines. When the spelling is irregular and pronunciation regular both are shown:

tab·leau /'tæbləʊ ‖ 'tæbləʊ, tæ'bləʊ/ *n* **-leaux** /ləʊz/ *or* **-leaus** ...

7.1.3 When the spelling is regular and pronunciation irregular both are shown:

say¹ /seɪ/ *v* **said**/ sed/, *3rd pers. pres. t.* **says** /sez/ ...

bath¹ /bɑːθ ‖ bæθ/ *n* **baths** /bɑːðz, bɑːθs ‖ bæðz, bæθs/ ...

7.1.4.1 When the final consonant of a word is doubled, or a *k* added to a final *c*, before an inflection is added, it is shown as follows:

beg /beg/ *v* **-gg-** ...

quiz² *v* **-zz-**...

picnic² *v* **-ck-** ...

7.1.4.2 If British English doubles the consonant and American English does not it is shown thus:

worship² *v* **-pp-** (*AmE* **-p-**) ...

7.1.5 If there are 2 possible forms of an INFLECTION both are shown and are divided by *or*:

cac·tus /'kæktəs/ *n* **-tuses** *or* **-ti** /taɪ/

7.1.6 An irregular INFLECTION has its own entry in the dictionary if it comes more than 10 dictionary places away from its base form.

7.1.7 Information is given in ITALICS about the relationship between the INFLECTION and its base form:

came /keɪm/ *past t. of* COME
feet /fiːt/ *pl* of FOOT

7.2 Noun inflections

7.2.1 No information is given for regular plurals of nouns when:

1. the plural is formed by adding *-s*: *part, parts*
2. the plural is formed by changing *-y* to *-ies*: *lady, ladies*
3. the plural is formed by adding *-es* to singular forms ending in any of the sounds /s, ʒ, ʃ, tʃ, dʒ/ (or by adding just *-s* if the word ends in *-e*): *church, churches*; *judge, judges*

The pronunciation of regular plural forms is the pronunciation of the base noun, with /z/ added if the base ends in a vowel sound or VOICED sound, /s/ added if the base ends in a VOICELESS sound, or /ɪz/ added if the base ends in /s, ʒ, ʃ, tʃ, dʒ/.

7.2.2 Irregular plural INFLECTION*s* and the plurals of nouns ending in *-o* are shown in the following way:

man¹ /mæn/ *n* **men** /men/ ...

ma·trix /'meɪtrɪks/ *n* **matrices** /-trɨsiːz/ *or* **matrixes** ...

7.2.3 When the plural is always or sometimes the same as the singular then it is shown by the following CODE*s*:

[Wn1]—these nouns usually form their plural in the regular way but sometimes (as with animals when talking about hunting) the plural is the same as the singular:

li·on /'laɪən/ ... *n* **1** [Wn1] a type of large yellow 4-footed animal of the cat family ...

[Wn2]—these nouns usually have a plural that is the same as the singular but they can also form the plural in the regular way (as when talking about different kinds of animals, esp. fish). The plural form is written out together with the CODE:

chub /tʃʌb/ *n* **chub** *or* **chubs** [Wn2] a type of small fish ...

When only one plural is shown the other is possible but very rare:

salm·on /'sæmən/ *n* **salmon 1** [Wn2;C] a type of large fish ...

[Wn3]—these nouns have a plural that is *always* the same as the singular. The plural form is written out together with the code:

sheep /ʃiːp/ *n* **sheep** [Wn3] a type of grass-eating animal ...

7.3 Adjective and adverb inflections

7.3.1 The COMPARATIVE and SUPERLATIVE forms of an adjective or adverb are shown when they are not formed by using *more* or *most*:

good¹ /gʊd/ *adj* **better** /'betəʳ/, **best** /best/ ...

bad¹ /bæd/ *adj* **worse** /wɜːs ‖ wɜrs/, **worst** /wɜːst ‖ wɜrst/ ...

7.3.2 The following CODE*s* are also used:

[Wa1]—the COMPARATIVE and SUPERLATIVE are formed by adding *-er* and *-est* (or *-r* and *-st* after a final *e*) or changing *-y* (when following a consonant) to *-ier* and *-iest*:

nice /naɪs/ *adj* [Wa1]...

This shows that the COMPARATIVE of *nice* is *nicer* and the SUPERLATIVE *nicest*.

[Wa2]—these usually longer adjectives and adverbs can form their COMPARATIVE and SUPERLATIVE either like the ones in [Wa1] or with *more* and *most*:

large-heart·ed /,· '··◂/ *adj* [Wa2] ...

This shows that *larger-hearted* or *more large-hearted* are acceptable COMPARATIVE*s* and *largest-hearted* or *most large-hearted* are acceptable SUPERLATIVES.

[Wa3]—in these adjectives and adverbs /ə/ is not pronounced when *-(e)r*, *-(e)st*, or *-ly* is added:

sim·ple¹ /'sɪmpəl/ *adj* [Wa3] ...

This shows that the COMPARATIVE *simpler* is pronounced /'sɪmpləʳ/ and the SUPERLATIVE *simplest* is pronounced /'sɪmplɨst/

[Wa5]—these adjectives and adverbs do not have a COMPARATIVE or SUPERLATIVE:

a·tom·ic /ə'tɒmɪk ‖ ə'tɒ-/ *adj* [Wa5] ...

7.4 Verb inflections

7.4.1 If only one INFLECTION is shown it is both the past tense and the past participle:

lay¹ /leɪ/ *v* **laid** /leɪd/ ...

7.4.2 If 2 are shown they are the past tense and the past participle, in that order:

come¹ /kʌm/ *v* **came** /keɪm/, **come** ...

7.4.3 The past tense or past participle are not usually shown if they are formed by the addition of *-ed* (or *-d* after *-e*, *-ee*, *-ye*, and *-oe*) or by changing *-y* to *-ied*. However, if there is a possibility of confusion they are shown:

visa² *v* **-saed** /zəd/ ...

7.4.4 The pronunciation of the past tense and past participle is the pronunciation of the base verb with:

1. /ɪd/ added after bases ending in /d/ or /t/:
   parted /'pɑːtɨd ‖ 'pɑrtɨd/, **gadded** /'gædɨd/
2. /d/ added after bases ending in VOICED sounds other than /d/:
   drugged /drʌgd/
3. /t/ added after bases ending in VOICELESS sounds other than /t/:
   taxed /tækst/

7.4.5.1 When other forms of the verb are irregular they are shown after the past tense and past participle and are explained in ITALICS:

> **do**[1] /duː/ *v* **did** /dɪd/, **done** /dʌn/, *3rd pers. sing. pres. t.* **does** /dəz; *strong* dʌz/, *pres. t. neg. except 3rd pers. sing.* **don't** /dəʊnt/, *3rd pers. sing. pres. t. neg.* **doesn't** /ˈdʌzənt/, *past. t. neg.* **didn't** /ˈdɪdənt/ ...

7.4.5.2 The 3rd person singular present tense is shown only when it is not formed in the same way as the regular plural of nouns.

7.4.5.3 The present participle is shown only if it is not formed in the usual way, by the addition of *-ing* or by the removal of the final *-e* (except for verbs ending in *-ee*, *-oe*, and *-ye*) and the addition of *-ing*. Thus:

> **singe**[1] /sɪndʒ/ *v* **singed,** *pres. p.* **singeing** ...
> **die**[1] /daɪ/ *v* **died,** *pres. p.* **dying** /ˈdaɪ-ɪŋ/ ...

7.4.6 Codes are also used to show verb INFLECTIONS:

[Wv1]—all the forms of this verb (**be**) appear in a table on page xxxviii.

[Wv2]—all the forms of these verbs (AUXILIARY verbs) appear in a table on page xxxviii.

[Wv3]—in these verbs /ə/ is not pronounced when *-ing* or *-er* is added:

> **coup·le**[1] /ˈkʌpəl/ *v* [Wv3] ...

This shows that the INFLECTED parts of this verb are **couples** /ˈkʌpəlz/, **coupling** /ˈkʌplɪŋ/, and **coupled** /ˈkʌpəld/, and that the noun **coupler** is pronounced /ˈkʌpləʳ/.

7.5 Pronoun inflections

These are shown by CODES:

[Wp1]—all the forms of personal PRONOUNS appear in a table on page xxxvii.

[Wp2]—all the forms of these other PRONOUNS appear in a table on page xxxviii.

8 Labels

8.0 Most of the words in this dictionary would be used, and understood, both in speaking and writing anywhere in the world. When the use of a word or phrase is limited in some way, this is shown by a short descriptive statement (LABEL). The LABELS give various kinds of information, and 2 or more of different kinds may be used together.

8.1 A word or phrase that belongs particularly to the English of one country or area is shown by one of these LABELS:

AmE	American English
AustrE	Australian English
BrE	British English
CanE	Canadian English
CarE	Caribbean English
Ind & PakE	Indian and Pakistani English
IrE	Irish English
NZE	New Zealand English
SAfrE	South African English
ScotE	Scottish English

More detail may be given by the use of the compass points, N, S, E, and W. The LABEL *NEngE* tells us that a word is used in the North of England. *London dial* means that a word belongs to the common local speech (DIALECT) of the London area; or *dial* may be used alone, of a word belonging to the common local speech of several places.

> **lakh** ... *n Ind & PakE* 100,000
> **beck**[1] ... *n NEngE* a stream ...
> **in back (of)** *AmE* behind

8.2 A word or phrase that is no longer used, but may be found in old books, is marked *obs* (=OBSOLETE) or, less strongly, *old use*. If a word seems to be passing out of use, it is marked *now rare* or *becoming rare*. The LABEL *rare* is used alone, of an uncommon word, particularly when a commoner word exists with the same meaning.

> **ve·loc·i·pede** ... *n* **1** ... **b** *obs or humor* a bicycle
> **wireless**[2] *n esp. BrE, becoming rare* **1** [U] the means of sending messages in sound ...

8.3 Words that belong particularly to literature or poetry are marked *lit* or *poet*. Words that appear mainly in the AUTHORIZED VERSION of the English Bible are marked *bibl*. Special words used in the law or in medicine are marked *law* or *med*, and words that would be used by specialists in various other subjects are marked *tech* (= TECHNICAL). Again, there is often a commoner word with the same meaning, which would be used by non-specialists.

> **lam·bent** ... *adj lit* ... having a soft light ...
> **ver·i·ly** ... *adv bibl or old use* really; truly
> **scap·u·la** ... *n med* SHOULDER BLADE
> **lar·ce·ny** ... *n* [U;C] *law* (an act of) stealing
> **quark** ... *n tech* the smallest possible piece of material ...

8.4 Words that would be used particularly on ceremonial occasions, in government writing, etc., are marked *fml* (= formal). Words that would seem unsuitable at this level of formality are marked *not fml*, and those that belong more particularly to friendly informal speech or private letters are marked *infml* (= informal). A word marked *sl* (= SLANG) would not often be used at all in writing or for serious purposes; it may be part of the private language of one social group, such as soldiers, criminals, or schoolchildren.

> **pray**[2] *adv fml or lit* ... please ...
> **get** ... *v* ... *not fml* **1** ... to receive
> **tel·ly** ... *n* ... *infml esp. BrE* television
> **fag**[3] *n sl* cigarette

8.5 Unpleasant words connected with sex or the bowels are marked *taboo*. These should be avoided in formal society, or when talking to strangers or children.

> **shit**[2] *n taboo* **1** [U] solid waste from the bowels ...

8.6 Some words show that the speaker dislikes the person or thing he is talking about. These are marked *derog* (= DEROGATORY). They include rude words, to be avoided, about race and nationality, of which the worst are also marked *taboo*. The opposite of this is *apprec* (= APPRECIATIVE). Polite words for things that are felt to be sad, dirty, or unpleasant are marked *euph* (= EUPHEMISTIC). Words or phrases that are used in a joking way are marked *humor* (= HUMOROUS); those that sound foolishly overimportant are marked *pomp* (= POMPOUS).

> **oth·er·world·ly** ... *adj sometimes derog* more concerned with the things of the spirit or mind ...

pom·my ... *n Austr & NZE sl, often derog* ... an Englishman ...
forward-look·ing...*adj* [Wa5] *apprec* planning for or concerned with the future
senior cit·i·zen ... *n euph* an old person ...
buck·et[1] ... *n* ... **4 kick the bucket** *humor sl* to die
pen[4] *v* ... *pomp* to write with a pen

8.7 Words or phrases marked *nonstandard* are perhaps widely used, but are considered by teachers and examiners to be incorrect.

no·how ... *adv nonstandard or humor* in no way ...
don't ... *contr. of* ... **2** *nonstandard, esp. AmE* does not

8.8 Words or phrases are labelled that are borrowed from foreign languages but are still felt to be foreign, and are often pronounced in a foreign way. They are marked according to their language of origin, *Fr* (French), *Ger* (German), *Sp* (Spanish), *It* Italian, *Lat* (Latin), and *Gk* (Greek).

dé·tente ... *n* ... *Fr* (a state of) easier and calmer political relations ...
zeit·geist ... *n* ... *Ger* ... the general spirit of a period in history

8.9 The official names (TRADEMARK*s*) under which products are sold are marked *tdmk* as a protection in law.

biro ... *n* ... *tdmk* BALLPOINT ...
land rov·er ... *n tdmk* (*often cap.*) a type of car ...

9 Punctuation in the dictionary

9.0 In order to use this dictionary properly, you should understand some of the special ways in which certain PUNCTUATION MARK*s* are used.

9.1 Round BRACKET*s* ( ) are used:

9.1.1 to show the kind of subject or object usually used with a verb, or the kind of noun an adjective gives information about:

lay[1] ... *v* ... **5** ... (of birds, insects, etc.) to produce (an egg or eggs) ...

This shows that *birds* and *insects* are the usual subjects of the verb **lay** and *eggs* are the usual objects, as in *The hen laid an egg.*

hand·some ... *adj* ... **1 a** (esp. of men) good-looking; of attractive appearance **b** (esp. of women) strong-looking; attractive with a firm large appearance rather than ...

The first meaning **a** usually REFER*s* TO men: meaning **b** usually REFER*s* TO women.

9.1.2 to show that a word or phrase or part of a word can be either included or left out.

For example, the verb **polish** has the code [T1 (UP)]: this means that one could say *He polished his shoes* or *He polished up his shoes.*

One of the explanations of **fry** is "to (cause to) be cooked in hot fat or oil". This means one could say *I fried an egg* or *The egg was frying.*

In the example sentence *He was commonly supposed (to be) foolish*, the BRACKET*s* mean that *to be* can be missed out.

N *abbrev. for:* North(ern)

This means **N** is the ABBREVIATION for *North* and *Northern.*

ma·gen·ta ... *n, adj* ... (of) the colour ...

This means that the word *of* is needed in the explanation of **magenta** only when the latter is used as an adjective.

9.1.3 to show various other kinds of information about a word or its grammar:

id ... *n* (in Freudian PSYCHOLOGY) ...
moo·cow ... *n* ... (*a child's word for*) a cow

See also **Meanings having more than one pattern** (page xxxv).

9.2 SQUARE BRACKET*s* [ ] are used only round the grammatical CODE*s*. (See page xxxviii).

9.3 The SLASH / means that either of 2 choices is possible. For example, the verb **argue** may be followed by *about* or *over* (a subject), or by *with* (a person), or by both. This state of affairs is shown in the CODE box in the form [IØ (*about/over* and/or *with*)], and in an example sentence as: *He argued about/over politics with George.* Under **clock** will be found the expression **put the clock on/forward,** another example of a choice between 2 words.

It also begins and ends pronunciations and surrounds pronunciation SYMBOL*s*.

9.4 The double bar ‖ divides a British pronunciation from an American one, as with **worse,** whose pronunciation is shown as /wɜːs ‖ wɜrs/.

9.5 A straight line | is used to separate examples of a single meaning:

hand˙o·ver *v adv* ... to give (somebody or something) into someone else's care: *The thief was handed over to the police.* | *Hand the money over*

9.6 A straight line — is used to introduce a CROSS-REFERENCE or related form:

hand·shake ... *n* an act of taking each other's right hand ... —see also GOLDEN HANDSHAKE

ma·lev·o·lent ... *adj* ... having or expressing a wish to do evil ... —**-lence** *n* [U]—~**ly** *adv*

This line — is also used after another name or spelling of a word:

lap·wing ... also **pewit, peewit**— *n* a type of small bird ...

9.7 The bent line ~ shows that some letters can be joined to the end of the word, as, for example, ~**ly** can be joined to **affectionate** to form **affectionately.** See also **Related words listed without explanation,** page xxvii.

9.8 The HYPHEN - indicates a PREFIX or SUFFIX that may be added to another word. See also **Related words listed without explanation,** and **Affixes and combining forms,** page xxvii.

It is also used to show the start and end of the pronunciation of part of a word where it is not shown in full, or to separate SYLLABLE*s*.

9.9 QUOTATION MARK*s* " " are used as in ordinary writing. They enclose especially conversations in examples and (parts of) example sentences from literature or the SEU (Survey of English Usage) collection of spoken and written material.

10 Examples

10.1 This dictionary contains a very large number of example phrases and sentences, many of them taken from the SEU (Survey of English Usage) collection of spoken and written material. They show how a word is actually used in English, and often give you additional information about it as well. They are printed in ITALICS and come after a COLON (:) at the end of an explanation individual examples in a group are separated from each other by a straight line (|).

10.2 Figurative examples Sometimes a word can be used, with the same meaning and in the same pattern, both for things in the real world and also for FIGURATIVE things in the mind that cannot be seen or touched. When this happens, the 2 are treated together as one meaning, and not as 2 separate ones. An example of a FIGURATIVE use is marked (fig.):

> **fat**[1] ... *adj* ... **3** thick and well-filled: *a fat book* | (fig.) *a fat bank account*

Here the book and the bank account are *fat* in the same way, though it is only the fatness of the book that can be measured in inches.

11 Cross-references

11.0 The reader's attention is drawn to related words in other parts of the dictionary in several ways.

11.1 Direct cross-reference When a word has the same meaning as, but is less common than, another word, and that other word is not in our special list of 2,000 words, we show the meaning of the less common word simply by printing the main word in small CAPITAL letters, like this:

> **pe·wit** ... *n* LAPWING

This means that to find the meaning of **pewit**, you should look up **lapwing.**

11.2 Cross-reference for explanation Often, in giving the meaning of a word, we have to use a word or a meaning that is not in our special list of 2,000 words. We print such a word in small CAPITAL letters, like this:

> **la·ma·se·ry** ... *n* a building or group of buildings where LAMA*s* live together

> **land breeze** ... *n* a light wind (BREEZE) blowing from the land to the sea

This means that to find out the meaning of **lama** and **breeze**, you should look them up in their own place in the dictionary.

11.3 "See" When a word in the dictionary is used only in combination with another word, forming a compound that is also given in the dictionary, all we do is to print that compound in small CAPITAL letters, with the word "see" in front of it, like this:

> **lau·re·ate** ... *adj* see POET LAUREATE

This tells you to look up **poet laureate,** where you will find out how **laureate** is used.

11.4 "Compare" This is an instruction to look up another word, which is printed in small CAPITAL letters, with the word "compare" in front of it, like this:

> **le·ga·to** ... *adj*, *adv* (of music) smoothly, with the notes sliding smoothly into each other —compare STACCATO

The reader is advised to look up this other word (here, **staccato**) in its own place, so that he may understand an important likeness to or difference from the word he originally looked up.

This instruction is used very often and in various ways. First, it is used for words related in meaning: after the def. of **macaroni** we find "—compare SPAGHETTI, VERMICELLI". Then, for words often confused or used wrongly: because they sound alike, as with "**etymology** ... —compare ENTOMOLOGY"; or because native speakers have difficulty with them, as with "**plausible** ... —compare FEASIBLE"; or because it has been found that foreign learners cannot easily recognize the difference between them, as with "**over** ... —compare ABOVE". For this last type we have drawn on the experience of many teachers, on language testing material, and on the findings of ERROR ANALYSIS studies.

11.5 "See also" This is a suggestion to look up another word, which is printed in small CAPITAL letters with the words "see also" in front of it, like this:

> **la·ma** ... *n* a Buddhist priest —see also DALAI LAMA

If the reader looks up this other word in its own place, he will find additional information that relates to the word he originally looked up. Lists of related PHRASAL verbs are often shown in this way at the end of the entry for the simple verb from which they are formed, like this:

> **rain**[2] *v* ... —see also RAIN DOWN, RAIN OFF, RAIN ON, RAIN OUT

11.6 "Opposite" The word which expresses the opposite meaning to that of a word you have looked up is printed in thick letters, with the word "opposite" in front of it, like this:

> **sign in** *v adv* to record one's name when arriving ... —opposite **sign out**

This tells you that **sign out** is the opposite in meaning of **sign in**, that is, it means "to record one's name when leaving". You do not need to look up **sign out** in its own place in order to use it correctly in relation to **sign in.**

11.7 Usage Notes These are described on page xxviii.

12 Idioms

12.0 An IDIOM is a fixed group of words with a special meaning that cannot be guessed from the combination of the actual words used. Thus, **to let one's hair down** is not connected with anything done to one's hair: it means to enjoy oneself or behave wildly. For the rules about whether a group of words is treated as an IDIOM under one of those words, or given its own place in the dictionary, see **Order of entries**, 2.0, page xiv.

12.1 In this dictionary IDIOM*s* are written in heavy black print thus: **let one's hair down.** They are listed in alphabetical order after all other meanings and each has a number.

12.2 An IDIOM is usually found under the word that

has the most IDIOMATIC meaning. Thus **a bone of contention** is under **bone** because *bone* is used in a more IDIOMATIC way than *contention*. If all the words are IDIOMATIC then it will be included under the most unusual word. Thus **a pig in a poke** is under **poke.** If you cannot find the IDIOM under the first word you choose, then look under the other words.

12.3 a, the, and the INFINITIVE marker **to** are not included at the beginning of an IDIOM unless they form a fixed part of it.

12.4 When an IDIOM includes **one, someone,** or **something** these are exchanged for a suitable noun or PRONOUN (word standing for a noun) when being used. Thus **someone** in **not know someone from Adam** becomes **him** in the sentence *I don't know him from Adam.*

12.5 When an IDIOM starts with **not** it need not always be introduced by *not* but must be used in a NEGATIVE way. Thus **not think much of** can be used in the sentence *I didn't expect to think much of the play.*

12.6 The sign / is used for dividing different possible forms of an IDIOM, as in **beat/run one's head against a brick wall**.

12.7 Where possessive forms of nouns or PRONOUN*s* are shown as **~'s** or **~s'** it means that **of ~** is usually possible. Where only **of ~** is shown then this form is fixed and the **~s'** or **~s'** form is wrong.

12.8 Possible additional wording is shown in round BRACKET*s* thus: **(buy) a pig in a poke.**

13 Collocations

13.1 A COLLOCATION is a group of words which are often used together to form a natural-sounding combination. In this dictionary COLLOCATION*s* are shown in 3 ways:
(1) by example in example sentences
(2) by explanation in the Usage Notes
(3) in heavy black type inside round BRACKET*s* if the COLLOCATION is found very often or if it has almost become a fixed phrase (but not an IDIOM). In this case, it is introduced by "in the phr." or "esp./sometimes/usu. in the phr." or "in such phrs. as".

ken[2] *n* ... knowledge; the limits of knowledge (esp. in the phrs. **beyond/outside/not within one's ken**) ...

13.2 Some words are explained in the course of explaining another related word, but do not appear again separately in the dictionary; like **lachrymal gland** in the following:

lach·ry·mal ... *adj* ... of or concerning tears or the organ (**lachrymal gland**) of the body that produces them

14 Related words listed without explanation

14.1 At the end of a word's explanation in this dictionary you will sometimes find words that can be formed by adding a SUFFIX to the word being explained. Such a related word is not explained because its meaning should be clear when the meaning of the SUFFIX is added to the meaning of the base word. It will always be followed by a part of speech, and may also have a pronunciation, a CODE, and an example sentence.

14.2 There are 3 ways of showing such words:

14.2.1—**~ness** *n* [U] as at the end of **crowded.** This means that **-ness** is added onto **crowded** to give **crowdedness** with the meaning "the state of being crowded".

14.2.2 —**-lation** *n* [U;C: (*of*)] as at the end of **violate.** This is used when the base word changes slightly before the SUFFIX is added, and means that **-lation** (= **-l** + **-ation**) is added onto a shortened form of **vi·o·late** (*vio*) to give **violation** with the meaning "(an example of) the act of violating".

14.2.3 curliness *n* [U] as at the end of **curly.** This is used when the base word is short and changes slightly before the SUFFIX is added, and means that **-ness** is added to **curly** to give **curliness** with the meaning "the state of being curly".

15 Affixes and combining forms

15.1 Many English words are built up by adding one or more AFFIXes to a base word; for example **unhappiness** is formed from **happy** by adding 2 AFFIXes: a PREFIX, **un-**, and a SUFFIX, **-ness**. These are parts of words. which cannot stand alone but which have either a meaning, or a use in the language, or both. All the more important AFFIXes can be found at their own alphabetical place in the dictionary, where, for example, the reader is told that **un-** is a PREFIX, used at the beginning of a word. It turns an adjective or an adverb into another adjective or adverb with the meaning "not", and this is shown in the style [*adj→adj*], [*adv→adv*]. It also turns a verb into another verb [*v→v*] with the meaning "showing the opposite action": **wrap** becomes **unwrap.**

15.2 The dictionary also shows that **-ness** is a SUFFIX, used at the end of a word. This form has no meaning when used alone, but is used for turning an adjective, like **happy,** into a noun [*adj→n*] like **happiness,** and means "the stated condition, quality, or degree". Examples are always given of words formed by the addition of these AFFIXes.

15.3 Other English words are built up by the use of COMBINING FORM*s*, which have their own meaning and are joined to another word or part of a word to make a new one. For example, the word **Russo-American** is formed from **American** by adding **Russo-**, a COMBINING FORM of the word **Russian.** The COMBINING FORM **-proof** has the same spelling as the word **proof,** but a different meaning. It turns nouns into adjectives [*n→adj*] with the meaning "giving protection against" and the dictionary gives examples such as **waterproof, soundproof.** These examples may or may not appear elsewhere in the dictionary.

15.4 This clear treatment of AFFIXes and COMBINING FORM*s* should enable you to guess the meanings of compound words that you may meet.

16 Usage Notes

16.1 This is another way, besides CROSS-REFERENCE, in which the connection of a word with others in the dictionary might be shown. In this case, 2 or more words of related meaning may be considered together, with an instruction such as "**rent** ... —see HIRE (USAGE)". A simple comparison might not be enough to show that in *BrE* a person **hires** an evening suit and **rents** a flat, while in *AmE* a person **rents** both. Another note shows the different ways in which **high** and **tall** are used, although both are for measuring distances from the ground. A number of words for games have USAGE Notes showing, for example, that a person plays **tennis** with a **racket** on a **court**. The note at **fire** shows that people **set fire** to things, and things **catch fire.**

16.2 The USAGE notes give a good deal of information about the grammar of words, and about fine differences of meaning. Sometimes this is expressed in the form of a table, as with **must** and **have to**; sometimes the words are compared in sentences, as with the set that includes **lonely**, **solitary**, and **alone**. Where the native speaker might feel real doubt about a question, such as whether to use a singular or plural verb after "**either** *of the men* ...", the Note explains what is the most common practice, and also advises on the best form for use in formal writing. Difficulties caused by changes in the language are dealt with in the same way, as with the use of **hopefully** to mean "It is hoped that ...". A good deal of language change in *BrE* is, like this example, the result of American influence, and some USAGE Notes point to cases where an *AmE* expression is particularly disliked by old-fashioned British speakers.

16.3 The USAGE Notes give many examples, and where it is necessary to show what is not acceptable they sometimes give an example of an incorrect sentence, marked * in accordance with the practice of modern writers on grammar. Although some teachers may be worried by this idea, in the belief that one should never show students examples of "wrong" English, many advanced students agree that this is the clearest way to show the working of a rule.

17 Grammar in the dictionary

17.0 Besides the familiar expressions "noun", "adjective", "verb", etc., this dictionary gives more detailed descriptions of the behaviour of words in English. This information, which is in the form of letters and numbers, is shown between SQUARE BRACKET*s*, [ ]. These letters and numbers are explained thoroughly in the following pages, which you should read with care if you want to get the most out of your dictionary. When you have done this, you will be able to remind yourself quickly of what the letters and numbers mean by looking at the tables inside the back cover.

17.1 THE BIG LETTERS

17.1.1 The big letters give information about the way a word works in a sentence or about the position it can fill: for example, they tell you whether a noun can or cannot have a plural, whether an adjective can come before or after a noun, or both, and whether a verb can have an OBJECT.

17.1.2 Positions

17.1.2.1 Positions I and II in the following explanations of the big letters show the position of nouns, adjectives, and adverbs round a main noun. Position I is *before* the noun: thus, in the sentence *He gave her a* **new** *car*, the adjective **new** is in position I, before the noun *car*. Position II is *after* the main noun: thus, in the sentence *She was* 47 *years* **old**, the adjective **old** is in position II, after the noun *years*.

17.1.2.2 Positions III and IV show the position of OBJECT*s* and COMPLEMENT*s* after a verb. Position III is the position directly after a verb, and position IV is the position that a second OBJECT or COMPLEMENT has after a first OBJECT OF COMPLEMENT: thus, in the sentence *The* **grateful** *president* **elect** *gave* **Margaret** *a new* **car, grateful** is in position I, **elect** is in position II, **Margaret** is in position III, and **car** is in position IV. **New** in *a* **new** *car* is in position I. In *My* **trouser** *legs got* **wet, trouser** is in position I, **wet** is in position III, and there is nothing in positions II and IV.

17.1.2.3 POSITION

	I	
She gave him a	**new**	coat.
His	**new**	coat was black.
	II	
The wood was 3 inches	**thick.**	
The president	**elect**	visited the factory.
	III	
She was	**happy.**	
He gave the	**boy**	a boat.
He kicked the	**ball.**	
	IV	
He made him	**king.**	
He gave the boy a	**boat.**	

17.1.3

[A] = adjectives and nouns that come in position I, before a noun.
Examples: *the* **main** (adj) *difficulty* | **General** (n) *Smith-Fortescue* | *a* **trouser** (n) *leg* | **atomic** (adj) *scientists*

[B] = adjectives that can come in position I or in positions III and IV as COMPLEMENT*s*. (Most English adjectives are of this type, so an adjective that can fill all these positions in all its meanings is not marked at all.)
Examples: *a* **happy** *man* | *The man became* **happy**. | *She made him* **happy**

[C] = nouns that can be counted, usually as UNIT*s* (*dog, box*), but in some cases as types (*wine*). They can be used with *one* or with *a/an*. (Most English nouns are of this type, so a noun that behaves in this way in all its meanings is not marked at all.)
Examples: *a/one* **dog** | *3* **dogs** | *4* **boxes** | *the 5 best* **wines** *of France* | *felt strong* **desires** | *become a* **general**

[D] = verbs that are followed by 2 nouns (*boy, book*; *wall, paint*), PRONOUN*s* (*him, them*), or nounlike expressions (*what to do*), which come in positions III and IV, often as INDIRECT OBJECT (*the boy*) + DIRECT OBJECT (*a book*). These nouns, PRONOUN*s*, etc., always represent (REFER TO) something else, not each other.
Examples:
(**Give** *the boy a book.*)
(**Give** *a book to the boy.*) } [D1 (*to*)]
(**Buy** *him a book.*)
(**Buy** *a book for him.*) } [D1 (*for*)]
Tell *the boy the truth.* [D1 (*to*)] | **Tell** *the boy what to do.* [D6b] |
(**Spray** *the wall with paint.*)
(**Spray** *paint on the wall.*) } [D1 + *with/on*] | *It* **cost** *me £6.* [D1] |
He **made** *her a good husband.* [D1 (*for*)] | *They* **put** *the difficulty* **down to** (v adv prep) *his failure* [D1]

[E] = adjectives, adverbs, and nouns that can come in position II.
Examples: *the president* **elect** (adj) | *3 years* **old** (adj) | *3 years* **ago** (adv) | *Saadi* **Pasha** (n)

[F] = adjectives and adverbs that come in positions III and IV as COMPLEMENT*s* (usu. after *be* or *seem*).
Examples: *She was* **asleep** (adj). | *He found her* **asleep** (adj). | *She was* **abroad** (adv). | *He found her* **abroad** (adv). | *The meeting was* **yesterday/upstairs** (adv). | *She was* **happy** *to do that* (adj). [F3] | *I'm not* **sure** *where to go* (adj) [F6b]

[GC] = nouns that usually represent groups. In the plural they take a plural verb, but in the singular they can take either a singular or (esp. in British English) a plural verb and plural PRONOUN.
Examples: *3 different* **committees** | *The* **committee** *is/are angry because it is/they are divided*

[GU] = nouns and adjectives that have no separate plural form. The nouns (*Admiralty*, *left*) usually represent groups, and can take either a singular or (esp. in British English) a plural verb. The adjectives (*the accused*) take a singular verb and PRONOUN for one person or thing, and a plural verb and PRONOUN for more than one.
Examples: *The* **Admiralty** (n) *is/are divided.* | *The* **left** (n) *is/are divided.* | *The* **accused** (adj) *is angry because he wants a new trial.* | *All the* **accused** (adj) *are angry because they want new trials*

[H] = adverbs that can be used with PREPOSITION*s* (*within*, *into*) and with other adverbs, esp. with those having the same form as PREPOSITION*s* (*through*).
Examples: *The bullet went* **right** *through* (*the wall*). | *It was ready* **well** *within the time*. | *It fell* **splash** *into the water*

[I] = verbs, most of which are INTRANSITIVE*s*, that need not be followed by anything in position III or IV, and need have no ADVERBIAL. An [I] verb followed by nothing at all is shown with the zero mark [Ø].
Examples: *We* **paused.** [IØ] | *We* **smoked.** [IØ] | *The sun* **rose**. [IØ] | *The bridge* **blew up** (v adv). [IØ] | *Yes, I* **can**. [IØ] | *They* **came**. [IØ] | *They* **came** *to hate her*. [I3] | *They* **came** *running*. [I4] | *If anyone asks you, don't* **let on** (v adv). [IØ] | *I* **helped**. [IØ] | *This factory* **is closing** *soon* [I4]

[L] = LINKing verbs, which are followed by something that represents (REFER*s* TO) the subject. This "something" may be a nounlike expression (*President* [L1]), or an adjective (*famous* [L7]) serving as COMPLEMENT in position III, or an ADVERBIAL (*here*, *to Harlow* [L9]).
Examples: *She* **became** *President*. [L1] | *She* **became** *famous*. [L7] | *She* **acted as** (v prep) *President*. [L1] | *It* **cost** *£6*. [L1] | *He* **ended up** (v adv) *rich*. [L7] | *The car's* **going** *up the hill* [L9]

[N] = nouns that are VOCATIVE*s*; they can be used in the singular in direct address to one person.
Examples: *Goodbye*, **doctor**! | *Goodbye*, **General**!

[P] = nouns and adjectives that are used only with plural verbs and PRONOUN*s*.
Examples: *The* **police** (n) *are here*. [P] | *The* **trousers** (n) *are here*. *They fit me*. [P] | *The* **dramatics** (n) *of the performance were interesting*. [P] | *Do the* **dead** (adj) *ever return?* [*the* + P]

[R] = nouns that are names (*God*, the *Earth*) or namelike (the *sack*). They are used either always with *the* or never with *the*.
Examples: **God** | *the* **Earth** | *got the* **sack**

[S] = nouns that are special singular nouns and can be used with *a* or *an* but not with *one*. They cannot be counted, and have no plural form.
Examples: *Have a* **think** *about it*. | *I heard a* **babble** *of voices*

[T] = verbs, many of which are TRANSITIVE*s*, that are followed by a noun or nounlike expression in position III as a DIRECT OBJECT which does not represent (REFER TO) the subject, unless REFLEXIVE.

Examples: *She* **kicked** *the boy/him.* [T1] | *She* **said** "*I'm here.*" [T1] | *She* **said** (*that*) *she was there.* [T5a] | *We* **looked at** (v prep) *the man.* [T1] | *She* **blew up** (v adv) *the bridge.* [T1] | **Tell** *the boy.* [T1] | **Tell** *the truth.* [T1] | *They* **considered** *him.* [T1] | *I* **helped** *him.* [T1] | *We* **put off** (v adv) *holding the meeting.* [T4] | *If anyone asks you, don't* **let on** (v adv) *that you know.* [T5] | *I can't* **put up with** (v adv prep) *all that noise.* [T1] | *The firm has* **decided** *to close its London branch* [T3]

[U] = uncountable nouns that cannot be counted as nouns of type [C] can. Nouns of type [U] take a singular verb and are not usually used with either *a/an* or *one*.

Examples: **Sugar/Love** *is sweet.* [U] | *He came by* **car.** [U] | *felt strong* **desire** [U] | *a lot of* **earth** [U] | *lots of* **wine** [U] | **Dramatics** *is interesting* [U]

[V] = verbs that are followed, in position III, by a 2-part DIRECT OBJECT. The first part is a nounlike expression, and the second part is an INFINITIVE with or without *to*, an *-ing* form, or a past participle. Note that *I* **saw** *the man leave* [V2] (without *to*) can become, in the PASSIVE, *The man was seen to leave* (with *to*).

Examples: *I* **saw** *the man leave* (= The man was seen to leave). [V2] | *I* **helped** *him clean the windows.* [V2] | *I* **helped** *him to clean the windows.* [V3] | **Tell** *the boy to do it.* [V3] | *I* **asked** *the man to do it.* [V3] | *I* **saw** *the man leaving.* [V4] | *to* **have** *a house built* [V8] | *We* **looked at** (v prep) *the man jumping.* [V4a] | *They* **inhibited** *her* **from** (v prep) *doing it* [V4b]

Some information about the forms of words is shown by the letters [Wa] (adjectives and adverbs), [Wn] (nouns), [Wp] (PRONOUN*s*), and [Wv] (verbs). (**Note** Numbers after the letter [W] do not have the same meaning as those numbers which may appear after any of the other letters, and which are explained below.)

[Wa] Some adjectives and adverbs have irregular forms of the COMPARATIVE and SUPERLATIVE (*good/well, better, best*). These irregular forms are given with the adjectives and adverbs themselves.

Most adjectives and adverbs form their COMPARATIVE and SUPERLATIVE with *more* and *most*; **(intelligent(ly),** *more* **intelligent(ly),** *most* **intelligent(ly)).** The letters [Wa] are used for adjectives and adverbs that do not belong to either of these 2 types, or that have special rules for the pronunciation of their COMPARATIVE or SUPERLATIVE.

[Wa1] = usually short adjectives and adverbs that form their COMPARATIVE and SUPERLATIVE in one of the following 3 ways:

nice, nice*r*, **nice***st* (+ *-r/-st*)
fast, fast*er*, **fast***est* (+ *-er/-est*)
angry, angr*ier*, **angr***iest* (*y* becomes *i* + *-er/est*).

[Wa2] = longer adjectives and adverbs that can form their COMPARATIVE and SUPERLATIVE either like those in [Wa1] or with *more* and *most*.

Examples: **secure** } **secure***r* **secure***st* / *more* **secure** *most* **secure**

large-hearted } **large***r***-hearted** **large***st***-hearted** / *more* **large-hearted** *most* **large-hearted**

well-known } **better-known** **best-known** / *more* **well-known** *most* **well-known**

[Wa3] = adjectives and adverbs in which /ə/ is not pronounced when *-(e)r*, *-(e)st*, or *-ly* is added.

Examples: **simple** /ˈsɪmpəl/, **simpler** /ˈsɪmpləʳ/, **simplest** /ˈsɪmplɨst/, **simply** /ˈsɪmpli/.

[Wa4] = adverbs in which the letters *-ally* are pronounced /li/.
Examples: **historically** /hɪ'stɒrɪkli/ (from **historical** /hɪ'stɒrikəl/)
poetically /pəʊ'etɪkli/ (from **poetic** /pəʊ'etɪk/).

[Wa5] = adjectives and adverbs that do not usually form a COMPARATIVE OF SUPERLATIVE.
Examples: *an* **atomic** *bomb* | *the* **main** *problem*

[Wn] Nouns of type [Wn] are usually the names of certain animals and plants. Some of these have 2 plurals, an ordinary plural with *-s* and a plural exactly like the singular; others have only one plural, exactly the same as the singular; the numbers show these facts about the word forms (INFLECTION*s*) of these nouns.

[Wn1] = nouns that usually change (add *-s*) in the plural, but sometimes (as with animals when talking about hunting) have a plural that is the same as the singular.
Examples: *He photographed several* **lions.** / *He shot several* **lion.** [Wn1]
There were 3 **pheasants** *for sale.* / *He went looking for* **pheasant** *because he was hungry.* [Wn1]

[Wn2] = nouns that usually or often do *not* change (add *-s*) in the plural, but can do so (as when talking about different kinds of animal, esp. fish, with the same name, or about insects or other small animals which cause disease or damage).
Examples: *He caught 5* **salmon.** / *The Atlantic and Pacific* **salmons** *are closely related.* [Wn2]
There were 2 **quails** *for sale.* / *He shot* **quail** *to make money.* [Wn2]
The plant was covered in **greenfly.** / *There are 2* **greenflies** *on my hand.* [Wn2]
This animal is infected with **hookworm.** / *2 large* **hookworms** *were found in his stomach.* [Wn2]

[Wn3] = nouns that never change in the plural. It is the same as the singular.
Examples: *There was a* **sheep** *in the garden.* / *The garden was full of* **sheep.** [Wn3]
He bought a **grouse**/*3* **grouse** *for dinner.* [Wn3]

[Wp] PRONOUN*s* marked [Wp] are shown in tables:

[Wp1] All the forms of these (personal) PRONOUN*s* appear on page xxxvii.

[Wp2] All the forms of these other (relative) PRONOUN*s* appear on page xxxviii.

[Wv] These letters show certain facts about the forms and pronunciation of verbs, or direct the reader to tables.

[Wv1] All the forms of this verb (**be**) appear on page xxxviii.

[Wv2] All the forms of these verbs (AUXILIARY verbs) appear on page xxxviii.

[Wv3] = verbs in which /ə/ is not pronounced when *-ing* or *-er* is added.
Examples: **couple** /'kʌpəl/, **coupling** /'kʌplɪŋ/, **coupler** /'kʌpləʳ/
(Compare **couples** /'kʌpəlz/, **coupled** /'kʌpəld/.)

[Wv4] = verbs that are often used in the *-ing* form as adjectives.
Example: *her* **flying** *feet*

[Wv5] = verbs that are often used in the *-ed* form as adjectives.
Example: **plaited** *hair*|**frozen** *fish*

[Wv6] = verbs that are not usually found in tenses that use the *-ing* form, with forms of the verb *be*.

Example: *He* **knows** *how to speak French*.

(The code [Wv6] means that you cannot say * *He's* **knowing** *French*. Compare *He's* **learning** *French*.

[X] = verbs that are followed in position III by a nounlike expression as DIRECT OBJECT and by a second expression that represents (REFERS TO) the DIRECT OBJECT. This second expression is a COMPLEMENT in position IV and may be a nounlike expression (*fool* [X1]) or an adjective (*foolish* [X7]), or an ADVERBIAL (*in the box, here* [X9]).

Examples: *They* **considered** *him a fool.* [X1] | *They* **regarded** *him* **as** (v prep) a *fool.* [X1] | *They* **considered** *him foolish.* [X7] | *They* **regarded** *him* **as** (v prep) *foolish.* [X7] | **Put** *it in the box.* [X9] | **Put** *it here.* [X9] | *He* **made** *her a good wife* [X1]

Note: An adjective without a letter is considered to be of type [B]. A noun without a letter is considered to be of type [C]. All verbs have at least one letter. Adverbs ending in *-ly* have no letters except sometimes [Wa], and few other adverbs have them.

Adjectives may be of one or more of the following types: [A], [B], [E], [F], [GU], [P], [Wa]

Adverbs may be of one or more of the following types: [E], [F], [H], [Wa]

Nouns may be of one or more of the following types: [A], [C], [E], [GC], [GU], [N], [P], [R], [S], [U], [Wn]

Verbs may be of one or more of the following types: [D], [I], [L], [T], [V], [Wv], [X]

(Note: These verb patterns are also listed in, G. Leech and J. Svartvik, *A Communicative Grammar of English* (Longman, 1975), 835–872, and you can find explanations of them in greater detail in, R. Quirk, S. Greenbaum, G. Leech and J. Svartvik, *A Grammar of Contemporary English*, (Longman, 1972) 12.29–70.)

Pronouns may have the letters [Wp], directing the reader to a table.

17.2 THE NUMBERS

17.2.1 The numbers give information about the way the rest of a phrase or CLAUSE is made up in relation to the word being described. They have the same meaning wherever they appear, except after the letters [Wa], [Wn], [Wp], and [Wv], which have their own rules.

[Ø] means that nothing need follow the verb in positions III or IV, or as an ADVERBIAL. It is used in [IØ].

Examples: *We* **paused.** [IØ] | *We* **smoked.** [IØ] | *The bridge* **blew up** (v adv). [IØ] | *Yes, I* **can.** [IØ] | *No,* I **haven't.** [IØ] | *They* **came.** [IØ] | *I* **helped** [IØ]

[1] means that a verb is followed by a nounlike expression in position III [L1]; [T1] or 2 nounlike expressions in positions III and IV [D1]; [X1].

Examples: *She* **became** *President.* [L1] | *She* **became** *what she wanted to be.* [L1] | *She* **kicked** *him.* [T1] | **Give** *the boy a book.* [D1] | *They* **considered** *him a fool.* [X1] | *She* **blew up** (v adv) *the bridge.* [T1] | *They* **regarded** *him* **as** (v prep) *a fool.* [X1] | *I* **helped** *her.* [T1] | *I* **told** *him.* [T1] | *We* **put off** (v adv) *the meeting* [T1]

[2] means that a verb is followed by the INFINITIVE without *to* (*fly, clean, leave*).

Examples: *I* **can** *fly.* [I2] | *I* **helped** *clean the windows.* [T2] | *I* **saw** *the man leave* [V2]

[3] means that a word is followed by the INFINITIVE with *to* (*to go, to see, to climb, to believe, to please, to answer, to know*).

Examples: *I* **want** *to go.* [T3] | *I* **came** *to see the truth.* [I3] | **Tell** *the boy to go.* [V3] | *I* **want** *him to go.* [V3] | *a* **yen** *to be alone* [S3] | *an* **attempt** *to climb the mountain* [C3] | *There is some* **reason** *to believe he will come.* [U3] | *John is* **eager** *to please.* [F3] | *John is* **easy** *to please; an* **easy** *person to please.* [B3] | *They* **called on** (v prep) *him to answer.* [V3] | *He* **turned out** (v adv) *to know the answer* [L3]

[4] means that a verb is followed by the *-ing* form (*singing, running, cooking, dancing*).

Examples: *I* **enjoyed** *singing/their singing.* [T4] | *She* **came** *running.* [I4] | *He* **watched** *mother cooking the dinner.* [V4] | *We* **put off** (v adv) *holding the meeting.* [T4] | *She* **ended up** (v adv) *dancing on the table* [L4]

[5] means that a word is followed by *that* + a CLAUSE.

Examples: *I* **know** (*that*) *he'll come.* [T5a] | **Tell** *the boy* (*that*) *it's time.* [D5a] | **Tell** *him so.* [D5b] | *He* **warned** *her* (*that*) *he would come.* [D5a] | *a* **desire** *that she* (*should*) *go* [C5c] | *Is there* **proof** *that he is here?* [U5] | *He is* **eager** *that she* (*should*) *go.* [F5c] | **happy** (*that*) *she did it* [F5a] | *If anyone asks you, don't* **let on** (v adv) *that you know* [T5]

[6] means that a word is followed in position III by a *wh*-word, *how*, or *as if*, + either a CLAUSE (*who should go; why he came*) or a phrase (*where to go*). (Note that any verb marked [1] can be followed by *what* + a CLAUSE. A verb is marked [6] only if it will take the other *wh*-patterns.)

Examples: *He* **decided** *who should go.* [T6a] | **Tell** *me where to go.* [D6b] | *the* **reason** *why he came* [C6a] | *I'm not* **sure** *where to go.* [F6b] | *She* **considered** *when to go.* [T6b] | *If anyone asks you, don't* **let on** (v adv) *where you live* [T6a]

[7] means that a verb is followed by an adjective (*famous, foolish*).

Examples: *She* **became** *famous.* [L7] | *They* **considered** *him foolish.* [X7] | *They* **regarded** *him* **as** (v prep) *foolish* [X7]

[8] means that a verb is followed by a past participle (*built, trapped*).

Examples: *to* **have** *a house built* [V8] | *He* **got** *trapped* [L8]

[9] means that a verb needs an ADVERBIAL, and that a noun or adjective needs a descriptive word or phrase.

Examples: *She* **lives** *here.* [L9] | **Put** *it in the box.* [X9] | *a film/tennis* **buff** [C9] | **jurisdiction** *over us all* [U9] | **located** *in Florida* [F9] | *She* **ended up** (v adv) *in China* [L9]

17.2.2 *Adjectives* may have one or more of the following numbers (apart from those following the letters [Wa]): [3], [5], [6], [9]
Nouns may have one or more of the following numbers (apart from those following the letters [Wn]): [3], [5], [6], [9]
Verbs always have one or more numbers, which may be any of those from [Ø] to [9]. (They may also have a number following the letters [Wv]).
Adverbs and PRONOUNS never have a number (except for those following the letters [Wa] and [Wp]).

17.3 THE LITTLE LETTERS

[a] In [1a] and [4a], [a] means that the adverb in a *v adv* marked [T1a, 4a] or the PREPOSITION in a *v prep* marked [V4a], comes just after the verb (even before a noun).

Examples: *They* **battened down** (v adv) *the hatches.* [T1a] | *He* **left off** (v adv) *working.* [T4a] | *We* **looked at** (v prep) *him jumping* [V4a]

In [5a], [a] means that the word *that* can be left out between a word and a following CLAUSE.

Examples: *I* **know** (*that*) *he'll come.* [T5a] | **Tell** *the boy* (*that*) *it's true.* [D5a] | *He was* **sure** (*that*) *she knew* [F5a]

In [6a], [a] means that a word is followed by a *wh*-word + a CLAUSE (*who should go, why he came*).

Examples: *He* **decided** *who should go.* [T6a] | *the* **reason** *why he came* [C6a] | *I'm not* **sure** *where I should go* [F6a]

[b] In [1b] and [4b], [b] means that the adverb in a *v adv* marked [T1b] or the PREPOSITION in a *v prep* marked [V4b] is separated from the verb, as by the noun phrase *foreign workers* or the PRONOUN *her* in these examples.

Examples: *They are* **keeping** *foreign workers* **under** (v adv). [T1b] | *They* **inhibited** *her* **from** (v prep) *doing it* [V4b]

In [5b], [b] means that a verb can be used with *so*, or sometimes with *not*.

Examples: *I* **believe** *so/not.* [T5b] | *So I* **see!** [T5b] | *I* **told** *you so* [D5b]

In [6b], [b] means that a word is followed by a *wh*- word + phrase including the INFINITIVE with *to* (*whom to see, where to go*).

Examples: *He* **decided** *whom to see.* [T6b] | **Tell** *me where to go.* [D6b] | *I'm not* **sure** *where to go* [F6b]

[c] In [5c], [c] means that a wish, desire, order, suggestion, etc., can be expressed by a verb used with *should* or (esp. in *AmE*) used in the INFINITIVE form as a SUBJUNCTIVE. [5c] is a formal pattern.

Examples: *I* **desire** *that she (should) go/not go.* [T5c] | *a* **desire** *that she (should) go/not go* [C5c] | *He is* **eager** *that she (should) go/not go* [F5c]

17.4 MEANINGS HAVING MORE THAN ONE PATTERN

17.4.0 When a word or a meaning of a word can be used in more than one pattern, all the patterns are shown together. Less important or rarer ones are enclosed within the signs ( ).

17.4.1

smoke[2] 1 is marked *v* [I∅;T1]. This means both the following patterns are possible: *We* **smoked.** [I∅] | *We* **smoked** *cigarettes* [T1]

The examples *felt a* **desire** [C] | *felt strong* **desire** [U] are shown together as **desire**[2] *n* [C;U].

Other examples: *through a* **lack** *of water* [C] | *for* **lack** *of water* [U] = **lack**[2] *n* [C;U]

She **became** *President.* [L1] | *She* **became** *famous* [L7] = **become** *v* **1** [L1,7]

They **regarded** *him* **as** (v prep) *a fool.* [X1] | *They* **regarded** *him* **as** (v prep) *foolish* [X7] = **regard as** *v prep* [X1,7]

He became a **general.** [C] | **General** *Smith-Fortescue came to tea.* [A] | *Have some more tea,* **General** [N] = **general**[2] *n* [C;A;N]

Dramatics *is an interesting art.* [U] | *The* **dramatics** *of her performance were interesting* = **dramatics** *n* [U;(P)]

If anyone asks you, don't **let on** (v adv). [I∅] | *Don't* **let on** (v adv) *that you know.* [T5] | *Don't* **let on** (v adv) *where you live.* [T6a] | *Don't* **let on** (v adv) *how to open it* [T6b] = **let on** *v adv* [I∅;T5,6a,b]

Forgive *us our sins.* [D1] | **Forgive** *us.* [T1] | **Forgive** *our sins* [T1] = **forgive** *v* [D1;T1]

17.4.2 Note: some, but not all, nouns that are titles of people and are marked [A;N] are used without *a* or *an* after [L] and [X] verbs: *She became* **chairman** [C;N;(A)]; but not **She became* **doctor** [C;A;(N)]

17.5 WORDS USED WITH PATTERNS

17.5.0 When a main word *must* or *may* be used with a less important word, and the less important word is *you, it, the, whether, if, to be*, an adverb (like UP), or a PREPOSITION (like *over*), then the less important word is shown together with the letter and number representing the pattern of the main word.

17.5.1 The sign + means that the less important word or words *must* be used with the main word.

Examples: *you* **fool** [*you*+N] | *It* **rains** *here every day*. [*it*+I∅] | *Do the* **dead** *ever return?* [*the*+P] | *landed on the* **Earth** [*the*+R] | *The* **Magi** *have come. bearing gifts.* [*the*+P] | *He was given the* **lash**. [*the*+R] | *He came by* **car**. [*by*+U] | *He was* **laden** (= deeply troubled) *with sorrow*. [F+ *with*] | *He* **divided** *2 into 6* = *He* **divided** *6 by 2*. [D1 + *into/by*] | *She* **argued** *him into/out of doing it*. [T1 + *into* or *out of*] | *He* **argued** *about/over politics with George* [I∅ (*about/over* and/or *with*)]

17.5.2 The signs ( ) enclose a less important word or words that may be used with the main word.

Examples: *the/a* **lash** *of waves on the rocks* [(*the*) S] | *The bushes were* **laden** (= heavily loaded) *with fruit*. [B (*with*)] | *I* **doubt** *whether/if he'll come*. [T6a (*whether*, *if*)] | *They* **congratulated** *him on/upon his success*. [T1 *on*, *upon*] | *He* **seems** (*to be*) *a fool/foolish*. [L (*to be*) 1,7] | *She* **ended up** (by) *dancing on the table*. [L4 (*by*)] | *The firm has decided to* **close** (*down*) *its London branch* [T1 (DOWN)]

17.5.3 The sign "esp." (= especially) introduces an adverb or PREPOSITION that may be used with a main word whose pattern includes the number 9.

Examples: *She* **sat** *down/in the chair/on the floor*. [L9, esp. DOWN] | **Lay** *it down/on the table/on the floor*. [X9, esp. DOWN] | *He* **lapped** *the edges over each other* [X9, esp. *over*]

17.6 USE OF THE COLON (:)

Words and numbers which come *after* the sign (:) are used with *all* the patterns which come *before* that sign.

close[1] is marked [T1; I∅: (DOWN)]. This means that DOWN can be used in both these examples:

The firm has decided to **close** (*down*) *its London branch*. [T1 (DOWN)] | *This factory is* **closing** (*down*) *soon* [I∅ (DOWN)]

lack[2] is marked [C;U: (*of*)]. This means that *of* can be used in both these examples:

The plants died through a **lack** *of water*. [C (*of*)] | *The plants died for* **lack** *of water* [U (*of*)]

desire is marked [C;U: (*for*, 3, 5c)]. This means *for* may follow *desire* whether it is a countable or an uncountable noun; so may a *that*- CLAUSE or a SUBJUNCTIVE:

a **desire** (*for beer*) [C (*for*)] | *some* **desire** (*for beer*) [U (*for*)] | *a* **desire** *to go* [C3] | *some* **desire** *to go* [U3] | *a* **desire** *that she go* [C5c] | *some* **desire** *that she go* [U5c]

17.7 TYPES OF VERB

17.7.0 This dictionary recognizes 5 degrees of dependence between a verb and an adverb, or between a verb and a PREPOSITION:

17.7.1 Some verbs, like *put*, must be used with an ADVERBIAL, but not necessarily with any one in particular.

Example: **put** [X9]: **Put** *it down/away/up here/over there/on the table*

17.7.2 Some verbs, like *lay*, must be used with an adverb or PREPOSITION, and especially with certain ones, like DOWN.

Example: **lay** [X9, esp. DOWN]: **Lay** *it down/down on the table/on the table*

17.7.3 Some verbs, like *close*, do not need any adverb or PREPOSITION, but are often used with certain ones, like DOWN.

Example: **close** [I∅ (DOWN)]: *This factory is* **closing** (*down*) *soon*

17.7.4 Some verbs, like *argue*, must be used with either of 2 words with opposite meanings, like *into* or *out of*.

Example: **argue** [T1 + *into* or *out of*]: *She* **argued** *him into/out of doing it*

17.7.5 Some verbs, like *divide*, are used with one of 2 or more words, like *into/by*, to produce sentences with closely related meanings.

Example: **divide** [D1 + *into/by*]: *He* **divided** *2 into 6* = *He* **divided** *6 by 2*

17.7.6 But when a verb, like *put*, and an adverb or PREPOSITION, like the adverb *off*, must be used together to form a combination like *put off*, with a special meaning, then the combination is treated in the dictionary as if it were a single verb. It may consist of a verb + adverb (*v adv*), a verb + PREPOSITION (*v prep*), a verb + adverb + PREPOSITION (*v adv prep*), or a verb + a word like *off* that is used both as an adverb and as a PREPOSITION (*v adv; prep*). (Note the difference between the ways in which these last 2 possibilities are shown: *v adv prep* and *v adv; prep*.)

Examples: *v* **blow** [T1]: *He* **blew** *his horn*

v adv **blow up** [T1;I∅]: *She* **blew up** *the bridge.* | *The bridge* **blew up**

v prep **lay into** [T1]: *We* **laid** *into them with words and blows*

v prep **look at** [T1;V4a]: *We* **looked at** *him.* | *We* **looked at** *him jumping*

v prep **regard as** [X1,7;V4b]: *They* **regarded** *him* **as** *a dead man/dead/having died*

v adv prep **put up with** [T1]: *They can't* **put up with** *him*

v adv prep **put down to** [D1]: *They* **put** *the difficulty* **down to** *his failure*/**put down** *the difficulty* **to** *his failure*

v adv prep **put up to** [D1;V4b]: *They* **put** *him* **up to** *it*/**put** *him* **up to** *doing it*

v adv; prep **lay off 1** [T1;D1]
- **lay off** *v adv* [T1]: *They* **laid off** *the men*/**laid** *the men* **off**
- **lay off** *v prep* [D1]: *They* **laid** *the men* **off** *work*

lay off 2 [I∅;T1]
- **lay off** *v adv* [I∅]: *The doctor told him to* **lay off** *for a few months*
- **lay off** *v prep* [T1]: *The doctor told him to* **lay off** *work for a few months*

Rule: In the case of a verb + adverb, the adverb usually comes *before* the *-ing* form of any following verb, *after* a short pronoun, and *before* or *after* a noun or long pronoun.

Examples:	
We **put off** *holding the meeting*	—
—	*We* **put** *it* **off**
We **put off** *the meeting*	*We* **put** *the meeting* **off**
We **put off** *everything*	*We* **put** *everything* **off**

17.8 PRONOUN TABLES

17.8.1 Personal Pronouns

[Wp1]	Person	Subject form	Object form	Poss. determiner	Poss. pron	Refl. pron
sing.	1st	I	me	my (*old use*) mine	mine	myself
	2nd	you (*old use*) thou	you thee	your thy (*old use*) thine	yours thine	yourself thyself
	3rd masc.	he	him	his	his	himself
	fem.	she	her	her	hers	herself
	NEUTER	it	it	its	—	itself
pl.	1st	we	us	our	ours	ourselves
	2nd	you (*old use*) ye	you	your	yours	yourselves
	3rd	they	them	their	theirs	themselves

17.8.2 Relative Pronouns

[Wp 2]	RESTRICTIVE (= limiting) and NON-RESTRICTIVE		RESTRICTIVE only
	personal	non-personal	personal and non-personal
Subject form	who	which	that
Object form	who(m)	which	that/(*or nothing at all*)
Poss. form	whose	of which/whose	

17.9 THE VERB "BE"

[Wv1] *Present*		With *not*	With *-n't*
1st pers. sing.	am, 'm	am not, 'm not	(See note[1] below)
2nd pers. sing.	are, 're (*old use*) art	are not, 're not	aren't
3rd pers. sing.	is, 's	is not, 's not	isn't
1st pers. pl.	are, 're	are not, 're not	aren't
2nd pers. pl.	are, 're	are not, 're not	aren't
3rd pers. pl.	are, 're	are not, 're not	aren't

(See note[2] below)

Past			
1st pers. sing.	was	was not	wasn't
2nd pers. sing.	were (*old use*) wert	were not	weren't
3rd pers. sing.	was	was not	wasn't
1st pers. pl. 2nd pers. pl. 3rd pers. pl.	were	were not	weren't
-ing form (pres. p.)	being	not being	
past p.	been		

Note[1]: the *-n't* form for the 1st pers. sing. is ***aren't*** and is only used in the phrase *aren't I?*
Note[2]: the nonstandard *-n't* form for all the present tense is *ain't*.

17.10 AUXILIARY VERBS

[Wv2]		With *not*	With *-n't*
can all pers. (2nd pers. sing. *old use*)	 can canst	cannot, can not	can't
could all pers. (2nd pers. sing. *old use*)	 could couldst	could not	couldn't
dare	dare (past t. *old use* durst)	dare not	daren't

		With *not*	With *-n't*
do			
Present			
all pers. sing. and pl.	do	do not	don't
except			
3rd pers. sing.	does	does not	doesn't
(2nd pers. sing. *old use*)	dost		
Past t.			
all pers.	did	did not	didn't
(2nd pers. sing. *old use*)	didst		
-ing *form*	doing		
Past p.	done	not done	
have			
Present			
all pers. sing. and pl.	have, 've	have not, 've not (*nonstandard*) ain't	haven't
except			
3rd pers. sing.	has, 's	has not, 's not (*nonstandard*) ain't	hasn't
(2nd pers. sing. *old use*)	hast		
Past t.	had, 'd	had not, 'd not	hadn't
-ing *form*	having	not having	
Past. p.	had		
may			
all pers.	may	may not	mayn't
(2nd pers. sing. *old use*)	mayst		
might	might	might not	mightn't
must	must	must not	mustn't
need	need	need not	needn't
ought to	ought to	ought not to	oughtn't to
shall			
all pers.	shall	shall not	shan't
(2nd pers. sing. *old use*)	shalt		
should			
all pers.	should	should not	shouldn't
(2nd pers. sing. *old use*)	shouldst		
used to	used to	used not to	didn't use(d) to, usedn't to
will			
all pers.	will, 'll	will not, 'll not	won't
(2nd pers. sing. *old use*)	wilt		
would			
all pers.	would, 'd	would not, 'd not	wouldn't
(2nd pers. sing. *old use*)	wouldst		

A, a

A, a /eɪ/ **A's, a's** *or* **As, as** **1** the first letter of the English alphabet **2 from A to Z** from beginning to end; including everything

A[1] (in Western music) **a** the 6th note (*AmE* also **tone**) in the row of notes which form the musical SCALE[5] (5) of C MAJOR[1] (3) **b** the musical KEY[1] (5) based on this note

A[2] *abbrev. for:* AMPERE

A[3] *n, adj* [Wa5;C;A] (in Britain) (a film) that may be unsuitable for children under 14 —compare AA, U[2], X[2]

a /ə; *strong* eɪ/ also (*before a vowel sound*) **an**—*indefinite article, determiner* **1** one: *I gave him a* THOUSAND *pounds|a* DOZEN *eggs.|I caught a fish yesterday* **2** (before certain DETERMINERs of quantity): *a few weeks|a little water|a great many|a bit much* **3** one member of a class: *I only know it was a dog and not a cat that bit me.|"I was a Burton before my marriage"* (changed from SEU S.) **4** any; every; the thing called: *A horse with a broken leg cannot run.|A bicycle has 2 wheels* **5** one like; another: *He is a (second) Caesar in speech and leadership* **6** (*before the name of an artist*) a work by: *What wonderful news: the painting on my wall is a Rembrandt!* —see AN (USAGE) **7** *often fml* (*showing that someone is unknown to the speaker*) a certain: *A Mrs. Smith wishes to speak to you.|a Christmas when it snowed* **8** *becoming rare* the same: *They are all songs of a type* **9** (*after* half/such/what/rather/(*lit*) many): *What a nice girl (she is)!|I've never met such a nice girl* **10** (*in the pattern* as/how/so/too+adj+a+countable or uncountable noun): *I've never met so nice a girl* **11** (*before uncountable* [U] *nouns*) a kind of: *Médoc is a very good wine* **12** (*before uncountable* [U] *nouns*) a container or UNIT (1) of: *I'd like a coffee, please.|I'd like a beer, please* **13** (*before the* -ing *form when used as a noun*) an example or case of: *Our work led to a setting up of 2 quite different systems of grammar* **14** a certain amount of; some **a** (before the "-ing" form when used as a noun): *I heard a crashing|a weeping in the kitchen* **b** (before singular [S] nouns with no plural form, including nouns related in meaning to the "-ing" form of verbs): *I had a weep|a think.|He has a knowledge of chemistry* **15** (*in the pattern* a+noun+of+poss. form): *a friend of mine|John's* (= one of my/John's friends) **16** (before the first one of a pair that seems to be a single whole): *a* BRACE AND BIT **17** each; every; per: *6 times a day|£2 a* DOZEN

a-[1] /ə/ *prefix* **1** in, to, at, or on: ABED|AFAR **2** in a stated condition: AFIRE **3** in a stated manner: *aloud*

a-[2] /eɪ, æ, ə/ *prefix* without; not: AMORAL|ASEXUAL

-a *suffix* **1** [*adj* (*-an, -ian*)→*n* P] a collection of facts, papers, etc., connected with: *Americana|Victoriana* **2** [*n*→*n*] (forms the plural of nouns ending in *-um*): *bacteria*

A-1 /ˌeɪ ˈwʌn/ *adj* **1** of the best quality; very good: *The service in that shop is really A-1* **2** in good health; working well: *Yesterday I was ill but today I am feeling A-1*

AA[1] /ˌeɪˈeɪ/ *n, adj* [Wa5;C;A] (in Britain) (a film) that children under 14 are not admitted to see in a cinema —compare A[3], U[2], X[2]

AA[2] *abbrev. for:* AUTOMOBILE ASSOCIATION

ab- /æb, əb/ *prefix* off; from, away: ABDUCT

a·back /əˈbæk/ *adv old use* backwards —see also TAKE ABACK

ab·a·cus /ˈæbəkəs/ *n* a frame holding wires on which small balls can be moved, used for teaching children how to count, or, esp. in eastern countries, for calculating

a·ban·don[1] /əˈbændən/ *v* [T1] **1** to leave completely and for ever; desert: *The sailors abandoned the burning ship* **2** to leave (a relation or friend) in a thoughtless or cruel way: *He abandoned his wife and went away with all their money* **3** to give up, esp. without finishing: *The search was abandoned when night came, even though the child had not been found* **4** [(*to*)] to give (oneself) up completely to a feeling, desire, etc.: *He abandoned himself to grief.|abandoned behaviour* —**-donment** *n* [U]

abandon[2] *n* [U] the state when one's feelings and actions are uncontrolled; freedom from control: *The people were so excited that they jumped and shouted with abandon|in gay abandon*

a·ban·doned /əˈbændənd/ *adj euph, now rare* given up to a life that is thought to be immoral —see also ABANDON[1] (2,4)

a·base /əˈbeɪs/ *v* [T1] to make (someone, esp. oneself) have less self-respect; make humble —**~ment** *n* [U]

a·bash /əˈbæʃ/ *v* [T1 *usu. pass.*] to cause to feel uncomfortable or ashamed in the presence of others: *The workman stood abashed as his mistakes were pointed out*

a·bate /əˈbeɪt/ *v* **1** [IØ] (of winds, storms, disease, pain, etc.) to become less strong; decrease: *The ship waited till the storm abated before sailing out to sea* **2** [T1 *often pass.*] *lit* to make less: *His pride was not abated by his many mistakes* **3** [T1] *law* to bring to an end (esp. in the phr. **abate a nuisance**) —**~ment** *n* [U]

ab·at·toir /ˈæbətwɑːʳ/ *n BrE* SLAUGHTERHOUSE

ab·bess /ˈæbɨs, ˈæbes/ *n* [C;N] a woman who is the head of a religious establishment (CONVENT), formerly called an ABBEY, for women —compare ABBOT

ab·bey /ˈæbi/ *n* **1** [C] (esp. formerly) a building in which Christian men (MONKs) or women (NUNs) live shut away from other people and work as a group for God; MONASTERY or CONVENT **2** [*the*+GU] the group of people living in such a building **3** [C *often cap. as part of a name*] a large church or house that was once such a building

ab·bot /ˈæbət/ *n* [A;C;N] a man who is the head of a religious establishment (MONASTERY), formerly called an ABBEY, for men —compare ABBESS

ab·bre·vi·ate /əˈbriːvieɪt/ *v* [T1] to make (a story, speech, visit, word, etc.) shorter

ab·bre·vi·a·tion /əˌbriːviˈeɪʃən/ *n* **1** [U] the act of making shorter **2** [C] a shortened form of a word, often one used in writing (such as *Mr*)

ABC /ˌ· · ˈ·/ *n* **1** [U] the alphabet, as taught to children: *Has the child learnt his ABC yet?* **2** [*the*+C (*of*)] the simplest facts about something which have to be learnt first: *classes in the ABC of cooking*

ab·di·cate /ˈæbdɪkeɪt/ *v* **1** [IØ (*from*);T1] to give up officially (an official position, esp. that of king or queen): *to abdicate (from) the* THRONE **2** [T1] *fml* to give up (a right or claim, esp. a responsibility): *He abdicated all responsibility for the care of the child* —**-cation** /ˌæbdɪˈkeɪʃən/ *n* [U;C]

ab·do·men /ˈæbdəmən, æbˈdəʊ-/ *n med* a main

part of the body in animals, being in man (and other MAMMALs) the part between the chest and legs, containing the stomach, bowels, etc., and in insects the end part of the body joined to the THORAX —see picture at INSECT —**-dominal** /æb'dɒmɨnəl‖-'dɑ-/ *adj* [Wa5]

ab·duct /æb'dʌkt, əb-/ *v* [T1] to take away (a person) unlawfully, often by force; KIDNAP: *The police think the missing woman has been abducted* —**abduction** /æb'dʌkʃən, əb-/ *n* [U]

a·bed /ə'bed/ *adj* [Wa5;F] *lit or old use* in bed

a·ber·rant /æ'berənt, ə-/ *adj* **1** changed from what is usual, expected, or considered to be right: *aberrant behaviour under the influence of drugs* **2** *tech* not true to type or class: *an aberrant example of a particular insect*

ab·er·ra·tion /ˌæbə'reɪʃən/ *n* **1** [U] a usu. sudden change away from the habitual way of thinking or acting; sudden forgetfulness: *She hit him in a moment of aberration* **2** [C] an example of this **3** [C] a sudden change, esp. for a short time, from health to illness of the mind or feelings

a·bet /ə'bet/ *v* **-tt-** [T1 (*in*)] **1** to encourage or give help to (a crime or criminal): *He abetted the thief in robbing the bank* **2 aid and abet** *law or humor* to help (someone) in crime —**~tor** *n*

a·bey·ance /ə'beɪəns/ *n fml* the condition of not being in force or in use, at or for a certain time (esp. in the phr. **in/into abeyance**): *an old custom that has fallen into abeyance*

ab·hor /əb'hɔːʳ, æb-/ *v* **-rr-** [T1] to feel very great hatred and dislike for; hate very much; DETEST: *Most people abhor cruelty to children*

ab·hor·rent /əb'hɒrənt‖-'hɔr-/ *adj* [(*to*)] **1** hateful; DETESTable: *Cruelty is abhorrent to him* **2** completely opposed in nature: *Cruelty is abhorrent to love* —**-rence** *n* [U]

a·bide¹ /ə'baɪd/ *v* **1** [T1,3,4] (usu. not in simple statements) to bear; TOLERATE: *I can't abide rude people.|I cannot abide to see such cruelty|seeing such cruelty* **2** [T1] *rare* to wait for

abide² *v* **abode** /ə'bəʊd/, **abided** [L9] *lit and old use* **1** to stay; remain: *"Abide with Me"* (famous HYMN) **2** to live (in or at a place)

abide by *v prep* **abided** [T1 *no pass.*] **1** to be faithful to; obey (laws, agreements, etc.): *If you join the club you must abide by its rules* **2** to wait for or accept: *You must abide by the results of your mistakes* —**abidance by** *n* [U] *fml*

a·bid·ing /ə'baɪdɪŋ/ *adj* [A] without end; lasting: *an abiding friendship*

a·bil·i·ties /ə'bɪlɨtiz/ *n* [P] powers and skills, esp. of the mind: *a job more suited to his abilities*

a·bil·i·ty /ə'bɪlɨti/ *n* [U] power and skill, esp. to do, think, act, make, etc.: *He has the ability to make a very good boat.|a man of great musical ability* —see GENIUS (USAGE)

-a·bil·i·ty, -ibility /ə'bɪlɨti/ *suffix* [*v, adj*→*n*] suitableness to act or be acted on in the stated manner: FLEXIBILITY

ab·ject /'æbdʒekt/ *adj* **1** (of a condition) as low as possible; deserving great pity: *abject slavery* **2** (esp. of people or behaviour) not deserving respect; showing lack of self-respect: *an abject slave* —**~ly** *adv* —**abjection** /æb'dʒekʃən, əb-/ *n* [U]

ab·jure /əb'dʒʊəʳ, æb-/ *v* [T1] *fml* to swear a solemn promise, esp. publicly, to give up (an opinion, belief, claim, faithfulness to someone or something, etc.) —**-juration** /ˌæbdʒʊ'reɪʃən‖-dʒə-/ *n*

ab·la·tive /'æblətɪv/ *adj, n* (of or concerning) a particular form of a Latin noun which carries the meaning of *by, with,* or *from* the noun

ab·laut /'æblaʊt (*Ger* 'aplaʊt)/ *n* [U] the way in which, in the system of some languages, the vowel of a word changes as the word is used in different ways (as in *drink, drank, drunk*)

a·blaze /ə'bleɪz/ *adj* [F] **1** on fire: *The wooden house was quickly ablaze* **2** [(*with*)] shining brightly; flashing: *The ladies were ablaze with jewels* **3** [+*with*] excited: *He was ablaze with anger*

a·ble /'eɪbəl/ *adj* **1** [F3] having the power, skill, knowledge, time, etc., necessary to do something: *As I had plenty of money I was (better/more) able to help her* —opposite **unable** **2** [Wa1;B] clever, skilled: *an abler actor than I thought* —see COULD (USAGE)

-a·ble, -ible /əbəl/ *suffix* **1** [*v*→*adj*] able or needing to be, fit for, worthy to, or likely to suffer the stated action: *bearable|payable|eatable* **2** [*n*→*adj*] having the quality of the stated condition: *knowledgeable|peaceable* —**-ably** *suffix* [→*adv*]

USAGE Adjectives formed with **-able**, **-ible** are often pass. in meaning: a *wash***able** garment is one that can be *washed.* (Compare a *washed* garment, which has been *washed.*) *Laugh***able** means "suitable to be *laughed* at" and *reli***able** is "able to be *relied* on" (RELY ON). Some common words where **-able** has a different meaning are *comfort***able**, which means (of a chair) "giving *comfort*" or (of a person) "in surroundings that provide *comfort*"; *knowledge***able** which means "having *knowledge*"; and *siz***able** which means "of a rather large *size*"; but it is not always possible to guess the meaning of such words from their parts.

able-bod·ied /ˌ·· '··◂/ *adj* strong and active in body

able sea·man /ˌ·· '··/ also **able-bodied seaman** /ˌ·· ·· '··/— *n* **-men** /mən/ (a trained man who holds) a naval rank below that of a NONCOMMISSIONED OFFICER

a·blu·tion /ə'bluːʃən/ *n* [U;C] *fml* the washing of part of the body as part of a religious ceremony

a·blu·tions /ə'bluːʃənz/ *n* [P] **1** *pomp or humor* the act of washing oneself **2** *fml* ABLUTION: *temple ablutions*

a·bly /'eɪbli/ *adv* in an able manner: *He could play the horn very ably*

ab·ne·ga·tion /ˌæbnɪ'geɪʃən/ also **self-abnegation** /ˌ· ··'··/— *n* [U] *usu. apprec* the action or quality of giving up, or not trying to get, things that one wants

ab·norm·al /æb'nɔːməl‖-'nɔr-/ *adj* different (usu. in a bad sense) from what is ordinary or expected; unusual; peculiar: *Is the child abnormal in any way?* —**~ly** *adv* —**~ity** /ˌæbnɔː'mælɨti‖-nər-/ *n* [C;U]

ab·o /'æbəʊ/ *n* **abos** *AustrE taboo derog sl* an Australian ABORIGINE

a·board /ə'bɔːd‖ə'bord/ *adv, prep* [F] on or into (a ship, train, aircraft, bus, etc.): *The boat is ready to leave. All aboard!|They went aboard the ship*

a·bode¹ /ə'bəʊd/ *n* [(*usu. sing.*)] **1** *lit, old use, or fml* place where one lives; home **2 of/with no fixed abode** *law* having no place as a regular home

abode² *past tense of* ABIDE²

a·bol·ish /ə'bɒlɪʃ‖ə'bɑ-/ *v* [T1] to bring to an end; stop: *There are many bad customs and laws that ought to be abolished*

ab·o·li·tion /ˌæbə'lɪʃən/ *n* [U] the act of putting an end to something: *the abolition of slavery* —**~ist** *n*

A-bomb /'eɪ bɒm‖-bɑm/ *n* ATOM BOMB

a·bom·i·na·ble /ə'bɒmɨnəbəl, -mənə-‖ə'bɑ-/ *adj* **1** causing great dislike; hateful; DETESTable: *Their cruel treatment of prisoners was abominable* **2** *infml* unpleasant; not liked: *The food in this hotel is abominable* —**-bly** *adv* [Wa3]

abominable snow·man /·ˌ···· '··/ *n* **-men** *infml* YETI

a·bom·i·nate /ə'bɒmɨneɪt‖ə'bɑ-/ *v* [T1] *fml* to have great hatred and dislike for; DETEST

a·bom·i·na·tion /əˌbɒmɨ'neɪʃən‖əˌbɑ-/ *n* **1** [U]

great hatred; DISGUST **2** [C] a very hateful or nasty thing or act

ab·o·rig·i·nal[1] /ˌæbəˈrɪdʒənəl/ *adj* of or about people or living things existing in a place from the earliest times or since the place was first described

aboriginal[2] *n* a member of a group, tribe, etc., that has lived in a place from the earliest times or since the place was first described

ab·o·rig·i·ne /ˌæbəˈrɪdʒəni/ *n* an ABORIGINAL[2], esp. of Australia

a·bort /əˈbɔːt‖-ɔrt/ *v* **1** [T1;IØ] to give birth too early to (a dead child) —compare MISCARRY (1) **2** [T1] to cause (a child) to be born too soon, or to end (a PREGNANCY) too soon, so that the child cannot live: *The doctor had to abort the baby/the* PREGNANCY **3** [T1;IØ] *tech* **a** to end (a job or plan, esp. a military or space flight) before the expected time because of some trouble **b** (of a job, plan, etc.) to end in this way

a·bor·tion /əˈbɔːʃən‖əˈbɔr-/ *n* **1** [U] the act of giving birth or causing to give birth before the baby is properly developed, esp. within the first 28 weeks of its existence inside a woman, so that the child cannot live **2** [C] an example of this, by accident or intention **3** [C] a badly-formed creature produced by such a birth **4** [C] a plan or arrangement which breaks down before it can develop properly —compare MISCARRIAGE (1); STILLBIRTH

a·bor·tion·ist /əˈbɔːʃənəst‖əˈbɔr-/ *n* a person, esp. a doctor, who intentionally causes an ABORTION

a·bor·tive /əˈbɔːtɪv‖əˈbɔr-/ *adj* coming to nothing; not developing; unsuccessful: *An abortive attempt to build that railway failed for lack of money* —**~ly** *adv*

a·bound /əˈbaʊnd/ *v* [L9] to exist in large numbers or great quantity: *wild animals abound in this park*

abound in also **abound with**— *v prep* [T1] to have in large numbers or great quantity: *The park abounds in wild animals*

a·bout[1] /əˈbaʊt/ *adv* [Wa5] **1** also (*esp. AmE*) **around**— *esp. BrE* here and there; in all directions or places; on all sides; around: *They go about together most of the time.|The visitors sat about on the floor* **2** [F] also (*esp. AmE*) **around**— *esp. BrE* in the area; in a near place: *Is there anybody about?* **3** near in number, time, degree, etc.; a little more or less than: *We walked about 5 miles* **4** *infml* almost; nearly: *I'm about ready* **5** also (*esp. AmE*) **around**— so as to face the opposite way: *The ship turned about and left the battle* —see also BRING ABOUT; COME ABOUT; see ON, ROUND[3] (USAGE)

about[2] *prep* **1** also (*esp. AmE*) **around**— *esp. BrE* here and there in; in all parts of; on all sides of; around: *They walked about the streets.|books lying about the room* **2** also (*esp. AmE*) **around**— *esp. BrE* in the area of; near: *I lost my pen about here* **3** also (*esp. AmE*) **around**— *lit, esp. BrE* surrounding: *the high wall about the prison* **4** with regard to; concerning: *Tell us about what happened.|Have you a book about the stars?* **5** on or near the body of: *There is a strange smell about him.|I have no money about me* **6** in the character of: *There is a sense of power about him* **7** busy or concerned with: *Do the shopping now, and while you're about it buy yourself a pair of shoes* **8 Be quick about it!** Do it quickly! **9 what/how about a** what news or plans have you concerning: *What about father? We can't just leave him here* **b** (making a suggestion): *How about a drink?* —see also SET ABOUT

about[3] *adj* [Wa5] **1** [F] moving from place to place, as after getting out of bed; active (esp. in the phr. **up and about**): *Is he about yet? He may still be asleep* **2** [F3] just ready (to do something): *We were about to start, when it rained* **3 not about to** *AmE sl* very unwilling to: *I'm not about to stop when I'm so close to success*

about-face /·ˌ· ˈ·, ·ˈ· ·/ *n* [*usu. sing.*] *esp. AmE* a complete change to the opposite position, direction or opinion

about turn /·ˌ· ˈ·/ *n, interj* (the action of obeying) a military order to turn round and face in the opposite direction

a·bove[1] /əˈbʌv/ *adv* [Wa5] **1** [F] in or to a higher place; OVERHEAD: *The clouds above began to get thicker.|A cry from above warned me of the danger* **2** on an earlier page or higher on the same page: *the facts mentioned above* **3** more: *20 and above* **4** higher (esp. in rank): *a military meeting for captains and above* **5** [F] in or to heaven

above[2] *prep* **1** higher than; over: *We flew above the clouds.|*(fig.) *There's nothing in this shop (at/for) above £5* —opposite **below**; compare OVER **2** more than: *She values safety above excitement* **3** higher in rank or power than: *The captain of a ship is above a seaman* **4** higher in quality than; not having (bad thoughts, plans, etc.) or doing (bad acts): *He wouldn't steal; he's above that.|He's above stealing* **5** out of reach of (because too great, good, etc.): *His behaviour is above praise* —compare **above someone's** HEAD[1] (21) **6** too good, proud, etc.: *He's not above doing what is necessary* **7 above all** most important of all **8 over and above** in addition; as well **9 above oneself a** having too much trust in one's own cleverness; SELF-SATISFIED **b** excited

above[3] *adj* [Wa5;B;E;*the*+GU] *fml* mentioned on an earlier page or higher on the same page: *For an explanation see the above sentence/see the sentence above.|The above is the most important fact.|The above are the most important facts*

a·bove·board /əˌbʌvˈbɔːd◂, əˈbʌvbɔːd‖əˈbʌvbord/ *adj* without any trick or attempt to deceive; honourable: *His part in the affair was quite (open and) aboveboard*

above-men·tioned /·ˌ· ˈ··◂/ *adj* [Wa5;A; *the*+GU] *fml* ABOVE[3]: *the above-mentioned facts*

ab·ra·ca·dab·ra /ˌæbrəkəˈdæbrə/ *n, interj* **1** (a word spoken to encourage the working of magic) **2** *derog* ceremonial nonsense without meaning

a·brade /əˈbreɪd/ *v* [IØ;T1] *tech* **a** (esp. of skin) to wear away by hard rubbing **b** to cause (esp. skin) to wear away by hard rubbing

a·bra·sion /əˈbreɪʒən/ *n tech* **1** [U] loss of surface by rubbing; wearing away **2** [C] a place where the surface, esp. of the skin, has been worn away

a·bra·sive[1] /əˈbreɪsɪv/ *adj* **1** causing the wearing away of a surface **2** tending to annoy; rough: *an abrasive voice* —**~ly** *adv*

abrasive[2] *n* [U;C] a substance, such as sand, used for polishing or removing a surface

a·breast /əˈbrest/ *adv* [F] **1** [Wa5] side by side, on a level, and facing the same direction: *lines of soldiers marching 5 abreast* **2 keep/be abreast of** to know all the time the most recent facts about (something non-material): *Read the papers if you want to keep abreast of the times*

a·bridge /əˈbrɪdʒ/ *v* [T1] **1** [Wv5] to make (something written or spoken) shorter by using fewer words; cut short **2** *lit* to make (a meeting, period of time, etc.) shorter

a·bridg·ment, abridgement /əˈbrɪdʒmənt/ *n* **1** [U] the act of making shorter **2** [C] something, such as a story, book, or play, that has been made shorter: *an abridgment for radio in 5 parts*

a·broad /əˈbrɔːd/ *adv* [Wa5;F] **1** to or in another country: *He lived abroad for many years* **2** over a wide area; widely; everywhere: *The news soon spread abroad that the examination results were* *ready* **3** *old use* out of doors: *There was no one abroad at that early hour*

ab·ro·gate /'æbrəgeɪt/ *v* [T1] *fml* to put an end to the force or effect of: *to abrogate a law/one's rights* —**-gation** /ˌæbrə'geɪʃən/ *n* [U;C]

a·brupt /ə'brʌpt/ *adj* [Wa2] **1** sudden and unexpected: *The train came to an abrupt stop, making many passengers fall off their seats* **2** (of behaviour, speech, character, etc.) rough and impolite; not wanting to waste time being nice **3** (of the ground) suddenly sloping up or down —**~ly** *adv* —**~ness** *n* [U9]

ab·scess /'æbses/ *n* a swelling on or in the body where a thick yellowish poisonous liquid (PUS) has gathered

ab·scond /əb'skɒnd, æb-‖æb'skɑnd/ *v* [IØ (*from, with*)] *fml* to go away suddenly and secretly because one has done something wrong or against the law

ab·sence /'æbsəns/ *n* **1** [U] the state of being away or of not being present: *Please look after my house during my absence* **2** [C] an occasion or period of being away **3** [U] non-existence; lack: *The police were delayed by the absence of information about the crime*

absence of mind /ˌ·· · '·/ *n* [U] loss of attention to what one is doing; state in which one forgets one's surroundings or what one is doing —compare PRESENCE OF MIND; ABSENT-MINDED

ab·sent[1] /'æbsənt/ *adj* **1** [B] not present: *How many students are absent today?* **2** [A] showing lack of attention to what is happening: *He had an absent look on his face* **3** [B] not in existence; lacking: *In the Manx type of cat, the tail is absent*

ab·sent[2] /əb'sent, æb-‖æb-/ *v* [T1 (*from*)] *fml* to keep (oneself) away: *He absented himself from the meeting*

ab·sen·tee /ˌæbsən'tiː/ *n* a person who stays away: *There were many absentees from the meeting*

ab·sen·tee·is·m /ˌæbsən'tiːɪzəm/ *n* [U] regular absence without good cause, esp. from work or duty

ab·sent·ly /'æbsəntli/ *adv* in an ABSENT-MINDED manner

absent-mind·ed /ˌ·· '··/ *adj* so concerned with one's thoughts as not to notice what is happening, what one is doing, etc. —**~ly** *adv* —**~ness** *n* [U]

ab·sinth, absinthe /'æbsɪnθ/ *n* **1** [U] a bitter green very strong alcoholic drink **2** [C] a glass of this

ab·so·lute /'æbsəluːt/ *adj* **1** complete; perfect: *He is a man of absolute honesty.|That's absolute nonsense!* **2** having complete power; without limit: *An absolute ruler can do just as he pleases* **3** not allowing any doubt; completely certain: *The police have absolute proof that he was the murderer* **4** without any conditions: *I have made you an absolute promise that I will help you* **5** not depending on or measured by comparison with other things —opposite **relative** —**~ness** *n* [U]

ab·so·lute·ly /'æbsəluːtli, ˌæbsə'luːtli/ *adv* **1** completely: *You are absolutely wrong* **2** without conditions: *You must agree absolutely and not try to change matters later* **3** *infml* certainly: *"Do you think so?" "Absolutely!"*

USAGE The adverbs **absolutely** and **altogether** are pronounced /'····/ when they come before the word they describe: *I* **absolutely** *refuse.*|**altogether** *different.* They are pronounced /ˌ··'··/ when they come after the word they describe, or when they stand alone: *different* **altogether**|**"Absolutely!"**

absolute ze·ro /ˌ··· '··/ *n* [U] the lowest temperature that is thought to be possible

ab·so·lu·tion /ˌæbsə'luːʃən/ *n* (esp. in the Christian religion) **1** [U] forgiveness for wrongdoing **2** [C] the words said by a priest in a church service when he declares that the people are forgiven

ab·so·lut·is·m /'æbsəluːtɪzəm/ *n* [U] the political principle that complete power should be in the hands of one ruler or a limited number of rulers

ab·solve /əb'zɒlv‖-ɑlv/ *v* [T1] **1** (of a priest) to give (a person) forgiveness for wrongdoing **2** [(*from*)] to free (someone) from fulfilling a promise or a duty, or from having to suffer for wrongdoing

ab·sorb /əb'sɔːb, əb'zɔːb‖-ɔrb/ *v* [T1] **1** to take or suck in (liquids) **2** to take in (knowledge, ideas, etc.) **3** [Wv5 (*in, by*)] to take up all the attention, interest, time, etc., of; ENGROSS (1): *I was absorbed in a book and didn't hear you call* **4** [Wv5 (*into, by*)] (of a big country, business, etc.) to make into a part of itself; take over: *Most little shops have been absorbed into big businesses*

ab·sor·bent /əb'sɔːbənt, -'zɔː-‖-ɔr-/ *n, adj* [B;C;U] (something) that is able to ABSORB

ab·sorb·ing /əb'sɔːbɪŋ, -'zɔː-‖-ɔr-/ *adj* taking all one's attention; very interesting; ENGROSSING

ab·sorp·tion /əb'sɔːpʃən, -'zɔː-‖-ɔr-/ *n* [U] **1** the act or action of ABSORBing or of being ABSORBed **2** [(*in*)] the taking up of all one's attention, interest, time, etc. **3** [(*into, by*)] the taking over of little countries, businesses, etc., by big ones

ab·stain /əb'steɪn/ *v* [IØ (*from*)] to keep oneself from eating, drinking, voting, etc.; REFRAIN[1] (from something) —**~er** *n*

ab·ste·mi·ous /əb'stiːmɪəs/ *adj* **1** allowing oneself only a little food, drink, or pleasure **2** having, being, or allowing only a little food, drink, or pleasure: *an abstemious meal* —**~ly** *adv* —**~ness** *n* [U]

ab·sten·tion /əb'stenʃən/ *n* **1** [U] the act of keeping oneself from doing something, esp. from voting **2** [C] an example of this: *50 votes for, 35 against, and 7 abstentions*

ab·sti·nence /'æbstɨnəns/ *n* [U (*from*)] the act of keeping away from pleasant things, esp. from alcoholic drink —**-nent** *adj*

ab·stract[1] /'æbstrækt/ *adj* **1** [Wa5] *tech* thought of as a quality rather than as an object or fact; not real or solid: *The word "hunger" is an* **abstract noun** **2** general as opposed to particular; not clear: *Your ideas on this matter seem a little abstract. Which piano shall we actually buy?* **3** (in art) connected with or producing ABSTRACTS[2] (2) **4 in the abstract** in general; apart from particular examples: *I like dogs in the abstract, but I can't bear this one*

abstract[2] /'æbstrækt/ *n* **1** a shortened form of a statement, speech, etc. **2** (in art) a painting, drawing, etc., that does not try to represent an object as it would be seen by a camera

ab·stract[3] /əb'strækt, æb-/ *v* [T1 (*from*)] **1** *tech* to remove by drawing out gently; separate **2** *euph* to steal

abstract[4] /'æbstrækt/ *v* [T1] to make a shortened account of (a statement, speech, etc.)

ab·stract·ed /əb'stræktɨd, æb-/ *adj* **1** inattentive to what is happening; deep in thought **2** that has been removed or separated —**~ly** *adv*

ab·strac·tion /əb'strækʃən, æb-/ *n* **1** [U] *tech* the act or action of ABSTRACTing[3] (1) or of being ABSTRACTed[3] (1) **2** [U] the state of not attending to what is going on; ABSENT-MINDEDness: *He wore a look of abstraction and I knew his thoughts were far away* **3** [C] an idea of a quality as separate from any object: *A good judge must consider all the facts of a case and not only be concerned with the abstraction "justice"*

ab·struse /əb'struːs, æb-/ *adj fml or humor* difficult to understand —**~ly** *adv* —**~ness** *n* [U]

ab·surd /əb'sɜːd‖-ɜrd/ *adj* **1** against reason or common sense; clearly false or foolish: *Even sensible men do absurd things* **2** funny because clearly unsuitable, false, foolish, or impossible: *You look absurd in your wife's hat!* —**~ly** *adv* —**~ity** /əb'sɜːdɪ̣ti, -'zɜː-‖-ɜr-/ *n* [U;C]

a·bun·dance /ə'bʌndəns/ *n* [S (*of*);*in* +U] a great quantity; plenty: *At the feast there was food and drink in abundance.*|*There was an abundance of corn last year*

a·bun·dant /ə'bʌndənt/ *adj* more than enough: *There are abundant supplies of firewood in the forest* —**~ly** *adv*

a·buse¹ /ə'bjuːz/ *v* [T1] **1** to say unkind, cruel, or rude things to (someone) or about (somebody or something) **2** to put to wrong use; use badly: *It is easy to abuse one's power* **3** *becoming rare* to handle without care; treat badly: *I'll lend you my camera but don't abuse it*

abuse² /ə'bjuːs/ *n* **1** [U] unkind, cruel, or rude words: *He greeted me with a stream of abuse* **2** [U; C] wrong use: *They talked about the uses and abuses of figures to prove things in politics* **3** [C] an unjust or harmful custom

a·bu·sive /ə'bjuːsɪv/ *adj* using or containing unkind, cruel, or rude language: *an abusive letter/person* —**~ly** *adv* —**~ness** *n* [U]

a·but·ment /ə'bʌtmənt/ *n* a support, esp. one on which a bridge or arch rests

a·but on /ə'bʌt/ *v prep* **-tt-** [T1 *no pass.*] *fml* (of land or buildings) to lie next to or touch (something, often land) on one side

a·bys·mal /ə'bɪzməl/ *adj not fml* very bad: *The food was abysmal*

a·byss /ə'bɪs/ *n* a great hole which appears to have no bottom: (fig.) *The sad man was in an abyss of hopelessness*

A/C *written abbrev. for*: account

a·ca·cia /ə'keɪʃə/ *n* **acacias** *or* **acacia** [Wn2] any of several trees, found mainly in hot countries, from which a substance (GUM² (1)) used for sticking is obtained

ac·a·dem·ic¹ /ˌækə'demɪk/ *adj* **1** concerning teaching or studying, esp. in a college or university **2** concerning those subjects taught to provide skills for the mind rather than for the hand —compare TECHNICAL (2) **3** [Wa5] of a college or university: *academic dress* **4** *derog* not concerned with practical examples; impractical: *The question of how many souls exist in heaven is academic*

academic² *n* a member of a college or university, esp. a person whose job is teaching

a·cad·e·mi·cian /əˌkædə'mɪʃən‖ˌækədə-/ *n* [C;A] a member of an ACADEMY (1)

a·cad·e·my /ə'kædəmi/ *n* (*often cap. as part of a name*) **1** a society of people interested in the advancement of art, science, or literature, to which members are usu. elected as an honour **2** a school for training in a special art or skill: *a military academy*|*an academy of music*

acc. *written abbrev. for:* **1** accompanied (by) (ACCOMPANY) **2** according (to) **3** A/C **4** ACCUSATIVE

ac·cede /ək'siːd, æk-/ *v* [IØ (*to*)] *fml* **1** to give approval to a suggestion, plan, demand, etc.; agree: *He acceded to our request* **2** to take a high post or position after someone has left it **3** to join a group of people, countries, etc., in an agreement

ac·cel·e·rate /ək'seləreɪt/ *v* **1** [T1;IØ] to (cause to) move faster **2** [T1] *fml* to cause to happen earlier

ac·cel·e·ra·tion /əkˌselə'reɪʃən/ *n* [U] **1** the act of increasing speed **2** the rate at which speed is increased in a certain time: *The new car has good acceleration*

ac·cel·e·ra·tor /ək'seləreɪtəʳ/ *n* **1** the piece of apparatus in a machine (esp. a car) which is used to increase the speed of the machine —see picture at CAR **2** *tech* a machine for producing power by making very small pieces of matter (PARTICLES (1b)) move very quickly

ac·cent¹ /'æksənt‖'æksent/ *n* **1** importance given to a word or part of a word (vowel or SYLLABLE) by saying it with more force or on a different musical note: *The accent in the word "important" is on the 2nd syllable* **2** the mark used, esp. above a word or part of a word, in writing or printing to show what kind of sound is needed when it is spoken: *In French there are 3 possible accents on the vowel "e"* **3** a particular way of speaking, usu. connected with a country, area, or class: *He speaks with a German accent*

ac·cent² /ək'sent‖'æksent/ *v* [T1] **1** to pronounce (a word or a part of a word) with added force or on a different musical note **2** to mark (a written word) with an accent **3** ACCENTUATE

ac·cen·tu·ate /ək'sentʃʊeɪt/ *v* [T1] **1** to pronounce with great force **2** to give more importance to; direct attention to: *The dark frame accentuates the brightness of the picture* —**-ation** /əkˌsentʃʊ'eɪʃən/ *n* [U;C]

ac·cept /ək'sept/ *v* **1** [T1;IØ] to take or receive (something offered or given), esp. willingly; receive with favour: *I cannot accept your gift.*|*He asked her to marry him and she accepted (him)* **2** [Wv5;T1, (*fml*) 5] to believe; admit; agree to: *I accept your reasons for being late.*|(*fml*) *I accept that the aircraft has no choice but to crash into the sea.*|*accepted principles of behaviour* **3** [T1] to take responsibility for: *I'll accept the bill only if you send it to my home address* —see REFUSE¹ (USAGE)

ac·cep·ta·ble /ək'septəbəl/ *adj* **1** good enough to be received: *Your work is not acceptable; do it again* **2** worth receiving; welcome: *The gift is very acceptable* —**-ability** /əkˌseptə'bɪlɪ̣ti/ *n* [U] —**-bly** /ək'septəbli/ *adv*

ac·cept·ance /ək'septəns/ *n* **1** [U;C] the act of accepting or being accepted **2** [U] favour; approval **3** [C] (in business) an agreement to pay

ac·cess /'ækses/ *n* **1** [C] means of entering; way in; entrance: *The only access to that building is along that muddy track* **2** [U] means or right of using, reaching, or entering: *Students need easy access to books* **3** [C] *lit or old use* a sudden attack, as of anger or a disease **4 easy/difficult of access** easy/difficult to reach

ac·ces·si·ble /ək'sesəbəl/ *adj* [B (*to*)] **1** easy to get or get into, to, or at: *The books are easily accessible as all the shelves are open* **2** easily persuaded or influenced —**-ibility** /əkˌsesə'bɪlɪ̣ti/ *n* [U]

ac·ces·sion /ək'seʃən/ *n fml* **1** [U (*to*)] the act of coming to a position, office, state, etc. **2** [U] increase or addition, as to a group or collection: *The collection of modern painting has become larger through accession* **3** [C (*to*)] something added; an addition: *an important new accession of scientific books to the library* **4** [U;C: (*to*)] agreement, as to a demand

ac·ces·so·ry /ək'sesəri/ *n* **1** [*usu. pl.*] something which is not a necessary part of something larger but which makes it more beautiful, useful, effective, etc.: *The accessories for a car include the heater and radio* **2** [*usu. pl.*] the hat, shoes, etc., that complete a woman's clothes: *a black dress with matching accessories* **3** also (*law*) **accessary**— a person who is not present at a crime but who helps another in doing something criminal, either before the act (**accessory before the fact**) or after the act (**accessory after the fact**)

ac·ci·dence /'æksɪ̣dəns/ *n* [U] *tech* the rules in language which are concerned with the INFLECTIONal (2a) changes in the form of words according to their work (as in *sing, sang, sung,* or in *body, bodies*) —compare MORPHOLOGY (1)

ac·ci·dent /ˈæksədənt/ *n* [C; *without*+U] **1** something, esp. something unpleasant, undesirable, or damaging, that happens unexpectedly or by chance: *I have had an accident in the kitchen and broken all the glasses.|We got back without accident* **2 by accident** ACCIDENTALly **3 by accident of** by the chance, luck, or fortune of: *By accident of birth he was rich*

ac·ci·den·tal /ˌæksəˈdentl/ *adj* not happening by plan or intention; happening by chance —**~ly** *adv* [Wa4]

accident-prone /ˈ··· ·/ *adj* (of a person) more likely to have accidents than most people are or than one usually is

ac·claim[1] /əˈkleɪm/ *v* **1** [T1] to greet with loud shouts of approval or praise **2** [T1 (*as*);X1] to declare to be or publicly recognize as, esp. with loud shouts of approval or praise: *They acclaimed him as the best writer of the year.|They acclaimed her their leader*

acclaim[2] *n* [U] strong expressions of approval and praise

ac·cla·ma·tion /ˌækləˈmeɪʃən/ *n* **1** [U] loud approval and praise, as for an idea or suggestion; ACCLAIM[2] **2** [C *usu. pl.*] loud shouts of welcome and honour **3 by acclamation** by the noise of shouts rather than by voting

ac·cli·ma·tize /əˈklaɪmətaɪz/ *v* [T1;IØ: (*to*)] **1** to cause (oneself, plants, animals, etc.) to become accustomed to the conditions of weather, in a new part of the world **2** to cause (oneself or another) to become accustomed to new conditions and places: *Country girls can't acclimatize themselves to working in an office* —**-tization** /əˌklaɪmətaɪˈzeɪʃən‖-tə-/ *n* [U]

ac·cliv·i·ty /əˈklɪvəti/ *n rare* an upward slope —compare DECLIVITY

ac·co·lade /ˈækəleɪd/ *n* **1** strong praise and approval: *His new book received accolades from the papers* **2** *old use* the act of giving a noble rank (KNIGHTHOOD) to a man by touching his shoulders with the flat blade of a sword

ac·com·mo·date /əˈkɒmədeɪt‖əˈkɑ-/ *v* [T1] *fml* **1** to provide with a room in which to live or stay **2** to have enough space for **3** [(*to*)] to bring (something) into agreement with something else: *a chair which accommodates its shape to a person's position* **4** [(*to*)] to change (oneself or one's habits, way of life, etc.) to fit new conditions **5** [(*with*)] to supply with something; help by doing something: *He asked his uncle to accommodate him (when he lost all his money)*

ac·com·mo·dat·ing /əˈkɒmədeɪtɪŋ‖əˈkɑ-/ *adj* **1** ready to change to suit new conditions; easy to deal with **2** willing to help —**~ly** *adv*

ac·com·mo·da·tion /əˌkɒməˈdeɪʃən‖əˌkɑ-/ *n* **1** [U] a place to live; room, flat, house, hotel room, etc.: *What sort of accommodation can you get in this city?* **2** [U] the act of changing something so that it suits new conditions **3** [U;C] the act of settling a business disagreement or the ending of a disagreement **4** [C] something that helps, or makes an action easier

ac·com·mo·da·tions /əˌkɒməˈdeɪʃənz‖əˌkɑ-/ *n* [P] *AmE* **1** lodging, food, and services **2** a seat or place to sleep, together with services and/or food

ac·com·pa·ni·ment /əˈkʌmpənimənt/ *n* **1** something which is usually or often found with something else **2** music played on a musical instrument to support singing or another instrument

ac·com·pa·nist /əˈkʌmpənəst/ *n* a person who plays a musical ACCOMPANIMENT

ac·com·pa·ny /əˈkʌmpəni/ *v* [T1] **1** to go with, as on a journey **2** to happen or exist at the same time as: *Lightning usually accompanies thunder* **3** to make supporting music for

ac·com·plice /əˈkʌmpləs‖əˈkɑm-, əˈkʌm-/ *n* a person who helps one to do wrong

ac·com·plish /əˈkʌmplɪʃ‖əˈkɑm-, əˈkʌm-/ *v* [T1] to succeed in doing; finish successfully; perform: *We tried to arrange a peace but accomplished nothing*

ac·com·plished /əˈkʌmplɪʃt‖əˈkɑm-, əˈkʌm-/ *adj* **1** skilled, clever; good at something, though not professional: *an accomplished singer* **2** *becoming rare* skilled in lady-like arts

accomplished fact /·,·· ˈ·/ *n* [S] something that has already happened, cannot be changed, and must be accepted

ac·com·plish·ment /əˈkʌmplɪʃmənt‖əˈkɑm-, əˈkʌm-/ *n* **1** [U] the act of finishing work completely and successfully **2** [C] something completely and successfully done: *She is known for her accomplishment in improving the country's hospitals* **3** [C] *polite becoming rare* a lady-like art **4 difficult/easy of accomplishment** *fml* difficult/easy to do

ac·cord[1] /əˈkɔːd‖-ɔrd/ *v* **1** [IØ (*with*)] to be of the same nature or quality; be in agreement: *What you have just said does not accord with what you told us yesterday.|His peaceful words and violent actions do not accord* **2** [D1 (*to*);(T1)] *fml* to give; allow: *He was accorded permission to use the library*

accord[2] *n* **1** [U] agreement (esp. in the phr. **in/out of accord (with)**) **2** [C] an agreement between countries, businesses, etc. **3 of one's own accord** without being asked; willingly; freely **4 with one accord** with everybody agreeing

ac·cord·ance /əˈkɔːdəns‖-ɔr-/ *n* [U] agreement (esp. in the phr. **in accordance with**): *In accordance with your orders I sold the boat*

ac·cord·ing as /əˈkɔːdɪŋ əz, -æz‖əˈkɔr-/ *conj* depending on whether: *They move into the next class, according as they pass or fail the examination*

ac·cord·ing·ly /əˈkɔːdɪŋli‖-ɔr-/ *adv* **1** in a way suitable to what has been said or what has happened: *You told me to lock the door and I acted accordingly (by locking it)* **2** therefore; so

according to /·ˈ·· ·/ *prep* **1** as stated or shown by: *According to my watch it is 4 o'clock* **2** in a way that agrees with: *Each man will be paid according to his ability*

ac·cor·di·on /əˈkɔːdɪən‖-ɔr-/ *n* a musical instrument that may be carried and whose music is made by pressing the middle part together and so causing air to pass through holes opened and closed by instruments (KEYs[1] (2)) worked by the fingers —compare CONCERTINA[1] —see picture at KEYBOARD[1]

ac·cost /əˈkɒst‖əˈkɔst, əˈkɑst/ *v* [T1] **1** to go up to and speak to (esp. a stranger) **2** (of a beggar or sexually immoral person) to go up to and ask for money or suggest sex

ac·count[1] /əˈkaʊnt/ *n* **1** [C] a written or spoken report; description; story: *Give us an account of what happened* **2** [U] *fml* importance; value; worth: *The doctor is a man of some account in the village* **3** [U] consideration; thought: *You must take into account the boy's long illness.|Leave their foolish remarks out of account* **4** [U] advantage; profit: *He put/turned his knowledge to (good) account* **5** [C] a record or statement of money received and paid out, as by a bank or business, esp. for a particular period or at a particular date: *The accounts show we have spent more than we received* **6** [C] a statement of money owed: *Will you add the cost of this skirt to my account as I haven't any money with me?*|(fig.) *I have an account to settle with you for calling me a thief* **7** [C] a sum of money kept in a bank which may be added to and taken from: *My account is empty* —see also

CURRENT ACCOUNT; DEPOSIT ACCOUNT; SAVINGS ACCOUNT **8 bring/call (someone) to account (for)** **a** to cause or force (someone) to give an explanation (of) **b** to punish (someone) (for) **9 by/from all accounts** according to what everyone, the papers, etc., say **10 of great/no account** of great/no importance **11 on account of** because of **12 on no account** also **not on any account**— not for any reason: *You must not go there on any account.|On no account must you go there* **13 on one's own account** **a** so as to advance one's own interests **b** at one's own risk **c** by oneself

account² *v* [X1,7] to consider: *He was accounted a wise man.|He accounted himself lucky to be alive*

ac·coun·ta·ble /ə'kaʊntəbəl/ *adj* **1** [F (*for*)] with the duty of having to give an explanation: *If anything happens to the boy I will hold you accountable (for it)* **2** [F (*to* and/or *for*)] responsible: *I am not accountable to you for my actions*

ac·coun·tan·cy /ə'kaʊntənsi/ *n* [U] the work or job of an ACCOUNTANT

ac·coun·tant /ə'kaʊntənt/ *n* a person whose job is to keep and examine the money accounts of businesses or people

account for *v prep* **1** [T1,6a: (*to*)] to give a statement showing how money or goods left in one's care have been dealt with: *He has to account to the chairman for all the money he spends* —compare ANSWER FOR **2** [T1,4,6a: (*to*)] to give an explanation or reason for: *He could not account for his foolish mistake* **3** [T1] *infml* to kill, shoot, or catch: *I think I accounted for 3 of the attackers*

ac·cou·tre·ments /ə'kuːtrəmənts/ also *AmE* **-terments** /ə'kuːtəmənts‖-tər-/— *n* [P] **1** everything a soldier carries, except his clothes and weapons **2** *humor* all the things except clothes that a traveller has with him, such as cameras and bags

ac·cred·it /ə'kredət/ *v* [T1 *usu. pass.*] **1** to send abroad as an official representing the government **2** [Wv5] to give the power to act for an organization: *an accredited representative of the firm* **3** [Wv5] to recognize or state that (something) is of a certain standard or quality **4** [(*with*)] to be regarded as having been responsible (for); CREDIT: *He was accredited with having said so*

ac·cre·tion /ə'kriːʃən/ *n fml* **1** [U] increase by natural growth or by the gradual addition of matter on the outside **2** [C] something added or the result of something having been added: *The thick dirt on the building was the accretion of ages.| towers and other accretions to the castle*

ac·crue /ə'kruː/ *v* [IØ] *fml* to become bigger or more by addition: *The interest on my bank account accrued over the years*

ac·cu·mu·late /ə'kjuːmjʊleɪt‖-mjə-/ *v* [T1;IØ] to make or become greater in quantity or size; collect or grow into a mass: *He quickly accumulated a large fortune*

ac·cu·mu·la·tion /əˌkjuːmjʊ'leɪʃən‖-mjə-/ *n* **1** [U] the act of accumulating (ACCUMULATE) **2** [C] matter, material, etc., that has come together or grown: *an accumulation of work while I was ill*

ac·cu·mu·la·tive /ə'kjuːmjʊlətɪv‖-mjəleɪ-, -lə-/ *adj* **1** CUMULATIVE **2** tending or trying to ACCUMULATE (esp. money or goods) —**~ly** *adv*

ac·cu·mu·la·tor /ə'kjuːmjʊleɪtəʳ‖-mjə-/ *n* **1** *esp. BrE* a box-like apparatus in which electrical power can be stored **2** a part of a COMPUTER (=calculating machine) where numbers are stored **3** *BrE* a set of BETs¹ on 4 or more horse races. The money won on each race is added to the money put on the next race until all the BETs have been won or one is lost

ac·cu·ra·cy /'ækjərəsi/ *n* [U] the quality of being ACCURATE; exactness or correctness

ac·cu·rate /'ækjərət/ *adj* **1** careful and exact: *This is an accurate statement of what happened* **2** free of mistakes; exactly correct —**~ly** *adv*

ac·curs·ed /ə'kɜːsəd, ə'kɜːst‖-ɜr-/ also **ac·curst** /ə'kɜːst‖-ɜr-/— *adj* **1** under a curse; suffering very bad fortune **2** hateful because causing bad fortune, suffering, great trouble, etc. —**~ly** /ə'kɜːsədli‖-ɜr-/

ac·cu·sa·tion /ˌækjʊ'zeɪʃən‖-kjə-/ *n* **1** [U] the act of accusing (ACCUSE) or of being accused **2** [C] a charge of doing wrong: *The accusation was that he had murdered a man*

ac·cu·sa·tive /ə'kjuːzətɪv/ *n, adj* [Wa5] (the CASE¹ (8) in the grammar of Latin, Greek, German, etc.) showing that the word is the DIRECT OBJECT of a verb

ac·cuse /ə'kjuːz/ *v* [Wv4,5;T1 (*of*)] to charge (someone) with doing wrong or breaking the law; blame: *The police accused him (of murder).|The angry man gave her an accusing look.|The judge asked the accused man to stand up* —**~r** *n* —**accusingly** *adv*

ac·cused /ə'kjuːzd/ *adj* [Wa5;*the*+GU] charged with doing wrong, a crime, etc.: *The judge asked the accused to stand up, and he stood up.|Several of the accused were found guilty*

ac·cus·tom /ə'kʌstəm/ *v* [T1 (*to*)] to make used to: *He had to accustom himself to the cold weather of his new country*

ac·cus·tomed /ə'kʌstəmd/ *adj* [Wa5] **1** [A] regular; usual: *her accustomed smile* **2** [F+*to*] being in the habit of; used to: *He is accustomed to working hard*

ace /eɪs/ *n* **1** [C] a playing card or other object (such as a DOMINO (1)), used in games, that has a single mark or spot and which usu. has the highest or the lowest value —see CARDS (USAGE) **2** [C9] *infml* a person of the highest class or skill in something: *He's an ace at cards* (=card games) **3** [C] (in tennis) a beginning shot (SERVE¹ (10)) that the opponent cannot hit back **4 within an ace of** *infml* very close to (a condition): *within an ace of success/victory/death*

a·cer·bi·ty /ə'sɜːbəti‖-ɜr-/ *n fml* **1** [U] bitterness, sourness of taste **2** [U] bitterness of speech, temper, or manner **3** [C] an example of this

ac·e·tate /'æsəteɪt/ *n* [U] a chemical made from ACETIC ACID

a·ce·tic /ə'siːtɪk/ *adj* [Wa5] of, concerning, or producing VINEGAR or ACETIC ACID

acetic ac·id /·ˌ·· '··/ *n* [U] the acid in a bitter liquid (VINEGAR) made from wine or beer

a·cet·y·lene /ə'setəliːn‖-lən, -liːn/ *n* [U] a colourless gas which burns with a very bright flame and is used in certain types of lamp and in cutting and joining pieces of metal

ache¹ /eɪk/ *v* **1** [IØ] to have or suffer a continuous dull pain: *I ache all over.|My head aches* **2** [IØ (*for, with*),3] to have a strong feeling or desire: *He was aching to go.|aching with desire to go*

ache² *n* (*often in comb.*) a continuous pain: *headache*|(fig.) *heartache*

USAGE 1 Note the word order in this fixed phr.: **aches and pains.** 2 Nouns formed from **ache** are treated as [U] when they mean a condition or state: *Chocolate gives me* **toothache**. When they mean a single attack of pain, they are usu. treated as [C] in *AmE* and [U] in *BrE*: *She very often gets (esp. AmE)* **stomachaches** *or (esp. BrE)* **stomachache**. But **headache** is always a [C] noun: *a nasty* **headache**.

a·chieve /ə'tʃiːv/ *v* [T1] **1** to finish successfully (esp. something, anything, nothing): *He will never achieve anything if he doesn't work harder* **2** to get as the result of action; gain (something non-material): *He hopes to achieve all his aims by the end of the year* —see COULD (USAGE) —**achievable** *adj*

a·chieve·ment /əˈtʃiːvmənt/ *n* **1** [U] the successful finishing or gaining of something **2** [C] something successfully finished or gained esp. through skill and hard work

A·chil·les' heel /əˌkɪliːz ˈhiːl/ *n* a weak point, esp. in a person's character

Achilles ten·don /·ˌ·· ˈ··/ *n* the stringlike TENDON which fixes the muscle at the back of the lower leg to the heel

a·choo /əˈtʃuː/ *interj AmE* ATISHOO

ac·id[1] /ˈæsɨd/ *adj* **1** having a sour or bitter taste like that of unripe fruit or VINEGAR **2** bad-tempered; angry in speech **3** of or concerning a chemical acid

acid[2] *n* **1** [U;C] a chemical substance containing a particular gas (HYDROGEN) the place of which may be taken by a metal to form another type of substance (a SALT[1] (3)) **2** [U] something (esp. a liquid) with an ACID[1] (1) taste **3** [U] *sl* LSD (1)

a·cid·i·fy /əˈsɪdɨfaɪ/ *v* [T1;I∅] to make into or become an acid

a·cid·i·ty /əˈsɪdɨti/ *n* [U] the quality of being acid; sourness

acid test /ˌ·· ˈ·/ *n* a test or trial which will prove whether something is as valuable as stated or will do what it is supposed to be able to do

a·cid·u·lat·ed /əˈsɪdʒʊleɪtɨd‖-dʒə-/ *adj tech* (esp. of sweets and drinks) made to have an acid taste

a·cid·u·lous /əˈsɪdʒʊləs‖-dʒə-/ *adj* **1** rather acid in taste **2** (of speech or manner) bitter; bad-tempered

ack-ack /ˌæk ˈæk‖ˈæk æk/ *n* [U;C *usu. pl.*] *infml now rare* an ANTIAIRCRAFT gun or fire from such a gun

ac·knowl·edge /əkˈnɒlɪdʒ‖-ˈnɑ-/ *v* **1** [T1,4,5 (*to*)] to agree to the truth of; recognize the fact or existence (of): *I acknowledge the truth of your statement.|They acknowledged* (*to us*) *that they were defeated.|They acknowledged having been defeated* **2** [T1 (*as*);X (*to be*) 1,7] to recognize, accept, or admit (as): *He was acknowledged to be the best player.|He was acknowledged as their leader.|They acknowledged themselves* (*to be*) *defeated* **3** [T1 (*with, by*)] to show that one is grateful for, as by giving or saying something: *His long service with the company was acknowledged with a present* **4** [T1] to state that one has received (something): *We must acknowledge his letter* **5** [T1] to show that one recognizes (someone) as by smiling, or waving: *My son walked right past me without even acknowledging me*

ac·knowl·edg·ment, -edgement /əkˈnɒlɪdʒmənt‖-ˈnɑ-/ *n* **1** [U] the act of acknowledging (ACKNOWLEDGE): *He was given a present in acknowledgment of his work for the business* **2** [C] something given, done, or said as a way of thanking **3** [C] a statement, letter, etc., saying that something has been received

ac·me /ˈækmi/ *n* [*usu. sing.*] the highest or greatest point of development, ability, success, etc.: *the acme of perfection*

ac·ne /ˈækni/ *n* [U] a disease (common among young people) in which small raised spots appear on the face and neck

ac·o·lyte /ˈækəlaɪt/ *n* **1** a person who helps a priest to perform religious ceremonies **2** *lit* an attendant

ac·o·nite /ˈækənaɪt/ *n* **1** [U;(C)] any of various plants usually having blue or bluish flowers and poisonous qualities **2** [U] a medicine made from one of these plants

a·corn /ˈeɪkɔːn‖-ɔrn, -ərn/ *n* the fruit or nut of the OAK tree, which grows in a cuplike holder —see picture at NUT[1], TREE[1]

a·cous·tic /əˈkuːstɪk/ *adj* [Wa5] **1** of or concerning sound or the sense of hearing **2** (esp. of a musical instrument) making its natural sound, not helped by electrical apparatus —**~ally** *adv* [Wa4]

a·cous·tics /əˈkuːstɪks/ *n* **1** [U] the scientific study of sound **2** [P] the qualities of a place, esp. a hall, which make it good, bad, etc., for hearing music and speeches: *The acoustics of the hall are so good that you can hear everything even from the cheapest seats* **3** [P] the qualities of sounds picked up by the ear

ac·quaint·ance /əˈkweɪntəns/ *n* **1** [S;U:+*with*] information or knowledge, as obtained through personal experience rather than careful study: *I have an/some acquaintance with the language* **2** [C] a person whom one knows, esp. through work or business, but who may not be a friend **3 make someone's acquaintance** also **make the acquaintance of someone**— to meet or get to know as by an introduction

ac·quaint·ance·ship /əˈkweɪntənsʃɪp/ *n* [S] **1** [(*with*)] the state of being socially acquainted (ACQUAINT WITH (2b)) **2** [(*among, with*)] the number of people with whom one is socially acquainted (ACQUAINT WITH (2b)): *He has a wide acquaintanceship among all sorts of people*

ac·quaint with /əˈkweɪnt/ *v prep* [D1] **1** to make (oneself or someone) familiar with (something) **2 be acquainted (with) a** to have knowledge (of): *I am already acquainted with the facts* **b** to have met socially: *We are acquainted* (*with each other*)

ac·qui·esce /ˌækwiˈes/ *v* [I∅ (*in*)] *fml* to agree, often unwillingly, without raising an argument; accept quietly: *He acquiesced in the plans his parents had made for him* —**-escence** *n* [U]

ac·qui·es·cent /ˌækwiˈesənt/ *adj* ready to agree without argument —**~ly** *adv*

ac·quire /əˈkwaɪəʳ/ *v* [T1] **1** to get for oneself by one's own work, skill, action, etc.: *He acquired a knowledge of the language by careful study* **2** to gain or come into possession of: *With the money he had won he was able to acquire some property*

acquired taste /·ˌ· ˈ·/ *n* [*usu. sing.*] something that one must learn to like: *Some alcoholic drinks are an acquired taste and are not liked at first*

ac·qui·si·tion /ˌækwɨˈzɪʃən/ *n* **1** [U] the act of acquiring (ACQUIRE) **2** [C] something or someone ACQUIREd: *This car is my latest acquisition.|He is a valuable acquisition to the firm*

ac·quis·i·tive /əˈkwɪzɨtɪv/ *adj* in the habit of acquiring (ACQUIRE) or collecting things: *He is very acquisitive and has filled his house with things he has bought* —**~ly** *adv* —**~ness** *n* [U]

ac·quit /əˈkwɪt/ *v* **-tt-** [T1] **1** [(*of, on*)] to give a decision as in a court of law that (someone) is not guilty of a fault or crime: *They acquitted him of murder.|He was acquitted on the charge* **2** *lit, usu. apprec.* to cause (oneself) to act in the stated (usu. favourable) way: *He acquitted himself rather badly*

ac·quit·tal /əˈkwɪtl/ *n* [C;U] the act of declaring or condition of being found not guilty, as in a court of law —opposite **conviction**

a·cre /ˈeɪkəʳ/ *n* a measure of land; 4,840 square yards or about 4,047 square metres: *The total area of a football field measures a little more than 2 acres* —see WEIGHTS & MEASURES TABLE

a·cre·age /ˈeɪkərɪdʒ/ *n* [S;U] the area of a piece of land measured in ACREs

ac·rid /ˈækrɨd/ *adj* **1** (of taste or smell) bitter; causing a stinging sensation: *the acrid smell of burning wood* **2** bitter in manner; bad-tempered: *an acrid speech*

ac·ri·mo·ny /ˈækrɨməni‖-məʊni/ *n* [U] bitterness,

as of manner or language —**-nious** /ˌækrᵻ-ˈməʊnɪəs/ *adj*: *an acrimonious quarrel* —**-niously** *adv*

ac·ro·bat /ˈækrəbæt/ *n* a person skilled in walking on ropes or swinging between ropes high in the air, balancing, walking on hands, etc., during a show, esp. at a CIRCUS (2) —see picture at THEATRE

ac·ro·bat·ic /ˌækrəˈbætɪk/ *adj* of or like an ACROBAT; moving or changing position quickly and easily, esp. in the air —**~ally** *adv* [Wa4]

ac·ro·bat·ics /ˌækrəˈbætɪks/ *n* **1** [U] the art and tricks of an ACROBAT: *Acrobatics is hard to learn but beautiful to watch* **2** [P] a group of ACROBATIC tricks considered as a performance: *His acrobatics yesterday were very clever*

ac·ro·nym /ˈækrənɪm/ *n* a word made up from the first letters of the name of something, esp. an organization (such as *NATO* from *N*orth *A*tlantic *T*reaty *O*rganization)

a·cross /əˈkrɒs‖əˈkrɔs/ *adv, prep* [Wa5] **1** from one side to the other (of): *The stream is 6 feet across.|They built a bridge across the river* **2** [F] to or on the opposite side (of): *Can you jump across?|We swam across the river.|They live just across the road (from us)* **3** so as to cross: *The 2 lines cut across each other* **4 across the board** concerning people or groups of all types, esp. within a business or industry: *It is an across-the-board pay rise* —see also COME ACROSS, CUT ACROSS, GET ACROSS, PUT ACROSS, RUN ACROSS

across from /·ˈ· ·/ *prep esp. AmE* opposite: *They live just across from us*

a·cros·tic /əˈkrɒstɪk‖əˈkrɔ-/ *n* a set or group of words or lines (as of a poem), written one below the other, in which all the first, last, or other particular letters form a word or phrase

a·cryl·ic fi·bre, *AmE* **-fi·ber** /əˌkrɪlɪk ˈfaɪbəʳ/ *n* [U;C] a type of threadlike material made by man, used for clothes

act[1] /ækt/ *v* **1** [T1;I∅] to represent (a part) or perform by action, esp. on the stage: *Olivier is acting ("Othello") tonight* **2** [L1] *derog* to play the part of, as in a play: *He is always acting the experienced man who has seen everything* **3** [I∅] *derog* to behave as if performing on the stage: *I can't take her seriously because she always seems to be acting* **4** [L9] (of a play) to be able to be performed as stated: *The play acts well* **5** [I∅ (*on, for*)] to take action: *Think before you act!|She acted favourably on our suggestion.|In this case I'm acting for my friend Mr. Smith* **6** [L9] to behave as stated: *to act foolishly|bravely and quickly* **7** [I∅ (*on, upon*)] to produce an effect; work: *Does the drug take long to act (on the pain)?* —see also ACT AS, ACT OUT, ACT UP, ACT UP TO

act[2] *n* **1** *fml* a thing done; deed (of the stated type): *a foolish act|an act of cruelty* **2** (*often cap.*) a law: *Parliament has passed an Act forbidding the killing of animals for pleasure* **3** (*often cap*) one of the main divisions of a stage play: *Hamlet kills the king in Act 5 Scene 2* **4** one of a number of short events in a theatre or CIRCUS (2) performance: *The next act will be a snake charmer* **5** *derog infml* an example of insincere behaviour used for effect (often in the phr. **put on an act**): *She doesn't really mean it, it's just an act* **6 act of grace** something done out of kindness and not because it is necessary by law or business agreement **7 catch (someone) in the (very) act of (doing)** to find (someone) actually doing (something wrong) **8 get in on the/someone's act** *infml* to get a share of an/someone's activity, and esp. any advantages that may come as a result **9 in the act of (doing)** while doing; at the moment of doing: *I was in the act of shooting him when I suddenly recognized him* —see also ACTS, ACT AS, ACT OUT, ACT UP, ACT UP TO

USAGE When **action** is used as a count noun it means the same thing as **act**: *a kind* **act/action**. Certain fixed phrs. use **act** and not **action**: *an* **act** *of cruelty|of mercy|caught in the* **act** *of stealing*.|**Action,** unlike **act**, is also used as a mass noun **a** to mean the way or effect of doing something: *the* **action** *of a runner|of a medicine* **b** in certain other fixed phrs.: *to take (quick)* **action** (=to act (quickly)).

act as *v prep* [L1] to fulfil the purpose of: *A trained dog can act as a guide to a blind man*

act·ing[1] /ˈæktɪŋ/ *adj* [Wa5;A] who has the office of, or is taking the place of: *the acting President*

acting[2] *n* [U] the art of representing a character, esp. on a stage or for a film

ac·tin·is·m /ˈæktᵻnɪzəm/ *n* [U] *tech* the ability of some of the sun's light to produce chemical changes, esp. on a film used in photography

ac·tion /ˈækʃən/ *n* **1** [U] movement using force or power for some purpose; doing things: *We must take action before it is too late* **2** [C] something done; deed: *Actions are more important than words* **3** [C *usu. sing.*] the way in which a body moves: *The horse had a fine action as it jumped the fence* **4** [C *usu. sing.*] the way in which a part of the body or a machine works: *Let's study the action of the heart* **5** [C *usu. sing.*] the moving parts of a machine or instrument: *The action of this piano is becoming stiff* **6** [C *usu. sing.*] effect: *Photographs are made possible by the action of light on film* **7** [C; U] a charge or a matter for consideration by a court of law: *If he doesn't pay us soon we will have to bring an action against him* **8** [C;U] fighting or a fight between armies or navies: *The action lasted 5 hours.|Many were killed in action* **9** [C *usu. sing.*] the main story or chain of events in a play or book rather than the characters in it: *The action took place in a mountain village* **10** [*the*+S] *sl* the most productive, interesting, or exciting activity in a particular field, area, or group: *London is great because that's where the action is!* **11 in/into action** in/into operation or a typical activity: *Things will be easier when we put the new system into action.|He is a very good tennis player: you ought to see him in action* **12 out of action** out of operation; no longer able to do a typical activity: *The storm put the telephones out of action* **13 take action** begin to act

ac·tio·na·ble /ˈækʃənəbəl/ *adj* giving enough cause for a charge in court

action paint·ing /ˈ·· ˌ··/ *n* [U] ABSTRACT painting where the paint is put on in various unusual ways, as by throwing or pouring

action sta·tions /ˈ·· ˌ··/ *interj* (an order to soldiers, sailors, etc., to take up or get into fighting positions, ready for battle or other urgent action)

ac·tiv·ate /ˈæktᵻveɪt/ *v* [T1] **1** to cause to be active; bring into use **2** to cause (a chemical action) to happen more quickly, as by heating **3** to cause to be RADIOACTIVE **4** to make pure (waste matter (SEWAGE)) by passing air through —**-ation** /ˌæktᵻˈveɪʃən/ *n* [U]

ac·tive[1] /ˈæktɪv/ *adj* **1** doing things or always ready to do things; able or ready to take action: *Although he is over 70 he is still active.|He leads an active life* **2** able to produce the typical effects or act in the typical way: *Be careful! That dangerous chemical is still active!* **3** [Wa5] (of a verb or sentence) having as the subject the person or thing doing the action (as in *The boy kicked the ball*) —compare PASSIVE[1] (4) —**~ly** *adv*

active[2] *n* [(*the*) S] also **active voice** /ˌ·· ˈ·/— the ACTIVE[1] (3) part or form of a verb: *Put this sentence into the active*

active ser·vice /ˌ·· ˈ··/ *n* [U] **on active service** *BrE* (in the armed forces) actually fighting

ac·tiv·ist /ˈæktɪvɪst/ *n* a person taking an active part, esp. in a political movement
ac·tiv·i·ty /ækˈtɪvɪti/ *n* **1** [U] the condition of being active **2** [C *often pl.*] something that is done or is being done, esp. for interest or education: *He has many activities that take up his time when he's not working* **3** [C *often pl*] action; deed: *Police fight against the activities of thieves*
act of God /ˌ· · ˈ·/ *n* a natural event, esp. something damaging, such as a violent storm or flood, whose happening can be neither prevented nor controlled
ac·tor /ˈæktəʳ/ *n* **1** a man who acts a part in a play —see picture at THEATRE **2** a person who takes part in something that happens
act out *v adv* [T1] to express (thoughts, unconscious fears, etc.) in actions and behaviour rather than in words
ac·tress /ˈæktrɪs/ *n* a female ACTOR[1] —see picture at THEATRE
Acts /ækts/ also **the Acts of the Apostles** /· ˌ· · · ·ˈ··/— *n* [R] one of the books in the Bible. It describes the deeds of the first followers of Christ
ac·tu·al /ˈæktʃʊəl/ *adj* [Wa5;A] **1** existing as a real fact: *The actual amount of money was not known although they knew it was large* **2 in actual fact** *not fml* in reality; in ACTUALITY; ACTUALLY
ac·tu·al·i·ty /ˌæktʃʊˈælɪti/ *n fml* **1** [U] the state of being real; existence **2** [C *usu. pl.*] something that is real; fact
ac·tu·al·ly /ˈæktʃʊəli, -tʃəli/ *adv* [Wa5] **1** in actual fact; really: *The people who actually have power are the owners of big industries.|Actually, you owe me more than this* **2** strange as it may seem: *He not only invited me into his house but he actually offered me a drink* —see PRESENTLY (USAGE)
ac·tu·a·ry /ˈæktʃʊəri‖-tʃʊeri/ *n* a person who advises insurance companies on how much to charge for insurance, after considering the risks of fire, death, etc. —**-arial** /ˌæktʃʊˈeərɪəl/ *adj* [Wa5;A]
ac·tu·ate /ˈæktʃʊeɪt/ *v* [T1] to cause to act: *He is actuated not by kindness but by a desire for fame*
act up also **play up**— *v adv* [IØ] *infml esp BrE* to behave or perform badly: *The car's engine is beginning to act up*
act up to *v adv prep* [T1] LIVE UP TO
a·cu·i·ty /əˈkjuːɪti/ *n* [U] *fml* fineness or sharpness, esp. of the mind or the senses of sight or hearing
ac·u·men /ˈækjʊmən, əˈkjuːmən‖əˈkjuː-/ *n* [U] *fml* ability to think and judge quickly and well: *His business acumen has made him very successful*
ac·u·punc·ture /ˈækjʊˌpʌŋktʃəʳ/ *n* [U] the method of stopping pain and curing diseases by pricking certain parts of the body with needles, used esp. in China
a·cute /əˈkjuːt/ *adj* **1** (of the mind or the senses) able to notice small differences, as of meaning or sound; working very well; sharp: *Dogs have an acute sense of smell* **2** severe; strong; deep: *She was in acute pain* **3** important enough to cause anxiety; very great: *There was an acute lack of food* **4** (of a disease) coming quickly to a dangerous condition —compare CHRONIC **5** (of a sound) so high as to be almost painful **6** (of an angle) being less than 90 degrees; narrow —see picture at GEOMETRY **7** [Wa5] (of a mark (ACCENT) put above a letter to show pronunciation) being the mark over é (as in *élite, café*) —compare GRAVE[3] —**~ly** *adv* —**~ness** *n* [U]
AD *abbrev. for*: (in the year) since the birth of Christ
ad /æd/ *n infml* advertisement
ad- /əd, æd/ *prefix* [v→v] towards; to: *to advance*| ADHERE
ad·age /ˈædɪdʒ/ *n* an old wise phrase; PROVERB
a·da·gio /əˈdɑːdʒəʊ/ *adv, adj, n* **-ios** (a piece of music) played slowly
Ad·am /ˈædəm/ *n* [R] **1** (according to the Bible) the first man whom God made —compare EVE **2 not know someone from Adam** *infml* to have no idea of what someone looks like
ad·a·mant[1] /ˈædəmənt/ *n* [U] hard stone, esp. a type that people used to consider too hard to be broken
adamant[2] *adj* [B;F(5, *in*)] *fml* (esp. of a person or behaviour) hard, immovable, and unyielding: *I am adamant that they should go* —**-mancy** /mənsi/ *n* [U] —**~ly** *adv*
Adam's ap·ple /ˌ·· ˈ··‖ˈ·· ˌ··/ *n* that part at the front of the throat that is seen to move when a person, esp. a man, talks or swallows —see picture at HUMAN[2]
a·dapt /əˈdæpt/ *v* [T1 (*to, for*)] to change so as to be or make suitable for new needs, different conditions, etc.: *He adapted an old car engine to drive his boat.|We adapted ourselves to the hot weather* —compare ADOPT
a·dap·ta·ble /əˈdæptəbəl/ *adj often apprec* able to change or be changed so as to be suitable for new needs, different conditions, etc.: *He is an adaptable man and will soon learn the new work* —**-ability** /əˌdæptəˈbɪlɪti/ *n* [U]
ad·ap·ta·tion /ˌædəpˈteɪʃən/ *n* **1** [U] the art of ADAPTing or the state of being ADAPTed: *The adaptation of the play for radio was easily done* **2** [C] something that has been ADAPTed
a·dapt·er, -or /əˈdæptəʳ/ *n* a person or thing that makes something suitable for a new purpose, esp. an apparatus (PLUG) that makes it possible to use more than one piece of electrical machinery from a single electricity supply point (SOCKET) —see picture at ELECTRICITY
ADC *abbrev. for*: AIDE-DE-CAMP
add /æd/ *v* **1** [T1 (*to*)] to put together with something else so as to increase the number, size, importance, etc.: *The fire is going out; will you add some wood?|He added some wood to increase the fire.|He added the wood to the fire* **2** [T1 (*to*, TOGETHER, UP);IØ] to join (numbers, amounts, etc.) so as to find the total: *If you add 5 and/to 3 you get 8* **3** [T5] to say also: *I should like to add that we are pleased with the result* **4 add fuel to the fire** *infml* to make someone feel even more strongly about something **5 add insult to injury** to make matters even worse, esp. by causing annoyance as well as harm —see also ADD TO, ADD UP, ADD UP TO
ad·den·dum /əˈdendəm/ *n* **-da** /də/ something that is added or is to be added, as at the end of a speech or book
ad·der /ˈædəʳ/ *n* a small poisonous snake found in northern Europe and northern Asia
ad·dict[1] /əˈdɪkt/ *v* [T1 (*to*) *usu. pass.*] to cause (someone) to need or be in the habit of having, taking, etc.: *He became addicted to the drug.*|(fig.) *He was addicted to reading* —compare DEVOTED (2)
ad·dict[2] /ˈædɪkt/ *n* a person who is unable to free himself from a harmful habit, esp. of taking drugs
ad·dic·tion /əˈdɪkʃən/ *n* **1** [U] the state of being ADDICTed **2** [C] an example of this: *Has he any other addictions besides smoking?*
ad·dic·tive /əˈdɪktɪv/ *adj* (of drugs, etc.) causing ADDICTION; habit-forming
ad·di·tion /əˈdɪʃən/ *n* **1** [U] the act of adding, esp. of adding numbers together **2** [C] something added: *A newly born child is often called an addition to the family* **3 in addition (to)** as well (as)
ad·di·tion·al /əˈdɪʃənəl/ *adj* [Wa5] in addition; added: *An additional charge is made for heavy bags* —**~ly** *adv* [Wa4]
ad·di·tive /ˈædɪtɪv/ *n* a substance added in small

quantities to something else, as to improve the quality, or add colour, taste, etc.

ad·dle /ˈædl/ *v* [Wv5;T1;I∅] **1 a** to cause (an egg) to go bad **b** (of an egg) to go bad **2** *infml* **a** to confuse (someone or someone's brain) **b** (of someone's brain) to become confused

ad·dress[1] /əˈdres/ *v* [T1] **1** [(*to*)] to write (on an envelope, parcel, etc.) the name of the person meant to be the receiver, usu. with the place where that person lives or works **2** to direct speech or writing to (a person or group) **3** [(*to*)] to direct (speech or writing) to a person or group **4** [(*to*)] *fml* to cause (oneself) to begin to speak to a person or group **5** [(*to*)] *fml* to put (oneself) to work at: *He addressed himself to the main difficulty* **6** [(*as*)] to speak or write to, using a particular title of rank: *Don't address me as "officer"*

address[2] /əˈdres/ *n* **1** [C] a speech, esp. one that has been formally prepared, made to a group of people (AUDIENCE) gathered especially to listen **2** [U] *fml* manner of expression; behaviour **3** [U] skill and readiness, esp. in conversation **4** [C] also **form of address**— the correct title or expression of politeness to be used to someone in speech or writing

address[3] /əˈdres‖əˈdres, ˈædres/ *n* **1** the number of the building, name of the street and town, etc., where a person works or esp. lives **2** such information written down, as on an envelope or parcel: *I can't read the address on this letter*

ad·dress·ee /ˌædreˈsiː, ə-/ *n* the person to whom a letter, parcel, etc., is addressed

add to *v prep* [T1] to increase

ad·duce /əˈdjuːs‖əˈduːs/ *v* [T1 (*for*)] *fml* to give (an example, proof, reason, etc.): *Can you adduce any reason at all for his strange behaviour, Holmes?*

add up *v adv* **1** [Wv6;I∅] *infml* to make sense; seem likely: *The various facts in the case just don't add up* **2** [T1;(I∅)] to add (numbers) together to get a total

add up to *v adv prep* [Wv6;L1] **1** *infml* to seem to be; amount to; mean: *Your long answer just adds up to a refusal* **2** (of numbers) to amount to (a total) when added together

-ade /eɪd/ *suffix* [*n*→*n* [U]] a usu. sweetened drink made from (the stated fruit): *orangeade*

ad·e·noid·al /ˌædɨˈnɔɪdl◂, ˌædnˈɔɪdl◂/ *adj* **1** [Wa5] of the ADENOIDS (1) **2** of ADENOIDS (2): *an adenoidal voice* —**~ly** *adv* [Wa4]

ad·e·noids /ˈædɨnɔɪdz, ˈædən-/ *n* **1** [P] the pair of soft growths between the back of the nose and the throat —compare TONSIL **2** [U;(P)] *infml* the condition in which these are swollen and sore —see picture at HUMAN[2]

ad·ept[1] /ˈædept/ *n* [(*at, in*)] a person who is highly skilled in something: *He is an adept in the art of stealing*

adept[2] /ˈædept, əˈdept‖əˈdept/ *adj* [B;F (*at, in*)] highly skilled: *He was adept at playing the piano* —**~ly** *adv*

ad·e·quate /ˈædɪkwɨt/ *adj* **1** [B (*for*)] enough for the purpose: *We took adequate food for the short holiday* **2** [B] only just enough: *We had adequate food but none to waste* **3** [F (*to*)] having the necessary ability or qualities: *I hope you will prove adequate to the job* **4** [B] only just good enough: *The performance was adequate, though hardly exciting* —**~ly** *adv* —**-quacy** /ˈædɪkwəsi/ *n* [U9 esp. *for*]: *He doubted her adequacy for the job*

ad·here /ədˈhɪəʳ/ *v* [I∅ (*to*)] to stick firmly (to another or each other): *The 2 surfaces adhered (to each other), and we couldn't get them apart*

ad·her·ence /ədˈhɪərəns/ *n* [U9, esp. *to*] **1** the act or condition of sticking to something firmly **2** the act or condition of favouring something strongly and remaining with it in spite of difficulties

ad·her·ent /ədˈhɪərənt/ *n* a person who favours and remains with a particular idea, opinion, or political party

adhere to *v prep* [T1] *often fml* to favour strongly and remain with; follow steadily; be faithful to (an idea, opinion, belief, etc.): *If you decide on a plan to win the game, you should adhere to it*

ad·he·sion /ədˈhiːʒən/ *n* **1** [U] the state of being stuck together or the action of sticking together **2** [U] the joining together of parts inside the body which should be separate **3** [C] an area of fleshlike body substance (TISSUE) that has grown round a diseased or damaged part

ad·he·sive[1] /ədˈhiːsɪv/ *adj* that can stick or cause sticking

adhesive[2] *n* an ADHESIVE substance, such as a sticky liquid (GLUE)

ad hoc /ˌæd ˈhɒk, -ˈhəʊk‖-ˈhɑk, -ˈhəʊk/ *adj Lat* made, arranged, etc., for a particular purpose: *An* **ad hoc committee** *is a committee specially established to deal with a particular subject*

a·dieu /əˈdjuː‖əˈduː/ *interj, n* **adieus** *or* **adieux** /əˈdjuːz‖əˈduːz/ *Fr* goodbye

ad in·fi·ni·tum /ˌæd ɪnfɨˈnaɪtəm/ *adv Lat* without end; for ever

ad·i·pose /ˈædɨpəʊs/ *adj tech* of or containing animal fat; fatty

adj *written abbrev. for:* adjective

ad·ja·cent /əˈdʒeɪsənt/ *adj* [(*to*)] *fml* very close; either touching or almost touching; next: *The 2 families live in adjacent streets*

ad·jec·tive /ˈædʒɪktɪv/ *n* a word which describes the thing for which a noun stands (such as *black* in the sentence *She wore a black hat*) —**-tival** /ˌædʒɪkˈtaɪvəl/ *adj*: *an adjectival phrase* —**-tivally** *adv* [Wa4]

ad·join /əˈdʒɔɪn/ *v* [Wv4;T1;I∅] to be next to, very close to, or touching (one another): *Our house adjoins theirs.|Our 2 houses adjoin.|the adjoining room|adjoining rooms*

ad·journ /əˈdʒɜːn‖-ɜrn/ *v* **1** [T1;I∅: (*for, till, until*)] **a** to bring (a meeting, trial, etc.) to a stop, esp. for a particular period or until a later time **b** (of people at a meeting, court of law, etc.) to come to such a stop **2** [I∅ (*to*)] *often humor* (of a group of people who are eating, talking, arguing, etc.) to go to another place, esp. for a rest: *We finished dinner and adjourned to the sunny garden* —**~ment** *n* [U;C]: *The court met again after an adjournment of 2 weeks*

ad·judge /əˈdʒʌdʒ/ *v fml or tech* **1** [T5;X (*to be*) 7,(1)] to decide or state officially or by law: *The court adjudged that he was guilty.|It adjudged him (to be) guilty* **2** [T1 (*to*)] to give, esp. as a prize or by a decision in law: *The court adjudged the dead man's house to his son*

ad·ju·di·cate /əˈdʒuːdɪkeɪt/ *v fml or tech* **1** [I∅ (*on, upon*)] to act as a judge (esp. in competitions between non-professionals in the arts): *Who will adjudicate (on this matter)?* **2** [T1 (*for*)] (of a court or judge) to make a decision about: *Who will adjudicate this matter (for us)?* **3** [X7,(1)] ADJUDGE (1) —**-cation** /əˌdʒuːdɪˈkeɪʃən/ *n* [U]: *The matter was brought up for adjudication*

ad·junct /ˈædʒʌŋkt/ *n* **1** something that is added or joined to something else but is not a necessary part of it **2** an ADVERBIAL word or phrase that limits or gives particular meaning to another word or part of a sentence (like *on Sunday* in *They arrived on Sunday*)

ad·jure /əˈdʒʊəʳ/ *v* [V3;(T1)] *fml* to urge solemnly: *She adjured him to tell the truth*

ad·just /əˈdʒʌst/ *v* **1** [T1;I∅: (*to*)] to change slightly, esp. in order to make suitable for a particular job or new conditions: *I must adjust my watch, it's slow.*|*He adjusted (himself) very quickly to the heat of the country* **2** [T1] to put into order; put in place; set right: *Your coat collar needs adjusting* —**~able** *adj* —**~ment** *n* [U;C]: *to make adjustments*

ad·ju·tant /'ædʒʊtənt‖'ædʒə-/ *n* **1** an army officer responsible for the office work in a body of soldiers (BATTALION) **2** also **adjutant bird** /'··· ·/— a large type of bird (STORK) found in India

ad lib /ˌæd 'lɪb/ *adv* [Wa5] *Lat infml* **1** without limit; freely: *a restaurant where you pay a fixed price and can eat ad lib* **2** [F] spoken, played, performed, etc., without preparation: *The best joke in the play was ad lib*

ad-lib[1] /ˌ· '·/ *adj* [Wa5;A] *infml* spoken, played, performed, etc., without preparation

ad-lib[2] /ˌ· '·/ *v* **-bb-** [T1;IØ] *infml* to invent and deliver (music, words, notes, etc.) without preparation, as in a play, performance, or meeting

ad·man /'ædmæn/ *n* **-men** /men/ *sl* a man employed in advertising

ad·mass /'ædmæs/ *n* [U] *BrE rare derog infml* **1** mass advertising, esp. in regard to its harmful effects on society **2** the mass of society influenced by large-scale advertising

ad·min·is·ter /əd'mɪnɪ̈stəʳ/ *v* [T1] **1** to control (esp. the business or affairs of a person or group) **2** [(*to*)] to put into operation; make work; give: *The courts administer the law.*|*She administered the medicine to the sick woman* **3** [(*to*)] *fml* to give (the official form of a promise or religious ceremony): *I administered the* OATH *to him*

administer to *v prep* [T1] *fml or tech* MINISTER TO

ad·min·is·tra·tion /ədˌmɪnɪ̈'streɪʃən/ *n* **1** [(*the*) U] the control or direction of affairs, as of a country or business **2** [(*the*) U] the act of putting something into operation, esp. by someone with the official power to do so: *the administration of the law* **3** [(*the*) U] *fml* the act of giving the official form of a promise or religious ceremony **4** [(*the*) C] *esp. AmE* (*often cap.*) the national government: *Not much was done by the last Administration*

ad·min·is·tra·tive /əd'mɪnɪ̈strətɪv‖-streɪtɪv/ *adj* [Wa5] of or concerning the control and direction of affairs, as of a country or business: *administrative responsibilities* —**~ly** *adv*

ad·min·is·tra·tor /əd'mɪnɪ̈streɪtəʳ/ *n* **1** a person who controls or directs the affairs, as of a country or business **2** a person who is good at arranging and directing **3** a person who is officially appointed to look after the business or property of another

ad·mi·ra·ble /'ædmərəbəl/ *adj* worthy of admiration; very good: *an admirable meal* —**-bly** *adv*

ad·mi·ral /'ædmərəl/ *n* [C;A;N] (a man who commands a large number of warships, and who holds) a very high rank or the highest rank in the navy

Ad·mi·ral·ty /'ædmərəlti/ *n BrE* **1** [(*the*) GU] the group of people appointed by the government to control the navy **2** [*the*+R] the building in which this group works

ad·mi·ra·tion /ˌædmər'eɪʃən/ *n* **1** [U] a feeling of pleasure and respect: *She was filled with admiration for his courage* **2** [*the*+S] a person or thing that causes such feelings: *His skill at games made him the admiration of his friends*

ad·mire /əd'maɪəʳ/ *v* [Wv4;T1] **1** [(*for*)] to regard with pleasure and respect; have a good opinion of: *I admire her for her bravery.*|*I gave her an admiring look* **2** to look at with pleasure —see WONDER (USAGE)

ad·mir·er /əd'maɪərəʳ/ *n* a person who admires, esp. a man who is attracted to a particular woman: *He is one of her many admirers*

ad·mis·si·ble /əd'mɪsəbəl/ *adj* **1** that can be allowed or considered: *an admissible excuse* **2** (of types of information) that may be allowed in a court of law —**-bility** /ədˌmɪsə'bɪlɪ̈ti/ *n* [(*the*) U]

ad·mis·sion /əd'mɪʃən/ *n* **1** [U] allowing or being allowed to enter or join a school, club, building, etc.: *Soon after his admission he became an officer of the society* **2** [C] an act of allowing someone to enter or join **3** [U] the cost of entrance: *Admission £1* **4** [C(5, *of*)] a statement saying or agreeing that something is true (usu. something bad); CONFESSION (1): *He made an admission that he was the thief* **5 by/on someone's own admission** (usu. of something bad) as someone has admitted or agreed himself

USAGE In the meaning "permission to go in" **admittance** is more formal than **admission**, which is the more ordinary word. The entrance price is the **admission**, not *the **admittance**. **Admittance** could not be used in an expression like *his* **admission** *of guilt*.

ad·mit /əd'mɪt/ *v* **-tt-** **1** [T1 (*in, into, to*)] to permit (a person or thing) to enter; let in: *I cannot admit you into the theatre yet.*|*There were no windows to admit air.*|*He was admitted to (the) hospital suffering from burns* **2** [T1] to have space or room for: *The church admits only 200 people* **3** [T1,4,5a;IØ: (*to*);V3 (*to be*)] to state or agree to the truth of (usu. something bad); CONFESS (1): *The thief admitted his crime.*|*He admitted to the murder.*|*He admitted (to) stealing.*|*I admit that it was difficult.*|*They admitted him to be mad* **4** [T1] to leave room for as possible; allow: *The facts admit no other explanation* —see REFUSE (USAGE)

admit of *v prep* [T1 *no pass.*] *fml* ADMIT (4)

ad·mit·tance /əd'mɪtəns/ *n* [U] allowing or being allowed to enter; right of entrance: *As the theatre was full I was unable to gain admittance* —see ADMISSION (USAGE)

ad·mit·ted /əd'mɪtɪ̈d/ *adj* [Wa5;A] *often derog* having admitted oneself to be (usu. something bad): *He is an admitted thief*

ad·mit·ted·ly /əd'mɪtɪ̈dli/ *adv* [Wa5] it must be admitted (that): *Admittedly, he is a thief, but he's also a great writer*

ad·mix·ture /əd'mɪkstʃəʳ/ *n* **1** a mixture **2** a substance that is added to another in a mixture

ad·mon·ish /əd'mɒnɪʃ‖-'mɑ-/ *v* [T1 (*against, for*)] *fml* to scold or warn gently —**~ing** *adj*: *an admonishing look* —**~ingly** *adv*

ad·mo·ni·tion /ˌædmə'nɪʃən/ *n* [C;(U)] gentle scolding or warning

ad·mon·i·to·ry /əd'mɒnɪ̈təri‖əd'mɑnɪ̈tori/ *adj fml* of or like warning advice or gentle scolding: *admonitory remarks*

ad nau·se·am /ˌæd 'nɔːziəm, -iæm/ *adv Lat* to an annoying degree, esp. through being repeated for a long time: *We have heard your complaints ad nauseam*

a·do /ə'duː/ *n* [U] **1** anxious activity; trouble; excitement (esp. in the phr. **without much/more/further ado**): *Without more ado he jumped into the water and swam off* **2 much ado about nothing** a lot of noise or talk about something that was really not serious or important

a·do·be /ə'dəʊbi/ *n* [U] a building brick made of earth and dried corn stems (STRAW) dried in the sun, used esp. in hot countries

ad·o·les·cent /ˌædə'lesənt/ *adj, n* **1** (of) a boy or girl in the period between being a child and being a grown person; young TEENAGER of about 13–16 **2** *derog* (of) a grown person who behaves like a young person of this age group: *I'm afraid I find Jim's humour a bit adolescent* —**-cence** /ˌædə'lesəns/ *n* [S;U]

a·dopt /ə'dɒpt‖ə'dapt/ *v* [T1] **1** to take (someone, esp. a child) into one's family as a relation for ever and to take on the full responsibilities in law of the parent —compare FOSTER **2** to take and use as one's own: *I adopted their method of making the machine* **3** to approve formally; accept: *The committee adopted his suggestions* **4** to choose, esp. as a representative —compare ADAPT

a·dop·tion /ə'dɒpʃən‖ə'dap-/ *n* **1** [U] the act of ADOPTing: *If you cannot have children of your own why not consider adoption?*|(fig.) *He was not born here, but this is now his country of adoption* **2** [C] an example of this

a·dop·tive /ə'dɒptɪv‖ə'dap-/ *adj* [Wa5] *fml* having ADOPTed (esp. a child): *Those are little Susan's adoptive parents*

a·dor·a·ble /ə'dɔːrəbəl‖ə'dor-/ *adj* **1** worthy of being loved deeply **2** *infml* charming or attractive: *What adorable curtains!*

ad·o·ra·tion /ˌædə'reɪʃən/ *n* [U] **1** religious worship **2** deep love and respect

a·dore /ə'dɔːʳ‖ə'dor/ *v* [Wv6] **1** [T1] to worship as God **2** [Wv4,5;T1] to love deeply and respect highly: *gave her an adoring look*|*He adores his elder brother.*|*his adored elder brother* **3** [T1,4] *infml* to like very much: *She adores the cinema/going to the cinema*

a·dorn /ə'dɔːn‖-ɔrn/ *v* [T1 (*with*)] **1** to add beauty or ornament to —see DECORATE (USAGE) **2** to add importance or attractiveness to: *He adorned his story with all sorts of adventures that never happened*

a·dorn·ment /ə'dɔːnmənt‖-ɔr-/ *n* **1** [U] the act of ADORNing **2** [C] an ornament; DECORATION (2)

a·dren·a·lin /ə'drenəlɨn/ *n* [U] **1** a chemical substance (HORMONE) made by the body during anger, fear, anxiety, etc., causing quick or violent action **2** a medical substance produced using this substance taken from animals

a·drift /ə'drɪft/ *adv, adj* [F] **1** (esp. of boats) not fastened, and driven about by the sea or wind; out of control; loose **2** left to the powers of fate; (esp. of people) without guidance or control: *The angry man turned his son adrift*

a·droit /ə'drɔɪt/ *adj* [B;F (*at, in*)] having or showing ability to use the skills of mind or hand, esp. quickly; clever —**~ly** *adv* —**~ness** *n* [U]

ad·u·late /'ædʒʊleɪt‖'ædʒə-/ *v* [T1 *often pass.*] *lit* to praise more than is necessary or truthful, esp. to win favour

ad·u·la·tion /ˌædʒʊ'leɪʃən‖ˌædʒə-/ *n* [U] praise that is more than is necessary or deserved, esp. to win favour —**-lator** /'ædʒʊleɪtəʳ‖'ædʒə-/ *n* —**-latory** /ˌædʒʊ'leɪtəri, 'ædʒʊleɪtəri‖'ædʒələtori/ *adj*

ad·ult /'ædʌlt, ə'dʌlt/ *adj, n* (of) a fully grown person or animal, esp. a person over an age stated by law, usu. 18 or 21

a·dul·ter·ate /ə'dʌltəreɪt/ *v* [T1 (*with*)] to make impure or of poorer quality by the addition of something of lower quality: *This milk has been adulterated with water* —**-ation** /əˌdʌltə'reɪʃən/ *n* [U;C]

a·dul·ter·er /ə'dʌltərəʳ/ *fem.* **adulteress** /-trɨs/— *n* a married person who has had sexual relations with someone outside the marriage

a·dul·ter·y /ə'dʌltəri/ *n* [U] sexual relations between a married person and someone outside the marriage —**-terous** *adj*

ad·um·brate /'ædʌmbreɪt/ *v* [T1] *fml* to give an incomplete or faint idea of (esp. future events) —**-bration** /ˌædʌm'breɪʃən/ *n* [U;C]

adv *written abbrev. for*: adverb

ad·vance¹ /əd'vɑːns‖əd'væns/ *v* **1** [IØ (*on, upon, against*)] to move or come forward: *The soldiers advanced on the enemy.*|*They advanced 20 miles* **2** [T1;IØ: (*to*)] to (cause to) improve or move forward: *He worked so well that his employer soon advanced him (to a higher position)* **3** [T1] to bring forward to an earlier date or time —opposite **postpone** **4** [IØ] to move forward; develop; change: *A month has passed and the work has not advanced* **5** [T1;IØ] *rare* to (cause to) increase; (cause to) rise

advance² *n* **1** [C *usu. sing.*] forward movement: *There were so many people that our advance was slow.*|*You cannot stop the advance of old age* **2** [C] a development; improvement: *There have been great advances in space travel in the last 20 years* **3** [C (*of*)] money that is paid before the proper time or lent: *I was given an advance of a month's pay* **4** [A] going or coming before: *An* **advance party** *is a group (as of soldiers) that travels ahead of the main group.*|*An* **advance copy** *is a copy of a book that comes out before the official date for sending out copies* **5** [C] *rare* an increase, as of price; rise **6 in advance (of) a** before in time: *paid the rent in advance* **b** in front (of): *walked (2 yards) in advance of her husband*

ad·vanced /əd'vɑːnst‖əd'vænst/ *adj* **1** far on in development: *He is spending a year in advanced studies* **2** modern (in ideas, way of living, etc.): *Most people find her advanced ideas difficult to accept* **3 advanced in years** *fml* old

advanced lev·el /·'· ˌ··/ *n* [C;*to*+U] (in British education) A LEVEL

ad·vance·ment /əd'vɑːnsmənt‖əd'væn-/ *n* [U] **1** the act of advancing; improvement **2** the obtaining of a higher position or rank

ad·vanc·es /ad'vɑːnsɨz‖əd'væn-/ *n* [P *sometimes sing.*] efforts made to become friends with or to gain favourable attention from; offers of friendship or love: *The association asked me to make advances to the minister.*|*She refused his advances*

ad·van·tage¹ /əd'vɑːntɪdʒ‖əd'væn-/ *n* **1** [C (*over*)] something that may help one to be successful or to gain a desired result: *He had the advantage (over other boys) of being born into a rich family* **2** [U] profit; gain; BENEFIT¹ (1): *It will be to his advantage if he studies hard* **3 Advantage X** (in tennis) (said when X has won the point after DEUCE): *Advantage Miss Evert* **4 You have the advantage of me** *BrE* You know something that I don't **5 take advantage of a** to make use of; profit from **b** to make use of somebody, as by deceiving them

advantage² *v* [T1] *fml* to be of profit to; BENEFIT

ad·van·ta·geous /ˌædvən'teɪdʒəs, ˌædvæn-/ *adj* helpful; useful; bringing a good profit —**~ly** *adv*

ad·vent /'ædvent/ *n* **the advent of** the arrival or coming of (an important event, period, person, etc.): *Society has changed rapidly since the advent of the car*

Advent *n* [R] **1** the coming of Christ to the world **2** the period of the 4 weeks before Christmas **3 the Second Advent** the future coming of Christ to the world

Ad·vent·ist /'ædvəntɨst‖əd'ven-/ *n* a person who believes that the 2nd coming of Christ to the world is near

ad·ven·ti·tious /ˌædvən'tɪʃəs, ˌædven-/ *adj fml* not expected or planned; coming by chance; accidental: *the adventitious birth of their 5th child* —**~ly** *adv*

ad·ven·ture /əd'ventʃəʳ/ *n* **1** [C] a journey, activity, experience, etc., that is strange and exciting and often dangerous: *I told them of my adventures in the mountains* **2** [U] excitement, as in a journey or activity; risk: *He lived for adventure* —see VENTURE (USAGE)

ad·ven·tur·er /əd'ventʃərəʳ/ *n* **1** a person who has or looks for adventures **2** a person who hopes to make a fortune by taking big risks with his money **3** a person who hopes to make a fortune or get a high place in society by dishonest, dangerous, or sexually immoral means

ad·ven·tur·ess /əd'ventʃərǝ̣s/ *n* a female ADVENTURER (1, esp. 3)

ad·ven·tur·ous /əd'ventʃərəs/ *adj* **1** eager for adventure; ready to take risks; daring; bold **2** full of danger; risky —**~ly** *adv*

ad·verb /'ædvɜːb‖-ɜrb/ *n* a word which describes or adds to the meaning of a verb, an adjective, another adverb, or a sentence, and which answers such questions as *how? when?* or *where?* (as in "He ran *slowly*." "It was *very* beautiful." "Come *tomorrow*." "Come *here*." "*Generally* (speaking), things are getting better.")

ad·ver·bi·al /əd'vɜːbɪəl‖-ɜr-/ *n, adj* (something) like, used as, or having qualities typical of an adverb: *an adverbial phrase* —**~ly** *adv*

ad·ver·sa·ry /'ædvəsəri‖'ædvərseri/ *n* a person or group to whom one is opposed; opponent or enemy

ad·verse /'ædvɜːs‖-ɜrs/ *adj* [(*to*)] *fml* not in favour of; going against; opposing: *The judge gave us an adverse decision.*|*in adverse conditions* —compare AVERSE —**~ly** *adv*

ad·ver·si·ty /əd'vɜːsǝ̣ti‖-ɜr-/ *n* **1** [U] bad fortune; trouble: *A good friend will not desert one in time of adversity* **2** [C] something unfortunate; misfortune: *to meet with adversities*

ad·vert /'ædvɜːt‖-ɜrt/ *n infml esp BrE* an advertisement: *I'm going to put an advert in the newspaper*

ad·ver·tise /'ædvətaɪz‖-ər-/ *v* **1** [T1;5;IØ] to make (something for sale, services offered, room to let, etc.) known to the public, as in a newspaper, or on film or television: *They advertised (that they had) a used car for sale* **2** [IØ (*for*)] to ask (for someone or something) by placing an advertisement in a newspaper, shop window, etc.: *We should advertise for someone to look after the garden* —**~r** *n*

ad·ver·tise·ment /əd'vɜːtǝ̣smənt‖,ædvər'taɪz-/ *n* **1** [C] also **ad**— a notice of something for sale, services offered, job position to be filled, room to let, etc., as in a newspaper, painted on a wall, or made as a film **2** [U] the action of advertising

ad·ver·tis·ing /'ædvətaɪzɪŋ‖-ər-/ *n* [U] the business which concerns itself with making known to the public what is for sale and encouraging them to buy, esp. by means of pictures in magazines, notices in newspapers, and messages on television (COMMERCIAL*s*)

ad·vert to /əd'vɜːt‖-ɜrt/ *v prep* [T1] *fml* to mention (something)

ad·vice /əd'vaɪs/ *n* **1** [U] opinion given by one person to another on how that other should behave or act: *I asked the doctor for his advice.*|*On his advice I am staying in bed* **2** [C *usu. pl.*] (esp. in business) a letter, note, or other report, esp. from a distant place giving information about delivery of goods

ad·vi·sab·le /əd'vaɪzəbəl/ *adj* that is advised or thought best to do; sensible; wise: *It is advisable to leave now*/*that you leave now* —**-sability** /əd,vaɪzə'bɪlǝ̣ti/ *n* [U9]

ad·vise /əd'vaɪz/ *v* **1** [T1 (*on*), 4,5b,c;IØ (*on*); D5,5b,6a,b;V3] to tell (somebody) what one thinks should be done; give advice to (somebody): *I advise waiting till the proper time.*|*I will do as you advise.*|*I advised her that she should wait.*|*I advised her where to stay.*|*I advise you to leave now* **2** [T1 (*of*);D5,5b,6a] *fml* to give notice to; inform: *I have advised her that we are coming.*|*Will you advise us (of) when the bags should arrive?* **3 ill-advised (to)** unwise (to) **4 well-advised (to)** wise (to): *You would be well-advised to stay at home today*

ad·vis·ed·ly /əd'vaɪzǝ̣dli/ *adv* after careful thought; purposely: *He cut down the tree advisedly, as it was diseased*

ad·vis·er, *AmE* also **-or** /əd'vaɪzəʳ/ *n* a person who gives advice, esp. one who is often asked for advice, as by a government or business

ad·vi·so·ry /əd'vaɪzəri/ *adj* **1** having the power or duty to advise **2** containing advice rather than orders

ad·vo·ca·cy /'ædvəkəsi/ *n* [U9, esp. *of*] the act or action of supporting an idea, way of life, person, etc.

ad·vo·cate[1] /'ædvəkǝ̣t, -keɪt/ *n* **1** [C] *law* a person, esp. a lawyer, who speaks in defence of or in favour of another person **2** [C9, esp. *of*] a person who speaks for or supports an idea, way of life, etc.: *He is an advocate of cold baths in the morning* —see also DEVIL'S ADVOCATE

ad·vo·cate[2] /'ædvəkeɪt/ *v* [T1,4] to speak in favour of; support (esp. an idea or plan): *I do not advocate building large factories*

adze, *AmE* also **adz** /ædz/ *n* an axe with the blade set at a right angle to the handle, used for shaping large pieces of wood —see picture at TOOL[1]

ae·gis, (*rare*) **egis** /'iːdʒǝ̣s/ *n* **under the aegis of** *lit* with the protection or support of

ae·on, eon /'iːən/ *n* a period of time too long to be measured

aer·ate /'eəreɪt/ *v* [Wv5;T1] **1** to put air or gas into (a liquid, esp. a drink) as by pressure **2** to allow air to act upon: *Blood is aerated in the lungs* —**-ation** /eə'reɪʃən/ *n* [U]

aer·i·al[1] /'eərɪəl/ *adj* [Wa5] **1** [A] of, in, from, or concerning the air **2** [A] moving or happening in the air, esp. through being supported by wires **3** [B] *lit or tech* of or like air or a gas; having no matter —**~ly** *adv*

aerial[2] *n* a wire, rod, or framework put up, often on top of a house, to receive radio or television broadcasts —see picture at HOUSE[1]

aer·ie, aery /'eəri, 'ɪəri/ *n* EYRIE

ae·ro- /'eərəʊ/ *comb. form* of or concerning aircraft: *an aeroengine*

aer·o·bat·ic /,eərə'bætɪk, ,eərəʊ-/ *adj* [Wa5] of or about AEROBATICS

aer·o·bat·ics /,eərə'bætɪks, ,eərəʊ-/ *n* **1** [U] the art of doing tricks in an aircraft, such as rolling over sideways or flying upside down **2** [P] a group of such tricks considered as a performance

aer·o·drome /'eərədrəʊm/ also (*esp. AmE*) **air·field**— *n esp. BrE* a small airport

aer·o·dy·nam·ic /,eərəʊdaɪ'næmɪk/ *adj* [Wa5;A;(B)] of or about AERODYNAMICS —**~ally** *adv* [Wa4]

aer·o·dy·nam·ics /,eərəʊdaɪ'næmɪks/ *n* **1** [U] the science that studies the forces of moving air and other gases and the forces that act on bodies moving through the air **2** [P] the qualities necessary for movement through the air

aer·o·naut·i·cal /,eərə'nɔːtɪkəl/ also **aer·o·naut·ic** /-'nɔːtɪk/— *adj* [Wa5] of or about AERONAUTICS

aer·o·nau·tics /,eərə'nɔːtɪks/ *n* [U] the science of the operation and flight of aircraft

aer·o·plane /'eərəpleɪn/ (*AmE* **air·plane**)— *n BrE* a flying vehicle that is heavier than air, that has wings, and has at least one engine

aer·o·sol /'eərəsɒl‖-sɑl/ *n* a small container from which liquid can be forced out in the form of a fine mist

aer·o·space /'eərəspeɪs, 'eərəʊ-/ *n* [A] of the air around the earth and the space beyond it: *an aerospace vehicle*

aer·tex /'eəteks‖'eər-/ *n* [U] *BrE tdmk* a loosely woven material used for shirts and underclothes

aer·y /'eəri, 'ɪəri/ *n* EYRIE

aes·thete, *AmE* also **es-** /'iːsθiːt‖'es-/ *n* a person who has a carefully developed sense of beauty, esp. beauty in art

aes·thet·ic, *AmE* also **es-** /iːsˈθetɪk, es-‖es-/ *adj* **1** of or concerning the sense of beauty, esp. beauty in art **2** having a developed sense of beauty **3** of or concerning AESTHETICS —**~ally** *adv* [Wa4]

aes·thet·ics, *AmE* also **es-** /iːsˈθetɪks, es-‖es-/ *n* [U] the study, science, or PHILOSOPHY (1) of beauty, esp. beauty in art

ae·ther /ˈiːθəʳ/ *n* [U] ETHER (2, 3)

ae·ti·ol·o·gy, *AmE* also **eti-** /ˌiːtiˈɒlədʒi‖-ˈɑ-/ *n* [U] the study of the causes of anything, esp. of diseases —**-gical** /ˌiːtɪəˈlɒdʒɪkəl‖-ˈlɑ-/ *adj*

a·far /əˈfɑːʳ/ *adv lit* **1** at a distance; far off **2 from afar** from a great distance

af·fa·ble /ˈæfəbəl/ *adj* easy to talk to; ready to be friendly; pleasant —**-bility** /ˌæfəˈbɪlɪ̈ti/ *n* [U] —**-bly** /ˈæfəbli/ *adv*

af·fair /əˈfeəʳ/ *n* **1** [*often pl.*] something that has been done or is to be done; something needing action; business: *The minister deals with important affairs of state.|Leave me alone; mind your own affairs* **2** a happening; event; action: *The meeting was a noisy affair* **3** a sexual relationship between 2 people not married to each other, esp. one that lasts for some time

af·fect¹ /əˈfekt/ *v fml often derog* **1** [T1,3] to pretend to feel, have, or do: *He affected illness so that he need not go to work.|He affected not to hear her* **2** [T1] to show a liking for; use: *He affects long words that few people can understand*

affect² *v* [T1] **1** to cause some result or change in; influence: *Smoking affects health* —compare EFFECT **2** to cause feelings of sorrow, anger, love, etc., in: *She was deeply affected by the news of his death* **3** (of a disease) to attack

af·fec·ta·tion /ˌæfekˈteɪʃən/ *n derog* **1** [U;C] behaviour which is not one's natural manner: *She is sincere and quite without affectation* **2** [C] a feeling or manner that is pretended

af·fect·ed /əˈfektɪ̈d/ *adj* **1** *derog* not real or natural; pretended: *She showed an affected interest in his art* **2** moved to sorrow, anger, love, etc.: *deeply affected by the sad story* **3** attacked by a disease —**~ly** *adv* —**~ness** *n* [U]

af·fect·ing /əˈfektɪŋ/ *adj* causing deep feeling: *an affecting experience*

af·fec·tion /əˈfekʃən/ *n* [U] gentle, lasting love, as of a parent for its child; fondness

af·fec·tion·ate /əˈfekʃənɪ̈t/ *adj* showing gentle love —**~ly** *adv*: *He signed the letter "Affectionately, your brother Bill"*

af·fi·ance /əˈfaɪəns/ *v* [T1 (*to*) *usu. pass.*] *old use* to promise in marriage

af·fi·da·vit /ˌæfɪ̈ˈdeɪvɪ̈t/ *n* a written statement made after an official promise (OATH) to tell the truth for use as proof in a court of law

af·fil·i·ate /əˈfɪlieɪt/ *v* [Wv5;T1;IØ: (*with, to*)] (esp. of a society or group) to join or connect: *All the affiliated organizations are in favour of the plan*

af·fil·i·a·tion /əˌfɪliˈeɪʃən/ *n* **1** [U] the act of affiliating or being affiliated (AFFILIATE) **2** [C] a connection or relationship, often official: *The local gardening club has affiliations with several societies in the town*

affiliation or·der /···ˈ·· ˌ··/ *n BrE* a decision made in a court of law ordering a man to pay for the support of his child born to a woman to whom he is not married

af·fin·i·ty /əˈfɪnɪ̈ti/ *n* **1** [U;C (*between, with*)] relationship, close likeness, or connection: *The French and Italian languages have many affinities (with each other)* **2** [C] a relationship through marriage, as of a man to his wife's relations **3** [C (*for, to, between*)] strong attraction: *He feels a strong affinity for/to her.|There is a strong affinity between them*

af·firm /əˈfɜːm‖-ɜrm/ *v* **1** [T1,5] to declare (usu. again, or in answer to a question): *He affirmed his love for her.|He affirmed that he was telling the truth* —compare DENY (1) **2** [IØ] to promise to tell the truth in a court of law, but without mentioning God or the Bible in the promise —**~ation** /ˌæfəˈmeɪʃən‖ˌæfɜr-/ *n* [U;C]

af·fir·ma·tive /əˈfɜːmətɪv‖-ɜr-/ *n, adj often fml* (a word) declaring "yes": *The answer was a strong affirmative.|It was an affirmative answer.|The answer was in the affirmative* —opposite **negative** —**~ly** *adv*

af·fix¹ /əˈfɪks/ *v* [T1 (*to*)] **1** to fix, fasten, or stick: *I affixed a stamp to the envelope* **2** to add by writing: *He affixed his name to the letter*

af·fix² /ˈæfɪks/ *n* a group of letters or sounds added to the beginning of a word (in the case of a PREFIX) or the end of a word (in the case of a SUFFIX) to change its meaning or its use (as in "*un*tie", "*mis*understood", "kind*ness*", "quick*ly*")

af·flict /əˈflɪkt/ *v* [T1 (*with*) *usu. pass.*] to cause to suffer in the body or mind; trouble

af·flic·tion /əˈflɪkʃən/ *n fml* **1** [U9] suffering; grief; trouble **2** [C] something which causes suffering: *Pains in the head were among the many afflictions she suffered*

af·flu·ent /ˈæfluənt/ *adj* having plenty of money or other possessions; wealthy —**-ence** *n* [U]

af·ford /əˈfɔːd‖-ord/ *v* **1** [T1] (*usu. with* can, could, able to) to be able to buy: *At last we can/are able to afford a house!* **2** [T1,3] (*usu. with* can, could, able to) to be able to do, spend, give, bear, etc., without serious loss or damage: *Can you afford £15,000 for a house?|Can you afford to lend me some money?|I can't afford 3 weeks away from work* **3** [D1;T1 (*to*)] *fml & lit* to provide with; supply with; give: *The tree afforded us shelter from the rain*

af·for·est /əˈfɒrɪ̈st‖əˈfɔ-, əˈfɑ-/ *v* [T1] to plant with trees in order to make a forest —**~ation** /əˌfɒrɪ̈ˈsteɪʃən‖əˌfɔr-, əˈfɑr-/ *n* [U]

af·fray /əˈfreɪ/ *n fml* a fight in a public place, esp. between small groups

af·fri·cate /ˈæfrɪkɪ̈t/ *n* a consonant sound combination consisting of a PLOSIVE (like /t/ or /d/) followed by a FRICATIVE pronounced in the same part of the mouth (like /ʃ/ or /ʒ/): *The word "church" contains the affricate /tʃ/*

af·front¹ /əˈfrʌnt/ *v* [T1] to be rude to or hurt the feelings of, esp. in public; offend

affront² *n* an act, remark, etc., that is rude to someone or hurts his feelings, esp. when intentional or in public

Af·ghan¹ /ˈæfgæn/ *n* **1** a person from Afghanistan —see NATIONALITY TABLE **2** a tall thin swift hunting dog native to the NEAR EAST, with a coat of thick silky hair —see picture at DOG¹

Afghan² *adj* of, from, or about Afghanistan

a·fi·cio·na·do /əˌfɪʃɪəˈnɑːdəʊ/ *n* **-dos** *Sp* a keen follower; FAN: *aficionados of cricket|a cinema aficionado*

a·field /əˈfiːld/ *adv* [Wa5;F] far away, esp. from home; to or at a great distance (esp. in the phr. **far afield**): *Do not go too far afield or we shall lose you*

a·fire /əˈfaɪəʳ/ *adv, adj* [Wa5;F (*with*)] on fire: *He set the house afire.*|(fig.) *He is afire with* ENTHUSIASM *for the new book he's reading*

a·flame /əˈfleɪm/ *adv, adj* [Wa5;F] on fire: *The house was aflame.*|(fig.) *The gardens were aflame with red and orange leaves*

a·float /əˈfləʊt/ *adv, adj* [Wa5;F] **1** on or as if on water; floating: *Help me get my boat afloat* **2** on ship; at sea: *How long did you spend afloat?* **3** covered with water; flooded **4** (of stories, talk about people, etc.) being told; getting around **5** out of debt: *Please lend me some money to keep me afloat*

a·foot /əˈfʊt/ *adv, adj* [Wa5;F] **1** *often derog* being prepared, made ready, or in operation: *There is a plan afoot to pull down the old building.|There is some strange business afoot* **2** *old use* on the move, esp. on foot

a·fore·said /əˈfɔːsed‖əˈfor-/ also **a·fore·men·tioned** /əˌfɔːˈmənʃənd‖əˌfor-/— *adj* [Wa5;A;GU] *fml* said or named before or above: *The aforesaid (person/people) was/were present at the trial*

a·fore·thought /əˈfɔːθɔːt‖əˈfor-/ *adj law* see MALICE

a for·ti·o·ri /ˌeɪ fɔːtiˈɔːraɪ, -ri‖-fɔrtiˈor-/ *adv* [Wa5] *Lat* for a still stronger reason; with greater reason: *A man with a quick temper is, a fortiori, not a patient man*

a·fraid /əˈfreɪd/ *adj* **1** [F (*of*,3,5a)] full of fear; FRIGHTENED: *Don't be afraid of dogs.|She was afraid to excite him in case he became dangerous.|She was afraid that it would bite* **2** [F (*of*,3,5a)] worried or anxious about possible results: *Don't be afraid of asking for help* **3** [F5a,b] *polite* sorry for something that has happened or is likely to happen: *I am afraid I've broken your pen.|"Are we late?" "I'm afraid so."|"Are we on time?" "I'm afraid not."*

a·fresh /əˈfreʃ/ *adv* [Wa5] *fml* once more; again: *I've spoiled the painting and must do it afresh*

Af·ri·can[1] /ˈæfrɪkən/ *n* a person from Africa

African[2] *adj* of, from, or about Africa

Af·ri·kaans /ˌæfrɪˈkɑːns/ *n* [R;U] a language of South Africa very much like Dutch

Af·ri·ka·ner /ˌæfrɪˈkɑːnəʳ/ *n* a South African whose native language is Afrikaans, esp. a descendant of the Dutch settlers of the 17th century

Af·ro /ˈæfrəʊ/ *n* **Afros** a hairstyle for men and women in which the hair is shaped into a large round bushy mass

Afro- *comb. form* **1** African; of Africa: *an Afro-American* **2** African and: *Afro-Asiatic*

aft /ɑːft‖æft/ *adv* [Wa5;F] *tech* in, near, or towards the back part (STERN) of a boat —opposite **fore**

af·ter[1] /ˈɑːftəʳ‖ˈæf-/ *adv* [Wa5;F;E] following in time or place; later; afterwards: *We arrived soon after.|"They lived happily ever after"* (phrase used in children's stories)

after[2] *prep* **1** following in time or order; later than; next: *We shall leave after breakfast.|They will return the day after tomorrow.|"after dark"* (SEU S.) **2** following continuously: *Year after year went by without hearing of him* **3** following in place or order: *He entered the room after his father.|Your name comes after mine in the list* **4** behind: *Shut the door after you* **5** as a result of; because of: *After the way he treated me I shall never want to see him again* **6** in spite of: *After all my care in packing it the clock arrived broken* **7** in the manner or style of: *It was a painting after the great master* **8** in accordance with: *You are a man after my own heart; we think and act alike in nearly all things* **9** in search of (esp. in order to punish); with a desire for: *The policeman ran after the thief.|They are after me.|"He's probably after you* (= with sexual intentions), *not that I blame him"* (SEU W.) **10** concerning; about: *Somebody asked after you today* **11** with the name of: *The boy was named after his uncle*

USAGE 1 **After** is properly used as a PREPOSITION (**after** *dinner*) or as a CONJUNCTION (**after** *he left*). In very informal English it is also used as an adverb with the same meaning as **afterwards** or **later**: *We had dinner and went home* **after**. Teachers and examiners do not like this use of after in an expression of time, though **after** (adv) can correctly be used when speaking of space or direction: *to follow* **after**. 2 **Later** can be followed by **than**: *He stayed* **later** *than I did.* Note: *just* **after/afterwards**| IMMEDIATELY **after/afterwards**|*a little/much* **later**.

after[3] *conj* at a later time than (when): *I found your coat after you had left the house*

after[4] *adj* [Wa5;A] **1** later in time: *He grew weak in after years* **2** in the back part, esp. of a boat: *the after* DECK

after- *prefix* [*n*→*n*] something that comes or happens after: AFTERBIRTH|*aftercare*

after all /ˌ·· ˈ·/ *conj, adv* **1** in spite of everything: *So you see I was right after all!* **2** it must be remembered (that): *I know he hasn't finished the work, but, after all, he is a very busy man*

af·ter·birth /ˈɑːftəbɜːθ‖ˈæftərbɜrθ/ *n* [U] the material that comes out of a woman just after she has given birth to a child

af·ter·care /ˈɑːftəkeəʳ‖ˈæftər-/ *n* [U] the care or treatment given to someone after a period in hospital, prison, etc.

af·ter·ef·fect /ˈɑːftərɪ̵fekt‖ˈæf-/ *n* [*often pl.*] an effect (usu. unpleasant) that follows some time after the cause or after the main effect

af·ter·glow /ˈɑːftəgləʊ‖ˈæftər-/ *n* [*usu. sing.*] **1** the light that remains in the western sky after the sun has set **2** a pleasant feeling that remains after the main feeling

af·ter·life /ˈɑːftəlaɪf‖ˈæftər-/ *n* **-lives** /laɪvz/ [*usu. sing.*] **1** the life that is thought by some people to follow death **2** the later part of one's life, esp. after a particular event

af·ter·math /ˈɑːftəmæθ‖ˈæftər-/ *n* [*usu. sing.*] the result or period following a bad event such as an accident, storm, war, etc.: *Life was much harder in the aftermath of the war*

af·ter·noon /ˌɑːftəˈnuːn‖ˌæftər-/ *adj, n* **1** (of) the period between midday and sunset: *I shall sleep in the afternoon.|I shall have an afternoon sleep* **2** a rather late period (as of time or life): *She spent the afternoon of her life in the South of France*

af·ter·noons /ˌɑːftəˈnuːnz‖ˌæftər-/ *adv AmE* in the afternoon repeatedly; on any afternoon

af·ters /ˈɑːftəz‖ˈæftərz/ *n* [P] *BrE infml* the part of a meal that comes after the main dish, usu. something sweet

af·ter·shave /ˈɑːftəʃeɪv‖ˈæftər-/ also (*fml*) **after-shave lo·tion** /ˈ·· · ˌ··/— *n* [U;C] a liquid with a pleasant smell for use on the face after shaving (SHAVE (1, 2))

af·ter·taste /ˈɑːftəteɪst‖ˈæftər-/ *n* a taste that stays in the mouth after the food that caused it is no longer there

af·ter·thought /ˈɑːftəθɔːt‖ˈæftər-/ *n* **1** an idea that comes later **2** something added later: *Surprisingly, the best part of the palace was an afterthought put on more than 20 years after the main part had been finished!*

af·ter·wards /ˈɑːftəwədz‖ˈæftərwərdz/ *AmE* also **af·ter·ward** /ˈɑːftəwəd‖ˈæftərwərd/— *adv* later; after that

a·gain /əˈgen, əˈgeɪn‖əˈgen/ *adv* [Wa5] **1** once more; another time: *Please say that again.|You must never do that again* **2** back to the place, condition, position, etc., that one was in before: *She was ill but now she is well again* **3** besides; further: *That wasn't much; I could eat as much again* **4** in addition: *Then again, do not forget you have no experience of travelling.|Again, there is another matter to consider* **5 again and again** also **time and time again**— very often; repeatedly **6 now and again** sometimes (but not very often); from time to time **7 once/yet again** one more time

a·gainst /əˈgenst, əˈgeɪnst‖əˈgenst/ *prep* **1** in an opposite direction to: *We sailed against the wind* **2** in opposition to: *We will fight against the enemy.|*

There were 20 votes for him and 12 against him.|The hotel has a rule against keeping animals in bedrooms **3** as a defence or protection from: *We are all taking medicine against the disease* **4** in the direction of and meeting: *The rain beat against the windows* **5** having as a background: *The picture looks good against that light wall* **6** touching, esp. for support: *I sat against the warm wall* **7** in preparation for: *We have saved some money against our old age* **8 over against** opposite to; facing: *We live over against the church*

a·gape /ə'geɪp/ *adv, adj* [F (*with*)] **1** wide open **2** in a state of wonder: *The children were agape (with excitement) as they watched the show*

a·gar-a·gar /ˌeɪgər 'eɪgəʳ‖ˌɑgɑr 'ɑgɑr/ also **agar** /'eɪgəʳ‖'ɑgɑr/— *n* [U] a jelly made from plants that live in the sea (SEAWEED) and used in soups and in the study of bacteria

ag·ate /'ægɨ̇t/ *n* [U;C] a hard stone with bands of colour, used in jewellery

age¹ /eɪdʒ/ *n* **1** [U;C] the period of time a person has lived or a thing has existed: *What is your age?|He is 10 years of age.|At your age you should know better.|What ages are your children?* **2** [U] one of the periods of life: *When a man has reached 40 he has reached middle age* **3** [U] an advanced or old period of life: *His back was bent with age* **4** [U; (C)] the particular time of life at which a person becomes able or not able to do something: *People who are either under age or over age may not join* **5** [C *usu. sing.*] (*in comb.*) (*usu. cap.*) a particular period of history: *The period in which man learnt to make tools of iron is called the Iron Age* **6** [C] all the people living at a particular time: *This age doesn't know what it is to be really poor.|We shall plan for the ages to come* **7** [C *often pl.*] *infml* a long time: *It's been ages/an age since we met* **8 (be/come) of age** (to be or reach) the particular age, usu. 18 or 21, when a person becomes responsible in law for his own actions, and is allowed to vote, get married, etc.

age² *v* **aged,** *pres. p.* **aging** *or* **ageing** [T1;I∅] **1** to (cause to) become old: *After his wife's death he aged quickly.|The fear of what might happen aged him* **2** to (cause to) become fitter for use with the passage of time; (cause to) have a fully-developed taste: *The wine aged well*

-age /ɪdʒ/ *comb. form* **1** [*n*→*n* U and/or S] (showing collection): *trackage*|BAGGAGE **2** [*v*→*n* U] (showing action): *road* HAULAGE **3** [*v*→*n* U and/or S] (showing end result, rate, or amount): BREAKAGE| COVERAGE **4** [*n*→*n* C] (showing a place or house of the stated type): ORPHANAGE **5** [*n*→*n* U and/or C] (showing state or rank): PEERAGE **6** [*v*→*n* U and/or S] (showing price or charge): POSTAGE *£5*

aged¹ /'eɪdʒd/ *adj* **1** [Wa5;F] being of the stated number of years: *My son is aged 10 years* **2** [B] (of wine, cheese, meat, etc.) having a fully-developed taste by having been left untouched in the proper conditions for some time

ag·ed² /'eɪdʒɨ̇d/ *adj* very old: *an aged man|He is aged.|The sick and the aged need our help*

age group /'· ·/ also **age bracket** /'· ˌ··/— *n* [GC] the people between 2 particular ages considered as a group

age·ing, aging /'eɪdʒɪŋ/ *n* [U] **1** the action of growing old **2** the changes that happen, as to wine, cheese, or a person's body, as time passes **3** the action of allowing or causing these changes

age·less /'eɪdʒləs/ *adj* **1** never growing old or never showing signs of growing old **2** never changing; ETERNAL: *ageless truth* —**~ness** *n* [U]

a·gen·cy /'eɪdʒənsi/ *n* **1** a business that makes its money esp. by bringing people into touch with others or the products of others: *I got this job in the factory through an employment agency* **2** the office or place of business of a person who represents a business: *The large firm has agencies all over the world* **3** [*usu. sing.*] the power or force which causes a result; influence: *Iron is melted by the agency of heat*

a·gen·da /ə'dʒendə/ *n* a list of the business or subjects to be considered at a meeting

a·gent /'eɪdʒənt/ *n* **1** a person who acts for another, esp. one who looks after or represents the business affairs of a person or firm: *Our agent in Rome deals with all our Italian business.|a secret agent* (= a political SPY) **2** a person who makes money by bringing people into touch with others or the products of others **3** a person or thing that works to produce a result: *Rain and sun are the agents which help plants to grow*

a·gent pro·voc·a·teur /ˌæʒɒ̃ prɒvɒkə'tɜːʳ‖ˌɑʒɑ̃ prəʊvɑ- (*Fr* aʒɑ̃ prɔvɔkatœr)/ *n* **agents provocateurs** (*same pronunciation*) *Fr* a person employed, esp. by the government or police, to encourage criminals or those working against the state, to take open action so that they can be caught

age of con·sent /ˌ· · ·'·/ *n* the age at which a person is considered to be old enough to marry or have sexual relations without breaking the law

ag·glom·er·ate¹ /ə'glɒməreɪt‖ə'glɑ-/ *v* [T1;I∅] to collect or gather into a mass or heap without organization —**-ation** /əˌglɒmə'reɪʃən‖əˌglɑ-/ *n* [U;C]: *Our towns are surrounded by agglomerations of ugly new houses*

ag·glom·er·ate² /ə'glɒmərɨ̇t‖ə'glɑ-/ *adj* gathered into a group or mass

agglomerate³ /əˌglɒmərɨ̇t‖əˌglɑ-/ *n* [U;S] a mass or heap, esp. of pieces of rock from an exploding mountain (VOLCANO) melted and united by heat

ag·glu·ti·na·tion /əˌgluːtɨ̇'neɪʃən/ *n* [U] **1** the action of sticking things together, or of becoming stuck together, esp. in a jelly-like form: *agglutination of bacteria/red blood cells* **2** the formation of new words by combining separate words (or parts of words) which each have their own meaning (as in "shipyard" from "ship" and "yard")

ag·glu·ti·na·tive /ə'gluːtɨ̇nətɪv‖-neɪtɪv/ *adj* tending to, or having the quality of, AGGLUTINATION (2): *an agglutinative language*

ag·gran·dize·ment, -isement /ə'grændɨ̇zmənt/ *n* [U] *often derog* increase or improvement in size, power, or rank: *He is willing to do anything for his own personal aggrandizement*

ag·gra·vate /'ægrəveɪt/ *v* [T1] **1** to make more serious or dangerous; make worse: *The lack of rain aggravated the already serious lack of food* **2** [Wv4] *infml or nonstandard* to annoy: *If he aggravates me any more I shall hit him.|I don't like your aggravating talk* —see ANGRY (USAGE)

ag·gra·va·tion /ˌægrə'veɪʃən/ *n* **1** [U] the action of aggravating or of being AGGRAVATED **2** [C] something that annoys one; trouble: *These continuous arguments are an aggravation*

ag·gre·gate¹ /'ægrɪgɨ̇t/ *adj* [Wa5;A;(B)] *fml* collected into one group, total, or mass: *What were your aggregate wages for this last year?*

ag·gre·gate² /'ægrɪgeɪt/ *v fml or tech* **1** [T1;I∅] to (cause to) come together into a group or mass **2** [L1;I∅ (*to*)] *rare* to amount as a whole to; add up to: *His various wages for the year aggregated (to) £10,000*

aggregate³ /'ægrɪgɨ̇t/ *n* **1** [U;C] *fml* a mass or total made up of small parts **2** [U;S] *tech* the materials, such as sand and small stones, that are added to a binding material (CEMENT) to form the very hard strong material (CONCRETE) used for roads, paths, floors, etc. **3 in the aggregate** *fml* considered as a whole group

ag·gre·ga·tion /ˌægrɪˈgeɪʃən/ *n* **1** [U] the collecting together into a mass of a number of different things **2** [C] a group or mass formed by this

ag·gres·sion /əˈgreʃən/ *n* **1** [U] the starting of a quarrel, fight, or war, esp. without just cause **2** [C] an attacking action made without just cause

ag·gres·sive /əˈgresɪv/ *adj* **1** *derog* always ready to quarrel or attack; threatening: *He is an aggressive person and likely to start a fight* **2** *apprec* not afraid of opposition: *If you want to be a successful businessman you must be aggressive and not worry about other people's feelings* **3** (of weapons) made for use in attack —**~ly** *adv* —**~ness** *n* [U]

ag·gres·sor /əˈgresəʳ/ *n derog* a person or country that begins a quarrel, fight, war, etc., with another, esp. without just cause

ag·grieved /əˈgriːvd/ *adj* **1** *fml* suffering from a personal offence, showing hurt feelings, etc. **2** *law* having suffered a wrong in law

ag·gro /ˈægrəʊ/ *n* [U] *BrE sl* trouble, esp. fighting, as between groups of young people

a·ghast /əˈgɑːst‖əˈgæst/ *adj* [F (*at*)] suddenly filled with surprise, fear, and wonder; shocked: *aghast at the thought of another war*

ag·ile /ˈædʒaɪl‖ˈædʒəl/ *adj* able to move quickly and easily; active —**~ly** *adv* —**-ility** /əˈdʒɪlə̇ti/ *n* [U]

ag·ing /ˈeɪdʒɪŋ/ *n* AGEING

ag·i·tate /ˈædʒə̇teɪt/ *v* **1** [T1] to shake (a liquid) or move (the surface of a liquid) about **2** [Wv5;T1] to cause anxiety to; trouble; worry **3** [IØ (*for*)] to argue strongly in public or to act for or against some political or social change

ag·i·ta·tion /ˌædʒə̇ˈteɪʃən/ *n* **1** [U] painful excitement of the mind or feelings; anxiety **2** [U;C: (*for*)] public argument, action, unrest, etc., for or against political or social change

ag·i·ta·tor /ˈædʒə̇teɪtəʳ/ *n* **1** a person who excites and influences other people's feelings esp. toward political or social change **2** a machine for shaking or STIRring[1] (1)

a·glow /əˈgləʊ/ *adj* [F (*with*)] bright with colour or excitement: *The sky was aglow with the setting sun.|Her face was aglow as she went to meet him*

ag·nos·tic /ægˈnɒstɪk, əg-‖-ˈnɑ-/ *n, adj* **1** (a person) who believes that one can only have knowledge of material things and that nothing is or can be known about God or life after death —compare ATHEIST **2** (a person) who claims that a particular point can neither be proved nor disproved —**~ism** /ægˈnɒstə̇sɪzəm, əg-‖-ˈnɑ/ *n* [U]

Ag·nus De·i /ˌægnʊs ˈdeɪ-iː‖ˌɑg-/ *n* [*the*+R] *Lat* the 6th part of the Roman Catholic religious service called the MASS, esp. when performed with music

a·go /əˈgəʊ/ *adv, adj* [E] back in time from now; in the past: *He left 10 minutes ago.|How long ago did he leave?*

USAGE **Ago** is not used with the perfect tense. One can say *I came here a year* **ago**, but not **I have/had come here a year* **ago**. But a sentence like this is possible: *"This would have been a couple of months* **ago**" (SEU S.).

a·gog /əˈgɒg‖əˈgɑg/ *adj* [F (*with*)] *infml* excited and expecting something to happen: *The children were all agog (with excitement) as the actor drew a gun from his pocket*

ag·o·nize, -ise /ˈægənaɪz/ *v* [IØ (*over*)] *infml* to suffer great pain or anxiety: *He agonizes over every decision he has to make*

ag·o·nized, -ised /ˈægənaɪzd/ *adj* expressing great pain: *She let out an agonized cry*

ag·o·niz·ing, -ising /ˈægənaɪzɪŋ/ *adj* causing great pain —**~ly** *adv*

ag·o·ny /ˈægəni/ *n* [U;C] **1** very great pain or suffering of mind or body: *He lay in agony until the doctor arrived.|He was in agonies of doubt.|He suffered agonies from his broken arm* **2 pile on/put on/turn on the agony** *sl derog* to say that one's sufferings, feelings, etc., are stronger, greater, or worse than they really are, esp. in order to influence others

agony col·umn /ˈ··· ˌ··/ *n humor* PERSONAL COLUMN

ag·o·ra·pho·bi·a /ˌægərəˈfəʊbɪə/ *n* [U] an unhealthy fear of open spaces

ag·o·ra·pho·bic /ˌægərəˈfəʊbɪk/ *n, adj* (a person) suffering from AGORAPHOBIA

a·grar·i·an /əˈgreərɪən/ *adj* of land, esp. farmland or its ownership

a·gree /əˈgriː/ *v* **1** [Wv5;IØ (*to*)] to accept an idea, opinion, etc., esp. after unwillingness or argument; approve: *He agreed to my idea.|We met at the agreed place* **2** [IØ (*on/about*);T3,5a: (*with*)] to have or share the same opinion, feeling, or purpose: *She agreed with me.|We agreed on the plan.|We agreed to leave at once.|They agreed that they should ask him.|We agreed on a price for the car.|We met at the agreed-on place* **3** [IØ (TOGETHER)] to be happy together; get on well together: *They will never agree* **4** [T1] *BrE nonstandard* to accept (an idea, opinion, etc.) esp. after unwillingness or argument: *The workers have agreed the government's plan* **5 agree to differ** to stop trying to persuade each other; remain friends in spite of having different opinions —see REFUSE (USAGE)

a·gree·a·ble /əˈgriːəbəl/ *adj* **1** [B] to one's liking; pleasant: *agreeable weather* **2** [F (*to*)] ready to agree; willing: *Are you agreeable?|He was agreeable to the suggestion*

a·gree·a·bly /əˈgriːəbli/ *adv* pleasantly: *I was agreeably surprised*

a·gree·ment /əˈgriːmənt/ *n* **1** [U] the state of having the same opinion, feeling, or purpose; thinking in the same way: *We are in agreement with their decision.|There is very little agreement about what to do* **2** [C] an arrangement or promise of action, as made between people, groups, businesses, or countries: *You have broken our agreement by not doing the work you promised* **3** [U] the use of matching forms of noun, adjective, verb, etc., in a sentence —compare CONCORD (3)

agree with *v prep* [T1 *no pass.*] **1** to be in accordance with: *Your story agrees with his in everything except small details* **2** *infml* to suit the health of: *The soup did not agree with me, and has given me a pain* —see also DISAGREE WITH **3** (of nouns, adjectives, verbs, etc.) to have the same number, person, CASE, etc., as

ag·ri·cul·ture /ˈægrɪˌkʌltʃəʳ/ *n* [U] the art or practice of farming, esp. of growing crops —**-tural** /ˌægrɪˈkʌltʃərəl/ *adj* —**-tur(al)ist** /ˌægrɪˈkʌltʃərələ̇st/ *n*

a·gron·o·my /əˈgrɒnəmi‖əˈgrɑ-/ *n* [U] the scientific study of soil and the growing of crops —**-mist** *n*

a·ground /əˈgraʊnd/ *adv, adj* [F] (of a ship) in, into, on, or onto the shore or bottom of a sea, lake, etc. (often in the phr. **run aground**)

a·gue /ˈeɪgjuː/ *n* [U;(C)] fever that begins with coldness and an uncontrollable shaking of the body, esp. when caused by the disease MALARIA

ah /ɑː/ *interj* a cry of surprise, pity, pain, joy, dislike, etc.: *Ah! I hurt my foot on that stone.|Ah, there you are!*

a·ha /ɑːˈhɑː/ *interj* a cry of surprise, satisfaction, amused discovery, etc.: *Aha, so it's you hiding there*

a·head /əˈhed/ *adv, adj* [F] **1** in or into a forward position; in advance; before: *One man went ahead to see if the road was clear.|The road ahead was full of sheep* **2** in or into the future: *to plan ahead* **3**

ahead of a in advance of **b** better than **4 get ahead** to do well; succeed

a·hem /m'hm; *spelling pronunciation* ə'hem/ *interj* a cough used to attract attention, give a slight warning, express doubts, etc.

a·hoy /ə'hɔɪ/ *interj* (a cry made by seamen as a greeting or warning)

aid[1] /eɪd/ *v* [T1 (*with, in*);V3] to give support to; help —see also **aid and** ABET (2) —see HELP (USAGE)

aid[2] *n* **1** [U] support; help: *He went to the aid of the hurt man.*|*What is the money in aid of?* **2** [C] a person or thing that supports or helps: *A dictionary is an important aid in learning a new language* —see also DEAF AID, HEARING AID, VISUAL AID **3 what ... in aid of?** *BrE infml* what ... for?: *"What's this little handle in aid of?" "It's for starting the machine."*| *"What's your new dress in aid of?" "It's spring!"*

aide /eɪd/ *n* a person who helps, esp. a person employed to help a government minister

aide-de-camp /ˌeɪd də 'kɒ̃ (*Fr* ɛd də kɑ̃)/ *n* **aides-de-camp** (*same pronunciation*) *Fr* a military or naval officer who helps an officer of higher rank in his duties

ail /eɪl/ *v* **1** [Wv4;I∅] *infml* to be ill and grow weak **2** [T1] *becoming rare* to cause pain to; trouble (esp. in the phr. **What ails you?**)

ai·le·ron /'eɪlərɒn‖-rɑn/ *n* the movable back edge of the wing of an aircraft, used esp. to keep the aircraft level or help it turn —see picture at AIRCRAFT

ail·ment /'eɪlmənt/ *n* an illness, esp. one that is not serious: *She is always complaining of some ailment or other*

aim[1] /eɪm/ *v* **1** [T1 (*at*);I∅ (*at, for*)] to point or direct (a weapon, shot, remark, etc.) towards some object, esp. with the intention of hitting it: *He aimed the gun carefully.*|*He aimed it at her head.*| *My remarks were not aimed at you* **2** [I3] to direct one's efforts (towards doing or obtaining something); intend (to): *I aim to be a writer*

aim[2] *n* **1** [U] the act of directing a weapon, remark, etc.: *The hunter took aim at the lion.*|*His aim was very good* **2** [C] the desired result of one's efforts; purpose; intention: *What is your aim in working so hard?*

aim at *v prep* [T1,4] to make an effort towards: *The factory must aim at increased production/at increasing production*

aim for *v prep* [T1] AIM AT

aim·less /'eɪmləs/ *adj* without any purpose; lacking intention: *his aimless life* —**~ly** *adv* —**~ness** *n* [U]

ain't /eɪnt/ *nonstandard* a shortened form of *am not, is not, are not, has not,* and *have not*: *We ain't coming.*|*They ain't got it*

air[1] /eəʳ/ *n* **1** [U] the mixture of gases which surrounds the earth and which we breathe: *The fresh air made him feel hungry* **2** [U] the sky or the space above the ground: *He jumped into the air* **3** [U] the sky as something through which to fly: *Air travel is now very fast.*|*I shall send the letter by air* **4** [C] the general character or appearance of something; appearance of, or feeling caused by, a person or place: *There was an air of excitement at the meeting* **5** [C] that part of a piece of music that is easily recognized and remembered; tune **6** [C] *rare* a very gentle wind; BREEZE[1] (1) **7 clear the air** *not fml* **a** to make the air in a place fresh again, as by opening the windows **b** to get rid of misunderstanding, doubt, etc., by stating the facts clearly **8 in the air** *infml* **a** (of stories, talk, RUMOURs, etc.) being passed on from one person to another **b** not fully planned or settled; uncertain **9 into thin air** *infml* completely out of sight or reach **10 on/off the air** broadcasting/not broadcasting: *We shall be on the air in 5 minutes* **11 take the air** *rather fml* to go for a walk, ride, etc., in order to breathe some fresh air —compare WIND[1] (1); see also AIRS

air[2] *v* **1** [T1;I∅] **a** to dry (clothes, sheets, beds, etc.) by putting them in a place that is warm or has plenty of dry air **b** (of clothes, sheets, beds, etc.) to become dry by this method **2** [T1;I∅] to (cause to) become fresh by letting in air: *We aired the room by opening the windows* **3** [T1] to make known to others (one's opinions, ideas, complaints, etc.), esp. in a noisy manner: *They were tired of the doctor airing his knowledge*

air·base /'eəbeɪs‖'eər-/ *n* a place where military aircraft land and take off

air·bed /'eəbed‖'eər-/ also **air mattress**— *n* a rubber or plastic bed or long bag filled with air rather than feathers or other material

air·blad·der /'eəblædəʳ‖'eər-/ *n* (in some animals, esp. fishes, and plants) a small fleshy bag containing air

air·borne /'eəbɔːn‖'eərborn/ *adj* [Wa5] **1** (esp. of seeds) carried about by the air **2** (esp. of aircraft) in the air; in flight **3** (of a group of soldiers) trained to fight in an area after being dropped by aircraft by means of PARACHUTEs

air·brake /'eəbreɪk‖'eər-/ *n* an apparatus for stopping a vehicle, such as a train or big car, that is worked by air under pressure

air·brick /'eəbrɪk‖'eər-/ *n* a brick with holes through it to allow air into and out of a room or building

air·bus /'eəbʌs‖'eər-/ *n* [C;*by*+U] an aircraft for carrying large numbers of passengers on short or middle-distance flights at regular times

air chief mar·shal /ˌ· · '··/ *n* [A;C] (in Britain) (a man who holds) the 2nd highest rank in the R.A.F.

air com·mo·dore /ˌ· '···/ *n* [A;C] (in Britain) (a man who holds) the 5th highest rank in the R.A.F.

air-con·di·tion·ing /'· ·ˌ···/ *n* [U] the system that uses one or more machines (**air-conditioners**) to keep air in a building cool and usu. dry in the summer —**-tioned** *adj*

air-cool·ing /'· ˌ··/ *n* [U] the system or apparatus that keeps something, such as an engine, cool by forcing air over or through it —**air-cooled** *adj*

air cor·ri·dor /'· ˌ···/ *n* a limited path through the air that an aircraft must follow

air·craft /'eəkrɑːft‖'eərkræft/ *n* **-craft** [Wn3;C; *by*+U] a flying machine of any type, with or without an engine

See next page for picture

aircraft car·ri·er /'·· ˌ···/ *n* a warship which can carry naval aircraft and which has a large flat surface where they can take off and land

air·craft·man /'eəkrɑːftmən‖'eərkræft-/ also **air·crafts·man** /-krɑːfts-‖-kræfts-/ **-men** /mən/— *n* [A; C] (in Britain) (a man who holds) the lowest rank in the R.A.F.

air·crew /'eəkruː‖'eər-/ *n* [GC] the pilot and others responsible for flying an aircraft, together with those who look after the comfort of any passengers

air·cush·ion /'eəkʊʃən‖'eər-/ *n* **1** a soft bag (CUSHION) to sit on, which is filled with air rather than feathers or other material **2** air forced out from under a vehicle (HOVERCRAFT) to support it

air·drop /'eədrɒp‖'eərdrɑp/ *n* the dropping of supplies or men from an aircraft, by means of a PARACHUTE, esp. to a place that is difficult to get to —**airdrop** *v* [T1 (*to*);(D1)]: *They airdropped supplies to us*

Aire·dale /'eədeɪl‖'eər-/ *n* a dog with a rough coat; type of large TERRIER

air·field /'eəfiːld‖'eər-/ *n* **1** *AmE* AERODROME **2** a place where aircraft may land and take off but which need not have any large buildings for

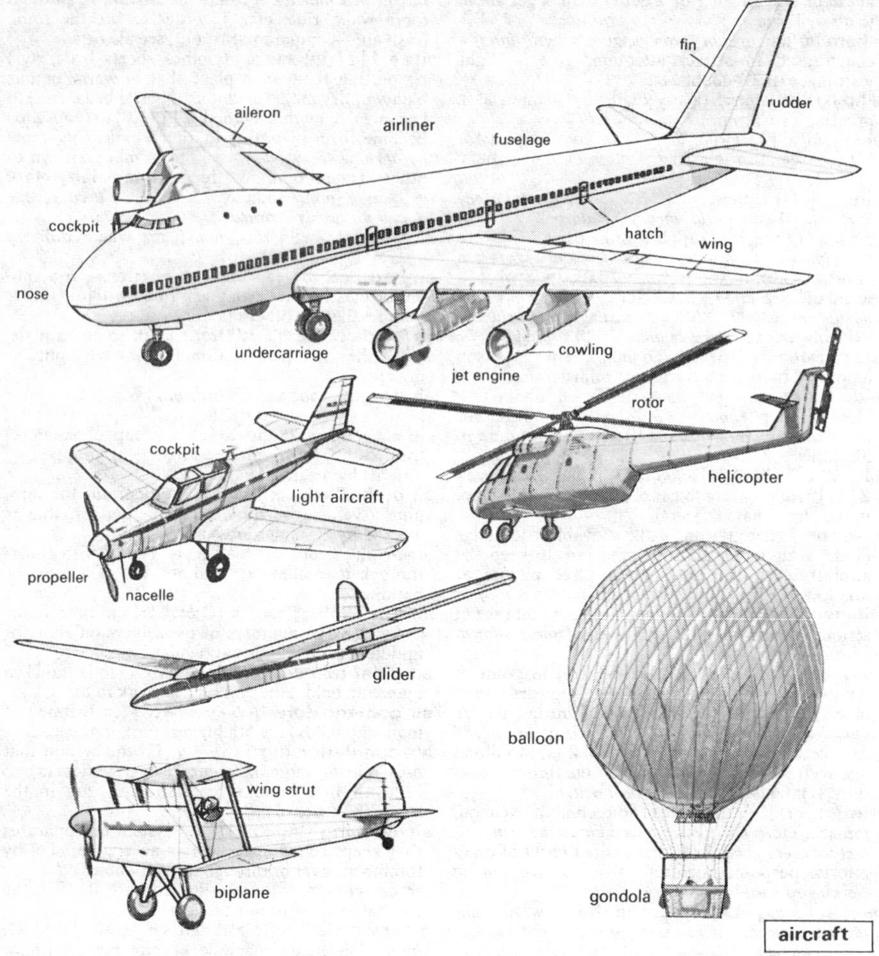

storing things or repairing the aircraft

air·flow /ˈeəfləʊ‖ˈeər-/ *n* [S;U] the movement of air over the surface of an aircraft in flight

air·force /ˈeəfɔːs‖ˈeərfors/ *n* that part of the military organization of a country that is concerned with attack and defence from the air

air·gun /ˈeəgʌn‖ˈeər-/ *n* **1** a gun which uses strong air pressure to fire a bullet **2** any apparatus that uses strong air pressure to force out a material, esp. paint

air·hole /ˈeəhəʊl‖ˈeər-/ *n* **1** a hole for air to pass through, as into places deep under the ground **2** a hole made by air, as in a cake or bread

air·host·ess /ˈeəˌhəʊstɪ̍s‖ˈeər-/ *n* a woman who looks after the comfort of the passengers of an aircraft during flight

air·i·ly /ˈeərɪ̍li/ *adv* **1** in a gay manner; not seriously **2** delicately; lightly

air·ing /ˈeərɪŋ/ *n* **1** [U] the leaving of clothes, sheets, etc., in the open air or in a warm place to get thoroughly dry **2** [U] the act of allowing fresh air into a room **3** [C *usu. sing.*] the making public of one's opinions, knowledge, ideas, etc.: *We had a meeting and gave our ideas a good airing* **4** [C *usu. sing.*] the act of going for a walk, ride, etc., in the fresh air

airing cup·board /ˈ·· ˌ··/ *n* a cupboard that is heated and used to make clothes, sheets, etc., thoroughly dry before use

air·lane /ˈeəleɪn‖ˈeər-/ *n* a path through the air regularly used by aircraft in flight

air·less /ˈeələs‖ˈeər-/ *adj* lacking fresh air; STUFFY (1)

air·let·ter /ˈeəˌletəʳ‖ˈeər-/ *n* [C;*by*+U] **1** a sheet of very thin paper (already stamped for posting) on which a letter can be written and which is then folded and stuck at the edges and sent by air without an envelope **2** any letter that is sent by air

air·lift /ˈeəˌlɪft‖ˈeər-/ *n* the carrying of large numbers of people or amounts of supplies by aircraft, esp. to or from a place that is difficult to get to —**airlift** *v* [T1 (*to*)]: *We airlifted food to them*

air·line /ˈeəlaɪn‖ˈeər-/ *n* a business that runs a regular service for carrying passengers and goods by air

air·lin·er /ˈeəˌlaɪnəʳ‖ˈeər-/ *n* a large passenger aircraft —see picture at AIRCRAFT

air·lock /ˈeəlɒk‖ˈeərlɑk/ *n* **1** a ball of air (BUBBLE) in a tube or pipe that prevents the passage of a liquid **2** an enclosed space or room into which or from which air cannot accidentally pass, as in a space vehicle or apparatus for working under water

air·mail /ˈeəmeɪl‖ˈeər-/ *n* [U] **1** letters, parcels, etc., sent by air **2** the system of sending things by air

air·man /ˈeəmən‖ˈeər-/ (*fem.* **airwoman**)— *n* **-men** /mən/ [A;C] *esp. BrE* any person in the airforce who is not above the rank of a NONCOMMISSIONED OFFICER

air mat·tress /ˈ· ˌ··/ *n* AIRBED

air·plane /ˈeəpleɪn‖ˈeər-/ *n AmE* AEROPLANE

air·pock·et /ˈeəˌpɒkɨt‖ˈeərˌpɑ-/ *n* a downward flow of air in the sky which causes an aircraft that is flying into it to lose height suddenly

air·port /ˈeəpɔːt‖ˈeərport/ *n* a place where aircraft can land and take off, which has several buildings, and which is regularly used by paying passengers

air raid /ˈ· ·/ *n* an attack by military aircraft: *an air-raid shelter*

airs /eəz‖eərz/ also **airs and grac·es** /ˌ· · ˈ··/— *n* [P] *derog* (esp. of a woman) unnatural manners or actions that are intended to make people think one is more important than one really is (esp. in the phrs. **give oneself airs, put on airs**)

air-sea res·cue /ˌ· · ˈ··/ *n* **1** [U] the work of saving people from aircraft that have crashed into the sea **2** [C] a case or example of this work

air·shaft /ˈeəʃɑːft‖ˈeərʃæft/ *n* an opening like a chimney for allowing fresh air into places deep under the ground, such as mines and TUNNELs

air·ship /ˈeəˌʃɪp‖ˈeər-/ *n* [C;*by*+U] *now rare* a flying vehicle that uses gas to make it lighter than air and an engine to make it move forward

air·sick /ˈeəˌsɪk‖ˈeər-/ *adj* being sick or ill through the effects of flying in an aircraft —**~ness** *n* [U]

air·space /ˈeəspeɪs‖ˈeər-/ *n* [U9] the air or sky above a country and regarded as the property of that country

air·speed /ˈeəspiːd‖ˈeər-/ *n* [S;U] the speed at which an aircraft travels through the air

air·strip /ˈeəˌstrɪp‖ˈeər-/ *n* a stretch of land that may be used by aircraft to take off and land, as in war or time of trouble, but not as a regular arrangement

air ter·mi·nal /ˈ· ˌ···/ *n* the building in which passengers for an aircraft flight come together before getting on board their aircraft or from which they leave at the end of their journey. It may be at the airport, or some distance away

air·tight /ˈeətaɪt‖ˈeər-/ *adj* not allowing air to pass in or out: *airtight containers*

air-to-air /ˌ· · ˈ·◂/ *adj* [Wa5;A] between aircraft in flight, esp. to be fired from one aircraft at another: *air-to-air weapons*

air vice-mar·shal /ˌ· · ˈ··◂/ *n* [A;C] (in Britain) (a man who holds) the 4th highest rank in the R.A.F.

air·way /ˈeəweɪ‖ˈeər-/ *n* **1** AIRLINE **2** AIRSHAFT

air·wom·an /ˈeəˌwʊmən‖ˈeər-/ *n* **-women** /ˌwɪmɪn/ [A;C] *esp. BrE* a female AIRMAN

air·wor·thy /ˈeəˌwɜːði‖ˈeərˌwɜrði/ *adj* (of aircraft) in proper and safe working condition —**-thiness** *n* [U]

air·y /ˈeəri/ *adj* [Wa2] **1** open to the fresh air: *The large window makes the room quite airy* **2** *derog* of or having AIRS; AFFECTED (1) **3** *derog* having little substance; empty: *Nothing results from his airy plans and promises* **4** light-hearted; gay; happy; careless **5** of, like, or in the air

aisle /aɪl/ *n* **1** a passage, usu. one of two, leading through the length of a church and divided from the central part (NAVE) by a row of pillars —see picture at CHURCH[1] **2** a narrow passage between rows of seats, shelves, etc., as in a theatre or large shop **3 roll in the aisles** (esp. of people at the theatre) to be helpless with laughter

aitch /eɪtʃ/ *n* **1** a way of spelling the name of the letter *H, h* **2 drop one's aitches** not to sound the letter *h* in one's speech, as by saying *'ome* for *home*

aitch-bone /ˈ· ·/ *n BrE* **1** a large bone at the back end (RUMP) of a cow **2** a piece of meat cut from over this bone

a·jar /əˈdʒɑːʳ/ *adv, adj* [F] (of a door) not quite closed; slightly open

a·kim·bo /əˈkɪmbəʊ/ *adj, adv* [Wa5;F] with arms bent at the elbows and hands on the sides (usu. on the HIPs[2]) (esp. in the phr. **with arms akimbo**)

a·kin /əˈkɪn/ *adj* [F (*to*)] **1** from the same family; related **2** having the same appearance, character, etc.; like: *His beautiful writing is akin to drawing*

-al /əl, əl/ *suffix* **1** [*n*→*adj*] of, concerning, or having the character of: *political*|DIRECTIONAL **2** [*v*→*n*] action of the stated type: *refusal*|*arrival*

à la /ˈæ lə, ˈɑː lɑː (*Fr* a la)/ *prep infml & Fr* in the manner of (esp. a person); like: *a plan for very great public spending à la Roosevelt*

al·a·bas·ter /ˈæləbɑːstəʳ‖-bæ-/ *n* **1** [U] a transparent soft mainly white stone used for making ornaments **2** [A] *lit* very white: *She has alabaster skin*

à la carte /ˌæ lə ˈkɑːt, ˌɑː lɑː-‖-ɑrt (*Fr* a ˌla kart)/ *adj, adv* [Wa5] *Fr* (of cooked food sold in a restaurant) according to a list (MENU) where each dish has its own separate price —compare TABLE D'HOTE

a·lack /əˈlæk/ *interj old use* a cry expressing sorrow

a·lac·ri·ty /əˈlækrɨti/ *n* [U] *fml* quick and willing readiness

à la mode /ˌæ lə ˈməʊd, ˌɑː lɑː- (*Fr* a la mɔd)/ *adv* [F] **1** according to the latest fashion or style **2** *AmE* (of food, esp. PIE) served with ice cream

a·larm¹ /əˈlɑːm‖əˈlɑrm/ also (*old use*) **a·lar·um** /əˈlærəm/— *n* **1** [C] a warning of danger, as by ringing a bell or shouting: *I gave/raised the alarm as soon as I saw what was happening.*|*There were several alarms during the night but no actual attacks* **2** [C] any apparatus, such as a bell, noise, flag, by which a warning is given **3** [C] (the apparatus that makes the noise in an) ALARM CLOCK **4** [U] sudden fear and anxiety as caused by the possibility of danger

alarm² also (*old use*) **alarum**— *v* [T1] **1** to excite with sudden fear and anxiety **2** to make conscious of danger

alarm clock /·ˈ· ·/ also **alarm**— *n* a clock that can be set to make a noise at any particular time to wake up sleepers: *What time shall I set the alarm clock for?* —see picture at CLOCK[1]

a·larm·ist /əˈlɑːmɨst‖əˈlɑr-/ *n derog* a person who raises an alarm when there is no reason for it, esp. a nervous person who always expects danger and says so to others

a·las /əˈlæs/ *interj lit* a cry expressing grief, sorrow, or fear

al·ba·tross /ˈælbətrɒs‖-trɔs, -trɑs/ *n* [Wn1] any of various large strong mostly white seabirds famous for their ability to fly long distances

al·be·it /ɔːlˈbiːɨt/ *conj fml* even though; although: *It was a very small albeit important mistake*

al·bi·no /ælˈbiːnəʊ‖ælˈbaɪ-/ *n* **-nos** **1** a person with a pale milky skin, very light hair, and eyes that are pink because of a lack of colouring matter **2** an animal or plant that lacks the typical colouring

al·bum /ˈælbəm/ *n* **1** a book whose pages have little or no writing and which is used for collecting photographs, stamps, pieces of newspaper, drawings, etc. **2** LONG-PLAYING RECORD

al·bu·men /ˈælbjʊmɨn‖ælˈbjuː-/ *n* [U] **1** the white or colourless part of an egg **2** also **albumin**— any of various substances (PROTEINs) contained in much animal and vegetable matter

al·che·mist /ˈælkəmɪst/ *n* a person who studied or practised ALCHEMY

al·che·my /ˈælkəmi/ *n* [U] (esp. in the MIDDLE AGES) the science concerned with finding a way to turn all metals into gold and which later developed into chemistry

al·co·hol /ˈælkəhɒl‖-hɔl/ *n* **1** [U] the pure colourless liquid present in drinks that can make one drunk, such as wine, beer, and SPIRITs[1] (12) **2** [U] the drinks containing this **3** [U;C] any of a class of chemical substances of which the alcohol in wine is one

al·co·hol·ic[1] /ˌælkəˈhɒlɪk‖-ˈhɔ-/ *adj* **1** containing alcohol **2** of, concerning, or caused by alcohol **3** suffering from ALCOHOLISM —**~ally** *adv* [Wa4]

alcoholic[2] *n* a person who cannot break the habit of drinking alcoholic drinks too much, esp. one whose health is damaged because of this

al·co·hol·is·m /ˈælkəhɒlɪzəm‖-hɔ-/ *n* [U] **1** the continued and habitual drinking of alcohol in great quantities **2** the diseased condition caused by this

al·cove /ˈælkəʊv/ *n* **1** a small partly enclosed space in a room for a bed, chairs, books, etc. **2** a space like this, as for a seat in a wall or row of bushes in a garden

al·der /ˈɔːldəʳ/ *n* [Wn2] a type of tree related to the BIRCH, which grows in wet places

al·der·man /ˈɔːldəmən‖-dər-/ *n* **-men** /mən/ **1** *BrE* a member of a town, city, or COUNTY (1) council who is of high rank and is chosen by the elected members **2** a local government officer having any of various duties —**~ic** /ˌɔːldəˈmænɪk‖-ər-/ *adj* [Wa5]

ale /eɪl/ *n* [U] any of various types of beer, esp. one that is pale in colour

ale·house /ˈeɪlhaʊs/ *n* **-houses** /ˌhaʊzɪz/ *old use* PUB

a·lert[1] /əˈlɜːt‖-ɜrt/ *adj* **1** watchful and ready to meet danger **2** *apprec* quick to see and act: *He is an alert boy* —**~ly** *adv* —**~ness** *n* [U]

alert[2] *n* **1** a warning to be ready for danger —opposite **all clear** **2** the period in which people remain especially watchful for danger **3 on the alert (for)** in a state of watchfulness for danger, as after a warning

alert[3] *v* [T1] **1** to put (esp. soldiers) on the ALERT[2] (3) **2** [(*to*)] to warn: *The doctor alerted me to the danger of not getting enough sleep*

A lev·el /ˈeɪ ˌlevəl/ also **advanced level**— *n* (*esp. in Britain*) **1** [U] the higher of the 2 standards of examinations (in the GCE), necessary for entrance to a university or most colleges **2** [C] an examination of this standard in a particular subject —compare O LEVEL

al·fal·fa /ælˈfælfə/ *n* [U] *AmE* LUCERNE

al·fres·co /ælˈfreskəʊ/ *adv, adj It* in the open air: *We ate alfresco during the summer.*|*We enjoyed an alfresco dinner*

al·gae /ˈældʒiː/ *n* [P] plants of a very simple form that live in or near water and are usu. very small —see picture at PLANT[2]

al·ge·bra /ˈældʒɪbrə/ *n* [U] a branch of MATHEMATICS in which signs and letters are used instead of numbers —**~ic(al)** /ˌældʒɪˈbreɪ-ɪk(əl)/ *adj* —**~ically** *adv* [Wa4]

al·go·rith·m /ˈælgərɪðəm/ *n tech* a list of instructions which are carried out in a fixed order to find the answer to a question or esp. to calculate a number —**~ic** /ˌælgəˈrɪðmɪk/ *adj*

a·li·as[1] /ˈeɪlɪəs/ *adv* (esp. of a criminal) also known as; also called: *The police said the thief's name was Henry Ford, alias Edward Ball, alias John Smith*

alias[2] *n* a name other than the usual or officially recognized name used by a person (esp. a criminal) on certain occasions; false name

al·i·bi /ˈælɪbaɪ/ *n* **-s** **1** an argument or defence that a person charged with a crime was in another place when the crime was done and that he therefore could not have done it: *They all had alibis when asked where they were on the day of the crime* **2** *infml* an excuse: *What's your alibi for being late this time Jones?* —see EXCUSE (USAGE)

a·li·en[1] /ˈeɪlɪən/ *adj* **1** [Wa5] belonging to another country or race; foreign: *alien people* **2** different in nature or character, esp. so different as to be opposed: *Their ideas are quite alien to our way of thinking*

alien[2] *n* a foreigner who has not become a citizen of the country where he or she is living

a·li·en·ate /ˈeɪlɪəneɪt/ *v* [T1 (*from*)] **1** to turn away the friendship of; cause to feel or become an enemy; make unfriendly **2** *tech* to take away (the ownership of land, a business, a right, etc.)

a·li·en·a·tion /ˌeɪlɪəˈneɪʃən/ *n* [U (*from*)] **1** the separation of a person or his friendship from a person with whom he was formerly friendly **2** a feeling of not belonging to or being part of one's surroundings: *The increasingly dull nature of many industrial jobs has led to the alienation of many workers* **3** *tech* the official taking of land, a business, a right, etc., from someone

a·li·en·ist /ˈeɪlɪənɪst/ *n old use* PSYCHIATRIST

a·light[1] /əˈlaɪt/ *v* **alighted** *or* **alit** /əˈlɪt/ [IØ (*from*)] *fml* to get off or down from, esp. at the end of a journey: *We alighted from the train soon after midday* —see DISMOUNT (USAGE)

alight[2] *adj* [F] **1** on fire; in flames **2** having the lights on; lit up

alight on also **alight up·on**— *v prep* [T1] **1** to come down from the air onto **2** *fml* to find unexpectedly; HAPPEN ON

a·lign, aline /əˈlaɪn/ *v* [T1;IØ] to come, bring, form, make, or arrange into a line

a·lign·ment, aline- /əˈlaɪnmənt/ *n* **1** [U] the act of forming or arranging into a line (esp. in the phrs. **into/out of alignment (with)**) **2** [C] the line or lines formed in this way **3** [U] (of people or countries with the same aims, ideas, etc.) the act of forming into groups **4** [C] a group formed in this way

align with *v prep* [T1] **1** to cause to come into the same line as: *Do you think you could align this picture with the one directly opposite it?* **2** to cause to come into accordance or agreement with: *We must align ourselves with the workers in the struggle for freedom*

a·like[1] /əˈlaɪk/ *adj* [F] being (almost) the same in appearance, quality, character, etc.; like one another: *The 2 brothers are very much alike.*|*You 2 are more alike than I thought*

alike[2] *adv* in (almost) the same way; equally: *She treats all her children alike*

al·i·men·ta·ry /ˌælɪˈmentəri/ *adj tech* concerning food and the way it is treated (DIGESTed[3] (1)) in the body

alimentary ca·nal /··ˌ··· ·ˈ·/ *n* the tubelike passage leading from the mouth to the stomach and onward —see picture at DIGESTIVE SYSTEM

al·i·mo·ny /ˈælɪməni‖-məʊni/ *n* [U;S] money that a man has been ordered to pay regularly to his (former) wife after they have been SEPARATEd[1] (6) or DIVORCEd[2] (1) in a court of law

alive /əˈlaɪv/ *adj* [F] **1** [Wa5] having life; not dead; living **2** full of life; active: *Although old he is still very much alive* **3** still in existence or operation: *The argument was kept alive by the politicians* **4 alive to** having full knowledge of: *He was alive to the dangers of the work* **5 alive with** covered with or full of (living things): *The dead dog is alive with insects*

al·ka·li /ˈælkəlaɪ/ *n* **-lis** *or* **-lies** [U;C] *tech* any of various substances that form chemical salts when combined with acids —opposite **acid**

al·ka·line /ˈælkəlaɪn‖-lə̇n/ *adj* of, concerning, or having the nature of an ALKALI

all[1] /ɔːl/ *predeterminer* **1** (*with v or sing. nouns*) the complete amount or quantity of; the whole of: *He ate all his food.|He ate it all.|We walked all the way.|We worked hard all last year* **2** (*with plurals*) every member or separate part of; every one of: *All these questions must be answered.|You must answer them all.|They must all be answered.|All the angles of a square are 90°* (= Each angle is 90°) **3** (*with plurals*) every member or separate part of, taken together; every one of, taken together: *All the angles of a square make 360°* (= The sum of the angles equals 360°) **4 all the . . . (that)** as much of (a) . . . as: *That ugly little house was all the home (that) I ever had* —see ALL[4] (USAGE)

all[2] *determiner* **1** (shows the complete amount or quantity of, or the whole of, an uncountable noun): *Not all food is good to eat.|We worked hard all year* **2** (includes every member or separate part of a group of countable nouns): *All children want presents on their birthdays.|Please answer all questions on this list.|"We've been looking at all kinds of new properties"* (SEU S.) **3** the greatest possible amount of: *The doctor came with all speed* **4** every; any: *He is a good musician beyond all doubt* **5** being influenced or controlled by or as if by (the stated quality or body organ): *I am listening carefully; I'm all ears.|I can't play the piano today; I feel awkward and am all thumbs.|He's such a kind man: he's all heart* **6 of all people** *infml* surprisingly; out of all the people who might be expected to be present, to be able to help, to be suitable, etc.: *To see George, of all people, in the Ritz Hotel!*
—see also ALL IN, ALL-IN, ALL-NIGHT, ALL-OUT, ALL-POWERFUL, ALL-PURPOSE, ALL RIGHT, ALL-ROUND, ALL-STAR, ALL-TIME

all[3] *adv* **1** [H] altogether; completely; wholly: *The table was all covered with papers.|I am all in favour of your suggestion.|She sat all alone* **2** to a very great degree; so much; much (in the phr. **all the**): *If we get help the work will get finished all the sooner.|And the rise in prices is all the more serious as/since we are not selling enough goods abroad* **3** for each side: *The result* (SCORE[1] (1)) *of the football match was 3 all; neither side won* **4 all along** *infml* all the time: *I knew that all along* **5 all but** almost; nearly: *I am all but ready* **6 all over a** everywhere (on an object or surface): *painted it green all over* **b** (*esp. AmE*) everywhere (in a place): *We've been hunting for her all over* **c** right across; to every part of (a place): *"travelled all over India"* (SEU S.) **7 (not) all there** *infml* (not) having a good quick mind **8 all the same** *infml* even so; in any case: *You say the bridge is safe; I shall take care all the same* **9 all the same to** *infml* not making any difference or causing any worry to: *If it's all the same to you, I'll turn the radio off.|It's all the same to me whether you stay or go* **10 all told** counting everyone or everything; altogether **11 all up (with)** *infml* at an end; ruined —see also ALL OUT, ALL OVER, ALL RIGHT, ALL ROUND

all[4] *pron* **1** everybody, everything, or everyone: *All enjoyed themselves.|He gave all he had.|The laws include all.|I brought all of them* **2 all in all** *infml* considering everything; on the whole, generally: *All in all we had a good time* **3 all of** fully: *It'll cost all of £5,000* **4 all that** *nonassertive, infml* so very: *"Things aren't all that good at the moment"* (SEU S.) **5 and all** *infml* and everything or everybody: *The whole of the fish may be eaten, head, tail, bones, and all* **6 (not) at all** (not) in any way: *I do not agree with you at all.|Do you feel ill at all?|Do you feel at all ill?* —see also NOT **at all 7 for all** in spite of: *They could not open the box for all their efforts* **8 for all one knows, cares, etc.** *infml* as far as one knows, cares, etc.: *For all I know he may well be guilty, but I really don't care* **9 in all** counting everyone or everything; altogether **10 it was all one could do (not) to** *infml* it was very difficult to: *It was all I could do not to cry* **11 not so/as good, cold, fast, etc., as all that** *infml* not so very good, cold, fast, etc. **12 once (and) for all** for the last time: *Once and for all I must ask you to be quiet*
USAGE 1 Americans, particularly when they are speaking, often prefer to say **all** *year (round)*, **all** *of the year*, **all** *of the food*; British speakers more often say **all** *the year (round)*, **all** *the food*. 2 **All** is sing. with [U] nouns: **All** *the money is spent*. It is pl. with pl. nouns: **All** *the people have gone*.

all[5] *n* **one's all** everything one possesses or considers valuable

all- *comb. form* **1** consisting or made only of: *an all-wool dress* **2** of, for, or concerning the whole of: *an all-England football team*

Al·lah /ˈælə/ *n* [R] (the Muslim name for) God

al·lay /əˈleɪ/ *v* [T1] *fml* to make (fear, anger, doubt, etc.) less

all clear /ˌ· ˈ·/ *n* a signal (such as a whistle or loud cry) that danger is past

all-day /ˌ· ˈ·◂/ *adj* [A] lasting all through the day: *an all-day event*

al·le·ga·tion /ˌælɪˈgeɪʃən/ *n fml* a statement that charges someone with doing something bad or criminal but which is not supported by proof: *allegations of cruelty unsupported by proof*

al·lege /əˈledʒ/ *v* [Wv5;T1,5,5b] *fml* to state or declare without proof or before finding proof: *The newspaper reporters allege that the man was murdered but they have given no proof.|So they allege, but have they any proof?*

al·leg·ed·ly /əˈledʒə̇dli/ *adv* according to charges made without proof: *He is allegedly a thief*

al·le·giance /əˈliːdʒəns/ *n* [U;C] loyalty, faith, and dutiful support to a king, country, idea, etc.: *His allegiances are divided*

al·le·gor·i·cal /ˌælə̇ˈgɒrɪkəl‖-ˈgɔ-, -ˈgɑ-/ *adj* of, concerning, or having the quality of an ALLEGORY —**~ly** *adv* [Wa4]

al·le·go·ry /ˈælə̇gəri‖-gori/ *n* **1** [C] a story, poem, painting, etc., in which the characters and actions represent good and bad qualities **2** [U] the style of such a story, poem, etc.

al·le·gret·to /ˌælə̇ˈgretəʊ/ *adv, adj, n* **-tos** (a piece of music) played fairly fast but not very fast

al·leg·ro /əˈlegrəʊ, əˈleɪ-/ *adv, adj, n* **-gros** (a piece of music) played in a rapid manner and full of life

al·le·lu·ia /ˌælə̇ˈluːjə/ *n, interj* HALLELUJA

al·ler·gic /əˈlɜːdʒɪk‖-ɜr-/ *adj* [(*to*)] **1** suffering from an ALLERGY (1): *He is allergic to the fur of cats* **2** *infml* having a strong dislike (for): *I am allergic to big dirty cities*

al·ler·gy /ˈælədʒi‖-ər-/ *n* [(*to*)] **1** a condition of being unusually sensitive to something eaten, breathed in, or touched, in a way that causes pain or suffering **2** *infml* a strong dislike (for)

al·le·vi·ate /əˈliːvieɪt/ *v* [T1] to make (pain, suffering, anger, etc.) less —**-ation** /əˌliːviˈeɪʃən/ *n* [U]

al·ley /ˈæli/ *n* **1** a narrow street or path between buildings in a town **2** a path in a garden or park, esp. one bordered by trees or bushes **3** a long narrow piece of ground, or floor along which heavy balls are rolled in order to knock over pieces (SKITTLE*s* or PIN*s*) of wood, plastic, etc., placed at the far end **4** a room or building containing one or many such long narrow areas —see also BLIND ALLEY

al·ley·way /ˈæliweɪ/ *n* ALLEY (1)

all fours /ˌ· ˈ·/ *n* **on all fours** down on one's hands and knees

all get-out /ˌ· ˈ· ·/ *n* **as all get-out** *AmE sl* to the highest or greatest possible degree

al·li·ance /əˈlaɪəns/ *n* **1** [U] the act of allying or the state of being allied (ALLY): (esp. in the phr. **in alliance (with)**: *They are in alliance (with each other)* **2** [C] a close agreement or connection between countries, groups, families, etc.: *We are hoping for an alliance with the workers of other factories* **3** [C] a group or association, esp. of countries, formed to look after the interests of its members **4** [C] *becoming rare* a union of families by marriage

al·lied /ˈælaɪd, əˈlaɪd/ *adj* [(*to*)] **1** joined by political agreement **2** related or connected, esp. by common qualities: *painting and other allied arts*

al·li·ga·tor /ˈælɪ̣geɪtəʳ/ *n* **1** [Wn1;C] a large cold-blooded fierce animal (like the CROCODILE) that lives on land and in lakes and rivers in the hot wet parts of America and China **2** [U] its skin turned into leather

all in /ˌ· ˈ·/ *adj* [F] *infml* worn out; very tired: *That job leaves me all in at the end of the day*

all-in /ˈ· ·/ *adj* [Wa5;A] **1** with everything included: *I'll sell you the car, tyres, and radio at an all-in price* **2** (esp. of the sport of wrestling (WRESTLE)) without limits on moves, holds, or methods

al·lit·er·a·tion /əˌlɪtəˈreɪʃən/ *n* [U] the appearance of the same sound or sounds at the beginning of 2 or more words that are next to or close to each other (as in "*R*ound the *r*ocks *r*uns the *r*iver")

al·lit·er·a·tive /əˈlɪtərətɪv‖-təreɪtɪv/ *adj* being, having, or using ALLITERATION —**~ly** *adv*

all-night /ˈ· ·/ *adj* [A] **1** lasting all through the night: *an all-night game of cards* **2** open all through the night: *an all-night shop*

al·lo·cate /ˈæləkeɪt/ also **allot**— *v* **1** [T1] to divide and give as shares: *We must allocate the money carefully* **2** [D1;T1 (*to*)] to give as a share: *We allocated the society some money* **3** [D1;T1 (*to*)] to set apart for somebody or some purpose: *That space has already been allocated for building a new hospital*

al·lo·ca·tion /ˌæləˈkeɪʃən/ *n* **1** [U] the giving of shares or places **2** [C] a share, as of money or space

al·lop·a·thy /əˈlɒpəθi‖əˈlɑ-/ *n* [U] *tech* the treatment of diseases by the use of medicines that produce effects different from or opposite to those of the disease being treated —**-thic(al)** /ˌæləˈpæθɪk(əl)/ *adj* —**-thically** *adv* [Wa4]

al·lot /əˈlɒt‖əˈlɑt/ *v* **-tt-** [D1;T1 (*to*)] ALLOCATE

al·lot·ment /əˈlɒtmənt‖əˈlɑt-/ *n* **1** [U] the giving of shares or places; ALLOCATION **2** [C] a share, as of money or space **3** [C] (in Britain) a small piece of land rented out, esp. by a town council, to people who will grow vegetables on it

all out /ˌ· ˈ·/ *adv infml* using all possible strength and effort

all-out /ˈ· ·/ *adj* [A] *infml* using all possible strength and effort; complete; total: *We made an all-out attempt to climb the mountain*

all o·ver /ˌ· ˈ··/ *adv* **1** in every part; everywhere: *He looked all over for the lost book* **2** at an end; finished **3** *infml* in every part or quality; thoroughly: *The man you have just described sounds like my father all over*

al·low /əˈlaʊ/ *v* **1** [T1,4;V3] to let (somebody) do something; let (something) be done; permit: *They do not allow it/smoking/you to smoke.|You are allowed into the room* **2** [T1;V3] to make possible (for); provide (for): *This plan allows 20 minutes for dinner.|Your gift allows me to buy a car* **3** [X9] to permit to be or to come: *She won't allow dogs in the house* **4** [D1;T1] to give, esp. money or time: *My father allows me some money for books.|The bank allows 5% on money kept with it* **5** [T5;X *to be* 1,7] *rare* to admit; accept: *We must allow that he is a brave man* **6** [T1] to permit as possible; admit: *The facts allow no other explanation*

al·low·a·ble /əˈlaʊəbəl/ *adj* that may be allowed or permitted —**-bly** *adv*

al·low·ance /əˈlaʊəns/ *n* **1** [C] **a** something, esp. money, provided regularly: *an allowance of £5,000 a year* **b** *AmE* POCKET MONEY (2) **2** [C] money provided for a special purpose: *Most people who travel in the course of their work are given travelling allowances* **3** [C] money taken off the cost of something, usu. for a special reason **4** [C;U] the taking into consideration of facts that may change something, esp. an opinion (esp. in the phr. **make (an) allowance for, make allowance(s) for**) **5** [C] share; part

allow for *v prep* [T1,4,6a;V3,4a] to take into consideration: *Allowing for the train being late, we should be back by 10.30.|Has everything been allowed for in your plan?*

allow of *v prep* [T1 *no pass.*] *fml* ALLOW (6)

al·loy[1] /ˈælɔɪ‖ˈælɔɪ, əˈlɔɪ/ *n* a metal made by mixing together 2 or more different metals

al·loy[2] /əˈlɔɪ‖əˈlɔɪ, ˈælɔɪ/ *v* [T1] **1** [(*with*)] to mix (one metal) with another **2** *lit* to lower in value or quality; spoil

all-pow·er·ful /ˌ· ˈ···/ *adj* having the power to do anything; OMNIPOTENT

all-pur·pose /ˈ· ˌ··/ *adj* [A;(B)] able to be used in all conditions or for all purposes: *an all-purpose cleaning liquid*

all right /ˌ· ˈ·/ *adv, adj* [Wa5;F] **1** safe, unharmed, or healthy: *Is the driver all right after the accident?* **2** *infml* satisfactory; acceptable; in a satisfactory or acceptable manner: *His work is all right (but he could be faster)* **3** (in answer to a suggestion, plan, etc.) I/we agree; yes: *All right! Let's go now* **4** *infml* beyond doubt; certainly: *He's ill all right: he has a very serious disease*

all round /ˌ· ˈ·/ *adv infml* in regard to everything; in every way: *Taken/considered all round it's not a bad car*

all-round /ˈ· ·/ *adj* [Wa5;A] having ability in many things, esp. in various sports —**~er** /ˌ· ˈ··/ *n*: *He's a good all-rounder who likes tennis, cricket, and swimming*

all·spice /ˈɔːlspaɪs/ *n* [U] a strong-tasting powder obtained from the berry of a West Indian tree and used in cooking

all-star /ˈ· ·/ *adj* [Wa5;A] (of a film, play, etc.) acted only or mostly by famous actors

all-time /ˈ· ·/ *adj* greatest, biggest, most, etc., ever known (esp. in the phrs. **all-time high, all-time low**): *The shop's sales have reached an all-time high in this very successful year*

al·lude to /əˈluːd/ *v prep* [T1,4] *fml* to speak of but without going straight to the point: *She did not say Mr. Smith's name, but it was clear she was alluding to him*

al·lure[1] /əˈlʊəʳ/ *v* [Wv4;T1 (*into*); V3] to attract by the offer of something pleasant; TEMPT

allure[2] *n* [U;S] attraction; charm: *The book has a certain allure for which it is hard to find a reason*

al·lure·ment /əˈlʊəmənt/ *n* **1** [C] something that attracts or charms: *The big cities are full of allurements on which to spend money* **2** [U] the act of attracting

al·lu·sion /əˈluːʒən/ *n* [U;C: (*to*)] *fml* the act of not speaking of something in an open manner, or something spoken of without directness, esp. while speaking about something else: *His allusions to my failures were unnecessary* —**-sive** /əˈluːsɪv/ *adj*: *an allusive style of poetry whose meaning is hard to understand because it is not directly expressed* —**-sively** *adv*

al·lu·vi·al /əˈluːvɪəl/ *adj* being, concerning, or made of soil put down by rivers, lakes, floods, etc.

al·lu·vi·um /əˈluːvɪəm/ *n* **-viums** *or* **-via** /vɪə/ [U;C] soil put down by rivers, lakes, floods, etc.

al·ly[1] /əˈlaɪ‖əˈlaɪ, ˈælaɪ/ *v* [Wv5;T1;IØ: (*with, to*)] to join or unite, as by political agreement or marriage: *The small country allied itself with/to the stronger power.*|*Will the workers of the factories ally against the big employers?*|*The allied countries fought together*

al·ly[2] /ˈælaɪ‖ˈælaɪ, əˈlaɪ/ *n* **1** a country that is joined to one's own by political agreement, esp. one that will provide support in war **2** a person who helps or supports one

al·ma ma·ter /ˌælmə ˈmeɪtəʳ, -ˈmɑː-‖-ˈmɑ-/ *n* [*usu. sing.*] *Lat fml & humor* **1** the school or university where a person was taught **2** *AmE* (*usu. caps*) the song of a school or university

al·ma·nac, (*old use*) **-nack** /ˈɔːlmənæk‖ˈɔl-, ˈæl-/ *n* a book giving a list of the days of a year, together with the times of various events such as sunrise and sunset, changes in the moon, and the rise and fall of the sea. Sometimes other information of general interest is given as well

al·might·y /ɔːlˈmaɪti/ *adj* **1** (*often cap.*) having the power to do anything; OMNIPOTENT: *God Almighty*|(*God,*) *the Almighty* **2** *infml* very big, strong, great, etc.: *an almighty crash*

al·mond /ˈɑːmənd‖ˈɑ-, ˈæ-, ˈæl-/ *n* **1** a fruit tree whose seeds are eaten as nuts **2** the nut of this tree —see picture at NUT[1]

almond-eyed /ˌ·· ˈ·ˈ/ *adj infml* having long narrow eyes, like those of people from the East

al·mo·ner /ˈɑːmənəʳ, ˈæl-‖ˈæl-, ˈɑ-/ *n BrE* an official in a hospital who looks after the material and social needs of the sick; a hospital SOCIAL WORKER (now officially called a **medical social worker**)

al·most /ˈɔːlməʊst‖ˈɔlməʊst, ɔlˈməʊst/ *adv* very nearly: *I almost dropped the cake.*|*She said almost nothing.*|*almost the longest piece*|*almost everybody*

USAGE Compare **almost, nearly**, and **practically**: 1 One can use any of them before **all, every, always**, or a neg. verb: **almost/nearly/practically** *all the boys*|**almost/nearly/practically** *every time*|**almost/nearly/practically** *always*|*I* **almost/nearly/practically** *didn't go.* 2 One can say *very/pretty/not* **nearly**: *I'm not* **nearly** *ready.*|*"Pretty* **nearly** *all the secrets of her married life."* (SEU S.), but one cannot use **almost** or **practically** after these words. 3 One can say **almost** *any/no/none/never*: **Almost** *any bus will do.*|*I* **almost** *never see her*; one can also use **practically** before these words, but not **nearly**.

alms /ɑːmz‖ɑmz, ɑlmz/ *n* [P;(U)] money, food, clothes, etc., given to poor people

alms-house /ˈ· ·/ *n* (in Britain) a house, usu. one of a group, provided in former times by a rich person, in which old or poor people could live without paying rent

al·oe /ˈæləʊ/ *n* **1** [C] a plant with thick pointed leaves **2** [U] also **bitter aloes**— a bitter medicine obtained from this plant

a·loft /əˈlɒft‖əˈlɔft/ *adv* [F] **1** at or to a great height: *The smoke rose aloft* **2** high up, as in the air or among the sails of a ship: *The flag was flying aloft*

a·lone /əˈləʊn/ *adv, adj* [F] **1** without others: *He lives/works alone.*|*The house stands alone on the hill.*|*I was alone in the house* **2** only: *You can't live on bread alone.*|*Time alone will show who was right* **3 leave/let alone a** to allow to be by oneself **b** to allow to remain as is; not INTERFERE (1) with: *Leave that alone: it's mine* —see also LET ALONE

USAGE **Alone** is neither good nor bad: *She lives on tea and cake when she's* **alone**. **Solitary** and **lone**, when used of things, mean that there is only one: *a* **solitary/lone** *tree in the garden*, but used of people they may show sadness, like **lonely** or (*esp. AmE*) **lonesome**: *Come over and see me; I'm feeling a bit* **solitary/lonely/lonesome. Forlorn** means great sadness because of being alone, and **desolate** is even stronger: *The death of his wife left him completely* **forlorn/desolate**.

a·long[1] /əˈlɒŋ‖əˈlɔŋ/ *prep* **1** in the direction of the length of; towards the end of: *We walked along the road* **2** in a line next to the length of: *Trees grew along the road* **3 along here/there** in this/that direction

along[2] *adv* **1** (used to strengthen the effect of using a verb of movement) forward; on: *She bicycled along, singing loudly* **2** with others or oneself: *When we went to Paris I took my sister along* (*with me*) **3** [F] here or there; over; across: *I'll be along soon.*|*Come along and visit us next week* **4 all along** all the time: *I knew the truth all along* **5 along with** together with: *There was a bill along with the parcel* **6 Get along (with you)!** *sl* —see GET ALONG **7 go along with** *infml* —see GO

a·long·side[1] /əˌlɒŋˈsaɪd‖əˌlɔŋ-/ *adv* close to and in line with the edge (of something); along the side: *We brought our boat alongside*

a·long·side[2] /əˌlɒŋˈsaɪd, əˈlɒŋsaɪd‖-lɔŋ-/ *prep* side by side with

a·loof /əˈluːf/ *adj, adv* [(*from*)] **1** [F] at a distance; not joining in (with); apart: *He held/kept himself aloof from the others* **2** [B] distant in feeling or interest; not very friendly; RESERVED (1) —**~ly** *adv* —**~ness** *n* [U (*from*)]

al·o·pe·cia /ˌæləˈpiːʃə/ *n* [U] *tech* the loss of hair from the head; BALDness (1)

a·loud /əˈlaʊd/ *adv* **1** in a voice that may be heard: *The teacher asked him to read the poem aloud* **2** in a loud voice; so as to be heard at a distance: *The pain caused him to cry aloud*

al·pac·a /ælˈpækə/ *n* **1** [C] a sheeplike animal of Peru, related to the LLAMA **2** [U] cloth made from the wool of this animal

al·pen·horn /ˈælpənhɔːn‖-ɔrn/ *n* a very long wooden horn formerly used in Switzerland, esp. to call sheep and cows

al·pen·stock /ˈælpənstɒk‖-stɑk/ *n* a long stick with a metal point used in climbing mountains

al·pha /ˈælfə/ *n* the first letter (A, α) in the Greek alphabet

alpha and o·me·ga /ˌ·· · ˈ···‖ˌ·· · ·ˈ··/ *n* [*the*+R] *lit* **1** the beginning and the end **2** the main or most necessary part

al·pha·bet /ˈælfəbet/ *n* the set of letters used in writing any language, esp. when arranged in order

al·pha·bet·i·cal /ˌælfəˈbetɪkəl/ also (*rare*) **al·pha·bet·ic** /ˌælfəˈbetɪk/— *adj* [Wa5] of, belonging to, or in the order of the alphabet: *In a dictionary the words are arranged in alphabetical order* —**~ly** *adv* [Wa4]

alpha par·ti·cle /ˈ·· ˌ···/ *n* a very small piece of matter (that is RADIOACTIVE and has a POSITIVE[1] (12) electric charge) that is thrown out when an atom breaks up

al·pine /ˈælpaɪn/ *adj* **1** of or concerning any high mountain **2** very high **3** (of plants) growing on parts of mountains that are too high for trees to grow on

al·read·y /ɔːlˈredi/ *adv* [Wa5] **1** by or before a stated or suggested time: *He had already gone*

(*when I arrived*) **2** sooner than expected: *Have you eaten your dinner already? What a good boy you are!* **3** before: *I've been there already and don't want to go again*
USAGE Note the difference between **already** and **all ready**: *We're* **all ready** means either that all of us are ready or that we are completely ready; **already** could not be used here. —see STILL, JUST (USAGE)

al·right /ˌɔːlˈraɪt/ *adv* all right
USAGE **Alright** is very common now, but some people think **all right** is better English.

Al·sa·tian /ælˈseɪʃən/ (*AmE* **German Shepherd**)— *n* *BrE* a large WOLFlike[1] (1) dog often used by police or to guard property —see picture at DOG[1]

al·so /ˈɔːlsəʊ/ *adv* [Wa5] **1** as well; besides; too: *Were you at the film? I was also there* (= I as well as you) **2 not only ... but (also) ...** both ... and ... : *The ceremony was not only colourful but (also) noisy*

also-ran /ˈ·· ·/ *n* **1** a horse that ran in a race but was not one of the first 3 at the end **2** a person who has failed to win, as at a particular sport or in an election

al·tar /ˈɔːltəʳ/ *n* **1** a table or raised level surface on which things are offered to a god **2** (in the Christian service of COMMUNION) the table on which the bread and wine are blessed —see picture at CHURCH[1] **3 lead (a woman) to the altar** *pomp* to marry (a woman) esp. in a church

altar boy /ˈ·· ·/ *n* a boy who helps the priest during ROMAN CATHOLIC religious services —compare ACOLYTE, SERVER (3)

al·tar·piece /ˈɔːltəpiːs‖-ər-/ *n* a painting or other work of art placed above and behind an ALTAR

al·ter /ˈɔːltəʳ/ *v* **1** [T1;I0] to (cause to) become different: *This shirt must be altered; it's too large.*| *You have altered since I last saw you* **2** [T1] *euph* CASTRATE —**~able** *adj*

al·ter·a·tion /ˌɔːltəˈreɪʃən/ *n* **1** [U] the act of making or becoming different: *My coat needs alteration* **2** [C] a change; something changed: *The alterations to your coat will take a long time*

al·ter·ca·tion /ˌɔːltəˈkeɪʃən‖-tər-/ *n fml* **1** [U] noisy disagreement; quarrelling **2** [C] a noisy disagreement; quarrel

al·ter e·go /ˌæltər ˈiːgəʊ, ˌɔːl-/ *n* **alter egos** *Lat lit* a very close and trusted friend

al·ter·nate[1] /ɔːlˈtɜːnɪ̵t‖ˈɔltər-, ˈæl-/ *adj* [Wa5] **1** (of 2 things) happening by turns; first one and then the other: *A week of alternate rain and sunshine* **2** one of every 2; every second: *He works on alternate days* **3** (esp. of leaves on a stem) growing first on one side of the stem and then on the other: *alternate leaves* —compare ALTERNATIVE —**~ly** *adv*

al·ter·nate[2] /ˈɔːltəneɪt‖-ər-/ *v* [I0 (*with, between*); T1] to (cause to) follow by turns: *We alternated periods of work and rest.*|*Farmers usually alternate their crops.*|*Work and sleep alternated without any changes.*|*Work alternated with sleep.*|*My life alternated between work and sleep* —**-nation** /ˌɔːltəˈneɪʃən‖-ər-/ *n* [U;C]

al·ter·nat·ing cur·rent /ˌ···· ˈ··/ *n* [U] flow or supply of electricity that changes direction with regularity and at a very rapid rate —compare DIRECT CURRENT

al·ter·na·tive[1] /ɔːlˈtɜːnətɪv‖ɔlˈtɜr-, æl-/ *adj* [Wa5] (of 2 things) that may be used, had, done, etc., instead of another; other: *We returned by the alternative road* —compare ALTERNATE —**~ly** *adv*

alternative[2] *n* **1** [(*the*) S;(C): (*to*)] something, esp. a course of action, that may be taken or had instead of one other: *The alternative to being taken prisoner was to die fighting.*|*We had to fight: there was no (other) alternative* **2** [(*the*) S;C] a choice between 2 or more courses or things: *You have the alternative of fighting or being taken prisoner* **3** [C (*to*)] one of 2 or more courses, ideas, things, etc.: *There are several alternatives to your plan*
USAGE Some writers do not like such sentences as *We have several* **alternatives** *to choose from* because they think there should be only 2 **alternatives**; but the word is quite often used like this.

al·ter·na·tor /ˈɔːltəneɪtəʳ‖ˈɔltər- ˈæl-/ *n* a machine (DYNAMO) for producing ALTERNATING CURRENT

al·though /ɔːlˈðəʊ/ *conj* in spite of the fact that; though: *They are generous although they are poor*

al·ti·me·ter /ˈæltɪˌmiːtəʳ‖ælˈtɪmɪ̵tər/ *n* an instrument (ANEROID BAROMETER) used, esp. in an aircraft, for recording height

al·ti·tude /ˈæltɪ̵tjuːd‖-tuːd/ *n* **1** [S;(C)] height, as of a mountain above sea level **2** [C *often pl.*] a high place or area: *At high altitudes it is difficult to breathe* **3** [S] the distance of the sun, the moon, a star, etc., above the horizon, measured as an angle

al·to[1] /ˈæltəʊ/ *n* **-tos 1** also **countertenor**— (a man with or a musical part for a man with) a high singing voice, between SOPRANO and TENOR **2** also **contralto**— (a woman with or a musical part for a woman with) a low singing voice, between SOPRANO and TENOR **3** (of a family of instruments) the instrument which plays notes in the area between SOPRANO and TENOR

alto[2] *adj* [Wa5] of, for, concerning, or having the range or part of an ALTO —see picture at NOTATION

al·to·geth·er[1] /ˌɔːltəˈgeðəʳ◂/ *adv* **1** completely; thoroughly: *It is not altogether bad* **2** considering all things; on the whole: *It was raining, but altogether it was a good trip* —see ABSOLUTELY (USAGE)

altogether[2] /ˌɔːltəˈgeðəʳ/ *n* **in the altogether** *humor* without clothes; NUDE[1] (1)

al·tru·is·m /ˈæltrʊ-ɪzəm/ *n* [U] consideration of the happiness and good of others before one's own; unselfishness —compare EGOISM

al·tru·ist /ˈæltrʊ-ɪ̵st/ *n* a person who is habitually good to others —compare EGOIST —**~ic** /ˌæltrʊˈɪstɪk/ *adj* —**~ically** *adv* [Wa4]

al·um /ˈæləm/ *n* [U] a chemical substance used in medicine and preparing leather

al·u·min·i·um /ˌæljʊˈmɪnɪəm, ˌælə-/ (*AmE* **a·lu·mi·num** /əˈluːmɪ̵nəm/)— *n* [U] *BrE* a silver-white metal that is a simple substance (ELEMENT (6)) light in weight, and easily shaped

a·lum·na /əˈlʌmnə/ *n* **-nae** /niː/ *AmE* a female ALUMNUS

a·lum·nus /əˈlʌmnəs/ *n* **-ni** /naɪ/ *AmE* a male former student of a school, college, or university

al·ve·o·lar /ˈælvɪələʳ, ˌælvɪˈəʊləʳ‖ælˈvɪələr/ *adj, n* (a consonant such as /t/ and /d/) made by putting the tongue on the hard bony areas at the top of the mouth just behind the front teeth

al·ways /ˈɔːlwɪ̵z, -weɪz/ *adv* [Wa5] **1** at all times; at each time: *The sun always rises in the east.*|*Do you sing in the bath? Always!* **2** for ever: *I will love you always*
USAGE When it is used with the *-ing* form of the verb, **always** often has a bad meaning: *He's* **always** *asking silly questions.*

al·ys·sum /ˈælɪsəm‖əˈlɪsəm/ *n* [C;U] a type of low-growing plant with yellow or white flowers

am /m, əm; *strong* æm/ [Wv1] *1st person sing. pres. t. of* BE: *I am (living) here now* —see AREN'T (USAGE)

AM /ˌeɪ ˈem/ amplitude modulation; a system of broadcasting in which the strength of the sound waves varies, so that the words and music provided for the listener are not always very clear: *an AM radio* —compare FM

a.m. /ˌeɪ ˈem/ *adv* (*often caps.*) (*used after numbers* *expressing time*) ante meridiem; before midday: *caught the 8 a.m.* (*train*) *from London* —opposite P.M.

a·mal·gam /ə'mælgəm/ *n* **1** [C] *fml* a mixture or combination **2** [U;(C)] *tech* a mixture of metals, one of which is MERCURY: *Fill the tooth with amalgam, not gold*

a·mal·gam·ate /ə'mælgəmeɪt/ *v* [T1;IØ: (*with*)] **1 a** (of businesses, societies, groups, etc.) to join; unite **b** to cause (businesses, societies, groups, etc.) to join or unite **2** to (cause to) mix; combine —**-ation** /əˌmælgə'meɪʃən/ *n* [U;C]: *The amalgamation of the 5 businesses into one company was a good idea*

a·man·u·en·sis /əˌmænjʊ'ensɪ̇s/ *n* **-ses** /siːz/ a person employed to write down what another is saying or to copy what another has written, esp. during the preparation of a book

a·mass /ə'mæs/ *v* **1** [T1] to gather or collect (money, goods, power, etc.) in great amounts **2** [IØ] *poet* to come together into a mass: *The clouds amassed above the hills*

am·a·teur[1] /'æmətəʳ, -tʃʊəʳ, -tʃəʳ, ˌæmə'tɜːʳ/ *n* **1** a person who paints pictures, performs plays, takes part in sports, etc., for enjoyment and without being paid for it —compare PROFESSIONAL[2] **2** a person without experience or skill in a particular art, sport, etc.

amateur[2] *adj* **1** of, by, or with AMATEURS: *amateur football|performances of plays* **2** being an AMATEUR or AMATEURS; not paid: *an amateur actor* **3** lacking skill; poor: *His piano performance was very amateur*

am·a·teur·ish /'æmətərɪʃ, ˌæmə'tjʊərɪʃ, -'tɜːrɪʃ‖ˌæmə'tʊʳ-, -'tɜr-/ *adj derog* lacking skill; not good; poor —**~ly** *adv* —**~ness** *n* [U]

am·a·to·ry /'æmətəri‖-tori/ *adj lit & poet* concerning or expressing love, esp. sexual love: *an amatory look*

a·maze /ə'meɪz/ *v* [T1] to fill with great surprise; cause wonder in: *Your knowledge amazes me.|It amazed me to hear that you were leaving* —**~ment** *n* [U]: *To my amazement I came first*

a·maz·ing /ə'meɪzɪŋ/ *adj usu. apprec* causing great surprise or wonder because of quantity or quality: *The new car goes at an amazing speed.|He has amazing skills.|Your wife is an amazing woman, George!* —**~ly** *adv*

am·a·zon /'æməzən‖-zɑn, -zən/ *n* a strong powerful woman, esp. one who is tall and likes sports —**~ian** /ˌæmə'zəʊnɪən/ *adj*

am·bas·sa·dor /æm'bæsədəʳ/ *fem.* **am·bas·sa·dress** /-drɪ̇s/— *n* a minister of high rank representing his country in another country either for a special occasion or for a longer period —**~ship** *n* [U;C]

am·bas·sa·do·ri·al /æmˌbæsə'dɔːrɪəl‖-'do-/ *adj* [Wa5] of an AMBASSADOR

am·ber /'æmbəʳ/ *n* [U] **1** a yellowish brown hard clear substance used for jewels, ornaments, etc. **2** its colour

am·ber·gris /'æmbəgriːs, -ɪs/ *n* [U] a waxy substance produced in part of the body (INTESTINES) of a large sea animal (WHALE), used in the production of pleasant-smelling liquids (PERFUMES)

am·bi- /'æmbɪ, æm'bɪ/ *prefix* [*adj→adj*] that has or is both, 2, or double: AMBIDEXTROUS|AMBIGUOUS|AMBIVALENT

am·bi·dex·trous /ˌæmbɪ'dekstrəs/ *adj* able to use either hand with equal skill —**~ly** *adv*

am·bi·ence /'æmbɪəns/ *n lit* the character, quality, feeling, etc., of a place: *The little restaurant has a pleasant ambience*

am·bi·ent /'æmbɪənt/ *adj* [Wa5] *lit* on all sides; completely surrounding: *ambient air*

am·bi·gu·i·ty /ˌæmbɪ̇'gjuːɪ̇ti/ *n* **1** [U] the condition of being AMBIGUOUS **2** [C] something that is AMBIGUOUS: *His reply was full of ambiguities*

am·big·u·ous /æm'bɪgjʊəs/ *adj* **1** able to be understood in more than one way; of unclear meaning: *an ambiguous reply* **2** uncertain; unclear —compare AMBIVALENT —**~ly** *adv* —**~ness** *n* [U]

am·bit /'æmbɪ̇t/ *n lit* range or limit of power or control

am·bi·tion /æm'bɪʃən/ *n* **1** [U;C] strong desire for success, power, riches, etc.: *That politician is full of ambition.|One of his ambitions is to become a minister* **2** [C] that which is desired in this way: *The big house on the hill is my ambition*

am·bi·tious /æm'bɪʃəs/ *adj* **1** [B;F (*to*)] having a strong desire for success, power, riches, etc.: *He is an ambitious man.|He is ambitious to succeed in politics* **2** [B] showing or demanding a strong desire for success, great effort, great skill, etc.: *an ambitious attempt to climb the dangerous mountain* —**~ly** *adv* —**~ness** *n* [U]

am·biv·a·lent /æm'bɪvələnt/ *adj* [(*towards, about*)] having opposing feelings towards, or opinions about, one person or thing —compare AMBIGUOUS —**-lence** *n* [U] —**~ly** *adv*

am·ble[1] /'æmbəl/ *v* [IØ (ABOUT, AROUND)] **1** to walk at an easy gentle rate **2** (of a horse) to move at an easy unhurried rate by lifting the 2 legs on one side and then the 2 on the other

amble[2] *n* [S] **1** *infml* a walk at an easy gentle rate **2** an easy gentle rate: *They came along at an amble*

am·bro·si·a /æm'brəʊzɪə‖-ʒə/ *n* [U] **1** (in ancient stories) the food of gods **2** *lit* something with a delightful taste or smell

am·bu·lance /'æmbjʊləns‖-bjə-/ *n* [C; *by*+U] a motor vehicle for carrying sick or wounded people, esp. to hospital —see picture at INTERCHANGE

am·bush[1] /'æmbʊʃ/ *v* [T1] to attack from a place where one has hidden and waited

ambush[2] *n* **1** [C; *by, from*+U] a surprise attack from a place of hiding **2** [C; *from, in*+U] the place where the attackers hide **3** [C; *in, into*+U] the act of hiding soldiers, police, etc., in order to make a surprise attack on passing enemies

AmE (*of a word or phrase in this dictionary*) American English

USAGE Do not confuse *AmE* and *BrE* with "(in Britain)" and "(in the US)". The first are words used, by speakers of these varieties of English, for things that exist all over the world: **cot** *AmE* CAMP BED|**knock up** *BrE infml* "to awaken by knocking". The second are for words used, by speakers of English all over the world, for things that exist in one country: **Inc** *abbrev. for:* (in the US) INCORPORATED|**employment exchange** (in Britain) a Government office. . . ."

a·me·ba /ə'miːbə/ *n AmE* AMOEBA —**-bic** *adj* [Wa5]

a·me·li·o·rate /ə'miːlɪəreɪt/ *v* [T1;IØ] *fml* to cause to become better or less bad; improve —compare ALLEVIATE —**-ration** /əˌmiːlɪə'reɪʃən/ *n* [U]

a·men /ɑː'men, eɪ-/ *interj* **1** (used at the end of a prayer or HYMN) may this be true; so be it **2 say amen to something** *infml* to agree very strongly with something

USAGE The pronunciation /eɪ'men/ is commonly used in speech outside church. In PROTESTANT churches in Britain, /ɑː'men/ is the usual form. In America, /eɪ'men/ is used at the end of a spoken prayer but /ɑː'men/ is common in singing.

a·me·na·ble /ə'miːnəbəl/ *adj* **1** [B;F (*to*)] able to be guided or influenced (by): *She is amenable to reason* **2** [F+*to*] *tech* in a position of having to obey a power or be punished by that power; responsible **3** [F+*to*] able to be tested by: *My scientific discoveries are amenable to the usual tests*

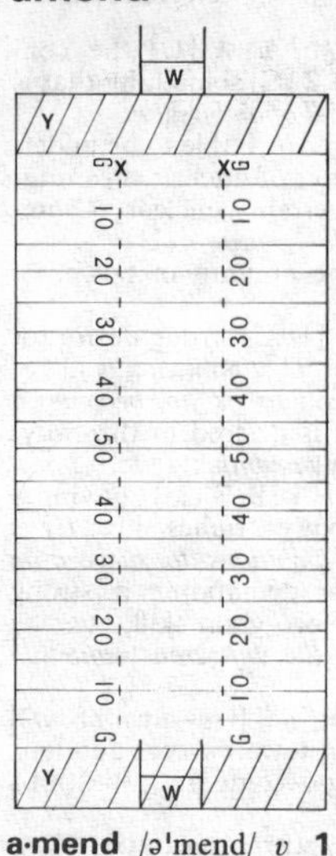

A halfback
B fullback
C quarterback
D wide receiver
E split end
F tackle
G guard
H centre
I tight end
J defensive end
K defensive tackle
L linebacker
M cornerback
N safety
O referee
P umpire
Q head linesman
R line judge
S field judge
T back judge
U down box
V yardage chain
W goal
X inbounds lines
Y end zone

American football

a·mend /ə'mend/ *v* **1** [T1;IØ] *lit* to (cause to) become better by getting rid of faults; (cause to) improve **2** [T1] to make changes in the words of (a rule or law) —compare EMEND

a·mend·ment /ə'mendmənt/ *n* **1** [U] the act of improving or changing: *Your plan needs some amendment before it can be made public* **2** [C] a change, made in or suggested for a rule, law, statement, etc.: *So many amendments were made to the rule that its original meaning was completely changed*

a·mends /ə'mendz/ *n* [P] something done to repair or pay for some harm, unkindness, damage, etc. (esp. in the phr. **make amends (to someone) (for something)**): *He made amends for his rudeness by giving her some flowers*

a·me·ni·ty /ə'miːnɪ̠ti‖ə'me-/ *n* **1** [C *often pl.*] a thing or condition in a town, hotel, place, etc., that one can enjoy and which makes life pleasant **2** [U9] pleasantness

A·mer·i·can /ə'merɪ̠kən/ *adj, n* (a person) belonging to North, Central, or South America, esp. the United States of America

American foot·ball /·,··· '··/ (*AmE* **football**)— *n* [U;R] *BrE* an American game (related to RUGBY) played by 2 teams of 11 players each, in which an ELLIPTIC ball is passed from one player to another in an attempt to get GOALs (3)

American In·di·an /·,··· '···/ also **A·mer·in·di·an** /,æmə'rɪndiən/— *n* INDIAN (2)

A·mer·i·can·is·m /ə'merɪ̠kənɪzəm/ *n* **1** [C] a word, phrase, speech sound, etc., of English as spoken in America **2** [U] *AmE* (loyalty to) the beliefs and aims of the United States of America

a·mer·i·can·ize, -ise /ə'merɪ̠kənaɪz/ *v* [T1;IØ] to (cause to) become American in character

am·e·thyst /'æmɪ̠θɪ̠st/ *n* **1** [C] a reddish-blue stone, used in jewellery **2** [U] reddish-blue; purple

a·mi·a·ble /'eɪmɪəbəl/ *adj* of a pleasant nature; good-tempered; friendly —**-bility** /,eɪmɪə'bɪlɪ̠ti/ *n* [U] —**-bly** /'eɪmɪəbli/ *adv*

am·i·ca·ble /'æmɪ̠kəbəl/ *adj* as suitable between friends; friendly; peaceful: *We reached an amicable agreement* —**-bility** /,æmɪ̠kə'bɪlɪ̠ti/ *n* [U] —**-bly** /'æmɪ̠kəbli/ *adv*

a·mid /ə'mɪd/ also **a·midst** /ə'mɪdst/— *prep fml & lit* in the middle of; among

a·mid·ships /ə'mɪd,ʃɪps/ *adv* [F] *tech* in the middle of the ship

a·mi·no ac·id /ə,miːnəʊ 'æsɪ̠d, ə,maɪ-/ *n* [C;(U)] a substance coming from, found in, and necessary to living matter

a·mir /ə'mɪəʳ/ *n* EMIR

a·miss[1] /ə'mɪs/ *adv* [Wa5;F] **1** in a bad way; wrongly or imperfectly: *You judge his character amiss* **2** *rare* out of the way; lost: *My watch has gone amiss* **3 take something amiss** to be angry at something, esp. because of a misunderstanding

amiss[2] *adj* [F] **1** wrong; imperfect: *The doctor said there was nothing amiss with her.|Is something amiss?* **2** (usu. with *no, not,* etc.) out of place; (a) bad (idea): *A few pleasant remarks may not be amiss*

am·i·ty /'æmɪ̠ti/ *n* [U] *fml* friendly relationship; friendship (often in the phr. **in amity (with)**)

am·me·ter /'æmɪtəʳ, 'æm,miːtəʳ/ *n* an instrument for measuring, in AMPEREs, the strength of an electric current —see picture at SCIENTIFIC

am·mo /'æməʊ/ *n* [U] *sl* AMMUNITION

am·mo·ni·a /ə'məʊnɪə/ *n* [U] a strong gas with a sharp smell, used in explosives, in machines (REFRIGERATORs) to keep things cold, in chemicals (FERTILIZERs) to help plants grow, etc.

am·mo·nite /'æmənaɪt/ *n* the rock-like shell (FOSSIL) of a type of sea animal that no longer exists but which has been preserved in various rocks —see picture at PREHISTORIC

am·mu·ni·tion /,æmjʊ'nɪʃən‖,æmjə-/ *n* [U] bullets, bombs, explosives, etc., esp. things fired from a weapon: (fig.) *The mistakes of the ministers provided perfect ammunition for their political enemies*

am·ne·si·a /æm'niːzɪə‖-ʒə/ *n* [U] loss of memory, either in part or completely

am·nes·ty /'æmnəsti/ *n* [U;C *usu. sing.*] (a) general act of forgiveness, esp. as allowed by a state to people who are guilty of political crimes against it

a·moe·ba /ə'miːbə/ also *AmE* **ameba**— *n* **-bas** *or* **-bae** /biː/ a very small form of living creature consisting of only one cell, found esp. in water and soil

a·moe·bic /ə'miːbɪk/ also *AmE* **amebic**— *adj* [Wa5] of or caused by AMOEBAs: *amoebic* DYSENTERY

a·mok /ə'mɒk‖ə'mak/ also **amuck**— *adv* **run amok** to go or run wild and out of control, esp. with a desire to kill people: (fig.) *If public spending runs amok our money will lose its value* —compare **run** RIOT

a·mong /ə'mʌŋ/ also **a·mongst** /ə'mʌŋst/— *prep* **1** in the middle of; surrounded by: *I live among the*

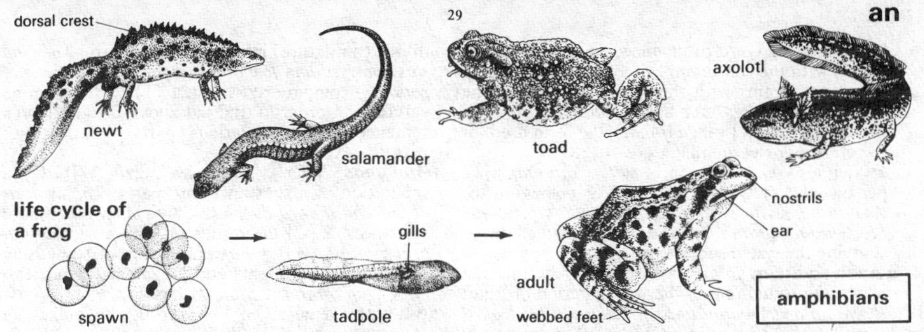

mountains.|I was among the crowd —see BETWEEN (USAGE) **2** in association with: *The minister was among those who attacked me* **3** in the class of; one of: *This mountain is among the highest in the world* **4** in shares to each of: *Divide this cake among them* **5** through the common action of: *They talked about the matter among themselves* (=together) —see BETWEEN (USAGE)

a·mor·al /eɪˈmɒrəl, æ-‖eɪˈmɔ-, -ˈmɑ-/ *adj* having no understanding of right and wrong: *Young children are amoral* —compare IMMORAL —**~ity** /ˌeɪmɒˈrælɨti, ˌæ-‖ˌeɪmə-/ *n* [U]

am·o·rous /ˈæmərəs/ *adj* of, concerning, expressing, or easily moved to love, esp. sexual love: *amorous looks|an amorous girl* —see EROTIC (USAGE) —**~ly** *adv* —**~ness** *n* [U]

a·mor·phous /əˈmɔːfəs‖-ɔr-/ *adj* having no fixed form or shape: *I can't understand his amorphous plans* —**~ly** *adv* —**~ness** *n* [U]

a·mor·tize, -ise /əˈmɔːtaɪz‖ˈæmər-/ *v* [T1] *tech* to pay off (a debt), esp. by regular small amounts

a·mount /əˈmaʊnt/ *n* **1** quantity or sum: *Large amounts of money were spent on the bridge* **2** total quantity or sum: *He could only pay half the amount he owed*
USAGE **Amount** is used with [U] nouns: *the* **amount** *of money*. With plurals it is better to use **number**: *the* **number** *of mistakes.*

amount to *v prep* [Wv6;L1] to be equal to: *Your words amount to a refusal.|His debts amount to over £1,000*

a·mour /əˈmʊəʳ/ *n becoming rare* **1** a sexual relationship, esp. one that is secret **2** a person, esp. a woman, with whom one has such a relationship

amp /æmp/ *n tech or infml* **1** AMPERE **2** AMPLIFIER

am·per·age /ˈæmpərɪdʒ/ *n* [S;U] the strength of an electric current measured in AMPs, as in an electricity system or as used by an electric instrument

am·pere, ampère /ˈæmpeəʳ‖ˈæmpɪər/ *n* the standard measure of the quantity of electricity that is flowing past a point —compare VOLT

am·per·sand /ˈæmpəsænd‖-ər-/ *n* the sign & for the word "and"

am·phet·a·mine /æmˈfetəmiːn, -mɨn/ *n* [C;(U)] a drug used in medicine and by people wanting a sense of speedy ability and excitement

am·phib·i·an /æmˈfɪbɪən/ *n* **1** an animal (such as a FROG) that is able to live both on land and in water **2** an aircraft that can land or take off on water **3** a motor vehicle that can travel both on land and in water

am·phib·i·ous /æmˈfɪbɪəs/ *adj* able to live or move both on land and in water

am·phi·the·at·re, *AmE* **-ter** /ˈæmfɨθɪətəʳ/ *n* a usu. roofless building with rows of seats on a slope that completely surrounds and rises above a central usu. circular area, esp. one built in ancient Rome used for competitions and theatre performances

am·pho·ra /ˈæmfərə/ *n* **-ras** *or* **-rae** /riː/ a narrow clay pot with 2 handles used, esp. in ancient Rome and Greece, for storing wine, oil, etc.

am·ple /ˈæmpəl/ *adj* [Wa2] **1** (*usu. before nouns of types* [U] *or* [P]) enough or more than is necessary: *We have ample money for the journey* **2** with plenty of space; large: *There is room for an ample garden* —**-ply** *adv*

am·pli·fi·er /ˈæmplɨfaɪəʳ/ *n* an instrument, as used in radios and RECORD PLAYERs, that makes electrical current or power stronger —see picture at SOUND[3]

am·pli·fy /ˈæmplɨfaɪ/ *v* **1** [T1;I∅ (*on, upon*)] to explain in greater detail: *He amplified (on) his remarks with drawings and figures* **2** [T1] to increase the strength of (something, esp. sound coming through electrical instruments) **3** [T1] to make larger or greater —**-fication** /ˌæmplɨfɨˈkeɪʃən/ *n* [S;U]

am·pli·tude /ˈæmplɨtjuːd‖-tuːd/ *n* **1** [U] largeness of space **2** [U] large amount; fullness **3** [S;U] *tech* the distance between the middle and the top (or bottom) of a wave (such as a sound wave)

am·poule /ˈæmpuːl/ also **am·pule** /ˈæmpjuːl/— *n* a small usu. glass container for medicine that is to be put (INJECTed) under a person's skin through a needle

am·pu·tate /ˈæmpjʊteɪt‖-pjə-/ *v* [T1;I∅] to remove (part of the body) by cutting off, esp. for medical reasons: *to amputate a leg|a finger|This is serious: I'm afraid we'll have to amputate* —compare EXCISE[2] —**-tation** /ˌæmpjʊˈteɪʃən‖-pjə-/ *n* [U;C]

am·pu·tee /ˌæmpjʊˈtiː‖-pjə-/ *n* a person who has had an arm or leg AMPUTATED

a·muck /əˈmʌk/ *adv* AMOK

am·u·let /ˈæmjʊlɨt, -let‖ˈæmjə-/ *n* an object worn in the belief that it will protect one against evil, disease, bad luck, etc.

a·muse /əˈmjuːz/ *v* [Wv4;T1] **1** to satisfy or excite the sense of humour of; cause laughter in: *Your story|behaviour amuses me.|I am amused to find you here.|an amused expression on one's face|an amusing story* **2** to cause to spend time in a pleasant or gay manner: *The new toys amused the child for hours.|The children amused themselves by playing games while their parents talked*

a·muse·ment /əˈmjuːzmənt/ *n* **1** [U] the state of being amused; enjoyment: *To everybody's amusement the actor fell off the stage.|I listened in amusement* **2** [U] the act of amusing **3** [C] something that causes one's time to pass in an enjoyable way: *Big cities have theatres, films, football matches, and many other amusements*

amusement ar·cade /·ˈ·· ·ˌ·/ *n* a room full of machines which spin numbers or with which one can play games after putting coins into them

amusement park /·ˈ·· ·/ *n AmE* FUNFAIR (2)

an /ən; *strong* æn/ *indef article, determiner* (used when the following word begins with a vowel sound) a: *an elephant, not a dog|an* R.A.F. *aircraft*
USAGE When putting **a** or **an** before a set of letters (an ABBREVIATION or ACRONYM) one must

know how they are pronounced in speech. R.A.F. begins with the consonant "r", but the name of the consonant begins with the vowel sound /ɑː/; one says *an R.A.F officer* but *a BBC broadcaster*.

an- /ən, æn/ *prefix* [*n→n, adj→adj*] (the form used for A- before a vowel sound): ANAESTHETIC

-an /ən/ also **-ean, -ian** /ɪən/— *suffix* **1** [*n→adj, n*] (a person who or thing that is) of or belonging to: *American|Christian* **2** [*n→adj*] like or typical of: *Mozartean music* **3** [*n→n*] a person skilled in or studying the stated subject: HISTORIAN —see also -A

a·nach·ro·nis·m /əˈnækrənɪzəm/ *n* **1** the mistake of placing something in the wrong period of time: *It was an anachronism to say "Julius Caesar looked at his watch"* **2** a person or thing that is or appears to be in the wrong period of time: *Sailing boats are an anachronism in this age of fast travel* —**-tic** /əˌnækrəˈnɪstɪk/ *adj* —**-tically** *adv* [Wa4]

an·a·con·da /ˌænəˈkɒndə‖-ˈkɑn-/ *n* a large South American snake that crushes its food to death

a·nae·mi·a /əˈniːmɪə/ also *AmE* **anemia**— *n* [U] the unhealthy condition of not having the proper number of red cells in the blood

a·nae·mic /əˈniːmɪk/ also *AmE* **anemic**— *adj* **1** suffering from ANAEMIA **2** lacking interest or excitement: *an anaemic meal/book*

an·aes·the·si·a /ˌænɪ̈sˈθiːzɪə‖-ʒə/ also *AmE* **anes-**— *n* [U] **1** the state of being unable to feel pain, heat, etc., esp. as produced by doctors, so that painful treatment can be given painlessly **2** the act or action of producing this state

an·aes·thet·ic¹ /ˌænɪ̈sˈθetɪk/ also *AmE* **anes-**— *adj* of, concerning, or causing ANAESTHESIA

anaesthetic² also *AmE* **anes-**— *n* [C;U] a substance that produces an inability to feel pain, heat, etc., either in a limited area (**local anaesthetic**) or in the whole body, together with unconsciousness (**general anaesthetic**)

a·naes·the·tist /əˈniːsθɪ̈tɪ̈st‖əˈnes-/ also *AmE* **anes-**— *n* a doctor who gives an ANAESTHETIC to a patient before he is treated by another doctor

a·naes·the·tize, -ise /əˈniːsθɪ̈taɪz‖əˈnes-/ also *AmE* **anes-**— *v* [T1] to make unable to feel pain, with or without producing unconsciousness

an·a·gram /ˈænəgræm/ *n* a word or phrase made by changing the order of the letters in another word or phrase: *"Silent" is an anagram of "listen"*

a·nal /ˈeɪnəl/ *adj* of, concerning, or near the ANUS

an·al·ge·si·a /ˌænəlˈdʒiːzɪə‖-ʒə/ *n* [U] *tech* the condition of being unable to feel pain even though conscious

an·al·ge·sic /ˌænəlˈdʒiːzɪk/ *n, adj* [B;C;U] (a substance, esp. one that is rubbed into the skin) causing ANALGESIA

a·nal·o·gize /əˈnælədʒaɪz/ *v* [T1;I∅: (*to, with*)] to explain by comparison

a·nal·o·gous /əˈnæləgəs/ *adj* [B;F (*to, with*)] *fml* like or alike in some ways

an·a·logue, -log /ˈænəlɒg‖-lɔg, -lɑg/ *n fml* something that is like or that may be compared with something else

analogue com·put·er /ˌ··· ·ˈ··/ *n* a COMPUTER (=electrical calculating machine) that works by measuring rather than by counting —compare DIGITAL COMPUTER

a·nal·o·gy /əˈnælədʒi/ *n* **1** [C (*to, with, between*)] a degree of likeness or sameness: *There is an analogy between the way water moves in waves and the way light travels* **2** [U] the act of explaining by comparing with another thing that has a certain likeness **3** [C] the state in which 2 things are alike in many ways **4** [U] (in the study of languages) the way in which the form of a word is changed or decided because of another word that is like it

an·a·lyse /ˈænəlaɪz/ also *AmE* **-lyze**— *v* [T1] **1** to divide (a mixture) into its separate parts: *The food was analysed and found to contain small amounts of poison* —compare SYNTHESIZE (1) **2** to examine carefully in order to find out about **3** to divide (a sentence) into its various parts **4** *esp. AmE* PSYCHOANALYSE

a·nal·y·sis /əˈnælɪ̈sɪ̈s/ *n* **-ses** /siːz/ **1** [C;U] a separation of a substance into parts: *The analysis of the food showed the presence of poison* —compare SYNTHESIS **2** [C] the results of such a separation, esp. as a list **3** [C] an examination of something together with thoughts and judgments about it **4** [U;C] *esp. AmE* PSYCHOANALYSIS

an·a·lyst /ˈænəlɪ̈st/ *n* **1** a person who makes an ANALYSIS, esp. of chemical materials: *a chemical analyst* **2** *esp. AmE* PSYCHOANALYST

an·a·lyt·ic /ˌænəˈlɪtɪk/ also **an·a·lyt·i·cal** /-kəl/— *adj* of, concerning, or using ANALYSIS (1) —**-ically** *adv* [Wa4]: *I enjoy music, but I don't listen to it analytically*

an·a·paest /ˈænəpest, -piːst/ also *AmE* **-pest** /-pest/— *n* a measure of poetry consisting of 2 weak (or short) beats followed by one strong (or long) beat —**~ic** /ˌænəˈpestɪk, -ˈpiː-‖-ˈpe-/ *adj, n* [Wa5]

a·nar·chic /æˈnɑːkɪk‖-ɑr-/ also **a·nar·chi·cal** /-kəl/— *adj* of, like, or causing ANARCHY —**~ally** *adv* [Wa4]

an·ar·chis·m /ˈænəkɪzəm‖-ər-/ *n* [U] the political belief that society should have no government, laws, police, etc., but should be a free association of all its members

an·ar·chist /ˈænəkɪ̈st‖-ər-/ *n* **1** a person who believes in ANARCHISM **2** *derog* a person who tries or wishes to destroy all forms of government and control and not put anything in their place —**~ic** /ˌænəˈkɪstɪk‖-ər-/ *adj* —**~ically** *adv* [Wa4]

an·ar·chy /ˈænəki‖-ər-/ *n* [U] **1** absence of government or control **2** lawlessness and social and political disorder caused by this **3** absence of order

a·nath·e·ma /əˈnæθɪ̈mə/ *n* **1** [C] a solemn curse, by the Christian church or one of its priests, by means of which someone is forbidden any rights as a Christian **2** [C] someone or something that has been cursed in this way **3** [C *usu. sing.*; U: (*to*)] something hated: *Those terrible ideas are (an) anathema to me*

a·nath·e·ma·tize /əˈnæθɪ̈mətaɪz/ *v* [T1] *fml or tech* to curse (someone or something)

an·a·tom·i·cal /ˌænəˈtɒmɪkəl‖-ˈtɑ-/ *adj* of or concerned with ANATOMY: *an anatomical description of the leg* —**-cally** *adv* [Wa4]

a·nat·o·mist /əˈnætəmɪ̈st/ *n* a person skilled in ANATOMY (1)

a·nat·o·my /əˈnætəmi/ *n* **1** [U] the scientific study of the bodies and body parts of animals **2** [C] the body or body parts of a person or animal **3** [C;U] the cutting into pieces of a body or body part of an animal for studying the way it is built; DISSECTION (1,2) **4** [C *usu. sing.*] the way something works, as discovered by careful examination: *The book studies the anatomy of modern society*

-ance, -ence /əns/ *suffix* **1** [*v, adj→n* [U]] action, state, or quality: *appearance|acceptance|importance* **2** [*v, adj→n* [C]] an example of this: *an appearance| a performance*

an·ces·tor /ˈænsəstəʳ, -ses-‖-ses-/ *fem.* **an·ces·tress** /-trɪ̈s/— *n* a person, esp. one living a long time ago, from whom another is descended

an·ces·tral /ænˈsestrəl/ *adj* [Wa5;A] belonging to or coming from one's ANCESTORS: *one's ancestral home*

an·ces·try /ˈænsəstri, -ses-‖-ses-/ *n* [U;C *usu. sing.*] the ANCESTORS of a person's family considered as a group or as a continuous line: *a person of noble ancestry*

an·chor[1] /ˈæŋkəʳ/ *n* **1** a piece of heavy metal, usu. a hook with 2 arms, at the end of a chain or rope, for lowering into the water to keep a ship from moving —see picture at FREIGHTER **2** a person or thing that provides strong support and a feeling of safety **3 cast/drop anchor** to lower the ANCHOR[1] (1) **4 come to anchor** to stop sailing and lower the ANCHOR[1] (1) **5 ride/lie/be at anchor** to float on the waves while held in place by an ANCHOR[1] (1) **6 weigh anchor** to pull up the ANCHOR[1] (1) and move off

anchor[2] *v* **1** [T1] to lower an ANCHOR[1] (1) to keep (a ship) from moving **2** [IØ] to stop sailing and lower the ANCHOR[1] **3** [T1;IØ] to (cause to) be fixed firmly

an·chor·age /ˈæŋkərɪdʒ/ *n* **1** [C] a place where ships may ANCHOR[2] (2) **2** [U;S] the money charged to ANCHOR[2] (2) in a harbour **3** [C;U] something to which something else is fixed in order to make it firm **4** [C;U] a means of making firm

an·cho·rite /ˈæŋkəraɪt/ *fem.* **anchoress** /-rɪ̣s, -res/— *n* a person who lives alone and avoids company in order to reach union with God; HERMIT (1)

an·cho·vy /ˈæntʃəvi‖ˈæntʃəʊvi/ *n* a small fish with a strong taste, often made into a paste —see picture at FISH[1]

an·cient[1] /ˈeɪnʃənt/ *adj* **1** in or of times long ago: *ancient Rome and Greece* **2** having existed since a very early time: *ancient customs* **3** *often humor* very old —see OLD (USAGE)

ancient[2] *n* **1** a person, esp. a Roman or Greek, who lived in times long ago **2** *old use* an old man

an·cients /ˈeɪnʃənts/ *n* [*the*+P] (*often cap.*) the civilized nations of long ago, esp. as represented by the writers of ancient Greece and Rome: *to study the writings of the ancients*

an·cil·la·ry[1] /ænˈsɪləri‖ˈænsɪ̣leri/ *adj fml or tech* providing help, support, or additional service

ancillary[2] *n fml or tech* a person who helps another in work

-an·cy, -ency /ənsi/ *suffix* [→*n*] state or quality: BUOYANCY

and /ənd, ən, *strong* ænd/ *conj* **1** (used to show connection or addition, esp. of words of the same type or sentences of the same importance) as well as; together with; with; also; besides: *He started to shout and sing.|The boy and girl went for a walk.|*(*a*) *knife and fork|John and I|He was cold and hungry* **2** (used in the pattern "A and B", where B is later in time than A) and then; and afterwards: *He came to tea and stayed to dinner.|I woke up and got out of bed* **3** (used to express result or explanation): *Water the seeds and they will grow.|She was sick and took some medicine* (compare *She took some medicine and was sick*) **4** (used to join repeated words and suggest continuing time, action, state, etc.) *We ran and ran.|We waited for hours and hours.|It came nearer and nearer* **5** (after *come, go, try,* etc.) to: *Come and have tea with me.|You'll go and see her* **6** (in saying numbers, used *before* the numbers 1 to 99 and *after* the word "HUNDRED", but sometimes left out in *AmE*): *one* MILLION, TWO HUNDRED *and* FIFTY-THREE THOUSAND, FOUR HUNDRED *and* TWENTY-SIX (=1,253,426) **7** *old use* (between the numbers 1 to 9 and the numbers 20, 30, 40, 50, 60, 70, 80, and 90, when counting from 1 to 100): *5 and 20* (= TWENTY-FIVE) (= 25) **8** (in descriptions of food) **a** served with: HAM[1] (1) *and eggs|meat and potatoes* **b** (used esp. after bread and bread products) covered or spread with: *bread and butter|a* ROLL[1] (2) *and cheese|fruit and cream* **9 and how!** *AmE sl* (used to strengthen an idea, or to express strong agreement) **10 and so forth/on a** and others of the same kind **b** and more in the same manner **c** and the rest **d** and various other things

an·dan·te /ænˈdænti, -teɪ‖ɑnˈdɑn-/ *n, adj, adv* ((a piece of music) played) rather slowly and evenly

an·di·ron /ˈændaɪən‖-ərn/ also **firedog**— *n* either of a pair of usu. metal supports for burning logs in a fire in a room

-an·dr- /ændr/ *comb. form* man or male: POLYANDRY

an·drog·y·nous /ænˈdrɒdʒɪ̣nəs‖-ˈdrɑ-/ *adj* (esp. of plants) being both male and female

an·ec·dot·al /ˌænɪkˈdəʊtəl/ *adj* of, containing, telling, or full of ANECDOTE*s*

an·ec·dote /ˈænɪkdəʊt/ *n* a short interesting or amusing story about a particular person or event

a·ne·mi·a /əˈniːmɪə/ *n esp. AmE* ANAEMIA —**-c** *adj* —**-cally** *adv* [Wa4]

an·e·mom·e·ter /ˌænɪ̣ˈmɒmɪ̣təʳ‖-ˈmɑ-/ *n* a machine for measuring the strength of wind —see picture at SCIENTIFIC

a·nem·o·ne /əˈneməni/ *n* **1** a plant that produces many red, white, or blue flowers **2** SEA ANEMONE

an·e·roid ba·rom·e·ter /ˌænərɔɪd bəˈrɒmɪ̣təʳ‖-ˈrɑ-/ *n* an instrument (BAROMETER) for measuring the changing pressure or force of the air by measuring how far the sides of a metal container emptied of air are pushed in by the air. It is used to tell what the weather is going to be or how high one is above the level of the sea —see picture at SCIENTIFIC

an·es·the·si·a /ˌænɪ̣sˈθiːzɪə‖-ʒə/ *n esp. AmE* ANAESTHESIA —**anesthetic** /ˌænɪ̣sˈθetɪk/ *adj, n* [Wa5] —**anesthetist** /əˈniːsθɪ̣tɪ̣st‖əˈnes-/ *n* —**anesthetize** /əˈniːsθɪ̣taɪz‖əˈnes-/ *v* [T1]

a·new /əˈnjuː‖əˈnuː/ *adv lit* in a new or different way; again

an·gel /ˈeɪndʒəl/ *n* **1** a messenger and servant of God, usu. represented as a person with large wings and dressed in white clothes **2** a spirit that watches and guards one —see also GUARDIAN ANGEL **3** a person, esp. a woman, who is very kind, good, beautiful, etc. —**~ic** /ænˈdʒelɪk/ *adj* —**~ically** *adv* [Wa4]

an·gel·i·ca /ænˈdʒelɪkə/ *n* **1** [U] a clear green sweet-smelling stem of a plant used, after being boiled in sugar, to ornament cakes **2** [U;C] the plant itself

an·ge·lus /ˈændʒɪ̣ləs/ *n* [*the*+R] (*often cap.*) **1** a prayer said 3 times a day by members of a branch of the Christian church (ROMAN CATHOLIC*s*) **2** the sound of a bell rung in churches to tell people when to say this prayer

an·ger[1] /ˈæŋgəʳ/ *n* [U] a fierce feeling of displeasure, usu. leading to a desire to hurt or stop the person or thing causing it

anger[2] *v* [T1] to make angry

an·gi·na pec·to·ris /ænˌdʒaɪnə ˈpektərɪ̣s/ also **angina** /ænˈdʒaɪnə/— *n* [U] a heart disease causing sudden sharp pains in the chest

an·gle[1] /ˈæŋgəl/ *n* **1** the space between 2 lines or surfaces that meet or cross each other, measured in degrees that represent the amount of a circle that can fit into that space: *An angle of 90° is called a right angle* —see picture at GEOMETRY **2** a corner, as of a building or piece of furniture **3** *infml* a point of view: *If you look at the accident from another angle you will see how funny it all was* **4 at an angle** not upright or straight; sloping or turning away

angle[2] *v* [T1] **1** to turn or move at an angle **2** *often derog* to represent (something) from a particular point of view: *She angles her reports to suit the people she is speaking to*

angle³ *v* [Wv3;I∅] (*usu. in* -ing *form*) to fish with a hook and line: *He loves* (*to go*) *angling on a fine summer day* —**~r** *n*
angle brack·et /ˈ·· ˌ··/ *n* **1** a metal support, used esp. in pairs for fixing a shelf to a wall **2** either of a pair of marks ⟨ ⟩ used for enclosing written material
angle for *v prep* [T1 *pass. rare*] *often derog.* to try to get (something) esp. by tricks or questions which are not direct: *Mary has been angling for an invitation to your party*
An·gli·can /ˈæŋglɪkən/ *n, adj* (a member) of a branch (CHURCH OF ENGLAND) of the Christian religion —**~ism** *n* [U]
an·gli·cis·m /ˈæŋglǝ̇sɪzəm/ *n* an English word or phrase that is in common use in another language
an·gli·cize, -ise /ˈæŋglǝ̇saɪz/ *v* [T1;(I∅)] to (cause to) become English in appearance, sound, character, etc.
an·gling /ˈæŋglɪŋ/ *n* [U] the sport of catching fish with a hook and line
An·glo- /ˈæŋgləʊ/ *comb. form* (*sometimes not cap.*) **1** British; of England or Britain: *an Anglo*PHILE **2** British or English and: *Anglo-American relations*
Anglo-A·mer·i·can¹ /ˌ·· ·ˈ···◂/ *adj* of or concerning both England and America, esp. the US: *Anglo-American trade*
Anglo-American² *n* an American, esp. of the US, descended from an English family
Anglo-Cath·o·lic /ˌ·· ˈ···◂/ *n, adj* (a member) of the part of the HIGH CHURCH branch of the CHURCH OF ENGLAND that worships rather like the ROMAN CATHOLIC church —**~ism** /ˌ·· ·ˈ····/ *n* [U]
Anglo-In·di·an /ˌ·· ˈ··◂/ *adj, n* **1** (of) an English person born or living in India **2** (of) a person descended from both English and Indian families
an·glo·phile /ˈæŋgləʊfaɪl, -glə-/ also **an·glo·phil** /ˈæŋgləʊfɪl, -glə-/— *n* a person interested in and liking English people and things
an·glo·phil·i·a /ˌæŋgləʊˈfɪlɪə, -glə-/ *n* [U] interest in and liking for English people, things, etc.
an·glo·phobe /ˈæŋgləʊfəʊb, -glə-/ *n* a person who hates English people and things
an·glo·pho·bi·a /ˌæŋgləʊˈfəʊbɪə, -glə-/ *n* [U] hatred of England and English people, things, etc.
Anglo-Sax·on /ˌ·· ˈ··◂/ *adj, n* **1** [B;C] (of or concerning) a member of the GERMANIC race of people who lived in England in early times **2** [B; U] (of or concerning) their language **3** [B;C] (of or concerning) a person who is very English
an·go·ra /æŋˈgɔːrə‖-ˈgo-/ *n* **1** [C] (*often cap.*) a goat or rabbit with long hair **2** [U] woollen material made from this hair **3** [C] (*often cap.*) a type of cat with long hair —see picture at CAT
an·gos·tur·a /ˌæŋgəˈstjʊərə‖-ˈstʊrə/ *n* [U] a bitter liquid made from the outer hard skin of a South American tree, used for adding taste to alcoholic drinks
an·gry /ˈæŋgri/ *adj* [Wa1;B;F (*with/at* and/or *at/about*)] **1** filled with anger: *I shall be angry if you break that.|I shall be angry with you.|I was angry about missing that film at the cinema* **2** (of the sky or clouds) stormy —**angrily** *adv*
USAGE Things, people, or events can **annoy**, **irritate**, or even (stronger and less modern) **vex** one without being bad enough to make one **angry** or (informal *AmE*) **mad**, still less to make one **furious** or drive one into a **rage**, which are stronger expressions still. **Aggravate** is often used informally to mean **annoy**, but some teachers do not like this use of the word. **Provoke** (formal) and **rile** (informal) have this same meaning. **Bother** means "worry", "displease" or "trouble": *Will it* **bother** *you if I put the radio on?* **Irk** and **irksome** are particularly for dull and annoying things that are often repeated: *It* **irk***ed him that she never stopped complaining.*
angst /æŋst/ *n* [U] *Ger* anxiety caused by considering the sad state of world affairs and/or the human condition
an·guish /ˈæŋgwɪʃ/ *n* [U] very great pain and suffering, esp. of mind: *She was in anguish over her missing child*
an·guished /ˈæŋgwɪʃt/ *adj* feeling or expressing very great pain, esp. of mind: *anguished cries*
an·gu·lar /ˈæŋgjʊləʳ‖-gjə-/ *adj* **1** having, forming, consisting of, or concerning an angle or angles **2** having sharp corners **3** (of a person) with the bones able to be clearly seen; having no curves on the body **4** (of a person's character) not easy to be friends with; awkward —**~ity** /ˌæŋgjʊˈlærǝ̇ti‖-gjə-/ *n* [U;C]
an·i·line /ˈænǝ̇liːn, -lǝ̇n‖ˈænəl-/ *n* [U] a chemical produced from coal and used in the production of colours, medicines, and plastics
an·i·mad·ver·sion /ˌænǝ̇mædˈvɜːʃən‖-ˈvɜrʒən/ *n* [(*on, upon*)] *pomp* a remark or opinion, esp. one showing the faults of something
an·i·mad·vert /ˌænǝ̇mædˈvɜːt‖-ɜrt/ *v* [I∅ (*on, upon, about*)] *pomp* to speak about or remark on, esp. in a way that finds fault
an·i·mal¹ /ˈænǝ̇məl/ *n* **1** a living creature, not a plant, having senses and able to move itself when it wants to: *Snakes, fish, and birds are all animals* **2** all this group except human beings: *Some people consider themselves quite different from animals* **3** a person considered as lacking a mind and behaving like a wild non-human creature **4** MAMMAL
animal² *adj* **1** [Wa5] of, concerning, or made from animals **2** *usu. derog* concerning the body, not the mind or the spirit: *animal desires*
an·i·mal·cule /ˌænǝ̇ˈmælkjuːl/ *n lit* an animal too small to be seen easily
an·i·mal·is·m /ˈænǝ̇məl-ɪzəm/ *n* [U] **1** the state of lacking higher or finer feeling and behaving like a wild animal **2** the belief that man has no soul
animal hus·band·ry /ˌ··· ˈ···/ *n* [U] *esp. AmE* the branch of farming concerned with the keeping of animals and the production of animal materials, such as milk and meat
animal king·dom /ˈ··· ˌ··/ *n* [*the*+R] one of the 3 divisions into which the world can be divided; all animal life considered as a group —compare VEGETABLE KINGDOM, MINERAL KINGDOM
an·i·mate¹ /ˈænǝ̇mǝ̇t/ *adj* **1** (of plants and animals) alive; living **2** (of animals rather than plants) moving or able to move: (fig.) *The clock was the only animate thing in the quiet room*
an·i·mate² /ˈænǝ̇meɪt/ *v* [Wv5;T1] **1** to give life to **2** to bring life or excitement to: *Laughter animated his face for a moment* **3** to cause to become active; urge on; interest: *His excitement animated us all*
animated car·toon /ˌ···· ·ˈ·/ *n fml* CARTOON
an·i·ma·tion /ˌænǝ̇ˈmeɪʃən/ *n* [U] **1** excitement; spirit; life: *They were full of animation as they talked of their holiday plans* **2** the making of CARTOONS
an·i·mis·m /ˈænǝ̇mɪzəm/ *n* [U] **1** a religion according to which all natural objects, all animals, and all plants have souls **2** the belief that the soul exists apart from the body —**animist** *n, adj*
an·i·mos·i·ty /ˌænǝ̇ˈmɒsǝ̇ti‖-ˈmɑ-/ *n* **1** [U (*against, towards, between*)] powerful, often active, hatred **2** [C] an example of this
an·i·mus /ˈænǝ̇məs/ *n* [S;U9] hatred; ANIMOSITY
a·nis /æˈniːs/ *n* [U] a type of strong alcoholic drink made with ANISEED
an·ise /ˈænǝ̇s/ *n* a plant producing strong-tasting seeds (ANISEED)
an·i·seed /ˈænǝ̇siːd/ *n* [U] the strong-tasting seeds

of the ANISE, used esp. in alcoholic drinks

an·kle /ˈæŋkəl/ *n* **1** the joint between the foot and the leg **2** the thin part of the leg just above the foot —see picture at HUMAN

an·klet /ˈæŋklɨ̇t/ *n* an ornamental ring, usu. of metal, worn round the ankle

an·nals /ˈænəlz/ *n* [P] **1** a history or record of events, discoveries, etc., produced every year, esp. by societies for the advancement of learning or science **2** historical records in general: *A great deal has been left unwritten in the annals of history* —**annalist** *n*

an·neal /əˈniːl/ *v* [T1] to make (metal, glass, etc.) hard by allowing to become cool slowly after heating until soft

an·nex /əˈneks‖əˈneks, ˈæneks/ *v* [T1] **1** [(*to*)] to join or add (a smaller thing) to a greater thing **2** [(*to*)] to take control and possession of (land, a small country, etc.) esp. by force **3** *infml humor* to take without permission: *Someone has annexed my pencil*

an·nex·a·tion /ˌænekˈseɪʃən/ *n* **1** [U] the act of taking control over or seizing lands **2** [C] an example of this

an·nexe, annex /ˈæneks/ *n* a building joined or added to a larger one: *a hospital annexe*

an·ni·hi·late /əˈnaɪəleɪt/ *v* [T1] to destroy completely: *We annihilated the enemy.*|(fig.) *His argument was annihilated* —**-lation** /əˌnaɪəˈleɪʃən/ *n* [U]

an·ni·ver·sa·ry /ˌænɨ̇ˈvɜːsəri‖-ɜr-/ *n* **1** a day which is an exact year or number of years after something has happened: *Next Friday is the anniversary of the day I first met you.*|*a wedding anniversary* —compare BIRTHDAY **2** a ceremony, feast, etc., held on this day

An·no Dom·i·ni /ˌænəʊ ˈdɒmɨ̇naɪ‖-ˈdɑ-/ *fml* AD

an·no·tate /ˈænəteɪt/ *v* [T1] to add short notes to (a book) to explain certain parts

an·no·ta·tion /ˌænəˈteɪʃən/ *n* **1** [U] the writing of notes of explanation **2** [C] a written note, esp. on the pages of a printed book

an·nounce /əˈnaʊns/ *v* **1** [T1,5] to make known publicly: *The government announced that they would pay their debts.*|*They announced the date of their wedding in the newspaper* **2** [T1] to state in a loud voice (the name of a person or thing on arrival, as of people at a party or aircraft at an airport) **3** [T1] to read (news) or introduce (a person or act) on the radio, television, etc. **4** [T1,5] to make clearly known: *The bright flowers and warm winds announced that spring was here*

an·nounce·ment /əˈnaʊnsmənt/ *n* a statement saying what has happened or what will happen

an·nounc·er /əˈnaʊnsəʳ/ *n* a person who reads news or introduces people, acts, etc., esp. on radio or television

an·noy /əˈnɔɪ/ *v* [Wv4;T1;(I∅)] to cause (someone) trouble; make a little angry, esp. by certain repeated acts: *These flies are annoying me.*|*I was annoyed because I missed the bus*

an·noy·ance /əˈnɔɪəns/ *n* **1** [U] the state of being annoyed **2** [U] the act of annoying **3** [C] something which annoys: *Those noisy cats are a great annoyance late at night*

an·nu·al[1] /ˈænjʊəl/ *adj* [Wa5] (happening, appearing, etc.) every year or once a year, esp. on or about the same date —**~ly** *adv*

annual[2] *n* **1** a plant that lives for only one year or season **2** a book or magazine produced once each year having the same title but containing different stories, pictures, information, etc.

an·nu·i·ty /əˈnjuːɨ̇ti‖əˈnuː-/ *n* **1** a fixed sum of money paid each year to a person for a stated number of years or until death **2** a type of insurance which provides a yearly income beginning at a certain age and continuing till death

an·nul /əˈnʌl/ *v* **-ll-** [T1] *tech* to cause (a marriage, agreement, law, etc.) to cease to exist —**annulment** *n* [U;C]

an·nu·lar /ˈænjʊləʳ‖-jə-/ *adj fml* shaped like a ring

an·nun·ci·a·tion /əˌnʌnsiˈeɪʃən/ *n* [(*the*) S] (*often cap.*) **1** the words of the ANGEL Gabriel to the VIRGIN Mary telling her that she was to give birth to CHRIST **2** the day (March 25th) on which some Christian churches remember this event

an·ode /ˈænəʊd/ also **positive pole**— *n tech* the part of an electrical instrument (such as a BATTERY) which collects ELECTRONs, often a rod or wire shown as (+) —compare CATHODE

an·o·dyne /ˈænədaɪn/ *n, adj* **1** (a medicine) which will lessen pain **2** (something) which comforts a troubled mind or turns the attention away from more important matters

a·noint /əˈnɔɪnt/ *v* [T1 (*with*); X1] to put oil on (a person, his head, or his body), esp. in a religious ceremony: *They anointed her with oil.*|*They anointed him king.*|*an anointed king* —**~ment** *n* [U;(C)]

a·nom·a·lous /əˈnɒmələs‖əˈnɑ-/ *adj fml or tech* different from what is the usual type or rule: *in an anomalous position* —**~ly** *adv*

a·nom·a·ly /əˈnɒməli‖əˈnɑ-/ *n fml* **1** unusual irregularity: *The anomaly of his position is that he is very famous, but still doesn't make much money* **2** a person or thing that is different from the usual type

a·non[1] /əˈnɒn‖əˈnɑn/ *adv old use or poet* **1** in a short time; soon **2 ever and anon** now and then; from time to time

anon[2] *abbrev. for*: (esp. at the end of a poem, letter, etc.) ANONYMOUS

an·o·nym·i·ty /ˌænəˈnɪmɨ̇ti/ *n* [U] the condition of being ANONYMOUS

a·non·y·mous /əˈnɒnɨ̇məs‖əˈnɑ-/ *adj* **1** (of a person) with name unknown **2** (of a piece of writing) without the writer's name: *It is unpleasant to receive anonymous letters* —**~ly** *adv*

a·noph·e·les /əˈnɒfɨ̇liːz‖əˈnɑ-/ *n tech* a kind of mosquito, esp. the sort that spreads a particular disease (MALARIA) —see picture at INSECT

an·o·rak /ˈænəræk/ *n* a short coat which has a protective cover (HOOD) for the head, and which keeps out wind and rain —compare PARKA

an·o·rex·i·a /ˌænəˈreksɪə/ *n* [U] *tech* a dangerous condition in which there is loss of the desire to eat

an·oth·er[1] /əˈnʌðəʳ/ *determiner* [Wa5] **1** being one more of the same kind: *another piece of cake*|*Have another one.*|*"Another £20,000"* (SEU S.) **2** different from the first or other: *Look at the difficulty another way* **3** some other: *I'm in a hurry, I'll see you another time*

another[2] *pron* **1** one more of the same sort; an additional one: *Your egg is bad; have another.*|*She has taken another of my books* **2** a person other than oneself: *Is it brave to die for another?* **3** a different one: *They went from one shop to another* **4 one another** each other: *They love one another* —see EACH (USAGE) **5 such another** *old use or poet* one more of the same sort, esp. one that is equally unusual

an·swer[1] /ˈɑːnsəʳ‖ˈæn-/ *n* **1** [C; *in*+U: (*to*)] a spoken or written reply, as to a question, request, letter or polite greeting: *Although I wrote a month ago I've had no answer yet.*|*I said good morning to him but he gave no answer* **2** [C; *in*+U: (*to*)] a reply in the form of action: *My answer to his threat was to hit him on the nose.*|*In answer to my shouts people ran to help* **3** [C; *in*+U: (*to*)] a reply to an argument or charge **4** [C] something, at first unknown, which is discovered as a result esp. of thinking, using figures, etc.: *I gave her all the necessary figures, and she found the answer quickly: the answer was 279* **5** [C] a piece of usu. written work to show knowledge or ability, as in an examination

answer² *v* **1** [(*for*); T1;I∅] to give an answer (to); reply (to): *You didn't answer his question.|Why didn't you answer?|Answer me this, will you?* **2** [T1; I∅: (*with*)] to do something as a reply (to): *I answered with a smile.|I answered his threat with a blow on his nose* **3** [T1;(I∅)] to attend or act in reply to (a sign, such as a telephone ringing, a knock on the door, or a whistle): *I telephoned this afternoon, but nobody answered (the telephone)* **4** [I∅ (*to*); T1] to act or move in reply; obey: *The dog answers to his name* **5** [I∅ (*for*); T1] to be satisfactory (for): *This tool will answer (for) our needs/will answer (our needs) very well* **6** [I∅ (*to*);T1] to be as described in; to equal; to fit: *He answers (to) the description you gave, so he must be the criminal* **7** [T1] to satisfy: *The government just didn't answer our hopes* **8** [I∅] *rare* (esp. of a plan) to succeed **9** [T1;I∅] to reply to (a charge or argument)
USAGE **Answer** and **reply** are the usual verbs for answering questions; **respond** is a rarer verb with the same meaning: *He* **answered** (not ***replied**) *the question/his mother.|"Are you coming?" "Yes," he* **answered/replied/responded.**|*I spoke, but he didn't* **answer/reply/respond**|*He* **answered/replied/responded** *that he was coming.* **Retort** or (*rare*) **rejoin** are angrier: *"Are you ready?" "Why should I be ready when you're not?" she* **retorted**.

an·swer·a·ble /'ɑːnsərəbəl‖'æn-/ *adj* **1** able to be answered **2** [F (*for*)] responsible: *I shall be answerable for what he does* **3** [F (*to* and/or *for*)] having to explain or defend one's actions: *I cannot do as I like but am answerable to the government for any decision I make* —**-bly** *adv*

answer back *v adv* [T1 *no pass.*; I∅] *infml* (esp. of children talking to grown-ups) to reply rudely (to): *Don't answer (your grandmother) back: it's not polite*

answer for *v prep* [T1 (*to*)] **1** to be or become responsible for: *I will answer for his safety* **2** to promise that (something) is good: *I will answer for the truth of what he has said* **3** to act, pay, or suffer as a result of: *You will have to answer for your violent behaviour in court*

ant /ænt/ *n* a small insect living on the ground in well-ordered groups and famous for hard work

-ant /ənt/ *suffix* **1** [*v*→*n, adj*] (a person or thing) that does (the stated action), is in (the stated condition), or causes (the stated effect): *defendant|pleasant* **2** [*v*→*n*] something, esp. a chemical, used or acted upon (in the stated way): *inhalant* (=a medicine that is INHALEd by the sick person)

ant·ac·id /æn'tæsɨd/ *n, adj* [U;C] (a medicine) preventing an acid condition, esp. in the stomach

an·tag·o·nis·m /æn'tægənɪzəm/ *n* **1** [U] active opposition or hatred between people or groups **2** [C] an example of this

an·tag·o·nist /æn'tægənɨst/ *n* a person who is opposed to another, esp. actively; opponent —**~ic** /æn,tægə'nɪstɪk/ *adj* —**~ically** *adv* [Wa4]

an·tag·o·nize /æn'tægənaɪz/ *v* [T1] to cause to become an enemy

ant·arc·tic /æn'tɑːktɪk‖-ɑr-/ *adj, n* [Wa5;B; *the*+R] (*often cap.*) (of or concerning) the most southern part of the world —compare ARCTIC

Antarctic Cir·cle /·,·· '··/ *n* [*the*+R] an imaginary (line of LATITUDE (1)) drawn round the world at a certain distance from the most southern point (south POLE³ (1) and below which there is no darkness for 6 months of each year and little light for the other 6 months —compare ARCTIC CIRCLE

an·te¹ /'ænti/ *n* [*usu. sing.*] **1** the money (STAKE) risked in a particular card game (POKER) and which must be put on the table after looking at one's cards and before taking more cards **2 raise the ante** *usu. sl* to increase the money or something else risked, as in a game of cards

ante² *v* see ANTE UP

ante- /'æntɪ/ *prefix* before in time, place, or order: ANTEROOM|ANTEDATE

ant·eat·er /'ænt,iːtəʳ/ *n* any of several animals that eat ants, esp. one with a long sticky tongue —see picture at MAMMAL

an·te·ced·ence /,æntɨ'siːdəns/ *n* [U] *fml* the act or state of going or being before, esp. in time; PRIORITY (1)

an·te·ced·ent¹ /,æntɨ'siːdənt/ *n* **1** *fml* a thing, event, etc., coming or being before another **2** *tech* the word, phrase, or sentence that comes before, and is represented by, another word (a PRONOUN)

antecedent² *adj* [(*to*)] *often fml* coming or being before

an·te·ced·ents /,æntɨ'siːdənts/ *n* [P] **1** past family; ANCESTORs: *a person of unknown antecedents* **2** the record of the history or past of a person, family, group, etc.: *the glorious antecedents of our nation*

an·te·cham·ber /'æntɪ,tʃeɪmbəʳ/ also **anteroom**— *n* a small room leading to a larger one

an·te·date /'æntɪdeɪt, ,æntɪ'deɪt/ *v* [T1] **1** to write too early a date on (a letter, paper, etc.) **2** to be earlier in history than —opposite **postdate**

an·te·di·lu·vi·an /,æntɪdɨ'luːvɪən/ *adj* **1** existing before the great flood of the earth which is reported in the Bible **2** *humor* old-fashioned; very old

an·te·lope /'æntɨləʊp‖'æntəl-/ *n* [Wn1] any of various types of graceful grass-eating animals like deer, having horns and able to run very fast —see picture at RUMINANT

ante me·rid·i·em /,æntɪ mə'rɪdɪəm, -dɪem/ *adv Lat, fml & rare* A.M.

an·te·na·tal¹ /,æntɪ'neɪtl/ also (*esp. AmE*) **prenatal**— *adj* [A;(B)] *tech, esp. BrE* existing or happening before birth: *An* **antenatal clinic** *is a place where women who are expecting babies go for medical examinations and exercises*

antenatal² *n esp. BrE* an ANTENATAL medical examination

an·ten·na¹ /æn'tenə/ *n* **-nae** /niː/ a long thin sensitive hairlike organ existing, esp. in pairs, on the heads of some insects and animals that live in shells, and used for feeling —see picture at CRUSTACEAN, INSECT

antenna² *n* **-nas** *esp. AmE* AERIAL

an·te·pe·nul·ti·mate /,æntɪpɨ'nʌltɨmət/ *n, adj fml* (something that is) third from the last: *In the set of words "walk," "run," "swim," "fly," the antepenultimate word is "run"* —compare PENULTIMATE

an·ter·i·or /æn'tɪərɪəʳ/ *adj* [Wa5; (*to*)] **1** earlier in time **2** *usu. tech* nearer the front —opposite **posterior**

an·te·room /'æntɪrʊm, -ruːm/ *n* **1** ANTECHAMBER **2** a room in which people wait, as before seeing a doctor

ante up *v adv* [T1a;I∅] *AmE sl* to pay (something)

an·them /'ænθəm/ *n* **1** a religious song to be sung in a church, esp. by a group of trained singers (CHOIR) **2** *lit* any ceremonial song of praise —see also NATIONAL ANTHEM

an·ther /'ænθəʳ/ *n* the part of a male flower which contains the substance (POLLEN) that makes the female flower bear fruit or seeds —see picture at FLOWER¹

ant·hill /'ænt,hɪl/ *n* a raised mass of earth, little pieces of wood, etc., in which ants live

an·thol·o·gy /æn'θɒlədʒi‖æn'θɑ-/ *n* a collection of

poems, or of other writings, often on the same subject, chosen from different books or writers —**-gist** *n* —**-gized, -gised** *adj*

an·thra·cite /ˈænθrəsaɪt/ *n* [U] a very hard kind of coal that burns slowly and without smoke

an·thrax /ˈænθræks/ *n* [U] a serious disease which attacks cattle, sheep, etc., and is sometimes caught from them by human beings

an·thro·po- /ˈænθrəpə/ *comb form* of or concerning human beings: ANTHROPOCENTRIC

an·thro·po·cen·tric /ˌænθrəpəˈsentrɪk/ *adj tech* regarding human beings as the reason for the existence of the world and/or as the measure of all value

an·thro·poid /ˈænθrəpɔɪd/ *adj* **1** (of an animal) like a man **2** *derog infml* (of a person) like an ANTHROPOID APE: *Please tell that anthropoid brother of yours to stand up straight and get his hair cut!*

anthropoid ape /ˌ··· ˈ·/ also **anthropoid**— *n* any of several types of very large monkey (such as the CHIMPANZEE and GORILLA) that have no tails and look very much like hairy men

an·thro·pol·o·gist /ˌænθrəˈpɒlədʒəst‖-ˈpɑ-/ *n* someone who studies ANTHROPOLOGY

an·thro·pol·o·gy /ˌænθrəˈpɒlədʒi‖-ˈpɑ-/ *n* [U] the scientific study of the nature of man, including the development of his body, mind, and society —see also SOCIAL ANTHROPOLOGY, PHYSICAL ANTHROPOLOGY, SOCIOLOGY —**-gical** /ˌænθrəpəˈlɒdʒɪkəl‖-ˈlɑ-/ *adj* [Wa5] —**-gically** *adv* [Wa4,5]

an·thro·po·mor·phic /ˌænθrəpəˈmɔːfɪk‖-ɔr-/ *adj* regarding a god, animal, or object as having the form and qualities of man

an·thro·po·mor·phis·m /ˌænθrəpəˈmɔːfɪzəm‖-ɔr-/ *n* [U] the idea that gods, animals, or objects have human forms or qualities

an·thro·poph·a·gous /ˌænθrəˈpɒfəgəs‖-ˈpɑ-/ *adj tech* of a person who eats human flesh (CANNIBAL)

an·thro·poph·a·gy /ˌænθrəˈpɒfədʒi‖-ˈpɑ-/ *n* [U] *tech* the eating of human flesh by other human beings; CANNIBALism

an·ti- /ˈænti‖æntaɪ/ also **ant-** /ænt/— *prefix* **1** showing feeling or opinion against: *antislavery* **2** being the opposite of: ANTICLIMAX **3** being opposite to: ANTIPODES **4** having an effect or activity against: ANTIAIRCRAFT|ANTIFREEZE|ANTISEPTIC

an·ti·air·craft /ˌæntiˈeəkrɑːft‖-ˈeərkræft/ *n, adj* [A;U] (gunfire) against enemy aircraft

an·ti·bi·ot·ic /ˌæntɪbaɪˈɒtɪk‖-ˈɑ-/ *n, adj* (a medical substance, such as PENICILLIN) produced by living things and able to stop the growth of, or destroy, harmful bacteria that have entered the body —**~ally** *adv* [Wa4]

an·ti·bod·y /ˈæntɪˌbɒdi‖-ˌbɑ-/ *n* a substance produced in the body and which fights against disease

an·tic /ˈæntɪk/ *adj lit* (of behaviour or movement of the body) strange, awkward, amusing, or foolish —see also ANTICS

an·tic·i·pate /ænˈtɪsəpeɪt/ *v* **1** [T1,4,5] *sometimes considered nonstandard* to expect: *We are not anticipating trouble when the factory opens again.|We anticipate (meeting) a lot of opposition to our new plan for traffic control.|We are not anticipating that there will be much trouble* **2** [T1] to do something before (someone else): *We anticipated our competitors by getting our book into the shops first* **3** [T1,5,6a] to see (what will happen) and act as necessary, often to stop someone else doing something: *We anticipated that the enemy would try to cross the river and so seized the bridge.|We anticipated where they would try to cross* **4** [T1] to prevent (someone) doing something by acting first: *They have anticipated us and seized the bridge* **5** [T1] to provide for the probability of (something) happening: *We anticipated their visit by buying plenty of food* **6** [T1] to make use of, deal with, or consider before the right or proper time: *Do not anticipate your earnings by spending a lot of money* **7** [T1,5,6a; I∅] to speak or write (something) before the proper time: *If I told you what is going to happen to the main character in the story I would be anticipating.|I won't anticipate the story*

an·tic·i·pa·tion /ænˌtɪsəˈpeɪʃən/ *n* [U (*of,* 5)] the act of anticipating (ANTICIPATE) (often in the phr. **in anticipation**): *We waited at the station in anticipation of her arrival.|Our anticipation of our competitors meant greater sales for our book*

an·tic·i·pa·to·ry /ænˌtɪsəˈpeɪtəri‖ænˈtɪsəpətori/ *adj* **1** that ANTICIPATEs: *anticipatory action* **2** done or happening in advance **3** done or happening too soon

an·ti·cler·i·cal /ˌæntɪˈklerɪkəl/ *adj* opposed to the influence of priests in public and political life —**~ism** *n* [U]

an·ti·cli·max /ˌæntɪˈklaɪmæks/ *n* **1** something unexciting coming after something exciting: *To be back in the office after climbing mountains for a week was an anticlimax for him* **2** *often humor* a sudden change from something noble, serious, exciting, etc., to something foolish, unimportant, or uninteresting

an·ti·clock·wise /ˌæntɪˈklɒkwaɪz‖-ˈklɑk-/ (*AmE* **counterclockwise**)— *adj, adv BrE* in the opposite direction to the hands of a clock —see picture at CLOCK[1]

an·tics /ˈæntɪks/ *n* [P9 *sometimes sing.*] strange or unusual behaviour, esp. with odd, amusing, or foolish movements of the body: *Everyone laughed at his foolish antics*

an·ti·cy·clone /ˌæntɪˈsaɪkləʊn/ *n tech* a mass of air that is heavy, causing settled weather, either hot or cold, in the area over which it moves

an·ti·dote /ˈæntɪdəʊt/ *n* **1** a substance to stop a poison working inside a person, or to prevent the effects of a disease **2** something used for preventing the bad effects of something else: *What is the antidote to our present political troubles?*

an·ti·freeze /ˈæntɪfriːz/ *n* [U] a chemical substance put in water to stop it from freezing in very cold weather, used esp. in the apparatus (RADIATOR (3)) which prevents a car's engine from becoming too hot

an·ti·gen /ˈæntɪdʒən/ *n* a substance which, when introduced into the body, causes the formation in the blood of another substance (an ANTIBODY) that fights against disease

an·ti·her·o /ˈæntɪˌhɪərəʊ/ *n* **-es** the main male character, esp. in a piece of modern literature, when represented as no braver, stronger, or cleverer than ordinary people —compare HERO, VILLAIN

an·ti·his·ta·mine /ˌæntɪˈhɪstəmiːn, -mən/ *n* [C;U] any of several chemical substances that work against the effects of HISTAMINE and are used in the treatment of colds and allergies (ALLERGY)

an·ti·knock /ˌæntɪˈnɒk‖-ˈnɑk/ *n* [U] any of several chemical substances added to petrol to make car engines run smoothly, without KNOCKing[1] (5)

an·ti·log·a·rith·m /ˌæntɪˈlɒgərɪðəm‖-ˈlɑ-, -ˈlɔ-/ also (*infml*) **an·ti·log** /ˈæntɪlɒg‖-lɑg, -lɔg/— *n* the number represented by a LOGARITHM

an·ti·ma·cas·sar /ˌæntɪməˈkæsə^r/ *n* a piece of ornamental cloth put on the back of a chair to protect it from marks left by hair oil

an·ti·mat·ter /ˈæntɪˌmætə^r/ *n* [U] *tech* material (MATTER) made of ELEMENTARY PARTICLEs opposite to the ordinary ones

an·ti·mo·ny /ˈæntəməni‖-məʊni/ *n* [U] a silver-white metal that is a simple substance (ELEMENT (6)), used esp. in the production of other metals

an·ti·pa·thet·ic /ˌæntɪpəˈθetɪk/ *adj* [(*to*)] **1** feeling or causing ANTIPATHY (1): *He is antipathetic to large dogs* **2** opposed in nature or character: *Those 2 ideas are completely antipathetic (to each other)* —**~ally** *adv* [Wa4]

an·tip·a·thy /æn'tɪpəθi/ *n* **1** [U (*to, towards, against, between*)] a fixed unconquerable dislike or hatred **2** [C] an example of this **3** [U;S] a difference between 2 substances, as between water and oil, that prevents them from combining

an·ti·per·son·nel /ˌæntɪpɜːsə'nel‖-ɜr-/ *adj euph* (of bombs) intended to hurt people, not destroy property, by exploding into small pieces

an·tip·o·dal /æn'tɪpədl/ also **an·tip·o·de·an** /ænˌtɪpə'dɪən/— *adj* of or at the ANTIPODES

An·tip·o·des /æn'tɪpədiːz/ *n* [*the*+P] *lit or humour* Australia (and New Zealand)

an·ti·quar·i·an[1] /ˌæntɪ'kweərɪən/ *n* a person who studies, collects, or sells objects that are very old

antiquarian[2] *adj* **1** of or concerning things that are very old or people who study, collect, or sell such things **2** selling old or rare books: *an antiquarian bookseller*

an·ti·qua·ry /'æntɪkwəri‖-kweri/ *n* ANTIQUARIAN[1]

an·ti·quat·ed /'æntɪkweɪtɪd/ *adj* old and not suited to present needs or conditions; not modern; old-fashioned —see OLD (USAGE)

an·tique[1] /æn'tiːk/ *adj fml or lit* **1** being old and therefore valuable **2** of or connected with the ancient world, esp. of Rome of Greece **3** being of an earlier period: *antique manners* **4** [Wa5; *the*+U] of the style of art of ancient Rome or Greece: *I really like the antique much better than modern art* —see OLD (USAGE)

antique[2] *n* **1** a piece of furniture, jewellery, etc., that is old and therefore becoming rare and valuable **2** a work of art or some other thing from the ancient world, esp. of Rome or Greece

an·tiq·ui·ty /æn'tɪkwɪti/ *n* **1** [U] the state of being very old; great age: *The nobleman was proud of his family's antiquity* **2** [U] the ancient world, esp. of Rome or Greece **3** [C *usu. pl.*] a building, work of art, etc., remaining from ancient times

an·tir·rhi·num /ˌæntɪ'raɪnəm/ *n* [Wn1] SNAPDRAGON

an·ti-Sem·i·tis·m /ˌæntɪ 'semɪtɪzəm/ *n* [U] hatred of Jews —**-Se·mit·ic** /sɪ'mɪtɪk/ *adj* —**-Se·mite** /'siːmaɪt‖'semaɪt/ *n*

an·ti·sep·tic /ˌæntɪ'septɪk/ *n, adj* (a chemical substance) able to prevent flesh, blood, etc., from developing disease, esp. by killing bacteria

an·ti·so·cial /ˌæntɪ'səʊʃəl/ *adj* **1** that causes damage to the way in which people live together peacefully: *Playing music so loudly that it annoys everyone else in the street is antisocial* **2** destroying, making dirty, etc., buildings or places used by the public **3** opposed to an orderly society or way of life **4** selfish **5** not liking to mix with other people

an·tith·e·sis /æn'tɪθɪsɪs/ *n* **-ses** /siːz/ **1** [(*between, to*) *usu. sing.*] complete difference; opposite nature; oppositeness: *The antithesis of death to life* **2** [(*of, to*) *usu. sing.*] the direct opposite: *The antithesis of death is life* **3** the putting together in speech or writing, of 2 opposite ideas: *Her speeches are full of antitheses like "We want deeds, not words!"*

an·ti·thet·ic /ˌæntɪ'θetɪk/ also **an·ti·thet·i·cal** /-kəl/— *adj* **1** of, concerning, or including ANTITHESIS **2** directly opposed: *Those 2 ideas are strongly antithetic (to each other)* —**-ically** *adv* [Wa4]

an·ti·tox·in /ˌæntɪ'tɒksɪn‖-'tɑk-/ *n* [C;U] a substance (either a SERUM (2) or something produced by the body) that cures or prevents a disease

ant·ler /'æntləʳ/ *n* either of the pair of branched horns of a male deer (STAG)

an·to·nym /'æntənɪm/ *n* a word opposite in meaning to another word: *"Pain" is the antonym of "pleasure"* —opposite **synonym**

a·nus /'eɪnəs/ *n tech* the hole through which solid food waste leaves the bowels —compare COLON[1], RECTUM —see picture at DIGESTIVE SYSTEM

an·vil /'ænvɪl/ *n* **1** a shaped iron block on which metals are hammered to the shape wanted **2** a small bone inside the ear which carries sound further inside it —see picture at EAR[1]

anx·i·e·ty /æŋ'zaɪəti/ *n* **1** [U (*for*)] fear, esp. as caused by uncertainty about something: *He felt strong anxiety (for her safety) when he heard she had gone* **2** [C] an example of this: *After listening to his advice she had no more anxieties* **3** [C] a cause of this: *Her sick child is a great anxiety to her* **4** [U,U3,5;C,C3,5] *infml* a strong wish to do something; eagerness: *anxiety to please*

anx·ious /'æŋkʃəs/ *adj* **1** [B (*for, about*)] feeling anxiety; troubled; fearful: *He was anxious for the safety of his money* **2** [B] causing anxiety or worry: *The period of his illness was anxious for us all* **3** [B (*for*) 3,5C] *infml* having a strong wish to do something; eager: *He was anxious to please his guests.|He was anxious that they should have all they want.|He was anxious for them to go* —see NERVOUS (USAGE) —**~ly** *adv*

an·y[1] /'eni/ *determiner* **1** one or some of whatever kind; every: *Any child would know that.|Ask any man you meet* **2** [*nonassertive*] one, some, or all, of whatever quantity; an unstated number or amount: *Have you got any money?|Are there any letters for me?|Come and see me if you have any time* **3** [*with neg.*] none at all: *I haven't any money.|There aren't any letters for you.|I never get any letters!|We haven't any ordinary fish* (=We have only special fish).|*We don't accept any students* (=We accept no students at all) **4** [*nonassertive*] of the usual or stated kind: *This isn't (any) ordinary fish* (=It's special fish).|*We don't accept just any students* (=We accept only very good students) **5** [*nonassertive*] the smallest or least possible amount or degree of: *There isn't any hope of finding the lost child.|It isn't any use looking for her* **6** no matter which, what, where, how, etc.: *We can make any size of shoe you wish.|Any room will do* **7** [*nonassertive*] *infml* a, an, or one: *This car hasn't any engine!* **8** as much as possible; all: *He will need any help he can get* **9 in any case** also **at any rate**— whatever may happen **10** unlimited or unmeasured in amount, number, etc. (esp. in the phrs. **any number/amount/quantity of**): *I have any number of things I must do today*

USAGE In the first meaning, *not* **any** *students/fish* means "no students/fish". In the 4th meaning **any** means "ordinary" as compared with "special", so that we can use it with **just**. Sometimes the difference is expressed only by the INTONATION tune: at the end of a sentence where **any** means "ordinary' the voice always rises. —see EITHER[2], SOME (USAGE)

any[2] *pron* **1** any person or persons; anybody: *His gift was unknown to any (of them) except himself* **2** any thing or things; any quantity or number: *They're all free: take any (of them) you like* **3 if any** if there is/are any at all; and perhaps no(ne): *There are very few trees, if any.|We have little if any water*

any[3] *adv* [Wa5 *nonassertive*] **1** in any degree; in the least degree; at all: *I can't stay any longer.|I don't feel any better for having had a holiday.|Do you feel any better?|(infml) He was never any good* **2** *AmE nonstandard* at all: *Poor old Billy Joe can't work any*

an·y·bod·y /'eniˌbɒdi, 'enibədi‖-ˌbɑdi/ also **an·y·one** /'eniwʌn/— *pron* **1** any person: *Is anybody* *listening?|There isn't anybody listening.|If anybody is listening, I hope he/they will say so.|It's simple: ask anybody!|He's better than anybody else* **2** a person of importance or influence: *If you want to be anybody you must work hard* **3 anybody's guess** *infml* a matter of uncertainty **4 if anybody** if there is anybody (of the type needed or stated): *Smith can do it if anybody (can)* —see EVERYBODY, SOME (USAGE)

an·y·how /ˈenihaʊ/ *adv* [Wa5] *infml* **1** without any regular order; in a careless manner: *His clothes were thrown down just anyhow* **2** in spite of that; in spite of everything; in any case: *He may not like my visit, but I shall go and see him anyhow (whether he likes it or not).|Well, anyhow, it's too late to do anything now* **3** (used to show a change of subject): *"John's a very good friend of mine. Well anyhow, I left for Messina the next morning"* **4 any old how** *sl* ANYHOW (1)

an·y·place /ˈenipleɪs/ *adv AmE* ANYWHERE (1,2)

an·y·road /ˈenirəʊd/ *adv BrE nonstandard* ANYWAY

an·y·thing¹ /ˈeniθɪŋ/ *pron* **1** [*nonassertive*] any one thing; something: *Is there anything in that box?|You can't believe anything she says.|Has anything strange happened?|"I wondered whether this had anything to do with the fact that . . ."* (SEU S.)|*"Do you want anything else?" "Just a black coffee, please."* (SEU W.) **2** no matter what: *He will do anything for a quiet life.|Anything will do to keep the door open* **3** [*nonassertive*] a thing of any kind, esp. something important or serious: *I was cut a little in the fight, but it wasn't anything.|"What's that strange noise?" "Don't worry: it isn't anything"* **4 anything but** not at all; far from: *That little bridge is anything but safe* **5 as easy/fast/strong, etc., as anything** *sl* very easy/fast/strong, etc. **6 if anything** if there is any difference: *If anything, my new job is harder than my old one* **7 like anything** *sl* (used to add force to a verb): *We ran like anything to get away* **8 not make/think anything of (something)** to think (something) not important **9 or anything** (suggests that there are other possibilities): *"If Bernard wants to call me or anything, I'll be here all day"* (SEU S.) —see SOME (USAGE)

anything² *adv* [Wa5] in any way, degree, or amount; at all: *Is this box anything like what you need?*

an·y·way /ˈeniweɪ/ *adv* [Wa5] *infml* ANYHOW (2,3): *He may not like my visit, but I shall go and see him anyway (whether he likes it or not)*

an·y·where /ˈeniweəʳ/ *adv* **1** [*nonassertive*] (in, at, or to) any place: *Did you go anywhere yesterday?|"too late to go anywhere"* (SEU W.)|*"I can't find it anywhere"* (SEU S.) **2** in, at or to no matter what place: *Sit anywhere you like* **3** (used before *from* and *between* to show free variation): *anywhere from 40 to 60 students|anywhere between 40 and 60 students* **4 anywhere near** *infml* **a** in any degree: *She isn't anywhere near as kind as he is* **b** at all near: *"This is not to say that we are anywhere near being able to . . ."* (SEU S.) **5 if anywhere** if there is ANYWHERE (1) of the type needed or stated; or else nowhere at all: *You will find it in London if anywhere* **6** [*nonassertive*] **or anywhere** or in/at/to some other place: *"If I suddenly decide to pack up and go to China or anywhere . . ."* (SEU W.) —see SOME (USAGE)

a·or·ta /eɪˈɔːtə‖-ˈɔr-/ *n* the largest blood vessel (ARTERY) in the body, taking blood from the heart —see picture at RESPIRATORY

a·pace /əˈpeɪs/ *adv lit & old use* at a great speed; quickly

ap·a·nage /ˈæpənɪdʒ/ *n* APPANAGE

a·part¹ /əˈpɑːt‖-ɑrt/ *adv* [Wa5] **1** [E (*from*)] separate; away; distant: *The 2 buildings are 3 miles apart.|We planted the trees wide apart.|The house stands apart (from the village).|He kept himself apart from the other children.|"a married man living apart from his wife"* (SEU S.) **2** to pieces: *He tore the cooked chicken apart and began to eat it* **3** [F] in or into a state of separation (from each other), independence, disconnection: *If I see the 2 boys apart I don't know which is which* **4** to or at one side, esp. for a certain purpose: *He took me apart to have a private talk with me* **5** not considering; aside: *A few little things apart, I am very pleased with the result.|Joking apart, we really do need a place to meet and talk* **6 apart from a** without considering; except for; aside from: *good work, apart from a few slight faults* **b** as well as: *Apart from the cost, the hat doesn't suit me* **7 tell/know apart** to be able to see the difference between

apart² *adj* [F] **1** separate; unconnected; independent: *He is a man apart from all others* **2** holding very different opinions; divided: *They look alike but in ideas they are very far apart* **3 worlds apart** *infml* very different: *In ideas those 2 political parties are worlds apart*

a·part·heid /əˈpɑːtheɪt, -teɪt, -taɪt, -taɪd‖-ɑr-/ *n* [U] the keeping separate of races of different colours in one country, esp. of Europeans and non-Europeans in South Africa

a·part·ment /əˈpɑːtmənt‖-ɑr-/ *n* **1** [*often pl.*] a room, esp. a large or splendid one, or one used by a particular person or group: *"The Royal or State Apartments may be seen every day from 1 to 5 o'clock"* **2** *esp. AmE* a flat **3** *BrE* a large and expensive flat

apartment house /·ˈ·· ·/ *n AmE* a block of flats

a·part·ments /əˈpɑːtmənts‖-ɑr-/ *n* [P] *esp. BrE* a set of rooms, usu. furnished, let to someone by the week, month, etc., esp. for holidays

ap·a·thet·ic /ˌæpəˈθetɪk/ *adj* without feeling or interest; lacking desire to act —**~ally** *adv* [Wa4]

ap·a·thy /ˈæpəθi/ *n* [U] lack of feeling or interest in something or everything; lack of desire or ability to act in any way: *He was sunk in apathy after his failure*

ape¹ /eɪp/ *n* **1** a large monkey without a tail or with a very short tail (such as a GORILLA or CHIMPANZEE) —see picture at PRIMATE² **2** *usu. derog* a person who copies the behaviour of others

ape² *v* [T1] to copy (a person or a person's behaviour, manners, speech, etc.); IMITATE

a·per·i·ent /əˈpɪərɪənt/ *n, adj* [C;(U);B] *tech, now rare* LAXATIVE

a·per·i·tif /əˌperɨˈtiːf/ *n* a small alcoholic drink taken before a meal

ap·er·ture /ˈæpətʃəʳ‖ˈæpərtʃʊər/ *n* **1** a hole, crack, or other narrow opening **2** the opening in a camera, TELESCOPE, etc., that admits light

a·pex /ˈeɪpeks/ *n* **-es** *or* **apices** /ˈeɪpɨsiːz/ [*usu. sing.*] **1** *tech or fml* the top or highest part of anything: *the apex of a* TRIANGLE **2** the highest point of power or success; CLIMAX¹ (1)

a·pha·sia /əˈfeɪʒə/ *n* [U] the loss of the ability to speak or to understand speech, caused by damage to the brain

a·pha·sic¹ /əˈfeɪzɪk/ *n* a person suffering from APHASIA

aphasic² *adj* concerning or suffering from APHASIA

a·phid /ˈeɪfɨd, ˈæfɨd/ also **a·phis** /ˈeɪfɨs, ˈæfɨs/— *n* any of various small insects (such as the GREENFLY) that live on the juices of plants

aph·o·ris·m /ˈæfərɪzəm/ *n* a true or wise saying or principle expressed in a few words; MAXIM

aph·o·ris·tic /ˌæfəˈrɪstɪk/ *adj* of, like, or containing APHORISMs

aph·ro·dis·i·ac /ˌæfrəˈdɪziæk/ *n, adj* [C;U;B] (a medicine, drug, etc.) causing sexual excitement

a·pi·a·rist /ˈeɪpɪərɪ̵st/ *n tech* a person who keeps bees

a·pi·a·ry /ˈeɪpɪəri‖ˈeɪpieri/ *n tech* a place where bees are kept, esp. a place in which there are several HIVES

a·pi·ces /ˈeɪpɪ̵siːz/ also **a·pex·es** /ˈeɪpeksɪ̵z/— *pl. of* APEX

a·pi·cul·ture /ˈeɪpɪ̵ˌkʌltʃəʳ/ *n* [U] *tech* the keeping of bees, esp. for profit

a·piece /əˈpiːs/ *adv* to, for, or from each person or thing; each: *They received 2 houses apiece from their father.|The apples cost 6 pence apiece*

ap·ish /ˈeɪpɪʃ/ *adj usu. derog* like an APE, esp. in trying foolishly to behave like others —**~ly** *adv* —**~ness** *n* [U]

a·plomb /əˈplɒm‖əˈplɑm/ *n* [U] power to remain calmly bold in appearance and behaviour in moments of difficulty; SELF-POSSESSION

a·poc·a·lypse /əˈpɒkəlɪps‖əˈpɑ-/ *n* the showing of hidden things, esp. the telling of what will happen when the world ends

a·poc·a·lyp·tic /əˌpɒkəˈlɪptɪk‖əˌpɑ-/ *adj* **1** *often derog* telling of great misfortunes in the future: *apocalyptic statements about the coming of wars and hunger* **2** of or like the end of the world: *apocalyptic scenes of death and destruction* **3** of or like an APOCALYPSE —**~ally** *adv* [Wa4]

A·poc·ry·pha /əˈpɒkrɪ̵fə‖əˈpɑ-/ *n* [*the*+GU] **1** a collection of Jewish and/or early Christian books sometimes, but usu. not, included in the Bible **2** pieces of literature which may or may not have been written by the stated person

a·poc·ry·phal /əˈpɒkrɪ̵fəl‖əˈpɑ-/ *adj* **1** of or connected with the APOCRYPHA **2** not regarded as true or certain, or as a real member of a group or class: *an apocryphal story about the minister's impatience* **3** (of a book, play, etc.) regarded as not having been written by the stated person

ap·o·gee /ˈæpədʒiː/ *n* [*usu. sing.*] **1** the point at which the moon, the sun, a space vehicle etc., is farthest from the earth —compare PERIGEE **2** the highest point of power or success

a·pol·o·get·ic[1] /əˌpɒləˈdʒetɪk‖əˌpɑ-/ *adj* **1** expressing sorrow for some fault or wrong **2** (of a person's manner) as if unwilling to cause trouble: *He asked in an apologetic voice if we would mind getting out of his way* —**~ally** *adv* [Wa4]

apologetic[2] *n* **1** [C (*for*)] an example of APOLOGETICS **2** [A] of APOLOGETICS

a·pol·o·get·ics /əˌpɒləˈdʒetɪks‖əˌpɑ-/ *n* [P;U] the art, science, or practice of arguing in defence or in explanation, as of an idea, belief, person, etc.

ap·o·lo·gi·a /ˌæpəˈləʊdʒɪə, -dʒə/ *n* [(*for, of*)] a formal defence or explanation, esp. of a belief

a·pol·o·gist /əˈpɒlədʒɪ̵st‖əˈpɑ-/ *n* [(*for*)] *often derog* a person who defends a belief or opinion by argument: *He is nothing but an apologist for the crimes of his political leaders!*

a·pol·o·gize, -ise /əˈpɒlədʒaɪz‖əˈpɑ-/ *v* [Iø (*to* and/or *for*)] to express sorrow, as for a fault or causing pain: *I apologized (to her) (for stepping on her foot)*

a·pol·o·gy /əˈpɒlədʒi‖əˈpɑ-/ *n* **1** a statement expressing sorrow for a fault, causing trouble or pain, etc.: *I must offer her an apology for not going to her party.|I must make an apology to her.|Please accept my apologies* **2** a defence or explanation of a belief, idea, etc.: *Shelley's "Apology for Poetry"* **3** *infml* a very poor example of something: *This bit of burnt potato is no more than an apology for a meal* —see EXCUSE (USAGE)

ap·oph·thegm /ˈæpəθem/ *n* APOTHEGM

ap·o·plec·tic /ˌæpəˈplektɪk/ *adj* **1** of, concerning, or having APOPLEXY **2** having a red face and easily made angry —**~ally** *adv* [Wa4]

ap·o·plex·y /ˈæpəpleksi/ *n* [U;(C)] the loss of the ability to move, feel, think, etc., usu. caused by too much blood in the blood vessels in the brain or by the bursting of one of these blood vessels; STROKE[2] (3)

a·pos·ta·sy /əˈpɒstəsi‖əˈpɑ-/ *n* **1** [U] desertion of one's religious faith, political party, beliefs, etc. **2** [C] an example of this

a·pos·tate /əˈpɒsteɪt, -stɪ̵t‖əˈpɑ-/ *n* a person guilty of APOSTASY

a·pos·ta·tize, -ise /əˈpɒstətaɪz‖əˈpɑ-/ *v* [Iø (*from*)] to be guilty of APOSTASY

a pos·ter·i·o·ri /ˌeɪ pɒsteriˈɔːraɪ, ˌɑː pɒsteriˈɔːriː‖ˌɑ pəʊstɪriˈəʊri, ˌeɪ pɑ-/ *adv, adj Lat* (of an argument) reasoned from effect to cause (as in the statement *The streets are wet so it must have rained*) —compare A PRIORI

a·pos·tle /əˈpɒsəl‖əˈpɑ-/ *n* **1** any of the 12 followers of Christ chosen by Him to spread His message to the world **2** any of the early Christians who introduced Christianity to a country, area, etc. **3** a leader of a new political or other belief or idea

ap·o·stol·ic /ˌæpəˈstɒlɪk‖-ˈstɑ-/ *adj* **1** of or concerning an APOSTLE (1,2), esp. one of the 12 **2** or concerning the leader (POPE) of one of the branches (ROMAN CATHOLIC CHURCH) of Christianity; PAPAL —**~ally** *adv* [Wa4]

a·pos·tro·phe[1] /əˈpɒstrəfi‖əˈpɑ-/ *n* (in a speech or piece of writing) words addressed to a person who is usu. absent or to an idea or quality as if it were a person

apostrophe[2] *n* the sign (') used in writing **a** to show that one or more letters or figures have been left out of a word or figure (as in *don't* and *'47* for *do not* and *1947*) **b** before or after *s* to show possession (as in *John's hat, James' hat, lady's hat, ladies' hats, children's hats*) **c** before *s* to show the plural of letters and figures (as in *There are 2 f's in off* and *Your 8's look like S's*)

a·pos·tro·phize /əˈpɒstrəfaɪz‖əˈpɑ-/ *v* [T1;Iø] to make an APOSTROPHE[1] to (someone or something)

a·poth·e·ca·ries' weight /·ˈ···· ·/ *n* [U] the system of weights used by those practising chemistry in mixing very small quantities of medicines

a·poth·e·ca·ry /əˈpɒθɪ̵kəri‖əˈpɑθɪ̵keri/ *n old use* a person with a knowledge of chemistry who mixed and sold medicines; PHARMACIST (2)

ap·o·thegm, apophthegm /ˈæpəθem/ *n rare* a short true or wise saying; APHORISM

a·poth·e·o·sis /əˌpɒθiˈəʊsɪ̵s‖əˌpɑ-, ˌæpəˈθiːəsɪ̵s/ *n* **-ses** **1** the act of raising or of being raised to the rank of a god **2** *lit* a state of the highest possible honour and glory reached by or given to someone or something **3** *lit* the perfect example; QUINTESSENCE: *She is the apotheosis of womanhood*

ap·pal, *AmE usu.* **appall** /əˈpɔːl/ *v* **-ll-** [T1] to shock deeply; fill with fear, hatred, terror, etc.

ap·pal·ling /əˈpɔːlɪŋ/ *adj* **1** causing fear; shocking, terrible **2** *infml* of very bad quality; having very little skill: *Mary is an appalling cook* —**~ly** *adv*: *appallingly bad*

ap·pa·nage, apanage /ˈæpənɪdʒ/ *n* **1** *lit* something, esp. property, that is claimed or received as a right by birth, office, position, etc. **2** *lit* something that naturally or necessarily goes with something else: *respect, an appanage of high rank* **3** *old use* land, or some other form of income, kept to support the younger children of kings

ap·pa·ra·tus /ˌæpəˈreɪtəs‖-ˈræ-/ *n* **-tuses** *or* **-tus** [U; C *pl. rare*] **1** a set of instruments, machines, etc., that work together for a particular purpose: *This electric heating apparatus is very clean.|a piece of apparatus|a lot of apparatus* **2** a set of instruments, machines, tools, materials, etc., needed for a particular purpose: *The television men set up their* *apparatus ready to film* **3** a group of parts that work together inside a body: *The breathing apparatus includes the nose, throat, and lungs* **4** an organization or system made up of many parts: *The political apparatus set up by the government is used to settle industrial trouble*

ap·par·el[1] /ə'pærəl/ *v* **-ll-** (*AmE* **-l-**) [Wv5;T1 (*in*)] *lit* to dress, esp. in fine or special clothes: *The king came out, apparelled in his finest clothing*

apparel[2] *n* [U] **1** *lit & old use* clothes, esp. of a fine or special sort: *priestly apparel* **2** *esp. AmE* (*in comb.*) clothes; clothing: *ladies' ready-to-wear apparel*

ap·par·ent /ə'pærənt/ *adj* **1** [(*to*)] easily seen or understood; plain: *Her anxiety was apparent to everyone* **2** according to what seems to be the case; not necessarily true or real; seeming: *Their apparent grief soon turned to laughter*

ap·par·ent·ly /ə'pærəntli/ *adv* [Wa5] **1** it seems (that); as it appears: *I wasn't there, but apparently she tried to drown him.*|*"Did she succeed?" "Apparently not"* **2** it is plain (that); EVIDENTLY: *Apparently she never got my letter after all* —compare EVIDENTLY, OBVIOUSLY

ap·pa·ri·tion /ˌæpə'rɪʃən/ *n* the spirit of a dead person moving in bodily form; GHOST[1] (1): *He fell unconscious when he saw the apparition of his dead wife*

ap·peal[1] /ə'piːl/ *n* **1** [U;C] (a) strong request for help, support, mercy, etc.: *His appeal for forgiveness went unanswered.*|*The appeal for money with which to build a new hall was very successful.*|*There was a look of appeal on her sad face* **2** [U] power to move the feelings; attraction; interest: *Films of that sort have lost their appeal for me.*|*sex appeal* **3** [C;U] a call to a higher court to change the decision of a lower court: *The right of appeal is an important part of good law.*|*a court of appeal* **4** [C] (esp. in sports) a call from a player for a decision from the person who judges the rules of the game (such as a REFEREE or UMPIRE)

appeal[2] *v* [I∅] **1** [(*to* and/or *for,* 3)] to make a strong request for help, support, mercy, etc.; beg: *He appealed to his attacker for mercy.*|*They are appealing for money to build a new hall.*|*The government is appealing to everyone to save water.*|*The police are appealing for anyone with information to come forward.*|*I don't like appealing, but I need help* **2** [(*to*)] to please, attract, or interest: *She appeals to me.*|*That music is too old-fashioned to appeal (to people) any longer* **3** [(*to* and/or *against*)] to call on a higher court to change the decision of a lower court: *I will appeal against being found guilty.*|*I intend to appeal (to a higher court)* **4** (esp. in sports) to call for a decision, as from the person with power to judge the rules of the game

ap·peal·ing /ə'piːlɪŋ/ *adj* **1** able to move the feelings: *the appealing eyes of the sad hungry child* **2** attractive or interesting: *the appealing appearance of the happy healthy child* —**~ly** *adv*

appeal to *v prep* [T1] **1** to look for support in: *By appealing to his better nature, we persuaded the boy to change his behaviour* **2** [*pass. rare*] to point to or show as reason or proof: *He appealed to the number of dead as a reason why the fighting should stop* **3** to settle or wish to settle a matter by the use of (reason, fighting, etc.): *If you do not obey me I shall appeal to force*

ap·pear /ə'pɪəʳ/ *v* **1** [I∅] to come into sight; come into view; be seen: *A car appeared over the hill.*|*In this disease spots appear on the skin* **2** [Wv6;I∅, 3; (*it*) L (*to be*) 1,7,9] to seem; look: *He appears to want to leave.*|*You appear well this morning.*|*He appears to be your friend but I doubt if he is.*|*It appears (to be) a true story* (=The story appears true).|*It appears true that she will win* (=That she will win appears true).|*He's guilty, it appears* **3** [Wv6; *it*+I5a,b,6a (**as if**)] to seem true: *It appears (that) she will win* (=It appears as if she will win).|*"Will she win?" "So it appears." "It appears so." "It appears not"* **4** [I∅] to come to a certain place, esp. in view of the public, as for attention or sale: *His new book will be appearing in the shops very soon.*|*If I fail to appear by 7 o'clock I will not be coming at all* **5** [I∅] to be present officially as in a court of law: *He had to appear before the committee to explain his behaviour* **6** [I∅ (*for*)] to perform duties as a lawyer in court: *Mr. Jones will appear for you in court tomorrow* **7** [Wv6;L9] to be found; exist: *The idea appears in many old books*

ap·pear·ance /ə'pɪərəns/ *n* **1** [C] the act of appearing, as to the eye, mind, or public: *My appearance at the party was not very welcome* **2** [U;C *usu. sing.*] that which can be seen; outward qualities; look: *He had an unhealthy appearance.*|*After being painted its appearance was quite different.*|*Appearance isn't everything in life, my boy* **3 put in/make an appearance (at)** to attend (a meeting, party, etc.), esp. for a short time only

ap·pear·anc·es /ə'pɪərənsɪ̵z/ *n* [P] **1** that which can be seen but which may be false; outward qualities; looks: *Don't judge by appearances* **2 keep up appearances** to keep looking the same as is usual or expected and hide what one doesn't want others to see or know **3 to/by/from all appearances** judging by all that can be seen or is known

ap·pease /ə'piːz/ *v* [T1] to make calm or satisfy, esp. by yielding to demands or by giving or doing something: *The angry man was appeased when they said they were sorry.*|*His hunger was not appeased until he reached the hotel*

ap·pease·ment /ə'piːzmənt/ *n* **1** [U;C] the act of appeasing (APPEASE) **2** [U] the political idea that peace can be obtained by giving an enemy what he demands

ap·pel·lant /ə'pelənt/ *n, adj* [Wa5] (a person) that calls on a higher court to change the decision of a lower court

ap·pel·late /ə'pelɪ̵t/ *adj* [Wa5;A] of or concerning APPEALS[1] (3) in courts of law: *an appellate court*

ap·pel·la·tion /ˌæpɪ̵'leɪʃən/ *n fml* a name or title, esp. one that is formal or descriptive

ap·pend /ə'pend/ *v* [T1 (*to*)] *fml* to add or join (esp. something written or printed onto the end of a larger piece of written material)

ap·pend·age /ə'pendɪdʒ/ *n* something added, joined to, or hanging from something, esp. something larger

ap·pen·dec·to·my /ˌæpɪ̵n'dektəmi/ *n* [C;U] the medical operation of removing the APPENDIX (1)

ap·pen·di·ci·tis /əˌpendɪ̵'saɪtɪ̵s/ *n* [U] the diseased state of the APPENDIX[1], usu. causing it to be medically removed

ap·pen·dix /ə'pendɪks/ *n* **-dixes** *or* **dices** /dɪ̵siːz/ **1** also **vermiform appendix**— a short wormlike organ leading off the bowel, and having little or no use —see picture at DIGESTIVE SYSTEM **2** something added, esp. additional information added at the end of a book

ap·per·tain to /ˌæpə'teɪn‖-əʳ-/ *v prep* [T1 *no pass.*] *fml* to belong to (usu. something rather than someone) by right: *the responsibilities appertaining to the chairmanship*

ap·pe·tite /'æpɪ̵taɪt/ *n* **1** [U;C] a desire or wish, esp. for food: *Don't eat anything that will spoil your appetite for dinner.*|(fig.) *He had no appetite for hard work* **2** [U;C] a desire to satisfy any bodily want: *sexual appetites* **3 whet someone's appetite a** to make someone eager to enjoy **b** to make someone eager for more of something —see DESIRE (USAGE)

ap·pe·tiz·er /ˈæpətaɪzəʳ/ *n* something small and attractive eaten at the beginning of a meal to increase the desire for food

ap·pe·tiz·ing /ˈæpətaɪzɪŋ/ *adj* causing desire, esp. for food —**~ly** *adv*: *food appetizingly cooked*

ap·plaud /əˈplɔːd/ *v* [T1;I∅] **1** to praise (a play, actor, performer, etc.) esp. by striking one's hands together (CLAPping) **2** to express strong agreement with (a person, idea, etc.)

ap·plause /əˈplɔːz/ *n* [U] loud praise for a performance or performer, esp. by striking the hands together (CLAPping)

ap·ple /ˈæpəl/ *n* **1** a hard round fruit with white juicy flesh and usu. a red, green, or yellow skin —see picture at FRUIT[1] **2 apple of discord** *lit* the cause of disagreement, argument, hatred, etc. **3 the apple of someone's eye** *infml* the person or thing most liked

apple cart /ˈ·· ·/ *n* **upset the/someone's apple cart** *infml* to spoil someone's plans

ap·ple·jack /ˈæpəldʒæk/ *n* [U] *AmE* very strong alcoholic drink (SPIRIT) made from apples

apple pie /ˌ·· ˈ·◂/ *n* **1** [C;U] apples cooked in pastry **2 in apple-pie order** *infml* in perfect arrangement or order

ap·pli·ance /əˈplaɪəns/ *n* an apparatus, instrument, or tool for a particular purpose, often one that is fitted to a larger machine

ap·plic·a·ble /əˈplɪkəbəl, ˈæplɪkəbəl/ *adj* **1** able to have an effect: *The new law is applicable from next Monday* **2** [(*to*)] able to have an effect on; directed towards: *This rule is not applicable to foreigners* **3** suitable for; proper; correct

ap·pli·cant /ˈæplɪkənt/ *n* a person who makes a request, esp. officially and in writing, for something such as a job, a place in a school, or tickets for the theatre

ap·pli·ca·tion /ˌæplɪˈkeɪʃən/ *n* **1** [U (*of* and/or *to*)] the putting to use: *The application of new scientific discoveries to industrial production methods usually makes jobs easier to do* **2** [U;C (*to*)] the quality of being useful or suitable: *That rule has no application to this particular case* **3** [U] the act of requesting, esp. officially and in writing: *Tickets may be bought on application to the theatre* **4** [C] such a request: *I wrote 5 applications for jobs but got nothing* **5** [U;C] the putting of one thing onto another, esp. medicine onto the skin: *The application of this medicine should be at night.|5 applications a day are necessary* **6** [C] the substance, esp. medicine, put on: *You will be able to get the application from the doctor* **7** [U] careful and continuous attention or effort: *He worked with great application to learn 3 musical instruments in one year*

ap·plied /əˈplaɪd/ *adj* [Wa5] (esp. of a science) put to practical use

ap·pli·qué[1] /əˈpliːkeɪ‖ˌæpləˈkeɪ (*Fr* aplike)/ *n* [U; (C)] (esp. in dress-making) ornamental work of one material sewn or stuck on to a larger surface of another material

appliqué[2] *v* [T1] to put (ornamental work) on a larger surface

ap·ply /əˈplaɪ/ *v* **1** [I∅ (*to* and/or *for*)] to request something, esp. officially and in writing: *I will apply for the job today* **2** [T1 (*to*)] to bring or put into use: *Apply as much force as is necessary.|Scientific discoveries are often applied to industrial production methods* **3** [T1 (*to*)] to put on or next to: *Apply some medicine to his wound* **4** [T1;I∅: (*to*)] to (cause to) have an effect; be directly related: *This rule does not apply.|This rule cannot be applied to every case* **5** [T1 (*to*)] to cause to work hard or with careful attention: *He applied himself to his new job.|He applied his mind to the difficulty*

ap·point /əˈpɔɪnt/ *v* **1** [T1 (*as*); X (*to be*) 1;(V3)] to put in or choose for a position, job (or purpose); make into an officer (of a business, club, etc.): *We must appoint a new teacher soon.|They appointed him (to be) chairman.|They appointed him as chairman.|They appointed him to catch all the rats in Hamelin* —see HIRE (USAGE) **2** [T1] to set up or make by choosing: *We must appoint a committee* **3** [T1] *fml* to arrange, settle; fix; decide: *Let's appoint a day to have dinner together* **4** [T5b,c] *becoming rare* to give orders

ap·point·ed /əˈpɔɪntəd/ *adj* [Wa5] **1** arranged, settled, fixed; decided: *She wasn't at the appointed meeting place* **2** chosen for a position or job **3** (*in comb.*) provided with necessary things; furnished: *The old hotel was not very well-appointed*

ap·point·ment /əˈpɔɪntmənt/ *n* **1** [U] the agreement of a time and place for meeting: *He will only see you by appointment* **2** [C] a meeting at an agreed time and place: *I have an appointment with the doctor* **3** [U (*of, as*)] the choosing of someone for a position, job, or office: *the appointment of John as chairman/to be chairman* **4** [C] a position or job: *I hope I shall get a teaching appointment at the new school*

USAGE When one arranges to see someone at a fixed time one *makes an* **appointment**. If one then actually sees the person as arranged, one is said to *keep the* **appointment**. If it will be impossible to meet after all, one should write or telephone to CANCEL (1) *the* **appointment**. —see JOB (USAGE)

ap·point·ments /əˈpɔɪntmənts/ *n* [P] furniture, esp. such things as gas fires, wash basins, etc., that are not easily removed

ap·por·tion /əˈpɔːʃən‖or-/ *v* [T1 (*between, among, amongst*)] to divide into and give as shares: *We must apportion the money fairly.|It was difficult to apportion the blame for the accident between the several drivers* —**~ment** *n* [C;U]

ap·po·site /ˈæpəzət/ *adj* [(*to, for*)] *fml* exactly suitable to the present moment, conditions, etc.

ap·po·si·tion /ˌæpəˈzɪʃən/ *n* [U;(C)] a state of affairs in grammar in which one simple sentence contains 2 or more noun phrases that describe the same person or thing and are used in the same way: *In the sentence "The rich man, a banker, was a criminal," the phrase "the rich man" and the phrase "a banker" are in apposition (to each other)*

ap·prais·al /əˈpreɪzəl/ *n* **1** the act of working out the value, quality, or condition of something **2** a statement of value, quality, or condition

ap·praise /əˈpreɪz/ *v* [T1] to judge the worth, quality, or condition of; find out the value of: *They all appraised the house carefully before offering to buy it* —**appraiser** *n*

ap·pre·cia·ble /əˈpriːʃəbəl/ *adj* enough to be felt, noticed, or considered important —**-bly** *adv*: *The temperature dropped appreciably last night*

ap·pre·ci·ate /əˈpriːʃieɪt/ *v* **1** [T1] to be thankful or grateful for: *I appreciate your help* **2** [T1] to understand and enjoy the good qualities of: *A sensitive mouth is necessary to appreciate good wine* **3** [T1] to understand fully: *I don't think you appreciate the dangers of this job* **4** [T1] to understand the high worth of: *His abilities were not appreciated in that school* **5** [I∅ (*in*)] (of property, possessions, etc.) to increase in value: *Houses in this area have all appreciated (in value) since the new road was built*

ap·pre·ci·a·tion /əˌpriːʃiˈeɪʃən/ *n* **1** [U] judgment, as of the quality, worth, or facts of something: *The teacher's appreciation of his pupils' chances of passing the examination was correct* **2** [C] a written account of the worth of something: *The pupils wrote an appreciation of the play they had just seen* **3** [U] understanding of the qualities or worth of something: *Their appreciation of the performance was expressed in loud cheers* **4** [U;S] grateful feelings: *He showed no appreciation of my advice|an appreciation of my help* **5** [U;S] rise in value, esp. of land or possessions: *an appreciation of 50% in property values*

ap·pre·cia·tive /ə'priːʃətɪv/ *adj* **1** grateful; thankful **2** feeling or showing understanding **3** feeling or showing admiration —**~ly** *adv*

ap·pre·hend /ˌæprɪ'hend/ *v* **1** [T1] *fml* to seize (a person who breaks the law); ARREST[1] (1) **2** [T1] *rare* to look forward to or expect with anxiety; fear **3** [T1,5,5b] *old use* understand

ap·pre·hen·sion /ˌæprɪ'henʃən/ *n* **1** [U *often pl. with sing. meaning*] anxiety, esp. about the future; fear: *She felt apprehension for the safety of her son.|Her apprehensions about an accident were not fulfilled* **2** [U;S] *fml* ability to understand; understanding **3** [U;C] the act of seizing (a person who breaks the law); ARREST

ap·pre·hen·sive /ˌæprɪ'hensɪv/ *adj* [(*of, for*)] fearful, esp. about the future; worried, anxious: *an apprehensive look|He was apprehensive of being killed.|She was apprehensive for her son's safety* —**~ly** *adv*

ap·pren·tice[1] /ə'prentɪ̈s/ *n* a person who is under an agreement to serve, for a number of years and usu. for low wages, a person skilled in a trade, in order to learn that person's skill: *an apprentice electrician|apprentice to an electrician*

apprentice[2] *v* [T1 (*to*)] to make or send as an APPRENTICE: *We apprenticed our son to an electrician*

ap·pren·tice·ship /ə'prentɪ̈sʃɪp/ *n* **1** [U] the condition of being an APPRENTICE **2** [C] the time or period this lasts **3** [C] an example of such a condition: *Several apprenticeships could not be filled*

ap·prise /ə'praɪz/ *v* [T1 (*of*), 5: *often pass.*] *fml becoming rare* to inform; tell: *He was apprised of our arrival.|He was apprised that we should arrive at mid-day*

ap·pro /'æprəʊ/ *n* **on appro** *BrE infml* on APPROVAL

ap·proach[1] /ə'prəʊtʃ/ *v* **1** [T1;I∅] to come near or nearer (to): *We approached the camp.|We approached with care.|The time is approaching when we must leave* **2** [T1] to come near or nearer to, in quality, condition, character, etc.: *His work is approaching perfection* **3** [T1 (*about*)] to speak to, esp. about something for the first time: *Did he approach you about lending him some money?* **4** [T1] to begin to consider or deal with (something non-material): *He approached the difficulty with great thought*

approach[2] *n* **1** [U] the act of APPROACHing: *Our approach drove away the wild animals.|The approach of winter brings cold weather* **2** [C] a means or way of entering: *All approaches to the town were blocked.|We left our car in the station approach* **3** [C *often pl.*] a speaking to someone for the first time, esp. in order to begin close personal relations: *I'm not very good at making approaches to strangers* **4** [C] a manner or method of doing something: *That player's approach to the music is quite different from anyone else's.|His book presents a new approach to the difficulty* **5** [U] likeness or nearness in quality, condition, character, etc.

ap·proa·cha·ble /ə'prəʊtʃəbəl/ *adj* **1** able to be reached **2** *infml* easy to speak to or deal with; friendly

ap·pro·ba·tion /ˌæprə'beɪʃən/ *n* [U] *fml* **1** praise **2** an official expression of agreement: *We have not yet received the approbation of the council for holding a dance in the town hall*

ap·pro·ba·to·ry /'æprəbeɪtəri‖'æprəbətori, ə'prəʊ-/ *adj fml* showing praise: *approbatory remarks*

ap·pro·pri·ate[1] /ə'prəʊprieɪt/ *v* [T1] **1** [(*for*)] to set aside for some purpose: *The government appropriated a large sum of money for building hospitals* **2** *euph* to take for oneself; steal: *The minister was found to have appropriated a great deal of government money*

ap·pro·pri·ate[2] /ə'prəʊprɪ-ɪ̈t/ *adj* [(*for, to*)] correct or suitable: *His bright clothes were not appropriate for a funeral* —**~ly** *adv* —**~ness** *n* [U]

ap·pro·pri·a·tion /əˌprəʊpri'eɪʃən/ *n* **1** [U (*for*)] the act of setting aside something for a special purpose: *The appropriation of public money for a new hospital* **2** [C] something, esp. money, set aside for a particular purpose: *an appropriation of £5,000,000 for a new hospital* **3** [U] *euph* the act of taking something for oneself; THEFT

ap·prov·al /ə'pruːvəl/ *n* **1** [U] the act of approving **2** [U;(C)] official permission **3 on approval** *BrE infml* also **on appro**— (of goods taken or sent from a shop) to be returned without payment if not found satisfactory, suitable, etc.

ap·prove /ə'pruːv/ *v* [T1] to agree officially to: *The minister approved the building plans* —**approvingly** /ə'pruvɪŋli/ *adv*

ap·proved school /·'· ·/ (*AmE* **reformatory, reform school**)— *n* [C;U] *BrE fml* a special school for boys or girls who have done things against the law, where they live and receive training

approve of *v prep* [T1,4;V4a] to consider good, right, wise, etc.: *I don't approve of (silly people) (wasting time)*

ap·prox *written abbrev. for:* APPROXIMATE(ly)[1]

ap·prox·i·mate[1] /ə'prɒksɪ̈mɪ̈t‖ə'prɑk-/ *adj* [Wa5] nearly correct but not exact: *The approximate number of boys in the school is 300—but remember that 300 is only an approximate figure!* —**~ly** *adv*: *approximately 300*

ap·prox·i·mate[2] /ə'prɒksɪ̈meɪt‖ə'prɑk-/ *v* [T1;L1] to bring or come near to: *Could you approximate the cost?|The cost will approximate £5,000,000*

approximate to /ə'prɒksɪ̈meɪt‖ə'prɑk-/ *v prep* [L1] *infml* to come near in amount, quality, condition, character, etc.: *What was said approximated to the facts but still left a great deal out*

ap·prox·i·ma·tion /əˌprɒksɪ̈'meɪʃən‖əˌprɑk-/ *n* **1** [C (*to, of*)] a result, calculation, description, drawing, etc., that is not exact but is good enough: *300 is only an approximation of the right number* **2** [U (*to, of*)] the state of being or getting near, as to a position, quality, or number

ap·pur·te·nance /ə'pɜːtɪ̈nəns, -tən-‖ə'pɜrtənəns/ *n* [*usu. pl.*] *law* **1** something belonging to or usu. connected with something else **2** any of various rights or responsibilities that go with the ownership of property

Apr. *written abbrev. for:* April

a·pri·cot /'eɪprɪ̈kɒt‖'æprɪ̈kɑt/ *n* **1** [C] a round soft pleasant-tasting but slightly sour fruit with a furry outside like a PEACH and a single large stone. It is orange or yellow and red in colour **2** [U] the colour of this fruit

A·pril /'eɪprəl/ *n* [R;(C)] the 4th month of the year

April fool /ˌ·· '·/ *n* a person who has been deceived or made fun of by a trick played on the morning of April 1st (**April Fools' Day, All Fools' Day**)

a pri·o·ri /ˌeɪ praɪ'ɔːraɪ, ˌɑː pri'ɔːriː‖-'or-/ *adj, adv Lat* (of an argument) reasoned from cause to effect (as in the statement *It is raining so the streets must be wet*) —compare A POSTERIORI

a·pron /'eɪprən/ *n* **1** a simple garment worn over the front part of one's clothes to keep them clean while working or doing something dirty or esp.

while cooking **2** also **apron stage** /ˌ·· ˈ·/— that part of a stage in a theatre that comes forward towards where the public sit **3** (in an airport) the hard surface on which planes are turned round, loaded, unloaded, etc.

apron strings /ˈ·· ·/ *n* [P] *infml* the strings of an APRON (1) regarded as a sign of control, as of a boy or man by his mother or wife (esp. in the phr. **tied to his mother's/wife's apron strings**)

ap·ro·pos¹ /ˌæprəˈpəʊ, ˈæprəpəʊ/ *adv Fr* **1** very suitably for the time, place, or state of affairs: *I thought he spoke very apropos* **2** (used to introduce a new subject connected with the earlier subject) by the way: *"John was here yesterday." "Apropos, did he mention his new job?"*

apropos² *adj Fr* very suitable for the time or conditions

apropos of /ˌ··ˈ· ·/ *prep Fr* with regard to; concerning: *Apropos of John's new job, did he tell you how much he is earning?*

apse /æps/ *n* the curved or many-sided arched end of a building, esp. the east end of a church —see picture at CHURCH¹

apt /æpt/ *adj* [Wa2] **1** [F3] having a tendency to do something; likely: *This kind of shoe is apt to slip on wet ground* **2** [B (*at*)] clever and quick to learn and understand: *He is an apt student.|He is apt at understanding difficult ideas* **3** [B] exactly suitable: *an apt remark* —**~ly** *adv* —**~ness** *n* [U9, esp. *for, at, of*]

ap·ti·tude /ˈæptɨtjuːd‖-tuːd/ *n* [U;C: (*for*)] natural ability or skill, esp. in learning: *He showed great aptitude for/in painting.|She shows an aptitude for writing.|The students had to take an aptitude test* —see GENIUS (USAGE)

aq·ua·lung /ˈækwəlʌŋ/ *n* an apparatus used by a swimmer under water to provide him with air, esp. a container of special air that is carried on the back and has a tube that takes the air to the mouth or nose

aq·ua·ma·rine /ˌækwəməˈriːn/ *n* **1** [C] a glass-like ornamental blue-green stone **2** [C] a jewel made from this **3** [U] the colour of this stone

aq·ua·plane¹ /ˈækwəpleɪn/ *n* a thin board on which a person stands while he is pulled quickly along the surface of the sea, a lake, etc., by a rope from a fast motorboat

aquaplane² *v* [IØ] **1** to ride on an AQUAPLANE for fun or sport **2** *esp BrE* (of cars and car tyres) to slide forwards without control on a wet road, not touching the real road surface at all

a·quar·i·um /əˈkweərɪəm/ *n* **-iums** *or* **-ia** /ɪə/ **1** a glass container for fish and other water animals **2** a building (esp. in a ZOO) containing many of these

A·quar·i·us /əˈkweərɪəs/ *n* **1** [R] the 11th division (sign) in a belt of stars (the ZODIAC), represented by a man pouring water **2** [R] the group of stars (CONSTELLATION) formerly in this division or sign **3** [C] a person born under this sign (during a month beginning January 21) —see picture at PLANET

a·quat·ic /əˈkwætɪk, əˈkwɒ-‖əˈkwæ-, əˈkwɑ-/ *adj* [Wa5] **1** living in or on water: *aquatic plants/animals* **2** happening in or on water: *aquatic sports including swimming and rowing* —**~ally** *adv* [Wa4,5]

aq·ua·tint /ˈækwətɪnt/ *n* **1** [U] the method of cutting a picture, ornamental surface, etc., into a flat piece of copper by letting a strong acid eat away the parts that have not been protected by wax or some other material **2** [C] a picture printed from such a piece of copper

aq·ua vi·tae /ˌækwə ˈvaɪtiː, -ˈviːtaɪ/ *n* [U] *Lat* any of various very strong alcoholic drinks (SPIRITs), esp. BRANDY

aq·ue·duct /ˈækwɨdʌkt/ *n* a pipe, bridge, or CANAL (1), that carries a water supply, esp. one that is built higher than the land around it or that goes across a valley

a·que·ous /ˈeɪkwɪəs, ˈækwɪəs/ *adj tech* of, like, containing, or in water —**~ly** *adv*

aq·ui·line /ˈækwɨlaɪn‖-laɪn, -lən/ *adj* of or like a particular bird (EAGLE) (esp. in the phrs. **aquiline nose/profile**): *An aquiline nose is one that is thin and curves like an* EAGLE*'s beak*

-ar /əʳ, ɑːʳ/ *suffix* **1** [*v→n*] (the form used for -ER in certain words): *beggar*|BURSAR|REGISTRAR **2** [*n→adj*] of or related to: MOLECULAR

Ar·ab /ˈærəb/ *n* **1** a person who speaks ARABIC, esp. one from North Africa or the ARABIAN PENINSULA **2** a type of fast graceful horse

ar·a·besque /ˌærəˈbesk/ *n* **1** a fancy ornamental pattern of twisted shapes of flowers, leaves, fruits, etc. **2** a flowing ornamental line, as in writing **3** a position in a particular kind of dancing (BALLET)

A·ra·bi·an /əˈreɪbɪən/ *adj* [Wa5] of Arabia, esp. the PENINSULA containing Saudi Arabia and several other countries: *the Arabian desert*

Ar·a·bic¹ /ˈærəbɪk/ *adj* of or concerning the language or writing of the ARABs (1): *Arabic literature*

Arabic² *n* [R;U] the SEMITIC language spoken by ARABs (1)

Arabic nu·me·ral /ˌ··· ˈ···/ *n* **1** any of the signs most commonly used for numbers in the English and many other alphabets (such as 1, 2, 3, 4, etc.) —compare ROMAN NUMERAL **2** any of the signs used for numbers in the ARABIC alphabet, on which the above number signs were based

ar·a·ble¹ /ˈærəbəl/ *adj* (of land) suitable or used for growing crops

arable² *n* [U] *tech* land that is used for growing crops —compare PASTURE

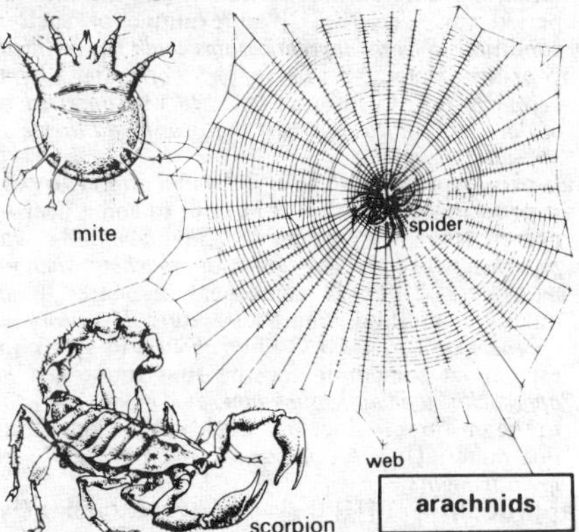

arachnids

a·rach·nid /əˈræknɪd/ *n* **-nids** *or* **-nidae** /nɨdiː/ the class of insect-like animals with 8 legs that includes SPIDERs and SCORPIONs

ar·bi·ter /ˈɑːbɨtəʳ‖ˈɑr-/ *n* **1** a person or group that has complete control or great influence over actions, decisions, etc.: *Beau Brummel was the arbiter of fashion in part of the 18th Century* **2** *rare* ARBITRATOR

ar·bi·tra·ry /ˈɑːbɨtrəri‖ˈɑrbɨtreri/ *adj* **1** of power that is uncontrolled and used without considering the wishes of others: *The arbitrary decisions of the factory owners caused anger among the workers* **2** *often derog* decided by or based on personal opinion or chance rather than reason: *I didn't know anything about any of the books so my choice was quite arbitrary* —**-rily** *adv* —**-riness** *n* [U]

ar·bi·trate /ˈɑːbɨtreɪt‖ˈɑr-/ *v* [T1;IØ] **1** [(*between*)] to act as a judge in (an argument), esp. at the request of both sides: *We must get someone to arbitrate (this difficulty).|Someone must arbitrate between them* **2** to settle (an argument, disagreement, etc.) by giving for consideration to a person chosen by both sides

ar·bi·tra·tion /ˌɑːbəˈtreɪʃən‖ˌɑr-/ *n* [U] **1** the settling of an argument by the decision of a person or group chosen by both sides **2 go to arbitration a** (of a business, group of workers, etc.) to give or choose to give an argument to a person chosen by both sides **b** (of an argument) to be given to a person chosen by both sides

ar·bi·tra·tor /ˈɑːbətreɪtəʳ‖ˈɑr-/ *n* a person chosen by both sides of an argument to examine the facts and make a decision to settle the argument

ar·bo·re·al /ɑːˈbɔːrɪəl‖ɑrˈbo-/ *adj* [Wa5] *tech* of, concerned with, or living in trees: *arboreal animals*

ar·bo·re·tum /ˌɑːbəˈriːtəm‖ˌɑr-/ *n* **-tums** *or* **-ta** /tə/ a garden of trees, esp. one for show or scientific study

ar·bour, *AmE* **arbor** /ˈɑːbəʳ‖ˈɑr-/ *n* a sheltered place, esp. with a seat, in a garden, usu. made by training trees or bushes to form an arch

arc¹ /ɑːk‖ɑrk/ *n* **1** part of a curved line or circle: *an arc of 110°* —see picture at GEOMETRY **2** the curved path that the sun, moon, or any star appears to move along when seen from the earth **3** a very powerful flow of electricity through the air or gas between 2 points, as in an **arc lamp** or ARC WELDING

arc² *v* **arced** *or* **arcked**; *pres. p.* **arcing** *or* **arcking** [IØ] **1** to make or follow a curved course **2** (of electricity) to make an ARC¹ (3) or flash, as at a bad connection

ar·cade /ɑːˈkeɪd‖ɑr-/ *n* a covered passage, esp. one with an arched roof or with a row of shops on one or both sides: *Burlington Arcade is a famous shopping passage in London*

Ar·ca·di·a /ɑːˈkeɪdɪə‖ɑr-/ *n* [R;C] an area or scene of simple pleasant country life

ar·cane /ɑːˈkeɪn‖ɑr-/ *adj lit* mysterious and secret: *arcane knowledge*

arch¹ /ɑːtʃ‖ɑrtʃ/ *n* **1** a curved top sometimes with a central point resting on 2 supports, as under a bridge or above a door: *The bridge had 7 arches* **2** something with this shape, esp. the middle of the bottom of the foot —see picture at HUMAN

arch² *v* **1** [T1] to make into the shape of an arch: *The cat arched her back in anger* **2** [L9, esp. *across, over*] to form an arch: *The trees arched over the path*

arch³ *adj* [Wa1] **1** (esp. of the behaviour of a woman or child) amused, gay, or intended to attract; COY: *an arch smile* **2** SUPERCILIOUS: *When he made that silly remark she gave him an arch look* —**~ly** *adv*

arch- /ɑːtʃ-, ɑːk-‖ɑr-/ *prefix* **1** [*n→n*] of the highest rank or class; chief: ARCHBISHOP|ARCHANGEL **2** [*n→n*] having the qualities of the type to the greatest degree: *arch*VILLAIN|*archenemy*

ar·chae·ol·o·gy, archeology /ˌɑːkiˈɒlədʒi‖ˌɑrkiˈɑ-/ *n* [U] the study of the buried remains of ancient times, such as houses, pots, tools, and weapons —**-gical** /ˌɑːkɪəˈlɒdʒɪkəl‖ˌɑrkɪəˈlɑ-/ *adj* —**-gically** *adv* [Wa4,5] —**-gist** /ˌɑkiˈɒlədʒəst‖ˌɑrkiˈɑ-/ *n*

ar·cha·ic /ɑːˈkeɪ-ɪk‖ɑr-/ *adj* belonging to the past; no longer used —see OLD (USAGE) —**~ally** *adv* [Wa4]

ar·cha·is·m /ɑːˈkeɪ-ɪzəm, ˈɑːkeɪ-‖ˈɑrki-/ *n* a word or phrase no longer in general use

arch·an·gel /ˈɑːkeɪndʒəl‖ˈɑrk-/ *n* a chief ANGEL (1) in the Jewish, Christian, and Muslim religions

arch·bish·op /ˌɑːtʃˈbɪʃəp◂‖ˌɑrtʃ-/ *n* (in some branches of the Christian church) a priest in charge of the churches and BISHOPs (1) in a very large area

arch·bish·op·ric /ˌɑːtʃˈbɪʃəprɪk‖ˌɑrtʃ-/ *n* the rank of, position of, period in office of, or church area (ARCHDIOCESE) governed by an ARCHBISHOP

arch·dea·con /ˌɑːtʃˈdiːkən◂‖ˌɑrtʃ-/ *n* (in the ANGLICAN branch of the Christian religion) a priest of high rank who directly serves under a priest of very high rank (BISHOP)

arch·dea·con·ry /ˌɑːtʃˈdiːkənri‖ˌɑrtʃ-/ *n* the rank, position, or house of an ARCHDEACON

arch·di·o·cese /ˌɑːtʃˈdaɪəsəs, -siːs‖ˌɑrtʃ-/ *n* (in several branches of the Christian religion) the church area under the government of an ARCHBISHOP

arch·duke /ˌɑːtʃˈdjuːk◂‖ˌɑrtʃˈduːk◂/ *n* [C;A] a prince of the royal family, esp. of the royal family of Austria in former times

ar·cher /ˈɑːtʃəʳ‖ˈɑr-/ *n* a person who shoots arrows from a piece of bent wood (BOW³ (1)), esp. as a sport or in war in former times

ar·cher·y /ˈɑːtʃəri‖ˈɑr-/ *n* [U] the art or sport of shooting arrows

ar·che·type /ˈɑːkɪtaɪp‖ˈɑr-/ *n* **1** the original idea or model of something, of which others are copies **2** a perfectly typical example of something —**-typal** /ˈɑːkɪtaɪpəl, ˌɑːkɪˈtaɪ-‖ˌɑrkɪˈtaɪ-/ *adj* —**-typical** /ˌɑːkɪˈtɪpɪkəl‖ˌɑr-/ *adj* —**-typically** *adv* [Wa4]

ar·chi·man·drite /ˌɑːkəˈmændraɪt‖ˌɑr-/ *n* the head of a group of holy men (MONK*s*) of an Eastern branch of the Christian church

ar·chi·pel·a·go /ˌɑːkəˈpeləgəʊ‖ˌɑr-/ *n* **-goes** *or* **-gos** **1** a number of small islands making a group **2** an area of sea containing such a group

ar·chi·tect /ˈɑːkətekt‖ˈɑr-/ *n* **1** a person who plans new buildings and sees that they are built properly **2** a person who makes an important plan of any kind

ar·chi·tec·ture /ˈɑːkətektʃəʳ‖ˈɑr-/ *n* [U] **1** the art and science of building, including its planning, making, and ornamentation **2** the style or manner of building, esp. as belonging to a particular country or period of history: *the architecture of ancient Greece* —**-tural** /ˌɑːkəˈtektʃərəl‖ˌɑr-/ *adj* —**-turally** *adv*: *Architecturally (speaking), Venice is very beautiful*

ar·chives /ˈɑːkaɪvz‖ˈɑr-/ *n* [P] **1** old papers, such as records, reports, lists, and letters of a particular group, family, country, etc., kept esp. for historical interest **2** the place where such papers are stored, esp. the place where government and national records are kept

ar·chi·vist /ˈɑːkəvəst‖ˈɑr-/ *n* a person who looks after ARCHIVES

arch·way /ˈɑːtʃweɪ‖ˈɑrtʃ-/ *n* **1** a passage with a roof, esp. one supported on arches **2** an entrance through an arch

-ar·chy /əki, ɑːki‖ərki, ɑrki/ *suffix* [→*n*] government or rule: ANARCHY|MONARCHY

arc·tic /ˈɑːktɪk‖ˈɑr-/ *adj* **1** of or concerning the most northern part of the world **2** very cold

Arctic *n* [*the*+R] the most northern part of the world —opposite **Antarctic**

Arctic Cir·cle /ˌ·· ˈ··/ *n* [*the*+R] an imaginary line (line of LATITUDE (1)) drawn round the world at a certain distance from the most northern point (the North POLE (1)), north of which line there is no darkness for 6 months of each year and little light for the other 6 months —see picture at GLOBE

arc weld·ing /ˌ· ˈ··/ *n* [U] the joining together of pieces of metal by means of an ARC¹ (3) of electricity

-ard /əd‖ərd/ also **-art** /ət‖ərt/— *suffix* [*adj*,(*v*)→*n*] being a person marked by the stated action or quality usu. one that is bad: DRUNKARD|DULLARD

ar·dent /ˈɑːdənt‖ˈɑr-/ *adj* strongly felt; strongly

active; eager; fierce: *He is an ardent supporter of our team* —**~ly** *adv*

ar·dour, *AmE* **ardor** /ˈɑːdəʳ‖ˈɑr-/ *n* [U;C] a strong burning feeling, because of something pleasing; excitement; eagerness: *His political ardour led him into many arguments*

ar·du·ous /ˈɑːdjʊəs‖ˈɑrdʒʊəs/ *adj fml* needing much effort; difficult: *an arduous climb|arduous work* —**~ly** *adv* —**~ness** *n* [U]

are[1] /əʳ; *strong* ɑːʳ/ [Wv1] *pres. t. pl. of* BE

are[2] /ɑːʳ/ *n* a measure of area, equal to 100 square metres (or 119.6 square yards) —see WEIGHTS & MEASURES TABLE

ar·e·a /ˈeərɪə/ *n* **1** [C] a particular space or surface: *You haven't cleaned the area under the table* **2** [C] a part or division of the world, esp. the one around one's home: *There aren't many wild birds in this area.|I am the area salesman for that part of the country* **3** [C;U] the size of a surface measured by multiplying the length by the width **4** [C] a subject or specialist field, as of ideas, work, or activity: *There have been many developments in the area of language teaching*

ar·e·ca /ˈærɪkə, əˈriːkə/ *n* a particular kind of tree (PALM) which grows in southeast Asia and which bears the **areca nut** —see also BETEL

a·re·na /əˈriːnə/ *n* **1** the middle part of a Roman AMPHITHEATRE, used for public sports and fights **2** an enclosed area used for public shows, sports, fights, amusements, etc. **3** a scene or place of activity, esp. of competition or fighting: *The small country became the arena of war between the 2 big powers*

aren't /ɑːnt‖ˈɑrənt/ [Wv1] *contr. of* **1** are not: *They aren't here* **2** *esp. BrE* am not (esp. in the phr. **aren't I**): *I'm your friend, aren't I?*
USAGE There is no completely natural *contr. of* "**am** *I not*?" Compare the following possibilities: 1) (*fml*) *I am your friend, am I not?* 2) (*infml*) *I'm your friend, aren't I?* 3) (*nonstandard*) *I'm your friend, ain't I?*—see CONTR. (USAGE)

a·rête /əˈret, əˈreɪt (*Fr* arɛt)/ *n Fr* a part of a mountain in the form of a long sharp edge with steep sides; RIDGE

ar·gent /ˈɑːdʒənt‖ˈɑr-/ *n* [U] *esp. poet* (the colour of) silver: *He carried an argent shield*

ar·gon /ˈɑːgɒn‖ˈɑrgɑn/ *n* [U] a chemically inactive gas that is a simple substance (ELEMENT (6)), found in the air, and used in some electric lights

ar·got /ˈɑːgəʊ‖ˈɑrgət (*Fr* argo)/ *n* [U;C] *Fr* speech spoken and understood by only a small class of people, esp. thieves

ar·gu·a·ble /ˈɑːgjʊəbəl‖ˈɑr-/ *adj* **1** [B] doubtful in some degree: *That their decision was the best one is arguable* **2** [B;F5] able to be supported with reasons: *It is arguable that the criminal is a necessary member of society* —**-bly** *adv*: *Arguably, the criminal is a necessary member of society*

ar·gue /ˈɑːgjuː‖ˈɑr-/ *v* **1** [I∅;T1,5] to provide reasons for or against (something), esp. clearly and in proper order: *He argues well.|They argued the case for hours.|He argued that she should not go* **2** [I∅ (*against; about/over* and/or *with*)] to reason strongly in defence of one's opinions and in opposition to those of others: *He is always ready to argue (about politics) (with George)* **3** [T1,5:X (*to be*) 1,7,9 *no pass.*] *lit* to show; SUGGEST (4): *The way he spends money argues him to be rich|a rich man|that he is rich* **4** [T5,5b] to give reasons to prove or try to prove: *The scientist argued that his discovery had changed the course of history* **5** [I∅ (*with, against, about*)] to disagree in words; fight with words; quarrel: *Do what you are told and don't argue (with me)* **6** [T1+*into* or *out of*] to persuade (someone) by showing reasons for or against, often with strong feeling: *She argued him into/out of his decision.|to argue Jim out of leaving his job*

ar·gu·ment /ˈɑːgjʊmənt‖ˈɑrgjə-/ *n* **1** [C (*for, against,* 5)] a reason given to support or disprove something: *There are many arguments against smoking/that one should not smoke* **2** [U] the use of reason to persuade someone: *We should try to settle this affair by argument not by fighting* **3** [C] a disagreement, esp. one that is noisy; quarrel: *The argument made her cry* **4** [C] *lit* a short account of the story or subject of a book, poem, etc.
USAGE This noun comes from both meanings of the verb **argue**; "quarrel" and "reason": *I had an* **argument** *with George over politics* (=a quarrel).|*I accepted his* **argument** *that we should increase taxation* (=reasoning).

ar·gu·men·ta·tive /ˌɑːgjʊˈmentətɪv‖ˌɑrgjə-/ *adj* (of a person) liking to argue —**~ly** *adv*: *She made her opinions known very argumentatively*

ar·gy-bar·gy /ˌɑːdʒi ˈbɑːdʒi‖ˌɑrdʒi ˈbɑr-/ *n* [C;U] *infml, esp. BrE* an argument or quarrel that is usu. noisy but not very serious

a·ri·a /ˈɑːrɪə/ *n* a song that is sung by only one person in a particular type of musical play (OPERA or ORATORIO)

-a·ri·an /eərɪən/ *suffix* [*n*→*adj, n*] (typical of) someone who practises or believes in: *very* AUTHORITARIAN|*a* VEGETARIAN

ar·id /ˈærɨd/ *adj* **1** (of land or a country) having so little rain as to be very dry and unproductive **2** not leading to any really new discoveries: *arid scientific studies concerned only with dry facts* **3** uninteresting; dull —**~ity** /əˈrɪdɨti/ *n* [U] —**~ly** /ˈærɨdli/ *adv*

Ar·ies /ˈeəriːz, ˈæri-iːz/ *n* **1** [R] the first division (sign) in a belt of stars (the ZODIAC), represented by a male sheep (RAM) **2** [R] the group of stars (CONSTELLATION) formerly in this division or sign **3** [Wn3;C] a person born under this sign (between March 21 and April 19) —see picture at PLANET

a·right /əˈraɪt/ *adv* [Wa5] *lit* correctly; properly: *Have I understood you aright?*

a·rise /əˈraɪz/ *v* **arose** /əˈrəʊz/, **arisen** /əˈrɪzən/ [I∅] **1** to come into being or to notice; happen; appear: *Difficulties will arise as we do the work.|A strong wind arose and blew our boat onto the rocks* **2** *rare* to move or go upward **3** *old use or poet* to get up, as from sitting or lying; stand up: *"I will arise and go now, and go to Innisfree"* (W. B. Yeats) —see RISE (USAGE)

ar·is·toc·ra·cy /ˌærɨˈstɒkrəsi‖-ˈstɑ-/ *n* **1** [(*the*) GC] the people of the highest social class, esp. people from noble families and with titles of rank —see also UPPER CLASS **2** [C] the finest, best, richest, or most powerful members of any group or class, in any activity **3** [U] government by people regarded as best or as belonging to the highest social rank, esp. a rank depending on birth or wealth

ar·is·to·crat /ˈærɨstəkræt, əˈrɪ-‖əˈrɪ-/ *n* **1** a member of an ARISTOCRACY, esp. a person from a noble family and with a title of rank **2** the finest example of a group or type: *Drink Rossignol, the aristocrat of table wines!*

ar·is·to·crat·ic /ˌærɨstəˈkrætɪk, əˌrɪ-‖əˌrɪ-/ *adj* of, like, or suitable for an ARISTOCRAT —**~ally** *adv* [Wa4]

a·rith·me·tic[1] /əˈrɪθmətɪk/ *n* [U] **1** the science of numbers —compare MATHEMATICS **2** the adding, subtracting, multiplying, etc., of numbers; calculation by numbers

ar·ith·met·ic[2] /ˌærɪθˈmetɪk/ also **-ical** /ɪkəl/— *adj* [Wa5] of or concerning ARITHMETIC —**~ally** *adv* [Wa4,5]: *We found the answer arithmetically*

a·rith·me·ti·cian /əˌrɪθməˈtɪʃən/ *n* a person who is skilled in or who studies ARITHMETIC

arithmetic pro·gres·sion /ˌ··ˌ·· ·ˈ··/ also **arithmetical progression** /ˌ··ˌ··· ·ˈ··/— *n* a set of numbers each of which is more or less than the one before it by a fixed amount (as in *2, 4, 6, 8, 10*)

ark /ɑːk‖ɑrk/ *n* (in the Bible) a large ship, esp. the one built by Noah (**Noah's ark**) in which he saved his family and 2 of every kind of animal from the flood that covered the world

Ark of the Cov·e·nant /ˌ· · · ˈ···/ *n* [*the*+R] a box that represented to the Jews the presence of God and which contained the laws of their religion

arm[1] /ɑːm‖ɑrm/ *n* **1** either of the 2 upper limbs of a human being or other animal that stands on 2 legs: *She carried the box under her arm* —see picture at HUMAN **2** something that is shaped like or moves like an arm: *a long narrow arm of the sea* —see pictures at EYE[1], SOUND[3] **3** the part of a garment, such as a coat, that covers the arm **4** the part of a chair on which the arm rests **5** a large branch of a tree **6** a part or division of a group that works at a particular activity, subject, etc. **7** power or force (esp. in the phr. **the (long) arm of the law**) **8 arm in arm** (of 2 people) with the arm of one person being passed through the bent arm of the other **9 at arm's length** as far away from the body as the length of an arm; at a safe distance away **10 keep somebody at arm's length** to avoid being friendly with somebody **11 in arms** (of a baby, child, etc.) not yet able to walk: *He's still only a* **babe in arms** **12 with open arms** gladly and eagerly: *She welcomed them with open arms* —**~less** *adj*

arm[2] *v* **1** [Wv5;T1;I∅: (*with*)] to supply with, fit with, or have, weapons or armour: *The crowd were armed with broken bottles.*|*I warn you that I am armed.*|*The country armed (itself) in preparation for war* **2** [T1 (*with*)] to supply with or give what is needed for a purpose: *The politician was armed with many facts and figures*

arm[3] *n* (*in comb.*) a division or branch of a country's armed forces, such as the air force, army, or navy: *Our air arm bombed the enemy*

ar·ma·da /ɑːˈmɑːdə‖ɑr-/ *n* [GC] *lit* a collection (FLEET) of armed ships: *The Spanish Armada sailed to England in 1588*

ar·ma·dil·lo /ˌɑːməˈdɪləʊ‖ˌɑr-/ *n* **-los** [Wn1] a small animal native to the warm parts of the Americas, covered in hard bands of bonelike shell

ar·ma·ment /ˈɑːməmənt‖ˈɑr-/ *n* **1** [C *often pl.*] the arms and other fighting material of an army, navy, etc. **2** [C *often pl.*] the weapons and armour for defence on a warship, aircraft, etc. **3** [C *often pl.*] an armed force or the total armed forces of a country **4** [U] the act of arming a country in preparation for war

ar·ma·ture /ˈɑːmətʃəʳ‖ˈɑr-/ *n* **1** the part of an electricity-making machine (DYNAMO) that moves and in which the electricity is made **2** the part of an electric motor in which the movement is produced **3** a piece of soft iron on the end of a MAGNET (1) to keep it strong **4** an iron bar in an instrument (such as an electric bell) moved by a MAGNET (1) **5** a frame that supports a figure of wax, clay, etc., while it is being made by the artist

arm·band /ˈɑːmbænd‖ˈɑrm-/ *n* a band of material worn round the arm to show official position, power, etc.

arm·chair /ˈɑːmtʃeəʳ, ˌɑːmˈtʃeəʳ‖ˈɑrm-, ˌɑrm-/ *n* a chair with supports for the arms —see picture at LIVING ROOM

armchair crit·ic /ˌ·· ˈ··/ *n often derog* a person who judges the work of others and gives advice without experiencing the practical difficulties

armed /ɑːmd‖ɑrmd/ *adj* [(*with, for*)] **1** carrying or supplied with weapons **2** having what is necessary, such as tools: *He was armed for the job*

armed forc·es /ˌ· ˈ··/ *n* [(*the*) P] the military forces of a country, usu. the army, navy, and air force

armed ser·vic·es /ˌ· ˈ···/ also **services**— *n* [(*the*) P] the armed forces, esp. during times of peace

arm·ful /ˈɑːmfʊl‖ˈɑrm-/ *n* all that a person can hold in one or both arms: *She brought in an armful of fresh flowers from the garden.*|*several armfuls*|*flowers by the armful!*

arm·hole /ˈɑːmhəʊl‖ˈɑrm-/ *n* a hole in a shirt, coat, etc., through which the arm is put

ar·mi·stice /ˈɑːmɨstɨs‖ˈɑrm-/ *n* an agreement made during a war to stop fighting, usu. for a limited period of time

arm·let /ˈɑːmlɨt‖ˈɑrm-/ *n* **1** a band of material worn round the arm for ornament or to show official position; ARMBAND **2** something shaped like a little arm: *an armlet of the sea*

ar·mo·ri·al /ɑːˈmɔːrɪəl‖ɑrˈmo-/ *adj* [Wa5] of or concerning a COAT OF ARMS

ar·mour, *AmE* **armor** /ˈɑːməʳ‖ˈɑr-/ *n* [U] **1** strong protective metal covering on fighting vehicles, ships, and aircraft **2** the vehicles with such covering, as compared with soldiers on foot or unprotected vehicles **3** strong protective metal or leather covering as worn in former times by noble fighting men and their horses **4** a protective covering of plants or animals of any type

armour-clad, *AmE* **armor-clad** /ˈ·· ·/ *adj* covered in ARMOUR PLATE: *armour-clad warships*

ar·moured, *AmE* **armored** /ˈɑːməd‖ˈɑrmərd/ *adj* **1** covered with or protected by armour: *armoured vehicles* **2** having fighting vehicles (such as TANKs (2)) and weapons protected by armour: *an armoured division*

armoured car /ˌ·· ˈ·/ *n* a military vehicle protected with light armour and usu. with a powerful gun (such as a MACHINEGUN)

ar·mour·er, *AmE* **armorer** /ˈɑːmərəʳ‖ˈɑr-/ *n* **1** a person who makes and repairs weapons and armour **2** a person in charge of weapons and other instruments of war

armour plate /ˌ·· ˈ·‖ˈ·· ·/ *n* [U] specially hardened metal used as a protective covering for vehicles of war —**armour-plated** /ˌ·· ˈ··‖ˈ·· ˌ··/ *adj*: *armour-plated warships*

ar·mour·y, *AmE* **armory** /ˈɑːməri‖ˈɑr-/ *n* a place where weapons and other instruments of war are stored

arm·pit /ˈɑːmˌpɪt‖ˈɑrm-/ *n* the hollow place under the arm at the shoulder —see picture at HUMAN

arms /ɑːmz‖ɑrmz/ *n* [P] **1** weapons of war **2** COAT OF ARMS **3 bear arms** *lit* to be or serve as a soldier **4 lay down one's arms** to stop fighting and yield; SURRENDER[1] (1) **5 take up arms** *lit* **a** to get ready to fight with weapons **b** to become a soldier **6 under arms** (of soldiers) having weapons; armed: *The country kept 50,000 men under arms at all times* **7 up in arms** *infml* **a** having weapons and being ready to show disobedience to a government or other force **b** very angry and ready to argue, quarrel, or fight: *The women are up in arms over/about their low rate of pay*

arms race /ˈ· ·/ *n* a struggle between unfriendly countries in which each tries to produce more and better weapons of war than the other

ar·my /ˈɑːmi‖ˈɑr-/ *n* **1** [(*the*)] the military forces of a country, esp. those trained to fight on land **2** a large body of people armed and trained for war **3** any large group, esp. one that is united for some purpose: *an army of workers/ants*

army corps /ˈ·· ·/ *n* **army corps** [Wn3;GC] one of the main parts into which an army is divided

army list /ˈ·· ·/ *n BrE* the official list of officers

within the British army COMMISSIONs

a·ro·ma /ə'rəʊmə/ *n* **1** a strong usu. pleasant smell: *the aroma of hot coffee* **2** an appearance, feeling, or sensation, considered typical of some quality: *There was an aroma of wealth in the room*

ar·o·mat·ic /ˌærə'mætɪk/ *adj* having a strong pleasant smell: *Aromatic plants are often used in cooking* —**~ally** *adv* [Wa4]

a·rose /ə'rəʊz/ *past t. of* ARISE

a·round[1] /ə'raʊnd/ *adv* [Wa5] *AmE or not fml* **1** on all sides; about; in every direction: *He looked around but could see nobody.|Why are all these books lying around?* **2** [F] in some place near; about; in the area: *She is around somewhere.|I'll wait around for a while* **3** all over the place or from one place to another; about; here and there: *I travelled around for a few years.|"Miss Baker suggested I show you around."* (SEU S.) **4** near in time, number, etc.; about: *around 10 o'clock|around 60 people* **5** *esp. AmE* so as to face the opposite direction; round: *He turned around when he heard a noise behind him* **6** *esp. AmE* so as to move in a circle; round: *turning around and around* **7** [E] *esp. AmE* in circular measurement; round: *a tree 5 feet around* **8** [F] *infml* being in existence or activity; about: *the most productive of the artists (who are) around today|"There just weren't any girls around at all"* (SEU S.) **9 get around to** *infml* to arrive at; find time for (talking about a subject, doing a job, etc.) **10 have been around** *infml* to have had lots of experience, esp. in different places: *Listen, my boy, I've been around and I know one or 2 things about life* **11 up and around** *infml esp. AmE* out of bed after illness; up and about —see also GET AROUND, GET AROUND TO

around[2] *prep* **1** on all sides of; all round; surrounding: *We sat around the table.|He put a frame around the picture* **2** *not fml* in some place near (to); in the area of: *He lives somewhere around London.|Stay around the garden* **3** from one place to another in; here and there in: *I travelled around the world for a few years* **4** so as to have a centre or base in: *The society was built around a belief in God* **5** so as to avoid or get past; round: *Let's go around the town, not through it.|(fig.) How can we get around the new taxes and keep some more money for ourselves?* —see ROUND (USAGE)

a·rouse /ə'raʊz/ *v* [T1] **1** to cause to wake; ROUSE (1): *We aroused him from his deep sleep* **2** to cause to become active; bring into being: *Her movements aroused him sexually*

ar·peg·gi·o /ɑː'pedʒiəʊ‖ɑr-/ *n* **-gios** the notes of a musical CHORD played separately, usu. from the lowest to the highest, rather than all at once

ar·que·bus /'ɑːkw$\frac{1}{3}$bəs‖'ɑr-/ also **harquebus**— *n* a kind of movable gun (used in former times) that had to be rested on a Y-shaped support when fired

arr. *written abbrev. for:* **1** ARRANGED (3) (by): *music by Mozart, arr. Britten* **2 a** arrive **b** arrival

ar·rack, arak /'ærək, -ək/ *n* [U] a very strong alcoholic drink (SPIRIT[1] (12)) made in Eastern countries

ar·raign /ə'reɪn/ *v* [T1 (*for*)] **1** to call or bring before a court of law, esp. to face a serious charge **2** to charge or attack in words —**~ment** *n* [U;C]

ar·range /ə'reɪndʒ/ *v* **1** [T1] to set in a good or pleasing order: *She arranged the flowers well.|He arranged his papers before starting to write* **2** [T1 (*for*), 3,5a,b,c;6a,b: (*with*)] also (*v prep* [T1,4 (*with*) *no pass.*]) **arrange about**— to plan in advance; prepare: *I have arranged a taxi (for us).|I arranged to meet them at 10 o'clock.|I arranged that I should meet them here.|I arranged with them to meet at 10 o'clock.|I've arranged (about the taxi) (with my firm)* **3** [T1 (*for*)] to set out (a piece of music) in a certain way, as for different instruments: *I have arranged this old piece of music for the piano*

arrange for *v prep* [T1;V3: (*with*)] to take action to cause or get: *I've arranged (with my firm) for a taxi (to pick us up at 10 o'clock)*

ar·range·ment /ə'reɪndʒmənt/ *n* **1** [U] the act of putting into or of being put into order: *The arrangement of the flowers only took a few minutes.|the art of flower arrangement* **2** [C] something that has been put in order: *There were some beautiful arrangements at the flower show.|a beautiful flower arrangement* **3** [C (*about, for, with,* 3)] something arranged, planned or agreed in a particular way: *I have an arrangement with my bank by which they let me use their money before I have been paid.|We could make an arrangement to meet at 10 o'clock.|Let's make arrangements for getting there on time* **4** [U] the act of making an agreement or settlement **5** [U] the setting out of a piece of music in a certain way, as for different instruments: *the arrangement of an old song for the piano* **6** [C] the result of this: *It is an arrangement by the musician himself*

ar·rant /'ærənt/ *adj* [A] *lit derog* very bad; complete: *an arrant thief|He talked arrant nonsense*

ar·ras /'ærəs/ *n old use* **1** a large cloth with pictures woven into it and hung on a wall in former times; TAPESTRY **2 behind the arras** *humor* in/into hiding; hidden

ar·ray[1] /ə'reɪ/ *v* [T1 *often pass.*] *fml or lit* **1** to set in order: *The soldiers were arrayed on the opposite hill* **2** to dress, esp. splendidly: *arrayed for her wedding*

array[2] *n* **1** a fine show or collection, as in a shop window: *a beautiful array of dress materials|(fig.) an array of information to support his claim* **2** an ordered force or army: *The crowd were met by an array of policemen* **3** [*usu. sing.*] clothes, esp. those that are splendid or for a special occasion: *She put on her finest array*

ar·rears /ə'rɪəz‖-ərz/ *n* [P] **1** money that is owed from the past and should have been paid **2** work that is still waiting to be done **3 in arrears a** in the state of owing money, esp. for something that should be paid regularly **b** (esp. of money) being owed

ar·rest[1] /ə'rest/ *v* [T1] **1** to seize in the name of the law and usu. put in prison: *The policeman arrested the thief* **2** to bring (a movement or development) to an end; stop: *The doctor arrested the growth of the disease* **3** [Wv4] to catch and fix (esp. somebody's attention): *The bright lights arrested the boy's attention.|an arresting statement*

arrest[2] *n* **1** [U;C] the act of ARRESTing[1] (1) or of being ARRESTed: *The arrest of the thief was quickly performed.|The police made several arrests* **2** *rare or tech* the act of stopping or the state of being stopped: *the arrest of the dangerous disease by means of the new drug* **3 under arrest** held as a prisoner, esp. by the police: *He is under arrest.|He was put/placed under arrest*

ar·rest·er wires /ə'restə waɪəz‖-tər waɪərz/ *n* [P] an arrangement of wires for reducing the speed of naval aircraft landing on a ship (AIRCRAFT CARRIER) when caught by the **arrester hook** on the aircraft —compare CATAPULT[1] (2)

ar·riv·al /ə'raɪvəl/ *n* **1** [U;(C)] the act of arriving: *The arrival of the aircraft has been delayed.|On (my) arrival home I was greeted by my parents* **2** [C] a person who or thing that arrives or has arrived: *There were several new arrivals in the school.|The new arrival was a large healthy baby boy*

ar·rive /ə'raɪv/ *v* [IØ] **1** to reach a place, esp. the end of a journey: *We arrived home late.|No letters arrived this morning* **2** to happen; come: *At last our holidays arrived* **3** (of a baby) to be born: *Her baby* *arrived during the night* **4** to win success or a high place in society: *Now that his books were sold in every shop he felt that he had arrived*

arrive at *v prep* [T1] to reach; come to: *After many hours' talk, the committee arrived at a decision*

ar·ro·gance /ˈærəgəns/ *n* [U] pride and self-importance shown in a way that is rude and disrespectful to others

ar·ro·gant /ˈærəgənt/ *adj* proud and self-important in a rude way that shows no respect for other people: *an arrogant official|arrogant manners* —**~ly** *adv*

ar·ro·gate /ˈærəgeɪt/ *v* [T1 (*to*)] *fml* to take or claim (for oneself) without the right of law: *Having seized power in the country, he arrogated to himself the right to change the law*

ar·row /ˈærəʊ/ *n* **1** a thin straight stick with a point at one end and usu. feathers at the other. It is shot in fighting or sport from a long piece of bent wood (BOW[3] (1)) **2** a sign like an arrow (→) used to show direction or the position of something

ar·row·head /ˈærəʊhed/ *n* a pointed piece of stone or metal fixed to the front end of an arrow

ar·row·root /ˈærəʊruːt, ˈærəruːt/ *n* [U] a kind of flour made from the root of a certain plant and used as a food for sick people and animals

arse /ɑːs‖ɑrs/ *n BrE taboo sl* **1** (*AmE* **ass**)—BOTTOM (5b) **2** a stupid annoying person

arse a·bout also **arse a·round**— *v adv* [I∅] *BrE taboo sl* to waste time: *Stop arsing about and get back to work*

ar·se·nal /ˈɑːsənəl‖ˈɑr-/ *n* **1** a government building where weapons and explosives are made or stored **2** a store of weapons: *The police found an arsenal of knives and guns in the murderer's house*

ar·se·nic¹ /ˈɑːsənɪk‖ˈɑr-/ *n* [U] **1** a grey simple substance (ELEMENT (6)) **2** a chemical form of this that is poisonous, used in medicine and for killing rats

ar·sen·ic² /ɑːˈsenɪk‖ɑr-/ also **-ical** /-kəl/— *adj* [Wa5;A;(B)] of or containing ARSENIC

ar·son /ˈɑːsən‖ˈɑr-/ *n* [U] the criminal act of setting fire to property in order to cause destruction —**~ist** *n*

art¹ /ɑːt‖ɑrt/ [Wv1] **thou art** *old use or bibl* (when talking to one person) you are

art² *n* **1** [U] the making or expression of what is beautiful or true, esp. in a manner that can be seen, as in a painting **2** [U] things produced in this way (esp. in the phr. **work of art**): *We studied the art of the early Japanese* **3** [U] fine skill in such making or expression, or in the making or doing of anything: *The art of painting well is not easily learnt.|He is good at the art of making friends* **4** [C] a skilful method of doing something, esp. something difficult: *There is an art to making bread*

-art /ət‖ərt/ *suffix* [*adj*, (*v*)→*n*] -ARD: BRAGGART

ar·te·fact /ˈɑːtɪ̈fækt‖ˈɑr-/ *n* ARTIFACT

ar·ter·i·al /ɑːˈtɪəriəl‖ɑr-/ *adj* [Wa5;A;(B)] **1 a** of or like an ARTERY (1) **b** (of blood) which is being sent from the heart: *Arterial blood is bright red* —compare VENOUS (1b) **2** (of a road, railway, etc.) main: *arterial roads leading into London*

ar·ter·i·o·scle·ro·sis /ɑːˌtɪəriəʊsklɪəˈrəʊsɪ̈s, -sklə-‖ɑr-/ *n* [U] a diseased condition in which the walls of certain blood-vessels become hard and thick and so prevent the easy flow of blood; hardening of the arteries (ARTERY (1))

ar·te·ry /ˈɑːtəri‖ˈɑr-/ *n* **1** a blood vessel that carries blood from the heart to the rest of the body —compare VEIN (1) —see picture at RESPIRATORY **2** a main road, railway, river, etc.

ar·te·si·an well /ɑːˌtiːziən ˈwel‖ɑrˌtiːʒən-/ *n* a well in which the water rises to the surface because of the force of the water coming down from the surrounding hills that are higher than the well

art·ful /ˈɑːtfəl‖ˈɑr-/ *adj* **1** cleverly deceitful; full of tricks; CUNNING: *He's very artful and usually succeeds in getting what he wants* —compare ARTLESS **2** skilfully put together; cleverly considered: *That artful arrangement of pieces of wood is made to catch mice* —compare ARTY —**~ly** *adv*: *artfully made* —**~ness** *n* [U]

ar·thri·tis /ɑːˈθraɪtɪ̈s‖ɑr-/ *n* [U] a disease causing pain and swelling in the joints of the body —**-tic** /ɑːˈθrɪtɪk‖ɑr-/ *adj, n*

ar·ti·choke /ˈɑːtɪ̈tʃəʊk‖ˈɑr-/ *n* [C;U] **1** a plant with a leafy kind of flower that may be eaten as a vegetable —see also GLOBE ARTICHOKE **2** also **Jerusalem artichoke**—a plant with a potato-like root that may be eaten as a vegetable

ar·ti·cle¹ /ˈɑːtɪkəl‖ˈɑr-/ *n* **1** a particular or separate thing or object, esp. one of a group: *I am wearing several articles of clothing* **2** a complete piece of writing in a newspaper, magazine, etc.: *Have you read the article on new industries?* **3** a complete or separate part in a written law agreement **4** the words "a" or "an" (**indefinite article**) and "the" (**definite article**)

article² *v* [T1 (*to, with*)] to place under agreement to serve a course of practical training under someone in a profession or trade, as by ARTICLES OF APPRENTICESHIP: *I am articled to a firm of lawyers*

ar·ti·cles /ˈɑːtɪkəlz‖ˈɑr-/ *n* [P] **1** also **articles of ap·pren·tice·ship** /ˌ··· · ·ˈ···/— a written agreement in law between someone learning a profession or job and the employer **2 in articles** working for, while learning from, an employer in accordance with the agreement made between them

ar·tic·u·late¹ /ɑːˈtɪkjʊlɪ̈t‖ɑrˈtɪkjə-/ *adj* **1** expressing or able to express thoughts and feelings clearly, esp. in words **2** (of speech) having clear separate sounds or words **3** having parts connected by joints: *an articulate insect* —**~ly** *adv*

ar·tic·u·late² /ɑːˈtɪkjʊleɪt‖ɑrˈtɪkjə-/ *v* **1** [T1;I∅] to speak: *He articulated (each word) carefully* **2** [T1] to express clearly and effectively: *He articulated his anger* **3** [Wv5;T1] to unite by joints that allow movements: *The bones of our fingers are articulated*

ar·tic·u·lat·ed /ɑːˈtɪkjʊleɪtɪ̈d‖ɑrˈtɪkjə-/ *adj esp. BrE* having parts joined in a way that allows easy movement

ar·tic·u·late·ness /ɑːˈtɪkjʊlɪ̈tnɪ̈s‖ɑrˈtɪkjə-/ *n* [U] the state or quality of being ARTICULATE¹ (1,2) or speaking ARTICULATEly¹ (1,2)

ar·tic·u·la·tion /ɑːˌtɪkjʊˈleɪʃən‖ɑrˌtɪkjə-/ *n* **1** [U] the production of speech sounds: *clear articulation* **2** [U] the expression of thoughts and feelings, esp. in words: *the articulation of one's real feelings* **3** [U] the act of uniting with a joint **4** [C] a joint, esp. in a plant

ar·ti·fact, arte- /ˈɑːtɪ̈fækt‖ˈɑr-/ *n* anything made by man, esp. something useful

ar·ti·fice /ˈɑːtɪ̈fɪ̈s‖ˈɑr-/ *n* **1** [C] a clever arrangement or thing: *The use of mirrors in a room is an artifice to make the room look larger* **2** [U] clever skill; CUNNING **3** [C] a skilful trick, esp. one intended to deceive **4** [U] inventive skill in deceiving

ar·tif·i·cer /ɑːˈtɪfɪ̈səʳ‖ɑr-/ *n* **1** *lit* a skilled workman **2** a naval officer of low rank who works in a ship's engine room

ar·ti·fi·cial /ˌɑːtɪ̈ˈfɪʃəl◂‖ˌɑr-/ *adj* **1** made by man; not natural: *artificial flowers* —see NATURAL (USAGE) **2** made to take the place of a natural product, esp. a clothing material: *artificial silk* **3** lacking true feelings; insincere; unreal: *She welcomed me with an artificial smile* —**~ly** *adv* —**~ity** /ˌɑːtɪ̈fɪʃiˈælɪ̈ti‖ˌɑr-/ *n* [U]

artificial in·sem·i·na·tion /ˌ···· ···ˈ··/ *n* [U;C] the putting of male seed into a female by hand or by means of an instrument, used esp. to improve the quality of cows and horses

artificial res·pi·ra·tion /ˌ···· ··ˈ··/ *n* [U;C] the attempt to make a person who is nearly dead (esp. through drowning) breathe again, as by pressing the chest and moving the arms —see also KISS OF LIFE

ar·til·le·ry /ɑːˈtɪləri‖ɑr-/ *n* [U] **1** large guns, esp. those that are connected to wheels or fixed in one place, as on a ship or in a fort **2** the part of the army trained to use such weapons

ar·ti·san /ˌɑːtɨ̆ˈzæn‖ˈɑrtɨ̆zən/ *n* a skilled workman, esp. in industry

art·ist /ˈɑːtɨ̆st‖ˈɑr-/ *n* **1** a person who practises or works in one of the FINE ARTS, esp. painting **2** a person who shows inventive skill in his work: *He is no ordinary thief; he's an artist* **3** a performer in a show, such as an actor or singer

ar·tiste /ɑːˈtiːst‖ɑr-/ *n* a professional singer, actor, dancer, etc.; ARTIST (3)

ar·tis·tic /ɑːˈtɪstɪk‖ɑr-/ *adj* **1** [Wa5] of, concerning, or typical of art or artists **2** *apprec* made or arranged with inventive skill and imagination; beautiful **3** liking what is well done in art or skilful in producing works of art: *He's very artistic* —**~ally** *adv* [Wa4]

art·ist·ry /ˈɑːtɨ̆stri‖ˈɑr-/ *n* [U] *apprec* inventive imagination and ability; artistic skill

art·less /ˈɑːtləs‖ˈɑr-/ *adj* not trying to deceive or influence others; simple, almost foolish; natural: *an artless village girl* —compare ARTFUL, ARTY —**~ly** *adv* —**~ness** *n* [U]

art nou·veau /ˌɑː nuːˈvəʊ‖ˌɑr- (*Fr* ar nuvo)/ *n* [U] *Fr* a style of art and ornament common at the end of the 19th century in Europe and America, using flowing lines and leaves

arts /ɑːts‖ɑrts/ *n* [P] those subjects or fields of study that are not considered to be part of science, esp. as taught at a university: *History is an arts subject* —see also BA, MA

arts and crafts /ˌ· · ˈ·/ *n* [P] the arts that are concerned with making objects by hand (such as weaving, binding books, making pots, etc.) in such a way that they are both useful and pleasing to look at

art·y /ˈɑːti‖ˈɑrti/ *adj* [Wa1] *often derog* making a show of being interested in art —compare ARTFUL, ARTLESS —**artiness** *n* [U]

art·y-craft·y /ˌɑːti ˈkrɑːfti‖ˌɑrti ˈkræfti/ *AmE usu.* **arts·y-crafts·y** /ˌɑːtsi ˈkrɑːftsi‖ˌɑrtsi ˈkræftsi/— *adj usu. derog* of, using, or making handmade objects or clothes, esp. to a degree that appears foolish: *That arty-crafty family make all their own clothes and look rather odd in them*

ar·um /ˈeərəm/ also **arum lil·y** /ˈ·· ˌ··/— *n* a tall white type of LILY

-a·ry¹ /-əri‖-eri/ *suffix* [→ *n*] **1** a thing belonging to or connected with; place for or of: LIBRARY|AVIARY|OVARY **2** a person belonging to, connected with, or working in or as: MISSIONARY|ADVERSARY|FUNCTIONARY

-ary² *suffix* [*n* → *adj*] of, concerning, or connected with: CUSTOMARY|BUDGETARY

as¹ /əz; *strong* æz/ *adv* **1** to the same degree or amount; equally: *Paul runs fast, but I run just as fast.|I don't run as/so fast.|Paul has a lot of money but I have as much/but I haven't as much/but I haven't so much* **2** *fml* for example, such as; like: *various animals, as cats and dogs* —see AS⁴ (USAGE) **3** (esp. before adjectives and participles) when considered in the stated way: *man as different from the other animals|man as described by scientists|man as compared with other animals* **4 I thought as much!** *infml* I thought so!

as² *conj* **1** (in the pattern *as . . . as . . .*) in or to the same degree in which: *She runs as fast as Paul (does)/me/I (do).|She runs as fast as possible.|She can run as fast as 20 miles an hour.|She doesn't run as/so fast as she used to.|I didn't think she could run as fast as that.|She is as clever as (she is) beautiful.|She works as carefully as she does quickly.|One is as light as the other is heavy.|She likes them as much as Paul* (= "as much as Paul likes them" OR "as much as she likes Paul").|*Those trees can be as big as 20 feet across.|I saw him as recently as last March/as long ago as 1920* —see AS⁴ (USAGE) **2** (in the pattern *the same . . . as . . .*): *This is the same as that.|This is the same as it was before.|This is the same one as/that you had before.|in the same building as my brother* —see also SAME **3** (in the pattern *such . . . as . . .*): *such animals as cats and dogs|animals such as cats and dogs|such guilt as to leave no doubt|such guilt as left no doubt of the court's decision* —see AS⁴ (USAGE); see also SUCH **4** (in the pattern *so . . . as . . .*): *so guilty as to leave no doubt|so as to leave no doubt|not so/as nice as Jean|He did it so as not to be caught* —see also SO **5** in the way or manner that: *Do as I say!* **6** while; when: *She dropped the glass as she stood up/was standing up.|He saw her as they were both getting off the bus* **7** because: *She stayed at home as she had no car.|He saw her, as they were both getting off the bus at the same time* **8** regardless of the degree to which; though: *Improbable as it seems, it's true* (*AmE* also *as improbable as it seems, it's true*) **9** (expressing a relation or PROPORTION) what; in the way that: *2 is to 4 as 8 is to 16.* (2:4 = 8:16)|*As 2 is to 4, (so) 8 is to 16.|As a man lives, so he dies* —see also SAME, SO, SUCH **10 as against** (used to introduce a comparison with something rather different) in comparison with: *The business done this year amounts to £20,000 as against £15,000 last year* **11 as from** on; at; not earlier or later than: *The agreement starts as from March 31* **12 as is** *infml* in the existing condition without change: *I'll sell it to you as (it) is, but don't complain if it doesn't work!* **13 as it is** in reality: *I thought things would get better, but as it is they are getting worse* **14 as it were** in a manner of speaking; so to speak: *He is my best friend, my second self, as it were* **15 as of** AS FROM **16 as of right** *BrE* by right; according to law: *All that money is now yours as of right* **17 as yet** so far; up to the present; up to now; until now: *I have received no answer from him as yet, but the answer will certainly come.|There has been no trouble—as yet!*

USAGE In comparisons, **as . . . as** can be used with or without *not*: *She's* **as** *pretty* **as** *her sister.|He's not* **as** *old* **as** *I am.* In comparisons of this type, **so . . . as** can be used only with *not*; one can say *She's not* **so** *pretty* **as** *her sister*, but one cannot say **She's* **so** *pretty* **as** *her sister.* —see THAN, ME (USAGE)

as³ *pron* **1** in accordance with what: *David, as you know, writes dictionaries.|As you know, David writes dictionaries.|He is a teacher, as is clear from his manner.|He is a teacher, as became clear from his manner.|As I was saying just now, . . .|It is as you told me.|It is just as you like* **2** (esp. before *go*) in accordance with the way in which: *He's quite good, as boys go.|It was very cheap as the prices of cars go these days* **3** *fml* and so: *David works hard, as do my brothers.|David is tall, as are my brothers*

as⁴ *prep* **1** like: *They all rose together as one man* **2** in the state, character, condition, job, etc. of (being): *Man (considered just) as man, without regard for race, religion, . . .|Speaking as a beginner,*

. . .|*He was famous as a soldier.*|*He works as a farmer.*|*They regard her as clever*
USAGE Before a list of examples, use **such as** rather than **as** by itself: *animals* **such as** *horses, cattle, and deer.* —see LIKE (USAGE)

as·bes·tos /æs'bestəs, æz-/ *n* [U] a soft grey material (like a mass of threads) that is dug out of the ground and made into clothes that protect against fire and solid sheets that prevent the spreading of heat

as·cend /ə'send/ *v often fml* **1** [IØ] to go, come, or move upward or to a higher position: *The stairs ascended in a graceful curve.*|*an ascending scale of (musical) notes* **2** [T1] to climb; go up along: *He ascended the stairs* **3 ascend the throne** to become king or queen

as·cen·dan·cy, -dency /ə'sendənsi/ *n* [U (*over*)] governing or controlling influence; power: *He slowly gained ascendancy over the group*

as·cen·dant¹, -dent /ə'sendənt/ *n* **in the ascendant a** having or nearly having a controlling power or influence: *Those ideas were in the ascendant in the 19th Century* **b** (of a sign of the ZODIAC (2)) above the eastern horizon at a particular time, such as someone's birth

ascendant², -dent *adj* **1** moving or directed upward; rising **2** greater in control or influence: *ascendant power*

as·cen·sion /ə'senʃən/ *n* [U] the act of going, coming, or moving upward or to a higher position

Ascension Day /·'·· ·/ *n* [R] the Thursday 40 days after EASTER

as·cent /ə'sent/ *n* **1** the act of going, moving, climbing, or travelling up; act of rising: *We made a successful ascent of the mountain.*|(fig.) *the ascent of man from his original state to modern civilization* **2** a way up; upward slope, path, etc.

as·cer·tain /ˌæsə'teɪn‖ˌæsər-/ *v* [T1,5a,b,6a,b] *fml* to discover (the facts of something); get to know: *I am going to ascertain the truth.*|*I ascertained that he was dead* —**~able** *adj*

as·cet·ic¹ /ə'setɪk/ also (*rare*) **-ical** /-kəl/— *adj* not allowing oneself bodily pleasures; in favour of great simpleness of manner, dress, food, etc. —**~ally** *adv* [Wa4]

ascetic² *n* a person who does not allow himself bodily pleasures, esp. for religious reasons —**~ism** /ə'setəsɪzəm/ *n* [U]

as·cor·bic ac·id /əˌskɔːbɪk 'æsəd‖əˌskɔr-/ *n* [U] VITAMIN C

as·cribe to /ə'skraɪb/ *v prep* [D1 *often pass.*] ATTRIBUTE TO (1,2): *He ascribes his success to skill and hard work.*|*No one knows who wrote that play, but it is usually ascribed to Cyril Tourneur* —**ascribable to** *adj prep*

as·crip·tion /ə'skrɪpʃən/ *n* [U (*to*)] *fml* the act of ascribing (ASCRIBE TO): *The ascription of their failure to lack of money is not honest*

a·sep·sis /eɪ'sepsəs, ə-/ *n* [U] *tech* absence of disease-causing bacteria

a·sep·tic /eɪ'septɪk, ə-/ *adj tech* (of a wound or something to cover a wound) free from bacteria; clean —**~ally** *adv* [Wa4]

a·sex·u·al /eɪ'sekʃʊəl, -'seksjʊəl/ *adj* [Wa5] **1** without sex or sexual organs **2** having no interest in sexual relations —**~ly** *adv* —**~ity** /ˌeɪsekʃʊ'æləti, ˌeɪseksjʊ-/ *n*

as for /'· ·/ *prep sometimes derog* with regard to; concerning: *Here I am; as for the others, they'll arrive later.*|*I could stay for one or 2 days, but as for staying a week—that would be impossible*
USAGE **As for** introduces a subject connected with what was being spoken of before, so it cannot come at the start of a conversation: *You can have a bed, but* **as for** *the children, they'll have to sleep on the floor.* In *BrE*, **as to** is also sometimes used in sentences like this. **With reference/respect/regard to** express the same idea in a more *fml* way, but they can also begin a new subject, especially in business letters: **With reference to** *your recent complaint . . .* —see also AS TO (USAGE)

as from /'· ·/ *prep* AS OF: *As from today you are in charge*

ash¹ /æʃ/ *n* **1** [C] a forest tree common in Britain that produces black BUDs (young unopened flowers) **2** [U] the hard wood of this tree

ash² *n* [U *often pl. with sing. meaning*] the soft grey powder that remains after something has been burnt: *Clean the ash/ashes from the fireplace.*|*The cigarette ash fell on her dress.*|*The house burnt to ashes* —see also SACKCLOTH **and ashes**

a·shamed /ə'ʃeɪmd/ *adj* **1** [F (*of*), F3,5a] feeling shame, guilt or sorrow (because of something done): *You should be ashamed (of yourself/your behaviour)!*|*You should be ashamed to tell such lies.*|*He was ashamed that he had lied.*|*He was ashamed of asking/having asked such a simple question* **2** [F3] unwilling to do something through fear of feeling shame or of being laughed at: *He was ashamed to ask such a simple question* —**~ly** /ə'ʃeɪmədli/ *adv*

ash·bin /'æʃˌbɪn/ *n esp. AmE* DUSTBIN

ash·can /'æʃkæn/ *n AmE* DUSTBIN

ash·en¹ /'æʃən/ *adj* [Wa5;A;(B)] made of ASH wood

ashen² *adj* **1** ash-coloured; pale grey: *His ashen face showed how much the news had shocked him* **2** [Wa5] consisting of ashes

ash·es /'æʃəz/ *n* [P] the remains of a dead body after burning (CREMATION): *Her ashes were scattered over the sea*

a·shore /ə'ʃɔːʳ‖ə'ʃor/ *adv* [F] **1** on, onto, or to the shore or land: *We came ashore from the boat* **2 all ashore that's going ashore** (an order to visitors to leave a ship before it sails)

ash·tray /'æʃtreɪ/ *n* a small dish for the ashes of cigarettes —see picture at LIVING ROOM

Ash Wednes·day /ˌ· '··/ *n* [R] the Wednesday which is the first day of LENT

ash·y /'æʃi/ *adj* **1** [Wa5] like, consisting of, or covered with ash **2** [Wa1] ash-coloured; grey; ASHEN² (1)

A·sian /'eɪʃən, 'eɪʒən‖'eɪʒən, 'eɪʃən/ also **A·si·at·ic** /ˌeɪʃi'ætɪk, ˌeɪzi-, ˌeɪʒi-‖ˌeɪʒi-, ˌeɪzi-/— *n, adj* (a native) of Asia

a·side¹ /ə'saɪd/ *adv* **1** to or towards the side: *She stepped aside to let him pass.*|(fig.) *The old leader stepped aside to allow an able young woman to be elected* **2** out of the way; away (esp. for a limited time): *He put his work aside* **3** being dismissed from one's thoughts; not being considered: *Joking aside, we really must do something* **4 aside from** APART from **5 set aside a** to put out of the way or out of one's thoughts **b** to make of no effect: *The decision of the court set aside the new law* **c** to put to one side for a special purpose: *a room set aside for playing card games*

aside² *n* **1** words spoken by an actor to those watching the play, and not intended to be heard by the other characters **2** a remark in a low voice not intended to be heard by everyone present **3** a remark or story told during a speech but which has no part in the speech; DIGRESSION

aside from /·'· ·/ *prep esp. AmE* APART FROM

as if /· '·/ also **as though**— *conj* **1** as it would be if: *It was (as hot) as if we were on the sun* **2** as one would do if: *He fought (as hard) as if his life was/were in danger.*|*He shook his head as if (he wanted) to say "No"* **3** that: *It seemed as if the night would never end.*|*Why doesn't she buy me a drink? It isn't as if she had no money!* (= The reason is not that she is without money) **4** (used for showing the neg. of what is said when expressing strong feeling): *As if I cared!* (=I don't care) **5 look as if** to seem that; seem to be: *"It looks as if you have got no admirers"* (SEU W.)

as·i·nine /ˈæsǝ̇naɪn/ *adj* foolish; stupid: *What an asinine remark!*

ask /ɑːsk‖æsk/ *v* **1** [T1,6a,6b;D1 ((*fml*) of), 6a,b; I∅] to call on (a person) for an answer (to); request (information) from someone: *Ask him!|I asked who he was/where to go.|Ask him who he is/where to go.|You must ask if you want to know something.|Ask him his name.|He asked her a question.|(fml) He asked a question of her.|She asked about his health* **2** [T1 (*for*), 3,5c;V3;I∅ (*for*)] to make a request for or to: *She asked his advice/him for advice.|They asked to go for a walk.|I asked that I (should) be allowed to see her.|She asked him to wake her at 6 o'clock.|She asked for his advice.|She asked to be woken at 6 o'clock.|She asked ((for) permission) to go.|Don't ask (me) for money!|Has anyone asked for me at the hotel?* **3** [T1 (*for, of*)] to demand (something, such as a price); expect: *He is asking a lot of money (for his house).|The job asks a great deal (of me)* **4** [T1;V3: (*for, to*)] to invite: *I have asked some friends (for dinner).|I have asked them to come (for dinner) (for/to tea).|I asked her to my house.|I asked her in/up/down for a drink.|I asked her (to come) out (with me) (for the evening).|I asked her (to come) over (to my home)*
USAGE **Ask** is the usual verb for questions: *He* **asked** *a question.|He* **asked** *(them) where they lived.|"Where do you live?" he* **asked**.*|If you don't know, you must* **ask**.|**Inquire** (=*enquire*) has the same meaning and could be used in the 3rd and 4th of these sentences, or in the 2nd without "them": *He* **inquired** *where they lived.|"Where do you live?" he* **inquired**. One **questions** or (more formal) **interrogates** a person, which means asking him many questions: *The police* **questioned/interrogated** *the prisoner.* (This may mean that they also used force.)

ask af·ter also (*fml*) **enquire after, inquire after**— *v prep* [T1 *pass. rare*] *infml* to enquire about the health or well-being of (someone): *"My mother asked after you." "How kind of her!"*

a·skance /ǝˈskæns, ǝˈskɑːns‖ǝˈskæns/ *adv* [Wa5] without liking or pleasure; with distrust (only in the phrase **look askance**): *She looked askance at the dirty man.|She looked at the dirty man askance*

a·skew /ǝˈskjuː/ *adv* [F] not straight or in the proper manner: *He wore his hat askew*

ask for *v prep* [T1 *no pass.*] *infml* (esp. in tenses with the *-ing* form) to behave so as to cause (something bad) (esp. in the phrs. **ask for trouble/it**): *If you climb mountains in misty weather, you're (really) asking for trouble!|When he went on calling me a fool, I said "You asked for it!" and hit him* —see also ASK, HEAD FOR

asking price /ˈ·· ·/ *n* [*usu. sing.*] the price that a seller states he wants for his goods

a·slant[1] /ǝˈslɑːnt‖ǝˈslænt/ *adv, adj* [F] not straight or level; sloping: *He wore his hat aslant*

aslant[2] *prep rare* across in a sloping position

a·sleep /ǝˈsliːp/ *adj* [Wa5;F] **1** sleeping: *He was asleep* **2** (of an arm or leg that has been in one position too long) unable to feel; NUMB **3 fall asleep a** to go into a state of sleep **b** *euph* to die **4 sound asleep** completely asleep

as long as /· ˈ· ·/ *conj* **1** also (*esp. BrE*) **so long as**— if and only if: *You may borrow this book as long as you promise to give it back* **2** *AmE* (usu. at the beginning of a sentence and used with *be* or the *-ing*-form) since; it being true that: *As long as you're up, get me a drink.|As long as you're going, I'll go too*

as of /ˈ· ·/ *prep* **1** also **as from**— from (the time stated): *As of today you are in charge* **2 as of right** *BrE* by right; according to law: *All that money is now yours as of right*

as op·posed to /· ·ˈ· ·/ *prep* as completely different from; in CONTRAST or opposition to: *John likes rice, as opposed to Mary, who hates it*

asp /æsp/ *n* a small poisonous snake of North Africa: *Cleopatra was bitten by an asp*

as·par·a·gus /ǝˈspærǝgǝs/ *n* **asparagus** [Wn3;U;C] a plant whose young green stems are eaten as a vegetable —see picture at VEGETABLE[1]

as·pect /ˈæspekt/ *n* **1** [C] *lit* appearance, esp. an expression of the face: *We became afraid of the angry aspect of the man* **2** [C] a particular side of a many-sided state of affairs, idea, plan, etc.: *You have only considered one aspect of the difficulty, but there are many* **3** [C9] the direction in which a window, room, front of a building, etc., faces: *The house has a south-facing aspect* —see VIEW (USAGE) **4** [C] the position of the stars in regard to each other, seen by some as influencing the affairs of man **5** [U;C] the form a verb takes to mark the difference in time, as between a continuing action (as in *is singing*) and a completed action (as in *sang*)

as·pec·tu·al /æˈspektʃʊǝl/ *adj* [Wa5] *tech* of or concerning the ASPECT (5) of a verb —**~ly** *adv*

as·pen /ˈæspǝn/ *n* [Wn1] a tall tree whose leaves move in the slightest wind

as·per·i·ty /æˈsperǝ̇ti, ǝ-/ *n fml* **1** [U] roughness of manner or temper: *He spoke with asperity about our bad work* **2** [C *usu. pl.*] a bitter unkind word or remark **3** [U;C *usu. pl.*] roughness, unpleasantness, bitterness, etc.: *We suffered the asperity of a northern winter.|The asperities of life in prison nearly killed me* **4** [U] roughness of surface; uneven appearance **5** [C] a rough spot or part

as·per·sion /ǝˈspɜːʃǝn, -ʒǝn‖-ɜr-/ *n fml, becoming pomp or humor* an unkind or harmful remark (esp. in the phr. **cast aspersions on/upon**): *The newspaper* CAST *aspersions on his ability to write good plays*

as·phalt[1] /ˈæsfælt‖ˈæsfɔlt/ *n* [U] a black sticky material that is firm when it hardens, used for the surface of roads: *an asphalt road (surface)*

asphalt[2] *v* [T1] to cover (esp. a road) with ASPHALT

as·pho·del /ˈæsfǝdel/ *n* **1** a plant with white, yellow, or pink flowers **2** a flower of this plant

as·phyx·i·a /æsˈfɪksɪǝ, ǝ-/ *n* [U] *rare or tech* asphyxiation (ASPHYXIATE)

as·phyx·i·ate /æsˈfɪksieɪt, ǝ-/ *v* [T1;I∅] *fml* to (cause to) be unable to breathe air; esp. to (cause to) die in this way; SUFFOCATE —**-ation** /æsˌfɪksiˈeɪʃǝn, ǝ-/ *n* [U]

as·pic /ˈæspɪk/ *n* [U] a clear brownish jelly made from meat bones

as·pi·dis·tra /ˌæspǝ̇ˈdɪstrǝ/ *n* [Wn1] a type of plant with broad green pointed leaves, often grown in houses

as·pi·rant /ǝˈspaɪǝrǝnt, ˈæspǝ̇rǝnt/ *n* [(*for, after*)] a person who hopes for and tries to get something great or important: *There are many aspirants for/after the president's job*

as·pi·rate[1] /ˈæspǝ̇reɪt/ *v* [T1] **1** to pronounce (a word or letter) with the sound of the letter H (as in (*a*) *human* but not in (*an*) *honour*) **2** [Wv5] *tech* to pronounce a consonant sound with a slight burst of air after it

as·pi·rate[2] /ˈæspǝ̇rǝ̇t/ *n* the sound of the letter H or the letter itself

as·pi·ra·tion /ˌæspǝ̇ˈreɪʃǝn/ *n* **1** [U;C] (a) strong desire to do something great or important **2** [C] an object of such desire **3** [U] the pronunciation of the letter H **4** [U] *tech* a slight burst of air that may follow a consonant sound —see ASPIRATE[1] (2)

as·pire /ə'spaɪəʳ/ *v* [IØ+*to* or *after*, 3] to direct one's hopes and efforts to some great or important aim: *He aspired after knowledge|to the highest positions|to become president*

as·pirin /'æsprɨn/ *n* **-rin** *or* **-rins** **1** [U] a medicine that lessens pain and fever **2** [C] this medicine in the form of a TABLET (1)

as re·gards /·ˑ'·/ *prep* **1** with regard to; regarding; AS FOR: *As regards (doing) that, I haven't decided yet* **2** according to; by: *correctly placed as regards size and colour*

ass[1] /æs/ *n* **1** any of a family of animals like horses but smaller and with longer ears, one of which animals is the donkey **2** *infml* a stupid foolish person **3 make an ass of oneself** *infml* to behave in a foolish manner

ass[2] *n AmE taboo sl* **1** ARSE **2 a bit of ass a** a girl **b** a sexual act with a woman

as·sail /ə'seɪl/ *v* [T1 (*with*)] *fml* **1** to attack violently, either with blows or words: *The army assailed the town.|I was assailed with rude words.|He was assailed with worries* **2** to attempt to be master of: *He assailed the difficulty with eagerness*

as·sai·lant /ə'seɪlənt/ *n fml* an attacker

as·sas·sin /ə'sæsɨn/ *n* a person who murders (a ruler or politician) for political reasons or reward

as·sas·sin·ate /ə'sæsɨneɪt‖-səneɪt/ *v* [T1] to murder (a ruler, politician, etc.) for political reasons or reward —**-ation** /əˌsæsɨ'neɪʃən‖-sən'eɪ-/ *n* [U;C]

as·sault[1] /ə'sɔːlt/ *n* **1** [C] a sudden violent attack: *He led an assault against the castle.*|(fig.) *Some music is an assault on the ears* **2** [U;C] *law* unlawful attack with blows against another person, or the threat of such an attack —compare INDECENT ASSAULT

assault[2] *v* [T1] to attack suddenly and violently

assault and bat·ter·y /·ˌ· · '···/ [U] *law* an attack which includes actual blows rather than just the threat of blows

assault craft /·'· ·/ *n* a small fast boat used esp. to get an attacking army from a large ship to the shore

as·say[1] /ə'seɪ, 'æseɪ/ *n* a test to discover the quality of or material in something, esp. something made of or containing metal

assay[2] /ə'seɪ/ *v* [T1] **1** to test (something, such as metal-bearing soil or a gold ring) for quality or to discover what materials are present **2** *lit* to attempt (something difficult): *to assay the impossible* —**~er** *n*

as·se·gai, assagai /'æsɨgaɪ/ *n* a long thin wooden spear with an iron point, used in southern Africa

as·sem·blage /ə'semblɪdʒ/ *n* **1** [C] a group of people or collection of articles, esp. one of high quality or on show **2** [U] the act of bringing, coming, or putting together

as·sem·ble /ə'sembəl/ *v* **1** [T1;IØ] to gather or collect together: *If we can assemble everybody then we can leave.|Pupils assemble for lessons at 8 o'clock* **2** [T1] to set in order: *The books are assembled on the shelves in alphabetical order* **3** [T1] to put together (something, such as a machine): *The people who assemble cars work very quickly*

as·sem·bly /ə'sembli/ *n* **1** [C] a group of people, esp. one gathered together for a special purpose such as worship **2** [U] a meeting together of people: *In some countries the right of assembly in public is not allowed for everybody* **3** [C;(U)] a call made by drum, horn, etc., to gather soldiers together **4** [C] a law-making body, esp. the lower of 2 such bodies

assembly line /·'·· ·/ *n* an arrangement of workers and machines in which each person has a particular job and the work is passed, often on a moving band, directly from one worker to the next until the product is complete

as·sem·bly·man /ə'semblimən/ *fem.* **assemblywoman** /-ˌwʊmən/— *n* **-men** /mən/ *AmE* a member of an ASSEMBLY (1) of law-makers

assembly room /·'·· ·/ *n* [*often pl.*] a room or set of rooms for public meetings, dances, etc.

as·sent[1] /ə'sent/ *v* [IØ (*to*);I3] *fml* to agree to a suggestion, idea, etc.: *I won't assent to her plan.|Why don't you assent?|I assented to listen to her*

assent[2] *n* **1** agreement: *Once we have his assent we can start* **2 with one assent** *fml* with the expressed agreement of all **3 by common assent** by general, often unspoken, agreement

as·sert /ə'sɜːt‖-ɜrt/ *v* **1** [T1, 5;X *to be* 1, 7] to state or declare forcefully: *She asserted her ideas loudly and clearly.|He asserted that he was not guilty.|She asserted her belief that he was not guilty.|She asserted the charge to be incorrect* **2** [T1] to make a claim to; defend in words: *He asserted his rights* **3** [T1] to show, esp. forcefully, the existence of: *He asserted his control by making them be quiet* **4 assert oneself a** to act in a way that shows one's power, control, etc. **b** to behave in a way that attracts notice

as·ser·tion /ə'sɜːʃən‖-ɜr-/ *n* **1** [U,U5] the act of ASSERTing **2** [C,C5] a forceful statement or claim: *He repeated his assertions that he was not guilty*

as·ser·tive /ə'sɜːtɪv‖-ɜr-/ *adj* marked by or expressing forceful statements or claims: *You couldn't fail to notice that assertive young man* —**~ly** *adv* —**~ness** *n* [U]

as·sess /ə'ses/ *v* [T1] **1** [(*at*)] to calculate the value of (property) or the amount of (income) for tax purposes: *They are assessing his house.|They assessed it at £15,000* **2** [(*at*)] to decide the amount of (a tax, money punishment (FINE), etc.) **3** to judge the quality or worth of

as·sess·ment /ə'sesmənt/ *n* **1** [U] the act of ASSESSing **2** [C] the value or amount at which something is calculated **3** [C] a judgment or opinion: *What is your assessment of this state of affairs?*

as·ses·sor /ə'sesəʳ/ *n* **1** a person whose job is to calculate the value of property or the amount of income or taxes **2** a person who advises a judge or official committee on matters that demand special knowledge

as·set /'æset/ *n* **1** [*usu. pl.*] something such as a house or furniture, that has value and that may be sold to pay a debt **2** a valuable quality or skill: *Beauty was her only asset*

as·sev·e·rate /ə'sevəreɪt/ *v* [T1,5] *fml* to declare solemnly and forcefully —**-ation** /əˌsevə'reɪʃən/ *n* [C;U]

as·si·du·i·ty /ˌæsɨ'djuːɨti‖-'du-/ *n fml* **1** [U] careful continual attention **2** [C] an example of this

as·sid·u·ous /ə'sɪdjʊəs‖-dʒʊəs/ *adj* having or showing careful and continual attention —**~ly** *adv*

as·sign /ə'saɪn/ *v* **1** [D1 (*to*)] to give as a share or for use: *They have assigned me a small room* **2** [D1 (*to*)] to give (property, rights, etc.): *I have assigned them my large house as I couldn't pay the debt* **3** [T1 (*for, to*)] to give, name, or fix as a time, place, reason: *We assigned a day in July for the performance* **4** [D1 (*to*);V3] to appoint to a job or duty; name: *I assigned you to wash the plates.|I assigned you the job* —**~able** *adj*

as·sig·na·tion /ˌæsɪg'neɪʃən/ *n fml* a meeting, esp. a secret meeting with a lover

as·sign·ment /ə'saɪnmənt/ *n* **1** [C] a position, office, or job which one is given or to which one is being sent: *I shall soon be leaving for an assignment* *in India.|The policeman's assignment was to discover the murderer* **2** [U] the act of ASSIGNing

as·sim·i·late /əˈsɪmɨleɪt/ *v* **1** [T1;IØ: (*to, into*)] to (allow to) become part of (a group, country, race, etc.): *America has assimilated many people from Europe.|Some foreigners assimilate easily into our way of life* **2** [T1;IØ] **a** to take (food) into the body after eating; DIGEST² (1) **b** (of food) to be taken into the body; be DIGESTed² (1) **3** [T1] to take as one's own; understand or use properly: *You have only remembered the facts well, not assimilated them*

assimilate to *v prep* [D1] to make like: *The laws of the defeated country were assimilated to those of the stronger country*

as·sim·i·la·tion /əˌsɪmɨˈleɪʃən/ *n* [U] **1** the act of assimilating or of being assimilated (ASSIMILATE) **2** the changing of a speech sound because of the influence of another speech sound next to it

as·sist /əˈsɪst/ *v* [T1;IØ:(*in*);V3] to help or support: *She assisted him in building the house.|She assisted in building it.|Good glasses will assist you to read* —see HELP (USAGE)

as·sist·ance /əˈsɪstəns/ *n* [U] help; support: *Can I be of any assistance?|She came to my assistance*

as·sis·tant /əˈsɪstənt/ *n* a person who helps another, as in a job, and is under that person's direction: *If I am to finish this work soon I must employ an assistant.|He is an assistant cook*

as·size /əˈsaɪz/ *n* **1** [U] the trial of a person by a judge and a group of people (JURY (1)) **2** [A] of or for ASSIZES

as·siz·es /əˈsaɪzɨz/ *n* **assizes** [Wn3;C *often pl. with sing. meaning*] (in Britain until 1971) a meeting or meetings of a special court held by an important judge travelling from one country town to another

assoc. *written abbrev. for:* **1** ASSOCIATED¹ **2** also **assn**— association

as·so·ci·ate¹ /əˈsəʊʃieɪt, əˈsəʊsi-/ *v* **1** [T1;IØ: (*with*)] to (cause to) join as friends or as partners in business: *If we can associate the 2 firms we will be much stronger.|We should associate ourselves with the larger firm.|He associates with criminals* **2** [T1 (*with*)] to connect in one's mind: *I don't associate the 2 ideas.|I associate politics with war*

as·so·ci·ate² /əˈsəʊʃiɨt, -ʃɨt/ *n* **1** a person connected with another, esp. in work: *He is not a friend but a business associate.|The thief and his associates were caught by the police.|John and Paul are associates (in business)* **2** a person who is a member of a society but with only limited rights

as·so·ci·a·tion /əˌsəʊsiˈeɪʃən, əˌsəʊʃi-/ *n* **1** [C (*of*); C3] a society of people joined together for a particular purpose: *Let's form an association to help blind people* **2** [U (*with*)] the act of joining or the state of being joined with somebody or something: *My association with that firm did not last long.|I am working in association with another person* **3** [U] the act of connecting things, esp. in the mind

Association Foot·ball /·ˌ····ˈ··/ *n* [U] *BrE* SOCCER

as·so·nance /ˈæsənəns/ *n* [U] the sounding alike of words, esp. the vowels of words (as in *born* and *warm*)

as·sort /əˈsɔːt‖-ɔrt/ *v* [T1] to divide into different sorts

as·sort·ed /əˈsɔːtɨd‖-ɔr-/ *adj* **1** of various types mixed together: *I took her a bag of assorted fruits* **2** (*in comb.*) suited by nature or character; matched: *That husband and wife are a well-assorted pair*

as·sort·ment /əˈsɔːtmənt‖-ɔr-/ *n* a group or quantity of mixed things or of various examples of the same type of thing; mixture: *This tin contains an assortment of sweets*

asst *written abbrev. for:* ASSISTANT

as·suage /əˈsweɪdʒ/ *v* [T1] *fml* to make (pain, suffering, desire, etc.) less

as·sume /əˈsjuːm‖əˈsuːm/ *v* **1** [Wv4;T1,5a,b;X (*to be*) 1,7] to take as a fact or as true without proof; suppose: *I assumed that he was there.|I assumed him (to be) able to read.|He was there—or so I assumed.|Assuming it rains tomorrow, what shall we do?* **2** [T1] to begin to use or perform (sometimes without the right); take upon oneself: *You will assume your new duties tomorrow.|The powerful criminal assumed control of the government* **3** [T1] to pretend to have or be: *He assumes a well-informed manner but in fact knows very little*

as·sump·tion /əˈsʌmpʃən/ *n* **1** [C (*of*), C5] something that is taken as a fact or as true without proof: *Our assumption that we would win was wrong* **2** [U;(C): (*of*)] the act of beginning to use or perform or of pretending to have or be: *His assumption of power was not liked by many*

as·sur·ance /əˈʃʊərəns/ *n* **1** [U] also **self-assurance**— strong belief in one's own ability and powers: *The teacher lacked assurance in front of his class* **2** [C (*of*), C5 *often pl. with sing. meaning*] a trustworthy statement; promise: *He gave me his assurance that he would come.|In spite of all his assurances, he did not come* **3** [U] *BrE* insurance: *life assurance*

as·sure /əˈʃʊəʳ/ *v* **1** [D5a;T1+*of*] to try to cause to believe or trust in something; promise; try to persuade: *I assure you that this medicine cannot harm you.|He assured us of his ability to work* **2** [D5a;T1+*of*] to make (oneself) sure or certain: *Before going to bed she assured herself that the door was locked* **3** [T1] to INSURE, esp. against death —see INSURE (USAGE) **4** [D1 (*for*);T1] to make certain the coming or obtaining of; ENSURE

as·sured¹ /əˈʃʊəd‖-ərd/ *adj* **1** also **self-assured**— having or showing certainty of one's own abilities and powers: *an assured manner* **2** having or showing certainty: *There is an assured demand for such goods*—**~ly** /əˈʃʊərɨdli/ *adv*: *Assuredly, he will come tomorrow.|He speaks very assuredly*

assured² *n* **-sured** *or* (*rare*) **-sureds** [*the*+C] *BrE* a person whose life has been INSUREd: *On the death of the assured his family will receive a large sum of money.|Money was paid for the lives of all (of) the assured*

as·ter /ˈæstəʳ/ *n* a garden flower with a bright yellow centre

as·te·risk¹ /ˈæstərɪsk/ also **star**— *n* a starlike mark (*) used **a** to call attention to a note at the bottom of a page **b** to mark that certain letters are missing from a word **c** to show that a word, phrase, sound, etc., is wrong or may never have existed (as in the example "In English we say *3 boys,* not **3 boy*")

asterisk² *v* [T1] to mark with an ASTERISK

a·stern /əˈstɜːn‖-ɜrn/ *adv* **1** [F] in or at the back part (STERN) of a ship **2** (of a ship) backwards **3** **fall astern (of)** (esp. of a ship or people on it) to come to be behind

as·te·roid /ˈæstərɔɪd/ also **minor planet**— *n* one of many small heavenly bodies (PLANET*s*) between MARS and JUPITER —see picture at PLANET

asth·ma /ˈæsmə‖ˈæzmə/ *n* [U] a diseased condition which makes breathing very difficult at times —**~tic** /æsˈmætɪk‖æz-/ *adj, n*: *He is (an) asthmatic* —**~tically** *adv* [Wa4]

as though /· ˈ·/ *conj* AS IF

as·tig·mat·ic /ˌæstɪgˈmætɪk/ *adj* suffering from, concerning, or curing ASTIGMATISM

as·tig·ma·tis·m /əˈstɪgmətɪzəm/ *n* [U] the inability of the eye to see properly or clearly because of its shape

a·stir /əˈstɜːʳ/ *adj* [F] **1** awake and out of bed **2** [(*at, with*)] in a state of excitement

as to /ˈ· ·/ *prep* **1** with regard to; AS REGARDS (1); AS FOR: *As to (doing) that, I haven't decided yet* **2**

esp. BrE (with doubts, arguments and questions) about: Nobody could decide (as to) what to do.| "doubts as to whether you've made the right decision" (SEU S.) **3** according to; by; AS REGARDS (2): *correctly placed as to size and colour*
USAGE It is *nonstandard,* but quite common in *BrE,* to use **as to** after a verb in the meaning of *"about": "We want to know from you* **as to** *whether you have ever experienced any cruelty."* (SEU S.) It is perfectly correct to use **as to** in *BrE* after nouns and adjectives expressing doubt or questioning: *"I'm terribly uncertain* **as to** *whether V. is the right girl for me".* (SEU W.) —see AS FOR (USAGE)

as·ton·ish /əˈstɒnɪʃ‖əˈstɑ-/ *v* [Wv4,5;T1 *often pass.*] to produce surprise or wonder in (someone): *We were astonished to hear what had happened.|He gave her an astonished look.|It was an astonishing performance for such a young musician*

as·ton·ish·ment /əˈstɒnɪʃmənt‖əˈstɑ-/ *n* [U] great surprise or wonder: *To my astonishment he was there before us*

as·tound /əˈstaʊnd/ *v* [Wv4;T1 *often pass.*] to shock with surprise: *He was astounded when he heard he had won.|Although small, he showed astounding strength*

as·tra·khan /ˌæstrəˈkæn◂‖ˈæstrəkən/ *n* [U] lamb's skin with the wool fixed in tight little curls: *astrakhan coats*

as·tral /ˈæstrəl/ *adj* of, from, or concerning stars

a·stray /əˈstreɪ/ *adj, adv* [F] **1** off the right path or way: *We missed the track and went astray* **2** away from the desirable or proper course; into bad or wrong ways: *The attractions of the big city soon led the young man astray.|I have gone astray somewhere in my calculations*

a·stride¹ /əˈstraɪd/ *adv* [F] with a leg on each side: *He rode astride*

astride² *prep* **1** with a leg on each side of: *He sat astride his father's legs.|astride a horse* **2** *rare* over; across: *The bridge astride the river*

as·trin·gent¹ /əˈstrɪndʒənt/ *adj* **1** able to tighten up the skin or stop bleeding **2** severe; bitter: *astringent remarks about that bad book* —**-gency** /əˈstrɪndʒənsi/ *n* [U] —**~ly** *adv*

astringent² *n* [C;U] *tech* a substance or medicine that tightens up the skin or the blood vessels and so stops bleeding

as·tro-¹ /ˈæstrəʊ, ˈæstrə/ *comb. form* concerning the stars or space: ASTRONAUT|ASTROPHYSICS

astro-² /əˈstrɒ‖əˈstrɑ/ *prefix* concerning the stars: ASTROLOGY|ASTRONOMER

as·tro·labe /ˈæstrəleɪb/ *n* an instrument used formerly for finding the positions of stars —compare SEXTANT

as·trol·o·ger /əˈstrɒlədʒəʳ‖əˈstrɑ-/ *n* a person who practises ASTROLOGY

as·trol·o·gy /əˈstrɒlədʒi‖əˈstrɑ-/ *n* [U] the art of understanding the supposed influence on events, character, and fate of the groups and positions of the sun, moon, stars, and PLANETs, and of telling the future from them —**-gical** /ˌæstrəˈlɒdʒɪkəl‖-ˈlɑ-/ *adj* —**-gically** *adv* [Wa4]

as·tro·naut /ˈæstrənɔːt‖-nɒt, -nɑt/ *n* a person who travels through space in a space vehicle

as·tro·nau·tics /ˌæstrəˈnɔːtɪks/ *n* [U] the science of the making and operation of space vehicles

as·tron·o·mer /əˈstrɒnəməʳ‖əˈstrɑ-/ *n* a person who studies the stars scientifically

as·tro·nom·i·cal /ˌæstrəˈnɒmɪkəl‖-ˈnɑ-/ also (*rare*) **as·tro·nom·ic** /ˌæstrəˈnɒmɪk‖-ˈnɑ-/— *adj* **1** of or concerning the stars or the study of the stars **2** *infml* (of an amount or number) very large: *Astronomical sums of money will be needed for this plan* —**~ly** *adv* [Wa4]

as·tron·o·my /əˈstrɒnəmi‖əˈstrɑ-/ *n* [U] the scientific study of the sun, moon, stars, and other heavenly bodies

as·tro·phys·ics /ˌæstrəʊˈfɪzɪks, ˌæstrə-/ *n* [U] the scientific study of the chemical nature of the stars and the natural forces that influence them —**-ical** /ˌæstrəʊˈfɪzɪkəl, ˌæstrə-/ *adj* —**-icist** /ˌæstrəʊˈfɪzɪ̆sɪ̆st, ˌæstrə-/ *n*

as·tute /əˈstjuːt‖əˈstuːt/ *adj* clever and able to see quickly something that is to one's advantage —**~ly** *adv* —**~ness** *n* [U]

a·sun·der /əˈsʌndəʳ/ *adv esp. lit* **1** apart from each other in position: *The war forced the parents and children asunder* **2** into pieces: *The boat was torn asunder by the storm*

a·sy·lum /əˈsaɪləm/ *n* **1** a place where a person can be safe or looked after **2** the protection and shelter given by such a place, esp. as given by one country to people who have left another for political reasons **3** *becoming rare* MENTAL HOSPITAL

a·sym·met·ric /ˌeɪsɪ̆ˈmetrɪk, ˌæ-/ also **-ical** /-kəl/— *adj* having sides that are not alike —opposite **symmetrical** —**~ally** *adv* [Wa4]

at /ət; *strong* æt/ *prep* **1** (used with something seen as a point in space): *He was at the door/at the shop/at the bus-stop/at the end of the road.|He went to the door and stood at the door until I came.|Our plane stopped at London (airport) on its way to New York.|I met him at Paul's (home).|I got it at the baker's (shop)* **2** (used with a point in time) *at 10 o'clock|at midnight|at Christmas|at the moment|at that time he was living in London* **3** (used with an intended aim, or object towards which a thing or action is directed): *He ran at her with a knife and drove it into her wicked heart.|After aiming (his gun) carefully at the bird, he missed it completely.|He shot at the General (but missed).* (Compare *He shot the General (and killed him)*).|*He threw the ball at me (intending to hit me).* (Compare *He threw the ball to me (hoping that I would catch it)*).|*He ran at me with a knife (but never reached me).* (Compare *He ran to me and kissed me).|He shouted at me (angrily).* (Compare *He shouted to me that I should be careful).|(infml) I don't really play tennis very well, you know—I just play at tennis (for amusement).|(infml) I'm leaving you, dearest, because—how shall I put it?—You always seem to be talking at me rather than to me.|"Up and at them, boys!" shouted the general as we attacked* **4** (used with words, actions, or ideas that are the cause of feeling or behaviour): *I was surprised/amused/pleased at* (= by) *his words.|I was angry at his behaviour.|I laughed at his foolishness* (and also: *I laughed at him*) **5** *AmE* (used with people and objects that are the cause of feeling or behaviour): *I was angry at* (= with) *John.|I was pleased at* (= with) *John's present* **6** (used with the field or area about which a judgment is made): *He's good/clever/bad at arranging things.|He's good/bad at games.|She's a* GENIUS¹ (2) *at chemistry.|She's getting on very well at her job* **7** (used before SUPERLATIVEs): *at best|at the best|at worst|at the worst* **8** (used before certain nouns to express states, conditions, feelings, etc.): *at work|at* LIBERTY|*at school* **9** (used with prices) for: *I bought 90 pencils at (a price or cost of) 10 cents each* —see FOR (USAGE) **10** (used before the rate, degree or position of something in a set or group): *at first|the temperature at 90°* **11** (used before ages): *at (the age of) 90* **12** (used before speeds and rates): *at (a speed or rate of) 90 miles an hour|He left at a run* **13** (used before levels): *The water stopped rising at (a level of) 90 feet* **14** (used before distances): *at (a distance of) 90 miles* **15 at a/an a** as a result of one; with or by means of one: *to reduce prices at a stroke|At a word from me she will* *come running* **b** during one; in the course of one: *2 at a time|He finished the drink at a* GULP

at all /· '·/ *adv* [(not in simple POSITIVE DECLARATIVE sentences)] **1** in any degree: *He doesn't smoke at all.|He doesn't seem at all interested in my plan* **2** ever: *Do you go there at all?* **3 Not at all a** (answering a question) No; Not a bit: *"The place itself doesn't encourage you?" "Not at all"* (SEU S.) **b** (answering an APOLOGY (1)) That's all right; It doesn't matter: *"I'm sorry to trouble you." "Not at all"*

at·a·vis·m /'ætəvɪzəm/ *n* **1** [U] the appearance in a person, animal, or plant of something that did not belong to its parents but to some earlier person, animal, or plant **2** [C] something that seems typical of a much earlier stage of development rather than the latest stage —**-vistic** /ˌætə'vɪstɪk/ *adj*

a·tchoo /ə'tʃuː/ *interj AmE* ATISHOO

ate /et, eɪt‖eɪt/ *past t. of* EAT

USAGE The most usual British pronunciation is /et/, though some people say /eɪt/. Most Americans say /eɪt/, and /et/ is thought to be non-standard by many Americans.

-ate /ɪ̵t, eɪt/ *suffix* **1** [*n→adj*] full of: *very* AFFECTIONATE **2** [*n→n*] the total group of people holding (the stated rank or office): *the* ELECTORATE **3** [*n, adj→v*] to act as; cause to become: *to* ACTIVATE **4** [*n→n*] *tech* a chemical salt formed from (the stated acid): PHOSPHATE —**-ately** *suffix* [*→adv*]: *fortunately*

a·tel·i·er /ə'telieɪ‖ˌætl'jeɪ (*Fr* atəlje)/ *n Fr & tech* a place where the skills of the hand are practised, such as painting, making pots or figures, etc.; STUDIO (1)

a·the·is·m /'eɪθi-ɪzəm/ *n* [U] disbelief in the existence of God

a·the·ist /'eɪθi-ɪ̵st/ *n* a person who disbelieves in the existence of God —compare AGNOSTIC (1) —**~ic(al)** /ˌeɪθi'ɪstɪk(əl)/ *adj* —**~ically** *adv* [Wa4]

ath·lete /'æθliːt/ *n* a person who is skilled in bodily exercises and who competes in games that need strength and speed, such as running and jumping

athlete's foot /ˌ·· '·/ *n* [U] a disease in which the skin cracks between the toes

ath·let·ic /æθ'letɪk, əθ-/ *adj* **1** of or concerning ATHLETES or ATHLETICS **2** (of people) strong in body, with plenty of muscle and speed

ath·let·ics /æθ'letɪks, əθ-/ *n* [U] the practice of bodily exercises and of sports demanding strength and speed, such as running and jumping

at home /· '·/ *n becoming rare* a party, esp. one that is small and informal, given at one's home: *I'm giving a small at home this evening: shall you come?*

a·thwart /ə'θwɔːt‖-ɔrt/ *prep rare* across, esp. in a sloping position: *The ship sailed athwart our path*

-a·tion /'eɪʃən/ *suffix* **1** [*v→n* U] (shows the active act or action of the stated verb): *Examination by that doctor is always very complete* (= The doctor examines someone) **2** [*v→n* U] (shows the PASSIVE (4) act or action of the stated verb): *At the end of my examination, the doctor said I was healthy* (= I was examined) **3** [*v→n* C or U] (shows the result of the stated verb, or something connected with it): *I've done 6 examinations today*

a·tish·oo /ə'tɪʃuː/ *AmE* **atchoo, achoo**— *interj BrE* the word used to represent an explosion in the nose (SNEEZE): *He went "atishoo!" into his handkerchief*

-a·tive /ətɪv/ *suffix* [*n, v→adj*] of, concerning, or connected with the noun or verb stated: ARGUMENTATIVE|IMAGINATIVE|INFORMATIVE

at·las /'ætləs/ *n* a book of maps

at·mo·sphere /'ætməsfɪəʳ/ *n* [*usu. sing.*] **1** the mixture of gases that surrounds any heavenly body, esp. the earth **2** the air, as in the sky or in an enclosed space **3** the feeling among a group or produced by the surroundings

at·mo·spher·ic /ˌætməs'ferɪk◂/ *adj* **1** [Wa5;A] of or concerning the earth's ATMOSPHERE (1) **2** [B] producing feelings of mysterious beauty, strangeness, etc.: *That music's very atmospheric*

atmospheric pres·sure /ˌ···· '··/ *n* [U;S] *fml* PRESSURE (4)

at·mo·spher·ics /ˌætməs'ferɪks/ *n* [P] a continuous light cracking noise in a radio caused by electrical forces in the ATMOSPHERE (1)

at·oll /'ætɒl‖'ætɑl, 'ætɔl, 'ætəʊl/ *n* a ring-shaped island (made of CORAL) partly or completely enclosing an area of sea water (LAGOON)

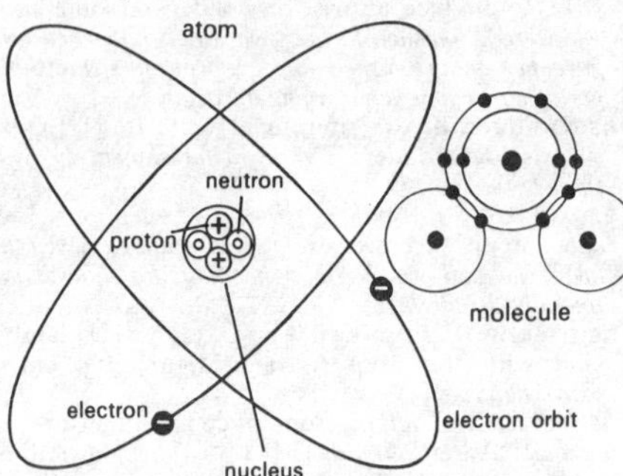

atomic structure

at·om /'ætəm/ *n* **1** the smallest piece of a simple substance (ELEMENT (6)) that still has the same qualities and can combine with other substances (to form MOLECULES) **2** *infml nonassertive* a very small bit: *There's not an atom of truth in that statement*

atom bomb /'·· ·/ also **atomic bomb** /·ˌ·· '·/— *n* a bomb whose very powerful explosion is caused by splitting an atom and setting free its force

a·tom·ic /ə'tɒmɪk‖ə'tɑ-/ *adj* [Wa5] **1** [B] of or concerning an atom or atoms **2** [B] working on or moving by ATOMIC ENERGY: *an atomic ship* **3** [A] working with or concerned in the making of ATOMIC ENERGY, ATOM BOMBS, etc.: *atomic scientists* **4** [A] possessing ATOM BOMBS —**~ally** *adv* [Wa4]

atomic en·er·gy /·ˌ·· '···/ *n* [U] also **nuclear energy**— the powerful force that is given out when the middle part (NUCLEUS) of an atom is changed, as by being split or by being joined to another atom. It is used to make electricity, to drive large ships, in ATOM BOMBS, etc.

atomic num·ber /·ˌ·· '··/ *n* the number of very small electrically charged pieces of matter (PROTONS) in the middle part (NUCLEUS) of an atom of a particular simple substance (ELEMENT (6))

atomic pile /·ˌ·· '·/ *n* NUCLEAR REACTOR

atomic weight /·ˌ·· '·/ *n* the weight of an atom of a single substance (ELEMENT) expressed as a comparison with the atomic weight of CARBON which is taken as 12

at·om·ize, -ise /'ætəmaɪz/ *v* [T1] to break (a liquid) into a mist or SPRAY[2] (2) of very little drops by forcing it through an instrument (**atomizer**) and out through a very small hole

a·ton·al /eɪ'təʊnl, æ-/ *adj* (of music) not based on any ordered set (SCALE[5] (5)) of notes —**~ly** *adv*

a·to·nal·i·ty /ˌeɪtəʊ'nælɪ̵ti, ˌæ-/ *n* [U] **1** (in music) the quality of being ATONAL **2** an ATONAL way of writing music: *Schoenberg used atonality in the music of his middle period*

a·tone /ə'təʊn/ *v* [IØ (*for*)] to make repayment (for

some crime, harm done to another, failure to act, etc.): *He tried to atone for his rudeness by sending her some flowers* —**~ment** *n* [U]

a·top /ə'tɒp‖ə'tɑp/ *prep esp. lit or pomp* on, to, or at the top of

-a·tor /eɪtəʳ/ *suffix* [*v* → *n*] a person or thing that acts in the stated manner

a·tro·cious /ə'trəʊʃəs/ *adj* **1** (of behaviour or an act) very cruel, shameful, shocking, etc. **2** *infml* very bad: *an atrocious meal* —**~ly**

a·troc·i·ty /ə'trɒsɪ̈ti‖ə'trɑ-/ *n* **1** [U] great evil, esp. cruelty **2** [C] a very evil, esp. cruel, act **3** [C] *infml* something that is very displeasing or ugly

at·ro·phy[1] /'ætrəfi/ *n* [U;S] **1** the decrease in size or wasting away of part of the body, esp. through lack of blood or lack of use **2** the weakening or coming to an end of some condition or course of development

atrophy[2] *v* [T1;I∅] to (cause to) suffer ATROPHY: *The disease atrophied her legs.|Her legs quickly atrophied*

at·tach /ə'tætʃ/ *v* [T1] **1** [(*to*)] to fix; fasten; join: *I attached a wire (to the radio)* **2** *law* to seize (a person or his goods) because of an unpaid debt

at·tach·é /ə'tæʃeɪ‖ˌætə'ʃeɪ (*Fr* ataʃe)/ *n Fr* a person who is employed to help the representative (AMBASSADOR) of one country in another country

attaché case /·'·· ·‖ˌ··'· ·/ *n* a thin hard case with a handle, for carrying papers

at·tach·ment /ə'tætʃmənt/ *n* **1** [U (*to*)] the act of attaching or of being attached (ATTACH (1); ATTACH TO (1)) **2** [C] something that is fixed to something else **3** [C] something that fixes or fastens **4** [C (*to*)] fondness or friendship **5** [C;U] *law* the seizure of a person or his goods in order to clear a debt

attach to *v prep* **1** [D1] to cause to join as a member of in action, esp. for a limited period of time: *He attached himself to the group of climbers.|His new firm attached him to the sales division of the business* **2** [T1] *fml* to come to: *No blame/guilt attaches to him for the accident* **3** [T1,4] *fml* to come from: *No blame/guilt attaches to (doing) that* **4** **attach importance to** to consider important **5** **be attached to** to be fond of: *I am very attached to her/the old customs*

at·tack[1] /ə'tæk/ *v* **1** [T1;I∅] to bring violence (on), esp. with weapons: *The enemy attacked us at night* **2** [T1] to speak or write strongly against: *The minister was attacked by the newspapers for promising to help the workers* **3** [T1] to harm, spoil, trouble, damage, etc., esp. by a continuing action: *The disease attacked his bones* **4** [T1] to begin (something) with eagerness and great interest: *He attacked the difficulties at once.|He attacked the food as if he had not eaten for a week* —**~er** *n*

attack[2] *n* **1** [U;C] (an act of) violence intended to harm: *The city came under attack during the night.|There have been many attacks against farmers recently* **2** [C (*on*)] writing or words intended to hurt or damage **3** [C;(U)] the act or manner of beginning something; start: *At the piano, his attack was full of life* **4** [C9 (*of*)] a sudden or unexpected period of suffering an illness, usu. a more serious one and esp. one which tends to return: *an attack of* MALARIA|*a* HEART ATTACK

at·tain /ə'teɪn/ *v* [T1] to succeed in arriving at, esp. after effort; reach: *He attained the position of minister* —**~able** *adj*

at·tain·der /ə'teɪndəʳ/ *n* [U] *law* the seizure of a person's property and the ending of his rights, as on being found guilty of certain crimes

at·tain·ment /ə'teɪnmənt/ *n* **1** [U] the act of ATTAINing **2** [C *usu. pl.*] something successfully reached or learnt, esp. a skill: *The ability to speak several languages was among his attainments*

attain to *v prep* [T1 *no. pass.*] *fml* to reach (a desired state or condition)

at·tar /'ætəʳ/ *n* [U] a pleasant-smelling oil obtained from flowers, esp. roses

at·tempt[1] /ə'tempt/ *v* [Wv5;T1,3,4] to make an effort at; try: *He attempted the examination but failed.|I attempted to speak but was told to be quiet.|I attempted walking until I fell over.|He was found guilty of attempted murder even though the other man did not die*

attempt[2] *n* [C (*at*), C3] **1** an effort made to do something: *We failed in our attempt (to climb the mountain)* **2** **attempt on someone's life** *fml* an effort to murder someone

at·tend /ə'tend/ *v* **1** [I∅ (*to*)] to give one's attention: *Listen and attend!|Are you attending to what is being said?* **2** [T1] to be present at; go to: *I shall be attending the meeting.|It will be well attended* **3** [I∅ (*on, upon*);T1] to look after; care for; serve: *I have a good doctor attending (on) me* **4** [T1] *fml* to go with: *Danger attended everything he did*

at·tend·ance /ə'tendəns/ *n* **1** [U9] the act of attending (esp. in the phr. **in attendance (on)**): *There is a doctor in attendance.|He is in attendance on the sick man* **2** [U;(C): (*at*)] the act of being present, esp. regularly: *Attendance at school is encouraged by law.|He missed 3 attendances this year* **3** [S (*at*)] the number of people present: *There was a large attendance at the meeting.|an attendance of 5,000*

at·tend·ant[1] /ə'tendənt/ *adj* [(*on*)] **1** connected with: *One of the attendant difficulties during the war was lack of food* **2** serving; on duty to help and look after: *He arrived with several attendant helpers*

attendant[2] *n* **1** [C] a person who goes with and serves or looks after another **2** [C;N] a person employed to look after and help visitors to a public place: *a* MUSEUM *attendant*

USAGE An **attendant** is not someone who **attends** a play, concert, or church service. Someone who works in a shop is a **shop assistant**.

attendant cir·cum·stanc·es /·ˌ·· '····/ *n* [P] conditions surrounding or going with an act or event

attend to *v prep* [T1] **1** to give help to: *You'd better attend to that thin dark girl: I think she's going to faint.|Are you being attended to, sir?* **2** to direct one's efforts and interest towards: *I have an urgent matter to attend to*

at·ten·tion[1] /ə'tenʃən/ *n* **1** [U] the act of fixing the mind on, esp. by watching or listening; full thought and consideration (often in the phr. **pay attention (to)**): *You must pay attention to the teacher. Do not let your attention wander.|Pay more attention in future!* **2** [U] particular care, notice, or action: *Old cars need a lot of attention to keep them working.|This letter is for the attention of the employer* **3** [C *often pl.*] *becoming rare* a kind, polite, or formal act, esp. one showing respect or love **4** [U] a military position in which a person stands straight and still: *The officer ordered the men to stand at attention during the whole ceremony*

attention[2] also **'shun**— *interj* a military order to come to ATTENTION[1] (4)

at·ten·tive /ə'tentɪv/ *adj* **1** taking careful notice; listening carefully **2** doing acts to satisfy the needs of another: *He was very attentive to the old lady and did everything for her* **3** polite —**~ly** *adv* —**~ness** *n* [U]

at·ten·u·ate /ə'tenjʊeɪt/ *v* [T1;I∅] *fml or tech* to (cause to) become thin, weak, less valuable, etc.: *a powerful drug, used in an attenuated form as a medicine* —**-ation** /əˌtenjʊ'eɪʃən/ *n* [U]

at·test /ə'test/ *v rare* **1** [T1,5,6a] to declare solemnly **2** [T1] *law* to make (somebody) promise to tell the truth, as in court **3** [T1] to be or give proof of: *His success attests his ability* **4** [T1] *law* to show to be true by signing as proof that one was present

at·tes·ta·tion /ˌæteˈsteɪʃən/ *n* **1** [U] the act of ATTESTing **2** [C] a statement which the maker solemnly declares to be true

at·test·ed /əˈtestɨ̍d/ (*AmE* **certified**)— *adj BrE* (of cows or milk) tested and shown to be free of disease —compare PASTEURIZEd

attest to *v prep* [T1] *fml* to be or give proof of: *His success attests to his ability*

at·tic /ˈætɪk/ *n* **1** that part of a building, esp. a house, just below the roof **2** this part made into a room

at·tire[1] /əˈtaɪəʳ/ *v* [T1 (*in*)] *fml* to put on clothes; dress: *attired in blue*

attire[2] *n* [U] *fml* dress; clothes: *in formal attire*

at·ti·tude /ˈætɨ̍tjuːd‖-tuːd/ *n* **1** the position or manner of standing of the body **2** a manner of feeling and behaving: *I dislike her unfriendly attitude* **3** judgment; opinion: *What is your attitude to this idea?* **4 strike an attitude** *lit* to put the body suddenly into an unnatural position and keep it there; behave unnaturally or in a way meant to draw attention

at·ti·tu·di·nize, -ise /ˌætɨ̍ˈtjuːdɨ̍naɪz‖-ˈtuːdən-aɪz/ *v* [IØ] *derog* to move, speak, or write in an unnatural way in order to gain attention

at·tor·ney /əˈtɜːni‖-ɜr-/ *n* **1** *esp. AmE* LAWYER **2 power(s) of attorney** power to act for another, esp. in matters of law and business, given by means of an official paper (**warrant/letters of attorney**)

attorney gen·er·al /·ˌ·· ˈ··/ *n* **attorneys general** *or* **attorney generals** (*usu. caps.*) the chief law officer of a state or nation —compare **Lord** CHANCELLOR

at·tract /əˈtrækt/ *v* [T1] **1** to cause to like, admire, notice, or turn towards: *He was attracted by her beauty.|Her beauty attracted him/his attention* **2** to draw towards one: *He attracted large numbers of followers.|Flowers attract bees* **3** to draw by unseen forces: *The moon attracts the earth's seas towards her/it(self)*

at·trac·tion /əˈtrækʃən/ *n* **1** [U] the act of attracting: *The attraction of the city's bright lights is hard to avoid.|Work has little attraction for me* **2** [C] something which attracts: *Her greatest attraction for me is her voice.|The city's bright lights, theatres, films, etc., are attractions that are hard to avoid*

at·trac·tive /əˈtræktɪv/ *adj* **1** having the power to attract: *The idea is very attractive* **2** (usu. of females, now increasingly of males) having good looks; pretty or HANDSOME —**~ly** *adv* —**~ness** *n* [U]

at·trib·u·ta·ble /əˈtrɪbjʊtəbəl‖-bjə-/ *adj* [F+*to*] that can be ATTRIBUTEd TO

at·tri·bute /ˈætrɨ̍bjuːt/ *n* **1** a quality belonging to or forming part of the nature of a person or thing: *Darkness is an attribute of night* **2** something regarded as a sign (or SYMBOL) of a person or position: *The sword is an attribute of the fighter*

at·trib·ute to /əˈtrɪbjuːt‖-bjət/ *v prep* **1** [D1,6 a ;V4b] to believe (something) to be the result of: *Jim attributes his success to hard work/to how hard he has always worked/to working hard* **2** [D1 *usu. pass.*] also **ascribe to**— to consider (something) to have been written by (someone): *This tune is usually attributed to J. S. Bach*

at·tri·bu·tion /ˌætrɨ̍ˈbjuːʃən/ *n* **1** [U] the act of attributing to (ATTRIBUTE TO): *The attribution of the play to that famous poet was shown to be wrong* **2** [C] a quality, typical thing, etc., that is regarded as part of the person or thing

at·trib·u·tive[1] /əˈtrɪbjʊtɪv‖-bjə-/ *adj* [Wa5] **1** of or concerning an ATTRIBUTE **2** (of an adjective, noun, or phrase) describing and coming before a noun (as *green* in *a green hat*) —compare PREDICATIVE —**~ly** *adv*

attributive[2] *n* an adjective, noun, or phrase that is ATTRIBUTIVE

at·tri·tion /əˈtrɪʃən/ *n* [U] **1** wearing away caused by rubbing **2** tiring and weakening in addition to fighting (esp. in the phr. **war of attrition**)

at·tune to /əˈtjuːn‖əˈtuːn/ *v prep* [D1 *usu. pass.*] to cause to become used to or ready for: *You have to attune your ears to modern music.|Are you attuned to new ways of thinking?*

a·typ·i·cal /eɪˈtɪpɪkəl/ *adj* not of the usu. kind or in the usu. manner; unusual; not typical —**~ly** *adv* [Wa4]

au·ber·gine /ˈəʊbəʒiːn‖-bər-/ *n* [C;U] *esp. BrE* EGGPLANT

au·brie·tia /ɔːˈbriːʃə/ *n* [Wn1] a type of low-growing plant with many small reddish-blue flowers

au·burn /ˈɔːbən‖-ərn/ *adj, n* [B;U] (esp. of hair) reddish-brown

auc·tion[1] /ˈɔːkʃən/ *n* **1** public sale of goods to the person who offers the most money: *a furniture auction|I shall sell my house by auction* —see also DUTCH AUCTION **2** (in some card games) the time when players compete to fix the CONTRACT[1] (3)

auction[2] *v* [T1 (OFF)] to sell by AUCTION[1] (1)

auction bridge /ˌ·· ˈ·/ *n* [U] BRIDGE[3]

auc·tio·neer /ˌɔːkʃəˈnɪəʳ/ *n* a person who is in charge of an AUCTION[1] (1) and who calls out the prices as they are reached

au·da·cious /ɔːˈdeɪʃəs/ *adj* **1** daring, often to a degree that is considered foolish; brave **2** daringly impolite or disrespectful, as to someone of high rank —**~ly** *adv*

au·dac·i·ty /ɔːˈdæsɨ̍ti/ *n* **1** [U] daring; boldness; bravery **2** [U] daring rudeness or CHEEK[1] (3) **3** [C] an act of daring or of showing no respect

au·di·ble /ˈɔːdɨ̍bəl/ *adj* able to be heard; hearable —**-bility** /ˌɔːdɨ̍ˈbɪlɨ̍ti/ *n* [U] —**-bly** /ˈɔːdɨ̍bli/ *adv*

au·di·ence /ˈɔːdɪəns‖ˈɔ-, ˈɑ-/ *n* **1** [GC] the people listening to or watching a performance, speech, television show, etc.: *The audience was/were very excited by the show.|an audience of 20,000* **2** [C] a formal meeting between somebody powerful and somebody less important: *The queen allowed him an audience of 20 minutes* **3** [U] *law* freedom to be heard, as in a court

au·di·o /ˈɔːdi-əʊ/ *adj* [Wa5;A] *tech* connected with or used in the broadcasting or receiving of sound radio signals —compare VIDEO (1)

audio- *comb. form* of or concerning hearing

audio fre·quen·cy /ˈ··· ˌ···/ *n* any of the various speeds of sound wave that can be heard by the human ear

au·di·om·e·ter /ˌɔːdiˈɒmɨ̍təʳ‖-ˈɑm-/ *n* an instrument used to measure ability to hear

audio-vis·u·al /ˌ··· ˈ···◂/ *adj* [Wa5] **1** of, for, or concerning both sight and hearing **2** made to help learning and teaching by using both sight and hearing: *The school's audio-visual apparatus includes films and records*

au·dit[1] /ˈɔːdɨ̍t/ *n* an official examination of the accounts of a business, society, etc., usu. done once each year

audit[2] *v* [T1] to examine (money accounts) officially

au·di·tion[1] /ɔːˈdɪʃən/ *n* **1** [C] a test performance requested of a singer, actor, etc., by the people from whom he hopes to get employment **2** [U] *tech* the act or power of hearing

audition[2] *v* **1** [T1;IØ] to cause (someone) to give an AUDITION **2** [IØ] to give an AUDITION: *I'm auditioning for a part in the play tomorrow, and I hope I get it!*

au·di·tor /ˈɔːdɪ̍təʳ/ *n* **1** a person whose work is to examine accounts, as of businesses **2** *rare* a person who listens; hearer

au·di·to·ri·um /ˌɔːdɪ̍ˈtɔːrɪəm‖-ˈto-/ *n* the space in a theatre, hall, etc., where people sit when listening to or watching a performance

au·di·to·ry /ˈɔːdɪ̍təri‖-tori/ *adj* [Wa5] *tech* of, by, or for hearing: *auditory difficulties for which an ear operation was necessary*

au fait /ˌəʊ ˈfeɪ (*Fr* o fɛ)/ *adj* [F (*with*)] *Fr* fully informed; familiar: *I was new at the college and not yet au fait with its customs*

au fond /ˌəʊ ˈfɔ̃ (*Fr* o fɔ̃)/ *adv Fr* at (the) bottom; in truth: *The quarrel is, au fond, personal and not political*

Aug. *written abbrev. for:* August

au·ger /ˈɔːgəʳ/ *n* an instrument for making large holes in wood or in the ground —see picture at TOOL[1]

aught /ɔːt‖ɔt, ɑt/ *pron* **for aught I know/care** *lit* for all I know/care; but I don't know/care: *I'm glad I haven't seen him for years. He might be dead for aught I care*

aug·ment /ɔːgˈment/ *v* [T1;(IØ)] *fml* to (cause to) become bigger, more valuable, better, etc.: *He augments his wages by working in his free time*

aug·men·ta·tion /ˌɔːgmenˈteɪʃən‖-mən-, -men-/ *n* **1** [U] the act of increasing or of being increased in size or amount **2** [C] that which is added to something; increase

au·gur[1] /ˈɔːgəʳ/ *n* (in ancient Rome) a religious official who could tell what would happen in the future

augur[2] *v* [T1 (*for*)] *lit* **1** to be a sign of (something) in the future: *The lack of rain augurs trouble* (*for the farmers*) **2** **augur well/ill (for)** to be a sign of good things/bad things in the future (for); BODE well/ill (for)

au·gu·ry /ˈɔːgjʊri‖ˈɔːgjəri/ *n* **1** [C] a declaration telling what the future will be **2** [C] a sign of coming events **3** [U] the art of telling the future, esp. as practised by the ancient Romans

au·gust /ɔːˈgʌst/ *adj lit* causing feelings of great respect; noble and grand —**~ly** *adv*

Au·gust /ˈɔːgəst/ *n* [R;(C)] the 8th month of the year

auk /ɔːk/ *n* a seabird with short wings, native to the northern parts of the world, which catches fish under water

auld lang syne /ˌɔːld-, ˌəʊld læŋ ˈzaɪn, -ˈsaɪn-/ *n* [U] *Scot E* (used esp. when singing or drinking) (the name of a song in praise of) the good old times

aunt /ɑːnt‖ænt/ also (*infml*) **aunt·ie, aunt·y** /ˈɑːnti‖ˈænti/— *n* [A;C;N] (*often cap.*) **1** the sister of one's father or mother, the wife of one's uncle, or a woman whose brother or sister has a child: —see TABLE OF FAMILY RELATIONSHIPS **2** a woman who is a friend or neighbour of a small child or its parents: *She is aunt to all the children in the street*

Aunt Sal·ly /ˌ· ˈ··/ *n* **Aunt Sallies** **1** a wooden figure of a woman at which people throw objects for fun **2** a person, group, or thing that is the object of complaints, funny remarks, etc.

au pair /ˌəʊ ˈpeəʳ (*Fr* o pɛr)/ *n Fr* a young foreigner, esp. a girl (an **au pair girl**), who lives with a family in return for doing light work in the house

au·ra /ˈɔːrə/ *n* **1** an effect or feeling that seems to surround and come from a person or place: *There was an aura of decay in the empty village* **2** a faintly shining shadow that some people claim to see surrounding the human body

au·ral /ˈɔːrəl/ *adj tech* of or received through hearing —**~ly** *adv*

USAGE In language teaching, **aural** is sometimes pronounced /ˈaʊrəl/ to show a difference with **oral** /ˈɔːrəl/, esp. in the phrase **oral/aural.**

au·re·ole /ˈɔːriəʊl/ also **au·re·o·la** /ɔːˈriːələ/— *n* HALO

au re·voir /ˌəʊ rəˈvwɑːʳ, ˌɒ-‖ˌəʊ-, ˌɔ-/ *interj Fr* till we meet again; goodbye for the present: *I won't say goodbye, but just au revoir*

au·ri·cle /ˈɔːrɪkəl/ *n* **1** the part of the ear that is on the outside of the head —see picture at EAR[1] **2** either of the 2 spaces in the top of the heart that receive blood from the main blood vessels (VEIN*s*) of the body and push it through into the VENTRICLE*s* (1) —see picture at RESPIRATORY

au·ric·u·lar /ɔːˈrɪkjʊləʳ‖-kjə/ *adj* [Wa5] *tech* of or concerning the ear

au·rif·e·rous /ɔːˈrɪfərəs/ *adj tech* containing gold: *auriferous rock*

au·ro·ra /əˈrɔːrə, ɔː-‖-ˈro-/ *n* **-ras** *or* **-rae** /riː/ bands or arches of coloured light in the night sky seen either in the most northern parts of the world (**aurora borealis** or **northern lights**) or in the most southern parts (**aurora australis** or **southern lights**)

aus·cul·ta·tion /ˌɔːskəlˈteɪʃən/ *n* **1** [U] the action of listening to the sounds coming from the organs inside the body as a method of discovering their health **2** [C] an act of this type

aus·pic·es /ˈɔːspɪ̍sɪ̍z/ *n* [P] help, support, and favour (esp. in the phr. **under the auspices of**): *This concert has been arranged under the auspices of the Queen*

aus·pi·cious /ɔːˈspɪʃəs/ *adj fml* **1** giving, promising, or showing signs of future success **2** of good fortune; lucky —**~ly** *adv*: *The year began auspiciously with good trade figures for January*

Aus·sie /ˈɒzi‖ˈɑsi, ˈɔsi/ *n sl* an Australian

aus·tere /ɔːˈstɪəʳ, ɒ-‖ɔ-/ *adj* [Wa2] **1** lacking comfort; hard: *We led an austere life in the mountains* **2** lacking the ability to enjoy life; self-controlled; serious: *an austere person/manner* **3** without ornament; plain: *an austere style of painting* —**~ly** *adv*

aus·ter·i·ty /ɒˈsterɪ̍ti, ɔː-‖ɔ-/ *n* **1** [U] the quality of being AUSTERE **2** [C *usu. pl.*] an AUSTERE act, practice, or manner: *We practised various austerities to make our money last longer* **3** [U] a way of life that does not cost much, esp. one forced on a country in time of war: *period of austerity*

Aus·tra·la·sian /ˌɒstrəˈleɪʒən, -ʃən‖ˌɔ-, ˌɑ-/ *n, adj* (a person, language, or thing) of Australia, New Zealand or the surrounding islands

Aus·tra·li·an /ɒˈstreɪlɪən‖ɔ-, ɑ-/ *n, adj* (a person, language, or thing) of Australia

Australian Rules foot·ball /·ˈ··· · ˌ··/ also (*AustrE*) **football**— *n* [U] an Australian game rather like RUGBY, which is played between 2 teams of 18 players

Aus·tro- /ˌɒstrəʊ‖ˌɔ-, ˌɑ-/ *comb. form* **1** Austrian; of Austria: *The Austro-Hungarian empire* **2** Austrian and: *the Austro-Italian border*

au·tar·chy /ˈɔːtɑːki‖-ɑr-/ *n* **1** [U] government of a country by one person **2** [C] a country so governed

au·tar·ky, -chy /ˈɔːtɑːki‖-ɑr-/ *n* **1** [U] the production by a nation of everything that it needs **2** [C] a nation that exists on this system

au·then·tic /ɔːˈθentɪk/ *adj* **1** known to have been made, painted, written, etc., by the person who is claimed to have done it; GENUINE **2** *infml* sincere —**~ally** *adv* [Wa4]

au·then·tic·ate /ɔːˈθentɪkeɪt/ *v* [T1] **1** to prove (something) to be AUTHENTIC (1): *Now that this painting has been authenticated as a Rembrandt, it's worth 10 times as much as I paid for it!* **2** to prove (a statement, account, etc.) to be true —**-ation** /ɔːˌθentɪˈkeɪʃən/ *n* [U9]

au·then·tic·i·ty /ˌɔːθenˈtɪsɨti/ *n* **1** [U9] the quality of being true or of being made, painted, written, etc., by the person claimed: *The painting's authenticity is not in doubt: it is a real Rembrandt* **2** [U] *infml* the quality of being sincere

au·thor /ˈɔːθəʳ/ *n* **1** the writer of a book, newspaper article, play, poem, etc. **2** the person who begins or thinks of anything, esp. an idea or plan

au·thor·ess /ˈɔːθərɨs/ *n becoming rare* a female AUTHOR

au·thor·i·tar·i·an[1] /ɔːˌθɒrɨˈteəriən‖ɔˌθɑ-, əˌθɔ-/ *adj* favouring or demanding obedience to rules and laws whether or not they are right: *Don't be so authoritarian! You can't order people about like that!|authoritarian government* —**~ism** *n* [U]

authoritarian[2] *n* **1** a person who believes that rules and laws of those in AUTHORITY (1), esp. over a country, should always be obeyed whether or not they are right **2** a person who is continually giving orders to others

au·thor·i·ta·tive /ɔːˈθɒrətətɪv, ə-‖əˈθɑrəteɪtɪv, əˌθɔ-/ *adj* **1** behaving as if giving orders; commanding: *Don't be so authoritative when you ask me to do something* **2** possessing the power to give orders: *There is no authoritative group here* **3** having the appearance of power: *an authoritative voice* **4** that may be used or trusted as having a respected store of knowledge or information: *We want a dictionary that will be an authoritative record of modern English* —compare DEFINITIVE —**~ly** *adv*

au·thor·i·ty /ɔːˈθɒrɨti, ə-‖əˈθɑ-, əˈθɔ-/ *n* **1** [U] the ability, power, or right, to control and command: *Who is in authority here?|A teacher must show his authority* **2** [C *often pl.*] a person or group with this power or right, esp. in public affairs: *The government is the highest authority in the country.|The authorities at the town hall are slow to deal with complaints* **3** [U] power to influence: *I have some authority with the young boy* **4** [U9] right or official power, esp. for some stated purpose: *What authority have you for entering this house?* **5** [C *usu. sing.*] a paper giving this right: *Here is my authority* **6** [C] a person, book, etc., whose knowledge or information is dependable, good, and respected: *He is an authority on plant diseases* **7** [C] a person, book, etc., mentioned as the place where one found certain information

au·thor·i·za·tion, -isation /ˌɔːθəraɪˈzeɪʃən‖ˌɔːθərə-/ *n* **1** [U] right or official power to do something: *I have the owner's authorization to use his house* **2** [C] a paper giving this right

au·thor·ize, -ise /ˈɔːθəraɪz/ *v* **1** [T1;V3] to give power to: *I authorized the man to act for me while I was away* **2** [T1] to give permission for: *I authorized the payment of this bill* **3** [T1 *pass. rare*] to give a good enough reason for; JUSTIFY (2)

Authorized Ver·sion /ˌ··· ˈ··/ also **King James Version**— *n* [*the*+R] the translation of the English Bible made in England in 1611, when James the First was king

au·thor·ship /ˈɔːθəʃɪp‖ˈɔːθər-/ *n* [U] **1** the personal origin (=IDENTITY (1) of the AUTHOR) of a book, play, poem, etc.: *The book's authorship is not known, but it was written in the 16th century* **2** the profession of writing, esp. of writing books for money

au·tis·m /ˈɔːtɪzəm/ *n* [U] an illness of the mind, esp. in children, in which the imagination becomes too important and good personal relationships cannot be formed

au·tis·tic /ɔːˈtɪstɪk/ *adj* suffering from AUTISM: *autistic children/behaviour* —**~ally** *adv* [Wa4]

au·to /ˈɔːtəʊ/ *n* **-tos** [C;*by*+U] *infml esp. AmE* a car

au·to- /ɔːtəʊ, ɔːtə/ *comb form* self; one's own; from oneself: AUTOBIOGRAPHY

au·to·bahn /ˈɔːtəbɑːn, ˈɔːtəʊ- (*Ger* ˈaʊtobaːn)/ *n Ger* a German (or Austrian) MOTORWAY

au·to·bi·o·graph·i·cal /ˌɔːtəbaɪəˈgræfɪkəl/ also **au·to·bi·o·graph·ic** /-ˈgræfɪk/— *adj* of or concerning the facts of one's own life, esp. as written in a book —**~ly** *adv* [Wa4]

au·to·bi·og·ra·phy /ˌɔːtəbaɪˈɒgrəfi‖-baɪˈɑ-/ *n* **1** [C] a book written by oneself about one's own life **2** [U] such books or the writing of such books —compare BIOGRAPHY

au·to-chang·er /ˈ·· ˌ··/ also **auto-change** /ˈ·· ·/— *n* an apparatus on a record player that causes one record after another to be played without the need to change the records by hand

au·toc·ra·cy /ɔːˈtɒkrəsi‖ɔˈtɑ-/ *n* **1** [U] rule by one person with unlimited power **2** [C] a country, group, etc., ruled in this way —compare AUTARCHY

au·to·crat /ˈɔːtəkræt/ *n* **1** a ruler with unlimited power **2** a person who orders things to be done without considering the wishes of others —**~ic** /ˌɔːtəˈkrætɪk/ *adj* —**~ically** *adv* [Wa4]

au·to·e·rot·i·cis·m /ˌɔːtəʊ-ɪˈrɒtɨsɪzəm‖-ˈrɑ-/ also **au·to·er·o·tis·m** /ˌɔːtəʊˈerətɪzəm/— *n* [U] *tech* the causing and satisfying of sexual excitement in and by oneself; MASTURBATION

au·to·graph[1] /ˈɔːtəgrɑːf‖-græf/ *n* a person's own writing done by hand, esp. his name (SIGNATURE) written in this way: *May I have your autograph, sir?*

autograph[2] *v* [T] to sign (a letter, statement, book, etc.) with one's own name to show that one has written it

autograph book /ˈ··· ·/ also **autograph al·bum** /ˈ··· ˌ··/— *n* a book of empty pages on which friends and famous people can write their names

au·to·mat /ˈɔːtəmæt/ *n tdmk* any one of a group of American restaurants where food can be obtained from machines into which coins are dropped: *Let's eat in the automat today*

au·to·mate /ˈɔːtəmeɪt/ *v* [T1;I∅] to make (something) work by machinery and without the work of men

au·to·mat·ic[1] /ˌɔːtəˈmætɪk◂/ *adj* **1** (esp. of a machine) able to work or move by itself without needing the operation of man: *The heating system here has an automatic temperature control* **2** done without thought, esp. as a habit: *The movements needed to ride a bicycle soon become automatic* **3** certain to happen: *You will get an automatic increase in pay every year* —**~ally** *adv* [Wa4]

automatic[2] *n* something, such as certain weapons (**automatic pistol, automatic rifle,** etc.) or cars in which some actions are done AUTOMATICally[1] (1)

automatic pi·lot /ˌ···· ˈ··/ *n* an instrument that guides aircraft, space vehicles, ships, etc., without needing operation by men

au·to·ma·tion /ˌɔːtəˈmeɪʃən/ *n* [U] the act or practice of using machines that need little or no human control, esp. in place of workers

au·tom·a·tis·m /ɔːˈtɒmətɪzəm‖ɔˈtɑ-/ *n* **1** [U;C] action done without conscious control, such as walking in one's sleep **2** [U] the idea that man's actions are the result of influences in the outside world only and not of consciousness

au·tom·a·ton /ɔːˈtɒmətən‖ɔˈtɑ-/ *n* **-ta** /tə/ *or* **-tons** **1** a thing or machine that moves or works by itself, esp. a manlike figure (ROBOT) that moves and acts as if alive **2** a person who acts without thought or feeling, as if he were a machine

au·to·mo·bile /ˈɔːtəməbiːl‖-məʊ-/ *n esp. AmE* car

Automobile Association /ˈ···· ···ˌ··/ *n* [*the*+R] a British club for motorists, providing various advantages such as help with repairs on the road

au·ton·o·mous /ɔːˈtɒnəməs‖ɔˈtɑ-/ *adj* governing

itself: *an autonomous country/group* —**~ly** *adv*

au·ton·o·my /ɔːˈtɒnəmi‖ɔˈtɑ-/ *n* [U] the condition of self-government, esp. of a state or group within a country

au·top·sy /ˈɔːtɒpsi‖-tɑp-/ *n* an examination of a dead body, esp. by cutting it open, to discover the cause of death; POSTMORTEM (1)

au·to·stra·da /ˈɔːtəʊstrɑːdə, ˈɔːtə-‖ˌaʊtəʊˈstrɑdə, ˌɔ-/ *n It* an Italian MOTORWAY

au·to·sug·ges·tion /ˌɔːtəʊsəˈdʒestʃən‖-səgˈdʒe-, -səˈdʒe-/ *n* [U] suggestion or influence directed towards himself coming from within a person rather than from another or from the outside world: *Can I really train myself out of my bad habits by autosuggestion?*

au·tumn /ˈɔːtəm/ *AmE* also **fall**— *n* [R;C;(U)] the season between summer and winter when leaves turn gold and fruits become ripe: (fig.) *He has reached the autumn of his life*

au·tum·nal /ɔːˈtʌmnəl/ *adj* of, like, or in autumn —**~ly** *adv*

aux·il·i·a·ry[1] /ɔːgˈzɪljəri, ɔːk-‖ɔgˈzɪljəri, -ˈzɪləri/ *adj* offering or giving help, esp. with lower rank or of less importance; adding support: *auxiliary workers/machinery*

auxiliary[2] *n* **1** a person (or thing) that offers or gives help: *The doctor is hoping to find 2 auxiliaries to work under him* **2** [*usu. pl.*] a foreign soldier or army in the service of a country at war **3** AUXILIARY VERB

auxiliary verb /·ˌ···· ˈ·/ *n* a verb that goes with another verb to show person, tense, VOICE[1] (8), ASPECT (5), etc. (such as *am, didn't,* and *have* in *"I am running", "I didn't climb", "they have heard"*)

av. *written abbrev. for:* **1** average **2** AVOIRDUPOIS

a·vail[1] /əˈveɪl/ *v* [Iø] *lit* **1** (esp. with *not*) to be of use: *The medicine did not avail against the disease* **2** **avail someone nothing** to be of no use to someone

avail[2] *n* [U] *lit* good result; profit; advantage; use (esp. in the phrs. **of no/little avail, without avail, to no avail**): *We tried and tried, but it was all to no avail: we failed*

a·vai·la·ble /əˈveɪləbəl/ *adj* **1** able to be got, obtained, used, etc.: *There is water available at the hut.|I'm sorry, sir, those shoes are not available in your size* **2** able to be visited or seen; not too busy: *The doctor is (not) available now* —**-ability** /əˌveɪləˈbɪlɪ̈ti/ *n* [U] —**-ably** /əˈveɪləbli/ *adv*

avail of *v prep* [D1 *no pass.*] *fml* to give (oneself) the advantage of: *You should avail yourself of every chance to improve your English*

av·a·lanche /ˈævəlɑːnʃ‖-læntʃ/ *n* **1** a large mass of snow and ice crashing down the side of a mountain **2** [*usu. sing.*] a large quantity that has arrived suddenly: *an avalanche of letters*

av·ant-garde[1] /ˌævɔːŋ ˈgɑːd◂‖ˌævɑŋ ˈgɑrd◂ (*Fr* avɑ̃ gard)/ *n* [(*the*) GU] *Fr* the people who produce the newest ideas, esp. in the arts

avant-garde[2] *adj Fr* being a member or product of the AVANT-GARDE: *avant-garde painters/painting*

av·a·rice /ˈævərɪ̈s/ *n* [U] *fml* too great eagerness and desire to get or keep wealth; GREED

av·a·ri·cious /ˌævəˈrɪʃəs/ *adj fml* having too great an eagerness and desire for wealth; GREEDY (1) —**~ly** *adv*

av·a·tar /ˌævəˈtɑːʳ/ *n* the appearance of a Hindu god in human or animal form: *an avatar of the god Vishnu*

a·vaunt /əˈvɔːnt‖əˈvɔnt, əˈvɑnt/ *interj old use* go away

Ave. *written abbrev. for:* AVENUE (2): *109 Lexington Ave.*

a·venge /əˈvendʒ/ *v* [T1 (*on, upon*)] **1** to get satisfaction for (a wrong) by punishing the wrong-doer(s): *They avenged his death by burning the village.|They avenged his death on the village* **2** to punish somebody for a wrong done to (oneself or somebody else): *I shall avenge my brother: the man who killed him shall die.|They avenged themselves on their enemy* —see REVENGE (USAGE) —**~r** *n*

av·e·nue /ˈævɪ̈njuː‖-nuː/ *n* **1** a road or way between 2 rows of trees, esp. one that leads to a house **2** a wide street in a town **3** the means of getting something; way to a result (often in the phr. **explore every avenue**)

a·ver /əˈvɜːʳ/ *v* **-rr-** [T1,5] *fml* to state forcefully; declare

av·e·rage[1] /ˈævərɪdʒ/ *n* **1** [C] the amount found by adding together several quantities and then dividing by the number of quantities: *The average of 3, 8, and 10 is 7* **2** [C;*above, below, on*+U] a level or standard regarded as usual or ordinary: *He is above average in his lessons.|On average we receive 5 letters each day*

average[2] *adj* [Wa5] **1** found by making an average: *What is the average rainfall for July?* **2** of the usual or ordinary kind: *There was nothing special about it, it was only average*

average[3] *v* **1** [L1] to be or come to an average: *My mail averages 20 letters a day* **2** [T1 *no pass.*] to do, get, or have as an average or usual quantity: *I average 8 hours work a day* **3** [T1;(Iø)] to calculate the average of (figures)

average out *v adv* [Iø (*at*)] *infml* to come to an average or ordinary level or standard, esp. after being higher or lower: *The good things and bad things in life average out in the end, don't they?*

a·verse /əˈvɜːs‖-ɜrs/ *adj* [F+*to*] *fml or humor* not liking; opposed: *I am averse to punishing people.|I am not averse to a good meal*

USAGE Both **averse** *to* and **averse** *from* exist, but some people think **averse** *from* is *nonstandard.* —compare ADVERSE

a·ver·sion /əˈvɜːʃən‖əˈvɜrʒən/ *n* **1** [U;S: (*to*)] strong dislike; hatred (often in the phr. **take an aversion to**): *My aversion to cruelty is very strong* **2** [C] a person or thing disliked (esp. in the phr. **someone's pet aversion(s)**)

a·ver·sive /əˈvɜːsɪv‖-ɜr-/ *adj* [Wa5;A] *tech* tending or causing to avoid something that is unpleasant or painful: *aversive training to get rid of bad habits by making them seem unpleasant* —**~ly** *adv*

a·vert /əˈvɜːt‖-ɜrt/ *v* [T1] **1** to prevent happening; avoid: *Accidents can be averted by careful driving* **2** [(*from*)] to turn away (one's eyes, thoughts, etc.): *She averted her eyes from the terrible sight*

a·vi·a·ry /ˈeɪvɪəri‖ˈeɪvieri/ *n* a large cage or enclosure for keeping birds in

a·vi·a·tion /ˌeɪviˈeɪʃən‖ˌeɪ-, ˌæ-/ *n* [U] **1** the act, art, or science of the operation or flight of aircraft **2** the aircraft, weapons, etc., of an airforce **3** the aircraft industry

a·vi·a·tor /ˈeɪvieɪtəʳ‖ˈeɪ-, ˈæ-/ *n old use* the pilot of an aircraft

av·id /ˈævɪ̈d/ *adj* [A;F (*for*)] eager; keen: *an avid reader|He is avid for praise* —**~ity** /əˈvɪdɪ̈ti/ *n* [U] —**~ly** *adv*

av·o·ca·do /ˌævəˈkɑːdəʊ◂/ also **avocado pear** /ˌ···· ˈ·/— *n* **-dos** *or* **-does** a green tropical fruit with a large seed and smooth oily flesh often eaten at the start of a meal

av·o·ca·tion /ˌævəˈkeɪʃən/ *n* work that is not one's usual job but is done for pleasure: HOBBY: *Reading is my avocation*

av·o·cet /ˈævəset/ *n* any of various birds with a long beak and long legs that live on the shores of seas and lakes

a·void /əˈvɔɪd/ *v* [T1,4] **1** to escape: *I avoided*

punishment by running away.|I avoided being punished **2** to miss or keep away from, esp. on purpose: *I avoided her by leaving by the back door.|She avoided answering my questions* —**~able** *adj*

a·void·ance /əˈvɔɪdəns/ *n* [U] the act of avoiding: *avoidance of danger*

av·oir·du·pois /ˌævədəˈpɔɪz, ˌævwɑːdjuːˈpwɑː‖ˌævərdəˈpɔɪz/ *n, adj* [U;E] *Fr* the system of weights used, esp. formerly in Britain, the standard measures being the OUNCE (1), pound, and TON (1): *16* OUNCE*s avoirdupois* —compare METRIC SYSTEM

a·vow /əˈvaʊ/ *v* [T1,5;X (*to be*) 1,7] *fml* to state openly; admit: *The prisoner avowed his guilt.|He avowed himself to be a supporter of the new group*

a·vow·al /əˈvaʊəl/ *n* [C;(U)] *fml* (an) open declaration or act of admitting: *He made (an) avowal of his real intentions*

a·vowed /əˈvaʊd/ *adj* [A] openly declared or admitted: *an avowed enemy* —**~ly** /əˈvaʊɪ̆dli/ *adv*: *He is avowedly my enemy*

a·vun·cu·lar /əˈvʌŋkjʊləʳ/ *adj* of, like, or concerning an uncle: *I really don't like avuncular advice from someone no older than I am!* —**~ly** *adv*

a·wait /əˈweɪt/ *v* [T1] **1** to wait for: *I am awaiting your reply* **2** to be in store for; be ready for: *A warm welcome awaits you* —see WAIT (USAGE)

a·wake¹ /əˈweɪk/ also **a·wak·en** /əˈweɪkən/— *v* **awoke** /əˈwəʊk/ *or* **awaked**, **awaked** *or* **awoken** /əˈwəʊkən/ **1** [T1;I∅,3] to (cause to) stop sleeping; wake: *The noise awoke me.|Byron awoke one morning to find himself famous* **2** [I∅ (*to*);T1] to (cause to) become conscious or active: *Her letter awoke old memories.|Old memories awoke in her when she read the letter* —see WAKE (USAGE)

awake² *adj* **1** [F] having woken; not asleep **2** [F+*to*] conscious (of): *He is awake to the difficulties* **3 wide awake a** not at all sleepy **b** not easily deceived

a·wak·en·ing /əˈweɪkənɪŋ/ *n* [*pl. rare*] **1** the act of waking from sleep **2** [(*to*)] the act of becoming conscious or concerned: *her awakening to social injustice* **3 rude awakening** sudden consciousness of an unpleasant state of affairs: *We had all been enjoying ourselves, but the rude awakening came when our firm started to lose money*

awaken to *v prep* **1** [D1] to cause to understand: *We must awaken the people to the dangers facing our country* **2** [T1] AWAKE TO

awake to also **awaken to**— *v prep* [T1 *no pass.*] to begin to understand: *We must awake to the dangers facing our country*

a·ward¹ /əˈwɔːd‖əˈwɔrd/ *v* [D1 (*to*);T1] **1** to give, esp. as the result of an official decision: *He was awarded the prize for being the fastest runner* **2** to give by a decision in a court of law: *The judge awarded a large sum of money to those hurt by the explosion*

award² *n* **1** something given as the result of an official decision, esp. a prize **2** a decision, or that which is given by a decision, in a court of law: *an award of £5,000 to those hurt in the explosion* **3** a sum of money given to a student so that he can afford to study

a·ware /əˈweəʳ/ *adj* **1** [F (*of*), F5,6a] having knowledge or consciousness: *Are you aware of the difficulty/that there is a difficulty?|I'm quite aware how you must feel* **2** [B9] having knowledge or consciousness of the stated type: *She is politically/artistically aware.|a politically/artistically aware person* **3** [B] having or showing understanding of oneself, one's surroundings, and other people: *It's nice to be with such an aware person* —**~ness** *n* [U (*of*, 5)]

a·wash /əˈwɒʃ‖əˈwɔʃ, əˈwɑʃ/ *adj* [F] **1** level with the water and washed over by the waves: *The river overflowed till the streets were awash* **2** loose in the waves and knocked about by them

a·way¹ /əˈweɪ/ *adv* **1** [F (*from*)] from this or that place; to or at another place; in another direction: *Go away!|He swam away from the ship.|I hope to get away early in the morning.|I shall be away 3 weeks.|"Thorpe's away is he?" "Yes, he's in Greece"* (SEU S.) **2** [E] at a distance: *Stand away from that hole.|He lives 3 miles away* **3** in another place, esp. in a place that is enclosed or locked: *I have put the gun away* **4** to an end; to nothing: *The sounds died away.|The water boiled away* **5** so as to pass (a period of time) completely as stated: *He slept away the day.|He slept the day away* **6** out of one's possession, control, use, etc.: *He gave everything away.|to sign away one's rights|to sign one's rights away* **7** so as to remove or separate: *He cut away a dead branch.|He cut a diseased part away* **8** [(*at*)] all the time; continuously: *to work away (all the time)|He cut away at the thick branch* **9** without delay (in the phrs. (*esp. AmE*) **right away** = (*BrE*) **straightaway**): *I'll do it right away* **10 away with!** *lit* take away; remove: *Away with the thief!* **11 far and away** very much; by far: *This is far and away the best example*

away² *adj* [A] (of a sports match) played at the place, sports field, etc., of one's opponent: *an away match* —opposite **home**

awe¹ /ɔː/ *n* [U] a feeling of respect mixed with fear and wonder: *He always stood in awe of his father*

awe² *v pres. p.* **aweing** [T1 (*into*)] to fill with AWE: *They were awed into silence by the great man*

awe-in·spir·ing /ˈ· ·ˌ··/ *adj* causing feelings of AWE —**~ly** *adv*

awe·some /ˈɔːsəm/ *adj* expressing or causing feelings of AWE (esp. when fear is present): *an awesome account of the terrors of war*

awe·struck /ˈɔːstrʌk/ also **awe·strick·en** /ˈɔːstrɪkən/— *adj* filled with, made silent by, or showing AWE: *We sat in awestruck silence after hearing the truth at last*

aw·ful /ˈɔːfəl/ *adj* **1** terrible; shocking: *The pain was awful* **2** *infml* very bad: *awful weather* **3** *lit & old use* causing feelings of AWE —**~ness** *n* [U]

aw·ful·ly /ˈɔːfəli/ *adv infml* (used to give more force to an expression) very: *awfully cold|awfully nice*

a·while /əˈwaɪl/ *adv esp. lit or fml* for a short time: *We rested awhile at the side of the road*

awk·ward /ˈɔːkwəd‖-ərd/ *adj* **1** lacking skill in moving the body or parts of the body easily; CLUMSY (1): *He is still awkward with a knife and fork and drops food at each meal* **2** not well made for use; difficult to use; causing difficulty: *This machine is awkward to handle.|(esp. BrE) Thursday is rather awkward for me; could we meet on Tuesday?* **3** *esp. BrE* (of a person) difficult to deal with; unwilling to agree: *Don't be awkward: we have to get this finished by 5 o'clock* **4** causing difficulty to those who are concerned and sensitive: EMBARRASSing: *There was a long awkward silence between them after his angry words* **5 awkward customer** *infml* a person or animal that is difficult or dangerous to deal with —**~ly** *adv* —**~ness** *n* [U]

awl /ɔːl/ *n* a small pointed tool (often with a broad handle) for making holes in leather —see picture at TOOL¹

aw·ning /ˈɔːnɪŋ/ *n* a movable covering, esp. one made of CANVAS, used to protect shop windows, ships' DECK*s*, etc., from sun or rain

a·woke /əˈwəʊk/ *past t. of* AWAKE

a·wok·en /əˈwəʊkən/ *past p. of* AWAKE

A.W.O.L. /ˌeɪ ˌdʌbəljuː əʊ ˈel, ˈeɪwɒl‖-wɔl/ *adj*

[Wa5;F] *infml* absent without leave; (of a member of the armed forces) absent from one's place of duty without permission

a·wry /əˈraɪ/ *adv, adj* [F] **1** not in the correct position or shape; twisted; bent **2** not as planned or intended; in a wrong manner: *Our plans have gone awry*

axe[1], *AmE* usu. **ax** /æks/ *n* **axes** /ˈæksɨz/ **1** [C] a tool with a heavy metal blade on the end of a long handle used to cut down trees or split logs —see picture at TOOL[1] **2** [*the*+R] *infml* (in the phrs. **give/get the axe**) **a** sudden ending of one's employment by an employer because of lack of money, an argument, etc. **b** the ending of a plan, esp. caused by a lack of money: *We were going to build a new school but it got the axe from the government* **3 have an axe to grind** *infml* to have private and often selfish reasons for one's actions

axe[2], *AmE* usu. **ax** *v* [T1] *infml* to remove suddenly and perhaps without warning from a job, a list of plans for completion, etc.

ax·i·om /ˈæksɪəm/ *n* a statement, esp. one that is short, that is generally accepted as true and doesn't need to be proved

ax·i·o·mat·ic /ˌæksɪəˈmætɪk/ *adj* **1** *tech* of, like, or containing one or more AXIOM*s* **2** not needing to be proved; SELF-EVIDENT —**~ally** *adv* [Wa4]

ax·is /ˈæksɨs/ *n* **axes** /ˈæksiːz/ **1** the line, usu. an imaginary line, around which a spinning body moves —see picture at GLOBE **2** a line that divides a regular shape into 2 equal parts with the same shape **3** a fixed line used as a reference point, esp. the HORIZONTAL and VERTICAL lines around a GRAPH

ax·le /ˈæksəl/ *n* a bar with a wheel on either end, around which the wheels turn or which turns with the wheels —see picture at CAR

ax·o·lot·l /ˌæksəˈlɒtl‖ˈæksəlɑtl/ *n* [Wn1] any of several types of small cold-blooded 4-legged creature (AMPHIBIAN*s* (1)) that live in the mountain lakes of Mexico and western US —see picture at AMPHIBIAN

ay·ah /ˈaɪə/ *n Ind & Pak E* an Indian nurse who looks after children

aye[1], **ay** /eɪ, aɪ/ *adv ScotE, esp. old use or poet* always; continually

aye[2] /aɪ/ *adv dial, poet, or naut* yes: *Aye, aye, sir; I'll do that at once*

aye[3], **ay** /aɪ/ *n* **1** a vote or voter in favour of an idea, plan, law, etc. **2 The ayes have it!** (said in Parliament to declare that more people have voted yes than no) —opposite **nay**; compare YEA[2]

a·za·le·a /əˈzeɪlɪə/ *n* **1** a type of bush with bright usu. strong-smelling flowers **2** a flower from this bush

az·i·muth /ˈæzɨməθ/ *n* the angle on the earth's surface between a north-south line and the position or direction of something, esp. a star, seen from a place on the earth

az·ure /ˈæʒəʳ, ˈæʒjʊəʳ, ˈæzjʊəʳ‖ˈæʒər/ *adj, n* [B;U] bright blue, as of the sky

B, b

B, b /biː/ **B's, b's** *or* **Bs, bs** the second letter of the English alphabet

b *written abbrev. for:* born: *b 1885*

B 1 a (in Western music) the 7th note (*AmE* also **tone**) in the row of notes which form the musical SCALE of C MAJOR **b** the musical KEY based on this note **2** the second level, as for an example of a student's work

BA *abbrev. for:* **1** Bachelor of Arts; (a title for someone who has) a first university degree: *Susan Potter, BA|a BA* **2** British Airways **3** Buenos Aires

baa[1] /bɑː/ also **ba**— *n* the sound made by a sheep or lamb

baa[2] *v* **baaed** [IØ] to make the sound that a sheep or lamb makes

bab·ble[1] /ˈbæbəl/ *v* **1** [IØ] to talk quickly and foolishly or in a way that is hard to understand: *During his fever he babbled without stopping* **2** [T1] to express by babbling: *She babbled her thanks in a great hurry* **3** [T1 (OUT)] to repeat foolishly; tell (secrets): *He babbled the secret (out) to his friends* —compare BLAB **4** [IØ (AWAY or ON)] to make continuous sounds like a baby learning to speak: *The baby babbled (away) for hours* **5** [Wv4;IØ (AWAY, ON, or ALONG)] to make continuous sounds like a stream running gently over rounded stones: *a babbling stream* —compare BURBLE

babble[2] *n* [U;S] **1** childish, disordered, or foolish talk **2** a confused sound of many people talking: *a babble of voices* **3** speech that is hard to understand because of its speed and pronunciation **4** a sound like that of water running gently over rounded stones: *What's that babble of running water I seem to hear?* —compare BURBLE

bab·bler /ˈbæbələʳ/ *n* a person who BABBLE*s*, esp. a baby learning to speak

babe /beɪb/ *n* **1** [C] *lit & poet* a baby **2** [N;(C)] *sl esp. AmE* a girl: HI *there, babe!*

ba·bel /ˈbeɪbəl/ *n* [S;U] a scene of confusion, noise of many voices, or disorder (as in the Bible story of the building of the tower of Babel) —compare BABBLE[2] (2)

ba·boon /bəˈbuːn‖bæ-/ *n* any of several types of large doglike monkeys of Africa or S. Asia —see picture at PRIMATE[2]

ba·bu, baboo /ˈbɑːbuː/ *n IndE* **1** [A] a former Hindu title, like Mr **2** [C] an Indian clerk

ba·by[1] /ˈbeɪbi/ *n* **1** [C] a very young child, esp. one who has not learnt to speak **2** [C;A] a very young animal or bird: *a baby monkey* **3** [C] **a** the youngest of a group: *the baby of the class* **b** a small member of a group: *a baby car* **4** [C] *usu. derog* a person who behaves like a baby: *Don't be such a baby!* **5** [N;(C)] *sl esp. AmE* a person, esp. a girl or woman: *I've got a gun here, baby, so you'd better just be a good boy and hand over all your money*

baby[2] *v* [T1] *infml* to treat like a baby; give a great deal of care or attention to

baby car·riage /ˈ·· ˌ··/ *n esp. AmE* PRAM

ba·by·hood /ˈbeɪbihʊd/ *n* [U] the period of time when one is a baby

ba·by·ish /ˈbeɪbi-ɪʃ/ *adj often derog* like a baby: *A big boy like you shouldn't be so babyish*

baby-mind·er /ˈ·· ˌ··/ *n esp. BrE* a person who takes care of babies while their mothers are away working

baby-sit /ˈ·· ·/ *v* **-sat**, *pres. p.* **-tt-** [IØ (*for*)] to act as a BABY-SITTER

baby-sit·ter /ˈ·· ˌ··/ also **sitter**— *n* a person who takes care of babies or children while their parents are out: *We'd love to go to your party, but baby-sitters are so hard to find these days!*

baby talk /ˈ·· ·/ *n* [U] **1** the speechlike sounds that babies make in the early stages of learning language **2** the things that fully grown people say to babies, intended to be like baby talk

baby tooth /'·· ·/ *n esp. AmE* MILK TOOTH

bac·ca·lau·re·ate /ˌbækə'lɔːrɪət/ *n fml* BACHELOR'S DEGREE: *He received his baccalaureate at an unusually early age*

bac·ca·rat, -ra /'bækərɑː‖ˌbækə'rɑ (*Fr* bakara)/ *n* [U] *Fr* a kind of card game usu. played for money

bac·cha·nal /ˌbækə'næl, 'bækənəl/ *n esp. lit* a noisy party with a lot of drinking and disorderly behaviour, perhaps including sex —**bacchanalian** /ˌbækə'neɪlɪən/ *adj*

bac·cy /'bæki/ *n* [U] *humor sl* tobacco

bach·e·lor /'bætʃələʳ/ *n* **1** an unmarried man **2** the holder, male or female, of a BACHELOR'S DEGREE

bachelor girl /'··· ˌ·/ *n euph* an unmarried woman, esp. a young independent one —compare SPINSTER

bachelor's de·gree /'··· ·ˌ·/ *n* a first university degree in any of several subjects, such as **Bachelor of Science** (B.Sc.)

ba·cil·lus /bə'sɪləs/ *n* **-cilli** /'sɪlaɪ/ **1** *tech* any of several kinds of rod-shaped bacteria **2** *infml* a bacterium

back[1] /bæk/ *n* **1** [C] the part of the body of a human or animal down the middle of which runs the BACKBONE: *lie on your back and look at the stars|You'll make your back ache if you carry those heavy buckets* **2** [*the*+R (*of*);(C)] the less important side or surface (of an object): *You must iron the backs of the shirts as well as the fronts.|There's another good song on the back of this record.|The back of the knife won't cut* **3** [(*the*) R (*of*);C] (of a building) the side opposite to the main entrance: *Let's go round to the back.|The back of the house looks out onto the river* **4** [*the*+R (*of*)] (of a vehicle) **a** the inside part behind the driver: *3 people can sit in the back of/on the back seat of this car* **b** the outside surface opposite to the usual direction of movement: *He wrote "Just Married" on the back of their car* **5** [*the*+R (*of*)] the furthest or last part (from the point towards which a group of people are facing or moving): *Sit at the back of the class/of the theatre/of the aircraft* **6** [*the*+R (*of*)] (of a chair) the part that one leans against when sitting —see picture at LIVING ROOM **7** [*the*+R (*of*)] (of a book or newspaper) the end: *There is a lot of useful information at the back of this dictionary* —compare BACK[2] (6) **8** [C;U] (in games like football) a player or position that defends the area to the left or right near the team's own GOAL: *John plays back/is one of the backs* —compare FORWARD[3], CENTRE[1] (5) and see picture at SOCCER **9 at the back (of)** *AmE not fml* also **in back (of) a** behind: *a garden at the back of the house* **b** on the less important side or surface (of): *a dress that buttons at the back* **10 at one's back** supporting or favouring one: *If you take this decision you will certainly have the President at your back* **11 back to back** with the backs facing each other: *Stand back to back and we'll see which of you is taller.|a row of back-to-back houses* **12 break the back of** to do most of; do the worst part of (something that must be done):*If we start very early, we can break the back of the journey before it gets hot* **13 be glad to see the back of someone** *infml* to be glad when someone goes away: *He's been living here for a month, and we'll be glad to see the back of him—he eats too much!* **14 have/with one's back to the wall** *infml* (to be) in a bad state of affairs, so that one must try very hard: *The trade figures are worse this month—the country's really got its back to the wall!* **15 on one's back** *infml* ill in bed: *He was (flat) on his back for 3 months* **16 put one's back into** to work very hard at: *If we really put our backs into the job we can finish it today* **17 put someone's back up** *infml* to annoy someone: *He always puts my back up by making those silly jokes* **18 turn one's back on** *often derog* to avoid; go away from (esp. when one should stay): *He's always been kind to me—I can't just turn my back on him now he's ill and poor* **19 know (esp. a place) like the back of one's hand** *infml* to know (esp. a place) very well —**~less** *adj* [Wa5]

back[2] *adv* **1** towards or at the back: *to tie one's hair back|Sit well back or you won't be able to fasten your seat belt* **2** away (from the front, the speaker, etc.): *Stand back! You're stepping on my skirt.|The house stood a little way back from the road* **3** where or how (one or something) was before: *Put the book back (on the shelf) when you've finished it.|Back in Nigeria (where I come from) we used to play a lot of tennis.|She came back to get the basket which she'd left behind.|Let me know when you're back/when you get back.|*(fig.) *Nobody wants Richard back as President.|"Welcome back to Old Trafford!"* (SEU S.) **4** *not fml* ago; in the past: *We met him 3 years back* **5** in return or reply: *Telephone me back when you know the answer* **6** towards the beginning (of a book): *You will find it 6 pages further back* —compare BACK[1] (7) **7** so as to be delayed or made slower: *The child's bad health has kept/held him back at school* **8** (of a clock) so as to show an earlier time: *to put the clock back an hour*

back[3] *adj* [Wa5;A] **1** long past: *The war is all back history now, and our 2 countries are good friends* **2** (of money) owed from an earlier time: *back pay/rent* **3** at the back: *the back door/back yard* —see also BACK DOOR (2) **4** earlier than the most recent one: *a back* NUMBER *of a magazine* —see also BACK NUMBER (2) **5** (in PHONETICS, of a vowel) made by raising the tongue at the back of the mouth —opposite **front 6** (in GOLF) being the last 9 holes of an 18-hole course

back[4] *v* **1** [IØ;T1] to (cause to) go backwards: *She backed the horse|The car backed through the gate* **2** [T1 (*in*)] to support and encourage, often with money: *If I back your plan I'll expect a share of the profits.|The union leaders decided to back the Government (in its action)* **3** [T1] to put money on the success of (a horse or dog in a race); BET on: *Jane backed the winner and won £5* **4** [T1] to write and sign a promise of payment on (a bill) **5** [T1 (*with*) *often pass*] to be or make the back of; LINE[1] the inside of: *You could back the dress with silk.|curtains backed with a plastic material* **6** [IØ] *tech* (of the wind) to change direction slowly, moving round the compass in the order North–West–South–East —compare VEER (5) **7 back the wrong horse** *not fml* to support the loser —see also BACK AWAY, BACK DOWN, BACK OFF, BACK ONTO, BACK OUT, BACK UP

back·ache /'bækeɪk/ *n* [C;U] (a) pain in the back: *He suffers from backache.|He is suffering from a backache* —see ACHE[2] (USAGE)

back a·way *v adv* [IØ] to move backwards, so as to allow space, or in fear, etc.

back·bench /ˌbæk'bentʃ◂/ *n* [*the*+GU] *esp. BrE* members of Parliament who do not hold official positions in the Government or Opposition, and who sit on the back seats: *a backbench member|on the backbench|backbench support for the plan* —compare FRONTBENCH —**backbencher** *n*: *angry backbenchers*

back·bite /'bækbaɪt/ *v* [IØ] *derog* to speak unkindly of an absent person —**~r** *n* —**-biting** *n* [U]

back·bone /'bækbəʊn/ *n* **1** [*the*+R (*of*)] the main support of a group, association, plan, etc.: *I tell you, Smith, the small farmer is the backbone of this country!* **2** [U] firmness of mind; strength of character: *"No backbone," said the old general. "That's the trouble with young people today!"* **3** [C; *the*+R] *not fml* SPINE (1) **4 to the backbone** completely; in all ways

back·break·ing /ˈbækbreɪkɪŋ/ *adj* (of work) very hard to do; heavy enough to "break one's back": *a backbreaking job/load* —**~ly** *adv*: *backbreakingly difficult*

back·chat /ˈbæktʃæt/ *n* [U] *BrE* rude talk in reply to someone: *Now listen to me carefully, and I don't want any backchat!*

back·cloth /ˈbæk-klɒθ‖-klɔθ/ *n BrE* BACKDROP (1)

back·comb /ˈbæk-kəʊm/ *v* [T1] to comb (hair) against the direction of growth, in order to produce a BOUFFANT effect

back crawl /ˌ·ˈ·/ *n* [*the*+R;C] BACKSTROKE

back·date /ˌbækˈdeɪt/ *v* [T1] to agree to give (something) a starting date earlier than the date of the agreement: *The increase in pay agreed in June will be backdated to January*

back dive /ˌ·ˈ·/ *n* a jump head first into the water (DIVE) for which one starts off facing the land

back door /ˌ·ˈ·/ *n* **1** the door at the back of a building **2 get in through/by the back door** to get a job through having some unfair advantage

back down *v adv* [I∅] to yield in argument, opinion, or claim; admit that one was wrong: *The speaker's forceful words persuaded his opponent to back down*

back·drop /ˈbækdrɒp‖-drɑp/ *n* **1** a painted cloth hung across the back of a stage —see picture at THEATRE **2** BACKGROUND (4): *The stormy political events of the 1930's provided the backdrop for the story of their love*

back·er /ˈbækəʳ/ *n* **1** someone who supports a plan with money; esp. someone who pays for a play to be performed in the theatre **2** someone who BACKs⁴ (3) a horse

back·fire¹ /ˈbækfaɪəʳ/ *n* an explosion in a petrol engine which comes too soon and makes a loud noise but does not drive the car forward

backfire² /ˌbækˈfaɪəʳ‖ˈbækfaɪəʳ/ *v* [I∅] **1** to produce a BACKFIRE¹ **2** to have an unexpected effect opposite to the effect intended: *His plan to get rich backfired (on him), and he lost all his money*

back for·ma·tion /ˈ· ·ˌ··/ *n tech* **1** [C] a word formed from another word that seems to be formed from it: *"To* POT*" is a back formation from "*POTTER*"* **2** [U] the formation of these words: *Back formation is something that enriches and modernizes English*

back·gam·mon /ˈbækgæmən/ *n* [U] an indoor board game for 2 players, using round wooden pieces and DICE

back·ground /ˈbækgraʊnd/ *n* **1** [C] the scenery or ground behind something **2** [C] the part of a painting or photograph that shows what is behind the main objects or people **3** [C *usu. sing.*] a position as unnoticeable as possible (in the phr. **in the background**): *She has a lot of power, but likes to remain in the background* **4** [C] the conditions existing when something happens or happened: *The election took place against a background of widespread unemployment* **5** [U] also **background information** /ˈ·· ··ˌ··/— information necessary for the understanding of something: *I'll need a bit more background (information) before I can help you* **6** [C] a person's family, experience, and education: *a young man of excellent background*

back·hand¹ /ˈbækhænd/ *n* **1** also **backhand stroke** /ˈ·· ·/— a stroke (as in tennis) made with the back of the hand turned in the direction of movement **2** the ability to make such strokes: *He's not really a very good player, but he's got an excellent backhand* —compare FOREHAND

backhand² *adv, adj* BACKHANDED

back·hand·ed /ˌbækˈhændɪ̈d‖ˈbækhændɪ̈d/ *adj, adv* **1** using or made with a BACKHAND (1) **2** using, made, or done with the back of the hand: *He struck the man a backhanded blow.|He struck the man backhanded* **3 a backhanded compliment** a remark that might cause either pleasure or displeasure: *He said my face was most unusual, which was rather a backhanded compliment*

back·hand·er /ˈbækhændəʳ/ *n* **1** a blow or stroke made with a BACKHAND (1) **2** *infml* BRIBE²

back·ing /ˈbækɪŋ/ *n* **1** [U] material or moral help: *The plan has plenty of backing, and will probably succeed* **2** [U;C] something that is used to make the back of an object: (*a*) *backing of cardboard* **3** [C] (esp. in popular music) the sound made by the instrument or instruments that support the main singer(s) or instrumentalist(s)

back·lash /ˈbæklæʃ/ *n* **1** a sudden violent backward movement after a forward one **2** a strong but usu. delayed movement against a growing belief or practice, esp. against a political or social development

back·log /ˈbæklɒg‖-lɔg, -lɑg/ *n* [C *usu. sing.*] a group of things to be done that were not done at the proper time: *After his holiday, he had a big backlog of work to get through*

back·most /ˈbækməʊst/ *adj* [Wa5;A] farthest back: *the backmost row of seats*

back num·ber /ˌ·ˈ··/ *n* **1** also **back is·sue** /ˌ·ˈ··/— a newspaper, magazine, etc., earlier than the most recent one **2** *derog* a person or thing that is out of date

back of /ˈ· ·/ *prep esp. AmE* at the back of

back of be·yond /ˌ· · ·ˈ·/ *n* [*the*+R] *BrE infml* a very distant place: *He lives somewhere at the back of beyond*

back off *v adv* [I∅] *AmE* BACK DOWN

back on·to *v prep* [T1] (of a place or building) to be near to at the back: *The house backs onto the river*

back out *v adv* [I∅ (*from, of*)] *not fml* to fail to fulfil (a promise, contract, etc.): *I hope I can depend on you not to back out at the last moment*

back pas·sage /ˌ·ˈ··/ *n euph* RECTUM

back·ped·al /ˌbækˈpedl‖ˈbækˌpedl/ *v* **-ll-** (*AmE* **-l-**) [I∅] **1** to PEDAL backwards, as on a bicycle **2** *infml* to take back a statement; undo something that has been done; draw back from some promised action

back·room boy /ˈbækrʊm ˌbɔɪ, -ruːm-/ *n* [*often pl.*] *esp. BrE infml* a person whose work is important but secret, esp. a scientist or planner

back seat /ˌ·ˈ·/ *n* **1** [C] a seat at the back of a car **2** [S] a less important position: *She won't take a back seat to anyone*

back-seat dri·ver /ˌ· ·ˈ··/ *n derog* a passenger in a motor vehicle who thinks he knows more than the driver and tells the driver what to do

back·side /ˈbæksaɪd/ *n sl* the part of the body on which one sits

back·slide /ˌbækˈslaɪd‖ˈbækslaɪd/ *v* [I∅] to fall back morally, in the practice of religion, etc.: *He kept away from strong drink for years, but recently I'm afraid he's begun to backslide* —**-slider** *n*

backspace¹ /ˈbækspeɪs/ *n* the part that one presses to make the roller of a TYPEWRITER move back towards the beginning of the line

back·space² /ˌ·ˈ·‖ˈ··/ *v* [I∅] to use the BACKSPACE¹

back·stage¹ /ˌbækˈsteɪdʒ/ *adv* **1** behind the stage in a theatre, esp. in(to) the dressing rooms of the actors **2** in secret: *That's what they say, but who knows what really goes on backstage?*

back·stage² /ˈbæksteɪdʒ/ *adj* [Wa5;A] of or about the private lives of theatre people: *"Backstage

Wife", the exciting story of the wife of a famous actor loved by 1000's of women!

back·stairs /ˈbæksteəz‖-steərz/ also **back·stair** /-steəʳ/— *adj* [Wa5;A] **1** secret and perhaps unfair: *backstairs influence* **2** full of news about the secret faults of others: *Let's have no more of this backstairs talk about the minister*

back·stay /ˈbæksteɪ/ *n* [*often pl.*] a rope that supports the MAST of a ship or boat against forward movement

back street /ˈ· ·/ *n* [*usu. pl.*] a street away from the main streets, esp. in a poor area of a town

back·stroke /ˈbækstrəʊk/ also **back crawl**— *n* [(*the*) S] **1** a swimming stroke done on one's back **2** the ability to do this stroke: *He's not a really good swimmer, but he's got a fine backstroke* **3** a swimming competition using only this stroke: *He won the backstroke again this year*

back talk /ˈ· ·/ *n* [U] *esp. AmE* BACKCHAT

back·track /ˈbæktræk/ *v* [I∅] **1** to go back over the same path **2** BACKPEDAL (2): *The government is backtracking from its more costly plans*

back·up /ˈbækʌp/ *n* **1** a thing or person ready to be used in place of another **2** a person or thing ready to help another

back up *v adv* [T1] **1** to support: *Most members were against Mr Jones, who would have lost his position if you hadn't backed him up* **2** (in sailing) to pull tight (the free end of a fastened rope)

back·ward /ˈbækwəd‖-ərd/ *adj* **1** [Wa5;A] directed towards the back, the beginning, or the past: *a backward look* **2** [Wa5;A] returning: *the backward journey* **3** [B] behind in development: *Some backward parts of the country do not have any electricity* **4** [F] unsure of oneself: *Come over and talk to me. Don't be so backward* —**~ly** *adv* —**~ness** *n* [U]

backward coun·try /ˌ·· ˈ··/ also **backward na·tion**— *n derog* DEVELOPING COUNTRY

back·wards /ˈbækwədz‖-ərdz/ also (*esp. AmE*) **backward**— *adv* **1** away from one's front; towards the back: *He looked backwards* **2** with the back first: *to walk backwards* **3** towards the past or an earlier state **4** in the opposite way to what is right or usual: *You've put on your hat backwards* **5 backwards and forwards** first in one direction and then in the opposite direction **6 bend/lean over backwards** to try as hard as possible or almost too hard: *"They would always bend over backwards to help them in any possible way"* (SEU S.) **7 know something backwards** to understand something perfectly: *"I've always been over it so many times that I know it backwards"* (SEU S.) —compare FORWARD²

back·wash /ˈbækwɒʃ‖-wɔʃ, -wɑʃ/ *n* [(*the*) S] **1** a backward movement (as of water or air) produced by a force pushing forward (like a boat engine) **2** *infml* the (usu. unpleasant) indirect result of an action: *He was left without money in the backwash of the failure of his business*

back·wa·ter /ˈbækwɔːtəʳ/ *n* **1** a part of a river, usu. a branch, out of the main stream, where the water does not move **2** a place (or state of mind) not influenced by outside events or new ideas

back·woods /ˈbækwʊdz/ *n* [*the*+GU] (esp. in N. America) uncleared land far away from towns

back·woods·man /ˈbækwʊdzmən/ *n* **-men** /mən/ **1** a man who lives in the BACKWOODS **2** *derog* a member of the British HOUSE OF LORDS who lives in the country and hardly ever attends its meetings

back·yard /ˌbækˈjɑːd◂‖-ˈjɑrd◂/ *n* **1** *BrE* a yard behind a house, covered with a hard surface **2** also **yard**— *AmE* a yard behind a house, usu. covered with grass

ba·con /ˈbeɪkən/ *n* [U] **1** *BrE* salted or smoked meat from the back or sides of a pig **2** *AmE* smoked meat from the sides of a pig, served in narrow thin pieces **3 bring home the bacon** *sl* to succeed, esp. in providing food and other necessary things for one's family **4 save one's bacon** *BrE infml* to escape with difficulty from loss, harm, blame: *I saved my bacon by arriving just in time for the meeting*

bac·te·ri·a /bækˈtɪərɪə/ *n sing.* **-rium** /rɪəm/ [P] very small living things (related to plants), some of which cause disease. They exist in water, soil, air, plants, and the bodies of men and animals —compare GERM (1), VIRUS —**-rial** *adj* [Wa5]

bac·te·ri·ol·o·gy /bækˌtɪəriˈɒlədʒi‖-ˈɑl-/ *n* [U] the scientific study of BACTERIA —**-ologist** /bækˌtɪəriˈɒlədʒɨst‖-ˈɑl-/ *n*

Bac·tri·an /ˈbæktrɪən/ *adj* [Wa5] see CAMEL (16)

bad¹ /bæd/ *adj* **worse** /wɜːs‖wɜrs/, **worst** /wɜːst‖wɜrst/ **1** not of acceptable quality; poor: *a bad worker|bad work* **2** unfavourable: *His behaviour has a bad effect on other people* **3** no longer of acceptable quality because of decay or disrepair: *bad fish|The house was in bad condition* **4** morally wrong: *bad behaviour* **5** disobedient: *a bad boy* **6** not suitable for a particular purpose; INEFFECTIVE: *very bad light in this room* **7** unpleasant: *bad news|a bad smell* **8** harmful: *Smoking is bad for your health* **9** not healthy; diseased: *bad teeth* **10** not feeling healthy or happy: *to feel bad* **11** serious; severe: *a bad cold|a bad defeat* **12** *infml* unfortunate; unpleasant (esp. in such phrs. as **It's a bad business, That's a bad business**) **13** not following the rules; incorrect: *bad grammar* **14** (of money) false; worthless: *a bad coin/cheque* **15** (of language or a word) not used in polite society **16 a bad lot/egg/hat/type** *old sl* a person of poor character **17 (act) in bad faith** (to act) dishonestly; without intending to carry out a promise **18 feel bad about** *infml* to be sorry or ashamed about: *I felt bad about not being able to come last night* **19 go from bad to worse** to keep getting worse **20 go bad** to become unfit to eat: *The fish has gone bad because of the hot weather* **21 have/get a bad name** to lose or have lost people's respect: *That kind of car has a bad name among motorists* **22 in a bad temper** angry **23 in a bad way** to be very ill or in serious trouble **24 (It's/That's) too bad** *infml* I'm sorry: *Too bad you couldn't come last night* **25 make the best of a bad job** *infml* to do as well as one can in a difficult position **26 not bad/not so bad/not half bad** *infml* really rather good (or well): *"How are you?" "Not bad."* **27 with (a) bad grace** unwillingly —**~ness** *n* [U]

bad² *n* [*the*+U] **1** that which is bad **2 go to the bad** *becoming rare* to begin living in a wrong, immoral, or evil way: *He's gone to the bad since he got rich* **3 take the bad with the good** to (learn to) accept both the good things and the bad things in life **4 to the bad** in debt: *I've spent so much that I'm £100 to the bad this month*

bad blood /ˌ· ˈ·/ also **bad feel·ing** /ˌ· ˈ··/— *n* [U] angry feeling: *There is a lot of bad blood between them. I think that one day they will quarrel openly*

bad debt /ˌ· ˈ·/ *n* a debt that is unlikely to be paid

bade /bæd, beɪd/ *past t. and p. of* BID¹

bad form /ˌ· ˈ·/ *n* [U] *esp. BrE* unacceptable behaviour: *It's bad form to get drunk*

badge /bædʒ/ *n* **1** a piece of metal or other material which shows a person's employment, rank, membership of a group, etc. **2** a sign of something, which sign can be seen: *Some officials wear chains round their necks as badges of office*

bad·ger¹ /ˈbædʒəʳ/ *n* **1** [C] any of several types of animal of the northern half of the world, which are black and have some white fur on their faces, live in holes in the ground, and are active at night

—see picture at CARNIVOROUS **2** [U] the skin or hair of this animal: *a badger brush*

badger² *v* [T1 (*with* or *into*);V3] to ask again and again: *You're always badgering me (with your silly questions)!*

bad·i·nage /ˈbædɪnɑːʒ‖ˌbædənˈɑʒ/ *n* [U] playful language making fun of somebody; BANTER²: *Enough of this badinage: let's talk seriously*

bad·ly /ˈbædli/ *adv* **1** in a bad manner: *badly made clothes|to play badly|badly wounded* **2** (esp. of competitions) by a great deal: *My horse was badly beaten in the race* **3** (*with* "want," "need," *etc.*) a great deal; very much: *They want help badly.|He is badly in need of a haircut*

badly-off /ˌ·· ˈ·/ *adj* **worse-off, worst-off** **1** [F] poor **2** [F3, 9, esp. *for*] unlucky; not provided with desirable things: *He's badly-off for friends* (=hasn't many friends) —opposite **well-off**; compare OFF¹ (11, 12)

bad·min·ton /ˈbædmɪntən/ *n* [U] a tennis-like game played by 2 or 4 people who hit a small feathered object (SHUTTLECOCK) over a high net
USAGE One plays a *game* of **badminton** on a *court*, using a **racket** to hit the **shuttlecock**, and *scoring* (SCORE) *points*. In an important *match*, the person in charge is called the **umpire.**

baf·fle¹ /ˈbæfəl/ *v* [Wv3;T1] to make effective action impossible by confusing: *The examination question baffled me completely and I couldn't answer it* —**~ment** *n* [U]

baffle² *n tech* a board or other means of controlling the flow of air, water, or sound coming into or going out of an enclosed space

baf·fling /ˈbæflɪŋ/ *adj* which BAFFLES¹: *a baffling question* —**~ly** *adv*: *a bafflingly difficult question*

bag¹ /bæg/ *n* **1** a container made of soft material such as cloth, paper, or leather, opening at the top **2** [(*usu. sing.*)] the quantity of usu. small birds or animals shot or caught on any one occasion: *We had a good bag that day* —compare KILL² (1) **3** BAGFUL **4 in the bag** *sl* as desired: *Don't worry. We've got the match in the bag.|We're sure to win. It's in the bag, I tell you!* **5 the whole bag of tricks** *sl* everything **6 a bag of bones** a very thin person (or animal)

bag² *v* **-gg-** **1** [T1] to put (material or objects in large quantities) into a bag or bags **2** [T1] *infml* to kill or catch (animals or birds): *We bagged a rabbit* **3** [T1] *sl* **a** to take without permission but not intending dishonesty: *He's bagged my pencil* **b** to take or keep (one of a limited number of spaces or places): *Try to bag seats at the back for us* **4** [IØ (OUT)] *infml* to hang loosely, like a bag: *His trousers bagged (out) at the knees*

bag and bag·gage /ˌ· · ˈ··/ *adv* with all one's belongings: *They threw her out of the house bag and baggage*

bag·a·telle /ˌbægəˈtel/ *n* **1** [U] a kind of game played with balls on a board with holes in it **2** [C] something considered to be small and unimportant; TRIFLE (1): *My book? Oh, nothing much, really—just a bagatelle* **3** [C] a small piece of music

bag·ful /ˈbægfʊl/ *n* **bagfuls** *or* **bagsful** the quantity in a bag

bag·gage /ˈbægɪdʒ/ *n* **1** [U] *BrE usu.* **luggage**— *esp. AmE* all the bags and other containers with which a person travels **2** [U] tents, beds, etc., esp. of an army, which they take with them **3** [C] *humor* a good-for-nothing young woman; MINX: *Come here, you little baggage, let me kiss you* **4** [C] *derog* an ugly annoying old woman: *You silly old baggage*

baggage room /ˈ·· ·/ *n AmE* LEFT LUGGAGE OFFICE

bag·gy /ˈbægi/ *adj* [Wa1] *infml* hanging in loose folds: *His trousers were baggy at the knees*

bag·pipes /ˈbægpaɪps/ also (*infml*) **pipes**— *n* [(*the*) P] any of several types of musical instrument played in Scotland and elsewhere, in which air stored in a bag is forced out through pipes to produce the sound: *to play the bagpipes|bagpipe music*

bags¹ /bægz/ *n* [P+*of*] *sl, esp. BrE* lots (of): *He has bags of money!*

bags² *n* [P] *BrE* wide trousers for men

bags³ *interj BrE sl* **Bags I!** (used by children) **a** It's mine; don't touch it **b** I'll do it, not you

bah /bɑː/ *interj* (shows a low opinion of someone or something)

bail¹ /beɪl/ *n* [U] **1** money left with a court of law so that a prisoner may be set free until he is tried **2 go bail for someone** to pay money so that someone may be set free in this way

bail² *n* (in cricket) either of 2 small pieces of wood laid on top of the STUMPS —see picture at CRICKET

bai·ley /ˈbeɪli/ *n* **1** the outer wall of a castle —see picture at CASTLE¹ **2** a courtyard inside these walls

Bailey bridge /ˈ·· ˌ·/ *n* a bridge made up of separate parts that can be carried to a river and put together quickly, used esp. in military operations

bai·liff /ˈbeɪlɪf/ *n* **1** *Br law* an official, esp. one who takes possession of goods or property when money is owed **2** *US law* an official in a law-court, esp. one who works as a messenger or door-keeper **3** *BrE* a man who looks after a farm or land for the owner

bail out *v adv* **1** [T1] to obtain (someone's) freedom by paying money (BAIL¹) to ensure appearance in court: *Clark was to be charged next month with robbing the bank, so his family paid £500 to bail him out* **2** [T1;IØ] also **bale out**— to remove water from (a boat) so as to prevent sinking: *When the storm rose on the lake, we had to bail out to reach the shore safely* **3** [T1] to pay money to save from failure: *The government can't hope to bail out all the companies* **4** [IØ (*of*)] *AmE* BALE OUT

bairn /beən‖beərn/ *n Scot & N Eng E* a child

bait¹ /beɪt/ *v* **1** [T1 (*with*)] to put BAIT² (1) on (a hook) to catch fish, or in (a trap) to catch animals **2** [T1] to make (an animal or a person) angry intentionally: *to bait a bear|At school they baited the boy because of his red hair*

bait² *n* [U;S] **1** food or something like food used to attract fish, animals, or birds which are then caught **2** something that attracts attention or causes desire **3 rise to the bait** **a** (of a fish) to come and take BAIT near the surface of the water **b** (of a person) to be influenced by something offered as BAIT, either by being attracted or by becoming angry

baize /beɪz/ *n* [U] thick woollen cloth, usu. green, used esp. to cover tables on which certain games are played

bake /beɪk/ *v* **1** [T1;IØ] to (cause to) cook using dry heat in a special box (an OVEN): *to bake bread|The bread is baking* **2** [T1;IØ] to (cause to) become hard by heating: *In former times, bricks were baked in the sun until they became hard* **3** [IØ] *infml* to become hot: *Open a window—I'm baking in here!* —see COOK² (USAGE)

Ba·ke·lite /ˈbeɪkəlaɪt/ *n* [U] *tdmk* any of several kinds of plastics or things related to plastics

bak·er /ˈbeɪkəʳ/ *n* a person who bakes bread and cakes, esp. professionally —see picture at STREET

baker's doz·en /ˌ·· ˈ··/ *n* 13: *I asked for 12, but he gave me a baker's dozen*

bak·er·y /ˈbeɪkəri/ *n* a place where bread and sometimes cakes are baked and/or sold

bak·ing pow·der /ˈ·· ˌ··/ *n* [U] a powder which forms small amounts of gas in bread and cakes while they are baking, and so makes them lighter

bak·sheesh /ˈbækʃiːʃ/ *n* [U] (in the Middle East) money given to someone who has done something for you, or to the poor

bal·a·cla·va /ˌbæləˈklɑːvə/ *n* a warm woollen head-covering that leaves the face free but covers the head, ears, and neck

bal·a·lai·ka /ˌbæləˈlaɪkə/ *n* a stringed musical instrument with a 3-sided body, played esp. in the USSR

bal·ance[1] /ˈbæləns/ *n* **1** [C] an instrument for weighing things by seeing whether the amounts in 2 hanging pans are equal —see picture at LABORATORY **2** [C] a weight or influence on one side which equals a weight or influence on the other: *The slow and steady Mr Smith acts as a balance to the clever but irresponsible Mr Jones* **3** [U;S] a state where all parts have their proper weight; EQUILIBRIUM: *Her character shows a perfect balance of mind and body* **4** [C *usu. sing.*] money or something else which remains or is left over: *My bank balance isn't very large any more.| May I take the balance of my holidays before the end of September?* **5 a favourable/unfavourable balance** a state of affairs in which more money is coming in than going out/going out than coming in **6 in the balance** uncertain(ly): *The future of the nation is/hangs in the balance* **7 keep/lose one's balance** to remain/cease to be steady: *She kept her balance and rode the bicycle. She lost her balance and fell over* **8 off balance** unsteady or unsteadily; in danger of falling **9 on balance** (with) all things considered; taking everything into consideration **10 strike a balance** to reach an arrangement which is fair to everybody

balance[2] *v* **1** [T1] to consider or compare **2** [T1; I∅] to (cause to) be steady, esp. in a difficult position: *to balance a ball on your nose* **3** [T1;I∅] to (cause to) be of equal weight, importance, or influence to (something/each other): *The weight here balances the weight there.|You have to balance the 2 weights* **4** [T1;I∅] **a** to make sure that no more money is going out of than coming into (an account): *Balance your accounts, young man!* **b** (of an account) to show no more money going out than coming in: *My accounts balance for the first time this year!*

bal·anced /ˈbælənst/ *adj apprec* having or showing a firm mind that does not suffer from unusual anxiety or worry —compare UNBALANCED

balanced di·et /ˌ·· ˈ··/ *n* a DIET[1] (1) with the right quantities and kinds of food needed for good health

balance of pay·ments /ˌ·· · ˈ··/ also **balance of trade** /ˌ·· · ˈ·/— *n* [(*the*) R] the amount of money coming into a country or area in comparison with the amount going out

balance of pow·er /ˌ·· · ˈ··/ *n* [*the*+R] **1** a position in which power, esp. political or military power, is evenly balanced on all sides **2** the power of one group in comparison with that of another **3 hold the balance of power** to be able to make either side more powerful than the other by favouring it: *The 2 big parties were so nearly equal in strength that a small party held the balance of power in Parliament*

balance sheet /ˈ·· ·/ *n* a statement of how much money has come in and how much has gone out

bal·co·ny /ˈbælkəni/ *n* **1** a shelflike place for people to stand or sit on built out from the wall of a house (or other building) and usu. enclosed **2** the seats upstairs in a theatre —see picture at THEATRE

bald /bɔːld/ *adj* [Wa1] **1** with little or no hair (on the head) **2** with little or no ornament; plain: *a bald statement* —**~ness** *n* [U]

bal·der·dash /ˈbɔːldədæʃ‖-dər-/ *n* [U] *infml* foolish talk or writing; nonsense

bald·ing /ˈbɔːldɪŋ/ *adj* becoming BALD (1): *a balding man/head*

bald·ly /ˈbɔːldli/ *adv* spoken plainly, even cruelly: *The doctor told him quite baldly that if he didn't stop smoking he'd be dead in a year*

bal·dric /ˈbɔːldrɪk/ *n* (esp. in former times) a belt for a sword, horn, etc.

bale /beɪl/ *n* [(*of*)] a large tightly tied mass of goods or material ready to be taken away

bale·ful /ˈbeɪlfəl/ *adj* (of appearance and behaviour) full of hate and desire to do harm; evil: *a baleful look* —**~fully** *adv*

bale out *v adv BrE* **1** [I∅ (*of*)] (*AmE* **bail out**)— to escape from an aircraft by PARACHUTE **2** [T1;I∅] BAIL OUT (2)

balk[1], **baulk** /bɔːk, bɔːlk/ *n* a thick rough wooden beam

balk[2], **baulk** *v* **1** [T1] to stop or get in the way of on purpose **2** [I∅ (*at*)] to be unwilling to face or agree to something difficult or unpleasant

ball[1] /bɔːl/ *n* **1** a round object used in play; anything of like shape: *to throw a ball|The Earth is a ball* **2** a ball as thrown or the ability to throw a ball in a certain way: *a fast ball|He throws a very fast ball* **3** a round bullet or SHELL[1] (4), now no longer used **4** a round mass: *a ball of clay|a snowball* **5** a rounded part of the body: *the ball of the foot*|EYEBALL —see picture at HUMAN[2] **6 on the ball** *infml* showing up-to-date knowledge and skill and readiness to act: *That book/writer is really on the ball, man!* **7 play ball a** *AmE* to (start to) play the game of BASEBALL **b** *infml* COOPERATE **8 start/keep the ball rolling** to begin/continue something **9 The ball is in your court** Now it's your turn to act or reply —see also BALLS

ball[2] *n* **1** [C] a large formal occasion for social dancing **2** [C] *sl* a very good time (esp. in the phr. **have a ball**)

bal·lad /ˈbæləd/ *n* **1** a short story told in the form of a poem **2** a simple song **3** a popular love song

bal·lade /bæˈlɑːd‖bə-/ *n* a special type of poem with usu. 3 groups of lines and a shorter 4th group all having the same last line and using a very small number of RHYMEs

bal·last[1] /ˈbæləst/ *n* [U] heavy material which a ship carries to keep it steady, which may be thrown from a BALLOON to make it rise higher, or which is put down under a road or railway

ballast[2] *v* [T1 (*with*)] to fill or supply with BALLAST

ball bear·ing /ˌ· ˈ··/ *n* **1** metal balls moving in a ring round a bar in a machine so that the bar may turn more easily, with less rubbing **2** any one of these metal balls

ball·cock /ˈbɔːlkɒk‖-kɑk/ *n* an apparatus for opening and closing a hole through which water passes, worked by a hollow floating ball which rises and falls with the level of the water

bal·le·ri·na /ˌbæləˈriːnə/ *n* a female BALLET dancer

bal·let /ˈbæleɪ‖bæˈleɪ, ˈbæleɪ/ *n* **1** [C] a dance in which a story is told without speech or singing **2** [C] the music for such a dance: *Tchaikovsky and Stravinsky each wrote several famous ballets* **3** [U; *the*+R] the art of doing such dances: *She has studied (the) ballet for 6 years* **4** [C] also **corps de ballet**— a group of ballet dancers who work together

bal·lis·tic /bəˈlɪstɪk/ *adj* [Wa5] of or about BALLISTICS

bal·lis·tics /bəˈlɪstɪks/ *n* [U] the scientific study of the movement of objects that are thrown or forced through the air such as bullets fired from a gun

bal·locks /ˈbɒləks‖ˈbɑ-/ *n, interj BrE taboo sl* BOLLOCKS

bal·loon[1] /bəˈluːn/ *n* **1** a large or small bag of strong light material filled with heated air or a gas lighter than air so that it can float in the air —see picture at AIRCRAFT **2** a small rubber bag that can be blown up, used as a toy **3** anything shaped like this (round or roundish), esp. the space round the words spoken by the figures in a CARTOON **4 the balloon goes up** the action starts

balloon[2] *v* **1** [I∅ (OUT or UP)] to get bigger and bigger, or rounder and rounder, like a BALLOON being blown up: *His cheeks ballooned (out) as he got fatter and fatter* **2** [L9] to travel softly through the air in a high curve: *The ball ballooned over the fielder's head, and he couldn't catch it*

bal·loon·ing /bəˈluːnɪŋ/ *n* [U] the sport of flying in a BALLOON[1] (1)

bal·loon·ist /bəˈluːnɪ̣st/ *n* a person who goes up in a BALLOON[1] (1)

bal·lot[1] /ˈbælət/ *n* **1** [C] a sheet of paper used to make a secret vote: *Don't spoil your ballot by writing in the wrong place* **2** [*the*+R] the action or system of secret voting: *The ballot is an important defence of political freedom* **3** [*the*+R] the right to vote: *"The ballot for women!" they cried as they marched on Parliament* **4** [C] a chance to vote: *Let's have a ballot on whether or not to do it* **5** [C] the number of votes recorded

ballot[2] *v* [I∅ (*for*)] to vote or decide by secret voting (about): *They've balloted for the new chairman, but nobody knows the result yet*

ballot box /ˈ·· ·/ *n* a box in which the voters put their BALLOTs[1] (1)

ball·point /ˈbɔːlpɔɪnt/ also (*BrE*) **biro**, (*fml*) **ball-point pen** /ˌ·· ˈ·/— *n* a pen which instead of a point at the end has a ball that rolls thick ink onto the paper

ball·room /ˈbɔːlrʊm, -ruːm/ *n* a large room or hall suitable for a BALL[2] (1)

balls /bɔːlz/ *n, interj taboo sl* **1** [P] TESTICLEs **2** [U] *derog* nonsense

balls up also (*AmE*) **ball up**— *v adv* [T1] *BrE taboo sl* to spoil —**balls-up** /ˈ· ·/ *n*

bal·ly /ˈbæli/ *adj, adv* [Wa5;A] *BrE, euph, becoming rare* BLOODY[2]

bal·ly·hoo /ˌbæliˈhuː‖ˈbælihuː/ *n* [U] *infml* ways of trying to gain public attention by making a lot of noise or through exciting kinds of advertising

balm /bɑːm‖bɑm, bɑlm/ *n* [U;C] **1** (an) oily liquid with a strong but pleasant smell, often from trees, used as medicine or to lessen pain **2** something that gives comfort to the spirit: *Your kind words come like balm to my hurt feelings*

balm·y /ˈbɑːmi‖ˈbɑmi, ˈbɑlmi/ *adj* [Wa1] **1** *apprec* (of air) soft and warm; MILD[1] (2) **2** *AmE* BARMY

ba·lo·ney /bəˈləʊni/ *n* [U] *esp. AmE* BOLONEY

bal·sa /ˈbɔːlsə/ *n* **1** [C] a tropical American tree with very light strong wood **2** [U] its wood, used esp. to make floating objects such as RAFTs

bal·sam /ˈbɔːlsəm/ *n* **1** [C] a type of flowering plant grown in gardens **2** [C] a tree that yields BALM (1) **3** [U;C] BALM (1)

bal·us·trade /ˌbæləˈstreɪd‖ˈbæləstreɪd/ *n* a row of upright pieces of stone or wood with a bar along the top, guarding the outer edge of stairs or steps, or of any place from which people might fall

bam·boo /ˌbæmˈbuː◂/ *n* **-boos** **1** [C;U] a tall plant of the grass family, found esp. in tropical areas, with hard, hollow, jointed stems, and of which some parts can be eaten when young **2** [U] the stems of this plant, used for making furniture and other things

bamboo cur·tain /ˌ·· ˈ··/ *n* [*the*+R] (*often caps.*) (a name for) the border between China and the rest of the world which cannot easily be crossed for purposes of trade, travel, etc. —compare IRON CURTAIN

bam·boo·zle /bæmˈbuːzəl/ *v* [T1 (*into* or *out of*)] *sl* to deceive; trick; HOODWINK

ban[1] /bæn/ *v* **-nn-** [T1] to forbid, esp. by law

ban[2] *n* [(*on*)] **1** an order BANning something: *to declare a ban on smoking in theatres* **2** a state of affairs in which something is BANned: *There is a ban on smoking in this theatre*

ba·nal /bəˈnɑːl, bəˈnæl/ *adj derog* uninteresting because very common: *a banal remark* —**banality** /bəˈnælɪ̣ti/ *n* [U;C]

ba·na·na /bəˈnɑːnə‖-ˈnæ-/ *n* any of several types of long curved tropical fruit, shaped like a thick finger, with a yellow skin and a soft, usu. sweet, inside —see picture at FRUIT[1], TREE[1]

banana re·pub·lic /·ˌ·· ·ˈ··/ *n* a small republic of Central or South America that is industrially undeveloped and politically unsteady

band[1] /bænd/ *n* **1** a thin flat narrow piece of material, esp. for fastening things together, or for putting round something to strengthen it **2** a thin flat narrow piece of material, forming part of an article of clothing: *neckband|wristbands* **3** a line of a different colour or pattern that stands out against the background on which it is painted or fixed **4** any of several areas of like shape into which a larger whole can be divided, such as a band of radio waves or of recorded music on a record

band[2] *v* [T1] to put a band or bands on —see also BAND TOGETHER

band[3] *n* **1** a group of people formed for some common purpose and often with a leader **2** a group of musicians (usu. not including players of stringed instruments) with a leader, esp. a group that plays "popular" rather than "serious" music —compare ORCHESTRA

ban·dage[1] /ˈbændɪdʒ/ *n* a narrow and usu. long piece of material, esp. cloth, for binding round a wound or round a part of the body that has been hurt —see picture at MEDICAL[1]

bandage[2] *v* [T1 (UP)] to tie up or bind round with a BANDAGE[1]: *The doctor bandaged (up) his broken ankle*

Band-Aid /ˈ· ˌ·/ *n tdmk AmE* a kind of STICKING PLASTER —see also ELASTOPLAST

ban·dan·na, -dana /bænˈdænə/ *n* a large handkerchief usu. with a brightly coloured pattern, worn round the neck or head

b and b /ˌ· · ˈ·/ *abbrev. for:* (*infml, esp. BrE*) bed and breakfast (=a bed for the night and breakfast the next morning), as offered in small hotels or private houses

band·box /ˈbændbɒks‖-bɑks/ *n* a light cardboard box for ladies' hats

ban·deau /ˈbændəʊ‖bænˈdəʊ/ *n* **-deaux** /dəʊz‖ˈdəʊz/ a band worn by a woman round her head to keep her hair in place

ban·dit /ˈbændɪ̣t/ *n* an armed robber, esp. one of an armed band

ban·dit·ry /ˈbændɪ̣tri/ *n* [U] the activity of BANDITs: *The national police are trying to stop all this banditry*

band·mas·ter /ˈbændˌmɑːstəʳ‖-ˌmæ-/ *n* a man who directs (CONDUCTs) a band that plays music (other than dance music)

ban·do·leer, bandolier /ˌbændəˈlɪəʳ/ *n* a belt that goes over a person's shoulder, and is used for carrying bullets

bands·man /ˈbændzmən/ *n* **-men** /mən/ a musician who plays in a band

band·stand /ˈbændstænd/ *n* a raised place, often with a roof, for a band when playing music in the open air

band to·geth·er *v adv* [I∅ (*against*)] to unite, usu. with some special purpose

band·wa·gon /ˈbænd,wægən/ *n* **jump on the bandwagon** to do or say something just because a lot of other people are doing or saying it

ban·dy[1] /ˈbændi/ *v* [T1] **1** to give and receive (words or blows) quickly **2 bandy words (with)** to quarrel (with)

bandy[2] *adj* [Wa1] **1** (of legs) curved outwards at the knees **2** also **bandy-legged** /,·· ˈ·◂‖ˈ·· ·/— (of a person or animal) having such legs

bandy a·bout *v adv* [T1 *often pass.*] **1** to spread (esp. unfavourable ideas) about by talking: *When the Websters' marriage failed, the news was quickly bandied about* **2** to talk about (something), often disrespectfully, not seriously, or without regard for truth: *Several different figures have been bandied about, but these are the only correct ones*

bane /beɪn/ *n* a cause of bad things (esp. in the phr. **the bane of one's existence/life**)

bane·ful /ˈbeɪnfəl/ *adj* causing bad things (often in the phr. **a baneful influence**) —**~ly** *adv*

bang[1] /bæŋ/ *v* **1** [T1] to strike sharply; BUMP[1] (1): *He fell and banged his knee* **2** [X9;L9] (to cause to) knock, beat, or push forcefully, often with a loud noise: *He banged the chair against the wall* **3** [L9] to make a sharp loud noise or noises: *There is someone banging about upstairs* **4** [T1] *taboo sl* (of a man) to have sex with —see also BANG AWAY, BANG INTO, BANG OUT, BANG UP

bang[2] *n* **1** a sharp blow **2** a sudden loud noise: *The door shut with a bang.* **3** a sudden strong effort: *This time, let's start off with a bang!* **4** *AmE* a lot of excitement: *What I'm trying to say, Marianne, is that I get a real bang out of seeing you* **5 go off** (*AmE* **over**) **with a bang** be very successful: *Gary Wonderful's latest record has really gone off with a bang over here*

bang[3] *adv* [H] *infml* right; directly; exactly: *We came bang up against more trouble.*|*Your answer's bang on* (=exactly correct).|*The lights went out bang in the middle of the performance*

bang[4] *n* [C *often pl. with sing. meaning*] hair cut straight across the forehead

bang[5] *v* [T1] to cut (the hair in front) straight across the forehead

bang a·way *v adv* [I∅ (*at*)] **1** *infml* to work very hard or with determined effort: *I haven't finished this work yet; I'll have to keep banging away at it until this evening* **2** *taboo sl* to have sex continuously: *They've been banging away all night*

bang·er /ˈbæŋəʳ/ *n BrE infml* **1** a SAUSAGE **2** any of several types of noisy FIREWORK **3** an old car, esp. one not in very good condition; JALOPY

bang in·to *v prep* [T1] BUMP INTO

ban·gle /ˈbæŋgəl/ *n* **1** a metal band worn round the arm or ankle as an ornament **2** an ornamental round flat object (DISC) that hangs loosely and often makes a noise when it moves

bang-on /,· ˈ·/ *interj infml* exactly correct; just right

bang out *v adv* [T1] *infml* **1** to perform (music) loudly: *Bob's at the piano again, banging out the latest popular tunes* **2** to write in haste, esp. on a TYPEWRITER: *Cyril's been hard at work all day, banging out a new story*

bang-up /,· ·/ *adj* [Wa5;A] *infml* very good: *You've done a bang-up job, my boy!*

bang up *v adv* [T1] *infml* to damage (something) or wound (a part of the body)

ban·i·an /ˈbænɪən/ *n* BANYAN

ban·ish /ˈbænɪʃ/ *v* [TI often+*from*] **1** to send away, usu. out of the country, as a punishment **2** to stop thinking about: *You can banish from your mind any idea of a holiday* —**~ment** *n* [U]

ban·is·ter /ˈbænɪ̣stəʳ/ *n* a row of upright pieces of wood or metal with a bar along the top guarding the outer edge of stairs

ban·jo /ˈbændʒəʊ/ *n* **-jos** *or* **-joes** a musical instrument with 4 or more strings, a long neck, and a body like a drum, used esp. to play popular music

bank[1] /bæŋk/ *n* **1** land along the side of a river, lake, etc. **2** earth which is heaped up in a field or garden, often making a border or division **3** a mass of snow, clouds, mud, etc.: *The banks of dark cloud promised a heavy storm* **4** a slope made at bends in a road or race-track, so that they are safer for cars to go round **5** SANDBANK: *The Dogger Bank in the North Sea can be dangerous for ships*

bank[2] *v* [I∅] (of a car or aircraft) to move with one side higher than the other, esp. when making a turn —see also BANK UP

bank[3] *n* a row, esp. of OAR*s* in an ancient boat or KEY*s* on a TYPEWRITER

bank[4] *n* **1** a place in which money is kept and paid out on demand, and where related activities go on —see picture at STREET **2** (*usu. in comb.*) a place where something is held ready for use, esp. ORGANIC products of human origin for medical use: *Hospital bloodbanks have saved many lives* **3** (a person who keeps) a supply of money or pieces for payment or use in a game of chance **4 break the bank** to win all the money that the BANK[4] (3) has in a game of chance

bank[5] *v* **1** [T1] to put or keep (money) in a bank **2** [L9, esp. *with*] to keep one's money (esp. in the stated bank): *Where do you bank?*

bank·book /ˈbæŋkbʊk/ also **passbook**— *n* a book in which a record of the money one puts into and takes out of a bank is kept

bank draft /ˈ· ·/ also **bank·bill** /ˈbænk-bɪl/, **banker's draft** /ˈ·· ·/— *n* an order by one bank to another (esp. a foreign bank) to pay a certain sum of money to someone

bank·er /ˈbæŋkəʳ/ *n* **1** a person who owns or controls or shares in the control of a BANK[4] (1): *Who are your bankers* (=which bank do you use)? **2** the player who keeps the BANK[4] (3) in various games of chance

banker's card /ˈ·· ·/ *n* an official card given to a bank's CUSTOMER and stating that the bank will always pay cheques up to a stated amount

banker's or·der /,·· ˈ··/ *n* STANDING ORDER (2)

bank hol·i·day /,· ˈ···/ *n* **1** *BrE* an official public holiday, not a Saturday or Sunday, when the banks are closed **2** *AmE* a period when banks are closed, usu. by government order, to prevent money difficulties

bank·ing /ˈbæŋkɪŋ/ *n* [U] the business of a bank or a banker

bank note /ˈ· ·/ *n* a piece of paper money printed for the national bank of a country for public use

bank on also (*fml*) **bank up·on**— *v prep* [T1,4;V3,4a *no pass.*] to depend on; trust in: *I'd like to come with you, but that's not a promise; don't bank on it.*|*I'm banking on you to help me with the arrangements*

bank rate /ˈ· ·/ *n* [(*the*) R;C] the rate of interest fixed by a central bank, such as the Bank of England

bank·rupt[1] /ˈbæŋkrʌpt/ *n* **1** a person who is unable to pay his debts **2** *derog* a person who is lacking in some usu. good quality: *a moral bankrupt, who will do anything for money*

bankrupt[2] *v* [T1] to make BANKRUPT[3] (1) or very poor

bankrupt[3] *adj* **1** [Wa5;B] unable to pay one's debts: *The company went bankrupt because it couldn't sell its products* **2** [B] *derog* lacking in some usu. good quality **3** [B] *derog* no longer able to produce anything good **4** [F+*in* or *of*] *derog* completely without (good things): *They seem to be bankrupt of all kind feelings*

bank·rupt·cy /ˈbæŋkrʌptsi/ *n* **1** [U] the quality or state of being BANKRUPT[3] **2** [C] an example of this: *There were many bankruptcies in the business world because it was hard to sell anything that year* **3** [U] *derog* complete failure or inability to produce anything good: *the bankruptcy of the government's plans became clear when prices rose steeply*

bank up *v adv* **1** [T1;IØ] to form into a mass: *The wind had banked the snow up against the wall* **2** [T1] to form (a fire) into a heap, so as to control the rate of burning: *At night we bank up the fire so that it's still burning in the morning* **3** [T1] to heap earth around, so as to control the flow of water: *Every spring we have to bank up the river to prevent flooding*

ban·ner[1] /ˈbænəʳ/ *n* **1** *lit* a flag **2** a long piece of cloth on which a sign is painted, usu. carried between 2 poles: *The marchers' banners all said "We want work"* **3 under the banner of** in the name of; for the cause of: *The new government came to power under the banner of change*

banner[2] *adj* [Wa5;A] *AmE apprec* very good: *a banner year for business*

banner head·line /ˌ·· ˈ··/ *n* a newspaper HEADLINE so big that it goes across several COLUMN*s*

ban·nock /ˈbænək/ *n* **1** (in N Eng & Scot) a kind of flat homemade loaf or cake made of OATMEAL **2** (in New England, US) a kind of flat homemade loaf or cake made of MAIZE

banns /bænz/ *n* [P] **1** a public declaration, esp. in church, of an intended marriage **2 publish the banns** to read this out in church

ban·quet[1] /ˈbæŋkwɨt/ *n* **1** a dinner for many people in honour of a special person or occasion, esp. one at which speeches are made **2** *apprec* a rich feast: *Everything you cook for me is a banquet, my dear*

banquet[2] *v* **1** [IØ] to take part in a BANQUET **2** [T1] to arrange a BANQUET for (someone): *They banqueted her like a queen when she became director of that company*

ban·shee /bænˈʃiː‖ˈbænʃiː/ *n* (esp. in Ireland) a spirit whose cry is believed to mean that there will be a death in the house

ban·tam /ˈbæntəm/ *n* any of various kinds of farm chicken, smaller than the standard kinds, but of which some of the males are fighters

ban·tam·weight /ˈbæntəmweɪt/ *n* a boxer (BOX[4]) who weighs more than 112 but not more than 118 pounds

ban·ter[1] /ˈbæntəʳ/ *v* [IØ] to speak or act playfully or jokingly —**~ing** *adj*: *bantering remarks* —**~ingly** *adv*

banter[2] *n* [U] light joking talk: *The actress exchanged banter with reporters*

ban·yan /ˈbænjən, ˈbænjæn/ also **banian, banyan tree** /ˈ·· ·/— *n* a kind of fruit tree growing in India, whose branches grow down towards the ground and form new roots

ba·o·bab /ˈbeɪəbæb‖ˈbaʊ-/ also **baobab tree** /ˈ··· ·/— *n* a type of African tree with a very broad trunk

bap·tis·m /ˈbæptɪzəm/ *n* **1** [U] a Christian religious ceremony in which a person is touched or covered with water to make him pure and show that he has been accepted as a member of the Church **2** [U] a ceremony in any other religion in which water is used to make people pure **3** [C] an example of these ceremonies: *There haven't been many baptisms in the village church this year* **4 baptism of fire a** a soldier's first experience of enemy gunfire, **b** any unpleasant first experience of something —**-tismal** /bæpˈtɪzməl/ *adj* [Wa5]

Bap·tist /ˈbæptɨst/ *n* a Christian who believes that BAPTISM should be only for people old enough to understand its meaning and that they should be covered completely with water

bap·tize, -ise /bæpˈtaɪz/ *v* **1** [T1] to perform the ceremony of BAPTISM on **2** [X1] to admit as a member of the stated church by BAPTISM: *He was baptized a* ROMAN CATHOLIC **3** [X1] to give (someone) a name at BAPTISM

bar[1] /bɑːʳ/ *n* **1** a length of wood or stiff metal across a door, gate, or window to keep it firmly closed **2** something that blocks things off or makes them difficult or impossible to do; BARRIER **3** a piece of solid material that is longer than it is wide: *a bar of soap/chocolate/gold/iron* **4** a bank of sand or stones under the water as in a river, parallel to a shore, at the entrance to a harbour, etc. **5** a narrow band of colour or light: *bars of sunlight* **6** (downward lines that mark off in writing) a few notes of music considered to form a group: *The new musical idea begins at the 50th bar* —see picture at NOTATION **7** a narrow band of metal or cloth worn on a military uniform or MEDAL esp. to show rank, service, or good performance **8** (in a court of law) a division marker between the part in which the business of the court is carried on and the part intended for the prisoner or the public **9** something that may try or judge a person: *Your acts will be judged at the bar of public opinion* **10** (room with) a COUNTER[1] **a** where alcoholic drinks are sold **b** where food and drinks are served and eaten: *a coffee bar* **c** where usu. cheap articles are offered for sale: *a hat bar* **11 behind bars** in prison **12 the prisoner at the bar** the person being tried in a court of law

bar[2] *v* **-rr-** **1** [T1] to close firmly with a bar: *to bar the door* **2** [X9] to keep in or out by barring a door, gate, etc.: *They barred themselves in.|She barred him out of her room* **3** [T1] to block (movement or action): *to bar the way to the city/to success* **4** [X9; (T1)] not to allow: *Guns are barred in Alice's restaurant.|My father barred smoking at the dinner-table* **5** [X9;(T1) *usu. pass.*] to mark with a band or a broad line: *The flag was barred in red and white*

bar[3] *prep* **1** except: *The whole group was at the party, bar John* **2 bar none** without any exceptions: *He's the best singer in the country, bar none* —see also BARRING

Bar *n* [*the*+GU] **1** *BrE* (the members of) the profession of BARRISTER **2** *AmE* (the members of) the profession of lawyer **3 be called to the Bar a** *BrE* to become a BARRISTER **b** *AmE* to become a lawyer

barb /bɑːb‖bɑrb/ *n* the sharp point of a fish hook, arrow, etc., with a curved shape which prevents it from being easily pulled out

bar·bar·i·an /bɑːˈbeərɪən‖bɑr-/ *n often derog* a person without civilization, esp. one who is rude and wild in behaviour: *"The barbarians have conquered Rome!" he shouted.|Only a barbarian like you would not like the work of such a great writer*

bar·bar·ic /bɑːˈbærɪk‖bɑr-/ *adj often derog* **1** of or like (that of) a BARBARIAN: *barbaric people/customs/ornaments* **2** very cruel: *a barbaric punishment* —**~ally** *adv* [Wa4]

bar·bar·is·m /ˈbɑːbərɪzəm‖ˈbɑr-/ *n derog* **1** [U] the state of being BARBARIC **2** [C] the act of a BARBARIAN, esp. a mistake in the use of language: *Some words which used to be considered barbarisms are now acceptable*

bar·bar·i·ty /bɑːˈbærɨti‖bɑr-/ *n derog* **1** [U] cruelty of the worst kind **2** [C] an example of this: *The barbarities of the last war must not be repeated*

bar·bar·ize, -ise /ˈbɑːbəraɪz‖ˈbɑr-/ *v* [T1] *derog* to make cruel, rude in manners or lacking in good judgment: *The people had been barbarized by years* *of bad treatment until they were like animals*

bar·bar·ous /ˈbɑːbərəs‖ˈbɑr-/ *adj derog* **1** BARBARIC (1); uncivilized **2** very cruel **3** offensive in behaviour or manners, esp. by making or showing many mistakes in the use of language: *a barbarous writer/style* —**~ly** *adv*

bar·be·cue[1] /ˈbɑːbɪkjuː‖ˈbɑr-/ *n* **1** a large framework on which to cook meat over an open fire, usu. outdoors **2** meat cooked in this way: *That was a really nice barbecue, John* **3** a feast or party at which meat is prepared in this way and eaten

barbecue[2] *v* [Wv5;T1] **1** to cook (meat) on a BARBECUE[1] (1) **2** to cook (meat) in a very hot SAUCE

barbed /bɑːbd‖bɑrbd/ *adj* **1** with one or more BARBs or short sharp points: *a barbed hook* **2** (esp. of speech) sharply funny, esp. about the faults of other people: *a barbed remark*

barbed wire /ˌ· ˈ·/ *n* [U] wire with short sharp points in it: *a barbed-wire fence*

bar·bel /ˈbɑːbəl‖ˈbɑr-/ *n* any of various types of large European fresh-water fish

bar·ber /ˈbɑːbəʳ‖ˈbɑr-/ *n* a person (usu. a man) who cuts men's hair and SHAVEs them —compare HAIRDRESSER

barber's pole /ˌ·· ˈ·/ *n* a pole with a red and white pattern going up it in a SPIRAL, often put outside a BARBER's shop as a sign

bar·bi·can /ˈbɑːbɪkən‖ˈbɑr-/ *n* something like a fort used for defence in former times, esp. a tower at a gate or bridge —see picture at CASTLE[1]

bar billiards /ˌ· ˈ··/ *n* [U] a game like BILLIARDS, but played on a smaller table and with a time limit after which balls are not returned

bar·bi·tu·rate /bɑːˈbɪtʃʊrɨ̍t‖bɑrˈbɪtʃərɨ̍t, -reɪt/ *n* [C;(U)] *med* any of various chemical substances that calm the nerves and put people to sleep

bar·ca·role, -olle /ˌbɑːkəˈrəʊl‖ˈbɑrkərəʊl/ *n* a piece of music like the songs of GONDOLIERs (=boatmen) in Venice), whose music has a beat like the beat of rowing

bard /bɑːd‖bɑrd/ *n lit & poet* **1** a poet **2 the Bard (of Avon)** Shakespeare

bare[1] /beəʳ/ *adj* **1** [Wa1;B] uncovered; empty **2** [Wa1;F+*of*] without; empty: *fields bare of grass|a room bare of furniture* **3** [Wa5;A] not more than; only; without addition: *I killed him with my bare hands.|A bare word would be enough for me* —**~ness** *n* [U]

bare[2] *v* [T1] **1** to take off a covering; bring to view **2 bare one's head** (esp. of men) to take one's hat off as a sign of respect **3 bare one's heart/soul** to make known one's deepest feelings: *I must bare my heart to someone, or I shall go mad!* **4 bare its teeth** (usu. of animals) to show the teeth, often as a sign of anger

bare·back /ˈbeəbæk‖ˈbeər-/ *adj, adv* [Wa5;A] riding without a SADDLE: *She was a bareback rider but she did not always ride bareback*

barebacked /ˌbeəˈbækt◂‖ˈbeərbækt/ *adj, adv* without a SADDLE (1): *a barebacked horse*

bare·faced /ˌbeəˈfeɪst◂‖ˈbeərfeɪst/ *adj* [Wa5] *derog* shameless: *It was a barefaced trick to get people to pay money for nothing* —**-facedly** /ˌbeəˈfeɪstli, -sɨ̍dli◂‖ˈbeərfeɪsɨ̍dli, -stli/ *adv*

bare·foot /ˈbeəfʊt‖ˈbeər-/ *adj, adv* [Wa5] without shoes or other covering on the feet

bare·head·ed /ˌbeəˈhedɨ̍d◂‖ˈbeərhedɨ̍d/ *adj, adv* [Wa5] with the head uncovered; without a hat

bare·leg·ged /ˌbeəˈlegɨ̍d, -ˈlegd◂‖ˈbeər-/ *adj, adv* [Wa5] with nothing on the legs; not wearing stockings

bare·ly /ˈbeəli‖ˈbeərli/ *adv* **1** in a bare way: *The room was furnished barely* (=with very little furniture) **2** almost not; only just; hardly: *He had barely arrived when he had to leave again.|We have barely enough money to last the week-end* —see HARDLY (USAGE)

bar·gain[1] /ˈbɑːgɨ̍n‖ˈbɑr-/ *n* **1** an agreement, esp. one to do something in return for something else: *He made a bargain with his wife: "You cook and I'll wash up"* **2** something that can be or has been bought for less than its real value: *These good shoes are a real bargain at such a low price* **3 A bargain's a bargain!** An agreement already made must be kept **4 a bargain hunter** a person who looks for ("hunts") bargains in the shops **5 drive a hard bargain** to get an agreement very much in one's own favour **6 a good/bad bargain** one that favours/does not favour the person who is making it **7 into the bargain** in addition: *She had to look after a house, a big garden—and 4 cats into the bargain* **8 It's/That's a bargain!** I agree **9 make the best of a bad bargain** to do one's best in difficult conditions

bargain[2] *v* **1** [IØ (*with* and/or *about*)] to talk about the conditions of a sale, agreement, or contract: *We bargained with her about the price* **2** [T5,(5c)] to get an agreement that: *The trade union bargained that its members should have another week's holiday*

bargain for also (*esp. AmE*) **bargain on**— *v prep* [T1;V3,4a: *nonassertive, pass. rare*] to take into account; consider: *I had not bargained for such heavy rain, and I got very wet without a coat*

barge[1] /bɑːdʒ‖bɑrdʒ/ *n* **1** a large low boat with a flat bottom, used mainly for carrying heavy goods on a CANAL or river —see picture at SHIP[1] **2** a motorboat carried by ships of the navy for the use of officers of high rank **3** a large rowing boat used chiefly on rivers for important people on ceremonial occasions

barge[2] *v* [L9;T9] to move in a heavy ungraceful way, perhaps hitting against things in addition: *He kept barging along/about, until I told him to stop*

barg·ee /bɑːˈdʒiː‖bɑr-/ *AmE* **barge·man** /bɑːdʒmən‖ˈbɑrdʒ-/— *n BrE* a man who is in charge of a BARGE, esp. on a CANAL

barge in *v adv* [IØ] to rush in rudely; interrupt: *The door burst open and the children barged in*

barge in·to *v prep* [T1 *usu. not pass.*] **1** to interrupt: *How rude of her to barge into the conversation!* **2** BUMP INTO

barge pole /ˈ· ·/ *n* **1** a long pole used in pushing along and guiding a BARGE **2 I wouldn't touch (something, someone) with a barge pole/(*AmE*) with a ten-foot pole** I want nothing to do with it/him

bar·i·tone /ˈbærɨ̍təʊn/ *n* (a man with) the male singing voice lower than TENOR and higher than BASS

bar·i·um /ˈbeərɪəm/ *n* [U] a soft silver-white metal that is a simple substance (ELEMENT (6)) and is found only in combination with other substances

barium meal /ˌ··· ˈ·/ *n* a chemical substance that people drink before they have X-RAYs, so that their inner organs will show up more clearly

bark[1] /bɑːk‖bɑrk/ *v* **1** [IØ (*at*)] to make the sound that dogs make, sharp and loud: *Don't bark like that, Hector!|The dog always barks at the postman* **2** [IØ] (of a gun) to sound when fired **3** [T1 (OUT),5] to say (something) in a sharp loud voice: *The officer barked (out) an order and then walked off* **4 bark up the wrong tree** *infml* to go to the wrong place or have a mistaken idea: *You're barking up the wrong tree if you ask her to help you, because she never helps anyone*

bark[2] *n* **1** the sound made by a dog **2** a sound like this: *the bark of the guns* **3** a voice like this, or words spoken in such a voice: *He always speaks in an angry bark* **4 His bark is worse than his bite** *infml* He sounds worse than he is

bark[3] *n* [U] the strong outer covering of a tree

bark[4] *v* [T1] **1** to take the BARK off: *to bark a tree* **2** to knock the skin off (the surface of a bone) as by falling (esp. in the phr. **bark one's shin**)

bark[5], **barque** *n* **1** a sailing ship with 3 MASTs, having square sails on the first 2 and a 3-cornered sail on the 3rd **2** *often lit* a small sailing ship of any type

bark·er /ˈbɑːkəʳ‖ˈbɑr-/ *n* a person (usu. a man) who stands outside a place of public amusement (esp. in a CIRCUS) shouting to people to come in

bar·ley /ˈbɑːli‖ˈbɑrli/ *n* [U] a grasslike grain plant grown as a food crop for people and cattle, and also used in the making of beer and SPIRITs —see picture at CEREAL

bar·ley·corn /ˈbɑːlikɔːn‖ˈbɑrlikɔrn/ *n* a grain of BARLEY —see also JOHN BARLEYCORN

barley sug·ar /ˈ·· ˌ··/ *n* [U;C] *BrE* a kind of sweet formerly made with BARLEY: *I'd like a barley sugar/a stick of barley sugar, please*

barley wa·ter /ˈ·· ˌ··/ *n* [U] *BrE* a drink made from PEARL BARLEY

barley wine /ˌ·· ˈ·/ *n* [U] *esp. BrE* a very strong beer

bar·maid /ˈbɑːmeɪd‖ˈbɑr-/ *n* [C;N] a female BARMAN

bar·man /ˈbɑːmən‖ˈbɑr-/ also **bartender**— *n* **-men** /mən/ [C;N] a man who serves drinks in a BAR[1] (10)

bar mitz·vah /ˌbɑː ˈmɪtsvə‖ˌbɑr-/ *n* **1** also **bar mitzvah boy** /ˌ· ˈ·· ·/— a Jewish boy who at 13 has reached the age of religious duty and responsibility **2** the Jewish religious ceremony that recognizes a boy as a BAR MITZVAH (1)

barm·y /ˈbɑːmi‖ˈbɑrmi/ also *AmE* **balmy**— *adj* [Wa5] *sl esp. BrE* foolish or a little mad: *You must be barmy to say that*

barn /bɑːn‖bɑrn/ *n* **1** a farm building for storing crops and food for animals —see picture at FARMYARD **2** *esp. AmE* a farm building for crops, food for animals, and the animals themselves **3** a big bare plain building: *You would never get me to live in a great barn of a house like that!*

bar·na·cle /ˈbɑːnəkəl‖ˈbɑr-/ *n* **1** a small SHELLFISH which collects in large numbers on rocks, on wood under water, and on the bottoms of ships, and which is hard to remove **2** someone who stays close to another person, or who is unwilling to leave

barn dance /ˈ· ·/ *n* **1** a gay social gathering at which country dances are performed, originally held in a BARN **2** *esp. BrE* a type of country dance performed at these gatherings

barn door /ˌ· ˈ·/ *n* **1** the large door of a BARN **2 He couldn't hit a barn door** He couldn't aim at and hit anything, not even something very large

barn·storm /ˈbɑːnstɔːm‖ˈbɑrnstɔrm/ *v* **1** [IØ] to go through country areas giving theatre performances in one place after another **2** [IØ] *esp. AmE* to travel from place to place making short stops to give political speeches **3** [T1] to travel across while doing this: *The actors/politicians are barnstorming the country* —**~er** *n*

barn·yard /ˈbɑːnjɑːd‖ˈbɑrnjɑrd/ *n* a yard on a farm, usu. enclosed by a fence, with BARNs and perhaps other buildings round it

ba·ro·graph /ˈbærəgrɑːf‖-græf/ *n* a BAROMETER that represents changes in the air pressure as a line on paper

ba·rom·e·ter /bəˈrɒmɪ̈təʳ‖-ˈrɑ-/ *n* **1** an instrument for measuring the pressure of the air in order to help to judge probable changes in the weather or to calculate height above sea level —see picture at SCIENTIFIC **2** something or someone that shows changes in public opinion —**-metric** /ˌbærəˈmetrɪk/ *adj* [Wa5] —**-metrically** *adv* [Wa4,5]

bar·on /ˈbærən/ *n* **1** [C;A] (in Britain) (the title of) a nobleman with the lowest rank in the House of Lords **2** [C] *esp. AmE* (*often in comb.*) a very important and powerful businessman: *an oil baron*|*a cattle baron* —see also BARONESS

bar·on·ess /ˈbærənɪ̈s/ *n* [C;A] (in Britain) (the title of) a woman who **a** is the wife of a BARON, or **b** is of noble rank in her own right

bar·on·et /ˈbærənɪ̈t, -net/ *n* (in Britain) (the rank of honour of) a KNIGHT[1] (2) whose title passes on to his son when he dies

bar·on·et·cy /ˈbærənɪ̈tsi/ *n* (in Britain) the rank of a BARONET: *A baronetcy is a rank of honour.*|*Several new baronetcies were made public in the New Year's Honours List*

ba·ro·ni·al /bəˈrəʊnɪəl/ *adj* **1** of, like, or about a BARON **2** large, rich, and noble: *a baronial hall*

bar·on·y /ˈbærəni/ *n* (in Britain) the rank of a BARON

ba·roque /bəˈrɒk, bəˈrəʊk/ *adj, n* **1** [B; *the*+R] (of, like, or about) a highly ornamental style of expression esp. common in all the arts in Europe and America during the 17th century **2** [B] (of buildings and works of art, music and literature) greatly, perhaps too greatly, ornamented

bar par·lour /ˈ· ˌ··/ *n* a room in an inn where private conversations may be held

barque /bɑːk‖bɑrk/ *n* BARK[5]

bar·rack /ˈbærək/ *v* [T1;IØ] *Br & AustrE infml* to interrupt by shouting or pretended cheering; shout against: *They barracked (the speaker) during the meeting*

bar·racks /ˈbærəks/ *n* **barracks** [Wn3;C *often pl. with sing. meaning*] **1** a building or group of buildings that soldiers live in **2** a big bare plain usu. ugly building; BARN (3): *You can't expect me to live in a barracks like that!*

bar·ra·cu·da /ˌbærəˈkjuːdə‖-ˈkuːdə/ *n* **-da** *or* **-das** [Wn2] any of several types of large fierce flesh-eating fish that live in warm seas

bar·rage[1] /ˈbærɑːʒ‖ˈbɑrɪdʒ/ *n* a manmade BAR[1] (4) built across a river usu. to provide water for farming

bar·rage[2] /ˈbærɑːʒ‖bəˈrɑʒ/ *n* **1** the firing of a number of heavy guns at once so that the exploding shells fall well forward in a line behind which soldiers are protected as they advance upon the enemy **2** (of speech or writing) a large number of things put forward at almost the same time or very quickly one after the other: *a barrage of questions*

barrage[3] *v* [T1 (*with*)] to deliver a BARRAGE[2] against: *They barraged the speaker with angry questions*

barred /bɑːd‖bɑrd/ *adj* **1** having bars, esp. of the stated number: *A 5-barred gate* **2** having bands of different colours: *barred feathers*

bar·rel /ˈbærəl/ *n* **1** a round wooden container with curved sides and a flat top and bottom: *a beer barrel* **2** also **barrelful** /-fʊl/— the amount of liquid contained in a barrel **3** [*often pl. with sing. meaning*] *infml* a great quantity: *a barrel/barrels of money* **4** a part of something that serves as a container and has the shape of a tube or CYLINDER **5 over a barrel** *infml* in a difficult position: *I have to obey him because he's got me over a barrel*

barrel or·gan /ˈ·· ˌ··/ *n* a big round musical instrument worked by machinery, which produces a sound rather like that of an ORGAN, is played usu. by turning a handle, can be moved from place to place, is played usu. by street musicians for money, and is common esp. in the Netherlands

bar·ren /ˈbærən/ *adj* **1** [Wa5] (of female animals) which cannot REPRODUCE their kind **2** [Wa5] (of trees or plants) bearing no fruit or seed **3** (of land) having poor soil that cannot produce a good crop

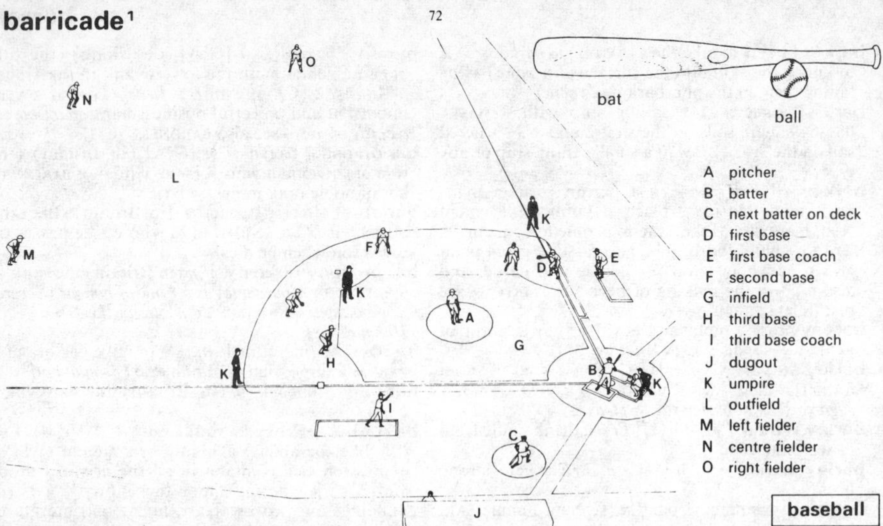

4 useless; empty; with no interest; which produces no result: *It is useless to continue such a barren argument* —**~ness** *n* [U]

bar·ri·cade¹ /ˈbærɨ̇keɪd, ˌbærɨ̇ˈkeɪd/ *v* **1** [T1] to block off or close off with a BARRICADE² **2** [T1] to prevent entrance to, by means of a BARRICADE² **3** [X9 esp. *in*] to put in a given place or condition by means of a BARRICADE²: *to barricade them in|to barricade oneself in one's room*

barricade² *n* a quickly-built wall of trees, earth, bricks, etc., put across a way or passage to block the advance of the enemy

bar·ri·cades /ˈbærɨ̇keɪdz, ˌbærɨ̇ˈkeɪdz/ *n* [P] a field or subject where there are sharp disagreements: *She fought on the barricades for women's rights*

bar·ri·er /ˈbærɪəʳ/ *n* something placed in the way in order to prevent or help to control people or things entering or moving forward: *The police put up barriers to control the crowd.|Deserts and high mountains have always been a barrier to the movement of people*|(fig.) *The colour of one's skin should be no barrier to success in life*

bar·ring /ˈbɑːrɪŋ/ *prep* **1** excepting: *The whole group was at the party, barring John* **2** without; if there is/are not: *We shall return at midnight, barring accidents* —see also BAR³

bar·ris·ter /ˈbærɨ̇stəʳ/ *n* (esp. in England) a lawyer who has the right of speaking and arguing in the higher courts of law —compare SOLICITOR

bar·row¹ /ˈbærəʊ/ *n* TUMULUS

barrow² *n* **1** a small HANDCART, with one or 2 wheels **2** a larger object with usu. 4 wheels, on which things are put to be sold in street markets **3** WHEELBARROW

barrow boy /ˈ·· ·/ also **barrow man**— *n esp. BrE* a man or boy who sells things from a BARROW² (2)

bar sin·is·ter /ˌ· ˈ···/ *n* **1** [C] a mark (as on a shield) showing that someone was born of unmarried parents **2** [*the*+R] *lit or euph* the fact or condition of being born of unmarried parents

Bart. /bɑːt‖bɑrt/ *written or humor abbrev. for:* BARONET

bar·tend·er /ˈbɑːˌtendəʳ‖ˈbɑr-/ *n* [C;N] *esp. AmE* BARMAN

bar·ter¹ /ˈbɑːtəʳ‖ˈbɑr-/ *v* [T1;IØ: (*for* and/or *with*)] to exchange goods for goods rather than goods for money: *They bartered farm products (with each other).|They bartered farm products for machinery.|bartering for food*

barter² *n* [U] the exchange of goods for goods rather than goods for money

barter a·way *v adv* [T1 (*for*)] BARGAIN AWAY: *He bartered away his freedom for a little comfort*

bar up *v* [T1] to shut completely with bars: *The empty house was barred up so that nobody could get in*

bas·alt /ˈbæsɔːlt, bəˈsɔːlt‖ˈbæ-, ˈbeɪ-/ *n* [U] a type of dark greenish-black IGNEOUS rock

base¹ /beɪs/ *n* **1** the bottom of something; the part of a thing on which the thing stands: *the base of a mountain/building/machine/pillar* —see picture at SCIENTIFIC **2** the starting point of something; the part from which something develops or originates: *the base of the thumb is where it joins the hand* **3** a centre from which a start is made in an activity, often one where supplies are kept and plans are made: *After we had reached the top of the mountain, we returned to our base camp* **4** a military camp, esp. one intended to remain in use for some time **5** (esp. in politics) a group or area favourable to a person, political party, plan, etc.: *How can she rise to power without a base (of support) in the working class?* **6** (in MATHEMATICS) a line on which a figure stands: *Draw a square on the base (line) "xy" as in the picture* —see picture at GEOMETRY **7** a line from which to calculate the distances and positions of distant points **8** *tech* the number in relation to which a number system or table is built up: *The number* e *is used as the base of the system of natural* LOGARITHMS.|*Ordinary numbers use base 10, but many* COMPUTERS *work to base 2* **9** the main part or substance of a mixture: *Several kinds of soup can be made using this vegetable base* **10** (in chemistry) a substance which combines with an acid to form a salt **11** (in the game of BASEBALL) any (esp. the first 3) of the 4 points which a player must touch in order to make a run —see picture at BASEBALL **12 not get to first base (with)** *AmE sl* to not even begin to succeed (with): *He was fond of Joan but he just couldn't get to first base with her* **13 off base** *AmE sl* **a** completely or foolishly mistaken: *Your idea is completely off base* **b** unprepared: *She caught me off base with that question*

base² *adj* [Wa1] *derog esp. lit* (of people, actions, etc.) low; dishonourable: *The soldiers were punished for their base conduct (=behaviour) in running away from the enemy* —**~ly** *adv* —**~ness** *n* [U]

base·ball /ˈbeɪsbɔːl/ *n* **1** [U] a game played with a BAT and ball between 2 teams of 9 players each on a large field of which the centre is 4 BASE*s*¹ (11)

that a player must touch in order to SCORE a run: *a baseball player/team/Baseball is the national game of the US* **2** [C] the ball used in this game
USAGE In **baseball** the **batter** tries to hit the ball thrown by the **pitcher**, and in an important game the person in charge is called the **umpire**.

base·board /ˈbeɪsbɔːd‖-bord/ *n AmE* SKIRTING BOARD

base-born /ˈ· ·/ *adj* [Wa5] *old use* having parents who were not noble and usu. poor: *Although base-born, he became rich*

-based /beɪst/ *comb. form* [*n→adj*] with something stated as a BASIS: *French is a Latin-based language*

base·less /ˈbeɪsləs/ *adj* without a good reason: *The charges made against him by the police were found to be baseless, so he was freed*

base·line /ˈbeɪslaɪn/ *n* **1** a line serving as a base **2** the back line at each end of a court in various games, such as tennis

base·ment /ˈbeɪsmənt/ *n* a room or rooms in a house which are below street level —compare CELLAR

base met·al /ˌ· ˈ··/ *n old use* a metal (like iron, lead, etc.) which is not regarded as precious (like gold or silver)

base on also **base up·on**— *v prep* [D1] to give (something) a reason or starting point in: *One should always base one's opinions on facts*

bas·es /ˈbeɪsiːz/ *pl. of* BASIS

bash[1] /bæʃ/ *v* [T1 (IN, UP)] *usu. infml* to hit hard (accidentally or on purpose), so as to crush, break, or hurt in some way: *He bashed his finger (with a hammer).|He bashed the door in and entered the room*

bash[2] *n usu. infml* **1** a hard or fierce blow: *He gave him a bash on the nose* **2 have a bash (at)** *BrE sl* to make an attempt (at): *I've never rowed a boat before, but I don't mind having a bash (at it)*

bash·ful /ˈbæʃfəl/ *adj* afraid to meet people; unsure of oneself; made unhappy by attention: *The bashful child was nervous with strangers* —**-fully** *adv* —**-fulness** *n* [U]

ba·sic /ˈbeɪsɪk/ *adj* of that which is more necessary than anything else, and on which everything else rests, depends, or is built: *the basic rules of good driving*

ba·sic·al·ly /ˈbeɪsɪkəli/ *adv* with regard to what is most important and BASIC, and in spite of surface behaviour or details; in reality; FUNDAMENTALLY: *Basically, he's a nice person, but he doesn't always show it.|He's basically nice.|He's basically a nice person*

Basic Eng·lish /ˌ·· ˈ··/ *n* [R] an international form of English worked out by C. K. Ogden, which uses a very small number of words to express a large number of ideas

ba·sics /ˈbeɪsɪks/ *n* [(*the*) P] *often infml* the simplest but most important parts of something usu. not material: *the basics of education (reading, writing, and simple calculations)*

bas·il /ˈbæzəl/ *n* [U] a type of sweet-smelling plant sometimes used in cooking

ba·sil·i·ca /bəˈsɪlɪkə, -ˈzɪl-/ *n* **1** (in ancient Rome) a long room round at one end with a roof resting on 2 lines of stone supports, used for law purposes **2** a ROMAN CATHOLIC church with special ceremonial rights, esp. a church with a form like this: *St Peter's Basilica is the largest* ROMAN CATHOLIC *church*

bas·i·lisk /ˈbæsɨlɪsk, ˈbæz-/ *n* **1** an imaginary snakelike creature, whose breath and look were thought to be able to kill: (fig.) *She gave him a basilisk look, and then walked away* **2** any of several kinds of LIZARD of South America with a hollow growth on their heads and back that they can fill with air

ba·sin /ˈbeɪsən/ *n* **1** a round hollow vessel, much wider than it is deep, for holding water or other liquid; bowl —see picture at KITCHEN **2** a round open container for various kinds of food **3** a hollow place containing water, or where water collects: *the basin of a* FOUNTAIN **4** a circular or egg-shaped valley; all that area of country from which water runs down into a river: *the Amazon Basin is very large* **5** *tech* a formation where the lines of rock all slope inwards towards the centre **6** the deep part of a harbour almost surrounded by land **7** a wide part of a CANAL where boats can be tied up

ba·sis /ˈbeɪsɨs/ *n* **bases** /ˈbeɪsiːz/ **1** that from which something (usu. not material) is started, built, developed, or calculated: *What is the basis of/for your opinion?* **2** the most necessary or important part of something such as a mixture: *The basis of this drink is orange juice*

bask /bɑːsk‖bæsk/ *v* [L9, esp. *in*] **1** to sit or lie in enjoyable heat and light: *I like to lie on the sand, basking in the sunshine* **2** to enjoy someone's favour, approval, etc.: *He wanted to bask in his employer's approval.|basking in her* REFLECT*ed glory*

bas·ket /ˈbɑːskɨt‖ˈbæ-/ *n* **1** a usu. light container which is made of bent sticks or other such material and used for carrying things **2** the contents of a basket: *Several baskets of fruit were eaten at the party* **3** an open net fixed to a metal ring high up off the ground, through which players try to throw the ball in the game of BASKETBALL **4** a point as counted in the game of BASKETBALL: *George Mikan made 102 baskets in the game last night!* **5 shoot a basket** *sl* to make a point in the game of BASKETBALL

bas·ket·ball /ˈbɑːskɨtbɔːl‖ˈbæs-/ *n* **1** [U] a usu. indoor game between 2 teams of usu. 5 players each, in which each team tries to throw a large ball through the other team's BASKET (3) **2** [C] the ball used in this game
USAGE One plays **basketball** on a *court, scoring* (SCORE) *points* by throwing the ball into a *net* or *basket*. In an important *match* the person in charge is called the **referee**.

bas·ket·ful /ˈbɑːskɨtfʊl‖ˈbæs-/ *n* BASKET (2)

bas·ket·ry /ˈbɑːskɨtri‖ˈbæs-/ *n* [U] **1** also **basket weav·ing** /ˈ·· ˌ··/— the art of making baskets and other such things **2** objects produced by this art

bas·ket·work /ˈbɑːskɨtwɜːk‖ˈbæskɨtwɜrk/ *n* [U] BASKETRY (2)

bas-re·lief /ˌbɑː rɪˈliːf, ˌbæs-/ *n Fr* **1** [U] a form of art in which figures are cut out of the stone or wood surface of a wall so that they stand out slightly from the background, which has been cut away —compare HIGH RELIEF **2** [C] an example of this kind of art: *a beautiful bas-relief*

bass[1] /bæs/ *n* **bass** *or* **basses** [Wn2] any of many kinds of fresh-water or salt-water fish that have prickly skins and that can be eaten

bass[2] /beɪs/ *adj* [Wa5] (of a male singing voice or musical instrument) deep or low in sound: *He has a fine bass voice.|a bass drum*

bass[3] /beɪs/ *n* **1** (a man with) the lowest male singing voice **2** also **bass line** /ˈ· ·/— the lowest part in written music —compare TREBLE[1] —see picture at NOTATION **3** a deep voice **4** DOUBLE BASS

bass clef /ˌbeɪs ˈklef/ *n* (in music) a sign (𝄢) showing that the following musical notes are lower in PITCH than MIDDLE C —compare TREBLE CLEF

bas·set /ˈbæsɨt/ also **basset hound** /ˈ·· ·/— *n* a type of sporting dog with a long body, short legs, and large ears, used at one time for hunting BADGER*s*

basset horn /ˈ·· ·/ *n* a type of early musical

instrument that is played by blowing and sounds rather like a CLARINET

bas·si·net /ˌbæsə̇ˈnet/ *n* **1** a baby's bed that looks like a basket, often with a covering at one end **2** a babycarriage (PRAM) like this in appearance

bas·soon /bəˈsuːn/ *n* a type of musical instrument, made of wood and played by blowing through a double REED (2) that makes a deep sound —see picture at WIND INSTRUMENT

bast /bæst/ also **bast fi·bre** /ˈ· ˌ··/— *n* [U] the inner skin, like a mass of threads, from certain trees, used for making floor-coverings, baskets, etc.

bas·tard¹ /ˈbæstəd, ˈbɑː-‖ˈbæstərd/ *n* **1** [C] a child of unmarried parents **2** [C;*you*+N] *sl* a man that one strongly dislikes: *I'm going to get* (=hurt, punish) *you, you bastard!* **3** [C;*you*+N:9] *sl* a man; fellow: *That dirty/lucky bastard!* **4 a bastard of a/an** *sl* a very troublesome: *a bastard of a snowstorm*

bastard² *adj* [Wa5;A] not according to the usual rule or law: *A bastard size of paper is not one of the sizes usually made or used by printers*

bas·tard·ize, -ise /ˈbæstədaɪz, ˈbɑː-‖ˈbæstər-/ *v* [T1] to reduce from a better to a worse state or condition: *I hate the way my ideas have been bastardized by the popular newspapers!* —**-ization** /ˌbæstədaɪˈzeɪʃən, ˌbɑː-‖ˌbæstər-/ *n* [U]

bas·tard·y /ˈbæstədi, ˈbɑː-‖ˈbæstər-/ *n* [U] *fml or law* the state of being a BASTARD¹ (1)

baste¹ /beɪst/ *v* [T1;I∅] to join (pieces of cloth) together in long loose stitches, in preparation for fine or machine sewing; TACK² (3)

baste² *v* [T1;I∅] to pour melted fat over (meat that is cooking) —see COOK² (USAGE)

baste³ *v* [T1] *sl* to hit hard, usu. with a stick

bas·ti·na·do¹ /ˌbæstə̇ˈneɪdəʊ, -ˈnɑː-/ *n* **-does** *old use* a beating with a heavy stick, esp. across the bottoms of the feet as a punishment

bastinado² *v* **-doed** [T1] *old use* to give a BASTINADO¹ to

bas·ti·on /ˈbæstɪən‖-tʃən/ *n* **1** a part of the wall of a castle or fort that stands out from the main part **2** *apprec* an especially strong point in defence: *a bastion of freedom during the war*

bat¹ /bæt/ *n* **1** any of several types of specially shaped wooden stick used for hitting the ball in various games —see BASEBALL, CRICKET², TABLE TENNIS (USAGE) **2** a strong solid stick **3** a sharp blow **4** BATSMAN: *one of the best bats in the game today* **5 at bat** (in BASEBALL) having a turn to hit the ball: *Who's at bat now?* **6 at full bat** *BrE sl* very fast: *He rode off at full bat* **7 off one's own bat** *sl* through one's own efforts; without being told or forced to: *Have you done all this work off your own bat?|I didn't invite them; they came off their own bat* **8 off the bat** *infml* without delay: *Speaking off the bat, I'd say you were right*

bat² *v* **-tt-** **1** [T1] to strike or hit with or as if with a BAT: *to bat a ball/a child|He batted the ball at least 300 feet* **2** [I∅] (in cricket and BASEBALL) to strike or hit a ball with a bat: *He's better at batting than at catching* **3** [I∅] (in cricket and BASEBALL) to have a turn to bat: *Who's batting now?* **4** [X9] (in BASEBALL) to advance (a runner) by batting: *Can Kluzewski bat the 2 runners home?* **5** [T1] (in BASEBALL) to have a batting average of: *He batted .326 last year* —**~er** *n*

bat³ *n* **1** any of several kinds of flying mouselike animals that usu. eat insects or fruit and are active at night —see picture at MAMMAL **2 as blind as a bat** *infml* not able to see well —see also BATS, BATTY

bat⁴ *v* [T1] **1** to close and open (the eyes) quickly, sometimes as a sexual invitation: *Don't bat your eyes at me, young lady!* **2 not bat an eyelid** *infml* to show no sign of one's feelings, esp. to show no surprise: *He heard the news without batting an eyelid*

batch /bætʃ/ *n* [C (*of*)] **1** *infml* a set; group: *a batch of orders|several batches of letters* **2** a quantity of material or number of things to be heated or cooked at one time: *a batch of bread/loaves*

bat·ed /ˈbeɪtə̇d/ *adj* **with bated breath** hardly breathing at all (because of fear, anxious waiting, or other strong feeling): *He waited for the news with bated breath*

bath¹ /bɑːθ‖bæθ/ *n* **baths** /bɑːðz, bɑːθs‖bæðz, bæθs/ **1** an act of washing one's whole body at one time: *to* (*BrE*) *have*/(*AmE*) *take a bath* **2** water for a bath: *to get into a cold bath*|(fig.) *a steam bath*|(fig.) *a bath of sunshine* **3** also (*esp. AmE*) **bathtub**— a container in which one sits to wash the whole body: *A solid gold bath!—I can't believe it* —see picture at BATHROOM **4** BATHROOM: *2 bedrooms, kitchen, and bath* **5** *tech* liquid in a container, which is used for some special purpose: *a chemical bath|an eyebath* **6** the quality or state of being covered with a liquid: *in a bath of* SWEAT —see also BATHS

bath² *v BrE* **1** [T1] to give a bath to (a person): *He's bathing the baby* **2** [I∅] to have a bath: *He can't see you now: he's bathing*

USAGE One **baths** so as to get clean: *He* **baths** *every morning.|When does she* **bath** *the baby?* We can also say *He has a* **bath** (or *esp. AmE takes a* **bath**) *every morning.* One **bathes** something to make it clean in a medical way: *to* **bathe** *a wound*/**bathe** *one's eyes.* **Bathe** is also the word for swimming: *to* **bathe** *in the sea|to have a* **bathe** *in the river.* (Note the spelling of **bathing, bathed**. When they are formed from **bath** they are pronounced /bɑːθɪŋ, bɑːθt‖ˈbæ-/ but when they are formed from **bathe** they are pronounced /beiðɪŋ, beɪðd/.) The large basin in which one **baths** is a **bath** (*AmE* usu. **bathtub**). A pool specially made for swimming is a **swimming pool** or (*BrE*) **swimming bath**.

bath chair /ˈ· ·/ *n* (*sometimes cap.* B) a wheeled chair with a covering for the top and sometimes for the sides, in which sick people can be pushed from place to place

bathe¹ /beɪð/ *v* **1** [I∅] *esp. BrE* to go into a body of water or swimming pool for pleasure; to go swimming: *I like to bathe in the sea* **2** [T1] to pour water or other liquid over; place in water or other liquid, usu. for medical reasons: *Bathe your twisted ankle twice a day* **3** [T1] to flow along the edge of: *The Mediterranean Sea bathes the sunny shores of Italy* **4** [I∅] *esp. AmE fml* BATH² (2) **5** [T1 *often pass.*] to spread over with (or as if with) light, water, etc.: *The shores of Italy were bathed in sunlight.|Her eyes were bathed with/in tears* —see BATH² (USAGE) —**~r** *n*

bathe² *n* [S] *BrE infml* the act of going into a body of water or swimming pool to bathe or swim: *Let's go for a bathe on this glorious day*

bath·ing /ˈbeɪðɪŋ/ *n* [U] the act or practice of going into water to bathe or swim: *Mixed bathing* (=by men and women) *is allowed in this swimming pool*

bathing beau·ty /ˈ·· ˌ··/ *n* a pretty girl dressed for bathing, esp. in a way that leaves the arms and legs uncovered

bathing cap /ˈ·· ·/ *n* a tight-fitting rubber cap worn esp. by women to keep their hair dry when swimming

bathing ma·chine /ˈ·· ·ˌ·/ *n* (in former times) a kind of moveable wooden hut placed in or near the sea to allow bathers to change clothes without being seen

bathing suit /ˈ·· ·/ also (*becoming rare*) **bathing cos·tume** /ˈ·· ˌ··/, **swimsuit, swimming costume**— *n BrE* the type of clothing worn by women for bathing or swimming: *a beautiful new bathing suit*

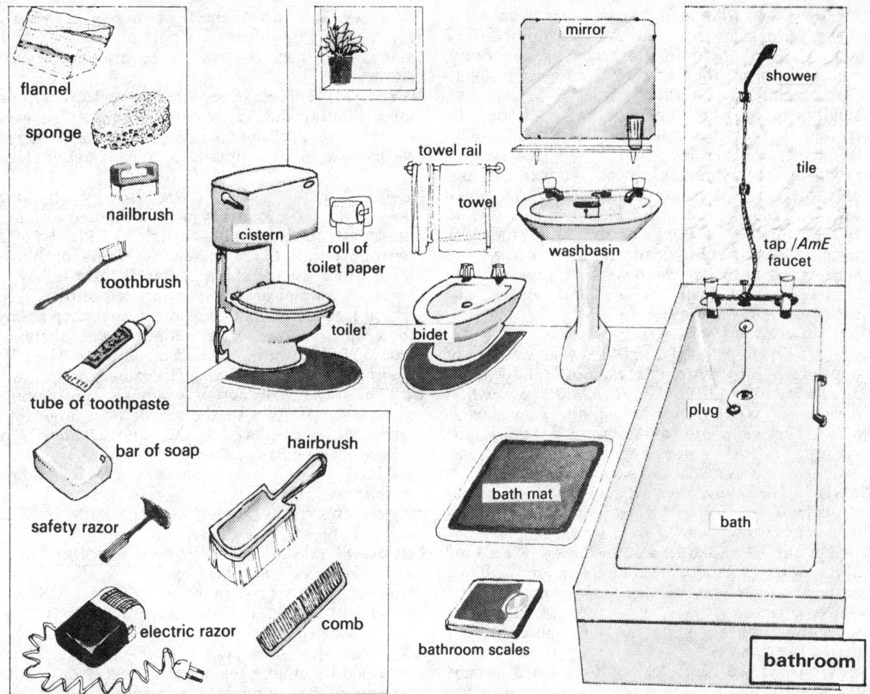

bath mat /'· ·/ *n* a usu. washable mat used in a BATHROOM (if of rubber, within the bath itself; if of cloth, beside the bath) —see picture at BATHROOM

ba·thos /'beɪθɒs‖-θɑs/ *n* [U] a sudden change from very beautiful or noble ideas, words, etc., to very common or foolish ones: *A bit of unintentional bathos spoiled the effect of his poem*

bath·robe /'bɑːθrəʊb‖'bæθ-/ *n* **1** a loose garment (usu. made of a material that takes in water easily) worn before and after bathing esp. by men **2** *AmE* a DRESSING GOWN, esp. as worn by men

bath·room /'bɑːθrʊm, -ruːm‖'bæθ-/ *n* **1** *BrE* a room containing a BATH[1] (3) (and possibly a TOILET) **2** *AmE* a room containing a TOILET (and possibly a BATH[1] (3)): *Is there a bathroom in this restaurant?*

baths /bɑːðz, bɑːθs‖bæðz, bæθs/ *n* **baths** [Wn3;C *often pl. with sing. meaning*] a public building with one or more rooms used for bathing or swimming: *the public baths*

bath·tub /'bɑːθtʌb‖'bæθ-/ also (*infml*) **tub**— *n esp. AmE* BATH[1] (3)

bath·y·sphere /'bæθɪsfɪə^r/ *n* a strong steel container used for going deep into the sea

ba·tik /bə'tiːk, 'bætɪk/ *n* [U] **1** a way of printing coloured patterns on cloth (usu. cotton cloth) by putting wax on the part not to be coloured, and melting it off afterwards **2** cloth ornamented in this way

ba·tiste /bæ'tiːst, bə-/ *n* [U] *Fr* thin fine cloth made of cotton or LINEN

bat·man /'bætmən/ *n* **-men** /mən/ *BrE* (in the armed services) an officer's personal servant

bat·on /'bætɒn‖bæ'tɑn, bə-/ *n* **1** a short thin stick used by a leader of music (CONDUCTOR) to show the beat of the music **2** a short stick showing that the person who carries it has some special office or rank **3** a short thick stick used as a weapon by a policeman **4** a hollow tube passed by one member of a team of runners to the next runner **5** a hollow metal rod usu. with a ball at one end, used for show by the leader of a public ceremonial march (PARADE)

bats /bæts/ *adj* [Wa5;F] *sl esp. BrE* mad; BATTY: *He's gone bats!*

bats·man /'bætsmən/ *n* **-men** /mən/ the player in cricket who tries to hit the ball with a BAT[1] (1)

bat·tal·i·on /bə'tælɪən/ *n* [GC] a group of usu. 500–1,000 soldiers trained for a particular kind of fighting, and made up of usu. 4 or more companies (COMPANY (5))

bat·ten /'bætn/ *n* a long board used for fastening other pieces of wood

batten down *v adv* [T1a] (on ships) to fasten with boards of wood (esp. in the phr. **batten down the hatches**): *There's a storm coming, so let's batten down the hatches* (= entrances to the lower parts of the ship)

batten on also **batten up·on**— *v prep* [T1 *pass. rare*] *esp. lit* to live well by using (someone) for one's own purposes: *It is not fair to batten on one's relatives*

bat·ter[1] /'bætə^r/ *v* **1** [IØ (AWAY, *at* or *on*)] to beat hard and repeatedly: *There's someone battering (away) at the door. You'd better let him in* **2** [X9] to cause to lose shape, break, or be badly damaged by continual hard beating: *The ship was battered to pieces by the storm* **3** [Wv5;T1] to wear out or cause to lose shape by continual use: *a battered old hat*

batter[2] *n* [U] a mixture of flour, eggs, and milk, beaten together and used in cooking

batter[3] *n* a person who BATs, esp. in BASEBALL —compare BATSMAN

bat·ter·ing ram /'··· ·/ also **ram**— *n* (in former times) a large heavy log with an iron end, used in war for breaking through the doors and walls of castles and towns

bat·ter·y /'bætəri/ *n* **1** [C] a number of big guns

together with the men and officers who serve them; set of guns mounted in a warship or fort **2** [C] a piece of apparatus for producing electricity, consisting of a group of connected electric CELLs —see picture at ELECTRICITY, CAR **3** [C] a line of small boxes in which hens are kept and specially treated so that they will grow fast and lay eggs frequently: *battery hens* **4** [C (*of*) *usu. sing.*] a group or set of things like tools, kitchen containers, knives, etc., that are kept together: *She had a battery of cooking pots in her kitchen* **5** [C (*of*) *usu. sing.*] a number of things of the same kind with which a person must deal: *He faced a battery of newspaper cameras/of questions* **6** [U] *law* striking another person (esp. in the phr. **assault and battery**): *guilty of battery*

batting crease /ˈ·· ·/ *n* POPPING CREASE

bat·tle[1] /ˈbætl/ *n* **1** [C] a fight between enemies or opposing groups; a struggle: *the Battle of Waterloo| a battle between 2 lions|I can't fight all your battles for you* **2** [U] fighting; struggling: *They died in battle.|They gave battle to the enemy* **3** [*the*+R] the victory: *In life the battle is not always to the strong, but often to the person who works hardest*

battle[2] *v* [IØ (AWAY, ON, *with, against*)] to fight or struggle: *The 2 fighters battled (with each other) for half an hour.|They battled away for a long time*

bat·tle-axe, *AmE* **bat·tle-ax** /ˈbætl æks/ *n* **1** a kind of heavy axe, formerly used as a weapon **2** *infml* a fierce and forceful, often unpleasant woman

battle cruis·er /ˈ·· ˌ··/ *n* a type of large fast warship with heavy guns, but with lighter armour than a BATTLESHIP

bat·tle·field /ˈbætlfiːld/ also **bat·tle·ground** /-graʊnd/— *n* **1** a place at which a battle is or has been fought **2** an area of strong disagreement: *Wages will be a political battlefield in the coming year*

bat·tle·ments /ˈbætlmənts/ *n* [(*the*) P] **1** a low wall round the flat roof of a castle or fort, with spaces to shoot through **2** the roof behind this wall —see picture at CASTLE[1]

battle roy·al /ˌ·· ˈ··/ *n* **battle royals** *or* **battles royal** a fierce battle or struggle

bat·tle·ship /ˈbætlˌʃɪp/ *n* the largest kind of warship, with the biggest guns and heaviest armour

bat·ty /ˈbæti/ *adj* [Wa1] *sl* mad —**battiness** *n* [U]

bau·ble /ˈbɔːbəl/ *n* **1** a cheap jewel **2** something pretty, bright, and ornamental, but of little real value: *Wealth and social position are only baubles; we cannot take them with us when we die*

baulk *n, v* BALK[1,2]

baux·ite /ˈbɔːksaɪt/ *n* [U] the clay (ORE) from which the metal ALUMINIUM is made

bawd /bɔːd/ *n old use or lit* a person in charge of PROSTITUTEs[2]

bawd·y /ˈbɔːdi/ *adj, n* [Wa1;B;U] fun(ny) about sex: *bawdy jokes* —**-dily** /ˈbɔːdəli/ *adv* —**-diness** /ˈbɔːdinəs/ *n* [U]

bawl /bɔːl/ *v* [T1 (OUT);IØ (AWAY)] **1** to shout or cry in a loud, rough, ugly voice: *Don't bawl like that: I can hear you.|He bawled at me/for his dinner.|The captain bawled (out) an order* **2** [X7] to cause (oneself) to become by doing this: *He bawled himself* HOARSE

bawl out *v adv* [T1] *AmE infml* to scold; TELL OFF (1)

bay[1] /beɪ/ *adj, n* [Wa5] (a horse whose colour is) reddish-brown

bay[2] also **bay tree**— *n* any of several trees like the LAUREL, whose leaves are sweet-smelling when crushed, and may be used in cooking

bay[3] *n* **1** any one of the chief parts into which a building or hall is divided: *In the library, the books on history are all kept in one bay* —see picture at WINDOW **2** a part of the floor or roof between 2 main beams or pillars **3** a part of a room which stands out from the rest —see also BOMB BAY, SICKBAY

bay[4] *v* [IØ] **1** to make repeatedly the deep cry of a large hunting dog (a HOUND): *The* HOUNDs *were baying as they followed the escaped prisoner* **2 bay at the moon** *infml* to complain continually and uselessly

bay[5] *n* **1** the deep cry or BARK made by a hunting dog (a HOUND) **2 at bay a** (of a hunted animal) under attack and having to fight for life **b** (of a person) under fierce attack by words or blows from which escape is impossible **3 bring to bay** to force an animal or a person into a position from which it is impossible to escape **4 hold/keep at bay** to keep someone or something some distance away: *He kept me at bay with a long knife.*|(fig) *He keeps illness at bay by eating lots of oranges*

bay[6] *n* (*often cap. as part of a name*) a wide opening along a coast; part of the sea or of a large lake enclosed in a curve of the land: *Botany Bay (Australia)|the Bay of Biscay*

bay leaf /ˈ· ·/ *n* a leaf of the BAY[2], used for adding taste in cooking

bay·o·net[1] /ˈbeɪənət, -net/ *n* a long knife fixed to the end of a soldier's gun (RIFLE)

bayonet[2] *v* [T1 (*in*)] to drive a BAYONET[1] into: *They bayoneted him in the back*

bay·ou /ˈbaɪuː/ *n* (esp. in the south-eastern US) any of various bodies of water with slow current and lots of water plants

bay rum /ˌ· ˈ·/ *n* [U] a sweet-smelling liquid obtained by mixing the juice of the BAY LEAF with an alcoholic spirit made from sugar

bay tree /ˈ· ·/ *n* BAY[2]

bay win·dow /ˌ· ˈ··/ *n* a window built outwards from the wall, often 3-sided, and built up from the ground —compare BOW WINDOW

ba·zaar /bəˈzɑːʳ/ *n* **1** (in Eastern countries) a marketplace or a group of shops **2** (in English-speaking countries) a sale to get money for some good purpose: *a church/hospital bazaar*

ba·zoo·ka /bəˈzuːkə/ *n* a type of long light gun that rests on the shoulder when fired and is used esp. against TANKs (2)

BBC *abbrev. for:* British Broadcasting Corporation: *the BBC*

BC *abbrev. for:* Before (the birth of) Christ: *Rome was begun in the year 753 BC* —compare AD

be[1] /bɪ; *strong* biː/ *v 1st pers. sing. pres. t.* **am** /əm, m; *strong* æm/, *contr.* **'m**; *2nd pers. sing. pres. t.* **are** /əʳ; *strong* ɑːʳ/, *contr.* **'re**, *neg. contr.* **aren't** /ɑːnt‖ɑrnt/; *3rd pers. sing. pres. t.* **is** /z, s, ɪz, *strong* ɪz/, *contr.* **'s**, *neg. contr.* **isn't** /ˈɪzənt/; *pl. pres. t.* **are** (as 2nd pers. sing.); 1st & 3rd pers. sing. past t. **was** /wəz, *strong* wɒz‖ˈwɑz/, *neg. contr.* **wasn't** /wɒzənt‖ˈwɑ-/; *2nd pers. sing. past t.* **were** /wəʳ; *strong* wɜːʳ/, *neg. contr.* **weren't** /wɜːnt‖wɜrnt/; *pl. past t.* **were** (as 2nd pers. sing.); *past part.* **been** /biːn, bɪn‖bɪn/; *past subj.* **were** (as 2nd pers. sing.) [Wv1 (as a helping verb)] **1** [I4] (forms the continuous tenses of verbs); *I'm going now.|You were saying something when I stopped you.|Have they been asking a lot of questions?|When will you be having dinner?* **2** [I4,8] (forms the pass. voice of verbs): *Smoking is not permitted.|He was told about it yesterday.|The house was being painted.|She has been invited to the party* **3** [I8] *old use* (used instead of "have" to form the perfect tenses of some verbs): *Christ is risen from the dead* **4** [I3] **a** (expresses what must or must not happen): *You are not to smoke in this room* **b** (expresses what should happen): *When am I to come?|Whatever am I to tell her when she finds out?|Those poor men are* *more to be pitied than blamed* **c** (expresses what is going to happen): *We are to be married in June.|We were to be married last week, but I changed my mind* **d** (expresses what cannot or could not happen): *We looked and looked, but the ring was nowhere to be found* **e** (expresses what had to and did happen): *As a young man, he did not know that he was to become famous later on* **5** [I3] (used in unreal conditional sentences): *If I were to do that, what would you say?|Were I to do that, what would you say?* **6** [I3] (introduces expressions of purpose): *The prize was to honour him for his great discoveries.|A knife is to cut with* —see also BEEN

be² *v* [Wv1 (as a connecting verb)] **1** [L1] (with nouns): *God is love.|Olivier is "Hamlet" tonight.|Let x be 10.|The first person I met was my father.|Horses are animals.|That book is £5.|The meeting was last week.|To do that is a good thing.|It's a good thing to do that* **2** [L1] (with PRONOUN*s*): *This book is mine.|I am the one.|(fml) It is I.|(infml) It's me.|If I were you, I shouldn't do it* **3** [L7] (with adjectives): *I'm ready.|He's happy.|To do that is good.|It's good to do that* **4** [L9] (with adverbs): *He is upstairs.|Has the postman been here yet?|If you want it that way, so be it!|You can be there in 10 minutes if you hurry* **5** [L9] (with PREPOSITIONAL phrases): *He is at home.|They are on the table.|The meeting was on Thursday.|A knife is for cutting with* **6** [L1] (*after* there): *Once there was an old man who . . . .|There is a book on the table* —see THERE¹ (USAGE) **7** [L5a,6a,b] (with CLAUSE*s*): *The trouble is (that) you know too much, my dear Bond.|It's as if we had never even started* **8** [L3] (with INFINITIVE*s*): *The difficulty is to know what to do* **9** [L4] (with the *-ing* form): *The trouble is knowing what to do* —see also BEEN

be³ *v* [Wv1;I∅] **1** to exist: *Whatever is, is right. "To be or not to be, that is the question"* (Hamlet) **2** (in the INFINITIVE) to remain untroubled: *Let him be, I tell you!* **3** (in short CLAUSE*s*): *"He was there." "Was he?"|He wasn't there, was he? He wasn't going, was he? It's raining hard, isn't it!|"He wasn't there." "Yes, he was!"* —see also BEEN

be- /bɪ/ *prefix* **1** [*v*→*v*] on; around; over: BEDAUB| BESMEAR **2** [*v*→*v*] to a great or greater degree; thoroughly: BEFUDDLE|BERATE **3** [*v*→*v*;*adj*→*adj*] too much; very showily: BEDECK **4** [*v*→*v*] about, to, at, upon; against; across: BESTRIDE|BESPEAK **5** [*adj*, *n*→*v*] to make; cause to be; treat as: BELITTLE| BEFRIEND **6** [*n*→*v*] to influence, trouble, treat, provide, or cover with, esp. too greatly: BEDEVIL| BECALMED

beach¹ /biːtʃ/ *n* **1** a shore of an ocean, sea, or lake or the bank of a river covered by sand, smooth stones, or larger pieces of rock **2** a seashore area, esp. one used for swimming and sunbathing —see SHORE¹ (USAGE)

beach² *v* [T1] to run or drive onto the shore: *to beach a boat*

beach ball /ˈ· ·/ *n* a large light ball, filled with air, for use at the BEACH¹

beach bug·gy /ˈ· ˌ··/ also **dune buggy**— *n* a motor vehicle with very large tyres for use on sand BEACHES

beach·comb·er /ˈbiːtʃˌkəʊməʳ/ *n* **1** a person who lives on or near the BEACH¹ and has no regular job **2** a long rolling wave coming in to a BEACH from the ocean

beach·head /ˈbiːtʃhed/ *n* a strong position (usu. on a BEACH¹) prepared by an attacking army that has landed, and from which it will try to advance further

beach·wear /ˈbiːtʃweəʳ/ *n* [U] clothing for wearing at a BEACH¹

bea·con /ˈbiːkən/ *n* **1** a signal fire commonly on a hill, tower, or pole **2** a tall object or a light on or near the shore, to act as a guide or warning to sailors **3** (in Britain) BELISHA BEACON **4** a flashing light to warn airmen of heights or to guide them at an airport **5** someone or something that provides guidance or sets a high standard to be followed: *The life of that great woman should be a beacon to us all*

bead¹ /biːd/ *n* **1** a small ball of glass or other material with a hole through it for a string or wire, worn with others on a thread, esp. round the neck, for ornament: *She was wearing a string of green beads* **2** any small body or drops of liquid in the shape of a ball: *beads of blood/of* SWEAT **3 draw a bead (on)** to take aim (at): *He drew a bead on the animal, and fired* **4 tell one's beads** *lit or old use* to say one's prayers

bead² *v* [Wv5;T1] **1** to ornament with BEAD*s* **2** to cover with small drops: *a face beaded with* SWEAT

bead cur·tain /ˌ· ˈ··/ *n* a curtain made by hanging side by side a large number of strings of BEAD*s*

bead·ing /ˈbiːdɪŋ/ *n* [U;C] a long narrow patterned piece of wood used for ornamenting walls, furniture, etc.

bea·dle /ˈbiːdl/ *n* **1** an officer who in former times helped a priest in keeping order in church, in giving money to the poor, etc., and today may walk with the head (MAYOR) of a town on important occasions **2** (in some British universities) a uniformed officer who may lead university processions and/or help to keep order, provide information, etc.

bead·y /ˈbiːdi/ *adj* [Wa2] (esp. of an eye) small, round, and shining, like a BEAD

bea·gle /ˈbiːgəl/ *n* a type of dog (a HOUND) with short legs, smooth hair, and large ears, used in the hunting of HARE*s* (like large rabbits) when the hunters are on foot rather than on horseback

bea·gling /ˈbiːglɪŋ/ *n* [U] hunting HARE*s* with BEAGLE*s*

beak¹ /biːk/ *n* **1** the hard horny mouth of a bird, a TURTLE, etc. —see picture at PREY¹ **2** anything pointed and sticking out like this, such as **a** a person's hooked nose **b** the pointed front end of a warship of former times, used as an attacking weapon

beak² *n BrE sl* **1** a judge in a lower court of law; MAGISTRATE **2** a schoolmaster, esp. the headmaster of a school

bea·ker /ˈbiːkəʳ/ *n* **1** a drinking cup with a wide mouth and usu. no handle **2** a small glass cup shaped for pouring, as used in a chemical LABORATORY —see picture at LABORATORY **3** also **beakerful**— the contents of such a vessel

be-all and end-all /ˌ· · · ˈ· ·/ *n* [*the*+R (*of*)] **1** the most important thing: *Dearest, you are the be-all and end-all of my life!* **2** the one thing that does the whole job: *If only this one action could be the be-all and the end-all of the whole affair!*

beam¹ /biːm/ *n* **1** a large long heavy piece of wood (usu. square), esp. one of the main ones used to support a building or to go from one side of a ship to the other **2** the main bar of a weighing scales **3** the long pole in front of a carriage, to which the horses are fastened **4 broad in the beam** *sl* (of a person) fat or wide across the lower back

beam² *n* **1** a line of light shining out from some bright object **2** radio waves sent out along a narrow path in one direction only, often to guide aircraft **3** a bright look or smile: *"How nice to see you!" she said, with a beam of welcome* **4 on/off the beam** *infml* **a** following a guiding beam correctly/ incorrectly **b** thinking or writing correctly/incorrectly

beam³ *v* **1** [L9] (of the sun or other shining

objects) to send out light (and heat): *The sun beamed through the clouds* **2** [IØ] to smile brightly and happily **3** [T1] to express by smiling: *He beamed a cheerful welcome as he opened the door* **4** [T1] (of the radio) to send out in a certain direction: *The (radio) news was beamed to East Africa*

beam-ends /ˌ· ˈ·‖ˈ· ·/ *n* **1 on her beam-ends** (esp. of a ship or boat) over on one side; nearly turned over **2 on one's beam-ends** *sl* (of a person or a business) almost without any money left: *Can you help me out with a bit of money? I'm on my beam-ends this week*

bean /biːn/ *n* **1** a seed of any of various upright climbing plants, esp. one that can be used as food **2** a plant bearing these seeds **3** a long container of these seeds (a POD), itself used as food when not yet fully grown **4** a seed of certain other plants, from which food or drink can be made: *coffee beans* **5** *sl* head; brain: *Use your bean, man!* **6** *infml* a valueless thing: *I don't care a bean.|It's not worth a bean/a row of beans* **7** *sl* the smallest possible coin: *I haven't a bean, so I can't pay you* **8 full of beans** *infml* full of active bodily strength and eagerness **9 old bean** *BrE old humor sl* (used to address a friend): *Have a look at this, old bean!* **10 spill the beans** *sl* to tell a secret, usu. unintentionally

bean·pole /ˈbiːnpəʊl/ *n* **1** a pole used for supporting the plants of the taller kinds of bean **2** *infml* a very tall thin person

bean·stalk /ˈbiːnstɔːk/ *n* a tall stem of a bean plant: *Most English-speaking children know the story "Jack and the Beanstalk"*

bear[1] /beəʳ/ *n* **1** [Wn1] any of various kinds of usu. large and heavy animals with thick rough fur that usu. eat fruit and insects as well as flesh —see picture at CARNIVOROUS **2** a rough, bad-mannered, bad-tempered man: *She's nice but her husband is such a bear that nobody likes him* **3** (on the STOCK EXCHANGE) a person who keeps selling shares so as to lower the price, and at last buys back at a lower price a larger amount than that sold —compare BULL[1] (5) **4 like a bear with a sore head** very bad-tempered, with no clear reason: *Don't talk to John this morning: he's like a bear with a sore head* —see also GREAT BEAR

bear[2] *v* **bore** /bɔːʳ‖bor/ **borne** /bɔːn‖born/ **1** [X9; (T1)] *fml* to carry from one place to another; carry away: *The sound of music was borne on the wind.|The vehicle bore me to the capital* **2** [T1;(IØ)] to support (a weight or load): *Will the ice on the lake bear your weight?*|(*rare*) *Will the ice bear?*|(fig.) *The captain of a ship bears a heavy load of duty and anxiety at all times.|All the costs of the repairs will be borne by our company* **3** [T1] to have or show: *Her face bore signs of tears.|This letter bears no date or signature* **4** [X9;D1 (*for*)] to keep (a feeling) in one's mind (in relation to someone): *Because of the love she bore him, she would have faced any danger.|I bear hatred against no man* **5** [T1,4] to be suitable for: *Such rude words won't bear repeating.|Her weak arguments won't bear examination* **6** [D1 (*to*);T1] to give birth to (a child or young animal): *His wife bore/has borne (him) 6 fine children* —see BORN[1] (USAGE) **7** [T1;IØ] to produce (a crop or fruit): *The young apple tree is bearing this year for the first time* **8** [T1] (in business) to produce (interest): *money that bears a low rate of interest* **9** [T1,4] to suffer: *He bears pain well.*|(fig) *I can't bear that dull friend of yours!*|(fig) *I can't bear sleeping in a cold bed* —see (USAGE) **10** [X9] to hold (oneself) in a certain way, usu. in a good way: *He bears himself very well when he is marching along* **11** [X9] *fml* to behave (oneself) in a certain way: *You have borne yourself bravely in this battle, Lord Faulconbridge* **12** [L9] to turn in the stated direction: *Cross the field, bear left, and you'll soon reach the village* **13** [T1] *often fml* to have: *to bear a famous name|x bears no relation to y* **14 bear in mind** to keep in one's memory; not forget —see also BEAR AWAY, BEAR DOWN, BEAR DOWN ON, BEAR OFF, BEAR ON, BEAR OUT, BEAR UP, BEAR WITH

USAGE Compare **bear, endure, stand, tolerate**. 1 **bear, stand,** and **endure** are all used in a *nonassertive* pattern with *can*: *I can't* **bear/stand/endure** *the new teacher*. Here they have almost the same meaning; **bear** and **stand** are commoner, **endure** is stronger. 2 They are also used, particularly **endure**, for great bodily hardship: *He* **endured/bore/stood** *the pain as long as he could*. 3 **Tolerate** is used of people or behaviour, but not of suffering: *I won't* **tolerate** *your rudeness.|You can* **tolerate** *him if you try*.

bear·a·ble /ˈbeərəbəl/ *adj* that can be borne or suffered without giving up one's courage: *The doctor said the pain would be just bearable* **—-bly** *adv*

bear a·way *v adv* [T1] *fml* CARRY OFF (1)

beard[1] /bɪəd‖-ərd/ *n* **1** hair on the face below the mouth, often including the jaws, chin, and neck: *Men and goats have beards.|John no longer wears a beard* —compare MOUSTACHE, WHISKERS **2** long hairs on a plant, as on BARLEY —see picture at CEREAL —**~less** *adj* [Wa5]

beard[2] *v* [T1] **1** to face or deal with (someone) boldly **2 beard the lion in his den** *lit* to face a person boldly on his own ground: *He's in his office, so let's beard the lion in his den now*

beard·ed /ˈbɪədɪ̣d‖ˈbɪər-/ *adj* having or wearing a beard: *I don't remember his name, but he was a tall, bearded man*

-bearded *comb. form* having a beard of a stated type: *a red-bearded man*

bear down *v adv* **1** [T1] to defeat: *His determined efforts at last bore down all opposition* **2** [IØ] to use effort: *The driver bore down with all his strength to control the car when the wheels slipped* **3** [IØ] to use effort to give birth to a child: *The nurse will tell you when to bear down*

bear down on also **bear down upon**— *v adv prep* [T1] **1** to come near threateningly: *The packed ice bore down on the ship* **2** to weigh heavily on: *Responsibility for his family bears down on a young man* **3** to punish severely: *The courts bear down (hard) on young criminals*

bear·er /ˈbeərəʳ/ *n* **1** [C] *fml* a person who bears or carries: *Please help the bearer of this letter.|the flagbearer* **2** [C] a person who helps to carry the body at a funeral **3** [C] a person who holds a note or cheque for the payment of money to himself: *The note says "payable to bearer on demand"* **4** [C] *esp. Ind. & PakE* a male servant **5** [C9] (*usu. in combs.*) a fruit-producing tree or plant: *a good/heavy/poor/light bearer*

bear hug /ˈ· ·/ *n infml* a rough tight HUG

bear·ing /ˈbeərɪŋ/ *n* **1** [U;S] manner of holding one's body or way of behaving: *upright, proud bearing* **2** [U;S] connection with or influence on something: *What you have said has no bearing on the subject under consideration* **3** [U] the ability to suffer, or to allow to continue without complaining: *Your rudeness is beyond/past all bearing, sir!* **4** [C] *tech* the part of a machine in which a turning rod is held, or which turns on a fixed rod —compare BALL BEARING **5** [C] *tech* a direction or angle as shown by a compass: *to take a (compass) bearing* **6** [U] giving birth (esp. in the phr. **child bearing**) **7** [U] producing fruit: *In a few years that young apple tree will be in full bearing*

bear·ings /ˈbeərɪŋz/ *n* [P] understanding of one's

position or the state of affairs: *In all this mass of facts I'm afraid I've rather lost my bearings*

bear·ish /ˈbeərɪʃ/ *adj* **1** rude; rough; bad-tempered **2** *tech* marked by, tending to cause, or hopeful of falling prices (as in a STOCK EXCHANGE) —**~ly** *adv* —**~ness** *n* [U]

bear off *v adv* [T1] *fml or lit* CARRY OFF (1)

bear on also **bear up·on**— *v prep* [T1 *no pass.*] to show some connection with: *How does your story bear on this case?*

bear out *v adv* [T1] to support the truth of: *The prisoner's story was borne out by his wife|by later information*

bear·skin /ˈbeəˌskɪn‖ˈbeər-/ *n* **1** [C;U] the skin of a bear: *a bearskin* RUG **2** [C] a tall fur cap worn on ceremonial occasions by certain soldiers in the British Army —see BUSBY (USAGE)

bear up *v adv* **1** [IØ (*under*)] to show courage or strength by continuing (in spite of difficulties) **2** [IØ (*under*)] to support something without becoming broken **3** [T1] to help (someone) to continue in a time of trouble; support **4** [IØ] *BrE* CHEER UP

bear with *v prep* [T1 *pass. rare*] to show patience towards; PUT UP WITH: *You must bear with his bad temper: he has recently been ill*

beast /biːst/ *n* **1** *lit* an animal, esp. a 4-footed one **2** a large 4-footed farm animal **3** [(*you*) N] *derog* a person (or sometimes a thing) that one doesn't like; BRUTE[2] (3): *a beast of a man|a beast of a job*

beast·ly[1] /ˈbiːstli/ *adj* [Wa2] **1** (of a person or non-material thing) that one does not like: *a beastly person|habit* **2** *esp. BrE infml* bad; nasty; unpleasant: *I've had a beastly cold all week* —compare BESTIAL —**-liness** *n* [U]

beastly[2] *adv* [Wa5] *esp. BrE infml* very (esp. unpleasantly or badly): *It's been beastly cold today, hasn't it?*

beast of bur·den /ˌ· · ˈ··/ *n* an animal (such as a horse or donkey) which carries things

beast of prey /ˌ· · ˈ·/ *n* an animal (such as a lion or tiger) which eats other animals

beat[1] /biːt/ *v* **beat, beaten** /ˈbiːtn/ *or* **beat** **1** [T1;L9] to hit many times, esp. with a stick: *His father beat the disobedient boy.|The rain was beating against the windows.|*(fig.) *The sun beat down all summer long* **2** [Wv5;T1] to shape by hitting; drive into place: *beautiful beaten copper* **3** [T1] to punish by hitting: *I'm sorry to say he beats his wife* **4** [T1;IØ] to hit or (cause to) move regularly: *to beat a drum|The bird beat its wings rapidly as it flew on.|The heart beats* **5** [T1] to mix by regular blows, as with a fork or spoon: *to beat 2 eggs* —see also BEAT UP (2) **6** [X9] to put into a stated condition by hitting; make (one's way) by hitting: *to beat the door down|to beat one's way out of a thick forest* **7** [T1] to defeat; do better than: *He beat his wife at tennis.|to beat the enemy|*(fig.) *That difficulty has beaten him.|*(fig.) *That strange story beats everything* (*I have ever heard*)*!|to beat the record* (*for the fastest race*) —see WIN[1] (USAGE) **8** [IØ] to drive wild birds or animals towards the guns of those waiting to shoot them **9 beat about the bush** also (*AmE*) **beat around the bush**— to fail or refuse to come to the point in talking **10 Beat it!** *sl* Go away at once! **11 beat one's breast** to show great, perhaps too great, grief **12 beat time** to make regular movements or noises by which the speed of music can be measured **13 Can you beat that/it!** *sl* Have you ever seen/heard anything as surprising as that! —see also BEAT ABOUT, BEAT DOWN, BEAT IN, BEAT OUT, BEAT UP

beat[2] *n* **1** [C] a single stroke or blow, esp. as part of a group: *one beat of the drum every 60 seconds|*(fig.) *a heartbeat* **2** [*the*+R (*of*)] a regular sound produced by or as if by repeated beating: *the beat of the drum|of my heart|of marching feet* **3** [*the*+R; C] time in music or poetry: *Every member of the band must follow the beat very closely* **4** [C] the usual path followed by someone on duty (esp. a policeman) **5 out of/off one's beat** *infml* different from one's usual activities: *Doing that is rather off my beat*

beat[3] *adj* [Wa5] **1** [F] *sl* very tired: *I'm* (*dead*) *beat after all that work!* **2** [A] *infml* BEATNIK: *the beat poets*

beat a·bout *v adv* **1** [IØ (*for*)] to search anxiously: *The prisoner beat about for a way to escape* **2** [IØ] (of a ship) to change direction

beat down *v adv infml* **1** [T1] to reduce by argument or other influence: *Competition should beat the price down* **2** [T1 (*to*)] to persuade (someone) to reduce a price: *The man was asking £5 for the dress, but I beat him down to £4.50*

beat·en /ˈbiːtn/ *adj* [Wa5] **1** [A;(B)] (of metal) made to take a certain shape by beating with a hammer: *The doors of the palace were of beaten gold* **2** [A;(B)] (*often in comb.*) (of a path, track, etc.) that is given shape by the feet of those who pass along it: *We followed a well-beaten path through the forest* **3** [B] conquered; defeated: *The beaten army ran before the victorious enemy* **4 off the beaten track** not well-known; not often visited: *Let's go somewhere off the beaten track this summer*

beat·er /ˈbiːtəʳ/ *n* **1** [(*often in comb.*)] a tool or instrument used for beating: *an egg beater* **2** a person who drives wild birds or animals towards the guns of those waiting to shoot them

be·a·tif·ic /bɪəˈtɪfɪk/ *adj* giving or showing great joy or peaceful happiness: *a beatific smile on the holy man's face* —**~ally** *adv* [Wa4]

be·at·i·fi·ca·tion /biˌætɪ̇fɪ̇ˈkeɪʃən/ *n* (in the ROMAN CATHOLIC church) **1** [U] the ceremony of BEATIFYing **2** [C] an example of this: *several beatifications last year*

be·at·i·fy /biˈætɪ̇faɪ/ *v* [T1] (in the ROMAN CATHOLIC church) to declare (a dead person) blessed

beat in *v adv* [T1] to break open by hitting repeatedly: *The boys robbed the old man and beat his head in*

beat·ing /ˈbiːtɪŋ/ *n* **1** [C;U] the act of giving repeated blows, usu. for punishment: *His father gave him a beating* **2** [C] a defeat: *I played him at tennis and I got a good beating*

be·at·i·tude /biˈætɪ̇tjuːd‖-tuːd/ *n* [U] a state of great happiness or blessedness

Be·at·i·tudes /biˈætɪ̇tjuːdz‖-tuːdz/ *n* [*the*+P] the statements about those who are blessed made by Jesus in the Bible (Matthew 5:3–12)

beat·nik /ˈbiːtnɪk/ *n* (in the late 1950's and early 1960's) HIPPIE

beat out *v adv* **1** [T1] to sound by beating: *The drummers beat out their tropical music, and we all danced* **2** [T1] to put out (a fire) by beating **3** [IØ] *tech* to sail into the wind: *The sailing ship beat out to sea*

beat up *v adv* [T1] **1** also **bash up** *sl*— to wound (someone) severely by hitting: *The boys robbed the old man and beat him up* **2** *BrE* to mix thoroughly: *Beat up the eggs and then cook* **3** *infml* DRUM UP

beau /bəʊ/ *n* **beaux** /bəʊz/ *or* **beaus** **1** *old use or lit* a man of fashion **2** *old use or dial* BOYFRIEND

Beau·jo·lais /ˈbəʊʒəleɪ‖ˌbəʊʒəˈleɪ (*Fr* boʒɔlɛ)/ *n* [U] a type of French red wine

beau monde /ˌbəʊ ˈmɔːnd‖-ˈmɑnd/ *n* [(*the*) R] *Fr* the world of high society and fashion

beaut[1] /bjuːt/ *n AmE & AustrE sl* BEAUTY (3)

beaut[2] *adj AustrE sl* (of a thing) nice; good: *The food|weather was beaut* —opposite **crook**

beau·te·ous /ˈbjuːtɪəs/ *adj poet* (used esp. of non-material things) beautiful: *"It is a beauteous evening, calm and free"* (Wordsworth) —**~ly** *adv*

beau·ti·cian /bjuː'tɪʃən/ *n* a person who gives beauty treatments (as to skin and hair)

beau·ti·ful /'bjuːtɪ̈fəl/ *adj* **1** having beauty —compare HANDSOME, PRETTY **2** *infml* very good: *a beautiful game|Your soup was really beautiful, Maude!* —**~ly** *adv*

beau·ti·fy /'bjuːtɪ̈faɪ/ *v* [T1] to make beautiful —see DECORATE (USAGE)

beau·ty /'bjuːti/ *n* **1** [U] qualities that give pleasure to the senses or lift up the mind or spirit: *a woman|a poem of great beauty* **2** [C] someone (usu. female) or something beautiful: *She is a great beauty.|the beauties of our fair city* **3** [C] *infml* someone or something very good (or bad): *That apple is a real beauty.|That black eye you got in the fight is a thorough beauty!* **4 the beauty (of something)** *not fml* the advantage (of something, esp. something not material): *The beauty of my idea is that it would cost so little!*

beauty par·lour, *AmE* **-lor** /'·· ˌ··/ also **beauty sal·on** /'·· ˌ··/, (*AmE*) **beauty shop** /'·· ·/— *n* a place where women are given beauty treatments, esp. of the face, skin, hair, and nails

beauty queen /'·· ·/ *n* the winner of a beauty competition

beauty sleep /'·· ·/ *n* [U] *usu. humor* sleep during the early part of the night, believed to be better for health and beauty: *I went to bed late last night and missed my beauty sleep*

beauty spot /'·· ·/ *n* **1** a dark-coloured spot (natural or otherwise) on a woman's face, formerly considered attractive; PATCH[1] (7) **2** a place known for the beauty of its scenery

bea·ver /'biːvəʳ/ *n* **1** [C] a type of water and land animal of the rat family with a broad flat tail and valuable fur. It builds DAMs across streams and is supposed to work very hard —see picture at MAMMAL **2** [U] its fur: *a beaver coat* **3** [C] *old sl* a thick beard **4 eager beaver** *infml* a person who is almost too keen on his job and who works very hard

beaver a·way *v adv* [IØ (*at*)] *esp. BrE humor sl* to work hard, but perhaps without much imagination: *They may look like clerks beavering away at unimportant work, but they will remind you that their job demands skill and experience*

be·bop /'biːbɒp‖-bɑp/ *n* [U] BOP (2)

be·calmed /bɪ'kɑːmd/ *adj* [Wa5] (of a sailing ship) unable to move forward because of the lack of wind

be·cause /bɪ'kɒz, bɪ'kəz‖bɪ'kɔz, bɪ'kəz/ *conj* for the reason that: *I do it because I like it.|"Why can't you do it now?" "Because I'm too busy"* —see REASON[1] (USAGE)

because of /·'· ·/ *prep* as a result of: *I came back because of the rain.|I went back not because of the rain, but because I was tired.|"It was because of the job that he had taken the flat"* (SEU W.)

beck[1] /bek/ *n NEngE* a stream, esp. a small hill-stream

beck[2] *n* **at someone's/one's beck and call** always ready to do everything someone/one asks: *He is at my beck and call*

beck·on /'bekən/ *v* [T1;V3;IØ] to make a silent sign, as with the finger, to call (someone): *She's beckoning (to) me.|She beckoned me to follow her.|He stood waiting until the policeman beckoned him on.|*(fig.) *I'd like to stay—but work beckons, you know!*

be·come /bɪ'kʌm/ *v* **became** /bɪ'keɪm/, **become 1** [L1,7,8] to come to be: *He became king.|The weather became warmer* **2** [T1] *rather fml* to suit or be suitable to: *That new dress becomes you, my dear* **3** [T1 *often neg.*] *rather fml* to be right or fitting for: *Those words do not become a person in your position* USAGE Compare **become, come, go**: **Become** is the most formal, and can be used of people or things: *Paul* **became** *famous.|The sky* **became** *cloudy.|It* **became** *clear that he was lying.* People can **go** or **become** *mad, blind,* LAME, *brown* (=from the sun) or *grey* (=grey hair) but one cannot say **He* **went** *famous/angry.* One can use **go** to mean **become** about things: *The meat* **went** *bad.|Everything's* **going** *wrong.|The sky* **went** *cloudy.* Note also the use of **come** in the phrs. *Her dream* **came true**.| *Everything will* **come right** *in the end.* —see GET[1], HAPPEN[1] (USAGE)

become of *v prep* [T1] (used with *what* or *whatever*) to happen to (usu. a person or material thing), often in a bad way: *I don't know what will become of the boy if he keeps failing his examinations.|What (ever) has become of my blue bag? I can't find it anywhere*

be·com·ing /bɪ'kʌmɪŋ/ *adj* **1** *apprec* (of a hat, dress, colour, etc.) looking very well on the wearer: *Blue always looks very becoming on her* **2** proper; suitable; right; fit; graceful: *His laughter was not very becoming on such a solemn occasion* —**~ly** *adv*: *The little girls were dressed becomingly/becomingly dressed*

bed[1] /bed/ *n* **1** [C;U] an article of furniture to sleep on: *a room with 2 beds|a comfortable bed for the night|It's time for bed.|It's bedtime.|You look ill, young man: bed is the place for you!* —see picture at BEDROOM **2** [U] *infml* sexual relations; lovemaking: *What's wrong with young people these days? They seem to think of nothing but bed!* **3** [C] (*often in comb.*) a piece of ground prepared for plants: *a flowerbed* —see picture at GARDEN[1] **4** [C] any prepared level surface, esp. one on which something rests; base: *The hut rests on a bed of cement* **5** [C] (*often in comb.*) the course of a river or the hollow in which a sea lies; bottom: *a riverbed|the seabed* **6** [C] a stretch of rock; STRATUM (1): *In this part of the country you can see the rock beds clearly, one on top of the other* **7 be brought to bed of** *lit & old use* to give birth to (a child) **8 bed of nails** *infml* a very uncomfortable position **9 a bed of roses** *infml* a happy comfortable state **10 die in one's bed** to die of natural causes rather than because of an accident, a fight, etc. **11 get out of bed on the wrong side** *infml* to be in a bad temper **12 go to bed with** *infml* to have sexual relations with **13 make the bed** to make the bed ready for sleeping by putting sheets, covers, etc., on it or by arranging them neatly **14 take to one's bed** to go to bed and stay there because of illness **15 you've made your bed and you must lie on it** you must accept the bad results of your actions

bed[2] *v* **-dd- 1** [T1] to fix on a base (or beneath the surface); EMBED: *The machine is bedded in cement* **2** [X9;(T1)] to plant in a bed or beds: *These young plants will soon be ready for bedding in these borders* —see also BED OUT **3** [T1] *infml* to have sexual relations with: *After many efforts he succeeded in bedding her* —see also BED DOWN, BED OUT

bed and board /ˌ· · '·/ *n* [U] lodging and food

bed and break·fast /ˌ· · '··/ *n* [U] *BrE* a night's lodging and breakfast the following morning

be·daub /bɪ'dɔːb/ *v* [T1 (*with*)] to make dirty with something wet and sticky; SMEAR[2] (1): *to bedaub a wall with mud*

bed·bug /'bedbʌg/ *n* a type of wingless blood-sucking insect that lives in houses and esp. beds

bed·clothes /'bedkləʊðz, -kləʊz/ *n* [(*the*) P] the sheets, covers, etc. put on a bed

bed·ding /'bedɪŋ/ *n* [U] **1** materials on which a person or animal can sleep: *This dried grass will*

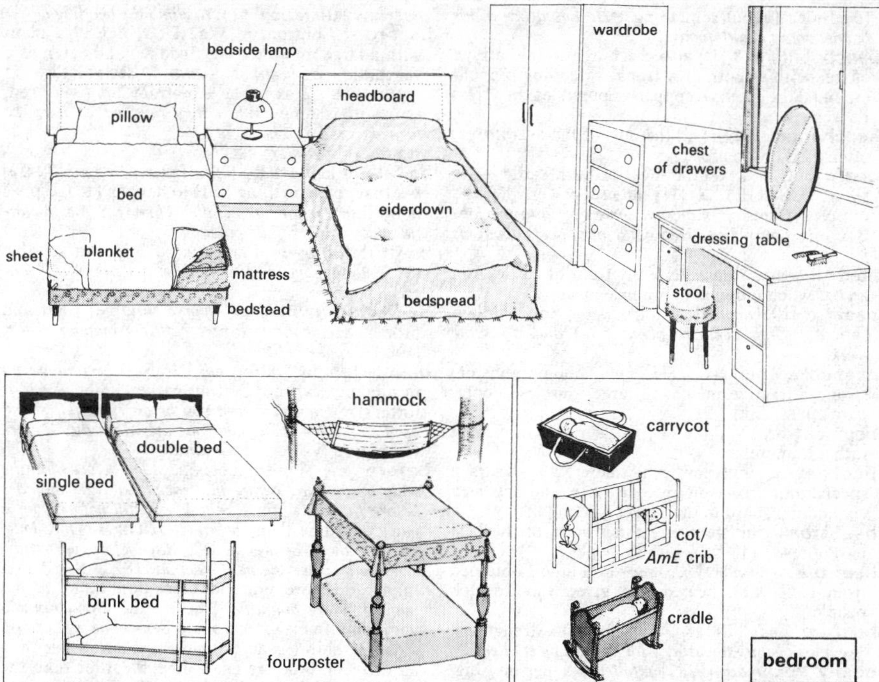

make good bedding for the animals **2** BEDCLOTHES

bed down *v adv* **1** [T1] to make (a person or animal) comfortable for the night **2** [IØ (*with*)] to make oneself comfortable for the night: *I'll bed down on the chairs*

be·deck /bɪˈdek/ *v* [Wv5;T1 (*with*)] to ornament; hang ornaments, jewels, flowers, etc. on: *The cars were all bedecked with flowers for the ceremony* —see DECORATE (USAGE)

be·dev·il /bɪˈdevəl/ *v* **-ll-** (*AmE* **-l-**) [T1] **1** to trouble greatly; have a bad effect upon: *The building of the bridge has been bedevilled by arguments over the plans* **2** to confuse: *That difficult question has been bedevilling me for some time* —**~ment** *n* [U]

be·dewed /bɪˈdjuːd‖bɪˈduːd/ *adj* [F (*with*)] *lit* made wet as with drops of water: *Her face was bedewed with tears*

bed·fel·low /ˈbedˌfeləʊ/ *n rare* **1** a person who shares a bed **2** a companion **3 Misfortune makes strange bedfellows** Bad times make very different people come together

be·dimmed /bɪˈdɪmd/ *adj* [F (*with*)] *lit* made less able to see or understand clearly: *Her eyes were bedimmed with tears*

bed·lam /ˈbedləm/ *n* **1** [U;S] *infml* a wild noisy place or activity **2** [C] *old use* a hospital for mad people

bed lin·en /ˈ· ˌ··/ *n* the sheets and PILLOWCASE*s* for a bed —compare BEDCLOTHES

bed·ou·in /ˈbedʊɪn/ *n* **bedouin** *or* **bedouins** [Wn2] (*often cap.*) a wandering Arab of the desert

bed out *v adv* [T1] to plant in enough space for growth: *Will you help me bed out the plants?*

bed·pan /ˈbedpæn/ *n* a low wide vessel used by a (usu. sick) person for emptying the bowels without getting out of bed —compare CHAMBER POT

bed·post /ˈbedpəʊst/ *n* **1** one of the main supports at the 4 corners of an old-fashioned bed **2 between you, me, and the bedpost/gatepost** *infml* without anyone else knowing: *Between you, me, and the bedpost, I think he's been drinking again*

be·drag·gled /bɪˈdrægəld/ *adj* with the clothes and hair in disorder: *a bedraggled appearance*

bed·rid·den /ˈbedˌrɪdn/ *adj* unable to get out of bed because of illness or old age

bed·rock /ˈbedrɒk‖-rɑk/ *n* [U] **1** the main stretch of solid rock in the ground supporting all the soil above it **2** the facts on which a belief or argument rests: *Let's get down to bedrock, and find out the truth*

bed·room /ˈbedrʊm, -ruːm/ *n* **1** [C] a room for sleeping in **2** [A] such a room used for sexual relations: *That new film has a lot of bedroom scenes*

bed·side /ˈbedsaɪd/ *n* [C *usu. sing.*] the side of a bed: *He has been called to the bedside of his father, who is seriously ill.*|*a bedside lamp*|*conversation*

bedside man·ner /ˌ·· ˈ··/ *n* the manner in which a doctor behaves when visiting a sick person

bed-sit·ter /ˌ· ˈ··/ also (*fml*) **bed-sit·ting room** /ˌ· ˈ·· ·/, (*infml*) **bed-sit** /ˌ· ˈ·/— *n BrE* a single room used for both living and sleeping in

bed·sore /ˈbedsɔːʳ‖-sor/ *n* a sore place on a person's skin, caused by having to lie in bed for a long time

bed·spread /ˈbedspred/ *n* an ornamental cloth spread over a bed —see picture at BEDROOM

bed·stead /ˈbedsted/ *n* the main framework (wooden or metal) of a bed —see picture at BEDROOM

bed·time /ˈbedtaɪm/ *n* [U;(C)] the right time for going to bed: *It's long past your bedtime, children!*|*If you go to bed now, I'll read you a bedtime story*

bee /biː/ *n* **1** a type of insect that makes sweet HONEY, lives in groups, can sting painfully, and is supposed to be very busy —see picture at INSECT **2** any of several related insects **3** *AmE infml* a meeting of neighbours for work **4** a friendly competition: *Who won the spelling bee?* **5 a bee in one's bonnet (about something)** *infml* a strange fixed idea (about something): *He has a bee in his bonnet about health foods*

beech /biːtʃ/ *n* **1** [C] also **beech tree** /ˈ· ·/— a type of tree with smooth grey trunk, spreading branches, and dark green or copper-coloured leaves **2** [U] its wood

beech mast /ˈ· ·/ *n* [U] the nuts of the BEECH tree, often used as food for pigs

beef[1] /biːf/ *n* **1** [U] the meat of farm cattle —see MEAT (USAGE) **2** [U] *infml* (power of) the muscles: *Come on, man, put some beef into the job!* **3** [C] *sl* a complaint: *He's got a lot of beefs about his job*

beef[2] *n* **beeves** /biːvz/ *tech* any form of cattle, esp. an OX, when fattened to produce meat

beef[3] *v* [IØ (*about*)] *sl often derog* to complain (about): *Stop beefing (about pay) and do some work!*

beef·cake /ˈbiːfkeɪk/ *n* [U] *infml* (photographs of) strong attractive men with large muscles —compare CHEESECAKE (2)

beef cat·tle /ˈ· ˌ··/ *n* [P] cattle raised for meat rather than milk

Beef·eat·er /ˈbiːfˌiːtəʳ/ *n* a soldier who wears a special uniform, as in ancient times, and acts as a ceremonial guard in the Tower of London

beef·steak /ˈbiːfsteɪk/ *n* a thick piece of the best part of BEEF[1] (1), usu. without bones

beef tea /ˌ· ˈ·/ *n* [U] *becoming rare* liquid obtained from BEEF[1] (1), heated and given esp. to sick people

beef up *v adv* [T1] *esp. AmE infml* to strengthen: *We must beef up the army with new young soldiers*

beef·y /ˈbiːfi/ *adj* [Wa2] *infml* (of a person) big, strong, and perhaps fat

bee·hive /ˈbiːhaɪv/ *n* HIVE (1a)

bee·line /ˈbiːlaɪn/ *n* **make a beeline for** *infml* to go quickly along a straight direct course for: *The hungry boy made a beeline for his dinner*

been /biːn, bɪn‖bɪn/ **1** *past p. of* BE **2** (to have) gone and come back from: *Have you ever been to India?* **3** *BrE* (to have) arrived and left: *I see the postman hasn't been yet* **4** *esp. BrE* (to have) happened: *I'm sorry, sir: the meeting's already been* **5 been and** (+past participles) *BrE infml* (expresses surprise): *He's been and won first prize!* —compare GO[1] (32b) —see GO[1] (USAGE)

beer /bɪəʳ/ *n* **1** [U] a type of bitter alcoholic drink made from grain **2** [C] a separate drink or container of this: *We had several beers* **3** [U] (*in comb.*) any of several kinds of drink, usu. non-alcoholic, made from roots or plants: GINGER *beer* **4 small beer** *sl* unimportant: *He thinks he's wonderful, but he's really rather small beer*

beer mon·ey /ˈ· ˌ··/ *n* [U] money set aside, usu. by a husband, for spending on small pleasures

beer·y /ˈbɪəri/ *adj* [Wa2] *often derog* of, like, or showing the effects of beer: *a beery smell|unpleasant beery breath*

bees·wax /ˈbiːzwæks/ *n* [U] wax made by bees, used for making furniture polish, candles, etc.

beet /biːt/ *n* **1** SUGAR BEET **2** *AmE* BEETROOT: *Beets are Hank's favorite vegetable*

bee·tle[1] /ˈbiːtl/ *n* **1** any of several types of insect with hard wing coverings —see picture at INSECT **2** *infml* any largish black insect **3** *sl or tdmk* (*often cap.*) a type of small German car made by the Volkswagen company

beetle[2] *n* a large wooden hammer

beetle[3] *v* [L9] *BrE sl* **1** (of people) to move off quickly: *After work we all beetled off for a drink* **2 Beetle off!** Go away at once!

beetle brows /ˌ·· ˈ·/ *n* [P] thick hairy EYEBROWs

bee·tling /ˈbiːtlɪŋ/ *adj* [Wa5;A] *esp. lit* (esp. of cliffs or high buildings) appearing to lean out over; OVERHANGing[1] (1): *to climb the beetling cliffs*

beet·root /ˈbiːtruːt/ *n* [Wn2;U;C] *BrE* **1** a plant with a large round red root, cooked and eaten as a vegetable: *a beetroot* SALAD —see picture at VEGETABLE[1] **2 as red as a beetroot** *infml* very red, esp. with shame: *When they laughed at her, she turned as red as a beetroot*

beeves /biːvz/ *pl. of* BEEF[2]

be·fall /bɪˈfɔːl/ *v* **-fell** /-ˈfel/, **-fallen** /-ˈfɔːlən/ [T1;IØ] *fml* (usu. of something bad) to happen (to), esp. as if by fate: *What has befallen (him)?|Some misfortune must have befallen them*

be·fit /bɪˈfɪt/ *v* **-tt-** [T1] *fml* to be proper or suitable to: *Your behaviour does not befit a person of your social position*

be·fit·ting /bɪˈfɪtɪŋ/ *adj apprec* suitable; right and proper: *He spoke in a very befitting manner* —**~ly** *adv*: *He spoke befittingly*

be·fore[1] /bɪˈfɔːʳ‖bɪˈfor/ *adv* [Wa5] **1** *becoming rare* in advance; ahead **2** at an earlier time; already; formerly: *Haven't I seen you before?|He fell silent, as before.|We had met on the Saturday before* (Compare *We met last Saturday*)

before[2] *prep* **1** in front of: *She stood before him.|the wide lands lying before the travellers|*(fig.) *the case before the court|*(fig.) *Your life is still before you* **2** earlier in time than: *before 1937|*(fig.) *before long|He got there before me.|the day before yesterday|"before or after the next election"* (SEU S.) **3** in a higher or more important position than: *to put quality before quantity* **4 before the Flood** *infml* a very long time ago; too old **5 before the mast** *lit* on a sailing ship (as an ordinary seaman rather than an officer) **6 before one's time a** earlier than the time in which one has lived: *The motorcar was invented before my time* **b** too soon to be accepted by the people among whom one lives: *Turner was before his time with many of his paintings* **7 before tax** when the tax has not been paid yet: *What does your husband earn before tax?* **8 carry all before one** to have complete victory or success: *The army defeated the enemy and carried all before it until it reached the city*

before[3] *conj* **1** earlier than the time when: *"We do want to buy something now before prices go up"* (SEU S.) **2** more willingly than; rather than: *He will die of hunger before he will steal*

be·fore·hand /bɪˈfɔːhænd‖-ˈfor-/ *adv* **1** in advance: *Please let me know your plans (well) beforehand.|"We got these little books of tickets paid beforehand"* (SEU S.) **2** too early; hasty: *Don't be beforehand in making up your mind*

be·friend /bɪˈfrend/ *v* [T1] to act as a friend to (someone younger, poorer, or weaker): *He befriended me when I was young*

be·fud·dle /bɪˈfʌdl/ *v* [T1] to confuse: *Don't befuddle me with all those masses of detail*

beg /beg/ *v* **-gg-** **1** [T1;IØ (*for*)] to ask humbly for (food, money, or other necessary things): *He lives by begging.|He begged (for) money (from the people in the street)* **2** [T1 (*of*), 5c;V3;IØ (*for*),3] to ask humbly (something not material): *to beg a favour (of someone)|to beg that one (should/may) be allowed to go|He begged and begged until I said yes.|to beg (for) forgiveness.|Do it, I beg (of) you* **3** [T3] to allow oneself: *I beg to point out that your facts are incorrect* **4** [IØ] (of a dog) to sit up with the front legs held against the chest **5** [T1] to avoid: *Your plan is interesting, but it seems to beg the real difficulties* **6 go begging** not to be bought or wanted by anyone: *Those blue hats went begging at the sale yesterday*

be·get /bɪˈget/ *v* **begot** /bɪˈgɒt‖bɪˈgat/, **begotten** /bɪˈgɒtn‖bɪˈgatn/ *or* **begot** [T1] **1** *bibl & old use* to become the father of: *"Abraham begat (=begot)*

Isaac" (*The Bible*, Matt. 1:2) **2** *fml* to produce: *Hunger begets crime*

beg·gar[1] /ˈbegəʳ/ *n* **1** a person who lives by BEGging (1) **2** *infml* fellow: *He's a cheerful little beggar, is your son!* **3 Beggars can't be choosers** *infml* You must take what you are offered

beggar[2] *v* [T1] **1** to make very poor: *They were beggared by trying to pay for their son's education* **2 beggar (all) description** *lit* to be beyond the powers of language to describe: *The valley was so beautiful as to beggar description*

beg·gar·ly /ˈbegəli‖-ərli/ *adj* **1** of or like a BEGGAR[1] (1) **2** much too little for the purpose —**-liness** *n* [U]

beg·gar·y /ˈbegəri/ *n* [U] the state of being very poor: *He was reduced to beggary by several business failures*

be·gin /bɪˈgɪn/ *v* **began** /bɪˈgæn/, **begun** /bɪˈgʌn/ [T1,3,4;IØ] **1** to start; take the first step: *"Are you sitting comfortably? Then I'll begin"* (BBC radio show for young children).|*to begin by dancing/with a story/on a new book/at the beginning* **2 to begin with** as the first reason: *We can't go. To begin with, it's too cold. Besides, we've no money* —see START[1] (USAGE)

be·gin·ner /bɪˈgɪnəʳ/ *n* a person who begins some activity, esp. a person without experience —compare STARTER

be·gin·ning /bɪˈgɪnɪŋ/ *n* [C *sometimes pl. with sing. meaning ;from*+U] the start; starting point; origin: *She knows that subject from beginning to end.*|*at/in the beginning* —see PREFACE[1] (USAGE)

beg off *v adv* [T1;IØ] to excuse (oneself or others): *Jane has just begged off, can you take her place in the team?*|*I'll have to beg Jane off, she's sick again*

be·gone /bɪˈgɒn‖bɪˈgɔn/ *v* [IØ] *poet usu. imper* to go away at once: *Begone, dull care!*

be·go·ni·a /bɪˈgəʊnɪə/ *n* any of a related group of tropical plants widely grown for their showy leaves and waxy flowers

be·gor·ra /bɪˈgɒrə‖bɪˈgɔrə/ *interj IrE infml* (used for giving force to an expression) by God!

be·got /bɪˈgɒt‖bɪˈgɑt/ *past t. of* BEGET

be·got·ten /bɪˈgɒtn‖bɪˈgɑtn/ *past p. of* BEGET

be·grudge /bɪˈgrʌdʒ/ *v* [D1 (*to*);T1,4] GRUDGE[1]

be·guile /bɪˈgaɪl/ *v* **1** [T1 (*into* or *out of*)] to deceive; cheat: *He beguiled me into lending him my bicycle* **2** [T1 (*by* or *with*)] to cause (time) to pass without being noticed: *We beguiled the time by telling jokes* **3** [T1] to charm: *Her voice and eyes beguiled me* —**-ling** *adj* —**-lingly** *adv* —**~ment** *n* [U]

be·gum /ˈbeɪgəm, ˈbiː-/ *n* (*often cap.*) (in India and Pakistan) a Muslim lady of high rank

be·gun /bɪˈgʌn/ *past p. of* BEGIN

be·half /bɪˈhɑːf‖bɪˈhæf/ *n* **on behalf of someone/someone's behalf** also (*AmE*) **in behalf of someone/someone's behalf**— (acting, speaking, etc.) for someone; in the interests of someone; as the representative of someone: *My husband can't be here today, so I'm going to speak on his behalf*

be·have /bɪˈheɪv/ *v* **1** [L9] to act; bear oneself: *She behaved with great courage.*|*He behaved badly to his wife* **2** [T1;IØ] to bear (oneself) in a socially-acceptable or polite way: *Learn how to behave.*|*Behave (yourself)!* **3** [L9] (of things) to act in a particular way: *It can behave either as an acid or as a salt.*|*My car has been behaving well since it was repaired*

-be·haved /bɪˈheɪvd/ *comb. form* behaving oneself in the stated way: *well-/badly-behaved*|*the best-/worst-behaved children I've ever seen*

be·hav·iour, *AmE* **-ior** /bɪˈheɪvɪəʳ/ *n* [U] **1** way of behaving **2 be on one's best behaviour** to try to show one's best manners **3 be of good behaviour** *law* to behave well

be·hav·iour·is·m, *AmE* **-ior-** /bɪˈheɪvɪərɪzəm/ *n* [U] the idea that the scientific study of the mind should be based on measurable facts about behaviour and body states, rather than on people's reports of their thoughts and feelings —**-ist** *n*

be·head /bɪˈhed/ *v* [T1] to cut off the head of, esp. as a punishment; DECAPITATE

Be·he·moth /bɪˈhiːmɒθ‖bɪˈhiːməθ, ˈbiːə-/ *n* **1** [R] a very large powerful animal described in the Bible **2** [C] something very large and powerful, but not governed by reason and perhaps dangerous

be·hest /bɪˈhest/ *n* [*usu. sing.*] *fml* an urgent request or command (esp. in the phr. **at the behest of**)

be·hind[1] /bɪˈhaɪnd/ *adv* **1** back; at the back; where (something or someone) was earlier: *to stay behind*|*If he can't go faster, leave him behind.*|*"I've left the keys behind"* (=I haven't got them) (SEU S.) **2** backwards; towards the back: *to go behind* **3** [(*with, in*)] late; slow; BEHINDHAND: *I'm afraid I'm a bit behind in/with my work.*|*She was never behind in offering advice* —compare AHEAD

behind[2] *prep* **1** at the back of; in a place, state, or time formerly held by: *We stayed (just) behind the advancing army.*|(fig.) *"What do you think was the intention behind writing the play?"* (SEU S.) **2** to or at the back, or further side or part, of: *We ran behind the house.*|*She stood behind a tree.*|*I ran out from behind it* **3** lower than (as in rank); below: *3 points behind the team in first place* **4** in support of; in favour of: *We're (right) behind you all the way!*|*"people like Ludendorff who had . . . no family or anything behind them"* (SEU S.) **5 behind someone's back** *infml* unknown to the person concerned **6 behind the scenes** in secret **7 behind the times** old-fashioned; out of date

behind[3] *n euph sl* the part of the body that a person sits on; BUTTOCKS: *I gave him a good swift kick in the behind*

be·hind·hand /bɪˈhaɪndhænd/ *adv* [(*with* or *in*)] *fml* **1** late: *Your rent was behindhand this month.*|*You were behindhand with your rent this month* **2** backward; slow: *She was never behindhand in offering advice*

be·hold /bɪˈhəʊld/ *v* **beheld** /bɪˈheld/ [T1] *lit & old use* **1** to have in sight; see: *He beheld the great city of Babylon* **2** (used in giving orders to direct the attention): *People, behold your king!* —**~er** *n*: *Beauty is in the eye of the beholder*

be·hold·en /bɪˈhəʊldn/ *adj derog* [F (*to*)] having to feel grateful (to): *I like to do things for myself and not feel beholden to anybody*

be·hove /bɪˈhəʊv‖bɪˈhuːv/ also (*AmE*) **be·hoove** /bɪˈhuːv/— *v* [*it*+V3] *fml* to be necessary, proper, or advantageous for: *It behoves you to work harder if you want to succeed here.*

beige /beɪʒ/ *n, adj* [U;B] a pale dull yellowish brown

be·ing[1] /ˈbiːɪŋ/ *n* **1** [U] existence; life: *What is the real nature of being?* **2** [U] the qualities or nature of a thing, esp. a living thing: *The news shook me to the very roots of my being* **3** [C] a living thing, esp. a person: *a human being* **4 in/into being** in/into existence: *to bring/call something into being*|*to come into being*|*A group of that sort is already in being*

being[2] *adj* **for the time being** for a limited period of time: *Let's do it just for the time being.*|*He wanted to stop but decided to continue for the time being*

be·la·bour, *AmE* **-bor** /bɪˈleɪbəʳ/ *v* **1** [T1] to work on or talk about to silly lengths: *He kept belabouring the point until we were all tired* **2** [T1 (*with*)] to attack with words or in writing: *They belaboured him on all sides with arguments* **3** [T1 (*with*)] *now* *rare* to beat heavily with repeated blows, as with a stick

be·lat·ed /bɪˈleɪtɨd/ *adj* delayed; arriving too late —**~ly** *adv*: *The letter arrived belatedly, when the wedding was over*

be·lay /bɪˈleɪ/ *v* [T1;IØ] *tech* (on ships) to fix (a rope) by winding under and over in the shape of an 8 on to a special hook (a **belaying pin**)

belch¹ /beltʃ/ *v* **1** [IØ] (of a person) to pass wind noisily from the stomach out through the throat **2** [T1 (OUT or (*fml*) FORTH)] to throw out with force or in large quantities: *Chimneys belch* (*out*) *smoke*

belch² *n* **1** the act or sound of BELCHing: *Everyone turned round when a loud belch came from the end of the room* **2** something BELCHed: *a belch of smoke*

be·lea·guer /bɪˈliːgəʳ/ *v* [Wv5;T1] **1** to surround with an army so as to prevent escape; BESIEGE (1): *a beleaguered city* **2** to worry and annoy continuously; HARASS (1): *beleaguered parents*

bel·fry /ˈbelfri/ *n* **1** a tower for a bell (as on a church) **2** the part of this tower in which the bell hangs —see picture at CHURCH¹ **3 be/have bats in the belfry** *infml* to be more than a little mad —see also BATS, BATTY

be·lie /bɪˈlaɪ/ *v* [T1] **1** to give a false idea of: *Her smile belied her real feelings of displeasure* **2** to show to be false: *The poor sales of the product belied our high hopes for it*

be·lief /bɨˈliːf/ *n* **1** [U;S: (*in*)] trust; a feeling that someone or something is good or able: *This has shaken my belief in doctors* **2** [U;S,S5: (*in*)] the feeling that something is true or that something really exists: (*a*) *belief in God|my belief that he is right|an idea not worthy of belief* **3** [C] something believed; an idea which is considered true, often one which is part of a system of ideas: *my religious beliefs* **4 beyond belief** too strange to be believed —see UNBELIEF (USAGE)

be·lie·va·ble /bɨˈliːvəbəl/ *adj* that can be believed —**-bly** *adv*

be·lieve /bɨˈliːv/ *v* [Wv6] **1** [IØ] to have a firm religious faith **2** [T1] to consider to be true or honest: *to believe someone|to believe someone's reports* **3** [T5a,b;V3;X (*to be*) 1, (*to be*) 7] to hold as an opinion; suppose: *I believe he has come.|He has come, I believe.|"Has he come?" "I believe so."|I believe him to have done it.|I believe him* (*to be*) *honest* —see UNBELIEF (USAGE)

believe in *v prep* **1** [T1] to have faith or trust in (someone): *Christians believe in Jesus* **2** [T1] to consider (something) to be true; consider (something or someone) to exist: *Do you believe in everything the Bible says?* **3** [T1,4a] to consider (something) to be of worth: *Jim believes in fresh air and exercise for his health*

be·liev·er /bɨˈliːvəʳ/ *n* **1** a person who has faith, esp. religious faith —compare UNBELIEVER **2** [+ *in*] a person who BELIEVES IN (3) (something or perhaps someone): *He's a great believer in fresh air as a cure for illness*

Be·li·sha bea·con /bəˌliːʃə ˈbiːkən/ also **beacon**— *n* (in Britain) a flashing orange light on a post that marks a street crossing place (a ZEBRA CROSSING) for walkers —see picture at STREET

be·lit·tle /bɪˈlɪtl/ *v* [T1] to cause to seem small or unimportant: *Don't belittle yourself/your efforts*

bell¹ /bel/ *n* **1** a round hollow metal vessel, which makes a ringing sound when struck —see picture at BICYCLE¹ **2** [(*usu.pl.*)] the sounding or stroke of a bell, as every half-hour on a ship to tell the time; the time shown in this way: *Leave the ship at 8 bells* (=12, 4, or 8 o'clock) **3** something with the form of a typical bell, hollow and widening towards the open end: *the bell of a flower/of a musical wind instrument* —see picture at WIND INSTRUMENT **4 as sound as a bell** *infml* **a** (of a person) without disease **b** (of a thing) in perfect condition **5 with bell, book, and candle** with all the necessary solemn ceremonies (as for declaring someone to be no longer a ROMAN CATHOLIC, or for driving out an evil spirit)

bell² *v* **bell the cat** *infml* to do something, in order to help others, which is as dangerous for oneself as it would be for a mouse to put a warning bell round a cat's neck

bel·la·don·na /ˌbeləˈdɒnə‖-ˈdɑnə/ *n* [U] a drug, used in medicine, obtained from a plant called the DEADLY NIGHTSHADE

bell-bot·toms /ˈ· ˌ··/ *n* [P] trousers with legs that grow wider at the bottom, such as those worn by some sailors —see PAIR¹ (USAGE)

bell·boy /ˈbelbɔɪ/ (*AmE* **bell·hop** /ˈbelhɒp‖-hɑp/)— *n esp. BrE* a boy or man employed by a hotel or club to take guests to their rooms, help them with their bags, and give them messages

belle /bel/ *n* a popular and attractive girl or woman, esp. one whose charm and beauty make her a favourite: *the belle of the* BALL (= dance)

belles-let·tres /ˌbel ˈletrə (*Fr* bɛl lɛtr)/ *n* [U] *Fr* literature that is of value for its beauty rather than for its practical importance

bell·flow·er /ˈbelˌflaʊəʳ/ *n* any of several related plants with usu. showy bell-shaped flowers

bel·li·cose /ˈbelɪkəʊs/ *adj fml* warlike; ready to quarrel or fight —**-cosity** /ˌbelɪˈkɒsɨti‖-ˈkɑs-/ *n* [U]

-bel·lied /-ˌbelid/ *comb. form* having a BELLY of the stated type: *a big-bellied man*

bel·lig·er·en·cy /bɨˈlɪdʒərənsi/ also **belligerence** /bɨˈlɪdʒərəns/— *n* [U] **1** the state of being at war **2** the state of being angry and appearing ready to fight: *I don't like your belligerency, Jones. Let's talk calmly!*

bel·lig·er·ent /bɨˈlɪdʒərənt/ *adj, n* **1** [Wa5;B;C] *tech* (a country or group that is) at war **2** [B] having or showing anger and readiness to fight: *I don't like your belligerent language, Jones!*

bel·low /ˈbeləʊ/ *v* **1** [IØ] to make the loud deep hollow sound typical of a BULL¹ (1) **2** [T1,5;IØ (*with*): (OUT)] to shout (something) in a deep voice: *to bellow* (*out*) *with excitement/pain/to bellow* (*out*) *orders/"Go away!" he bellowed* —**bellow** *n*

bel·lows /ˈbeləʊz/ *n* **bellows** [Wn3;C *often pl. with sing. meaning*] **1** an instrument used for blowing air into a fire to make it burn quickly —see PAIR¹ (USAGE) **2** an instrument like this used for supplying a musical ORGAN with air

bell push /ˈ· ·/ *n* a small button that one presses in order to ring an electric bell

bel·ly /ˈbeli/ *n* **1** *infml* the part of the human body, between the chest and the legs, which contains the stomach and bowels **2** a surface or object curved or round like this part of the body

bel·ly·ache¹ /ˈbeli-eɪk/ *n* **1** [C;U] an ache in the BELLY (esp. the stomach or bowels) **2** [C] *sl often derog* a complaint, perhaps not deserved: *He's got a lot of bellyaches about the job, but he earns a lot of money*

bellyache² *v* [IØ (*about*)] *sl often derog* to complain, perhaps unjustly: *Stop bellyaching and get on with the job!*

belly but·ton /ˈ·· ˌ··/ *n sl* NAVEL (1)

belly dance /ˈ·· ·/ *n* a sexy dance performed by a woman that makes use of movements of the BELLY —**~r** *n*

belly flop /ˈ·· ·/ *n infml* an act of falling (DIVE), in which the front of the body strikes flat against a surface of water

bel·ly·ful /ˈbelifʊl/ *n* [*usu. sing.*] *sl* too much: *I've had a bellyful of your silly advice*

belly-land /ˈ·· ·/ *v* [T1;IØ] *infml* to land (a plane) on the undersurface without use of the landing apparatus —**belly landing** *n* [U;C]

belly laugh /ˈ·· ·/ *n infml* a deep full laugh, as if coming from the BELLY

belly out *v adv* [T1;IØ] to (cause to) swell or become full: *The wind bellied out the sail.|The sail bellied out in the wind*

be·long /bɪˈlɒŋ‖bɪˈlɔŋ/ *v* **1** [L9] to be suitable or advantageous: *A telephone belongs in every home.|A man of his ability belongs in teaching* **2** [IØ] to be in the right place: *That chair belongs in the other room.|After years of living here, I feel that I belong*

be·long·ings /bɪˈlɒŋɪŋz‖bɪˈlɔŋ-/ *n* [P9] those things which belong to one, which are one's property

belong to *v prep* [T1 *no pass.*] **1** to be the property of: *That dictionary belongs to me* **2** to be a member of (an organization): *What party do you belong to?* **3** to be connected with: *As a writer, he really belongs to the 18th century*

be·loved¹ /bɪˈlʌvd/ *adj* [F (*by* or (*fml*) *of*)] dearly loved: *beloved by/of all her many, many friends* —see LOVELY¹ (USAGE)

be·lov·ed² /bɪˈlʌvɪ̵d/ *adj, n* **1** [A;S9;N] (a person) whom one loves very much: *His beloved (wife) had died* **2** [N] *fml* (*esp. in religious language*) dear people; dear friends: *Beloved, we have met here today to witness the marriage of these 2 young people* —see also DEARLY BELOVED

be·low¹ /bɪˈləʊ/ *adv* **1** in a lower place; on a lower level: *to come up from below|to be down below| He looked down from the mountain to the valley below* —opposite **above** —compare UNDERNEATH **2** in, to, or at a lower rank or number: *officers of the rank of captain and below* **3** on or to a lower floor or DECK of a ship: *the captain told the sailors to go below* **4** on earth: *"My words fly up, my thoughts remain below. Words without thoughts never to heaven go"* (Shakespeare, *Hamlet*) **5** lower on the same page or on a following page: *See p. 85 below* —opposite **above 6** under the surface of the water or earth: *miners working below*

below² *prep* **1** in a lower place than; on a lower level than: *below the knee|(a mile) below the village| (just) below/beneath the surface of the water* **2** lower in amount, rank, etc. than: *below $5|below the age of 17|below the average income|A captain is below a general* —opposite **above** —compare UNDER², BENEATH²

below³ *adj* [Wa5;E] written or mentioned lower on the same page or on a following page: *The information below was provided by my good friend Captain Smith-Fortescue* —opposite **above**

belt¹ /belt/ *n* **1** a band worn around the waist: *a nice new leather belt* **2** a long circular piece of leather or other such material used for driving a machine or for carrying materials —compare FAN BELT **3** an area that has some special quality: *The Corn Belt* (=where corn grows)|*The Bible Belt* (=where people are very religious)|*The Green Belt* (=where grass and trees must not be replaced by buildings) **4** *esp. BrE sl* a very fast car trip: *Let's go for a belt down the* MOTORWAY! **5 hit below the belt** *infml* to give an unfair blow (to) or attack in an unfair way **6 tighten one's belt** *infml* to live more cheaply: *In a period of mass unemployment a lot of people must learn to tighten their belts*

belt² *v* **1** [T1 (UP)] to fasten with a belt: *She belted (up) her raincoat* **2** [X9] to fasten (to something) with a belt: *He belted on his sword* **3** [T1] to hit with a belt: *Jones really belted his son that time!* **4** [T1] *infml* to hit very hard, esp. with the hand: *I belted him in the eye.|The tennis player was so annoyed that he belted the ball right out of the court* **5** [L9] *esp. BrE sl* to travel fast: *really belting along/down the* MOTORWAY

belt·ed /ˈbeltɪ̵d/ *adj* [Wa5] **1** [B] provided with a belt: *a belted raincoat* **2** [A] having the right to wear a belt as a sign of rank or honour (in the phr. **a belted earl**)

belt·ing /ˈbeltɪŋ/ *n* [U] *tech* **1** belts: *This shop carries quite a wide variety of belting* **2** material for belts

belt out *v adv* [T1] *infml* to sing loudly: *to belt out a song*

belt up *v adv* [IØ] *sl not polite* (usu. used in giving or reporting orders) to be quiet: *Belt up, you boys, Father's asleep* —see also SHUT UP (1,2)

belt·way /ˈbeltweɪ/ *n AmE* RING ROAD

be·moan /bɪˈməʊn/ *v* [T1] *fml* to be very sorry because of: *He bemoaned his bitter fate.|She bemoaned the lack of money for many good ideas*

be·mused /bɪˈmjuːzd/ *adj* having or showing inability to think properly: *a bemused person/expression|bemused by/with all the questions*

ben /ben/ *n ScotE* (*often cap. as part of a name*) a mountain or hill: *Ben Nevis|They were climbing the ben*

bench /bentʃ/ *n* **1** [C] a long seat for 2 or more people: *a park bench* **2** [*the*+R] the seat where a judge sits in court: *to speak from the bench* **3** [*the*+R] the judge himself: *The bench declared . . .* **4** [*the*+GU] judges as a group: *What are the feelings of the bench about this?* **5** [C] a long worktable

bench·er /ˈbentʃəʳ/ *n* any of the chief or governing members of one of the Inns of Court, or societies of lawyers in England —see also BACKBENCHer, FRONTBENCHer

bench mark /ˈ· ·/ *n* a mark made on something fixed at a point of known height, from which heights and distances can be measured in mapmaking (SURVEYing)

bend¹ /bend/ *v* **bent** /bent/ **1** [T1;IØ] to (cause to) be forced into or out of a curve or angle: *to bend the wire|*(fig.) *He is very firm about it: I cannot bend him* **2** [L9;(T1)] to (cause to) slope or lean away from an upright position: *to bend over/down/forward/back|bent down with age|to bend one's head in worship* **3** [X9] to direct (one's efforts) to, as in aiming with a BOW³ (1) and arrow: *He bent his mind to the job* —see also BENT, BENT ON, **bend over** BACKWARDS

bend² *n* **1** the act or action of bending or the state of being bent **2** something that is bent, such as a curved part of a road or stream **3 round the bend** *infml, often humor* mad: *Her behaviour really drives me round the bend!*

bend be·fore *v prep* [T1] BOW TO (1)

bend·ed /ˈbendɪ̵d/ *adj* **on bended knee(s)** *lit* kneeling, esp. to ask a favour humbly

bends /bendz/ *n* [*the*+(U;P)] a painful disease caused by gas in the blood vessels, suffered esp. by deep-sea divers who come to the surface too soon

bend to *v prep* [T1] BOW TO (2)

be·neath¹ /bɪˈniːθ/ *adv fml* **1** in or to a lower position; below: *the sky above, the earth beneath* **2** directly under; underneath: *up from beneath* —compare BELOW¹, UNDER¹

beneath² *prep* **1** in or to a lower position than; below; directly under or at the foot of, and often close or touching: *everything beneath the moon|a village beneath the hills|"down in the ditch beneath the churchyard wall"* (SEU W.) **2** not suitable to the rank of; not worthy of: *Such behaviour is beneath you* **3** under the control or influence of: *We shall do well beneath his guiding hand* —compare BELOW², UNDER²

ben·e·dic·tine /ˌbenɪ̵ˈdɪktiːn/ *n* [U] (*often cap.*) a strong alcoholic drink (LIQUEUR) first made by members of the BENEDICTINE order

Ben·e·dic·tine /ˌbenʒ'dɪktɪn/ *n* a male or female member of a Christian religious order obeying the rules of SAINT Benedict

ben·e·dic·tion /ˌbenʒ'dɪkʃən/ *n* (the act of giving) a blessing: *The priest pronounced a benediction over the happy pair*

Ben·e·dic·tus /ˌbenʒ'dɪktəs/ *n* [*the*+R] the 5th part of the ROMAN CATHOLIC religious service called the MASS, esp. when performed with music

ben·e·fac·tion /ˌbenʒ'fækʃən/ *n* **1** [U] doing good or giving money for a good purpose **2** [C] a sum of money so given

ben·e·fac·tor /'benʒˌfæktəʳ/ *fem.* **ben·e·fac·tress** /-trʒs/— *n* a person who does good or who gives money for a good purpose

ben·e·fice /'benʒfʒs/ *n* the pay and position of the Christian priest of an area (PARISH): *He holds a comfortable benefice in Yorkshire*

be·nef·i·cent /bɪ'nefʒsənt/ *adj fml apprec* doing good; kind —**-cence** *n* [U] —**~ly** *adv*

ben·e·fi·cial /ˌbenʒ'fɪʃəl/ *adj* (of non-living things) helpful; useful: *His holiday has had a beneficial effect* —**~ly** *adv*

ben·e·fi·cia·ry /ˌbenʒ'fɪʃəri‖-'fɪʃieri/ *n* [C (*of*)] the receiver of a BENEFIT, esp. a person who receives money or property left by someone who has died: *His eldest son was the main beneficiary when he died.|Our competitors will be the chief beneficiaries of all this trouble in our firm*

ben·e·fit¹ /'benʒfɪt/ *n* **1** [U] advantage; profit; good effect: *He has had the benefit of a first-class education.|I've done it for his benefit.|It is of great benefit to everyone* **2** [U;C] money provided by the government as a right, esp. in sickness or unemployment: *collecting unemployment benefit|unemployment and sickness benefits* **3** [C] an event, esp. a theatrical performance, to raise money for some person or special purpose: *a benefit for old actors|It's this cricketer's benefit match* (=when the money the public pays to see the match is given to him as a reward for his years of service in the game) **4** [U] *AmE* RELIEF (6)

benefit² *v* [T1] (of non-living things) to be useful, profitable, or helpful to: *Such foolish behaviour will not benefit your case*

benefit from also **benefit by**— *v prep* [T1] to gain by; receive BENEFIT¹ from: *Who would be most likely to benefit from the old man's death?*

benefit of cler·gy /ˌ··· · '··/ *n* [U] **1** *old use* the special rights of priests in the law **2** *humor euph* the official approval of the church, esp. as expressed in the marriage ceremony: *John and Mary are living together without benefit of clergy*

benefit of the doubt /ˌ··· · · '·/ *n* [*the*+U] the right to favourable consideration in the absence of complete proof of wrongness or guilt (esp. in the phrs. **give/have the benefit of the doubt**): *He must have the benefit of the doubt until we are certain he's guilty.|Let's give this new plan the benefit of the doubt*

be·nev·o·lence /bʒ'nevələns/ *n* [U;(S)] the desire to do good: *Giving that money was an act of benevolence*

be·nev·o·lent /bʒ'nevələnt/ *adj* having or showing BENEVOLENCE —**~ly** *adv*

be·night·ed /bɪ'naɪtʒd/ *adj lit* lost in moral darkness; untaught: *benighted minds* —**~ly** *adv*

be·nign /bɪ'naɪn/ *adj* **1** having or showing a kind or gentle nature **2** *med* (of a disease) not dangerous to life; not MALIGNANT (2) —**~ly** *adv*: *to smile benignly*

be·nig·ni·ty /bɪ'nɪgnʒti/ *n* [U] *fml* kindness; gentleness

bent¹ /bent/ *adj BrE sl* **1** dishonest, esp. in the meaning of allowing oneself to be influenced by money or gifts (BRIBEs): *a bent* COPPER (=policeman)—opposite **straight** **2** mad **3** HOMOSEXUAL

bent² *n* [(*for*)] **1** a tendency of mind; special natural skill or cleverness (in): *He has a bent for art* **2** **follow one's bent** to do the work which one is interested and skilled in

bent³ *past t. and p. of* BEND

bent on also **bent up·on**— *adj* [F,F4] with one's mind set on; determined on: *Jim seems bent on becoming a musician*

be·numbed /bɪ'nʌmd/ *adj* having all sense of feeling taken away, esp. by cold

Ben·ze·drine /'benzʒdriːn/ *n* [U] *tdmk* a drug which excites the higher centres of the brain and clears a blocked-up nose

ben·zene /'benziːn, ben'ziːn/ also **ben·zol** /'benzɒl‖-zɫ/— *n* [U] a colourless liquid (C_6H_6), obtained chiefly from coal, that burns quickly and changes easily into a gas. It is used to make certain types of engine run, and in making various chemical products

ben·zine /'benziːn, ben'ziːn/ *n* [U] a mixture of liquids, obtained from PETROLEUM, that burns quickly and changes easily into a gas. It is used to make certain types of engine run, and for cleaning

be·queath /bɪ'kwiːð, bɪ'kwiːθ/ *v* [D1 (*to*);T1] *fml* to give or pass on to others after death: *They bequeathed him a lot of money*

be·quest /bɪ'kwest/ *n fml* that which is given or left to others after death: *a bequest of £5,000 to his eldest son*

be·rate /bɪ'reɪt/ *v* [T1 (*for*)] *fml* to scold

be·reave /bʒ'riːv/ *v* **bereaved** *or* **bereft** /bʒ'reft/ [Wv5;T1 (*of*)] *fml* to take away, esp. by death: *He was bereaved (of his wife).|bereaved of all hope*

USAGE **Bereaved** is a much stronger and sadder word than **bereft**, although both words mean that one has lost something: to be **bereft** *of one's senses|a* **bereaved** *mother* (= one whose child has died).

be·reaved /bʒriːvd/ *adj* [Wa5;*the*+GU] *fml* whose close relative or friend has just died: *The bereaved was full of grief for his dead wife.|The bereaved were full of grief for their dead child*

be·reave·ment /bʒ'riːvmənt/ *n* [U] the state of having been BEREAVED: *Bereavement is often a time of great grief*

be·reft /bʒ'reft/ *adj* [Wa5;F+*of*] completely without: *bereft of all hope*

be·ret /'bereɪ‖bə'reɪ/ *n* a round usu. woollen cap with a tight headband and a soft full flat top. It has no PEAK at the front, and is considered typical of artists, Frenchmen, Spaniards, and soldiers

ber·i·ber·i /ˌberi'beri/ *n* [U] a disease that attacks nerves in all parts of the body including the brain

berk /bɜːk‖bɜrk/ *n* [C; *you*+N] *BrE derog sl* (usu. of men) a fool

ber·ry /'beri/ *n* **1** a small soft fruit, esp. one that can be eaten **2** the dry seed of some plants (such as coffee)

See next page for picture

ber·serk /bɜː'sɜːk, bə-‖bɜr'sɜrk, 'bɜrsɜrk/ *adj* [F] mad with violent anger: *On hearing the terrible news he went berserk*

berth¹ /bɜːθ‖bɜrθ/ *n* **1** a place where a ship can stop and be tied up, as in a harbour **2** a sleeping place in a ship or train **3** *infml* a job **4** **give someone/something a wide berth** *infml* to stay at a safe distance from someone or something dangerous or unpleasant

berth² *v* [T1;IØ] **a** (of a ship) to come into port to be tied up **b** to bring (a ship) into port to be tied up: *The captain berthed his ship at midday*

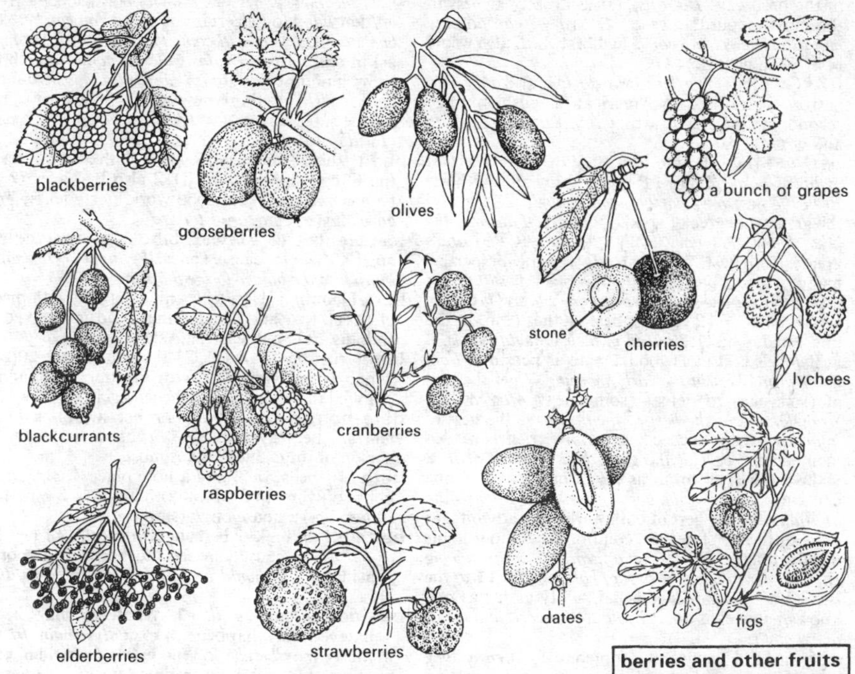

berries and other fruits

ber·yl /ˈberəl/ *n* [U;C] a type of precious stone, usu. green

be·seech /bɪˈsiːtʃ/ *v* **besought** /bɪˈsɔːt/ *or* **beseeched** [Wv4;T1 (*of*);V3] *fml or lit* to ask eagerly and anxiously: *He besought a favour of the judge*

be·seem /bɪˈsiːm/ *v* [T1] *fml or old use* to suit: *It ill beseems you to do that* = *To do that ill beseems you* (= It is not proper for you to do that)

be·set /bɪˈset/ *v* **beset;** *pres. part.* **besetting** [T1 (*with*)] **1** [(*usu. pass.*)] to trouble from all directions; attack without ceasing: *He was beset by doubts.|The plan was beset with difficulties from the beginning* **2** (in war) to surround and prepare to attack: *The enemy beset the city with a strong army*

be·set·ting /bɪˈsetɪŋ/ *adj* [Wa5;A] (of something bad) continuously present: *a besetting difficulty*

be·side /bɪˈsaɪd/ *prep* **1** at or close to the side of; next to: *sitting beside the driver|a town beside the sea* —compare SIDE¹ **by side 2** in comparison with: *Beside last year's results, the figures for this year have fallen* **3 beside the point** having nothing to do with the main point or question: *I want to do it in any case: the cost is beside the point* **4 beside oneself (with)** almost mad (with trouble or excitement) —see BESIDES² (USAGE)

be·sides¹ /bɪˈsaɪdz/ *adv* [Wa5] in addition; also: *I don't want to go; (and) besides, I'm tired.|This car belongs to Smith, and he has 2 others besides.|I don't like those blue socks: what have you got besides?*

besides² *prep* as well as; in addition to: *There were 3 others present at the meeting besides Mr Day.|"Mr K was on the Guards* RESERVE *besides being in the police"* (SEU W.)

USAGE Compare **beside, besides, except**: 1 **Beside** can be used at the end of a sentence: *That's the girl you were sitting* **beside. Besides²** cannot. 2 **Besides²** means "as well as"; **except** means "but not; leaving out", and follows **all, none**, etc.: *All of us passed* **besides** *John* means that John passed too, but *All of us passed* **except** *John* means that John did not pass.

be·siege /bɪˈsiːdʒ/ *v* [T1] **1** to surround with armed forces **2** [(*with*)] to press with questions, requests, letters, etc.: *The crowd besieged the minister with questions about their taxes.|They were besieged with invitations to parties* **3** to cause worry or trouble to: *doubts that besieged him*

be·smear /bɪˈsmɪəʳ/ *v* [T1 (*with*)] **1** to cover with dirty, sticky, or oily marks: *After his work on the car his hands were besmeared with dirt* **2** BESMIRCH

be·smirch /bɪˈsmɜːtʃ‖-ɜrtʃ/ *v* [T1] to damage (a person or his character) in the opinion of others

be·som /ˈbiːzəm/ *n* a brush made of sticks tied together on a long handle

be·sot·ted /bɪˈsɒtəd‖bɪˈsɑ-/ *adj* [F (*with*)] made dull, stupid, or foolish by strong drink or powerful feeling; drunk: *besotted with drink|love|power*

be·sought /bɪˈsɔːt/ *past t. and p. of* BESEECH

be·spat·tered /bɪˈspætəd‖-ərd/ *adj* [(*with*)] SPATTERed (1)

be·speak /bɪˈspiːk/ *v* **bespoke** /bɪˈspəʊk/, **bespoken** /bɪˈspəʊkən/ [T1] *fml* to show; be a sign of: *His skill at singing bespeaks much good training*

be·spoke /bɪˈspəʊk/ *adj* [Wa5] *BrE* (of clothes) specially made to someone's measurements; MADE-TO-MEASURE

best¹ /best/ *adj* (*superl. of* GOOD) [Wa5] **1** the most skilful: *the best rider* **2** the most moral: *the best man I ever knew* **3** of the highest quality: *the best wine|Of all of them, she's (the) best.|(fml) The wine was of the best* **4** most effective: *What is the best thing to do?|"The best way to get a job is not to care whether you get it or not"* (SEU S.) **5 the best part of** most of: *I haven't seen her for the best part of a week*

best² *adv* (*superl. of* WELL) [Wa5] **1** in the best way: *The boy or girl who does best will get the prize* **2** (*esp. in combs.*) most: *the best-loved singer|"A Wednesday would suit me best"* (SEU S.) **3 as best**

in the best way: *Do it as best you can* **4 at best** in the most favourable case: *At best we can do only half as much as last year* **5 had best** *AmE* also **would best**— had BETTER³ (4)
USAGE Both *You had* **best** *do it* and *You would* **best** *do it* are used in American English, but the second is considered wrong by British speakers and writers.

best³ *n* **1** [*the*+R] the best state or part: *The best of life is past!* **2** [*the*+R] something that is best: *Even the best may not be good enough* **3** [*the*+R] the greatest degree of good or quality: *I demand the best of any dictionary I buy!* **4** [*the*+R;R9] one's greatest, highest, or finest effort, state or performance: *to do one's best|to try one's best (to get there)|to look one's best|to be at one's best|This is the best I can do* **5** [R9] one's best clothes (esp. in the phr. **Sunday best**): *dressed in their (Sunday) best* **6 at its/one's best** in as good a state as possible: *I am never at my best in the early morning* **7 get the best of (someone)** to defeat (someone): *After a long struggle, we got the best of them* **8 have the best of** *infml* to win or succeed at/in: *We tried hard, but they had the best of the game|had the best of it* **9 make the best of** to do as much or as well as one can with: *to make the best of oneself|of a bad state of affairs* **10 the best of both worlds** the advantages of 2 different states or conditions without their disadvantages: *He lives on a farm and works in a big city in order to have the best of both worlds* **11 to the best of one's knowledge/belief/ability** as far as one knows/believes/is able: *I will do the work to the best of my ability*

best⁴ *v* [T1] to defeat (someone): *After a long struggle, we bested them*

bes·ti·al /ˈbestɪəl‖ˈbestʃəl/ *adj derog* **1** (of human beings and their behaviour) of or like an animal in being nasty or shameful **2** very cruel; BRUTAL (2): *bestial cruelty* —**~ly** *adv*

bes·ti·al·i·ty /ˌbestiˈælɪ̇ti‖ˌbestʃi-/ *n* [U] **1** *derog* the state or condition of being BESTIAL **2** sexual relations between a human being and an animal

bes·ti·ar·y /ˈbestɪəri‖ˈbestʃiːeri/ *n* a book (esp. of the MIDDLE AGES in Europe) with information about animals that is intended to amuse people or to teach them proper behaviour

be·stir /bɪˈstɜːʳ/ *v* **-rr-** [T1;(V3)] *fml* to cause (oneself) to move quickly or become active: *We must bestir ourselves (to take the necessary action)*

best man /ˌ· ˈ·/ *n* [*usu. sing.*] (at a marriage ceremony) the friend and attendant of the man who is to be married (BRIDEGROOM)

be·stow /bɪˈstəʊ/ *v* [T1 (*on* or *upon*)] *fml* to give: *Several gifts were bestowed on the royal visitors* —**~al** *n* [U9]

be·strew /bɪˈstruː/ *v* **bestrewed, bestrewn** /bɪˈstruːn/ *or* **bestrewed** [T1] *fml* **1** to lie scattered over: *Flowers bestrewed the grave of the dead child* **2** [(*with*)] STREW (1): *to bestrew the grave with flowers*

be·stride /bɪˈstraɪd/ *v* **bestrode** /bɪˈstrəʊd/, **bestridden** /bɪˈstrɪdn/ [T1] *fml* to sit or stand on or over (a thing) with legs apart, as in sitting on a horse: *to bestride a horse|a fence*

best-sel·ler /ˌ· ˈ··/ *n* something (esp. a book) that sells in very large numbers

bet¹ /bet/ *n* [C] **1** an agreement to risk money on the result of a future event: *Let's make a bet on the next election.|to place a bet (with a* BOOKMAKER*)|to win|lose a bet* **2** a sum of money so risked: *a £5 bet* **3 hedge/cover one's bets** *infml* to protect oneself against loss by risking money on more than one possible result

bet² *v* **bet** *or* **betted;** *pres. p.* **betting** [D1,5a;T1 (*on*), 5a;I∅ (*on*)] **1** to risk (money) on the result of a future event: *I('ll) bet (you) (£5) that they'll win the next election* **2 bet one's boots/bottom dollar/shirt on/that** *infml* to be certain of/that: *You can bet your boots on that|that he'll come late again* **3 I bet** *infml* **a** I'm sure: *I bet it rains|will rain tomorrow!* **b** (to show humorous doubt): *"He'll do it tomorrow." "I bet he will!"* (=I think he won't)" **4 You bet** *sl* You can be sure; certainly: *"Will you tell her?" "You bet (I will)"*

be·ta /ˈbiːtə‖ˈbeɪtə/ *n* [R;(C)] **1** the 2nd letter of the Greek alphabet (Β, β) **2** also B— a mark for between average and good work by students: *They gave him (a) beta for history*

be·take /bɪˈteɪk/ *v* **betook** /bɪˈtʊk/, **betaken** /bɪˈteɪkən/ [X9] *lit* to cause (oneself) to go: *He betook himself to the palace to see the King*

be·tel /ˈbiːtl/ *n* [U] a leaf which is filled with pieces of BETEL NUT and other things, and is CHEWed by Indians and Southeastern Asians

betel nut /ˈ·· ·/ *n* [U;C] the nut of the ARECA, which is red and hard with a bitter taste, and is CHEWed in India and Southeast Asia

bête-noire /ˌbet ˈnwɑːʳ (*Fr* bɛt nwar)/ *n* **bêtes-noires** /ˌbet ˈnwɑːz‖-ɑrz (*Fr* bɛt nwar)/ *Fr* the person or thing one dislikes most

beth·el /ˈbeθəl/ *n* **1** *bibl* a holy place **2** *esp. BrE* a house of worship for NONCONFORMISTS **3** *esp. AmE* (*often cap.*) a house of worship for sailors

be·think /bɪˈθɪŋk/ *v* **bethought** /bɪˈθɔːt/ [T1 (*of*)] *lit or old use* to cause (oneself) to be reminded or to consider: *You should bethink yourself of your duty, my Lord!*

be·tide /bɪˈtaɪd/ *v lit* **1 Whatever may betide** Whatever may happen: *We shall remain friends whatever may betide* **2 Woe betide (you, him, etc.)** you, he, etc., will be in trouble: *Woe betide them if they're late!*

be·times /bɪˈtaɪmz/ *adv lit or humor* early; in good time

be·to·ken /bɪˈtəʊkən/ *v* [T1] *fml* to be a sign (of): *All those black clouds betoken a storm*

be·tray /bɪˈtreɪ/ *v* **1** [T1 (*to*)] to be disloyal or unfaithful to: *I thought he would be too loyal to betray his friends!* **2** [T1 (*to*)] to give away or make known (esp. a secret): *He betrayed the news to all his friends* **3** [T1 (*to*), 5,6a (esp. **what**);(V3)] to be a sign of (something one would like to hide): *Her red face betrayed her nervousness|betrayed (the fact) that she was nervous|betrayed what she was thinking about* **4** [T1] to show the real feelings or intentions of (someone/oneself): *He tried to seem angry, but his smile betrayed him|but he betrayed himself by smiling* —**~er** *n*

be·tray·al /bɪˈtreɪəl/ *n* **1** [U] the act of BETRAYing **2** [C] an example of this: *a betrayal of my principles*

be·troth /bɪˈtrəʊð, bɪˈtrəʊθ/ *v* [Wv5;T1 (*to*)] *becoming rare* **1** to promise to give in marriage: *Her father betrothed her to him at an early age* **2** (esp. of a woman) to promise to give (oneself) in marriage: *She betrothed herself to him*

be·troth·al /bɪˈtrəʊðəl/ *n* **1** [U] the act of BETROTHing **2** [C] an example of this —compare ENGAGEMENT (1)

be·trothed /bɪˈtrəʊðd, bɪˈtrəʊθt/ *n* **1** [S9] the person to whom one has been BETROTHed: *She was here with her betrothed* **2** [*the*+P] 2 people who are BETROTHed to each other: *The betrothed stood before the priest* —compare FIANCÉ(E)

bet·ter¹ /ˈbetəʳ/ *adj* (*compar. of* GOOD) [Wa5] **1** of higher quality, moral value, usefulness, etc.: *You're a better man than I am!|a better wine|This new medicine is better for a cold* **2 be better than one's word** *infml* to do more than one has promised **3 Better luck next time!** (said to encourage someone who has done badly *this* time) **4 for better or (for) worse** (*as said in the Christian marriage ceremony*) whatever happens; even if there are difficulties: *He promised to take her for better or for worse* **5 have seen better days** *infml* to be in a worse condition now than formerly: *That poor old man/That old house has seen better days* **6 little/no better than** almost the same as (someone or something not good): *He is no better than a thief* **7 no better than she should be** *old infml euph* of doubtful character sexually **8 one's better half** *infml pomp* one's wife **9 the better part of** more than half: *I haven't seen him for the better part of a month!*

better² *adj* (*compar. of* WELL) **1** [Wa5;F] completely well again after an illness: *Now that he's better he can play football again* **2** [F9] improved in health: *Are you feeling any better?|I'm a little/no/much better (than I was)*

USAGE The first meaning is not used with **than** or with adverbs like **much**. One is either **better**, in this meaning, or one is not: *I'm nearly/I'm completely* **better** *now.*

better³ *adv* (*compar. of* WELL) **1** in a more excellent manner: *He swims better than I do* **2** to a higher or greater degree: *She knows the story better than I do* **3 go one better (than)** *infml* to do better (than): *That was a good story, but I can go one better* **4 had better** ought to; should: *"I thought I'd better warn you, just in case David should ever mention it"* (SEU W.).|*"I'd better not go round at* LUNCH *time"* (SEU S.)

better⁴ *n* **1** [S] *fml* something better: *That's my idea: can you think of a better?* (=a better one) **2 get the better of** to defeat (someone) or deal successfully with (a difficulty): *to get the better of one's opponents*

better⁵ *v* **1** [T1;(I0)] to (cause to) improve: *They tried to better their living conditions.|Living conditions have bettered a great deal* **2** [T1] to go beyond in quality: *to better last year's results|to better a sports record* **3 better oneself a** to earn more money **b** to educate oneself

better⁶, bettor *n* a person who BETs

bet·ter·ment /ˈbetəmənt‖-tər-/ *n* [U] the action of making or becoming better; improvement

bet·ters /ˈbetəz‖-ərz/ *n* [P9] people of higher rank or greater worth (than someone) (often in the phr. **one's elders and betters**): *Don't speak that way to your betters, young man!*

be·tween¹ /bɪˈtwiːn/ *prep* **1** (of position or time): *standing (in) between Mr A and Mr B|between 5 and 6 o'clock|between 5 and 6 miles away|(fig.) A girl is between a child and a woman* **2** (showing connection): *a railway between 2 cities|regular air service between the 2 cities|a marriage between Mr A and Miss B* **3** (showing division): *Divide it between the 2 children.|a choice between 2 possibilities|What's the difference between this and that?|a quarrel between Mr A and Mr B|a football match between Manchester United and Sheffield United* **4** (showing the result of the shared activity of several people): *They all did the job between them.|Between them they collected $50* **5** taking together the total effect of (a set of things): *Between cooking, cleaning, washing, sewing, and writing, she was very busy* **6 between you and me** also **between you, me, and the gatepost, between ourselves** *infml*— without anyone else knowing: *Between you and me, (I think) he's rather stupid* **7 come/stand between (people)** to separate (people): *I hope that nothing ever comes between us!* **8 little/nothing to choose between them** (almost) no difference between them **9 there is no love lost between them** *infml* they dislike each other —see also IN BETWEEN

USAGE Compare **among** and **between**: 1 **Between¹** must be followed by 2 things. It is right to say **between** *the 2 houses* or **between** *each house and the next.* It is common, but nonstandard, to say ***between** *each house.* 2 Some books say that **between¹** should be followed by 2 things only, and **among** by 3 or more: *Divide it* **between** *the 2/***among** *the 3 children.* But when we speak of clear and exact position we always use **between**: *Ecuador lies between Colombia, Peru, and the Pacific Ocean.*

between² *adv* **1** in or into a space, or period of time, that is between: *There's only the tree and the rock, captain: I can see nothing between!* **2 few and far between** *infml* rare and infrequent —see also IN BETWEEN

be·twixt /bɪˈtwɪkst/ also **'twixt**— *prep, adv old use or poet* between

betwixt and be·tween /·ˌ· · ·ˈ·/ *adv* in a middle position; neither one thing nor the other

bev·el¹ /ˈbevəl/ *n* **1** the slope of a surface at an angle other than a right angle, usu. along the edge of wood or glass **2** a tool for making such a sloping edge or surface

bevel² *v* **-ll-** (*AmE* **-l-**) [Wv5;T1] to make a sloping edge on (wood or glass)

bevel gear /ˈ·· ·/ *n* toothed wheels with sloping edges to work at right angles to each other —see picture at MACHINERY

bev·er·age /ˈbevərɪdʒ/ *n fml* a liquid for drinking, esp. one that is not water, medicine, or alcohol

bev·y /ˈbevi/ *n* [(*of*)] **1** a large group or collection, esp. of girls or women: *a bevy of beauties* **2** a group of certain kinds of birds, esp. QUAIL

be·wail /bɪˈweɪl/ *v* [T1] *fml* to express deep sorrow for, esp. by or as if by weeping

be·ware /bɪˈweəʳ/ *v* [I0(*of*);T6 (esp. **what**)] (used in giving or reporting orders) to be careful: *Beware of the dog*

USAGE **Beware** does not change its form.

be·wil·der /bɪˈwɪldəʳ/ *v* [Wv4,5;T1] to confuse, esp. by the presence of lots of different things at the same time: *Big city traffic bewilders me.|the bewildering traffic of a big city|a bewildered look* —**~ment** *n* [U]: *Imagine my bewilderment when she said that!*

be·witch /bɪˈwɪtʃ/ *v* [T1] **1** to have a magic effect, often harmful, on: *Shakespeare's character "Bottom" was bewitched and given the head of a donkey in "A Midsummer Night's Dream"* **2** [Wv4] to charm as if by magic: *The girl's sweet smile had bewitched him, and he could refuse her nothing.|a bewitching smile* —compare ENCHANT

bey /beɪ/ *n* (*often cap.*) **1** [C] (the title of) a governor or officer esp. in the Middle East **2** [E] (the Turkish word for) Mr: *Ahmet Bey* —compare EFFENDI

be·yond¹ /bɪˈjɒnd‖bɪˈjɑnd/ *adv* on or to the further side; further: *If we cross the mountains we may find people living in the valley beyond.|I will go with you to the bridge, but not a step beyond.|(fig.) ". . . to prepare for the changes of the 1970's and beyond"* (SEU W.)

beyond² *prep* **1** on or to the further side of: *What lies beyond the mountains?* **2** [*usu. nonassertive*] (of time) later than; past; after: *Don't stay there beyond midnight* **3** out of reach of; much more than; outside the limits of: *The high fruit was beyond my reach.|That strange idea is beyond belief.|"blame ourselves for something that's quite beyond our control"* (SEU S.) **4** [*nonassertive*] besides; except (for): *I own nothing beyond the clothes on my back.|Beyond that, there is nothing more I can say* **5 beyond compare/all praise** wonderfully good **6 beyond one's hopes/one's wildest dreams** better than one could possibly have expected

beyond³ also **great beyond**— *n* [*the*+R] (*often cap.*) life after death; HEREAFTER²: *What can we*

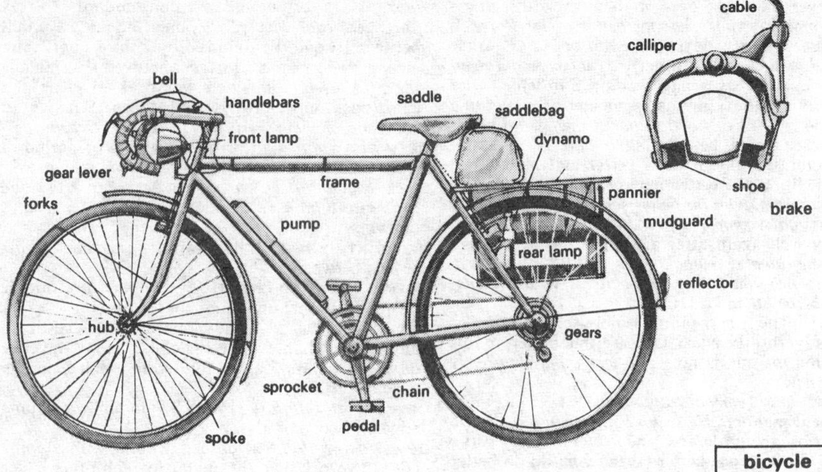

bicycle

poor human beings know of the beyond? —see also BACK OF BEYOND

be·zique /bə̱ˈziːk/ *n* [U] a card game for 2 or more players, played with 64 cards

bhang /bæŋ/ *n* [U] the form of CANNABIS (2) used in India, sometimes in a drink, sometimes smoked in cigarettes, which is not very powerful in its effect. It is the leaves, stem, and (sometimes) fruit of the plant

bi- /baɪ/ *prefix* 2, twice, both, etc.: *bi*ANNUAL (=once every 2 years or twice in one year)| BIMETALLISM (=concerning both gold and silver) USAGE Expressions like **bi***weekly* are confusing, because they may mean "twice in one week/month/year" or "once in 2 weeks/months/years".

bi·as¹ /ˈbaɪəs/ *n* [C;U] **1** (that which causes) the movement of a rolled ball (in the game of BOWLS) away from the straight course **2** a tendency to be in favour of or against something or someone without knowing enough to be able to judge fairly PREJUDICE¹ (1,2): *a bias towards/against something* **3** a tendency of mind: *Her scientific bias showed itself in early childhood* **4 cut (cloth) on the bias** to cut (cloth) across, from one corner towards the opposite one; cut DIAGONALly

bias² *v* **-s-** *or* **-ss-** [Wv5;T1] to cause to form settled favourable or unfavourable opinions without enough information to judge fairly; PREJUDICE² (1): *His background biases him against foreigners*

bias bind·ing /ˌ·ˈ··/ *n* [U] material in the form of a narrow band, cut on the BIAS¹ (4), for use when sewing curved edges or corners of cloth

bib /bɪb/ *n* **1** a cloth or plastic shield tied under a child's chin to protect its clothes **2** the upper part of an APRON or OVERALLS, above the waistline

bi·ble /ˈbaɪbəl/ *n* (a copy of) a holy book: (fig.) *This dictionary should be your bible when studying English*

Bible *n* [C;*the*+R] **1** (a copy of) the holy book of the Christians, consisting of the OLD TESTAMENT and the NEW TESTAMENT **2** (a copy of) the holy book of the Jews; the OLD TESTAMENT

bib·li·cal /ˈbɪblɪkəl/ *adj* (*sometimes cap.*) of, like, or about the Bible, esp. the AUTHORIZED VERSION (=English translation of 1611): *trying to write in a biblical style* —**~ly** *adv* [Wa4]

biblio- /ˈbɪbliəʊ/ *comb. form* book: BIBLIOGRAPHY

bib·li·og·ra·pher /ˌbɪbliˈɒgrəfəʳ‖-ˈɑg-/ *n* **1** a person who studies BIBLIOGRAPHY (1) **2** a person who makes a BIBLIOGRAPHY (2)

bib·li·og·ra·phy /ˈbɪbliˈɒgrəfi‖-ˈɑg-/ *n* **1** [U] the history or description of books or writings **2** [C] a list of writings which share some quality: *a bibliography of writings by/about Byron* **3** [C] a list of all writings used in the preparation of a book or article, usu. appearing at the end

bib·li·o·phile /ˈbɪblɪəfaɪl/ *n* a person who loves books

bib·u·lous /ˈbɪbjʊləs‖-bjə-/ *adj humor or pomp* (typical of a person) that likes to drink a lot or too much

bi·cam·er·al leg·is·la·ture /baɪˈkæmərəl/ *n* a law-making body consisting of 2 parts (HOUSE*s*¹ (6), CHAMBER*s* (2)), like the SENATE and the House of Representatives in the US CONGRESS

bi·carb /baɪˈkɑːb, ˈbaɪkɑːb‖-ɑrb/ *n* [U] *infml* BICARBONATE, esp. as used for settling the stomach

bi·car·bon·ate /baɪˈkɑːbənə̱t, -neɪt‖-ˈkɑr-/ also **bi·carbonate of so·da** /·,··· · ˈ··/— *n* [U] a chemical substance used esp. in baking and taken with water to settle the stomach

bi·cen·te·na·ry /ˌbaɪsenˈtiːnəri‖-ˈtenəri, -ˈsentəneri/ *n* the day or year exactly 200 years after a particular event: *Longman's bicentenary fell in the year 1924*

bi·cen·ten·ni·al¹ /ˌbaɪsenˈtenɪəl/ *n esp. AmE* BICENTENARY

bicentennial² *adj* [Wa5] 200th (esp. in the phr. **bicentennial anniversary**)

bi·ceps /ˈbaɪseps/ *n* **biceps** [Wn3;C *often pl. with sing. meaning*] the large muscle on the front of the upper arm —see picture at HUMAN²

bick·er /ˈbɪkəʳ/ *v* [IØ (*about/over* and/or *with*)] to quarrel, esp. about small matters: *The 2 children were always bickering* (*with each other*) (*over/about small matters*)

bi·cy·cle¹ /ˈbaɪsɪkəl/ also **cycle,** (*infml*) **bike**— *n* [C; *by*+U] a 2-wheeled vehicle which one rides by pushing its PEDAL*s* with the feet USAGE One **rides** (*on*) a **bicycle**, **horse**, **scooter**, or **motorbike**. One **mounts** (*it*), **gets on** (*it*), or **gets onto** *it*, and later **dismounts** (*from it*) or **gets off** (*it*).

bicycle² also **cycle,** (*infml*) **bike**— *v* [IØ (ALONG)] to travel by bicycle —**bicyclist** *n*

bid¹ /bɪd/ *v* **bade** /bæd, beɪd/ *or* **bid, bidden** /ˈbɪdn/ *or* **bid;** *pres. p.* **bidding** *old use or lit* **1** [D1 (*to*);T1] to say or wish (a greeting or goodbye to someone): *He bid me good morning as he passed* **2** [V2,3;(T1)] to order or tell (someone to do something): *She would never do as she was bidden* **3** [X9] to invite:

guests bidden to a wedding —**~der** *n* [C]

bid² *v* **bid** **1** [T1;IØ (*on*): (*for*)] to offer (a price) whether for payment or acceptance, as at an AUCTION: *He bid £5 for an old book.|What am I bid for this old book?* (= what will people bid for it?) **2** [IØ (*for*)] to try to get approval or support by making offers, promises, etc.: *They are bidding for our favour by making wild promises that they can't keep* **3** [T1;IØ] (in playing cards) to declare one's intention of winning (a certain number of games): *Have you bid yet?|I bid 2* SPADES³ —**~der** *n*

bid³ *n* **1** an offer to pay a certain price at a sale, esp. at an AUCTION: *a bid of £5 for that old book* **2** an offer to do some work at a certain price; TENDER³ (1): *Bids for building the bridge were invited from British and American firms* **3** a declaration of the number of games (TRICK*s*) a cardplayer says he intends to win: *a bid of 2* SPADES³ **4** a chance or turn to make such a declaration: *It's your bid now, Mr Jones* **5** an attempt or effort to get, win, or attract: *The criminal made a bid for freedom by trying to run away*

bid·da·ble /ˈbɪdəbəl/ *adj esp. BrE* (of a person) easily led, taught, or controlled

bid·ding /ˈbɪdɪŋ/ *n* [U] **1** order; command (esp. in the phrs. **at one's bidding, do someone's bidding**) **2** the act or action of making BID*s*

bide /baɪd/ *v* **bide one's time** to wait, usu. for a long time, until the right moment: *He seems to be doing nothing, but really he's just biding his time*

bi·det /ˈbiːdeɪ‖bɪˈdeɪ (*Fr* bidɛ)/ *n* a kind of small low bath for sitting across to wash the lower parts of the body —see picture at BATHROOM

bid fair *v adv* [I3] to seem likely: *The day bids fair to stay fine and sunny*

bi·en·ni·al /baɪˈeniəl/ *adj* [Wa5] **1** (of events) happening once every 2 years: *A biennial art show was held in the city in 1970, 1972 and 1974* **2** (of plants) living for 2 years and producing seed in the second year —**~ly** *adv*

bier /bɪəʳ/ *n* a movable frame like a table, sometimes with wheels, for supporting a dead body or COFFIN, or for taking it to the graveside

biff¹ /bɪf/ *n sl* a quick hard blow

biff² *v* [T1] *sl* to give a BIFF¹ to: *He biffed me on the head!*

bi·fo·cals /baɪˈfəʊkəlz‖ˈbaɪfəʊ-/ *n* [P] eyeglasses having an upper part made for looking at distant objects, and a lower part made for reading —see PAIR¹ (USAGE) —**bifocal** *adj* [Wa5]

bi·fur·cate¹ /ˈbaɪfəkeɪt‖-ər-/ *v* [IØ] *fml* (of roads, branches, rivers, etc.) to divide into 2 branches or parts: *A mile further on, the river bifurcates; one branch flows east, and the other flows southeast* —**-cation** /ˌbaɪfəˈkeɪʃən‖-ər-/ *n* [U;(C)]

bi·fur·cate² /baɪˈfɜːkɪ̈t‖-ɜr-/ also **bi·fur·cat·ed** /ˈbaɪfəkeɪtɪ̈d‖-ər-/— *adj* [Wa5] *tech* having divided into 2 parts: *a bifurcate river*

big¹ /bɪg/ *adj* **-gg-** [Wa1] **1** [B] of more than average size, weight, force, importance, etc.: *a big box|How big is it?|no bigger than a pin|a big mouse|That child is big for his age.|The big question is what to do next.|a big-boned person|*(fig.) *big-hearted|Don't cry: you're a big boy/girl now.|The big moment has come at last!* **2** [A] (esp. of people) doing a great deal of some activity: *a big eater|a big spender* **3** [F (*with*)] *lit* (of a woman) PREGNANT (1): *big with child* **4** [F;(B)] *esp. AmE sl* very popular: *Frank Sinatra is very big in Las Vegas* **5 have big ideas** *infml* to want to do something important or to become someone important **6 too big for one's boots/breeches** *infml* believing oneself to be more important than one really is —see also **big** NOISE, **big** SHOT¹ **7 that's big of (you, him, etc.)** *infml* that's generous of you, him, etc. —**~ness** *n* [U]

big² *adv* [Wa1] *sl* **1 talk big** to talk as if one were more important than one really is **2 think big** to plan to do a great deal in spite of all possible difficulties

big·a·mist /ˈbɪgəmɪ̈st/ *n* a person who is guilty of BIGAMY

big·a·mous /ˈbɪgəməs/ *adj* [Wa5] of or belonging to the crime of BIGAMY —**~ly** *adv*

big·a·my /ˈbɪgəmi/ *n* [U] the state of being married to 2 people at the same time: *Bigamy is considered a crime in many countries*

big bang the·o·ry /ˌ· ˈ· ˌ···/ *n* [*the*+R] the idea that everything began with the explosion of a single mass of material so that the pieces are still flying apart —compare STEADY STATE THEORY

big broth·er /ˌ· ˈ··/ *n* **1** one's elder brother **2** (*usu. caps.*) a government leader who has too much power and allows no freedom

big busi·ness /ˌ· ˈ··/ *n* [U;(C)] *infml* business with a lot of money and influence, employing many people

big deal /ˌ· ˈ·/ *interj esp AmE sl* (showing that one considers something unimportant): *"He's got a house and a car!" "Big deal! I've got a house and 2 cars!"*

Big Dip·per /ˌ· ˈ··/ *n* [*the*+R] *AmE* PLOUGH

big end /ˌ· ˈ·/ *n* [*usu. sing.*] *BrE tech* (in a car engine) the part of a connecting rod which joins onto the CRANK¹ (1) —see picture at PETROL

big game /ˌ· ˈ·/ *n* [U] the largest wild animals hunted for sport, such as lions and elephants, but not usu. including deer or ANTELOPE: *a big-game hunter in Africa*

big·head /ˈbɪghed/ *n* [C; (*you*) N] *infml* a person who thinks too highly of his own importance

bight /baɪt/ *n* **1** a bend or curve in a coast larger than, or curving less than, a BAY (6) **2** a bend (LOOP) made in the middle of a rope

big name /ˌ· ˈ·/ *n infml* an important person or group: *He's a big name in the music world*

big·ot /ˈbɪgət/ *n derog* a person who thinks strongly and unreasonably that his own opinion or belief is correct, esp. about matters of religion, race, or politics

big·ot·ed /ˈbɪgətɪ̈d/ *adj derog* (typical of a person) that believes strongly and unreasonably that he and people like him are right or best, esp. in matters of religion, race, or politics: *bigoted people/opinions* —**~ly** *adv*

big·ot·ry /ˈbɪgətri/ *n* [U] *derog* **1** the state of mind of a BIGOT **2** acts or beliefs typical of a BIGOT

big sis·ter /ˌ· ˈ··/ *n* one's elder sister

big stick /ˌ· ˈ·/ *n* [*the*+R] the threat of using military or political force to get what one wants

big time /ˈ· ·/ *n* [*the*+R] *sl* the top rank (esp. in sports or the amusement business): *Don't worry—you're in the big time now!* —**big-timer** *n*

big top /ˌ· ˈ·/ *n* [(*the*)] a very large tent used by a CIRCUS (= a show with performing animals, people, etc.)

big·wig /ˈbɪgwɪg/ *n humor or derog sl* an important person

bi·jou /ˈbiːʒuː/ *n* **bijoux** /ˈbiːʒuːz/ *Fr* **1** a jewel **2** something small and pretty: *a nice little bijou theatre*

bike /baɪk/ *n, v* [C;IØ] *infml* BICYCLE

bi·ki·ni /bɪ̈ˈkiːni/ *n* a very small 2-piece bathing suit for women

bi·la·bi·al /baɪˈleɪbiəl/ *adj, n* [Wa5] (a consonant) produced with both lips: *The English sound for* b *is a bilabial*

bi·lat·er·al /baɪˈlætərəl/ *adj* [Wa5] of, on, or with 2 sides; between or concerning 2 parties: *a bilateral agreement (between country A and country B)* —**~ly** *adv*

bil·ber·ry /ˈbɪlbəri‖-ˌberi/ *n* **1** a low bushy plant growing on hillsides and in high woods in Northern Europe **2** its bluish fruit, which can be eaten

bile /baɪl/ *n* [U] **1** a bitter green-brown liquid formed in the LIVER[1] and poured into the bowel (through the **bile duct**), where it breaks up fat into very small bits which are more easily used by the body —see picture at DIGESTIVE SYSTEM **2** bad temper

bilge /bɪldʒ/ *n* **1** [C] the broad bottom of a ship **2** [U] also **bilge wa·ter** /ˈ·ˌ··/— dirty water in the bottom of a ship **3** [U] *sl* foolish talk: *Don't give me that bilge!*

bi·lin·gual[1] /baɪˈlɪŋgwəl/ *adj* [Wa5] **1** of, containing, or expressed in 2 languages: *a bilingual French-English dictionary* **2** able to speak a second language as well as one speaks one's first language

bilingual[2] *n* a person who is able to speak a second language as well as he can speak his first language

bil·i·ous /ˈbɪlɪəs/ *adj* **1** having too much BILE (1) in the body, which causes sickness and pains in the head: *Fatty food makes some people bilious* **2** bad-tempered —**~ness** *n* [U]

bilk /bɪlk/ *v* [T1 (*out of*)] to cheat (someone) (out of something, usu. money)

bill[1] /bɪl/ *n* **1** *tech* the beak of a bird —see picture at BIRD **2** *BrE* (*usu. cap. as part of a name*) a long narrow piece of land sticking out into the sea, and shaped like a beak: *Portland Bill*

bill[2] *v* **bill and coo** *infml* (of lovers) to kiss and speak softly to each other: *They sat there billing and cooing till after midnight!*

bill[3] *n* **1** [C] a plan for a law, written down for the government to consider **2** [C] a list of things bought and their price **3** [C] a printed notice: *Stick No Bills* (a public warning on a wall, fence, etc.) **4** [C9] *AmE* a piece of paper money; NOTE[2] (6): *a 5-dollar bill|I'm sorry: I have nothing to pay with except some big bills* **5 fill the bill** *infml* to be suitable: *Who's the right person for the job? Who will fill the bill?* **6 foot the bill (for)** *infml* to pay and take responsibility (for), esp. for something important: *Who's going to foot the bill for the failure of the new aircraft?* **7 top/head the bill** *infml* to be mentioned first in a list as the most important

bill[4] *v* **1** [T1 (*for*)] *esp. tech* to send a bill to: *I can't pay now: please bill me (for it) later* **2** [T1 (*as*);V3] to advertise in printed notices: *billed (to appear) as Hamlet*

bill·board /ˈbɪlbɔːd‖-ord/ *n AmE* HOARDING (2)

bil·let[1] /ˈbɪlɨ̠t/ *n* **1** a lodging-house for a soldier **2 a good billet** *infml becoming rare* a good job

billet[2] *v* [T1 (*on*)] to provide (a soldier) with a BILLET[1]: *The captain billeted his soldiers on old Mrs Smith* (=in old Mrs Smith's house)

bil·let-doux /ˌbɪleɪ ˈduː (*Fr* bije du)/ *n* **billets-doux** /-ˈduːz (*Fr* -du)/ *Fr, humor or lit* a love letter

bill·fold /ˈbɪlfəʊld/ *n AmE* WALLET (1)

bill·hook /ˈbɪlhʊk/ also **bill**— *n* a tool consisting of a blade with a hooked point and a handle, used esp. in cutting off unwanted branches of trees and cutting up wood for fires

bil·li·ard /ˈbɪljəd‖-ərd/ *n* [A] of or for BILLIARDS: *a billiard table|billiard balls*

bil·li·ards /ˈbɪljədz‖-ərdz/ *n* [U] a game played on a cloth-covered table with balls knocked with long sticks (CUEs) against each other or into pockets at the corners and sides: *Billiards is my favourite game* USAGE One plays **billiards** on a **billiard table**, scoring (SCORE) *points*. In an important *match* the person in charge is called the **referee.**

bil·li·on /ˈbɪljən/ *determiner, n, pron* **billion** *or* **billions** [see NUMBER TABLE 2] **1** (the number) 1,000,000,000; 10^9 **2** *BrE old use* (the number) 1,000,000,000,000; 10^{12} —**~th** *determiner, n, pron, adv* [see NUMBER TABLE 3]

Bill of Ex·change /ˌ· · ·ˈ·/ *n* **Bills of Exchange** a written order to pay money at a certain date

bill of fare /ˌ· · ˈ·/ *n* **bills of fare** a list of dishes to be served; MENU

bill of health /ˌ· · ˈ·/ *n* **a clean bill of health** a favourable report **a** on someone's health **b** about something: *The school was given a clean bill of health by the government*

bill of lad·ing /ˌ· · ˈ··/ *n* **bills of lading** a list of things carried, esp. on a ship

bill of rights /ˌ· · ˈ·/ *n* **bills of rights** (*usu. caps.*) a written list of the most important rights of the citizens of a country: *The Bill of Rights of the US* CONSTITUTION|(fig.) *This new law is going to be the unmarried mother's bill of rights*

bill of sale /ˌ· · ˈ·/ *n* **bills of sale** an official written statement that something has been sold by one person to another

bil·low[1] /ˈbɪləʊ/ *n* **1** a wave, esp. a very large one **2** a rolling mass (as of flame or FOG) like a large wave —**~y** *adj*

billow[2] *v* [Wv4] **1** [IØ] to rise and roll in waves **2** [IØ (OUT)] to swell out, as a sail: *billowing sails/skirts*

bill·post·er /ˈbɪlˌpəʊstə^r/ also **bill·stick·er** /ˈbɪlˌstɪkə^r/— *n* a worker who sticks printed notices onto walls —**billposting** *n* [U]

bil·ly /ˈbɪli/ also **bil·ly·can** /ˈbɪlikæn/— *n* a tin vessel used for cooking or boiling water, when camping —see picture at CAMP[2]

billy goat /ˈ·· ·/ *n* (*used esp. by or to children*) a male goat —compare NANNY GOAT

billy-o /ˈ·· ·/ also **billy-oh** /ˈ·· ·/— *n* **like billy-o** *BrE sl* a lot; very strongly, fast, or fiercely: *to run like billy-o*

bil·tong /ˈbɪltɒŋ‖-tɔŋ/ *n* [U] *SAfrE* meat dried in the sun

bi·me·tal·lic /ˌbaɪmɨ̠ˈtælɪk/ *adj tech* **1** having to do with BIMETALLISM **2** made of 2 metals

bi·met·al·lis·m /baɪˈmetəl-ɪzəm/ *n* [U] *tech* the idea that the money system should be based on 2 metals (esp. silver as well as gold) whose values should have a fixed relation to each other

bi·month·ly /baɪˈmʌnθli/ *adv, adj* [Wa5] **1** appearing or happening every 2 months: *a bimonthly magazine* **2** *nonstandard* appearing or happening twice a month —see BI- (USAGE)

bin /bɪn/ *n* **1** [C] (*often in comb.*) a large wide-mouthed container (esp. one with a lid) for bread, flour, coal, etc., or for waste —see also DUSTBIN —see picture at STREET, KITCHEN **2** [*the*+R] *sl* LOONY BIN

bi·na·ry /ˈbaɪnəri/ *adj* [Wa5] *tech* **1** consisting of 2 things or parts; double: *A* **binary star** *is a double star, consisting of 2 stars turning round each other* **2** using the 2 numbers, 0 and 1, as a base: *A* **binary system of numbers** *is used in many* COMPUTERs

bind[1] /baɪnd/ *v* **bound** /baʊnd/ **1** [T1 (UP)] to tie: *Bind the prisoner with rope.|Bind the prisoner's arms.|*(fig.) *He stood there, bound by the magic of her voice* **2** [X9] to put into a given state by tying: *Bind the prisoner to his chair with rope.|Bind the prisoner's arms together* **3** [T1 (UP)] to tie together: *She bound (up) her hair* **4** [T1 (UP)] BANDAGE[2]: *to bind (up) wounds* **5** [T1] to fasten together and enclose in a cover: *to bind a book* **6** [T1] to strengthen or ornament with a band of material: *The edges of the floor mat are coming undone because they have not been bound properly* **7** [T1;IØ] to (cause to) stick together: *This flour mixture isn't wet enough to bind properly* **8** [IØ;(T1)] to make it hard for (someone) to move the bowels: *Eggs are considered a binding food* **9** [T1] to cause to obey esp. by a law or a solemn promise: *I am bound by my promise.|I have bound myself by an agreement.|a binding agreement* **10** [V3] to make or declare it necessary for (someone) to do something: *They bound me to remain silent about it.|I bound myself to pay back the debt I owed* **11** [T1 (TOGETHER)] to unite: *Many things bind us (together)* **12** [I∅] to have a uniting, limiting, or controlling effect: *Promises, agreements, etc., that bind* —see also BOUND³

bind² *n* [S] *sl* an annoying state of affairs (often in the phr. **a bit of a bind**)

bind down *v adv* [T1] (*often pass.*) to limit (esp. a person): *The young scientist felt bound down by a lot of useless and confusing rules*

bind·er /ˈbaɪndəʳ/ *n* **1** [C] a person who binds, esp. books: *Your book is still at the binder's* **2** [C] a machine that binds things together, esp. one that binds corn when it is cut **3** [C;U] a substance that causes things to stick together **4** [C] a usu. removable cover, esp. for holding sheets of paper, magazines, etc.

bind·er·y /ˈbaɪndəri/ *n* a workshop where books are bound

bind·ing¹ /ˈbaɪndɪŋ/ *n* **1** [U] the action of a person or machine that binds: *Binding (books) is hard to learn* **2** [C] a book cover: *The binding of this book is torn* **3** [U] material sewn or stuck along the edge of something for strength or ornament: *with silk binding at the edges*

binding² *adj* that must be obeyed: *a binding agreement|This promise is binding on everyone who signed it*

bind on *v adv* [T1] to put on by binding: *He bound it on with rope*

bind o·ver *v adv* [T1] *Br law* to declare it necessary for (someone) to cause no more trouble under threat of punishment (often in the phr. **bind (someone) over to keep the peace**): *The judge bound over the 2 criminals for a year*

bind to *v prep* [D1] to declare (the stated kind of behaviour) necessary for (someone): *We must bind the members of the committee to secrecy*

bind·weed /ˈbaɪndwiːd/ *n* [U] a type of unwanted plant (WEED) which grows along the ground and curls itself round other plants

binge /bɪndʒ/ *n sl* SPREE: *They went on a binge last night and didn't get back till 3 in the morning!*

bin·go /ˈbɪŋgəʊ/ *n, interj* **1** [U] a game played for money or prizes by covering rows of numbered squares on a card **2** *sl* an expression of joy at a sudden successful result

bin·na·cle /ˈbɪnəkəl/ *n* a box with a glass top in which a ship's compass is kept, with a lamp for use at night

bi·noc·u·lar /bɪˈnɒkjʊləʳ, baɪ-‖-ˈnɑkjə-/ *adj* [Wa5] **1** [B] of, related to, or made for the use of both eyes: *binocular* VISION **2** [A] of or for BINOCULARS: *a binocular case*

bi·noc·u·lars /bɪˈnɒkjʊləz, baɪ-‖-ˈnɑkjələrz/ *n* [P] a pair of glasses like short TELESCOPE*s* for both eyes, used for looking at distant objects: *I watched the horse-race through my binoculars* —see PAIR¹ (USAGE) and picture at OPTICS

bi·no·mi·al /baɪˈnəʊmɪəl/ *n, adj* [Wa5] *tech* (an expression) consisting of 2 numbers, letters, etc., connected by the sign + or the sign − (like $a+b$ or $x-7$)

bi·o- /ˈbaɪəʊ, baɪˈɒ‖ˈbaɪəʊ, baɪˈɑ/ *comb. form* (of) life and living things: BIOLOGY

bi·o·chem·is·try /ˌbaɪəʊˈkemɪ̣stri/ *n* [U] (the scientific study of) the chemistry of living things: *to study biochemistry at university*

bi·o·de·gra·da·ble /ˌbaɪəʊdɪˈgreɪdəbəl/ *n tech, usu. apprec* able to be broken down esp. into harmless products by the action of living things (such as MICROORGANISM*s*): *She wants all bottles to be biodegradable after they've been used*

bi·og·ra·pher /baɪˈɒgrəfəʳ‖-ˈɑg-/ *n* a writer of BIOGRAPHY: *Boswell was the biographer of Dr Johnson*

bi·o·graph·i·cal /ˌbaɪəˈgræfɪkəl/ also **bi·o·graph·ic** /-ˈgræfɪk/— *adj* [Wa5] of BIOGRAPHY: *Those facts about his early life are of great biographical interest* —**~ly** *adv* [Wa4]

bi·og·ra·phy /baɪˈɒgrəfi‖-ˈɑg-/ *n* **1** [C] a written account of a person's life: *Boswell's famous biography of Dr. Johnson* **2** [U] this branch of literature: *I like poetry better than biography*

bi·o·log·i·cal /ˌbaɪəˈlɒdʒɪkəl◂‖-ˈlɑ-/ *adj* [Wa5] of BIOLOGY: *biological studies* —**~ly** *adv* [Wa4]

biological war·fare /ˌ····· ˈ··/ also **germ warfare**— *n* [U] methods of fighting a war in which living things such as bacteria are used for harming the enemy or his cattle and crops: *Biological warfare is probably the most terrible form of war*

bi·ol·o·gy /baɪˈɒlədʒi‖-ˈɑl-/ *n* [U] **1** the scientific study of living things: *to study biology* **2** the scientific laws of the life of a certain type of living thing: *the biology of bacteria can be quite hard to understand* —**-gist** *n*

bi·on·ic /baɪˈɒnɪk‖-ˈɑn-/ *adj infml* having powers (such as speed, strength, etc.) that are greater than those of ordinary human beings

bi·o·sphere /ˈbaɪəsfɪəʳ/ *n* [*the*+R] *tech* the part of the world in which life can exist

bi·o·tech·nol·o·gy /ˌbaɪəʊtekˈnɒlədʒi‖-ˈnɑ-/ *n* [U] *AmE* ERGONOMICS

bi·par·ti·san /ˌbaɪpɑːtɪ̣ˈzæn‖baɪˈpɑrtɪ̣zən/ *adj* [Wa5] representing or consisting of members of 2 political parties: *a bipartisan committee*

bi·par·tite /baɪˈpɑːtaɪt‖-ˈpɑr-/ *adj* [Wa5] **1** being in 2 parts **2** shared by 2 parties: *a bipartite agreement*

bi·ped /ˈbaɪped/ *n tech* a 2-footed creature

bi·plane /ˈbaɪpleɪn/ *n* an aircraft with 2 sets of wings, one above the other —compare MONOPLANE —see picture at AIRCRAFT

birch¹ /bɜːtʃ‖bɜrtʃ/ *n* **1** [C] any of several kinds of tree, common in northern countries, with smooth wood and thin branches **2** [U] its wood **3** [C] a rod made from its wood, or a handful of sticks tied together, used for punishing

birch² *v* [T1] to whip or hit, esp. with a BIRCH¹ (3), esp. as a punishment

bird /bɜːd‖bɜrd/ *n* **1** [C] a creature with wings and feathers **2** [C] *infml* a person: *He's|She's a dear old bird* **3** [C] *BrE sl* a woman: *Who is that beautiful bird I saw you with last night?* **4** [*the*+R] *sl* a rude noise made as a sign of disapproval: *They started to give the actor the bird when they saw his performance was bad* **5** [U] *BrE sl* a period of time spent in prison (esp. in the phr. **do bird**) **6 A bird in the hand (is worth 2 in the bush)** *infml* Something which one has really got (is better than a lot of nice things which one hasn't got) **7 Birds of a feather (flock together)** *infml* People of the same kind (often bad) (like each other's company): *I'm not surprised those 2 are such friends; they're birds of a feather!* **8 early bird** *infml* a person who gets up or arrives early **9 kill 2 birds with one stone** *infml* to get 2 results (esp. good ones) with one action **10 (strictly) for the birds** *AmE sl* worthless; silly **11 The early bird gets/catches the worm** A person who gets up or arrives early will be successful
See next page for picture

bird-brained /ˈ· ·/ *adj infml* stupid; silly

bird dog /ˈ· ·/ *n AmE* GUNDOG

bird fan·ci·er /ˈ· ˌ···/ *n* a person who is interested in birds, esp. one who keeps and breeds them

bird·ie /ˈbɜːdi‖ˈbɜrdi/ *n* **1** (used to or by children)

a bird; little bird **2** (in GOLF) an act of hitting the ball into the hole, taking one stroke fewer than is average for that particular hole —compare BOGEY (4), EAGLE (2), PAR[1] (3)

bird·lime /ˈbɜːdlaɪm‖ˈbɜr-/ also **lime**— *n* [U] sticky material spread on branches to catch birds

bird of par·a·dise /ˌ·· ˈ···/ *n* any of a large number of brightly-coloured birds of the New Guinea area

bird of pas·sage /ˌ·· ˈ··/ *n* **1** a bird that flies from one country or area to another, according to the season **2** *infml* a person who never stays in one place very long

bird of prey /ˌ·· ˈ·/ *n* any bird that kills other birds and small animals for food

bird·seed /ˈbɜːdsiːd‖ˈbɜr-/ *n* [U] a mixture of small seeds used chiefly for feeding birds that are kept in cages

bird's-eye view /ˌ·· ˈ·/ *n* [C (*of*) *usu. sing.*] **1** a view seen from high up, as if by a flying bird **2** *infml* a general view of a subject: *a bird's-eye view of chemistry*

bird-watch·er /ˈ· ˌ··/ *n* a person who watches wild birds in their natural surroundings, and tries to recognize different types; ORNITHOLOGIST

bi·ret·ta /bə̇ˈretə/ *n* a square cap worn esp. by ROMAN CATHOLIC priests

bi·ro /ˈbaɪərəʊ/ *n* **biros** [C; *in*+U] *tdmk* BALLPOINT: *written in biro*

birth /bɜːθ‖bɜrθ/ *n* **1** [C;U] the act or time of being born, of coming into the world esp. out of the body of a female parent: *the birth of a child| birth, marriage, and death|Last year there were more births than deaths.|She weighed 8 pounds at birth* **2** [U;(C)] the act or fact of producing forth young (often in the phr. **give birth to**): *She gave birth to a fine healthy baby.|Birth need not be unpleasant for the mother* **3** [U] family origin: *of noble birth| French by birth* **4** [C] beginning; start; origin: *the birth of a new political party*

birth con·trol /ˈ· ·ˌ·/ *n* [U] various methods of limiting the number of children born, esp. by preventing them from coming into being —see also CONTRACEPTIVE

birth·day /ˈbɜːθdeɪ‖ˈbɜr-/ *n* **1** the date on which someone was born: *When is your birthday?* **2** the day when this date falls: *Happy birthday to you!| Let me wish you a happy birthday!*

birth·mark /ˈbɜːθmɑːk‖ˈbɜrθmɑrk/ *n* an unusual mark on the body at birth

birth·place /ˈbɜːθpleɪs‖ˈbɜr-/ *n* the place of birth or origin: *Stratford-upon-Avon was Shakespeare's birthplace.|Cooperstown, New York, is said to be the birthplace of* BASEBALL

birth·rate /ˈbɜːθreɪt‖ˈbɜr-/ *n* the number of births for every 100 or every 1000 people in a given area or group during a given time: *a birthrate of 3 per 100*

birth·right /ˈbɜːθraɪt‖ˈbɜr-/ *n* [C *usu. sing.*; *by*+U] that which belongs to a person because of his/her birth or as a member of a certain nation: *Englishmen, remember your birthright of freedom: it is yours by birthright*

bis·cuit /ˈbɪskə̇t/ *n* **1** [C] *BrE* any of many types of flat thin dry cake, sweetened or unsweetened, usu. sold in tins or packets **2** [C] *AmE* SCONE **3** [U] a light greyish yellowish brown colour, or a greyish yellow **4** [U] cups, plates, etc., made of baked clay, after their first heating in the fire but before the GLAZE is put on **5 take the biscuit** *BrE sl* to be the best/worst thing one has ever seen or heard of

bi·sect /baɪˈsekt‖ˈbaɪsekt/ *v* [T1] *tech* to divide into 2 usu. equal parts —**~ion** /baɪˈsekʃən‖ˈbaɪsek-/ *n* [U]

bi·sex·u·al[1] /baɪˈsekʃʊəl/ *adj* [Wa5] **1** possessing qualities of both sexes **2** sexually attracted to people of both sexes: *bisexual love* **3** of or related to both sexes —**~ity** /baɪˌsekʃʊˈælə̇ti/ *n* [U] —**~ly** *adv* [Wa5]

bisexual[2] *n* [C] a person who is sexually attracted to people of both sexes

bish·op /ˈbɪʃəp/ *n* **1** [C;A;N] (*often cap.*) (in some branches of the Christian church) a priest in charge of the churches and priests in a large area **2** [C] (in CHESS) a piece that can be moved any number of squares from one corner towards the opposite corner —see CHESS (USAGE)

bish·op·ric /ˈbɪʃəprɪk/ *n* DIOCESE

bis·muth /ˈbɪzməθ/ *n* [U] a grey-white metal ELEMENT (6), easily broken, used in medicine

bi·son /ˈbaɪsən/ *n* [Wn2;C] any of several large wild cowlike animals formerly very common in Europe and North America, with a very large head and shoulders covered with lots of hair —see picture at RUMINANT

bisque /bɪsk/ *n* [U] thick cream soup

bis·tro /ˈbiːstrəʊ/ *n* **-tros** (esp. in France) a small or simple BAR[1] (10), restaurant, or NIGHTCLUB

bit[1] /bɪt/ *n* **1** a metal bar, part of a BRIDLE, that is put in the mouth of a horse and used for controlling its movements —see picture at HORSE **2** a part of a tool for cutting or making holes —see also BRACE AND BIT **3 take the bit between its/one's teeth a** (of a horse) to run away out of control **b** (of a person) to begin with perhaps too much determination

bit[2] *n* **1** [C (*of*)] a small piece or quantity: *every bit of the food|He read all the interesting bits in the newspaper.|"did a bit of Christmas shopping"* (SEU S.) **2** [S] a short time: *"The marks I'm afraid will just be there for a bit"* (SEU S.) *". . . and then we walked a bit"* (SEU S.) **3** [C9] *BrE infml* a small coin, esp. one worth 3 or 6 old pence: *a sixpenny bit* **4** [C] *AmE sl* 12½ cents (esp. in the phr. **2 bits** (=25 cents or a quarter)): *I wouldn't give you 2 bits for that old book!* **5** [S+*of*] *not fml* some (in the phrs. **a bit of luck/advice/news**) **6 a bit** (**of**) *infml* **a** to some degree; rather: *a bit tired|That's a bit (too) much to pay.|Your article is a bit long for our paper.|I'm afraid your friend is a bit of a thief.*|(*BrE*) *That's a bit of all right* (=very good) **b** [*nonassertive*] to any degree; at all: *"He's not a bit like that really"* (SEU W.) —see USAGE **7 a** (**nice**) **bit of goods/stuff/fluff** *BrE sl* a (pretty) girl **8 bits and pieces** *infml* small things of various kinds: *Let me get my bits and pieces together* **9 bit by bit** also **a bit at a time**— *infml* by degrees; little by little; a little at a time; gradually **10 every bit as** *infml* just as; quite as: *He's every bit as clever as you are* **11 not a bit** (**of it**) *infml* not at all; not in the least: *It didn't hurt a bit when my tooth was pulled out* **12 to bits** into small pieces: *The bridge was blown to bits by the explosion.*|(fig.) *My nerves have gone (all) to bits lately*

USAGE Although one can use **a bit** before adjectives: *I'm a (little)* **bit** *tired,* it cannot be used before nouns. Do not say **a* **bit** *money* but *a* **bit** *of money.*

bit[3] *n* the standard measure of COMPUTER information

bitch[1] /bɪtʃ/ *n* **1** [C] a female dog **2** [C; *you*+N] *derog* a woman —see also SON OF A BITCH

bitch[2] *v* [I∅ (*about*)] *sl* to complain: *Don't bitch all day long about the heat: do some work!*

bitch·y /ˈbɪtʃi/ *adj* [Wa1] having or showing a tendency to make nasty jokes about other people and find fault with everything —**bitchily** *adv* —**bitchiness** *n* [U]

bite[1] /baɪt/ *v* **bit** /bɪt/, **bitten** /ˈbɪtn/ **1** [T1;I∅] to cut, crush, or seize (something) with the teeth or to attack (someone or something) with the teeth: *My monkey doesn't often bite.|The boy bit into the piece of cake.|The hungry dog bit on a bone/at the meat.|The fierce dog bit the postman on the leg* **2** [X9; (T1)] to make in this way: *The dog has bitten a hole in my trousers* **3** [X9] to put into the stated condition in this way: *The dog has bitten off a piece of meat.|The dog bit away a large piece of the meat.|He's bitten his fingernails to pieces.|The dog bit the criminal to death* **4** [T1;I∅] (of insects and snakes) to prick the skin (of) and draw blood: *The mosquitoes are really biting this evening!|A snake will not bite you if you leave it alone* **5** [I∅] (of fish) to accept food on a fisherman's hook: *I've sat here for hours but the fish just aren't biting today.*|(fig.) *I hoped she would be interested in my plan, but she didn't bite* **6** [I∅] to take hold of something firmly: *The ice on the road was so hard that the car wheels would not bite* **7** [I∅] to have or show an effect, unpleasant to some: *The government's new higher taxes are really beginning to bite* **8 be bitten with** *infml* to have (a desire for something or a strong interest in something): *Ever since he was 16 years old, he has been bitten with a love of motorcycles* **9 bite one's lips** to try to hide one's anger or displeasure **10 bite someone's head off** *infml* to speak to or answer someone rudely and angrily **11 bite the dust** *sl* **a** to be killed (esp. in a fight) **b** to be completely defeated **12 bite the hand that feeds one** to harm someone who has been good to one

bite[2] *n* **1** [C] an act of biting: *The cat gave its owner a playful bite.|He took a bite at the apple* **2** [C] a piece bitten off: *A large bite had been taken out of the apple* **3** [S] *infml* something to eat: *He's hungry because he hasn't had a bite (to eat) all day* **4** [C; (U)] a wound made by biting, esp. by animals, insects or snakes: *Your face is covered with insect bites!|He was taken to the hospital to be treated for snake bite* **5** [C] an act of taking food from a fisherman's hook (by a fish): *Sometimes when I go fishing I sit for hours without (having/getting) a bite* **6** [U] the action of holding or cutting into or the ability to do this: *You need a tool with a good deal of bite to it for making holes in hardwood* **7** [U;S] sharpness; bitterness: *There's a bite in this cold wind.|This cheese has no taste: I like cheese with more bite in it.|His words had a cruel bite to them which we all felt keenly*

bite back *v adv* [T1] *infml* to control; prevent from being expressed: *Peter was about to tell the secret, but he bit his words back*

bite on *v prep* [T1] *infml* to consider; work at: *Jim likes to have some difficult question to bite on*

bit·ing /ˈbaɪtɪŋ/ *adj* painful; cruel: *a cold and biting wind|He had some biting things to say about my weak efforts to draw* —**~ly** *adv*: *a bitingly cold wind*

bit part /ˈ· ·/ *n* a small, unimportant part for an actor in a play

bit·ter[1] /ˈbɪtəʳ/ *adj* [Wa1] **1** having a peculiar sharp, biting taste, like beer or black coffee without sugar —opposite **sweet** **2** (of cold, wind, etc.) very sharp, keen, cutting, biting, etc.: *a bitter winter wind* **3** causing pain or grief: *It was a bitter disappointment to him when he failed his examination* **4** filled with, showing, or caused by hate, anger, unfulfilled expectation, sorrow, or other unpleasant feelings: *bitter enemies|bitter tears* **5 to the bitter end** *infml* to the end in spite of all unpleasant difficulties; until no more effort is possible: *to struggle to the bitter end* —**~ly** *adv* —**~ness** *n* [U]

bitter[2] *adv* to a bitter degree; bitterly

bitter[3] *n* [U] *BrE* bitter beer; *A half of bitter, please*

bit·tern /ˈbɪtən‖-ərn/ *n* [Wn1;C] any of several kinds of brown long-legged waterbird, found esp. in Europe, which make a deep hollow sound

bit·ters /ˈbɪtəz‖-ərz/ *n* [U;P] a usu. alcoholic mixture of bitter-tasting plant products used esp. in mixing drinks

bit·ter·sweet /ˌbɪtər-ˈswiːt◂/ *adj* **1** [B] pleasant, but mixed with sadness: *bittersweet memories of my childhood* **2** [A;(B)] *AmE* of, like, or related to a type of chocolate made with very little sugar

bit·ty /ˈbɪti/ *adj* [Wa1] **1** *often derog* consisting of or containing little bits: *a bitty collection of short stories* **2** *AmE dial* very little: *a little bitty baby* —**-tiness** *n* [U]

bi·tu·men /ˈbɪtʃʊmə̇n‖bə̇ˈtuː-/ *n* [U] any of various sticky substances (such as ASPHALT or TAR), esp. as used in road-making

bi·tu·mi·nous /bə̇ˈtjuːmə̇nəs‖bə̇ˈtuː-/ *adj* of, like, or related to BITUMEN

bituminous coal /·ˌ··· ˈ·/ also (*not fml*) **soft coal**— *n* [U] a type of coal that gives off a lot of smoke when burning —opposite **anthracite**

bi·valve /ˈbaɪvælv/ *n tech* any of many types of shellfish with 2 shells joined together, such as an OYSTER

biv·ou·ac[1] /ˈbɪvʊ-æk/ *n* a soldiers' camp without tents

bivouac[2] *v* **-ck-** [IØ] (esp. of soldiers) to spend the night in the open without tents: *They have/are bivouacked behind those trees*

bi·week·ly[1] /baɪˈwiːkli/ *adv, adj* [Wa5] **1** appearing or happening every 2 weeks: *a biweekly magazine* **2** *nonstandard* appearing or happening twice a week; SEMIWEEKLY —see BI- (USAGE)

biweekly[2] *n* a newspaper, magazine, etc., appearing BIWEEKLY[1]

bi·zarre /bə̇ˈzɑːʳ/ *adj* (esp. of appearance or happenings) strange; peculiar; odd —**~ly** *adv*

blab /blæb/ *v* **-bb-** [IØ] *sl* to tell a secret: *Here come the police! Someone must have blabbed!*

blab·ber /ˈblæbəʳ/ *v* [IØ] *derog* to talk foolishly or too much

blab·ber·mouth /ˈblæbəmaʊθ‖-ər-/ *n* [C; (*you*) N] *derog sl* a person who tells secrets by talking too much

black[1] /blæk/ *adj* **1** [Wa1;B] of the colour of night; without light; having the colour black —opposite **white** **2** [Wa5;B] (of coffee) without milk or cream: *I'll have my coffee black, please* **3** [Wa5;A] (*in comb.*): *The black bear is a type of bear* **4** [Wa5; B] *no longer derog* (of a person) of a black-skinned race: *a black scientist* **5** [Wa1;B] very dirty: *Your hands are black! Go and wash them* **6** [Wa1;B] (of feelings, behaviour, news, etc.) very bad: *The bad news we've been getting means that things look very black for us* **7** [Wa1;B] very angry: *He gave me a black look* **8** [Wa1;A;(B)] *lit* evil: *black-hearted* **9** [Wa1;A] (of humour) funny about unpleasant or dangerous people or states of affairs (in the phrs. **black humour**, **black comedy**) **10 not be as black as one is painted** to be a better person than one is said to be **11 go black** (of a scene) to disappear from view as someone faints or becomes unconscious: *Suddenly everything went black and that's the last thing I can remember* —**~ness** *n* [U]

black[2] *n* **1** [U] the darkest colour: *After her husband died, she dressed in deep black for the rest of her life* **2** [U] black paint or colouring: *She puts a lot of black round her eyes* **3** [C] *no longer derog* a person of a black-skinned race **4 in the black** having money in a bank account: *We are/Our account is (nicely) in the black this month* —opposite **in the red**

black[3] *v* [T1] **1** to make black, as with a blow or by covering with a black substance: *to black shoes|to black someone's eye*—see also BLACK OUT **2** *BrE* (esp. of a trade union) to declare it wrong to work with (goods, a business firm, etc.): *blacked a firm that refused to pay proper wages*

black·a·moor /ˈblækəmʊəʳ/ *n old use or humor* a BLACK[1] (4) person, esp. a man

black and blue /ˌ· · ˈ·◂/ *adj* [Wa5] (having the skin) darkly discoloured (BRUISED) as the result of a blow: *a black-and-blue mark on his skin|After the fight, he was black and blue all over*

black and tan /ˌ· · ˈ·/ *n* **black and tans** **1** a dog; a type of TERRIER **2** (*usu. cap.* B & T) a soldier from Great Britain who fought against the armed movement for Irish independence in 1920–21 in the Royal Irish CONSTABULARY **3** *esp. BrE* a type of alcoholic drink which is a mixture of BITTER[3] and a kind of STOUT[2]

black and white /ˌ· · ˈ·◂/ *n* [U] **1** writing (esp. in the phr. **in black and white**): *I want this agreement in black and white as soon as possible* **2** the showing of pictures in black, white, and grey, without additional colours: *On television, I like colour for some things and black and white for others.|black-and-white television*

black art /ˌ· ˈ·/ *n* [*the*+R;C *usu. pl.*] magic that is used for evil purposes; BLACK MAGIC

black·ball /ˈblækbɔːl/ *v* [T1] to vote against (a person who wants to join a group): *Will you blackball her if she tries to join our club?*

black belt /ˌ· ˈ·/ *n* (a person who holds) a high rank in the practice of certain types of Eastern self-defence, esp. JUDO and KARATE: *She is/has a black belt in* KARATE

black·ber·ry /ˈblækbəri‖-beri/ *n* **1** the berry of various types of BRAMBLE, black or purple when ripe, and eatable though full of small seeds **2** a plant bearing this fruit —see picture at BERRY —**~ing** *n* [U]: *to go blackberrying*

black·bird /ˈblækbɜːd‖-ɜrd/ *n* any of various types of European and American birds of which the male is largely or completely black, including a European singing bird with a yellow beak —see picture at BIRD

black·board /ˈblækbɔːd‖-ord/ *n* a dark smooth surface (usu. black or green) used esp. in schools for writing or drawing on, usu. with chalk

black box /ˌ· ˈ·/ *n* an apparatus for controlling or recording information about a system, which can be put in or taken out as a single whole: *When we took out the black box, we found out why the plane had crashed*

black cap /ˌ· ˈ·/ *n* (in Britain, in former times) a cap worn by a judge when ordering a prisoner's death

Black Coun·try /ˈ· ˌ··/ *n* [*the*+R] an industrial area of about 50 square miles in the west MIDLANDS of England (including parts of Staffordshire, Worcestershire, Warwickshire), considered wealthy but formerly made black by industrial smoke —compare POTTERIES

black·cur·rant /ˌblækˈkʌrənt◂‖-ˈkɜr-/ *n* **1** a type of European garden fruit with small round blue-black berries: *blackcurrant jelly* **2** the low bush that bears this fruit —see picture at BERRY

Black Death /ˌ· ˈ·/ *n* [*the*+R] the illness (probably BUBONIC PLAGUE) that killed large numbers of people in Europe and Asia in the 14th century

black·en /ˈblækən/ *v* **1** [T1;IØ] to (cause to) become black or dark: *The smoke had blackened the white walls of the kitchen* **2** [T1] to speak or write bad things about (esp. someone's character): *Don't blacken my good name by spreading lies*

black eye /ˌ· ˈ·/ *n* [C] the condition in which the skin round someone's eye is made black by a blow: *If he says that again I'll give him a black eye*

black-eyed /ˌ· ˈ·◂/ *adj* [Wa5] having eyes in which the coloured part (IRIS) is nearly black: *a beautiful black-eyed girl*

black flag /ˌ· ˈ·/ *n* [*the*+R;(C)] the flag of a PIRATE, all black —compare JOLLY ROGER

black frost /ˌ· ˈ·/ *n* [U] *esp. BrE* hard slippery FROST without any white covering: *Black frost made the roads dangerous*

black·guard /'blægɑːd, -gəd‖-gərd, -gɑrd/ *n* [C; *you*+N] *derog* a man of bad character, quite without honour
black·head /'blækhed/ *n* a kind of spot on the skin with a black centre
black hole /,· '·/ *n* **1** an area in outer space into which everything near it, including light itself, is pulled **2** a nasty crowded enclosed space with too little room or air
black ice /,· '·/ *n* [U] hard slippery ice that does not appear different from the surface of the road it covers: *Black ice made the roads dangerous*
black·ing /'blækɪŋ/ *n* [U] a substance (such as a paste or polish) that is put on an object to make it black
black·jack /'blækdʒæk/ *n* **1** [U] PONTOON **2** [C] a winebottle made of black leather **3** [C] *AmE* COSH[1]
black-lead /,blæk 'led/ *v* [T1] to put BLACK LEAD on (metal, esp. the metal parts of a fireplace); polish with BLACK LEAD
black lead /,· '·/ *n* [U] PLUMBAGO[2]
black·leg[1] /'blækleg/ *n BrE derog* a person who continues to work when others are on STRIKE[2] (1) for better pay, working conditions, etc.; SCAB[1] (3)
blackleg[2] *v* **-gg-** [IØ] *BrE derog* to act as a BLACKLEG[1]
black·list[1] /'blæk,lɪst/ *n* a list of people, groups, countries, etc. about whom something unfavourable is known, or who have done something wrong, or who are to be punished: *to be on the blacklist for non-payment of debts*
blacklist[2] *v* [T1] to put on a BLACKLIST[1] and to avoid, not give help or work to, not trade with, etc.: *blacklisted for non-payment of debts|for political reasons*
black·ly /'blækli/ *adv* **1** angrily **2** sadly or unfavourably **3** *lit* evilly: *crimes blackly done*
black mag·ic /,· '··/ *n* [U] magic believed to be done with the help of the devil or of evil spirits
black·mail[1] /'blækmeɪl/ *n* [U] the obtaining of money or advancement by threatening to make known unpleasant facts about a person or group
blackmail[2] *v* [T1 (*into*)] to obtain money or advancement from (someone) by BLACKMAIL[1]: *Don't think you can blackmail me* (*into doing that*)*: I'll report you to the police!* —**~er** *n* [C]
Black Ma·ri·a /,blæk mə'raɪə/ *n sl* a vehicle used by the police to carry prisoners
black mar·ket /,· '··◂/ *n* [*usu. sing.*] the unlawful buying and selling of goods, foreign money, etc., when such trade is controlled, esp. during or after a war: *They bought butter on the black market.|black-market butter*
black mar·ket·eer /,· ··'·/ *n* a person who sells things on the BLACK MARKET
Black Mass /,· '·/ *n* a ceremony in which worshippers of the devil use forms like those of Christian worship
Black Mus·lim /,· '··/ *n* a member of a black group that believes in the religion of Islam and wants the establishment of a separate black society
black·out /'blækaʊt/ *n* **1** a period of darkness enforced during wartime as a protection against air attack: *The streets were not lighted at night during the blackout* **2** a period of darkness caused by a failure of the electric power supply: *the famous blackout of New York City in 1977* **3** a sudden turning off of stage lighting to signal the end of (part of) a play **4** a loss of consciousness for a short time: *He had had a blackout after the accident and could not remember what happened* **5** an intentional prevention of the reporting of certain facts: *a blackout of news about the attack*
black out *v adv* **1** [T1] to darken so that no light is seen: *During the war we had to black out all our windows* **2** [T1] to cover (esp. writing) so as to hide completely: *The advertisement for the concert said where it was to take place, but the date had been blacked out* **3** [IØ] to faint: *After the accident he blacked out and couldn't remember what happened*
Black Pan·ther /,· '··/ *n* a member of an organization of black Americans that is in favour of self-help and BLACK POWER
black pep·per /,· '··/ *n* [U] a type of PEPPER[1] (1a) made from crushed PEPPER seeds from which the dark outer covering has not been removed
black pow·er /,· '··/ *n* [R] (*often cap.*) **1** the belief that in any country black people should have a share of political and ECONOMIC power which is in accordance with the number of black people in that country **2** any of several political movements in favour of this belief
black pud·ding /,· '··/ *n* [C;U] *BrE* a kind of SAUSAGE, black or nearly black in colour, made of animal blood and fat, and grain
black sheep /,· '·/ *n* [Wn3;C] a worthless member of a respectable group
Black·shirt /'blækʃɜːt‖-ɜrt/ *n* a member of a political organization having a black shirt as part of its uniform, esp. a member of the former Italian FASCIST party
black·smith /'blæk,smɪθ/ also **smith**— *n* a metalworker who makes and repairs things made of iron, esp. one who makes horseshoes
black spot /'· ·/ *n* a stretch of road where an unusually large number of accidents have happened
black·thorn /'blækθɔːn‖-ɔrn/ *n* [C;U] **1** a type of European plant with sharp prickles and small berries, often planted in rows. It flowers in early spring, when the weather is often still quite cold **2** any of several American HAWTHORNs
black tie /,· '·◂/ *adj* [Wa5] (of parties and other social occasions) having as a condition that all men who come should wear rather formal clothes: *a black-tie dinner-dance* —compare WHITE TIE
black·wa·ter fe·ver /,··· '··/ *n* [U] a very severe form of the disease MALARIA esp. in West Africa
blad·der /'blædəʳ/ *n* **1** a bag of skin inside the body of human beings or animals, in which waste liquid collects before it is passed out —see picture at DIGESTIVE SYSTEM **2** a bag of skin, leather, or rubber which can be filled with air or liquid
blade /bleɪd/ *n* **1** the flat cutting part of a knife, sword, or other cutting tool or weapon such as a RAZOR —see picture at TOOL[1] **2** the flat wide part of an OAR, a PROPELLER, a cricket BAT, etc. **3** a long flat leaf of grass or grasslike plants such as WHEAT **4** *now rare* a gay sharp amusing fellow: *He is quite a gay blade*
blae·ber·ry /'bleɪbəri‖-beri/ *n ScotE* BILBERRY
blah /blɑː/ *n* [U] *sl* (*often repeated*) empty but often high-sounding talk or writing: *the blah-blah-blah of noisy conversation|the Minister's usual blah about everybody working harder*
blame[1] /bleɪm/ *v* [D1+*on*/*for*;T1 (*for*)] **1** to consider (someone) responsible for (something bad): *They blamed the failure on George.|They blamed George* (*for the failure*) **2 A bad workman always blames his tools** People should be willing to admit responsibility for their own mistakes **3 be to blame for** to be guilty (of): *The children were not to blame for the accident. They were in no way to blame*
blame[2] *n* **1** [(*the*) U (*for*)] responsibility for something bad: *The judge laid/put the blame for the accident on the driver of the car.|We were ready to take/bear the blame for what had happened* **2** [U] bad opinion: *You will bring the blame of others upon yourself if you fail in this* —see WRONG[1] (USAGE)

blame·less /ˈbleɪmləs/ *adj* free from blame; guiltless: *a blameless life* —**~ly** *adv* —**~ness** *n* [U]

blame·wor·thy /ˈbleɪmˌwɜːði‖-ɜr-/ *adj fml* deserving blame: *blameworthy behaviour* —**-thiness** *n* [U]

blanch /blɑːntʃ‖blæntʃ/ *v* **1** [T1] to make (a plant or plant product) colourless, as by removing the skin or keeping out of the light: *blanched* ALMOND*s of cake* **2** [I∅,3 (*with, at*)] to become white with fear, cold, etc.: *Her face blanched with fear at the bad news.|She blanched to hear the bad news*

blanc·mange /bləˈmɒnʒ, -ˈmɒndʒ‖-ˈmɑ-/ *n* [C;U] a mixture of CORN FLOUR, sugar, milk, and other sweet materials which sets and is eaten when cold: *She was so afraid that she was shaking like a blancmange*

bland /blænd/ *adj* [Wa1] **1** (of people and behaviour) not giving offence or being unusual in any way; not showing strong feelings **2** (of food) not hurting the stomach and without much taste: *The doctor says that the sick woman must have only bland food.|This soup is too bland for me* —**~ly** *adv* —**~ness** *n* [U]

blan·dish·ments /ˈblændɪʃmənts/ *n* [P] acts of pleasing used to make a person agree, usu. to a wrong act: *She refused to yield to his blandishments*

blank[1] /blæŋk/ *adj* [Wa1] **1** without writing, print, or other marks: *a blank page|Please write your name in the blank space at the top of the page* **2** expressionless; without understanding; without interest: *I tried to explain, but he just gave me a blank look.|Every day seemed blank and meaningless* —**~ly** *adv* —**~ness** *n* [U]

blank[2] *n* **1** an empty space: (fig.) *When I tried to remember his name, my mind was a complete blank* **2** a piece of paper with spaces for putting in information: *When you have completed the blank, send it back to me* **3** BLANK CARTRIDGE: *The gun fired a blank* **4 draw a blank** *infml* to be unsuccessful

blank car·tridge /ˌ· ˈ··/ *n* a CARTRIDGE (1) that contains an explosive but no bullet

blank cheque, *AmE* **check** /ˌ· ˈ·/ *n* **1** a cheque signed and given to someone to write in whatever amount he wishes to receive **2** *infml* complete freedom to do as one wants about something; CARTE BLANCHE: *The minister was given a blank cheque to get the nation moving again*

blan·ket[1] /ˈblæŋkɨt/ *n* **1** [C] a thick esp. woollen covering used esp. on beds to protect from cold —see picture at BEDROOM **2** [C (*of*) *usu. sing.*] a thick covering, as of snow or darkness: *The valley was covered with a blanket of mist* **3** [A] including all cases, classes, or possible happenings; unlimited: *a blanket rule* **4 born on the wrong side of the blanket** *BrE euph now rare* born of unmarried parents

blanket[2] *v* [T1 (*with*) *usu.pass.*] to cover as if with a blanket: *The country was blanketed with snow*

blank verse /ˌ· ˈ·/ *n* [U] unRHYMEd poetry: *Most of Shakespeare's plays are written in blank verse*

blare[1] /bleəʳ/ *v* [I∅ (OUT)] (of a horn or other loud sound-producing instrument) to sound sharply, loudly, and unpleasantly: *The radio is blaring: turn it off!*

blare[2] *n* [(*the*) S] a loud sharp unpleasant noise as of a horn: *the blare of a brass band|the blare of the radio|a blare of horns*

blare out *v adv* [T1] (esp. of a machine) to produce (sounds or words) loudly and unpleasantly: *The radio blared out the news*

blar·ney /ˈblɑːni‖-ɑr-/ *n* [U] **1** *infml* soft pleasant speech telling someone how beautiful, clever, etc., he is; FLATTERY (1): *She refused to listen to his smooth blarney* **2 kiss the Blarney Stone** *infml* to gain the power to persuade by skilful speech: *You must have kissed the Blarney Stone to be able to talk like that!*

bla·sé /ˈblɑːzeɪ‖blɑˈzeɪ/ *adj Fr* (typical of a person who is) tired of all forms of pleasure and not able to obtain further enjoyment: *You're being very blasé about it: aren't you glad you won the prize?*

blas·pheme /blæsˈfiːm/ *v* [I∅ (*against*);T1] to speak without respect of or use bad language about (God or religious matters): *He can hardly speak without blaspheming (against) God* —**~r** *n*

blas·phe·mous /ˈblæsfɨməs/ *adj* **1** (of people) having the habit of speaking against God or things considered holy **2** (of words, pictures, etc.) showing God or holy things as bad or foolish —**~ly** *adv*

blas·phe·my /ˈblæsfɨmi/ *n* **1** [U] disrespectful or bad language about God or holy things: *They charged him with blasphemy (against religion)* **2** [C] an example of this: *Their conversation was full of blasphemies*

blast[1] /blɑːst‖blæst/ *n* **1** [C] an unexpected quick strong movement of wind or air: *the icy blast(s) of the north wind|a blast of wind* **2** [C;U] an explosion or the very powerful rush of air caused by an explosion: *During the bombing, many people were killed or wounded by (the) blast* **3** [C] a very loud usu. unpleasant sound of a brass wind instrument: *He blew several loud blasts on his horn* **4 (at) full blast** (of work, activity, etc.) fully: *He was working (at) full blast in order to complete the order before the holidays*

blast[2] *v* **1** [I∅;X9] to break up (esp. rock) by explosions: *The road is closed because of blasting.|They're trying to blast away the face of this rock* **2** [T1] to strike with explosives: *The planes blasted the port until all the boats were sunk* **3** [T1] *lit* to cause to dry up and die esp. by great heat or cold, or lightning: *Every green thing had turned brown, blasted by the icy breath of winter* **4** [T1] *fml* to kill; destroy: *His future was blasted by his having been in prison* **5** [T1] *euph* DAMN[1] (7): *You can't take my own car away from me, blast it all!*

blast[3] *interj* (used for expressing great annoyance)

blast·ed /ˈblɑːstɨd‖ˈblæstɨd/ *adj* **1** [B] *lit* struck by lightning: *the blasted* OAK **2** [B] *fml* destroyed: *blasted hopes* **3** [Wa5;A] *euph* DAMN[3] (1): *Make that blasted dog keep quiet*

blast fur·nace /ˈ· ˌ··/ *n* a steel container, about 25 metres high, where iron is separated from iron ORE by the action of heat and air blown through at great pressure

blast-off[1] /ˈ· ·/ *n* [R;(C)] (of a space vehicle) TAKEOFF

blast off[2] *v adv* [I∅] (of a space vehicle) TAKEOFF

bla·tant /ˈbleɪtənt/ *adj* rough; shameless; offensively noticeable: *He showed blatant disregard for the law by taking my car without permission.|blatant satisfaction* —**~ly** *adv*

blath·er /ˈblæðəʳ/ *n, v* [U;I∅] BLETHER

blaze[1] /bleɪz/ *n* [C *usu.sing.*] **1** the sudden sharp shooting up of a flame; a very bright fire: *The fire burned slowly at first, but soon burst into a blaze* **2** brightly shining light or bright colour: *The whole building was a blaze of light.|The flowers made a blaze of red.|(fig.) a blaze of glory* **3** a big dangerous fire: *The dry grass was on fire, and we had to try to put out the blaze* **4** a sudden explosion of angry feeling: *In a blaze of anger he shouted at them* —see also ABLAZE, BLAZES

blaze[2] *v* **1** [I∅ (AWAY, UP, *with*)] to (begin to) burn with a bright flame: *A wood fire was blazing (away), but there was no other light in the room.|(fig.) Her eyes were blazing with anger* **2** [I∅] to show very bright colour; shine brightly or warmly: *Lights were blazing in every room*

blaze[3] *v* [T1 *usu.pass.*] to spread (news) about: *The* *news was blazed in great letters across the tops of the daily papers*

blaze⁴ *n* a white mark, esp. one on the front of a horse's head

blaze⁵ *v* **blaze a/the trail a** to make marks along a path (TRAIL) for others to follow **b** to be the first in some direction or activity: *Our company has blazed a trail in new methods of advertising*

blaze a·way *v adv* [I∅ (*at*)] to fire guns rapidly and continuously: *The soldiers were surrounded, but they kept on blazing away at the enemy*

blaz·er /ˈbleɪzəʳ/ *n* a JACKET esp. for men or boys, sometimes with the special sign of a school, club, etc., on it

blaz·es /ˈbleɪzɨ̌z/ *n euph sl* (used for adding force to various expressions) HELL¹ (3): *Go to blazes!|What the blazes do you think you're doing?!*

blaz·ing /ˈbleɪzɪŋ/ *adj* **1** [B] brightly burning: *People were led out of the blazing building* **2** [Wa5; A] *infml* (shamelessly) clear for everyone to see: *His story was just one blazing lie from start to finish.|a blazing quarrel*

bla·zon¹ /ˈbleɪzən/ *n* COAT OF ARMS

blazon² *v* [T1] to paint (ARMS (2)) in colours or for ornamental purposes —see also EMBLAZON

bla·zon·ry /ˈbleɪzənri/ *n* **1** [U] the art of describing COATS OF ARMS **2** [U9;S] a bright show of colour, ARMS (2), etc.

bleach¹ /bliːtʃ/ *v* [T1;(I∅)] to (cause to) become white or whiter: *There were only a few dry bones left, bleached by the sun*

bleach² *n* [U] a substance used in BLEACHing

bleach·ers /ˈbliːtʃəz‖-ərz/ *n* [P] *AmE* a part of the seating arrangement for watching a BASEBALL game, with cheap seats open to the sun: *There's nothing like sitting in the bleachers on a hot summer day, watching my favourite team play!*

bleaching pow·der /ˈ·· ˌ··/ *n* [U] a substance made from CHLORINE and lime, used for whitening cloth

bleak /bliːk/ *adj* [Wa1] **1** (of weather) cold and cheerless: *The weather in early December was bleak and unpleasant* **2** (of places) without shelter from cold winds: *a bleak hillside struck by the full force of the east wind* **3** (of future events) cold; cheerless; uninviting; discouraging: *The future of this firm will be very bleak indeed if we keep losing money* —**~ly** *adv*

blear·y /ˈblɪəri/ *adj* [Wa1] (esp. of eyes) red and unable to see well because of tiredness, tears, etc.: *A bad cold has made him bleary-eyed* —**blearily** *adv* —**bleariness** *n* [U]

bleat¹ /bliːt/ *v* **1** [I∅] to make the sound of a sheep, goat, or CALF¹ (1a) **2** [I∅;T1 (OUT)] *infml* to speak or say (something) in a weak, shaking voice: *You've got enough to eat! What are you bleating about?|He's always bleating (out) some complaint or other*

bleat² *n* [C *usu. sing.*] **1** the sound made by a sheep, goat, or CALF **2** a sound like this: *the bleat of the old man's high shaky voice*

bleed /bliːd/ *v* **bled** /bled/ **1** [I∅] to lose blood: *Your nose is bleeding* **2** [I∅ (*for*)] (of the heart) to feel as if wounded by sorrow: *My heart bled for the poor unhappy children* **3** [T1] to draw blood from (esp. as was done by doctors in former times) **4** [T1 (*for*)] to make (someone) pay too much money: *He bled them for every penny they'd got* **5 bleed someone white** *infml* to take all someone's money

bleed·er /ˈbliːdəʳ/ *n sl* **1** [C] a person who bleeds easily, esp. a HEMOPHILIAC **2** [C; *you*+N] *BrE derog* a man one does not like: *I told that bleeder not to come here again!* **3** [C9; *you*+N9] *BrE* (a) man; fellow: *That lucky bleeder!|You poor old bleeder!* **4 a bleeder of a/an** *BrE derog* a very troublesome: *a (real) bleeder of a snowstorm*

bleed·ing /ˈbliːdɪŋ/ *adj* [Wa5;A] *BrE sl* BLOODY²

bleeding heart /ˌ·· ˈ·/ *n* any of various plants, esp. the WALLFLOWER

bleep¹ /bliːp/ *n* a high, usu. repeated, sound sent out by a machine to attract someone's attention

bleep² *v* **1** [I∅(*for*)] to send out one or more BLEEPs¹: *The machine bleeped.|They're bleeping for you, doctor* **2** [T1] to call by means of one or more BLEEPs¹: *They're bleeping you, doctor*

blem·ish¹ /ˈblemɪʃ/ *v* [T1] to spoil the beauty or perfection of: *Her beautiful face was blemished by the marks of an old wound.*|(fig.) *His character had been blemished by a newspaper article suggesting he'd been dishonest*

blemish² *n* a mark that spoils beauty or perfection: *The only blemish on the baby's skin was a red mark on its neck.*|(fig.) *The court declared him not guilty, and he was set free without the least blemish on his character*

blench /blentʃ/ *v* [I∅] to make a sudden movement in fear; RECOIL¹ (1): *He blenched as the bright light suddenly shone on him where he was hiding*

blend¹ /blend/ *v* **1** [T1;I∅: (TOGETHER, *with*)] to (cause to) mix: *Some kinds of tobacco do not blend well with each other.|Blend the sugar, flour, and eggs (together)* **2** [Wv5;T1] to produce (tea, coffee, WHISKY, etc.) out of a mixture of several varieties: *blended* WHISKY **3** [I∅ (WELL, *with*)] to go well together; HARMONIZE (3): *These houses seem to blend well with the trees and the* COUNTRYSIDE.|*Their voices blend well with each other* **4** [I∅ (*into*)] to become combined into a single whole: *These houses seem to blend into the* COUNTRYSIDE.|*The* COUNTRYSIDE *and the houses seem to blend (into each other)*

blend² *n* a product of BLENDing¹: *We've been selling a great deal of this blend of coffee.|His manner was a blend of friendliness and respect*

blend·er /ˈblendəʳ/ *n* **1** a person or machine that BLENDs¹ **2** *esp. AmE* LIQUIDIZER

blend in *v adv* **1** [I∅ (*with*)] to come together as a BLEND²; HARMONIZE (3): *The colours blend in nicely.|The house blends in with its surroundings* **2** [T1] to bring in as part of a BLEND²; mix in: *When you have mixed the eggs and the water together, blend in a little flour*

bless /bles/ *v* **blessed** *or* **blest** /blest/ [T1] **1** to ask God's favour for: *The priest blessed the ship before it left port* **2** to make holy, esp. for use in connection with religion: *The priest blessed the bread and wine in preparation for the ceremony* **3** to praise or call holy: *Bless the name of the Lord!* **4** *becoming rare* (in expressions of good-humoured surprise): *Bless me! He's won again!|Well, bless my stars!|Well, I'm blest!* —compare DAMN¹

bless·ed /ˈblesɨ̌d/ *adj* **1** [B] holy; favoured by God: *Blessed be the name of the Lord!|Blessed are the peacemakers|The blessed live on in heaven* **2** [A] *apprec* happy; desirable: *The villagers lived their lives in blessed calmness.|a few moments of blessed silence* **3** [Wa5;A] *euph sl* (used to give force to expressions of displeasure): *They've sold the whole blessed lot, and now there isn't a single apple left.|"No one gave us a blessed penny"* (Saturday Review) —compare DAMNed —**~ly** *adv*: *blessedly free from pain* —**~ness** *n* [U]: *to live in* **single blessedness** (=to live unmarried)

Blessed Sac·ra·ment /ˌblesɨ̌d ˈsækrəmənt/ also **Sacrament**— *n* [*the*+R] (used in the CATHOLIC church) (the holy bread eaten at) the Christian ceremony of the EUCHARIST

bless·ing /ˈblesɪŋ/ *n* **1** [C] an act of asking or receiving God's favour, help, or protection: *The blessing of the Lord be upon you all.|Blessings fell* *from heaven* **2** [C] a gift from God; something one is glad of: *When you feel sad, count* (=remember) *your blessings* **3** [U9] *infml* approval; encouragement: *The government has given its blessing to the new plan, and will provide the necessary money* **4 ask a blessing** to say a prayer of thanks to God at a meal **5 a blessing in disguise** something not very pleasant, which however is really a good thing after all: *The storm was a blessing in disguise because it kept us at home when you telephoned*

bless with *v prep* **be blessed with** to be favoured with; be fortunate enough to possess: *I have never been a rich man, but I have always been blessed with good health*

bleth·er /ˈbleðəʳ/ also **blather**— *v* [Wv4;I∅] *esp. Scot and NBrE sl* to talk foolishly and without meaning: *Do stop blethering and talk sensibly* —**blether** *n* [U]

blew /bluː/ *past t. of* BLOW[1,3]

blight[1] /blaɪt/ *n* [U] **1** any of several diseases of plants marked by the drying up and fading of the diseased parts **2** a condition of disorder and ugliness: *the blight of the centre of so many of our big cities* **3 cast/put a blight on/upon** to have a DESTRUCTIVE or saddening effect on/upon: *The failure of his marriage cast a blight on his whole life*

blight[2] *v* [T1] to spoil or attack with BLIGHT[1]: *The fruit trees were badly blighted*

blight·er /ˈblaɪtəʳ/ *n BrE sl becoming rare* **1** [C] a man one does not like: *I told that blighter not to come here again!* **2** [C9; *you*+N9] (a) man; fellow; boy: *You lucky blighter!|Poor little blighter! What is the matter with him?*

bli·mey /ˈblaɪmi/ *interj BrE sl* (used for expressing surprise)

blimp /blɪmp/ *n* an AIRSHIP filled with a light gas

Blimp *n* COLONEL BLIMP —**~ish** *adj*

blind[1] /blaɪnd/ *adj* **1** [Wa1;B; *the*+P] unable to see: *blind from birth|The blind deserve our help.|He is blind in one eye* **2** [Wa5;A] intended for those who cannot see: *a blind school* **3** [Wa1;F (*to*)] of poor judgment or understanding: *He is blind to the probable results of his behaviour* **4** [Wa1;B] careless; thoughtless; uncontrolled: *blind haste/anger* **5** [Wa1;B] without reason or purpose: *the blind forces of nature* **6** [Wa5;B] done wholly by using instruments within an aircraft and without looking outside: *blind flying|flying blind|a blind landing* **7** [Wa5;B] in or into which it is difficult to see: *a blind corner|a blind turning where the road ahead cannot be seen* **8** [Wa5;A] *sl* slightest (esp. in the phr. **not take a blind bit of notice**) **9 turn a blind eye (to)** to take no notice of; pretend not to see (something): *You shouldn't really drink here, but I'm willing to turn a blind eye* (*to it*) **10 (a case of) the blind leading the blind** people with little information advising people with even less —**~ly** *adv* —**~ness** *n* [U]

blind[2] *v* [T1] **1** [Wv4] to make unable to see, either for a time or for always: *He was blinded by the smoke from the burning leaves.|The soldier was blinded in battle.|blinded in one eye|a blinding flash of light* **2** [(*to*)] to make unable to notice or understand: *His desire to do it blinded him to all the difficulties.|blinded by his desire to do it*

USAGE **Blinded** and **deafened** are only used when there is a clear cause: *He was* **blinded** *by dust*/**blinded** *in the war.|The music was so loud I was nearly* **deafened**. Otherwise use the adjectives **blind, deaf**: *He became* **blind/deaf**.|*a* **deaf/blind** *child.*

blind[3] *n* **1** [C *often pl. with sing. meaning*] also (*AmE*) **window shade**— cloth or other material pulled down from a roller to cover a window **2** [C *usu. sing.*] a way of hiding the truth by giving a false idea: *His newspaper job was only a blind for his real business, which was receiving stolen goods* **3** [C] *esp. AmE* HIDE[3]: *We watched the animals from the safety of a blind*

blind al·ley /ˌ· ˈ··/ *n* a little narrow street with no way out at the other end: *to be trapped in a blind alley.*|(fig.) *We tried one idea after another, but they all seemed to be blind alleys*

blind date /ˌ· ˈ·/ *n infml* **1** a social meeting (DATE) between a man and a woman (or a boy and a girl) who have not met before: *I met my wife on a blind date* **2** either of the 2 people who take part in such a meeting: *She was my blind date*

blind drunk /ˌ· ˈ·/ *adj* [Wa1;F] *sl* very drunk

blind·er /ˈblaɪndəʳ/ *n BrE sl* **1** a wild party with a lot of drinking (esp. in the phr. **go/be on a blinder**) **2** something unusually difficult or good, esp. an excellent piece of play in cricket or football: *That catch was a blinder.|He took a blinder of a catch.|You played a blinder today, Bruce* (=played very well)

blind·ers /ˈblaɪndəz‖-ərz/ *n* [P] *AmE* BLINKERS (1, 2)

blind·fold[1] /ˈblaɪndfəʊld/ *v* [T1] to cover (the eyes) of (a person) with or as if with a piece of material: *The prisoner was blindfolded, placed against a wall, and shot.|They blindfolded his eyes*

blindfold[2] *n* something that covers the eyes to prevent seeing, such as a piece of material

blind man's buff /ˌ· · ˈ·/ *n* [U] a game played by children in which one child, whose eyes are covered with a cloth, tries to catch the others

blind spot /ˈ· ·/ *n* **1** the point in the eye where the nerve enters, which is not sensitive to light **2** a part of an area that cannot be seen easily, esp. the part of the road slightly behind and to the side of the driver of a motorcar **3** something that a person is never able to understand: *I have a blind spot where modern art is concerned*

blink[1] /blɪŋk/ *v* **1** [T1;I∅] to shut and open (the eyes) quickly, once or several times: *She blinked* (*her eyes*) *as the bright light shone on her* **2** [I∅] (of distant lights) to seem to be unsteady; seem to go rapidly on and off: *As the ship drew near to port in the darkness, we could see the lights blinking on land* **3** [T1;I∅] *AmE* WINK[1] (3) **4 blink the fact** *BrE infml* to refuse to think about the fact; hide the fact from oneself: *It's no use blinking the fact* (*that we have no money left*)

blink[2] *n* **1** an act of BLINKing[1] **2 on the blink** *infml* (of machinery) not working properly: *The radio has been on the blink all day: I must have it repaired*

blink at *v* [T1,4] *infml* to show surprise at: *He didn't blink at* (*the idea of*) *leaving his home and going far away*

blink a·way *v* [T1] to try to cause to go away by BLINKing[1]: *She blinked away her tears*

blink·ered /ˈblɪŋkəd‖-ərd/ *adj* **1** [Wa5] (of a horse) wearing BLINKERS (1) **2** having or showing an inability to see or understand: *blinkered opinions*

blink·ers /ˈblɪŋkəz‖-ərz/ *n* [P] **1** also (*AmE*) **blinders**— a pair of flat pieces of leather fixed beside a horse's eyes to prevent sight of objects at his sides **2** also (*AmE*) **blinders**— an inability to see or understand: *He has blinkers on when it comes to politics* **3** *AmE* WINKERS

blink·ing /ˈblɪŋkɪŋ/ *adj* [Wa5;A] *BrE euph* BLOODY[2]: *Don't be such a blinking fool!*

blip /blɪp/ *n* **1** a very short sound, as if produced by a machine —compare BLEEP[1] **2** an image produced by a RADAR apparatus

bliss /blɪs/ *n* [U] complete happiness, as if one were in heaven: *What bliss to be able to lie in bed instead of working!* —**~ful** *adj* —**~fully** *adv* —**~fulness** *n* [U]: *the blissfulness of not having to work!*

blis·ter[1] /ˈblɪstəʳ/ *n* **1** a thin watery swelling under the skin, caused by rubbing, burning, etc.: *His heavy shoes raised blisters on his feet* **2** a swelling on the surface of things such as painted wood or a rubber tyre

blister² *v* **1** [T1] to cause one or more BLISTERs¹ to form on: *The heat had blistered the paint on the building* **2** [I∅] to form one or more BLISTERs¹: *He is not used to hard work, and his hands blister easily*

blis·ter·ing /ˈblɪstərɪŋ/ *adj* **1** raising BLISTERs¹, esp. by great heat: *the blistering sun* **2** very angry and intended to hurt: *blistering words|a blistering look|a blistering tongue* —**~ly** *adv*: *blisteringly hot*

blithe /blaɪð‖blaɪð, blaɪθ/ also (*lit*) **blithe·some** /-səm/— *adj* (of behaviour, language, spirits, etc.) happy; gay; free from care: *a blithe spirit* —**~ly** *adv*: *She continued blithely on in spite of all difficulties*

blith·er·ing /ˈblɪðərɪŋ/ *adj* [A] *derog sl* talking nonsense; BLOODY²: *a blithering fool*

blitz¹ /blɪts/ *n* **1** a sudden heavy attack, esp. from the air, or a period of such attacks: *During the blitz everyone used to spend the night in special shelters* **2** *sl* a period of great activity for some special purpose: *an advertising blitz to get people to buy more cigarettes*

blitz² *v* [T1] to make one or more BLITZ¹ attacks on: *The East End of London was badly blitzed in 1940*

bliz·zard /ˈblɪzəd‖-ərd/ *n* a long severe snowstorm

bloat·ed /ˈbləʊtɪ̈d/ *adj* **1** unpleasantly swollen: *the bloated body of a drowned animal* **2** much larger than what is proper: *bloated figures for the cost of the plan*

bloat·er /ˈbləʊtəʳ/ *n* a large fat fish (esp. a HERRING) that has been treated lightly with salt and quickly with smoke

blob /blɒb‖blɑb/ *n* a drop or small round mass: *His modern paintings look like a mass of blobs to me*

bloc /blɒk‖blɑk/ *n Fr* **1** a group of people (esp. politicians), political parties, or nations that act together **2 en bloc** /ˌɒn ˈblɒk‖ˌɑn ˈblɑk/ all together; all at once: *Let's consider all the difficulties en bloc*

block¹ /blɒk‖blɑk/ *n* **1** [C] a solid mass or piece of wood, stone, etc.: *The floor was made of wooden blocks* **2** [C] a quantity of things considered as a single whole: *a block of seats in a theatre|a block of shares in a business* **3** [C] a piece of wood or metal with words or line drawings cut into the surface of it, for printing **4** [C] a large building divided into separate parts (esp. flats or offices): *a block of flats|an office block* —see picture at STREET **5** [C] (the distance along one of the sides of) a building or group of buildings built between 2 streets: *The Radio City Music Hall is about 4 blocks from here* **6** [C] something that gets in the way, that makes it difficult to move forward, or that stops activity: *a memory block|a heart block|a block in the pipes somewhere* **7** [*the*+R] the large piece of wood, with a hollow for the head, on which people's heads were cut off as a punishment in former times **8** [C] *AmE* BRICK (3) **9 knock someone's block off** *sl* to knock someone's head off: *If you don't stop saying that I'm going to knock your block off!*

block² *v* [T1] **1** to prevent (movement, activity, or success): *to block an opponent's move|to block the enemy's advance* **2** to prevent the success of: *Someone is blocking our plan.|The player tried to block his opponent* **3** to prevent, or make difficult, movement through or action by: *to block the door|one's heart* **4** [Wv5] to limit or prevent the use of a certain kind of money for a political or other reason: *blocked* CURRENCY

block·ade¹ /blɒˈkeɪd‖blɑ-/ *n* **1** the shutting up of a place by warships or soldiers to prevent any people or goods from coming or going **2 break a blockade** to force a way through the blockade **3 raise/lift a blockade** to end a blockade: *We raised our blockade of the enemy's port when peace was established* **4 run a blockade** to go through a blockade, taking things out or bringing things in

blockade² *v* [T1] to put under a BLOCKADE¹: *The ships blockaded the enemy harbours*

block·age /ˈblɒkɪdʒ‖ˈblɑ-/ *n* **1** a state of being blocked: *There has been a blockage in supplies of food because no ships have been sailing* **2** something that causes a block: *a blockage in the pipe somewhere*

block and tack·le /ˌ· · ˈ··/ *n* [U;C *usu. sing.*] an arrangement of wheels and ropes for lifting heavy things: *He raised the fallen tree trunk with (a) block and tackle*

block·bust·er /ˈblɒkˌbʌstəʳ‖ˈblɑk-/ *n* **1** a very heavy and powerful (non-atomic) bomb to be dropped from an aircraft **2** *infml* a person or thing that is very effective or violent: *The new James Bond picture is going to be a real blockbuster* **3** *esp. AmE infml* a person who gets white people to sell their houses to him cheaply by telling them that black people are going to move into the area

block·head /ˈblɒkhed‖ˈblɑk-/ *n* [C; *you*+N] *infml* (usu. used by males to or about males) a foolish brainless person: *Why did you destroy it, you blockhead! It was an important letter!*

block·house /ˈblɒkhaʊs‖ˈblɑk-/ *n* **-houses** /ˌhaʊzɪ̈z/ a small strong building used as a shelter (as from enemy fire) or for watching dangerous operations (such as powerful explosions)

block in also **block out**— *v adv* [T1] to make a quick drawing showing the general idea of: *I have blocked in a plan of the house but have given no details*

block let·ters /ˌ· ˈ··/ also **block cap·i·tals** /ˌ· ˈ···/— *n* [P] *BrE* the hand printing of words in which each letter is formed separately and written in its big (CAPITAL) form: *Please write your name in block letters*

bloke /bləʊk/ *n BrE infml* a man; fellow

blond /blɒnd‖blɑnd/ *adj n* [Wa1] **1** [B;C] (*fem.* **blonde**) (a person) with light-coloured hair (usu. yellowish) and skin **2** [B] (of hair) light-coloured (usu. yellowish)

blood¹ /blʌd/ *n* **1** [U] red liquid which flows round the body **2** [U9] family relationship: (*lit.*) *They are not of the same blood.|of noble blood* **3** [U9] strong esp. bad, angry, or unpleasant feeling: *There is bad blood between them, and they are always fighting* **4** [C] *old use* a young man of fashion; rich young man of spirit: *The young bloods drank and sang gaily* **5 of the blood (royal)** related to the ruling king or queen; of the royal family: *a prince of the blood* **6 blood and thunder** full of meaningless action, violence (and noise): *Do all small boys like blood-and-thunder pictures?* **7 Blood is thicker than water** Relatives are really more important than friends **8 fresh/new blood** a new person or new people (in a firm, group, etc.): *What we need here is some fresh blood with new ideas* **9 in cold blood** cruelly and on purpose: *They killed the harmless old man in cold blood!* **10 make someone's blood boil** to make someone greatly and suddenly angry **11 make someone's blood run cold** to make someone greatly and suddenly afraid —compare **in cold** BLOOD **12 run/be in the blood** to be a quality with which many members of the same family are born: *Acting runs in their blood: they have been actors for more than 150 years*

blood² *v* [T1 *often pass.*] **1** to give (someone) a first experience of some activity: *Young Jeremy's just being blooded, so we don't expect him to be very* *good at the game yet* **2** to allow (hunting dogs) to taste the blood of a killed fox **3** to mark with the blood of a killed fox (a person who has gone hunting for the first time)

blood bank /ˈ· ·/ *n* a store of human blood for use in hospital treatment

blood·bath /ˈblʌdbɑːθ‖-bæθ/ *n* the killing at one time of many men, women, and children

blood broth·er /ˌ· ˈ··/ *n* one of 2 or more men who have made a solemn promise to treat each other as brothers during a ceremony in which their blood is mixed together: *How can I hurt him? He's my blood brother!*

blood count /ˈ· ·/ *n* a medical examination of the blood to see if it contains all the right substances in the right amounts

blood·cur·dling /ˈblʌdˌkɜːdlɪŋ‖-ɜr-/ *adj* causing a feeling of fear to run through the whole body: *bloodcurdling cries*

-blood·ed /ˌblʌdɨ̣d/ *comb. form* having or showing blood or a character of the stated type: *warm-blooded animals*

blood feud /ˈ· ·/ *n* an old quarrel between people or families, with murders on both sides

blood group /ˈ· ·/ also **blood type**— *n* any of the 4 classes into which human beings can be separated in accordance with the presence or absence in their blood of certain substances: *What is your blood group?*

blood heat /ˈ· ·/ *n* [U] a temperature about that of the human body

blood·hound /ˈblʌdhaʊnd/ *n* a kind of large hunting dog with a very sharp sense of smell, used for tracking people or animals

blood·less /ˈblʌdləs/ *adj* **1** [Wa5] without blood **2** without killing or violence: *a bloodless victory* **3** lacking in spirit or eager interest in life: *bloodless young people with no sense of fun* **4** lacking in human feeling —**~ly** *adv* —**~ness** *n* [U]

blood·let·ting /ˈblʌdˌletɪŋ/ *adj* [U] **1** the former medical practice of treating sick people by removing some of their blood **2** BLOODSHED

blood lust /ˈ· ·/ *n* [C;U] a strong desire to kill or wound

blood mon·ey /ˈ· ˌ··/ *n* [U] **1** money obtained as a result of murdering or as a reward for murdering someone or for giving murderers information about where the person they want can be found **2** money paid to the family of a person who has been murdered

blood plas·ma /ˈ· ˌ··/ *n* [U] PLASMA

blood poi·son·ing /ˈ· ˌ···/ also (*tech*) **septicaemia**— *n* [U] a dangerous condition in which an infection spreads from a small area of the body through the BLOODSTREAM

blood pres·sure /ˈ· ˌ··/ *n* [U;C] the measurable force with which blood travels through the BLOODSTREAM: *I'm afraid your blood pressure is a little high, young man*

blood red /ˌ· ˈ·◂/ *adj* [Wa5] red like blood

blood re·la·tion /ˈ· ·ˌ··/ *n* a relative by direct family connections rather than by marriage: *John is a blood relation of mine: he is my brother's son.*|*John and Mary are blood relations*

blood·shed /ˈblʌdʃed/ *n* [U] killing, usu. in fighting: *There was a lot of bloodshed when the 2 countries went to war*

blood·shot /ˈblʌdʃɒt‖-ʃɑt/ *adj* (of the eyes) having the white part coloured red: *His eyes were bloodshot after too much drinking*

blood sport /ˈ· ·/ *n* [*usu. pl.*] *derog* the hunting and killing of birds and animals for pleasure: *He is against all blood sports, especially foxhunting*

blood·stain /ˈblʌdsteɪn/ *n* a mark or spot of blood: *There were bloodstains on the floor where the men had been fighting* —**bloodstained** *adj*: (*fig.*) *This castle has a bloodstained history*

blood·stock /ˈblʌdstɒk‖-stɑk/ *n* [U] THOROUGHBRED (=racially pure) horses collectively, esp. when used for racing: *a lot of first-class bloodstock at the races*

blood·stream /ˈblʌdstriːm/ *n* [(*the*) R;(C)] the blood as it flows through the blood vessels of the body: *Blood poisoning is a dangerous infection of the bloodstream*

blood·suck·er /ˈblʌdˌsʌkəʳ/ *n* **1** any insect that bites and then sucks blood from the wound **2** *derog infml* a person who tries to get as much money as possible from other people: *a real bloodsucker of an employer*

blood·thirst·y /ˈblʌdˌθɜːsti‖-ɜr-/ *adj* having or showing eagerness to kill or too much interest in violence —**-ily** *adv* —**-iness** *n* [U]

blood trans·fu·sion /ˈ· ·ˌ··/ *n* [C;U] transfusion (TRANSFUSE)

blood type /ˈ· ·/ *n* BLOOD GROUP

blood ves·sel /ˈ· ˌ··/ *n* any of the tubes of various sizes through which blood flows in the body

blood·y[1] /ˈblʌdi/ *adj* [Wa1] **1** covered with blood: *He escaped from the fight with nothing worse than a bloody nose* **2** connected with wounding and killing: *a bloody battle* —**bloodily** *adv* —**bloodiness** *n* [U]

bloody[2] *adj, adv* [Wa5;A] *esp. BrE sl not polite* **1** (used for giving force to a value judgment): *Don't be a bloody fool!*|*It's bloody wonderful!* **2** (used as an almost meaningless addition to angry speech): *I got my bloody foot bloody caught in the bloody chair, didn't I?* **3 Not bloody likely** (often showing anger) No: *"Will you lend me £10?" "Not bloody likely!"*

bloody mar·y /ˌblʌdi ˈmeəri/ *n* a drink made by mixing VODKA and TOMATO juice

bloody-mind·ed /ˌ·· ˈ··◂/ *adj* [Wa5] *BrE sl, usu. derog* having or showing a desire to oppose the wishes of others, often unreasonably: *She's so bloody-minded that she wouldn't give me the newspaper, even though she didn't want it herself!* —**~ness** *n* [U]

bloom[1] /bluːm/ *n* **1** [C] *apprec* a flower: *What beautiful blooms!* **2** [U] a covering of fine powder on ripe GRAPEs, PLUMs, etc. **3 in (full) bloom** in (full) flower: *The roses are in bloom* —compare **in** BLOSSOM[1] **4 in the bloom of** at the best time of/for: *in the bloom of youth/beauty* **5 take the bloom off (something)** *infml* to take away the best part or freshness of (something): *Many angry quarrels have taken the bloom off their friendship*

bloom[2] *v* [IØ] **1** to produce flowers, yield flowers, come into flower or be in flower: *The roses are blooming* **2** to be or become rich in plant life: *to make the desert bloom* **3** [(*with*)] (esp. of women) to show a healthy colour: *blooming with health and beauty* **4** to develop; BLOSSOM[2] (2): *The friendship between them bloomed when they found out how many interests they shared* —compare BLOSSOM

bloom·er[1] /ˈbluːməʳ/ *n BrE humor sl* a big mistake

bloomer[2] *n* [A] of or like BLOOMERS

bloom·ers /ˈbluːməz‖-ərz/ *n* [P] a woman's garment of short loose trousers gathered at the knee, worn in Europe and America in the latter part of the 19th century —see PAIR[1] (USAGE)

bloom·ing /ˈbluːmɪŋ, ˈblʊmɨ̣n/ *adj, adv* [Wa5;A] *esp. BrE euph sl* BLOODY[2]

blos·som[1] /ˈblɒsəm‖ˈblɑ-/ *n* **1** [C] the flower of a flowering tree or bush: *apple blossoms* **2** [U] the mass of such flowers on a single plant, tree, or bush: *a tree covered in blossom* **3 in blossom a** (esp. of a tree or bush) bearing flowers **b** at a high point or stage of development: *a friendship in full blossom*

blossom[2] *v* **1** [IØ (FORTH, OUT)] (of a seed plant, esp. a tree or bush) to produce or yield flowers; BLOOM[2] (1): *The apple trees are blossoming* **2** [Wv4;IØ (OUT, INTO)] to develop: *Their friendship blossomed when they discovered their shared interests* **3** [Wv4;IØ (OUT, INTO)] (esp. of a girl or woman) to grow and develop: *Jane is blossoming (out) (into a beautiful girl)* **4** [IØ (FORTH, OUT)] to become LIVELY and gay: *He used to be very quiet, but he has really blossomed out since he came to live here* —compare BLOOM

blot[1] /blɒt‖blɑt/ *n* **1** a spot or mark that spoils or makes dirty, esp. as of ink dropped accidentally from a pen: *a blot of ink on the paper* **2** a fault or shameful act, esp. by someone usually of good character: *a blot on one's character|a blot on an otherwise clean driving record* **3 blot on one's/the escutcheon** *lit* something shameful that spoils someone's record **4 blot on the landscape** something ugly (such as a building) that spoils the look of its surroundings

blot[2] *v* **-tt- 1** [T1;IØ] to make one or more BLOTs[1] (on): *She blotted the paper with ink spots.|She blotted her driving record by having an accident.|This pen blots easily* **2** [T1] to dry or remove with or as if with BLOTTING PAPER: *Blot the page before you begin the next one* **3 blot one's copybook** *infml* to spoil one's record: *She was a good driver until she blotted her copybook by having an accident*

blotch /blɒtʃ‖blɑtʃ/ *n* **1** a spot or larger reddened mark on the skin, of no special shape **2** a large spot of ink or colour: *a blotch of ink on your dress|a blotch of red* —**~y** *adj* [Wa1]: *a blotchy skin*

blot out *v adv* [T1] **1** to cover; hide: *The mist blotted out the view* **2** to destroy or remove completely: *Whole families blotted out in a moment!*

blot·ter /ˈblɒtəʳ‖ˈblɑ-/ *n* **1** a large piece of BLOTTING PAPER on which writing paper can be pressed face down to dry the ink **2** a curved piece of wood to which BLOTTING PAPER has been fastened **3** *AmE* a book where records are first written, before the information is stored elsewhere (esp. in the phr. **police blotter**)

blotting pa·per /ˈ·· ˌ··/ *n* [U] special thick soft paper which can take up liquids and which is used to dry wet ink marks on the surface of paper after writing

blot·to /ˈblɒtəʊ‖ˈblɑ-/ *adj* [F] *BrE sl* drunk: *Old John was really blotto at the party last night*

blouse /blaʊz‖blaʊs/ *n* **blouses** /ˈblaʊzɨz/ **1** a usu. loose garment for women, reaching from the neck to about the waist **2** the upper part of a soldier's or AIRMAN'*s* uniform, usu. with outside pockets

blow[1] /bləʊ/ *v* **blew** /bluː/, **blown** /bləʊn/ **1** [(*it*) IØ] (esp. of the wind, air, etc.) to move; be active: *The wind is blowing hard.|It's blowing hard tonight* **2** [IØ (*on*);(T1)] to send out a strong current of air (esp. from the lungs): *He blew and blew, but nothing happened.|to blow on one's food to make it cool|to blow (on) one's fingers to make them warm* **3** [L9; X9;(IØ (*in*);T1)] to (cause to) move (usu. into the stated condition) by the force of a current of air: *The wind has blown my hat off.|My papers are blowing about.|I blew the dust off the book.|The wind blew her hair.|Her hair blew (in the wind)* **4** [D1 (*for*);T1] to make or give shape to by the action of a current of moving air: *to blow glass|He blew me a beautiful glass animal* **5** [T1;IØ] to (cause to) sound by the action of a strong current of moving air: *to blow a horn|The horn blew (loudly)* **6** [IØ] to take short quick breaths, usu. because of effort or strong feeling: *He was (*PUFF*ing and) blowing as he climbed the stairs* **7** [IØ;T1] **a** (of an electrical FUSE[2]) to suddenly stop working because a part has melted **b** to cause (a FUSE[2]) to do this: *If you put on the radio, the television, and the iron, it will blow the fuses* **8** [T1] *sl* to lose (money or a favourable chance) as the result of foolishness: *I blew £10 at cards the other night.|I've blown my chances with her by saying that* **9** [IØ] *sl* to leave suddenly and quickly: *Let's blow before they catch us!* **10** [T1] *euph sl* DAMN[1] (7): *Blow it! I've missed my train.|Well, I'll be blowed! He's won again!|Well, blow me (down)!* **11 blow hot and cold (about)** *infml* to be favourable (to) at one moment and unfavourable (to) at the next moment **12 blow one's nose** to clean the nose by sending a strong breath through it into a handkerchief **13 blow one's own trumpet/horn** *infml* to say good things about oneself, perhaps immodestly, so that others will know them **14 blow one's top/stack** *sl* to become violently angry **15 blow someone a kiss** also **blow a kiss to someone**— (esp. of or to children) to kiss one's hand and then breathe over it towards the person one would like to receive the kiss **16 blow someone's mind** *sl* to fill someone with strong feelings of wonder or confusion —see also MIND-BLOWING **17 blow the whistle on** *sl* to cause to stop esp. by bringing unfavourable to public notice: *It's about time someone blew the whistle on his dishonest practices* **18 blow town** *AmE sl* to leave a town suddenly and quickly **19 It's blowing (up) a storm/gale** *infml* There is or is going to be a storm **20 There she blows!** (supposed to be said on a ship by the first person who sees a WHALE) —see also BLOW BACK, BLOW DOWN, BLOW IN, BLOW INTO, BLOW OFF, BLOW OUT, BLOW OVER, BLOW UP

blow[2] *n* **1** *infml* a strong wind or windy storm **2** an act or example of blowing: *Give your nose a good blow*

blow[3] *v* **blew, blown** [Wv5;IØ] *lit* BLOOM[2] (1): *a full-blown rose*

blow[4] *n* **1** a hard stroke with the open or closed hand, a weapon, etc.: *a blow on the head* **2** a shock or misfortune: *It was a great blow to her when her mother died* **3 at/with one blow** also **at/with a single blow**— with only one stroke or effort: *He knocked them both down with one blow* **4 come to blows** also **exchange blows**— to start fighting **5 get a blow in** *infml* **a** to succeed in hitting **b** to make a point in an argument **6 strike a blow for/against** *lit* to do something important for or against something, esp. in some sort of struggle: *Strike a blow for freedom by fighting this unjust new law* **7 without (striking) a blow** without having to fight

blow back *v adv* [IØ] to blow in the wrong direction: *If the gas blows back you must turn off the supply, as it is dangerous*

blow-by-blow /ˌ· · ˈ·/ *adj* [Wa5;A] with many details; describing all the events in the order in which they happen(ed) (esp. in the phr. **blow-by-blow account**): *a blow-by-blow account of the match/the meeting*

blow down *v adv* [T1;IØ] to (cause to) fall by blowing: *The storm blew several trees down in the park*

blow·er /ˈbləʊəʳ/ *n* **1** a person who blows **2** an apparatus for producing a current of air or gas: *to use a snow blower to clear snow from the roads* **3** *BrE sl* telephone: *Get on the blower to him at once!*

blow·fly /ˈbləʊflaɪ/ *n* any of various flies that lay their eggs esp. on meat or in wounds

blow·gun /ˈbləʊgʌn/ *n* BLOWPIPE

blow·hard /ˈbləʊhɑːd‖-ɑrd/ *n AmE infml* a noisy person with a good, perhaps too good, opinion of himself; BRAGGART

blow·hole /ˈbləʊhəʊl/ *n* **1** a hole in solid metal caused by air or gas during the melted state **2** a hole in the ice to which water animals come to breathe **3** a nosehole (NOSTRIL) in the top of the head of a WHALE

blow in *v adv* [I∅] **1** *sl* to arrive unexpectedly: *Jim has just blown in: we weren't expecting him till Tuesday* **2** *tech* (of an oil well) to start producing

blow in·to *v prep* [T1] *sl* to arrive unexpectedly in (esp. in the phr. **blow into town**)

blow·lamp /ˈbləʊlæmp/ also **blow·torch** /-tɔːtʃ‖-tɔrtʃ/— *n* a lamp (or gas-pipe) from which a mixture of gas and air is blown out under pressure so as to give a small area of very hot flame

blown /bləʊn/ *past p. of* BLOW[1,3]

blow off *v adv* **blow off steam** *infml* to give expression to anger or excitement

blow·out /ˈbləʊaʊt/ *n* **1** *sl* a very gay noisy party with a lot of eating and drinking **2** the bursting of a container (esp. a tyre) by pressure of the contents (esp. air) on a weak spot **3** a hole made in a container by such bursting **4** a case of uncontrolled activity of an oil or gas well

blow out *v adv* **1** [T1;I∅] to (cause to) stop burning: *Jane blew the flame out* **2** [T1;I∅] (esp. of a tyre) to (cause to) burst: *The tyre blew out as I was driving to work, and I had to stop* **3** [T1;I∅] **a** (of electrical machinery) to stop working **b** to cause (electrical machinery) to stop working **4** [I∅ (*in*);T1] to (cause to) be driven out by the force of air or other gas: *The explosion blew the windows out*

blow o·ver *v adv* [I∅] (of bad weather) to stop blowing; cease: *The storm has blown over.*|(fig.) *I hope your troubles will soon blow over*

blow·pipe /ˈbləʊpaɪp/ also **blowgun**— a tube used for blowing small stones or poisoned arrows (DARTS), used by some wild tribes as a weapon

blow-up /ˈ· ·/ *n* **1** an explosion **2** a sudden moment of anger **3** a photographic enlargement: *Look at this blow-up of the child's picture*

blow up *v adv* **1** [T1;I∅] to (cause to) explode or be destroyed by exploding: *blow up the bridge* **2** [I∅;T1] to (cause to) become firm by filling with air: *We've got a rubber boat that blows up.*|*Be sure to blow up the tyres before you set off* **3** [T1] to enlarge (a photograph): *The photographer blew the child's picture up and entered it in a competition.*|(fig.) *This small matter has been blown up in order to cause difficulty between the 2 nations* **4** [I∅] to become suddenly angry: *Her father blew up when she arrived home in the morning* **5** [I∅] (of bad weather) to start blowing; arrive: *There's a storm blowing up.*|(fig.) *Our old argument has blown up again*

blow·y /ˈbləʊi/ *adj* [Wa1] *infml* windy: *a blowy day*

blow·zy, blowsy /ˈblaʊzi/ *adj usu. derog* (of a woman or her appearance) fat, dirty, red-faced, and untidily dressed

blub·ber[1] /ˈblʌbəʳ/ *n* [U] **1** the fat of sea creatures, esp. WHALES, from which oil is obtained **2** crying: *Stop that blubber!*

blubber[2] *v* [I∅] *usu. derog* to weep noisily: *Do stop blubbering! I can't hear what you're saying*

blubber out *v adv* [T1,5,6] to say while weeping

blud·geon[1] /ˈblʌdʒən/ *n* a heavy-headed stick used as a weapon

bludgeon[2] *v* [T1 (*to*);X7] to hit (someone) repeatedly with a BLUDGEON[1]: *The thieves bludgeoned the old man senseless/to death*

bludgeon in·to *v prep* [V4b] to force (someone) to do (something): *He was bludgeoned into paying the money*

blue[1] /bluː/ *adj* [Wa1] **1** [B] having the colour blue: *The sky is deep blue.*|*She wore a light blue dress.*|*He painted the door blue.*|*Your hands are blue with cold* **2** [F] *infml* (of people and conditions) sad and without hope: *I'm feeling rather blue today* **3 scream/shout blue murder** to complain loudly: *When the doctor pushed the needle into her arm she shouted blue murder* **4 till one is blue in the face** unsuccessfully for ever: *You can call that dog till you're blue in the face but he'll never come* —**~ness** *n* [U] —**bluish** *adj*

blue[2] *n* **1** [C;U] (a variety of) the colour of the clear sky or of the deep sea on a fine day: *dressed in blue*|(*A*) *light blue would be a nice colour for the curtains* **2** [C] *AustrE sl* a fight **3 a bolt from the blue** *infml* something unexpected and unpleasant: *The news of the accident came as a bolt from the blue* **4 out of the blue** unexpectedly: *John arrived out of the blue*

blue[3] *v* [T1] to colour blue

blue ba·by /ˈ· ˌ··/ *n* a baby whose skin is blue when it is born because there is something wrong with its heart

blue·bag /ˈbluːbæg/ *n* [C;U] (a small bag of) blue powder which is used to improve the colour when washing white clothes

blue·beard /ˈbluːbɪəd‖-ərd/ *n* (*usu. cap.*) (from the name of a character in a children's story) a husband who marries and kills one wife after another: *King Henry VIII of England was a real Bluebeard*

blue·bell /ˈbluːbel/ *n* any of various blue bell-shaped flowers, as **a** (in Scotland) the HAREBELL **b** (in England) the wild HYACINTH

blue·ber·ry /ˈbluːbəri‖-beri/ *n* (the fruit of) any of several types of small bush in North America —compare BILBERRY

blue·bird /ˈbluːbɜːd‖-ɜrd/ *n* any of several types of small blue singing birds in North America

blue-black /ˌ· ˈ·◂/ *adj* [Wa5] between blue and black; very dark blue

blue blood /ˌ· ˈ·‖ˈ· ·/ *n* [U] the quality of being a nobleman by birth: *A member of a noble family is said to have blue blood in his* VEINS

blue-blood·ed /ˌ· ˈ··◂/ *adj* [Wa5] (of a person) having BLUE BLOOD

blue book /ˈ· ·/ *n* an official report printed by the British Government

blue·bot·tle /ˈbluːˌbɒtl‖-bɑtl/ *n* any of several types of large blue fly; the meat fly or BLOWFLY

blue cheese /ˌ· ˈ·/ *n* [C;U] (any of several types of) cheese marked with blue lines of decay

blue chip /ˌ· ˈ·/ *n adj* [Wa5] (an industrial share) that is costly and of good quality: *buy a lot of blue chips*|*The shares of this company are blue chip*

blue·coat /ˈbluːkəʊt/ *n* someone that wears a blue coat, such as (in the US) a Northern soldier during the Civil War

blue-col·lar /ˌ· ˈ··◂/ *adj* [Wa5;A] *esp. AmE* of or relating to workers who do hard or dirty work with their hands: *blue-collar workers*|*The Miners' Union is a blue-collar union* —compare WHITE-COLLAR

blue film /ˌ· ˈ·/ *n* a cinema film about sex, esp. one that is shown at a private club

blue·fish /ˈbluːˌfɪʃ/ *n* **bluefish** [Wn3;C] any of several types of blue sea fish which are caught for sport and food off the coast of N. America

blue gum /ˈ· ·/ *n* any of several Australian trees of the EUCALYPTUS family

blue·jack·et /ˈbluːˌdʒækɪ̈t/ *n pomp* a sailor in the navy

blue law /ˈ· ·/ *n AmE infml* a law to control sexual morals

blue moon /ˌ· ˈ·/ *n* [S] *infml* a very long time (in such phrs. as **once in a blue moon**): *Where have you been? I haven't seen you in a blue moon*

blue-pen·cil /ˌ· ˈ··/ *v* [T1] *infml* to cross out (anything not to be permitted) from (a piece of writing); CENSOR[2]: *to blue-pencil* (*the dirty words in*) *a play*

blue pe·ter /ˌ· ˈ··/ *n* [*the* +R] (*sometimes cap.*) a blue flag with a white square, flown on a ship just before it leaves port

blue·print /ˈbluːˌprɪnt/ *n* a photographic copy, in

white on blue paper, of a plan for making a machine or building a house: (fig.) *The plans for improving the educational system have only reached the blueprint stage so far*

blue rib·bon /ˌ· ˈ··/ *n* an honour given to the winner of the first prize in a competition

blues /bluːz/ *n* **1** [(*the*) GU;S] a piece or type of slow, sad music from the Southern US: *The blues was/were first performed by the black people of New Orleans.|a well-known blues singer|Play us another blues* **2** [*the*+GU] *infml* the state of being sad: *suffer from the blues|a sudden attack of the blues*

blue·stock·ing /ˈbluːˌstɒkɪŋ‖-ˌstɑ-/ *n derog* a woman who is thought to be too highly educated

bluff¹ /blʌf/ *adj* **1** (of a person or his manner) rough, plain, and cheerful, perhaps without considering the feelings of others: *Charles has a very kind heart in spite of his bluff way of speaking* **2** (of a ship or of cliffs) having a steep broad flat front —**~ly** *adv* —**~ness** *n* [U]

bluff² *n* a high steep bank or cliff: *They sat on a bluff and watched the sea*

bluff³ *v* **1** [I∅] to deceive by pretending to be stronger, cleverer, surer of the truth, etc., than one is: *He says he'll make the letters public, but he's only bluffing because he hasn't really got them* **2** [T1 (*through, out of*)] to find or make (one's way) by doing this: *He could bluff his way through any difficulty* **3 bluff it out** *infml* to escape trouble by continuing a deception: *George, here comes my husband; do you think we can bluff it out?*

bluff⁴ *n* [U] **1** the action of BLUFFing³ (1): *He threatened to dismiss me from my job, but it's all bluff* **2 call someone's bluff** to tell someone who is BLUFFing³ (1) to do what he threatens to do, guessing that he will not be able to: *When he threatened to dismiss me I called his bluff*

bluff in·to *v prep* [D1;V4b] to persuade (someone) into (doing something) by BLUFFing³ (1): *He bluffed me into thinking that his stick was a gun*

blun·der¹ /ˈblʌndəʳ/ *v* **1** [I∅] to make a BLUNDER²: *The officer must have blundered when he told the soldiers to attack in the wrong place* **2** [L9] to move awkwardly or unsteadily, as if blind: *He blundered through the dark forest* —**~er** *n* [C; *you*+N]: *you blunderer! Look what you've done*

blunder² *n* a very stupid or unnecessary mistake: *to make a blunder*

blun·der·buss /ˈblʌndəbʌs‖-ər-/ *n* an old kind of gun with a wide mouth to the barrel, which fires a quantity of small SHOT for a short distance

blunder on also **blunder up·on**— *v prep* [T1] HAPPEN ON

blunt¹ /blʌnt/ *adj* **1** (of a knife, pencil, etc.) not sharp: (fig.) *Too much alcohol makes your senses blunt* **2 a** (of a person) speaking roughly and plainly, without trying to be polite or kind: *a blunt man* **b** (of speech) rough and plain: *He told her the sad truth in a few blunt words* —**~ness** *n* [U]

blunt² *v* [T1] to make BLUNT¹ (1)

blunt·ly /ˈblʌntli/ *adv* roughly and plainly: *To speak bluntly, that student is sure to fail*

blur¹ /blɜːʳ/ *n* [S] something whose shape is not clearly seen: *The houses appeared as a blur in the mist.|*(fig.) *My memory of the accident is only a blur*

blur² *v* **-rr-** [Wv5 (*by, with*);T1] to make difficult to see (through or with) clearly: *Tears blur my eyes.| windows blurred with rain|a very blurred photograph*

blurb /blɜːb‖blɜrb/ *n infml* a short description by the PUBLISHER of the contents of a book, printed on its paper cover or in advertisements

blurt out /blɜːt‖blɜrt/ *v adv* [T1] to say (something which should not be said) suddenly and without thinking: *Peter blurted out the news before he considered its effect*

blush¹ /blʌʃ/ *v* **1** [Wv4;I∅ (*at, for, with*);L7] to become red in the face, from shame or because people are looking at one: *She blushed as red as a rose for/with shame.|He blushed at their praises.|a blushing girl* **2** [I∅ (*for*),3] to be ashamed: *When I see the prices that tourists are charged, I blush.|She blushed to admit that . . .* —**~ingly** *adv*

blush² *n* **1** a case of BLUSHing¹ (1): *His remark brought a blush into the young girl's cheeks* **2 at first blush** *lit* at the first sight: *It seemed a good idea at first blush, but there were several faults in it* **3 put someone to the blush** *old use* to make someone ashamed: *He put me to the blush by his foolish behaviour when we were out together* **4 spare someone's blushes** *infml* to avoid making someone BLUSH¹ (1): *You shouldn't say all these nice things about me; spare my blushes!*

blus·ter¹ /ˈblʌstəʳ/ *v* [I∅] **1** to speak loudly and roughly, with noisy threats, often to hide lack of real power **2** (of wind) to blow roughly —**~er** *n*

bluster² *n* [U] **1** noisy threatening talk **2** the noise of rough wind or waves: *the bluster of the storm*

bluster out *v adv* [T1,6a] to express (threats or angry words) in a BLUSTERing¹ (1) way: *bluster out threats/what he would do if he caught us*

blus·ter·y /ˈblʌstəri/ *adj* (of weather) rough windy and violent: *a blustery winter day*

b o /ˌbiː ˈəʊ/ *abbrev. for:* (*often caps*) body odour; an unpleasant smell from a person's body, esp. as caused by SWEAT² (1)

bo·a¹ /ˈbəʊə/ also **boa con·stric·tor** /ˈ·· ·ˌ··/— *n* any of several types of large non-poisonous South American snake, that kills creatures by crushing them —see picture at REPTILE

boa² also **feather boa**— *n* a long snake-shaped garment (STOLE) made of feathers, worn by women about the neck esp. in former times

boar /bɔː/ *n* **1** a male pig on a farm that is kept for breeding (= is not CASTRATEd) —compare HOG¹ (1,2), SOW¹ **2** WILD BOAR

board¹ /bɔːd‖bord/ *n* **1** [C] a long thin flat piece of cut wood; PLANK¹ (1) **2** [C] (*often in comb.*) a flat surface with patterns, used for playing a (stated) game on: *I want to play* CHESS *but I can't find the board.|I'm looking for the* CHESS*board* **3** [C] (*often in comb.*) a flat piece of hard material used for putting a (stated) food on: *Put the bread on the (bread)board before cutting it* **4** [C] also **notice-board**— a flat piece of hard material fastened to the wall in a public place to pin notices on **5** [C] BLACKBOARD **6** [U] (the cost of) meals: *I pay £10 a week for board and lodging* **7** [GC (*often cap.*)] a committee or association, as of company directors or government officials, set up for a special responsibility: *He has joined/been elected to the board of a new company.|Mary is a workers' representative on the Board* **8 above board** (usu. of an action in business) completely open and honest: *There's nothing secret about what we're doing, it's all perfectly above board* **9 across the board** including all groups or members, as in an industry: *a wage increase of £10 a week across the board* **10 go by the board** (of plans, arrangements, etc.) to come to no result; fail completely **11 on board a** in (a ship or public vehicle): *go/get on board the train/the aircraft/the ship|He enjoys life on board the "Queen Anne"* **b** on a ship: *As soon as I'm on board I always feel sick* —compare ABOARD **12 sweep the board** to win nearly everything: *Our party swept the board in the election* (=won nearly all the seats in parliament)

board² *v* **1** [T1 (OVER, UP)] to cover with BOARDs¹ (1): *a boarded floor|Board the windows up* **2** [T1] **a** to go on BOARD¹ (11) (a ship or public vehicle): *We'd better board the train now* **b** (in old naval

fighting) to jump onto (an enemy ship) **3** [T1; L9,esp. *at, with*] to get or supply meals and usu. lodging for payment: *She arranged to board some students from the university.|I'm boarding with a friend/at a friend's house*

-board *comb form* **1** [*n,adj→n*[U]] material (of the stated type) formed as a thin flat firm sheet: *a box made of* CARDBOARD|*a* HARDBOARD *floor* **2** [*n,v→n*[C]] a BOARD¹ (1) used for the stated purpose: FLOORBOARD*s* **3** [*adv→adj;prep→adv*] ship's side: *He fell* OVERBOARD.|*An* OUTBOARD MOTOR *is outside the boat that it drives*

board·er /ˈbɔːdəʳ‖ˈbor-/ *n* **1** a person who pays to live and receive meals at another person's house; lodger: *Mrs Brown takes in boarders for a living* **2** a schoolchild who lives at the school **3** (in old naval fighting) a man who jumps onto an enemy ship

board·ing /ˈbɔːdɪŋ‖ˈbor-/ *n* [U] BOARD*s*¹ (1) laid side by side: *The windows were covered with boarding*

boarding card /ˈ·· ·/ *n* an official card to be given up when one enters an aircraft

board·ing·house /ˈbɔːdɪŋhaʊs‖ˈbor-/ *n* **-houses** /ˌhaʊzɪ̇z/ **1** a private lodging house (not a hotel) that supplies meals **2** a house for children to live in at a BOARDING SCHOOL

boarding school /ˈ·· ·/ *n* [C;U] a school at which children live instead of going there daily from home: *a small country boarding school*

board out *v adv* [IØ;T1] to (cause to) get food (and usu. live) regularly away from home: *We'll have to board the cat out while we're on holiday*

board·room /ˈbɔːdruːm, -rʊm‖ˈbord-/ *n* a room in which the directors of a company hold meetings

boards /bɔːdz‖bordz/ *n* **1** [P] the covers of a book: *a book in cloth boards* **2** [*the*+P] *old use and pomp* the theatre; the stage: *He has been on the boards* (= been an actor) *all his life*

board·walk /ˈbɔːdwɔːk‖ˈbord-/ *n AmE* a footpath, often made of boards, usu. beside the sea

boast¹ /bəʊst/ *n* [C,C5] **1** *usu. derog* an expression of self-praise: *His boast that he was the strongest man in the village turned out not to be true* **2** *not derog* a cause for being proud: *It is one of their proudest boasts that nobody is sent to prison without trial*

boast² *v* **1** [IØ (*about, of*)] *usu. derog* to talk (too) proudly: *He boasted of/about the big fish he had caught.|Don't believe him; he's just boasting* **2** [T5] *usu. derog* to say proudly **3** [T1] *not derog* (usu. not of people) to be lucky enough to own: *This village boasts 3 shops*

boast·er /ˈbəʊstəʳ/ *n derog* someone who BOASTs² (1)

boast·ful /ˈbəʊstfəl/ *adj derog* (of a person or his words) full of self-praise —**~ly** *adv* —**~ness** *n* [U]

boat¹ /bəʊt/ *n* **1** [C; *by*+U] (*often in comb.*) a small open vessel for travelling across water: *a small fishing/sailing/rowing boat|cross the river by boat/in a boat* **2** [C; *by*+U] *infml* any ship: *Are you going to America by boat or by air?* **3** a boat-shaped dish for serving liquid food at meals: *a* GRAVY *boat* **4 in the same boat** in the same unpleasant conditions; facing the same dangers: *If you lose your job I'll lose mine, so we're both in the same boat* **5 push the boat out** *infml BrE* to make a special effort to enjoy oneself and have a good time, esp. by spending more money than usual: *They really pushed the boat out for their daughter's wedding, and invited 100 people* **6 rock the boat** *infml* to make matters worse for a group, at a difficult time, by expressing differences of opinion: *The leader of the party asked Tony not to rock the boat until after the election* **7 take to the boats** (of the people on a ship) to escape in the ship's boats because the ship is sinking

USAGE Boats are usually smaller than ships, though the word may be used informally of a large passenger vessel. Large naval vessels are always called ships.—see TRAIN¹, VESSEL (USAGE)

boat² *v* [IØ] to use a small boat for pleasure (often in the phr. **go boating**): *Let's go boating on the lake*

boat·er /ˈbəʊtəʳ/ *n* a stiff hat made of dried corn stems (STRAW)

boat hook /ˈ· ·/ *n* a long pole with an iron hook on the end, to pull or push a small boat

boat·house /ˈbəʊthaʊs/ *n* **-houses** /ˌhaʊzɪ̇z/ a small building by the water in which boats are kept

boat·man /ˈbəʊtmən/ *n* **-men** /mən/ [C;N] a man who has small boats for hire, or who rows or sails small boats for pay

boat race /ˈ· ·/ *n* a race between rowing boats

boat·swain, bosun /ˈbəʊsən/ *n* [C;N] (the rank of) a chief seaman on a ship, who calls the men to work and looks after the boats, ropes, etc.

boat train /ˈ· ·/ *n* a train that takes people to or from ships in port

bob¹ /bɒb‖bɑb/*v* **-bb-** **1** [T1;IØ (UP or DOWN)] to move (something) quickly and repeatedly up and down, as on water: *The small boat was bobbing on the rough water of the lake* **2** [T1;IØ] (of a woman) to make (a CURTSY (=bending of the knees to show respect)) quickly: *She bobbed a* CURTSY.|*The little girl bobbed politely at me*

bob² *n* a BOBbing¹ movement, esp. a CURTSY

bob³ *n* a BOBbed⁴ haircut: *to wear one's hair in a bob*

bob⁴ *v* **-bb-** [Wv5;T1] to cut (a woman's hair) so as to be hanging loosely to shoulder-length or shorter: *have one's hair bobbed*

bob⁵ *n* **bob** [Wn3;C] *infml* a former British coin, the shilling (=5p): *It'll cost you 4 bob*

Bob *n* **Bob's your uncle!** /ˌ· · ˈ··/ (used for showing satisfaction that a way of avoiding or preventing some difficult state of affairs has been found): *I needed to get to town but I haven't got a car: my friend has a car but he doesn't know the way: and so we agreed to travel together—Bob's your uncle!*

bob·bin /ˈbɒbɨn‖ˈbɑ-/ *n* a small roller on which thread is wound, as in a sewing machine —compare REEL¹

bob·by /ˈbɒbi‖ˈbɑbi/ *n infml BrE* a policeman

bobby pin /ˈ·· ·/ *n AmE* a HAIRGRIP

bob·cat /ˈbɒbkæt‖ˈbɑb-/ *n* a type of small short-tailed usu. brown American wild cat (LYNX)

bob·o·link /ˈbɒbəl-ɪŋk‖ˈbɑ-/ *n* a type of small North American singing bird

bob·sleigh /ˈbɒbsleɪ‖ˈbɑb-/ also **bob·sled** /-sled/— *v n* [C;IØ] (to ride in) a small vehicle that runs on metal blades, is large enough to carry 3 or 4 people, has a movable front part to control direction, and is used for sliding down snowy slopes (TOBOGGANing)

bob·tail /ˈbɒbteɪl‖ˈbɑb-/ *n* a horse or dog with its tail cut short: *Here comes Captain Jones on his black bobtail* —see also RAGTAG

bob·tailed /ˈbɒbteɪld‖ˈbɑb-/ *adj* [Wa5] with a short tail

bob up *v adv* [IØ] to float quickly to the surface: *If you try to sink an apple in water it keeps bobbing up.*|*He lost all his money, but soon bobbed up again*

bock /bɒk‖bɑk/ *n* [C;U] (a glass of) strong dark German beer

bod /bɒd‖bɑd/ *n infml BrE* a person, esp. a man

bode¹ /bəʊd/ *v lit* **1** [D1 *no pass.*;L1] to be a sign of; FORETELL: *These weaknesses in his character boded (him) no good for the future* **2** [IØ+WELL or ILL (*for*)] AUGUR WELL/ILL (for)

bode² *past t. of* BIDE

bod·ice /ˈbɒdɨs‖ˈbɑ-/ *n* the (usu. close-fitting) upper part of a woman's dress or undergarment above the waist

-bod·ied /ˌbɒdid‖ˌbɑ-/ *comb. form* having the stated type of body: *big-bodied* —see also ABLE-BODIED

bod·i·ly¹ /ˈbɒdɨli‖ˈbɑ-/ *adj* [Wa5;A] of the human body: *He likes to be sure of his bodily comforts* —see also PHYSICAL (4)

bodily² *adv* (esp. of movement) in a body or as a whole; completely: *He picked the child up bodily and carried it to bed*

bod·ing /ˈbəʊdɪŋ/ *n* [C;U] *rare* FOREBODING

bod·kin /ˈbɒdkɨn‖ˈbɑd-/ *n* a long thick needle without a point

bod·y /ˈbɒdi‖ˈbɑdi/ *n* **1** [C] the whole of a person or animal as opposed to the mind or soul: *You can imprison my body but not my mind* —see picture at HUMAN² **2** [C] this without the head or limbs: *He had a wound on his leg and 2 more on his body* **3** [C] this when it is dead: *Where did you bury the/his body?* **4** [C (*of*)] a large amount: *a body of information*|*The oceans are large bodies of water* **5** [GC (*sometimes cap.*)] a number of people who do something together in a planned way: *The House of Commons is an elected body.*|*The Governing Body of the College meet/meets every Thursday* **6** [C] *infml* a person, usu. a woman: *Mrs Jones was a dear old body* **7** [C] *tech.* an object; piece of matter: *The sun, moon, and stars are heavenly bodies.*|*The speed at which a falling body travels*|*a foreign body* (=something that ought not to be there) *in one's eye* **8** [U] (of wine) full strong quality: *I like a wine with plenty of body* **9** [C (*of*)] the main part (esp. in the phr. **the body of**): *We sat in the body of the hall and the actors performed on the stage.*|*The important news comes in the body of the letter* **10** [C] the part (of a car) in which one sits, as opposed to the engine, wheels, etc. —see picture at CAR **11 in a body** (of a group of people) all as one; all together: *They marched in a body to the minister's house and demanded to see him* **12 keep body and soul together** to remain alive (by getting money or food): *She hardly eats/earns enough to keep body and soul together* **13 own someone body and soul** to own someone completely: *My husband thinks he owns me body and soul*
USAGE For practical purposes your **body** is you, so it is better to say *I* in an expression like *I am healthy*, rather than **My body is healthy*. One's **figure** is the shape of one's body, esp. in relation to clothes: *She has a good/bad/*LOVELY **figure**. **Body** could be used here only by a painter or a lover.

body blow /ˈ·· ·/ *n* **1** (in BOXING) a blow that strikes one's opponent above the waist and below the breast **2** a serious SETBACK

bod·y·guard /ˈbɒdigɑːd‖ˈbɑdigɑrd/ *n* **1** [C] a man whose duty is to guard an important person: *The Queen's 2 bodyguards were very tall men* **2** [GC] a group of men with this job: *The President's bodyguard is/are waiting in the hall*

bod·y·line bowl·ing /ˌbɒdilaɪn ˈbəʊlɪŋ‖ˌbɑ-/ also (*infml*) **bodyline** /ˈbɒdilaɪn‖ˈbɑ-/— *n* [U] (*in cricket*) the BOWLing of the ball in a dangerous manner towards the body of the man who is to hit it

body pol·i·tic /ˌ·· ˈ···/ *n* [*the*+R] citizens as forming a state under a government

body snatch·er /ˈ·· ˌ··/ *n* (in former times) a person who dug up dead bodies and sold them to doctors for scientific study (DISSECTION)

body stock·ing /ˈ·· ˌ··/ *n* a closely-fitting garment in one piece that covers the body and often the arms and legs

bod·y·work /ˈbɒdiwɜːk‖ˈbɑdiwɜrk/ *n* [U] the main parts of a motor vehicle, esp. the polished outside parts, as opposed to the engine, wheels, etc.: *repaint the bodywork of the bus*

Bo·er /bəʊəʳ, bɔːʳ, bʊəʳ/ *adj* [Wa5;A] of or related to the white people of South Africa who came there from Holland —see also AFRIKAANS

bof·fin /ˈbɒfɨn‖ˈbɑ-/ *n infml BrE* a scientist

bog /bɒg‖bɑg, bɔg/ *n* **1** [C;U] (an area of) soft wet ground into which the feet sink, containing a great deal of decaying vegetable matter: *the bogs of Ireland* **2** [C] *BrE sl* LAVATORY

bog as·pho·del /ˌ· ˈ···/ *n* [U;C] either of 2 types of small BOG (1) plants in Europe and the US, having bright yellow flowers

bog down *v adv* **-gg-** [IØ;T1 *usu.pass.*] to (cause to) sink (as if) into a BOG (1): *The car (got) bogged down in the mud.*|(fig.) *The talks with the men (got) bogged down on the question of working hours*

bo·gey¹, bogy, bogie /ˈbəʊgi/ *n* **1** also **bogey man** /ˈ·· ˌ·/— (used by or to children) an imaginary evil spirit used for threatening children **2** an imaginary fear: *State ownership of industry is a political bogey to many people* **3** (used by or to children) a bit of dirty MUCUS in the nose **4** (in GOLF) an act BOGEYing² —compare BIRDIE¹ (2), EAGLE (2), PAR¹ (3)

bogey² *v* [T1] (in GOLF) to hit the ball into (a

hole), taking one stroke more than is average

bog·gle /ˈbɒgəl‖ˈbɑ-/ *v* [IØ (*at*)] to make difficulties (about something) esp. owing to fear or surprise: *He's always boggled at murder/at killing people.|What an impossible job! The/My mind boggles* (=I can't imagine doing it) —see also MIND-BOGGLING

bog·gy /ˈbɒgi‖ˈbɑgi, ˈbɔgi/ *adj* [Wa1] (of ground) soft and wet —see BOG (1)

bogie, bogey, bogy /ˈbəʊgi/ *n* **1** a set of 4 or 6 wheels set in a frame under a railway engine or carriage, that make it able to go round curves **2** a small light cart (TROLLEY)

bo·gus /ˈbəʊgəs/ *adj derog* pretended; false

bo·he·mi·an /bəʊˈhiːmɪən, bə-/ *adj, n* [B;C] (a person) that does not follow the usual rules of social life, though obeying the law: *Many writers, artists, and musicians are thought to be bohemians/to lead bohemian lives*

boil¹ /bɔɪl/ *n* a painful infected swelling under the skin, which bursts when ripe

boil² *v* **1** [T1;IØ] **a** to cause (a liquid or the vessel containing it) to reach the temperature at which liquid changes into a gas: *Peter boiled the* KETTLE.*|I'm boiling the baby's milk* **b** (of a liquid or the vessel containing it) to reach this temperature: *Is the kettle/the milk boiling yet?*|(fig.) *Robert was boiling with anger* **2** [DI (for);T1] to cook (food) in water at 100°C: *Boil the potatoes for 20 minutes.|Shall I boil you an egg?* **3** [IØ (AWAY)] **a** (of food) to (continue to) cook in water at 100°C: *The potatoes have been boiling* (*away*) *for 20 minutes* **b** (of a liquid or the vessel containing it) to (continue to) be at this temperature: *The pot/the water is boiling* (*away*) *on the fire* **4** [X7] to cause to reach the stated condition by cooking in water: *Please boil my egg hard.|soft-boiled eggs* **5 boil dry a** (of a liquid) to disappear by changing into a gas: *The water all boiled dry* **b** to become dry because the liquid has disappeared in this way: *Don't let the pot/the vegetables boil dry* **6 make someone's blood boil** to make someone very angry: *Injustice makes my blood boil* —see also HARD-BOILED —see COOK² (USAGE)

boil³ *n* **1** [S] an act or period of BOILing² (3): *Give the clothes a good boil and they'll come white* **2** [*the*+R] BOILING POINT: *The pot/The water is just on the boil.|The milk has nearly come to the boil.|Bring the soup to the boil*

boil a·way *v adv* [IØ] to be reduced to nothing (as if) by boiling: *The water had all boiled away and the pan was burned.*|(fig.) *His excitement soon boiled away when the work actually started*

boil down *v adv* [IØ;T1 (*to*)] to (cause to) become less by boiling: *Put a lot of the vegetable in the pan because it boils down.|She boiled the bones down* (*to jelly*).|(fig.) *boil the story down* (*to a few sentences*)

boil down to *v adv prep* [L1] *infml* to be or mean (something), leaving out the unnecessary parts: *The whole matter boils down to a power struggle between the trade union and the directors*

boil·er /ˈbɔɪləʳ/ *n* **1** [C] a container for boiling, as in a steam engine, or to make hot water in a house **2** [C9] a person who boils the stated substance: *a soap boiler*

boiler suit /ˈ·· ·/ *n* a garment made in one piece, worn for dirty work; OVERALLS

boiling hot /ˌ·· ˈ·◂/ also **boiling**— *adj infml* very hot: *boiling hot weather*

boiling point /ˈ·· ·/ *n* **1** [C] the temperature at which a liquid boils: *Water and oil have different boiling points* **2** [R] the point at which high excitement, anger, etc., breaks into action

boil o·ver *v adv* [IØ] **1** (of a liquid) to swell as it boils and flow over the sides of a container: *Turn off the gas, the milk is boiling over* **2** [(*into*)] to get out of control (and develop into): *The argument boiled over into open war*

boil up *v adv* **1** [D1 (*for*);T1] to make hot and cook: *I'll boil you up some nice fish soup* **2** [IØ] (of troubles) to arise and reach a dangerous level: *Trouble was boiling up in the Middle East*

bois·ter·ous /ˈbɔɪstərəs/ *adj* **1** (of a person or his behaviour) noisily cheerful and rough **2** (of weather) wild and rough —**~ly** *adv* —**~ness** *n* [U]

bold /bəʊld/ *adj* **1** [Wa1] (of a person or his behaviour) daring; courageous; adventurous: *a very bold action* **2** [Wa1] *derog* (of a person, esp. a woman, or her behaviour) without shame: *a bold girl* **3** [Wa1] (of the appearance of something) strongly marked; clearly formed: *the bold shape of the cliffs|a drawing done in a few bold lines* **4** [Wa5] (of printing) in BOLDFACE **5 as bold as brass** rude(ly); without respect: *He sat there as bold as brass and refused to leave* **6 be/make (so) bold (as) to** (esp. in social matters) to dare to: *I made* (*so*) *bold* (*as*) *to ask the great man if I could take his photograph* **7 make bold with** —see make FREE¹ with —**~ly** *adv* —**~ness** *n* [U]

bold·face /ˈbəʊldfeɪs/ *n* [U] (in printing) thick black letters: *The words being explained are entered in this dictionary in boldface*

bold·faced /ˌbəʊldˈfeɪst◂/ *adj* **1** (of a person or his behaviour) BOLD (2): *a boldfaced attempt to rob the bank* **2** [Wa5] (of printing) in BOLDFACE: *boldfaced* TYPE

bole /bəʊl/ *n* the main stem (TRUNK) of a tree

bo·le·ro¹ /bəˈleərəʊ/ *n* **-ros** (a piece of music written for) a type of Spanish dance

bol·e·ro² /ˈbɒlərəʊ‖bəˈleərəʊ/ *n* **-ros** a (woman's) short coat (JACKET) open at the front

boll /bəʊl/ *n* the seed case of the cotton plant

bol·lard /ˈbɒləd‖ˈbɑlərd/ *n* a short thick post **a** *BrE* in the middle of a street, where walkers wait **b** on a ship or beside the water, for tying ships' ropes to **c** at the end of streets closed to cars so that they may not enter

bol·locks /ˈbɒləks‖ˈbɑ-/ also **ballocks**— *n, interj BrE taboo sl* **1** [P] TESTICLEs **2** [U] nonsense —compare BALLS

bollocks up *AmE* **bol·lix up** /ˈbɒlɪks‖ˈbɑ-/— *v adv* [T1] *BrE taboo sl* BALLS UP —**bollocks-up** /ˈ·· ·/ *n*

boll wee·vil /ˌ· ˈ··/ *n* a type of small grey insect that attacks the cotton plant

bo·lo·ney, *AmE* also **baloney** /bəˈləʊni/ *n* [U] *sl* silly talk for the purpose of deceiving: *He says he'll help us but that's a lot of boloney; he won't*

Bol·she·vik /ˈbɒlʃɪ̈vɪk‖ˈbəʊl-/ *n, adj* [C;B] **1** (a supporter) of the system of government introduced in the USSR in 1917 **2** (a supporter) of any system like this; (a) MARXIST

Bol·she·vis·m /ˈbɒlʃəvɪzəm‖ˈbəʊl-, ˈbɔl-, ˈbɑl-/ *n* [U] **1** the BOLSHEVIK (1) system **2** BOLSHEVIK (2) ideas

bol·shy /ˈbɒlʃi‖ˈbəʊlʃi, ˈbɔl-, ˈbɑl-/ *adj* [Wa1] *BrE infml derog* (of a person or his behaviour) against the established social order; showing unwillingness to help in a common aim: *I asked her to help me but she's being a bit bolshy about it*

bol·ster /ˈbəʊlstəʳ/ *n* a long round PILLOW (=bag filled with feathers) that goes under the other ones at the head of a bed, stretching right across it

bolster up *v adv* [T1] to give necessary support and encouragement (to a person or his feelings or beliefs): *bolster up someone's pride*

bolt¹ /bəʊlt/ *n* **1** a screw with no point, which fastens onto a NUT¹ (2) to hold things together —see picture at MACHINERY **2** a metal bar that slides across to fasten a door or window —see picture at DOOR **3** a quantity of cloth rolled into a pipe shape, as it comes from the factory **4** (in former times) a short heavy arrow to be fired from a CROSSBOW **5** THUNDERBOLT (1) **6 shoot one's (last) bolt** to make a last effort; be unable to continue: *He's shot his bolt; he'll have to give up now* —see also **a bolt from the** BLUE²

bolt² *v* **1** [IØ] (esp. of a horse) to run away suddenly, as in fear: *My horse bolted and threw me in the mud* **2** [IØ] *infml* (of a person) to hurry away: *The thief bolted when he saw the policeman* **3** [T1 (DOWN)] to swallow hastily: *He bolted (down) his breakfast* **4** [L9;X9] to (cause to) stay in a given state with a BOLT¹ (1): *These 2 metal parts bolt together; this one bolts onto that one.|I bolted the 2 parts together* **5** [IØ;T1] to (cause to) fasten with a BOLT¹ (2): *She bolted the door.|This door bolts on the inside* **6** [X9] to keep in a given state with a BOLT¹ (2): *Let me out! I'm bolted in* **7** [T1] *AmE* to break away from (a political party): *He bolted the Republicans*

bolt³ *adv* straight and stiffly (in the phr. **bolt upright**): *He made the children sit bolt upright*

bolt⁴ *n* [S] **1** an act of running away: *The horse did a bolt* **2 make a bolt for** to try to escape quickly by means of: *He made a bolt for the door* **3 make a bolt for it** to run away

bolt⁵ *v* [T1] *tech* to SIFT (flour) usu. through fine cloth

bolt·hole /ˈbəʊlthəʊl/ *n* a place to which one can BOLT² (2) for safety

bomb¹ /bɒm‖bɑm/ *n* **1** [C] a hollow metal container filled with explosive, or with other chemicals of a stated type or effect: *plant a bomb in the post office|A time bomb explodes some time after it is placed in position* **2** [*the* + R] the atomic bomb, or the means of making and using it, seen from a political point of view: *Has that country got the bomb now?* **3 (go) like a bomb** *BrE infml* (to go) **a** (of a vehicle) very fast: *My new car goes like a bomb* **b** very successfully: *The party went like a bomb* **4 spend/cost a bomb** *infml* to spend/cost a lot of money

bomb² *v* [IØ;T1] to attack with bombs, esp. by dropping them from aircraft

bom·bard /bɒmˈbɑːd‖bɑmˈbɑrd/ *v* [T1 (*with*)] **1** to keep attacking heavily (as if) with gunfire: *The warships bombarded the port.|The speaker was bombarded with questions* **2** (in science) to direct a stream of fast-moving PARTICLE*s* (1b) at (an atom)

bom·bar·dier /ˌbɒmbəˈdɪəʳ‖ˌbɑmbər-/ *n* **1** [C;N] the man on a military aircraft who drops the bombs **2** [C;N;A] (a member of) a low rank in the part of the army using big guns (ARTILLERY)

bom·bard·ment /bɒmˈbɑːdmənt‖bɑmˈbɑrd-/ *n* [C *usu. sing.*;U] (an) attack with big guns: *a noise of heavy bombardment|a bombardment which lasted a week*

bom·bast /ˈbɒmbæst‖ˈbɑm-/ *n* [U] *derog* high-sounding insincere words with little meaning —**~ic** *adj*: *a bombastic person|speech* —**~ically** *adv* [Wa4]

bomb bay /ˈ· ·/ *n* the part underneath a military aircraft where the bombs are carried

bomb dis·pos·al squad /ˈ··ˌ·· ·/ *n* [GC] a group of people trained to deal with unexploded bombs

bomb·er /ˈbɒməʳ‖ˈbɑ-/ *n* **1** an aircraft that carries and drops bombs —compare FIGHTER (2) **2** a person who puts bombs into buildings and other places, in order to kill people, cause damage, etc.

bomb out *v adv* [T1 *usu. pass*] to make homeless by dropping bombs

bomb·proof /ˈbɒmpruːf‖ˈbɑm-/ *adj* giving protection against bombs: *a bombproof shelter*

bomb·shell /ˈbɒmʃel‖ˈbɑm-/ *n* [*usu. sing.*] *infml* a great and often unpleasant surprise: *The news of the defeat was a bombshell*

bomb·sight /ˈbɒmsaɪt‖ˈbɑm-/ *n* an apparatus for aiming bombs, in an aircraft

bomb·site /ˈbɒmsaɪt‖ˈbɑm-/ *n* an open space in a town, where a large bomb has destroyed all the buildings

bomb up *v adv* [IØ;T1] **a** (of a plane) to load with bombs **b** to load (a plane) with bombs

bo·na fi·de /ˌbəʊnə ˈfaɪdi‖ˈbəʊnə faɪd/ *adj, adv Lat law* real(ly); sincere(ly); in good faith: *Bona fide travellers may leave their cars at the station*

bona fi·des /ˌbəʊnə ˈfaɪdiz/ *n* [GU] *Lat law* sincerity; honest intentions: *His bona fides is/are unquestionable*

bo·nan·za /bəˈnænzə, bəʊ-/ *n esp. AmE* **1** a lucky find in digging for gold, silver, or oil **2** something very profitable

bon·bon /ˈbɒnbɒn‖ˈbɑnbɑn/ *n Fr* **1** a sweet made **a** of sugar, in a fancy shape **b** of chocolate with a soft filling **2** CHRISTMAS CRACKER

bond¹ /bɒnd‖bɑnd/ *n* **1** [C] a paper in which a government or an industrial firm promises to pay back with interest money that has been lent (INVESTED): *4½% National Savings bonds* **2** [C] a written agreement or promise with the force of law: *enter into a bond with one's neighbour* **3** [C *often pl.*] a feeling, likeness, etc., that unites 2 or more people or groups: *2 countries united in the bonds of friendship* **4** [S] a state of being stuck together: *This new paste makes a firmer bond* **5 in/out of bond** (of goods brought into a country) in/out of a BONDED WAREHOUSE: *place the silk in bond|take the wine out of bond* **6 one's word is (as good as) one's bond** one's spoken promise can be completely trusted

bond² *v* **1** [Wv5;T1] to put (goods) into a BONDED WAREHOUSE **2** [IØ;T1 (TOGETHER, *to*)] to (cause to) stick together as with paste: *These 2 substances won't bond together*

bond- *comb. form* **1** [*n*→*n*] in BONDAGE: *bond(s) man|bondwoman|bondservant|bondslave* **2** [*n*→*n*] BOND¹ (1): BONDHOLDER

bond·age /ˈbɒndɪdʒ‖ˈbɑn-/ *n* [U (*to*)] *lit* the condition of being a slave, (esp.) from which one cannot escape, or any state which seems like this: *Moses led the Israelites out of their bondage in Egypt*

bond·ed /ˈbɒndɪ̣d‖ˈbɑn-/ *adj* [Wa5] **1** made of 2 or more thicknesses of material stuck together: *bonded wood* **2** (of goods brought into a country) on which tax has not yet been paid —see BONDED WAREHOUSE

bonded ware·house /ˌ·· ˈ··/ *n* an official store for BONDED (2) goods

bond·hold·er /ˈbɒndˌhəʊldəʳ‖ˈbɑnd-/ *n* someone who holds government or industrial BOND*s*¹ (1)

bonds /bɒndz‖bɑndz/ *n* [P] *lit* chains, ropes, etc., used for tying up a prisoner: *escape from one's bonds|His bonds were too tight*

bone¹ /bəʊn/ *n* [C;U] **1** (one of) the hard parts of the body, which protect the organs within and round which are the flesh and skin: *He broke a bone in his leg* —see also SKELETON (1) **2 all skin and bone** *infml* (of a creature) very thin: *The poor horse looked all skin and bone* **3 as dry as a bone** *infml* perfectly dry: *You can put on your socks now, they're as dry as a bone* —see also BONE-DRY **4 big/strong-boned** having big/strong bones **5 a bone of contention** something that causes argument: *That island has been a bone of contention between our 2 countries for years* **6 chilled/frozen to the bone** *infml* feeling cold right through the body: *Let's go home! I'm chilled to the bone* **7 cut to the bone** to reduce (costs, services, etc.) as much as possible: *The bus service has been cut to the bone* **8 feel in**

one's bones to believe strongly though without proof: *I'm going to fail the examination! I can feel it in my bones* **9 have (got) a bone to pick with someone** *infml* to have something to complain about to someone: *I've got a bone to pick with you. Why did you take my bicycle?* **10 make no bones about (doing) something** to feel no doubt or shame about (doing) something: *I made no bones about telling her the truth* **11 not make old bones** not to live to be old: *If he drinks so much he won't make old bones* —**~less** *adj* [Wa5]

bone² *v* [T1] **1** to take the bones out of: *Will you bone this piece of fish for me?* **2** *old sl* to steal

bone chi·na /ˌ· ˈ··/ *n* [U] (cups, plates, etc., made of) fine white clay mixed with crushed animal's bones

boned /bəʊnd/ [Wa5] **1** with the bones taken out: *boned meat* **2** (of clothes) stiffened (as if) with pieces of bone

bone-dry /ˌ· ˈ·/ *adj infml* perfectly dry

bone·head /ˈbəʊnhed/ *n* [C; *you*+N] *sl* a stupid person —**~ed** *adj*

bone-i·dle /ˌ· ˈ··/ also **bone-la·zy**— *adj derog* (of a person or his behaviour) completely lazy

bone meal /ˈ· ·/ *n* [U] substance made from crushed bones, for improving the soil

bon·er /ˈbəʊnəʳ/ *n old & AmE sl* a schoolboy's foolish mistake: *I've just made the most terrible boner*

bone·set·ter /ˈbəʊnˌsetəʳ/ *n* a person, not a doctor, who puts people's broken bones back into place

bone·shak·er /ˈbəʊnˌʃeɪkəʳ/ *n infml, often humor* an uncomfortable shaky old vehicle, esp. a bicycle

bone up on also **mug up**— *v adv prep* [T1] *infml* to study hard, esp. for a special purpose

bon·fire /ˈbɒnfaɪəʳ‖ˈbɑn-/ *n* a large fire built in the open air, for pleasure, as a CELEBRATION, or to burn unwanted things

bon·go /ˈbɒŋgəʊ‖ˈbɑŋ-/ also **bongo drum** /ˈ·· ·/— *n* **-gos** *or* **-goes** either of a pair of small drums played with the hands, used in popular western music

bon·ho·mie /ˈbɒnəmi‖ˌbɑnəˈmiː/ *n* [U] *Fr* cheerfulness; easy friendliness

bo·ni·to /bəˈniːtəʊ/ *n* **-tos** *or* **-to** [Wn2] any of several types of middle-sized Atlantic fish of the TUNA family, that can be eaten

bon·kers /ˈbɒŋkəz‖ˈbɑŋkərz/ *adj* [F] *BrE sl* mad: *Charles is completely bonkers*

bon mot /ˌbɒn ˈməʊ‖ˌbəʊn- (*Fr* bɔ̃ mo)/ *n* **bons mots** /ˌbɒn ˈməʊz‖ˌbəʊn- (*Fr* bɔ̃ mo)/ *Fr* a clever saying; joke

bon·net /ˈbɒnǰt‖ˈbɑ-/ *n* **1** a round head-covering tied under the chin, and often with a piece in front (BRIM) that shades the face, worn by babies and in former times by women **2** a soft flat cap worn by men, esp. soldiers, in Scotland **3** (*AmE* **hood**)— *BrE* a metal lid over the front of a car —see picture at CAR —see also **a BEE in one's bonnet**

bon·ny /ˈbɒni‖ˈbɑni/ *adj* [Wa1] *apprec, esp. Scot E* **1** [B] pretty and healthy: *a bonny baby*|*It's good to see her looking so bonny* **2** [A] satisfactory; skilful in the stated way: *a bonny fighter* —**bonnily** *adv*

bon·sai /ˈbɒnsaɪ, ˈbəʊ-‖bəʊnˈsaɪ, ˈbəʊnsaɪ/ **bonsai** [Wn3;C] a plant in a pot, esp. a tree, that has been prevented from growing large by a special Japanese method

bo·nus /ˈbəʊnəs/ *n* **1** an additional payment beyond what is usual, necessary, or expected, such as a share of the profits paid to those who hold shares in or work for a business or are INSURED with an insurance company: *The workers got a Christmas bonus* **2** *infml* anything pleasant in addition to what is expected: *Her unexpected visit was a pure bonus* **3 cost-of-living bonus** an amount of additional money paid to workers because of rising prices **4 no claims bonus** a reduction made in the charge for insurance on a motor vehicle, because there have been no claims

bon vi·vant /ˌbɒn viːˈvɒnt‖ˌbɑn viːˈvɑnt (*Fr* bɔ̃ vivɑ̃)/ *n Fr* a person who likes good wine and food and cheerful companions

bon·y /ˈbəʊni/ *adj* [Wa1] **1** very thin so that the bones can be seen: *her bony hand* **2** (of food) full of bones: *bony fish*

bon·zer /ˈbɒnzəʳ‖ˈbɑn-/ *adj AustrE apprec* good; nice; fine: *a bonzer new car*

boo¹ /buː/ *interj, n* **boos** **1** a shout of disapproval or strong disagreement **2 can't/couldn't say boo to a goose** *infml* to be very fearful: *He won't defend us; he can't say boo to a goose*

boo² *v* **1** [T1;I∅] to express disapproval (of) or strong disagreement (with), esp. by saying "BOO¹": *The crowd booed (the speaker)* **2** [X9] to send (away) by making this sound: *The crowd booed the speaker off the stage*

boob¹ /buːb/ *n sl* a foolish mistake

boob² *v sl* **1** [I∅] to make a foolish mistake **2** [T1] to fail; do (something) badly: *He boobed his examinations twice*

boobs /buːbz/ *n* [P] *infml* a woman's breasts

boo·by /ˈbuːbi/ *n* **1** also (*AmE sl*) **boob**— *infml* a silly or foolish person **2** any of several kinds of seabird

booby hatch /ˈ·· ·/ *n AmE sl* a hospital for the mad

booby prize /ˈ·· ·/ *n* a prize given (esp. as a joke) for the worst performance in a competition

booby-trap /ˈ·· ·/ *v* [T1] to provide with a BOOBY TRAP: *He booby-trapped the door with a bag of flour*

booby trap *n* **1** a hidden bomb which explodes when some harmless-looking object is touched **2** any harmless trap used for surprising someone

boo·dle /ˈbuːdl/ *n esp. AmE sl* **1** money dishonestly paid or received, esp. for political reasons or favours **2** a lot of money

boo·hoo /ˌbuː ˈhuː/ *v, n, interj* (to make) the sound of loud childish weeping

book¹ /bʊk/ *n* **1** a collection of sheets of paper fastened together as a thing to be read, or to be written in **2** one of the main divisions or parts of a larger written work (as of a long poem or the Bible) **3** the words of a light musical play: *Oscar Hammerstein II wrote the book of "Oklahoma", and Richard Rodgers wrote the music* —compare LIBRETTO **4** any collection of things fastened together, esp. one with its own covers: *a book of stamps/tickets/matches* **5** *esp. BrE infml* a book listing names and telephone numbers: *We have a telephone but we're not in the book yet* **6 a closed book (to)** a subject about which one knows very little: *Politics is a closed book to me, so don't ask me questions about it* **7 bring (someone) to book** to punish or make (someone) pay: *Don't worry, he will be brought to book for his wickedness one day* **8 It suits my book** It suits my plans **9 like a book** in a way that suggests written rather than spoken language: *How do you expect me to fall in love with someone who speaks like a book all the time?* **10 make (a) book on** to offer to receive and pay out money on the results of a competition, esp. a race **11 take a leaf out of someone's book** to behave as someone else has done, or would probably do: *Take a leaf out of my book: start saving for your holidays now* **12 throw the book at (someone)** (esp. of the police or a judge) to make all possible charges against (someone) —see also BOOKS

book² *v* **1** [D1 (*for*);T1;I∅ (UP)] also (*esp. AmE*) **reserve**— *esp. BrE* to arrange in advance to have (something): *to book seats on a plane*|*You'll have to book (up) early if you want to see that show* **2** [T1] *infml* to enter charges against, esp. in the police records: *On the night of June 24 you were booked on a charge of speeding.|He's been booked twice this year for kicking players in the other team*

book·a·ble /ˈbʊkəbəl/ *adj* [Wa5] that can be BOOKed[2] (1) in advance: *bookable seats in a theatre*

book·bind·er·y /ˈbʊkˌbaɪndəri/ *n* **1** [U] the art of binding covers on books **2** [C] a place where this is done —**bookbinder** *n*

book·bind·ing /ˈbʊkˌbaɪndɪŋ/ *n* [U] BOOKBINDERY (1)

book·case /ˈbʊk-keɪs/ *n* a piece of furniture consisting of shelves to hold books —see picture at LIVING ROOM

book club /ˈ· ·/ *n* a club that offers books cheap to its members

book·end /ˈbʊkend/ *n* [*usu. pl.*] one of a pair of supports to hold up a row of books

book in *v adv esp. BrE* **1** [T1;IØ: (*at*)] to (cause to) have a place kept for one at a hotel: *I've booked you in at the Grand Hotel, I hope you approve* **2** [IØ] to report one's arrival, as, at a hotel desk, an AIRPORT, etc.; CHECK IN (1): *We booked in as soon as we arrived*

book·ing /ˈbʊkɪŋ/ also (*esp. AmE*) **reservation**— *n* [C;U] *esp. BrE* **1** a case or the act of BOOKing[2] (1), esp. a seat: *All bookings must be made at least 3 weeks in advance* **2** a case or the act of BOOKing[2] (2)

booking clerk /ˈ·· ·/ *n BrE* a person who sells tickets for journeys, esp. at a railway station

booking of·fice /ˈ·· ˌ··/ *n BrE* an office where tickets are sold, esp. at a railway station

book·ish /ˈbʊkɪʃ/ *adj often derog* having or showing more interest in ideas from books than in practical matters —**~ly** *adv* —**~ness** *n* [U]

book·keep·ing /ˈbʊkˌkiːpɪŋ/ *n* [U] the act of keeping the accounts of money of a business company, a public office, etc. —**bookkeeper** *n*

book learn·ing /ˈ· ˌ··/ *n* [U] *infml and often derog* that which is learnt from books rather than by experience of life

book·let /ˈbʊklət/ *n* a small book, usu. with a paper cover; PAMPHLET

book·mak·er /ˈbʊkˌmeɪkəʳ/ also (*infml*) **book·ie** /ˈbʊki/, **turf accountant**— *n* a person who takes money (BETs (1)) risked on the results of competitions, esp. horse races

book·mark /ˈbʊkmaːk‖-ark/ also **book·mark·er** /ˈbʊkmaːkəʳ‖-ar-/— *n* something put between the pages of a book to find a place in it

book·mo·bile /ˈbʊkməʊˌbiːl/ *n esp. AmE* a vehicle that serves as a travelling library

book·plate /ˈbʊkpleɪt/ *n* a piece of paper (a LABEL) placed in a book to show who owns it

books /bʊks/ *n* [P] **1** written records of money, names, etc.: *How many names are there on your books?* **2 at one's books** studying: *He'll succeed because he's always at his books* **3 in someone's good books** *infml* in favour with someone **4 in someone's bad/black books** *infml* in disfavour with someone **5 on/off the books** in/no longer in the list of members: *They have taken his name off the books of that club* —see also BOOK[1]

book·sell·er /ˈbʊkˌseləʳ/ *n* a person who sells books to the public

book·shop /ˈbʊkʃɒp‖-ʃap/ (*AmE* **book·store**)— *n esp. BrE* a shop where books are sold

book·stall /ˈbʊkstɔːl/ *n* a table or small shop open at the front, where books, magazines, etc., are shown for sale, esp. on railway stations

book through *v adv* [IØ (*to*)] to buy a ticket for the whole of a divided journey: *If you have to change trains in London, you may be able to book through* (*to your last station*)

book to·ken /ˈ· ˌ··/ *n* a small card that can be exchanged for books at a bookshop: *I gave him a £5 book token for his birthday*

book up *v adv* [T1 *usu. pass.*] to keep (a place or time) for people who have made arrangements in advance: *I'm sorry, the hotel is* (*fully*) *booked up.*| (fig.) *The singer is always booked up for a year ahead*

book·work /ˈbʊkwɜːk‖-ɜrk/ *n* [U] the study of books or of rules as opposed to doing practical work: *He's not good at bookwork, but he likes working with his hands*

book·worm /ˈbʊkwɜːm‖-ɜrm/ *n* **1** an insect that eats the binding and paste of a book **2** *often derog* a person who is very fond, perhaps too fond, of reading and study

boom[1] /buːm/ *n* **1** a long pole on a boat, to which a sail is fastened **2** a long pole used on an apparatus for loading and unloading (DERRICK) **3** a long pole on the end of which a camera or MICROPHONE can be moved about **4** a heavy chain fixed across a river to stop things (such as logs) floating down or prevent ships sailing up **5 lower the boom on someone** *infml* to attack someone suddenly and forcefully

boom[2] *v* [IØ] **1** to make a deep hollow sound; RESOUND (1): *The guns boomed* **2** to grow rapidly, esp. in value, in importance, or in the opinion of others: *Business is booming these days: we shall all grow rich!*

boom[3] *n* **1** a BOOMing[2] (1) sound or cry **2** a rapid growth or increase: *How long can the present business boom last?*

boo·mer·ang[1] /ˈbuːməræŋ/ *n* a curved stick which makes a circle and comes back when thrown. It is used by Australian natives (ABORIGINEs) to kill birds, some animals, etc.

boomerang[2] *v* [IØ (*on*)] to come back to the starting point suddenly, unexpectedly, and usu. with bad effects: *His plan to reduce the number of workers boomeranged* (*on him*), *and he lost his own job*

boom out *v adv* [T1;IØ] to (cause to) come out with a deep hollow sound: *He boomed out his answer.|His answer boomed out*

boom town /ˈ· ·/ *n* a town experiencing a sudden growth in business activity, wealth, and population

boon /buːn/ *n* **1** something favourable; a comfort; a help: *The radio is a great boon to the blind* **2** *old use* a favour: *to ask a boon of someone*

boon com·pan·ion /ˌ· ·ˈ··/ *n* [*usu. pl.*] (used esp. of a relationship between men) a good, close, esp. fun-loving friend

boor /bʊəʳ/ *n derog* a rude ungraceful ungentlemanly person, esp. a man —**~ish** *adj* —**~ishly** *adv* —**~ishness** *n* [U]

boost[1] /buːst/ *v* **1** [T1 (UP)] to push up from below: *If you boost me up, I can just reach the window* **2** [T1] *infml* to increase; raise: *to boost prices|plans to boost production by 30% next year* **3** [T1] *infml* to help to advance or improve: *We need a holiday to boost our spirits* **4** [T1] *infml esp. AmE* to favour the interests of, esp. by speech and writing: *He is always boosting his home town* **5** [T1] *tech* to increase (esp. the supply of electricity or water) in force, pressure, or amount

boost[2] *n* **1** a push upwards **2** an increase in amount **3** an act that brings help or encouragement: *That holiday has been a boost to our spirits*

boost·er /ˈbuːstəʳ/ *n* **1** a person who BOOSTs[1] **2** *esp. AmE infml* a person who is very much in favour of something or someone: *a great booster of his home town* **3** *tech* an apparatus that helps to increase force, power, or pressure **4** a substance that increases the effectiveness of a drug or medicine:

This medicine will protect you against the disease, but after 6 months you'll need a booster

booster rock·et /ˈ·· ˌ··/ *n tech* a ROCKET[1] (2) that provides additional power to help to get a MISSILE (1) off the ground

boot[1] /buːt/ *n* **to boot** (often of something unpleasant) besides; in addition: *He is dishonest, and a coward to boot*

boot[2] *n* **1** [C *usu. pl.*] a covering of leather or rubber for the foot, usu. heavier and thicker than a shoe, and with a part for supporting the ankle **2** [C] (*AmE* **trunk**)— *BrE* an enclosed space at the back of a car for bags and boxes —see picture at CAR **3** [C] *infml* a blow given by or as if by a foot wearing a boot: *He jumped out from the bushes, gave me a boot in my stomach, and ran away with my money* **4** [*the*+R] *sl* the act of sending someone away rudely, esp. from a job: *They gave him the boot for coming late.*|*He got the boot* —compare SACK[1] (2) **5 the boot is on the other foot** *infml* the state of affairs has changed to the opposite of what it was **6 die in one's boots/with one's boots on** *infml* to die while still working **7 have one's heart in one's boots** *infml* to be afraid **8 lick someone's boots** *infml derog* to try to gain favour from someone in a higher position or rank by being too polite and too obedient **9 make someone lick one's boots** *infml* to defeat someone completely and make him lose his self-respect **10 put the boot in** *esp BrE sl* to kick someone hard, usu. when he is already on the ground **11 too big for one's boots** *infml* too proud

boot[3] *v infml* **1** [X9] to kick **2** [T1] BOOT OUT

boot·black /ˈbuːtblæk/ also **shoeblack**— *n becoming rare* a person who cleans and polishes shoes, esp. in the street for money

boot·ed /ˈbuːtɨ̞d/ *adj* [Wa5] having boots, esp. of a stated type: *black-booted soldiers*

boot·ee /ˈbuːtiː, buːˈtiː/ *n* [C *usu. pl.*] a boot or sock with a short leg, esp. a baby's woollen boot

booth /buːð‖buːθ/ *n* **1** (at a market) a covered movable shop **2** (at a FAIR[3]) a tent or small building where goods are sold or games are played **3** an enclosed place big enough for one person at a time: *a telephone booth*|*a voting booth*|*a listening booth in a record shop* **4** an enclosed place for one person selling something: *a ticket booth* **5** an enclosed place in a restaurant, esp. one with a table between 2 long seats

boot·lace /ˈbuːtleɪs/ *n* **1** [*usu. pl.*] a LACE[1] (1) for boots **2** *BrE* SHOELACE

boot·leg[1] /ˈbuːtleg/ *adj* [Wa5;A;(B)] (of or about alcoholic drink) unlawful

bootleg[2] *v* **-gg-** [T1;IØ] to make, carry, or sell (alcoholic drink) unlawfully —**-legger** *n*

boot·less /ˈbuːtləs/ *adj* [Wa5] *fml or lit* (of non-material things) useless: *bootless care*

boot out *v adv* [T1] *infml* to send away rudely and sometimes with force, esp. to dismiss from a job: *They booted him out for coming late*

boots /buːts/ *n* **boots** [Wn3;C;N] *BrE becoming rare* a male hotel servant who cleans shoes and carries bags

boot·straps /ˈbuːtstræps/ *n* [P] *infml* one's own efforts, without outside help (in the phr. **by one's own bootstraps**): *He lost all his money and all his friends deserted him, but he pulled himself up by his own bootstraps, and now he owns quite a successful business*

boot·y /ˈbuːti/ *n* [U] goods stolen by thieves or taken by a victorious army

booze[1] /buːz/ *v* [IØ] *sl* to drink alcohol, esp. too much alcohol: *He spends every night boozing with his friends*

booze[2] *n sl* **1** [U] alcoholic drink **2 on the booze** drinking alcohol heavily

booz·er /ˈbuːzəʳ/ *n sl* **1** a person who BOOZEs **2** *BrE* PUB

booze-up /ˈ· ·/ *n BrE sl* a party with a lot of drinking

booz·y /ˈbuːzi/ *adj* [Wa1] showing signs of heavy drinking of alcohol: *a boozy party* —**boozily** *adv* —**booziness** *n* [U]

bop /bɒp‖bɑp/ *n* **1** [C] *esp. AmE sl* a blow that strikes a person **2** [U] also **bebop**— a type of JAZZ music

bop·per /ˈbɒpəʳ‖ˈbɑpər/ *n* TEENYBOPPER

bo·rac·ic /bəˈræsɪk/ *adj* [Wa5] *tech* of or containing BORAX

boracic ac·id /·ˌ·· ˈ··/ *n* [U] *tech* BORIC ACID

bor·age /ˈbɒrɪdʒ‖ˈbɔ-, ˈbɑ-/ *n* [U] a type of blue-flowered European garden plant with hairy leaves which are used for giving a special taste to food and drink

bo·rax /ˈbɔːræks‖ˈbo-/ *n* [U] a white saltlike powder used in glass-making

Bor·deaux /bɔːˈdəʊ‖bɔr-/ *n* [U] white or red wine of the Bordeaux area of southern France —compare CLARET[1]

bor·del·lo /bɔːˈdeləʊ‖ˈbɔr-/ *n* **-os** BROTHEL

bor·der[1] /ˈbɔːdəʳ‖ˈbɔr-/ *n* **1** an edge: *His handkerchief had a white border* —see picture at GARDEN[1] **2** (land near) the dividing line between 2 countries: *soldiers guarding the border*|*within our borders*|*over the border*

border[2] *v* [T1] **1** [(*with*)] to put a border on: *to border a dress with silk* **2** to be a border to: *fields bordered by woods* **3** to have a common border with: *France borders Germany along parts of the Rhine.*|*France and Germany border each other*

Border *n* [*the*+R] the border between England and Scotland

bor·der·er /ˈbɔːdərəʳ‖ˈbɔrdərər/ *n* a person who lives near a country's borders, esp. near the border between England and Scotland

bor·der·land /ˈbɔːdəlænd‖ˈbɔrdər-/ *n* **1** [C] land at or near the border of 2 countries **2** [*the*+R;(S)] a condition between 2 other conditions and like each of them in certain ways: *the borderland between sleeping and waking*

bor·der·line[1] /ˈbɔːdəlaɪn‖ˈbɔrdər-/ *n* [C *usu. sing.*] (a line marking) a border: *the borderline between France and Germany*|*between sleeping and waking*

borderline[2] *adj* [Wa5;A] **1** almost below accepted standards of quality or behaviour: *Those borderline jokes of yours are almost rude* **2** that may or may not belong to a certain type: *a borderline case*

border on also **border up·on**— *v prep* [T1] to be very much like: *Your remarks border on rudeness, sir!*

bore[1] /bɔːʳ‖bor/ *v* **1** [L9;(IØ)] to make a round hole or passage in something: *This machine can bore through solid rock* **2** [L9] to move steadily ahead, usu. through difficulties: *The ship bored on through the big waves* **3** [T1] to make in either way: *to bore a hole*|*a well*|*to bore one's way through a crowd of people*

bore[2] *n* a hole made by boring (BORE[1] (1)), esp. for oil, water, etc.

bore[3] *past t. of* BEAR[2]

bore[4] *n* a very large wave caused by a movement of the sea (by a TIDE) running up a narrow river

bore[5] *n* **1** [C] *derog* a person who causes others to lose interest in him, esp. by continual dull talk **2** [S] *esp BrE infml* something which is rather unpleasant: *It's a bore having to go out again on a cold night like this*

bore[6] *v* [Wv4;T1;IØ] to make (someone) tired or uninterested, esp. by continual dull talk: *The* *teacher bored his students.|The lesson was boring, and the students were bored (by it)* —**~dom** *n* [U]

-bore *comb form* (a measurement of the width of the hollow inside a gun barrel): *12-bore|small-bore*

bore·hole /ˈbɔːhəʊl‖ˈbor-/ *n* BORE²

bor·er /ˈbɔːrəʳ‖ˈbo-/ *n* a person, tool, or insect that makes round holes

bo·ric ac·id /ˈbɔːrɪk‖ˈbo-/ also **boracic acid**— *adj* [U] a white acid powder made from BORAX

born¹ /bɔːn‖born/ *adj* [Wa5] **1** [F] brought into existence by or as if by birth: *The baby was born at 8 o'clock.*|(fig.) *The new political party was born at a small meeting.|I feel as if I have been born again* **2** [F] at birth; originally: *Carlos Gardel was born French, but grew up in Argentina* **3** [A] having a stated quality from or as if from birth: *a born leader* **4** [F] being in a stated condition from birth or by birth: *nobly born* **5** [F3] fated from or as if from birth: *born to succeed* **6 born and bred** to come into the world and grow up: *He was born and bred in Yorkshire.|He was Yorkshire born and bred* **7 born of** owing existence to: (fig.) *His wish to become a doctor was born of a desire to help sick people* **8 born with a silver spoon in one's mouth** to have money and social advantages from birth **9 in all my born days** *infml* in all my life

born² *past p. of* BEAR²
USAGE This is one of the 2 past p. of **bear** when it means "to give birth to". Compare: *He was* **born** *in 1950*/**born** *of French parents.|She has* **borne** *3 children.*

-born *comb. form* **1** native: *American-born* **2** born in a stated condition (or sometimes in a stated way): *the rich, the well-born, and the able* **3** coming or resulting from: *war-born crime*

borne /bɔːn‖born/ *past p. of* BEAR² —see BORN² (USAGE)

-borne *comb. form* carried as stated: *airborne diseases*

borne in on /ˌ·ˈ··/ also **borne in up·on** /·ˈ··ˌ·/— *adj* [Wa5;F] brought firmly to the consciousness of: *Slowly it was borne in on the citizens that the enemy had surrounded them*

bo·ron /ˈbɔːrɒn‖ˈboran/ *n* [U] *tech* a type of simple chemical substance (ELEMENT (6)) in the form of a brown powder, best known for its use in BORIC ACID and BORAX

bo·rough /ˈbʌrə‖-rəʊ/ *n* a town, or a division of a large town, with certain rights: *the Royal Borough of Kensington and Chelsea|the Borough of Brooklyn*

bor·row /ˈbɒrəʊ‖ˈba-, ˈbɔ-/ *v* **1** [T1;IØ: (*from*)] to take or receive (something) for a certain time and with intention to return: *to borrow (£5) from a friend* —compare LEND, LOAN¹,² **2** [T1] *euph* to take without permission: *Somebody seems to have borrowed my watch when I wasn't looking* **3** [T1;IØ: (*from*)] to take or copy (esp. ideas, words, etc.): *English has borrowed (words) from many languages* **4 live on borrowed time** to be alive after the time when one should probably have died —**~er** *n*

bor·row·ing /ˈbɒrəʊɪŋ‖ˈba-, ˈbɔ-/ *n* **1** [U] the act or action of borrowing **2** [C] something (esp. non-material) which has been borrowed: *English has many borrowings from other languages*

borscht, borshcht /bɔːʃt‖borʃt/ also **borsch** /bɔːʃ‖borʃ/— *n* [U] **1** a BEETROOT soup (of East European origin) usu. served cold, often with sour cream **2** a thick CABBAGE soup (of East European origin) served hot

bor·stal /ˈbɔːstl‖ˈbɔr-/ *n* [C;U] *BrE* (*often cap.*) a prison school for young offenders: *He was sent to borstal for stealing*

bor·zoi /ˈbɔːzɔɪ‖ˈbɔrzɔɪ/ *n* a type of large long-haired swift dog developed in Russia to hunt wolves (WOLF) —see picture at DOG¹

bosh /bɒʃ‖baʃ/ *n, interj* [U] *esp. BrE sl* empty talk; nonsense

bo·s'n, bo's'n /ˈbəʊsən/ *n* BOATSWAIN

bos·om¹ /ˈbʊzəm/ *n* **1** *often euph or lit* the front of the human chest, esp. the female breasts: *She had a well-developed bosom.|She held the child to her bosom* **2** the part of a garment covering the breast(s): *She carried his letter in the bosom of her dress.*|(*AmE*) *the bosom of his shirt* **3** *lit* the seat of secret thoughts and feelings: *Her bosom was torn by sorrow* **4** *lit* a broad surface, esp. of a sea or lake: *the calm bosom of the lake* **5 in the bosom of** in a close relationship with: *He spent his last years in the bosom of his family*

bosom² *adj* [Wa5;A] very close (esp. in the phr. **bosom friend**)

bos·om·y /ˈbʊzəmi/ *adj infml* having well-developed breasts: *a bosomy actress*

boss¹ /bɒs‖bɔs/ *n* **1** a round metal ornament which stands out from the surface of something, such as a shield **2** (esp. in churches) a raised stone ornament, part of the pattern of the inside roof

boss² *n* [C;N] *infml* **1** a master; employer; person having control over others: *to ask the boss for more money|Have you got a match, boss?|The trouble with my wife is that she doesn't know who's (the) boss* (=she thinks she's in charge, but I think I am) **2** *AmE usu. derog* a political party chief

boss³ *v* [T1 (ABOUT or AROUND);(IØ)] to be the person in control (of); give orders (to): *Tom likes to boss (younger children) (about)*

boss⁴ *adj* **make a boss shot (at)** *BrE sl* to make a first, probably not very good, attempt (at)

boss-eyed /ˈ··/ *adj BrE derog sl* with eyes looking in different directions; CROSS-EYED

boss·y /ˈbɒsi‖ˈbɔsi/ *adj* [Wa1] *infml derog* having or showing fondness for giving orders: *a bossy person/manner* —**bossiness** *n* [U]

bo·sun /ˈbəʊsən/ *n* BOATSWAIN

bo·tan·i·cal /bəˈtænɪkəl/ *adj* [Wa5;A] **1** of or related to plants or BOTANY: *a beautiful botanical garden with plants from all over the world* **2** obtained from plants: *botanical drugs*

bot·a·nist /ˈbɒtənəst‖ˈba-/ *n* a specialist in BOTANY; professional student of plants

bot·a·nize, -ise /ˈbɒtənaɪz‖ˈba-/ *v* **1** [IØ] to study plant life and collect examples of plants: *to botanize in Ecuador* **2** [T1] to travel into (a place) in order to do this: *to botanize Ecuador*

bot·a·ny /ˈbɒtəni‖ˈba-/ *n* [U] the scientific study of plants

botch¹ /bɒtʃ‖batʃ/ *v infml* [Wa5;T1 (UP)] to do (something) badly; esp. to repair (something) badly: *I tried to cook a nice dinner, but I'm afraid I've rather botched it (up).|a botched job*

botch² also **botch-up** /ˈ··/— *n infml* a bad piece of work (esp. in the phr. **make a botch of something**)

both¹ /bəʊθ/ *predeterminer determiner* being the 2; having to do with the one and the other: *both feet|both his eyes|both these armies*

both² *pron* **1** the one as well as the other: *both of us|both of his eyes|We are both well.|Both (of us) are well.|John and Mary have both won prizes.|John and Mary both have won prizes.*|(*AmE*) *He likes John and Mary both.|Why not use both?|Why not do both?* **2 the both of** *AmE nonstandard* the 2 of; both of: *the both of us* —see EACH¹ (USAGE)

both³ *conj* **both . . . and . . .** not only . . . but also . . .: *both New York and London|She spoke with both kindness and understanding.|He both speaks and writes Swahili.|She is well known both for her kindness and for her understanding.|both now and always*

both·er¹ /ˈbɒðəʳ‖ˈba-/ *v* **1** [T1] to cause to be nervous; annoy or trouble, esp. in little ways: *I'm* *busy: don't bother me.|That's what bothers me most* **2** [T1] (in polite expressions) to cause inconvenience to: *I'm sorry to bother you, but can you tell me the time?* **3** [IØ (*with* or *about*),3] to cause inconvenience to oneself; trouble oneself: *Don't bother with/about it* **4** [T1;IØ] *euph derog* (used for adding force to expressions of displeasure): *Bother! I've missed my train!|Bother the lot of you! Go away at once!* —see ANGRY (USAGE) **5 bother oneself/one's head about** to trouble oneself; be anxious about: *Don't bother yourself about that just because of me!*

bother² *n* **1** [U] trouble, inconvenience, or anxiety (usu. caused by small matters and lasting a short time): *We had a lot of bother finding our way here* **2** [C *usu. sing.*] something (or someone) that causes this: *I don't want to be a bother to you, but could I possibly stay here for the night?* **3** [U] *BrE sl* BOVVER

both·er·a·tion /ˌbɒðəˈreɪʃən‖ˌbɑ-/ *interj rare* (used for expressing slight annoyance)

both·er·some /ˈbɒðəsəm‖ˈbɑðər-/ *adj* that causes BOTHER² (1): *bothersome demands/people*

bot·tle¹ /ˈbɒtl‖ˈbɑtl/ *n* **1** [C] a container, typically of glass or plastic, with a rather narrow neck or mouth and usu. no handle **2** [C] also **bottleful**— the quantity held by a bottle: *He drank 3 bottles of wine!* **3** [the+R] alcoholic drink: *Poor John's on the bottle again!* **4** [*the*+R;S] milk in bottles used in place of mother's milk: *Which is better: the breast or the bottle?* **5 hit the bottle** *sl* to (start to) drink a lot of alcohol

bottle² *v* [T1] **1** to put into one or more bottles: *an apparatus for bottling wine* **2** [Wv5] to preserve in bottles as by heating: *bottled fruit*

bottle-feed /ˈ·· ·/ *v* **-fed** /-fed/ [Wv5;T1;IØ] to feed (as a baby) with a bottle, rather than with the breast: *She is against bottle-feeding (babies).|a bottle-fed baby*

bot·tle·ful /ˈbɒtlfʊl‖ˈbɑ-/ *n* BOTTLE¹ (2)

bottle green /ˌ·· ˈ·/ *n, adj* [Wa5;U;B] the dark green colour of the glass used esp. in making beer bottles

bot·tle·neck /ˈbɒtlnek‖ˈbɑ-/ *n* **1** a narrow space in a road which slows down cars **2** a condition or state of affairs that slows down free movement or the rate of advance: *I hope the book will come out on time in spite of all the bottlenecks*

bottle up *v adv* [T1] to control in an unhealthy way: *Bottling up your feelings leads to trouble*

bot·tom /ˈbɒtəm‖ˈbɑ-/ *n* **1** [C (*of*)] the base on which something stands; the lowest part, inside or outside: *at the bottom of the stairs|the bottom of his trouser legs|the flat bottom of the glass|at/in/on the bottom of your cup* **2** [(*the*)R(*of*)] the ground under the sea, a lake, or a river: *at the bottom of the sea.|They sent the enemy ship to the bottom (of the sea).|the river-bottom|This part is too deep for swimming: I can't touch bottom* **3** [(*the*)R(*of*)] the least important or least worthy part of anything: *He is always at the bottom of the class.|He started life at the bottom, and worked his way up (to success)* **4** [*the*+R(*of*)] the far end: *I'll walk with you to the bottom of the road.|(BrE) We grow vegetables at the bottom of our garden* **5** [C] **a** the part of a chair on which one sits **b** the part of the body on which one sits: *to fall on one's bottom* **6** [*the*+R+*of*] *often derog* the starting point; the cause; that on which everything else rests: *Who is at the bottom of all this trouble?* **7** [C] (the lowest part of) a ship **8** [C *usu. pl.*] low-lying grassland along a river or stream **9** [A] lowest; last: *in the bottom row* **10 at bottom** really; in spite of appearances: *He pretends to be very hard, but he's a kind man at bottom* **11 bet one's bottom dollar** *infml* to be sure: *You can bet your bottom dollar that he'll get there before anyone else* **12 bottom up** upside down **13 Bottoms up!** *infml* Empty your glasses! Finish your drinks! **14 from the bottom of one's heart** truly; with real feeling; without deceiving: *I want to tell you from the bottom of my heart that I am truly sorry* **15 knock the bottom out of** *infml* to take away the necessary support on which something rests: *The bad news knocked the bottom out of market prices* **16 start at the bottom of the ladder** *infml* to begin in the least important position: *He started at the bottom of the ladder and worked his way up (to success)* **17 the top and bottom of it** *infml* **a** the whole of it, with nothing more to be said: *You're wrong, and that's the top and bottom of it* **b** the explanation: *He did it for the money, and that's the top and bottom of it* —compare TOP¹·³

bottom drawer /ˌ·· ˈ·/ (*AmE* **hope chest**)— *n* [*usu. sing.*] *BrE old infml* (the place for) the clothes, sheets, etc., which a girl collects before getting married: *Give her something for her bottom drawer*

bot·tom·less /ˈbɒtəmləs‖ˈbɑ-/ *adj* [Wa5] with no bottom or limit; very deep: (fig.) *His kindness seems bottomless, but in fact he will soon have no more money to give away*

bottom out *v adv* [IØ] **1** to be at its lowest position: *The valley bottomed out by the river* **2** to reach the lowest point before rising again: *House prices bottomed out in 1974*

bot·u·lis·m /ˈbɒtʃʊlɪzəm‖ˈbɑtʃə-/ *n* [U] a serious form of food poisoning caused by bacteria that are found in preserved meat and vegetables

bou·doir /ˈbuːdwɑːʳ/ *n* a woman's dressing room, bedroom, or private sitting room

bouf·fant /ˈbuːfɒŋ, -fɒnt‖buːˈfɑnt (*Fr* bufɑ̃)/ *adj* (of hair or a dress) PUFFed out

bou·gain·vil·lae·a, *AmE usu.* **-lea** /ˌbuːgənˈvɪlɪə/ *n* a type of climbing plant with big red and purple flowers which grows in hot countries

bough /baʊ/ *n* a branch of a tree, esp. a main branch

bought /bɔːt/ *past t. and p. of* BUY¹

bouil·la·baisse /ˌbuːjəˈbes‖-ˈbeɪs/ *n* [C;U] *Fr* a strong-tasting dish made from fish

bouil·lon /ˈbuːjɒn‖-jɑn (*Fr* bujɔ̃)/ *n* [C;U] *Fr* a clear soup made by boiling meat and vegetables in water

boul·der /ˈbəʊldəʳ/ *n* a large stone or a mass of rock

boule·vard /ˈbuːlvɑːd‖ˈbuːləvɑrd, ˈbʊ-/ *n* **1** a broad street, usu. having trees on each side **2** *AmE* (*often cap. as part of a name*) a wide main road: *Sunset Boulevard* —compare AVENUE (1,2)

bounce¹ /baʊns/ *v* **1** [T1;IØ] **a** (of a ball) to spring back or up again from the ground **b** to cause (a ball) to do this **2** [T1;L9] to (cause to) jump or spring up and down like a ball; (cause to) move with a springing movement, often angrily or noisily: *She bounced out of the house and never came back.|She bounced the baby (on her knee)* **3** [IØ] *sl* (of a cheque) to be returned by a bank as worthless

bounce² *n* **1** [U] the act or action of bouncing (BOUNCE¹): *The ball has plenty of bounce, and goes up very high after it hits the ground* **2** [C] an example of this: *The ball gave a high bounce* **3** [U] behaviour which is full of life, but may be too noisy: *She has a lot of bounce, but not everybody likes that* **4 on the bounce** after a ball has BOUNCED¹ (1): *to catch a ball on the bounce*

bounce back *v adv* [IØ] to improve after one's feelings have been hurt

bounc·er /ˈbaʊnsəʳ/ *n* **1** a person or thing that BOUNCEs¹: *That rubber ball is a good bouncer* **2** *infml* a strong man employed (esp. at a club or inn)

to throw out unwelcome visitors **3** BUMPER² (2)
bounc·ing /ˈbaʊnsɪŋ/ *adj* [Wa5;A] *apprec* (esp. of babies) fine; strong; healthy; active: *2 bouncing baby boys*
bounc·y /ˈbaʊnsi/ *adj* [Wa2] **1** (showing that one is) full of life and eager (perhaps too eager) for action: *a bouncy person/manner* **2** that BOUNCEs well: *a bouncy ball* —**-ily** *adv* —**-iness** *n* [U]
bound¹ /baʊnd/ *adj* [Wa5;F+*for*;F9] intending to go (to); going (to): *bound for home|college-bound*
bound² *v* [T1 *usu. pass.*] to mark the edges of; keep within a certain space: *The US is bounded on the north by Canada and on the south by Mexico*
bound³ *adj* [Wa5] **1** [F (*to*)] fastened by or as if by a band; kept close to: *bound to one's job|bound to a post* —see also -BOUND **2** [F3] certain; sure: *It's bound to rain soon.|You're bound to succeed* **3** [F3] placed under the lawful or moral need to act: *I am duty-bound to tell you* **4** [B] (of a book) fastened within covers: *a leather-bound book|a book bound in leather* **5** [F3] determined; having a firm intention: *He is bound to go, and nothing can stop him* **6** [B] held in a chemical combination: *salts bound in water* **7** [B] (in grammar) always found in combination with another form (esp. in the phr. **bound form**): *"un-" and "er" are bound forms which are found in the words "unknown" and "speaker"* **8** **bound up in** busy with; very interested in: *She is bound up in her work with old people* **9** **bound up with** dependent on; connected with: *His future is closely bound up with that of the company he works for* **10** **I'll be bound!** *infml* I'm quite certain: *He'll have some good reason for being late, I'll be bound!*
bound⁴ *n* **1** a jump or LEAP² **2** BOUNCE² (2)
bound⁵ *v* [L9] **1** to jump or LEAP¹: *He bounded away* **2** to spring or BOUNCE¹ back from a surface
-bound *comb. form* **1** limited, kept in, or controlled in the stated way: *We were snow-bound and couldn't go out of the house.|desk-bound pilots* **2** (esp. of earth) made to stick together by the stated conditions: FROST-*bound earth*
bound·a·ry /ˈbaʊndəri/ *n* **1** the limiting or dividing line of surfaces or spaces; border: *The new boundaries of the country were fixed after the war.|A river forms the boundary (line) between the 2 countries* **2** the outer limit of anything, esp. of a system of thought or knowledge: *The boundaries of human knowledge are being pushed further out* **3** (in cricket) **a** the line which marks the limit of the field of play: *A ball hit to or over the boundary is worth 4 or 6 runs* **b** (a hit to (or over) this line, that is worth) 4 (or 6) runs: *He hit 6 boundaries in his 37* —see picture at CRICKET²
bound·en /ˈbaʊndən/ *adj* [Wa5;A] *fml becoming rare* necessary (in the phr. **bounden duty**)
bound·er /ˈbaʊndəʳ/ *n* [C;*you*+N] *BrE old sl* a man who does not behave in a socially acceptable way; CAD
bound·less /ˈbaʊndləs/ *adj* without limits: *boundless wealth/imagination* —**~ly** *adv* —**~ness** *n* [U]: *the boundlessness of his imagination*
bounds /baʊndz/ *n* [P] **1** the furthest limits or edges of something; the limits beyond which one may not go: *There were no bounds to his foolishness.|His foolishness was without bounds.|Unwise behaviour of that sort goes beyond the bounds of reason.|We must put/set bounds to our spending.|It is within the bounds of possibility that he is guilty* **2** **out of bounds** (**to**) forbidden to be visited (by): *That part of town is out of bounds (to soldiers)*
boun·te·ous /ˈbaʊntɪəs/ *adj fml or lit* **1** ready and willing to give freely: *a bounteous giver* **2** given freely: *bounteous gifts* —**~ly** *adv* —**~ness** *n* [U]
boun·ti·ful /ˈbaʊntɪfəl/ *adj fml or lit* **1** freely given; plentiful: *bountiful gifts* **2** BOUNTEOUS (1) —**~ly** *adv*
boun·ty /ˈbaʊnti/ *n* **1** [U] generosity: *a rich lady famous for her bounty to the poor* **2** [C] something that is given generously **3** [C] money given by a government for some special act or service
bou·quet¹ /bəʊˈkeɪ, buː-/ *n* **1** flowers picked and fastened together in a bunch **2** words of praise: *In his speech there were bouquets for everyone who had helped him*
bouquet² *n* [C;U] the smell of wine, etc.: *a rich bouquet*
bour·bon /ˈbʊəbən‖ˈbɜr-/ *n* [U] a type of American strong alcoholic drink (WHISKY)
bour·geois¹ /ˈbʊəʒwɑː‖bʊərˈʒwɑ/ *n* **bourgeois** *Fr* **1** a member of the MIDDLE CLASS **2** a member of the CAPITALIST class **3** *derog* a person more concerned with possessions and good manners than with ideas and feelings
bourgeois² *adj Fr* **1** [WA5] of, related to, or typical of the MIDDLE CLASS **2** [Wa5] CAPITALIST²: *What is the future of bourgeois society?* **3** *derog* having or showing more interest in possessions and good manners than in ideas and feelings: *She is the most bourgeois person I know*
bour·geoi·sie /ˌbʊəʒwɑːˈziː‖-ər-/ *n* [(*the*) GU;(C)] *Fr* **1** the MIDDLE CLASS **2** the CAPITALIST class
bourn¹, bourne /bɔːn‖born/ *n old use* (now used mainly in placenames) a small stream: *Eastbourne*
bourn², bourne *n old use or lit* limit; border: *". . . death/The undiscovered country from whose bourn/No traveller returns . . ."* (Shakespeare, *Hamlet*)
bourse /bʊəs‖bʊərs/ *n Fr* a European STOCK EXCHANGE, esp. in France
bout /baʊt/ *n* **1** a short period of activity: *bouts of fierce activity followed by periods of rest|bouts of drinking (alcohol)* **2** an attack of illness: *several bouts of fever* **3** a BOXING match
bou·tique /buːˈtiːk/ *n Fr* **1** a small shop (usu. for women) selling up-to-date clothes and other personal articles of the newest kind **2** a department of this kind within a large department store
bou·zou·ki /bʊˈzuːki/ *n* a long-necked stringed musical instrument of Greek origin, which is like a MANDOLIN: *bouzouki music*
bo·vine /ˈbəʊvaɪn/ *adj* **1** *tech* like a cow or OX **2** *derog* slow-thinking and slow-moving
Bov·ril /ˈbɒvrɪl‖ˈbɑv-/ *n* [U] *tdmk* a substance obtained from meat and mixed with hot water to make a drink
bov·ver /ˈbɒvəʳ‖ˈbɑ-/ *n* [U] *BrE sl* violence or threatening behaviour, esp. by groups of boys or young men wearing heavy boots for kicking (**bovver-boots** /ˈ·· ·/)
bow¹ /baʊ/ *v* **1** [IØ (DOWN, *to*)] to bend forward the upper part of the body to show respect or yielding: *Everyone bowed as the Queen walked into the room.|*(fig.) *We must bow to fate and accept what cannot be avoided* **2** [T1] to express (something) in this way: *He bowed his thanks* **3** [X9] to lead while doing this: *He bowed me to the door.|He bowed them out (of the room)* **4** [T1 (DOWN)] to bend (esp. the head): *The guilty man bowed his head in shame* **5** **bow and scrape** *usu. derog* to behave to someone with a politeness that is too great and may be false **6** **bow down (to), bow the neck/the knee (to)** to admit defeat and agree to serve: *We shall never bow down to our enemies!* **7** **bow to nobody** to claim the first or highest place for oneself: *I bow to nobody in my love for the plays of Shakespeare* **8** **bow to someone's opinion, knowledge, etc.** to accept that someone's opinion, knowledge, etc., is of more value than one's own
bow² *n* **1** a bending forward of the upper part of the body to show respect or yielding: *He moved*

aside for her with a polite bow **2 make one's/its/their bow** *infml* to appear publicly for the first time: *The new book will make its bow in the spring* **3 take a bow** to come on stage to receive praise at the end of a performance

bow³ /bəʊ/ *n* **1** a piece of wood held in a curve by a tight string and used for shooting arrows —see also CROSSBOW, LONGBOW **2** a long thin piece of wood with a tight string fastened along it, used for playing musical instruments that have strings —see picture at STRINGED INSTRUMENT **3** a knot formed by doubling a line into 2 or more round or curved pieces, and used for ornament in the hair, in tying shoes, etc. **4 have more than one string/have 2 strings to one's bow** *infml* to have several possibilities from which to choose: *Don't think he's just a person who writes books: he has more than one string to his bow*

bow⁴ *v* **1** [IØ] *tech* to bend or curve **2** [T1;IØ] to play (a piece of music) on a musical instrument with a BOW³ (2)

bow⁵ /baʊ/ *n* [*often pl. with sing. meaning*] the forward part of a ship —see picture at FREIGHTER

Bow bells /ˌbəʊ ˈbelz/ *n* **born within the sound of Bow bells** born in the City of London, or near enough to be a true Londoner (COCKNEY)

bowd·ler·ize, -ise /ˈbaʊdləraɪz/ *v* [T1;IØ] *usu. derog* to remove from (a book, play, etc.) those parts considered unfit for children or ladies: *This dictionary has not been bowdlerized*

bowed /baʊd/ *adj* bent down or over: *He stood with bowed head at the funeral.|bowed (down) with age/with snow*

bow·el /ˈbaʊəl/ *n* [*the*+R;(C)] *med* BOWELS (1)

bow·els /ˈbaʊəlz/ *n* [P] **1** a long pipe continuing down from the stomach and leading the waste matter out of the body —compare INTESTINE **2** *lit* the place where kind personal feelings are said to come from: *the bowels of* COMPASSION/*of pity* **3** [+*of*] the inner, lower part (of anything) (esp. in the phr. **the bowels of the earth**)

bow·er /ˈbaʊəʳ/ *n lit* **1** (a summer house in) a pleasant shaded place under the trees **2** BOUDOIR

bow·er·bird /ˈbaʊəbɜːd‖-ərbərd/ *n* any of several types of bird that live in or near Australia, the male of which builds a special tubelike framework of grass, ornamented with brightly-coloured objects, to attract the female

bow·ie knife /ˈbəʊi naɪf‖ˈbuːi-, ˈbəʊi-/ *n* a strong single-edged hunting knife of American origin, which has part of the back edge curved upwards to a point and sharpened

bow·ing /ˈbəʊɪŋ/ *n* [U] **1** the manner of using the BOW³ (2) in music **2** the way in which a piece of music is to be played using the BOW³ (2)

bowl¹ /bəʊl/ *n* **1** [C] (*often in comb.*) a deep round container for holding liquids, flowers, sugar, etc.: *a sugar bowl* —see picture at KITCHEN **2** [C] the contents of a bowl: *There are 2 bowls of sugar left* **3** [*the*+R] *lit* a drinking vessel, representing merry-making **4** [C] anything in the shape of a bowl: *the bowl of a pipe (for smoking)*

bowl² *n* **1** a ball for rolling in the game of BOWLS **2** an act of rolling the ball in the games of BOWLS or BOWLING

bowl³ *v* **1** [X9;IØ;(T1)] to roll (a ball) in the games of BOWLS or BOWLING: *He bowls (the ball) very fast* **2** [T1] to obtain by doing this: *He bowled 300 last night!* **3** [L9;(IØ)] to play the games of BOWLS or BOWLING: *He goes bowling every Saturday* **4** [X9;IØ;(T1)] (in cricket) to throw (the ball) towards the hitter (BATSMAN) by swinging the arm above the head without bending the elbow: *He bowled the first ball too wide* —see CRICKET² (USAGE) and picture **5** [L9;(IØ)] (in cricket) to be the person who throws the ball in this way: *He bowls for the Nottingham team* **6** [T1 (OUT)] (in cricket) to force (a BATSMAN) to leave the field by hitting the WICKET behind him with a ball thrown in this way: *He bowled his man (out) with the very first ball!* **7** [X9] to cause to roll: *The wind bowled his hat down the street*

bowl a·long *v adv* [IØ] to move smoothly (and often quickly) along: *Work is bowling along nicely now*

bow-legged /ˈbəʊˌlegd, -ˌlegə̇d/ *adj* (esp. of people) having the legs curving outwards at the knee; BANDY²

bowl·er¹ /ˈbəʊləʳ/ *n* a person who BOWLS³ esp. in cricket: *the best bowler in the team* —see CRICKET² (USAGE)

bowler² also **bowler hat** /ˌ·· ˈ·/, (*AmE* **derby**)— *n esp. BrE* a man's round hard hat, usu. black: *He wears a bowler to go to his office in the City (of London)*

bowl·ful /ˈbəʊlfʊl/ *n* BOWL¹ (2)

bow·line /ˈbəʊlə̇n/ *n* **1** also **bowline knot** /ˈ·· ·/—a special sort of knot which does not slip, used esp. by sailors **2** a rope running from the edge of a sail to the BOW⁵

bowl·ing /ˈbəʊlɪŋ/ *n* [U] **1** any of various games in which balls are rolled at an object or a group of objects **2** also **tenpin bowling**— an indoor game of American origin in which a large heavy ball is rolled along a wooden track in an effort to knock down as many as possible of a set of 10 bottle-shaped wooden objects

bowling al·ley /ˈ·· ˌ··/ *n* a place for BOWLING, esp. the game of BOWLING (2)

bowling green /ˈ·· ·/ *n* an area of short smooth grass for playing the game of BOWLS

bowl o·ver *v adv* [T1] **1** to knock (someone) down by running: *Someone ran round the corner and nearly bowled me over* **2** to give a great surprise to (someone): *Your sudden news has quite bowled me over*

bowls /bəʊlz/ *n* [U] an outdoor game in which one tries to roll a big ball as near as possible to a small ball called "the JACK"

bow·man /ˈbəʊmən/ *n* **-men** /mən/ ARCHER

bow out /baʊ/ *v adv* [IØ (*of*)] to leave, or stop doing something: *The old leader decided to bow out now instead of fighting to keep his position*

bow·ser /ˈbaʊzəʳ/ *n* a special vehicle used for carrying petrol to an aircraft at an AIRPORT

bow·shot /ˈbəʊʃɒt‖-ʃɑt/ *n* [*usu. sing.*] *esp. lit* the distance from the place where an arrow is fired, to the place where it lands: *The castle lies not a bowshot from here, my lord*

bow·sprit /ˈbəʊˌsprɪt‖ˈbaʊ-, ˈbəʊ-/ *n* a pole sticking out from the front of a ship (BOW⁵), to which ropes from the sails are fastened

bow tie /ˌbəʊ ˈtaɪ/ *n* a TIE fastened at the front with a knot in the shape of a BOW³ (3)

bow to /baʊ/ *v prep* [T1] **1** to yield to: *I bow to your opinion, and will take your advice* **2** to obey

bow win·dow /ˌbəʊ ˈwɪndəʊ/ *n* a window built outwards from the wall in a curve, and built up from the ground —compare BAY WINDOW

bow·wow¹ /ˌbaʊˈwaʊ/ *interj infml* a word meant to be like the sound a dog makes

bowwow² /ˈbaʊwaʊ/ *n* (a child's word for) a dog

box¹ /bɒks‖bɑks/ *n* **boxes** *or* **box** **1** [Wn1;C;U] a type of small tree with dark stiff leaves that do not fall during the winter, often planted in rows as a wall or fence **2** [U] BOXWOOD

box² *n* **1** [C] (*often in comb.*) a container for solids, usu. with stiff sides and often with a lid: *a wooden box|a shoebox* **2** [C] the contents of a box: *She's eaten a whole box of chocolates* **3** [C] a small room or enclosed space: *a box at the theatre|the witness box in a law-court|the signal box on a railway line* —see picture at THEATRE **4** [C] (in cricket) a rounded piece of metal or plastic worn by the hitter (BATSMAN) over the lower part of the body, to protect the TESTICLEs from being hit by the ball **5** [*the*+R] *BrE sl* television: *I hate all these old films they keep showing on the box every night*

box[3] *v* [T1] **1** to put in one or more boxes: *The oranges were boxed and sent off quickly* **2 box the compass a** to name all 32 points of the compass in their correct order **b** to change course completely, or come to do the opposite of what was done at the beginning —see also BOX OFF

box[4] *v* [IØ (*with* or *against*);T1] **1** to fight (someone) with the closed hands (FISTs): *John and Paul boxed* (*with*) *each other* **2 box someone's ears** *infml* to hit someone on the ears with the hands —**~er** *n*

box[5] *n* **give someone a box on the ear** *infml* to BOX[4] (2) someone's ears

Box and Cox /ˌbɒks ən ˈkɒks‖ˌbɑks ən ˈkɑks/ *v* [IØ] *BrE infml* to take turns in doing something

box·er /ˈbɒksəʳ‖ˈbɑk-/ *n* a type of largish short-haired dog of German origin, usu. light brown in colour

box·ful /ˈbɒksfʊl‖ˈbɑks-/ *n* BOX[2] (2)

box in also **box up**— *v adv* [T1] to enclose in a small space: *Living in that small flat in the middle of all those high buildings, she feels boxed in*

box·ing /ˈbɒksɪŋ‖ˈbɑk-/ *n* [U] the sport of fighting with the tightly closed hands (the FISTs)
USAGE One *boxes* (BOX[4]) in a **ring** wearing special **gloves** and wins *on* **points**, by winning more **rounds** than the other man, or by a **knockout** or **technical knockout**. In an important *match* the person in charge is called the *judge* or **referee**.

Boxing Day /ˈ·· ·/ *n* [R] a public holiday in England and Wales, which is the first day after Christmas that is not a Sunday

box kite /ˈ· ·/ *n* a tailless KITE for flying, consisting of 2 or more open-ended connected boxes

box num·ber /ˈ· ˌ··/ *n* a number used as a mailing address, esp. in replying to newspaper advertisements

box off *v adv* [T1 (*from*)] to separate by putting into an enclosed space: *Each of us is boxed off* (*from the others*) *in his own little office.*|(fig.) *He keeps those 2 very different ideas boxed off from each other in his mind*

box-of·fice /ˈ· ˌ··/ *adj* [Wa5;A] of or about the ability of a play, film, etc., to make a profit by continuing to attract ticket-buyers: *The play was a box-office success, but I didn't like it*

box of·fice *n* a place in a theatre, cinema, concert hall, etc., where tickets are sold

box span·ner /ˈ· ˌ··/ *n* a SPANNER with a special head that fits over a NUT[1] (2)

box up *v adv* **1** [IØ *usu. imper.*] *infml* to keep quiet **2** [T1] BOX IN

box·wood /ˈbɒkswʊd‖ˈbɑks-/ also **box**— *n* [U] the hard wood of the BOX[1] tree

boy[1] /bɔɪ/ *n* **1** [C;N *often pl.*] a young male person: *When the child was born, the nurse said, "It's a boy!"|"Come here, boy!" shouted the old man.|a boy actor* **2** [C] a son, esp. young **3** [C] a male person of any age who acts as if he were still a boy **4** [C] *infml esp. AmE* a male person, of any age, from a given place: *John Smith? Yes—he's a local boy, I believe* **5** [C;N] (now considered offensive) a male servant of a different race: *Don't carry that trunk—I'll get one of the boys to do it* **6** [N9] *becoming rare* (used in forming phrases for addressing men): *Thank you, my boy/dear boy/old boy* **7 (one's) blue-eyed boy** /ˌ· · ˈ·/ (one's) favourite person

boy[2] *interj infml esp. AmE* (expressing excitement): *Boy, what a game!*

-boy *comb. form* a boy or young man working in a given place or at a given job: *an office-boy|a delivery-boy|a tea-boy*

boy·cott[1] /ˈbɔɪkɒt‖-kɑt/ *v* [T1] **1** (usu. of a group of people) to refuse to do business with: *They're boycotting the shop because the people who work there aren't allowed to join a union* **2** to refuse to attend or take part in: *to boycott a meeting*

boycott[2] *n* an act of BOYCOTTing[1]: *They have declared a boycott of/against that shop*

boy·friend /ˈbɔɪfrend/ *n* a male companion, usu. young, with whom a woman spends time and shares amusements

boy·hood /ˈbɔɪhʊd/ *n* [U;C *usu. sing.*] the state or period of being a boy: *Did you have a happy boyhood, father?*

boy·ish /ˈbɔɪ-ɪʃ/ *adj often apprec* of or like a boy: *his boyish laughter|her boyish movements* —**~ly** *adv* —**~ness** *n* [U]

boys /bɔɪz/ *n* [P;N] *apprec* men who are thought of as young and as forming a group in some way: *to spend a night with the boys|Up and at them, boys!*

boy scout /ˌ· ˈ·‖ˈ· ·/ (*fem.* **girl guide**, *AmE* **girl scout**) also (*infml*) **scout**— *n* (*often cap.*) a member of an association (the **(boy) scouts**) for training boys in character and self-help through camping, giving help to others, etc.

Br *written abbrev. for:* **1** [A] BROTHER[1] (3) (in a religious society): *Br Maurice, Br Theodore, and Br Charles* **2** also **Brit**— British

BR *abbrev. for:* British Rail (the British railway system)

bra /brɑː/ also (*fml*) **brassiere**— *n* a woman's close-fitting undergarment worn to support the breasts

brace[1] /breɪs/ *n* **1** something used for supporting, stiffening, or fastening **2** a rope used on a sailing ship to tighten a sail **3** a support sometimes worn by a person with a weak back **4** a wire worn inside the mouth, usu. by children, to make right the irregular growth of teeth **5** a mark } or { used for connecting information printed on more than one line —compare BRACKET[1] (2) **6 in a brace of shakes** *BrE sl* very quickly —see also SPLICE **the main brace**

brace[2] *v* [T1] **1** to make stronger: *Let's brace this wall!* **2** to provide or support with a brace: *His weak back was heavily braced* **3** to put or set firmly: *He braced his foot against the edge of the wall* **4** to prepare (oneself), usu. for something unpleasant or difficult: *Brace yourself for the shock!*

brace[3] *n* **brace** [Wn3;C (*of*)] (usu. in hunting or shooting) 2 of a kind; a pair: *We brought back several brace of wild birds.|Those 2 are a brace of thieves!* —compare PAIR[1], COUPLE[2]

brace and bit /ˌ· · ˈ·/ *n* a tool used for making holes in wood —see picture at TOOL

brace·let /ˈbreɪslɪ̈t/ *n* a band or ring, usu. of metal, worn round the wrist or arm as an ornament

brace·lets /ˈbreɪslɪ̈ts/ *n* [P] *infml* HANDCUFFS

brac·es /ˈbreɪsɪ̈z/ *n* [P] *esp. BrE* **1** (*AmE* **suspenders**)— elastic cloth bands worn over the shoulders to hold up men's trousers: *a pair of braces* —see PAIR[1] (USAGE) **2 wear a belt and braces** *infml* to be too worried about one's own safety; take no risks

brace up *v adv* [T1;IØ] to (cause to) have more courage, spirit, and cheerfulness

brac·ing /ˈbreɪsɪŋ/ *adj apprec* (esp. of air) fresh and health-giving: *How I love this bracing sea air!*

brack·en /ˈbrækən/ *n* [U] **1** a kind of plant (a FERN) which grows in forests, on waste land, and on the slopes of hills, and becomes a rich red-brown colour in autumn —see picture at PLANT[2] **2** a mass of such plants

brack·et[1] /ˈbrækɨt/ *n* **1** a piece of metal or wood put in or on a wall to support something: *a lamp bracket* **2** [*usu. pl.*] **a** also **square bracket**— either of the pair of signs [ ] used for enclosing a piece of information: *The information about the grammar of this word is in brackets* **b** also **angle bracket**— either of the pair of signs ⟨ ⟩ used for enclosing a piece of information **c** *infml* PARENTHESIS (2) **d** BRACE[1] (5) **3** a group of people who share some quality: *the upper income bracket|the 16–25 age bracket*

bracket[2] *v* [T1] **1** [(OFF)] to enclose in BRACKETs[1] (2) **2** [(TOGETHER)] to regard as belonging together: *Don't bracket Smith and Jones (together): they're really very different*

brack·ish /ˈbrækɪʃ/ *adj* (of water) not pure; a little salty —**~ness** *n* [U]

bract /brækt/ *n* a leaflike part of a plant, often brightly coloured and growing in groups of a flowerlike appearance

brad·awl /ˈbrædɔːl/ *n* a small tool with a sharp point for making holes

brae /breɪ/ *n Scot E* a hillside or the slope at the side of a river valley

brag[1] /bræg/ *v* **-gg-** [IØ (*of* or *about*);T5] **1** to speak in praise of oneself, perhaps falsely; BOAST[2] (1,2): *Don't brag!|He bragged of having won first prize 10 years ago/bragged that he had won first prize* **2** **nothing to brag about** *infml* not very good: *His performance was nothing to brag about, and he won't be coming back*

brag[2] *n* [U] a type of card game

brag·ga·do·ci·o /ˌbrægəˈdəʊʃiəʊ/ *n It* **1** [U] noisy BRAGging[1] **2** [C] BRAGGART

brag·gart /ˈbrægət‖-ərt/ *n derog* a noisy fellow with a good opinion of himself, who BRAGs[1] a lot

Brah·man /ˈbrɑːmən/ also **Brahmin** /ˈbrɑːmɨn/— *n* a Hindu of the highest rank (CASTE)

braid[1] /breɪd/ *v* [T1] **1** *esp. AmE* to twist together into one string or band; PLAIT[2]: *She braided her hair neatly* **2** to ornament with an edging of BRAID[2] (2)

braid[2] *n* **1** [C *usu. pl.*] *esp. AmE* a band of hair made by twisting several lengths over and under each other; PLAIT[1]: *She wears her hair in braids down her back* **2** [U] a number of threads of silk, cotton, gold, etc., twisted together to make a narrow edging to put on material: *gold braid for a military officer's uniform*

braille /breɪl/ *n* [U] (*sometimes cap.*) (a way of) printing with raised round marks which blind people can read by touching them

brain[1] /breɪn/ *n* **1** [C] *med* the organ of the body in the upper part of the head, which controls thought and feeling: *The brain is the centre of higher nervous activity* **2** [C;U] the mind; INTELLIGENCE (1): *a good brain|He's nice, but he hasn't got much brain* **3** [C] *infml* a person with a good mind: *Some of the best brains in the country are here tonight* **4** **have something on the brain** *infml* to think about something continually, or too much: *From the way he acts, you'd think he had sex on the brain*

brain[2] *v* [T1] **1** to kill by knocking out the BRAINS of: *He brained his enemy with one blow* **2** *infml* to hit hard on the head

brain·child /ˈbreɪntʃaɪld/ *n infml* somebody's idea or (usu.) invention, esp. if successful: *This brainchild of mine has saved us a lot of money*

brain drain /ˈ· ·/ *n* the movement of large numbers of highly-skilled or professional people from the country where they were trained to other countries where they can earn more money

-brained /breɪnd/ *comb. form* having a brain or brains of the stated type: *My silly bird-brained friend* (= with a brain as small as a bird's) *can't spell*

brain·less /ˈbreɪnləs/ *adj derog* foolish; silly; stupid —**~ly** *adv*

brain·pan /ˈbreɪnpæn/ *n med* the case of bone in which the brain is contained

brains /breɪnz/ *n* [U] **1** the material of which the brain consists: *Sheep's brains is my favourite dish* **2** *infml* the ability to think: *He's got a lot of brains* **3** **blow out one's brains** *infml* to shoot oneself through the head **4** **pick someone's brains** *infml* to make use of someone's knowledge **5** **rack/beat/cudgel one's brains (about something)** *infml* to think very hard (about something)

brain·storm /ˈbreɪnstɔːm‖-stɔrm/ *n infml* **1** *BrE* a sudden great disorder of the mind: *I don't know why I forgot those papers: I must have had a brainstorm or something* **2** *AmE* BRAINWAVE

brains trust /ˈ· ·/ *AmE* **brain trust**— *n BrE infml* a group of people with special knowledge and experience who answer questions or give advice

brain·wash /ˈbreɪnwɒʃ‖-wɔʃ, -wɑʃ/ *v infml derog* [T1 (*into*)] to cause (someone) to change beliefs by means which are not limited to reason or force: *Don't let all those television advertisements brainwash you into buying that soap*

brain·wash·ing /ˈbreɪnˌwɒʃɪŋ‖-ˌwɔ-, -ˌwɑ-/ *n infml derog* **1** [U] the act or action of BRAINWASHing **2** [C *usu. sing.*] an example of this

brain·wave /ˈbreɪnweɪv/ *n BrE infml* a sudden clever idea: *Listen: I've just had a brainwave. Here's what we should do . . .*

brain·y /ˈbreɪni/ *adj* [Wa1] *infml* clever —**braininess** *n* [U]

braise /breɪz/ *v* [T1] to cook (meat) slowly in fat and a little liquid in a covered dish —see COOK[2] (USAGE)

brake[1] /breɪk/ *n* an apparatus for slowing or lessening movement and bringing to a stop (as of a wheel or car): (fig.) *The government put the brakes on all our plans by giving us less money* —see picture at BICYCLE[1]

brake[2] *v* **1** [T1] to cause to slow or stop (or as if by) a BRAKE[1]: *to brake a car* **2** [IØ] to use a BRAKE[1]: *He braked suddenly*

brake[3] *n* **1** [C] an area of rough or wet land with many low-growing wild bushes and plants **2** [U] BRACKEN

brake horse·pow·er /ˌ· ˈ···/ *n* [U] the HORSEPOWER developed by an engine and measured by the amount that the BRAKE[1] has to be used

bram·ble /ˈbræmbəl/ *n* any of a large number of common wild prickly bushes of the rose family, esp. one which bears a red fruit which later becomes black; the wild form of BLACKBERRY

bran /bræn/ *n* [U] the crushed skin of wheat and other grain separated from the flour

branch[1] /brɑːntʃ‖bræntʃ/ *n* **1** an armlike stem growing from the trunk of a tree or from another such stem **2** an armlike part or division of some material thing: *a branch of a river|a branch road|a branch railway* **3** a division of a non-material thing: *a branch of knowledge/of government.|Our business has branches in many cities.|He comes from a branch of our family that settled in America*

branch[2] *v* [IØ (OFF)] **1** to become divided into branches: *Follow the main road until it branches, and then turn to the right* **2** to form such a division: *Follow the main road to the end, and then take the road that branches (off) to the right*

branch out *v adv* [IØ (*into*)] to add to the range of one's activities: *The book firm has decided to branch out into selling music and records*

brand[1] /brænd/ *n* **1** a class of goods which is the product of a particular firm or producer: *What is* *your favourite brand of soap?* **2** a special kind: *He has his own brand of humour* **3** *fml* a piece of burnt or burning wood **4** a mark made (as by burning) usu. to show ownership: *These cattle have my brand on them* **5** *poet* a piece of wood burnt to give light; TORCH (2) **6** *poet* a sword

brand[2] *v* **1** [T1] to mark by or as if by burning, esp. to show ownership: *Farmer Brown's cattle are branded with the letter B* **2** [T1] (of bad experiences) to leave a mark on: *These bad experiences have branded him for life* **3** [X1] to give a lasting bad name to: *Those people/Those actions have branded him a thief*

brand as *v prep* [X1] BRAND[2] (3): *They have branded him as a thief*

bran·dish /ˈbrændɪʃ/ *v* to wave (something, esp. a weapon) about: *He brandished a newspaper at me and said, "Have you read this exciting news?"*

brand name /ˈ· ·/ *n* TRADE NAME

brand-new /ˌ· ˈ·◂/ *adj apprec* clearly new and unused

bran·dy[1] /ˈbrændi/ *n* **1** [U] a strong alcoholic drink usu. made from wine **2** [C] a type or single drink of this

brandy[2] *v* [Wv5;T1] to preserve (certain fruits) in BRANDY[1]: *brandied* PEACH*es*

brandy snap /ˈ·· ·/ *n* a thin sticky kind of sweet tasting of GINGER[1]

brash /bræʃ/ *adj* [Wa1] **1** *derog* rudely disrespectful and proud **2** hasty and too bold, esp. from lack of experience —**~ly** *adv* —**~ness** *n* [U]

brass /brɑːs‖bræs/ *n* **1** [U] a very hard bright yellow metal, a mixture of COPPER[1] and ZINC **2** [C] an object made of this metal, esp. a musical wind instrument: *Our band has some of the best brass players in the country* **3** [C] (esp. in Britain) a flat piece of this metal fixed to the floor or wall of a church in memory of a dead person **4** [U] *sl, esp. NEngE* money: *plenty of brass* **5** [U] *sl* shameless daring: *How did she have the brass to do that?*

brass band /ˌ· ˈ·/ *n* a band consisting mostly of BRASS (2) (musical) instruments

brassed off /ˌbrɑːst ˈɒf‖ˌbræst ˈɔf/ *adj* [F (*with*); (A)] *BrE sl* tired and annoyed; FED UP

bras·se·rie /ˈbræsəri‖ˌbræsəˈri (*Fr* brasri)/ *n Fr* a restaurant that sells beer

brass hat /ˌ· ˈ·/ *n sl* a military officer of high rank

bras·siere /ˈbræzjəʳ‖brəˈzɪər/ *n fml* BRA

brass knuck·les /ˌ· ˈ··/ *n* [P] *AmE* KNUCKLE-DUSTER

brass-mon·key /ˌ· ˈ··◂/ *adj* [Wa5;A] *BrE sl* (of weather) very cold

brass plate /ˌ· ˈ·/ *n* a flat piece of brass put up outside an office to give the name of the person or group whose office it is

brass tacks /ˌ· ˈ·/ *n* **get down to brass tacks** *infml* to come to the really important facts or the real business

brass·y /ˈbrɑːsi‖ˈbræsi/ *adj* [Wa1] **1** like brass in colour **2** like brass or brass musical instruments in sound **3** (esp. of a woman) shameless and loud in manner

brat /bræt/ *n derog* a child, esp. a bad-mannered one

bra·va·do /brəˈvɑːdəʊ/ *n* [U] the (often unnecessary) showing of courage or boldness

brave[1] /breɪv/ *adj* [Wa1] *apprec* **1** [B] (of a person who is) courageous, fearless, and ready to suffer danger or pain: *brave soldiers|brave actions|Let us remember the brave who died in the last war* **2** [A] *now rare* fine: *a brave new world* —**~ly** *adv* —**~ry** /ˈbreɪvəri/ *n* [U]

brave[2] *v* [T1] to meet (danger, pain, or trouble) without showing fear: *He braved his father's displeasure by marrying the girl*

brave[3] *n* a young North American Indian WARRIOR (fighting man)

brave out *v adv* **brave it out** to face trouble or blame bravely: *The director's called me into his office; I'd better go and brave it out* —compare BLUFF[3] **it out**, BRAZEN OUT

bra·vo /ˈbrɑːvəʊ, brɑːˈvəʊ/ *interj, n* **-vos** a shout of joy because someone (esp. a performer) has done well

bra·vu·ra /brəˈvjʊərə/ *n* [U] *It* a very showy style of performing something, esp. music: *the bravura of her performance|a bravura performance*

brawl[1] /brɔːl/ *v* [IØ] to take part in a BRAWL[2] —**~er** *n*

brawl[2] *n* a noisy quarrel, often in a public place, which usu. includes fighting

brawn /brɔːn/ *n* **1** [U] human muscle; MUSCULAR strength **2** [U;(C)] (*AmE* **headcheese**)— *BrE* (pieces of) pig-meat boiled and pressed in a pot with jelly

brawn·y /ˈbrɔːni/ *adj* (of people who are) strong; MUSCULAR: *The muscles of his brawny arms are strong as iron* —**-iness** *n* [U]

bray[1] /breɪ/ *v* [IØ] to make the sound that a donkey makes: (fig.) *The horns made a braying noise*

bray[2] *n* the sound a donkey makes

bra·zen /ˈbreɪzən/ *adj* **1** *lit* like brass, esp. in producing a loud unmusical sound as brass does when struck: *the brazen notes of the horns* **2** shameless; immodest —**~ly** *adv*

brazen out *v adv* **brazen it out** to face trouble or blame with shameless daring —compare BLUFF[3] **it out**, BRAVE OUT

bra·zier /ˈbreɪzjəʳ‖-ʒər/ *n* a container for burning coals

BrE (*of a word or phrase in this dictionary*) BRITISH ENGLISH —see AmE (USAGE)

breach[1] /briːtʃ/ *n* **1** [C;U] an act of breaking, not obeying, or not fulfilling a law, promise, custom, etc.: *Your action is a breach of our agreement.|You are in breach of your contract* **2** [C] an opening, esp. one made in a wall by attackers **3 stand in the breach** to bear the worst or heaviest part of the attack **4 throw oneself into the breach** to go at once to the help of those in trouble or danger

breach[2] *v* [T1] to break an opening in; break through

breach of con·fi·dence /ˌ· · ˈ···/ *n fml* the telling of a secret

breach of prom·ise /ˌ· · ˈ··/ *n* [U;C] *law* a failure to fulfil a promise, esp. a promise to marry someone

breach of the peace /ˌ· · · ˈ·/ *n law* unlawful fighting in a public place: *sent to prison for a breach of the peace*

bread /bred/ *n* [U] **1** a common food made of baked flour: *a loaf of bread* **2** food generally: *our daily bread* **3** means of staying alive: *to beg one's bread|to earn one's bread as a labourer* **4** *sl* money **5 bread and** bread spread with: *bread and butter|bread and cheese* —see USAGE **6 bread and butter** *infml* way of earning money: *He doesn't just write for fun: writing is his bread and butter* **7 (cast/throw one's) bread upon the waters** *infml* (to spend) money or (perform) good deeds without the expectation of anything in return **8 break bread with** *pomp* to eat with **9 know which side one's bread is buttered** *infml* to know who or what will be of most gain to oneself **10 take the bread out of someone's mouth** *infml* to make it impossible for someone to earn enough money

USAGE When **bread and** *butter* means pieces of bread with butter spread on them, it takes a singular verb: *This* **bread and** *butter is too thick.*

Compare *I bought* **bread** *and butter at the shop, and they cost 50p.*

bread-and-but·ter /ˌ· · ˈ··◂/ *adj* [Wa5;A] **1** concerned with the things that are necessary for life: *low wages, bad houses to live in, and other bread-and-butter political questions* **2** that can be depended upon: *"Hamlet" and "Othello" are the bread-and-butter plays of our theatre group* **3** sent or given as thanks for being treated well by one's host or hostess (esp. in the phr. **a bread-and-butter letter**)

bread·bas·ket /ˈbredˌbɑːskɪ̣t‖-ˌbæ-/ *n* [(*the*) *usu. sing.*] **1** *infml* an important grain-producing area: *The Ukraine is the breadbasket of the Soviet Union* **2** *sl* the stomach: *Hit him in the breadbasket, Maxie!*

bread·board /ˈbredbɔːd‖-bord/ *n* a special piece of flat smooth wood on which to cut a loaf of bread into SLICE*s* (thin pieces)

bread·crumb /ˈbredkrʌm/ *n* [*often pl.*] a very small bit of the soft inner part of a loaf of bread: *breadcrumbs to feed the birds|breadcrumbs for cooking*

bread·ed /ˈbredɪ̣d/ *adj* [Wa5] (esp. of meat or fish) covered with BREADCRUMB*s* and cooked

bread·fruit /ˈbredfruːt/ *n* **1** [C;U] a type of round usu. seedless tropical fruit that looks and feels like bread when baked **2** [C] also **breadfruit tree** /ˈ·· ·/— a tall tropical tree that bears this fruit

bread·line /ˈbredlaɪn/ *n* **1** a line of people waiting to be given food which they are too poor to buy: *Do you remember the mass unemployment and breadlines of the 1930s?* **2 on the breadline** very poor

breadth /bredθ, bretθ/ *n fml* **1** [U;C] (the) distance from side to side; width: *What is the breadth of this river? The breadth is 16 metres.|It's 16 metres in breadth.|a breadth of 16 metres|rivers of different breadths* **2** [C] a wide stretch (of land, water, etc.) **3** [U] the quality of taking everything or many things into consideration; range (as of knowledge, experience, etc.): *The great breadth of Dr. Plunkett's learning made his book the standard work on the subject* **4** [U] the ability to consider other people's opinions even if different from one's own: *a woman of great breadth of mind/opinions* **5 the length and breadth of** *pomp* every part of: *I have travelled through the length and breadth of this nation* —see also HAIR'S BREADTH

breadth·ways /ˈbredθweɪz, ˈbretθ-/ also **breadth·wise** /-waɪz/— *adj, adv* with the broad side nearest the viewer: *Look at this piece of wood breadthways.|a breadthways view*

bread·win·ner /ˈbredˌwɪnəʳ/ *n* [(*the*)] the person who works to supply a family with food, money, etc.: *Who is the breadwinner in your family?*

break¹ /breɪk/ *v* **broke** /brəʊk/, **broken** /ˈbrəʊkən/ **1** [T1;IØ] to (cause to) separate into parts suddenly or violently, but not by cutting or tearing: *to break a window/a leg|The rope broke when they were climbing.|The window broke into pieces* **2** [X9;L9] to (cause to) become separated from the main part suddenly or violently, but not by cutting or tearing: *to break a branch off a tree|A large piece of ice broke away from the main mass* **3** [T1;IØ] to (cause to) become unusable by damage to one or more parts: *He broke his wristwatch by dropping it.|This machine is broken and must be repaired* **4** [X7;L7] to (cause to) become, suddenly or violently: *The prisoner broke free/loose.|The box broke open when it fell.|They broke the door down* **5** [T1] to open the surface of: *to break the skin/the soil* **6** [T1] to disobey; not keep; not act in accordance with: *to break the law/a promise* **7** [L9] to force a way (into, out of, or through): *He broke into the shop and stole £100* **8** [T1] to bring under control: *to break a horse/a child's spirit* **9** [T1] to do better than: *to break a record in sports* **10** [T1] to ruin: *If that young man tries to marry my daughter, I'll break him!* **11** [T1] to destroy as an effective force: *We broke the enemy at the battle of Harlow Fields* **12** [T1] to make known (esp. something bad): *Break the bad news to him gently, please* **13** [T1;L9] to interrupt (an activity): *We broke our journey to Rome at Venice.|The bushes will break his fall.|Let's break for a meal and begin again afterwards.|The red flowers break the green of the picture* **14** [T1;IØ] to (cause to) come to an end: *to break the silence with a cry.|The cold weather at last broke at the end of March* **15** [IØ] to come esp. suddenly into being or notice: *as day breaks|The storm broke.|The news broke* **16** [IØ] to fail as a result of pressure from inside or outside: *His health broke.|He may break under continuous questioning* **17** [IØ;(T1)] to (cause to) change suddenly in direction, level, loudness, etc.: *The ball broke away from the person trying to hit it.|His voice broke with strong feeling/when he was 15 years old* **18** [T1] to discover the secret of: *She broke their* CODE (=secret writing).*|The police broke the case and caught the criminal* **19 break the back of** *infml* to finish the main or the worst part of: *It took them all day to break the back of the job* **20 break the bank** to win all the money as at a game of cards: *I'm the man who broke the bank at Monte Carlo!* (old popular song) **21 break camp** to pack up everything and leave a camping place **22 break cover** (of an animal) to run out from a hiding place **23 break someone's heart**/(of someone's heart) **break** to make/become very sad: *The bad news broke my heart.|It was heart-breaking news.|My heart is broken|I am heart-broken* **24 break the ice** *infml* **a** to make a beginning **b** to get through the first difficulties in starting a conversation **25 break new/fresh ground** to make new discoveries: *Scientists are breaking fresh ground every day in their search for new medicines* **26 break one's neck** *infml* to kill oneself by doing something dangerous or foolish: *You'll break your neck if you aren't more careful!* **27 break short** to cause to end earlier than intended: *The visit was broken short because there was talk of war* **28 break step** to march irregularly, not always keeping the same beat **29 break wind** *euph* to let out gases from the stomach and bowels —see also BREAK AWAY, BREAK DOWN, BREAK EVEN, BREAK IN, BREAK IN ON, BREAK INTO, BREAK OF, BREAK OFF, BREAK OUT, BREAK THROUGH[1,2], BREAK UP, BREAK WITH

break² *n* **1** an opening made by breaking or being broken: *a break in the clouds* **2** a pause for rest; period of time between activities: *a break in the concert|a coffee break|a tea break* **3** a change from the usual pattern or custom: *a break from/with the past|a break in the weather* **4** the time of day before sunrise when daylight first appears: *the break of day|at break of day|at daybreak* **5** an escape, esp. from prison **6** (in cricket) a change of direction of the ball on first hitting the ground after being thrown **7** (in the game of BILLIARDS) the number of points made by one player during one continuous period of play **8** (in tennis) a case of winning a game from the opponent who began it: *Cox had 2 breaks in the first set, but still lost it* **9** *infml* a chance (esp. to make things better); piece of luck, esp. of good luck: *Give him a break and he'll succeed.|He's had a good year with several big breaks/lucky breaks* **10 make a break for it** *infml* to try to escape by running away **11 without a break** continuously: *She's worked for 27 hours without a break*

break·age /ˈbreɪkɪdʒ/ *n* **1** [U] the action of breaking **2** [C] a broken place or part: *a breakage in the gas pipes* **3** [U;C *usu. pl. with sing. meaning*] the articles or value of the articles broken: *breakage/ breakages of £37*

break·a·way /ˈbreɪkəweɪ/ *adj, n* [Wa5] **1** [C] a person or thing that BREAKS AWAY **2** [C] an act or example of BREAKing AWAY (as from a group or custom) **3** [A] favouring independence from an association of some kind: *A breakaway group within the old political party formed a new one* **4** [C] *esp. AustrE* a sudden mad rush of horses or cattle; STAMPEDE[1] (1) **5** [C] *esp. AustrE* an animal that escapes from control **6** [A;C] *AmE* an object made so that it breaks easily when hit: *breakaway road signs for safety in car accidents*

break a·way *v adv* [IØ (*from*)] **1** to escape (from someone): *The criminal broke away from the 2 policemen who were holding him* **2** to cease (often political or religious) connection with, or loyalty or obedience to: *Modern music has broken away from 18th-century rules*

break·down /ˈbreɪkdaʊn/ *n* **1** a sudden failure in operation: *Our car had a breakdown on the road.|an electricity breakdown* **2** a sudden weakening or loss of powers of the body or mind: *a nervous breakdown* **3** a (usu. sudden) failure and stopping: *a breakdown of talks between workers and employers* **4** a division by types or into smaller groups; explanation in simple language: *I'd like a breakdown of these figures, please*

break down *v adv* **1** [T1] to destroy (something); reduce to pieces: *The police broke the door down.| The old cars were broken down for their metal and parts* **2** [T1;IØ] to (cause to) be defeated: *The police tried to break down the prisoner's opposition.| His opposition broke down* **3** [IØ] (of machinery) to fail to work: *The car broke down* —see also BROKEN-DOWN **4** [IØ] to fail: *The peace talks have broken down* **5** [IØ] (of a person) to lose control of one's feelings: *Peter broke down and wept when his mother died* **6** [T1;IØ: (*into*)] to (cause to) have a chemical change: *Chemicals in the body break down our food into useful substances* **7** [T1;IØ (*into*)] to (cause to) separate into different kinds or divide into types: *The figures must be broken down into several lists*

break·er /ˈbreɪkəʳ/ *n* a large wave with a white top that rolls onto the shore

-breaker *comb. form* a person or thing that breaks something: *Law-breakers must be punished*

break e·ven *v adv* [IØ] to do business without making either a profit or a loss

break·fast[1] /ˈbrekfəst/ *n* [C;U] the first meal of the day: *It happened at/during breakfast.|She likes eggs for breakfast.|Would you like breakfast now?*

breakfast[2] *v* [IØ (*on*)] to eat breakfast: *We breakfasted early (on orange juice, eggs, and coffee)*

break-in /ˈ· ·/ *n* **1** the unlawful entering of a building, using force: *15 break-ins in the last week* **2** the first use or performance of something new, done in especially easy conditions in preparation for more difficult ordinary conditions

break in *v adv* **1** [IØ] to enter a building by force: *He broke in and stole my money* **2** [IØ] to interrupt: *He broke in with some ideas of his own* **3** [T1] to bring under control; teach (a horse) to obey; help (someone) to become accustomed to work: *When horses are about 6 months old, they have to be broken in.|2 weeks in the new office should be enough to break you in*

breaking and en·ter·ing /ˌ·· · ˈ···/ *n* [U] the crime of HOUSEBREAKING

break in on also **break in up·on**— *v adv prep* [T1] to interrupt: *break in on someone's dreams/thoughts*

break in·to *v prep* [T1] **1** also **burst into**— to enter by force: *to break into a house* **2** to interrupt: *to break into a conversation|to break into the afternoon* **3** also **burst into**— to begin suddenly to give voice to: *to break into song/laughter* **4** to begin suddenly: *break into a run* **5** to use part of, unwillingly: *to break into the money one has saved*

break·neck /ˈbreɪknek/ *adj* [Wa5;A] very fast or dangerous: *breakneck speed*

break of *v prep* [D1] to cure (someone) of (a habit): *Doctors keep trying to break him of smoking/of his dependence on the drug*

break off *v adv* **1** [T1,4;IØ: (*with*)] to (cause to) end: *Those 2 countries have broken off relations (with each other) again.|He broke off (speaking) to answer the telephone.|Let's break off (work) and have some tea* **2** [T1;IØ] to (cause to) become separated from the main part with suddenness or violence, but not by cutting or tearing: *He broke off a branch and gave it to me.|A branch broke off (the tree) and I picked it up*

break·out /ˈbreɪkaʊt/ *n* a violent or forceful break from an enclosed space or a difficult state of affairs, esp. **a** a military attack to break from being surrounded **b** an escape from prison, usu. of several prisoners at once

break out *v adv* **1** [IØ] to begin suddenly: *War/A fire broke out* **2** [IØ (*in*)] to show or give voice to, suddenly: *His face broke out in spots.|She broke out in curses* **3** [IØ (*of*)] to escape (from): *to break out of prison* **4** [T1a] to open, unfold, etc.

break·through /ˈbreɪkθruː/ *n* **1** the action of forcing a way through the enemy: *a military breakthrough made at night* **2** the action of making a discovery (often suddenly and after earlier failures) that will lead to other discoveries: *Scientists have made a breakthrough in their treatment of that disease* **3** a discovery of this sort: *an important medical breakthrough*

break through[1] *v adv* [IØ] **1** to appear: *It was a cloudy day, but the sun at last broke through* **2** to make a new discovery that will lead to other discoveries: *Scientists hope to break through soon in their fight against heart disease* **3** to advance in spite of opposition: *Janet at last broke through and established herself as an important member of the government*

break through[2] *v prep* [T1] **1** to force a way through: *Have our soldiers broken through the enemy's defences yet?|The sun broke through the clouds* **2** to conquer, by discoveries: *Scientists have recently broken through another* BARRIER *to knowledge*

break·up /ˈbreɪkʌp/ *n* **1** (esp. of a relationship or association) a coming to an end: *the breakup of a marriage/of a firm* **2** a division into smaller parts: *the breakup of the large farms*

break up *v adv* **1** [T1;IØ] to (cause to) divide into smaller pieces: *Freezing weather will break up the soil* **2** [T1;IØ] *tech* **a** to take (a ship) apart; DISMANTLE **b** (of a ship) to be destroyed: *The ship broke up on the rocks* **3** [T1;IØ] to (cause to) come to an end: *The police broke up the fight.|The party broke up when the police arrived.|Their marriage broke up* **4** [IØ] to cease to be together: *The crowd broke up* **5** [IØ] *BrE* (of a school or pupil) to begin the holidays: *When does your school break up?|We break up early this year* **6** [IØ] also **split up**— to separate: *What will happen to the children if Jim and Mary break up?* **7** [T1;IØ] to (cause to) suffer severe anxiety and pain: *The bad news will break him up.|He may break up under all this trouble* —compare BREAK DOWN (5) **8** [T1] *AmE* to amuse greatly: *His funny story really broke me up*

break·wa·ter /ˈbreɪkˌwɔːtəʳ‖-ˌwɔ-, -ˌwɑ-/ *n* a thick wall built out into the sea to lessen the force of the waves near a harbour

break with *v prep* [T1] to cease one's connection

with: *to break with one's former friends/with old ideas*

bream /briːm/ *n* [Wn2] **1** a kind of freshwater fish with a thick flat body **2** a kind of salt-water fish (the **sea bream**)

breast¹ /brest/ *n* **1** either of the 2 parts of a woman's body that produce milk, or the smaller parts like these on a man's body: *a baby still at its mother's breast/at the breast* **2** *lit* the upper front part of the body between the neck and the stomach —see picture at HUMAN², BIRD **3** *lit* the part of the body where the feelings are supposed to be: *a troubled breast* —compare HEART (2), BOSOM¹ (3) **4 beat one's breast** *infml* to make a noisy open show of sorrow that may be partly pretence **5 make a clean breast of something** to tell the whole truth about something, esp. something unpleasant for oneself

breast² *v* [T1] **1** *lit* to stand up fearlessly against: *We must breast the storms of life* **2** *fml* to meet and push aside with one's chest: *The winner of the race breasted the* TAPE¹ (2).|(fig.) *The ship breasted the waves*

breast·bone /ˈbrestbəʊn/ *n* the upright bone in the front of the chest, to which the top 7 pairs of RIBs are connected —see picture at SKELETON

breast-feed /ˈ· ·/ *v* **-fed** /fed/ [Wv5;T1;I∅] to feed (a baby) with milk from the breast, not from a bottle: *Are breast-fed babies really happier?* —compare SUCKLE

breast·plate /ˈbrestpleɪt/ *n* a piece of armour worn to protect the chest

breast pock·et /ˌ· ˈ··/ *n* a pocket on the breast of a JACKET, esp. one worn by men

breast·stroke /ˈbrest-strəʊk/ *n* [(*the*) S] a way of swimming with one's chest downwards, by putting the arms in front of the head while drawing the knees forward and outwards and then sweeping the arms back while kicking backwards and outwards

breast·work /ˈbrestwɜːk‖-ɜrk/ *n* a defensive earth wall (EARTHWORK) built as high as a man's chest

breath /breθ/ *n* **1** [U] air taken into and breathed out of the lungs: *The horse's breath hung like a cloud over their heads on that cold day.|After all that running I have no breath left* **2** [C] an act of breathing air in and out once: *Take a deep breath, stick out your tongue, and say* "AH!"|(fig.) *Let's go out for a breath of fresh air* **3** [U] *lit* life: *I shall love you as long as I have breath* **4** [C *usu. sing.*] a movement of air; very slight wind: *Hardly a breath of air was moving* **5** [S+*of*] a word about or slight sign of (something): *There's a breath of spring in the air today* **6** [S] a moment (in the phrs. **in one breath, in the same breath, in the next breath**): *In one breath he said "yes" and in the next he said "no"!* **7 below/under one's breath** in a low voice or a whisper **8 the breath of life** something very necessary: *Admiration is the breath of life to a man like Jones* **9 catch one's breath a** to stop breathing suddenly (often under the influence of strong feeling): *The song was so beautiful it made me catch my breath* **b** to get one's BREATH (12): *Let me catch my breath after running so fast!* **10 draw/take breath** to have a rest or make a pause: *After running, they stopped to take breath* **11 first draw breath** *lit* to be born **12 get one's breath (back) (again)** to return to one's usual rate of breathing: *I need time to get my breath after running* **13 have no breath left** to find breathing hard (as after exercise) **14 hold one's breath** to stop breathing for a time: (fig.) *All Europe held its breath to see who would win the election* **15 one's last/dying breath** one's last moment of life **16 out of breath** breathing very rapidly (as from tiring exercise); BREATHLESS (2) **17 take one's breath away** to make one unable to speak (from surprise, pleasure, etc.): *She was so beautiful, it took my breath away* **18 waste one's breath** to talk uselessly, without effect **19 with bated breath** anxiously

breath·a·lyse /ˈbreθəl-aɪz/ *v* [T1] *infml* to test (a driver) with a BREATHALYSER

breath·a·lys·er /ˈbreθəl-aɪzəʳ/ *n infml* an apparatus used by the police in Britain to measure the amount of alcohol that the driver of a car has drunk

breathe /briːð/ *v* **1** [T1;I∅] to take into (and send out of) the lungs (air, gas, etc.): *It's healthy to breathe deeply.|He became ill after breathing coal dust for many years* **2** [I∅] *lit* to live: *I shall love you as long as I breathe!* **3** [T1] to say softly or whisper: *He breathed a prayer/a warning/words of love into her ear* **4** [T1 (*into*)] to give or send out (a smell, a feeling, etc.): *The new general was able to breathe courage/new life into the army.*|(fig.) *He really breathes fire when he gets angry!* **5** [I∅] (of flowers, wine, cloth, etc.) to take in air: *Open the wine so that it can breathe before we drink it* **6 As I live and breathe!** *infml* (an expression of surprise): *As I live and breathe, he's here again after 20 years!* **7 (be able to) breathe again** to feel calm after feeling anxious: *As soon as the policeman walked away we could breathe (freely) again* **8 breathe down someone's neck** *infml* to keep too close a watch on what someone is doing: *I can't work properly when you are breathing down my neck all the time* **9 breathe one's last** *fml or euph* to die

breathe in *v adv* **1** [T1;I∅] to take (air, gas, etc.) into the lungs: *Lie down on your back and breathe in, Mr. Jones. Good, good.|He became ill after breathing in a lot of coal dust* **2** [T1] to listen to closely, with great interest: *She breathed in every word he was saying*

breathe out *v adv* [I∅] to send air out of the lungs

breath·er /ˈbriːðəʳ/ *n* **1** (*usu. in comb.*) a person (or animal) that breathes: *a heavy breather* **2** *infml* a short pause for a rest: *We've been working quite a long time now: let's have/take a breather*

breath·ing /ˈbriːðɪŋ/ *n* [U] (*often in comb.*) the act or action of breathing: *heavy breathing*

breathing space /ˈ·· ·/ *n* [C;U] (a) period of inactivity, esp. for rest and getting ready for further efforts

breath·less /ˈbreθləs/ *adj* **1** [Wa5] not breathing; dead: *The body lay breathless on the bed: there was no sign of life* **2** breathing with difficulty; needing to breathe rapidly: *By the time I got to the top I was completely breathless* **3** causing one to breathe with difficulty: *breathless haste/hurry/speed* **4** causing one to stop breathing (because of excitement, fear, or other strong feeling): *a breathless silence during the exciting last game of the tennis match* **5** *rare* with no movement of air or wind: *The afternoon was hot and breathless, as if a storm were coming* —**~ly** *adv* —**~ness** *n* [U]

breath·tak·ing /ˈbreθˌteɪkɪŋ/ *adj* **1** very exciting: *a breathtaking horse race* **2** very unusual: *breathtaking beauty* —**~ly** *adv*: *breathtakingly beautiful*

breath·y /ˈbreθi/ *adj* [Wa2] (esp. of the voice) not clear or strong; with noticeable noise of breath: *a breathy voice* —**breathily** *adv* —**breathiness** *n* [U]

breech /briːtʃ/ *n* the end of a gun into which the shot or bullet is put

breech·es, *AmE* also **britches** /ˈbrɪtʃ½z/ *n* [P] **1** short trousers esp. for men, fastened at or below the knee: *knee-breeches* **2** *humor* trousers —see PAIR¹ (USAGE); see also RIDING BREECHES

breeches buoy /ˈ·· ˌ·/ *n* a means of saving a

person's life at sea, by which something like a pair of BREECHES of strong material, to hold the person, is pulled along a rope to bring him to the shore or to a boat

breech-load·er /ˈ· ˌ··/ *n* a gun which is loaded at the BREECH (the back end of the barrel), instead of through the MUZZLE (the front end of the barrel) as in earlier times

breed[1] /briːd/ *v* **bred** /bred/ **1** [IØ] (of animals) to produce young: *Some animals will not breed when kept in cages.*|(fig.) (*derog*) *Those people breed like rabbits* **2** [T1] to keep (usu. animals or fish) for the purpose of producing young, esp. where the choice of parents is controlled: *He breeds cattle* **3** [T1] to train; educate; cause to develop; bring up: *Northern countries breed people who can live in cold weather* **4** [T1] to cause or be the beginning of: *Flies in foodshops breed disease* **5 born and bred** /ˌ· · ˈ·/ by birth and training or education: *He is a countryman born and bred, and he doesn't like big cities*

breed[2] *n* a kind or class of animal (or plant) usu. developed under the influence of man: *a breed of dog*|(fig.) *a fine breed of man*

breed·er /ˈbriːdəʳ/ *n* **1** a person who BREEDs[1] (2) animals, birds, or fish **2** an animal, bird, or fish that produces young: *Cows of that type are good breeders*

breed·ing /ˈbriːdɪŋ/ *n* [U] **1** the producing of young by animals, birds, or fish (or plants) **2** the business of keeping animals, birds, or fish for the purpose of obtaining new and better kinds, or young for sale: *cattle-breeding* **3** (training in) polite social behaviour: *A person of fine breeding behaves well on all occasions* **4 birth and breeding** good birth, education, and social behaviour: *a gentleman by birth and breeding*

breeding-ground /ˈ·· ·/ *n* **1** a place where the young, esp. of wild creatures, are produced: *Sea cliffs are the breeding-ground of many sea-birds* **2** the place or point of origin (often of something bad): *Dirt is the breeding-ground of disease*

breeze[1] /briːz/ *n* **1** a light gentle wind **2** *tech* a wind of from 4 to 31 miles per hour **3** *esp AmE sl* something easily done: *Learning English is a breeze? You must be joking!* **4 in a breeze** *sl, esp. AmE* easily: *He won the competition in a breeze* **5 shoot the breeze** *AmE sl* to have a light conversation: *Hank and Gus were shooting the breeze while Chuck poured the drinks*

breeze[2] *v* [L9] *infml* to move swiftly and unceremoniously: *He just breezed in, asked me to lend him £50, and, when I said "no", breezed out again!*|*She breezed along, smiling at everyone*

breeze·block /ˈbriːzblɒk‖-blɑk/ *n BrE* a lightweight building-block made of cement and small pieces of burnt coal (CINDERs) —see picture at SITE[1]

breeze through also **sail through**— *v prep* [T1] *infml* to go through or pass easily: *She breezed through that difficult book with no trouble at all!*|*You should breeze through the examination if you know the subject well*

breez·y /ˈbriːzi/ *adj* [Wa1] **1** of or having fairly strong BREEZEs: *It's quite breezy today, so it will be a good day to dry the wet washing* **2** quick, cheerful, and unceremonious; merry, light, and bright in manner: *His breezy manner made him popular with the other workers, but not with his employer* —**breezily** *adv* —**breeziness** *n* [U]

Bren gun /ˈbren gʌn/ *n* a type of light rapid-firing gun (MACHINEGUN)

breth·ren /ˈbreðrən/ *n* [P;N] (usu. in formal or solemn address or in speaking of the members of a profession, association, or religious group) brothers: *dearly* BELOVED *brethren*

breve /briːv/ *n* **1** a curved mark ◡ used for showing that a sound or part of a word is pronounced short, esp. in poetry **2** a long musical note equal to 2 SEMIBREVEs —see picture at NOTATION

brev·et /ˈbrevɨt‖brɨˈvet/ *n* a written official statement giving a military officer a higher rank without an increase in pay

bre·via·ry /ˈbriːvɪəri, ˈbre-‖-ieri/ *n* a book used in the ROMAN CATHOLIC church, containing the prayers to be said on each day by priests

brev·i·ty /ˈbrevɨti/ *n* [U] (of non-material things) shortness: *the brevity of his writing/his life*

brew[1] /bruː/ *v* **1** [T1;(IØ)] to make (beer) **2** [T1; IØ: (UP)] **a** to mix (tea or coffee) with hot water and prepare for drinking **b** (of tea or coffee) to become ready for drinking after being mixed with hot water **3** [T1 (UP)] to prepare (esp. something bad): *He's brewing some sort of trouble for us all* **4** [IØ] (esp. of something bad) to be in preparation or ready to happen; develop: *Trouble/A storm was brewing*

brew[2] *n* **1** the result of BREWing[1]: *Is this brew to your taste? Do you like it?* **2** the amount of liquid BREWed[1] at one time: *You'll need a big brew for all those people* **3** the nature or quality of what is BREWed[1]: *I like a stronger brew (of tea)*

brew·er /ˈbruːəʳ/ *n* a person who makes beer

brewer's droop /ˌ·· ˈ·/ *n* [U] *BrE humor* the inability of a man to make his sexual organ become larger (ERECT[1]), owing to drinking too much alcohol

brew·er·y /ˈbruːəri/ *n* a place where beer is made

brew-up /ˈ· ·/ *n BrE infml* the act or action of making tea (or sometimes coffee): *Let's have a brew-up: how do you like your tea?*

bri·ar /ˈbraɪəʳ/ *n* **1** [C] a tobacco pipe made from the root of a BRIER **2** [C;U] BRIER

bribe[1] /braɪb/ *v* **1** [T1 (*with* or *into*);V3] to influence unfairly (esp. someone in a position of trust) by favours or gifts: *He bribed the policeman (to let him go free/into letting him go free).*|(fig.) *The child was bribed with a piece of cake to go to bed quietly* **2** [X9] to get or make in this way: *He bribed himself/his way onto the committee*

bribe[2] *n* something offered or given in bribing (BRIBE[1]): *The official was charged with taking bribes from people who wanted favours in return*

brib·er·y /ˈbraɪbəri/ *n* [U] the act or practice of giving or taking a BRIBE[2]

bric-a-brac /ˈbrɪk ə ˌbræk/ *n* [U] small ornaments in a house

brick /brɪk/ *n* **1** [C;U] (a hard piece of) baked clay used for building: *He used yellow bricks to build his house.*|*a red brick house*|*The house is brick, not wood.*|*The colour is brick-red* —see picture at SITE[1] **2** [C] something in the shape of a brick (esp. in the phr: **a brick of ice cream**) **3** [C] (*AmE* **block**)— *BrE* a small building block as a child's toy **4** [C] *BrE sl* a very nice trustworthy person (esp. a man); good friend **5 beat/run one's head against a brick wall** *infml* to hurt oneself or waste one's efforts by trying to do something impossible **6 (come down) like a ton of bricks** *sl* (to come down) with sudden crushing weight or force or in sudden anger: *He came down on me like a ton of bricks when I asked to use his car* **7 drop a brick** *BrE sl* to make a foolish remark which hurts someone's feelings; make a GAFFE **8 make bricks without straw** to do work without the necessary materials or money

brick·bat /ˈbrɪkbæt/ *n* **1** a piece of something hard (like a brick), esp. when thrown in anger **2** *infml* an attack using words: *The minister was at the* *receiving end of a lot of parliamentary brickbats for his handling of the affair*

brick·field /ˈbrɪkfiːld/ also (*esp. AmE*) **brick·yard** /-jɑːd‖-jard/— *n* a place where bricks are made

brick·lay·er /ˈbrɪkˌleɪəʳ/ *n* a workman who lays bricks (=puts bricks in place) —**-laying** *n* [U]

brick o·ver *v adv* [T1] to cover completely with bricks: *In former times, people bricked over some of their windows to avoid the window tax*

brick up *v adv* [T1] **1** also **brick in**— to fill completely with bricks: *They've bricked up the space between the 2 rooms* **2** to enclose behind a wall of bricks: *When he'd murdered his wife, he bricked her body up in the kitchen*

brick·work /ˈbrɪkwɜːk‖-ɜrk/ *n* [U] any piece of building work in which bricks are used; bricks put together in the form of a wall or ornament: *ornamental brickwork round the windows*

brid·al /ˈbraɪdl/ *adj* [Wa5] of the BRIDE or the marriage ceremony: *a bridal dress|ceremony*

bride /braɪd/ *n* a girl or woman about to be married, or just married: *Here comes the bride, all dressed in white* (wedding song) —see WOMAN (USAGE)

bride·groom /ˈbraɪdgruːm, -grʊm/ also **groom**— *n* a man about to be married, or just married

brides·maid /ˈbraɪdzmeɪd/ *n* an unmarried girl or woman (usu. one of several) who attends the BRIDE on the day of the marriage ceremony: *Poor girl! She's always a bridesmaid, never a* BRIDE (old saying)

bride-to-be /ˌ·· ˈ·/ *n* **brides-to-be** a future BRIDE

bridge[1] /brɪdʒ/ *n* **1** something that carries a road over a valley, river, etc., and is usu. built of wood, stone, iron, etc. **2** the raised part of a ship on which the captain and other officers stand when on duty —see picture at FREIGHTER **3** the bony upper part of the nose, between the eyes —see picture at HUMAN[2] **4** the part of a pair of glasses for the eyes that joins them and rests on or above the nose —see picture at EYE[1] **5** a small movable part of a stringed musical instrument, used for keeping the strings stretched —see picture at STRINGED INSTRUMENT **6** a small piece of metal for keeping false (man-made) teeth in place. It is fastened to the natural teeth **7 A lot of water has flowed under the bridge (since then)** A great deal has happened (since then) **8 Don't cross your bridges before you come/get to them** Don't waste time thinking about difficulties which may never arise

bridge[2] *v* [T1] to build a bridge across: *to bridge a river*

bridge[3] *n* [U] a card game for 4 players developed from the game of WHIST and usu. played as CONTRACT BRIDGE or sometimes AUCTION BRIDGE

bridge·head /ˈbrɪdʒhed/ *n* **1** a strong position far forward in enemy land from which an attack will be made on the enemy **2** a position well forward, from which further advances can be made: *This discovery will be a bridgehead for additional discoveries in science* —compare BEACHHEAD

bridge o·ver *v adv* **1** [T1a] to find a way to deal with, at least for a short time: *to bridge over someone's difficulties* **2** [T1b] to help (someone) at least for a short time: *This money should bridge you over till next month*

bridge·work /ˈbrɪdʒwɜ‖-ɜrk/ *n* [U] *esp. AmE* the BRIDGE*s*[1] (6) in a mouth

bri·dle[1] /ˈbraɪdl/ *n* leather bands put on a horse's head for controlling its movements —see picture at HORSE

bridle[2] *v* **1** [T1] to put a BRIDLE[1] on: *When the horse has been bridled we can start the journey* **2** [T1] to hold back; bring under control: *Bridle your tongue and be more careful what you say* **3** [IØ (*at*)] to show anger or displeasure, esp. by making a proud upward movement of the head and body: *I asked her to do it, but she bridled* (*with anger*) (*at the suggestion*)

bridle path /ˈ·· ·/ *n* a path made especially for horseback riding, but not for vehicles

Brie /briː/ *n* [U] a type of soft French cheese

brief[1] /briːf/ *adj* [Wa1] **1** *fml* short, esp. in time: *Life is brief.|a brief look at the newspaper|a brief letter* **2 in brief** in a shortened form; in as few words as possible: *It's a long letter, but in brief, he says "No"* **3 brief and to the point** (of speech or writing) short and exactly expressing the intended meaning: *The letter was brief and to the point: it said "No"* —**~ly** *adv*: *He spoke briefly.|Briefly, he said "No"*

brief[2] *n* **1** a short spoken or written statement, esp. one giving facts or arguments about a law case **2** *esp. BrE* a set of instructions setting limits to someone's powers or duties: (fig.) *It's not part of my brief to tell him what to do, but . . .* **3 hold no brief for** not be in favour of: *I hold no brief for severe punishment, but we must get the child to obey somehow!*

brief[3] *v* [T1] to give last instructions or necessary information to: *to brief a bombing pilot and his men before the attack.|Before the meeting, let me brief you on what to expect*

brief·case /ˈbriːfkeɪs/ *n* a flat usu. soft leather case for carrying papers or books, which opens at the top —compare ATTACHÉ CASE

brief·ing /ˈbriːfɪŋ/ *n* [C;U] an act or the action of giving last instructions or necessary information: *Before the meeting, let me give you a briefing*

briefs /briːfs/ *n* [P] very short close-fitting UNDERPANTS or PANTIES —see PAIR[1] (USAGE)

brier, briar /braɪəʳ/ *n* **1** [C] a wild bush covered with prickles (THORN*s*), esp. the wild rose bush **2** [U] a group or mass of such bushes

brig /brɪg/ *n* **1** a ship with 2 MAST*s* (=poles carrying sails) and large square sails on both of them **2** *AmE infml* a room or building where soldiers or sailors are locked up as punishment; military prison

bri·gade /brɪˈgeɪd/ *n* **1** a part of an army, of about 5,000 soldiers **2** a group of people, usu. with a special uniform, who have certain duties, such as putting out fires: *the Fire Brigade*

brig·a·dier /ˌbrɪgəˈdɪəʳ/ *n* an officer of middle rank in the British army, commanding a BRIGADE

brigadier-gen·eral /ˌ··· ˈ··/ *n* **1** an officer of high rank in the British army **2** an officer of middle rank in the American army, AIRFORCE, or MARINE CORPS

brig·and /ˈbrɪgənd/ *n fml or lit* an armed thief, esp. one of a band of thieves living in mountains; BANDIT

brig·and·age /ˈbrɪgəndɪdʒ/ *n* [U] the activities of BRIGAND*s*; lawlessness

brig·an·tine /ˈbrɪgəntiːn/ *n* a ship like a BRIG (1), but with fewer sails

bright /braɪt/ *adj* [Wa1] **1** giving out or throwing back light very strongly; full of light; shining: *The sun is brighter than the moon.|What a bright sunny day!* **2** (of a colour) strong, clear, and easily seen: *bright red/yellow* **3** famous; glorious: *one of the brightest moments in our country's history* **4** full of life; cheerful; happy; gay: *Her face was bright with happiness|bright eyes* **5** (of a person who is) clever; quick at learning: *a bright child/idea* **6** showing hope or signs of future success: *You have a bright future ahead of you, my boy!* **7 look on/at the bright side (of things)** to be cheerful and hopeful in spite of difficulties —**~ly** *adv* —**~ness** *n* [U]

bright·en /ˈbraɪtn/ *v* [T1;I∅: (UP)] to (cause to) become bright: *The day/The future is brightening* (*up*).|*She has brightened* (*up*) *my whole life*

Bright's di·sease /ˈ· ·ˌ·/ *n* [R] a serious disease of the KIDNEY*s*, with pain and swelling

brill /brɪl/ *n* [Wn2] a type of European flat seafish like the TURBOT

bril·lian·cy /ˈbrɪlɪənsi/ *n* [U] the quality of being BRILLIANT

bril·liant[1] /ˈbrɪlɪənt/ *adj* **1** very bright, splendid, or showy in appearance: *brilliant blue|brilliant stars* **2** very clever; causing great admiration or satisfaction: *a brilliant speaker/scientist* **3** having or showing great skill (esp. in playing a musical instrument) but perhaps not enough feeling or understanding: *a brilliant piece of music|a brilliant style of playing* —**-liance** *n* [U] —**~ly** *adv*

brilliant[2] *n* **1** a precious stone cut in a pointed shape **2** a common stone cut to make it look like a precious stone

bril·lian·tine /ˈbrɪlɪəntiːn/ *n* [U] an oily mixture for making men's hair shine and lie flat

brim[1] /brɪm/ *n* **1** the top edge of a cup, glass, bowl, etc., esp. with regard to the quantity of the contents: *The glass was full to the brim* **2** the bottom part of a hat which turns outwards to give shade or protection against rain —compare CROWN[1] (7)

brim[2] *v* **-mm-** [I∅ (OVER)] to be BRIMFUL: *Her eyes brimmed* (*over*) *with tears.|a brimming cup of coffee*

brim·ful, -full /ˈbrɪmˌfʊl/ *adj* [Wa5;F (*of* or *with*)] full to the top (or BRIM[1] (1)); overflowing: *She filled the bowl brimful with sugar.|Her eyes were brimful of tears.*|(fig.) *He was brimful of suggestions*

-brimmed /brɪmd/ *comb form* (of hats) having a BRIM[1] (2) of the stated kind: *a broad-brimmed hat*

brim o·ver *v adv* [I∅ (*with*)] to express a lot of (usu. a good feeling): *brimming over* (*with joy*) —compare BUBBLE[1] (3)

brim·stone /ˈbrɪmstəʊn, -stən/ *n* [U] **1** the chemical substance SULPHUR **2 fire and brimstone** the fires of HELL, believed to be a punishment after death for those who have done wrong

brin·dled /ˈbrɪndəld/ *adj* (esp. of cows and cats) having brownish or reddish-brown fur or hair with marks or bands of another colour

brine /braɪn/ *n* [U] **1** water containing quite a lot of salt, used for preserving food **2** *lit* seawater —**briny** *adj* [Wa2]

bring /brɪŋ/ *v* **brought** /brɔːt/ **1** [D1 (*to, for*);T1] to come with or lead: *Bring me the book.|Bring your friend to the party.|Bring an answer.|The prisoner was brought before the judge.|The soldier's brave deeds brought him honour and glory.|The beauty of the music brought tears to her eyes* —see USAGE **2** [T1;V3] to cause or lead to: *Spring rains bring summer flowers.|What brought you to do it?|He could never bring himself to kill an animal or bird* **3** [D1;T1] to sell or be sold for: *This old car will bring about £10.|What/How much would a new car bring?|The pictures he sells bring him £12,000 a year* **4** [T1 (*against*)] *law* to make officially: *The policeman brought a charge against the fast driver.|The neighbours brought a complaint against that noisy family* **5** [T1;V4] to cause to come: *Her cries brought the neighbours* (*running*).|*One sad letter from his wife brought many offers of help/brought him crying home* **6** [X9] to cause to reach a certain state: *Bring them in/out/back/together.|to bring something into being/into action/to an end|to bring someone low* (*in defeat*)|*to bring someone to his knees* (*in defeat*) **7 bring to book** to force to give an explanation, or to be punished: *He was at last brought to book for his crimes* —see also BRING ABOUT, BRING AROUND, BRING BACK, BRING DOWN, BRING DOWN ON, BRING FORTH, BRING FORWARD, BRING IN, BRING INTO, BRING OFF, BRING ON[1,2], BRING OUT, BRING OVER, BRING ROUND, BRING THROUGH[1,2], BRING TO, BRING TOGETHER, BRING UNDER[1,2], BRING UP, BRING UP AGAINST

USAGE **Bring** means "cause to come with one, towards or with the speaker": **Bring** *the scissors/your mother here.|I* **brought** *this book away with me.* The opposite of this meaning is **take away. Take** means "cause to go with one": *Let's* **take** *Mary to the cinema.* **Carry** means "cause to come or go with one by giving support": *He* **carried** *the child/the bag on his back.|A bus* **carries** *passengers.* **Fetch** means "go and get and bring back": *Please* **fetch** *the scissors from my bedroom/the children from school.*

bring a·bout *v adv* **1** [T1a,(1)] to cause: *Science has brought about many changes in our lives* **2** [T1b] also **bring around, bring round**— to change the direction of (a boat) so as to face the opposite way: *If the wind changes, you'll have to bring the boat/her about*

bring a·round *v adv* [T1] **1** [(*to*)] also **bring over, bring round**— to persuade into a change of opinion: *We must bring him around to our point of view* **2** BRING ABOUT (2) **3** BRING ROUND (1)

bring back *v adv* **1** [D1 (*to*);T1] to return or cause to return: *All library books must be brought back before June 20.|If you go to the meeting, would you mind bringing me back?|Bring us back our books, please.|Bring us our books back, please* **2** [D1 (*for*); T1] to obtain and return with: *When you go to the post office, will you please bring me back some stamps?|Will you please bring me some stamps back?|Will you please bring some stamps back for me?* **3** [T1] to cause to return to the mind: *The Beatles singing "Yesterday": that certainly brings back memories!* **4** [T1 (*to*)] to cause to return (to health, existence, etc.): *They want to bring back hanging as a punishment*

bring down *v adv* [T1] **1** to cause to fall or come down: *The pilot brought the plane down gently* **2** to cause to fall or come down by force: *to bring down a plane with gunfire|He brought the deer down with one shot* **3** [(*to*)] **a** to reduce (prices): *to bring down the price* **b** to cause to reduce prices: *to bring the salesman down to a lower price* **4** to move (a figure) from one list to another, when dividing: *to bring down the next 2 figures* **5** to cause to continue (from earlier to later times): *To bring our story down to the present day . . .* **6** [(*to*)] to reduce or lower (to): *to bring someone down to your own level* **7 bring the house down/bring down the house** *infml* to give a performance that everybody likes very much

bring down on *v adv prep* [D1] to cause (something bad) to happen to: *to bring down trouble/bring trouble down on the whole family*

bring forth *v adv* [T1a] *old use* to produce, esp. give birth to: *"Bring forth men children only"* (Shakespeare, *Macbeth*)

bring for·ward *v adv* [T1] **1** (in BOOKKEEPING) to move to the top of a list of figures (the total at the bottom of an earlier page), before adding in the figures on the new page: *The total at the top of the page, is marked "brought forward"* **2** also **put forward**— to bring nearer the time of: *The election will be brought forward to June, as so many people are on holiday in July* **3** to introduce; suggest: *A plan was brought forward to allow workers to share in the profits* **4** to produce (esp. something not material): *Can the prisoner bring forward any proof of his story?*

bring in *v adv* **1** [T1;D1] to produce as profit or earnings; earn: *The sale brought* (*us*) *in over £200.*|

The boys are bringing in £60 a week **2** [T1] to introduce: *to bring in a* BILL[3] *(in Parliament)|to bring in a new fashion* **3** [T1;V3] to ask (someone) to come to one's help: *to bring in experienced people to advise* **4** [T1] to give a decision in court: *to bring in a* VERDICT *of guilty or not guilty* **5** [T1] to take to a police station: *The policeman brought in 2 boys whom he had caught stealing*

bring in·to *v prep* [D1] to cause (an activity or condition) to start: *to bring (something) into being/into play/into force*

bring off *v adv* [T1] **1** to take (usu. a person) from a dangerous place: *to bring off the shipwrecked sailors* **2** to succeed in (something difficult): *to bring off a big business deal*

bring on[1] *v adv* [T1] **1** to cause: *Going out in the rain brought on a fever* **2** to cause to advance, grow, or come earlier: *This warm weather should bring on the crops* **3** [(*in*)] to help or improve: *More study should bring on your English.|More study should bring you on in English*

bring on[2] also **bring up·on**— *v prep* [D1] to cause (something, usu. unpleasant) to happen to (esp. oneself): *You've brought the trouble on yourself*

bring out *v adv* **1** [T1;D1] to produce: *to bring out a new kind of soap* **2** [T1] also **draw out**— to cause to develop; cause to be seen: *Difficulties can bring out a person's best qualities.|to bring out the meaning|to bring out the worst in someone* **3** [T1] also **draw out**— to encourage, esp. to encourage to talk: *Mary is very quiet: try to bring her out at the party* **4** [T1] to cause to stop working for a purpose (STRIKE[1]): *We'll bring the workers out for more pay* **5** [T1] *becoming rare* to introduce (usu. a young lady) into the social life of a great city —see also COME OUT (7)

bring o·ver *v adv* [T1] **1** (on a boat) to cause (sails) to swing to the other side **2** BRING AROUND (1)

bring round *v adv* [T1] **1** also **bring to**— to cause to regain consciousness: *Peter has fainted: try to bring him round* **2** to cause (a boat or ship) to face the opposite way: *They brought the boat/her round* **3** BRING ABOUT (2) **4** [(*to*)] BRING AROUND (1)

bring through[1] *v adv* [T1] to save the life of (someone very ill): *Can the doctor bring Mother through?* —see also PULL THROUGH (1)

bring through[2] also **carry through**— *v prep* [D1] to save (someone) from: *The doctor brought Mother through a serious illness.|The people's courage brought them through the war*

bring to *v adv* **1** [T1;I∅] also **bring up**— **a** to cause a ship or boat to stop **b** (of a ship or boat) to stop **2** [T1] BRING ROUND (1)

bring to·geth·er *v adv* [T1b] to cause (esp. a man and a woman) to meet: *I'm so glad to have been the means of bringing you 2 together —you are so right for each other!*

bring un·der[1] *v adv* [T1b] to control and defeat, usu. by political force: *Those who oppose our wishes will be brought under* —compare KEEP UNDER

bring under[2] *v prep* [D1] to include in a type: *We can bring your suggestions under several headings* —compare COME UNDER (3)

bring up *v adv* **1** [T1] to educate and care for in the family until grown-up: *to bring up children* **2** [T1] to raise or introduce (a subject): *to bring up the question of* —compare COME UP (1) **3** [T1;(I∅)] *esp. BrE* to be sick; VOMIT[2] (one's food) **4** [T1 *usu. pass.*] to cause to stop suddenly: *John was about to enter the room, when he was brought up short by a note on the door* **5** [T1] to cause to arrive: *to bring up more soldiers* **6** [T1 (*to*)] to cause to reach: *That brings the total up (to £200)* **7** [T1 (*for*)] *esp. BrE infml* to speak severely to: *Mother is always bringing the boy up for his bad behaviour* **8** [T1] HAVE UP **9** [T1;I∅] BRING TO **10 bring up the rear** to be the last in a line or in a group of soldiers

bring up a·gainst *v adv prep* [D1] **1** [*usu. pass.*] to cause to meet (opposition): *Things were working well when we were brought up against unexpected delays* **2** [*often pass.*] to raise to the disadvantage of: *Your prison record may be brought up against you*

brink /brɪŋk/ *n* [*usu. sing.*] **1** an edge at the top of a cliff or other steep high point **2** a state of dangerous nearness (usu. something unpleasant or exciting); VERGE (2) (esp. in the phrs. **on/to the brink of**): *His failures brought him to the brink of ruin* **3 to/on the brink of the grave** very near death

brink·man·ship /ˈbrɪŋkmənʃɪp/ also (*rare*) **brinks·man·ship** /ˈbrɪŋks-/— *n* [U] *infml* the art or practice of pushing a dangerous state of affairs to the limit of safety before stopping

briny deep /ˌ·· ˈ·/ also (*infml*) **briny**— *n* [*the*+R] *lit or pomp* the sea

bri·oche /ˈbriːɒʃ, briːˈəʊʃ‖briːˈəʊʃ, -ˈɔʃ (*Fr* briɔʃ)/ *n Fr* a small cake made with a lot of eggs and butter

bri·quette, briquet /brɪˈket/ *n* coal dust mixed with a substance that binds it together (such as TAR) pressed into a block for burning in a fireplace

brisk /brɪsk/ *adj* [Wa2] **1** quick and active: *a brisk walker/walk* **2** (esp. of wind and air) filling with desire for activity; pleasantly cold and strong: *a brisk wind* —**~ly** *adv* —**~ness** *n* [U]

bris·ket /ˈbrɪskɨt/ *n* [C;U] the breast or lower chest of a 4-footed animal, esp. as meat for eating

bris·tle[1] /ˈbrɪsəl/ *n* [C;U] (a) short stiff coarse hair: *His face was covered with bristles*

bristle[2] *v* [I∅ (UP, *with*)] (esp. of hair, fur, etc.) to stand up stiffly: *His hair bristled (up) with anger*

bristle with *v prep* [T1] **1** to show (as anger and/or a strong desire not to yield): *He bristled with anger* **2** to have plenty of (usu. something unpleasant): *This job bristles with difficulties*

bris·tly /ˈbrɪsli/ *adj* [Wa2] **1** like or full of BRISTLES[1]: *This brush is too hard and bristly: please give me a softer one* **2** (esp. of people) difficult to deal with because quick to become angry

bris·tols /ˈbrɪstlz/ *n* [P] *BrE sl* a woman's breasts

Brit BR (2)

britch·es /ˈbrɪtʃɨz/ *n* [P] *AmE* BREECHES

Brit·ish /ˈbrɪtɪʃ/ *adj* [Wa5] **1** of Britain or the British COMMONWEALTH: *a British citizen|I'm German, but my wife is British* **2** of Britain: *The British drink a great deal of tea*

British Eng·lish /ˌ·· ˈ··/ *n* [U] the English spoken by British people (as being different from that spoken by Americans, Australians, etc.)

Brit·ish·er /ˈbrɪtɪʃəʳ/ *n AmE* a native of Britain

British therm·al u·nit /ˌ·· ˈ·· ··/ *n* the quantity of heat needed to raise one pound of water one degree FAHRENHEIT

Brit·on /ˈbrɪtn/ *n* a native of Britain: *The ancient Britons used to paint themselves blue*

brit·tle /ˈbrɪtl/ *adj* [Wa2] **1** hard but easily broken: *brittle glass* **2** easily damaged or destroyed: *a brittle friendship|a brittle agreement* **3** easily hurt or offended: *a brittle nature* **4** lacking WARMTH or depth of feeling: *a brittle, cold person|brittle gayness or humour*

broach /brəʊtʃ/ *v* [T1] **1 a** to open (an unopened bottle) **b** *tech* to put a TAP in (a barrel) in order to draw off the liquid inside **2** [(*to*)] to introduce as a subject of conversation (esp. in the phr. **broach a/the subject**): *At last he broached the subject of their marriage (to her)*

broad[1] /brɔːd/ *adj* [Wa1] **1** [B] wide; measuring a good deal from side to side or between limits: *broad shoulders|a broad river* **2** [E] (after an expression of measurement) in width; across: *12 feet/4 metres broad* **3** [B] stretching out far and wide: *broad fields* **4** [B] not limited; generous in thought: *broad opinions* **5** [A] general; not particular: *I have a broad general idea of your plan: now give me the details* **6** [B] (of a work of art) bold in effect; showing great imagination: *the broad sweep of the painter's brushwork/imagination* **7** [B] plain; easy to see or understand: *a broad suggestion* **8** [A] full and clear (esp. in the phr. **broad daylight**) **9** [B] *esp. BrE* of a way of speaking typical of a part of Great Britain, and different from standard English: *He spoke broad Scots* **10** [B] (esp. of subjects for laughter) too bold and rude, esp. about sexual matters; not acceptable in polite society: *broad jokes/broad* COMEDY **11 it's as broad as it's long** *BrE* it makes no difference; it does not matter: *"Shall we go by bus or train?" "I don't mind; it's as broad as it's long"* —**~ly** *adv*: *Broadly (speaking), I agree with you* —**~ness** *n* [U]

broad² *n* **1** *AmE sl* a woman **2** [*usu. pl.*] (*usu. cap. as part of a name*) a lakelike stretch of water formed where a river broadens out, esp. in eastern England: *the Norfolk Broads*

broad bean /ˌ· ˈ·‖ˈ· ·/ *n* a large flat kind of bean grown to be eaten as a fresh vegetable —compare LIMA BEAN

broad·cast¹ /ˈbrɔːdkɑːst‖-kæst/ *adj* [Wa5;A] **1** made public by means of radio (or television): *broadcast news* **2** of or related to radio (or television) broadcasting: *broadcast time*

broadcast² *n* a single radio (or television) presentation: *He gave a group of broadcasts*

broadcast³ *v* **broadcast** **1** [T1] to make widely known: *to broadcast the news to all one's friends* **2** [T1] to send out or give as a radio (or television) presentation: *The BBC will broadcast the news at 10 o'clock* **3** [I∅] to send out one or more radio (or television) presentations: *The BBC broadcasts every day* **4** [I∅] to speak or perform on radio (or perhaps television): *He's broadcasting very often these days* —**~er** *n*

broad·cast·ing /ˈbrɔːdˌkɑːstɪŋ‖-ˌkæs-/ *n* [U] the action or activity of sending out sound (or images) by means of radio (or television)

Broad Church /ˌ· ˈ·/ *adj* of, about, or belonging to a group within the CHURCH OF ENGLAND (during the later 19th century) who favoured greater freedom in matters of official belief —**~man** *n*

broad·cloth /ˈbrɔːdklɒθ‖-klɔθ/ *n* [U] thick cloth, made of wool, of very good quality

broad·en /ˈbrɔːdn/ *v* [T1;I∅ (OUT)] to (cause to) become broad or broader: *Travel broadens the mind.|The river broadens (out) at this point*

broad gauge /ˌ· ˈ·/ *adj tech* (of a railway track) of greater than standard width

broad jump /ˈ· ·/ *n* [*the*+R;(C)] *AmE* LONG JUMP

broad·loom /ˈbrɔːdluːm/ *adj, n tech* (a floor covering (CARPET)) which is woven on a wide LOOM¹, esp. in one single colour

broad·mind·ed /ˌbrɔːdˈmaɪndɪ̈d◂/ *adj* having or showing willingness to respect the opinions (and actions) of others even if very different from one's own —**~ly** *adv* —**~ness** *n* [U]

broad·sheet /ˈbrɔːdʃiːt/ *n* **1** *old use* a sheet of paper printed on one or both sides and folded **2** something (as a poem or an advertisement) printed on such a sheet

broad·side /ˈbrɔːdsaɪd/ *n* **1** the side of a ship above the WATERLINE **2** *rare* a broad or unbroken surface **3** the firing of all the guns on one side of a ship at the same time **4** a forceful attack in words, spoken or printed **5** BROADSHEET

broad·sword /ˈbrɔːdsɔːd‖-ord/ *n old use or lit* a sword with a broad flat cutting blade, esp. one held and swung with both hands

broad·ways /ˈbrɔːdweɪz/ also **broad·wise** /-waɪz/— *adv* with the broadest side or part in the front

bro·cade¹ /brəˈkeɪd‖brəʊ-/ *n* [U] ornamental cloth usu. of silk often with a raised pattern of gold or silver threads

brocade² *v* [Wv5;T1] to ornament (cloth) with a raised pattern

broc·co·li /ˈbrɒkəli‖ˈbrɑ-/ *n* a type of open branching CAULIFLOWER whose young flower heads are eaten as a vegetable

bro·chure /ˈbrəʊʃəʳ, -ʃʊəʳ‖brəʊˈʃʊər/ *n* a small thin book (BOOKLET; PAMPHLET), esp. one giving instructions or details of a service offered for money: *a holiday brochure|an advertising brochure*

brogue¹ /brəʊg/ *n* [*usu. pl.*] a strong thick shoe, esp. one with a pattern made in the leather, worn by men or women

brogue² *n* [*usu. sing.*] the way in which the Irish speak English: *a strong rich musical (Irish) brogue*

broil¹ /brɔɪl/ *v* **1** [T1] *esp. AmE* GRILL¹ (1) (esp. chicken, meat, or fish) —see COOK² (USAGE) **2** [Wv4,5;T1;I∅] to (cause to) be very hot or too hot: *It's really broiling today!|I'm broiling in this hot sun!|I really got broiled beside the sea yesterday* **3 broiling hot** /ˌ·· ˈ·◂/ very or too hot

broil² *n lit* a noisy quarrel or argument

broil·er /ˈbrɔɪləʳ/ *n* **1** *AmE* a person or kitchen apparatus that cooks by BROILing¹ **2** a young small chicken raised esp. to be cooked by BROILing¹ (or GRILLing¹) **3** *infml* a very hot day: *Yesterday was a real broiler!* **4** *lit* a noisy quarreller

broke¹ /brəʊk/ *adj* [Wa5;F] *sl* completely without money (often in the phrs. **flat**/(*BrE*) **stony broke**): *He/His firm is (flat/stony) broke.|His firm has gone broke*

broke² *past t. of* BREAK¹

bro·ken¹ /ˈbrəʊkən/ *adj* [Wa5] **1** violently separated into smaller pieces: *a window broken by a ball* **2** damaged, spoilt, or made useless by breaking: *a broken clock/leg* **3** (of land surfaces) irregular, interrupted, or full of stones, etc.: *broken fields* **4** (of agreements, laws, etc.) disobeyed or not fulfilled: *a broken law/promise* **5** where man and wife are no longer living together: *a broken marriage|a broken home* **6** discontinuous; interrupted: *a broken journey* **7** made weak; crushed: *broken dreams|a broken spirit|a broken man* **8** imperfectly spoken or written: *broken English* —**~ly** *adv* —**~ness** *n* [U]

broken² *past p. of* BREAK¹

broken-down /ˌ·· ˈ·◂/ *adj* worn out in body or mind; in a state of disrepair or decay: *a broken-down old car/horse*

broken-heart·ed /ˌ·· ˈ··◂/ *adj* (of a person who is) unable to struggle against deep grief —**~ly** *adv*

bro·ker /ˈbrəʊkəʳ/ *n* **1** a person who does business for another, esp. in buying and selling foreign money or shares in business **2** *BrE* an officer of the law whose duty is to sell the goods of people who cannot pay their debts

brol·ly /ˈbrɒli‖ˈbrɑli/ *n BrE sl* UMBRELLA

bro·mide /ˈbrəʊmaɪd/ *n* **1** [C;U] any of several chemical compounds, used in medicine to calm excitement **2** [C] a statement or idea without newness or freshness: *tired old bromides about the weather*

bro·mine /ˈbrəʊmiːn/ *n* [U] a simple substance (ELEMENT (6)) that is usu. in the form of a red poisonous liquid, used in photography and in medicine

bron·chi·al /ˈbrɒŋkɪəl‖ˈbrɑŋ-/ *adj* [Wa5;A] of or about the BRONCHIAL TUBEs: *bronchial disease*

bronchial tube /ˌ·· ˈ·‖ˈ·· ·/ *n* [*usu. pl.*] either of the 2 branches connecting the WINDPIPE (=breath tube) with the lungs —see picture at RESPIRATORY

bron·chi·tis /brɒŋˈkaɪtɡ̇s‖braŋ-/ *n* [U] an illness (INFLAMMATION) of the BRONCHIAL TUBE*s* —**-tic** *adj*

bron·co /ˈbrɒŋkəʊ‖ˈbraŋ-/ *n* **-cos** a wild or half-wild horse of the western US; MUSTANG

bron·to·sau·rus /ˌbrɒntəˈsɔːrəs‖ˌbran-/ *n* **-ri** /raɪ/ any of various types of very large 4-footed and probably plant-eating DINOSAUR*s* —see picture at PREHISTORIC

Bronx cheer /ˌbrɒŋks ˈtʃɪəʳ‖ˈbraŋks tʃɪər/ *n AmE sl* RASPBERRY (3)

bronze[1] /brɒnz‖branz/ *v* [T1] to give the appearance or colour of BRONZE[2] to: *bronzed by the sun*

bronze[2] *n* **1** [U] a hard mixture (ALLOY[1]) mainly of copper and tin: *a bronze ornament* **2** [U] the colour of this mixture; dark reddish-brown **3** [C] a work of art made of bronze: *many fine bronzes in this collection*

Bronze Age /ˈ· ·/ *n* [*the*+R] the time when men used tools made of BRONZE[2] before iron was known, about 4–6,000 years ago

brooch /brəʊtʃ/ *n* an ornament worn on women's clothes, fastened on by means of a pin

brood[1] /bruːd/ *n* [GC] **1** a family of young birds **2** a family of other young creatures all produced at the same time **3** *usu. derog* a group having a common nature or origin: *the Devil and his brood*

brood[2] *v* [IØ] **1** to sit on eggs as a hen does **2** to continue to think angrily or sadly (about something bad): *Don't just sit there brooding: do something!* —**~er** *n*

brood[3] *adj* [Wa5;A] kept for giving birth to young: *a brood hen|a brood* MARE[1]

brood o·ver *v prep* [T1] **1** also **brood a·bout**— to think deeply, quietly, and long about: *She brooded over the plan, trying to find some mistake in it* **2** also **brood a·bout**— to continue to think angrily or sadly about: *Don't just sit there brooding over your troubles: do something!* **3** to hang closely over: *A thundercloud had been brooding over the hills all afternoon.|Trouble seems to be brooding over this family*

brood·y /ˈbruːdi/ *adj* [Wa2] **1** like a mother bird wanting to sit on her eggs **2** having or showing sadness and silence, as with self-pity or unhappy thoughts —**-dily** *adv* —**-diness** *n* [U]

brook[1] /brʊk/ *v* [T1 *used with neg.*] *fml* to allow or accept without complaining; bear willingly: *He would brook no interruptions from his listeners.|This important matter brooks no delay. We must talk about it now!*

brook[2] *n* a small stream

broom /bruːm, brʊm/ *n* **1** [U] a type of large bushy plant with yellow flowers that grows on sandy or waste land **2** [C] a large sweeping brush, usu. with a long handle —see picture at HOUSEHOLD **3 A new broom sweeps clean** A person newly appointed is always eager to make great changes

broom·stick /ˈbruːmˌstɪk, ˈbrʊm-/ *n* the long thin handle of a BROOM (2)

Bros. *written abbrev. for:* Brothers: *Jones Bros. sell the best men's suits*

broth /brɒθ‖brɔθ/ *n* [U;(C)] **1** soup in which meat, fish, rice, or vegetables have been cooked: *chicken broth* **2 a broth of a boy** *IrE infml* a fine fellow

broth·el /ˈbrɒθəl‖ˈbra-, ˈbrɔ-/ *n* a house of PROSTITUTE*s*[2], where sex can be had for money

broth·er[1] /ˈbrʌðəʳ/ *n* **1** [C] a male relative with the same parents: *John and Peter are brothers.|John is Peter's brother.|John has a brother.|You've been like a brother to me* —see TABLE OF FAMILY RELATIONSHIPS **2** [C;N] a male member of the same group: *a brother doctor|We must all stand together, brothers!* **3** [C;N;A] (*often cap.*) (a title for) a male member of a religious group, esp. a MONK: *a Christian Brother|Brother John will read the evening prayers* **4 brothers in arms** /ˌ·· · ˈ·/ soldiers who have served together —**~ly** *adj*: *brotherly love* —**~liness** *n* [U]

brother[2] *interj esp. AmE* (an expression of slight annoyance and/or surprise) (esp. in the phr. **oh brother!**)

broth·er·hood /ˈbrʌðəhʊd‖-ər-/ *n* **1** [U] the quality or state of being brothers **2** [C] an association for a particular purpose **3** [C9 *usu. sing.*] *usu. infml* the whole body of people in a business or profession: *the medical brotherhood* **4** [C] a group of men, usu. MONK*s*, living a religious life, usu. together in one place

brother-in-law /ˈ·· · ˌ·/ *n* **brothers-in-law** **1** the brother of one's husband or wife **2** the husband of one's sister **3** the husband of the sister of one's husband or wife —see TABLE OF FAMILY RELATIONSHIPS

brough·am /ˈbruːəm/ *n* a one-horse light closed carriage with 4 wheels, used in former times

brought /brɔːt/ *past t. and p. of* BRING

brou·ha·ha /ˈbruːhaːhaː‖bruːˈhaha/ *n* [U] *infml* disorderly or unnecessary noise and activity

brow /braʊ/ *n* **1** [*usu. pl.*] EYEBROW **2** FOREHEAD **3** *poet* facial expression: *an angry brow* **4** the upper part of a slope or a hill; the edge of a steep place **5 knit one's brows** to show displeasure, worry, or deep thought by FROWNing

brow·beat /ˈbraʊbiːt/ *v* **-beat, -beaten** /biːtn/ [T1 (*into* or *out of*)] to cause to be afraid or force to obey by using fierce looks or words: *to browbeat someone (into doing something)*

brown[1] /braʊn/ *n, adj* [Wa1;U;(C);B] (of) the colour of earth: *brown shoes|He is very brown after his holiday.|dark brown|a dark brown|The brown in my paint box is too dark.|She likes to wear brown*

brown[2] *v* [T1;IØ] to (cause to) become brown or browner: *browned by the sun|This meat takes some time to brown properly when cooking*

brown·ie /ˈbraʊni/ *n* a good-natured little fairy believed to perform helpful services at night

Brownie *n* **1** (in Britain) a member of the GIRL GUIDE*s* from 8 to 11 years old **2** (in the US) a member of the GIRL SCOUT*s* from 7 to 9 years old

brown off *v adv* [Wv5;T1] *BrE sl* to cause to lose interest and/or become angry: *Hearing him say that really browned me off.|I'm really browned off*

brown rice /ˌ· ˈ·/ *n* [U] unpolished rice which still has its outer covering

brown·stone /ˈbraʊnstəʊn/ *n* **1** [U] a soft reddish-brown stone used in building **2** [C] a house with a front of this stone, esp. common in New York City

brown stud·y /ˌ· ˈ··/ *n* **in a brown study** *infml* deep in thought

browse[1] /braʊz/ *n* [*usu. sing.*] a period of time spent in browsing (BROWSE[2]): *While you were out I had a good browse through your books*

browse[2] *v* [IØ] **1** to feed on young plants, grass, etc.: *cows browsing in the fields* **2** to read here and there in books, esp. for enjoyment: *to browse through/among someone's books*

bru·cel·lo·sis /ˌbruːsɡ̇ˈləʊsɡ̇s/ *n* [U] a disease of farm animals and man

Bru·in /ˈbruːɡ̇n/ *n* [R;N] a bear, esp. in children's stories

bruise[1] /bruːz/ *v* **1** [T1] to cause one or more BRUISE*s*[2] on: *She fell and bruised her knee.|a bruised knee* **2** [IØ] to show one or more BRUISE*s*[2]: *Her skin/The skin of a soft fruit bruises easily*

bruise[2] *n* a discoloured place where the skin of a human, animal, or fruit has been INJURED by a blow but not broken

bruis·er /ˈbruːzəʳ/ *n infml* a big rough strong man: *a big bruiser*

bruis·ing /ˈbruːzɪŋ/ *adj infml* very severe; needing a lot of bodily effort: *a bruising battle between the 2 fighters*

bruit a·broad /bruːt/ also **bruit a·bout**— *v adv* [T1,5] *fml or pomp* to mention to many people; make known widely: *It's been bruited abroad that you're going to get married*

brunch /brʌntʃ/ *n* [C;U] *infml* a late breakfast, an early LUNCH, or a combination of the 2

bru·nette, *AmE* also **-net** /bruːˈnet/ *n* a white woman with dark hair

brunt /brʌnt/ *n* **bear the brunt of** to suffer the heaviest part of (an attack): *I had to bear the brunt of his anger alone, until my friends joined me*

brush¹ /brʌʃ/ *n* [U] **1** also **brushwood**— small branches broken off from trees or bushes **2** (land covered by) small rough trees and bushes

brush² *n* **1** (*often in comb.*) an instrument for cleaning, smoothing, or painting, made of sticks, stiff hair, nylon, etc.: *a clothesbrush|a toothbrush|a hairbrush|a paintbrush* —see picture at HOUSEHOLD **2** the tail of a fox **3** an act of brushing: *I'll just give my coat/hair a quick brush* **4** a quick light touch in passing: *He felt the brush of her silk dress against him as she passed*

brush³ *v* **1** [T1] to clean or smooth with a brush: *to brush one's coat/the floor/one's teeth/one's hair* **2** [X7] to remove with or as if with a brush: *to brush away a fly (with one's hand)|to brush dirt off* **3** [X7,9] to put into the stated condition with or as if with a brush: *to brush one's teeth clean|to brush a piece of paper off a table*

brush⁴ *v* **1** [T1;L9;(I∅)] to pass lightly over or across (someone or something); touch lightly against (someone or something) in passing: *The light wind gently brushed his cheek.|It brushed against/over/across his cheek* **2** [L9] to move lightly or carelessly: *I wanted to speak to her, but she just brushed past (me)*

brush⁵ *n* a short and unimportant meeting or battle: *a brush with the police/with the enemy*

brush a·side also **brush a·way**— *v adv* [T1] to refuse to pay attention to: *to brush difficulties/opposition aside*

brush down *v adv* [T1b] to remove dust and dirt from, with hands or brush: *to brush someone/oneself down* —compare DUST² **down**

brush-off /ˈ· ·/ *n* **brush-offs** [*the*+R;(C)] *sl* a clear refusal to be friendly or to listen; rude dismissal: *I wanted to speak to her/to ask her for more pay, but she gave me the brush-off*

brush off¹ *v adv* [T1b] to refuse to listen to or have a relationship with (someone)

brush off² *v adv* [I∅] to disappear or come off with brushing: *Don't worry: the dirt will brush off easily*

brush up also **polish up**— *v adv* [T1a] to improve one's knowledge of (something known but partly forgotten) by study: *I must brush up my French before going to Paris* —**brush-up** /ˈ· ·/ *n*

brush up on *v adv prep* [T1] BRUSH UP

brush·wood /ˈbrʌʃwʊd/ *n* [U] BRUSH¹ (1)

brush·work /ˈbrʌʃwɜːk‖-ɜrk/ *n* [U] an artist's way of putting on paint with his brush: *Frans Hals' brushwork is certainly excellent!*

brusque /bruːsk, brʊsk‖brʌsk/ *adj* [Wa1] quick and rather impolite: *a brusque person/manner|brusque behaviour* —**~ly** *adv* —**~ness** *n* [U]

brus·sels /ˈbrʌsəlz/ *n* [P] *infml BrE* (*sometimes cap.*) BRUSSELS SPROUT*s*

brussels sprout /ˌ·· ˈ·/ also (*infml*) **sprout**— *n* [*usu. pl.*] (*often cap.* B) a small tight bunch of leaves, used as a vegetable, which grows in groups on the sides of a high stem —see picture at VEGETABLE¹

bru·tal /ˈbruːtl/ *adj* **1** having or showing no fine or tender human feeling: *a brutal lie/person* **2** cruel: *a brutal attack/attacker* **3** severe; very hard to bear: *brutal weather* **4** unpleasantly correct: *the brutal truth* —**-tally** /ˈbruːtəli/ *adv*

bru·tal·i·ty /bruːˈtælɪ̈ti/ *n* **1** [U] the quality or state of being BRUTAL: *the brutality of the attack* **2** [C] a BRUTAL act or course of action: *the brutalities of war*

bru·tal·ize, -ise /ˈbruːtəlaɪz/ *v* [T1] to make BRUTAL or unfeeling —**-ization** /ˌbruːtəlaɪˈzeɪʃən‖-lə-/ *n* [U]

brute¹ /bruːt/ *adj* [Wa5;A] like an animal in being unreasonable, cruel, or very strong: *brute force|brute strength|a brute* BEAST

brute² *n* **1** *often derog* an animal, esp. a large one: (fig.) *War can really bring out the brute in a man* **2** an unfortunate animal: *The horse broke its leg when it fell and the poor brute had to be destroyed* **3** *sometimes humor* a rough, cruel, insensitive, or bad-mannered person, esp. a man: *He is an unfeeling brute!|a great brute of a man*

brut·ish /ˈbruːtɪʃ/ *adj derog* **1** suitable for animals rather than people: *In uncivilized conditions, the life of man is "nasty, brutish, and short"* (Thomas Hobbes) **2** having or showing strong socially unacceptable feeling: *to eat with brutish enjoyment* **3** insensitive; unreasoning: *a brutish lack of understanding* —**~ly** *adv*

B.Sc. /ˌbiː es ˈsiː/ (*AmE* **B.S.**)— *abbrev. for:* (*BrE*) Bachelor of Science; (a title for someone who has) a first university degree in a science subject: *He is/has a B.Sc. in Chemistry.|Mary Jones, B.Sc.*

bub·ble¹ /ˈbʌbəl/ *v* **1** [L9;(I∅)] to form, produce, or rise as BUBBLE*s*² **2** [L9;(I∅)] to make the sound of BUBBLE*s*² rising in liquid: *We could hear the pot bubbling (away) quietly on the fire* **3** [I∅ (OVER, *with*)] (usu. of women) to express a lot of a good feeling: *Mary was really bubbling (over) (with joy)* —compare BRIM OVER

bubble² *n* **1** [C *often pl.*] a hollow ball of liquid containing air or gas: *bubbles on a boiling liquid|several bubbles in the glass of this ornament|to blow (soap) bubbles for fun* **2** [U] the sound or appearance of a steadily boiling mixture: *We could hear the bubble of the cooking pot* **3** [C] something empty or not lasting; a plan or idea which is undependable and fails suddenly: *It seemed a good idea, but a few sharp questions soon pricked the bubble*

bubble and squeak /ˌ·· · ˈ·/ *n* [U] *BrE* a dish consisting of potatoes, green vegetables (esp. CABBAGE), and sometimes meat, all cooked in fat together

bubble gum /ˈ·· ·/ *n* [U] CHEWING GUM that can be blown into large BUBBLE*s*²

bub·bly¹ /ˈbʌbli/ *adj* [Wa1] **1** full of BUBBLE*s*² **2** showing good feelings freely: *bubbly people at a party*

bubbly² *n* [U] *sl* CHAMPAGNE

bu·bon·ic plague /bjuːˌbɒnɪk ˈpleɪg‖buːˌbɑ-/ *n* [U] a disease (sometimes very common in former times) that spreads quickly from rats to man, produces swellings under the arms and elsewhere, and usu. causes death

buc·ca·neer /ˌbʌkəˈnɪəʳ/ *n* a sea-robber; PIRATE¹ (1): (fig.) *That businessman claims to be a captain of industry, but really he's more of a buccaneer*

buck¹ /bʌk/ *n* **1** [Wn1] (*fem.* **doe**)—the male of certain animals, esp. the deer, the rat, and the rabbit **2** [Wn1] ANTELOPE **3** *old infml* a fine, gay, well-dressed man, usu. young, esp. in early 19th-century England **4** *sl, esp. AmE* an American dollar

buck² *v* **1** [I∅] (esp. of a horse) to jump up with all 4 feet off the ground: *when they tried to ride the horse, it bucked wildly* **2** [X9] (esp. of a horse) to throw off (esp. a rider) by doing this: *The wild horse bucked its first rider off* **3** [T1] *esp. AmE infml* to oppose: *Don't try to buck every new tendency* —see also BUCK UP

buck³ *n* [*the*+R] *sl* responsibility (esp. in the phr. **pass the buck (to someone)**): *I don't know enough about it to decide, so I'll pass the buck (to you).|"The Buck Stops Here"* (sign on Pres. Truman's desk)

buck·board /ˈbʌkbɔːd‖-ord/ *n* (esp. in the US in the 19th century) a kind of light 4-wheeled vehicle pulled by a horse

bucked /bʌkt/ *adj* [F] *infml BrE* made more cheerful; pleased: *We were bucked by the good news*

buck·et¹ /ˈbʌkɪ̈t/ *n* **1** a type of container for liquids; PAIL —see picture at HOUSEHOLD **2** also **bucketful** /ˈbʌkɪ̈tfʊl/— its contents: *She poured a bucket of water over me* **3** *infml* a large quantity: *The rain came down in buckets* **4 kick the bucket** /ˌ· · ˈ··/ *humor sl* to die

bucket² *v* **1** [I∅ (DOWN)] *infml BrE* **a** to rain very hard: *It's been bucketing down all day* **b** (of rain) to fall very hard: *The rain's really bucketing down* **2** [L9] to move very roughly and irregularly: *The car bucketed down the steep road*

bucket seat /ˈ·· ·/ *n* a small separate folding seat sometimes found in cars and aircraft

buck·le¹ /ˈbʌkəl/ *n* **1** a metal fastener used for joining the ends of 2 leather bands (STRAPs), or for ornament **2** *tech* a bend or wavy effect, esp. in metal, produced by heat or other conditions

buckle² *v* **1** [T1;I∅: (UP or TOGETHER)] to (cause to) fasten with a BUCKLE¹: *He buckled (up) his belt tightly.|The belt buckled (up) easily.|The 2 ends buckle (together) at the back.|These new shoes tie up; those old ones buckle* **2** [X9;L9] to (cause to) stay in a stated place with a BUCKLE¹: *He buckled on his sword.|The sword buckled on easily.|He buckled himself into his seat* **3** [T1;I∅] to (cause to) become bent or wavy through heat, shock, pressure, etc.: *The shock buckled the wheel of my bicycle.|The wheel buckled* **4** [I∅] to begin to yield: *The defenders buckled (under the attack) and in the end they ran away*

buckle down *v adv* [I∅ (*to*)] to begin to work seriously (at): *to buckle down to writing the book*

buck·ler /ˈbʌkləʳ/ *n* a small circular shield with a raised centre

buckle to *v adv* [I∅] to put effort into work: *If we all buckle to, we'll soon get the job done*

buck·ram /ˈbʌkrəm/ *n* [U] stiff cloth used for covering books, stiffening hats and parts of coats, etc.

buck·shee /ˌbʌkˈʃiː◂/ *adj, adv BrE sl* free; without payment: *2 buckshee tickets for the dance tonight|We can get in buckshee*

buck·shot /ˈbʌkʃɒt‖-ʃɑt/ *n* [U] coarse lead shot used esp. for hunting

buck·skin /ˈbʌkˌskɪn/ *n* [U] strong soft yellowish leather made from the skin of a deer or goat

buck·tooth /ˌbʌkˈtuːθ/ *n* **-teeth** /ˈtiːθ/ [*usu. pl.*] a large front tooth that sticks out

buck up *v adv* **1** [T1a] to try to improve: *You'd better buck up your ideas* **2** [I∅] HURRY UP **3** [I∅] CHEER UP

buck·wheat /ˈbʌkwiːt/ *n* [U] small black grain much used as food for hens, and in America for making cakes

bu·col·ic /bjuːˈkɒlɪk‖-ˈkɑ-/ *adj lit* having to do with the country and countrymen —**~ally** *adv* [Wa4]

bud¹ /bʌd/ *n* [C; *in*(*to*)U] a young tightly rolled-up flower (or leaf) before it opens: *The new buds begin to appear in the spring, when plants come into bud* —see also NIP¹ **in the bud** and picture at FLOWER¹

bud² *v* **-dd-** [I∅] to produce BUDs¹: *The trees are budding and spring is near*

bud³ *n* [N] *sl, esp. AmE* BUDDY (2)

Bud·dhis·m /ˈbʊdɪzəm‖ˈbuː-, ˈbʊ-/ *n* [U] a religion of east and central Asia growing out of the teaching of Gautama Buddha that pureness of spirit is the answer to suffering —**Buddhist** *n*

bud·ding /ˈbʌdɪŋ/ *adj* [Wa5;A] beginning to develop: *a budding poet*

bud·dy /ˈbʌdi/ *n* **1** [C] *infml* (esp. of a man) companion; partner: *He's my buddy.|We're buddies* **2** [N] *sl, esp. AmE* (used as a form of address, often in anger) fellow: *Get out of my way, buddy!*

budge /bʌdʒ/ *v* [T1;I∅ *usu. negative*] to (cause to) move a little: *I can't budge this rock.|*(fig.) *She won't budge from her opinions*

bud·ger·i·gar /ˈbʌdʒərigɑːʳ/ also (*infml*) **bud·gie** /ˈbʌdʒi/— *n* a small bright-coloured bird of Australian origin, often kept as a cage bird in British houses

bud·get¹ /ˈbʌdʒɪ̈t/ *n* **1** [C] a plan of how to spend money: *a family/business/weekly budget* **2** [C] a plan of how much money to take in (as by taxation) and how to spend it: *a government budget* **3** [C] the quantity of money stated in either type of plan: *a budget of £10,000,000,000* **4** [A] *euph* cheap: *Enjoy our budget prices now!* **5 balance the budget** to make sure that no more money is going out than coming in

budget² *v* [I∅] to plan private or public spending within the limits of a certain amount of money: *He saves a lot of money by careful budgeting*

bud·get·ar·y /ˈbʌdʒɪ̈təri‖-teri/ *adj* [Wa5] of or belonging to a BUDGET¹

budget for *v prep* [T1,4a] to plan to save enough money for: *He budgeted for the coming year/for a holiday/for buying a new car*

buff¹ /bʌf/ *n, adj* **1** [U;B] a faded yellow colour: *buff yellow* **2** [U] a yellow leather made from cowskin **3 in the buff** *infml, esp. BrE* with no clothes on **4 strip to the buff** *infml, esp. BrE* to take off all one's clothes

buff² *v* [T1 (UP)] to polish (metal) with something soft

buff³ *n* [C9] *infml* a person who is very interested in and knowledgeable about the stated subject: *a film buff*

buf·fa·lo /ˈbʌfələʊ/ *n* **-loes** *or* **-lo** [Wn1] **1** any of several kinds of very large black cattle with long flattish curved horns, found mainly in Asia and Africa —see picture at RUMINANT **2** BISON

buff·er¹ /ˈbʌfəʳ/ *n* **1** a spring put on the front and back of a railway engine or carriage to take the shock when it knocks against or runs into anything **2** a person or thing that lessens the shock of a blow or a difficulty: *A little money can be a useful buffer in time of need* **3** *tech* a substance used to make slower a change in the chemical nature of another substance, esp. a change from an acid to an ALKALINE state or the opposite

buffer² *v* **1** [X9] to act as a BUFFER¹ (2) to: *She buffered him against all difficulties* **2** [T1] to treat with a BUFFER¹ (3)

buf·fer³ *n infml BrE* a foolish old man (esp. in the phr. **old buffer**)

buff·er state /ˈ·· ·/ also **buffer**— *n* a smaller peaceful country between 2 larger ones, serving to lessen the chance of war between them

buf·fet¹ /ˈbʌfɪ̈t/ *n* a blow or sudden shock: *the buffets of fate*

buffet² *v* [T1] **1** to strike sharply, esp. with the hand **2** to strike repeatedly: *We were buffeted by the wind and the rain* **3** *lit* to struggle against: *The swimmer buffeted the waves*

buf·fet³ /ˈbʊfeɪ‖bəˈfeɪ/ *n* **1** (a place, esp. a long table, where one can get) food, usu. cold, to be eaten standing up or sitting down somewhere else **2** SIDEBOARD
buffet a·bout /bʌf½t/ *v adv* [T1b] to hit and/or throw from side to side: *We were buffeted about during the rough train ride*
buf·foon /bəˈfuːn/ *n* a rough and noisy fool: *to play the buffoon at a party*
buf·foon·er·y /bəˈfuːnəri/ *n* **1** [U] the silly awkward behaviour of a BUFFOON **2** [C *usu. pl.*] an example of this
bug¹ /bʌg/ *n* **1** [C] *AmE* any small insect, creeping or flying —compare BEETLE¹ **2** [C] *infml* a small living thing causing disease; GERM: *I'm not feeling well: I must have picked up a bug somewhere* **3** [*the*+R9] *infml* an eager but sometimes foolish or not lasting interest in something: *bitten by the travel bug|the photography bug* **4** [C9] *infml* a person who is very interested in something: *a photography bug* **5** [C] *infml* a fault or difficulty, esp. something wrong with a machine: *a bug in the works* **6** [C] *sl* an apparatus for listening secretly to other people's conversations: *There's a bug in this room somewhere* **7** [C] BEDBUG
bug² *v* **-gg-** [T1] *sl* **1** to fit with a secret listening apparatus: *The police have bugged my office* **2** *esp. AmE* to trouble (someone) continually: *Stop bugging me, man!*
bug·a·boo /ˈbʌgəbuː/ *n* **-boos** *infml, esp. AmE* an imaginary cause of fear: *childish bugaboos*
bug·bear /ˈbʌgbeəʳ/ *n* a cause of concern, perhaps without reason: *the national bugbear of rising prices*
bug·ger¹ /ˈbʌgəʳ/ *n sl, esp. BrE* **1** *taboo* a person thought to be foolish and/or annoying: *You silly bugger!* **2** *taboo* SODOMITE **3** (used in expressions of good or kind feeling) fellow or animal: *Poor bugger!* **4** something that causes a lot of trouble or difficulty: *That job's a real bugger!|a bugger of a job*
bugger² *v* [T1] *BrE* **1** *taboo or law* to be guilty of SODOMY against **2** *sl* (used for adding force to expressions of displeasure): *Bugger it! I've missed my train!|Bugger the lot of you! Go away at once!*
bugger a·bout *v adv BrE taboo sl* **1** [IØ (*with*)] to behave foolishly **2** [T1b] to cause difficulties to (someone): *Stop buggering me about!*
bug·gered /ˈbʌgəd‖-ərd/ *adj* [F] *BrE taboo sl* very tired
bugger off *v adv* [IØ] *BrE taboo sl* (used esp. in giving or reporting orders) to go away: *He told me to bugger off!*
bugger up *v adv* [T1] *BrE taboo sl* to spoil; ruin: *We lost our cases on the journey; it really buggered up our holiday*
bug·ger·y /ˈbʌgəri/ *n* [U] *BrE taboo or law* SODOMY
bug·gy /ˈbʌgi/ *n* **1** a light carriage pulled by one horse **2** *AmE* a vehicle for pushing babies about in; PRAM **3 the horse-and-buggy days** *infml* time before the motorcar: *Things were different in the horse-and-buggy days*
bug·house /ˈbʌghaʊs/ *n* **-houses** /haʊz½z/ *AmE derog sl* a hospital for the mad
bu·gle /ˈbjuːgəl/ *n* a brass musical instrument, played by blowing, like a TRUMPET¹ but shorter, used esp. for army calls —see picture at WIND INSTRUMENT —**~r** *n*
bug·rake /ˈbʌgreɪk/ *n BrE humor sl* a comb
buhl /buːl/ *n* [U] *now rare* fine tables, cupboards, etc., in which a pattern of metal, shell, or bone (IVORY) is set into the surface as an ornament
build¹ /bɪld/ *v* **built** /bɪlt/ **1** [D1 (*for*);T1:(*out of*); IØ] to make (one or more things) by putting pieces together: *That house is built of brick(s).|They're building (houses) in that area now.|He built me a model ship out of wood* **2** [T1 (UP)] to bring into being or develop: *Hard work builds (up) character.|Reading builds the mind* —see also BUILD IN, BUILD INTO, BUILD ON¹·², BUILD UP
build² *n* [U;C] shape and size, esp. of the human body: *a powerful build|We are of the same build*
build·er /ˈbɪldəʳ/ *n* **1** a person who builds (esp. houses): *a firm of local builders* **2** (*in combs.*) something that brings into being or develops: *Hard work is a great character-builder*
build in *v adv* [T1 *usu. pass.*] **1** to make a fixed part of usu. a room: *These cupboards are built in* **2** to cause to be a part of something which cannot be separated from it: *The difficulties seem built in*
build·ing /ˈbɪldɪŋ/ *n* **1** [C] something usu. with a roof and walls that is intended to stay in one place and not to be moved or taken down again: *Houses and churches are buildings* **2** [U] the art or business of making objects of this sort
building block /ˈ·· ·/ *n* any of the pieces out of which or on which something is built: *Those facts are the building blocks of his argument*
building so·ci·e·ty /ˈ·· ·ˌ···/ *n* (in Britain) an association into which people put money which is then lent to those who want to buy or build houses
build in·to *v prep* [D1 *usu. pass.*] **1** to fix to something so as to make a part of it: *The cupboards are built into the walls* **2** to cause to be a part of something: *The rate of pay was built into her contract*
build on¹ *v adv* [T1 *often pass.*] to make as an additional building: *This part of the hospital was built on later*
build on² also **build up·on**— *v prep* **1** [D1] to base (something) on (something): *The insurance business is built on trust.|His argument is built on facts* **2** [T1,4a] BANK ON
build·up /ˈbɪld-ʌp/ *n* **1** the act or action of BUILDing UP: *the buildup of our military forces* **2** something produced by BUILDing UP: *the buildup of traffic on the road*
build up *v adv* **1** [T1;IØ] to (cause to) increase; develop: *to build up one's strength|The clouds are building up* **2** [T1;IØ] to (cause to) form steadily, become larger, or become stronger: *He has built up a good business over the years* **3** [Wv5;T1 *usu. pass.*] to cover with buildings: *The area has been built up since I lived here.|It has become a built-up area* **4** [T1 (*into*)] to praise (someone or something) so as to influence the opinion of others: *The singer has been built up into a great success*
-built /bɪlt/ [*comb. form* [→*adj*]] formed or shaped in a stated way: *a well-built house/man*
built-in /ˌ· ˈ·◂/ *adj* forming a part of something that cannot be separated from it: *built-in difficulties|a built-in cupboard*
built-up /ˌ· ˈ·◂/ *adj* **1** made of several parts or sheets fastened together **2** covered with buildings: *a built-up area*
bulb /bʌlb/ *n* **1** a round root of certain plants **2** any object of this shape, esp. the glass part of an electric lamp that gives out light: *We'll have to change the bulb again* —see pictures at ELECTRICITY and MEDICAL¹
bul·bous /ˈbʌlbəs/ *adj often derog* shaped like a BULB; fat and round: *a bulbous nose*
bul·bul /ˈbʊlbʊl/ *n* any of several types of small bird that live in Asia and Africa
bulge¹ /bʌldʒ/ *n* **1** a swelling of a surface caused by pressure from within or below: *What is that bulge I see in your pocket?* **2** a sudden unusual increase in quantity, which does not last: *The population bulge after the war made more schools necessary* —**bulgy** *adj* [Wa2]—**bulgily** *adv* —**bulginess** *n* [U]
bulge² *v* [IØ (*with*, OUT)] to swell out: *His stomach bulged (out).|His pockets were bulging with presents*

bulk¹ /bʌlk/ *n* **1** [U] great size, shape, mass, or quantity: *Great bulk does not always mean great weight* **2** [C] an unusually large, fat, or shapeless body: *The elephant lowered its great bulk* **3** [*the*+R (*of*)] the main or greater part: *The bulk of the work has already been done* **4** [U] rough food materials often eaten to help the movement of the bowels: *There isn't enough bulk in the food you eat* **5** [U] goods carried in the lower part of a ship **6 in bulk** not divided into parts; not packed in separate parcels: *to buy/sell in bulk*

bulk² *v* **bulk large** to appear important or play an important part

bulk·head /ˈbʌlkhed/ *n* [*often pl.*] any of several walls which divide a ship into separate parts, so that, if one part is damaged, water will not fill the whole ship

bulk·y /ˈbʌlki/ *adj* [Wa2] **1** having BULK¹ (1), esp. if large of its kind or rather fat **2** having great size or mass in comparison with weight: *a bulky woollen garment* —**-ily** *adv* —**-iness** *n* [U]

bull¹ /bʊl/ *n* **1** the male form of cattle, supposed to be fierce and hard to control, kept on farms to be the parent of young cattle —see picture at FARMYARD **2** a man like one of these animals, esp. in being big and strong **3** *sl, esp. AmE* a policeman **4** the male of the elephant and certain other large land or sea animals: *This elephant is a bull.|a bull elephant* **5** a person who buys business shares or goods in expectation of a price rise or who acts to cause such a rise: *a bull market* —compare BEAR¹ (3) **6 take the bull by the horns** *infml* to face difficulties without fear

bull² *v* [T1] **1** to advance by forcing: *He bulled his way through the crowd* **2** to try to raise the prices of: *to bull shares|to bull the market*

bull³ *n* a solemn official letter from the POPE (the head of the Roman Catholic Church)

bull⁴ *n* [U] *BrE sl* (in the army) too great attention paid to the need for cleaning, polishing, and other unpleasant duties

bull⁵ *n, interj* [U] *sl* foolish rude talk; nonsense: *a load/a lot of bull!* —see also SHOOT¹ **the bull**

Bull *n* [*the*+R;C] TAURUS: *He was born under the Bull*

bull·dog /ˈbʊldɒg‖-dɔg/ *n* **1** any of several types of dog of English origin with a short neck and front legs set far apart. They are often shown as representing Britain —see picture at DOG¹ **2** a man like one of these animals, esp. in having courage and determination **3** also **bulldog clip** /ˈ·· ·/— a small metal apparatus with a spring, used in offices to hold papers together as in a tightly closed mouth

bull·doze /ˈbʊldəʊz/ *v* **1** [T1] to push out of the way with a special heavy machine (a BULLDOZER): *to bulldoze the ground before building* **2** [X9] to force insensitively, without regard for the feelings or opinions of others: *He bulldozed his plan through Parliament.|He bulldozed his way through the opposition* **3** [T1 (*into*)] to cause to agree or to obey by force or threat: *They bulldozed him (into agreeing)*

bull·doz·er /ˈbʊldəʊzəʳ/ *n* a powerful machine used for pushing heavy objects, earth, etc., out of the way when a level surface is needed —see picture at SITE¹

bul·let /ˈbʊlǝ̣t/ *n* **1** a type of shot fired from a gun, usu. long and with a rounded or pointed end —compare SHOT¹ (6), SHELL¹ (4) **2** something that looks like this **3 bite (on) the bullet** to suffer something unpleasant bravely

bullet-head·ed /ˈ·· ˌ··◂/ *adj* (esp. of a person) having a small round solid-looking head

bul·le·tin /ˈbʊlətǝ̣n/ *n* **1** a short public usu. official notice: *Here is the latest bulletin about the President's health* **2** a short news report intended to be made public without delay: *to read the news bulletins* **3** a printed NEWSSHEET, esp. one produced by an association or group

bulletin board /ˈ··· ·/ *n AmE* **notice** BOARD

bul·let·proof /ˈbʊlǝ̣tpruːf/ *adj* that stops bullets from passing through it: *a bulletproof car/garment*

bull·fight /ˈbʊlfaɪt/ *n* a ceremonial fight between men and a BULL¹, esp. as practised as a sport in Spain, Portugal, and Latin America

bull·fight·ing /ˈbʊlˌfaɪtɪŋ/ *n* [U] the art, as seen in a BULLFIGHT, of exciting a BULL¹ to attack, avoiding its charge, and, in Spain and Spanish America, killing it ceremonially —**-ter** *n*

bull·finch /ˈbʊlˌfɪntʃ/ *n* a type of small European songbird with a bright reddish breast and a strong rounded beak

bull·frog /ˈbʊlfrɒg‖-frɑg, -frɔg/ *n* a type of large-headed American FROG (1) with a loud unpleasant cry (CROAK²)

bull·head·ed /ˌbʊlˈhedǝ̣d◂/ *adj often derog* (of a person) going after what one wants without regard for the opinion of others —**~ly** *adv* —**~ness** *n* [U]

bul·lion /ˈbʊljən/ *n* [U] bars of gold or silver: *gold bullion*

bull·necked /ˌbʊlˈnekt◂/ *adj* (of a person) with a short and very thick neck (like a BULL'*s*¹)

bul·lock /ˈbʊlək/ *n* a young BULL¹ which cannot breed, often used for pulling vehicles —compare STEER¹

bull·ring /ˈbʊlˌrɪŋ/ *n* a circular place (an ARENA) for BULLFIGHT*s*, surrounded by rows of seats

bull's-eye /ˈ· ·/ *n* **1** the circular centre of a TARGET that people try to hit when shooting: (fig.) *Your last remark really hit the bull's-eye: it was exactly right* **2** a shot that hits the centre and has the highest value **3** a kind of large hard round sweet **4** a circular opening for light or air **5** a thick round piece of glass usu. forming part of a larger surface

bull·shit /ˈbʊlˌʃɪt/ *n, interj* [U] *taboo sl* BULL⁴·⁵

bull ter·ri·er /ˌ· ˈ···/ *n* a type of short-haired dog of English origin which is a mixture of BULLDOG and TERRIER

bul·ly¹ /ˈbʊli/ *n* a person, esp. a schoolboy, who uses his strength to hurt weaker people or make them afraid

bully² *adj* [Wa5;F+*for*] *humor sl* very good: *"I've done it!" "Well, bully for you"*

bully³ *v* [T1 (*into*);V3] to act like a BULLY¹ towards, often with the intention of forcing someone to do something: *bullying smaller boys (into doing things)*

bully⁴ also **bully beef** /ˈ·· ·/— *n* [U] a kind of pressed cooked BEEF¹ (1) in tins

bul·ly·boy /ˈbʊlibɔɪ/ *n infml* a rough fellow, esp. one employed to beat people up

bully off *v adv* [IØ] to start a game of HOCKEY (1) —**bully-off** /ˈ·· ·/ *n*

bul·rush /ˈbʊlrʌʃ/ *n* any of several kinds of tall grasslike waterside plants

bul·wark /ˈbʊlwək‖-ərk/ *n* **1** [*often pl.*] a strong wall built for defence or protection **2** [(*of*)] a strong support or protection in danger: *Our country is a bulwark of freedom*

bum¹ /bʌm/ *n sl, esp. BrE* the part of the body on which a person sits; BUTTOCK*s*

bum² *v* **-mm-** [T1 (*off*)] *sl* to beg: *Can I bum a cigarette off you?*

bum³ *n Am & AustrE derog sl* **1** [C] a wandering beggar **2** [*the*+R] the life of this sort of person: *John lost his job and went on the bum* **3** [C] a person who does his job poorly: *calling the judge a bum* **4** [C] a person who spends a lot of time on some game or amusement: *a* BEACH *bum*

bum⁴ *adj* [Wa5;A] *sl* **1** very bad: *some bum advice* **2** not working properly: *a bum knee*

bum a·long *v adv; prep* [T1;IØ] *sl* to move (along) steadily, usu. in a car: *We were just bumming along (the road)*

bum a·round also **bum a·bout**— *v adv* [IØ] *sl* **1** to spend time lazily **2** to spend time travelling for amusement

bum·ble /ˈbʌmbəl/ *v* [IØ (ON, *about*)] *sl* to speak without making much sense, or so that the words are hard to hear clearly: *He kept bumbling on about something I couldn't understand properly*

bum·ble·bee /ˈbʌmbəlbiː/ *n* a type of large hairy bee which makes a loud noise when flying

bum·boat /ˈbʌmbəʊt/ *n rare* a boat which brings fresh vegetables and other articles from the shore for sale to larger ships

bumf, bumph /bʌmf/ *n* [U] *BrE derog sl* uninteresting written material that must be read, signed, or otherwise dealt with

bum·mer /ˈbʌməʳ/ *n sl* something bad, esp. a drug experience

bump¹ /bʌmp/ *v* **1** [T1] to strike or knock with force or violence: *The car bumped the tree.|The 2 cars bumped each other.|I've bumped my knee (against/on the wall)* **2** [IØ (TOGETHER)] to strike or knock against each other: *The 2 cars bumped (together)* **3** [L9;(IØ)] to strike something with force: *Something bumped against me.|It kept bumping (down the stairs)* **4** [X9] to move by striking with force: *bumping the glass off the table* **5** [L9] to move (along) with much sudden upward shaking, as of a wheeled vehicle over uneven ground: *We bumped along/up and down* —see also BUMP INTO, BUMP OFF, BUMP UP

bump² *n* **1** a sudden forceful blow or shock **2** a raised round swelling, often as caused by a blow

bump³ *adv* [H] suddenly; hard; with a sudden BUMPing¹ noise: *He wasn't looking, and ran bump into a tree*

bum·per¹ /ˈbʌmpəʳ/ *n* **1** [C] *now rare* a very full cup or glass: *a bumper of* MEAD **2** [A] something that is very full or large (esp. in the phr. **a bumper crop**)

bumper² *n* **1** a bar fixed on the front or back of a car to protect the car when it knocks against anything —see picture at CAR **2** also **bouncer**— (in cricket) a fast ball that springs up sharply and might hit the BATSMAN on the head or body **3** *AmE* BUFFER¹ (1)

bumper-to-bumper /ˌ·· · ˈ··◂/ *adj* [Wa5] (of cars) very close together one after another; with BUMPERs² (1) almost touching: *The traffic was bumper-to-bumper all the way home*

bump in·to *v prep* [T1] *infml* to meet by chance

bump·kin /ˈbʌmpkɪ̥n/ *n derog infml* an awkward foolish fellow, usu. from the country

bump off *v adv* [T1] *sl* to kill; murder

bump·tious /ˈbʌmpʃəs/ *adj derog* having or showing a habit of putting forward one's own opinions or interests noisily and with little regard for the feelings of others: *a bumptious person/manner* —**~ly** *adv* —**~ness** *n* [U]

bump up *v adv* [T1] *infml* to increase; raise: *You need a good result to bump up your average*

bump·y /ˈbʌmpi/ *adj* [Wa1] **1** with many BUMPs²: *a bumpy road/ride/head* **2** *infml* with parts that are high (or good) and parts that are low (or bad): *We've had rather a bumpy time (of it) since the war* **3** (of music, poetry, etc.) with uneven time: *bumpy dance music* —**-ily** *adv* —**-iness** *n* [U]

bun /bʌn/ *n* **1** a small round sweet cake **2** a mass of (esp. woman's) hair twisted and fastened into a tight round shape, usu. at the back of the head: *She wears her hair in a bun* **3 have a bun in the oven** *humor (used esp. by men)* (of a woman) to have an unborn child in the body; be PREGNANT (1)

bunch¹ /bʌntʃ/ *n* [(*of*)] **1** [(*of*)] a number of things (usu. small and of the same kind) fastened, held, or growing together at one point: *a bunch of flowers/fruit/keys* **2** *infml, often humor or derog* a group: *a nice bunch of girls|a bunch of thieves|My friend John is the best of the bunch*

bunch² *v* [T1;IØ: (UP)] **1** to (cause to) form into one or more bunches: *The captain told the players not to bunch (up) together, but to spread out over the field* **2** (of cloth or clothes) to (cause to) gather into folds: *I don't like the way this cloth bunches up*

bun·dle¹ /ˈbʌndl/ *n* **1** [C (*of*)] a number of articles tied, fastened, or held together, usu. across the middle **2** [C] a number of fine threadlike parts lying closely together, esp. consisting of nerves, muscles, or the inner substances of plant stems **3** [S+*of*] *infml* a mass (of): (fig.) *I'm so anxious I'm just a bundle of nerves this morning*

bundle² *v* **1** [L9;X9] to (cause to) move or hurry in a rather quick and rough manner: *They bundled the minister into a car and drove away before anyone could stop them.|We all bundled into a car* **2** [X9] to put together or store in a disordered way: *Don't bundle all the clothes into that bag so carelessly*

bundle off *v adv* [T1b (*to*)] to cause to go away or off quickly, usu. after trouble: *The family were so ashamed of the youngest son that they bundled him off (to Canada).|They bundled the children off to school*

bundle up *v adv* **1** [T1] to gather or tie in one or more BUNDLEs: *Can you bundle up the sheets for me, please?* **2** [T1;IØ] to dress (oneself) in a lot of heavy warm clothing: *to bundle (oneself) up against the cold*

bung¹ /bʌŋ/ *n* a round piece of wood or other such material used to close the hole in a container —see picture at LABORATORY

bung² *v BrE infml* **1** [X9;D1] to throw: *He picked up a stone and bunged it over the fence.|Bung me a cigarette, will you?* **2** [X9] to put or push, esp. roughly; cause to go: *Look what the postman's just bunged through the letter box*

bun·ga·low /ˈbʌŋgələʊ/ *n* a type of house which is all on one level —see VILLA (USAGE) and picture at HOUSE¹

bung·hole /ˈbʌŋhəʊl/ *n* a hole for emptying or filling a barrel

bun·gle¹ /ˈbʌŋgəl/ *v* [T1;(IØ)] to do (something) badly: *to bungle a job* —**~r** *n*

bungle² *n* a failure caused by lack of skill: *The job was a bungle*

bung up *v adv* [T1 *often pass.*] *infml* to block; stop up: *to bung up a hole|My nose is bunged up with a cold*

bun·ion /ˈbʌnjən/ *n* a painful red swollen lump on the first joint of the big toe

bunk¹ /bʌŋk/ *n* **1** a bed usu. fixed to the wall (as on a ship) and that is often one of 2 or more placed one above the other **2** BUNK BED

bunk² *v* [L9 (DOWN)] *infml* to sleep in one or more BUNKs¹ (or beds): *We bunked (down) with some friends for the night*

bunk³ *n* [U] *sl* nonsense: *a load of bunk*

bunk⁴ *n* **do a bunk** *BrE sl* to run away; leave, esp. when one should not

bunk bed /ˈ· ·/ also **bunk**— *n* either of usu. 2 beds fixed one above the other and used esp. by children —see picture at BEDROOM

bun·ker /ˈbʌŋkəʳ/ *n* **1** a place to store coal, esp. on a ship or outside a house **2** *AmE* **sand trap**—*BrE* (in GOLF) a place dug out and filled with sand, from which it is hard to hit the ball **3** a strongly-built shelter for soldiers, esp. one built underground

bun·kered /ˈbʌŋkəd‖-ərd/ *adj* [Wa5;F] *BrE* (in GOLF) (of a player) having hit the ball into a BUNKER (2)

bunk·house /ˈbʌŋkhaʊs/ *n* **-houses** /ˌhaʊzɪ̈z/ a building where workers sleep

bunk off *v adv* [IØ] *BrE sl* to run away, esp. from school; play TRUANT

bun·kum /ˈbʌŋkəm/ *n* [U] *sl* BUNK[3]

bunk-up /ˈ· ·/ *n* [*usu. sing.*] *infml BrE* help in climbing: *I want to look over this wall; will you give me a bunk-up?*

bunk up *v adv* [IØ (*with*)] *BrE sl* to have sexual relations (with)

bun·ny /ˈbʌni/ *n* (*used esp. by or to children*) a rabbit

bunny girl /ˈ·· ·/ also **bunny**— *n* a young woman dressed in a garment that shows off the sexually attractive parts of her body, with the addition of false rabbit's ears and a tail, who serves drinks in certain NIGHTCLUB*s*

Bun·sen burn·er /ˌbʌnsən ˈbɜːnəʳ‖-ər-/ *n* a burner used in practical scientific work, in which gas is mixed with air before burning —see picture at LABORATORY

bun·ting[1] /ˈbʌntɪŋ/ *n* any of several types of small bird

bunting[2] *n* [U] **1** a light loosely-woven cloth used mainly for flags and ornamental hangings for special occasions **2** ornamental hangings, esp. in the colours of the national flag

buoy[1] /bɔɪ‖ˈbuːi, bɔɪ/ *n* **1** a floating object fastened to the bed of the sea to show ships where there are rocks **2** LIFE BUOY

buoy[2] *v* [T1 (UP) *usu. pass.*] **1** to keep (someone or something) floating: *buoyed by the water* **2** to support; keep high: *wealth buoyed by increased production*

buoy·an·cy /ˈbɔɪənsi‖ˈbɔɪənsi, ˈbuːjənsi/ *n* [U;S] **1** the tendency of an object to float, or to rise when pushed down into a liquid: *the buoyancy of light wood* **2** the power of a liquid to force upwards an object pushed down into it: *the buoyancy of water* **3** the ability to return quickly to high spirits after being in low spirits or receiving bad news: *a buoyancy of spirit that keeps her going* —**-ant** *adj* —**-antly** *adv*

buoy up *v adv* [T1] to raise the spirits of; to raise (spirits): *Her spirits were buoyed up by hopes of success*

bur /bɜːʳ/ *n* BURR[3]

Bur·ber·ry /ˈbɜːbəri‖ˈbɜrbəri, -beri/ *n tdmk* a RAINCOAT of the type made by Burberry's of London

bur·ble /ˈbɜːbəl‖ˈbɜr-/ *v* **1** [IØ (ON)] to make a sound like a stream flowing over stones **2** [IØ (ON, AWAY)] to talk quickly but foolishly or in a way that is hard to hear clearly **3** [T1] to express in this way

bur·den[1] /ˈbɜːdn‖-ɜr-/ *n fml* **1** a heavy load **2** a duty which is hard to do properly; heavy responsibility: *the burdens of (high public) office*

burden[2] *v* [T1 (*with*)] to load or trouble: *I will not burden you with a lengthy account.|burdened with heavy taxation*

burden[3] *n* **1** [C] *lit or tech* a part of a song which is repeated often **2** [*the*+R (*of*)] the main subject or point (esp. in the phr. **the burden of the story**)

burden of proof /ˌ·· · ˈ·/ *n* [*the*+R] the duty or responsibility of proving something: *The burden of proof lies on/with the person who brings/makes the charge*

bur·den·some /ˈbɜːdnsəm‖ˈbɜr-/ *adj* causing or being a BURDEN[1] (esp. 2): *burdensome duties* —**~ness** *n* [U]

bur·dock /ˈbɜːdɒk‖ˈbɜrdɑk/ *n* BURR[3] (2)

bu·reau /ˈbjʊərəʊ/ *n* **bureaux** /ˈbjʊərəʊz/ **1** *BrE* a large desk or writing-table with a wooden cover which slides over the top to close it **2** *AmE* a chest of drawers for bedroom use **3** a government department **4** a business office, esp. one that collects and/or keeps facts: *an information bureau*

bu·reauc·ra·cy /bjʊˈrɒkrəsi, bjʊə-‖-ˈrɑ-/ *n usu. derog* **1** [S] government officers who are appointed rather than elected **2** [S] a group of people like this in a business or other type of organization: *the company bureaucracy* **3** [U] government by such officers rather than by those who are elected, often supposed to be ineffective and full of stupid unnecessary rules

bu·reau·crat /ˈbjʊərəkræt/ *n usu. derog* **1** a member of a BUREAUCRACY **2** an officer of government (or business) who tries to centre power in himself

bu·reau·crat·ic /ˌbjʊərəˈkrætɪk/ *adj usu. derog* of, related to, or having the qualities of a BUREAUCRACY or a BUREAUCRAT: *bureaucratic government* —**~ally** *adv* [Wa4]

burg /bɜːg‖bɜrg/ *n AmE sl* a city or town

bur·geon /ˈbɜːdʒən‖ˈbɜr-/ *v* [Wv4;IØ] *fml* to grow; begin to develop: *the burgeoning cities of Asia and Africa*

bur·gess /ˈbɜːdʒɪ̈s‖ˈbɜr-/ *n old use or pomp* a free man of a city or country, having the right to elect representatives to the government

burgh /ˈbʌrə‖bɜrg, ˈbʌrəʊ/ *n ScotE* BOROUGH

bur·gher /ˈbɜːgəʳ‖ˈbɜr-/ *n* a man who lives in a town

bur·glar /ˈbɜːgləʳ‖ˈbɜr-/ *n* a thief who breaks into houses, shops, etc., esp. during the night —compare HOUSEBREAKER

burglar a·larm /ˈ·· ·ˌ·/ *n* an apparatus that makes a loud warning noise when a thief breaks into a building

bur·glar·y /ˈbɜːgləri‖ˈbɜr-/ *n* [C;U] (an example of) the crime of entering a building (esp. a home) by force with the intention of stealing

bur·gle /ˈbɜːgəl‖ˈbɜr-/ *AmE* also **bur·glar·ize** /ˈbɜːgləraɪz‖ˈbɜr-/— *v* [T1;(IØ)] to break into a building and steal from (it or the people in it): *Help! I've been burgled*

bur·go·mas·ter /ˈbɜːgəˌmɑːstəʳ‖ˈbɜrgəˌmæstər/ *n* the chief man (MAYOR) of a town esp. in Germany or Holland

Bur·gun·dy /ˈbɜːgəndi‖ˈbɜr-/ *n* [U] a type of French red (or white) wine

bur·i·al /ˈberɪəl/ *n* [U;C] the act, action, or ceremony of putting a dead body into a grave

bur·lap /ˈbɜːlæp‖ˈbɜr-/ *n* [U;A] a kind of coarse cloth used esp. for making large bags (SACK*s*[1])

bur·lesque[1] /bɜːˈlesk‖bɜr-/ *n* **1** [C;(U)] speech, acting, or writing in which a serious thing is made to seem foolish or a foolish thing is treated solemnly so as to make people laugh: *a burlesque of a famous poem* **2** [U] (formerly in the US) VAUDEVILLE usu. including STRIPTEASE

burlesque[2] *v* [T1] to cause to appear amusing by means of BURLESQUE[1] (1): *to burlesque someone/someone's poem*

bur·ly /ˈbɜːli‖ˈbɜrli/ *adj* [Wa5] (of a person) strongly and heavily built —**-liness** *n* [U]

burn[1] /bɜːn‖bɜrn/ *n esp. ScotE* a small stream

burn[2] *v* **burnt** /bɜːnt‖bɜrnt/ *or* **burned** **1** [IØ] to be on fire: *The house is burning! Help!|*(fig.) *He's burning* (*with fever*) **2** [IØ] to (be able to) become on fire: *Paper burns easily* **3** [IØ (AWAY)] to contain a fire: *a little heater burning* (*away*) *in the corner* **4** [IØ] to give off light; shine: *a light burning in the window* **5** [Wv4;IØ] to produce or experience an unpleasant hot feeling: *That medicine burns so!|ears burning after being in a strong wind|the burning* *sand* **6** [I∅ (*with*),3] (esp. in *-ing* form) to experience a very strong feeling: *burning with anger/desire|She is burning to tell you the news* **7** [L9;X9] to force or make (a way) by or as if by fire or great heat: *Her words burnt (their way) into his heart* **8** [I∅;L7] to change for the worse or be destroyed by fire or heat: *The potatoes have burnt (black) and we cannot eat them!|All his papers burnt (in the great fire)* **9** [T1] to destroy by fire: *He burnt all his old papers* **10** [T1] to kill by fire: *Joan of Arc was burnt (at the* STAKE[1]*)* **11** [T1] to hurt or damage by fire or heat: *to burn one's hand* **12** [T1] to use for power, heating, or lighting: *ships that burn coal| lamps that burn oil* **13** [X9] to change by fire or heat: *They are burning clay to make bricks.|The papers were burnt to ashes* **14** [X9] to produce by fire: *He burnt a hole in his shirt.|She burnt her name into the wood* **15 burn one's boats/bridges** *infml* to destroy all means of going back, so that one must go forward **16 burn one's fingers** also **get one's fingers burnt**—*infml* to suffer the unpleasant results of a risky or thoughtless action: *If you give him all your money, you're likely to burn your fingers!* **17 burn someone's ears** *sl* to scold someone strongly **18 burn the candle at both ends** *infml* to use up all one's strength by trying to do too many different things, esp. by being active by night as well as by day **19 burn the midnight oil** *infml* to work or study till late at night **20 have money to burn** *infml* to have enough money to remain rich even after wasting some of it **21 Money burns a hole in his pocket** *infml* Whenever he has money, he spends it —see also BURN AWAY, BURN DOWN, BURN OFF, BURN INTO, BURN OUT, BURN UP

USAGE The British use **burned** as the past tense and participle of **burn**, only when it is 1 INTRANSITIVE: *The fire burned brightly*. 2 (fig.): *The desire for freedom burned in their hearts.* Otherwise the British past tense and participle is **burnt**: *I('ve) burnt the dinner!* Americans can use **burned** all the time, but may also use **burnt**, esp. as an adjective: *burnt bread.*

burn³ *n* **1** [C;(*the*+U)] a hurt place, effect, or sensation produced by burning: *burns on her hand| the burn of the medicinal cream on a cut* **2** [C] an act of firing the motors of a space vehicle: *a short burn* **3 a slow burn** *sl, esp. AmE* a steady change from calmness into greater and greater anger: *to do a slow burn*

burn a·way *v adv* [T1;I∅] to destroy or be destroyed by burning: *The skin on his foot was burnt away.| The pile of paper burnt away to nothing*

burn down *v adv* **1** [T1 *often pass.*;I∅] to destroy (usu. a building) or be destroyed by fire: *The building (was) burnt down and only ashes were left* **2** [I∅] also **burn low**— (esp. of a fire) to flame less brightly or strongly as the coal, wood, etc., is used up —compare BURN OUT, BURN UP

burn·er /ˈbɜːnəʳ‖ˈbɜr-/ *n* a person or thing that burns, esp. the part of a cooker, heater, etc., that produces flames —see also CHARCOAL BURNER

-burner *comb. form* **1** having BURNERs of the stated number or type: *a 2-burner heater* **2** that burns material of the stated type for power, heat, or light: *an oil-burner*

burn·ing /ˈbɜːnɪŋ‖ˈbɜr-/ *adj* [A] **1** being on fire: *a burning house|(fig.) burning cheeks* **2** (of feelings) very strong: *a burning interest in science* **3** producing (a sensation of) great heat or fire: *a burning fever|a burning sensation on the tongue* **4** having very great importance; having to be dealt with at once; urgent: *Mass unemployment is one of the burning questions of our time*

burn in·to *v prep* [D1] **1** to fix (as a mark) by burning, so that removal is impossible: *The owner's mark was burnt into the animal's skin* **2** *usu. pass.* to fix (as an idea) in the mind, so that removal is impossible: *The habit of obedience was burned into me as a child*

bur·nish /ˈbɜːnɪʃ‖ˈbɜr-/ *v* [T1] to polish (esp. metal), usu. with something hard and smooth

burn off *v adv* **1** [T1] to destroy by burning: *His hair was burnt off.|The farmers are burning off the* STUBBLE **2** [T1a] to remove the remains of grain crops from, by burning: *The farmers are burning off the fields*

bur·nous, burnouse, *AmE* also **burnoose** /bɜːˈnuːs‖bɜr-/ *n* a long one-piece loose outer garment worn by Arabs and Moors, with a soft covering for the head, neck, and shoulders

burn out *v adv* **1** [T1 *usu. pass.*] to make hollow by fire: *The building was burnt out and only the walls remained* —compare BURN DOWN (1) **2** [T1b (*of*) *usu. pass.*] (*usu. pass.*) to cause to leave by fire: *The family were burnt out of their home twice last year* **3** [T1b;I∅] to stop burning because there is nothing left to burn: *That small fire can be left to burn (itself) out* **4** [T1;I∅] to stop working through damage caused by heat: *The engine has/is burned out* **5** [T1;I∅] to cease to be active: *You'll burn yourself out if you work too hard*

burnt /bɜːnt‖bɜrnt/ *past t. & p. of* BURN² —see BURN² (USAGE)

burnt of·fer·ing /ˌ· ˈ···/ *n* **1** *humor* a piece of food which has been burnt by being cooked too much **2** something (usu. a plant or animal) which is burnt as an offering to a god

burnt-out /ˌ· ˈ·◂/ also **burned-out**— *adj* **1** worn out by too much use or improper use: *burnt-out machines* **2** no longer active: *a burnt-out poet*

burn up *v adv* **1** [I∅] to flame more brightly or strongly: *Put some more wood on the fire to make it burn up* **2** [T1] to destroy completely by fire: *All the wood has been burnt up* **3** [I∅] to be destroyed by great heat: *The* ROCKET *burned up when it re-entered the earth's* ATMOSPHERE **4** [T1;I∅] *sl* to travel at high speed (along): *to burn up (the road)* **5** [T1] *AmE sl* to cause to be very angry **6** [T1] *AmE sl* TELL OFF (1)

burp¹ /bɜːp‖bɜrp/ *n sl* BELCH² (1)

burp² *v* **1** [T1] *infml* to help (a baby) to get rid of stomach gas, esp. by rubbing or gently striking the back **2** [I∅] *sl* BELCH¹ (1)

burr¹ /bɜːʳ/ *n* [(*the*)S] **1** a long loud HUM² **2** a way of pronouncing English with a strong "r"-sound, esp. in Northumbria or North-West Scotland

burr² *v* [I∅ (AWAY, ON)] to produce a BURR¹

burr³, bur *n* **1** a seed-container of certain plants, covered with prickles which make it stick onto clothes **2** a type of plant which has such seed-containers

bur·ro /ˈbʊrəʊ‖ˈbɜrəʊ/ *n* **-ros** *esp. AmE* a donkey, usu. small

bur·row¹ /ˈbʌrəʊ‖ˈbɜrəʊ/ *n* a hole in the ground made by an animal, esp. a rabbit, in which it lives or hides

burrow² *v* **1** [X9;(T1)] to make by or as if by digging: *to burrow a hole in the sand|to burrow a way through the sand* **2** [L9] to move ahead by or as if by digging: *to burrow into/through the sand* **3** [X9;L9] to (cause to) move as if looking for warmness, safety, or love: *She burrowed her head into my shoulder.|He burrowed against her back for warmness*

bur·sar /ˈbɜːsəʳ‖ˈbɜr-/ *n* a person in a college or school who has charge of money, property, etc.

bur·sa·ry /ˈbɜːsəri‖ˈbɜr-/ *n* **1** a BURSAR's office **2** SCHOLARSHIP (1)

burst¹ /bɜːst‖bɜrst/ *v* **burst 1** [T1;I∅] to (cause to) break suddenly, esp. by pressure from within: *The* *bottle/tyre burst.|He burst a blood vessel.|He burst the chains that held him.|The storm burst and we all got wet.*|(fig.) *My heart will burst* (*with grief/joy*) **2** [X9;L9] to (cause to) come into the stated condition suddenly, often with force: *He burst free* (*from the chains*).|*He burst out of the chains.|She burst through the door into the room.|In spring the young flowers burst open.|The police burst open the door* **3** [I∅ (*with*),3] (in the *-ing* form) to be filled to the breaking point (with a substance or usu. pleasant feeling): *That bag is bursting* (*with potatoes*).|*I am bursting with joy.|He is bursting to tell you the news*

burst² *n* a sudden outbreak of effort: *a burst of laughter/of speed*

burst in on also **burst in up·on**— *v adv prep* [T1] **1** to interrupt (someone), usu. noisily: *It was very rude of you to burst in on Father while he was working* **2** BREAK IN ON

burst in·to *v prep* [T1] **1** to enter hurriedly (usu. a room) **2** BREAK INTO (3)

burst out *v adv* **1** [I4] to begin suddenly (to use the voice without speaking): *They burst out laughing/crying/into song* **2** [T1] to say suddenly: *"I don't believe it!" burst out the angry old man*

bur·then /ˈbɜːðən‖ˈbɜr-/ *n, v lit* BURDEN[1,2,3]

bur·ton /ˈbɜːtn‖ˈbɜrtn/ *n* (*often cap.*) **gone for a burton** *BrE sl* **a** not to be found; missing **b** broken; no longer working **c** killed

bur·y /ˈberi/ *v* **1** [T1] to put into the grave: *to bury a dead person*|(fig.)|to bury quarrels and forget the past **2** [T1] to hide away: *The dog has buried a bone.*|(fig.) *They've buried themselves in the country.|The facts are buried in a few old books.|with one's head buried in a book* **3** [X9] to push deep into or under: *He buried his hands in his pockets.|He buried his head in his hands*

bus¹ /bʌs/ *n* [C; *by*+U] a large passenger-carrying motor vehicle, esp. one which carries the public on payment of small amounts: *to travel by bus|I saw him on the bus.|to catch/miss the bus* —see TRAIN¹ (USAGE) and picture at STREET

bus² *v* **-ss-** **1** [X9;L9] to carry (or travel) by bus **2** [T1;(I∅)] *esp. AmE* to carry (pupils) by bus to a school in a distant area, where the pupils are of a different race

bus·by /ˈbʌzbi/ *n* **1** a type of small fur hat worn by certain soldiers **2** *infml* BEARSKIN (2)
USAGE The tall black fur hats worn by the 5 GUARDS REGIMENTs of the British army are officially called **bearskins**, but most people call them **busbies**. Officially, only the shorter fur hat worn by certain other REGIMENTs can be called a **busby**.

bush /bʊʃ/ *n* **1** [C] a small low tree —see picture at GARDEN¹ **2** [*the*+R] uncleared wild country, esp. in Australia or Africa **3 beat about the bush** *infml* to avoid coming to the main point: *Tell me the truth: don't beat about the bush, man!*

bush·ba·by /ˈbʊʃbeɪbi/ *n* a type of small monkey-like African animal, sometimes kept as a pet

bushed /bʊʃt/ *adj* [F] *infml* very tired

bush·el /ˈbʊʃəl/ *n* a measure, esp. of grain; about 36.5 LITREs —see WEIGHTS & MEASURES TABLE

bush tel·e·graph /ˌ· ˈ···/ *n* [U] the sending of messages over long distances by such methods as smoke signals, beating drums, etc.

bush·whack /ˈbʊʃwæk/ *v not fml* **1** [I∅] to live out in the BUSH (2) **2** [T1] to attack (someone) from hiding; AMBUSH¹ —**~er** *n*

bush·y /ˈbʊʃi/ *adj* [Wa1] (of hair) growing thickly: *a bushy beard/tail* —**bushiness** *n* [U]

busi·ness /ˈbɪznɪ̀s/ *n* **1** [C;U] one's work or employment: *Other people's quarrels are a lawyer's business.|I'm here on business, not for pleasure* **2** [U] trade and the getting of money: *How's business? Business is good.|They've done* (*some*) *business together.|It's a pleasure to do business with you.|After school she went into business* **3** [C] a particular money-earning activity or place, such as a shop: *How's the business?|to sell one's business* **4** [S] a duty: *It's a teacher's business to make children learn* **5** [S] an affair; event; matter; thing: *I don't understand this business* (*of the additional money*).|*The business before the meeting tonight is . . .|a strange business* **6** [U] (in acting a play) things done by an actor other than speaking, such as movements of the hands, the look on the face, etc.: *stage business* **7 Business is business** When dealing with money we must not think of other matters, such as friendship **8 have no business to do something** also **have no business doing something**— to have no right to do something **9 like nobody's business** *sl* very fast or very well: *That man plays the piano like nobody's business* **10 Mind your own business** *infml* Don't ask about things that don't concern you **11 no business of yours** *infml* nothing to do with you; nothing that concerns you

business end /ˈ·· ·/ *n* [*the*+R (*of*)] *infml* the end (of something) which is dangerous, is used for causing harm, etc.: *the business end of a gun* (=the barrel)

business hours /ˈ·· ·/ *n* [P] the time during which business is done: *Our business hours are from 9 to 5*

busi·ness·like /ˈbɪznɪ̀s-laɪk/ *adj* having or showing the ability to succeed in business or to do things calmly and with common sense: *a businesslike person/manner*

busi·ness·man /ˈbɪznɪ̀smən/ (*fem.* **busi·ness·wom·an** /-ˌwʊmən/)— *n* **-men** /mən/ **1** a person in business, esp. as the director of a business firm **2** a person who would be successful in business, who knows how to get and save money

busk /bʌsk/ *v* [I∅] *BrE infml* to play music in the street in order to earn money

busk·er /ˈbʌskəʳ/ *n BrE infml* a street musician

bus·man /ˈbʌsmən/ *n* **-men** /mən/ *BrE* a man who works on the public buses, esp. a busdriver

busman's hol·i·day /ˌ·· ˈ···/ *n* [*usu. sing.*] a holiday spent in doing one's usual work

bus stop /ˈ· ·/ *n* a fixed place where buses stop for passengers: *Let me off at the next bus stop, please* —see picture at STREET

bust¹ /bʌst/ *n* **1** the human head, shoulders, and chest, esp. as shown in SCULPTURE¹ **2** *euph* a woman's breasts; BOSOM¹ (1) **3** a measurement round a woman's breasts and back: *rather big round the bust*

bust² *v* **busted** *or* **bust** [T1] *infml* to break, esp. with force: *I bust*(*ed*) *my watch this morning* —see also BUST OUT, BUST UP

bust³ *v* [T1] *sl* **1** (of the police) to take to a police station; ARREST¹ (1): *He was busted for having unlawful drugs* **2** (of the police) to enter without warning to look for something unlawful; RAID²: *His house was busted this morning and some drugs were taken away* **3** to lower (esp. a military man) in rank; DEMOTE

bust⁴ *n sl* **1** a complete failure: *His new play was a complete bust!* **2** a police ARREST² (1) or RAID¹ (4): *The bust was made at 3 o'clock in the morning*

bust⁵ *adj* [Wa5] *infml* **1** broken: *My watch is bust; I must take it to the repairer's* **2 go bust** (of a business) to fail

bus·tard /ˈbʌstəd‖-ərd/ *n* [Wn1] the largest type of land bird of Europe and Australia

bus·ter /ˈbʌstəʳ/ *n* [N] *sl, often derog, esp. AmE* fellow: *Come here, buster!*

-buster /ˌbʌstəʳ/ *comb. form* [*n*→*n*] *sl* a person who

BUSTS[3] or breaks: *Our crimebusters will catch those criminals*

bus·tle[1] /ˈbʌsəl/ *v* [Wv3;I∅] to be busy, often with much noise: *She is always bustling about the house*

bustle[2] *n* [(*the*)S9] activity with plenty of noise and movement: *the bustle of the big city|a bustle of activity*

bustle[3] *n* a frame used for holding out the back part of a woman's dress in former times

bustle with *v prep* [T1 *no pass.*] to have lots of (noisy, busy activity): *The big city is bustling with life*

bust out *v adv AmE* **1** [I∅] *infml* to show flowers and leaves suddenly: *"June is busting out all over"* (song) **2** [I∅] *sl* BREAK OUT (3): *"Tom, have you bust out?"* (Steinbeck, *The Grapes of Wrath*) **3** [I4] *infml* BURST OUT (1)

bust-up /ˈ· ·/ *n sl* **1** a quarrel, noisy and sometimes with fighting: *quite a bust-up last night* **2** *AmE* BREAKUP (1): *the bust-up of their marriage*

bust up *v adv sl* **1** [I∅] to have a quarrel **2** [T1] *AmE* to damage; destroy; spoil: *The travel company's failure bust up their holiday* **3** [I∅] *AmE* BREAK UP (6)

bus·y[1] /ˈbɪzi/ *adj* [Wa1] **1** [B (*with*),B4] working; not free: *He is busy now and cannot see you.|He is busy writing.|to be busy with some important work|a busy man* **2** [B] full of work or activity: *a busy day| a busy town* **3** [B] *AmE* (of telephones) in use; ENGAGED (2): *I'm sorry, sir, the (telephone) line is busy* **4** [B] *derog* full of details that lead the eye away from the main pattern: *This wallpaper's too busy for our bedroom, don't you think?* **5 as busy as a bee/bees** very busy —**busily** *adv* —**busyness** *n* [U]: *Her never-ending busyness made him tired*

USAGE Compare **busy, employed, occupied**, which in one meaning are very close: 1 One can be *very* **busy**, or **busier** *than before*, but one cannot be **very* **occupied** or **more* **employed**. 2 Both **busy** and **occupied** (a more formal word) mean that one has a lot to do and is not free. **Employed** usually means that one is working at a paid job, which may not mean that one is *very* **busy** or *fully* **occupied** at any particular moment. But one can say *She was* **occupied/employed** *in cooking the dinner*.

busy[2] *v* [T1 (*with*)] to make or keep (esp. oneself) busy: *To forget his troubles, he busied himself with answering letters/in his garden*

bus·y·bod·y /ˈbɪzi,bɒdi‖-,badi/ *n derog* a person who takes too much interest in the affairs of others

but[1] /bət; *strong* bʌt/ *conj* **1** rather; instead: *not one, but 2!* **2** yet; in spite of this: *It's not cheap, but it's very good.|He would like to go, but he can't* **3** except for the fact that; however: *He would like to go, but he's busy.|We were coming to see you, but it rained (so we didn't).|They would have written to you, but you told them not to.|He would have said no, but he was afraid* **4** yet also; and at the same time: *I came home sadder but wiser.|They are poor but proud* **5** (after certain NEGATIVES[2]) without it being true that: *I never see her but I want to kiss her.|Hardly a week passes but I get another good idea* **6** (after certain NEGATIVES[2]) that: *There's no doubt/no question but he's the guilty one* **7** (shows disagreement): *"I'll give you £5." "But that's not enough!"* **8** (shows surprise) *"She's won first prize." "But that's wonderful!"* **9** (introduces a new subject): *But now to our next question* **10 not only . . . but (also) . . .** both . . . and . . . —see also BUT THAT, BUT THEN

but[2] *prep* **1** (after **no, all, nobody, who, where**, etc.) other than; except: *There's no one here but me.|Who but George would do such a thing?|Anything but that!|everywhere but in Scotland* **2 the first/next/last but one/two/three** *esp. BrE* one/2/3 from the first/next/last: *His house is the last but one in this street* —see also BUT FOR

USAGE Compare **but, except**, and **save**. In this sentence we can use all 3: *We're all here* **but/except/(*fml*) save** *Mary*. But in this sentence **but** cannot be used: *The window is never opened* **except/save** *in summer*. Use **but** only after words like *no, all, nobody, anywhere, everything*, or after question-words like *who?, where?, what?* It is usually followed by a noun or PRONOUN: *everywhere* **but** *in Scotland|Who* **but** *John would say that?* —see ME (USAGE)

but[3] *adv* **1** *lit* only; just: *He is still but a child!* **2** *AmE sl* and do it; and let it be: *Go there but fast!* **3 all but** very nearly; almost: *The job is all but finished!*

but[4] *pron* (after certain NEGATIVES[2]) that . . . not; who . . . not: *Not a man but had tears in his eyes* (=There was no one without tears in his eyes.)

but[5] /bʌt/ *n* **1 But me no buts** *humor or lit* Don't argue with me; Don't give me excuses **2 ifs and buts** *infml* unwanted arguments against something; unnecessary doubts: *I'm tired of your ifs and buts. Do what I tell you!* **3 (There are) no buts about it** *infml* (There is) no doubt about it; There's no reason for not doing it

bu·tane /ˈbjuːteɪn/ *n* [U] a natural gas used for cooking, heating, and lighting

butch[1] /bʊtʃ/ *adj BrE sl* showing a lot of male tendencies: *a butch woman*

butch[2] *n BrE sl* a BUTCH[1] woman

butch·er[1] /ˈbʊtʃəʳ/ *n* **1** a person who kills animals for food or one who sells meat —see picture at STREET **2** a person who causes blood to flow unnecessarily: *That general/doctor is a real butcher!*

butcher[2] *v* [T1] **1** to kill (animals) and prepare for sale as food **2** to kill bloodily or unnecessarily

butch·er·y /ˈbʊtʃəri/ *n* [U] **1** the preparation of meat for sale **2** cruel and unnecessary killing of human beings

but for /ˈ· ·/ *prep* without; if not for: *But for my brother's help, I would not have finished the work* —compare EXCEPT FOR, SAVE[3]

but·ler /ˈbʌtləʳ/ *n* the chief male servant of a house

butt[1] /bʌt/ *v* [T1;I∅] to strike or push against (someone or something) with the head or horns: *He butted (his head) against the wall* —see also BUTT IN —**butt** *n*: *He gave me a butt in the stomach!*

butt[2] *n* a person (or perhaps thing) that people make fun of: *Poor John was the butt of all their jokes*

butt[3] *n* **1** a large, thick, or bottom end of something: *the butt-end* **2** *sl* the part of the body on which a person sits **3** the last unsmoked end of a cigarette

butt[4] *n* a large barrel for holding liquids

but·ter[1] /ˈbʌtəʳ/ *n* [U] **1** yellow fat made from milk, spread on bread, used in cooking, etc. **2** (*in combs.*) a substance like butter made from something else: *apple butter* **3 Butter wouldn't melt in his/her mouth** *infml* He/She pretends to be kind and harmless but is not really so! —**~y** *adj*

butter[2] *v* [T1] **1** to spread with or as if with butter: *to butter bread* **2 know on which side one's bread is buttered** *infml* to know who will help one most, or bring one most gain —see also BUTTER UP

butter bean /ˈ·· ·/ *n* [*usu. pl.*] any of several types of large broad bean often sold dried, and used as food

but·ter·cup /ˈbʌtəkʌp‖-ər-/ *n* a type of yellow wild flower

but·ter·fin·gers /ˈbʌtə,fɪŋgəz‖ˈbʌtər,fɪŋgərz/ *n* **butterfingers** [Wn3;C;N] *infml* a person who is likely to let things fall or slip through his/her fingers

but·ter·fly /ˈbʌtəflaɪ‖-ər-/ *n* **1** any of several insects that fly by day and often have large beautifully-coloured wings —see picture at INSECT **2** a person who is not serious but spends most of his/her time running after pleasure **3 have butterflies in one's stomach** *infml* to feel very nervous before doing something

but·ter·milk /ˈbʌtəˌmɪlk‖-ər-/ *n* [U] the liquid that remains after butter is made from milk

but·ter·scotch /ˈbʌtəskɒtʃ‖-ərskɑtʃ/ *n* [U] **1** a sweet food made from sugar and butter (and perhaps sweet SYRUP) boiled together **2** a yellowish brown colour

butter up *v adv* [T1] *sl* to FLATTER (someone)

but·ter·y /ˈbʌtəri/ *n* (in some British universities) a room from which food and drink are served

but that /ˈ· ·/ *conj fml* **1** BUT[1] (3): *He would have said no but that he was afraid* **2** (after certain NEGATIVEs[2]) that: *There's no doubt/no question but that he's the guilty one* **3** whether perhaps: *Who knows but that he may succeed?*

but then /ˌ· ˈ·/ also **but then a·gain** /ˌ· · ·ˈ·/— *conj* but on the other hand: *It doesn't go very well, but then what do you expect from a £50 car?*

butt in *v adv* [I∅ (*on, to*)] *sl often derog* to interrupt, usu. by speaking: *I wish you wouldn't keep butting in on our conversation!*

but·tock /ˈbʌtək/ *n* either of the 2 fleshy parts on which a person sits: *the left/right buttock*

but·tocks /ˈbʌtəks/ *n* [(*the*) P] the part of the body on which a person sits —see picture at HUMAN[2]

but·ton[1] /ˈbʌtn/ *n* **1** a small usu. round or flat thing that is fixed to a garment or other object and usu. passed through an opening (BUTTONHOLE[1] (1)) to act as a fastener: *a row of buttons down the front of his shirt|a button nose* (=a small broad flattish nose) **2** a button-like part, object, or piece of apparatus **3** also **push button**— a button-like object used for starting, stopping, or controlling a machine, an apparatus, etc.: *Push the button to start the machine/to turn on the light* **4** *esp. AmE* BADGE (1): *wearing his club's button|wearing a button saying "Make Love Not War"* **5 on the button** *sl, esp. AmE* exactly right

button[2] *v* [T1;I∅] to (cause to) close or fasten with buttons: *to button (up) one's shirt|My shirt doesn't button (up) easily*

button-down /ˈ·· ·/ *adj* [Wa5;A] **1** (of a collar) having the ends fastened to the garment with buttons **2** (of a shirt) having a collar of this type

buttoned up /ˌ·· ˈ·◂/ *adj* **1** quiet; not talking much **2** having or showing difficulty in feeling or expressing oneself freely **3** (of a piece of work) successfully completed: *That is another job buttoned up*

but·ton·hole[1] /ˈbʌtnhəʊl/ *n* **1** a hole for a button: *This buttonhole is torn* **2** *BrE* a flower to wear on one's coat or dress: *wearing a beautiful buttonhole*

buttonhole[2] *v* [T1] to stop and force to listen: *She buttonholed me outside the Minister's Office*

but·ton·hook /ˈbʌtnhʊk/ *n* a hook used in former times for drawing small buttons through BUTTONHOLEs[1] (1), esp. in boots

but·tons /ˈbʌtnz/ *n* **buttons** [Wn3;C] *now rare* BELLBOY

button up *v adv* **1** [I∅] *sl* (usu. in giving or reporting an order) to keep quiet **2** [T1] *infml* to complete successfully: *Let's button up this job*

but·tress[1] /ˈbʌtrəs/ *n* **1** a support for a wall —see picture at CHURCH[1] **2** something that supports or strengthens: *Our country is a great buttress of world peace*

buttress[2] *v* [T1 (UP, *with* or *by*)] to support or strengthen with or as if with a BUTTRESS[1]: *She buttressed her argument with lots of solid facts*

bux·om /ˈbʌksəm/ *adj apprec* (of a woman) attractively fat and healthy-looking

buy[1] /baɪ/ *v* **bought** /bɔːt/ **1** [D1 (*for*);T1;X7;I∅: (*for* or *from*)] to obtain (something) by giving money (or something else of value): *He bought me a book from/(sl) off them for £5.|He bought that car new/cheap.|When prices are low, he buys* **2** [T1 (*with*)] to obtain in exchange for something, often something of great value: *They bought peace with their freedom* **3** [T1] to be exchangeable for: *Our money buys less than it used to* **4** [T1] *sl, esp. AmE* accept; believe: *I don't buy that nonsense* **5 buy time** *infml* to delay an action or decision that seems to be coming too soon: *He tried to buy time by doing a lot of talking* **6 I'll buy it!** *not fml* I can't answer that, so will you tell me?

buy[2] *n infml* **1** an act of buying **2** something of value at a low price; BARGAIN[1] (2): *It's a real buy at that price!*

buy·er /ˈbaɪə[r]/ *n* a person who buys, esp. the head of a department in a department store: *a buyer for Harrod's*

buyer's mar·ket /ˌ·· ˈ··, ˈ·· ˌ··/ *n* [*usu. sing.*] a state of affairs in which goods are plentiful, buyers have a lot of choice, and prices tend to be low —compare SELLER'S MARKET

buy in *v adv* [T1] BID IN

buy off *BrE* also **buy o·ver**— *v adv* [T1] BRIBE[1] (1)

buy out *v adv* [T1] **1 a** to gain control of by buying the whole of: *to buy out a business* **b** to buy the business of: *We bought out the owners for £600,000* **2** [(*of*)] to gain (someone's) freedom from usu. the armed forces, by paying money: *to buy someone out (of the army)*

buy up *v adv* [T1] **1** to buy all the supplies of: *to buy up all the sugar in London* **2** BUY OUT (1)

buzz[1] /bʌz/ *v* **1** [I∅] to make a low HUM, as bees do **2** [I∅ (*with*)] to make or be filled with a low confused whisper: *The crowd/room buzzed (with excitement)* **3** [T1;V3;I∅ (*for*)] to call (someone) by using a BUZZER: *She buzzed (for) her secretary (to come).|I came as soon as you buzzed* **4** [T1] *infml* to fly low and fast over: *Planes buzzed the crowd as a warning*

buzz[2] *n* **1** [C] a noise of BUZZing[1]: *I heard a buzz just now.|I heard the buzz of their voices all night* **2** [C] a signal made by a BUZZER **3** [S] *sl* a telephone call: *I'll just give him a buzz*

buz·zard /ˈbʌzəd‖-ərd/ *n* **1** [C] (in Britain) a type of heavy slow-flying bird that kills and eats other creatures (a HAWK[1]) **2** [C] (in America) a type of heavy slow-flying black bird that eats dead flesh (a VULTURE)

buzz·er /ˈbʌzə[r]/ *n* **1** a thing that BUZZes[1], esp. an electric signalling apparatus **2** the sound of such an apparatus: *At the buzzer you will both come 10 feet forward*

buzz off *v adv* [I∅] *sl, esp. BrE* (in giving or reporting orders) to go away: *Buzz off, you nasty little child!*

by[1] /baɪ/ *prep* **1** near; beside: *standing by the window|to run by the river* **2** by way of; through: *to enter by the door|to leave by the first train out* **3** past: *He walked/passed by me without noticing me.|I go by the house every day.|to run by the tree* **4** already . . . (at/on/in); not later than; before: *By this time tomorrow he'll be here.|Be here by this time tomorrow.|He won't be here by this time tomorrow.|By this time tomorrow I'll have finished the job.|Do you think you'll have finished by 4 o'clock?* **5** (usu. with the PASSIVE[1] form of verbs) as a result of action on the part of; through; by means of: *written by Shakespeare|struck by lightning|taken by force* **6** in accordance with: *to play by the rules* **7** to the amount or degree of: *His horse won by a* *nose.|They paid him too little by £3.|It's better by far* **8** (giving the reason for a judgment): *I can see by your face.|I'd know you anywhere by your laugh.|It's dangerous to judge by appearances* **9** (showing the part seized, held, etc.): *to lead by the hand|to seize the hammer by the handle* **10** (in expressions of strong feeling and solemn promises): *By God he's done it!|I* SWEAR *by everything I believe in* **11** (in measurements and operations with numbers, quantities, etc.): *a room 15 feet by 20 feet|to divide X by Y* **12** (often with plurals or *the*+singular) (showing a measure or a rate): *paid by the hour|by result(s)|berries by the handful|to move along by inches* **13** (showing the size of groups that follow each other): *little by little|The animals went in 2 by 2* **14** (with the *-ing* form): *to earn money by writing|I can tell by looking at you* **15** (without *the*) (in expressions of the following types): **a**: *to go by land|sea|air|made by hand|to send by letter|by mistake|to call someone by name|to know someone by name|sight|day by day* **b** during: *Cats sleep by day and hunt by night* **c** with regard to: *a doctor by profession|French by birth* **d** (showing the type of TRANSPORT²): *to go by car|boat|plane* **16** *tech* having (the stated male animal, esp. a horse) as a father: *Golden Trumpet, by Golden Rain out of Silver Trumpet* —compare OUT OF (8) **17 (all) by oneself** (completely) alone: *He was by himself.|He did it all by himself!* **18 have/keep (something) by one** to have/keep (something) close to one, for easy use

by² *adv* **1** past: *to run by|Please let me (get) by.|A lot of time has gone by since then.|He walked|passed by without noticing me* **2** *infml, esp. AmE* at or to another's home: *Stop|Come by for a little talk after work* **3 be by** to be near: *Do it when nobody is by* **4 lay/put/set (something) by** to keep or store (something, esp. money) for the future

by-, bye- *prefix* less important: SECONDARY (1): BY-PRODUCT|BY-ELECTION|BYWAY

by and by /ˌ·· ˈ·/ *adv infml* before long; soon: *He'll come back by and by*

by and large /ˌ· · ˈ·/ *adv sometimes considered nonstandard* on the whole; in general: *By and large, your idea is a good one*

bye¹ /baɪ/ *n* (in cricket) a run made off a ball that the hitter (BATSMAN) did not touch —see also LEG BYE

bye² also **bye-bye** /ˌ· ˈ·‖ˈ· ·/, (*esp. AmE*) **bye now** /ˈ· ·/— *interj infml* goodbye

bye-byes /ˈbaɪbaɪz/ *n* **go to bye-byes** (*used by or to children*) to go to sleep

by-e·lec·tion /ˈ· ·ˌ··/ *n* a special election held between regular elections to fill a position whose former holder has left it or died

by·gone¹ /ˈbaɪgɒn‖-gɔn/ *adj* [Wa5;A] gone by; past: *in bygone days of long ago*

bygone² *n* an interesting object no longer in use, as sold in special shops, shown to the public, etc.

by·gones /ˈbaɪgɒnz‖-gɔnz/ *n* **let bygones be bygones** *infml* to forget (and forgive) the bad things in the past

by·law, byelaw /ˈbaɪlɔː/ *n* **1** *BrE* a special law or rule made not by the government of the whole country, but by a local council, a railway, etc. **2** *AmE* a rule made by an organization for governing its own affairs

by-line /ˈ· ·/ *n* a line at the beginning of a newspaper or magazine article giving the writer's name

by·pass¹ /ˈbaɪpɑːs‖-pæs/ *n* **1** a passage or road to one side, esp. a way round a town: *Take the bypass to avoid the traffic in the centre of town* **2** *tech* an instrument for sending a flow of gas, liquid, etc., round, instead of through, a part of a machine

bypass² *v* [T1] to avoid: *Let's bypass the town with all its traffic!*

by·play /ˈbaɪpleɪ/ *n* [U] action of less importance going on at the same time as action of more importance, esp. on stage: *a lot of byplay between the speakers that radio listeners couldn't see*

by-prod·uct /ˈ· ˌ··/ *n* **1** something formed in addition to the main product: *Silver is often obtained as a by-product during the separation of lead from rock* **2** an additional result, sometimes unexpected or unintended

byre /baɪəʳ/ *n BrE dial, now rare* a farm building for cattle; COWSHED

by·stand·er /ˈbaɪˌstændəʳ/ *n* a person standing near, but not taking part in, what is happening; ONLOOKER: *The police asked some of the bystanders about the accident*

by the way /ˌ· · ˈ·/ also (*becoming rare*) **by the bye** /ˌ· · ˈ·/— *adv infml* (introducing a new subject or one that has not been mentioned earlier): *By the way, what happened to all the money I gave you?*

by vir·tue of /ˌ· ˈ·· ·/ *prep* as a result of: *He knows it very well by virtue of continual practice*

by·way /ˈbaɪweɪ/ also **by·path** /ˈbaɪpɑːθ‖-pæθ/, **by·road** /ˈbaɪrəʊd/— *n* a smaller road or path which is not much used or known

by·ways /ˈbaɪweɪz/ *n* [*the*+P (*of*)] the less well-known parts (of something, esp. the study of a subject): *the byways of English literature*

by·word /ˈbaɪwɜːd‖-ɜrd/ *n* **1** a common saying or PROVERB **2** [(*for*)] (the name of) a person, place, or thing that is taken as representing some quality, often bad: *The general's name had become a byword for cruelty in war*

by·zan·tine /baɪˈzæntaɪn, -tiːn, bɪ-‖ˈbɪzəntiːn, -taɪn/ *adj* [Wa5] *fml or lit, often derog* **1** difficult to understand because there are too many thoughts, ideas, etc.; COMPLICATED (2); labyrinthine (LABYRINTH) **2** of or practised by people who delight in inventing new and painful ways of making others suffer: *byzantine cruelty*

C, c

C, c /siː/ **C's, c's** *or* **Cs, cs**— **1** the third letter of the English alphabet **2** the ROMAN NUMERAL (number) for 100

c *abbrev. for:* **1** cent(s) **2** CA (about) **3** CUBIC **4** CENTIMETRE(*s*)

C¹ **1** (in Western music) **a** the note (*AmE* also **tone**) beginning the row of notes which form the musical SCALE of C MAJOR **b** the musical KEY based on this note **2** the third level, as for an example of a student's work

C² *written abbrev. for:* CENTIGRADE (=CELSIUS): *Water boils at 100°C*

ca *written abbrev. for:* CIRCA (about)

cab /kæb/ *n* **1** [C; *by*+U] *esp. AmE* taxi: *Shall we walk or take a cab?|Shall we walk or go by cab?* **2** [C; *by*+U] (in former times) a horse-drawn carriage for hire **3** [C] the part of a bus, railway engine, etc., in which the driver sits or stands

ca·bal /kəˈbæl/ *n* [GC] *derog now rare* a small group

of people who make secret plans for (esp. political) action

cab·a·ret /ˈkæbəreɪ‖ˌkæbəˈreɪ/ *n* **1** [U;C] a performance of popular music and dancing while guests in a restaurant have a meal, usu. at night **2** [C] a restaurant that presents such performances

cab·bage /ˈkæbɪdʒ/ *n* **1** [C] a type of large round vegetable with thick green leaves wrapped round its short stem —compare LETTUCE **2** [U] the leaves of this vegetable used (usu. cooked) as food **3** [C] *BrE infml* an inactive person who takes no interest in anything—see picture at VEGETABLE[1]

cab·by, cab·bie /ˈkæbi/ *n* [C;N] *infml* a taxi driver

cab·driv·er /ˈkæbˌdraɪvəʳ/ *n esp. AmE* a taxi driver

ca·ber /ˈkeɪbəʳ/ *n* **1** a long heavy wooden pole used in Scotland in games which test skill and strength **2 tossing the caber** a Scottish game in which a person throws this pole into the air and tries to make it land in a particular place

cab·in /ˈkæbɪ̣n/ *n* **1** a small room on a ship usu. used for sleeping **2** the room at the front of an aircraft in which the pilot sits **3** a small roughly built usu. wooden house: *One of our greatest presidents was born in a little log cabin*

cabin boy /ˈ·· ·/ *n* a boy who is a servant on a ship: *At 15 he was a cabin boy, at 50 commander of the navy*

cabin class /ˈ·· ·/ *n* [U] (on a ship) the travelling conditions which are better and dearer than TOURIST CLASS but worse and cheaper than FIRST CLASS: *I always travel cabin class.|How much is a cabin-class ticket?*

cabin cruis·er /ˈ·· ˌ··/ *n* [C; *by*+U] a large motor boat with one or more CABIN*s* (1) —see picture at BOAT[1]

cab·i·net /ˈkæbɪ̣nɪ̣t, ˈkæbnɪ̣t/ *n* **1** [C] **a** a fine piece of usu. wooden furniture, often with glass doors, used for storing or showing small objects of value or interest **b** a container for a television, record player, etc. **2** [C] FILING CABINET **3** [C] *old use* a small private room **4** [GC] (in various countries) the most important ministers of the government, who meet as a group to make decisions or to advise the head of the government **5** [C;U] *esp. BrE* a meeting of this group: *2 cabinets were held in London last week but no decision was made.|We'll decide that question in cabinet*

cabinet-mak·er /ˈ··· ˌ··/ *n becoming rare* a workman who makes fine furniture

ca·ble[1] /ˈkeɪbəl/ *n* **1** [C;U] (a length of) **a** thick heavy strong rope esp. used on board ships **b** strong wire rope or metal chain used for supporting or pulling objects —see picture at FREIGHTER **2** [C; *by*+U] a set of wires put underground or under the sea which carry telegraph and telephone messages: *Telegrams go to America by cable* **3** [C] *not formal* a telegraphed message **4** [A] having a twisted and knotted pattern of thread, used in KNITting: *She made me some woollen clothes using a cable stitch pattern* **5** [C] *infml* CABLE'S LENGTH

cable[2] *v* [D1 (*to*), 5a;T1,5a;V3;I∅] to send (someone) (something) by telegraph: *I cabled* (*him*) (*some money*).|*He cabled her* (*to come*)

cable car /ˈ·· ·/ *n* a car which is supported in the air and pulled by a continuous CABLE[1] (1) and which usu. travels from the top of a mountain to its foot or to the top of another mountain

ca·ble·gram /ˈkeɪbəlgræm/ *n fml* CABLE[1] (3)

cable rail·way /ˈ·· ˌ··/ *n* a railway along which vehicles are pulled by a continuous CABLE fastened to a motor, used esp. where there are very steep slopes

cable's length /ˈ·· ·/ also **cable length**— *n naut* 600 ft; 100 FATHOM*s*; 1/10 of a NAUTICAL MILE

ca·boo·dle /kəˈbuːdl/ *n* **the whole caboodle** *sl* the whole lot; everything

ca·boose /kəˈbuːs/ *n* **1** a ship's kitchen; GALLEY **2** *AmE* a small carriage at the back of a goods train for people who work on the train —compare GUARD'S VAN

cab rank /ˈ· ·/ also **cab·stand** /ˈkæbstænd/— *n esp. AmE* TAXI RANK

cab·ri·o·let /ˈkæbrɪəleɪ‖ˌkæbrɪəˈleɪ/ *n* **1** CONVERTIBLE[2] **2** a 2-wheeled one-horse carriage (used esp. in former times) with a roof that can be folded back

ca·ca·o /kəˈkɑːəʊ‖kəˈkaʊ/ *n* **cacaos 1** a seed from which COCOA and chocolate are made **2** the South American tree which produces this seed

cache[1] /kæʃ/ *n* **1** a secret place for keeping provisions or valuable, esp. stolen, things **2** the contents of this: *The cache was worth a fortune*

cache[2] *v* [T1] to store (something) in a CACHE[1] (1): *The thieves cached the stolen money*

cach·et /ˈkæʃeɪ‖kæˈʃeɪ/ *n* **1** [C] a special mark to show that an article is of very high quality **2** [U] high social position: *He is a man of cachet* **3** [C] a small case (CAPSULE) for medicine that is swallowed together with its contents

ca·chou /kəˈʃuː/ *n* a sweet eaten to hide a smell on the breath

cack·le[1] /ˈkækəl/ *v* [I∅] **1** to make the noise made by a hen after laying an egg **2** to laugh or talk loudly and unpleasantly with henlike sounds: *Why do you always cackle instead of laughing properly?* —**cackler** /ˈkækləʳ/ *n*

cackle[2] *n* **1** [(*the*) S] the sound of cackling (CACKLE[1]) **2** [C] a short high laugh: *cackles of amusement* **3** [U] *infml* foolish useless talk **4 cut the cackle** *BrE sl* to stop talking (when important action needs to be taken)

ca·coph·o·ny /kəˈkɒfəni‖kəˈkɑ-/ *n* [U;C] a mixture of unpleasant usu. loud sounds which are out of tune: *What* (*a*) *cacophony!* —**-onous** *adj*

cac·tus /ˈkæktəs/ *n* **-tuses** *or* **-ti** /taɪ/ any of a number of desert plants protected by sharp prickles, with thick fleshy stems and leaves —see picture at PLANT[2]

cad /kæd/ *n* [C; *you*+N] *derog, now rare* a man who behaves dishonourably: *That man is a cad; have nothing to do with him!* —**~dish** *adj*

ca·dav·er /kəˈdeɪvəʳ, kəˈdæ-‖kəˈdæ-/ *n esp. med* a dead human body

ca·dav·er·ous /kəˈdævərəs/ *adj* looking like a dead body; very pale; thin and unhealthy

cad·die[1], **caddy** /ˈkædi/ *n* a person who carries GOLF CLUB*s* for someone else who is playing

caddie[2] *v* [I∅ (*for*)] to act as a CADDIE[1]

cad·dy /ˈkædi/ *n* TEA CADDY

ca·dence /ˈkeɪdəns/ *n* **1 a** a regular beat of sound; RHYTHM **b** a set of CHORD*s* at the end of a phrase of music **2** the rise and fall of the human voice esp. in reading poetry

ca·den·za /kəˈdenzə/ *n* (in a piece of music played by several musicians) an ornamental part, played by a single musician, usually near the end of a piece of music, esp. a CONCERTO

ca·det /kəˈdet/ *n* **1** [C] **a** a person studying to become an officer in one of the armed forces or the police **b** a person who is a member of a CADET CORPS **2** [A] (of a part of a family) descended from a younger member: *The prince was from the cadet branch of the royal family*

cadet corps /·ˈ· ·/ *n* **cadet corps** [Wn3;GC] an organization which gives simple military training to pupils in some British schools

cadge[1] /kædʒ/ *v* [I∅ (*from*); T1 (*from and/or for*)] *not fml & derog* to get or try to get (something) by asking, often seeming to be taking advantage of someone: *He cadged 20p for cigarettes yesterday* —**cadger** *n*

cadge² *n* **on the cadge** *not fml & derog* cadging (CADGE¹): *He's on the cadge for money again*

ca·di /ˈkɑːdi/ *n* (in some Muslim countries) the judge (MAGISTRATE) of various towns or villages

cad·mi·um /ˈkædmiəm/ *n* [U] a bluish-white metal that is a simple substance (ELEMENT (6)), used esp. for covering metal objects with a protective surface

ca·dre /ˈkɑːdə, -drə, ˈkeɪdə‖ˈkædri, ˈkɑdrə/ *n* **1** [*usu. pl.*] an inner group of highly trained and active people in a political party or military force **2** a highly trained and active member of a political party or military force

Caer·phil·ly /keəˈfɪli, kɑː-‖kɑr-/ *n* [U] a type of creamy-white Welsh cheese with a delicate taste

cae·sar·e·an sec·tion, ce-, -ian /sə̇ˌzeəriən ˈsekʃən/ also **caesarean**— *n* [C; *by*+U] (in a difficult birth) an operation in which parts of a woman's body (ABDOMEN and UTERUS) are cut to allow the baby to be taken out: *Our first baby was born by caesarean section because my wife had difficulty giving birth*

cae·su·ra /sɪˈzjʊərə‖sɪˈʒʊərə, sɪˈzʊərə/ *n* **1** a pause **a** in the middle of a line of poetry **b** showing a dividing point in a piece of music **2** *fml* a break; interruption

caf·e, café /ˈkæfeɪ‖kæˈfeɪ, kə-/ *n* a small restaurant where light meals and drinks (in Britain only nonalcoholic drinks) are served —compare RESTAURANT

USAGE Some British people use nonstandard pronunciations /keɪf/ and /kæf/ in humour. The nonstandard spelling *caff* is sometimes also used in humour.

caf·e·te·ri·a /ˌkæfə̇ˈtɪəriə/ *n* a restaurant where people collect their own food and drink, often in a factory, college, etc.

caf·feine /ˈkæfiːn‖kæˈfiːn/ *n* [U] a chemical substance found in coffee and tea, often used in medicines as a STIMULANT (something which makes people feel more active)

caf·tan, kaftan /ˈkæftæn‖kæfˈtæn/ *n* a long loose garment usu. of cotton or silk, worn by men in the Near and Middle East and by esp. women in Western countries

cage¹ /keɪdʒ/ *n* **1** a framework of wires or bars in which animals or birds may be kept or carried **2** an enclosure which has the form or purpose of such a framework **3** an enclosed area for prisoners or prisoners of war **4** (in a mine) the framework in which men and apparatus are raised to or lowered from the surface

cage² *v* [Wv5;T1] to put (something) into a cage: *caged birds*

cage in *v adv* [T1 *often pass.*] to enclose or limit the freedom of (someone): *Mothers of young children often feel caged in at home*

cag·ey /ˈkeɪdʒi/ *adj* [Wa1] *infml* careful; secretive; unwilling to talk or to be friendly: *She's very cagey about her past life* —**cagily** *adv* —**caginess** *n* [U]

ca·hoots /kəˈhuːts/ *n* **in cahoots (with)** *sl, esp. AmE* in partnership (with); **in** LEAGUE² (5) **(with)**

cai·man, cayman /ˈkeɪmən/ *n* [Wn1] a type of Central and South American CROCODILE-like animal

ca·ique /kɑːˈiːk/ *n* a type of small boat or ship used in the Eastern Mediterranean

cairn /keən‖keərn/ *n* a heap of stones piled up, esp. on mountain tops, to mark a place or remind people of someone or something

cais·son /ˈkeɪsən, kəˈsuːn‖ˈkeɪsɑn, -sən/ *n* **1** a large box (usu. on 2 wheels) in which AMMUNITION (=explosives, bullets for guns, etc.) is carried **2** a large box filled with air, which allows men to work under water **3** a floating box used for raising sunken ships to the surface

ca·jole /kəˈdʒəʊl/ *v* [T1+*into* or *out of*] to persuade by praise or deceit: *She's always cajoling people (into giving her money).|She cajoled me (out of going)*

cake¹ /keɪk/ *n* **1** [U] a food made by baking a sweet mixture of flour, eggs, sugar, etc. **2** [C] a piece of this food baked into a certain shape or size: *The cook has made you a splendid birthday cake* **3** [C9] (*often in comb.*) a round flat shaped piece of food: *a potato cake* **4** [C (*of*)] a dried flattened solid block of a substance: *a cake of soap|a cake of mud* **5 (be) a piece of cake** *sl, esp. BrE* (to be) very easy **6 (sell) like hot cakes** very quickly: *Those pictures are going like hot cakes, there will be none left soon* **7 have one's cake and eat it (too)** also **eat one's cake and have it**— *infml* to have the advantages of something without the disadvantages that go with it: *You spend all your money on beer and then complain about being poor, but you can't expect to have your cake and eat it (too), you know* **8 take the cake** see **take the** BISCUIT

cake² *v* **1** [D1+*with/on*] to (cause to) cover thickly; ENCRUST: *We caked the wall with mud.|We caked mud on the wall* **2** [I∅] to become a solid mass: *The food had caked in the pan*

cal·a·bash /ˈkæləbæʃ/ *n* **1** a large hard fruit of tropical American origin **2** the tree on which this fruit grows **3** the dried shell of this fruit used as a bowl

cal·a·boose /ˌkæləˈbuːs‖ˈkæləbuːs/ *n AmE* a small prison

cal·a·mine lo·tion /ˌkæləmaɪn ˈləʊʃən/ *n* [U] a liquid used for putting on skin that has been burnt by the sun, to make it less painful

ca·lam·i·tous /kəˈlæmə̇təs/ *adj* having the nature of or causing a CALAMITY: *In the calamitous flood 200 people died* —**~ly** *adv*

ca·lam·i·ty /kəˈlæmə̇ti/ *n* a terrible or very bad event; serious misfortune: *50 people were killed in the calamity*

cal·ci·fy /ˈkælsə̇faɪ/ *v* [T1;I∅] to (cause to) become hard by the addition of lime

cal·ci·na·tion /ˌkælsə̇ˈneɪʃən/ *n* [U] the heating of a chemical to a high temperature to remove unwanted contents or to change its nature, esp. to a dry or powdery condition

cal·cine /ˈkælsɪn, -saɪn‖kælˈsaɪn/ *n* a product of CALCINATION

cal·ci·um /ˈkælsiəm/ *n* [U] a silver-white metal that is a simple substance (ELEMENT) and is found, in combination with other chemicals, in bones, teeth, and chalk

calcium car·bide /ˌ··· ˈ··/ *n* [U] the combination of 2 chemicals (CALCIUM and CARBON) from which a gas (ACETYLENE) can be made by adding water

cal·cu·la·ble /ˈkælkjʊləbəl, -kjə-‖-kjə-/ *adj* **1** that can be worked out from known facts **2** that can be measured —**-bly** *adv*

cal·cu·late /ˈkælkjʊleɪt, -kjə-‖-kjə-/ *v* **1** [Wv4; T1,5a,6a;I∅] to work out or find out (something) by using numbers; COMPUTE: *Have you calculated the result?|I calculated that we would arrive at 6.00 p.m.|The scientist could not calculate when the spaceship would reach the moon.|The new calculating instrument is very simple but quick to use* **2** [T1,5a,6a,b;I∅] to work out by using one's judgment; ESTIMATE: *Did she calculate the cost?|Yes, she calculated that it would cost £100.|I'll calculate what it will cost.|Have you finished calculating yet?* **3** [Wv5;T1,5a,6a,b] to plan; intend: *That was a calculated threat: she meant to annoy you*

calculate on *v prep* [T1,4;V4a] to depend on

(something), usu. for a purpose: *If you want to borrow money from George, you can't calculate on his/him being in a good temper before dinner*

cal·cu·lat·ing /ˈkælkjʊleɪtɪŋ, -kjə-‖-kjə-/ *adj usu. derog* coldly planning and thinking about future actions and esp. whether they will be good or bad for oneself; SHREWD; CRAFTY

calculating ma·chine /ˈ····· ·ˌ·/ also **calculator**— *n* a machine which can carry out number operations and which usu. has a small memory —compare COMPUTER

cal·cu·la·tion /ˌkælkjʊˈleɪʃən, -kjə-‖-kjə-/ *n* **1** [U] the act of calculating **2** [C] the result of an act of calculating: *His calculation was correct but hers was wrong* **3** [U] the condition of being a CALCULATING person: *There was calculation behind his choice of friends; he wanted people useful to him in business*

cal·cu·la·tor /ˈkælkjʊleɪtəʳ, -kjə-‖-kjə-/ *n* **1** a person who calculates **2** a CALCULATING MACHINE, esp. a small one —see picture at MATHEMATICAL

cal·cu·lus /ˈkælkjʊləs, -kjə-‖-kjə-/ *n* **-li** /laɪ/ *or* **-luses** **1** [C] *med* a stone of chalky matter which sometimes forms in the body **2** [U] (in MATHEMATICS) a way of making calculations about quantities which are continually changing, such as the speed of a falling stone or the slope of a curved line —see also DIFFERENTIAL CALCULUS, INTEGRAL CALCULUS

cal·dron /ˈkɔːldrən/ *n* CAULDRON

cal·en·dar /ˈkælɪ̈ndəʳ/ *n* **1** [C] a system which names, arranges, and numbers each day of each month of the year: *In the 18th century Britain stopped using the* JULIAN CALENDAR *and started using the* GREGORIAN CALENDAR **2** [C] a set of tables or sheets on which this system is printed **3** [C *usu. sing.*] a list of important events in the year of a particular organization: *According to the university calendar your examinations will be in June*

calendar month /ˌ··· ˈ·/ *n* **1** a month measured according to the CALENDAR (1), such as one of the 12 months of the modern European system: *You'll be paid by the calendar month* —compare LUNAR MONTH **2** a period of time from a given date in one month to the same date in the next month: *From January 4 to March 4 is 2 calendar months*

calendar year /ˌ··· ˈ·/ *n* **1** YEAR (2) **2** a period of time from a given date in one year to the same date in the next year: *From 4 March 1976 to 4 March 1978 is 2 calendar years*

cal·en·der¹ /ˈkælɪ̈ndəʳ/ *v* [T1] *tech* to put between rollers in order to press smooth

calender² *n tech* a machine for rolling, pressing and smoothing paper, cloth, etc.

cal·ends, kalends /ˈkælɪ̈ndz/ *n* [P;(U)] the first day of the month according to the ancient Roman CALENDAR —compare IDES

calf¹ /kɑːf‖kæf/ *n* **calves** **1** [C] **a** the young of the cow **b** the young of some other large animals such as the elephant —see MEAT (USAGE) **2** [U] CALFSKIN **3 in/with calf** (of an animal) PREGNANT (1); expecting a CALF

calf² *n* **calves** the fleshy back part of the human leg between the knee and the ankle —see picture at HUMAN²

calf love /ˈ· ·/ *n* [U] PUPPY LOVE

calf·skin /ˈkɑːfˌskɪn‖ˈkæf-/ *n* [U] leather made from the skin of the CALF¹ (1a)

cal·i·brate /ˈkælɪ̈breɪt/ *v* [T1] **1** to measure the inside size (DIAMETER) of (a tube or gun) **2** to correct or mark degrees and dividing points on (the scale of a measuring instrument)

cal·i·bra·tion /ˌkælɪ̈ˈbreɪʃən/ *n* **1** [U] the act of calibrating (CALIBRATE¹ (1, 2)) **2** [C] a set of degrees or measurement marks

cal·i·bre, *AmE* also **-ber** /ˈkælɪ̈bəʳ/ *n* **1** [C] the inside size (DIAMETER) of a tube or gun **2** [C] the size of a bullet: *a 32-calibre bullet* **3** [S;(U)] the quality of something or someone: *This work's of a very high calibre.|This doctor's of a very different calibre to the other.|people of (a) very different calibre*

cal·i·co /ˈkælɪkəʊ/ *n* [U] a type of heavy cotton cloth

cal·i·per /ˈkælɪ̈pəʳ/ *n AmE* CALLIPER

ca·liph, khalif /ˈkeɪlɪf/ *n* (*often cap.*) (a title formerly given to) a Muslim ruler who followed Muhammed as a leader of the Muslims: *the caliph of Baghdad*

ca·li·phate, khalifate /ˈkeɪlɪ̈feɪt/ *n* the office, length of rule (REIGN), or country of a CALIPH

cal·is·then·ic /ˌkælɪ̈sˈθenɪk/ *n* [A] CALLISTHENIC

cal·is·then·ics /ˌkælɪ̈sˈθenɪks/ *n* [U;(P)] CALLISTHENICS

calk¹ /kɔːk/ *n tech* a rough iron plate on a boot or horseshoe to prevent slipping

calk² *v* [T1] *tech* to put a CALK on (something)

calk³ *v* [T1] CAULK

call¹ /kɔːl/ *v* **1** [T1;I∅ (*to, for*): (OUT)] to shout; speak or say in a loud clear voice: *He called for help.|They called for an hour but no one heard.|"Stop," he called out.|The fishermen called (out) to the men on the shore.|Are they still calling?* **2** [I∅ (*at, in, on, for*)] **a** to make a short visit to someone: *Let's call (in) on John for 10 minutes.|She called (on me) (on Tuesday).|He called to take her to the theatre.|Do you think we should call at Bob's while we're in London?|Please call again* **b** (of people esp. selling things) to make regular visits: *The milkman calls once a day* **3** [T1;I∅] to (try to) telephone or radio to (someone or something): *I called him this morning but he was out.|I'll call again later* **4** [T1 (OUT, OFF)] to speak (a list): *I'll call the numbers.|Please call out the names of all the people who are present* **5** [T1] to (try to) cause to come by speaking loudly or officially or by sending an order or message: *Mother is calling me.|He called me over/down (from the tree)/in (from outdoors).|The minister called the union leaders to a meeting.|The king called Parliament (together)* **6** [T1] to cause to happen by making an official declaration: *The president called an election* **7** [T1] to waken (someone): *She called me early today* **8** [I∅ (*to*); T1] **a** (of an animal) to make the usual cry to (another animal): *The birds are calling (each other)* **b** to signal to (someone or something) with typical sounds: *The drums are calling (me)* **c** to attract (someone or something): *The sea is calling him* **9** [X1] to name: *We'll call the baby Jean.|Let's call the new town Harlow* **10** [X1;7] to consider: *I call him a fool.|I don't call Russian a hard language* **11** [X1,7,9] **a** to say that (someone) is (something): *She called me fat.|Call me what you like.|Did he call the ball out or in?* **b** to claim (perhaps falsely) that (one) is (something): *How could you do such a nasty thing and still call yourself my friend?* **12** [X1] to agree to (an amount or quantity) calculated for practical purposes, but not calculated very exactly: *I don't know how much it is but let's call it £5* **13** [I∅;T1] (in card games) **a** BID² (3): *He called last.|What did she call?|It's his turn to call* **b** to say what will be TRUMPS² (1): *What did you call?* **14** *NEng & ScotE sl* to say nasty things about (someone): *She's always calling me* —see also **call to** ARMS; **call someone's** BLUFF⁴ (2); **call it a** DAY; **call to** MIND¹ (8); **call something in** QUESTION¹ (5); **call it** QUITS (2); **call one's** SHOT¹ (17); **call a** SPADE **a** SPADE¹ (3); **call the** TUNE¹ (2)

call² *n* [C] **1** a shout; cry: *They heard a call for help* **2** the cry of an animal: *The call of this bird is very loud* **3** an instrument which makes a sound like the cry of, and which attracts, a bird or animal:

When hunting wild duck he always uses a call **4 a** a short usu. formal visit: *The princess makes a call on the king every morning.|You must return his call soon* **b** a business or professional visit: *When does the milkman make his call at your house?* **5** a demand; claim: *He has many calls on his time* **6** [(*to*, 3)] a command to meet, come, or do something; SUMMONS: *The minister waited for a call to the palace.|The call was for 6 o'clock so the actors had to be there by 5.|In the war many people answered the call of their country.|He felt a call (from God) to become a priest* **7** (in card games) BID² (3): *Is he making his call?|It's your call now* **8** (in sports and games) the decision of an UMPIRE¹ (1): *The players disagreed with his call* **9** an attempt to ring someone on the telephone; conversation over the telephone: *I have a call for you from London.|He gave his wife a call but she was out* **10** (on the STOCK EXCHANGE (1)) a notice that a payment of money (INSTALMENT) must be made **11** the attraction of a particular activity or state: *He felt the call of the sea* **12** the instructions in a dance: *Listen to the call and you won't make mistakes* **13** [C;(U)] a need: *You have no call for more money* **14** ROLL CALL **15 at/on call a** ready for use: *The company car is always on call to take you to our meetings* **b** ready to work at a command: *The nurse is on call tonight.|Our leader has great numbers of men at his call* **16 pay a call** *euph* URINATE **17 within call** near enough to hear a call —see also PORT OF CALL; CLOSE CALL; **call of** NATURE (5)

cal·la /ˈkælə/ *n* a type of tall white plant of the LILY family —compare ARUM

call back *v adv* **1** [T1] to cause (someone) to return: *Mrs. Jones was about to leave when her secretary called her back* **2** [I∅] to pay another visit: *The salesman will call back later* **3** [T1;I∅] to return a telephone call: *I'll call (you) back*

call box /ˈ· ·/ also **telephone booth, phone booth;** *BrE* also **telephone kiosk, phone box, telephone box**— *n* a small hut or enclosure containing a telephone for use by the public —see picture at STREET

call·boy /ˈkɔːlbɔɪ/ *n* a boy who tells actors when it is time for them to go onto the stage

call by *v adv* [I∅] *infml* to visit when passing: *I'll call by at the shops on the way home*

call down *v adv* [T1] **1** to ask for something to come down from or as if from heaven: *The priest called down God's anger on the disobedient people* **2** *sl* to say bad things about: *The newspapers called down his latest book* **3** *AmE sl* to scold; TELL OFF **4** *sl, esp. AmE* (*BrE* **call out**) to invite (someone) to fight

call·er /ˈkɔːləʳ/ *n* **1** [C] a person who makes a short visit: *The priest is a regular caller* **2** [C;(*esp. BrE*) N] a person making a telephone call: *I'm sorry, caller, their telephone seems to be broken* **3** [C] a person who calls out numbers in a game (such as BINGO (1)) or instructions in a dance

call for *v prep* [T1] **1** to demand: *to call for the waiter|to call for the bill* **2** to need; deserve: *Your remark was not called for.|It was an uncalled-for remark* **3** to collect (someone or something): *I'll call for you at 9 o'clock*

call forth *v adv* [T1] *fml* to cause to be seen or used: *Trouble can call forth a person's best qualities*

call girl /ˈ· ·/ *n* a woman who arranges on the telephone for men to meet her for paid sex —see also PROSTITUTE

cal·lig·ra·phy /kəˈlɪgrəfi/ *n* [U] (the art of producing) beautiful writing by hand —**-pher, -phist** *n*

call in *v adv* [T1] **1** to ask to attend: *call the doctor in* **2 a** to request the return of: *The makers have called in some cars with dangerous faults* **b** to demand payment of: *I'm going to call in the money I lent* **3** to remove from general use (CIRCULATION): *The government called in all old £5 notes* **4 call in question** to doubt

call-in /ˈ· ·/ *n AmE* PHONE-IN

call·ing /ˈkɔːlɪŋ/ *n* **1** [C] *fml* profession; trade: *"What was his calling?" "He was a teacher"* **2** [C (*to, for*), C3] a strong desire or feeling of duty to do a particular job; VOCATION: *My son has a calling to become a priest*

cal·li·per, *AmE* also **caliper** /ˈkælɪ̵pəʳ/ *n* [A] of or for CALLIPERS

cal·li·pers, *AmE* also **calipers** /ˈkælɪ̵pəz‖-ərz/ [P] **1** an instrument with 2 legs used for measuring thickness, the distance between 2 surfaces, and inner width (DIAMETER) —see PAIR (USAGE) and picture at TOOL¹ **2** metal supports fixed to the legs of a person with weak legs to help him to walk

cal·lis·then·ic, calisthenic /ˌkælɪ̵sˈθenɪk/ *n* [A] of or for CALLISTHENICS

cal·lis·then·ics, calisthenics /ˌkælɪ̵sˈθenɪks/ *n* [U;P] bodily exercises intended to develop healthy, strong, and beautiful bodies

call loan /ˈ· ·/ also **call mon·ey** /ˈ· ˌ··/— *n* a money LOAN which must be repaid at the demand of the lender or borrower

call off *v adv* [T1] **1** to cause not to take place **2** to cause to keep away

call on also **call up·on**— *v prep* **1** [T1] to visit (someone): *We can call on Mary tomorrow* **2** [T1 (*for*); V3] to ask (someone) to do something: *I will now call on Jean (for an answer).|I call on the people of this country to work hard for national unity* **3** [T1] to need to use: *to call on all one's strength*

cal·lous /ˈkæləs/ *adj* **1** *med* (of the skin) hard and thick; having CALLUSes **2** unkind; without feelings for the sufferings of other people —**~ly** *adv* —**~ness** *n* [U]

call out *v adv* [T1] **1** to order officially (someone) to come to one's help: *Call out the firemen/the army* **2** CALL FORTH **3** to cause to stop work (to STRIKE): *The miners' leader called out his men* **4** *sl BrE* (*AmE* **call down**) to invite (someone) to fight

callow /ˈkæləʊ/ *adj* [Wa2] **1** (of a bird) without feathers; young **2** *derog* (of a person or behaviour) young; without experience; IMMATURE

call sign /ˈ· ·/ *n* **1** a ship's signal (in MORSE CODE) to attract attention **2** a sound sent out by a radio station at the beginning of a broadcast, to show which station it is

call-up /ˈ· ·/ *AmE* **draft**— *n BrE not fml* **1** an order to serve in the armed forces: *He got his call-up papers in July* **2** a period in which such orders are given out: *There was a call-up in 1916* **3** the number of people, esp. men, who receive such orders: *There was a large call-up in 1916*

call up *v adv* **1** [T1] to bring back to memory **2** [T1] (*AmE* **draft**)— *BrE infml* to order (someone) to join the armed forces: *He was called up in 1917* **3** [T1;I∅] *AmE* to telephone: *I'll call you up this evening.|I called up, but she wasn't there* **4** [T1] to cause to arrive: *The magician claims to be able to call up spirits from the dead* **5** [T1;I∅] to send a message to (a particular radio station)

cal·lus /ˈkæləs/ also **cal·los·i·ty** /kəˈlɒsɪ̵ti‖kəˈlɑ-/— *n* an area of thick hard skin: *calluses on his hands|callused hands*

calm¹ /kɑːm‖kɑm, kɑlm/ *n* [S;(U)] **1 a** (of weather) an absence of wind or rough weather **b** (of water) a period of stillness: *There was a calm on the sea* **2** a time of peace and quiet; absence of excitement or worry

calm² *adj* [Wa1] **1 a** (of weather) not windy: *After the storm it was calm* **b** (of water) not rough; smooth; still: *The sea was calm* **2** free from excitement; quiet; untroubled: *Even after her husband died she was calm* — **~ly** *adv*

calm³ *v* [T1] to make calm: *The mother calmed her child*

calm down *v adv* **1** [IØ] (of a living being or something active) to become calm: *The excited girl quickly calmed down.|At last the wild wind calmed down* **2** [T1] to make (a living being) calm: *I'll go and calm the excited dogs/your angry brother down*

cal·o·mel /'kæləmel‖-məl/ *n* [U] a white tasteless chemical substance (a COMPOUND of MERCURY and CHLORINE) used in medicine

cal·or gas /'kælə gæs/ *n* [U] *tdmk* (*sometimes cap.*) a type of gas (BUTANE) usu. sold in metal containers for use in houses, factories, etc., where there is no gas supply: *When we camp we usually cook with Calor gas*

cal·o·rie /'kæləri/ *n* **1** a measure of heat; the amount of heat needed to raise the temperature of one gram of water by one degree CENTIGRADE² (1) **2** a measure used when stating the amount of heat or ENERGY (3) that a food will produce: *One thin piece of bread has 90 calories*

cal·o·rif·ic /ˌkælə'rɪfɪk/ *adj tech* heat-producing: *This coal has a high calorific value*

ca·lum·ni·ate /kə'lʌmni-eɪt/ *v* [T1] to speak calumnies (CALUMNY) about (someone)

cal·um·ny /'kæləmni/ *n* **1** [C] an incorrect and unjust thing said about a person with the intention of destroying the good opinion people have of him: *The calumnies against him were soon shown to be false* **2** [U] the act of saying these things

cal·va·ry /'kælvəri/ *n* **1** a model which represents the CRUCIFIXION (death of CHRIST): *There is a calvary outside the church* **2** a very bad experience which causes great suffering: *Her husband's death was her calvary*

calve /kɑːv‖kæv/ *v* [IØ] (of animals) to give birth to a CALF

calves /kɑːvz‖kævz/ *pl. of* CALF

Cal·vin·ism /'kælvɪ̆nɪzəm/ *n* [U] the teachings of John Calvin (1509–64), accepted by a branch of the Christian religion —**-ist** *adj, n*: *the Calvinist church|He was a Calvinist*

ca·lyp·so /kə'lɪpsəʊ/ *n* **-sos** *or* **-soes** a type of song based on a subject of interest in the news and sung in a West Indian manner

ca·lyx /'kælɪks, 'keɪ-‖'keɪ-/ *n* **calyces** /'kælɪ̆siːz, 'keɪ-‖'keɪ-/ *or* **calyxes** *tech* a ring of leaves (SEPALs) which protects a flower before it opens and later supports the opened flower —see picture at FLOWER¹

cam /kæm/ *n* a wheel or part of a wheel shaped to change circular movement into up-and-down (VERTICAL) or side-to-side (HORIZONTAL) movement —see picture at PETROL

ca·ma·ra·de·rie /ˌkæmə'rɑːdəri‖-'ræ-, -'rɑ-/ *n* [U] the fellowship and good will shown to each other by COMRADEs (1), esp. people who spend time together at work, in the army, etc.

cam·ber¹ /'kæmbəʳ/ *v* **1** [T1] to give a CAMBER to (something) **2** [IØ] to have a CAMBER

camber² *n* [C;U] a slight upward curve in the shape of a road or other surface which causes water to run off: *A slight camber keeps the road free of water and also makes driving easier*

cam·bric /'keɪmbrɪk/ *n* [U] a fine white cloth originally of LINEN (1), now usu. of cotton

came /keɪm/ *past t. of* COME

cam·el /'kæməl/ *n* **1** [C] either of 2 large long-necked animals used for riding or carrying goods in desert countries— **a** the Arabian camel (DROMEDARY) with one large HUMP¹ (2) on its back **b** the Asian BACTRIAN camel with two large HUMPs¹ (2) on its back —see pictures at RUMINANT **2** [C] a floating box used esp. to raise sunken ships to the surface **3** [U] a light yellow-brown colour

cam·el·hair /'kæməlheəʳ/ also **camel's hair** /'·· ·/— *n* [U] **1** a thick yellowish brown cloth made from a mixture of wools, usu. used for making coats **2** fine hair used in making artists' brushes

ca·mel·li·a /kə'miːlɪə/ *n* **1** a type of East Asian bush with shiny leaves and large roselike flowers **2** a flower which grows on this bush

Cam·em·bert /'kæməmbeəʳ/ *n Fr* **1** [U] a type of soft rich French cheese with a greyish-white outside and a yellowish inside **2** [C] an amount of this cheese shaped like a wheel, prepared, packed, and sold separately

cam·e·o /'kæmi-əʊ/ *n* **-eos** **1** a piece of women's ornamental jewellery consisting of a raised shape or figure on the background of a small fine flat stone of a different colour **2** a short piece of fine writing or acting usu. concerned with showing the character of one person, place, or event

cam·e·ra /'kæmərə/ *n* **1** an apparatus for taking photographs or moving pictures **2** the part of the television system which changes images into electrical signals **3** **in camera** *fml* in secret; privately: *The court met in camera*

cam·e·ra·man /'kæmərəmən/ *n* **-men** /mən/ **1** a person who works a camera, esp. for films or television **2** a person who sells cameras

cam·i-knick·er /'kæmi ˌnɪkəʳ/ *n* [A] of or for CAMI-KNICKERS

cami-knick·ers /'kæmi ˌnɪkəz‖-ərz/ also **cami-knicks** /'kæmi nɪks/— *n* [P] a woman's garment combining CAMISOLE and KNICKERS¹ (1): *She was wearing a pair of cami-knickers*

cam·i·sole /'kæmɪ̆səʊl/ *n* (esp. in former times) a short undergarment worn by women on the top half of the body

cam·o·mile, chamomile /'kæməmaɪl/ *n* **1** [C] a type of plant with sweet-smelling white and yellow flowers —compare DAISY **2** [U] a medicine made from the dried flowers of this plant

cam·ou·flage¹ /'kæməflɑːʒ/ *n* [C;U] a way of using colouring or shape which makes it difficult to see or find something; the use of branches, paint, nets, smoke, etc., to hide a usu. military object: *Many animals have a natural camouflage which hides them from their enemies.|Camouflage is necessary if we are to deceive the enemy*

camouflage² *v* [T1] to try to hide (something) by using CAMOUFLAGE: *The military vehicles were camouflaged*

camp¹ /kæmp/ *n* **1** [C;U] a place where people live in tents or huts for a short time usu. for pleasure: *When we were on holiday we stayed in a camp.|The climbers had a camp near the top of the mountain.|We were in camp by 6 o'clock.|Let's go back to camp* **2** [C] (*usu. in comb.*) a place where people live often unwillingly: *a labour camp|an army camp* **3** [C] a group of people or organizations with the same esp. political or religious ideas —compare SCHOOL OF THOUGHT **4** [U] life or work in the armed forces **5** **break/strike camp** to take up and put away the tents one has been living in when one is preparing to go somewhere else

camp² *v* **1** [IØ] to set up (PITCH) or live in a camp: *The hunters camped near the top of the mountain.|We go camping every summer* **2** [IØ (*out*)] to sleep outdoors in a tent: *We camped out last night*
See next page for picture

camp³ *adj* **1** HOMOSEXUAL **2** (of a man) behaving or looking like a woman **3** once thought beautiful but now considered so unfashionable as to be amusing: *He still likes the cinema films he liked as a child: then he thought they were good; now he thinks they are camp* **4** **high camp** (intentionally made)

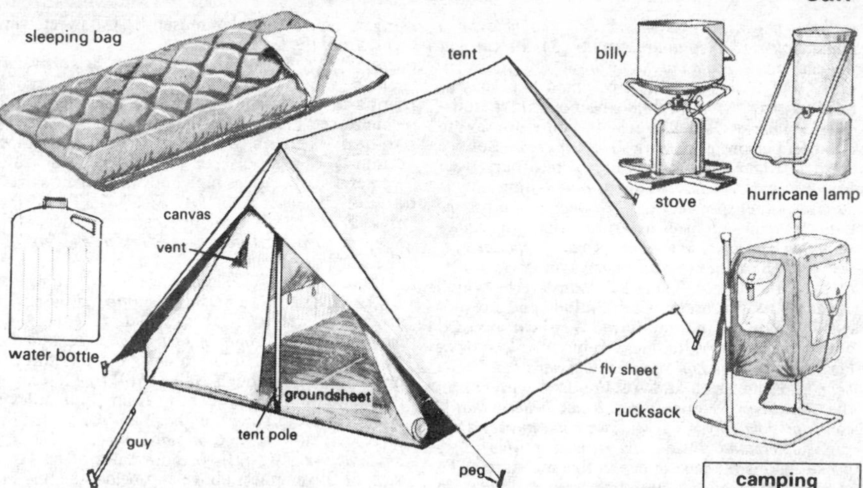

artistically very bad, but in an interesting or stylish way

cam·paign¹ /kæm'peɪn/ *n* [C; *on*+U] **1** a connected set of military actions with a particular purpose: *The Spanish campaign and the campaign to seize Moscow were both failures* **2** a connected set of actions intended to obtain a particular result in politics or business: *The Leader of the Opposition is on campaign in Scotland.|The campaign succeeded and he won the election*

campaign² *v* [IØ (*for*)] to lead, take part in, or go on a CAMPAIGN: *Joan is campaigning for equal rights for women* —**~er** *n*

cam·pa·ni·le /ˌkæmpə'niːli/ *n* a high bell tower which stands separately from any other building

cam·pa·nol·o·gy /ˌkæmpə'nɒlədʒi‖-'nɑ-/ *n* [U] the art of making or esp. of ringing bells —**-gist** *n*

cam·pan·u·la /kæm'pænjʊlə‖-jələ/ *n* any of various types of plant with bell-like flowers, such as the HAREBELL

camp bed /ˌ· '·‖'· ·/ *AmE* **cot**— *n* a light narrow usu. single bed which folds flat and is easily carried

camp chair /ˌ· '·‖'· ·/ *n* a light chair which folds flat and is easily carried —compare DECK CHAIR

camp·er /'kæmpəʳ/ *n* **1** a person who camps **2** *AmE* a motor vehicle big enough to live in when on holiday, usu. having apparatus for cooking and sleeping in the back part

camp·fire /'kæmpfaɪəʳ/ *n* a usu. wood fire made in the open air by campers

camp fol·low·er /'· ˌ··/ *n* **1** a person (esp. a PROSTITUTE) who is not a soldier but who follows the army from place to place for business reasons **2** a politician who joins a party or movement for personal gain

camp·ground /'kæmpgraʊnd/ *n* **1** CAMPSITE **2** *esp. AmE* a place used for outdoor religious meetings

cam·phor /'kæmfəʳ/ *n* [U] a strong-smelling white substance obtained from trees, used in medicine to prevent unconsciousness, in industry in the making of plastics, and also used to keep insects away

cam·phor·at·ed /'kæmfəreɪtɪ̣d/ *adj* containing CAMPHOR: *camphorated oil*

camphor ball /'·· ·/ *n* a small ball of CAMPHOR used to keep insects away from clothes —compare MOTHBALL

cam·pi·on /'kæmpɪən/ *n* [Wn1] any of several types of small plant with small white, red, or blue flowers, commonly found in Britain

camp meet·ing /'· ˌ··/ *n AmE* a religious meeting lasting several days, usu. held in a large tent or in the open air, and attended by people who camp in the surrounding area

camp out *v adv* [IØ] **1** to camp outdoors **2** [(*with*)] *sl esp BrE* to live for a short time (with): *Jim and Mary had to camp out with her parents in their house in Dorset*

camp·site /'kæmpsaɪt/ also **campground**— *n* a place, such as a field, used for camping or for a camp

camp up *v adv* **camp it up** *sl* to act with too much movement of the hands and speak with too much movement of the voice, in a way that seems funny and unnatural: *The actors camped it up last night* —see also HAM UP

cam·pus /'kæmpəs/ *n* **1** [C;U] the grounds of a university, college, or school **2** [A] a university: *Do you like campus life?* **3** [C] *esp. AmE* a separate branch of a university: *Is Berkeley the biggest campus of the University of California?*

cam·shaft /'kæmʃɑːft‖-ʃæft/ *n* a rod to which a CAM is fastened

can¹ /kən; *strong* kæn/ *v* **could** /kəd; *strong* kʊd/, *3rd pers. sing. pres. t.* **can**, *pres. t. neg. contr.* **can't** /kɑːnt‖kænt/ *or* **cannot** /'kænət, -nɒt‖-nɑt/, *past t. neg. contr.* **couldn't** /'kʊdnt/ [Wv2;IØ,2] **1** to know how to: *I can swim well.|I couldn't/wasn't able to do that new job; it was too difficult* **2** to be able to: *I can see you easily from here.|This man could cure all diseases.|Let's go where we can practise our religion freely.|I'll see what can be done.|Everything that money can buy* **3** to be allowed to (by rules): *You can't pick the ball up in football* **4** [*nonassertive*] to allow oneself to: *You can hardly blame him for doing that.|I can't take your coat without paying you for it* **5** to have permission to; may: *The teacher said we could go to the shops for sweets.|*(*infml*) *Can we go to the shops for sweets, please, Miss?* **6** (used for expressions of surprise in question form): *What(ever) can it possibly be?* **7** to have to; must: *If you don't be quiet you can leave the room* **8** (expressing doubt about a possibility) may; might: *What can the police want with me; I've done nothing wrong.|Can he still be alive after all these years?* **9** (with verbs expressing actions of the 5 senses and of the mind): *I can see you easily from here.|I couldn't understand him when he spoke very fast* **10** (with requests) will: *"Can you put it in lots of*

well-salted water?" (SEU S.).|*Can you hold on a minute, please?* —compare COULD (3) **11 can but** *fml* can only: *I could but do my duty*
USAGE 1 **Can** is now more common than **may** or **might** to express informally the idea of "permission", since we do not feel it polite to say to another person: *You may (not) do this.* But we often use **may** when talking about ourselves: **May/(Might)** *I help you?* or in *fml* writing: *If the Minister is satisfied that it is reasonable to do so, he* **may** . . . or in sentences like this: *"What right have we to tell somebody in Germany what he* **may** *or* **may** *not do?"* (SEU S.) (Here the speaker disapproves of the whole idea of **may**.) 2 Many verbs which concern the 5 senses and the mind, and are not usually found in the -ing form [Wv6] can be used with **can** to express the idea of -ing: *I'm looking at him and I* **can** *see him.*|*I'm listening hard but I can't hear it.* **Taste, smell** and **feel** are used with **can** in the same way. Notice also: *I* **can** *believe that.*|*I* **can't** *imagine why.*|**Can** *you guess the answer?*|*She* **can't** *understand it.*|**Can** *you remember where they live?* **Could** is the past of **can** in this meaning. 3 To express "possibility", use **may, could, might**, in sentences that mean "perhaps"; otherwise use **can**. Compare: *The road* **can** *be blocked* (=it is possible to block it) and *The road* **may/could/might** *be blocked* (=perhaps it is blocked). Use **can** in questions about possibility: *This* **may** *be true*→**Can** *this be true?* and usually in statements about impossibility. Compare: *This* **may** *not be true* (=perhaps it is not true) and *This* **can't** *be true* (=it is not possible that it is true). —see COULD (USAGE)

can² /kæn/ *n* **1** a usu. round metal container with an open top or removable lid and sometimes with handles, used for holding milk, coffee, oil, waste, ashes, etc. **2** *esp. AmE* a closed metal container in which foods are preserved without air; TIN **3** *esp. AmE* also **canful** /ˈkænfʊl/— the contents of such a container: *Add 2 cans of juice to the mixture and it will taste better* **4** *sl* prison; JAIL; CLINK (esp. in the phr. **in the can**) **5 carry the can** *infml esp. BrE* to take the blame: *Why do I always have to carry the can when something goes wrong?* **6 in the can** *infml* (of films) completed; ready for showing to the public

can³ /kæn/ *v* **-nn-** [T1] **1** to preserve (food) by putting in a closed metal container without air: *In this factory they can fish to be sent abroad* **2** [Wv5] *sl* to record (music): *In this shop they always play canned music*

ca·nal /kəˈnæl/ *n* **1** a watercourse dug in the ground **a** to allow ships or boats to travel along it: *The Panama canal joins 2 oceans* **b** to bring water to or remove water from an area: *Canals have been built to take water to the desert* **2** *med* a narrow passage in the body through which liquids pass

canal boat /·ˈ· ·/ *n* a long narrow boat for use on a CANAL

can·a·lize, -ise /ˈkænəlaɪz/ *v* [T1] **1** to deepen, straighten, or widen (a river): *By canalizing the river they prevented flooding* **2** to direct (water) in one direction **3** to direct (a variety of actions) to one particular end: *If we want to influence the government we must canalize our efforts* —**-lization** /ˌkænəlaɪˈzeɪʃən‖-lə-/ *n* [U]

can·a·pé /ˈkænəpeɪ‖-pi, -peɪ/ *n* a small piece of bread spread with cheese, fish, or meat and usu. served with drinks at a party

ca·nard /kæˈnɑːd‖kəˈnɑrd (*Fr* kanar)/ *n Fr* a false piece of news

ca·nar·y¹ /kəˈneəri/ *n* **1** [C] a type of small yellow bird usu. kept as a pet **2** [C] *sl, esp. AmE* a female singer, esp. of popular music **3** [U] sweet white wine from the Canary Islands

canary² *n, adj* [Wa5] (having) a bright yellow colour

ca·nas·ta /kəˈnæstə/ *n* [U] a type of card game in which 2 sets (PACK*s*) of cards are used

can·can /ˈkænkæn/ *n* (esp. in France in the 19th century) a type of gay stage dance in which women kick their legs high and shake their skirts

can·cel /ˈkænsəl/ *v* **-ll-** (*AmE* **-l-**) **1** [T1;(I∅)] to give up or call off (a planned activity, idea, etc.): *She cancelled her trip to New York as she felt ill* **2** [T1;(I∅)] to declare that (something) is to be without effect: *She cancelled her order for a new car* **3** [T1] to mark (a postage stamp) officially to prevent re-use **4** [T1] to balance; equal: *The increase in the strength of their navy is cancelled by that in our army* **5** [T1] to cross out (writing) by drawing a line through **6** [T1 (*by*)] *tech* to remove the same number or quantity from (both sides of an EQUATION (1) or from above and below the line in a FRACTION (2)): *Can you cancel 2xy=4xp by anything?* **7** [I∅ (*by*)] (of both sides of an EQUATION or the numbers above and below the line in a FRACTION) to permit division by the same number or quantity: *Does anyone in the classroom think that 2xy=4xp will cancel by anything?*

can·cel·la·tion /ˌkænsəˈleɪʃən/ *n* **1** [U] the act of CANCELling (1) or of having been CANCELled (1): *The cancellation of the order for planes led to the closure of the factory* **2** [C] an example of this: *Because there have been cancellations you can now come on the trip* **3** [C] the mark used when CANCELling (3) a postage stamp: *Some rare cancellations are very valuable*

cancel out *v adv* [I∅;T1] (of figures) to balance (each other); be equal to (each other): *The £1 I owed him and the £1 he owes me cancel (each other) out*

can·cer /ˈkænsəʳ/ *n* **1** [C;U] (a) diseased growth in the body: *He's got a cancer in his throat.*|*He's got cancer of the throat* **2** [C] (a) spreading evil in a person or in society: *Violence is the cancer of our society*

Cancer *n* **1** [R] **a** the ancient sign, a sea animal (CRAB), representing the 4th division of the ZODIAC belt of stars **b** the group of stars (CONSTELLATION) formerly in this division —see picture at PLANET **2** [C] a person born under the influence of this sign —see also TROPIC OF CANCER

can·cer·ous /ˈkænsərəs/ *adj* of or like CANCER: *He had a cancerous growth on his neck* —**~ly** *adv*

can·de·la /kænˈdiːlə, -ˈdelə, ˈkændələ/ *n* **-las** *tech* a measure of the strength of light

can·de·la·brum /ˌkændəˈlɑːbrəm/ also **can·de·la·bra** /-brə/— *n* **-brums** *or* **-bra** /brə/ an ornamental holder for several candles or lamps

can·did /ˈkændəd/ *adj* **1** [B] directly truthful, even when telling the truth is uncomfortable or unwelcome **2** [A] (of a camera) secretly used for photographing people who do not know they are being photographed

can·di·date /ˈkændədət‖-deɪt, -dət/ *n* **1** a person taking an examination **2** a person who wants, or whom others want, to be chosen for a position, esp. in an election: *John was the strongest candidate for the job.*|*He claimed he would be a candidate in the presidential election*

can·di·da·ture /ˈkændədətʃəʳ/ also (*esp. AmE*) **can·di·da·cy** /ˈkændədəsi/— *n* **1** [U] the state of being a CANDIDATE: *He made known his candidature for the next election* **2** [C] an example of this: *Several candidatures have been made public for next year's elections*

can·did·ly /ˈkændədli/ *adv* **1** in a sincerely honest truthful way: *He spoke to me very candidly about his humble origin; he isn't ashamed of his family* **2** speaking in a CANDID way

can·died /ˈkændid/ *adj* **1 a** having a covering of shiny sugar **b** cooked in sugar until shiny: *candied fruit* **2** (of words) friendly but deceptive: *candied praise*

can·dle /ˈkændl/ *n* **1** a usu. round stick of wax containing a length of string (the WICK) which gives light when it burns **2 burn a/the candle at both ends** *infml* to work very early and very late; spend too much time on work or pleasure; get too little rest: *Young people like to enjoy life, and they often burn the candle at both ends* **3 can't/is not fit to hold a candle to** *infml* to be much less able than (someone): *He can't hold a candle to John when it comes to learning foreign languages* **4 The game's not worth the candle** *infml, esp. BrE* the difficulties resulting from a certain course of action are greater than the advantages it will bring **5 hold a candle to the devil** *lit* to help in doing evil

can·dle·light /ˈkændl-laɪt/ *n* [U] the light produced by candles

Can·dle·mas /ˈkændlməs/ *n* [R] a Christian feast held on February 2nd

can·dle·pow·er /ˈkændlˌpaʊəʳ/ *n* [(*the*) S] the amount of light coming from an object (measured in CANDELA*s*): *What is the candlepower of this lamp?*

can·dle·stick /ˈkændlˌstɪk/ *n* a holder for usu. one candle —compare CANDELABRUM and see picture at CHURCH[1]

can·dle·wick /ˈkændlˌwɪk/ *n* **1** [C;U] (a piece of) the string (WICK) contained in candles and burned to give light **2** [U] an ornamental pattern (esp. on bed covers) made of rows of raised short threads (TUFT*s*) separated from other rows by bare material **3** [U] material having such a pattern: *The covering was made of candlewick*

can·dour, *AmE* **-dor** /ˈkændəʳ/ *n* [U] the state or quality of being sincerely honest, undeceptive, and truthful (CANDID)

can·dy[1] /ˈkændi/ *n* **1** [C;U] *esp. AmE* (a shaped piece of) various types of boiled sugar sweets or chocolate **2** [U] a very sweet soft sugary food

candy[2] *v* **1** [T1] to preserve (food) by cooking in sugar **2** [T1] to boil (sugar) until hard and shiny **3** [I∅] to become covered with sugar; CRYSTALLIZE[2] (1) into sugar

can·dy·floss /ˈkændiflɒs‖-flɑs, -flɔs/ *n* **1** [U] *AmE* usu. **cotton candy**— fine sticky often coloured sugar threads eaten as a sweet and usu. served on a stick: *I like eating candyfloss* **2** [C] *BrE* a single serving of this: *Can I have a candyfloss, please?*

can·dy·tuft /ˈkændɪtʌft/ *n* [C;U] a type of plant with white, pink, and purple bunches of flowers

cane[1] /keɪn/ *n* **1** [C] **a** the hard smooth thin often hollow stem of certain plants (tall grasses such as SUGAR CANE or BAMBOO) **b** the stem of certain fruit-producing plants that grow straight from the root, such as the BLACKBERRY **2** [U] lengths of this used as a material for making furniture: *cane chairs* **3** [C] a length of this used for supporting weak plants, for helping weak people to walk, or for punishing people **4** [*the*+R] a punishment (esp. in schools) in which a person is struck with this (often in the phr. **get/give the cane**)

cane[2] *v* [T1] **1** to punish (someone) by striking with a CANE[1] (3); give the CANE[1] (4) to (someone): *The teacher used to cane me when I behaved badly.|I got a good caning for coming to school late* **2** to repair (furniture) by using pieces of CANE[1] (2)

ca·nine /ˈkeɪnaɪn, ˈkæ-‖ˈkeɪ-/ *adj, n tech* (of, for, typical of) a dog or related animal

canine tooth /ˈ·· ·/ *n* one of 4 sharp pointed teeth in the mouth —see picture at TOOTH[1]

can·is·ter /ˈkænɪ̇stəʳ/ *n* **1** a usu. metal container used for holding a dry substance **2** a small container which bursts and scatters its contents when fired from a gun: *a canister of* TEARGAS —compare GRENADE

can·ker[1] /ˈkæŋkəʳ/ *n* **1** [C;U] a sore or area of soreness caused by a disease which attacks the wood of trees and the flesh (esp. the mouth and ears) of animals and people: *Our cat has a canker in its ear.|This tree is suffering from canker* **2** [C] (a) spreading evil in a person or society: *Violence is the canker in our society* —compare CANCER (2) **3** [U] GANGRENE —**~ous** *adj*

canker[2] *v* **1** [T1] to destroy by CANKER[1] (1) **2** [I∅] (esp. of plants) to develop or have CANKER[1] (1)

canker worm /ˈ·· ·/ *n* [Wn2] any of various types of insects which destroy the leaves of plants

can·na /ˈkænə/ *n* **1** any of various types of tropical plants with large leaves and bright red, orange, or yellow flowers **2** a flower from the plant

can·na·bis /ˈkænəbɪ̇s/ *n* [U] **1** the parts of the INDIAN HEMP plant which can be made into a drug sometimes smoked in cigarettes to give a feeling of pleasure, leading to sleepiness **2** also **(Indian) hemp**, (*sl*) **pot**, (*sl*) **grass**— the drug produced (in the stronger form of HASHISH or esp. the less strong form of MARIJUANA, or as BHANG)

canned /kænd/ *adj* **1** [Wa5] *esp. AmE* (of food) preserved in a tin **2** *sl* drunk

can·nel·lo·ni /ˌkænɪ̇ˈləʊni/ *n* [U;(P)] meat or cheese with a covering of PASTA

can·ne·ry /ˈkænəri/ *n* a factory where food is CANned[3] (1)

can·ni·bal /ˈkænɪ̇bəl/ *n* **1** a person who eats human flesh **2** an animal which eats the flesh of its own kind

can·ni·bal·is·m /ˈkænɪ̇bəlɪzəm/ *n* [U] (esp. of people who eat human flesh) the act or practice of eating one's own kind —**-tic** /ˌkænɪ̇bəˈlɪstɪk/ *adj*

can·ni·bal·ize, -ise /ˈkænɪ̇bəlaɪz/ *v* [T1] to use (a broken machine) to provide parts for the repair of another faulty machine of the same kind

can·non[1] /ˈkænən/ *n* **cannons** *or* **cannon** **1** a big gun fixed to the ground or onto a usu. 2-wheeled carriage: *The general decided to use cannon against the enemy.|In this castle there are cannons from the 15th century* **2** a powerful gun to be fired from an aircraft: *Our fighter planes are all armed with cannon*

cannon[2] *v* [L9] to strike forcefully; knock: *He came running round the corner, cannoned into me, and knocked me over*

can·non·ade /ˌkænəˈneɪd/ *n* a continuous heavy firing by large guns: *Much of the city was destroyed in the cannonade*

can·non·ball /ˈkænənbɔːl/ *n* (used in former times) a heavy iron ball fired from a CANNON[1] (1)

cannon fod·der /ˈ·· ˌ··/ *n* [U] soldiers thought of as nothing but "food" for CANNON*s*[1] (1), as military material which can be used without regard for their lives

can·not /ˈkænət, -nɒt‖-nɑt/ [Wv2] *fml* **1** (*commonly used in writing*) can not: *Mr Smith is sorry that he cannot accept your kind invitation to dinner* **2** (*used as the opposite of* must, *to say that something is impossible*): *They cannot have gone out because the light's on!* (compare *They must have gone out, because the light's not on*) —compare MUST (2) **3** **cannot (help/choose) but** *fml* must: *I cannot (help) but admit the truth of your remarks, although they go against my interests.|We could not but weep at the sad news*

can·ny /ˈkæni/ *adj* [Wa1] **1** clever; not easily deceived esp. in money matters: *That old lady's* *canny for her age* **2** *N E EngE apprec* nice; good; lucky: *He's a canny boy.|It's a canny little dog* **3** *ScotE* careful —**cannily** *adv*

ca·noe¹ /kə'nuː/ *n* [C; *by*+U] a long light narrow boat, pointed at both ends, and moved by a PADDLE¹ (1) held in the hands: *We crossed the lake by canoe*
USAGE One **paddles** a **canoe** and *gets into* or *out of* it. —see picture at BOAT¹

canoe² *v* **canoed,** *pres. p.* **canoeing** **1** [IØ] to travel by CANOE **2** [T1] to pass over or through by CANOE: *We canoed the lake in less than an hour* **3** [T1;IØ] to carry (goods) from one place to another by CANOE —**~ist** *n*

can·on¹ /'kænən/ *n* **1** [C] an established law of the Christian Church **2** [*the*+R] the central and holiest part of the Christian religious service called the MASS (1) **3** [C] an official list of the writings accepted as being truly the work of a certain writer or as forming part of a certain collection of writings such as the Bible **4** [C] *fml* a generally accepted standard of behaviour or thought: *His behaviour offends against the canons of good manners*

canon² *n* [C;A] a Christian priest with special duties in connection with the chief church (CATHEDRAL) of an area

ca·non·i·cal /kə'nɒnɪkəl‖kə'nɑ-/ *adj* **1** according to CANON LAW **2** in accordance with a general rule

ca·non·i·cals /kə'nɒnɪkəlz‖kə'nɑ-/ *n* [P] *tech* the garments worn by a Christian priest when leading a religious service in church

can·on·ize, -ise /'kænənaɪz/ *v* [T1] to declare (a dead person) a SAINT (2): *Joan of Arc was canonized in 1920*

canon law /ˌ·· '·/ *n* [U] the established law of the Christian Church

ca·noo·dle /kə'nuːdl/ *v* [IØ] *BrE sl* (of a man and a woman) to hold each other lovingly; to CUDDLE each other

can·o·py /'kænəpi/ *n* **1** a cover usu. of cloth fixed above a bed or seat or carried on posts above a person on ceremonial occasions **2** the enclosure over the front (COCKPIT) of a plane **3** anything which seems like a cover: *The canopy of the heavens.|A canopy of branches*

canst /kənst; *strong* kænst/ [Wv2] **thou canst** *old use or bibl* (when talking to one person) you can

cant¹ /kænt/ *n* **1** a sloping surface: *Ships usually have a cant so that water will run off* **2** a sudden movement which causes sloping: *The bus gave a cant and an old lady fell and hurt herself*

cant² *v* [T1;IØ] to (cause to) slope —see also CANT OVER

cant³ *n* [U] **1** special words used by a particular group of people esp. with the intention of keeping the meaning secret from others not in their group; JARGON: *thieves' cant* **2** *derog* talk meant to deceive people about oneself, esp. about one's religious practices: *Every word she said was cant: she's not been inside a church for years*

can't /kɑːnt‖kænt/ [Wv2] *contr. of* **1** (*commonly used in speech*) can not: *You can swim, can't you?* —see MUST (USAGE), CONTR. (USAGE), CANNOT **2** **I can't think** I don't in the least know: *I can't think why you like her*

Can·tab /'kæntæb/ *abbrev* (*used esp. after the title of a degree*) of Cambridge University: *John Smith, M.A. Cantab*

Can·ta·bri·gi·an /ˌkæntə'brɪdʒɪən/ *n infml, now rare* a student or former student of Cambridge University

can·ta·loup, *AmE* **-loupe** /'kæntəluːp‖-ləʊp/ *n* [C;U] a type of large round fruit (MELON) with a hard green skin and juicy reddish-yellow flesh; sort of MUSKMELON: *Have a/some cantaloup!|a cantaloup* MELON

can·tan·ker·ous /kæn'tæŋkərəs/ *adj infml* bad-tempered; quarrelsome —**~ly** *adv* —**~ness** *n* [U]

can·ta·ta /kæn'tɑːtə, kən-‖kən-/ *n* a usu. religious musical work for several single (SOLO) voices and a mixed group of singers (CHORUS). It is shorter than an ORATORIO

can·teen /kæn'tiːn/ *n* **1** a place in a factory, military camp, etc., where people may buy and eat food, meals, drinks, sweets, etc. **2** a collection consisting of a knife, fork, spoon, cup, and tin plate from which a soldier eats when on the march **3** *BrE* a set of knives, forks, and spoons (CUTLERY) usu. for 6 or 12 people **4** a small usu. leather container in which water or other drink is carried

can·ter¹ /'kæntəʳ/ *n* [*usu. sing.*] **1** (of a horse) a movement which is fast but slower than a GALLOP **2** a ride on a horse which is moving at this speed: *I'm going for a canter round the field*

canter² *v* [T1;IØ] to (cause to) move at the speed of a CANTER

can·ti·cle /'kæntɪkəl/ *n* a short religious song usu. taken from the Bible

can·ti·le·ver /'kæntˌɪ̈ˌliːvəʳ/ *n* an armlike beam standing out from an upright supporting post or wall and used for supporting a shelf, one end of a bridge, etc.: *A* **cantilever bridge** *is built on supports from which cantilevers stand out and join together*

can·to /'kæntəʊ/ *n* **-tos** one of the main divisions of a long poem

can·ton /'kæntɒn, kæn'tɒn‖'kæntən, -tɑn/ *n* a small political division of certain countries, esp. of Switzerland

can·ton·ment /kæn'tuːnmənt‖-'təʊn-, -'tɑn-/ *n* a collection of buildings where soldiers live; military camp

can·tor /'kæntəʳ, -tɔːʳ/ *n* **1** the man who leads the people in prayer and who sings the music in a Jewish religious service **2** the leader of a group of singers (CHOIR) esp. in a church

cant o·ver *v adv* [IØ] (esp. of a movable object) to lean over: *The leg of the chair broke and the chair canted over*

can·vas /'kænvəs/ *n* **1** [U] strong rough cloth used for tents, sails, bags, etc. —see picture at CAMP² **2** [C] **a** a piece of this used for an oil painting **b** a completed oil painting **3** **under canvas** **a** in tents **b** (of a ship) with sails spread open

can·vass¹, -vas /'kænvəs/ *v* **1** [IØ;T1: (*for*)] to go through (an area) or to (people) to ask for (political support or orders for one's goods) or to find out (people's opinions): *The Labour party has canvassed all of this town but it won't win the election.|I'm canvassing tonight* **2** [T1] to examine and consider (something, such as an idea) in detail

can·vass², -vas *n* an act of CANVASSing¹ (1)

can·yon /'kænjən/ *n* a deep narrow steep-sided valley usu. with a river flowing through —see VALLEY (USAGE)

cap¹ /kæp/ *n* **1** a type of soft flat tight-fitting head-covering worn by men and boys —compare HAT (1) **2** this given officially as a sign of honour or rank: *He has 2 caps for playing cricket for England.|She wore the white cap of a nurse* **3** an often white head-covering of no particular shape sometimes worn by women servants and old women **4** (*sometimes in comb.*) a protective covering for the end or top of an object: *Put the cap back on the bottle.|*TOE CAP **5** a natural covering: *This hill has been formed into such a shape because a cap of hard rock at the top has protected the soft rock underneath* **6** a small paper container holding enough explosive to cause a very small explosion, usu. used in toy guns **7** also **Dutch cap, diaphragm**— (*often in comb.*) a small round object fitted inside a woman to allow her to have sex without having children —see CONTRACEPTIVE **8 cap in hand** *not fml* humbly: *I hope the unions don't go cap in hand to the government again* **9 a feather in one's cap** *not fml* something to be proud of **10 put on one's thinking cap** *infml* to start to think seriously **11 set one's cap at (someone)** *infml* (of a woman) to try to attract (a man)

cap² *v* **-pp-** [T1] **1** to put a cap on (someone or something); cover with a cap **2** to give a cap to (someone) as a sign of honour or rank: *He's been capped 3 times for playing in British sports teams* **3** to form a cap over (something): *Clouds capped the hills* **4** to improve on (what someone has said or done)

cap. caps. *abbrev. for:* CAPITAL¹ (3) letter

cap·a·bil·i·ties /ˌkeɪpəˈbɪlətiz/ *n* [P] undeveloped qualities or abilities which can be developed: *She has capabilities as a singer; she is worth training*

ca·pa·bil·i·ty /ˌkeɪpəˈbɪləti/ *n* **1** [C;U] the quality of being CAPABLE (1): *We compared the capabilities of the 2 boys and found the first to be the cleverer.*| *But the second boy still has some capability for improvement* **2** [C9;U9] the quality or condition of having the skills and apparatus necessary for fighting the stated type of war: NUCLEAR (1) *capability*

ca·pa·ble /ˈkeɪpəbəl/ *adj* **1** [F+*of*] having the ability of doing or the power to do: *She's capable of any crime* **2** [F+*of*] ready for; open to: *That's capable of being misunderstood* **3** [B] able; clever, esp. at something needing practical skill: *a very capable doctor*|*My son's capable as a driver* —**-bly** *adv*

ca·pa·cious /kəˈpeɪʃəs/ *adj fml* able to hold a lot: *a capacious bottle*|(fig.) *a capacious memory* —**~ly** *adv* —**~ness** *n* [U]

ca·pac·i·ty /kəˈpæsəti/ *n* **1** [S;U9] the amount that something can hold or produce: *The seating capacity of this theatre is 500.*|*This bottle has half the capacity of that.*|*This is a building of very large capacity.*|*This factory has a productive capacity of 200 cars a week* —see WEIGHTS & MEASURES TABLE **2** [C;U: (*for*)] ability; power: *He has a big capacity for enjoying himself.*|*Her capacity for remembering is very interesting.*|*Has he the capacity to be king?*|*This book is beyond my son's capacity* —see GENIUS (USAGE) **3** [C] character; position: *I'm speaking in my capacity as minister of trade* **4** [U] *tech* fitness according to the law **5 filled to capacity** completely full: *The theatre was filled to capacity*

cap and bells /ˌ· · ˈ·/ *n* [U] *old use* the typical dress of a JESTER in former times

cap-a-pie /ˌkæp ə ˈpiː/ *adv Fr & lit* from head to foot: *He was armed cap-a-pie* (=wearing full armour)

ca·pa·ri·son¹ /kəˈpærəsən/ *n* (esp. in former times) an ornamental cloth covering for a horse, or for horse and rider

caparison² *v* [Wv5 (*in*);T1] **1** to put a CAPARISON on (a horse), as was done in former times **2** *lit* to dress (someone, esp. oneself) in richly ornamental clothing: (fig.) *Her ideas were caparisoned in beautiful poetry*

cape¹ /keɪp/ *n* (often in names) a piece of land joined to the coast and standing out into the sea: *We sailed round the cape to shelter from the storm.*| *the Cape of Good Hope*

cape² *n* a long loose outer garment fastened at the neck and hanging from the shoulders: *A cape gives good protection in wet weather* —compare CLOAK

Cape Col·oured /ˌ· ˈ··/ also **Coloured**— *n* (according to South African law) a person of mixed blood

ca·per¹ /ˈkeɪpəʳ/ *n* **1** a small dark-coloured flower-BUD¹ (1) used for giving a special sourish taste to food **2** a type of Mediterranean prickly bush on which this grows

caper² *v* [IØ] to jump about in a joyful manner: *The lambs were capering in the fields*

caper³ *n* **1** a gay jumping movement **2** *infml* a childish trick; PRANK **3** *sl* an unlawful activity; crime: *The government will soon stop their caper of not paying taxes* **4 cut a caper/capers** *not fml* **a** to behave foolishly **b** to jump about in a joyful manner.

cap·il·la·ri·ty /ˌkæpəˈlærəti/ *n* [U;S] *tech* the power of CAPILLARY ATTRACTION

ca·pil·la·ry /kəˈpɪləri‖ˈkæpəleri/ *n* a very fine hair-like tube with very narrow width such as the smaller bloodvessels in the body —see picture at SCIENTIFIC and TOOTH

capillary at·trac·tion /·ˌ··· ·ˈ··‖ˈ···· ·ˌ··/ *n* [U] the force which causes a liquid to rise up a narrow tube: *Capillary attraction causes water to rise from the roots to the branches of trees*

cap·i·tal¹ /ˈkæpətl/ *adj* [Wa5;A] **1** punishable by death **2** *BrE now rare* excellent; very good **3** (of a letter) written or printed in its large form (such as A, B, C) rather than its usual (LOWER CASE) form (such as a, b, c) **4 of capital importance** very important —see also CAPITALS

capital² *n* **1** [C] a town which serves as the centre of government: *Paris is one of the world's most beautiful capitals* **2** [U] wealth, esp. when used to produce more wealth; the machines, buildings and goods used in a business: *"We must understand the difference between* **fixed capital** *(machinery, factories) and* **circulating capital** *(half-finished goods)" said the teacher* **3** [S;U] (a sum of) money used for starting a business: *This business was started with a capital of £10,000* **4** [S;U] *infml* (a sum of) money: *He saved every week and after 20 years had a capital of £10,000* **5** [C] a CAPITAL¹ (3) letter, esp. one at the beginning of a word **6 make capital of** to use to one's advantage: *The leader of the Opposition made (political) capital of the government's difficulties*

capital³ *n* the top part of a pillar

capital⁴ *interj BrE pomp* excellent; very good: *You'll do what I ask? Capital!*

capital as·sets /ˌ··· ˈ··/ *n* [P] *tech* everything that has money value in a business, such as machines, buildings, goods, etc.

capital ex·pen·di·ture /ˌ··· ·ˈ···/ *n* [U;S] *tech* (an amount of) money spent to improve machinery, buildings, etc., belonging to a business: *More capital expenditure is necessary if the railways are to compete successfully with the roads*

capital gains /ˌ··· ˈ·/ *n* [P] profits made by selling possessions

cap·i·tal·is·m /ˈkæpətl-ɪzəm/ *n* [U] the type of production and trade based on the private ownership of wealth, the free market, and little industrial activity by the government

cap·i·tal·ist¹ /ˈkæpətl-əst/ *n* **1** a person who owns or controls much wealth (CAPITAL² (2,3,4)) and esp. who lends it to businesses, banks, etc., at interest **2** *rare* a person who favours and supports CAPITALISM

cap·i·tal·ist² also **cap·i·tal·is·tic** /ˌkæpətl-ˈɪstɪk/— *adj* [Wa5] **1** [Wa5;A] owning or controlling a large amount of wealth **2** [B] practising or supporting CAPITALISM: *the capitalist countries of the West* **3** [B] practising or supporting activities intended to increase profit without much regard for other effects

cap·i·tal·i·za·tion, -isation /ˌkæpȷ̊tl-aɪˈzeɪʃən‖-tl-ə-ˈzeɪ-/ *n* **1** [U] the act of capitalizing (CAPITALIZE (1,2)) **2** [S] a sum of money resulting from this: *a capitalization amounting to £5,000* **3** [S] all the wealth (CAPITAL² (2,3)) used in a business **4** [U] the use of CAPITAL letters in writing or printing

cap·i·tal·ize, -ise /ˈkæpȷ̊tl-aɪz/ *v* **1** [IØ;T1] **a** (of a number of future payments) to (cause to) change into one amount of money to be paid now: *Have you decided to capitalize your interest repayments?* **b** (of goods, property, etc.) to (cause to) change into money: *This bank capitalizes at £100,000.|He's decided to capitalize all his property* **2** [T1] to supply money to (a firm) for (something): *The bank has promised to capitalize our new business* **3** [T1] to write with a CAPITAL¹ (3) letter

capitalize on *v prep* [T1] to use (something) to one's advantage: *She capitalized on his mistake and won the game*

capital lev·y /ˌ··· ˈ··/ *n* a tax on private or industrial wealth (CAPITAL) paid to the government usu. in addition to income tax

capital pun·ish·ment /ˌ··· ˈ···/ *n* [U] punishment by death according to law; the death PENALTY

cap·i·tals /ˈkæpȷ̊tlz/ *n* [P] (the style of) printing or writing in large letters: *The word* DICTIONARY *is printed here in capitals* —compare ITALICS, ROMAN (1)

cap·i·ta·tion /ˌkæpȷ̊ˈteɪʃən/ *n* **1** a tax paid equally by all people —compare POLL TAX **2** a payment made esp. to a society according to the number of members

Cap·i·tol /ˈkæpȷ̊tl/ *n* [*the*+R] (in the United States) the building in Washington where CONGRESS meets

ca·pit·u·late /kəˈpɪtʃʊleɪt‖-tʃə-/ *v* [IØ] to yield to the enemy, usu. on agreed conditions; SURRENDER

ca·pit·u·la·tion /kəˌpɪtʃʊˈleɪʃən‖-tʃə-/ *n* [C;U] (an example of) the act of yielding usu. on agreed conditions; SURRENDER

ca·pit·u·la·tions /kəˌpɪtʃʊˈleɪʃənz‖-tʃə-/ *n* [P] an agreement between 2 governments which allows a country's citizens to remain under that country's laws when living in the other country —compare EXTRATERRITORIAL RIGHTS

ca·pon /ˈkeɪpən‖-pɑn, -pən/ *n* a male chicken with its sex organs removed in order to make it grow big and fat and thus suitable for eating

ca·pric·ci·o /kəˈpritʃiəʊ/ also **caprice**— *n* a piece of music that is free in form, quick, and full of movement

ca·price /kəˈpriːs/ *n* **1** [C] a sudden often foolish change of mind or behaviour usu. without any real cause; sudden wish to have or do something; WHIM **2** [U] the natural qualities of mind and character (DISPOSITION) which cause one to have such changes of mind and behaviour: *His lack of money was the result of caprice in spending on unnecessary things* **3** CAPRICCIO

ca·pri·cious /kəˈprɪʃəs/ *adj* being likely to change suddenly; often changing; untrustworthy; governed by CAPRICE: *We can't go camping while the weather is so capricious* —**~ly** *adv* —**~ness** *n* [U]

Cap·ri·corn /ˈkæprɪkɔːn‖-ɔrn/ *n* **1** [R] **a** the ancient sign, a goat, representing the 10th division of the ZODIAC belt of stars **b** the group of stars (CONSTELLATION) formerly in this division —see picture at PLANET **2** a person born under the influence of this sign —see also TROPIC OF CAPRICORN

cap·si·cum /ˈkæpsɪkəm/ *n* [C;U] *tech* PEPPER¹ (2)

cap·size /kæpˈsaɪz‖ˈkæpsaɪz/ *v* [IØ;T1] **a** (esp. of a boat or ship) to turn over **b** to turn (esp. a boat or ship) over: *The large wave capsized the boat, causing many people to drown*

cap·stan /ˈkæpstən/ *n* a round drumlike machine turned by hand or some other type of power in order to wind up a rope that pulls or raises heavy objects —compare WINCH and see picture at FREIGHTER

cap·sule /ˈkæpsjuːl‖-səl/ *n* **1** a measured amount of medicine inside an outer covering, the whole of which is swallowed **2** the part of a spaceship in which the pilots live and work and from which the engine is separated when the take-off is completed **3** *tech* the seed container of a plant **4** *med* a cover (MEMBRANE or SAC) over part of the body, such as a joint

cap·tain¹ /ˈkæptȷ̊n/ *n* **1** [C] the leader of a team or group **2** [A;C;N] the person in command of a ship or aircraft **3** [A;C;N] **a** an officer of middle rank in the navy **b** an officer of low rank in the army or US air force **4 captain of industry** a man who holds an important position in the industrial life of a country

captain² *v* [T1] to be captain of; command; lead

cap·tion /ˈkæpʃən/ *n* **1** words shown or printed with a picture, drawing, etc., to explain the subject or give further information: *I didn't understand the drawing until I read the caption* **2** a heading, esp. of part of an article or official paper; title: *I read no further than the caption because the subject of the article seemed uninteresting*

cap·tious /ˈkæpʃəs/ *adj* marked by too great a readiness to find fault; too CRITICAL: *a captious woman, difficult to please* —**~ly** *adv* —**~ness** *n* [U]

cap·ti·vate /ˈkæptȷ̊veɪt/ *v* [T1] to charm, excite, and attract (someone or something): *Venice's beauty captivated the old man so much that he swore he would never leave for fear he might die elsewhere* —**-vation** /ˌkæptȷ̊ˈveɪʃən/ *n* [U9]

cap·tive¹ /ˈkæptɪv/ *adj* [Wa5] **1** taken prisoner esp. in war **2** not allowed to move about freely; imprisoned: *Many people would like to see all captive animals set free* **3** *lit* of or relating to CAPTIVITY: *these captive chains* **4 hold someone captive** to keep someone as a prisoner

captive² *n* **1** a person taken prisoner esp. in war **2** a person who has been CAPTIVATED: *He was Helen's captive, a prisoner of her charms*

captive au·di·ence /ˌ·· ˈ···/ *n* a group of people who are not able or not allowed to stop listening or watching: *People watching television are a captive audience for advertisers*

captive bal·loon /ˌ·· ·ˈ·/ *n* a large gas-filled bag (BALLOON) held to the ground by a rope or chain

cap·tiv·i·ty /kæpˈtivȷ̊ti/ *n* [U] the state of being CAPTIVE¹ (1,2): *Many animals breed better when they are free than they do when in captivity*

cap·tor /ˈkæptəʳ/ *n usu. fml* a person who has CAPTURED² (1) someone or something: *I soon escaped from my captors*

cap·ture¹ /ˈkæptʃəʳ/ *n* **1** [U] the act of taking or being taken by force **2** [C] something that has been taken, caught, or won by force: (fig.) *She's got the president in love with her now. What a capture!*

capture² *v* [T1] **1** to take (a person or animal) prisoner: *He was captured trying to escape from the country.|The cat has captured a mouse* **2** to take control of (something) by force from an enemy; win; gain **3** to preserve (something) in an unchanging form on film, in words, etc.: *I captured my baby daughter's first smile on film.|In his book he tried to capture the beauty of Venice* **4** to hold the interest of (someone); CAPTIVATE: *Her beauty captured him and he swore to stay with her for ever*

car /kɑːʳ/ *n* **1** [C; *by*+U] also (*BrE*) **motor car**, (*AmE*) **automobile**, (*AmE infml*) **auto**— a vehicle with 3 or usu. 4 wheels and driven by a motor, esp.

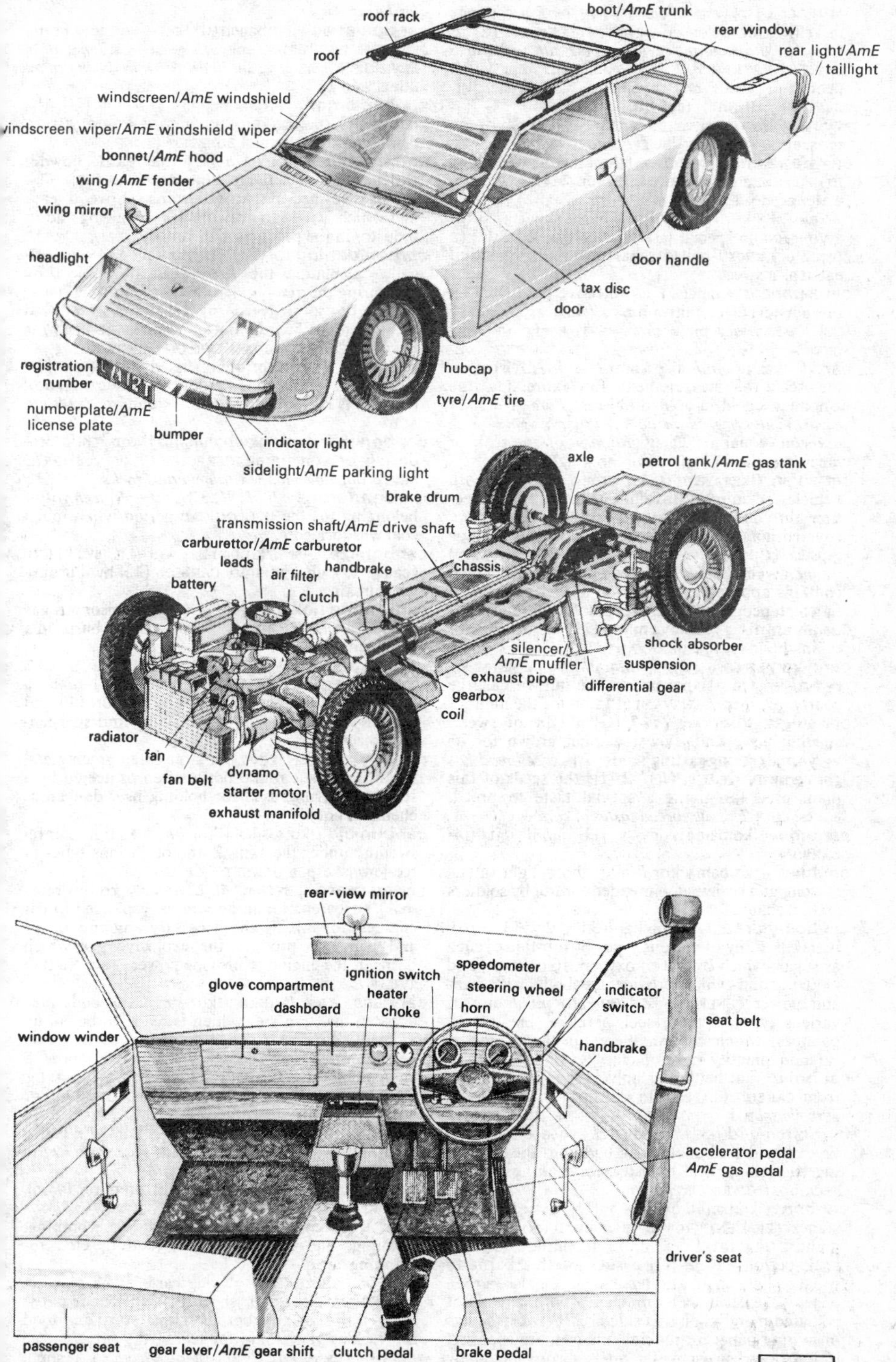

roof rack
boot/*AmE* trunk
rear window
rear light/*AmE* taillight
roof
windscreen/*AmE* windshield
windscreen wiper/*AmE* windshield wiper
bonnet/*AmE* hood
wing /*AmE* fender
wing mirror
headlight
door handle
tax disc
door
registration number
hubcap
tyre/*AmE* tire
numberplate/*AmE* license plate
bumper
indicator light
sidelight/*AmE* parking light

axle
petrol tank/*AmE* gas tank
brake drum
transmission shaft/*AmE* drive shaft
carburettor/*AmE* carburetor
leads
handbrake
chassis
battery
air filter
clutch
silencer/*AmE* muffler
shock absorber
suspension
exhaust pipe
differential gear
gearbox
coil
radiator
fan
fan belt
dynamo
starter motor
exhaust manifold

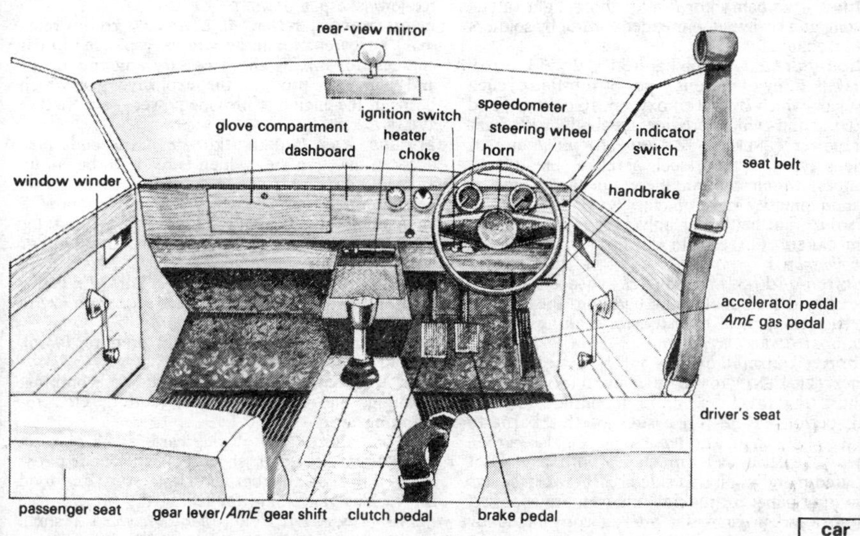

one for carrying people —see also picture at PETROL **2** [C] (*esp. in comb.*) *esp. AmE* a carriage or vehicle for use on railways or CABLE*s*[1] (1b): *This train has a restaurant car|a sleeping car* —see also CABLE CAR; TRAM **3** [C] any small vehicle in which people or goods are carried as part of a LIFT, BALLOON, AIRSHIP, etc.
USAGE One **drives** a **car** or a **taxi**, and the passengers *ride in it*. One *gets into* or *out of* it.

ca·rafe /kəˈræf, kəˈrɑːf/ *n* (the amount contained in) an ornamental bottle used for serving wine or water at meals

car·a·mel /ˈkærəməl/ *n* **1** [U] burnt sugar used for giving food a special taste and colour **2** [C;U] (a piece of) sticky boiled sugar containing this and eaten as a sweet

car·a·pace /ˈkærəpeɪs/ *n* a protective hard shell on the outside of certain animals, such as CRAB*s* or TORTOISE*s* —see pictures at REPTILE and CRUSTACEAN

car·at /ˈkærət/ *AmE* also **karat**— *n* **1** a division on the scale of measurement for expressing the amount of gold in golden objects: *Pure gold is 24 carats.|This ring is made of 18-carat gold* **2** a division (equal to 200 MILLIGRAM*s*) on the scale of measurement for expressing the weight of jewels

car·a·van /ˈkærəvæn/ *n* **1** a group of people with vehicles or animals travelling together for protection through unfriendly esp. desert areas **2** a covered horse-drawn cart in which people such as gipsies (GIPSY) live or travel **3** (*AmE* **trailer**) —*BrE* a vehicle which can be pulled by car, which contains apparatus for cooking and sleeping, and in which people live or travel usu. for holidays

car·a·van·ning /ˈkærəvænɪŋ/ *n* [U] the practice of taking holidays in a CARAVAN (3)

car·a·van·se·rai /ˌkærəˈvænsəraɪ/ also **car·a·van·sa·ry** /-ri/— *n* (in Asian countries) an inn with a large courtyard where CARAVAN*s* (1) stop for the night

car·a·way /ˈkærəweɪ/ *n* **1** [C] a type of sweet-smelling usu. white-flowered plant grown for its very small strong-tasting seeds: *This nice bread has got caraway seeds in (it)!* **2** [U] the seeds of this plant used for giving a special taste to bread, cakes, etc.: *This nice bread tastes of caraway!*

car·bide /ˈkɑːbaɪd‖ˈkɑr-/ *n* [U] *infml* CALCIUM CARBIDE

car·bine /ˈkɑːbaɪn‖ˈkɑr-/ *n* a short light RIFLE (=long gun) originally intended for use by soldiers on horseback

car·bo·hy·drate /ˈkɑːbəˈhaɪdreɪt, -drɨt‖ˌkɑr-/ *n* [C;(U)] **1** any of various types of substance, such as sugar, which consist of oxygen, HYDROGEN, and CARBON, and which provide the body with heat and power (ENERGY) **2** [*usu. pl.*] *infml* any of various types of food, such as cake, bread, and potatoes, which contain these substances and if eaten in quantity make one fat

car·bol·ic /kɑːˈbɒlɪk‖kɑrˈbɑlɪk/ *adj* [Wa5] coming from CARBON (1), esp. in the form of COAL TAR: *carbolic soap*

carbolic ac·id /·ˌ·· ˈ··/ also (*tech*) **phenol**— *n* [U] a type of acid used in cleaning buildings for destroying bacteria and, in industry, for making plastics —compare CARBONIC ACID

car·bon /ˈkɑːbən‖ˈkɑr-/ *n* **1** [U] a simple substance (ELEMENT) found in a pure form as diamonds, GRAPHITE, etc., or in an impure form as coal, petrol, etc. **2** [C] a stick of this burnt to produce light in an ARC **lamp** **3** [U;C] also **carbon paper**— (a sheet of) thin paper with a coat of coloured material on one side used between sheets of writing paper for making one or more copies **4** [C] also **carbon cop·y** /ˌ·· ˈ··/— a copy made by using this paper; DUPLICATE: *I want one original and 2 carbons, please.*|(fig.) *John is a carbon copy of his father*

car·bon·at·ed /ˈkɑːbəneɪtɨd‖ˈkɑr-/ *adj* containing CARBON DIOXIDE: *Many drinks are carbonated to make them more pleasant to drink by producing small* BUBBLE*s*[2] (1)

car·bon·a·tion /ˌkɑːbəˈneɪʃən‖ˌkɑr-/ *n* [U] the putting of CARBON DIOXIDE into a liquid, esp. a drink, to produce small BUBBLE*s*[2] (1)

carbon black /ˌ·· ˈ·/ *n* [U] fine black powder which contains a large amount of CARBON (1), which is formed by partly burning oil, wood, etc., and which is used in drawing as a colouring and in industry in the production of rubber

carbon dat·ing /ˌ·· ˈ··/ *n* [U] a method of scientifically calculating the age of an old object by measuring the amount of CARBON (1) in it

carbon di·ox·ide /ˌ·· ·ˈ··/ *n* [U] the gas produced when animals breathe out or when CARBON (1) is burned in air —compare CARBON MONOXIDE

car·bon·ic ac·id /kɑːˌbɒnɪk ˈæsɨd‖kɑrˌbɑ-/ *n* [U] a type of weak acid produced when CARBON DIOXIDE is mixed with water —compare CARBOLIC ACID

car·bon·if·er·ous /ˌkɑːbəˈnɪfərəs‖ˌkɑr-/ *adj* producing or containing CARBON (1) or coal: *The miners dug down to the carboniferous rocks*

Carboniferous *adj, n* [Wa5;B; *the*+R] *tech* (of or belonging to) the GEOLOGICAL period when much coal was formed

car·bon·ize, -ise /ˈkɑːbənaɪz‖ˈkɑr-/ *v* [IØ;T1] to (cause to) change into CARBON (1) by burning without air

carbon mo·nox·ide /ˌ·· ·ˈ··/ *n* [U] a poisonous gas produced when CARBON (1) (esp. petrol) burns in a small amount of air

carbon pa·per /ˈ·· ˌ··/ *n* [U;C] CARBON (3)

car·bo·run·dum /ˌkɑːbəˈrʌndəm/ *n* [U] *tdmk* a hard solid substance (made from CARBON (1) and SILICON) and used esp. for polishing and sharpening objects

car·boy /ˈkɑːbɔɪ‖ˈkɑr-/ *n* a large often green glass, metal, or plastic round bottle often protected by a special covering, used for holding usu. dangerous chemical liquids

car·bun·cle /ˈkɑːbʌŋkəl‖ˈkɑr-/ *n* **1** a large painful swelling under the skin **2** any of various types of red jewels, esp. a GARNET

car·bu·ret·tor, -retter, *AmE* **-retor** /ˌkɑːbjʊˈretəʳ, -bə-‖ˈkɑrbəreɪtəʳ/ *n* an apparatus, esp. used in car engines, for mixing the necessary amounts of air and petrol to produce the explosive gas which burns in the engine to provide power —see picture at CAR

car·cass, -case /ˈkɑːkəs‖ˈkɑr-/ *n* **1** the body of a dead animal, esp. one which is ready to be cut up as meat **2** *derog sl* the body of a dead or living person: *Move your carcass: I want to sit down!* **3** *derog infml* the decaying remains of something: *the carcass of an old car* **4** the framework of an old or unfinished ship

car·cin·o·gen /kɑːˈsɪnədʒən‖kɑr-, ˈkɑrsɨ-/ *n med* a substance which tends to produce a CANCER (2) in the body

card[1] /kɑːd‖kɑrd/ *v* [IØ;T1] to prepare (wool, cotton, etc.) with a CARD[2]

card[2] *n* a comblike instrument used for combing, cleaning, and preparing wool, cotton, etc., for spinning

card[3] *n* **1** also (*fml*) **playing card**— one of a set (PACK) of 52 small sheets of stiffened paper marked to show number and class (SUIT) and used for various games and for telling the future —see CARDS (USAGE) **2 a** (*often in comb.*) a small sheet of stiffened paper usu. with information printed on it and having various uses: *a membership card* **b** *not fml* VISITING CARD: *He didn't leave a message, but here's his card* **3 a** a piece of stiffened paper usu. with a picture on the front and a message inside sent to a person by post on special occasions, such as on a birthday, at Christmas, etc.: *I sent her a get-well card when she was in hospital* **b** POSTCARD **4** *infml* an odd or amusing person; WAG: *John's a real card; he always makes me laugh* **5** a list of events, esp. at a sports meeting **6 have a card up one's sleeve** *infml* to have a secret plan or intention **7 make a card** (in card games) to win a TRICK¹ (7) with a particular card **8 one's best/strongest card** *not fml* one's strongest and most effective argument —see also CARDS

card⁴ *adj* [Wa5;A] made of stiffened paper —compare CARDBOARD

card⁵ *n* [A] of or for CARDS (1, 2): *a card-table|card-players*

car·da·mom /ˈkɑːdəməm‖ˈkɑr-/ *n* **1** [C;U] (one of) the seeds of a type of East Indian fruit used in medicine and for giving a special taste to food **2** [C] the fruit which contains these seeds

card·board¹ /ˈkɑːdbɔːd‖ˈkɑrdbord/ *n* [U] a thick stiff paperlike usu. brownish or greyish material used for making boxes, the backs of books, etc. —compare CARD⁴

cardboard² *adj* [Wa5] **1** made from CARDBOARD¹: *a cardboard box* **2** unreal; unnatural: *Her new book's full of cardboard characters* —compare WOODEN (2)

card-car·ry·ing /ˈ· ˌ···/ *adj* [Wa5;A] being a full member of a (usu. political) organization: *Jean's a card-carrying member of the Labour party*

car·di- /ˈkɑːdi‖ˈkɑrdi/ also **car·di·o-** /-əʊ/— *comb. form med* heart: CARDIAC

car·di·ac /ˈkɑːdi-æk‖ˈkɑr-/ *adj* [Wa5;A] *med* connected with the heart or with heart disease

car·di·gan /ˈkɑːdɪgən‖ˈkɑr-/ *n* a KNITted (=made of wool twisted together with special stitches) woollen men's or women's short coat with SLEEVEs (1) but usu. without collar and usu. fastened at the front with buttons or a belt

car·di·nal¹ /ˈkɑːdənəl‖ˈkɑr-/ *adj* [Wa5] most important; chief; main: *The cardinal idea of the Labour party's political thought is that all people should be equal.|a cardinal* SIN² (1)

cardinal² *adj, n* [B;U] (having) a deep rich red colour

cardinal³ *n* **1** [A;C;N] a priest with one of the highest ranks of the ROMAN CATHOLIC church, who is a member of the group (**Sacred College**) which elects the head of the church (the POPE) **2** any of various types of North American birds (FINCHes) of which the male is bright red in colour **3** CARDINAL NUMBER

cardinal num·ber /ˌ··· ˈ··/ *n* one of the numbers 1, 2, 3, etc. —compare ORDINAL number (first, second, third, etc.)

cardinal point /ˌ··· ˈ·/ *n* POINT¹ (9)

card in·dex /ˈ· ˌ··/ *n* **1** (a case containing) a number of cards each carrying a particular piece of information and arranged in a special order **2** the information kept in this form

card·punch /ˈkɑːdpʌntʃ‖ˈkɑrd-/ *n* a machine that puts information onto cards in such a way that calculating machines with memories (COMPUTERs) can read and understand it

cards /kɑːdz‖kɑrdz/ *n* [P] **1** also (*fml*) **playing cards**— a set (PACK) of 52 CARDs³ (1) **2** games played with such a set; card playing: *Let's play cards tonight* **3 get one's cards** *BrE infml* to be dismissed from one's job **4 house of cards** *not fml* a plan with little chance of success **5 lay/put one's cards on the table** *not fml* to be completely honest; say openly what one hopes and intends to do **6** (*BrE*) **on**/(*AmE*) **in the cards** *infml* probable: *They say war's on the cards* **7 play one's cards well** *not fml* to act in the most effective manner to get what one wants

USAGE One plays the various card games on a *card table,* and in many of them one SCOREs² (1) **tricks**. The **cards** themselves come in 2 red **suits**, **hearts** and **diamonds**; and 2 black ones, **clubs** and **spades**. Each **suit** has an **ace**, a **king**, a **queen**, and a **jack** or **knave**: *the* **king** *of* **hearts**|*the* **jack** *of* **clubs**.

card·sharp /ˈkɑːdʃɑːp‖ˈkɑrdʃɑrp/ also **card·sharp·er** /-ˌʃɑːpəʳ‖-ˌʃɑrpər/— *n* a person who plays cards deceitfully and dishonestly, esp. to make money

card vote /ˈ· ·/ *n* a vote taken at a meeting of representatives of various organizations for which each organization's representative has the same number of votes as his organization's total membership —compare PROXY

care¹ /keəʳ/ *n* **1** [U] worry; anxiety; sorrow; grief; suffering of the mind: *free from care* **2** [C] an anxiety; worry; cause of sorrow, grief, etc. **3** [U] charge; keeping; protection; responsibility: *under the doctor's care|People who are seriously ill are kept in a hospital's* INTENSIVE *care* UNIT **4** [U] serious attention; effort: *You must do your work with more care if you want to be successful* **5** [U] carefulness in avoiding harm, damage, etc.: *Glass; handle with care!|Cross the road with care* **6** [C] a person or thing for which one is responsible; object of one's special attention **7 care of** also **c/o**, (*AmE*) **in care of**— (used when addressing letters to mean) at the address of: *John Smith, care of Mary Jones, 14, High Street* **8 have a care!** *infml* be more careful! *"Have a care, sir!" said the old gentleman when I stood on his toe* **9 take care of (someone or something) a** be responsible for (someone or something): *Take care of the baby while I'm out* **b** *sl* to beat; kill: *If you don't give me the money I'll send my boys to take care of you* —see CARE² (USAGE) **10 take into care** to put (esp. a child) into a home owned and controlled by the state to make sure of proper treatment: *John's parents used to come home drunk and beat him, so he was taken into care by the local council*

care² *v* **1** [T3] to like; want: *I don't care to play football; I'd rather go for a walk* **2** [IØ (*about*); T6] to mind; be worried, anxious, or concerned (about): *When his mother died Allan didn't seem to care at all.|After our argument my wife said she didn't care where I went or what I did* **3 care a damn** give a DAMN² (2)

USAGE Compare **care about**, **care for**, and **take care (of)**: To **care about** something is to think it important, whether or not one likes it: *I don't* **care about** *what people think.* To **care for** now usually means "to have a liking for", or "to want", and is *nonassertive*: *Would you* **care for** *some tea?* To **take care** is to be **careful**: **Take care** *not to drop it!* To **take care of** means "to look after": *Please* **take care of** *the baby for me.*

ca·reen /kəˈriːn/ *v* **1** [IØ;T1] **a** (of a ship) to lean to one side **b** to cause (a ship) to lean to one side **2** [T1] to turn (a ship) on one side for cleaning or repairing **3** [L9, esp. ALONG] *esp. AmE* to go forward rapidly while making sudden movements from side to side: *As the carriage careened (along) down the hill, the passengers were thrown roughly from side to side* —compare CAREER³

ca·reer¹ /kəˈrɪəʳ/ *n* **1** [C] a job or profession for which one is trained and which one intends to follow for the whole of one's life **2** [C] (a part of) the general course of a person's working life: *Churchill's career proves he was a great man* **3** [C; (*at*) U9] fast violent speed: *The horse went down* *the hill at full career, crashed into a wall, and killed itself*

career[2] *adj* [Wa5;A] *esp. AmE* professional: *He's a career teacher; it's the only job he's ever done.*|*The position of* AMBASSADOR *to France is not a career position, but is filled by political appointment*

career[3] *v* [L9, esp. ABOUT, ALONG] to go at full speed; rush wildly: *The car careered uncontrollably down the hill.*|*He's always careering about and breaking things*

career girl /·ˈ· ·/ *n* a woman who puts advancement in her profession before all other things, such as getting married or having children

ca·reer·ist /kəˈrɪərɪ̣st/ *n usu. derog* a person who puts advancement in his profession before all other things, such as friends, family, etc., and who may be willing to act unfairly to gain advancement —**-ism** *n* [U]

care for *v prep* [T1] **1** [*nonassertive no pass.*] to like: *I don't really care for tea; I like coffee better* **2** [*nonassertive no pass.*] (*often in suggestions with* would *or* should) to like to have: *Would you care for some tea?* **3** to nurse or attend (someone or something); look after: *He's very good at caring for sick animals* —see CARE[2] (USAGE)

care·free /ˈkeəfriː‖ˈkeər-/ *adj* **1** *apprec* free from anxiety; happy; without sorrow or fear: *On a fine spring day like this I feel quite carefree* **2** *derog* irresponsible: *He's carefree with his money*

care·ful /ˈkeəfəl‖ˈkeər-/ *adj* **1** [B;F3,6a] taking care (with the intention of avoiding danger): *If you'd been more careful crossing the road you wouldn't have been hit by the car* **2** [B] showing attention to details: *He's a careful worker* **3** [B] done with care; showing care: *Doctors made a careful examination and found nothing wrong* **4** [B] *infml* not wanting to spend money; ungenerous; TIGHT: *He's too careful with his money; he never buys a drink for anyone* —**~ly** *adv*: *Hold this glass carefully, I don't want it broken* —**~ness** [U]

care·less /ˈkeələs‖ˈkeər-/ *adj* **1** [B] not taking care; inattentive: *A careless driver is a danger to us all* **2** [A;(B)] not showing care or thought; done without care **3** [A] free from care; untroubled **4** [F (*about*); (B)] thoughtless; not worried: *He's careless about his family/about money matters* —**~ly** *adv* —**~ness** *n* [U]

ca·ress[1] /kəˈres/ *n* a light tender touch or kiss showing one's love for someone

caress[2] *v* [T1] to give a CARESS to (someone): *He caressed his wife lovingly*

car·et /ˈkærɪ̣t/ *n tech* the mark used in writing and printing to show where something is to be added

care·tak·er /ˈkeəˌteɪkəʳ‖ˈkeər-/ *n* **1** also (*esp. AmE and ScotE*) **janitor**— a person employed to look after a school or other usu. large public building and to be responsible for small repairs, cleaning, etc. **2** a person who looks after a house or land when the owner is absent

caretaker gov·ern·ment /ˈ··· ˌ···/ *n* a government which holds office for the usu. short period between the end of one government and the appointment of a new government

care·worn /ˈkeəwɔːn‖ˈkeərworn/ *n lit* showing the effect of grief, worry, or anxiety: *the careworn face of the mother of a large poor family*

car·go /ˈkɑːgəʊ‖ˈkɑr-/ *n* **-goes** [C;U] (one load of) the goods (FREIGHT) carried by a ship, plane, or vehicle: *We sailed from Newcastle with a cargo of coal*

car·i·bou /ˈkærɪ̣buː/ *n* [Wn1] a type of North American REINDEER

car·i·ca·ture[1] /ˈkærɪkətʃʊəʳ/ *n* **1** [C] a representation of a person in literature or art made so that parts of his character appear more noticeable, odd, or amusing than they really are: *Newspapers often contain caricatures of well-known politicians.*|(fig.) *a caricature of a government that can do nothing right* **2** [C] an amusing representation by one person of another's voice, manners, character: *After dinner Ted amused the company with caricatures of his friends* **3** [U] the art of doing this: *John's more skilled at caricature than he is at acting*

caricature[2] *v* [T1] to represent in CARICATURE —**-turist** /ˈkærɪkətʃʊərɪ̣st/ *n*

car·ies /ˈkeəriz/ *n* [U] *med* decay of the bones and esp. teeth

car·ill·on /ˈkærɪ̣ljən, kəˈrɪ-‖ˈkærəljɑn, -lən/ *n* (tune played on) a set of bells (often in a tower) sounded by hammers controlled from a row of keys (as on a piano KEYBOARD[1] (1))

car·i·ous /ˈkeərɪəs/ *adj med* decaying; having CARIES

Car·mel·ite /ˈkɑːmɪ̣laɪt‖ˈkɑr-/ *n* a man or woman who is a member of the ROMAN CATHOLIC religious society (ORDER) of **Our Lady of Mount Carmel**

car·mine /ˈkɑːmɪ̣n, -maɪn‖ˈkɑr-/ *n, adj* [U] (having) a deep purplish red colour

car·nage /ˈkɑːnɪdʒ‖ˈkɑr-/ *n* [U] the killing and wounding of many animals or esp. people: *The battlefield was a scene of carnage*

car·nal /ˈkɑːnl‖ˈkɑrnl/ *adj* [A] *usu. derog* of the flesh, bodily, or esp. sexual: *Carnal pleasures can destroy a man's soul*

car·na·tion[1] /kɑːˈneɪʃən‖kɑr-/ *n* **1** a type of small garden plant with sweet-smelling white, pink, or red flowers **2** a flower from this plant

carnation[2] *adj, n* [U] (having) a bright pink colour

car·ne·li·an /kɑːˈniːlɪən‖kɑr-/ *n* CORNELIAN

car·ni·val /ˈkɑːnɪ̣vəl‖ˈkɑr-/ *n* **1** [U] public rejoicing with feasting, dancing, drinking, and often processions and shows: *carnival time in Rio de Janeiro* **2** [C] **a** a period when this takes place esp. in ROMAN CATHOLIC countries in the weeks before LENT: *Rio de Janeiro's carnival is the best in the world* **b** a period of such activities, esp. at a particular time of year: *the winter carnival*

car·ni·vore /ˈkɑːnɪ̣vɔːʳ‖ˈkɑrnɪ̣vor/ *n* **1** a flesh-eating animal: *Lions are carnivores; rabbits are not* **2** *rare* an insect-eating plant

car·niv·o·rous /kɑːˈnɪvərəs‖kɑr-/ *adj* (esp. of animals) flesh-eating: *Sheep are not carnivorous but tigers are.*|*carnivorous plants*
See next page for picture

car·ob /ˈkærəb/ also **locust**— *n* **1** a type of Mediterranean tree with red flowers and beanlike fruit **2** the fruit of this tree

car·ol[1] /ˈkærəl/ *n* **1** a religious song of joy and praise esp. sung at Christmas **2** *lit or poet* a joyful song (as of birds)

carol[2] *v* **-ll-** (*AmE* **-l-**) **1** [IØ (AWAY)] to sing joyfully **2** [IØ] to sing CAROL*s*[1] (1) (esp. going from house to house): *The children went carolling during the week before Christmas* **3** [T1] to praise (someone or something) with CAROL*s*[1] (1): *The thankful people carolled their king*

ca·rot·id /kəˈrɒtɪ̣d‖-ˈrɑ-/ *adj* [Wa5;A] of or being the main blood vessel (ARTERY) or vessels that pass up the neck and supply the head

ca·rous·al /kəˈraʊzəl/ *n* [U;(S)] *lit* drinking and merry-making

ca·rouse[1] /kəˈraʊz/ *n* [S] *lit* an act of carousing (CAROUSE)

carouse[2] *v* [IØ] *lit* to make merry, esp. by drinking large amounts of alcoholic drink

car·ou·sel, carr- /ˌkærəˈsel/ *n* **1** *AmE* ROUNDABOUT (1) **2** *esp. AmE* a circular moving belt on which bags, cases, etc., from a plane are placed for collection by passengers

carnivorous mammals

carp[1] /kɑːp‖kɑrp/ *v* [Wv4;I∅ (ON, *at*)] *derog infml* to find fault and complain continuously and unnecessarily: *Please stop carping (on) at the way I dress*

carp[2] *n* **carp** *or* **carps** [Wn2] **1** [C] a type of large FRESHWATER fish that lives in lakes, pools, and slow-moving rivers and is believed to live a long time —see picture at FISH[1] **2** [C;U] this fish cooked and eaten as food

car·pal /ˈkɑːpəl‖ˈkɑr-/ *adj* [Wa5;A;(B)] *med* belonging to or connected with the wrist or the bones in the wrist —see picture at SKELETON

car park /ˈ· ·/ *n esp. BrE* **1** *AmE* **parking lot**— an open place where cars and other vehicles may be parked, sometimes for a small payment —compare COACH PARK **2** an enclosed place used for this purpose: *My car is on the 3rd floor of a* MULTISTOREY (=with many floors) *car park*

car·pen·ter /ˈkɑːpɨntəʳ‖ˈkɑr-/ *n* a person who is skilled at making and repairing wooden objects —compare JOINER (1)

car·pen·try /ˈkɑːpɨntri‖ˈkɑr-/ *n* [U] the art or work of a CARPENTER

car·pet[1] /ˈkɑːpɨt‖ˈkɑr-/ *n* **1** [U] heavy woven often woollen material for covering floors or stairs **2** [C] a shaped piece of this material, usu. fitted to the size of a particular room —see picture at LIVING ROOM **3** [C] anything which covers the ground like this: *a carpet of flowers* **4 on the carpet** *infml* **a** blamed (REPRIMANDed) for having done something wrong: *You'll be on the carpet if mother finds out you've broken that plate* **b** *BrE* under consideration: *My plan will be on the carpet at today's meeting* **5 sweep (something) under the** *BrE* **carpet**/*AmE* **rug** *infml* to keep (something) secret: *I know what you did; you can't sweep things under the carpet to keep them hidden from me*

carpet[2] *v* [T1] **1** to cover with or as if with a CARPET[1] (1,2) **2** *infml esp. BrE* to blame (REPRIMAND) (someone): *He was carpeted for bad work*

car·pet·bag /ˈkɑːpɨtbæg‖ˈkɑr-/ *n* a bag made from CARPET[1] (1) and used, esp. in former times, by travellers

car·pet·bag·ger /ˈkɑːpɨtˌbægəʳ‖ˈkɑr-/ *n derog* a person from one area who tries to take an active part in the political life of another area, esp., in the United States, a Northerner politically active in the South in the 1860's and '70's

car·pet·ing /ˈkɑːpɨtɪŋ‖ˈkɑr-/ *n* [U] heavy woven often woollen material used for making CARPETs[1] (1,2)

carpet slip·per /ˈ·· ˌ··/ *n fml* SLIPPER

carpet sweep·er /ˈ·· ˌ··/ *n* a hand machine for sweeping CARPETs[1] (1,2) —compare VACUUM CLEANER —see picture at HOUSEHOLD

car pool /ˈ· ·/ *n* an agreement made by a number of car owners to take turns driving each other to work, school, church, etc.: *By being in a car pool I save £2 a week on petrol money*

car·port /ˈkɑːpɔːt‖ˈkɑrport/ *n* a shelter, having only a roof and one or 2 sides, often built against a side of a house, and in which a car is kept —compare GARAGE[1] (1)

car·pus /ˈkɑːpəs‖ˈkɑr-/ *n* **carpi** /-paɪ/ *med* the wrist or the 8 bones which make up the wrist

car·riage /ˈkærɪdʒ/ *n* **1** [C] a wheeled vehicle, esp. a private horse-drawn vehicle **2** (*AmE* **car**)— *BrE* a railway passenger vehicle: *I'll be sitting in the 3rd carriage from the front of the train* **3** [U] (the cost of) the act of moving goods from one place to another **4** [C] a wheeled support for moving a heavy object, esp. a gun **5** [C] a movable part of a machine: *This printing machine has a carriage which holds and moves the paper* **6** [C *usu. sing.*;U] the manner of holding one's head, limbs, and body when standing or walking; DEPORTMENT **7 carriage and pair** a wheeled vehicle pulled by 2 horses, as in former times **8 carriage forward** *tech* the cost of carrying (the goods) is to be paid by the receiver **9 carriage paid/free** *tech* the cost of carrying (the goods) has been paid by the sender

car·riage·way /ˈkærɪdʒweɪ/ *n BrE* the part of a road's surface on which vehicles travel —see also DUAL CARRIAGEWAY

car·ri·er /ˈkærɪəʳ/ *n* **1** [C] a person or business that carries goods or passengers from one place to another for payment **2** [C] *med* a person or thing that carries and passes diseases to others without himself or itself suffering from the disease **3** [C9] a military vehicle or ship which carries soldiers, planes, weapons, etc. **4** [C] a usu. metal framework fixed to a vehicle to hold bags, goods, etc. **5** [C] a person employed to carry messages; messenger: *He worked as a carrier between banks in the city*

carrier bag /ˈ··· ·/ (*AmE* **shopping bag**)— *n BrE* a cheap strong paper or plastic bag for carrying goods away from a shop

carrier pi·geon /ˈ··· ˌ··/ also **homing pigeon**— *n* a PIGEON (a type of bird) that has been trained to carry small messages from one place to another

car·ri·on /ˈkærɪən/ *n* [U] dead and decaying flesh

carrion crow /ˈ··· ·/ *n* a type of largish black European bird (CROW) that eats dead flesh and small animals

car·rot /ˈkærət/ *n* **1** [C] a type of plant with a fairly long orange-red pointed root and grown as a vegetable —see picture at VEGETABLE[1] **2** [C;U] the root of this plant eaten as food: *Have another carrot.|Would you like some more carrot?* **3** [C] *infml* a promised reward or advantage for doing something: *Which shall it be: the carrot (reward) or the stick (punishment)?*

car·rot·y /ˈkærəti/ *adj* (esp. of the hair) having an orange-red colour

car·ry[1] /ˈkæri/ *v* **1** [T1] to bear (someone or something) in one's arms, on one's back, etc., while moving: *The monkey carried her baby on her back* —see BRING (USAGE) **2** [T1] to act as the means by which (a person or thing) is moved from one place to another; TRANSPORT; CONVEY: *A taxi carried me to the station.|Pipes carry oil across the desert* —see BRING (USAGE) **3** [T1] to bear the weight of (something) without moving: *This pillar carries the whole roof* **4** [T1] *tech* to support with food: *This field can carry up to 10 cows* **5** [T1] *infml* to keep or support with money, help, personal effort, etc.: *The company will carry you until your illness is over* **6** [T1] to keep or hold (something) with one; wear: *In Britain police do not usually carry guns* **7** [X9 *no pass.*] to move or hold (oneself) in a certain way: *Janet carries herself very nicely and attracts all the men* **8** [T1] to pass from one person to another; spread: *Many serious diseases are carried by insects* **9** [IØ] to be able to reach a certain distance; TRANSMIT; cover space: *She could never be a great singer because her voice does not carry!|How far does this gun carry?* (=how far will it fire?) **10** [T1] (of a shop) to have (goods) for sale: *This shop carries a very wide variety of clothes* **11** [T1;IØ] (of a female) to be expecting (a child or young animal): *Our cow's carrying again* **12** [T1;IØ] to put (a number) into the next upright row to the left as when doing addition: *Write 4 and carry 1* **13** [T1] to print or broadcast: *All the newspapers carried articles about the government's plans* **14** [T1] *infml* to hold (alcoholic drink) without showing bad effects: *He can't carry more than 4 glasses of beer without getting drunk* **15** [T1] to contain: *The report carried a serious warning of future trouble* **16** [T1] to have as a usual or necessary result: *Such a crime carries a serious punishment* **17** [T1 *no pass.*] to win the sympathy, support, or agreement of: *The government carried the country and won the election* **18** [IØ;T1] **a** (esp. of a law or plan) to be approved; PASS[1] (15): *The law carried by 310 votes to 306* **b** to cause (esp. a law or plan) to be approved; (cause to) PASS[1] (15): *The law was carried by 310 votes to 306.|The government succeeded in carrying its plan through Parliament* **19** [X9] to increase, enlarge, or continue (someone or something) in space, time, or degree; take: *This building will be carried up to 16 floors.|His ability carried him to the top of his profession* **20** [T1] to succeed in not showing: *He carries his age very well. He looks 40 but in fact he's 60* **21 carry all/everything before one** to be completely successful; win a complete victory **22 carry (something) too far** to do (something) for too long or to too great a degree: *If you pretend to the police that you've discovered a bomb, you may find you've carried the joke too far* **23 carry the ball** *infml* to have the chief post; have most work **24 carry the can** *BrE infml* to take the blame; be responsible **25 carry the day** to win; be completely successful **26 carry weight (with)** to have influence (with)

carry[2] *n* **1** [S;U] the distance an object such as a bullet will travel after being fired or thrown; RANGE of a gun: *This gun has plenty of carry.|a carry of 500 yards* **2** [C] one of the methods of holding a RIFLE (=long gun) while marching **3** [S;U] the act of carrying a boat across land between 2 rivers or lakes; PORTAGE **4** [C] a place where this is done

car·ry·all /ˈkæri-ɔːl/ *n* a large, usu. soft, bag or case —compare HOLDALL

carry a·way *v adv* [T1 *usu. pass.*] to excite: *Marsha got so carried away when arguing with her husband that she killed him*

carry back *v adv* [T1 (*to*)] to take back in memory: *The old picture carried me back 35 years to my wedding day*

car·ry·cot /ˈkærikɒt‖-kɑt/ *n esp. BrE* a small boxlike container, usu. having 2 handles and easily carried, in which a baby can sleep —see picture at BEDROOM

carry for·ward also **carry over**— *v adv* [T1] (when adding up accounts) to make a total at the bottom of an upright row of figures, ready to be moved to the top of the next page for further addition

car·ry·ings-on /ˌkæri-ɪŋz ˈɒn‖-ˈɑn/ *n* [P] *infml* foolish excited usu. noisy behaviour: *There were carryings-on in the camp when the lights had been put out*

carry off *v adv* [T1] **1** to cause the death of (someone) **2** to perform or do (a part, action, duty, etc.) easily and successfully **3** to win (the prize, honour, etc.): *Jean carried off all the prizes in the competition*

carry-on /ˌ·· ˈ·/ *n* **1** [S] *infml* a piece of silly usu. annoying behaviour **2** [C] a small bag which can be carried on board a plane and which holds what one needs for the journey

carry on *v adv* **1** [T1a,4;IØ] to continue, esp. in spite of an interruption or difficulties: *Even after the king had entered the room she carried on talking.|Carry on the good work!|The government must carry on, whatever the cost.|We'll carry on our conversation tomorrow* **2** [IØ] *infml* to behave in a very excited and anxious manner: *Mother did carry on so when she heard the bad news!*

carry on with *v adv prep* [T1 *not pass.*] **1** *infml* to have a love affair with (someone) **2 to carry/be carrying on with** for the present time; for now; for the time being: *Here's £5 to be carrying on with, I'll give you more tomorrow*

car·ry·out /ˈkæri-aʊt/ *adj, n Am & ScotE* TAKEAWAY

carry out *v adv* [T1] to fulfil; complete: *He carried out his threat to kill his enemy.|to carry out a plan, order, duty, etc.*

carry-o·ver /ˈ·· ˌ··/ *n* **1** [C *usu. sing.*] the total of one page of an account carried forward to the top of the next page **2** [C;U] (a piece of) business left until a later date or left from an earlier date **3** [C] an influence on something by something else, often by something finished: *There's quite a carry-over from my work on dictionaries to the poetry I write*

carry o·ver *v adv* **1** [Wv6;L9 (*from*)] to remain; continue: *The habit carries over from my childhood* **2** [T1] CARRY FORWARD

carry through[1] *v adv* **1** [T1] CARRY OUT: *In spite of a long struggle we succeeded in carrying most of our plans through* **2** [IØ (*to*)] to continue to exist: *feelings that carry through to the present*

carry through[2] *v adv; prep* [T1;D1] to help (someone) to continue in an effective way during (an illness, difficult period, etc.): *His courage carried him through (his illness)*

car·sick /ˈkɑːˌsɪk‖ˈkɑr-/ *adj* sick when in a moving car —**~ness** *n* [U]

cart¹ /kɑːt‖kɑrt/ *n* **1** a usu. 2-wheeled wooden vehicle drawn by an animal, esp. a horse, and used for farming or for carrying goods **2** any of various types of small light wooden vehicle with 2 or 4 wheels and moved by hand **3 be in the cart** *sl, esp. BrE* to be in an awkward, difficult, or losing position **4 put the cart before the horse** *not fml* to put things in the wrong order; mistake cause for effect and effect for cause

cart² *v* [T1] **1** to carry in a cart **2** [(*off*)] *derog infml* to carry as if in a cart, usu. in a disrespectful manner: *The police carted the prisoners off to prison* **3** *infml* to carry by hand: *Do you have to cart that bag round all day?*

cart·age /ˈkɑːtɪdʒ‖ˈkɑr-/ *n* [U;S] the cost of having goods carried from one place to another in a cart

carte blanche /ˌkɑːt ˈblɑːnʃ‖ˌkɑrt- (*Fr* kart blɑ̃ʃ)/ *n* **cartes blanches** /ˌkɑːts ˈblɑːnʃ‖ˌkɑrts- (*Fr* kart blɑ̃ʃ)/ [U (*in*); U3] *Fr* full freedom, esp. in politics and in spending money: *The king gave his minister carte blanche in foreign affairs*

car·tel /kɑːˈtel‖kɑr-/ *n* **1** a combination of independent companies in order to limit competition and increase profits **2** a combination of political groups for common action

cart·er /ˈkɑːtəʳ‖ˈkɑr-/ *n* a person whose job is driving carts

cart·horse /ˈkɑːthɔːs‖ˈkɑrthɔrs/ *n* a heavy powerful horse, esp. used for heavy work and pulling carts

car·ti·lage /ˈkɑːtəlɪdʒ‖ˈkɑr-/ *n* [C;U] (a piece of) strong elastic substance found instead of bone in young animals and, esp. round the joints, in older animals: *Cartilage protects the joints.|There is a cartilage in the nose* —compare GRISTLE

car·ti·lag·i·nous /ˌkɑːtəˈlædʒənəs‖ˌkɑr-/ *adj med* of or like CARTILAGE

car·tog·ra·pher /kɑːˈtɒgrəfəʳ‖kɑrˈtɑ-/ *n* a person who makes maps; map-maker

car·tog·ra·phy /kɑːˈtɒgrəfi‖kɑrˈtɑ-/ *n* [U] the science or art of making maps

car·ton /ˈkɑːtn‖ˈkɑrtn/ *n* a box made from stiff paper (CARDBOARD) used for holding goods

car·toon /kɑːˈtuːn‖kɑr-/ *n* **1** a humorous drawing, often dealing in an amusing (SATIRICAL) way with something of interest in the news **2** a drawing used as a model for a painting or other work of art **3** also (*fml*) **animated cartoon**— a cinema film made by photographing a set of drawings —see also STRIP CARTOON —**~ist** *n*

car·tridge /ˈkɑːtrɪdʒ‖ˈkɑr-/ *n* **1** a usu. metal or paper tube containing explosive and a bullet for use in a gun, or enough explosive to set off an explosion (BLAST) **2** (in a record player) a small case containing the needle (STYLUS) that changes needle movement into electrical power **3** a container holding, usu. recorded MAGNETIC TAPE used esp. with a TAPE RECORDER —compare CASSETTE (2)

cartridge belt /ˈ·· ·/ *n* a band of leather or strong cloth worn round the waist or over the shoulder to carry a number of CARTRIDGE*s* (1)

cartridge pa·per /ˈ·· ˌ··/ *n* [U] a type of strong thick whitish paper used for **a** making CARTRIDGE*s* (1) **b** drawing on in pencil and ink

cart track /ˈ· ·/ *n* a narrow road with a rough surface

cart·wheel¹ /ˈkɑːt-wiːl‖ˈkɑrt-/ *n* a circular movement in which a person stretches his arms above himself then moves sideways off his feet, onto one hand, then onto the other hand (so that his feet are above and his head below), and then back onto his feet: *Jean learned how to* **turn cartwheels** *at school* —compare SOMERSAULT

cartwheel² *v* [I∅] to move sideways like a turning wheel; to turn CARTWHEEL*s*

carve /kɑːv‖kɑrv/ *v* **1** [T1 (*into*)] to cut (usu. wood or stone) in order to make a special shape **2** [D1 (*for*);T1: (*from, in, into, out of*)] to make (a special shape) by cutting usu. wood or stone: *The artist carved you an interesting ornament from this piece of wood.|What did she carve (for) you?* **3** [I∅] to work as a SCULPTOR: *"What's her job?" "She carves"* **4** [T1;I∅] to cut (cooked meat) into pieces or SLICE*s*, esp. at a meal **5** [D1 (*for*); T1] to cut (one or more pieces or SLICE*s*) from cooked meat: *He carved me some very nice pieces of chicken* **6** [D1 (*for*); T1: (OUT)] to make or get (a social position, famous name, etc.) by hard work: *He carved out a name for himself.|He carved himself (out) a nice position in the business*

carv·er /ˈkɑːvəʳ‖ˈkɑr-/ *n* **1** a person who CARVE*s* (1,2,3,4) **2** CARVING KNIFE

carve up *v adv* [T1] **1** *derog* to divide **2** *sl* to wound (someone) with a knife

carv·ing /ˈkɑːvɪŋ‖ˈkɑr-/ *n* **1** [C] something shaped or made by carving (CARVE (1)) **2** [U] the work, art, or skill of a person who CARVE*s*

carving fork /ˈ·· ·/ *n* a large fork used to hold meat in place for cutting with a CARVING KNIFE

carving knife /ˈ·· ·/ *n* a long sharp knife used for cutting large pieces of meat into smaller pieces

car·y·at·id /ˌkæriˈætəd/ *n tech* a pillar shaped like a clothed female figure

cas·cade¹ /kæˈskeɪd/ *n* **1** a steep high usu. small waterfall, esp. one part of a bigger waterfall **2** anything that seems to pour or flow downward: *Climbing plants with their bright flowers hung in cascades over the garden wall.|Her hair fell over her shoulders in a cascade of curls*

cascade² *v* [L9;X9] to (cause to) pour in quantity: *When it rained, water would cascade down the window*

cas·ca·ra /kæˈskɑːrə‖kæˈskærə/ *n* [U] a type of not very strong LAXATIVE

case¹ /keɪs/ *n* **1** [C] an example: *It was a case of stupidity, not dishonesty* **2** [C] a particular occasion or state of affairs: *Pauline and Mary haven't finished their work; in the first case because she* (=Pauline) *couldn't do it, in the second case* (=Mary) *because of laziness.|Pauline's stupid, but it's different in the case of Mary; she's just lazy* **3** [C] **a** (of diseases) a single example: *This is a case of fever* **b** a person suffering from an illness **4** [C] **a** a combination or set of events needing police or other inquiry or action: *a case of robbery with violence* **b** a person being dealt with by the police, a SOCIAL WORKer, etc. **5** [C] a question to be decided in a court of law: *My case against Mr. Smith is to be heard* (=judged) *today* **6** [C *usu. sing.*] the facts and arguments supporting one side in a disagreement or in a question brought before a court of law: *The police have a clear case against the prisoner* **7** [C] *derog sl* a silly person; fool: *He's a real case* **8** [C;U] (in grammar) (changes in) the form of a word (esp. of a noun, adjective, or PRONOUN) showing its relationship with other words in a sentence: *"Me" is the object case of "I".| "Mine" is the* POSSESSIVE *case of "I".|Case is an important part of the grammar of many languages.| case endings* **9 be the case** *fml* be true: *She thought she was hurt but it wasn't really the case* **10 in any case** whatever happens: *In any case, catch the train tomorrow* **11 in case a** for fear that; because . . . might; LEST: *Take your coat in case it rains/(just) in case it should rain* **b** (of events in the future) because . . . perhaps; because . . . might: *Take your* *dancing shoes in case you decide to go dancing* **c** *esp. AmE* if: *In case the house burns down, we'll get the insurance money* **d** for fear that something that is not mentioned should happen: *"I will keep some of these unused in case"* (SEU W.) **12 just in case** *tech esp. AmE* only if: *Q is true just in case P is true* **13 in case of a** for fear that (that stated event) should happen: *We'd better insure the house in case of fire* (=for fear that there should be a fire) **b** if (the stated event) should happen: *"In case of fire, break the glass"* (on a notice) **14 in this/that case** if this/that is so; if this/that happens: *In that case come a little earlier* **15 make out a/one's case (for)** to put arguments in favour of (something) **16 put the case (that)** to suggest (that)

case² *n* **1** a large box in which goods can be stored or moved **2** also **caseful**— the amount such a box holds **3** a box or container for holding and protecting something **4** the frame of a door or window **5** SUITCASE **6 upper case** (of letters of the alphabet) large (CAPITAL): *The letter "E" is upper case* **7 lower case** (of letters of the alphabet) small: *The letter "e" is lower case*

case³ *v* [T1] **1** to enclose or cover with a case **2** *sl* to examine, esp. with the intention of robbing: *The thief was* **casing the joint** (=examining the place he intended to rob)

case·book /ˈkeɪsbʊk/ *n* a written record kept by doctors, police, SOCIAL WORKers, etc., of the cases they have dealt with

case end·ing /ˈ· ˌ··/ *n* the change in the end of a word which shows CASE¹ (8): *"'s" is the* POSSESSIVE *case ending of most English nouns in the singular*

case his·tory /ˌ· ˈ··/ *n* a record of the past history of someone suffering from an illness, social difficulties, etc.

ca·se·in /ˈkeɪsɪən, -siːn‖keɪˈsiːn, ˈkeɪsɪən/ *n* [U] a whitish body-building food substance (PROTEIN) found in milk and cheese —**caseous** /ˈkeɪsɪəs/ *adj*

case law /ˈ· ·/ *n* [U] *tech* that part of the law which is based on former judgments, usu. used when there is doubt over the exact meaning of a law passed by parliament —compare STATUTE LAW

case·ment win·dow /ˌkeɪsmənt ˈwɪndəʊ/ also **casement**— *n* a window that opens like a door

case stud·y /ˈ· ˌ··/ *n* the study of a person or group of people in order to learn about their social development and relationship with other people in society

case·work /ˈkeɪswɜːk‖-ɜrk/ *n* [U] SOCIAL WORK concerned with direct consideration of the difficulties of a particular person, family, etc. —**~er** *n*

cash¹ /kæʃ/ *n* [U] **1** money in coins and notes, rather than cheques: *I've no cash on me, can I pay you tomorrow?* **2** *infml* money in any form **3 cash down** payment must be made for goods in the form of notes and coins before they leave the shop **4 cash on delivery** C.O.D. **5 cash on the barrelhead** *infml humor, esp. AmE* CASH¹ (1): *We don't accept cheques: we want cash on the barrelhead* **6 hard cash** *infml* CASH¹ (1): *We don't accept cheques: we want hard cash* **7 ready cash** CASH¹ (1) that can be used for payment at once: *I've no ready cash on me: can I pay you tomorrow?*

cash² *v* [D1 (*for*); T1] to exchange (a cheque or other order to pay) for CASH (1): *Can you cash this postal order for that old lady please?|Where can I get this cashed?*

cash and car·ry /ˌ· · ˈ··/ *n, adj* [Wa5;A] (a usu. large shop where goods are) sold at low prices if paid for at once and if taken away by the buyer

cash crop /ˈ· ·/ *n* a crop produced for sale rather than for use by the grower —compare SUBSISTENCE CROP

cash desk /ˈ· ·/ *n* (in a shop) the desk where payments are made

ca·shew /ˈkæʃuː, kəˈʃuː/ *n* **1** also **cashew tree** /ˈ·· ·/— a type of tropical American tree **2** the small curved nut of this tree —see picture at NUT¹

cash flow /ˈ· ·/ *n* [S;U] the flow of money payments to, from, or within a firm or business: *Cash-flow difficulties in our company make it impossible to raise wages at the moment.|a cash flow of £50,000 per month*

cash·ier¹ /kæˈʃɪəʳ/ *n* a person in charge of money receipts and payments in a bank, hotel, shop, etc.

cashier² /kæˈʃɪəʳ, kə-/ *v* [T1] to dismiss (someone, usu. an officer) with dishonour from service in the armed forces

cash in *v adv* [IØ (*on*)] to take advantage or profit (from): *Let's cash in on the fine weather and go out for the day*

cash·mere /ˈkæʃmɪəʳ‖ˈkæʒ-, ˈkæʃ-/ *n* [U] fine soft wool made from the hair of a type of goat which lives in Kashmir

cash reg·is·ter /ˈ· ˌ···/ *n* a business machine, esp. used in shops for calculating and recording the amount of each sale and the money received, and sometimes for giving change

cas·ing /ˈkeɪsɪŋ/ *n* **1** a protective covering, esp. the outer rubber covering of a car tyre: *This wire has a rubber casing* **2** the frame of a door or window

ca·si·no /kəˈsiːnəʊ/ *n* **-nos** a building used for social activities, esp. playing games for money

cask /kɑːsk‖kæsk/ *n* **1** a barrel-shaped container for holding and storing liquids **2** the amount contained in this

cas·ket /ˈkɑːskɪ̈t‖ˈkæs-/ *n* **1** a small usu. ornamental box for holding jewels, letters, and other small valuable things **2** *euph, esp. AmE* COFFIN

casque /kæsk/ *n* (in former times) a protective metal covering worn by soldiers over their heads; HELMET

cas·sa·va /kəˈsɑːvə/ also **manioc**— *n* **1** [C] a type of tropical plant with thick fleshy roots —see picture at VEGETABLE¹ **2** [U] flour made from the roots of this plant, used in preparing several foods (including TAPIOCA)

cas·se·role /ˈkæsərəʊl/ *n* **1** [C] a deep usu. covered dish in which food, esp. meat may be cooked and served **2** [C;U] the food cooked in this: *Would you like some more casserole?*

cas·sette /kəˈset/ *n* **1** a container for photographic film which can be fitted into a camera **2** a container, usu. holding MAGNETIC TAPE, which can be fitted into a TAPE RECORDER —see picture at SOUND³ —compare CARTRIDGE (3)

cas·sock /ˈkæsək/ *n* a heavy ankle-length usu. black, red, or purple garment worn by some priests and by people helping at religious services

cas·so·wa·ry /ˈkæsəweri/ *n* any of various types of large Australian or New Guinean birds which are unable to fly and which are like but smaller than the OSTRICH

cast¹ /kɑːst‖kæst/ *v* **cast 1** [T1] to throw or drop: *The fishermen cast their nets into the sea* **2** [T1 (*off*)] to throw off; remove: *Every year the snake casts (off) its skin* **3** [T1] to give (a vote) **4** [X9; (T1)] to turn or direct: *The evening sun cast long shadows (across the garden).|This misuse of public money has cast doubts on the actions of the whole government* **5** [T1 (*as, in*)] to give an acting part to (a person): *The director cast me as a mad scientist/cast me in that new play* **6** [T1] to choose actors for parts in (a play) **7** [T1] to make (an object) by pouring hot metal (or plastic) into a specially shaped container (MOULD) **8** [T1] to pour (hot metal) into a specially shaped container (MOULD) to make a CAST² (4): *to cast* BRONZE² (1) **9** [L9]

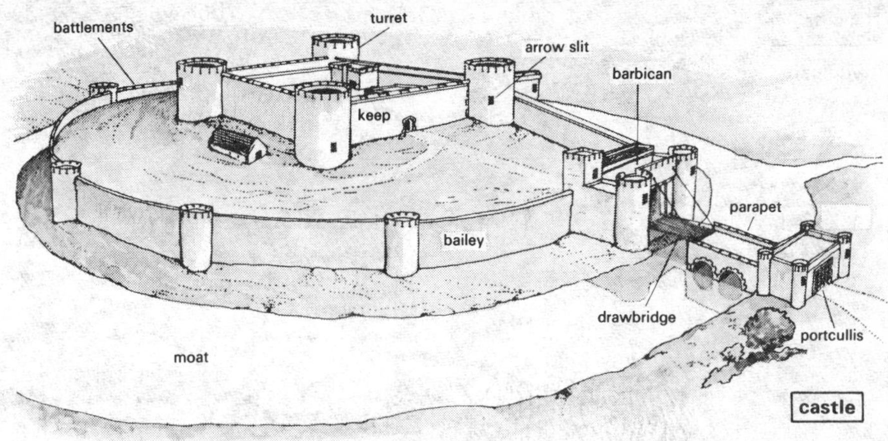

(of metal) to be fit or suitable for making a CAST² (4): *Iron casts better than copper* **10** [T1] (in KNITting (1)) to make (a stitch) **11** [T1] to calculate: *to cast accounts|to cast a* HOROSCOPE **12** [T1] to make and put into effect (a SPELL¹)

cast² *n* **1** [C] an act of throwing: *The fisherman's cast reached right to the middle of the lake* **2** [GC] the actors in a play, moving picture, etc. **3** [C] a hard stiff protective covering of cloth and cement, for holding a broken bone in place while it gets better **4** [C] an object CAST¹ (7) in a specially shaped container (MOULD) **5** [(*the*) S] general shape or quality: *the noble cast of his head|an inquiring cast of mind* **6** [S] a slight addition (of one colour) mixed with or spread over another: *green with a faint yellowish cast* **7** [C *usu. sing.*] *becoming rare* a slight SQUINT² (1) **8** [C] a small pile of earth thrown out of the ground by worms when they make a hole

cast a·bout for also **cast a·round for**— *v adv prep* [T1 *no pass.*] to search or look for in all directions

cas·ta·nets /ˌkæstəˈnets/ *n* [P] a musical instrument made from 2 shells of hard wood, plastic, etc., fastened to the thumb by a string and played by being knocked together by the other fingers

cast a·side *v adv* [T1] to get rid of; DISCARD: *As soon as she became rich she cast aside all her old friends|all her old habits*

cast·a·way /ˈkɑːstəweɪ‖ˈkæst-/ *n* **1** a person saved from death in a shipwreck by reaching the shore of a strange country or lonely island **2** a person made to leave a ship by force and left on a piece of land

cast a·way *v adv* [T1 *usu. pass.*] to leave (someone) somewhere as the result of a shipwreck: *We were cast away on an island without food or water*

cast down *v adv* [T1 *usu. pass.*] to lower in spirit; UPSET: *Father was very cast down by the news of our aunt's death*

caste /kɑːst‖kæst/ *n* **1** [U] division of society based on class differences of wealth, rank, rights, profession, or job **2** [C] any of the groups resulting from this division, in which a person usu. finds himself at birth, esp. one of the social classes of Hinduism: *He belonged to the lowest caste and so he could not marry the princess.|The caste system is still very strong in India today* **3** [U] social position; PRESTIGE **4 lose caste** to come down in social rank; lose respect

cas·tel·lat·ed /ˈkæstɪ̈leɪtɪ̈d/ *adj tech* (of a building) having defences like a castle; made to look like a castle

cast·er, -or /ˈkɑːstəʳ‖ˈkæs-/ *n* **1** a small metal or plastic wheel fixed to the base of a piece of furniture so that it can be easily moved **2** a small glass and metal or plastic container with small holes in the top so that sugar, salt, etc., may be evenly spread over foods —compare SALTCELLAR

caster sug·ar /ˈ·· ˌ··/ *n* [U] very fine white sugar

cast·i·gate /ˈkæstɪ̈geɪt/ *v* [T1] *fml* **1** to punish or scold severely in order to correct **2** to express strong disapproval of (a person, behaviour, or someone's ideas) —**-gation** /ˌkæstɪ̈ˈgeɪʃən/ *n* [U]

cast·ing /ˈkɑːstɪŋ‖ˈkæstɪŋ/ *n* **1** [C] a usu. metal or plastic object shaped by having been CAST¹ (7) **2** [U] the act of choosing actors for a play or film **3** [U] (in fishing) the act of throwing the hook, fastened to the line, into the water at a place where one thinks there are fish

casting vote /ˌ·· ˈ·/ *n* a deciding vote (usu. by a chairman) used when there is a TIE (=when both sides have an equal number of votes)

cast-iron /ˌ· ˈ··◂/ *adj* [Wa5] **1** made of CAST IRON **2** hard; strong; unbreakable; unyielding: *She has a cast-iron stomach; she can eat anything*

cast i·ron /ˌ· ˈ··/ *n* [U] a hard but easily breakable type of iron, made by pouring hot liquid iron mixed with CARBON (1) and SILICON into a cold shaped container (MOULD)

cas·tle¹ /ˈkɑːsəl‖ˈkæ-/ *n* **1** a large strongly-built building or set of buildings made in former times to be defended against attack **2** also **rook**— (in the game of CHESS) one of the powerful pieces placed on the corner squares of the board at the beginning of each game—see CHESS (USAGE) **3** **build castles in the air/in Spain** *not fml* to make plans which will probably not succeed; DAYDREAM

castle² *v* [I∅] (in the game of CHESS) to move the king 2 squares towards either of his own CASTLEs¹ (2) and put the CASTLE¹ (2) on the square that the king has moved across

cast-off /ˈ· ·/ *adj* [Wa5] (esp. of clothes) unwanted by someone else; thrown away —**castoff** /ˈkɑːstɒf‖ˈkæstɔf/ *n* [*usu. pl.*]

cast off *v adv* **1** [T1;I∅] **a** (of a boat or ship) to be set free on the water by a rope being untied **b** to set (a boat or ship) free by untying a rope **2** [T1] to give or throw away (clothes no longer wanted) **3** [I∅] (in a SQUARE DANCE) to turn one's partner and pass round the outside of the set **4** [I∅;T1] (in

KNITting (1)) to finish making something of woollen thread by removing (stitches) from the needle in such a way that the garment does not come undone **5** [T1] CAST ASIDE

cast on *v adv* [IØ;T1] (in KNITting) to start making something of woollen thread by putting (the first stitches) onto a needle

castor /ˈkɑːstəʳ‖ˈkæs-/ *n* CASTER

castor oil /ˌ·· ˈ·◂/ *n* [U] a thick fatty yellowish medicinal oil made from the poisonous seeds of the **castor-oil plant** and used esp. as a LAXATIVE

castor sug·ar /ˈ·· ˌ··/ *n* [U] CASTER SUGAR

cast out *v adv* [T1 (*of*) *often pass.*] to drive out or away; EXPEL

cas·trate /kæˈstreɪt‖ˈkæstreɪt/ *v* [T1] to remove all or part of the sex organs of (a male animal or person) —compare EMASCULATE —**-tration** /kæˈstreɪʃən/ *n* [U;C]

cas·u·al¹ /ˈkæʒʊəl/ *adj* **1** [B] resulting from chance: *a casual meeting* **2** [B] showing or feeling little sense of responsibility; uninterested: *a casual host* **3** [A;(B)] not serious or thorough: *A casual newspaper reader wouldn't like articles on politics every day* **4** [B] informal; not for special use: *casual clothes* **5** [A;(B)] not close: *a casual friendship* **6** [Wa5;A] (of workers) employed for a short period of time —**~ly** *adv* —**~ness** *n* [U]

casual² *n* a person employed for a short period of time: *John's a casual, he can't find a proper job anywhere*

cas·u·al·ty /ˈkæʒʊəlti/ *n* **1** [C] a person hurt in an accident: *There were 10 serious casualties in the train crash* **2** [C] a person or thing defeated or destroyed **3** [C] a military person lost through death, wounds or illness **4** [R] also **casualty ward, department**— a place in a hospital where people hurt in accidents are taken for treatment: *They rushed her to casualty but she was dead on arrival*

cas·u·ist /ˈkæʒʊɪ̇st/ *n derog & fml* a person skilled in CASUISTRY —**-istic** /ˌkæʒʊˈɪstɪk/ *adj* —**-istical** *adj* —**-istically** *adv* [Wa4]

cas·u·is·try /ˈkæʒʊɪ̇stri/ *n* [U] *often derog & fml* false but clever use of principles, esp. when dealing with cases of conscience, law, or right and wrong behaviour: *Your casuistry can't make me believe that our defeat was really a victory*

ca·sus bel·li /ˌkɑːsəs ˈbeliː, ˌkeɪsəs ˈbelaɪ/ *n* **casus belli** [Wn3] *tech Lat* an event or political action which directly causes a declaration of war

cat /kæt/ *n* **1** [C] a small animal with soft fur and sharp teeth and CLAWs (nails), often kept as a pet or in buildings to catch mice and rats **2** [C] any of various types of animals related to this, such as the lion or tiger **3** [C] *derog* a nasty woman **4** [C] a strong apparatus used to lift heavy objects, esp. ANCHORs¹ (1) onto a ship **5** [C] *sl, becoming rare* (a) man: *Are you cats coming in to hear my new records?* —compare GUY² (1) **6** [*the*+R;C] *infml* CAT-O'-NINE TAILS **7** [C] *BrE infml* CAT BURGLAR **8** [C] *infml* CATERPILLAR TRACTOR **9 cat and dog life** *infml* a life full of quarrels and arguments **10 enough to make a cat laugh** *infml* very funny **11 (Even) a cat may look at a king** *not fml* (Even) the lowest rank of people have some rights **12 let the cat out of the bag** *infml* to tell a secret (often unintentionally) **13 like a cat on hot bricks** (*AmE* **like a cat on a hot tin roof**)— *BrE infml* very nervous or anxious: *You're like a cat on hot bricks today. What's wrong?* **14 there's not enough/no room to swing a cat** *BrE sl* This is a very small, narrow, or crowded place **15 rain cats and dogs** *infml* to rain very heavily **16 wait for the cat to jump** also **see which way the cat jumps**— *infml* to do nothing until one sees how events develop

cat·a- /ˈkætə/ *prefix tech* down

cat·a·clys·m /ˈkætəklɪzəm/ *n* a violent and sudden change or event, esp. a serious flood or EARTHQUAKE —**~ic** /ˌkætəˈklɪzmɪk/ *adj*

cat·a·comb /ˈkætəkuːm‖-kəʊm/ *n* [C *usu. pl.*] an

underground burial place made up of many passages and rooms

cat·a·falque /ˈkætəfælk/ *n* an ornamented raised framework on which a dead body may be placed before an official funeral

cat·a·lep·sy /ˈkætəlepsi/ *n* [U] *med* a type of illness (probably a severe form of SCHIZOPHRENIA) in which there is loss of will-power and the limbs either become stiff as in death or else remain in whatever position they are placed —**-tic** /ˌkætəˈleptɪk/ *adj* [Wa5]

cat·a·logue[1], *AmE* also **-log** /ˈkætəlɒg‖-lɔg, -lɑg/ *n* a list of places, names, goods, etc. (often with information about them) put in a special order so that they can be found easily

catalogue[2], *AmE* also **-log** *v* [T1;(I∅)] **1** to make a CATALOGUE[1] of (a list of goods, places, names, etc.): *Can you catalogue the furniture you sell and send me a copy of it?* **2** to enter (a book, place, name, etc.) into a CATALOGUE[1]

ca·tal·pa /kəˈtælpə/ *n* any of several types of American and Asian tree with broad heart-shaped leaves and pale showy flowers

ca·tal·y·sis /kəˈtæləsəs/ *n* [U] the act of quickening a chemical activity by adding a CATALYST

cat·a·lyst /ˈkætl-əst/ *n* [C;(U)] a substance which, without itself changing, causes chemical activity to quicken: (fig.) *The workers' demand for higher wages was a catalyst in a difficult state of affairs, and led to important social changes* —**-lytic** /ˌkætəˈlɪtɪk/ *adj*

cat·a·ma·ran /ˌkætəməˈræn/ *n* **1** a type of boat with a flat usu. wooden surface (DECK) supported by 2 narrow parallel HULLS (floating surfaces) with a space between them, and moved by sails or an engine —see picture at SAIL[2] **2** a rough flat floating object (RAFT) made by tying logs of wood together, and moved by sails or PADDLES[1] (1)

cat-and-mouse /ˌ· · ˈ·/ *adj* [Wa5;A] *not fml* consisting of continuous chasing, near-seizures and escapes, and waiting for the right moment to attack

cat·a·pult[1] /ˈkætəpʌlt/ *n* **1** (*AmE* **slingshot**)— *BrE* a small Y-shaped stick with a rubber band fastened between the forks, used by children to shoot small stones at objects **2** a powerful apparatus for helping planes take off from a ship —compare ARRESTER WIRES **3** a machine for throwing heavy stones, balls, etc., into the air, used, in former times, as a weapon for breaking down defensive walls

catapult[2] *v* **1** [T1] to hit (something or someone) with something fired from a CATAPULT[1] (1): *The bad boy tried to catapult the old man's window* **2** [X9] to fire from a CATAPULT[1] (1): *The bad boy tried to catapult a stone through the old man's window* **3** [L9;X9] to (cause to) move quickly as if fired from a CATAPULT[1] (1): *When I tried to catch the thief he catapulted through the window, over the wall, and escaped.|When the bus hit the tree one of the passengers was catapulted through the window* **4** [T1] to use a CATAPULT[1] (2) to help (a plane) take off from a ship

cat·a·ract /ˈkætərækt/ *n* **1** a large waterfall **2** [*usu. pl.*] a stretch of a river where the current flows very fast DOWNHILL[2] (1) **3** *med* a diseased growth on the eye causing a slow loss of sight by preventng light from entering

ca·tarrh /kəˈtɑːʳ/ *n* [U;(C)] a disease, esp. of the nose and throat, causing a flow of thick liquid and discomfort, as when one has a cold —**~al** *adj* [Wa5]

ca·tas·tro·phe /kəˈtæstrəfi/ *n* a sudden, unexpected, and terrible event that causes great suffering, misfortune, or ruin: *The war was a terrible catastrophe in which many people died* —**-phic** /ˌkætəˈstrɒfɪk‖-ˈstrɑ-/ *adj* —**-phically** *adv*

cat·a·ton·ic /ˌkætəˈtɒnɪk‖-ˈtɑ-/ *n, adj* [Wa5] (a person suffering from the disease) of CATALEPSY: *catatonic* SCHIZOPHRENIA

cat bur·glar /ˈ· ˌ··/ also (*infml*) **cat** (*AmE* **second-story man**)— *n BrE* a thief who enters and leaves a building by climbing up walls, pipes, etc.

cat·call /ˈkætkɔːl/ *v, n* [I∅;C] (to make) a loud whistle or cry expressing disapproval or displeasure, as at the theatre, a sports match, etc.

catch[1] /kætʃ/ *v* **caught** /kɔːt/ [(*rare in tenses with* -ing *form*)] **1** [T1] to get hold of (something moving in the air); seize: *The dog caught the ball in its mouth* **2** [T1] to trap (esp. an animal) after chasing or hunting; take: *Cats like to catch mice* **3** [T1;V4] to find unexpectedly; come upon suddenly; discover by surprise: *Mother caught me stealing from the shop and scolded me severely* **4** [L9] to become stuck: *My skirt caught in the door* **5** [T1] to be in time for: *We had to drive very quickly in order to catch the train* —opposite **miss** **6** [T1] to get (an illness); become infected with: *You'll catch cold if you don't put a coat on* **7** [T1] to cause to become hooked, held, fastened, or stuck, accidentally or on purpose: *I caught my dress on a nail* **8** [X9] to hit (a person or animal); strike: *I caught him on the head with a heavy blow* **9** [T1] to attract (esp. interest or attention): *The boy knocked on the window to catch my attention* **10** [Wv6;T1] to get or notice for a moment (note the phr. **catch sight of**): *I caught sight of my old friend in town today.|I thought I caught a smell of burning but I must have been mistaken* **11** [I∅] to start to burn, work, operate: *The wind was so strong that the fire caught quickly.|The plane's engine is having difficulty in catching so the flight will be late in leaving* **12** [Wv6; T1] to hear; understand: *I didn't catch what you said. Please repeat it* **13** [T1 (OUT) *often pass.*] (in cricket) to send (a player) off the field by taking and holding a ball knocked off the BAT[1] (1) before it touches the ground **14 catch fire** to start to burn **15 catch it** *infml* to be in trouble with someone for doing something wrong: *You'd better hurry home. You'll catch it from mother if you're late* **16 catch one's breath a** to stop breathing for a moment from surprise, fear, shock, etc.: *The news was so unexpected I caught my breath from shock* **b** to rest for a short while after hard work so as to be able to continue later: *Let me sit down for a moment while I catch my breath* **17 catch someone's eye** to attract someone's attention by looking at him

catch[2] *n* **1** [C] an act of seizing and holding a ball **2** [C] (the amount of) something caught: (*infml*) *Her husband was a good catch. They say he's got a fortune in the bank* **3** [C] a hook or other apparatus for fastening something or holding it shut: *The catch on this door seems to be broken. It won't open* **4** [C] *infml* a hidden or awkward difficulty: *That house is for sale very cheaply; there must be a catch in it somewhere!* **5** [U] a simple game in which 2 or more people throw a ball to each other, esp. played by children

catch at *v prep* [T1] to try to take, seize, or hold: *A drowning man will catch at anything, even a* STRAW (1)

catch crop /ˈ· ·/ *n* a quick-growing vegetable crop planted between 2 rows of another crop to use soil not otherwise used

catch·er /ˈkætʃəʳ/ *n* a person or thing that catches

catch·ing /ˈkætʃɪŋ/ *adj* [F;(B)] *infml* **1** (of a disease) infectious **2** CATCHY

catch·ment ar·e·a /ˈkætʃmənt ˌeərɪə/ *n* **1** also **catchment ba·sin** /ˈ·· ˌ··/, **catchment**— the area from which a lake or river gets its water **2** also **catchment**— the area from which people are sent to a central school, hospital, etc.

catch on *v adv* [IØ] **1** to become popular **2** [(*to*)] to understand: *Do you mind repeating what you said, I didn't quite catch on (to what you meant)?*

catch out *v adv* [T1] to show (someone) to be at fault

catch·pen·ny /ˈkætʃˌpeni/ *adj* [Wa5;A] *derog* worthless, but made to appear attractive, esp. through cheapness or showiness

catch·phrase /ˈkætʃfreɪz/ *n* a phrase, often with little meaning, which becomes popular for a time, so that everyone uses it

catch up *v adv* **1** [IØ (*with*); *BrE* also T1] to come up from behind; draw level with: *When will Britain catch up with Japan in industrial production?|You walk on and I'll catch up with you later* (*BrE* also *catch you up later*) **2** [IØ (*on*)] to bring or come up to date: *I have to catch up on writing letters tonight so I can't come out* **3 caught up in a** completely interested in: *I was caught up in conversation with Mrs Jones when you rang* **b** included in, often against one's wishes; INVOLVED in: *The government seems to have got caught up in the difficulties between the employers and the trade unions*

catch·word /ˈkætʃwɜːd‖-ɜrd/ *n* a word or phrase repeated so regularly that it becomes representative of a political party, newspaper, etc.; SLOGAN

catch·y /ˈkætʃi/ *adj* [Wa1] tending to catch the interest or attention —**catchily** *adv*

cat·e·chis·m /ˈkætɪ̈ˌkɪzəm/ *n* **1** [C] a set of questions and answers, often written in the form of a small book, used esp. for Christian religious instruction **2** [U] instruction, esp. about religion, taught by using the question-and-answer method —**catechist** *n*

cat·e·chize, -ise /ˈkætɪ̈kaɪz/ *v* [T1] to give (someone) esp. religious instruction by question, answer, explanation, and example: *The priest went abroad to catechize the nonbelievers*

cat·e·gor·i·cal /ˌkætɪ̈ˈgɒrɪkəl‖-ˈgɔ-, -ˈgɑ-/ *adj* unconditional; wholly fixed; made without any doubt in the mind of the speaker or writer: *One should never make a categorical statement without being sure of one's facts* —**~ly** *adv* [Wa4]: *Our king has categorically refused to meet the enemy leader*

cat·e·go·rize, -ise /ˈkætɪ̈gəraɪz/ *v* [T1 (*as*)] to put in a CATEGORY

cat·e·go·ry /ˈkætɪ̈gəri‖-gori/ *n* a division or class in a system for dividing objects into groups according to their nature

ca·ter /ˈkeɪtəʳ/ *v* **1** [IØ (*at*)] to provide and serve food and drinks, usu. for payment, at a public or private party rather than a restaurant: *Who's catering at your daughter's wedding?* **2** [T1] *AmE infml* to provide and serve food and drinks, usu. for payment, at (a public or private party rather than a restaurant): *Who's catering your daughter's wedding?*

ca·ter·er /ˈkeɪtərəʳ/ *n* a person or firm hired to supply food and drinks at public or private parties

cater for *v prep* [T1] *BrE* **1** to take account of; consider **2** (*AmE* **cater to**)— to take account of and provide with what is necessary: *Our newspapers and magazines try to cater for all opinions*

cat·er·pil·lar /ˈkætəˌpɪləʳ‖-tər-/ *n* a type of small long many-legged wormlike creature (LARVA of the BUTTERFLY and other insects) which feeds on the leaves of plants —see picture at INSECT

caterpillar trac·tor /ˌ···· ˈ··/ also (*infml*) **cat**— *n* a large heavy vehicle which moves along on an endless chain of metal plates fastened over the wheels (**caterpillar**), and is used for farm work, road repair, or building work

cater to *v prep* [T1] **1** to provide with what is necessary, specialize in satisfying: *Those newspapers and magazines cater to the lowest and most evil feelings of their readers* **2** *AmE* CATER FOR (2)

cat·er·waul /ˈkætəwɔːl/ *v* [IØ] **1** to make a loud unpleasant catlike sound **2** *infml* to quarrel loudly and angrily —**caterwaul** *n* [S;(C)]

cat·fish /ˈkætˌfɪʃ/ *n* [Wn2] any of various types of large-headed fish with long fleshy hairlike growths around the mouth —see picture at FISH[1]

cat·gut /ˈkætgʌt/ *n* [U] strong cord made from the bowel skin of animals and used for making the strings of musical instruments

ca·thar·sis /kæˈθɑːsɪ̈s‖-ɑr-/ *n* **-ses** /siːz/ *fml or tech* **1** [U] the action of getting rid of troublesome feelings by expressing them, as **a** under the influence of art **b** under the influence of drugs **c** by reliving early experiences, esp. painful ones **d** in the course of a strong relationship with one or more other people **2** [C] an example of this

ca·thar·tic[1] /kæˈθɑːtɪk‖-ɑr-/ *adj* **1** *fml or tech* of, related to, or producing CATHARSIS **2** of, for, or having the effect of a strong LAXATIVE

cathartic[2] *n* [C;(U)] a strong LAXATIVE

ca·the·dral /kəˈθiːdrəl/ *n* the chief church of a DIOCESE (an area with a BISHOP (1)), typically a large building for worship, usu. ornamented inside and out with art and/or wood-and-stone work in beautiful patterns

cath·er·ine wheel /ˈkæθərɪ̈n wiːl/ *n* a type of circular FIREWORK that is pinned to an upright surface and turns round when set on fire

cath·e·ter /ˈkæθɪ̈təʳ/ *n* a thin tube that is put into blood vessels or other passages in the body, used esp. for putting in or taking out liquids

cath·ode /ˈkæθəʊd/ also **negative pole**— *n* the part of an electrical instrument (such as a BATTERY (2)) from which ELECTRONs leave, often a rod or wire represented by the sign [−] —compare ANODE

cathode ray tube /ˌ·· ˈ· ·/ *n* a glass instrument in which streams of ELECTRONs from the CATHODE (**cathode rays**) are directed onto a flat surface where they give out light, as in a television receiver

cath·o·lic /ˈkæθəlɪk/ *adj fml* (esp. of likings and interests) general; widespread; broad

Catholic[1] *adj* [Wn5] of, being, or connected with a church which claims to be the historical descendant of the early Christian church, esp. the ROMAN CATHOLIC church: *The priest favoured sending Catholic children to Catholic schools.|Is he Catholic or* PROTESTANT*?*

Catholic[2] *n* ROMAN CATHOLIC[1] (1): *Is he a Catholic or a* PROTESTANT*?*

Ca·thol·i·cis·m /kəˈθɒlɪ̈sɪzəm‖keˈθɑ-/ *n* [U] Roman Catholicism

cath·o·lic·i·ty /ˌkæθəˈlɪsɪ̈ti/ *n* [U] *fml* the quality of being general, widespread, or broad, esp. with regard to likings and interests

Catholicity *n* [U] the state of being in agreement with the teachings of the ROMAN CATHOLIC[1] (1) church

cat·kin /ˈkætkɪn/ *n* a stringlike bunch of soft small furry flowers that grows on certain trees (such as the WILLOW or BIRCH)

cat·nap /ˈkætnæp/ *n infml* a very short light sleep

cat·nip /ˈkætnɪp/ *n* [U] a type of strong-smelling small green plant (MINT), the smell of which is attractive and pleasing to cats

cat-o'-nine tails /ˌkæt ə ˈnaɪn teɪlz/ *n* **-tails** [Wn3] a whip of 9 knotted cords fastened to a handle, formerly used for punishing people

cat's cra·dle /ˌ· ˈ··/ *n* [U] a game played with string wound round the fingers and passed from one finger to another to make various shapes

cat's eye /'· ·/ *n* **1** a small object fixed in the road which shines when lit by car lights in the dark and is used in groups set in straight lines down the middle of the road —see picture at INTERCHANGE² **2** any of various QUARTZlike valuable stones
cat's paw /'· ·/ *n* **1** *infml* a person who does nasty or dangerous things with no profit to himself at the command of another person **2** a light wind **3** *tech* a type of knot used by sailors
cat suit /'· ·/ *n infml* a close-fitting garment for the whole body usu. worn by women or children, esp. when playing games —compare LEOTARD, WET SUIT
cat·sup /'kætsəp/ *n* [U] KETCHUP
cat·tle /'kætl/ *n* [P] large 4-legged farm animals, esp. cows, kept as property or bred for use: *He has 20* **(head of) cattle** *on his farm.*|(fig.) *Those poor soldiers died like cattle, without a struggle*
cattle cake /'·· ·/ *n* [U] food made from various substances and fed to cattle
cattle grid /'·· ·/ *n* a set of poles put over a hole in the road, which cars can go across but cattle cannot
cat·ty /'kæti/ also **cat·tish** /'kætɪʃ/— *adj* [Wa2] *derog infml* (esp. of a woman or her behaviour) marked by hatred or anger that is not openly or directly expressed; SPITEful —**cattiness** *n* [U] —**cattily** *adv*
cat·walk /'kætwɔːk/ *n* **1** a narrow raised way or passage, esp. as along a bridge or round a large machine **2** a long narrow stage sticking out into a room, on which fashion shows are held
cau·cus¹ /'kɔːkəs/ *n* [GC] **1** a meeting of representatives elected by the members of a political party, usu. to decide POLICY (=the party's ideas on how to govern) or choose CANDIDATEs (=the people who are to represent the party at an election) **2** a group of people in a political party strong enough to control or have an effect on the party's POLICY (=the party's ideas on how to govern)
caucus² *v* [IØ] *AmE* to hold or meet in a CAUCUS
cau·dal /'kɔːdl/ *adj tech* of, near, or concerning the tail or tail-end of the body —**~ly** *adv*
caught /kɔːt/ *past t. & p. of* CATCH
caul /kɔːl/ *n* a skin which covers a baby before birth, part of which is often seen covering the baby's head when it is being born
caul·dron, cal- /'kɔːldrən/ *n old use or lit* a large open metal pot for boiling liquids over an open fire, used esp. in former times: (fig.) *His heart was a cauldron of powerful feelings*
cau·li·flow·er /'kɒlɪˌflaʊəʳ‖'kɔ-, 'kɑ-/ *n* **1** [C] a type of garden vegetable with green leaves around a large white head of undeveloped flowers —compare CABBAGE and see picture at VEGETABLE¹ **2** [U] the white part of this vegetable cooked and eaten as food
caulk, calk /kɔːk/ *v* [T1] **1** to stop (usu. a ship) from letting in water by pressing oily or sticky WATERPROOF material into cracks in the wood **2** to block up (cracks in wood) with oily or sticky WATERPROOF material
caus·al /'kɔːzəl/ *adj* [Wa5] **1** of or showing the relationship of cause and effect **2** being a cause: *the causal force that produced all these effects* **3** *rare* arising from a cause **4** (in grammar) expressing a cause: *Causal phrases usually begin with the word "because", as in "because of her illness"* —**~ly** *adv*
cau·sal·i·ty /kɔː'zælɪ̣ti/ *n* [U] the relationship between a cause and its effect; principle that events have causes: *The* **law of causality** *says that all effects have a cause*
cau·sa·tion /kɔː'zeɪʃən/ *n* [U] **1** the action of causing or producing **2** the relationship of cause and effect; CAUSALITY
caus·a·tive¹ /'kɔːzətɪv/ *adj* **1** acting as a cause; producing an effect **2** (in grammar) showing that the subject of a verb is the cause of an action or state: *The causative verb "to* FELL*" means "to cause to fall"* —**~ly** *adv*
causative² *n* (in grammar) a CAUSATIVE¹ (2) word or form: *The verb "to* FELL² (1,2)*" may be called a causative*
cause¹ /kɔːz/ *n* **1** [C (*for*);C3] something which produces an effect; a person, thing, or event that makes something happen **2** [U] reason: *Don't complain without (good) cause* —compare REASON¹ (5) **3** [C] a principle or movement strongly defended or supported **4** [C] *law* the reason for action in a court of law; a matter over which a person goes to law **5 make common cause (with)** to take action together for a particular purpose **6 show cause** *law* to give a good reason
cause² *v* [D1 (*to*, (*for*)); T1;V3] to lead to; be the cause of: *What caused his illness?*| *I think you like causing trouble to/for people*
cause cé·lè·bre /ˌkəʊz se'lebrə, ˌkɔːz- (*Fr* koz selɛbr)/ *n* **causes célèbres** (*same pronunciation*) *Fr* **1** an action in a court of law that receives a great deal of public attention and interest **2** something unfavourable which is likely to attract great public attention
cause·less /'kɔːzləs/ *adj* having no known cause —**~ly** *adv*
cause·way /'kɔːzweɪ/ *n* a raised road or path esp. across wet ground or water
caus·tic¹ /'kɔːstɪk/ *n* [C;U] (any of various types of) chemical substance able to burn or destroy (CORRODE) by chemical action
caustic² *adj* **1** able to burn or destroy by chemical action; CORROSIVE **2** bitter; unpleasant; sour; nasty: *John's always making caustic remarks about other people* —**~ally** *adv* [Wa4]
cau·ter·ize, -ise /'kɔːtəraɪz/ *v* [T1] *med* to burn (a wound, snake bite, etc.) with a very hot iron or CAUSTIC² (1) substance to destroy infection
cau·tion¹ /'kɔːʃən/ *n* **1** [C] a spoken warning usu. given by a policeman, judge, etc., when a person has broken the law or done something wrong but when the crime is not serious **2** [U] great care; the act of paying attention or of taking care **3** [S] *old sl* a person or thing whose behaviour or appearance causes amusement
caution² *v* **1** [T1 (*about, against*); V3;D5] to warn against possible danger: (*law*) *The policeman said, "I must caution you that anything you say may be used against you (at your trial)"* **2** [(*for, about*)] to warn about something bad already done, often with the threat of future punishment for doing it again
cau·tion·ar·y /'kɔːʃənəri‖-neri/ *adj* [Wa5] *fml or humor* giving advice or a warning: *cautionary* TALES (=stories) *intended to warn us*
cau·tious /'kɔːʃəs/ *adj* careful; paying attention; having or showing CAUTION¹ (2): *She is cautious of telling secrets* —**~ly** *adv*: *She opened the door cautiously so as not to wake the baby* —**~ness** *n* [U]
cav·al·cade /ˌkævəl'keɪd, 'kævəlkeɪd/ *n* a ceremonial procession of riders, carriages, vehicles, etc.
cav·a·lier¹ /ˌkævə'lɪəʳ/ *n* **1** *old use* a gentleman trained in arms and horsemanship; KNIGHT **2** (in mid 17th century England) a royalist; supporter of Charles I in the war against Parliament —compare ROUNDHEAD
cavalier² *adj* **1** proud; selfish; thoughtless **2** informal and easy in manners, esp. towards ladies; DEBONAIR
cav·al·ry /'kævəlri/ *n* [(*the*) GU] **1** (esp. in former times) soldiers who fight on horseback **2** *esp. AmE*

lighter and faster armoured vehicles used for protecting larger slower forces

cav·al·ry·man /ˈkævəlrimən/ *n* **-men** /mən/ (esp. in former times) a soldier who fights on horseback

cave /keɪv/ *n* a deep natural hollow place **a** underground, usu. with an opening to the surface **b** in the side of a cliff or hill

ca·ve·at /ˈkeɪviæt, ˈkæv-/ *n* **1** *law & fml* a notice that no action must be taken in a law court concerning a question until the opposition has been heard **2** *fml* a warning against certain acts or practices

caveat emp·tor /ˌkeɪviæt ˈemptɔːʳ, ˌkæv-/ *Lat* (a warning principle in buying and selling) let the buyer take the risk of buying something of bad quality

cave-in /ˈ· ·/ *n* **1** an act of caving in (CAVE IN) **2** a place where earth has caved in (CAVE IN (1))

cave in *v adv* **1** [IØ;T1] **a** (of a roof or the covering over a hollow place) to fall in or down: *The roof of the old house caved in during the severe storm* **b** to cause (a roof or the covering over a hollow place) to fall in or down: *They caved in the roof of the underground passage with powerful explosives* **2** [IØ] *infml* (of business, firm, etc.) to fail **3** [IØ] *infml* to yield

cave·man /ˈkeɪvmæn/ *n* **-men** /men/· **1** a person or early manlike creature who lived in a cave in very ancient (PREHISTORIC) times —compare NEANDERTHAL MAN **2** [C; *you*+N] *infml* a man who acts in a rough strong violent rude manner

cav·ern /ˈkævən‖-ərn/ *n* a large deep cave

cav·ern·ous /ˈkævənəs‖-ərnəs/ *adj* **1** containing many caves or CAVERNs **2** very large and deep; being or suggesting a CAVERN **3** (of a sound) hollow-sounding —**~ly** *adv*

cav·i·ar, -are /ˈkæviɑːʳ/ *n* [U] **1** the salted eggs (ROE) of various large fish, esp. the STURGEON, eaten as food, often at the very beginning of a meal. It is highly regarded and very costly **2 caviar to the general** *lit or humor* something liked and understood only by a well-bred person of sensitivity and good education

cav·il /ˈkævəl/ *v* **-ll-** (*AmE* **-l-**) [IØ (*at*)] to find fault unnecessarily —**~er** *n*

cav·i·ty /ˈkævɨti/ *n* a hole or hollow space in a solid mass

cavity wall /ˈ··· ·/ *n* a wall, made up of 2 walls with a small space between them, used in buildings to keep out noise, cold, etc.

ca·vort /kəˈvɔːt‖-ɔrt/ *v* [IØ] *infml* (esp. of a person) to jump or dance about noisily —compare CAPER²

ca·vy /ˈkeɪvi/ *n* GUINEA PIG (1)

caw /kɔː/ *v, n* [IØ (OUT); C] (to make) the loud rough natural cry of various large birds (such as CROWs)

cay /keɪ, kiː/ *n* KEY³

cay·enne pep·per /ˌkeɪen ˈpepəʳ/ also **cayenne** /ˌkeɪˈen◂/— *n* **1** [C] a type of PEPPER¹ (2) with long thin very hot-tasting red fruit **2** [U] a very hot-tasting red powder made from the crushed seeds of this, used for giving a special taste to food

cay·man /ˈkeɪmən/ *n* [Wn1] CAIMAN

cc *abbrev. for:* **1** CUBIC CENTIMETRE: *a 200 cc engine* **2** CUBIC CAPACITY

cease¹ /siːs/ *v* [IØ;T(1),3,4] *fml* **1** to stop (esp. an activity): *Cease fire!* (=Stop shooting!).|*At last they have ceased work(ing)* **2 cease and desist** *law* to stop

cease² *n fml* **without cease** continuously; without ceasing

cease-fire /ˈ· ·/ *n* an act of stopping fighting for a long or short period

cease·less /ˈsiːsləs/ *adj* [Wa5] *fml* unending; continuous; without ceasing: *Ceaseless enemy activity has forced us to leave that area* —**~ly** *adv*: *She cried ceaselessly*

ce·dar /ˈsiːdəʳ/ *n* **1** [C] a type of tall EVERGREEN tree (a tree that keeps its leaves in winter) with hard reddish sweet-smelling wood —see picture at PLANT² **2** [U] also **ce·dar·wood** /ˈsiːdəwʊd‖-ər-/— the wood of this tree used for making pencils, ornamental boxes, furniture, etc.

cede /siːd/ *v* [D1 (*to*); T1] to yield (usu. land or a right) to (another country or person), esp. after losing a war: *In 1871 France ceded Germany Alsace–Lorraine, in 1918 Germany ceded it back to France*

ce·dil·la /sɪˈdɪlə/ *n* (when writing certain languages) a mark put under a letter (as ç in French) to show that it has a special sound

cei·ling /ˈsiːlɪŋ/ *n* **1** the inner surface of the top of a room —compare ROOF¹ (1) **2** *tech* the greatest height at which a plane can safely fly **3** *tech* the height above ground of the bottom of the lowest clouds **4** a usu. official upper limit on wages, rents, etc.

cel·an·dine /ˈseləndaɪn/ *n* [Wn2] a type of small plant with yellow or white star-shaped flowers

cel·e·brant /ˈselɨbrənt/ *n tech* the priest who performs the actions at the holiest part of the MASS (=a church service of the Christian religion)

cel·e·brate /ˈselɨbreɪt/ *v* **1** [IØ] to enjoy oneself, usu. on a special occasion **2** [T1] to mark (an event or special occasion) with public or private rejoicings **3** [T1] to praise (someone or something) in writing, speech, etc. **4** [T1;IØ] *tech* (of a priest) to perform (esp. the holiest part of the Christian religious service called the MASS) solemnly and officially

cel·e·brat·ed /ˈselɨbreɪtɨd/ *adj* [(*for*)] well-known; famous: *Venice is celebrated for its beautiful buildings*

cel·e·bra·tion /ˌselɨˈbreɪʃən/ *n* **1** [U] the act of celebrating (CELEBRATE) **2** [C] an occasion of celebrating (CELEBRATE (1,2))

ce·leb·ri·ty /sɨˈlebrɨti/ *n* **1** [C] a famous person **2** [U] the state of being famous; fame

ce·ler·i·ty /sɨˈlerɨti/ *n* [U] *fml* speed; quickness

cel·e·ry /ˈseləri/ *n* [U] **1** a type of small plant with bunched greenish-white stems grown as a vegetable: *He dug up a* **head of celery** *and gave it to the cook* —see picture at VEGETABLE¹ **2** the stems of this plant eaten cooked or uncooked as food: *The cook put a* **stick of celery** *on everyone's plate*

ce·les·ti·al /sɨˈlestɪəl‖-tʃəl/ *adj fml* **1** [Wa5] of or belonging to the sky or heaven: *The sun, the stars, and the moon are celestial bodies* **2** heavenly; having the qualities of a god

cel·i·ba·cy /ˈselɨbəsi/ *n* [U] the state of being unmarried, esp. as the result of a religious promise —compare CHASTITY

cel·i·bate /ˈselɨbɨt/ *adj, n* [Wa5] (a person, esp. a priest, who is) unmarried, esp. as the result of a religious promise

cell /sel/ *n* **1** a small room **a** in a prison for one person or a small number of people **b** in a MONASTERY or CONVENT for one person **2** one of the groups of people in a secret, esp. political organization **3** one small part of a larger whole, as one of the divisions of a HONEYCOMB (2) **4** an apparatus for making a current of electricity by chemical action **5** a very small division of living matter, with one centre of activity (NUCLEUS), able alone or with others to perform all the operations necessary for life, and being the smallest division of living matter able to act independently

cel·lar /ˈseləʳ/ *n* **1** [C] an underground room, usu.

used for storing goods; BASEMENT **2** [*the*+R] *infml* (esp. in sport) the lowest rank in a list based on success **3** [C] a person's store of wine

cel·lar·age /ˈselərɪdʒ/ *n* [U;S] **1** the amount of CELLAR (1) space, esp. used for storing goods **2** the charge made for storing something in a CELLAR (1)

cel·list /ˈtʃeləst/ also (*fml*) **violoncellist**— *n* a person who plays the CELLO

cel·lo /ˈtʃeləʊ/ also (*fml*) **violoncello**— *n* **-los** **1** [C] a type of 4-stringed musical instrument, like the VIOLIN and VIOLA¹ (1) but larger and producing a deeper sound, that is held between the knees and played with a BOW³ (2) —see picture at STRINGED INSTRUMENT **2** [C *usu. pl.*] *infml* a person who plays this instrument in a band

cel·lo·phane /ˈseləfeɪn/ *n* [U] *tdmk* thin transparent material used for wrapping goods

cel·lu·lar /ˈseljʊləʳ‖-jə-/ *adj* **1** of, containing, or consisting of CELLs (3) **2** *tech* (of materials) loosely woven: *A cellular material is usually warmer than a solid one* **3** having many holes; able to hold much liquid; POROUS: *This cellular rock holds much water*

cel·lu·loid /ˈseljʊlɔɪd‖-jə-/ *n* [U] *tdmk* **1** a strong easily burnt plastic substance made mainly from CELLULOSE and formerly used for making photographic film **2** **on celluloid** on cinema film

cel·lu·lose /ˈseljʊləʊs, -əʊz‖-jə-/ *n* [U] **1** the material from which the cell walls of plants are made, used in making paper, plastic, many man-made materials, etc. **2** also (*tech*) **cellulose ac·e·tate** /ˌ··· ˈ···/— a type of plastic material used for many industrial purposes, esp. making photographic films or explosives

Cel·si·us /ˈselsɪəs/ *n, adj* [R;A;E] CENTIGRADE: *10° Celsius*

cel·tic /ˈkeltɪk, ˈseltɪk/ *adj* [Wa5] of (the languages of) the Celts, an often small dark-haired European people who include the Welsh and the Bretons

ce·ment¹ /sɪˈment/ *n* [U] **1** a grey powder, made from a burned mixture of lime and clay, which becomes hard like stone after having been mixed with water and allowed to dry **2** any of various types of thick sticky hard-drying chemical liquids (ADHESIVEs) used for filling holes, as in the teeth, or for joining things together

cement² *v* [T1] **1** [(TOGETHER)] to join together or make firm with or as if with CEMENT¹ (1,2) **2** [(OVER)] to cover (something) with CEMENT (1): *We've decided to cement our garden as we don't like flowers*

cement mix·er /·ˈ· ˌ··/ *n* a drumlike machine which turns round and round, in which CEMENT¹ (1), sand, and water are mixed to make CONCRETE² (1) —see picture at SITE¹

cem·e·tery /ˈsemətri‖-teri/ *n* an area of ground, usu. not belonging to a church, set aside for the burial of dead people —compare CHURCHYARD

cen·o·taph /ˈsenətɑːf‖-tæf/ *n* an object (MONUMENT (1)) built as a lasting reminder of a dead person or people, esp. those killed in war

cen·sor¹ /ˈsensəʳ/ *n* **1** an official who examines printed matter, films, or (sometimes in war) private letters with the power to remove anything offensive or (in war) helpful to the enemy **2** (in ancient Rome) either of 2 officials whose duties included taking the CENSUS (=a list of all the people and the taxes they pay) and watching and directing public morals **3** *tech* (in PSYCHOLOGY (1,2)) something which prevents unacceptable memories, ideas, and wishes from coming into consciousness by REPRESSION (2)

censor² *v* [T1] to examine (books, films, letters, etc.) with the intention of removing anything offensive

cen·so·ri·ous /senˈsɔːrɪəs‖-ˈsor-/ *adj* having the habit of fault-finding; eager to judge unfavourably; severely CRITICAL: *censorious people/behaviour* —**~ly** *adv* —**~ness** *n* [U]

cen·sor·ship /ˈsensəʃɪp‖-ər-/ *n* [U] the acts, practice, or duties of a CENSOR¹ (1)

cen·sure¹ /ˈsenʃəʳ/ *n fml* **1** [U] the act of blaming, severely and unfavourably judging, or expressing strong disapproval: *The opposition failed to pass a vote of censure on the government* **2** [C] *rare* a usu. official expression of disapproval; unfavourable judgment: *He received a public censure for his dishonourable behaviour*

censure² *v* [T1] *fml* to express strong disapproval of (someone or their behaviour or actions); judge severely and unfavourably

cen·sus /ˈsensəs/ *n* **censuses** **1** an official count of a country's total population **2** an official count of anything of importance for governmental planning

cent¹ /sent/ *n* 0·01 of any of certain money standards, such as the dollar

cent² *abbrev. for:* **1** CENTIGRADE **2** CENTURY

cent- also **centi-**— *prefix* **1** 100 or 100th: CENTIMETRE|CENTENNIAL|CENTIPEDE **2** 100th part: *centisecond* —see WEIGHTS & MEASURES TABLE

cen·taur /ˈsentɔːʳ/ *n* (in Greek and Roman MYTHOLOGY (1)) one of a race of animals said to be half man and half horse

cen·ta·vo /senˈtɑːvəʊ/ *n* **-vos** a coin of small value used in various Spanish- and Portuguese-speaking countries

cen·te·nar·i·an /ˌsentəˈneərɪən/ *n* (a person who is) at least 100 years old

cen·te·na·ry /senˈtiːnəri‖-ˈte-, ˈsentəneri/ also (*esp. AmE*) **centennial**— *n* the day or year exactly 100 years after a particular event

cen·ten·ni·al /senˈtenɪəl/ *adj* [Wa5;A] 100th (esp. in the phr. **centennial anniversary**)

cen·ter /ˈsentəʳ/ *n, v AmE* CENTRE

center bit /ˈ·· ·/ *n AmE* CENTRE BIT

cen·ter·board /ˈsentəbɔːd‖-tərbord/ *n AmE* CENTREBOARD

center for·ward /ˌ·· ˈ··/ *n AmE* CENTRE FORWARD

center of grav·i·ty /ˌ·· · ˈ···/ *n AmE* CENTRE OF GRAVITY

cen·ter·piece /ˈsentəpiːs‖-ər-/ *n AmE* CENTREPIECE

cen·ti- /ˈsentə/ *prefix* CENT-

cen·ti·grade¹ /ˈsentəgreɪd/ also **Celsius**— *adj* [Wa5;B;E] (*often cap.*) of, in, or related to the CENTIGRADE scale of temperature: *0° Centigrade equals 32°* FAHRENHEIT

centigrade² also **Celsius**— *n* (*often cap.*) a scale of temperature in which water freezes at 0° and boils at 100° —see WEIGHTS & MEASURES TABLE —compare FAHRENHEIT and see picture at SCIENTIFIC

cen·ti·gram, -gramme /ˈsentəgræm/ *n* a weight equal to a 100th part of a gram —see WEIGHTS & MEASURES TABLE

cen·time /ˈsɒntiːm‖ˈsɑn- (*Fr* sɑ̃tim)/ *n Fr* **1** 0·01 of any of certain money standards, such as the FRANC **2** a coin of this value

cen·ti·me·tre, *AmE* **-ter** /ˈsentəˌmiːtəʳ/ *n* a measure of length equal to 0·01 metres or 0·4 inches —see WEIGHTS & MEASURES TABLE

cen·ti·pede /ˈsentəpiːd/ *n* a type of small insect-like creature with a long thin many-jointed body, each joint having a pair of legs

cen·tral¹ /ˈsentrəl/ *adj* **1** [Wa5;A] being the centre: *This is the central city of the whole area* **2** [B] being at, in, or near the centre: *The central shops are conveniently reached from all parts of the city* **3** [Wa5;A] chief; main; of greatest importance: *The central aim of this government is social equality* **4** [F] convenient; easily reached: *Our house is very* *central for the shops and theatres* **5** [Wa5;A] *med* of or related to the CENTRAL NERVOUS SYSTEM —**~ly** *adv*

central² *n* [C;N] *AmE now rare* (the people working at) a telephone EXCHANGE¹ (2)

central gov·ern·ment /ˌ·· ˈ···/ *n* the government of the country as a whole

central heat·ing /ˌ·· ˈ··/ *n* [U] a system of heating buildings in which heat is produced and controlled at a single point and carried by pipes or DUCTs to the various parts of the building in the form of hot air or water

cen·tral·is·m /ˈsentrəlɪzəm/ *n* [U] the practice of gathering power into the central body of an organization (as in a political or educational system)

cen·tral·ize, -ise /ˈsentrəlaɪz/ *v* [Wv4,5;IØ;T1: (*in*)] **a** (esp. of the controlling power of government) to gather under central control: *Under the old political system wealth and power centralized in the hands of a few noble families* **b** to cause (esp. the controlling power of government) to gather under central control: *The king is trying to centralize all power in his own hands* —**-ization** /ˌsentrəlaɪˈzeɪʃən‖-lə-/ *n* [U]

central nerv·ous sys·tem /ˌ·· ˈ·· ˌ··/ *n* the part of the NERVOUS SYSTEM which consists of the brain and the SPINAL CORD

cen·tre¹, *AmE* **-ter** /ˈsentəʳ/ *n* **1** [C] a middle part or point; point equally distant from all sides; the exact middle esp. the point around which a circle is drawn: *Although London is Britain's capital it is not at the centre of the country* —see picture at GEOMETRY **2** [C9] a point, area, person, or thing that is the most important in relation to an interest, activity, or condition: *a shopping centre*| *She likes to be the centre of attention all the time* **3** [C9] an area filled with many people (esp. in the phr. **urban centre**) **4** [*the*+R] (*often cap.*) having a middle (MODERATE) position esp. in politics: *The centre parties are opposed to forming a new government and want an election* **5** [C; *the*+R] (in sport) a player in a team who plays in or near the middle of the playing field —compare BACK¹ (8), FORWARD³ (1); see MIDDLE (USAGE)

centre², *AmE* **-ter** *v* **1** [L9;X9: esp. *on, upon, round, around*] to (cause to) gather to a centre; (cause to) have a centre: *Our thoughts centred on the young girl about to be married* **2** [L9;X9: esp. *on, upon, round, around*] to (cause to) have as a main subject: *Attention centred on the priest* **3** [T1] to place in or at the centre: *Centre this picture on the wall please* **4** [T1] (in sports) to pass (a ball) to the centre of a field: *If he'd centred that ball we might have won the match*

centre bit /ˈ·· ·/ *n* a tool for making holes in wood

cen·tre·board, *AmE* **-ter-** /ˈsentəbɔːd‖-ərbord/ *n* a board (KEEL) which can be raised or lowered through the bottom of a sailing boat, used for keeping the boat steady when in the water

centre for·ward /ˌ·· ˈ··/ *BrE infml* also **striker**— *n* (in football) the player from each team who plays in the centre of the field

centre of grav·i·ty /ˌ·· · ˈ···/ *n* that point in any object on which it will balance

cen·tre·piece, *AmE* **-ter-** /ˈsentəpiːs‖-ər-/ *n* **1** an ornament, esp. an ornamental arrangement of flowers, placed in the middle of a table **2** the showiest or most important thing in a group

cen·tri·fu·gal /ˌsentrɪˈfjuːgəl◂, senˈtrɪfjʊgəl‖senˈtrɪfjəgəl/ *adj* [Wa5] tending to move in a direction away from the centre —opposite **centripetal**

centrifugal force /ˌ···· ˈ·, ·ˌ··· ˈ·‖·ˌ··· ˈ·/ *n* [U;(C)] the force which pushes away from the centre of a mass when it is spun very quickly —opposite **centripetal force**

cen·tri·fuge /ˈsentrɨfjuːdʒ/ *n* an apparatus for spinning a container round very quickly so that CENTRIFUGAL FORCE forces the heavier liquids and any solids to the outer edge or bottom of the container

cen·trip·e·tal /senˈtrɪpɨtl/ *adj* [Wa5] tending to move in a direction towards the centre —opposite **centrifugal**

centripetal force /·ˌ··· ˈ·/ *n* [U;(C)] the force which pulls an object towards a central point —opposite **centrifugal force**

cen·trist /ˈsentrɨst/ *n, adj* (of) a person who opposes the opinions of far right and far left political parties; MODERATE

cen·tu·ri·on /ˌsenˈtʃʊəriən‖-ˈtʊ-/ *n* (in the army of ancient Rome) an officer commanding a company of about 100 men

cen·tu·ry /ˈsentʃəri/ *n* **1** a period of 100 years **2** (*sometimes cap.*) one of the 100-year periods counted forwards or backwards from the supposed year of CHRIST'*s*¹ (1) birth **3** (in cricket) 100 runs made by one player in one INNINGS (1) **4** (in the army of ancient Rome) a company of about 100 men

ce·phal·ic /sɨˈfælɪk/ *adj* [Wa5;A] *tech* of or connected with the head: *The* **cephalic index** *shows the size and shape of the human head*

ce·ram·ic /sɨˈræmɪk/ *adj* [A;(B)] of or connected with CERAMICS

ce·ram·ics /sɨˈræmɪks/ *n* **1** [U] the art or practice of making bricks, pots, etc., by shaping bits of clay and baking until hard **2** [P] articles produced in this way

ce·re·al /ˈsɪəriəl/ *n* **1** [C] any kind of grain **2** [C] a plant which is grown to produce grain for food, such as wheat, rice, etc. **3** [U;C] (any of various types of) food made from grain, esp. eaten at breakfast

See next page for picture

cer·e·bel·lum /ˌserɨˈbeləm/ *n* **-lums** *or* **-la** /lə/ *med* a small part of the back of the brain, concerned with the movement of muscles

cer·e·bral /ˈserɨbrəl‖səˈriː-, ˈserɨ-/ *adj* **1** *med* (often of illnesses) of or connected with the brain **2** *esp. fml or humor* tending to or showing (too much) serious thinking: *a rather cerebral person whom many people considered cold and unfeeling* —**~ly** *adv*

cer·e·bra·tion /ˌserɨˈbreɪʃən/ *n* **1** [U] *tech* the working of the brain **2** [U;(C)] *fml or humor* the act of thinking very seriously

ce·re·brum /səˈriːbrəm/ *n* **-brums** *or* **-bra** /brə/ *med* the front part of the brain, concerned with thought and decision

cer·e·mo·ni·al¹ /ˌserɨˈməʊniəl/ also **ceremonious**— *adj* marked by or done according to ceremony —**~ly** *adv*

ceremonial² *n* **1** [U] the special order and formal rules of ceremony, esp. as in social or religious life: *According to church ceremonial the priest kisses the Bible before reading from it* **2** [C] a ceremony: *Tonight there will be a tribal ceremonial of great importance to mark the chief's birthday*

cer·e·mo·ni·ous /ˌserɨˈməʊniəs/ *adj* **1** fond of ceremony and formal behaviour; formally polite **2** CEREMONIAL¹ —**~ly** *adv* —**~ness** *n* [U]

cer·e·mo·ny /ˈserɨməni‖-məʊni/ *n* **1** [C] a special formal, solemn, and well-established action or set of actions used for marking an important private or public, social or religious event: *The wedding ceremony was beautiful* **2** [U] the special order and formal behaviour demanded by social customs on particular occasions: *The queen was crowned with proper ceremony* **3 Master of Ceremonies a** the person who directs activity on a formal occasion

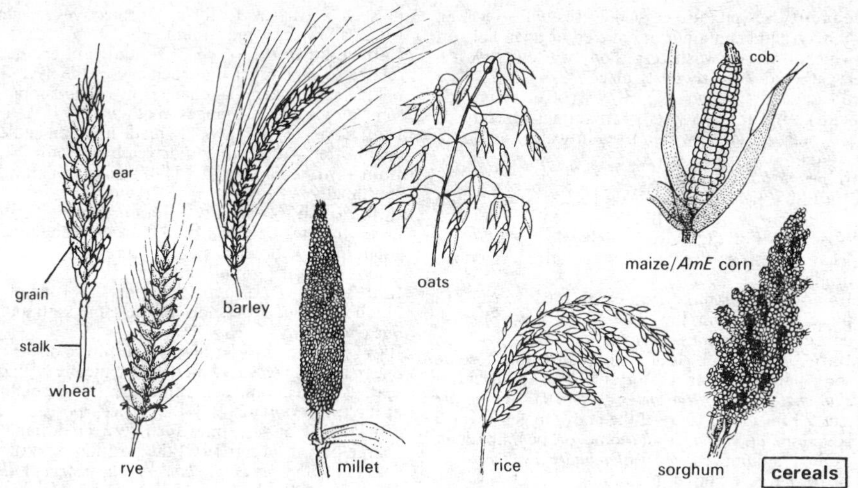

b *esp. AmE* the person who presents a show on radio or television **4 stand on/upon ceremony** to follow the formal rules of behaviour

ce·rise /sə'ri:z/ *adj, n* [B;U] (having) a clear red colour

cert¹ /sɜ:t‖sɜrt/ *n esp. BrE sl* a certainty; something considered certain to happen or succeed: *It's a (dead) cert that this horse will win the race*

cert² *n abbrev. for:* CERTIFICATE

cer·tain¹ /'sɜ:tn‖'sɜrtn/ *adj* **1** [B] sure; established beyond all doubt or question; known: *There's no certain cure for this illness* **2** [F] sure; having no doubt: *I'm certain she saw me yesterday* **3** [B;F3,5] sure to happen: *It's almost certain that the government will lose the next election* **4** [F3,5a] (of people) sure: *Be certain you catch your train on time.|She's certain to do well in the examination.|Are you certain that you'll get there in time?* **5** [F] *rare* clever; practised; unfailing: *His ear for music was certain* **6 make certain a** to enquire and make sure: *Make certain (that) you know what time the train goes* **b** to do something in order to be sure (of getting something): *We went to the theatre early and made certain we all got seats/made certain of getting seats* —see SURE (USAGE)

certain² *determiner* **1** not named or described but taken as known: *There are certain laws about drinking and driving, you know!* **2** not named or described but existing: *The government has a plan which for certain reasons it's against the national interest to make public* **3** named, but not well known: *A certain Mrs Jones rang me up today but she'd got the wrong number* **4** a limited (quantity or number of); small (amount of); some but not a lot of: *He makes a certain profit from his business but he'll never be rich*

certain³ *pron* [+*of*] certain ones; some but not all (of): *"... certain of the questions raised in Feb. 1975 ..."* (SEU W.)

cer·tain·ly /'sɜ:tnli‖'sɜr-/ *adv* **1** without doubt; surely **2** (as a polite or strong way of answering a question) yes; of course: *"Will you help me?" "Certainly I will"* **3 certainly not** (as a strong way of answering a question) no; of course not: *"Will you lend me your comb?" "Certainly not!"* —see SURE (USAGE)

cer·tain·ty /'sɜ:tnti‖'sɜr-/ *n* **1** [U] the state of being certain; freedom from doubt: *I can't say with certainty what my plans are* **2** [C] a clearly established fact: *It's a certainty that this horse will win the race*

cer·ti·fi·ab·le /'sɜ:tɪ̆faɪəbəl‖'sɜr-/ *adj* **1** [B] that can be certified (CERTIFY) **2** [F] *BrE infml* mad: *If you ask me, she's certifiable: she's completely mad*

cer·tif·i·cate /sə'tɪfɪkət‖sər-/ *n* an official sheet of paper (DOCUMENT) on which is written or printed a statement, usu. made by a person officially given power to make it, that a certain fact or facts are true: *a birth/marriage/death certificate*

cer·tif·i·cat·ed /sə'tɪfɪkeɪtɪ̆d‖sər-/ *adj* [Wa5] *esp. BrE* having successfully completed a course of training for a particular profession: *a certificated nurse*

certified mail /ˌ··· '·/ *n* [U] *AmE* mail sent by RECORDED DELIVERY

certified milk /ˌ··· '·/ *n* [U] *AmE* milk produced under official medical control

certified pub·lic ac·coun·tant /ˌ··· ˌ·· ·'··/ *n AmE* CHARTERED ACCOUNTANT

cer·ti·fy /'sɜ:tɪ̆faɪ‖'sɜr-/ *v* **1** [T1] to declare that (something) is correct or true: *The bank certified my accounts* **2** [X7;T5] to declare, esp. after some kind of test: *The doctor certified me mad.|The minister certified that his trip abroad was necessary* **3** [Wv5;T1] to give a CERTIFICATE to (someone) declaring successful completion of a course of training for a particular profession: *a certified teacher* **4** [T1] *BrE infml* to officially declare (someone) mad (INSANE): *You should be certified; you're mad*

cer·ti·tude /'sɜ:tɪ̆tju:d‖'sɜrtɪ̆tu:d/ *n* [U,U5] the state of being or feeling certain; freedom from doubt

ce·ru·le·an /sɪ̆'ru:lɪən/ *adj* deep blue, like a clear sky

cer·vi·cal /'sɜ:vɪkəl‖'sɜr-/ *adj* [Wa5] *med* of or related to a neck or CERVIX

cer·vix /'sɜ:vɪks‖'sɜr-/ *n* **-vices** /vɪsi:z/ or **-vixes** *med* a narrow necklike opening into an organ, esp. into the WOMB

ce·sar·e·an sec·tion, -ian- /sɪ̆ˌzeərɪən 'sekʃən/ *n* CAESAREAN SECTION

ces·sa·tion /se'seɪʃən/ *n* a short pause or a stop: *We arranged a week-long cessation of fighting with the enemy.|a momentary cessation of breathing*

ces·sion /'seʃən/ *n* [C;U] *law* (an example of) the act of ceding (CEDE = to yield) property or rights, usu. by agreement

cess·pit /ˈses,pɪt/ also **cess·pool** /ˈses-puːl/— *n* **1** an underground container or covered or open hole, in which a house's waste, esp. body waste (SEWAGE), is gathered **2** a dirty nasty place

ce·tac·ean /sɪˈteɪʃən/ *adj, n tech* (of or connected with) a fishlike MAMMAL (=an animal which feeds its young on milk) which lives in water, such as a WHALE

cf. *abbrev. for:* (*Lat*) compare

Chab·lis /ˈʃæbli (*Fr* ʃabli)/ *n* [U] a type of non-sweet white wine from Burgundy, France

cha-cha /ˈtʃɑː tʃɑː/ also **cha-cha-cha** /ˌ· · ˈ·/— *n* **-chas** a fast spirited dance of Latin American origin

cha·conne /ʃæˈkɒn‖-ˈkɔn, -ˈkɑn/ *n* (*often cap.*) (a piece of music in the style of) a slow Spanish dance: *Bach's famous chaconne for* VIOLIN

chafe[1] /tʃeɪf/ *v* **1** [IØ;T1] to (cause to) become sore, painful, or uncomfortable by rubbing: *Her skin chafes easily.|Her shoes chafed the skin on her feet* **2** [T1] to rub (part of the body) to get warm **3** [L9, esp. *at, under*] to become or be impatient, excited, or annoyed: *He chafed under his illness*

chafe[2] *n* a sore caused by rubbing

chaff[1] /tʃɑːf‖tʃæf/ *n* [U] **1** the outer seed covers (HUSK*s*), separated from the grain when it is being THRESHed (=prepared for use as food) **2** dried grasses and plant stems used as food for farm animals **3** *lit* something worthless **4 separate the wheat from the chaff** to separate the important parts from the worthless parts

chaff[2] *n* [U] *infml* good-humoured fun, talking, or joking; BANTER

chaff[3] *v* [T1 (*about*)] *infml* to make fun of (someone) in a good-humoured way

chaf·finch /ˈtʃæ,fɪntʃ/ *n* a type of small bird, with a cheerful song, common in Europe

chaf·ing dish /ˈtʃeɪfɪŋ dɪʃ/ *n* a container with a heater underneath, used for cooking or keeping food warm, esp. at the table

chag·rin[1] /ˈʃægrɪn‖ʃəˈgrɪn/ *n* [U] a feeling of sorrow, anger, annoyance, or disappointment, caused by unfulfilled hopes or failure

chagrin[2] *v* [T1] to cause (someone) to feel CHAGRIN[1]; annoy, anger, or disappoint (someone) greatly: *It chagrined me greatly to be told of her complaints*

chain[1] /tʃeɪn/ *n* **1** [C;U] (a length of) usu. metal rings, connected to or fitted into one another, used for fastening, supporting, ornamenting, etc.: *The bridge was supported by heavy iron chains hanging from 2 towers.|The head of the council wore her chain of office.|a lot of chain* —see picture at TOOL[1] **2** [C9] a number of connected things, such as events, shops, restaurants, mountains, etc. **3** [C] an old measurement of length usu. equal to 66 feet (20 m) —see WEIGHTS & MEASURES TABLE **4 in chains** kept in prison or as a slave; not free: *"Man is born free yet everywhere he is in chains"* (Rousseau)

chain[2] *v* [X9, esp. UP, TOGETHER, DOWN] to limit the freedom of (someone or something) with or as if with a chain: *It's time the dogs were chained up for the night.*|(fig.) *I'd feel chained down with a wife, a house, and children*

chain bridge /ˈ· ·/ *n* a type of bridge supported from towers by large heavy strong chains

chain gang /ˈ· ·/ *n* a group of prisoners chained together for work outside their prison

chain let·ter /ˈ· ˌ··/ *n* a letter sent to several people who are asked to send copies to several more people

chain mail /ˈ· ·/ also **chain ar·mour** /ˈ· ˌ··/— *n* [U] armour made by joining small metal rings together in such a way as to form a protective garment which allows easy movement

chain re·ac·tion /ˌ· ·ˈ··/ *n* **1** a number of events so related to each other that each causes the next **2** a related set of chemical changes in which action in some atoms causes changes in others

chain saw /ˈ· ·/ *n* a SAW[1] (1) made up of an endless chain fitted with teeth and driven by a motor

chain-smoke /ˈ· ·/ *v* [IØ;T1] to smoke (cigarettes) continually —**~r** *n*

chain stitch /ˈ· ·/ *n* [U;C] **1** an ornamental stitch in sewing, which gives the effect of a chain **2** a stitch in CROCHET in which the thread is pulled by a hook into the form of a chain

chain store /ˈ· ·/ also **multiple store**— *n* (one of) a number of usu. large shops of the same kind under one ownership

chair[1] /tʃeəʳ/ *n* **1** [C] a piece of furniture on which one person may sit, which has typically a back, seat, usu. 4 legs, and sometimes arms —see picture at LIVING ROOM **2** [C] the office, position, or official seat of someone, such as a chairman, in charge of a meeting **3** [C] the position of PROFESSOR (1): *She holds a chair of chemistry in that university* **4** [C] *tech* (on railways) a metal block fastened to the SLEEPER (=a large piece of wood which supports the rails) to hold the rail in place **5** [*the*+R] also **electric chair**— a chairlike machine used in the United States for killing certain criminals, esp. murderers, by giving them a powerful electric shock: *He got the chair for killing the old lady* **6** [C] SEDAN CHAIR —see also ARMCHAIR, WHEELCHAIR, BATH CHAIR

chair[2] *v* [T1] **1** to be chairman of (a meeting) **2** *BrE* to lift up and carry (someone), usu. as a sign of admiration: *When he won the race his supporters chaired him round the field*

chair lift /ˈ· ·/ *n* an apparatus which carries people, esp. SKIers, up and down steep slopes by means of chairs hung from and fixed to a moving wire above the chair

chair·man /ˈtʃeəmən‖ˈtʃeər-/ *n* **-men** /mən/ **1** [C; N;(A)] a person **a** in charge of a meeting: *She's one of our best and most experienced chairmen* **b** who directs the work of a committee, department, etc.: *He was elected (the) chairman of the education committee* **2** [C] (in former times) a man employed to help carry a SEDAN CHAIR

chair·man·ship /ˈtʃeəmənʃɪp‖ˈtʃeər-/ *n* **1** [C *usu. sing.*] the rank, position, or period in office of chairman **2** [U] the abilities or qualities of a chairman: *You must learn chairmanship if you want to control meetings effectively*

chair·per·son /ˈtʃeə,pɜːsən‖ˈtʃeər,pɜrsən/ *n* CHAIRMAN (1) or CHAIRWOMAN

chair·wom·an /ˈtʃeə,wʊmən‖ˈtʃeər-/ *n* **-women** /ˌwɪmɪn/ [C;(N)] a female chairman

chaise /ʃeɪz/ *n* [C; *by*+U] any of several types of small light usu. 2-wheeled carriages, used esp. in former times, in which 2 people could ride, drawn by one horse

chaise longue /ˌʃeɪz ˈlɒŋ‖-ˈlɔŋ/ *n* **chaises longues** *or* **chaise longues** (*same pronunciation*) *Fr* a COUCH, with an arm at only one end, on which one can sit and stretch out one's legs

chal·et /ˈʃæleɪ‖ʃæˈleɪ/ *n* **1** a usu. wooden house with a steeply sloping roof, esp. common in Switzerland **2** a small hut used by SHEPHERD*s* (people who guard sheep) in the Alps during the summer **3** a small house (BUNGALOW) or hut, esp. as in a holiday camp

chal·ice /ˈtʃælɪ̈s/ *n* a gold or silver ornamental cup, used esp. to hold wine in Christian religious services such as the MASS —see picture at CHURCH[1]

chalk[1] /tʃɔːk/ *n* **1** [U] a type of soft white rock

(LIMESTONE) formed in ancient times from the shells of very small sea animals, used for making lime and various writing materials **2** [C;U] (a piece of) this material, white or coloured, used for writing or drawing: *The teacher wrote with a stick/piece of chalk.|Do you need some more chalk?|coloured chalks* **3 as different as chalk and cheese** also **as like as chalk to cheese**— *infml* completely unlike each other

chalk[2] *v* [T1;IØ] to write, mark, or draw with chalk

chalk out *v adv* [T1] **1** to make a drawing or plan of (something) **2** to describe (something) in words in a general way: *The general chalked out his plan of attack*

chalk up *v adv* [T1] *infml* **1** to succeed in getting (esp. points in a game): *We've chalked up more points than any other team this year* **2** to charge to someone's or one's own account; record on someone's or one's own account: *Anything you do wrong will be chalked up against you*

chalk·y /ˈtʃɔːki/ *adj* [Wa1] of or like chalk: *I don't like this cake; it's got a chalky taste* —**-iness** *n* [U]

chal·lenge[1] /ˈtʃælǰndʒ/ *v* **1** [T1 (*to*); V3] to call (someone) to compete against one, esp. in a fight, match, etc.: *I challenged him to a game of tennis* **2** [T1] to demand official proof of the name and aims of (someone): *The soldier on guard challenged the stranger as soon as she appeared* **3** [T1] to question the lawfulness or rightness of (someone or something): *She challenged the justice of the new law* **4** [T1;V3] to call (a person or thing) to competitive action or effort; test the abilities of (a person or thing): *This difficulty challenges my mind to find an answer.|I only like to study something if it really challenges me* **5** [T1;V3] to ask or demand as of right: *The soldier challenged the stranger to say who she was.|*(*lit*) *This event challenges an explanation* **6** [T1] *law* to declare that one will not accept (a JUROR) before the beginning of a case: *We have decided to challenge Mr. Brown because we do not believe he will be fair to the person we are representing in court* —**~er** *n*

challenge[2] *n* **1** [C;C3] an invitation to compete in a fight, match, etc.: *He accepted his friend's challenge to swim across the river* **2** [C;C3] a demand usu. by a soldier, to stop and prove who and what one is: *The stranger was met with a challenge at the town gates* **3** [U] the quality of demanding competitive action, interest, or thought: *This job is too dull; I want one with more challenge* **4** [C] something with this quality: *To build a bridge in a day was a real challenge* **5** [C] an expression of doubt about the lawfulness of something: *The election of the new government was met by a challenge from its opponents* **6** [C] *law* a statement that one will not accept a JUROR (=one of the 12 people who decide if a person is guilty or not in a court of law), made before the beginning of a case

chal·leng·ing /ˈtʃælǰndʒɪŋ/ *adj* **1** causing competitive interest, action, or thought, esp. because new, unusual, or difficult: *His new book is full of challenging ideas* **2** causing great interest; fascinating (FASCINATE): *She's a challenging woman, isn't she!* —**~ly** *adv*

cham·ber /ˈtʃeɪmbəʳ/ *n* **1** [C] *old use* a room, esp. a bedroom **2** [C; *the*+R] a usu. elected law-making body: *In Britain the upper chamber is the* **House of Lords**, *the lower the* **House of Commons** **3** [*the*+R] the hall in which such a body meets **4** [C] a room set aside for a special purpose: *This is the death chamber where murderers wait to be put to death* **5** [C] an enclosed space, esp. in a body or machine: *The heart has 4 chambers.|Put the bullet into the firing chamber of your gun* —see also CHAMBERS

chambered nau·ti·lus /ˌ·· ˈ···/ *n* NAUTILUS

cham·ber·lain /ˈtʃeɪmbəlǰn‖-bər-/ *n* [C;N] an important official appointed to direct the housekeeping affairs of a king or nobleman's court

cham·ber·maid /ˈtʃeɪmbəmeɪd‖-ər-/ *n* a female servant employed to clean and tidy bedrooms and make beds, as in a hotel

chamber mu·sic /ˈ·· ˌ··/ *n* music written for a small group of instruments and suitable for performance in a private home or small hall

chamber of com·merce /ˌ·· · ˈ··/ *n* [GC] a group of businessmen working together for the purpose of improving trade

chamber or·ches·tra /ˈ·· ˌ···/ *n* a small group of musicians, usu. with one player for each instrumental part

chamber pot /ˈ·· ·/ *n* a round vessel for liquid and solid body waste, usu. used in the bedroom by an old or sick person and kept under the bed

cham·bers /ˈtʃeɪmbəz‖-ərz/ *n* [P] *law* **1** a room or set of rooms where a judge deals with matters which need not be raised in court **2** *not AmE* rooms set aside for a special purpose, esp. as offices

cha·me·le·on /kəˈmiːlɪən/ *n* **1** any of various types of small 4-legged long-tailed animals (LIZARD*s*) able to change their colour to match their surroundings —see picture at REPTILE **2** a person who changes his behaviour, ideas, etc., to suit his own purposes

cham·ois[1] /ˈʃæmwɑː, ˈʃæmi/ *n* **chamois** /ˈʃæmwɑːz, ˈʃæmiz/ [Wn3] a type of small wild goatlike animal from the mountain areas of Europe and south-west Asia

chamois[2] /ˈʃæmi/ also **cham·my, shammy** /ˈʃæmi/— *n* **chamois** /ˈʃæmiz/ **1** [U] also **chamois leather** /ˈ·· ˌ··/— a type of soft leather prepared from the skin of CHAMOIS[1], sheep, or goats **2** [C] a piece of this used as a cloth for washing and polishing objects

cham·o·mile /ˈkæməmaɪl/ *n* CAMOMILE

champ[1] /tʃæmp/ *v* **1** [IØ (*on, at*); T1] also **chomp**— (of a horse) to bite (food, the BIT[1] (1)), etc.), noisily: *The horse is champing* (*at*) *his food* **2** [IØ, 3] *infml* to be impatient; be eager: *The train was late and the passengers were champing to get home* **3** **champ at the bit** *infml* to be impatient; be eager

champ[2] *n* [C;N] *infml* CHAMPION[1] (2,3): *You can tell this dog's a champ by the way it walks*

cham·pagne /ʃæmˈpeɪn/ *BrE infml* also **cham·pers** /ˈʃæmpəz‖-ərz/— *n* [U] a type of costly French white wine containing a lot of little balls of air (BUBBLE*s*), usu. drunk on special occasions

cham·paign /ʃæmˈpeɪn/ *n lit* an area of open country without forests or towns

cham·pi·on[1] /ˈtʃæmpɪən/ *n* **1** a person who fights for, supports strongly, or defends a principle, movement, person, etc. **2** a person or animal unbeaten in competitions of courage, strength, or skill **3** a person or animal that shows signs of being better than others: *This dog's only young but already you can tell he's a champion*

champion[2] *v* [T1] to fight for, support strongly, or defend (a principle, movement, person, etc.)

champion[3] *adj* [Wa5] *BrE infml apprec* very good; better than most: *"How do you feel?"—"Champion, thank you!"*

champion[4] *adv NEEngE infml apprec* in a CHAMPION[3] manner

cham·pi·on·ship /ˈtʃæmpɪənʃɪp/ *n* **1** [U] the act of CHAMPIONing[2]: *His championship of women's rights is well known* **2** [C *often pl. with sing. meaning*] a competition held to find the CHAMPION[1] (2,3) **3** [C] the position, title, rank, or period of being CHAMPION[1] (2,3): *I don't think this new fighter can take the championship from him*

chance¹ /tʃɑːns‖tʃæns/ *n* **1** [U] the force that seems to make things happen without cause or reason; luck; good or bad fortune: *Chance plays an important part in many card games* **2** [A] accidental; not planned **3** [C;U: (*of*) *often pl. with sing. meaning*] (a) possibility; likelihood that something will happen: *You'd have more chance of catching the train if you got a bus to the station instead of walking* **4** [C (*of*), C3] a favourable occasion; OPPORTUNITY: *I never miss a chance of playing football.|If I give you a second chance will you promise to be good?* **5** [C (*of*)] a risk: *That's a chance I'll have to take!* **6** [C] a ticket in a RAFFLE or LOTTERY (1) **7 by chance** accidentally; by accident; unintentionally **8 on the (off) chance** in view of the (unlikely) possibility; in the hope: *We went to the cinema on the (off) chance of seeing Paul there* **9 (the) chances are (that)** *infml* It is likely (that): *Chances are he's already heard the news* —see also RUN¹ (31) **the chance/danger of,** STAND¹ (21) **a chance,** STAND **a good/fair chance**
USAGE Compare **chance, opportunity,** and **occasion**: One *has* a **chance** or **opportunity** *to do something/of doing something*, which means that it is luckily possible for one at a favourable moment: *I had the* **chance/opportunity** *of visiting Paris.|I had no* **opportunity/chance** *to see him.|I wish I'd had your* **chances/opportunities**! We also say *There is a* **chance** (=possibility) *that I will see him*, and **opportunity** could not be used here. An **occasion** is either the moment when something happens: *on the* **occasion** *of her wedding*, or (*fml*) a reason: *I had* **occasion**/*had no* **occasion** *to visit Paris.*

chance² *v* [Wv6] **1** [I3; *it*+I5] to take place by chance; happen by accident: *She chanced to be in the park when I was there.|If it should chance to rain we'll take a taxi home* **2** [T1,4;(V4)] to take a chance with; risk: *You shouldn't chance all your money at once.|I'll chance another game of cards if you will* **3 chance it** also (*rare*) **chance one's arm**— *infml* to take a chance of success, though failure is possible; take a risk: *I don't know if we can get it, but let's chance it*

chance³ *adj* [Wa5;A] accidental; unplanned: *I had a chance meeting with your brother today; he seemed glad to see me*

chan·cel /ˈtʃɑːnsəl‖ˈtʃæn-/ *n* the eastern part of a church, where the priests and CHOIR (=singers) usu. sit —see picture at CHURCH¹

chan·cel·ler·y /ˈtʃɑːnsələri‖ˈtʃæn-/ *n* **1** [C] the position, rank, or office of a CHANCELLOR **2** [C] the building in which the CHANCELLOR has his offices **3** [GC] the officials who work in a CHANCELLOR'*s* office: *The chancellery are opposed to any move which might lead to war* **4** [C] *tech* also **chancery**— the offices of an official representative (AMBASSADOR or CONSUL (1)) of a foreign country

chan·cel·lor /ˈtʃɑːnsələʳ‖ˈtʃæn-/ *n* **1** [C;N;A] (*often cap.*) (in various countries) the chief minister of state: *The chancellor is the most powerful man in the Austrian government* **2** [C;N] (*often cap.*) a state or law official of high rank: *The most important judge in Britain is the* **Lord Chancellor**.|*In Britain the* **Chancellor of the Exchequer** *deals with taxes and government spending* **3** [C;N] the official head of various universities —compare VICE-CHANCELLOR

chance on also **chance up·on**— *v prep* [T1] to meet by chance; find by chance

chan·ce·ry /ˈtʃɑːnsəri‖ˈtʃæn-/ *n* **1** (in Britain) the LORD CHANCELLOR'*s* division of the **High Court of Justice** dealing with EQUITY (2) **2** (in the United States) a court dealing with EQUITY (2) **3** an office for the collection and safe-keeping of official papers **4 ward in chancery** *law* a young person whose affairs are in the charge of the LORD CHANCELLOR, usu. because of the death of both parents

chanc·y /ˈtʃɑːnsi‖ˈtʃænsi/ *adj* [Wa1] *infml* risky; uncertain as to the result: *That was a chancy thing to do; you could have been killed* **—-iness** *n* [U9]

chan·de·lier /ˌʃændəˈlɪəʳ/ *n* a branched ornamental holder for electric lights or candles, usu. hanging from the CEILING (=the inside roof of a room)

chand·ler /ˈtʃɑːndləʳ‖ˈtʃæn-/ *n old use* a person who makes or sells candles —see also SHIP'S CHANDLER

change¹ /tʃeɪndʒ/ *v* **1** [Wv5;T1;IØ] to (cause to) become different: *In Autumn the leaves change from green to brown.|You've changed such a lot since I last saw you.|He's been a changed man since his wife died* **2** [T1 (*for*)] to give, take, or put something in place of (something else, usu. of the same kind): *Her new dress didn't fit so she took it back to the shop and changed it (for another)* **3** [IØ (*into, out of*); T1] to put (different clothes) on oneself: *I'm just going to change into something more comfortable.|Why does it take women so long to change a dress?* **4** [T1] to put (fresh clothes or coverings) on a baby, child, bed, etc. **5** [T1] to put fresh clothes or covers on (a baby, child, bed, etc.): *How often do you change your bed?* **6** [T1] to exchange (2 things): *to change sides in an argument* **7** [T1] to give (money) in exchange for money of a different type: *Where can I change English money (for foreign money)?* **8** [IØ (*from, to*); T1] to leave and enter (different vehicles) in order to continue or complete a journey: *I had to change from a train to a bus for part of the journey* **9** [IØ (UP or DOWN; *into, to*)] also (*esp. AmE*) **shift**— to cause the engine of a vehicle to be in a different (higher or lower) GEAR¹ (3), usu. to go faster or slower: *Change into second* GEAR¹ (3) *when you go up the hill.|***Change down** *before going up the hill and then* **change up** *at the top* **10 change gear(s)** also (*esp. AmE*) **shift gear(s)**— to make a change in speed and power by causing the engine of a vehicle to be in a different GEAR¹ (3): *Change gear at the bottom of the hill.|*(fig.) *After beginning the speech seriously he changed gear and told some jokes* **11 change hands** to go from the ownership of one person to another **12 change one's mind** to come to have a new opinion **13 change one's tune/note** to become humble, sad, sorry: *You say you won't speak to me again but you'll soon change your tune* **14 change step** (when marching in a group) to move from keeping time with one foot to keeping time with the other —compare EXCHANGE

change² *n* **1** [C;U] (an example of) the act or result of changing: *If we are to avoid defeat we need a change of leadership.|The doctor said the girl had taken a change for the better but was still seriously ill* **2** [C] something different done for variety, excitement, etc. (note the phr. **for a change**): *Let's have breakfast early for a change* **3** [C9 (*of*)] **a** a fresh set of clothes to put on in place of those being worn **b** something new and fresh used in place of something old: *Your car could do with a change of oil* **4** [U] the money returned when the amount given is more than the cost of the goods being bought: *If it cost 25 pence and you gave her a pound you should get 75 pence change* **5** [U] **a** coins of low value: *How much have you got in change?* **b** money in low-value coins or notes exchanged for a coin or note of higher value: *Can you give me change for a 50-penny piece?* **6** [C] an order in which a set of bells is rung **7** [*the*+R] *infml* CHANGE OF LIFE **8 get no change out of (someone)** *infml* to get no help from (someone) **9 ring the changes a** to ring church bells in every possible order **b** *BrE* to change the way something is done: *It's time you* *rang the changes and changed the way you dress*

change·a·ble /ˈtʃeɪndʒəbəl/ *adj* **1** (esp. of the weather) likely to change **2** often changing; variable: *His temper's been very changeable this week so don't annoy him* —**-bility** /ˌtʃeɪndʒəˈbɪlɪ̈ti/ *n* [U] —**-bly** /ˈtʃeɪndʒəbli/ *adv*: *I wish you'd behave less changeably* —**~ness** /ˈtʃeɪndʒəbəlnɪ̈s/ *n* [U]

change in·to *v prep* **1** [L1] to become (something different): *When the prince kissed the cat it changed into a beautiful princess* **2** [D1] to cause (someone or something) to become (something different): *The scientist tried to change iron into gold*

change·less /ˈtʃeɪndʒləs/ *adj* marked by the absence of change —**~ly** *adv*

change·ling /ˈtʃeɪndʒlɪŋ/ *n* **1** a stupid or ugly child left in place of a beautiful clever one supposedly by fairies **2** any child secretly exchanged for another while still a baby

change of life /ˌ· · ˈ·/ *n* [*the*+R] *not fml* MENOPAUSE

change·o·ver /ˈtʃeɪndʒˌəʊvəʳ/ *n* a change from one activity or system of working to another; an important change

change o·ver *v adv* [I∅ (*from* and/or *to*)] to make a complete change: *In 1971 Britain changed over from pounds, shillings, and pence to the new decimal money system*

change ring·ing /ˈ· ˌ··/ *n* [U] the art or practice of ringing a set of bells (as in the tower of a church) in continually varying order

chan·nel[1] /ˈtʃænl/ *n* **1** the bed of a stream of water **2** the deepest part of a river, harbour, or sea passage: *Ships must follow the channel into the port* **3** a narrow sea passage connecting 2 seas or oceans: *The English Channel separates England and France and connects the Atlantic Ocean and North Sea* **4** a passage for liquids: *There's a channel in the middle of the old street to help water flow away when it rains* **5** *often pl. with sing. meaning* any course or way along which information travels: *You should go through the official channels if you want the government to help* **6** a particular band of radio waves used for broadcasting television; television station: *Which channel will you be broadcasting on tonight?* **7** the shows, information, news, advertisements, etc., broadcast on a particular television station **8** a way, course, or direction of thought or action: *He needs a new channel for his activities*

chan·nel[2] *v* **-ll-** (*AmE* **-l-**) [T1] **1** to direct: *Try to channel your abilities into something useful* **2** to form a CHANNEL[1] (1,2,4) in: *We ought to channel this street so that water can flow away easily* **3** to take in a CHANNEL[1] (1,4): *Water was channelled into the garden* **4** to go in a CHANNEL[1] (1): *The water channelled its way through the desert into the lake*

chant[1] /tʃɑːnt‖tʃænt/ *v* [I∅;T1] **1** to sing (words) to a CHANT[2] (1) **2** to continuously repeat (words) in time: *The crowd chanted "Down with the government"*

chant[2] *n* [C;S] **1** an often-repeated tune, often with many words sung on one note, in which the time is largely controlled by the words, esp. used in religious services **2** words continuously repeated in time: *The chant of the crowd was "Equal rights for all"*

chan·te·relle /ˌʃɒntəˈrel‖ˌʃæn-, ˌʃɑn-/ *n Fr* a type of eatable yellow FUNGUS (1)

Chan·ti·cleer /ˌtʃæntɪ̈ˈklɪəʳ/ *n* [R] *lit* (the name of a) COCK[1] (1)

chan·try /ˈtʃɑːntri‖ˈtʃæn-/ *n* **1** a sum of money (ENDOWMENT) given to a church to provide for priests to pray or say religious services, usu. for the soul of the giver **2** a CHAPEL (=a small church or part of a church) paid for by such a gift of money

chan·ty, *AmE* also **-tey** /ˈʃænti/ *n* SHANTY[2]

cha·os /ˈkeɪ-ɒs‖-ɑs/ *n* **1** [U;S] a state of complete and thorough disorder and confusion: *After the failure of electricity supplies the city was in chaos* **2** [U] *poet* the state of the universe before there was any order

cha·ot·ic /keɪˈɒtɪk‖-ˈɑtɪk/ *adj* in a state of complete disorder and confusion; confused: *The capital was in a chaotic state after the enemy had seized the airport* —**~ally** *adv* [Wa4]

chap[1] /tʃæp/ *n infml esp. BrE* a man or boy; FELLOW: *John's a nice chap, he'll always help a friend*

chap[2] *v* **-pp-** [Wv5;I∅;T1] **a** (of human skin) to become sore, rough, and cracked **b** to cause (human skin) to become sore, rough, and cracked: *You'll chap your hands if you use that soap; use this: it's smoother on your skin.* | *chapped hands*

chap[3] *n* a small rough crack or sore in the skin or lip

chap[4] also **chop**— *n* **1** [*usu. pl.*] the fleshy covering of a jaw: *The fox had blood on its chaps* —see picture at DOG[1] **2 lick one's chaps** *infml* to think of or look forward to something hungrily or eagerly

chap·el[1] /ˈtʃæpəl/ *n* **1** [C] a place, such as a small church, a room in a hospital, prison, etc., but not a PARISH CHURCH, used for Christian worship **2** [C] a part of a church with its own ALTAR (2) and used esp. for private prayer and small religious services **3** [C] (esp. in England and Wales) a church or place of Christian worship used by NONCONFORMISTS (=those who do not belong to the established state or ROMAN CATHOLIC church) **4** [U] the religious services held in such places: *He goes to chapel every Sunday night* **5** (in Scotland) a ROMAN CATHOLIC church **6** [GC] an association of people employed in a printing office; branch of the printers' union: *Whether the paper is printed tonight depends on the vote in the chapel*

chapel[2] *adj* [Wa5;F] *BrE becoming rare* (esp. in England and Wales) NON-CONFORMIST: *He's chapel but his wife's a member of the* CHURCH OF ENGLAND

chap·el·goer /ˈtʃæpəlˌgəʊəʳ/ *n* (esp. in England and Wales) a person who regularly goes to CHAPEL[1] (4)

chap·er·on[1], **-one** /ˈʃæpərəʊn/ *n* **1** an older person (usu. a woman) who goes with a young unmarried woman in public **2** an older person present at a young people's party to be responsible for correct behaviour

chaperon[2], **-one** *v* [T1;I∅] to act as a CHAPERON[1] (1,2) to (a person or people)

chap·fall·en /ˈtʃæpˌfɔːlən/ also **chopfallen**— *adj infml* unhappy; in low spirits

chap·lain /ˈtʃæplɪ̈n/ *n* a priest or other religious minister responsible for the religious needs of a club, a part of the armed forces, an important person, etc. —see also PADRE

chap·lain·cy /ˈtʃæplɪ̈nsi/ *n* **1** the building or office in which a CHAPLAIN works: *I'm just going to the chaplaincy to see the priest* **2** the position, or period in office of a CHAPLAIN

chap·let /ˈtʃæplɪ̈t/ *n* **1** a part of the Christian ROSARY (2) consisting of 5 DECADES: *Every night she finished her prayers with a chaplet* **2** any string of small ornamental, usu. glass balls (BEADS) **3** an ornamental band of flowers worn on the head

chaps /tʃæps, ʃæps/ *n* [P] protective leather covers worn over trousers, esp. when riding a horse

chap·ter /ˈtʃæptəʳ/ *n* **1** [C] one of the main divisions of a book or long article, usu. having a number or title **2** [C] a special period in history; number of connected happenings: *Was the period of the empire the finest chapter in British history?* **3** [GC] (a general meeting of) **a** all the priests connected with a CATHEDRAL **b** all the members of a religious group: *Are you going to the chapter next* *week?* **4** [C] *esp. AmE* a local branch of a society, club, etc. **5 chapter and verse** /ˌ·· · ˈ·/ the exact place where information can be found: *He told me chapter and verse where I could find information about the political power of the royal family* **6 chapter of accidents** *BrE* many unfortunate happenings, one coming quickly after another

chapter house /ˈ·· ·/ *n* the building or rooms where a CHAPTER (3) meets

char[1] /tʃɑːʳ/ *v* **-rr-** [Wv5;IØ;T1] to (cause to) become black by burning: *There was charred wood on the ground so we knew there'd been a fire*

char[2] *v* **-rr-** [IØ] *BrE* (of a woman) to work as a cleaner in a house, office, public building, etc., usu. for payment by the hour or day

char[3] *n BrE* CHARWOMAN

char[4] *n* [U] *BrE sl* tea

char·a·banc /ˈʃærəbæŋ/ *n* [C; *by*+U] *becoming rare, not AmE* a large public motor vehicle (COACH), esp. used for pleasure trips

char·ac·ter[1] /ˈkærᵻktəʳ/ *n* **1** [C] **a** (in writing systems which do not use letters) a sign used for representing a word in writing: *Chinese has no alphabet and is written in characters* **b** a written or printed mark (as a letter or figure) having a recognized meaning: *I wish this book were written in bigger characters: these are so difficult to read* **2** [C; U: (*of*)] the combination of qualities which makes a thing, event, place, etc., different from another: *This town isn't interesting–let's go somewhere else with more character* **3** [C;U] the qualities which make a person different from another; moral nature: *The king is a man of good and noble character* **4** [U] moral strength; honesty; INTEGRITY **5** [C] *infml* a person: *Some character just walked up and stole her bag* **6** [C] a person in a book, play, etc.: *I find all the characters in his new play amusing and interesting* **7** [C] official position; CAPACITY: *He was there in his character as a town official* **8** [C] *esp. BrE* a usu. written statement of a person's qualities and abilities; REFERENCE: *My new employer asked for a character of me from my old teacher* **9** [C] *rare* fame, good or bad; REPUTATION: *He's got himself the character of a thief* **10** [C] *infml* an odd or humorous person: *She's a real character, she makes everyone laugh* **11 in character** like one's usual nature **12 out of character** unlike one's usual nature —compare CHARACTERISTIC[2], REPUTATION

character[2] *adj* [Wa5;A] **1** (of a person) able to play an unusual, odd, or difficult part in a play: *a character actress* **2** (of a part in a play) needing the qualities of such a person: *a character part*

char·ac·ter·is·tic[1] /ˌkærᵻktəˈrɪstɪk/ *adj* [B (*of*), B5] typical; representing a person's or thing's usual character —**~ally** *adv* [Wa4]: *Characteristically, he behaved badly*

characteristic[2] *n* [(*of*)] a special and easily recognized quality of someone or something: *A useful characteristic of the cat is its ability to catch and kill mice* —compare CHARACTER[1] (2,3), REPUTATION

char·ac·ter·i·za·tion /ˌkærᵻktəraɪˈzeɪʃən‖-ər-/ *n* [C;U] (an example of) the act or practice of characterizing (CHARACTERIZE (1)): *His characterization of me as untrustworthy is totally false*

char·ac·ter·ize, -ise /ˈkærᵻktəraɪz/ *v* [T1] **1** to describe the character of (someone or something) **2** to be typical of (someone or something): *A rabbit is characterized by its long ears*

char·ac·ter·less /ˈkærᵻktələs‖-tər-/ *adj derog* without character; ordinary

cha·rade /ʃəˈrɑːd‖ʃəˈreɪd/ *n* an act or position which is easily seen to be false or foolish

cha·rades /ʃəˈrɑːdz‖ʃəˈreɪdz/ *n* [U;(P)] a game in which words are acted by players, often part (SYLLABLE) by part, until guessed by other players

char·coal /ˈtʃɑːkəʊl‖ˈtʃɑr-/ *n* **1** [U] (pieces of) the black substance made by burning wood in a closed container with little air, burnt in fires to give heat or used in sticks for drawing with **2** [C] also **charcoal draw·ing** /ˌ·· ˈ··/— a picture made by drawing on paper with this material: *That's a beautiful charcoal you did of my wife*

charcoal burn·er /ˈ·· ˌ··/ *n* a person (esp. in former times) whose job is burning wood to make CHARCOAL (1)

chard /tʃɑːd‖tʃɑrd/ also **Swiss chard**— *n* **1** [C] a type of plant with a large root and large juicy leaves and stems, grown as a vegetable **2** [U] the leaves and stems of this plant cooked and eaten as food, like SPINACH

charge[1] /tʃɑːdʒ‖tʃɑrdʒ/ *v* **1** [IØ;T1;D1: (*for*)] to ask in payment: *How much do you charge for your eggs?|This hotel charged me £5 for a room for the night.|They've always charged a tax on bottles of wine brought into this country* —see COST, ORDER (USAGE) **2** [T1] to record (something) to someone's debt: *Don't forget to charge the money to my account* **3** [IØ (*at*); T1] to rush in or as if in an attack: *Suddenly the wild animal charged at us* **4** [T5,5b] to declare officially and openly (that something is wrong): *The king charged that his minister had disobeyed instructions.|So he charged, but I don't believe it* **5** [V3] to command; give as a responsibility: *The judge charged me to be silent.|He charged me to look after his daughter* **6** [T1] **a** to load (a gun): *The soldiers charged their guns and prepared to fire* **b** *lit* to fill (a glass): *Charge your glasses and drink to my health!* **7** [Wv5 (*with*); IØ;T1] to (cause to) take in the correct amount of electricity: *Does your car* BATTERY (2) *charge easily?|*(fig.) *My husband is always charged with strength and power*

charge[2] *n* **1** [C] the price asked or paid for an article or service: *The charge for a front-row seat is £5* **2** [U (*of*)] care; control; responsibility: *I've got charge of your class tomorrow so you must do as I tell you* **3** [C] **a** a person or thing for which one is responsible: *I became my uncle's charge after my father's death* **b** a duty; responsibility: *My charge is to win the souls of men* **4** [C] an order; command: *The old servant died happy, having fulfilled his master's charge* **5** [C] a spoken or written statement blaming a person for a crime, for breaking the law, or for doing something morally wrong: *The charge was murder* **6** [C] a rushing forceful attack **7** [C] the amount of explosive to be fired at one time **8** [C;U] (a quantity of) electricity put into a BATTERY (2) or other electrical apparatus **9** [C *usu. sing.*] *sl* (a piece of) excitement: *They seem to get a charge out of playing this game* **10 bring a charge against**: to blame (someone) officially for having broken the law: *The police brought a charge of murder against me* **11 face a charge** to have to reply to a statement of one's guilt, usu. in a court of law **12 give in charge** *esp. BrE* to hand (someone) over to the police **13 in charge of** responsible for: *I'll be in charge of the whole factory next week when the director's away* **14 in/under someone's/something's charge** under someone's or something's control, someone's or something's responsibility: *This hospital's in her charge until the director comes back* **15 priest/curate in charge** a priest responsible for a church where there is no regular VICAR (2) **16 take charge of** to be or become responsible for (someone or something): *Can you take charge of this class please, Miss Jones?*

charge·a·ble /ˈtʃɑːdʒəbəl‖-ɑr-/ *adj* **1** [Wa5;B (*with*)] that can be charged, blamed, held responsible, or ACCUSED: *If you kill her you'll be chargeable with murder* **2** [Wa5;F (*on, to*)] (of money costs) that can be added to an account or paid by someone: *These debts are chargeable to me/my account.|To whom is this chargeable?*

charge ac·count /ˈ· ·ˌ·/ *n AmE* CREDIT ACCOUNT

charged /tʃɑːdʒd‖-ɑr-/ *adj* **1** [(*with*)] having strong feelings or purpose: EMOTIONAL*ly-charged* **2** tending to cause strong feelings or much argument: *Whether changes should be made in the voting system is a highly-charged political question*

char·gé d'af·faires /ˌʃɑːʒeɪ dæˈfeəʳ‖ˌʃɑr-/ *n* **chargés d'affaires** (*same pronunciation*) *tech & Fr* an official below the rank of minister who **a** takes the place of his government's representative (AMBASSADOR) during the latter's absence **b** represents his government in a country to which no AMBASSADOR has been appointed

charg·er¹ /ˈtʃɑːdʒəʳ‖-ɑr-/ *n old use* a large flat plate used for carrying and serving food, esp. meat

charger² *n old use or lit* an army officer's horse, esp. ridden in battle

charge sheet /ˈ· ·/ *n* a record kept in a police station of all people against whom a charge has been made, with information about the charge

charge with *v prep* **1** [D1;V4b] (esp. of an official or an official group) to bring a charge against (someone) for (something wrong); ACCUSE of: *The police are going to charge me with murder/with having murdered him* **2** [V4b] to give (someone) the duty or responsibility of: *He charged me with looking after his daughter while he was away*

char·i·ot /ˈtʃærɪət/ *n* a 2-wheeled horse-drawn seatless vehicle used in ancient times in battles, races, and processions

char·i·o·teer /ˌtʃærɪəˈtɪəʳ/ *n* the driver of a CHARIOT

cha·ris·ma /kəˈrɪzmə/ *n* **-mas** *or* **-mata** /mətə/ **1** [U] the special charm or personal magical qualities which cause a person to win and keep the interest and love of ordinary people **2** [C] *tech* one of the favours of the spirit (GRACE*s*) given by God to a person, usu. for the good of the Church, such as the power of curing diseases

cha·ris·ma·tic /ˌkærɪ̇zˈmætɪk/ *adj* **1** having CHARISMA (1) **2** *rare* favoured by God —**~ally** *adv* [Wa4]

char·i·ta·ble /ˈtʃærɪ̇təbəl/ *adj* **1** [B] full of goodness and kind feelings towards others **2** [B] generous, esp. in giving help to the poor **3** [B] merciful in judging others; forgiving **4** [Wa5;A] (of organizations) concerned with giving help to the poor: *a charitable club* —**-bly** *adv*

char·i·ty /ˈtʃærɪ̇ti/ *n* **1** [U] kindness; the feeling of generosity: *Charity made her give food to the old woman* **2** [U] Christian love for God and man **3** [U] help to the poor; ALMS: *She was always very generous in her charity* **4** [C] a society or organization that gives help to the poor **5** [U] sympathy and kindness shown when judging others **6 charity begins at home** one's first duty is to one's family; after that, to others **7 (as) cold as charity** unfeeling; cold; unfriendly **8 Sister of Charity** a member of a woman's religious society (ORDER)

charity school /ˈ··· ·/ *n* (in former times) a place where poor children were given free lodgings and education

char·la·dy /ˈtʃɑːˌleɪdi‖ˈtʃɑr-/ *n* CHARWOMAN

char·la·tan /ˈʃɑːlətn‖ˈʃɑr-/ *n derog* a person who deceives others by falsely claiming to have a special knowledge or skill, esp. medical knowledge: *That new doctor's a charlatan; he couldn't tell I had a broken arm* —compare QUACK³

Charles·ton /ˈtʃɑːlstən‖-ɑr-/ *n* a type of quick spirited dance, esp. popular in the 1920's

char·lock /ˈtʃɑːlɒk‖ˈtʃɑrlɑk/ *n* [Wn2] a type of wild yellow-flowered plant of the MUSTARD family

char·lotte /ˈʃɑːlət‖ˈʃɑr-/ *n* [U;C] cooked apple or other fruit covered with very fine pieces of bread (CRUMB*s*), baked and eaten as food

charlotte russe /ˌʃɑːlət ˈruːs‖ˌʃɑr-/ *n* **charlotte russes** (*same pronunciation*) [C;U] a dish of cake filled with whipped cream, usu. eaten as the last part of a meal

charm¹ /tʃɑːm‖tʃɑrm/ *n* **1** [C] an act, expression, or phrase believed to have magical powers **2** [C] an object worn to keep away evil or bring good luck **3** [C] a small ornament worn on a chain (**charm bracelet**) round the wrist **4** [C;U] the power or ability to please, win over, or delight: *This town has a charm you couldn't find in a big city.|He needed all his charms to persuade her he was right* **5 work like a charm** *not fml* to happen or take place with complete success: *Her plan to persuade him to buy her a new dress worked like a charm*

charm² *v* [T1] **1** to please; win over; delight: *She charms every man she meets* **2** to control (something) as if by magic **3** [Wv5] to protect with or as if with a charm: *It seemed as if he had a charmed life, and his enemies could never harm him*

charm·er /ˈtʃɑːməʳ‖-ɑr-/ *n* **1** a young man or woman who charms others **2** a person who can make snakes obey him, esp. by playing a pipelike instrument

charm·ing /ˈtʃɑːmɪŋ‖-ɑr-/ *adj* very pleasing; delightful: *What a charming young man, I do like him* —**~ly** *adv*

char·nel house /ˈtʃɑːnl haʊs‖ˈtʃɑr-/ also **charnel**— *n lit* a place where the bodies and bones of dead people are placed

chart¹ /tʃɑːt‖tʃɑrt/ *n* **1** a map, esp. a detailed map of a sea area **2** (a sheet of paper with) information written or drawn in the form of a picture, GRAPH, etc., usu. with the intention of making it easily understood

chart² *v* [T1 (OUT)] **1** to make a map or CHART¹ (1, 2) of; show or record on a CHART¹ (1,2): *The scientist hoped to chart the sea area between France and Britain* **2** *infml* to make a rough plan, in words or writing

char·ter /ˈtʃɑːtəʳ‖-ɑr-/ *n* **1** [C; *by*+U] a written or printed signed statement from a ruler, government, etc., giving rights, freedoms, etc., to the people, an organization, or a person: *The rights of our citizens are governed by charter* **2** [C; *by*+U] a written or printed statement giving the principles, duties, and forms of a governing body or organization: *We must change our charter if we decide to allow foreigners to join our organization* **3** [A;(U)] the practice of hiring or renting cars, buses, planes, etc., for special use: *This travel firm specializes in charter (flights)*

charter² *v* [T1] **1** to give a CHARTER¹ (1,2) to (a country, firm, organization, etc.) **2** to hire or rent (a plane, train, bus, etc.) for a special use

chartered ac·coun·tant /ˌ·· ·ˈ··/ (*AmE* **certified public accountant**)— *n BrE* an ACCOUNTANT who has successfully completed his training, passed the official examinations, and has full professional recognition

charter mem·ber /ˌ·· ˈ··/ *n esp. AmE* FOUNDER MEMBER

char·treuse¹ /ʃɑːˈtrɜːz‖ʃɑrˈtruːz (*Fr* ʃartrøz)/ *n* [U] a type of strong sweet green or yellow alcoholic drink made by members of the **Carthusian** religious group

chartreuse² *adj, n* [B;U] (having) a yellow-green colour

char·wom·an /ˈtʃɑːˌwʊmən‖ˈtʃɑr-/ also **charlady**, **char**— *n* **charwomen** /-ˌwɪmɪn/ *esp. BrE* a woman who works as a cleaner in a house, office, or public building

char·y /ˈtʃeəri/ *adj* [Wa1;F (*of*)] *fml* careful; unwilling to take risks; CAUTIOUS: *She's chary of crossing a busy main road* —**charily** *adv*

Cha·ryb·dis /kəˈrɪbdɨs/ *n* see SCYLLA

chase¹ /tʃeɪs/ *v* **1** [T1] to follow rapidly in order to catch: *The cat chased the mouse but could not catch it.*|(fig.) *Why do modern people chase material possessions?* **2** [X9] to drive away; cause to leave: *We must chase the enemy from our country* **3** [T1 (DOWN, UP)] to try to find: *The police have been trying to chase the dead man's sister up but they have no idea where she lives*

chase² *n* **1** [C] an act of chasing something: *The criminal gave us a long chase before we caught him* **2** [*the*+R] the sport of hunting esp. foxes: *Do you like riding in the chase?* **3** [C] the person or thing being chased: *Our fastest ship can catch up with the chase in 2 hours* **4** [C] (often in place names) an area of land set aside for the breeding of wild animals for hunting and shooting **5 give chase** to chase someone: *The old lady saw the thief running up the street and gave chase on her bicycle*

chase³ *v* [T1] *tech* to ornament (wood or metal) by marking with a tool without a cutting edge —**~r** *n*

chase⁴ *n tech* **1** the barrel of a gun **2** a long hollow passage in a wall, floor, etc., for holding wires and pipes

chase a·bout *v adv; prep* [I∅;T1] *infml* to rush or hurry about (in): *Stop chasing about (the house) and sit down!*

chase af·ter *v prep* [T1] *infml* to try to draw level with by running: *Chase after Anne and ask her to get some eggs while she's at the shops*

chas·er /ˈtʃeɪsəʳ/ *n* a weaker alcoholic drink drunk after a stronger alcoholic drink, or between stronger alcoholic drinks

chas·m /ˈkæzəm/ *n* a very deep crack or opening in the surface of the earth or ice: (fig.) *There was a (deep) political chasm between the 2 countries which nearly led to war*

chas·sis /ˈʃæsi/ *n* **chassis** /ˈʃæsiz/ [Wn3] **1** the framework on which the body and working parts of a vehicle, radio, etc. are fastened or built **2** the frame and working parts of a car, radio, etc., as opposed to its body—see picture at CAR **3** the landing apparatus of a plane **4** *humor* a human body, esp. that of an attractive woman: *She's got quite a chassis!*

chaste /tʃeɪst/ *adj* [Wa1] **1** pure in word, thought, and deed, esp. being without sexual activity: *The priest was chaste in mind and body* **2** *apprec* simple; not too ornamented: *He wrote in a pure, chaste style* —**~ly** *adv*

chas·ten /ˈtʃeɪsən/ *v* [T1] **1** to make (a person who has done wrong, or wrong behaviour) correct by punishment: *5 years in prison had not chastened him.*|*Failure will chasten your pride* **2** [Wv4,5] to make (a person or behaviour) pure; cause to improve: *He had been chastened by various experiences in life but especially by the death of his wife*

chas·tise /tʃæˈstaɪz/ *v* [T1] *fml* **1** to punish severely, usu. by beating: *Parents don't chastise their children as much as they used to do* **2** to blame (CENSURE) severely: *Parliament intends to chastise the slowness of the government in making a new prices and incomes agreement with the unions*

chas·tise·ment /ˈtʃæstɨzmənt‖tʃæsˈtaɪz-/ *n* [C;U] *fml* (a) severe punishment

chas·ti·ty /ˈtʃæstɨti/ *n* [U] the state of being sexually pure: *Defend your chastity if you want to stay morally pure*

chastity belt /ˈ··· ·/ *n* a special belt worn by a woman in former times to prevent her from having sexual relations

chas·u·ble /ˈtʃæzjʊbəl‖-jə-/ *n* a loose-fitting garment without arms worn by some Christian priests at religious services, esp. the MASS (1)

chat¹ /tʃæt/ *v* **-tt-** [I∅ (*about*, AWAY)] *infml* to talk in a friendly familiar informal manner: *The 2 friends sat in a corner and chatted away to each other about the weather*

chat² *n infml* **1** [C] a friendly informal conversation **2** [U] the action of CHATting¹ (1): *We need less chat and more work if we're to finish this job today* **3** *esp. BrE* worthless and sometimes unkind talk, GOSSIP

chât·eau, chat- /ˈʃætəʊ‖ʃæˈtəʊ/ *n* **-teaus** *or* **-teaux** /ˈʃætəʊz‖ʃæˈtəʊz/ *Fr* a castle or large country house in France

chat·e·laine /ˈʃætl-eɪn/ *n Fr* **1** the female owner, or wife of the owner, of a large country house or castle **2** *rare* a set of ornamental chains fastened to a woman's belt for carrying small articles such as keys

chat·tel /ˈtʃætl/ *n law* **1** an article of movable property (esp. in the phr. **goods and chattels**) **2** (esp. in former times) a slave

chat·ter¹ /ˈtʃætəʳ/ *v* [I∅] **1** [(AWAY, ON, *about*)] (of people) to talk rapidly and at length, usu. about something unimportant: *I wish you'd stop chattering on about things you don't understand* **2** [(AWAY)] (of certain animals and birds) to make rapid speechlike sounds: *The monkeys were chattering away in the trees* **3** (of the teeth or machines) to knock together, esp. through cold or fear: *I was so cold my teeth were chattering.*|*You could hear guns chattering in the distance* —**~er** *n*

chatter² *n* [U] **1** rapid informal unimportant conversation: *I dislike chatter at the best of times but especially when I'm trying to work* **2** a rapid knocking sound made by teeth, machines, etc., or the rapid speechlike sounds made by certain animals and birds: *The chatter of the enemy's guns could be heard in the city*

chat·ter·box /ˈtʃætəbɒks‖-tərbɑks/ *n not fml* a person, esp. a child, who talks a lot

chat·ty /ˈtʃæti/ *adj* [Wa1] *infml* **1** fond of talking: *I wish she weren't so chatty; she's always annoying me when I'm trying to read* **2** having the style and manner of informal conversation

chat up *v adv* [T1] *BrE infml* (esp. of men) to make friends with by talking to (esp. a woman): *He's always trying to chat up the girls*

chauf·feur¹ /ˈʃəʊfəʳ, ʃəʊˈfɜːʳ/ *n* [C;(N)] a person employed to drive someone's car

chauffeur² *v* **1** [I∅] to work as a CHAUFFEUR¹ **2** [T1 (AROUND, ABOUT)] to take (a person) from place to place in one's car as if one were a CHAUFFEUR¹

chau·vin·is·m /ˈʃəʊvɨnɪzəm/ *n* [U] **1** very great and often blind admiration of one's country; proud belief that one's country is politically, morally, and militarily, better than all others **2** unreasoned belief that the sex to which one belongs is better than the other sex: *People who favour equal rights for women must fight against* **male chauvinism** *wherever it appears*

chau·vin·ist /ˈʃəʊvɨnɨst/ *n, adj* (a person or organization) favouring, feeling, or showing CHAUVINISM: *I think our chauvinist government wants to rebuild the empire.*|*Her husband's such a chauvinist that he won't even let her vote the way she wants* —**~ic** /ˌʃəʊvɨˈnɪstɪk/ *adj* —**~ically** *adv* [Wa4]

cheap¹ /tʃiːp/ *n* **on the cheap** *infml* cheaply; without paying the full cost: *She got some new trousers on the cheap down at the market*

cheap² *adj* [Wa1] **1 a** low in price; costing little: *Fresh vegetables are very cheap in the summer* **b** worth more than the cost; good value for money: *Bread is cheap in this shop, it costs twice as much over the road* **c** *BrE* reduced in price for quick sale

2 charging low prices: *This is the cheapest restaurant in town* **3** needing little effort: *The army won a cheap victory over the enemy who had few guns and soldiers* **4** worth little; of or considered of little value: *100 years ago life was a lot cheaper than it is today* **5 a** of poor quality; SHODDY: *Her shoes looked cheap and nasty to me* **b** of a low or offensively unpleasant sort; VULGAR: *I hate his kind of cheap humour* **6** *esp. AmE* careful with money; TIGHT: *He's the cheapest man in town, he's never bought any of his friends a drink* **7 dirt cheap** *infml* at a very low price: *That dress was dirt cheap in the other shop, I wish I'd bought it there* **8 feel cheap** *infml* to feel ashamed: *After giving in to his desires she said she felt cheap* **9 hold (something) cheap** to put a low value on something: *He held his wife's love cheap so she left him* **10 make oneself cheap** to do something that lowers one's worth in one's own or other people's judgment: *He's made himself cheap by his unpleasant behaviour* —**~ly** *adv* —**~ness** *n* [U]

cheap[3] *adv* [Wa1] **1** at a very low price: *I was very lucky to get it so cheap* **2** in a cheap way: *I wish she wouldn't act so cheap*

cheap·en /ˈtʃiːpən/ *v* **1** [T1;I∅] to (cause to) become cheaper in price or value **2** [T1] to make (esp. oneself) less attractive or good: *By your nasty behaviour you've cheapened yourself in everyone's opinion*

cheap-jack /ˈ· ·/ *adj* [A] **1** of bad quality, cheap, or worthless: *cheap-jack films that I don't want to see* **2** wanting to make money by producing or selling goods that are of bad quality and usu. cheap

cheap·skate /ˈtʃiːpskeɪt/ *n* [C;(N); *you*+N] *derog, esp. AmE* a person who spends or gives unwillingly

cheat[1] /tʃiːt/ *n* **1** [C; *you*+N] a person who cheats; dishonest person **2** [C] an example of cheating; dishonest, deceitful trick: *These sheets I've bought are a cheat; they're too short for the bed* **3** [U] *rare* the act of cheating **4** [U] a type of card game in which 2 or more players try to win by acting deceitfully

cheat[2] *v* **1** [T1 (*of, out of*)] to take from (someone) unfairly, dishonestly or deceitfully: *He cheated the old woman ((out) of her money) by making her sign a paper she didn't understand* **2** [I∅ (*at*)] to act dishonestly or deceitfully to win an advantage esp. in a game: *I always cheat at cards, it's the only way I can win* **3** [T1] *lit* to avoid or escape as if by deception: *The swimmers cheated death in spite of the storm* **4** [I∅ (*on*)] *infml* to be sexually unfaithful, esp. to one's husband or wife: *They've been married for only 6 months, and already she's started cheating (on him)!*

check[1] /tʃek/ *n* **1** [S (*on*); *in*+U] a stop; control; RESTRAINT: *We've kept the disease in check for a year now* **2** [C (*on*)] something which stops, controls, or RESTRAINS: *The woods and the river were a check on the army's advance* **3** [C (*on*)] an examination to make certain that something is correct: *a check on the quality of all goods leaving the factory* **4** [C] *AmE* a mark or sign to show that something is correct; TICK **5** [C] a standard against which something can be examined: *Don't copy my answers completely; just use them as a check to see if yours are right* **6** [C] a receipt; ticket or object for claiming something: *I've lost the check for my coat* **7** [C;U] a pattern of squares: *She wore a pretty blue and white check* **8** [C] any of the squares in such a pattern **9** [U] (in CHESS) the position of the king when under direct attack from an opponent's piece(s) —see CHESS (USAGE) **10** [C] *AmE & ScotE* a bill at a restaurant **11** [C] *AmE* CHEQUE

check[2] *v* **1** [T1] to stop; control; hold back; RESTRAIN: *A change of wind checked the fire* **2** [I∅; T1,5,6a,b] to test, examine, or mark to see if something is correct; make sure; VERIFY: *Have you checked the examination papers yet, sir?|When I checked my shopping list I found I'd forgotten to buy eggs.|"Is the baby asleep?" "I'll just go and check"* **3** [T1] to find out and note: *He checked the temperature each day before leaving home* **4** [T1] (in CHESS) to move one's pieces so as to put (the opponent's king) under direct attack —see CHESS (USAGE) **5** [T1] *AmE* to place (something) somewhere to be looked after: *They checked their coats before taking their seats in the theatre* **6** [T1] *AmE* TICK

check·book /ˈtʃekbʊk/ *n AmE* CHEQUEBOOK

checked /tʃekt/ *adj* having a pattern of squares (CHECKs[1] (8)): *Do you like my new checked curtains?*

check·er[1] /ˈtʃekəʳ/ *v esp. AmE* CHEQUER

checker[2] *n AmE* DRAUGHT (8)

check·er·board /ˈtʃekəbɔːd‖ˈtʃekərbord/ *n* **1** *esp. AmE* DRAUGHTBOARD **2** something with a pattern of squares like this

check·ers /ˈtʃekəz‖-ərz/ *n* [U] *AmE* DRAUGHTS

check in *v adv* **1** [I∅ (*at, to*)] to report one's arrival, as at a hotel desk, an airport, etc.: *You must check in at the airport an hour before your plane leaves* **2** [T1] *esp. AmE* to have the return of (an article) recorded: *I'm just going to check in these books at the library* —compare CHECK OUT (2)

checking ac·count /ˈ·· ·ˌ·/ *n AmE* CURRENT ACCOUNT

check·list /ˈtʃekˌlɪst/ *n* a complete list of books, goods, voters, etc., so arranged as to provide an easy means of finding information about these things; CATALOGUE

check·mate[1] /ˈtʃekmeɪt/ *v* [T1] **1** (in CHESS) to win the game by moving one's pieces so as to put (the opponent's king and therefore the opponent) under direct attack from which escape is impossible: *He checkmated my king in 6 moves and so won the game.|You've checkmated me 3 times in 6 games!* —see CHESS (USAGE) **2** to stop; completely defeat

checkmate[2] *n* [C;U] **1** (in CHESS) the position of a king when under direct attack from an opponent's pieces from which escape is impossible: *The game ended with a checkmate.|I can force (you into) checkmate in 6 moves* —see CHESS (USAGE) **2** (a) complete defeat

check·off /ˈtʃek-ɒf‖-ɔf/ *n* [U] *tech* the removal of trade union payments from a worker's pay by the employer at the request of the union

check off *v adv* [T1] *tech* to take (union payments) from a worker's pay before the worker gets it

check·out /ˈtʃek-aʊt/ *n* **1** a desk in a self-service shop where one shows the goods one has chosen and pays for them **2** the time at which a guest must leave a hotel room or be charged for another day: *Checkout is at midday in this hotel*

check out *v adv* **1** [I∅ (*of*)] to leave a hotel after paying the bill **2** [T1 (*of*)] *esp. AmE* to have the removal of (a thing) recorded: *To check a book out of the library* **3** [I∅] *infml* to be found to be true after inquiries have been made: *How does this story check out with the facts?* —compare CHECK IN

check o·ver *v adv* [T1] to examine: *Please check this piece of work over and say if you see any mistakes*

check·point /ˈtʃekpɔɪnt/ *n* a place where a CHECK[1] (3) is made on people, traffic, goods, etc.: *There are a number of checkpoints on the border between East and West Berlin*

check·rail /ˈtʃek-reɪl/ *n* GUARDRAIL (2)

check·rein /ˈtʃek-reɪn/ *n tech* a short leather belt

(REIN) used for **a** preventing a horse from lowering its head **b** for joining together the REINs of 2 horses, working as a team
check·room /ˈtʃek-rʊm, -ruːm/ *n esp. AmE* **1** CLOAKROOM (1) **2** LEFT-LUGGAGE OFFICE
check·up /ˈtʃek-ʌp/ *n infml* a general medical examination: *You look tired and ill; why don't you have a checkup?|His doctor gave him a checkup and found nothing wrong*
check up on *v adv prep* [T1] *infml* to make thorough inquiries about (something or someone): *She felt the police were checking up on her so she left the country*
ched·dar /ˈtʃedəʳ/ *n* [U] (*often cap.*) a type of firm smooth usu. yellowish cheese
cheek[1] /tʃiːk/ *n* **1** [C] a fleshy part on either side of the face below the eye, esp., in human beings: *Her cheeks went red after she ran up the stairs* —see picture at HUMAN[2] **2** [C] *infml* either of the 2 soft fleshy parts at the back lower end of the body, esp. in human beings; BUTTOCK **3** [U] *infml* bold disrespectful rude behaviour **4 say something/speak/talk with (one's) tongue in (one's) cheek** to say one thing and mean the opposite, esp. in a bad way: *"How beautiful you look!" she said to the ugly girl, with (her) tongue in (her) cheek* **5 cheek by jowl (with) a** in close association: *They say the unions and this government are cheek by jowl* **b** very close together; tightly packed: *You'll never get through that crowd of people; they're packed in there cheek by jowl*
cheek[2] *v* [T1] *infml, esp. BrE* to behave boldly, disrespectfully, or rudely towards (someone): *Pupils should never cheek their teachers* —compare SASS
cheek·bone /ˈtʃiːkbəʊn/ *n* the bone above the cheek, just below the eyes
-cheeked /tʃiːkt/ *comb form* having cheeks of the stated kind: *After running to school the boys were red-cheeked*
cheek·y /ˈtʃiːki/ *adj* [Wa1] *infml* disrespectful; rude —**cheekily** *adv* —**cheekiness** *n* [U]
cheep /tʃiːp/ *v, n* [I∅;S] (to make) the weak high noise made by young birds
cheer[1] /ˈtʃɪəʳ/ *n* **1** [C] a shout of praise, encouragement, etc.: *You can hear the cheers of the crowd 2 miles away from the football ground* **2** [U] happiness of mind; good spirits; gaiety: *He's always full of cheer in summer* **3 good cheer** feasting and merry-making **4 of good cheer** *lit* cheerful: *Be of good cheer*
cheer[2] *v* **1** [I∅] to shout in praise, approval, or support: *Every time an English runner won a race the crowd cheered* **2** [T1 (*on*)] to encourage by shouting praise, approval, or support: *The crowd cheered their favourite horse (on)* **3** [T1] to give encouragement, hope, help, or support to: *The trapped miners were cheered when they heard the shouts of their friends*
cheer·ful /ˈtʃɪəfəl‖-ər-/ *adj* **1** happy; gay; in good spirits **2** *apprec* pleasant; causing a happy feeling: *You could never be unhappy in such a cheerful house* **3** *apprec* willing: *His cheerful acceptance of responsibility encouraged us all* —**~ly** *adv* —**~ness** *n* [U]
cheer·ing /ˈtʃɪərɪŋ/ *adj* encouraging; gladdening: *The government's cheering news about the reduction in taxes pleased everyone*
cheer·i·o /ˌtʃɪəriˈəʊ/ *interj BrE infml* **1** goodbye **2** *becoming rare* CHEERS (3)
cheer·lead·er /ˈtʃɪəˌliːdəʳ‖-ər-/ *n* (esp. in the US) a person who calls for and directs cheering, as at a football match
cheer·less /ˈtʃɪələs‖-ər-/ *adj* dull; without comfort; saddening: *I don't feel like going to work on such a cheerless day* —**~ly** *adv* —**~ness** *n* [U]: *The cheerlessness of this old cold house makes me want to leave at once*
cheers /tʃɪəz‖tʃɪərz/ *interj infml* **1** *esp. BrE* (when drinking someone's health) good health **2** *BrE* thank you: *"That's just what I want. Cheers!" she said when I gave her the present* **3** *BrE* (esp. on the telephone) good-bye: *"See you tonight, then. Cheers!" I said, and put down the receiver*
cheer up also **buck up**— *v adv* [I∅;T1] *infml* to (cause to) become happier, more cheerful: *Cheer up! The news isn't too bad*
cheer·y /ˈtʃɪəri/ *adj* [Wa2] bright; gay; cheerful: *He gave us a cheery greeting* —**cheerily** *adv* —**cheeriness** *n* [U]
cheese /tʃiːz/ *n* **1** [U;C] (any of many kinds of) soft or firm solid food made from pressed and sometimes ripened milk solids (CURDs): *cheese made from the milk of cows, sheep, or goats|a very good cheese* **2** [C] usu. a large shaped and wrapped quantity of this **3 green cheese** newly made cheese
cheese·cake /ˈtʃiːzkeɪk/ *n* **1** [C;U] a type of cake in or on a sweet pastry case, made from a mixture containing soft or unripe cheese **2** [U] *sl becoming rare* photographs of pretty women with few clothes on —compare BEEFCAKE
cheese·cloth /ˈtʃiːzklɒθ‖-klɔθ/ *n* [U] **1** a very light thin cotton cloth used for putting round some kinds of cheeses **2** a heavier, thicker cotton cloth used for making garments, esp. shirts
cheese off *v adv* [Wv5;T1 (*with*)] *BrE sl* to tire (someone) thoroughly; annoy: *You look cheesed off with life; what's wrong?* —compare BROWN OFF
cheese·par·ing /ˈtʃiːzˌpeərɪŋ/ *adj, n* [A;U] *derog* (marked by) great carefulness when giving or spending money
chee·tah /ˈtʃiːtə/ *n* a type of long-legged swift-moving spotted African animal of the cat family, about the size of a small LEOPARD and able to be trained to hunt deer or other animals —see picture at CAT
chef /ʃef/ *n* a skilled male cook, esp. the chief cook in a hotel or restaurant
chef d'oeu·vre /ˌʃeɪ ˈdɜːvrə‖-ˈdɜr- (*Fr* ʃɛ dœvrə)/ *n* **chefs d'oeuvre** (*same pronunciation*) *Fr* the best piece of work by an artist, writer, etc.; MASTERPIECE
chem *written abbrev. for:* **1** chemical **2** CHEMIST **3** chemistry
chem·i·cal[1] /ˈkemɪkəl/ *adj* of, connected with, used in, or made by chemistry: *A chemical change takes place in paper when it burns* —**~ly** *adv*
chemical[2] *n* any substance used in or produced by chemistry; any of the substances known as ELEMENTs (6) or the COMPOUNDs[3] (1) formed from them
che·mise /ʃəˈmiːz/ *n* a woman's simple dress that hangs straight from the shoulder
chem·ist /ˈkemɪ̣st/ *n* **1** a scientist who specializes in chemistry **2** also (*fml*) **pharmacist**, (*AmE* **druggist**)— *BrE* a person skilled in the making of medicine **3** also (*fml*) **pharmacist**, (*AmE* **druggist**) *BrE*— a person who owns or runs a shop ((*fml*) **pharmacy**, *BrE* **chemist's**, (*AmE*) **drugstore**) where esp. medicines are sold
chem·is·try /ˈkemɪ̣stri/ *n* [U] **1** the science which studies the substances (ELEMENTs) which make up the earth, universe, and living things, how these substances combine with each other, and how they behave under different conditions **2** the chemical make-up and behaviour of a substance: *He's trying to learn more about the chemistry of lead*
chem·o·ther·a·py /ˌkeməʊˈθerəpi‖ˌkiː-/ *n* [U] the use of chemical substances to treat and control diseases
che·nille /ʃəˈniːl/ *n* [U] **1** twisted thread which is

wool, cotton, silk or man-made, having a soft smooth brush-like surface and used for ornamenting dresses, curtains, etc. **2** material made from this thread

cheque, *AmE* **check** /tʃek/ *n* **1** [C; *by*+U] a written order to a bank, usu. made on a specially printed sheet of paper supplied by the bank, to pay a certain sum of money from one's bank account to another person: *I'd like to pay by cheque, please, rather than in* CASH (1) **2** [C] a small printed sheet of paper supplied by a bank to someone who has an account with it, on which such an order can be written: *Can you please let me have 30 cheques?* **3 crossed cheque** *esp. BrE* a cheque which must be put into a bank account before being paid **4 blank cheque a** CARTE BLANCHE: *I gave him a blank cheque to do as he pleased* **b** a signed cheque given to the person to whom it is payable and who writes on it the amount to be paid later

cheque·book, *AmE* **checkbook** /ˈtʃekbʊk/ *n* a book of new cheques supplied by a bank to a person who has an account with it

cheque card, *AmE* **check card** /ˈ· ·/ *n* a card given by a bank to those who have an account with it, which promises that the bank will pay out the money written on their cheques up to a certain amount

chequ·er, *AmE* **checker** /ˈtʃekəʳ/ *v* [Wv5;T1] **1** to cover with a pattern of differently coloured squares **2** to mark by changes of good and bad luck; vary: *He'd had a chequered past in the government but was now determined to be successful in the armed forces*

cher·ish /ˈtʃerɪʃ/ *v* [T1] **1** to care for tenderly; love: *The old man cherished the girl as if she were his daughter* **2** to keep (hope, feelings, love, etc.) in mind deeply and with strongly favourable feelings: *He cherished the memory of his dead wife*

che·root /ʃəˈruːt/ *n* **1** *tech* a CIGAR with both ends cut square **2** *sl* CIGAR

cher·ry[1] /ˈtʃeri/ *n* **1** [C] a type of small soft fleshy red, yellow, or black round fruit with a stonelike seed in the middle —compare GRAPE and see picture at BERRY **2** [C] also **cherry-tree** /ˈ·· ·/— the tree on which this fruit grows **3** [U] the wood of this tree: *Is that chair made of cherry?* **4** [C *usu. sing.*] *sl* VIRGINITY (esp. in the phr. **lose one's cherry**) **5 a second/another bite at the cherry** a second chance to do or get something

cherry[2] *adj, n* [Wa5;B;U] (having) a varying but usu. middle red colour

cher·ub[1] /ˈtʃerəb/ *n* **-ubs** *or* **-ubim** /əbɪm/ *bibl & lit* one of God's winged attendants (ANGEL*s*) described in the Bible as having various forms, usu. shown in paintings as a beautiful fat child

cherub[2] *n* **1** [C] a beautiful and usu. winged child in paintings **2** [C;N] a sweet pretty guiltless-looking person, esp. a child —**~ic** /tʃəˈruːbɪk/ *adj* —**~ically** *adv* [Wa4]

cher·vil /ˈtʃɜːvəl‖-ɜr-/ *n* [U] **1** any of several types of strong-smelling garden plants (HERB*s*) with divided leaves **2** the dried leaves of this plant used to give a special taste to food

Chesh·ire cat /ˌtʃeʃə ˈkæt‖-ər-/ *n* **grin like a Cheshire cat** *infml* to smile very widely all the time: *I wish you'd stop grinning like a Cheshire cat and try to be serious*

chess /tʃes/ *n* [U] a game for 2 players each of whom starts with 16 pieces (**chessmen**) which can be moved according to fixed rules across a **chessboard** in an attempt to trap (CHECKMATE) the opponent's king
USAGE One plays a game of **chess** on a *board*, using **chessmen** or **pieces**. These are either *black* or *white*, and are called **king, queen, bishop, knight, rook** (or **castle**) and **pawn**. One attacks the king by saying **"Check!"** and wins the game when one can say **"Checkmate!"**

chess·board /ˈtʃesbɔːd‖-ord/ *n* a square board with 64 black and white squares, each square being next to a square of a different colour, on which CHESS or DRAUGHTS is played

chess·man /ˈtʃesmæn, -mən/ *n* **-men** /men, mən/ any of the 32 pieces used in playing CHESS

chest /tʃest/ *n* **1** the upper front part of the body enclosing the heart and lungs —see picture at HUMAN[2] **2** a large strong box in which valuable objects are kept, goods packed, etc. **3** the quantity contained in such a box: *a chest of tea* **4 get (something) off one's chest** to bring (a worry) out into the open by talking

-chest·ed /ˈtʃestɪ̈d/ *comb. form* having a chest of the stated kind: *She was flat-chested*

ches·ter·field /ˈtʃestəfiːld‖-ər-/ *n* **1** a type of SINGLE-BREASTED coat for men made so that buttons do not show and having a smooth soft (VELVET) collar **2** a type of long seat (COUCH) with a back and sides, thickly covered with comfortable soft material

chest·nut[1] /ˈtʃesnʌt/ *n* **1** [C] a smooth reddish-brown nut that stays enclosed in a prickly case until ripe, eaten raw or cooked —see picture at NUT[1] **2** [C] also **chestnut tree** /ˈ·· ˌ·/— the tree on which this nut grows **3** [U] the wood of this tree: *Is that table made of chestnut?* **4** [C] a reddish-brown horse **5** [C] *infml* a joke or story so old and well-known that it is not funny: *His speeches are always full of old chestnuts*

chestnut[2] *adj, n* [Wa5;B;U] (having) a deep reddish-brown colour

chest of drawers /ˌ· · ˈ·/ *AmE* also **bureau**— *n* a piece of furniture with several drawers usu. used for holding clothes —see picture at BEDROOM

chest·y /ˈtʃesti/ *adj* [Wa1] *infml* **1** (esp. of women) having a large or well-developed chest **2** sounding as if coming from the chest (esp. in the phr. **chesty cough** /ˌ·· ˈ·/) —**chestily** *adv*

che·val glass /ʃəˈvæl glɑːs‖-glæs/ *n* a long movable mirror held in an upright frame

chev·a·lier /ˌʃevəˈlɪəʳ/ *n rare* **1** a member of certain honourable groups or ORDER*s*[1] (16): *a Chevalier of the* LEGION *of Honour in France* **2 a** KNIGHT **b** a male member of the lowest rank of French noblemen **3** a brave polite honourable (CHIVALROUS) man

chev·ron /ˈʃevrən/ *n* a piece of cloth in the shape ^ or ∨, one (or more) of which, on the SLEEVE*s* (1) of a police or armed forces uniform, shows the wearer's rank

chev·y, chevvy /ˈtʃevi/ *v BrE sl* CHIVY

chew[1] /tʃuː/ *v* [T1 (UP); IØ (*on*)] **1** to crush (food or tobacco) with, or as if with, the teeth: *You must chew your food well before you swallow it* **2 bite off more than one can chew** *infml* to attempt more than one can deal with or succeed in finishing: *I told him that if he tried to build his own house he'd be biting off more than he could chew* **3 chew the fat** *infml* CHAT[1] (1): *We sat there drinking beer and chewing the fat until it was time to go home* **4 chew the rag** *infml* **a** *BrE* to complain: *I wish you'd stop chewing the rag and get on with your work* **b** *AmE* CHEW[1] (3) the fat

chew[2] *n* **1** [S] the act of CHEWing: *I'll think about it while I have a chew* **2** [C] a sweet or piece of tobacco made to be CHEWed but not swallowed: *a chew of tobacco*

chewed up /ˌ· ˈ·/ *adj* [F (*about*)] *AmE sl* worried; anxious; BOTHERed: *Don't get all chewed up about it: everything will be all right*

chewing gum /ˈ·· ·/ also **gum**— *n* [U] a sweet

sticky plastic substance usu. having a special taste made to be CHEWed[1] (1) but not swallowed

chew out *v adv* [T1b] *infml, esp. AmE* to scold: *The teacher chewed me out for being late*

chew o·ver *v adv* [T1b] *infml* to think about (a question, difficulty, etc.): *I'll chew it over for a few days and let you know my opinion*

chi /kaɪ/ *n* [(C);R] the 22nd letter of the Greek alphabet

Chi·an·ti /kiˈænti‖kiˈɑnti/ *n* [U] *It* a red Italian table wine which is neither sweet nor BUBBLY[1] (1)

chi·a·ro·scu·ro /ki,ɑːrəˈskʊərəʊ/ *n* **-ros** *It* **1** [U] representation of something in art, using light and shadow without regard to colour, esp. so as to give a feeling of depth **2** [U] the arrangement or treatment of light and dark parts in a picture **3** [C] a painting made using only black, brown, and white

chic /ʃiːk/ *adj, n* [Wa2;B;U] (showing) good style: *I like your chic hat.|She wears her clothes with chic* —**~ly** *adv*

chi·ca·ne·ry /ʃɪˈkeɪnəri/ *n* **1** [U] deception by false reasoning in order to gain an advantage —see also SOPHISTRY **2** [C;U] (a piece of) deceitful practice, esp. in law

Chi·ca·no /tʃɪˈkɑːnəʊ/ *n* **-nos** a Mexican-American

chi·chi /ˈʃiːʃiː/ *adj infml & slightly derog* **1** pretending to be fashionable but appearing showy or too ornamental: *Her chichi dress amused everyone* **2** fashionable: *The actors went to a chichi party in a chichi part of town*

chick /tʃɪk/ *n* **1** [C] a young chicken **2** [C] the young of any bird **3** [C;N] *sl* a young woman: *I like the look of that chick*

chick·en[1] /ˈtʃɪkɪ̣n/ *n* **1** [C] a hen (or perhaps COCK[1] (1)), esp. when young but older than a CHICK (1) —see picture at DOMESTIC ANIMAL **2** [C] one of the young of any bird **3** [U] the meat of the young hen (or COCK[1] (1)) cooked and eaten as food: *Do you like boiled chicken?* —see MEAT (USAGE) **4** [C;N] *sl* (*used esp. by children*) a person who lacks courage; COWARD: *You're a chicken; that's why you won't climb the tree* **5** [U] *infml* a children's game to test one's courage **6** **count one's chickens before they're hatched** to make plans depending on something which has not yet happened: *"My horse is sure to win the race, so I'm going to spend the money now." "Don't count your chickens before they're hatched!"* **7** **no (spring) chicken** *sl* (esp. of women) no longer young: *She needs lots of make-up to hide the fact that she's no spring chicken*

chicken[2] *adj* [F] *sl* lacking courage

chick·en·feed /ˈtʃɪkɪ̣nfiːd/ *n* [U] *sl* a small unimportant amount of money: *The bank offered to lend us £1000 but it's chickenfeed compared to what we need*

chick·en·heart·ed /,tʃɪkɪ̣nˈhɑːtɪ̣d◂‖-ɑr-/ also **chicken-liv·ered** /,·· ˈ··◂/— *adj* lacking courage; cowardly —**~ness** *n* [U]

chicken out *v adv* [IØ (*of*)] *derog sl* to decide not to do something because of being afraid: *He chickened out of climbing up the tree*

chicken pox /ˈ·· ·/ *n* [U] a disease, caught esp. by children, that is marked by a slight fever and spots on the skin

chick·pea /ˈtʃɪkpiː/ *n* **1** [Wn2] a type of small bushy plant grown for its small round PEAlike (1) seeds **2** a seed of this plant, larger than the common PEA and eaten as food

chick·weed /ˈtʃɪk-wiːd/ *n* [U] any of various types of low-growing small-leaved usu. white-flowered plants, liked and eaten by birds

chic·le /ˈtʃɪkəl/ *n* [U] the thickened juice (GUM) of a tropical American tree used in making CHEWING GUM

chic·o·ry /ˈtʃɪkəri/ *n* [U] **1** a type of thick-rooted blue-flowered European plant grown for its roots and leaves **2** the leaves of this plant eaten raw as a vegetable **3** a powder made from the dried crushed roots of this plant and added to coffee to give a special taste

chide /tʃaɪd/ *v* **chided** *or* **chid** /tʃɪd/, **chid** *or* **chidden** /ˈtʃɪdn/ [IØ (*for, with*)] *lit* to scold: *The king chided Sir Lancelot for his unfaithfulness/with unfaithfulness*

chief[1] /tʃiːf/ *n* **1** [C;N;A] a leader; ruler; person with highest rank; head of a party, organization, etc.: *The king is chief of the armed forces by right.|The chief of (the) police (department) demanded severe punishments for criminals* **2** [C;N;A] *sl* BOSS **3** [N] *infml* (used as a polite form of address by one man to another): *"Where to, chief?" the taxi-driver asked me* **4** [C] (in HERALDRY (1)) the top part of a personal shield **5** **-in-chief** /,· ˈ·/ (*used as a comb form*) having the highest rank: *In World War 2 Eisenhower was commander-in-chief of the armed forces* **6** **in chief** *lit* most of all; in particular

chief[2] *adj* [Wa5;A] **1** highest in rank: *the chief clerk|chief priest* **2** most important; main: *What is the chief town of Norway?|Rice is the chief crop of India*

chief con·stab·le /,· ˈ···/ *n* (in Britain) an officer in charge of the police in a large area

chief in·spect·or /,· ·ˈ··◂/ *n* [C;A] (esp. in Britain) a police officer of middle rank

chief jus·tice /,· ˈ··◂/ *n* [C;A] the head judge of a court of justice

chief·ly /ˈtʃiːfli/ *adv* **1** mainly; mostly but not wholly: *Bread is chiefly made of flour* **2** above all; particularly; especially: *Chiefly, I ask you to remember to write to your dear mother*

chief of staff /,· · ˈ·/ *n* **1** a high ranking officer in the armed forces who serves as main adviser to a commander **2** (in the US armed forces) the commanding officer of the army or air force: *He became (the) chief of staff in 1976*

chief su·per·in·ten·dent /,· ···ˈ··◂/ *n* [C;A] (in Britain) a police officer of high rank

chief·tain /ˈtʃiːftɪ̣n/ *n* the leader of a tribe or other such group, esp. of a Scottish CLAN (1); chief

chief·tain·ship /ˈtʃiːftɪ̣nʃɪp/ **1** also **chief·tan·cy** /-si/— the position, rule, rank, or period in office of a CHIEFTAIN: *During your father's chieftainship no one would have dared disobey* **2** the art and practice of being a chieftain

chif·fon /ˈʃɪfɒn‖ʃɪˈfɑn/ *n* [U] a soft smooth thin transparent silky material used for scarves (SCARF), dresses, etc.

chif·fo·nier, -fonnier /,ʃɪfəˈnɪəʳ/ *n* **1** a narrow ornamental piece of furniture with several drawers (CHEST OF DRAWERS), often with a movable mirror fixed on the top **2** a low movable cupboard with a top that can be used as a side table at meals

chig·ger /ˈtʃɪgəʳ/ also **chigoe** /ˈtʃɪgəʊ/— *n esp. AmE* JIGGER (1)

chi·gnon /ˈʃiːnjɒn‖-jɑn/ *n Fr* a knot of hair worn by a woman at the back of the head

chi·hua·hua /tʃɪ̣ˈwɑːwə/ *n* a type of very small dog

chil·blain /ˈtʃɪlbleɪn/ *n* a red painful swelling or sore usu. on the toes, ears, or fingers, caused by coldness and poor blood supply

child /tʃaɪld/ *n* **children** /ˈtʃɪldrən/ **1** [C] an unborn or recently born person: *My wife lost her first child a month before it should have been born* **2** [C; *my*+N] a young human being from the time of birth to the completion of bodily development **3** [C] a son or daughter: *We've got 5 children.|(fig.) Moses led the children of Israel out of Egypt* **4** [C] **a** *derog* someone who behaves childishly: *He might be 50* *but he's still a child.|Don't be such a child!* **b** an inexperienced person: *I'm a child when it comes to money matters|a child in money matters* **5** [C9] a person very influenced by another person, place, or state of affairs: *At university one could tell he was Marx's child just from hearing him speak* **6** [C9] product; result: *The atomic bomb is the child of 20th century scientific developments* **7 get someone/be with child** *lit* to make someone/be PREGNANT **8 great/heavy with child** *lit* (of a woman) near the time of giving birth

child·bear·ing /ˈtʃaɪldˌbeərɪŋ/ *n* [U] the act of giving birth to children: *The woman was too old for childbearing when she married* —**childbearing** *adj* [A]

child·birth /ˈtʃaɪldbɜːθ‖-ɜrθ/ *n* [U] the act of giving birth to a child

child·hood /ˈtʃaɪldhʊd/ *n* [U;C] **1** the time or condition of being a child: *The Russian nobles taught their children from childhood to speak French* **2 second childhood** weakness of mind caused by old age; DOTAGE

child·ish /ˈtʃaɪldɪʃ/ *adj* **1** of, typical of, or for a child: *The little girl spoke in a high childish voice* **2** *derog* having a manner unsuitable for a grown up; IMMATURE (2) —compare CHILDLIKE —**~ly** *adv* —**~ness** *n* [U]

child·like /ˈtʃaɪldlaɪk/ *adj often apprec* of or typical of a child, esp. having a natural guiltless lovable quality —compare CHILDISH (2)

child prod·i·gy /ˌ· ˈ···/ *n* INFANT PRODIGY

child's play /ˈ· ·/ *n* [U] **1** something very easy to do: *Driving a car isn't child's play even when you've had practice* **2** something not very important: *His illness is child's play when you think of how serious it might have been*

chill¹ /tʃɪl/ *v* **1** [Wv5;IØ;T1] to (cause to) become cold esp. without freezing: *I want this wine to chill so I'll leave it in a cold place for an hour.|chilled beer* **2** [Wv5;T1] to preserve (food) by keeping cold but not frozen: *chilled meat* **3** [IØ;T1] *tech* (of the surface of hot liquid metal) to (cause to) harden by making cool suddenly **4** [Wv4;IØ;T1] to (cause to) **a** have a feeling of cold as from fear: *Our hearts chilled when we heard the news. | a chilling murder story* **b** become discouraged or low in spirits: *Failure chilled his hopes*

chill² *adj* [Wa1] **1** cold: *a chill wind* **2** unfriendly; discouraging: *The union leaders and employers had a chill meeting and reached no satisfactory agreement*

chill³ *n* **1** an illness marked by coldness and shaking of the body **2** [*usu. sing.*] a certain coldness: *There was a chill in the air this morning, wasn't there?* **3** [*usu. sing.*] a discouraging feeling, often of fear; a lowering of spirits: *The bad news put a chill into us all*

chill·er /ˈtʃɪləʳ/ *n* **1** an apparatus (such as a MOULD² (1)) for quickly making cold the surface of hot liquid metal **2** *infml* a story of murder, violence, etc., that causes fear, anxiety, and uncertainty in the mind (SUSPENSE)

chil·li, *AmE* usu. **chile, chili** /ˈtʃɪli/ *n* **chillies** (*AmE* usu. **chiles, chilies**) **1** [C] the very hot-tasting seed case of the PEPPER plant **2** [U] a hot red powder made from this, used for giving a special taste to food —compare PEPPER¹ (1) **3** [U] also **chilli con car·ne** /ˌtʃɪli kən ˈkɑːni‖-ɑrni/— a cooked dish of meat and beans given a special taste by the addition of this powder, and common in the western US

chill·y /ˈtʃɪli/ *adj* [Wa1] **1** noticeably cold; cold enough to be uncomfortable: *It grew chilly when the fire went out.|I feel chilly without a coat* **2** unfriendly; discouraging; cold: *The king was given a chilly welcome when he arrived on the island* —**chilliness** *n* [S;U]

chime¹ /tʃaɪm/ *n* **1** [*usu. pl.*] the sound made by a set of bells: *Listen to the chimes of the church bells* **2** a musical sound like this: *The chime of the clock woke him up* **3** [*usu. pl.*] a set of bells, each having a different note, rung to produce a musical tune **4** a musical instrument which makes a bell-like sound when struck **5** *lit* agreement; HARMONY: *There was a happy chime of belief and practice in everything she did*

chime² *v* **1** [IØ;T1] to (cause to) make musical bell-like sounds **2** [T1] to call, declare, or show (the time) by making a bell-like ringing sound: *The clock chimed one o'clock* **3** [IØ (*with*)] to be or act in accordance: *Her beliefs and practice chime well together*

chime in *v adv infml* **1** [IØ (*with*); T5] to interrupt or join in a conversation by expressing (an opinion): *He's always ready to chime in with his opinion* **2** [IØ (*with*)] to suit; match: *Do the president's ideas chime in with yours?*

chi·me·ra, -maera /kaɪˈmɪərə, kɪ̆-/ *n* **1** an imaginary terrible creature (MONSTER) made up of parts of different animals **2** a hope, idea, dream, etc., that can never become true; unreal fancy **3** *tech* a plant or animal produced by mixing cells from different types of plant, animals, etc., together

chi·me·ri·cal /kaɪˈmerɪkəl, kɪ̆-/ also **chi·me·ric** /kaɪˈmerɪk, kɪ̆-/— *adj* existing only as the product of unreal imagination; imaginary; fanciful: *chimerical ideas that can never become real* —**~ly** *adv* [Wa4]

chim·ney /ˈtʃɪmni/ *n* **1** a hollow passage often rising above the roof of a building which allows smoke and gases to pass from a fire or very hot substance: *Every northern town seems to have lots of factory chimneys pouring smoke into the air* —see picture at ROOF¹ **2** a glass tube often wide at the centre and narrow at the top, put around a flame as in an oil lamp **3** *tech* a deep narrow upward passage in a cliff or rock —see picture at MOUNTAIN

chim·ney·breast /ˈtʃɪmnibrest/ *n esp. BrE* the wall which stands out into a room, with the fire at its centre —compare MANTELPIECE

chimney cor·ner /ˈ·· ˌ··/ *n esp. BrE* a space built into an old-fashioned CHIMNEYBREAST with enough room for a seat on either side of the fire: *The ancient inn had a chimney corner where old men could sit close to the fire* —compare INGLENOOK

chim·ney·piece /ˈtʃɪmnipiːs/ *n becoming rare* a wooden or brick ornamental covering fixed onto or built into the wall above and around the fire

chim·ney·pot /ˈtʃɪmnipɒt‖-pɑt/ *n* a short EARTHENWARE or metal pipe sometimes fixed to the top of a chimney, esp. to carry off the smoke —see picture at ROOF¹

chim·ney·stack /ˈtʃɪmnistæk/ *n* **1** (*AmE* usu. **smokestack**)— the tall part of a chimney which rises above the roof of a building such as a factory **2** *BrE* a group of several small chimneys sticking up from the roof of a house

chim·ney·sweep /ˈtʃɪmni-swiːp/ also **chim·ney·sweep·er** /-ˌswiːpəʳ/, (*infml*) **sweep**— *n* a person whose job is cleaning the insides of chimneys (esp. a young boy in former times)

chim·pan·zee /ˌtʃɪmpænˈziː, -pən-/ also (*infml*) **chimp** /tʃɪmp/— *n* a large dark-haired African monkey-like animal (APE) smaller and less fierce than a GORILLA —see picture at PRIMATE²

chin /tʃɪn/ *n* **1** the front part of the face (esp. of a human being) where it stands out slightly below the mouth —see picture at HUMAN² **2 (Keep your)**

chin up! *infml* Keep your spirits high; Don't give up

chi·na /ˈtʃaɪnə/ *n* [U] **1** a hard white substance made by baking fine clay at high temperatures —compare PORCELAIN **2** plates, cups, etc., made from this or a substance like this; CROCKERY: *Please lay the table with the best china* **3 a bull in a china shop** *infml* a rough and careless person in a place where skill and care are needed: *John's like a bull in a china shop: he's always knocking things over*

china clay /ˌ·· ˈ·ˈ/ *n* [U] a type of very fine clay used in making CHINA (1); KAOLIN

china clos·et /ˈ·· ˌ··/ *n* a cupboard, often with glass doors, where CHINA (2) is stored or shown

Chi·na·town /ˈtʃaɪnətaʊn/ *n* [C;R] an area in a city where there are Chinese shops, restaurants, and clubs, and where many Chinese people live

chi·na·ware /ˈtʃaɪnəweəʳ/ *n* [U] CHINA (2)

chin·chil·la /ˌtʃɪnˈtʃɪlə/ *n* **1** [Wn1;C] a type of small South American SQUIRREL-like animal with a long tail, strong back legs, and soft pale grey fur **2** [U] the fur of this animal **3** [U] *AmE* a heavy woollen material used esp. for making coats

chine /tʃaɪn/ *n tech* **1** the BACKBONE (set of bones down the centre of the back) of an animal body prepared for sale as meat **2** part of this with the flesh around it used as meat

Chinese /ˌtʃaɪˈniːzˈ/ *adj* of or related to China, its people, or their language

Chinese che·quers, *AmE* **-ckers** /ˌ·· ˈ··/ *n* [U;(P)] a game for 2–6 players in which small balls are moved from hole to hole on a board in the shape of a 6-pointed star

Chinese lan·tern /ˌ·· ˈ··/ also **Japanese lantern**— *n* a folding LANTERN or LANTERN-like ornament of thin coloured paper

chink[1] /tʃɪŋk/ *n* **1** a narrow crack or opening: *He watched the girls through a chink in the wall* **2** a narrow beam of light shining through such a crack: *There was not even a chink of light to lighten the darkness of the room*

chink[2] *v* [T1] to close (narrow cracks or spaces) by filling with a hard-drying substance: *He chinked the hole in the wall with clay*

chink[3] *n* CLINK[2]

chink[4] *v* [I∅;T1] CLINK[1]

Chink *n taboo derog sl* a Chinese person

chin·less /ˈtʃɪnləs/ *adj* **1** having a chin that is small or that slopes inwards **2** *BrE infml* of a weak and cowardly nature **3 chinless wonder** /ˌ·· ˈ··/ *BrE sl* a foolish person, often of noble birth

chi·nook /tʃʲəˈnʊk, -ˈnuːk/ *n* **1** a warm wet wind that blows off the sea onto the northwest coast of America **2** a warm dry wind that blows down the eastern slopes of the Rocky Mountains

chin·strap /ˈtʃɪnstræp/ *n* the band hanging down to the chin, which helps to keep a military protective hat (HELMET) firmly in place on the owner's head

chintz /tʃɪnts/ *n* [U] a type of cotton cloth printed with brightly coloured patterns, used for making curtains, furniture covers, etc.

chin·wag /ˈtʃɪnwæg/ *n* [S] *sl* an informal conversation; CHAT

chin-wag·ging /ˈ· ˌ··/ *n* [U] *sl* CHINWAG

chip[1] /tʃɪp/ *n* **1** a small piece as of brick, wood, paint, etc., broken off something: *a chip of wood* **2** a crack or mark left when a small piece is broken off or knocked out of an object: *I was annoyed to find a chip in my new table* **3** a flat plastic object (COUNTER) used for representing money in certain games **4** [*usu. pl.*] (*AmE* **French fry**)— *BrE* a long thin piece of potato cooked in deep fat **5** [*usu. pl.*] *AmE & AustrE* CRISP[3] **6 chip off the old block** *infml often apprec* (usu. said by and about males) a person very like his father: *You're a chip off the old block, my boy* **7 have a chip on one's shoulder** *infml* to feel quarrelsome, usu. as a result of feeling badly treated; be in a bad temper: *He's got a chip on his shoulder today; I think he's had an argument with his wife* **8 pass/cash in one's chips** *infml & euph* to die **9 when the chips are down** *infml* when a very important point is reached: *When the chips are down, you have only yourself to depend on*

chip[2] *v* **-pp-** **1** [I∅;T1] to (cause to) lose a small piece from the surface or edge: *This rock chips easily.|Someone's chipped my best glass* **2** [X9, esp. OFF, *off*] to cause (a small piece) to be broken off a surface or edge: *I've chipped a piece out of your table, I'm sorry.|I've chipped off a piece of your table.|I've chipped a piece off your table* **3** [T1] *esp. BrE* to cut (potatoes) into small pieces ready to be cooked as CHIPS[1] (4)

chip at *v prep* [T1 (AWAY)] to (try to) break small pieces off (something): *Your son was chipping (away) at the table when I came in*

chip a·way *v adv* **1** [T1] to destroy (something) bit by bit, by breaking small pieces off: *After a great deal of effort, he succeeded in chipping away the stone that held the door open* **2** [I∅ (*at*)] to (try to) break small pieces off something: *All my life, little by little, you've tried to chip away at my hopes!*

chip·board /ˈtʃɪpbɔːd‖-ord/ *n* [U] a type of board made from waste pieces of wood, used as a building material

chip in *v adv infml* **1** [I∅ (*with*); T5] to enter a conversation suddenly with an opinion: *John chipped in that it was time to go home* **2** [I∅;T1a] to add (one's share of money or activity): *I could only afford to chip in a few pounds*

chip·munk /ˈtʃɪpmʌŋk/ *n* a type of small American SQUIRRELlike animal with a long bushy tail, strong back legs, and bands of black and white colour along its back, often seen in trees

Chip·pen·dale[1] /ˈtʃɪpəndeɪl/ *adj, n* [Wa5;B;R] (of, being, or related to) an 18th-century English furniture style known for its graceful shape and fine ornamentation

Chippendale[2] *n* [U] furniture in the CHIPPENDALE style: *He owns a lot of fine Chippendale*

chip·ping /ˈtʃɪpɪŋ/ *n esp BrE* [*usu. pl.*] small rough piece of stone used when putting new surfaces on roads, railway tracks, etc.: *Remember to drive carefully; they're putting new chippings down on the roads*

chip·py /ˈtʃɪpi/ *n N EngE sl* a shop which sells cooked fish and CHIPS[1] (4)

chi·ro·man·cy /ˈkaɪrəmænsi/ *n* [U] *lit* PALMISTRY

chi·rop·o·dy /kʲəˈrɒpədi, ʃʲə-‖-ˈrɑ-/ *AmE* also **podiatry**— *n* [U] the professional care and treatment of the human foot in health and disease —**-dist** *n*

chi·ro·prac·tic /ˈkaɪrəpræktɪk/ *n* [U] the treatment of diseases by feeling and pressing by hand the bones, esp. those of the back and neck —compare OSTEOPATHY —**-tor** *n*

chirp[1] /tʃɜːp‖tʃɜrp/ also **chirrup** /ˈtʃɪrəp‖ˈtʃɪ-, ˈtʃɜ-/— *v* **1** [I∅ (AWAY)] to make the short sharp sound(s) of small birds or some insects **2** [T1 (OUT); I∅] to say or speak in a way that sounds like this: *She chirped (out) her thanks*

chirp[2] also **chirrup**— *n* the short sharp sound made by small birds or some insects

chirp·y /ˈtʃɜːpi‖ˈtʃɜrpi/ *adj* [Wa1] *infml esp. BrE* (of people) in good spirits; cheerful: *You seem chirpier than usual today* —**chirpily** *adv* —**chirpiness** *n* [U]

chis·el[1] /ˈtʃɪzəl/ *n* a metal tool with a sharp cutting edge at the end of a blade, used for cutting into or shaping a solid material (such as wood, stone, etc.) —see picture at TOOL[1]

chisel[2] *v* **-ll-** (*AmE* **-l-**) **1** [I∅ (AWAY); D1 + *into/out of*; T1] to cut or shape with a CHISEL[1]: *He chiselled* *that rock into the figure of a woman.|He chiselled the figure of a woman out of that rock* **2** [I∅] *sl* to get (something) by deceitful or unfair practices: *He seems able to get anything by chiselling* **3** [T1 (*out of*)] *sl* to trick; deceive: *He's chiselled me out of £5!*

chis·el·ler, *AmE* also **-eler** /ˈtʃɪzələʳ/ *n sl* a person who uses deceitful and unfair practices to get what he wants: *Don't trust him: he's a chiseller!*

chit¹ /tʃɪt/ *n infml* **1** a young child **2** *often derog* a spirited, bold, and sometimes disrespectful young woman: *a chit of a girl*

chit² *n* a short letter, esp. a signed note showing a sum of money owed (for drinks, food, etc.)

chit·chat /ˈtʃɪt-tʃæt/ *n* [U] *infml* informal conversation

chiv·al·rous /ˈʃɪvəlrəs/ *adj* **1** of or relating to CHIVALRY **2** (esp. of men) marked by bravery, honour, generosity, and good manners **3** (esp. of men) being polite and helpful, esp. to women and weak people —**~ly** *adv*

chiv·al·ry /ˈʃɪvəlri/ *n* **1** [U] (in the MIDDLE AGES) the beliefs or practices of noble soldiers (KNIGHT*s*) as a group **2** [U] the qualities (such as bravery, honour, generosity, and kindness to the weak and poor) which this system aimed at developing in noble soldiers (KNIGHT*s*) **3** [U] (when speaking of a man) good manners, esp. towards women **4** [P] *old use* all the noble soldiers (KNIGHT*s*) of a country

chive /tʃaɪv/ *n* **1** a type of plant related to the onion and having narrow grasslike leaves **2** [*usu. pl.*] (pieces of) the leaves of this plant used for giving a special taste to food

chiv·y, chivvy /ˈtʃɪvi/ also **chevy, chevvy**— *v* [T1] *infml* to annoy (someone) by continually arguing, scolding, etc.: *She chivvied me so much that I hit her*

chlo·ride /ˈklɔːraɪd‖ˈklor-/ *n* **1** [C;U] a chemical mixture (COMPOUND) of CHLORINE with another substance **2** [U] such a mixture used for cleaning and disinfecting

chlo·ri·nate /ˈklɔːr̩neɪt‖ˈklo-/ *v* [Wv5;T1] to disinfect by putting CHLORINE into (a substance, esp. water): *Water is usually chlorinated in public swimming baths to keep it pure.|chlorinated water* —**-nation** /ˌklɔːr̩ˈneɪʃən‖ˌklo-/ *n* [U]

chlo·rine /ˈklɔːriːn‖ˈkloriːn/ *n* [U] a gas that is a simple substance (ELEMENT) greenish-yellow, strong-smelling, and used for making cloth white and water pure

chlor·o·form¹ /ˈklɒrəfɔːm‖ˈklorəfɔrm/ *n* [U] a colourless strong-smelling poisonous chemical liquid that becomes gas at a low temperature, used as an ANAESTHETIC (=a substance that makes people unconscious) and in industry as a SOLVENT (=a substance that softens or melts other substances)

chloroform² *v* [T1] to treat with CHLOROFORM¹ in order to make unconscious or to kill

chlo·ro·phyll /ˈklɔːrəfɪl‖ˈklor-/ *n* [U] the green-coloured substance in the stems and leaves of plants that has the ability to change chemicals into the substances necessary for growth when sunlight is present —see PHOTOSYNTHESIS

choc-ice /ˈtʃɒk aɪs‖ˈtʃɑk-, ˈtʃɔk-/ also **choc-bar** /ˈ· ·/— *n BrE* a shaped piece of ice cream with a covering of chocolate

chock¹ /tʃɒk‖tʃɑk/ *n* a shaped piece of wood placed under something, such as a door, boat, barrel, or wheel to prevent it from moving

chock² *v* [T1 (UP)] to use a CHOCK¹ to prevent (something) from moving: *Chock that barrel (up) or else it will roll over*

chock-a-block /ˌtʃɒk ə ˈblɒk◂‖ˈtʃɑk ə ˌblɑk/ *adj, adv* [F (*with*)] *infml* very crowded; packed tightly: *The road was chock-a-block with cars again today*

chock-full /ˌ· ˈ·◂/ *adj* [Wa5;F (*of*)] *infml* completely full: *The train was chock-full of travellers*

choco·late¹ /ˈtʃɒkl̩t‖ˈtʃɑkəl̩t, ˈtʃɔk-/ *n* **1** [U] a solid sweet usu. brown substance made from the crushed seeds of a tropical American tree (CACAO), eaten as a sweet **2** [C] a small sweet made by covering a centre, such as a nut, with this substance: *Never eat chocolates before dinner* **3** [U] a sweet brown powder made by crushing this substance, used for giving a special taste to sweet foods and drinks **4** [C;U] (a cupful of) a drink made from hot milk (and water) mixed with this powder

chocolate² *adj, n* [B;U] (having) a variable usu. brownish grey colour: *At the windows she had chocolate curtains*

choice¹ /tʃɔɪs/ *n* **1** [C] the act of choosing: *What influenced you when you made your choice?* **2** [U] the power, right, or chance of choosing: *Have I any choice but to do as you tell me?* **3** [C] someone or something chosen: *I don't like her but if she's the people's choice for president I will obey her* **4** [C] a variety from which to choose: *There was a big choice of shops in the small town* **5 Hobson's choice** /ˌ·· ˈ·/ no choice at all because there is only one course of action possible

choice² *adj* [Wa1] **1** (esp. of food) worthy of being chosen; of high quality: *The shop was selling choice apples so I bought a pound* **2** *lit* well chosen: *He told the story in choice phrases* **3** *humor* (of language) very strong and offensive: *She swore at him angrily but he used even choicer phrases in reply* —**~ly** *adv* —**~ness** *n* [U]

choir /ˈkwaɪəʳ/ *n* **1** [GC] a group of people who sing together esp. during religious services: *a church/school choir* **2** [C *usu. sing.*] that part of a church building where such a group of people sit: *The procession of priests moved through the choir to greet the faithful (people)* —see picture at CHURCH¹

choir·boy /ˈkwaɪəbɔɪ‖-ər-/ *n* a boy who sings in a church CHOIR (1)

choir·mas·ter /ˈkwaɪəmɑːstəʳ‖-ərmæ-/ *n* the director of a CHOIR (1)

choir school /ˈ· ·/ *n* a school connected with the chief church (CATHEDRAL) of an area

choir screen /ˈ· ·/ *n* an ornamental framework which divides the CHOIR (2) from the main part of some church buildings

choke¹ /tʃəʊk/ *v* **1** [I∅;T1] to (cause to) struggle to breathe or (cause to) stop breathing because of blocking of or damage to the breathing passages: *Water went down his throat and he started to choke.|His death was sudden: he choked on a fish bone.|*(fig.) *plants choked by long grass* **2** [Wv5;T1 (UP, *with*)] to fill (a space or passage) completely: *The roads into London were so choked up with traffic that even the fire engines couldn't get through.|*(fig.) *all choked up with a strong feeling, and unable to speak* **3** [T1] to use the CHOKE² (2) to reduce the amount of air to (an engine) in order to make starting easier

choke² *n* **1** [C] the act of choking (CHOKE¹ (1)): *One quick choke, and the old man was dead* **2** [C] an apparatus that controls the amount of air going into a car engine —see picture at CAR **3** [*the*+R] *BrE sl* CHOKY

choke back *v adv* [T1] to control (esp. violent or very sad feelings) as if by holding in the throat: *She tried to choke back her anger/her tears, but failed*

choke down *v adv* [T1] **1** to swallow quickly or with difficulty: *He had to choke down his breakfast in order to catch his bus* **2** CHOKE BACK

choke off *v adv* [T1] **1** *sl esp. BrE* to get rid of (someone) by discouragement: *As soon as we'd choked Joan off by telling her it was too cold to go* *out, we all went for a drink* **2** CHOKE BACK

chok·er /ˈtʃəʊkəʳ/ *n* **1** a narrow band of material with a small ornament or jewel at the centre, worn very tightly round a woman's neck **2** a high tight-fitting old-fashioned stiff collar

chok·y, chokey /ˈtʃəʊki/ *n* [*the*+R] *BrE sl* prison: *He's not in the choky again, is he?*

chol·er /ˈkɒləʳ‖ˈkɑ-/ *n* [U] *becoming rare* anger

chol·e·ra /ˈkɒlərə‖ˈkɑ-/ *n* [U] an infectious disease of tropical countries which attacks esp. the stomach and bowels, and often leads to death

chol·e·ric /ˈkɒlərɪk‖ˈkɑ-/ *adj* easily made angry; bad-tempered —**~ally** *adv* [Wa4]

cho·les·te·rol /kəˈlestərɒl‖-rol/ *n* [U] a white soapy substance found in all cells of the body, which helps to carry fats, produce oil for the skin and hair, and make body-controlling substances (HORMONE*s*)

chomp /tʃɒmp‖tʃɑmp, tʃɔmp/ *v* [I∅ (*on, at*)] CHAMP¹ (1)

choose /tʃuːz/ *v* **chose** /tʃəʊz/, **chosen** /tʃəʊzən/ **1** [T1,4,6a,b;V3;D1 (*for*); X (*to be*) 1;I∅ (*between, from*)] to pick out from a greater number; show (what one wants) by taking: *Have you chosen a hat yet?|If you had to choose (between) staying here alone or going with me, what would you do?|Will you help me choose myself a new coat?|Who did you choose to be/as your new member of parliament?|Who was chosen (to be/as) king?|There are 10 to choose from* **2** [T3,5c,6a,b;I∅] to decide: *He chose not to go home until later.|He chose that we should stay.|Who's going to choose what to do?|Will you choose, please?* **3 There's little/not much to choose between them** They are very much alike

choos·y, choosey /ˈtʃuːzi/ also (*esp. AmE*) **picky**— *adj* [Wa1] careful in choosing; hard to please: *Jean's very choosy about what she eats*

chop¹ /tʃɒp‖tʃɑp/ *v* **-pp- 1** [I∅ (AWAY); X9] to cut by repeatedly striking with or as if with a heavy sharp-ended tool, such as an axe: *I'm tired of chopping: will you do it now?|He chopped the block of wood in 2 with a single blow* **2** [X9] to make by doing this: *We had to to chop a path through the thick forest before we could come to the river* **3** [T1 (UP)] to cut into very small pieces: *Chop the onions up, please* **4** [T1] to strike (a ball) with a quick downward stroke **5** [I∅ (AWAY, *at*)] to try to CHOP (1,3,4): *I've been chopping ((away) (at this tree)) for half an hour with no results.|He chopped at me with his knife, but missed.|He chopped at the ball but missed, and the game was lost* **6** [T1 *often pass.*] *sl* to cause (esp. a plan or effort) to stop suddenly: *"Plans for New Schools Chopped for Lack of Money," said the newspaper*

chop² *n* **1** [C] a quick short cutting blow as with an axe: *The mad murderer cut off her head with just one chop of the axe* **2** [C] a short quick downward stroke or blow, directed at a ball or an opponent **3** [C] a small piece of meat usu. containing a bone: *We're having lamb chops for dinner* **4** [(*the*) S] short quick movements as of waves: *We could feel the chop of the waves moving the boat up and down* **5 get the chop** *sl* to be dismissed from work: *He got the chop for being late*

chop³ *v* **-pp-** [L9, esp. ABOUT, ROUND] **1** (esp. of the wind) to change direction suddenly: *The wind keeps chopping about, so it might be dangerous to go sailing* **2 chop and change** to keep changing (direction, one's opinion, plans, etc.): *I wish you wouldn't chop and change your mind like this; either buy a new car or don't, but leave me in peace* **3 chop logic** to use arguments which seem reasonable but which are in fact false

chop⁴ *n* **1** (esp. in India and China) **a** an official stamp or mark (SEAL) **b** an official mark on goods or coins to show the quality **2** a kind or group of goods of the same quality **3 first chop** top quality: *first-chop tea*

chop⁵ *n* CHAP

chop-chop /ˈ· ·/ *adv* [Wa5] *sl* quickly; without delay

chop down *v adv* [T1] to cause to fall by CHOPping¹ (1): *to chop down a tree*

chop·fal·len /ˈtʃɒpfɔːlən‖ˈtʃɑp-/ *adj* CHAPFALLEN

chop·house /ˈtʃɒphaʊs‖ˈtʃɑp-/ *n* **-houses** /haʊzɨz/ a restaurant specializing in meat dishes, esp. STEAK or CHOP*s*² (3)

chop off *v adv; prep* [T1;D1] to remove by CHOPping¹ (2): *She chopped off a big piece of wood for the fire.|She chopped a big piece of wood off the tree for the fire*

chop·per /ˈtʃɒpəʳ‖ˈtʃɑ-/ *n* **1** a heavy sharp-ended tool used for cutting meat; axe —see picture at TOOL¹ **2** *sl* HELICOPTER **3** *tech* an apparatus that interrupts an electric current, beam of light, etc., at a fixed time **4** *sl* MOTORCYCLE

chop·pers /ˈtʃɒpəz‖ˈtʃɑpərz/ *n* [P] *sl* teeth

chop·py /ˈtʃɒpi‖ˈtʃɑpi/ *adj* [Wa1] **1** (of water) covered with many short rough waves: *The sea was choppy today although there was hardly any wind* **2** (of wind) variable **3** *infml* disconnected; changing quickly from one thing to another: *I thought his book was written in too choppy a style* —**choppiness** *n* [U]

chop·stick /ˈtʃɒp-stɪk‖ˈtʃɑp-/ *n* [*usu. pl.*] either of a pair of narrow sticks held between the thumb and fingers and used in East Asian countries for lifting food to the mouth: *When we go to a Chinese restaurant we always use chopsticks instead of a knife and fork*

chop su·ey /ˌtʃɒp ˈsuːi‖ˌtʃɑp-/ *n* [U] a dish in Chinese style made of bits of vegetables and meat or fish, and served hot with rice —compare CHOW MEIN

cho·ral /ˈkɔːrəl‖ˈko-/ *adj* [Wa5;A;(B)] of, related to, or sung by a CHOIR or CHORUS: *a choral group|a choral society|a choral dance*

cho·rale /kɒˈrɑːl‖kəˈræl, -rɑl/ *n* **1** (a tune for) a song of praise (HYMN) sung in a church: *a Bach chorale* **2** CHOIR (1); CHORUS¹ (1)

chord¹ /kɔːd‖kɔrd/ *n* a combination of 2 or more musical notes sounded at the same time

chord² *n* **1** a straight line joining 2 points on a curve —see picture at GEOMETRY **2** a string of a stringed musical instrument **3** CORD¹ **4 strike a chord** to call up memory or feelings in the mind; RING³ (7) **a bell 5 touch the right chord** to make clever use of someone's feelings: *He touched the right chord and she gave him £10*

chore /tʃɔːʳ‖tʃor/ *n* **1** a small bit of regular work, quickly and easily done; daily necessary job, esp. in a house or on a farm: *Each morning she would get up, do the chores, then go next door for a talk with her neighbour* **2** a piece of uninteresting, difficult, or disliked work: *It's such a chore to do the shopping every day!*

chor·e·og·ra·pher /ˌkɒriˈɒgrəfəʳ, ˌkɔː-‖ˌkoriˈɑg-/ *n* a person who plans, arranges, and directs dances for the stage

chor·e·og·ra·phy /ˌkɒriˈɒgrəfi, ˌkɔː-‖ˌkoriˈɑg-/ *n* [U] the art of dancing or of arranging dances for the stage

cho·rine /ˈkɔːriːn‖ˈkor-/ *n AmE infml* CHORUS GIRL

chor·is·ter /ˈkɒrɪstəʳ‖ˈkor-, ˈkɑr-/ *n* a member of a group of people who sing together (CHOIR), esp. in a church

chor·tle¹ /ˈtʃɔːtl‖ˈtʃɔrtl/ *v* [I∅] to give a laugh of pleasure or satisfaction; CHUCKLE: *He chortled with delight when I told him my news*

chortle² *n* [S;(C)] a laugh of pleasure or satisfaction

cho·rus¹ /ˈkɔːrəs‖ˈkorəs/ *n* **1** [GC] a group of people who sing together: *The chorus were very good, weren't they?* **2** [C] a piece of music written to be sung by such a group **3** [GC] a group of dancers, singers, or actors who play a supporting part in a film or show **4** [C] a piece of music played or sung after each group of lines (VERSE) of a song **5** [C] something said by many people at one time: *The minister's speech was met with a chorus of shouts* **6** [C] *tech* **a** (in ancient Greek plays) a group of actors who used poetry and music to explain or give opinions on the action of the play **b** (in Elizabethan plays) a person who makes a speech before, after, or during the play explaining or giving opinions on the action of the play **7 in chorus** all together: *The people shouted in chorus "Long live the king!"*

chorus² *v* [T1,5;(I∅)] to sing or speak at the same time: *The papers all chorused the praises of the president*

chorus girl /ˈ·· ·/ *n* a young woman who sings or dances in a CHORUS¹ (3)

chose /tʃəʊz/ *past t. of* CHOOSE

cho·sen /ˈtʃəʊzən/ *past p. of* CHOOSE

chow¹ /tʃaʊ/ *n* [U] *sl* food

chow² also **chow chow** /ˈ· ·/— *n* a type of dog originally bred in China —see picture at DOG

chow·der /ˈtʃaʊdəʳ/ *n* [U] **1** a thick soup prepared from bits of sea animals (SHELLFISH), vegetables, meat, and often milk **2** a thick soup like this

chow mein /ˌtʃaʊ ˈmeɪn/ *n* [U] a dish in Chinese style made of bits of meat and cooked vegetables served hot, often with cooked NOODLE*s* —compare CHOP SUEY

Christ¹ /kraɪst/ *n* **1** [R;N] also **Jesus Christ**— the man who established Christianity, considered by Christians to be the son of God and to be still alive in heaven where he forms one of the 3 persons of the TRINITY **2** [R; (*the*+R);N] MESSIAH (1)

Christ² *interj infml* **1** also **Jesus Christ, Jesus**— (used before a whole phrase or sentence to show unwelcome surprise): *Christ! I've forgotten the keys!* **2** (used before *no* or *yes* to add force): *Christ, no!*

chris·ten /ˈkrɪsən/ *v* **1** [T1] to make (someone esp. a child) a member of a Christian church by BAPTISM (1) and, typically, the giving of a name: *The baby was christened by the priest* **2** [X1] to give (someone) a name at BAPTISM (1): *We christened our baby John* **3** [T1;X1] to name (esp. a ship) at an official ceremony: *We asked the Queen to christen the ship.|The ship was christened the Queen Mary* **4** [T1] *infml esp. BrE* to use for the first time: *Have you christened your new car yet?*

Chris·ten·dom /ˈkrɪsəndəm/ *n* [U] **1** all Christian people in general **2** *old use* the Christian countries of the world

chris·ten·ing /ˈkrɪsənɪŋ/ *n* [C;U] the Christian ceremony of BAPTISM or of naming a person, usu. a child

Chris·tian¹ /ˈkrɪstʃən, -tɪən/ *n* **1 a** a person who believes in the teachings of Jesus Christ **b** *infml* (*used by and of believers in these teachings*) a good person **2** a person who is a member of a Christian church by BAPTISM (1)

Christian² *adj* **1** [Wa5] believing in or belonging to any of the various branches of Christianity: *The Christian people of England must speak out against this crime* **2** [Wa5] of or related to CHRIST¹ (1), Christianity, or Christians: *"I don't like the way Christian ideas work in practice," said the angry politician* **3** *usu. apprec* following the example of Christ; having qualities such as kindness, generosity, etc.: *He behaved in a Christian way to all, even his enemies*

Christian e·ra /ˌ·· ˈ··/ *n* [*the*+R] the period of history from the birth of Christ to the present day

Chris·ti·an·i·ty /ˌkrɪstiˈænɜ̱ti/ *n* **1** [R] the religion based on the life and teachings of CHRIST¹ (1) **2** [U] the condition or fact of being a follower of any of the various branches of this religion: *I have never doubted his Christianity although he's always been unkind to me* **3** [U] CHRISTENDOM (1)

Christian name /ˈ·· ·/ *n* (of a Christian) FIRST NAME

Christian Sci·ence /ˌ·· ˈ··/ *n* [R] a branch of Christianity including belief in curing illness by means of faith —**-entist** *n*

christ·like /ˈkraɪstlaɪk/ *adj usu. apprec* being like CHRIST¹ (1) in character, spirit, or action

Christ·mas /ˈkrɪsməs/ *n* [C;R] **1** also **Christmas Day** /ˌ·· ˈ·/— a Christian holy day usu. held on December 25th (or in some churches January 6th) in honour of the birth of Christ, usu. kept as a public holiday **2** the period just before, and the 12 days just after, this

Christmas box /ˈ·· ·/ *n not AmE* a small gift of money to the postman, milkman, etc., for their services during the year

Christmas cake /ˈ·· ·/ *n* [C;U] (a) heavy cake containing much dried fruit and usu. having a covering of ornamented hard sugar (ICING), made to be eaten at Christmas —compare CHRISTMAS PUDDING

Christmas card /ˈ·· ·/ *n* an ornamental GREETING CARD sent from one person to another at Christmas

Christmas crack·er /ˌ·· ˈ··/ also **cracker**— *n* a tube of brightly coloured paper which makes a harmless exploding sound when both ends are pulled at the same time, used esp. at Christmas parties

Christmas Eve /ˌ·· ˈ·/ *n* [R] the day, and esp. the evening, before Christmas

Christmas pud·ding /ˌ·· ˈ··/ *n* [C;U] (a) heavy sweet dish (PUDDING) containing much dried fruit and often covered with burning alcohol (BRANDY), served esp. at the end of dinner on Christmas day —compare CHRISTMAS CAKE

Christmas stock·ing /ˌ·· ˈ··/ *n* a stocking (esp. hung by a fireplace or a bed) into which small Christmas presents are put (esp. for children)

Christ·mas·time /ˈkrɪsməstaɪm/ also (*lit*) **Christ·mas·tide** /-taɪd/— *n* [R] the period just before and the 12 days just after Christmas; the Christmas season

Christmas tree /ˈ·· ·/ *n* a real or man-made tree ornamented at Christmas with candles, lights, coloured paper, etc., often brought into the home

chro·mat·ic /krəʊˈmætɪk, krə-/ *adj* **1 a** of or related to colour or colours **b** highly coloured **2** of or related to the musical SCALE⁵ (5) (**chromatic scale** /·ˌ·· ˈ·/) which consists completely of half steps (SEMITONE*s*) —**~ally** *adv* [Wa4]

chrome /krəʊm/ *n* [U] **1** a hard metal combination (ALLOY) of CHROMIUM with other metals, esp. used for covering objects with a thin shiny protective metal plate **2** *infml* CHROMIUM **3** a yellow colouring substance (PIGMENT (1)): *chrome yellow*

chrome steel /ˌ· ˈ·/ *n* [U] a metal combination (ALLOY) of CHROMIUM and steel

chro·mi·um /ˈkrəʊmɪəm/ *n* [U] a blue–white metal that is a simple substance (ELEMENT) found only in combination with other chemicals, used for covering objects with a thin shiny protective plate

chro·mo·some /ˈkrəʊməsəʊm/ *n tech* a threadlike body found in all living cells, which passes on and controls the nature, character, etc., of a young plant, animal, or cell. Each type of animal or plant has a certain number of these, fixed for that type

chron- also **chrono-**— *comb. form* (of) time: CHRONOMETER|CHRONOLOGY

chron·ic /ˈkrɒnɪk‖ˈkrɑ-/ *adj* **1** [B] (of diseases or illnesses) continual; lasting a long time: *a chronic cough* **2** [A] (of a sufferer from a disease or illness) seriously suffering from a disease or illness which has lasted a long time: *a chronic alcoholic* **3** [B] *BrE nonstandard sl* very bad; terrible: *She's got a chronic sense of humour* —**~ally** *adv* [Wa4]

chron·i·cle /ˈkrɒnɪkəl‖ˈkrɑ-/ *n* a record of historical events, arranged in order of time, usu. without any judgment as to their causes, effects, nature, etc.

chronicle² *v* [Wv3;T1] to record as in a CHRONICLE: *Before the 15th century most history students just wanted to chronicle events rather than make judgments about them* —**~r** *n*

chron·o·graph /ˈkrɒnəgrɑːf‖ˈkrɑnəgræf/ *n tech* an instrument for measuring and recording periods of time

chron·o·log·i·cal /ˌkrɒnəˈlɒdʒɪkəl‖ˌkrɑnəˈlɑ-/ *adj* [Wa5] arranged according to the order of time: *The teacher gave the pupils a chronological list of events which in his opinion had caused the First World War* —**~ly** *adv* [Wa4]

chro·nol·o·gy /krəˈnɒlədʒi‖-ˈnɑ-/ *n* **1** [U] the science which measures time and gives dates to events **2** [C] a list or table arranged according to the order of time: *a chronology of man's history since the 10th century* **3** [C] the arrangement of events according to the order of time: *Do you agree with his chronology of events in the 13th century?*

chro·nom·e·ter /krəˈnɒmɪ̈təʳ‖-ˈnɑ-/ *n tech* a very exact clock or other instrument for measuring time, esp. as used for scientific purposes

chrys·a·lis /ˈkrɪsəlɪ̈s/ *n* **chrysalises** /-siːz/ a hard case-like shell in which a PUPA (=an insect in its inactive wormlike stage) is enclosed —compare COCOON and see picture at INSECT

chry·san·the·mum /krɪˈsænθɪ̈məm/ *n* **1** any of various types of garden plant with large showy brightly-coloured flowers **2** a flower of this plant

chub /tʃʌb/ *n* **chub** *or* **chubs** [Wn2] a type of small fish which lives in rivers and lakes but not in sea-water

chub·by /ˈtʃʌbi/ *adj* [Wa1] *not fml* (of animals or people) having a full round usu. pleasing form; slightly fat —**chubbiness** *n* [U]

chuck¹ /tʃʌk/ *v* **1** [D1;X9] *infml* to throw (something), esp. with a short movement of the arms: *Chuck me the ball.*|*Let's chuck all these old papers away!*|(fig.) *Don't be so noisy, or the driver will chuck us off (the bus)* **2** [T1 (IN, UP)] *sl* to give up; leave: *He's decided to chuck his old job (in)* **3 chuck it (in)** *sl* to stop it: *Chuck it or I'll hit you* **4 chuck (someone) under the chin** to touch or STROKE (rub lovingly and gently) under the chin

chuck² *n* **1** [C] a gentle or loving stroke under the chin **2** [*the*+R] *sl* dismissal from a job (in the phrs. **get/give the chuck**): *He gave me the chuck last week: can you find me a new job?*

chuck³ *n* **1** [U] meat, esp. BEEF, taken from the side of an animal just above the top of the front legs **2** [C] an apparatus for holding a tool or a piece of work in a machine

chuck·le¹ /ˈtʃʌkəl/ *v* [Wv3;I∅] to laugh quietly: *I could hear him chuckling to himself as he read that funny article*

chuckle² *n* a quiet laugh

chuck out *v adv* [T1] *infml* **1** [(*of*)] to force (a person) to leave: *The waiter threatened to chuck us out of the restaurant if we got drunk* **2** to throw out; throw away; get rid of; stop using —**chucker-out** /ˌ·· ˈ·/ *n*

chug¹ /tʃʌg/ *n* [S;(C)] a knocking sound of or as if of an engine running slowly: *I heard the chug of the engine as it struggled up the hill*

chug² *v* **-gg-** [L9, esp. ALONG, AWAY] to move while making a knocking sound: *I heard the engine chugging along*

chuk·ker /ˈtʃʌkəʳ/ also **chukka** /-kə/— *n* one of the periods of 7 minutes each into which the game of POLO is divided

chum¹ /tʃʌm/ *n* [C;N] *infml* a good friend, esp. among boys

chum² *v* **-mm-** [I∅ (*with*, TOGETHER)] *BrE old sl* to share a room (with someone): *He's going to chum with a friend next year instead of having a room to himself.*|*They'll be chumming (together) next year*

chum·my /ˈtʃʌmi/ *adj* [Wa1] *infml* friendly or ready to be friends

chump /tʃʌmp/ *n* **1** *sl* a fool **2** a short thick block of wood **3** also **chump chop** /ˈ· ·/— a thick piece (CHOP) of meat with a bone through one end **4 (go) off one's chump** *BrE old sl* (to become) mad: *If you continue to behave like that, people will think you've gone off your chump!*

chum up *v adv* **-mm-** [I∅ (*with*)] *infml* to make friends with: *I've only been here a few days but I've already chummed up with quite a lot of people, so don't worry about me being lonely*

chunk /tʃʌŋk/ *n* **1** *not fml* a short thick piece or lump that is bigger than the pieces into which something is usually cut **2** *infml* a fairly large amount

chunk·y /ˈtʃʌŋki/ *adj* [Wa1] **1** (of people and animals) short and rather fat: *a chunky little man* **2** (of materials, clothes, etc.) having a thick knotted pattern: *She's making her boyfriend a chunky woollen coat for winter* **3** (esp. of food) containing thick solid pieces of food: *chunky* MARMALADE

church¹ /tʃɜːtʃ‖tʃɜrtʃ/ *n* **1** [C] a building made for public Christian worship **2** [U] such a building, esp. when used for religious purposes: *I'm just going to church to see the priest* **3** [U] public Christian worship **4** [*the*+R] the profession of the CLERGY (priests and people employed for religious reasons) of a religious body: *When he was 30 he joined the church and became a priest* **5** [U] religious power (as compared with state power): *Do you agree with the separation of church and state?* **6** [C (*usu. cap.*)] the organization of Christian believers as **a** all the Christian believers in the world **b** the members of any of the various branches of Christianity: *She lived and died a member of the true Church* **c** the body of Christians in a town or area: *Paul went to address the Church at Rome* **7 Established Church** /·ˌ·· ˈ·/ a form of Christianity officially supported by the state

See next page for picture

church² *adj* [Wa5;F] *infml, becoming rare* (in England and Wales) being a member of the established state church: *My uncle's church but none of the rest of us are* —compare CHAPEL²

church³ *v* [Wv5;T1 *usu. pass.*] (in the CHURCH OF ENGLAND) to take (a woman who has just had a child) to a religious service in which God is thanked for the birth of the child: *Very few women are churched today; it's an old custom which is dying out*

church·go·er /ˈtʃɜːtʃˌgəʊəʳ‖-ɜr-/ *n* a person who regularly attends public Christian worship in a church

church·ing /ˈtʃɜːtʃɪŋ‖-ɜr-/ *n* [C;U] (in the CHURCH OF ENGLAND) a religious service in which a woman who has just had a child thanks God for the safe birth of her child

Church of Eng·land /ˌ· · ˈ··/ *n* [*the*+R] the state church which is established by law in England,

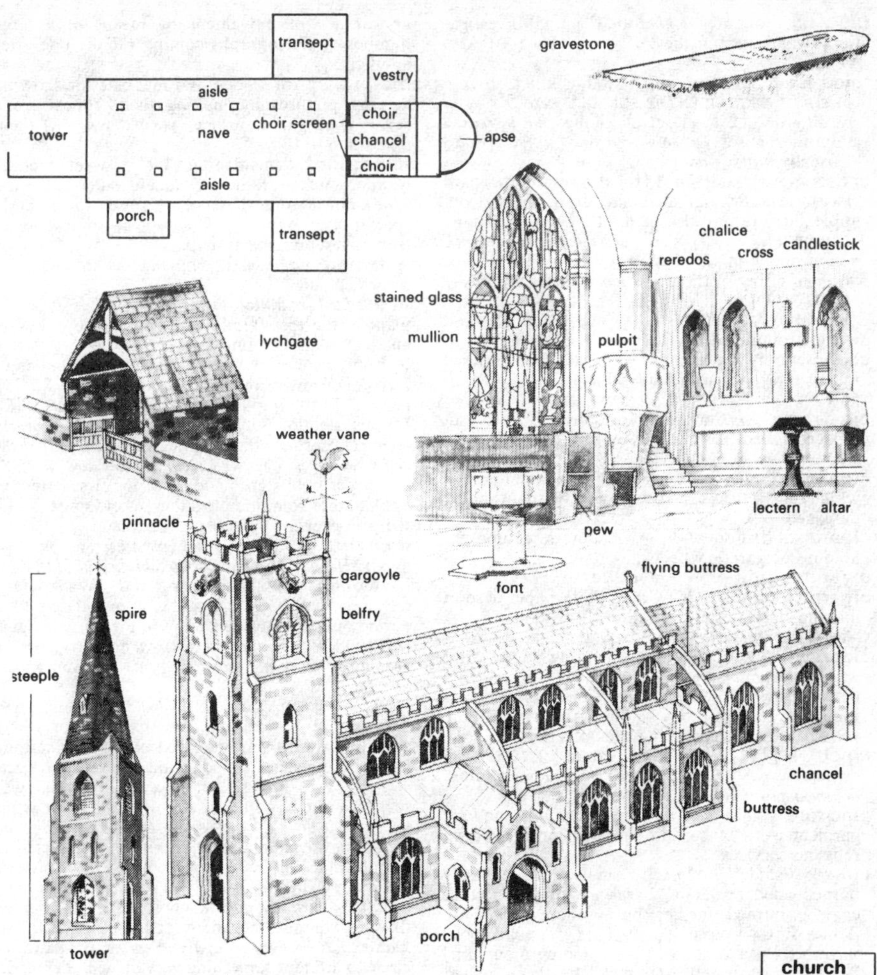

church

was separated from the ROMAN CATHOLIC church in the 16th century, has married priests and BISHOPs, and whose head is the King or Queen

Church of Scot·land /ˌ· · ˈ··/ *n* [*the*+R] the official established PRESBYTERIAN church in Scotland

church·war·den /ˌtʃɜːtʃˈwɔːdn‖ˈtʃɜrtʃwɔrdn/ *n* (in a CHURCH OF ENGLAND church) either of 2 officers elected, by the people who attend church, to be responsible for the church's property and money

church·yard /ˈtʃɜːtʃjɑːd‖ˈtʃɜrtʃjɑrd/ *n* an open space around and belonging to a church, in which dead members of that church can usu. be buried —compare CEMETERY, GRAVEYARD

churl /tʃɜːl‖tʃɜrl/ *n* **1** *derog* a rude person with bad manners **2** *old use* a person of low birth, esp. a PEASANT

churl·ish /ˈtʃɜːlɪʃ‖-ɜr-/ *adj lit derog* bad-tempered —**~ly** *adv* —**~ness** *n* [U]

churn[1] /tʃɜːn‖tʃɜrn/ *n* **1** a container in which milk is moved about violently until it becomes butter **2** *not AmE* a large metal container in which milk is stored or carried from the farm

churn[2] *v* **1** [T1] to make butter by beating (milk) **2** [T1 (UP); I∅] to (cause to) move about violently: *The ship churned the water up as it passed.|My stomach started to churn as soon as we left port*

churn out *v adv* [T1] *infml* to produce a large quantity of (something), as if by machinery: *This factory churns out lots and lots of cars a day*

chute /ʃuːt/ *n* **1** a sloped passage along which something may be passed, dropped, or caused to slide **2** a steep part of a riverbed along which water flows rapidly **3** *infml* PARACHUTE

chut·ney /ˈtʃʌtni/ *n* [U] a sour-tasting mixture of various fruits, hot-tasting seeds, and sugar, which is eaten with other dishes

CI /ˌsiː ˈaɪ/ *abbrev. for:* Channel Islands: *Jersey, CI*

CIA /ˌsiː aɪ ˈeɪ/ *abbrev. for:* the Central Intelligence Agency of the US

ci·ca·da /sɪ̇ˈkɑːdə‖sɪ̇ˈkeɪdə, -ˈkɑ-/ also **ci·ca·la** /sɪ̇ˈkɑːlə/— *n* a type of tropical insect with a large wide head and large transparent wings. It makes a special noise, esp. in hot weather

cic·a·trice /ˈsɪkətrɪs/ also **cic·a·trix** /-trɪks/— *n* **cicatrices** /ˌsɪkəˈtraɪsiːz/ *lit or med* SCAR

ci·ce·ro·ne /ˌsɪsəˈrəʊni, ˌtʃɪtʃə-/ *n* **-roni** /-ˈrəʊniː/ *It & lit* a guide who shows and describes places and objects of interest to tourists and sightseers

CID /ˌsiː aɪ ˈdiː/ *abbrev. for:* the Criminal Investigation Department in the UK —see also SCOTLAND YARD

-cide /saɪd/ *suffix* [*n*→*n*[C;U]] **1** a killer: *It is a powerful* INSECTICIDE.|*The* SUICIDEs *were buried in special graves* **2** (an) act of killing: *the increased* SUICIDE *rate*|MATRICIDE —**-cidal** *suffix* [→*adj*] —**-cidally** *suffix* [→*adv*]

ci·der, cyder /ˈsaɪdəʳ/ *n* **1** [U] also (*esp. AmE*) **hard cider**— *esp. BrE* an alcoholic drink made from apple juice. It may also be used for making a type of VINEGAR **2** [U] also **soft cider**— *esp. AmE* non-alcoholic apple juice **3** [C] a drink, glass, or bottle of either of these: *I'd like 2 ciders and a beer please*

CIF /ˌsiː aɪ ˈef/ *abbrev. for:* Cost, Insurance, and Freight (all included): *The price is £27 CIF*

ci·gar /sɪˈgɑːʳ/ *n* a tightly-packed solid tube-shaped roll of uncut tobacco leaves for smoking —compare CIGARETTE

cig·a·rette, *AmE* also **-ret** /ˌsɪgəˈret/ *n* finely cut tobacco rolled in a narrow tube of thin paper for smoking —compare CIGAR

cigarette case /ˌ··ˈ· ·/ *n* a small usu. metal case in which cigarettes can be carried without being damaged

cigarette hol·der /··ˈ· ˌ··/ *n* a narrow tube for holding a cigarette when smoking it

cigarette light·er /··ˈ· ˌ··/ *n* LIGHTER[2] (2)

cigarette pa·per /··ˈ· ˌ··/ *n* [U] thin paper used in making cigarettes

C-in-C *abbrev. for:* COMMANDER IN CHIEF

cinch[1] /sɪntʃ/ *n* **1** [S] *sl* **a** something done easily: *My examination was a cinch; I'll pass easily* **b** something certain: *It's a cinch that that horse will win the race* **2** [C] *tech* a belt used for fastening the SADDLE (rider's seat) to the back of a horse

cinch[2] *v* [T1] *sl* to make certain of: *The king cinched his party's victory in the election by imprisoning the opposition leaders*

cinc·ture /ˈsɪŋktʃəʳ/ *n tech* the belt round the long garment worn by certain Christian priests during religious services

cin·der /ˈsɪndəʳ/ *n* **1** [C] a small piece of partly burned wood, coal, etc., that is not yet ash and that can be burned further but without producing flames **2** [C] a piece of LAVA (2) (grey solid rock) thrown from a VOLCANO (an exploding mountain) **3** [U] the waste left after metal has been melted from ORE (stone rich in minerals); SLAG

Cin·de·rel·la /ˌsɪndəˈrelə/ *n* a woman or girl whose qualities and abilities have not been recognized: (fig.) *Chemistry is the Cinderella of the sciences in our school: it gets hardly any attention at all*

cin·ders /ˈsɪndəz‖-ərz/ *n* [P] ashes: *Before making the fire remember to empty out yesterday's cinders*

cin·e- /ˈsɪni/ *comb. form esp. BrE* of, for, or related to CINEMATOGRAPHY or the film industry: *cinecamera*|*cinefilm*

cine *n* [U] *infml esp. BrE* CINEMATOGRAPHY

cin·e·ma /ˈsɪnɪ̵mə/ *n* **1** [C] (*AmE* **movie theater**)— *BrE* a theatre in which moving pictures are shown **2** [*the*+R] also (*infml, esp. BrE*) **pictures**, (*esp. AmE*) **movies**— *esp. BrE* a showing of a moving picture: *Let's go to the cinema tonight* **3** [*the*+R] also (*esp. AmE*) **movies**— *esp. BrE* the moving picture industry: *He's worked in the cinema all his life* **4** [*the*+R] also (*esp. AmE*) **movies**— *esp. BrE* the art of making moving pictures: *The cinema is the most exciting and developing art form at present*

cin·e·mat·o·graph /ˌsɪnɪ̵ˈmætəgrɑːf‖-græf/ *n old use esp. BrE* a PROJECTOR or camera used in CINEMATOGRAPHY

cin·e·ma·to·gra·phy /ˌsɪnɪ̵məˈtɒgrəfi‖-ˈtɑ-/ *n* [U] *tech* the art or science of films that give the appearance of movement by means of a large number of photographs coming rapidly one after another

cine-pro·jec·tor /ˈ·· ·ˌ··/ *n* a machine for showing moving pictures by making them appear on a specially-prepared surface (PROJECTing[2] (3) them on a SCREEN[1] (3))

cin·na·mon[1] /ˈsɪnəmən/ *n* **1** [U] sweet-smelling powder made from the tough outer covering (BARK) of a tropical Asian tree, used for giving a special taste to food **2** [C] a type of tropical Asian tree from which this is made

cinnamon[2] *adj, n* [B;U] (having) a light yellowish brown colour

cinque·foil /ˈsɪŋkfɔɪl/ *n* any of various types of plant of the rose family with small yellow flowers and leaves divided into 5 parts

ci·pher[1], **cypher** /ˈsaɪfəʳ/ *n* **1** [C] the number 0; zero **2** [C] any of the numbers from 1 to 9 **3** [C] a person of little importance and no influence **4** [C; U] (a system of) secret writing; CODE: *The government changes the official cipher every day so that the enemy never knows which cipher they are using* **5** *rare* a personal sign made up of the first letters of one's names combined together; MONOGRAM

cipher[2], **cypher** *v* [T1;(IØ)] ENCIPHER

cir·ca /ˈsɜːkə‖ˈsɜr-/ *prep fml* (used esp. with dates) about: *He was born circa 1060 and died in 1118*

cir·ca·di·an /sɜːˈkeɪdɪən‖sɜr-/ *adj* [Wa5;A;(B)] *tech* (esp. of body changes) of or related to a period of about 24 hours (esp. in the phr. **circadian rhythm**): *By studying his circadian* RHYTHMs, *a person can learn at what time of day he works most effectively*

cir·cle[1] /ˈsɜːkəl‖ˈsɜr-/ *n* **1** (a flat round area enclosed by) a curved line that is everywhere equally distant from one fixed point **2** something having the general shape of this line; ring: *a circle of trees* **3** an upper floor in a theatre, usu. with seats set in curved lines: *Are we going to sit in the upper circle or in the* DRESS CIRCLE? **4** [*sometimes pl. with same meaning*] a group of people connected in an informal way because of common interests: *He has a large circle of friends.*|*In political circles there is talk of war* **5** *poet* a chain of events which finishes where it began; CYCLE: *The circle of the seasons has brought us again to spring* **6 square the circle** to attempt something very difficult or impossible —see also GREAT CIRCLE, VICIOUS CIRCLE, FULL CIRCLE, TRAFFIC CIRCLE

circle[2] *v* [Wv3] **1** [T1] to draw or form a circle around (something): *The teacher circled the pupils' spelling mistakes in red ink* **2** [T1] to move or travel in a circle around (something): *The plane circled the airport before landing* **3** [IØ (*around, round,* AROUND, ROUND)] to move or travel in a circle: *The birds circled around in the air*

cir·clet /ˈsɜːklɪ̵t‖ˈsɜr-/ *n* a narrow round band as of gold, silver, jewels, etc., worn (esp. by women) on the head, arms, or neck as an ornament

cir·cuit /ˈsɜːkɪ̵t‖ˈsɜr-/ *n* **1** [C] *tech* a closed curve such as a circle or ELLIPSE **2** [C] *tech* the area enclosed by this **3** [C] a complete ring: *We made/did the circuit of the old city walls* **4** [C] the complete circular path of an electric current: *A break in the circuit had caused the lights to go out* **5** [C] a set of electrical parts or apparatus intended for some special purpose: *a television circuit* —see picture at ELECTRICITY **6** [C; *on*+U] a regular journey from place to place made by a judge to hear law cases: *The judge is on circuit for most of the year* **7** [C] the area covered by this journey: *He has the smallest circuit in the country* **8** [C] (in some religious organizations) an area in which the churches share religious leaders —compare DIOCESE **9** [C] *infml* an association of related groups, such as teams; LEAGUE[2] (1) **10** [GC; *on*+U] a group of establishments offering the same films, plays, etc. —see also CLOSED CIRCUIT TELEVISION, SHORT CIRCUIT

circuit break·er /ˈ·· ˌ··/ *n tech* a SWITCH or other apparatus which interrupts an electric current when the need arises

cir·cu·i·tous /sɜːˈkjuːɪ̈təs‖sɜr-/ *n fml* going a long way round instead of in a straight line: *the river's circuitous course* —**~ly** *adv*

cir·cu·lar[1] /ˈsɛːkjʊləʳ‖ˈsɜrkjə-/ *adj* **1** round; being shaped like or nearly like a circle **2** forming or moving in a circle **3** going a long way round; not direct: *Stop giving me circular explanations and tell me what really happened* **4** intended to be sent to a large number of people

circular[2] *n* a printed advertisement, paper, or notice intended to be given to a large number of people for them to read: *Did you see that circular from the government telling us about their attack on high prices?*

cir·cu·lar·ize, -ise /ˈsɜːkjʊləraɪz‖ˈsɜrkjə-/ *v* [T1] to send CIRCULARs[2] to (a group of people)

circular saw /ˌ··· ˈ·/ *n* a power-driven tool which can cut wood very quickly by means of the sharp teeth on its round metal blade

cir·cu·late /ˈsɜːkjʊleɪt‖ˈsɜrkjə-/ *v* **1** [IØ;T1] to (cause to) move or flow along a closed path: *Blood circulates round the body.|The heart circulates blood round the body* **2** [IØ;T1] to (cause to) spread widely: *The news of the enemy's defeat quickly circulated round the town.|The unions have started to circulate false stories about the government* **3** [IØ] *infml* to move about freely: *The prince circulated from group to group at the party* —**-latory** /-lətəri‖-tori/ *adj*

circulating li·bra·ry /ˈ···· ˌ···/ *n* a library from which books may be borrowed by people who pay regularly for the right to do so

cir·cu·la·tion /ˌsɜːkjʊˈleɪʃən‖ˌsɜrkjə-/ *n* **1** [U;C] the flow of gas or liquid around a closed system, esp. the movement of blood through the body: *A person with poor circulation ought to see his doctor regularly* **2** [U] the movement of something such as news or money from place to place or from person to person: *I wanted to buy his book but it's been taken out of circulation* —compare TRAFFIC **3** [S9 (*of*)] the average number of copies of a newspaper, magazine, book, etc., sold or read over a certain time: *This magazine has a circulation of 400,000 mainly in the North of England*

cir·cu·la·to·ry sys·tem /ˈsɜːkjʊlətəri ˌsɪstɪ̈m‖ˈsɜrkjələˌtori-/ *n* the system of blood, blood vessels, and heart, concerned with the movement (CIRCULATION (1)) of blood round the body

cir·cum- /ˌsɜːkəm‖ˌsɜr-/ *prefix* around; about: *circumference|to* CIRCUMNAVIGATE *the world*

cir·cum·cise /ˈsɜːkəmsaɪz‖ˈsɜr-/ *v* [T1] to cut off the skin (FORESKIN) at the end of the sex organ of (a man) or part of the sex organ (CLITORIS) of (a woman)

cir·cum·ci·sion /ˌsɜːkəmˈsɪʒən‖ˌsɜr-/ *n* [C;U] the act of circumcising (CIRCUMCISE), esp. as part of a Jewish or Muslim religious ceremony

cir·cum·fer·ence /səˈkʌmfərəns‖sər-/ *n* **1** the length round the outside of a circle; distance round a round object: *The earth's circumference is nearly 25,000 miles* —see picture at GEOMETRY **2** the line round the outside edge of a figure, object, or place; PERIPHERY —**-ential** /səˌkʌmfəˈrenʃəl‖sər-/ *adj* [Wa5]

cir·cum·flex /ˈsɜːkəmfleks‖ˈsɜr-/ *n, adj* [Wa5] ((of) a mark (ACCENT (2)) put above a letter to show pronunciation) being the mark over ê —compare GRAVE[3], ACUTE (7)

cir·cum·lo·cu·tion /ˌsɜːkəmləˈkjuːʃən‖ˌsɜr-/ *n fml* **1** [U] the use of a large number of unnecessary words to express an idea needing fewer words, esp. when trying to avoid directly answering a difficult question **2** [C] an example of this; way of saying something that is longer than necessary —**-tory** /-ˈlɒkjətəri‖-ˈlɑkjətori/ *adj*

cir·cum·nav·i·gate /ˌsɜːkəmˈnævɪ̈geɪt‖ˌsɜr-/ *v* [T1] *fml* to sail completely round (esp. the earth) —**-gation** /ˌsɜːkəmnævɪ̈ˈgeɪʃən‖ˌsɜr-/ [C;U]

cir·cum·scribe /ˈsɜːkəmskraɪb‖ˈsɜr-/ *v* [T1] **1** [Wv5] *fml* to keep within narrow limits; limit: *His activities have been severely circumscribed since his serious illness* **2** *tech* to draw a circle passing through all the outside corner points of (a GEOMETRICAL figure): *The teacher asked the pupils to circumscribe the square* **3** [Wv5] *tech* (of a line) to pass through all the outside corner points of (a GEOMETRICAL figure): *This square is circumscribed by the circle*

cir·cum·scrip·tion /ˌsɜːkəmˈskrɪpʃən‖ˌsɜr-/ *n* [U; (C)] *fml or tech* the act of circumscribing or the state of having been CIRCUMSCRIBED (1,2,3)

cir·cum·spect /ˈsɜːkəmspekt‖ˈsɜr-/ *adj fml* **1** (of a person) careful; making a careful consideration of the state of affairs before acting; CAUTIOUS **2** (of actions) done after much thought; not risky; CAUTIOUS —**~ly** *adv* —**~ion** /ˌsɜːkəmˈspekʃən‖ˌsɜr-/ *n* [U]

cir·cum·stance /ˈsɜːkəmstæns, -stəns‖ˈsɜr-/ *n* **1** [C] a fact, detail, condition, or event concerned with and usu. influencing another event, person, or course of action: *The police want to consider each circumstance in turn* **2** [U] formal usu. official ceremony: *I love the pomp and circumstance of these great ceremonies of church and state*

cir·cum·stances /ˈsɜːkəmstænsɪ̈z, -stənsɪ̈z‖ˈsɜr-/ *n* [P] **1** the state of a person's material affairs, esp. with regard to the amount of money he has: *He seems to be in easy circumstances since he had his pay increase* **2** the state of affairs, esp. the sum of all conditions, facts, or events which are beyond one's control: *The circumstances forced me to accept a very low price when I sold the house* **3 in/under no circumstances** never; regardless of events: *Under no circumstances will there be wage control while I am head of the government!* **4 in/under the circumstances** because of the conditions; because things are as they are: *I wanted to leave quickly but under the circumstances (my uncle had just died) I decided to stay another night*

cir·cum·stan·tial /ˌsɜːkəmˈstænʃəl‖ˌsɜr-/ *adj* **1** *fml* of or dependent on CIRCUMSTANCEs (1) **2** *fml* (esp. of a description) containing all the details **3** *law* (of information concerning a crime) worth knowing but not directly important; INCIDENTAL (esp. in the phr. **circumstantial evidence**) —**~ly** *adv*

cir·cum·vent /ˌsɜːkəmˈvent‖ˌsɜr-/ *v* [T1] **1** to defeat, esp. as the result of cleverness; FRUSTRATE: *The king tried to circumvent his enemies in the government, but his cleverly prepared plan failed and he lost his crown* **2** to avoid by or as if by passing round: *Don't try to circumvent the new tax laws: it's better to pay honestly and avoid punishment* —**~ion** *n* [U]

cir·cus /ˈsɜːkəs‖ˈsɜr-/ *n* **1** a group of performers who travel from place to place with their acts, earning money by performing for the public **2** a public performance by such a group, with various acts of skill and daring by people and animals **3** a tent-covered place with seats for the public round one or more rings in the middle, in which this performance takes place **4** *BrE* a round open area where a number of streets join together: *Oxford Circus* **5** *derog* a noisy badly behaved meeting or other such activity **6** (in Ancient Rome) a round or 4-sided space surrounded by seats for the public in which sports, races, etc., took place

cirque /sɜːk‖sɜrk/ *n tech* a steep-sided bowl-shaped hollow basin on a mountain side, originally formed by ice

cir·rho·sis /sɨ̣ˈrəʊsɨ̣s/ *n* [U] *med* a serious disease of esp. the LIVER (=an important body organ), which often leads to death

cir·rus /ˈsɪrəs/ *n* [U] a type of very light feathery white cloud made of very small drops of frozen water, usu. at a height of 20–40,000 feet above the earth's surface

cis·sy /ˈsɪsi/ *n* [C; (*you*) N] *BrE derog infml* SISSY

cis·tern /ˈsɪstən‖-ərn/ *n* a container with a pipe leading in and out, used in the garden for storing rainwater or in the house as part of the system which washes (FLUSHes) body waste from the TOILET —see picture at BATHROOM

cit·a·del /ˈsɪtədl, -del/ *n* **1** a strong heavily-armed fort, usu. commanding a city, built to be a last place of safety and defence in time of war **2** a very heavily-armed and strongly defended place; STRONGHOLD (1); BASTION: (fig.) *Our country has become a citadel of freedom in the modern world*

ci·ta·tion /saɪˈteɪʃən/ *n* **1** [C] an official call (SUMMONS) to appear before a court of law **2** [C] a formal statement of a person's qualities, esp. bravery in battle **3** [U] the act of citing (CITE (2)) **4** [C] *tech* a short passage taken from something written or spoken by someone else; QUOTATION: *People who write dictionaries use citations to study or show the meaning of words*

cite /saɪt/ *v* [T1] **1** [(*for*)] to call (someone) to appear before a court of law; SUMMONS: *He was cited for* CONTEMPT OF COURT **2** to mention (a passage written or spoken by someone else) or (the person who wrote or spoke such a passage); QUOTE: *It's no use citing the Bible to someone who doesn't believe in God* **3** [(*for*)] to officially declare (someone or something) worthy of praise: *The soldier was cited by the king for his bravery* **4** to mention, esp. as an example in a statement, argument, etc.: *The minister cited the latest crime figures as proof of the need for more police*

cit·i·zen /ˈsɪtɨ̣zən/ *n* **1** a person who lives in a particular city or town, esp. one who has certain voting or other rights in that town **2 a** a person who is a member of a particular country by birth or NATURALIZATION (=being officially allowed to become a member) **b** a person who belongs to and gives his loyalty to a particular country and who expects protection from it: *She's a British citizen but lives in India*

cit·i·zen·ry /ˈsɪtɨ̣zənri/ *n* [GU] the whole body of citizens

cit·i·zen·ship /ˈsɪtɨ̣zənʃɪp/ *n* [U] the state of being a citizen: *Citizenship brings duties as well as rights*

cit·ric ac·id /ˌsɪtrɪk ˈæsɨ̣d/ *n* [U] a type of weak acid that is found in some fruits, such as oranges and LEMONs

cit·ron /ˈsɪtrən/ *n* **1** [C] a type of pale-yellow thick-skinned fruit like the LEMON but larger and less sour **2** [C] the type of small tree on which this fruit grows **3** [U] the skin of this fruit preserved in sugar and used, when baking, for giving a special taste to cakes

cit·rus[1] /ˈsɪtrəs/ also **citrus tree** /ˈ·· ·/— *n* any of various types of prickly tree that never lose their leaves, grown in warm countries for their juicy fruits

citrus[2], *BrE* also **-trous** *adj* [Wa5] (of fruits) soft and juicy with a sour or sour-sweet taste; coming from a CITRUS: *I love eating citrus fruits, especially oranges*

cit·y /ˈsɪti/ *n* **1** a usu. large and important group of houses, buildings, etc., esp. with a centre where amusements can be found and business goes on. It is usu. larger and more important than a town, and in Britain it will usually have a CATHEDRAL **2** [*usu. sing.*] all the people who live in such a place

City *n* [*the*+R] the influential British centre for money matters and for the buying and selling of business shares, which is a part of London —compare WALL STREET

city fa·ther /ˌ·· ˈ··/ *n* [*usu. pl.*] *pomp esp. AmE* a member of the governing body of a city

city hall /ˌ·· ˈ·/ *n esp. AmE* **1** [C] a public building used for a city's local government offices and meetings **2** [R] the local government of the city: *He had to fight city hall before he was allowed to build his new house* —compare TOWN HALL

city-state /ˌ·· ˈ·‖ˈ·· ·, ˌ·· ˈ·/ *n* (esp. in former times) a city which, with the surrounding country area, forms an independent state: *Athens was one of the most powerful city-states of ancient Greece*

civ·et /ˈsɪvɨ̣t/ *n* [U] **1** a strong-smelling liquid produced from near the sexual organs of the CIVET CAT and used in making PERFUME (=pleasant smelling liquid) **2** [C] CIVET CAT

civet cat /ˈ·· ·/ *n* a small long-bodied short-legged catlike animal usu. found in Asia or Africa

civ·ic /ˈsɪvɪk/ *adj* **1** of a city or town: *The president's visit was the most important civic event of the year* **2** of a citizen: *civic pride|civic duties*

civ·ics /ˈsɪvɪks/ *n* [U] a social science dealing with the rights and duties of citizens, the way government works, etc.

civ·ies /ˈsɪviz/ *n* CIVVIES

civ·il /ˈsɪvəl/ *adj* **1** [Wa5] of, belonging to, or consisting of the general population; not military or religious: *The soldiers thought it would be a long time before civil government would be re-established* **2** [Wa5] of or belonging to all citizens: *The judge ordered that the prisoner should lose his civil rights* **3** [Wa5] (of law) dealing with the rights of private citizens; concerned with judging private quarrels between people rather than with criminal offences: *It was a civil case so there was no question of him being sent to prison* **4** [Wa2] polite enough to be acceptable, esp. if not friendly: *Try to be civil to her, even if you don't like her.|Keep a civil tongue in your head!* (=stop speaking rudely) —see also CIVILLY

civil de·fence /ˌ·· ·ˈ·/ *n* [U] the protection of the population of a country against military attack, esp. from the air, usu. carried out by an official organization of citizens (**civil defence corps**) who are not in the armed forces

civil dis·o·be·di·ence /ˌ·· ··ˈ···/ *n* [U] a non-violent way of forcing the government to change its position by refusing to pay taxes, obey laws, etc.: *If the government does not change its unpopular plans there'll be an increase in civil disobedience*

civil en·gi·neer·ing /ˌ·· ··ˈ··/ *n* [U] the planning, building, and repair of public works, such as roads, bridges, large public buildings, etc.

ci·vil·i·an /sɨ̣ˈvɪlɪən/ *n, adj* [Wa5] (a person) not of the armed forces: *Does Ruritania have a civilian or a military government?*

ci·vil·i·ty /sɨ̣ˈvɪlɨ̣ti/ *n* **1** [U] politeness; the quality of having good manners; helpfulness; COURTESY **2** [C] an act or expression of politeness, helpfulness, COURTESY, etc.

civ·i·li·za·tion, -sation /ˌsɪvəl-aɪˈzeɪʃən‖-vəl-ɨ̣ˈzeɪ-/ *n* **1** [U] an advanced stage of human social development with a high level of art, religion, science, government, etc., and a written language

2 [C] the type of advanced society of a particular time or place: *The history student hoped to compare the civilizations of ancient China and Japan* **3** [U] *infml* modern society with all its comforts **4** [U] the act of civilizing or of being civilized: *The civilization of these tribes will not take a long time*

civ·i·lize, -lise /ˈsɪvəl-aɪz/ *v* [T1;(I∅)] **1** to (cause to) come from a lower stage of development to an (esp. industrially) highly developed stage of social organization: *The Romans hoped to civilize all the tribes of Europe and thus make them want to join their empire* **2** [Wa4] *not fml* to (cause to) improve in education and manners: *Under the civilizing influence of the great city, the country boy soon became a gentleman*

civil law /ˌ·· ˈ·/ *n* [U] **1** the body of law concerned with judging private quarrels between people and dealing with the rights of private citizens, rather than with military or criminal cases **2** also **Roman Law**— the body of law belonging to Ancient Rome and the modern systems of law based upon it —compare COMMON LAW (1) . **3** the law of a particular state as opposed to other kinds of law, such as international law —compare COMMON LAW, CANON LAW

civil lib·er·ty /ˌ·· ˈ···/ *n* [U;C *usu. pl.*] complete freedom of opinion, thought, speech, action, etc., so long as this does not harm other people —compare CIVIL RIGHTS

civil list /ˈ·· ·/ *n* (in Britain) a sum of money voted yearly by Parliament to the King or Queen as head of state, and to certain other people

civ·il·ly /ˈsɪvəl-i/ *adv* **1** politely; helpfully; in a CIVIL (4) manner: *He civilly offered his seat to an old lady* **2** in accordance with CIVIL LAW (1,3): *The judge agreed that since no one had seen her husband for 7 years he was civilly dead*

civil mar·riage /ˌ·· ˈ··/ *n* **1** [C] also **civil ceremony** /ˌ·· ˈ····/— a marriage ceremony performed in a government office by a government official rather than in a church by a priest **2** [C] a marriage begun with such a ceremony: *Their civil marriage lasted many years* **3** [U] the practice of getting married in such a way: *Civil marriage is increasing in Britain*

civil rights /ˌ·· ˈ·/ *n* [P] the nonpolitical rights, such as freedom, equality, etc., which belong to a person because he is a citizen and without regard to his race, religion, colour, sex, etc.: *Do blacks and whites have the same civil rights in your country?|Are there equal civil rights for men and women?* —compare CIVIL LIBERTY

civil ser·vant /ˌ·· ˈ··/ *n* a person employed in the CIVIL SERVICE —see OFFICER (USAGE)

civil ser·vice /ˌ·· ˈ··/ *n* **1** [*the*+R;(C)] all the various departments of the esp. national government except the armed forces, law courts, and religious organizations: *She works in the civil service and got her job through a civil service examination* **2** [GU] all the people who are employed in this: *The civil service ought to obey the elected government*

civil war /ˌ·· ˈ·/ *n* [C;U] (a) war between opposing groups of people from the same country fought within that country

civ·vies, civies /ˈsɪviz/ *n* [P] *sl* clothes worn by ordinary people as opposed to a military uniform

civ·vy street /ˈsɪvi striːt/ *n* [R] *sl now rare* (*often caps.*) the life of ordinary people as opposed to life in the armed forces: *"I'll be glad to get back to civvy street," said the soldier*

clack /klæk/ *v* **1** [I∅;T1] to (cause to) make one or more sudden quick sounds: *The teacher told the children to stop clacking their pencils* **2** [I∅] *sl* to talk quickly and continuously; CHATTER: *Don't pay attention to clacking tongues* **3** [I∅] CLUCK —**clack** *n* [S]

clad /klæd/ *adj* [Wa5;F9, esp. *in*] *lit* (*often in comb.*) covered; clothed: *The old lady was clad in a fur coat.|The mountain was clad in mist.|ill-/poorly-clad|an armour-clad ship*

claim¹ /kleɪm/ *v* **1** [I∅ (*on, for*); T1] to ask for or demand (a title, property, money, etc.) as the rightful owner or as one's right: *Did you claim on the insurance after your car accident?* **2** [T1] to take (a title, property, money, etc.) as the rightful owner: *The prince hoped to claim the English crown with the help of a foreign army* **3** [T1] to call for; deserve; need; REQUIRE (often in the phr. **claim attention**): *This difficulty claims our undivided attention* **4** [T3.5a] to declare to be true; state esp. in the face of opposition; MAINTAIN (5): *Jean claims to own a car but I don't believe her.|The prince claimed (that) he was the lawful King of England*

claim² *n* **1** [C (*for, on*)] a demand for something as one's own by right: *The government would not even consider his claim for money* **2** [C (*to, on*)] a right to something: *The poor have a claim to our sympathy* **3** [C,C3,5] a statement of something as fact: *The government's claim that war was necessary was clearly mistaken.|His claim to know the answer was not believed* **4** [C] something claimed, esp. an area of land **5** [C] a sum of money claimed, esp. from an insurance company **6 jump a claim** to take land that another person has claimed as his own —see also STAKE **a claim, claim** DAMAGES **7 lay claim to** to state one's right to be owner of: *He laid claim to his father's crown*

clai·mant /ˈkleɪmənt/ *n* [(*to*)] *fml or law* a person who makes a claim

clair·voy·ance /kleəˈvɔɪəns‖kleər-/ *n* [U] the supposed power of seeing and understanding objects and events not directly present to the senses

clair·voy·ant /kleəˈvɔɪənt‖kleər-/ *adj, n* (of or related to the powers of) a person who has the power of CLAIRVOYANCE

clam¹ /klæm/ *n* **1** any of various types of soft-bodied sea animals with a double shell (BIVALVE*s*), that live in sand or mud —see picture at MOLLUSC **2** *sl* a quiet secretive person

clam² *v* **-mm-** *esp. AmE* **go clamming** to gather CLAM*s*¹ (1), esp. by digging in the sand or mud —see also CLAM UP

clam·bake /ˈklæmbeɪk/ *n esp. AmE* **1** an informal meal (PICNIC) by the sea, esp. one where CLAM*s*¹ (1) and other things are cooked together in a special way and eaten **2** *sl* a noisy, gay, or high-spirited event, esp. **a** a social party **b** a political meeting

clam·ber¹ /ˈklæmbəʳ/ *v* [L9 (ABOUT), esp. *over*] to climb usu. using both feet and hands and usu. with difficulty or effort: *Stop clambering (about) over my new furniture*

clamber² *n* [S] a difficult usu. rough climb

clam·my /ˈklæmi/ *adj* [Wa1] being unpleasantly sticky, DAMP (=slightly wet), and usu. cold: *clammy hands/weather* —**-mily** *adv* —**-miness** *n* [U]

clam·or·ous /ˈklæmərəs/ *adj* marked by confused noise and shouting or by loud demands and complaints: *The clamorous demand of opposition politicians was met by silence from the government* —**~ly** *adv*

clam·our¹, *AmE* **-or** /ˈklæməʳ/ *n* [C *usu. sing.*] **1** a loud continuous usu. confused noise or shouting; DIN: *a clamour of voices/of bells* **2** [(*for*)] a continuous loud strong demand or complaint: *In spite of the public clamour for lower taxes the government decided not to call an election*

clamour², *AmE* **-or** *v* **1** [I∅] to make a CLAMOUR¹ (1) **2** [I∅ (*for*); T1,3,5] to express (a demand) continually, loudly, and strongly: *The baby is clamouring to be fed*

clamp¹ /klæmp/ *n* **1** an apparatus for fastening or holding things firmly together, usu. consisting of 2 parts that can be moved nearer together by turning a screw **2** a band of metal for tightening or holding 2 or more things firmly together, used esp. at sea

clamp² *v* [X9, esp. TOGETHER] to fasten with a CLAMP¹: *Clamp these 2 pieces of wood together*

clamp³ *n tech* a pile of vegetables, esp. potatoes, stored under a covering of earth

clamp·down /ˈklæmpdaʊn/ *n infml* a sudden usu. official limitation or prevention of doing or saying something: *The government has decided that a clampdown on the sale of foreign cars is to the country's advantage*

clamp down *v adv* [IØ (*on*)] *infml* to become more firm; make limits: *The police are going to clamp down on criminal activity in this area*

clam·shell /ˈklæmʃel/ *n* either of the 2 shells of a CLAM¹ (1)

clam up *v adv* **-mm-** [IØ] *sl* to become silent: *She clammed up whenever I mentioned her husband*

clan /klæn/ *n* [GC] **1** (esp. in the Scottish HIGHLANDS) a group of families, all originally descended from one family; tribe **2** *humor* a large family

clan·des·tine /klænˈdestɨn/ *adj* done secretly or privately often for an unlawful reason —**~ly** *adv* —**~ness** *n* [U]

clang¹ /klæŋ/ *v* [IØ;T1] to (cause to) make a loud ringing sound, such as when metal is struck: *The metal tool clanged when it hit the ground* —**clang** *n* [S]

clang·er /ˈklæŋəʳ/ *n BrE sl* **1** a very noticeable mistake or unfortunate remark **2 drop a clanger** to make such a mistake or remark: *It's just like you to drop a clanger in front of the president by calling her "sir"!*

clan·gor, *BrE* also **-gour** /ˈklæŋəʳ/ *n* [(*the*) S] a loud long sound, such as when pieces of metal are struck together: *We could hear the clangor of the men's hammers even with the windows closed* —**~ous** *adj* —**~ously** *adv*

clank¹ /klæŋk/ *v* [IØ;(T1)] to (cause to) make a short loud sound, like that of a heavy moving metal chain: *The prisoners' ankle chains clanked as they walked* —**clank** *n* [S]

clan·nish /ˈklænɪʃ/ *adj often derog.* (of a group of people) having the habit of keeping together as a group, esp. supporting each other against those from outside —**~ly** *adv* —**~ness** *n* [U]

clans·man /ˈklænzmən/ *n* **-men** /mən/ a member of a CLAN

clap¹ /klæp/ *v* **-pp-** **1** [T1 (TOGETHER); IØ] to strike (one's hands) together with a quick movement and loud sound: *The teacher clapped to attract the class's attention* **2** [IØ] to show one's approval by doing this; APPLAUD (1): *The people in the theatre enjoyed the play and clapped loudly* **3** [X9, esp. *on*] to strike lightly with the open hand usu. in a friendly manner: *He clapped his son on the back* **4** [X9] *infml* to put, place, or send usu. quickly and effectively: *The judge clapped the criminal in prison* **5 clap eyes on** *BrE infml* to see (someone or something): *It's many years since I clapped eyes on him*

clap² *n* **1** [C] a loud explosive sound: *a clap of thunder* **2** [S] the sounds of hands being CLAPped¹ (1) **3** [S (*on*)] a light friendly hit, usu. on the back, with an open hand: *He gave me a clap on the back and invited me for a drink*

clap³ *n* [*the*+R] *euph sl* the disease GONORRHEA

clap·board /ˈklæpbɔːd‖ˈklæbərd, ˈklæpbord/ *n* [U] *AmE* WEATHERBOARD (1): *a clapboard house in America*

clap on *v adv* **-pp-** [T1] *infml* to put (something) on quickly: *He clapped his hat on and ran out*

clapped-out /ˌ· ˈ·◂/ *adj infml esp. BrE* **1** [F] (of a person) very tired: *I feel really clapped-out tonight after working all day* **2** [Wa5;B] (of a thing) old and worn out: *She bought a clapped-out old car*

clap·per /ˈklæpəʳ/ *n* **1** the hammerlike object hung inside a bell which strikes the bell to make it ring **2** an apparatus that makes a repeated loud noise: *Many farmers use clappers to stop birds eating the crops* **3** *sl* the tongue of a person who talks a lot **4** a person or thing that CLAPs¹ (1,2)

clap·per·board /ˈklæpəbɔːd‖-ərbord/ *n* (when starting to film a scene for the cinema) a board on which the details of the scene to be filmed are written, held up in front of the camera

clap·pers /ˈklæpəz‖-ərz/ *n* **run like the clappers** *BrE infml* to run very fast, often in order to escape

clap·trap /ˈklæptræp/ *n* [U] *infml* **1** empty, insincere, and worthless speech or writing intended only to win praise and attention **2** nonsense; foolish talk

claque /klæk/ *n* a group of people hired to APPLAUD (=show approval by making a noise with the hands) at the end of a performance in a theatre or a political meeting

clar·et¹ /ˈklærət/ *n* [U] red wine, esp. from the Bordeaux area of France

claret² *adj, n* [B;U] (being) a deep purplish red colour

clar·i·fi·ca·tion /ˌklærɨfɨˈkeɪʃən/ *n* [C;U] (an example of) the act or action of CLARIFYing (1): *We need more clarification of your plans before we can promise to support you*

clar·i·fy /ˈklærɨfaɪ/ *v* **1** [IØ;T1] to (cause to) become clearer and more easily understood: *When will the government clarify its position on equal pay for women?* **2** [T1] to make (a liquid, butter, etc.) clear or pure by removing unwanted substances

clar·i·net /ˌklærɨˈnet/ *n* [C] any of a number of long tubelike usu. wooden musical instruments, played by blowing through —see picture at WIND INSTRUMENT

clar·i·net·tist, -netist /ˌklærɨˈnetɨst/ *n* a person who plays the CLARINET

clar·i·on /ˈklærɪən/ *n* **1** a type of instrument used in former times for making a loud clear very high sound and played by blowing **2** the sound made when this instrument is blown: (fig.) *the clarion call of duty*

clar·i·ty /ˈklærɨti/ *n* [U] clearness: *clarity of thinking*

clarts /klɑːts‖klɑrts/ *n* [U] *NE & ScotE* mud; dirt when wet —**clarty** *adj* [Wa1]

clash¹ /klæʃ/ *v* **1** [IØ (*with*)] to come into opposition: *The enemy armies clashed near the border.*| *Those colours she's wearing clash* (=don't match) **2** [IØ (*with*)] (of events) to be at the same time on the same date and therefore cause difficulty: *Her wedding clashed with my examination so I couldn't go* **3** [IØ;T1 (TOGETHER)] to (cause to) make a loud confused noise: *Mother clashed 2 pans together to wake us up*

clash² *n* **1** [S] a loud confused noise: *The soldiers were woken by the clash of weapons* **2** [C] an example of opposition or disagreement: *clash of interests* **3** [C (*between*)] a fight; battle: *A border clash between the 2 armies started the war*

clasp¹ /klɑːsp‖klæsp/ *n* **1** [C] a usu. metal fastener for holding 2 things or parts of one thing together: *The clasp on his belt had broken, so he had to hold his trousers up* **2** [C *usu. sing.*] **a** a tight firm hold, esp.

by the hand; GRIP **b** a tight holding of the body, esp. by someone's arms; EMBRACE

clasp² *v* [T1] **1** to take or seize firmly; enclose and hold, esp. with the fingers or arms: *He clasped the money in his hands* **2** [(TOGETHER)] to fasten with a CLASP¹ (1)

clasp knife /ˈ· ·/ *n* a knife which has a blade or blades that fold into the handle; JACK KNIFE

class¹ /klɑːs‖klæs/ *n* **1** [U] the fact that there are different social groups with different social and political positions and points of view: *Class differences can divide a nation.|Is education class-based?* **2** [GC9 *sometimes pl. with sing. meaning*] a social group whose members have the same political, social, and ECONOMIC position and rank: *Are the ruling classes the enemies of the people?|lower-class life|the upper class* —see also MIDDLE CLASS, WORKING CLASS **3** [C] a division of people or things according to rank, behaviour, etc. **4** [C] a division of living things (such as MAMMALs) below a PHYLUM and usu. including several ORDERs¹ (13) **5** [C] *not AmE* a division of university degrees or examination results, according to their quality: *What class (of degree) did you get: first, second, or third?* **6** [C] (in education) a group of pupils or students taught together **7** [C;U] (in education) a period of time during which pupils or students are taught: *What time does the next class begin?* **8** [C] *esp. AmE* a number of pupils or students in a school or university doing the same course in the same year: *We were both members of the class of (19)68* **9** [C] a level of quality of travelling conditions on a train, plane, boat, etc.: *(a) first-class (ticket) to Birmingham, please* **10** [U] *apprec infml* the quality that makes one look as though one has high social rank: *I like the look of that girl; she's got real class*

class² *v* [T1] **1** to put into a class; CLASSIFY **2** [(*as*)] *infml* to consider: *I class that as wickedness*

class-con·scious /ˌ· ˈ··◂/ *adj* **1** actively conscious of belonging to a particular social class: *Don't be class-conscious: accept people at their true worth* **2** believing in and actively conscious of a struggle between classes: *The class-conscious workers will destroy the old society and build a new one* —**~ness** *n* [U]

clas·sic¹ /ˈklæsɪk/ *adj* [Wa5;A] **1** having the highest quality; of the first or highest class or rank **2** serving as a standard, model, or guide; well known, esp as the best example **3** of or belonging to an established set of artistic or scientific standards or methods with a long history; well known in the stated way: *a classic example of love at first sight*

classic² *n* **1** a piece of literature or art, a writer, or an artist of the first rank and of lasting importance: *Shakespeare's plays were all classics.|(fig.) That joke's a classic; it really is very funny* **2** a famous event usu. with a long history, esp. (in horse races) one of the 5 chief English flat races

clas·si·cal /ˈklæsɪkəl/ *adj* **1** (*sometimes cap.*) being in accordance with ancient Greek or Roman models in literature or art or with later systems and standards based on them; simple but good; influenced by CLASSICISM **2** [Wa5] (of music) put together and arranged (COMPOSEd) with serious artistic intentions; having an attraction that lasts over a long period of time (as opposed to popular or FOLK music): *Bach and Beethoven wrote classical music.|the classical music of India* **3** [Wa5] (of music, esp. that before 1800) following established rules of style, contents, and RHYTHM —compare ROMANTIC¹ (3) **4** of or related to a form or system established before modern times; TRADITIONAL: *Classical scientific ideas about light were changed by Einstein* **5** concerned with the study of the HUMANITIES (esp. Greek and LATIN) and general sciences as opposed to TECHNICAL subjects: *He was given a classical education* **6** CLASSIC¹ (3)

clas·si·cis·m /ˈklæsǰsɪzəm/ also **clas·sic·al·is·m** /ˈklæsǰkəl-ɪzəm/— *n* [U] **1** the principles, ideas, and style (esp. with regard to balance, regularity, and simpleness of form) of the art or literature of ancient Greece or Rome **2** (*often cap.*) (in art and literature) the quality of being simple, balanced, and controlled, not giving way to feeling, and following ancient models **3** the use of such principles or the presence of such qualities in art or literature: *the classicism of 16th century art* —compare ROMANTICISM, REALISM (2)

clas·si·cist /ˈklæsǰsǰst/ *n* **1** a person who **a** favours the study of the CLASSICS in schools, colleges, etc. **b** is skilled in the study of the CLASSICS **2** a person who favours or uses CLASSICISM (1,2) in literature or art —compare ROMANTICIST

clas·sics /ˈklæsɪks/ *n* [*the*+P] (*often cap.*) the languages and literature of ancient Greece and Rome

clas·si·fi·ca·tion /ˌklæsǰfǰˈkeɪʃən/ *n* **1** [U] the act or result of CLASSIFYing, esp. the placing of plants and animals into groups (class, PHYLUM, ORDER, etc.) according to their origins, characters, etc. **2** [C] a group, division, class, or CATEGORY into which something is placed **3** [C] (esp. in libraries) a system for arranging titles of books, magazines, etc., according to broad fields of knowledge and to particular subjects within each field

clas·si·fied /ˈklæsǰfaɪd/ *adj* [Wa5] **1** divided or arranged in classes; placed according to class: *If you look in the classified part of the telephone book you'll find plenty of hotels* **2** *esp. AmE* (of government, esp. military, information) officially secret: *This information is classified; only the president can see it*

classified ad /ˌ··· ˈ·/ *BrE* also **small ad**— *n* a usu. small advertisement placed in a newspaper by a person wishing to sell or buy something, offer or get employment, etc.

clas·si·fy /ˈklæsǰfaɪ/ *v* [T1] **1** to arrange or place (animals, plants, books, etc.) into classes; divide according to class: *People who work in libraries spend a lot of time classifying books* **2** *esp. AmE* to officially mark or declare (information) secret

class·less /ˈklɑːsləs‖ˈklæs-/ *adj* **1** (of societies) not divided into special classes **2** belonging to no particular social class: *spoke a classless variety of English* —**~ness** *n* [U]

class list /ˈ· ·/ *n not AmE* a list dividing people who have taken university examinations into classes according to their results

class·mate /ˈklɑːsmeɪt‖ˈklæs-/ *n* a member of the same class in a school, college, etc.

class·room /ˈklɑːs-rʊm, -ruːm‖ˈklæs-/ *n* a room in a school, college, etc., in which a class meets for a lesson

class strug·gle /ˌ· ˈ··/ also **class war** /ˌ· ˈ·/— *n* [(*the*) U] **1** disagreement and opposition between different classes in a society **2** (in Marxist political thought) the struggle for political and ECONOMIC power carried on between the ruling class and the ruled classes, esp. in modern times between the CAPITALIST class and the PROLETARIAT

class·y /ˈklɑːsi‖ˈklæsi/ *adj* [Wa1] *infml* stylish; fashionable; of high class or rank

clat·ter¹ /ˈklætəʳ/ *v* [IØ;(T1)] to (cause to) move with a number of rapid short knocking sounds: *The metal dish clattered down the stone stairs*

clatter² *n* **1** [S] a number of rapid short knocking sounds; RATTLE: *The clatter came from the kitchen where pans were being washed.|a clatter of metal* *plates* **2** [U] noise, busy activity: *the busy clatter of the city*

clause /klɔːz/ *n* **1** (in grammar) a group of words containing a subject and FINITE verb, forming a sentence or part of a sentence, and often doing the work of a noun, adjective, or adverb —compare PHRASE, SENTENCE **2** a separate part or division of a written agreement or DOCUMENT with its own separate and complete meaning

claus·tro·pho·bi·a /ˌklɔːstrəˈfəʊbɪə/ *n* [U] *med* fear of being enclosed in a small closed space —opposite **agoraphobia**

claus·tro·pho·bic /ˌklɔːstrəˈfəʊbɪk/ *n, adj med* (a person) suffering from CLAUSTROPHOBIA —opposite **agoraphobic**

clav·i·chord /ˈklævəkɔːd‖-ɔrd/ *n* an early type of piano-like musical instrument in which small metal hammers strike wire strings to produce notes

clav·i·cle /ˈklævɪkəl/ *n med* (esp. in human beings) the bone forming the front part of the shoulder; COLLARBONE —see picture at SKELETON

claw¹ /klɔː/ *n* **1** a sharp usu. curved nail on the toe of an animal or bird —see pictures at CAT and BIRD **2** *becoming rare* the foot of an animal with such nails, esp. of a bird: *A hen's claw has 3 toes* **3** a limb of certain insects and sea animals, such as CRABS, used for attacking, catching, and holding objects; PINCER **4** (of tools, esp. hammers) a split curved forklike end, usu. used for pulling nails out of wood

claw² *v* **1** [T1] to tear, seize, pull, etc., with or as if with CLAWS **2** [X9] to put into the stated condition by doing this: *She clawed the door open* **3** [IØ (AWAY, *at*)] to try to do this: *The climber clawed at the cliff surface as he felt himself slipping* **4** [T1] to make by doing this: *She clawed a hole in my shirt in her temper*

claw ham·mer /ˈ· ˌ··/ *n* a hammer with a split curved forklike end, esp. used for pulling nails out of wood

clay /kleɪ/ *n* [U] heavy firm earth, soft when wet, becoming hard when baked at a high temperature, and from which bricks, pots, EARTHENWARE, etc., are made —**~ey** /ˈkleɪ-i/ *adj* [Wa2]

clay·more /ˈkleɪmɔːʳ‖-or/ *n* **1** a large 2-edged sword used in former times by the people who lived in the Scottish HIGHLANDS **2** also **claymore mine** /ˌ·· ˈ·/— a type of explosive weapon (MINE³ (3)) for setting into the ground, being aimed to explode in only one direction (as at an advancing enemy)

clay pi·geon /ˌ· ˈ··/ also **pigeon**— *n* a plate-shaped piece of baked clay thrown up into the air to be shot at, esp. as a sport (**clay pigeon shooting**)

clean¹ /kliːn/ *adj* [Wa1] **1 a** free from dirt or unwanted matter; pure **b** free from disease or infection **2** not yet used; fresh: *clean clothes* **3** without mistakes; readable: *a clean copy of the report|a clean piece of work* **4 a** morally or sexually pure; honourable; free from guilt: *a clean life|(infml) a clean joke* **b** obeying the rules; fair; sportsmanlike: *a clean fighter* **5 a** well-formed; STREAMLINED: *The clean shape of the railway engine meant it could travel very fast* **b** having a smooth edge or surface; even; regular: *a clean cut* **c** clear; PRECISE: *a clean writing style* **6** skilful; clever; not CLUMSY: *a clean throw* **7** *bibl* (esp. in the Jewish religion) **a** (of people) pure in heart and mind: *All who are clean may enter God's house* **b** (of animals) that can lawfully be eaten: *Jews must only eat meat from clean animals* **8** complete; thorough: *a clean escape* **9** [Wa5] *sl* **a** empty: *The ship returned home clean; no fish had been caught* **b** having no hidden weapons: *The police searched me but I was clean* **10 clean sweep a** a complete change: *We want to make a clean sweep of all the old ideas and start again* **b** a complete victory: *Our party made a clean sweep of all the places at the last election* **11 come clean** *infml* to admit one's guilt; tell the unpleasant truth: *Why doesn't the government come clean and tell us its plans?* —**~ness** *n* [U]

clean² *adv* **1** [Wa5;H] all the way; completely: *The bullet went clean through (his arm)* **2** [Wa5;H] *infml* completely: *I'm clean out (of food); I forgot to go to the shops* **3** [Wa1] *infml* in a clean way: *Play the game clean* **4 clean bowled** (in cricket) BOWLed by a ball which hits the WICKET without touching the BAT

clean³ *v* **1** [T1;IØ] to (cause to) become clean: *Please clean the windows as I can hardly see out.|Metal ornaments clean easily* **2** [T1] to cut out the bowels and inside parts of the body from (birds and animals that are to be eaten): *I have to clean the chicken before I can cook it* —see also CLEAN DOWN, CLEAN OUT, CLEAN UP

clean⁴ *n* [S] an act of cleaning dirt, esp. from the surface of something: *She gives the room a good clean every day.|It needs a (good) clean now*

clean-cut /ˌ· ˈ·◂/ *adj* **1** well shaped; having a smooth surface; regular; neat: *a clean-cut hair style* **2** clear in meaning; DEFINITE: *a clean-cut explanation that was quickly understood* **3** neat and clean in appearance: *a clean-cut young boy*

clean down *v adv* [T1] to brush or wash (a wall, car, etc.) from top to bottom: *I'm going to clean down the car this afternoon as it's getting very dirty*

clean·er /ˈkliːnəʳ/ *n* **1** a person whose job is cleaning offices, houses, etc. **2** a machine, apparatus, or substance used in cleaning **3** *AmE* CLEANER'S **4** CLEANING WOMAN

clean·er's *n* **1** a place where clothes, material, etc., can be taken to be cleaned, usu. with chemicals, for payment —see also DRY CLEANER'S **2 take (someone) to the cleaner's** *infml* to cause (someone's) ruin: *If we don't make a profit this year we're going to get taken to the cleaner's by the people we owe money to*

cleaning wom·an /ˈ·· ˌ··/ also **cleaning lady**— *n* a woman who is hired, esp. by the hour, to clean private houses, offices, public buildings, etc.

clean-limbed /ˌ· ˈ·◂/ *adj apprec or humor* (esp. of a young man) tall, well-made and active-looking: *a group of clean-limbed young cricketers*

clean·li·ness /ˈklenlinəs/ *n* [U] habitual cleanness

clean·ly¹ /ˈklenli/ *adj* [Wa1] personally neat; careful to keep clean; always clean: *Cats are among the cleanliest animals there are*

clean·ly² /ˈkliːnli/ *adv* in a clean manner

clean out *v adv* [T1] **1** to make (the inside of usu. a room, box, drawer, etc.) clean and tidy **2 a** to take all the money of (someone) by stealing or by winning: *I got cleaned out playing cards* **b** to steal everything from (a place): *The thieves cleaned out the store*

cleanse /klenz/ *v* **1** [T1] to make (usu. a cut, wound, etc.) clean or pure: *The nurse cleansed the wound before stitching it* **2** [D1+*from/of*; T1 (*of*)] to remove (an illness or something bad) from (a person) by or as if by cleaning: *May God cleanse me of my wickedness*

cleans·er /ˈklenzəʳ/ *n* [C;U] a substance, such as a chemical liquid or powder, used for making cleaning easier and more effective

clean-shav·en /ˌ· ˈ··◂/ *adj* with all hair on the face SHAVED off: *He used to wear a beard, but now he is clean-shaven*

clean·up /ˈkliːn-ʌp/ *n* **1** [S] the act of CLEANing UP: *I'm going to have a good cleanup today* **2** [C] *sl* a very large profit

clean up *v adv* **1** [T1;IØ] to clean thoroughly: *It's* *your turn to clean (the bedroom) up.*|(fig.) *The new government has promised to clean up the town by getting rid of all the criminals* **2** [T1;I∅] to remove by cleaning: *Clean up the pieces of this broken bottle* **3** [T1] *infml* to gain (money) as profit: *He cleaned up a fortune playing cards*

clear[1] /klɪəʳ/ *adj* **1** [Wa1;B] bright; free from anything that darkens; transparent: *a clear sky*|*clear eyes* **2** [Wa1;B] (esp. of sounds, people, writing, etc.) easily heard, seen, read, or understood: *a clear speaker*|*a clear article on modern politics* **3** [Wa1;B] (esp. of the mind or a person) thinking without difficulty; understanding clearly: *a clear thinker* **4** [Wa1;F (*about*), F5,6a,b] (of a person) certain; CONFIDENT: *She seems quite clear about her plans.*|*I'm not clear (about) where she lives/what to do.*|*Are you clear that you don't want to buy it?* **5** [Wa1;B (*of*)] free from guilt or blame; untroubled: *a clear conscience*|*clear of guilt* **6** [Wa1;B (*of*)] open; free from blocks, dangers, or OBSTRUCTIONs: *a clear road*|*a clear view*|*The road's clear of snow now* **7** [Wa1;B] empty; with nothing on it: *I've finished my work and my desk is clear.*|(fig.) *I see that next week is clear: let's meet then* **8** [Wa1;B] of a pure and even colour; free from marks: *a clear skin*|*a clear wine* **9** [Wa1;B] plain; noticeable; OBVIOUS: *a clear case of murder*|*It's clear from his actions that he loves her* **10** [Wa5;A] *infml* complete; without limit: *a clear victory* **11** [Wa5;F (*of*)] free; rid; no longer touching: *We're clear of danger now.*|*The ship is now clear (of the shore)* **12** [Wa5;B;E] *tech* (esp. of wages or profit) remaining after all taxes, trade union payments, etc., have been paid; NET[3] (1): *I get a clear £50 a week.*|*I get £50 a week clear.*|*I earn £50 clear a week* —**~ness** *n* [U]

clear[2] *adv* **1** [Wa1] in a clear manner: *Speak loud and clear* **2** [Wa5] out of the way; so as to be no longer inside or near: *She jumped clear (of the train)* **3** [Wa5;H] *infml* completely; all the way: *You can see clear to the mountains today!*|*The prisoner got clear away* —see also STEER **clear of**

clear[3] *v* **1** [I∅;T1] to (cause to) become clear: *After the storm the sky cleared.*|*This soap should help clear your skin* **2** [I∅;T1:(AWAY)] to (cause to) go away: *Soldiers! Clear the people away from the palace gates* **3** [T1 (*from*)] to remove; take away; get rid of: *I'll just clear the plates away, then I'll have a rest.*|*Whose job is it to clear snow from the road?* **4** [T1 (*of*)] to remove unwanted objects from (the land, a road, an object, etc.): *We must clear the area of enemy soldiers as soon as possible* **5** [T1 (*of*)] to free from blame (a person wrongly thought to have done something wrong): *The judge cleared the prisoner of any crime and set him free* **6** [T1] to pass by or over (something) without touching: *The horse easily cleared every fence* **7** [T1] *not fml* to satisfy all the official conditions of (a government body, official person, etc.): *The car cleared* CUSTOMS (3) *and was soon across the border* **8** [T1] to give official permission for (a ship, plane, person, etc.) to leave or enter a country: *The plane took off as soon as it was cleared* **9** [T1] to pass, give official permission to, or favour (a plan, planned activity, etc.): *The plans for the new road have not yet been cleared by the local council* **10** [T1;I∅] **a** to pass (a cheque) from one bank to another through a CLEARINGHOUSE: *It takes 3 days to clear a cheque* **b** (of a cheque) to pass from one bank to another through a CLEARINGHOUSE: *How long does it take for a cheque to clear?* **11** [T1] *infml* to earn (a large amount of money) as CLEAR[1] (10) profit or wages: *He clears £10,000 a year easily* **12** [T1] to repay (a debt) in full: *I like to clear my debts as quickly as possible as I don't like owing people money* **13** [T1] *tech* DECODE **14 clear the air** to remove doubt and bad feeling by honest explanation, usu. by having an argument: *We had been annoyed with each other for weeks before we cleared the air* **15 clear the decks a** (on a ship) to prepare for a fight **b** *infml* to get ready for action: *Let's clear the decks and start work; it has to be finished today, you know* —see also CLEAR AWAY, CLEAR OFF, CLEAR OUT, CLEAR UP

clear[4] *n not fml* **in the clear a** free from danger, guilt, blame, etc.: *The police have gone so we're in the clear* **b** free from debt: *I'll be in the clear after I get paid*

clear·ance /ˈklɪərəns/ *n* **1** [C;U] the act or result of CLEARing[3]: *Clearance of this cheque could take a week.*|*The ship sailed as soon as it got clearance* **2** [C;U] the distance between one object and another passing beneath or beside it: *The clearance between the bridge and the top of the car was only 10 feet* **3** [U] also **security clearance**— official acceptance that one is in no way an enemy of one's country: *You need clearance before you can work with the president*

clearance sale /ˈ·· ·/ *n* a time when a shop sells goods at reduced prices in order to get rid of as many as possible: *This shop's having a clearance sale next week: we'll be able to get some cheap clothes*

clear a·way *v adv* [T1] to make an area tidy by removing (esp. objects not firmly fastened to anything): *Let's clear away the plates now that dinner is over* —compare CLEAR OFF

clear-cut /ˌ· ˈ·◂/ *adj* **1** having a smooth regular neat shape (OUTLINE) **2** clear in meaning; DEFINITE: *The minister provided Parliament with clear-cut plans for future action*

clear-head·ed /ˌ· ˈ··◂/ *adj* [Wa2] having or showing a clear understanding; sensible —**~ly** *adv* —**~ness** *n* [U]

clear·ing /ˈklɪərɪŋ/ *n* **1** [C] an area of land cleared of trees but surrounded by other trees **2** [U] the passage of a cheque through a CLEARINGHOUSE

clear·ing·house /ˈklɪərɪŋhaʊs/ *n* **-houses** /ˌhaʊz½z/ an establishment where banks exchange cheques and settle their accounts: (fig.) *My office is a sort of clearinghouse where people bring their difficulties*

clear·ly /ˈklɪəli‖ˈklɪərli/ *adv* **1** in a clear manner: *He spoke so clearly that I could hear every word* **2** undoubtedly; OBVIOUSly: *That's clearly a mistake.*|*Clearly, he's a very stupid person*

clear off *v adv* **1** [I∅] *sl* to leave a place, often quickly: *When the 2 boys saw the policeman they cleared off as quickly as they could* **2** [T1] *not fml* to make empty by removing unfastened objects: *Let's clear off the table now that dinner is over* —compare CLEAR AWAY

clear out *v adv* **1** [I∅ (*of*)] *infml* to leave esp. a building or enclosed space, often quickly: *When the police arrived the thieves quickly cleared out of the house* **2** [T1] to collect and throw away (unwanted objects): *I decided to clear out all the old clothes that we never wear* **3** [T1] to clean thoroughly: *I'm going to clear out your bedroom today: don't let it get so untidy again*

clear·out /ˈklɪəraʊt/ *n* [S] *infml esp. BrE* the act of CLEARing OUT (2,3)

clear-sight·ed /ˌ· ˈ··◂/ *adj* [Wa2] **1** having clear sight; able to see clearly **2** able to make good judgments about the future —**~ly** *adv* —**~ness** *n* [U]

clear up *v adv* **1** [T1 a] to find an answer to; explain: *to clear up the mystery* **2** [T1;I∅] to put in order; tidy up; finish: *I've lots of work to clear up by the weekend.*|*Don't expect me to clear up after you all the time!* **3** [I∅] to become less bad or come to an end: *I hope your troubles clear up soon*

clear·way /ˈklɪəweɪ‖-ər-/ *n esp. BrE* a stretch of road which is not a MOTORWAY but on which cars can only stop when in difficulties

cleat /kliːt/ *n* **1** [*usu. pl.*] any of several pieces of leather, rubber, iron, etc., fastened to the bottom (SOLE) of a shoe to preserve it and to prevent slipping **2** a piece of wood, metal, etc., fixed to a usu. wooden article, such as the seat of a chair, to prevent it from splitting **3** a piece of wood or metal in the form of a small bar with 2 short arms, around which ropes can be tied tightly

cleav·age /ˈkliːvɪdʒ/ *n* **1** [C] a division or break caused by splitting: *a sharp cleavage in society between rich and poor* **2** [U] the act of splitting **3** [U] the ability or tendency of certain rocks and minerals to split along usu. straight lines and to have regular smooth surfaces where this has happened **4** [C;U] *infml* the space between a woman's breasts, esp. that which can be seen when she is wearing a low-cut dress —compare DÉCOLLETÉ

cleave /kliːv/ *v* **cleaved** *or* **cleft** /kleft/ *or* **clove** /kləʊv/, **cleaved** *or* **cleft** *or* **cloven** /ˈkləʊvən/ **1** [T1] to divide or cut by a cutting blow: *The axe cleaved the piece of wood.|The murderer clove the man's head open with an axe* **2** [X9] to make by or as if by cutting: *The hunters tried to cleave a path through the tropical forest* **3** [L9] to split or come apart easily, esp. along natural lines of division: *Western society cleaves along class lines* **4** **(caught) in a cleft stick** *not fml* (caught) in an awkward position, from which it is difficult to escape: *With the unions on one side and the employers on the other, the government is in a cleft stick over its prices and incomes plan*

cleav·er /ˈkliːvəʳ/ *n* a heavy sharp-bladed short-handled axelike tool, used esp. for cutting up large pieces of meat

cleave to /kliːv/ *v prep* **cleaved to** *or* **clove to** [T1] *lit or old use* to remain loyal or faithful to (someone or an idea): *The tribes clove to their old beliefs even after the Europeans arrived*

clef /klef/ *n* a special sign put at the beginning of a line (STAVE) of written music to show the height (PITCH) at which the notes should be played —see picture at NOTATION

cleft /kleft/ *n* a space, crack, opening, or split: *The climber fell down a cleft in the rocks.|a sharp cleft in society between rich and poor*

cleft pal·ate /ˌ· ˈ··/ *n* **1** [C] an unnatural crack or separation in the PALATE (1), with which people are sometimes born: *He has a cleft palate and speaks with difficulty* **2** [U] this condition considered as a disease: *Cleft palate can be treated by an operation*

clem·a·tis /ˈklemətɪ̵s, klɪˈmeɪtɪ̵s/ *n* [U] any of various types of climbing plants (VINE*s*) with bunches of white, yellow, or purple flowers

clem·en·cy /ˈklemənsi/ *n* **1** [U] mercy, esp. when used to make a punishment less severe **2** [U9] (esp. of the weather) gentleness; MILDness

clem·ent /ˈklemənt/ *adj* **1** *lit* merciful; LENIENT: *a clement judge, sympathetic to young offenders* **2** (esp. of the weather) gentle; not severe; MILD —**~ly** *adv*

clench /klentʃ/ *v* [T1] **1** to close tightly: *She clenched her teeth* **2** to hold firmly: *He clenched his money in his hand*

clere·sto·ry /ˈklɪəstəri‖ˈklɪərˌstori/ *n* the upper part of the wall of a building, esp. a church, rising above the roof of a lower part of the same building and in which there are usu. a number of windows

cler·gy /ˈklɜːdʒi‖-ɜr-/ *n* [(the) P] the people who are members of esp. the Christian priesthood and who are allowed to perform religious services

cler·gy·man /ˈklɜːdʒimən‖-ɜr-/ also (*old use*) **cleric** /ˈklerɪk/— *n* **-men** /mən/ a Christian priest or MINISTER

cler·i·cal /ˈklerɪkəl/ *adj* [Wa5] **1** of or concerning the CLERGY: *wearing a clerical collar* **2** of or concerning a clerk: *clerical work in an office* —**~ly** *adv* [Wa4,5]

cler·i·hew /ˈklerɪhjuː/ *n* a short 4-lined humorous poem about a usu. well-known person

clerk[1] /klɑːk‖klɜrk/ *n* **1** a person employed in an office, shop, etc., to keep records, accounts, etc., and to do written work **2** an official in charge of the records of a court, town council, etc. **3** also **salesclerk**— *esp. AmE* a person who works in a shop, esp. selling things **4** *rare & law* a priest; CLERGYMAN —see OFFICER (USAGE)

clerk[2] *v* [L9] *infml esp. AmE* to act or work as a CLERK[1] (1,2,3)

clerk of works /ˌ· · ˈ·/ *n BrE* the person in charge of building operations in a particular place

clev·er /ˈklevəʳ/ *adj* [Wa1] **1** quick at learning and understanding; having a quick, effective, and able mind: *a clever student* **2** skilful, esp. at using the hands or body: *a clever worker* **3** being the result of a quick able mind; showing ability and skill: *a clever idea* **4** *derog infml* (often of an insincere person) appearing able or skilful but not really being so; SUPERFICIAL **5** **clever clever** *infml usu. derog* wanting or intended to appear clever even if not really so **6** **too clever by half** *infml derog esp. BrE* too clever (esp. for one's own good): *That new boy offended everyone by being too clever by half* —**~ly** *adv* —**~ness** *n* [U]

clever dick /ˈ·· ·/ *n* [C;N] *derog sl esp. BrE* someone who likes to show that he is cleverer than other people: *I hate you, you clever dick. You think you're better than me just because you get higher marks*

clew[1], **clue** /kluː/ *n* **1** a ball of thread, wool, etc. **2** *tech* a lower corner of a ship's sail **3** *tech* a circle of metal fastened to each of the lower corners of a ship's sail

clew[2], **clue** *v* **1** [T1] to roll (wool, thread, etc.) into a ball **2** [T1 (UP)] *tech* to raise or lower (the sails of a ship) by means of a rope fastened to the CLEW*s*[1] (3)

clew[3] *n now rare* CLUE

cli·ché /ˈkliːʃeɪ‖kliːˈʃeɪ/ *n derog* an unchanging idea or expression used so commonly that it has lost much of its expressive force —**~d** *adj*

click[1] /klɪk/ *n* **1** a slight short sound, such as when a key turns in a lock **2** a sound made by pressing 2 speech organs together (esp. the tongue against the roof of the mouth) and then moving them rapidly apart, thus drawing air into the mouth

click[2] *v* **1** [T1;IØ] to (cause to) make a slight short sound: *The door clicked shut* **2** [IØ (*with*)] *infml* to fall into place; be understood: *Her joke suddenly clicked (with us) and we all laughed* **3** [IØ (*with*)] *infml* to be a success: *That film's really clicked (with young people); it's very popular* **4** [IØ (*with*)] *infml* to be a quick success, esp. with members of the opposite sex: *They clicked with each other as soon as they met*

click·e·ty-click /ˌklɪkɪ̵ti ˈklɪk/ also **clinkety-clank**— *n* [(*the*) S] a repeated slight short quick sound, usu. in time: *The clickety-click of train wheels on the lines is an almost musical sound*

cli·ent /ˈklaɪənt/ *n* **1** a person who **a** pays a professional person, esp. a lawyer, for help and advice **b** gets help or advice from any of the government's social services **2** CUSTOMER —see CUSTOMER (USAGE)

cli·en·tele /ˌkliːənˈtel‖ˌklaɪənˈtel, ˌkliː-/ *n* [GU] those who use the services of a business, shop, professional man, etc.: *My clientele has always* *favoured quality rather than quantity.|Do your clientele like the new fashions?*

client state /ˌ·· ˈ·ˈ/ *n* [C9] a state which is dependent upon the support and protection of another larger and more powerful state —compare SATELLITE (3)

cliff /klɪf/ *n* a high very steep face of rock, ice, earth, etc., esp. on a coast: *the white cliffs of Dover*

cliff·hang·er /ˈklɪfˌhæŋəʳ/ *n not fml* **1** a competition or fight of which the result is in doubt until the very end **2** (esp. on the radio and on television) an event, scene, or part (EPISODE) of a play, story, etc., which ends with a moment of uncertainty (SUSPENSE) about what will happen next

cli·mac·ter·ic /klaɪˈmæktərɪk, ˌklaɪmækˈterɪk/ *n lit* **1** an important turning point; period in life when important changes take place in the human body **2** MENOPAUSE

cli·mac·tic /klaɪˈmæktɪk/ *adj* of or forming a CLIMAX —compare CLIMATIC

cli·mate /ˈklaɪmɨt/ *n* **1** the average weather conditions at a particular place over a period of years: *a tropical climate* **2** the general temper or opinions of a group of people or period of history: *I wouldn't have liked the moral/political climate of Britain before the First World War*

cli·mat·ic /klaɪˈmætɪk/ *adj* [Wa5] of or related to CLIMATE (1) —compare CLIMACTIC —**~ally** *adv* [Wa4,5]

cli·ma·tol·o·gy /ˌklaɪməˈtɒlədʒi‖-ˈtɑ-/ *n* [U] the science that studies CLIMATE (1)

cli·max¹ /ˈklaɪmæks/ *n* **1** that part in a related set or list of events, ideas, expressions, etc., which is most powerful, interesting, and effective, and which usu. comes near the end **2** (of a play, book, film, etc.) the most interesting and important part, usu. near the end **3** (when having sex) the best part; ORGASM **4** *tech* CLIMAX COMMUNITY

climax² *v* [L9, esp. *in*; T1 (*with*)] to (cause to) reach a CLIMAX¹ (1): *a life of service to the nation, climaxing in her appointment as President*

climax com·mu·ni·ty /ˈ·· ·ˌ···/ *n tech* all the plant life which will grow in an area if it is left alone

climb¹ /klaɪm/ *v* **1** [IØ;T1] to go esp. from a lower to a higher position up, over, or through, esp. by using the hands and feet: *The old lady climbs up the stairs with difficulty.|Do you think you can climb that tree?|The child climbed into/out of the car* **2** [IØ;T1] to go esp. from a lower to a higher position up or over (esp. mountains) as a sport **3** [IØ] to rise to a higher point; go higher: *It became hotter as the sun climbed in the sky* **4** [IØ] to slope upwards: *The road climbed steeply* **5** [IØ;T1] (esp. of a plant) to grow upwards, esp. along a supporting surface: *The rose tree has climbed right up the side of the house* **6** [IØ + *into* or *out of*] *infml* to get into or out of clothing usu. with haste or some effort: *The soldiers climbed into their uniforms at the sound of the warning bell*

climb² *n* [C *usu. sing.*] **1** a journey upwards made by climbing; act of climbing: *The minister's climb to power had taken 20 years* **2** a place to be climbed; very steep slope; place where climbing is necessary: *There was a steep climb on the road out of town*

climb down¹ *v adv; prep* [IØ;T1] to go down, esp. by using the hands and feet: *We easily climbed down (the side of the cliff)*

climb down² *v adv* [IØ] *infml esp. BrE* (esp. in order to make a difficult state of affairs easier) to admit that one has been wrong, has made a mistake, etc.; BACK DOWN

climb-down /ˈ· ·/ *n* an act of admitting that one has been wrong, made a mistake, etc. (done esp. in order to make a difficult state of affairs easier): *Your country's climb-down at the last minute saved us all from war*

climb·er /ˈklaɪməʳ/ *n* **1** a person or thing that climbs: *This plant is a good climber.|My son's a very good climber; he hopes to climb Everest next year* **2** *infml* a person trying to reach a higher social position (esp. in the phr. **social climber**)

climb·ing i·ron /ˈ·· ·/ *n* [*usu. pl.*] CRAMPON

clime /klaɪm/ *n* [C9 *usu. pl.*] *poet* CLIMATE (1): *travelled to sunny southern climes*

clinch¹ /klɪntʃ/ *v* **1** [Wv5;T1] to fix (a nail) firmly in place by bending the point over: *The pieces of wood were fastened together with a clinched nail* **2** [T1 (TOGETHER)] to fasten (esp. pieces of wood) tightly together by or as if by doing this **3** [T1] *infml* to settle (a business matter or an agreement) firmly (esp. in the phr. **clinch a deal**): *The 2 businessmen clinched the deal quickly* **4** [IØ] (of 2 BOXers⁴) to hold each other tightly with the arms: *The fighters clinched in the corner*

clinch² *n* **1** [S] (in the sport of BOXING) the position of the 2 fighters when holding each other tightly, with the arms: *The fighters were in a clinch* **2** [S] *sl* the position of 2 lovers holding each other very tightly **3** [C] a nail, screw, etc., which has been CLINCHed¹ (1) **4** [S] a firm hold (as if) with a CLINCHed¹ (1) nail or screw: *He held his money in a clinch*

clinch·er /ˈklɪntʃeʳ/ *n infml* a last point, fact, or remark which ends and usu. successfully decides an argument

cline /klaɪn/ *n tech* CONTINUUM: *According to some students of grammar, certain expressions form a cline from "most nounlike" to "most verblike"*

cling /klɪŋ/ *v* **clung** /klʌŋ/ **1** [IØ (*to*)] to hold tightly; refuse to let go; stick firmly: *The smell of onions clings, doesn't it?|She clung tightly to her few remaining possessions* **2** [L9;(IØ)] to stay near; remain close: *Little children always cling to their mothers.|The 2 friends cling together wherever they go* **3** [L9, esp. *to*] to remain faithful to or in favour of an idea, belief, etc.: *She clung to the hope that her son was not dead*

cling·ing /ˈklɪŋɪŋ/ *adj* **1** (esp. of clothes) tight-fitting; sticking tightly and closely to the body **2** too dependent upon the presence of another person: *That clinging child refuses to leave its mother*

cling·y /ˈklɪŋi/ *adj* [Wa1] *not fml* CLINGING

clin·ic /ˈklɪnɪk/ *n* **1** a building or part of a hospital where a group of people, esp. doctors, give usu. specialized medical treatment and advice: *The clinic is near the station.|an eye clinic* **2** the people who work in such a place: *What did the clinic say about your illness?* **3** an occasion in a hospital when medical students are taught by looking at ill people: *At Mr Spingarn's clinic you will receive a very thorough examination, but a number of students will be present*

clin·i·cal /ˈklɪnɪkəl/ *adj* **1** (of medical teaching) given in a hospital and using ill people as examples: *He found his clinical training more interesting than that he'd done in class* **2** of or connected with a CLINIC or hospital **3** cold; appearing more interested in the scientific than the personal details of a case: *He seemed to have a rather clinical way of looking at the break-up of his own marriage, and would describe it as "a very interesting state of affairs"* —**~ly** *adv* [Wa4]

clinical ther·mom·e·ter /ˌ··· ·ˈ···/ *n tech* a THERMOMETER used for measuring the temperature of the human body

clink¹ /klɪŋk/ *v* [IØ;TI] to (cause to) make a slight knocking sound like that of pieces of glass or metal lightly hitting each other

clink² *n* [S] a slight knocking noise, like that of

pieces of glass or metal lightly hitting each other

clink³ *n* [*the*+R] *sl* prison: *The police will send you to the clink if you steal*

clink·er /ˈklɪŋkəʳ/ *n* **1** [C;U] (a lump of) the partly burnt matter left after coal or other minerals have been burned; (a piece of) SLAG (1) **2** [C] *sl* a failure: *In spite of our efforts, the play was a real clinker!*

clinker-built /ˌ·· ˈ·ˈ/ *adj* [Wa5] *tech* (esp. of boats) made from boards of wood or plates of metal whose bottom parts cover the top parts of the next lower boards or plates

clink·e·ty-clank /ˌklɪŋkǝ̵ti ˈklæŋk/ *n* [S] CLICKETY-CLICK

clip¹ /klɪp/ *v* **-pp-** [X9;L9: esp. ON, *to*, TOGETHER] to (cause to) fasten onto something with a CLIP² (1): *Clip these sheets of paper together please.|Will this map clip to the wall?|Does your jewellery clip on?*

clip² *n* **1** a small variously-shaped plastic or usu. metal object for holding things tightly together or in place: *Fasten these sheets of paper together with a clip, please* **2** a container (MAGAZINE (3)) in or fastened to a gun and from which bullets and explosive can be rapidly passed into the gun for firing

clip³ *v* **-pp-** [T1] **1** to cut with scissors or another sharp instrument: *I'm going to clip this picture out of the paper.*|(fig.) *The king tried to clip the powers of his ministers* **2 a** to leave out (parts of a word or sentence) when writing or speaking: *He annoys me by clipping the ends off his words* **b** to shorten (a word or sentence) in this way: *clipped speech* **3** to put a hole in (a ticket): *The bus driver clipped our tickets to show we'd used them* **4** *infml* to strike with a short quick blow: *I'll clip your ears if you don't behave* **5 clip someone's wings** *not fml* to prevent someone being as active as before, esp. someone who has wasted time and money

clip⁴ *n* **1** [C] the act of CLIPping **2** [C] *tech* the quantity of wool cut from a group (FLOCK) of sheep at one time **3** [C] *infml* a short quick blow **4** [S] *infml esp. AmE* a fast speed: *He moved at a good clip*

clip·board /ˈklɪpbɔːd‖-ord/ *n* a small hard board with a usu. metal fastener (CLIP) at the top so that sheets of writing paper can be held firmly in place

clip joint /ˈ· ·/ *n derog sl* a business, esp. a restaurant or NIGHTCLUB, that regularly charges too much and may make use of other dishonest practices as well

clip-on /ˈ· ·/ *adj* [Wa5;A] that can be fastened on to something with a CLIP: *She wore a piece of clip-on jewellery on her coat*

clip·per /ˈklɪpəʳ/ *n* **1** [C] a sailing ship built in former times to travel very quickly, esp. over long distances —see picture at SAIL² **2** [C] a person who CLIPs or cuts **3** [A;C] CLIPPERS: *a clipper blade|Is the clipper in the cupboard?*

clip·pers /ˈklɪpəz‖-ərz/ *n* [P] a usu. scissor-like tool or instrument used for CLIPping³ (1), esp. the nails and hair: *The clippers are on the shelf* —see PAIR (USAGE)

clip·pie /ˈklɪpi/ *n BrE sl* a woman employed to take the passengers' payments on a bus

clip·ping /ˈklɪpɪŋ/ *n* **1** a piece cut off or out of something: *nail clippings* **2** *AmE* CUTTING (2): *Have you saved that newspaper clipping about my old friend?*

clique /kliːk/ *n derog* a closely united usu. small group of people who do not allow others easily to join their group

cli·quey /ˈkliːki/ *adj* [Wa1] *derog infml* CLIQUISH

cli·quish /ˈkliːkɪʃ/ *adj derog* of, related to, or being like a CLIQUE —**~ness** *n* [U]

clit·o·ris /ˈklɪtərǝ̵s/ *n* a small part of the female sex organ which is rather like the male sex organ (PENIS) in that it becomes bigger when the female is sexually excited

clo·a·ca /kləʊˈeɪkə/ *n* **-cae** /kiː/ **1** the last part of the bowels of some animals, such as birds, from which body wastes and eggs leave the body **2** *lit* SEWER

cloak¹ /kləʊk/ *n* **1** a loose, outer garment, usu. without arm-coverings (SLEEVE*s*), which is sometimes worn instead of a coat **2** something which covers, hides or keeps secret; DISGUISE: *His friendly behaviour was a cloak for his evil intentions*

cloak² *v* [T1 (*with*)] to hide, keep secret, or cover (ideas, thoughts, beliefs, etc.)

cloak-and-dag·ger /ˌ· · ˈ··/ *adj* [Wa5;A] (esp. of plays, films, stories, etc.) dealing with adventure, mystery, and/or ESPIONAGE (=the stealing of official secrets): *I like to read a good cloak-and-dagger story*

cloak·room /ˈkləʊkrʊm, -ruːm/ *n* **1** *AmE* also **checkroom**— a room, as in a theatre, where hats, coats, bags, etc., may be left for a short time, usu. under guard **2** *euph esp. BrE* a LAVATORY (2), esp. in a public building

clob·ber¹ /ˈklɒbəʳ‖ˈklɑ-/ *v* [T1] *sl* **1** to strike severely and repeatedly: *I'll clobber you if you don't do what you're told* **2** to defeat completely **3** to attack fiercely and continually: *The government's going to clobber the unions if they don't agree to the new prices and incomes plan*

clobber² *n* [U] *sl esp. BrE* **1** the belongings that one carries around with one: *I'll just get my clobber, then I'll be ready to go* **2** clothes: *I like your new clobber*

cloche /klɒʃ‖kləʊʃ/ *n* **1** an often bell-shaped glass or transparent plastic cover put over young plants to protect them **2** a close-fitting bell-shaped woman's hat popular esp. in the 1920s

clock¹ /klɒk‖klɑk/ *n* **1** an instrument (not worn like a watch) for measuring and showing time usu. by means of 2 or 3 hands moving around a round numbered face (DIAL) to mark the hour, minute, and, sometimes, second **2** *infml* **a** MILEOMETER **b** SPEEDOMETER **3** *BrE sl* someone's face: *I'll hit you in your clock if you keep on annoying me!* **4 around/round the clock** all day and all night usu. without stopping: *People with very important jobs sometimes have to work around the clock* **5 put the clock back a** (in countries which officially change the time at the beginning of winter and summer) to move the hands of a clock back one or 2 hours: *In Italy they put the clock back 2 hours every October* **b** to set aside modern laws, ideas, plans, etc., and stay with old-fashioned ones: *The government's put the clock back with its new plans for education* **6 put the clock on/forward** (*AmE* also **ahead**) (in countries which officially change the time at the beginning of winter and summer) to move the hands of the clock one or 2 hours forward: *In Britain they put the clock on an hour in spring* **7 run out/kill the clock** *AmE* (when one is winning a game, such as football) to keep possession of the ball until the end of the game to prevent the opposition from winning any more points **8 sleep the clock round** *BrE* to sleep for at least 12 hours —compare ROUND-THE-CLOCK **9 watch the clock** *derog not fml* to think continually of how soon work will end: *He's a bad worker who's always watching the clock* **10 work against the clock** to work very quickly in order to finish a job before a certain time —see also O'CLOCK

USAGE If a **clock** or **watch** says 11.50 at 12 o'clock, then it is (*10 minutes*) *slow*; if it says 12.05, it is (*5 minutes*) *fast*. If it gets *faster* every day, it *gains* (time); if it gets slower every day it *loses*

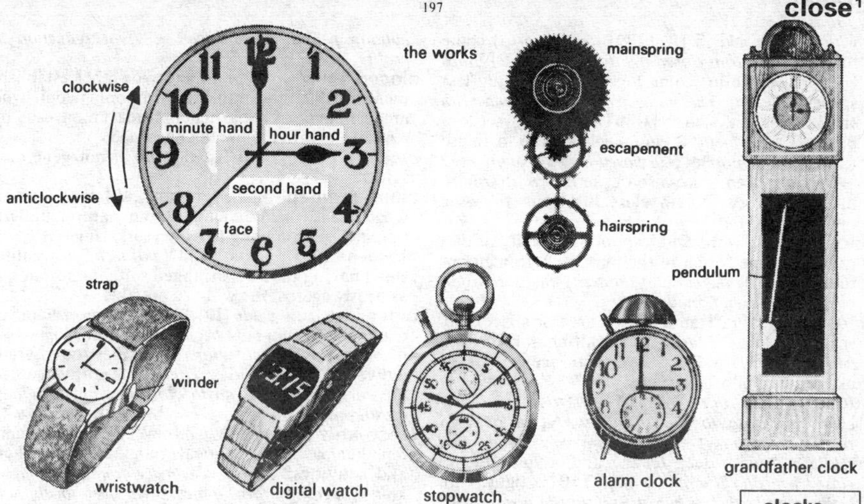

(time). When one puts it to the right time one *sets* it: *I set my* **watch** *by the radio* (= by listening to the radio time signal).

clock² *v* [T1] **1** TIME² (3): *I clocked him while he ran a mile* **2** *BrE sl* to strike: *I'll clock you if you annoy me again!* **3 clock (somebody) one** *BrE sl* to strike: *I'll clock you one if you annoy me again!*

clock³ *n* an ornamental pattern on the side of a sock or stocking esp. at the ankle

clock golf /ˌ· ˈ·/ *n* [U] a game in which one or more players try to knock a ball into a small hole in the ground from 12 points equally distant from the hole

clock in also **clock on**— *v adv* [IØ] **1** to start work, esp. at a regular time: *I usually clock in at 8 o'clock* **2** to record the time when one arrives at work, usu. on a special card —compare CLOCK OUT

clock out also **clock off**— *v adv* [IØ] **1** to finish work, esp. at a regular time **2** to record the time when one leaves work, usu. on a special card —compare CLOCK IN

clock tow·er /ˈ· ˌ··/ *n* a usu. 4-sided tower often forming part of a building, such as a church, and with a clock face on each of the sides, near the top

clock up *v adv* [T1a] *infml* **1** to record (a distance travelled, points won, etc.): *We clocked up 1,000 miles coming here* **2** to reach (a certain speed): *I can clock up 100 miles an hour in my new car!* **3** ACCUMULATE; CHALK UP: *He clocked up a lot of debts when he was living in Paris*

clock-watch·er /ˈ· ˌ··/ *n derog not fml* a student, worker, etc., who shows lack of interest in his work by thinking continually of how soon work will end —**-watching** *n* [U]

clock·wise /ˈklɒk-waɪz‖ˈklɑk-/ *adj, adv* [Wa5] in the direction in which the hands of a clock move if looked at from the front: *You must turn the lid clockwise if you want to fasten it tightly.*|*a clockwise movement of the lid* —opposite **anticlockwise**; see picture at CLOCK¹

clock·work /ˈklɒk-wɜːk‖ˈklɑk-wɜrk/ *n* [U] **1** [A; (U)] **a** the machinery that works a clock **b** machinery like this, that can usu. be wound up with a key, and that is used esp. in toys: *The children played happily with their clockwork toys* **2 like clockwork** smoothly; easily; regularly; without trouble

clod /klɒd‖klɑd/ *n* **1** [C] a lump or mass, esp. of clay or earth **2** [C; (*you*) N] *not fml* a stupid person; fool

clod·dish /ˈklɒdɪʃ‖ˈklɑd-/ *adj* like a CLOD (2) —**~ly** *adv* —**~ness** *n* [U]

clod·hop·per /ˈklɒdˌhɒpəʳ‖ˈklɑdˌhɑ-/ *n* **1** *not fml* an awkward careless rough country person **2** [*usu. pl.*] *humor* a big heavy strong shoe

clog¹ /klɒg‖klɑg/ *n* **1** [*usu. pl.*] a kind of shoe **a** with a thick usu. wooden bottom (SOLE) **b** completely made from one piece of wood **2** something that makes movement or action difficult, esp. a heavy block of wood fastened to an animal's leg to stop it wandering

clog² *v* **-gg- 1** [T1;IØ: (UP)] to (cause to) become blocked: *Don't clog your memory (up) with useless information.*|*A machine won't work properly if it is clogged with dirt* **2** [T1] to make movement difficult by means of a CLOG¹ (2): *Farmers used to clog their cows before fences were built to enclose fields*

clog dance /ˈ· ·/ *n* (esp. in industrial areas of the North of England) a dance in which the performers wear CLOGs¹ (1) and loudly beat time on the floor —**clog dancer** *n* —**clog dancing** *n* [U]

clog·gy /ˈklɒgi‖ˈklɑgi/ *adj* [Wa1] lumpy and sticky

cloi·son·né /klwɑːˈzɒneɪ‖ˌklɔɪzənˈeɪ/ *adj, n* [B;U] *Fr* (of or related to) ornamental work in which different colours of ENAMEL (=a glasslike substance often used for covering metal objects) are kept apart by thin metal bands

clois·ter¹ /ˈklɔɪstəʳ/ *n* **1** [C *usu. pl.*] a covered passage which encloses an open square garden or courtyard, which has open archways on one side facing into the garden or courtyard, and which usu. forms part of a church, MONASTERY, or CONVENT **2** [C *usu. sing.; the*+R] a place of religious peace and quiet; CONVENT; MONASTERY

cloister² *v* [Wv5;T1] to shut away from the world in or as if in a CONVENT or MONASTERY: *He had led a cloistered life in one of our older universities, and knew little of practical affairs*

clone /kləʊn/ *n tech* the nonsexually-produced descendants of a single plant or animal

clop /klɒp‖klɑp/ *v, n* **-pp-** [IØ;S] (to make) a sound like horses' feet (HOOFS)

close¹ /kləʊz/ *v* **1** [T1;IØ] to (cause to) shut: *Close the windows and keep out the cold air* **2** [T1;IØ] to (cause to) be not open to the public: *When does the shop close?* **3** [T1;IØ: (DOWN)] to (cause to) stop operation: *The firm has decided to close (down) its London branch.*|*This factory is closing (down) soon* **4** [T1] to bring to an end: *She closed her speech* *with a funny joke* **5** [I∅;(T1)] to (cause to) come together: *His arms closed tightly round her* **6** [T1;I∅ (UP)] to (cause to) come together by making less space between: *The nurse closed the wound with stitches* **7** **close a deal (with)** *not fml* to settle a business agreement **8** **close one's eyes to** to refuse to consider or notice: *She closed her eyes to my need* —opposite **open** —see also CLOSE DOWN, CLOSE IN, CLOSE UP, CLOSE WITH, **close the** DOOR **to** —see OPEN (USAGE)

close² /kləʊz/ *n* the end, esp. of an activity or of a period of time (often in the phrs. **bring/come/draw to a close**): *At the close of the party there were few guests who weren't drunk*

close³ /kləʊs/ *n* **1** an enclosed area or space, esp. the area around a large important church (CATHEDRAL); courtyard **2** a narrow entrance or passage usu. leading into a courtyard

close⁴ /kləʊs/ *adj* [Wa1] **1** [B (*to*)] near: *The church is close to the shops* **2** [A] **a** near in relationship: FIRST COUSINs *are considered close relations* **b** with deep feeling and/or importance: *close friends|a close relationship* **3** [B] **a** tight; with little or no space: *When she sewed she always used close stitches* **b** narrow; limited: *They had only a very close space to sleep in* **4** [B] thorough; careful: *We kept a close watch on the prisoners* **5** [B] **a** lacking fresh or freely moving air: *It's very close in here today* **b** heavy OPPRESSIVE (2): *the closest weather for a long time* **6** [B] (esp. of competition) in which the competitors are almost equal; decided by a very narrow edge (MARGIN (3)) **7** [F (*about*)] secretive: *She's always been very close about her past life* **8** [F (*with*)] not generous; STINGY: *close with money* **9** [B] (in PHONETICS) pronounced with little space above the tongue: *close vowels* **10** **keep/lie close** to stay hidden; not show oneself —see also **close** SHAVE²; NEAR (USAGE) —**~ly** *adv* —**~ness** *n* [U]

close⁵ /kləʊs/ *adv* [F (TOGETHER, *to*)] **1** near: *Stay close together* **2** **close to** also (*infml*) **close on**— (esp. before numbers) almost: *close to 90 years ago| Close on 90 people came* **3** **close to home** *not fml* near the (often unpleasant) truth, so that one is strongly concerned or influenced: *Everyone felt that the speaker's remarks hit close to home* —see also **close to the** WIND

close call /ˌkləʊs ˈkɔːl/ *n infml* a narrow escape

close-cropped /ˌkləʊs ˈkrɒpt◂‖-ˈkrɑpt◂/ *adj* [Wa2] **1** having hair which is cut short **2** also **close-cut**— (of the hair) short

closed /kləʊzd/ *adj* [Wa5] **1** [(*to*)] (esp. of a shop or public building) not open to the public **2** only open to a special few: *a closed membership* **3** (in PHONETICS) ending in a consonant: *a closed* SYLLABLE

closed book /ˌ· ˈ·/ *n infml* **1** something of which one knows nothing **2** something which is completed or finished with

closed cir·cuit /ˌ· ˈ··◂/ *n* **1** an uninterrupted path round which electricity can flow **2** (in television) a system which sends signals by wire to a limited number of receivers

closed-door /ˌ· ˈ·◂/ *adj* [Wa5;A] *not fml* (esp. of meetings) not open to the newspapers and public

close down /kləʊz/ *v adv* [I∅;T1] **a** (of a radio or television station) to stop broadcasting for the night **b** to cause (a radio or television station) to stop broadcasting for the night —see also CLOSE¹ (3)

close·down /ˈkləʊzdaʊn/ *n* **1** *esp. BrE* (in radio and television) the end of a time of broadcasting **2** (in a factory, business, etc.) a general stopping of work; SHUTDOWN: *A complete closedown over the holiday period would mean a great reduction in profits*

closed shop /ˌ· ˈ·◂/ *n* a factory or other establishment in which the employer hires only people who are members of a particular trade union usu. by agreement with the union concerned

close·fist·ed /ˌkləʊsˈfɪstɪ̈d◂/ *adj sl* not generous; STINGY

close-grained /ˌkləʊs ˈgreɪnd◂/ *adj* [Wa2] (esp. of wood or leather) having a fine natural pattern (GRAIN⁵), esp. having narrow yearly rings

close-hauled /ˌkləʊs ˈhɔːld◂/ *adj tech* (of a sailing ship) having the sails arranged so that one can sail as nearly against the wind as possible

close in /kləʊz/ *v adv* [I∅] **1** to have fewer hours of daylight: *The days are beginning to close in now that it's Autumn* **2** [(*on, upon*)] to gather round gradually, usu. from all sides: *The people ran away when the enemy army began to close in.*|(fig.) *Night is closing in*

close-knit /ˌkləʊs ˈnɪt◂/ *adj* [Wa2] tightly bound together by social, political, religious, etc., beliefs and activities: *People who move from small close-knit villages to large cities often feel lonely and friendless*

close-lipped /ˌkləʊs ˈlɪpt◂/ *adj* silent or saying little

closely-knit *adj* CLOSE-KNIT

close out /kləʊz/ *v adv* [T1;I∅] *AmE* to try and get rid of (goods) by selling at reduced prices: *This shop is closing out everything next week* —**closeout** /ˈkləʊzaʊt/ *n*

close sea·son /ˈkləʊs ˌsiːzən/ also (*esp. AmE*) **closed season**— *n* the period of each year when certain animals, birds, or fish may not by law be killed for sport —opposite **open season**

close-set /ˌkləʊs ˈset◂/ *adj* set close together: *close-set houses*

clos·et¹ /ˈklɒzɪ̈t‖ˈklɑ-, ˈklɔ-/ *n* **1** *AmE* a cupboard built into the wall of a room and going from floor to CEILING (1) **2** *now rare* a small private room for thought, prayer, etc. **3** *old use* LAVATORY (1,2)

closet² *adj* [Wa5;A] *old use* suited for use or enjoyment in private (esp. in the phr. **closet drama**)

closet³ *v* [T1 (TOGETHER, *with*)] *often pass.* to enclose (esp. oneself) in a private room: *The king and his ministers closeted themselves together while they talked about the government's difficulties*

close thing /ˌkləʊs ˈθɪŋ/ *n* **1** something bad that nearly happened, but didn't: *That was a close thing! We nearly hit the other car!* **2** also **close-run thing** /ˌ· · ˈ·/— a battle, election, or competition which was nearly lost, but won in the end

close-up /ˈkləʊs ʌp/ *n* **1** a usu. large-scale photograph taken from very near **2** *not fml* a close or personal (INTIMATE (2)) view or description of something: *His book was meant as a close-up of life in London*

close up /kləʊz/ *v adv* **1** [T1] to close completely; block: *The old road has now been closed up* —see also **close up** SHOP **2** [I∅;T1] to (cause to) come nearer each other: *Close up the ranks!|The general ordered his soldiers to close up*

close with /kləʊz/ *v prep* [T1] **1** *BrE* to come to an agreement with: *The 2 ministers didn't close with each other until late in the evening* **2** *BrE* to agree to: *The businessman quickly closed with the new offer* **3** *lit* to begin to fight: *The 2 armies closed with each other and started a fierce battle*

closing price /ˈ·· ˌ·/ *n* the price of the business shares of a firm, business, etc., when trade on the STOCK EXCHANGE stops at the end of the day

closing time /ˈ·· ·/ *n* [R;C] the time, usu. fixed by law, at which a business establishment stops doing

business, esp. the time at which a PUB stops serving drinks
clo·sure /ˈkləʊʒəʳ/ *n* **1** [C;U] (an example of) the act of closing **2** [C *usu. sing.*] also (*esp. AmE*) **cloture**— *tech* (in a parliament or other law-making body) a method of stopping further talk about a question in order to take a vote on it —compare GUILLOTINE[1] (4)
clot[1] /klɒt‖klɑt/ *n* **1** [C] a thickened or half-solid mass or lump, usu. formed from a liquid, esp. blood **2** [C; *you*+N] *sl esp. BrE* a stupid person; fool
clot[2] *v* **-tt-** [IØ;T1] to (cause to) form into CLOTs[1] (1)
cloth /klɒθ‖klɔθ/ *n* **cloths** /klɒθs‖klɔðz, klɔθs/ **1** [U] material made from wool, hair, cotton, etc., by weaving, and used for making garments, coverings, etc.: *I need a lot of cloth if I'm going to make a new dress* **2** [C] (*often in comb.*) a piece of this used for a special purpose: *a* **tablecloth**|*Pass the cloth, please: I want to clean the windows* **3** [*the* + R] *fml* the priestly profession: *a man of the cloth* (= a priest)
clothe /kləʊð/ *v* [T1] **1** to provide clothes for (a person or people): *He has to work hard to feed and clothe his large family* **2** *lit* to cover (something) as if with clothing: *Mist clothed the hills*
clothes /kləʊðz, kləʊz/ *n* [P] garments, such as trousers, dresses, shirts, etc., worn on the body —compare CLOTHING
clothes·bas·ket /ˈkləʊðzbɑːskɨt, ˈkləʊz-‖-bæs-/ *n* a basket in which clothes are kept before or after washing
clothes hang·er /ˈ· ˌ··/ *n* HANGER
clothes·horse /ˈkləʊðzhɔːs, ˈkləʊz-‖-ɔrs/ *n* **1** a framework on which clothes are hung to dry, usu. indoors **2** *AmE sl* a person who dresses very showily
clothes·line /ˈkləʊðzlaɪn, kləʊz-/ also **line**— *n* a rope or cord on which clothes are hung to dry, usu. outdoors
clothes peg /ˈ· ˌ·/ also **peg**, *AmE* **clothes·pin** /ˈkləʊðzˌpɪn, ˈkləʊz-/— *n BrE* a small forked instrument made of one or 2 small pieces of wood or plastic used for holding wet washed clothes on a CLOTHESLINE for drying
clothes tree /ˈ· ˌ·/ *n* a wooden pole with hooks branching from the top on which coats, hats, etc., may be hung
cloth·i·er /ˈkləʊðɪəʳ/ *n fml becoming rare* a person who makes or sells men's clothes or cloth
cloth·ing /ˈkləʊðɪŋ/ *n* [U] *often fml & tech* the garments, such as trousers, dresses, shirts, etc., worn together on different parts of the body: *warm winter clothing*|*food, clothing, and shelter* —compare CLOTHES
clotted cream /ˌ·· ˈ·/ *n* [U] thick cream made mainly in England by slowly heating milk and taking the cream from the top
clo·ture /ˈkləʊtʃəʳ/ *n* [*usu. sing.*] *esp. AmE* CLOSURE (2)
cloud[1] /klaʊd/ *n* **1** [C;U] (a variously-shaped weightless mass of) very small drops of water floating high in the air: *When there are black clouds you can tell it's going to rain.*|*There's more cloud today than yesterday* **2** [C] a variously-shaped weightless mass of dust, smoke, etc., which floats in the air: *Clouds of smoke rose above the bombed city* **3** [C] a large number of small things moving through the air as a mass: *a cloud of insects* **4** [C; U] (an area of) darkness in something otherwise transparent: *There was a/some cloud in the bottom of the beer* **5** [C9] something that causes unhappiness or fear: *The sad news of her father's death was the only cloud on an otherwise happy year* **6 have one's head in the clouds** *infml* to be not thinking about everyday matters; be not paying attention; be in a dreamlike state **7 under a cloud** out of favour; looked on with distrust
cloud[2] *v* **1** [T1;IØ (OVER)] to (cause to) become covered with or as if with clouds: *The thick mist clouded the mountain tops* **2** [T1] to make uncertain, unclear, confused, etc.: *Age clouded his memory* **3** [T1;IØ: (UP)] to (cause to) become less transparent or darker: *You'll cloud the beer if you shake the barrel.*|*The steam has clouded the windows up*
cloud·bank /ˈklaʊdbæŋk/ *n* a thick mass of low cloud
cloud·burst /ˈklaʊdbɜːst‖-ɜr-/ *n* a sudden very heavy fall of rain
cloud-capped /ˈ· ·/ *adj* [Wa5] *lit* (of mountains, hills, etc.) having the top surrounded by clouds
cloud cham·ber /ˈ· ˌ··/ *n tech* a vessel full of dust-free air and steam in which a scientist can watch the behaviour of IONs of gas
cloud-cuck·oo-land /ˌ· ˈ·· ·/ *n* [R] *derog* (*sometimes caps*) an imaginary place of unreal dreams and perfection
cloud·less /ˈklaʊdləs/ *adj* [Wa5] without clouds; clear
cloud nine /ˌ· ˈ·/ *n* **on cloud nine** *sl, esp. AmE* very happy: *He was on cloud nine after his wife had the baby*
cloud·y /ˈklaʊdi/ *adj* [Wa1] **1** full of clouds; OVERCAST: *a cloudy day*|*a cloudy sky* **2** not clear or transparent: *cloudy beer*|*a cloudy mirror* **3** uncertain: *the cloudy beginnings of modern history*|*His memory has always been cloudy* —**cloudiness** *n* [U]
clout[1] /klaʊt/ *n* **1** [C] *sl* a blow or knock esp. given with the hand **2** [C *often pl.*] *NEngE sl* an article of clothing **3** [U] *AmE sl* influence, esp. political influence: *had a lot of clout with the governor*
clout[2] *v* [T1] **1** *sl* to strike, esp. with the hand **2** *AmE infml* to hit (esp. a ball) with force
clove[1] /kləʊv/ *n* the dried unopened flower of a tropical Asian plant, used whole or as a powder for giving a special taste to food
clove[2] *n* any of the smallest pieces into which the usu. round fleshy root (BULB) of the GARLIC plant can be divided: *a clove of* GARLIC
clove[3] *past t. of* CLEAVE
clove hitch /ˈ· ·, ˌ· ˈ·/ *n* a type of knot used esp. at sea for fastening a rope around a bar of wood
clo·ven /ˈkləʊvən/ *past p. of* CLEAVE
cloven hoof /ˌ·· ˈ·/ also **cloven foot**— *n* a foot, such as that of a cow, sheep, goat, etc., divided into 2 parts: *The devil is sometimes supposed to have cloven hoofs*
clo·ver /ˈkləʊvəʳ/ *n* [U;C] **1** any of various types of small usu. 3-leafed plants with pink, purple, or white flowers, often grown as food for cattle **2 in clover** *infml* living in comfort —see also FOUR-LEAF CLOVER
clo·ver·leaf /ˈkləʊvəliːf‖-vər-/ *n* **-leafs** *or* **-leaves** /liːvz/ **1** the leaf of a CLOVER **2** something that looks like this, esp. the network of curved roads which connect 2 very important roads (MOTORWAYs) where they cross each other
clown[1] /klaʊn/ *n* **1** a performer, esp. in the CIRCUS (1), who dresses funnily and tries to make people laugh by his jokes, tricks, or actions **2** *derog* a person who continually tells jokes or acts stupidly
clown[2] *v* [IØ (ABOUT)] *derog* to behave like a CLOWN[1] (2); act stupidly or foolishly
clown·ish /ˈklaʊnɪʃ/ *adj derog* of or like a CLOWN[1] (2): *clownish dress*|*silly clownish behaviour* —**~ly** *adv* —**~ness** *n* [U]
cloy /klɔɪ/ *v* [IØ;(T1)] *becoming rare* (esp. of sweet sticky food) to become unpleasant to (someone)

by being taken in too great a quantity: *Chocolates start to cloy if you eat too many*

club¹ /klʌb/ *n* **1** a society of people who join together for a certain purpose, esp. sport or amusement: *a working-men's club|a cricket club* **2** a building where such a society meets **3** a heavy wooden stick, thicker at one end than the other, suitable for use as a weapon **4** a specially shaped stick for striking a ball in certain sports, esp. GOLF —see GOLF (USAGE) **5** a playing card with one or more 3-leafed figures printed on it in black: *I have 4 clubs in my hand* —compare DIAMOND, HEART, SPADE —see CARDS (USAGE) **6 in the club** *sl* (esp. of an unmarried woman) expecting a baby: *Jean's in the club again* **7 Join the club!** *sl esp. BrE* (said in order to suggest that other people are in the same position): *"I have a bad cold" "Join the club: I have one, too"*

club² *v* **-bb-** [T1] to beat or strike with a heavy stick (CLUB)

club·ba·ble /ˈklʌbəbəl/ *adj BrE* fit to be a member of a club; likely to be popular in a club; SOCIABLE

club·foot /ˈklʌbfʊt/ *n* **1** [C] a badly shaped foot twisted out of position from birth **2** [U] the condition of having such a foot —**~ed** /ˌklʌbˈfʊtɪ̈d◂/ *adj*

club·house /ˈklʌbhaʊs/ *n* **-houses** /haʊzɪ̈z/ a CLUB¹ (2), esp. one used by a sports group

club to·geth·er *v adv* **-bb-** [IØ] to share the cost of something with others: *The family clubbed together to buy a new car*

cluck¹ /klʌk/ *v* **1** [IØ] to make a CLUCK² **2** [T1] to express usu. with interest, approval, or disapproval: *She clucked her disapproval*

cluck² *n* the low short noise that a hen makes when calling her chickens or sitting on her eggs

clue¹ /kluː/ *n* **1** something that helps to find an answer to a question, difficulty, etc.: *Have any clues been found that can help the police find the criminal?* **2 not have a clue** *infml* to be unable to understand; know nothing

clue² *n, v* CLEW

clue in *v adv* [T1b] *infml* to give (someone) help in understanding or finding an answer: *I can't imagine where you've hidden it: please clue me in*

clue·less /ˈkluːləs/ *adj* [Wa5] *sl esp. BrE* helpless; stupid

clue up *v adv* **(all) clued up (about/on)** *infml* very well-informed; knowing a lot

clump¹ /klʌmp/ *n* **1** [C] a group of trees, bushes, plants, etc., growing together **2** [C] a heavy solid lump or mass of **a** dirt, soil, mud, etc. **b** *tech* bacteria **3** [S] a heavy slow sound, such as made by slow footsteps

clump² *v* **1** [L9] to walk with slow heavy noisy footsteps **2** [IØ;T1: (TOGETHER)] *tech* to (cause to) gather into or form a mass (CLUMP¹ (2b)): *The bacteria clumped together*

clum·sy /ˈklʌmzi/ *adj* [Wa1] *derog* **1** awkward and ungraceful in movement or action; without skill or grace: *A clumsy dog knocked the cup over* **2** done or made in an awkward fashion: *Her clumsy speech annoyed everyone* **3** difficult to handle or control: *You shouldn't wear such clumsy shoes* —**clumsily** *adv* —**clumsiness** *n* [U]

clung /klʌŋ/ *past t. and past p. of* CLING

clus·ter¹ /ˈklʌstəʳ/ *n* a number of things of the same kind growing or being close together in a group: *a cluster of bees|a cluster of stars*

cluster² *v* [IØ (*around, round,* TOGETHER); T1 (TOGETHER)] to (cause to) gather or grow in one or more CLUSTERS¹: *The men clustered together round the fire and sang songs*

clutch¹ /klʌtʃ/ *v* [T1] to hold tightly: *The mother clutched her baby in her arms*

clutch² *n* **1** [S] the fingers or hands in the act of CLUTCHing¹ **2** [C *usu. sing.*] the act of CLUTCHing¹; a tight hold: *His clutch was not tight enough and he fell from the branch* **3** [C] an apparatus, as in a car, which allows working parts of machinery to be connected or disconnected at the driver's will —see picture at CAR

clutch³ *n* **1** a number of eggs laid by a bird, esp. a hen, at one time **2** the group of chickens born from these eggs

clutch at *v prep* [T1] to try to seize: *He clutched at the branch but he could not reach it*

clutch·es /ˈklʌtʃɪ̈z/ *n* [P] control; power; possession: *Once he was in the clutches of the enemy he knew he'd never escape*

clut·ter¹ /klʌtəʳ/ *v* [T1 (UP)] to make untidy or confused: *Don't clutter up your room.|The room was cluttered with furniture*

clut·ter¹ /ˈklʌtəʳ/ *v* [T1 (UP)] to make untidy or confused: *Don't clutter up your room.|The room was cluttered with furniture*
I had to tidy it up

cm *written abbrev. for:* CENTIMETRE(*s*)

co- /kəʊ/ *prefix* **1** with; together; JOINT(ly)²: *to coexist|a* CO*HEIR|*COETERNAL|COEDUCATION *of boys and girls* **2** joined in an action with another **a** as an equal: COAUTHOR|*codirector* **b** with less responsibility: *copilot*

c/o /ˌsiː ˈəʊ◂/ *abbrev. for:* (in) care of (esp. used when writing addresses): *Send it to John Smith c/o Dorothy Smith: that's his mother*

Co.¹ *written abbrev. for:* COUNTY (1): *Sunderland, Co. Durham*

Co.² /kəʊ/ *n* **and Co.** and Company: *James Smith & Co.*

C.O. /ˌsiː ˈəʊ◂/ *abbrev. for:* Commanding Officer

coach¹ /kəʊtʃ/ *n* **1** [C] a large enclosed 4-wheeled horse-drawn carriage, used esp. in former times or in official ceremonies **2** [C; *by*+U] *BrE* a bus used for long-distance travel or touring: *We went by coach* —see picture at INTERCHANGE² **3** [C] a railway passenger carriage, esp. for day travel **4** [C] a person **a** who trains sportsmen for games, competitions, etc.: *a football coach* **b** employed privately to train a pupil or student for an examination: *an English coach* **5** [C] *AustrE* a farm cow used for attracting wild cattle into a trap **6 coach class** *AmE now rare* SECOND CLASS (2) **7 drive a coach and (four) horses through** *infml* to defeat completely (a law, plan, intention, etc., esp. of a government)

coach² *v* **1** [T1 (*for, in*)] to train or teach (a person or a group of people); give instruction or advice to (a person or a group of people): *I coach people for English examinations* **2** [IØ] to act or be employed as a COACH¹ (4)

coach·build·er /ˈkəʊtʃˌbɪldəʳ/ *n* a skilled worker who builds the bodies of motor vehicles, railway carriages, etc.

coach·man /ˈkəʊtʃmən/ *n* **-men** /mən/ [C;N] a person employed to drive a horse-drawn COACH¹ (1)

coach park /ˈ· ·/ *n BrE* an open place where COACHes¹ (2) may be parked sometimes for a small payment —compare CAR PARK

coach·work *n* the outside body of a car

co·ad·ju·tor /kəʊˈædʒʊtəʳ‖ˌkəʊəˈdʒuːtər, kəʊˈædʒətər/ *n* a helper, esp. a person who helps a BISHOP (= high ranking priest); ASSISTANT

co·ag·u·lant /kəʊˈægjʊlənt‖-gjə-/ *n* [C;U] (a) substance that causes a liquid to COAGULATE

co·ag·u·late /kəʊˈægjʊleɪt‖-gjə-/ *v* [IØ;T1] **a** (esp. of an ORGANIC (1) liquid) to change from a liquid into a solid or nearly solid mass, esp. by chemical action: *Blood coagulates when it meets air* **b** to cause (esp. an ORGANIC (1) liquid) to change in this way: *Air can coagulate blood* —**-lation** /kəʊ-ˌægjʊˈleɪʃən‖-gjə-/ *n* [U]

coal¹ /kəʊl/ *n* **1** [U] a black or dark brown mineral which is dug (MINEd) from the earth, which can be burned to give heat, and from which gas, COAL TAR, and many other products can be made **2** [C] a flaming, burning, or already burnt piece of this mineral or wood; EMBER: *A coal fell from the fire and burned the mat* **3 carry/take coals to Newcastle** *not fml* to take goods to a place where they are plentiful already **4 heap coals of fire on someone's head** *lit* to return good for evil and so cause feelings of guilt —compare KILL **someone with kindness 5 haul over the coals** *infml* to scold (someone) for doing something wrong

coal² *v* **1** [T1] to supply (a ship, engine, etc.) with coal **2** [IØ] (of ships, engines, etc.) to take in a supply of coal

coal·bun·ker /ˈkəʊlˌbʌŋkəʳ/ *n* **1** a small low usu. brick or cement building in which coal is stored **2** a space in a ship or engine where coal is stored

co·a·lesce /ˌkəʊəˈles/ *v* [IØ] to grow together or unite so as to form one group, body, mass, etc. —**coalescence** *n* [U]

coal·face /ˈkəʊlfeɪs/ *n* the part of a COAL SEAM (=a thick bed of coal in a mine) from which coal is cut

coal·field /ˈkəʊlfiːld/ *n* an area in which there are a lot of coalmines

coal gas /ˈ· ·, ˌ· ˈ·/ *n* [U] gas used esp. for lighting and heating, produced by burning coal: *a coal-gas fire*

coal·hole /ˈkəʊlhəʊl/ *n* **1** a small room, usu. beneath the surface of the ground, where coal is stored **2** a usu. round hole through which coal is poured into this room

coal·house /ˈkəʊlhaʊs/ *n* **-houses** /haʊzɪ̇z/ a hut or small building (SHED) where coal is stored

coaling sta·tion /ˈ·· ˌ··/ *n* a place at which coal is supplied to ships or engines

co·a·li·tion /ˌkəʊəˈlɪʃən/ *n* **1** [U] the act of uniting into one body or mass **2** [GC] a union of political parties for a special purpose, usu. for a limited period of time: *During the war Britain was ruled by a coalition*

coal·mine /ˈkəʊlmaɪn/ also **coal pit** /ˈ· ·/, **pit**— *n* a mine from which coal is obtained

coal·scut·tle /ˈkəʊlˌskʌtl/ also **scuttle**— *n* a bucket in which coal is carried and from which it can be poured —see picture at LIVING ROOM

coal seam /ˈ· ·/ also **coal mea·sure** /ˈ· ˌ··/— *n* a thick bed of coal in a mine

coal tar /ˈ· ·, ˌ· ˈ·/ *n* [U] a thick black sticky liquid made by heating coal without air, from which many drugs and chemical products may be obtained

coarse /kɔːs‖kors/ *adj* [Wa1] **1** not fine; lumpy; rough: *coarse grains of sand* **2** having a rough surface; not smooth: *The priest wore a coarse woollen garment next to his skin* **3** rough in manner; not delicate in action: *coarse behaviour|a coarse joke* **4** (esp. of food) of low quality: *coarse food* —**~ly** *adv* —**~ness** *n* [U]

coarse fish /ˈ· ·/ *n* **coarse fish** *or* **coarse fishes** [Wn2;C;U] *BrE* (the meat of) any fish that lives in lakes or rivers, except the SALMON

coars·en /ˈkɔːsən‖ˈkor-/ *v* [IØ;T1] to (cause to) become coarse: *The wrong kind of soap can coarsen the skin*

coast¹ /kəʊst/ *n* **1** [C] the land next to the sea; seashore **2** [*the*+R] an area bordering the sea **3** [C] *AmE* a hill or slope down which one may roll or slide **4** [S] *AmE* a trip down such a hill or slope **5 the coast is/was/will be clear** *infml* all danger has/had/will have gone: *When the coast was clear the 2 thieves escaped* —see SHORE¹ (USAGE)

coast² *v* **1** [IØ (*along*, ALONG)] to keep moving after effort has ceased, esp. to travel down a hill without using any power: *The children were enjoying coasting along on their bicycles* **2** [IØ] to sail along from port to port on the coast; sail near the coast **3** [T1] to sail along the coast of (a country)

coast·al /ˈkəʊstl/ *adj* [Wa5;A] of or related to the COAST¹ (1): *Ships should not enter rocky coastal waters*

coast·er /ˈkəʊstəʳ/ *n* **1** a ship which sails from port to port along a coast **2** a small round mat placed under a bottle, glass, etc., to protect a table top or other surface **3** *AmE* a small vehicle used for COASTing² (1) **4** *AmE* ROLLER-COASTER

coast·guard /ˈkəʊstgɑːd‖-ɑrd/ *n* a person serving in the COAST GUARD

coast guard /ˈ· ·/ *n* [GU] (*often caps.*) a naval or police organization intended to watch for ships in danger and prevent unlawful activity at sea

coast·guards·man /ˈkəʊstgɑːdzmən‖-ɑr/ *n* **-men** /mən/ [C;A] *AmE* COASTGUARD

coast·line /ˈkəʊstlaɪn/ *n* the shape (OUTLINE) of a coast, esp. as seen from sea

coast·wise /ˈkəʊstwaɪz/ *adj, adv* [Wa5] *infml* following the coast

coat¹ /kəʊt/ *n* **1** an outer garment with long SLEEVE*s*, often fastened at the front with buttons, and usu. worn to keep warm or for protection **2** a long-SLEEVEd outer garment worn on the upper part of the body as the top half of a suit; JACKET (1): *a coat and skirt* **3** an animal's fur, wool, hair, etc. **4** a covering spread over a surface: *a coat of paint|a coat of dust* **5 cut one's coat according to one's cloth** to avoid spending more than one earns: *The government must cut its coat according to its cloth if it wants to lower taxes next year* —see also DRESS³ (2) coat

coat² *v* [T1] to cover with a COAT¹ (4): *The table was coated in/with dust*

coat hang·er /ˈ· ˌ··/ *n* HANGER

coat·ing /ˈkəʊtɪŋ/ *n* **1** [C] a covering of any substance spread over a surface: *2 coatings of paint|a cake with a coating of chocolate* **2** [U] cloth from which coats are made

coat of arms /ˌ· · ˈ·/ *n* a group of patterns or pictures, usu. painted on a shield or shield-like shape, used by a noble family, town council, university, etc., as their special sign

coat of mail /ˌ· · ˈ·/ *n* a protective garment made from metal rings or plates, worn as armour by soldiers in former times

coat tails /ˈ· ·/ *n* [P] **1** the long divided piece of material which hangs down from the back of a man's DRESS³ (2) coat **2 on someone's coat tails** *not fml esp. AmE* (esp. in politics) with the help of another

coax /kəʊks/ *v* **1** [T1 (*into, out of*); V3] to persuade (someone) by gentle kindness or patience: *I coaxed him into taking me to the theatre* **2** [X9] to obtain (something) by gently persuading: *I coaxed a kiss from the little girl* —**~ingly** *adv*

cob /kɒb‖kɑb/ *n* **1** also **corncob**— the long hard central part of an ear of corn (MAIZE) —see picture at CEREAL **2** a male SWAN **3** a strong short-legged horse, usu. trained to walk in a showily stylish fashion **4** a type of large nut, esp. one from the HAZEL tree

co·balt /ˈkəʊbɔːlt/ *n* [U] a strong shiny silver-white MAGNETIC metal that is a simple substance (ELEMENT) used in blue colouring materials and in making metals

cob·ber /ˈkɒbəʳ‖ˈkɑ-/ *n* [N] *Austr & NZE, infml* friend; MATE² (1)

cob·ble¹ /ˈkɒbəl‖ˈkɑ-/ *v* [T1] *rare* to repair (shoes)

cobble² *v* [Wv5;T1] to cover (PAVE) the surface of (a road) with COBBLESTONE*s*: *Streets were first cobbled in the 19th century.*|*old cobbled streets*

cob·bler /ˈkɒbləʳ‖ˈkɑ-/ *n* **1** a person who earns money by repairing shoes **2** *derog* a careless workman

cob·blers /ˈkɒbləz‖ˈkɑblərz/ *n BrE sl* [U] foolish talk; nonsense (esp. in the phr. **a load of old cobblers**): *I've never heard such a load of old cobblers in my whole life!*

cob·ble·stone /ˈkɒbəlstəʊn‖ˈkɑ-/ also **cobble**— *n* [*often pl*] a naturally rounded or specially shaped stone, esp. used for covering the surface of roads in former times

co·bra /ˈkɒbrə, ˈkəʊ-‖ˈkəʊ-/ *n* a type of African or Asian poisonous snake that can spread the skin of its neck to make itself look bigger and more dangerous

cob·web /ˈkɒbweb‖ˈkɑb-/ *n* **1** a very fine network of sticky threads made by a SPIDER (=a small 8-legged insect-like animal) to catch insects **2** a single thread from such a network **3** anything which seems to be hidden or confused **4 blow the cobwebs away** *infml* to make (someone or something, esp. oneself) fresher, clearer, or better: *Let's go for a walk and blow the cobwebs away*

Co·ca-Co·la /ˌkəʊkə ˈkəʊlə/ also (*infml*) **coke** /kəʊk/— *n* [C;U] *tdmk* (a small bottle or glass of) a popular non-alcoholic dark-coloured BUBBLY drink of American origin

co·caine /kəʊˈkeɪn/ *n* [U] a type of drug sometimes used for preventing pain in medical operations, or taken first for pleasure and then from habit by ADDICT*s* (=people unable to stop taking drugs)

coc·cyx /ˈkɒksɪks‖ˈkɑk-/ *n* **coccyxes** *or* **coccyges** /kɒkˈsaɪdʒiːz‖ˈkɑksə-/ *med* the bones showing the remains of a tail in man, found at the bottom of the BACKBONE (=the line of bones that runs down the back) —see picture at SKELETON

coch·i·neal /ˌkɒtʃəˈniːl‖ˌkɑ-/ *n* **1** [C] a type of tropical American insect **2** [U] bright red colouring matter made from the dried body of this insect

coch·le·a /ˈkɒklɪə‖ˈkɑ-/ *n* **-leas** *or* **-leae** /-li-iː/ *med* a SPIRAL-shaped tube-like part of the inner ear where the nerves necessary for hearing are found —see picture at EAR¹

cock¹ /kɒk‖kɑk/ *n* **1** [C] (*AmE* **rooster**)— a fully-grown male chicken —see picture at DOMESTIC BIRD **2** [C] (*often in comb.*) a fully-grown male of any type of small bird or bird used for food **3** [C] an apparatus such as a TAP, VALVE, etc., for controlling the flow of liquid in a pipe **4** [C] the hammer of a gun **5** [C;U] the position of a gun's hammer when drawn back for firing **6** [N] *sl BrE* (used by men to men): *Excuse me, cock, can you change me a pound note?* **7** [C] *taboo sl* PENIS **8 cock of the walk** *infml often derog* the ruling and most influential person among a group of people, esp. one who is too proud **9 go off at half cock** *infml* to begin too early and ineffectively **10 live like fighting cocks** *infml, esp. BrE* to live very well, esp. eating the best food

cock² *v* **1** [T1] to set (the hammer of a gun) in the correct position for firing **2** [IØ;T1: (UP)] **a** (of parts of the body) to stand up: *The horse's ears cocked up* **b** to cause (parts of the body) to stand up: *The horse cocked its ears when it heard the noise* **3** [T1] to cause (a hat, head, etc.) to slope slightly; TILT: *The man cocked his hat in the latest fashion* **4 cock one's snook/snoot (to/at)** *BrE infml* to put one's thumb to one's nose to offend (someone)

cock³ *n* **1** [*usu. sing.*] the act of COCKing² (2,3) **2** a slight slope; TILT

cock⁴ *n* **1** [C] a small pile of HAY (=dried grass) **2** [U] *sl* foolishness; stupidity (esp. in the phr. **a load of old cock**) **3** [U] *infml esp. BrE* bold behaviour: *I don't like his cock*

cock⁵ *v* [T1] to pile (HAY) into COCK*s*⁴ (1)

cock·ade /kɒˈkeɪd‖kɑ-/ *n* an ornamental ROSETTE (=knot of material) worn on the hat as a sign of rank, membership of a particular society, etc.

cock-a-doo·dle-doo /ˌkɒk ə ˌduːdl ˈduː‖ˌkɑk-/ *n* **-doos** the loud long cry made by a COCK¹ (1)

cock-a-hoop /ˌkɒk ə ˈhuːp‖ˌkɑk-/ *adj* [F] *infml* **1** very happy and pleased: *He was cock-a-hoop about his new job* **2** *AmE* in disorder: *Everything's all cock-a-hoop in this office and no one can find anything*

cock-a-leek·ie, cocka- /ˌkɒk ə ˈliːki‖ˌkɑk-/ also **cocky-leeky**— *n* [U] *esp. ScotE* a soup made from boiled chicken and vegetables, esp. LEEK*s*

cock-and-bull sto·ry /ˌ· · ˈ· ˌ··/ *n infml* a foolish improbable story told as if it were true —compare BULL⁵

cock·a·too /ˌkɒkəˈtuː‖ˈkɑkətuː/ *n* **-toos** **1** [Wn1] a type of Australian bird (PARROT) having on the top of its head a number of large feathers (CREST) which can be raised or lowered at will —see picture at EXOTIC **2** *AustrE infml* the owner of a small farm

cock·chaf·er /ˈkɒktʃeɪfəʳ‖ˈkɑk-/ *n* a type of European insect (BEETLE) which attacks and destroys trees and plants

cock·crow /ˈkɒk-krəʊ‖ˈkɑk-/ *n* [C; *at*+U] early morning; sunrise; the time at which COCK*s* (=male chickens) CROW (make loud long sounds): *He woke up at cockcrow*

cocked hat /ˌ· ˈ·/ *n* **1** a 3-cornered hat with turned-up edges, worn in former times or with special uniforms **2 knock into a cocked hat** *sl* **a** to defeat completely: *He'll knock all the other competitors into a cocked hat* **b** to cause to fail: *Her refusal knocked all my plans into a cocked hat*

cock·e·rel /ˈkɒkərəl‖ˈkɑ-/ *n* a young COCK¹ (1)

cock·er span·i·el /ˌkɒkə ˈspænɪəl‖ˌkɑkər-/ also **cocker** /ˈkɒkəʳ‖ˈkɑ-/— *n* a type of dog with long ears and silky coat, trained for use in hunting or kept as a pet

cock·eyed /ˌkɒkˈaɪd◂‖ˌkɑk-/ *adj sl* **1** *derog* foolish; stupid: *I hate him and his cockeyed plans!* **2** turned or twisted to one side; CROOKED (1): *The picture on the wall's cockeyed*

cock·fight /ˈkɒkfaɪt‖ˈkɑk-/ *n* a fight between 2 fully-grown male chickens (COCK*s*¹ (1)) with sharp metal instruments (SPUR*s*) fastened to their heels, watched as a sport —**~ing** *n* [U]

cock·horse /ˌkɒkˈhɔːs‖ˈkɑkhɔrs/ *n rare* **1** a stick with a model horse's head fastened to the top, which children pretend to ride **2** ROCKING HORSE

cock·le /ˈkɒkəl‖ˈkɑ-/ *n* **1** a type of European soft-bodied sea animal that lives inside a pair of heart-shaped shells (COCKLE SHELL*s*) and is eaten —compare SCALLOP and see picture at MOLLUSC **2** also **cockleshell** /ˈkɒkəlʃel‖ˈkɑ-/— *lit* a small light boat **3 warm the cockles of someone's/the heart** *infml* to make someone happier

cock·le·shell /ˈkɒkəlʃel‖ˈkɑ-/ *n* **1** a type of heart-shaped shell with thin lines marked on its outer surface **2** COCKLE (2)

Cock·ney /ˈkɒkni‖ˈkɑkni/ *n* a Londoner, esp. one from the EAST END: *A true Cockney is born within the sound of the bells of St Mary-Le-Bow church*

cock·pit /ˈkɒkˌpɪt‖ˈkɑk-/ *n* **1** a small enclosed space in which COCKFIGHT*s* take place: (fig.) *Poland has been the cockpit of modern history* **2** the part of a plane or racing car in which the pilot and COPILOT sit —see picture at AIRCRAFT **3** (in former times) a space on the lower floor (DECK) of a warship for the treatment of people wounded in battle

cock·roach /ˈkɒk-rəʊtʃ‖ˈkɑk-/ *n* any of several types of large black insect, some of which live in dirty houses —see picture at INSECT

cocks·comb /ˈkɒks-kəʊm‖ˈkɑks-/ *n* **1** also **cox·comb**— *lit* the cap of a professional fool (JESTER) **2** a type of plant with bunches of red, purple, or yellow featherlike flowers **3** the red fleshy growth at the top of a COCK's[1] (1) head

cock·sure /ˌkɒkˈʃʊəʳ‖ˌkɑk-/ *adj infml & derog* too sure of oneself; offensively sure of oneself

cock·tail /ˈkɒkteɪl‖ˈkɑk-/ *n* **1** [C] a mixed alcoholic drink **2** [C9;(U9)] a small quantity of specially prepared SEAFOOD eaten at the start of a meal: *a* SHRIMP/PRAWN *cocktail* —see also FRUIT COCKTAIL

cocktail dress /ˈ·· ·/ *n* a short (woman's) dress worn on formal occasions

cocktail lounge /ˈ·· ·/ *n* a public room, in a hotel, restaurant, club, etc., where COCKTAIL*s* (1) and other drinks may be bought

cock-up /ˈ· ·/ *n* **1** *BrE taboo sl* a confused state of affairs; example of complete disorder **2** *tech* a slightly raised letter or number such as in M^r^

cock·y /ˈkɒki‖ˈkɑki/ *adj* [Wa1] *infml derog* too sure of oneself: *I don't like him; he's far too cocky* —**cockiness** *n* [U]

cock·y-leek·y /ˌkɒki ˈliːki‖ˌkɑki-/ *n* [U] *esp. ScotE* COCK-A-LEEKIE

co·co /ˈkəʊkəʊ/ *n* **cocos** COCONUT PALM

co·coa /ˈkəʊkəʊ/ *n* **1** [U] a dark brown powder made by crushing the cooked seeds of a tropical American tree (CACAO), used for giving a special chocolate-like taste to sweet foods and drinks **2** [C;U] (a cupful of a) drink made from hot milk or water mixed with this powder

co·co·nut /ˈkəʊkənʌt/ *n* **1** [C] a very large brown hard-shelled nutlike fruit from a tropical tree (COCONUT PALM), having hard white flesh and a hollow centre filled with a milky juice —see picture at FRUIT[1] **2** [U] the flesh of this seed eaten raw as food

coconut mat·ting /ˌ··· ˈ··/ *n* [U] heavy material made from the coarse hair which surrounds and protects the outside of the COCONUT (1), used for making mats

coconut palm /ˈ··· ·/ also **coco**— *n* a type of tall tropical tree (PALM) on which the COCONUT grows

coconut shy /ˈ··· ·/ *n* a game at a FAIR[3] (1), in which people pay to throw balls at COCONUT*s* in order to win a prize by knocking them off posts

co·coon[1] /kəˈkuːn/ *n* a protective case of silky threads in which a PUPA (=an insect in its inactive stage) is enclosed —compare CHRYSALIS

cocoon[2] *v* [T1] *rare* to keep (a car, plane, etc.) in a protective covering, esp. for storing

cod /kɒd‖kɑd/ also **cod·fish** /ˈkɒdˌfɪʃ‖ˈkɑd-/— *n* **1** [Wn2;C] a type of large North Atlantic sea fish —see picture at FISH[1] **2** [Wn2;C] any of several other types of fish like this, esp. a closely-related type from the Pacific **3** [U] the flesh of this fish cooked and eaten as food

cod[2] *v* **-dd-** [T1] *BrE sl* to make a fool of (someone): *You're codding me!*

C.O.D. /ˌsiː əʊ ˈdiː/ *abbrev. for:* Cash on Delivery; with payment to be made at the time and place of delivery

co·da /ˈkəʊdə/ *n* **1** a usu. independent passage that ends a piece of music **2** a partly independent passage that ends a work of literature

cod·dle /ˈkɒdl‖ˈkɑdl/ *v* [Wv3,5;T1] **1** to cook (eggs, fruit, etc.) slowly in water just below boiling point: *coddled eggs* **2** *not fml* also **mollycoddle**— to treat (a person or animal) too tenderly; spoil: *I think your daughter's been coddled too much; she expects us to do everything she wants*

code[1] /kəʊd/ *n* **1** [C; *in*+U] a system of secret words, letters, numbers, etc., used instead of ordinary writing to keep messages secret **2** [C;*in*+U] a system of signals used instead of letters and numbers in a message that is to be broadcast, telegraphed, etc.: *a telegraphic code* —see also MORSE CODE **3** [C] a body of established social customs: *a code of behaviour|Christianity's moral code* **4** [C] a collection of laws: *the Napoleonic code*

code[2] *v* [T1] **1** also **encode**— to translate into a CODE[1] (1,2) **2** to give a special CODE[1] to something: *You've not coded these books yet; how can I put them in order?*

co·deine /ˈkəʊdiːn/ *n* [U] a drug made from OPIUM, used as a pain-killing medicine, esp. for headaches and colds

co·dex /ˈkəʊdeks/ *n* **codices** /ˈkəʊdɪsiːz/ *tech* an original form, esp. of an ancient or holy book

cod·ger /ˈkɒdʒəʳ‖ˈkɑ-/ *n infml* an odd or peculiar old man

cod·i·cil /ˈkəʊdɪsɪl‖ˈkɑdɪsəl, -sɪl/ *n law* an addition to a WILL (=a paper stating who is to have one's possessions after one's death)

co·di·fy /ˈkəʊdɪfaɪ‖ˈkɑ-/ *v* [T1] to arrange (esp. laws) into a CODE (=an ordered system): *The new government promised to codify the laws* —**-fication** /ˌkəʊdɪfɪˈkeɪʃən‖ˌkɑ-/ *n* [C;U]

cod·ling[1] /ˈkɒdlɪŋ‖ˈkɑd-/ *n* a young COD[1] (1)

codling[2] also **cod·lin** /ˈkɒdlɪn‖ˈkɑd-/— *n* a type of small unripe apple used in cooking

cod-liver oil /ˌ· ·· ˈ·/ *n* [U] oil obtained from the LIVER (=an organ of the body) of the COD and other related fishes

cod·piece /ˈkɒdpiːs‖ˈkɑd-/ *n* an often ornamented piece of material used esp. in the 15th and 16th centuries to cover the opening in the front of men's tight-fitting trousers

cods·wal·lop /ˈkɒdzwɒləp‖ˈkɑdzwɑ-/ *n* [U] *sl, esp. BrE* nonsense; foolish talk

co·ed[1] /ˌkəʊˈed◂‖ˈkəʊed/ *n AmE infml* a female student in a college or university open to both sexes

coed[2] *adj* [Wa5] *infml* (of education, a school, college, etc.) COEDUCATIONal

co·ed·u·ca·tion /ˌkəʊedʒʊˈkeɪʃən‖-dʒə-/ *n* [U] the system of educating boys and girls together in the same buildings and classes —**~al** *adj* [Wa5]

co·ef·fi·cient /ˌkəʊɪˈfɪʃənt/ *n tech* **1** a number written before and multiplying another number or quantity: *In 8pz=4 the coefficient of pz is 8* **2** (a number that is) a measure of the quality possessed by a substance under fixed conditions

coefficient of ex·pan·sion /··ˌ·· · ·ˈ··/ *n tech* the number that shows the amount by which a substance EXPAND*s* (=grows in size) for a given change in temperature

coe·la·canth /ˈsiːləkænθ/ *n* a type of sea fish which was thought to have died out 70,000,000 years ago until one was caught near South Africa in 1938 —see picture at PREHISTORIC

co·e·qual /ˌkəʊˈiːkwəl/ *n, adj* [Wa5;B;C: (*with*)] (any of 2 or more people who are) equal with one another in rank, ability, power, etc. —**~ly** *adv*

co·erce /kəʊˈɜːs‖-ˈɜrs/ *v* [T1] **1** [(*into*)] to make (an unwilling person or group of people) do something, by using force, threats of punishment, etc.: *The government coerced the unions into accepting the pay limit by threatening to call an election* **2** [*often pass.*] to keep (a person, group of people, or activity) under control by using force, threats of punishment, etc.; REPRESS (2): *The working people have been coerced by their employers for too long!* **3** [*often pass.*] to gain acceptance for (a course of action) by force or the threat of force: *Our agreement to the plan was coerced: we were not free to say no to it!*

co·er·cion /kəʊˈɜːʃən‖-ˈɜrʒən/ *n* [U] **1** the act of coercing (COERCE) or of being COERCEd **2** government by force

co·er·cive /kəʊˈɜːsɪv‖-ˈɜr-/ *adj* serving or intended to COERCE: *coercive measures* —**~ly** *adv* —**~ness** *n* [U]

co·ter·nal /ˌkəʊɪˈtɜːnl‖-ɜr-/ *adj* [Wa5;B (*with*)] *esp. bibl* equally ETERNAL (=lasting for ever) with one another —**~ly** *adv*

co·e·val /kəʊˈiːvəl/ *n, adj lit* (a person) of the same age

co·ex·ist /ˌkəʊɪgˈzɪst/ *v* [IØ (*with*)] **1** to exist together at the same time: *Can love and hate coexist in the same person?* **2** (of countries with opposed political systems) to live together in peace with one another

co·ex·ist·ence /ˌkəʊɪgˈzɪstəns/ *n* [U (*with*)] **1** the state of existing together **2** (of countries with opposed political systems) the state of peacefully existing together —**-ent** *adj*

C of E /ˌsiː əv ˈiː/ *abbrev. for:* CHURCH OF ENGLAND

cof·fee /ˈkɒfi‖ˈkɔfi, ˈkɑfi/ *n* **1** [U] a brown powder made by crushing COFFEE BEAN*s*, used for making drinks or giving a special taste to food **2** [C;U] (a cupful of) a hot brown drink made by adding hot water and/or milk to this powder

coffee bar /ˈ·· ·/ *n BrE* a place where light meals, sweets, and nonalcoholic drinks are served. It does not usu. serve breakfast —compare COFFEE SHOP —see COFFEE HOUSE (USAGE)

coffee bean /ˈ·· ·/ *n* the dark brown seed of the COFFEE TREE, crushed and used for making drinks or giving a special taste to food

coffee break /ˈ·· ·/ *n esp. AmE* TEA BREAK

coffee house /ˈ·· ·/ *n* (in Central Europe and in former times in England) a place where nonalcoholic drinks, cakes, and light meals are served, often used as an informal meeting place

USAGE This is a much older word than **coffee bar**. Today, a place called a **coffee house** is usually of a higher class than one called a **coffee bar**. —compare COFFEE SHOP

coffee mill /ˈ·· ·/ *n* an apparatus for crushing COFFEE BEAN*s* into powder (COFFEE (1))

cof·fee·pot /ˈkɒfipɒt‖ˈkɔfipɑt, ˈkɑ-/ *n* a container in which coffee is made or served

coffee shop /ˈ·· ·/ *n* **1** *AmE* a small restaurant, esp. one that serves sweet food, simple meals, and breakfast —compare COFFEE BAR **2** a shop that sells various kinds of COFFEE BEAN*s*

coffee ta·ble /ˈ·· ˌ··/ *n* a small long low table on which coffee may be served, magazines arranged, etc.

coffee-table book /ˈ·· ·· ˌ·/ *n often derog or humor* a large costly book, usu. having many pictures, placed so that visitors to a house can see and admire it

coffee tree /ˈ·· ·/ *n* a type of tropical bush or tree on which dark brown seeds (COFFEE BEAN*s*) grow

cof·fer /ˈkɒfəʳ‖ˈkɔfər, ˈkɑ-/ *n* **1** a large strong chest for holding money, jewels, or other valuable objects **2** *tech* an ornamental enclosed sunken area (PANEL¹ (1)) on the inside roof of a room **3** CAISSON (2,3)

cof·fer·dam /ˈkɒfədæm‖ˈkɔfər-, ˈkɑ-/ also **coffer**— *n* CAISSON (2,3)

cof·fers /ˈkɒfəz‖ˈkɔfərz, ˈkɑ-/ *n* [P] *infml* the quantity of money ready for use, imagined as if stored in COFFER*s*

cof·fin /ˈkɒfɨn‖ˈkɔ-/ *n* **1** the box in which a dead person is buried **2 nail in someone's coffin** *infml* something bad which will bring a person's ruin nearer

cog /kɒg‖kɑg/ *n* **1** any of the teeth round the edge of a wheel that cause it to move or be moved by another wheel —see picture at MACHINERY **2 cog in the machine** *infml* an unimportant person or branch of a firm in a very large business or organization: *I didn't want to be just a cog in the machine so I started my own business and now find work much more interesting*

co·gen·cy /ˈkəʊdʒənsi/ *n* [U] the power to prove or produce belief; quality of being COGENT: *The cogency of the priest's arguments made me believe in God*

co·gent /ˈkəʊdʒənt/ *adj* having the power to prove or produce belief; forceful in argument; CONVINCING: *I have cogent reasons for voting for the workers' party* —**~ly** *adv*

cog·i·tate /ˈkɒdʒɨteɪt‖ˈkɑ-/ *v* [IØ (*about, on, upon*)] *fml* to think carefully and seriously about something

cog·i·ta·tion /ˌkɒdʒɨˈteɪʃən‖ˌkɑ-/ *n* [U *often pl. with sing. meaning*] *fml* the act of thinking carefully and seriously

co·gnac /ˈkɒnjæk‖ˈkəʊ-, ˈkɑ-/ *n* [C;U] (a glass of) a type of fine strong alcoholic drink (BRANDY) made in Southwestern France

cog·nate¹ /ˈkɒgneɪt‖ˈkɑg-/ *adj* [(*with*)] **1** *tech* related in origin: *Italian and Spanish are cognate languages* **2** *fml or tech* related; sharing many qualities: *Do you think chemistry is cognate with any other science?*

cognate² *n tech or fml* a person or thing related in origin or having much in common with another

cog·ni·tion /kɒgˈnɪʃən‖kɑg-/ *n* [U] *tech or fml* the act or action of knowing, including consciousness of things and judgment about them

cog·ni·tive /ˈkɒgnɨtɪv‖ˈkɑg-/ *adj* [Wa5] *tech or fml* of, about, or needing COGNITION: *cognitive* PSYCHOLOGY (1,2) —**~ly** *adv*

cog·ni·zance /ˈkɒgnɨzəns‖ˈkɑg-/ *n* **take cognizance of** *fml or law* to take notice of; take into consideration: *The judge has taken cognizance of the new facts in your case*

cog·ni·zant /ˈkɒgnɨzənt‖ˈkɑg-/ *adj* [F+*of*] *fml or law* conscious; AWARE: *The judge said he was not cognizant of the case*

cog·no·men /kɒgˈnəʊmən‖kɑg-, ˈkɑgnə-/ *n* **1** *tech* a person's family name (SURNAME), esp. the 3rd and usu. last name of an ancient Roman citizen **2** *pomp* any name, esp. a descriptive NICKNAME

co·gno·scen·ti /ˌkɒnjəʊˈʃentiː‖ˌkɑnjə-/ *n* [(*the*) P] *It* people with very good knowledge of or experience in fashion, art, food, etc.; CONNOISSEUR*s*

cog·wheel /ˈkɒg-wiːl‖ˈkɑg-/ *n* a toothed wheel (wheel with teeth (COG*s*) round the edge) that can move or be moved by another wheel of the same type

co·hab·it /ˌkəʊˈhæbɨt/ *v* [IØ (*with*)] *tech or fml* (of one or more unmarried people) to live as a married person or married people: (fig.) *Can peace and freedom cohabit in the modern world?* —**~ation** /kəʊˌhæbɨˈteɪʃən/ *n* [U]

co·here /kəʊˈhɪəʳ/ *v* [Wv6;IØ] **1** to stick together; be united **2** to be reasonably and naturally connected, esp. in thought: *Do his religious and political beliefs cohere?*

co·her·ence /kəʊˈhɪərəns/ also **co·her·en·cy** /-rənsi/— *n* [U] natural or reasonable connection, esp. in thoughts or words; CONSISTENCY¹

co·her·ent /kəʊˈhɪərənt/ *adj* (esp. of speech, thought, ideas, etc.) being naturally or reasonably connected; easily understood; CONSISTENT —**~ly** *adv*

co·he·sion /kəʊˈhiːʒən/ *n* [U] **1** the act or state of sticking together tightly: *We need more moral cohesion if we're to defeat the enemy* **2** (in science) the force which holds parts of a solid or liquid together

co·he·sive /kəʊˈhiːsɪv/ *adj* **1** producing COHESION: *cohesive forces in society* **2** *tech* tending to stick together: *Is water cohesive by nature or not?* —**~ly** *adv* —**~ness** *n* [U]

co·hort /ˈkəʊhɔːt‖-hɔrt/ *n* **1** (in the ancient Roman army) a group of between 300 and 600 soldiers under one commander, being a 10th part of a LEGION **2** any group or company of people, esp. soldiers joined together **3** *often derog esp. AmE* a companion: *That criminal and all his cohorts must be brought to justice*

coif /kɔɪf/ *n* a close-fitting cap covering the top, sides, and back of the head, worn, esp. in former times by both men and women and today by some NUNs (=members of female religious groups) under their VEILs (=long loose head coverings)

coif·feur /kwɒˈfɜːʳ‖kwɑ-/ *n fml* HAIRDRESSER

coif·fure /kwɒˈfjʊəʳ‖kwɑ-/ *n* a style of arranging and combing a woman's hair —**-fured** *adj*

coil¹ /kɔɪl/ *v* [T1 (UP);L9, esp. UP] to (cause to) wind or twist into a ring or continuous circular shape (SPIRAL): *Will you coil the rope up please?|The snake coiled (itself) around the tree/coiled itself into a ball/coiled up*

coil² *n* **1** [C] a connected set of rings or twists into which a rope, wire, etc., can be wound; continuous circular shape made by winding rope, wire, etc.: *a coil of rope* **2** [C] a single one of these rings or twists: *a loose coil of hair* **3** [C] *tech* an electrical apparatus made by winding wire into a continuous circular shape, used for carrying an electric current —see picture at CAR **4** [C; *the*+R] a plastic or metal object fitted inside a woman to prevent her having more children; INTRAUTERINE DEVICE

coin¹ /kɔɪn/ *n* **1** [C] a piece of metal, usu. flat and round, made by a government for use as money **2** [*in/with*+U] such pieces in number: *He paid me in coin* **3 pay someone in his own/the same coin** *infml* to treat someone as he has treated others

coin² *v* [T1] **1** to make (metal) into coins **2** to make (coins) from metal: *The government has decided to coin more 50-penny pieces/-pence pieces* **3** to invent (a word or phrase): *Who coined that word?* **4 coin (the) money (in)** also **coin it (in)**— *infml* to make or earn a lot of money very quickly —**~er** *n*

coin·age /ˈkɔɪnɪdʒ/ *n* **1** [U] the act of making coins: *Only the government has the right of coinage today* **2** [U] metal coins in large numbers; CURRENCY (2): *What sort of coinage do they use in France?* **3** [U] the coins made by COINing² (2) **4** [C] a word or phrase recently invented: *That's an interesting coinage* **5** [U] the act of inventing new words or phrases

co·in·cide /ˌkəʊɪ̵nˈsaɪd/ *v* [IØ (*with*)] **1** to happen at the same time or during the same period of time **2** (of ideas, opinions, etc.) to be in agreement: *My religious beliefs and yours don't coincide*

co·in·ci·dence /kəʊˈɪnsɪ̵dəns/ *n* **1** [C] a combination of events, happening by chance, but in such a way that it seems planned or arranged: *What a coincidence it was to be in London just when you were!* **2** [U] the condition or fact of coinciding (COINCIDE): *Is there any coincidence between his opinions and your own?*

co·in·ci·dent /kəʊˈɪnsɪ̵dənt/ *adj* [Wa5] **1** *tech or fml* existing or happening in the same position and time **2** *fml* having like natures; being in complete agreement

co·in·ci·den·tal /kəʊˌɪnsɪ̵ˈdentl/ *adj* resulting from a COINCIDENCE (1) —**~ly** *adv*

coir /kɔɪəʳ/ *n* [U] a thick hard-wearing material made from the coarse hair that covers the COCONUT (1), used for making ropes, mats, etc.

co·i·tus /ˈkɔɪtəs, *med* ˈkəʊɪ̵təs/ also **co·i·tion** /kəʊˈɪʃən/— *n* [U] *med or fml* the act of sex; SEXUAL INTERCOURSE —**coital** /ˈkɔɪtl, *med* ˈkəʊɪ̵tl/ *adj* [Wa5]

coitus in·ter·rup·tus /ˌkɔɪtəs ɪntəˈrʌptəs, *med* ˌkəʊɪ̵-/ *n* [U] *Lat & fml* the practice of taking the man's sex organ out of the woman's sex organ before the sex act is completed, to prevent the woman having a baby

coke¹ /kəʊk/ *n* [U] the solid substance that remains after gas has been removed from coal by heating. It is burnt to give great heat, esp. when making steel

coke² *v* [T1] to change (coal) into COKE¹

coke³ *n* **1** [U] *sl* COCAINE **2** [C;U] *infml tdmk* COCA-COLA

col /kɒl‖kɑl/ *n* a low place between 2 high points in a mountain range, esp. where people, animals, and vehicles can cross the range easily —see picture at MOUNTAIN

col. *written abbrev. for:* COLONEL

col- /kəl, kɒl‖kəl, kɑl/ *prefix* (the form used for CON- before l-): COLLATERAL

co·la /ˈkəʊlə/ *n* [U] any of several types of non-alcoholic BUBBLY dark-coloured drink

col·an·der /ˈkʌləndəʳ, ˈkɒ-‖ˈkʌ-, ˈkɑ-/ also **cullender**— *n* a bowl-shaped pan with many small holes in the bottom, used for separating liquid from food

cold¹ /kəʊld/ *adj* [Wa1] **1** [B] having a low temperature: *a cold day|a cold wind* **2** [B] having a lower temperature than normal: *It's a cold day for July isn't it?* **3** [B] not feeling warm: *I'm very cold today; I should have put a coat on* **4** [F] *infml* (in games) still a long way from finding an object, the answer, etc.: *You're getting colder; you'll never find it* **5** [F] *infml* unconscious; esp. as the result of a severe blow to the head (esp. in the phr. **out cold**): *I knocked him (out) cold with one blow* **6** [B] (of people or their actions) showing a lack of (friendly) feelings; unkind **7** [B] (esp. of a woman) FRIGID (3) **8** [B] (of food) cooked but not eaten hot —see also **cold** TURKEY, **have cold feet** (FOOT), **in cold** BLOOD, **to make someone's** BLOOD **run cold** —**~ly** *adv* —**~ness** *n* [U]

cold² *n* **1** [*the*+R] the absence of heat; low temperature; cold weather: *It's nice to put on a warm coat and go for a walk in the cold* **2** [C;(U)] an illness, esp. of the nose and/or throat, which is common in winter and may cause headaches, coughing, slight fever, and general discomfort (esp. in the phrs. **catch cold, the common cold**) **3 (out) in the cold** *infml* not considered; seemingly unwanted: *I felt I was out in the cold at the party so I thought I'd come home*

cold³ *adv infml* completely; thoroughly: *When he asked her to marry him she refused him cold*

cold-blood·ed /ˌ· ˈ··◂/ *adj* **1** [Wa5] having a body temperature that changes according to the temperature of the surroundings: *Snakes are cold-blooded* **2** *derog* showing complete lack of feeling; cruel: *a cold-blooded murder* **3** *infml* being very sensitive to cold: *Joan's cold-blooded: she always feels cold, even with a coat on*

cold chis·el /ˌ· ˈ··/ *n* a strong narrow sharp-ended steel tool (CHISEL) used for cutting metal

cold com·fort /ˌ· ˈ··/ *n* [U] something that gives little sympathy or comfort; little CONSOLATION: *My wife is ill in a foreign prison, and it is cold comfort to know that the foreign government may fall in a few years' time*

cold cream /ˈ· ·/ *n* [U] a thick white sweet-smelling oily cream used, esp. by women, for cleaning and smoothing the skin of the face, neck, and hands

cold cuts /ˈ· ·/ *n* [P] *esp. AmE* thinly cut pieces of various types of cold meat

cold feet /ˌ· ˈ·/ *n* [P] *not fml* loss of courage; doubt strong enough to prevent a planned course of action (in the phrs. **get/have cold feet**)

cold fish /ˌ· ˈ·/ *n* a person who deals with others in a cold way

cold frame /ˈ· ·/ *n* a small glass-covered frame and the soil it encloses, used for protecting young plants

cold front /ˌ· ˈ·‖ˈ· ·/ *n* an advancing edge of a cold air mass

cold-heart·ed /ˌ· ˈ··◂/ *adj derog* lacking sympathy or feeling; unkind: *a cold-hearted refusal* —**~ly** *adv* —**~ness** *n* [U]

cold saw /ˈ· ·/ *n* a SAW used for cutting metal

cold shoul·der /ˌ· ˈ··/ *n* [*the*+R] *infml* intentionally cold or unsympathetic treatment (esp. in the phrs. **give/get the cold shoulder**): *Don't give me the cold shoulder: I didn't mean to make you angry*

cold-shoulder *v* [T1] *infml* to give the COLD SHOULDER to

cold snap /ˈ· ·/ *n* a sudden short period of very cold weather

cold sore /ˈ· ·/ also **fever blister**— *n* a sore on or near the lips, or within the mouth, that often comes with a cold or fever

cold steel /ˌ· ˈ·/ *n* [U] *lit* one or more cutting weapons, such as a knife or a sword: *"One more word from you, sir," said Sir Percival, "and you'll feel my cold steel in your heart!"*

cold stor·age /ˌ· ˈ··/ *n* [U] **1** STORAGE (as of food or furs) in a cold place **2** *not fml* the condition of being put aside for future action, rather than being put into action at once as was originally planned

cold store /ˈ· ·/ *n* a building or place where food, furs, etc., can be kept in COLD STORAGE (1)

cold sweat /ˌ· ˈ·/ *n* [S] a state in which one SWEATs and feels cold because of fear or nervousness

cold war /ˌ· ˈ·◂/ *n* (*sometimes caps.*) a severe political struggle between states with opposed political systems, which struggle, although very unfriendly, does not lead to actual fighting

cole·slaw /ˈkəʊlslɔː/ *n* [U] finely cut CABBAGE (=a leafy vegetable) in a DRESSING (=a thick tasty liquid), eaten as a SALAD

co·ley /ˈkəʊli/ *n* **1** [Wn2;C] any of several types of sea fish **2** [U] the flesh of this fish eaten as food

col·ic /ˈkɒlɪk‖ˈkɑ-/ *n* [(*the*) U] a severe pain in the stomach and bowels (esp. of children)

col·ick·y /ˈkɒlɪki‖ˈkɑ-/ *adj* **1** like or related to COLIC **2** suffering from COLIC

co·li·tis /kəˈlaɪtɪ̈s/ *n* [U] redness and swelling of the COLON (=part of the bowels) causing severe discomfort

col·lab·o·rate /kəˈlæbəreɪt/ *v* [IØ] (*with* and/or *on*) **1** to work together or with someone else: *Quirk and Greenbaum collaborated* (*on the new grammar*) **2** [(*with*)] *derog* to help an enemy country which has entered and taken control of one's own: *Anyone who collaborates should be shot* —**-rator** *n*

col·lab·o·ra·tion /kəˌlæbəˈreɪʃən/ *n* [U] the act of collaborating (COLLABORATE) (often in the phr. **in collaboration (with)**)

col·lab·o·ra·tion·ist /kəˌlæbəˈreɪʃən-ɪ̈st/ *n, adj derog* (of) a person that favours or practises working together with an enemy that has entered and taken control of a country: *Collaborationists will be severely punished* —**-ism** *n* [U]

col·lage /ˈkɒlɑːʒ‖kəˈlɑːʒ/ *n* **1** [C] a picture made by sticking various materials or objects onto a surface **2** [U] the art of making such pictures

col·lapse[1] /kəˈlæps/ *v* **1** [IØ;(T1)] to (cause to) fall down or inwards suddenly: *The weight of snow collapsed the roof* **2** [IØ;T1] **a** (of an object) to fold into a shape that takes up less space: *This table collapses, so I can store it easily when I'm not using it* **b** to cause (an object) to fold into a shape that takes up less space: *Collapse the table and put it away, please* **3** [IØ] to fall helpless or unconscious: *This man's collapsed: call for the doctor!* **4** [IØ] to fail suddenly and completely; break down: *All opposition to the government has collapsed* **5** [IØ;T1] *med* **a** (of a lung or blood vessel) to fall into a flattened mass: *We must take him to hospital at once: his right lung seems to have collapsed and he can't breathe!* **b** to cause (a lung or blood vessel) to fall into a flattened mass: *The doctors had to collapse her right lung to save her life*

collapse[2] *n* **1** [S;(U)] (an example of) the act of falling down or inwards: *The storm caused the collapse of the roof* **2** [S;(U)] (an example of) the act of suddenly and completely failing or breaking down: *The pound's collapse was caused by the bankers.|Collapse of the empire can't be prevented* **3** [C;U] (an example of) the act of suddenly and completely losing strength and/or will: *a state of near collapse|He suffered from a nervous collapse*

col·lap·si·ble /kəˈlæpsəbəl/ *adj* that can be COLLAPSEd[1] (2) for easy storing

col·lar[1] /ˈkɒləʳ‖ˈkɑ-/ *n* **1** the part of a shirt, dress, or coat, that stands up or folds down round the neck: *The collar comes off this shirt and can be washed separately* **2** a close-fitting ornamental band worn round the neck, esp. by women **3** a leather or metal band put round an animal's neck —see picture at DOG[1] **4** a round leather object put round the shoulders of a horse to help it pull a vehicle or other object: *The horse won't move until its collar's comfortable* **5** *tech* a band or coloured marking round the neck: *This animal has a black collar and is therefore a different type from that* **6** any of various ring-like machine parts —see also BLUE-COLLAR, WHITE-COLLAR

collar[2] *v* [T1] **1** *infml* to seize; catch and hold as if by the collar: *Mrs Brown collared me as I was going to work and she talked for such a long time that I was late* **2** *sl* to take without permission: *Did you collar my book?*

col·lar·bone /ˈkɒləbəʊn‖ˈkɑlər-/ also (*med*) **clavicle**— *n* either of a pair of bones joining the RIBs to the shoulders —see picture at SKELETON

collar stud /ˈ·· ·/ *n* a small buttonlike object for fastening a collar to a shirt

col·late /kəˈleɪt/ *v* [T1] **1** to examine and compare (copies of books, notes, etc.) carefully in order to find the differences between them: *I'm going to collate this new copy with an earlier one to see what changes have been made* **2** *tech* to arrange (the sheets) of (esp. a book) in the proper order: *Have you collated this book yet?*

col·lat·e·ral[1] /kəˈlætərəl/ *adj* [Wa5] *fml or tech* **1** side by side; parallel **2** additional, but with less importance; supporting: *A collateral aim of the government's industrial plan is to increase employment* **3** descended from the same person but through a different line: COUSINs *are collateral relatives but brothers are directly related* **4** of, related to, based on, or being COLLATERAL[2]

collateral[2] *n* [S;U] *tech* property or something valuable promised to a person if one is unable to repay money one has borrowed from that person: *He used his house as* (*a*) *collateral for a large debt* —compare SECURITY[3]

col·la·tion /kəˈleɪʃən/ *n* **1** [U] the act of collating (COLLATE): *Have you completed the collation of this book?* **2** [C] *fml* a usu. cold light meal

col·league /ˈkɒliːg‖ˈkɑ-/ *n* a fellow worker, esp. in a profession

col·lect[1] /ˈkɒlɪkt, -lekt‖ˈkɑ-/ *n* a short prayer,

varying from day to day, read near the beginning of certain Christian religious services

col·lect² /kə'lekt/ *v* **1** [T1;I∅] to (cause to) gather together: *Collect the books and put them in a pile on my desk.|A crowd of people collected to cheer the new king* **2** [T1] to gather (objects) as a sport, HOBBY, for study, etc.: *John collects foreign coins* **3** [T1] to call for and take away (someone or something) **4** [T1] to regain control of (oneself, one's thoughts, senses, etc.): *I tried to collect my thoughts but was too excited* **5** [T1;I∅] to obtain payment of (money): *The government could save money by improving the way it collects taxes*

collect³ *adj, adv* [Wa5] *AmE* to be paid for by the receiver: *Call me collect as soon as you get home.|I sent you the books collect*

col·lect·ed /kə'lektɨd/ *adj* having control of oneself, one's thoughts, senses, etc.; calm: *She was calm, cool and collected.|How can you stay so collected after an argument?* —**~ly** *adv*

col·lec·tion /kə'lekʃən/ *n* **1** [U] the act of collecting **2** [C] the emptying of a post-box by a postman: *What time's the next collection?* **3** [C] a group of objects collected as a HOBBY, for study, etc.: *Janet has a very good collection of foreign coins* **4** [C] a sum of money collected, esp. at a religious service: *What does the church do with the money it gets from collections?* **5** [C] the gathering of such money: *When the time came for the collection the priest asked the people to be generous* **6** [C *usu. sing.*] a pile of material, paper, dust, dirt, etc., often unwanted and unplanned: *There was a collection of dust in the corner*

col·lec·tive¹ /kə'lektɪv/ *adj* [Wa5] **1** formed by collection; considered as a whole: *We must turn our collective mistakes to our advantage* **2** of or related to a number of people or groups of people considered or acting as one: *It is the collective opinion of the governments of Western Europe that peace is always better than war* **3** shared by all members of a group: *collective ownership* **4** (in grammar) that is COLLECTIVE² (3): —**~ly** *adv "*FLOCK*" is a collective word for a group of birds*

collective² *n* **1** a group; a body of people considered as a whole: *The workers' collective won't like the new industrial plan* **2** a business or firm owned and controlled by the people who work in it **3** (in grammar) a noun (also **collective noun**)— that stands for a group of people or things: *"Committee" and "*FLOCK*" are collectives*

collective bar·gain·ing /·,·· '···/ *n* [U] talks between unions and employers about working conditions, rules, wages, etc.

collective farm /·,·· '·/ *n* a large farm, usu. in SOCIALIST countries, made by joining a number of small farms together, owned by the state, and controlled by the farm workers in the service of society as a whole

collective lead·er·ship /·,·· '···/ *n* [U] (esp. in COMMUNIST countries) control of the government by more than one man

collective noun /·,·· '·/ *n tech* a noun singular in form but naming a collection of people, animals, or things as a group: "FLOCK" *is a collective noun for a group of birds or sheep*

col·lec·ti·vis·m /kə'lektɪvɪzəm/ *n* [U] *tech* the system under which the means of production are owned and controlled by the state or the people as a whole

col·lec·tiv·ize, -ise /kə'lektɪvaɪz/ *v* [Wv5;T1;I∅] *tech* to bring (private industry, farms, etc.) under state ownership and control according to the principles of COLLECTIVISM: *When did the Soviet government decide to collectivize the farms?|If we decide to collectivize, will there be much opposition?|collectivized industry* —**-ization** /kə,lektɪvaɪ'zeɪʃən‖-və-/ *n* [U]

col·lec·tor /kə'lektəʳ/ *n* [(*often in comb.*)] **1** a person employed to collect taxes, tickets, debts, etc. **2** a person who collects stamps, coins, furniture, etc., for pleasure or interest: *a stamp-collector*

collector's i·tem /·'·· ,··/ (*BrE* also **collector's piece** /·'·· ·/)— *n* an object of interest to COLLECTOR*s* (2) because of its beauty or rarity

col·leen /'kɒliːn, kɒ'liːn‖kɑ'liːn, 'kɑliːn/ *n IrE* a girl

col·lege /'kɒlɪdʒ‖'kɑ-/ *n* **1** [C;U] a school for higher and professional education, often connected to a university **2** [C;U] (in the United States) a school of higher learning giving a BACHELOR'*s* degree **3** [C] (in Britain) a body of teachers and students forming a separate part of certain universities **4** [C;U] (in Britain) any of certain large public or private schools **5** [C] the building or buildings used by any of these educational groups: *The college is just over the road from the station* **6** [C9] *tech* a body of people with a common profession, purpose, duties, or rights: *She's a member of the Royal College of Nurses.|the* ELECTORAL *college|The College of* CARDINAL*s elects and advises the* POPE

college pud·ding /,·· '··/ *n* [C;U] a sweet cake-like mixture containing dried fruit, cooked by steam or baked

col·le·gi·ate /kə'liːdʒɪət/ *adj* [Wa5] **1** of or related to a college or college students **2** having a college or colleges: *Durham is a collegiate university*

collegiate church /·,·· '·/ *n tech* a Christian church (not a CATHEDRAL) with more than one regular priest or MINISTER

col·lide /kə'laɪd/ *v* [I∅ (*with*)] **1** to meet and strike (together) violently: *Many people were hurt when the 2 buses collided on the corner* **2** to disagree strongly; be opposed: *The government collided with Parliament over its industrial plans*

col·lie /'kɒli‖'kɑli/ *n* a type of dog much used for tending sheep or kept as a pet —see picture at DOG¹

col·li·er /'kɒlɪəʳ‖'kɑ-/ *n esp. BrE* **1** a person employed to cut coal in a mine **2** a ship for carrying coal

col·lie·ry /'kɒljəri‖'kɑl-/ *n esp. BrE* a coal mine and the buildings, machinery, etc., connected with it

col·li·sion /kə'lɪʒən/ *n* [C;U] (an example of) the act of colliding (COLLIDE): *Many people were killed in the collision between the bus and the car.|A collision with Parliament could ruin the government's plans*

collision course /·'·· ,·/ *n* a course likely to end in COLLISION: *The employers' organization is on a collision course with the unions*

col·lo·cate /'kɒləkeɪt‖'kɑ-/ *v* [I∅ (*with*)] *tech* (of words) to go together or with another word in a way which sounds natural: *"Strong" collocates with "coffee" but "powerful" does not.|The words "strong" and "coffee" collocate*

col·lo·ca·tion /,kɒlə'keɪʃən‖,kɑ-/ *n* **1** [U] the act of collocating (COLLOCATE) **2** [C] *tech* an arrangement of words which sounds natural: *"Strong coffee" is an English collocation but "powerful coffee" is not*

col·lo·qui·al /kə'ləʊkwɪəl/ *adj* (of words, phrases, expressions, style, etc.) of, suitable for, or related to ordinary, informal, or familiar conversation; not formal or special to literature —**~ly** *adv*

col·lo·qui·al·is·m /kə'ləʊkwɪəlɪzəm/ *n* **1** [C] an expression used in, or suitable for, ordinary, familiar, or informal conversation **2** [U] COLLOQUIAL style

col·lo·quy /ˈkɒləkwi‖ˈkɑ-/ *n fml* a formal conversation

col·lude /kəˈluːd/ *v* [IØ (*with*)] *fml or law* to act together or with someone else through a secret agreement intended to cheat or deceive others: *colluded with the secret police*

col·lu·sion /kəˈluːʒən/ *n* [U] *fml or law* secret agreement between 2 or more people with the intention of cheating or deceiving others —**-sive** /-ˈluːsɪv/ *adj*

col·ly·wob·bles /ˈkɒliˌwɒbəlz‖ˈkɑliˌwɑ-/ *n* [*the*+P] *infml* a slight stomach-ache usu. caused by a feeling of nervousness and fear: *My wife failed her driving test because she had the collywobbles*

co·logne /kəˈləʊn/ also **eau de cologne**— *n* [U] a sweet-smelling liquid made from alcohol and special oils, put on the wrists, behind the ears, etc., to make one feel fresh and smell pleasant

co·lon[1] /ˈkəʊlən/ *n* the lower part of the large bowel (the LARGE INTESTINE) in which food changes into solid waste matter and passes into the RECTUM

colon[2] *n* a mark (:) used in writing and printing to introduce a statement, example, etc.

colo·nel /ˈkɜːnəl‖ˈkɜr-/ *n* [C;A;N] an officer of middle rank in the army or American air force

Colonel Blimp /ˌ·· ˈ·/ also **Blimp**— *n derog* an old man with old-fashioned political ideas, who thinks himself important without reason

co·lo·ni·al[1] /kəˈləʊnɪəl/ *adj* [Wa5] **1** [A;(B)] of or related to colonies (COLONY (1,2)): *The African people have successfully fought against colonial rule* **2** [A;(B)] of or related to a COLONIST: *colonial ideas* **3** [A;(B)] (*often cap.*) of or related to the 13 British colonies (COLONY (1)) which formed the United States: *a beautiful old colonial house near Boston* **4** [A9;(B9)] of or related to the time when another country was a COLONY: *a beautiful old Spanish colonial house near Bogotá, built when Colombia was ruled by Spain* **5** [B] *tech* living in, consisting of, or forming a COLONY (3): *colonial plants*

colonial[2] *n* a person living or having lived for a long time in a COLONY (1,2), who is not a member of the native population —compare COLONIST

co·lo·ni·al·is·m /kəˈləʊnɪəlɪzəm/ *n* [U] the principles or practice of having or keeping colonies (COLONY (1,2)) abroad: *British colonialism led to the establishment of a large empire* —compare IMPERIALISM, NEOCOLONIALISM

co·lo·ni·al·ist /kəˈləʊnɪəlɨst/ *adj, n* (a supporter) of COLONIALISM; (a person) in favour of having or keeping colonies (COLONY (1,2)): *The Ruritanians feared the colonialist plans of the Flatland government*

Col·o·nies /ˈkɒləniz‖ˈkɑ-/ *n* [*the*+P] the 13 British colonies (COLONY (1)) which originally formed the United States

col·o·nist /ˈkɒlənɨst‖ˈkɑ-/ *n* a person who settled in a new COLONY soon after it was established: *American colonists* —compare COLONIAL[2]

col·o·nize, -ise /ˈkɒlənaɪz‖ˈkɑ-/ *v* [T1;IØ] to make (a country, area, etc.) into a COLONY: *The British first colonized Australia in the 18th century.|This area has recently been colonized by trees of many sorts* —**-nization** /ˌkɒlənaɪˈzeɪʃən‖ˌkɑlənə-/ *n* [U] —**~r** /ˈkɒlənaɪzəʳ‖ˈkɑ-/ *n*

col·on·nade /ˌkɒləˈneɪd‖ˌkɑ-/ *n* a row of pillars with equal spaces between, usu. supporting a roof or row of arches —**-naded** *adj* [Wa5]

col·o·ny /ˈkɒləni‖ˈkɑ-/ *n* **1** a country or area under the control of a distant country and settled by people from that country **2** a country or area controlled and developed by a distant country **3** a group of people from the same country or with the same religion, interests, profession, etc., living together: *the French colony in Saigon|an artists' colony|the Greek colony in Istanbul* **4** a group of the same kind of animals or plants living or growing together in close association: *a colony of plants* **5** all the bacteria growing together as the descendants of a single cell

col·or *AmE* COLOUR

Col·o·ra·do bee·tle /ˌkɒləraːdəʊ ˈbiːtl‖ˌkɑləræ-/ *AmE* also **Colorado po·ta·to beetle**— *n* [Wn2] a type of black-and-yellow insect that attacks potatoes

col·o·ra·tion /ˌkʌləˈreɪʃən/ *n* [U] **1** arrangement of colours; colouring: *This flower has beautiful coloration* **2** the beliefs, principles, practices, etc., belonging to a person, group, or country

col·o·ra·tu·ra /ˌkɒlərəˈtʊərə, -ˈtjʊ-‖ˌkʌ-/ *n* **1** [U] rapid and difficult musical passages meant to ornament sung music **2** [U] music with much of this ornamentation **3** [C] a female singer, esp. a SOPRANO, who specializes in singing such music

co·los·sal /kəˈlɒsəl‖kəˈlɑ-/ *adj* very large in size or quantity: *a colossal building|a colossal rate of interest*

co·los·sal·ly /kəˈlɒsəli‖kəˈlɑ-/ *adv* **1** *infml* very: *That was colossally interesting.|They had a colossally big house* **2** in a COLOSSAL manner: *a colossally planned palace*

co·los·sus /kəˈlɒsəs‖kəˈlɑ-/ *n* **-suses** *or* **-si** /saɪ/ a person or thing of very great size, importance, or ability: *China is a colossus when compared to Hong Kong.|Rembrandt was an artistic colossus*

co·los·trum /kəˈlɒstrəm‖kəˈlɑ-/ *n* [U] the liquid produced by a woman's breasts for the first few days after a baby is born, different in various ways from later mother's milk

col·our[1], *AmE* **color** /ˈkʌləʳ/ *n* **1** [U] the quality which allows the eyes to see the difference between (for example) a red flower and a blue flower when both are the same size and shape **2** [C] red, blue, green, black, brown, yellow, white, etc.: *"What colour is this paint?" "It's red."|What colour did you paint the door?* **3** [C;U] (a) substance used for giving one of these special qualities to something; paint; DYE: *The artist painted in water-colours* **4** [U] the general appearance of the skin; COMPLEXION: *As she became more annoyed Jean's colour changed* **5** [C] the COLOUR[1] (2) of a person's skin **6** [U] the COLOUR[1] (2) of a person's skin, if not white: *a person of colour* **7** [U] details or behaviour of a place, thing, or person, that interest the mind or eye and excite the imagination: *He's such a well-known politician because he has a great deal of colour.|She loved the life, noise, and colour of the market* **8** [U] (in music) variety of expression: *a piece with much colour* **9 be/feel/look off colour** *not fml* to be rather ill: *You look a little off colour today, are you ill?* **10 give/lend colour to** to make (something, esp. something unusual) appear likely or true: *Her wet hair and clothing lent colour to her claim that she had been thrown into the lake by a madman* **11 give a false colour to** to give a false account of **12 have a high colour** to appear very red in the face **13 lose colour** to become pale: *As her illness got worse she lost more and more colour*
USAGE This word is often used in questions: *What* **colour** *is it/the car?* (not **What* **colour** *has it?*) The answer will usually be *It/The car is red*, rather than **a red* **colour** or **red in* **colour**.

colour[2], *AmE* **color** *v* **1** [T1;X(1),7] to cause (something) to have colour or a different colour esp. with a CRAYON or pencil rather than a brush: *The child is colouring the picture* **2** [IØ] to take on or change colour: *The leaves have already started to colour; it will soon be winter* **3** [T1] to give a special effect or feeling to (a person, event, etc.): *Personal* *feelings coloured his judgment.|a highly-coloured account of his difficulties* **4** [I0] to become red in the face; BLUSH: *As soon as he started to argue he coloured quickly.|She coloured with annoyance*

colour bar /'·· ·/ *AmE* also **color line**— *n* the set of customs, laws, or political, historical, and social differences which prevent people of different colours from mixing freely: *They couldn't find anywhere to live because of the colour bar in that area*

colour-blind /'·· ·/ *adj* unable to see the difference between certain colours: *I first knew my son was colour-blind when he thought roses and grass were the same colour* —**colour blindness** /'·· ,··/ *n* [U]

col·oured¹, *AmE* **colored** /'kʌləd‖-ərd/ *adj* **1** (*esp. in comb.*) the stated colour: *She wore a cream-coloured dress* **2** *becoming rare* belonging to a race that does not have a white skin: *Many coloured people live in Bradford.|coloured politics*

coloured², *AmE* **colored** *n often derog* **1** [(*the*) P] people of COLOUR¹ (6); people who do not have a white skin **2** [*usu. pl.*] any person belonging to a race that does not have a white skin **3** (*often cap.*) CAPE COLOURED

col·our·fast, *AmE* **colorfast** /'kʌləfɑːst‖'kʌlərfæst/ *adj* having colour which will not fade or run —**~ness** *n* [U]

col·our·ful, *AmE* **colorful** /'kʌləfəl‖-ər-/ *adj* **1** showily coloured; full of colour or colours; bright; gay: *a bird with colourful wings* **2** likely to excite the senses or imagination; rich in expressive variety or detail: *a colourful period of history|a colourful language*

colour in *v adv* [T1] to colour (a certain area, figure, or shape): *The child decided to colour in the picture in his book*

col·our·ing, *AmE* **coloring** /'kʌlərɪŋ/ *n* **1** [C;U] a substance used for giving a special colour to another substance, esp. food; DYE: *Have we got any colouring? I want to make this cake pink* **2** [U] the act or method of giving a special colour to something: *The colouring of food is against the law in some countries* **3** [U] healthy or ill appearance as expressed by skin colour: *People always think I'm ill because of my colouring*

col·our·less, *AmE* **colorless** /'kʌlələs‖-ər-/ *adj* **1** without colour: *Water is colourless.|a colourless liquid* **2** having less than usual colour; pale: *He was so colourless we thought he was ill* **3** dull; lacking variety, interest, strongly marked personal character, excitement, etc.: *John's wife is one of the most colourless people I've ever met.|a colourless existence* —**~ly** *adv* —**~ness** *n* [U]

col·ours, *AmE* **colors** /'kʌləz‖-ərz/ *n* [P] **1** the official flag of a country, ship, part of the army, etc.: *The general was proud that his men had taken the enemy colours in battle.|I am always ready to serve the colours* (=my country) **2** a dress, cap, piece of material, etc., worn as a sign of one's club, school, team, etc.: *I was glad to see our colours come first in the race* **3 get/win one's colours** to be chosen to play on a sports team **4 in its true colours** as it really is **5 lower one's colours** to give up one's demands or position: *After a week of arguing I decided to lower my colours and buy my wife the new car she wanted* **6 nail one's colours to the mast** to make a decision, express it, and keep firmly to it **7 sail under false colours** to express feelings or opinions in favour of something which one really opposes; be a HYPOCRITE **8 show one's true colours** to show one's real nature or character, esp. for the first time **9 stick to one's colours** to keep firmly to one's opinions, decisions, etc. **10 with flying colours** with great success: *He passed his examination with flying colours*

colour scheme /'·· ·/ *n* the arrangement of various colours in a room, garden, painting, etc., to produce a desired effect: *I think your colour scheme would have been better if you'd chosen red curtains instead of blue*

colt /kəʊlt/ *n* **1** a young male horse or related animal **2** *infml & often derog* a young inexperienced person

Colt *n tdmk* a type of PISTOL

col·ter /'kəʊltəʳ/ *n* COULTER

colt·ish /'kəʊltɪʃ/ *adj* **1** *often derog* playful in an awkward uncontrolled manner; high-spirited: *the boy's coltish attempts at dancing* **2** of, related to, or like a COLT (1) —**~ly** *adv* —**~ness** *n* [U]

col·um·bine /'kɒləmbaɪn‖'kɑ-/ *n* [Wn2] any of several types of plants with colourful 5-pointed downward-hanging flowers

col·umn /'kɒləm‖'kɑ-/ *n* **1** a pillar used in a building as a support or ornament or standing alone as a MONUMENT **2** anything looking like a pillar in shape or use: *a column of smoke* **3** one of 2 or more divisions of a page, lying side by side and separated from each other by a narrow space, in which lines of print are arranged: *the advertising columns of "The Times"* **4** an article by a particular writer, that regularly appears in a newspaper or magazine: *I always read Max Forsyth's column in the "Flatland Times"* **5 a** a large number of rows of people, vehicles, animals, etc., following one behind the other: *a column of soldiers* **b** a long line of ships one behind the other **6** a list of numbers arranged one under the other: *It took a long time to add up the long column (of figures)* —see also FIFTH COLUMN

col·umn·ist /'kɒləmɪ̵st, -ləmnɪ̵st‖'kɑ-/ *n* a person who writes a regular article for a newspaper or magazine

com- /kəm, ˌkɒm‖ˌkɑm/ *prefix* (the form used for CON- before *b-*, *p-*, or *m-*): *combination*

co·ma¹ /'kəʊmə/ *n* **1** a state of long unnatural deep unconsciousness, from which it is difficult to wake up, caused by disease, poisoning, a severe blow, etc. **2 go into a coma** to become unconscious in such a way: *After she drank the poison she went into a coma*

coma² *n* **comas** or **comae** /'kəʊmiː/ *tech* the shining cloud around the head of a COMET

co·ma·tose /'kəʊmətəʊs/ *adj* **1** *tech* in a COMA¹; deeply unconscious: *Is the poisoned girl conscious or comatose?* **2** *fml* of or like a COMA¹: *a deep comatose sleep* **3** inactive and sleepy: *feeling a bit comatose after dinner*

comb¹ /kəʊm/ *n* **1 a** a toothed piece of bone, metal, plastic, etc., used for cleaning, tidying, and straightening, the hair —see picture at BATHROOM **b** a thing like this in shape, which is worn in a woman's hair as an ornament **2** a thing like this in shape or use, such as an object used for CARDing (=straightening and cleaning) wool, cotton, etc. **3** [S] an act of combing: *Your hair needs a good comb* **4** the red growth of flesh on top of the head of a COCK (=a fully-grown male chicken) —see picture at DOMESTIC ANIMAL **5** HONEYCOMB (1)

comb² *v* **1** [T1] to clean, tidy, straighten, or arrange (esp. the hair) with a comb: *If you combed your hair more often you wouldn't look so untidy.|She combed out the knots in the cat's long fur* **2** [T1 (*for*)] to search (a place) thoroughly: *The police combed the woods for the missing boy*

comb. *written abbrev. for:* combination(s)

com·bat¹ /'kɒmbæt, kəm'bæt‖kəm'bæt, 'kɑmbæt/ *v* **-tt-** (*AmE* **-tt-** *or* **-t-**) [T1;I0 (*with, against*)] to fight or struggle against: *We must combat the enemy everywhere until victory is ours.|The priest swore to combat evil wherever it appeared.|The* *doctor spent his life combatting disease.|The ship combatted with the wind and waves*

com·bat² /ˈkɒmbæt‖ˈkɑm-/ *n* [C;U] **1** (a) struggle between 2 men, armies, ideas, etc.: *The combat between good and evil will continue for ever.|We can only settle our differences by armed combat* **2 single combat** a fight between 2 people only

com·ba·tant /ˈkɒmbətənt‖kəmˈbætənt/ *n* a person playing or ready to play a direct part in fighting: *In the last war as many noncombatants as combatants were killed.|The Irish government refused to allow combatant ships to enter its ports*

com·ba·tive /ˈkɒmbətɪv‖kəmˈbætɪv/ *adj* ready, willing, or eager to fight: *He is combative by nature: he enjoys an argument* —**~ly** *adv*

comb·er /ˈkəʊməʳ/ *n* **1** a person or machine that combs wool, cotton, etc. **2** a long curling wave

comb. form *written abbrev. for:* COMBINING FORM

com·bi·na·tion /ˌkɒmbɪ̆ˈneɪʃən‖ˌkɑm-/ *n* **1** [U] the act of combining **2** [U] the state of being combined **3** [C] a number of people or things that are combined or united in a common purpose: *The church is supported by a combination of people from all social classes.|A combination of parties formed the new government as no single party was in control of Parliament.|The* **Combination Acts** *of the last century limited a worker's right to join a union* **4** [C] a MOTORCYCLE and SIDECAR **5** [C] the list of special numbers or letters needed to open a COMBINATION LOCK **6** [C] something that results from 2 or more things, esp. chemicals, being combined: *An* ALLOY *is a combination of 2 or more different metals* **7** [C] *tech* one of the sets into which a list of numbers, letters, etc., can be arranged or ordered: *The teacher said he could make 6 different combinations with the letters a, b, and c, using each letter only once* **8** [A] COMBINATIONS: *This looks very good combination material*

combination lock /··ˈ·· ·/ *n* a special lock which can only be opened when its control is turned in accordance with a special list of numbers or letters particular to that lock

com·bi·na·tions /ˌkɒmbɪ̆ˈneɪʃənz‖ˌkɑm-/ also (*infml*) **coms** /kɒmz‖kɑmz/— *n* [P] any of various types of undergarments worn, esp. by men, to cover the upper and lower parts of the body and legs —see PAIR (USAGE)

com·bi·na·to·ri·al /ˌkɒmbɪ̆nəˈtɔːrɪəl‖ˌkɑmbɪ̆nəˈtorɪəl/ *adj* [Wa5] *tech* belonging to that part of the science of numbers which deals with the arrangement of numbers, objects, letters, etc., in COMBINATIONs (7)

com·bine¹ /kəmˈbaɪn/ *v* **1** [IØ (*against*); T1 (*with,* TOGETHER)] to (cause to) come together, unite, act together, or join together: *2 political parties have combined to form a government as no single party had control of Parliament.|The 2 countries combined together against their enemy* **2** [IØ;T1: (TOGETHER, *with*)] to (cause to) enter into a chemical union: *What chemicals combine together to make water?|What do we produce when we combine copper and iron?*

com·bine² /ˈkɒmbaɪn‖ˈkɑm-/ *n* **1** a group of people, businesses, companies, political parties, etc., joined or acting together for a shared purpose **2** also **combine har·vest·er** /ˌ·· ˈ···/— a machine that REAPs (=cuts), THRESHes (=separates the seed from the stem), and cleans grain

combined op·e·ra·tions /·ˌ· ··ˈ··/ also **combined ex·er·cis·es** /·ˌ· ˈ····/— *n* [P] war operations in which air, land, and sea forces work together

combining form /·ˈ·· ·/ *n tech* a form that combines with a word or a part of a word to make a new word: *The combining form* "RUSSO" *combines with "American" to make the word "*RUSSO-*American"*

com·bo /ˈkɒmbəʊ‖ˈkɑm-/ *n* **-bos** *infml* a small band that usu. plays JAZZ or dance music

comb-out /ˈ· ·/ *n* [S;(C)] *infml* an act of COMBing OUT: *The government hopes to save money by the latest comb-out of government officials.|Her hair needs a good comb-out*

comb out *v adv* [T1a] *infml* **1** to find and get rid of (unnecessary officials, things, etc.) from a department, organization, etc., usu. with the intention of saving money: *The government hopes to cut costs by combing out unnecessary officials from the armed forces* **2** to find and get rid of unnecessary things, officials, etc., from (a department, organization, etc.): *We must comb out the university if we are to save money* **3** to search among books, records, etc., for (facts, information, etc.): *The student spent many hours in the library combing out the facts she wanted* **4** to remove (unwanted twists) from (hair or fur) by combing: *combed out the* TANGLEs*|combed out her hair*

com·bus·ti·ble¹ /kəmˈbʌstɪ̆bəl/ *adj* **1** that can catch fire and burn easily: *Petrol is highly combustible so don't smoke while you're handling it* **2** (of a person or a person's character) that becomes excited easily: *My son has a very combustible nature and often loses his temper when he doesn't mean to*

combustible² *n* [C;(U)] a substance that can catch fire and burn easily

com·bus·tion /kəmˈbʌstʃən/ *n* [U] **1** the act of catching fire and burning **2** *tech* the chemical activity, usu. in the presence of oxygen, that produces light and heat

come¹ /kʌm/ *v* **came** /keɪm/, **come** **1** [IØ,4] to move towards the speaker or a particular place: *Why don't you come when you know your dinner's ready?|The little girl came running to her mother for sympathy* **2** [IØ] to arrive where the speaker is or at a particular place: *The train slowly came into the station* **3** [IØ] to arrive as expected or in the course of time: *Uncle's birthday is coming so we must remember to get him a present* **4** [L9, esp. *up to, down to*] to reach: *The water came (up) to my neck.|Her hair came (down) to her knees.|The floods came through to/as far as my garden* **5** [L9] to exist in a particular place: *In this list of goods the price comes next to the article* **6** [L9] to be (in a particular place in an ordered set): *Your family should always come before your job.|My wife comes first, my children second.|Monday comes after Sunday* **7** [I3] **a** to happen: *How did Jean come to be invited to this party?* **b** begin: *In time I came to love her* **8** [L9, esp. *from, of*] to happen as a result of the stated cause: *This accident came of your carelessness.|Success comes when you work hard* **9** [L7] to become: *The buttons on my coat came unfastened.|The door came open* —compare COME AWAY, COME OFF —see BECOME (USAGE) **10** [L9] to be offered, produced, etc.: *Shoes come in many shapes and sizes.|Milk comes from cows or other animals* **11** [L9] to move into view: *The sun came and went but mostly it was cloudy.|Darkness came at 6 o'clock* **12** [IØ] *sl* to have an ORGASM: *My wife never seems to come when we have sex* **13 come face to face with** to meet (someone or something) directly: *We came face to face with a very serious difficulty* **14 come full circle** to end at the place where one started; be back at the beginning **15 come home to** *infml* to be fully understood by (someone): *It suddenly came home to me what he meant by his strange behaviour* **16 come and go** to pass or disappear quickly; change: *Fashions come and go but the long dress is always popular* **17 come it (with/over)** *sl esp. BrE* to act boldly or disrespectfully with someone: *Don't* *come it with/over me or else I'll hit you* **18 come it a bit (too) strong** *infml esp. BrE* to go beyond the truth of something; to say or do more than is necessary: *It would be coming it a bit too strong if I said I hated my sister, but it's true I dislike her* **19 come out right** *BrE* also **come right**— to end in a satisfactory manner: *I hope everything will come (out) right (for you) in the end* **20 come unstuck** to meet with difficulties or failure: *The government's going to come unstuck if prices keep rising* —see also **come** CLEAN, **come a** CROPPER **21 how come** *infml* how did it happen (that): *How come you got that job at the factory?* **22 to come** in the future: *The years/days to come* —see also COME ABOUT, COME ACROSS, COME ACROSS WITH, COME ACROSS AS, COME AGAIN, COME ALONG, COME APART, COME AROUND, COME AT, COME AWAY, COME BACK, COME BEFORE, COME BETWEEN, COME BY, COME DOWN, COME DOWN ON, COME DOWN TO, COME DOWN WITH, COME FORWARD, COME FROM, COME IN, COME IN FOR, COME IN ON, COME INTO, COME OF, COME OFF, COME ON, COME OUT, COME OUT AGAINST, COME OUT FOR, COME OUT IN, COME OUT WITH, COME OVER, COME ROUND, COME THROUGH, COME TO, COME UNDER, COME UP, COME UP AGAINST, COME UPON, COME UP TO, COME UP WITH

come² *n* [U] *taboo sl* the liquid produced by a man's or woman's sex organ during ORGASM

come a·bout *v adv* **1** [IØ,I5] to happen: *How did this dangerous state of affairs in Europe come about?| I'll never understand how it came about that you were an hour late on such a short journey* **2** [IØ] (of a ship or the wind) to change direction: *The wind has come about to the north*

come a·cross¹ also **come upon**— *v prep* [T1 *no pass.*] to meet or discover, esp. by chance: *I've just come across a beautiful poem in this book*

come across² *v adv* [IØ] to be effective and well received: *Your speech came across very well; everyone understands your opinion now*

come across as *v adv prep* [L1,4,7] *infml* to seem to be (judging from behaviour or actions): *He came across (to me) as (being) quite a nice person, really*

come across with *v adv prep* [T1 *no pass.*] *sl* to provide (money or information) when needed: *"Wealthy relatives . . . who would come across with a* COUPLE *of* THOUSAND *pounds"* (SEU S.)

come a·gain *v adv* [IØ] **1** to return **2 Come again?** *infml* What did you say?

come a·long *v adv* [IØ] **1** also **come on**— to advance; improve: *How's your work coming along?* **2** also **come on**— to improve in health: *Mother's coming along nicely, thank you* **3** to happen; arrive by chance: *Take every chance that comes along* **4** also **come on**— to follow: *You go now, I'll come along later* **5 Come along!** also **Come on (now)!**— *infml* Try harder!; Make more effort!: *Come along, someone must know the answer to my question*

come a·part *v adv* [IØ] to break into pieces without the need of force: *I picked up the old book and it just came apart in my hands*

come a·round *v adv* [IØ] **1** COME ROUND **2** *sl* MENSTRUATE

come at *v prep* [T1 *no pass.*] **1** GET AT (1): *Put the food where the cat can't come at it* **2** GET AT (2): *It was a long time before we came at the truth* **3** COME FOR: *I saw the lion just as it was going to come at me.|She came at me with a knife*

come-at-a·ble /ˌkʌm ˈæt əbəl/ *adj sl* ACCESSIBLE; GET-AT-ABLE

come a·way *v adv* [IØ] **1** *BrE* to leave: *When did you come away from the party?* **2** [(*from*)] to become disconnected without being forced: *I touched the handle and it came away from the door in my hands*

come·back /ˈkʌmbæk/ *n* **1** a return to a former position of strength, importance, or high rank, after a period of absence: *The team made a comeback in the second half of the match* **2** a clever quick reply: *Your comeback certainly made his remark look foolish; I wish I could answer him as quickly and cleverly as you did!*

come back *v adv* **1** [IØ] to become fashionable or popular again: *Do you think long dresses will ever come back?* **2** [IØ (*to*)] to return to memory: *It's suddenly come back to me where I saw you last* **3** [L9] to reply, usu. forcefully (in the phrs. **come back at** and/or **with**): *After John's unkind remark about her clothes, Jean came back at him with an angry remark*

come be·fore *v prep* [*no pass.*] **1** [T1,4] to be of more importance than (someone or something): *One's family comes before one's job* **2** [T1] to be dealt with by: *Your matter comes before the committee this week*

come be·tween *v prep* [T1 *no pass.*] to interrupt (2 people or things); cause trouble between (2 people or things): *John lets nothing come between himself and his work.|What came between Hazel and Paul to make them separate?*

come by *v prep* [T1] **1** to obtain: *Jobs are hard to come by with so many people out of work.|Did you come by that money honestly?* **2** to receive by accident or chance; get: *How did you come by that wound in your arm?* **3** COME ACROSS¹

Com·e·con /ˈkɒmikɒn‖ˈkɑmikɑn/ *n* [R] Council for Mutual Economic Aid; an ECONOMIC organization established to encourage trade and friendly relations among 9 COMMUNIST countries, including the Soviet Union —compare COMMON MARKET

co·me·di·an /kəˈmiːdɪən/ *n* **1** [C] an actor who **a** tells jokes or does amusing things to make people laugh **b** acts in funny plays or films **2** [C] *infml* a person who amuses others or who tries to be amusing: *Paul's a real comedian; he's always fun to be with* **3** [C;(*you*+)N] *derog* a foolish person who cannot be taken seriously

co·me·di·enne /kəˌmiːdiˈen/ *n* a female COMEDIAN (1)

come·down /ˈkʌmdaʊn/ *n infml* **1** a fall in importance, rank, or respect: *She used to have servants: now she finds it a comedown to have to do the work herself* **2** a disappointment: *That film was a real comedown: it wasn't interesting at all*

come down *v adv* **1** [L9, esp. *to*] to be passed on from one period of history to another: *This song comes down to us from the 10th century* **2** [IØ] to be reduced in price: *I don't think meat will come down this year, do you?* **3** [IØ] *sl* to cease to feel the effects of a drug that influences the mind: *Mary looked so bad after she'd come down that I thought she was going to die* **4** [L9, esp. *in*] to lose position, respect, or social rank: *John came down in my opinion after his bad behaviour at the dance* **5** [IØ] to fall: *The roof came down on our heads* **6** [IØ (*from, to*)] to leave a big city for a small town or the country: *The landowner comes down from London twice a year to visit his farms* **7** [IØ (*from*)] *BrE* to leave university (esp. Oxford or Cambridge) usu. after finishing all or part of one's course **8 come down in favour of/on the side of (someone or something)** to decide to support: *The industrial court came down on the side of the employers* **9 come down in the world** to be reduced to a humbler standard of living or social rank —opposite **come up in the world** **10 come down to earth** to return to reality —see DOWN (USAGE)

come down on *v adv prep* [*no pass.*] **1** [X9, esp.

for; V3] to ask (someone) forcefully: *Mother came down on me to clean my room.|The debt collector came down on us for payment* **2** [T1] to punish: *The courts are going to come down heavily on young criminals* **3** [T1 (*for*)] to scold severely: *The teacher came down on me for talking in class*

come down to *v adv prep* [T1,4 *no pass.*] to be able to be reduced to: *What do our choices in this matter come down to?|Our choices come down to going or staying*

come down with *v adv prep* [T1 *no pass.*] *infml* to get; catch (an infectious illness): *I think I'm coming down with a cold*

com·e·dy /ˈkɒmə̇di‖ˈkɑ-/ *n* **1** [C] a funny play, film, or other work in which the story and characters are amusing and which ends happily **2** [U] this type of play, film, etc.: *The actor liked working in comedy because he loved to make people laugh* **3** [C;(U)] an event, activity, or type of behaviour in real life that is funny or amusing **4** [U] the amusing quality of a play, film, book, person's behaviour, etc.: *I like Shakespeare's comedy, even in his most serious plays*

comedy of man·ners /ˌ··· · ˈ··/ *n* a play or other work of literature which makes the behaviour and fashions of a particular social class or group look foolish and amusing

come for *v prep* [T1] to advance towards in a threatening manner

come for·ward *v adv* [I∅] **1** to offer oneself to fill a position, give help to the police, etc.: *No one has come forward with information about the murder.|Only 2 people have come forward for election to the committee* **2** *tech* to become ready for sale or for use: *How many pigs are expected to come forward this month?*

come from *v prep* [Wv6;T1 *no pass.*;L9] to have as a place of origin: *I come from Newcastle but have spent most of my life in London.|Where do you come from?*

come-hith·er /ˌ·ˈ··◂/ *adj* [Wa5;A] *infml* purposefully attractive in a sexual way: *She looked at me with come-hither eyes and my excitement grew.|a come-hither look*

come in *v adv* **1** [I∅] to become fashionable, seasonal, etc.: *When did the short skirt first come in?* **2** [I∅] to take one's position or start to take part in a game or at work: *All the people watching the cricket game hoped the next man to come in would save his team* **3** [L7,9] to take place in a race: *to come in third* **4** [I∅] also **get in**— to be elected; come into power: *If the Workers' Party comes in at the next election a lot of industry will be state owned* **5** [I∅] to arrive as expected: *Has the train come in yet?* **6** [I∅] (of the sea) to rise: *The sea's coming in so don't stay on the sand too long* **7** [I∅] to be received as income: *There's very little money coming in at present so we'll have to be careful what we spend* **8** [L7] to be (esp. in the phrs. **come in handy, come in useful**): *This material will come in useful one day, so don't throw it away* **9** [Wv6;I∅] to take part; gain advantage: *I heard you talking about sharing out the money but where do I come in?* —see also **when one's SHIP comes in**

come in for *v adv prep* [T1 *no pass.*] **1** to receive as a share or as a right: *She came in for a fortune when her mother died.|Why do I only come in for a small share?* **2** to receive (esp. blame): *The government's industrial plan has come in for much of the blame for the price rise in raw materials*

come in on *v adv prep* [T1 *no pass.*] *infml* to join; take part in: *Let's ask Alice to come in on the plan*

come in·to *v prep* [T1] **1** to gain (a sum of money), esp. by INHERITANCE after someone's death: *He came into a fortune when his mother died* **2** (*before nouns of type* [U]) to begin to be in (a state or activity): *to come into fashion/existence/force/flower/consideration|When the house came into sight we were all pleased because it was so cold and rainy outside* **3 come into one's own** to gain respect, power, independence, praise, etc., by showing one's true worth: *She didn't really come into her own until she'd won the election for party leader*

come·ly /ˈkʌmli/ *adj* [Wa2] *lit* attractive; having a pleasing appearance: *a comely young woman* —**comeliness** *n* [U]

come of *v prep* [T1 *no pass.*] **1** to be descended from: *She comes of a good family* **2** to result from: *I don't know if any good will come of your actions* **3 come of age** to reach an age (usu. 18, 19 or 21) when one is considered by law to be responsible for oneself and for obedience to the law

come off¹ *v adv* **1** [I∅] to become unfastened or disconnected: *A button came off as I was climbing over the wall* **2** [I∅] to take place; happen: *The wedding came off as planned* **3** [I∅] to succeed: *Their attempt to shoot the king did not come off* **4** [I∅] to cease public performance: *This play's been such a failure that it's coming off next week* **5** [L7,9] to get on: *John came off best in the fight*

come off² *v prep* [T1 *no pass.*] **1** to come unfastened or disconnected from: *A button came off my coat: can you sew it back on?* **2 Come off it!** *infml* (*usu. in giving or reporting an order*) to stop lying or pretending: *Come off it; tell the truth!|He told me to come off it, as I had no right to give him orders*

come-on /ˈ· ·/ *n* **1** *infml esp. AmE* an action meant to persuade someone to do something, esp. buy particular goods **2 give (someone) the come-on** *sl* (esp. of a woman) to behave in a sexually exciting way towards (someone): *She gave me the come-on as soon as her husband was out of the room*

come on¹ *v adv* **1** to appear in turn or at the appointed time: *The next player came on 5 minutes late* **2** *infml* to be dealt with: *When does this boy's case come on?* **3** [I∅, (*esp. BrE*) 3] *infml* to start: *The rain's just about to come on so let's get home quickly.|I can feel a cold coming on.|There is a storm coming on.|(esp. BrE) It came on to snow* **4** COME ALONG (1,2,4,5)

come on² *v prep* [T1 *no pass.*] COME ACROSS¹

come out *v adv* **1** [I∅] to appear: *The stars came out as soon as it was dark* **2** [I∅] to become known: *It came out that she'd been stealing from her friend* **3** [I∅] (of meaning) to become clear: *The meaning of his speech didn't come out well* **4** [L9] to be seen, as in a photograph: *Mary always comes out well in pictures* **5** [I∅] (of a photograph) to be DEVELOPed: *The pictures I took of the baby didn't come out* **6** [I∅] to be made public; be PUBLISHed: *When does John's new book come out?* **7** [I∅] (of a young lady of the upper classes) to be officially introduced in upper-class society, usu. at a formal, showy, and costly dance: *Amanda is coming out next spring* **8** [I∅] (of colour, a mark, etc.) to be removed; disappear: *I've washed this shirt twice and the ink still hasn't come out* **9** [I∅] to refuse to work: *Workers in every factory are coming out in support of the dismissed men* **10** [I∅ (*at*)] *infml* to reach a total: *This sum won't come out* **11** [L9] to gain a certain position: *I came out first in the examinations.|I came out in the top 3* **12** [L7] to end in the stated way: *The answer to the sum came out wrong/right*

come out a·gainst *v adv prep* [T1;T4 *no pass.*] to declare one's opposition to (someone or something): *The American government came out against the new British plane*

come out for *v adv prep* [T1 *no pass.*] to declare one's support for (someone or something): *In the* *mid-1640s Oxford came out for the king, London for Parliament*

come out in *v adv prep* [T1 *no pass.*] *infml* to be partly covered by (marks caused by an illness or disease): *Jean has come out in spots so I'm keeping her off school*

come out with *v adv prep* [T1 *no pass.*] *infml* **1** to say, esp. suddenly or unexpectedly: *John came out with a foolish remark which annoyed his old uncle* **2** PUBLISH: *We're going to come out with a great new dictionary next year*

come o·ver[1] *v adv* **1** [IØ (*to, from*)] to come from a distance: *When did you first come over to England?* **2** [IØ (*to*)] to change sides or opinions; COME ROUND (2): *He'll never come over to our way of thinking* **3** [IØ] to make a short informal visit: *Come over and see us sometime* **4** [L7] *esp. BrE* (*esp. followed by adjectives of feeling or illness*) to become: *I came over ill, so I had to lie down* **5** [IØ] COME ACROSS[2]

come over[2] *v prep* [T1 *no pass.*] (of a sudden strong feeling) to trouble or annoy (someone): *A feeling of faintness and sickness came over me, so I had to lie down*

com·er /ˈkʌməʳ/ *n infml* **1** *esp. AmE* a person who appears to be very successful or likely to succeed in his job or in society —compare GOER **2 all comers** everyone who comes or tries

-comer *comb. form* a person who comes or arrives in the stated way or at the stated time: *John and Jean are newcomers to our town.|I hate latecomers to a party*

come round *v adv* [IØ] **1** also **come to, come around**— to regain consciousness **2** [(*to*)] to change sides or opinions: *He'll come round to our way of thinking: just leave him alone* **3** to settle an argument: *Jim and Mary often argue but it doesn't take them long to come round* **4** to happen regularly: *Birthdays come round too quickly when one is older* **5** also **come about**— (of a ship or the wind) to change direction: *The ship came round to sail into port* **6** to travel a longer way than usual: *We came round by the fields as we didn't want to go through the woods in the dark* **7** to become calmer after being in a bad temper: *Leave him alone and he'll soon come round* **8** COME OVER[1] (3)

co·mes·ti·ble /kəˈmestəbəl/ *n, adj fml* (a substance) fit to be eaten as food: *rare comestibles, on sale at Christmas time*

com·et /ˈkɒm̩ɪ̣t‖ˈkɑ-/ *n* a heavenly body with a very bright head and a long less bright tail that moves round the sun in a very long thin path (ORBIT)

come through[1] *v adv* [IØ] **1** to arrive as expected: *Have your examination results come through yet?* **2** [(*with*)] to do what is needed or expected: *I knew that in the end John would come through (with the money we needed)*

come through[2] *v adv; prep* [IØ;T1 *no pass.*] to continue to live after (something dangerous): *John was so ill he was lucky to come through (his operation)*

come to[1] *v prep* **1** [T1,4 *no pass.*] to concern: *When it comes to politics I know nothing* **2** [T1 *no pass.*] to reach; arrive at: *When it came to my knowledge that you'd been stealing I decided to catch you in the act.|to come to an end* —see also **come to** GRIEF, **come to** GRIPS **with, come to** LIFE **3** [T1 *no pass.*] to reach all the way to; reach as far as: *The water came to my waist* **4** [L1] to amount to: *The bill came to £5.50* **5** [T1 *no pass.*] to enter the mind suddenly: *Suddenly the words of the song came to me* **6** [T1 *no pass.*] to be received by or given to (a person): *You've got a big surprise coming to you.|The house came to me on my father's death* —compare COME INTO (1) **7 come to heel a** (of a dog) to follow closely just behind the owner **b** (of a person) to obey; agree **8 come to oneself a** to regain self-control **b** *lit* to regain consciousness **9 come to pass** *usu. fml* to happen **10 What is X coming to?** (asked when X is becoming worse)| What is going to happen to X?: *What's it all coming to?*

come to[2] *v adv* COME ROUND (1)

come un·der *v prep* [T1 *no pass.*] **1** to be governed or controlled by: *This committee will come under the new Education Department* **2** to receive: *We came under heavy enemy gunfire* **3** to be able to be found below or after (a key word, heading, etc.): *What heading does this come under?|What word does this* IDIOM *come under?* **4 come under the hammer** to be sold at an AUCTION **5 come under the knife** *infml* to have a medical operation

come up *v adv* [IØ] **1** to come to attention or consideration: *Your question came up at the meeting* **2** *infml* to be chosen: *My number will never come up* **3** to happen: *I'll let you know if anything comes up* **4** to rise in society or in rank **5** to come near: *He came up and said, "Pleased to see you"* **6** to become, esp. after cleaning: *The silk dress came up beautifully* **7 come up in the world** to reach a higher standard of living or social rank —opposite **come down in the world**

come up a·gainst *v adv prep* [T1 *no pass.*] to meet (usu. a difficulty or opposition): *The workers came up against their employer's unwillingness to pay higher wages*

come upon *v prep* [T1 *no pass.*] COME ACROSS[1]

come-up·pance /ˌkʌm ˈʌpəns/ *n* [*usu. sing.*] *infml* a well-deserved punishment or misfortune

come up to *v adv prep* [L1] to equal: *Your recent work hasn't come up to your earlier standards*

come up with *v adv prep* [T1 *no pass.*] *infml* to think of (a plan, answer, reply, etc.); produce: *He couldn't come up with an answer when I asked him why he was late*

com·fit /ˈkʌmf̩ɪ̣t/ *n becoming rare* a sweet covered in sugar usu. with a fruit or nut centre

com·fort[1] /ˈkʌmfət‖-ərt/ *n* **1** [U] the state of being free from anxiety, pain, or suffering, and of having all one's bodily wants satisfied; complete contentment **2** [U] strengthening help, kindness, sympathy, etc., given to a person who is suffering, grieving, or unhappy: *The priest spoke a few words of comfort to the dying man* **3** [C] a person or thing that gives strength or hope, or that makes grief or pain easier for an unhappy person: *My husband was a great comfort to me when I was ill* —**~less** *adj*

comfort[2] *v* [T1] to give COMFORT[1] (2) to (an unhappy, ill, or anxious person or animal): *I tried to comfort Jean after her mother's death*

com·for·ta·ble /ˈkʌmftəbəl, ˈkʌmfət-‖ˈkʌmfərt-, ˈkʌmft-/ *adj* **1** [B] giving comfort, esp. to the body: *a comfortable chair* **2** [B] having or providing comfort: *a comfortable income|a comfortable job* **3** [F] not experiencing (too much) pain, grief, anxiety, etc.: *The doctor said that mother was comfortable after her operation* **4** [F;(B)] fairly rich; not poor: *We're comfortable, but can't afford to buy some of the things we'd like* **5** [A] simple and undemanding: *His life had settled into a comfortable pattern that never seemed to change* —**-bly** /-təbli/ *adv*

com·for·ta·bly off /ˌ···· ˈ·/ *adj* [F] *euph* fairly rich: *They're comfortably off, so they can afford a new car every year*

com·fort·er /ˈkʌmfətəʳ‖-fər-/ *n* **1** a person who gives comfort **2** a length of usu. woollen material worn around the neck to keep it warm **3** *esp. AmE* a warm thick outer covering for the bed; QUILT —see also JOB'S COMFORTER

Comforter *n* [*the*+R] *bibl* HOLY SPIRIT

comfort sta·tion /ˈ·· ˌ··/ *n AmE euph* PUBLIC CONVENIENCE

com·frey /ˈkʌmfri/ *n* a type of tall wild plant with rough hairy leaves and purple or white flowers

com·fy /ˈkʌmfi/ *adj* [Wa2] *infml* comfortable

com·ic¹ /ˈkɒmɪk‖ˈkɑ-/ *adj* **1** funny; causing laughter; intended to amuse; humorous: *a comic performance* **2** of or marked by COMEDY (1,2,4)

comic² *n* **1** [C] *infml* a person who is funny or amusing, esp. a professional COMEDIAN (1) **2** [C; (*you*+) N] *derog* a foolish person who cannot be taken seriously **3** [C] *AmE* usu. **comic book**— a magazine for children containing COMIC STRIP*s* **4** [A] COMICS: *a newspaper's comic page*

com·i·cal /ˈkɒmɪkəl‖ˈkɑ-/ *adj slightly derog & infml* amusing in an odd way; strange; odd: *That's a comical hat you're wearing, with all those flowers!* —**~ly** *adv* [Wa4]

comic book /ˈ·· ·/ *n AmE* COMIC² (3): *comic-book adventures*

comic op·era /ˌ·· ˈ··/ *n* an OPERA with an amusing story, speaking as well as singing, and usu. a happy ending

com·ics /ˈkɒmɪks‖ˈkɑ-/ *n esp. AmE* **1** [P] COMIC BOOK*s* **2** [*the*+P] COMIC STRIP*s*: *In the newspaper I read the comics before I even look at the political news*

comic strip /ˈ·· ·/ *BrE* also **strip cartoon** /ˈ· ·ˌ·/— *n* a set of drawings telling a short story, often with words showing the speech of the characters in the pictures

Com·in·form /ˈkɒmɪ̀nfɔːm‖ˈkɑmɪ̀nfɔrm/ *n* [*the*+R] Communist Information Bureau; an international COMMUNIST political organization established in 1947

com·ing¹ /ˈkʌmɪŋ/ *n* [(*the*) S] **1** arrival: *With the coming of winter days get shorter* **2 comings and goings** *infml* the acts of arriving and leaving: *We watched the comings and goings of the guests from our bedroom window*

coming² *adj* [Wa5;A] **1** arriving; that is coming or will come: *During the coming joyful season we must remember the poor and those without homes* **2** *infml* having the ability to succeed in work or in society: *a coming young man*

coming-out /ˌ·· ˈ·/ *n* [(*the*) S] the formal introduction of a young upper-class woman to upper-class society, usu. at a showy and costly dance: *We've arranged a coming-out party for Amanda next spring*

Com·in·tern /ˈkɒmɪ̀ntɜːn‖ˈkɑmɪ̀ntɜrn/ *n* [*the*+R] Communist International; the Third INTERNATIONAL, which lasted from 1929 to 1943

com·i·ty /ˈkɒmɪ̀ti‖ˈkɑ-/ *n fml & rare* **1** [U] friendly, polite, and respectful behaviour and manners **2** [C] a society built on such behaviour and manners

comity of na·tions /ˌ··· · ˈ··/ *n law* **1** [U] the respect shown by one country for another, esp. as regards each other's laws, customs, and governmental organization **2** [(*the*) S] the group of nations showing this sort of respect for each other

com·ma /ˈkɒmə‖ˈkɑmə/ *n* the mark (,) used in writing and printing, for showing a short pause

com·mand¹ /kəˈmɑːnd‖kəˈmænd/ *v* **1** [T1,5b,c; V3;I∅] to direct (a person or people), with the right to be obeyed; order: *The general commanded his men to attack the city.|Our leader is not fit to command* (*us*).*|She commanded that we* (*should*) *attack at once.|So she commanded.|The king commands the armed forces.|She commanded us to come at once* —see ORDER (USAGE) **2** [T1] to deserve and get: *This great man is able to command everyone's respect* **3** [T1] *fml* to be in a position to use; have at one's service: *The employers command great wealth but we have nothing* **4** [T1] to be in a position to control (a city, area, place, etc.): *This fort commands the whole valley*

command² *n* **1** [C] an order: *All his commands were quickly obeyed* **2** [U9, esp. *of*; (S)] control: *The army is under the king's direct command* **3** [C] a division of the army, air force, etc., under separate control or the control of one person: *pilots of the Southern Air Command* **4** [C9] a group of officers or officials with the power to give orders: *the German High Command* **5** [S;U] the ability to control and use: *He has* (*a*) *good command of spoken French* **6 at someone's command** *lit* ready to obey someone: *I'm at your command* **7 at the word of command** when the order is given

com·man·dant /ˌkɒmənˈdænt‖ˈkɑməndænt/ *n* [C;A] the chief officer in charge of a military organization: *The prisoners of war hated the commandant of their camp*

com·man·deer /ˌkɒmənˈdɪəʳ‖ˌkɑ-/ *v* [T1] to seize (private property) for public, esp. military use: *The soldiers commandeered the house and used it for offices*

com·mand·er /kəˈmɑːndəʳ‖kəˈmæn-/ *n* **1** [C;A; N] an officer of middle rank in the navy **2** [C] the officer of any rank who is in charge of a group of soldiers: *He became* (*the*) *commander of our group at the age of 25*

com·mand·er in chief /·ˌ·· · ˈ·/ *n* an officer in control of all the armed forces of a country, area, etc.: *The Queen is commander in chief of the British armed forces*

com·mand·ing /kəˈmɑːndɪŋ‖kəˈmæn-/ *adj* **1** [Wa5;A] having command; being in charge: *Who's your commanding officer?* **2** [Wa5;A] controlling, because of a strong position: *We must have state ownership of the* **commanding heights of the economy** (=the banks, railways, mines, large-scale industry, etc.).*|The castle has a commanding position on a steep hill* **3** [B] deserving or expecting respect and obedience: *My wife has such a commanding voice that everyone obeys her*

com·mand·ment /kəˈmɑːndmənt‖kəˈmænd-/ *n* **1** *lit* a command; order **2** *often cap.* any of the 10 laws (**Ten Commandments**) which according to the Bible were given by God to the Jews on Mount Sinai

command mod·ule /·ˈ· ˌ··/ *n tech* the part of a space vehicle from which operations are controlled

com·man·do /kəˈmɑːndəʊ‖kəˈmæn-/ *n* **-dos** *or* **-does** (a member of) a small fighting force specially trained for making quick attacks into enemy areas

command pa·per /·ˈ· ˌ··/ *n tech* a paper laid before Parliament by royal command

command per·form·ance /·ˌ· ·ˈ··/ *n* a special performance at a theatre given at the request of, and usu. attended by, the head of state

command post /·ˈ· ·/ *n* the place at which the commander of a fighting army group receives orders from above and gives orders to the soldiers he controls

comme il faut /ˌkɒm iːl ˈfəʊ‖ˌkɑm- (*Fr* kɔm il fo)/ *adj* [Wa5;F] *Fr* according to proper social standards: *You can't wear those old trousers for the wedding—it's not comme il faut*

com·mem·o·rate /kəˈmeməreɪt/ *v* [T1] **1** to give honour to the memory of (someone or something); remember, esp. by a public ceremony **2** to be in memory of (someone or something): *This building was built to commemorate the Fire of London*

com·mem·o·ra·tion /kəˌmeməˈreɪʃən/ *n* [(*of*)] **1** [U] the act of commemorating (COMMEMORATE): *Commemoration of the last war plays an important* *part in Soviet political life* **2** [C] (a part of) a formal religious service in memory of a person or event **3** [C] something built to COMMEMORATE (2) a particular person, event, or occasion; MEMORIAL: *This building is a commemoration of the battle of Waterloo*

com·mem·o·ra·tive /kəˈmemərətɪv/ *adj* [Wa5] *adj* produced in honour of a particular person, event, or occasion: *This stamp is commemorative of the Queen's wedding*

com·mence /kəˈmens/ *v* [I∅;T1,3,4] *fml or tech* to begin; start: *Should we commence the attack?|After the election the new government commenced to develop/developing the roads*

com·mence·ment /kəˈmensmənt/ *n* [U;C *usu. sing.*] **1** *fml* the act of commencing (COMMENCE); beginning **2** *esp. AmE* (a) ceremony at which university or college students are given their degrees or DIPLOMA*s*

com·mend /kəˈmend/ *v* [T1 (*to*)] *fml* **1** to officially recognize (someone or something) as being worthy of praise, notice, etc.; speak favourably of (someone or something): *I can commend this man's work to you.|Our shop has always been very highly commended* **2** to put (someone or something, esp. oneself) into the care or charge of someone else: *The dying man commended his soul/himself to God*

com·men·da·ble /kəˈmendəbəl/ *adj* worthy of or deserving praise: *commendable efforts* —**-bly** *adv*

com·men·da·tion /ˌkɒmənˈdeɪʃən‖ˌkɑ-/ *n* **1** [U] *fml* praise; approval: *Have I earned your commendation?* **2** [C (*for*)] an official prize or honour given because of one's good qualities: *He was given a commendation for bravery after he saved the little children from the fire*

com·men·da·to·ry /kəˈmendətəri‖-tori/ *adj fml* serving to COMMEND (1): *a commendatory letter*

com·men·su·ra·ble /kəˈmenʃərəbəl/ *adj* [(*to, with*)] *fml* **1** that can be measured by the same standard: *The journey from New York to Los Angeles in 1976 is not commensurable with the same journey in 1876* **2** COMMENSURATE —**-bly** *adv*

com·men·su·rate /kəˈmenʃərɪ̈t/ *adj* [(*with*)] *fml* **1** equal in size, quality, or length of time **2** fitting; suitable: *He was given a job commensurate with his abilities*

com·ment¹ /ˈkɒment‖ˈkɑ-/ *n* [C;U] (an) opinion, explanation, or judgment written or spoken about an event, book, person, state of affairs, etc.: *What comments have you about my son's behaviour?|No comment!* (= I've nothing to say)

comment² *v* [I∅ (*on, upon*); T5] to make a remark; give an opinion: *The king refuses to comment on the election results.|Jean commented that she thought it was time for us to go home*

com·men·ta·ry /ˈkɒməntəri‖ˈkɑmənteri/ *n* **1** [C] a written collection of opinions, explanations, judgments, etc., on a book, event, person etc. **2** [C;U] (a number of) opinions or descriptions spoken during an event, occasion, football match, etc.: *His spirited commentary makes a match very interesting even on the radio*

com·men·tate /ˈkɒmənteɪt‖ˈkɑ-/ *v* [I∅ (*on*)] **1** to give a COMMENTARY (2) **2** to be a COMMENTATOR: *Alfred commentates on football matches for television*

com·men·ta·tor /ˈkɒmənteɪtəʳ‖ˈkɑ-/ *n* a broadcaster who gives opinions or descriptions during an event, occasion, football match, etc.

com·merce /ˈkɒmɜːs‖ˈkɑmɜrs/ *n* [U] the buying and selling of goods, esp. between different countries; trade: *Our country has grown rich because of its commerce with other nations*

com·mer·cial /kəˈmɜːʃəl‖kəˈmɜr-/ *adj* **1** of, related to, or used in COMMERCE: *Our commercial laws are very old-fashioned* **2 a** likely to produce profit: *Oil has been found in commercial quantities in the North Sea* **b** having or showing a desire to make a big profit without regard for other considerations: *This musician only makes commercial records* **3** (of television or radio) paid for by charges made for advertising goods and services —**~ly** *adv*

commercial² *n* an advertisement on television or radio

com·mer·cial·is·m /kəˈmɜːʃəlɪzəm‖kəˈmɜr-/ *n* [U] *often derog* the principles, methods, and practices of COMMERCE, esp. those concerned with making profits: *I dislike the heartless commercialism of many of our big companies*

com·mer·cial·ize, -ise /kəˈmɜːʃəlaɪz‖kəˈmɜr-/ *v* [T1] to make (something) a matter of profit: *Do you agree with me that Christmas is too commercialized these days?*

commercial trav·el·ler /·ˌ·· ˈ···/ (*AmE* **traveling salesman**)— *n BrE now rare* a person who travels from place to place trying to get orders for his firm's goods

commercial ve·hi·cle /·ˌ·· ˈ···/ *n* a vehicle used for carrying goods from place to place

com·mie /ˈkɒmi‖ˈkɑ-/ *n* [C; (*you*) + N] *sl usu. derog* COMMUNIST

com·mis·e·rate with /kəˈmɪzəreɪt/ *v prep* [T1] to feel or express sympathy, sorrow, or pity for (a person): *I commiserated with my friend after his accident*

com·mis·e·ra·tion /kəˌmɪzəˈreɪʃən/ *n* [U;(C)] (an expression of) sorrow, sympathy, or pity for the misfortune of another

com·mis·sar /ˌkɒmɪ̈ˈsɑːʳ‖ˌkɑ-/ *n* **1** [C;A;N] the official name of a minister in the Soviet government until 1946 **2** [C] (in the Soviet Union) an official of the COMMUNIST party who works in the armed forces to teach its principles and make sure of loyalty to it

com·mis·sar·i·at /ˌkɒmɪ̈ˈseərɪət‖ˌkɑ-/ *n tech* **1** [GC] a department in the army dealing with the supply of provisions **2** [U] the supply of provisions to the army **3** [GC] (the official name of) a government department in the Soviet Union until 1946: *The People's Commissariat for Iron and Steel*

com·mis·sa·ry /ˈkɒmɪ̈səri‖ˈkɑmɪ̈seri/ *n* **1** *esp. AmE* **a** a shop owned by the army, a firm (FILM COMPANY), etc., where soldiers, actors, etc., can buy provisions, usu. cheaply **b** a place where soldiers, people employed by a firm, esp. a moving-picture firm, etc., can buy and eat food **2** an officer with duties in the COMMISSARIAT (1) **3** *now rare* a person to whom a special duty or responsibility has been given by a person of higher rank; DEPUTY

commissary gen·e·ral /ˌ···· ˈ···/ *n* the officer in charge of a COMMISSARIAT (1)

com·mis·sion¹ /kəˈmɪʃən/ *n* **1** [U] the act of giving special powers or certain duties to a person or group of people **2** [C,C3] the job, duty, or power, given in such a way: *The commission for the new theatre was given to a well-known* ARCHITECT (1) **3** [GC] *often cap.* a group of people appointed to perform certain duties: *to establish a commission to suggest improvements in the educational system* **4** [U9] the act of doing something wrong or unlawful: *Commission of a crime followed by speedy punishment* **5** [C;U] (an amount of) money, usu. related to the value of goods sold, paid to a salesman for his services: *He gets 10% commission on everything he sells: if he sells goods worth £100 his commission is £10* **6** [C] (an official paper appointing someone to) any of several high ranks in the armed forces **7 in commission** (of a ship) sea-worthy; ready for active service **8 out of commission** (esp. of a ship) not ready for active service; waiting for repair; out of ORDER¹ (3): *With so many ships out of commission how can we win this war?*

commission² *v* **1** [T1;V3;X1] to give a COMMISSION¹ (2,6) to (a person or group of people): *The King commissioned an artist to paint a picture of the Queen.|I was commissioned a general in 1939* **2** to place a special order for (something): *The king commissioned a new piece of music for his daughter's wedding* **3** to bring (a ship) into active service

com·mis·sion·aire /kəˌmɪʃəˈneəʳ/ *n esp. BrE* a uniformed attendant at the entrance to a cinema, theatre, hotel, etc.

commissioned of·fic·er /·ˌ·· ˈ···/ *adj* a middle- or high-ranking officer in the armed forces appointed by a COMMISSION¹ (6) signed by the head of state —compare NONCOMMISSIONED OFFICER

com·mis·sion·er /kəˈmɪʃənəʳ/ *n* **1** [C;N] *often cap.* a member of a COMMISSION¹ (3) **2** [C;N] *often cap.* a representative of a government in a country with which it has special relations **3** [C;N;A] *often cap.* an official in charge of a certain government department **4** [C;N;A] *AmE* (esp. in BASEBALL) a person employed as head of a professional sports organization **5** *sl esp. BrE* BOOKMAKER

com·mit /kəˈmɪt/ *v* **-tt-** [T1] **1** to do (something wrong, bad, or unlawful): *to commit a crime/an* ERROR **2** [(*to*)] *usu. pass.* to order (someone) to be placed under the control of another, esp. in prison or in a MENTAL (3) hospital: *He was found guilty and committed.|The evil murderer was committed to the flames* (=to be burnt) **3** [(*to*)] to promise (esp. oneself, one's property, etc.) to a certain cause, position, opinion, or course of action: *The government can't commit any more money to improving the National Health Service* **4 commit oneself (on)** to make one's opinions known (on): *He refused to commit himself (on women's rights)* **5 commit to memory** *fml* MEMORIZE: *He committed the whole Bible to memory* **6 commit to print** *fml* to write down

com·mit·ment /kəˈmɪtmənt/ *n* **1** [C (*to*); C3] a promise to follow a certain course of action: *We must honour our commitments to smaller nations.|Come and look round our shop without commitment* **2** [C] a responsibility: *I don't want to get married because I don't want any commitments* **3** [U9] loyalty to a system of thought and action: *political/religious commitment* **4** [U] the act of COMMITting (2): *the commitment of the criminal to a special hospital*

com·mit·tal /kəˈmɪtl/ *n* [C;U] *esp. AmE* (an example of) the act of sending a person to prison or to a MENTAL (3) hospital

com·mit·ted /kəˈmɪtɪ̣d/ *adj* [(*to*)] **1** having given one's whole loyalty to a particular aim, job, or way of life: *Jean's a committed nurse/Christian/teacher.|Allan has been committed to equal rights for women for many months* **2** [F] (in a state of) having promised: *Allan has been committed to going there for a long time now*

com·mit·tee /kəˈmɪti/ *n* [GC] a group of people chosen to do a particular job or for special duties: *He's on the committee that controls council spending*

com·mit·tee·man /kəˈmɪtimæn/ (*fem.* **committee-woman**)— *n* **-men** /men/ [C;A] a member of a committee

committee stage /·ˈ·· ·/ *n* [C;U] *law* (in either house of the British Parliament) the stage between the second and third consideration (READING) of a suggested law (BILL), when it is closely examined by a small committee

commit to *v prep* [D1] **1** to trust (someone or something) to the special care of (someone else): *The dying priest committed his soul to God* **2** to put (something) in (a special form or condition) as for future use or preservation: *Don't commit your promises to paper if you're not certain you can keep them*

com·mode /kəˈməʊd/ *n* **1** a piece of furniture containing drawers or shelves **2** a movable piece of bedroom furniture containing a vessel to be used as a LAVATORY (1) or for holding water **3** *AmE euph* LAVATORY (1)

com·mo·di·ous /kəˈməʊdɪəs/ *adj usu. lit or fml* **1** having plenty of space for the purpose: *She could put all her clothes in one commodious drawer.|a commodious house* **2** *esp. old use* convenient or satisfactory for the purpose: *Although the house was small it was commodious* —**~ly** *adv*

com·mod·i·ty /kəˈmɒdɪ̣ti‖kəˈmɑ-/ *n* **1** a thing of use or advantage, esp. something sold for profit: *Commodities are exchanged for money* **2** an article of trade or COMMERCE, esp. a farm or mineral product: *Wine is one of the many commodities that France sells abroad*

com·mo·dore /ˈkɒmədɔːʳ‖ˈkɑmədor/ *n* [C;A;N] **1** an officer of middle rank in the navy **2** the captain in charge of a group (FLEET) of MERCHANT ships (=ships carrying goods, materials, etc.) **3** the president of a club for people who go sailing

com·mon¹ /ˈkɒmən‖ˈkɑ-/ *adj* **1** [Wa5] **a** belonging to or shared equally by 2 or more; united; JOINT (2): *It is the common desire of France and Britain to defeat the enemy, let us therefore make common cause against him* **b** of or belonging to society as a whole; public: *The common good would best be served by keeping prices from rising too quickly* **2** [Wa2] found or happening often and in many places; usual: *Rabbits and foxes are common in Britain* **3** [Wa5] widely known; general; ordinary: *It's common knowledge among politicians that an election will soon be called* **4** [Wa5] of no special quality; ordinary; having no special rank; average; plain: *Does the common man oppose the idea of political union between European countries?|Common salt is very cheap.|the* **common cold** **5** [Wa2] *derog* coarse in manner; typical of the bad qualities or behaviour of people who have no feeling for art, beauty, good manners, etc.; VULGAR: *The way you speak is very common.|I don't like her; she's* **as common as muck/dirt** (= very common) **6** *tech* having the same relationship to 2 or more quantities: *5 is a common* FACTOR (2) *of 10 and 20* —**~ness** *n* [U]

common² *n* **1** [C] (*often in names*) an area of grassland with no fences which all people are free to use: *Every Saturday Jean went riding on the village common.|Harlow Common is very beautiful in winter* **2 in common** in shared possession: *The men of this tribe hold their women in common.|In common with many other young men he likes older women better than young ones* **3 out of the common** unusual

com·mon·age /ˈkɒmənɪdʒ‖ˈkɑ-/ *n* [U] *law* the right of leaving one's animals to feed on COMMON LAND

com·mon·al·ty /ˈkɒmənəlti‖ˈkɑ-/ *n* [*the*+GU] *fml* the common people; ordinary citizens

common car·ri·er /ˌ·· ˈ···/ *n tech* a person or company that carries goods, people, or messages from one place to another for payment

com·mon·er /ˈkɒmənəʳ‖ˈkɑ-/ *n* a person who is not a member of a noble family; person without a title —compare NOBLE²

common ground /ˌ·· ˈ·/ *n* [U] **1** shared belief or interest **2 on common ground** in an area of shared beliefs: *When it comes to prices and incomes agreements, we're on common ground* **3 Common ground!** *BrE* I agree with you!

common land /ˈ·· ·/ *n* [U] land that may be used by everyone: *There was much common land outside the village*

common-law /ˌ·· ˈ·◂/ *adj* [Wa5;A] **1** according to COMMON LAW (but not STATUTE LAW): *She's his common-law wife because she's lived with him for 20 years without marrying him.|common-law marriage* **2** related to COMMON LAW (2): *Common-law principles were established at an early date in English history*

common law /ˌ·· ˈ·/ *n* [(*the*) U] *tech* **1** the body of law originating in England and the modern systems of law based upon it —compare CIVIL LAW (2) **2** the unwritten law, esp. of England, based on custom and court decisions rather than on laws made by Parliament —compare STATUTE LAW

com·mon·ly /ˈkɒmənli‖ˈkɑ-/ *adv* **1** usually; generally; ordinarily **2** *derog* in a COMMON[1] (5) manner: *Don't behave so commonly, you nasty girl!*

Common Mar·ket /ˌ·· ˈ··◂/ also (*tech & usu. fml*) **European Economic Community**— [*the*+R] a West European political and ECONOMIC organization established to encourage trade and friendly relations between its 9 member states —compare COMECON

common noun /ˌ·· ˈ·◂/ *n tech* a noun that is not the name of a particular person, place, or thing: *"Book" and "sugar" are common nouns in English* —opposite **proper noun**

common-or-gar·den /ˌ·· · ˈ··◂/ (*AmE* **common-or-gar·den-va·ri·e·ty** ˌ·· · ·· ·ˈ···)— *adj* [A;(B)] *BrE infml* ordinary: *They've got a common-or-garden house just like anyone else*

com·mon·place[1] /ˈkɒmənpleɪs‖ˈkɑ-/ *n* a well-known statement or remark worn out by too much use: *I'm tired of listening to her political speeches; they're full of commonplaces*

commonplace[2] *adj* **1** common; ordinary: *Soon it will be commonplace for men to travel to the moon* **2** *not fml* common and uninteresting: *a commonplace person* **3** *derog* (of statements or remarks) well-known and worn out by too much use: *The fashionable remarks of today often become the commonplace expressions of tomorrow*

common room /ˈ·· ·/ *n* (in schools, colleges, etc.) a room for the use of teachers and/or students when they are not teaching or studying

com·mons /ˈkɒmənz‖ˈkɑ-/ *n* **1** [*the*+P] *old use* the common people as opposed to their rulers or people of noble birth **2** [U] *lit or pomp* food provided at meals for a large group of people who eat together, esp. at a college **3 short commons** *BrE* less food than is deserved or necessary

Commons *n* **1** [*the*+P] the members of the HOUSE OF COMMONS as a group: *The Commons feel annoyed at the way the government has treated them* **2** [*the*+R] HOUSE OF COMMONS

common sense /ˌ·· ˈ·◂/ *n* [U] *not fml* practical good sense and judgment gained from experience, rather than special knowledge from school or study: *Although she's not very clever she's got lots of common sense*

com·mon·weal /ˈkɒmənwiːl‖ˈkɑ-/ *n fml or lit* **1** [*the*+R] the general good of all the people living in a state **2** [C] COMMONWEALTH (3)

com·mon·wealth /ˈkɒmənwelθ‖ˈkɑ-/ *n tech, fml, or lit* **1** [GU] all the people of a country or state **2** [C] also (*fml or lit*) **commonweal**— a country or state

Commonwealth *n* **1** [*the*+R] also (*fml*) **Commonwealth of Nations**— an organization of independent states which were formerly parts of the British Empire, established to encourage trade and friendly relations among its members **2** [C] the official title of **a** some states of the United States, such as Virginia, Maryland, etc. **b** some countries or states in association with other states, such as Australia, Puerto Rico, etc.: *The Commonwealth of Puerto Rico* **3** [*the*+R] England from 1649 to 1660, esp. under Cromwell

com·mo·tion /kəˈməʊʃən/ *n* **1** [U] great and noisy confusion or excitement; violent and noisy movement: *"Why is there so much commotion coming from this room?" asked the angry teacher* **2** [C] an example of social or political disorder; violent DISTURBANCE: *The imprisonment of the union leaders caused a commotion right through the country*

com·mu·nal /ˈkɒmjʊnəl‖kəˈmjuː-/ *adj* **1** [Wa5] of or shared by a COMMUNITY: *communal life* **2** marked by group ownership and use of property: *communal ownership of property* **3** [Wa5] shared or used by members of a group: *We had a communal television in our college which everyone could watch if they wanted to* **4** [Wa5] of, related to, or based on racial, religious, or language groups: *There are serious communal difficulties in Ruritania*

com·mune[1] /kəˈmjuːn/ *v* [IØ] **1** [(*with*, TOGETHER)] *esp. lit & poet* to exchange thoughts, ideas, or feelings: *The friends communed together until darkness fell.*|(fig.) *I often walk by the sea to commune with nature* **2** *esp. AmE* to receive COMMUNION

commune[2] /ˈkɒmjuːn‖ˈkɑ-, kəˈmjuːn/ *n* **1** (a house for) a group of people who live together, though not of the same family, and who share their lives and possessions: *He became dissatisfied with modern life and man's selfish wish for private wealth, so he went and joined a* HIPPIE *commune* **2** (esp. in COMMUNIST countries) a group of people who work as a team for the general good, esp. in raising crops and animals. They usually own and control the means of production together **3** the area of land owned and used by such a group of people **4** (in some countries, such as France and Belgium) the smallest division of local government **5** a group of people working together to protect and help local interests

com·mu·ni·ca·ble /kəˈmjuːnɪkəbəl/ *adj* (of thoughts, illnesses, ideas, etc.) that can be (easily) COMMUNICATEd (=passed from one person to another): *a communicable disease* —**-bly** *adv*

com·mu·ni·cant /kəˈmjuːnɨkənt/ *n* a person who (regularly) receives COMMUNION: *John's a frequent communicant; he receives* COMMUNION *every day*

com·mu·ni·cate /kəˈmjuːnɨkeɪt/ *v* **1** [T1 (*to*)] *fml* to make (news, opinions, feelings, etc.) known: *I don't think the leader of the Opposition communicates his thoughts clearly* **2** [T1 (*to*)] *fml* to pass on (a disease, heat, movement, etc.) **3** [IØ (*with*, TOGETHER)] *fml* to share or exchange opinions, news, information, etc.: *Has the Minister of Foreign Affairs communicated with the American President yet?* **4** [IØ (*with*)] *fml* (esp. of rooms) to join; connect; be connected: *Our bedroom communicates with the bathroom* **5** [IØ] *tech* to receive COMMUNION: *The old lady communicated every Sunday*

com·mu·ni·ca·tion /kəˌmjuːnɨˈkeɪʃən/ *n* **1** [U] the act or action of communicating (COMMUNICATE (1,2,3)): *All communication with France was stopped when the enemy gained control of the sea.|Radio and television are important means of communication* **2** [U] the exchange of information, news, ideas, or opinions: *Speech and writing are man's most important methods of communication* **3** [C] something COMMUNICATEd; message: *This communication is secret so no one but you must see it* —see also COMMUNICATIONS

communication cord /·ˌ··ˈ·· ·/ *n esp. BrE* a chain running the length of a train which a passenger may pull to stop the train in a sudden dangerous state of affairs (EMERGENCY)

com·mu·ni·ca·tions /kə,mjuːnǰˈkeɪʃənz/ *n* [P] the various ways of travelling, moving goods and people, and sending information, between 2 places or in an area; roads, railways, radio, telephone, television, etc.: *Moscow has excellent communications with all parts of the Soviet Union.*|*London has poor road communications with the surrounding area, but the railway network is excellent*

com·mu·ni·ca·tive /kəˈmjuːnǰkətɪv/ *adj* readily and eagerly willing to talk or give information; not secretive

com·mu·nion /kəˈmjuːnɪən/ *n* **1** [C] a group of people or religious organizations having the same (esp. Christian) religious beliefs; DENOMINATION: *He belongs to the* ANGLICAN *communion* **2** [U9 (*with*)] the state of sharing religious beliefs and practices: *Our church is in communion with the* POPE **3** [U9 (*with*)] *lit & poet* the sharing or exchange of thoughts, ideas, feelings, etc.; the act of communing (COMMUNE[1]): *Wordsworth had a great feeling of the communion between himself and the hills and lakes* **4 hold communion with oneself** *poet or fml* to think seriously and deeply, esp. about moral questions

Communion also **Holy Communion**— *n* [R;(C)] the religious service in PROTESTANT churches in which bread and wine are shared in a solemn ceremony as a sign of CHRIST'*s* body and blood in remembrance of his death; EUCHARIST (often in the phrs. **take/receive Communion**): *Are you going to Communion today?* —compare MASS

com·mu·ni·qué /kəˈmjuːnǰkeɪ‖kə,mjuːnǰˈkeɪ/ *n Fr* an official report or declaration, usu. to the public or newspapers: *In its latest communiqué the government suggests that both sides will soon reach an agreement*

com·mu·nis·m /ˈkɒmjʊnɪzəm‖ˈkɑmjə-/ *n* a classless social and political system in which the means of production are owned and controlled by the state or the people as a whole, and the goods and wealth produced shared according to the principle "from each according to his ability to each according to his needs" —compare SOCIALISM

Communism *n* [U] **1** the belief that COMMUNISM is the best possible form of society and that it will one day be established in accordance with the principles and practices of MARXISM-LENINISM **2** the international political movement aimed at establishing COMMUNISM **3** the present political and ECONOMIC (=production and trade) system of any country ruled by the COMMUNIST party: *Under Communism there is usually state ownership and control of the means of production*

com·mu·nist /ˈkɒmjʊnǰst‖ˈkɑmjə-/ *adj, n* (of or related to) a person who favours the general principles of COMMUNISM: *Many people who are not members of the* COMMUNIST *party have communist beliefs.*|*You must learn that there's a difference between "communist" spelt with a small "c" and "*COMMUNIST*" spelt with a large "C"* —**~ic** *adj*

Communist *adj, n* (of or related to) a person who believes that COMMUNISM is the best possible form of society and that it will one day be established in accordance with the principles of MARXISM-LENINISM: *The Communist party favours central ownership and control of the means of production* —**~ic** *adj*

com·mu·ni·ty /kəˈmjuːnǰti/ *n* **1** [C] a group of people living together and/or united by shared interests, religion, nationality, etc.: *The Polish community in Britain has succeeded in keeping its language and way of life alive for 30 years* **2** [C] *tech* a group of plants or animals living together in the same surroundings, usu. dependent on each other for the means of existence **3** [C;U] (a) closeness; nearness; likeness: *They were united by community of interests* **4** [U] shared possession: *community of property* **5** [C] *tech* also **religious community** /·,·· ·ˈ···/— a group of men and/or women who lead a shared life of prayer and work according to a set of religious rules they have promised to obey **6** [*the*+R] the public; people in general: *The job of a politician is to serve the community* —see SOCIETY (USAGE)

community cen·tre /·ˈ··· ,··/ *n* a building where people from a certain area or group can meet for social, educational, or other purposes

community chest /·ˈ··· ·/ *n esp. AmE* an amount of money collected by the people and businesses of an area to help people in need

community sing·ing /·,··· ˈ··/ *n* [U] informal singing in which all present may take part

com·mu·ta·ble /kəˈmjuːtəbəl/ *adj* [Wa5] that can be COMMUTED

com·mu·ta·tion /,kɒmjʊˈteɪʃən‖,kɑmjə-/ *n* **1** [C; U] (a) reduction in the severity of a punishment: *The court ordered a commutation of his punishment from death to life imprisonment* **2** *fml esp. AmE* the act or action of commuting (COMMUTE (3)) **3** [U (*of* and/or *for*)] *tech* the act of exchanging one thing for another, esp. one form of payment for another, such as a money payment for a payment by service **4** [C] *tech* a payment of one sort made instead of an equal payment of another sort

commutation tick·et /,··ˈ·· ,··/ *n esp. AmE* a ticket sold at a reduced price by a railway or bus company for a fixed number of trips between 2 places during a certain period of time —compare SEASON TICKET

com·mu·ta·tive /kəˈmjuːtətɪv‖ˈkɑmjəteɪtɪv/ *adj* [Wa5] of or related to COMMUTATION

com·mu·ta·tor /ˈkɒmjʊteɪtəʳ‖ˈkɑmjə-/ *n tech* an apparatus used in electric motors, machines, etc., for changing the direction of flow of an electric current

com·mute /kəˈmjuːt/ *v* **1** [T1 (*from* and/or *to*)] to make (a punishment) less severe: *His punishment was commuted from death to life imprisonment by the judge* **2** [T1 (*into, for*)] *fml* to exchange (one thing, esp. one kind of payment) for another **3** [IØ (*between; from* and/or *to*)] to travel regularly a long distance between one's home and work (esp. by train): *She commutes from Cambridge to London every day*

com·mut·er /kəˈmjuːtəʳ/ *n* a person who makes a regular journey of some distance between home and work, esp. by train

com·pact¹ /kəmˈpækt/ *adj* **1** firmly and closely packed together; solid: *The trees grew in a compact mass* **2** (esp. of writing) expressed in a short space; CONCISE: *His book was written in a compact style* **3** arranged in or filling a small space: *Jean's got a compact little flat* —**~ly** *adv* —**~ness** *n* [U]

com·pact² /ˈkɒmpækt‖ˈkɑm-/ *n* **1** a small flat usu. round container for a woman's FACE POWDER, a POWDER PUFF, and a mirror **2** also **compact car** /,·· ˈ·/— *esp. AmE* a small car

compact³ /ˈkɒmpækt‖ˈkɑm-/ *n tech* an agreement between 2 or more parties, countries, etc.

compact⁴ /ˈkɒmpækt‖ˈkɑm-/ *v* [IØ (*with*)] to make a COMPACT³: *In 1733 France compacted with Spain*

com·pact·ed /kəmˈpaktǰd/ *adj* pressed, joined together, or united firmly and closely: *a compacted mass*

com·pan·ion /kəmˈpænɪən/ *n* **1** [C] a person who spends time with another, because he is a friend or by chance, as when travelling: *My fellow travellers made/were good companions*|(fig.) *If you decide to join our party remember that fear of imprisonment* *will be your daily companion* **2** [C9] a person who willingly or unwillingly shares the work, pleasures, worries, etc., of another: *They were working companions* **3** [C] a person, esp. a woman, hired to help, live with, or travel with another, esp. older or ill person: *I worked as a companion to an old princess* **4** [C] either of a pair or set of things; one thing that matches another: *I used to have a companion (piece) to that ornament, but I broke it* **5** [C9] (usu. in titles) a book which gives one instructions on how to do something; guide; HANDBOOK: *the Motorist's Companion* **6** [C] *tech* (used in some British titles of honour): *Benjamin Britten,* **C.H.** (=Companion of Honour)

com·pan·io·na·ble /kəm'pænɪənəbəl/ *adj* friendly; likely to be a good companion

com·pan·ion·ship /kəm'pænɪənʃɪp/ *n* [U] the relationship of companions; friendly company; fellowship: *He missed the companionship he'd enjoyed in the navy*

com·pan·ion·way /kəm'pænɪənweɪ/ *n* the steps leading from the DECK (=any of the floors on a ship) to the area below —compare GANGWAY

com·pa·ny /'kʌmpəni/ *n* **1** [U] companionship; fellowship: *I was grateful for Jean's company when I travelled up to Edinburgh* **2** [U] companions; the people with whom a person spends time **3** [U] one or more guests: *No, you can't go out tonight; we're expecting company* **4** [GC] a group of people together for some purpose: *A company of travellers are/is expected to arrive soon* **5** [GC] a body of (usu. about 120) soldiers, usu. part of a REGIMENT or BATTALION **6** [GC] an organization of musical performers or actors and actresses who work together: *The theatre company make/makes a tour of the country every summer* **7** [GC] the officers and men of a ship **8** [GC] a group of people combined together for business or trade; firm: *a bus company|Which company do you work for?* **9** [U] the members of such a group of people whose names do not appear in a firm's official name (in the phr. **and Company**): *Jean Robinson and Company* **10 be good/bad/excellent company** to be a good/bad/excellent person to be with: *John's poor company when he's at home but when Jean arrives he changes completely* **11 in company** when other people, esp. visitors or guests are present: *If you had good manners you wouldn't swear in company* **12 keep company (with)** (esp. of members of the opposite sex) be friendly and go out together: *John and Jean are keeping company but I don't think they'll ever marry* **13 part company (with/from)** to finish a relationship: *After 2 years of marriage they parted company as good friends*

company man·ners /'··· ,··/ *n* [P] *infml* very polite behaviour used in front of visitors for whom one feels great respect

com·par. *written abbrev. for:* COMPARATIVE

com·pa·ra·ble /'kɒmpərəbəl‖'kɑm-/ *adj* [(*with, to*)] *fml* **1** that can be compared: *A comparable car would cost far more abroad* **2** worthy of comparison: *Our house is not comparable with yours. Ours is just a small hut while yours is a palace* —**-bly** *adv*

com·par·a·tive¹ /kəm'pærətɪv/ *adj* [Wa5] **1** based on or making a comparison: *a comparative study of European languages* **2** measured or judged by comparison: *a study of the comparative wealth of the British and Dutch Royal Families* **3** of or related to the form of adjectives or adverbs expressing an increase in quality, quantity, or degree: *"Bigger" is the comparative form of "big".|"Worse" is the comparative form of "bad"* —**~ly** *adv*

comparative² *n tech* **1** also **comparative degree** /·,··· ·'·/— the form of an adjective or adverb that shows some increase in quality, quantity, or degree: *"Worse" is the comparative of "bad".|"Bigger" is the comparative of "big"* **2** an adjective or adverb in this form: *How many comparatives are there in this sentence?*

com·par·a·tive·ly /kəm'pærətɨvli/ *adv* **1** to a certain degree; RELATIVELY: *Man is a comparatively new creature on the face of the earth* **2** in a COMPARATIVE way: *These 2 languages must be studied comparatively*

com·pare¹ /kəm'peəʳ/ *v* **1** [T1 (*to, with*)] to examine or judge (one thing) against another in order to show the points of likeness or difference: *If you compare Marx's work with Hegel's you'll find many differences.|If you compare both of our cars you'll find they're very much alike* **2** [T1 (*to, with*)] to show the likeness or relationship of (one thing) and another: *It's impossible to compare Buckingham Palace and my little house* **3** [T1] *tech* (in grammar) to form the degrees of comparison of (an adjective or adverb): *"Compare the adjective 'nice'." "Nice, nicer, nicest"*

USAGE **Compare** can be followed by *to* or *with*: *He* **compared** *London to/with Paris.|London is large,* **compared** *to/with Paris. With* is more often used if we are speaking of a long detailed study: *a book that* **compares** *the human brain with that of the elephant. In/by* **comparison** is followed by *with*, not *to*: *Paris is small* **in comparison** (*with London*)

compare² *n* [U] comparison (in the phrs. **beyond/past/without compare**): *beautiful beyond compare*

compare with *v prep* [T1,4] to be worthy of comparison with: *Her poor early works don't even begin to compare with her wonderful later productions.|Walking can't compare with flying*

com·pa·ri·son /kəm'pærɨsən/ *n* **1** [U] the act of comparing **2** [C] the result of comparing; a statement of the points of likeness and difference between 2 things —see COMPARE (USAGE) **3** [U] likeness (esp. in the phr. **no comparison**): *There is no comparison between frozen and fresh food* **4** (in grammar) the changing of the form of an adverb or adjective to show the 3 degrees of POSITIVE, COMPARATIVE, and SUPERLATIVE

com·part·ment /kəm'pɑːtmənt‖-ɑr-/ *n* one of the parts into which an enclosed space is divided, such as one of the small rooms in a railway carriage or one of the small box-like containers inside the front of a car: *We sat in the third compartment from the front of the carriage.|The driver kept his maps in a small compartment in the front of his car*

com·part·men·tal·ize, -ise /,kɒmpɑːt'mentl-aɪz‖kəm,pɑrt-/ *v* [Wv5;T1] to divide into separate COMPARTMENT*s*

com·pass¹ /'kʌmpəs/ *v* [T1] ENCOMPASS¹ (2)

compass² *n* **1** an instrument for showing direction, usu. consisting of a freely-moving MAGNETIC needle which always moves to point to the north —see picture at SCIENTIFIC **2** any of several other instruments used for this purpose **3** [*usu. pl. with sing. meaning*] a V-shaped instrument used for drawing circles, measuring distances on maps, etc. —see PAIR (USAGE) —see picture at MATHEMATICAL **4** [*usu. sing.*] *fml* area; range; limit: *To help the old is well within the compass of the government's social responsibility*

com·pas·sion /kəm'pæʃən/ *n* [U (*on, for*)] sorrow, pity, or sympathy for the sufferings and misfortunes of others, causing a desire to give help or show mercy: *The world's main religions all teach us to have compassion on/for the poor, hungry, and those in need*

com·pas·sion·ate /kəm'pæʃənɨt/ *adj* feeling or showing COMPASSION —**~ly** *adv*

compassionate leave /·,··· '·/ *n* [U] *BrE* special

permission to leave work or military service for a limited time for personal reasons: *When the soldier's mother died he was given compassionate leave to attend her funeral*

compass point /'·· ·/ *n* POINT[1] (9)

com·pat·i·bil·i·ty /kəm,pætə'bɪlǝ̀ti/ *n* [U (*with*)] the state of being COMPATIBLE

com·pat·i·ble /kəm'pætəbəl/ *adj* [Wa3;F (*with*); (B)] that can exist or work in agreement together or with another: *Do you think that religion is compatible with science?|They aren't really compatible people/ideas/blood groups* (=compatible with each other) —**-bly** *adv*

com·pat·ri·ot /kəm'pætrɪət‖-'peɪt-/ *n* a person who was born in or who is a citizen of the same country as another: *John and Jean are compatriots because they both come from Scotland*

com·peer /'kɒmpɪəʳ‖'kɑm-/ *n fml* **1** a person of equal rank **2** a companion; COMRADE

com·pel /kəm'pel/ *v* **-ll-** **1** [V3] to make (a person or thing) do something by or as if by force: *The rain compelled us to stay indoors* **2** [T1] to cause by or as if by force; demand; make necessary: (fig.) *His cleverness and skill compel our admiration* —**compelling** *adj* —**compellingly** *adv*

com·pen·di·ous /kəm'pendɪəs/ *adj fml* (of writers, books, etc.) giving the main information and details about a subject in a short but complete form —**~ly** *adv*

com·pen·di·um /kəm'pendɪəm/ *n tech* a short but detailed and complete account of facts, information, a subject, etc.: *a compendium of useful information*

com·pen·sate /'kɒmpənseɪt‖'kɑm-/ *v* [X9;(T1)] to provide (someone or something) with a balancing effect for some loss or something lacking; make a suitable payment for some loss: *Many firms compensate their workers if they are hurt at work*

compensate for *v prep* [D1;V4a;T1,4] to COMPENSATE (someone or onself) for the bad effect of (something): *Nothing can compensate* (*me*) *for the loss of my husband/for losing my husband*

com·pen·sa·tion /,kɒmpən'seɪʃən‖,kɑm-/ *n* [(*for*)] **1** [U;S] something given to COMPENSATE: *Did you get any compensation when you were dismissed from your job?*|(fig.) *Her beautiful hair and figure are some compensation for her ugly face* **2** [U] the act of compensating (COMPENSATE) —compare CONSOLATION, RECOMPENSE

com·pen·sa·to·ry /kəm'pensətəri, ,kɒmpən'seɪ-‖kəm'pensətori/ *adj* serving to COMPENSATE: *compensatory payments*

com·pere[1] /'kɒmpeəʳ‖'kɑm-/ *n BrE* a person who introduces the various acts in a stage or television show

compere[2] (*AmE infml* **emcee**)— *v* [T1;I∅] *esp. BrE* to act as a COMPERE[1] in (a television or stage show): *Who compered last night's show?*

com·pete /kəm'piːt/ *v* [I∅,3] to try to win something in competition with someone else: *John competed for a place at their school, but didn't get in.|Although there were only 4 horses competing it was an exciting race*

com·pe·tence /'kɒmpǝ̀təns‖'kɑm-/ also (*now rare*) **com·pe·ten·cy** /-tənsi/— *n* **1** [U] ability to do what is needed; skill: *Gordon drives with competence* —see GENIUS (USAGE) **2** [S] *fml, lit & becoming rare* enough money for one to live on comfortably, esp. without having to work **3** [U] *law* **a** (of courts of law) ability to act: *This case is beyond this court's competence* **b** (of people) the qualities necessary to be admitted to a court of law; the state of having the necessary age, citizenship, etc., to enter and speak in a court of law

com·pe·tent /'kɒmpǝ̀tənt‖'kɑm-/ *adj* **1** [B] having the ability or skill to do what is needed **2** [F,F3] *esp. law* having the power to deal with something: *This court is not competent to deal with your case/competent with regard to your case* **3** [B] very satisfactory: *He did a competent job* —**~ly** *adv*

com·pe·ti·tion /,kɒmpǝ̀'tɪʃən‖,kɑm-/ *n* **1** [U] the act of competing (often in the phr. **in competition with**): *He was in competition with 10 others, so he did well to win the race* **2** [C] a test of strength, skill, ability, etc.: *a beer-drinking competition* **3** [U] the struggle to gain advantage, profit, or success, from another or others: *There was keen competition between the various teams fighting for first place* **4** [U] the person or people against whom one competes: *The players nervously wondered what sort of competition there'd be at the match*

com·pet·i·tive /kəm'petǝ̀tɪv/ *adj* **1** of, related to, based on, or decided by competition: *the competitive nature of British society* **2** liking to compete: *Jane's a very competitive person* —**~ly** *adv* —**~ness** *n* [U]

com·pet·i·tor /kəm'petǝ̀təʳ/ *n* a person, team, business organization, firm, etc., competing with another or others; opponent; RIVAL: *There were 10 competitors in the race.|There are many competitors hoping to increase their trade with China*

com·pi·la·tion /,kɒmpǝ̀'leɪʃən‖,kɑm-/ *n* **1** [U] the act or action of compiling (COMPILE) **2** [C] something that has been COMPILEd, such as a report, collection of writings, mass of information, etc.

com·pile /kəm'paɪl/ *v* [T1] **1** to put (facts, information, etc.) together in a single collection: *He compiled enough information on his tour of South American capitals to write a book* **2** to make (a report, book, etc.) from facts and information found in various places: *It takes years of hard work to compile a good dictionary* —**-piler** *n*

com·pla·cen·cy /kəm'pleɪsənsi/ also **com·pla·cence** /-səns/— *n* [U] *often derog* a feeling of quiet pleasure, contentment, or satisfaction with oneself: *With the state of affairs in Lancashire so dangerous I see no reason for the government's complacency*

com·pla·cent /kəm'pleɪsənt/ *adj often derog* pleased or contented with oneself; self-satisfied; without anxiety; untroubled: *However many matches a team wins it should never be allowed to get complacent* —**~ly** *adv*

com·plain /kəm'pleɪn/ *v* **1** [I∅ (*about* and/or *to*), T5] to express feelings of annoyance, pain, unhappiness, dissatisfaction, grief, etc.; speak in an unhappy, annoyed, dissatisfied way: *Mary is always complaining about something. Why can't she be pleasanter?* **2** [I∅ (*about* and/or *to*)] to make a formal report about someone or something one considers annoying, wrong, etc.: *Our next-door neighbour said he'd complain about us to the police if we made any more noise* —**~er** *n* —**~ing** *adj* —**~ingly** *adv*

com·plain·ant /kəm'pleɪnənt/ *n fml & law* PLAINTIFF

com·plaint /kəm'pleɪnt/ *n* **1** [C] a statement expressing annoyance, unhappiness, pain, dissatisfaction, grief, etc. **2** [C] a cause or reason for complaining: *The workers made a list of their complaints* **3** [C] a formal statement about a person or thing causing trouble, annoyance, or dissatisfaction: *The police received complaints about the noise from our party from 2 of our neighbours* **4** [C] something, such as an illness, causing pain or discomfort: *a chest complaint* **5** [U] the act of complaining: *If your neighbours are too noisy then you have cause for complaint* **6 lodge a complaint (against)** *law* COMPLAIN (2) (about): *A complaint* *has been lodged against you with the police*

com·plai·sance /kəm'pleɪzəns/ *n* [U] *fml* willingness to do what pleases others

com·plai·sant /kəm'pleɪzənt/ *adj fml* ready and willing to please others; ready to agree —compare COMPLACENT —**~ly** *adv*

com·ple·ment¹ /'kɒmpl̥əmənt‖'kɑm-/ *n* **1** [C (*to*)] something that completes or makes perfect: *A fine wine is a complement to a good meal* **2** [C; *to*+U] *tech* the number or quantity needed to make something complete, esp. the full number of officers and men needed for a ship **3** [C] (in grammar) a word or phrase (esp. a noun or adjective) that follows a verb and describes esp. a noun or PRONOUN that comes before it: *The words "cold" and "chairman" are complements in the sentences "John is cold," "John became chairman," "John considers the weather cold," and "John named me chairman"* —compare COMPLIMENT

com·ple·ment² /'kɒmpl̥əment‖'kɑm-/ *v* [T1] to make (something) complete; be the COMPLEMENT¹ (1) of (something): *This wine complements the food perfectly* —compare COMPLIMENT

com·ple·men·ta·ry /ˌkɒmpl̥ə'mentəri‖ˌkɑm-/ *adj* [(*to*)] serving to complete; supplying what is lacking or needed by another or each other for completion: *Irish farming and British industry are complementary. Each provides what the other needs*

complementary an·gles /··ˌ··· '··/ *n* [P] 2 angles which when added together equal 90°

complementary col·ours /··ˌ··· '··/ *n* [P] colours which when mixed make white or grey

com·plete¹ /kəm'pliːt/ *adj* **1** [B] having all necessary, usual, or wanted parts; whole and in order; lacking nothing: *John's birthday did not seem complete without his father there* **2** [B] finished; ended: *When will work on the new railway be complete?* **3** [A] thorough; full: *It was a complete surprise to see you on the bus yesterday morning* **4** [Wa5;F+*with*] fully or additionally supplied: *We bought a house complete with furniture* **5** [A] *now rare* (of people) skilful —**~ness** *n* [U]

complete² *v* [T1] **1** to make (something) whole or perfect; add what is missing or needed to (something) to form a finished whole: *I need one more stamp before my collection is completed* **2** [Wv5] to finish (something): *When will work be completed on the new road?|The Queen will be the first person to travel along the completed new road* **3** to succeed in finishing: *The army completed a successful attack on the enemy capital*

com·plete·ly /kəm'pliːtli/ *adv* wholly; altogether; in every way; totally: *The army made a completely successful attack on the enemy capital*

com·ple·tion /kəm'pliːʃən/ *n* **1** [U] the act of completing something: *Completion of this bridge is expected in 1980* **2** [C] an example of this: *A lot of people used to leave the course before the end, but lately we've been getting more and more completions* **3** [U] the state of being complete: *The road is near completion, it should be finished soon*

com·plex¹ /'kɒmpleks‖ˌkɑm'pleks◂/ *adj* **1** consisting of many closely related or connected parts: *There is a complex network of roads connecting Glasgow and Edinburgh* **2** difficult to understand or explain: *His political ideas were too complex to get support from ordinary people* **3** [Wa5] (of a word or sentence) consisting of a main part and one or more other parts: *"Childish" is a complex word consisting of a main part, "child", and another part, "-ish".|"If it rains, I won't go" is a complex sentence with a main part, "I won't go," and another part, "If it rains"* —compare COMPOUND

complex² /'kɒmpleks‖'kɑm-/ *n* **1** [C9] a system consisting of a large number of closely related parts: *a sports complex with everything needed for many different activities* **2** [C] *tech* a closely connected group of unconscious images, wishes, fears, feelings, etc., which influence a person's behaviour without him knowing it —see INFERIORITY COMPLEX; SUPERIORITY COMPLEX **3** [C (*about*)] *infml* a fixed, often confused idea or feeling about something: *Andrew's complex about sex made his marriage a failure*

com·plex·ion /kəm'plekʃən/ *n* **1** the natural colour and appearance of the skin, esp. of the face: *a good/dark/fair/pale complexion* **2** [*usu. sing.*] general character or nature: *The dismissal of the minister for foreign affairs has changed the whole complexion of the government*

com·plex·i·ty /kəm'pleks̥əti/ *n* [U;C] (an example of) the state of being COMPLEX¹ (1,2)

com·pli·ance /kəm'plaɪəns/ *n* [U (*with*)] **1** obedience: *Compliance with the laws is expected of all citizens* **2** the tendency to yield (too) willingly to the wishes of others: *His compliance with everything we suggest makes it hard to know what he really feels*

com·pli·ant /kəm'plaɪənt/ *adj* readily acting in accordance with a rule, order, demand, the wishes of others, etc.: *I don't respect people who are too compliant* —**~ly** *adv*

com·pli·cate /'kɒmpl̥əkeɪt‖'kɑm-/ *v* [T1] **1** to make (something) difficult to understand or deal with **2** to make (something) more COMPLEX¹ (1) **3** [*often pass.*] to make (a state of affairs, esp. an illness) worse or more severe: *a serious disease complicated by an additional bacterial infection*

com·pli·cat·ed /'kɒmpl̥əkeɪt̥əd‖'kɑm-/ *adj* **1** containing or consisting of many closely related or connected parts: *a complicated machine* **2** difficult to understand or deal with: *Don't ask me such complicated questions* —**~ly** *adv* —**~ness** *n* [U]

com·pli·ca·tion /ˌkɒmpl̥ə'keɪʃən‖ˌkɑm-/ *n* **1** [U] the act of complicating (COMPLICATE (1)): *We cannot allow further complication of this matter if we want to find a quick and satisfactory answer* **2** [C] something that adds new difficulties: *The union's demand for higher wages was a complication that the government had not expected* **3** [C *often pl. with sing. meaning*] a confused relationship of parts: *The complications of this machine make it difficult to handle correctly* **4** [C] a new illness that arises during the course of another illness, thus making treatment more difficult: *The doctors were sure they could cure my husband's disease, but when complications arose they lost hope*

com·plic·i·ty /kəm'plɪs̥əti/ *n* [U (*in*)] the act of taking part with another person in some wrongful action, esp. a crime —see also ACCOMPLICE

com·pli·ment¹ /'kɒmpl̥əmənt‖'kɑm-/ *n* **1** an expression of praise, admiration, or respect: *That young man is always ready to pay compliments to a pretty young lady* **2** **fish/angle for compliments** *often derog* to try by deceptive means to get someone to say something nice about you: *"I'm sorry this is just a quick meal." "But mother, you know your cooking is always wonderful," he said, and asked himself why she always had to fish for compliments* —compare COMPLEMENT **3** **return a/the compliment** to say something nice about or to someone who has said something nice about you

com·pli·ment² /'kɒmpl̥əment‖'kɑm-/ *v* [T1 (*on*)] to praise someone with a COMPLIMENT¹; pay a COMPLIMENT¹ to (someone): *John complimented Jean on her beautiful new dress* —compare COMPLEMENT

com·pli·men·ta·ry /ˌkɒmpl̥ə'mentəri‖ˌkɑm-/ *adj* **1** expressing admiration, praise, respect, etc. **2** [Wa5] given free, out of kindness or respect: *complimentary tickets* —compare COMPLEMENTARY

com·pli·ments /ˈkɒmplᵻmənts‖ˈkɑm-/ *n* [P] good wishes: *That was an excellent dinner, Pierre: my compliments to the* CHEF!
com·pline, -plin /ˈkɒmplᵻn‖ˈkɑm-/ *n* [R] *tech* (esp. in the ROMAN CATHOLIC church) a short religious service read or sung in the evening
com·ply /kəmˈplaɪ/ *v* [IØ (*with*)] to act in accordance with a demand, order, rule, etc.: *People who refuse to comply with the law will be punished*
com·po /ˈkɒmpəʊ‖ˈkɑm-/ *n* **-pos** [U;C] *tech abbrev. for:* (*esp. as the name of various substances used in industry*) COMPOSITION
com·po·nent /kəmˈpəʊnənt/ *n* any of the parts that make up or are needed for a whole (esp. for a machine or system)
com·port /kəmˈpɔːt‖-ort/ *v* [X9] *fml* to behave (oneself): *That little girl comported herself very well at the party last night*
com·port·ment /kəmˈpɔːtmənt‖-or-/ *n* [U] *fml often pomp* behaviour; manner
com·pose /kəmˈpəʊz/ *v* **1** [T1] to make up (something); form (something): *The chemistry teacher asked the pupils what water was composed of* —compare COMPRISE **2** [T1] to make or form (something) by putting parts together: *The artist composed an interesting picture by putting the variously-coloured shapes together* **3** [T1;IØ] to write (music, poetry, etc.) **4** [T1] to make (esp. oneself) calm, quiet, etc.: *Jean was nervous at first but soon composed herself* **5** [T1] to settle (a point of disagreement): *The 2 leaders composed their disagreement and were soon the best of friends again* **6** [T1] *tech* (in printing) to form (words, sentences, pages, etc.) ready for printing
com·pos·er /kəmˈpəʊzəʳ/ *n* a person who writes music
com·pos·ite /ˈkɒmpəzᵻt‖kɑmˈpɑ-/ *adj, n* [Wa5] (something) made up of a number of different parts or materials
composition /ˌkɒmpəˈzɪʃən‖ˌkɑm-/ *n* **1** [U] the act of putting together parts to form something; act of composing (COMPOSE): *a piece of music of his own composition* **2** [C] an example of this, such as a piece of music or art or a poem: *I like his earlier poems but not his later compositions* **3** [C;U] the arrangement of the parts of something; way in which parts are combined to produce something: *The composition of the committee favours the government* **4** [U] the various parts of which something is made up **5** [C] a short piece of writing (ESSAY) done as an educational exercise **6** [C] something consisting of a mixture of various substances: *a chemical composition* **7** [U] the arrangement of words, sentences, pages, etc., for printing; work of a COMPOSITOR
com·pos·i·tor /kəmˈpɒzᵻtəʳ‖-ˈpɑ-/ *n tech* a person who arranges words, sentences, pages, etc., for printing
com·pos men·tis /ˌkɒmpəs ˈmentᵻs‖ˌkɑm-/ *adj* [F] *law lat* having the ability to think clearly and be responsible for one's actions: (*infml*) *I hope you're feeling compos mentis today; we've got an examination this afternoon* —opposite **non compos mentis**
com·post¹ /ˈkɒmpɒst‖ˈkɑmpəʊst/ *n* [U] a mixture of decayed plant or animal matter, such as cut grass or leaves, used for making the soil richer
compost² *v* [T1] **1** to cover with COMPOST¹ **2** to make COMPOST¹ from
com·po·sure /kəmˈpəʊʒəʳ/ *n* [U] complete control over one's feelings; calmness; steady manner or state of mind: *Keep calm: don't lose your composure*
com·pote /ˈkɒmpəʊt‖ˈkɑm-/ *n* [U] fruit cooked in sweetened water, usu. served at the end of a meal
com·pound¹ /kəmˈpaʊnd/ *v* [T1] **1** [(*from, of*)] to make (a substance or state) by combining various parts, qualities, etc.: *The old lady's charm was compounded of beauty and kindness* **2** [(*into*)] to put together (various parts, qualities, etc.) to form a whole: *He compounded various substances into an effective medicine* **3** *tech* to calculate (interest) on the original sum of money lent or borrowed and on all the unpaid interest already earned **4** [*often pass.*] to add to or increase (something bad): *Our mistakes were compounded by other people's lack of judgment*
com·pound² /ˈkɒmpaʊnd‖ˈkɑm-/ *adj* [Wa5] **1** (of a single whole) consisting of 2 or more separable parts, substances, etc. **2** (of a word or sentence) consisting of 2 or more main parts: *"Childcare" is a compound word consisting of the 2 main parts "child" and "care"* —compare COMPLEX
compound³ /ˈkɒmpaʊnd/ *n* **1** something consisting of a combination of 2 or more parts, substances, etc., esp. a chemical substance consisting of at least 2 different simple substances (ELEMENTs (6)) combined in such a way that it usu. has qualities different from those of the substances from which it is made —compare ELEMENT, MIXTURE **2** a COMPOUND word or sentence
compound⁴ *n* a group of buildings enclosed by a wall, fence, etc.
compound eye /ˌ·· ˈ·/ *n* an eye, as in an insect, made up of very many small parts each of which sees part of the whole
compound frac·ture /ˌ·· ˈ··/ *n med* a broken or cracked bone which cuts through the surrounding flesh, thus making an open wound
compound in·terest /ˌ·· ˈ··/ *n* [U] interest calculated on the original sum of money lent or borrowed and on all the unpaid interest already earned
compound leaf /ˌ·· ˈ·/ *n tech* a leaf consisting of several small leaves joined to a single stem
com·pre·hend /ˌkɒmprɪˈhend‖ˌkɑm-/ *v fml* **1** [T1;IØ] to understand: *The child read the story but did not comprehend its meaning* **2** [T1] to include: *The park comprehends all the land on the other side of the river*
com·pre·hen·si·ble /ˌkɒmprɪˈhensəbəl‖ˈkɑm-/ *adj* that can be (easily) understood: *One often finds a writer's books more comprehensible if one knows about his life and the time when he was alive* —**-bility** /ˌkɒmprɪhensəˈbɪlᵻti‖ˌkɑm-/ *n* [U]
com·pre·hen·sion /ˌkɒmprɪˈhenʃən‖ˌkɑm-/ *n* **1** [U (*of*)] the act of understanding **2** [U (*of*)] the ability of the mind to understand **3** [C;U] (in schools) an exercise to test and improve the pupil's ability to understand language
com·pre·hen·sive¹ /ˌkɒmprɪˈhensɪv‖ˌkɑm-/ *adj* **1** thorough; broad; including much: *The government gave a very comprehensive explanation of its plans for industrial development* **2** [Wa5] *BrE* (of education) teaching pupils of all abilities and from all social classes in the same school —**~ly** *adv*
comprehensive² also **comprehensive school** /ˌ··ˈ·· ·/— *n BrE* a school where pupils of all abilities and from all social classes are taught from the age of 11
com·press¹ /kəmˈpres/ *v* [T1 (*into*)] **1** [Wv5] to force (a substance) into less space; press together: *In her anger she compressed her lips so tightly that they went white* **2** to put (thoughts, ideas, etc.) into fewer words
com·press² /ˈkɒmpres‖ˈkɑm-/ *n* a small thick mass (PAD) of soft firmly packed material pressed to part of the body, esp. a wound, to stop bleeding, reduce fever, etc.
com·pres·si·ble /kəmˈpresəbəl/ *adj* that can be (easily) COMPRESSed: *Air is a compressible gas* —**-bility** /kəmˌpresəˈbɪlᵻti/ *n* [U]

com·pres·sion /kəm'preʃən/ *n* [U] **1** the act of COMPRESSing[1] **2** the state of being COMPRESSed[1]
com·pres·sor /kəm'presəʳ/ *n* an apparatus, usu. part of a machine, for COMPRESSing[1] (1) gas or air
com·prise /kəm'praɪz/ *v* [Wv6] **1** [L1] to consist of; include; be made up of: *The United Kingdom comprises England, Wales, Scotland, and Northern Ireland* **2** [T1 *pass. with* of *not* by] to make up; form: *15 separate republics comprise the Soviet Union* —compare COMPOSE
com·pro·mise[1] /'kɒmprəmaɪz‖'kam-/ *n* **1** [U] the act of settling an argument or differences of opinion between opposing sides by each side yielding some of its demands and agreeing to some of the demands of the other; act of settling an argument by taking a middle course acceptable to all sides: *We should settle our differences by compromise not by war* **2** [C] an agreement reached in this way: *She wanted the comfort of a large car and the low cost of a small one, so she bought a size in between the 2 as a compromise*
compromise[2] *v* **1** [IØ (*on*)] to settle an argument or differences of opinion by taking a middle course acceptable to all sides: *Jean didn't know whether to wear formal dress or informal trousers so she compromised and wore a skirt* **2** [Wv4;T1] to make (someone or something) open to dishonour, danger, etc.: *John felt compromised by what Jean had said about his friendship with the criminal*
comp·tom·e·ter /kɒmp'tɒmɪ̈təʳ‖kamp'ta-/ *n tdmk* a calculating machine
comp·trol·ler /kən'trəʊləʳ, kəmp-/ *n* [C;A;N] *fml* (sometimes used as an official title for a) CONTROLLER
com·pul·sion /kəm'pʌlʃən/ *n* **1** [U] force or influence that makes a person do something: *The governor had to use compulsion to make the people pay taxes.|I will pay nothing under compulsion* **2** [C,C3] a strong usu. unreasonable desire that is difficult to control: *Drinking is a compulsion with her*
com·pul·sive /kəm'pʌlsɪv/ *adj* [A;(B)] resulting from a COMPULSION (2): *Compulsive smoking is bad for one's health* —**~ly** *adv* —**~ness** *n* [U]
com·pul·so·ry /kəm'pʌlsəri/ *adj* [Wa5] put into force by the law, orders, etc.: *Education is compulsory for all children in Britain* —**-rily** /-sərɪ̈li/ *adv*
com·punc·tion /kəm'pʌŋkʃən/ *n* [U] (*often in neg. sentences*) an awkward feeling of guilt; shame for one's wrong actions: *That woman didn't have the slightest compunction about telling me a lie*
com·pu·ta·tion /ˌkɒmpjʊ'teɪʃən‖ˌkampjə-/ *n* [C; U *often pl. with sing. meaning*] (the result of) the act of calculating: *According to my computation(s), the bank should pay me £100 interest this year*
com·pute /kəm'pjuːt/ *v* [T1;IØ] to calculate (a result, answer, sum, etc.)
com·put·er /kəm'pjuːtəʳ/ *n* an electric calculating machine that can store and recall information and make calculations at very high speeds
com·put·er·ize /kəm'pjuːtəraɪz/ *v* **1** [T1] to store (information) in a COMPUTER **2** [T1;(IØ)] to use a COMPUTER to control (an operation, system, etc.): *The firm has decided to computerize its wages department.|Our firm computerized years ago!*
com·rade /'kɒmrɪ̈d, -reɪd‖'kamræd/ *n* **1** [C] a close companion, esp. a person who shares difficult work or troubles **2** [C;A;N] (esp. used as a title in COMMUNIST countries) a citizen; fellow member of a union, political party, etc.: *We were met at the airport by 3 comrades from the local council.|Comrades, please be quiet* **3** [C *usu. pl.*] *usu. derog* COMMUNIST (esp. in the phr. **the comrades**)
com·rade·ship /'kɒmrɪ̈dʃɪp, -reɪd-‖'kamræd-/ *n* [U;(C)] companionship; friendship

coms /kɒmz‖kamz/ *n* [P] *infml* COMBINATIONS
con[1] /kɒn‖kan/ *v* **-nn-** [T1] *old use* to study or examine (something) very carefully, esp. in order to learn or keep in one's memory
con[2] *adv* **1** (of arguing) against (something) (esp. in the phr. **pro and con**): *We must be fair and consider the reasons* PRO *and con* **2 He's very con (it)** *infml* He's very strongly against (it)
con[3] *n* [C *usu. pl.*] **1** an argument or reason against (something) (esp. in the phr. **pros and cons**) **2** a person who or vote that is against (a suggestion) (esp. in the phr. **pros and cons**): *There are more* PROs *than cons.|There are 10* PROs *and 8 cons*
con[4] *n sl* CONFIDENCE TRICK
con[5] *v* **-nn-** [T1 (*into, out of*)] *sl* to trick (a trusting person) in order to make money: *They've conned me out of all my money!*
con[6] *n sl* a prisoner; CONVICT
con- /kən, kɒn‖kən, kan/ *prefix* together; with: CONDUCT —see also COL-, COM-, COR-
con·cat·e·nate /kɒn'kætɪ̈neɪt‖kan-/ *v* [Wv5;T1] *fml or tech* to join together; unite as in a chain
con·cat·e·na·tion /kɒnˌkætɪ̈'neɪʃən‖kan-/ *n fml or tech* **1** [U] the act of concatenating (CONCATENATE) **2** [U] the state of being CONCATENATED **3** [C] a number of things or events joined together as in a chain: *a concatenation of misfortunes*
con·cave /ˌkɒn'keɪv◂, kən-‖ˌkan'keɪv◂, kən-/ *adj* curved inward, like the inside surface of a hollow ball: *a concave mirror* —opposite **convex**; see picture at OPTICS
con·cav·i·ty /kən'kævɪ̈ti/ *n* **1** [U] the state of being CONCAVE **2** [C] a CONCAVE place
con·ceal /kən'siːl/ *v* [T1 (*from*), 4] to hide; keep from being seen or known: *It is wrong for a man to conceal his feelings from his wife*
con·ceal·ment /kən'siːlmənt/ *n* [U] **1** the act of CONCEALing **2** the state of being CONCEALed (often in the phr. **in concealment**): *The criminals stayed in concealment until the police had passed*
con·cede /kən'siːd/ *v* **1** [T1,5;IØ;D1 (*to*)] to admit as true, just, or proper, often unwillingly (often in the phr. **concede defeat**): *The government conceded defeat as soon as the election results were known.|I'm willing to concede that a larger car would have cost more, but I still think we should have bought one.|I concede you that point, but I still think you're wrong* **2** [D1 (*to*); T1] to give as a right; allow; yield: *After the First World War Germany conceded her neighbours much valuable land.|The* CHAMPION *conceded 10 points to me at the start of the game, but, even so, he beat me!* **3** [IØ] to end a game or match by admitting defeat: *I conceded when I saw I had lost*
con·ceit /kən'siːt/ *n* **1** [U] also **conceitedness**— too high an opinion of one's own abilities, value, etc.: *That girl's* **full of conceit** **2** [C] *tech* an unusual cleverly-expressed comparison, esp. in poetry, showing fancy rather than imagination: *the use of conceits in Elizabethan poetry*
con·ceit·ed /kən'siːtɪ̈d/ *adj* having or showing CONCEIT (1): *Joan became very conceited after she passed those examinations* —**~ly** *adv* —**~ness** *n* [U]
con·cei·va·ble /kən'siːvəbəl/ *adj* [B,B5] that can be thought of or believed; imaginable: *It is conceivable that my wife missed the train, but it's very unlikely* —**-bly** *adv*
con·ceive /kənsiːv/ *v* **1** [T1;IØ] *tech or bibl* to become PREGNANT with (a child): *Our first child was conceived in March and born in December* **2** [T1,5a,6b] to think of; imagine; consider: *Scientists first conceived the idea of the atomic bomb in the 1930s.|Until I saw you I'd never conceived that such beauty existed* —see PERCEIVE (USAGE)
conceive of *v prep* [T1,4: (*as*)] to think of;

imagine; consider: *It's difficult to conceive of travelling to the moon.|In ancient times the world was conceived of as flat*

con·cen·trate¹ /ˈkɒnsəntreɪt‖ˈkɑn-/ *v* **1** [IØ;T1: (*on, upon*)] to keep or direct (all one's thoughts, efforts, attention, etc.): *I'm never able to concentrate so early in the morning.|If you don't concentrate more on your work you'll be dismissed!* **2** [L9;X9] to (cause to) come together in or around one place: *Industrial development is being concentrated in the South of the country.|The crowds concentrated in the centre of the town near the royal palace* **3** [T1] *tech* to strengthen by reducing the per cent of water in a SOLUTION (=a mixture of some substance and water)

concentrate² *n* [C;U] a CONCENTRATED¹ (3) form of something: *orange juice concentrate*

con·cen·trat·ed /ˈkɒnsəntreɪtɨ̣d‖ˈkɑn-/ *adj* **1** [A] very strong: *This pupil has made a concentrated effort to improve his work* **2** [B] increased in strength by the removal of liquid or the addition of more of a substance

con·cen·tra·tion /ˌkɒnsənˈtreɪʃən‖ˌkɑn-/ *n* **1** [U] close or complete attention: *This book will need all your concentration* **2** [C] a close gathering: *There is a concentration of industry in the South of the country* **3** [S] *tech* the measure of the amount of a substance contained in a liquid: *What is the concentration of salt in sea water?* **4** [U] the act of concentrating (CONCENTRATE¹)

concentration camp /ˌ··ˈ·· ·/ *n* a large enclosed area where political prisoners or people considered as threats to the state are imprisoned

con·cen·tric /kənˈsentrɪk/ *adj* [Wa5 (*with*)] *tech* having the same centre: *concentric circles|Is this circle concentric with that?* —see picture at GEOMETRY

con·cept /ˈkɒnsept‖ˈkɑn-/ *n* [C (*of*); C5] a general idea, thought, or understanding

con·cep·tion /kənˈsepʃən/ *n* **1** [U] the act of forming an idea, plan, etc.: *At the moment of its conception, every detail of a great musical work would become clear in Mozart's mind* **2** [U,U5,(6b); C: (*of*)] (a) general understanding; idea: *Different people have different conceptions of what he means.|Having studied history I have some/a conception of what life was like in the past.|I have no conception (of) why you left home* **3** [C;U] *tech* the starting of a new life by the union of a male and a female sex cell

con·cep·tu·al /kənˈseptʃʊəl/ *adj* [Wa5] of, related to, or based on (the formation of) CONCEPTs: *Is conceptual ability limited to man?* —**~ly** *adv*

con·cep·tu·al·ize, -ise /kənˈseptʃʊəlaɪz/ *v* [T1;IØ] to form a CONCEPT of (something)

con·cern¹ /kənˈsɜːn‖-ɜrn/ *v* [T1] **1** [*no pass.*] to be about: *This story concerns a good girl and a wicked fairy* **2** to be of importance or interest to; have an effect on: *The marriage of a queen concerns all the people who live in her country* **3** to worry (a person); cause anxiety; make unhappy or troubled **4** [(*about, with*)] to worry (esp. oneself); interest (esp. oneself): *A good doctor should always concern himself with your health* **5 To whom it may concern** (the beginning of a letter that may be read by anyone who receives or sees it)

concern² *n* **1** [C] a matter that is of interest or importance to someone: *The fact that you have left your wife isn't my concern* **2** [U (*for*)] serious care or interest: *a nurse's concern for a sick man* **3** [U] worry; anxiety: *There is no cause for concern; the storm was not too serious* **4** [C] a business; firm: *Our concern only makes shoes for children* **5** [C] *tech* a share: *He has a small concern in our business* **6 going concern** a business that is in active and usu. profitable operation, not just planned **7 paying concern** a business that makes enough profits

con·cerned /kənˈsɜːnd‖-ɜr-/ *adj* **1** [B (*about*), B3] anxious; worried: *The concerned mothers anxiously waited for their children.|I was very concerned about my mother's illness* **2** [Wa5;E] interested; taking part: *All concerned very much enjoyed their afternoon visit to the country* **3 as far as I'm concerned** (esp. with an expression of unfavourable feeling or opinion) in my opinion **4 be concerned with** to be about: *This story is concerned with fairies and wicked magicians* **5 where X is/are concerned** In matters that have an effect on X; when it comes to X: *Where work is concerned, I always try to do my best*

con·cern·ed·ly /kənˈsɜːnɨ̣dli‖-ɜr-/ *adv* in a CONCERNED (1) way

con·cern·ing /kənˈsɜːnɪŋ‖-ɜr-/ *prep* about; with regard to: *Concerning your letter, I am pleased to inform you that your plans are quite acceptable to us*

con·cert /ˈkɒnsət‖ˈkɑnsərt/ *n* **1** a musical performance given by a number of singers or musicians or both —compare RECITAL **2 in concert a** working together; in agreement: *The various governments decided to act in concert over this matter* **b** playing or singing at a concert: *Tonight you can see "The Rolling Stones" in concert*

con·cert·ed /kənˈsɜːtɨ̣d‖-ɜr-/ *adj* **1** [Wa5] planned or done together by agreement; combined: *a concerted effort of all governments to stop crime* **2** *nonstandard* very strong (esp. in the phr. **concerted effort**): *This pupil has made a concerted effort to improve his work* —**~ly** *adv*

con·cert·go·er /ˈkɒnsətgəʊəʳ‖ˈkɑnsərt-/ *n* a person who frequently goes to concerts

concert grand /ˌ·· ˈ·/ *n* a piano of the largest size, played esp. at concerts

con·cer·ti·na¹ /ˌkɒnsəˈtiːnə‖ˌkɑnsər-/ *n* a type of small musical wind instrument of the ACCORDION family, held and played in the hands by pressing in from both ends

concertina² *v* [IØ] *BrE infml* (of a vehicle) to get all pressed together like a CONCERTINA¹ as the result of a crash: *the heavy* LORRY *concertinaed when it crashed into the wall*

con·cert·mas·ter /ˈkɒnsətˌmɑːstəʳ‖ˈkɑnsərtˌmæstər/ *n AmE* LEADER (4)

con·cer·to /kənˈtʃɜːtəʊ‖-ˈtʃertəʊ/ *n* **-tos** a piece of music for one or more SOLO instruments and ORCHESTRA

concert pitch /ˌ·· ˈ·/ *n* **1** *tech* the PITCH (=the degree of highness or lowness of music) used as the standard for all instruments **2 at concert pitch (for)** *infml* in a state of complete (and perhaps anxious) readiness or fitness: *The navy and army were at concert pitch for war*

con·ces·sion /kənˈseʃən/ *n* **1** [U (*of*)] the act of yielding **2** [C] a point or thing yielded, esp. after a disagreement: *The firm's promise to increase our pay was a concession to union demands* **3** [C (*from*), C3] a right given or yielded by a government, owner of land, etc., to do something special: *oil concessions in the North Sea*

con·ces·sion·aire /kənˌseʃəˈneəʳ/ *n fml* a person who has been given a CONCESSION (3); holder of a CONCESSION (3)

con·ces·sive /kənˈsesɪv/ *adj fml* of, related to, or being a CONCESSION (3)

concessive clause /ˌ·,·· ˈ·/ *n* a CLAUSE (1), often introduced by "although", which shows willingness to admit (CONCEDE) a point that goes against the main argument of a sentence: *A concessive clause begins the sentence "Although you are right about that, you are wrong about everything else"*

conch /kɒntʃ, kɒŋk‖kɑ-/ *n* **1** a type of SNAIL-like

tropical sea animal with a large twisted often brightly coloured shell **2** the shell of this animal

con·chol·o·gy /kɒŋ'kɒlədʒi‖kaŋ'ka-/ *n* [U] *tech* the scientific study of shells and the animals that live in them

con·ci·erge /ˌkɒnsi'eəʒ‖ˌkansi'erʒ (*Fr* kɔ̃sjɛrʒ)/ *n* *Fr* (esp. in France) a CARETAKER; person (usu. a woman) who looks after the entrance to a block of flats

con·cil·i·ate /kən'sɪlieɪt/ *v* [T1] to make (someone or a group of people) calm; win the support or friendly feelings of (a person or a group of people); remove the anger or distrust of (a person or a group of people)

con·cil·i·a·tion /kənˌsɪli'eɪʃən/ *n* [U] the act of conciliating (CONCILIATE): *Conciliation is the best way of regaining a person's trust after an argument*

con·cil·i·a·to·ry /kən'sɪliətəri‖-tori/ *adj* tending or intending to CONCILIATE: *He was very conciliatory but I still can't forgive him*

con·cise /kən'saɪs/ *adj* short and clear; expressing much in few words: *a concise speech/book/speaker* —**~ly** *adv*

con·ci·sion /kən'sɪʒən/ also **con·cise·ness** /kən'saɪsnɪ̵s/— *n* [U] the quality or state of being CONCISE: *the admirable concision of David's latest book*

con·clave /'kɒŋkleɪv‖'kaŋ-/ *n* **1** *tech* a private meeting of CARDINALs to elect the POPE: (fig.) *Should the party leader be elected by all the members of the party or by a conclave of those lucky enough to have been elected to Parliament?* **2 sit in conclave** to hold a private or secret meeting in order to consider some matter

con·clude /kən'klu:d/ *v* **1** [T1;IØ: (*by*)] *fml* to (cause to) come to an end: *We concluded the meeting at 8 o'clock with a prayer* **2** [T1 (*with*)] to arrange or settle (something): *We concluded an agreement with the enemy and soon made peace* **3** [T5] to come to believe after consideration of known facts: *The judge concluded that the prisoner was guilty*

con·clu·sion /kən'klu:ʒən/ *n* **1** the end; closing part: *I found the conclusion of his book very interesting indeed* **2** a judgment or decision: *What conclusions did you come to/draw/reach?* **3** an arrangement or agreement that introduces a changed state of affairs which is likely to last for some time: *The conclusion of peace is in the interests of both countries* **4 a foregone conclusion** something decided in advance; something very likely to happen **5 in conclusion** as the last thing: *In conclusion, I'd like to say how much I've enjoyed staying here* **6 jump to conclusions/a conclusion** to form a judgment too quickly **7 try conclusions with** to compete against (someone) to find who is the stronger, more skilful, etc.

con·clu·sive /kən'klu:sɪv/ *adj* putting an end to doubt or uncertainty: *conclusive proof that he was the murderer* —**~ly** *adv*

con·coct /kən'kɒkt‖-'kakt/ *v* [T1] **1** to make (something) by mixing or combining parts: *Although there was little food in the house Jean concocted a splendid meal* **2** to invent (usu. something false, a lie, etc.); make up: *John concocted an excuse for being late and the teacher believed him*

con·coc·tion /kən'kɒkʃən‖-'kak-/ *n* **1** [C;U] something CONCOCTed **2** [U] the act of CONCOCTing

con·com·i·tance /kən'kɒmɪ̵təns‖-'ka-/ *n* *fml* **1** [U] the state of being CONCOMITANT[1] **2** [C] CONCOMITANT[2]

con·com·i·tant[1] /kən'kɒmɪ̵tənt‖-'ka-/ *adj* [Wa5; B (*with*)] *fml* existing or happening together (with something else): *war with all its concomitant sufferings* —**~ly** *adv*

concomitant[2] *n* [*usu. pl.*] *fml* something that exists or happens together with something else; something that often or naturally goes with something else

con·cord /'kɒŋkɔ:d‖'kaŋkɔrd/ *n* **1** [U] friendly relationship; complete peace and agreement: *The 2 tribes had lived in concord for many centuries* **2** [C] *tech* an agreement, esp. a TREATY, establishing peace and friendly relations: *Both sides willingly signed the concord which ended the disagreement between them* **3** [U] (in grammar) agreement between words, esp. with regard to their number: *Doctor Smith spent many years studying verb and noun concord*

con·cor·dance /kən'kɔ:dəns‖-ɔr-/ *n* **1** [U] *fml* agreement; state of being CONCORDANT **2** [C] *tech* an alphabetical list of the words used in a book or collection of books by one writer, with information about where they can be found and usu. about how they are used

con·cor·dant /kən'kɔ:dənt‖-ɔr-/ *adj* [(*with*)] *fml* being in agreement; being of the same regular pattern

con·cor·dat /kɒn'kɔ:dæt‖kan'kɔr-/ *n* *tech* an agreement between the church and a state settling matters of religious importance

con·course /'kɒŋkɔ:s‖-ors/ *n* **1** an act of coming, gathering, moving, or happening together: *an interesting concourse of events|a large concourse of people* **2** a hall or open place where passages or roads meet and crowds of people can gather

con·crete[1] /'kɒŋkri:t‖kan'kri:t/ *adj* **1** [Wa5] *tech* existing as something real or solid; actual: *Light is not concrete but a window is* **2** particular as opposed to general; clear; DEFINITE: *Have you any concrete thoughts on how to deal with this difficulty?* —**~ly** *adv*

con·crete[2] /'kɒŋkri:t‖'kaŋ-/ *n* [U] a building material made by mixing sand, very small stones, cement, and water

concrete[3] /'kɒŋkri:t‖'kaŋ-/ *v* [T1;IØ] to cover (a path, wall, etc.) with CONCRETE[2]: *The workman is still busy concreting the road*

concrete mix·er /'·· ˌ··/ *n* a machine consisting of a barrel which turns slowly round and round, in which CONCRETE[2] is mixed

con·cu·bi·nage /kɒn'kju:bɪ̵nɪdʒ‖kan-/ *n* [U] the practice of 2 people living as husband and wife without being married according to law

con·cu·bine /'kɒŋkjʊbaɪn‖'kaŋ-/ *n* a woman who lives with a man as his wife, sometimes in addition to his lawful wife: *The king had 4 wives and 20 concubines*

con·cu·pis·cence /kən'kju:pɪ̵səns‖kan-/ *n* [U] sexual desire; LUST —**-cent** *adj*

con·cur /kən'kɜ:ʳ/ *v* **-rr-** *fml* **1** [IØ (*with*)] to agree: *Our opinions on this matter concur* **2** [IØ,3] to happen at the same time: *Everything concurred to produce the desired effect*

con·cur·rence /kən'kʌrəns‖-'kɜr-/ *n* **1** [C,C5] an agreement of opinion: *the concurrence of all 3 judges that the man was guilty* **2** [C] an example of actions, events, etc., happening at the same time: *an interesting concurrence of events* **3** [U] the act of CONCURring

con·cur·rent /kən'kʌrənt‖-'kɜr-/ *adj* **1** [Wa5; (*with*)] existing or happening at the same time **2** [Wa5] *tech* having one and only one common point **3** [(*with*)] being in agreement: *My opinions are concurrent with yours as regards this matter* —**~ly** *adv*

con·cuss /kən'kʌs/ *v* [Wv5;T1 *often pass.*] to

damage (the brain) with a heavy blow, shock, or violent shaking

con·cus·sion /kən'kʌʃən/ *n* **1** [U] damage of the brain caused by a heavy blow, shock, or violent shaking: *He's suffering from concussion after falling out of a window* **2** [C] a violent blow, shock, or shaking: *a concussion caused by the explosion*

con·demn /kən'dem/ *v* **1** [T1 (*as*)] to express strong disapproval of (someone or some action): *Most people are willing to condemn violence of any sort (as evil)* **2** [T1 (*for*)] to judge (a person) guilty: *He was condemned and imprisoned in a day* **3** [Wv5;X9;V3] to state the punishment for (a guilty person), esp. a punishment of death or long imprisonment: *The prisoner was condemned to death.|The court condemned her to spend all her life in prison* **4** [X9;V3] to force (someone) into an unhappy state of affairs: *His bad leg condemned him to a wheelchair* **5** [Wv5;T1 (*as*)] to declare (something) officially unfit for use: *Although this house is condemned (as unfit), an old lady still lives here* **6** [T1] to show the guilt of (a person): *His evil face condemned him*

con·dem·na·tion /ˌkɒndəm'neɪʃən, -dem-‖ˌkɑn-/ *n* **1** [U (*of*)] the act of CONDEMNing **2** [C (*of*)] an example of the act of CONDEMNing (1,2) **3** [C *usu. sing.*] a cause or reason for being CONDEMNed (2,6): *His evil face was his condemnation*

condemned cell /·,· '·, ·'· ·/ *n* a room where prisoners are kept who are to be punished by death

con·den·sa·tion /ˌkɒnden'seɪʃən, -dən-‖ˌkɑn-/ *n* **1** [U] change from a gas to a liquid or, sometimes, to a solid: *condensation of steam to water* **2** [U] small drops of a liquid or solid substance formed in this way; drops of liquid formed when steam becomes cool: *There was condensation on the windows* **3** [C; U] (an example or result of) the act of making a book, speech, report, etc., shorter: *A condensation of that famous book printed in our magazine last month*

con·dense /kən'dens/ *v* **1** [I∅;T1] **a** (of a gas) to become liquid, or sometimes solid, esp. by becoming cooler **b** to cause (a gas) to become liquid, or sometimes solid, esp. by making cooler **2** [Wv5; T1] to put into a smaller or shortened form: *a condensed report*

condensed milk /·,· '·/ *n* [U] milk which is thickened by taking away some of its water, and which is sweetened and sold in tins

con·dens·er /kən'densəʳ/ *n* an apparatus that makes a gas change into a liquid

con·de·scend /ˌkɒndɪ'send‖ˌkɑn-/ *v* **1** [Wv4;I3] to agree to do something beneath one's social rank: *The general condescended to eat with the soldiers* **2** [Wv4;I∅ (*to*)] to act in a manner that makes one appear of a higher social rank than others: *Mrs Smith condescends to all her neighbours.|I dislike people who are condescending*

con·de·scen·sion /ˌkɒndɪ'senʃən‖ˌkɑn-/ *n* [U] the act or habit of CONDESCENDing

con·dign /kən'daɪn/ *adj fml* (esp. of punishment) fitting; well deserved —**~ly** *adv*

con·di·ment /'kɒndɨmənt‖'kɑn-/ *n* [C *often pl.*; (U)] *fml* a powder or liquid used for giving a special taste to food: *Pepper and salt are condiments*

con·di·tion¹ /kən'dɪʃən/ *n* **1** [C (*of*)] a state of being or existence: *The* ASTRONAUT*s soon got used to the condition of weightlessness* **2** [U] the state of general health or fitness: *You could improve your condition by running every day* **3** [U] readiness for use; the state of being fit for use: *This car's in poor condition* **4** [C] a disease; illness: *This is an interesting condition. I've never seen this illness before* **5** [C (*of, for*), C5c] something stated as necessary or desirable for something else (often in phrs. of the form **on . . . condition**): *What are her conditions for joining us?|She will join us on one condition: that we divide all the profits equally* **6** [C] position in society; rank (often in the phr. **people of every condition**) **7 in/out of condition** thoroughly healthy or fit/not fit: *Walk to work every day and you'll soon be back in condition* **8 on condition that** if; PROVIDING: *I'll come on condition that John is invited, too* **9 on no condition** never; not at any time; in no state of affairs: *You must on no condition climb that high wall!*

condition² *v* **1** [Wv4,5;T1] to put (esp. oneself or an animal) into good health or proper working order: *You need to condition yourself if you're to play in the football match on Friday.|Your dog looks very well conditioned* **2** [Wv5;T1] to settle; decide; govern: *The amount of money I spend is conditioned by the amount I earn* **3** [Wv5;V3;T1] *esp. tech or derog* to train: *Society has conditioned each one of us.|The scientist conditioned the dog to jump each time it heard a bell*

con·di·tion·al¹ /kən'dɪʃənəl/ *adj* [Wa5] **1** [(*on, upon*)] depending on a certain condition or conditions: *His agreement to buy our house was conditional on us leaving all the furniture in it* **2** (in grammar) expressing a condition or supposition: *A conditional sentence often begins with the words "if" or "unless"* —**~ly** *adv*

conditional² *n* (in grammar) a CONDITIONAL (2), form, esp. a sentence or CLAUSE (1): *How many conditionals are there on page 42?*

conditioned re·flex /·,·· '··/ also **conditioned response** /·,·· ·'·/— *n tech* a REFLEX that is developed as the result of repeated treatment or training

con·di·tions /kən'dɪʃənz/ *n* **1** [P] CONDITION (1): *We were interested in working conditions in Africa.|What are conditions like in your country now?* **2** [P9] CIRCUMSTANCES: *Even under the best conditions, we couldn't get there in less than 3 days* **3** [P9] TERMS of payment: *I can let you have it on very favourable conditions: only £2 now and the rest in easy payments spread out over 15 months*

USAGE Compare **conditions** and **situation**: Besides their other meanings they can both mean "state of affairs; CIRCUMSTANCES": *the* ECONOMIC **conditions/situation**. Perhaps **conditions** here means daily matters like food, work, and houses, while **situation** might be concerned with the international balance of payments.

con·do·lence /kən'dəʊləns/ *n* [C *often pl.* (*on*); U] (an expression of) sympathy for someone who has experienced sadness, sorrow, misfortune, etc.: *Please accept my condolences on your mother's death*

con·dole with /kən'dəʊl/ *v prep* [T1 (*on, over*)] to express sympathy to (someone who has experienced sadness, sorrow, misfortune, etc.)

con·dom /'kɒndəm‖'kɑn-, 'kʌn-/ *n* a usu. rubber covering worn over the male sex organ during sexual relations, used as a means of birth control and/or a protection against disease

con·do·min·i·um /ˌkɒndə'mɪnɪəm‖ˌkɑn-/ *n tech* **1** [U] rule of a country by 2 or more other states acting together **2** [C] a country ruled by 2 or more other states acting together: *the English-French Condominium of the New Hebrides* **3** [C] *AmE* (a flat in) a block of flats of which each is owned by the people who live in it

con·done /kən'dəʊn/ *v* [T1] to forgive (wrong action or behaviour); treat (a wrong action or behaviour) as harmless

con·dor /'kɒndɔːʳ‖'kɑndər, -dɔr/ *n* a type of very large Californian or South American VULTURE (=a large bird that feeds on dead bodies) —see picture at PREY¹

con·duce to /kən'djuːs‖-'duːs/ also **conduce to·**

wards— *v prep* [T1,(4)] *fml* to help to produce: *Does plenty of exercise conduce to good health?*

con·du·cive /kən'djuːsɪv‖-'duː-/ *adj* [F+*to*] *fml* likely to produce: *Plenty of exercise is conducive to good health* —**~ness** *n* [U9 (*to*)]

con·duct¹ /'kɒndʌkt, -dəkt‖'kɑn-/ *n* **1** [U] *fml* behaviour: *I'm glad to see your conduct at school has improved* **2** [U9] direction of the course of (a business, activity, etc.)

conduct² /kən'dʌkt/ *v* **1** [T1] *fml* to behave (oneself): *I like the way your children conduct themselves. Their behaviour is very good* **2** [T1] to direct the course of (a business, activity, etc.) **3** [T1] to lead or guide (a person, tour, etc.) **4** [T1; IØ] to stand before and direct the playing of (musicians or a musical work) **5** [T1] to act as the path for (electricity, heat, etc.): *Plastic and rubber won't conduct electricity* **6** [IØ] to collect payments from the passengers on (a public vehicle): *She's conducted on London buses for 20 years*

con·duc·tion /kən'dʌkʃən/ *n* [U] the passage of electricity along wires, water through pipes, etc.

con·duc·tive /kən'dʌktɪv/ *adj tech* able to act effectively as a path for electricity, heat, etc.: *Copper is a very/highly conductive metal*

con·duc·tiv·i·ty /ˌkɒndʌk'tɪvəti‖ˌkɑn-/ also **con·duc·tance** /kən'dʌktəns/— *n* [U] *tech* the ability of a substance to act as a path for electricity, heat, etc.: *The high conductivity of copper makes it a much needed metal*

con·duc·tor /kən'dʌktəʳ/ *n* **1** [C] a person who directs the playing of a group of musicians **2** [C; N] a person employed to collect payments from passengers on a public vehicle **3** [C] a substance that readily acts as a path for electricity, heat, etc.: *Wood is a poor conductor of heat* **4** *esp. AmE* the guard on a train

conductor rail /·'·· ·/ *n tech* the rail from which electricity is passed to electric engines on some railway systems

con·duit /'kɒndɪt, 'kɒndjʊət‖'kɑnduːət/ *n* a pipe or passage for carrying water, gas, a number of electric wires, etc.

cone /kəʊn/ *n* **1** a solid object with a round base and a point at the top —see picture at GEOMETRY **2** a hollow or solid object shaped like this: *Many children would rather eat ice cream from cones than from dishes* **3** the fruit of a PINE or FIR, consisting of several partly separate seed-containing pieces laid over each other, shaped rather like this

co·ney /'kəʊni/ *n* CONY

con·fab·u·late /kən'fæbjʊleɪt‖-bjə-/ also (*infml*) **con·fab** /kən'fæb/— *v* [IØ (*with*)] *pomp* to talk together

con·fab·u·la·tion /kənˌfæbjʊ'leɪʃən‖-bjə-/ also (*infml*) **con·fab** /'kɒnfæb‖'kɑn-/— *n pomp* a private conversation

con·fec·tion /kən'fekʃən/ *n fml* a sweet-tasting dish

con·fec·tion·er /kən'fekʃənəʳ/ *n* a person who makes or sells sweets, ice cream, cakes, etc.

con·fec·tion·e·ry /kən'fekʃənəri/ *n* **1** [U] sweet foods, cakes, sweets, etc.: *You eat too much confectionery; that's why you're fat* **2** [U] the work of a CONFECTIONER: *He studied confectionery for several years* **3** [C] a CONFECTIONER*'s* shop or place of work

con·fed·e·ra·cy /kən'fedərəsi/ *n* **1** *tech* a political union of several peoples or states **2** a combination or group of people

con·fed·e·rate¹ /kən'fedərət/ *adj* [Wa5] belonging to a CONFEDERACY: *The 11 southern states which left the United States in 1860 and 1861 called themselves the Confederate States of America*

confederate² *n* **1** a member of a CONFEDERACY **2** *derog* a person who shares in a crime **3** [*usu. cap.*] a supporter of the 11 southern states which left the United States in 1860 and 1861

con·fed·e·rate³ /kən'fedəreɪt/ *v* [T1;IØ] to (cause to) combine in a CONFEDERACY: *If we confederate we can establish a country strong enough to be politically independent*

con·fed·e·ra·tion /kənˌfedə'reɪʃən/ *n* **1** [U] the act of confederating (CONFEDERATE) **2** [C] *tech* CONFEDERACY: *The 4 states combined to form a powerful confederation*

con·fer /kən'fɜːʳ/ *v* **-rr-** *fml* **1** [T1 (*on, upon*)] to give (a gift, title, honour, favour, etc.): *The queen conferred a noble title on her faithful minister* **2** [IØ (*on, with*)] to talk together; compare opinions: *The ministers are still conferring on this matter* —**~ment** *n* [C;U]

con·fe·rence /'kɒnfərəns‖'kɑn-/ *n* [C; *in*+U] a meeting held so that opinions and ideas on a subject, or a number of subjects, can be exchanged: *A conference of West European states today decided that political union between them was unlikely before 1980* —see also PRESS CONFERENCE

con·fess /kən'fes/ *v* **1** [T1,4,5a,6a;IØ (*to*)] to admit (a fault, crime, something wrong): *The prisoner has confessed her crime.|I confessed (to) hating the king.|Jean confessed she'd eaten all the cakes* **2** [T1,4,5a,6a;IØ (*to*)] *tech* to make (one's faults) known to a priest or God: *Won't you confess and be at peace with God?* **3** [X (*to be*) 1,7] to declare (oneself) to be: *The minister confessed himself guilty/to be a thief* **4** [T1] *tech* (of a priest) to hear the CONFESSION (2) of (a person): *The priest confessed 90 people on Saturday morning* **5 must/ have to confess** to admit: *I must confess I hate this government*

con·fessed /kən'fest/ *adj* not secretive; open; by one's own admittance or declaration: *Mrs Jones is a (self-) confessed alcoholic* —**~ly** /-'fesədli/ *adv*

con·fes·sion /kən'feʃən/ *n* **1** [U;C] (an example of) the act of admitting one's crimes, serious faults, etc. **2** [U] *tech* a religious service at which a person tells his faults to a priest **3** [C] *fml* a declaration of esp. religious belief: *a confession of faith* **4** [C] a religious group (usu. Christian) with its own organization and a shared system of belief: *the many confessions of the Netherlands*

con·fes·sion·al /kən'feʃənəl/ *n* **1** [C] a usu. enclosed place in a church where the priest hears people make their CONFESSION (1) **2** [*the*+R] the practice of admitting faults to a priest: *A good priest always keeps the secrets of the confessional to himself*

con·fes·sor /kən'fesəʳ/ *n* [C9,(C)] *tech* the priest to whom a person regularly makes his CONFESSION (1)

con·fet·ti /kən'feti/ *n* [U] small pieces of coloured paper thrown about on happy occasions, esp. weddings

con·fi·dant /'kɒnfədænt, ˌkɒnfə'dænt‖'kɑnfədænt/ (*fem.* **confidante**)— *n* [C9,(C)] a person to whom one tells one's secrets or with whom one talks about personal matters

con·fide /kən'faɪd/ *v* [T4,5,6a: (*to*)] to tell (information, secrets, personal matters, etc.) secretly to a person one trusts

confide in *v prep* [T1] to (feel able to) talk freely to (a person) esp. about one's secrets: *Allan felt he could confide in the priest*

con·fi·dence /'kɒnfədəns‖'kɑn-/ *n* **1** [U9] faith; full trust: *You have won my confidence; I know I can trust you* **2** [U] belief in one's own or another's ability: *Jean lacks confidence in herself* **3** [C] a secret; some personal matter told secretly to a person: *The 2 girls told each other confidences about their boyfriends* **4** [C] CONFIDENCE TRICK **5 in**

confidence privately; secretly: *I told you that in confidence so why did you tell Jean about it?* **6 take (someone) into one's confidence** to tell (a person one considers trustworthy) one's secrets

confidence trick /'··· ·/ also *sl* **con**— *n* a trick played in order to cheat a trusting person of money

con·fi·dent /'kɒnfɪ̈dənt‖'kɑn-/ *adj* [B;F (*of*, 5)] feeling or showing CONFIDENCE (1,2): *a confident smile|The politician spoke in a confident voice* —**~ly** *adv*

con·fi·den·tial /ˌkɒnfɪ̈'denʃəl‖ˌkɑn-/ *adj* **1** spoken or written in secret; to be kept secret: *confidential information* **2** trusted with private matters: *a confidential secretary* **3** showing full trust: *He spoke in a confidential voice.|a confidential look* —**~ity** /ˌkɒnfɪ̈denʃi'ælɪ̈ti‖ˌkɑn-/ *n* [U] —**~ly** /ˌkɒnfɪ̈'denʃəli‖ˌkɑn-/ *adv*

confide to *v prep* [D1] **1** to tell (something) to (someone) CONFIDENTIALly: *Alice confided her dislike of her husband to Jean* **2** *lit* to give (someone or something) into (the charge or care of (someone)); ENTRUST: *Let us confide our souls to (the care of) God*

con·fid·ing /kən'faɪdɪŋ/ *adj* trustful —**~ly** *adv*

con·fig·u·ra·tion /kənˌfɪgjʊ'reɪʃən‖-jə-/ *n* the arrangement of the various parts of something; shape: *Scientists know little about the configuration of the moon's surface*

con·fine /kən'faɪn/ *v* [T1 (*to*)] **1** [Wv5] to enclose within limits: *Please confine your remarks to the subject we're talking about* **2** to shut or keep in a small space: *John was confined to bed for a week with his cold* **3** [*usu. pass.*] *med* to keep (a woman about to give birth to a baby) in bed: *She was confined on the 20th and the baby was born on the 21st*

con·fine·ment /kən'faɪnmənt/ *n* **1** [C;U] also **lying-in**— the time during which a woman about to give birth to a child is kept in bed **2** [U (*to*)] the act of confining or state of being confined (CONFINE (1,2)): *Their confinement to such a small area could not be carried out without the use of force*

con·fines /'kɒnfaɪnz‖'kɑn-/ *n* [P] limits; borders: *within the confines of one country|This is outside the confines of human knowledge*

con·firm /kən'fɜːm‖-ɜrm/ *v* **1** [T1,5a,6a] to support; make certain; give proof (of): *Please confirm your telephone message in writing.|The king confirmed that the election would be on June 20th* **2** [T1] to give approval to (a person, agreement, position, etc.); agree to: *When do you think the President will confirm you in office?* **3** [T1] *tech* to admit (a person) to full membership of a church

con·fir·ma·tion /ˌkɒnfə'meɪʃən‖ˌkɑnfər-/ *n* **1** [U] the act of CONFIRMing (2) **2** [U;C;U5;C5] (a) proof; something that CONFIRMS (1): *Your news was really confirmation for my beliefs* **3** [C;U] *tech* a religious service in which a person is made a full member of the church

con·firmed /kən'fɜːmd‖-ɜr-/ *adj* [A] firmly settled in a particular way of life: *He'll never get married: he's a confirmed* BACHELOR

con·fis·cate /'kɒnfɪ̈skeɪt‖'kɑn-/ *v* [Wv5;T1 (*from*)] to seize (private property) from someone without payment in order to keep, destroy, give to others, etc.: *The teacher confiscated my radio because she heard me playing it in class.|Confiscated property should be kept by the state for public use* —**-cation** /ˌkɒnfɪ̈s'keɪʃən‖ˌkɑn-/ *n* [U;C]

con·fis·ca·to·ry /'kɒnfɪ̈skeɪtəri, kən'fɪskətəri‖kən'fɪsketori/ *adj* **1** that CONFISCATEs **2** that take(s) away too much in a severe manner: *Confiscatory taxes will ruin the industry of this country*

con·fla·gra·tion /ˌkɒnflə'greɪʃən‖ˌkɑn-/ *n fml* a very large fire that destroys much property, esp. buildings or forests

con·flate /kən'fleɪt/ *v* [T1;(I∅)] *tech* to combine —**conflation** /kən'fleɪʃən/ *n* [U;C]

con·flict¹ /'kɒnflɪkt‖'kɑn-/ *n* [C;U] **1** (a) war; battle; struggle: *Armed conflict could start at any time.|There is a possibility of a serious conflict in North America* **2** (an example of) the meeting of opposing ideas or beliefs: *Some people feel there is a great deal of conflict between religion and science* **3** (a) disagreement; argument; quarrel: *There is no conflict between church and state in Britain today but there were many conflicts in the past*

con·flict² /kən'flɪkt/ *v* [Wv4;I∅ (*with*)] to be in opposition (to another or each other); disagree; vary: *Do British laws conflict with any international laws?*

con·flu·ence /'kɒnfluəns‖'kɑn-/ *n fml* **1** [U;C] the flowing together of 2 or more streams: (fig.) *a confluence of ideas* **2** [C] the place where 2 or more streams flow together: *The city of Koblenz was established at the confluence of the Rhine and the Mosel*

con·form /kən'fɔːm‖-ɔrm/ *v* [I∅ (*to*)] to be obedient to, be in agreement with, or act in accordance with established patterns, rules, etc.: *Most people willingly conform to the customs of society.|Do you conform to your state's official religion?*

con·for·ma·ble /kən'fɔːməbəl‖-ɔr-/ *adj* **1** [F (*to*)] *fml* obedient: *I've tried to be conformable to your wishes* **2** [F+*to*] *fml* acting in agreement: *Government actions should always be conformable to the will of the people* **3** [B (*to*)] *tech* (of beds of rock) having the same general shape as beds above and below: *conformable beds of rock* —**-bly** *adv*

con·for·ma·tion /ˌkɒnfɔː'meɪʃən‖ˌkɑnfɔr-/ *n* [U;C] *fml or tech* the way something is formed; shape: *the unusual conformation of the clouds*

con·form·ist /kən'fɔːmɪ̈st‖-ɔr-/ *adj, n sometimes derog* (of, concerning, or being) a person who acts and thinks in accordance and agreement with the established rules, values, and customs, of society

con·for·mi·ty /kən'fɔːmɪ̈ti‖-ɔr-/ also **con·form·ance** /kən'fɔːməns‖-ɔr-/— *n* [U] **1** action or behaviour that is in agreement with established rules, customs, etc.: *Conformity to society's customs is advisable if you want a happy life* **2 in conformity (with)** in agreement (with): *I always try to dress in conformity with the latest fashions*

con·found /kən'faʊnd/ *v* [T1] **1** to confuse and surprise (a person or group of people): *The poor election results confounded the government* **2** *becoming rare* to fail to tell the difference between (2 things): *How could you confound these 2 pairs of shoes?|It's impossible to confound pain and pleasure* **3** *old use* to defeat (an enemy, plan, etc.); put to shame **4** *euph* DAMN: *Confound it/you/him/that silly fool, etc.!*

con·found·ed /kən'faʊndɪ̈d/ *adj* **1** [B] confused and deeply troubled: *I felt confounded by your bad manners.|a confounded look* **2** [A] *euph* DAMNed: *That confounded boy's bad behaviour annoys me. He's a confounded fool* —**~ly** *adv*

confound with *v prep* [X1] *fml* to mistake (one thing) for another: *To confound the spelling of "their" with that of "there" is a common mistake*

con·fra·ter·ni·ty /ˌkɒnfrə'tɜːnɪ̈ti‖ˌkɑnfrə'tɜr-/ *n* [GC] a group of religious people who are not priests, who work together for some good purpose

con·frère /'kɒnfreəʳ‖'kɑn- (*Fr* kɔ̃frɛr)/ *n pomp & Fr* a companion (esp. male), esp. a person who shares in one's job or interests: *One of John's confrères at the office is getting married today*

con·front /kən'frʌnt/ *v* [T1] to face boldly or

threateningly: *The soldiers were confronted by 2 terrorists as they left their camp*

con·fron·ta·tion /ˌkɒnfrənˈteɪʃən‖ˌkɑn-/ *n* [C;U] **1** (an example of) the act of CONFRONTing: *The Arab-Israeli confrontation is causing our firm serious difficulties* **2** [+*with*] (an example of) the act of CONFRONTing WITH

confront with *v prep* [D1] to bring face to face; cause to meet: *A good teacher should not confront his pupils with too much information in one lesson*

Con·fu·cian /kənˈfjuːʃən/ *adj* of or related to Confucius (Kung Fu-Tse) or his teachings or his followers

Con·fu·cian·is·m /kənˈfjuːʃənɪzəm/ *n* [U] the beliefs and practices of those who follow the teachings of Confucius

Con·fu·cius /kənˈfjuːʃəs/ *n* an important Chinese thinker, alive about 2,500 years ago, who taught that one should be loyal to one's family, friends, and rulers, and treat others as one would like to be treated

con·fuse /kənˈfjuːz/ *v* [T1] **1** to make less clear; make more difficult to understand **2** to mix up; mislead; cause to be mistaken: *We tried to confuse the enemy by swimming along the river and hiding* **3** [(*with*)] to fail to tell the difference between (2 things): *I'm always confusing salt and/with sugar* —**~d** *adj* —**-fusedly** /kənˈfjuːzɨ̣dli/ *adv* —**-fusing** *adj* —**-fusingly** *adv*

con·fu·sion /kənˈfjuːʒən/ *n* [U;S] **1** disorder: *Your room is in complete confusion; tidy it up at once!* **2** the act of confusing: *If you write more clearly you'll prevent the confusion of your readers* **3** the state of being confused: *There was confusion as to whether we had won the battle or not*

con·fute /kənˈfjuːt/ *v* [T1] to prove (a person or argument) to be wrong —**-futation** /ˌkɒnfjuːˈteɪʃən‖ˌkɑn-/ *n* [C;U]

con·ga /ˈkɒŋgə‖ˈkɑŋgə/ *n* **1** a spirited dance of Latin American origin, in which the dancers form a long winding chain **2** the music for this dance

con·gé /ˈkɒnʒeɪ‖kɒnˈʒeɪ, ˈkɑnʒeɪ (*Fr* kɔ̃ʒe)/ *n Fr & pomp* **1** formal and respectful DEPARTURE (in the phr. **take one's congé**): *The minister took his congé of the royal lady* **2 give someone his/her congé** to dismiss someone suddenly from one's presence or favour

con·geal /kənˈdʒiːl/ *v* [Wv5;I∅;T1] **a** (of a liquid) to become thick or solid: *The blood congealed* **b** to cause (a liquid) to become thick or solid: *They congealed the liquid by freezing it*

con·ge·ni·al /kənˈdʒiːnɪəl/ *adj fml* **1** [(*to*)] (of a person or people) liked because of having the same behaviour, customs, etc.: *I met few people congenial to me in that city.|congenial company/companions* **2** pleasant; in agreement with one's nature: *congenial work|congenial weather* —**~ly** *adv*

con·gen·i·tal /kənˈdʒenɨ̣tl/ *adj* [Wa5] *med* (of diseases) existing at or from one's birth —**~ly** *adv*

con·ger eel /ˌkɒŋgər ˈiːl‖ˌkɑŋ-/ also **conger**— *n* **1** [C] a type of large EEL **2** [U] this, cooked and eaten as food

con·gest /kənˈdʒest/ *v* [Wv5] **1** [I∅;T1] *med* **a** (of a blood vessel or part of the body) to become very full of liquid **b** to cause (a blood vessel or part of the body) to become very full of liquid: *His lungs seem to be congested* **2** [T1] to cause (a street, city, narrow place, etc.) to become very full or blocked, esp. because of traffic: *Buses and cars congested every street in the centre of London*

con·ges·tion /kənˈdʒestʃən/ *n* [U] **1** *med* a condition in which too much liquid collects in a blood vessel or other part of the body: *He's suffering from congestion of the lungs* **2** the condition of being too full or blocked up, esp. because of traffic: *I don't like driving through London because there's too much congestion*

con·glom·e·rate /kənˈglɒmərɨ̣t‖-ˈglɑ-/ *n* **1** a rounded mass of various materials gathered together **2** *tech* a rock consisting of many small round stones (PEBBLEs) held together by hardened clay **3** a large business firm that controls the production of goods of very different kinds

con·glom·e·ra·tion /kənˌglɒməˈreɪʃən‖-ˌglɑ-/ *n* a collection of many different things gathered together: *His pockets were full of a strange conglomeration of objects*

con·grats /kənˈgræts/ *interj infml* CONGRATULATIONS

con·grat·u·late /kənˈgrætʃʊleɪt‖-tʃə-/ *v* [T1 (*on*)] **1** to speak to (a person) with praise and admiration for a happy event or something successfully done: *We congratulated him on having passed the examinations.|Let me congratulate you on the birth of your daughter.|I hear you're to be congratulated* **2** to have pleasure or pride in (oneself) for something successfully done: *You really should congratulate yourself on your appearance; you look charming* —**-lation** /kənˌgrætʃʊˈleɪʃən‖-tʃə-/ *n* [U]

con·grat·u·la·tions /kənˌgrætʃʊˈleɪʃənz‖-tʃə-/ *interj, n* [P (*on*)] an expression of joy for someone's success, good fortune, luck, etc.: *It's your birthday today? Congratulations!|We thanked him for his congratulations and left*

con·grat·u·la·to·ry /kənˌgrætʃʊˈleɪtəri‖-ˈgrætʃələtori/ *adj* [Wa5] serving to CONGRATULATE: *The day after my daughter was born I received a congratulatory letter and present from my friends at work*

con·gre·gate /ˈkɒŋgrɨ̣geɪt‖ˈkɑŋ-/ *v* [I∅;(T1)] to (cause to) gather together: *The crowds congregated in the square in front of the palace when they heard the news of the king's death*

con·gre·ga·tion /ˌkɒŋgrɨ̣ˈgeɪʃən‖ˌkɑŋ-/ *n* **1** [C] a group of people gathered together **2** [GC] a group of people who worship regularly in a particular church or the group present for worship at any one time

con·gre·ga·tion·al /ˌkɒŋrɨ̣ˈgeɪʃənəl‖ˌkɑŋ-/ *adj* [Wa5] of or related to a religious CONGREGATION (2)

Congregational *adj* [Wa5] of or related to CONGREGATIONALISM: *He's a member of the Congregational church*

Con·gre·ga·tion·al·is·m /ˌkɒŋgrɨ̣ˈgeɪʃənəlɪzəm‖ˌkɑŋ-/ *n* the system of government and religious beliefs of one of the branches of the Christian church, in which each local church governs its own affairs —**-ist** *n*

con·gress /ˈkɒŋgres‖ˈkɑŋgrɨ̣s/ *n* **1** [C] the elected law-making body of certain countries: *There will soon be elections to our congress* **2** [(G);C] this body as it exists between elections to it: *Our last congress was/were unable to decide this question* **3** [C] a formal meeting of representatives of societies, countries, etc., to exchange information and opinions: *The Congress of Vienna|a medical congress* **4** [U] *fml* the act of coming together, esp. for the sex act

Congress *n* [R] **1** the highest law-making body of the US: *Congress has been asked to pass a law about that* **2** this body as it exists for the 2 years between elections to it: *the 71st Congress* **3** a political party in India

con·gres·sion·al /kənˈgreʃənəl/ *adj* (*often cap.*) of or related to a CONGRESS[1], esp. to the United States CONGRESS (1): *congressional elections|a congressional committee*

con·gress·man /ˈkɒŋgrɨ̣smən‖ˈkɑŋ-/ (*fem.* **congress·wo·man** /-ˌwʊmən/)— *n* **-men** /mən/ (*often* *cap.*) **1** [C;A;N] a member of a CONGRESS (1), esp. of the US CONGRESS (1) **2** [C;A;N] a member of the US HOUSE OF REPRESENTATIVES

con·gru·ent /ˈkɒŋgruənt‖ˈkɑŋ-/ *adj* **1** [Wa5 (*with, to*)] *tech* (of one or more figures in GEOMETRY) having the same size and shape as another or each other: *congruent* TRIANGLE*s* **2** [(*with*)] *fml* CONGRUOUS —**~ly** *adv* —**-ence** /əns/ *n* [U]

con·gru·i·ty /kənˈgruːǰti/ *n fml* **1** [U] the state or quality of being of like character or in agreement **2** [C *usu. pl.*] a point of agreement

con·gru·ous /ˈkɒŋgruəs‖ˈkɑŋ-/ also **congruent**— *adj* [(*with, to*)] *fml* fitting; suitable: *Your behaviour is not congruous with your social rank*

con·ic /ˈkɒnɪk‖ˈkɑ-/ *adj* [Wa5] *esp. tech* of, related to, or shaped like a CONE (1): *A* **conic section** *is a figure made on the surface of a* CONE *by an imaginary flat surface* (PLANE⁴ (1)) *passing through it*

con·i·cal /ˈkɒnɪkəl‖ˈkɑ-/ *adj* shaped like a CONE (1): *a conical hat|huts with conical roofs* —**~ly** *adv* [Wa4]

co·ni·fer /ˈkəʊnǰfəʳ, ˈkɒ-‖ˈkɑ-/ *n* any of various types of tree which bear CONE*s* (3), most of which are EVERGREEN (=keeping their leaves in winter) —see picture at PLANT²

co·nif·er·ous /kəˈnɪfərəs‖kəʊ-, kə-/ *adj* [Wa5] of, related to, or being a CONIFER: *coniferous trees|coniferous wood* —see picture at TREE¹

conj *written abbrev. for:* CONJUNCTION

con·jec·tur·al /kənˈdʒektʃərəl/ *adj* based on CONJECTURE: *I lack some necessary information so my opinion on this matter can only be conjectural*

con·jec·ture¹ /kənˈdʒektʃəʳ/ *n* **1** [U] the formation of an idea, opinion, etc., from incomplete or uncertain information: *The origin of the human race is a matter for pure conjecture* **2** [C,C5] a guess; opinion based on incomplete or uncertain information: *I don't agree with his conjecture that prices will rise next year*

conjecture² *v* [T5,5b,(1);IØ] *fml* to form (an opinion) from incomplete or uncertain information: *I think you're only conjecturing when you say the government will lose the next election*

con·join /kənˈdʒɔɪn/ *v* [T1;IØ] *fml & tech* to (cause to) join together or unite for a common purpose

con·joint /kənˈdʒɔɪnt/ *adj* [Wa5] *fml* joined together; united; combined —**~ly** *adv*

con·ju·gal /ˈkɒndʒʊgəl‖ˈkɑndʒə-/ also **connubial**— *adj* [Wa5;A] *fml* concerning the relationship between husband and wife: *the conjugal bed|conjugal rights*

con·ju·gate¹ /ˈkɒndʒʊgeɪt‖ˈkɑndʒə-/ *v tech* **1** [T1] to give the various forms of (a verb) that show number, person, tense, etc.: *Can you conjugate "to have" in all its tenses?* **2** [IØ] (of a verb) to have various forms to show number, person, tense, etc.: *In English "to have" conjugates irregularly* **3** [IØ] (of single-celled simple forms of life) to join together with another living thing of the same kind in CONJUGATION (4)

con·ju·gate² /ˈkɒndʒʊgǰt‖ˈkɑndʒə-/ *adj* [Wa5] *tech* joined together as a pair: *2 conjugate cells*

con·ju·ga·tion /ˌkɒndʒʊˈgeɪʃən‖ˌkɑndʒə-/ *n tech* **1** [C] a class of verbs which CONJUGATE¹ (2) in the same way: *There are 4 conjugations in Latin but also many irregular verbs* **2** [C] the way that a particular verb CONJUGATE*s*¹ (2): *In English "to be" has an irregular conjugation* **3** [U] the method of conjugating (CONJUGATE¹ (1,2)): *You must learn conjugation before you can use verbs correctly* **4** the exchange of NUCLEAR material between 2 single-celled simple forms of life just before each cell divides

con·junc·tion /kənˈdʒʌŋkʃən/ *n* **1** [C] (in grammar) a word such as "but" or "and" that connects parts of sentences, phrases, etc. **2** [C9] *fml* a combination of events in time and space; CONJUNCTURE **3** [U] *tech* the meeting or passing of 2 heavenly bodies in the same division of the ZODIAC: *This month Mars is in conjunction with Venus* **4** [C;U] *fml* (an example of) the act of CONJOINing; combination: *a pleasing conjunction of ability and beauty* **5 in conjunction with** in combination with; together with; along with: *The army is acting in conjunction with the police to hunt and find terrorists*

con·junc·ti·va /ˌkɒndʒʌŋkˈtaɪvə‖ˌkɑn-/ *n* **-vas** *or* **-vae** /viː/ *med* a very fine transparent skin that covers and helps to protect the inside surface of the eyelid and the surface of the eye —see picture at EYE¹

con·junc·tive /kənˈdʒʌŋktɪv/ also **con·junct** /ˈkɒndʒʌŋkt, kənˈdʒʌŋkt‖ˈkɑn-, kən-/— *n, adj* [Wa5] *tech* (a word) joining or serving to join phrases together: *The word "however" although an adverb can be used as a conjunctive. It is therefore a conjunctive adverb*

con·junc·ti·vi·tis /kənˌdʒʌŋktɪvˈaɪtǰs/ *n* [U] *med* a painful disease of the CONJUNCTIVA of the eye, with redness and swelling (INFLAMMATION)

con·junc·ture /kənˈdʒʌŋktʃəʳ/ *n* [C9] a combination of events or a particular state of affairs, usu. producing serious difficulties: *The new government was faced by a very serious conjuncture (of events) which threatened the country's future*

con·jure¹ /ˈkʌndʒəʳ‖ˈkɑn-/ *v* **1** [X9] to cause (something) to appear by or as if by magic: *The clever magician conjured a rabbit out of his hat* **2** [IØ] to do clever tricks which seem magical, esp. by very quick movement of the hands: *Jean conjures so well that many people think she really does do her tricks by magic* **3 a name to conjure with** the name of a very influential or important person or thing

con·jure² /kənˈdʒʊəʳ/ *v* [V3] *fml & old use* to ask (someone) solemnly for help, mercy, obedience, etc.: *I conjure you with my dying breath always to serve God faithfully*

con·jur·er, -or /ˈkʌndʒərəʳ‖ˈkɑn-/ *n* **1** a person who CONJURE*s*¹ (2) to amuse others, esp. for payment —see picture at THEATRE **2** a person who practises the magic arts, WIZARD, esp. one who CONJURE*s* UP (3) the spirits of dead people

conjure up /ˈkʌndʒəʳ‖ˈkɑn-/ *v adv* [T1] **1** to imagine (something): *Try to conjure up a picture of life in Ancient Egypt* **2** to cause (something) to be remembered: *Even after 20 years his name conjures up such beautiful memories* **3** CONJURE¹ (1): (fig.) *Jean can conjure up a good meal in half an hour*

conk¹ /kɒŋk‖kɑŋk, kɔŋk/ *n sl* a nose: *I hit him on his conk*

conk² *v* [T1] *sl* **1** to strike (someone), esp. on the head, with a heavy blow: *I'll conk you if you annoy me again* **2 conk (someone) one** to strike (someone), esp. on the head, with a heavy blow: *I'll conk you one if you annoy me again!*

conked-out /ˌkɒŋkt ˈaʊt◂‖ˌkɑŋkt-/ *adj sl* broken down; in very bad condition: *I can only afford to buy a conked-out old car*

con·ker /ˈkɒŋkəʳ‖ˈkɑŋ-/ *n infml esp. BrE* the shiny brown nut-like seed of the HORSE CHESTNUT (=a type of tree) —see picture at TREE¹

con·kers /ˈkɒŋkəz‖ˈkɑŋkərz/ *n* [U] (esp. in Britain) a children's game in which one person swings a CONKER which has been fastened to a piece of string in an attempt to break his opponent's CONKER

conk out *v adv* [IØ] *sl* **1** to fail suddenly; break down: *Our car conked out on the way home so we had to walk* **2** to become unconscious or fall asleep suddenly, esp. from great tiredness

con·nect /kə'nekt/ *v* **1** [Wv4;T1;(L9)] to join; unite; LINK: *They hired 2 rooms with connecting doors.|This road connects London and Edinburgh.|The scientist connected the wires and started the apparatus working* **2** [Wv5;T1 (*with*)] to think of as related: *connected events|I always considered your brother to be connected with the crime* **3** [T1] to join by telephone: *I was again connected to the wrong person* **4** [T1] to connect (something) to an electricity supply: *Make sure the machine's connected properly before you press the button* **5** [IØ (*with*)] (of one or more trains, buses, etc.) to be so planned that passengers can change to another or from one to the other: *This flight connects with a flight for Bratsk at Irkutsk*

con·nect·ed /kə'nektɨd/ *adj* **1** [B] joined or related: *connected events* **2** [Wa5;B (*to, with*)] related by birth or marriage: *Most European royal families are connected (with each other)* **3** [B] having the various parts reasonably joined together: *a long but properly connected sentence* **4** [B9] having social, professional, or business relationships of the stated kind: *You must be very well-connected: you seem to know all the right people*

connecting rod /·'·· ·/ *n* a rod that joins 2 moving parts; esp. one connecting the PISTON to the CRANKSHAFT in an INTERNAL-COMBUSTION ENGINE —see picture at PETROL

con·nec·tion, *BrE* also **con·nex·ion** /kə'nekʃən/ *n* **1** [U] the act of connecting: *the connection of the house pipes to the water supply* **2** [C;U] (an example of) the state of being connected; relationship: *Is there a connection between the sun and the seasons?* **3** [C] **a** an example of the act of moving from one vehicle to another to continue a journey: *I made a connection at Irkutsk for Bratsk* **b** a plane, train, bus, etc., planned to take passengers arriving by another one: *There are connections at Paris for all European capitals* **4** [C] anything that connects: *excellent road and railway connections with the coast|a bad telephone connection* **5** [C *usu. pl.*] a social, professional, or business person with whom one has a working relationship **6** [C *usu. pl.*] a person connected to others as by family: *She's English but has Irish connections* **7** [C] a place where 2 things are connected: *The machine won't work because of a faulty connection* **8 in connection with** with regard to: *In connection with your request of March 18th we are sorry to tell you . . .* **9 in this/that connection** in this/that state of affairs; in this/that CONTEXT

con·nec·tive /kə'nektɪv/ *n, adj* [Wa5] **1** (a word) joining or serving to join phrases, parts of sentences, etc.: *"And" is a frequently used connective in English* **2** (something) joining or serving to join things together

con·ning tow·er /'kɒnɪŋ ˌtaʊəʳ‖'kɑ-/ *n tech* **1** a raised enclosed place on a SUBMARINE (=an underwater ship), which is used as an entrance and from which sailors can keep watch **2** a heavily armoured raised place on a warship, from which the commander directs operations

con·niv·ance /kə'naɪvəns/ *n* [U (*at, with*)] the act of conniving (CONNIVE) or of conniving at (CONNIVE AT) something: *The criminals could not have escaped without your connivance*

con·nive /kə'naɪv/ *v* [IØ,3: (*with*)] to work together secretly for some wrong or unlawful purpose: *The 2 criminals connived with the police to rob a bank.|The criminals and the police connived to rob the bank*

connive at *v prep* [T1;V4a] to avoid noticing or reporting (that which one ought to oppose): *The policeman connived at the prisoners' escape*

con·nois·seur /ˌkɒnə'sɜːʳ‖ˌkɑ-/ *n* [C (*of*)] a person with a good understanding of a subject for which knowledge and good judgment are needed: *My uncle is a connoisseur of fine wines/old furniture/art*

con·no·ta·tion /ˌkɒnə'teɪʃən‖ˌkɑ-/ *n* [*often pl. with sing. meaning*] a meaning or idea suggested by a word or thing in addition to the formal meaning or nature of the word or thing: *The bad connotations of the word* "SKINNY" *are quite different from the good connotations of the word* "SLIM"

con·no·ta·tive /'kɒnəteɪtɪv, kə'nəʊtətɪv‖'kɑnə-/ *adj* of, concerning, or being a CONNOTATION —**~ly** *adv*: "SKINNY" *and* "SLIM" *are 2 words for the same thing, but connotatively they are different*

con·note /kə'nəʊt/ *v* [T1] (of a word) to suggest (a meaning) in addition to the formal meaning: *Hunger connotes unhappiness*

con·nu·bi·al /kə'njuːbɪəl‖-'nuː-/ *adj fml* CONJUGAL

con·quer /'kɒŋkəʳ‖'kɑŋ-/ *v* **1** [Wv4,5;T1;IØ] to take (land) by force; win (land) by war: *The Normans conquered England in 1066.|a conquering army|a conquered city* **2** [Wv4,5;T1;IØ] to defeat (an enemy); be victorious over (an enemy) **3** [T1] *lit* to succeed in gaining the favour, praise, love, attention, etc., of (a person, place, profession, etc., originally unfavourable to one): *John went to Paris to conquer the artistic world* **4** [T1] to gain control over (something unfriendly or difficult): *Man has yet to conquer the stars.|When will scientists conquer the weather?* —**~or** *n*

con·quest /'kɒŋkwest‖'kɑŋ-/ *n* **1** [U] the act of conquering: *This land is ours by right of conquest* **2** [C] something conquered, esp. land gained in war: *French conquests in Asia* **3** [C] a person whose favour or love has been won: *He's one of pretty Jane's many conquests* **4 make a conquest (of)** to win the love or favour of (someone): *John seems to have made a real conquest of Janet. They're always together.*

con·quis·ta·dor /kɒn'kwɪstədɔːʳ‖kɑn'kiː-/ *n* **-dores** /kɒnˌkwɪstə'dɔːreɪz‖kɑnˌkiː-/ *or* **-dors** *Sp* a Spanish conqueror of Mexico and Peru in the 16th century

con·san·guin·e·ous /ˌkɒnsæŋ'gwɪnɪəs‖ˌkɑn-/ *adj fml* related by birth

con·san·guin·i·ty /ˌkɒnsæŋ'gwɪnɨti‖ˌkɑn-/ *n* [U] *fml* relationship by birth: *People may not marry within certain degrees of consanguinity*

con·science /'kɒnʃəns‖'kɑn-/ *n* [C;U] **1** an inner sense that knows the difference between right and wrong, judges one's actions according to moral laws, and makes one feel guilty, good, evil, etc.: *My conscience is clear* **2 for conscience' sake** in order to satisfy one's conscience: *She gave him back the money she'd stolen, for conscience' sake* **3 have no conscience** to be unable to tell the difference between right and wrong: *Jean's got no conscience, she'd steal anything from anybody* **4 in all conscience** without offending one's conscience: *I couldn't do such a wicked thing in all conscience* **5 matter of conscience** a question which only one's conscience can decide: *I can't advise you on such a question; it's a matter of conscience* **6 on one's conscience** causing one to feel guilty: *How can you sleep with such a wicked crime on your conscience?* —see CONSCIOUS (USAGE)

conscience clause /'·· ˌ·/ *n* a part of a law that says that the law need not be obeyed by people whose consciences will not allow them to obey it

conscience mon·ey /'·· ˌ··/ *n* [U] money paid to cover the cost of something wrongly taken, in order to satisfy one's guilty conscience

conscience-smit·ten /'·· ˌ··/ *adj* sorry for having done something wrong

con·sci·en·tious /ˌkɒnʃi'enʃəs‖ˌkɑn-/ *adj* showing or done with great care, attention, or seriousness of purpose: *a conscientious worker|a conscientious piece of work* —see CONSCIOUS (USAGE) —**~ly** *adv* —**~ness** *n* [U]

conscientious ob·jec·tor /··ˌ·· ·ˈ··/ *n* a person who refuses to serve in the armed forces because of moral or religious beliefs —**conscientious objection** *n* [U]

con·scious /ˈkɒnʃəs‖ˈkɑn-/ *adj* **1** [F] able to understand what is happening; awake: *He is badly hurt but still conscious.*|*Is he conscious enough to answer questions?* **2** [B] able to think and will: *Man is a conscious animal* **3** [F (*of*), F5] knowing; understanding; seeing with the mind: *John isn't conscious of his bad manners.*|*Jean's always been very conscious that she annoys many people* **4** [A] intentional: *Anne spoke with conscious nastiness to the old lady* —**~ly** *adv*

USAGE The opposite of **conscious** is **unconscious** in both the following meanings: **a** *He's still* **unconscious**/*He's not* **conscious** *yet after the accident.* **b** *I was* **conscious/unconscious** *of her presence.* In PSYCHOLOGY, **conscious** is compared with **subconscious** or **unconscious**: *the* **conscious/subconscious/unconscious** (*mind*)|*a* **conscious/subconscious/unconscious** *dislike.* None of these words should be confused with **conscientious**, which is related in meaning to **conscience**.

con·scious·ness /ˈkɒnʃəsnɪ̇s‖ˈkɑn-/ *n* **1** [U] the condition of being awake or able to understand what is happening: *John lost consciousness at 8 o'clock in the evening and died in the night.*|*We all lose consciousness when we go to sleep* **2** [U] all the ideas, feelings, opinions, etc., held by a person or a group of people: *the moral consciousness of a country* **3** [U] inward knowledge of something, esp. of one's own existence, rights, etc.: *The class consciousness of the workers made them unite in the struggle* **4** [S;U: (*of*, 5)] knowledge or feeling, esp. of a not very clear kind; AWAREness: *a consciousness that someone else was in the dark room*

con·script[1] /ˈkɒnskrɪpt‖ˈkɑn-/ *n* a person made to serve in one of the armed forces by law

cons·cript[2] /kənˈskrɪpt/ *v* [T1 (*into*)] to make (someone) serve in one of the armed forces by law

con·scrip·tion /kənˈskrɪpʃən/ *n* [U] the practice of forcing people by law to serve in the armed forces

con·se·crate /ˈkɒnsɪ̇kreɪt‖ˈkɑn-/ *v* **1** [Wv5;T1] to declare, make, or set apart in a special ceremony as holy: *When was this church consecrated?*|*The priest held the consecrated bread and wine high so that the people might worship* **2** [X9 (*to*)] to set apart solemnly for a particular purpose: *The priest promised God he would consecrate his life to helping the poor*

con·se·cra·tion /ˌkɒnsɪ̇ˈkreɪʃən‖ˌkɑn-/ *n* **1** [U (*of*)] (an example of) the act of consecrating (CONSECRATE): *Have you ever been to the consecration of a new church?* **2** [*the*+R] the time during the MASS (=a Christian religious service) when bread and wine are made holy by the actions and words of the priest

con·sec·u·tive /kənˈsekjʊtɪv‖-kjə-/ *adj* [Wa5] following in regular or unbroken order: *The numbers 4, 5, 6 are consecutive* —**~ly** *adv*

con·sen·sus /kənˈsensəs/ *n* [*usu. sing.*] a general agreement; collective or group opinion: *What is the consensus of opinion, gentlemen?*|*Can we reach a consensus on this matter?*

con·sent[1] /kənˈsent/ *v* [IØ (*to*); I3] to agree; give permission: *Jean tried to persuade her father but he refused to consent.*|*John consented to help the old lady*

consent[2] *n* [U] **1** agreement; permission: *Governments should rule only with the consent of the governed.*|*Jean's parents refused their consent to her marriage* **2 age of consent** the age at which one may lawfully marry or have sex **3 with one consent** with complete agreement; UNANIMOUSly

con·se·quence /ˈkɒnsɪ̇kwəns‖ˈkɑnsɪ̇kwens/ *n* **1** [C] something that follows from an action or condition; result **2** [U] *fml* importance: *Is it of much consequence to you that the government has lost the election?* **3 in consequence (of)** also **as a consequence (of)**— *fml* as a result (of): *In consequence of your bad work I am forced to dismiss you*

con·se·quent /ˈkɒnsɪ̇kwənt‖ˈkɑn-/ *adj* [(*on, upon*)] *fml* following as a result: *The flooding of large areas of land was consequent upon the heavy rain*

con·se·quen·tial /ˌkɒnsɪ̇ˈkwenʃəl‖ˌkɑn-/ *adj fml* **1** important: *a consequential decision* **2** CONSEQUENT

con·se·quent·ly /ˈkɒnsɪ̇kwəntli‖ˈkɑn-/ *adv* as a result; therefore: *The rain was heavy—(and) consequently the land was flooded*

con·ser·van·cy /kənˈsɜːvənsi‖-ɜr-/ *n* [GC] *BrE* a body of officials appointed to control and protect esp. a river or other watercourse: *the Thames Conservancy*

con·ser·va·tion /ˌkɒnsəˈveɪʃən‖ˌkɑnsər-/ *n* [U] **1** the act of conserving (CONSERVE[1]); preservation **2** the controlled use of a limited supply of natural things, to prevent waste or loss: *Most people have come to accept the need for conservation if we are to make sure of a supply of minerals, food, forests, etc., for the future*

con·ser·va·tion·ist /ˌkɒnsəˈveɪʃənɪ̇st‖ˌkɑnsər-/ *n* an active supporter of CONSERVATION (2)

conservation of en·er·gy /··ˌ·· · ˈ···/ *n* [(*the*) U] *tech* the scientific principle that the total amount of ENERGY within the universe can never vary

conservation of mass /··ˌ·· · ˈ·/ also **conservation of mat·ter** /··ˌ·· · ˈ··/— *n tech* the scientific principle that the total MASS[2] (3) within the universe can never vary

con·ser·va·tis·m /kənˈsɜːvətɪzəm‖-ɜr-/ *n* [U] **1** the belief that the established order of society should be kept as it is for as long as possible and then changed only slowly **2** the principle and practices of those people or political parties that tend towards this belief: *the conservatism of certain old officials* **3** dislike of change, esp. sudden change: *conservatism in matters of language*

con·ser·va·tive[1] /kənˈsɜːvətɪv‖-ɜr-/ *adj* **1** favouring the established order of society: *I have a very conservative uncle who still thinks that a woman's place is in the home* **2** liking old ways; not liking change, esp. sudden change: *very conservative in matters of language* **3** not showy; modest: *That's a very conservative hair style; but I think it suits you* **4** careful; kept within reasonable limits: *He made a conservative guess at the population of London* —**~ly** *adv*

conservative[2] *n* a CONSERVATIVE person: *Aunt Mary's a real conservative. She's totally opposed to women going out to work.*|*Why are you such a conservative in the way you dress, Jim?*

Conservative *adj, n* (of, concerning, or being) a member of a CONSERVATIVE PARTY: *The present Conservative government does not seem very* CONSERVATIVE[1] (1)

Conservative and U·nion·ist Par·ty /·ˌ··· · ˈ··· ˌ··/ *n* [*the*+R] *fml* the British CONSERVATIVE PARTY

Conservative Par·ty /·ˈ··· ˌ··/ *n* any of several political parties, such as one in Britain, that tend to be opposed to great or sudden changes in the established order of society and (now) favour increased competition as the way to bring industrial wealth

con·ser·va·toire /kənˈsɜːvətwɑːʳ‖-ɜr-/ *n lit* CONSERVATORY (2): *She played the piano for years before her mother decided to send her to a conservatoire*

con·ser·va·to·ry /kənˈsɜːvətəri‖-ˈsɜrvətori/ *n* **1** a glass enclosed room where delicate plants are grown —see picture at HOUSE[1] **2** a school where people are trained in music or acting

con·serve¹ /kən'sɜːv‖-ɜrv/ *v* [T1] **1** to use (a supply) carefully without waste; preserve: *We must conserve our forests if we are to make sure of a future supply of wood* **2** *fml* to preserve (fruit) by cooking in sugar: *Mother always conserves a variety of fruits from our garden in summer*

con·serve² /'kɒnsɜːv‖'kɑnsɜrv/ *n* [U;C *often pl.*] *fml* fruit preserved by being cooked in sugar; JAM[3]

con·sid·er /kən'sɪdə^r/ *v* **1** [T1,4,6a,b;I∅] to think about; examine: *I'm considering changing my job.|We've decided to move and are considering a new house in London.|I considered employing Mr Smith but decided that Mr Jones was more suited to the job* **2** [Wv6;X (*to be*) 1,7;V3] to regard as; think of in a stated way: *I consider you a fool* (=I regard you as a fool).|*I consider it a great honour to be here with you today.|He said he considered me (to be) too lazy to be a good worker.|The Shetland Islands are usually considered a part of Scotland* **3** [T1,5,6a] to take into account: *If you consider (the fact) that she's only been studying English a year, she speaks it very well*

con·sid·e·ra·ble /kən'sɪdərəbəl/ *adj* fairly large or great in amount, size, or degree: *When her father died Jean became head of a very considerable business empire*

con·sid·e·ra·bly /kən'sɪdərəbli/ *adv* much; a great deal: *It's considerably windier today than it was yesterday*

con·sid·er·ate /kən'sɪdərɪ̈t/ *adj apprec* thoughtful of the rights or feelings of others: *a very considerate young man|considerate towards old people* —**~ly** *adv* —**~ness** *n*

con·sid·e·ra·tion /kən,sɪdə'reɪʃən/ *n* **1** [U (*to*)] careful thought; thoughtful attention: *We shall give your request careful consideration.|I've sent them my poem for (their) consideration* **2** [U (*for*)] thoughtful attention to the wishes and feelings of others: *John never showed any consideration for his mother's feelings.|Have you no consideration for others, you nasty boy?* **3** [C] a fact to be considered when making a decision; reason: *Time is an important consideration.|A number of considerations have led me to refuse your request* **4** [C *pl. rare*] a payment for a service; reward: *For a small consideration I'll help you move your belongings to your new house.|John will do anything for a consideration* **5** [U] *rare* importance: *Don't worry about breaking that cup; it's of no consideration* **6 in consideration of** in return for; on account of; because of: *a small payment in consideration of many kind services* **7 leave out of consideration** to fail to consider (something) **8 on no consideration** in no case: *On no consideration must you be seen visiting the police station* **9 take into consideration** take (something) into account: *Your teacher will take your recent illness into consideration when judging your examination* **10 taking everything into consideration** all things CONSIDERED (3)

con·sid·ered /kən'sɪdəd‖-ərd/ *adj* **1** [Wa5;A] reached after careful thought: *It is my considered opinion that you should be shot* **2** [B9] highly regarded: *a very highly considered general* **3 all things considered** when one considers everything that might have produced a different result: *"The ground was muddy, and she hadn't run for a month." "Yes: her speed was really quite good, all things considered"*

con·sid·er·ing¹ /kən'sɪdərɪŋ/ *prep* if one takes into account the rather surprising fact (of): *He did poorly in his examinations considering that he had studied hard for them.|He did poorly in his examinations, considering how hard he had studied for them*

considering² *conj* if one takes into account the rather surprising fact that: *Considering he's only been learning English a year he speaks it very well.|He did poorly in his examinations, considering he had studied hard for them*

considering³ *adv not fml* (*in end position only*) **all things** CONSIDERED (3): *Yes: her speed was really quite good, considering*

con·sign /kən'saɪn/ *v* **1** [T1 (*to*)] to send (something) to a person or place for sale: *The goods were consigned to you by railway and should have arrived by now* **2** [X9, esp. *to*] *fml* to give (something or someone) into the care of another; hand over: *The evil man consigned his soul to the devil.|Before her death my mother consigned me into my uncle's care*

con·sign·ee /,kɒnsaɪ'niː, -sɪ̈-‖,kɑn-/ *n fml* the person to whom something is delivered

con·sign·ment /kən'saɪnmənt/ *n* **1** [U] the act of CONSIGNing (1) **2** [C (*of*)] a number of goods CONSIGNed (1) together **3 on consignment** sent to a person or shop that pays only for what is sold and returns what is unsold: *We only have a small shop in a small village so we usually only order goods on consignment*

con·sign·or, -er /kən'saɪnə^r/ *n* a person who CONSIGNs goods

con·sis·ten·cy /kən'sɪstənsi/ also **con·sis·tence** /-təns/— *n* **1** [U] the state of always keeping to the same principles or course of action: *The government's actions completely lack consistency* **2** [C;U] the degree of firmness, stiffness, or thickness: *To make this cake you must first mix butter and sugar to the consistency of thick cream*

con·sis·tent /kən'sɪstənt/ *adj* **1** [B] (of a person, behaviour, beliefs, etc.) continually keeping to the same principles or course of action; having a regular pattern: *The government hasn't been too consistent in the way it's treated unemployment and rising prices* **2** [F (*with*)] in agreement: *This statement is not consistent with the ones you made earlier* —**~ly** *adv*

con·sist in /kən'sɪst/ *v prep* [Wv6;T1,4 *no pass.*] to have as a base; depend on: *True freedom consists in the absence of laws.|The beauty of Venice consists in the style of its ancient buildings*

consist of *v prep* [Wv6;T1 *no pass.*] to be made up of: *The United Kingdom consists of Great Britain and Northern Ireland*

con·sis·to·ry /kən'sɪstəri/ *n tech* **1** a solemn meeting of the official governing body of a church to deal with church business **2** the place where this meeting takes place —**-rial** /,kɒnsɪs'tɔːrɪəl‖,kɑnsɪs'torɪəl/ *adj* [Wa5]

con·so·la·tion /,kɒnsə'leɪʃən‖,kɑn-/ *n* **1** [U] comfort during a time of sadness or disappointment: *I got many letters of consolation when mother died* **2** [C] a person or thing that CONSOLEs: *Your presence was a consolation to me at such a sad time*

consolation prize /,··'·· ·/ *n* a prize given to someone who has not won a competition, esp. to someone who has come second

con·sol·a·to·ry /kən'sɒlətəri, -'səʊlə-‖-'səʊlətori, -'sɑ-/ *adj* comforting; intended to CONSOLE

con·sole¹ /kən'səʊl/ *v* [T1 (*with*)] to give comfort or sympathy to (someone) in times of disappointment or sadness: *After fire had destroyed my home I consoled myself with the thought that it might have been worse*

con·sole² /'kɒnsəʊl‖'kɑn-/ *n* **1** an ornamental BRACKET (=a support fastened to a wall) for supporting a shelf or other object **2** a flat surface containing the controls for a machine, electrical apparatus, ORGAN (4), etc. **3** a radio or television set made to stand on the floor rather than on a table or on legs

con·sole ta·ble /'·· ˌ··/ *n tech* a narrow table fixed to the wall and supported by BRACKETs (=supports fastened to the wall)

con·sol·i·date /kən'sɒlǰdeɪt‖-'sɑ-/ *v* [T1;IØ] **1** to (cause to) become strong or firm: *Britain is trying to consolidate her position in the North Atlantic* **2** [(*into*)] to (cause to) combine into fewer or one: *The government hoped to consolidate 10 states to form 3 new ones.*|*Several small businesses consolidated to form a large powerful company* —**-dation** /kənˌsɒlǰ'deɪʃən‖-ˌsɑ-/ *n* [C;U]: *The 3 small businesses formed one large one by consolidation.*|*the consolidation of the 3 firms*

consolidated fund /·ˌ···· '·/ *n tech* (in Britain) money collected from taxation in order to pay the interest on the national debt

con·sols /kən'sɒlz‖-'sɑlz/ also (*fml*) **consolidated an·nu·i·ties** /·ˌ···· ·'···/— *n* [P] *tech* interest-bearing British government BONDs repayable on demand

con·som·mé /kən'sɒmeɪ, 'kɒnsəmeɪ‖ˌkɑnsə'meɪ/ *n* [U] *Fr* clear soup made from meat and/or vegetables

con·so·nance /'kɒnsənəns‖'kɑn-/ *n* **1** [U (*with*)] *fml* agreement among parts (often in the phr. **in consonance (with)**) **2** [C;U] *tech* a pleasant-sounding combination of musical notes —opposite **dissonance** **3** [U (*with*)] *tech* the likeness in sound of the last consonants of 2 or more words: *The words "home" and "game" show consonance*

con·so·nant¹ /'kɒnsənənt‖'kɑn-/ *n* **1** any of the speech sounds made by partly or completely stopping the flow of air as it goes through the mouth **2** a letter representing a consonant sound; any of the letters of the English alphabet except a, e, i, o, u

consonant² *adj* **1** [(*to, with*)] *fml* being in agreement: *Your actions do not appear to be consonant with your principles* **2** *tech* of or marked by musical CONSONANCE (2) —opposite **dissonant** **3** [(*with*)] *tech* (of a word or words) marked by CONSONANCE (3): *"Home" and "game" are consonant (with each other)*

con·sort¹ /'kɒnsɔːt‖'kɑnsɔrt/ *n* [C9] the wife or husband, esp. of a ruler: —compare PRINCE CONSORT, QUEEN CONSORT

consort² *n fml & rare* **1** a group, esp. of old musical instruments of the same family or of musicians who perform old music: *a consort of* VIOLs **2** **in consort (with)** together (with): *The young prince ruled in consort with his father the king*

con·sor·ti·um /kən'sɔːtɪəm‖-ɔr-/ *n* **-tiums** *or* **-tia** /tɪə/ *tech* a combination of a number of companies, banks, businesses, etc., for a common purpose

con·sort to·geth·er /kən'sɔːt‖-ɔrt/ *v adv* [IØ] *often derog* to CONSORT WITH (1) each other: *Thieves and other criminals often consort together*

consort with /kən'sɔːt‖-ɔrt/ *v prep* [T1] **1** *often derog* to spend time in the company of (esp. bad people): *You consort too much with wild young men* **2** [Wv6 *no pass.*] *fml* to suit; fit: *Your actions do not consort with your principles*

con·spec·tus /kən'spektəs/ *n fml* a report, set of tables, etc., giving a general view of a subject

con·spic·u·ous /kən'spɪkjʊəs/ *adj* [(*for*)] noticeable; attracting attention; easily seen: *She's always conspicuous because of her fashionable clothes.*|*He was conspicuous for his bravery.*|*That was a very conspicuous mistake.*|(fig.) *You were conspicuous by your absence yesterday* —**~ly** *adv* —**~ness** *n* [U]

conspicuous con·sump·tion /·ˌ··· ·'··/ *n* [U] wasteful spending intended to attract attention and done as proof of one's high social position

con·spi·ra·cy /kən'spɪrəsi/ *n* **1** [C] a secret plan to do something unlawful: *The police discovered the general's conspiracy to seize control of the government* **2** [U] the act of secretly planning to do something unlawful: *My grandfather was hanged for conspiracy in 1845*

conspiracy of si·lence /·ˌ··· · '··/ *n* **conspiracies of silence** a secret agreement to keep silent about something, esp. for selfish personal advantage (as when a business firm knowingly sells a dangerous drug without warning the public)

con·spi·ra·tor /kən'spɪrətəʳ/ *n* a person who takes part in a CONSPIRACY (1): *The conspirators met secretly in a ruined building far from the town*

con·spi·ra·to·ri·al /kənˌspɪrə'tɔːrɪəl‖-'tor-/ *adj* of, related to, or concerning a CONSPIRACY (1) —**~ly** *adv*

con·spire /kən'spaɪəʳ/ *v* **1** [IØ,3: (*with, together*)] to plan together secretly (something unlawful or bad): *The criminals conspired to rob a bank* **2** [I3] (of events) to combine: *Events conspired to produce great difficulties for the government*

con·sta·ble /'kʌnstəbəl‖'kɑn-/ *n* **1** [C;A;N] *esp. BrE* a policeman of the lowest rank —compare P.C., POLICEMAN, POLICEWOMAN, PATROLMAN (2) **2** *tech* the governor of a royal castle **3** *tech* (in former times) an important official in a royal or noble household

con·stab·u·la·ry /kən'stæbjʊləri‖-jəleri/ *n* [GC] the police force of a particular town, area, or country

con·stan·cy /'kɒnstənsi‖'kɑn-/ *n* [U] **1** firmness of mind; freedom from change: *He spoke in parliament with constancy of purpose* **2** faithfulness; loyalty: *constancy between husband and wife*

con·stant¹ /'kɒnstənt‖'kɑn-/ *adj* **1** unchanging; fixed: *He drove at a constant speed* **2** happening all the time: *I dislike these constant arguments* **3** continuous; without break: *We make constant use of our new car* **4** *lit* loyal; faithful: *a constant friend* —**~ly** *adv*

constant² *n tech* something, esp. a number or quantity, that never varies

con·stel·la·tion /ˌkɒnstǰ'leɪʃən‖ˌkɑn-/ *n* **1** a group of fixed stars often having a name, such as the Great Bear **2** *lit* a group, collection, or gathering of usu. related people, qualities, or things: *a constellation of the most famous television performers of the year*

con·ster·na·tion /ˌkɒnstə'neɪʃən‖ˌkɑnstər-/ *n* [U] great surprise, shock, and fear

con·sti·pate /'kɒnstǰpeɪt‖'kɑn-/ *v* **1** [Wv4,5;T1] to cause CONSTIPATION in (a person or animal): *I'm constipated again* **2** [IØ] *infml* to get CONSTIPATION: *I constipate very easily so I can't eat eggs*

con·sti·pa·tion /ˌkɒnstǰ'peɪʃən‖ˌkɑn-/ *n* [U] the (medical) condition of being unable to empty the bowels frequently enough and/or effectively

con·sti·tu·en·cy /kən'stɪtʃʊənsi/ *n* **1** [C] a parliamentary division whose people elect one or a number of people to represent them in a law-making body **2** [GC] the body of voters living in such a division: *My constituency are/is opposed to the government's plan to limit wages, so I must vote against it*

con·sti·tu·ent¹ /kən'stɪtʃʊənt/ *n* **1** a voter; member of a CONSTITUENCY (2) **2** any of the parts that make up a whole: *the constituent parts of society*

constituent² *adj* [Wa5] being one of the parts that make a whole: *What are the constituent parts of an atom?*

constituent as·sem·bly /·ˌ··· ·'··/ *n* (*often caps.*) a body of representatives elected to establish or change the CONSTITUTION (1) of a country

con·sti·tute /'kɒnstǰtjuːt‖'kɑnstǰtuːt/ *v fml* **1** [Wv6;L1] to make up; form; be: *7 days constitute a week* **2** [T1] to establish: *Governments should be* *constituted by the will of the people* **3** [X1] to appoint: *Who has the king constituted his representative to the court of France?*

con·sti·tu·tion /ˌkɒnstǀ̩ˈtjuːʃən‖ˌkɑnstǀ̩ˈtuː-/ *n* **1** [C] the body of laws and principles according to which a country is governed: *According to the American constitution presidential elections are held every 4 years* **2** [C] the general condition of a person's body or mind: *an old man with a weak constitution* **3** [C (*of*)] the way in which something is made up **4** [U] the act of constituting (CONSTITUTE)

con·sti·tu·tion·al[1] /ˌkɒnstǀ̩ˈtjuːʃənəl‖ˌkɑnstǀ̩ˈtuː-/ *adj* [Wa5] **1** established or limited by a CONSTITUTION (1): *There are severe constitutional limits on the queen's power* **2** allowed according to the CONSTITUTION (1): *Is this new law constitutional?* **3** of or related to the CONSTITUTION (2) of a person's body or mind: *a constitutional weakness*

constitutional[2] *n* a walk taken for one's health

con·sti·tu·tion·al·is·m /ˌkɒnstǀ̩ˈtjuːʃənəlɪzəm‖ˌkɑnstǀ̩ˈtuː-/ *n* belief that a government should be based on established laws and principles —**-ist** *n*

con·sti·tu·tion·al·ly /ˌkɒnstǀ̩ˈtjuːʃənəli‖ˌkɑnstǀ̩ˈtuː-/ *adv* in accordance with a political CONSTITUTION (1): *The government must always act constitutionally.|Constitutionally, the government has no right to do that*

con·sti·tu·tive /ˈkɒnstǀ̩tjuːtɪv‖ˈkɑnstǀ̩tuː-/ *adj* CONSTITUENT[1] (2)

con·strain /kənˈstreɪn/ *v* [V3 *esp. pass.*] to make (someone) do something by force or by strongly persuading: *I felt constrained to do what he told me*

con·strained /kənˈstreɪnd/ *adj* awkward; unnatural: *a constrained manner* —**~ly** /-nǀ̩dli/ *adv*

con·straint /kənˈstreɪnt/ *n* **1** [U] the threat or use of force to direct the action of others: *We acted under constraint* **2** [C (*on*)] something that limits one's freedom of action: *lawful constraints on immoral behaviour*|(*tech*) *constraints on the rules of grammar* **3** [U] a forced or unnatural manner; the condition of hiding one's natural feelings and behaviour: *The servants showed constraint in the queen's presence*

con·strict /kənˈstrɪkt/ *v* [Wv5;T1] to make (esp. a blood vessel) narrower, smaller, or tighter: (fig.) *Your point of view seems very constricted to me* —**~ive** *adj*

con·stric·tion /kənˈstrɪkʃən/ *n* **1** [U] the act of CONSTRICTing **2** [U] a feeling of pressure or tightness: *He's suffering from constriction of the chest* **3** [C] something that CONSTRICTs: *He seems to have a constriction in the chest*

con·stric·tor /kənˈstrɪktəʳ/ *n tech* **1** a muscle that reduces or increases the size of an organ in the body **2** a snake, such as a BOA, that kills animals by winding round and crushing them

con·struct[1] /kənˈstrʌkt/ *v* [Wv5;T1] **1** to build; make by putting together or combining parts: *a difficult sentence to construct* **2** *tech* to draw (a GEOMETRICAL figure) using suitable instruments: *to construct a square on this line*

con·struct[2] /ˈkɒnstrʌkt‖ˈkɑn-/ *n tech* a general idea of something formed in the mind by combining a number of pieces of information; CONCEPT: *forms a construct of a real object by putting information from the senses together in the mind*

con·struc·tion /kənˈstrʌkʃən/ *n* **1** [U] the act or manner of CONSTRUCTing[1] (1): *There are 2 new hotels near here under construction.|A chair is an object of simple construction* **2** [U] the business or work of building; building industry: *My husband works in the construction industry.|a construction firm* **3** [C] a meaning or sense given to a statement, action, etc.: *Please don't put the wrong construction on his behaviour* **4** [C] something CONSTRUCTed[1] (1), esp. a building: *a peculiarly shaped construction* **5** [C] *tech* the arrangement and relationship of words in a phrase or sentence: *A good dictionary should give the meanings of words and examples of the constructions they are used in* —**~al** *adj* [Wa5]

con·struc·tive /kənˈstrʌktɪv/ *adj* serving a useful purpose; helping to improve or develop something; helpful: *John made a number of very constructive suggestions at the meeting* —**~ly** *adv* —**~ness** *n* [U]

con·struc·tor /kənˈstrʌktəʳ/ *n* a builder: *a firm of constructors*

con·strue /kənˈstruː/ *v* **1** [X9] to place a certain meaning on (a sentence, statement, action, etc.); understand: *You can construe what he said in a number of different ways* **2** [T1] *tech* to explain the relationship of (words in a sentence), esp. when translating Latin or Greek

con·sub·stan·ti·a·tion /ˌkɒnsəbstænʃiˈeɪʃən‖ˌkɑn-/ *n tech* the belief that the body and blood of Christ exist together with the bread and wine offered by the priest during the MASS (=a Christian religious service) —compare TRANSUBSTANTIATION

con·sul /ˈkɒnsəl‖ˈkɑn-/ *n* **1** a person appointed by a government to protect and help its citizens who live or work in or around a foreign city **2** either of the 2 chief public officials of the ancient Roman republic, each elected for one year **3** any of the 3 chief public officials of the French republic between 1799 and 1804 —**~ship** *n*

con·su·lar /ˈkɒnsjʊləʳ‖ˈkɑnsələʳ/ *adj* of or related to a CONSUL or his work

con·su·late /ˈkɒnsjʊlǀ̩t‖ˈkɑnsəlǀ̩t/ *n* **1** the official building or offices in which a CONSUL (1) lives or works **2** the office, rank, or position of a CONSUL; CONSULship: *He gained the consulate in 1799*

con·sult /kənˈsʌlt/ *v* **1** [T1] to go to (a person, book, etc.) for information, advice, an opinion, etc.: *Have you consulted your doctor about your illness?* **2** [IØ (*for*)] to work as a CONSULTANT (2): *John consults for a large building firm*

con·sul·tan·cy /kənˈsʌltənsi/ *n* the job of a CONSULTANT (1) in a hospital: *He was appointed to a consultancy only recently*

con·sul·tant /kənˈsʌltənt/ *n* **1** *esp. BrE* a high ranking hospital doctor who gives specialist advice in addition to that given by an ordinary doctor **2** a person who gives specialist professional advice to others: *an industrial relations consultant|a firm of consultants*

con·sul·ta·tion /ˌkɒnsəlˈteɪʃən‖ˌkɑn-/ *n* **1** [C;U: (*with*) *often pl. with sing. meaning*] (an example of) the act of CONSULTing (often in the phr. **in consultation (with)**): *The minister of foreign affairs today had consultations with the president of France* **2** [C] a meeting held to exchange opinions and ideas: *The employers held a consultation to decide whether to increase their workers' wages*

con·sul·ta·tive /kənˈsʌltətɪv/ *adj* [Wa5] that can give advice or make suggestions; ADVISORY: *a consultative committee*

con·sult·ing /kənˈsʌltɪŋ/ *adj* [Wa5;A] **1** providing specialist or professional advice: *a consulting lawyer* **2** of or related to CONSULTing or a CONSULTANT (esp. 1): *a doctor's consulting room*

consult with *v prep* [T1 *pass. rare*] to exchange opinions, information, etc., with (a person or people): *Before we can accept the firm's offer we must consult with the workers*

con·sume /kənˈsjuːm‖-ˈsuːm/ *v* [T1] **1** to eat or drink **2** to use; use up: *Arguing about details consumed many hours of the committee's valuable* *time* **3** [Wv4] (of a fire) to destroy: *The fire soon consumed the wooden buildings.*|(fig.) *She was consumed by hate* **4** [(AWAY)] to spend wastefully: *He consumed all his money on women and drink*

con·sum·er /kən'sjuːmə^r‖-'suː-/ *n* a person who buys and uses goods and services: *The price increases were passed on by the firm to the consumers.*|*a consumer advice and protection centre*

con·sum·mate[1] /kən'sʌmȝt/ *adj fml* **1** [Wa5;B] perfect; complete: *Their happiness was consummate* **2** [Wa5;A] skilled: *a consummate musician* —**~ly** *adv*: *consummately happy*

con·sum·mate[2] /'kɒnsəmeɪt‖'kɑn-/ *v* [T1] *fml* **1** to make perfect: *His happiness was consummated when she agreed to marry him* **2** to make (a marriage) complete by having sex

con·sum·ma·tion /ˌkɒnsə'meɪʃən‖ˌkɑn-/ *n* **1** [C *usu. sing.*] the point at which something is made complete or perfect: *the consummation of 10 years' work* **2** [U] the act of consummating (CONSUMMATE[2]), esp. a marriage

con·sump·tion /kən'sʌmpʃən/ *n* **1** [U] the act of consuming (CONSUME): *Consumption of cotton increased even after it rose in price* **2** [U;S] the amount CONSUMEd: *There's too great a consumption of alcohol in Britain* **3** [U] *old use* TUBERCULOSIS of the lungs (a disease)

con·sump·tive[1] /kən'sʌmptɪv/ *adj old use* of, related to, or suffering from TUBERCULOSIS of the lungs

consumptive[2] *n old use* a person suffering from TUBERCULOSIS of the lungs

cont. *written abbrev. for:* **1** containing **2** contents **3** CONTINENT **4** continued

con·tact[1] /'kɒntækt‖'kɑn-/ *n* **1** [U] the condition of meeting, touching or coming together with **2** [U] relationship; connection: *Have you been in contact with your sister recently?*|*That poor madman has lost all contact with reality* **3** [C] *infml* a social, professional, or business connection; person one knows in a position to be of help to one **4** [C] an electrical part that can be moved to touch or not touch a like part, therefore completing or interrupting an electrical CIRCUIT **5 make contact** to get in touch, esp. after much effort: *Our generals have made contact with the enemy and asked for peace* **6 make/break contact** to complete or interrupt an electrical CIRCUIT

contact[2] *v* [T1] to get in touch with (someone); reach (someone) by message, telephone, etc.

contact[3] *adj* [Wa5;A] caused or made active by touch: *contact poisons*

contact lens /'·· ·/ *n* [*often pl.*] a very small thin LENS specially shaped to fit closely over the eye to improve eyesight

con·ta·gion /kən'teɪdʒən/ *n* **1** [U] the act of spreading a disease by touch **2** [C] a disease spread in such a way **3** [C9] a harmful influence that spreads from person to person: *A contagion of fear seems to be spreading all through the city*

con·ta·gious /kən'teɪdʒəs/ *adj* **1** [B] (of a disease) that can be spread by touch **2** [F] (of a person) having a CONTAGIOUS (1) disease **3** [B] tending to spread easily from person to person: *Her laughter's contagious!* **4** [B] *infml* infectious —**~ly** *adv* —**~ness** *n* [U]

con·tain /kən'teɪn/ *v* [T1] **1** to hold; have within itself: *This bottle contains 2 glasses of beer.*|*Beer contains alcohol.*|*This book contains all the information you need* **2** to hold back; keep under control: *Try to contain your anger/yourself!*|*The demand for free elections can be contained no longer* **3** *tech* to enclose (esp. an angle): *How big is the angle contained by these 2 sides?*

con·tained /kən'teɪnd/ *adj* calm; quiet; controlled: *Her feelings seem very contained*

con·tain·er /kən'teɪnə^r/ *n* **1** anything such as a box, barrel, bottle, etc., used for holding something **2** *tech* a very large usu. metal box in which goods are packed to make it easy to lift or move them —see picture at INTERCHANGE[2]

con·tain·er·ize, -ise /kən'teɪnəraɪz/ *v* [Wv5;T1] *tech* to use CONTAINERs (2) for the movement of (goods) —**-ization** /kənˌteɪnəraɪ'zeɪʃən‖-rə-/ *n* [U]

container port /·'·· ·/ *n tech* a port specially built to handle CONTAINERs (2) of goods

container ship /·'·· ·/ *n tech* a ship specially built to carry CONTAINERs (2) of goods —see picture at SHIP[1]

con·tain·ment /kən'teɪnmənt/ *n* [U] the political principle and practice of using means other than war to prevent an unfriendly state from becoming more powerful and influential

con·tam·i·nate /kən'tæmȝneɪt/ *v* [Wv4,5;T1] to make impure or bad by or as if by mixing in/with impure, dirty, or poisonous matter: *Don't eat this food: it may have been contaminated by the flies.*|*The river was contaminated with waste from the factory.*|(fig.) *Our students are being contaminated by foreign ideas!* —**-nator** *n*

con·tam·i·na·tion /kənˌtæmȝ'neɪʃən/ *n* **1** [U] the act of contaminating (CONTAMINATE): *contamination of the river by industrial waste* **2** [U] the state of being CONTAMINATED **3** [C] something which CONTAMINATEs

contd. *written abbrev. for:* continued

con·tem·plate /'kɒntəmpleɪt‖'kɑn-/ *v* **1** [T1] to look at quietly and solemnly **2** [T1,4,6a,b;IØ] to think deeply about; consider with continued attention: *The doctor contemplated the difficult operation he had to perform.*|*I hope your mother isn't contemplating coming to stay with us!* **3** [T1] to expect: *The police contemplated various kinds of trouble after the football match*

con·tem·pla·tion /ˌkɒntəm'pleɪʃən‖ˌkɑn-/ *n* [U (*of*)] the act of thinking deeply and quietly; deep thought: *Each morning the priest spent an hour in quiet contemplation.*|*She seemed lost in contemplation*

con·tem·pla·tive /kən'templətɪv, 'kɒntəmpleɪtɪv‖kən'templətɪv, 'kɑntəmpleɪtɪv/ *adj* [Wa5] marked by or spending much time in CONTEMPLATION: *a contemplative look*

con·tem·po·ra·ne·ous /kənˌtempə'reɪnɪəs/ *adj* [Wa5; (*with*)] *fml* originating, existing, or happening during the same period of time as another or each other —**~ly** *adv*

con·tem·po·ra·ry[1] /kən'tempərəri, -pəri‖-pəreri/ *adj* **1** [Wa5] of or belonging to the same (stated) time: *In 1066 William landed in England, and a contemporary Englishman wrote the following report of his landing: . . .* **2** modern; of or belonging to the present: *contemporary history/art/furniture*

contemporary[2] *n* **1** a person born or living at the same time as another **2** a person of the same age as another: *John is my contemporary, we're both 55* **3** a person of the present period: *Is this musician a contemporary?*

con·tempt /kən'tempt/ *n* [U] **1** the feeling that someone or something is of a lower rank and undesirable: *I feel nothing but contempt for such dishonest behaviour* **2** lack of respect or admiration: *I treat those fools with the contempt they deserve* **3** the condition of being thought of low rank or undesirable: *People who smoke and drink too much should be held in contempt*

con·temp·ti·ble /kən'temptəbəl/ *adj* that ought to be treated with CONTEMPT (1,2): *That was a contemptible trick to play on a friend!* —**-bly** *adv*

contempt of court /·ˌ· · '·/ *n* [U] the offence of behaving badly in words or speech in a court of law, esp. by disobeying a judge's order

con·temp·tu·ous /kən'temptʃʊəs/ *adj* [(*of*)] showing, feeling, or expressing CONTEMPT (1,2): *She's contemptuous of my humble home and poor surroundings* —**~ly** *adv*

con·tend /kən'tend/ *v* **1** [I∅ (*against, for, with*)] to compete as in a race or against difficulties: *Britain contended for control of the sea in the 17th century* **2** [T5] to claim; say with strength: *The police contended that the difficulties they faced were too severe*

con·tend·er /kən'tendəʳ/ *n* [(*for*)] (esp. in sports) a person who takes part in a competition, esp. in order to win a title or prize

con·tent¹ /kən'tent/ *adj* [F (*with*); F3] satisfied; happy: *John seems content just to sit in front of the television all night*

content² /kən'tent/ *v* [T1 (*with*)] to make (a person or oneself) happy or satisfied: *John contented himself with 2 glasses of beer even though he could have had more*

content³ /kən'tent/ *n* [U] *lit* contentment

con·tent⁴ /'kɒntent‖'kɑn-/ *n* **1** [U] the subject matter of a book, paper, etc.: *I like the style of this book but I don't like the content* **2** [S9] the amount of a substance contained in something: *Eggs have a very high food content*

con·tent·ed /kən'tentɪ̈d/ *adj* [B (*with*), B3] satisfied; happy: *Jean seems contented just to sit and sew in front of a warm fire* —**~ly** *adv*

con·ten·tion /kən'tenʃən/ *n* **1** [U] the act of CONTENDING: *This is no time for contention. We are in severe trouble and must help each other* **2** [C,C5,5c] *fml* a claim; argument; point of view: *My contention is that the government's plan would never have been successful whatever had happened* —see also BONE **of contention**

con·ten·tious /kən'tenʃəs/ *adj fml* **1** (of a person) tending to argue **2** likely to cause argument —**~ly** *adv* —**~ness** *n* [U]

con·tent·ment /kən'tentmənt/ *n* [U] happiness; the state of being satisfied; satisfaction: *complete contentment|the contentment of a well-fed, well-cared-for baby*

con·tents /'kɒntents‖'kɑn-/ *n* **1** [P] a table at the front of a book with details of what the book contains **2** [P;(U)] that which is contained in an object: *He emptied the bottle of its contents* **3** [P] the subject matter of a book, paper, etc.: *I like the style of this book but I don't like the contents.|a magazine of varied contents*

con·test¹ /kən'test/ *v* [T1;(I∅)] *fml* **1** to compete for; fight for: *How many people are contesting this seat on the town council?* **2** to question the truth or rightness of (something): *I intend to contest the judge's decision in another court*

con·test² /'kɒntest‖'kɑn-/ *n* **1** a struggle or fight in which 2 or more people compete for victory: *a contest of skill|A contest developed for the position of minister of foreign affairs* **2** a competition, esp. one judged by a PANEL (=a group) of specially chosen judges: *a beauty contest|a dancing contest*

con·tes·tant /kən'testənt/ *n* someone competing in a CONTEST: *There are 50 contestants from all parts of the country in this dancing competition*

con·text /'kɒntekst‖'kɑn-/ *n* **1** the setting of a word, phrase, etc., among the surrounding words, phrases, etc., often used for helping to explain the meaning of the word, phrase, etc.: *In some contexts "mad" means "foolish", in some "angry", and in others* "INSANE".|*You should be able to tell the meaning of this word from its context* **2** the general conditions in which an event, action, etc., takes place: *In the context of late 19th century Italy it was difficult to be both a practising Christian and a politician*

con·tex·tu·al /kən'tekstʃʊəl/ *adj* [Wa5] of, according to, or resulting from the CONTEXT: *This word has a special contextual meaning here* —**~ly** *adv*

con·ti·gu·i·ty /ˌkɒntɪ̈'gju:ɪ̈ti‖ˌkɑn-/ also **con·tig·u·ous·ness** /kən'tɪgjʊəsnəs/— *n* [U] *fml* the state of being CONTIGUOUS

con·tig·u·ous /kən'tɪgjʊəs/ *adj* [Wa5; (*to, with*)] **1** touching; next (to); having a common border: *England is the only country contiguous to/with Wales* **2** next or near in time or order: *Were these events contiguous?* —**~ly** *adv*

con·ti·nence /'kɒntɪ̈nəns‖'kɑn-/ *n* [U] *fml* the ability to control oneself, esp. one's bodily desires and feelings

con·ti·nent¹ /'kɒntɪ̈nənt‖'kɑn-/ *adj fml* able to control oneself, esp. one's bodily desires and feelings

continent² *n* any of the 7 main unbroken masses of land on the earth: *Africa is a continent, Greenland is not* —see picture at GLOBE

Continent *n* [*the*+R] Europe without the British Isles: *He's gone for a holiday on the Continent, but I'm not sure whether to France or Italy*

USAGE When Americans speak of "Europe" they mean Britain and the CONTINENT: *We're going to Europe this summer.* A British speaker who is going to France says *We're going to the* CONTINENT.

con·ti·nen·tal¹ /ˌkɒntɪ̈'nentl◂‖ˌkɑn-/ *adj* **1** of, related to, or typical of a very large mass of land: *The weather in Eastern Siberia is typically continental* **2** [Wa5] of, related to, or typical of Europe without the British Isles **3** *AmE* of, related to, or typical of North America: *The continental United States does not include Hawaii*

continental² *n* **1** a person who lives in Europe but not in the British Isles: *She met a charming continental while on holiday* **2 not worth a continental** *AmE infml* worthless

continental break·fast /ˌ···· '··/ *n* [C;(U)] a light breakfast usu. consisting of bread, butter, JAM, and coffee, typically eaten in various European countries —compare ENGLISH BREAKFAST

continental drift /ˌ···· '·/ *n* [U] *tech* the very slow movement of the CONTINENTs² across the surface of the earth: *Most scientists now believe that the shape of the* CONTINENTs *can be explained by continental drift*

continental quilt /ˌ···· '·/ *n* DUVET

continental shelf /ˌ···· '·/ *n* a plain of varying width under the sea forming the border to a CONTINENT², typically ending in a very steep slope to the ocean's depths

con·tin·gen·cy /kən'tɪndʒənsi/ *n* a possibility; event that might happen, but which is unlikely: *We must always be prepared for all contingencies/every contingency.|We have contingency plans ready in case there is a flood*

con·tin·gent¹ /kən'tɪndʒənt/ *adj* **1** [F+*on, upon*] dependent on something uncertain or that has not yet happened: *Whether or not we arrive on time is contingent on the weather* **2** [B] happening by chance; accidental —**~ly** *adv*

contingent² *n* **1** [C9,(C)] a group of soldiers, ships, etc., gathered together to help a larger force: *The northern army has been strengthened by a large contingent from New York* **2** [GC9] a representative group forming part of a large gathering: *Have the Scottish contingent arrived at the meeting yet?*

con·tin·u·al /kən'tɪnjʊəl/ *adj* repeated; regular; frequent: *He hates these continual arguments with his wife* —**~ly** *adv*

USAGE **Continual** is often used of bad things: **continual** *hammering|these* **continual** *interruptions.* **Continuous** is used of things or events that are connected without a break, but may have a beginning and end: *3 days'* **continuous** *flight|2 rivers connected to form one* **continuous** *waterway.*

con·tin·u·ance /kənˈtɪnjʊəns/ *n* **1** [U;S] the act of continuing: *Continuance of the war will mean short food supplies at home* **2** [(*the*) S] the time for which something continues: *We were unable to buy bread for the continuance of the war*

con·tin·u·a·tion /kənˌtɪnjʊˈeɪʃən/ *n* **1** [U] the act of continuing: *The large profits made by the arms trade is the main reason why that government favours its continuation* **2** [C] something which continues from something else: *The Baltic Sea is a continuation of the North Sea*

con·tin·ue /kənˈtɪnjuː/ *v* **1** [I∅;T1,3,4] to (cause to) go on happening: *The fighting around the airport continued for a week before the enemy were defeated* **2** [I∅;T1] to (cause to) last, go forward: *The road continues in a straight line for 5 miles* **3** [I∅;T1,3,4] to (cause to) start again after an interruption: *After a short break the play continued.|Will you continue gardening after dinner?* **4** [L9] to remain; stay: *This animal can continue in this state for a month.|We continued in Cairo while John was in Alexandria* **5** [X9 *often pass.*; L9] to (cause to) stay in a particular job or office: *The king decided to continue Pitt as chief minister* **6** [T1,5;I∅] to say in continuation: *The politician continued that he thought the government should call an election.|"We must fight for freedom and racial equality," continued the speaker.|And did she continue after saying that?*

con·ti·nu·i·ty /ˌkɒntɪ̈ˈnjuːɪ̈ti‖ˌkɑntɪ̈ˈnuː-/ *n* [U] **1** the state of being continuous: *There's no continuity between the parts of his book* **2** the arrangement of the parts of a film, radio or television broadcast, etc., in correct uninterrupted order: *If you work as a continuity girl you are responsible for making sure that the film is properly arranged* **3** the music, words, etc., that connect the various parts of a radio or television broadcast, film, etc.: *I enjoyed the acting but thought the continuity was bad*

con·tin·u·o /kənˈtɪnjʊəʊ/ also **figured bass**— *n* **-os** (in music esp. of the 17th and 18th centuries) a musical part consisting of a set of low notes together with special figures showing all the higher notes (CHORD*s*) to be played with them

con·tin·u·ous /kənˈtɪnjʊəs/ *adj* continuing without interruption; unbroken: *The brain needs a continuous supply of blood.|The sign "continuous performance" means that there is only a short pause between the end of one showing of the film and the beginning of the next* —see CONTINUAL (USAGE) —**~ly** *adv*

con·tin·u·um /kənˈtɪnjʊəm/ *n* **-uums** *or* **-ua** /jʊə/ **1** something which is without parts and the same from beginning to end: *the continuum of time* **2** anything that changes only by regular degrees and keeps a common character from beginning to end: *a continuum from the lowest to the highest forms of life*

con·tort /kənˈtɔːt‖-ɔrt/ *v* [Wv5 (*with*); T1;I∅] to (cause to) twist violently out of shape: *Her face was contorted with anger.|You should see how her face contorts when she's annoyed.|trees with contorted branches*

con·tor·tion /kənˈtɔːʃən‖-ɔr-/ *n* **1** [U] the act of CONTORTING: *contortion of the body caused by poison* **2** [C] a twisted position or movement: *the contortions of a snake*

con·tor·tion·ist /kənˈtɔːʃənɪ̈st‖-ɔr-/ *n* a person who earns money by twisting his body into unnatural shapes and positions to amuse others —see picture at THEATRE

con·tour¹ /ˈkɒntʊəʳ‖ˈkɑn-/ *n* **1** [*often pl. with sing. meaning*] the shape of the outer limits of an area: *the contour of the British coast*|(fig.) *the contours of the present political state of affairs* **2** also **contour line** /ˈ·· ·/— an imaginary line drawn on a map to show the limits of the areas at or above a certain height above sea level

contour² *v* [Wv5;T1;(I∅)] **1** to build (a road) along the CONTOUR*s*¹ (1) of a hill: *If we contour this road it will be longer but have fewer steep slopes* **2** to show the CONTOUR*s*¹ of (an area) as on a map

contour³ *adj* [Wa5;A] related to or following the CONTOUR*s*¹ of the land: *contour farming*

contour map /ˈ·· ·/ *n* a map on which CONTOUR*s*¹ (2) are shown

contr. *written abbrev. for:* CONTRACTION

USAGE The shortened forms marked *contr.* in this dictionary are now used everywhere except in the most *fml* or *tech* writing.

con·tra- /ˈkɒntrə‖ˈkɑn-/ *prefix* **1** against: CONTRACEPTION|CONTRAINDICATE **2** *tech* set at a musical PITCH (=level) below the usual BASS: CONTRABASS

con·tra·band /ˈkɒntrəbænd‖ˈkɑn-/ *adj, n* [B;U] (of, concerning, or being) goods or possessions which it is unlawful to bring into or send out of a country or to own: *He was seized by the police because contraband goods were found in his house.|contraband trade|to trade in contraband*

con·tra·bass /ˌkɒntrəˈbeɪs‖ˌkɑn-/ *n* DOUBLE BASS

con·tra·cep·tion /ˌkɒntrəˈsepʃən‖ˌkɑn-/ *n* [U] birth control; the act or practice of preventing sex from resulting in the birth of a child, and/or all the methods for preventing this: *They did not practise contraception because they wanted a baby.|Most doctors give advice on contraception*

con·tra·cep·tive /ˌkɒntrəˈseptɪv‖ˌkɑn-/ *adj, n* [Wa5] (of, concerning, or being) a drug or any object or material used inside or outside the sex organs as a means of preventing an act of sex from resulting in the birth of a child: *I get regular contraceptive advice from my doctor.|Some people think that using contraceptives makes sex less pleasant* —see also CAP; CONDOM; INTRAUTERINE DEVICE; PILL; SHEATH

con·tract¹ /ˈkɒntrækt‖ˈkɑn-/ *n* **1** [C,C3] a formal agreement, having the force of law, between 2 or more people or groups: *Our shop has entered into/made a contract with a clothing firm to buy 100 coats a week* **2** [C] a signed paper on which the conditions of such an agreement are written: *Never sign a contract until you have read it from beginning to end and are sure you can fulfil all its conditions* **3** [C] *tech* (in the card game BRIDGE) an agreement between partners to try and win a stated number of TRICK*s*

con·tract² /kənˈtrækt/ *v* **1** [T1,3;I∅] to settle or arrange by formal agreement: *A foreign firm has contracted to build a new railway across Africa.|Our shop contracted with a local clothing firm for 100 coats a week* **2** [T1] to get (something unwanted): *My son's contracted a severe fever* **3** [I∅;T1] to (cause to) become smaller in size: *Metal contracts as it becomes cool.|In conversational English "is not" often contracts to "isn't"*

contract bridge /ˌkɒntrækt ˈbrɪdʒ‖ˌkɑn-/ *n* [U] —see BRIDGE³

con·trac·tile /kənˈtræktaɪl‖-tl/ also **con·trac·ti·ble** /kənˈtræktəbəl/— *adj tech* (esp. of a muscle) that can CONTRACT² (3) or be CONTRACTED² (3): *The heart is a highly contractile organ*

contract in /ˈkɒntrækt‖ˈkɑn-/ *v adv* [I∅ (*to*)] to promise, esp. officially, to take part

con·trac·tion /kənˈtrækʃən/ *n* **1** [U] the act of CONTRACTING² (esp. 2,3) **2** [C] the shortened form of a word or words: *"Won't" is a contraction of "will not"* **3** [C] *tech* a very strong and often painful narrowing, tightening, and shortening of a muscle, esp. of the muscles around the baby inside a woman who is about to give birth to a child: *When you feel the next contraction push very hard and the birth will be very quick*

con·trac·tor /kən'træktə^r‖'kɑntræk-/ *n* a person, business, or firm, that provides building materials or labour for building jobs

contract out /'kɒntrækt‖'kɑn-/ *v adv* [IØ (*of*)] to promise, esp. officially, not to take part

con·trac·tu·al /kən'træktʃʊəl/ *adj* [Wa5] of, related to, or agreed in a contract: *You have a contractual duty to provide this shop with 100 coats a week* —**~ly** *adv*

con·tra·dict /ˌkɒntrə'dɪkt‖ˌkɑn-/ *v* **1** [T1;IØ] to declare (a person, opinion, something written or spoken) to be wrong or untruthful: *Young children should never contradict what their parents say.|Don't contradict!* **2** [T1] (of a statement, action, fact, etc.) to be opposite in nature or character to (a statement, action, fact, etc.): *Your actions contradict your declared moral principles*

con·tra·dic·tion /ˌkɒntrə'dɪkʃən‖ˌkɑn-/ *n* **1** [U] **a** the act of CONTRADICTing (1): *My father punishes contradiction severely* **b** the state of being CONTRADICTed (1): *Contradiction makes my teacher angry* **2** [U] direct opposition between things compared; disagreement: *There is no contradiction between my behaviour and my principles.|They are not in contradiction* **3** [C] a statement, action, or fact that CONTRADICTs (2) another or itself: *It is a contradiction to say you support the government but would not vote for it in an election*

con·tra·dic·to·ry /ˌkɒntrə'dɪktəri‖ˌkɑn-/ *adj* [Wa5] **1** [(*to*)] serving to CONTRADICT: *The politician's statement was contradictory to the one he'd made earlier in the same week* **2** having the habit of CONTRADICTing (1): *Allan has a nasty contradictory nature*

con·tra·dis·tinc·tion /ˌkɒntrədɪ'stɪŋkʃən‖ˌkɑn-/ *n fml* **in contradistinction to** as opposed to; in CONTRAST to: *plants in contradistinction to animals*

con·trail /'kɒntreɪl‖'kɑn-/ *n tech* a line of white water VAPOUR (=steam) made in the sky by planes flying at a great height: *I couldn't see the plane but I saw its contrail*

con·tra·in·di·ca·tion /ˌkɒntrəˌɪndʒ̇'keɪʃən‖ˌkɑn-/ *adj tech* a sign that a medicine should not be used: *High blood pressure is a contraindication for this new drug* —**-cated** /-'ɪndʒ̇keɪtʒ̇d/ *adj*

con·tral·to /kən'træltəʊ/ *n* **-tos** ALTO[1] (2)

con·trap·tion /kən'træpʃən/ *n infml* a strange-looking machine or apparatus: *I don't understand how this contraption works*

con·tra·pun·tal /ˌkɒntrə'pʌntl‖ˌkɑn-/ *adj* [Wa5] of, using, or related to musical COUNTERPOINT —**~ly** *adv*

con·tra·ri·e·ty /ˌkɒntrə'raɪʒ̇ti‖ˌkɑn-/ *n* **1** [U] the state of being CONTRARY[2] **2** [C] something CONTRARY[2]; CONTRADICTION

con·tra·ri·wise /'kɒntrəriwaɪz, kən'treəri-‖'kɑntreri-/ *adv* in the opposite manner or direction; VICE VERSA; CONVERSEly: *I am happy when the sun shines, and, contrariwise, I am unhappy when it rains*

con·tra·ry[1] /'kɒntrəri‖'kɑntreri/ *n* **1** [*the*+R] the opposite: *They say he is guilty, but I believe the contrary* **2 by contraries** in an opposite way to what was expected: *Things at work seem to be going by contraries at present, I can't get anything right* **3 on the contrary** (*used for expressing strong opposition to what has just been said*) not at all; no: *"I believe you like your job." "On the contrary, I hate it!"* **4 to the contrary a** to the opposite effect: *If you don't hear (something) to the contrary I'll meet you at 7.00 o'clock outside the cinema* **b** NOTWITHSTANDING: *I know she's unhappy, all her brave talk to the contrary*
USAGE Compare **on the contrary, on the other hand, in contrast**: **On the contrary** is used when one says a statement is not true: *"It's cold". "***On the contrary,** *it's hot."* Use **on the other hand** when adding a new and different fact to a statement: *It's cold, but* **on the other hand** *it's not raining.* **In contrast** is also used of 2 very different facts that are both true, but it points out the surprising difference between them: *It was cold yesterday, but* **in contrast** *it's very hot today.*

con·trar·y[2] /kən'treəri/ *adj* (of a person or their character) difficult to handle or work with; unreasonably keeping to one's own opinions or plans, in opposition to the wishes of others: *Old Mrs Smith is far too contrary to make friends easily* —**-ily** /-rʒ̇li/ *adv* —**-iness** *n* [U]

con·tra·ry[3] /'kɒntrəri‖'kɑntreri/ *adj* **1** [(*to*)] completely different; wholly opposed: *contrary opinions* **2** unfavourable: *Our sailing boat was delayed by contrary winds*

contrary to /'··· ·/ *prep* in opposition to: *Contrary to all advice he started to climb the mountain during a storm*

con·trast[1] /'kɒntrɑːst‖'kɑntræst/ *n* **1** [U] the act of CONTRASTing[2]; comparison of unlike objects, esp. to show differences: *In contrast with/to your belief that we shall fail, I know we shall succeed* **2** [C;U: (*between*)] (a) difference or unlikeness, esp. of colour or brightness: *such a contrast between brother and sister|This artist uses contrast skilfully* **3** [C] something noticeably different from something else: *The black paint on the door provides a suitable contrast for the white walls*

con·trast[2] /kən'trɑːst‖-'træst/ *v* [(*with*)] **1** [T1] to compare (2 things or people or one thing or a person with another) so that differences are made clear: *In this book the writer contrasts good with/and evil* **2** [IØ] to show a difference when compared: *Your actions contrast unfavourably with your principles*

con·tra·vene /ˌkɒntrə'viːn‖ˌkɑn-/ *v* [T1] **1** to act in opposition to; break (a law, rule, custom, etc.): *Your behaviour contravenes established social customs* **2** to question the truth of (a statement, principles, etc.)

con·tra·ven·tion /ˌkɒntrə'venʃən‖ˌkɑn-/ *n* [C;U] (an example of) the act of breaking the law, rules, customs, etc.: *To steal is a contravention of the law/is an act in contravention of the law*

con·tre·temps /'kɒntrətɑ̃‖'kɑn- (*Fr* kɔ̃trətɑ̃)/ *n* **-temps** /-tɑ̃z (*Fr* -tɑ̃)/ [Wn3] *Fr* an unlucky, unfortunate, or unexpected accident or happening

con·trib·ute /kən'trɪbjuːt/ *v* **1** [T1;IØ: (*to*)] to join with others in giving or supplying (money, help, etc.): *Although he has plenty of money Allan didn't contribute to Jane's present when she left the office* **2** [IØ (*to*)] to help in bringing about; have a share in: *Plenty of fresh air contributes to good health.|Too much alcoholic drink will contribute to your ruin* **3** [T1;IØ: (*to*)] to supply (a written article) to a magazine, newspaper, etc.: *I make most of my money by writing books but I do contribute to magazines sometimes*

con·tri·bu·tion /ˌkɒntrʒ̇'bjuːʃən‖ˌkɑn-/ *n* **1** [U] the act of contributing (CONTRIBUTE) **2** [C] something CONTRIBUTED (1,3): *I give a small contribution to the church each week*

con·trib·u·tor /kən'trɪbjʊtə^r‖-jə-/ *n* a person who CONTRIBUTEs (1,3): *a regular contributor to our magazine*

con·trib·u·to·ry /kən'trɪbjʊtəri‖-jətori/ *adj* [Wa5] **1** helping to bring about a result: *Your stupidity was a contributory cause of the fire* **2** (of a PENSION or insurance plan) paid for by workers as well as by their employers

con·trite /'kɒntraɪt‖'kɑn-/ *adj* caused by, feeling,

or showing guilt: *a humble and contrite heart|contrite tears* —**~ly** *adv*

con·tri·tion /kən'trɪʃən/ *n* [U] sincere sorrow for one's wrong actions and thoughts

con·triv·ance /kən'traɪvəns/ *n* **1** [C] something CONTRIVED (2), esp. a machine or apparatus: *The scientist invented a new contrivance for milking cows* **2** [C *usu. pl.*] a clever, often deceitful, plan: *Ann's many contrivances to get herself invited to people's houses* **3** [U] the act of contriving (CONTRIVE (2)); ability to invent: *Such a machine is beyond the contrivance of ordinary people*

con·trive /kən'traɪv/ *v* **1** [T1,3] to plan, usu. with skill: *The prisoner contrived a way of escaping/to escape* **2** [T1] to form or make in a clever or skilful way; invent: *to contrive a dress from a piece of old cloth* **3** [T1,3] to cause (something) to happen in accordance with one's plans or in spite of difficulty: *Can you contrive to be here early?|After much difficulty I contrived to escape*

con·trived /kən'traɪvd/ *adj* unnatural and forced: *the contrived gaiety of a worried hostess*

con·trol[1] /kən'trəʊl/ *v* **-ll-** **1** [T1] to have power over (someone or something); rule: *This fort controls the whole valley. It must be defended whatever the cost.|You try to control me as though I were your slave* **2** [Wv4;T1] to have directing influence over (someone or something); direct; fix the time, amount, degree or rate of (an activity): *The pressure of steam in the engine is controlled by this button.|Try to control your temper!|Control yourself! Don't shout!* **3** [Wv5;T1] to test (esp. a scientific study or EXPERIMENT) by comparison with a chosen standard: *a controlled* EXPERIMENT **4** [Wv5;T1] to make sure of the correctness of (figures, accounts, etc.): *The accounts of the whole company are controlled in this one department*

control[2] *n* **1** [U (*of, over*)] the power to control, command, influence, or direct: *We must not allow the enemy control of this valley.|Which party has political control of the town council? Our party took control after the last election.|I lost control (of myself) and hit him* **2** [U (*on, over*)] guidance; the fixing of the time, amount, degree, or rate of an activity; act of controlling: *There's little government control over industrial organization in this country.|wage control* **3** [C *often pl. with sing. meaning*] the place from which a machine, activity, system, etc., is controlled: *the control tower of an airport|Who's at the controls today?* **4** [C] *tech* something used as a standard against which the results of a scientific study or EXPERIMENT can be judged or compared **5** [C *usu. pl.*] a means of controlling: *The government's wage controls will be a failure if they don't get union support.|Parliament uses its power to vote money supplies as a control over the government* **6** *tech* (in SPIRITUALISM) the dead person who guides a MEDIUM **7 in control** in command; in charge **8 in the control of** controlled by: *I was in the control of evil men who forced me to do wicked things* **9 out of control** in(to) a state of not being controlled: *The car went out of control and crashed over the cliff* **10 under control** working properly; in order; controlled in the correct way: *It took the teacher months to bring her class under control*

con·trol·ler /kən'trəʊlə^r/ *n* **1** [C;A;N] also (*fml*) **comptroller**— a business or government official responsible for money matters **2** [C] a person who directs a division of a large organization

control tow·er /·'· ·/ *n* a building at an airport, which instructs planes when to land and take off

con·tro·ver·sial /ˌkɒntrə'vɜːʃəl‖ˌkɑntrə'vɜrʃəl/ *adj* likely to cause or causing much argument or disagreement: *a controversial speech/decision/person/politician/book* —**~ly** *adv*

con·tro·ver·sy /'kɒntrəvɜːsi, kən'trɒvəsi‖'kɑntrəvɜrsi/ *n* [C;U] (an) argument about something over which there is much disagreement: *The new government appointments have caused much controversy.|The point in controversy is not whether we should do it, but whether we can do it*

con·tro·vert /'kɒntrəvɜːt, ˌkɒntrə'vɜːt‖'kɑntrəvɜrt, ˌkɑntrə'vɜrt/ *v* [T1] *rare* to oppose (an idea, opinion, etc.) by reasoning

con·tu·ma·cious /ˌkɒntjʊ'meɪʃəs‖ˌkɑntə-/ *adj fml* unreasonably disobedient, esp. to an order of court —**~ly** *adv*

con·tu·ma·cy /'kɒntjʊməsi‖kən'tuː-/ *n* [U] *fml* unreasonable disobedience, esp. to an order of court —compare CONTEMPT OF COURT

con·tu·me·li·ous /ˌkɒntjʊ'miːlɪəs‖ˌkɑntə-/ *adj fml* too bold in a disrespectful way —**~ly** *adv*

con·tume·ly /'kɒntjuːmli, kən'tjuːmḷli‖kən'tuːmḷli/ *n fml* **1** [U] disrespectful and offensive behaviour, language, or treatment **2** [C] an example of this; INSULT

con·tuse /kən'tjuːz‖-'tuːz/ *v* [Wv5;T1] *med* to hurt or damage (part of the body) esp. without breaking the skin; BRUISE

con·tu·sion /kən'tjuːʒən‖-'tuː-/ *n* *med* **1** [C] BRUISE **2** [U] the act of contusing (CONTUSE)

co·nun·drum /kə'nʌndrəm/ *n* a question which can only be answered by guessing; trick question asked for fun; RIDDLE

con·ur·ba·tion /ˌkɒnɜː'beɪʃən‖ˌkɑnər-/ *n* a number of cities and towns that have spread and joined together to form one network, often with a large city as its centre

con·va·lesce /ˌkɒnvə'les‖ˌkɑn-/ *v* [IØ] to spend time getting well after an illness

con·va·les·cence /ˌkɒnvə'lesəns‖ˌkɑn-/ *n* [U;S] the length of time a person spends getting well after an illness

con·va·les·cent /ˌkɒnvə'lesənt‖ˌkɑn-/ *adj, n* [Wa5] (for, related to, or being) a person spending time getting well after an illness: *a convalescent nursing home*

con·vec·tion /kən'vekʃən/ *n* [U] the movement in a gas or liquid caused by warm gas or liquid rising, and cold gas or liquid sinking: *a convection heater|Warm air rises by convection*

con·vec·tor /kən'vektə^r/ *n* a heating apparatus in which air becomes hot by passing over hot surfaces and then moves about an enclosed space, room, etc., by CONVECTION

con·vene /kən'viːn/ *v* [IØ;T1] **a** (of a group of people, committee, etc.) to meet or gather **b** to call (a group of people, committee, etc.) to meet or gather

con·ven·er, -or /kən'viːnə^r/ *n esp. BrE* a member of a society, committee, club, etc., whose duty it is to call meetings

con·ve·ni·ence /kən'viːnɪəns/ *n* **1** [U] fitness; suitableness; the quality of being convenient: *We bought this house for its convenience. It's very near the shops and where I work* **2** [U9] a suitable time: *Please come at your earliest convenience* **3** [C] an apparatus, machine, service, etc., which gives comfort or advantage to its user: *This house has all the modern conveniences* **4** [U] personal comfort or advantage: *He thinks only of his own convenience* **5** [C] *BrE fml* PUBLIC CONVENIENCE **6 at one's convenience** where and when it suits one: *Do this at your convenience*

con·ve·ni·ent /kən'viːnɪənt/ *adj* **1** suited to one's needs: *a convenient house/time/place|convenient tools* **2** [(*for*)] near; easy to reach: *Our house is very convenient for the shops* —**~ly** *adv*

con·vent /'kɒnvənt‖'kɑnvent/ *n* a house or set of

buildings in which NUNs live according to their religious promises

con·ven·ti·cle /kən'ventɪkəl/ *n* (in England in former times) (a building used for) an unlawful secret meeting of NONCONFORMISTs (=Christians in disagreement with the established state religion)

con·ven·tion /kən'venʃən/ *n* **1** [C] a formal agreement: *The various countries all agreed to sign the convention* **2** [C;U] (an example of) generally accepted practice, esp. with regard to social behaviour: *It is a matter of convention that men should open doors for ladies.*|(*a*) *political convention* **3** [C] (a meeting of) a group of people gathered together with a shared, often political purpose: *a teachers' convention*

con·ven·tion·al /kən'venʃənəl/ *adj* **1** *often derog* following accepted practices, customs, and standards, sometimes too closely: *I wish you weren't so conventional in the clothes you wear.*|*Jean's got very conventional opinions about food, so she won't eat anything new or foreign* **2** [Wa5] (of a weapon) not atomic —**~ly** *adv*

con·ven·tion·al·i·ty /kənˌvenʃə'næləti/ *n fml* **1** [U] acceptance of CONVENTIONAL standards: *The conventionality of his clothes makes him look old-fashioned* **2** [C] a CONVENTIONAL practice, standard, or thing

con·verge /kən'vɜːdʒ‖-ɜr-/ *v* [IØ (*on*)] to come together towards a common point: *Railway lines seem to converge when one looks at them from a distance.*|*The 2 armies converged on the enemy capital for the last battle of the war* —**-vergent** *adj* [Wa5] —**-vergence** *n* [C;U]

con·ver·sant /kən'vɜːsənt‖-ɜr-/ *adj* [F+*with*] familiar; having knowledge or experience: *I can't claim to be very conversant with any of the sciences because I've never studied them*

con·ver·sa·tion /ˌkɒnvə'seɪʃən‖ˌkɑnvər-/ *n* [C;U] (an) informal talk in which people exchange news, feelings, and thoughts: *Mrs Smith spends a lot of time in conversation with her neighbour*

con·ver·sa·tion·al /ˌkɒnvə'seɪʃənəl‖ˌkɑnvər-/ *adj* (of a word, phrase, manner, etc.) of or commonly used in conversation: *Business letters are not usually written in conversational style.*|*conversational French* —**~ly** *adv*

con·ver·sa·tion·al·ist /ˌkɒnvə'seɪʃənələst‖ˌkɑnvər-/ *n* a person who spends much time in conversation or whose conversation is clever and interesting

con·ver·sa·zi·o·ne /ˌkɒnvəsætsi'əʊni‖ˌkɑnvərsɑ-/ *n* **-ones** *or* **-oni** /'əʊni/ *fml & It* a meeting for conversation, esp. about art, literature, science, etc.

con·verse[1] /kən'vɜːs‖-ɜrs/ *v* [IØ (*on/about* and/or *with*)] to talk informally: *After a year studying at university I feel able to converse with anyone about anything*

con·verse[2] /'kɒnvɜːs‖kən'vɜrs/ *adj* [Wa5] (esp. of opinions, beliefs, statements, etc.) opposite: *I hold the converse opinion* —**~ly** /kən'vɜːsli‖-ɜr-/ *adv*

converse[3] /'kɒnvɜːs‖-ɜrs/ *n* [*the*+R (*of*)] **1** the opposite of something: *"Empty" is the converse of "full".*|*I disagree with your opinion, in fact I believe the converse to be true* **2** *tech* (in LOGIC) a statement made by changing the order of some of the words in another statement: *"It's windy but not wet" is the converse of "It's wet but not windy"*

con·ver·sion /kən'vɜːʃən‖-'vɜrʒən/ *n* **1** [U (*of, from* and/or *into/to*)] the act of CONVERTing: *When the new system of measurement is introduced many old people will find conversion of yards to metres difficult.*|*Conversion of your heating system from coal to gas will be costly* **2** [C (*of, from* and/or *into/to*)] a change from one use or purpose to another: *Some people favour the conversion of royal palaces into flats for ordinary people.*|*Do you know a firm that can do house conversions?* **3** [C (*from, to*)] a change in which a person accepts completely a new religion, political belief, etc.: *There were many conversions to Christianity among the ancient Romans.*|*His conversion from Hinduism to Buddhism worried his mother* **4** [C;U] *tech* (in RUGBY and American football) (an example of) the act of kicking the ball over the bar of the GOALPOSTs

con·vert[1] /kən'vɜːt‖-ɜrt/ *v* **1** [T1 (*to*) *usu. pass.*] to persuade a person to accept a particular religion, political belief, etc.: *John was converted to Buddhism by a Chinese priest.*|*Give me time and I'll convert her to our political party* **2** [IØ (*from* and/or *to*)] *AmE* to change one's religion: *John has converted to Buddhism* **3** [Wv5;T1;IØ: (*to, into*)] to (cause to) change to or into another form, substance, or state, or from one use or purpose to another: *Coal can be converted to gas by burning.*|*This seat converts into a bed.*|*Does electricity convert easily to other forms of power?*|*We have converted (our house) to North Sea gas* (=We are now using North Sea gas) **4** [L9;T1: (*for, into, to*)] **a** (of one type of money) to change into another type of money of equal value: *At what rate does the dollar convert into pounds?* **b** to cause (one type of money) to change into another of equal value: *Foreign money can be converted at this bank* **5** [T1; IØ] *tech* (in RUGBY and American football) to kick (a ball) over the bar of the GOALPOSTs

con·vert[2] /'kɒnvɜːt‖'kɑnvɜrt/ *n* a person who has been persuaded to accept a particular religion, political belief, etc.

con·vert·er /kən'vɜːtəʳ‖-ɜr-/ *n tech* **1** a FURNACE in which steel is made according to the **Bessemer process** **2** also **convertor**— an apparatus that changes the direction of electric currents **3** also **convertor**— an apparatus that changes the wave length of a radio signal **4** also **convertor**— an apparatus that changes the form in which information is written so that it can be accepted and dealt with by a COMPUTER (=a calculating machine with a memory)

con·ver·ti·ble[1] /kən'vɜːtəbəl‖-ɜr-/ *adj* [Wa5] **1** [(*into*)] (of a type of money) that can be freely exchanged for other types of money: *The dollar is convertible, the* ROUBLE *is not* **2** (of a car) having a roof that can be folded back **3** that can be CONVERTed: *a convertible bed that changes into a seat* —**-bility** /kənˌvɜːtə'bɪləti‖-ɜr-/ *n* [U]

convertible[2] *n* a car with a roof that can be folded back

con·vex /ˌkɒn'veks◂, kən-‖ˌkɑn'veks◂, kən-/ *adj tech* curved outward, like the outside edge of a circle: *a convex mirror that makes you look fat* —see picture at OPTICS —**~ly** *adv*

con·vex·i·ty /kən'veksəti/ *n tech* **1** [U] the state of being CONVEX **2** [C] a CONVEX surface, or shape

con·vey /kən'veɪ/ *v* **1** [T1 (*from* and/or *to*)] to take or carry from one place to another: *Wires convey electricity from power stations to the user.*|*We conveyed our goods to market in an old car* **2** [T1,5: (*to*)] to make (feelings, ideas, thoughts, etc.) known: *I can't convey my feelings in words.*|*Words convey meaning* **3** [T1 (*to*)] *law* to give the rights to (a property) to someone else: *When was this land conveyed to you?*

con·vey·ance /kən'veɪəns/ *n* **1** [U] the act of CONVEYing **2** [C] *law* an official paper by which the right to ownership of a property is given by one person to another **3** [C] *fml* a carriage or other vehicle

con·vey·anc·er /kən'veɪənsəʳ/ *n law* a lawyer who prepares CONVEYANCEs (2)

con·vey·anc·ing /kən'veɪənsɪŋ/ *n* [U] *law* the branch of law concerned with preparing CONVEYANCE*s* (2)
con·vey·er, -or /kən'veɪəʳ/ *n* **1** a person whose business is CONVEYing (1,3) **2** CONVEYER BELT
conveyer belt /·'·· ·/ *n* [C; *by*+U] an endless moving belt that carries objects from one place to another
con·vict¹ /kən'vɪkt/ *v* [T1 (*of*)] to find (someone) guilty of a crime, esp. in a court of law: *The criminal was convicted of murder*
con·vict² /'kɒnvɪkt‖'kɑn-/ *n* a person who has been found guilty of a crime and sent to prison, esp. for a long time: *an escaped convict*
con·vic·tion /kən'vɪkʃən/ *n* **1** [U] the act of CONVICTing¹: *Conviction of the prisoner for a political crime will cause great unrest all through the country* **2** [C] an occasion on which one has been CONVICTed¹: *This was her 3rd conviction* **3** [C,C5; U,U5] (a) very firm and sincere belief: *I speak in the full conviction that our cause is just.*|*From the way she spoke you could tell she was speaking from conviction*
con·vince /kən'vɪns/ *v* [T1 (*of*); V3;D5] to cause (someone) to believe or feel certain; to persuade (someone): *It took many hours to convince John of his wife's guilt.*|(esp. *AmE*) *We convinced Anne to go by train rather than plane.*|*It's going to be hard to convince my wife that we can't afford a new car* —compare PERSUADE
con·vinced /kən'vɪnst/ *adj* **1** [A] full of CONVICTION (3): *a convinced supporter of his political party* **2** [F (*of*), F5] certain; sure: *convinced that war would come*|*convinced of it*
con·vinc·ing /kən'vɪnsɪŋ/ *adj* serving to CONVINCE: *a convincing speaker/speech*|*Their claim to have developed atomic weapons is not very convincing* —**~ly** *adv*
con·viv·i·al /kən'vɪvɪəl/ *adj* **1** (of a person) friendly; fond of eating, drinking, and good company **2** (of an event, behaviour, etc.) merry: *a very convivial party* —**~ly** *adv* —**~ity** /-ˌvɪvɪ'ælɪ̣ti/ *n* [U]
con·vo·ca·tion /ˌkɒnvə'keɪʃən‖ˌkɑn-/ *n* **1** [U] the act of convoking (CONVOKE) **2** [GU] (*often cap.*) an organization of church officials usu. of the Church of England, that holds formal meetings to talk about church business: *Convocation could not agree on the question of women priests* **3** [GU] (*often cap.*) (in certain universities) an organization of GRADUATE*s* that holds regular formal meetings: *Are you a member of Convocation?*
con·voke /kən'vəʊk/ *v* [T1] *fml* to call together for a meeting: *When is the king going to convoke the new Parliament?*
con·vo·lut·ed /'kɒnvəluːtɪ̣d‖'kɑn-/ *adj* **1** *fml* twisted; curved: *Some sheep have convoluted horns* **2** difficult to understand or follow: *convoluted arguments* —**~ly** *adv*
con·vo·lu·tion /ˌkɒnvə'luːʃən‖ˌkɑn-/ *n* **1** [*usu. pl.*] *fml* a fold; twist: *the convolutions of a long snake*|(fig.) *the convolutions of her difficult argument* **2** *med* a fold on the brain's surface
con·vol·vu·lus /kən'vɒlvjʊləs‖-'vɑlvjə-/ *n* [U;C *pl. rare*] any of various types of climbing plants like the MORNING GLORY
con·voy¹ /'kɒnvɔɪ‖'kɑn-/ *v* [T1] (of an armed ship, vehicle, soldiers, etc.) to go with and protect (a group of ships, vehicles, etc.)
convoy² *n* [GC] **1** a group of ships or vehicles, esp. if protected by an armed ship, vehicle, etc. **2** a protecting force of armed ships, vehicles, soldiers, etc. **3 in convoy** in a large group for protection (or other reasons): *We sailed in convoy because we thought the enemy might attack* **4 under convoy** protected by armed ships, vehicles, etc.
con·vulse /kən'vʌls/ *v* [Wv5 (*with*); T1] to shake (a person, animal, society, etc.) violently as if with CONVULSION*s*: *News that the king had imprisoned many parliamentary officials threatened to convulse the country*
con·vul·sion /kən'vʌlʃən/ *n* [*usu. pl.*] an unnaturally violent and sudden movement: *The child's nervous illness often threw her into convulsions*
con·vul·sive /kən'vʌlsɪv/ *adj* [Wa5] being, having, or producing a CONVULSION: *a convulsive movement of the muscles* —**~ly** *adv*
co·ny, coney /'kəʊni/ *n* **1** [Wn1;C] *tech* a rabbit **2** [U] rabbit fur, esp. when made to look like the fur of some other animal
coo¹ /kuː/ *v* **1** [IØ] to make the low soft cry of a DOVE OR PIGEON, or a sound like this **2** [IØ;T1] to speak softly and lovingly: *The parents cooed to their baby* —see also BILL **and coo**
coo² *n* **coos** the low soft cry of a DOVE OR PIGEON
cook¹ /kʊk/ *n* a person who prepares and cooks food: *John's a cook in the army but one day he hopes to be a* CHEF —compare CHEF —see KITCHEN (USAGE)
cook² *v* **1** [Wv5;T1;IØ] to prepare (food) for eating by using heat; make (a dish): *If I cook the meat this morning we can have it cold this evening.*|*Do you want your vegetables cooked or raw?*|*I'm going to cook all day tomorrow* **2** [L9] (of food) to be prepared in this way: *Make sure this meat cooks for at least an hour* **3** *infml* to change (facts, numbers, etc.) dishonestly for one's own advantage: *Jean was dismissed from the bank for cooking the books* (= stealing money by making changes in the accounts) —see also **cook someone's** GOOSE
USAGE Food is **stewed** or **boiled** in a pot with water, on top of the fire. One eats all the contents of a pot of **stewed** food, while the water is poured away before one eats, for example, **boiled** potatoes. If an inner vessel is used, so that the water does not directly touch the food, the food is **steamed**. **Simmering** is very gentle slow boiling, and **braising**, which is used only of meat, means cooking slowly in a covered pot with a little fat and water. **Frying** means cooking on top of the fire in fat or oil. Cooking by direct heat (usually under the **grill** in a modern kitchen) is called **grilling** (compare (*esp. AmE*) **broiling**), unless the direct heat is used on bread or bread-like foods that are already cooked, to make them hard and brown, when the word is **toasting**. To cook inside the **oven** is to **bake**, but a large piece of meat is said to be **roasted** whether it is cooked in the oven or, as often in former times, over a fire. One **bastes** a piece of meat while it is being **roasted** by pouring some of its own juice back over it from time to time, with a spoon.
cook·er /'kʊkəʳ/ *adj* **1** *esp. BrE* an apparatus on which food is cooked; STOVE; OVEN —see picture at KITCHEN **2** [*usu. pl.*] a fruit intended to be cooked: *These apples are good cookers*
cook·e·ry /'kʊkəri/ *n* [U] the preparation of food: *Boys as well as girls are taught cookery in school these days*
cookery book /'··· ˌ·/ also (*esp. AmE*) **cook·book** /'kʊkbʊk/— *n* a book which gives information on how to prepare and cook food
cook·house /'kʊkhaʊs/ *n* **-houses** /ˌhaʊzɪ̣z/ a kitchen, either in or out of doors, where food is cooked in a camp
cook·ie /'kʊki/ *n* **1** [C] also **cooky**— *esp. AmE* a small flat sweet cake; BISCUIT **2** [C] *ScotE* BUN (1) **3** [C9] a type of sweet BISCUIT, believed to be of American origin, that contains small pieces of chocolate (esp. in the phrs. **Maryland/chocolate-chip/tollhouse cookie**) **4** [C9] also **cooky**— *AmE sl* a person, esp. a man: *a clever cookie* **5** [C9] also

cooky— *AmE sl* an attractive woman

cook·ing /ˈkʊkɪŋ/ *adj* [Wa5;A] suitable for or used in cooking: *cooking apples|cooking* SHERRY

cook·out /ˈkʊk-aʊt/ *n infml esp. AmE* a meal cooked and eaten outdoors

cook up *v adv* [T1] *infml* to invent falsely: *Jean cooked up a story to explain why she was late for work but her employer did not believe her*

cool[1] /kuːl/ *adj* [Wa1] **1** neither warm nor cold; pleasantly cold: *a cool day* **2** giving a feeling between warm and cold; helping to keep one from feeling too warm: *As it was a hot day she wore a cool dress.|A cool wind blew off the sea* **3** (esp. of a person) calm; unexcited: *Even when you argue you should try and keep cool.|John has a very cool head* (=he never gets too excited) **4** [(*towards*)] (of a person, manner, behaviour, etc.) lacking warm feelings; not as friendly as usual: *Charles seemed very cool towards me today. I wonder if I've offended him.|The president was given a cool welcome when he visited London* **5** *infml & derog* (of a person, manner, behaviour, etc.) disrespectful: *I don't like the cool way you took my book without asking me first* **6** *sl becoming rare* very good: *You look real(ly) cool in that new dress* **7** [A] *infml* (used to give force to an expression, esp. to amounts of money): *This businessman earns a cool £1000 a month* —**~ish** *adj* [Wa5] —**coolly** /ˈkuːl-li/ *adv* —**~ness** *n* [U]

cool[2] *v* [IØ;T1: (DOWN)] **1** to (cause to) become cool: *Open the windows to cool the room.|Let your tea cool a little before you drink it* **2 cool it** to keep calm; calm down **3 cool one's heels** to be forced to wait

cool[3] *n* **1** [*the*+R] something that is neither warm nor cold: *the cool of the evening* **2** [U9] *sl* calmness of temper: *Even if John annoys you try and keep your cool* **3 blow/lose one's cool** *sl* to lose one's calmness

cool[4] *adv* **play it cool** to act in a calm and unexcited way

coo·lant /ˈkuːlənt/ *n* [C;U] *tech* (a type of) liquid used for cooling down part of a machine or apparatus that tends to get hot, such as the cutting edge of a tool

cool down also **cool off**— *v adv* [IØ;T1] **a** (of an angry or excited person) to become calmer and less excited: *She didn't cool down for hours after that argument* **b** to cause (an angry or excited person) to become calmer or less excited: *I tried to cool her down but she was still very angry when she left*

cool·er /ˈkuːləʳ/ *n* **1** [C] a container in which something is cooled or kept cool: *a wine cooler* **2** [*the*+R] *sl* prison

cool-head·ed /ˌ· ˈ··◂/ *adj* [Wa2] calm; hard to excite

coo·lie /ˈkuːli/ *n* (esp. in Asia) an unskilled worker

cooling-off pe·ri·od /ˌ·· ˈ· ˌ···/ *n* a period before a STRIKE (2) when unions and employers must try to come to an agreement

coon /kuːn/ *n* **1** *taboo derog sl* a black person **2** *infml* RACCOON

coop /kuːp/ *n* a cage for small creatures, esp. hens: *the chicken coop*

coo·per /ˈkuːpəʳ/ *n* a person who makes or repairs barrels

co·op·e·rate, co-operate /kəʊˈɒpəreɪt‖-ˈɑp-/ *v* [IØ (*with, in*); I3] to work or act together for a shared purpose: *The British cooperated with the French in building a plane that neither country could afford by itself.|Let's all cooperate to get the work done quickly* —**-rator** *n*

co·op·e·ra·tion, co-op- /kəʊˌɒpəˈreɪʃən‖-ˌɑp-/ *n* [U] **1** the act of working together for a shared purpose **2** willingness to work together **3** support; help: *I need your cooperation in this matter*

co·op·e·ra·tive[1], co-op- /kəʊˈɒpərətɪv‖-ˈɑp-/ *adj* **1** helpful: *The teacher thanked her pupils for being so cooperative* **2** [Wa5] made, done, or worked by people acting together: *The farmer and his neighbours decided to establish a cooperative farm* —**~ly** *adv*

cooperative[2], co-op- also **co-op** /ˈkəʊ ɒp‖-ɑp/— *n* a firm, building, farm, shop, etc., owned and controlled by the people who work in it (**producers' cooperative**) or use its services (such as a **consumers' cooperative**): *The farmers were too poor to buy a new machine each so the government helped them establish a cooperative and now they share a number of machines*

Cooperative, Co-op- also **Co-op**— *n* any of a large chain of British shops (**Cooperative Wholesale Society**) originally intended to provide goods cheaply and share the profits among the people who bought there

co-opt /ˌkəʊ ˈɒpt‖-ˈɑpt/ *v* [T1 (*into*)] (of the members of an elected group) to choose (someone not elected) as a fellow member: *I wasn't elected to the committee: I was co-opted onto it so that I could give them my specialist professional advice*

coop up *v adv* [T1 *usu. pass.*] to enclose; limit the freedom of (a person or animal): *How long are we going to stay cooped up in here? Let's get out for some fresh air!*

co·or·di·nate[1] /kəʊˈɔːdɪ̣nɪ̣t‖-ˈɔr-/ *adj* **1** equal in importance, rank, or degree: *coordinate* CLAUSE*s in a sentence* **2** of or based on COORDINATE*s*[2] (2) —**~ly** *adv*

coordinate[2] /kəʊˈɔːdɪ̣nɪ̣t‖-ˈɔr-/ *n* **1** *fml* any of a number of people or things that are equal in importance, rank, or degree **2** *tech* any of an ordered set of numbers and/or letters that give the exact position of a point, as on a map: *You can't find the city on the map if you don't know the coordinates*

co·or·di·nate[3] /kəʊˈɔːdɪ̣neɪt‖-ˈɔr-/ *v* [Wv5;T1;IØ] to (cause to) work together, esp. to increase effectiveness: *If we coordinate our efforts we should be able to defeat the enemy*

co·or·di·nates /kəʊˈɔːdɪ̣nɪ̣ts‖-ˈɔr-/ *n* [P] separate women's garments that can be worn together, esp. in matching colours, such as a shirt and skirt or a coat and trousers

co·or·di·na·tion /kəʊˌɔːdɪ̣ˈneɪʃən‖-ˌɔr-/ *n* [U] **1** the act of coordinating (COORDINATE) **2** the way in which muscles work together when performing a movement: *You would be a good horseback rider if only you could improve your coordination*

coot /kuːt/ *n* **1** [C] a type of water bird with dark grey feathers and a short beak —see picture at WATER[1] **2** [C;*you*+N] *sl* a foolish person **3 bald as a coot** *sl* completely BALD

cop[1] /kɒp‖kɑp/ *v* **-pp-** [T1;V4] **1** *sl esp. BrE* to catch (someone who has done or is doing something wrong): *Mother copped me stealing cakes from the kitchen and beat me severely* **2 cop a plea** *sl esp. AmE* **a** to admit being guilty of a lesser charge in order to avoid being put on trial for a more serious one **b** to admit a fault and ask for mercy **3 cop it** *sl esp. BrE* to be in serious trouble: *You'll cop it if mother catches you in the kitchen again*

cop[2] *n infml* a policeman

cop[3] *n BrE sl* **1 a fair cop** a fair or just ARREST, esp. when the police have been chasing the criminal for a long time **2 not much cop** worthless; valueless: *I wish we'd not come to this dance, it's not much cop*

cope[1] /kəʊp/ *n* a long loose garment worn by priests on special occasions

cope[2] *v* [IØ (*with*)] to deal successfully with something: *Jean felt unable to cope with (driving in) heavy traffic after her accident.|(Esp. BrE) After her* *nervous illness Janet lost the ability to cope*

co·peck /ˈkəʊpek/ *n* KOPECK

Co·per·ni·can sys·tem /keʊˈpɜːnɪ̵kən ˌsɪstɪ̵m‖-ɜr-/ *n* [*the*+R] the idea, first put forward by Copernicus (1473–1543), that all the chief heavenly bodies (PLANET*s*), including the earth, travel round the sun —compare PTOLEMAIC SYSTEM

cop·i·er /ˈkɒpɪəʳ‖ˈkɑ-/ *n* a person or machine that copies, esp. a machine for making copies of drawings, pictures, or paintings

co·pi·lot /ˈkəʊˌpaɪlət/ *n* [C;N] a pilot who shares in the control of a plane with another

cop·ing /ˈkəʊpɪŋ/ *n* a protective covering of stone or brick on top of a wall or roof —see picture at ROOF[1]

cop·ing·stone /ˈkəʊpɪŋstəʊn/ also **cope·stone** /ˈkəʊpstəʊn/— *n* **1** *lit* the finishing act of a piece of work **2** any of the stones used in a COPING

co·pi·ous /ˈkəʊpɪəs/ *adj* **1** plentiful: *copious tears* **2** (of a writer) having written much: *Agatha Christie was one of the most copious of British writers* —**~ly** *adv*

cop-out /ˈ· ·/ *n sl usu. derog* a failure to take the responsibility of making a difficult decision or of doing what one thinks right

cop out *v adv* **-pp-** [IØ (*of, on*)] *sl often derog* to avoid one's responsibilities: *You've got to do it: don't try to cop out* (*of it*) *by telling me you're too busy!*

cop·per[1] /ˈkɒpəʳ‖ˈkɑ-/ *n* **1** [U] a soft reddish metal that is a simple substance (ELEMENT), easily shaped, and allows heat and electricity to pass through it easily **2** [C;U] *BrE infml* a coin of low value made of this or of BRONZE: *He had only a few coppers in his pocket* **3** [C] *esp. BrE* a metal vessel, esp. in which clothes are boiled **4** [C] a type of small BUTTERFLY, usu. with reddish-brown wings —**~y** /ˈkɒpəri‖ˈkɑ-/ *adj*

copper[2] *v* [T1] to cover (an object, esp. the bottom of a ship) with copper

copper[3] *n, adj* [B;U] (having) a reddish-brown colour

copper[4] *n infml* a policeman

copper beech /ˌ·· ˈ·/ *n* a type of BEECH tree with reddish brown leaves

copper-bot·tomed /ˌ· ·ˈ··◂/ *adj* [Wa5] **1** *infml* safe in every way: *copper-bottomed promises* **2** (of a ship) having its bottom covered in copper and therefore fit to sail in seawater

cop·per·head /ˈkɒpəhed‖ˈkɑpər-/ *n* a type of poisonous North American snake

cop·per·plate /ˈkɒpəpleɪt‖ˈkɑpər-/ *n* **1** [C;U] (a) polished copper plate on which a picture or pattern is cut **2** [C] a print on paper made from this **3** [U] neat regular curving handwriting, usu. with all the letters of a word joined together

cop·per·smith /ˈkɒpəˌsmɪθ‖ˈkɑpər-/ *n* a person skilled at working in copper

cop·pice /ˈkɒpɪ̵s‖ˈkɑ-/ also **copse** /kɒps‖kɑps/— *n* a wood of small trees or bushes

cop·ra /ˈkɒprə‖ˈkɑprə/ *n* [U] the dried flesh of the coconut, from which oil is pressed for making soap

Cop·tic /ˈkɒptɪk‖ˈkɑp-/ *adj* [Wa5] of, belonging to, or related to the COPTIC CHURCH, or the language used in its religious services

Coptic Church /ˌ·· ˈ·/ *n* [*the*+R] a branch of the Christian Church based in Ethiopia and Egypt

cop·u·la /ˈkɒpjʊlə‖ˈkɑpjələ/ *n tech* an INTRANSITIVE verb which joins (LINK*s*) the subject of a sentence with the PREDICATE: *In the sentence "The house seems big", "seems" is a copula.*|*In this dictionary, copulas are marked* [L]

cop·u·late /ˈkɒpjʊleɪt‖ˈkɑpjə-/ *v* [IØ (*with*)] *fml* **1** (of a human) to have sex **2** (of an animal) to MATE[3] —**-lation** /ˌkɒpjʊˈleɪʃən‖ˌkɑpjə-/ *n* [U]

cop·u·la·tive[1] /ˈkɒpjʊlətiv‖ˈkɑpjəleɪ-/ *adj* [Wa5] **1** *tech* serving to connect words or word groups and expressing addition of their meanings: *a copulative* CONJUNCTION **2** *fml* of or related to copulation (COPULATE)

copulative[2] *n tech* a COPULATIVE[1] (1) word

cop·y[1] /ˈkɒpi‖ˈkɑpi/ *n* **1** [C] a thing made to be exactly like another: *John asked his secretary to make him 4 copies of the letter* **2** [C] a single example of a magazine, book, newspaper, etc.: *Did you get your copy of "The Times" today?* **3** [U] *tech* written material ready to be printed: *The printers are waiting for more copy* **4 good copy** interesting news: *The dismissal of the minister of foreign affairs will make good copy in the newspapers* —see also KNOCK UP **copy**

copy[2] *v* **1** [T1 (*for*)] to make a copy of (something) **2** [T1] to follow (someone or something) as a standard or pattern: *Jean always copies the way I dress. What I wear today she wears tomorrow* **3** [T1; IØ: (*from, off*)] *derog* to cheat by writing or doing (exactly the same thing) as someone else: *You copied this work off Paul. I know because you've made exactly the same mistakes*

cop·y·book /ˈkɒpibʊk‖ˈkɑ-/ *n* **1** a book containing examples of good handwriting, formerly used in schools as a standard for pupils learning to write **2 blot one's copybook** *infml esp. BrE* to spoil one's record: *Gordon blotted his copybook by getting drunk and being sick*

cop·y·boy /ˈkɒpibɔɪ‖ˈkɑ-/ (*fem.* **cop·y·girl** -gɜːl‖-ɜrl)— *n* a young person who does unskilled jobs in a newspaper office

cop·y·cat /ˈkɒpikæt‖ˈkɑ-/ *n* [C;N] *derog infml* **1** a person who regularly and without thought copies other people's behaviour, dress, manners, etc. **2** a child who regularly copies the work of other children at school

cop·y·desk /ˈkɒpidesk‖ˈkɑ-/ *n AmE tech* a desk in a newspaper office where written material (COPY[1] (3)) is checked and prepared for printing

copy ed·i·tor /ˈ·· ˌ···/ *n* a person in a newspaper office who reads through written material (COPY[1] (3)) and prepares it for the printer

cop·y·hold /ˈkɒpihəʊld‖ˈkɑ-/ *n tech* **1** [U] (in former times) the ownership of land on conditions agreed with the lord of the MANOR **2** [C] (in former times) a piece of land held in this way —**~er** *n*

cop·y·ist /ˈkɒpi-ɪ̵st‖ˈkɑ-/ *n* a person who makes written copies; TRANSCRIBER

copy out *v adv* [T1] to write (something) exactly as written elsewhere: *The teacher asked the children to copy out notes from their history book*

cop·y·right[1] /ˈkɒpiraɪt‖ˈkɑ-/ *n* [C;U] the right in law to be the only producer, seller, or broadcaster, of a book, play, film, record, etc., for a fixed period of time: *Who has the copyright of/on/for your book—you or the* PUBLISHER?

cop·y·writ·er /ˈkɒpiraɪtəʳ‖ˈkɑ-/ *n* a person who writes the words for advertisements

coq·ue·try /ˈkɒkɪ̵tri‖ˈkəʊ-/ *n* **1** [U] (of a woman) behaviour intended to attract the attention and admiration of men; FLIRTATIOUS behaviour **2** [C] an example of this

co·quette /kəʊˈket, kɒ-‖kəʊ-/ *n* a woman who tries to attract the attention and admiration of men without having sincere feelings for them; woman who FLIRT*s* with men —**-quettish** *adj* —**-quettishly** *adv*

cor /kɔːʳ/ *interj BrE sl* (an expression used for showing great surprise)

cor- *prefix* (the form used for CON- before *r*-): CORRELATE

cor·a·cle /ˈkɒrəkəl‖ˈkɔ-, ˈkɑ-/ *n* a small light round

boat, built like a WICKER basket and covered with animal skins, sometimes used by fishermen on Irish and Welsh lakes

cor·al[1] /ˈkɒrəl‖ˈkɔ-, ˈkɑ-/ *n* **1** [U] a white, pink, or reddish stonelike or hornlike substance formed from the bones of very small sea animals (POLYPs (1)) which gather together in great numbers. It is often used for making jewellery **2** [C] a piece of this substance **3** [C;Wn2] *infml* POLYP (1)

coral[2] *adj, n* [B;U] (having) a pink or reddish orange colour: *coral lips*

coral is·land /ˌ· ˈ··/ *n* an island formed by a large mass of CORAL[1] (1)

coral reef /ˈ·· ·, ˌ·· ˈ·/ *n* a large mass of CORAL[1] (1) that rises above, or close to, the surface of the sea

cor an·glais /ˌkɔːr ˈɒŋgleɪ‖-ɔŋˈgleɪ/ *AmE* **English horn**— *n* **cors anglais** /ˌkɔːr-/ *Fr* a type of long wooden musical instrument played by blowing. It is like the OBOE but produces a lower note

cor·bel /ˈkɔːbəl‖ˈkɔr-/ *n tech* a piece of stone or wood built out from a wall as a support for a beam or other heavy object

cor bli·mey /ˌkɔː ˈblaɪmi‖ˌkɔr-/ also **blimey**— *interj BrE sl* (an expression used for showing surprise)

cord[1] /kɔːd‖kɔrd/ *n* **1** [C;U] (a length of) thick string or thin rope **2** [C] also **chord**— a part of the body, such as a nerve or number of bones joined together, that is like a length of this in appearance: *the* VOCAL CORDS **3** [C] a raised line on the surface of cloth, such as on CORDUROY **4** [U] cloth, such as corduroy, with raised lines on its surface **5** [C;U] (a piece of) wire with a protective covering, for joining electrical apparatus to a supply of electricity

cord[2] *v* [T1;(IØ)] to tie, bind, or connect with cord

cord·age /ˈkɔːdɪdʒ‖ˈkɔr-/ *n* [U] **1** rope or cord in general **2** the ropes used on board a ship

cor·di·al[1] /ˈkɔːdɪəl‖ˈkɔrdʒəl/ *adj* warmly friendly: *a cordial smile/welcome/invitation*

cordial[2] *n* **1** [U9] fruit juice which is added to water and drunk to make one feel fresher **2** [C;U] LIQUEUR

cor·di·al·i·ty /ˌkɔːdiˈælǝ̣ti‖ˌkɔrdʒiˈæ-/ *n* [U] warm friendliness

cor·di·al·ly /ˈkɔːdɪəli‖ˈkɔrdʒəli/ *adv* **1** in a CORDIAL[1] manner **2 to dislike/hate/etc. each other cordially** to dislike/hate/etc. each other very strongly

cor·dil·le·ra /ˌkɔːdǝ̣lˈjeərə‖ˌkɔr- (*Sp* korðihera)/ *n Sp* a system of mountain ranges, often consisting of several chains of mountains side by side

cor·dite /ˈkɔːdaɪt‖ˈkɔr-/ *n* [U] *tech* smokeless explosive powder

cor·don /ˈkɔːdn‖ˈkɔrdn/ *n* **1** a line or ring of police, soldiers, military vehicles, ships, etc., placed around an area to protect or enclose it **2** *tech* a fruit tree with its branches cut so that it grows as a single stem, esp. against a wall **3** an ornamental band or cord worn as a sign of honour, rank, or membership of an ORDER

cor·don bleu /ˌkɔːdɒŋ ˈblɜː‖ˌkɔrdɔŋ- (*Fr* kɔrdɔ̃ blø)/ *n Fr* **1** *not fml* a very good cook: *She's a real cordon bleu (cook)!* **2** a prize given to a cook or restaurant for high quality cooking: (fig.) *What a splendid meal! It's really cordon bleu (cooking)!*

cordon off *v adv* [T1] to enclose (an area) with a line of police, soldiers, military vehicles, etc.

cords /kɔːdz‖kɔrdz/ also **corduroys** /ˈkɔːdərɔɪz‖ˈkɔr-/— *n* [P] *infml* trousers made from CORDUROY —see PAIR (USAGE)

cor·du·roy /ˈkɔːdərɔɪ‖ˈkɔr-/ *n* [U] thick strong cotton cloth with thin raised lines on it, used esp. for making outer clothing

corduroy road /ˌ··· ˈ·/ *n* (esp. in the US) a rough road made from tree trunks or logs laid side by side

core[1] /kɔːʳ‖kor/ *n* **1** the hard or solid central part containing the seeds of certain fruits, such as the apple —see picture at FRUIT[1] **2** the most important or central part of anything **3** a bar of soft iron or other MAGNETIC metal used in an electric motor to provide a path for the MAGNETIC field and increase its strength **4 rotten to the core** thoroughly bad **5 to the core a** right to the centre **b** thoroughly; completely —see also HARD CORE

core[2] *v* [T1] to remove the CORE[1] (1) from (a fruit)

co·re·li·gion·ist /ˌkəʊrǝ̣ˈlɪdʒənǝ̣st/ *n* [(*of*)] a member of the same religion

cor·er /ˈkɔːrəʳ‖ˈkorər/ *n* a specially shaped knife for coring (CORE[2]) apples

co·re·spon·dent /ˌkəʊrǝ̣ˈspɒndənt‖-ˈspɑn-/ *n law* a person charged with ADULTERY (=sex outside marriage) with the wife or husband (the RESPONDENT) of a person wanting a DIVORCE (=an end to the marriage) —compare CORRESPONDENT

cor·gi /ˈkɔːgi‖ˈkɔrgi/ *n* **corgis** a type of small dog with short legs, a long back, and a foxlike head

co·ri·an·der /ˌkɒriˈændəʳ‖ˌko-/ *n* **1** [C;U] a type of small plant with hot-tasting seeds **2** [U] the seeds of this plant, dried and used to give a special taste to food

Co·rin·thi·an /kəˈrɪnθɪən/ *adj* [Wa5] of, related to, like, or typical of the most richly ornamented style of ancient Greek ARCHITECTURE (=building) —compare DORIC, IONIC

cork[1] /kɔːk‖kɔrk/ *n* **1** [U] the light springy outer covering (BARK) of the **cork oak** (=a tree from Southern Europe and North Africa) **2** [C] **a** a round piece of this material fixed into the neck of a bottle to close it tightly **b** an object like this made from rubber or plastic

cork[2] *v* [T1 (UP)] to close (the neck of a bottle or other object) tightly with a CORK[1] (2)

cork·age /ˈkɔːkɪdʒ‖ˈkɔr-/ *n* [U] *BrE* the charge made by a hotel or restaurant owner for opening and serving wine which people have brought with them

corked /kɔːkt‖kɔrkt/ *adj BrE* **1** (of wine) having an unpleasant taste because of a bad or decaying CORK[1] (2) **2** *sl* very drunk

cork·er /ˈkɔːkəʳ‖ˈkɔr-/ *n infml* **1** a very interesting, noticeable, or excellent person or thing **2** *BrE* an unanswerable argument; point of view which puts an end to a course of action or conversation **3** *BrE* a daring lie

cork·screw /ˈkɔːkskruː‖ˈkɔrk-/ *n* **1** an apparatus of twisted metal with a metal, plastic, or wooden handle, used for drawing CORKs[1] (2) out of bottles **2** SPIRAL

cork up *v adv* [T1] *infml* BOTTLE UP

corm /kɔːm‖kɔrm/ *n* the thick round underground stem of certain plants, from which the flowers and leaves grow in the spring

cor·mo·rant /ˈkɔːmərənt‖ˈkɔr-/ *n* a type of large black fish-eating seabird with a long neck and a beak shaped like a hook —see picture at WATER[1]

corn[1] /kɔːn‖kɔrn/ *n* [U] **1** *BrE* (the seed of) any of various types of grain plants, esp. wheat **2** also (*esp. BrE*) **maize, Indian corn**— *esp. AmE & AustrE* (the seed of) a type of tall plant grown, esp. in America and Australia, for its ears of yellow seeds: SWEET CORN —see picture at CEREAL

corn[2] *v* [Wv5;T1] to preserve (meat) by preserving in salt or covering with salty water

corn[3] *n* **1** a painful area of thick hard skin on the foot, usu. on or near a toe **2 tread on someone's corns** *infml* to hurt someone's feelings; offend someone personally

corn bread /ˈ· ·/ *n* [U] (esp. in the US) coarse

bread made from crushed CORN[1] (2)

corn·cob /ˈkɔːnkɒb‖ˈkɔrnkɑb/ *n* the woody central part of an ear of CORN[1] (2): *smoked a corncob pipe*

corn·crake /ˈkɔːnkreɪk‖ˈkɔrn-/ *n* a type of common European bird with a loud sharp cry

cor·ne·a /ˈkɔːnɪə‖ˈkɔr-/ *n* a strong transparent protective covering on the front outer surface of the eye —see picture at EYE[1] —**~l** *adj* [Wa5]

cor·ne·li·an /kɔːˈniːlɪən‖kɔr-/ also **carnelian**— *n* a type of reddish, reddish-brown, or white stone used in jewellery or ornaments

cor·ner[1] /ˈkɔːnəʳ‖ˈkɔr-/ *n* **1** (the inside or outside of) the point at which 2 lines, surfaces, or edges meet: *the bottom corners of the page|He fell and hit his head on the corner of a box* **2** the area formed where 2 lines, surfaces, or edges, meet: *The number is in the top right-hand corner of the page* **3** the place where 2 roads, paths, or streets, meet: *I'll meet you on/at the corner of Smith Street and Beach Road* **4** [*often pl.*] a part of the world, esp. a distant one: *People have come from all the corners of the world to hear this lady sing* **5** [C (*on*)] a position which allows complete control over the production, buying, or selling, of certain goods: *a corner on the cotton* MARKET **6** [C] also **corner kick** /ˈ·· ·/ (in football) a kick taken from the corner of the field **7 around/round the corner** very near **8 cut corners** *infml* to do something in the easiest or quickest way, by paying no attention to rules, using simpler methods, etc. **9 cut off a/the corner** *esp. BrE* to go across a piece of grass, special area, etc., instead of walking round it **10 drive/force/put (someone) into a corner** to put (someone) into a difficult or threatening position from which to escape is difficult **11 be in a tight corner** to be in a difficult or threatening position from which escape is difficult **12 turn the corner** to become better after an illness, period of difficulties, etc.

corner[2] *v* **1** [Wv5;T1] to force (a person or animal) into a difficult or threatening position: *fought like a cornered animal* **2** [T1] to gain control of (the buying, selling, or production of goods): *By defeating their main competitor this firm has cornered the wheat market* **3** [IØ] (of a vehicle, driver, etc.) to turn a corner: *My car corners well even in bad weather*

corner[3] *adj* [Wa5;A] **1** used or shaped for use in a corner: *a corner table* **2** being at a corner: *a corner shop|a corner seat* **3** (in certain games, such as football) of or related to the corners of a playing area: *a corner kick*

-cor·nered /ˌkɔːnəd‖ˌkɔrnərd/ *comb. form* [→adj] having the stated number or kind of corners: *a 3-cornered hat*

cor·ner·stone /ˈkɔːnəstəʊn‖ˈkɔrnər-/ *n* **1** [C] a stone set at one of the bottom corners of a building, often put in place at a special ceremony **2** [C9] something of first importance

cor·net /ˈkɔːnɪ̧t‖kɔrˈnet/ *n* **1** a small brass musical instrument, played by blowing, very like a TRUMPET but with a softer sound **2** *BrE* also (*esp. AmE*) **cone**— a specially shaped thin pastry container, round at one end and pointed at the other, for ice-cream, eaten together with its contents **3** *BrE* also (*esp. AmE*) **cone**— this container and the ice-cream it holds

corn ex·change /ˈ· ·ˌ·/ *n* a place where corn is bought and sold WHOLESALE

corn·field /ˈkɔːnfiːld‖ˈkɔrn-/ *n* a field where corn is grown

corn·flakes /ˈkɔːnfleɪks‖ˈkɔrn-/ *n* [P] small FLAKEs made from coarsely crushed corn, usu. eaten at breakfast, often with milk, sugar, and fruit added

corn flour /ˈ· ·/ *AmE* **corn·starch** /ˈkɔːnstɑːtʃ‖ˈkɔrnstɑrtʃ/— *n* [U] a fine white flour made from crushed corn, rice, or other grain, used in cooking to thicken liquids

corn·flow·er /ˈkɔːnflaʊəʳ‖ˈkɔrn-/ *n* a type of small wild European plant sometimes grown in gardens for its showy blue, white, or pink flowers

cor·nice /ˈkɔːnɪ̧s‖ˈkɔr-/ *n* **1** [C;(U)] an ornamental border at the top edge of the front of a building or pillar or round the top inside edges of the walls in a room **2** [C] a mass of snow, ice, rocks, etc., hanging over the edge of a cliff, roof, etc., and seeming likely to fall

Cor·nish /ˈkɔːnɪʃ‖ˈkɔr-/ *adj* [Wa5] of Cornwall or its language

Cornish pas·ty /ˌ·· ˈ··/ *n* a folded piece of pastry baked with meat and potatoes in it, usu. enough for one person to eat

Corn Laws /ˈ· ·/ *n* [*the*+P] a number of laws in force in the United Kingdom before 1846, intended to keep grain prices high by preventing the bringing of foreign grain into the country

corn pone /ˈ· ·/ *n* [U] *AmE* PONE

cor·nu·co·pi·a /ˌkɔːnjʊˈkəʊpɪə‖ˌkɔrnə-/ *n* a horn-shaped ornamental container overflowing with fruit, flowers, grain, etc., used in art as a sign of plenty; horn of plenty

corn·y /ˈkɔːni‖ˈkɔrni/ *adj* [Wa1] *infml* old-fashioned; simple; said or repeated too often: *a corny joke/film/play|corny acting*

co·rol·la /kəˈrɒlə‖-ˈrɑ-/ *n tech* the part of a flower formed by the PETALs, usu. brightly coloured to attract insects —see picture at FLOWER[1]

co·rol·la·ry /kəˈrɒləri‖ˈkɔrəleri, ˈkɑ-/ *n fml* **1** something that naturally follows from something else; result **2** a statement that follows, without needing further proof, from another statement for which proof exists

co·ro·na /kəˈrəʊnə/ *n* **-nas** *or* **-nae** /niː/ the shining irregularly-shaped circle of light seen round the sun when the moon passes in front of it

cor·o·na·ry /ˈkɒrənəri‖ˈkɔrəneri, ˈkɑ-/ *adj* [Wa5; A;(B)] *med* **1** *tech* of or related to either of the blood vessels that supply blood directly to the heart **2** of or related to the heart

coronary throm·bo·sis /ˌ···· ·ˈ··/ also (*infml*) **coronary**— *n* **-ses** a medical condition in which there is a blood CLOT in either of the blood vessels supplying blood directly to the heart; HEART ATTACK

cor·o·na·tion /ˌkɒrəˈneɪʃən‖ˌkɔ-, ˌkɑ-/ *n* the ceremony at which a king, queen, ruling prince, etc., is crowned

cor·o·ner /ˈkɒrənəʳ‖ˈkɔ-, ˈkɑ-/ *n* a public official who inquires into the cause of a person's death when it is not clearly the result of natural causes

coroner's in·quest /ˌ··· ˈ··/ also **inquest**— *n* an official inquiry at which a CORONER tries to find out the cause of a person's death

cor·o·net /ˈkɒrənɪ̧t‖ˌkɔrəˈnet, ˌkɑ-/ *n* **1** a crown worn by princes or noblemen, like that of a king or queen, but smaller **2** a band of precious metal and jewels worn on the head by rich women on special occasions; TIARA (1)

Corp. /kɔːp‖kɔrp/ *abbrev. for:* **1** CORPORAL **2** CORPORATION

cor·po·ra /ˈkɔːpərə‖ˈkɔr-/ *pl. of* CORPUS

cor·po·ral[1] /ˈkɔːpərəl‖ˈkɔr-/ *adj* [Wa5] *fml* of, on, or related to the body; bodily: *corporal punishment*

corporal[2] *n* [C;A;N] a NONCOMMISSIONED OFFICER of low rank in the army or British air force

cor·po·rate /ˈkɔːpərɪ̧t‖ˈkɔr-/ *adj* **1** [B] of, belonging to, or shared by all the members of a group; COLLECTIVE: *corporate responsibility/effort* **2** [Wa5; B] of, belonging to, or related to a CORPORATION (1,2) **3** [Wa5;B;E] being or forming a single body: *the university became a body corporate/a corporate body* —**~ly** *adv*

cor·po·ra·tion /ˌkɔːpəˈreɪʃən‖ˌkɔr-/ *n* **1** [GC] *not fml* a group of people (COUNCIL) elected to govern a town **2** [GC] a body of people permitted by law to act as a single person, esp. for purposes of business, with rights and duties separate from those of its members: *John works for a large American chemical corporation* **3** [C] *sl* a very large fat stomach

corporation tax /ˌ‥ˈ‥ ·/ *n* [C;U] *tech* a tax on a firm's profits

cor·po·re·al /kɔːˈpɔːrɪəl‖kɔrˈpor-/ *adj* [Wa5] *fml* **1** of or for the body as opposed to the spirit **2** that can be touched; material; PHYSICAL —**~ly** *adv*

corps /kɔːʳ‖kor/ *n* **corps** /kɔːz‖korz/ **1** [GC] *often cap.* a trained army group with special duties and responsibilities: *the medical corps* **2** [GC] *often cap.* a branch of the army equal in size to 2 DIVISIONs **3** [GC9] a group of people united in the same activity: *the president's* PRESS *corps|the* DIPLOMATIC *corps*

corps de bal·let /ˌkɔː də ˈbæleɪ‖ˌkor də bæˈleɪ, -ˈbæleɪ/ *n* [GC] *Fr & tech* BALLET (4)

corpse /kɔːps‖korps/ *n* a dead body, esp. of a person

cor·pu·lence /ˈkɔːpjʊləns‖ˈkorpjə-/ also **cor·pu·len·cy** /-lənsi/— *n* [U] the state of being very fat

cor·pu·lent /ˈkɔːpjʊlənt‖ˈkorpjə-/ *adj* very fat

cor·pus /ˈkɔːpəs‖ˈkor-/ *n* **corpora** /ˈkɔːpərə‖ˈkor-/ *or* **corpuses** a collection **a** of all the writings of a special kind, on a special subject, or by a certain person: *the corpus of Shakespeare's works* **b** of material or information for study: *The dictionary is based on a corpus of 10,000,000 words taken from English books and newspapers*

cor·pus·cle /ˈkɔːpəsəl, kɔːˈpʌ-‖ˈkorpə-/ *n* any of the red or white cells in the blood

corpus de·lic·ti /ˌkɔːpəs dɪˈlɪktaɪ‖ˌkor-/ *n* **corpora delicti** /ˌkɔːpərə-‖ˌkor-/ *Lat* the facts which together show that a criminal act has taken place

cor·ral¹ /kɒˈrɑːl, kə-‖kəˈræl/ *n* **1** (esp. in Western America) an enclosed area where cattle, horses, etc., are kept **2** an enclosed area within a ring of carts for protection against attack

corral² *v* **-ll-** [T1] **1** to drive (animals) into a CORRAL¹ (1) **2** to arrange (carts) into a ring for protection against attack

cor·rect¹ /kəˈrekt/ *v* [T1] **1** to make right; mark the mistakes in: *Correct my spelling if it's wrong* **2** to cure of a fault, esp. by punishing: *Parents seem unwilling to correct their children these days*

correct² *adj* **1** right; without mistakes: *a correct answer|correct spelling* **2** keeping to proper standards of manners, behaviour, etc.: *It is not correct to speak while one's mouth is full* —**~ly** *adv* —**~ness** *n* [U]

cor·rec·tion /kəˈrekʃən/ *n* **1** [U] the act of CORRECTing¹ **2** [C] a change that corrects something; improvement: *Teachers usually make corrections in red ink* **3** [U] *euph* punishment: *The prisoner was sent to a labour camp for correction*

cor·rec·ti·tude /kəˈrektɪ̈tjuːd‖-tuːd/ *n* [U] *fml* correctness of behaviour

cor·rec·tive /kəˈrektɪv/ *adj, n* [Wa5] (something) intended or tending to correct: *The criminals were sent to prison for corrective punishment* —**~ly** *adv*

cor·re·late¹ /ˈkɒrɪ̈leɪt‖ˈkɔ-, ˈkɑ-/ *n* either of 2 very closely or causally connected things: *Smoking and diseases of the lungs are thought to be correlates*

correlate², **corelate** *v* [IØ;T1 (*with*)] to (show to) have a close shared relationship or causal connection: *It is interesting to correlate the history of the 19th century with its literature*

cor·re·la·tion /ˌkɒrɪ̈ˈleɪʃən‖ˌkɔ-, ˌkɑ-/ *n* **1** [C (*between*)] a shared relationship or causal connection: *a high correlation between unemployment and crime* **2** [U] *fml* (an example of) the act of correlating (CORRELATE²) **3** [C] *tech* a GRAPH showing the closeness of the relationship between 2 sets of figures

cor·rel·a·tive /kəˈrelətɪv/ *adj, n* [Wa5] **1** *fml* (any of 2 or more things that are) naturally related **2** *tech* (either of 2 words) regularly used together but rarely used next to each other: *"Either" and "or" are correlative* CONJUNCTIONs

cor·re·spond /ˌkɒrɪ̈ˈspɒnd‖ˌkɔrɪ̈ˈspɑnd, ˌkɑ-/ *v* [IØ] **1** [(*with, to*)] to be in agreement; match: *These goods don't correspond with/to the list of those I ordered* **2** [(*to*)] to be like or equal; match closely: *Does the Irish word "*COLLEEN*" correspond to the English word "girl"?* **3** [(*with*)] to exchange letters regularly: *Janet and Bob corresponded for many years before they met*

cor·re·spon·dence /ˌkɒrɪ̈ˈspɒndəns‖ˌkɔrɪ̈ˈspɑn-, ˌkɑ-/ *n* [U;C] **1** agreement between particular things; likeness **2** the act of exchanging letters **3** the letters exchanged between people: *The library bought all the correspondence between Queen Victoria and her daughters*

correspondence course /ˌ‥ˈ‥ ·/ *n* an educational course for people who cannot attend a school or college. Information and work are exchanged between the teacher and student by post

cor·re·spon·dent¹ /ˌkɒrɪ̈ˈspɒndənt‖ˌkɔrɪ̈ˈspɑn-, ˌkɑ-/ *adj* [Wa5] **1** [(*with*)] *fml* being in agreement; fitting; matching: *The result was correspondent with my wishes* **2** CORRESPONDING

correspondent² *n* **1** a person with whom another person exchanges letters regularly **2** someone employed by a newspaper, television or radio station, etc., to report news from a distant area: *a war correspondent|news from our own correspondent* **3** a person or firm that has regular business relations with a person or firm abroad

cor·re·spon·ding /ˌkɒrɪ̈ˈspɒndɪŋ‖ˌkɔrɪ̈ˈspɑn-, ˌkɑ-/ *adj* matching; related: *All rights carry with them corresponding responsibilities* —**~ly** *adv*

cor·ri·dor /ˈkɒrɪ̈dɔːʳ‖ˈkɔrɪ̈dər, ˈkɑ-/ *n* **1** a passage, esp. enclosed: *You'll find Room 101 at the end of the corridor* **2** a narrow piece of land that passes through a foreign country: *the Polish Corridor (to the sea)* —*see also* AIR CORRIDOR

corridor train /ˈ‥· ·/ *n* a train with carriages divided into COMPARTMENTs, with a corridor down one side

cor·rie /ˈkɒri‖ˈkɔri, ˈkɑri/ *n ScotE* CIRQUE

cor·ri·gen·dum /ˌkɒrɪ̈ˈdʒendəm‖ˌkɔ-, ˌkɑ-/ *n* **-da** /də/ *tech* something to be made correct, esp. in a printed book

cor·rob·o·rate /kəˈrɒbəreɪt‖kəˈrɑ-/ *v* [T1] to support or strengthen (an opinion, belief, idea, etc.) by fresh information or proof: *A person who saw the road accident corroborated the driver's statement* —**-rator** *n*

cor·rob·o·ra·tion /kəˌrɒbəˈreɪʃən‖kəˌrɑ-/ *n* [U] **1** the act of corroborating (CORROBORATE) **2** (additional) information which CORROBORATEs an opinion, belief, idea, etc.

cor·rob·o·ra·tive /kəˈrɒbərətɪv‖kəˈrɑ-/ *adj* (of a person, information, etc.) intending or tending to CORROBORATE an opinion, belief, etc.

cor·rob·o·ree /kəˈrɒbəriː‖kəˈrɑ-/ *n AustrE* **1** a ceremonial dance done by Australian ABORIGINEs on special occasions **2** *infml* a noisy party, dance, etc.

cor·rode /kəˈrəʊd/ *v* [T1;IØ: (AWAY)] to (cause to) become worn or be destroyed slowly, esp. by chemical action: *Acid causes metal to corrode*

cor·ro·sion /kəˈrəʊʒən/ *n* [U] **1** the act of corroding (CORRODE) **2** a substance, such as RUST, produced by this act: *The corrosion on the car's* *body showed it had been badly treated*

cor·ro·sive /kəˈrəʊsɪv/ *adj* **1** able or tending to CORRODE **2** weakening or destroying society, a person's feelings, etc.: *the corrosive influence of industrial society* **3** (of language) very fierce: *a corrosive attack on the government's plans, printed in a newspaper* —**~ly** *adv* —**~ness** *n* [U]

cor·ru·gate /ˈkɒrəgeɪt‖ˈkɔ-, ˈkɑ-/ *v* [Wv5;T1;IØ] to (cause to) have wavelike folds: *Sheets of corrugated iron are often used by builders for roofs and fences* —see picture at ROOF[1]

cor·ru·ga·tion /ˌkɒrəˈgeɪʃən‖ˌkɔ-, ˌkɑ-/ *n* **1** [U] the act of corrugating (CORRUGATE) **2** [C] a fold in a CORRUGATEd surface

cor·rupt[1] /kəˈrʌpt/ *v* **1** [T1;IØ] to make morally bad; cause to change from good to bad: *Complete power corrupts completely* **2** [T1] to influence (a person, esp. a public official) improperly; BRIBE: *He was sent to prison for trying to corrupt a policeman with money* **3** [Wv5;T1] to change the original form of (a language, set of teachings, etc.) in a bad way: *Has English been corrupted or made richer by the introduction of foreign words?* —**~ible** *adj* —**~ibility** /kəˌrʌptəˈbɪlᵻti/ *n* [U]

corrupt[2] *adj* **1** immoral; wicked; bad: *a corrupt film, full of sex and violence* **2** dishonest; open to BRIBERY (=the buying and selling of favours for gifts or money): *a corrupt judge* **3** containing mistakes; different from the original: *They spoke a corrupt form of French* —**~ly** *adv* —**~ness** *n* [U]

cor·rup·tion /kəˈrʌpʃən/ *n* **1** [U] the act of CORRUPTing[1] **2** [U] dishonesty; immoral behaviour; the state of being CORRUPT[2] (2): *the corruption of the ancient Roman court* **3** [U] decay; impurity: *The corruption of the body after death* **4** [C *usu. sing.*] a movement away from the pure original form of a language, set of teachings, etc.: *This is not true Christianity but a corruption of it*

cor·sage /kɔːˈsɑːʒ‖kɔr-/ *n* **1** *tech* the upper part of a woman's dress, esp. round the breasts **2** a small bunch of flowers worn by a woman at the neck or waist of her dress

cor·sair /ˈkɔːseəʳ‖ˈkɔr-/ *n* **1** a PIRATE from North Africa who sailed the seas stopping and robbing ships in former times **2** the ship sailed by a group of such PIRATE*s*

corse /kɔːs‖kɔrs/ *n old use & poet* CORPSE

corse·let[1] /ˈkɔːslət‖ˈkɔr-/ *n* a piece of armour worn in former times on the upper part of the body, but not usu. covering the arms

cor·se·let[2] /ˈkɔːslᵻt‖ˌkɔrsəˈlet/ *n* a light CORSETlike undergarment for women

cor·set /ˈkɔːsᵻt‖ˈkɔr-/ *n* a very tight-fitting undergarment worn, esp. by women, to give shape to the waist and HIP*s* —**~ed** *adj* [Wa5]

cor·tege, -tège /kɔːˈteɪʒ‖kɔrˈteʒ/ *n* [GC] *fml* a procession of attendants, esp. at a funeral

cor·tex /ˈkɔːteks‖ˈkɔr-/ *n* **-tices** /tᵻsiːz/ *tech* **1** the outer covering of an organ or part of the body, esp. the grey matter covering the outer surface of the brain **2** the part of a plant's stem or root between the skin and the wood in the middle, such as the BARK of a tree —**cortical** /ˈkɔːtɪkəl‖ˈkɔr-/ *adj* [Wa5]

cor·ti·sone /ˈkɔːtᵻzəʊn‖ˈkɔrtᵻsəʊn/ *n* [U] a powerful substance used esp. in treating RHEUMATIC diseases

co·run·dum /kəˈrʌndəm/ *n* [U] a very hard mineral used in powder form for polishing and sharpening tools

cor·us·cate /ˈkɒrəskeɪt‖ˈkɔ-, ˈkɑ-/ *v* [Wv4;IØ] *fml* **1** to flash; shine: *a coruscating jewel* **2** to be clever or showy in style: *coruscating humour* —**-cation** /ˌkɒrəˈskeɪʃən‖ˌkɔ-, ˌkɑ-/ *n* [U]

cor·vée /ˈkɔːveɪ‖ˈkɔr-/ *n* [U; *the*+R;C] *tech* (in former times) unpaid work done instead of paying taxes to one's lord or the government

cor·vette /kɔːˈvet‖kɔr-/ *n* **1** *tech* a small fast warship used for protecting other ships from attack, esp. by SUBMARINE*s* (=underwater vessels) **2** (in former times) a small sailing warship with one row of guns along each side

cos[1] /kəz/ *conj infml* because

cos[2] /kɒs‖kɑs/ *abbrev. for:* COSINE

cosh[1] /kɒʃ‖kɑʃ/ *n infml esp. BrE* a short metal pipe or rubber tube, usu. filled with a heavy material such as wood, metal, or stone, used as a weapon

cosh[2] *v* [T1] *infml esp. BrE* to strike (someone or something) with a COSH[1]

co·sig·na·to·ry /ˌkeʊˈsɪgnətəri‖-tori/ *n fml* a person signing together with others: *Britain, France, and Germany were all cosignatories of the agreement*

co·sine /ˈkəʊsaɪn/ *n tech* the FRACTION (2) calculated for an angle by dividing the length of the side next to it in a right-angled TRIANGLE by the length of the side opposite the right angle —see picture at TRIGONOMETRY

cos let·tuce /ˌkɒs ˈletᵻs‖ˌkɑs-, ˌkəʊs/ also **cos**— *n* [C;(U)] a type of LETTUCE with long leaves

cos·met·ic[1] /kɒzˈmetɪk‖kɑz-/ *n* [*usu. pl.*] a preparation such as a face-cream, body-powder, etc., intended to make the skin or hair more beautiful: *Mother has a special cosmetic(s) bag for keeping her cosmetics in*

cosmetic[2] *adj* **1** [Wa5] of, related to, or causing increased beauty of the skin or hair: *a cosmetic cream* **2** *derog* dealing only with the noticeable part of a matter or difficulty; intended to hide something bad

cos·me·ti·cian /ˌkɒzməˈtɪʃən‖ˌkɑz-/ *n* a person professionally trained in the use of COSMETIC*s*[1]

cos·mic /ˈkɒzmɪk‖ˈkɑz-/ *adj* [Wa5] of or related to the whole universe —**~ally** *adv* [Wa4,5]

cosmic dust /ˌ·· ˈ·/ *n* [U] very small pieces of matter floating freely in space

cosmic ray /ˌ·· ˈ·/ *n* [*usu. pl.*] a stream of RADIATION reaching the earth from outer space

cos·mog·o·ny /kɒzˈmɒgəni‖kɑzˈmɑ-/ *n* **1** [U] the study of the origin and development of the universe **2** [C] a set of principles intended to explain the origin and development of the universe

cos·mol·o·gy /kɒzˈmɒlədʒi‖kɑzˈmɑ-/ *n* **1** [U] the study of the origin and arrangement of the universe **2** [C] a set of principles intended to explain the origin and arrangement of the universe

cos·mo·naut /ˈkɒzmənɔːt‖ˈkɑz-/ *n* a Soviet ASTRONAUT

cos·mo·pol·i·tan[1] /ˈkɒzməˈpɒlᵻtn‖ˈkɑzməˈpɑ-/ *adj* **1** consisting of people from many different parts of the world: *a cosmopolitan crowd at a meeting of United Nations representatives* **2** (of a person, belief, opinion, etc.) not narrow-minded; showing wide experience **3** *tech* (of an animal or plant) existing in most parts of the world, under various natural conditions

cosmopolitan[2] *n* **1** a person who has gained wide experience of the world by travelling widely **2** *derog or apprec* a person with wide interests and international opinions, who would feel at home anywhere, or who feels at home nowhere: *rootless cosmopolitans|an amusing cosmopolitan*

cos·mos[1] /ˈkɒzmɒs‖ˈkɑzməs/ *n* [*the*+R;(C)] the whole universe considered as an ordered system

cosmos[2] *n* **cosmos** *or* **cosmoses** [Wn2] a type of garden plant with showy pink, white, or red flowers

cos·set /ˈkɒsᵻt‖ˈkɑ-/ *v* **-tt-** [Wv5;T1] to pay a great deal of attention to making (a person) comfortable and contented; treat very kindly

cost[1] /kɒst‖kɔst/ *n* **1** [C *often pl. with sing. meaning*] the price of making or producing something: *Their prices are high because production costs are very great* **2** [(*the*) S] the amount paid or asked for goods or services; price: *If you buy more than 10 books we will reduce the cost of each book by 10%* **3** [(*the*) S;U] something needed, given, or lost, to obtain something: *He saved his daughters from the fire but at the cost of his own life* **4 count the cost** to consider all the disadvantages before doing something **5 to one's cost** to one's disadvantage or loss; from one's own unpleasant experience: *I know to my cost that a broken leg can be very painful* —see also COSTS

cost[2] *v* **cost 1** [L1;D1 *no pass.*] to have (an amount of money) as a price: *It will cost you £50 to fly to Paris.|The best goods usually cost most* **2** [D1 *no pass*] to cause (a person) (loss or disadvantage): *Your crime will cost you your life* **3** [T1 *no pass.*] *sl esp. BrE* to be costly for (someone): *It will cost you to go by train, why not go by bus*

USAGE The **price** of a thing is what it **costs** to you, or what the person who is selling it **charges** you for it: *What is the* **price** *of this watch?|What does it* **cost**? The **value** of a thing is what it is worth: *He sold it at a* **price** *below its real* **value**. **Cost**, not **price**, is used **a** for services: *the* **cost** *of having the house painted.* **b** for more general things: *the* **cost** *of living.* **Expense** is used like **cost**, esp. when this is thought of as too large: *the terrible* **expense** *of having the house painted.* A person **charges** a **charge**, a **price**, or (for professional services) a **fee**. A thing **costs** a sum of money: *This watch* **costs** *£10.*

cost[3] *v* [T1] to calculate the price to be charged for (a job, someone's time, etc.): *The job was costed by the builder at about £150*

cost ac·coun·tant /ˈ· ·ˌ··/ *BrE* also **cost clerk** /ˈ· ·/— *n* a person who keeps a record of all the costs of production in a business, firm, etc. —**cost accounting** *n* [U]

co-star[1] /ˈkəʊ stɑːʳ/ *n* a famous actor or actress who appears together with another famous actor or actress in a moving picture or television play

co-star[2] *v* **-rr- 1** [IØ (*with*)] to appear as a CO-STAR[1] in a moving picture: *Who's co-starring with Robert Redford in this new moving picture?* **2** [T1] (of a moving picture or television play) to have (someone) as a CO-STAR[1]: *"Co-starring Glenda Jackson and Richard Burton"*

cos·ter·mon·ger /ˈkɒstəˌmʌŋgəʳ‖ˈkɑstərˌmɑŋ-/ also **coster** /ˈkɒstəʳ‖ˈkɑ-/— *n BrE* a person who sells fruit and vegetables from a cart in the street, esp. in London

cost·ive /ˈkɒstɪv‖ˈkɑ-/ *adj* [Wa5] *rare* suffering from or causing CONSTIPATION

cost·ly /ˈkɒstli‖ˈkɔstli/ *adj* [Wa2] **1** having a high price; EXPENSIVE **2** gained or won at a great loss: *the costliest war in our history* —**-liness** *n* [U]

cost of liv·ing /ˌ· · ˈ··/ *n* [(*the*) R9;(S9)] the cost of buying the goods and services thought necessary to provide a person with the average accepted standard of living: *As the cost of living goes up my* **standard of living** *goes down*

cost price /ˌ· ˈ·/ *n* [C; *at*+U] the price a shopkeeper pays for an article, as opposed to the price he charges the buyer

costs /kɒsts‖kɔsts/ *n* [P] **1** the cost of taking a matter to a court of law, esp. as ordered to be paid to the winning side by the losers in the case **2 at all costs** whatever may/might happen

cos·tume /ˈkɒstjʊm‖ˈkɑstuːm/ *n* **1** [U] the clothes or style of dress typical of a certain period, country, rank or profession, esp. as worn on the stage by an actor or actress: *actors in policemen's costumes* **2** [C] a suit or dress of this sort **3** [C] *becoming rare* a woman's suit consisting of a skirt and short coat made from the same material

costume ball /ˈ·· ˌ·/ *n* FANCY DRESS BALL

costume jew·elle·ry /ˈ·· ˌ···/ *n* [U] precious-looking jewellery made from cheap materials

cos·tu·mi·er /kɒˈstjuːmɪəʳ‖kɑˈstuː-/ also **cos·tum·er** /ˈkɒstjuːməʳ‖ˈkɑstuː-/— *n* a person who makes or deals in COSTUMEs, esp. for the stage

co·sy[1], *AmE* usu. **cozy** /ˈkəʊzi/ *adj* [Wa1] *apprec* warm and comfortable: *a cosy little house* —**cosily** *adv* —**cosiness** *n* [U]

cosy[2], *AmE* usu. **cozy** *n* a covering put over a boiled egg or teapot to keep the contents warm: *a tea cosy*

cot[1] /kɒt‖kɑt/ *n poet* a small house; hut; COTTAGE

cot[2] *n* **1** *AmE* **crib**— a small bed for a young child, usu. with movable sides so that the child cannot fall out —see picture at BEDROOM **2** *AmE* CAMP BED

cot[3] *abbrev. for:* COTANGENT

co·tan·gent /kəʊˈtændʒənt/ *n tech* the FRACTION calculated for an angle by dividing the length of the sides next and opposite to it in a right angled TRIANGLE —see picture at SINE

cote /kəʊt/ *n* (*often in comb.*) a hut or shelter for small animals, esp. birds, kept as pets or for profit: *a* DOVE-*cote*

co·te·rie /ˈkəʊtəri/ *n* a close group of people with common interests, tastes, etc.; CLIQUE: *a small coterie of artists*

co·ter·mi·nous /kəʊˈtɜːmɪ̣nəs‖-ɜr-/ *adj* [Wa5; (*with*)] *fml* touching; sharing the same border: *England is the only country coterminous with Wales* —**~ly** *adv*

co·til·li·on /kəˈtɪlɪən/ *n* **1** a spirited dance of 18th century French origin **2** the music for this **3** *esp. AmE* a formal dance party, esp. one at which young girls are introduced to society

cot·tage /ˈkɒtɪdʒ‖ˈkɑ-/ *n* a small house, esp. in the country

cottage cheese /ˌ·· ˈ·‖ˈ·· ·/ *n* [U] soft white cheese made from sour milk

cottage hos·pi·tal /ˌ·· ˈ···/ *n* a small hospital, usu. in the country

cottage in·dus·try /ˌ·· ˈ···/ *n* [C;U] (an) industry whose labour force consists of people working at home with their own tools or machinery: *Weaving used to be England's most important cottage industry*

cottage loaf /ˌ·· ˈ·/ *n* a loaf of bread made in 2 round pieces with the smaller one stuck on top of the larger one

cottage pie /ˌ·· ˈ·/ *n* [U] *BrE* SHEPHERD'S PIE

cot·tag·er /ˈkɒtɪdʒəʳ‖ˈkɑ-/ *n rare* a person who lives in a country COTTAGE

cot·tar, cotter /ˈkɒtəʳ‖ˈkɑ-/ *n ScotE* a person who lives in a small house owned by a farmer and works on the farm instead of paying rent

cot·ton /ˈkɒtn‖ˈkɑtn/ *n* [U] **1** a type of tall plant grown in warm areas for the soft white hair that surrounds its seeds **2** the soft white hair of this plant used for making thread, cloth, COTTON WOOL, etc. **3** thread or cloth made from this: *a cotton dress|a* REEL *of white cotton*

cotton can·dy /ˌ·· ˈ··/ *n* [U] *AmE* CANDY FLOSS

cotton gin /ˈ·· ·/ *n* a machine that separates seeds and other unwanted objects from COTTON (2)

cotton on *v adv* [IØ (*to*)] *infml* to understand: *He'd been speaking for half an hour before I cottoned on (to what he meant)*

cot·ton·seed /ˈkɒtnsiːd‖ˈkɑtn-/ *n* [U;(C)] (a) seed of the COTTON (1) crushed to obtain **cottonseed oil** /ˌ··· ˈ·/ from which soap, paint, and cooking oil is made

cot·ton·tail /ˈkɒtnteɪl‖ˈkɑtn-/ *n esp. AmE* a small rabbit with a white tail
cotton to *v prep* [T1] *esp. AmE infml* to become friendly with (someone): *John's very friendly and will cotton (up) to anyone easily*
cotton waste /ˌ·· ˈ·/ *n* [U] material left over from cotton production, and used for cleaning machinery
cotton wool /ˌ·· ˈ·/ *n* [U] a soft mass of COTTON (2) used for cleaning parts of the body or putting medical liquids onto it
cot·y·le·don /ˌkɒtəˈliːdn‖ˌkɑ-/ *n tech* a leaflike part within a seed. It contains food for the plant when it starts to grow and protects the stem when it first appears above the soil
couch[1] /kaʊtʃ/ *v* **1** [X9 *usu. pass*] to express (words, a reply, etc.) in a certain way: *The government's refusal was couched in unfriendly language* **2** [T1;IØ] (of an animal) to lay (itself) down in hiding, rest or readiness to attack: *The cat couched (itself) ready to spring*
couch[2] *n* **1** a long piece of furniture, usu. with a back and arms, on which more than one person may sit; SOFA **2** a bed-like piece of furniture on which a person lies when being examined by a doctor
couch·ant /ˈkaʊtʃənt/ *n* [Wa5;E] *tech* (of an animal in a COAT OF ARMS) lying down with the head raised up: *a lion couchant*
cou·chette /kuːˈʃet/ *n not AmE* a narrow shelf-like bed which folds up to the wall when not in use, on which a person can sleep when on a train
couch grass /ˈ· ·/ also **couch**— *n* [U] any of several types of coarse grass that spread by long creeping roots
cou·gar /ˈkuːgəʳ/ also **mountain lion, puma,** *AmE* also **panther**— *n* [Wn1] a large powerful brown wild cat from the mountainous areas of Western North America and South America —see picture at CAT
cough[1] /kɒf‖kɔf/ *v* **1** [IØ] to push air out from the throat suddenly, with a rough explosive noise, one or more times, esp. because of discomfort in the lungs or throat during a cold or other infection **2** [T1 (*up*)] to clear (something) from the throat by doing this: *I knew she was seriously ill when she started to cough up blood* **3** [IØ] to make a sound like a cough: *The engine coughed but would not start* **4** [IØ] *BrE sl* to admit that one has done something wrong or unlawful: *Even after the police threatened him Smith refused to cough*
cough[2] *n* **1** [S] a (medical) condition marked by frequent or repeated coughing: *John had a bad cough this morning but felt well enough to go to work* **2** [C] an act or sound of coughing: *She gave a nervous cough*
cough up *v adv* [T1a] *sl* to produce (esp. money or information) unwillingly
could /kəd; *strong* kʊd/ *v neg. contr.* **couldn't** /ˈkʊdnt/ [Wv2;IØ,2] **1** *past t. of* can: *I can't sing now, but I could when I was young.|I couldn't get the tickets yesterday* (Compare: *Luckily, I was able to get the tickets yesterday*) **2** (used instead of *can* in reported speech): *"I can't go." "He said he couldn't go"* **3** (used, often with *if*, to say that something would or might be possible): *I could come tomorrow (if you like)* (Compare: *I can come tomorrow*, which shows more desire to come).|*You could earn more if you could work a little harder.|"The car won't start", "Couldn't you try pushing it?"* **4** (with requests) would (*more polite than* can):*Could you please hold on a minute?* —compare CAN[1] (10) **5** (suggesting that a person should do something, behave in a certain way, etc.) should; ought to (have): *You could at least have met me at the station, couldn't you?* —compare MIGHT (4) **6** (in CLAUSE*s* expressing purpose) might; would be able to: *I wrote down his telephone number so that I could remember it* —compare MIGHT (3)
USAGE **Could** is the past tense of **can** meaning "permission": *He said we* **could** *smoke*. To express the idea of succeeding in doing something difficult because of one's own powers or efforts, use **manage** *to* or *be* **able** *to*: *I* **managed** *to/was* **able** *to finish my homework in an hour* (=I could and I did). **Could** can be used when we wish only to say that someone had the power or ability: *He* **could**/*was* **able** *to play the piano when he was 3* (not ***managed to** here). Note that as **manage** *to* and **be able** *to* mean "doing" something, they are not usually used in the *pass.*, so that we can say *I was* **able** *to make myself heard* but not **I was* **able** *to be heard.* **Succeed** *in* and **achieve** have the same meaning as **manage** *to*: *to* **succeed** *in finishing the job|to* **achieve** *a good result.* —see CAN (USAGE)
couldn't [Wv2] *contr. of* could not: *"Couldn't you see?" "No, I couldn't"* —see CONTR. (USAGE)
couldst /kʊdst/ **thou couldst** *old use or bibl* (when talking to one person) you could
coul·ter, colter /ˈkəʊltəʳ/ *n tech* a sharp metal blade fixed to the front of a PLOUGH (=a machine for breaking up the soil) to cut the soil ready for lifting and turning by the PLOUGHSHARE (=the main cutting blade)
coun·cil[1] /ˈkaʊnsəl/ *n* [GC; *in*+U] a group of people appointed or elected to make laws, rules, or decisions, for a town, church, etc., or to give advice: *The council of ministers advised the king to dismiss the generals.|Councillor Smith is in council now and won't be free for at least 2 hours*
council[2] *adj* [Wa5;A] **1** *esp. BrE* (of houses, flats, etc.) built, owned, and controlled by the local government of an area **2** used for council meetings: *Official meetings of the town council are always held in the* **council chamber**
coun·cil·lor /ˈkaʊnsələʳ/ *n* [C;A;N] a member of a council —**~ship** *n*
coun·sel[1] /ˈkaʊnsəl/ *n* **1** [U] advice: *They refused to listen to the old man's counsel* **2** [P;(C)] *law* (a group of) one or more lawyers (BARRISTER*s*) acting for someone in a court of law: *The judge asked counsel for the* DEFENCE *to explain his point.|Counsel are agreed* **3 hold/take counsel with (someone)** to ask (someone) for advice: *She took counsel with her lawyer* **4 keep one's own counsel** to keep one's own plans, opinions, etc., secret **5 take counsel together** to ask each other's advice and opinions on a matter of importance
counsel[2] *v* **-ll-** (*AmE* **-l-**) [T1;V3;L9] *fml* to advise: *I have waited for 6 months yet you still counsel patience.|They counselled against travelling at night in such dangerous country*
coun·sel·lor, *AmE* **counselor** /ˈkaʊnsələʳ/ *n* **1** [C] an adviser: *a beauty counsellor|a marriage guidance counsellor* **2** [C;A] *esp. AmE* a lawyer
count[1] /kaʊnt/ *v* **1** [IØ (UP, *to*)] to say or name the numbers in order, one by one or by groups: *He closed his eyes, counted to 100 and then came to look for us.|John's only 4 but he can already count to 20* **2** [T1] to say or name the numbers in regular order up to and including (a particular number): *Count 20 then come and find me* **3** [T1,6] to say or name (objects) one by one in order to find the whole number in a collection; total; add up: *Count the apples in this box.|Have the votes been counted yet?* **4** [T1] to include: *There are 6 people in my family counting my mother and father* **5** [X1] to consider; regard: *After such a bad accident you should count yourself lucky you're alive.|Janet was counted among the greatest dancers of the century.*

6 [I∅] to have value, force, or importance: *It is not how much you read but what you read that counts* **7 count the cost** to consider all risks before making a decision or doing something **8 count for nothing/little** to be of little worth or importance —~**able** *adj*

count² *n* **1** [C] an act of counting; total reached by counting **2** [C (*of*)] one of a number of crimes of which a person is thought to be guilty: *The prisoner was found not guilty on all counts* **3** [U] *infml* account; notice: *I never take any count of what people say about me* **4 keep/lose count** to know/fail to know the exact number: *I've lost count of how many times that actress has been married* **5 take the count** also **be out for the count**—(in BOXING) to be COUNTed OUT

count³ *n* [C;A;N] (*often cap.*) (the title of) a European (not British) nobleman with the rank of EARL

count·a·ble /ˈkaʊntəbəl/ *adj* that can be counted: *A* **countable noun** *can also be called a* COUNT NOUN *and is often marked* [C] *in this dictionary* —opposite **uncountable**

count·down /ˈkaʊntdaʊn/ *n* an act of COUNTing DOWN: *With only 10 seconds to go the scientists had to stop the countdown because of a fault in the spaceship's oxygen supply*

count down *v adv* [I∅] to count backwards in seconds to zero, esp. before sending a space vehicle into space

coun·te·nance¹ /ˈkaʊntɪ̈nəns/ *n fml* **1** [C] the appearance or expression of the face: *a sad/fierce/angry countenance* **2** [U] support; approval: *Your father refuses to give countenance to your plans to marry*

countenance² *v* [T1,4;V4] to give support or approval to; permit; allow: *We will never countenance violence, however serious the threat against us| Your father won't countenance you/your marrying a foreigner*

coun·ter¹ /ˈkaʊntəʳ/ *n* **1** a narrow table or flat surface on which goods are shown or at which people in a shop, bank, etc., are served **2 over the counter** (when buying drugs) without a PRESCRIPTION (=a special note written by a doctor): *You can buy medicine to cure your headache over the counter at many shops* **3 under the counter** privately, secretly, and often unlawfully: *During the war some shopkeepers made a lot of money by selling scarce goods under the counter at high prices*

count·er² *n* **1** a person or machine that counts, esp. an electrical apparatus that records the number of times an event happens **2** a small flat object of metal, plastic, wood, etc., used in games instead of money

counter³ *v* **1** [T1] to oppose; move or act in opposition to (something): *My employer countered my request for more money by threatening to dismiss me* **2** [T1] to make of no value; NULLIFY (2): *The government is trying to counter the general opinion that its actions favour the rich, by increasing income tax on higher incomes* **3** [T1;I∅] to meet (an attack, or blow) with another attack or blow; RETALIATE: *Try to counter with your left* (=left hand)

counter⁴ *adv, adj* [Wa5;F+*to*] (in a manner or direction that is) opposed or opposite: *He acted counter to all advice*

counter⁵ *n* **1** something that is opposed; OPPOSITE **2** a piece of stiff material fitted into the heel of a shoe to give it lasting shape **3** (in BOXING or FENCING) a blow or movement intended to stop and return one's opponent's attack

counter- *prefix* **1** opposite in direction: COUNTERCLOCKWISE|COUNTERMARCH **2** matching; CORRESPONDING: COUNTERPART **3** opposing; done in return: COUNTERATTACK|COUNTERPLOT

coun·ter·act /ˌkaʊntəˈrækt/ *v* [T1] to lessen, reduce, or oppose the effect of (something) by opposite action: *This drug should counteract the snake's poison* —~**ion** /-ˈrækʃən/ *n* [C;U]

coun·ter·at·tack¹ /ˈkaʊntərətæk/ *n* an attack made to stop, oppose, or return an enemy attack

counterattack² *v* [I∅;T1] to make a COUNTERATTACK¹ (on) —~**er** *n*

coun·ter·at·trac·tion /ˌkaʊntərəˈtrækʃən/ *n* an attraction that competes with another

coun·ter·bal·ance¹ /ˈkaʊntəˌbæləns‖-tər-/ also **counterpoise**— *n* **1** a weight or force that acts as a balance for another weight or force **2** a force or influence that stops or opposes another: *His wife's calm nature acts as a counterbalance to his excitability*

counterbalance² /ˌkaʊntəˈbæləns‖-tər-/ also **counterpoise**— *v* [T1] to oppose or balance with an equal weight or force: *The man used his weight to counterbalance the load and prevent it from slipping*

coun·ter·blast /ˈkaʊntəblɑːst‖-tərblæst/ *n* (*used as in newspapers*) a quick violent reply; BACKLASH: *"Minister's Charge Brings Quick Counterblast from Leader of Opposition"* (title of newspaper story)

coun·ter·claim /ˈkaʊntəkleɪm‖-tər-/ *n* an opposing claim, esp. in law

coun·ter·clock·wise /ˌkaʊntəˈklɒkwaɪz‖-tərˈklɑk-/ *adj, adv AmE* ANTICLOCKWISE

coun·ter·es·pi·o·nage /ˈkaʊntərˈespɪənɑːʒ, -nɪdʒ/ *n* [U] ESPIONAGE (= the act of secretly obtaining information about the activities of foreign governments) directed towards uncovering and opposing enemy ESPIONAGE

coun·ter·feit¹ /ˈkaʊntəfɪt‖-tər-/ *v* [T1] to copy (something) closely in order to deceive: *It is against the law to counterfeit money* —~**er** *n*

counterfeit² *adj* [Wa5] made exactly like something real in order to deceive: *a counterfeit coin*

coun·ter·foil /ˈkaʊntəfɔɪl‖-tər-/ *n* a part of a cheque, money order, etc., kept by the sender as a record; STUB

coun·ter·in·tel·li·gence /ˌkaʊntərɪnˈtelɪ̈dʒəns/ *n* [U] activity intended to keep valuable information from the enemy, to deceive the enemy, to prevent SABOTAGE (=activity meant to weaken the state), or to gather political and military information

coun·ter·ir·ri·tant /ˌkaʊntəˈrɪrɪ̈tənt/ *n* [C;U] *med* something put on the skin to produce a slight pain with the intention of reducing a stronger pain

coun·ter·mand /ˌkaʊntəˈmɑːnd, ˈkaʊntəmɑːnd‖ˈkaʊntərmænd/ *v* [T1] **1** to declare (a command already given) ineffective, often by giving a different order **2** to take back (an order for goods): *Mrs Brown wishes to countermand her order for this electric fire*

coun·ter·march /ˈkaʊntəmɑːtʃ‖-tərmɑrtʃ/ *v* [I∅] *tech* (of a group of soldiers) to change direction while continuing to march in the same order —**countermarch** *n* [C]

coun·ter·mea·sure /ˈkaʊntəmeʒəʳ‖-ər-/ also **coun·ter·move** /ˈkaʊntəmuːv‖-ər-/— *n* an action intended to oppose another action or state of affairs: *Government countermeasures against rising prices*

coun·ter·of·fen·sive /ˌkaʊntərəˈfensɪv/ *n* a large-scale attack made to stop, oppose, or return an enemy attack

coun·ter·pane /ˈkaʊntəpeɪn‖-ər-/ *n* BEDSPREAD

coun·ter·part /ˈkaʊntəpɑːt‖-ərpɑrt/ *n* a person or thing that serves the same purpose as another: *The queen is the counterpart of the German president. They are both nonpolitical heads of state*

coun·ter·point /ˈkaʊntəpɔɪnt‖-ər-/ *n* **1** [U] the musical practice of combining 2 or more tunes so that they can be played together as a single whole

2 [C] a tune added to another in this way

coun·ter·poise[1] /ˈkaʊntəpɔɪz‖-ər-/ *v* [T1] COUNTERBALANCE[2]

counterpoise[2] *n* **1** [U] the condition of being balanced; EQUILIBRIUM **2** [C] COUNTERBALANCE[1]

coun·ter-rev·o·lu·tion /ˌkaʊntərevəˈluːʃən/ *n* [C;U] (a movement arising from) political or military opposition to a REVOLUTION or to a government established by REVOLUTION —**~ary** /-nəri‖-neri/ *adj, n* [Wa5]

coun·ter·sign[1] /ˈkaʊntəsaɪn‖-ər-/ *n* a secret sign or signal that one has to know before being allowed to pass a military guard, enter a building, etc.; PASSWORD

countersign[2] *v* [T1] to sign (a paper already signed by someone else): *When you have signed the agreement, it will be countersigned by a director of the firm*

coun·ter·sink[1] /ˈkaʊntəsɪŋk‖-ər-/ *v* **-sank** /sæŋk/, **-sunk** /sʌŋk/ [T1] *tech* **1** to enlarge (the top of a hole) so that the head of a screw will fit level with the surface **2** to fit (a screw) into such an enlarged hole —see picture at MACHINERY

countersink[2] *n tech* a tool for COUNTERSINKing[1] (1) the tops of holes

coun·ter·ten·or /ˌkaʊntəˈtenəʳ‖ˈkaʊntərˌtenər/ *n* ALTO[1] (1)

coun·ter·vail /ˌkaʊntəˈveɪl‖-er-/ *v* [Wv4;T1] to act against (something) with equal force: *The government was opposed by the countervailing power of parliament*

coun·tess /ˈkaʊntɨs/ *n* [C;A;N] **1** (the title of) the wife of an EARL or COUNT **2** a noblewoman who holds in her own right the rank of EARL or COUNT

count in *v adv* [T1b] *infml* to include: *If you're planning a trip to London count me in* —opposite **count out**

counting frame /ˈ·· ·/ *n* ABACUS

coun·ting·house /ˈkaʊntɪŋhaʊs/ *n* **-houses** /ˌhaʊzɨz/ (esp. in former times) a business office where accounts and money are kept: *"The king was in his countinghouse counting out his money"* (from a children's song)

count·less /ˈkaʊntləs/ *adj* very many; too many to be counted

count noun /ˈ· ·/ *n tech* a noun that has a plural and that can be used with numbers and words such as **many**, **few**, etc., or with **a** or **an**: *In this dictionary, count nouns are often marked* [C]

count off *v adv* [IØ] *AmE tech* NUMBER[2] (3)

count on also **count up·on**— *v prep* [T1,4;V3,4a] **1** to depend on (someone, something, or something happening): *You can't count on the weather being fine* **2** to expect; take into account: *I didn't count on John arriving so early; we've not even started preparing dinner yet* —see RELY ON (USAGE)

count out *v adv* [T1b] **1** to put down in turn while counting: *He counted out 10 £5 notes* **2** to declare (a BOXer[4] who fails to rise from the floor after 10 seconds) to be loser of a fight **3** [*often pass*] *tech* to declare that there are too few members present for (Parliament) to do business: *The* HOUSE OF COMMONS *was counted out last night because only 10* MPs *were present* **4** *infml* leave out by choice: *If you're playing football in this rainy weather you can count me out* —opposite **count in**

coun·tri·fied /ˈkʌntrifaɪd/ *adj often derog* of, like, or belonging to the country or country people; UNSOPHISTICATED

coun·try[1] /ˈkʌntri/ *n* **1** [C] a nation or state with its land or population: *Some parts of this country are much warmer than others* **2** [C] the nation or state of one's birth or citizenship: *After many years abroad he wanted to return home to his country* **3** [*the*+R] the people of a nation or state: *The country is opposed to war* **4** [U] land with a special nature or character: *good farming country* **5** [*the*+R] the land outside cities or towns; land used for farming or left unused: *We're hoping to go for a day in the country if the weather's fine tomorrow* **6 go to the country** *esp. BrE* to call a general election: *If they're defeated in Parliament on this matter the government will be forced to go to the country* —see FOLK (USAGE)

country[2] *adj* [Wa5;A] of, in, from, or related to the COUNTRY[1] (5): *country life|country speech|a country house*

country and west·ern /ˌ·· · ˈ··/ also **country music** /ˌ·· ˈ··/— *n* [U] popular music in the style of the southern and western US: *Nashville, Tennessee, is considered the centre of country-and-western* (*music*), *but it is written and played in many other places, too*

country club /ˈ·· ·/ *n* a sports and social club with land in the country

country cous·in /ˌ·· ˈ··/ *n derog* a simple inexperienced person confused by busy city life

country dance /ˌ·· ˈ·‖ˈ·· ·/ *n* any of several native English dances for several pairs of dancers arranged in rows or circles

coun·try·man /ˈkʌntrimən/ *fem.* **coun·try·wom·an** /-ˌwʊmən/— *n* **-men** /mən/ **1** a person from one's own country; COMPATRIOT **2** a person living in the country or marked by country ways

country par·ty /ˈ·· ˌ··/ *n* a political party supporting the interests of farmers and country people

country seat /ˌ·· ˈ·/ *n* the country house of a wealthy landowner

coun·try·side /ˈkʌntrisaɪd/ *n* [U] land outside the cities and towns, used for farming or left unused; country areas

coun·ty /ˈkaʊnti/ *n* **1** [C] a large area divided from others for purposes of local government. British counties have important powers regarding education, social services, planning, etc. **2** [C] the people who live in a COUNTY (1) **3** [*the*+GU] *BrE old use* the rich landowners of a COUNTY (1) as a group

county bor·ough /ˌ·· ˈ··/ *n* (in Britain until 1973) a large town with the same local government powers as a COUNTY

county coun·cil /ˌ·· ˈ··/ *n* [GC] (in Britain) a body of people elected to govern a COUNTY

county court /ˌ·· ˈ·/ *n* [C; *in*+U] **1** (in Britain) a local court of law that deals with CIVIL (=not criminal) cases, esp. concerning money matters **2** (in some states of the US) a local court of law that deals with CIVIL and criminal cases

county town /ˌ·· ˈ·/ *AmE* **county seat**— *n* the chief town of a COUNTY

coup /kuː/ *n* **1** a clever move or action that obtains the desired result: *It would be quite a coup for you if you were appointed a member of the government. You'd really have the power you want, then* **2** COUP D'ETAT **3 pull off a coup** to succeed in getting the desired result by one's own cleverness

coup de grace /ˌkuː də ˈgrɑːs/ *n* **coups de grace** (*same pronunciation*) *Fr* a blow or shot intended to kill a suffering person or animal: (fig.) *Her chances in the next election were given the coup de grace when she lost the support of her most influential followers*

coup d'é·tat /ˌkuː deɪˈtɑː‖-deˈtɑ/ also **coup**— *n* **coups d'état** (*same pronunciation*) a sudden or violent seizure of state power by a small group

cou·pé[1] /ˈkuːpeɪ‖kuːˈpeɪ/ *n* an enclosed 4-wheeled horse-drawn carriage used esp. in former times, with 2 seats inside and an outside seat at the front for the driver

coupé[2] also **coupe** /kuːp/— *n* an enclosed motor vehicle with 2 doors and a sloping back, made in different styles by various firms —see picture at INTERCHANGE²

cou·ple¹ /ˈkʌpəl/ *v* [Wv3] **1** [T1 (TOGETHER)] to join together; connect: *The train will be ready to leave when all the carriages have been coupled* **2** [I∅ (*with*)] (of animals) to unite sexually; MATE

couple² *n* **1** 2 things related in some way but not necessarily matched or part of a set; 2 things of the same kind: *I found a couple of socks in the bedroom but they don't make a pair* **2** a man and a woman together, esp. a husband and wife **3** [(*of*)] *infml* a few; several; small number: *I'll just have a couple of drinks and then I'll come home*

USAGE A set of 2 things like *shoes* is a **pair**. Anything made in 2 parts like *trousers* or SPECTACLES is also a **pair**. Any 2 things of the same kind can be spoken of as a **couple**: *a* **couple** *of cars/of cats*, but **pair** means a closer joining: *a* **pair** *of criminals* have been working together, *a* **pair** *of houses* are joined together. A husband and wife are spoken of as a **couple**. —compare BRACE, PAIR

couple on *v adv* [Wv3;T1 (*to*)] to fasten (one thing) to another: *The train was very full so they coupled 2 more carriages on at Crewe*

coup·let /ˈkʌplɨt/ *n* 2 lines of poetry, one following the other, that are of equal length and end in the same sound

couple with *v prep* [Wv3;D1;V4b] **1** to join (one thing or set of things) to another: *Working too hard, coupled with not getting enough sleep, made him ill* **2** to think of as being related: *I've always coupled the word "America" with freedom and equality*

coup·ling /ˈkʌplɪŋ/ *n* something that connects 2 things, esp. 2 railway carriages

cou·pon /ˈkuːpɒn‖-pɑn/ *n* **1** a ticket that shows the right of the holder to receive some payment; service, etc. VOUCHER: *I have a coupon for 10 pence off that packet of soap* **2** *tech* one of a number of small forms fixed to a BOND¹ (1) (=a receipt for money lent to a firm or the government) that represent sums of interest that can be collected on certain dates **3** a printed form on which goods can be ordered, an enquiry made, a competition entered, etc.

cour·age /ˈkʌrɪdʒ/ *n* [U] **1** the quality of mind or spirit that makes a person able to control fear in the face of danger, hardship, pain, misfortune, etc.; bravery: *Courage is the ability to control fear, not the absence of fear.|The man was highly praised for having the courage to go into the burning house to save the 2 little girls* **2 have the courage of one's convictions** to be brave enough to do or say what one thinks is right **3 take one's courage in both hands** to gather enough courage to do something that needs a lot

cou·ra·geous /kəˈreɪdʒəs/ *adj* brave; fearless; marked by courage: *It was courageous of you to try and save the drowning man* —**~ly** *adv* —**~ness** *n* [U]

cour·gette /kʊəˈʒet‖kʊr-/ *n* a small green MARROW (=a type of long round vegetable with a thin dark-green skin and soft light-green flesh) eaten cooked as a vegetable —compare ZUCCHINI

cou·ri·er /ˈkʊrɪəʳ/ *n* **1** a messenger, esp. one on urgent or official business **2** someone who goes with and looks after travellers on a tour

course¹ /kɔːs‖kors/ *n* **1** [(of) *usu. sing.*] movement from one point to another; continuous movement in space or time: *The enemy should be defeated in the course of* (=during) *the year.|During the course of the flight we shall be serving meals and drinks* **2** the path over which something moves; direction of movement taken by someone or something (note the phrs. **on/off course**): *Our course is directly south.|the course of a stream|The ship was blown off course* **3** an area of land or water on which a race is held or certain types of sport played: *a* GOLF *course* **4** a plan of action; method of moving forward; way of behaving: *Your best course of action is to forget about the whole unfortunate matter* **5** a set of lessons on one subject: *a French course|an evening course* **6** a complete body of studies in a college, university, etc.: *a 4-year history course|a course of study* **7** *esp. BrE* a set of events of a planned or fixed number, as of medical treatment: *a course of drugs/treatment|a course of French lessons/of lessons at evening classes* **8** any of the several parts of a meal: *We had a 3-course dinner. The first course was soup, the second meat and potatoes, and the third baked apples and cream* **9** a continuous level line of bricks, stone, or some other building material, all along a wall —compare DAMP COURSE **10 a matter of course** that which one expects to happen; something done without any great effort; something natural **11 in the course of time** when enough time has passed **12 in due course** without too much delay **13 in the ordinary course of events/things** usually: *In the ordinary course of events you'd have been able to borrow money from the bank, but this year even banks have little money to lend* **14 of course** also (*infml*) **course**— **a** certainly; NATURALLY (4): *Of course I'll still love you when you're old* **b** (*often followed by* but) it is at least true (that): *A competitive firm must, of course, make a fair profit.|Of course parts of it are funny but it's not really a good film* **15 run/take its/their course** (of an illness, state of affairs, number of events, etc.) to continue to its natural end; develop naturally **16 stay the course** to continue something through to the end in spite of difficulties

course² *v* **1** [I∅] (of liquid) to flow or move rapidly: *Tears coursed down his cheeks* **2** [T1;I∅] to cause (a rabbit or HARE) to be chased by dogs as a sport

cours·er /ˈkɔːsəʳ‖ˈkor-/ *n poet* a swift horse

cours·ing /ˈkɔːsɪŋ‖ˈkor-/ *n* [U] the sport of chasing HAREs or rabbits with dogs

court¹ /kɔːt‖kort/ *n* **1** [C; *from, in, out of, to*+U] a room or building in which law cases can be heard and judged: *The case was settled out of court* (=without having to be heard by a judge) **2** [*the*+R; *of*+U] (the judge) law officials, and people attending, gathered together to hear and judge a law case: CONTEMPT *of court|The court will stand for the judge* **3** [C; *at, to*+U] the chief royal palace: *The British court is in London* **4** [C] the officials, noblemen, servants, etc., who attend a king or queen: *the royal courts of Europe* **5** [C;U] (an official meeting of) the body of ministers and officials who advise a king or queen **6** [C; *off, on, out of*+U] (a part of) an area specially prepared and marked for various ball games, such as TENNIS: *Are the players on court yet?|She knocked the ball right out of court/into the far court* —see picture at TENNIS **7** [C] a short street enclosed by buildings on 3 sides: *lived in Westbury Court* **8** also **courtyard**— an open space wholly or partly enclosed by buildings **9 pay court to** *becoming rare* to pay attention to (a woman, influential person, etc.) in order to gain favour, advantage, love, approval, etc.: *Jean's so pretty that many men pay court to her* **10 rule/put out of court** to prevent (a person, matter, or subject) from being considered or taken into account by a court of law **11 take (someone) to court** to start an action in law against (someone) —see also **the** BALL **is in your court**

court² *v* **1** [T1] to pay attention to (an important or influential person) in order to gain favour, advantage, approval, etc.: *He's courting his rich old* *aunt in the hope that he'll get her money when she dies* **2** [T1] (of a man) to spend time with or pay attention to (a woman one hopes to marry): *John courted Mary for years before she agreed to marry him* **3** [L9] (of a man and woman) to be in a relationship that may lead to marriage: *Jean and Bob courted in secret because their parents opposed their plans to marry* **4** [T1] to try to obtain (a desired state): *The teacher tried to court popularity by giving his pupils very little work* **5** [T1] to risk (something bad), often foolishly or without enough thought: *to court danger/defeat/*DISASTER

court card /'· ·/ *n* the king, queen, or JACK in a set (PACK) of playing cards

cour·te·ous /'kɜːtɪəs‖'kɜr-/ *adj* polite and kind; marked by good manners and respect for others —opposite **discourteous** —**~ly** *adv* —**~ness** *n* [U]

cour·te·san /ˌkɔːtə̇'zæn‖'kortə̇zən/ *n* (esp. in former times) a woman who takes payment for sex from noble and socially important people —compare PROSTITUTE

cour·te·sy /'kɜːtə̇si‖'kɜr-/ *n* **1** [U] polite behaviour; good manners **2** [C] a polite or kind action or expression **3 by courtesy of** because of the kindness of or permission given by (someone) usu. without payment: *This picture was lent to us by courtesy of the National Art Collection*

court·house /'kɔːthaʊs‖'kort-/ *n* **-houses** /ˌhaʊzə̇z/ *esp. AmE* a building in which a court of law meets

court·ier /'kɔːtɪə^r‖'kor-/ *n* (esp. in former times) a noble who attended at the court of a king or other ruler

court·ing /'kɔːtɪŋ‖'kor-/ *adj* [Wa5] in a relationship that may lead to marriage: *a courting* COUPLE/*pair*

court·ly /'kɔːtli‖'kortli/ *adj* [Wa1] suitable for a royal court; worthy of respect; polite: *courtly behaviour*|*a courtly procession* —**-liness** *n* [U]

court-mar·tial¹ /ˌ· '··‖'· ˌ··/ *n* **courts-martial** *or* **court martials** [C; *by*+U] **1** a military court of officers appointed to try people for offences against military law **2** a trial before such a court

court-martial² *v* **-ll-** (*AmE* also **-l-**) [T1] to try (someone) in a military court for an offence against military law

court of in·quir·y /ˌ· · ·'··‖ˌ· · '···/ *n* **courts of inquiry** [GC] a body of people appointed to find out the facts or causes of a particular event, esp. an accident

Court of Ses·sion /ˌ· · '··/ *n* [*the*+R] *law* [X] the highest court of law in Scotland for dealing with CIVIL (=noncriminal) cases

court·room /'kɔːt-rʊm, ˌ-ruːm‖'kort-/ *n* a room in which a court of law meets

court·ship /kɔːt-ʃɪp‖'kort-/ *n* **1** [C;U] (the length of time taken by) the act of COURTing² (2) **2** [U] special behaviour, dancing, or activity, used by animals to attract each other before mating (MATE)

court·yard /'kɔːtjɑːd‖'kortjɑrd/ *n* a space enclosed by walls or buildings, next to or within a castle, large house, etc.

cous·cous /'kuːskuːs/ *n* [U;C] a North African dish, made of coarse flour cooked in steam, served with cooked meat, esp. lamb, and vegetables

cous·in /'kʌzən/ *n* **1** [C;A;(*fml*) N] the child of one's uncle or aunt —see TABLE OF FAMILY RELATIONSHIPS **2** [C] a person or thing of a closely related type: *The Polish and Russian languages are cousins*

cou·ture /kuː'tjʊə^r‖-'tʊər/ *n* [U] the business of making and selling fashionable women's clothes —**couturier** /kuː'tjʊərieɪ‖-'tʊərɪər/ *n*

cove¹ /kəʊv/ *n* a small sheltered opening in the coastline; small BAY

cove² *n BrE old sl* a man

cov·en /'kʌvən/ *n* a gathering of usu. 13 WITCHes

cov·e·nant¹ /'kʌvənənt/ *n* **1** a formal solemn agreement between 2 or more people or groups: *God's covenant with His people* **2** a written promise to pay a regular sum of money to a church, CHARITY, etc.

covenant² *v* [T1 (*for*), 3,5: (*with*)] to promise in writing: *I covenanted to pay £1 a week to the church*

Cov·en·try /'kʌvəntri, 'kɒv-‖'kʌv-, 'kɑv-/ *n* **send (someone) to Coventry** *not fml* (of a group of workers, people, etc.) to refuse to speak to (someone) as a sign of disapproval or as a punishment

cov·er¹ /'kʌvə^r/ *v* **1** [T1 (OVER)] to place or spread something upon, over, or in front of (something) in order to protect, hide, etc.: *The noise was so loud that she covered her ears with her hands* **2** [T1] to be or lie on the surface of (something); spread over (something): *Dust covered all the furniture* **3** [T1] to have as a size: *The town covers 5 square miles* **4** [T1 *no pass.*] to travel (a distance): *I want to cover 100 miles by dark* **5** [Wv5;T1] to watch (a place, building, area, etc.) for possible trouble: *The police have got all the roads out of town covered* **6** [T1] to report the details of (an event, particular state of affairs, etc.) as for a newspaper: *I want our best reporters sent to cover the political trials* **7** [T1] to be enough money for: *Will £10 cover the cost of a new skirt?* **8** [Wv5;T1] to protect as from loss; INSURE: *You should get yourself covered as soon as possible* **9** [T1] to protect (a person) by aiming a gun at an enemy: *You run to the garage and start the car while I cover you from the upstairs window* **10** [T1] to keep a gun aimed at (someone): *The police covered the dangerous criminal with a gun until the other man arrived* **11** [T1] (of a gun, castle, fort, etc.) to command; control: *This fort covers the entrance to the harbour* **12** [T1] (in sport) **a** to guard the play of (an opponent) **b** to defend (an area or position) against attack by the other team **13** [T1;I0] to act in place of (someone who is absent): *John's ill today so will you cover for him Jean?* **14** [T1] to include; consist of; take into account: *The doctor's talk covered the history of medicine from Roman times to the present day*

cover² *n* **1** [C] anything that protects by covering, esp. a piece of material: *I always put a cover on the chair before I let the cat sit on it* **2** [C] something placed on top of another thing; lid; top **3** [C] the outer front or back page of a magazine or PAPERBACK (=soft backed book): *I only bought this magazine because of the pretty girl on the cover* **4** [C] a cloth used on a bed to make it warmer: *If you're cold in the night get some more covers from the cupboard* **5** [C] an envelope or wrapper for mail **6** [C] *tech* a place for one person set at a table with a knife, fork, etc. **7** [U] shelter or protection for soldiers or military activity: *The flat land gave the soldiers no cover from enemy fire* **8** [U] shelter of any kind: *We tried to find cover from the storm* **9** [U] insurance against loss, damage, etc: *cover against fire* **10** [(*the*) R] the plant life of an area: *What is the natural cover of England?* **11** [C] something that hides or keeps something secret: *This business is a cover for unlawful activity* **12 break cover** to come out of hiding **13 read from cover to cover** to read (a book) from beginning to end **14 take cover** to hide or protect oneself: *As soon as it started to rain we took cover under a tree* **15 under plain cover** in a plain envelope **16 under separate cover** in a separate envelope: *"This is a receipt. The goods will be sent later under separate cover"*

cov·er·age /'kʌvərɪdʒ/ *n* **1** [U;S] the amount of protection given by insurance; risks covered by insurance **2** [U] **a** the amount of time and space given by television, a newspaper, etc., to report a particular piece of news or event **b** the way in which a particular piece of news or event is reported

cover charge /ˈ·· ·/ *n* a charge made by a restaurant or NIGHTCLUB in addition to the cost of the food and drinks

covered wag·on /ˌ·· ˈ··/ *n* a large horse-drawn vehicle with an arch-shaped cloth-covered top, in which settlers crossed North America in the 19th century

cover girl /ˈ·· ·/ *n* a pretty girl whose picture appears on the cover of a magazine

cov·er·ing /ˈkʌvərɪŋ/ *n* [C;(U)] something that covers or hides: *We always put a covering over our pet rabbit's cage at night to keep out the cold*

covering let·ter /ˌ··· ˈ··/ *n* a letter or note containing an explanation or additional information, sent with a parcel or another letter

cov·er·let /ˈkʌvəlɪ̆t‖-vər-/ *n* BEDSPREAD

cover note /ˈ·· ·/ *n* a short printed record proving that insurance money has been paid. It protects one until a proper insurance contract (POLICY) is ready

cover point /ˈ·· ˌ·/ *n tech* **1** [R] a fielding position facing and slightly in front of the hitter (BATSMAN) and just over ⅓ of the way to the edge of the playing area **2** [C] a player in this position, or who usually fields there

cov·ert[1] /ˈkʌvət‖ˈkəʊvərt/ *adj* [Wa5] secret; hidden; not openly shown: *covert reasons|covert dislike* —**~ly** *adv*

cov·ert[2] /ˈkʌvət‖-ərt/ *n* **1** a thick growth of bushes and small trees in which animals can hide, esp. when being hunted **2 draw a covert** to search through such an area for foxes, rabbits, etc.

cover up *v adv* [T1a] to prevent (something) from being noticed: *She tried to cover up her nervousness as she waited to make her speech* —**cover-up** /ˈ·· ·/ *n* [S]

cover up for *v adv prep* [T1] *not fml* to hide something wrong or shameful in order to save (someone else) from punishment, blame, etc.: *He says he's guilty of the crime, but I think he's trying to cover up for a friend*

cov·et /ˈkʌvɪ̆t/ *v* [Wv5;T1;I∅] *bibl & derog* to desire eagerly to possess (something, esp. something belonging to another person): *Never covet wealth and power*

cov·et·ous /ˈkʌvɪ̆təs/ *adj derog* marked by a too eager desire for wealth, possessions, or what belongs to someone else —**~ly** *adv* —**~ness** *n* [U]

cov·ey /ˈkʌvi/ *n* **1** a small group of PARTRIDGE*s*, GROUSE, or other birds **2** *humor* a group

cow[1] /kaʊ/ *n* **1** [C] the fully-grown female form of cattle, kept on farms esp. to provide milk —see pictures at FARMYARD and RUMINANT **2** [C] the female form of the elephant and certain other large sea and land animals: *a cow elephant|That elephant's a cow* **3** [C;*you*+N] *derog sl* a woman **4 till the cows come home** *infml* for ever —see also SACRED COW —compare BULL, CALF —see MEAT (USAGE)

cow[2] *v* [Wv5;T1] to conquer or bring under control by violence or threats: *The generals tried to cow opposition to their military rule by imprisoning a number of leading politicians*

cow·ard /ˈkaʊəd‖-ərd/ *n* [C;*you*+N] a person unable to face danger, pain, or hardship because he lacks courage; person who shows fear in a shameful way

cow·ard·ice /ˈkaʊədɪ̆s‖-ər-/ also **cow·ard·li·ness** /ˈkaʊədlinɪ̆s‖-ərd-/— *n* [U] lack of courage

cow·ard·ly /ˈkaʊədli‖-ər-/ *adj* typical of a COWARD

cow·bell /ˈkaʊbel/ *n* a bell hung from the neck of a cow to make a sound so that the cow can be easily found

cow·boy /ˈkaʊbɔɪ/ *n* **1** a man, usu. working on horseback, employed to look after cattle, esp. in the western part of the United States and Canada **2** *BrE sl* a wild irresponsible fellow

cow·catch·er /ˈkaʊˌkætʃəʳ/ *n* a strong metal frame fastened to the front of a railway engine or TRAM to push objects off the track, thus preventing accidents

cow·er /ˈkaʊəʳ/ *v* [I∅ (DOWN)] to bend low and draw back as from fear, pain, shame, cold etc.; CRINGE: *The dog cowered when its master beat it*

cow·girl /ˈkaʊgɜːl‖-ɜrl/ *n* a girl who dresses in the style of a COWBOY and who may also work on a cattle RANCH

cow·hand /ˈkaʊhænd/ *n* **1** a person hired to tend cows **2** COWBOY

cow·heel /ˈkaʊhiːl/ *n* [C;U] (esp. in the North of England) the heel (=foot) of a cow cooked as food: TRIPE *and cowheel*

cow·herd /ˈkaʊhɜːd‖-ɜrd/ *n* COWHAND (1)

cow·hide /ˈkaʊhaɪd/ *n* **1** [C;U] the skin of a cow, esp. with the hair on it **2** [U] leather made from this **3** [C] a strong heavy whip made from a cord of knotted leather

cowl /kaʊl/ *n* **1** a loose head covering (a HOOD), for the whole of the head but not the face, esp. worn by MONK*s* **2** a long loose garment with such a head covering, esp. worn by MONK*s* **3** a metal chimney-top covering moved by the wind to point in the direction that allows smoke to escape most easily **4** COWLING

cow·lick /ˈkaʊˌlɪk/ *n* a small mass of hair that stands up from the head and will not lie flat

cowl·ing /ˈkaʊlɪŋ/ also **cowl**— *n* a removable metal cover for an aircraft engine —see picture at AIRCRAFT

cow·man /ˈkaʊmən/ *n* **-men** /mən/ COWHAND (1)

co-work·er /ˌkəʊ ˈwɜːkəʳ‖ˈkəʊ ˌwɜrkər/ *n* a fellow-worker

cow·pat /ˈkaʊpæt/ *n euph* a lump of cow DUNG (=waste matter passed out from the bowels)

cow·pox /ˈkaʊpɒks‖-pɑks/ *n* [U] a disease of the cow, which is not serious, but, when given to man, as by VACCINATION, protects against SMALLPOX

cow·rie, cowry /ˈkaʊri/ *n* a shiny brightly-marked tropical shell, formerly used as money in parts of Africa and Asia

cow·shed /ˈkaʊʃed/ also **cow·house** /-haʊs/— *n* a building to which cows are taken to be milked or in which they live during the coldest winter months —see picture at FARMYARD

cow·slip /ˈkaʊˌslɪp/ *n* [Wn2] any of several types of small wild plant, esp. a member of the PRIMROSE family which is common in Britain and has sweet-smelling yellow flowers —see picture at FLOWER[1]

cox[1] /kɒks‖kɑks/ also (*fml*) **cox·swain** /ˈkɒksən, -sweɪn‖ˈkɑk-/— *n* **1** a person who guides and controls a rowing boat, esp. in races **2** the sailor in charge of a ship's boat

cox[2] also (*fml*) **coxswain**— *v* [T1;I∅] to guide and control (a rowing boat), esp. in races —see also BOX **and** COX

cox·comb /ˈkɒkskəʊm‖ˈkɑks-/ *n* **1** [C;*you*+N] a foolish man who spends too much time and money on his clothes and appearance **2** [C] COCKSCOMB

coy /kɔɪ/ *adj* [Wa1] (esp. of a woman or her behaviour) prettily modest or humble in the presence of others so as to attract attention —**~ly** *adv* —**~ness** *n* [U]

coy·ote /ˈkɔɪ-əʊt, kɔɪˈəʊti‖ˈkaɪ-əʊt, kaɪˈəʊti/ *n* [Wn1] a type of small WOLF native to western North America and Mexico

coy·pu /ˈkɔɪpuː/ *n* a large water rat, native to South America, kept on fur farms for its valuable fur —compare NUTRIA
coz·en into /ˈkʌzən/ *v prep* [V4a] *esp. lit* to cause (someone) to (do something), esp. by tricks or by skilfully persuading: *He cozened the old lady into trusting him with her money*
cozen out of *v adv prep* [D1] *esp. lit* to get (something) from (someone), esp. by tricks or by skilfully persuading: *The pretty child could cozen anything out of her old grandfather*
co·zy /ˈkəʊzi/ *adj* [Wa1] *AmE* COSY —**cozily** *adv* —**coziness** *n* [U]
CP *n* [*the*+GU] *infml* COMMUNIST party —**CP'er** /ˌsiːˈpiːəʳ/ *n*
CPA *n AmE* CERTIFIED PUBLIC ACCOUNTANT: *My brother is a CPA, so I always let him do my taxes for me*
crab¹ /kræb/ *n* **1** [C] a type of sea animal with a broad roundish flattened shell-covered body and 5 pairs of legs, of which the front pair are large powerful PINCERS used for seizing food —see picture at CRUSTACEAN **2** [U] the flesh of this animal cooked as food **3 catch a crab** (in rowing) to lose balance through putting one's OAR too deeply into the water
crab² *v* **-bb- go crabbing** to fish for CRABS¹
crab³ *v* **-bb- 1** [IØ (*about*)] *infml* to complain in a bad-tempered way **2** [T1] *lit* to make bad-tempered, bitter, or sour
crab⁴ *n* [C;*you*+N] *infml* a bad-tempered bitter complaining person
crab ap·ple /ˈ· ˌ··/ also **crab**— *n* **1** a small sour apple **2** the tree that bears this fruit
crab·bed /ˈkræbɨd/ *adj* **1** (of a person, actions, or behaviour) bitter; bad-tempered; sour **2** (of writing done by a person) difficult to read because the letters are too close together **3** (of writings, a style of writing, or a writer) difficult to read or understand —**~ly** *adv* —**~ness** *n* [U]
crab·by /ˈkræbi/ *adj* [Wa1] CRABBED (1)
crab·grass /ˈkræbgrɑːs‖-græs/ *n* [U] a type of wild grass that grows quickly by means of its creeping roots
crab louse /ˈ· ·/ also **crab**— *n* a type of LOUSE that lives on the human body in the hair around the sexual organs
crab·wise /ˈkræbwaɪz/ also **crab·ways** /ˈkræbweɪz/— *adv* sideways, esp. in an awkward manner
crack¹ /kræk/ *v* **1** [IØ;T1] to (cause to) make a sudden explosive sound: *The whip cracked threateningly* **2** [Wv5;IØ;T1] to (cause to) break without dividing into separate parts; split: *Don't pour hot water into the glass or it will crack.|I don't like drinking from cracked cups* **3** [IØ;T1: (OPEN)] to (cause to) break open: *The plant will not grow until the seed has cracked open.|Although the criminals used explosives they were unable to crack the* SAFE **4** [IØ;T1] to (cause to) change suddenly or sharply in direction, level, loudness, etc.: *His voice cracked with grief as he spoke about his dead brother at the funeral* **5** [T1] *infml* to tell (a joke) in a clever or very amusing way **6** [IØ (UP)] to fail as a result of difficulties from inside or outside; lose control or effectiveness: *Pressure of work caused John to crack up* **7** [T1] to strike with a sudden blow: *The teacher cracked the disobedient pupil's fingers with his ruler* **8** [T1;IØ (*against*)] to (cause to) strike with a sudden blow: *The boy fell and cracked his head against the wall* **9** [T1] to discover the sécret of **10** [T1] *infml* to open (a bottle) for drinking **11** [T1; IØ] *tech* to (cause to) separate into simpler compounds: *This is a* **cracking plant** *where oil is cracked by heating under pressure* **12 crack a crib** *BrE sl* to rob a house **13 cracked up to be** *infml* believed to be: *This inn's not all it's cracked up to be. The beer's bad and the service unfriendly* **14 get cracking** also **get weaving**— *infml esp. BrE* to be or become busy doing something in a hurried way
crack² *n* **1** [C] a loud long explosive sound: *a crack of thunder* **2** [(*the*) S] a sudden (repeated) explosive sound: *the crack of the guns* **3** [C] a narrow space or opening: *The door was opened just a crack* **4** [C] a line of division caused by splitting; very narrow thin mark or opening caused by breaking, but not into separate parts: *a crack in the window|a crack in the ice* **5** [C] a sudden sharp blow: *She gave him a crack on the head for disobedience* **6** [C (*at*)] *infml* an attempt: *This is her first crack at writing a book* **7** [C] a clever quick forceful joke, reply, or remark: *He's always making cracks about my big feet* **8** [C] a sudden change in the level or loudness of the voice **9 at the crack of dawn** at the first light of day; at first morning light **10 the crack of doom** *becoming rare & often humor* the end of the world: *This house is very well built. It should last till the crack of doom* **11 a fair crack of the whip** *BrE infml* a fair chance of doing something: *Instead of making the government's job harder the opposition should give them a fair crack of the whip* **12 paper/paste/cover over the cracks** *infml* to hide faults or difficulties, esp. in a hasty or careless way
crack³ *adj* [Wa5;A] of high quality or good ability; skilful: *a crack force of soldiers|a crack cricket player|a crack shot* (=someone who hits what he shoots at)
crack·brained /ˈkrækbreɪnd/ *adj* foolish; stupid; CRAZY: *a crackbrained idea*
crack·down /ˈkrækdaʊn/ *n* [(*on*)] an action taken to stop an unlawful or disapproved activity: *a crackdown on drunken driving*
crack down *v adv* [IØ (*on*)] to become more severe: *The military government declared its intention of cracking down on all political activity*
cracked /krækt/ *adj infml* (of a person) stupid; foolish; ill in the mind; mad
crack·er /ˈkrækəʳ/ *n* **1** a small thin round or square well-baked unsweetened cake of a breadlike mixture: *cheese and crackers* **2** a small harmless explosive charge wrapped in strong paper, used for making loud noises as on special occasions **3** *BrE infml* a very nice-looking woman: *a real cracker* **4** *AmE infml usu. derog* a poor white person, esp. a man, usu. from the south-eastern US **5** CHRISTMAS CRACKER
crack·ers /ˈkrækəz‖-ərz/ *adj* [F] *BrE infml* (of a person) mad; CRACKED: *Anyone who supports your football team must be crackers*
crack·le¹ /ˈkrækəl/ *v* [Wv3;T1;IØ] to (cause to) make small sharp sudden repeated sounds: *The fire crackled*
crackle² *n* **1** [(*the*) S] the noise of repeated small sharp sudden sounds: *the crackle of burning logs|of* STATIC *electricity* **2** [U] a network of fine lines on the surface of some types of CHINA (=cups, plates, etc.) **3** [U] CRACKLEWARE
crack·le·ware /ˈkrækəlweəʳ/ *n* [U] CHINA (=cups, plates, etc.) made to have a network of fine lines on the surface
crack·ling /ˈkræklɪŋ/ *n* [U] **1** the firm hard easily broken brown skin of baked PORK **2** CRACKLE² (1): *the crackling of the fire*
crack·pot /ˈkrækpɒt‖-pɑt/ *adj, n* [A;C;*you*+N] *infml & often humor* (of, belonging to, or being) a person with very strange, foolish, or mad ideas: *a crackpot scientist*
cracks·man /ˈkræksmən/ *n* **-men** /mən/ a person who steals things from houses esp. by breaking into SAFEs
crack·up /ˈkræk-ʌp/ *n infml* a sudden failure of the

mind; state where one loses control of one's feelings; BREAKDOWN

-c·ra·cy /krəsi/ also **-ocracy** /'ɒkrəsi‖'ɑk-/— *suffix* **-cracies** **1** [→*n*[U]] government by the stated social class or principle: THEOCRACY|DEMOCRACY|BUREAUCRACY **2** [→*n*[C]] a society so governed **3** [→*n*] the (powerful) social class of: ARISTOCRACY

cra·dle[1] /'kreɪdl/ *n* **1** [C] a small bed for a baby, usu. made so that it can be moved gently from side to side —see picture at BEDROOM **2** [C] the place where something begins; origin: *Greece was the cradle of western civilization* **3** [*the*+R] the earliest years of one's life: *From the cradle to the grave* (=all through life) *man is the most unfortunate of all creatures* **4** [C] any of various frameworks of wood and/or metal used for supporting something being built or repaired, for holding something in place, or for doing certain jobs: *Window cleaners are pulled up and down tall buildings on cradles.*| *Ships are held in cradles while they're being built.*| *Remember to put the telephone back in the cradle when you've finished*

cradle[2] *v* [T1] to hold gently as if in a CRADLE[1] (1): *John cradled his baby daughter in his arms.*|(fig.) *cradled in sleep*

craft[1] /krɑːft‖kræft/ *n* **1** [C] a job or trade needing skill, esp. with one's hands: *the jewellers' craft* **2** [GC] all the members of a particular trade or profession as a group **3** [U] skill in deceiving people for a bad purpose: *Don't trust her; she's full of craft.*|*craft and* GUILE

craft[2] *n* **craft** [Wn3] **1** a boat, esp. of a small size; vessel: *The harbour was full of pleasure craft* **2** an aircraft **3** SPACECRAFT

craft[3] *v* [T1] *esp. AmE* to make by or as if by hand: *a carefully crafted story*

-craft *comb. form* **1** [*n*→*n*[U]] skill in the stated kind of work: *housecraft* **2** [*n*→*n*[U]] *often derog* skill typical of the stated kind of person: *priestcraft* **3** [*n*→*n* [Wn3; C; *by*+U]] a vehicle of the stated kind: AIRCRAFT

crafts·man /'krɑːftsmən‖'kræ-/ *n* **-men** /mən/ a highly skilled worker: *jewellery made by the finest craftsmen* —**~ship** *n* [U]

craft u·nion /'· ,··/ *n* a trade union with membership limited to workers of the same CRAFT[1] (2): *Craft unions have few members today*

craft·y /'krɑːfti‖'kræf-/ *adj* [Wa1] cleverly deceitful: *That politician is as crafty as a fox* —**craftily** *adv* —**craftiness** *n* [U]

crag /kræg/ *n* a high steep rough rock or mass of rocks

crag·gy /'krægi/ *adj* [Wa1] **1** steep and rough; having many CRAGs **2** (esp. of a man's face) rough in appearance; strongly marked: *I was attracted by Abraham Lincoln's craggy face*

crake /kreɪk/ *n* [Wn1] any of various types of bird with short wings, a narrow body, and strong legs, native to wet land in most parts of the world

cram[1] /kræm/ *v* **-mm-** **1** [X9, esp. *in, into,* DOWN] to force or press (a person or thing) into a small space: *to cram people into a railway carriage*|*Have you seen the way he crams food down* (*his mouth*)? **2** [T1 (*with*)] to fill (something) too full (note the phr. **cram full**): *Don't cram your bag too full of clothes.*|*Stop cramming your face with food!* **3** [T1] to prepare (a pupil or student) for an examination by hastily giving as much information and facts as possible **4** [IØ (*for*)] to prepare oneself for an examination by working very hard and learning hastily

cram-full /,· '·◂/ *adj* [F (*of*)] *BrE infml* CHOCK-FULL

cram·mer /'kræmə^r/ *n* **1** a person who is CRAMMing[1] (4) for an examination **2** *usu. infml* a person or thing that helps such a person, esp. a teacher, a special school, or a specially prepared book

cramp[1] /kræmp/ *n* [*esp. BrE* U; *esp. AmE* C] severe pain from the sudden tightening of a muscle, which is usu. caused by the cold or too much exercise, and which makes movement difficult: *The swimmer was seized with cramp and had to be lifted from the water*

cramp[2] *n* **1** also **cramp i·ron** /'· ,··/— a metal bar bent at both ends used for holding together blocks of stone or pieces of wood, metal, etc. **2** a frame or tool with a movable part which can be screwed tightly in place, used for holding things together

cramp[3] *v* [T1] **1** to fasten tightly with a CRAMP[2] **2** to prevent the natural growth or development of (something) **3** **cramp someone's style** *infml* to prevent someone from showing his abilities to the full or from doing as well as he could

cramped /kræmpt/ *adj* **1** limited in space: *a cramped little flat* **2** (of writing) having badly-formed letters written too closely together: *Cramped writing is difficult to read*

cram·pon /'kræmpən/ *n* **1** [*usu. pl.*] also **climbing iron**— a metal framework with sharp points (SPIKEs) underneath, fastened to the bottom of boots to make climbing less difficult, esp. on ice **2** a movable pair of curved iron bars (LEVERs) used for lifting and raising heavy weights

cramps /kræmps/ also **stomach cramps**— *n* [P] sharp pains in the stomach

cran·ber·ry /'krænbəri‖-beri/ *n* **1** a small red sour-tasting berry used for making a jelly that is eaten with cooked chicken and other bird flesh —see picture at BERRY **2** the type of small bush on which this berry grows

crane[1] /kreɪn/ *n* **1** a machine for lifting and moving heavy objects by means of a very strong rope or wire fastened to a movable arm (JIB) —see picture at SITE[1] **2** a type of large tall bird with very long legs and neck, which spends much time walking in water catching fish in its very long beak

crane[2] *v* [T1;IØ] to stretch out (one's neck) esp. to get a better view: *Jane craned her neck to look for her husband in the crowd*

crane fly /'· ·/ *n fml* DADDY LONGLEGS

cra·ni·al /'kreɪnɪəl/ *adj* [Wa5] *med* of or related to the CRANIUM —**~ly** *adv*

cra·ni·um /'kreɪnɪəm/ *n* **-niums** *or* **-nia** /nɪə/ *med* the bony framework of the animal or human head; part of the SKULL that covers the brain

crank[1] /kræŋk/ *n* **1** [C] an apparatus for changing movement in a straight line into circular movement or for passing circular movement on, consisting, in its simplest form, of a handle fixed at right-angles to a rod **2** [C] *sometimes humor & infml* a person with very strange, odd, or peculiar ideas: *a food crank* **3** [C; *you*+N] *AmE infml* a nasty bad-tempered person

crank[2] *v* [T1] **1** to use a CRANK[1] (1) to turn (a rod) **2** [(UP)] to use a CRANK[1] (1) to start (a car): *My car's so old that I have to crank it on cold mornings*

crank·shaft /'kræŋkʃɑːft‖-ʃæft/ *n* a rod turning, or driven by, a CRANK[1] (1), esp. in a railway engine —see picture at PETROL

crank·y /'kræŋki/ *adj* [Wa1] *infml* **1** very strange; peculiar; odd: *a cranky old scientist with cranky ideas* **2** (of a machine or apparatus) unsteady; shaky; in need of repair **3** *AmE* bad-tempered; nasty: *a cranky unfriendly old lady*

cran·ny /'kræni/ *n esp. humor or lit* a small narrow opening in a wall, rock, etc.; small crack: *a mouse hiding in a cranny in the stone wall* —**-nied** *adj* —see also NOOKs **and crannies**

crap¹ /kræp/ *n taboo sl* **1** [U] solid waste matter passed from the bowels **2** [S] an act of passing waste matter from the bowels: *to have a crap* **3** [U] nonsense: *His speech was just a load of crap* **4** [U] unwanted things: *Clear all this crap off the table*

crap² *v* **-pp-** [IØ] *taboo sl* to pass waste matter from the bowels

crap³ *interj sl* nonsense

crap⁴ *n* [A] CRAPS: *a crap player*

crape /kreɪp/ *n* [C;U] **1** also **crepe**— a band of black material worn on the hat or arm as a sign of grief at someone's death **2** CREPE

crap·py /ˈkræpi/ *adj* [Wa1] *sl* of very low quality: *a crappy dance*

craps /kræps/ *n* [U;(P)] **1** an American game played with 2 DICE for money **2 shoot craps** to play this game

crap up *v adv* [T1] *sl* to do very badly; spoil: *If you crap up the work again, you'll be out of a job!*

crash¹ /kræʃ/ *v* **1** [IØ;T1] to (cause to) have a sudden, violent, and noisy accident: *The car crashed on the bend, killing its driver and 2 passengers.|The car would not stop so the driver had to crash it into the wall* **2** [T1;IØ] to (cause to) fall or strike the ground noisily and violently: *She crashed the plates angrily down on the table* **3** [L9] to move violently and noisily: *The angry elephant crashed through the forest towards the hunters' camp* **4** [IØ] to make a sudden loud noise: *The lightning flashed and thunder crashed* **5** [IØ] (in the world of business and money matters) to fail suddenly; come to ruin: *The New York* STOCK EXCHANGE *crashed in 1929* **6** [T1;(IØ)] *infml* also **gatecrash**— to join (a party) without having been invited **7** [L9] *sl* to spend the night in a particular place; sleep: *Can I crash on your floor tonight?*

crash² *n* **1** a sudden loud noise as made by a violent blow, fall, break, etc.: *a crash of thunder|the crash of breaking glass* **2** a violent vehicle accident: *All the passengers were killed in the train/plane/car crash* **3** a sudden severe business failure: *the Wall Street crash*

crash³ *adj* [Wa5;A] marked by a very great effort to reach quickly the desired results: *She wanted to lose weight so she went on a crash* DIET*|a crash course in conversational French*

crash⁴ *n* [U] coarse cloth made from rough lumpy irregular thread

crash⁵ *adv* [H] with a crash: *The heavy box landed crash on his head!*

crash bar·ri·er /ˈ· ˌ···/ *n* a strong fence or wall built to keep vehicles and/or people apart where there is a possibility of danger or accident: *Since crash barriers were put down the centre of the busiest main roads, accidents have been less severe* —see picture at INTERCHANGE²

crash-dive /ˈ· ·/ *v* [IØ;T1] **a** (of a SUBMARINE) to sink to a great depth to escape attack by ships or planes **b** to take (a SUBMARINE) down to a great depth to escape attack by ships or planes —**crash dive** *n*

crash hel·met /ˈ· ˌ··/ *n* a very strong protective head covering (HELMET) worn on the head by racing car drivers, MOTORCYCLE riders, etc.

crash·ing /ˈkræʃɪŋ/ *adj* [Wa5;A] *infml* very great; complete: *a crashing fool*/BORE⁵

crash-land /ˈ· ·/ *v* [IØ;T1] **a** (of a plane) to crash in a controlled way so that as little damage as possible is done **b** to cause (a plane) to crash in this way —**crash landing** /ˌ· ˈ··/ *n* [C;U]

crass /kræs/ *adj* **1** stupid; unfeeling; coarse: *crass behaviour* **2** (of stupidity, foolishness, etc.) complete; very great: *crass stupidity*/IGNORANCE —**~ly** *adv* —**~ness** *n* [U]

-crat /ˌkræt/ also **-ocrat** /əˌkræt/— *suffix* [*n*] **1** a believer in (the stated principle of government): *a* DEMOCRAT **2** a member of (a usu. powerful social class or group): *a* BUREAUCRAT*|the* ARISTOCRAT*s* —**-cratic** /ˈkrætɪk/ *comb. form* [→*adj*] —**-cratically** /ˈkrætɪkəli/ *comb. form* [→*adv* [Wa4]]

crate¹ /kreɪt/ *n* **1** a box or framework, esp. made of wood, for holding fruit, bottles, furniture, etc.: *a milk crate|a crate of apples* **2** also **crateful** /ˈkreɪtfʊl/— the amount held in one of these: *He drank a whole crate of beer!* **3** *infml & sometimes humor* an old car or plane in great need of repair

crate² *v* [T1] to pack into a CRATE¹

cra·ter /ˈkreɪtəʳ/ *n* **1** the round bowl-shaped mouth of a VOLCANO **2** a round hole in the ground formed by an explosion: *a bomb crater* **3** a flat-bottomed steep-sided round hole on the moon's surface, sometimes having a mountain right in the centre

cra·vat /krəˈvæt/ *n* a piece of material loosely folded and worn round the neck by men

crave /kreɪv/ *v* [T1;L9, esp. *for, after*; I3] **1** to have a very strong desire for (something): *She craves (after) admiration.|I'm craving for a cup of tea, I've not had one all day.|(lit) The tired boy craved after rest* **2** [T1] *fml & pomp* to ask seriously for: *May I crave your attention?*

cra·ven /ˈkreɪvən/ *n, adj derog* (a person) completely lacking courage —**cravenness** *n* [U] —**cravenly** *adv*

crav·ing /ˈkreɪvɪŋ/ *n* [C (*for*),C3] a very strong desire: *a craving for sweets*

crawl¹ /krɔːl/ *v* [IØ] **1** to move slowly with the body close to the ground or floor, or on the hands and knees: *The baby crawled across the room.|There's an insect crawling up your back!* **2** to go very slowly: *The roads were very busy so traffic crawled along at 10 miles an hour* **3** [(*with*)] to be completely covered by worms, insects, or other such animals: *Don't eat that apple, it's crawling with worms.*|(fig.) *After the explosion the town was crawling with soldiers* **4** to have an unpleasant sensation, as of worms, insects, etc., creeping over one's skin: *The sight of snakes makes my flesh crawl* **5** *infml* to try to win the favour of someone of higher rank by being too nice to them, doing small jobs for them, etc.: *She's not very clever but the teacher likes her because she crawls to him*

crawl² *n* **1** [S] a very slow movement **2** [(*the*) S] also **Australian crawl** /·ˈ··· ·/— a rapid way of swimming while lying on one's stomach, moving first one arm and then the other over one's head, and kicking the feet up and down —see also PUB-CRAWL

crawl·er /ˈkrɔːləʳ/ *n* **1** [C; *you*+N] *sl* a person who tries to win the favour of someone of higher rank by being too nice to them, doing jobs for them, etc. **2** [A] CRAWLERS

crawl·ers /ˈkrɔːləz‖-ərz/ *n* [P] ROMPERS

cray·fish /ˈkreɪˌfɪʃ/ also **craw·fish** /ˈkrɔ-/— *n* [Wn2] **1** [C] a type of small LOBSTER-like animal with 4 pairs of walking limbs, a pair of powerful arms (PINCER*s*) used for seizing food, and a shell-covered body, that lives in rivers and streams —see picture at CRUSTACEAN **2** [U] the flesh of this animal cooked as food

cray·on¹ /ˈkreɪən, -ɒn‖-ɑn, -ən/ *n* a stick of coloured wax or chalk used for writing or drawing, esp. on paper

crayon² *v* [T1;IØ] to draw with a CRAYON¹

craze¹ /kreɪz/ *v* [Wv5;T1 *usu. pass.*] **1** to make very excited, angry, or mad: *a crazed expression|The climber was crazed by the many hours he'd spent in the freezing cold* **2** *tech* to make small fine cracks on the surface of (a cup, plate, etc.)

craze² *n* [(*for*)] a very popular fashion, usu. for a

very short time: *This new toy is the latest craze in America*

cra·zy /ˈkreɪzi/ *adj* [Wa1] *not fml* **1** [B;F3] mad; ill in the mind: *You're crazy to go out in this stormy weather* **2** [B] impractical; foolish: *a crazy idea* **3** [F+*about*] wildly excited; very fond (of) or interested (in): *She's crazy about dancing* **4 like crazy** *sl* wildly and/or very actively: *You'll have to work like crazy to get this finished* —**-zily** *adv* —**-ziness** *n* [U]

crazy pav·ing /ˌ·· ˈ··/ *n* [U] irregular pieces of stone fitted together to make a path or flat place for walking

creak[1] /kriːk/ *v* [IØ] to make the sound of a badly-oiled door when it opens: *We must oil this door to stop it creaking.|creaking with age*

creak[2] *n* [(*the*) S;(C)] the sound made by a badly-oiled door when it opens

creak·y /ˈkriːki/ *adj* [Wa1] that CREAK*s*: *Remember to oil that creaky door* —**creakily** *adv* —**creakiness** *n* [U]

cream[1] /kriːm/ *n* **1** [U] the thick fatty slightly yellowish liquid that separates from and rises to the top of milk when left to stand, and is eaten as food, esp. with sweet dishes: *Have some cream in your coffee.|a cream cake* **2** [U] a substance made to look and taste like this: ARTIFICIAL cream **3** [C9;U9] food made of or containing a sweet soft smooth substance, like this: *a chocolate cream|cream of chicken (soup)* **4** [C9;U9] a preparation made thick and soft like CREAM (1), esp. used for softening and improving the skin: *a skin cream|face cream* **5** [U;C] a preparation like this used as medicine: *Put some of this cream on that burn* **6** [*the*+R (*of*)] the best part of anything: *the cream of society*|(fig.) *the cream of the cream*

cream[2] *adj, n* [B;U] (having) the colour of CREAM[1] (1); (having) a yellowish-white colour: *She wore a cream dress*

cream[3] *v* [T1] **1** to beat (food) until creamy: *Cream your butter well before adding the sugar and flour* **2** [Wv5] to prepare (a vegetable, meat, etc.) with cream or a creamy liquid: *creamed chicken|creamed potatoes* **3** to take cream from the surface of (milk) **4** *sl* to defeat completely

cream cheese /ˌ· ˈ·‖ˈ· ·/ *n* [U] a soft white smooth cheese made from milk and sometimes cream

cream·er /ˈkriːməʳ/ *n* a small vessel for holding cream

cream·e·ry /ˈkriːməri/ *n* a place where milk, butter, cream, and cheese are produced or sold; DAIRY

cream horn /ˌ· ˈ·/ *n* a hollow horn-shaped pipe of sweet pastry baked and filled with cream

cream off *v adv* [T1] to remove (the best): *I'm opposed to the idea of creaming off the cleverest pupils and sending them to a special school*

cream of tar·tar /ˌ· · ˈ··/ *n* [U] TARTAR[1] (3)

cream puff /ˌ· ˈ·/ *n* **1** [C] a hollow pipe of sweet pastry baked and filled with cream **2** [C; *you*+N] a weak and ineffective person, esp. a man

cream so·da /ˌ· ˈ··/ *n* [U] a sweet gassy VANILLA-flavoured drink

cream·y /ˈkriːmi/ *adj* [Wa1] **1** thick, soft, and smooth like cream: *Our new creamy soap will keep your skin soft and smooth* **2** containing cream; tasting of cream: *creamy milk* —**creaminess** *n* [U]

crease[1] /kriːs/ *n* **1** a line made on cloth, paper, etc., by crushing, folding, or pressing: *You've got a crease in your dress where you've been sitting* **2** a straight thin line down the front and back of each leg in a pair of trousers **3** a white or black line marked on the ground to show special areas or positions in certain games —see picture at CRICKET

crease[2] *v* **1** [Wv5;T1] to make a line or lines appear on (a garment, paper, cloth, etc.) by folding, crushing, or pressing: *Don't sit for too long or you'll crease your new dress.|She wanted to wear her black dress but it was too creased* **2** [Wv5;T1] to make a thin straight line appear down the back and front of each leg of (a pair of trousers): *Don't put those trousers on until I've creased them* **3** [IØ] to allow such lines to form: *This new material won't crease* **4** [Wv5;T1 (*with*)] *sl* to cause to laugh a lot: *That joke really creased me (with laughter)!*

cre·ate /kriˈeɪt/ *v* **1** [T1] to cause (something new) to exist; produce (something new): *We've created a beautiful new house from out of an old ruin.|Her new dress created much excitement.*|(fig.) *In the play "Death of a Salesman", the part of Willy Loman was created* (=acted for the first time) *by Lee J. Cobb* **2** [X1;(T1)] to appoint (someone) to a special rank or position: *The Queen's son was created Prince of Wales at a ceremony in Caernarvon castle* **3** [IØ] *infml* to be noisily angry: *I wish the baby would stop creating and go to sleep*

USAGE **Create** is used esp. 1. when speaking of God: *God* **created**/*made man.* 2. with certain words, or types of object: one **creates** the *characters* in a book one writes; one **creates** a *sensation,* or a PRECEDENT; one **creates** (or *makes*) a DISTURBANCE or a *difficulty.*

cre·a·tion /kriˈeɪʃən/ *n* **1** [U] the act of creating (CREATE (1,2)): *Does the government oppose the creation of an independent Scottish parliament?* **2** [C] something CREATEd; something produced by man's invention or imagination: *an artist's creation* **3** [C] a noticeably fashionable garment or hat: *the latest creations from Paris* **4** [U] the universe, world, and all living things: *Man is the lord of creation*

Creation *n* [*the*+R] the story of the earth's origin as told esp. in the Bible: *Haydn's* ORATORIO *"The Creation" is based on the Bible*

cre·a·tive /kriˈeɪtɪv/ *adj* **1** having the ability to produce, or producing, new and original ideas and things: *creative thinking* **2** resulting from newness of thought or expression: *useful and creative work* —**~ly** *adv*

cre·a·tiv·i·ty /ˌkriːeɪˈtɪvɪ̈ti/ also **cre·a·tive·ness** /kriˈeɪtɪvnɪ̈s/— *n* [U] the ability to produce new and original ideas and things; inventiveness: *Someone with creativity is needed for this job*

cre·a·tor /kriˈeɪtəʳ/ *n* a person who CREATE*s* (1)

Creator *n* [R9] God: *gave thanks to the/her Creator*

crea·ture /ˈkriːtʃəʳ/ *n* **1** [C] an animal of any kind **2** [C9] (*used in expressions of feeling*) a person, esp. female: *The poor creature had no home, family, or friends* **3** [C9, esp. *of*] a person whose rank or position is dependent on his total obedience to another: *Don't trust him! He's the military governor's creature* **4** [C] a strange or terrible being: *creatures from outer space* **5 (all) God's creatures (great and small)** animals and human beings

creature com·forts /ˌ·· ˈ··/ *n* [P] the material goods, such as food, clothes, etc., that increase bodily comfort

crèche /kreɪʃ‖kreʃ (*Fr* krɛʃ)/ *n Fr* **1** a place where babies and young children are cared for by specially-trained people while their mothers work; DAY NURSERY **2** *AmE* CRIB[1] (3)

cre·dence /ˈkriːdəns/ *n* [U] acceptance as true; belief: *The newspapers are giving no credence to the government's latest statements*

cre·den·tials /krɪˈdenʃəlz/ *n* [P] a letter or other written proof of a person's position, trustworthiness, etc.

cred·i·bil·i·ty /ˌkredɪ̈ˈbɪlɪ̈ti/ *n* [U] the state or quality of being CREDIBLE

credibility gap /ˌ··ˈ··· ·/ *n* the difference between

what someone, esp. a politician, says and what he means or does

cred·i·ble /'kredəbəl/ *adj* deserving or worthy of belief; trustworthy: *a credible news report|After this latest affair he hardly seems credible as a politician* —**-bly** *adv*

cred·it¹ /'kredɨt/ *n* **1** [U] belief; trust; faith: *I place full credit in the government's abilities.|This story is gaining credit* **2** [U] public attention; approval; praise; favourable notice or regard: *Although the invention was mine, I was given no credit for it* **3** [C *usu. sing.*] a cause of honour: *You're a credit to your team* **4** [U] a system of buying goods or services when they are wanted and paying for them later: *You can always buy the furniture on credit if you can't pay the full price now: buy now, pay later* —compare HIRE PURCHASE **5** [U] a period of time during which the full price of an article bought under this system must be paid: *Our shop only allows people 6 months' credit* **6** [U] the quality of being likely to repay debts and be honest with money: *His credit is good. You can trust him* **7** [U] (the amount of) money in a person's account, as at a bank: *on the credit side of the account*—compare DEBIT **8** [C] (esp. in the US) a measure of a student's work, esp. at a university, often equal to one hour of class time per week: *French 101 is a 3-credit course that meets Mondays, Wednesdays, and Fridays from 9 to 10 o'clock* **9 do (someone) credit** to be a cause of honour to someone: *Our armed forces do us credit. They're the finest in the world* **10 to someone's credit a** in someone's favour: *It is to the king's credit that he opposed the establishment of a military government* **b** to/in someone's name; belonging to someone: *She's not yet 30 years old, and already she has 5 books to her credit!* (=she's written 5 books)

credit² *v* [T1] to believe: *Do you really credit the government's statement?*

cred·i·ta·ble /kredɨtəbəl/ *adj* deserving praise, honour, approval, etc.: *a creditable effort to establish peace* —**-bly** *adv*

credit ac·count /'·· ·,·/ *AmE* **charge account** /'· ·,·/— *n* an account with a shop which allows one to take goods at once and pay for them later

credit card /'·· ·/ *n* a card provided by a business firm allowing the holder to obtain goods and services without payment of cash, the cost being charged to his account and paid later

credit note /'·· ·/ *n* a note given by a shop when goods have been returned as faulty, allowing one to buy other goods of the same value

cred·i·tor /'kredɨtə^r/ *n* a person or firm to whom money is owed

credit squeeze /'·· ·/ *n* a period of time during which the government makes the borrowing of money and the buying of goods on CREDIT¹ (4) difficult, usu. in an effort to reduce spending and increase saving

credit ti·tles /'·· ,··/ *n* [P] the names of the actors and other people responsible for a cinema or television show, which appear in a list at the beginning or end

credit to *v prep* [D1] to place (the stated amount of money) in (an account): *Please credit £10 to my account|to me*

credit with *v prep* **1** [D1,V4b] to give CREDIT¹ (2) to (someone) for (something): *Please credit me with some sense!* **2** [D1] to increase (an account) by (the stated amount of money): *Please credit my account|me with £10*

cre·do /'kri:dəʊ, 'kreɪ-/ *n* **-dos** **1** [*the*+R] (*usu. cap.*) the third part of the Christian religious service called the MASS, esp. when performed with music **2** [C] a statement of beliefs and principles: *a credo of* SOCIALIST *principles*

cre·du·li·ty /krɪ'dju:lɨti‖-'du:-/ *n* [U] too great a willingness to believe, esp. without certain proof

cred·u·lous /'kredjʊləs‖-dʒə-/ *adj* too willing to believe, esp. without real proof —**~ly** *adv* —**~ness** *n* [U]

creed /kri:d/ *n* **1** a short statement of religious belief, esp. the formal statement of Christian belief said at certain church services **2** a system of beliefs or principles: *In our country all men are treated equally without regard to race, social origin, or creed*

creek /kri:k/ *n* **1** *BrE* a long narrow body of water reaching from the sea, a lake, etc., into the land **2** *AmE* a small narrow stream **3 up the creek** *sl* in trouble; very bad; wrong: *His driving's up the creek*

creel /kri:l/ *n* a basket used for carrying fish

creep¹ /kri:p/ *v* **crept** /krept/ **1** [IØ] to move slowly and quietly with the body close to the ground: *The cat crept silently towards the mouse* **2** [L9] to move or advance slowly and quietly: *The sea crept noiselessly up the shore.|One hardly notices the way old age creeps up on one* **3** [Wv4;IØ] to grow along the ground or a surface: *a garden full of creeping plants* **4** [IØ] (of the body) to have an unpleasant sensation, as of worms, insects, etc., moving over the skin; CRAWL¹ (4): *His story about dead people leaving their graves at night really made my flesh creep*

creep² *n* **1** [C; *you*+N] *sl* an unpleasant person who tries to win the favour of a person of higher rank, esp. by praising insincerely **2** [U] the slow movement of loose soil, rocks, etc.

creep·er /'kri:pə^r/ *n* **1** [C;U] any of various types of plant which climb up trees and walls or grow along the ground: *My foot got caught in a creeper and I fell down from the tree.|a Virginia creeper* —see picture at GARDEN¹ **2** [C] any of various types of bird or insect that creep or climb in trees **3** [A] CREEPERS

creep·ers /'kri:pəz‖-ərz/ *n* [P] **1** shoes with thick rubber bottoms **2** *AmE* ROMPERS

creep in *v adv* [IØ] to begin to happen: *Mistakes are creeping in which could have been avoided*

creep in·to *v prep* [T1 *no pass.*] to begin to happen in: *You must stop these mistakes creeping into your work!*

creeps /kri:ps/ *n* [P] *infml* an unpleasant sensation of fear, as of worms, insects, etc., creeping over one's skin: *The old castle gives me the creeps*

creep·y /'kri:pi/ *adj* [Wa1] *infml* causing or feeling an unpleasant sensation of fear, as of worms, insects, etc., creeping over one's skin: *a creepy old house* —**creepily** *adv* —**creepiness** *n* [U]

creepy-crawl·y /,·· '··/ *n infml* a creeping insect

cre·mate /krɨ'meɪt‖'kri:meɪt/ *v* [T1] to burn (a dead person) at a special funeral ceremony —**cremation** /krɪ'meɪʃən/ *n* [C;U]

crem·a·to·ri·um /,kremə'tɔ:rɪəm‖,kri:mə'to-/ also **crem·a·to·ry** /'kremətəri‖'kri:mətori/— *n* **-iums** *or* **-ia** /ɪə/ a building, usu. surrounded by a pleasant garden, in which dead people are CREMATED

crème de menthe /,krem də 'mɒnθ‖,krɪ:m də 'menθ (*Fr* krɛm də mɑ̃t)/ *n* [C;U] *Fr* (a glass of) thick sweet green PEPPERMINT-flavoured alcoholic drink

cren·el·lat·ed, *AmE* **crenelated** /'krenəl-eɪtɨd/ *adj tech* protected by BATTLEMENTS: *a crenellated castle*

cre·ole /'kri:əʊl/ *adj, n* (*often cap.*) **1** [C;U] (of, being, or related to) a language which is formed by the combination of a European language with one or more others, and which has become the native language of its speakers —compare PIDGIN **2** [C] (of, being, or related to) a person of mixed

European and African blood **3** [C] (of, being, or related to) any person of pure European blood born in the West Indies or parts of Spanish America **4** [C] (of, being, or related to) a descendant of a freed slave resettled in West Africa **5** [C] (of, being, or related to) a descendant of the original French settlers in the southern United States **6** [U;(C)] (of, being, or related to) food prepared in the hot strong-tasting style of these descendants: *Creole cooking*|SHRIMP *creole*

cre·o·sote[1] /ˈkriːəsəʊt/ *n* [U] thick brown oily liquid used for preserving wood and as a DISINFECTANT

creosote[2] *v* [IØ;T1] to paint (something) with CREOSOTE[1]

crepe, crêpe /kreɪp/ *n Fr* **1** [U] also **crape**— light soft thin cloth, with a finely lined and folded surface, made from cotton, silk, wool, etc., esp. worn in former time at funerals **2** [U] also **crepe rub·ber** /ˌ· ˈ··/— rubber tightly pressed to have a finely lined and folded surface, used esp. for making the bottoms of shoes **3** [C] CRAPE (1) **4** [C] a small very thin PANCAKE

crepe pa·per /ˌ· ˈ··‖ˈ· ˌ··/ also **crepe**— *n* [U] thin brightly coloured paper with a finely lined and folded surface, esp. used for making ornamental paper chains, STREAMERs, etc.

crêpe su·zette /ˌkreɪp sʊˈzet/ *n* **crêpes suzette** /ˌkreɪps sʊˈzet/ *or* **crepe suzettes** /ˌkreɪp sʊˈzets/ *Fr* a thin soft flat cake (PANCAKE) made from a mixture of milk, eggs, and flour, usu. eaten hot with a thick sweet alcoholic liquid poured over

crept /krept/ *past t. and past p. of* CREEP

cre·pus·cu·lar /krɪˈpʌskjʊləʳ‖-kjə-/ *adj* **1** *lit* of, like, related to the time when day is changing into night or night into day; not bright; faint **2** *tech* (of an animal) active only during the time when day is changing into night or night into day

cre·scen·do[1] /krɪ̵ˈʃendəʊ/ *n* **-dos** **1** a gradual increase of force or loudness, esp. of music **2** a piece of music showing such an increase in loudness **3** *infml* the point of greatest excitement; CLIMAX: *The demands for an election rose to a crescendo in the later part of the year*

crescendo[2] *adj, adv* [Wa5] gradually increasing in force or loudness

cres·cent[1] /ˈkresənt/ *n* **1** the curved shape of the moon during its first and last quarters, when it forms less than ½ a circle **2** something shaped like this, esp. a curved row of houses, curved street, etc. **3** *often cap.* this shape as a sign of the faith and religion of Muslims: *the* CROSS *and the Crescent* —compare CROSS[1] (6)

crescent[2] *adj* [Wa5;A] (of the moon) increasing; growing; WAXing

cress /kres/ *n* [U] any of several types of very small plants whose leaves are eaten raw with other vegetables or between pieces of bread and butter, or put on food to make it look more attractive

crest /krest/ *n* **1** a showy growth of feathers on top of a bird's head **2** something like this worn, esp. in former times, on top of soldiers' HELMETs as an ornament **3** the top of something, esp. of a mountain, hill, or wave **4** a special ornamental picture used as a personal mark on letters, envelopes, one's plates, etc., or put above the shield on one's COAT OF ARMS

crest·ed /ˈkrestɪ̵d/ *adj* [Wa5] having a CREST (1,2,4): *the bird's crested head*|*The prince always writes on crested writing paper*

crest·fal·len /ˈkrestˌfɔːlən/ *adj* disappointed; low in spirits; sad

cre·ta·ceous /krɪˈteɪʃəs/ *adj* [Wa5] *tech* **1** of the nature of, like, or containing chalk **2** (*usu. cap.*) of the period of time about 140,000,000 to 170,000,000 years ago, when the chalk-rocks were formed

cret·in /ˈkretɪ̵n‖ˈkriːtn/ *n* **1** [C] *med* a person whose development of mind and body has been stopped in early childhood because of a weakness in the THYROID **2** [C; *you*+N] *sl* a stupid foolish person: *You silly cretin! Why didn't you catch the ball when I threw it?* —**~ous** *adj*

cret·onne /kreˈtɒn, ˈkretɒn‖ˈkriːtɑn, krɪˈtɑn/ *n* [U] heavy cotton cloth with printed patterns on it, used for curtains, furniture covers, etc.

cre·vasse /krɪˈvæs/ *n* a deep open crack, esp. in thick ice —see picture at MOUNTAIN

crev·ice /ˈkrevɪ̵s/ *n* a narrow crack or opening, esp. in rock

crew[1] /kruː/ *n* [GC] **1 a** all the people working on a ship, plane, etc. **b** all the people working on a ship, plane, etc., except the officers **2** a group of people working together: *a train track repair crew*|*the stage crew for the new play* **3** a rowing team **4** *infml* a gathering of people: *We were such a happy crew on our day in London*

crew[2] *v* [IØ] to act as the CREW[1]: *crewed on the winning boat*

crew[3] *old use a past t. of* CROW

crew cut /ˈ· ·/ *n* a very closely cut style of hair for men

crew·man /ˈkruːˌmən/ also **crewmember** /ˈkruːˌmembəʳ/— *n* **-men** /mən/ a member of a CREW: *We need 2 more crewmen before we can leave port*

crib[1] /krɪb/ *n* **1** [C] *esp. AmE* COT[2] (1) **2** [C] an open box or wooden framework holding food for animals; MANGER **3** [C] *AmE* **creche**— a representation of the birth of Christ as seen in a church at Christmas **4** [C] *AmE* a box, metal container, or small building for storing grain **5** [C] *infml* something copied dishonestly from another's work: *The teacher would have given me a high mark, but he noticed some of my answers were cribs from yours* **6** [C] *infml* a book supplying a translation, esp. to a Latin schoolbook **7** [U] CRIBBAGE **8** [C] (in the game of CRIBBAGE) a set of cards belonging to the person who shares out the cards, made up of cards from each player **9** [C] *BrE sl* a house one intends to rob

crib[2] *v* **-bb-** [T1;IØ] *infml* to copy (something) dishonestly from someone else: *I didn't know the answers to the teacher's questions so I cribbed them off John*

crib·bage /ˈkrɪbɪdʒ/ also (*infml*) **crib**— *n* [U] a card game in which the number of points made by each player is shown by placing very small pieces of wood in holes arranged in rows on a small board (**cribbage board**)

crick[1] /krɪk/ *n* a painful stiffening of the muscles, esp. in the back or the neck, making movement difficult: *You'll get a crick in your neck if you sleep with your hair wet*

crick[2] *v* [T1] to cause (part of the body) to have a CRICK[1]

crick·et[1] /ˈkrɪkɪ̵t/ *n* **1** a type of small brown insect, the male of which makes loud short noises by rubbing its leathery wings together **2 as chirpy/lively as a cricket** *sl* very happy and active

cricket[2] *n* **1** an outdoor game, popular in Britain, played with a ball, BAT, and WICKETs, by 2 teams of 11 players each **2 not cricket** *old use or humor* (of a thing) unfair or not honourable: *I could have got what I wanted by telling her that, but it wouldn't have been cricket*

USAGE One plays **cricket** on a **pitch/wicket**, which is in the middle of a *field*. The **bowler bowls** the ball at the **wicket**, and the **batsman** SCOREs *runs*.

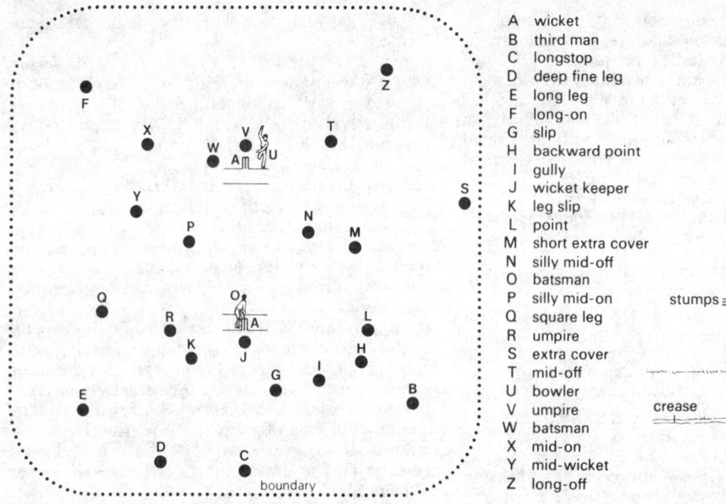

cricket

In a *match* the person in charge is called the **umpire**.

crick·et·er /ˈkrɪkɨtəʳ/ *n* a person who plays cricket

cried /kraɪd/ *past t. and p. of* CRY

cri·er /ˈkraɪəʳ/ *n* **1** an official who calls out publicly in a court of law **2** a person, esp. a young child, who cries a lot **3** TOWN CRIER

cries /kraɪz/ *3rd pers. sing. pres. t. of* CRY

cri·key /ˈkraɪki/ *interj BrE sl* (expresses surprise)

crime /kraɪm/ *n* **1** [C] an offence which is punishable by law: *If you* COMMIT (=do) *a crime you must expect to be punished.|the crime of not telling the truth in a court of law* **2** [U] unlawful activity in general: *It is the job of the police to prevent crime* **3** [C] a bad immoral act: *It isn't a crime to steal food when your children are hungry* **4** [S] *infml* a shame; pity: *It's a crime that this food should be wasted when so many people are hungry|It's a crime the way he treats her* —compare SIN

crim·i·nal[1] /ˈkrɪmɨnəl/ *adj* **1** [Wa5;A] of or related to crime or its punishment: *A criminal lawyer is a specialist in criminal law* **2** [B] of the nature of a crime: *a criminal act* **3** [Wa5;B] guilty of crime **4** [F] *infml* very bad: *It's criminal that some people should have 4 houses while others have nowhere to live* —**~ly** *adv*

criminal[2] *n* a person who is guilty of crime: *The judge sent the criminal to prison for 4 years*

crim·i·nol·o·gy /ˌkrɪmɨˈnɒlədʒi‖-ˈnɑ-/ *n* [U] the scientific study of crime and criminals —**-gist** *n*

crimp /krɪmp/ *v* [Wv5;T1] **1** to press (something) into small regular folds: *crimped material* **2** to curl (hair), esp. by using a rod of hot iron

crim·plene /ˈkrɪmpliːn/ *n* [U] *tdmk* a type of man-made material that tends not to become lined (CREASED) when crushed, folded, or pressed

crim·son[1] /ˈkrɪmzən/ *adj, n* [Wa5;B;U] (having) a deep slightly purplish red colour

crimson[2] *v* [T1;I∅] to (cause to) become CRIMSON[1]: *The light from the fire crimsoned the sky.|Her face crimsoned from shame*

crimson lake /ˌ·· ˈ·/ *n* [U] LAKE[2]

cringe /krɪndʒ/ *v* [I∅] **1** to bend and move back, esp. from fear or humbleness: *The slaves cringed every time their angry master raised his whip* **2** [Wv4; (*before, to*)] to behave towards a person of higher rank with humbleness and lack of self-respect: *Enough of this cringing: Let's behave like men!* **3** [(*at*)] *infml* to have a feeling of dislike or great annoyance: *Your foolish talk makes me cringe*

crin·kle[1] /ˈkrɪŋkəl/ *v* [Wv3;I∅;T1] [Wv5] to (cause to) become covered with fine lines by crushing or pressing: *I can't wear this dress to the dance – it's all crinkled*

crinkle[2] *n* [C] a thin line or fold made on cloth or paper by crushing or pressing

crin·kly /ˈkrɪŋkli/ *adj* [Wa2] **1** having many thin lines or folds made by pressing or crushing **2** (of hair) curly —**crinkliness** *n* [U]

cri·noid /ˈkraɪnɔɪd, ˈkrɪ-/ *n* any of many types of simple sea animals with featherlike arms

crin·o·line /ˈkrɪnəlɨn/ *n* a woman's undergarment of stiff material worn in former times under a dress to make it swell out

cripes /kraɪps/ *interj sl* (expresses surprise)

crip·ple[1] /ˈkrɪpəl/ *n* a person partly or wholly unable to use one or more of his limbs, esp. the legs

cripple[2] *v* [Wv3;T1] **1** [Wv4,5] to hurt or wound (a person) in such a way that use of one or more of the limbs is made difficult or impossible **2** *infml* to make useless; weaken seriously

cri·sis /ˈkraɪsɨs/ *n* **-ses** /siːz/ **1** the turning point in a serious illness, at which there is a sudden change for better or worse: *As soon as he reaches the crisis we'll know if he's going to live or die* **2** a turning point in the course of anything; uncertain time or state of affairs; moment of great danger or difficulty: *a governmental/political crisis|the crisis in Southern Africa*

crisp[1] /krɪsp/ *adj* [Wa1] **1** hard; dry; easily broken: *crisp pastry* **2** firm; fresh: *a crisp apple|crisp vegetables* **3** newly made or prepared; fresh: *a crisp pound note* **4** (of hair) tightly curled **5** (of style, manners, etc.) quick; showing no doubts or slowness; clear: *a quick crisp reply|a crisp manner of speaking* **6** (of the air, weather, etc.) cold; dry; fresh: *a crisp winter day|the crisp autumn wind* —**~ly** *adv* —**~ness** *n* [U]

crisp[2] *v* [I∅;T1] to (cause to) become CRISP[1] (esp. 1,2), esp. by cooking or heating: *If you cook this pastry at a high temperature it should crisp nicely*

crisp[3] also **potato crisp** (*AmE & AustrE*) **potato chip**— *n BrE* a thin piece of potato cooked in very hot fat, dried, and usu. sold in packets

crisp·y /ˈkrɪspi/ *adj* [Wa1] CRISP[1] (1,2) —**crispiness** *n* [U]

criss·cross[1] /ˈkrɪskrɒs‖-krɔs/ *n* a mark or pattern

made by crossing a number of straight lines; network of lines

crisscross² *v* **1** [T1] to mark with a pattern of crossing lines: *Train tracks crisscross the country* **2** [IØ] to form a CRISSCROSS³ pattern: *Animal tracks crisscross in the snowy fields*

crisscross³ *adj* [Wa5;A;(B)] marked by crossed lines: *a crisscross pattern|crisscross lines*

crisscross⁴ *adv* [Wa5] in crossing directions; in a CRISSCROSS³ manner: *His socks had been thrown crisscross on the floor*

cri·te·ri·on /kraɪˈtɪərɪən/ *n* **-ria** /rɪə/ *or* **-rions** an established rule, standard, or principle, on which a judgment is based: *What criteria do you use when judging the quality of a student's work?*

crit·ic /ˈkrɪtɪk/ *n* **1** a person skilled in forming and expressing judgments about the good and bad qualities of something, esp. art, music, etc. **2** a person who (regularly) finds fault with someone or something: *Jean's her own severest critic. She's always finding fault with herself*

crit·i·cal /ˈkrɪtɪkəl/ *adj* **1** [B (*of*)] finding fault; judging severely: *If you really understood the difficulties facing the government you wouldn't be so critical of its spending reductions.|Janet's only critical of Alice because she doesn't like her* **2** [B] marked by careful attention and judgment: *a critical thinker* **3** [B] of, related to, or being, the deciding turning point (CRISIS) in the course of anything: *a critical stage of the fever|of critical importance* **4** [B] very serious or dangerous: *a critical illness|His condition is reported as being critical* **5** [Wa5;A] of or related to the work of a CRITIC (1): *critical writings on art|critical opinions on this latest play* **6** [Wa5;B] *tech* (in science) of, being, or related to a fixed value as of pressure, temperature, etc., at which a substance changes suddenly: **Critical pressure** *is the smallest amount of pressure that can make a gas at critical temperature into a liquid.|***Critical temperature** *is the temperature above which a gas cannot become liquid even if the pressure changes* —**~ly** *adv* [Wa4]

crit·i·cis·m /ˈkrɪtɪ̈sɪzəm/ *n* **1** [U] the act of forming and expressing judgments about the good or bad qualities of anything, esp. artistic work; work of a CRITIC (1) **2** [U;(C)] such (a) judgment **3** [U] unfavourable judgment; disapproval; the act of finding fault: *The military government intends to stop unfavourable criticism by controlling newspapers and broadcasting* **4** [C] an unfavourable opinion or remark: *Your criticisms seem to have offended him* —see also TEXTUAL CRITICISM

crit·i·cize, -ise /ˈkrɪtɪ̈saɪz/ *v* [T1 (*for*); IØ] **1** to find fault with (someone or something); judge severely: *Although he praised my work in general the minister criticized my handling of this particular matter* **2** to make judgments about the good and bad points of (someone or something): *Would you like to read and criticize my new book?*

cri·tique /krɪˈtiːk/ *n* **1** [C] an article, book, set of remarks, etc., criticizing (CRITICIZE (2)) esp. an idea or a person's system of thought: *Marx's critique of Hegel* **2** [U] the art or practice of CRITICISM (1)

crit·ter /ˈkrɪtəʳ/ *n sl AmE* creature

croak¹ /krəʊk/ *v* **1** [IØ] to make a deep low noise such as a FROG (1) makes **2** [IØ;T1] to speak with a rough voice as if one has a sore throat **3** [IØ] *euph sl* to die

croak² *n* **1** [C] a deep low noise such as a FROG (2) makes **2** [S] a rough sound as produced by a sore throat: *to speak with a croak*

cro·chet¹ /ˈkrəʊʃeɪ‖krəʊˈʃeɪ/ *n* [U] **1** work, esp. fancy work, done with a needle having at one end a small hook (**crochet-hook** /ˈ·· ·/) used for making new stitches by drawing thread through other stitches **2** examples of work done in this way

crochet² *v* [D1 (*for*); T1;IØ] to make by means of CROCHET¹: *crochet a dress for a baby*

crock¹ /krɒk‖krɑk/ *n* a vessel made from baked earth

crock² *n infml* **1** *esp. BrE* an old motor car **2** an old person who is too weak to work: *an old crock*

crock·e·ry /ˈkrɒkəri‖ˈkrɑ-/ *n* [U] cups, plates, pots, etc., esp. made from baked earth

croc·o·dile /ˈkrɒkədaɪl‖ˈkrɑ-/ *n* [Wn1] **1** [C] any of several types of large animal (REPTILE) that live on land and in lakes and rivers in the hot wet parts of the world and have a long hard-skinned body and a long mouth with many strong teeth —compare ALLIGATOR, CAIMAN; see picture at REPTILE **2** [U] the skin of this animal used as leather **3** [C] a line of people, esp. schoolchildren, walking in pairs

crocodile tears /ˈ··· ˌ·/ *n* [P] tears or other signs of sorrow that are insincere

cro·cus /ˈkrəʊkəs/ *n* a type of small low-growing garden plant with a single purple, yellow, or white flower, which opens in early spring —see picture at FLOWER¹

croft /krɒft‖krɔft/ *n BrE* **1** (esp. in Scotland) a very small farm **2** a small enclosed field

croft·er /ˈkrɒftəʳ‖ˈkrɔf-/ *n BrE* a person who rents (or sometimes owns) a CROFT (1)

crois·sant /ˈkrwɑːsɒŋ‖krwɑːˈsɔŋ (*Fr* krwɑsɑ̃)/ *n Fr* a piece of buttery breadlike pastry, shaped like a CRESCENT¹ (1), baked, and eaten, esp. as part of a CONTINENTAL BREAKFAST

crom·lech /ˈkrɒmlek‖ˈkrɑm-/ *n tech* **1** a circle of upright stones built in ancient times in Britain and France **2** DOLMEN

crone /krəʊn/ *n* [C;*you*+N] a bent old woman

cro·ny /ˈkrəʊni/ *n* [C9] *infml* a friend or companion, esp. of someone old: *John's gone out with some of his cronies*

crook¹ /krʊk/ *n* **1** [C] a long stick or tool with a bent or curved end: *a* SHEPHERD'*s crook* **2** [C] a bend or curve: *She carried the parcel in the crook of her arm* —see picture at HUMAN² **3** [C; *you*+N] *infml* a thief

crook² *v* [T1;IØ] to (cause to) bend: *She crooked her arm to make carrying the parcel easier*

crook³ *adj AustrE not fml* (of things) nasty; bad: *The food/weather was crook* —opposite BEAUT

crook·ed /ˈkrʊkɪ̈d/ *adj* **1** not straight; twisted; bent: *a crooked street* **2** *infml* dishonest —**~ly** *adv* —**~ness** *n* [U]

croon /kruːn/ *v* **1** [T1;IØ] to sing with (too) much feeling **2** [IØ;T1] to sing gently in a low soft voice **3** [X9] to produce a stated effect on (someone) by doing this: *The mother crooned her baby to sleep*

croon·er /ˈkruːnəʳ/ *n old use or humor* a person who sings old popular songs with too much feeling

crop¹ /krɒp‖krɑp/ *n* **1** [*often pl.*] a plant or plant product such as grain, fruit, or vegetables grown or produced by a farmer: *Wheat is a widely grown crop in Britain* **2** the amount of such a product produced and gathered in a single season or place: *We've had the biggest wheat crop ever this year because of the hot summer|*(fig.) *a fine crop of hair* **3** [*usu. sing.*] a group or quantity appearing at any one time: *a whole new crop of college students* **4** a baglike part of a bird's throat where food is stored and partly DIGESTed **5** also **hunting crop, riding crop**— a short riding whip consisting of a short fold of leather fastened to a handle —see picture at HORSE **6** the handle of a whip **7** [*usu. sing.*] hair cut very short

crop² *v* **-pp-** **1** [T1;X7] (of an animal) to bite off and eat the tops of (grass, plants, etc.): *The sheep* *cropped the grass short* **2** [T1] to cut (a person's hair or a horse's tail) short **3** [T1] to remove the outer parts of (a horse's ear) by cutting **4** [T1 (*with*)] to plant (an area of land) with a crop: *The farmer decided to crop 3 fields with wheat and 2 with potatoes* **5** [L9] to bear a crop: *The potatoes and beans have cropped well this year, but the wheat badly*

crop dust·ing /ˈ· ˌ··/ also **crop spray·ing** /ˈ· ˌ··/— *n* [U] the act of shaking insect-killing chemical powders and liquids over crops, esp. done from a low-flying plane or from a specially shaped gunlike tool

crop out also **crop up**— *v adv* [IØ] (of rocks, minerals, etc.) to show above the earth's surface

crop·per[1] /ˈkrɒpəʳ‖ˈkrɑ-/ *n* **1** [C9] a plant bearing a crop: *Beans were good croppers this year* **2** [C] a person or thing that CROP*s*[2] (2,3)

cropper[2] *n sl* **come a cropper a** to fall heavily **b** to fail completely

crop up *v adv* [IØ] *infml* **1** to arise, happen, or appear, unexpectedly: *Some difficulties have cropped up at work so I'll be late coming home tonight* **2** CROP OUT

cro·quet /ˈkrəʊkeɪ, -ki‖krəʊˈkeɪ/ *n* [U] an outdoor game played on grass in which players knock wooden balls through a number of small metal arches (HOOP*s*) with a long-handled wooden hammer (MALLET)

cro·quette /krəʊˈket/ *n* [*often pl.*] a small rounded mass of crushed meat, fish, vegetables, etc., covered with beaten egg and/or very small pieces of bread (BREADCRUMB*s*), cooked in deep fat, and eaten as food

crore /krɔːʳ‖kror/ *determiner, n* **crore** *or* **crores** [Wn2] *Ind & PakE* (*plural esp.* crore *after* numbers) 10,000,000; 100 LAKH*s*

cro·sier, crozier /ˈkrəʊʒəʳ, -zɪəʳ/ *n* a long stick with an ornamented curved end, carried by a BISHOP on formal occasions

cross[1] /krɒs‖krɔs/ *n* **1** [C] an upright post with a shorter bar crossing it near the top on which people were nailed by their hands and feet and left to die as a punishment in ancient times **2** [C] any of various representations of this, used for ornament, in art, HERALDRY, etc.: *a Latin cross|St George's cross|a Maltese cross* **3** [C] a small silver or gold object shaped like this, worn round the neck on a chain as an ornament or sign of Christian faith **4** [C9] an ornament of this shape worn as an honour (a MEDAL), esp. for military bravery **5** [C] an act of making this shape by moving one's hand on one's chest as a religious act in church, before saying one's prayers, etc.: *to make the sign of the cross* **6** [C *often cap.*] this shape as the sign of the Christian faith or religion —compare CRESCENT[1] (3) **7** [*the*+R *often cap.*] Christ's death as the act that saved the world: *"It is by the Cross that we were set free from death," said the priest* **8** [C] an example of sorrow or suffering as a test of one's patience or goodness: *Everyone has his own cross to bear in this life* **9** [C] an object of this shape built in a public place or at the end of a grave to remind people of the dead **10** [C] a figure or mark formed by one straight line crossing another, as X, often used **a** as a sign of where something is **b** as a sign that something is incorrect **c** the signature of a person who can't write **11** [C9, esp. *between*] an animal or plant that is a mixture of breeds: *A* **tiglon** *is a cross between a tiger and a lion* —see also HYBRID **12** [C9, esp. *between*] a combination of 2 different things: *The drink tasted like a cross between coffee and hot chocolate* **13 on the cross** DIAGONALly; from corner to corner: *Cut the cloth on the cross* **14 take the cross** to become a CRUSADER (=a Christian soldier who fought against Muslims in former times) **15 take up one's cross** to accept sufferings and sorrow and bear them with patience

cross[2] *v* **1** [T1;(IØ)] to go, pass, or reach across: *The soldiers took 3 days to cross the desert.|The bridge crosses the river at its narrowest point* **2** [IØ] to lie or pass across each other: *I'll meet you at the place in the forest where the paths cross* **3** [Wv5;T1] to place or fold across each other: *Jean sat on the floor with her legs crossed* **4** [T1] to oppose (someone or his plans, wishes, etc.): *Anne hates being crossed so don't argue with her* **5** [T1] to draw a line across: *Remember to cross your 't's when you're writing* **6** [Wv5;T1] (in Britain) to draw 2 lines across (a cheque) to show that it must be paid into a bank account —compare OPEN[1] (16) **7** [T1] to make a movement of the hand forming a cross on (oneself) as a religious act: *The old lady crossed herself as she left the church* **8** [IØ;T1] (of letters in the post, people travelling, etc.) to meet and pass: *We posted our letters on the same day so they crossed in the post* **9** [T1] to cause (an animal or plant) to breed with one of another kind: *I crossed a tiger with/and a lion and bred a* **tiglon** **10 cross one's heart (and hope to die)** *sl* to promise **11 cross one's mind** to come into one's thoughts **12 cross one's 't's and dot one's 'i's** *infml* to be very careful; pay careful attention to detail **13 cross someone's palm (with silver) a** to give money to someone to say what is going to happen to one in the future **b** to give money to someone for an improper favour; BRIBE someone **14 cross swords with (someone)** to argue with (someone) **15 cross someone's path** to meet someone **16 keep one's fingers crossed** *infml* to hope that nothing will happen to upset one's plans: *He's keeping his fingers crossed that it won't rain on Saturday when he wants to play football* —see also **don't cross your** BRIDGE*s* **before you come to them**

cross[3] *adj* [Wa1;B] angry; bad-tempered: *The old lady was really cross when the boy's ball broke her window* —**~ly** *adv* —**~ness** *n* [U]

Cross *n* [(*the*) R] the cross on which Christ died

cross- *comb. form* **1** lying, passing, or moving across the general direction of movement: *cross-traffic*‖CROSSWINDS‖CROSSCURRENTS‖*cross-*CHANNEL *ships*|CROSSTOWN **2** opposed: CROSS-PURPOSES **3** lying across; TRANSVERSE: CROSSBEAM|CROSSBENCHES

cross·bar /ˈkrɒsbɑːʳ‖ˈkrɔs-/ *n* a bar joining 2 upright posts, esp. the bar joining 2 GOALPOST*s*

cross·beam /ˈkrɒsbiːm‖ˈkrɔs-/ *n* a beam lying across and helping to support a number of other beams

cross·bench·es /ˈkrɒsˌbentʃ½z‖ˈkrɔs-/ *n* [P] seats in both houses of the British Parliament on which members sit who do not belong to the official government or opposition parties —**-bencher** *n*

cross·bones /ˈkrɒsbəʊnz‖ˈkrɔs-/ *n* [P] see SKULL AND CROSSBONES

cross·bow /ˈkrɒsbəʊ‖ˈkrɔs-/ *n* a powerful weapon combining a BOW and a gun. It consists of a length of wood or metal held in a curve by a piece of strong tight string and fastened across a wooden handle that is specially shaped for firing arrows, and was used in former times

cross·bred /ˈkrɒsbred‖ˈkrɔs-/ *n, adj* [Wa5] produced by mixing breeds: *crossbred sheep*

cross·breed[1] /ˈkrɒsbriːd‖ˈkrɔs-/ *n* an animal or plant which is a mixture of breeds

crossbreed[2] *v* [T1;IØ] **a** to cause (an animal or plant) to breed with one of another breed **b** (of an animal or plant) to breed with one of another breed

cross·check /ˌkrɒsˈtʃek‖ˌkrɔs-/ *v* [T1] to find out the correctness of (a calculation, answer, etc.) by using a different method or information from different places

cross-coun·try[1] /ˌ· ˈ··◂/ *adj, adv* [Wa5] across the fields or open country: *a cross-country race*

cross-country[2] *n* [C;U] a race run not on a track but across open country and fields

cross·cur·rent /ˈkrɒsˌkʌrənt‖ˈkrɔskɜr-/ *n* a current as in the sea, a river, etc., moving across the general direction of the main current: (fig.) *the crosscurrents of public opinion*

cross·cut /ˈkrɒskʌt‖ˈkrɔs-/ *n* a direct course between 2 points, esp. a DIAGONAL cut or path

crosscut saw /ˌ·· ˈ·/ *n* a thin flat blade of metal with a row of sharp teeth down one side and a handle at each end, used by 2 men as a tool for cutting down trees

crosse /krɒs‖krɔs/ *n* a specially-shaped long-handled RACKET with a net at the end, used in the game of LACROSSE

cross-ex·am·ine /ˌ· ·ˈ··/ also **cross-question**— *v* [T1;(I∅)] **1** to question (a witness already questioned by the opposing side in a court of law) to test the answers and information given **2** to question (someone) very closely or severely, esp. in order to compare the answers with other answers given before —**cross-examination** /ˌ· ···ˈ··/ *n* [C;U] —**cross-examiner** /ˌ· ·ˈ···/ *n*

cross-eyed /ˈ· ·/ *adj* having one or both eyes turned in towards the nose

cross-fer·ti·lize, -ise /ˌ· ˈ···/ *v* [T1] **1** to cause male sex cells (POLLEN) from one plant to unite with female sex cells from (another plant) **2** [*often pass.*] *often apprec.* to influence with ideas from different areas or fields of study: *During those important years Europe was cross-fertilized with/by ideas from many other societies* —**-lization** /ˌ· ···ˈ··/ *n* [U]

cross·fire /ˈkrɒsfaɪəʳ‖ˈkrɔs-/ *n* [U] one or more lines of gunfire firing across the direction of movement

cross-grained /ˌ· ˈ·◂/ *adj* **1** (of wood) having the GRAIN running across rather than along; having an irregular GRAIN **2** *infml* difficult to please; ARGUMENTATIVE

cross-hatch·ing /ˈ· ˌ··/ *n* [U] lines drawn across part of a DIAGRAM (=an informational picture or figure) to show that it is made of different material or to produce the effect of shade in a drawing

cross-in·dex /ˌ· ˈ··/ *v* [T1] to provide one or more CROSS-REFERENCES*s* for (information) in (a book, article, etc.) —**cross-index** *n*

cross·ing /ˈkrɒsɪŋ‖ˈkrɔ-/ *n* **1** a journey across the sea **2** a place where 2 lines, tracks, etc., cross **3** a place at which a road, river, etc., may be crossed **4** *tech* (in a church) the place where the NAVE and the TRANSEPT cross

cross-legged /ˌkrɒs ˈlegd◂‖ˌkrɔs ˈlegɪ̈d◂/ *adj, adv* [Wa5] **1** sitting with ankles crossed and legs wide apart **2** having one leg placed over and across the other

cross off *v adv; prep* [D1;T1] to remove (from) by drawing a line through: *If you don't want to come, cross your name off (the list)*

cross out *v adv* [T1] to draw a line through (writing): *As I'd made 2 mistakes in my sentence I crossed them out and wrote it again*

cross·o·ver /ˈkrɒsəʊvəʳ‖ˈkrɔs-/ *n esp. BrE* **1** an arrangement of lines by which a train may move from one track to another **2** a road passing over another road; FLYOVER

cross·patch /ˈkrɒspætʃ‖ˈkrɔs-/ *n* [C;N] *humor sl* a bad-tempered person

cross·piece /ˈkrɒspiːs‖ˈkrɔs-/ *n* a piece of anything lying across something else

cross·ply /ˈkrɒsplaɪ‖ˈkrɔs-/ *adj* [Wa5] (of a motor tyre) made stronger by cords pulled tightly across each other inside the rubber

cross-pol·li·nate /ˌ· ˈ···/ *v* [T1] CROSS-FERTILIZE (1) —**cross-pollination** /ˌ· ··ˈ··/ *n* [U]

cross-pur·pos·es /ˌ· ˈ···/ *n* **1 at cross purposes** with different and opposing purposes in mind: *talk at cross-purposes* **2 be at cross-purposes** (of 2 people) to misunderstand each other's purpose; have different and opposing purposes

cross-ques·tion /ˌ· ˈ··/ *v* [T1] CROSS-EXAMINE —**~er** *n*

cross-re·fer /ˌ· ·ˈ·/ *v* [T1;I∅: (*from* and/or *to*)] to direct (the reader) from one place in a book to another place in the same book: *In this dictionary* CAPITAL[1] (3) *letters are used to cross-refer from one word to another*

cross-ref·erence /ˌ· ˈ··‖ˈ· ˌ··/ *n* a note directing the reader from one place in a book to another place in the same book: *In this dictionary cross-references are shown in* CAPITAL[1] (3) *letters*

cross·road /ˈkrɒsrəʊd‖ˈkrɔs-/ *n* a road that crosses another road

cross·roads /ˈkrɒsrəʊdz‖ˈkrɔs-/ *n* **crossroads** [Wn3] **1** a place where 2 or more roads cross **2** a point at which an important decision must be taken

cross-sec·tion /ˈ· ˌ··/ *n* **1** (a drawing of) a surface made by cutting across something, esp. at right angles to its length: *a cross-section of a worm| cross-section of a plant stem* **2** a typical or representative example of the whole: *a cross-section of British society*

cross-stitch /ˈ· ·/ *n* **1** [C] a stitch shaped like an X made by crossing one stitch over another at right angles **2** [U] ornamental sewing in which this stitch is used

cross talk /ˈ· ·/ *n* [U] **1** rapid exchange of clever remarks, esp. between 2 COMEDIANS (=actors who try to make people laugh) or between members of different parties in Parliament **2** interruption of a radio or telephone conversation by unwanted signals from elsewhere

cross·tree /krɒs-triː‖ˈkrɔs-/ *n tech* either of the 2 beams of wood or metal fastened across the top part of a MAST (=an upright pole for carrying a ship's flags or sails) to hold the ropes, keep the sails spread open, etc.

cross·walk /ˈkrɒswɔːk‖ˈkrɔs-/ *n AmE* a specially marked path where people on foot may cross a road

cross·wind /ˈkrɒsˌwɪnd‖ˈkrɔs-/ *n* a wind blowing (nearly) at right angles to the line of flight of a plane, direction of movement of traffic on a road, etc.

cross·wise /ˈkrɒsˌwaɪz‖ˈkrɔs-/ *adv, adj* **1** so as to cross something; across: *a wind blows crosswise* **2** crossing another or each other; in the form of a cross: *logs laid crosswise on the floor*

cross·word /ˈkrɒsˌwɜːd‖ˈkrɔsˌwɜrd/ also **crossword puz·zle** /ˈ·· ˌ··/— *n* a game in which words are fitted into a pattern of numbered squares in answer to numbered CLUES (=pieces of information about the necessary word) in such a way that words can be read across as well as down when the game is completed

crotch /krɒtʃ‖krɑtʃ/ *n* **1** the place where a branch separates from a tree **2** also **crutch**— the place between the tops of the legs of the human body —see picture at HUMAN[2] **3** also **crutch**— (a piece of cloth used to strengthen) the place where the legs of a pair of trousers, undergarment, etc., join

crotch·et /ˈkrɒtʃɪ̈t‖ˈkrɑ-/ *n* **1** *AmE* **quarter note**—

tech a musical note, sign ♩, having a quarter of the value of a SEMIBREVE —see picture at NOTATION **2** an odd, strange, or unreasonable idea **3** a small hook or hooked instrument

crotch·et·y /ˈkrɒtʃɨ̣ti‖ˈkrɑ-/ *adj* **1** having or being a CROTCHET (2) **2** *infml* (esp. of someone old) bad-tempered; liking to argue or complain

crouch[1] /kraʊtʃ/ *v* [I∅ (DOWN)] to lower the body close to the ground by bending the knees and back: *The cat saw the bird and crouched down ready to jump.|The tall man had to crouch to get into the small car*

crouch[2] *n* [S] the act of CROUCHing[1]: *The car was so small that the tall man had to sit in a crouch*

croup[1] /kruːp/ *n* the fleshy part above the back legs of certain animals, esp. the horse —see picture at HORSE

croup[2] *n* [(*the*) U] *med* a disease of the throat, esp. in children, that makes breathing difficult and noisy and causes coughing —**croupy** *adj*

crou·pi·er /ˈkruːpɪəʳ/ *n* a person who collects the money lost and pays out the money won at a table where games are played for money

crou·ton /ˈkruːtɒn‖-tɑn/ *n Fr* a small square piece of bread TOASTed or cooked in fat and eaten in soup

crow[1] /krəʊ/ *n* **1** any of various types of large shiny black birds with a low loud cry —see picture at BIRD **2 as the crow flies** in a straight line **3 eat crow** *AmE infml* to be forced to admit humbly that one was wrong **4 have a crow to pluck** *infml* to have an unpleasant matter to talk about **5 stone the crows** *BrE sl & becoming old use* (expresses surprise, disbelief, etc.): *Stone the crows, I don't believe that!*

crow[2] *v* [I∅] **1** to make the loud high cry of a COCK (=a fully-grown male chicken) **2** [(*with*)] (esp. of a baby) to make wordless sounds of happiness or pleasure: *The baby crowed with pleasure when its father picked it up* **3** [(*about*)] *infml* to speak proudly: *I wish John would stop crowing about his examination results* —see also CROW OVER

crow[3] *n* **1** [(*the*) S] the loud high cry of a COCK (=a fully-grown male hen) **2** [S;(C)] a loud wordless sound of pleasure or happiness as made by babies

crow·bar /ˈkrəʊbɑːʳ/ *n* an iron bar with a bent V-shaped end put under heavy objects and pressed to raise them off the ground

crowd[1] /kraʊd/ *v* **1** [Wv5 (*with*); T1;L9] (esp. of people) to fill: *In the week before the holidays shoppers crowded the stores* **2** [L9] (esp. of people) to come together in large numbers: *People crowded round the scene of the accident.|They crowded round/in* **3** [X9, esp. IN] to press tightly, as into a small space: *He crowded as many books as possible on to the shelf.|He crowded them in* **4** [T1] *BrE sl* to put pressure on; begin to threaten: *to crowd a debtor for payment* **5 crowd (on) sail** *tech* to spread more sails to make a ship go faster

crowd[2] *n* **1** [GC] a large number of people gathered together: *a crowd waiting for a bus|There were crowds of people at the theatre* **2** [C9] a particular social group: *I don't like the college crowd; that's why I never go to college dances* **3** [C] a large number of things in disorder: *a crowd of books and papers on his desk* **4** [*the*+R] people in general: *He writes all his books for the crowd rather than for specialists* **5 follow/move with/go with the crowd** to do or say the same as other people: *I do what I want to do; I don't follow the crowd* **6 to pass in a crowd** *not fml* to be satisfactory if not examined too closely **7 raise oneself/rise above the crowd** to show oneself to be better than most other people

crowd·ed /ˈkraʊdɨ̣d/ *adj* **1** completely full; filled with a crowd: *a crowded bus|crowded streets* **2** uncomfortably close together: *passengers crowded (together) on a bus* —**~ness** *n* [U]

crowd out *v adv* [T1b *usu. pass.*] to make entrance impossible because of lack of space: *Your article was crowded out of the magazine; I'm sorry*

crow·foot /ˈkrəʊfʊt/ *n* **crowfoot** *or* **crowfoots** [Wn2] any of various types of plant with divided leaves that look like birds' feet

crown[1] /kraʊn/ *n* **1** [C] an ornamental head covering, usu. made of gold with jewels in, worn by a king or queen as a sign of royal power **2** an ornament of this shape used in art, ornaments, HERALDRY, etc. **3** [*the*+R *usu. cap.*] the governing power of a kingdom that has limited the personal political power of its king or queen: *Land belonging to the crown does not belong to the queen personally but to the state* **4** [*the*+R] the rank of king or queen: *He won the crown by killing the old king in battle* **5** [C] a circle of flowers or leaves worn on the head as a sign of victory, honour, or rank **6** [*the*+R] a CHAMPIONSHIP title: *He won the crown in 1973* **7** [C] the top or highest part of anything, as of the head, hat, mountain, etc.: *the crown of a hill* —see picture at HUMAN[2] **8** [C] the head itself: *"Jack fell down and broke his crown"* (old children's poem) **9** [C] a British coin worth 25 pence used in former times as money but now made only on ceremonial occasions to be kept not spent **10** any of several standards of money, used esp. in countries of Northern Europe **11** [C] the part of the tooth which can be seen **12** [C] the most perfect point of anything

crown[2] *v* **1** [T1;X1] to give royal power to by solemnly placing a crown on the head of (a person) **2** [T1] to place a circle of flowers or leaves on someone's head as a sign or victory **3** [T1] to cover the top of (something): *Mist crowned the mountain.|Trees crowned the hill* **4** [Wv4;T1] to complete worthily: *Success in the peace talks has crowned this government's period in power* **5** [Wv5; T1] to put a protective covering on (a decayed tooth): *I have 2 crowned teeth* **6** [T1] *infml* to hit (someone) on the head: *Be quiet or else I'll crown you!* **7 to crown it all** to complete good or bad fortune: *His house burnt down and his car was stolen and to crown it all he lost his job*

crown cap /ˌ· ˈ·/ *n* a metal cap for a bottle

crown col·o·ny /ˌ· ˈ···/ *n* (*often caps.*) a British COLONY ruled by a governor appointed by the British government, not elected by the people

crown court /ˌ· ˈ·/ *n* [C;U] a British law court for judging criminal cases

crowned head /ˌ· ˈ·/ *n* a king or queen: *All the crowned heads of Europe were at the dead queen's funeral*

crown jew·els /ˌ· ˈ··/ *n* [P] the crowns, swords, jewels, etc., worn by a king or queen on great state occasions

crown prince /ˌ· ˈ·◂/ *n* [C;A] the man who has the lawful right to be king after the death of the present king or ruling queen

crown prin·cess /ˌ· ·ˈ·◂‖ˌ· ˈ··◂/ *n* **1** the woman who has the lawful right to be ruling queen after the death of the present king or ruling queen **2** the wife of a CROWN PRINCE

crow o·ver *v prep* [T1 *no pass.*] to delight in (the defeat or misfortune of someone): *The nasty boy crowed over his enemy's failure*

crow's foot /ˈ· ·/ *n* **crow's feet** **1** [*usu. pl.*] a line (WRINKLE) at the outer corner of a person's eye **2** CROWFOOT

crow's nest /ˈ· ·/ *n* a small box or shelter near the top of a ship's MAST (=an upright pole for holding the sails) from which a man can watch for danger, land, etc.

cro·zier /ˈkrəʊʒəʳ, -zɪəʳ/ *n* CROSIER

cru·cial /ˈkruːʃəl/ *adj* [(*to, for*)] of deciding importance: *at a crucial moment|a crucial point in the talks* —**~ly** *adv*

cru·ci·ble /ˈkruːsəbəl/ *n* **1** a vessel in which substances are heated to very high temperatures **2** the hollow part at the bottom of a FURNACE in which melted metal collects **3** a severe searching test

cru·ci·fix /ˈkruːsɨ̣fɪks/ *n* a cross with a figure of Christ on it

cru·ci·fix·ion /ˌkruːsɨ̣ˈfɪkʃən/ *n* **1** [C;U] (an example of) the act of CRUCIFYing **2** [C] a picture or other representation of Christ on the Cross

Crucifixion *n* [*the*+R] the death of Christ on the Cross

cru·ci·form /ˈkruːsɨ̣fɔːm‖-fɔrm/ *adj* [Wa5] cross-shaped

cru·ci·fy /ˈkruːsɨ̣faɪ/ *v* [T1] **1** to kill (someone) by nailing or binding to a cross and leaving to die **2** to be very cruel or unpleasant to (someone or something) esp. by unfair public attack: *crucified by public opinion*

crude¹ /kruːd/ *adj* [Wa1] **1** in a raw or natural state; unprepared; untreated: *crude oil|crude rubber* **2** lacking grace, education, or sensitive feeling: *the crude behaviour of his brother|crude people* **3** not skilfully made, done, or finished: *a crude shelter in the forest|crude methods|crude ideas* —**~ly** *adv*

crude² *n* [U] CRUDE¹ (1) oil: *1,000 barrels of crude*

cru·di·ty /ˈkruːdɨ̣ti/ *n* **1** [U] also **crudeness** /kruːdnɨ̣s/— the state or quality of being CRUDE¹: *The crudity of his jokes annoyed the priest* **2** [C] a CRUDE¹ (2) act, remark, or other example of this state or quality

cru·el /ˈkruːəl/ *adj* [Wa1] **1** liking to cause pain or suffering; taking pleasure in the pain of another; unkind; merciless: *The cruel master beat his slaves mercilessly with a whip.|Anyone who likes watching animals suffer is cruel* **2** painful; causing suffering: *a cruel punishment/disease/remark|*(fig.) *a cruel wind* —**~ly** *adv* —**~ness** *n* [U]

cru·el·ty /ˈkruːəlti/ *n* **1** [U] also **cruelness** /ˈkruːəlnɨ̣s/— the state or quality of being cruel: *cruelty to animals|the cruelty of war* **2** [C] a cruel act, expression, or other example of this state or quality: *Kicks and blows are undeserved cruelties to a harmless little dog*

cru·et /ˈkruːɨ̣t/ *n* **1** also **cruet stand** /ˈ·· ·/— a set of containers for pepper, salt, oil, MUSTARD, VINEGAR, etc., standing on a specially shaped holder of glass or metal, for use at meals **2** any of these containers, esp. a small glass bottle for oil or VINEGAR

cruise¹ /kruːz/ *v* [IØ] **1** to sail in an unhurried way searching for enemy ships or for pleasure **2** [Wv4] (of a car, plane, etc.) to move at a practical rather than high speed in order to make best use of petrol, oil, etc.: *a cruising speed of 60 miles an hour* **3** *sl* to look (as in public places) for a sexual partner

cruise² *n* a sea voyage for pleasure

cruis·er /ˈkruːzəʳ/ *n* [C; *by*+U] **1** a large fast warship **2** CABIN CRUISER

crumb /krʌm/ *n* **1** [C] a very small piece of dry food, esp. bread or cake: *Sweep up the crumbs from under the table* **2** [C] a small amount: *crumbs of knowledge/information* **3** [C; *you*+N] *AmE sl* a worthless person

crum·ble¹ /ˈkrʌmbəl/ *v* [Wv3] **1** [T1;IØ] to (cause to) break into very small pieces: *The cook crumbled the bread and added it to the soup* **2** [Wv4;IØ] to decay; come to ruin: *a crumbling church|The Roman empire crumbled under pressure from uncivilized northern tribes.|*(fig.) *All her hopes crumbled to nothing*

crumble² *n* **1** [C9;U9] a cooked dish of sweetened fruit covered with a mixture of flour, fat and sugar **2** [U] the mixture of flour, fat, and sugar cooked in this dish

crum·bly /ˈkrʌmbli/ *adj* [Wa2] easily CRUMBLEd¹ (1)

crum·my /ˈkrʌmi/ *adj* [Wa1] *sl* **1** of poor quality; worthless: *a crummy book|What a crummy idea!* **2** rather ill: *I've felt crummy all morning so I'm staying at home this afternoon*

crum·pet /ˈkrʌmpɨ̣t/ *n* **1** [C] (esp. in Britain) a small thick round breadlike cake with holes in one side, usu. eaten hot with butter spread over the side with the holes in —compare MUFFIN **2** [U] *BrE infml & often humor* women considered as sexual objects: *Jean's a nice piece of crumpet!* (=Jean's a sexually attractive woman)

crum·ple /ˈkrʌmpəl/ *v* [Wv3] **1** [Wv5;IØ;T1: (UP)] to (cause to) become full of irregular folds by pressing, crushing, etc.: *Take care not to crumple your dress by packing it carelessly.|a crumpled dress* **2** [IØ (UP)] *infml* to fall down; lose strength: *The enemy army crumpled up under our attacks*

crunch¹ /krʌntʃ/ *v* **1** [T1;IØ (AWAY, *on*)] to crush (food) noisily with the teeth: *The dog lay in front of the fire crunching (on) a bone* **2** [Wv4;IØ] to make a crushing noise as of eating nuts, walking through fallen leaves, etc.: *Our feet crunched on the frozen snow.|The stones crunched under the car tyres* —**crunchy** *adj* [Wa1]

crunch² *n* **1** [(*the*) S] a crushing sound: *We could hear the crunch, crunch, crunch of the bear as it walked over the frozen snow* **2** [*the*+R] *infml* a difficult moment at which an important decision must be made (esp. in the phr. **when/if it comes to the crunch**): *They're against our plan now but when it comes to the crunch they'll support us*

crup·per /ˈkrʌpəʳ/ *n* a leather belt passing under a horse's tail and fastened to the SADDLE (=a seat on the horse's back) to prevent it from slipping forward

cru·sade¹ /kruːˈseɪd/ *n* **1** (*usu. cap.*) any of the Christian wars to win back the Holy Land (Palestine) from the Muslims in the 11th, 12th, and 13th centuries **2** [(*of, for*)] a struggle or movement for the defence or advancement of an idea, principle, etc.: *a crusade against crime|a crusade for women's rights*

crusade² *v* [Wv4;IØ (*against, for*)] to take part in a CRUSADE¹: *to crusade for women's rights|a crusading young lawyer* —**~r** *n*

cruse /kruːz/ *n bibl & old use* a small pot or jar for holding oil, wine, etc.

crush¹ /krʌʃ/ *v* **1** [T1] to press with great force so as to break, hurt, or destroy the natural shape or condition: *Don't crush this box, there are flowers inside!|The tree fell on top of the car and crushed it* **2** [T1] to break into a powder by pressure: *This machine crushes wheat grain to make flour* **3** [IØ;T1] to press tightly; CROWD: *The people crushed through the gates as soon as they were opened* **4** [Wv4;T1] to destroy completely, esp. by using force: *10 years of marriage had not crushed his spirit.|The military government has successfully crushed all opposition* **5** [T1;IØ] CRUMPLE (1)

crush² *n* **1** [S] uncomfortable pressure caused by a great crowd of people: *There was such a crush on the train that I could hardly breathe* **2** [C *usu. sing.*] *infml* a social gathering attended by an uncomfortably great number of people **3** [U9] *esp. BrE* a drink made by crushing the juice from fruit:

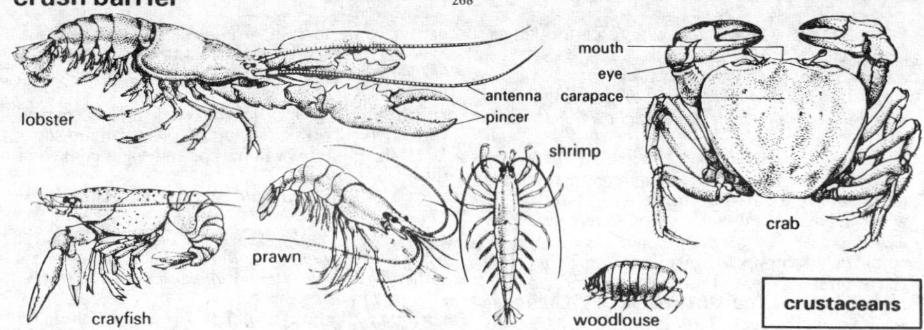

Would you like some more orange crush? **4** [C (*on*)] *infml* a strong foolish and short-lived liking or love for someone

crush bar·ri·er /ˈ· ˌ···/ *n* a fence or something else put in the way to control or prevent forward movement

crust /krʌst/ *n* **1** [C;U] the hard usu. brown outer surface of baked bread **2** [C] a piece of bread with this on one side **3** [C;U] the baked pastry on a PIE **4** [C;U] a hard outer covering (as of earth or snow): *the earth's crust|a thin crust of ice* **5 off one's crust** *sl* mad —see also UPPER CRUST

crus·ta·cean /krʌˈsteɪʃən/ *adj, n* [Wa5] (of, belonging to, or being) any of a group of animals with a hard outer shell that are closely related to the insects: LOBSTER*s*, CRAB*s, and* SHRIMP *are crustaceans*

crust o·ver *v adv* [IØ] to become covered with a CRUST (4): *The snow crusted over during the freezing weather*

crust·y /ˈkrʌsti/ *adj* [Wa1] **1** having a hard well-baked CRUST (1): *a crusty loaf* **2** bad-tempered; bad-mannered: *a crusty man with bad manners|a crusty old general* —**crustily** *adv* —**crustiness** *n* [U]

crutch /krʌtʃ/ *n* **1** a stick of wood, metal, or other material, with a piece that fits under the arm, for supporting a person who has difficulty in walking —see picture at MEDICAL[1] **2** a support like this in shape or use: (fig.) *Religion/John was her crutch in times of sorrow* **3** CROTCH (2,3)

crux /krʌks/ *n* the part of a matter that is the most difficult to understand or deal with satisfactorily

cry[1] /kraɪ/ *v* **1** [IØ;(T1)] to produce (tears) from the eyes with or without sounds expressing grief, sorrow, sadness, etc.: *She cried with grief when she heard news of her friend's death.|Paul was crying for some more cake* (=because he wanted some more cake).|*On the day of mother's funeral my father cried real tears for the first time in his life* **2** [IØ (OUT)] to make loud sounds expressing fear, sadness, or some other feeling: *The little boy cried out with pain when he burnt his fingers* **3** [IØ (*for*); T1: (OUT)] to call loudly; shout: *The trapped woman cried out for help.|"Run, run!" cried the citizens as enemy soldiers entered their city* **4** [IØ] (of certain animals and birds) to make one's natural sound **5** [T1;IØ] to make known by shouting out **6 cry for the moon** *infml* to demand something impossible **7 cry (oneself) to sleep** to cry until one falls asleep **8 cry one's eyes/heart out** to cry very bitterly: *When her pet dog died my daughter cried her eyes out* **9 for crying out loud** *sl* (used to give strength to a demand, request, etc.): *For crying out loud shut that door!* **10 give (someone) something to cry about** *infml* to punish (someone) more severely for crying after having been less severely punished —see also **cry** WOLF; **cry over spilt** MILK; CRY DOWN; CRY OFF; CRY OUT AGAINST; CRY OUT FOR; CRY UP

cry[2] *n* **1** [C (*of*)] any loud sound expressing fear, pain, etc.: *a cry of anger/hunger/pain/fear* **2** [C] a loud call; shout: *the cry of a newspaper seller|a cry of "Stop, thief!"|I miss the old street cries* (=the shouts made by people offering goods for sale) *of London* **3** [S] a period of crying: *Don't worry about Jean. She'll be better after she's had a (good) cry* **4** [C (*for*), C3] a general public demand or complaint: *a national cry for lower taxes* **5** [C9] a call to action: *an Indian war cry|a battle cry* **6** [C] the natural cry of certain animals or birds **7 a far/long cry from** a great deal different from (something): *The state of affairs in industry is a far cry from what it was last year* **8 in full cry a** (of a group of dogs) making loud noises as they hunt an animal: *The dogs were in full cry after a fox* **b** (of a person) eagerly demanding or attacking: *After the government's defeat in Parliament the opposition were in full cry*

cry·ba·by /ˈkraɪˌbeɪbi/ *n* [C; *you*+N] a person, esp. a child, who cries or complains too readily with little cause

cry down *v adv* [T1] to express a poor opinion of (something) —opposite **cry up**

cry·ing /ˈkraɪ-ɪŋ/ *adj* [Wa5;A] *infml* (esp. of something bad) that demands attention: *There's a crying need for new schools in the big cities*

cry off *v adv* [IØ] to fail to fulfil a promise or agreement: *He tried to cry off after swearing he would do it!*

cry out a·gainst *v adv prep* [T1,4 *pass. rare*] to express one's disapproval of (something)

cry out for *v adv prep* [T1 *no pass.*] to be in great need of (something); demand (something): *The garden is crying out for rain*

crypt /krɪpt/ *n* an underground room, esp. under a church

cryp·tic /ˈkrɪptɪk/ *adj* hidden; secret; mysterious: *The words in a completed* **cryptic crossword** *can be read to give a special message* —**~ally** /-tɪkəli/ *adv* [Wa4]

cryp·to- /ˈkrɪptəʊ/ *comb. form* hidden; secret: *For 10 years he lived as a crypto-Christian in a country where to be a Christian was a crime.|a crypto-*COMMUNIST

cryp·to·gram /ˈkrɪptəgræm/ *n* a message or writing in secret letters

cryp·to·gra·phy /krɪpˈtɒgrəfi‖-ˈtɑ-/ *n* [U] the study of secret writing and CODE*s* —**-pher** *n* —**-phic** /ˌkrɪptəˈgræfɪk/ *adj* —**-phically** *adv* [Wa4]

crys·tal /ˈkrɪstl/ *n* **1** [U] a transparent natural mineral that looks like pure ice **2** [C] a shaped piece of this used as an ornament or jewel **3** [U] transparent colourless glass of very high quality: *a crystal wine glass* **4** [C] a very small regular shape with surfaces in even arrangement, formed naturally by a substance on becoming solid: *sugar and salt crystals* **5** [C] *AmE* the transparent cover over the face of a clock or watch

crystal gaz·ing /ˈ·· ˌ··/ *n* [U] the practice of looking steadily into a CRYSTAL (1) ball in an

attempt to see what is going to happen in the future —**crystal gazer** /'·· ˌ··/ *n*
crys·tal·line /'krɪstəlaɪn, -li:n‖-lən/ *adj* [Wa5] **1** of or like CRYSTAL (1); very clear; transparent **2** made of CRYSTALs (4): *crystalline rocks*
crys·tal·lize, -ise /'krɪstəlaɪz/ *v* **1** [T1;I∅] to (cause to) form CRYSTALs (4): *At what temperature does sugar crystallize?* **2** [T1;I∅] to (cause to) become clear, settled, or fixed in form: *The minister is at present trying to crystallize his ideas into a practical plan* **3** [Wv5;T1] to preserve (fruit) by covering the surface with sugar and leaving to harden —**-lization** /ˌkrɪstəlaɪ'zeɪʃən‖-lə-/ *n* [U]
crystal set /'·· ·/ *n* (esp. in former times) a simple radio receiver
cry up *v adv* [T1] to praise highly —opposite **cry down**
cu. *written abbrev. for:* CUBIC
cub /kʌb/ *n* **1** the young of various types of meat-eating wild animals, such as the lion, bear, etc.: *a fox and her cubs* **2** a member of the CUBS **3** a young and inexperienced person, esp. male
cub·by·hole /'kʌbihəʊl/ *n* a small enclosed space
cube[1] /kju:b/ *n* **1** a solid object with 6 equal sides: *a sugar cube|a cube of apple* —see picture at GEOMETRY **2** the number made by multiplying a number by itself twice: *The cube of 3 is 27* $(3\times3\times3=27)$
cube[2] *v* **1** [Wv5;T1] to multiply a number by itself twice: *3 cubed* (written 3^3) *is 27* **2** to cut (something) into CUBEs[1] (1): *Cube the apples before putting them in the pan*
cube root /ˌ· '·‖'· ·/ *n* the number which when multiplied by itself twice equals the given number: *If 3 is the cube root of 27* (written $\sqrt[3]{27}$) *then* $3\times3\times3=27$
cu·bic /'kju:bɪk/ *adj* [Wa5] **1** being a measurement of the space that would fit into a CUBE[1] (1) with edges of the stated length: *a cubic inch/foot/mile/metre* —see WEIGHTS & MEASURES TABLE **2** CUBICAL
cu·bi·cal /'kju:bɪkəl/ *adj* also **cubic**— [Wa5] having the form of a CUBE[1] (1)
cu·bi·cle /'kju:bɪkəl/ *n* a very small enclosed division of a larger room, as for dressing or undressing at a swimming pool
cub·is·m /'kju:bɪzəm/ *n* [U] (*often cap.*) a 20th century art style in which the subject matter is represented by GEOMETRIC shapes —**cubist** *n*
cu·bit /'kju:bɨt/ *n bibl* an ancient measurement of length equal to the length of the arm between the wrist and the elbow, usu. between 18 and 22 inches (=between 45 and 56 CENTIMETREs)
cub re·port·er /ˌ· ·'··/ *n* a young inexperienced newspaper reporter
cubs /kʌbz/ *n* [*the*+P; *at, to*+U] a division of the BOY SCOUTs for younger boys
cuck·old[1] /'kʌkəld, 'kʌkəʊld‖-kəld/ *n humor derog now rare* a man whose wife has had sex with another man since she has been married
cuckold[2] *v* [T1] *humor now rare* to make (a husband) into a CUCKOLD[1]
cuck·old·ry /'kʌkəldri/ *n* [U] *humor now rare* the state of being a CUCKOLD[1]
cuck·oo[1] /'kʊku:‖'ku:ku:, 'kʊ-/ *n* **-oos** **1** a type of grey European bird that lays its eggs in other birds' nests, flies south for winter, and has a call that sounds like its name **2** the call of this bird
cuckoo[2] *adj sl* stupid; mad; foolish: *a cuckoo boy|cuckoo ideas|You're cuckoo*
cuckoo clock /'·· ·/ *n* a small wall clock with a wooden bird inside that appears to tell each hour with the call of a CUCKOO[1] (1)
Cuckoo-spit /'·· ·/ *n* [U] the whitish liquid produced on the stems and leaves of plants by a certain insect
cu·cum·ber /'kju:kʌmbəʳ/ *n* **1** [C] a type of long round vegetable with a dark green skin and very light green watery flesh, usu. eaten raw with cold food or PICKLEd —see picture at VEGETABLE[1] **2** [U] pieces of this eaten as food
cud /kʌd/ *n* [U9] **1** food that has been swallowed and brought up again to the mouth from the first stomach of certain animals, such as the cow, sheep, etc., for further CHEWing (=crushing in the mouth) (esp. in the phr. **chew the cud**=RUMINATE (1)) **2 chew the cud** *infml* to think deeply before making a decision
cud·dle[1] /'kʌdl/ *v* [Wv3;T1;I∅] to hold (someone, something, or each other) lovingly and closely in the arms: *The little girl picked up her pet dog and cuddled it.|Jean and John were cuddling in the back row of the cinema last night*
cuddle[2] *n* [S] an act of cuddling (CUDDLE[1]): *As soon as I opened the door my little daughter ran up to me for a cuddle*
cud·dle·some /'kʌdlsəm/ *adj* CUDDLY
cuddle up *v adv* [Wv3;I∅ (*to,* TOGETHER)] to lie close and comfortably: *The children cuddled up to each other in bed*
cud·dly /'kʌdli/ *adj* [Wa1] lovable; suitable for cuddling (CUDDLE[1])
cud·gel[1] /'kʌdʒəl/ *n* **1** a short thick heavy stick or other such object used as a weapon; short heavy CLUB **2 take up the cudgels for** to begin to support or act strongly in favour of: *took up the cudgels for women's rights*
cudgel[2] *v* **-ll-** (*AmE* **-l-**) [T1] to strike or beat with a CUDGEL[1]
cue[1] /kju:/ *n* **1** (esp. in a play) a word, phrase, or action serving as a signal for the next person to speak or act: *The actor missed his cue and came onto the stage late* **2** an example of how to behave, what to do, etc.; guiding standard: *Follow the general's cue and fight more bravely* **3 take one's cue from** *infml* to use the practice of (another person) as a standard for one's own actions
cue[2] *n* **1** a long straight wooden rod, slightly thicker at one end than the other, used for pushing the ball in BILLIARDS, SNOOKER, etc. **2** QUEUE[1] (2)
cue in *v adv* [T1b] to give (someone) a sign to be ready to do something: *The director will cue you in when it's your turn to sing*
cuff[1] /kʌf/ *n* **1** the end of a SLEEVE (=the arm of a garment) **2** *AmE* TURN-UP **3 off the cuff** without preparation
cuff[2] *v* [T1] to strike (a person or animal) lightly with the open hand: *Mother cuffed the dog when she found it asleep on a chair*
cuff[3] *n* a light blow with the open hand
cuff link /'· ·/ *n* [*usu. pl.*] a buttonlike object that passes through 2 small holes (BUTTONHOLEs) on a shirt CUFF to fasten it
cuffs /kʌfs/ *n* [P] *infml* HANDCUFFS
cui·rass /kwɪ'ræs/ *n* a piece of armour covering the upper half of the body but not the arms
cui·sine /kwɪ'zi:n/ *n* [U;(C)] *Fr* a style of cooking: *French cuisine|This hotel has excellent cuisine*
cul-de-sac /'kʌl də ˌsæk, 'kʊl-‖ˌkʌl də 'sæk, ˌkʊl-/ *n* **cul-de-sacs** *or* **culs-de-sac** /kʌl-, kʊl-/ **1** a street with only one way in or out; BLIND ALLEY **2** DEAD END (1)
cul·i·na·ry /'kʌlɨnəri‖'kʌlɨneri, 'kju:l-/ *adj* [Wa5] of, related to, or suitable for the kitchen or cooking
cull[1] /kʌl/ *v* **1** [T1] to choose (something) from among others: *to cull the prettiest flowers* **2** [T1;I∅] to take from a group and kill (a weak or unproductive animal): *We culled that hen because she wasn't*

laying any eggs **3** [T1;IØ] to search through (a group of animals) and kill the weakest and least productive: *Every year the groups of* SEALS *that live off our coasts are culled because they eat too much fish*

cull² *n* **1** an act of CULLing¹ (3): *Because of the decrease in fish supplies 2* SEAL *culls will be necessary this year* **2** an animal killed because it is weak or unproductive

cul·len·der /ˈkʌlɨndəʳ/ *n* COLANDER

cul·mi·nate in /ˈkʌlmɨneɪt/ *v prep* [T1,(4);V4a] to reach the highest point, degree, or development in: *All his efforts culminated in failure.|The army's brave fighting culminated in total victory*

cul·mi·na·tion /ˌkʌlmɨˈneɪʃən/ *n* the highest point: *The culmination of the doctor's life's work was his discovery of a cure for the cold*

cu·lotte /kjuːˈlɒt‖kjʊˈlɑt/ *n* [A] CULOTTES

cu·lottes /kjuːˈlɒts‖kjʊˈlɑts/ *n* [P] short skirtlike trousers worn by women; trousers shaped to look like a skirt —see PAIR (USAGE)

cul·pa·ble /ˈkʌlpəbəl/ *adj* deserving blame; guilty: *culpable behaviour|They held him culpable for the offence* —**-bility** /ˌkʌlpəˈbɪlɨti/ *n* [U] —**-bly** /ˈkʌlpəbli/ *adv*

cul·prit /ˈkʌlprɨt/ *n* the person guilty or believed to be guilty of a crime or offence

cult /kʌlt/ *n* **1** [C] (the group of people believing in) a particular system of religious worship, with its special customs and ceremonies: *When did he join the cult?|an ancient tribal cult* **2** [C9] worship of or loyalty to a person, principle, etc.: *The leadership cult developed in a number of European countries between the wars* **3** [C9] (the group of people following) a popular fashion or a particular interest

cul·ti·va·ble /ˈkʌltɨvəbəl/ *adj* [Wa5] that can be cultivated

cul·ti·vate /ˈkʌltɨveɪt/ *v* [T1] **1** to prepare (land) for the growing of crops **2** to plant, grow, and raise (a crop) by preparing the soil, providing with water, etc. **3** to improve or develop by careful attention, training, or study: *to cultivate a love of art* **4** to encourage the growth of friendship with or the good will of (a person): *John always tries to cultivate people who are useful to him professionally*

cul·ti·vat·ed /ˈkʌltɨveɪtɨd/ *adj* **1** having or showing good education and manners, sensitivity, etc. **2** [Wa5] (of land) used for growing crops

cul·ti·va·tion /ˌkʌltɨˈveɪʃən/ *n* [U] **1** the act of cultivating (CULTIVATE): *to bring new land under cultivation|The cultivation of cotton has fallen in recent years* **2** the state or quality of being CULTIVATED (3)

cul·ti·va·tor /ˈkʌltɨveɪtəʳ/ *n* **1** a person who cultivates **2** a tool or machine for loosening the earth around growing plants, destroying unwanted plants, etc.

cul·tu·ral /ˈkʌltʃərəl/ *adj* [Wa5] of or related to CULTURE: *cultural independence|the cultural difficulties of children coming to a new society* —**~ly** *adv*

cul·ture /ˈkʌltʃəʳ/ *n* **1** [U] artistic and other activity of the mind and the works produced by this: *The aim of our library service is to bring culture to the people* **2** [U] a state of high development in art and thought existing in a society and represented at various levels in its members: *the development of culture|a man of little culture* **3** [C;U] the particular system of art, thought, and customs of a society; the arts, customs, beliefs, and all the other products of human thought made by a people at a particular time: *ancient Greek culture|a tribal culture, never studied before* **4** [U] development and improvement of the mind or body by education or training **5** [U] the practice of raising animals and growing plants or crops: *bee culture|The culture of this uncommon flower is increasing in Britain* **6** [C; U] (a group of bacteria produced by) the practice of growing bacteria for scientific use or use in medicine

cul·tured /ˈkʌltʃəd‖-ərd/ *adj* **1** [Wa5] grown or produced by man: *a cultured* PEARL **2** having or showing good education, good manners, sensitivity, etc.; CULTIVATED: *cultured minds that like good books and painting*

cul·vert /ˈkʌlvət‖-ərt/ *n* **1** a pipe for waste water that passes under a road, railway line, bank of earth, etc. **2** an underground pipe for electric wires, gas, etc.

-cum- /kʊm, kʌm/ *comb. form* combined with; together with: *a bed-cum-*SITTING ROOM (=a BED-SITTER)|*Chorlton-cum-Hardy is a part of Manchester*

cum·ber /ˈkʌmbəʳ/ *v* [T1 (*with*)] *becoming rare* ENCUMBER

cum·ber·some /ˈkʌmbəsəm‖-bər-/ also (*rare*) **cum·brous** /-brəs/— *adj* heavy and awkward to carry, wear, etc.: *a cumbersome parcel*

cum·in /ˈkʌmɨn/ *n* [U] **1** a type of small plant whose pleasant-smelling seedlike fruit is used in cooking and medicine **2** the fruit of this plant

cum·mer·bund /ˈkʌməbʌnd‖-ər-/ *n* a broad belt of cloth worn round a man's waist, esp. as part of formal evening dress

cu·mu·la·tive /ˈkjuːmjʊlətɪv‖-mjə-/ *adj* [Wa5] increasing steadily in amount by one addition after another: *cumulative interest payable on a debt* —**~ly** *adv*: *Cumulatively, the effects of the drug are quite bad*

cu·mu·lo·nim·bus /ˌkjuːmjʊləʊˈnɪmbəs‖-mjə-/ *n* [U;C] a type of very thick dark cloud with a flat base, that usu. forms at a height of 4 miles and produces heavy rain

cu·mu·lus /ˈkjuːmjʊləs‖-mjə-/ *n* [U;C] a type of thick white feathery cloud with a flat base, that forms at an average height of 2 miles

cu·nei·form /ˈkjuːnifɔːm, ˈkjuːni-ɨfɔːm‖kjuːˈnɪəfɔrm/ *adj, n* [Wa5;B;U] (of, related to, or written in) WEDGE-shaped letters used in writing by the Babylonians, Assyrians, and other peoples of ancient Mesopotamia

cun·ni·lin·gus /ˌkʌnɪˈlɪŋgəs/ also **cun·ni·linc·tus** /-ˈlɪŋktəs/— *n* [U] the practice of touching a woman's sex organs with the lips and tongue in order to give sexual pleasure

cun·ning¹ /ˈkʌnɪŋ/ *adj* **1** showing or having cleverness in deceiving; clever: *as cunning as a fox* **2** *old use* skilful: *a cunning worker* **3** *infml esp. AmE* attractive; pretty; CUTE: *a cunning little girl/smile* —**~ly** *adv*

cunning² *n* [U] **1** cleverness, esp. in deceiving: *The fox showed its cunning by swimming along the stream so that the hunting dogs wouldn't be able to smell it* **2** *old use* skill: *In spite of his great age he could still show much cunning at handling an axe*

cunt /kʌnt/ *n taboo* **1** [C] VAGINA **2** [C; *you*+N] a foolish or nasty person

cup¹ /kʌp/ *n* **1** [C] a small round container, usu. with a handle, from which liquids are drunk, esp. hot liquids such as tea or coffee **2** [C] this container with the liquid in it: *If you're making a pot of tea I'd love a cup* **3** [C] also **cupful** /ˈkʌpfʊl/— the amount held by one CUP¹ (1): *Add one cup of flour to half a cup of sugar and mix* **4** [C] a small circular object: *the cup of a flower* —see picture at NUT¹ **5** [C; *the*+R] a specially shaped ornamental vessel, usu. made of gold or silver, given as a prize in a competition: *Which team do you think will win the cup this year?* **6** [U9;C9] a specially prepared drink of wine or another alcoholic drink: CIDER *cup*|CLARET *cup* **7** [C9] that which comes to a person in life; experience: *When her child died her cup of sorrow seemed complete* **8** [C] (in religious use) CHALICE **9 in one's cups** when drunk —see also **one's cup of** TEA

cup² *v* **-pp-** [T1] **1** to form (esp. the hands) into the shape of a cup: *He cupped his cold hands round the cup of hot chocolate* **2** *med* to press a glass cup against the skin of (a person) so that the air pressure inside the cup is reduced and the blood inside the body therefore drawn to the surface

cup·bear·er /ˈkʌpˌbeərəʳ/ *n* an official in a royal or noble court who serves wine on special occasions

cup·board /ˈkʌbəd‖-ərd/ *n* a set of shelves enclosed by doors, where clothes, cups, plates, food, etc., may be stored —compare CLOSET¹ (1)

cupboard love /ˈ·· ·/ *n* [U] love shown with the intention of gaining something by it

cup cake /ˈ· ·/ *n* a small round cake, often covered with chocolate, baked and/or served in a cup-shaped container

cup fi·nal /ˈ· ˌ··/ *n BrE* (esp. in football) the last match to decide the winning team in a competition —compare CUP-TIE

cu·pid /ˈkjuːpɨd/ *n* a beautiful winged boy carrying a BOW and arrows, used in art for representing love

cu·pid·i·ty /kjʊˈpɪdɨti/ *n* [U] very great desire, esp. for money and property

cu·po·la /ˈkjuːpələ/ *n* a small DOME forming (part of) a roof

cup·pa /ˈkʌpə/ *n* [*usu. sing.*] *BrE infml* a cup of tea: *I'm so thirsty I'm almost dying for a cuppa*

cup·ping /ˈkʌpɪŋ/ *n* [U] *med* the act of pressing a glass cup tightly against the skin in order to draw blood to the surface

cu·pric /ˈkjuːprɪk/ *adj* [Wa5] containing copper

cup-tie /ˈ· ·/ *n BrE* (esp. in football) a match between 2 teams competing in a competition —compare CUP FINAL

cur /kɜːʳ/ *n* **1** [C] a worthless bad-tempered dog, esp. of mixed breed —compare MONGREL **2** [C; *you*+N] a badly behaved worthless person; nasty person who likes to quarrel; coward

cu·ra·ble /ˈkjʊərəbəl/ *adj* [Wa5] that can be cured: *a curable disease* —**-bly** *adv* [Wa3]

cu·ra·çao /ˈkjʊərəsəʊ, ˌkjʊərəˈsəʊ/ *n* [U] a thick sweet alcoholic drink given a special orange taste by the addition of the skin of the bitter **curaçao orange**

cu·ra·cy /ˈkjʊərəsi/ *n* the office or work of a CURATE

cu·rate /ˈkjʊərɨt/ *n* a priest of the lowest rank appointed to help the priest of a PARISH

cu·ra·tive /ˈkjʊərətɪv/ *n, adj* [Wa5] (something) serving to cure an illness: *A rest in the mountains is the best curative for breathing difficulties*

cu·ra·tor /kjʊˈreɪtəʳ/ *n* **1** the person in charge of a MUSEUM, library, etc. **2** *AustrE* a GROUNDSMAN —**~ship** *n*

curb¹ /kɜːb‖kɜrb/ *n* **1** a length of chain or leather passing under a horse's jaw and fastened to the BIT **2** a controlling influence; CHECK: *Keep a curb on your anger* **3** *AmE* KERB

curb² *v* [T1] **1** to control (one's feelings, temper, spending, etc.) **2** *tech* to control (a horse) by pulling the CURB¹ (1)

curd /kɜːd‖kɜrd/ *n* [U;C *usu. pl. with sing. meaning*] the thick soft almost solid substance that separates from milk when it becomes sour, eaten as food or used for making cheese —see also LEMON CURD; compare WHEY

cur·dle /ˈkɜːdl‖ˈkɜrdl/ *v* [Wv3;T1;IØ] to (cause to) form into CURDS; (cause to) thicken: (fig.) *His blood curdled with terror at the sight* —see also BLOODCURDLING

cure¹ /kjʊəʳ/ *v* [T1;(IØ)] **1** [(*of*)] to bring health to (a person) in place of disease or illness, esp. by medical treatment: *This medicine should cure you of your cold.*|(fig.) *Parents try to cure their children of bad habits* **2** to make (a disease, illness, etc.) go away, esp. by medical treatment **3** to remove (something bad): *Government action to cure unemployment* **4** to preserve (food, skin, tobacco, etc.) by drying, hanging in smoke, covering with salt, etc.

cure² *n* **1** a course of medical treatment: *The president went to the south of France for a cure at a famous hospital* **2** a drug or medicine that cures an illness, disease, etc.: *Scientists have so far failed to provide a cure for the common cold* **3** a return to health after illness: *This drug should bring about a cure* **4** something that cures something bad: *At present there seems no cure for rising prices and falling living standards* **5** *tech* the priestly office; position as a priest

cu·ré /ˈkjʊəreɪ‖kjʊˈreɪ (*Fr* kyre)/ *n Fr* a PARISH PRIEST in France

cure-all /ˈ· ·/ *n* something that makes all bad things better; PANACEA

cu·ret·tage /kjʊəˈretɪdʒ‖ˌkjʊrəˈtɑːʒ/ *n* [U] the act of removing diseased flesh and skin from body wounds by using a special medical instrument (**curette**)

cur·few /ˈkɜːfjuː‖ˈkɜr-/ *n* **1** a rule that all people should be indoors by a stated time **2** the time during which people must be indoors according to this rule **3** (in former times) (the ringing of a bell to mark the beginning of) a time of night, at which lights and fires had to be put out

cu·ri·a /ˈkjʊərɪə/ *n* **-iae** /ɪiː/ **1** (in former times) the king's court of justice **2** (*often cap.*) the POPE and the officials assisting him responsible for the organization of the church

cu·ri·o /ˈkjʊərɪəʊ/ *n* **-ios** an object, valuable because of its age, rarity, or beauty

cu·ri·os·i·ty /ˌkjʊəriˈɒsɨti‖-ˈɑs-/ *n* **1** [U,U3;S,S3] the desire to know or learn: *The boy burned with* (*a*) *curiosity to know what was in the letter addressed to his mother* **2** [C] a strange, interesting, or rare object, custom, etc.

cu·ri·ous /ˈkjʊərɪəs/ *adj* **1** [F3] eager to know or learn: *A good student should always be curious to learn* **2** [B;F3] too eager to know or learn, esp. about what does not concern one; having or showing too much interest in other people's affairs: *He was so curious to know what was in the letter that he opened it, even though it was addressed to his father* **3** [B] odd; strange; peculiar: *a curious state of affairs* **4** [B] interesting because rare; unusual: *a curious piece of 19th century art* —**~ly** *adv*: *Curiously* (*enough*), *he seemed to know that already*

curl¹ /kɜːl‖kɜrl/ *v* **1** [Wv5;T1;IØ] **a** (of hair) to twist into or form a curl or curls: *"Plenty of bread makes your hair curl," said the old man jokingly* **b** to cause (hair) to twist into or form a curl or curls: *I don't like my hair straight so I'm going to have it curled* **2** [T1;IØ: (UP)] to (cause to) form one or more curls or twists: *In autumn the leaves on trees become brown, curl up, and die* **3** [IØ;T1] to (cause to) wind: *The plant's stem curled round the branches of the tree* **4** [IØ] to move in a curve or SPIRAL (=a shape like the lines on a screw): *Smoke curled above the fire*

curl² *n* **1** [C; *in* + U] a small hanging mass (LOCK¹) of twisted hair; small mass of hair twisting upwards **2** [C] something with the shape of the lines on a screw; SPIRAL: *a curl of smoke* **3** [U] the state of having this shape or being in masses of this type: *How do you keep your hair in curl?*

curl·er /ˈkɜːləʳ‖ˈkɜr-/ *n* [*often pl.*] a specially-made round object round which hair is twisted to make it curl

cur·lew /ˈkɜːljuː‖ˈkɜrluː/ *n* a type of bird with brownish feathers and a long curved beak

cur·li·cue, curlycue /ˈkɜːlɪkjuː‖ˈkɜr-/ *n* an ornamental twisted pattern, as made with a pen under one's signature

curl·ing /ˈkɜːlɪŋ‖ˈkɜr-/ *n* [U] a Scottish winter sport played by sliding flat heavy stones over ice towards a mark called the **tee**

curling i·ron /ˈ·· ˌ··/ also **curling tong** /ˈ·· ·/— *n* [*usu. pl.*] a heated instrument used for curling or straightening the hair

curling stone /ˈ·· ·/ *n* a heavy round flat stone with a handle, slid across the ice in the sport of CURLING

curl up *v adv* [I0;(T1)] to (cause to) lie comfortably with the limbs drawn close to the body: *In the long winter evenings I like to curl up in front of the fire with a good book*

curl·y /ˈkɜːli‖ˈkɜrli/ *adj* [Wa1] having curls or tending to curl —**curliness** *n* [U]

cur·mud·geon /kɜːˈmʌdʒən‖kɜr-/ *n* [C; *you*+N] *infml* a bad tempered man, esp. old

cur·rant /ˈkʌrənt‖ˈkɜr-/ *n* **1** a small dried seedless GRAPE, esp. used in baking cakes **2** (*esp. in comb.*) any of various types of small bushes grown for their small fruits: *a* BLACKCURRANT *bush* **3** (*esp. in comb.*) the small black, red, or white juicy fruit that grows in bunches on such bushes: *a* REDCURRANT

cur·ren·cy /ˈkʌrənsi‖ˈkɜr-/ *n* **1** [U] the state of being in common use or general acceptance: *Reports that the general is to be dismissed are gaining currency among government ministers* **2** [C;U] the particular type of money in use in a country: *The German currency is among the strongest in the world*

cur·rent[1] /ˈkʌrənt‖ˈkɜr-/ *adj* **1** [Wa5] belonging to the present time; of the present day: *current fashions/events/prices/the current month's account* **2** commonly accepted; in general use: *This word is no longer in current use* **3** (esp. of money) passing from one person to another; used as money: *The English 10-shilling note is no longer current* —**~ly** *adv*

current[2] *n* **1** [C] a continuously moving mass of liquid or gas, esp. one flowing through slower-moving liquid or gas: *The current is strongest in the middle of the river.|air currents* **2** [C;U] the flow of electricity past a fixed point —see also ALTERNATING CURRENT, DIRECT CURRENT **3** [C] *tech* the rate of flow measured in AMPERE*s* **4** [C] a general tendency or course of movement of events; opinions: *The military government hopes to control the current of public opinion by controlling broadcasting*

current ac·count /ˈ·· ·ˌ·/ *AmE* **checking account** /ˈ·· ·ˌ·/— *n* a bank account which usu. does not earn interest and from which money can be taken out at any time by cheque —compare DEPOSIT ACCOUNT, SAVINGS ACCOUNT

current as·sets /ˌ·· ˈ··/ *n* [P] money ready for use, and other ASSET*s* which can be changed into money when needed

cur·ric·u·lum /kəˈrɪkjʊləm‖-kjə-/ *n* **-la** /lə/ *or* **-lums** a course of study offered in a school, college, etc.

curriculum vi·tae /kəˌrɪkjʊləm ˈvaɪtiː, ˈviːtaɪ‖-kjə-/ also (*esp. AmE*) **résumé**— *n* **curricula vitae** /-kjʊlə-‖-kjələ-/ [*usu. sing.*] *Lat, fml* a short written account of one's education and past employment, used esp. when looking for a new job

cur·rish /ˈkɜːrɪʃ/ *adj* cowardly; nasty; of, related to, or being a CUR —**~ly** *adv*

cur·ry[1] /ˈkʌri‖ˈkɜri/ *v* [T1] **1** to rub and clean (a horse) with a special comb (**currycomb**) **2 curry favour** to try and win favour or attention, often by insincere means: *to curry someone's favour*

curry[2] *n* [C;U] (a dish of) meat, vegetables, or eggs, etc., cooked in a thick often hot-tasting liquid made from CURRY POWDER, usu. eaten with rice or special bread

curry[3] *v* [Wv5;T1] to cook (meat, vegetables, eggs, etc.) in a thick often hot-tasting liquid made from CURRY POWDER: *curried chicken*

curry pow·der /ˈ·· ˌ··/ *n* [U] a mixture of SPICE*s* (=hot-tasting dried vegetable parts) crushed into a fine powder, used for giving a special hot taste to food

curse[1] /kɜːs‖kɜrs/ *n* **1** [C (*on*)] a word or sentence asking God, heaven, a spirit, etc., to bring down evil or harm on someone or something **2** [C (*on*)] the evil or harm called down in this way: *Our tribe is under a curse* **3** [C] a cause of misfortune, evil, etc.: *Foxes can be a curse to farmers* **4** [C] a word or words used in swearing; word or words expressing anger, hate, etc. **5** [*the*+R] *sl* (a period of) MENSTRUATION: *to have the curse* **6 not give/care a (tinker's) curse** (*AmE* **not give/care a (tinker's) damn**)— *BrE sl* to be quite unworried (about): *I don't care a tinker's curse what he thinks of me!*

curse[2] *v* **1** [T1] to call down God's anger, evil, misfortune, etc., upon (someone): *The priest cursed the hunters for daring to stand on holy ground* **2** [T1] to swear at: *The rider cursed his unwilling horse* **3** [I0] to swear; use bad language **4 cursed with** suffering misfortune or great harm because of (someone or something): *My mother is cursed with blindness and difficulty in hearing*

curs·ed /ˈkɜːsɪ̈d‖ˈkɜr-/ also **curst** /kɜːst‖kɜrst/— *adj* **1** hateful: *I hate the cursed fool!* **2** *infml* annoying: *I wish that cursed dog would be quiet* —**~ly** *adv*

cur·sive /ˈkɜːsɪv‖ˈkɜr-/ *adj* (of writing) written in a flowing rounded style with the letters joined together; in the style of handwriting rather than printing —**~ly** *adv*

cur·so·ry /ˈkɜːsəri‖ˈkɜr-/ *adj* (of work, reading, etc.) not thorough; done without attention to details —**-rily** *adv*

curt /kɜːt‖kɜrt/ *adj* [Wa1] (of a person, his manner, what he says, etc.) too short in speech to be polite; rudely short in speech, manner, etc.: *a curt speaker/reply/answer/manner* —**~ly** *adv* —**~ness** *n* [U]

cur·tail /kɜːˈteɪl‖kɜr-/ *v* [T1] to cut short; reduce; limit: *The government hopes to curtail public spending in the next tax year* —**~ment** *n* [C;U]

cur·tain[1] /ˈkɜːtn‖ˈkɜrtn/ *n* **1** a piece of hanging cloth that can be drawn to cover a window or door, to divide a room in 2, etc. —see picture at LIVING ROOM **2** a sheet of heavy material drawn or lowered across the front of a stage in a theatre: *As the curtain rises a dead body is seen on the stage. . . .* —see picture at THEATRE **3** something like this that covers, protects, hides, etc.: *The castle was hidden behind a curtain of smoke* **4 draw a curtain over (something)** to say no more about (something) —see also BAMBOO CURTAIN; IRON CURTAIN

curtain[2] *v* [Wv5;T1] to provide (a window, house, etc.) with a curtain: *I bought enough material to curtain the house*

curtain call /ˈ·· ·/ *n* the appearance of actors and actresses at the end of a performance to be APPLAUDed

curtain off *v adv* [T1] to separate or divide off with a curtain: *We can curtain off each bed in the hospital for private examination*

curtain rais·er /ˈ·· ˌ··/ *n* a short play acted before the main play

cur·tains /ˈkɜːtnz‖ˈkɜr-/ *n* [P] *sl* the end, esp. of a life: *If your work doesn't improve it will be curtains for you*

curt·sy¹, **curtsey** /ˈkɜːtsi‖ˈkɜr-/ *n* a woman's act of respect to someone of higher rank, done by bending the knees and lowering the head and shoulders —compare BOW

curtsy², **curtsey** *v* [IØ (*to*)] (of a woman or girl) to bend the knees and lower the head and shoulders as an act of respect to someone of higher rank —compare BOW

cur·va·ceous, **-cious** /kɜːˈveɪʃəs‖ˈkɜr-/ *adj sl* (of a woman) having a pleasingly well-developed figure, with attractive curves —**~ly** *adv*

cur·va·ture /ˈkɜːvətʃəʳ‖ˈkɜr-/ *n* [C;U] **1** the degree to which something is curved; state of being curved: *The moon's surface has more curvature than the earth's* **2** *med* (an) unnatural curving of a body part, usu. causing pain or illness: *curvature of the* SPINE

curve¹ /kɜːv‖kɜrv/ *v* [IØ;T1] to (cause to) bend in the shape of a curve: *The road curved to the right*

curve² *n* **1** a line of which no part is straight and which contains no angles; rounded bend: *to take the curve in a road|a curve in the road* **2** also **curve ball** /ˈ· ·/— (in BASEBALL) a throw (PITCH) in which the ball spins so that it curves, as to the left when thrown by the right hand: (fig.) *The newspaper reporter threw the politician a curve by asking him an unexpected question he couldn't answer*

cush·ion¹ /ˈkʊʃən/ *n* **1** a bag filled with a soft substance on which a person can lie, sit, or rest comfortably: *The priest knelt on a cushion to pray* **2** something like this in shape or purpose: HOVERCRAFT*s ride on a cushion of air* **3** the soft rubber border on the inside edge of a BILLIARD table

cushion² *v* [Wv5;T1] **1** to lessen the force of: *Nothing can cushion the severity of the electoral defeat* **2** to protect from hardship or sudden change: *The princess led a cushioned life in her country palace* **3** to provide with a CUSHION¹ or CUSHION*s*: *a cushioned seat*

cush·y /ˈkʊʃi/ *adj* [Wa1] *infml* (of a job, style of life, work, etc.) needing little effort; easy —**cushiness** *n* [U]

cusp /kʌsp/ *n tech* **1** a pointed end, esp. of a tooth **2** the point formed by 2 curves meeting: *the cusp of the moon in its first quarter|the cusp of a* CRESCENT

cus·pi·dor /ˈkʌspɪ̈dɔːʳ/ *n AmE* SPITTOON

cuss¹ /kʌs/ *n sl* **1** a man: *a peculiar old cuss* **2** a curse

cuss² *v* [T1;IØ] *sl* to curse

cuss·ed /ˈkʌsɪ̈d/ *adj sl* **1** too unwilling to change one's opinions, actions, etc., even when they are clearly mistaken; OBSTINATE **2** CURSED —**~ly** *adv* —**~ness** *n* [U]

cus·tard /ˈkʌstəd‖-ərd/ *n* [U] **1** *esp. BrE* a thick sweet yellow liquid made by adding CUSTARD POWDER to boiling sweetened milk, poured over sweet foods and eaten **2** EGG CUSTARD

custard pow·der /ˈ·· ˌ··/ *n* [U] a powder made from a mixture of dried eggs, fine flour, and sugar, added to boiling sweetened milk to make CUSTARD

cus·to·di·al /kʌˈstəʊdɪəl/ *adj* [Wa5] of or related to CUSTODY

cus·to·di·an /kʌˈstəʊdɪən/ *n* **1** a person in charge of a public building; keeper of a library, castle, MUSEUM, etc.: (fig.) *He says that film should not be shown, but he has no right to act as a custodian of public morals* **2** *fml* a person with CUSTODY (1) over someone or something —**~ship** *n* [U]

cus·to·dy /ˈkʌstədi/ *n* [U] **1** the act or right of caring for someone, esp. when this right is given in a court of law: *The father was given custody of the children because the mother was always drinking* **2** the state of being cared for or guarded: *She kept her jewels in custody at the bank.|The stolen car is now in police custody* **3** imprisonment; DETENTION: *The criminal was seen at the airport and taken into custody by the police*

cus·tom /ˈkʌstəm/ *n* **1** [C;U] (an) established socially accepted practice: *tribal customs|Social customs vary greatly from country to country* **2** [U] *fml* regular support given to a shop or person trading by those who buy their goods or services: *We lost a great deal of custom when that new shop opened across the road* **3** [C] the habitual practice of a person: *His custom was to get up early and have a cold bath every morning* —see HABIT (USAGE)

custom- *comb. form* (done) in accordance with the buyer's (CUSTOMER*'s*) wishes: *a custom-built car|custom-made clothes*

cus·tom·a·ry /ˈkʌstəməri‖-meri/ *adj* established by or according to custom; usual; habitual: *It is customary to give people gifts on their birthday* —**-rily** /-mərɪ̈li‖ˌkʌstəˈmerɪ̈li/ *adv*

cus·tom·er /ˈkʌstəməʳ/ *n* **1** [C] a person who buys goods or services from a shop or person trading, esp. regularly: *The new shop across the road has taken away some of my best customers* **2** [C9] *sl* a person one has to deal with; fellow: *an odd customer*

USAGE One is a **customer** if one gets things for one's money, as in a shop. If one gets services, as from a lawyer, a bank, or a HAIRDRESSER, one is a **client**, except in the case of **a** medical services, when one is a **patient b** hotels, at which one is a **guest**.

cus·toms /ˈkʌstəmz/ *n* [P] **1** taxes paid in accordance with the law on goods entering or (less often) leaving a country **2** (*often cap.*) the government organization established to collect these taxes **3** (*often cap.*) a place where travellers' belongings are searched when leaving or entering a country: *As soon as I'd got through customs I felt at home*

customs du·ty /ˈ·· ˌ··/ *n* [C *often pl.*; U] (a) tax paid in accordance with the law on goods entering or (less often) leaving a country

customs house /ˈ·· ·/ also (*esp. AmE*) **cus·tom·house** /ˈkʌstəmhaʊs/— *n* a government office, esp. at a port or border, where CUSTOMS (1) are collected

customs un·ion /ˈ·· ˌ··/ *n* an arrangement between independent states to remove taxes charged on goods moving between them and to charge broadly equal taxes on goods entering them from elsewhere

cut¹ /kʌt/ *v* **cut**, *pres. p.* **cutting** [T1;IØ] to make a narrow opening in (something) with a sharp edge or instrument, accidentally or on purpose: *Don't cut your fingers on the broken glass.|This knife won't cut. Perhaps it needs sharpening* **2** [T1 (UP)] to divide (something) by separating with a sharp edge or instrument: *The boys cut the cake in 2 and ate half each.|After they'd killed the woman the murderers cut up her body and burned it* **3** [T1] to make (something) by using a sharp instrument: *The hunters cut their way through the forest with axes.|to cut a hole in something* **4** [IØ] to be able to be separated, divided, or marked as with a sharp instrument: *A freshly baked cake doesn't cut easily.|This material seems to have cut very nicely* **5** [X9, esp. AWAY, OFF, OUT] to separate (something) from the main part of something with a sharp instrument; remove with a sharp instrument: *The murderer's head was cut off with an axe.| Cut the dead wood away from the trees* **6** [D1 (*for*);(T1)] to separate (a part of something) for (someone): *The old lady cut the priest a piece of cake* **7** [T1] to shorten or improve with a sharp instrument (note the phrs. **cut short/long**): *Your finger nails need cutting.|"With his tail cut short and ears cut long,/*OH *where can my little dog be?"* (old song) **8** [T1] to make less: *Your story is too long: it needs cutting* **9**

[T1] to grow (a tooth): *Our baby's just cutting her first teeth so she needs some medicine to reduce the pain* **10** [T1 (OFF)] to interrupt (a supply of gas, electricity, etc.): *The water was cut for 2 hours yesterday while the road was being repaired* **11** [T1 (BACK)] to make (esp. a public service) smaller, less frequent, etc.: *Where I live they're cutting (back) train services, postal deliveries, and school meals* **12** [T1 (OUT)] to remove (parts (of)), so as to improve: *All the scenes showing sex or violence were cut from the moving picture before it was shown on television* **13** [Wv4;T1;L9] to hurt the feelings of (someone): *His cruel remark cut me deeply.|a cutting remark* **14** [T1] *infml* to be absent on purpose from (a class, school, etc.): *I felt tired this morning so I stayed in bed and cut school* **15** [X9, esp. DOWN] to cause (a tree) to fall; bring down (a tree) with an axe, SAW, etc.: *We must not let them cut down such fine trees just to build a road!* **16** [T1] to gather in (corn, wheat, etc.) **17** [L9] to change direction suddenly: *The player ran for the ball but suddenly cut to the left to get a better position* **18** [I∅;T1] to divide (a pile of playing cards) in 2 before DEALing **19** [T1] to cross: *The line AC is cut by line PQ at point Z* **20** [T1] to make (a ball) spin by striking: *The player confused his opponent by cutting the ball to the right* **21** [I∅] to stop photographing a scene when making a moving picture: *"Cut!" shouted the director* **22** [T1] to walk across rather than round (a corner): *A path had been worn in the grass where people had cut the corner* **23** [T1] *infml* to make (a record): *When did this singer cut his first record?* **24** [X9] to set (someone or something) free or loose by CUTting¹ (2) a rope, metal, etc. (note the phr. **cut free**): *I cut myself free with my axe* **25 cut and run** *sl* to escape by running **26 cut both ways** (of an action) to have disadvantages as well as advantages **27 cut corners** to do something in a less than perfect way in order to save time, money, etc. **28 cut it fine** to leave oneself little time, money, etc., to do what is needed **29 cut no/not much ice (with)** to have little or no effect or influence (on someone) **30 cut one's coat according to one's cloth a** to spend in accordance with one's income **b** to be practical in limiting one's plans **31 cut one's losses** to stop taking part in a failing business, firm, etc., before one loses too much money **32 cut one's teeth on/in (something)** to gain one's first experience from doing (something) **33 cut (somebody) dead/cold** to refuse to recognize (somebody one knows) in order to be rude or show displeasure: *I saw Jean in town today but she cut me cold* **34 cut (something) short a** to make (something) shorter: *to cut a long story short* **b** to cause to finish before completion, and usu. suddenly: *I was trying to tell him what really happened, but he cut me short.*

cut² *n* **1** the result of cutting; opening; wound: *a cut in the cloth|How did you get that cut in your hand?* **2** something obtained by cutting, esp. a piece of meat cut from an animal: *cuts of fresh lamb|a nice cut off the joint* **3** [(*in*)] a reduction in size, amount, etc.: *cuts in government spending* **4** the style in which clothes are made: *I don't like the cut of his new suit* **5** [(*at*)] a stroke or blow with a sword, knife, etc.: *The soldier made a cut at his enemy with his sword* **6** an act of removing a part, esp. to improve or shorten: *Before this play is broadcast several cuts must be made in order not to offend people* **7** the part that is cut out: *I don't think there's anything in this cut that would have offended anyone* **8** [(*of, in*)] *infml* a share: *The government plans to take a 50% cut of oil profits* **9** a quick sharp stroke in cricket, tennis, etc. **10** the act of cutting (dividing) a pile of playing cards in 2 before DEALing **11** *tech esp. AmE* the quantity of wood (TIMBER) cut down in a particular period of time **12** *rare* a refusal to recognize someone one knows **13 a cut above** *infml* better; of higher quality or rank: *Mrs Smythe considers herself a cut above other people. That's why she treats them so rudely* **14 cut and thrust** spirited argument

cut a·cross *v prep* [T1] **1** to take a shorter way across (a field, corner, etc.) **2** to go beyond or across the limits of: *a new group of members of parliament that cuts across party lines|broader areas of study that cut across the divisions between school subjects* (example based on SEU S.) **3** to be opposed to: *The minister's speech cut across what he'd said before and pointed the way to a change in government thinking*

cut-and-dried /ˌ· · ˈ·◂/ also **cut-and-dry**— *adj* **1** already prepared and unlikely to be changed; fixed or settled in advance **2** being or done according to a plan, standard method, or well-known simple rule; ROUTINE

cut at *v prep* [T1] to aim a blow at (someone): *The soldier cut at his enemy with his sword*

cut·a·way /ˈkʌtəweɪ/ *n* TAILCOAT

cut·back /ˈkʌtbæk/ *n* a planned decrease; reduction to an earlier rate

cut back *v adv* **1** [T1] to cut (a plant) close to the stem; PRUNE **2** [T1;I∅ (*on*)] to reduce in size or amount: *The unions strongly oppose any plans to cut back (on) industrial production*

cut down *v adv* **1** [T1] to bring down by cutting; FELL: *to cut down a tree with an axe* **2** [T1a,4;I∅: (*on*)] to reduce in quantity or amount: *The doctors have told me to cut down (on) smoking and drinking* **3** [T1] to knock down or kill (someone) esp. by striking with a sword or sharp weapon **4** [T1] (of a disease) to kill or make unable to walk: *The prince on whom the people placed such great hopes was cut down by a rare disease when only 20* **5** [T1b] to persuade (someone) to reduce a price: *At first they wanted £100 but we cut them down to £65* **6** [T1] to reduce the length of a garment: *If you cut down this old pair of trousers you can go swimming in them* **7 cut down to size** *infml* to reduce from too great importance to true or suitable importance

cute /kjuːt/ *adj* [Wa1] delightfully pretty and often small: *She wore the cutest little dress you ever did see* —**~ly** *adv* —**~ness** *n* [U]

cut glass /ˌ· ˈ·◂/ *n* [U] glass specially ornamented or shaped by having patterns cut on it

cu·ti·cle /ˈkjuːtɪkəl/ *n* an outer covering of hard skin, esp. surrounding the lower edges of the nails on the toes and fingers —see picture at HUMAN²

cut in *v adv* [I∅ (*on*)] *infml* **1** to interrupt: *Don't cut in while I'm talking. You can say what you want later* **2** to drive into a space between cars in a dangerous way likely to cause an accident: *You nearly caused a crash by cutting in (on me) like that!*

cut·lass /ˈkʌtləs/ *n* **1** a short sword with a slightly curved blade **2** *CarE* MACHETE

cut·ler /ˈkʌtləʳ/ *n* a person who makes, sells, or repairs knives or other cutting instruments

cut·le·ry /ˈkʌtləri/ *n* [U] knives and other cutting instruments, esp. those used when eating —compare SILVERWARE

cut·let /ˈkʌtlɪ̥t/ *n* **1** a small piece of meat for one person **2** a flat CROQUETTE

cut·off /ˈkʌtɒf‖-ɔf/ *n* **1** a fixed limit or stopping point **2** an apparatus for stopping or controlling the flow of water, gas, steam, etc. in a pipe

cut off *v adv* [T1] **1** [T1;(D1 (*for*))] to separate by cutting: *She cut off a small piece of cake and gave it to me* **2** to disconnect: *We were cut off in the middle of our telephone conversation* **3** [T1 *usu. pass.*] to kill or seriously hurt: *How sad! He was cut off when he* *was still very young, with all his work still ahead of him* **4** to take from (a person) the right to have one's property when one is dead: *If you marry that girl I'll cut you off completely without a penny!* **5** [(*from*)] to block off or surround so that further movement out or in is impossible: *When the city was cut off, everyone knew that total defeat was certain*

cut·out /ˈkʌtaʊt/ *n* **1** a figure (to be) cut out of wood or paper **2** something that interrupts or disconnects an electric CIRCUIT, esp. when too heavy a current is passing through

cut out *v adv* **1** [T1 (*of*)] to remove by or as if by cutting: *She cut the advertisement out of the newspaper so that she would remember it* **2** [T1] to cut paper, cloth, etc., into a smaller shape as desired: *to cut out a dress|a sewing pattern* **3** [T1] to make by cutting: (fig.) *She has cut out a place for herself in the world of politics.|The rain and wind have cut out a deep valley* **4** [T1,4] *infml* to leave out; stop: *My doctor says I must cut out smoking and strong drinks* **5** [T1] *infml* to stop: *Let's cut out the talking and get back to work!* **6** (esp. of a car) to move suddenly out to the other side of the road, esp. in order to pass a slower vehicle **7** [IØ] (of a motor) to stop suddenly: *Every time I got my car started the engine cut out after a few minutes* **8** [T1] *tech* to separate (one animal) from a group of animals **9** **cut it/that out** *infml* to stop it: *John and Jean were arguing so their father told them to cut it out or go to bed* **10** **cut out (the) dead wood** *infml* to remove the ineffective or useless parts from something, esp. an organization **11** **cut out for something/to do something** naturally well-suited for something **12** **have one's work cut out for one** *infml* to have a lot of work to do

cut-price /ˌ· ˈ·◂/ *adj* [Wa5;A;(B)] **1** (of goods) cheap; sold at reduced prices: *cut-price food|cut-price petrol* **2** (of a shop) selling goods at reduced prices: *a cut-price garage*

cut·purse /ˈkʌtpɜːs‖-ɜrs/ *n old use* PICKPOCKET

cut-rate /ˌ· ˈ·◂/ *adj* [Wa5;A;(B)] sold at a price or rate below the standard charge

cut·ter /ˈkʌtəʳ/ *n* **1** a small fast boat belonging to a larger ship, esp. used for moving supplies or passengers to or from the land **2** a lightly-armed government ship used for preventing smuggling (SMUGGLE) **3** an instrument used for cutting: *a pair of wire-cutters* **4** a worker whose job is cutting cloth, glass, stone, metal, etc.

cut·throat¹ /ˈkʌtθrəʊt/ *n* **1** [C; *you* + N] a murderer; fierce criminal **2** [C] also **cutthroat razor** /ˌ·· ˈ··/— a RAZOR with a very sharp open blade

cutthroat² *adj* [Wa5;A;(B)] very fierce; merciless; unprincipled

cut·ting¹ /ˈkʌtɪŋ/ *n* **1** a stem, leaf, etc., cut from a plant and put in soil or water to form roots and grow into a new plant **2** *AmE* **clipping**— a piece cut out from a newspaper, magazine, etc., such as an article, advertisement, or photograph **3** something produced by cutting, esp. a passage cut through higher land so that a road, railway, etc., can pass

cutting² *adj* **1** [B] bitter; severe: *After the government's cutting attack on the unions there seems little chance of industrial peace this winter* **2** [B] (esp. of the wind) uncomfortably strong and cold **3** [Wa5; A] sharp-edged; very sharp: *Where's your cutting knife?* —**~ly** *adv*

cutting room /ˈ·· ·/ *n* a room where unwanted parts are removed from cinema films, TAPEs¹ (3), etc.

cut·tle·fish /ˈkʌtlˌfɪʃ/ *n* **cuttlefish**— [Wn3] a type of SQUIDlike sea animal with long arms (TENTACLEs) that puts out a black inky liquid when attacked —see picture at MOLLUSC

cut up *v adv* **1** [T1] to cut into little pieces **2** [T1] to destroy; defeat severely **3** [T1b *usu. pass*] to cause suffering to (someone): *Jean was really cut up when her husband left her* **4** [T1] *sl* to judge severely: *The writer's latest book was so cut up in the newspapers that few people bought it*

cut·worm /ˈkʌtwɜːm‖-ɜrm/ *n* a type of CATERPILLAR that eats through the stems of plants near the ground, esp. during the night

cwm /kuːm/ *n* a short valley or hollow place in the side of a mountain —see VALLEY (USAGE)

cwt *written abbrev. for:* HUNDREDWEIGHT

-cy /si/ *suffix* [*n, adj*→*n*] **1** the state or quality of: ACCURACY|BANKRUPTCY **2** (the period of time in) the rank or office of: *a* BARONETCY —compare -CRACY

cy·a·nide /ˈsaɪənaɪd/ *n* [U] a type of very strong poisonous substance

cy·ber·net·ics /ˌsaɪbəˈnetɪks‖-bər-/ *n* [U] the scientific study of the way in which information is moved about and controlled in machines, the brain, and the nervous system —**-ic** *adj* [Wa5] —**-ically** *adv* [Wa4,5]

cy·cla·mate /ˈsaɪkləmeɪt/ *n* [C;U] any of various man-made sweeteners, used (esp. formerly) instead of sugar, esp. by people trying to lose weight

cyc·la·men /ˈsɪkləmən/ *n* **cyclamen** [Wn3] any of various types of plant of the PRIMROSE family, with thick fleshy roots and white, purple, pink, or very red flowers

cy·cle¹ /ˈsaɪkəl/ *n* **1** [C] a number of related events happening in a regularly repeated order: *the trade cycle|the cycle of the seasons* **2** [C] the period of time needed for this to be completed: *a 50-second cycle* **3** [C] a group of songs, poems, etc., connected with some central event or person **4** [C; *by*+U] a bicycle or MOTORCYCLE

cycle² *v, n* BICYCLE

cy·clic /ˈsaɪklɪk/ also **cy·cli·cal** /-klikəl/— *adj* happening in CYCLEs¹ (1) —**~ally** *adv* [Wa4]

cy·clist /ˈsaɪklɪ̈st/ *n* BICYCLIST

cy·clone /ˈsaɪkləʊn/ *n* a very violent wind moving very rapidly in a circle round a calm central area; TORNADO —see TYPHOON (USAGE)

cy·clo·pae·di·a, *AmE* **cyclopedia** /ˌsaɪkləˈpiːdɪə/ *n now rare* ENCYCLOPAEDIA

cy·clops /ˈsaɪklɒps‖-klɑps/ *n pl. rare* (in ancient Greek stories) a one-eyed GIANT

cy·clo·style¹ /ˈsaɪkləstaɪl/ *n* a special apparatus consisting of a pen with a small toothed wheel that cuts very fine holes in special paper to make a STENCIL from which copies are made

cyclostyle² *v* **1** [IØ] to use a CYCLOSTYLE¹ **2** [Wv5;T1] to produce copies of (something written) by using a CYCLOSTYLE¹

cy·clo·tron /ˈsaɪklətrɒn‖-trɑn/ *n* a special scientific apparatus for producing electric PARTICLEs moving at very high speeds; atom-SMASHer

cy·der /ˈsaɪdəʳ/ *n* CIDER

cyg·net /ˈsɪgnɪ̈t/ *n* a young SWAN

cyl·in·der /ˈsɪlɪ̈ndəʳ/ *n* **1** a long round hollow or solid body —see picture at GEOMETRY **2** an object or container shaped like this, esp. a hollow metal tube **3** the vessel within which a PISTON moves back and forward as in an engine —see picture at PETROL

cy·lin·dri·cal /sɪ̈ˈlɪndrɪkəl/ *adj* [Wa5] of, related to, or having the form of a CYLINDER (1) —**~ly** *adv* [Wa4,5]

cym·bal /ˈsɪmbəl/ *n* either of a pair of round thin metal plates struck together to make a loud ringing noise, used in music —see picture at PERCUSSION —**~ist** *n*

cyn·ic /ˈsɪnɪk/ *n sometimes derog* a person who thinks that all men act selfishly in their own interests, who sees little or no good in anything, and who shows this by making unkind and unfair remarks about people and things

cyn·i·cal /ˈsɪnɪkəl/ *adj sometimes derog* like, related to, or belonging to a CYNIC: *cynical remarks|behaviour* —**~ly** *adv* [Wv4]

cyn·i·cis·m /ˈsɪnɪ̇sɪzəm/ *n sometimes derog* **1** [U] the state of mind or feelings of a CYNIC; character of a CYNIC **2** [C] a remark or action expressing this

cy·no·sure /ˈsɪnəzjʊəʳ‖ˈsaɪnəʃʊəʳ/ *n fml* a centre of attention

cy·pher /ˈsaɪfəʳ/ *n, v* CIPHER

cy·press /ˈsaɪprɪ̇s/ *n* **1** [C] a type of tree with dark green leaves and hard wood, that does not lose its leaves in winter —see picture at TREE[1] **2** [U] the wood of this tree

Cy·ril·lic /sɪ̇ˈrɪlɪk/ *adj, n* [Wa5;B;U] (of, related to, written in, or being) the alphabet used for Russian, Bulgarian, various other Slavonic languages, Mongolian, etc.

cyst /sɪst/ *n* an enclosed hollow growth in or on the body, containing liquid matter

cyst·i·tis /sɪˈstaɪtɪ̇s/ *n* [U] a disease of the BLADDER, esp. of women, in which water must be passed frequently from the body, often with pain and difficulty

cy·tol·o·gy /saɪˈtɒlədʒi‖-tɑ-/ *n* [U] the scientific study of cells —**-gist**

czar /zɑːʳ/ *n* [C;A] TSAR

cza·ri·na /zɑːˈriːnə/ *n* [C;A] TSARINA

Czech /tʃek/ *adj* of Czechoslovakia

D,d

D, d /diː/ **D's, d's** *or* **Ds, ds** **1** the 4th letter of the English alphabet **2** the ROMAN NUMERAL (=number) for 500

d *written abbrev. for:* died: *d 1937*

D (in Western music) **a** the second note (*AmE* also **tone**) in the row of notes which form the musical SCALE of C MAJOR **b** the musical KEY based on this note

-d *suffix* (the form used for -ED after a vowel)

-'d [Wv2] *contr. of* **1** would: *I asked if he'd go* **2** had: *I asked if he'd gone.|Where'd he gone?* —see CONTR. (USAGE) **3** *infml* (*in questions after* where, what, when, *etc.*) did: *Where'd he go?* —see 's (USAGE)

dab[1] /dæb/ *n* [(*at*)] a slight or light touch: *He made a few dabs at the fence with the paint but didn't really paint it*

dab[2] *v* **-bb-** [X9] **1** also **dab at**— to touch lightly or gently, usu. several times: *She dabbed the wound with a wet cloth* **2** to cover with light quick strokes and usu. carelessly and incompletely: *He dabbed paint on the fence*

dab[3] *n infml* a small amount: *I'd just like a dab more butter on this bread if you don't mind*

dab[4] *n* **dab** *or* **dabs** [Wn2] any of several kinds of flat fish

dab[5] also **dab hand** /ˌ· ˈ·/— *n* [(*at*)] *BrE sl* a person who is very clever or good (at something): *She's a dab at sailing*

dab·ble /ˈdæbəl/ *v* [Wv3] **1** [IØ (*at, in*)] to work at or study something with some interest but without serious intentions: *to dabble in politics* **2** [L9] to PADDLE[2] (2)—**-bler** *n*: *sometimes derog*

dab·chick /ˈdæbˌtʃɪk/ *n* any of several kinds of small waterbird

dabs /dæbz/ *n* [P] *BrE sl* FINGERPRINTs

da ca·po /ˌdɑː ˈkɑːpəʊ/ *adj, adv* [Wa5;A] (in music) (to be played) once again, starting from the beginning

dace /deɪs/ *n* **dace** [Wn3] any of several types of small fish found in fresh (not salt) water

dachs·hund /ˈdækshʊnd, -sənd/ *n* a type of small dog with short legs, a long body, and long hanging ears

dac·tyl /ˈdæktɪl‖-tl/ *n* a measure of poetry consisting of one strong (or long) beat followed by 2 weak (or short) beats —**~ic** /dækˈtɪlɪk/ *adj, n* [Wa5]

dad /dæd/ *n* [C;R;N] *infml* father —see TABLE OF FAMILY RELATIONSHIPS

dad·dy /ˈdædi/ *n* [C;R;N] *infml* (*used esp. by or to children*) father —see TABLE OF FAMILY RELATIONSHIPS

daddy long·legs /ˌdædi ˈlɒŋlegz‖-ˈlɔŋ-/ also (*fml*) **crane fly**— *n* **daddy longlegs** [Wn3;C] a type of flying insect with long legs

da·do /ˈdeɪdəʊ/ *n* **-dos** (*AmE* **-does**) a band of different-coloured paint on wood round the lower part of a wall of a room

dae·mon /ˈdiːmən/ *n lit.* **1** (in ancient Greek stories) a being like a spirit, halfway between gods and men **2** a spirit that fills a person with the power to think, do, or make new things —compare DEMON —**~ic** /dɪˈmɒnɪk‖-ˈmɑ-/ *adj* —**~ically** /dɪˈmɒnɪkli‖-ˈmɑ-/ *adv* [Wa4]

daf·fo·dil /ˈdæfədɪl/ *n* a type of yellow flower of early spring —see picture at FLOWER[1]

daft /dɑːft‖dæft/ *adj* [Wa1] *infml, esp. BrE* silly; wild; foolish: *a daft person|a daft thing to do* —**~ly** *adv* —**~ness** *n* [U]

dag·ger /ˈdægəʳ/ *n* **1** a short pointed knife used as a weapon **2** also **obelisk**— a sign like a small dagger or cross (†) used in printing to draw the reader's attention to something **3 at daggers drawn (with someone)** about to fight (with someone) **4 look daggers at someone** to look angrily at someone

da·go /ˈdeɪgəʊ/ *n* **-gos** *or* **-goes** *derog infml* a person from Spain, Portugal, or Italy
USAGE This word is considered much ruder in the US than in Britain.

da·guer·reo·type /dəˈgerəʊtaɪp‖-rə-/ *n* [C;U] an early (type of) photograph

dah·li·a /ˈdeɪlɪə‖ˈdælɪə/ *n* any of several types of brightly-coloured big garden flowers

Dail Ei·reann /ˌdaɪl ˈeərən, dɔɪl ˈeɪrən/ also (*infml*) **Dail**— *n* [*the*+R] the lower house of the Irish parliament

dai·ly[1] /ˈdeɪli/ *adj, adv* [Wa5] (happening, appearing, etc.) once a day or every day or every day except Sunday and perhaps Saturday: *a daily journey|goes there twice daily|a daily newspaper called "The Daily News"|He gets paid daily.|He gets a daily wage*

daily[2] *n* **1** a newspaper printed and sold every day except Sunday and perhaps Saturday **2** also **daily help** /ˌ·· ˈ·/— *infml esp. BrE* a woman servant who comes to clean a house daily but does not live there

daily bread /ˌ·· ˈ·/ *n* [U] *infml* food, money, and other things necessary for life (esp. in the phr. **earn one's daily bread**)

daily doz·en /ˌ·· ˈ··/ *n* [U] bodily exercises done

every day (in the phr. **do one's daily dozen**)

dain·ty¹ /ˈdeɪnti/ *n* an especially nice piece of food, usu. small and sweet, like a little cake

dainty² *adj* [Wa1] **1** small, pretty, clean, and delicate: *a dainty child|dress|movement|piece of furniture* **2** not easy to please, esp. about food: *a dainty eater* —**-tily** *adv* —**-tiness** *n* [U]

daiqu·i·ri /ˈdaɪkə̇ri, ˈdæk-/ *n* a type of sweet COCKTAIL (=alcoholic mixed drink)

dair·y /ˈdeəri/ *n* **1** (on a farm) a place where milk is kept and butter and cheese are made **2** a farm where milk, butter, and cheese (**dairy products**) are produced **3** a shop where milk, butter, cheese, and sometimes eggs and other food products are sold

dairy cat·tle /ˈ·· ˌ··/ *n* [P] cattle kept for milk rather than for meat

dairy farm /ˈ·· ·/ *n* DAIRY (2) —**dairy farmer** *n*

dair·y·ing /ˈdeəri-ɪŋ/ also **dairy farm·ing** /ˈ·· ˌ··/— *n* [U] the business of running a DAIRY (2)

dair·y·maid /ˈdeərimeɪd/ also **milkmaid**— *n old use* a woman who works in a DAIRY (2)

dair·y·man /ˈdeərimən/ *n* **-men** /mən/ **1** a man who works in a DAIRY (2) **2** a man who buys and sells DAIRY products

da·is /ˈdeɪə̇s, deɪs/ *n* [*usu. sing.*] a raised part of the floor at one end of a hall or meeting room, for speakers or other important people

dai·sy /ˈdeɪzi/ *n* **1** a very common type of small flower, yellow in the centre and white round it, growing wild or in gardens —see picture at FLOWER¹ **2 fresh as a daisy** in a healthy and active state; not tired: *He woke up fresh as a daisy after his long sleep* **3 push up the daisies** *humor* to be dead and buried

dak bun·ga·low /ˌdɑːk ˈbʌŋgələʊ, ˌdæk-/ *n* a rest-house for travellers in India

Dal·ai La·ma /ˌdælaɪ ˈlɑːmə/ also **Grand Lama** /ˌ· ˈ··/— *n* the head of the religion of LAMAISM

dale /deɪl/ *n N EngE & poet* a valley

dal·li·ance /ˈdæliəns/ *n* [U;(C)] (an act of) DALLYing WITH (2) someone

dal·ly /ˈdæli/ *v* [IØ (ABOUT, *over*)] to be slow or waste time: *Don't dally or we'll be late.|The children dallied about in the garden and forgot about dinner.|Don't dally over your food*

dally with *v prep* [T1] **1** to play with (an idea); TOY WITH (1): *Father often dallies with the thought of going to live on a tropical island* **2** to play at a love relationship with (someone, usu. of the opposite sex): *Never dally with a woman you don't intend to marry*

dal·ma·tian /dælˈmeɪʃən/ *n* (*usu. cap.*) a type of large dog, white with black spots

dam¹ /dæm/ *n* the mother of a 4-legged animal —compare SIRE¹ (1)

dam² *n* a wall or bank built to keep back water: *The Aswan Dam helps to control the River Nile in Egypt*

dam³ *v* **-mm-** [T1 (UP)] **1** to build a dam across: *to dam (up) the river* **2** to keep back by means of a dam: *to dam (up) the water* —see also DAM UP

dam·age¹ /ˈdæmɪdʒ/ *n* **1** [U] harm; loss: *The storm caused great damage|did a lot of damage.|damage to his marriage* **2** [*the* +R] *infml* the price, esp. of something done for you rather than of an object bought (esp. in the phr. **What's the damage?**)

damage² *v* [Wv4;T1] to cause damage to

dam·ag·es /ˈdæmɪdʒə̇z/ *n* [P] *law* money that must be paid for causing damage: *The court ordered him to pay £1500 damages to the person he had hurt*

dam·a·scene /ˈdæməsiːn, ˌdæməˈsiːn/ *adj* [Wa5] *esp. lit* of DAMASK (1)

dam·ask /ˈdæməsk/ *n, adj* [Wa5;U;B] **1** (a kind of cloth) ornamented with a special pattern: *with a beautiful damask cloth on the table* **2** *poet* the pink colour of a DAMASK ROSE: *her damask cheek*

damask rose /ˈ·· ·/ *n* **1** [C] a type of large sweet-smelling pink rose **2** [U] its colour

dame /deɪm/ *n AmE sl* a woman: *What a dame!*

Dame *n* [C;A] (the title of) a woman who has been given a rank of honour by the King or Queen of England (which is equal to that of KNIGHT): *Dame Ellen (Terry) was a famous actress.*|(fig.) *Dame Nature|Dame Fortune*

dame school /ˈ· ·/ *n old use* a small private school for young children, often kept by an old woman

damn¹ /dæm/ *v* [T1] **1** (esp. of God) to send to punishment without end after death **2** to declare to be very wrong or bad: *The play was bad and the newspapers all damned it* **3** to ruin or be the ruin of: *With this latest foolish action he had damned himself in everyone's opinion* **4** to curse at: *It's as likely that he'll damn you as (that he'll) say "Good morning"* **5 I'll be damned if I will!** *infml* (a strong way of saying) I won't **6 Well, I'll be damned!** *infml* (a strong way of saying) I'm very surprised **7 (God) Damn it/you/that silly fool, etc.!** *sl* (a strong way of expressing anger, meaning) May God damn it/you/that silly fool, etc.! **8 damn with faint praise** to praise slightly, suggesting real disapproval

damn² *n* **1** [C] the word "DAMN"⁴ as a curse: *His speech is full of "damns" and worse curses* **2** [S *nonassertive*] *infml* (not) even a small unimportant amount: *I don't care|give a damn what he does.|His promise isn't worth a damn*

damn³ also **(God)damn(ed)**— *adj, adv* [Wa5;A] *sl* **1** (used for giving force to an expression, good or bad): *a damn fool|damn foolish|He ran damn fast* **2 damn all** nothing: *He's the most ungenerous person I know; you'll get damn all out of him*

damn⁴ also **damnation**— *interj sl* (an expression of strong anger or disappointment)

dam·na·ble /ˈdæmnəbəl/ *adj* **1** bad enough for God to DAMN¹ (1) **2** *infml* very bad: *this damnable weather!* —**-bly** *adv*: *infml*

dam·na·tion /dæmˈneɪʃən/ *n* [U] **1** the act of DAMNing¹ (1) or state of being damned: *to fear damnation* **2 (May) damnation take you!** *sl* (God) DAMN¹ (7) you! **3 in damnation** *sl* (used for giving strength to an expression of anger): *What in damnation do you mean by that?*

damned·est¹ /ˈdæmdə̇st/ *n* **do one's damnedest** *infml* to do everything possible: *She's doing her damnedest to succeed*

damnedest² *adj* [*the*+A] *infml* the most unusual, surprising, etc.: *Isn't that the damnedest thing you've ever heard?*

damn·ing /ˈdæmɪŋ/ *adj* that is very strongly against: *Some damning information against them was discovered*

damn well /ˌ· ˈ·/ also **damned well**— *adv* (used for giving force to a verb, usu. about something bad) beyond doubt or question; certainly: *You knew damn well what was going to happen when you said that*

Dam·o·cles /ˈdæməkliːz/ *n* **sword of Damocles** something bad that may happen at any time: *The possibility of another attack of his illness hung over his happiness like a sword of Damocles*

damp¹ /dæmp/ also **dampness**— *n* [U] wetness: *The damp in the air makes my old bones hurt*

damp² *v* [T1] **1** [(DOWN)] to make ((the strings of) a musical instrument) sound less loudly **2** DAMPEN (2)

damp³ *adj* [Wa1] rather wet: *damp air|a damp room* —**~ly** *adv*

damp course /ˈ· ·/ also **damp-proof course** /ˈ·· ·/— *n* a thickness of material in a wall to prevent wetness from coming up through the bricks

damp down also **dampen down**— *v adv* [T1] **1** to make (a fire) burn more slowly, often by covering with ash or by controlling the flow of air **2** to control so as to reduce: *A few weeks' hard work should damp down his keenness*

damp·en /ˈdæmpən/ *v* **1** [T1;I∅] to (cause to) become DAMP[3]: *The rain hardly dampened the ground* **2** [T1] to make (feelings) less happy: *Nothing can dampen my spirits on this glorious morning*

damp·er /ˈdæmpəʳ/ *n* **1** a metal plate, door, etc., that can be moved to control the amount of air that reaches a burning fire and so make it burn more or less brightly **2** an apparatus that stops the shaking of a piano string —see picture at KEYBOARD[1] **3** an influence that makes dull or sad (esp. in the phr. **put a damper on something**): *His sad face put a damper on our party*

damp·ish /ˈdæmpɪʃ/ *adj* rather DAMP or wet

dam·sel /ˈdæmzəl/ *n* **1** *old use & lit* a young unmarried woman of noble birth **2** *pomp or humor* a girl

dam·son /ˈdæmzən/ *n* **1** a type of PLUM tree, grown for its small acid purple fruit **2** its fruit

dam up *v adv* [T1] to control (a feeling) in an unhealthy way: *Damming up your anger leads to trouble*

dance[1] /dɑːns‖dæns/ *v* **1** [I∅ (*to*)] to move to music: *She loves to dance to fast music* **2** [T1] to move to the music of (a type of dance): *She danced the* WALTZ *with me* **3** [X9] to cause to dance: *She danced her little daughter round the room* **4** [T1;X9] to express or bring into the stated condition by dancing: *She danced her thanks.*|*She danced her way into the hearts of all who saw her* **5** [I∅] to move quickly up and down, or about: *The waves danced in the sunlight* **6 dance attendance on/upon someone** to always do what someone else wants one to do without asking questions —**dancer** *n*

dance[2] *n* **1** [C] an act or example of dancing: *to do a little dance* **2** [C] (the name of) a set of movements performed to music, usu. including leg movements: *The* WALTZ *is a beautiful dance* **3** [C] a social meeting or party for dancing: *Let's give/have a dance tomorrow.*|*to go to a dance* **4** [C] a piece of music for dancing: *The band played a slow dance* **5** [*the*+R] (*sometimes cap.*) the art of dancing: *Her whole life has been given to the study of the dance* **6 lead someone a (pretty, merry, etc.) dance** to cause someone a lot of trouble, as by making him follow you about from place to place without any advantage to himself

dan·de·li·on /ˈdændɨlaɪən/ *n* a type of small wild bright-yellow flower with leaves that have deep V-shaped cuts in them, sometimes eaten but often considered a useless plant (WEED)

dan·der /ˈdændəʳ/ *n* **get one's/someone's dander up** *infml* to make oneself/someone angry: *Her angry words really got my dander up*

dan·di·fied /ˈdændɪfaɪd/ *adj rather derog* (dressed) like a DANDY[1]: *a dandified person/appearance*

dan·dle /ˈdændl/ *v* [T1] to move (esp. a baby) up and down in one's arms or on one's knee in play

dan·druff /ˈdændrəf, -drʌf/ *n* [U] a common disease in which bits of dead skin form on the head and can be seen in the hair

dan·dy[1] /ˈdændi/ *n rather derog becoming rare* a man who spends too much time and money on his clothing and personal appearance

dandy[2] *adj* [Wa1] *infml esp. AmE becoming rare* **1** very good: *That's a dandy idea; let's do it* **2 fine and dandy** OKAY: *"Let's go out tonight." "Fine and dandy; I'll see you at 8"*

dan·ger /ˈdeɪndʒəʳ/ *n* **1** [U] the possibility of harm or loss: *The sign says "Danger! Falling rocks".*|*a danger signal*|*a place where children can play without danger*|*The sick man's life had been in danger, but now he was out of danger.*|*He is in (great, real, etc.) danger of losing all his money if he continues to buy useless objects* **2** [C] a case or cause of danger: *the dangers of smoking*

danger mon·ey /ˈ·· ˌ··/ *n* [U] additional pay for dangerous work

dan·ger·ous /ˈdeɪndʒərəs/ *adj* [B,B3] able to or likely to cause danger: *a dangerous person/place/drug/illness*|*It's dangerous to smoke* —**~ly** *adv*: *Don't drive dangerously.*|*He is dangerously ill*

dan·gle /ˈdæŋgəl/ *v* **1** [I∅] to hang loosely: *keys dangling from a chain* **2** [T1;I∅] to (cause to) swing loosely: *He dangled the keys on his chain* **3** [X9, esp. *in front of* or *before*] to try to attract someone by promising or describing; offer as an attraction: *He dangled a trip to Paris in front of her to get her to work for him* **4 keep someone dangling** *infml* to keep someone waiting and not knowing what the result will be: *She likes to keep her lovers dangling.*|*Don't keep me dangling: tell me if I passed the test*

Da·nish /ˈdeɪnɪʃ/ *adj* [Wa5] of Denmark, its people, or their language —see NATIONALITY TABLE

Danish pas·try /ˌ·· ˈ··/ *n* **1** [U] pastry made from a rich light DOUGH (1) **2** [C] a piece of this

dank /dæŋk/ *adj* [Wa1] unpleasantly wet and usu. cold: *an unhealthy house with dank stone walls* —**~ness** *n* [U]

dap·per /ˈdæpəʳ/ *adj* (esp. of small men) (perhaps too) neat in appearance and quick in movements: *a dapper person/appearance*

dap·pled /ˈdæpəld/ *adj* **1** marked with many usu. cloudy and roundish spots of a type of colour different from their background: *a dappled horse* **2** marked with many spots of sun and shadow: *We rested in the dappled shade of a tree*

dapple-grey, *AmE* also **dapple-gray** /ˌ·· ˈ··/ *n, adj* [Wa5] (a horse that is) grey with spots of darker grey or with spots of a different colour

Dar·by and Joan /ˌdɑːbi ən ˈdʒəʊn‖ˌdɑrbi-/ *n* [P] *BrE* **1** any happily married elderly husband and wife: *Those 2 are like Darby and Joan* **2 Darby and Joan club** a social club for elderly people

dare[1] /deəʳ/ *v pres. t. neg. contr.* **daren't** **1** [Wv2,6; I∅,2] to be brave (or rude) enough to: *I dare not/daren't go there.*|*Dare you ask him?*|*I don't know whether he dare try.*|*He dare not/daren't come.*|*How dare you say such a thing?*|*That is as much as I dare spend on it* **2** [Wv6;I∅;T2,3] to be brave (or rude) enough (to): *He does not/doesn't dare (to) answer.*|*Don't (you) dare (to) touch it!*|*He would never dare (to) come.*|*I wonder how he dared (to) say that* **3** [T1] to be brave enough to face: *He dared the anger of her family* **4** [T1] to be brave enough to try (esp. something new): *The actress dared a new way of playing that famous character* **5** [V3;(T1)] to say that (someone) is not brave enough (to do something); CHALLENGE: *I dared him to jump.*|*I dared him (to), but he didn't*

dare[2] *n* a statement that someone is not brave enough to do something; CHALLENGE

dare·dev·il /ˈdeədevəl‖ˈdeər-/ *n, adj* [Wa5;A] (a person) who is very brave but not properly careful: *That daredevil is going to jump into the water from a great height.*|*What a daredevil person he is!*

daren't /deənt‖deərnt/ [Wv2] *contr. of* dare not —see CONTR. (USAGE)

dare·say /deəˈseɪ‖ˈdeər-/ *v esp. BrE* (*only with* "I") **1** [T5a] (I) suppose (that); perhaps: *I daresay you're right.*|*I daresay it will come later* **2** [I∅] (I) suppose so; no doubt; of course: *You're right, I daresay*

dar·ing[1] /ˈdeərɪŋ/ *adj* **1** very brave (in a good or bad sense): *a daring person/action*|*a daring effort to* *save the city|a daring crime* **2** unusual; new in ideas: *a daring idea/plan* **3** shocking: *a daring film* —**~ly** *adv*: *He spoke daringly.|a film that's daringly different!*

daring² *n* [U] **1** bravery: *a person/an action of great daring* **2** newness in ideas: *a plan of great daring* **3** ability to shock: *a sex film of great daring*

dark¹ /dɑːk‖dark/ *adj* [Wa1] **1** partly or completely without light: *too dark to read|In winter it gets dark here early* **2** tending towards black: *dark hair|dark green|dark clothes|a tall dark good-looking man* **3** evil: *the dark powers that lead to war* **4** sad; unfavourable: *dark days ahead|Don't always look on the dark side of things* **5 a** secret; hidden: *He kept his plans dark* **b** not easy to understand: *There is some dark meaning in his words* **6** (of voices) deep and rich —**~ly** *adv*: *He spoke darkly of trouble to come* —**~ness** *n* [U]

dark² *n* **1** [*the*+R] the absence of light; darkness: *Can cats really see in the dark?|Some children are afraid of the dark* **2** [(*the*) R] the time of day when there is no light (esp. in the phrs. **after dark, before dark**): *We don't go out after dark.|Get home before dark* **3** [U] a dark or deep colour: *the dark of her eyes* **4 in the dark a** in secrecy: *business done in the dark* **b** without knowledge: *They kept the public in the dark about their agreement*

Dark Ag·es /ˈ· ˌ··/ *n* [*the*+P] the period in European history from about AD 476 (the fall of Rome) to about AD 1000, believed to be lacking in knowledge and art

Dark Con·ti·nent /ˌ· ˈ···/ *n* [*the*+R] *now rare* Africa, esp. before Europeans knew much about it

dark·en /ˈdɑːkən‖ˈdar-/ *v* [T1;I∅] **1** to (cause to) become dark: *The sky quickly darkened after sunset.|Darken the green paint by adding black paint.|This terrible event will darken the rest of our lives.|His face darkened with anger when he heard the bad news* **2 Never darken my door/these doors again** *humor pomp* Don't come back here again

dark horse /ˌ· ˈ·/ *n* a competitor who may be successful although not much is known about him: *Everyone thinks Mary will get the job, but John and Elizabeth are among the dark horses for it*

dark·room /ˈdɑːkruːm, -rʊm‖ˈdark-/ *n* a dark room in which photographs can be given their proper form (DEVELOPed)

dark·y, darkey /ˈdɑːki‖ˈdarki/ *n taboo derog* (*often cap.*) a black man or woman

dar·ling¹ /ˈdɑːlɪŋ‖ˈdar-/ *n* [C;N] a person who is very much liked or loved: *My grand-daughter is a little darling.|Darling, will you please hurry up!*

darling² *adj* [A;(B)] **1** dearly loved: *my darling husband/wife/child* **2** *infml* (*usu. used by women*) charming; very nice: *What a darling dress!*

darn¹ /dɑːn‖darn/ *v* [T1;I∅] to repair (a hole in cloth or a garment with a hole in it) by passing threads through and across (by needle-weaving): *Please darn my sock/the hole in my sock*

darn² *n* a place in cloth that has been DARNed: *socks full of darns*

darn³ *n, adj, adv, interj,* (*v*) *euph* DAMN⁴

darn·ing /ˈdɑːnɪŋ‖ˈdar-/ *n* [U] **1** the work or skill of DARNing **2** clothes that need to be or are being DARNed: *Put all the darning in that basket*

dart¹ /dɑːt‖dart/ *n* **1** [C] a small sharp-pointed object to be thrown, shot, etc., esp. one used as a weapon or in games: *a poisoned dart|(fig.) Her words were filled with darts of anger* **2** [S9] a quick movement in a particular stated direction: *The prisoner made a dart for the door* **3** [C] a fold made to make a garment fit better, and held together by sewing

dart² *v* **1** [L9] to move suddenly and quickly: *He darted out/towards the door.|Insects were darting about before the storm* **2** [X9] to throw or send out suddenly and quickly: *The snake darted out its tongue.|He darted an angry look at his enemy*

dart·board /ˈdɑːtbɔːd‖ˈdartbord/ *n* a circular board at which DARTS¹ (1) are thrown in games

Dart·moor /ˈdɑːtmʊəʳ‖ˈdart/ *n* [R] a prison in south-west England

darts /dɑːts‖darts/ *n* [U] any of several games in which DARTS¹ (1) are thrown at a DARTBOARD

dash¹ /dæʃ/ *v* **1** [L9;(I∅)] to run quickly and suddenly: *I must dash (off) to catch a train.|He suddenly dashed into the street.|They've been dashing about all day* **2** [X9;L9] to (cause to) strike with great force: *The waves dashed the boat against the rocks.|The waves dashed against the rocks* **3** [X9; L9] to (cause to) break by throwing with great force: *The glass bowl dashed to pieces against the stone floor* **4** [T1] to destroy or ruin (hopes, spirits, etc.): *The angry letter dashed my hopes that we could remain friends* **5** [T1] *BrE euph* DAMN: *Dash it all, I've lost again!*

dash² *n* **1** [S] a sudden quick run: *The prisoners made a dash for freedom* **2** [C *usu. sing.*] a short race for runners: *the 100-yard dash* —compare SPRINT **3** [(*the*) S] (the sound of) liquid, or loose solids, striking liquid or solids: *the dash of the waves against the side of the ship* **4** [C (*of*)] a small amount of something mixed with or added to something else: *a dash of pepper/wine/colour* **5** [U] a combination of bravery and style: *a man of great dash and spirit* **6** [C] a mark (—) used in writing and printing: *The dash is longer than the* HYPHEN **7** [C] a long sound used in sending messages by telegraph: *The message consisted of dots and dashes* **8 cut a dash** to have a strong effect on other people that makes them remember you, esp. because of your appearance and style

dash·board /ˈdæʃbɔːd‖-bord/ *n* an instrument board in a car, where many of the controls are —see picture at CAR

dashed /dæʃt/ *adj* **1** [B] disappointed; discouraged: *You look a bit dashed. What's wrong?* **2** [Wa5;A] *BrE euph* DAMN⁴ed: *That dashed cat! He's here again!*

dash·ing /ˈdæʃɪŋ/ *adj* having a lot of DASH² (5): *a dashing young officer* —**~ly** *adv*

dash off *v adv* [T1] to write or draw in haste: *dash off a letter*

da·ta /ˈdeɪtə, ˈdɑːtə/ *n* [P;(U)] facts; information: *The data are/is all ready for examination*

USAGE This is now coming to be used as a [U] noun: *This* **data** *is very interesting.* Many people do not like this use of the word.

data bank /ˈ·· ·/ *n* a collection of DATA, esp. for use by a COMPUTER

data pro·cess·ing /ˌ·· ˈ···/ *n* [U] the use of DATA by COMPUTERs

date¹ /deɪt/ *n* **1** a small brown sweet fruit with a long stone, from hot dry countries —see picture at BERRY **2** also **date palm** /ˈ· ·/— the tree that produces this fruit

date² *n* **1** [C] time shown by one or more of the following: the number of the day, the month, and the year (but not usu. by month alone) **2** [C] a written or printed date: *This book has no date on it.|The date on the coin is 1921* **3** [U] a period of time in history (esp. in the phr. **of early/late date**): *This Greek dish is of very early date* **4** [C] an arrangement to meet at a particular time and place: *They made a date to meet soon* **5** [C] *infml* a social meeting between an unmarried man and woman, or boy and girl: *Does your mother let you go out on dates?* **6** [C] *infml esp. AmE* a person with whom one has such a meeting: *Of course you can bring your date to my party* **7 out of date** not generally used at a given date; not modern; old fashioned: *A lot of new words go* (= become) *out of date very quickly.|out-of-date methods* **8 to date** until today; yet: *He left 3 weeks ago and we haven't had one single letter from him to date.|To date he has done half the work* **9 up to date** modern; as new as anything in a given period: *We want our methods to be up to date.|up-to-date methods* —see also BLIND DATE

date³ *v* **1** [T1] to (allow to) know the date of: *I can't date that house exactly, but it must be very old.|The unusual shape of this pot dates it at about AD 400* **2** [T1] to write the date on: *Please date your letters to me in future* **3** [T1;I∅] to (cause to) seem no longer in fashion: *This type of music is beginning to date.|Her clothes date her, I'm afraid* **4** [T1;I∅] *infml esp. AmE* to go on or have a DATE² (5) with (another or each other): *She's been dating him for months but it's not serious yet.|They've been dating (each other) for months* —**datable, dateable** *adj*

date back to *v adv prep* [T1 *no pass.*] to have lasted since (the date of building or origin): *This church dates back to 1173*

dat·ed /ˈdeɪtɨd/ *adj* out of DATE² (7): *Those words all seem rather dated: I haven't heard them since the 1940's*

date from *v prep* [T1 *no pass.*] DATE BACK TO: *The custom dates from the time when men wore swords*

date·less /ˈdeɪtləs/ *adj* that will never end or go out of DATE² (7): *Her dateless fame will never die.|the play's dateless subject*

date·line /ˈdeɪtlaɪn/ *n* a line in a newspaper article that gives its date and place of origin

dates /deɪts/ *n* [P] the dates of a person's birth and death, or of the beginning and end of something: *Michelangelo's dates are 1475 to 1564*

da·tive /ˈdeɪtɪv/ *adj, n* [Wa5] (of or being) (a special form for) the INDIRECT OBJECT

daub¹ /dɔːb/ *v* **1** [D1 + *with/on*] to cover with something soft and sticky: *to daub the wall with paint|He daubed paint on the wall.|His clothes were daubed with mud and oil* **2** [I∅] *infml* to paint pictures without much skill: *I'm not a good painter but I like to daub* —**~er** *n*

daub² *n* **1** [U;C] (a) soft sticky material for covering surfaces like walls **2** [C] a small bit of soft sticky material: *a daub of paint/of butter* **3** [C] a badly painted picture

daugh·ter /ˈdɔːtəʳ/ *n* **1** someone's female child: *Mr and Mrs Jones have 3 daughters.*|(fig.) *Joan of Arc was one of France's greatest daughters* —see TABLE OF FAMILY RELATIONSHIPS **2** something thought of as a daughter: *French is a daughter (language) of Latin* —**~ly** *adj*

daughter-in-law /ˈ·· · ·/ *n* **daughters-in-law** the wife of one's son —see TABLE OF FAMILY RELATIONSHIPS

daunt /dɔːnt/ *v* [Wv4;T1 *often pass.*] **1** to cause to lose courage or the will to act: *He felt completely daunted by the difficulties that faced him.|The examination questions were rather daunting, and I was afraid to start writing* **2 nothing daunted** *fml* not having lost courage or the will to act in spite of difficulties: *The fire had almost completely destroyed the village, but, nothing daunted, the people began building again at once*

daunt·less /ˈdɔːntləs/ *adj* not DAUNTed; fearless: *dauntless courage/soldiers* —**~ly** *adv*

dau·phin /ˈdɔːfɨn (*Fr* dofɛ̃)/ *n* [*the* + R;(C)] *Fr* (*often cap.*) the eldest son of the king of France

dav·it /ˈdævɨt, ˈdeɪvɨt/ *n* a long curved pole (usu. one of a pair) that hangs or swings out over the side of a ship and is used for lowering and raising boats, goods, etc. —see picture at FREIGHTER

Da·vy Jones's lock·er /ˌdeɪvi dʒəʊnzɨz ˈlɒkəʳ‖-ˈlɑkər/ *n* [R] *infml* the bottom of the sea

Da·vy lamp /ˈdeɪvi læmp/ *n* an early kind of miner's SAFETY LAMP

daw·dle /ˈdɔːdl/ *v* [Wv3;I∅] *infml* to spend time doing nothing; move or do something very slowly, wasting time and effort: *He dawdled all morning/all the way to school* —**-dler** *n*

dawdle a·way *v adv* [T1] *infml* to waste (something such as time)

dawn¹ /dɔːn/ *v* [I∅] (of the day, morning, etc.) to begin to grow light just before the sun rises: *The morning dawned fresh and clear after the storm at night*

dawn² *n* **1** [C;U] the time of day when light first appears; the first appearance of light in the sky before the sun rises: *They take the boat out every day at dawn.|The dawns here in the mountains are beautiful* **2** [*the* + R(*of*)] (of something not material) the beginning or first appearance: *the dawn of civilization/of history/of hope* **3 at (the) break of dawn** when light was just beginning to appear **4 dawn is breaking** light is just beginning to appear

dawn on also **dawn up·on**— *v prep* [T1 *no pass.*] to become gradually known by (someone): *It dawned on me where I'd seen him before*

day /deɪ/ *n* **1** [C;U] a period of light: *I can see by day, but not by night.|He worked all day* **2** [C] a period of 24 hours: *There are 7 days in a week.|the day before yesterday|the day after tomorrow* —see USAGE **3** [C] (*often cap.*) a special date: *Christmas Day was a Wednesday this year* **4** [*the* + R;C9] a period of time: *In my day things were different.|He's the man of the day.|in the days of Good Queen Bess|in those days* **5** [C] a period of work: *She works an 8-hour day and a 5-day week.|She's paid by the day* **6** [C9] a period of success or fame (esp. in the phr. **to have (had) one's day**): *He was a very good actor, but I'm afraid he's had his day now* **7** [*the* + R] a (period of) struggle, battle, or competition: *We've won/lost the day* **8** [S] a point of time; occasion: *We must get together again some day.|We have lost 100 times, but one day we shall win!* **9 by day** *esp. lit* during the day (esp. when compared with **by** NIGHT (8)): *He works in an office by day and drives a taxi by night* **10 the other day** in the recent past: *I saw your friend the other day* **11 call it a day** *infml* to finish working for the day; decide to stop work (esp. in the phr. **let's call it a day**) **12 day after day/day in day out** continuously **13 day and night** all the time **14 Every dog has his day** Everyone has at least one period of success —see also DAYS¹ **15 fall on evil days** *fml or lit* to experience a difficult period; fall on hard times **16 from day to day/day by day** each day; as time goes on **17 from one day to the next** 2 days in a row: *I never know her plans from one day to the next* **18 He doesn't know the time of day** He isn't clever at all **19 It's all in a day's work** It's all part of one's job **20 make someone's day** *infml* to give someone a completely happy day: *It makes the old lady's day when the children come to see her* **21 pass the time of day with someone** to have a short conversation with someone, not about serious subjects **22 this day week/today week/a week today** *BrE* a week from today —see also WEEK (3,4) **23 to the day** exactly (in time): *We left Spain one year ago to the day* (= exactly one year ago) **24 to this day** until now: *I haven't told him the whole story to this day!*

USAGE If today is Wednesday, then Monday was *the* **day** *before yesterday* and Friday will be *the* **day** *after tomorrow.* One cannot leave out *the* **day** in these expressions.

day·boy /ˈdeɪbɔɪ/ *fem.* **day·girl** /-gɜːl‖-gɜrl/— *n* a pupil who lives at home but goes to a school where some children live —opposite **boarder**

day·break /ˈdeɪbreɪk/ *n* [U] DAWN² (1)

day-care /ˈ· ·/ *adj* [Wa5;A] caring for children during the day, while their parents are away working: *We need more day-care centres*

day·dream¹ /ˈdeɪdriːm/ *n* a pleasant dreamlike set of thoughts (often about the future) during waking hours, often drawing attention away from present surroundings

daydream² *v* [I∅] to have DAYDREAM*s*: *That pupil's always daydreaming: he never listens to what the teacher's saying* —**~er** *n*

day·light /ˈdeɪlaɪt/ *n* [U] **1** the light of day: *You look different by daylight from at night* **2** the "light" of understanding or public knowledge **3** DAWN² (1)

daylight sav·ing time /ˌ·· ˈ·· ·/ *n* [U] *AmE* SUMMER TIME

day nur·se·ry /ˈ· ˌ··/ *n* a place where small children can be left during the day while their parents are away working

day of reck·on·ing /ˌ· · ˈ···/ *n* [*the* +R;(C)] a time when the results of mistakes or misdeeds are felt, or when offences are punished

day re·lease course /ˌ· ·ˈ· ·/ *n BrE* an educational course attended by workers during the usual working day

day re·turn /ˌ· ·ˈ·/ also **day tick·et** /ˈ· ˌ··/— (*AmE* **round-trip ticket**)— *n BrE* a ticket that one can use to go and come back again on the same day, usu. cheaper than 2 separate single tickets

day·room /ˈdeɪruːm, -rʊm/ *n* a room for reading, writing, and amusement, used only during the day, not at night, and found esp. in schools, military camps, prisons, hospitals, etc. —compare COMMON ROOM

days¹ /deɪz/ *n* [P] life: *He began his days in a village and ended his days in a great city*

days² *adv esp. AmE* by day repeatedly; during any day: *She works days*

day school /ˈ· ·/ *n* [C;U] a school whose pupils attend only during the day on weekdays, returning home at night and at weekends

day·time /ˈdeɪtaɪm/ *n* [U;*the* +R] DAY (1): *I cannot sleep in the daytime.|daytime flights*

day-to-day /ˌ· · ˈ·◂/ *adj* [Wa5;A] **1** taking place, made, or done during several days coming one after the other: *life's day-to-day difficulties* **2** planning for one day at a time with little thought for the future: *They lived an aimless day-to-day existence* —compare EVERYDAY

daze¹ /deɪz/ *v* [T1 *often pass.*] to cause to be unable to think or feel clearly, esp. by a blow: *After the accident John was dazed.*|(fig.) *The news left him dazed* —**~dly** /ˈdeɪzɨdli/ *adv*

daze² *n* **in a daze** in a DAZEd condition

daz·zle¹ /ˈdæzəl/ *v* [Wv3,4;T1] **1** to cause to be unable to see by throwing a strong light in the eyes: *The lights of the car dazzled me on the dark road* **2** to cause wonder to: *The splendid room dazzled the young girl.|She was dazzled by her sudden success*

dazzle² *n* [(*the*) S] **1** brightness; splendid quality: *the dazzle of light|of her smile* **2** a brightly shining whole or object: *The theatre was a dazzle of bright lights* **3 in a dazzle** in a DAZZLED¹ condition

DC *abbrev. for:* **1** DIRECT CURRENT **2** District of Columbia, the area which contains Washington, the capital of the USA

D-day /ˈ· ·/ *n* [R] **1** 6 June 1944, the day on which British, American, Canadian, French, and Polish soldiers landed on the shores of northern France during World War 2 **2** a day on which an operation or planned action is to begin

DDT /ˌ· · ˈ·/ *n* [U] a type of chemical that kills insects

de- /diː-, dɪ-/ *prefix* **1** [*v→v*] to do the opposite of: *de*ACTIVATE|*de*VITALIZE|*de*EMPHASIZE **2** [*n→n*] the opposite of: *de*EMPHASIS **3** [*n→v*] to remove: *to debone* **4** [*n→v*] to remove from: *to* DETHRONE *a king* **5** [*v→v*] to reduce: DEVALUE **6** [*adj→adj*] (esp. in grammar) coming from something else: *a deverbal noun* **7** [*n→v*] *fml* to get off: DETRAIN

dea·con /ˈdiːkən/ *fem.* **dea·con·ess** /-kənɨs/— *n* an officer of various Christian churches, below a priest

dead¹ /ded/ *adj* [Wa5,(1)] **1** [B; *the*+P] no longer alive: *a dead man/plant/leaf|Do the dead ever come back to life?*|(fig.) *His love for you is now dead* —see USAGE **2** [A;(F)] without life; not able to live: *dead rocks and stones|dead matter* **3** [F] unable to feel: *It's so cold outside that my fingers feel dead.*|(fig.) *That cruel man is dead to pity* **4** [B] not in use: *a dead language|dead ideas* —compare LIVING¹ (2) **5** [B] without the necessary power: *This cigarette has gone dead.|dead matches|a dead* BATTERY|*The television's been dead since the storm* (=it doesn't work) —compare LIVE² (3,4) **6** [B] without movement or activity: *a dead weight*|(fig.) *The place seemed dead* **7** [F] *infml* very tired: *After all that work, I'm really dead!* **8** [B] **a** (of a ball) out of PLAY¹ (13) **b** (of a ball) unable to BOUNCE¹ (1a) **c** (of ground where ball games are played) on which the ball does not roll fast **9** [B] (of sounds) dull; hollow; not ringing clearly **10** [B] (of colours) dull; without brightness **11** [A] complete: *a dead stop|dead silence| a dead loss* **12 beat/flog a dead horse** to keep mentioning something that no longer interests anyone else **13 dead to the world** very deeply asleep or unconscious —**~ness** *n* [U]
USAGE If a person or other creature is no longer alive, one can say either that he/she/it is **dead**, or that he/she/it has **died**: *Our old dog* **died** *years ago/has just* **died**/*will soon* **die**.|*Our old dog has been* **dead** *for years/is* **dead** *now/will soon be* **dead**.|*a* **dead** *dog.*

dead² *n* **in the dead of** in the quietest or least active period of: *in the dead of night/winter*

dead³ *adv* **1** suddenly and completely: *She stopped dead* **2** [H] *infml* completely: *dead certain|dead tired* **3** [H] *infml* directly: *dead ahead*

dead-beat /ˌ· ˈ·◂/ *adj infml* tired out

dead beat /ˈ· ·/ *n* **1** a lazy person **2** *derog* BEATNIK

dead cen·tre /ˌ· ˈ··/ *n* [(*the*) R] the exact centre: *He wanted to hit the dead centre.|He hit it dead centre!*

dead·en /ˈdedn/ *v* [T1] to cause to lose (strength, force, feeling, brightness): *to deaden the pain|Thick walls deaden noise*

dead end /ˌ· ˈ·/ *n* **1** an end (as of a street) with no way out **2** a position, state, or course of action that leads to nothing further: *We've come to a dead end in our efforts to reach agreement.|I want to leave this dead-end job of mine* **3 dead-end kids** *infml esp. AmE* children from poor areas who have to fight to stay alive

dead heat /ˌ· ˈ·/ *n* a race in which there is no single winner: *The race was a dead heat, and first prize was divided*

dead let·ter /ˌ· ˈ··/ *n* **1** a letter that cannot be delivered or returned to the sender: *Perhaps it's in the dead-letter office* **2** a law that still exists but that people no longer obey: *That law was passed in 1603 and it's become a dead letter*

dead·line /ˈdedlaɪn/ *n* a date or time before which something must be done, esp. the time after which material is not accepted for a particular number of a newspaper, magazine, etc.: *I hope we can finish this before the deadline!*

dead·lock /ˈdedlɒk‖-lɑk/ *n* a disagreement which cannot be settled

dead·ly[1] /ˈdedli/ *adj* [Wa2] **1** [B] likely to cause or able to produce death: *a deadly disease/weapon* **2** [A] aiming to kill or destroy: *a deadly enemy* **3** [B] highly effective against something or someone: *a deadly argument against his plan* **4** [A] marked by determination or very great seriousness: *deadly seriousness* **5** [A] like death in appearance: *deadly paleness* **6** [B] *derog* like death in dullness or lack of activity: *a deadly conversation* **7** [A;(B)] making it impossible for the spirit or soul to advance further (esp. in the phr. **the 7 deadly sins**) —compare MORTAL SIN, VENIAL **sin** —**-liness** *n* [U]

deadly[2] *adv* **1** suggesting death: *deadly pale* **2** very: *deadly serious|deadly dull*

deadly night·shade /ˌ·· ˈ··/ *n* [U;C] a type of poisonous European plant of the potato family (with dark purple flowers and black berries), from which the drug BELLADONNA is obtained

dead man's han·dle /ˌ· · ˈ··/ *n* a handle which controls the speed of a train or other vehicle and will bring it to a stop if not held continually by the driver

dead march /ˈ· ·/ *n* a solemn slow march for a funeral

dead·pan /ˈdedpæn/ *adj, adv infml* with no show of feeling, esp. when telling jokes as if they were serious: *deadpan humour|The actor played his part completely deadpan*

dead reck·on·ing /ˌ· ˈ···/ *n* [U;C] the mapping of the position of a ship or aircraft from the record of earlier positions, the distance sailed or flown, etc., and without looking at the sun, moon, or stars

dead shot /ˌ· ˈ·/ *n* **1** a shot that hits exactly what is aimed at **2** a person who can fire such shots

dead·weight /ˈdedˈweɪt/ *n* [S;(U)] the whole weight of something that does not move at all, which is a weight supposed to be particularly heavy

dead wood /ˌ· ˈ·/ *AmE* **dead·wood** /ˈdedwʊd/— *n* [U] *esp. BrE* **1** wood dead on the tree **2** useless people or things

deaf /def/ *adj* [Wa1] **1** [B; *the*+P] unable to hear at all or to hear well: *deaf people|The deaf find social life difficult* **2** [F (*to*)] unwilling to hear or listen: *deaf to all my prayers* **3** **turn a deaf ear to** to be unwilling to hear or listen to —**~ness** *n* [U]

deaf-aid /ˈ· ·/ *n BrE infml* HEARING AID

deaf·en /ˈdefən/ *v* [Wv4;T1] to make deaf: *This noise will deafen us all!*

deaf-mute /ˌ· ˈ·‖ˈ· ·/ *n, adj* [Wa5] (a person) who is deaf and cannot speak

deal[1] /diːl/ *n* **1** [S (*of*)] a quantity or degree, usu. large or not known exactly: *A deal of money was spent.|a great deal of support|a good deal faster* **2** [*the*+R;C] the act or right of giving out cards to players in a card game: *Who has the deal now?|The next 2 deals will be interesting*

deal[2] *v* **dealt** /delt/ **1** [D1 (*to*);T1: (OUT)] to give as one's share: *I tried to deal justice to all men.| I dealt out 3 pieces to each guest.| I dealt (them) (out) 3 pieces each* **2** [D1 (*to*); T1: (OUT); I∅] to give out (playing cards) to players in a game: *I dealt (them) (out) good cards, I did!| Who deals next?* **3** [D1 (*to*)] to strike (in the phr. **deal someone a blow**) —see also DEAL IN, DEAL WITH

deal[3] *n* **1** [C] an act of dealing **2** [S9] *infml* treatment received: *a dirty/raw deal* (= bad treatment) **3** [C] an arrangement to the advantage of both sides, often in business: *Let's (esp. AmE) make/(BrE) do a deal with each other and stop fighting*

deal[4] *n* [U] *esp BrE* FIR or PINE wood: *made of deal*

deal at *v prep* [T1] to deal with (a business establishment): *I've dealt at this store for 20 years*

deal·er /ˈdiːləʳ/ *n* **1** a person who deals playing cards **2** a person in a given type of business: *a used-car dealer*

deal in *v prep* [T1 *usu. not pass.*] to buy and sell; trade in: *This shop deals in woollen goods*

deal·ing /ˈdiːlɪŋ/ *n* [U] method of business; manner of behaving: *I'm all in favour of plain honest dealing —but is it practical?*

deal·ings /ˈdiːlɪŋz/ *n* [P] personal or business relations: *I've had dealings with him, but I don't know him very well*

deal with *v prep* [T1] **1** to do business, esp. trade, with: *I've dealt with this store/person for 20 years* **2** to treat; take action about (someone or something): *Children are tiring to deal with.|How do you deal with a drunken husband?|There are too many difficulties for us to deal with* **3** to be concerned with: *Tom's new book deals with the troubles in Ireland*

dean /diːn/ *n* **1** [C;N;A] (in several Christian churches) an officer in charge of several priests or church divisions **2** [C;N] (in some universities) a person in charge of a division of study or in charge of students and their behaviour **3** [C] DOYEN

dean·e·ry /ˈdiːnəri/ *n* **1** the area controlled by a DEAN (1) **2** the office or official home of a DEAN

dear[1] /dɪəʳ/ *adj* [Wa1] **1** [B] much loved: *He's my dearest friend* **2** [A] (*usu. cap.*) as an address, expressing fondness, or as a formality at the beginning of a letter: *Dear Jane|Dear Sir* **3** [F+*to*; (A)] precious: *Life is very dear to him.|He holds life (very) dear* **4** [B] *esp. BrE* costly: *It's too dear: I can't afford it* —**~ness** *n* [U]

dear[2] *adv* a lot (in the phr. **cost someone dear**) of pain and effort

dear[3] *n* [C;N] a person who is loved or lovable: *Be a dear and buy me some cigarettes, won't you?|I love you, (my) dear*

dear[4] *interj* (used for expressing surprise, sorrow, slight anger, discouragement): OH *dear! I've lost my pen.|"Mr. Smith is ill again." "Dear me! Dear! Dear! I'm sorry to hear that"*

USAGE This expression is "stronger" in *BrE* than in *AmE*.

dear·est /ˈdɪərɪ̵st/ *n* [N] a much-loved person: *I love you, (my) dearest* —see also **nearest** (NEAR[3] (3)) **and dearest**

dear·ly /ˈdɪəli‖ˈdɪərli/ *adv* **1** with much feeling, usu. good feeling: *I should dearly love to go back to Scotland.|He loves his wife dearly* **2** at a high price or terrible cost in time, effort, pain, etc.: *He paid dearly for his experience*

dearly be·lov·ed /ˌ·· ·ˈ··/ *n* [N] (used as a form of address by a priest to a man and a woman about to be married): *Dearly beloved, we have come together in the sight of God . . .*

dearth /dɜːθ‖dɜrθ/ *n* [S+*of*] *fml* a lack (of); SHORTAGE (of)

dear·y, -ie /ˈdɪəri/ *n* [N;(C)] *infml* DEAR[3]

death /deθ/ *n* **1** [U;C] the last end of life; time or manner of dying: *He was happy to the day of his death.|Car accidents have caused many deaths* **2** [(*the*) R (*of*)] the cause or occasion of loss of life (often in the phr. **be the death of**): *Drinking was the death of him.|If you go out without a coat, you'll catch your death of cold.|*(fig.) *You'll be the death of me with your funny jokes! You'll make me die laughing!* **3** [R] (*usu. cap.*) the destroyer of life, usu. shown as a SKELETON: *In that picture you can see Death leading a dance of dead people to the next world* **4** [U] the state of being dead: *Kiss me while we're young, for death lasts a long time.|as still as death* **5** [*the*+R+*of*] the end or destruction (of something not alive): *That defeat meant the death* *of all my hopes* **6 to death** beyond all acceptable limits: *He works the people in his shop to death.|I am sick to death of your complaints* **7 put to death** to kill, esp. with official permission: *The prisoners were all put to death* **8 a natural death** death from natural causes like illness or old age, not as the result of an accident, murder, etc.: *She lived a long happy life and died a natural death* **9 in at the death** present at the death of a hunted animal or at the defeat of a person, plan, etc. **10 at death's door** about to die; in danger of dying: *That very sick man is at death's door, I'm afraid*

death·bed /ˈdeθbed/ *n* [C9 *usu. sing.*] the bed on which someone dies or is expected to die: *I'm afraid that very sick man is on his deathbed*

death·blow /ˈdeθbləʊ/ *n* [*usu. sing.*] **1** a killing blow or shock **2** an act, action, or event that destroys or ends someone or something: *His refusal to help us dealt a deathblow to our plans*

death du·ty /ˈ· ˌ··/ (*AmE* **death tax** /ˈ· ·/)— *n BrE* a sum of money that must be paid to a government on land, money, goods, etc., left to a person on the death of the original owner

death·less /ˈdeθləs/ *adj* [Wa5] unforgettable; IMMORTAL: *Shakespeare's deathless fame* —**~ly** *adv*

death·like /ˈdeθlaɪk/ *adj* like death or like that of death: *a deathlike paleness/stillness*

death·ly[1] /ˈdeθli/ *adv* in a deathlike way: *a deathly cold body*

deathly[2] *adj* DEATHLIKE

death mask /ˈ· ·/ *n* a copy of a dead person's face made by pressing soft wax down over the face

death rate /ˈ· ·/ *n* the number of people per 1,000 who die in a particular year in a particular place

death rat·tle /ˈ· ˌ··/ *n* an unusual sound (like a RATTLE[2] (2)) sometimes heard from the throat of a person near death

death roll /ˈ· ·/ *n* a list of the names of dead people whose deaths have something in common, such as time, place, or manner

death's-head /ˈ· ·/ *n* a human SKULL representing death

death toll /ˈ· ·/ *n* the number of people who died in a particular way: *I'm afraid there will be a large death toll from that railway accident*

death trap /ˈ· ·/ *n* something or some state that may be very dangerous to life: *the risk of going to sea in a boat that was a death trap*

death war·rant /ˈ· ˌ··/ *n* **1** a written official order to kill (EXECUTE(4)) someone **2** a sure sign of failure: *The news that there would be no more money from the government was a death warrant for all our great plans for the future*

death·watch /ˈdeθwɒtʃ‖-wɑtʃ/ *n* **1** also **death-watch bee·tle** /ˌ·· ˈ··/— any of various small insects that make a sound like the TICK of a clock, esp. some which are common in old buildings, where they dig into furniture and other things made of wood **2** a period of time watching beside a person who is soon going to die

death wish /ˈ· ·/ *n* a conscious or unconscious desire for the death of another person or esp. of oneself

deb /deb/ *n infml* DEBUTANTE

dé·bâ·cle /deɪˈbɑːkəl, dɪ-/ *n Fr* **1** a sudden and disorderly rush of people, of an army away from the enemy, etc. **2** a sudden break-down or failure

de·bar from /dɪˈbɑːʳ/ *v prep* **-rr-** [V4b] to prevent (someone) from (doing or having something): *Until recently, women were debarred from owning land here*

de·bark /dɪˈbɑːk‖-ɑrk/ *v* [I∅] *becoming rare* DISEMBARK —**debarkation** /ˌdiːbɑːˈkeɪʃən‖-ɑr-/ *n* [C;U]

de·base /dɪˈbeɪs/ *v* [T1] **1** to lower in personal quality or in the opinion of others: *Such unkind action debases you* **2 a** to lower the real value of (coins) by making them with less valuable metal **b** *derog becoming rare* DEVALUE —**~ment** *n* [U;C]

de·ba·ta·ble /dɪˈbeɪtəbəl/ *adj* **1** that can be DEBATED[2] because doubtful, questionable, perhaps not true, etc.: *a debatable statement/argument* **2** claimed by more than one country: *a debatable border area*

de·bate[1] /dɪˈbeɪt/ *n* a usu. public meeting in which a question is talked over by at least 2 people or groups, each expressing a different point of view: *There will be a long debate in Parliament before the new law is passed*

debate[2] *v* **1** [I∅ (*upon* or *about*);T1: (*with*)] to argue about (something) with (someone), usu. in an effort to persuade other people: *We debated until the bar closed.|I debated (upon/about) the question (with Mary).|I debated with Mary (upon/about the question)* **2** [T1] to consider in one's own mind the arguments for and against something: *I debated the idea in my mind until I fell asleep*

de·bat·er /dɪˈbeɪtəʳ/ *n* **1** a person who is skilled in or fond of giving arguments for or against ideas **2** a person who takes part in DEBATES[1], esp. as a member of a team

de·bauch[1] /dɪˈbɔːtʃ‖dɪˈbɔtʃ, dɪˈbɑtʃ/ *v* [T1] to lead away from socially approved forms of behaviour, esp. in relation to sex and alcohol

debauch[2] *n* an act or occasion of going beyond socially-approved limits of behaviour, esp. in relation to sex and alcohol; wild party or ORGY

de·bauch·ee /ˌdebɔːˈtʃiː, -ʃiː‖dɪˌbɔˈtʃiː, dɪˌbɑ-/ *n derog* a DEBAUCHED[1] person

de·bauch·e·ry /dɪˈbɔːtʃəri/ *n derog* **1** [U] behaviour that goes beyond socially-approved limits, esp. in relation to sex and alcohol **2** [C *usu. pl.*] an example or occasion of this

de·ben·ture /dɪˈbentʃəʳ/ *n* a written promise by a government or a business company to pay a debt and a fixed rate of interest on the debt

de·bil·i·tate /dɪˈbɪlɨteɪt/ *v* [T1] to make (a person or a person's health) weak: *Heat debilitates many people.|a debilitating disease*

de·bil·i·ty /dɪˈbɪlɨti/ *n* [U] weakness, esp. as the result of disease

deb·it[1] /ˈdebɨt/ *n* **1** a record (in a book of accounts) of money spent or owed —compare CREDIT[1] (7) **2** also **debit side** /ˈ·· ·/— the left-hand side of an account book on which debits are written

debit[2] *v* **1** [T1 (*against*)] to enter in the left-hand or "DEBIT"[1] side of an account: *Debit £10 against Mr. Smith/Mr. Smith's account* **2** [T1 (*with*)] to charge with a DEBIT[1]: *Debit Mr. Smith/Mr. Smith's account with £10* —compare CREDIT[1] (7)

deb·o·nair /ˌdebəˈneəʳ/ *adj apprec* (usu. of men) gay and charming, but also polite and well-dressed: *a debonair manner/young man*

de·bone /ˌdiːˈbəʊn/ *v* [Wv5;T1] to remove the bones from (esp. chicken, duck, meat rather than fish): *deboned chicken*

de·bouch /dɪˈbaʊtʃ‖-ˈbuːʃ/ *v* [L9] to come out from a narrow place (such as a valley) into a broader place (such as a stream): *The river debouches into a wide plain*

de·brief /ˌdiːˈbriːf/ *v* [T1] to find out information from (someone on one's own side), esp. by thorough questioning about the results of an action: *We debriefed our pilot after she had flown over the enemy's land*

deb·ris /ˈdebriː, ˈdeɪ-‖dəˈbriː, deɪ-/ *n* [U] *Fr* **1** the remains of something broken to pieces or destroyed; ruins: *After the bombing there was a lot of debris everywhere* **2** *esp. tech.* heaps of pieces of rock

debt /det/ *n* **1** [C;U] something owed to someone

else: *a debt of £10|to pay one's debts|*(fig.) *a debt of* GRATITUDE *for your help* **2** [U] the state of owing; the duty of repaying that which is owed (often in phrs. like **in debt, out of debt**): *He was in debt when he was poor, but has been out of debt since he got rich.|in debt to you for £10|your help* **3 run into debt** to begin to owe money **4 debt of honour** a debt that a gentleman will pay although the law does not force him to

debt·or /ˈdetəʳ/ *n* a person who owes money

de·bug /ˌdiːˈbʌg/ *v* **-gg-** [T1] *infml* to remove the BUGS[1] (5,6) from: *Let's debug the machine so that it works properly.|Let's debug the room so that we can talk freely*

de·bunk /ˌdiːˈbʌŋk/ *v* [T1] *infml* to point out the truth about (over-praised people, things, ideas, etc.): *A lot of people used to believe that, but now it's been quite thoroughly debunked* —**~er** *n*

de·but¹ /ˈdeɪbjuː, ˈdebjuː‖deɪˈbjuː, dɪ-/ *n Fr* **1** a first public appearance: *The singer made his debut as Mozart's Don Giovanni* **2** a formal entrance into upper-class society made by a young woman: *At 18 she made her debut at a big party at the Ritz* **3** a first attempt or appearance: *Tonight's dinner is my husband's debut as a cook*

debut² *v* [IØ (*as*)] *infml* to make a DEBUT

deb·u·tante /ˈdebjʊtɑːnt/ also (*infml*) **deb**— *n* a woman who is about to make or has just made her DEBUT[1] (2)

Dec. *written abbrev. for:* December

dec·a- /ˈdekə-/ also **dec-** /dek-/— *prefix* 10: DECALOGUE—see WEIGHTS & MEASURES TABLE

dec·ade /ˈdekeɪd, deˈkeɪd/ *n* a period of 10 years: *Prices have risen steadily during the past decade.|The 1920's are remembered as a particularly gay decade*

dec·a·dence /ˈdekədəns/ *n* [U] (a period or state marked by) a fall to a lower or worse level from a former higher or better level

dec·a·dent¹ /ˈdekədənt/ *adj* marked by DECADENCE —**~ly** *adv*

decadent² *n* (in France and England in the 1890's) any of a group of writers and painters whose subjects were considered morally offensive

Dec·a·logue /ˈdekəlɒg‖-lɔg, -lɑg/ *n* [*the* +R] *tech* the TEN COMMANDMENTS

de·camp /dɪˈkæmp/ *v* [IØ] **1** (esp. of soldiers) to leave a place where one has camped **2** *infml* to leave any place quickly (and usu. in secret): *The lodger has decamped without paying his bill*

de·cant /dɪˈkænt/ *v* [T1] **1** to pour (liquid, esp. wine) from one container into another, esp. so as to leave all the undrinkable parts (SEDIMENT) in the first container **2** *sl* to move (people) from one living or working place into another, esp. for a limited time

de·cant·er /dɪˈkæntəʳ/ *n* a bottle or related container (usu. of glass and ornamented) for holding liquid (esp. wine) which has been DECANTed into it

de·cap·i·tate /dɪˈkæpɪteɪt/ *v* [T1] to cut off the head of (esp. as a punishment); BEHEAD —**-tation** /dɪˌkæpɪˈteɪʃən/ *n* [U;C]

de·cath·lon /dɪˈkæθlɒn‖-lɑn, lən/ *n* a competition in out-of-door games (ATHLETICS) consisting of 10 separate events: *Who won the decathlon at this year's games?*

de·cay¹ /dɪˈkeɪ/ *v* **1** [T1;IØ] to (cause to) go through destructive chemical changes or go bad: *Sugar can decay the teeth.|Her decayed tooth had to be taken out* **2** [IØ] to fall to a lower or worse state; lose health, power, strength, activity, etc.: *History sometimes seems to teach us that all nations decay in the course of time*

decay² *n* [U] **1** the action or state of decaying: *That university has fallen into decay in the last 100 years* **2** (esp. of the teeth) the decayed parts

de·cease /dɪˈsiːs/ *n* [U] *fml & law* death: *Upon your decease the house will pass to your wife*

de·ceased¹ /dɪˈsiːst/ *adj* [Wa5] *fml & law* (of people) no longer living, esp. recently dead

deceased² *n* **deceased** [Wn3] *fml & law* the dead (person or people): *The deceased left a large sum of money to his wife*

de·ceit /dɪˈsiːt/ *n derog* **1** [U] the quality of being dishonest **2** [C] DECEPTION (2)

de·ceit·ful /dɪˈsiːtfəl/ *adj derog* dishonest —**~ly** *adv* —**~ness** *n* [U]

de·ceive /dɪˈsiːv/ *v* [Wv4;T1 (*in, into*);IØ] to cause (someone) to accept as true or good what is false or bad: *I trust him because I know he would never deceive me.|Do my eyes deceive me, or is that really an elephant pulling a carriage?* —**deceiver** *n*

de·cel·e·rate /ˌdiːˈseləreɪt/ *v* [T1;IØ] to (cause to) go slower: *We decelerated (the engine) long before we came to a stop* —compare ACCELERATE (1)

De·cem·ber /dɪˈsembəʳ/ *n* [R;(C)] the 12th and last month of the year

de·cen·cies /ˈdiːsənsiz/ *n* [*the*+P] *becoming rare* the standards of socially-acceptable behaviour (esp. in the phr. **observe** (= behave in accordance with) **the decencies**)

de·cen·cy /ˈdiːsənsi/ *n* [U] the quality of being DECENT: *I know you didn't like him, but at least have the decency to go to his funeral!*

de·cent /ˈdiːsənt/ *adj* **1** fitting; proper; socially acceptable; not causing shame or shock to others: *I tell you decent people just don't do things like that!|decent behaviour|clothing|living conditions* **2** *infml* rather good: *You can get quite a decent meal there without spending too much money* —**~ly** *adv*

de·cen·tral·ize, -ise /ˌdiːˈsentrəlaɪz/ *v* [T1;IØ] to (cause to) move from one big place to several smaller places —**-ization** /ˌdiːsentrəlaɪˈzeɪʃən‖-lə-/ *n* [U]

de·cep·tion /dɪˈsepʃən/ *n* **1** [U] the act or state of deceiving or being deceived **2** [C] also **deceit**— something that deceives; a trick

de·cep·tive /dɪˈseptɪv/ *adj* tending or having power to deceive; misleading —**~ly** *adv*: *deceptively simple, but really difficult* —**~ness** *n* [U]

dec·i- /ˈdesɪ/ *prefix* 10th part: DECIMAL —see WEIGHTS & MEASURES TABLE

dec·i·bel /ˈdesɪbel/ *n tech* a measure of the loudness of sound

de·cide /dɪˈsaɪd/ *v* **1** [T1,6a,b] to arrive at an answer or way out that ends uncertainty or disagreement about: *to decide the question|to decide where to go|where they should go* **2** [T3,5a] to come to hold or declare a stated belief: *She decided to go|(that) he should go* **3** [T1] to bring to a clear or certain end: *One blow decided the fight* **4** [T1;V3] to cause to make a choice: *Your words have decided me (to help you)* **5** [IØ] to make a choice or judgment: *I've been waiting all day for them to decide!|They decided in favour of him and against me.|They have decided about it* —see also DECIDE ON

de·cid·ed /dɪˈsaɪdɪd/ *adj* **1** very clear and easily seen or understood: *a decided change for the better|a decided turn to the left* **2** having or showing no doubt; sure of oneself: *a man of very decided opinions|His character is very decided*

de·cid·ed·ly /dɪˈsaɪdɪdli/ *adv* in a very DECIDED manner: *She was very decidedly angry.|He spoke so decidedly that none of us dared question him*

decide on *v prep* [T1,4] to decide in favour of: *I've decided on a new car|on going there*

de·cid·u·ous /dɪˈsɪdʒʊəs/ *adj* [Wa5] *tech* **1** falling off seasonally or at a certain stage of development of life: *deciduous leaves* **2** having parts that fall off, esp. leaves: *deciduous trees* —see picture at TREE[1]

dec·i·mal[1] /ˈdesɨməl/ *adj* [Wa5] having to do with the number 10 —**-mally** *adv*: *to count decimally*
decimal[2] also **decimal frac·tion**— *n* a number like .5, .375, .06, etc.
dec·i·mal·ize, -ise /ˈdesɨməlaɪz‖ˈdesəmə-/ *v* [T1; IØ] to change to a DECIMAL system —**-ization** /ˌdesɨməlaɪˈzeɪʃən‖-lə-/ *n* [U]
decimal point /ˌ··· ˈ·/ *n* the dot at the left of a DECIMAL[2]
dec·i·mate /ˈdesɨmeɪt/ *v* [T1] to destroy a large part of: *Disease decimated the population* —**-mation** /ˌdesɨˈmeɪʃən/ *n* [U]
USAGE **Decimate** used to mean "to kill at least $\frac{1}{10}$ of". It now often means "to kill at least $\frac{9}{10}$ of", but many people feel that this use is bad English.
de·ci·pher /dɪˈsaɪfəʳ/ *v* [T1] to discover the meaning of (something difficult or secret, esp. a CODE)
de·ci·sion /dɪˈsɪʒən/ *n* **1** [U] the act of deciding: *In political matters, decision can be very difficult* **2** [C] a choice or judgment: *Who made the decision to go there?|Whose decision was it?|The judge will give his decision tomorrow.|Come to a decision soon* **3** [C] a report of that which has been decided: *The decision appeared in all the newspapers* **4** [U] the quality of being able to make choices or judgments quickly and to act on them with firmness —opposite **indecision**
de·ci·sive /dɪˈsaɪsɪv/ *adj* **1** having the power or quality of deciding: *a decisive influence* **2** marked by or showing determination or firmness: *A decisive person acts quickly and often succeeds* **3** unquestionable: *a decisive advantage* —**~ly** *adv* —**~ness** *n* [U]
deck /dek/ *n* **1** [C; *on, below, above*+U] a usu. wooden floor built across a ship over all or part of its length —see picture at FREIGHTER **2** [C] a surface like this, such as the floor or level of a bus: *A double-deck bus has 2 levels: you can smoke on the upper deck* **3** [C] *esp. AmE* a set of playing cards; PACK[1] (4) **4 on deck** *esp. AmE* **a** ready for duty **b** next in order **5 clear the decks a** to get everyone off the DECK*s* of a ship **b** to remove everything from a given place, esp. so as to make it ready for action
deck·chair /ˈdek tʃeəʳ/ *n* a folding chair with a long seat of cloth (usu. CANVAS) on which one may stretch out one's legs. It is used on the open part of the DECK of a ship, and also in gardens and in the sunshine —see picture at GARDEN[1]
-deck·er /ˈdekəʳ/ *comb. form* [*n* → *adj, n*] having a stated number of levels, floors, or DECK*s* (1,2): *A double-decker (bus) has 2 floors*
deck·hand /ˈdekhænd/ *n* a man or boy who is hired to do cleaning and other unskilled work on a ship
deck·le-edged /ˌdekəl ˈedʒd◂/ *adj* [Wa5] (of paper, photographs, etc.) having rough irregularly-cut edges —**deckle edge** *n*
deck out *v adv* [T1 (*in*) *often pass.*] to make (someone or something) more beautiful or gay: *The street was decked out in flags* —see DECORATE (USAGE)
deck with *v prep* [D1 (OUT) *often pass.*] to ornament (someone or something) with (pretty things): *The Christmas tree was decked with gifts* —see DECORATE (USAGE)
de·claim /dɪˈkleɪm/ *v often derog* **1** [T1 (*to*)] to say (something) loud and clear, with pauses and usu. hand movements to increase the effect of the words **2** [IØ] to speak in this way: *I wish you wouldn't declaim all the time: just speak naturally!*
dec·la·ma·tion /ˌdekləˈmeɪʃən/ *n sometimes derog* **1** [U] the act or art of DECLAIMing **2** [C] something which is DECLAIMed —**declamatory** /dɪˈklæmətəri‖-tori/ *adj*
dec·la·ra·tion /ˌdekləˈreɪʃən/ *n* **1** [C;(U)] the act of declaring: *a declaration of war* **2** [C] a statement giving information in a court of law **3** [C] (a written statement containing a record of) something declared: *Please make a written declaration of all the goods you bought abroad*
de·clare /dɪˈkleəʳ/ *v* **1** [T1;X1,7] to make known publicly or officially, according to rules, custom, etc.: *Our government has tonight declared war on Ruritania.|Jones was declared the winner of the fight.|I declare Alvin B. Schiff elected!* **2** [T1,5a;X (*to be*) 1, (*to be*) 7] to state (or show) with great force so that there is no doubt about the meaning: *He declared his position.|He declared (that) he was right.|He declared himself (to be) a member of their party.|They declared themselves (to be) for/against the plan.|His actions declared him (to be) an honest man* **3** [T1] to make a full statement of (property for which money may be owed to the government): *Have you anything to declare?* **4** [IØ;X7] (of the captain of a cricket team) to end the team's INNINGS before all its members have been put out: *Do you think Brearley will declare before tea?* **5** [T1;IØ] (in the game of BRIDGE[3]) to say which type of card will be played as (TRUMPS) **6 declare oneself** to state clearly one's point of view or intentions **7 (well,) I declare!** (an expression of slight surprise or slight anger) —**declarable** *adj*: *Have you any declarable goods?* —**declaratory** /dɪˈklærətəri‖-tori/ *adj*
declare a·gainst *v prep* [T1,4] to state one's opposition to (someone, something, or doing something)
de·clared /dɪˈkleəd‖-ərd/ *adj* (esp. of people) openly admitted, stated to be, or described as: *a declared enemy of mine|a declared supporter of the government* —**declaredly** /dɪˈkleərɨdli/ *adv*: *declaredly a supporter of the government*
declare for *v prep* [T1,4] to state one's support for (someone, something, or doing something)
de·clas·si·fy /ˌdiːˈklæsɨfaɪ/ *v* [T1] to declare (esp. political and military information) no longer secret —**-fication** /ˌdiːklæsɨfɨˈkeɪʃən/ *n* [U]
de·clen·sion /dɪˈklenʃən/ *n* (*in grammar*) **1** [U] the act of giving the different forms of a noun, PRONOUN, or adjective **2** [C] a class of nouns and/or adjectives which have the same forms: *In Latin, the 4th and 5th declensions are smaller than the first 3* —compare CONJUGATION (1)
dec·li·na·tion /ˌdeklɨˈneɪʃən/ *n* **1** [U;C] *tech* the distance of a star north or south of an imaginary line round the middle of the sky **2** *tech* the angle of a compass needle, east or west, from true north: *a declination of 15 degrees* **3** [C] a formal refusal
de·cline[1] /dɪˈklaɪn/ *v* **1** [IØ] *fml or lit* to slope or move downwards: *About 2 miles east, the land begins to decline towards the river* **2** [IØ] to move from a better to a worse position, or from higher to lower: *His power/health/influence has begun to decline now that he is old.|The old man declined rapidly and soon died.|That old lady wants to spend her declining years by the sea* **3** [T1,3;IØ] to refuse, usu. politely; be unwilling: *We asked them to come to our party, but they declined (the invitation).|The minister declined to make a statement to the newspapers* **4** [T1] (in grammar) to give the different forms of (a noun, PRONOUN, or adjective) —see REFUSE (USAGE)
decline[2] *n* **1** [C *usu. sing.*] a period of declining (DECLINE[1] (2)), esp. as something or someone gets near the end: *There is a sharp decline in interest in sports in our town.|She went into a decline and soon died* **2 on the decline** declining (DECLINE[1] (2)): *In our town, interest in sports is on the decline*
de·cliv·i·ty /dɪˈklɪvɨti/ *n fml or tech* a downward slope

de·clutch /ˌdiːˈklʌtʃ/ *v* [IØ] to step on the CLUTCH² (3) of a car, esp. before changing GEAR¹ (3)
de·coc·tion /dɪˈkɒkʃən‖-ˈkɑk-/ *n* a liquid obtained by boiling something for a long time in water
de·code /ˌdiːˈkəʊd/ *v* [T1] to discover the meaning of (a message in a secret language (a CODE)): *We decoded the enemy's telegram and were able to win a famous victory*
dé·colle·tage /ˌdeɪkɒlˈtɑːʒ‖deɪˌkɑləˈtɑʒ/ *n Fr* a top edge of a woman's dress that is cut very low, so that part of the shoulders, chest, and breasts is not covered
dé·col·leté /deɪˈkɒlteɪ‖deɪˌkɑləˈteɪ/ *adj Fr* (of a woman or a dress) leaving uncovered part of the shoulders, chest, and breasts
de·col·o·nize, -ise /ˌdiːˈkɒlənaɪz‖-ˈkɑ-/ *v* [T1] to give political independence to —**-nization** /ˌdiːkɒlənaɪˈzeɪʃən‖-kɑlənə-/ *n* [U]
de·com·pose /ˌdiːkəmˈpəʊz/ *v* [T1;IØ] **1** to (cause to) break up and separate into simple parts **2** to (cause to) decay —**-position** /ˌdiːkɒmpəˈzɪʃən‖-kɑm-/ *n* [U]
de·com·press /ˌdiːkəmˈpres/ *v* [T1] to reduce the pressure of or on —**~ion** /-ˈpreʃən/ *n* [U]
de·con·gest·ant /ˌdiːkənˈdʒestənt/ *n* [C;U] a medicine that reduces swelling and blocking, esp. in the nose
de·con·tam·i·nate /ˌdiːkənˈtæmɪ̈neɪt/ *v* [T1] to remove dangerous impure substances from: *Decontaminate the room where the sick man died* —**-nation** /-ˌtæmɪ̈ˈneɪʃən/ *n* [U]
de·con·trol¹ /ˌdiːkənˈtrəʊl/ *v* **-ll-** [T1] to end control of: *As soon as the government decontrolled prices, everything became dearer in the shops*
decontrol² *n* [U;(C)] the removal of control(s)
dé·cor /ˈdeɪkɔːʳ‖deɪˈkɔr/ *n* [C;U] *Fr* the ornamental furnishing and arranging of a place, esp. a room, house, or stage: *Who did the décor for the new play at the Globe Theatre?*
dec·o·rate /ˈdekəreɪt/ *v* **1** [T1 (*with*)] to provide with something ornamental, esp. for a special occasion: *The streets were decorated with flags* **2** [T1;IØ] to paint or put a surface covering on the walls or the outside of a house: *After the house is built, how much will it cost to decorate (it)?* **3** [T1] to be or serve as an ornamentation to: *Those pictures decorate the walls very well* **4** [T1 (*for*)] to give (someone) an official mark of honour, such as a MEDAL
USAGE Many verbs mean "to add something to, so as to make more attractive". **Adorn** is particularly used of people: *She* **adorned** *herself with jewels.* **Decorate** can be used of a room or house as in def. 2: *They're having the kitchen* **decorated**. Otherwise **decorate**, like **adorn**, **embellish**, **deck out**, **deck with**, and **bedeck** (*lit*), may or may not have the bad sense of adding too much, perhaps so as to hide ugliness: *a fat old woman* **bedecked** *with jewels.* **Decorate**, **ornament**, **embellish** and **garnish** cannot be used of people, and **garnish** is most often used of cooking: *a boiled fish* **garnished** *with pieces of potato.* **Beautify** cannot have a bad sense, but means that something is really made beautiful.
dec·o·ra·tion /ˌdekəˈreɪʃən/ *n* **1** [U] the act or art of decorating; the state of being DECORATED **2** [C] an ornament; something that DECORATES: *gay decorations for a party* **3** [C] something given as a sign of honour, esp. military: *There are only a few public occasions on which it is correct to wear all one's decorations*
dec·o·ra·tive /ˈdekərətɪv‖ˈdekərə-, ˈdekəreɪ-/ *adj apprec* ornamental; used for decorating (DECORATE (1,3)): *a decorative gold table* —**~ly** *adv*
dec·o·ra·tor /ˈdekəreɪtəʳ/ *n* **1** a person who paints houses inside and out **2** INTERIOR DECORATOR
dec·o·rous /ˈdekərəs/ *adj* (of appearance or behaviour) correct; not unpleasant to the feelings of others; properly serious in manner according to the customs of society —**~ly** *adv*
de·co·rum /dɪˈkɔːrəm‖-ˈko-/ *n* [U] DECOROUS behaviour or appearance: *To preserve decorum, they said they were husband and wife*
de·coy¹ /ˈdiːkɔɪ/ *n* **1** a figure of a bird which is used for attracting wild birds within range of guns **2** a trick which is used for getting a person into a dangerous position
de·coy² /dɪˈkɔɪ/ *v* [T1 (*into*)] to deceive (a person) into coming into danger: *They decoyed him into (going into) a dark street, where they robbed him*
de·crease¹ /dɪˈkriːs/ *v* [T1;IØ] to (cause to) become less in size, number, strength, amount, or quality: *Our sales are decreasing.|I shall have to decrease your wages*
de·crease² /ˈdiːkriːs/ *n* **1** [C;(U)] the act or action of decreasing; the state of being decreased **2** [C (*of, in*)] the amount by which something decreases
de·cree¹ /dɪˈkriː/ *n* **1** [C,C5; *by*+U] an official command or decision (by a king, government, church, etc.) **2** [C] *esp. AmE* a judgment (of certain types) in a court of law
decree² *v* **1** [T1] to cause or bring into being by DECREE¹: *They have decreed an end to all this fighting* **2** [T5b;(IØ)] to state (something) officially, with the force of law: *They have decreed that all this fighting should end.|*(fig.) *God decreed that we should meet, my dear* **3** [T1,5b] *esp. AmE* (of a judge, court of law, etc.) to order officially: *to decree a punishment|to decree that a criminal should be punished*
decree ni·si /dɪˌkriː ˈnaɪsaɪ/ *n law* (in former times) an order by a court that a DIVORCE (=end of a marriage) should have effect at a certain future time except if a cause is shown why it should not
de·crep·it /dɪˈkrepɪ̈t/ *adj* weak or in bad condition from old age or hard use
de·crep·i·tude /dɪˈkrepɪ̈tjuːd‖-tuːd/ *n* [U] the quality or state of being DECREPIT
de·cry /dɪˈkraɪ/ *v* [T1] *fml* to speak ill of; say bad things about (something powerful or dangerous to the public)
ded·i·cate /ˈdedɪ̈keɪt/ *v* [T1] to set apart for a holy purpose, often with a solemn ceremony: *The new church will be dedicated on Sunday*
ded·i·cat·ed /ˈdedɪ̈keɪtɪ̈d/ *adj* (esp. of people) very interested in or working very hard for an idea, a purpose, a field of activity, etc. —**~ly** *adv*
dedicate to *v prep* [D1;V4b] **1** to set apart or give to a particular cause, purpose, or action: *The doctor dedicated his life/himself to finding a cure* **2** to declare (a book, performance, etc.) to be in honour of (esp. a person): *He dedicated his first book to his mother*
ded·i·ca·tion /ˌdedɪ̈ˈkeɪʃən/ *n* **1** [C;U] the act of dedicating (DEDICATE) **2** [C;U] the state of being DEDICATED: *The dedication of that scientist to his work is wonderful to see* **3** [C] the words used in dedicating (DEDICATE TO)
de·duce /dɪˈdjuːs‖dɪˈduːs/ *v* [T1,5] **1** to determine or decide (something) from general principles in relation to a particular thing, fact, or event: *From the fact that Socrates was a man and the principle that all men will die I deduced that Socrates would die* **2** *nonstandard* INFER —**-ducible** *adj*
de·duct /dɪˈdʌkt/ *v* [T1 (*from*)] to take away (an amount, a part) from a total —**~ible** *adj*
de·duc·tion /dɪˈdʌkʃən/ *n* **1** [U;C] the act or action of deducing (DEDUCE) **2** [C,C5] that which is DEDUCED: *All her deductions were correct.|The deduction that he was guilty worried them* **3** [U;C]

the act or action of DEDUCTing **4** [C] that which is DEDUCTed: *Several deductions were made from her wages every week*

de·duc·tive /dɪˈdʌktɪv/ *adj* by reasoning from a general idea or set of facts to a particular idea or facts —**~ly** *adv*

deed /diːd/ *n* **1** [C; *in*+U] something done on purpose: *good deeds|an honourable man in word and in deed* **2** [C] *law* a written or printed and signed paper that is both proof and an official record of an agreement, esp. an agreement concerning ownership of land and/or building

deed of cov·e·nant /ˌ· · ˈ···/ *n* a written and signed agreement usu. concerning the ownership of land or property

deed poll /ˈ· ·/ *n* **deed polls** *or* **deeds poll** [C; *by*+U] *law* a DEED (2) signed by one person only, as when making a gift of land to another person, when changing one's name, etc.

deem /diːm/ *v* [T5a;X (*to be*) 1, (*to be*) 7] *fml* to consider; have the opinion: *Do you deem this plan (to be) sensible?|He would deem it an honour if the minister came to see him*

deep[1] /diːp/ *adj* [Wa1] **1** [B] going far downward: *a deep well|the deep sea* **2** [B] going well inward from an outer surface: *a deep wound|a deep chest* **3** [B] not near the surface of the body: *deep organs of the body* **4** [B] well below the level of the conscious mind: *a deep disorder of the character* **5** [B] going well back from a front surface: *a deep cupboard* **6** [B] near the outer limits of the playing area: *a hit to deep right field* **7** [B] going far from the side towards the centre: *deep borders of bright red silk* **8** [F] towards the centre and far from the entrances or outer limits: *a house deep in the forest* **9** [E] going a stated amount in an understood direction, usu. downward or backward: *a shelf 20 inches deep|cars parked 3 deep* **10** [B] (*esp. in comb.*) covered, enclosed, or filled to a stated degree: *ankle-deep in mud* **11** [B] difficult to understand: *deep scientific principles* **12** [B] *BrE* (of people) difficult to get to know well: *a deep person* **13** [A] mysterious and strange: *a deep dark secret* **14** [B] having or showing a fine ability to understand things thoroughly: *a deep mind/understanding/thinker* **15** [B] strong; difficult to change: *a deep sleep|deep feelings|a deep influence* **16** [B] seriously bad or damaging: *in deep debt/dishonour* **17** [B] (of a colour) strong and full but not bright: *a deep blue sky* **18** [B] (of a sound or of breath) low; coming from far down in the chest **19** [F] distant in time or space: *deep in the Middle Ages* **20 deep waters** new, unknown, and probably difficult parts of a subject **21 go off the deep end** *sl* to lose one's temper suddenly or violently **22 in deep water** in serious trouble **23 the deep end** the most difficult end or part **24 thrown in at the deep end** suddenly and unexpectedly faced with a difficult piece of work, a new job, etc. —**~ly** *adv* —**~ness** *n* [U]

deep[2] *adv* [Wa5] **1** [H] to a great depth; deeply: *He pushed his stick deep (down) into the mud* **2** [H] far into; late: *They danced deep into the night* **3** near the outer limits of the playing area **4 Still waters run deep** Not much shows on the surface (of a person), but there may be a lot going on deep down inside

deep[3] *n* [*the*+R] *poet* the sea

deep·en /ˈdiːpən/ *v* [T1;I0] to (cause to) become deep or deeper: *We'll have to deepen the well if we want more water.|"The mystery deepens, my friends," said Sherlock Holmes*

deep freeze /ˌ· ˈ·‖ˈ· ·/ *n* FREEZER (1)

deep fry /ˈ· ·/ *v* [Wv5;T1] to FRY (food) totally covered in oil or fat

deep in /ˈ· ·/ *prep* with the mind so completely fixed on (something) that one notices little else

deep-laid /ˌ· ˈ·◂/ *adj* [Wa2] planned in secret: *deep-laid plans*

deep-root·ed /ˌ· ˈ··◂/ also **deeply rooted** /ˌ·· ˈ··◂/— *adj* [Wa2] having firm roots or strongly fixed in one's nature, esp. for a long time: *For some people, smoking is a deep-rooted habit*

deep-seat·ed /ˌ· ˈ··◂/ *adj* [Wa2] **1** existing far below the surface: *a deep-seated illness, with no signs on the surface* **2** DEEP-ROOTED

deer /dɪəʳ/ *n* **deer** [Wn3] any of several types of rather large fast 4-footed animal, of which the males usu. have wide branching horns (ANTLERs) —see picture at RUMINANT

deer·stalk·er /ˈdɪəstɔːkəʳ‖ˈdɪər-/ also **deerstalker hat** /ˌ··· ˈ·/— *n* a kind of soft hat pointed in front and at the back, with ear-coverings that can be worn up or down

de-es·ca·late /ˌdiː ˈeskəleɪt/ *v* [T1;I0] to (cause to) decrease in area, force, range, or rate: *We've de-escalated (our bombing), but the enemy hasn't* —**-lation** /ˌdiːeskəˈleɪʃən/ *n* [U]

def *written abbrev. for:* **1** DEFINITE **2** DEFINITION

de·face /dɪˈfeɪs/ *v* [T1] **1** to spoil or damage the surface or appearance of, as by writing or making marks on **2** to make no longer readable by destroying important details —**~ment** *n* [U]

de fac·to /ˌdeɪ ˈfæktəʊ‖ˌdɪ-, ˌdeɪ/ *adj, adv* [Wa5] *Lat* in actual fact, though not perhaps justly or according to law —compare DE JURE

de·fame /dɪˈfeɪm/ *v* [T1] to damage the good name of (a person or group), usu. by unfair means —**defamatory** /dɪˈfæmətəri‖-tori/ *adj* —**defamation** /ˌdefəˈmeɪʃən/ *n* [U]

de·fault[1] /dɪˈfɔːlt/ *n* [U] *esp. law* **1** failure to do something demanded by duty or law **2** failure to pay one's debts **3** failure to appear at the proper time in a court of law **4** failure to take part in or finish a competition: *She won by default, because her opponent refused to play* **5 in default of** in the absence of; without; lacking

default[2] *v* [I0] to fail to fulfil a contract, agreement, or duty, esp. **a** to fail to pay a debt **b** to fail to appear in a court of law **c** to fail to take part in or finish a competition —**~er** *n*

de·feat[1] /dɪˈfiːt/ *v* [T1] **1** to beat; win a victory over (a person or group) in any kind of struggle: *Our team/army/political party has defeated our opponents!*|(fig.) *I've tried to understand your idea, but I'm afraid it's defeated me* —see WIN (USAGE) **2** to cause to fail; FRUSTRATE (1): *It was lack of money, not of effort, that defeated their plan*

defeat[2] *n* **1** [U] the act of defeating: *the defeat of the losing army* **2** [U] the act or state of being defeated: *their defeat by the winning army* **3** [C] a case of being defeated

de·feat·is·m /dɪˈfiːtɪzəm/ *n* [U] the practice of thinking, acting, or talking in a way that shows an expectation of being defeated —**-ist** *n*

def·e·cate /ˈdefɪ̈keɪt/ *v* [I0] *fml* to pass waste matter from the bowels —**-cation** /ˌdefɪ̈ˈkeɪʃən/ *n* [U]

de·fect[1] /ˈdiːfekt, dɪˈfekt/ *n* something lacking or imperfect; fault: *The machine is unsafe because of the defects in it.|He suffers from a hearing defect*

de·fect[2] /dɪˈfekt/ *v* [I0 (*from* and/or *to*)] to desert a political party, group, or movement, esp. in order to join an opposing one —**~or** *n*

de·fec·tion /dɪˈfekʃən/ *n* **1** [U] the act of DEFECTing[2] **2** [C] a case of DEFECTing[2]

de·fec·tive /dɪˈfektɪv/ *adj* **1** lacking something necessary; faulty: *defective machinery/hearing* **2** lacking one or more of the usual forms of grammar: *"Must" and "can" are often defective verbs: for example, they have no -ing forms* **3** (of a person) well below the average, esp. in mind —**~ly** *adv* —**~ness** *n* [U]

de·fence, *AmE* usu. **defense** /dɪˈfens/ — *n* **1** [U] the act or action of defending: *the defence of one's country|He spoke in defence of justice.|the art of self-defence* **2** [U] the ability to defend oneself effectively: *Defence costs are rising every day* **3** [C] means, methods, or things used in defending: *The defences of the city are strong.|Mountains are a defence against the wind* **4** [C] a group of moves or plays used in defending, esp. in CHESS **5** [C *usu. sing.*] (a speech containing) arguments used in defending oneself, esp. in a court of law: *The prisoner's defence was rather weak* **6** [*the*+GU] one or more lawyers who defend someone in court **7** [GC] the part of a team that tries to defend its own GOAL (2) in a match —**~less** *adj*

de·fend /dɪˈfend/ *v* **1** [T1 (*from* or *against*)] to keep safe from harm; protect against attack: *The fort cannot be defended against an air attack* **2** [T1; I∅] to play at (a position) so as to keep an opponent from advancing, making points, or winning: *They defended (their side of the field) very well* **3** [T1,4] to support, protect, or show the rightness of, by argument: *How can you defend killing someone like that?* **4** [T1] to act as a lawyer for (the person who has been charged) **5** [I∅] to oppose attack: *He's better at defending than attacking*

de·fen·dant /dɪˈfendənt/ *n* a person in a law trial against whom a charge is brought —compare PLAINTIFF

de·fen·si·ble /dɪˈfensəbəl/ *adj* that can be defended: *a defensible position* —**-bly** *adv*

de·fen·sive¹ /dɪˈfensɪv/ *adj* **1** that defends; that is for defence: *defensive weapons/play|a defensive position* **2** *sometimes derog* (of the language or behaviour of someone) who always seems to be expecting attack: *I wonder why he's so defensive about his wife?* —**~ly** *adv* —**~ness** *n* [U]

defensive² *n* **on the defensive** *sometimes derog* prepared for an expected attack

de·fer /dɪˈfɜːʳ/ *v* **-rr-** [T1] **1** to put off or hold back until a later date; delay; POSTPONE: *Let's defer action for a few weeks.|His military service was deferred until he finished college* **2** *AmE* to allow to put off military service until a later date —**~ment** *n* [U;C]

def·er·ence /ˈdefərəns/ *n* [U] **1** the act of DEFERring TO someone; regard for another's wishes, opinions, etc., shown because of respect or love, or because of the other's higher position or greater power **2** **out of/in deference to** because of respect for —**-ential** /ˌdefəˈrenʃəl/ *adj* —**-entially** *adv*

defer to *v prep* **-rr-** [T1] to yield to, esp. in opinion: *defer to more experienced people|defer to your advice*

de·fi·ance /dɪˈfaɪəns/ *n* [U] **1** DEFIANT behaviour: *His defiance of the law cost him his life* **2** **in defiance of** in open disregard for: *In defiance of the law you drove your car much too fast* **3** **set (something) at defiance** to show open disrespect for (something)

de·fi·ant /dɪˈfaɪənt/ *adj* showing no fear or respect; fearlessly refusing to obey —**~ly** *adv*

de·fi·cien·cy /dɪˈfɪʃənsi/ *n* **1** [U] the quality or state of being DEFICIENT **2** [C] a case of this; lack: *The deficiencies in this plan are very clear and it can't possibly succeed*

deficiency dis·ease /·ˈ··· ·ˌ·/ *n* [C;U] (a) disease caused by a lack of one or more substances necessary for health

de·fi·cient /dɪˈfɪʃənt/ *adj* [(*in*)] having none or not enough (of); lacking (in): *food deficient in iron|a deficient supply of water|deficient in skill* —**~ly** *adv*

def·i·cit /ˈdefɨsɨt/ *n* **1** an amount which is too small in quantity or too low in quality: *a deficit in/of rain* **2** (the amount of) a disadvantage: *Our team won in spite of a deficit of several runs at the beginning of the last day of the match* **3** the amount by which money that goes out is more than money that comes in

de·file¹ /dɪˈfaɪl/ *v* [T1] to make unclean or destroy the pureness of: *Evil books defile the mind.|Our beautiful country is being defiled by advertising* —**~r** *n* —**~ment** *n* [U]

de·file² /dɪˈfaɪl, ˈdiːfaɪl/ *n* a narrow passage, esp. through mountains

de·fine /dɪˈfaɪn/ *v* **1** [T1;I∅] to give the meaning(s) of (a word or idea); describe exactly: *Some words are hard to define because they have many different uses* **2** [T1] to show or explain the qualities, nature, duties, etc., of: *This book attempts to define the position of the state government in city affairs* **3** [T1] to set, mark, or show the limits, edge, or shape of: *I saw a clearly defined shape outside the window in a flash of light* **4** [T1 (*as*)] to show the character or nature of: *Good manners define the gentleman.|What defines us as human?*

def·i·nite /ˈdefɨnɨt, ˈdefənɨt/ *adj* **1** having very clear limits: *to set definite standards for our students* **2** without any uncertainty or unclearness: *We demand a definite answer* **3** unquestionable; undoubted: *That book of his will be a definite success* **4** having or showing firmness of opinion and willingness to act quickly: *definite people/behaviour* —compare DEFINITIVE

definite ar·ti·cle /ˌ··· ˈ···/ *n* (*in grammar*) **1** (in English) the word THE **2** (in other languages) a word or form with uses or meanings like those of the English word "the": *Russian has no definite article* —compare INDEFINITE ARTICLE

def·i·nite·ly /ˈdefɨnɨtli, ˈdefənɨtli/ *adv* **1** in a DEFINITE way: *He speaks very definitely, and I hope he acts definitely too* **2** without doubt; clearly: *That answer is definitely true.|That was definitely the best play I've seen all year.|He is definitely coming/definitely not coming.|(very) definitely yes* **3** (in answer to a question) Yes, indeed: *"Is he coming?" "Definitely!"* **4** **Definitely not!** (in answer to a question) No indeed

def·i·ni·tion /ˌdefɨˈnɪʃən/ *n* **1** [U;C] the act or action of defining (DEFINE) **2** [C] an exact statement of the meaning, nature, or limits of something **3** [U] clearness of shape, colour, or sound: *This photograph lacks definition.|Your new radio certainly has/gives good definition*

de·fin·i·tive /dɪˈfɪnɨtɪv/ *adj* **1** that provides a last decision that cannot be questioned: *a definitive victory* **2** that cannot be improved as a treatment of a particular subject: *She's written the definitive life of Byron* —compare DEFINITE —**~ly** *adv*

de·flate /ˌdiːˈfleɪt, dɪ-/ *v* **1** [T1;I∅] to (cause to) become smaller by losing air or gas **2** [T1] to cause to seem and/or feel less important or good (usu. suddenly): *He keeps saying how wonderful he is, but one sharp remark should be enough to deflate him* **3** [T1;I∅] to reduce the supply of money (of) or lower the level of prices (of)

de·fla·tion /ˌdiːˈfleɪʃən, dɪ-/ also **disinflation**— *n* **1** [U] the act of deflating or the state of being DEFLATEd **2** [U;C] a decrease in the amount of money (esp. money to be lent), which is meant to produce lower prices —compare INFLATION (2), REFLATION

de·fla·tion·a·ry /ˌdiːˈfleɪʃənri, dɪ-‖-neri/ also **disinflationary**— *adj* that produces, may produce, or is supposed to produce DEFLATION (2) of money or prices

de·flect /dɪˈflekt/ *v* [T1;I∅: (*from*)] to (cause to) turn from a straight course or fixed direction: *Mary threw a stone at John but it was deflected away from him when it hit a tree*

de·flec·tion /dɪˈflekʃən/ *n* [U;C] **1** a turning aside; turning off course: *the deflection of the stone by the tree* **2** a movement away from 0 (or the base position) by the pointer, needle, etc., of a measuring instrument **3** the amount of such a turning or movement: *a deflection of 30°*

de·flow·er /ˌdiːˈflaʊəʳ, dɪ-/ *v* [T1] *esp. lit* to have sex with (someone, usu. female, who has not had sex before)

de·fo·li·ant /ˌdiːˈfəʊlɪənt, dɪ-/ *n* [C;(U)] (a) chemical substance used on plants in order to cause their leaves to drop off too soon

de·fo·li·ate /ˌdiːˈfəʊlieɪt, dɪ-/ *v* [T1] to use DEFOLIANT on —**-ation** /-ˌfəʊliˈeɪʃən/ *n* [U]

de·for·est /ˌdiːˈfɒr$\frac{1}{2}$st, dɪ-‖-ˈfɔ-, -ˈfɑ-/ *v* [T1] *esp. AmE* DISAFFOREST —**~ation** /diːˌfɒr$\frac{1}{2}$ˈsteɪʃən, dɪ-‖-ˌfɔ-, -ˌfɑ-/ *n* [U]

de·form /dɪˈfɔːm‖-ɔrm/ *v* [Wv5;T1] **1** to spoil the form of **2** to spoil the appearance of: *a face deformed by disease/anger* **3** to make very ugly

de·for·ma·tion /ˌdiːfɔːˈmeɪʃən‖-ɔr-/ *n* **1** [U] the action of DEFORMing or the state of being DEFORMed: *the deformation of a solid by pressure* **2** [U;C] (a) change for the worse **3** [U;C] (a) change of form or shape **4** [C] a result of such a change: *a body full of deformations*

de·for·mi·ty /dɪˈfɔːm$\frac{1}{2}$ti‖-ɔr-/ *n* **1** [U] the state of being DEFORMed: *He's very attractive in spite of his slight deformity* **2** [C] an imperfection of the body, esp. an imperfection that can be seen **3** [C] a moral or artistic fault: *deformities of style*

de·fraud /dɪˈfrɔːd/ *v* [T1 (*of*)] to deceive so as to get or keep something wrongly and usu. unlawfully

de·fray /dɪˈfreɪ/ *v* [T1] *fml* to provide for the payment of; pay: *They will defray the cost of my trip if I do them a favour*

de·frock /ˌdiːˈfrɒk‖-ˈfrɑk/ *v* [T1] UNFROCK

de·frost /ˌdiːˈfrɒst‖-ˈfrɔst/ *v* **1** [T1;I0] to (cause to) become unfrozen: *to defrost meat|Don't let the meat defrost too quickly* **2** [T1] to remove ice from: *to defrost a* REFRIGERATOR **3** [T1] *AmE* DEMIST —**~er** *n*

deft /deft/ *adj* [Wa1] *apprec* effortlessly skilful: *a deft performance* —**~ly** *adv* —**~ness** *n* [U]

de·funct /dɪˈfʌŋkt/ *adj fml or law* having finished the course of life or existence; dead: *a letter from her defunct aunt|defunct ideas*

de·fuse /ˌdiːˈfjuːz/ *v* [T1] **1** to remove the FUSE[1] (2) from (something explosive) so as to prevent an explosion: *to defuse a bomb* **2** to make less dangerous; make calmer: *to defuse a dangerous* SITUATION *or* CRISIS

de·fy /dɪˈfaɪ/ *v* **1** [T1] to be ready to fight against; show no fear of nor respect for: *I defy you, you devil!|How long can those criminals continue to defy the law!* **2** [V3] to ask, very strongly, to do something considered impossible; dare; CHALLENGE: *I defy you to give me one good reason for believing you* **3** [T1,(4)] to remain unreachable by all efforts at or from: *It defies description.|His strange behaviour defies understanding*

de·gauss /ˌdiːˈgaʊs/ *v* [T1] *tech* to remove the MAGNETISM from: *They degaussed the ship*

de·gen·e·ra·cy /dɪˈdʒenərəsi/ *n* [U] **1** the state of being DEGENERATE[1] **2** the action of becoming DEGENERATE[1] **3** sexual behaviour that is not considered proper or natural

de·gen·e·rate[1] /dɪˈdʒenər$\frac{1}{2}$t/ *adj* **1** having become worse (as in nature, character, quality, appearance, or use) in comparison with a former state: *Will too much freedom make them degenerate?|Just what do you mean by "degenerate art"?* **2** having sunk to a condition below that which is proper for a given type: *a degenerate* SPECIES

degenerate[2] *n* a person who is DEGENERATE[1], esp. a man considered guilty of serious sexual misbehaviour

de·gen·e·rate[3] /dɪˈdʒenəreɪt/ *v* [I0 *from* and/or *into*] **1** to pass from a higher to a lower type or condition: *The wide road degenerated into a poor little path* **2** to sink into a low state of mind or morals: *That fine young man has degenerated under the influence of evil company* **3** to become worse in quality: *Her beautiful voice has degenerated into an unpleasant whisper* **4** to fall below a condition or standards proper to a given group or type

de·gen·e·ra·tion /dɪˌdʒenəˈreɪʃən/ *n* [U] **1** becoming or being DEGENERATE[1]: *the degeneration of his character/his art* **2** a DEGENERATE[1] condition, esp. of diseased material of a plant or animal: *Fatty degeneration of an organ like the heart can be dangerous*

de·gen·e·ra·tive /dɪˈdʒenərətɪv‖-nəreɪtɪv/ *adj* of, related to, or tending to cause DEGENERATION: *a degenerative disease of the heart* —**~ly** *adv*

de·grade /dɪˈgreɪd/ *v* **1** [T1] to bring down in the opinion of others, in self-respect, in personal quality, or in behaviour: *A dishonest action like that will degrade you.|Don't degrade yourself by answering such foolish charges against you* **2** [T1;I0] *tech* to (cause to) change from a higher to a lower kind of living matter, or from a compound chemical to a simpler one —**degradation** /ˌdegrəˈdeɪʃən/ *n* [U]

de·gree /dɪˈgriː/ *n* **1** [C;U] (the size of) a step or stage in a set of steps or stages rising in order from lowest to highest: *The students have different degrees of ability.|To what degree can he be trusted?|He can be trusted to some/a certain degree.|He cannot be trusted in the slightest degree.|He is getting better by degrees, but it will be some time before he is completely well* **2** [C] *tech* any of various measures: *Water freezes at 32 degrees* FAHRENHEIT *(32°F) or 0 degrees* CENTIGRADE *(0°C).|an angle of 90 degrees (90°)* LONGITUDE —see WEIGHTS & MEASURES TABLE **3** [C] a title given by a university: *She has the degree of PhD* **4** [U] *esp. old use* a rank or place in society: *She was a lady of high degree/a woman of low degree*

de·horn /ˌdiːˈhɔːn‖-ˈhɔrn/ also **dishorn**— *v* [T1] to remove the horns from or prevent them from growing on (cattle)

de·hu·man·ize, -ise /ˌdiːˈhjuːmənaɪz/ *v* [T1] to remove some or all of the human qualities from: *Cruel and unnecessary punishment dehumanizes both the punisher and the punished* —**-ization** /ˌdiːhjuːmənaɪˈzeɪʃən‖-mənə-/ *n* [U]

de·hy·drate /ˌdiːˈhaɪdreɪt/ *v* **1** [T1] to dry; remove all the water from: *to dehydrate eggs to make egg powder* **2** [I0] to lose water from the body: *That sick man will dehydrate and die if we don't get medical help* **3** [T1] *derog* to cause to become dry and uninteresting in style, character, etc. —**~d** /ˌdiːhaɪˈdreɪt$\frac{1}{2}$d/ *adj*: *I don't like that dehydrated old fool telling us what to do!* —**-dration** /ˌdiːhaɪˈdreɪʃən/ *n* [U]

de·ice /ˌdiːˈaɪs/ *v* [T1;I0] *tech* to make or stay free of ice

de·i·fi·ca·tion /ˌdiː$\frac{1}{2}$f$\frac{1}{2}$ˈkeɪʃən, ˌdeɪ-/ *n* [U] the act of DEIFYing: (fig.) *The deification of all those young singers can't be healthy*

de·i·fy /ˈdiː$\frac{1}{2}$faɪ, ˈdeɪ-/ *v* [T1] **1** to make a god of **2** to take as an object of worship: *deifying objects of wood and stone* **3** to consider and treat as of the very highest value: *to deify money*

deign /deɪn/ *v* [T3] *sometimes derog* to be gracious enough or lower oneself to; not be too proud to: *Now that she is married to a rich and famous man, she no longer deigns to visit her former friends* —compare CONDESCEND (1)

de·is·m /ˈdiːɪzəm, ˈdeɪ-/ *n* [U] (*often cap.*) the belief in a god whose existence can be proved by looking at the world he made rather than by considering some message he delivered to man personally —**deist** *n*

de·i·ty /ˈdiːɨti, ˈdeɪ-/ *n* **1** [U] the rank or real nature of a god **2** [C] a god or goddess: *the deities of ancient Greece* **3** [C] a person considered and treated as good and/or powerful in the highest degree

Deity *n* [*the*+R] God

dé·jà vu /ˌdeɪʒɑːˈvjuː, -ˈvuː (*Fr* deʒa vy)/ *n* [U] *Fr* the feeling of remembering something that one is in fact experiencing for the first time

de·jec·ted /dɪˈdʒektɨd/ *adj* having or showing low spirits; sad: *a dejected look/person* —**~ly** *adv*

de·jec·tion /dɪˈdʒekʃən/ *n* [U] lowness of spirits; sadness

de ju·re /ˌdiː ˈdʒʊəri/ *adj, adv* [Wa5] *Lat* by right; of right; lawful(ly) —compare DE FACTO

dek·ko /ˈdekəʊ/ *n* **have a dekko (at)** *BrE sl* to have a look (at)

de·lay¹ /dɪˈleɪ/ *n* **1** [U] the act of delaying or the state of being delayed: *Do it without (any) delay!* **2** [C] an example of being delayed: *There will be some delays on all roads because of heavy traffic this morning* **3** [C] the time during which something or someone is delayed: *Delays of up to 2 hours were reported on all roads this morning*

delay² *v* **1** [T1,4] to do something later than planned: *We decided to delay (going on) our holiday until next month* **2** [T1] to stop for a time or cause to be late: *What delayed you so long?* **3** [I∅] to move or act slowly, esp. on purpose: *They're trying to delay until help arrives.|Don't delay: act today!*

de·lec·ta·ble /dɪˈlektəbəl/ *adj apprec* very pleasing; delightful: *What delectable food you cook!* —**-bly** *adv*

de·lec·ta·tion /ˌdiːlekˈteɪʃən/ *n* [U] enjoyment; delight; pleasure; amusement: *For the delectation of his friends, he did special magic tricks*

del·e·ga·cy /ˈdelɨgəsi/ *n* **1** [U] the appointment of someone as a DELEGATE¹ **2** [U] the system of delegating (DELEGATE²) **3** [C] a body or group of delegates: *This decision should be made by a delegacy acting for the officers of the university*

del·e·gate¹ /ˈdelɨgɨt/ *n* a person acting for one or more others, such as a representative to a meeting or an organization

del·e·gate² /ˈdelɨgeɪt/ *v* **1** [T1 (*to*)] to give (part of one's power, rights, etc.) for a certain time: *I have delegated my command to Captain Roberts* **2** [T1; V3] to appoint as one's representative: *I have delegated Captain Roberts (to serve in my place)*

del·e·ga·tion /ˌdelɨˈgeɪʃən/ *n* **1** [U] the act of delegating (DELEGATE²) or the state of being DELEGATED² **2** [C] a group of DELEGATEs¹

de·lete /dɪˈliːt/ *v* [T1 (*from*)] to take, rub, strike, or cut out (esp. something written or printed): *If you delete 50 words, we can put the whole story on one page.|Delete his name from the list of members*

del·e·ter·i·ous /ˌdelɨˈtɪəriəs/ *adj fml* having an often unclear or unexpected harmful effect on the body, mind, or spirit: *the possible deleterious effects of being weightless for a long time/of bad books* —**~ly** *adv*

de·le·tion /dɪˈliːʃən/ *n* **1** [U] the act of deleting (DELETE) or the state of being DELETED **2** [C] something DELETED: *several deletions in your letter*

delft /delft/ also **delf** /delf/, **delft·ware** /ˈdelftweəʳ/— *n* [U] (*usu. cap.*) **1** a kind of POTTERY with bright, often blue, ornamentation, first made in Delft, Holland **2** POTTERY like this

de·lib·e·rate¹ /dɪˈlɪbərɨt/ *adj* **1** carefully considered; thoroughly planned: *The government is taking deliberate action to lower prices* **2** intentional; on purpose: *That shooting was not accidental, but a deliberate attempt to kill him!* **3** (of speech, thought, or movement) slow; careful; unhurried: *The old man rose from his chair in a deliberate way and left the room* —**~ly** *adv* —**~ness** *n* [U]

de·lib·e·rate² /dɪˈlɪbəreɪt/ *v* [T1,6a,b;I∅ (*upon, about*)] to consider (important and difficult questions) carefully, often in formal meetings with other people: *The judges are deliberating (the question).|They are deliberating (upon/about) what to do*

de·lib·e·ra·tion /dɪˌlɪbəˈreɪʃən/ *n* **1** [U] the act of deliberating (DELIBERATE²) **2** [U;C] careful consideration; thorough examination of a matter: *After much deliberation, we found that nothing could be done.|Our deliberations were useless* **3** [U] the quality of being slow, careful, unhurried in speech, thought, or movement

de·lib·e·ra·tive /dɪˈlɪbərətɪv‖-bəreɪtɪv/ *adj* [Wa5] for the purpose of deliberating; having the power of deliberating (DELIBERATE²): *Parliament is a deliberative body*

del·i·ca·cy /ˈdelɪkəsi/ *n* **1** [U] the quality of being DELICATE **2** [C] something pleasing to eat that is considered rare or costly: *That food is a great delicacy*

del·i·cate /ˈdelɪkɨt/ *adj* **1** finely made; delightful: *a delicate piece of silk* **2** finely made; needing careful handling; easily broken or hurt: *The body is a delicate machine* **3** needing careful treatment or TACT; likely to go wrong at any moment: *a delicate affair/position/subject* **4** easily made ill; easily yielding to illness: *a delicate child|in delicate health* **5** very pleasing but not strong and perhaps not easy to recognize, taste, smell, see, etc.: *delicate tastes/smells/colours* **6** sensitive: *That delicate instrument can record even very slight changes* **7** sensitive to bad manners in oneself or in others: *Some delicate people don't like to offend; others don't like to be offended.|delicate feelings* —**~ly** *adv*

del·i·ca·tes·sen /ˌdelɪkəˈtesən/ *n* **1** [U] delicacies (DELICACY (2)), esp. those which are ready to eat when sold **2** [C] a shop that sells them

de·li·cious /dɪˈlɪʃəs/ *adj* **1** giving great pleasure; delightful **2** pleasing to one of the body's senses, esp. those of taste or smell: *What delicious food you've cooked!* —**~ly** *adv* —**~ness** *n* [U]

de·light¹ /dɪˈlaɪt/ *n* **1** [U] a high degree of pleasure or satisfaction; joy: *I read your new book with real delight* **2** [C] something or someone that gives great pleasure: *Your daughter/new book/little dog is a real delight!|the delights of London's night life* **3** **take delight in** to receive great pleasure from

delight² *v* **1** [T1;I∅] to cause (someone) to receive great satisfaction, enjoyment, or joy: *a book that is certain to delight|He delighted them with his performance* **2** [I3] to take great pleasure in doing something: *"Let dogs delight to* BARK *and bite, for God has made them so"* (old poem) **3** **I shall be delighted (to come)** *polite* I shall be very happy (to come)

de·light·ful /dɪˈlaɪtfəl/ *adj* highly pleasing: *a delightful little house* —**~ly** *adv*

delight in *v prep* [T1,4 *no pass.*] to take or receive great pleasure in: *He delights in (looking at) pictures by Holman Hunt*

de·lim·it /dɪˈlɪmɨt/ also **de·lim·i·tate** /-mɨteɪt/— *v* [T1] to fix the limits of —**~ation** /dɪˌlɪmɨˈteɪʃən-/ *n* [U]

de·lin·e·ate /dɪˈlɪnieɪt/ *v* [T1] **1** to draw; show by drawing lines in the shape of **2** to describe in usu. sharp or lifelike detail —**-ation** /dɪˌlɪniˈeɪʃən/ *n* [U]

de·lin·quen·cy /dɪˈlɪŋkwənsi/ *n* **1** [U] the quality or state of being DELINQUENT² **2** [U] (a tendency towards) behaviour that is not in accordance with accepted social standards or with the law **3** [C] *fml* an example or case of being DELINQUENT² —see also JUVENILE DELINQUENCY

de·lin·quent¹ /dɪˈlɪŋkwənt/ *n* a person who is DELINQUENT² (1), esp. if young

delinquent² *adj* **1** not having obeyed the law or done one's duty; having broken a law, esp. one which is not very important; having a tendency to break the law or to do socially unacceptable things **2** (of debts, accounts, etc.) not having been paid or paid into in time **3** of, like, or typical of DELINQUENTs¹

del·i·ques·cent /ˌdelɪˈkwesənt/ *adj fml or tech* taking up water from the air and so becoming liquid: *Table salt becomes deliquescent in wet weather* —**-cence** *n* [U]

de·lir·i·ous /dɪˈlɪərɪəs/ *adj* **1** of, related to, or typical of DELIRIUM **2** suffering from or marked by DELIRIUM —**~ly** *adv*: (fig.) *deliriously happy*

de·lir·i·um /dɪˈlɪərɪəm/ *n* **1** [C;U] an excited dreamy state in serious illness **2** [S] a very excited state: *a delirium of joy*

delirium tre·mens /dɪˌlɪərɪəm ˈtremənz‖-ˈtriː-/ *n* [U] *fml* DT's

de·liv·er /dɪˈlɪvəʳ/ *v* **1** [T1 (*from*)] to set free **2** [T1 (UP, *to*)] to hand over: *When will the letter be delivered?|to deliver the town up to the enemy|We can deliver goods to your door* **3** [T1] **a** to help in giving birth: *They delivered the woman* **b** to help in the birth of: *They delivered the child* **4** [T1] to say; read aloud: *He delivered his speech effectively* **5** [X9] to send (something aimed or guided) to the intended place: *She delivered a hard blow to his jaw* **6** [D1 (*to*);T1] to bring (votes, influence, etc.) to the support of a political movement, a person trying to get elected, etc.: *They'll deliver me all their support* **7** [IØ (*on*)] to produce the promised, desired, or expected results: *Make sure he delivers (on his promise)* **8 be delivered of** *fml* to give birth to, with medical help **9 deliver the goods** *sl* DELIVER (7) **10 Stand and deliver!** (said, in former times, by armed robbers to travellers in carriages) Stop and give me your valuable possessions!

de·liv·er·ance /dɪˈlɪvərəns/ *n* [U (*from*)] *fml* the act of saving from danger or freeing from bad conditions, or the state of being saved from danger or freed from bad conditions —**-er** *n*

de·liv·er·y /dɪˈlɪvəri/ *n* **1** [U (*from*)] *fml* the act of setting free or the state of being set free; DELIVERANCE **2** [U;C: (*to*)] the act of handing over or the state of being handed over: *The next postal delivery is at 2 o'clock.|The delivery of our town to the enemy was a great shock to us all.|the delivery of goods to your door* **3** [C] the birth of a child: *The mother/The child had an easy delivery* **4** [C;(U)] the act of speaking in public or throwing a ball in a game; style of speaking in public or throwing a ball in a game: *a good/fast/slow delivery*

de·liv·er·y·man /dɪˈlɪvərimən/ *n* **-men** /mən/ *esp. AmE* a man who delivers goods to people who have bought or ordered them, usu. locally

delivery note /·ˈ··· ·/ *n esp. BrE* a receipt, usu. in 2 copies, that comes with goods that are delivered and is to be signed by the person who receives them

dell /del/ *n* a small valley with grass, and with trees on its sides

de·louse /ˌdiːˈlaʊs/ *v* [T1] to remove LICE (*pl. of* LOUSE) or creatures of this kind from

Del·phic /ˈdelfɪk/ also **Del·phi·an** /-fɪən/— *adj* **1** [Wa5] of, like, or concerning the ancient Greek city of Delphi or its famous ORACLE (1) **2** *lit* not clearly understood; seeming to have more than one possible meaning

del·phin·i·um /delˈfɪnɪəm/ also **larkspur**— *n* **1** any of a large group of upright branching plants **2** a flower of such a plant, usu. blue, which grows on long stems

del·ta /ˈdeltə/ *n* **1** [R;(C)] the 4th letter of the Greek alphabet (Δ, δ) **2** [C] a piece of low land shaped like a Δ where a river branches out towards the sea: *the Nile Delta in Egypt*

delta wing /ˈ·· ·/ *n* an aircraft wing or pair of wings with a shape like that of the Greek letter Δ: *a delta-wing aircraft*

de·lude /dɪˈluːd/ *v* [T1 (*with, into*)] to mislead the mind or judgment of; deceive; trick: *He deluded everyone into following him.|Don't delude yourself with false hopes*

del·uge¹ /ˈdeljuːdʒ/ *n* **1** a great flood: *the Deluge described in the Bible*|(fig.) *a deluge of questions* **2** a very heavy rain: *You'll be wet through in that deluge!*

deluge² *v* [T1] **1** *fml* to cover with a great flood of water **2** [(*with*) *usu. pass.*] to pour out a great flood of things over (someone): *The minister was deluged with questions/cries/shouts*

de·lu·sion /dɪˈluːʒən/ *n* **1** [U] the act of deluding or the state of being DELUDED **2** [C] a false belief, esp. if strongly held: *She is under the delusion that I'm going to give her a lot of money.|That sick man is under the delusion that he is Napoleon.|to suffer from delusions* (*of* GRANDEUR) —see ILLUSION (USAGE)

de·lu·sive /dɪˈluːsɪv/ also **de·lu·so·ry** /-səri/— *adj* **1** likely to DELUDE: *a delusive act/person* **2** that is a DELUSION; misleading: *a delusive belief* —**~ly** *adv*

de luxe /də ˈlʌks‖-ˈlʊks/ *adj Fr* of especially good quality, as if intended for the wealthy: *The de luxe model costs a lot more*

delve /delv/ *v* **1** [IØ (*into* or *among*)] to search deeply: *He delved into lots of old books and papers for the facts* **2** [T1;IØ] *poet or old use* to dig

de·mag·ne·tize, -ise /ˌdiːˈmægnətaɪz/ *v* [T1] **1** to take away the MAGNETIC qualities of **2** *tech* to remove sounds from (a MAGNETIC TAPE) —**-tization** /ˌdiːmægnətaɪˈzeɪʃən‖-nətə-/ *n* [U]

dem·a·gog·ic /ˌdeməˈgɒgɪk‖-ˈgɑ-/ *adj* of or like a DEMAGOGUE: *demagogic speeches* —**~ally** *adv* [Wa4]

dem·a·gogue /ˈdeməgɒg‖-gɑg/ *n derog* a leader who tries to gain, or has gained, power by exciting popular feelings rather than by reasoned argument

dem·a·gogu·e·ry /ˈdeməgɒgəri‖-gɑ-/ also **dem·a·gog·y** /ˈdeməgɒgi, -dʒi‖-gɑ-/— [U] *derog* the principles or practices of a DEMAGOGUE

de·mand¹ /dɪˈmɑːnd‖dɪˈmænd/ *n* **1** [C (*for*), C5] an act of demanding; claim: *The workers' demand for higher wages seems reasonable.*|(fig.) *This work makes great demands on my time* **2** [S;U: (*for*)] the desire of people for particular goods or services; the ability and willingness of people to pay for them: *Is there much demand/a great demand for teachers in this town?|Oil is in great demand these days* **3 on demand** when payment is demanded

demand² *v* **1** [T1,3,5c;(IØ)] to claim as if by right; ask or ask for and not take "No" for an answer: *I demand my rights/my money!|I demanded his name/a clear answer.|I demand to know the truth!|I demand that John (should) go there at once!* **2** [T1] to need urgently: *This work demands your attention without delay!*

de·mand·ing /dɪˈmɑːndɪŋ‖dɪˈmæn-/ *adj* that needs a lot of attention or effort: *A new baby and a new job can both be very demanding*

de·mar·cate /ˈdiːmɑːkeɪt‖dɪˈmɑr-/ *v* [T1] **1** to mark the limits of **2** to set apart; separate

de·mar·ca·tion /ˌdiːmɑːˈkeɪʃən‖-ɑr-/ *n* [U;(C)] limitation; separation: *a row of trees on the line of demarcation between the 2 pieces of land*

demarcation dis·pute /··ˈ·· ·ˌ·/ *n* a disagreement

between different trades unions about which jobs should be done by the members of each union

de·mean /dɪˈmiːn/ *v* [T1] *fml* to lower in the opinion of oneself or others: *Such behaviour demeans you in my eyes.|Don't demean yourself by doing anything dishonourable*

de·mea·nour, *AmE* **-nor** /dɪˈmiːnəʳ/ *n fml* behaviour towards others; outward manner: *His demeanour has always been that of a perfect gentleman*

de·men·ted /dɪˈmentɪ̣d/ *adj* mad; of unbalanced mind —**~ly** *adv*

dem·e·ra·ra sug·ar /ˌdeməˌreərə ˈʃʊgəʳ/ *n* [U] brown sugar, usu. from the West Indies

de·mer·it /diːˈmerɪ̣t/ *n* a fault or failing: MERITS (= good qualities) *and demerits*

de·mesne /dɪˈmeɪn/ *n* **1** land round a great house; land owned and for the use of a lord or king: *the Royal Demesne* **2** *law or humor* land that is one's own property

dem·i- /ˈdemi/ *prefix* **1** half **2** a person or thing that partly belongs to (a stated type or class): DEMIGOD

dem·i·god /ˈdemigɒd‖-gɑd/ *fem.* **dem·i·god·dess** /-dɪ̣s/— *n* **1** (in ancient stories) someone greater than a man but less than a god **2** a person who is, is believed to be, or believes himself to be more like a god than a man

dem·i·john /ˈdemidʒɒn‖-dʒɑn/ *n* a narrow-necked bottle enclosed in basketwork and holding from about 5 to 45 litres

de·mil·i·ta·rize, -rise /ˌdiːˈmɪlɪ̣təraɪz/ *v* [Wv5;T1] to take away the military power of; prevent (esp. a border area) from being used for military purposes —**-rization** /ˌdiːmɪlɪ̣təraɪˈzeɪʃən‖-tərə-/ *n* [U]

de·mise /dɪˈmaɪz/ *n* [U] **1** *law or euph* death: *Upon his demise the title passed to his son, who became Lord Tweedsmuir* **2** *humor* the ending of existence or activity: *The demise of that dishonest newspaper has brought no tears to my eyes!*

de·mist /ˌdiːˈmɪst/ (*AmE* **defrost**)— *v* [T1] *BrE* to clean steam from (the windows of a car)

de·mist·er /ˌdiːˈmɪstəʳ/ (*AmE* **defroster**)— *n BrE* an apparatus which uses heat from the engine to keep the windows of a car clear of steam

dem·o /ˈdeməʊ/ *n* **demos** *infml* DEMONSTRATION (2)

de·mo- /ˈdemə, dɪˈmɒ‖ˈdemə, dɪˈmɑ/ *prefix* the people, esp. the common people: DEMOGRAPHY| DEMOCRACY

de·mob¹ /diːˈmɒb‖-ˈmɑb/ *v* **-bb-** [T1] *BrE infml* DEMOBILIZE

demob² *n* [A;(U)] *BrE infml* demobilization (DEMOBILIZE): *His demob suit didn't fit very well, but he felt good in it after so many years at war*

de·mo·bi·lize, -lise /diːˈməʊbɪ̣laɪz/ *v* **1** [T1 *often pass.*] to send (members of an army) back to peacetime life **2** [I∅;T1 *often pass.*] **a** (of an army or other official armed group) to allow all members to go home **b** to send home all the members of (an army or other official armed group) —**-lization** /dɪˌməʊbəlaɪˈzeɪʃən‖-bələ-/ *n* [U]

de·moc·ra·cy /dɪˈmɒkrəsi‖dɪˈmɑ-/ *n* **1** [U] "government of the people, by the people, and for the people" (A. Lincoln): *direct democracy* **2** [U] government by elected representatives of the people: *representative democracy* **3** [C] a country governed by its people or their representatives **4** [U] social EQUALITY and the right to take part in decision-making: *How close have we come to industrial democracy?*

dem·o·crat /ˈdeməkræt/ *n* a person who believes in or works for DEMOCRACY

Democrat *n* a member or supporter of the DEMOCRATIC party of the United States of America —compare REPUBLICAN

dem·o·crat·ic /ˌdeməˈkrætɪk/ *adj* **1** of, related to, or favouring DEMOCRACY **2** of, related to, or intended to please the broad masses of the people: *democratic art* **3** favouring and practising social EQUALITY, esp. by mixing socially with people of the lower classes —**~ally** *adv* [Wa4]: *the democratically-elected government*

Democratic *adj* [Wa5] of, related to, or favouring one of the 2 largest political parties of the US (the **Democratic party**) —compare REPUBLICAN

de·moc·ra·tize, -tise /dɪˈmɒkrətaɪz‖dɪˈmɑ-/ *v* [T1; I∅] to (cause to) become (more) DEMOCRATIC —**-tization** /dɪˌmɒkrətaɪˈzeɪʃən‖dɪˌmɑkrətə-/ *n* [U]

dé·mo·dé /ˌdeɪˈməʊdeɪ‖ˌdeɪməʊˈdeɪ/ *adj Fr* no longer in fashion: *I'm afraid your clothes/your ideas are a bit démodé, my dear*

de·mog·ra·phy /dɪˈmɒgrəfi‖-ˈmɑ-/ *n* [U] the study of information in figures (STATISTICS) about the population of an area or country and how these figures vary with time —**-pher** /dɪˈmɒgrəfəʳ‖-ˈmɑ-/ *n* —**-phic** /ˌdeməˈgræfɪk, ˌdiː-/ *adj* [Wa5]

de·mol·ish /dɪˈmɒlɪʃ‖dɪˈmɑ-/ *v* [T1] **1** to destroy; pull or tear down: *They're going to demolish that old building and put up a new one.*|(fig.) *We've demolished all her arguments and she has nothing more to say* **2** *sl* to eat up hungrily: *to demolish 2 big platefuls of chicken*

dem·o·li·tion /ˌdeməˈlɪʃən/ *n* **1** [U] the action of DEMOLISHing **2** [C] a case of this: *several demolitions in our street*

de·mon /ˈdiːmən/ *n* **1** an evil spirit **2** something or someone considered as being like an evil spirit: *the demon hatred|When angry, he's a real demon.|That child is a little demon* **3** *infml* a person of unusual force, activity, or singleness of purpose: *a demon for work|a demon card-player* —compare DAEMON

de·mon·e·tize, -tise /diːˈmʌnɪ̣taɪz‖diːˈmɑ-/ *v* [T1] **1** to stop using (a metal) as a standard of money: *When was gold demonetized?* **2** to declare that (something) is of no value for official payment

de·mo·ni·a·cal /ˌdiːməˈnaɪəkəl/ also **de·mo·ni·ac** /dɪˈməʊniæk/— *adj* **1** [Wa5] possessed or influenced by a DEMON **2** of, related to, or like a DEMON: *demoniacal cruelty* —**demoniacally** *adv* [Wa4]

de·mon·ic /dɪˈmɒnɪk‖dɪˈmɑ-/ *adj* of, by, or like a DEMON; DEMONIACAL (2): *demonic possession|a demonic spirit* —**demonically** *adv* [Wa4]

de·mon·stra·ble /dɪˈmɒnstrəbəl, ˈdemən-‖dɪˈmɑn-/ *adj* **1** that can be DEMONSTRATED: *a demonstrable truth* **2** easily clear; that can be seen as true without difficulty —**-bly** *adv*: *But that idea is demonstrably false!* —**-bility** /dɪˌmɒnstrəˈbɪlɪ̣ti‖dɪˌmɑn-/ *n* [U]

dem·on·strate /ˈdemənstreɪt/ *v* **1** [T1,5,6a,b] to show clearly: *Please demonstrate how the machine works* **2** [T1,5] to prove or make clear, esp. by reasoning or giving many examples: *She demonstrated that 2 and 2 are 4* **3** [T1] to show the value or use of, esp. to a possible buyer **4** [I∅] to arrange or take part in a public show of strong feeling or opinion, often with marching, big signs, etc.

dem·on·stra·tion /ˌdemənˈstreɪʃən/ *n* **1** [U;C,C5] the act of demonstrating (DEMONSTRATE): *the demonstration of a machine* **2** [C] also (*infml*) **demo**—a public show of strong feeling or opinion, often with marching, big signs, etc.: *a demonstration against the war*

de·mon·stra·tive /dɪˈmɒnstrətɪv‖dɪˈmɑn-/ *adj* **1** [Wa5] that DEMONSTRATES **2** that shows feelings openly: *a demonstrative person/action* —**~ly** *adv*: *She welcomed him demonstratively—with a kiss*

demonstrative pro·noun /·ˌ··· ˈ··/ also **demonstrative**— *n* a PRONOUN that points out the one meant and separates it from others of the same class: *"This", "that", "these" and "those" can be demonstrative pronouns*

dem·on·stra·tor /ˈdemənstreɪtəʳ/ *n* **1** a person who DEMONSTRATES **2** a person who takes part in a DEMONSTRATION: *The demonstrators attacked the police* **3** (esp. in British universities) a person who helps a PROFESSOR by doing practical work with students

de·mor·al·ize, -ise /dɪˈmɒrəlaɪz‖dɪˈmɔ-, dɪˈmɑ-/ *v* [Wv4;T1] to lessen or destroy the courage and self-respect of: *Bad weather and many defeats demoralized our army* —**-ization** /dɪˌmɒrəlaɪˈzeɪʃən‖dɪˌmɔrələ-, dɪˈmɑ-/ *n* [U]

de·mote /dɪˈməʊt/ *v* [T1] to lower in rank or position —**demotion** /dɪˈməʊʃən/ *n* [U;C]

de·mot·ic /dɪˈmɒtɪk‖dɪˈmɑ-/ *adj* [Wa5] *fml* belonging to or used by the common people

de·mur¹ /dɪˈmɜːʳ/ *v* **-rr-** [IØ (*at* or *to*)] *fml* to show signs of being against something, esp. because of a feeling that it might be wrong: *They demurred at the idea of not paying*

demur² *n* **without demur** *fml* with no sign of disagreement or disapproval

de·mure /dɪˈmjʊəʳ/ *adj* [Wa2] **1** (esp. of women and children) quiet, serious, and not mixing easily with other people: *a demure young lady* **2** pretending to be so: *trying to attract with demure behaviour* —**~ly** *adv* —**~ness** *n* [U]

de·mys·ti·fy /ˌdiːˈmɪstɨ̞faɪ/ *v* [T1] to remove the mystery from; make clear (what is (often intentionally) kept hard to understand) —**-fication** /ˌdiːmɪstɨ̞fɨ̞ˈkeɪʃən‖-fə-/ *n* [U]

den /den/ *n* **1** the home of a usu. large fierce wild animal, esp. a lion **2** a centre of secret, esp. unlawful, activity: *a den of thieves* **3** *infml* a small quiet room in a house, where a person, usu. a man, can be alone: *Father's in his den now, Johnny*

de·na·tion·al·ize, -ise /diːˈnæʃənəlaɪz/ *v* [T1] to remove from state ownership —**-ization** /ˌdiːnæʃənəlaɪˈzeɪʃən‖-nələ-/ *n* [U;C]

de·ni·al /dɪˈnaɪəl/ *n* **1** [U] the act of DENYing **2** [C] an example of this: *a denial of justice* **3** [C] a statement DENYing something: *The minister asked the newspaper to print a denial of the untrue story* **4** [U] SELF-DENIAL: *a life of denial*

den·i·er /ˈdenɪəʳ/ *comb. form* a measure of the fineness of the threads (YARN) of silk, cotton, etc.: *15-denier stockings*

den·i·grate /ˈdenɨ̞greɪt/ *v* [T1] *fml* to declare to be not very good or not important —**-gration** /ˌdenɨ̞ˈgreɪʃən/ *n* [U]

den·im /ˈdenɨ̞m/ *n* [U] a strong cotton cloth used esp. for JEANS

den·ims /ˈdenɨ̞mz/ *n* [P] trousers made of DENIM; JEANS

den·i·zen /ˈdenɨ̞zən/ *n* [+*of*] *lit or humor* an animal or plant, or sometimes a person, that lives or grows in a particular place

de·nom·i·nate /dɪˈnɒmɨ̞neɪt‖dɪˈnɑ-/ *v* [X1] *fml or pomp* to give a name to: *the later part of the day, which the common people denominate "the afternoon"* (changed from Shakespeare)

de·nom·i·na·tion /dɪˌnɒmɨ̞ˈneɪʃən‖dɪˌnɑ-/ *n* **1** [U] *fml* the act of denominating (DENOMINATE) **2** [C] *fml* a name, esp. a general name for a class or type **3** [C] a particular religious body with special beliefs different from those of others with the same religious faith: *Among Christians there are many denominations* **4** [C] a standard of quantity, size, measurement, or esp. of value: *coins of many denominations*

de·nom·i·na·tion·al /dɪˌnɒmɨ̞ˈneɪʃənəl‖dɪˌnɑ-/ *adj* [Wa5] of, controlled by, or being a religious DENOMINATION: *a denominational school*

de·nom·i·na·tor /dɪˈnɒmɨ̞neɪtəʳ‖dɪˈnɑ-/ *n* the number below the line in a FRACTION; DIVISOR: *4 is the denominator in 1/4*

de·no·ta·tion /ˌdiːnəʊˈteɪʃən/ *n* **1** [U] the act or action of denoting (DENOTE) **2** [C] the thing pointed to by a word (rather than the feelings or ideas connected with the word) —compare CONNOTATION —**-tive** /dɪˈnəʊtətɪv‖ˈdiːnəʊteɪtɪv, dɪˈnəʊtə-/ *adj* [Wa5]

de·note /dɪˈnəʊt/ *v* **1** [T1] to be a name of: *The word "lion" denotes a certain kind of animal* **2** [T1,5] to be a mark of or that: *The sign "=" denotes that 2 things are equal.|A smile often denotes pleasure* —compare CONNOTE

de·noue·ment /deɪˈnuːmɑ̃‖ˌdeɪnuːˈmɑ̃ *Fr* denumɑ̃/ *n Fr* the end of a story when everything comes out right or is explained

de·nounce /dɪˈnaʊns/ *v* **1** [T1 (*to* and/or *as*)] to speak or write against: *They denounced him to the police as a criminal.|The minister's action was denounced in the newspapers* **2** [T1] to declare publicly and officially the end of (an agreement, esp. one between nations)

dense /dens/ *adj* [Wa1] **1** (having parts that are) closely packed or crowded together: *a dense crowd|dense trees* **2** difficult to see through: *a dense mist* **3** difficult to understand because packed with ideas: *dense writing* **4** stupid; difficult to reach with ideas: *a dense mind|a dense boy* —**~ly** *adv*: *densely packed* —**~ness** *n* [U]

den·si·ty /ˈdensɨ̞ti/ *n* **1** [U] the quality of being DENSE (1,2,3) **2** [U;C] *tech* the relation of the amount of matter (the mass) to the space into which the matter is packed (its VOLUME)

dent¹ /dent/ *n* **1** a small or hollow place in the surface of something man-made, which is the result of a blow or pressure: *a dent in one's car|* (fig.) *a dent in one's pride* **2 make a dent in** *infml* to make a first step towards success in: *It is already 6 o'clock and we haven't made a dent in this pile of work*

dent² *v* [T1;IØ] to (cause to) show one or more DENTs

den·tal¹ /ˈdentl/ *adj* [Wa5] of or related to the teeth: *dental decay*

dental² also **dental con·so·nant** /ˌ·· ˈ···/— *n* a sound formed with the end or blade of the tongue against the upper front teeth

dental plate /ˌ·· ˈ·/ *n* PLATE¹ (8a)

den·ti·frice /ˈdentɨ̞frɨ̞s/ *n* [U;C] *fml* TOOTHPASTE or TOOTH POWDER

den·tist /ˈdentɨ̞st/ also (*fml*) **dental sur·geon** /ˌ·· ˈ··/— *n* a person professionally trained to treat the teeth

den·tis·try /ˈdentɨ̞stri/ *n* [U] the work of a DENTIST

den·ture /ˈdentʃəʳ/ *n fml* PLATE¹ (8b)

den·tures /ˈdentʃəz‖-ərz/ also (*infml*) **false teeth**— *n* [P] a pair of pieces of pink plastic (PLATEs¹ (8a)) fitted with upper and lower sets of man-made teeth, worn by people who have few or no natural teeth left

de·nude /dɪˈnjuːd‖dɪˈnuːd/ *v* [T1 (*of*)] **1** to remove the covering from: *Wind and rain had denuded the mountainside of soil* **2** to remove an important possession or quality from: *denuded of all pride|self-respect*

de·nun·ci·a·tion /dɪˌnʌnsiˈeɪʃən/ *n* [C;U] (an example of the act of) denouncing (DENOUNCE): *the denunciation of evil*

de·ny /dɪˈnaɪ/ *v* **1** [T1,4,5;V3] to declare untrue; refuse to accept (as true, as a fact): *Can you deny the truth of his statement?|He denied it to be the case.|He denied telling me/that he had told me* —opposite **affirm** **2** [T1] to disclaim connection with or responsibility for: *Don't tell me he has* *denied his country and his principles!* **3** [D1] to refuse to give or allow: *He denied his children nothing and gave them everything they wanted* **4** [T1] to refuse to allow (oneself) too much pleasure: *He has denied himself all his life* —see REFUSE (USAGE)

de·o·do·rant /diː'əʊdərənt/ *n* [U;C] a man-made chemical substance that destroys or hides unpleasant smells, esp. those of the human body

de·o·do·rize, -rise /diː'əʊdəraɪz/ *v* [T1] to remove or prevent the unpleasant smell of

de·part /dɪ'pɑːt‖-ɑrt/ *v* [I∅ (*from*)] **1** *fml* to leave (esp. a place): *The royal train departed from the capital at 12 o'clock* **2 depart this life** *euph* to die

de·part·ed /dɪ'pɑːtɪ̇d‖-ɑr-/ *adj* [Wa5] **1** gone for ever: *to remember one's departed youth/fame* **2** *euph* dead: *The departed was a good friend of mine.|Let us pray for all the faithful departed who gave their lives for God*

depart from *v prep* [T1] to turn or move away from (something followed or done formerly): *I'd like to depart from the main subject of my speech for a few moments*

de·part·ment /dɪ'pɑːtmənt‖-ɑr-/ *n* **1** [C] any of the important divisions or branches of a government, business, school or college, etc.: *the History Department of a university|the children's clothing department of a large store* **2** [C] (in various countries) a political division rather like a COUNTY in Britain or a state in the U.S.A. **3** [S9] *infml BrE* an activity or subject for which a person is particularly responsible: *"I'm not going to repair the clock; that's your department," she said to her husband* —**~al** *adj* [Wa5]

department store /-'·· ·/ *n* a large shop divided into departments, in each of which a different type of goods is sold

de·par·ture /dɪ'pɑːtʃə^r‖-ɑr-/ *n* [U;C] **1** the action of DEPARTing; an act of DEPARTING: *What is the departure time of the flight?|The new system is a departure from our usual way of keeping records* **2 take one's departure (from)** *fml* to leave

de·pend /dɪ'pend/ *v* **That (all) depends/It all depends** I have certain doubts about that/it —see also DEPEND ON

de·pen·da·ble /dɪ'pendəbəl/ *adj* that can be depended on or trusted —**-bly** *adv* —**-bility** /dɪˌpendə'bɪlɪ̇ti/ *n* [U]

de·pen·dant /dɪ'pendənt/ also **dependent**— *n* **1** a person who depends on another for material support (food, clothing, money, etc.) **2** *old use* a servant

de·pen·dence /dɪ'pendəns/ *n* [U (*on, upon*)] **1** the quality or state of being dependent, esp. the quality or state of being influenced, controlled, or materially supported by another person, thing, or force **2** trust: *I place/put a lot of dependence on that woman's abilities* **3** the need to have certain drugs regularly, esp. dangerous or unlawful ones; ADDICTION

de·pen·den·cy /dɪ'pendənsi/ *n* **1** [C] a country controlled by another **2** [U] *now rare* dependence

de·pen·dent /dɪ'pendənt/ *adj* [(*on*)] that depends on: *a dependent child/area|Success is dependent on the results of this examination*

dependent clause /·,·· '·/ also **subordinate clause**— *n* a CLAUSE which cannot stand by itself, but can help to make a sentence when part of, or joined to, a main CLAUSE: *"When I came" is a dependent clause in the 2 sentences "When I came, she had left" and "She wants to know when I came"*

depend on also **depend up·on**— *v prep* **1** [T1;V3,4a] to trust (usu. someone): *I depend on you to do it.|I depended on the map, but it was wrong* **2** [T1] to be dependent on: *My wife and children depend on me* **3** [T1,6a *no pass.*] to vary according to: *Whether the game will be played depends on the weather* **4 depend (up)on it** (at the beginning or end of a sentence) be quite sure; have no doubt

de·pict /dɪ'pɪkt/ *v* [T1] *fml* **1** to represent by a picture: *This painting depicts the Battle of Waterloo* **2** to describe: *The song depicts the love of Margarethe for Faust* —**depiction** /dɪ'pɪkʃən/ *n* [U;C (*of*)]

de·pil·a·to·ry /dɪ'pɪlətəri‖-tori/ *adj, n* [Wa5;C;U] (a substance) that gets rid of unwanted hair, esp. on the human body

de·plete /dɪ'pliːt/ *v* [T1] **1** to lessen greatly in quantity, contents, power, or value: *The cost of this journey has depleted our small store of money* **2** [(*of*)] *rare* to empty of something important—**depletion** /dɪ'pliːʃən/ *n* [U]

de·plor·a·ble /dɪ'plɔːrəbəl‖dɪ'plo-/ *adj* **1** that should be DEPLOREd **2** very bad: *The condition of this dirty room is deplorable.|a deplorable performance* —**-bly** *adv*

de·plore /dɪ'plɔː^r‖-or/ *v* [T1] to be very sorry about (and consider wrong): *One must deplore such (bad) behaviour*

de·ploy /dɪ'plɔɪ/ *v* [T1] to spread out, use, or arrange for action, esp. for military action: *We must deploy all our soldiers correctly in order to win the battle.|We must deploy all our skill in order to succeed in business* —**~ment** *n* [U;C]

de·po·nent /dɪ'pəʊnənt/ *n law* a person who makes a written statement (a DEPOSITION) for use in a court of law

de·pop·u·late /ˌdiː'pɒpjʊleɪt‖-'pɑpjə-/ *v* [Wv5;T1] to reduce greatly the population of —**-lation** /ˌdiːpɒpjʊ'leɪʃən‖-pɑpjə-/ *n* [U]

de·port[1] /dɪ'pɔːt‖-ort/ *v* [T1] to send out of the country (an undesirable person who is not a citizen) —**deportation** /ˌdiːpɔː'teɪʃən‖-por-/ *n* [U; C]

deport[2] *v* [T1] *fml* to behave (oneself)

de·por·tee /ˌdiːpɔː'tiː‖-or-/ *n* a person who has been DEPORTed[1] or who is to be DEPORTed[1]

de·port·ment /dɪ'pɔːtmənt‖-or-/ *n* [U] *fml* **1** *BrE* the way a person, esp. a young lady, stands and walks: *She learnt (good) deportment when she was quite young* **2** *AmE* the way a person, esp. a young lady, behaves in the company of others

de·pose /dɪ'pəʊz/ *v* **1** [T1] to remove from a high official position, esp. from that of ruler: *The head of state was deposed by the army* **2** [T(1),3,5;I∅] to state solemnly in a court of law (the information that one believes true): *He deposed to having seen the criminal*

de·pos·it[1] /dɪ'pɒzɪ̇t‖dɪ'pɑ-/ *v* **1** [X9;(T1)] to put down (usu. in a stated place): *Where can I deposit this load of sand?* **2** [T1] (esp. of wind and liquids) to let fall and leave lying (a sheet or thickness of solid matter): *A fine soil was deposited by winds carrying desert dust* **3** [T1] to place in a bank or SAFE[2] (1): *He's deposited quite a lot of money recently* **4** [T1] to pay (part of a sum due as a sign that the rest will be paid later)

deposit[2] *n* **1** [C;U] something DEPOSITed: *There are rich deposits of gold in those hills.|There's some deposit at the bottom of this bottle of wine* **2** [C *usu. sing.*] a part payment of money, which is made so that the seller will not sell the goods to anyone else: *You must pay a deposit to the hotel if you want them to keep a room free for you* —compare EARNEST[3] (1) **3** [U;C] an act or action of DEPOSITing: *The rate of the river's deposit of mud is about one inch a year*

deposit ac·count /-'·· ·,·/ *n* a bank account which earns interest and usu. from which money can be taken out only if advance notice is given —compare SAVINGS ACCOUNT, CURRENT ACCOUNT

dep·o·si·tion /ˌdepə'zɪʃən, ˌdiː-/ *n* **1** [U] the act of deposing (DEPOSE) or removing someone from high office: *the deposition of the king by the army* **2** [U] the act of deposing (DEPOSE) or making a usu. written statement to a court of law which is solemnly declared to be true **3** [C] a statement so made

de·pos·i·tor /dɪˈpɒzətəʳ‖dɪˈpɑ-/ *n* a person who DEPOSITs money in a bank account

de·pos·i·to·ry /dɪˈpɒzətəri‖dɪˈpɑzətori/ *n* a person or place that keeps things safely stored: (fig.) *That old man is the depository of a great deal of knowledge*

dep·ot /ˈdepəʊ‖ˈdiːpəʊ/ *n* **1** a storehouse for goods **2** a place where soldiers' stores are kept, and where new soldiers are trained **3** *AmE* a railway station

de·prave /dɪˈpreɪv/ *v* [Wv5;T1] to make bad in character: *His evil friends have depraved him* —**depravation** /ˌdeprəˈveɪʃən/ *n* [U]

de·prav·i·ty /dɪˈprævəti/ *n* **1** [U] the quality or state of being DEPRAVED **2** [C] a DEPRAVED act, practice, or habit

dep·re·cate /ˈdeprəkeɪt/ *v* [T1] *fml* to express disapproval of; DEPLORE: *Such waste of money is to be deprecated at a time like this* —**-catingly** /ˈdeprəkeɪtɪŋli/ *adv* —**-cation** /ˌdeprəˈkeɪʃən/ *n* [U]

dep·re·ca·to·ry /ˈdeprəkeɪtəri‖-kətori/ *adj* **1** trying to prevent disapproval: *He admitted his mistake with a deprecatory smile* **2** serving to express disapproval; APOLOGETIC: *his deprecatory words against the minister*

de·pre·ci·ate /dɪˈpriːʃieɪt/ *v* **1** [T1] to represent as of little value and esp. of less value than usu. supposed; DENIGRATE **2** [IØ] (esp. of money) to fall in value —**depreciation** /dɪˌpriːʃiˈeɪʃən/ *n* [U]

de·pre·ci·a·to·ry /dɪˈpriːʃɪətəri‖-ʃətori/ *adj* tending to DEPRECIATE: *I don't like your depreciatory remarks about her wonderful new book*

dep·re·da·tion /ˌdeprəˈdeɪʃən/ *n* [*usu. pl.*] *fml* an act of destroying, ruining, or taking by force: *The depredations of war/of the storm can still be seen several years after the event*

de·press /dɪˈpres/ *v* [T1] **1** *fml* to press down: *Depress this button in case of fire* **2** to cause to sink to a lower level or position: *Does mass unemployment depress wages?* **3** to lessen the activity or strength of: *The bad news depressed his spirits* **4** to sadden; discourage: *The bad news depressed me* —**depressing** *adj*: *depressing news* —**depressingly** *adv*

de·pressed /dɪˈprest/ *adj* **1** low in spirits; sad **2** flattened **3** having the central part lower than the edges **4** suffering from low levels of business activity: *depressed areas of the country* **5** being below the standard: *His reading level is depressed in comparison with other boys of his age*

de·pres·sion /dɪˈpreʃən/ *n* **1** [U;C] an act of pressing down or the state of being pressed down **2** [C] a part of a surface lower than the other parts: *The rain collected in several depressions on the ground* **3** [C] an area where the pressure of the air is low in the centre and higher towards the outside: *A depression usually brings bad weather* **4** [U;C] a feeling of sadness and hopelessness: *His depression came to an end when she kissed him* **5** [C] a period of reduced business activity and high unemployment: *Many people still remember the great depression of the 1930s*

dep·ri·va·tion /ˌdeprəˈveɪʃən/ *n* **1** [U] the act of depriving (DEPRIVE OF) **2** [U] the state or feeling of being DEPRIVED **3** [C] a lack or loss: *the many deprivations from which the poor suffer*

de·prived /dɪˈpraɪvd/ *adj* (esp. of people) marked by lack of the things that make life worth living; poor and uneducated: *Are we doing enough to help the deprived?*

de·prive of /dɪˈpraɪv/ *v prep* [D1] to take away from; prevent from using: *They deprived the criminal of his rights.|She has been deprived of sight (=blind) for some years*

dept. *written abbrev. for:* DEPARTMENT

depth /depθ/ *n* [U;C *usu. sing.*] **1** the state of being deep: *What is the depth of this lake?|a depth of 30 feet|the depth of his voice/of her feeling* **2 out of/beyond one's depth a** in water that is deeper than one's height **b** beyond one's ability to understand: *I'm out of my depth when it comes to natural sciences* **3 in depth a** stretching out for some distance **b** going beneath the surface appearance of things, esp. if done with great thoroughness: *a study in depth of the poems|an in-depth study*

depth charge /ˈ· ·/ also **depth bomb** /ˈ· ·/— *n* a bomb that explodes under water and is used esp. against SUBMARINEs

depths /depθs/ *n* [*the*+P] the deepest or most central part of: *in the depths of the ocean*|(fig.) *in the depths of winter/of his character*

dep·u·ta·tion /ˌdepjʊˈteɪʃən‖-pjə-/ *n* **1** [U] the act of deputing (DEPUTE) **2** [C] a group of people DEPUTED: *The minister agreed to receive a deputation from the railwaymen's trade union*

de·pute /dɪˈpjuːt/ *v fml* **1** [T1;V3] to allow to act for one with part of one's power: *I deputed John to take charge of the younger boys at the concert* **2** [T1 (*to*)] to give (part of one's power) to someone else: *I have deputed the keeping of the accounts to John while I am in hospital*

dep·u·tize, -tise /ˈdepjʊtaɪz‖-pjə-/ *v* **1** [IØ (*for*)] to act as DEPUTY **2** [T1;V3] *AmE* to appoint as DEPUTY; DEPUTE

dep·u·ty /ˈdepjʊti‖-pjə-/ *n* **1** a person who has the power to act for another: *John will be my deputy while I am away* **2** a member of the lower house of parliament in certain countries, such as France **3** (in the US) a person who has been appointed to help a SHERIFF, esp. to catch criminals

de·rail /ˌdiːˈreɪl, dɪ-/ *v* [T1;(IØ)] to (cause to) run off the RAILs (= the railway line): *The train was derailed by the accident* —**~ment** *n* [U;C]

de·range /dɪˈreɪndʒ/ *v* [Wv5;T1] to put into a state of disorder, esp. in relation to the mind: *The poor woman's mind has been deranged for many years.|She is deranged* —**~ment** *n* [U;C]

der·by /ˈdɑːbi‖ˈdɜrbi/ *n AmE* BOWLER[2] (1)

Derby *n* [*the*+R] a famous race for horses in England

der·e·lict[1] /ˈderəlɪkt/ *adj* left to decay: *a derelict old house too dangerous to live in*

derelict[2] *n* a damaged ship with no one in it

der·e·lic·tion /ˌderəˈlɪkʃən/ *n* **1** [U] the state of being DERELICT **2** [U;C] failure to do as one ought (esp. in the phr. **dereliction of duty**)

de·ride /dɪˈraɪd/ *v* [T1,4: (*as*)] to laugh at or make fun of as of no value

de ri·gueur /də riːˈgɜːʳ (*Fr* də rigœr)/ *adj* [F] *Fr* proper and necessary according to fashion or custom: *That sort of clothing is de rigueur at a formal ceremony*

de·ri·sion /dɪˈrɪʒən/ *n* [U] the act of deriding or the state of being derided (DERIDE): *Everyone held the old man in derision*

de·ri·sive /dɪˈraɪsɪv/ *adj* showing DERISION: *derisive laughter* —**~ly** *adv*

de·ri·so·ry /dɪˈraɪsəri/ *adj* **1** deserving DERISION because useless, ineffective, or not enough: *a derisory offer of £10 for something worth £100* **2** DERISIVE —**-rily** *adv*

de·riv·a·tive[1] /dɪˈrɪvətɪv/ *adj usu. derog* not original or new: *Her paintings are really quite derivative, you know: they show a strong influence of the French school* —**~ly** *adv*

derivative² *n* **1** something coming from something else: *French is a derivative of Latin* **2** the limit of the relation of the change in a FUNCTION to the change in its independent variable as the latter change comes closer to 0

de·rive from /dɪ'raɪv/ *v prep* **1** [D1] to obtain from: *He derives a lot of pleasure from meeting new people.|The word "DERIDE" is derived from the Latin "de" ("down") and "ridere" ("to laugh")* **2** [T1] to come from: *The word "DERIDE" derives from Latin* —**derivable** *adj* —**derivation** /ˌderɪ̇'veɪʃən/ *n* [U;C]

-derm- /dɜːm‖dɜrm/ *comb. form* having to do with the skin: DERMATITIS; EPIDERMIS

der·ma·ti·tis /ˌdɜːmə'taɪtɪ̇s‖ˌdɜr-/ *n* [U] a disease of the skin, marked by redness, hotness, swelling, and pain

der·ma·tol·o·gy /ˌdɜːmə'tɒlədʒi‖ˌdɜrmə'tɑ-/ *n* [U] the scientific study of the skin, esp. of its diseases and their treatment —**-ogist** *n*

der·o·gate /'derəgeɪt/ *v* [T1] *fml* DEPRECIATE —**derogation** /ˌderə'geɪʃən/ *n* [U]

derogate from *v prep* [T1] *fml* to lessen (a good quality, a right, etc.): *Such shameful behaviour will certainly derogate from his fame*

de·rog·a·to·ry /dɪ'rɒgətəri‖dɪ'rɑgətori/ *adj fml* showing or causing lack of respect: *I can't bear his derogatory remarks about my character* —**-rily** /dɪ'rɒgətərɪ̇li‖dɪˌrɑgə'torɪ̇li/ *adv*

der·rick /'derɪk/ *n* **1** a form of CRANE for lifting and moving heavy weights, for example into or out of a ship —see picture at FREIGHTER **2** a tower built over an oil well to raise and lower the DRILL and move other apparatus

der·ring-do /ˌderɪŋ 'duː/ *n* [U] *old use or humor* daring; courageous action without thought of danger (often in the phr. **deeds of derring-do**)

derv /dɜːv‖dɜrv/ *n* [U] *BrE tdmk* an oil product used in DIESEL ENGINEs

der·vish /'dɜːvɪʃ‖'dɜr-/ *n* **1** a member of any of a number of Muslim religious groups, some of which are famous for spinning around, shouting loudly, etc. **2** a person who dances or spins about with strong feeling and without minding what other people think

de·sal·i·nize, -nise /diː'sælɪ̇naɪz/ also **de·sal·i·nate** /-neɪt/, **de·salt** /-'sɔːlt/— *v* [T1] to remove salt from: *to desalinize sea water to make it drinkable* —**-nization** /diːˌsælɪ̇naɪ'zeɪʃən‖-lɪ̇nə-/ *n* [U] —**-nation** /diːˌsælɪ̇-'neɪʃən/ *n* [U]

de·scale /ˌdiː'skeɪl/ *v* [T1] to remove unwanted chalky matter (SCALE³ (2b)) from the inside of: *These old pipes need to be descaled*

des·cant /'deskænt/ *n* **1** [U;C] music sung or sometimes played at the same time as other music and usu. higher, meant to ornament the main music and increase its effect **2** [U;C] (that which can produce) high music; SOPRANO; TREBLE **3** [C] *poet* a song

des·cant on /des'kænt, dɪs-/ also **descant up·on**— *v prep* [T1] **1** to sing or play a DESCANT (1) at the same time as (other music) **2** *fml* to say something further about (a subject)

de·scend /dɪ'send/ *v* [T1;I∅] *often fml* to come, fall, or sink from a higher to a lower level; go down (along): *The sun descended behind the hills.|She descended the stairs.|I want to talk about all these points in descending order of importance* —compare ASCEND (1,2)

de·scen·dant /dɪ'sendənt/ *n* [C (*of*)] a person or other living thing that has another as grandfather or grandmother, great-grandfather, etc.: *He says he is a descendant of Julius Caesar, but I doubt it*

de·scend·ed /dɪ'sendɪ̇d/ *adj* [Wa5;F+*from*] having the stated person or other living thing as grandfather or grandmother, great-grandfather, etc.

descend on also **descend up·on**— *v prep* [T1] **1** to arrive suddenly at: *The whole family descended on us at Christmas* **2** (of a group of people) to attack: *Thieves descended on the traveller*

descend to *v prep* [T1,4] to lower oneself to: *I'm surprised that he should descend to cheating*

de·scent /dɪ'sent/ *n* **1** [C;U] the act or fact of going or coming down: *The road makes a sharp descent just past the lake.|his descent into a life of crime* **2** [U9] family origins: *She is of German descent* **3** [U;S] a sudden unwelcome attack (or visit): *We can expect the usual descent of relatives at Christmas*

de·scribe /dɪ'skraɪb/ *v* **1** [T1,6a,b] to give a picture (of someone or something) in words: *to describe a man/a place/an event|Try to describe exactly what happened just before the accident* **2** [T1] *tech* to draw the shape of: *to describe a circle within a square* **3** [T1] to move in the shape of: *The falling star described a long curve in the sky*

describe as *v prep* [D1] to call; regard; consider: *I should describe the attempt as a failure/as unsuccessful*

de·scrip·tion /dɪ'skrɪpʃən/ *n* **1** [U] the act of describing or giving a picture in words: *The play was dull beyond description.|Her powers of description are very great* **2** [C] a statement or account that describes: *This book gives a good description of life on a farm* **3** [C] *not fml* a sort or kind (esp. in the phrs. **of that description**; **of every description**; **of all descriptions**): *A person of that description should never be trusted*

de·scrip·tive /dɪ'skrɪptɪv/ *adj* **1** [Wa5] that describes: *descriptive writing* **2** that describes well: *the most descriptive writing I have ever read.|Your words are very descriptive: I understand exactly* **3** [Wa5] describing how a language is used: *a descriptive grammar of English* —compare PRESCRIPTIVE (2) —**~ly** *adv* —**~ness** *n* [U]

de·scry /dɪ'skraɪ/ *v* [Wv6;T1] *lit* to notice something a long way off: *Our host descried a gentleman of unusual appearance standing at the far end of the hall*

des·e·crate /'desɪkreɪt/ *v* [T1] **1** to use (something holy, such as a church) for purposes which are not holy **2** to put to a bad or improper use: *Don't desecrate my love for you by comparing it with anything ordinary* —**-cration** /ˌdesɪ'kreɪʃən/ *n* [U; (C)]

de·seg·re·gate /diː'segrɪgeɪt/ *v* [T1;(I∅)] to end SEGREGATION, esp. racial SEGREGATION (in): *Children of all races go to our school now that we've desegregated it* —**-ation** /diːˌsegrɪ'geɪʃən/ *n* [U]

de·sen·si·tize, -tise /diː'sensɪ̇taɪz/ *v* [T1] to make less sensitive to light, pain, feelings, etc.: *to desensitize photographic material* —**-tization** /diːˌsensɪ̇taɪ'zeɪʃən‖-tə-/ *n* [U]

des·ert¹ /'dezət‖-ərt/ *n* a large sandy piece of land where there is very little rain and less plant life than elsewhere: *the Sahara Desert|a hot desert wind*

de·sert² /dɪ'zɜːt‖-ɜrt/ *v* **1** [Wv5;T1] to leave empty or leave completely: *the silent deserted streets of the city at night* **2** [T1] to leave at a difficult time or leave in a difficult position: *All my friends have deserted me!*|(fig.) *When he had to speak to her his courage suddenly deserted him* **3** [T1;I∅] to leave (military service) without permission

de·sert·er /dɪ'zɜːtəʳ‖-ɜr-/ *n* a person who leaves his duty or his leader, esp. one who leaves military service without permission

de·ser·tion /dɪ'zɜːʃən‖-ɜr-/ *n* [C;U] (an example of) the act of leaving one's duty, one's family, or military service without permission, esp. if without the intention of returning

de·serts /dɪˈzɜːts‖-ɜrts/ *n* [P] that which is deserved, esp. if bad or painful (esp. in the phr. **just deserts**)

de·serve /dɪˈzɜːv‖-ɜrv/ *v* [Wv6;T1,3] **1** to be worthy of; be fit for: *Such bad behaviour deserves a beating.|She deserved to win because she was the best* **2 deserve well/ill of** *fml* to deserve to be treated well/badly by

de·serv·ed·ly /dɪˈzɜːvɪ̈dli‖-ɜr-/ *adv* rightly: *Rembrandt is a deservedly famous artist*

de·serv·ing /dɪˈzɜːvɪŋ‖-ɜr-/ *adj* [F+*of*;A] worthy of support or help: *We must help the deserving poor.|(fml) He is deserving of all praise for his great efforts* —**~ly** *adv*

dés·ha·bil·lé /ˌdeɪzæˈbiːeɪ (*Fr* dezabije)/ *n* [U] *Fr* DISHABILLE

des·ic·cant /ˈdesɪ̈kənt/ *n tech* a chemical substance that makes things dry

des·ic·cate /ˈdesɪ̈keɪt/ *v* **1** [T1;I∅] *fml* to (cause to) dry up **2** [Wv5;T1] *tech* to preserve (a food) by drying; DEHYDRATE

de·sid·e·ra·tum /dɪˌzɪdəˈreɪtəm, -ˈrɑː-, dɪˌsɪ-/ *n* **-ta** /tə/ *fml* something desired as necessary: *Time and money are desiderata for a successful holiday*

de·sign¹ /dɪˈzaɪn/ *v* **1** [T1] to imagine and plan out in the mind: *He designed the perfect crime* **2** [T1; V3: *often pass.*] to develop for a certain purpose or use: *a book designed mainly for use in colleges|This weekend party was designed to bring the 2 leaders together* **3** [T1;I∅] to make a drawing or pattern of (something); to draw the plans for (something): *to design dresses for a famous shop|She designs for a famous shop*

design² *n* **1** [C] a plan in the mind **2** [C] a drawing or pattern showing how something is to be made **3** [U] the art of making such drawings or patterns: *She attended a school of dress design* **4** [U] the arrangement of parts that go into human productions: *This cheap machine looks good but it is of very bad design and doesn't work well* **5** [C] an ornamental pattern **6** [U] purpose; purposeful planning: *Do you think the house was burnt down by accident or design?* —see also DESIGNS, DESIGNEDLY

des·ig·nate¹ /ˈdezɪgnɪ̈t, -neɪt/ *adj* [Wa5;E] *fml* chosen for an office but not yet officially placed in it: *the minister designate*

des·ig·nate² /ˈdezɪgneɪt/ *v* **1** [T1] *fml* to point out or call by a special name: *These x-marks on the drawing designate all the possible entrances to the castle grounds* **2** [T1 (*for*);V3] to appoint (for special work): *I am designating you to act for me while I am away*

designate as *v prep* [D1 *often pass.*] to name officially as: *The school has been designated as the meeting place for the evening art club.|She has been designated as the Minister for Education*

des·ig·na·tion /ˌdezɪgˈneɪʃən/ *n* **1** [U (*of* and *as*)] the act of designating (DESIGNATE): *the designation of Smith as the man for the job* **2** [C] *fml* a name, title, or description of a particular thing or person

de·sign·ed·ly /dɪˈzaɪnɪ̈dli/ *adv* on purpose; intentionally

de·sign·er /dɪˈzaɪnəʳ/ *n* a person who makes plans or patterns: *a designer of dresses/shoes/cars|an aircraft designer*

de·sign·ing¹ /dɪˈzaɪnɪŋ/ *adj derog* intending to deceive: *Designing people always try to get what they want and don't care how they get it*

designing² *n* [U] DESIGN² (3)

de·signs /dɪˈzaɪnz/ *n* [P (*on, upon,* or *against*)] evil plans (esp. for stealing something): *They have designs on your money/your life*

de·sir·a·ble /dɪˈzaɪərəbəl/ *adj* **1** worth having, doing, or desiring: *For this job it is desirable to know something about medicine* **2** causing desire, esp. sexual desire: *a beautiful and desirable woman* —**-bility** /dɪˌzaɪərəˈbɪlɪ̈ti/ *n* [U] —**-bly** /dɪˈzaɪərəbli/ *adv*

de·sire¹ /dɪˈzaɪəʳ/ *v* [Wv6] **1** [T1,3,5c;V3] *fml* to wish or want very much: *I desire happiness.|I desire to be happy.|The Queen desires that you (should) come at once.|She desires you to come at once.|Give our guests whatever they desire* **2** [T1] to wish to have sexual relations with

desire² *n* **1** [C;U: (*for,* 3,5c)] a strong wish: *I am filled with desire to go back there.|He has a strong desire to succeed/for success.|many unsatisfied desires|his desire that you should do it* **2** [C;U: (*for*)] a strong wish for sexual relations with: *Antony's desire for Cleopatra* **3** [C (*for*), C3,5] an expressed wish or order: *I shall try to act according to your desires.|He expressed a desire to see the papers* **4** [C9 *usu. sing.*] something or someone desired: *What is your greatest desire/your heart's desire?*
USAGE One can feel **desire** for anything. **Appetite** is only for things of the body, esp. food, and **lust** (*derog*) is a very strong word, particularly for sex.

de·sir·ous /dɪˈzaɪərəs/ *adj* [F + *of,* F5] *fml* feeling or having a desire: *She has always been desirous of fame/of being famous.|The president is strongly desirous that you should attend the meeting*

de·sist /dɪˈzɪst, dɪˈsɪst/ *v* [I∅ (*from*)] *fml* to cease doing; not do any more: *I told him not to do it any more, and he desisted*

desk /desk/ *n* a table, often with drawers, at which one reads, writes, or does business

desk clerk /ˈ· ·/ *n AmE* RECEPTIONIST

desk·work /ˈdeskwɜːk‖-ɜrk/ *n* [U] *often derog* office work, esp. that done at a desk: *He likes teaching better than deskwork*

des·o·late¹ /ˈdesələt/ *adj* **1** (of a place) sad and without people in it: *a desolate old house* **2** (of a person) sad and deserted by friends —**~ly** *adv* —**-lation** /ˌdesəˈleɪʃən/ *n* [U]

des·o·late² /ˈdesəleɪt/ *v* [T1 *usu. pass.*] to make very sad: *She was desolated by the death of her husband*

de·spair¹ /dɪˈspeəʳ/ *v* [I∅ (*of*)] to lose all hope (of): *Don't despair: things will get better soon!|During the war, the soldier despaired of ever coming home alive*

despair² *n* [U (*of*)] **1** complete lack or loss of hope: *Defeat after defeat filled us with despair.|His despair of becoming a great artist made him stop painting* **2** the cause of this feeling (esp. in the phr. **the despair of**): *Every year my roses are the despair of all the village gardeners because I always win first prize at the flower show*

de·spair·ing /dɪˈspeərɪŋ/ *adj* [A] showing or causing DESPAIR²: *He gave a despairing cry at the bad news* —**~ly** *adv*

de·spatch /dɪˈspætʃ/ *n, v* [C;U;T1] DISPATCH

de·spatch·es /dɪˈspætʃɪ̈z/ *n* DISPATCHES

des·pe·ra·do /ˌdespəˈrɑːdəʊ/ *n* **-does** *or* **-dos** a bold, merciless lawbreaker who cares nothing about the results of his actions and fears no danger; DESPERATE criminal

des·per·ate /ˈdespərɪ̈t/ *adj* **1** (of a person) ready for any wild act because of loss of hope: *a desperate criminal|He was desperate for work to provide food for his children* **2** (of an action) wild or dangerous; done as a last attempt: *a last desperate effort to win* **3** (of a state of affairs) very difficult and dangerous: *The country is in a desperate state and we must all work hard* —**~ly** *adv*

des·per·a·tion /ˌdespəˈreɪʃən/ *n* [U] **1** the state of being DESPERATE: *He kicked at the locked door in desperation* **2** *infml* a state of angry nervousness that cannot long be controlled: *If you don't stop this* *continual arguing, you will drive me to desperation*

des·pic·a·ble /dɪˈspɪkəbəl, ˈdespɪ-/ *adj* that should be or deserves to be DESPISEd: *It is despicable of you to leave your wife and family without any money* —**-bly** *adv*

de·spise /dɪˈspaɪz/ *v* [T1] to regard as worthless, low, bad, etc.; dislike very angrily

de·spite /dɪˈspaɪt/ *prep fml* in spite of: *He came to the meeting despite his serious illness*

de·spoil /dɪˈspɔɪl/ *v* [T1 (*of*)] *fml* to steal from; take away from, using force: *The army despoiled the village.|They despoiled the villagers of their belongings*

de·spon·dent /dɪˈspɒndənt‖dɪˈspɑn-/ *adj* feeling or showing a complete loss of hope and courage, and a belief that nothing can happen or be done to improve matters: *despondent about his poor health* —**~ly** *adv* —**-dency** /dənsi/ *n* [U]

des·pot /ˈdespɒt, -ət‖ˈdespət, -ɑt/ *n often derog* a person who has all the power of government and uses it unjustly or cruelly: *That mother rules her family like a real despot*

des·pot·ic /dɪˈspɒtɪk, de-‖-ˈspɑ-/ *adj derog* of or like a DESPOT —**~ally** *adv* [Wa4]

des·pot·is·m /ˈdespətɪzəm/ *n* [U] *derog* rule by a DESPOT

des·sert /dɪˈzɜːt‖-ɜrt/ *n* [C;U] sweet food served at the end of a meal

des·sert·spoon /dɪˈzɜːtspuːn‖-ɜrt-/ *n esp. BrE* a spoon of the same shape as a TEASPOON and TABLESPOON but between them in size, used for eating DESSERT

des·sert·spoon·ful /dɪˈzɜːtspuːnfʊl‖-ɜr-/ also **des-sertspoon**— *n* **-spoonfuls** *or* **-spoonsful** **1** the contents of a DESSERTSPOON **2** a measure used in cooking, equal to about 2 TEASPOONfuls

dessert wine /·ˈ· ·/ *n* [U;C] a usu. sweet wine often served with DESSERT or between meals

des·ti·na·tion /ˌdestɪ̵ˈneɪʃən/ *n* a place which is set for the end of a journey or to which something is sent: *The parcel was sent to the wrong destination*

des·tined /ˈdestɪ̵nd/ *adj* [Wa5;B;F (*by* or *for*), F3] intended for some special purpose; intended by fate; willed by God: *He was destined by his parents for life in the army.|His work was destined never to succeed.|I never thought I would marry her, but I suppose it was destined*

des·ti·ny /ˈdestɪ̵ni/ *n* **1** [C] fate; that which must or had to happen: *It was the great man's destiny to lead his country to freedom* **2** [R] (*often cap.*) that which seems to decide man's fate, thought of as a person or a force: *Destiny is sometimes cruel*

des·ti·tute /ˈdestɪ̵tjuːt‖-tuːt/ *adj* **1** [B] lacking the simplest necessary things of life (food, clothing, shelter), or the means to buy or get them **2** [F+*of*] lacking in; completely without: *The cruel man was destitute of human feeling* —**-tution** /ˌdestɪ̵ˈtjuːʃən‖-ˈtuː-/ *n* [U]

de·stroy /dɪˈstrɔɪ/ *v* **1** [T1;(I∅)] to tear down or apart; ruin; put an end to the existence or effectiveness of (something): *The enemy destroyed the city.*|(fig.) *You have destroyed my life and all my hopes* **2** [T1] *euph* to kill (esp. an animal in a home or ZOO): *The dog is mad and ought to be destroyed*

de·stroy·er /dɪˈstrɔɪəʳ/ *n* **1** a person who destroys **2** a type of small fast warship

de·struc·tion /dɪˈstrʌkʃən/ *n* [U] **1** the act of destroying or state of being destroyed: *the destruction of the forest by fire|The army left the enemy town in complete destruction* **2** that which destroys: *Pride was her destruction, for it caused the loss of all her friends*

de·struc·tive /dɪˈstrʌktɪv/ *adj* **1** causing destruction: *a destructive storm* **2** wanting or tending to destroy —**~ly** *adv* —**~ness** *n* [U]

des·ue·tude /ˈdeswɪ̵tjuːd, dɪˈsjuːɪ̵-‖-tuːd/ *n* [U] *fml* disuse: *Those strange old laws still exist, but have fallen into desuetude*

des·ul·to·ry /ˈdesəltəri, ˈdez-‖-tori/ *adj fml* passing from one thing to another without plan or purpose: *If she continues to work in that desultory way, she will never finish anything* —**-rily** /ˈdesəltərɪ̵li, ˈdez-‖ˌdesəlˈtorɪ̵li, ˌdez-/ *adv*

de·tach /dɪˈtætʃ/ *v* [T1 (*from*)] to separate esp. from a larger mass and usu. without violence or damage —**~able** *adj*

de·tached /dɪˈtætʃt/ *adj* **1** separate; not connected **2** [Wa5] (of a house) not connected on any side with any other building; free-standing —compare SEMIDETACHED and see picture at HOUSE[1] **3** (of a person or an opinion) not influenced by other people's opinions; not showing much personal feeling

de·tach·ed·ly /dɪˈtætʃɪ̵dli/ *adv* in a DETACHED (3) way

de·tach·ment /dɪˈtætʃmənt/ *n* **1** [U] the act of DETACHing **2** [U] the state of being DETACHED (3) **3** [C] a group of soldiers (or ships) sent from the main group on special duty

de·tail[1] /ˈdiːteɪl‖dɪˈteɪl/ *n* **1** [C] a small point or fact: *Everything in her story is correct (down) to the smallest detail* **2** [U] such small parts considered together: *He has a good eye for detail and notices almost everything.|The colour in that picture is very good, but there's too much detail* **3** [C] a small working party of soldiers or sailors **4 in . . . detail** giving a lot of facts **5 go into . . . detail(s)** to give a lot of facts: *That's very interesting, but could you go into a little more detail about it?*

detail[2] *v* **1** [T1;V3] appoint to do some special duty: *He detailed the soldiers to look for water* **2** [T1 (*to*)] *rare* give a lot of facts about

de·tailed /ˈdiːteɪld‖dɪˈteɪld/ *adj* with a lot of facts given: *He gave me a detailed account of his work*

de·tain /dɪˈteɪn/ *v* [T1] **1** to keep (a person) from leaving during a certain time: *The police have detained 2 men for questioning at the police station* **2** to delay: *This matter isn't very important, and shouldn't detain us very long*

de·tain·ee /ˌdiːteɪˈniː/ *n* a person DETAINed officially, esp. for political reasons, and often held in a camp rather than a prison

de·tect /dɪˈtekt/ *v* [T1] to find out; notice: *Small quantities of poison were detected in the dead man's stomach.|I seemed to detect some anger in his voice*

de·tec·tion /dɪˈtekʃən/ *n* [U] **1** the act or action of DETECTing: *Many important mistakes have been escaping detection, and a lot of money has been lost as a result* **2** the work of a DETECTIVE: *The detection of crime is not always easy*

de·tec·tive /dɪˈtektɪv/ *n* a policeman whose special job is to find out information that will lead to criminals being caught

de·tec·tor /dɪˈtektəʳ/ *n* any instrument used for finding out the presence of something: *a gas detector*

dé·tente /ˈdeɪtɒnt, deɪˈtɒnt‖-ɑnt (*Fr* detɑ̃t)/ *n* [C;U] *Fr* (a state of) easier and calmer political relations, esp. between countries

de·ten·tion /dɪˈtenʃən/ *n* **1** [U] the act of preventing a person from going away during a limited period of time, or the state of being prevented from going away **2** [U] the state of being kept in school after school hours as a punishment: *He was kept in detention for talking during class* **3** [C] an example of either of these

de·ter /dɪˈtɜːʳ/ *v* **-rr-** [T1 (*from*)] to turn aside, discourage, or prevent from acting (as by fear, threats, or the possibility of something unpleasant): *The fact that we have these big bombs will deter our enemies from attacking us*

de·ter·gent /dɪ'tɜːdʒənt‖-ɜr-/ *n* [C;U] a chemical product used for cleaning esp. clothing and dishes

de·te·ri·o·rate /dɪ'tɪərɪəreɪt/ *v* [I∅;(T1)] to (cause to) become worse: *his deteriorating health* —**-ration** /dɪˌtɪərɪə'reɪʃən/ *n* [U]

de·ter·mi·nant /dɪ'tɜːmɪnənt‖-ɜr-/ *n fml* something that decides, fixes, settles, or limits: *Is cost or comfort the determinant in choosing a new car?*

de·ter·mi·na·tion /dɪˌtɜːmə̇'neɪʃən‖-ɜr-/ *n* **1** [U (*of*), U3] firm intention: *He came with the determination of staying/to stay only one week* **2** [U] the ability to make firm decisions and act in accordance with them; strong will to succeed: *a woman of great determination who always gets what she wants* **3** [U] the fixing of the limits of something **4** [U] the finding (of the exact position or nature of something) **5** [C] a formal decision, esp. by a judge

de·ter·mine /dɪ'tɜːmə̇n‖-ɜr-/ *v* **1** [T3,5;V3] to (cause to) form a firm intention in the mind: *He determined to go at once/that he would go at once.|That determined me to do it* **2** [T1,6a,b] to decide: *to determine the rights and wrongs of the case|to determine where to go* **3** [T1] to limit; fix; be the cause of; control: *Weather determines the size of the crop* **4** [T1] to fix exactly; find out and fix: *to determine the position of a star*

de·ter·mined /dɪ'tɜːmə̇nd‖-ɜr-/ *adj* [B;F3] firm; having or showing a strong will: *a very determined woman who always gets what she wants|I am determined to go and nothing will stop me*

de·ter·min·er /dɪ'tɜːmə̇nəʳ‖-ɜr-/ *n tech* a word that limits the meaning of a noun and comes before adjectives that describe the same noun: *In the phrase "his new car", the word "his" is a determiner*

de·ter·min·is·m /dɪ'tɜːmə̇nɪzəm‖-ɜr-/ *n* [U] the belief that acts of the will, natural events, or social changes are settled and decided by earlier causes —**-tic** /dɪˌtɜːmə̇'nɪstɪk‖-ɜr-/ *adj*: *But your deterministic beliefs leave no room for my free will!*

de·ter·rent /dɪ'terənt‖-'tɜr-/ *n, adj* (something) that DETERs: *Our bombs will be a deterrent to the enemy.|the deterrent effect of the bad weather* —**-rence** /dɪ'terəns‖-'tɜr-/ *n* [U]

de·test /dɪ'test/ *v* [T1, 4] to hate with very strong feeling: *I detest people who deceive and tell lies.|They detest all that shooting and killing* —**~able** *adj* —**~ably** *adv* —**~ation** /ˌdiːte'steɪʃən/ *n* [U]

de·throne /dɪ'θrəʊn/ *v* [T1] to remove (a king or queen) from power: (fig.) *The chairman of that big company was dethroned by a forceful young woman* —**~ment** *n* [U;C]

det·o·nate /'detəneɪt/ *v* [T1;I∅] to (cause to) explode suddenly: *The soldiers placed the bomb carefully, detonated it, and destroyed the bridge*

det·o·na·tion /ˌdetə'neɪʃən/ *n* **1** [U] the act or action of detonating (DETONATE) **2** [C] the noise of an explosion

det·o·na·tor /'detəneɪtəʳ/ *n* an apparatus or small quantity of explosive used to DETONATE a larger quantity of strong explosive

de·tour¹ /'diːtʊəʳ/ *n* a way round something: *They made a detour to avoid the busy centre of the town*

detour² *v* [I∅ (*round* or (*AmE*) *around*)] to make a DETOUR

de·tract from /dɪ'trækt/ *v prep* [T1] **1** to take something away from; make less the value of: *All the ornamental work detracts from the beauty of the building's shape* **2** to say evil things about: *He always tries to detract from the work of other people in the same field* —**detraction** /dɪ'trækʃən/ *n* [U;S]: *It is no detraction from the value of his work to say that I had the same idea 10 years earlier*

de·trac·tor /dɪ'træktəʳ/ *n* a person who says bad things, often unjustly, in order to lessen the value or good quality of something or someone

de·train /ˌdiː'treɪn/ *v* [I∅] *fml* to get off a railway train: *to detrain at Reading*

det·ri·ment /'detrə̇mənt/ *n* **1** [U] harm; damage (esp. in the phrs. **without detriment to** and **to the detriment of**): *He did hard work without detriment to his health.|He smoked a lot, to the detriment of his health* **2** [C *usu. sing.*] a cause of harm or damage: *Smoking is a detriment to health* —**~al** *adj*: *Union membership should not be detrimental to your future in that company* —**~ally** *adv*

de·tri·tus /dɪ'traɪtəs/ *n* [U] *tech* **1** heavier matter which falls down to the bottom, as from SEWAGE (waste matter of a city) when it is being treated chemically **2** substances rubbed away from rocks by the wind or by water, such as sand

de trop /də 'trəʊ (*Fr* də tro)/ *adj* [Wa5;F] *Fr pomp* too much or too many: *A heavy coat was de trop when it was so hot*

deuce /djuːs‖duːs/ *n* **1** [C] a card or a DICE of the value of 2 **2** [U] (in tennis) 40–40; 40 points to each player **3** [(*the*) R] *old euph sl* (used for adding force to an expression) devil: *Who the deuce did that?|What the deuce happened?* **4 a deuce of a/an** *old euph sl* causing great trouble: *They got into a deuce of a fight* **5 the deuce to pay** *old euph sl* **the** DEVIL¹ (14) **to pay** **6 The deuce you will/won't, he can/can't, etc.** *old euph sl* **The** DEVIL (15) **you will** **7 Deuce take it!** *old euph sl* **The** DEVIL (12) **take it!**

deuc·ed /'djuːsə̇d, djuːst‖'duː-/ *adj, adv* [A] *old euph sl* very bad(ly); unfortunate(ly): *You seem to be in a deuced hurry.|This bag is deuced heavy!* —**~ly** *adv*: *This bag is deucedly heavy!*

Deu·te·ron·o·my /ˌdjuːtə'rɒnəmi‖ˌduːtə'rɑ-/ *n* [R] the 5th book of the OLD TESTAMENT of the Bible

de·val·u·a·tion /diːˌvæljʊ'eɪʃən/ *n* [U] **1** a reduction in the exchange value of money **2** a lessening esp. of value or quality

de·val·ue /diː'væljuː/ *v* **1** [T1;I∅] to begin the DEVALUATION of (money): *We had to devalue (our money) last year* —compare REVALUE (2) **2** [T1] to cause or be responsible for a DEVALUATION of (as a person or a work of art): *Let's not devalue his work unjustly*

dev·a·state /'devəsteɪt/ *v* [T1] to destroy completely; make impossible to live in; LAY WASTE —**-station** /ˌdevə'steɪʃən/ *n* [U]

dev·a·stat·ing /'devəsteɪtɪŋ/ *adj* **1** completely destructive: *a devastating storm*|(fig.) *a devastating argument against our new plan* **2** *infml* very good; able to obtain the desired result: *You look devastating tonight, my dear.|His jokes were completely devastating* (= very funny) —**~ly** *adv*

de·vel·op /dɪ'veləp/ *v* **1** [T1;I∅: (*from* or *into*)] to (cause to) grow, increase, or become larger or more complete: *to develop from a seed into a plant|to develop a business/one's mind|That engine develops a lot of heat* **2** [T1] to study or think out fully, or present fully: *I'd like to develop this idea a little more fully before I go on to my next point* **3** [T1;L9] (in photography) to (cause to) appear on a film or photographic paper: *I think these photographs will look nice when they're developed.|These photographs haven't developed very well* **4** [T1] to bring out the ECONOMIC possibilities of (esp. land or natural substances): *We must develop all the natural substances in our country which can make us rich!* **5** [T1;I∅] to (cause to) begin to be seen, become active, or show signs of: *Trouble is developing among the sailors.|He seems to be developing an illness*

de·vel·op·er /dɪˈveləpəʳ/ *n* **1** [C;U] (in photography) a chemical substance used for bringing out the image on a photographic plate or film after a picture has been taken on it **2** [C] a person who hopes to make a profit from developing land (esp. by building on it) or buildings (esp. by improving them)

de·vel·op·ing coun·try /·,··· ˈ··/ also **developing nation** /·,··· ˈ··/— *n euph* a poor country that is trying to become richer and to improve the living conditions of its people

de·vel·op·ment /dɪˈveləpmənt/ *n* **1** [U] the act or action of developing or the state of being developed; a gradual unfolding: *the development of a seed into a plant/of his shop into a big business* **2** [U] the amount of such developing: *the great development of the chest muscles in birds* **3** [C] a result of developing: *This new rose is a development from a very old kind of rose* **4** [C] a developed piece of land, esp. one that has houses built on it: *This new development is very modern, but there's nothing to do here on Saturday night* **5** [C] a new event or piece of news: *the latest developments in the murder trial*

de·vel·op·men·tal /dɪˌveləpˈmentl/ *adj* [Wa5] *fml* of or about the development of the mind or body —**~ly** *adv*

de·vi·ance /ˈdiːvɪəns/ also **de·vi·an·cy** /-si/— *n* [U; C] DEVIANT quality, state, or behaviour: *sexual deviance*

de·vi·ant /ˈdiːvɪənt/ also (*AmE*) **de·vi·ate** /-ɪ̣t/— *adj, n* (a person or thing) that is different or moves away from an accepted standard: *Sexually deviant behaviour is sometimes against the law.|Deviant children need help*

de·vi·ate /ˈdiːvieɪt/ *v* [IØ (*from*)] to be different or move away (from an accepted standard of behaviour, or from a correct or straight path): *Don't deviate from the rules*

de·vi·a·tion /ˌdiːviˈeɪʃən/ *n* **1** [C;U] (a) noticeable or marked difference from accepted standards of behaviour: *sexual deviation* **2** [C] *derog* a difference from an established system of political beliefs by people who claim to accept the main beliefs of the system **3** [C] the difference between the north as shown by a MAGNETIC COMPASS (as on a ship) and true north: *a deviation of 5°* **4** [C] (in STATISTICS) the difference between a measure and the average of all the measures: *a deviation of 5*

de·vi·a·tion·ist /ˌdiːviˈeɪʃənɪ̣st/ *n derog* a person who claims to share the main points of a system of political beliefs but who disagrees about some other points also considered important, esp. about the best ways to gain the desired results —**-ism** *n* [U]

de·vice /dɪˈvaɪs/ *n* **1** an instrument, esp. one that is cleverly thought out: *a device for sharpening pencils* **2** something (such as a special phrase or group of words) which is intended to produce a particular artistic effect in a work of literature **3** a drawing or picture, esp. one used by a noble family as their special sign **4** *becoming rare* a plan, esp. for a purpose not wholly good **5 leave someone to his own devices** to leave (someone) alone, without help

dev·il[1] /ˈdevəl/ *n* **1** [*the*+R] (*usu. cap.*) the most powerful evil spirit; Satan **2** [C] an evil spirit **3** [C] an evil person **4** [C] *infml* a high-spirited person, usu. a man, who is ready for adventure: *He's a devil with the ladies.|Be a devil and have another drink.|a devil of a fellow* **5** [C9] *infml* (in expressions of strong feeling) fellow; man; boy: *He failed his examination, (the) poor devil.|You lucky devil!* **6** [*the*+R] *sl* (used to give force to various expressions of displeasure): *What the devil happened?* **7 between the devil and the deep (blue) sea** *infml* facing 2 choices, both of which are bad **8 Give the devil his due** Be just even to a bad person **9 go to the devil** to be ruined **10 Go to the devil!** *sl* Go away at once! **11 play the devil with** *infml* to do a lot of harm to: *These high winds are playing the devil with my new hairstyle* **12 The devil take it!** *sl becoming old use* (an expression of strong displeasure) **13 the/a devil of a/an** *sl* causing great trouble: *It's the devil of a business dealing with him* **14 the devil to pay** *sl* a great deal of trouble: *There'll be the devil to pay if we're caught taking these cakes* **15 The devil you will/won't, he can/can't,** (etc. with other verbs in [I2]) *sl becoming old use* (used as a rude reply showing strong disagreement): *"John says he'll go to town." "The devil he will!"* **16 the very devil** *infml* very difficult or painful: *Our new machine is wonderful, but it's the very devil to get started*

devil[2] *v* **-ll-** (*AmE* **-l-**) [Wv5;T1] to cook in a very hot-tasting thick liquid: *devilled chicken/eggs*

dev·il·ish /ˈdevəlɪʃ/ *adj* evil; like the devil: *Those devilish tricks of yours will get you into prison some day, young man!* —**~ness** *n* [U]

dev·il·ish·ly /ˈdevəlɪʃli/ *adv* **1** also (*nonstandard*) **devilish**— *infml* (showing displeasure) very: *It was devilish(ly) hard work climbing the mountain* **2** in a DEVILISH manner

devil-may-care /ˌ·· · ˈ·/ *adj* gay, careless, and wild in behaviour

dev·il·ment /ˈdevəlmənt/ also **dev·il·ry** /-ri/— *n* **1** [U] evil behaviour or (usu.) behaviour that causes trouble **2** [U] wildly gay behaviour **3** [C] a case or example of either of these: *That child is always busy with some devilment or other*

devil's ad·vo·cate /ˌ·· ˈ···/ *n* a person who says the opposite of what he believes in order to play with, or test out, ideas

de·vi·ous /ˈdiːvɪəs/ *adj* **1** *derog* not direct and probably not completely honest: *Mary is a devious person and I don't trust her* **2** not going in the straightest or most direct way: *Let's take this devious path to avoid the other people* —**~ly** *adv* —**~ness** *n* [U]

de·vise /dɪˈvaɪz/ *v* [T1] **1** to plan or invent (esp. cleverly): *He devised a plan for getting the jewels out of the country.|He devised an instrument to measure light waves* **2 devise and bequeath** *law* BEQUEATH

de·vi·tal·ize, -ise /ˌdiːˈvaɪtl-aɪz/ *v* [T1] to take the strength or life force from —**-ization** /diːˌvaɪtl-aɪˈzeɪʃən‖-əˈzeɪ-/ *n* [U]

de·void /dɪˈvɔɪd/ *adj* [Wa5;F+*of*] *fml* empty (of); lacking (in): *This house is totally devoid of furniture.|He is devoid of human feeling!*

de·vo·lu·tion /ˌdiːvəluːʃən/ *n* [U] the giving of part of one's power, work, duties, etc., to another person or group

de·volve on /dɪˈvɒlv‖dɪˈvɑlv/ also **devolve upon**— *v prep* [T1 *no pass.*] (of power, work, duties, etc.) to go to (another person or group); be passed to

devolve to *v prep* [T1 *no pass.*] *law* (of land, goods, etc.) to become the property of, on the death of the owner

de·vot·ed /dɪˈvəʊtɪ̣d/ *adj* **1** [B (*to*)] loyal; loving; caring a great deal: *a devoted father/friend|He is very devoted to his wife* **2** [F (*to*)] spending a great deal of time and/or effort (on); fond (of): *devoted to Bach/football/helping others* —**~ly** *adv*

dev·o·tee /ˌdevəˈtiː/ *n Fr* **1** [C (*of*)] a person who admires someone or something: *a devotee of Bach (=Bach's music)/football|Every great artist has his devotees—and enemies* **2** [C] a person who DEVOTEs himself TO religion; a very religious person: *The temple was full of devotees wanting to pray to the god*

de·vote to /dɪˈvəʊt/ *v prep* [D1] to set apart for; give wholly or completely to: *He has devoted his life* *to helping blind people.|I don't think we should devote any more time to this question*

de·vo·tion /dɪˈvəʊʃən/ *n* [U (*to*)] **1** the act of devoting or the condition of being DEVOTED TO: *The devotion of too much time to sports leaves too little time for studying* **2** great fondness **3** attention to religion; DEVOUTness

de·vo·tion·al /dɪˈvəʊʃənəl/ *adj* [Wa5;A;(B)] of, about, or used in religious DEVOTIONS: *devotional literature*

de·vo·tions /dɪˈvəʊʃənz/ *n* [P] religious acts, esp. prayers

de·vour /dɪˈvaʊəʳ/ *v* **1** [T1] to eat up quickly and hungrily: *The lion devoured the deer.*|(fig.) *She devoured the new book* **2** [Wv4;T1 *usu. pass.*] (of a feeling) to possess (a person); completely take up the attention of: *a devouring jealousy|He was devoured by hate*

de·vout /dɪˈvaʊt/ *adj* **1** [B; *the*+P] (of people) seriously concerned with religion: *a devout Hindu| The devout were all hurrying to the mosque* **2** [A] full of serious purpose; feeling or felt very deeply: *It is my devout hope that he will not come back* —**~ness** *n* [U]

de·vout·ly /dɪˈvaʊtli/ *adv* **1** in a DEVOUT (1) way **2** (with verbs of hoping, believing, etc.) deeply and sincerely: *I devoutly hope that we shall succeed*

dew /djuː‖duː/ *n* [U] the small drops of water which form on cold surfaces during the night

dew·drop /ˈdjuːdrɒp‖ˈduːdrɑp/ *n* **1** a drop of DEW **2** *BrE humor* a drop of liquid on the end of someone's nose, esp. coming from inside the nose

dew·lap /ˈdjuːlæp‖ˈduː-/ *n* a hanging fold of loose skin under the throat of a cow, dog, etc.

dew·pond /ˈdjuːpɒnd‖ˈduːpɑnd/ *esp. BrE* a small hollow, either natural or man-made, in which DEW collects

dew·y /ˈdjuːi‖ˈduːi/ *adj* [Wa1] wet (as if) with DEW: *She looked at him all dewy-eyed with love* —**dewily** *adv* —**dewiness** *n* [U]

dex·ter·i·ty /dekˈsterɪ̇ti/ *n* [U] *apprec* the quality of ability, cleverness, and skill, esp. in the use of the hands: *the dexterity with which he plays the piano| The lawyer showed great dexterity in preparing his arguments*

dex·ter·ous /ˈdekstərəs/ also **dex·trous** /ˈdekstrəs/— *adj apprec* having or showing DEXTERITY: *She untied the knots with dexterous fingers* —**~ly** *adv*

dex·trose /ˈdekstrəʊz, -strəʊs/ *n* [U] a form of sugar (GLUCOSE) found in many sweet fruits

dho·ti /ˈdəʊti/ *n* a cloth worn, esp. in former times, between the legs and round the lower part of the body by Hindu men

dhow /daʊ/ *n* a ship with one large sail, used esp. by Arab sailors for trade round the coasts —see picture at BOAT

di- /daɪ, dɪ/ *comb. form* [*n*→*n*; *adj*→*adj*] double; into or between 2: *A di*TRANSITIVE *verb has 2 objects* —see also BI-

di·a·be·tes /ˌdaɪəˈbiːtiːz, -tɪ̇s/ *n* [U] a disease of the PANCREAS, in which there is more sugar in the blood than can be used

di·a·bet·ic /ˌdaɪəˈbetɪk/ *adj, n* [Wa5;B;C] (typical of or suitable for) a person suffering from DIABETES

di·a·bol·ic /ˌdaɪəˈbɒlɪk‖-ˈbɑlɪk/ also (*rare*) **diabolical**— *adj* [Wa5] of or coming from the devil

di·a·bol·i·cal /ˌdaɪəˈbɒlɪkəl‖-ˈbɑ-/ also (*rare*) **diabolic**— *adj derog* **1** very cruel and evil: *What a diabolical plan!* **2** *infml* very unpleasant and annoying: *I've been waiting for this train for 45 minutes, and still it hasn't come. It's really diabolical!* —**~ly** *adv* [Wa4]

di·a·crit·ic /ˌdaɪəˈkrɪtɪk/ *n* a mark placed over, under, or through, a letter, to show a sound value different from that of the same letter when unmarked

di·a·crit·i·cal /ˌdaɪəˈkrɪtɪkəl/ also **diacritic**— *adj* [Wa5] concerning or being a DIACRITIC: *diacritical marks*

di·a·dem /ˈdaɪədem/ *n lit* **1** a royal crown of jewels **2** a circle of flowers or leaves worn round the head

di·ae·re·sis, di·e- /daɪˈɪərɪ̇sɪ̇s, -ˈe-‖-ˈe-/ *n* **-ses** /siːz/ a sign (¨) placed over the 2nd of 2 vowels to show that it is pronounced separately from the 1st

di·ag·nose /ˈdaɪəgnəʊz‖-nəʊs/ *v* [T1 (*as*)] to discover the nature of (a disease): *The doctor diagnosed my illness* (*as a rare skin disease*)

di·ag·no·sis /ˌdaɪəgˈnəʊsɪ̇s/ *n* **-ses** /siːz/ [C;U: (*of*)] (a statement which is the result of) diagnosing (DIAGNOSE): *Diagnosis is one of the most important parts of the doctor's work.|The 2 doctors made/gave different diagnoses of my disease* —compare PROGNOSIS (1)

di·ag·nos·tic /ˌdaɪəgˈnɒstɪk◂‖-ˈnɑ-/ *adj* [Wa5] **1** of or relating to diagnosing (DIAGNOSE) **2** [F (*of*)] (of medical signs) helping to DIAGNOSE: *Your appearance and condition are diagnostic of yellow fever*

di·ag·o·nal /daɪˈægənəl/ *n, adj* [Wa5;B;C] **1** (in the direction of) a straight line joining 2 opposite corners of a square, or other 4-sided flat figure: *The 2 diagonals of a square cross in the centre.|Draw a diagonal line to divide the square into 2* —see picture at GEOMETRY **2** (any straight line) which runs in a sloping direction: *a cloth with a diagonal pattern* —**~ly** *adv*

di·a·gram /ˈdaɪəgræm/ *n* a plan or figure drawn to explain an idea; drawing which shows the arrangement of something rather than what it actually looks like —**~matic** /ˌdaɪəgrəˈmætɪk/ *adj* —**~matically** *adv* [Wa4]

di·al[1] /daɪəl/ *n* **1** the front or face of any of various instruments such as a clock showing measurements of time, speed, pressure, etc., by means of a pointer and figures —see also SUNDIAL **2** the plate on the front of a radio set, with a pointer and names or numbers, which is used to find a particular radio station **3** the wheel on a telephone with holes for the fingers, which is moved round when one makes a telephone call —see picture at LIVING ROOM

dial[2] *v* **-ll-** (*AmE* **-l-**) [I0;T1] to make a telephone call; call (a number, person, or place) on a telephone with a DIAL[1] (3): *How do I dial Paris?| To get the police, dial 999.|Put in the money before dialling*

di·a·lect /ˈdaɪəlekt/ *n* [C;U] a variety of a language, spoken in one part of a country, which is different in some words, grammar, or pronunciation from other forms of the same language: *the Yorkshire and Lancashire dialects|a poem written in Scottish dialect* —**~al** /ˌdaɪəˈlektl/ *adj* —**~ally** *adv*

di·a·lec·tic /ˌdaɪəˈlektɪk/ also **di·a·lec·tics** /ˌdaɪəˈlektɪks/— *n* [U] *tech* the art or method of arguing, and of examining the ideas and activities in the mind, according to certain rules of question and answer —**~al** *adj*

di·a·lec·ti·cian /ˌdaɪəlekˈtɪʃən/ *n* a person skilled in DIALECTIC

dial·ling code, *AmE* **area code** /ˈ·· ·/ *n* the group of numbers that one must DIAL[2] to call the country or city in which a person is, before one DIALs[2] the person's own number

dialling tone /ˈ·· ·/ *AmE* **dial tone** /ˈ··/— *n* [*the*+R] the sound made by a telephone receiver to show that one may now DIAL[2] the number that one wants

di·a·logue, *AmE* **-log** /ˈdaɪəlɒg‖-lɔg, -lɑg/ *n* [C;U] **1** (a) written conversation in a book or play: *a* *short dialogue between Hamlet and the grave-digger* **2** (a) conversation which examines differences of opinion, as between leaders: *At last there can be (a) reasonable dialogue between our 2 governments*

di·am·e·ter /daɪ'æmɪ̵tə^r/ *n* **1** (the length of) a straight line going from side to side through the centre of a circle or other curved figure: *Measure the diameter of this circle* —see picture at GEOMETRY **2** a measurement of how many times bigger an object looks, when seen through a microscope or MAGNIFYing glass: *This glass magnifies 20 diameters*

di·a·met·ri·cally /ˌdaɪə'metrɪkli/ *adv* completely; directly (in the phrs. **diametrically opposite, diametrically opposed**): *I am diametrically opposed to* (= I completely diagree with) *his ideas on politics and education*

di·a·mond /'daɪəmənd/ *n* **1** [C;U] a very hard, valuable, precious stone, usually colourless, which is used for cutting things and also in jewellery: *a diamond ring|a diamond mine* **2** [C] an ornament set with one or more of these stones: *Shall I wear my diamonds tonight?* **3** [C] a figure with 4 straight sides of equal length that stands on one of its points **4** [C] a playing card with one or more of these figures printed on it in red: *the 4 of diamonds|I've only one diamond left in my hand* —compare SPADE[3] (1), CLUB[1] (5), HEART (4); see CARDS (USAGE) **5** [C] (in BASEBALL) **a** the area of the field inside the 4 BASES **b** the whole playing field **6 rough diamond** *infml* a very kind person with rough manners

diamond ju·bi·lee /ˌ··· '···/ *n* the 60th yearly return of the date of some important personal event, esp. of becoming a king or queen —compare SILVER JUBILEE, GOLDEN JUBILEE

diamond wed·ding /ˌ··· '··/ also **diamond wedding an·ni·ver·sa·ry** /ˌ··· '·· ··ˌ···/— *n* the 60th yearly return of the date of a wedding —compare SILVER WEDDING, GOLDEN WEDDING

di·a·per /'daɪəpə^r‖'daɪpə^r/ *n* **1** [U] (fine cotton or LINEN cloth with) a pattern of straight lines which cross each other so as to form small DIAMOND (3) shapes **2** [C] *AmE* NAPPY

di·aph·a·nous /daɪ'æfənəs/ *adj* (esp. of cloth) so fine and thin that it can be seen through

di·a·phragm /'daɪəfræm/ *n* **1 a** the muscle that separates the lungs from the stomach **b** the front part of the chest above the waist **2** any thin plate or piece of stretched skin which makes or is moved by sound: *The diaphragm of a telephone is moved by the sound of the voice* **3** the group of small plates lying one above the other which control the amount of light entering a camera —see picture at PHOTOGRAPHIC **4** CAP[1] (7)

di·a·rist /'daɪərɪ̵st/ *n* the writer of a DIARY: *Samuel Pepys was a famous English diarist of the 17th century*

di·ar·rhoe·a, -rhe·a /ˌdaɪə'rɪə/ *n* [U] the type of illness in which the bowels are emptied too often and in too liquid a form

di·a·ry /'daɪəri/ *n* **1** (a book containing) a daily record of the events in a person's life: *Mary keeps* (= writes) *a diary.|Have you been reading my diary again?* **2** a book with marked separate spaces for each day of the year, in which one may write down things to be done in the future: *I'll look in my diary to see if I'm free next Wednesday*

Di·as·po·ra /daɪ'æspərə/ also **Dispersion**— *n* [*the*+R] **1** the scattering of the Jews in various countries outside Palestine, after they were sent out of Babylon **2** (the Jews living in) those countries, then and today: *the people|the countries of the Diaspora*

di·a·tom /'daɪətɒm‖-tɑm/ *n* any of several types of very small plants that live in water

di·a·ton·ic scale /ˌdaɪətɒnɪk 'skeɪl‖-tɑ-/ *n* [*the*+R;(C)] (in music) a set (SCALE) of 8 musical notes using a fixed pattern of spaces (INTERVALs) between the notes

di·a·tribe /'daɪətraɪb/ *n* [(*against*)] *fml* a long violent attack in speech or writing

dib·ble[1] /'dɪbəl/ also **dib·ber** /'dɪbə^r/— *n* a small pointed tool which is used to make holes in the earth for small plants

dibble[2] *v* **1** [T1 (*in, into*)] to plant (plants) with a DIBBLE **2** [IØ;T1] to make holes in (the earth) with a DIBBLE

dice[1] /daɪs/ *n* **dice 1** [Wn3] a small 6-sided block of wood, bone, plastic, etc., with a different number of spots from 1–6 on the various sides, used in games of chance: *throw the dice|a pair of dice|A dice|One of the dice has rolled under the table.|*(fig.) *Cut the meat into small dice* **2** [U] any game of chance which is played with these: *to play dice* **3 no dice** *infml, esp. AmE* no use

USAGE The old singular form **die** is not used now in *BrE* except in the old saying **The die is cast** = The decision has been made and cannot now be changed.

dice[2] *v* **1** [IØ (*for, with*)] to play DICE[1] (2) (with someone, for money, possessions, etc.): *spend his time drinking and dicing|They were dicing for drinks* **2** [X9 (*into, out of*) *no pass.*] to put, bring, etc., into or out of a state or the possession of something by playing DICE[1] (2): *He diced himself out of a large fortune* **3** [T1] to cut (food) into small square pieces: *The meat should be finely diced* **4 dice with death** to take a great risk

dice a·way *v adv* [T1] **1** to lose (money or possessions) by playing DICE[1] (2): *He diced away all his money* **2** to fill (time) by playing DICE[1] (2)

dice for *v prep* [D1,6a (**who, which**)] to play DICE[1] (2) with (someone) for: *I'll dice you for it.|He diced me for which of us should marry the girl* —compare TOSS FOR

dic·ey /'daɪsi/ *adj* [Wa1] *infml* risky and uncertain

di·chot·o·my /daɪ'kɒtəmi‖-'kɑ-/ *n* [(*between*)] a division into 2 parts or groups, esp. 2 that are opposite in nature or cannot both be real or true

dick /'dɪk/ *n taboo sl* PENIS

dick·ens /'dɪkɪ̵nz/ *n* [*the*+R] *infml* (used for giving force to an expression): *What|Who|Where the dickens is that?* —compare DEUCE (3), DEVIL[1] (6)

USAGE **Who the dickens?** etc. is more polite than **Who the devil?**

dick·er /'dɪkə^r/ *v* [IØ (*for, with*)] *infml* to argue about the price (with someone, for something one wants to buy); HAGGLE

dick·y[1], **-ey, -ie** /'dɪki/ *n* **1** a small piece of cloth worn to fill in the open neck of a coat; false shirt-front **2** *esp. BrE* a small third seat at the back of an old-fashioned 2-seat car **3** DICKYBIRD (1)

dicky[2] *adj* [Wa1] *infml BrE* weak; likely to break or go wrong: *My father has a dicky heart.|Be careful up there! The ladder's a bit dicky*

dick·y·bird /'dɪkibɜːd‖-ɜrd/ *n esp. BrE* **1** also **dicky**— (*used esp. by or to children*) any small bird **2 not say a dickybird** *infml* to remain silent

Dic·ta·phone /'dɪktəfəʊn/ *n tdmk* an office machine into which one can DICTATE[1] (1)

dic·tate[1] /dɪk'teɪt‖'dɪkteɪt/ *v* **1** [IØ;T1 (*to*)] to say (words) for someone else to write down: *He can't write but he can dictate.|She dictated a letter to her secretary* **2** [T1 (*to*)] to state (demands, conditions, etc.) with the power to enforce: *We're now in a position to dictate our own demands (to our employers)*

dic·tate[2] /'dɪkteɪt/ *n* [(*of*) *usu. pl.*] an order which should be obeyed, esp. one that comes from within ourselves: *follow/obey the dictates of your own conscience*

dictate to *v prep* [T1 *often pass.*;D6: *usu. neg.*] to give orders to: *I refuse to be dictated to!*

dic·ta·tion /dɪk'teɪʃən/ *n* **1** [U] **a** the act of dictating (DICTATE[1] (1)) **b** the act of writing down what is DICTATED[1] (1) **2** [C] something DICTATED[1] (1) to test one's ability to hear and write a foreign language correctly: *The teacher gave us 2 French dictations today*

dic·ta·tor /dɪk'teɪtəʳ‖'dɪkteɪtər/ *n derog* a ruler who has complete power over a country, esp. if he has gained the power by force

dic·ta·to·ri·al /ˌdɪktə'tɔːrɪəl‖-'tor-/ *adj derog* **1** [Wa5] (of people or behaviour) (typical) of a DICTATOR: *a dictatorial ruler|dictatorial power* **2** like (that of) a DICTATOR: *dictatorial manners|Don't be so dictatorial!* —**~ly** *adv*

dic·ta·tor·ship /dɪk'teɪtəʃɪp‖-'teɪtər-/ *n derog* **1** [C; U] **a** the position or power of a DICTATOR; government by a DICTATOR **b** the period during which a DICTATOR rules a country **2** [C] a country ruled by a DICTATOR

dic·tion /'dɪkʃən/ *n* [U] **1** the choice of words and phrases **2** the way in which a person pronounces words: *Actors need training in diction* —compare ENUNCIATION (1) **3 poetic diction** the use of special words and phrases in poetry which are not used in PROSE or speech

dic·tion·a·ry /'dɪkʃənəri‖-neri/ *n* **1** a book that gives a list of words in alphabetical order, with their pronunciations and meanings: *This book is a dictionary* **2** a book like this that gives, for each word, one in another language with the same meaning: *a German-English dictionary* **3** a book like this that deals with words and phrases concerning a special subject: *a science dictionary|a dictionary of place names*

dic·tum /'dɪktəm/ *n* **-ta** /-tə/ *or* **-tums** **1** a formal statement of opinion, made (as if) with full knowledge; wise saying **2** *law* an opinion expressed by a judge in court —compare RULING[1]

did /dɪd/ [Wv2] *past t. of* DO

di·dac·tic /daɪ'dæktɪk/ *adj* **1** [Wa5] (of speech or writing) meant to teach, esp. to teach a moral lesson **2** *derog* (typical of a person) too eager to teach —**~ally** *adv* [Wa4]

did·dle /'dɪdl/ *v* [T1 (*out of*)] *infml* to get something from (someone) by dishonest means; cheat

did·n't /'dɪdnt/ [Wv2] *contr. of* did not —see CONTR. (USAGE)

didst /dɪdst/ [Wv2] **thou didst** *old use or bibl* (when talking to one person) you did

die[1] /daɪ/ *v* **died,** *pres. p.* **dying** /'daɪ-ɪŋ/ **1** [I∅; L1,7,9;T1] (of creatures and plants) to stop living: *He'll die if he doesn't eat.|She's very ill and I'm afraid she's dying.|He died happy.|She died a rich woman.|die for one's country|"What did he die of?" "He died of a fever/of thirst/in an accident/by drowning/from a wound"* **2** [I∅] to cease; to end gradually: *My love for you will never die.|The day is dying in the west* **3** [I∅] (of knowledge, ideas, etc.) to become lost and forgotten: *His secret died with him, for he never told anyone* **4 be dying for/to** *infml* to have a great wish for/to: *I'm dying for a cigarette.|We're dying to hear what happened* **5 die by one's own hand** to kill oneself **6 die hard** (of old beliefs, customs, etc.) to take a long time to disappear **7 die in harness** to die while still working at one's job **8 die in one's bed** to die quietly at home of old age or illness **9 die with one's boots on** to die while still active or while fighting **10 dying wish** a wish made just as one is dying **11 to one's dying day** as long as one lives —see DEAD (USAGE)

die[2] *n* **1** a metal block used for pressing or cutting metal, plastic, etc., into shape **2** an instrument used for making a screw (THREAD) on a BOLT **3** *old or AmE sing. of* DICE[1] (1)

die a·way *v adv* [I∅] (esp. of sound, wind, light) to fade and become less and less and cease

die back *v adv* [I∅] (of a plant) to die but remain alive in the roots

die-cast·ing /'· ˌ··/ *n* [C;U] the method or result of making metal objects by forcing (not pouring) the liquid metal under pressure into a hollow container (MOULD): *These engine parts are die-castings*

die down *v adv* [I∅] **1** to become less strong or violent: *The fire is dying down. Please get more coal.|It took a long time for the excitement to die down* **2** (of a plant) DIE BACK

die·hard /'daɪhɑːd‖-ɑrd/ *n* a person who opposes change and refuses to take up new ideas even when they are good: *a diehard politician|It's no good asking Father to join the union; he's a real diehard*

die off *v adv* [I∅] (of a group of living things) to die one by one: *The deer in the forest are all dying off from disease*

die out *v adv* [I∅] (of families, races, practices, and ideas) to disappear completely: *The practice of educating the eldest son to be a priest is dying out*

di·e·re·sis /ˌdaɪ'ɪərɪ̈sɪ̈s, -'e-‖-'e-/ *n* **-ses** /siːz/ DIAERESIS

die·sel en·gine /'diːzəl ˌendʒɪ̈n/ also **diesel**— *n* a type of oil-burning engine in which hot air sets fire to heavy oil, often used for buses and trains —compare PETROL ENGINE

diesel oil /'·· ·/ also **diesel fu·el** /'·· ˌ··/— *n* [U] heavy oil used in DIESEL ENGINEs

di·et[1] /'daɪət/ *n* **1** [C;U] the sort of food and drink usually taken (by a person or group): *Proper diet and exercise are both important for health.|The Irish used to live on a diet of potatoes* **2** [C] a limited list of food and drink that one is allowed, esp. by a doctor: *The doctor ordered him a diet without sugar* **3 (be/go) on a diet** (to be, start) living on a limited list of food and drink: *I mustn't have chocolate—I'm on a diet*

diet[2] *v* [I∅;T1] to (cause to) live on a DIET[1] (2)

diet[3] *n* **1** [C] a meeting to talk about political or church matters **2** [(*the*) C;R] (*often cap.*) a name given to parliament in certain countries

di·e·ta·ry /'daɪətəri‖-teri/ *adj* [Wa5] of or concerning DIET[1] (1)

di·e·tet·ic /ˌdaɪə'tetɪk/ *adj* [Wa5;A] concerned with DIETETICS: *dietetic studies*

di·e·tet·ics /ˌdaɪə'tetɪks/ *n* [U] the science of DIET[1] (1) —see -ICS (USAGE)

di·e·ti·cian, -tian /ˌdaɪə'tɪʃən/ *n* a person trained in DIETETICS

diet sheet /'·· ·/ *n* a list of the food and drink a sick person is allowed to eat

dif·fer /'dɪfəʳ/ *v* **1** [I∅ (*from*) (*in, as to*)] to be unlike: *Nylon and silk differ.|Nylon differs from silk in/as to origin and cost* **2** [I∅ (*with*) (*about, on, over*)] (of people) to have an unlike or opposite opinion; disagree: *My husband and I often differ, but we're quite happy together.|He differed with his brother about/on/over a political question* **3 agree to differ** to stop trying to persuade each other **4 I beg to differ** *fml* I disagree with you

dif·fe·rence /'dɪfərəns/ *n* **1** [C (*between*)] a way of being unlike: *There are several important differences between cricket and football. One difference is . . .* **2** [S;U: (*between, in, of, to*)] (an) amount of unlikeness: *The difference between 5 and 11 is 6.|"What's the difference in temperature between the day and the* *night?" "There's a difference of 30 degrees."|Flowers make no/a/a lot of/some/all the difference to a room.|It doesn't make much/any/the least difference to me what you do/whether you go or stay* **3** [C *often pl.*] a slight disagreement **4 split the difference** to agree on an amount halfway between: *You say £10 and I say £12, so let's split the difference and call it £11*

dif·fe·rent /ˈdɪfərənt/ *adj* **1** [B (*from, than, to*)] unlike; not of the same kind: *Mary and Jane are quite different.|Mary is different from/than/to Jane.|She is different than Jane is.|He's a different man from what he was 10 years ago* **2** [A (*from, than, to*)] separate; other: *John and Peter belong to different age-groups.|This is a different car from the one I drove yesterday* **3** [A] (with *pl.*) various; several; that are not the same: *We make this dress in (3/a lot of) different colours* **4** [B] *infml* unusual; special: *Buy Sloppo, the soap that is different!* (advertisement) —**~ly** *adv*

USAGE 1 **different(ly) from** is correct in both *BrE* and *AmE*. Some *BrE* speakers also say **different to**: *He is different to me,* and some *AmE* speakers say **different than**: *He is different than I am*; but teachers and examiners do not really like either of these. **indifferent** can only be followed by **to**: *I am indifferent to this question.* 2 **different** and **various** both mean "not the same" but **various** means "several not the same", so it needs a plural noun: **various** *reasons/people* **Different** can also be used with a singular or [U] noun, and it then means that the noun is compared with something else that may or may not be mentioned: *You look* **different** *(from before) with your hair cut.|They each wanted to see a* **different** *film (from each other.)|The weather is* **different in India**.

dif·fe·ren·tial¹ /ˌdɪfəˈrenʃəl◂/ *adj* depending on a DIFFERENCE (1,2): *They pay differential rents according to their income*

differential² *n* **1** the amount of difference between things, esp. difference in wages between workers at different levels in the same industry **2** DIFFERENTIAL GEAR

differential cal·cu·lus /ˌ···· ˈ···/ *n* [*the*+R] (in MATHEMATICS) a way of measuring the speed at which an object is moving at a particular moment; one of the 2 ways of making calculations about quantities which are continually changing —compare INTEGRAL CALCULUS

differential gear /ˌ···· ˈ·/ *n* an arrangement of GEAR*s* between the back wheels of a car that allows one back wheel to turn faster than the other when the car goes round a corner —see picture at CAR

dif·fe·ren·ti·ate /ˌdɪfəˈrenʃieɪt/ *v* **1** [T1 (*from*);IØ (*between*)] to see or express a difference (between): *I can't differentiate (between) these 2 flowers.|Can you differentiate this kind of rose from the others?* **2** [T1 (*from*)] (of a quality) to make different by its presence: *What is it that differentiates these 2 substances?|Its strange way of making a nest differentiates this bird from others* —**-ation** /ˌdɪfərenʃiˈeɪʃən/ *n* [C;U]

dif·fi·cult /ˈdɪfɪkəlt/ *adj* **1** [B,B3] not easy; hard to do, make, understand, etc.: *English is difficult.|a difficult language to learn|It was very difficult to put the tent up because of the wind* **2** [B] (of people) unfriendly and always quarrelling; not easily pleased: *a difficult child|Don't be so difficult!*

dif·fi·cul·ty /ˈdɪfɪkəlti/ *n* **1** [U (*in*)] the quality of being difficult; trouble: *She had/found great difficulty in understanding him.|He spoke with difficulty.|He did it without much/any difficulty* **2** [C *often pl.*] something difficult; a trouble: *I'm in a bit of a difficulty over paying my rent.|He's having* FINANCIAL (= money) *difficulties.|Jones keeps raising/making difficulties over my new plan*

dif·fi·dent /ˈdɪfɪ̵dənt/ *adj* [(*about*)] having or showing a lack of belief in one's own powers, and therefore unwilling to speak or act with force: *He is diffident about expressing his opinions* —opposite **confident** —**~ly** *adv* —**-dence** /dəns/ *n* [U]

dif·fract /dɪˈfrækt/ *v* [T1] to break up (a beam of light) so as to form a number of dark and light or coloured bands (the SPECTRUM) —**~ion** /dɪˈfrækʃən/ *n* [U]

dif·fuse¹ /dɪˈfjuːs/ *adj* **1** DIFFUSEd²: *Direct light is better for reading than diffuse light* **2** *derog* (of speaking or writing, or of a speaker or writer) using too many words and not keeping to the point —**~ly** *adv* —**~ness** *n*

dif·fuse² /dɪˈfjuːz/ *v* [IØ;T1] to (cause to) spread out freely in all directions: *to diffuse knowledge/a smell/a feeling of happiness|The drop of blood diffused in the bowl of water, which became pink*

dif·fu·sion /dɪˈfjuːʒən/ *n* [(*the*) U (*of*)] the state or action of being DIFFUSEd²: *Clouds cause (the) diffusion of light from the sun*

dig¹ /dɪg/ *v* **dug** /dʌg/; *pres. p.* **digging** **1** [IØ;T1] to break up and move (earth): *The dog has been digging in that corner for an hour.|We must dig the vegetable garden* **2** [IØ;T1] to make (a hole) by taking away the earth: *We shall have to dig under the river/through the mountain/into the hill to lay this pipe.|The prisoners escaped by digging an underground passage* **3** [T1] to uncover (esp. root vegetables) by taking away the earth **4** [T1] *sl* to like or understand: *Do you dig modern music?* **5 dig someone in the ribs** to touch someone with one's elbow, as to share a joke —see also DIG AT, DIG FOR, DIG IN, DIG INTO, DIG OUT, DIG OVER, DIG UP

dig² *n infml* **1** a quick push: *John's falling asleep, just give him a dig!|*(fig.) *That last remark was a dig at me* (= addressed to me, to annoy me) **2 a** an ancient place, town, or building being uncovered and studied by ARCHAEOLOGIST*s* (= students of ancient times) **b** the digging up of a place like this: *go on a dig*

dig at *v prep* [T1] to speak to (someone) in an unpleasant way: *Stop digging at me!*

di·gest¹ /ˈdaɪdʒest/ *n* a short account (of a piece of writing) which gives the most important facts: *a digest of Roman laws*

di·gest² /daɪˈdʒest, dɪ̵-/ *v* **1** [IØ;T1] to (cause to) be changed into a form that the body can use: *Cheese doesn't digest easily.|Mary can't digest fat.|* (fig.) *His rudeness is hard to digest* **2** [T1] to think over and arrange in the mind —**~ible** *adj* —**~ibility** /daɪˌdʒestəˈbɪlɪ̵ti, dɪ̵-/ *n*

di·ges·tion /daɪˈdʒestʃən, dɪ̵-/ *n* [C;U] (a) power of DIGESTing² (1) food: *have a good/weak digestion|Cheese is bad for their digestions.|Digestion is more difficult for old people* —compare INDIGESTION

di·ges·tive¹ /daɪˈdʒestɪv, dɪ̵-/ *adj* [A] connected with or helping in the DIGESTing² (1) of food

digestive² *n tdmk* a type of plain usu. unsweetened BISCUIT

digestive sys·tem /·ˈ·· ˌ··/ *n* the whole length of the pipe (ALIMENTARY CANAL) down which food travels through the body while it is being DIGESTed² (1)

See next page for picture

dig for *v prep* [T1] to look for by digging: *dig for gold*

dig·ger /ˈdɪgəʳ/ *n* **1** a person or machine that DIGs¹ (1,2,3) **2** *AustrE infml* an Australian soldier

dig·ging /ˈdɪgɪŋ/ *n* **1** [U] the action of DIGging¹ (1,2,3) **2** [C *often pl.*] a place where people dig for metal, esp. gold

dig·gings /ˈdɪgɪŋz/ *n* [P] *now rare* DIGS

dig in *v adv* **1** [IØ;T1] to dig a protective place for

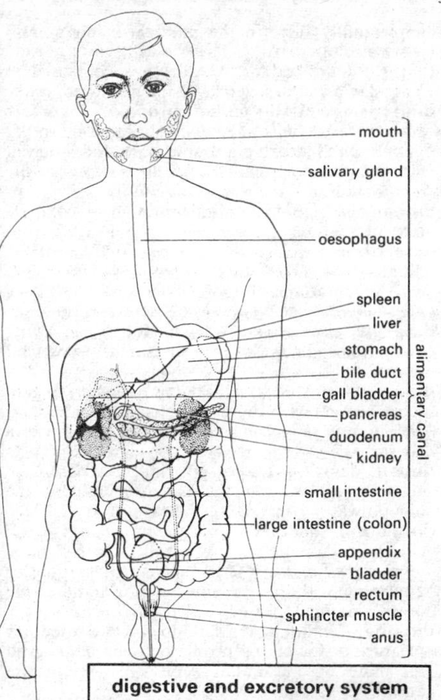

digestive and excretory system

(oneself): *The soldiers were ordered to dig (themselves) in* **2** [T1] *infml* to make certain of (one's) position; get (oneself) firmly settled: *I had plenty of time to dig myself in when I started the new job. I'm well dug in now* **3** [T1] to mix (something) into the soil by digging **4** [I∅] also **dive in**— *infml* to help oneself to food and start eating: *Here's your breakfast, so dig in!* **5 dig one's heels in** *infml* to refuse to do something

dig in·to *v prep* **1** [T1] *infml* to start eating (something) **2** [T1] to examine thoroughly: *The police are digging into this case* **3** [D1] to push (something) into: *dig a fork into the meat* **4** [D1] to make certain of (one's) position in: *I had plenty of time to dig myself into the new job*

di·git /ˈdɪdʒ$\frac{1}{2}$t/ *n* **1** any of the numbers from 0 to 9: *The number 1978 contains 4 digits* **2** a finger or toe

di·gi·tal /ˈdɪdʒ$\frac{1}{2}$tl/ *adj* [Wa5;A] **1** relating to calculation with DIGITs (1) **2** relating to the fingers and toes

digital com·put·er /ˌ··· ·ˈ··/ *n* a COMPUTER (=electrical calculating machine) that performs operations by counting rather than by measuring —compare ANALOGUE COMPUTER

dig·ni·fied /ˈdɪgn$\frac{1}{2}$faɪd/ *adj* (of people and behaviour) having or showing DIGNITY (1,2): *a dignified manner|a dignified old man* —opposite **undignified**

dig·ni·fy /ˈdɪgn$\frac{1}{2}$faɪ/ *v* [T1 (*by, with*)] to give DIGNITY (1,2) to: *Don't try to dignify those few hairs on your face by calling them a beard*

dig·ni·ta·ry /ˈdɪgn$\frac{1}{2}$təri‖-teri/ *n* a person holding a high position, esp. in the church

dig·ni·ty /ˈdɪgn$\frac{1}{2}$ti/ *n* **1** [U] true worth and nobleness of character **2** [U] calm, formal, and grand behaviour **3** [C] a high position, rank, office, or title **4 beneath one's dignity** below one's standard of moral and social behaviour **5 stand on one's dignity** to demand to be treated with proper respect

dig out *v adv* **1** [T1 (*of*)] to find by searching: *I dug out these old trousers to give to the boy.*|(fig.) *dig the truth out (of him)* **2** [T1 (*of*)] to get out by digging; free from being buried **3** [I∅ (*for*)] *AmE* (esp. of animals) to move quickly: *The fox dug out for the forest* **4** [I∅] *esp. CanE* to free oneself from being buried in snow: *3 towns in northern Canada are digging out this morning*

dig o·ver *v adv* [T1] *infml* to reconsider: *I'd like some time to dig over the questions raised in today's meeting*

di·graph /ˈdaɪgrɑːf‖-græf/ *n* a pair of letters that represent one sound: *"ea" in "head" and "ph" in "phrase" are digraphs*

di·gress /daɪˈgres/ *v* [I∅ (*from*)] (of a writer or speaker) to turn aside or wander away (from the subject): *I'll tell you a funny story, if I may digress (from my subject) for a moment*

di·gres·sion /daɪˈgreʃən/ *n* [C;U] (a case of) DIGRESSing

digs /dɪgz/ *n* [P] *BrE infml* lodgings: *When his family left London, Tom moved into digs*

dig up *v adv* [T1] **1** to find or take out of the ground, by digging: *Father dug up an old coin in the garden.*|(fig.) *The newspapers have dug up that unpleasant old story* **2** *infml* to collect by searching: *Between us we should be able to dig up enough money for your ticket*

dike¹, dyke /daɪk/ *n* **1** a thick bank or wall built to control water and prevent flooding: *Hurry! The dike has broken* —compare DAM² **2** a narrow passage dug to carry water away **3** *ScotE* a wall, esp. round a field

dike², dyke *v* **1** [I∅] to work at making a DIKE¹ **2** [T1] to protect (land) with a DIKE¹

→**dike³, dyke** *n sl* a woman who is sexually attracted to other women; LESBIAN

di·lap·i·dat·ed /d$\frac{1}{2}$ˈlæp$\frac{1}{2}$deɪt$\frac{1}{2}$d/ *adj* (of things) broken and old; falling to pieces: *a dilapidated car|castle*

di·lap·i·da·tion /d$\frac{1}{2}$ˌlæp$\frac{1}{2}$ˈdeɪʃən/ *n* [U] the state of being DILAPIDATED

di·lap·i·da·tions /d$\frac{1}{2}$ˌlæp$\frac{1}{2}$ˈdeɪʃənz/ *n* [P] *BrE* the money that one must pay for damage done to a furnished house that one has been renting

di·late /daɪˈleɪt/ *v* [I∅;T1] **a** (esp. of parts of the body) to become wider or further open by stretching: *Her eyes dilated with terror* **b** to cause (esp. parts of the body) to become wider or further open: *The cat dilated its eyes* —**-lation** /daɪˈleɪʃən/ *n* [U]

dilate on also **dilate up·on**— *v prep* [T1] *fml* to speak or write at length on (a subject): *She kept dilating on her son's cleverness* —see also EXPATIATE UPON

dil·a·to·ry /ˈdɪlətəri‖-tori/ *adj* (of people and behaviour) slow in action; causing delay: *It was rather dilatory of him not to answer such an important letter*

→**dil·do** /ˈdɪldəʊ/ *n* -os an object shaped like the male sex organ (PENIS) that can placed inside the female sex organ (VAGINA) for sexual pleasure

di·lem·ma /d$\frac{1}{2}$ˈlemə, daɪ-/ *n* a difficult choice to be made between 2 courses of action, both undesirable: *She was in a dilemma as to whether to marry Paul, who was poor, or Charles, who was ugly* —see also **on the** HORN **s of a dilemma**

USAGE Many people feel that **dilemma** should mean a choice between only 2 possibilities: *Jill was in a* **dilemma** *whether to go out with Bill or Joe.* They do not like it to be used, as it often is, where there are more than 2 possibilities: . . . *whether to go out with Bill or Joe or Tom or Peter.*

dil·et·tan·te /ˌdɪl$\frac{1}{2}$ˈtænti‖-ˈtɑnti/ *n, adj* **-tes** *or* **-ti** /ti/ *usu. derog* (typical of) a person who amuses himself with an art or branch of knowledge, but without taking it seriously —compare AMATEUR

dil·i·gence /ˈdɪlǰdʒəns/ *n* **1** [U] the quality of being DILIGENT **2** [C] (in former times) a public carriage: *They crossed the mountains in a diligence*
dil·i·gent /ˈdɪlǰdʒənt/ *adj* (of people and behaviour) hardworking; showing steady effort: *He's a diligent worker and deserves more pay* —**~ly** *adv*
dill /dɪl/ *n* [U] a plant whose seeds are used in medicine and to give a special taste to food
dil·ly·dal·ly /ˈdɪliˌdæli/ *v* [IØ] *infml* to waste time, usu. by being unable to make up one's mind
di·lute[1] /daɪˈluːt/ *v* [T1 (*with*)] to make (a liquid) weaker or thinner (by mixing another liquid with it): *He diluted the paint with oil.|The water will dilute the wine.|*(fig.) *The effect of the speech was diluted by the speaker's nervousness*
dilute[2] /ˌdaɪˈluːt/ *adj* that has been DILUTEd: *a very dilute mixture*
di·lu·tion /daɪˈluːʃən/ *n* **1** [U] the act of diluting (DILUTE) or state of being DILUTEd: *They charged him with unlawful dilution of the beer* **2** [C] something that is DILUTEd
dim[1] /dɪm/ *adj* [Wa1] **1** (of a light) not bright: *The light is too dim for me to see* **2** not easy to see: *the dim shape of a large animal in the mist* **3** (of the eyes) not able to see clearly: *The old man's eyesight was dim* **4** *infml* (of people) stupid **5 take a dim view of** *infml* to think badly of; not to approve of —**~ly** *adv* —**~ness** *n* [U]
dim[2] *v* **-mm-** [IØ;T1] to (cause to) become DIM[1] (1,2,3): *The lights in the theatre began to dim.|The smoke dimmed his eyes*
dime /daɪm/ *n* **1** a coin of the US and Canada, worth 10 cents or 1/10 of a dollar **2 a dime a dozen** *infml AmE* TEN **a penny**
di·men·sion /daɪˈmenʃən, dǰ-/ *n* **1** a measurement in any one direction: *A line has one dimension and a square has 2 dimensions* **2** (in ALGEBRA) one of the unknown quantities in a set of numbers to be multiplied: *a^3, a^2b and abc are expressions of 3 dimensions*
-di·men·sion·al /daɪˈmenʃənəl, dǰ-/ *comb. form* having the stated number of DIMENSIONs: *A 3-dimensional* (*abbrev.* **3D**) *cinema film is one that seems to have depth as well as breadth and height*
di·men·sions /daɪˈmenʃənz, dǰ-/ *n* [P9 (esp. *of*)] size: *a box of large dimensions|The dimensions of this difficulty have only recently been recognized*
di·min·ish /dǰˈmɪnɪʃ/ *v* [IØ;T1] to (cause to) become or seem smaller: *His illness diminished his strength*
di·min·u·en·do /dǰˌmɪnjʊˈendəʊ/ *n* **-dos** *It* (in music) a decrease in loudness —opposite **crescendo**
dim·i·nu·tion /ˌdɪmǰˈnjuːʃən‖-ˈnuː-/ *n* [C;U] a case or the state of DIMINISHing or being DIMINISHed: *suffer a diminution in income*
di·min·u·tive[1] /dǰˈmɪnjʊtɪv‖-njə-/ *n* a word formed by adding a DIMINUTIVE SUFFIX: *The word* "DUCKLING" *is a diminutive, formed from the word "duck"*
diminutive[2] *adj* very small, and sometimes also lovable: *The dog is so diminutive that it can be carried in my pocket*
diminutive suf·fix /·ˌ··· ˈ··/ *n* an ending which is added to a word to express smallness: -LING *is a diminutive suffix, and a* DUCKLING *is a small duck*
dim·i·ty /ˈdɪmǰti/ *n* [U] strong cotton material with a raised pattern, used for bed covers and curtains
dim·ple /ˈdɪmpəl/ *n apprec* a little hollow place on the skin, esp. one formed in the cheek when a person smiles —see picture at HUMAN[2]
dim·wit /ˈdɪmwɪt/ *n* [C;(*you*) N] *infml* a stupid person —**dim-witted** /ˌ· ˈ··◂/ *adj*
din[1] /dɪn/ *n derog* **1** a loud, continuous, confused, and unpleasant noise **2 kick up a din** to make a noise of this kind
din[2] *v* **-nn-** [IØ] (of a sound) to be heard loudly and unpleasantly (esp. in the phr. **din in one's ears**) —see also DIN INTO
di·nar /ˈdiːnɑːʳ‖dɪˈnɑr, ˈdiːnɑr/ *n* a coin used in Yugoslavia and in several Muslim countries
dine /daɪn/ *v* **1** [IØ] *fml* to eat dinner: *Don't talk about business while we're dining.|dine with Peter/at Peter's* **2** [T1] to give a dinner party for (often in the phr. **wine and dine**): *When we go to town, my brother wines and dines us splendidly*
dine in *v adv* [IØ] to eat dinner at home —compare DINE OUT
dine off *v prep* [T1 *usu. not pass.*] **1** to eat for dinner (food): *They dined off bread and cheese* **2** to eat dinner at the cost of (a person): *He's been dining off his brother for weeks* **3** DINE OUT ON
dine out also **eat out**— *v adv* [IØ] to eat dinner away from home, esp. in a restaurant —compare DINE IN
dine out on *v adv prep* [T1 *usu. not pass.*] to gain social success with (news or a story): *Ever since his adventure in the mountains, he's been dining out on the story*
din·er /ˈdaɪnəʳ/ *n* **1** a person who DINEs **2** *AmE* a small restaurant beside the road, often in the shape of a railway carriage **3** *AmE* DINING CAR
ding·dong /ˌdɪŋˈdɒŋ◂‖ˈdɪŋdɔŋ/ *adv, adj, n* **1** [A;U] (like) the noise made by a bell: *The bells rang dingdong all morning* **2** [A] *infml* ((of) a fight or argument) with first one side winning and then the other winning, repeatedly: *a dingdong battle*
din·ghy /ˈdɪŋgi/ *n* a small open boat, used for pleasure or for taking people between a ship and the shore —see also RUBBER DINGHY —see picture at SAIL[2]
din·gle /ˈdɪŋgəl/ *n* a small wooded valley
din·go /ˈdɪŋgəʊ/ *n* **-goes** a type of Australian wild dog
din·gy /ˈdɪndʒi/ *adj* [Wa2] (of things and places) dirty and faded: *a dingy street|The curtains are getting rather dingy* —**dingily** *adv*: *She was dingily dressed in dull brown* —**dinginess** *n* [U]
din·ing car /ˈ·· ·/ also **restaurant car**— *n* a carriage on a train where meals are served
dining room /ˈ·· ·/ *n* a room where meals are served and/or eaten
dining ta·ble /ˈ·· ˌ··/ *n* a table esp. for having meals on: *write letters on the dining table* —compare DINNER TABLE
din in·to *v prep* [D1] *infml* to repeat (something) forcefully over and over again to (someone): *I ought to remember that rule; I've had it dinned into me often enough by our old teacher*
dink /dɪŋk/ *n* a softly-hit tennis shot, that just goes over the net
din·kum /ˈdɪŋkəm/ *adj infml AustrE* honest; real; GENUINE (esp. in the phr. **fair dinkum**)
din·ky /ˈdɪŋki/ *adj* [Wa1] **1** *BrE* (*used esp. by women*) small and charming: *Look at that dinky little spoon!* **2** *AmE derog* small and unimportant: *This room is too dinky for me*
din·ner /ˈdɪnəʳ/ *n* **1** [C;(*the*) R;U] the main meal of the day, eaten either at midday or in the evening: *I'm busy cooking* (*the*) *dinner.|It's dinner time/time for dinner.|I've cooked you a nice hot dinner.|He ate very little dinner.|Dinner's ready!|We're having fish for* (*our*) *dinner.|What time do you have/*(*AmE*) *eat dinner?|Don't telephone John while he's at/having dinner.|The children have to pay for their school dinners* (=dinner provided by the school) **2** [C] a formal occasion in the evening when this meal is eaten: *The firm are giving/holding an important dinner*
USAGE If **dinner** is at midday, the evening meal is called **tea** or **supper.** If **dinner** is in the evening, the midday meal is called **lunch**

dinner bell /ˈ·· ·/ *n* a bell rung to let people know that dinner is ready

dinner jack·et /ˈ·· ˌ··/ also (*esp. AmE*) **tuxedo**— *n* **1** a man's black coat for rather formal evening occasions **2** a complete suit of clothes including this coat, black trousers, a white shirt and black BOW tie —compare TAILS

dinner ser·vice /ˈ·· ˌ··/ also **dinner set** /ˈ·· ·/— *n* a complete set of plates and dishes for dinner

dinner ta·ble /ˈ·· ˌ··/ *n* a table on which dinner is being served: *Don't talk about these nasty subjects at the dinner table* (= while we're having dinner) —compare DINING TABLE

di·no·saur /ˈdaɪnəsɔːʳ/ *n* any of several types of very large long-tailed creatures (REPTILE*s*) that lived in very ancient times and no longer exist

dint /dɪnt/ *n* **1** *esp. poet* a hollow place on the surface of something hard, made by a blow; DENT **2 by dint of** by means of: *He reached the top by dint of great effort*

di·o·cese /ˈdaɪəsɪ̵̈s/ *n* (in the Christian religion) the area under the government of a BISHOP (=priest of very high rank) —**-cesan** /daɪˈɒsɪ̵̈sən‖-ˈɑ-/ *adj* [Wa5;A]

di·ox·ide /daɪˈɒksaɪd‖-ˈɑk-/ *n* a chemical compound containing 2 atoms of oxygen to every one of another (stated) simple substance (ELEMENT)

dip¹ /dɪp/ *v* **-pp-** **1** [T1 (IN, *into*)] to put (something) in/into a liquid for a moment and then take out: *dip one's hand into the water* **2** [T1] to put (an animal) quickly into a chemical liquid that kills insects **3** [T1] to put (a garment) into a liquid (DYE) to change the colour **4** [I0;T1] to (cause to) drop slightly, perhaps just for a moment: *Grain prices dipped yesterday.|The sun dipped below the western sea.|You should dip the car's* HEADLIGHT*s* (=lights at the front) *when you meet another car at night*

dip² *n* **1** [C] *infml* a quick bathe in the sea, a lake, etc. **2** [C] a slope down; slight drop in height: *The road takes a sudden dip just round the corner* **3** [C; U] (a liquid for) DIPping¹ (2) animals: *Give the sheep a dip tomorrow.|a bucket of strong dip* **4** [C] a candle made by DIPping¹ (1) a string (WICK) into melted wax or fat **5** [U] any of several types of thick liquid mixture into which BISCUIT*s* or bits of vegetables can be DIPped¹ (1) before being eaten at parties: *Try some of this sour cream dip*

diph·ther·i·a /dɪfˈθɪərɪə, dɪp-/ *n* [U] a serious infectious disease of the throat which makes breathing difficult

diph·thong /ˈdɪfθɒŋ, ˈdɪp-‖-θɔŋ/ *n* **1 a** a compound vowel made by pronouncing 2 vowels quickly one after the other: *The vowel sound in "my" is a diphthong* **b** the way of writing such a sound in PHONETICS: *The vowel sound in "my" is written with the diphthong* aɪ **2** DIGRAPH

dip in *v adv* [I0] to take one's share of things offered: *Put the presents in the middle of the room so that everyone can dip in*

dip in·to *v prep* [T1] **1** to read or study for a short time or without much attention; LOOK INTO: *I haven't read that book properly, I've only dipped into it* **2** to put one's hand into (a place) and take something out: *She keeps dipping into the bag of sweets* **3 dip into one's pocket/purse/savings** to spend or provide money **4 dip into the future** to try to see what the future will be like

di·plo·ma /dɪ̵̈ˈpləʊmə/ *n* an official paper showing that a person has successfully finished a course of study or passed an examination

di·plo·ma·cy /dɪ̵̈ˈpləʊməsi/ *n* [U] **1** the art and practice of establishing and continuing relations between nations **2** skill at dealing with people and getting them to agree

dip·lo·mat /ˈdɪpləmæt/ *n* a person employed in DIPLOMACY (1)

dip·lo·mat·ic /ˌdɪpləˈmætɪk◂/ *adj* **1** [Wa5;A] of or related to DIPLOMACY (1): *Nigel joined the diplomatic service* **2** [B] of or related to DIPLOMACY (2): *Try to be diplomatic when you refuse her invitation, so as not to cause bad feeling* —opposite **undiplomatic** **3** [Wa5;A] *tech* **a** of or related to the study of the form of ancient writings **b** copying exactly the form of the original: *a diplomatic* EDITION *of an ancient piece of writing*

dip·lo·mat·i·cally /ˌdɪpləˈmætɪkli/ *adv* **1** [Wa5] in connection with DIPLOMACY (1): *Diplomatically speaking, it would be very dangerous to offend the king just now* **2** showing DIPLOMACY (2): *He told the artist diplomatically that his ugly picture was "unusual"*

diplomatic re·la·tions /ˌ···· ·ˈ··/ *n* [P (*with*)] the connection between 2 countries that keep some of their representatives at an EMBASSY in the other country

di·plo·ma·tist /dɪ̵̈ˈpləʊmətɪ̵̈st/ *n* **1** a person who is skilled in DIPLOMACY (2) **2** *rare* DIPLOMAT

dip·per /ˈdɪpəʳ/ *n* **1** a vessel like a cup with a long handle, used for taking up liquid out of a container **2** a type of European, North American, and Asian bird that feeds on the bottom of streams

Dipper *n* [*the*+R] *esp. AmE* PLOUGH

dip·so·ma·ni·a /ˌdɪpsəˈmeɪnɪə/ *n* [U] an uncontrollable desire for alcoholic drinks

dip·so·ma·ni·ac /ˌdɪpsəˈmeɪniæk/ *n* a person suffering from DIPSOMANIA

dip·stick /ˈdɪpˌstɪk/ *n* a stick used for measuring the depth of liquid in a container, esp. for measuring the amount of oil in a car's engine

dip·switch /ˈdɪpˌswɪtʃ/ *n BrE* an instrument in a car for lowering the beam of the HEADLIGHT*s* so that drivers coming in the opposite direction may see the road clearly

dip·tych /ˈdɪptɪk/ *n tech* a (holy) picture made in 2 parts which fold together like the pages of a book —compare TRIPTYCH

dire /daɪəʳ/ *adj* [Wa1] **1** [B] (of needs and dangers) very great; terrible: *be in dire need of food* **2** [A] causing great fear for the future: *a dire warning*

di·rect¹ /dɪ̵̈ˈrekt, daɪ-/ *v* **1** [T1 (*to*)] to tell (someone) the way (to a place): *"I'm lost. Can you direct me to Times Square?" "I'm sorry, I can't direct you. My friend will direct you there"* **2** [T1] to control and be in charge of (the way something is done): *Who directed that new Italian film?|He directed the building of the new bridge* **3** [T5c;V3] *fml* to order (someone to do something, or that something shall be done): *The policeman directed the crowd to move back.|The general directed that the prisoners should be set free* —see ORDER (USAGE) **4** [T1 (*to*)] to write the address on (a letter) **5** [X9 esp. *to, at*] to turn or aim (attention, remarks, etc.) (in the stated direction): *This warning is directed at you.|Please direct your complaints to the President* **6** [T1] to influence: *Her action was directed by pity* **7** [X9 esp. *towards*] to aim (movement) (in the stated direction): *He directed his eyes heavenward.|We directed our steps towards the house*

direct² *adj* **1** [Wa2;B] straight; going from one point to another without turning aside: *Which is the most direct way to London?|The bomb made a direct hit on the school* **2** [Wa5;B] leading from one point to another without stopping and without anything coming between: *a direct flight from London to Los Angeles|as a direct result of this event* **3** [Wa5;A] (of family relationships) passing in a straight line from parent to child **4** [B] (of people and behaviour) honest and easily understood: *He gave a direct answer to my question.|She's always* *very direct and open in her manner, so I know exactly what she's thinking* **5** [Wa5;A] exact: *He's the direct opposite of his brother* —**~ness** *n* [U]

direct³ *adv* in a straight line; without stopping or turning aside: *The next flight doesn't go direct to Rome, it goes by way of Paris*

direct ac·tion /·,· '··/ *n* [U] *euph* the use for political purposes of action which may be against the law, such as a STRIKE (=refusal to work)

direct cur·rent /·,· '··/ *n* [U] a flow of electricity that moves in one direction only —compare ALTERNATING CURRENT

di·rec·tion /dɨ'rekʃən, daɪ-/ *n* **1** [U] the action of DIRECTING¹; control: *The singing group is under the direction of Mr. Blair* **2** [C] the course on which a person or thing moves or is aimed: *He drove away in the direction of London.|Shots were fired about in all directions* **3** [C] the point towards which a person or thing faces: *What direction does this house face?* **4 sense of direction** knowledge as to which way one is facing or moving

di·rec·tion·al /dɨ'rekʃənl‖daɪ-/ *adj* [Wa5] connected with direction in space; suitable for finding out where radio signals come from (esp. in the phr. **directional aerial**)

direction find·er /·'·· ,··/ *n* a receiver for radio waves (AERIAL) that shows where radio signals are coming from

di·rec·tions /dɨ'rekʃənz, daɪ-/ *n* [P,P6b,P9 esp. *as to*] instructions on what to do or how to do something: *Follow the directions on the medicine bottle.|His directions (as to) how to get to the farm were quite clear*

di·rec·tive¹ /dɨ'rektɪv, daɪ-/ *adj* [Wa5;A] meant to instruct and direct

directive² *n* an official order

di·rect·ly¹ /dɨ'rektli, daɪ-/ *adv* **1** in a direct manner: *He lives directly opposite the church.|She answered me very directly and openly* —opposite **indirectly** **2** at once: *Answer me directly!* **3** *infml* soon; almost at once: *He should be here directly if you don't mind waiting*

directly² *conj infml* as soon as: *I came directly I got your message*

direct ob·ject /·,· '··/ *n* the noun or noun phrase needed to complete the meaning of a statement using a TRANSITIVE verb: *In "I saw Mary", "Mary" is the direct object; in "I gave Mary the money", "the money" is the direct object*

di·rec·tor /dɨ'rektəʳ, daɪ-/ *n* **1** a person who directs an organization **2** a member of the board of directors who run a company **3** a person who directs a play or esp. a film, instructing the actors, cameramen, etc. —see picture at THEATRE

di·rec·tor·ate /dɨ'rektərɨt, daɪ-/ *n* **1** [GC] a board of directors: *The directorate is/are very worried about the drop in sales* **2** [C] DIRECTORSHIP

Director of Pub·lic Pros·e·cu·tions /·,··· ,·· ··'··/ *n* [*the*+R] (in Britain) the government lawyer who decides in certain doubtful cases whether a person shall be tried by a court of law

di·rec·tor·ship /dɨ'rektəʃɪp, daɪ-‖-ər-/ *n* (the period of holding) the position of a DIRECTOR (1,2)

di·rec·to·ry /daɪ'rektəri, dɨ-/ *n* a book or list of names, facts, etc., usu. arranged in alphabetical order: *The telephone directory gives people's names, addresses, and telephone numbers*

direct speech /·,· '·/ *n* [U] *tech* the actual words of a speaker, repeated without changes in the grammar: *In "He said he was hungry", his actual words in direct speech were "I'm hungry"* —opposite **indirect/reported speech**

direct tax /·,· '··/ *n* [C;U] (a) tax such as income tax which is actually collected from the person who pays it, rather than on the sale of goods or services (as with VAT) —opposite **indirect tax** —**~ation** *n* [U]

dire·ful /'daɪəfəl‖-ər-/ *adj lit* threatening or producing terrible effects —**~ly** *adv*

dirge /dɜːdʒ‖dɜrdʒ/ *n* **1** a slow sad song sung over a dead person **2** *derog* any slow sad song or piece of music

dir·i·gi·ble /'dɪrɨdʒəbəl, dɨ'rɪ-/ *n* a BALLOON which can be guided on its way; AIRSHIP

dirk /dɜːk‖dɜrk/ *n* a short sword used in Scotland in former times; kind of DAGGER

dirn·dl /'dɜːndl‖'dɜr-/ *n* a wide skirt with a tight waist, or with a close-fitting upper part (BODICE)

dirt /dɜːt‖dɜrt/ *n* [U] **1** unclean matter, esp. in the wrong place: *wash the dirt off the floor/off the child's knees* **2** soil; loose earth: *The children were outside playing happily in the dirt* **3** nasty talk or writing about sex; PORNOGRAPHY: *a good story with a bit of dirt in it* **4** *infml* nasty talk about people: *She enjoys hearing a bit of dirt about her neighbours* **5 as cheap as dirt** (esp. of a woman) low class; not a lady **6 dirt cheap** *infml* very cheap **7 fling/throw dirt at** to say nasty things (about) **8 treat someone like dirt** to treat someone as though he were worthless

dirt farm·er /'· ,··/ *n AmE* a farmer who earns his living by farming his own land, esp. without hired help

dirt road /,· '·/ *n AmE* a road of hard earth without a made up surface

dirt track /'· ·/ *n* a track used for motorcycle races

dirt·y¹ /'dɜːti‖'dɜr-/ *adj* [Wa1]· **1** not clean: *dirty hands|My dress is getting dirty and needs washing* **2** causing people or things to become unclean: *Repairing cars is a dirty job* **3** (of thoughts or words) concerned with sex in an unpleasant way: *They sat up drinking and telling dirty stories* **4** *infml* (of the weather) rough and unpleasant: *The fishermen won't go out on such a dirty night* **5** (of an atomic bomb) having a large amount of FALLOUT **6 do the dirty on someone** *infml* to treat someone in a mean way **7 give someone a dirty look** *infml* to look at someone with great disapproval **8 wash one's dirty linen in public** to make unpleasant subjects public which ought to be kept private —**dirtily** *adv*

dirty² *v* [IØ;T1] to (cause to) become dirty: *Don't dirty your hands.|White shoes dirty very quickly*

dirty³ *adv sl* very: *a dirty big house*

dirty trick /,·· '·/ *n* a mean ugly trick: *He played a dirty trick on me by refusing to do what he had promised*

dirty work /'·· ·/ *n* [U] **1** work that makes one DIRTY (1) **2** work that nobody wants to do: *Why do you always leave me to do all the dirty work?* **3** *infml* dishonest behaviour: *There's been some dirty work with the club accounts, and some money is missing*

dis- /dɪs/ *prefix* **1** [*adj→adj; n→n; v→v*] not (to) (forms the opposite of the word): DISAPPROVE|DISCONTENTED|DISHONEST(ly)|DISAGREEMENT|DISORDER|DISLOYAL(ty) **2** [*v→v*] to undo the action of: DISCONNECT|DISINFECT **3** [*n→v*] to take away: DISFOREST|DISFRANCHISE

dis·a·bil·i·ty /,dɪsə'bɪlɨti/ *n* **1** [U] the state of being DISABLED **2** [C] something that DISABLEs: *He gets money* (a **disability pension**) *from the Government because of his disabilities.|To work under disabilities*

dis·a·ble /dɪs'eɪbəl/ *v* **1** [Wv5;T1 (*often pass.*)] to make (a person) unable to use his body properly: *a disabled soldier|He was disabled in the war; he lost his left arm* **2** [T1 (*from*)] *fml* to take away (from a person) a power or right; DISQUALIFY —**~ment** *n* [C;U]

dis·a·bled /dɪs'eɪbəld/ *n* [*the*+P] DISABLED (1)

people: *The disabled are to receive more money*

dis·a·buse /ˌdɪsəˈbjuːz/ *v* [T1 (*of*)] *fml* to free (a person) from a wrong idea: *If you think I'm going to lend you money I must disabuse you*

dis·ad·van·tage /ˌdɪsədˈvɑːntɪdʒ‖-ˈvæn-/ *n* **1** an unfavourable condition or position; anything which makes one less successful than other people: *His bad health is a great disadvantage to him* —opposite **advantage 2 at a disadvantage** in an unfavourable position: *I feel rather at a disadvantage talking to her, because she's so clever* **3 to someone's disadvantage** so as to cause someone loss or damage: *Her height will be very much to her disadvantage if she wants to be a dancer*

dis·ad·van·ta·geous /ˌdɪsædvənˈteɪdʒəs, -væn-/ *adj* [(*to*)] causing or being a DISADVANTAGE —opposite **advantageous** —**~ly** *adv*

dis·af·fect·ed /ˌdɪsəˈfektɨd/ *adj* [(*to, towards*)] politically discontented; lacking loyalty (esp. to/towards a government): *The people are becoming disaffected to/towards the chief minister*

dis·af·fec·tion /ˌdɪsəˈfekʃən/ *n* [U (*to, towards*)] the state of being DISAFFECTED

dis·af·fil·i·ate /ˌdɪsəˈfɪlieɪt/ *v* [IØ;T1: (*from*)] (of a person or organization) to break (one's) connection with an organization; end an AFFILIATION

dis·af·for·est /ˌdɪsəˈfɒrɨst‖-ˈfɑ-, -ˈfɔ-/ also **disforest**— *v* [T1] to cut down the forests of or on (a place) —opposite **afforest** —**~ation** /ˌdɪsəfɒrɨˈsteɪʃən‖-fɑ-, -fɔ-/ *n* [U]

dis·a·gree /ˌdɪsəˈgriː/ *v* [IØ (*with*)] **1** (of people) to have different opinions; quarrel slightly: *Bill and I often disagree but we're good friends.|I disagree with him about/over/as to what we ought to do* —opposite **agree 2** (of statements, reports, etc.) to be unlike: *These 2 reports of the accident disagree. The newspaper report disagrees with the account on the radio* —opposite **agree**

dis·a·gree·a·ble /ˌdɪsəˈgriːəbəl/ *adj* **1** unpleasant; causing discomfort: *Sweeping chimneys is a disagreeable job* —opposite **agreeable 2** (of people) bad-tempered and unfriendly: *Smile at me, and stop being so disagreeable* —opposite **agreeable** —**~ness** *n* [U] —**-ably** *adv*

dis·a·gree·ment /ˌdɪsəˈgriːmənt/ *n* **1** [C;U] the fact or a case of DISAGREEing (1): *There has been serious disagreement between the 2 political parties over this question.|Bill and I have been having a few disagreements lately* **2** [U] (of statements, reports, etc.) unlikeness; DISAGREEing (2): *There is some disagreement between these 2 statements* —opposite **agreement 3 in disagreement (with) a** in the state of DISAGREEing (1): *I am in total disagreement with you as to the value of your plan* **b** in the state of DISAGREEing (2): *The 2 sets of figures are in disagreement*

disagree with *v prep* [T1 *no pass.*] (of food or weather) to have a bad effect on; make ill: *Chocolate always disagrees with me* —opposite **agree with**

dis·al·low /ˌdɪsəˈlaʊ/ *v* [T1] *fml* to refuse officially to recognize or allow: *disallow a* GOAL|*disallow a claim* —opposite **allow**

dis·ap·pear /ˌdɪsəˈpɪəʳ/ *v* [IØ] **1** to go out of sight: *The sun disappeared behind a cloud* —opposite **appear 2** to cease to exist; become lost: *These beautiful birds are fast disappearing.|My keys have disappeared off the table* —opposite **appear**

dis·ap·pear·ance /ˌdɪsəˈpɪərəns/ *n* [C;U] a case or the event of DISAPPEARing; the state of having DISAPPEARed

dis·ap·point /ˌdɪsəˈpɔɪnt/ *v* [T1] **1** to fail to fulfil the hopes of (a person): *I'm sorry to disappoint you, but I can't come after all* **2** to defeat (a plan or hope): *I'm sorry to disappoint your hopes*

dis·ap·point·ed /ˌdɪsəˈpɔɪntɨd/ *adj* **1** [B (*about, at, in, with*);F3] (of a person) unhappy at not seeing hopes come true: *Since he lost the election he's a disappointed man.|Are you very disappointed about/at losing the race?|My parents will be disappointed in/with me if I fail the examination* **2** [B] (of a plan or hope) defeated: *his disappointed hopes for his future* —**~ly** *adv*

dis·ap·point·ing /ˌdɪsəˈpɔɪntɪŋ/ *adj* causing one to be unhappy at not seeing hopes come true: *What disappointing news!|Your examination marks are rather disappointing; I hoped you would do better* —**~ly** *adv*

dis·ap·point·ment /ˌdɪsəˈpɔɪntmənt/ *n* **1** [U] the state of being disappointed: *He left the station in great disappointment, for she wasn't on the train* **2** [C] someone or something disappointing: *Our son has been a disappointment to us.|He suffered various disappointments in his attempts to get work* **3 to someone's disappointment** which makes someone feel disappointed

dis·ap·pro·ba·tion /ˌdɪsæprəˈbeɪʃən/ *n* [U] *fml* disapproval: *He showed great disapprobation at my suggestion* —opposite **approbation**

dis·ap·prov·al /ˌdɪsəˈpruːvəl/ *n* [U] **1** the state of disapproving: *He spoke with disapproval of your behaviour.|She shook her head in disapproval* (= as a sign of disapproval) —opposite **approval 2 to someone's disapproval** which makes someone disapprove

dis·ap·prove /ˌdɪsəˈpruːv/ *v* [IØ (*of*)] to have a bad opinion for moral reasons (of): *He disapproves of mothers going out to work; in fact he disapproves very strongly* —opposite **approve** —**-provingly** *adv* —opposite **approvingly**

dis·arm /dɪsˈɑːm‖-ˈɑrm/ *v* **1** [IØ] (esp. of a country) to give up one's weapons; reduce the size and strength of armed forces —opposite **arm 2** [T1] to take the weapons away from —opposite **arm 3** [Wv4;T1] *apprec* to drive away anger from; make harmless: *We didn't trust him at first, but his friendliness disarmed all opposition.|a disarming smile*

dis·ar·ma·ment /dɪsˈɑːməmənt‖-ˈɑr-/ *n* [U] the act or principle of DISARMing (1): *new plans for disarmament*

dis·ar·range /ˌdɪsəˈreɪndʒ/ *v* [T1] to upset the arrangement of —**~ment** *n* [U]

dis·ar·ray /ˌdɪsəˈreɪ/ *n* [U] the state of disorder: *She rushed out of the burning house with her clothes in disarray*

dis·as·so·ci·ate /ˌdɪsəˈseʊʃieɪt, -sieɪt/ *v* [T1 (*from*)] DISSOCIATE

di·sas·ter /dɪˈzɑːstəʳ‖dɪˈzæ-/ *n* [C;U] (a) sudden great misfortune: *The loss of the ship was a disaster.|The election results will bring political disaster*

di·sas·trous /dɪˈzɑːstrəs‖dɪˈzæ-/ *adj* being a DISASTER: *a disastrous mistake|The results were disastrous* —**~ly** *adv*

dis·a·vow /ˌdɪsəˈvaʊ/ *v* [T1] *fml* to say that one knows nothing of; refuse to admit (knowledge, a connection, etc.) —**~al** *n* [C;U]

dis·band /dɪsˈbænd/ *v* [IØ;T1] **a** (of a group) to break up and separate: *The club has disbanded* **b** to break up and separate (a group): *The officers disbanded the club* —**~ment** *n* [U]

dis·bar /dɪsˈbɑːʳ/ *v* **-rr-** [T1 *often pass.*] to make (a BARRISTER) leave the profession (the BAR) —**~ment** *n* [U]

dis·be·lief /ˌdɪsbɨˈliːf/ *n* [U (*in*)] lack of belief: *He listened to my story with an air of growing disbelief* —opposite **belief** —see UNBELIEF (USAGE)

dis·be·lieve /ˌdɪsbɨˈliːv/ *v* [T1] to refuse to believe; hold (a statement) not to be true or (a person) not to be truthful: *I was forced to disbelieve him* —**-liever** *n*

USAGE **disbelieve, disbelieve in** are not often used in statements. People more often say: *I don't believe you.|I don't believe (in) that story.* They are not used as the opposite of **believe** when it means **approve of**. People say: *I don't believe in mothers going out to work.* —see UNBELIEF (USAGE)

disbelieve in *v prep* [T1] to refuse to believe in; hold (a statement) not to be true or real: *I was forced to disbelieve in his story/in the existence of God*

dis·bur·den /dɪs'bɜːdn‖-ɜr-/ *v* [T1] **1** to free from a load: *disburden the donkey* —opposite **burden 2** UNBURDEN

dis·burse /dɪs'bɜːs‖-ɜrs/ *v* [I∅;T1] *fml* to pay out (money) esp. from a sum saved or collected for a purpose

dis·burse·ment /dɪs'bɜːsmənt‖-ɜr-/ *n* [C;U] *fml* (an act of) disbursing (DISBURSE): *after the disbursement of £20|make several small disbursements*

disc, *AmE* **disk** /dɪsk/ *n* **1** something round and flat **2** a ball-shaped surface that looks flat: *the disc of the full moon* **3** (GRAMOPHONE) RECORD[2] (6) **4** a flat piece of strong bendable material (CARTILAGE) between the bones (VERTEBRAE) of one's back (esp. in the phr. **a slipped disc**)

dis·card[1] /dɪs'kɑːd‖-ɑrd/ *v* **1** [T1] to get rid of as useless: *discard an old coat/one's old friends* **2** [I∅; T1] (in card games) to give up (unwanted cards): *to discard the Queen of Hearts*

dis·card[2] /'dɪskɑːd‖-ɑrd/ *n* a card DISCARDed (2) in a card game

disc brakes /'· ·/ *n* [P] BRAKE*s* (=apparatus for stopping the wheels of a vehicle) which work by the pressure of a pair of DISC*s* (1) against another one in the centre of a car wheel

di·scern /dɪ'sɜːn‖-ɜrn/ *v* [Wv6;T1,5a,6] to see, notice, or understand, esp. with difficulty: *He was just able to discern the road in the dark.|I soon discerned that the man was lying.|It was difficult to discern which of them was to blame* —**~ible** *adj* —**~ibly** *adv*

di·scern·ing /dɪ'sɜːnɪŋ‖-ɜr-/ *adj* [B; *the*+P] *apprec* having or showing the power to decide and judge; having good taste: *a discerning man/mind|The discerning like to buy their clothes at my shop*

di·scern·ment /dɪ'sɜːnmənt‖-ɜr-/ *n* [U] *apprec* the quality of being DISCERNING: *He showed great discernment in his choice of wine*

dis·charge[1] /dɪs'tʃɑːdʒ‖-ɑr-/ *v* **1** [I∅;T1] to send, pour, or let out (gas, liquid, etc.): *The chimney discharges smoke.|The River Rhine discharges (itself) into the North Sea* **2** [T1 (*from*)] to allow (a person) to go: *The judge discharged the prisoner.|The aircraft discharged its passengers* **3** [T1 (*from*)] to dismiss (a person) from a job **4** [T1] to pay (a debt) **5** [T1] to perform (a duty or promise) **6** [T1 (*at, into*)] to fire or shoot (a gun, arrow, etc.) **7** [I∅] (of a wound) to send out infected liquid matter (PUS) **8** [I∅;T1] **a** (of a ship) to unload **b** to unload (a ship) **9** [I∅;T1] **a** (of an electrical apparatus) to send out electricity **b** to remove electricity from (an electrical apparatus) **10** [T1] *law* to put an end to (a court order)

dis·charge[2] /dɪs'tʃɑːdʒ, 'dɪstʃɑːdʒ‖-ɑr-/ *n* **1** [U] the action of discharging (DISCHARGE); the state or event of being DISCHARGEd: *the discharge of one's debts/of the guns/of one's duty/of gas from a container|After my discharge from the army I went into business* **2** [C] an order or paper that DISCHARGE*s* (2,4,10) **3** [C] that which is DISCHARGEd (1,7,9): *a discharge of electricity*

discharged bank·rupt /·,· '··/ *n* a BANKRUPT (= person who is unable to pay his or her debts) who has obeyed the orders of the court and is now free to do business again

disc har·row /'· ,··/ *n* a machine with a set of DISC*s* on a frame, which is rolled over the ground to break it up so that crops can be planted

di·sci·ple /dɪ'saɪpəl/ *n* **1** a follower of any great teacher (esp. religious): *Martin Luther King considered himself a disciple of Gandhi* **2** (*often cap.*) one of the 12 first followers of Christ; APOSTLE

di·sci·ple·ship /dɪ'saɪpəlʃɪp/ *n* [U] the state or time of being a DISCIPLE

dis·ci·pli·nar·i·an /,dɪsəplə'neərɪən/ *n* a person who is good at making people obey orders: *a good/severe/poor disciplinarian|He's a good teacher but he's not much of a disciplinarian*

dis·ci·pli·na·ry /'dɪsəplɪnəri, ,dɪsə'plɪ-‖'dɪsəpləneri/ *adj* **1** of or relating to DISCIPLINE[1] (1,2): *We must take strong disciplinary action against the wrongdoers* **2** of or relating to DISCIPLINE[1] (5) (usu. in the phr. **interdisciplinary studies**)

dis·ci·pline[1] /'dɪsəplən/ *n* **1** [U] training of the mind and body to produce obedience and self-control: *school/military discipline* **2** [U] control gained as a result of this training: *The teacher can't keep discipline in her classroom* **3** [U] punishment: *That child needs discipline. Send her to bed without any dinner* **4** [C] a method of training: *Learning poetry is a good discipline for the memory* **5** [C] a branch of learning studied at a university: *You're no good at history, so you'd better choose one of the other disciplines*

discipline[2] *v* [T1] **1** to provide DISCIPLINE[1] (1,2) for; train: *You must learn to discipline yourself* **2** to punish in order to train: *She never disciplines her children and they are uncontrollable* **3** to punish (a worker) for disobeying orders, breaking rules, etc.

disc jock·ey /'· ,··/ *n* a broadcaster who introduces records of popular music on a radio or television show

dis·claim /dɪs'kleɪm/ *v* [T1, 4] to say that one does not own or does not claim; DENY

dis·claim·er /dɪs'kleɪmər/ *n* a (written) statement which DISCLAIM*s*

dis·close /dɪs'kləʊz/ *v* **1** [T1,5,6] to make known: *He disclosed the truth/that he had been in prison* **2** [T1] to show by uncovering: *The curtain opened, to disclose an empty stage*

dis·clo·sure /dɪs'kləʊʒər/ *n* **1** [U] the act of disclosing (DISCLOSE (1)) **2** [C] a secret which is DISCLOSEd (1): *She made several surprising disclosures about her past life*

dis·co /'dɪskəʊ/ *n* **-cos** *infml* DISCOTHEQUE

dis·col·o·ra·tion, -ouration /dɪs,kʌlə'reɪʃən/ *n* **1** [U] the act of DISCOLOURing or state of being DISCOLOUREd **2** [C] a DISCOLOUREd place; mark or STAIN

dis·col·our, *AmE* also **discolor** /dɪs'kʌlər/ *v* [Wv5; I∅;T1] to (cause to) change colour for the worse: *his discoloured teeth*

dis·com·fit /dɪs'kʌmfət/ *v* [T1] *fml* **1** to cause a little shame or annoyance to (a person): *She was rather discomfited when the rain spoiled her new hat* **2** to upset (a plan)

dis·com·fi·ture /dɪs'kʌmfətʃər/ *n* [U] the act of DISCOMFITing or state of being DISCOMFITed

dis·com·fort /dɪs'kʌmfət‖-ərt/ *n* **1** [U] lack of comfort: *the discomfort of camping in the mountains* **2** [U] slight anxiety or shame: *She turned red with discomfort when the teacher spoke* **3** [C] something that makes one uncomfortable: *the discomforts of travel*

dis·com·mode /,dɪskə'məʊd/ *v* [T1] *fml or lit* INCOMMODE

dis·com·pose /,dɪskəm'pəʊz/ *v* [T1] *fml* to cause

(someone) to lose control and become worried —**-posure** /ˌdɪskəm'pəʊʒəʳ/ *n* [U]

dis·con·cert /ˌdɪskən'sɜːt‖-ɜrt/ *v* [Wv4;T1 *often pass.*] to cause (someone) to feel doubt and anxiety: *She was disconcerted to hear that she would have to make a speech* —**~ingly** *adv*: *The baby is disconcertingly like Mr Jones*

dis·con·nect /ˌdɪskə'nekt/ *v* [T1] **1** [(*from*)] to undo the connection of (material things): *disconnect the telephone|disconnect a waterpipe from the main supply* **2** to break the telephone connection between (2 people): *I think we've been disconnected. Will you ring that number again, please?*

dis·con·nect·ed /ˌdɪskə'nektǰd/ *adj* (of thoughts and ideas) badly connected; not well planned: *make a few disconnected remarks* —**~ly** *adv*

dis·con·nec·tion /ˌdɪskə'nekʃən/ *n* [C;U] a case or the quality of being DISCONNECTED

dis·con·so·late /dɪs'kɒnsəlǰt‖-'kɑn-/ *adj* [(*about/at*)] (typical of a person) hopelessly sad, esp. at the loss of something, and unwilling to be comforted: *his disconsolate face|She is disconsolate about/at the death of her cat* —**~ly** *adv*

dis·con·tent¹ /ˌdɪskən'tent/ *adj* [F (*with*)] DISCONTENTED: *She always seems discontent with life* —opposite **content**

discontent² *v* [T1] to make (someone) DISCONTENTED: *Has something happened to discontent you?*

discontent³ also **dis·con·tent·ment** /-mənt/— *n* **1** [U (*with*)] lack of contentment; dissatisfaction —opposite **content(ment)** **2** [C *usu. pl.*] a reason for lacking contentment: *They explained their various discontentments to the President*

dis·con·tent·ed /ˌdɪskən'tentǰd/ *adj* [(*with*)] (typical of a person) dissatisfied and restlessly unhappy: *She has a discontented look, as if she never enjoys life.|He's discontented with his wages* —opposite **contented** —**~ly** *adv*

dis·con·tin·ue /ˌdɪskən'tɪnjuː/ *v* [I∅;T1,4] *fml* to stop or end: *His visits soon discontinued.|He will discontinue (teaching) his class until after the summer* —**-tinuance** *n* [U]

dis·con·ti·nu·i·ty /ˌdɪskɒntǰ'njuːǰti‖-ɑntǰ'nuː-/ *n* **1** [U] the quality of not being continuous: *There has been discontinuity in the boy's education* —opposite **continuity** **2** [C] *fml* a breaking or space between

dis·con·tin·u·ous /ˌdɪskən'tɪnjʊəs/ *adj* not continuous in space or time: *Following is a discontinuous line* – – – – —opposite **continuous** —**~ly** *adv*

dis·cord /'dɪskɔːd‖'dɪskɔrd/ *n* [C;U] **1** (a case of) disagreement between people: *A good deal of discord has/various discords have arisen in the university over this question* **2** (esp. in music) (a) lack of agreement heard when sounds are made or notes played which do not sound well together —opposite **harmony**

dis·cord·ance /dɪs'kɔːdəns‖-ɔr-/ *n* [U] DISCORD

dis·cord·ant /dɪs'kɔːdənt‖-ɔr-/ *adj* in a state of DISCORD: *discordant opinions/music* —**~ly** *adv*

dis·co·theque /'dɪskətek, ˌdɪskə'tek/ also (*infml*) **disco**— *n* a club where young people dance to recorded popular music

dis·count¹ /'dɪskaʊnt/ *n* **1** a reduction made in the cost **a** when buying goods in a shop: *a discount of 10% on new cars* **b** *tech* when buying a BILL OF EXCHANGE (= a written order to pay money) before it is due to be paid **2 at a discount a** below the usual price **b** *fig.* not valuable or wanted: *Honesty seems to be rather at a discount today*

dis·count² /dɪs'kaʊnt‖'dɪskaʊnt/ *v* [T1] **1** to pay little attention to; believe (a story or piece of news) to be unimportant or not completely true: *Much of what he says must be discounted; he imagines things* **2** *tech* to give less than the stated price for (a BILL OF EXCHANGE)

discount brok·er /'·· ˌ··/ *n tech* a person who is paid to help in arrangements between buyers and sellers

dis·coun·te·nance /dɪs'kaʊntǰnəns/ *v* [T1] *fml* to look with disfavour on (behaviour or actions)

discount store /'·· ·/ also **discount house**— *n* a shop where goods are sold below the price suggested by the makers

dis·cour·age /dɪs'kʌrɪdʒ‖-kɜr-/ *v* **1** [Wv4,5;T1] to take away courage and spirit from: *It discourages me/It's very discouraging that every time I try to ride a bicycle I fall off* **2** [T1,4] to try to prevent (an action) esp. by showing disfavour; put difficulties in the way of: *We discourage smoking in this school* **3** [T1 (*from*)] to try to prevent (someone from doing something) esp. by showing disfavour: *His mother discouraged him from joining the navy, saying that it was a hard life, but he refused to be discouraged* —opposite **encourage** —**-agingly** *adv*

dis·cour·age·ment /dɪs'kʌrɪdʒmənt‖-'kɜr-/ *n* **1** [U] the action of discouraging or state of being discouraged **2** [C] something that discourages: *He finished the job in spite of many discouragements* —opposite **encouragement**

dis·course /'dɪskɔːs‖-ors/ *n fml* **1** [C (*on, upon*)] a serious speech or piece of writing: *The priest delivered a long discourse on/upon the evils of untruthfulness* **2** [U] serious conversation: *The judges held solemn discourse together*

dis·course up·on /dɪs'kɔːs‖-ors/ also **discourse on**— *v prep* [T1] *fml* to make a long formal speech about: *Our teacher discoursed for hours upon/on Greek literature*

dis·cour·te·ous /dɪs'kɜːtɪəs‖-ɜr-/ *adj fml* (of people or their behaviour) not polite —opposite **courteous** —**~ly** *adv* —**~ness** *n* [U]

dis·cour·te·sy /dɪs'kɜːtəsi‖-ɜr-/ *n* [C;U] *fml* (an act of) DISCOURTEOUSness: *You showed great discourtesy by not asking him to sit down* —opposite **courtesy**

dis·cov·er /dɪs'kʌvəʳ/ *v* **1** [T1] to find (something existing but not known before, often a place or a scientific fact): *Columbus discovered America in 1492.|I discovered a fly in my coffee* —compare INVENT **2** [T1,5,6;V3] to find out (a fact, or the answer to a question): *We soon discovered the truth.|We discovered her to be a good cook* (= that she was a good cook).*|Did you ever discover who sent you the flowers?|We never discovered how to open the box.|Scientists have discovered that this disease is carried by rats* —**~able** *adj* —**~er** *n*

dis·cov·e·ry /dɪs'kʌvəri/ *n* **1** [*the*+U5,9 esp. *of*] the event of discovering: *The discovery of oil on their land made the family rich.|She was shocked at the discovery that he was a thief* **2** [C] a case of discovering something: *make an important scientific discovery* **3** [C] something discovered: *A collector of rare insects will show us some of his latest discoveries*

dis·cred·it¹ /dɪs'kredǰt/ *v* [T1] **1** [(*with*)] to cause people to lack faith in; stop people believing in: *The idea that the sun goes round the earth has long been discredited* **2** to refuse to believe in: *One should discredit a good deal of what is printed in newspapers*

discredit² *n* **1** [U] loss of belief and trust **2** [S+*to*] someone or something that is harmful (to the good name of the stated person or group); a DISGRACE: *That bad boy is a discredit to his family* —opposite **credit** **3** [U] doubt and disbelief: *He threw discredit on his brother's story*

dis·cred·i·ta·ble /dɪs'kredǰtəbəl/ *adj* (of behaviour) shameful; bringing DISCREDIT² (2) —**-bly** *adv*

di·screet /dɪˈskriːt/ *adj* (of people or their behaviour) careful and polite, esp. in what one chooses (not) to say; showing good sense and judgment: *a discreet silence|It wasn't very discreet of you to ring me up at the office* —opposite **indiscreet** —**~ly** *adv*

di·screp·an·cy /dɪˈskrepənsi/ *n* [C;U: (*between*)] difference; lack of agreement (between stories, amounts, etc.): *You said you paid £5 and the bill says £3; how do you explain the discrepancy?*

di·screte /dɪˈskriːt/ *adj* [Wa5] *esp. tech or fml* separate; discontinuous: *The picture consisted of a lot of discrete spots of colour* —**~ly** *adv* —**~ness** *n* [U]

di·scre·tion /dɪˈskreʃən/ *n* [U] **1** the quality of being DISCREET —opposite **indiscretion** **2** the ability to decide what is most suitable to be done: *I won't tell you what time to leave—you're old enough to use your own discretion* **3 at someone's discretion** according to someone's decision: *The hours of the meetings will be fixed at the chairman's discretion* **4 years of discretion** the/an age when one is considered old enough to take one's own decisions **5 discretion is the better part of valour** it is better to be careful than to take risks

di·scre·tion·a·ry /dɪˈskreʃənəri‖-neri/ *adj fml* allowing DISCRETION (2) (esp. in the phr. **discretionary powers**)

di·scrim·i·nate /dɪˈskrɪmɪ̣neɪt/ *v* [Wv6;IØ] to see or make a difference: *Death does not discriminate; it comes to everyone.|discriminate in favour of white people*

discriminate a·gainst *v prep* [T1] *derog* to treat (someone) as worse than others

discriminate be·tween *v prep* [Wv6;T1] **1** to tell the difference between (2 or more things or people), esp. so as to choose the best: *The elephant can discriminate between food and money* **2** *often derog* to treat (2 or more things or people) differently: *The new law discriminates between men and women/between people employed in the same firm*

discriminate from *v prep* [Wv6;D1] to tell the difference between (one thing or person) and (another) esp. so as to choose the best

di·scrim·i·nat·ing /dɪˈskrɪmɪ̣neɪtɪŋ/ *adj* **1** [B] *apprec* (typical of a person) able to choose the best by seeing small differences **2** [Wa5;A] *often derog* showing DISCRIMINATION (2); DISCRIMINATORY

di·scrim·i·na·tion /dɪˌskrɪmɪ̣ˈneɪʃən/ *n* [U] **1** *apprec* ability to choose the best by seeing small differences **2** [(*against*)] *often derog* treating different things or people in different ways: *Pay us all the same! There must be no discrimination*

di·scrim·i·na·to·ry /dɪˈskrɪmɪ̣nətəri‖-tori/ *adj* [Wa5;A] *often derog* showing DISCRIMINATION (2): *introduce a discriminatory law*

di·scur·sive /dɪˈskɜːsɪv‖-ɜr-/ *adj* (of a person or his words or writing) passing from one subject or idea to another in an informal way, without any clear plan: *write in a discursive style* —**~ly** *adv* —**~ness** *n* [U]

dis·cus /ˈdɪskəs/ *n* a heavy plate of wood, metal, or stone, which is thrown as far as possible, as a sport

di·scuss /dɪˈskʌs/ *v* [T1,6a,b: (*with*)] to talk about (with someone) from several points of view: *The women were discussing hats.|We discussed what to do and where we should go*

di·scus·sion /dɪˈskʌʃən/ *n* [C;U] **1** a case or the action of DISCUSSing: *have/hold a discussion about/as to our future plans|settle the matter with as little discussion as possible* **2 come up for discussion** *fml* (of a subject) to be DISCUSSed according to plan, as in the arrangements (AGENDA) for a committee meeting **3 under discussion** *fml* (of a subject) being DISCUSSed

dis·dain[1] /dɪsˈdeɪn/ *n* [U] lack of respect; the feeling that someone or something is low and worthless —compare CONTEMPT, SCORN[1]

disdain[2] *v* [Wv6] **1** [T1] to regard with DISDAIN: *Why do you disdain my offer of friendship?* —compare DESPISE **2** [T3,4 *no pass.*] to refuse (to do an action) because of DISDAIN: *She disdained to answer/answering his rude remarks*

dis·dain·ful /dɪsˈdeɪnfəl/ *adj* [(*of, towards*)] showing DISDAIN: *She gave me a disdainful smile.|He is very disdainful of/towards stupid people* —compare CONTEMPTUOUS, SCORNful —**~ly** *adv*

dis·ease /dɪˈziːz/ *n* [C;U] (an) illness or disorder caused by infection or unnatural growth, not by an accident: *catch/die of/suffer from/cure a disease|Many diseases are/Some disease is caused by bacteria.|plant diseases|A wound is not a disease.|*(fig.) *diseases of the mind/of society* —**-eased** *adj*: *a diseased bone|diseased plants|*(fig.) *a diseased imagination*

USAGE Though **illness** and **disease** are often used alike, **illness** is really a state, or length of time, of being unwell, which may be caused by a **disease**. It is **diseases** that can be caught and passed on if they are infectious or CONTAGIOUS, and that are the subjects of medical study.

dis·em·bark /ˌdɪsɪ̣mˈbɑːk‖-ɑrk/ also **debark**— *v* [IØ;T1: (*from*)] **a** (of people) to go on shore from a ship **b** to put on shore (people or goods) —opposite **embark** —**~ation** /ˌdɪsembɑːˈkeɪʃən‖-ɑr-/ *n* [U]

dis·em·bar·rass of /ˌdɪsɪ̣mˈbærəs/ *v prep* [D1] *fml or pomp* to free (oneself or another) of (a charge, job, responsibility, etc.): *Let me disembarrass you of that heavy box, sir* —**~ment** *n* [U+*of*]

dis·em·bod·ied /ˌdɪsɪ̣mˈbɒdid‖-ˈbɑ-/ *adj* [Wa5;A] **1** (of a soul) existing without a body: *the disembodied spirits of the dead* **2** coming from someone who cannot be seen: *disembodied voices*

dis·em·bowel /ˌdɪsɪ̣mˈbaʊəl/ *v* **-ll-** (*AmE* **-l-**) [T1] to take out the bowels of

USAGE When one prepares a bird for cooking, the word is **clean**: *Will you clean this chicken for me, please?*

dis·em·broil /ˌdɪsɪ̣mˈbrɔɪl/ *v* [T1 (*from*)] *fml* to set free (from a condition of confusion and difficulty): *He tried to disembroil himself (from the argument between Robert and Jean)* —opposite **embroil**

dis·en·chant /ˌdɪsɪ̣nˈtʃɑːnt‖-ˈtʃænt/ *v* [Wv5;T1 (*with*)] to set free from being charmed (ENCHANTed); show (someone) that something is not worthy or valuable; DISILLUSION —**~ment** *n* [U]

dis·en·cum·ber /ˌdɪsɪ̣nˈkʌmbə^r/ *v* [T1 (*from, of*)] *fml* to free (someone) (from something heavy or inconvenient) —opposite **encumber**

dis·en·dow /ˌdɪsɪ̣nˈdaʊ/ *v* [T1] to take away from (esp. a church) the money or land (ENDOWMENTs) given in the past to provide an income —opposite **endow** —**~ment** *n* [U]

dis·en·gage /ˌdɪsɪ̣ŋˈgeɪdʒ/ *v* [IØ;T1: (*from*)] **1** **a** (esp. of parts of a machine) to come loose and separate **b** to loosen and separate (esp. parts of a machine): *Disengage the GEARs when you park the car* **2** (of soldiers, ships, etc.) to stop fighting and go or take (oneself) away: *They disengaged (themselves) without loss of men* —opposite **engage** —**~ment** *n* [U (*from*)]

dis·en·gaged /ˌdɪsɪ̣ŋˈgeɪʒd/ *adj* [Wa5;F] *fml* (of people) free from social or official arrangements: *I should like to see the President if he is disengaged* —opposite **engaged**

dis·en·tan·gle /ˌdɪsɪ̣nˈtæŋgəl/ *v* **1** [IØ;T1: (*from*)] **a** to remove knots from and straighten out (rope, hair, etc.) **b** (of rope, hair, etc.) to become straight and free from knots **2** [T1 (*from*)] to free from confusion, esp. to find out by doing this: *How can I* *disentangle the truth from all these lies?* —opposite **entangle** —**~ment** *n* [U]

dis·e·qui·lib·ri·um /ˌdɪsekwə̇ˈlɪbrɪəm, ˌdɪsiː-/ *n* [U] *fml* the loss or lack of balance (EQUILIBRIUM)

dis·es·tab·lish /ˌdɪsə̇ˈstæblɪʃ/ *v* [T1] to take away the official position from (a national church such as the CHURCH OF ENGLAND) —**~ment** *n* [U]

dis·fa·vour, *AmE* **-vor** /dɪsˈfeɪvəʳ/ *n* [U] *fml* **1** dislike; disapproval: *Mary seems to look upon/regard/*VIEW *John with disfavour* **2** [(*with*)] the state of being disliked: *John seems to be/have fallen into disfavour (with Mary)* —opposite **favour**

dis·fig·ure /dɪsˈfɪgəʳ‖-ˈfɪgjər/ *v* [Wv4;T1] to spoil the beauty of: *Those spots on her face are very disfiguring* —**~ment** *n* [C;U]

dis·for·est /dɪsˈfɒrə̇st‖-ˈfɑ-, -ˈfɔ-/ *v* [T1] DISAFFOREST —**~ation** /-ˌfɒrə̇ˈsteɪʃən‖-ˌfɑ-, -ˌfɔ-/ *n* [U]

dis·fran·chise /dɪsˈfræntʃaɪz/ *v* [T1] to take away the rights of citizenship, esp. the right to vote (the FRANCHISE) from —opposite **enfranchise** —**~ment** /-tʃɪz-‖-tʃaɪz-/ *n* [U]

dis·frock /ˌdɪsˈfrɒk‖-ˈfrɑk/ *v* [T1] UNFROCK

dis·gorge /dɪsˈgɔːdʒ‖-ɔr-/ *v* **1** [T1] to throw out of the stomach through the mouth: *The dog disgorged the bone it had swallowed* **2** [Wv6;L9;X9: esp. *at, into*] (of a river) to flow out; pour out (its water): *The Mississippi disgorges (its waters) into the Gulf of Mexico/at New Orleans* **3** [I0;T1] *infml* to give back (something stolen) to the owner

dis·grace¹ /dɪsˈgreɪs/ *v* [T1] **1** to be a DISGRACE² (2) to: *He disgraced himself last night by drinking too much* **2** [*usu. pass.*] to put (a public person) out of favour with DISGRACE² (1): *The dishonest minister was publicly disgraced*

disgrace² *n* **1** [U] shame; loss of honour and respect: *His actions brought disgrace on his family.| Being poor is no disgrace* **2** [S (*to*)] a cause of shame and loss of respect: *Doctors like that are a disgrace to our hospitals.|My dear! That old dress of yours is a disgrace* **3 be in disgrace** *infml* (esp. of a child) to be regarded with disapproval by the grown-up people because of something that one has done: *Harry's in disgrace because he won't eat his vegetables* **4 fall into disgrace (with)** to come to be regarded with disapproval because of something that one has done

dis·grace·ful /dɪsˈgreɪsfəl/ *adj* bringing DISGRACE² (1): *What a disgraceful thing to do!* —**~ly** *adv*

dis·grun·tled /dɪsˈgrʌntld/ *adj* [*at, with*] annoyed and disappointed, esp. at not having got what he wants

dis·guise¹ /dɪsˈgaɪz/ *v* [T1] **1** [(*as*)] to change the usual appearance etc. of, so as to hide the truth: *She disguised herself as a man, but she couldn't disguise her voice* **2** to hide (the real state of things): *There's no disguising the fact/It is impossible to disguise the fact that business is bad*

disguise² *n* **1** something that is worn to hide who one really is: *The thief wore a false beard and glasses as a disguise.|Nobody saw through his disguise* **2 in disguise a** DISGUISEd¹ (1) **b** hidden but real: *His illness was a blessing in disguise, because he afterwards married his nurse*

dis·gust¹ /dɪsˈgʌst, dɪz-/ *n* [U (*at*)] strong feeling of dislike caused by an unpleasant sight, sound, or smell, or by bad behaviour: *The food at the hotel filled him with disgust*

disgust² *v* [Wv4,5 (*at, with*);T1] to cause a feeling of DISGUST¹ in: *Your rude behaviour disgusts me.| I'm completely disgusted at/with you.|What a disgusting smell!*

dish¹ /dɪʃ/ *n* **1** a large flat (often round or OVAL) vessel from which food is put onto people's plates: *A ˈmeat dish is a dish for meat, a ˌwooden ˈdish is a dish made of wood* (note the STRESS) **2** (an amount of) cooked food of one kind: *Baked apples are his favourite dish/a sweet dish* **3** any object shaped like a DISH (1), esp. the large REFLECTOR of a radio TELESCOPE **4** *infml apprec (said by men)* a pretty girl: *Jean's really quite a dish, isn't she?* **5** DISHFUL

dish² *v* [T1] *infml, esp. BrE* to ruin (a person or his hopes): *If his shoe comes untied it'll dish his chances in the race* —see also DISH OUT, DISH UP

dis·ha·bille /ˌdɪsəˈbiːl/ also **déshabillé**— *n* [(*in*) U] *Fr* the state of being only partly dressed (usu. said of a woman): *She opened the door in (a state of) dishabille*

dis·har·mo·ny /dɪsˈhɑːməni‖-ɑr-/ *n* [U] disagreement; lack of HARMONY: *bring disharmony into the family* —**-monious** /ˌdɪshɑːˈməʊnɪəs‖-ɑr-/ *adj*

dish·cloth /ˈdɪʃklɒθ‖-klɔθ/ *n* a cloth for washing or drying DISHES

dis·heart·en /dɪsˈhɑːtn‖-ɑr-/ *n* [Wv4;T1] to cause to lose hope; discourage: *He's easily disheartened by difficulties.|This bad news will dishearten them* —**~ment** *n* [C;U]

dish·es /ˈdɪʃə̇z/ *n* [(*the*) P] all the dishes, plates, cups, knives, forks, etc., used for a meal: *Let's wash/do the dishes*

di·shev·elled /dɪˈʃevəld/ *adj* (of a person or his appearance, esp. his hair) untidy

dish·ful /ˈdɪʃfʊl/ *n* the amount that a DISH¹ (1) will hold

dis·hon·est /dɪsˈɒnə̇st‖-ˈɑ-/ *adj* (of a person or his behaviour) not honest; deceiving: *a dishonest politician|get money by dishonest means* —**~ly** *adv*

dis·hon·est·y /dɪsˈɒnə̇sti‖-ˈɑ-/ *n* [U] the quality of being dishonest: *I can forgive a mistake but I can't forgive dishonesty*

dis·hon·our¹, *AmE* **-or** /dɪsˈɒnəʳ‖-ˈɑ-/ *n* [S;U (*to*)] (something or someone that causes) loss of honour: *His desertion from the army was a dishonour to his family/brought dishonour on his family*

dishonour², *AmE* **-or** *v* [T1] **1** to bring DISHONOUR to **2** (of a bank) to refuse to pay out money (a cheque) —compare BOUNCE¹ (3)

dis·hon·ou·ra·ble, *AmE* **-orable** /dɪsˈɒnərəbəl‖-ˈɑ-/ *adj* (of behaviour) shameful; not honourable: *a dishonourable action* —**-rably** *adv*

dish out *v adv* [T1] *infml* to serve out to several people; HAND OUT (2): *dish out the examination papers|He likes dishing out good advice*

dish up *v adv* **1** [I0;T1] to put (the food for a meal) into dishes, ready to be eaten: *Hurry! I'm just dishing up now.|Help me dish up the vegetables/the dinner* **2** [T1] *infml* to produce (facts or arguments): *Our history teacher has been dishing up the same old lessons for 20 years*

dish·wash·er /ˈdɪʃˌwɒʃəʳ‖-ˌwɔ-, -ˌwɑ-/ *n* a person or machine that washes DISHES —see picture at KITCHEN

dish·wa·ter /ˈdɪʃˌwɔːtəʳ‖-ˌwɔ-, -ˌwɑ-/ *n* [U] *often derog* water in which dirty dishes have been washed: *This tea tastes like dishwater*

dish·y /ˈdɪʃi/ *adj* [Wa1] *infml* (of a person) having sexual charm: *She's just married this simply dishy man* —compare DISH¹ (4)

dis·il·lu·sion /ˌdɪsə̇ˈluːʒən/ *v* [T1] to free from a wrong idea (ILLUSION); tell or show the (esp. unpleasant) truth to: *She doesn't know her father is a thief, and I don't want to disillusion her* —compare DISABUSE

dis·il·lu·sioned /ˌdɪsə̇ˈluːʒənd/ *adj* [(*at, about, with*)] (of a person) feeling bitter and unhappy as a result of having been DISILLUSIONed: *He's very disillusioned with the present Government/at the Government's behaviour*

dis·il·lu·sion·ment /ˌdɪsə̇ˈluːʒənmənt/ also **disillusion**— *n* [U] the state of having been DISILLUSIONed

dis·in·cen·tive /ˌdɪsɪn'sentɪv/ *n* [(*to*)] a practice, system, etc., that discourages action or effort —opposite **incentive**
dis·in·cli·na·tion /ˌdɪsɪŋklɪ'neɪʃən/ *n* [S+*for*, S3; U+*for*, U3] (a) lack of willingness; slight dislike: *I feel a/some disinclination to travel/for travelling now I'm older*
dis·in·clined /ˌdɪsɪn'klaɪnd/ *adj* [F+*for*, F3] unwilling: *I feel disinclined for exercise/to go out in this weather*
dis·in·fect /ˌdɪsɪn'fekt/ *v* [T1] to clean (things and places) so as to destroy bacteria —**~ion** *n* [U]
dis·in·fec·tant /ˌdɪsɪn'fektənt/ *n* [C;U] (a) DISINFECTing substance
dis·in·fest /ˌdɪsɪn'fest/ *v* [T1] *tech* to free (esp. a place) from rats, mice, insects, etc. (VERMIN) —**~ation** /-fes'teɪʃən/ *n* [U]
dis·in·gen·u·ous /ˌdɪsɪn'dʒenjuəs/ *adj* (of a person or his behaviour) not open or sincere; slightly dishonest and untruthful: *It was disingenuous of him to praise me just because he wanted money from me* —compare INGENUOUS —**~ly** *adv* —**~ness** *n* [U]
dis·in·her·it /ˌdɪsɪn'herɪt/ *v* [T1] to take away from (usu. one's child) the lawful right to receive (INHERIT) one's goods after one's death —**~ance** *n* [U]
dis·in·te·grate /dɪs'ɪntɪgreɪt/ *v* [I∅;T1] to (cause to) break up (as if) into small pieces: *ancient walls disintegrated by time and weather|Is society beginning to disintegrate?* —**-gration** /dɪsˌɪntɪ'greɪʃən/ *n* [U]
dis·in·ter /ˌdɪsɪn'tɜːʳ/ *v* **-rr-** [T1 *often pass.*] *fml* to dig up (esp. a body from a grave) —opposite **inter** —**~ment** *n* [C;U]
dis·in·terest·ed /dɪs'ɪntrɪstɪd/ *adj* **1** *apprec* (typical of a person) willing to judge or act fairly because not influenced by personal advantage: *His action was not disinterested because he hoped to make money out of the affair* **2** [(*in*)] *usu. considered nonstandard* not caring; uninterested: *She seems completely disinterested (in her work)* —**~ly** *adv* —**~ness** *n* [U]
dis·joint /dɪs'dʒɔɪnt/ *v* [T1] *fml* JOINT³ (2): *disjoint this duck*
dis·joint·ed /dɪs'dʒɔɪntɪd/ *adj* (of words or ideas) not well connected; not following in reasonable order: *He gave a rather disjointed account of the battle* —**~ly** *adv* —**~ness** *n* [U]
dis·junc·tive /dɪs'dʒʌŋktɪv/ *adj* [Wa5] *tech* (of a word which joins other words (CONJUNCTION)) expressing a choice or opposition between 2 ideas: *"Or" is disjunctive/is a disjunctive* CONJUNCTION, *but "and" is not*
disk /dɪsk/ *n AmE* DISC
dis·like¹ /dɪs'laɪk/ *v* [Wv6;T1,4] to consider unpleasant; not to like: *I dislike big cities/wearing stockings/being spoken to like that*
dislike² /ˌdɪs'laɪk/ *n* [C;U: (*of, for*)] **1** (a) feeling of disliking (DISLIKE): *She spoke of him with great dislike.|have a dislike of/for cats* **2 likes and dislikes** /ˌ· · '··/ feelings of liking and disliking **3 take a dislike to** to begin to dislike
dis·lo·cate /'dɪsləkeɪt‖-ləʊ-/ *v* [T1] **1** [Wv5] to put (a bone) out of place **2** to put (plans, business, machinery, etc.) out of order; DISRUPT
dis·lo·ca·tion /ˌdɪslə'keɪʃən‖-ləʊ-/ *n* **1** [C;U] (a case of) being DISLOCATED (1): *The doctor treated all the people suffering from dislocations and broken bones* **2** [S;U] (a case or period of) being DISLOCATED (2): *The storm caused considerable/a 6-hour dislocation of traffic*
dis·lodge /dɪs'lɒdʒ‖dɪs'lɑdʒ/ *v* [T1 (*from*)] to force out of a position: *dislodge a fishbone from a cat's throat|The enemy are in the forest and must be dislodged* —**~ment** *n* [U]
dis·loy·al /dɪs'lɔɪəl/ *adj* [(*to*)] not loyal —**~ly** *adv* —**~ty** *n* [U;C: (*to*)]
dis·mal /'dɪzməl/ *adj* showing or causing sadness; lacking comfort: *a dismal song|dismal weather|The future looks pretty dismal* —**~ly** *adv*
dis·man·tle /dɪs'mæntl/ *v* **1** [I∅;T1] **a** to take (a machine or article) to pieces **b** (of a machine or article) to be able to be taken to pieces **2** [T1] to take away the furniture, machines, etc., from (a building or ship) —**~ment** *n* [U]
dis·mast /dɪs'mɑːst‖-'mæst/ *v* [T1] to take away the MAST(*s*) (=upright poles which carry the sails) from (a ship)
dis·may¹ /dɪs'meɪ/ *v* [Wv5;T1] to fill with DISMAY
dismay² *n* [(*in, with*) U] **1** strong feeling of fear and hopelessness: *They listened in/with dismay to the news.|The news filled/struck them with dismay* **2 to one's dismay** causing fear and hopelessness
dis·mem·ber /dɪs'membəʳ/ *v* [T1] **1** to cut or tear (a body) apart, limb from limb **2** to divide (a country or piece of land) into parts —**~ment** *n* [U]
dis·miss /dɪs'mɪs/ *v* [T1] **1** [(*from*)] *fml* to send away (from employment): *If you're late again you'll be dismissed (from your job)* —compare SACK¹ (2) **2** [(*from*)] to allow to go: *The teacher dismissed the class 10 minutes early* **3** [(*as, from*)] to put away (a subject) (from one's mind); treat (a subject) as not serious: *Let's dismiss this subject and talk of something else.|He just laughed, and dismissed the idea as unimportant* **4** (of a judge) to stop (a court case): *The judge dismissed all the charges (against Smith), saying "Case dismissed!"* **5** [(*for*)] (in cricket) to end the INNINGS of (a player or team)
dis·miss·al /dɪs'mɪsəl/ *n* [C;U] an act or the action of DISMISSing; event of being DISMISSed
dis·mount /dɪs'maʊnt/ *v* **1** [I∅ (*from*)] to get down (as from a horse or bicycle) **2** [T1] to throw off (from a horse): *The 2 men in armour each tried to dismount the other* **3** [T1] to take down (esp. a gun) from the base or carriage
USAGE One **dismounts** from anything that one **rides** with one's legs hanging down on each side, such as horses, bicycles, motorcycles, and SCOOTERs; one **gets off** or (*fml*) **alights** from a bus or train, and **gets out of** a car or taxi.
dis·o·be·di·ent /ˌdɪsə'biːdɪənt, ˌdɪsəʊ-/ *adj* [(*to*)] (of a person or his behaviour) failing to obey: *a disobedient child|He was disobedient to his mother* —**~ly** *adv* —**-ence** *n* [U (*to*)]
dis·o·bey /ˌdɪsə'beɪ, ˌdɪsəʊ-/ *v* [I∅;T1] to fail to obey: *Don't dare to disobey!|disobey one's mother/the rules*
dis·o·blige /ˌdɪsə'blaɪdʒ/ *v* [Wv4;T1] *fml* to go against the wishes of; cause inconvenience to: *It was very disobliging of him to refuse to help* —**-bligingly** *adv*
dis·or·der¹ /dɪs'ɔːdəʳ‖-ɔr-/ *v* [Wv5;T1] to put into DISORDER² (1,3): *a disordered mind/brain* (=ill)
disorder² *n* **1** [U] lack of order; confusion: *The house was in (a state of) disorder because of the young children* **2** [C;U] (a) violent public expression of political dissatisfaction **3** [C;U] slight disease or illness: *suffering from (a) stomach disorder/from disorders of the bowels*
dis·or·der·ly /dɪs'ɔːdəli‖-ɔrdər-/ *adj* **1** untidy; confused: *a disorderly room* **2** (of people or their behaviour) violent in public: *Everybody started shouting and the meeting became very disorderly* —see DRUNK¹ —**-liness** *n* [U]
disorderly house /·'··· ·/ *n law* a BROTHEL (=house where women can be hired for sexual pleasure) or a house where games of chance are played for money without proper permission: *His*

sister keeps a disorderly house in Buenos Aires

dis·or·gan·ize, -ise /dɪsˈɔːgənaɪz‖-ɔr-/ *v* [T1] to throw into disorder (arrangements, a system, etc.) —**-ization** /dɪsˌɔːgənaɪˈzeɪʃən‖-ɔrgənə-/ *n* [U]

dis·or·i·en·tate /dɪsˈɔːrɪənteɪt‖-ˈor-/ also (*esp. AmE*) **dis·or·i·ent** /-rɪənt/— *v* [T1 *usu. pass.*] to cause (someone) to lose the sense of direction: *I'm quite disorientated. Which way is north?*|(fig.) *He seems disorientated since he left the army, and doesn't know what to do next* —opposite **orientate** —**-tation** /dɪsˌɔːrɪənˈteɪʃən‖-ˌor-/ *n* [U]

dis·own /dɪsˈəʊn/ *v* [Wv6;T1] to refuse to accept as one's own; say that one has no connection with: *Peter's father disowned him when he robbed that bank*

di·spar·age /dɪˈspærɪdʒ/ *v* [Wv4;T1] to speak without respect of; make (someone or something) sound of little value or importance: *In spite of your disparaging remarks, I think he sings beautifully* —**-agingly** *adv* —**~ment** *n* [C;U: (*of*)]

dis·pa·rate /ˈdɪspərɪ̈t/ *adj* [Wa5] (of 2 or more things) quite different; that cannot be compared in their qualities: *Chalk and cheese are disparate substances* —**~ly** *adv*

di·spar·i·ty /dɪˈspærɪ̈ti/ *n* [C;U: (*between, in, of*)] (an example of) difference or INEQUALITY: *There is (a) great disparity of/in age between him and his wife*

dis·pas·sion·ate /dɪsˈpæʃənɪ̈t/ *adj apprec* (of a person or his behaviour) calm and fair; not taking sides in an argument —**~ly** *adv* —**~ness** *n* [U]

di·spatch[1], **despatch** /dɪˈspætʃ/ *v* [T1] **1** [(*to*)] to send off (to a place or for a stated purpose): *dispatch letters/invitations|dispatch a boy to the shop to buy beer* **2** to finish quickly; get through (work, food, etc.): *We soon dispatched the chocolate cake* **3** *euph* to kill (usu. officially and according to plan)

dispatch[2], **despatch** *n* **1** [U] DISPATCHing[1]: *After the dispatch of the messenger, we waited* **2** [C] a message carried by a government official, or sent to a newspaper by one of its writers: *send/carry a dispatch from Rome to London* **3** [U] speed and effectiveness: *He did the job with great dispatch*

dispatch box /ˈ·ˈ· ·/ *n* a box for official papers

di·spatch·es, despatches /dɪˈspætʃɪ̈z/ *n* [P] messages sent to a government to describe a battle: *He had the honour of being mentioned in dispatches for his bravery*

dispatch rid·er /ˈ·ˈ· ˌ··/ *n* a man who carries DISPATCHES usu. on a motorcycle

di·spel /dɪˈspel/ *v* **-ll-** [T1] to drive away (as if) by scattering: *The sun soon dispelled the mist.|His calm words dispelled our fears*

di·spen·sa·ble /dɪˈspensəbəl/ *adj* not necessary; that can be DISPENSED WITH

di·spen·sa·ry /dɪˈspensəri/ *n* a place where medicines are DISPENSED (2) and where medical attention is given, esp. in a hospital or school

dis·pen·sa·tion /ˌdɪspənˈseɪʃən, -pen-/ *n* **1** [U] *fml* the act of dispensing (DISPENSE (1)) **2** [C;U] (in the ROMAN CATHOLIC Church) (a case of) permission to disobey a general rule or break a promise **3** [C] an event that seems specially arranged by God or Nature: *The death of the nasty old man seemed a wonderful dispensation to his children* **4** [C] a particular religious system, esp. considered as controlling human affairs during a period: *during the Christian dispensation*

di·spense /dɪˈspens/ *v* [T1] **1** [(*to*)] to deal out; give out (to a number of people): *A judge dispenses justice.|This machine dispenses coffee to anyone who puts in a coin* **2** to mix and give out (medicines)

di·spens·er /dɪˈspensəʳ/ *n* **1** a person who DISPENSEs medicines **2** a container from which liquids or solids can be obtained by pushing or by pressing a handle

dispense with *v prep* [T1] **1** to do without: *We shall have to dispense with the car; we can't afford it* **2** to make unnecessary; allow the lack of: *This new office machine will dispense with the need for a secretary*

di·spens·ing chem·ist /·ˌ·· ˈ··/ *n* (in Britain) a person who both sells medicines and is trained to DISPENSE (2) them

di·sper·sal /dɪˈspɜːsəl‖-ɜr-/ *n* [U] the act of dispersing or the event of being DISPERSEd: *After the dispersal of the crowd, 5 people were found to be hurt* —compare DISPERSION (1)

di·sperse /dɪˈspɜːs‖-ɜrs/ *v* **1** [IØ;T1] to (cause to) scatter in different directions: *After school the children dispersed to their homes.|The wind dispersed the smoke.|A* PRISM *disperses light* **2** [T1] to place at different points: *Groups of police were dispersed all along the street where the Queen was to pass*

di·sper·sion /dɪˈspɜːʃən‖dɪˈspɜrʒən/ *n* [U] *tech* DISPERSAL: *the dispersion of light by a* PRISM

Dispersion *n* [*the*+R] DIASPORA (1)

di·spir·it /dɪˈspɪrɪ̈t/ *v* [Wv5;T1] to discourage; take away the hopeful spirit of

dis·place /dɪsˈpleɪs/ *v* [T1] **1** to force out of the usual place: *He displaced a bone in his knee while playing football* **2** [(*as*)] to take the place of (as if) by pushing out

USAGE Compare **displace**, **replace**, and **substitute**: **Replace** can mean **a** to put back in the same place as before: *to* **replace** *the books on the right shelf* **b** to fill or take the place of: *using oil to* **replace** *coal|* **replacing** *coal with/by oil.* **Displace** and **substitute** have only this second meaning. When **displace** is used of people, it usually gives a feeling of sadness, anger, or lack of justice: *I don't want to be* **displaced** *in your heart by that young fool.* The grammar of **substitute** is rather different: **substituting** *oil for coal|If you want to go out, I can* **substitute** *for you.*

displaced per·son /·ˌ· ˈ··/ *n* **displaced persons** a person forced to leave his/her own country

dis·place·ment /dɪsˈpleɪsmənt/ *n* **1** [U] the act or action of displacing or the state of being DISPLACEd **2** [S] *tech* the weight of water pushed aside by a ship floating in the water

di·splay[1] /dɪˈspleɪ/ *v* [T1] to show: *to display fruit in a shop|to display one's true feelings*

display[2] *n* **1** [C;(U)] the act or action of DISPLAYing: *a display of skill* **2** [C] a collection of things DISPLAYed: *a display of fruit|to put things in a display case* **3** **on display** being shown publicly

dis·please /dɪsˈpliːz/ *v* [T1] to cause DISPLEASURE to

dis·plea·sure /dɪsˈpleʒəʳ/ *n* [U] angry dislike and disapproval

dis·port /dɪˈspɔːt‖-ort/ *v* [T1;IØ] to amuse (oneself) actively: *disporting (themselves) on the seashore*

dis·po·sa·ble /dɪˈspəʊzəbəl/ *adj* [Wa5] **1** that can be freely used, esp. after taxes have been paid: *What was your disposable (personal) income last year?* **2** intended to be used once and then thrown away: *disposable paper plates*

dis·pos·al /dɪˈspəʊzəl/ *n* [U9] **1** arrangement **2** the act or action of getting rid of: *waste disposal* **3** the power or right to use freely (esp. in the phr. **at someone's disposal**): *I put my car at his disposal*

dis·pose /dɪˈspəʊz/ *v* **1** [T1 (*for*)] to put in place; set in readiness: *disposing soldiers for the battle* **2** [IØ] to settle a matter

dis·posed /dɪˈspəʊzd/ *adj* [F3] willing: *You can help me if you feel so disposed/disposed to.|I don't feel disposed to help you*

dispose of *v prep* [T1] to get rid of; throw away; finish with: *Dispose of these old newspapers.|I can dispose of your argument*

dispose to *v prep* [D1] **1** to give a tendency to: *He* *is disposed to sudden periods of anger* **2** also **dispose to·wards**—*fml* to give a feeling of the stated type towards: *He was well/favourably/unfavourably disposed to his secretary*

dis·po·si·tion /ˌdɪspəˈzɪʃən/ *n* **1** [U3,9;C3,9 *usu. sing.*] a general tendency of character, behaviour, etc.: *He has a happy disposition.|She has a disposition to that disease* **2** [S3,9] a general feeling: *We all felt a disposition to leave at once* **3** [U9] the settlement at the end: *the disposition of the law case* **4** [U9] DISPOSAL: *My car was at his disposition*

dis·pos·sess /ˌdɪspəˈzes/ *v* [T1 (*of*)] *fml* to take the right of possession or use away from: *They've dispossessed me (of my house)!* —**~ion** *n* [U9]

dis·pos·sessed /ˌdɪspəˈzest/ *adj* [Wa5;B;F (*of*); *the*+P] *fml* having been forced to give up the right to homes, possessions, etc.: *Sir, the dispossessed are demanding their rights!|people dispossessed of all they had*

dis·proof /dɪsˈpruːf/ *n* [U9] **1** the act or action of disproving (DISPROVE): *The disproof of his story will take a lot of effort* **2** something that DISPROVEs: *The disproof of his story was the fact that he was in Edinburgh, not Glasgow, at the time*

dis·pro·por·tion /ˌdɪsprəˈpɔːʃən‖-or-/ *n* [C;U: (*between*)] a lack of PROPORTION; lack of proper relation between the parts: *a disproportion between the wealth of some and the low standard of living of others*

dis·pro·por·tion·ate /ˌdɪsprəˈpɔːʃənɨ̍t‖-or-/ *adj* [B;F (*to*)] showing DISPROPORTION; unequal; with too much on one side and too little on the other: *His great anger was disproportionate to the small quarrel they had* —**~ly** *adv*

dis·prove /dɪsˈpruːv/ *v* [T1] to prove (something) to be false

di·spu·ta·ble /dɪˈspjuːtəbəl, ˈdɪspjʊ-‖dɪˈspjuː-, ˈdɪspjə-/ *adj* not necessarily true; open to question —**-tably** *adv*

dis·pu·tant /ˈdɪspjʊtənt, dɪˈspjuː-‖ˈdɪspjə-, dɪˈspjuː-/ *n fml or law* a person who DISPUTEs, esp. one who is arguing or quarrelling

dis·pu·ta·tion /ˌdɪspjʊˈteɪʃən‖ˌdɪspjə-/ *n* **1** [U; (C)] *fml* the act or action of disputing (DISPUTE), arguing, or quarrelling **2** [C] *old use* a speech in defence of something or an argument about something, made according to certain rules of reasoning

dis·pu·ta·tious /ˌdɪspjʊˈteɪʃəs‖ˌdɪspjə-/ *adj* **1** tending to DISPUTE[1] or argue **2** *now rare* causing DISPUTEs[2] or arguments —**~ly** *adv*

di·spute[1] /dɪˈspjuːt/ *v* **1** [T1,6a,b;I∅ (*about*)] to argue (about something), esp. angrily and for some time: *They disputed for hours (about) where to go* **2** [T1] to disagree about; call into question; doubt **3** [T1] to struggle against (esp. in defence): *Our soldiers disputed the advance of the enemy* **4** [T1] to struggle over or about (esp. in defence): *The defending army/The 2 armies disputed every inch of ground*

dispute[2] /dɪˈspjuːt, ˈdɪspjuːt/ *n* **1** an argument or quarrel: *a long dispute about where to go* **2 beyond/past (all) dispute** such as cannot be doubted **3 in dispute (with)** in a state of disagreement (with) **4 in/under dispute** being argued about; in disagreement **5 without dispute** undoubted(ly)

dis·qual·i·fi·ca·tion /dɪsˌkwɒlɨ̍fɨ̍ˈkeɪʃən‖-kwɑ-/ *n* **1** [U] the act of disqualifying or the state of being disqualified (DISQUALIFY) **2** [C] something that disqualifies (DISQUALIFY): *His quick temper and unfriendliness are disqualifications for the job of hotel-keeper*

dis·qual·i·fy /dɪsˈkwɒlɨ̍faɪ‖-kwɑ-/ *v* [T1 (*for* or *from*)] to make or declare unfit, unsuitable, or unable to do something: *Her youth disqualifies her from becoming president.|His criminal past disqualified him for the job he wanted.|He won the game, but was disqualified because of his bad behaviour*

dis·qui·et[1] /dɪsˈkwaɪət/ *v* [Wv4;T1] to make anxious: *His mother is disquieted that/because she has received no letters from him for 4 months*

disquiet[2] *n* [U] anxiety and/or dissatisfaction

dis·qui·e·tude /dɪsˈkwaɪətjuːd‖-tuːd/ *n* [U] *fml or old use* DISQUIET[2]

dis·qui·si·tion /ˌdɪskwɨ̍ˈzɪʃən/ *n sometimes derog* a long (perhaps too long) speech or written report about some subject

dis·re·gard[1] /ˌdɪsrɪˈgɑːd‖-ɑrd/ *v* [T1] to pay no attention to; treat as not worthy of regard or notice

disregard[2] *n* [U9 (*for* or *of*)] **1** the act of DISREGARDing or the state of being DISREGARDed: *disregard for my instructions* **2** lack of proper attention to someone or something; NEGLECT: *His disregard of his personal appearance made him unattractive*

dis·rel·ish[1] /dɪsˈrelɪʃ/ *v* [T1] *fml or pomp* to dislike; dislike the taste of

disrelish[2] *n* [U] *fml* lack of pleasure; feeling of dislike

dis·re·mem·ber /ˌdɪsrɪˈmembəʳ/ *v* [T1,6a,b;I∅] *dial, Am&IrE* to forget: *I disremember . . . what I did*

dis·re·pair /ˌdɪsrɪˈpeəʳ/ *n* [U] the state of being in need of repair (esp. in the phrs. **in/into disrepair**)

dis·rep·u·ta·ble /dɪsˈrepjʊtəbəl‖-pjə-/ *adj* having or showing a bad character; having a bad name: *disreputable people/behaviour/a disreputable-looking person*|(fig.) *a disreputable old coat* —**~ness** *n* [U] —**-tably** *adv*

dis·re·pute /ˌdɪsrɪˈpjuːt/ *n* [U] loss or lack of people's good opinion; bad REPUTE (esp. in the phrs. **in/into disrepute**): *The hotel fell into disrepute after they began to serve alcohol*

dis·re·spect /ˌdɪsrɪˈspekt/ *n* [U] lack of respect or politeness —**~ful** *adj* —**~fully** *adv*

dis·robe /dɪsˈrəʊb/ *v* [I∅;(T1)] *fml* to take off (esp. ceremonial outer) clothing: *Don't disrobe in public.|After the trial, the judge disrobed and left the court*

dis·rupt /dɪsˈrʌpt/ *v* [T1] to bring or throw into disorder: *An accident has disrupted railway services into and out of the city* —**~ion** /-ˈrʌpʃən/ *n* [U;C] —**~ive** /-ˈrʌptɪv/ *adj*: *the disruptive influence of trouble-makers* —**~ively** *adv*

dis·sat·is·fac·tion /dɪˌsætɨ̍sˈfækʃən, dɪsˌsæ-/ *n* [U,U5] lack of satisfaction: *her dissatisfaction that he arrived late/at his late arrival*

dis·sat·is·fy /dɪˈsætɨ̍sfaɪ, dɪsˈsæ-/ *v* [T1] to fail to satisfy; displease

dis·sect /dɪˈsekt, daɪ-/ *v* **1** [T1;I∅] to cut up (something) into parts, esp. to cut up (the body of a plant or animal) in such a way as to find the shape and relationship of the parts, as medical students do **2** [T1] to study very carefully, part by part (esp. to find the faults in); ANALYSE

dis·sec·tion /dɪˈsekʃən, daɪ-/ *n* **1** [U] the act or action of DISSECTing or the state of being DISSECTed **2** [C] an example of this **3** [C] a part of an animal or plant that has been DISSECTed

dis·sem·ble /dɪˈsembəl/ also (*fml*) **dissimulate**— *v* [Wv3;T1;I∅] to hide (esp. one's true feelings, intentions, etc.) —**~r** *n*

dis·sem·i·nate /dɪˈsemɨ̍neɪt/ *v* [T1] *fml* to spread (news, ideas, etc.) widely, like scattering seed —**-nation** /dɪˌsemɨ̍ˈneɪʃən/ *n* [U]

dis·sen·sion /dɪˈsenʃən/ *n* **1** [U] disagreement, esp. leading to argument and quarrelling **2** [C] an example of this

dis·sent[1] /dɪˈsent/ *v* [I∅ (*from*)] to disagree; refuse to agree: *I dissent altogether (from such an unwise idea)*

dissent[2] *n* **1** [U] disagreement; difference of opinion: *When I asked for agreement there was no dissent* **2** [U] *now rare* (*often cap.*) religious separation from the CHURCH OF ENGLAND; NONCONFORMITY: *Is Dissent stronger in Wales or in Cornwall?* **3** [C] *esp. AmE* also **dissenting o·pin·ion** /·,·· ·'··/— a judge's opinion disagreeing with that of most of the other judges of a law case

dis·sent·er /dɪ'sentəʳ/ *n* **1** a person who DISSENTs **2** (*often cap.*) a member of a church that has become separate from the CHURCH OF ENGLAND; NONCONFORMIST

dis·sent·ing /dɪ'sentɪŋ/ *adj* **1** of or like a person who DISSENTs **2** [Wa5] (*often cap.*) of or like a church that has become separate from the CHURCH OF ENGLAND; NONCONFORMIST

dis·ser·ta·tion /ˌdɪsə'teɪʃən‖ˌdɪsər-/ *n* a long usu. written treatment of a subject, esp. one written for a higher university degree

dis·ser·vice /dɪ'sɜːvəs, dɪs'sɜː‖-ɜr-/ *n* [U;S] harm or a harmful action: *You will be doing yourself a disservice if you send that angry letter to such a powerful person*

dis·sev·er /dɪ'sevəʳ/ *v* [T1] *fml* to disunite; SEVER

dis·si·dent /'dɪsədənt/ *adj, n* (a person) openly and often strongly disagreeing with an opinion or a group: *political dissidents* —**-dence** *n* [U]

dis·sim·i·lar /dɪ'sɪmələʳ, dɪs'sɪ-/ *adj* unlike; not SIMILAR —**~ly** *adv*

dis·sim·i·lar·i·ty /dɪˌsɪmə'lærəti, dɪsˌsɪ-/ also (*fml*) **dis·si·mil·i·tude** /ˌdɪsə'mɪlətjuːd, ˌdɪs-sə-/— *n* [U] the state or degree of being DISSIMILAR: *How great is the dissimilarity between the 2 plans?*

dis·sim·u·late /dɪ'sɪmjʊleɪt‖-mjə-/ *v* [T1;I∅] *fml* DISSEMBLE —**-lation** /dɪˌsɪmjʊ'leɪʃən‖-jə-/ *n* [U;C]

dis·si·pate /'dɪsəpeɪt/ *v* **1** [T1;I∅] to (cause to) disappear or scatter: *He tried to dissipate the smoke by opening a window.|When it started to rain, the crowd quickly dissipated* **2** [T1 *often pass.*;I∅] *tech* to (cause to) lose (heat, electricity, etc.) without the possibility of more being provided **3** [T1] to spend, waste, or use up foolishly: *He dissipated his large fortune in a few years of heavy spending*

dis·si·pat·ed /'dɪsəpeɪtəd/ *adj* (typical of a person) that spends his/her life in search of foolish or dangerous pleasure: *a dissipated person/life*

dis·si·pa·tion /ˌdɪsə'peɪʃən/ *n* [U] **1** the act of dissipating or the state of being DISSIPATED **2** the continual search for foolish or dangerous pleasure

dis·so·ci·ate /dɪ'səʊʃieɪt, -sieɪt/ also **disassociate**— *v* [T1 (*from*)] to separate from association or union with something or someone else; disconnect: *Can the private and public lives of a politician ever be dissociated?|You have no right to dissociate yourself from the actions of your friends* —**-ation** /dɪˌsəʊʃi'eɪʃən, -si'eɪʃən/ *n* [U]

dis·sol·u·ble /dɪ'sɒljʊbəl‖dɪ'sɑljə-/ *adj* that can be DISSOLVEd —**-bility** /dɪˌsɒljʊ'bɪləti‖dɪˌsɑljə-/ *n* [U]

dis·so·lute /'dɪsəluːt/ *adj* (typical of a person) that leads a bad life: *a dissolute person/life* —**~ly** *adv* —**~ness** *n* [U]

dis·so·lu·tion /ˌdɪsə'luːʃən/ *n* [U] **1** the separation of a thing into its parts **2** decay, esp. death: *the dissolution of the Roman Empire* **3** the ending or breaking up of an association, group, partnership, etc.: *the dissolution of a marriage|the dissolution of Parliament before a general election*

dis·solve /dɪ'zɒlv‖dɪ'zɑlv/ *v* **1** [T1;I∅] to separate into simple parts **2** [T1;I∅] **a** to cause (a solid or a gas) to become liquid by putting into liquid **b** (of a solid or a gas) to become liquid by being put into liquid: *Sugar dissolves in water* **3** [T1;I∅] **a** to cause (an association, group, etc.) to end or break up **b** (of an association, group, etc.) to end or break up **4** [I∅] to waste or fade away: *His strength dissolved* **5** [I∅] (of things seen) to fade out gradually: *The mountains dissolved behind a thick curtain of clouds* **6** [L9] to lose one's self-control under the influence of strong feeling: *to dissolve in/into tears*

dis·so·nance /'dɪsənəns/ *n* **1** [U] the sounding at the same time of musical notes which do not sound pleasant when played or sung together **2** [C] a combination of musical notes which do not sound pleasant when sounded together **3** [S;U] a lack of agreement among beliefs, or between beliefs and actions

dis·so·nant /'dɪsənənt/ *adj* marked by DISSONANCE —**~ly** *adv*

dis·suade /dɪ'sweɪd/ *v* [T1 (*from*)] to prevent from doing something by giving reasons: *I tried to dissuade her* (*from joining the club*) —**-suasion** /dɪ'sweɪʒən/ *n* [U]

dist. *written abbrev. for:* **1** distance **2** DISTRICT

dis·taff /'dɪstɑːf‖'dɪstæf/ *n* **1** *now rare* the stick from which the wool is pulled in spinning **2 on the distaff side** on the woman's side of the family

dis·tal /'dɪstəl/ *adj tech* far from the point of joining or origin —opposite **proximal** —**~ly** *adv*

dis·tance[1] /'dɪstəns/ *n* **1** [C;U] (the amount of) separation in space or time: *What is the distance to London/between London and Glasgow/from London to Glasgow?|It is some distance away|a good distance away|within* (*easy*) *walking distance of home.|I can hardly remember him at this distance of/in time.|a distance of 20 miles* **2** [(*the*) S (*of*)] a distant point or place: *One can see the ancient ruins from a distance of 20 miles/at a distance of 20 miles/in the distance* **3** [C *usu. pl.*] large empty spaces: *The distances stretched away as far as the eye could see* **4** [C;U] social separation or coldness in personal relations: *There has been a great distance between us since our quarrel* **5 go the distance** (in sports, esp. BOXING) to keep playing, running, or fighting till the end of the match **6 keep one's distance (from)** to stay far enough away (from): *The lion looked dangerous, so I decided to keep my distance from it* **7 keep someone at a distance** to treat someone without much friendliness

distance[2] *v* [T1] OUTDISTANCE

dis·tant /'dɪstənt/ *adj* **1** [B;E] separate in space or time; far off; away: *distant lands|the distant sound of a bell|at some far distant time|100 years distant|the distant past* **2** [A] coming from or going to a distance: *a distant journey* **3** [A] (of people) not closely related: *Those 2 boys don't look alike, but they are distant relations* **4** [B] not very close: *There is a distant relationship between those 2 ideas* **5** [B] showing social distance or lack of friendliness

dis·tant·ly /'dɪstəntli/ *adv* **1** in a manner that shows inattention, social separation, or lack of friendliness: *He looked at me distantly* **2** not closely: *Those 2 people/ideas are distantly related* **3** at a distance; far away: *an object distantly seen on the horizon*

dis·taste /dɪs'teɪst/ *n* [S;U: (*for*)] dislike; displeasure

dis·taste·ful /dɪs'teɪstfəl/ *adj* [B;F (*to*)] causing DISTASTE: *The very idea of cheating him is distasteful to me* —**~ly** *adv* —**~ness** *n* [U]

dis·tem·per[1] /dɪ'stempəʳ/ *n* [U] a disease of animals, esp. dogs and rabbits, causing fever, disordered breathing, and general weakness

distemper[2] *v* [T1;X7] *esp. BrE* to paint with DISTEMPER[3]

distemper[3] *n* [U] *esp. BrE* a paint for walls and other surfaces that can be made thinner by mixing with water

dis·tem·pered /dɪ'stempəd‖-ərd/ *adj lit or old use* mad: *a distempered mind*

dis·tend /dɪ'stend/ *v* [T1;I∅] *fml* to (cause to) swell
dis·ten·sion /dɪ'stenʃən/ *n* [U] *fml* swelling: *distension of the stomach*
dis·til, *AmE* usu. **-till** /dɪ'stɪl/ *v* **-ll-** **1** [T1] to make (a liquid) into gas and then make the gas into liquid, as when separating alcohol from water: *Water can be made pure by distilling it.|distilled water* **2** [T1 (OUT)] to remove in this way: *Sea water can be made fit to drink by distilling out the salt* **3** [T1;I∅] to (cause to) fall drop by drop: *In certain conditions, water distils through hard rock and appears in drops on the surface* **4** [T1] to get or take the most important part(s) of (a book, an idea, a subject, etc.): *This book gives you the distilled ideas of the ancient Greeks in a form that is easy to understand*
dis·til·la·tion /ˌdɪst̮ˈleɪʃən/ *n* **1** [U] the act or action of DISTILling or the state of being DISTILled: *the distillation of pure water/of* WHISKY **2** [C;U] a liquid or other product got by DISTILling
dis·til·ler /dɪ'stɪlə^r/ *n* a person who DISTILs, esp. strong alcoholic drink such as WHISKY
dis·til·le·ry /dɪ'stɪləri/ *n* a factory or business firm where DISTILling is done, esp. the DISTILling of WHISKY
dis·tinct /dɪ'stɪŋkt/ *adj* **1** [B;F (*from*)] different; separate: *Those 2 ideas are quite distinct (from each other).|They wanted to form a new and completely distinct political party* **2** [B] clearly seen, heard, understood, etc.; plain; noticeable: *a distinct smell of burning* —**~ly** *adv* —**~ness** *n* [U]
USAGE Anything clearly noticed is **distinct**: *There's a* **distinct** *smell of beer in this room.* A thing or quality that is clearly different from others of its kind is **distinctive**, or **distinct** *from*: *Beer has a very* **distinctive** *smell; it's quite* **distinct** *from the smell of wine.*
dis·tinc·tion /dɪ'stɪŋkʃən/ *n* **1** [C;U: (*between*)] difference: *Can you make/draw a distinction between these 2 ideas?* **2** [S;U] the quality of being unusual, esp. of being unusually good in mind or spirit; worth: *a writer of true distinction* **3** [C] a special mark of honour: *These are the highest distinctions that have ever been given by our government*
dis·tinc·tive /dɪ'stɪŋktɪv/ *adj* clearly marking a person or thing as different from others: *Each rank in the army has a distinctive sign to wear* —see DISTINCT (USAGE) —**~ly** *adv* —**~ness** *n* [U]
dis·tin·guish /dɪ'stɪŋgwɪʃ/ *v* **1** [T1] to recognize by some mark or typical sign: *I can distinguish them by their uniforms* **2** [Wv6;T1] to hear or see clearly: *I can distinguish objects at a great distance* **3** [T1 (*from*);I∅ (*between*)] to make or recognize differences: *I can distinguish (between) those 2 objects/ideas.|I can distinguish (between) right and wrong.|I can distinguish right from wrong* **4** [Wv6;T1] to set apart or mark as different: *Elephants are distinguished by their long noses* (TRUNKs) **5** [T1] to make unusually good: *He distinguished himself by his performance in the examination*
dis·tin·gui·sha·ble /dɪ'stɪŋgwɪʃəbəl/ *adj* **1** [B] that can be clearly seen, heard, understood, etc.: *A black object is not easily distinguishable on a dark night* **2** [B;F (*from*)] that can be clearly recognized as different: *Those 2 objects/ideas are not easily distinguishable (from each other)*
dis·tin·guished /dɪ'stɪŋgwɪʃt/ *adj* [B;F (*for*)] *apprec* marked by excellent quality or deserved fame
dis·tort /dɪ'stɔːt‖-ɔrt/ *v* [T1] **1** to twist out of the true meaning: *Stop distorting what I've said.|He gave a distorted account of what had happened* **2** to twist out of a natural, usual, or original shape or condition: *a face distorted by/with anger* **3** (of a radio or television set, cinema camera, etc.) to show, play, etc., improperly: *a radio that distorts sound*
dis·tor·tion /dɪ'stɔːʃən‖-ɔr-/ *n* **1** [U] the act or action of distorting or the state of being DISTORTed **2** [C] something that is DISTORTed
dis·tract /dɪ'strækt/ *v* [Wv4;T1 (*from*)] to take (a person, a person's mind) off something: *Don't distract me (from working).|Don't distract my attention*
dis·tract·ed /dɪ'strækt̮d/ *adj* [B;F (*by* or *with*)] (typical of a person who is) anxious or unable to think clearly by being troubled about many things: *He gave me a distracted look and ran out of the room* —**~ly** *adv*
dis·trac·tion /dɪ'strækʃən/ *n* **1** [U] the act of DISTRACTing or the state of being DISTRACTed **2** [U] an anxious confused state of mind near madness: *Her continual talking drove him to distraction* **3** [C] something (or someone) that DISTRACTs; amusement: *There are too many distractions here to work properly.|The cinema is my favourite distraction*
dis·train /dɪ'streɪn/ *v* [I∅ (*upon*)] *law* to take goods from someone in order to force payment of a debt: *If he doesn't pay, will the court distrain (upon his house)?*
dis·traint /dɪ'streɪnt/ *n* [U] *law* the act of DISTRAINing
dis·trait /dɪ'streɪ (*Fr* distrɛ)/ *adj Fr* (typical of a person who is) not paying close attention to the surroundings
dis·traught /dɪ'strɔːt/ *adj* [B;F (*with*)] (typical of a person who is) very anxious and troubled almost to the point of madness
dis·tress[1] /dɪ'stres/ *n* **1** [U] great suffering of the mind or body; pain or great discomfort: *The sick man showed signs of distress.|Your dishonest actions have caused us all a great deal of distress* **2** [S] something that causes great suffering of the mind: *The girl's leaving home was a great distress to her family* **3** [U] the state of suffering caused by a lack of money or of the necessary things of life: *Someone must help these poor people in their (great) distress* **4** [U] a state of danger or great difficulty: *If the storm continues on the mountain, the climbers will be in distress by morning.|Send out a distress signal*
distress[2] *v* [T1] to cause DISTRESS[1] to
dis·tressed ar·e·a /·ˌ· '···/ *n BrE now rare* an area of continuing high unemployment
dis·tress·ing /dɪ'stresɪŋ/ also **dis·tress·ful** /dɪ'stresfəl/— *adj* causing DISTRESS[1]: *distressing news* —**~ly** *adv*
dis·trib·ute /dɪ'strɪbjuːt/ *v* [T1] **1** [(*to* or *among*)] to divide among several or many: *to distribute the books to the students|to distribute the prizes among the winners* **2** [(*over*)] to spread out; scatter: *This new machine distributes seed evenly and quickly (over the whole farm)* **3** [(*to*)] to give out or deliver (the same thing to many people): *to distribute written material about the election to every voter* **4** to supply (goods) in a particular area, esp. to shops
dis·tri·bu·tion /ˌdɪstr̮ˈbjuːʃən/ *n* **1** [U9] the act or action of distributing or the state of being DISTRIBUTEd **2** [U;S] the way in which the members of a group are DISTRIBUTEd: *Why has the distribution of these animals changed so much in our part of the world?* **3** [C] an example or act of distributing (DISTRIBUTE) —**~al** *adj* [Wa5]
dis·trib·u·tive /dɪ'strɪbjʊtɪv‖-bjə-/ *adj* [Wa5;A;(B)] **1** distributing (DISTRIBUTE): *The distributive trades of* TRANSPORT *and selling are as important as those which actually produce goods* **2** *tech* (of a word) concerning each single member of a group: *Distributive words in English include "each", "every", "either", and "neither"* —**~ly** *adv*

dis·trib·u·tor /dɪ'strɪbjʊtə^r^‖-bjə-/ *n* **1** a person or thing that DISTRIBUTES **2** an instrument which sends electric current in the right order to each SPARKING PLUG in a motorcar engine —see picture at CAR and PETROL

dis·trict /'dɪstrɪkt/ *n* **1** a fixed land division of a country, a city, etc., made officially for particular purposes: *a postal district|a district council* **2** a part of a country with a special and particular quality, or of a particular kind: *the Lake District of England* **3** an area of a town: *the Garden District of New Orleans*

dis·trust[1] /dɪs'trʌst/ *v* [T1] to lack trust in; mistrust

USAGE **Distrust** is perhaps a little stronger than **mistrust**. Otherwise they have the same meaning, but **mistrust** is the only one that can be used about oneself: *She* **mistrusted** *herself/***mistrusted** *her ability to do the job.*

distrust[2] *n* [U;S] lack of trust; mistrust: *He keeps his money at home because he has a great distrust of banks* —see DISTRUST (USAGE)

dis·trust·ful /dɪs'trʌstfəl/ *adj* having or showing DISTRUST[2]; mistrustful —**~ly** *adv* —**~ness** *n* [U]

dis·turb /dɪ'stɜːb‖-ɜrb/ *v* [T1] **1** to change the usual or natural condition of: *A light wind disturbed the surface of the water* **2** to break in upon (esp. a person who is working) **3** [Wv4] to cause (a person) to become anxious: *disturbing news* **4** to break (a person's peace of mind, sleep, etc.) **5** **disturb the peace** *law* to cause public disorder

dis·turb·ance /dɪ'stɜːbəns‖-ɜr-/ *n* **1** [U9] the act of DISTURBing or the state of being DISTURBed **2** [C] a case of this: *Those men were charged by the police with causing a disturbance* **3** [U9;C] something that DISTURBs: *The noise of cars passing along the road is a continual disturbance to our quiet at home*

dis·turbed /dɪ'stɜːbd‖-ɜr-/ *adj* having or showing signs of an illness of the mind or the feelings: *The* EMOTIONALLY *disturbed are often difficult to treat*

dis·u·ni·on /dɪs'juːnɪən/ *n* [U] **1** the act of disuniting or the state of being DISUNITED **2** DISUNITY

dis·u·nite /ˌdɪsjuː'naɪt/ *v* [T1;(I∅)] to divide; separate

dis·u·ni·ty /dɪs'juːnɪ̈ti/ *n* [U] lack of unity, esp. with disagreement and quarrelling

dis·use /dɪs'juːs/ *n* [U] the state of no longer being used: *That law has fallen into disuse*

dis·used /ˌdɪs'juːzd◂/ *adj* [Wa5] *esp. BrE* no longer used: *a disused mine*

di·syl·lab·ic /ˌdɪsɪ̈'læbɪk, ˌdaɪ-/ *adj* [Wa5] *tech* consisting of 2 SYLLABLEs

di·syl·la·ble /dɪ'sɪləbəl, daɪ-/ *n tech* a word or other language form consisting of 2 SYLLABLEs: *The word "language" is a disyllable*

ditch[1] /dɪtʃ/ *n* a long narrow not very deep V- or U-shaped passage cut into the ground, as for water to flow through

ditch[2] *v* [T1] *sl* to get rid of; leave suddenly; ABANDON: *His old car stopped working and he decided to ditch it.|He promised to drive us to London but he ditched us 50 miles away*

dith·er[1] /'dɪðə^r^/ *v* [I∅ (ABOUT, *about*)] *infml* to act nervously or be unable to decide

dither[2] *n* [S] *infml* a state of nervous excitement and inability to make decisions

dith·ers /'dɪðəz‖-ərz/ *n* [*the*+P] *infml, esp. BrE* DITHER[2]: *He's got the dithers about the choice*

dit·to /'dɪtəʊ/ *n* **-tos** **1** *infml* the same: *"He said we should do it." "And I say ditto (to that)"* **2** a mark (") meaning the same: *one black pencil at 12p " blue " " 15p* (=one black pencil at 12p, one blue pencil at 15p)

dit·ty /'dɪti/ *n* a short simple song

di·u·ret·ic /ˌdaɪjʊ'retɪk/ *n, adj* [U;C;B] (a medicine) that causes a flow of URINE

di·ur·nal /daɪ'ɜːnəl‖-'ɜr-/ *adj* [Wa5] *fml or tech* of, related to, happening in, or active in the daytime rather than the nighttime —opposite **nocturnal** —**~ly** *adv*

div. *written abbrev. for*: **1** divided **2** DIVINE **3** DIVIDEND **4** (*infml pronounced as* /dɪv/) division

di·va·gate /'daɪvəgeɪt/ *v* [I∅ (*from*)] *fml* to go off the point in speech or writing —**-gation** /ˌdaɪvə'geɪʃən/ *n* [U;C]

di·van /dɪ'væn‖'daɪvæn/ *n* **1** a long soft seat on a wooden base, usu. without back or arms, placed against a wall **2** also **divan bed** /·,· '·‖,·· '·/— the same used for sleeping: *We have a divan bed in the spare room* **3** (*often cap.*) (in former times) (a room used for) a council of state in some Eastern countries, esp. Turkey

dive[1] /daɪv/ *v past t.* also (*esp. AmE*) **dove** /dəʊv/ **1** [I∅ (IN, OFF, *off, from,* or *into*)] to jump head first into the water: *The boy ran to the side of the swimming pool and dived off* **2** [I∅ (DOWN, *for*)] to go under the surface of the water; SUBMERGE: *They are diving for gold from the Spanish wreck* **3** [I∅ (DOWN)] (of a plane or bird) to go down steeply and swiftly **4** [L9] (on land) to move quickly, esp. downwards, head first, or out of sight: *The rabbit dived into its hole.|to dive suddenly into a little doorway* **5** [L9] to put one's hand(s) quickly and suddenly deep into something, esp. in order to get something out: *He dived into the bag and brought out 2 red apples* **6** [L9 esp. IN] to enter quickly and suddenly into some matter or activity: *He had never studied French before, but he just dived in and started trying to speak it*

dive[2] *n* **1** an act of diving (DIVE): *a beautiful dive into the pool|When the shots sounded in the street, we made a dive for the nearest doorway* **2** *infml* a not very respectable place, esp. for meeting, eating, or amusement: *He had his money stolen in a low dive* **3** **take a dive** *sl* to agree to lose a match dishonestly, esp. a BOXING match

dive-bomb /'· ·/ *v* [T1;I∅] (of a plane or its pilot) to dive and then bomb: *to dive-bomb a crowd of women and children* —**~er** *n*

div·er /'daɪvə^r^/ *n* a person who DIVEs, esp. one who works at the bottom of the sea in special dress with a supply of air

di·verge /daɪ'vɜːdʒ, dɪ̈-‖-ɜr-/ *v* [I∅ (*from*)] to go out in different directions: *I'm afraid our opinions diverge (from each other) (from a common starting point)*

di·ver·gence /daɪ'vɜːdʒəns, dɪ̈-‖-ɜr-/ also **di·ver·gen·cy** /-dʒənsi/— *n* [U;C] (an example of) the action or amount of diverging (DIVERGE) —**-gent** *adj* —**-gently** *adv*

di·vers /'daɪvəz‖-ərz/ *adj* [Wa5;A] *old use or humor* many different: *Divers persons were present, of all stations in life*

di·verse /daɪ'vɜːs‖dɪ̈'vɜrs, daɪ-/ *adj* different; various: *many diverse interests* —**~ly** *adv often fml*

di·ver·si·fy /daɪ'vɜːsɪ̈faɪ‖dɪ̈'vɜr-, daɪ-/ *v* [T1;I∅] to make different or various in form or quality; vary: *That factory is trying to diversify its products to sell in different markets.|Our factory diversified several years ago!* (=started to make many different sorts of product)

di·ver·sion /daɪ'vɜːʃən, dɪ̈-‖-ɜrʒən/ *n* **1** [U;C] a turning aside from a course, activity, or use: *the diversion of a river to supply water somewhere else|the diversion of someone's attention* **2** [C] something that turns someone's attention away from something else that one does not wish to be noticed: *I claim that your last argument was a diversion to make us forget the main point* **3** [C] something that

DIVERTs or amuses: *London offers lots of diversions for every type of person*

di·ver·sion·a·ry /daɪ'vɜːʃənəri, dʒ-‖-ɜrʒəneri/ *adj* intended to form a DIVERSION from the principal operation or main point

di·ver·si·ty /daɪ'vɜːsʒti, dʒ-‖-ɜr-/ *n* [S;U: (*of*)] the condition of being different or having differences; variety: *Mary has a great diversity of interests: she likes sports, travel, photography, and making radio sets*

di·vert /daɪ'vɜːt, dʒ-‖-ɜr-/ *v* [T1] **1** [(*from, to*)] to cause to turn aside or from one use or direction to another: *They diverted the river to supply water somewhere else* **2** [(*from*)] to turn (a person or a person's attention) away from something, with good or bad result: *A loud noise diverted my attention (from cooking) and everything was burnt* **3** [Wv4] to amuse: *He can always invent a new game to divert the children*

di·ver·ti·men·to /dɪˌvɜːtʒ'mentəʊ‖-ɜr-/ *n* **-tos, -ti** /ti/ a musical work for a small number of instruments, in several parts (MOVEMENTs) and often of a light character

di·ver·tisse·ment /dɪ'vɜːtʒsmənt‖-ɜr- (*Fr* divɛrtismɑ̃)/ *n Fr* **1** an amusing thing to do **2** DIVERTIMENTO

di·vest of /daɪ'vest, dʒ-‖-ɜr-/ *v prep* [D1] *fml* **1** to take off (the ceremonial clothes) of: *They divested the king of his* ROBEs *of state* **2** to take away (the official position or special rights) of: *They divested the king of all his power* **3** to cause (oneself) to get rid of (esp. false ideas): *If you wish to be a happy man, you must divest yourself of pride*

di·vide[1] /dʒ'vaɪd/ *v* **1** [T1;I∅: (*into*)] to (cause to) separate into parts: *"Does this table divide?" "Yes. It divides into 2 separate parts."|This class is too large. We shall have to divide it.|Divide this line into 20 equal parts.|Divide it in half* **2** [T1 (*from*)] to be that which separates (2 things) or comes between (2 parts of one thing): *The new road will divide the farm.|A low brick wall divides our garden from/and our neighbour's garden* **3** [T1 (*between*)] to use (different amounts of the same thing) for different purposes: *He divides his time between reading and writing* **4** [T1 (*by* or *from*)] to separate into groups according to some system: *Divide the books according to subject/by subject.|Divide the younger children and/from the older children* **5** [T1 (UP, *between, among* or *with*)] to separate and give out or share: *Divide the cake (up) between/among you.|Divide the cake with your sister* **6** [D1+*by/into*;T1;I∅ (*into*)] to find out how many times one number contains or is contained in another number, as shown in the following expressions: *Divide 15 by 3. 15 divided by 3 is 5.|Divide 3 into 15. 3 divides into 15 5 times* **7** [T1] to be an important cause of disagreement between; to separate into opposing groups: *I hope this disagreement will not divide us* **8** [T1;I∅] to (cause to) vote by separating into one group for and one group against: *Parliament divided on the question, and the Government won narrowly*

divide[2] *n* **1** *tech* a line of high land that comes between 2 different river systems; WATERSHED (1) **2 the Great Divide** *lit* the border between life and death

div·i·dend /'dɪvʒdənd, -dend/ *n* **1** that part of the money made by a business which is divided among those who own shares in the business: *The company declared a large dividend at the end of the year* **2** the amount of this money which goes to each person who owns a share of the business: *What dividend did you receive?* **3** a number to be divided by another: *When 15 is divided by 3, the number 15 is the dividend* —compare DIVISOR **4 pay dividends** to produce an advantage; be useful in the future: *I'm sure that new idea will pay dividends some day*

di·vid·ers /dʒ'vaɪdəz‖-ərz/ *n* [P] an instrument for measuring or marking off lines, angles, etc. —see PAIR (USAGE) and picture at MATHEMATICAL

div·i·na·tion /ˌdɪvʒ'neɪʃən/ *n* **1** [U] the act or action of telling the unknown or the future **2** [C] an example of this

di·vine[1] /dʒ'vaɪn/ *adj* **1** [Wa5] of, related to, or being God or a god **2** *infml* (*used esp. by women*) very very good: *That play we saw last night was just simply divine!* —**~ly** *adv*

divine[2] *n now rare* a priest, esp. of the Christian religion, with special training and interest in religious studies

divine[3] *v* **1** [T1,6a,b;I∅] to discover or guess (the unknown, esp. the future) by or as if by magic **2** [T1;I∅ (*for*)] to be able to find (water or minerals) under ground: *He divined (for) water on my farm*

di·vin·er /dʒ'vaɪnəʳ/ *n* a person who DIVINEs[3], esp. one who can find water under ground —compare DOWSER

divine right /·ˌ· '·/ *n* [U] the idea that a king receives his right to rule directly from God and not from the people: *the divine right of kings*|(fig.) *You seem to think you can do anything you want by divine right! Well, you can't!*

divine ser·vice /·ˌ· '··/ *n* [C;U] a service of Christian worship

div·ing bell /'·· ·/ *n* a bell-shaped metal container let down into the water in which men work under water

div·ing·board /'daɪvɪŋbɔːd‖bord/ *n* a board fixed at one end, esp. high off the ground, off which people DIVE (1) into the water —compare SPRINGBOARD

diving suit /'·· ·/ *n* a special suit worn by DIVERs, which keeps water out and has a supply of air

di·vin·ing rod /·'·· ·/ *n* DOWSING ROD

di·vin·i·ty /dʒ'vɪnʒti/ *n* **1** [U] the quality or state of being DIVINE[1] **2** [C] (*often cap.*) a DIVINE[1] being; god or goddess **3** [U] THEOLOGY

Divinity *n* [*the*+R] God

di·vis·i·ble /dʒ'vɪzəbəl/ *adj* [Wa5] that can be divided: *15 is divisible by 3*

di·vi·sion /dʒ'vɪʒən/ *n* **1** [U] separation or DISTRIBUTION **2** [C] one of the parts or groups into which a whole is divided **3** [GC] a large military or naval group, esp. one able to fight on its own without needing additional support or supplies **4** [C] an important group having a special purpose within a governmental, business, or educational organization **5** [C] something that divides or separates: *The river forms the division between the old and new parts of the city* **6** [U] disagreement; lack of unity **7** [U] the act or action of finding out how many times one number or quantity is contained in another: *the division of 15 by 3|Have you learnt division?* **8** [C] (in Britain) a vote in Parliament in which all those in favour go to one place and all those against go to another: *to force a division*

division bell /·'·· ·/ *n* (in Britain) a bell that is rung in the Parliament building to let members who are not in the main meeting room know that a DIVISION (8) is to take place

division lob·by /·'·· ˌ··/ *n* (in Britain) either of the 2 places to which a Member of Parliament goes to vote for or against something in a DIVISION (8)

division of la·bour /·ˌ·· · '··/ *n* [(*the*) U] a system in which each member of a group specializes in a different type of work, in the hope that total production will be increased

di·vi·sive /dʒ'vaɪsɪv/ *adj* tending to divide people, make them argue amongst themselves, etc.; causing disunity —**~ly** *adv* —**~ness** *n* [U]

di·vi·sor /dʒ'vaɪzəʳ/ *n* the number by which another

number is divided: *When 15 is divided by 3, the number 3 is the divisor* —compare DIVIDEND (3)

di·vorce¹ /d$\frac{1}{2}$'vɔːs‖-ors/ *n* **1** [U;C] a complete breaking up of a marriage declared by a court of law: *Is divorce allowed in your country?|She obtained a divorce after years of unhappiness* **2** [C *usu. sing.*] a separation: *There is a growing divorce between desire and possibility in today's world*

divorce² *v* **1** [T1;I∅] to end a marriage between (a husband and wife) or to (a husband or a wife): *The court divorced them.|They divorced (each other).|She divorced him.|a divorced woman* **2** [T1 (*from*)] to separate: *It is hard to divorce love and duty/love from duty in one's mind*

di·vor·cée /d$\frac{1}{2}$'vɔːsiː‖d$\frac{1}{2}$,vor'seɪ, -'siː/ *n Fr* a DIVORCEd woman

div·ot /'dɪvət/ *n* a small piece of earth and grass dug out accidentally by a player hitting a GOLF ball

di·vulge /daɪ'vʌldʒ, d$\frac{1}{2}$-/ *v* [T1 (*to*), 5,6a] *fml* to tell (what has been secret): *Who divulged our plans (to the secret police)?|Newsmen divulged that the President had been considering the idea for some time before making it public yesterday* —**-ence** *n* [U;C]

div·vy¹ /'dɪvi/ *v* [T1 (UP)] *sl* to divide: *Divvy it up between us*

divvy² *n* [C;U] *BrE sl* (esp. in former times) a DIVIDEND (2), esp. one paid by a COOPERATIVE Society

Dix·ie /'dɪksi/ *n* [R] *infml AmE* the Southern states of the US, esp. the south-eastern states where slaves were owned before the War Between the States (the CIVIL WAR): *back home in Dixie*

dix·ie·land /'dɪksilænd/ also **dixieland jazz** /,··· '·/— *n* [U] old-style (TRADITIONAL) JAZZ

DIY abbrev. for: DO **it yourself**

diz·zy¹ /'dɪzi/ *adj* [Wa1] **1** [B] having or showing an unpleasant feeling that things are going round and round **2** [A] causing this feeling; DIZZYing² (esp. in the phr. **a dizzy height**) **3** [F (*with*)] having a pleasant feeling of excitement and lightness, as if floating **4** [B] *infml* silly —**dizzily** *adv* —**dizziness** *n* [U]

dizzy² *v* [Wv4;T1] to make DIZZY¹ or confused

DJ *abbrev. for:* **1** DISC JOCKEY **2** DINNER JACKET

DNA *abbrev. for: tech* deoxyribonucleic acid; the acid which carries GENETIC information in a cell

do¹ /duː/ *v* **did** /dɪd/, **done** /dʌn/, *3rd pers. sing. pres. t.* **does** /dəz; *strong* dʌz/, *1st pers. sing. pres. t. neg.* **don't** /dəʊnt/, *3rd pers. sing. pres. t. neg.* **doesn't** /'dʌzənt/, *past. t. neg.* **didn't** /dɪdənt/ [Wv2] **1** [I2] (a helping verb, as in): *Did he go?|Did he do it?|Why didn't he do it?|"Didn't he sing well?" she asked* **2** [I2] (a helping verb, as in): *Why don't you come for the weekend?* (= Please come for the weekend) **3** [I2] (a helping verb, as in): *"Didn't he sing well!" she shouted* **4** [I2] (a helping verb, as in): *Not only did he come, but he saw her* **5** [I2] (a helping verb, as in): *He didn't come* **6** [I2] (a helping verb, as in): *He owns, or did own, a Rolls-Royce* **7** [I2] (a helping verb, as in): *Don't go.|Don't be silly!|(esp. BrE) Don't let's go.|(nonstandard AmE) Let's don't go* **8** [I2] (a helping verb, to strengthen or support another verb, as in): *"He never comes." "You're wrong. He does come!"|"Go. Yes, do go!"|"Be seated. Please do be seated"* **9** [I∅] (in place of another verb, as in): *He likes it, and so does she.|He doesn't like it, and neither does she* **10** [I∅] (in place of another verb, to agree with a remark made by someone else, as in): *"He looks hungry." "So he does!"* **11** [I∅] (in place of another verb, as in): **a** *fml "Have you visited her?" "Yes, I have done so (many times)"* **b** *BrE "Have you visited her?" "Yes, I have (done)."|"Will you come for the weekend?" "Yes, I may (do)"* **12** [I∅] (in place of another verb, as in): *"Did he come?" "Yes, he did"* **13** [I∅] (in place of another verb, as in): **a** *He likes it, doesn't he?* **b** *He likes it, doesn't he!* **c** (*esp. BrE*) *He likes it, does he?* **14** [I∅] (in place of another verb, as in): *He knows English better than he did.|He rose early, as he had always done* **15** [T1] (in place of another verb, as in): *What he does is (to) teach.|What John did to his suit was (to) ruin it* **16** [T1] (in place of another verb, as in): *"What are you doing?" "(I'm) cooking"|"What have you done?"* **17** **What . . . doing** (often expressing disapproval) Why?: *What is that book doing on the floor?*

do² *v* **1** [T1] (with actions and nonmaterial things): *to do woodwork(ing)|to do repairs|to do a lesson|to do science at school|to do 80 miles an hour|to do time (in prison)|I shan't do anything to you.|There's nothing more to do/to be done.|Look at what a little hard work can do!|What are you doing?* —see DO WITH (USAGE) **2** [T1] (with action nouns ending in *-ing*): *He does the cooking and she does the washing.|Does he do (the/any) cooking?|It's teaching that he does* **3** [T1] *infml* (with places) to visit and see everything interesting in: *Do Oxford in 3 days? I wonder . . .* **4** [T1;L7,9;D1] (with certain particular nonmaterial expressions): *I did my best (to help him).|I used to do business with him.|Those who do good will find peace.|This medicine will do you good.|I hope you will do better in future.|You did right (in telling me).|He had only done his duty, after all.|That won't do (you) any harm.|I have some work to do.|I hope you will do me the honour of paying me a visit.|Will you do me a kindness?* **5** (with people and nonmaterial things) to give or provide with: **a** [D1 (*to*); T1]: *That picture of her doesn't do her justice* **b** [D1 (*for*); T1]: *Do me a favour* **6** [T1 *no pass.*;I∅] *esp. BrE* (with people) to be enough (for): *"Will £5 do you?" "Yes, that will do (me) nicely"* **7** [T1] *esp. BrE* (with people) to cheat; HAVE: *I'm afraid he's done you on that sale, my friend! You've been done!* **8** [T1] *infml, esp. BrE* to punish; hurt: *If you don't stop talking, I'll do you!* **9** [T1 *usu. not pass.*] *esp. BrE* (with people) to serve by means of action with things: *The* BARBER (=man who cuts hair) *will do you next.|They did me very well at that hotel (with their good food and clean rooms)* **10** [T1] (with people) to perform as or copy the manner of (IMITATE): *Olivier did "Othello" last night.|He does Harold Wilson very well* **11** [T1] (with things) to arrange: *to do one's hair|to do the flowers* **12** [T1] (with things) to clean: *to do one's teeth|to do the room|to do the dishes* **13** [T1] (with things) to cook: *They do fish very well in that restaurant* **14** [D1 (*for*);T1] (with things) to prepare: *to do (us) a report|to do a book|to do a complete suit in only 3 days!* **15** [L9] to behave; act: *When in Rome, do as the Romans do.|Do as you're told!|You did well in coming to see me quickly* **16** [L9] to advance towards a desired state: *After the birth, mother and child are doing well/nicely.|They did poorly in the examination* **17** [I∅ (*for*), *usu. infin.*] to be suitable: *That won't do.|How would this do?|It does not do to work too much.|This little bed will do for our youngest daughter.|Will £5 do?|How will £5 do?* **18** [I∅] (in the *-ing*-form) happening: *What's doing at your place tonight?|There's nothing doing in this town at night* **19** **That will do!** That's enough!: *That will do! It's perfect as it is.|That will do! I order you to stop before it's too late* **20** **be up and doing** *infml* to be active: *He's up and doing by 5 o'clock in the morning!* **21** **do it yourself** *infml* the idea of doing repairs and building things oneself, instead of paying workmen: *She's very interested in do it yourself.|She's a great do-it-yourself-er* **22** **do or die** *fml* to succeed or die; do everything possible to succeed **23** **do to death** to kill: (fig.) *That song has* *been done to death by being repeated so often* **24 do (oneself) proud** *infml* to be successful **25 do (someone) proud** to give (someone) cause for pride or satisfaction **26 do one's (own) thing** *sl* to do what is personally satisfying, even though others may disapprove **27 How are you doing?** *infml, esp. AmE* (an informal greeting to a friend) **28 How do you do?** *polite* (a form of words used when introduced to someone: in later meetings, say "How are you?") **29 make do (with something)** also **make (something) do**— *infml* to use (something) even though it may not be perfect or enough: *We haven't got meat, so we'll have to make do with bread* **30 nothing doing** *sl* no: *"Will you lend me £5?" "Nothing doing"* **31 That does it!** (an expression showing that enough, or too much has been done): *That does it: it's perfect.|That does it! I refuse to go on* **32 What do you do (for a living)?** What is your work? —see MAKE (USAGE); see also **do in the** EYE[1] (11), DO AWAY WITH, DO BY, DO DOWN, DO FOR, DO IN, DO OUT, DO OUT OF, DO OVER, DO UP, DO WITH, DO WITHOUT

do[3] *n* **dos** *or* **do's** /duːz/ *infml* **1** *esp. BrE* a big party **2** *BrE* a cheat: *If you knew the whole thing was a do, why did you go along with it?* **3 dos and don'ts** rules of behaviour **4 fair dos!** *BrE sl* (used esp. when complaining of unfair treatment) let's all have fair shares!

do[4], doh /dəʊ/ *n* [R] **1** the first (lowest) note in the (SOL-FA) musical scale: *Sing do!* **2** the 8th (highest) note in the same scale

do a·way with *v adv prep* [T1] **1** to cause to end; ABOLISH **2** also **make away with**— *infml* to kill or murder (someone or oneself)

dob·bin /ˈdɒbɪ̣n‖ˈdɑ-/ *n* [N] *lit* a name for a working horse (not a race horse)

do by *v prep infml* **1 do well by** treat well **2 hard done by** treated badly **3 Do as you would be done by** Treat others as you would like them to treat you **4 do (something) by halves** to do (something) in a careless or unfinished way or not thoroughly

doc /dɒk‖dɑk/ *n* [N; (*the*)+R; (*AmE*) A] *infml* DOCTOR[1] (2)

doc. *abbrev. for*: DOCUMENT[1]

do·cile /ˈdəʊsaɪl‖ˈdɑsəl/ *adj* easily taught or led —**docility** /dəʊˈsɪlɪ̣ti‖dɑ-/ *n* [U]

dock[1] /dɒk‖dɑk/ *n* [C;U] a common broad-leafed plant that grows by the roadside in England and other northern countries

dock[2] *v* [T1] **1** to cut off the end of; cut short: *docking a horse's tail* **2** to take away a part of: *to dock a man's wages* **3** [(OFF, *off*, or *from*)] to take away (something) (from something else, esp. wages): *to dock £5 from a man's wages*

dock[3] *n* a place where ships are loaded and unloaded, or repaired: *the docks of London|London's dockland by the Thames*

dock[4] *v* [T1;IØ: (*at*)] to (cause to) sail into, or remain at, a DOCK[3]

dock[5] *n* [(*the*) *usu. sing.*] the place in a court of law where the prisoner stands

dock·er /ˈdɒkəʳ‖ˈdɑ-/ (*AmE* **longshoreman**)— *n* a person who works at a DOCK[3], loading and unloading ships

dock·et[1] /ˈdɒkɪ̣t‖ˈdɑ-/ *n fml or tech* **1** a list of things to be done, esp. a list of law cases to be tried **2** a short description of the contents of a long report or a set of papers **3** a copy of a receipt given to someone, which shows the details written on it **4** a LABEL tied to a parcel of goods showing where it is to be taken to

docket[2] *v* [T1] *fml or tech* to put on or in a DOCKET[1] (1,2): *to docket a law case*

dock·yard /ˈdɒkjɑːd‖ˈdɑkjɑrd/ *n* a place where ships are built or repaired; SHIPYARD

doc·tor[1] /ˈdɒktəʳ‖ˈdɑk-/ *n* **1** [C;A] a person holding one of the highest degrees given by a university (such as a PHD, DSC, D LITT, etc.) **2** [C;A;N] a person whose profession is to attend to sick people (or animals): *an animal doctor|You should see a doctor.|Doctor Smith will see you now.|Good morning, doctor* **3** [C9] *infml* a person who repairs the stated things; REPAIR MAN: *a radio/bicycle doctor* **4** [A;N] *AmE* DENTIST **5 under the doctor (for)** *BrE infml* being treated by a doctor (for)

doctor[2] *v* [T1] *infml* **1** to give medical treatment to **2** to repair **3** [(UP)] *derog* to change for some purpose: *doctoring the play to suit the public* **4** [(UP)] *derog* to change in a dishonest way: *charged with doctoring the election results* **5** *euph* to make (esp. an animal) unable to breed; NEUTER[3]

doc·tor·al /ˈdɒktərəl‖ˈdɑk-/ *adj* [Wa5;A] of or related to the university degree of DOCTOR[1] (1): *a doctoral degree*

doc·tor·ate /ˈdɒktərɪ̣t‖ˈdɑk-/ *n* the degree, title, or rank of a DOCTOR[1] (1), esp. a nonmedical one

Doctor of Phi·los·o·phy /ˌ·· · ·ˈ···/ *n* also (*infml*) **D Phil, PhD**— (a person who has gained) an advanced university degree

doc·tri·naire[1] /ˌdɒktrɪ̣ˈneəʳ‖ˌdɑk-/ also **doc·tri·nar·i·an** /-ˈneəriən/— *n derog, rare* a person who tries to put into action some system of ideas (some DOCTRINE) without considering the practical difficulties

doctrinaire[2] *adj derog* of, related to, or typical of a DOCTRINAIRE: *The members of that political party have very doctrinaire beliefs*

doc·tri·nal /dɒkˈtraɪnəl‖ˈdɑktrɪ̣nəl/ *adj* [Wa5;A; (B)] of, related to, or concerning DOCTRINE

doc·trine /ˈdɒktrɪ̣n‖ˈdɑk-/ *n* **1** [C;U] something that is taught **2** [C;U] a principle, esp. religious, or the whole body of principles in a branch of knowledge or system of belief **3** [C] a principle of law established through past decisions **4** [C] *esp. AmE* a statement of official government opinions and intentions, esp. in international relations: *the Monroe Doctrine*

doc·u·ment[1] /ˈdɒkjʊmənt‖ˈdɑkjə-/ *n* a paper that gives information, proof, or support of something else: *Let me see all the official documents concerning the sale of this land*

doc·u·ment[2] /ˈdɒkjʊment‖ˈdɑkjə-/ *v* [T1] to prove or support with DOCUMENTs: *That's a very interesting claim, but can you document it?|The history of this area is very well documented*

doc·u·men·ta·ry[1] /ˌdɒkjʊˈmentəri‖ˌdɑkjə-/ *adj* [Wa5;A] **1** of or related to DOCUMENTs[1]: *documentary proof* **2** presenting facts through art: *documentary films*

documentary[2] *n* a presentation of facts through art, esp. on the radio or in the cinema: *We saw a documentary about Yorkshire coal miners*

doc·u·men·ta·tion /ˌdɒkjʊmənˈteɪʃən, -men-‖ˌdɑkjə-/ *n* [U] **1** the act or action of DOCUMENTing[2]: *The documentation of his claim took a long time* **2** proof or support in the form of DOCUMENTs: *His claim is still without documentation*

dod·der /ˈdɒdəʳ‖ˈdɑ-/ *v* [IØ] *infml* **1** (of a person) to become or act as if weak and shaky, usu. from age: *Poor old Aunt Mary is beginning to dodder* **2** (of a person) to walk slowly and shakily, usu. from age: *The old fellow doddered down the street* —**~er** *n*

dod·der·ing /ˈdɒdərɪŋ‖ˈdɑ-/ also **dod·der·y** /-dəri/— *adj infml* weak, shaky, and slow, usu. from age —**-ingly** *adv*

dod·dle /ˈdɒdl‖ˈdɑdl/ *n* [*usu. sing.*] *infml BrE* something that is very easy to do: *That driving test was a real doddle*

dodge[1] /dɒdʒ‖dɑdʒ/ *v* **1** [IØ] to move suddenly

aside **2** [T1] to avoid by so doing **3** [T1] *infml* to avoid by a trick or in some dishonest way: *tax-dodging*

dodge[2] *n* **1** an act of avoiding by a sudden movement of the body **2** *infml* a clever way of avoiding something or of deceiving or tricking someone: *a tax dodge*

dodg·ems /ˈdɒdʒəmz‖ˈdɑ-/ *n* [*the*+P] *BrE infml* (in places of public amusement) small electric cars (**dodgem cars**) that people try to drive skilfully in an enclosed space, so as to avoid hitting each other

dodg·er /ˈdɒdʒəʳ‖ˈdɑ-/ *n infml* a person who DODGES, esp. one who uses clever and perhaps dishonest tricks to avoid duties or payments: *a tax dodger*

dodg·y /ˈdɒdʒi‖ˈdɑ-/ *adj* [Wa1] *infml, esp. BrE* **1** risky and possibly dangerous: *a dodgy plan* **2** cleverly and perhaps dishonestly tricky: *a dodgy person* **3** not safe to use; in a dangerous condition: *Don't sit on that chair; it's a bit dodgy*

do·do /ˈdəʊdəʊ/ *n* **dodoes** *or* **dodos** **1** a large flightless bird that no longer exists **2** (**as**) **dead as a dodo** *infml* dead: *That strange plan of yours is now as dead as a dodo: nobody is interested in it any more*

do down *v adv* [T1] *BrE infml* **1** to cheat **2** to cause to feel ashamed or less proud of oneself **3** to say bad things about (someone, esp. someone who is not present)

doe /dəʊ/ *n* **1** a fully-grown female deer (or rabbit) **2** the female of any animal of which the male is called a BUCK

do·er /ˈduːəʳ/ *n infml* (esp. in comparisons) a person who does things or is active: *She's a doer, not just a thinker or a talker*

-doer *comb. form* a person who does things of the stated type: *an evil-doer|a wrong-doer*

does /dəz; *strong* dʌz/ *neg. contr.* **doesn't** /ˈdʌzənt/ *3rd pers. sing. pres. of* DO

doe·skin /ˈdəʊˌskɪn/ *n, adj* [Wa5] **1** [C] the skin of a DOE **2** [U;B] leather made from such a skin: *a doeskin bag* **3** [U;B] soft leather like this

doff /dɒf‖dɑf, dɔf/ *v* [T1] *old use or pomp* to take off (clothes, esp. outer garments, and hats) —opposite **don**

do for *v prep* [T1] **1** *BrE infml* to keep house or do cleaning for (someone) **2** *BrE sl* to kill; murder **3** **done for** *infml* finished or worn out or very tired or about to die, etc.: *At the end of a long day I'm just about done for.*|(fig.) *Don't say our team is done for!* **4** **What/(*BrE*)How will you do for (something)?** What arrangements will you make for (something)?: *What will you do for food when you are camping?*

dog[1] /dɒg‖dɔg/ *n* **1** [C] a common 4-legged flesh-eating animal, esp. any of the many varieties used by man as a companion or for hunting, working, guarding, etc. It is often called "man's best friend" **2** [C] the male of this animal and of certain animals like it, esp. the fox and the WOLF **3** [C] *infml* a worthless evil man **4** [C9; *you*+N9] *infml* a fellow: *a gay dog|You lucky dog!* **5** [C] *AmE sl* something not of good quality **6** **die like a dog** to die in trouble, in shame, alone, or unhappy **7** **dressed up like a dog's dinner** *BrE infml* dressed in fine clothes which one thinks very splendid, but which other people consider rather silly **8** **Every dog has his/its day** A time of good fortune comes at least once to everyone **9** **Give a dog a bad name (and hang him)** If people think someone is bad, then nothing can help him **10** **lead a dog's life** *infml* to have an unhappy life with many troubles **11** **lead someone a dog's life** *infml* to cause someone trouble all the time **12** **Let sleeping dogs lie** Leave alone things which may cause trouble **13** **Love me, love my dog** Accept my friends as yours **14** **not have a dog's chance** *infml* to have no chance at all **15** **put on the dog** *sl* to act as though one were more important than one is, in the hope of gaining the admiration or respect of others **16** **top dog** *infml* the person on top, who has power —compare UNDERDOG **17** **treat someone like a dog** *infml* to treat someone very badly **18** **You can't teach an old dog new tricks** Old people can't change their ways or habits easily —see also DOGS, **dog in the** MANGER[2]

See next page for picture

dog[2] *v* **-gg-** [T1 *often pass.*] (esp. of nonmaterial things) to follow closely (like a dog); PURSUE: *We were dogged by bad luck during the whole journey*

dog bis·cuit /ˈ· ˌ··/ *n* a small dry hard piece of baked breadlike food made for dogs

dog·cart /ˈdɒgkɑːt‖ˈdɔgkɑrt/ *n* **1** a 2-wheeled vehicle, pulled by a horse, with 2 seats across the vehicle, back to back **2** a small cart made to be pulled by a large dog

dog·catch·er /ˈdɒgˌkætʃəʳ‖ˈdɔg-/ *n* an official of a town, city, etc., whose duty it is to catch wandering dogs and take them off the streets

dog col·lar /ˈ· ˌ··/ *n* **1** a neckband for a dog, onto which a LEASH can be fastened **2** *humor* a priest's collar, stiff and fastened at the back

dog days /ˈ· ·/ *n* [(*the*) P] (*often caps.*) the hottest days of the year (in July and August)

doge /dəʊdʒ/ *n* the highest government official in Venice and in Genoa in former times

dog-eared /ˈ· ·/ *adj* (esp. of books and papers) having the corners of the pages bent down with use, like a dog's ears

dog-eat-dog /ˌ· · ˈ·/ *adj* [A] having, showing, or marked by cruel merciless self-interest: *In this dog-eat-dog world you must fight to stay on top*

dog·fight /ˈdɒgfaɪt‖ˈdɔg-/ *n* **1** a fight between dogs, or any cruel uncontrolled fight without proper rules **2** a fight between armed aircraft

dog·fish /ˈdɒgˌfɪʃ‖ˈdɔg-/ *n* [Wn2] any of several kinds of small SHARKS —see picture at FISH[1]

dog·ged /ˈdɒgɪ̣d‖ˈdɔ-/ *adj* having or showing a character which refuses to yield or give up in the face of difficulty or opposition: *She was not very clever, but by dogged effort she learnt a good deal at school* —**~ly** *adv* —**~ness** *n* [U]

dog·ge·rel /ˈdɒgərəl‖ˈdɔ-, ˈdɑ-/ *n* [U] poetry that is silly, often not intended to be serious, and often irregular or too regular in beat

dog·go /ˈdɒgəʊ‖ˈdɔ-/ *adv* **lie doggo** *BrE sl* to lie or hide quietly without moving or making a noise; remain in hiding until the fear of being discovered is past

dog·gone /ˈdɒgɒn‖ˈdɔgɔn/ *v* [T1] *AmE euph sl* God DAMN!: *Doggone it, I've lost again!* —**doggoned, doggone** *adj* [A]: *That doggoned cat has upset the milk again!*

dog·gy, doggie /ˈdɒgi‖ˈdɔgi/ *n* (*used esp. to or by children*) a dog

dog·house /ˈdɒghaʊs‖ˈdɔg-/ *n* **in the doghouse** *infml* in a state of disfavour or shame

do·gie /ˈdəʊgi/ *n AmE* a motherless CALF (baby cow) in a group of cattle

dog·leg /ˈdɒgleg‖ˈdɔg-/ *n* a sharp bend in a road, a racetrack, or esp. part of a GOLF course: *a dogleg to the right*

dog·ma /ˈdɒgmə‖ˈdɔgmə, ˈdɑgmə/ *n* **1** [C;U] an important belief or set of beliefs taught officially by a church **2** [C] *usu. derog* a belief or principle that people are expected to accept without reasoning

dog·mat·ic /dɒgˈmætɪk‖dɔg-, dɑg-/ *adj* **1** of or based on DOGMA **2** *usu. derog* (typical of a person) who puts forward without proof beliefs that other people are expected to accept without question: *a dogmatic opinion/manner/person* —**~ally** *adv* [Wa4]

dog·mat·ics /dɒg'mætiks‖dɔg-, dɑg-/ *n* [U] the study of religious DOGMA

dog·ma·tis·m /'dɒgmətɪzəm‖'dɔg-, 'dɑg-/ *n* [U] *usu. derog* the quality or practice of being DOGMATIC (2) —**-tist** *n*

do-good·er /ˌ· '··‖'· ˌ··/ *n* **do-gooders** *usu. derog* a person who tries to do good things for others, but may be impractical or ineffective

dog pad·dle /'· ˌ··/ *n* [*usu. sing.*] *infml* a simple swimming stroke in which the legs are kicked while the arms make short quick movements up and down near the head

dogs /dɒgz‖dɔgz/ *n* **1** [*the*+P] a sports event at which dogs (esp. GREYHOUNDs) race and money is won or lost: *We always win some money at the dogs* **2** [P] *humor sl* feet: *I've walked so much today that my dogs are really killing me* **3** [P] also **firedogs** ANDIRONs **4 go to the dogs** to lead a wasteful bad life or to become ruined

dogs·bod·y /'dɒgzˌbɒdi‖'dɔgzˌbɑdi/ *n BrE infml* a person in a low position who has to do the least interesting work

dog-tired /ˌ· '·◂/ *adj infml* very tired

dog·tooth /'dɒgtuːθ‖'dɔg-/ *n* **-teeth** /tiːθ/ an ornamental band of connected V-shaped figures, or a pattern like this, used esp. on old European stone churches

dog·trot /'dɒgtrɒt‖'dɔgtrɑt/ *n* [*usu. sing.*] a quick easy way of moving along that is faster than walking but slower than running

dog·wood /'dɒgwʊd‖'dɔg-/ *n* any of several kinds of flower-bearing bush

doh /dəʊ/ *n* [R] DO⁴

doi·ly, doyley, doyly /'dɔɪli/ *n* a small round or square ornamented piece of cloth or paper used under a bowl, dish, etc. esp. to protect the surface of a table

do in *v adv* [T1] **1** *sl* to kill: *If he tells the police again I'm really going to do him in* **2** [Wv6] *infml* to tire completely: *I'm really done in after walking all day!*

do·ings /'duːɪŋz/ *n* **doings** *infml* **1** [P] things that are done, things that happen, or social activities: *a lot of doings at Smith's house tonight* **2** [Wn3;C] *BrE* any small thing, esp. the name of which one forgets or does not know: *Put the doings on the table*

dol·drums /'dɒldrəmz‖'dəʊl-, 'dɑl-, 'dɔl-/ *n* [*the*+P] **1** a place on the ocean where ships cannot move because there is no wind **2 in the**

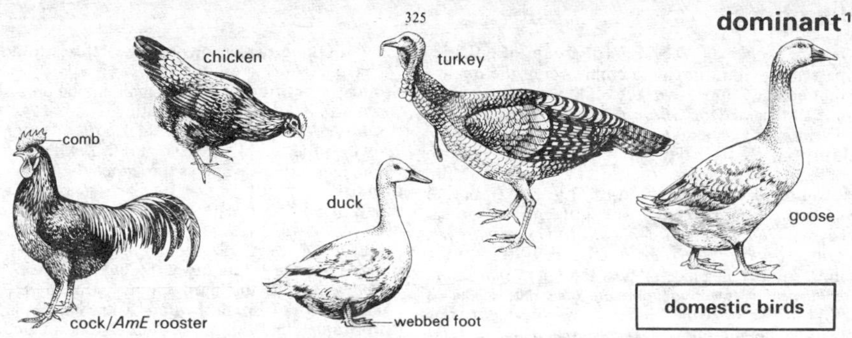

doldrums *infml* **a** in a low and sad state of mind **b** in a state of inactivity

dole /dəʊl/ *n* [*usu. sing.*] **1** something DOLED OUT: *a dole of soup* **2 go/be on the dole** *BrE infml* to start to receive/to receive money from the government because one is unemployed

dole·ful /ˈdəʊlfəl/ *adj* **1** sad in a self-pitying way **2** causing or expressing unhappiness or low spirits —**~ly** *adv* —**~ness** *n* [U]

dole out *v adv* [D1 (*to*);T1] to give (esp. money or food in small quantities) (to people in need)

doll /dɒl‖dɑl, dɔl/ *n* **1** a small figure of a person, esp. of a baby, esp. for a child to play with **2** *infml* a pretty but silly young woman who dresses too finely **3** *sl* a young girl or woman, esp. one with charm: *My grand-daughter is a little doll* **4** *AmE sl* a person that one likes: *You'll lend me £5? You're a real doll, Bill!*

dol·lar /ˈdɒləʳ‖ˈdɑ-/ *n* **1** [*usu. sing.*] any of various standards of money, as used in the US, Canada, Australia, New Zealand, Hong Kong, etc. It is worth 100 cents and its sign is $ **2** a piece of paper, a coin, etc. of this value

dol·lop /ˈdɒləp‖ˈdɑ-/ *n* [(*of*)] *infml* **1** a shapeless mass, esp. of food: *a dollop of soft potatoes* **2** an unmeasured amount, esp. of liquid: *coffee with a dollop of alcohol added* **3** a small amount: *In her writing there isn't a single dollop of self-pity*

doll's house /ˈ· ˌ·/ also (*esp. AmE*) **doll·house** /ˈdɒlhaʊs‖ˈdɑl-, ˈdɔl-/— *n* **-houses** /haʊzǝ̇z/ **1** a child's toy house in which small DOLLS (1), toy furniture, etc., can be put **2** a house so small that it makes one think of a child's toy house

doll up *v adv* [T1 *often pass.*] *infml* to dress (someone or oneself) prettily

dol·ly /ˈdɒli‖ˈdɑli, ˈdɔli/ *n* **1** (used esp. by and to children) DOLL (1) **2** *tech* a flat surface or frame on wheels for moving heavy objects, such as a television or cinema camera

dolly bird /ˈ·· ·/ also **dolly**— *n infml BrE, usu. apprec* a pretty young woman, esp. one wearing fashionable clothes

dol·men /ˈdɒlmen, -mǝ̇n‖ˈdəʊlmǝ̇n, ˈdɔl-, ˈdɑl-/ also **cromlech**— *n* a group of upright stones supporting a large flat piece of stone, built in ancient times in Britain and France

dol·or·ous /ˈdɒlərəs‖ˈdəʊ-/ *adj poet* sad; causing or showing DOLOUR —**~ly** *adv*

dol·our, *AmE* **-or** /ˈdɒləʳ‖ˈdəʊ-/ *n* [U] *poet, esp. BrE* sorrow; pain of the mind or spirit

dol·phin /ˈdɒlfǝ̇n‖ˈdɑl-, ˈdɔl-/ *n* a type of toothed sea animal 2–3 metres long, which swims about very quickly in groups, going over and under the surface of the water in curves —see picture at SEA

dolt /dəʊlt/ *n* [C; *you*+N] *derog* a slow-thinking foolish fellow —**~ish** *adj* —**~ishly** *adv*

-dom /dəm/ *suffix* **1** [*adj→n*] the state of being (something): *freedom* **2** [*n→n*] the stated rank: *He received the* DUKEDOM *on the death of his father* **3** [*n→n*] the area ruled by a person of the stated rank: *a kingdom* **4** [*n→n*] *infml* the group of people each of whom has the stated rank, job, interest, or character: OFFICIALDOM

do·main /dəˈmeɪn, dəʊ-/ *n* **1** land(s) owned or controlled by one person, a government, etc. **2** a subject of activity, interest, or knowledge: *I can't answer your question about photography. It's not in my domain*

dome /dəʊm/ *n* **1** a rounded top on a building or room **2** something of this shape: *the blue dome of the sky* **3** *old use or poet* a large grand building, such as a palace **4** *sl* the human head, esp. when hairless

domed /dəʊmd/ *adj* [Wa5] (*often in comb.*) covered with or shaped like a DOME

Domes·day Book /ˈduːmzdeɪ bʊk/ *n* [(*the*) R] a record of all the lands of England, showing their size, value, ownership, etc., made in 1086 on the orders of William the Conqueror

do·mes·tic¹ /dəˈmestɪk/ *adj* **1** of the house, home, or family **2** liking home duties and pleasures **3** of one's own country or some particular country; not foreign —**~ally** *adv* [Wa4]

domestic² *n* a DOMESTIC servant, usu. female

domestic an·i·mal /·ˌ·· ˈ···/ *n* an animal that is not wild, esp. one kept on a farm

do·mes·ti·cate /deˈmestǝ̇keɪt/ *v* [T1] **1** to make (an animal) able to live with man and serve him, esp. on a farm —compare TAME² (1) **2** [Wv5] to cause to be interested in and enjoy home life and duties —**-cation** /dəˌmestǝ̇ˈkeɪʃən/ *n* [U]

do·mes·tic·i·ty /ˌdəʊmesˈtɪsǝ̇ti/ *n* **1** [U] (a liking for) home or family life **2** [C *usu. pl.*] home and family affairs

domestic sci·ence /·ˌ·· ˈ··/ *n* [U] the name given in some schools to the study of the skills of housekeeping, cooking, etc.

domestic ser·vice /·ˌ·· ˈ··/ *n* [U] the work of a servant in a house, esp. cleaning

dom·i·cile¹ /ˈdɒmǝ̇saɪl‖ˈdɑ-, ˈdəʊ-/ *n* **1** *fml* one's home; the place where one lives **2** *law* the place where for official purposes one is considered to live, whether or not one really spends much time there

domicile² *v* [Wv5;T1] *fml or law* to establish in or provide with a DOMICILE: *He travels about a lot but he is domiciled in London*

dom·i·cil·i·a·ry /ˌdɒmǝ̇ˈsɪliəri‖ˌdɑmǝ̇ˈsɪlieri, ˈdəʊ-/ *adj* [Wv5;A;(B)] *fml* of, like, to or at a home; as in a home: *a domiciliary visit|domiciliary care*

dom·i·nance /ˈdɒmǝ̇nəns‖ˈdɑ-/ *n* [U] the fact or state of dominating (DOMINATE); importance, power, or controlling influence: *the director's dominance of the firm*

dom·i·nant¹ /ˈdɒmǝ̇nənt‖ˈdɑ-/ *adj* **1** dominating (DOMINATE): *My sister had a very dominant nature; we all did what she wanted.|The Town Hall was built in a dominant position on a hill where everyone could see it* **2** (of one of a pair of body parts) being stronger than the other: *The right hand is dominant* *in most people* **3** [Wa5] *tech* (of groups of qualities passed on from parent to child) being the quality that actually appears in the child when more than one are passed on: *Brown eyes are dominant and blue eyes are* RECESSIVE

dominant² *n* [(*the*)] the 5th note of a musical scale of 8 notes —compare TONIC² (3)

dom·i·nate /ˈdɒmɪ̈neɪt‖ˈdɑ-/ *v* **1** [T1;IØ (*over*)] to have or exercise controlling influence or power (over): *Her desire to dominate* (*other people*) *has caused trouble in her family* **2** [T1;L9] to have the most important place or position (in): *Sports, and not learning, seem to dominate* (*in*) *that school* **3** [T1] to rise or to be higher than; provide a view from a height above: *The church dominated the whole town*

dom·i·na·tion /ˌdɒmɪ̈ˈneɪʃən‖ˈdɑ-/ *n* [U] the act or fact of dominating or the state of being DOMINATEd

dom·i·neer /ˌdɒmɪ̈ˈnɪəʳ‖ˌdɑ-/ *v* [Wv4;IØ (*over*)] *usu. derog* to show a desire to control others, usu. without any consideration of their feelings or wishes: *I wouldn't work for someone who tries to domineer* (*over everyone*) *as Mr. Smith does.*|*a domineering person*/*manner*

Do·min·i·can /dəˈmɪnɪkən/ *adj, n* [Wa5] (a member) of a ROMAN CATHOLIC religious order established by St. Dominic in 1215 and esp. interested in PREACHing

do·min·ion /dəˈmɪnɪən/ *n* **1** [U (*over*)] *esp. lit* the power or right to rule: *Alexander the Great held dominion over a large area* **2** [C] the land(s) held in complete control by one person, ruler, or government: *the King's dominion*(*s*) **3** [C] (*often cap.*) a self-governing nation of the British COMMONWEALTH: *the Dominion of Canada*

dom·i·no /ˈdɒmɪ̈nəʊ‖ˈdɑ-/ *n* **-noes** one of a set of flat pieces of wood, bone, etc., with a different number of spots on each, used for playing a game

dom·i·noes /ˈdɒmɪ̈nəʊz‖ˈdɑ-/ *n* [U] any of several games played with a set of usu. 28 DOMINOes

don¹ /dɒn‖dɑn/ *n* **1** (in the Universities of Oxford and Cambridge) a teacher **2** *BrE* a university teacher

don² *v* **-nn-** [T1] *old use or pomp* to put on (clothing and hats) —opposite **doff**

Don *n* [N] (in Spanish-speaking countries) a polite title used before a man's first name: *Don Miguel*

do·nate /dəʊˈneɪt‖ˈdəʊneɪt/ *v* [T1;IØ: (*to*)] to make a gift of (something), esp. for a good purpose —see also DONOR

do·na·tion /dəʊˈneɪʃən/ *n* the act of donating or something DONATEd: *She made a donation of £1,000 to the Children's Hospital*

done /dʌn/ **1** finished: *When you have*/*are done, come back!* **2 Done!** Agreed!; I accept!: *"I'll give you £5 for it." "Done!"* **3 Have done (with it)!** *fml* Finish (it)! **4 (It's) easier said than done** talk is easier than action **5 No sooner said than done** It can be done at once, without delay **6 over and done with** ended; finished: *That affair's now over and done with* (=there is nothing more to be said or done about it) **7 That isn't done** Such behaviour is not socially acceptable **8 What's done cannot be undone** It's too late to change what has already happened **9** *past p. of* DO

don·jon /ˈdɒndʒən, ˈdʌn-‖ˈdɑn-, ˈdʌn-/ *n* a massive inner tower of a castle as built in former times

Don Ju·an /ˌdɒn ˈhwɑːn, -ˈwɑːn, -ˈdʒuːən‖ˌdɑn- (*Span.* don ˈxwan)/ *n infml* a man who is a great lover; LADY-KILLER: *He thinks he's a Don Juan, but none of the girls like him*

don·key /ˈdɒŋki‖ˈdɑŋki/ *n* **1** a type of animal of the horse family, but smaller and with longer ears, used by man to carry loads; ASS¹ **2** a foolish slow-thinking person or one who refuses to do as he is told

donkey en·gine /ˈ·· ˌ··/ *n* a small engine on a ship used esp. in loading and unloading

donkey jack·et /ˈ·· ˌ··/ *n* a thick JACKET reaching down to the top of the legs, and usu. with a piece of leather or plastic across the shoulders

donkey's years /ˈ·· ·/ *n* [U] *BrE sl* a very long time: *That was donkey's years ago.*|*I haven't seen him for donkey's years.*|*It's donkey's years since I've seen him*

don·key·work /ˈdɒŋkiwɜːk‖ˈdɑŋkiwɜrk/ *n* [U] *infml, esp. BrE* the hard uninteresting part of a piece of work (esp. in the phr. **do the donkeywork**)

don·nish /ˈdɒnɪʃ‖ˈdɑnɪʃ/ *adj esp. BrE* of, related to, or typical of a university DON, esp. in being more interested in ideas than in real life —**~ly** *adv*

do·nor /ˈdəʊnəʳ/ *n* **1** a person who gives, DONATEs, or presents **2** (*often in comb.*) a person who permits a substance or part of his body to be put into someone else for medical purposes: *a blood donor*

don't /dəʊnt/ [Wv2] *contr. of* **1** do not —see CONTR. (USAGE) **2** *nonstandard, esp. AmE* does not

doo·dle /ˈduːdl/ *v* [IØ] to draw irregular lines, figures, etc., aimlessly while thinking about something else —**doodle** *n*: *making doodles on paper while the teacher is talking*

doo·dle·bug /ˈduːdlbʌg/ *n infml BrE* a V-1 (a flying bomb)

doom¹ /duːm/ *n* [U;C *usu. sing.*] **1** a terrible fate; unavoidable destruction or death: *to meet one's doom*|*to go*/*be sent to one's doom*|*the day of doom* **2 pronounce someone's doom** to say that punishment or misfortune is to be suffered by someone **3 the crack of doom** the beginning of the end of the world

doom² *v* [Wv5;T1 (*to*);V3] to cause to experience or suffer something unavoidable and unpleasant, such as death or destruction: *From the start, the plan was doomed* (*to failure*/*to fail*)

Dooms·day /ˈduːmzdeɪ/ *n* [R] **1** the last day of the world's existence, when God will judge all men **2 till Doomsday** *infml* forever

door /dɔːʳ‖dor/ *n* **1** a movable flat surface that opens and closes the entrance to a building, room, or piece of furniture: *to knock at the door*|*to open*/*close the door*|*a wooden door*|*the kitchen*/*cupboard door*|*Most houses have a* **front door** *at the front and a* **back door** *at the back.*|(fig.) *Good luck is often the door to success.*|(fig.) *This agreement opens the door to advances in every field* **2** [*usu. sing.*] DOORWAY: *to come through the door* **3** (in certain fixed phrases) house; building: *My sister lives only 2*/*a few doors away.*|*The taxi will take us from door to door so we won't have to walk at all.*|*He sells books* (*from*) *door to door.*|*He is a door-to-door salesman.*|*My brother lives next door* (*to us*).|(fig.) *Knocking down and killing someone when driving after drinking alcohol is next door to murder!* **4 answer the door** *infml* to go to the door and open it, to see who has knocked or rung **5 at death's door** *lit* near death **6 be on the door** *infml* to have some duty at the door, such as collecting tickets **7 by the back door** secretly or by a trick **8 lay (something) at someone's door** to blame (something) on someone **9 out of doors** OUTDOORS **10 show someone the door** to make it clear that someone is not welcome and should leave **11 show someone to the door** to go politely to the door with someone who is leaving **12 shut the door in someone's face a** not to allow someone to enter **b** not to allow someone to carry out a plan **13 shut/close the door to/on** to make impossible: *The workers' behaviour has shut*

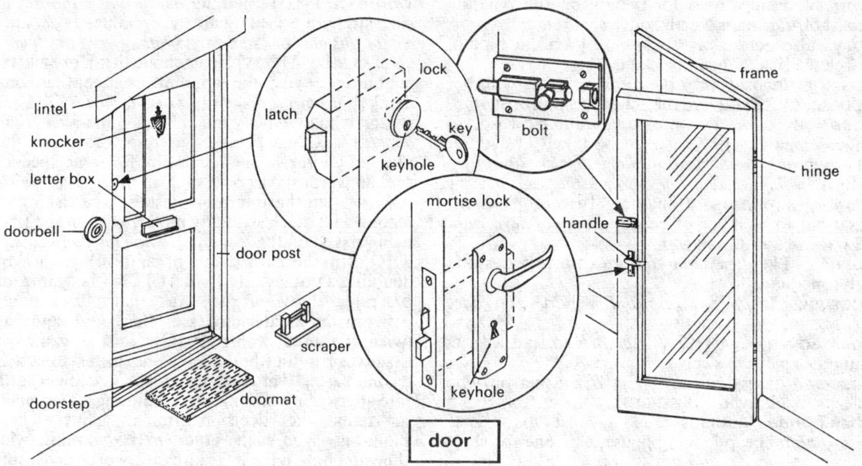

the door to/on any new agreement on higher wages **14 within doors** *fml* INDOORS

door·bell /ˈdɔːbəl‖ˈdor-/ *n* a bell provided for visitors to a house to ring for attention —see picture at DOOR

door·frame /ˈdɔːfreɪm‖ˈdor-/ also **door·case** /-keɪs/— *n* the frame into which a door fits when closed

door·keep·er /ˈdɔːˌkiːpəʳ‖ˈdor-/ *n* a person who guards the main door of a large building and lets people in and out —compare DOORMAN

door·knob /ˈdɔːnɒb‖ˈdornɑb/ *n* a usu. round handle (KNOB (2)) on a door that, when turned, allows the door to be opened

door·knock·er /ˈdɔːnɒkəʳ‖ˈdorˌnɑkər/ *n* KNOCKER (2)

door·man /ˈdɔːmæn, -mən‖ˈdor-/ *n* **-men** /men, mən/ a man in a large or official building (such as a hotel or theatre) who watches the door, helps people to find taxis, sometimes lets people in and out, and usu. wears a uniform

door·mat /ˈdɔːmæt‖ˈdor-/ *n* a mat placed in front of or inside a door for cleaning dirt from the bottom of shoes —see picture at DOOR

door·nail /ˈdɔːneɪl‖ˈdor-/ *n* **dead as a doornail** *infml* dead

door·plate /ˈdɔːpleɪt‖ˈdor-/ *n* a flat piece of metal fixed to a door and bearing a name, esp. the name of the person living or working inside

door·scrap·er /ˈdɔːskreɪpəʳ‖ˈdor-/ *n* a piece of thin shaped metal placed in front of an outer door, with an upper edge on which people can remove mud from their shoes before entering

door·step /ˈdɔːstep‖ˈdor-/ *n* **1** a step before an outer door —see picture at DOOR **2** *BrE sl* a very thick piece of bread cut from a loaf

door·stop·per /ˈdɔːˌstɒpəʳ‖ˈdorˌstɑ-/ also **door·stop** /-stɒp‖-stɑp/— *n* **1** an apparatus for holding a door open **2** something sticking out from a wall or floor (and usu. having a rubber end) intended to prevent damage to the wall when the door is opened quickly

door·way /ˈdɔːweɪ‖ˈdor-/ *n* an opening for an entrance door into a building or room (not into a piece of furniture): *She stood in the doorway, unable to decide whether or not to enter.*|(fig.) *Exercise is a doorway to good health*

do out *v adv* [T1] *infml, esp. BrE* to clean thoroughly: *to do out a room*

do out of *v adv prep* [D1 *often pass.*] *infml* to prevent (someone) from having (something) by cheating: *I've been done out of my rights*

do o·ver *v adv* **1** [T1] to repaint (a room, wall, etc.) **2** [T1] *AmE* to remake **3** [T1b] *AmE* to repeat **4** [T1b] *sl* to attack and wound

dope¹ /dəʊp/ *n* **1** [U] any of various thick liquids used for making machines run easily **2** [U] protective paint used on the wings of (esp. small) aircraft **3** [U] *infml* a drug whose use is forbidden by law except on the orders of a doctor, taken to improve the performance of people or animals, to produce unconsciousness, or because of a pleasant effect on the body or mind **4** [U] *sl* information, esp. from someone who can be trusted **5** [C] *sl* a stupid person

dope² *v* [T1 (UP)] *infml* to give DOPE¹ (3) to or put DOPE in: *to dope a person/a horse/oneself/a drink*

dop·ey, dopy /ˈdəʊpi/ *adj* [Wa1] **1** *infml* having or showing a dullness of the mind or feelings caused or as if caused by alcohol or a drug; sleepy and unable to think clearly **2** *sl* stupid

Dor·ic /ˈdɒrɪk‖ˈdɔ-, ˈdɑ-/ *adj* [Wa5] of, related to, like, or typical of the oldest and simplest style of ancient Greek building: *a Doric pillar* —compare IONIC, CORINTHIAN

dor·mant /ˈdɔːmənt‖ˈdɔr-/ *adj* inactive, esp. not actually growing or producing typical effects: *dormant animals asleep for the winter*|(fig.) *Many people disliked the plan, but opposition remained dormant because nobody could think of a better one*

dor·mer /ˈdɔːməʳ‖ˈdɔr-/ also **dormer win·dow** /ˈ‥ ˌ‥/— *n* a window built upright in a sloping roof —see picture at ROOF¹

dor·mi·to·ry¹ /ˈdɔːmɪ̈təri‖ˈdɔrmɪ̈tori/ also (*infml*) **dorm** /dɔːm‖dɔrm/— *n* **1** a room for sleeping, esp. a large room containing a number of beds **2** *AmE* a building, esp. of a university, where students whose home is far away live, sleep, and study, usu. 2 to a room

dormitory² *adj* [Wa5;A] being a place from which people travel to work in a larger place, esp. a city, every day: *a dormitory town*

dor·mouse /ˈdɔːmaʊs‖ˈdɔr-/ *n* **-mice** /maɪs/ a type of small European forest animal about the size of a mouse, having a long furry tail and looking rather like a SQUIRREL

dor·sal /ˈdɔːsəl‖ˈdɔr-/ *adj* [Wa5;A;(B)] of, on, or near the back, esp. of an animal: *the dorsal* FIN *of a fish*

do·ry¹ /ˈdɔːri‖ˈdori/ *n* a flat-bottomed rowing boat

with high sides used for fishing on the Atlantic coast off northern North America

dory² also **John Dory** /ˌ· ˈ··/— *n* [Wn2] a type of large sea fish that can be eaten

dos·age /ˈdəʊsɪdʒ/ *n* **1** [C *usu. sing.*] the amount of a DOSE¹ (1) **2** [U] *rare* the act of dosing (DOSE²)

dose¹ /dəʊs/ *n* **1** a measured amount (esp. of liquid medicine) given or to be taken at a time: *There is only one dose of medicine left in this bottle.*| (fig.) *In the accident, the workers received a heavy dose of* RADIATION **2** anything (usu. unpleasant) that has to be taken or borne: *a dose of hard work* **3** *sl* a case of GONORRHEA

dose² *v* [T1] *often derog* to give a DOSE¹ to, esp. to give medicine to

doss /dɒs‖dɑs/ *n* [S] *sl, esp. BrE* a short sleep: *have a doss*

doss down *v adv* [IØ] *sl, esp. BrE* to find a (usu. humble) place to sleep

doss·er /ˈdɒsəʳ‖ˈdɑ-/ *n sl, esp. BrE* a person who sleeps regularly in a DOSSHOUSE

doss·house /ˈdɒshaʊs‖ˈdɑs-/ *n* **-houses** /haʊzɨ̇z/ *sl, esp. BrE* a cheap lodging house, esp. one for short stays

dos·si·er /ˈdɒsieɪ‖ˈdɔsjeɪ, ˈdɑ-/ *n* a set of papers containing a detailed report or detailed information: *The police keep dossiers on all well-known thieves*

dost /dʌst/ [Wv2] **thou dost** *old use or bibl* (when talking to one person) you do

dot¹ /dɒt‖dɑt/ *n* **1** a small spot: *The horse and rider moved further and further away until they became only a dot in the distance* **2** a small round mark made with or as if with a pen: *a dot on the letter i* **3** a short sound or flash of light forming a letter or part of a letter (as in sending messages by telegraph) **4 on the dot** *infml* at the exact point in time (or space): *The 3 o'clock train arrived on the dot.*|*It was here on the dot of 3* **5 the year dot** *BrE sl, often derog* a very long time ago

dot² *v* **-tt- 1** [T1] to mark with a dot: *to dot an i* **2** [T1 *often pass.*] to cover with or as if with dots: *a lake dotted with boats*|*a dotted dress* **3** [T1;(D1)] to hit sharply: *He dotted me (one) on the nose* **4 dot the i's and cross the t's** *infml* to give or settle all possible details —see also DOTTED LINE

do·tage /ˈdəʊtɪdʒ/ *n* [U9] a state of weakness of the mind caused by old age; SECOND CHILDHOOD (esp. in the phr. **in one's dotage**)

dote on /dəʊt/ also **dote up·on**— *v prep* [T1] to have or show too much fondness for (esp. a person)

doth /dʌθ/ [Wv2] *old use or bibl* does

dot·ing /ˈdəʊtɪŋ/ *adj* [A] having or showing (too) much fondness: *a doting husband* —**~ly** *adv*

dot·ted line /ˌ·· ˈ·/ *n* **1** a line of dots on paper, on which something is to be written, such as one's name or the answer to a question **2 sign on the dotted line** *infml* to agree to something quickly and unconditionally

dot·tle /ˈdɒtl‖ˈdɑtl/ *n* [U] partly burnt tobacco left in a hard mass at the bottom of a pipe

dot·ty /ˈdɒti‖ˈdɑti/ *adj* [Wa1] *infml* weak-minded, foolish, or mad

doub·le¹ /ˈdʌbəl/ *adj* [Wa5] **1** having or made up of 2 parts that are alike: *double doors*|*a ship with a double bottom*|*a double lock on the door* —compare SINGLE¹ (2) **2** folded once: *Is this cloth just 18 inches wide or is it double?* **3** made for or serving 2 people, animals, etc.: *a double bed*|*a double room in a hotel* **4** having 2 different qualities, uses, or ways in which to be considered: *a double purpose*|*a double meaning* **5** dishonest; seeming one thing while being another (esp. in the phr. **double dealing**) **6** (of a flower) having many more PETALs than the usual flower of its kind: *a double rose*

double² *n* **1** [U] something that is twice another in size, strength, speed, quantity, or value: *I paid only £2 for this old book and Mr. Smith offered me double (= £4) for it* **2** [C;A] an alcoholic drink of SPIRITS, containing twice the amount usu. sold as one drink: *I'll have a double* (SCOTCH), *please* **3** [C] a person who looks very much like another: *He is my double* **4** [C] an actor or actress who takes the place of another in a cinema film for some special, esp. dangerous, purpose (such as riding a horse) **5** [C] a sudden sharp turn or twist **6** [C] a risking of money on 2 races, with any money won on the first being risked on the second: *He won the daily double* **7** [C] (in the card game of BRIDGE) an act of doubling (DOUBLE⁵ (6)) **8** [C] (in the game of DARTS) a throw of the DART that hits a point between the 2 outer circles on the board, and has twice the usual value **9** [C] (in the game of BASEBALL) a hit that allows the hitter to reach second BASE **10 at the double** (esp. of soldiers) at a rate between walking and running **11 double or quits** the decision (in a game where money is risked, such as DICE) to risk winning twice the amount one has already won, or losing it all **12 on the double** *infml* very quickly —see also DOUBLES

double³ *predeterminer, adv* twice (the amount, size, or quality): *10 is double 5.*|*double the amount of milk*|*His weight is double what it was 10 years ago*

double⁴ *adv* [Wa5] 2 together; in groups of 2 or in pairs: *Mary and Jane can sleep double tonight and you can have one of their beds.*|*When one drinks too much, sometimes one sees double*

double⁵ *v* **1** [T1;IØ] to make, be, or become twice as great or as many: *I must double the amount, or it won't be enough.*|*Sales doubled in 5 years* **2** [T1] (of an actor or actress) to act (2 parts in one play): *Mary agreed to double the 2 parts of the dancer and the mother* **3** [IØ (BACK)] to make a sudden sharp turn or twist: *He started running towards the street but suddenly doubled (back) and ran in the opposite direction* **4** [T1] to sail round by changing direction quickly **5** [T1;IØ] (to cause to) fold or bend sharply or tightly over: *Double the cover and put it over the child* **6** [IØ] (in the card game of BRIDGE) to make twice as great what the opponents will lose if they lose (or win if they win) **7** [IØ] (in the game of BASEBALL) to hit a DOUBLE² (9) —see also DOUBLE AS, DOUBLE BACK, DOUBLE OVER, DOUBLE UP

double as *v prep* [L1] to be or act as in addition to being or acting as something else: *In the play, Mary is playing the part of the dancer, but agreed to double as the mother*

double back *v adv* **1** [IØ] to return along the same path: *He started running towards the street but suddenly doubled back to the house* **2** [T1] DOUBLE OVER (1)

double-bar·relled, *AmE* **-reled** /ˌ·· ˈ··◂/ *adj* [Wa5] **1** (of a gun) having 2 barrels fixed side by side **2** *infml* (of a statement) having a double purpose **3** *BrE infml* (of family names) connected by a HYPHEN (as in *Smith-Fortescue*)

double bass /ˌdʌbəl ˈbeɪs/ also **bass**— *n* the largest and deepest instrument of the VIOLIN family —see picture at STRINGED INSTRUMENT

double bed /ˌ·· ˈ·/ *n* a bed big enough for 2 people —see picture at BEDROOM —**double-bedded** /ˌ·· ˈ··◂/ *adj* [Wa5]: (*esp. BrE*) *We'd like a double-bedded room, please*

double bluff /ˌ·· ˈ·/ *n* a double PRETENCE: *If I say I'm going to Pinsk he'll guess I'm really going to Minsk, so I'll admit that I'm going to Minsk and then he'll think I'm lying, which will be a double bluff* —see BLUFF³ (1)

double-breast·ed /ˌ·· ˈ··◂/ *adj* [Wa5] **1** (of a coat or JACKET) made so that one side of the front is brought across the other side of the front and usu. having a double row of buttons and a single row of buttonholes **2** (of a suit) having a JACKET made in this way

double-check /ˌ·· ˈ·/ *v* [T1;IØ] **1** to examine (something) twice for exactness or quality **2** (in the game of CHESS) to CHECK (a player or a player's king) with 2 pieces at the same time

double chin /ˌ·· ˈ·/ *n* a fold of loose skin between the face and neck, considered a sign of fatness in people

double cream /ˌ·· ˈ·/ *n* [U] *BrE* specially thick cream

double-cross /ˌ·· ˈ·/ *v* [T1] *sl* to cheat by pretended friendship —**double cross** *n* —**double-crosser** *n*

double date /ˌ·· ˈ·/ *n infml, esp. AmE* a DATE[2] (5) for 2 men and 2 women

double-deal·er /ˌ·· ˈ··/ *n* a deceiver; dishonest person —**-dealing** *n* [U]

double-deck·er /ˌ·· ˈ··◂/ *n* [C; *by*+U] **1** a bus with 2 floors —compare SINGLE-DECKER **2** a SANDWICH made with 3 pieces of bread leaving 2 spaces that are filled with food

double-de·clutch /ˌ·· ·ˈ·/ *v AmE* **double-clutch** /ˈ·· ·/ [IØ] (in a motor vehicle) to step twice on the CLUTCH when changing from one GEAR to another

double-dutch /ˌ·· ˈ·/ *n* [U] *humor derog* speech (or writing) that one cannot understand

double-dyed /ˌ·· ˈ·◂/ *adj* [Wa5] *esp. lit* (of a person) having a usu. bad quality very strongly: *a double-dyed thief/liar*

double-edged /ˌ·· ˈ·◂/ *adj* [Wa5] **1** having 2 edges that can be used **2** having 2 purposes or meanings, usu. quite different from each other

double en·ten·dre /ˌduːblɒn ˈtɒndrə‖-blɑn ˈtɑn- (*Fr* dublɑ̃tɑ̃dr)/ *n Fr* a word or phrase that may be understood in 2 different ways, one of which is usu. sexual

double-en·try book-keep·ing /ˌ·· ·· ˈ· ··/ *n* [U] a way of keeping accounts in which everything is written twice, once as an outgoing and once as an incoming amount

double fea·ture /ˌ·· ˈ··/ *n* a cinema performance in which 2 main films are shown

double first /ˌ·· ˈ·/ *n* (the holder of) a British university BACHELOR's degree with results at the highest level in 2 subjects or examinations

double-glaze /ˌ·· ˈ·/ *v* [Wv5;T1] to provide (a window) of (a room) with an additional sheet of glass —**-zing** *n* [U]: *We're having double-glazing fitted*

double Glouces·ter /ˌdʌbəl ˈglɒstəʳ‖-glɑ-/ *n* [(C); U] (an) orange cheese rather like CHEDDAR

double-joint·ed /ˌ·· ˈ··◂/ *adj* having joints that allow movement (esp. of the fingers) backwards as well as forwards: *He's double-jointed.|a double-jointed elbow*

double o·ver *v adv* **1** [T1] also **double back**— to fold (something) in half **2** [T1;IØ] DOUBLE UP (1)

double-park /ˌ·· ˈ·/ *v* [T1;IØ] to block a road by parking (a vehicle) beside a vehicle already parked: *Double-parking is usually unlawful*

double-quick /ˌ·· ˈ·◂/ *adj, adv* [Wa5] *infml* very quick(ly): *Get the doctor double-quick! The baby has swallowed a pin*

doub·les /ˈdʌbəlz/ *n* **doubles** [Wn3;C] a match or competition made up of matches (esp. of tennis) played between 2 pairs of players: *Who'll win the men's/women's doubles at Wimbledon this year?* —see also MIXED DOUBLES —compare SINGLES

double-stop /ˌ·· ˈ·/ *v* [T1;IØ] to play (a stringed musical instrument) with fingers on 2 strings, playing both strings at the same time

doub·let /ˈdʌblɪ̆t/ *n* **1** a man's tight-fitting garment for the upper half of the body, with or without arm coverings, worn in Europe from about 1400 to the middle 1600s **2** one of 2 (or more) words with the same origin but different forms and/or meanings (such as *shirt* and *skirt*)

double take /ˌ·· ˈ·/ *n infml, esp. AmE* a quick but delayed movement of surprise usu. for humorous effect (esp. in the phr. **do a double take**)

double-talk /ˈ·· ·/ *v* [IØ;(T1)] *infml* **1** to use language that appears to be serious and have meaning but in fact is a mixture of sense and nonsense: *You can't double-talk your way out of this difficulty!* **2** to use language that is unnecessarily hard to understand —**double-talk** *n* [U] —**double-talker** *n*

double·think /ˈdʌbəlˌθɪŋk/ *n* [U] *derog* the ability to believe 2 opposing ideas at the same time

double time /ˌ·· ˈ·/ *n* [U] double wages paid to people who work at weekends or on public holidays

double up *v adv* **1** [IØ;T1] also **double over**— **a** (of a person) to bend (usu. with pain or laughter) **b** to cause (a person) to bend (usu. with pain or laughter) **2** [IØ] to share a bedroom **3** [T1] DOUBLE OVER (1)

dou·bloon /dʌˈbluːn/ *n* a former gold coin of Spain and Spanish America

doub·ly /ˈdʌbli/ *adv* [Wa5] **1** to twice the degree: *Her life is doubly interesting because she became famous so young* **2** in 2 ways: *He is doubly troubled, first because he is ill and secondly because he is poor*

doubt[1] /daʊt/ *v* **1** [T1, 5a, 6a (**whether, if**)] to be uncertain (about): *I doubt the truth of it.|I doubt whether it's true.|I don't doubt that John will come on time* **2** [T1, 6a (**whether, if**)] to mistrust: *I doubt his honesty.|I doubt if he's honest.|He says he can cure me, but I still doubt him* **3** [T5a] to consider unlikely: *I doubt that John will come* —**~er** *n*

USAGE Some people think *I* **doubt** *whether he'll come* is better than *I* **doubt** *if he'll come.* In the neg. form this verb must be followed by *that*: *I don't* **doubt** *that he'll come.*

doubt[2] *n* **1** [C;U:(5,6a (**whether, if**), *about*)] (a feeling of) uncertainty of belief or opinion: *troubled by religious doubt/doubts.|There is some doubt (as to/about) whether John will come on time.|There's no doubt that he'll come* **2** [C;U: (*about*)] (a feeling of) mistrust: *He says he can cure me, but I still have my doubts (about him/it)* **3** [U] a tendency not to believe or accept **4 in doubt** in a condition of uncertainty **5 without doubt** it is certain —see also NO DOUBT

USAGE 1 **Doubt** is followed by *that* after *no* or *not*: *There is some* **doubt** *(as to) whether he is guilty.|There is no* **doubt** *that he is guilty.* 2 *Without* **doubt** and **undoubtedly** express a stronger sense of knowing the real truth than **no doubt** or **doubtless**, which can be used as an adverb meaning not much more than "I think" or "I agree."

doubt·ful /ˈdaʊtfəl/ *adj* **1** [B (*about*);F6a,b] (of a person) full of doubt; not trusting: *I feel very doubtful about this/about whether to go.|Are you doubtful of/about Mr. Smith?|I'm doubtful where to go/whether he's still alive* **2** [B] uncertain; not settled: *The future is too doubtful for us to make plans* **3** [B] not probable; unlikely: *It is doubtful if we can get the engine working before morning* **4** [B] questionable as to honesty, properness, or value: *The new servant seems a doubtful fellow to me: can we trust him?* —**~ly** *adv*

doubt·ing Thom·as /ˌ·· ˈ··/ *n humor* a person, esp. a man, who does not easily believe things

doubt·less /ˈdaʊtləs/ *adv* [Wa5] **1** without doubt: *John will doubtless come on time as he always does* **2**

probably: *It will doubtless rain on the day of the garden party* —see DOUBT[2] (USAGE)

douche /duːʃ/ *n* **1** (an instrument for forcing) a stream of water into or onto any part of the body to wash it **2** (**like**) **a cold douche** *infml* (like) an unpleasant surprise or sudden discouragement

dough /dəʊ/ *n* [U] **1** flour mixed with water ready for baking **2** *sl, esp. AmE* money

dough·nut /ˈdəʊnʌt/ *n* a small round cake fried in fat and covered with sugar. It is often ring-shaped, esp. in the US

dough·ty /ˈdaʊti/ *adj* [Wa1] *old use or humor* able; strong; brave

dough·y /ˈdəʊi/ *adj* [Wa1] **1** like DOUGH (1) **2** (of bread, cake, etc.) not cooked enough; soft or too soft **3** (of human skin) unhealthily lacking in clearness and colour; PASTY

do up *v adv* [T1] **1** to fasten: *Do up your buttons/my dress/this knot* **2** to repair; improve: *to do up the house/an old skirt* **3** to wrap: *to do up a parcel* **4** to make (oneself) more beautiful: *Mary has done herself up for the party* **5 done up** *BrE infml* very tired

dour /dʊəʳ‖daʊər, dʊər/ *adj* [Wa1] hard and cold in one's nature; unfriendly; unsmiling —**~ly** *adv*

douse, dowse /daʊs/ *v* [T1] **1** [(*with, in*)] to put into water or throw water over **2** *infml* to put out; turn off (a light)

dove[1] /dʌv/ *n* **1** any of various types of PIGEON; soft-voiced bird often used as a sign of peace **2** *esp. AmE* a person, esp. a politician, in favour of peace —opposite HAWK[1] (2) **3** (**as**) **gentle as a dove** very gentle

dove[2] /dəʊv/ *a past t.* (*esp. AmE*) *of* DIVE

dove·cote /ˈdʌvkəʊt, -kɒt‖-keʊt, -kɑt/ also **-cot** /-kɒt‖-kɑt/— *n* **1** a box or house built for DOVEs[1] (1) to live in **2 flutter the dovecotes** *humor or pomp* to do something which causes unexpected excitement among people who are usually quiet

dove·tail[1] /ˈdʌvteɪl/ *n* **1** a way of joining 2 pieces esp. of wood with a shaped piece sticking out at the end of one piece fitting closely into a cut-out place in the other piece **2** a joint formed in this way

dovetail[2] *v* **1** [T1 (TOGETHER)] to join (esp. pieces of wood) by means of DOVETAILs **2** [I∅ (*with, into*)] to fit skilfully together to form a whole

dow·a·ger /ˈdaʊədʒəʳ/ *n* **1** a woman of rank who has land or a title received from her husband who is dead **2** *infml* a grand-looking rich old lady

dow·dy /ˈdaʊdi/ *adj* [Wa1]·*derog* **1** (esp. of a woman) badly, dully dressed **2** (of clothes, esp. dresses) uninteresting; old-fashioned —**-dily** *adv* —**-diness** *n* [U]

dow·el /ˈdaʊəl/ *n* a pin (often of wood) in one part which fits into a hole in the other part

dow·er[1] /ˈdaʊəʳ/ *n* **1** *fml* money, lands, etc., that a woman has a lawful right to receive on her husband's death **2** *lit* a desirable quality which one has at birth: *a dower of good health* **3** *lit* DOWRY

dower[2] *v* [T1 (*with*)] *fml or lit* to provide with a DOWER —compare ENDOW

do with *v prep* **1** [T1,4: *no pass.*] (*usu. after* could *or sometimes* can) to need or want: *I could do with a cup of tea.|This room could do with (a) cleaning* **2** [T1,4: *no pass.*] *BrE infml* (*with neg.*) to bear; allow; experience willingly: *I can't do with loud music.|He couldn't do with waiting any longer, so he left* **3** [D1 *no pass.*] to cause (oneself) to spend time doing: *The boys didn't know what to do with themselves when school ended* **4** [T1 *no pass.*] (*with* have *or* be) to finish with: *Have you/Are you done with the newspaper?|I've done with that silly crowd* **5** [D1] (in questions with "what") to do with regard to: *"What have you done with my pen?" "Put it away."|"What shall we do with Aunt Maud?" "Take her to see a play."* **6** [T1 *no pass.*] to make DO[2] (29) with: *I'm afraid you'll have to do with a lot less now that our money's gone* **7 have/be to do with** to have a connection with: *His job has/is to do with telephones* **8 have/be something/nothing/anything/a lot, etc., to do with** to have some/no/any/a lot of, etc., connection with: *His job has nothing to do with telephones.|Don't have anything to do with those people* **9 over and done with** (*esp. of bad things*) past; finished with **10 What is x doing with** Why has x got: *What was that little boy doing with a book on chemistry?*
USAGE Compare **do** *to* and **do with**: *What have you* **done with** *my wife?* means "Where is she?" (It would be sensible to answer *She's in the kitchen,* but not **I've done a lot with her,* or **We've done the shopping together.*) *What have you* **done** *to my wife?* suggests that you have hurt her.

do with·out *v adv; prep* [T1;I∅] to succeed, live, etc., well enough in the absence of (someone or something); DISPENSE WITH: *I haven't enough money to buy a car, so I'll just have to do without (one)*

down[1] /daʊn/ *adv* [Wa5] **1** towards or into a lower position; from above to a lower place: *Can you lift that box down from the shelf for me?|The boy climbed down to a lower branch on the tree.|It gets cold quickly when the sun goes down.|The man bent down to kiss the child.|"children who are always falling down"* (SEU S.) **2** at or in a lower position or place of less importance: *What's that down there in the corner?|"How are we going to keep them down on the farm after they've seen Paris?"* (song) **3** to or into a sitting or lying position: *Please sit down.|You may feel better if you go and lie down* **4** to or onto a surface: *Please put that cup down (on the table)* **5** to or towards the floor, the ground, the ground floor, or the bottom: *Put your bags down anywhere.|He was knocked down by a car.|The telephone wires were blown down by the storm.|Go down and see what the noise is.|Down, dog!|"a modern building* ENTIRE*ly burnt down."* (SEU S.)|(fig.) *Our team went down (to defeat) fighting hard* **6** into the body by swallowing: *Can't you get the medicine down?* **7** in or towards the south: *He's flying down to London from Glasgow. Then he intends to take the train from London down to Brighton.|down South|I'll be down in London all the week* —compare UP[1] (10) **8** *BrE* (esp. from London or a university) from a city or place of importance to one supposed to be of less importance: *We usually go (from London) down to Bath for a week every summer.|When is John coming down from Oxford?* —see USAGE **9** to or towards a point away from the speaker, esp. a point at a lower level: *Will you walk down to the shop with me?|I'll meet you down in the market in an hour* **10** (with verbs of fixing or fastening) firmly; tightly; safely: *Have you stuck down the back of the envelope?*|(fig.) *"I know this job of mine isn't much, but on the other hand I don't feel tied down"* (SEU W.) **11** on paper; in writing: *"Did you write/copy/mark/put down the telephone number?" "I have it down somewhere."|Put me down (on the list) for 25 pence for Anne's present.|I think I am down (on the list) to introduce the main speaker at the meeting* **12** (of that part of a sum of money to be paid at once) in CASH: *You can buy this car for £30 down and £5 a week for 3 years* **13** (showing or making a decrease or lower level of price, quantity, or quality): *Production has gone down this year.|Let's mark down the prices.|We must hold our spending down* **14** to the moment of catching, getting, or discovering: *The men rode/hunted the lion down.|The police ran the thief down* **15** into silence: *The speaker was shouted/*HOWL*ed down* **16** to a state of less activity, force, strength, power, etc.: *Let the fire burn down.|*

Can you quieten the children down?|Please turn the radio down (= lower) *a bit* **17** to or in a lower or worse condition: *The cruel rulers had kept the people down for many years.|That family has certainly come down in the world* (= socially) **18** from an earlier or past time: *This old idea has appeared and reappeared in various places down through the ages.| These jewels have been passed down in our family from mother to daughter for 300 years* **19** until thicker, (thinner), different, smaller, lower, weaker, or powdery: *Boil it down.|Water this drink down.|The heels of his shoes had worn down.|He got his report down to only 3 pages* **20** until clean: *washed/HOSEd the car down/rubbed down the horse* **21** seriously (esp. in the phr. **get down to work**) **22 down to** to and including a lower degree or position in a set: *Everyone works, from the President down to the boy who sweeps the floors.|I have only read down to the middle of the page* **23 down to the ground** *infml* perfectly; completely: *That suits me down to the ground* **24 down under** *infml* in or to Australia or New Zealand **25 down with** ill with: *Mother has gone/come down with a cold* **26 Down with** I/We don't want: *Down with the laws that have kept us slaves!*
USAGE When a person leaves university, he **goes down**, whether it is for a holiday or for ever: *We go* **down** *on the 3rd June.|I went* **down** *in 1972* —opposite **go up**. A student who is dismissed from a university is **sent down**.

down² *adj* [Wa5] **1** [F] in a low position, esp. lying on the ground: *The fighter is down!|The telephone wires are down!* **2** [F] below the horizon (esp. in the phr. **The sun is down**) **3** [F] downstairs: *It's very early in the morning, and no one is down yet* **4** [A;E] directed or going down: *the road down|the down stairs|(BrE) the down train (=from London;* compare *the up train)* **5** [F] being at a lower level: *The water is down.|Sales are down* **6** [F] being in a state of reduced or low activity: *The fire is down* **7** [F] sad; in low spirits: *I feel down today* **8** [F] behind an opponent (by): *Billie Jean King was down (by) 15–40 in the 3rd game, but went on to win the match* **9** [F] *infml, esp. AmE* finished; done: *8 down and 2 to go* **10 down for** entered on the list for (a race, school, etc.) **11 down on** *infml* having a low opinion of or dislike for: *Don't be down on him* **12 hit/kick someone when he's down** *infml* to take an unfair advantage of someone

down³ *prep* **1** to or in a lower or descending position; along; to the far end of: *He ran down the hill.|He looked down the barrel of the gun.|down the stairs|down the road|go down the garden* **2** to or in the direction of the current of: *to go/be down the river* **3** from an earlier to a later point in time; along: *We can't look ahead down the years and know what the future will bring* **4** *BrE nonstandard* to; down to: *I'm just going down the shops/down the town*

down⁴ *n* **1** (in American football) one of 4 attempts to advance a football 10 yards **2 have a down on someone** *infml* to have a low opinion of, or feel dislike for, someone —see also UPS AND DOWNS

down⁵ *v* [T1] **1** to knock to the ground **2** to defeat: *The government easily downed the opposition* **3** to swallow quickly (esp. a liquid) **4 down tools** *BrE* (of workers) to stop working, esp. to STRIKE¹ (16)

down⁶ *n* [U] **1** fine soft feathers **2** fine soft hair **3** any fine soft substance like these

down- *prefix* **1** *[v,-ed,-ing→v,adj,n]* so as to be underneath or in a lower position: *to* DOWNGRADE| DOWNTRODDEN|*a* DOWNPOUR —see USAGE **2** *[n→adj,adv]* being or going (farther) down: DOWNHILL|DOWNSTREAM|DOWNSTAIRS
USAGE These words are often formed from a *v adv*, or from a verb that can be followed by **down**: *fall down→downfall.*

down-and-out /ˌ· · ˈ·◂/ *adj, n* **down-and-outs** (a person who is) suffering from bad fortune, lack of money and work, etc., and seeming to be unable to do anything about it —**~er** *n*

down at heel /ˌ· · ˈ·◂/ *adj* **1** (of shoes) worn away underneath the heels **2** (of a person) wearing shoes with worn-down heels and, more generally, clothes whose condition suggests lack of money

down·beat /ˈdaʊnbiːt/ *n* the downward stroke of the director (CONDUCTOR) of a group of musicians, showing the first note of a measure (BAR) of music

down·cast /ˈdaʊnkɑːst‖-kæst/ *adj* **1** having or showing low spirits or sadness **2** directed downwards: *with downcast eyes*

down·draught, *AmE* **-draft** /ˈdaʊndrɑːft‖-dræft/ *n* a current of air moving downwards, esp. through a chimney into a room

down·er /ˈdaʊnəʳ/ *n infml* **1** a drug that lowers the spirits or makes feelings dull **2** an experience or state of affairs that is saddening —compare UPPER³

down·fall /ˈdaʊnfɔːl/ *n* **1** a sudden fall (esp. from high rank); ruin **2** a person or thing that causes this: *Drink|A disloyal friend was his downfall* **3** a fall (esp. of rain), esp. when sudden or heavy

down·grade /ˈdaʊngreɪd, daʊnˈgreɪd‖ˈdaʊngreɪd/ *v* [T1] to lower in rank, position, or importance —opposite **upgrade**

down·heart·ed /ˌdaʊnˈhɑːtɨ̣d◂‖-ɑr-/ *adj* having or showing low spirits or sadness —**~ly** *adv*

down·hill¹ /ˌdaʊnˈhɪl/ *adv* [Wa5] **1** [E] towards the bottom of a hill: *to run downhill|the road downhill* **2** towards a lower or worse state or level (esp. in the phr. **go downhill**)

down·hill² /ˌdaʊnˈhɪl◂/ *adj* [Wa5] **1** [A] sloping or going towards the bottom of a hill **2** [A] of or related to SKIing or running down hills **3** [B] *infml* easy: *The hardest part of the work is over and the rest is downhill*

Dow·ning Street /ˈdaʊnɪŋ striːt/ *n* [R] **1** the London street in which (at Number 10) the PRIME MINISTER officially lives **2** the government of Great Britain: *What does Downing Street think?*

down pay·ment /ˌ· ˈ··/ *n* a part of the full price paid at the time of buying or delivery, with the rest to be paid later

down·pour /ˈdaʊnpɔːʳ‖-por/ *n* a heavy fall of water, esp. rain

down·right¹ /ˈdaʊnraɪt/ *adv* [Wa5] *infml* (esp. with something bad) thoroughly: *It makes me downright angry to see food thrown away*

downright² *adj* [Wa5;A] *infml* **1** plain; direct; honest: *a downright kind of man who says just what he thinks* **2** (esp. with something bad) thorough: *a downright shame| You're a downright cheat*

downs /daʊnz/ *n* [P] *BrE* (*often cap. as part of a name*) low rounded hills (esp. chalk hills) covered with grass, esp. as in the South of England: *the North/South Downs*

down·stage¹ /ˌdaʊnˈsteɪdʒ◂/ *adv* [F] towards or at the front of a theatrical stage: *The actor came/is downstage.|action downstage|downstage right/left*

down·stage² *adj* [A] at the front of a theatrical stage: *downstage action*

down·stairs¹ /ˌdaʊnˈsteəz‖-ərz/ *adv* [Wa5;F] on or to a lower floor and esp. the main or ground floor: *to come downstairs|Is anyone downstairs yet?*

down·stairs² /ˌdaʊnˈsteəz◂‖-ər-/ *adj* [Wa5;A] on a lower floor and esp. the main or ground floor: *the downstairs part of the house* —**downstairs** *n* [Wn3;C]: *The downstairs isn't interesting, but the upper floors are nice*

down·stream /ˌdaʊnˈstriːm◂/ *adv, adj* [Wa5] (moving) with the current, towards the mouth of a river, stream, etc.
down-to-earth /ˌ· · ˈ·◂/ *adj* practical; in accordance with reality
down·town[1] /ˌdaʊnˈtaʊn/ *adv* [Wa5;F] *esp. AmE* to, towards, or in the lower part or business centre of a town or city: *to go/be downtown* —compare UPTOWN
down·town[2] /ˌdaʊnˈtaʊn◂/ *adj* [Wa5;A] *esp. AmE* of the lower part or business centre of a town or city
down·trod·den /ˈdaʊnˌtrɒdn‖-ˌtrɑ-/ *adj rather lit* treated badly by those in positions of power
down·ward /ˈdaʊnwəd‖-wərd/ *adj* [Wa5;A] towards or in a lower place or condition: *a downward movement of prices/of the head*|(fig.) *the downward path to ruin*
down·wards /ˈdaʊnwədz‖-ər-/ *AmE* usu. **-ward** /-wəd‖wərd/— *adv* **1** from a higher to a lower place or condition **2** towards the ground or floor: *He lay on the floor face downwards* **3** from an earlier time: *downwards through the years*
down·wind /ˌdaʊnˈwɪnd/ *adj, adv* (going or being) in the direction that the wind is moving
down·y /ˈdaʊni/ *adj* [Wa1] like or covered with DOWN[6]
dow·ry /ˈdaʊəri/ *n* the property that a woman brings to her husband in marriage
dowse[1] /daʊs/ *v* [T1 (*with*)] DOUSE
dowse[2] /daʊz/ *v* [I∅ (*for*)] to try to find underground streams or minerals with the help of a DOWSING ROD —**dowser** *n* —**dowsing** *n* [U]
dows·ing rod /ˈdaʊzɪŋ rɒd‖-rɑd/ also **divining rod**— *n* a Y-shaped stick which is believed to point down towards a place where there is underground water or minerals, when held by a person with special ability
dox·ol·o·gy /dɒkˈsɒlədʒi‖dɑkˈsɑ-/ *n* a usu. short song of praise to God, esp. one sung in churches
doy·en /ˈdɔɪən/ (*fem.* **doy·enne** /dɔɪˈen/)— *n* the oldest, longest-serving, or most experienced member of a group, often a group of government representatives in a foreign country
doy·ley, doyly /ˈdɔɪli/ *n* DOILY
doze /dəʊz/ *v* [I∅] to sleep lightly —**doze** *n* [S]: *He likes* (*to have*) *a doze after dinner*
doze a·way *v adv* [T1] to spend (time) dozing (DOZE)
doz·en /ˈdʌzən/ *abbrev.* **doz.** /dʌz/— *determiner, n* **dozen** *or* **dozens** [see NUMBER TABLE 4A] **1** a group of 12 **2 dozens (and dozens) of** *infml* lots (and lots) of: *"I've been there dozens of times." "How many?" "20 or 30 times at least"* **3 talk, speak, etc., nineteen/twenty/forty to the dozen** *infml* to talk quickly and continuously, never stopping —see also BAKER'S DOZEN, DAILY DOZEN
doze off also **drop off, nod off**— *v adv* [I∅] to fall asleep unintentionally
doz·y /ˈdəʊzi/ *adj* [Wa1] **1** sleepy: *a dozy person|a dozy feeling* **2** making one sleepy: *a dozy summer afternoon* **3** *infml BrE* stupid; lacking understanding —**-ily** *adv* —**-iness** *n* [U]
D Phil /ˌdiː ˈfɪl/ *n* PHD
dpt *written abbrev. for:* department
Dr *written abbrev. for:* Doctor
drab[1] /dræb/ *n old use derog* **1** SLATTERN **2** HARLOT
drab[2] *adj* [Wa1] **1** of a muddy yellowish brown or green colour **2** uninteresting; cheerless; dull: *drab lives* —**~ly** *adv* —**~ness** *n* [U]
drabs /dræbz/ *n* see DRIBS
drachm /dræm/ *n* **1** DRAM **2** DRACHMA
drach·ma /ˈdrækmə/ *n* **-mas** *or* **-mae** /-miː/ **1** an ancient Greek silver coin and weight of different amounts at different times **2** the standard of money of modern Greece —see MONEY TABLE
dra·co·ni·an /drəˈkəʊnɪən, dreɪ-/ *adj* very severe or cruel: *draconian laws*
draft[1] /drɑːft‖dræft/ *n* **1** [C; *in*+U] the first rough written form of anything or a rough plan: *I've made a first draft of my speech for Friday, but it still needs a lot of work.|a draft plan for a new law|a plan still only in draft* **2** [C; *by*+U] a written order for money to be paid by a bank, esp. from one bank to another: *a draft on the Glasgow branch of our bank for £50 for Mr. Smith.|to get money from Paris to Rome by draft* **3** [*the*+R] *AmE* CONSCRIPTION **4** [(*the*) U] *esp. AmE* a group of people chosen by CONSCRIPTION **5** [C;U] *AmE* DRAUGHT
draft[2] *v* [T1] **1** to make a DRAFT of **2** [(*into*)] *AmE* CONSCRIPT
draft·ee /drɑːfˈtiː‖dræfˈtiː/ *n AmE* a man who has been CONSCRIPTed into the armed forces
drafts·man /ˈdrɑːftsmən‖ˈdræfts-/ *n* **-men** /mən/ **1** also (*esp. BrE*) **draughtsman**— a person who makes drawings of all the parts of a new building or machine **2** a person who puts a suggested law or a new law into proper words **3** *AmE* DRAUGHTSMAN[2] (1)
draft·y /ˈdrɑːfti‖ˈdræfti/ *adj* [Wa1] *AmE* DRAUGHTY
drag[1] /dræg/ *n* **1** [C;U] the action or an act of dragging **2** [C] something that is dragged along over a surface **3** [C (*on, upon*)] something or someone that makes it harder to advance towards a desired end **4** [U;S] the force of the air that acts against the movement of an aircraft **5** also **drag hunt** /ˈ· ·/— a hunt in which trained dogs (**draghounds**) follow the smell of a cloth that has been pulled over the ground **6** [S] *sl* something dull and uninteresting: *The party was a drag, so we left early* **7** [C] *sl* an act of breathing in cigarette smoke **8** [U] *sl* woman's clothing worn by a man: *in drag*
drag[2] *v* **-gg-** **1** [T1] to pull (a heavy thing) along: *dragging a great branch along|dragging his foot* **2** [X9] to cause to come or go unwillingly: *Why must you drag me out to a concert on this cold night!* **3** [I∅ (ON)] to move along too slowly in space or time: *He dragged behind the others.|The meeting dragged* (*on*).*|The play dragged a bit in the 3rd act* **4** [I∅ (ALONG)] to move along while touching the ground: *The bottom of her long dress dragged* (*along*) *in the dust* **5** [T1 (*for*)] to look for something by pulling a heavy net along the bottom of (a body of water): *They're dragging the river for the body of the missing girl* **6 drag one's feet/heels** *infml* to act intentionally in a slow or ineffective way —see also DRAG DOWN, DRAG IN, DRAG ON, DRAG OUT, DRAG UP
drag down *v adv* [T1] **1** to cause (someone) to feel weak after illness **2** to reduce (someone) to a lower social or behavioural level
drag·gled /ˈdrægəld/ *adj* BEDRAGGLED
drag·gy /ˈdrægi/ *adj* [Wa1] *infml* unpleasantly dull
drag in *v adv* [T1] to introduce (something unconnected with the subject) —compare DRAG UP (1)
drag·net /ˈdrægnet/ *n* **1** a net that is pulled along the bottom of a river or lake, to bring up anything that may lie there **2** a network of actions and methods for catching criminals
drag·o·man /ˈdrægəmən, -gəʊ-/ *n* **-mans** a person who is a guide and translator in the NEAR EAST and MIDDLE EAST
drag·on /ˈdrægən/ *n* **1** an imaginary fire-breathing animal in children's stories **2** a fierce older woman, esp. one who allows too little freedom to a young girl in her charge
drag on *v adv* [I∅] to last an unnecessarily long time: *The meeting dragged on all day*
drag·on·fly /ˈdrægənflaɪ/ *n* any of a group of large

harmless brightly-coloured insects, with a long thin body and 2 pairs of large thin wings —see picture at INSECT

dra·goon[1] /drəˈguːn/ *n* a member of a European army group formerly consisting of heavily armed soldiers on horseback

dragoon in·to *v prep* [D1;V4b] to force or attempt to force into obeying by violent measures: *I was dragooned into helping*

drag out *v adv* **1** [T1;I∅] to (cause to) last an unnecessarily long time: *They dragged out the meeting with long speeches* **2** [T1 (*of*)] to force (something) to be told: *to drag the truth out of the prisoner*

drag up *v adv* [T1] *infml* **1** to raise (a subject) unnecessarily: *Don't drag that question up again!* **2** *BrE* to bring up (a child) in a poor way, esp. without good manners

drain[1] /dreɪn/ *v* **1** [T1;I∅ (AWAY, OFF, OUT)] to (cause to) flow off gradually or completely: *to drain all the water out|The water drained (off/away).*|(fig.) *money draining away in silly spending* **2** [T1 (OFF, *of*);I∅ (*of*)] to (cause to) become gradually dry or empty: *Let the wet glasses drain (dry) before you put them away.|She was so afraid/angry that her face (was) drained of blood.*|(fig.) *war that drains a nation of youth and wealth* **3** [T1] to carry away the surface water of: *They want to drain the land to make crops grow better on it* **4** [T1 (OFF)] to empty by drinking the contents of **5** [T1 (*of*)] to make weak and tired by using up the forces of body, mind, or feelings **6 drain dry** to drain until dry; drain completely: *Let the wet glasses drain dry before you put them away.|Drain the glasses dry.|I feel drained dry (of feeling)* **7 drain the cup of** *lit* to experience fully (esp. something unpleasant)

drain[2] *n* **1** [C] a means of DRAINing, such as a pipe or tube: *The drains are blocked up* —see picture at HOUSE[1] **2** [C] something that DRAINs, empties, or uses up: *All this spending is a drain on the money I have saved* **3** [U;S] the act of DRAINing **4 laugh like a drain** *BrE sl* to laugh noisily **5 down the drain** *infml* used wastefully or brought to nothing: *Years of work went down the drain in the fire*

drain·age /ˈdreɪnɪdʒ/ *n* [U] **1** the act or action of DRAINing **2** something that is DRAINed off, such as liquid or waste **3** a means for DRAINing, such as a pipe or tube **4** an area DRAINED

drainage ba·sin /ˈ·· ˌ··/ also **basin**— *n* DRAINAGE (4): *the great drainage basin of the Amazon*

drain a·way also **drain off**— *v adv* [T1;I∅] **1** to (cause to) flow away: *to let the water drain away|to drain the blood away*|(fig.) *All my money is draining away in silly spending* **2** [(*to*)] to (cause to) leave as a result of attractive offers: *Some of the cleverest people in Britain (were) drained away to other countries* —compare BRAIN DRAIN **3** to (cause to) weaken: *My strength is draining away*

drain·ing board /ˈ·· ·/ *n* a sloping board with a wavy surface, on which dishes are placed after washing to allow them to dry —see picture at KITCHEN

drain·pipe /ˈdreɪnpaɪp/ *n* a pipe for DRAINAGE, esp. of water and waste from buildings —see picture at HOUSE[1]

drainpipe trou·sers /ˌ·· ˈ··/ *n* [P] *infml* narrow pipelike trousers for men, that fit the body and legs tightly —see PAIR (USAGE)

drake /dreɪk/ *n* a male duck

dram /dræm/ *n* **1** a small measure of weight —see WEIGHTS & MEASURES TABLE **2** a small measure of liquid **3** *infml* a small alcoholic drink

dra·ma /ˈdrɑːmə/ *n* **1** [C] a serious work of literature that can be acted or read as a PLAY **2** [(*the*) U] PLAYS: *Which do you like better: music or (the) drama?* **3** [U9] a group of events concerning forces in opposition to each other: *the drama of international politics*

dra·mat·ic /drəˈmætɪk/ *adj* **1** [Wa5] of or related to the DRAMA (2) **2** exciting **3** catching and holding the imagination by unusual appearance or effects: *a very dramatic woman with flashing eyes and a long black dress* —**~ally** *adv* [Wa4]

dra·mat·ics /drəˈmætɪks/ *n* [U;(P)] **1** the study or practice of theatrical arts such as acting **2** *often derog* DRAMATIC behaviour or expression

dram·a·tis per·so·nae /ˌdræmətɪ̣s pɜːˈsəʊnaɪ, pə-ˈsəʊniː‖-pərˈsəʊniː/ *n Lat* **1** [(*the*) P] the characters (or actors) in a play **2** [(*the*) C *usu. sing.*] a list of these characters (or actors)

dram·a·tist /ˈdræmətɪ̣st/ *n* a writer of plays, esp. serious ones; PLAYWRIGHT

dram·a·tize, -ise /ˈdræmətaɪz/ *v* **1** [T1] to change (a book, report, etc.) so that it can be acted or read as a play: *He's dramatizing the story of his own life* **2** [T1;I∅] to present (something) in a DRAMATIC manner: *Don't dramatize so much, Johnny, just give us the facts!* —**-tization** /ˌdræmətaɪˈzeɪʃən‖-mətə-/ *n* [U9;C]

drank /dræŋk/ *past t. of* DRINK[1]

drape[1] /dreɪp/ *v* **1** [D1+*with, in, (a)round, over*;T1] to cover or ornament (something) with or as if with (folds of cloth): *Let us drape this picture of our leader with/in the national flag.|Let us drape the national flag round this picture of our leader* **2** [T1 (*over, (a)round*)] to cause to hang or stretch out loosely or carelessly: *He draped his legs over the arm of the chair*

drape[2] *n* [*usu. sing.*] **1** an arrangement in or of folds: *The piece of silk in the shop window had a beautiful drape* **2** the way clothing is cut or hangs: *His suit has a fashionable drape*

drap·er /ˈdreɪpəʳ/ *n BrE* a person who sells women's clothes, cloth, curtains, etc.

drap·er·y /ˈdreɪpəri/ *n* **1** [U] (*AmE* **dry goods**)— *BrE* the trade of or goods sold by a DRAPER: *My uncle deals in drapery.|The drapery department of the store* **2** [U] the arrangement of cloth in folds **3** [U;C] cloth or a garment arranged in folds: *a photograph taken against a background of drapery* **4** [U] *AmE* heavy cloth used as curtains

dras·tic /ˈdræstɪk/ *adj* strong, sudden, and often violent or severe: *Drastic changes are necessary to improve the government of the country* —**~ally** *adv* [Wa4]

drat /dræt/ *v* **-tt-** [T1] *euph sl* DAMN: *Drat it! I forgot my keys!|Drat!|Drat you! You're 10 minutes late!|Stop that dratted noise!*

draught, *AmE usu.* **draft** /drɑːft‖dræft/ *n* **1** [C] a current of air: *You may catch (a) cold if you sit in a draught* **2** [C] the flow of air through a chimney or FURNACE **3** [C] an act of swallowing liquid or the amount of liquid swallowed at one time **4** [C] *lit* a liquid for drinking, esp. a medicine: *a sleeping draught* **5** [C] the depth of water needed by a ship so that it will not touch bottom **6** [*on*+U;A] the drawing of a liquid from a large container such as a barrel: *Haven't you got beer on draught here?|I want draught beer, not bottled beer!* —see also DRAFT[1] (5) **7** [A] (*esp. in comb.*) (of animals) used for pulling loads: *a draught horse* **8** [C] (*AmE* **checker**)— *BrE* a small round piece used in playing DRAUGHTS

draught·board /ˈdrɑːftbɔːd‖ˈdræftbord/ (*AmE* **checkerboard**)— *n BrE* a board on which DRAUGHTS is played

draughts /drɑːfts‖dræfts/ (*AmE* **checkers**)— *n* [U] *BrE* a game played by 2 people, each with 12 round pieces, on a board of 64 squares

draughts·man¹ /ˈdrɑːftsmən‖ˈdræfts-/ *n* **-men** /mən/ *BrE* DRAUGHT (8)
draughtsman² *n AmE usu.* **drafts- 1** a person (esp. a man) who draws well: *Ingres was one of the greatest draughtsmen in the history of French painting* **2** *esp. BrE* DRAFTSMAN (1)
draught·y /drɑːfti‖dræfti/ *adj* [Wa1] with cold DRAUGHT*s* (1) blowing through
draw¹ /drɔː/ *v* **drew** /druː/, **drawn** /drɔːn/ **1** [T1] to pull: *to draw a net through the water|a cart drawn by a horse* **2** [X9] to cause to go in a stated direction: *to draw someone aside|to draw one's socks on* **3** [L9] *rather lit* to move or go steadily or gradually: *Night draws near.|The car drew ahead of the others* **4** [T1] to attract: *The play is drawing big crowds.|I feel drawn towards him* **5** [L9;(IØ)] to attract a paying public: *The play is drawing well* **6** [T1] to cause to come (as the direct result of an action): *to draw enemy fire by making a noise|Her shouts drew the attention of the police* **7** (of people) to take (a breath) in **8** [T1] to cause (blood) to flow **9** [T1] to bring or pull out, esp. with effort: *to draw a nail/a tooth* **10** [T1] to remove the bowels from: *to draw a chicken* **11** [IØ] (esp. of tea) to yield the full taste and smell **12** [T1] to collect (liquid) in a container: *to draw water from the well* **13** [T1] (of a ship) to need (a stated depth of water) in order to float **14** [T1] (of money, business shares, etc.) to earn: *money drawing interest in a bank* **15** [X9; (T1)] to take (money) from a bank or other such place: *to draw money from one's account|to draw a lot of money out* **16** [T1] to receive regularly esp. from a particular place: *to draw one's wages every Friday* **17** [T1] to receive or take by chance: *to draw a winning card/number* **18** [T1] to bend (a BOW) by pulling back the string, ready to shoot an arrow **19** [T1;IØ] to pull out (a weapon) ready for use: *to draw a sword|He drew (his gun) and fired* **20** [Wv5;T1;IØ] to end (a game, battle, etc.) without either side winning: *They drew (the game) 5 points to 5 (= 5 all).|We've had several drawn matches this year* **21** [IØ] to make pictures with a pencil or pen: *to draw very well* **22** [T1] **a** to make with a pencil or pen: *to draw a line/a map* **b** to make a picture of in this way: *to draw one's daughter|(fig.) Shakespeare draws his characters well* **23** [T1 (*on*)] to prepare (esp. a cheque) properly: *to draw a cheque on one's New York bank* **24** [T1] to make or get by reasoning: *to draw a comparison/a lesson/a* CONCLUSION **25** [L9;(IØ)] to produce or allow a current of air: *The chimney draws well* **26 draw the/a line a** to decide the exact difference between things that lack fixed borders: *to try to draw the line between science and art in medicine* **b** to fix a border shutting out what one will not do or agree to: *I'm sorry: that's where I draw the line.|to draw the line at stealing* **27 draw the curtain/the blinds a** to close the curtain or the BLIND*s*³ (1) **b** to pull open the curtain —see also DRAW APART, DRAW ASIDE, DRAW AWAY, DRAW BACK, DRAW DOWN, DRAW FOR, DRAW IN, DRAW INTO, DRAW OFF, DRAW ON, DRAW OUT, DRAW UP
draw² *n* **1** an act or example of DRAWing¹ (17): *He picked a winning number on the first draw.|He won and I lost: that's the luck of the draw* **2** an act of DRAWing ON a cigarette, pipe, etc. **3** a state of affairs in which neither side wins: *The game was/ended in a draw* **4** a person or thing that attracts esp. a paying public **5 quick/fast on the draw** *infml* quick at pulling out a hand gun
draw a·part *v adv* [IØ] to get further and further away (from each other): *The 2 boats/political parties are drawing apart*
draw a·side also **take aside**— *v adv* [T1] to lead to a place where private conversation is possible: *I drew him aside and whispered the truth in his ear*
draw a·way *v adv* **1** [T1;IØ: (*from*)] to move (something) away, usu. quickly: *She drew away from him when he tried to kiss her* **2** [IØ (*from*)] to get further and further ahead (of)
draw·back /ˈdrɔːbæk/ *n* a difficulty or disadvantage; something that can cause trouble: *The only drawback of the plan is that it costs too much*
draw back *v adv* **1** [IØ (*from*)] to hold oneself at a distance **2** [IØ (*from*)] to be unwilling to consider or fulfil (something): *The firm drew back from (fulfilling) its agreement and wanted to talk about a new contract* **3** [T1;IØ: (*from*)] DRAW AWAY (1)
draw·bridge /ˈdrɔːˌbrɪdʒ/ *n* a bridge that can be pulled up to let ships pass, to protect a castle from attack, etc. —see picture at CASTLE¹
draw down *v adv* [T1a] to attract; invite: *to draw down blame on our heads*
draw·er¹ /ˈdrɔːəʳ/ *n* a person who draws
drawer² /drɔːʳ/ *n* **1** a sliding boxlike container with an open top (as in a table or desk) **2 (not) out of the top drawer** *infml* (not) from the best class of society —see also BOTTOM DRAWER
drawers /drɔːz‖drɔrz/ *n* [P] an undergarment for the lower part of the body, worn esp. by women, but no longer common —see PAIR (USAGE)
draw for *v prep* [T1,6a] to draw LOT*s* for: *Let's draw for the right to go first/for who will be leader*
draw in *v adv* **1** [IØ] (of a single day) to become dark **2** [IØ] to arrive: *The train/car drew in* **3** [IØ] to move to one side of the road: *The bus drew in to let the cars pass* **4** [T1] (of people) to take in (a breath) **5** [IØ] CLOSE IN (1) —compare DRAW OUT (2)
draw·ing /ˈdrɔːɪŋ/ *n* **1** [U] the art of drawing with lines made with a pen, pencil, etc.: *good at drawing* **2** [C] a picture made by drawing: *a drawing of a cat* **3** [C] an act or example of drawing, esp. an occasion when something is decided or won in a chance way by drawing LOT*s*
drawing board /ˈ·· ·/ *n* **1** a flat piece of wood on which paper is laid to draw on esp. with pen or pencil **2 go back to the drawing board** *infml* to start again after one's first attempt has failed
drawing pin /ˈ·· ·/ (*AmE* **thumbtack**)— *n BrE* a short nail with a broad flat head for pressing with one's thumb into a board or wall, to hold a notice or picture in place
drawing room /ˈ·· ·/ *n* **1** *AmE* a private room in a railway train, in which 3 people can sleep **2** *fml* LIVING ROOM
draw in·to *v prep* [D1] to encourage (someone unwilling) to join: *My brother was drawn into a fight*
drawl¹ /drɔːl/ *v* [T1 (OUT);IØ (ON)] to speak or say slowly, with vowels greatly lengthened
drawl² *n* a slow way of speaking, with the vowels greatly lengthened
drawn¹ /drɔːn/ *adj* **1** (esp. of the face) changed as if by pulling or stretching: *a face drawn with sorrow* **2** [Wa5] (of games, competitions, etc.) ended with neither side winning: *a drawn game|The match was drawn 5–5*
drawn² *past p. of* DRAW¹
draw off *v adv* **1** [T1] to remove: *to draw off some water|(fml) to draw off one's socks* **2** [IØ] to move away
draw on¹ *v adv* **1** [T1] *fml* to put on by pulling: *to draw on socks* **2** [IØ] to come near in time: *Winter is drawing on* **3** [T1b;V3] to encourage (someone), esp. to talk: *He drew the prisoner on to tell his story.|They drew the poor child on with false promises*
draw on² *v prep* [T1] **1** also **draw up·on**— to make use of (often money): *I shall have to draw on the money I've saved.|A writer has to draw on his*

imagination and experience **2** to pull out a weapon and threaten to use it against: *He drew on me, and I was forced to defend myself*

draw out *v adv* **1** [T1] to stretch (something) in space or time: *to draw out the wire|to draw out the speech|a long-drawn-out speech* **2** [I∅] to have more hours of daylight: *The days are drawing out now that it's Spring* —compare CLOSE IN, DRAW IN **3** [T1;I∅: (*of*)] to (cause to) leave: *The train drew out (of the station)* **4** [T1 (*of*)] to take (money) from a bank or other account **5** [T1] to show the general idea of: *The committee drew out a plan for the reorganization, without showing any details* **6** [T1 (*of*)] to get (something) told: *I was able to draw his story out of him* **7** [T1] BRING OUT (3) **8** [T1] BRING OUT (2)

draw·string /ˈdrɔːˌstrɪŋ/ *n* [*often pl.*] a string or cord that can be made tighter or looser, used for fastening clothes, bags, etc.

draw up *v adv* **1** [T1] to form and usu. write: *to draw up a plan|a contract* **2** [T1 *often pass.*] to place in prepared order: *The soldiers were drawn up, ready to fight the enemy* **3** [I∅ (*to*)] (of a vehicle) to get to a certain point and stop: *The car drew up (to me) and 3 men got out* **4** [T1] to make (oneself) stand straight, often proudly: *to draw oneself up to one's full height*

dray /dreɪ/ *n* a low strong flat 4-wheeled cart without sides, used for carrying heavy loads

dread¹ /dred/ *v* [Wv5;T1,3,4,5] to fear greatly: *I dread him|to see him|seeing him|that he will come*

dread² *n* **1** [U;S] a great fear, esp. of some harm to come: *She suffers from (a) great dread of heights* **2** [C *usu. sing.*] the cause of great fear: *Illness is the great dread of his life*

dread³ *adj* [A] *lit* **1** causing great fear or anxiety: *the dread return of the cruel ruler* **2** causing a solemn mixture of honour and fear: *God's dread judgment*

dread·ful /ˈdredfəl/ *adj* **1** causing great fear or anxiety; terrible: *the dreadful news of the accident|dreadful pain* **2** very unpleasant or shocking: *There's a dreadful noise in this room* **3** *infml* not enjoyable; uninteresting: *The play last night was just dreadful!* —**~ness** *n* [U9]

dread·ful·ly /ˈdredfəli/ also (*nonstandard*) **dreadful**— *adv* **1** in a DREADFUL manner: *dreadfully hurt* **2** *infml polite* very: *I'm dreadfully sorry, old man: I didn't mean to step on your toe*

dread·nought, -naught /ˈdrednɔːt/ *n* a type of BATTLESHIP used at the beginning of the 20th century

dream¹ /driːm/ *n* **1** a group of thoughts, images, or feelings experienced during sleep **2** a group of thoughts, images, or feelings like these, experienced when half-awake or when the mind is not completely under conscious control; DAYDREAM **3** [*usu. sing.*] a state of mind in which one has such experiences frequently and does not pay much attention to the real world **4** something imagined, not real, but believed in or greatly and hopefully desired: *She thinks he is in love with her, but it's only a dream* **5** *infml* a thing or person notable for beauty, excellence, or enjoyable quality: *Their new house is a real dream*

dream² *v* **dreamed** *or* **dreamt** /dremt/ [T1,5a;I∅ (*of, about*)] **1** to have (a dream) (about something): *Do you dream at night?|to dream something strange|I dreamt he would come* **2** to imagine (something): *I never said that! You must have been dreaming!|I never dreamt that such a thing could happen!* **3 not dream of** *infml* not consider; not be able to, esp. for moral reasons: *I wouldn't dream of hurting the child!* USAGE 1 **Dreamed** and **dreamt** are both correct in *BrE*, for both the past tense and the past participle, but Americans more often use **dreamed** for both. 2 Avoid saying ***I dreamed/dreamt** *a dream.* It is better to say *I had a dream,* or *I* **dreamed/dreamt** (*that* . . .).

dream a·way *v adv* [T1] to spend (time) in dreaming or inactivity

dream·boat /ˈdriːmbəʊt/ *n sl* a very attractive person of the opposite sex

dream·er /ˈdriːməʳ/ *n* **1** a person who dreams **2** a person who has ideas or plans that are considered impractical

dream·land /ˈdriːmlænd/ *n* **1** [U;(C)] a beautiful and happy place that exists only in a dream or in one's imagination: *Stop living in (a) dreamland and do some work!* **2** [U] *humor or lit* sleep

dream·less /ˈdriːmləs/ *adj* (of sleep) without dreams; peaceful —**~ly** *adv*

dream·like /ˈdriːmlaɪk/ *adj* as in a dream; unreal

dream up *v adv* [T1] *sl often derog* to think of or imagine (something unusual or surprising): *She can always dream up some new reason for not doing anything unpleasant*

dream world /ˈ· ·/ *n* **1** a world of false and unreal ideas **2** DREAMLAND

dream·y /ˈdriːmi/ *adj* [Wa1] **1** (of a person) living more in the imagination than in the real world **2** peaceful and beautiful: *dreamy eyes* **3** not clear, sharp, or exact: *soft and dreamy music|The misty scene had a dreamy quality about it* **4** *young girls' sl* wonderful; desirable; beautiful: *Isn't that dress dreamy!* —**-ily** *adv* —**-iness** *n* [U]

drear /drɪəʳ/ *adj* [Wa1] *poet* DREARY (1)

drear·y /ˈdrɪəri/ *adj* [Wa1] **1** sad or saddening: *a dreary day, cold and without sunshine* **2** *infml* dull; uninteresting: *Addressing envelopes all the time is dreary work* —**-ily** *adv* —**-iness** *n* [U]

dredge¹ /dredʒ/ *n* DREDGER (1)

dredge² *v* [T1;I∅ (*for*)] to use a DREDGER (1) (in, on, or for something): *They are dredging for the dead body.|Can we dredge the river to make it deeper?*

dredge³ *v* [D1+*over/with*;T1] to cover (food) lightly by scattering (something powdery) over it: *to dredge a fish with flour|She dredged a little sugar over the cooked pastry*

dredg·er /ˈdredʒəʳ/ *n* **1** also **dredge**— a machine or ship used for digging or sucking up mud and sand from below water —see picture at SHIP¹ **2** a person who DREDGES²

dredge up *v adv* [T1] **1** to bring to the surface of water **2** *infml* to produce or bring up (usu. something unpleasant): *to dredge up the sad facts of the past|to dredge up an old quarrel*

dregs /dregz/ *n* [P] **1** bitter bits of matter in a liquid that sink to the bottom and are thrown away **2** the most worthless part of anything: *Murderers and thieves belong to|are the dregs of society*

drench /drentʃ/ *v* [T1 (*to, with*) *often pass.*] to make (usu. people, animals, or clothes) thoroughly wet: *I am drenched to the skin! I had no coat on when the rain started.|a drenching rain|I got a good drenching in the rain*

dress¹ /dres/ *v* **1** [T1;I∅] to put clothes on (oneself or someone else): *I'll be ready in a moment: I'm dressing.|Please dress the baby, George* —see USAGE **2** [T1;I∅] to provide (oneself or someone else) with clothes: *She dresses well on very little money.|She's very well-dressed* **3** [T1] to make or choose clothes for: *The princess is dressed by a famous dressmaker* **4** [I∅] to put on special correct formal clothes for the evening: *He said he would go to the party if he didn't have to dress* **5** [Wv5;L9] to wear clothes of the stated colour or type: *an old lady dressed in black* —see USAGE **6** [T1] to

arrange (hair) **7** [L9;X9] to (cause to) form a straight line: *Officer, dress those men to the right!*| *Soldiers, dress right!* **8** [T1] *tech* to give a desired finished surface to (cloth or building stones) **9** [T1] *tech* to clean and prepare (meat, birds) for market or for cooking **10** [T1] *tech* to prepare (ground) for planting, esp. by spreading FERTILIZER **11** [T1] to add a tasty liquid to (a SALAD) **12** [T1] to clean and put medicine and a protective covering on (a wound) **13** [T1] to make interesting or pretty by adding ornaments: *to dress a Christmas tree* **14** [T1] to arrange goods interestingly in (esp. a shop window) **15 dressed in one's (Sunday) best** *infml* wearing one's best clothes **16 dressed (up) to kill** *infml* wearing very showy clothes, esp. to attract the opposite sex
USAGE To **dress** means **a** "to put on clothes": *I can* **dress** (=*get* **dressed**) *in 5 minutes.*|*She* **dressed** *the baby.* We can say: **Dress** *at once!*|*Get* **dressed** *at once!*|**Put on** *your clothes at once!* but not **Wear your clothes at once!* **Dress** also means **b** "to have on or wear clothes of the stated colour or type." Compare: *She always* **dresses** *in black*/**wears** *black.*| *He's not* **dressed** *in his uniform*/**wearing** *his uniform.* —see also DRESS DOWN, DRESS UP

dress² *n* **1** [U] clothing, esp. outer clothing: *In this old play, the actors wear the dress of 100 years ago* **2** [C] a woman's or girl's outer garment that covers the body from shoulder to knee or below **3** [U9] (*in comb.*) clothing worn on special occasions or by special types of people: *evening dress*

dress³ *adj* [Wa5;A] **1** related to or used for a dress: *dress material* **2** (of clothing) suitable for a formal occasion: *a dress shirt/coat/suit* **3** requiring or permitting formal dress: *a dress affair*

dres·sage /ˈdresɑːʒ‖drəˈsɑːʒ/ *n* [U] the performance by a horse of various actions as a result of slight but skilful movements of the rider's hands, legs, and weight

dress cir·cle /ˈ· ˌ··/ *n* the first row of raised seats in a theatre, where it was once the custom to wear special clothes for the evening

dress down *v adv* **1** [T1] to make (leather or a horse's skin) soft or clean by brushing, cleaning, or rubbing **2** [IØ] to dress in a suitably humble fashion for some occasion or company **3** [T1] to scold; TELL OFF (1) —**dressing-down** /ˌ·· ˈ·/ *n*: *That disobedient child needs a good dressing-down*

dress·er¹ /ˈdresəʳ/ *n* **1** *esp. BrE* a piece of furniture for holding dishes and other articles used in eating, having open shelves above and cupboards below **2** *AmE* a chest of drawers, used esp. for clothing, often with a mirror on top

dresser² *n* (*esp. in comb.*) a person who dresses, esp. in the stated way: *a fashionable dresser*

dress·ing /ˈdresɪŋ/ *n* **1** [U] the act or action of a person who dresses **2** [U;C] a usu. liquid mixture for adding to a dish, esp. a SALAD **3** [U;(C)] *AmE* a usu. solid mixture for putting inside a chicken, duck, piece of rolled meat, etc. before cooking; STUFFING **4** [C] material used to cover a wound

dressing gown /ˈ·· ·/ *n* a garment rather like a long loose coat, worn after rising from bed and before putting on outer clothes, or when resting during the day

dressing ta·ble /ˈ·· ˌ··/ *n* a low table with a mirror, usu. in a bedroom, at which a woman sits while arranging her hair, making up her face, etc. —see picture at BEDROOM

dress·mak·er /ˈdresˌmeɪkəʳ/ *n* a person, usu. a woman, who makes dresses —**-making** *n* [U]

dress re·hears·al /ˈ· ·ˌ··/ *n* the last practice performance (REHEARSAL) of a play before its official public performance. The actors wear the special clothes needed for the play, rather than ordinary clothes

dress up *v adv* **1** [T1;IØ] to make (something, or oneself) more attractive, esp. with clothing **2** [IØ (*in*)] (usu. of children) to wear someone else's clothes for fun and pretence: *My daughter likes dressing up* (*in her mother's clothes*) **3** [T1 (*as, in*)] to make (something or someone) seem different or more attractive: *He dressed the facts up in amusing details* **4** [T1] to make (an idea) seem more pleasant or acceptable

dress·y /ˈdresi/ *adj* [Wa1] **1** (of a person) showy in dress **2** (of clothes) showy or ornamental, not for ordinary wear

drew /druː/ *past t. of* DRAW¹

drib·ble¹ /ˈdrɪbəl/ *v* **1** [IØ (AWAY)] (of a liquid, esp. SALIVA, or a powdery solid) to flow or fall out in drops little by little: (fig.) *Our money seems to be dribbling away now that everything costs more* **2** [IØ; (T1)] to let (a liquid, esp. SALIVA) fall or flow out slowly drop by drop: *The baby is dribbling: wipe its mouth* **3** [IØ;T1] to move (esp. a ball) by a number of short kicks, strokes, or BOUNCE with foot, hand, or stick

dribble² *n* **1** a small slowly-moving stream or flow **2** a very small or unimportant bit or quantity **3** an act or example of dribbling (DRIBBLE) esp. a ball

drib·let /ˈdrɪblət/ *n* **1** a very small or unimportant sum or part **2** a drop of liquid

dribs /drɪbz/ *n* **dribs and drabs** *infml* small and unimportant amounts: *He's paying me back in dribs and drabs*

dried /draɪd/ *past t. and past p. of* DRY²

dried fruit /ˌ· ˈ·/ *n* [U] raw fruit preserved by drying

dried milk /ˌ· ˈ·/ *n* [U] MILK POWDER

dried-up /ˌ· ˈ·◂/ *adj* having become smaller and older-looking through or as if through loss of liquid

dri·er /ˈdraɪəʳ/ *n* DRYER

drift¹ /drɪft/ *n* **1** [U;C] the movement or course of something DRIFTing²: *the aimless drift of the former government* **2** [C] a mass of matter (such as snow or sand) blown up by wind: *snow in great drifts* **3** [U] earth, sand, stones, and rock left by running water or a GLACIER **4** [C;U] a general tendency or movement: *the drift of young people from the country to the city* **5** [S9] the general meaning: *I'm sorry: I can't quite catch the drift of what you're saying*

drift² *v* **1** [IØ] to float or be driven along by wind, waves, or currents: *They drifted* (*out to sea*).|(fig.) *She just drifts from job to job.*|(fig.) *They had been married for a long time but gradually drifted apart until they separated* **2** [T1;IØ] to pile up under the force of the wind or water: *The snow lay drifted in great piles against the house*

drift·age /ˈdrɪftɪdʒ/ *n* **1** [U;S] the act or amount of DRIFTing of some object, esp. through the action of wind or water **2** [U;S] movement away from a set course because of DRIFTing **3** [U] material that has DRIFTed

drift·er /ˈdrɪftəʳ/ *n* **1** *often derog* a person who DRIFTs, esp. one who travels or moves about aimlessly **2** a boat from which fish are caught in a DRIFTNET

drift ice /ˈ· ·/ *n* [U] ice broken off large ice masses and carried along by wind and moving water on the sea, a river, etc.

drift·net /ˈdrɪftnet/ *n* a large net spread in water to catch fish which DRIFTs as the water moves

drift·wood /ˈdrɪftwʊd/ *n* [U] wood blown onto the shore by wind

drill¹ /drɪl/ *v* **1** [T1] to make or remove with or as if with a DRILL² (1): *to drill a hole in wood*|*to drill the bad bits out of someone's teeth* **2** [T1 (UP);IØ] to use a DRILL[2] (1) on (something): *to drill (up) a road|to drill someone's teeth* **3** [T1;IØ] **a** to train (soldiers) in military movements **b** to practise military movements under instruction **4** [T1;IØ: (*in*)] to instruct and exercise by repeating: *Let's drill them in English pronunciation* **5** [T1] to shoot a bullet through

drill² *n* **1** [C] a tool or machine for making holes: *a road drill|a* DENTIST'*s drill* **2** [U] the training of soldiers **3** [U;C] training and instruction in a subject, esp. by means of repeating and following exact orders **4** [C] practice in how to deal with a dangerous state of affairs: *a fire drill* **5** [*the*+R] *BrE infml* the approved or correct way of doing something effectively: *What's the drill for getting money after 4 o'clock?*

drill³ *n* a type of large monkey, rather like a MANDRILL

drill⁴ *n* **1** a machine used for planting seeds in rows **2** a row of seeds planted in this way

drill⁵ *v* [T1] to plant (seeds) in rows

drill⁶ *n* [U] a type of strong cotton cloth: *drill trousers*

drill in *v adv* [T1] HAMMER IN

drill in·to *v prep* [D1] HAMMER INTO

dri·ly /ˈdraɪli/ *adv* see DRY

drink¹ /drɪŋk/ *v* **drank** /dræŋk/, **drunk** /drʌŋk/ **1** [T1;IØ: (DOWN, OFF, UP)] to swallow (liquid) **2** [T1] to take in or suck up: *drinking air into his lungs* **3** [T1 (*to*)] to give or join in (a TOAST[2] (2)) —see HEALTH (3) **4** [IØ] to use alcohol, esp. too much: *He doesn't smoke or drink.|He drinks like a fish* **5** [X9] to bring to a stated condition by taking alcohol: *He drank himself into unconsciousness.|He drank his troubles away* —see also **drink someone under the** TABLE

drink² *n* **1** [U;C] a liquid suitable for swallowing **2** [U;C] the habit or an act of drinking alcohol: *Have another drink!|strong drink|Her frequent quarrelling drove him to drink* **3** [*the*+R] *sl* the sea

drin·ka·ble /ˈdrɪŋkəbəl/ *adj* suitable or safe for drinking

drink·er /ˈdrɪŋkəʳ/ *n* **1** a person who drinks **2** a person who drinks alcohol, esp. too much: *a heavy drinker*

drink in *v adv* [T1] to take in through the senses, esp. eagerly

drinking foun·tain /ˈ·· ˌ··/ *n* an apparatus, usu. in a public place, in which water for drinking is forced up through a small hole either in a continuous stream or when a button is pushed

drinking wa·ter /ˈ·· ˌ··/ *n* [U] water for drinking

drink to *v prep* [T1 *pass. rare*] to wish (someone or something) good health or success; drink a TOAST[2] (2) to —see HEALTH (3)

drip¹ /drɪp/ *v* **-pp- 1** [IØ (DOWN);T1] to fall or let fall in drops: *Water is dripping (down) from the roof.|The roof is dripping water.|*(fig.) *Her voice dripped false sweetness* **2** [Wv4;IØ] to let fall drops of liquid: *a dripping roof* **3** [IØ (*with*)] to overflow with or as if with liquid: (fig.) *a uniform dripping with* DECORATIONS|(fig.) *a voice that dripped with false sweetness*

drip² *n* **1** [(*the*) S] the action or sound of falling in drops: *All night I heard the drip drip drip of the water* **2** [C;(U)] (an apparatus for) liquid put into a blood vessel at a slow rate **3** [C; *you* + N] *sl* a dull and unattractive person

drip-dry¹ /ˈ· ·/ *v* [T1;IØ] to (cause to) dry smoothly after hanging when wet

drip-dry² /ˌ· ˈ·◂/ *adj* [Wa5] (of clothing) that will dry smooth and needs no ironing when hung while wet: *a drip-dry shirt*

drip·ping¹ /ˈdrɪpɪŋ/ *n* [U] fat and juices that have come from meat during cooking

dripping² *adv* [Wa5] **dripping wet** very or completely wet

drive¹ /draɪv/ *v* **drove** /drəʊv/, **driven** /ˈdrɪvən/ **1** [X9;(T1)] to force to go: *to drive trade away|to drive cattle along the road|*(fig.) *He drives his workers (very hard)* **2** [T1;L9;IØ] to guide and control (a horse or vehicle): *to drive a horse/a cart/a car|She drives well.|He/They drove to the station/in the park.|Don't drink and drive* —see LEAD (USAGE), RIDE (USAGE) **3** [X9] to take (someone) in a vehicle as stated: *Can you drive me to the station?* **4** [L9] (of a vehicle) to perform or go in the stated way: *This car drives easily* **5** [T1] to direct force onto (a thing): *The engines drive the ship.|to drive a ball|to drive a nail|An oil engine drives the pump* **6** [X9] to put into the stated condition in this way: *to drive the nail through the wood* **7** [X9] to produce by opening a way: *to drive a tunnel/a railway through a mountain* **8** [T1;V3] (esp. of something unpleasant) to force (someone) to work hard or act as stated: *Pride drove her (to succeed)* **9** [X7;9] to force (someone) into the stated, usu. unpleasant, condition: *to drive him out of his senses|to drive someone mad|to drive someone to drink* **10** [Wv4;IØ] (esp. of rain) to move along with great force **11** [Wv5;T1] to collect (esp. snow) into large heaps: *as pure as the driven snow* **12 drive someone into a (tight) corner** *infml* to force someone into a real or imaginary position from which escape is difficult **13 drive something home (to)** to make something unmistakably clear (to) **14 let drive at** to aim a blow at

drive² *n* **1** [C] a journey in a vehicle **2** [C] an act of forcing animals to move together so as to make it easier to catch or kill them **3** [C;U] an act of hitting a ball, the distance a ball is hit, or the force with which it is hit: *to hit a long high drive to the right* **4** [C] a road for vehicles, esp. one through a public park or to a private house —see picture at HOUSE[1] **5** [C] an attacking move, esp. by an army into land held by an enemy **6** [C] a strong well-planned effort by a group for a particular purpose: *The club is having a membership drive* **7** [C9] *BrE* a competition of the stated type, esp. of a card game: *a* WHIST *drive* **8** [C] an important need which is part of a person's nature and which urges him to act in order to fulfil it: *Hunger, thirst, and sex are among the strongest human drives* **9** [U] a forceful quality of mind or spirit that gets things done: *He's clever but he won't succeed because he lacks drive* **10** [U;C] the apparatus by which a machine is set or kept in movement: *This car has (a) front-wheel drive*

drive at *v prep* [T1, 6 (what) *no pass.*] *infml* (*in* -ing *form*) to mean: *What are you driving at?* (= What do you mean?)

drive-in /ˈ· ·/ *n, adj* [Wa5;C;A] (a place) that people can use while remaining in their cars: *a drive-in (restaurant/cinema)*

drive in *v adv* [T1] to teach (something) with effort

drive in·to *v prep* [D1] **1** to teach (something) with effort to (someone) **2** to force (someone) into: *driving me into a nervous illness*

driv·el¹ /ˈdrɪvəl/ *v* **-ll-** (*AmE* **-l-**) [IØ (ON)] to talk stupidly, carelessly, or in a childish way —**~ler** *n*

drivel² *n* [U] nonsense: *I've never heard such silly drivel in all my life!*

drive off *v adv* **1** [T1] to force away or back; REPEL **2** [IØ] (in the game of GOLF) to make or hit the first stroke

driv·er /ˈdraɪvəʳ/ *n* **1** [C;N] a person who DRIVEs: *Who was the driver of the car when the accident happened?|a cattle-driver* **2** [C] a GOLF CLUB (2) with a wooden head, for hitting the ball long

distances at the beginning of play —see also SCREWDRIVER
drive·way /ˈdraɪvweɪ/ *n* a short private road leading from the street to a house, garage, or car-park; DRIVE² (4)
driv·ing /ˈdraɪvɪŋ/ *adj* [Wa5;A] **1** passing on force: *a driving wheel* **2** producing a strong effect: *a driving influence* **3** having great force: *a driving rain* **4** of or about guiding and controlling vehicles, esp. cars: *a driving school|a driving test*
driving li·cence /ˈ·· ˌ··/ (*AmE* **driver's license**)— *n* a LICENCE to drive a motor vehicle, obtained after success in a **driving test** /ˈ·· ·/
driving wheel /ˈ·· ·/ *n* the wheel turned by an engine (such as a railway engine)
driz·zle¹ /ˈdrɪzəl/ *v* [*it*+IØ] to rain in very small drops or very lightly
drizzle² *n* [U;S] a fine misty rain —**drizzly** *adj*: *a drizzly rain|a drizzly day*
drogue /drəʊg/ *n* **1** an open-ended bag made of stiff cloth (or a frame of wood in the same shape) which is put into the sea so as to keep the front of the ship into the wind **2** something pulled behind an aircraft for other aircraft to shoot at **3** also **drogue par·a·chute** /ˌ· ˈ···/—a small PARACHUTE that pulls out a larger one or that slows down the speed of a falling object or of a landing aircraft
droll /drəʊl/ *adj* [Wa1] having a humorously odd or unusual quality: *a droll person/expression* —**drolly** /ˈdrəʊl-li/ *adv* —**~ness** /ˈdrəʊlnəs/ *n* [U]
droll·e·ry /ˈdrəʊləri/ *n* **1** [U] DROLL humour **2** [C] an example of this
-drome /drəʊm/ *comb. form* a large specially prepared space for the stated purpose: *an* AERODROME
drom·e·da·ry /ˈdrʌmədəri, ˈdrɒm-‖ˈdrɑməderi/ *n* a type of camel with one HUMP¹ (2) —see picture at RUMINANT
drone¹ /drəʊn/ *n* **1** a male bee, esp. a male HONEYBEE **2** *derog* a person who lives on the labour of others; PARASITE **3** a pilotless aircraft or ship controlled by radio
drone² *v* **1** [IØ] to make a continuous low dull sound like that of bees **2** [IØ;(T1)] to speak or say (something) in a low dull voice without variety of level or speed
drone³ *n* [(*the*) S] **1** a continuous dull low sound like that of bees: *the drone of the enemy aircraft* **2** **a** a fixed deep note sounded continuously during a piece of music **b** the pipe in a set of BAGPIPES that makes a sound like this
drone on also **drone a·way**— *v adv* [IØ] **1** [(*about*)] to continue to speak in a low dull voice without variety of level or speed: *He always drones on about high prices* **2** to continue in a dull uninteresting manner: *The meeting droned on for hours*
drool /druːl/ *v* [IØ] *derog* **1** to let liquid flow from the mouth: *At the sight of the food he started drooling* **2** to talk foolishly **3** [(*over, about*)] to show pleasure in a foolish way: *I don't like all those girls drooling over that singer*
droop¹ /druːp/ *v* [Wv4;IØ] **1** to hang or bend downwards: *His shoulders drooped with tiredness.|The flowers drooped and faded* **2** to become sad or weakened; LANGUISH: *His spirits drooped*
droop² *n* [(*the*) S] the condition or appearance of DROOPing: *the droop of his shoulders/of the flowers*
drop¹ /drɒp‖drɑp/ *n* **1** [C] the amount of liquid that falls in one round mass: *a drop of oil|a tear drop|*(fig.) *He's had a drop too much* (*of alcohol*) *to drink* **2** [C] the smallest possible amount of liquid **3** [C9] a small round sweet: *He likes to eat fruit drops/chocolate drops* **4** [S;(C)] a fall: *a long drop down into the hole|a drop in temperature/quantity/quality|a drop of 10 feet* **5** [C] *esp. AmE* a place where something may be dropped, put, or left: *a mail drop* **6** [C] that which is dropped: *a drop of food from an aircraft to the hungry people on the island* **7 get the drop on someone** *sl* **a** to draw a gun and point it at someone **b** to get quickly into a more favourable position than someone —see also DROPS **8** (**only**) **a drop in the bucket/the ocean** something too small to have the desired effect
drop² *v* **-pp-** **1** [IØ;T1] to fall or let fall in drops: *The water dropped down slowly|The wet leaves dropped water* **2** [T1] to let fall or lower: *to drop a handkerchief|to drop one's voice* **3** [IØ (OFF, AWAY)] to go lower; become less: *Prices dropped.|His voice dropped to a lower note.|The wind has dropped* **4** [IØ (DOWN)] to fall unexpectedly or suddenly or let oneself fall: *The fruit dropped* (*down*) *from the tree.|* (fig.) *They worked until they dropped* **5** [T1] to lose: *He's been dropping a lot of money at horse races lately* **6** [X9] *infml* to allow (someone) to get out of a vehicle: *Drop me at the corner* **7** [T1 (*from*)] to leave out (from a team): *I've been dropped* (*from the football team*) *for next Saturday's match* **8** [T1] to say softly or in passing: *She dropped a valuable suggestion at the party last night* **9** [T1] to discontinue seeing, talking about, using, or practising; give up: *to drop the subject|He's dropped all his old friends* **10** [T1] to leave out: *He often drops his "h's" when he speaks* **11** [T1] *infml* to knock down; cause to fall: *dropped him with one blow* **12** [T1] *drug-users' sl* to take (drugs) **13** [L9 esp. *in, by, over, round*] to come or go unexpectedly or informally: *Drop in and see us when you're next in London!* **14** [L9 esp. AWAY, BACK, BEHIND, OFF] to get further away from a moving object by moving more slowly than it: *Our boat started the race well, but soon dropped off/away* (*from the others*)*/behind* (*the others*)*.|We dropped to last place* **15 drop a brick/clanger** *BrE infml* to do or say something that is socially unacceptable **16 drop dead** *sl* (*often used in the imper. as an* INSULT) to die suddenly **17 drop someone a line/note** to write a short letter to someone **18 drop something like a hot potato/coal** *infml* to quickly stop dealing with something that has suddenly become unpleasant
drop ham·mer /ˈ· ˌ··/ also **drop press** /ˈ· ·/— *n* a heavy power-driven hammer raised and then dropped esp. on metal resting on a hard surface
drop in on *v adv prep* [T1 *no pass.*] to visit (someone) without warning, informally
drop·kick¹ /ˈdrɒpˌkɪk‖ˈdrɑp-/ *n* (in RUGBY or AMERICAN FOOTBALL) a kick made by dropping the ball onto the ground and kicking it as it rises —compare PLACEKICK, PUNT⁵
dropkick² *v* **1** [IØ] to make a DROPKICK **2** [T1] **a** to kick (a ball) by this means **b** to kick (a GOAL) by this means
drop·let /ˈdrɒplət‖ˈdrɑp-/ *n* a very small drop (as of a liquid)
drop off *v adv* **1** [IØ] also **drop away**— to lessen; become fewer: *Interest in the game has dropped off* **2** [T1] *infml* to allow (someone) to get out of a vehicle **3** [IØ] *infml* DOZE OFF
drop·out /ˈdrɒp-aʊt‖ˈdrɑp-/ *n* **1** a person who DROPs OUT of school or college without completing the course **2** a person who DROPs OUT of ordinary society and tries to practise another life-style
drop out *v adv* [I|(*of*)] to stop attending or taking part: *He dropped out of ordinary society because it was driving him mad*
drop·per /ˈdrɒpəʳ‖ˈdrɑ-/ *n* **1** a person who drops **2** a short glass tube often with a rubber part (BULB) at one end for pressing, used for measuring out liquids, esp. liquid medicine, by drops —see picture at MEDICAL¹
drop·pings /ˈdrɒpɪŋz‖ˈdrɑ-/ *n* [P] waste matter from the bowels of animals and birds

drops /drɒps‖drɑps/ *n* [P] (*often in comb.*) liquid medicine intended to be taken drop by drop: *eyedrops|Here is some medicine to drink, and here are some drops*

drop·sy /ˈdrɒpsi‖ˈdrɑpsi/ *n* [U] a gathering of liquid under the skin (or in the organs) because of various diseases —**-sical** *adj*

dross /drɒs‖drɑs, drɔs/ *n* [U] **1** useless material (metal OXIDEs) which comes to the surface of melted metal **2** waste or impure matter

drought /draʊt/ *n* a long period of dry weather, when there is not enough water: *The crops died during the drought*

drove¹ /drəʊv/ *n* **1** a group of esp. farm animals driven or moving in a body **2** a crowd of people moving or acting together **3** a large group of things of the same sort

drove² *past t. of* DRIVE

drov·er /ˈdrəʊvəʳ/ *n* a person who drives cattle or sheep, esp. to market

drown /draʊn/ *v* **1** [I∅] to die by being under water for a long time **2** [T1] to kill by holding under water for a long time **3** [T1] to cover completely with water, esp. by a rise in the water level: *streets and houses drowned by the floods* **4** [T1 (*with, in*)] to make thoroughly wet: *drowning the bananas with cream* **5** [T1 (*in*)] to cause (oneself) to become very active or deeply interested in something: *He drowned himself in work* **6** [T1 (OUT)] to cover up (a sound) by making a loud noise **7 drown one's sorrows** to drink alcohol in an attempt to forget one's troubles

drowse¹ /draʊz/ *v* [I∅] **1** [(OFF)] to fall into a light sleep **2** to be inactive

drowse² *n* [S] the act or a case of drowsing (DROWSE); DOZE

drowse a·way *v adv* [T1] to spend (time) in a light sleep or in peaceful inactivity

drow·sy /ˈdraʊzi/ *adj* [Wa1] **1** ready to fall asleep **2** making one sleepy: *a drowsy summer afternoon* **3** giving the appearance of peaceful inactivity: *a drowsy village* —**-sily** *adv* —**-siness** *n* [U]

drub /drʌb/ *v* **-bb-** [T1] *infml* **1** to beat severely (with or as if with a stick) **2** to defeat thoroughly: *We gave the other team a good drubbing*

drudge¹ /drʌdʒ/ *v* [I∅] to do hard, humble, or uninteresting work

drudge² *n* a person who DRUDGEs: "LEXICOGRAPHER: *a writer of dictionaries; a harmless drudge*" (Dr Johnson)

drudg·e·ry /ˈdrʌdʒəri/ *n* [U] hard dull humble uninteresting work

drug¹ /drʌg/ *n* **1** a medicine or material used for making medicines **2** a habit-forming substance: *Tobacco and alcohol can be dangerous drugs* **3 a drug on the market** *infml* goods which no one wants to buy

drug² *v* **-gg-** [T1] **1** to add drugs to, esp. so as to produce unconsciousness: *a drugged drink* **2** to influence with drugs or give drugs to, esp. so as to produce unconsciousness: *to drug a sick man in pain|a drugged sleep*

drug·get /ˈdrʌgɪ̥t/ *n* **1** [U] rough heavy woollen material used esp. as a floor covering **2** [C] a floor covering made of this

drug·gist /ˈdrʌgɪ̥st/ *n AmE* PHARMACIST

drug·store /ˈdrʌgstɔːʳ‖-stor/ *n esp. AmE* a PHARMACY, esp. one which sells not only medicine, beauty products, film, etc., but also simple meals

dru·id /ˈdruːɪ̥d/ *n* (*often cap.*) a member of the ancient CELTIC priesthood of Britain, Ireland, and France, before the Christian religion

drum¹ /drʌm/ *n* **1** [C] a musical instrument consisting of a skin or skinlike surface stretched tight over one or both sides of a hollow circular frame, and struck by hand or with a stick **2** [(*the*) S] a sound like that of such an instrument: *the drum of the rain against my window* **3** [C] something that looks like such an instrument, esp. a part of a machine, a large container for liquids, or a hollow frame on which to wind string, rope, or wire: *an oil drum* **4** EARDRUM **5 beat the drum** *infml* to do everything possible to draw public attention to something

drum² *v* **-mm-** **1** [I∅] to beat or play a drum **2** [X9] to beat a drum for (someone moving into or out of a given state): *They drummed the captain off the ship* **3** [I∅;(T1)] to make (drum-like noises), esp. by continuous beating or striking: *He drummed on the table with his fingers.|to drum a strange loud beat* —see also DRUM INTO, DRUM OUT, DRUM UP

drum·beat /ˈdrʌmbiːt/ *n* a stroke on a drum or its sound

drum·fire /ˈdrʌmfaɪəʳ/ *n* [(*the*) S] the continuous quick firing of big heavy guns that sounds like the beating of a big drum

drum·head /ˈdrʌmhed/ *n* the material (such as skin or plastic) stretched over each end of a drum

drumhead court-mar·tial /ˌ·· · ˈ··/ *n* a COURT-MARTIAL¹ (1) that tries offences on the battlefield

drum in·to *v prep* [D1] *infml* to put (an idea) firmly into (someone or someone's mind) by steady effort or continuous repeating

drum ma·jor /ˌ· ˈ··‖ˈ· ˌ··/ *n* **1** a soldier (a SERGEANT (1)) in charge of the drummers of a military band, who leads the band when they march and play **2** *AmE* the male leader of any band of marching musicians

drum ma·jor·ette /ˌ· ··ˈ·/ *n* (esp. in the US) a showily-dressed girl who marches in front of a musical band

drum·mer /ˈdrʌməʳ/ *n* **1** a person who plays a drum **2** *AmE sl* COMMERCIAL TRAVELLER

drum out *v adv* [T1] **1** [(*of*)] to send away formally and disapprovingly: *He was drummed out of the army* **2** to send out (a message) by or as if by beating a drum

drum·stick /ˈdrʌmˌstɪk/ *n* **1** a stick for beating a drum **2** *infml* the lower meaty part of the leg of a bird, eaten as food

drum up *v adv* [T1] *infml* **1** to call together by or as if by beating a drum: *Let's drum up some buyers for our new product* **2** to obtain by continuous effort and esp. by advertising: *Let's drum up some more business* **3** to invent; originate: *Let's drum up a new time-saving method*

drunk¹ /drʌŋk/ *adj* [Wa1;F] **1** under the influence of alcohol: *The police charged him with being drunk and disorderly.|He got drunk on only 2 drinks.|That's the drunkest I've ever seen him* **2** [(*with*)] controlled by some feeling as if under the influence of alcohol: *drunk with power* **3** (**as**) **drunk as a lord** *infml* very drunk **4 dead/blind drunk** *infml* completely drunk **5 drunk and disorderly** *law* (the official charge in a court against someone who is said to have been) drunk

drunk² *n often derog* a person who is drunk

drunk³ *past p. of* DRINK¹

drunk·ard /ˈdrʌŋkəd‖-ərd/ *n derog* a person who is drunk often or most of the time —compare ALCOHOLIC²

drunk·en /ˈdrʌŋkən/ *adj* [A] **1** drunk **2** resulting from or marked by too much drinking of alcohol: *a drunken sleep|a drunken party* —**~ly** *adv* —**~ness** *n* [U]

drupe /druːp/ *n tech* any type of fruit with a hard stone surrounded by juicy flesh, such as the CHERRY, PEACH, or PLUM

dry¹ /draɪ/ *adj* [Wa1] **1** not wet; not having water or liquid in any form on or below the surface: *The* *clothes are dry.|The soil is too dry for planting* **2** (of parts of the earth) emptied of water: *The well has gone dry.|a dry lake* **3** no longer liquid or sticky: *The paint on this door is not yet dry: be careful!* **4** no longer giving milk: *a dry cow* **5** using no liquid: *a dry method of doing it* **6** without tears or other liquid substances from the body: *dry* SOBs*|a dry wound* **7** having or producing thirst: *I always feel dry in this hot weather.|dry work in the sun* **8** (esp. of bread) without butter or not fresh: *dry bread/cake* **9** (of alcoholic drinks, esp. wine) not sweet; not fruity in taste **10** without rain or wetness: *dry weather|dry heat* **11** not allowing the sale of alcoholic drink: *Are any parts of the US still dry?* **12** dull and uninteresting: *The book was as dry as dust* **13** cold in manner; according to the rules but without personal warmness or feeling: *dry politeness|a dry style of painting* **14** plain and simple: *the dry facts and nothing else* **15** amusing without appearing to be so; quietly IRONIC: *I like his dry humour* **16 (as) dry as a bone** also **bone-dry**— *infml* very dry **17 (as) dry as dust** *infml* **a** very uninteresting **b** very thirsty —**dryly, drily** *adv* —**dryness** *n* [U]

dry² *v* **1** [IØ (OUT);T1] to (cause to) become dry: *Dry your wet hands.|The wet clothes will soon dry (out) in the sun* **2** [Wv5;T1] to preserve (food) by removing liquid: *dried fruit/milk* —see also DRY OUT, DRY UP

dry·ad /ˈdraɪæd/ *n* (in ancient Greek stories) a spirit who lived in a tree, and whose life ended when the tree died; wood NYMPH

dry bat·te·ry /ˈ· ˌ···/ also **dry cell** /ˈ· ·/— *n* an electric BATTERY (2) containing chemicals made into a paste rather than a liquid

dry-clean /ˌ· ˈ·/ *v* [T1] to clean (clothes, material, etc.), without using water

dry clean·er's /ˌ· ˈ··/ *n* a shop where clothes, materials, etc., can be taken to be DRY-CLEANed

dry clean·ing /ˌ· ˈ··/ *n* [U] **1** the action or industry of DRY-CLEANing clothes **2** clothes that need to be, or have just been, DRY-CLEANed: *I took my dry cleaning home*

dry dock /ˈ· ·/ *n* [C; *in*+U] a place in which a ship is held in position while the water is pumped out, leaving the ship dry for repairs

dry·er, drier /ˈdraɪəʳ/ *n* **1** a person who dries **2** a machine that dries: *to sit under the hair dryer* **3** a chemical substance that dries

dry-eyed /ˌ· ˈ·◂/ *adj* [Wa2] (of a person) not weeping; not showing sadness

dry goods /ˈ· ·/ *n* [P] *esp. AmE* DRAPERY (1)

dry ice /ˌ· ˈ·/ *n* [U] CARBON DIOXIDE in a solid state, used mainly to keep food and other things cold

dry land /ˌ· ˈ·/ *n* [U] land that is not under water: *After 3 weeks at sea we were happy to get onto dry land again*

dry out *v adv* [T1;IØ] **1** to (cause to) give up dependence on alcoholic drink **2** to (cause to) become completely dry

dry rot /ˌ· ˈ·/ *n* [U] **1** diseased growth in wood (as in wooden floors) which turns wood into powder **2** decay of the mind or spirit of a group, which is hard to see at first but has bad effects in the end

dry-shod /ˌ· ˈ·/ *adj* [F] without getting the shoes or feet wet

dry up *v adv* **1** [T1;IØ] to (cause to) become completely dry **2** [IØ] *sl* SHUT UP (1)

dry wall /ˌ· ˈ·/ also **dry wall·ing** /ˌ· ˈ··/, **dry-stone wall** /ˌ· ˈ··, ˌ· ·ˈ·/— *n* [C;(U)] a wall made of stones put together without any sticky substance (MORTAR²) to hold them together, set up esp. to separate fields

d t's /ˌdiː ˈtiːz/ also (*fml*) **delirium tremens**— *n* [(*the*) P] an excited state in which unreal things are seen, caused by much drinking of alcohol

du·al /ˈdjuːəl‖ˈduːəl/ *adj* [Wa5;A;(B)] **1** consisting of 2 parts or having 2 parts like each other; double **2** having a double character or nature

dual car·riage·way /ˌ·· ˈ···/ *n BrE* a main road on which the traffic travelling in opposite directions is kept apart by a central band or separation of some sort

dub¹ /dʌb/ *v* **-bb-** [X1] **1** *lit or old use* to make (someone) a KNIGHT by a ceremonial touch on the shoulder with a sword while kneeling **2** *humor* (or in newspapers) to name humorously or descriptively: *They dubbed him Fatty because he was so fat.|She was dubbed "The Queen of the Tennis Court"*

dub² *v* [T1] to give new or different sound effects to, or change the original spoken language of (a cinema film, radio show, or television show)

dub·bin¹ /ˈdʌbɨ̣n/ also **dub·bing** /dʌbɪŋ/— *n* [U] a type of thick oily paste used for making leather softer

dubbin² *v* [T1] to put DUBBIN on (a leather article); treat with DUBBIN

du·bi·e·ty /djuːˈbaɪəti‖duː-/ *n fml* **1** [U] a feeling of uncertainty or doubt; DUBIOUSness **2** [C] a doubtful matter: *the dubieties of his position*

du·bi·ous /ˈdjuːbɪəs‖ˈduː-/ *adj* **1** causing doubt; of uncertain value or meaning **2** feeling doubt; undecided: *I'm still dubious about that plan* **3** possibly dishonest: *a rather dubious fellow who may be a criminal|dubious behaviour* —**~ly** *adv* —**~ness** *n* [U]

du·cal /ˈdjuːkəl‖ˈduː-/ *adj* of, like, or fit for a DUKE

duc·at /ˈdʌkət/ *n* [N;C] a gold coin of various values formerly used in several countries of Europe

duch·ess /ˈdʌtʃɨ̣s/ *n* [N;C] (*often cap.*) (the title of) **a** the wife of a DUKE: *The Duchess of Denver was the mother of Lord Peter Wimsey* **b** a woman of DUCAL rank in her own right

duch·y /ˈdʌtʃi/ *n* (*often cap.*) (used esp. in names) the lands of a DUKE or DUCHESS: *the Duchy of Cornwall*

duck¹ /dʌk/ *n* **1** [Wn1;C] (*masc.* **drake**)— any of various common swimming birds with short legs, short necks, and a wide beak, some wild, some kept for meat, eggs, and soft feathers —see picture at DOMESTIC ANIMAL **2** [U] the meat of this bird as food **3** [C;(N)] *infml, esp. BrE* (*used by men to or about children, and by women to or about everybody*) a person one likes: *She's a sweet old duck.|a perfect duck* **4** [C] also (*now rare*) **duck's egg** /ˈ· ·/— (in cricket) the failure to make any runs at all when hitting the ball **5 break one's duck** (in sports) to succeed in making one's first run, point, etc. **6 like water off a duck's back** *infml* having no effect **7 sitting duck** *infml* a thing or person with no defences or protection; easy TARGET **8 take to something like a duck to water** *infml* to learn or get used to something naturally and very easily —see also LAME DUCK

duck² *v* **1** [T1;IØ] to lower (one's head or body) quickly, esp. so as to avoid being hit **2** [T1 (*in*)] to push under water: *He ducked his head in the stream to get cool* **3** [L9] to try to escape by hiding quickly: *He saw a policeman coming, and ducked behind a car* **4** [T1] *infml* to try to avoid (a difficulty or unpleasant responsibility); DODGE —**duck** *n*

duck³ *n* [U] a heavy strong usu. cotton cloth

duck-billed plat·y·pus /ˌdʌkˌbɪld ˈplætɨ̣pəs/ also **duck·bill** /ˈdʌkˌbɪl/— *n* a type of egg-laying Australian animal with a beak like a duck's

duck·boards /ˈdʌkbɔːdz‖-bordz/ *n* [P] *BrE* narrow boards with spaces between, nailed on crosspieces, for walking over muddy ground

duck·ing stool /ˈ·· ·/ *n* a seat on one end of a long pole, to which bad-tempered and unpleasant women were tied in former times in order to be DUCKed² (2) in water as a punishment

duck·ling /ˈdʌklɪŋ/ *n* **1** [C] a small young duck **2** [U] the meat of a young but almost fully-grown duck as food

duck out of *v adv prep* [T1,4] *infml* to escape one's responsibility for: *Don't try to duck out of doing that unpleasant job!*

ducks /dʌks/ *n* [P] trousers of DUCK³: *dressed in white ducks* —see PAIR (USAGE)

ducks and drakes /ˌ· · ˈ·/ *n* [U] **1** a children's game in which one makes flat stones jump along the surface of water **2 play ducks and drakes with money** *infml* to waste money wildly

duck·weed /ˈdʌkwiːd/ *n* [U] any of various plants that grow on the surface of water that is not very deep, often eaten by water birds

duck·y /ˈdʌki/ also **ducks**— *n* [N] *infml, esp. BrE* (*used esp. by women*) dear; LUV; DUCK¹ (3)

duct /dʌkt/ *n* **1** a thin, narrow tube in the body which carries liquids, esp. from GLANDs: *tearducts* **2** a thin, narrow tube in plants which carries water, air, etc. **3** any kind of pipe in the ground for carrying liquids or other substances, or electric power lines —see also AQUEDUCT, VIADUCT **4** a pipe for carrying air into, out of, or inside a building, ship, etc.

duc·tile /ˈdʌktaɪl‖-tl/ *n* **1** (esp. of metals) that can be pressed or pulled into shape without needing to be heated **2** (of other substances) whose shape can be changed easily **3** *lit* (of a person or behaviour) easily influenced or controlled; MALLEABLE —**-tility** /dʌkˈtɪlǝ̇ti/ *n* [U]

duct·less gland /ˌ·· ˈ·/ *n* ENDOCRINE GLAND

dud /dʌd/ *n sl* a person or thing that is worthless, valueless, useless, or unable to serve a desired purpose: *a dud cheque*

dude /djuːd‖duːd/ *n AmE sl now rare* **1** a man who loves to wear fine clothes; DANDY **2** a city man, esp. an Easterner in the West

dude ranch /ˈ· ·/ *n* (in America) a holiday place that offers activities (such as horse riding) typical of western RANCHes (cattle farms)

dud·geon /ˈdʌdʒǝn/ *n* **in high dudgeon** *fml* in a state of bad temper or anger caused by hurt feelings

duds /dʌdz/ *n* [P] *sl* clothes

due¹ /djuː‖duː/ *adj* **1** [F (*to*)] *fml* owed or owing as a debt or right: *A great deal of money is due to you.|Our grateful thanks are due to you* —see DUE TO (USAGE) **2** [A] *fml* proper; suitable; enough: *driving with due care and attention* **3** [F] payable: *a bill due today* **4** [F (*for*);F3] (showing arrangements made in advance) expected; supposed (to): *The next train to London is due here at 4 o'clock.|I am due to leave quite soon now.|I am due for an increase in pay soon* **5 in due course/time** in or at the proper time —see also DULY

due² *n* [C9 *usu. sing.*] **1** something that rightfully belongs to someone, esp. something non-material (esp. in the phr. **give someone his due**): *I don't like him, but, to give him his due, he is a good singer* **2 give the devil his due** *infml* to be fair even to those we dislike

due³ *adv* (*before* north, south, east, *and* west) directly; exactly: *due north* (*of here*)

due⁴ *prep fml, esp. AmE* owed or owing as a debt or right to: *our grateful thanks are due you*

du·el¹ /ˈdjuːǝl‖ˈduːǝl/ *n* **1** a fight with hand guns or swords, arranged between 2 people because of a quarrel: *to fight a duel* **2** a struggle or argument between any 2 opposed people, groups, animals, ideas, etc.

duel² *v* **-ll-** (*AmE* **-l-**) [IØ (*with*);T1] to fight a DUEL with (another person or each other) —**dueller** *n*

du·en·na /djuːˈenǝ‖duː-/ *n* **1** (esp. in Spanish- and Portuguese-speaking countries) an older woman who watches over and trains the daughters of a family **2** *rare* CHAPERON¹ (1)

dues /djuːz‖duːz/ *n* [P] official charges or payments: *harbour dues*

du·et /djuːˈet‖duːˈet/ *n* a piece of music for 2 performers

due to /ˈ· ·/ *prep* because of; caused by: *His illness was due to bad food*

USAGE Compare **due to** and **owing to**: As **due** is an adjective, it seems that **due to** should really be used only with nouns: *His absence was* **due to** *the storm.* But educated speakers are now beginning to use **due to** with verbs, thus treating **due to** like **owing to** or **because of**: *He arrived late* **due to/owing to** *the storm.*

duff /dʌf/ *n* see PLUM DUFF

duf·fel, duf·fle /ˈdʌfǝl/ *n* [U] a rough heavy woollen cloth with a soft furry surface

duffel bag, duffle bag /ˈ·· ·/ *n* a long round bag made of strong cloth, for carrying clothes and other belongings on a journey —compare KIT BAG

duffel coat, duffle coat /ˈ·· ·/ *n* a loose coat made of DUFFEL, usu. fastened with long tubelike buttons (TOGGLEs) and often having a baglike headcovering joined to the neck

duf·fer /ˈdʌfǝʳ/ *n infml* [(*at*)] a foolish person or slow learner: *She is a duffer at games, who never improves*

dug¹ /dʌg/ *n* **1** UDDER **2** (of a female animal) TEAT (2)

dug² *past t. and p. of* DIG¹

dug·out /ˈdʌgaʊt/ *n* **1** a small light boat made by cutting out a deep hollow in a log **2 a** a (usu. military) shelter dug in a hillside **b** a (usu. military) shelter dug in the ground with an earth roof —compare TRENCH¹ (2)

duke /djuːk‖duːk/ *n* (*often cap.*) (the title of) a nobleman of the highest rank outside the Royal Family: *the Duke of Norfolk|He became a duke on the death of his father* —see also DUCHESS

duke·dom /ˈdjuːkdǝm‖ˈduːk-/ *n* **1** the rank or position of a DUKE **2** the period during which a DUKE holds his title **3** DUCHY

dukes /djuːks‖duːks/ *n* [P] *sl* FISTs: *Put your dukes up and fight!*

dul·cet /ˈdʌlsǝ̇t/ *adj lit* (esp. of sounds) sweet; pleasant; calming

dul·ci·mer /ˈdʌlsǝ̇mǝʳ/ *n* a small European musical stringed instrument of former times, played with light hammers held in the hands

dull¹ /dʌl/ *adj* [Wa1] **1** (of colour or surfaces) not bright, strong, or sharp; not shining: *a dress of some uninteresting dull colour|dull grey* **2** (of sound) not clear; low: *a dull knocking sound somewhere in the house* **3** (of weather, the sky, etc.) cloudy; grey; dark: *It's dull today: we shall have rain* **4** (of the senses) not of good quality: *The old man's hearing has become dull, and you must speak clearly to him* **5** (of things having edges or points) not sharp **6** (of pain) not sharply or clearly felt **7** having or showing slowness in thinking and understanding: *He couldn't teach such dull children.|a dull answer* **8** uninteresting; unexciting; lacking in imagination; boring (BORE⁶): *I slept through her dull speech* **9** having or showing lowness of spirit, lack of cheerfulness, or lack of desire for action: *If you go to bed late you will feel too dull to work the next morning* **10** (of trade, business, etc.) not active **11 (as) dull as ditchwater/**(*AmE*) **dishwater** *infml* very dull or uninteresting —**~y** *adv* —**~ness** *n* [U]

dull² *v* [T1;(IØ)] to (cause to) become dull: *eyes*

and ears dulled by age|Give me something to dull the pain

dull·ard /ˈdʌləd‖-ərd/ *n* [C;*you*+N] a dull slow-thinking person

du·ly /ˈdjuːli‖ˈduːli/ *adv* [Wa5] in a DUE manner, time, or degree; properly: *The carriage that he had ordered duly arrived, and we drove off.|Your suggestion has been duly noted*

dumb /dʌm/ *adj* **1** [Wa5;*the*+P] unable to speak: *dumb animals|special schools for the* DEAF *and dumb|The terrible news struck us all dumb* **2** [Wa1] unwilling to speak; silent: *The prisoner remained dumb during his trial* **3** [Wa1] *infml* stupid —**~ly** *adv* —**~ness** *n* [U]

dumb·bell /ˈdʌmbel/ *n* **1** [C *usu. pl.*] a weight consisting of 2 rounded ends connected by a short bar and usu. used in pairs for exercises **2** [C; *you*+N] *sl, esp. AmE* a stupid person, usu. male

dumb·found, dumfound /dʌmˈfaʊnd/ *v* [Wv5;T1] to make unable to speak because of wonder, surprise, or lack of understanding

dumb show /ˈ· ·/ *n* [C;U] something performed with actions only, and without any speaking: *to tell a story in dumb show*

dumb·wait·er /ˌdʌmˈweɪtəʳ/ *n* **1** *esp. BrE* a small table that turns round on a fixed base, put on a larger table and used for serving food **2** a small LIFT[2] (4) used for moving food, plates, etc., from one level of a building (such as a restaurant) to another; food LIFT

dum-dum /ˈdʌm dʌm/ also **dum-dum bul·let** /ˌ· · ˈ··/— *n* a soft-nosed bullet that spreads out upon hitting an object

dum·my /ˈdʌmi/ *n* **1** an object made to look like and take the place of a real thing: *a dummy gun made of wood* **2** something like a human figure made of wood or wax and used to make or show off clothes: *a dressmaker's dummy* **3** (*AmE* **pacifier**)— *BrE* a rubber thing for sucking, put in a baby's mouth to keep it quiet **4** (a player with) open cards on the table in the game of BRIDGE **5** *sl, esp. AmE* a stupid fool **6** a person who seems to be acting for himself but is really acting for another **7** *AmE* a drawing or pasted arrangement of words, pictures, etc., used as a guide for setting up a page or part of a page in printing

dummy run /ˌ·· ˈ·/ *n* a practice attempt made before the real thing

dump[1] /dʌmp/ *v* **1** [T1;(I∅)] to drop or unload (something) in a heap or carelessly: *Don't dump that sand in the middle of the path!|They dumped their bags on my floor and left!|No dumping here* **2** [T1] *sl* to get rid of suddenly and perhaps impolitely **3** [T1;I∅] *derog* to sell (goods) in a foreign country at a very low price

dump[2] *n* **1** a place for DUMPing something (such as waste material) **2** (a place for) a stored supply of military materials **3** *derog sl* a dirty and untidy place: *This town's a real dump*

dump·er /ˈdʌmpəʳ/ also **dumper truck** /ˈ·· ˌ·/, *AmE* **dump truck** /ˈ· ·/— *n* a vehicle with a large movable container on the front, that is used for carrying and emptying heavy loads (of soil, stones, etc.) at places where building is being done —see picture at SITE[1]

dump·ling /ˈdʌmplɪŋ/ *n* **1** a lump of boiled DOUGH, often served with meat or having meat inside it **2** a sweet food made of pastry with fruit inside it: *apple dumplings* **3** *infml* a short round usu. nice person: *a little round dumpling of a man*

dumps /dʌmps/ *n* **(down) in the dumps** *infml* sad and spiritless

dump·y /ˈdʌmpi/ *adj* [Wa1] *infml* (esp. of a person) short and thick or fat: *a dumpy little woman* —**-iness** *n* [U]

dun /dʌn/ *adj, n* **1** [Wa1;B;U] (of) a brownish-grey colour that lacks brightness **2** [C] a horse of this colour

dunce /dʌns/ *n* [C;*you*+N] a slow learner; stupid person

dunce's cap /ˈ·· ·/ also **dunce cap** /ˈ· ·/— *n* a tall round pointed paper hat formerly placed on the heads of dull slow pupils at school

dun·der·head /ˈdʌndəhed‖-ər-/ *n* [C; *you*+N] a stupid person

dune /djuːn‖duːn/ also **sand dune**— *n* a sandhill (often long and low) piled up by the wind on the seashore or in a desert

dune bug·gy /ˈ· ˌ··/ *n* BEACH BUGGY

dung /dʌŋ/ *n* [U] solid waste material passed from the bowels of animals (esp. cows and horses), often mixed with soil to make the soil produce more plants; animal MANURE

dun·ga·ree /ˌdʌŋgəˈriː/ *n* [A] of, about, or like DUNGAREES: *My right dungaree leg is torn*

dun·ga·rees /ˌdʌŋgəˈriːz/ *n* [P] trousers or work clothes made of heavy cotton cloth, usu. blue —see PAIR (USAGE)

dun·geon /ˈdʌndʒən/ *n* a close dark prison, commonly underground, beneath a castle

dung·hill /ˈdʌŋˌhɪl/ *n* **1** a heap of DUNG, esp. on a farm **2** something (such as a condition or state of affairs) that is very bad, esp. morally bad

dunk /dʌŋk/ *v* [T1;(I∅): (*in*)] *infml* **1** to dip (esp. food) into liquid while eating **2** to put or cause (someone, oneself, or something) to go under water, usu. for a limited time: *It is nice to dunk oneself in a pool on a hot day* —**dunk** *n*

du·o /ˈdjuːəʊ‖ˈduːəʊ/ *n* **duos** **1 a** DUET **b** 2 musicians who play DUETs **2** *infml* a pair: *They make a good duo, don't you think?*

du·o·dec·i·mal /ˌdjuːəˈdesɪ̈məl‖ˌduː-/ *adj* [Wa5] *tech* of 12 or 12's; concerning calculation by 12's (rather than by 10's as in the decimal system)

du·o·de·num /ˌdjuːəˈdiːnəm‖ˌduː-/ *n* **-na** /nə/ *or* **-nums** *tech* the first part of the bowel (about 12 inches long) below the stomach —see picture at DIGESTIVE SYSTEM —**-nal** *adj* [Wa5]: *a duodenal* ULCER

du·o·logue /ˈdjuːəlɒg‖ˈduːəlɔg, -lɑg/ *n* a DIALOGUE between 2 people

dupe[1] /djuːp‖duːp/ *n* [(*of*)] a person who is tricked or deceived (by someone else): *The old lady was the dupe of a dishonest man*

dupe[2] *v* [T1 (*into*) *often pass.*] to trick or deceive: *The old lady was duped by a dishonest man, who duped her into thinking he was honest*

du·plex /ˈdjuːpleks‖ˈduː-/ *adj* [Wa5;A;(B)] **1** *tech* double; having 2 **2** *AmE* (of a usu. costly flat) having rooms on 2 floors of a building, with inside stairs connecting them

du·pli·cate[1] /ˈdjuːplɪ̈kɪ̈t‖ˈduː-/ *adj* [Wa5;A] **1** consisting of or existing in 2 parts that are exactly alike: *duplicate keys to the front door* **2** being the same as another: *I'll have a duplicate key to the front door made for your 21st birthday*

duplicate[2] /ˈdjuːplɪ̈kɪ̈t‖ˈduː/ *n* something that is exactly like another in appearance, pattern, or contents; copy: *If you've lost your key, I can give you a duplicate.|These 2 keys are duplicates* (*of each other*)

du·pli·cate[3] /ˈdjuːplɪ̈keɪt‖ˈduː-/ *v* [T1] **1** to copy exactly: *Can you duplicate this key for me?|All the members received duplicated notices of the meeting* **2** to make again; make double —**-cation** /ˌdjuːplɪ̈ˈkeɪʃən‖ˌduː-/ *n* [U]

du·pli·ca·tor /ˈdjuːplɪ̈keɪtəʳ‖ˈduː-/ *n* a machine that makes copies of written, printed, or drawn material

du·plic·i·ty /djuːˈplɪsɪ̇ti‖duː-/ *n* [U] deceit; deception

dur·a·ble /ˈdjʊərəbəl‖ˈdʊ-/ *adj* long-lasting: *durable clothing|We must make a durable peace* —**-bly** *adv* —**-bility** /ˌdjʊərəˈbɪlɪ̇ti‖ˌdʊ-/ *n* [U]

du·ra·tion /djʊˈreɪʃən‖dʊ-/ *n* [U] **1** continuance in time: *an illness of short duration* **2** the time during which something exists or lasts, usu. something non-material: *He will be in hospital for the duration of the school year* **3 for the duration** *infml* **a** as long as the war lasts **b** as long as something lasts: *We're in this together for the duration*

dur·bar /ˈdɜːbɑːʳ‖ˈdɜr-/ *n Ind & Pak E* a court or ceremonial gathering held by Indian princes in former times

du·ress /djʊˈres‖dʊ-/ *n* [U] unlawful or unfair threats: *A promise made under duress need not be kept*

dur·ex /ˈdjʊəreks‖ˈdʊ-/ *n tdmk, BrE* (*often cap.*) SHEATH (4)

dur·ing /ˈdjʊərɪŋ‖ˈdʊ-/ *prep* **1** through the whole course of: *He swims every day during the summer.|"We're open from 10 o'clock until 6 o'clock during the week and then on Saturdays from 10 o'clock until 2 o'clock"* (SEU S.) **2** at some point in the course of: *He came in during the night.|"Only 2 trains left during the morning"* (SEU W.) —compare FOR (USAGE)

durst /dɜːst‖dɜrst/ [Wv2] *old use past t. of* DARE: *He durst not do it*

dusk /dʌsk/ *n* [U] the time when daylight is fading; darker part of TWILIGHT (1,2), esp. at night: *The lights go on at dusk*

dusk·y /ˈdʌski/ *adj* [Wa1] **1** darkish in colour: *dusky brown* **2** *euph or taboo derog* having dark skin: *the dusky races* **3** shadowy: *in the dusky light of the deep forest* —**-iness** *n* [U]

dust¹ /dʌst/ *n* **1** [U] powder made up of very small pieces of waste matter: *There was half an inch of dust on the books before I cleaned them* **2** [U] finely powdered earth: *There is no grass here and in the summer we have a great deal of dust* **3** [S] a cloud of this: *The car raised quite a dust as we drove off* **4** [U] powder made up of small pieces of some substance: *gold dust* **5** [U] *lit* the earthly remains of bodies once alive: *Respect the dust of our great leader* **6** [U] the earth as a place of burial: *He has been in the dust for 100 years* **7** [U] a state of dishonour and loss of self-respect: *He rose again from the dust of past defeats* **8** [U] something worthless (often in the phr. **dust and ashes**): *Success in the world was dust to him* **9 kick up/raise a dust (about)** *infml* to argue and shout (about) **10 lay the dust** to stop clouds of powdery earth from rising by making the ground wet **11 shake the dust off one's feet** *BrE infml* to go away in anger **12 throw dust in someone's eyes** *infml* to deceive someone **13 when the dust has settled** *infml* when the confusion is over —see also BITE¹ (11) **the dust** —**~less** *adj*: *dustless coal*

dust² *v* **1** [T1 (OFF, DOWN);IØ] to clean the dust from; remove dust: *Please dust all the books on the bottom shelf* **2** [D1+*with*/*over* (*onto*);T1] to cover with dust or fine powder: *to dust the crops with a substance that would kill insects.|Dust this new powder lightly over (onto) the roses.|to dust a cake with sugar*

dust·bin /ˈdʌstˌbɪn/ (*AmE* **garbage can**)— *n BrE* a container with a lid, for holding waste materials such as empty tins and bottles until they can be taken away

dust·bowl /ˈdʌstbəʊl/ *n* an area that suffers from dust storms and long periods without rain

dust·cart /ˈdʌstkɑːt‖-kɑrt/ (*AmE* **garbage truck**)— *n BrE* a LORRY which goes from house to house in a town to collect the contents of DUSTBINs

dust·coat /ˈdʌstkəʊt/ *n* a light coat worn over clothes (esp. in former times) to protect them from dust, as when travelling

dust·er /ˈdʌstəʳ/ *n* a cloth or tool for dusting furniture: *She held her* **feather duster** *by the handle*

dust jack·et /ˈ· ˌ··/ also **dust cov·er, jacket**— *n* a loose paper cover put as a protection round the hard cover of a book, often having writing or pictures describing the book

dust·man /ˈdʌstmən/ (*AmE* **garbage collector**)— *n* **-men** /mən/ *BrE* one of the men employed (as by a town) to remove waste material from DUSTBINs

dust off *v adv* [T1] to begin to use or practise again, after a period of not doing so: *Dust off your old skills and prepare for new responsibilities!*

dust·pan /ˈdʌstpæn/ *n* a flat pan with a handle into which house dust can be brushed —see picture of HOUSEHOLD

dust·sheet /ˈdʌst-ʃiːt/ *n* a large sheet used for throwing over furniture, shop goods, etc., in order to keep the dust off

dust·up /ˈdʌst-ʌp/ *n BrE sl* a quarrel or esp. a fight

dust·y /ˈdʌsti/ *adj* [Wa1] **1** dry and covered or filled with dust: *In the summer the town becomes dusty* **2** like dust or in the form of dust **3** (of colour) like dust or not bright: *dusty brown* **4** lacking life or spirit; dry **5 not so dusty** *infml BrE* fairly good; quite well: *"How are you feeling today?" "Not so dusty"*

dusty an·swer /ˌ·· ˈ··/ *n* an answer which is not likely to please or satisfy the questioner

Dutch¹ /dʌtʃ/ *adj* **1** of or related to the people, country, or language of the Netherlands (Holland) —see NATIONALITY TABLE **2 go Dutch (with someone)** to share expenses: *Charles and Kate always go Dutch at the restaurant* —see also DOUBLE-DUTCH

Dutch² *n* **one's Dutch** *London dial or humor* one's wife

Dutch auc·tion /ˌ· ˈ··/ *n* [C; *by*+U] a public sale at which the price is gradually reduced until somebody will pay it

Dutch barn /ˌ· ˈ·/ *n* a wall-less building with a curved roof supported on a frame, used for storing crops

Dutch cap /ˌ· ˈ·/ *n* CAP¹ (7)

Dutch cour·age /ˌ· ˈ··/ *n* [U] *infml* the courage that comes from being drunk

Dutch elm dis·ease /ˌ· ˈ· ·ˌ·/ *n* [R] a disease caused by a type of FUNGUS that attacks and kills ELM trees

Dutch ov·en /ˌ· ˈ··/ *n* **1** an upright metal shield that throws the heat forward onto things baked in front of a fire **2** an iron pot with a lid for baking things in a fire **3** a brick oven whose walls are heated before baking things

Dutch treat /ˌ· ˈ·/ *n* [U;C] *pomp* a meal in a restaurant, trip, etc., at which everybody pays his own bill —see also **go** DUTCH¹ (2)

Dutch un·cle /ˌ· ˈ··/ *n* a person who scolds firmly and seriously (esp. in the phr. **talk to someone like a Dutch uncle**)

du·ti·a·ble /ˈdjuːtɪəbəl‖ˈduː-/ *adj* (of goods) on which one must pay DUTY (2)

du·ti·ful /ˈdjuːtɪfəl‖ˈduː-/ also (*fml*) **du·te·ous** /-tɪəs/— *adj* (of people and their behaviour) having or showing a sense of DUTY (1); with proper respect and obedience —**~ly** *adv* —**~ness** *n* [U]

du·ty /ˈdjuːti‖ˈduːti/ *n* **1** [C;U] what one must do either because of one's job or because one thinks it right: *do my duty|It's my duty to help you.|pay a duty visit* (= because of conscience) **2** [C *often pl. with sing. meaning*;U] any of various types of tax: CUSTOMS *duties are paid on goods entering the* *country, death duties on property when the owner dies, and stamp duty when one sells a house* **3 do duty for** (of things) to (be able to) be used instead of **4 heavy duty** (as of a machine) able to do hard work: *This vehicle has heavy duty tyres* **5 (as) in duty bound** (as) required by one's job or esp. by conscience: *I'm in duty bound to visit my old aunt* **6 on/off duty** (esp. of soldiers, nurses, etc.) required/not required to work: *When I'm off duty I play tennis*

duty-free /ˌ·· ˈ·ˈ/ *adj, adv* (concerning the sale of goods) allowed to come into the country without tax: *You can bring in one bottle duty-free.|the duty-free shop at the airport*

du·vet /ˈduːveɪ/ also **continental quilt**— *n Fr* a large bag filled with feathers, used on a bed to take the place of all the other coverings

dwarf[1] /dwɔːf‖dwɔrf/ *n* **1** a person, animal, or plant of much less than the usual size: *Their 2nd son is a dwarf.|a dwarf apple tree* **2** any of various small imaginary manlike creatures in fairy stories: *the story of Snow White and the 7 Dwarfs*

dwarf[2] *v* [T1] **1** to prevent the proper growth of: *the Japanese art of dwarfing trees* **2** to cause to appear small by comparison: *The new tall building dwarfs all the little shops*

dwell /dwel/ *v* **dwelt** /dwelt/ *or* **dwelled** [L9] *fml* to live: *dwell in a forest/on an island* —see LIVE (USAGE)

-dwell·er /ˈdwelər/ *comb. form* a person or animal that lives (in the stated place): *town-dwellers|cave-dwellers|These lions are forest-dwellers*

dwell·ing /ˈdwelɪŋ/ *n fml and humor* a house, flat, etc., where people live: *Welcome to my humble dwelling!*

dwelling house /ˈ·· ·/ *n esp. law* a house which is lived in rather than being used as a shop, office, etc.

dwell on also **dwell up·on**— *v prep* [T1] to think, speak, or write a lot about: *Don't dwell so much on your past*

dwin·dle /ˈdwɪndl/ *v* [IØ (AWAY)] to become gradually fewer or smaller: *The number of people on the island is dwindling*

dy·ar·chy /ˈdaɪɑːki‖-ɑr-/ *n AmE* DIARCHY

dye[1] /daɪ/ *n* [C;U] **1** a vegetable or chemical substance, usu. liquid, used to colour things esp. by dipping —compare PAINT[2] (1) **2 of the deepest/blackest dye** of the worst kind

dye[2] *v* **dyed,** *pres.p.* **dyeing** [T1;IØ;X7;L7] to give or take (a stated) colour by means of DYE: *She dyed the dress (red).|Will this dress dye?|The dress will dye red/dye very well.|*(fig.) *Sunset dyed the sky red* —**dyer** *n: a professional dyer*

USAGE Compre **die** (verb): **died, dying**.

dyed-in-the-wool /ˌ· · · ˈ·ˈ/ *adj often derog* impossible to change (as to the stated or known quality): *Charles is a dyed-in-the-wool Republican*

dye·stuff /ˈdaɪstʌf/ *n* [C *often pl.*;U] a substance used to give colour: *This factory makes dyestuff(s)*

dye·works /ˈdaɪwɜːks‖-ɜr-/ *n* **dyeworks** [Wn3;C] a factory where things are coloured or where colouring materials are made: *John works at a dyeworks.|several important dyeworks*

dyke /daɪk/ *n, v* DIKE

dy·nam·ic[1] /daɪˈnæmɪk/ *adj* **1** [Wa5] *tech* of or relating to force or power that causes movement —opposite **static** **2** *often apprec* (of people, ideas, etc.) full of or producing power and activity: *a dynamic person|a dynamic period in history* —**~ally** *adv* [Wa4]

dynamic[2] *n* [(*the*) S9] *fml* a force of history or of the mind that produces action or change

dy·nam·ics /daɪˈnæmɪks/ *n* [P;U] **1** the science that deals with matter in movement **2** (in music) changes of loudness —see -ICS (USAGE)

dy·na·mis·m /ˈdaɪnəmɪzəm/ *n* [U] **1** (in a person) the quality of being DYNAMIC[1] (2) **2** a system of thought that explains everything in the world as the result of natural forces acting upon each other

dy·na·mite[1] /ˈdaɪnəmaɪt/ *n* [U] **1** a powerful explosive used in MINING, made of NITROGLYCERINE mixed with earth **2** *infml* something or someone that will cause great shock, surprise, admiration, etc.: *That news story/that new singer is really dynamite*

dynamite[2] *v* [T1] to blow up with DYNAMITE[1] (1)

dy·na·mo /ˈdaɪnəməʊ/ *n* **-mos** a machine (esp. small) which turns some other kind of power into electricity: *the dynamo on my bicycle|*(fig.) *Randolph is a real dynamo; he never stops working* —compare GENERATOR —see picture at BICYCLE

dyn·a·sty /ˈdɪnəsti‖ˈdaɪ-/ *n* **1** a line of kings all of the same family: *a dynasty of Welsh kings* **2** the time during which the same family of kings rule a country: *during the Ming dynasty in China* —**dynastic** /dɪˈnæstɪk‖daɪ-/ *adj*: *dynastic rule*

d'you /djʊ, dʒə/ *contr. of* (*not fml*) do you: *D'you see what I mean?*

dys·en·te·ry /ˈdɪsəntəri‖-teri/ *n* [U] a painful disease of the bowels that causes them to be emptied more often than usual and to produce blood and MUCUS

dys·lex·i·a /dɪsˈleksɪə/ also (*not fml*) **word blindness**— *n* [U] *tech* inability to read, considered by modern educational thinkers as a condition to be treated and cured like an illness —**dyslexic** *adj*

dys·pep·si·a /dɪsˈpepsɪə, -ˈpepʃə/ *n* [U] difficulty in DIGESTing food (changing it into a form in which it can be built into the body); INDIGESTION

dys·pep·tic[1] /dɪˈspeptɪk/ *adj* (typical of a person) suffering from DYSPEPSIA

dyspeptic[2] *n* a person who suffers from DYSPEPSIA

E, e

E, e /iː/ **E's, e's** *or* **Es, es** the 5th letter of the English alphabet

E[1] (*in Western music*) **1** the third note (*AmE* also **tone**) in the row of notes which form the musical SCALE of C MAJOR **2** the musical KEY based on this note

E[2] *abbrev. for:* **1** east(ern) **2** (*esp. BrE*) EARTH[1] (5)

e /iː/ *tech* the sign used in MATHEMATICS for the base of the system of natural LOGARITHMs, having a value of about 2.71828

each[1] /iːtʃ/ *determiner* every one separately **a** (esp. before a singular [C] noun): *She cuts the cake into pieces and gives one to each (good) child* **b** (after esp. plural nouns or PRONOUNs): *(The boys) John, Peter, and Bill each say they came first in the race.|They each want to do something different*

USAGE Compare **both** and **each**: 1 In the most exact use, **both** is used for 2 things taken together, **each** for any number of things taken separately. Compare: **Both** *of us won a prize* (=1 prize or 2 prizes). **Each** *of us won a prize* (=2 prizes). 2 **Both** always takes a plural verb: **Both** *these books are*

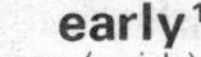

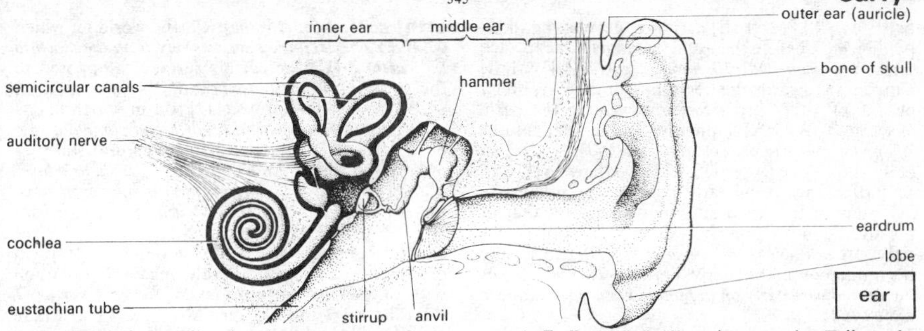

mine. **Each** is usually singular, except **a** after a plural subject: *They* **each** *have beautiful daughters.|They've* **each** *decided, haven't they?* **b** *not fml* to avoid using *his or her*, or to avoid using *his* to mean women as well as men: **Each** *member of the party must do their* (=*fml his/her his or her*) *share*, **c** sometimes when the PRONOUN form is followed by **of**+(something long and plural); **Each** *of the 2 beautiful girls upstairs is/are married*. —see ALL[4], EVERY (USAGE)

each² *pron* [(*of*)] every one (of 2 or more) separately: *She cuts the cake into pieces and gives one to each of the (good) children.|"He tells each of us only what we have to know"* (SEU W.)

each³ *adv* [Wa5] for or to every one: *The tickets are £1 each*

each oth·er /ˌ· ˈ··/ also **one another**— *pron* [(*not subject*)] (means that each of 2 or more does something to the other(s)): *Susan and Robert kissed each other* (=Susan kissed Robert and Robert kissed Susan)

USAGE Some people like to say **each other** about 2 people or things, and **one another** about more than 2, but this is not a fixed rule.

each way /ˌ· ˈ·◂/ *adv tech* (in gambling (GAMBLE)) to win if the horse or dog BACKed[4] (9) comes first, second, or third, in a race: *I put £1 each way on Red Rum, so I won some money though he came second*

ea·ger /ˈiːgəʳ/ *adj* [Wa2;B (*for, about*); F3,5c] keen; full of interest or desire: *He listened to the story with eager attention.|He is eager for success.|I am eager for you to meet my new friends.|(fml) The head is eager that all workers shall/should come in time* —see also **eager** BEAVER —**~ly** *adv* —**~ness** *n* [U (*for*, 3,5c, *about*)]

ea·gle /ˈiːgəl/ *n* **1** any of various types of very large strong meat-eating birds with hooked beaks and very good eyesight —see picture at PREY[1] **2** (in GOLF) an act of hitting the ball into the hole, taking 2 strokes fewer than is average for that particular hole —compare BIRDIE, BOGEY, PAR

eagle-eyed /ˌ·· ˈ·◂/ *adj* **1** having very good eyesight **2** looking very keenly (at something): *Peter watched eagle-eyed while Bill counted the money* —compare HAWK-EYED **3** noticing details: *an eagle-eyed employer, who sees the smallest mistake*

ea·glet /ˈiːglɪ̈t/ *n* a young EAGLE

ear¹ /ɪəʳ/ *n* **1** [C] the organ of hearing, of which there are two, one on each side of the head: *You needn't shout into my ear like that; I can hear you perfectly well* —see picture at HUMAN[2] **2** [C] the outer part of that organ: *The rabbit pricked up its long pink ears when it saw me* **3** [S9] sympathetic attention or notice (note the phr. **catch someone's ear**): *She caught the minister's ear and persuaded him to accept her plan* **4** [S9, esp. *for*] keen recognition of sounds, esp. in music and languages: *He doesn't like concerts because he has no ear for music* **5 all ears** *infml* listening eagerly: *Tell us what happened; we're all ears* **6 by ear** to play (music) from memory without having seen it printed: *Peter can play the most difficult piano music by ear* **7 go in (at) one ear and out (at) the other** *infml* (of news, orders) to have no effect because not listened to: *I told the children to go to bed, but it went in at one ear and out at the other, and they're still here* **8 out on (one's) ear** *sl* suddenly thrown out of a place or esp. dismissed from a job, because of misbehaviour **9 play it by ear** *infml* to act as things develop from moment to moment, rather than making plans in advance, esp. in a difficulty —compare **by** EAR[1] (6) **10 prick up one's ears** *infml* to begin suddenly to pay attention: *I heard you talking about dinner, so I pricked up my ears because I'm hungry too* **11 (someone's) ears are/must be burning** *infml* we have been talking (esp. unkindly) about him: *Everybody at the party was talking about you and Mary. Are your ears burning?* **12 up to (one's) ears in** *infml* deep in or very busy with: *I haven't time to go out tonight; I'm up to my ears in work* **13 wet behind the ears** *sl* very young and without experience

ear² *n* the head of a grain-producing plant such as corn or wheat, used for food —see picture at CEREAL

ear·ache /ˈɪəreɪk/ *n* [(*esp. BrE*)U;(*esp. AmE*)C] (an) ache or pain in the inside part of the ear —see ACHE (USAGE)

ear·drum /ˈɪədrʌm‖ˈɪər-/ *n* a tight thin skin inside the ear, which makes one hear the sound waves that beat against it

eared /ɪəd‖ɪərd/ *adj* **1** having outside ears that can be seen: *The fur of the eared* SEAL *is very beautiful* —compare EAR[1] (2) **2** having 2 parts shaped like ears, such as the handles of a PITCHER **3** (of corn or wheat) having ears —compare EAR[2]

-eared *comb. form* [*adj→adj*] **1** having EARs[1] (1) (of a particular kind): *The sharp-eared little boy heard everything that his parents were saying* **2** having EARs[1] (2) (of a particular kind): *a pink-eared rabbit* **3** (of corn or wheat) having EARs[2] (of a particular kind): *full-eared corn*

ear·ful /ˈɪəfʊl‖ˈɪər-/ *n* [S] *infml* as much talk, esp. angry and unwanted, as one can bear: *If he comes here again and tries to make trouble, he'll get an earful from me!*

earl /ɜːl‖ɜrl/ *n* a British nobleman of high rank: *The Earl of Warwick lives in a castle* —see also COUNTESS —**~dom** *n*

ear·li·est /ˈɜːlɪ̈st‖ˈɜr-/ *n* **at the earliest** and no earlier: *The letter will not reach him until Monday at the very earliest* —opposite **at the latest**

ear·lobe /ˈɪələʊb‖ˈɪər-/ *n* LOBE (1)

ear·ly¹ /ˈɜːli‖ˈɜrli/ *adv* [Wa1] **1** before the usual, arranged, or expected time —compare LATE[2] (1) **2** towards the beginning of a period: *The bush was planted early in the season* —compare LATE[2] (2)

early² *adj* **1** [Wa1;B;E] arriving, developing, happening, etc., before the usual, arranged, or expected time: *The train was 10 minutes early* **2** [Wa1;B] happening towards the beginning of the day, life, a period of time, etc.: *She returned in the early morning* **3** [Wa5;A] happening in the near future: *I hope for an early answer to my questions* —see also **early** BIRD —see LATE (USAGE) —**-liness** *n* [U]

early clos·ing /ˌ·· ˈ··/ **early closing day** /ˌ·· ˈ·· ·/— *n* [S] a day in the week on which shops are shut in the afternoon

early on *adv* [Wa1 *no superl.*] *esp. BrE* near the beginning or at an early period: *The wheel was discovered very early on in human history* —compare EARLY² (2)

early warn·ing sys·tem /ˌ·· ˈ·· ˌ··/ *n* a network of RADAR stations which give information in advance, when an enemy air attack comes near

ear·mark¹ /ˈɪəmɑːk‖ˈɪərmɑrk/ *n* **1** a mark on the ear of a farm animal to show whom it belongs to **2** [*often pl.*] sign(s) that tell(s) you what something is: *He has all the earmarks of a fool*

earmark² *v* [T1] to set aside (something, esp. money) for a particular purpose

ear·muff /ˈɪəmʌf‖ˈɪər-/ *n* [*usu. pl.*] either of a pair of ear coverings connected by a band over the top of the head, and worn to protect a person's ears, esp. from cold —see PAIR (USAGE)

earn /ɜːn‖ɜrn/ *v* **1** [T1 (*by*)] to get (money) by working: *He earns £3,000 a year* (*by writing stories*) **2** [T1 (*by*)] to get (something that one deserves) because of one's qualities: *He earned the title of "The Great" by his victories in the war* **3** [D1] to cause (someone) to get or be worthy of: *His victories in the war earned him the title of "The Great"* —see WIN (USAGE) —**~er** *n*

ear·nest¹ /ˈɜːnɪ̇st‖ˈɜr-/ *n* [U] seriousness (esp. in the phr. **in earnest**): *It soon began to snow in real earnest* (=very hard)

earnest² *adj* determined and serious, perhaps too serious: *He made an earnest attempt to persuade her* —**~ly** *adv* —**~ness** *n* [U]

earnest³ *n* **1** [S] a part payment of money, as a sign that one will pay the full amount later —compare DEPOSIT¹ (4) **2** [S9, esp. *of*] something which comes first to show what will come after: *He has been working harder today as an earnest of his good intentions for the future*

earnest mon·ey /ˈ·· ˌ··/ *n* [U] EARNEST³ (1)

earn·ings /ˈɜːnɪŋz‖ˈɜr-/ *n* [P] **1** money which is earned by working **2** money made by a company; profits

earnings-re·la·ted /ˌ·· ·ˈ··◂/ *adj esp. BrE* (of money payments or plans) higher as one earns more: *an earnings-related* PENSION

ear·phone /ˈɪəfəʊn‖ˈɪər-/ *n* **1** [*usu. pl.*] either of the 2 pieces that fit over the ears in a HEADSET, and turn electrical signals or radio waves into sound —compare EARPIECE (3) —see PAIR (USAGE) **2** a single piece of apparatus of this kind, for one ear, as on some telephones

ear·piece /ˈɪəpiːs‖ˈɪər-/ *n* **1** [*usu. pl.*] either of 2 pieces, as of a hat or cap, which cover the ears to keep them warm **2** [*usu. pl.*] either of the 2 pieces of a pair of glasses which hold the glasses on to the ears **3** EARPHONE

ear·plug /ˈɪəplʌg‖ˈɪər-/ *n* [*usu. pl.*] either of 2 pieces of soft material which are put into the openings of the outer ears to keep out water or noise —see PAIR (USAGE)

ear·ring /ˈɪəˌrɪŋ/ *n* [*often pl.*] an ornament worn on the ear —see PAIR (USAGE)

ear·shot /ˈɪəʃɒt‖ˈɪərʃɑt/ *n* **within/out of earshot** within/beyond the distance up to which a sound can be heard

earth¹ /ɜːθ‖ɜrθ/ *n* **1** [(*the*) R9] the world on which we live: *They returned successfully from the moon to the earth* **2** [U] the earth's surface as opposed to the sky: *She is the most beautiful woman on earth* —see LAND (USAGE) **3** [U] soil in which plants grow: *He filled the pot with earth and planted a rose in it* **4** [*the*+R] the world in its natural state, as opposed to what man has made of it: *She is a lover of the earth and believes that man is ruining it* —see LAND (USAGE) **5** [(*the*) C *usu. sing.*] also (*abbrev.*) **E**— *BrE* the wire which connects a piece of electrical apparatus to the ground **6** [C] (in chemistry) an OXIDE (=chemical combination with oxygen) of certain metals: *the rare earths* **7** [C *usu. sing.*; *to*+U] *esp. BrE* the hole where certain wild animals live, such as foxes **8 come back/down to earth** to stop dreaming and return to practical matters **9 down to earth** honest, direct, and practical; saying what one thinks **10 on earth** *infml* (used for giving force to an expression): *What on earth are you doing?* —compare EVER (4) **11 run (something/someone) to earth** to find (something/someone) by searching everywhere

earth² *v* [T1] *BrE* to connect a piece of electrical apparatus to the ground —compare EARTH¹ (5)

Earth *n* [R] the name of our world: *the* PLANET *Earth* —see picture at PLANET

earth·bound /ˈɜːθbaʊnd‖ˈɜrθ-/ *adj* [Wa5] **1** unable to leave the surface of the earth **2** unable to rise above ordinary practical matters: *too earthbound to be a poet*

earth·en /ˈɜːθən, -ðən‖ˈɜr-/ *adj* [Wa5] **1** made of earth: *an earthen floor* **2** made of baked clay: *an earthen pot* —compare EARTHENWARE

earth·en·ware /ˈɜːθənweəʳ, -ðən‖ˈɜr-/ *n* [U] cups, dishes, pots, etc., that are EARTHEN (2): *This factory makes earthenware*

earth·ling /ˈɜːθlɪŋ‖ˈɜrθ-/ *n* [C;N] *lit* (in SCIENCE FICTION) (used of or to a human being by a creature from another world): *"Take me to your leader, earthling," said the green creature from the spaceship*

earth·ly /ˈɜːθli‖ˈɜrθli/ *adj* [Wa5;A] **1** of this world as opposed to heaven; material **2** [*nonassertive*] *infml* possible: *There's no earthly reason for me to go* **3 have an earthly** *BrE* [*nonassertive*] *infml* to have the slightest chance/hope/idea: *Will John win the prize? No, he hasn't an earthly*

earth·nut /ˈɜːθnʌt‖ˈɜrθ-/ also **pignut**— *n* **1** any of various European plants with small TUBERs like nuts, which can be eaten **2** the TUBER of such a plant

earth·quake /ˈɜːθkweɪk‖ˈɜrθ-/ *n* a sudden shaking of the earth's surface, which may be violent enough to cause great damage

earth·shak·ing /ˈɜːθˌʃeɪkɪŋ‖ˈɜrθ-/ *adj* of the greatest importance to the whole world: *The murder of the President was an earthshaking event* —**~ly** *adv*

earth up *v adv* [T1] to cover (the roots and part of the stems of a plant) with earth: *It's time to earth up those potatoes*

earth·work /ˈɜːθwɜːk‖ˈɜrθwɜrk/ *n* [*usu. pl.*] a bank of earth used (esp. formerly) as a protection against enemy attack

earth·worm /ˈɜːθwɜːm‖ˈɜrθwɜrm/ *n* a common kind of long thin worm which lives in the soil

earth·y /ˈɜːθi‖ˈɜrθi/ *adj* [Wa1] more concerned with things of the body than with things of the mind: *Peter is a very earthy person, interested only in beer and sex* —**earthiness** *n*

ear·wax /ˈɪəwæks‖ˈɪər-/ *n* [U] yellow wax which is formed in the outer ear and prevents one from hearing clearly

ear·wig /ˈɪəˌwɪg‖ˈɪər-/ *n* a type of insect with 2 curved toothlike parts on its tail

ease[1] /iːz/ *n* [U] **1** the state of being comfortable and without worry or anxiety: *Gloria is a rich woman now, and leads a life of (the greatest) ease* **2** the ability to do something without difficulty: *The wall is so low that they can jump over it with ease* —compare EASILY (1) **3 at (one's) ease** without worry or nervousness **4 ill at ease** worried and nervous **5 put someone at his ease** to free someone from worry or nervousness **6 (stand) at ease** (*used esp. as a military command*) (to stand) with feet apart —compare **stand** EASY, **at** ATTENTION[1] (4) **7 take one's ease** rest from work or effort

ease[2] *v* **1** [T1] to take away (pain or worry): *I gave him some medicine to ease the pain* **2** [T1] to make more comfortable: *I eased her mind by telling her that the children were safe* **3** [T1 (*of*)] to free (someone) from pain or worry: *I eased him (of his difficulty) by telling him what to do* **4** [T1] to make looser: *My new coat is too tight and must be eased under the arms* **5** [IØ] to become less troublesome or difficult: *The relationship between these 2 countries has eased* **6** [X9] to cause (something) to move as stated, esp. slowly and gently by using skill and care: *The drawer in my desk was stuck fast, but I eased it open with a knife*

ea·sel /ˈiːzəl/ *n* a wooden frame to hold a BLACKBOARD, or to hold a picture while it is being painted

ease up also **ease off**— *v adv* [IØ] *infml* **1** to work less hard: *My father has had a hard life and it's time he eased up a bit* **2** [(*on*)] to become less severe: *You should ease up on the child and stop scolding her*

eas·i·ly /ˈiːzə̇li/ *adv* **1** without difficulty: *I can easily finish it today* —compare EASE[1] (2), EASY[1] (1) **2** without doubt: *She is easily the prettiest girl in the class*

east[1] /iːst/ *adv* [Wa5] (*often cap.*) **1** towards the east: *The room faces East, so we get the morning sun* **2 out East** *BrE* in/to Asia: *Smith-Fortescue went out East as a young man* —compare EAST (1) **3 back East** *AmE* in/to the eastern United States, as seen from the western United States: *Homer B. Stroud has gone back East to study*

east[2] *n* (*often cap.*) **1** [(*the*) R] (to, facing or in) the direction in which the sun rises —compare EASTERN **2** [(*the*) R] one of the 4 main points of the compass, which is on the right of a person facing north **3** [*the*+R;(A)] (of a wind) (coming from) this direction: *The wind is in the east*—compare EASTERLY

East *n* [*the*+R] **1** the eastern part of the world, esp. Asia —compare ORIENT **2** (*sometimes not cap.*) the part of a country which is further east than the rest —see NORTH (USAGE)

east·bound /ˈiːstbaʊnd/ *adj* [Wa5] travelling towards the east: *an eastbound ship*

East End /ˌ· ˈ·◂/ *n* [*the*+R] the eastern part of London, lived in mostly by poor people, and which is the industrial area near the sea-port —**East Ender** *n*

Eas·ter /ˈiːstəʳ/ *n* **1** [R;(C)] the yearly feast-day when Christians remember the death of Christ and his rising from the grave **2** [A] happening at that time of the year: *the Easter holidays*

Easter egg /ˈ·· ·/ *n* (*often not cap.*) **1** an egg to be eaten at EASTER, made of chocolate, sugar, etc. **2** a hen's egg, painted in bright colours, to be eaten at EASTER

eas·ter·ly /ˈiːstəli‖-ərli/ *adj* [Wa5] **1** towards or in the east: *the easterly shore of the lake|in an easterly direction* **2** (of a wind) coming from the east: *a strong easterly wind*

east·ern /ˈiːstən‖-ərn/ *adj* (*often cap.*) of or belonging to the east part of the world or of a country —see NORTH (USAGE)

East·ern·er /ˈiːstənəʳ‖-ərnər/ *n AmE* someone who lives in or comes from the eastern United States

east·ern·most /ˈiːstənməʊst‖-ərn-/ *adj* [Wa5] *fml* farthest east

East Side /ˌ· ˈ·◂/ also **Lower East Side**— *n* [*the*+R] the south-eastern part of Manhattan (New York), lived in mostly by poor people

east·ward /ˈiːstwəd‖ˈiːstwərd/ *adj* going towards the east

east·wards /ˈiːstwədz‖ˈiːstwərdz/ *AmE* also **eastward** — *adv* towards the east; east

eas·y[1] /ˈiːzi/ *adj* [Wa1;B,B3] **1** not difficult: *an easy book|John is easy to please* (= it is not difficult to please him) —compare EASE[1] (2), EASILY (1) **2** comfortable and without worry or anxiety: *He leads a very easy life.|with an easy mind* —compare EASE[1] (1) **3 by easy stages** (on a journey) only short distances at a time **4 easy on the ear/eye** *infml* nice to listen to/look at **5 easy touch** SOFT TOUCH **6 easy victim/mark** somebody who can easily be cheated or treated badly: *Susan was an easy* VICTIM *of Sir John's wicked intentions* **7 easy virtue** *old use* low sexual morals: *a woman of easy virtue* **8 I'm easy** *infml esp. BrE* I'll willingly accept what you decide **9 on easy terms** (when buying a car, furniture, etc.) (to pay) a little at a time instead of all at once —**easiness** *n* [U]

easy[2] *adv* [Wa1] **1 easier said than done** harder to do than to talk about **2 Easy!** (command) Go gently! —compare EASE UP (1) **3 Easy come, easy go** what we get without difficulty is quickly lost **4 easy does it** *not fml* Do it less quickly and/or with less effort!; RELAX! **5 go easy** to work less hard —compare EASE UP (1) **6 go easy on** (someone) to be less severe with (someone) —compare EASE UP (2) **7 go easy on** (something) not to use too much of it **8 stand easy** (*used esp. as a military command*) stand more comfortably than when **at** EASE[1] (6) **9 take it/things easy** to not work too hard

easy chair /ˌ·· ˈ·/ *n* a big soft chair with arms, that is comfortable to sit in

eas·y·going /ˌiːziˈgəʊɪŋ◂/ *adj* [Wa2] taking life easily: *Our teacher is very easygoing*

eat /iːt/ *v* **ate** /et, eɪt‖eɪt/, **eaten** /ˈiːtn/ **1** [T1 (UP); IØ] to take in through the mouth and swallow (solid food or soup): *Eat your dinner!*|(fig.) *That big house eats up money* **2** [Wv6;T1] to use regularly as food: *Tigers eat meat.|What do horses eat?* **3** [IØ] to have a meal: *What time do we eat?* **4** [X9, esp. AWAY;L9] to use up, damage, or destroy (something), esp. by chemical action: *The acid ate away the metal.|The acid has eaten into/through the metal* **5** [T1] to make by or as if by doing this **6 eat out of someone's hand** *infml* to be very willing to obey or agree with someone **7 eat one's head off** *infml* (of people and esp. of animals) to eat large and costly quantities of food **8 eat one's heart out (for)** to be very unhappy (about) or have great desire (for someone or something) without talking about it: *She was eating her heart out for a soldier who was away at the war* **9 eat someone out of house and home** *infml* (of people) to eat a lot of food to someone else's cost **10 be eaten up with** (jealousy, desire, etc) to be completely and violently full of **11 eat one's words** to take back what one has said; say that one is sorry for having said something

USAGE /et/ is not considered to be the correct way of pronouncing the past tense of **eat** in *AmE* For the British, /eɪt/ and /et/ are both used though perhaps more people say /et/.

ea·ta·ble /ˈiːtəbəl/ *adj* [*often neg.*] (of food) in a fit condition to be eaten

USAGE A food is **eatable** if it is fresh, and satisfactorily prepared: *The bread was so old that it* *was hardly* **eatable**/*was* **uneatable**. A substance is **edible** if it is possible to treat it as food: *Are these berries* **edible**, *or are they poisonous?*

ea·ta·bles /ˈiːtəbəlz/ *n* [P] food, esp. raw: *We went to the country for the day with a basket of eatables* —compare EATS

eat·er /ˈiːtəʳ/ *n* **1** [C9] a person who eats in the particular stated way: *He's a big/heavy eater* (=he eats a lot) **2** [C] *infml* EATING APPLE

eating apple /ˈ·· ˌ··/ *n* an apple of the kind that one eats raw

eating-house /ˈ·· ·/ also **eating-place**— a restaurant

eat in·to *v prep* [T1] to use part of (something): *Our holiday has eaten into the money we saved* —compare EAT (4)

eats /iːts/ *n* [P] *infml* cooked or prepared food, ready for eating: *It's dinner-time, and we've got lots of good eats on the table tonight!* —compare EATABLES

eau de co·logne /ˌəʊ də kəˈləʊn/ *n* [U] *Fr* COLOGNE

eaves /iːvz/ *n* [P] the edges of a usu. sloping roof which come out beyond the walls —see picture at HOUSE[1]

eaves·drop /ˈiːvzdrɒp‖-drɑp/ *v* **-pp-** [IØ (*on*)] to listen secretly (to other people's conversation) —**-dropper** *n*

ebb¹ /eb/ *n* [U] **1** the flow of the sea away from the shore; the going out of the TIDE: *The* TIDE *is on the ebb* —see also EBB TIDE, FLOOD TIDE **2** decay; failure; low state (esp. in the phr. **at a low ebb**): *Fred's courage seems to be at rather a low ebb; let's try to make him a bit more cheerful*

ebb² *v* [IØ (AWAY)] **1** (of the sea) to flow away from the shore **2** to grow less; become slowly lower and lower

ebb tide /ˌ· ˈ·/ *n* the flow of the sea away from the shore: *The ship sailed out of harbour on the ebb tide and came back on the* FLOOD TIDE

eb·o·ny¹ /ˈebəni/ *n* [U] a kind of hard heavy black wood

ebony² *n, adj* [Wa5;B;U] (having) the colour of EBONY

e·bul·li·ence /ɪˈbʌlɪəns, ɪˈbʊ-/ *n* [U] *lit* the quality of being full of happiness and excitement; the overflowing expression of joy: *Randolph was in a state of ebullience, laughing and singing and buying drinks for us all* —see also EXUBERANCE

e·bul·li·ent /ɪˈbʌlɪənt, ɪˈbʊ-/ *adj* showing or feeling EBULLIENCE —**~ly** *adv*

ec·cen·tric¹ /ɪkˈsentrɪk/ *adj* **1** (of a person or his behaviour) peculiar; unusual; rather strange: *If you go to the palace in tennis shoes, they will think you are eccentric* **2** [Wa5] (of 2 or more circles) not drawn round the same centre —compare CONCENTRIC and see picture at GEOMETRY **3** (of movement) not (moving) in a regular circle: *Mars, Venus, and the other* PLANETs *move in eccentric paths* (ORBITs) —**~ally** *adv* [Wa4]

eccentric² *n* **1** an ECCENTRIC person **2** *tech* a piece of apparatus which changes circular movement into backwards-and-forwards movement

ec·cen·tri·ci·ty /ˌeksenˈtrɪsɪ̈ti, -sən-/ *n* **1** [U (*of*)] the quality of being ECCENTRIC: *You must expect some eccentricity of behaviour in a very old lady.|the eccentricity of these circles* **2** [C] an example of ECCENTRIC behaviour: *eccentricities in dress*

ec·cle·si·as·tic /ɪˌkliːziˈæstɪk/ *n* a priest, usu. in the Christian Church

ec·cle·si·as·ti·cal /ɪˌkliːziˈæstɪkəl/ also **ecclesiastic**— *adj* connected with a Christian church, esp. with its formal and established organization: *ecclesiastical history|ecclesiastical music* —**-cally** *adv* [Wa4]

ECG *AmE* also **EKG**— *abbrev. for:* **1** ELECTR DIOGRAM: *The doctor ordered an ECG* **2** ELI CARDIOGRAPH

ech·e·lon /ˈeʃəlɒn‖-lɑn/ *n* **1** [U;C] *tech* an ai ment of ships, soldiers, planes, etc., like rather than in a single line. Each one is behind and partly beside the next one **2** [*pl. with sing. meaning*] (in a group of people or organization) a level: *the lower echelons of the* BUREAUCRACY

ech·o¹ /ˈekəʊ/ *n* **-oes** **1** a sound sent back or repeated, as from a wall of rock or inside a cave **2** a person or thing that copies or repeats: *Millicent is only an echo of her husband's opinions, and has no ideas of her own* **3 to the echo** *old use* very loudly

echo² *v 3rd pers. sing. pres. t.* **echoes** [IØ (*with, to*); T1] **1** to (cause to) come back as an ECHO¹ (1): *Their voices echoed in the big empty hall.|The room echoed with the sound of music* **2** to copy or repeat: *"The system of taxation here is terrible," said Frederick. "Terrible," echoed Millicent* —compare ECHO¹ (2)

é·clair /ɪˈkleəʳ, eɪ-/ also **chocolate éclair** /ˌ·· ·ˈ·/— *n Fr* a small finger-shaped cake made of pastry, with cream inside and chocolate on top

é·clat /ˈeɪklɑː‖eɪˈklɑ/ *n* [U] *Fr* great success; splendid effect, producing praise from everyone

e·clec·tic¹ /ɪˈklektɪk/ *adj fml* (of people, methods, ideas, etc.) not following any one system or set of ideas, but using parts of many different ones: *an eclectic style of art* —**~ism** /-tɪsɪzəm/ *n* [U] —**~ally** /-tɪkli/ *adv* [Wa4]

eclectic² *n* a person who thinks or works in an ECLECTIC way

e·clipse¹ /ɪˈklɪps/ *n* **1** [C] the disappearance, complete or in part, of the sun's light when the moon passes between it and the earth, or of the moon's light when the earth passes between it and the sun **2** [C;U] the loss of fame, power, success, etc.: *She used to be a famous actress, but she's now in eclipse; she never appears on the stage now*

eclipse² *v* [T1 *often pass.*] **1** (of the moon or earth) to cause an ECLIPSE¹ (1) (of sun or moon): *The moon is partly eclipsed* **2** to do or be much better than; to make (someone or something) lose fame and appear dull by comparison: *She is quite eclipsed by her sister, who is cleverer, prettier, and more amusing* **3** to make a shadow on; make dark or troubled: *Our happiness was soon eclipsed by the terrible news*

e·clip·tic /ɪˈklɪptɪk/ *n* [*the*+R] *tech* the path along which the sun seems to move

ec·logue /ˈeklɒg‖ˈeklɔg, -lɑg/ *n* a short poem about country life, often in the form of a conversation —see also PASTORAL

e·co·lo·gi·cal /ˌiːkəˈlɒdʒɪkəl‖-ˈlɑ-/ *adj* [Wa5] of or concerning ECOLOGY: *an ecological study of the neighbourhood*

e·co·lo·gi·cally /ˌiːkəˈlɒdʒɪkli‖-ˈlɑ-/ *adv* **1** in an ECOLOGICAL way: *studied the neighbourhood ecologically* **2** from an ECOLOGICAL point of view: *Ecologically (speaking), this dirty treeless park is a failure*

e·col·o·gy /ɪˈkɒlədʒi‖ɪˈkɑ-/ *n* [U] (the scientific study of) the pattern of relations of plants, animals, and people to each other and to their surroundings —**-gist** *n*

ec·o·nom·ic /ˌekəˈnɒmɪk, iː-‖-ˈnɑ-/ *adj* [Wa5] **1** [A] connected with trade, industry, and wealth; of or concerning ECONOMICS: *The country is in a bad economic state, so we must reduce profits* **2** [B] profitable; not resulting in a loss of money: *She was able to let her house at an economic rent, which paid for the repairs and made a small profit* —opposite **uneconomic**

ec·o·nom·i·cal /ˌekəˈnɒmɪkəl, ˌiː-‖-ˈnɑ-/ *adj* not wasteful; using money, time, goods, etc., carefully:

She is an economical housekeeper and feeds her family cheaply

ec·o·nom·i·cally /ˌekəˈnɒmɪkli, ˌiː-‖-ˈnɑ-/ *adv* **1** not wastefully: *Mary dresses very economically because she makes all her clothes herself* —compare EXTRAVAGANTly **2** in a way which is connected with ECONOMICS: *Economically (speaking), the country is in a very bad state because we are spending more than we produce*

ec·o·nom·ics /ˌekəˈnɒmɪks, ˌiː-‖-ˈnɑ-/ *n* **1** [U] (*sometimes cap.*) the science of the way in which industry and trade produce and use wealth **2** [P] the principles of making profit, saving money, and producing wealth: *The economics of national growth are of the greatest importance to all modern governments*

economic sanc·tions /ˌ···· ˈ··/ *n* [P] the means used by one or more nations to force another nation to obey them, not by military power but by refusing to buy from or sell to the other nation

e·con·o·mist /ɪˈkɒnəmɪ̈st‖ɪˈkɑ-/ *n* a person who has studied and understands the science of ECONOMICS

e·con·o·mize, -mise /ɪˈkɒnəmaɪz‖ɪˈkɑ-/ *v* [I∅ (*on*); T1] to use or spend less (money, time, goods, etc.) than before: *to economize on petrol* —compare ECONOMICAL

e·con·o·my¹ /ɪˈkɒnəmi‖ɪˈkɑ-/ *n* **1** [C;U] (an example of) the careful use of money, time, strength, etc.: *economy of effort* —compare ECONOMICAL **2** [(*the*) C9] the ECONOMIC (1) life of a country; the operation of a country's money supply, industry, and trade: *The new oil that we have found will improve the state of the economy* **3** [C9] an ECONOMIC (1) system: *the different economies of the US and the USSR* —compare COMMUNISM, CAPITALISM

economy² *adj* [Wa5;A] **1** cheap: *Enjoy our economy prices now!|An* **economy class** *air ticket costs much less* **2** big (and good value for money): *Buy the large economy size!* **3** intended to save money: *In our office we had an economy* DRIVE *with economy* MEASURE*s like turning off the lights whenever we went out*

e·co·sys·tem /ˈiːkəʊˌsɪstɪ̈m/ *n* an ECOLOGICAL system which relates all the plants, animals and people in an area to their surroundings, considered as a whole

éc·ru /ˈekruː, ˈeɪ-/ *adj, n* [Wa5;B;U] *Fr* BEIGE

ec·sta·sy /ˈekstəsi/ *n* [U;C] **1** a state of very strong feeling, esp. of joy and happiness: *in an ecstasy of delight/grief/admiration* **2** a religious state in which the soul is said to leave the body and be united with God

ec·stat·ic /ɪkˈstætɪk, ek-/ *adj* causing or experiencing ECSTASY —**~ally** *adv* [Wa4]

ECT *abbrev. for:* (*BrE*) electro-convulsive therapy; ELECTRIC SHOCK THERAPY

ec·to·plas·m /ˈektəplæzəm, ˈektəʊ-/ *n* [U] a mist-like substance which supposedly appears when the spirit of a dead person is brought back

e·cu·men·i·cal, oecu- /ˌiːkjʊˈmenɪkəl‖ˌekjə-/ *adj* favouring, or tending towards, Christian unity all over the world —**-cally** *adv* [Wa4]

e·cu·men·i·cal·is·m, oecu- /ˌiːkjʊˈmenɪkəlɪzəm‖ˌekjə-/ *n* [U] belief in, or efforts towards, Christian unity all over the world

ec·ze·ma /ˈeksɪ̈mə‖ˈeksɪ̈mə, ˈegzɪ̈mə, ɪgˈziːmə/ *n* [U] **1** a red swollen condition of the skin **2** a skin condition which appears in some families, seen esp. in babies

-ed /d, ɪ̈d, t/ also (*after vowels*) **-d**— *suffix* **1** [*v*→*v, adj*] (forms the regular past tense and past participle of verbs. The past participle form is often used as an adjective): *want, wantèd, wanted|walked|played|show, showed, shown|a wanted criminal* **2** [*n*→*adj*] (forms adjectives from nouns and noun phrases): *a bearded man|a* KIND-HEARTED *woman* USAGE **-d** and **-ed** added to the end of a verb to make the past tense or past participle (*loved, failed*) have the sound /d/ except **a** after verbs ending with the sounds /p, k, f, θ, s, ʃ, tʃ/. Here **-ed** is pronounced /t/ as in *watched* /wɒtʃt/ **b** after verbs ending with the sounds /t, d/. Here **-ed** is pronounced /ɪd/ in *BrE* and /əd/ in *AmE,* as in *needed* (ˈniːdɪ̈d). —see -ING (USAGE)

E·dam /ˈiːdəm, -dæm/ *n* [U;(C)] a yellow pressed cheese from the Netherlands, made in balls

ed·dy¹ /ˈedi/ *n* a circular movement of water, wind, dust, mist, smoke, etc.: *The little paper boat was caught in an eddy and spun round and round in the water*

eddy² *v* [I∅] to move round and round: (fig.) *The crowd eddied about in the market-place*

e·del·weiss /ˈeɪdlvaɪs/ *n* [U] *Ger* a type of plant with flowers, growing in the Alps

E·den /ˈiːdn/ *n* **1** [R] (in the Bible) the garden where Adam and Eve lived before their disobedience to God **2** [C] a beautiful place which gives joy

edge¹ /edʒ/ *n* **1** [C] the thin sharp cutting part of a blade, a tool, etc.; cutting line where 2 sides meet: *Please sharpen the edge of this axe* **2** [C; *on*+U] the narrowest part along the outside of a solid: *Can you stand a coin up on edge?|the edge of a plate* **3** [C] the outer limit of an area: *the edge of the cliff|the water's edge* **4 give the edge of one's tongue** *sl* to speak sharply (to); speak angrily and roughly (to) **5 have the edge on** *not fml, esp. AmE* be better than: *He has the edge on the other students* **6 on edge** *not fml* nervous; EDGY **7 put an edge on** to sharpen **8 set someone's teeth on edge** *not fml* to give an unpleasant feeling to someone **9 take the edge off** *not fml* make less sharp: (fig.) *Eating bread and butter took the edge off his hunger*

edge² *v* **1** [Wv5;T1 (*with*)] to place an edge or border on: *a white handkerchief edged with blue|We need an edged tool to cut with* **2** [X9;L9] to (cause to) move sideways little by little; (cause to) move with the edge in front: *We edged the large cupboard through the door.|He edged (himself/his way) to the front of the crowd* **3** [T1] (in cricket) to hit (the ball) off the edge of the BAT: *He edged the ball away for 3 runs*

-edged /edʒd/ *comb. form* [→*adj*] with one or more edges of the stated type or number: *a sharp-edged blade|a 2-edged sword*

edge out *v adv* [T1] **1** to cause (someone) to lose gradually an official position or powers: *That forceful young woman edged out the former chairman and is now chairman herself* **2** to defeat (someone) by only a small amount

edge·ways /ˈedʒweɪz/ also **edge·wise** /-waɪz/— *adv* [Wa5] **1** in the direction of the edge; sideways **2 get a word in edgeways** [*nonassertive*] *infml* to get a chance to speak (when someone else is speaking)

edg·ing /ˈedʒɪŋ/ *n* [U;C] something that forms an edge or border: (*a*) *white handkerchief with a blue edging*

edg·y /ˈedʒi/ *adj* [Wa2] *infml* nervous: *She's been a bit edgy lately, waiting for the examination* —**edgily** *adv*

ed·i·ble /ˈedəbəl/ *adj* fit to be eaten; eatable: *the difference between edible and poisonous berries* —see EATABLE (USAGE) —**edibility** /ˌedəˈbɪlɪ̈ti/ *n* [U]

ed·i·bles /ˈedəbəlz/ *n* [P] things fit to be eaten; eatables

e·dict /ˈiːdɪkt/ *n* **1** (in former times) an official public order having the force of law DECREE **2** an order or command: *We always obeyed grandmother's edict(s)*

ed·i·fi·ca·tion /ˌedɪ̈fɪ̈ˈkeɪʃən/ *n* [U] *fml* the improvement of character or the mind: *He read books more for edification than for pleasure*

ed·i·fice /ˈedɪ̈fɪ̈s/ *n fml or pomp* a large, fine building, such as a palace or church

ed·i·fy /ˈedɪ̈faɪ/ *v* [Wv4;T1] *fml* to improve (the character or mind of): *He read edifying books to improve his mind*

ed·it /ˈedɪ̈t/ *v* [T1] **1** to prepare for printing (esp. the writing of another person): *to edit his friend's book|a Shakespeare play* **2** *now rare* to direct and take responsibility for the organization and opinions of (a newspaper, magazine, etc., or a special part of one) **3** to prepare from collected material (a cinema film, radio performance, or recording)

e·di·tion /ɪˈdɪʃən/ *n* **1** one printing of a book, newspaper, magazine, etc.: *an edition of 20,000|a very large first edition* **2** the form in which a book is printed: *A paper-back edition of a book* (= in paper covers) *is much cheaper than a* **hard-back** *edition* (= in hard cardboard covers)

ed·i·tor /ˈedɪ̈təʳ/ *n* a person who EDITs —**~ship** *n* [U]

ed·i·to·ri·al¹ /ˌedɪ̈ˈtɔːrɪəl‖-ˈtor-/ *adj* of or related to an EDITOR: *an editorial office|She's made a lot of editorial changes in their book* —**~ly** *adv*

editorial² *BrE* also **leader, leading article**— *n* a part of a newspaper (supposed to be written by the EDITOR) giving an opinion on some question of the day (rather than news)

ed·i·to·ri·al·ize, -ise /ˌedɪ̈ˈtɔːrɪəlaɪz‖-ˈtor-/ *v* [I∅] *AmE* **1** to express an opinion in the form of an EDITORIAL² **2** *often derog* to introduce opinion into the reporting of facts: *In that newspaper, it is hard to see where reporting stops and editorializing begins* **3** to express an opinion (as on a question about which there is sharp disagreement)

edit out *v adv* [T1] to remove (words) when preparing something for printing

ed·u·cate /ˈedjʊkeɪt‖ˈedʒə-/ *v* [T1] to teach; train the character or mind of: *He was educated at a very good school*

ed·u·cat·ed /ˈedjʊkeɪtɪ̈d‖ˈedʒə-/ *adj* (*often in comb.*) having been educated: *self-educated|half-educated|educated tastes|an educated ear for music*

educated guess /ˌ···· ˈ·/ *n infml* a guess based on a certain amount of information, and therefore likely to be right

ed·u·ca·tion /ˌedjʊˈkeɪʃən‖ˌedʒə-/ *n* **1** [U;C *pl. rare*] (the results of) teaching or the training of mind and character: *She has had a good education* **2** [U] a field of knowledge dealing with how to teach effectively: *He trained to be a teacher at a college of education*

ed·u·ca·tion·al /ˌedjʊˈkeɪʃənəl‖ˌedʒə-/ *adj* **1** [Wa5] of or about education: *an educational establishment* **2** providing education: *the most educational experience I have ever had* —**~ly** *adv*

ed·u·ca·tion·ist /ˌedjʊˈkeɪʃənɪ̈st‖ˌedʒə-/ also **ed·u·ca·tion·al·ist** /-ʃənəlɪ̈st/— *n* a specialist in how to make education effective

ed·u·ca·tor /ˈedjʊkeɪtəʳ‖ˈedʒə-/ *n* a person who educates, esp. as a profession

e·duce /ɪˈdjuːs‖ɪˈduːs/ *v* [T1] *fml* **1** to arrive at usu. through reasoning from known facts: *to educe a powerful argument against a new plan* —compare DEDUCE **2** *now rare* to bring, draw, or lead out (as a hidden power or skill)

-ee /iː/ *suffix* **1** [*v→n*] a person to whom the stated action is done: PAYEE|TRAINEE|EMPLOYEE **2** [*n, adj, v→n*] a person who acts in the stated way: ABSENTEE|REFUGEE|ESCAPEE **3** [*n→n*] a very small kind of: *the baby's* BOOTEEs

EEC /ˌiː iː ˈsiː/ *abbrev. for:* European Economic Community; COMMON MARKET

EEG /ˌiː iː ˈdʒiː/ *abbrev. for:* (*med*) **1** ELECTROENCEPHALOGRAM **2** ELECTROENCEPHALOGRAPH

eel /iːl/ *n* any of various types of fish that are shaped like snakes and are hard to hold —see picture at FISH¹

e'en /iːn/ *adv contr. of* (*poet*) even

e'er /eəʳ/ *adv contr. of* (*poet*) ever

-eer /ɪəʳ/ *suffix often derog* **1** [*n→n*] -ER²: *a* PROFITEER|*a* RACKETEER **2** [*n→v*] -IZE: *to* PROFITEER|PROFITEER*ing*|ELECTIONEER*ing*

ee·rie /ˈɪəri/ *adj* [Wa2] causing fear because strange: *It's eerie to walk through a dark wood at night* —**eerily** *adv* —**eeriness** *n* [U]

ef·face /ɪˈfeɪs/ *v* [T1] **1** to rub out; destroy the surface of: *Someone has effaced part of the address on this letter* **2** to forget (esp. in the phr. **efface the memory of**): *She could never efface the memory of her dead child* **3** [Wv4] to behave (oneself) so as not to be noticed by other people: *a very quiet modest self-effacing person* —**~ment** *n* [U]

ef·fect¹ /ɪˈfekt/ *n* [U;C (*on, upon*)] **1** a result: *the effects of an illness* **2** a result produced on the mind or feelings: *Her new red dress produced quite an effect on everyone.|Don't look at the details, consider the general effect* **3 give effect to** to carry out: *He gave effect to his dead brother's wishes by having him buried properly* **4 in effect a** in (esp. lawful) operation: *The old system of taxation will remain in effect until next May* **b** for all practical purposes; it is more or less true to say: *Her brother is king, but she is, in effect, the real ruler of Ruritania* **5 into effect** into (esp. lawful) operation: *A new system of taxation will come/go/be brought/be put into effect next May* **6 take effect a** to come into (esp. lawful) operation: *The new system of taxation will take effect next May* **b** to begin to produce results: *The medicine quickly took effect* **7 to . . . effect** with . . . general meaning: *He called me a fool, or words to that effect.|He has made a declaration to the effect that all fighting must cease at once*

effect² *v* [T1] *fml* to cause, produce, or have as a result: *I will effect my purpose: no-one shall stop me!* —compare AFFECT²

ef·fec·tive /ɪˈfektɪv/ *adj* **1** having a noticeable or desired effect; producing the desired result: *He made an effective speech.|His efforts to improve the school have been very effective* **2** [Wa5] actual; real; able to work, serve, or take part: *the effective strength of our army|Her brother is king, but she is the effective ruler of Ruritania* —compare EFFICACIOUS, EFFICIENT

ef·fec·tive·ly /ɪˈfektɪvli/ *adv* **1** in an effective way **2** [Wa5] for all practical purposes; it is more or less true to say; in effect

ef·fec·tive·ness /ɪˈfektɪvnɪ̈s/ *n* [U] the ability or power to have a noticeable or desired effect

ef·fec·tives /ɪˈfektɪvz/ *n* [P] *esp. AmE* armed men ready to serve: *There are 5,000 soldiers in camp, but only 4,000 effectives*

ef·fects /ɪˈfekts/ *n* [P] *fml or law* belongings; personal property: *He died poor, and left no (personal) effects*

ef·fec·tu·al /ɪˈfektʃʊəl/ *adj fml* (of actions but not of the people who do them) producing the complete effect intended; effective: *effectual action against unemployment* —**~ness** *n* [U]

ef·fec·tu·al·ly /ɪˈfektʃʊəli/ *adv fml* **1** in an EFFECTUAL way: *to fight effectually against unemployment* **2** for all practical purposes; it is true to say

ef·fec·tu·ate /ɪˈfektʃʊeɪt/ *v* [T1] *fml* to carry out successfully: *Our organization has effectuated the return to their countries of all the political prisoners*

ef·fem·i·na·cy /ɪ̇ˈfemɪ̇nəsi/ *n* [U] the state of being EFFEMINATE
ef·fem·i·nate /ɪ̇ˈfemɪ̇nɪ̇t/ *adj derog* (of a man or his behaviour) like a woman; soft; weak; unmanly; lacking in courage —**~ly** *adv*
ef·fen·di /eˈfendi/ *n* [E;(N)] (in Turkey and some Eastern Mediterranean countries) a title of respect put after the name of a man
ef·fer·vesce /ˌefəˈves‖ˌefər-/ *v* [IØ (*with*)] **1** (of a liquid) to have balls of gas forming inside, usu. by chemical action **2** (of people) to be gay and excited, full of spirit: *The crowd waiting to see the Queen effervesced with excitement* —**-vescence** *n* [U] —**-vescent** *adj* —**-vescently** *adv*
ef·fete /ɪˈfiːt‖e-/ *adj* **1** weak; worn out; with no more force: *The Roman empire was once strong, but it grew effete when there were enough slaves to do all the work* **2** EFFEMINATE —**~ness** *n* [U]
ef·fi·ca·cious /ˌefɪ̇ˈkeɪʃəs/ *adj fml* (esp. of medicines and medical treatment) producing the desired effect; effective —compare EFFECTIVE, EFFICIENT —**~ly** *adv*
ef·fi·ca·cy /ˈefɪ̇kəsi/ also **ef·fi·ca·ci·ty** /ˌefɪ̇ˈkæsɪ̇ti/— *n* [U] *fml* the state or quality of being EFFICACIOUS
ef·fi·cien·cy /ɪˈfɪʃənsi/ *n* [U] the state or quality of being EFFICIENT
ef·fi·cient /ɪˈfɪʃənt/ *adj* working well and without waste: *Our efficient new machines are much cheaper to run* —compare EFFECTIVE, EFFICACIOUS —**~ly** *adv*
ef·fi·gy /ˈefɪ̇dʒi/ *n* **1** *fml* the figure or picture of a person: *On November 5 our children burn an effigy of Guy Fawkes* **2** **in effigy** in the form of such a figure rather than as a real person
ef·flo·res·cence /ˌefləˈresəns/ *n* [U] **1** *fml* the period or action of the forming and developing of flowers on a plant **2** *fml* the act or action of developing and unfolding as if coming into flower: *periods of efflorescence in science and art* **3** *tech* a sheet of powder or CRYSTALs formed by chemical action —**-cent** *adj*
ef·flu·ent /ˈefluənt/ *n tech* **1** [C] a stream flowing out from a lake **2** [U;C] (a type of) liquid waste that flows out esp. from a factory and may be harmful: *a law against dangerous effluent being poured into our rivers* **3** [U] the liquid that comes out from an establishment for the chemical treatment of waste material (SEWAGE)
ef·flux /ˈeflʌks/ *n* **-es** **1** [U] the outward flow of gas or liquid: *the increased efflux of salt water from the lake* **2** [C] a gas or liquid that flows out
ef·fort /ˈefət‖ˈefərt/ *n* **1** [U] the use of strength; trying hard with mind or body: *He is strong enough to lift the heavy box without effort* **2** [C,C3] an example of this: *The prisoner made an effort to escape, but he couldn't climb the prison wall* **3** [C] the result of trying: *Finishing the work in one day was a very good effort*
ef·fort·less /ˈefətləs‖ˈefərt-/ *adj* making and needing no EFFORT (1) when doing something: *He is a skilful and effortless performer on several musical instruments* —**~ly** *adv* —**~ness** *n* [U]
ef·fron·te·ry /ɪˈfrʌntəri/ *n* **1** [U (*of*), U3] bold rudeness and wrong-doing without any sensation of shame: *You damaged my bicycle last week and now you have the effrontery to want to use my car!* **2** [C *often pl.*] an example of this: *his many daring effronteries*
ef·ful·gence /ɪˈfʌldʒəns‖ɪˈfʊl-, ɪˈfʌl-/ *n* [U;S] *lit* (a) strong, glorious light; stream of bright light, as from the sun: *the effulgence of the tropical sun at midday*
ef·ful·gent /ɪˈfʌldʒənt‖ɪˈfʊl-, ɪˈfʌl-/ *adj lit* having EFFULGENCE —**~ly** *adv*
ef·fu·sion /ɪˈfjuːʒən/ *n* **1** [C] *derog* an example of the expression of strong feelings in words, often in the form of bad poetry: *They laughed at his poetic effusions* **2** [C;U] *fml* a strong outward flow of liquid or gas, as when escaping or being poured out; EFFLUX: *a dangerous effusion of gas through a hole in the pipe*
ef·fu·sive /ɪˈfjuːsɪv/ *adj often derog* pouring out feelings without control: *Her effusive welcome made us feel most uncomfortable* —**~ly** *adv* —**~ness** *n* [U]
eft /eft/ *n* NEWT
e.g. *abbrev. for:* (*Lat*) **exempli gratia**; for example: *You must avoid sweet foods, e.g. cake, chocolate, sugar, and ice cream*
e·gal·i·tar·i·an /ɪˌgælɪ̇ˈteərɪən/ *adj often apprec* holding or showing the belief that all men are equal and should have equal rights and advantages —**~ism** *n* [U]
egg /eg/ *n* **1** [C] a rounded object containing new life, which comes out of the body of a female bird, snake, etc.: *This hen lays beautiful brown eggs* **2** [C; U] (the contents of) this when used for food: *After breakfast the baby had egg all over his face* **3** [C] the seed of life in a woman or female animal, which joins with the male seed (SPERM) to make a baby —see also FERTILIZE, OVUM **4** **a bad egg** a worthless and dishonest person; a wrong-doer **5** **as sure as eggs are/is eggs** *infml* without any doubt **6** **have egg on one's face** *infml esp. BrE* to seem foolish: *The government has egg on its face over the failure of its prices and incomes plan* **7** **put all (one's) eggs in one basket** *infml* to make all (one's) plans depend on the success of one thing; risk everything on one attempt, as by putting all one's money into one business **8** **teach (one's) grandmother (to suck eggs)** *infml* to give advice to a person who knows all about the matter already: *"John, don't drive so fast!" "I've been driving a car for 30 years, so don't try to teach your grandmother to suck eggs"*
egg-bound /ˈ· ·/ *adj* (of a bird, esp. a hen) unable to allow an egg to leave the body
egg·cup /ˈeg-kʌp/ *n* a small container to hold an egg that has been boiled in its shell, so that it can be eaten
egg cus·tard /ˌ· ˈ··/ *n* [U;(C)] a boiled or baked mixture of eggs and sweetened milk
egg·head /ˈeghed/ *n usu. derog* a highly educated person, perhaps too highly educated; HIGHBROW
egg·nog /ˌegˈnɒg‖ˈegnɑg, ˌegˈnɑg/ *n* [U] an alcoholic drink to which egg, sugar, and SPICEs have been added
egg on *v adv* [T1;V3] to encourage (someone) strongly (to do something): *Mary egged her husband on to save up some money and start his own business*
egg·plant /ˈegplɑːnt‖ˈegplænt/ *BrE* usu. **aubergine**— *n* **1** [C] a type of plant with a large purple fruit that is eaten as a vegetable, usu. cooked **2** [C;U] the fruit of this plant —see picture at VEGETABLE[1]
egg roll /ˈ· ·/ *n AmE* SPRING ROLL —see also ROLL[1] (2, 3)
egg·shell /ˈegʃel/ *n* **1** [C] the shell, or hard outside part, of a bird's egg **2** [A] very thin and delicate (esp. in the phr. **eggshell china**) **3** [A] neither very shiny nor very dull (esp. in the phr. **eggshell paint**)
egg tim·er /ˈ· ˌ··/ *n* a small glass container, like a small HOURGLASS, through which sand runs in about 3 minutes, which is used for measuring the time when boiling eggs —compare HOURGLASS
egg whisk /ˈ· ·/ also (*esp. AmE*) **egg·beat·er** /-ˌbiːtəʳ/— *n esp. BrE* a tool used in the kitchen to mix up eggs for cooking and make them light and full of air
e·gis /ˈiːdʒɪ̇s/ *n* [S9] AEGIS
eg·lan·tine /ˈegləntaɪn, -tiːn/ also **sweetbrier,**

-briar— *n* [C;U] a kind of wild rose

e·go /ˈiːɡəʊ, ˈeɡəʊ/ *n* **egos** **1** the self, esp. as seen in relation to other selves or to the outside world **2** (in Freudian PSYCHOLOGY) the one of the 3 parts of the mind that connects a person to the outside world, because it can think and act; conscious self —compare ID, SUPEREGO

e·go·cen·tric /ˌiːɡəʊˈsentrɪk, ˌe-/ *adj derog* selfish; thinking only about (one)self, rather than about other people or society —**~ally** *adv* [Wa4] —**~ity** /ˌiːɡəʊsenˈtrɪsɪ̈ti, ˌe-/ *n* [U]

e·go·is·m /ˈiːɡəʊɪzəm, ˈe-/ *n* [U] *usu. derog* the quality or state of always thinking about (one)self, and about what will be the best for (one)self; continued selfishness —compare EGOTISM, ALTRUISM

e·go·ist /ˈiːɡəʊɪ̈st, ˈe-/ *n* **1** *derog* a person who shows EGOISM —compare EGOTIST, ALTRUIST **2** a believer in the idea of EGOISM —**~ic** /ˌiːɡəʊˈɪstɪk, ˌe-/ *adj* —**~ical** /-kəl/ *adj* —**~ically** *adv* [Wa4]

eg·o·tis·m /ˈeɡətɪzəm, ˈiː-‖ˈiː-/ *n* [U] *derog* the quality or state of talking too much about oneself and believing that one is more important than other people —compare EGOISM

eg·o·tist /ˈeɡətɪ̈st, ˈiː-‖ˈiː-/ *n derog* a person who shows EGOTISM —compare EGOIST —**~ic** /ˌeɡəˈtɪstɪk, ˌiː-‖ˌiː-/ *adj* —**~ically** *adv* [Wa4] —**~ical** /-kəl/ *adj*

ego trip /ˈ·· ·/ *n sl* an act or set of acts that gives selfish pleasure to the EGO

e·gre·gious /ɪˈɡriːdʒəs/ *adj* [A;(B)] *derog* (*used with words with bad or unfavourable meanings*) especially and noticeably bad: *You made an egregious mistake when you spoke so rudely to the president* —**~ly** *adv*

e·gress /ˈiːɡres/ *n* **1** [U] *fml or law* the act, power, or right of going out, esp. from a building or a closed place **2** [C] *fml* a way out; EXIT

e·gret /ˈiːɡrɪ̈t, -et/ *n* any of various birds (HERONs) with beautiful long white feathers which are sometimes worn as an ornament

E·gyp·tian /ɪˈdʒɪpʃən/ *adj* [Wa5] that belongs to, or is a native of, Egypt

eh /eɪ/ *interj infml* (used for showing surprise or doubt, or when asking someone to agree, or when asking for something to be repeated): *Let's have another drink, eh?|"I'm cold!" "Eh?" "I said I'm cold!"*

ei·der·down /ˈaɪdədaʊn‖-dər-/ *n* a thick warm covering for a bed filled with the soft feathers (DOWN[6]) of a large black and white bird (**eider duck**) —see picture at BEDROOM

eight /eɪt/ *determiner, n, pron* **1** [see NUMBER TABLE 1] (the number) 8 **2** [C] a rowing-boat for racing that holds 8 men **3 have had one over the eight** also **be one over the eight** *infml* to be drunk: *Listen to John singing! He must have had/must be one over the eight* —**eighth** /eɪtθ/ *determiner, n, pron, adv* [see NUMBER TABLE 3]

eigh·teen /eɪˈtiːn◂/ *determiner, n, pron* [see NUMBER TABLE 1] (the number) 18 —**~th** *determiner, n, pron, adv* [see NUMBER TABLE 3]

eighth note /ˈ· ·/ *n AmE* QUAVER[2] (2)

eight·some /ˈeɪtsəm/ *n* **1** also **eightsome reel** /ˌ·· ˈ·/— a quick, cheerful Scottish dance (REEL) for 8 dancers **2** a group of 8 people who are performing this dance —see also -SOME[2]

eigh·ty /ˈeɪti/ *determiner, n, pron* [see NUMBER TABLE 1] (the number) 80 —**eightieth** /ˈeɪtɪəθ/ *determiner, n, pron, adv* [see NUMBER TABLE 3]

ei·stedd·fod /aɪˈstedfəd (*Welsh* aɪˈsteðvɒd)/ *n* (*often cap.*) a meeting in Wales at which poets, singers, and musicians compete in many activities in Welsh

ei·ther[1] /ˈaɪðəʳ‖ˈiː-/ *determiner* **1** one or the other of 2: *He's lived in London and Manchester, but he doesn't like either city very much* —compare NEITHER[1], ANY[1] **2** one and the other of 2; each: *He sat in the car with a policeman on either side of him* —compare BOTH[1]

either[2] *pron* one or the other of 2: *He has lived in London and Manchester, but he doesn't like either (of them)*

USAGE **Either** and **neither** as PRONOUNs are usually singular in *fml* writing, but often plural in speech when they are followed by a plural: **Neither** *of the books are* (fml *is*) *very interesting.*|*Are* (fml *Is*) **either** *of the boys ready?* **None** is now usually plural in such sentences, and **any** is always plural before a plural: **None** *of the books are/is very interesting.*|*Are* **any** *of the boys ready?*|**None** *of us wants to be killed young.*

either[3] *conj* (used before the first of 2 or more choices which are expressed by like noun phrases, verb phrases, etc., separated by *or*): *It's either a boy or a girl.*|*"You either love him or hate him"* (SEU S.)

USAGE 1 **Either** . . . **or** and **neither** . . . **nor** are plural **a** when the word next to the verb is plural. Compare **Either** *my father or my brothers are coming.*|**Either** *my brothers or my father is coming.* **b** *not fml* to avoid saying *he or she*, since there is no one word for this in English: *If* **either** *David* **or** *Janet come, they will want a drink.* (fml *If* **either** *David* **or** *Janet comes, he or she . . . .*) 2 Be careful to put **either** next to the part of the sentence that it concerns. Compare: **Either** *you must improve your work* **or** *I shall dismiss you.*|*You must improve* **either** *your work* **or** *your appearance*

either[4] *adv* (*used with* neg. *expressions*) also: *I haven't read this book, and my brother hasn't either* (=both haven't read it).|*"I can't swim!" "I can't, either!"* (=I, too, am unable to swim)|*"They're not going down but they're not going up either; they're sort of steady"* (SEU S.) —compare NEITHER[4], TOO (2)

either-or /ˌ·· ˈ·/ *n* **either-ors** *infml* an unavoidable choice between only 2 possibilities: *We fight, or we don't—it's an either-or decision*

e·jac·u·late /ɪˈdʒækjʊleɪt‖-kjə-/ *v* [T1;I∅] **1** *fml* to cry out or say (something) suddenly and shortly **2** *med* to throw out suddenly and with force from the body (esp. the male seed (SPERM))

e·jac·u·la·tion /ɪˌdʒækjʊˈleɪʃən‖-kjə-/ *n* **1** [C] something which is said suddenly and with feeling: *I heard John shout an ejaculation which sounded like "God!"* **2** [C;U] *med* an act or the action of throwing out liquid with force from the body, esp. the male seed (SPERM)

e·ject /ɪˈdʒekt/ *v* [T1 (*from*)] to throw out with force: *The young men were making such a noise in the restaurant that the police came and ejected them* —**~ion** /ɪˈdʒekʃən/ *n* [U;C]

e·jec·tor /ɪˈdʒektəʳ/ *n* an apparatus which EJECTs something

ejector seat /·ˈ·· ·/ also (*esp. AmE*) **ejection seat**— *n esp. BrE* a type of seat which throws out the pilot from a plane, when he can no longer control it and must reach the ground by PARACHUTE

eke out /iːk/ *v adv* [T1 (*with, by*)] **1** to cause (a small supply of something) to last longer, by being careful or by adding something else: *She eked out her small income by washing clothes for other people* **2 eke out a living** to get by hard work the small amount of money and goods necessary for a poor life

EKG *AmE* ECG

el /el/ *n* [*usu. sing.*] *infml esp. AmE* ELEVATED RAILWAY

e·lab·o·rate[1] /ɪˈlæbərət/ *adj* full of detail; carefully worked out and with a large number of parts: *an elaborate machine|curtains with an elaborate pattern of flowers* —**~ly** *adv* —**~ness** *n* [U]

e·lab·o·rate² /ɪˈlæbəreɪt/ *v* [I∅ (*on*); T1] to add more detail to (something): *Just tell us the facts and don't elaborate (on them)*

e·lab·o·ra·tion /ɪˌlæbəˈreɪʃən/ *n* **1** [U] the act of making ELABORATE¹: *Just tell us the plain facts without wasting time on elaboration* **2** [C] the result of making ELABORATE¹; (too much) detail and ornament

é·lan /ˈeɪlɒn‖eɪˈlɑn (*Fr* elɑ̃)/ *n* [U] *Fr* eagerness, quickness, and high spirits: *The soldiers rushed into the attack with great élan* —compare ÉCLAT

e·land /ˈiːlənd/ *n* [Wn1] a type of large African deerlike animal (ANTELOPE)

e·lapse /ɪˈlæps/ *v* [I∅] *fml* (of time) to pass away: *He went away in June, and now 3 months have elapsed and it's September*

e·las·tic¹ /ɪˈlæstɪk/ *adj* **1** (of material such as rubber) which springs back into the original or natural shape after being stretched: *an elastic band*| (fig.) *Lions move with elastic grace* **2** not stiff or fixed; able to be changed to fit all cases: *elastic rules|With his elastic character he will soon be cheerful again*

elastic² *n* [U] (a piece of) ELASTIC¹ (1) material, esp. rubber: *This toy plane will fly if you wind up the elastic that drives it*

elastic band /·ˌ·· ˈ·/ *n BrE* RUBBER BAND

e·las·ti·ci·ty /ˌiːlæˈstɪsɪ̇ti, ɪˌlæ-/ *n* [U] the state or quality of being ELASTIC¹

E·las·to·plast /ɪˈlæstəplɑːst‖-plæst/ *n tdmk BrE* a kind of STICKING PLASTER —see also BAND-AID

e·late /ɪˈleɪt/ *v* [T1 (*by*) *usu. pass.*] to fill (someone) with pride and joy: *He was elated by his son's success*

e·lat·ed /ɪˈleɪtɪ̇d/ *adj* [B (*at*); F3,5] filled with ELATION: *The people seem elated at the victory*

e·la·tion /ɪˈleɪʃən/ *n* [U] the state or quality of being filled with pride and joy: *the people's elation at the good news*

el·bow¹ /ˈelbəʊ/ *n* **1** the joint where the arm bends, esp. the outer point of this —see picture at HUMAN² **2** the part of a garment which covers this arm joint **3** an L-shaped joint shaped like this arm joint, in a pipe, chimney, etc. **4 at someone's elbow** close to someone and ready to help **5 lift one's elbow** *infml* to drink too much alcohol: *John's out, lifting his elbow as usual, and he'll probably come home drunk* **6 out at elbow(s) a** (of a person) badly dressed and poor-looking **b** (of a garment) worn out and with holes in it

elbow² *v* [X9] **1** to push with the elbows: *I tried to stop him, but he elbowed me out of the way* **2** to make (one's way) by doing this: *He elbowed his way through the crowd*

elbow grease /ˈ·· ·/ *n* [U] *infml* hard work with the hands, esp. polishing and cleaning

el·bow·room /ˈelbəʊrʊm, -ruːm/ *n* [U] space in which to move freely

el·der¹ /ˈeldəʳ/ *n* **1** [C] also **elder tree**— a type of small tree, with white flowers in large flat groups, and red or black berries **2** [A] ELDERBERRY

elder² *adj* [Wa5] **1** [A] (of people, esp. in a family) older, esp. the older of 2: *my elder brother* (=I have one brother, who is older than I am)|*Her elder daughter is married* (=she has 2 daughters).| *the elder members of the party* —compare OLDer (2) **2** [*the*+A; *the*+E] older than another person (esp. a son) of the same name: *William Pitt the elder was a politician, like his son.|the elder Pitt* —compare YOUNGER

USAGE One can say: *He is older than I am, but not: *He is elder than I am.*

elder³ *n* **1** [(*the*) S9] the older of 2 people: *Which is the elder (of the 2 sisters)?|He is my elder by 10 years* (=He is 10 years older than I am) **2** [C] (*often cap.*) a man who holds an official position in some Christian churches **3 one's elders** people who are older than one

el·der·ber·ry /ˈeldəbəri‖ˈeldərˌberi/ *n* the fruit of the ELDER¹ tree —see picture at BERRY

el·der·flow·er /ˈeldəflaʊəʳ‖-dər-/ *n* the flower of the ELDER¹ tree

el·der·ly /ˈeldəli‖ˈeldərli/ *adj often euph* (of a person) getting near old age: *My father is getting elderly now and can't walk very fast*

elder states·man /ˌ·· ˈ··/ *n* an old and respected politician, usu. no longer in an official position, who is asked for advice because of his long experience

el·dest /ˈeldɪ̇st/ *adj, n* [Wa5] (a person, esp. in a family, who is) oldest of 3 or more: *She has 3 children, and her eldest has just started school*

El Do·ra·do /ˌel dəˈrɑːdəʊ/ *n* [R] *Sp* an imaginary city or country, supposed to be in South America, which is full of gold

e·lect¹ /ɪˈlekt/ *adj* [Wa5;E] *fml* **1** chosen (for) but not yet at work (in an official position) **2** elected to an office but not yet officially placed in it

elect² *n* [(*the*) P] *fml* (in some forms of the Christian religion) people who are chosen by God to go to heaven: *the elect|God's elect*

elect³ *v* **1** [T1 (*as, to*); X1] to choose (someone) by voting: *They elected a President.|They elected Nixon (as) President.|They elected him to represent them.|They elected me to the Board of Directors* **2** [T3] *fml* to decide (to do something), esp. when making an important decision about the future: *He elected to become a doctor*

e·lec·tion /ɪˈlekʃən/ *n* [C;U] (an example of) the choosing of representatives to fill a position, esp. a political office, by vote: *The Government have decided on the date of the next general election.|The election results will be broadcast tonight.|Trade Union representatives are chosen by election; all the members have a vote*

Election Day /·ˈ·· ˌ·/ *n* [R] (in the US) a day when public officials are elected, esp. the day in November when national elections are held

e·lec·tion·eer /ɪˌlekʃəˈnɪəʳ/ *v* [I∅] (*usu. in tenses with the* -ing *form*) to work at ELECTIONEERING —see also CANVASS

e·lec·tion·eer·ing /ɪˌlekʃəˈnɪərɪŋ/ *n* [U] the work of persuading people to vote for a political party by visiting voters, making speeches, etc.

e·lec·tive¹ /ɪˈlektɪv/ *adj* [Wa5] **1** *fml* (of a position) filled by election: *The office of President of the US is an elective one, but the position of Queen of England is not* **2** having the power to elect **3** *AmE* (of a course, esp. at university) freely chosen; not REQUIRED; OPTIONAL

elective² *n AmE* an ELECTIVE¹ (3) course which is studied at school or college

e·lec·tor /ɪˈlektəʳ‖-tər, -tɔr/ *n fml* **1** a person who has the right to vote in any particular ELECTION **2** (in the US) a member of the ELECTORAL COLLEGE

e·lec·to·ral /ɪˈlektərəl/ *adj* [Wa5;A] connected with **a** an election **b** the electors: *the electoral system in this country*

electoral col·lege /·ˌ··· ˈ··/ *n* [*the*+GU] the national body elected by the voters of each state to choose the President of the US

electoral roll /·ˌ·· ˈ·/ also **electoral re·gis·ter** /·ˌ··· ˈ···/— *n* [(*the*) *usu. sing.*] the list of people in an area who have the right to vote in elections

e·lec·to·rate /ɪˈlektərɪ̇t/ *n* [(*the*) GC] all the people in the country who have the right to vote, seen as a group

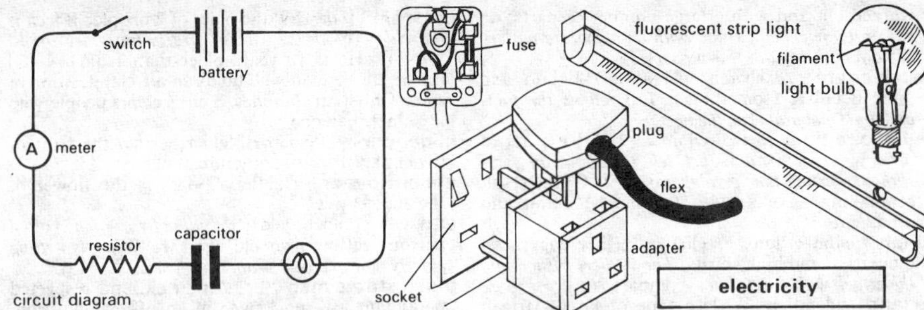

E·lec·tra Com·plex /ɪˈlektrə ˌkɒmpleks‖-ˌkɑm-/ *n* (in FREUDIAN PSYCHOLOGY) (of a young girl) unconscious sexual desire for one's father combined with hatred of one's mother

e·lec·tric /ɪˈlektrɪk/ *adj* **1** [Wa5;A] (of machines) producing electricity: *They have an electric* GENERATOR *which uses oil and makes all the electricity for the farm.|an electric storm* **2** [Wa5;A] produced by electricity: *electric power|an electric shock* **3** [Wa5; B] worked by electricity: *an electric clock|an electric fire* **4** [Wa5;A] being electricity: *an electric* SPARK[1] (2) **5** [B] very exciting: *His speech had an electric effect upon all the listeners, and they rushed into the streets* —**~ally** *adv* [Wa4]
USAGE Anything either worked by or producing electricity is **electric**: *an* **electric** *clock/shock/light/* GENERATOR. Otherwise, the word is **electrical**. It expresses the idea of a less close connection with electricity, and is used **a** of people or their work: *an* **electrical** *engineer* **b** in other expressions where the connection is more general: **electrical** *apparatus|an* **electrical** *fault in the system.* —compare ELECTRICAL, ELECTRONIC

e·lec·tri·cal /ɪˈlektrɪkəl/ *adj* [Wa5] **1** [A] concerned with electricity: *an electrical* ENGINEER **2** [B] using electricity in some way: *electrical apparatus* —compare ELECTRIC, ELECTRONIC —**~ly** *adv* [Wa4]

electric blan·ket /·ˌ·· ˈ··/ *n* a BLANKET with electric wires passing through, used for making a bed warm

electric chair /·ˌ·· ˈ·/ *n* **1** [C] a machine used for killing murderers in some states of the US **2** [*the*+R] also (*infml*) **chair**— the punishment of death by this means —see also ELECTROCUTE

electric eye /·ˌ·· ˈ·/ *n infml* PHOTOELECTRIC CELL (2)

electric fence /·ˌ·· ˈ·/ *n* a wire fence through which electricity is passed, so as to give an electric shock to creatures that touch it

el·ec·tri·cian /ɪˌlekˈtrɪʃən/ *n* a person whose job is to fit and repair electrical apparatus

e·lec·tri·ci·ty /ɪˌlekˈtrɪsɪ̇ti/ *n* [U] **1** the power which is produced by rubbing (FRICTION) or by chemical means (a BATTERY) or by a machine called a GENERATOR, and which gives us heat, light and sound, and drives machines **2** electric current **3** a feeling of keen excitement, esp. one that spreads through a group of people

electric shock /·ˌ·· ˈ·/ *n* a shock caused by electricity: *I got an electric shock when I touched that wire*

electric shock ther·a·py /·ˌ·· ˈ· ˌ···/ also **e·lec·tro·con·vul·sive therapy** /ɪˌlektrəʊkənˌvʌlsɪv ˈθerəpi/— *n* [U] *med* the treatment of diseases of the mind by giving ELECTRIC SHOCK*s*

e·lec·tri·fy /ɪˈlektrɪ̇faɪ/ *v* [Wv5;T1] **1** to pass an electric current through (something): *electrified wires* **2** to change (something) to a system using electric power: *The national railway system used to run on steam, but now it has nearly all been electrified* **3** to excite and surprise greatly: *She electrified her family by appearing on television with no clothes on* —**-fication** /ɪˌlektrɪ̇fɪ̇ˈkeɪʃən/ *n* [U]

e·lec·tro- /ɪˌlektrəʊ/ *comb. form tech* **1** connected with electricity: ELECTROCARDIOGRAM, ELECTROLYSIS **2** electric and: *electro-chemical*

e·lec·tro·car·di·o·gram /ɪˌlektrəʊˈkɑːdɪəgræm‖-ˈkɑr-/ *n med* the drawing that is made by an ELECTROCARDIOGRAPH —compare ELECTROENCEPHALOGRAM

e·lec·tro·car·di·o·graph /ɪˌlektrəʊˈkɑːdɪəgrɑːf‖-ˈkɑrdɪəgræf/ *n med* a piece of apparatus that records in the form of a drawing the electrical changes that take place in the heart as it beats —compare ELECTROENCEPHALOGRAPH

e·lec·tro·cute /ɪˈlektrəkjuːt/ *v* [T1 *often pass.*] to kill by passing electricity through the body —**-cution** /ɪˌlektrəˈkjuːʃən/ *n* [U;C]

e·lec·trode /ɪˈlektrəʊd/ *n* [*often pl.*] either of the 2 points (the TERMINAL*s*) at which the current enters and leaves a BATTERY, or other electrical apparatus —see also ANODE, CATHODE

e·lec·tro·en·ceph·a·lo·gram /ɪˌlektrəʊɪnˈsefələgræm, -trəʊen-/ *n med* the drawing that is made by an ELECTROENCEPHALOGRAPH —compare ELECTROCARDIOGRAM

e·lec·tro·en·ceph·a·lo·graph /ɪˌlektrəʊɪnˈsefələgrɑːf, -trəʊen-‖-græf/ *n med* a piece of apparatus that records in the form of a drawing the electrical activity of the brain —compare ELECTROCARDIOGRAPH

e·lec·trol·y·sis /ɪˌlekˈtrɒlɪ̇sɪ̇s‖-ˈtrɑ-/ *n* [U] **1** the separation of a liquid into its chemical parts by passing electricity through it (from an ANODE to a CATHODE) **2** the destruction of hair roots by means of an electric current: *You can have the hairs on your chin removed by electrolysis*

e·lec·tro·lyte /ɪˈlektrəlaɪt/ *n* any of various liquids, such as COPPER SULPHATE, which can be broken down into their chemical parts by passing electricity through them

e·lec·tron /ɪˈlektrɒn‖-trɑn/ *n* one of the parts which all together make up an atom; "bit" of NEGATIVE electricity moving round one "bit" of POSITIVE electricity (PROTON) inside an atom —see also NEUTRON and picture at ATOM

el·ec·tron·ic /ɪˌlekˈtrɒnɪk‖-ˈtrɑ-/ *adj* [Wa5] **1** connected with ELECTRON*s* **2** [*tech*] connected with any apparatus that works by ELECTRONICS (2) **3** (of music) produced by means of ELECTRONICS (2): *He turned on the record-player, producing a crash of electronic sound*

el·ec·tron·ics /ɪˌlekˈtrɒnɪks‖-trɑ-/ *n* [U] **1** the branch of science that deals with the behaviour of ELECTRON*s* **2** the branch of industry that makes such products as radio, television, and recording apparatus, whose operation depends on the behaviour of ELECTRON*s*

electron mi·cro·scope /·ˌ·· ˈ···/ *n* a type of

microscope which uses a beam of ELECTRONs to make very small things large enough to see

e·lec·tro·plate /ɪˈlektrəʊpleɪt‖-trə-/ *v* [Wv5;T1] to cover with a thin surface of metal, usu. silver, as a result of ELECTROLYSIS (1): *"Are these spoons solid silver?" "No, they're electroplated"*

e·lec·tro·shock ther·a·py /ɪˈlektrəʊʃɒk ˌθerəpi‖-ʃɑk-/ *n* [U] *AmE* ELECTRIC SHOCK THERAPY

el·e·e·mos·y·na·ry /ˌelɪ-ɪˈmɒsənəri‖ˌelɪˈmɑsənəri/ *adj fml* (of work or gifts) given or received without payment: *Beggars are people who live by eleemosynary or* CHARITABLE *gifts*

el·e·gant /ˈelɪgənt/ *adj apprec* **1** having the qualities of grace, beauty, and fashion: *an elegant woman|elegant in her manners/her speech* **2** (of things) beautiful and well made: *an elegant room|an elegant piece of furniture* **3** (of ideas) neat and simple: *an elegant piece of reasoning|an elegant scientific proof* —**~ly** *adv* —**-ance** /ˈelɪgəns/ *n* [U;S]

el·e·gi·ac¹ /ˌeləˈdʒaɪək/ also **el·e·gi·a·cal** /-əkəl/— *adj* **1** [Wa5] **a** (of a person) who writes or wrote ELEGIACs **b** (of a poem) written in the form of an ELEGIAC **2** connected with elegies (ELEGY), esp. expressing sorrow for something that is lost: *His description of his youth at the end of the 19th century has an elegiac quality* —**~ally** *adv* [Wa4]

elegiac² *n* [*often pl.*] a form of poetry or POETIC METRE invented in ancient Greece for expressing sorrow. It has 6 feet (FOOT¹ (7)) in the first line and 5 in the second

el·e·gy /ˈelədʒi/ *n* a type of poem or song written to show sorrow for the dead or for something lost

el·e·ment /ˈeləmənt/ *n* **1** [S9, esp. *of*] a quality or amount which can be noticed: *There is an element of truth* (=some truth) *in what you say* **2** [C] a necessary part of a whole: *Honesty is an important element in the character of a postman* **3** [C *often pl. with sing. meaning*] (of people, often in a political sense) a group: *the lawless elements in society* **4** [C] the heating part of a piece of electrical apparatus: *the element of an electric fire* **5** [C] *old use* any of the 4 substances earth, air, fire, and water, from which (it was believed) everything material was made **6** [C] any of more than 100 simple substances that consist of atoms of only one kind and that, alone or in combination, make up all substances: *Both* HYDROGEN *and oxygen are elements, but water, which is formed when they combine, is not* **7 in/out of (one's) element** in/out of (one's) proper surroundings

el·e·men·tal /ˌeləˈmentl/ *adj* **1** of or being like a great force of nature: *the elemental violence of the storm* **2** (of a person's character) having simple and strong feelings: *She killed herself when her lover left her, because of her elemental nature* **3** [Wa5] *old use* concerned with the 4 ELEMENTs (5)

el·e·men·ta·ry /ˌeləˈmentəri/ *adj* **1** (of a question) simple and easy to answer **2** concerned with the beginnings, esp. of education and study: *some elementary exercises for the piano*

elementary par·ti·cle /ˌ····· ˈ···/ *n tech* any of the 20 or more smallest pieces of any substance (including ELECTRONs, PROTONs, and NEUTRONs) which make up atoms

el·e·ments /ˈeləmənts/ *n* [*the*+P] **1** (of a school subject) the beginnings; the first steps **2** (*often cap.*) the weather, esp. bad weather: *In spite of the terrible storm he walked on, quite careless of the elements* —see also ELEMENTAL (1) **3** *fml* (*usu. cap.*) (in the Christian religion) the bread and wine which Christians eat and drink in the ceremony called the MASS, COMMUNION, or the EUCHARIST

el·e·phant /ˈeləfənt/ *n* [Wn1] the largest 4-footed animal now living, with 2 long curved teeth (TUSKs) and a long nose called a TRUNK with which it can pick things up —see picture at RUMINANT

el·e·phan·ti·a·sis /ˌeləfənˈtaɪəsəs, -fæn-/ *n* [U] a disease, esp. of tropical countries, which causes the skin and flesh to grow very thick

el·e·phan·tine /ˌeləˈfæntaɪn‖-tiːn/ *adj often humor* heavy and awkward like an elephant: *The big fat man walked with slow elephantine steps*

el·e·vate /ˈeləveɪt/ *v* [T1] **1** [Wv4] to make (the mind, soul, etc.) better, higher, or more educated: *An elevating book is better for you than a light love story* **2** *fml* to raise or lift up: *He elevated his voice slightly* **3 elevate someone to the peerage** to make someone a lord (PEER)

el·e·vat·ed /ˈeləveɪtəd/ *adj* **1** (of thoughts, language, etc.) fine and noble **2** *infml old use* slightly drunk: *My dear! The gentlemen seem a little elevated. Let us leave them to their wine*

elevated rail·way /ˌ···· ˈ··/ also (*infml esp. AmE*) **el**— *n* a railway which runs on a kind of continuous bridge above the street in a town

el·e·va·tion /ˌeləˈveɪʃən/ *n* **1** [U9,(U)] *fml* (the state resulting from) the act or action of elevating (ELEVATE): *His elevation to the rank of a lord has made him very proud* **2** [(*the*) U (*of*); S] *fml* (of thoughts, language, etc.) the quality of being fine and noble: *the elevation of his style in literature* **3** [C] *fml* a hill: *We climbed to the top of a small elevation, from which we could look at the town* **4** [S] height above sea-level: *Their house is at an elevation of 2,000 metres* —compare ALTITUDE **5** [C] (a drawing of) a flat upright side of a building: *This drawing shows what the front elevation of the house will look like when it is built* —compare PLAN¹ (3), PERSPECTIVE, FACADE **6** [S] The angle made with the horizon by some pointing apparatus, such as a gun: *The gun was fired at an elevation of 60 degrees* —see also TRAJECTORY

Elevation of the Host /··ˌ·· · · ˈ·/ *n* [*the*+R] (in the ROMAN CATHOLIC church) the ceremony of lifting up the holy bread and wine so that the people can look at them with solemn respect

el·e·va·tor /ˈeləveɪtəʳ/ *n* **1** *AmE* LIFT² (4) **2** a machine consisting of a moving belt with buckets, used for raising grain and liquids, unloading ships, etc. **3** a storehouse for grain **4** one of the 2 movable parts in the tail of an aircraft which make it able to climb and descend —compare AILERON

e·lev·en /ɪˈlevən/ *determiner, n, pron* [see NUMBER TABLE 1] **1** (the number) 11: *eleven years old|a boy of eleven* **2** [GC] a complete team of 11 players in football, cricket, etc.: *a member of the school football eleven* —**~th** *determiner, n, pron, adv* [see NUMBER TABLE 3]

eleven-plus /·ˌ·· ˈ·/ *n* [the+R] (in Britain until the introduction of COMPREHENSIVE education) an examination which each 11 year old child took, the result of which decided whether he went to a GRAMMAR SCHOOL or SECONDARY MODERN school

e·lev·en·ses /ɪˈlevənzəz/ *n BrE infml* tea, coffee, or a light meal, which is taken at about 11 o'clock in the morning

eleventh hour /·ˌ·· ˈ·/ *n* [*the*+R] the very last moment: *War, which seemed certain, was prevented at the eleventh hour*

elf /elf/ *n* **elves** /elvz/ a type of small fairy which is said to play tricks on people

el·fin /ˈelfən/ *adj* **1** [Wa5] ELFlike: *the fairies at their elfin dances in the moonlight* **2** *apprec* having a quality of magical charm: *silvery elfin laughter*

elf·ish /ˈelfɪʃ/ also **elvish**— *adj becoming rare* (of people or behaviour) having the quality or habit of playing tricks on people like an ELF; MISCHIEVOUS —**~ly** *adv* —**~ness** *n* [U]

e·li·cit /ɪˈlɪsɨt/ *v* [T1 (*from*)] *fml* to get, draw out, cause to come out (facts, information, etc.): *He elicited the truth at last, by questioning all the boys in the school* —**~ation** /ɪˌlɪsɨˈteɪʃən/ *n* [U;C]

e·lide /ɪˈlaɪd/ *v* [Wv5;T1] to leave out the sound of (a letter or part of a word) in pronunciation: *We elide the "d" in "Wednesday" when we're talking quickly* —**elision** /ɪˈlɪʒən/ *n* [U;C]

el·i·gi·ble /ˈelɨdʒəbəl/ *adj* **1** [B] suitable to be chosen, esp. as a husband: *She knows a lot of eligible young men who are all rich and attractive.|an eligible place for a holiday* **2** [F (*as, for*), F3+*as, for*] belonging to the group from which a choice must be made: *Anyone who can speak French is eligible to join this club* —**-bility** /ˌelɨdʒəˈbɪlɨti/ *n* [U]—**-bly** /ˈelɨdʒəbli/ *adv* [Wa3]

e·lim·i·nate /ɪˈlɪmɨneɪt/ *v* **1** [T1 (*from*)] to remove or get rid of: *eliminate the mistakes from your writing|eliminate waste material from the body* **2** [T1] to show that (a possibility) does not exist and so need not be considered **3** [T1] *infml* and *euph* or *humor* to kill —**-nation** /ɪˌlɪmɨˈneɪʃən/ *n* [U]

e·lite /eɪˈliːt, ɪ-/ *n* [(*the*) GC] *Fr* the best or most important people in a social group: *the power elite inside the government*

e·lit·is·m /eɪˈliːtɪzəm, ɪ-/ *n* [U] **1** **a** leadership or rule by an ELITE **b** belief in the leadership of an ELITE **2** consciousness of belonging to an ELITE: *The new President's elitism will make him unpopular with the mass of the people* —**elitist** /eɪˈliːtɨst, ɪ-/ *adj, n*

e·lix·ir /ɪˈlɪksəʳ/ *n* [C;(U)] *lit* **1** an imaginary liquid which scientists once hoped would change other metals into gold, or make life last for ever **2** an imaginary cure for all evils

E·liz·a·be·than¹ /ɪˌlɪzəˈbiːθən/ *adj* [Wa5] (in Britain) of the period of Queen Elizabeth I of England, 1558–1603

Elizabethan² *n* a person who lived in the ELIZABETHAN age

elk /elk/ *n* [Wn1] **1** *BrE* any of several types of deer of Europe and Asia of the largest kind, with very big flat ANTLERS (branching horns) **2** also **wapiti**— *AmE* a type of large North American deer, like the RED DEER but larger

elk·hound /ˈelkhaʊnd/ *n* a type of dog bred in Norway, with a short body, short, pointed ears, and a very thick grey coat, originally bred in Norway for hunting ELKS

el·lipse /ɪˈlɪps/ *n* the curve that is seen when one looks at a circle sideways; regular OVAL

el·lip·sis /ɪˈlɪpsɨs/ *n* **-ses** /siːz/ [C;U;(*of*)] (an example of) the leaving out of a word or words from a sentence when the meaning can be understood without them: *There is an ellipsis of "was" in the following sentence: "In the accident the child was hurt and the mother killed"* (=was killed)

el·lip·tic /ɪˈlɪptɪk/ also **el·lip·ti·cal** /-tɪkəl/— *adj* **1** [Wa5] having the shape of an ELLIPSE: *The Earth's path round the sun is elliptical* **2** having the quality of ELLIPSIS **3** (of speech or literature) difficult to understand because more is meant than is actually said: *"It's getting late." "What an elliptic remark. Do you mean you're hungry?"* —compare CRYPTIC —**~ally** *adv* [Wa4]

elm /elm/ *n* **1** also **elm tree** /ˈ· ·/— any of several types of large, tall, broad-leaved tree **2** [U] the hard heavy wood of this tree

el·o·cu·tion /ˌeləˈkjuːʃən/ *n* [U] the art of good clear speaking in public, with proper attention to the control of the voice and the making of the sounds

el·o·cu·tion·a·ry /ˌeləˈkjuːʃənəri‖-ʃəneri/ *adj* [Wa5] of or concerning ELOCUTION

el·o·cu·tion·ist /ˌeləˈkjuːʃənɨst/ *n* **1** a person who is good at ELOCUTION, or who teaches it **2** a person who gives public performances of speech, esp. of poetry, from memory

e·lon·gate /ˈiːlɒŋgeɪt‖ɪˈlɔŋ-/ *v* [Wv5;T1] to make (a material thing) longer: *This picture that you've painted isn't like me. The nose is much too elongated*

e·lon·ga·tion /ˌiːlɒŋˈgeɪʃən‖ɪˌlɔŋ-/ *n* **1** [U] (of material things) the act or action of elongating (ELONGATE) **2** [C] something that has been ELONGATEd; EXTENSION

e·lope /ɪˈləʊp/ *v* [IØ] **1** [(*with*)] (esp. of a woman) to run away secretly with a lover **2** (of a man and woman) to run away secretly with the intention of getting married usu. without parental approval —**~ment** *n* [C;U]

el·o·quence /ˈeləkwəns/ *n* [U] *fml, usu. apprec* the state or quality of being ELOQUENT

el·o·quent /ˈeləkwənt/ *adj fml* **1** *apprec* **a** (of a person) able to make good speeches that influence the hearers **b** (of a speech) of a kind that influences the hearers **2** [(*of*)] expressing or showing (something) very strongly though without words: *The healthy appearance of the children is eloquent of the wealth of the nation* —**~ly** *adv*

else /els/ *adv* [Wa5; (*but*)] **1** (*after question words, some* PRONOUNs *and adverbs*) **a** besides; in addition: *I've said I'm sorry. What else can I say?* (=what more)|*Who else* (=which other person) *did you see?|Does anybody else want to look at this book?|I don't know the answer. You must ask somebody else* **b** in/at a different place, time, or way; apart from that mentioned: *I can't come on Tuesday. When else can we meet?|Everybody else but me has gone to the party* **2** **or else** **a** or otherwise; or if not: *He must pay £100 or else go to prison.|The book must be here, or else you've lost it* **b** (used alone for expressing a threat): *Do what I tell you or else!*

else·where /elsˈweəʳ, ˈelsweəʳ‖ˈelsweər/ *adv* [Wa5;(*than*)] at, in, or to another place: *This hotel is full. We must look for rooms elsewhere*

e·lu·ci·date /ɪˈluːsɨdeɪt/ *v* [T1] *fml* to explain or make clear (a difficulty or mystery): *We cannot understand why you did this. Please elucidate the reasons for your action* —**-dation** /ɪˌluːsɨˈdeɪʃən/ *n* [U;(C)]

e·lu·ci·da·to·ry /ɪˈluːsɨdeɪtəri‖-tori/ *adj fml* that ELUCIDATES: *In a few elucidatory words he explained the scientific work he was doing*

e·lude /ɪˈluːd/ *v* [T1] **1** to escape from (somebody or something), esp. by means of a trick: *The fox succeeded in eluding the hunters by running back in the opposite direction* **2** (of a fact) to escape from the memory of (somebody): *I remember his face very well, but his name eludes me for the moment* (=I can't remember it)

e·lu·sive /ɪˈluːsɪv/ also **e·lu·so·ry** /ɪˈluːsəri/— *adj* difficult to catch, find, or remember: *He's such an elusive person; you never know where he is when you want him* —**~ly** *adv* —**~ness** *n* [U]

el·ver /ˈelvəʳ/ *n* a young EEL

elves /elvz/ *pl. of* ELF

elv·ish /ˈelvɪʃ/ *adj* ELFISH

E·lys·i·an /ɪˈlɪzɪən‖ɪˈlɪʒən/ *adj* of ELYSIUM: (fig.) *The 2 lovers lived together in a state of Elysian happiness*

E·lys·i·um /ɪˈlɪzɪəm‖ɪˈlɪʒɪəm, -zɪ-/ *n* **-siums, -sia** /zɪə/ **1** [R] (according to the ancient Greeks) the home of the happy dead **2** [C] *lit* any place or state of great happiness

em- /ɨm; *strong* em/ *prefix* (the form used for EN- before *b-, m-,* or *p-*): EMPOWER|EMBITTER

'em /əm/ *pron infml or dial* THEM

e·ma·ci·ate /ɪˈmeɪʃieɪt/ *v* [Wv5;T1] to cause to become very thin: *By the time the prisoners were set* *free, they were terribly emaciated and could hardly walk* —**-ation** /ɪˌmeɪsiˈeɪʃən/ *n* [U]

em·a·nate from /ˈeməneɪt/ *v prep* [T1 *no pass.*] *fml* **1** (of ideas, orders, suggestions, etc.) to come originally from: *The suggestion that there should be more street lamps emanated from the citizens' committee* **2** (of gas, light, etc.) to come out from: *A bad smell emanated from the dead dog in the road* —**emanation** /ˌeməˈneɪʃən/ *n* [U;C: (*of, from*)]

e·man·ci·pate /ɪˈmænsəpeɪt/ *v* [T1 (*from*)] to make free socially, politically, and in law: (*fig.*) *This new machine will emancipate us from all the hard work we once had to do* —**-pator** *n*

e·man·ci·pa·tion /ɪˌmænsəˈpeɪʃən/ *n* [U] **1** the act of emancipating (EMANCIPATE) **2** the condition of being EMANCIPATEd: *She showed her emancipation by drinking beer and piloting an aircraft*

e·mas·cu·late /ɪˈmæskjʊleɪt‖-skjə-/ *v* [T1 *often pass.*] *med* **1** to take away the power of becoming a father from; CASTRATE **2** to make weak; take away all the life and strength from —**-lation** /ɪˌmæskjʊˈleɪʃən‖-skjə-/ *n* [U]

em·balm /ɪmˈbɑːm/ *v* [T1] to prevent (a dead body) from decaying by treating it with chemicals or sweet-smelling plants; preserve from being forgotten —**~er** *n* —**embalmment** /ɪmˈbɑːm-mənt/ *n* [U]

em·bank·ment /ɪmˈbæŋkmənt/ *n* a wide wall of stones or earth, which is built to keep a river from overflowing its banks, or to carry a road or railway over low ground: *We must throw up an embankment to stop the river from flooding the town.*|*We walked along the Thames Embankment*

em·bar·go[1] /ɪmˈbɑːgəʊ‖-ɑr-/ *n* **-goes** **1** an official order forbidding an action, esp. the movement of ships, or trade: *to lay an embargo on trade with an enemy country* **2 to lay something under an embargo** (of a government) to take something by force for the good of the country

embargo[2] *v* **-goed,** *pres. p.* **-going** [T1] to lay an EMBARGO on (something)

em·bark /ɪmˈbɑːk‖-ɑrk/ *v* [T1;I∅] to go, put, or take on a ship: *We embarked at Liverpool for New York.*|*The ship embarked passengers and wool at an Australian port*

em·bar·ka·tion /ˌembɑːˈkeɪʃən‖-ɑr-/ *n* **1** [U;C] (an example of) the act or action of EMBARKing **2** [U+*on* or *upon*] the act or action of EMBARKing ON: *her embarkation on a new way of life*

embark on also **embark up·on**— *v prep* [T1] to start (something new or difficult): *to embark on a new way of life/on a new profession*

em·bar·rass /ɪmˈbærəs/ *v* [T1 *often pass.*] **1** [Wv4] to cause to feel ashamed or socially uncomfortable: *She was embarrassed when they asked her age.*|*I don't like making speeches in public; it's so embarrassing* **2** to cause to feel anxious about money: *He was embarrassed by many debts* —**~ingly** *adv*

em·bar·rass·ment /ɪmˈbærəsmənt/ *n* **1** [U] **a** the act of EMBARRASSing **b** the state of being EMBARRASSed (1) **2** [C] a difficulty about money: *his many* FINANCIAL *embarrassments* —compare EMBARRASS (2) **3** [C] a person or thing that EMBARRASSes: *That nasty child is an embarrassment to his parents*

em·bas·sy /ˈembəsi/ *n* **1** a group of officials, usu. led by an AMBASSADOR, who are sent by a government to do its business with the government of another country **2** (*sometimes cap.*) **a** the official building where an AMBASSADOR and those who work with him live in a foreign country **b** the group of people who work and live in this building —compare RESIDENCY

em·bat·tled /ɪmˈbætld/ *adj* **1** surrounded by enemies **2** (of a person) continually troubled by annoying or harmful influences

em·bed /ɪmˈbed/ *v* **-dd-** [D1+*in/with usu. pass.*] to fix (something) firmly and deeply in (a mass of surrounding matter): *a gold crown embedded with jewels*|(fig.) *That terrible day will be for ever embedded in my memory*

em·bel·lish /ɪmˈbelɪʃ/ *v* [T1 (*with*)] **1** to make more beautiful, esp. by adding ornaments: *a white hat embellished with pink roses* **2** to add details, perhaps untrue, to (a statement or story): *I asked him to tell the simple truth and not to embellish it with ideas of his own* —see DECORATE (USAGE) —**~ment** *n* [U;C]

em·ber /ˈembəʳ/ *n* [*usu. pl.*] a red-hot piece of wood or coal, esp. in a fire that is no longer burning with flames

ember day /ˈ·· ·/ *n tech* one of 12 days in the year which in some Christian churches are spent in prayer and FASTing[3] (not eating meat)

em·bez·zle /ɪmˈbezəl/ *v* [T1,I∅] to take and use for oneself in a wrong way (money that is placed in one's care): *The clerk embezzled several thousand pounds from the bank where he worked* —**~ment** *n* [U] —**-zler** *n*

em·bit·ter /ɪmˈbɪtəʳ/ *v* [Wv5;T1 *often pass.*] to fill with painful or bitter feelings; make sad and angry: *He was embittered by his many disappointments* —**~ment** *n* [U]

em·bla·zon /ɪmˈbleɪzən/ *v* [Wv5;D1+*on/with usu. pass*] to ornament (a shield or flag) with (the signs that belong to a particular family (a COAT OF ARMS)): *a flag with the family* ARMS *emblazoned on it*

em·blem /ˈembləm/ *n* [(*of*)] an object which is the sign of something: *The national emblem of England is a rose* —compare SYMBOL

em·ble·mat·ic /ˌembləˈmætɪk/ *adj* [(*of*)] acting as an EMBLEM: *The crown is emblematic of the power of a king* —**~ally** *adv* [Wa4]

em·bod·i·ment /ɪmˈbɒdɪmənt‖ɪmˈbɑ-/ *n* someone or something in which something is embodied (EMBODY (1)) (esp. in the phr. **the embodiment of**): *His enemies called him the embodiment of evil*

em·bod·y /ɪmˈbɒdi‖ɪmˈbɑdi/ *v* [T1] **1** (of works, writings, etc.) to express: *Words embody thought.*|*The letter embodied all his ideas* **2** [Wv5] to give a body to (a spirit): *the embodied spirits of the dead* **3** (of things) to contain or include: *The new car embodies many improvements*

embody in *v prep* [D1 *usu. pass.*] **1** (of people) to give (something) form or expression in: *She embodies her principles in her behaviour* **2** to include (something) in: *Many improvements are embodied in the new car*

em·bold·en /ɪmˈbəʊldən/ *v* [V3] to help (somebody to do something) by giving the necessary courage: *She smiled, and this emboldened him to speak to her*

em·bo·lis·m /ˈembəlɪzəm/ *n med* **1** a blocking of a blood vessel **2** something which causes this, such as a hard mass of blood or an amount of air

em·bon·point /ˌɑ̃bɔ̃ˈpwæ̃ (*Fr* -pwɛ̃)/ *n* [U] *Fr euph* (pleasant) fatness (usu. of women): *As you have a tendency to—how shall I put it?—embonpoint, you really shouldn't eat so many chocolates*

em·bos·omed /ɪmˈbʊzəmd/ *adj* [Wa5;F9, esp. *in, among*] *poet* enclosed or surrounded: *a house embosomed in trees*

em·boss /ɪmˈbɒs‖ɪmˈbɑs, -ˈbɔs/ *v* [Wv5;D1+*on/with*] to cause (an ornamental raised pattern) to appear on (metal, paper, etc.) by pressing; ornament (metal, paper, etc.) with a raised pattern: *The name and address of the firm are embossed on its paper*

em·bow·ered /ɪmˈbaʊəd‖-ərd/ *adj* [Wa5;F9, esp.

in, among] *poet* enclosed or surrounded, esp. by plants and trees: *a little house embowered among roses*

em·brace¹ /ɪm'breɪs/ *v* **1** [T1;I∅] to take and hold (another or each other) in the arms as a sign of love: *She embraced her son tenderly.|The 2 sisters met and embraced* **2** [T1] (of things) to contain or include: *This book embraces many different subjects* **3** [T1] *fml* to make use or take willingly: *He embraced at once my offer to employ him* **4** [T1] to become a believer in: *He embraced the Muslim religion when he went to live in the East*

embrace² *n* the act of embracing (EMBRACE¹ (1))

em·bra·sure /ɪm'breɪʒə^r/ *n* **1** an opening, wider on the inside than on the outside, in the wall of a fort or castle, through which the defenders can shoot **2** an opening, wider on the inside than on the outside, on the inner side of a door or window, esp. in a castle

em·bro·ca·tion /ˌembrə'keɪʃən/ *n* [C;U] *fml* a liquid medicine used for rubbing any part of the body that is stiff or aching from exercise —compare LINIMENT

em·broi·der /ɪm'brɔɪdə^r/ *v* **1** [I∅;T1: (*with, in, on*)] to do ornamental needlework on (cloth): *a dress embroidered with flowers in silk thread* **2** [T1 (*on*)] to make in this way: *to embroider a pattern on a cloth* **3** [T1 (*with*)] *often euph* to improve (a story) by adding ornamental details from the imagination

em·broi·der·y /ɪm'brɔɪdəri/ *n* [U] **1** the act or result of EMBROIDERing (1): *She sat quietly at her embroidery* **2** the act or result of EMBROIDERing (3): *Just tell me the truth without a lot of embroidery!*

em·broil /ɪm'brɔɪl/ *v* [T1 *often pass.*] to cause (oneself or another) to join in (a quarrel): *John and Peter were quarrelling, but Mary refused to get embroiled*

embroil in *v prep* [D1 *often pass.*] to cause (oneself or another) to join in (a quarrel): *She embroiled herself in their argument*

em·bry·o /'embriəʊ/ *n* **-os** **1** the young of any creature in its first state before birth, or before coming out of an egg **2 in embryo** still undeveloped: *His plans are still in embryo*

em·bry·on·ic /ˌembri'ɒnɪk‖-'ɑnɪk/ *adj* in an undeveloped or very early state of growth; in the condition of an EMBRYO

e·mend /ɪ'mend/ *v* [Wv5;T1] to take the mistakes out of (written matter) before printing —compare AMEND

e·men·da·tion /ˌiːmen'deɪʃən/ *n* **1** [U (*of*)] the act of EMENDing **2** [C *often pl.*] the change(s) made when something is EMENDed: *A list of emendations is included at the beginning of some books*

em·e·rald¹ /'emərəld/ *n* a bright green precious stone

emerald² *adj, n* [B;U] (of) the colour of an EMERALD; clear bright green

e·merge /ɪ'mɜːdʒ‖-ɜr-/ *v* [I∅] **1** [(*from, out of*)] to come or appear (from/out of somewhere): *The sun emerged from behind the clouds* **2** [(*from*)] to become known as a result of inquiry

e·mer·gence /ɪ'mɜːdʒəns‖-ɜr-/ *n* [U9] *fml* the act of emerging (EMERGE (1)): *the emergence of many new nations since the war*

e·mer·gen·cy /ɪ'mɜːdʒənsi‖-ɜr-/ *n* an unexpected and dangerous happening which must be dealt with at once: *Ring the bell in an emergency.|emergency* EXIT|*emergency* RATIONs

e·mer·gent /ɪ'mɜːdʒənt‖-ɜr-/ *adj* [Wa5;A] emerging (EMERGE (1)), esp. from a poor and dependent state into a richer independent state: *the emergent countries of Africa*

e·mer·i·tus /ɪ'merɪtəs/ *adj* [Wa5;A;E] *Lat* (*often cap.*) (of a teacher in a university or, esp., PROFESSOR) who is no longer holding office but keeps his title: *the emeritus* PROFESSOR *of chemistry*

em·e·ry /'eməri/ *n* [U] (*usu. in comb.*) the powdered form of a very hard metal, which is used for polishing things and making them smooth —see also CARBORUNDUM

e·met·ic /ɪ'metɪk/ *n, adj* [C;U] (something, esp. medicine) eaten or drunk to cause a person to bring up food from the stomach through the mouth: *If someone drinks poison, give him an emetic at once*

em·i·grant /'emɪgrənt/ *n* [(*from* and/or *to*)] a person who EMIGRATEs —compare IMMIGRANT

em·i·grate /'emɪ̈greɪt/ *v* [I∅ (*from* and/or *to*)] to leave one's own country in order to go and live in another —**-ion** /ˌemɪ̈'greɪʃən/ *n* [C;U]

USAGE Some birds **migrate** twice a year between hot and cold countries, and this word can also be used of people who regularly go to and fro between countries. The people or birds are **migrants**, and the practice is called **migration**: **migrant** *workers|the spring* **migration** *of the wild ducks.* If someone leaves one country to go and become a citizen of another, he **emigrates** or is an **emigrant** from the country that he leaves, and the practice is called **emigration**: *a ship full of* **emigrants** *leaving Liverpool|to* **emigrate** *to Australia.* From the point of view of the country he enters, the same person is an **immigrant,** or **immigrates** (not a common word) and the practice is called **immigration**: *to pass through* **Immigration** *Control at the port|English language classes for* **immigrants**. —compare IMMIGRATE

ém·i·gré /'emɪgreɪ/ *n Fr* a person who leaves his own country, usu. for political reasons, esp. one who left France after the French Revolution or Russia after the Russian Revolution

em·i·nence /'emɪnəns/ *n* **1** [U] the quality of being famous and of a high rank, esp. in learning, science, the arts, etc.: *to reach/win eminence as a painter/a scientist* **2** [C] *fml* a hill or high ground: *The tower had been built on a small eminence*

Eminence *n* [C9;N9,(N)] the title given to a man holding high religious rank (a CARDINAL) in the ROMAN CATHOLIC church (esp. in the phrs. **His/Your Eminence**; **Their Eminences**)

em·i·nent /'emɪnənt/ *adj* (of people) famous and admired; having EMINENCE (1): *The most eminent doctors treated the king in his illness*

em·i·nent·ly /'emɪnəntli/ *apprec* (of qualities or abilities) unusually: *Your decision was eminently fair*

e·mir /e'mɪə^r/ *n* (*often cap.*) a Muslim ruler, esp. in Asia and parts of Africa

e·mir·ate /e'mɪəreɪt, -rɪ̈t/ *n* the position, state, power, lands, etc., of an EMIR

em·is·sa·ry /'emɪ̈səri‖-seri/ *n* [(*of*)] a person who is sent with an official message, often secret, or who is sent to do special work, often unpleasant

e·mis·sion /ɪ'mɪʃən/ *n* **1** [C;U] an act or the action of EMITting: *the sun's emission of light|the emission of smoke and ashes from Vesuvius* **2** [C] something which is EMITted **3** [U;C] the passing out of male sexual liquid (SEMEN) from the male organ, or the liquid itself

e·mit /ɪ'mɪt/ *v* **-tt-** [T1] to send out (esp. heat, light, smell, sound): *The chimney emitted a cloud of smoke.|*(fig.) *John emitted a few curses*

Em·men·ta·ler, -thaler /'eməntɑːlə^r/ also **Swiss cheese**— *n* [U] a type of cheese of Swiss origin with a not very strong nutlike taste and large holes

e·mol·li·ent /ɪ'mɒliənt‖ɪ'mɑ-/ *n, adj* [Wa5;B;C;U] (something, esp. a medicine) which softens the skin and cures it when it is sore: *an emollient against sunburn*

e·mol·u·ment /ɪˈmɒljʊmənt‖ɪˈmɑljə-/ *n* [*usu. pl.*] *fml* money or other form of profit received for work; wage: *a small weekly emolument|Emoluments connected with this position include free education for the children* —compare SALARY; see PAY² (USAGE)

e·mote /ɪˈməʊt/ *v* [I∅] *infml* to express feelings in a violent manner, as if in a play or film: *The actress was emoting in front of the cameras*

e·mo·tion /ɪˈməʊʃən/ *n* **1** [C] any of the strong feelings of the human spirit: *Love, hatred, and grief are emotions.|His speech had an effect on our emotions rather than on our reason* **2** [U] strength of feeling; excited state of the feelings: *He described the accident in a voice shaking with emotion* —**~less** *adj* —**~lessly** *adv* —**~lessness** *n* [U]

e·mo·tion·al /ɪˈməʊʃənəl/ *adj* **1** (of people) having feelings which are strong or easily moved: *Women are often said to be more emotional than men* —opposite **unemotional** **2** (of words, literature, music, etc.) **a** showing strong feeling **b** able to cause strong feeling; EMOTIVE **3** with regard to the EMOTIONs (1): *He has emotional difficulties*

e·mo·tion·al·is·m /ɪˈməʊʃənəlɪzəm/ *n* the quality of feeling or showing too much EMOTION (2), and of yielding too much to it —**-ist** *n*

e·mo·tion·al·ly /ɪˈməʊʃənəli/ *adv* **1** [Wa5] with regard to the EMOTIONs (1): *Emotionally (speaking), I feel great sympathy with you, but I still think you are wrong* **2** in an EMOTIONAL (2) manner: *She wept loudly and behaved very emotionally*

e·mo·tive /ɪˈməʊtɪv/ *adj* which causes or may cause strong feeling; EMOTIONAL (2b): *"Home" is a much more emotive word than "house"* —**~ly** *adv*

em·pan·el, im- /ɪmˈpænl/ *v* **-ll-** (*AmE* **-l-**) [T1] *fml* **1** [(*for, as*)] to put (a person's name) on the list (PANEL) of people who will serve on a JURY (=12 people in a court of law who decide whether the prisoner is guilty) **2** to choose (a JURY) from the list (PANEL): *The judge said that they would have to empanel a new* JURY

em·pa·thy /ˈempəθi/ *n* [S;U: (*with*)] **1** the power or state of imagining oneself to be another person, and so of sharing his ideas and feelings: *She feels great empathy with her little son* —compare SYMPATHY (1) **2** the power or state of imagining that a work of art or an object of nature shares one's own feelings, and therefore of understanding and enjoying it: *His acting of "Hamlet" showed great empathy with the character*

em·pe·ror /ˈempərəʳ/ *n* (*fem.* **empress**) the head of an empire

em·pha·sis /ˈemfəsɨs/ *n* **-ses** /siːz/ [C;U: (*on, upon*)] special force given to certain words, ideas, or details, in speaking, writing, drawing, etc., to show that they are particularly important: *This dictionary places/lays/puts a special emphasis on grammar.|"You're not coming, are you?" he said, with great emphasis on "you're"* (=he said the word slowly and loudly)

em·pha·size, -ise /ˈemfəsaɪz/ *v* [T1] to place EMPHASIS on: *The band emphasized the beats in the music to show that it was a marching tune*

em·phat·ic /ɪmˈfætɪk/ *adj* **1** expressed with EMPHASIS: *He answered the question with an emphatic "No"* **2** (of ideas, beliefs, etc.) strongly held: *It is my emphatic opinion that . . .* **3** (of events) perfectly certain and noticeable: *an emphatic success/honour/victory*

em·phat·ic·al·ly /ɪmˈfætɪkəli/ *adv* **1** in a manner that shows EMPHASIS: *"Certainly not," he said emphatically* **2** most certainly: *It is emphatically necessary to build more houses*

em·phy·se·ma /ˌemfɨˈsiːmə/ *n* [U] *med* a diseased condition in which the lungs become swollen with air, causing difficulty in breathing and often preventing the proper action of the heart

em·pire /ˈempaɪəʳ/ *n* **1** [C] (*often cap.*) a group of countries under one government, usu. ruled by an EMPEROR: (fig.) *the industrial empire of Standard Oil* **2** [U] the power that holds such a group together: *the cares and anxieties of empire*

Empire *n* [A] **1** (esp. of dress and furniture) (belonging to, fashionable in) the period of Napoleon I of France, 1804–15 **2 the First Empire** (in France) the period of Napoleon I **3 the Second Empire** (in France) the period of Napoleon III, 1852–70

em·pir·i·cal /ɪmˈpɪrɪkəl/ *adj* (of people or methods) guided only by practical experience rather than by scientific ideas out of books —**-cally** *adv* [Wa4]

em·pir·i·cis·m /ɪmˈpɪrɨsɪzəm/ *n* [U] the system of working by EMPIRICAL methods —**-cist** *n*

em·place·ment /ɪmˈpleɪsmənt/ *n* a special position prepared for a heavy gun to stand on

em·plane /ɪmˈpleɪn/ also (*esp. AmE*) **enplane**— *v* [I∅;T1] *fml* to (cause to) get onto an aircraft

em·ploy¹ /ɪmˈplɔɪ/ *v* **1** [T1 (*as*); V3] to use (a person) as a paid worker: *The firm employs about 100 men.|We employ her as an adviser* —compare UNEMPLOYED (1) **2** [T1,V3] to take on or appoint (a person) as a paid worker: *We're employing 3 new secretaries next Monday* **3** [T1 (*as*)] *fml* to use: *The police had to employ force (in order) to break up the crowd.|This bird employs its beak as a weapon* **4** [T1 (*in*)] *fml* to spend (time): *She employs all her free time in sewing* —see BUSY (USAGE), HIRE² (USAGE)

employ² *n* [U] *fml* employment

em·ploy·a·ble /ɪmˈplɔɪəbəl/ *adj* (of a person) suitable to be employed —opposite **unemployable**

em·ploy·ee /ɪmˈplɔɪ-iː, ˌemplɔɪˈiː/ *n* [(*of*)] a person who is employed: *a Government employee* —see OFFICER (USAGE)

em·ploy·er /ɪmˈplɔɪəʳ/ *n* a person who employs others

employ in *v prep* [V4b *often pass.*] *fml* to keep (oneself or another) busy in (doing something): *She was employed in watering the garden*

em·ploy·ment /ɪmˈplɔɪmənt/ *n* **1** [U] the state of being EMPLOYed (1) —opposite **unemployment** **2** [U9] the act of EMPLOYing (3) **3** [C] *fml* a way of EMPLOYing oneself IN doing something: *Gardening is a pleasant employment for Sunday afternoon*

employment a·gen·cy /ˈ·ˈ·· ˌ···/ *n* a private business which makes a profit by helping people to find work or workers

employment ex·change /·ˈ·· ·ˌ·/ also **labour exchange**— *n fml* (in Britain) a Government office which helps those who want work or workers

em·po·ri·um /ɪmˈpɔːrɪəm‖ɪmˈpor-/ *n* **-riums** *or* **-ria** /rɪə/ *fml* **1** a market; large shop or (*esp. AmE*) store **2** a centre for trade: *Singapore, a great emporium of the East*

em·pow·er /ɪmˈpaʊəʳ/ *v* [V3 *often pass.*] *fml* to give (someone) the power or lawful right (to do something): *The new law empowered the police to search private houses* —compare ENABLE (2), ENTITLE (2)

em·press /ˈemprɨs/ *n* [(*of*)] **1** the wife of an EMPEROR **2** a female EMPEROR

emp·ti·ly /ˈemptɨli/ *adv* in an EMPTY¹ (5) way

emp·ty¹ /ˈempti/ *adj* **1** [Wa5] containing nothing: *an empty cup* **2** [Wa5] (of a house or building) with nobody in it; in which nobody is living: *There are 3 empty houses in our street* **3** [Wa1; (*of*)] not having the contents which are usually there: *He drove through streets empty of traffic* **4** [Wa5] *infml* hungry (in the phr. **to feel empty**) **5** [Wa5; (*of*)] *derog* (of words, talk, etc.) without sense or purpose; meaningless, unreal: *empty promises* **6 on an empty stomach** not having eaten anything, esp. breakfast —**emptiness** *n* [U]

empty² *v* **1** [T1] to make EMPTY¹ (1): *They emptied the bottle* (=drank all that was in it) **2** [I∅ (*into*)] (of a place, a container, etc.) to send or move its contents somewhere else: *The room emptied very quickly.*|*The River Nile empties* (*flows*) *into the Mediterranean Sea* **3** [(OUT, *into, onto*)] to put or move (the contents of a container) somewhere else: *He emptied out all his pockets onto the table*

empty³ *n* [*usu. pl*] a container or vehicle that has been emptied: *He took all the empties* (=empty bottles) *back to the shop*

empty-hand·ed /ˌ·· ˈ··/ *adj* [Wa5] (of people) with nothing in the hands, esp. because nothing has been gained or obtained

empty-head·ed /ˌ·· ˈ··◂/ *adj infml* (of people) foolish and silly

empty set /ˌ·· ˈ·/ *n* [*the*+R] *tech* NULL SET

em·pur·pled /ɪmˈpɜːpəld‖-ɜr-/ *adj lit* that has become purple

em·py·re·al /ˌempɪˈriːəl, ˌempaɪ-/ also **empyrean**— *adj* [Wa5;A] *lit* of the EMPYREAN: *empyreal heights*

em·py·re·an /ˌempɪˈriːən, ˌempaɪ-/ *n* [*the*+R] *lit* (*often cap.*) the highest part of heaven, where (in former times) God was said to live; sky

e·mu /ˈiːmjuː/ *n* [Wn1] a large Australian bird, smaller than the OSTRICH, which runs well but cannot fly

em·u·late /ˈemjʊleɪt‖ˈemjə-/ *v* [T1] to try to do as well as or better than (another person)

em·u·la·tion /ˌemjʊˈleɪʃən‖ˌemjə-/ *n* [U (*of*)] the act or state of emulating (EMULATE): *The young man worked hard in emulation of his famous father*

e·mul·si·fy /ɪˈmʌlsǰfaɪ/ *v* [T1] *tech* to make into an EMULSION

e·mul·sion¹ /ɪˈmʌlʃən/ *n* [C;U] **1 a** a creamy mixture of liquids which do not really unite, such as oil and water **b** a medicine that is made in this way **2** the substance on the surface of a photographic film which makes it sensitive to light **3** *infml* EMULSION PAINT —**-sive** /ɪˈmʌlsɪv/ *adj*

emulsion² *v* [I∅;T1;X7] *infml* to paint (something) with EMULSION PAINT; *We emulsioned the bathroom yellow*

emulsion paint /·ˌ·· ˈ·/ *n* [C;U] any of several types of paint in which the colour is mixed into an EMULSION, and which are not shiny when they dry

en- /ɪn/ *prefix* **1** [*n, v→v*] to put or get into: ENDANGER|ENTRAIN **2** [*n, adj→v*] to cause to be: ENRICH|ENLARGE|ENSLAVE

-en /ən/ *suffix* **1** [*n→adj*] made of: EARTHEN *pots*|*a* GOLDEN *crown* **2** [*n, adj→v*] also (*after* -e) **-n**— to cause to be or have; become: DARKEN|STRENGTHEN|RIPEN

en·a·ble /ɪˈneɪbəl/ *v* [Wv3] **1** [V3] to make (a creature) able (to do something): *This bird's large wings enable it to fly very fast* **2** [V3] to give (someone) the power, means, or right (to do something): *The new law enables a man to claim money from the State if he has no work* —compare EMPOWER, ENTITLE **3** [T1] to make (something) possible or easy: *This dictionary will enable better international understanding* **4** [T1] to allow (something): *a new law enabling the opening of shops on Sundays* —compare EMPOWER, ENTITLE

en·a·bling /ɪˈneɪblɪŋ/ *adj* [Wa5;A] (of a law) that allows or makes possible (esp. in the phr. **enabling legislation**=the law that allows a new State to join the US)

en·act /ɪˈnækt/ *v* [T1] **1** [*often pass.*] (of the Government) to make or pass (a law) (note the phr. **Be it further enacted that . . .**) **2** to perform or represent (a part of a play)

en·act·ment /ɪˈnæktmənt/ *n fml* **1** [U (*of*)] the act or practice of ENACTing: *the enactment of a scene from a play* **2** [C] a law: *The following enactments have been passed . . .*

e·nam·el¹ /ɪˈnæməl/ *v* **-ll-** (*AmE* **-l-**) [Wv5;T1] to cover or ornament with ENAMEL

enamel² *n* [U] **1** a glassy substance which is melted at a very high temperature, and put as an ornament or protection onto objects made of metal or clay, such as kitchen pots and pans or car bodies **2** a kind of paint which is used esp. on wood to produce a very shiny (GLOSSY) surface when it dries —compare EMULSION PAINT **3** the hard smooth outer surface of the teeth —see picture at TOOTH

e·nam·el·ware /ɪˈnæməlweəʳ/ *n* [U] metal pots and pans for the kitchen which are covered with ENAMEL² (1)

en·am·oured, *AmE* **enamored** /ɪˈnæməd‖-ərd/ *adj* [F9, esp. *of, with*] very fond of; liking very much; charmed by: *He's so* (*much*) *enamoured of his own plan that he won't listen to me*

en·camp /ɪnˈkæmp/ *v* [I∅ (*at, on, in*)] **1** to make a camp: *We'd better encamp for the night* **2 be encamped** to be in one's camp; have encamped: *The soldiers are encamped on the hill, where they have been encamped for months*

en·camp·ment /ɪnˈkæmpmənt/ *n* a large camp, esp. military; place where soldiers are encamped

en·cap·su·late /ɪnˈkæpsjʊleɪt‖-sə-/ *v* [T1 (*in*)] **1** to enclose in or as if in a small case (CAPSULE) **2** to reduce to a short form (facts, information, etc.)

en·case /ɪnˈkeɪs/ *v* [T1 (*in*) *often pass.*] to cover completely (as) with a case: *His body was encased in shining armour*

en·caus·tic /ɪnˈkɔːstɪk/ *adj* [Wa5] (of bricks, TILEs, etc.) with the colours burnt in

-ence /əns/ *suffix* [*v→n*] -ANCE: REFERENCE| *existence*|OCCURRENCE| *an* OCCURRENCE

en·ceph·a·li·tis /ɪnˌsefəˈlaɪtǰs/ *n* [U] *med* INFLAMMATION of the brain

en·chain /ɪnˈtʃeɪn/ *v* [T1 (*in, with, by*)] **1** to put or hold in chains **2** to hold (the attention, the will, etc.) as if in chains —**~ment** *n* [U]

en·chant /ɪnˈtʃɑːnt‖ɪnˈtʃænt/ *v* [Wv5;T1] **1** [(*by, with*) *often pass.*] to fill (someone) with delight: *He was enchanted by/with the idea* **2** to use magic on: *a palace in an enchanted wood*

en·chant·er /ɪnˈtʃɑːntəʳ‖ɪnˈtʃæn-/ *fem.* **en·chant·ress** /-trǰs/— *n* a person who **a** uses magic or **b** is ENCHANTING

en·chant·ing /ɪnˈtʃɑːntɪŋ‖ɪnˈtʃæn-/ *adj apprec* delightful: *an enchanting child* —**~ly** *adv*

en·chant·ment /ɪnˈtʃɑːntmənt‖ɪnˈtʃænt-/ *n* **1** [C] the act or result of using a piece of magic to ENCHANT: *A wicked woman laid an enchantment on the princess* **2** [U;C] a delightful influence: *The beauty of the scene filled us with enchantment*

en·ci·pher /ɪnˈsaɪfəʳ/ also **cipher**— *v* [T1;(I∅)] to put (a message) into secret writing (a CIPHER) —compare DECIPHER

en·cir·cle /ɪnˈsɜːkəl‖-ɜr-/ *v* [T1 (*by, with, in*) *often pass.*] to surround; make a circle round: *a house encircled by/with trees*|*He encircled her in his arms* —**~ment** *n* [U]

en·clave /ˈenkleɪv, ˈeŋ-/ *n Fr* a part of a country, or a group of people of a separate race or nation, which is completely surrounded by another

en·close /ɪnˈkləʊz/ *v* [Wv5;T1 (*by, in*) *often pass.*] **1** to surround with a fence or wall so as to shut in or close: *an enclosed religious* ORDER¹ (16) *with few visits from outsiders* **2** to put (esp. something sent with a letter) inside: *I enclose a cheque for £50.00 (with this letter)*

en·clo·sure /ɪn'kləʊʒəʳ/ *n* **1** [U (*of*)] the act of enclosing a piece of land: *People must fight against the enclosure of land that is not privately owned* **2** [C] a piece of land that is enclosed **3** [C] something that is put in with a letter

en·code /ɪn'kəʊd/ *v* [Wv5;T1] to turn (a message) into CODE (an agreed arrangement by which certain signs are given a special secret meaning) —compare DECODE

en·co·mi·um /ɪn'kəʊmɪəm/ *n* **-miums** *or* **-mia** /mɪə/ *fml* an expression of very high praise

en·com·pass /ɪn'kʌmpəs/ *v* [T1] *fml* **1** [(*with*) *often pass.*] to surround on all sides: *He is encompassed with doubts.|The enemy encompassed the city* **2** also **compass**— to succeed in causing (usu. a bad result): *He encompassed by a trick the ruin of his enemies*

en·core[1] /'ɒŋkɔːʳ‖'ɑŋ-/ *n Fr* **1** a call (=Please do it again!) which is made by listeners who are pleased with a song or other performance **2** a song or other performance which is given again because it is asked for —**encore** *interj*

encore[2] *v* [T1] to express approval of (a performer or a performance) by shouting "ENCORE!"

en·coun·ter[1] /ɪn'kaʊntəʳ/ *v* [T1] *fml* **1** to meet or be faced by (something bad, esp. a danger or a difficulty): *He encountered many difficulties* **2** to meet unexpectedly: *He encountered a friend on the road*

encounter[2] *n* [*with*] a sudden meeting (usu. either unexpected or dangerous)

encounter group /'·'·· ·/ *n* a group of people who meet together for training in greater sensitivity to their own and one another's feelings

en·cour·age /ɪn'kʌrɪdʒ‖ɪn'kɜr-/ *v* [Wv4:T1 (*in*); V3] to give courage or hope to (someone); urge (someone) on to fresh efforts: *They encourage the children to paint pictures.|Don't encourage her laziness by doing things for her* —**-agingly** *adv*

en·cour·age·ment /ɪn'kʌrɪdʒmənt‖ɪn'kɜr-/ *n* **1** [U] the act of encouraging: *He owed his success to his wife's encouragement* **2** [C] something which encourages: *Your words were a great encouragement to me*

en·croach /ɪn'krəʊtʃ/ *v* [I∅ (*on, upon*)] to go beyond, or take more than, what is right, usual, or natural: *The sea is encroaching upon the land all along the coast*

en·croach·ment /ɪn'krəʊtʃmənt/ *n* [U;C:(*on, upon*)] the act or result of ENCROACHing

en·crust /ɪn'krʌst/ *v* [T1 (*with*) *usu. pass.*] to cover (a surface) with a thin hard outer covering, sometimes for ornament: *a gold crown encrusted with jewels|boots encrusted in mud*

en·cum·ber /ɪn'kʌmbəʳ/ *v* [T1 (*with*) *often pass.*] **1** to make free action or movement difficult for (someone): *He is encumbered with debts* **2** to fill (a place) inconveniently full: *The room was encumbered with heavy furniture*

en·cum·brance /ɪn'kʌmbrəns/ *n* a person or thing that ENCUMBERs (1)

-en·cy /ənsi/ *suffix* [→*n*] -ANCY: *a tendency*

en·cyc·li·cal /ɪn'sɪklɪkəl/ also **encyclical let·ter** /·,···'··/— *n* a letter sent round by the head of the Church of Rome (the POPE) to all his churches

en·cy·clo·pe·di·a, -paedia /ɪn,saɪklə'piːdɪə/ *n* a book or set of books dealing with every branch of knowledge, or with one particular branch, in alphabetical order: *A dictionary explains words and an encyclopedia explains facts*

en·cy·clo·pe·dic, -paedic /ɪn,saɪklə'piːdɪk/ *adj approv* (of knowledge, memory, etc.) wide and full, like the contents of an ENCYCLOPEDIA —**~ally** *adv* [Wa4]

end[1] /end/ *n* [(*of*)] **1** [C] the point(s) where something stops, or beyond which it does not exist: *the ends of a rope/of a stick/of a box|the end of the road/of the railway line* **2** [C] the furthest point from here: *the ends of the earth* (=the furthest parts, most difficult to reach)|*He's down at the end of the garden* **3** [C] the latest point in time or in order: *the end of the year/of his life* **4** [C *often pl.*] a little piece that is left over: *cigarette ends* —see also ODDS AND ENDS **5** [C *often pl.*] an aim or purpose: *He wants to buy a house, and is saving money to/for this end* **6** [C] *euph* death: *His end was peaceful* **7** [C9] a particular part of a business: *My partner looks after the advertising end* **8 at a loose end** *AmE* **at loose ends**— having nothing to do: *Can I help you? I'm at a loose end this morning* **9 at an end** finished **10 at the deep end** in the most difficult part (of a job) **11 begin/start at the wrong end** to begin/start in the wrong place, or not at the proper beginning **12 come/draw to an end** (of something which goes on for some time) to finish: *The year was drawing to an end* **13 the (absolute) end** *infml* (used as an expression of amused or weak disapproval) a very bad thing or person: *The party was the absolute end. There wasn't even enough to drink* **14 end on** with the points or the narrow sides hitting each other: *The 2 trains hit each other end on* **15 end to end** with the points or the narrow sides touching each other: *We can provide seats for 10 people if we place these 2 tables end to end* —compare END[1] (14) **on 16 get (hold of) the wrong end of the stick** to get a wrong idea which is exactly opposite to the right idea; misunderstand completely **17 get one's end away** *BrE euph sl* to have sex **18 get the dirty end of the stick** *infml*— to be unfairly treated or given the most unpleasant job **19 go off the deep end** to lose control of oneself; become angry **20 in the end** at last: *He tried many times to pass the examination, and in the end he succeeded* **21 keep one's end up** *infml esp. BrE* to go on facing difficulties bravely and successfully **22 loose ends** parts not properly completed: *The committee's report was very good, but there are just a few loose ends* **23 make an end of** *fml* to finish (esp. something one is doing oneself): *Let us make an end of this foolish quarrel!* —compare **put an** END[1] (27) **to 24 make (both) ends meet** to get just enough money for one's needs **25 no end of** *infml* **a** an endless amount of; very great deal of: *It'll cost no end of money!* **b** (used for giving force to an expression): *They're having no end of a good time* **26 on end a** (of time) continuously: *He sat there for hours on end* **b** upright: *We had to stand the table on end to get it through the door* **27 put an end to** to stop from happening any more —compare **make an** END[1] (23) **of 28 without end** endless; never finishing

end[2] *v* [I∅;T1] to (cause to) finish: *The party ended at midnight.|The war ended in 1975.|He ended his letter with good wishes to the family* —see also END IN, END OFF, END UP

en·dan·ger /ɪn'deɪndʒəʳ/ *v* [T1] to cause danger to: *You will endanger your health if you work so hard*

en·dear·ing /ɪn'dɪərɪŋ/ *adj* that ENDEARs one TO someone: *an endearing smile* —**~ly** *adv*

en·dear·ment /ɪn'dɪəmənt‖ɪn'dɪər-/ *n* [C;U] (an expression of) love: *He was whispering endearments to her*

en·dear to /ɪn'dɪəʳ/ *v prep* [D1 *no pass.*] to cause (someone, esp. oneself) to be loved (by someone): *His kindness endeared him to everyone*

en·deav·our[1], *AmE* **-or** /ɪn'devəʳ/ *v* [I3] *fml* to try: *He endeavoured to climb the mountain*

endeavour², *AmE* **-or** *n* [C;U:(3)] *fml* an effort; attempt: *The sick man made no endeavour to get better*

en·dem·ic /en'demɪk, ɪn-/ *adj* [Wa5; (*in, to*)] (esp. of diseases) found regularly in a particular place: *an endemic disease of the chest among miners* —compare EPIDEMIC

end game /'· ·/ *n* the last stage in the game of CHESS, when most of the playing pieces have been taken from the board

end in *v prep* [L1;V4a] to result in: *The battle ended in a victory|in everyone going home*

end·ing /'endɪŋ/ *n* the end, esp. of a story, film, play, or word: *Children like stories with happy endings*

en·dive /'endɪv‖'endaɪv/ *n* **1** [C] a type of plant with curly green leaves which are eaten raw **2** [C; U] *AmE* CHICORY

end·less /'endləs/ *adj* [Wa5] **1** never finishing: *The journey seemed endless* **2** *tech* (of a belt, a chain, etc.) circular; with the ends joined: *The machine drives an endless belt* —**~ly** *adv*

en·do·crine /'endəʊkrɪn, -kraɪn/ *adj* [Wa5;A] *med* making substances (HORMONE*s*) which are poured directly into the BLOODSTREAM of the body

endocrine gland /ˌ··· '·/ also **ductless gland**— *n* *med* any of several organs of the body (the PITUITARY, THYROID, etc., GLAND*s*) which pour HORMONE*s* into the BLOODSTREAM of the body

end off *v adv* [T1 (*by, with*)] to finish (something), esp. suitably

en·dorse, in- /ɪn'dɔːs‖-ɔrs/ *v* [T1] **1** to write one's name on (the back of) (a cheque, bill, etc.) **2** [*usu. pass.*] *esp. BrE* to write a note on (a driving LICENCE) to say that the driver has broken the law **3** *fml* to express approval or support of (opinions, actions, etc.): *I fully endorse your opinions on this subject* —**~ment** *n* [U;C]

en·dow /ɪn'daʊ/ *v* [T1] to give (as to a school) a large amount of money which brings in a yearly amount for use: *He spent all his large fortune on endowing a hospital*

en·dow·ment /ɪn'daʊmənt/ *n* **1** [U] the act of ENDOWing: *He spent his money on the endowment of schools* **2** [C *usu. pl.*] the money that an organization receives when it has been ENDOWed **3** [C *usu. pl.*] the natural qualities that a person is ENDOWed WITH

endowment pol·i·cy /·'·· ˌ···/ *n tech* an arrangement by which a person pays money regularly over a number of years so that an agreed amount will be paid to him at the end of that time, or to his family if he dies first; type of insurance

endow with *v prep* [DI *usu. pass.*] *apprec* to make rich from birth with (any good quality or ability): *She is endowed with both beauty and brains*

end·pa·per /'endˌpeɪpə^r/ *n* [*usu. pl.*] a piece of paper, usu. without any printing on it, which is stuck inside the cover at the beginning or end of a book

end prod·uct /'· ˌ··/ *n tech* something which is produced as the result of a number of operations: *Our raw material is oil, and our end product is nylon stockings* —compare BY-PRODUCT

en·due with, in- /ɪn'djuː‖ɪn'duː/ *v prep* [DI *often pass.*] *fml* to supply (someone) with (a good quality): *He prayed to God night and day to endue him with the spirit of holiness*

end up *v adv* [L1,4,7,9] to finish (esp. in a particular place or way): *He ended up (as) head of the firm.|We may end up in China*

en·dur·ance /ɪn'djʊərəns‖ɪn'dʊər-/ *n* [U] **1** the state or power of enduring (ENDURE (1)): *Long-distance races are won by the runners with the greatest endurance* **2 beyond/past endurance** impossible to bear any longer

endurance test /·'·· ·/ *n* a test of one's power to ENDURE (2b) under difficult conditions

en·dure /ɪn'djʊə^r‖ɪn'dʊə^r/ *v* **1** [T1,3,4 *often nonassertive*] to bear (pain, suffering, etc.): *Be quiet! I can't endure that noise a moment longer* —see BEAR² (USAGE) **2** [IØ] *fml* **a** to last: *He is a great writer, and his books will endure for ever* **b** to remain alive and unweakened: *They had spent 3 days in the desert without water, and could not endure much longer* —**-durable** *adj* [*often nonassertive*]

en·dur·ing /ɪn'djʊərɪŋ‖ɪn'dʊər-/ *adj* that ENDURE*s* (2a): *He has enduring memories of her kindness to him* —**~ly** *adv*

end·ways /'endweɪz/ also **end·wise** /-waɪz/— *adv* [Wa5; (ON)] **1** with the end forward; not sideways: *The box is quite narrow when you look at it endways (on)* **2** end to end (END¹ (15)): *Put the tables together endways*

en·e·ma /'enɨmə/ *n* (an instrument used for) the action of introducing liquid (such as medicine) into the bowels, through the RECTUM

en·e·my /'enəmi/ *n* **1** a person who hates or dislikes another person; one of 2 or more people who hate or dislike each other: *His behaviour made him many enemies* (=made many people dislike him).|*John and Paul are enemies* (=of each other) **2** someone or something that hurts, wants to harm, or is against (someone or something): *The army advanced to meet the enemy.|William Wilberforce was the enemy of slavery*

en·er·get·ic /ˌenə'dʒetɪk‖-ər-/ *adj* full of ENERGY (1): *an energetic tennis player* —**~ally** *adv* [Wa4]

en·er·gize, -ise /'enədʒaɪz‖-ər-/ *v* [T1] *tech* to give ENERGY to

en·er·gy /'enədʒi‖-ər-/ *n* [U] **1** (of people) the quality of being full of life and action; power and ability to do a lot of work: *Young people usually have more energy than the old* **2** [*often pl. with same meaning*] the power which one can use in working: *to* APPLY/DEVOTE *all one's energies to a job|to* CONCENTRATE *one's energy on it* **3** the power which does work and drives machines: *atomic/electrical energy|the energy of the sun*

en·er·vate /'enəveɪt‖-ər-/ *v* [Wv4;T1] (of non-material things) to make weak: *He was enervated by his long illness*

en fa·mille /ˌɒn fæ'miː‖ˌɑn- (*Fr* ɑ̃ famij)/ *adv* [F] *Fr* at home; among the family

en·fant ter·ri·ble /ˌɒnfɒn te'riːblə‖ˌɑnfɑn- (*Fr* ɑ̃fɑ̃ tɛribl)/ *n* **enfants terribles** (*same pronunciation*) *Fr* **1** a shocking but also often amusing person **2** a child who makes himself socially troublesome by asking awkward questions, telling people's secrets in public, etc.

en·fee·ble /ɪn'fiːbəl/ *v* [T1 *often pass.*] to make (someone) weak: *He was enfeebled by his long illness* —**~ment** *n* [U]

en·fi·lade¹ /'enfɨleɪd, -lɑːd/ *n* [U;S] *Fr* gunfire directed from end to end of a line of soldiers in battle

enfilade² *v* [T1] *Fr* to direct ENFILADE gunfire on

en·fold /ɪn'fəʊld/ *v* [T1 (*in*)] *fml* **1** to enclose, esp. in one's arms: *She enfolded the child lovingly in her arms* **2** [*often pass.*] to wrap up: *The old lady was enfolded in a heavy woollen garment*

en·force /ɪn'fɔːs‖-ors/ *v* [T1] **1** to cause (a rule or law) to be carried out effectively: *Governments make laws and the police enforce them* **2** [Wv5; (*on, upon*)] to make (something) happen, esp. by threats or force: *The shipwrecked sailor spent a year of enforced silence alone in the desert* **3** to give greater force to (an argument, a piece of advice, etc.); REINFORCE: *He enforced his statement by producing facts and figures* —**~able** *adj* —**~ment** *n* [U]

en·fran·chise /ɪn'fræntʃaɪz/ *v* [T1 *often pass.*] **1** to give FRANCHISE (the right to vote at elections) to —see also SUFFRAGE (1) **2** to free (slaves) —**~ment** /-tʃɪ̈zmənt/ *n* [U]

en·gage /ɪn'geɪdʒ/ *v* **1** [T1 (*as*); V3] to arrange to employ (someone): *to engage a new secretary* —see HIRE[2] (USAGE) **2** [T1] *fml* to order (a room, seat, etc.) to be kept for one: *I've engaged a room at the hotel* **3** [IØ (*with*); T1] **a** (of parts of a machine) to fasten onto, fit into, or lock together: *This wheel engages with that wheel and turns it* **b** to cause (parts of a machine) to do this: *You must engage the* CLUTCH (*of a car*) **4** [T3,5;V3] *fml* to bind (oneself) by a promise: *He engaged* (*himself*) *to pay back the money* **5** [T1] to take up (time, thought, attention, etc.): *The spots of blood on the floor engaged the attention of the police* **6** [T1 (*in*)] *fml* to attack: *They engaged the enemy* (*in battle*)

en·ga·gé /ˌɒŋgæ'ʒeɪ‖ˌɑŋgɑ- (*Fr* ɑ̃gɑʒe)/ *adj* [F] *Fr* actively concerned with political questions (esp. on the LEFT[2] (3)); COMMITTED

en·gaged /ɪn'geɪdʒd/ *adj* [Wa5] **1** [F (*in, on*)] (of people) busy: *Can you come on Monday? No, I'm engaged* (=I've arranged to do something).|*engaged in writing the history of Rome/on a long study of Roman history* —see also ENGAGE IN (1), ENGAGE UPON **2** [F] *AmE* **busy**— (of a telephone line) in use: *Sorry! The line/the number is engaged* **3** [F] (of seats, tables, and rooms in public places) kept for someone to use later; RESERVED: *Is this seat engaged?* **4** [F (*to*) (F3)] having agreed to marry (note the phr. **an engaged couple**): *My daughter is engaged* (*to a nice young doctor*).|*Edward and I have got engaged.*|*They're engaged* (*to be married*)

engage for *v prep* [T1 *no pass.*] *fml* to take responsibility for: *I will engage for John's good behaviour should you decide to employ him*

engage in *v prep* **1** [T1;D1;V4b] to make oneself busy in; to (start to) spend one's time in: *to engage in politics/trade*|*The old lady engaged herself in making clothes for her neighbours' children* **2** [D1] to make (someone) join with one in: *I engaged him in conversation*

en·gage·ment /ɪn'geɪdʒmənt/ *n* **1** [C] an agreement to marry: *Have you heard that John has broken off his engagement to Mary?* (=said he no longer wishes to marry her) **2** [C] a promise to meet or go out with a person, or to do something: *I can't come out on Monday because I have an engagement* **3** [C] *fml* a formal promise, esp. in writing: *The Government has broken all its engagements* **4** [C] a battle: *Although it was only a short engagement, a lot of men were killed or wounded* **5** [U] (of parts of a machine) the act or result of engaging (ENGAGE (3a))

engagement ring /·'·· ·/ *n* a ring, usu. containing precious stones, which a man gives to a woman when they decide to marry

engage up·on *v prep* [T1] *fml* to begin: *engaged upon a new profession*

en·gag·ing /ɪn'geɪdʒɪŋ/ *adj apprec* charming: *engaging manners*|*an engaging smile* —**~ly** *adv*

en·gen·der /ɪn'dʒendəʳ/ *v* [T1] *fml* to produce or be the cause of (a state, condition, etc.): *Flies carry dirt, and dirt engenders disease*

en·gine /'endʒɪ̈n/ *n* **1** a piece of machinery with moving parts which changes power (from steam, electricity, oil, etc.) into movement: *the engine of a car* —see MACHINE[1] (USAGE) and picture at PETROL **2** also **locomotive**— a machine which pulls a railway train **3** FIRE ENGINE

-en·gined /ˌendʒɪ̈nd/ *comb. form* with ENGINEs (1) of a stated type or number: *a 4-engined aircraft*

engine driv·er /'·· ˌ··/ *AmE* **engineer**— *n BrE* a man who drives a railway engine

en·gi·neer[1] /ˌendʒɪ̈'nɪəʳ/ *n* **1** a person who plans and understands the making of machines, roads, bridges, harbours, etc.: *an electrical/a* CIVIL/*mining/*MECHANICAL *engineer*|*I'm in the* **Royal Engineers** (=branch of the British Army) **2** *AmE* ENGINE DRIVER **3** a skilled person who controls an engine or engines, esp. on a ship **4** *esp. BrE* a person who works with machines in a factory: *Fred is a member of the Engineers' Union*

engineer[2] *v* [T1] **1** [*often pass.*] to plan and make as an engineer does: *The mountain road is very well engineered* **2** to arrange or cause by clever secret planning: *He had powerful enemies who engineered his ruin*

en·gi·neer·ing /ˌendʒɪ̈'nɪərɪŋ/ *n* [U] **1** the science or profession of an ENGINEER[1] (1) **2** the act or result of ENGINEERing[2] (1): *The Queen admired the engineering of the new railway*

En·glish[1] /'ɪŋglɪʃ/ *adj* belonging to England, its people, etc.: *an English village*|*My father is English, but my mother is Scottish; they're both British*

English[2] *n* **1** [*the*+P] the people of England: *Why can't the English teach their children how to speak?* ("My Fair Lady") **2** [U;R] the language of England, the US, etc.: *This dictionary is written in English* **3 the Queen's/King's English** *apprec* good correct English, as spoken and written by educated people

English break·fast /ˌ·· '··/ *n* [C;(U)] a breakfast usu. consisting of cooked BACON and eggs followed by TOAST and MARMALADE, commonly eaten in England —compare CONTINENTAL BREAKFAST

English horn /ˌ·· '·/ *AmE* COR ANGLAIS

En·glish·man /'ɪŋglɪʃmən/ *fem.* **En·glish·wo·man** /-ˌwʊmən/— *n* **-men** /mən/ a British citizen born in England or of English parent(s)

English set·ter /ˌ·· '··/ *n* a type of fairly large, (partly) white dog, with a long head, a smooth silky coat and hairy tail and legs, used for hunting birds —compare IRISH SETTER

en·graft /ɪn'grɑːft‖ɪn'græft/ *v* [T1 (*into, on, onto, upon*)] **1** to join (a living branch or stem (SCION)) onto a living branch of another usu. stronger bush or tree of a related kind (STOCK(s)) in order to produce further growth: *to engraft a new rose onto a wild rose* **2** IMPLANT

en·grave /ɪn'greɪv/ *v* [D1+*with/on*; T1] **1** to cut (words, pictures, etc.) on wood, stone, or metal: (fig.) *The terrible memory was engraved on his mind/in his memory* **2** to prepare (special plates of metal) in this way, for printing —**engraver** *n*

en·grav·ing /ɪn'greɪvɪŋ/ *n* **1** [C;U] the art or work of an ENGRAVEr (1) **2** [C] a picture printed from an ENGRAVED (2) metal plate: *I bought an old engraving of London Bridge*

en·gross /ɪn'grəʊs/ *v* [T1] **1** [(*in*) *usu. pass.*] to fill completely the time and attention of: *He was so engrossed in his work that he completely forgot the time* **2** *tech* to copy (esp. law papers) in large handwriting or in formal style

en·gross·ing /ɪn'grəʊsɪŋ/ *adj* (not of a person) very interesting: *an engrossing book* —**~ly** *adv*

en·gulf /ɪn'gʌlf/ *v* [T1] (of the earth, the sea, etc.) to destroy by swallowing up: *The stormy sea engulfed the small boat*

en·hance /ɪn'hɑːns‖ɪn'hæns/ *v* [T1] to increase (good things such as value, power, or beauty): *The moonlight enhanced the beauty of the scene* —**~ment** *n* [C;U:(9)]

e·nig·ma /ɪ'nɪgmə/ *n* a person, thing or event that is mysterious and very hard to understand: *"The* *whole purpose of life," he said, "is an enigma. Why are we born?"*

en·ig·mat·ic /ˌenɪgˈmætɪk/ *adj* (of things, events or behaviour) mysterious and very hard to understand —**~ally** *adv* [Wa4]

en·join /ɪnˈdʒɔɪn/ *v* **1** [T1 (*on*), 4,5c;V3] *fml* to order (someone to do something or something to be done): *His religion enjoins praying.*|*He enjoined obedience on the soldiers* —see ORDER² (USAGE) **2** [T1 (*from*)] *AmE or law* to forbid (someone to do something or something to be done) by an official order: *The judge enjoined him from selling alcohol* —compare INJUNCTION

en·joy /ɪnˈdʒɔɪ/ *v* **1** [T1,4] to get happiness from (things and experiences): *enjoyed your dinner/a party/listening to music* **2** [T1] to possess or use (something good): *He has always enjoyed* (=had) *very good health* **3 enjoy oneself** to be happy; experience pleasure: *Did you enjoy yourself at the party?*
USAGE A verb after **enjoy** always ends in **-ing**: *I enjoyed meeting him.*

en·joy·a·ble /ɪnˈdʒɔɪəbəl/ *adj* (of things and experiences) pleasant: *an enjoyable holiday* —**-bly** *adv*

en·joy·ment /ɪnˈdʒɔɪmənt/ *n* **1** [C;U] the state or an example of ENJOYing (1): *He found great enjoyment in his work* **2** [(*the*) U9] the state of ENJOYing (2): *The enjoyment* (=possession) *of good health is a great advantage*

en·kin·dle /ɪnˈkɪndl/ *v* [T1] *lit* to cause (strong feelings such as anger or desire) to increase and burst out

en·large /ɪnˈlɑːdʒ‖-ɑr-/ *v* [IØ;T1] to (cause to) grow larger or wider: *This photograph probably won't enlarge well*

en·large·ment /ɪnˈlɑːdʒmənt‖-ɑr-/ *n* **1** [S9;U9] the act, state, or result of enlarging (ENLARGE): *After the enlargement of the farm, there was more work to do* **2** [C] a photograph that has been printed in a larger size than the original

enlarge on also **enlarge up·on**— *v prep* [T1] to add more length and detail to what has been said or written

en·light·en /ɪnˈlaɪtn/ *v* [T1] to cause to understand; free from false beliefs: *Peter thought the world was flat until I enlightened him!*

en·light·ened /ɪnˈlaɪtənd/ *adj apprec* not keeping to false beliefs; having true understanding: *to hold enlightened opinions*

en·light·en·ment /ɪnˈlaɪtənmənt/ *n* [U] **1** the act of ENLIGHTENing: *This law is so difficult to understand that only a lawyer can provide enlightenment* **2** *apprec* the state of having been ENLIGHTENed: *The family owed a great deal to the enlightenment of their mother's opinions about the bringing up of children*

Enlightenment *n* [*the*+R] the period in the 18th century in Europe, when certain thinkers taught that science and the free use of reason would improve the human condition

en·list /ɪnˈlɪst/ *v* **1** [T1;IØ] to (cause to) enter the armed forces: *He enlisted when he was 18.*|*We must enlist more men* **2** [T1] to obtain (help, sympathy, etc.): *Can I enlist your help in collecting money for the people made homeless by the flood?* —**~ment** *n* [C;U]

enlisted man /·ˈ·· ·/ *n AmE* a man (or woman) in the armed forces whose rank is below that of an officer

en·liv·en /ɪnˈlaɪvən/ *v* [T1] to make (people or events) more active, spirited, or cheerful

en masse /ˌɒn ˈmæs‖ˌɑn-/ *adv Fr* all together, in a mass or crowd

en·mesh /ɪnˈmeʃ/ *v* [T1 (*in*) *usu. pass.*] to catch in or as if in a net: (fig.) *He was enmeshed in his own lies*

en·mi·ty /ˈenmɪ̈ti/ *n* [C;U] the state or feeling of being an enemy or enemies: *He felt great enmity towards his brother.*|*John and Bill are at enmity (with each other)*

en·no·ble /ɪˈnəʊbəl/ *v* [T1] **1** to make (someone) a nobleman **2** to make (someone or something) better and more honourable: *His character has been ennobled by all his sufferings* —**~ment** *n* [U]

en·nui /ɒnˈwiː‖ɑn-/ *n* [U] *Fr* tiredness caused by lack of interest and having nothing to do: *Since he stopped working he has been suffering badly from ennui* —compare BOREdom⁶

e·nor·mity /ɪˈnɔːmɪ̈ti‖-ɔr-/ *n* **1** [U9] evil, greater than could ever be expected: *the enormity of his behaviour in murdering his wife and children* **2** [C *usu. pl.*] a very evil action: *Enormities have been* COMMIT*ted* (=done) *in some countries against black people* **3** [U9] the quality of ENORMOUSness, esp. of any difficulty: *the enormity of the job of feeding the whole world*

e·nor·mous /ɪˈnɔːməs‖-ɔr-/ *adj* [Wa5] very large indeed: *an enormous house/meal/amount of money* —**~ness** *n* [U]

e·nor·mous·ly /ɪˈnɔːməsli‖-ɔr-/ *adv* very much indeed: *enormously rich*|*it interests me enormously*

e·nough¹ /ɪˈnʌf/ *determiner* **1** [A;E: (*for*, 3)] as much of (a quantity) or as many of (a plural) as may be necessary: *We have enough seats for everyone.*|*enough money/money enough (for John) to buy a car* **2 fool enough** foolish ENOUGH² (1): *I was fool enough to believe him* **3 man enough** manly ENOUGH² (1): *Are you man enough for this dangerous job?*
USAGE 1 **Enough** can come before or after a plural or a mass noun (**enough** *money/people, money/people* **enough**) but must come after a singular count noun (*fool* **enough**). 2 **Enough**+*that* (*he's old* **enough** *that he can do it*) is quite common, particularly in *AmE*, but teachers and examiners do not like it. 3 **Sufficient** has the same meaning as **enough¹·³**, but is more formal. It is more often used for degree (**sufficient** *reason*) while **enough** is used for quantity. **Sufficiently** has the same meaning as **enough²**.

enough² *adv* **1** [(*for*, 3)] to the necessary amount or degree: *It's warm enough (to swim).*|*"a big enough house"* (SEU S.)|*He didn't run fast enough (to catch the train)* **2** not very but only rather: *She cooks well enough, and she would cook very well indeed if she took more trouble* **3 oddly/curiously/strangely enough**— although this is ODD/CURIOUS/strange: *He's lived in France for years, but strangely enough he can't speak a word of French* **4 fair enough** *infml* all right; satisfactory and reasonable: *"You can eat the ones I don't want." "That's fair enough!"* **5 sure enough** *infml* as expected: *He said he would come, and sure enough he came*

enough³ *pron* **1** a quantity or number which satisfies need: *I have enough to do.*|*Not enough is known about this subject.*|*I've had enough of your rudeness!* (=too much) **2 enough and to spare** more than is necessary **3 enough of a fool** foolish ENOUGH² (1) **4 enough of a man** manly ENOUGH² (1) **5 more than enough a** more than is necessary **b** too much

en pas·sant /ˌɒn ˈpæsɑ̃‖ˌɑn pɑˈsɑ̃ (*Fr* ɑ̃ pasɑ̃)/ *adv* [Wa5] *Fr* **1** in passing; by the WAY¹ (11b) **2** (in the game of CHESS) (used of the taking of a PAWN, as it makes a first move of 2 squares, by another PAWN that is in a position to threaten the first of these squares)

en·plane /ɪnˈpleɪn/ *v* [IØ;T1] *fml esp. AmE* EMPLANE

en·quire /ɪnˈkwaɪəʳ/ *v* [T1,6a,b (*fml of*); IØ (*about,*

after, concerning, for or *into*)] INQUIRE —see ASK (USAGE)
en·qui·ry /ɪn'kwaɪəri‖'ɪnkwaɪəri, ɪn'kwaɪəri, 'ɪn-kwə̇ri/ *n* INQUIRY
en·rage /ɪn'reɪdʒ/ *v* [T1] to make very angry: *Her behaviour enraged him* —**enraged** *adj* [B (*at, by*); F3,5]
en·rap·ture /ɪn'ræptʃəʳ/ *v* [T1] to fill (someone) with great joy or delight (RAPTURE) —**enraptured** *adj* [B (*at, by*); F3,5]
en·rich /ɪn'rɪtʃ/ *v* **1** [T1 (*by*)] to make rich: *The discovery of oil will enrich the nation* **2** [T1 (*by, with*)] to improve (by adding something): *This dish is enriched with cream* —**~ment** *n* [U (*of*)]
en·rol, enroll /ɪn'rəʊl/ *v* **-ll-** [Wv5;IØ (*as, in*); T1 (*as, in*)] to make (oneself or another person) officially a member of a group
en·rol·ment, enroll- /ɪn'rəʊlmənt/ *n* **1** [U;(C): (*as, in*)] (an example of) the act or state of ENROLling or of being ENROLled: *His enrolment as a member of the cricket club surprised us very much* **2** [S;(C): (*of*)] the number of people ENROLled: *The school has an enrolment of 2,000 pupils*
en route /ˌɒn 'ruːt‖ˌɑn-/ *adv* [F (*for, from, to*)] *Fr* on the way: *We were en route from London to New York*
en·san·guined /ɪn'sæŋgwə̇nd/ *adj lit* covered with blood
en·sconce /ɪn'skɒns‖ɪn'skɑns/ *v* [T1] *fml or humor* to place or seat (esp. oneself) comfortably in a safe place: *He ensconced himself in a comfortable chair* —**ensconced** *adj* [Wa5;F (*on, in, among*)]
en·sem·ble /ɒn'sɒmbəl‖ɑn'sɑm- (*Fr* ɑ̃sɑ̃bl)/ *n Fr* **1** also **tout ensemble**— a set of things that successfully combine with or match each other to make a whole: *Some of the buildings are ugly, but if you look at the town from a distance the ensemble* (=the effect of the whole) *is pleasing* **2** (*often cap.*) a small group of musicians who regularly play together —compare ORCHESTRA **3 a** a piece of music written for a small number of players of different instruments **b** (in OPERA) a piece of combined singing by all the performers who are on stage **4** *tech* a complete matching set of women's clothes, such as a dress, coat, and shoes, to be worn together
en·shrine /ɪn'ʃraɪn/ *v* [T1] *fml* to put or keep in or as if in a holy place (SHRINE) —**enshrined** *adj* [Wa5;F (*in, among*)]
en·shroud /ɪn'ʃraʊd/ *v* [T1] *fml* to cover and hide, as a dead body is covered with a SHROUD —**enshrouded** *adj* [Wv5;F (*in, by*)]
en·sign /'ensaɪn, -sən‖'ensən/ *n* **1** [C] a flag on a ship, which acts as a special sign, esp. to show what nation the ship belongs to **2** [C;A] (in Britain before 1871) an officer of the lowest rank in the army, who carried the flag **3** [C;A] (in the US) an officer of the lowest rank in the navy
en·slave /ɪn'sleɪv/ *v* [Wv5;T1] to make into a slave —**~ment** *n* [U]
en·snare /ɪn'sneəʳ/ *v* [T1 (*by, in, into*) *often pass.*] to catch (a person or creature) in or as if in a trap (SNARE)
en·sue /ɪn'sjuː‖ɪn'suː/ *v* [Wv4;IØ (*from*)] *fml* to happen afterwards (often as a result): *They said the building would be finished during the ensuing* (=the following) *year*
en·sure /ɪn'ʃʊəʳ/ *v* **1** [T1,5] to make (something) certain (to happen): *He wrote one poem which ensured his undying fame* **2** [D1;T1] to make (someone) certain to get (something good) or avoid (something bad): *This medicine will ensure you* (=make certain that you get) *a good night's sleep* —see INSURE (USAGE)
-ent /ənt/ *suffix* [*v*→*adj, n*] -ANT: *different*|RESIDENT
en·tail¹ /ɪn'teɪl/ *v* **1** [T1] to make (an event or action) necessary: *Writing a history book entails a lot of work* **2** [T1 (*on, upon*) *often pass.*] *law* (esp. in former times) to leave (land) allowing passage at death only from father to son (or as arranged) but not sale to a stranger: *The castle and the land are entailed on the eldest son*
en·tail² /'enteɪl/ *n* [U;(C)] *law* (esp. in former times) the arrangement of ENTAILing land
en·tan·gle /ɪn'tæŋgəl/ *v* [T1 (*among, in, with*) *often pass.*] to cause (string, rope, hair, etc.) to become twisted or mixed (with something else), or to cause (something) to become twisted or mixed (with string, rope, hair, etc.): *The bird entangled itself in the net.*|*The sailor's legs got entangled with the ropes* —compare TANGLE
en·tan·gle·ment /ɪn'tæŋgəlmənt/ *n* **1** [U] the act or state of entangling or being ENTANGLEd: (fig.) *to avoid entanglement in dishonest business dealings* **2** [C] something which ENTANGLEs: (fig.) *This famous painter never married, because he believed that a wife and children would be entanglements and would interrupt his work* **3** [C *often pl.*] a fence made of BARBED WIRE, placed so as to make the advance of enemy forces difficult
en·tente /ɒn'tɒnt‖ɑn'tɑnt/ *n Fr* **1** [C;U] a friendly relationship between 2 or more countries: *the entente between Britain and France* **2** [(*the*) GU] (*sometimes cap.*) 2 or more countries that have a friendly relationship: *Our Entente have/has decided to declare war*
en·ter /'entəʳ/ *v* **1** [T1] to come or go into: *to enter a room/a house* **2** [IØ] **a** to come in: *Please do not enter without knocking on the door* **b** to come on the stage: *Enter Romeo/Romeo enters* (order to an actor in a printed play) **3** [T1] to become a member of (esp. a profession): *to enter the army* **4** [T1 (UP, *in*)] to write down (names, amounts of money, etc.) in a book: *You must enter up the £5 you spent in the account book*
enter for *v prep* [D1;T1] to put the name (of oneself or another) on a list for: *John entered (himself) for the examination*
enter in·to *v prep* [T1] **1** [(*with*)] to begin: *to enter into a contract with a firm* **2** to understand and take part in: *He entered into the spirit of the game with great excitement* **3** [*no pass.*] to be a part of: *John's accident didn't enter into our plans. We shall have to go without him now*
en·te·ri·tis /ˌentə'raɪtə̇s/ *n* [U] a painful infection of the bowels
enter on also **enter up·on**— *v prep* [T1] **1** *fml* to begin: *The new teacher entered upon his duties in the autumn* **2** to take possession of (property) according to law: *When he was 18 he entered on the large fortune that his rich father had left him*
en·ter·prise /'entəpraɪz‖-ər-/ *n* **1** [C] a plan to do something, esp. to do something daring or difficult **2** [U] the courage that is needed to do something daring or difficult **3** [U9] the way of arranging and carrying on business: *Some people believe in private enterprise, while others believe in government ownership of industry* **4** [C] an organization, esp. a business firm: *one of the largest enterprises of its kind*
en·ter·pris·ing /'entəpraɪzɪŋ‖-ər-/ *adj apprec* having or showing ENTERPRISE (2) —**~ly** *adv*
en·ter·tain /ˌentə'teɪn‖-ər-/ *v* **1** [IØ;T1] to give a party (for); to provide food and drink in one's house (for): *He does most of his entertaining in restaurants* **2** [IØ;T1] to amuse and interest: *A teacher should entertain as well as teach* **3** [T1] to be ready and willing to think about (an idea, doubt, suggestion, etc.)
en·ter·tain·er /ˌentə'teɪnəʳ‖-ər-/ *n* a person who

ENTERTAINs (2) professionally: *She may not be a great actress but she's a very popular entertainer*

en·ter·tain·ing /ˌentəˈteɪnɪŋ‖-ər-/ *adj apprec* amusing and interesting: *an entertaining story* —**~ly** *adv*

en·ter·tain·ment /ˌentəˈteɪnmənt‖-ər-/ *n* **1** [U] the act of ENTERTAINING (1): *He gets an entertainment* ALLOWANCE (*compare* EXPENSE ACCOUNT) *for the entertainment of foreign business men* **2** [U;C] (a) public amusement: *A cinema is a place of entertainment* **3** [U] amusement: *Old Uncle John is getting married again, greatly to the entertainment of his family*

en·thral, enthrall /ɪnˈθrɔːl/ *v* **-ll-** [T1] to hold as if by magic the complete attention and interest of (someone), esp. by using words: *The little boy was enthralled by the soldier's stories of battles* —**enthralled** *adj* [B;F3] —**enthralling** *adj* —**~ingly** *adv*

en·throne /ɪnˈθrəʊn/ *v* [T1] to place (a king, queen, or BISHOP) on a THRONE (official seat): *The Queen was enthroned in the city's most ancient church* —**~ment** *n* [C;U]

en·throned /ɪnˈθrəʊnd/ *adj* [Wa5;F (*in*); (B)] seated on or as if on a THRONE: (fig.) *Shakespeare wrote that the quality of mercy is enthroned in the hearts of kings*

en·thuse /ɪnˈθjuːz‖ɪnˈθuːz/ *v* [I∅ (*about* or *over*)] *infml* to show ENTHUSIASM: *"Listen to Marigold, enthusing as usual!" "What's she enthusing about this time?"*

en·thu·si·as·m /ɪnˈθjuːziæzəm‖ɪnˈθuː-/ *n* [C;U: (*for, about*)] a strong feeling of interest and admiration: *Among his many enthusiasms is a great fondness for Eastern music*

en·thu·si·ast /ɪnˈθjuːziæst‖ɪnˈθuː-/ *n* [C9, esp. *about*: (C)] a person who is habitually full of ENTHUSIASM (about something): *a bicycling enthusiast|He's a real enthusiast about wild flowers* —**~ic** /ɪnˌθjuːziˈæstɪk‖ɪnˌθuː-/ *adj* —**~ically** *adv* [Wa4]

en·tice /ɪnˈtaɪs/ *v* [V3;X9, esp. AWAY, *from, into*] to persuade (someone) to do a (usu. wrong) action by offering something pleasant or by argument: *He enticed her away from her husband* —**-ticing** *adj* —**-ticingly** *adv*

en·tice·ment /ɪnˈtaɪsmənt/ *n* **1** [U] the act of enticing (ENTICE), esp. of enticing a young person away for sexual reasons **2** [U] the quality of being ENTICING: *The idea of living on a sunny island has great enticement for me* **3** [C *often pl.*] something which ENTICEs

en·tire /ɪnˈtaɪəʳ/ *adj* [Wa5;A] **1** with nothing left out; complete: *an entire set of Shakespeare's plays* **2** complete in degree: *I am in entire agreement with you* —**~ly** *adv* [Wa5]

en·tir·e·ty /ɪnˈtaɪərəti/ *n* [U9] *fml* **1** the state of being complete (ENTIRE (1)) (esp. in the phr. **in its entirety**) **2** the total or whole: *the entirety of the population*

en·ti·tle /ɪnˈtaɪtl/ *v* [Wv5 *often pass.*] **1** [X1] to give (to a book, play, etc.) (a title): *This book is entitled "Crime And Punishment"* **2** [V3] to give (someone) the right (to do something): *Officers are entitled to travel first class* —**~ment** *n* [U,U3]

entitle to *v prep* [D1] to give the right to: *This ticket entitles you to a free seat at the concert*

en·ti·ty /ˈentəti/ *n* [C;(U)] (the quality of having) a single separate and independent existence: *Since Germany was divided it is no longer one political entity*

en·tomb /ɪnˈtuːm/ *v* [T1 (*in* or *among*)] *often pass. fml & lit* to put or contain in or as if in a grave (TOMB): *60 men were entombed by the mine explosion* —**~ment** *n* [C;U]

en·to·mol·o·gy /ˌentəˈmɒlədʒi‖-ˈmɑ-/ *n* [U] the scientific study of insects —compare ETYMOLOGY (1) —**-gist** *n* —**-gical** /-məˈlɒdʒɪkəl‖-ˈlɑ-/ *adj*

en·tou·rage /ˈɒntʊrɑːʒ‖ˈɑn-/ *n* [GC] *Fr* all the people who surround and follow an important person

en·tr'acte, entracte /ˈɒntrækt‖ˈɑn-/ *n Fr* (a piece of music or other performance given during) the time between acts in a play

en·trails /ˈentreɪlz/ *n* [P] the inside parts of an animal, esp. the bowels

en·train /ɪnˈtreɪn/ *v* [I∅;T1] *tech* to get or put (esp. soldiers) into a train

en·trance[1] /ˈentrəns/ *n* **1** [C] a gate, door, or other opening by which one enters: *the entrance to the railway station* —compare ENTRY (3) **2** [C;U] the act of entering: *The young actor made only 2 entrances (onto the stage)* **3** [U] the right to enter: *a school entrance examination|the entrance money* (=money which must be paid) *to join a tennis club*
USAGE In *BrE, an* **entrance** is a gate or door by which one enters: *selling tickets at the* **entrance** *to the cinema*; *an* **entry** is either **a** the act of **enter**ing: *Britain's* **entry** *into the EEC* or **b** a narrow passage between houses: *to hide in a dark* **entry**. Americans may use **entry** for all 3 of these. Both words are used, with the same meaning, before other nouns, in expressions like **entrance/entry** *form*|**entrance/entry** FEE.

en·trance[2] /ɪnˈtrɑːns‖ɪnˈtræns/ *v* [Wv4;T1] *apprec* to fill (someone) with great wonder and delight —**entranced** *adj* [B (*at, by, with*); F3,5]

entrance fee /ˈentrəns fiː/ *n* the money which one pays to enter

en·trant /ˈentrənt/ *n* **1** a person who enters a profession: *They are now accepting women as entrants to the Government service* **2** a person or animal that enters for a race or competition

en·trap /ɪnˈtræp/ *v* **-pp-** [T1 (*by, in, into*) *often pass.*] *fml* to catch as if in a trap; deceive or trick (into) —**~ment** *n* [U;(C)]

en·treat /ɪnˈtriːt/ *v* [I∅;T1 (*for*), 5c;V3] *fml* to beg humbly or very seriously: *"Forgive me," she entreated (him).*|*I entreat your help* —**~ingly** *adv*

en·trea·ty /ɪnˈtriːti/ *n* [C;U:(3,5c)] *fml* (an example of) the action of ENTREAT*ing*: *She could not influence him by entreaty*

en·trée /ˈɒntreɪ‖ˈɑn-/ *n Fr* **1** [C;U: (*into*)] the right or freedom to enter: *His wealth gave him the entrée into upper-class society* **2** [C] a small carefully prepared meat dish, served after the fish and before the main dish of meat in a formal dinner

en·trench, intrench /ɪnˈtrentʃ/ *v* **1** [I∅] to dig a long deep ditch (TRENCH) in the ground to protect a place or an army **2** [X9, esp. *against, behind, in*] to place (oneself) in a safe position as if in a hole: *He entrenched himself behind his newspaper*

en·trenched /ɪnˈtrentʃt/ *adj* **1** (of rights, customs, beliefs, etc.) firmly established **2** (of a place that is being defended) protected by TRENCHes

en·trench·ment /ɪnˈtrentʃmənt/ *n* **1** [C] a system of TRENCHes dug for defence **2** [U] the quality of being ENTRENCHED

en·tre·pôt /ˈɒntrəpəʊ‖ˈɑn-/ *n Fr* a centre, often a seaport, where goods are collected and stored before being sent where they are needed —compare DEPOT (1)

en·tre·pre·neur /ˌɒntrəprəˈnɜːʳ‖ˌɑn-/ *n Fr* **1** a person who makes the plans for a business or a piece of work and gets it going **2** *AmE* **producer**— a person who arranges for the performance of plays or musical shows —compare IMPRESARIO (2)

en·tre·sol /ˈɒntrəsɒl‖ˈɑntrəsɑl/ *n* an additional floor between 2 main floors of a building; MEZZANINE

en·tro·py /ˈentrəpi/ *n* [U] **1** a measure of the difference between the temperatures of something which heats and something which is being heated:

Entropy increases as the heat becomes the same all through a system, such as the inside of a steam engine **2** the state which the universe will reach when all the heat is spread out evenly **3** the tendency of heat and other forms of ENERGY to spread out and gradually disappear

en·trust, intrust /ɪn'trʌst/ *v* [D1+*with*/*to*] to give (someone) the charge of (something) with complete trust: *I entrusted the child to your care*

en·try /'entri/ *n* **1** [C (*into*)] the act of coming or going in; ENTRANCE[1] (2): *Great Britain's entry into the war* **2** [U] the right to enter: *You mustn't drive into a street with a "No Entry" sign* —compare ENTRÉE (1) **3** [C] *esp. AmE* a door, gate, or passage by which one enters: *Leave the boxes in the entry and we'll carry them up later* **4** [C;U] the act or result of writing something down on a list, as in an account of money or in a dictionary: *Entry of a word in a dictionary does not mean approval of the word entered* **5** [C] a person, thing, or group entered in a race or competition: *This pot of apple jelly is Mrs Smith's entry for the cooking competition*

entry vi·sa /'·· ˌ··/ *n* a mark or signature which is put on the official paper which allows one to travel (PASSPORT) giving permission to enter a particular country

en·twine /ɪn'twaɪn/ *v* [T1] **1** to make by twisting 2 or more things together: *She entwined a crown of roses for herself* **2** [(*in*, (*a*)*round*)] to twist together, round, or in: *They walked along with their fingers entwined* —compare ENTANGLE

e·nu·me·rate /ɪ'njuːməreɪt‖ɪ'nuː-/ *v* [T1] to name (things on a list) one by one: *He enumerated all his reasons* **—-ration** /ɪˌnjuːmə'reɪʃən‖ɪˌnuː-/ *n* [C;U]

e·nun·ci·ate /ɪ'nʌnsieɪt/ *v* **1** [T1;I∅] to pronounce (a (part of a) word) (clearly): *An actor must learn to enunciate clearly* **2** [T1] to express (ideas, opinions, etc.) clearly and firmly: *He enunciated his views on the subject of crime*

e·nun·ci·a·tion /ɪˌnʌnsi'eɪʃən/ *n* **1** [U] the way of pronouncing (words) **2** [C9;U9] a clear expression (of ideas, opinions, etc.)

en·vel·op /ɪn'veləp/ *v* [Wv4,5;T1 (*in*)] to wrap up or cover completely: *He'd enveloped himself in various garments to keep out the cold.|The building was soon enveloped in flames* **—~ment** *n* [U]

en·ve·lope /'envələʊp/ *n* a covering which contains something, esp. the paper cover of a letter: *the envelope of air around the earth*

en·ven·om /ɪn'venəm/ *v* [Wv5;T1] **1** *lit* to put poison in or on (esp. a weapon) **2** to fill with hatred

en·vi·a·ble /'enviəbəl/ *adj* **1** (of a person) causing ENVY: *He has everything he wants; he's an enviable young man* **2** (of someone's position, possessions, etc.) very desirable: *He faced his enemies with enviable courage.|an enviable job* —opposite **unenviable** **—-bly** *adv*

en·vi·ous /'enviəs/ *adj* [(*of*)] feeling or showing ENVY: *She was envious of her sister's beauty* —see JEALOUS (USAGE) **—~ly** *adv*

en·vi·roned /ɪn'vaɪərənd/ *adj* [Wa5;F9, esp. *by*, *with*] *fml* (of places) surrounded: *a lake environed by/with woods*

en·vi·ron·ment /ɪn'vaɪərənmənt/ *n* **1** [C] all the surrounding conditions which influence growth and development: *Children need a happy home environment* **2** [*the*+R] the natural conditions, such as air, water, and land, in which man lives: *They are passing new laws to prevent the* POLLUTION (=spoiling and making dirty) *of the environment*
USAGE One's **surroundings** are the place which surrounds one, and so is one's **environment**, but here it is considered from the point of view of its influence on one's feelings, morals, and ideas. Compare *to grow up in beautiful* **surroundings**/*in a happy* **environment**. **Environs** are the area surrounding a place, not a person: *in the* **environs** *of Manchester.* —see also ECOLOGY

en·vi·ron·men·tal /ɪnˌvaɪərən'mentl/ *adj* [Wa5] **1** of, or caused by someone's or something's ENVIRONMENT (1): *Should we take this boy away from the bad environmental influences in which he lives?* **2** of the ENVIRONMENT (2): *environmental science|the environmental effects of pouring industrial waste into rivers* **—-tally** /-təli/ *adv*

en·vi·ron·men·tal·ist /ɪnˌvaɪərən'mentəl¹₃st/ *n* a person who tries to prevent the ENVIRONMENT (2) from being spoilt —compare ECOLOGY **—-ism** *n* [U]

en·vi·rons /'envɪrənz, ɪn'vaɪərənz‖ɪn'vaɪərənz/ *n* [P9] the neighbourhood surrounding a town: *The environs of Vienna are very beautiful* —see ENVIRONMENT (USAGE)

en·vis·age /ɪn'vɪzɪdʒ/ *AmE* also **en·vi·sion** /ɪn'vɪʒən/— *v* [T1,4,5] to see in the mind as a future possibility (events, actions, etc.): *Henry Ford envisaged an important future for the motor car*

en·voy[1], envoi /'envɔɪ/ *n* the end of a poem or piece of writing esp. the last 4 lines of a BALLADE, which are addressed to some important person and express the main idea of the poem

envoy[2] *n* **1** a messenger, esp. one sent by one government to do business with another government **2** an official in the foreign service of a country, second in rank to an AMBASSADOR

en·vy[1] /'envi/ *n* [U (*at*, *of*)] **1** also (*rare*) **enviousness**— a feeling one has towards someone when one wishes that one had his qualities or possessions: *The boy's new bicycle was an object of envy to all his friends* (=it made them feel envy) —compare JEALOUSY **2 the envy of (someone)** a thing or person that makes someone wish to own the thing or be like the person: *Their beautiful garden is the envy of all the neighbours*

envy[2] *v* [Wv4,5;D1;T1] to feel ENVY (1) for or of: *I don't envy you your journey in this bad weather* **—~ingly** *adv*

en·zyme /'enzaɪm/ *n* a chemical substance (CATALYST) produced by certain living cells, which can cause or hasten chemical change in plants or animals without itself being changed

e·on /'iːən/ *n* AEON

ep·au·let, -lette /ˌepə'let/ *n* a shoulder ornament, esp. on a military or naval uniform

é·pée /'epeɪ/ *n* a sharp-pointed stiff narrow sword, with a bowl-shaped guard for the hand, used in FENCING —see FENCING (USAGE)

e·phem·e·ral /ɪ'femərəl/ *adj* living only for a day; having a very short life: *My other writings are very ephemeral, but this book will be remembered for ever* **—-rally** *adv*

ep·ic[1] /'epɪk/ *adj* [Wa5] *usu. apprec* (of stories, events, etc.) full of brave action and excitement, like an EPIC[2]: *the epic fight of one small ship against 6 enemy ships* **—~ally** *adv* [Wa4]

epic[2] *n* a long poem telling the story of the deeds of gods and great men, or the early history of a nation: *The Ramayana is an epic of ancient India, and the Odyssey is an epic of ancient Greece.*|(fig.) *His book about his travels in the desert is an epic*

ep·i·cen·tre, *AmE* **-ter** /'epɪˌsentəʳ/ *n tech* the place on the Earth's surface which is just over the part inside the Earth where an earth-movement (EARTHQUAKE) begins

ep·i·cure /'epɪkjʊəʳ/ *n* a person who takes great interest in the pleasures of food and drink, and regards cooking as an art; GOURMET

ep·i·cu·re·an /ˌepɪkjʊ'riːən/ *adj*, *n* [Wa5] (being or typical of) a person who particularly enjoys the

more delicate pleasures of the senses
Epicurean *adj, n* [Wa5] (a person) believing in or concerned with the teaching which states that pleasure is good and pain is evil —compare STOIC, HEDONIST
ep·i·dem·ic[1] /ˌepȧˈdemɪk/ *adj* [Wa5] (esp. of an infectious disease) very common in one place for a time: (fig.) *Violence is reaching epidemic levels in the city* —compare ENDEMIC
epidemic[2] *n* a large number of cases of the same infectious disease during a single period of time: *an epidemic of* CHOLERA/*a* CHOLERA *epidemic*
ep·i·der·mis /ˌepȧˈdɜːmȧs‖-ɜr-/ *n* [U;C] *med* the outside part of a creature's skin
ep·i·di·a·scope /ˌepȧˈdaɪəskəʊp/ *n* a type of lamp which throws pictures of transparent or other objects, such as photographic film or pages from a book, onto a surface
ep·i·glot·tis /ˌepȧˈglɒtȧs‖-ˈglɑ-/ *n med* a little shield at the back of the tongue, which closes to prevent food or drink from entering the lungs —see picture at RESPIRATORY
ep·i·gram /ˈepȧgræm/ *n* a short clever amusing poem or saying: *Who invented the epigram "Everything I like is either unlawful, immoral, or fattening"?*
ep·i·gram·mat·ic /ˌepȧgrəˈmætɪk/ *adj* of or like an EPIGRAM —**~ally** *adv* [Wa4]
ep·i·lep·sy /ˈepȧlepsi/ *n* [U] a disease of the brain which causes sudden attacks of uncontrolled violent movement and loss of consciousness
ep·i·lep·tic /ˌepȧˈleptɪk/ *adj, n* [Wa5] (being, typical of, dealing with, or concerning) a person who suffers from EPILEPSY: *She has 2 epileptic children.*|*the epileptic department of the hospital*
ep·i·logue /ˈepȧlɒg‖-lɑg/ *n* the last part of a piece of literature, which finishes it off, esp. a speech made by one of the actors at the end of a play —opposite **prologue**
E·piph·a·ny /ɪˈpɪfəni/ *n* [R] the feast of the Christian church, on January 6th, in memory of the coming of the 3 kings from the East to see the baby Jesus Christ
e·pis·co·pa·cy /ɪˈpɪskəpəsi/ *n* **1** [U] *fml* the rank or office of a BISHOP (=a high official and priest of the Christian church) or the time he spends in that position: *During the whole 37 years of my episcopacy I have never heard such nonsense!* **2** [*the*+GU] the whole body of BISHOPs, as in a particular country
e·pis·co·pal /ɪˈpɪskəpəl/ *adj* [Wa5;A;(B)] **1** *fml* of or concerning BISHOPs **2** (*often cap.*) (of a church) governed by BISHOPs (esp. in the phrs. **the Episcopal Church** (in Britain), **the Protestant Episcopal Church** (in the US))
e·pis·co·pa·li·an /ɪˌpɪskəˈpeɪlɪən/ *adj, n* [Wa5] (*often cap.*) (a member) of an EPISCOPAL (2) church: *George always goes to the mosque, but Ali and I are Episcopalians*
ep·i·sode /ˈepȧsəʊd/ *n* (an account in a play or book of) one separate event, esp. an important or serious one: *one of the funniest episodes in my life*
ep·i·sod·ic /ˌepȧˈsɒdɪk‖-ˈsɑ-/ *adj derog* (of a story, play, etc.) made up of separate, esp. loosely connected EPISODEs: *Your new book is too episodic. It should contain one continuous story* —**~ally** *adv* [Wa4]
e·pis·tle /ɪˈpɪsəl/ *n fml or humor* a letter, esp. a long and important one
Epistle *n* [*often pl.*] any of the letters written by the first followers (APOSTLEs) of Christ, in the Bible
e·pis·to·la·ry /ɪˈpɪstələri‖-təleri/ *adj* [Wa5;A] *fml or pomp* **1** of letters or the writing of letters **2** carried on by, or in the form of, letters
ep·i·taph /ˈepȧtɑːf‖-tæf/ *n* a short description of a dead person, often written on a stone above his grave
ep·i·thet /ˈepȧθet/ *n* an adjective or descriptive phrase, esp. of praise or blame used of a person: *He cursed me, using a lot of rude epithets like "bloody"*
e·pit·o·me /ɪˈpɪtəmi/ *n* [(*of*)] **1** a thing or person that shows, to a very great degree, a quality or set of qualities (esp. in the phr. **the epitome of**): *My cat is the epitome of laziness* (=is very lazy) **2** *rare* a short account of a book or speech
e·pit·o·mize, -mise /ɪˈpɪtəmaɪz/ *v* [T1] **1** to be an EPITOME (1) of **2** *rare* to give an EPITOME (2) of
e·poch /ˈiːpɒk‖ˈepək/ *n* **1** a period of historical time, or an age in the history of the earth, during which events or developments of a stated kind happened —compare ERA **2** an important event which seems to begin a whole new period: *Meeting George was an epoch in Mary's life*
epoch-mak·ing /ˈ·· ˌ··/ *adj* (esp. of an event) very important; being or beginning an EPOCH (2)
e·pon·y·mous /ɪˈpɒnȧməs‖ɪˈpɑ-/ *adj* [Wa5] (of a character in literature) being the character after whom the (stated) book, play, etc., is named (esp. in the phr. **eponymous hero**)
Ep·som salt /ˌepsəm ˈsɔːlt/ *n* [U *usu. pl. with sing. meaning*] a bitter colourless or white powder, used medically to empty the bowels
eq·ua·bil·i·ty /ˌekwəˈbɪləti/ *n* [U] the state of being EQUABLE: *Even John's equability was upset by what happened*
eq·ua·ble /ˈekwəbəl/ *adj* **1** (of temperature, or a person's character) without great changes; even and regular: *an equable temperature, neither very hot nor very cold* **2** (of a person) of even temper; not easily annoyed: *I like working with John because he's so calm and equable* —compare EQUITABLE —**-bly** *adv*
e·qual[1] /ˈiːkwəl/ *adj* **1** [Wa5;B (*in, to*)] (of 2 or more) the same in size, number, value, rank, etc.: *Cut the cake into 6 equal pieces.*|*Women demand equal pay for equal work* (=equal to men).|*Mary is quite equal to Bill in brains* **2** [F+*to*] (of a person) having enough strength, ability, etc. (for): *Bill is quite equal to (the job of) running the office* **3 equal to the occasion** able to meet or deal with whatever happens **4 on equal terms** (meeting or speaking) as equals; without difference of rank —see also **on an** EQUALITY (2)
equal[2] *n* [C9] a person that is equal (to another or to oneself): *I'm not Mary's equal/the equal of Mary in beauty.*|*He feels that they are his equals/that he and they are equals*
equal[3] *v* **-ll-** (*AmE* **-l-**) [Wv6] **1** [L1] (of sizes or numbers) to be the same (as): *"x=y" means that x equals y* **2** [T1 (*in, as*)] to be as good, clever, etc. (as): *None of us can equal her, either in beauty or as a dancer*
USAGE The EQUATION x=y can be read in 2 ways: "x equals y" or "x is equal to y".
e·qual·i·tar·i·an /ɪˌkwɒlȧˈteərɪən‖ɪˌkwɑ-/ *adj* EGALITARIAN
e·qual·i·ty /ɪˈkwɒlȧti‖ɪˈkwɑ-/ *n* [U] **1** the state of being equal: *the equality of man* **2 on an equality (with)** the same in rank: *Now I've passed the examination I'm on an equality with my teacher. Yes, we're on an equality at last!*
e·qual·ize, -ise /ˈiːkwəlaɪz/ *v* [T1] to make equal in size or numbers: *to equalize incomes* —**-ization** /ˌiːkwəlaɪˈzeɪʃən‖-lə-/ *n* [U]
eq·ual·ly /ˈiːkwəli/ *adv* **1** [Wa5] as (much); to an equal degree: *They're both equally pretty and they can both run equally fast* **2** in equal shares: *They shared the work equally between them* **3** [Wa5] (*comparing 2 ideas*) at the same time and in spite of that: *We must help people to find jobs and houses outside the city. But equally, we must remember that*

some city people want to remain where they are

eq·ua·nim·i·ty /ˌiːkwəˈnɪmǰti, ˌekwə-/ *n* [U] calmness of mind: *He received the bad news with surprising equanimity*

e·quate /ɪˈkweɪt/ *v* [T1 (*with*)] to consider or make (2 or more things or people) equal: *You can't equate his poems and/with his plays*

e·qua·tion /ɪˈkweɪʒən/ *n* **1** [C] a statement that 2 quantities are equal: *x+2y=7 is an equation* **2** [U] the act or fact of equating (EQUATE): *The equation of political terror with/and firm government is dangerously misleading*

e·qua·tor /ɪˈkweɪtəʳ/ *n* [*the*+R] (*often cap.*) an imaginary line (line of LATITUDE) drawn round the world halfway between its most northern and southern points (POLEs)—see picture at GLOBE

eq·ua·to·ri·al /ˌekwəˈtɔːrɪəl‖ˌiːkwətor-/ *adj* **1** [Wa5] of, concerning or near the EQUATOR **2** very hot: *equatorial weather* —**-ally** *adv*

e·quer·ry /ɪˈkweri, ˈekwəri‖ˈekwəri/ *n* a male official in a royal court, in attendance on the king or a member of the royal family

e·ques·tri·an /ɪˈkwestrɪən/ *adj, n* [Wa5;A;C] (a person) riding on a horse; (of) a rider on a horse: *an equestrian* STATUE (=stone figure) *of King Richard Lionheart|Susan is a very keen equestrian*

e·qui- /ˌekwǰ, ˌiːkwǰ/ *comb. form* equal or equally: *Cairo and Oslo are about* EQUIDISTANT *from Rome.|An* EQUILATERAL TRIANGLE *has 3 sides of equal length*

e·qui·dis·tant /ˌiːkwǰˈdɪstənt/ *adj* [Wa5;F (*from*)] equally distant: *Rome is about equidistant from Cairo and Oslo*

e·qui·lat·e·ral /ˌiːkwǰˈlætərəl/ *adj* [Wa5] (of a TRIANGLE) having all 3 sides equal —see picture at GEOMETRY

e·qui·lib·ri·um /ˌiːkwǰˈlɪbrɪəm/ *n* [U] a state of balance: *He lost his equilibrium and fell into the lake*

eq·uine /ˈekwaɪn, ˈiː-/ *adj* of or like horses: *her long, equine face*

eq·ui·noc·tial /ˌiːkwǰˈnɒkʃəl‖-ˈnɑk-/ *adj* [Wa5;A] of or at the time of the EQUINOX: *equinoctial* GALEs (=strong winds at this time)

eq·ui·nox /ˈiːkwǰnɒks, ˈe-‖-nɑks/ *n* [(*the*) C] one of the 2 times in the year (about March 21 and September 22) when all places in the world have day and night of equal length: *the* VERNAL (=spring) *and autumnal equinoxes*

e·quip /ɪˈkwɪp/ *v* **-pp-** **1** [T1 (*with, for*)] to provide (oneself or another) with what is necessary (for doing something): *They can't afford to equip their army properly* **2** [T1 (*for*); V3] to make (oneself or another) able (to do something) or prepared (for something): *Your education will equip you to earn a good living* —**equipped** *adj* [B9]: *well-equipped travellers*

eq·ui·page /ˈekwǰpɪdʒ/ *n* (in former times) the carriage of a rich person, with its horses and attendants

e·quip·ment /ɪˈkwɪpmənt/ *n* [U] **1** the things needed to do something: *modern office equipment* **2** the act of EQUIPping: *The complete equipment of the new hospital will take a year*

eq·ui·poise /ˈekwǰpɔɪz/ *n tech* [U] a state of balance or EQUILIBRIUM, when there is no change or movement because 2 opposing forces are equal: *To weigh out a quantity of sugar correctly, the scales should be in equipoise*

eq·ui·ta·ble /ˈekwǰtəbəl/ *adj* fair and just: *an equitable division of the money* —opposite **inequitable** —**-bly** *adv*

eq·ui·ta·tion /ˌekwǰˈteɪʃən/ *n* [U] *fml* the art of riding horses

eq·ui·ties /ˈekwǰtiz/ *n* [P] a company's ordinary shares, which carry no fixed interest: *Julian's father left him a nice little packet of equities*

eq·ui·ty /ˈekwǰti/ *n* [U] **1** the quality of being EQUITABLE: *They shared the work of the house with perfect equity* **2** (esp. in the law systems of English-speaking countries) the principle of justice which may be used to correct a law, when that law would cause hardship in special cases

e·quiv·a·lence /ɪˈkwɪvələns/ *n* [U] the state or quality of being EQUIVALENT

e·quiv·a·lent[1] /ɪˈkwɪvələnt/ *adj* [Wa5;B (*to*)] (of time, amount, number, etc.) same; equal: *He changed his pounds for the equivalent/an equivalent amount of dollars* —**~ly** *adv*

equivalent[2] *n* that which is EQUIVALENT: *Some American words have no British equivalents*

e·quiv·o·cal /ɪˈkwɪvəkəl/ *adj* **1** (of words) having a double or doubtful meaning **2** (of behaviour or events) questionable; mysterious —opposite **unequivocal** —**~ly** *adv*

e·quiv·o·cate /ɪˈkwɪvəkeɪt/ *v* [I∅] to speak in an EQUIVOCAL way on purpose to deceive people: *Answer yes or no, but don't equivocate*

e·quiv·o·ca·tion /ɪˌkwɪvəˈkeɪʃən/ *n* [C;U] an act or the action of speaking in an EQUIVOCAL way: *The minister never answers a question plainly; he's a master of equivocation*

er /ɜːʳ, əʳ/ *interj* (a HESITATION noise): *And then he—er—er—just suddenly seemed to—er—disappear!*

-er[1] /əʳ/ also (*after* -e) **-r**— *suffix* (used to form the COMPARATIVE of many shorter adjectives and adverbs): *hot, hotter|dry, drier|My car is fast but his is faster/goes faster*

-er[2] also (*after* -e) **-r**— *suffix* **1** [*v→n*] a person who: *A dancer dances and a waiter waits (at table). Dancing and waiting are their professions.|A* DINE*r may be a person who is dining* (DINE=have dinner) **2** [*v→n*] a thing that: *A telephone receiver receives an electrical signal.|A screwdriver drives in screws* **3** [*v→n*] something acted upon: *A cooker (esp. BrE) is a kind of apple that one cooks* **4** [*n→n*] a person who makes: *A* GLOVE*r makes* GLOVE*s* **5** [*n→n*] a person who lives in: *A Londoner lives in London* **6** [*n→n*] a person having, being, or connected with: *A* TEENAGER *is a young person of* TEENAGE (13–19).*|A* **forty-niner** *was a person who went to California in 1849* **7** [*n→n*] a thing having: *A 3-wheeler is a car with 3 wheels* **8** [*n→n*] a person who knows about or works at: *A* GEOGRAPHER *has studied* GEOGRAPHY

USAGE Although **-er** is joined onto verbs to form a noun meaning someone who performs the action of the verb, nobody will say *I'm a* **writer**/*a* **dancer** if it is not his profession. One may ask, about sports and interests, *"Are you a* **footballer**?/*a* **photographer**?*"* (=Do you practise the art? Are you keen on it?) but if someone answers *"Yes!"* he is claiming to have professional skill. One can, however, say *He's a very keen* **footballer**/*a very good* **dancer** without suggesting that he does it professionally.

e·ra /ˈɪərə/ *n* **1** a set of years which is counted from a particular point in time: *The Christian era is counted from the birth of Christ* —compare EPOCH (1) **2** a period of time in history named after an important event or development: *The era of space travel has begun* —compare EPOCH (1)

e·rad·i·cate /ɪˈrædǰkeɪt/ *v* [T1] to destroy completely and put an end to (something bad): *to eradicate crime/disease/bad habits* —**-cation** /ɪˌrædǰˈkeɪʃən/ *n* [U]

e·rad·i·ca·tor /ɪˈrædǰkeɪtəʳ/ *n* [U] a chemical that removes ink marks

e·rase /ɪˈreɪz‖ɪˈreɪs/ *v* [T1] **1** to rub out or remove (something, esp. a pencil mark) **2 erase a blackboard** *AmE* to clean a BLACKBOARD by rubbing out the chalk marks

e·ras·er /ɪˈreɪzəʳ‖-sər/ *n* **1** *fml or AmE* a piece of rubber used to rub out writing **2** also **blackboard eraser**— *AmE* a piece of clothlike material with a stiff back which is used to ERASE (2) **a blackboard**

e·ra·sure /ɪˈreɪʒəʳ‖-ʃər/ *n* **1** [U (*of*)] the act of erasing (ERASE) **2** [C] a place marked by erasing (ERASE) something: *The pupil's exercise was full of erasures*

ere /eəʳ/ *prep, conj poet or old use* before: *ere morning*

e·rect[1] /ɪˈrekt/ *adj* **1** upright; standing straight up on end, not leaning over or lying down: *Hold your head erect* **2** *med* (of the PENIS) being in a state of ERECTION (3) —**~ly** *adv* —**~ness** *n* [U]

erect[2] *v* [T1] **1** *fml* to build or establish (a solid thing which was not there before): *This* MONUMENT *was erected to Queen Charlotte* (=in honour of the memory of Queen Charlotte) **2** to fix or place in an upright position (a solid thing which was lying flat): *to erect a tent*

e·rec·tile /ɪˈrektaɪl‖-tl/ *adj med* (of parts of the body, esp. the PENIS (=male sex organ)) that can fill with blood, which makes the part stand upright: *erectile* TISSUE (=flesh)

e·rec·tion /ɪˈrekʃən/ *n* **1** [U] the act or fact of building something: *The erection of the new hospital so near the main road was a mistake* **2** [C] a building: *The new college building is a most peculiar erection* **3** [C;U] (an example of) the state of the PENIS when upright: *Just thinking about her gave him an erection*

er·e·mite /ˈer$\frac{1}{2}$maɪt/ *n rare* HERMIT

erg /ɜːg‖ɜrg/ *n* a measure of work: *It takes about 350 ergs to lift a pin one inch*

er·go /ˈɜːgəʊ‖ˈɜr-/ *adv Lat, usu. humor* (*used for introducing the result of an argument*) therefore

er·go·nom·ics /ˌɜːgəˈnɒmɪks‖ˌɜrgəˈnɑ-/ *AmE* also **biotechnology**— *n* [U] the study of the conditions in which people work most effectively with machines

er·mine /ˈɜːm$\frac{1}{2}$n‖ˈɜr-/ *n* **1** [Wn1;C] (the name given in winter, when its fur turns white, to) a STOAT **2** [U] the white fur of this animal, often worn, esp. formerly, by important people such as kings and judges

e·rode /ɪˈreʊd/ *v* **1** [T1 (AWAY)] (of acids, water, wind, etc.) to eat into; to wear or rub away: *The sea erodes the rocks* **2** [IØ] to be or become worn away or rubbed away: *The coast is slowly eroding away*

e·ro·ge·nous /ɪˈrɒdʒənəs‖ɪˈrɑ-/ *adj* [Wa5] *tech* (of parts of the body) sexually sensitive: *The female breasts are an erogenous* ZONE

e·ro·sion /ɪˈrəʊʒən/ *n* [U] the action or result of eroding (ERODE): *soil erosion by rain and wind|* (fig.) *the slow erosion of royal power* —**-sive** /ɪˈrəʊsɪv/ *adj* —**-siveness** *n* [U]

e·rot·ic /ɪˈrɒtɪk‖ɪˈrɑ-/ *adj* of or concerning sexual love and desire: *erotic feelings|an erotic picture* —**~ally** *adv* [Wa4]

USAGE **Erotic** is used particularly for works of art: *an* **erotic** *film|some* **erotic** *Japanese pictures.* **Sexual** just means "connected with or in regard to sex": *the* **sexual** *organs|the* **sexual** *habits of the British.* **Amorous, lecherous,** and (*infml*) **sexy** can all be used of people or their thoughts or behaviour, but **amorous** is concerned with love rather than sex: *a long* **amorous** *letter*, while **lecherous** is rather *derog* and usually used of men, and **sexy** may mean "making other people think of sex"! Compare: *a nasty* **lecherous** *old man|She looks very* **sexy** *in those trousers.*

e·rot·i·ca /ɪˈrɒtɪkə‖ɪˈrɑ-/ *n* [P] *often derog* EROTIC books, pictures, etc.: *This nasty old man has a valuable collection of erotica*

e·rot·i·cis·m /ɪˈrɒt$\frac{1}{2}$sɪzəm‖ɪˈrɑ-/ *n* [U] the state or quality of being EROTIC

err /ɜːʳ/ *v* [IØ] **1** *fml* to make a mistake; to do something wrong: *To err is human* (old saying).|*He erred in supposing that the house was empty* **2 err on the side of** to go too far in the direction of: *It is better to err on the side of mercy* (=to be too merciful rather than not merciful enough)

er·rand /ˈerənd/ *n* **1** a short journey made to get something or to carry a message (note the phr. **run errands for**): *I've no time to go on/run errands for you!* —see also FOOL'S ERRAND **2** the purpose of such a journey: *I've got a few errands to do in the town*

er·rant /ˈerənt/ *adj* [A] **1** mistaken; ERRing: *An errant husband is one who leaves his wife and chases other women* **2** wandering away from home and doing bad things in distant places: *She went to London to bring back her errant daughter* —see also KNIGHT-ERRANT

er·rat·ic /ɪˈrætɪk/ *adj* changeable without reason; not regular in movement or behaviour —**~ally** *adv* [Wa4]

er·ra·tum /eˈrɑːtəm/ *n* **-ta** /tə/ [*usu. pl*] *Lat* a mistake in printing or writing, esp. one noted in a list at the beginning of a printed book

er·ro·ne·ous /ɪˈrəʊnɪəs/ *adj fml* (of a statement, a belief, etc.) incorrect: *the erroneous belief that the world is flat* —**~ly** *adv*

er·ror /ˈerəʳ/ *n* **1** [C] a mistake; something done wrongly, or an example of bad behaviour: *It wasn't all Jane's fault when she left Bill; there were errors on both sides* **2** [U] the state of being wrong in behaviour or beliefs: *The accident was caused by human error.*|*I did it in error* (=by mistake)

USAGE An **error** is the same as a **mistake**, except **a** in moral matters: *the* **errors** (not **mistakes**) *of his youth* **b** in certain fixed phrs., such as **by mistake** or **an error of judgment.**

er·satz /ˈeəzæts‖ˈeərzɑts/ *adj Ger derog* which is used instead of something else, either because of cost or because the real thing cannot be obtained: *ersatz flour made from potatoes|ersatz coffee*

Erse /ɜːs‖ɜrs/ *n* [U] GAELIC

e·ruc·ta·tion /ɪˌrʌkˈteɪʃən/ *n* [C;U] *fml* (an example of) the action of BELCHing[1] (1)

er·u·dite /ˈerʊdaɪt‖ˈerə-/ *adj fml* (of a person or a book) full of learning: *He has written many erudite works on the history of the Roman Empire* —**~ly** *adv* —**-dition** /ˌerʊˈdɪʃən‖ˌerə-/ *n* [U]

e·rupt /ɪˈrʌpt/ *v* [IØ] (of a mountain with fire inside it (VOLCANO)) to explode and pour out fire: *Mount Vesuvius hasn't erupted for a good many years* (fig.) *Violence erupted in the city after the football match*

e·rup·tion /ɪˈrʌpʃən/ *n* [C;U] **1** (an example of) the action of ERUPTing: *a* VOLCANO *in a state of eruption*|(fig.) *eruptions* (=sudden cases) *of infectious disease* **2** (the sudden appearance of) an unhealthy spot or area on the skin

-e·ry /əri/ *suffix* **1** [*n, (adj)*→*n*[U]] also (*after* -d, -t, -l, -n, -e) **-ry**— **a** the art, behaviour, or condition of: SLAVERY|BRAVERY|DEVILRY **b** a collection of: *a lot of* CROCKERY|*modern* MACHINERY|*in all her* FINERY **2** [*n*→*n*[C]] also (*after* -e) **-ry**— a place where the stated thing lives, or is done, made, or sold: BAKERY|ROOKERY|REFINERY

er·y·sip·e·las /ˌer$\frac{1}{2}$ˈsɪpələs/ *n* [U] a type of infectious skin disease

-es /$\frac{1}{2}$z/ *suffix* (the form used for -s when added to a word ending with -s, -z, -ch, -sh or -y): BLESS*es*|*watches|glasses|ladies*

es·ca·late /ˈeskəleɪt/ *v* **1** [IØ;T1] **a** (of war) to spread and get more serious by stages **b** (of a government, an army, etc.) to cause (a war) to spread and get more serious **2** [I∅] (of prices and wages) to rise, one after the other: *The cost of living is escalating* —**-lation** /ˌeskəˈleɪʃən/ *n* [U]

es·ca·la·tor /ˈeskəleɪtəʳ/ *BrE* also **moving staircase**— *n* a set of moving stairs, as in an underground railway system or a large city shop

es·ca·lope /ˈeskələʊp/ *n* a thin boneless piece of PORK, BEEF, or esp. VEAL (=meat from a young cow), cooked in hot fat in a coating of egg and BREADCRUMBs

es·ca·pade /ˈeskəpeɪd/ *n* a wild, exciting, and sometimes dangerous act, esp. one that disobeys rules or causes some trouble (such as one carried out for fun by young people)

es·cape¹ /ɪˈskeɪp/ *v* **1** [I∅ (*from, out of*)] (of a person) to reach freedom: *escape from/out of the burning house|The prisoners have escaped* **2** [I∅ (*from, out of*)] (of liquids or gases) to come out; to find a way out: *Some gas is escaping from the pipe* **3** [I∅;T1,4] (of a person) to avoid (a stated evil): *escaped death|escaped his fate|to go south to escape the English winter|He narrowly* (=only just) *escaped being drowned* **4** [T1] (of an event, a fact, etc.) to be unnoticed or forgotten by: *I'm afraid your name escapes me* (=I've forgotten it).|*Nothing escaped his attention* **5** [T1] (of a noise, words, etc.) to be produced or made, usu. unconsciously, by (a person): *A whistle of surprise escaped him*

escape² *n* **1** [C;U: (*from, out of*)] (an example of) the act of escaping or fact of having escaped: *my successful escape from prison|The thief jumped into a car and made his escape* **2** [C (*of, from, out of*)] a case of the act of escaping by a liquid or gas: *an escape of gas* (*from the pipe*) **3** [S;U] something that frees one from unpleasant or dull reality: *She reads love stories as an escape* —see also ESCAPISM **4** **narrow escape** a case of only just avoiding (stated) evil

es·cap·ee /ˌeskeɪˈpiː, ɪˌskeɪˈpiː/ *n* a prisoner who has escaped from prison

es·cape·ment /ɪˈskeɪpmənt/ *n* the part of a clock or a watch which controls the moving parts inside —compare ESCARPMENT and see picture at CLOCK¹

escape ve·lo·ci·ty /·ˈ· ·ˌ···/ *n* [S9;U] the speed at which an object moves fast enough to get free from the pull of the Earth, or from another PLANET, and not fall back

es·cap·is·m /ɪˈskeɪpɪzəm/ *n* [U] *derog* activity intended to provide escape from unpleasant or dull reality: *That story about 3 beautiful girls in a spaceship is pure escapism! You should read a serious book about the war, like me* —**escapist** *adj, n*

es·ca·pol·o·gy /ˌeskəˈpɒlədʒi‖-ˈpɑ-/ [U] the art or practice of escaping, esp. from bags, chains, etc., as a theatrical performance —**-gist** *n*

e·scarp·ment /ɪˈskɑːpmənt‖-ɑr-/ *n* **1** a long cliff on a mountain-side **2** a steep slope just below the wall of a fort

es·cha·tol·o·gy /ˌeskəˈtɒlədʒi‖-ˈtɑ-/ *n* [U] (in religious, esp. Christian, teaching) the subject of the 4 Last Things, which are the end of the world, God's last judgment of man, and rewards and punishments after death —compare SCATOLOGICAL —**-gical** /ˌeskətəˈlɒdʒɪkəl‖-ˈlɑ-/ *adj*

es·chew /ɪsˈtʃuː/ *v* [T1] *fml* to avoid on purpose (something thought to be evil): *eschew bad company/alcoholic drinks*

es·cort¹ /ˈeskɔːt‖-ɔrt/ *n* **1** [GC] a person or people, often in ships or aircraft, who go with another as a guard or as an honour: *The prisoner travelled under police escort* (=with some policemen) **2** [C] a man who takes a woman out for the evening: *Mary's escort arrived at 7 o'clock with a bunch of red roses*

e·scort² /ɪˈskɔːt‖-ɔrt/ *v* [T1 (*to*)] to go with (someone) as an ESCORT¹: *May I escort you to the dance?*

escort a·gen·cy /ˈ·· ˌ···/ *n* an organization which provides young men or women as social companions for an evening

es·cri·toire /ˌeskrɪ̌ˈtwɑːʳ/ *n tech* a small writing-desk, usu. old and valuable, with drawers for papers and a lid which closes when it is not in use

e·scutch·eon /ɪˈskʌtʃən/ *n* **1** a ceremonial shield on which the sign (COAT OF ARMS) of a noble family is painted **2** **blot on one's escutcheon** *pomp* a dishonourable action or event that harms one's good name

-ese /iːz/ *suffix* **1** [*n*→*adj* [Wa5], *n*] (the people or language) belonging to (a country): *to learn* JAPANESE|JAPANESE *art|The* JAPANESE *are so polite!* —see LANGUAGE TABLE **2** [*n*→*n*] *usu. derog* literature written in the (stated) style: *Johnsonese*| JOURNALESE

Es·ki·mo /ˈeskɪ̌məʊ/ *adj* [Wa5;A] of or related to a race of people living in the far north of North America, eastern Siberia, and the surrounding islands

e·soph·a·gus /ɪˈsɒfəgəs‖ɪˈsɑ-/ *n* OESOPHAGUS

es·o·ter·ic /ˌesəˈterɪk, ˌiːsə-/ *adj* **1** secret and mysterious; having deep and secret meanings which are only understood by a few chosen people **2** (of knowledge, interests, etc.) limited to a small circle of people: *Some words are really too esoteric for this dictionary* —**~ally** *adv* [Wa4]

ESP /ˌiː es ˈpiː/ *abbrev. for:* EXTRASENSORY PERCEPTION

esp. /esp/ *abbrev. for:* especially: *In this dictionary, the expression "esp. in the phr. . . ." means "especially in the phrase . . ."*

es·pal·i·er /ɪˈspælɪəʳ (*Fr* ɛspalje)/ *n* [A] *Fr* a wooden or wire frame in a garden, on which fruit trees are trained to grow

es·pe·cial /ɪˈspeʃəl/ *adj* [A] *fml* SPECIAL¹ (2)

es·pe·cial·ly /ɪˈspeʃəli/ *adv* **1** also **specially**— to a particularly great degree: *"Do you like chocolate?" "Not especially."|not especially hot|I love Italy, especially in summer* **2** also **specially**— in particular; above all: *Noise is unpleasant, especially when you're trying to sleep* **3** SPECIALLY (1): *This crown was made especially for the King*

Es·pe·ran·to /ˌespəˈræntəʊ/ *n* [R] an invented language, intended for international use

es·pi·o·nage /ˈespɪənɑːʒ/ *n* [U] *Fr* the action of SPYing; work of finding out the political secrets of countries to be passed on to their enemies: *Industrial espionage is the stealing of knowledge about another firm's business*

es·pla·nade /ˈespləneɪd‖-nɑd/ *n* a level open space for walking, often along the seafront of a seaside town

es·pous·al /ɪˈspaʊzəl/ *n fml* **1** [C;U] the giving of one's support to an aim, idea, etc.: *John's espousal of violent political beliefs annoyed his father very much* **2** [C *often pl. with sing. meaning*] *old use* a marriage or a promise of marriage

es·pouse /ɪˈspaʊz/ *v* [T1] *fml* **1** to (decide to) support an aim, idea, etc.: *He espoused the* CAUSE (=political idea) *of equal rights for women* **2** *old use* (of a man) to (promise to) marry (a woman) **3** [(*to*)] *old use* (of a woman's parents) to promise (a woman) to a man in marriage

es·pres·so /eˈspresəʊ, ɪˈspre-/ *n* **-sos** [C;U] *It* (a cup of) a kind of coffee made by forcing steam through crushed coffee beans

es·prit de corps /eˌspriː də ˈkɔːʳ/ *n* [U] *Fr* loyalty among the members of a group

es·py /ɪˈspaɪ/ *v* [T1] *fml* to see suddenly, usu. from a distance or unexpectedly: *One day Robinson Crusoe espied a footprint in the sand*

Esq., also (*rare*) **Es·quire** /ɪ'skwaɪəʳ‖'esk-, ɪ'skwaɪər/ *n* [E] *esp. BrE* (used as a title of politeness usu. written in its shortened form after the full name of a man): *The envelope is addressed to Peter Jones, Esq.*

-esque /esk/ *suffix* [*n→adj*] **1** in the manner or style of: ROMANESQUE|*Kafkaesque* (=in the manner or style of the writer Franz Kafka) **2** like: PICTURESQUE|STATUESQUE

-ess /es/ *suffix* [*n→n*] a female (of the stated kind): *a* GIANTESS|*an actress|a waitress|2* LIONESSes
USAGE A serious woman writer does not like to be called an AUTHORess or *poetess*. It is not polite to call a black woman a NEGRess, or a Jewish woman a *Jewess*.

es·say¹ /e'seɪ/ *v* [T1,3] *fml* to try (to do something): *to essay a* TASK (= piece of work)

es·say² /'eseɪ/ *n* a piece of writing, not poetry, or a story, usu. short and on one subject —**~ist** *n*

es·say³ /'eseɪ, e'seɪ/ *n* [(*at*)] *fml* an attempt or effort: *She made her first essays at cooking*

es·sence /'esəns/ *n* **1** [U (*of*)] the central or most important quality of a thing, which makes it what it is; the inner nature of a thing, by which it can be recognized or put into a class: *The essence of his religious teaching is love for all men* **2** [C;U] the best part of a substance, taken out and reduced to a jelly, liquid, etc.: *essence of roses|meat essence* **3 in essence** in its/one's nature; ESSENTIALLY (1) **4 of the essence** very important: *We must hurry. Time is of the essence*

es·sen·tial¹ /ɪ'senʃəl/ *adj* **1** [B (*to, for*)] **a** necessary: *We can live without clothes, but food and drink are essential to life/for the preservation of life* **b** forming the central part of: *Her most essential quality is kindness* **2** [Wa5;A] *tech* of an ESSENCE (2): *essential oils*

essential² *n* [*often pl.*] **1** something that is necessary, or ESSENTIAL¹ (1a): *The room was furnished with the simplest essentials: a bed, a chair and a table* **2** something that forms the ESSENCE (1) (of something): *the essentials of grammar|One of the essentials of her character is kindness*

es·sen·tial·ly /ɪ'senʃəli/ *adv* **1** in reality, though perhaps not in appearance; BASICally: *She's essentially kind* **2** necessarily: *"Must I do it today?" "Not essentially"*

est. /est/ *abbrev. for:* **1** established: *H. Perkins and Company, est. 1869* **2** ESTIMATE

-est /ɪ̵st/ *suffix* **1** also (*after* -e) **-st**— (forms the SUPERLATIVE of many shorter adjectives and adverbs): *cold, colder, coldest|dry, drier, driest|Which soap washes whitest?* **2** also **-st**— *old use or bibl* (forms the second person singular of English verbs): THOU *goest*|THOU *didst*

es·tab·lish /ɪ'stæblɪʃ/ *v* [Wv5] **1** [T1] to set up (an organization): *established a shop/school/business/new state* **2** [T1 (*as, in*)] to place (oneself or another) in a (stated) firm or good position: *He established his son in business.|He established himself as the most powerful minister in the new government* **3** [T1,5,6a] to find out or make certain of (a fact, answer, etc.): *to establish the truth of a story* **4** [T1] to make (a rule): *We've established a rule in this club that everyone buys his own drinks* **5** [T1] to cause people to believe in or recognize (a claim, fact, etc.): *She established her fame as an actress* **6** [Wv5;T1] to make (a religion) official for a nation: *The established religion of Egypt is Islam*

es·tab·lish·ment /ɪ'stæblɪʃmənt/ *n* **1** [U9] the act of ESTABLISHing: *the establishment of new industry by the Government* **2** [GC] (a group of people that form) a business organization: *These 2 hotels are both excellent establishments*

Establishment *n esp. BrE, often derog* **1** [*the*+GU] the powerful organizations and people who are said to control public life and support the established order of Society: *The Establishment is/are trying to stop the spreading of this new habit* **2** [*the*+GU9] (*sometimes not cap.*) a controlling group of the stated kind: *Will the musical Establishment allow your new songs to be performed?*

es·tam·i·net /e'stæmɪneɪ‖e,stæmɪ'neɪ/ *n Fr* a small French or French-style restaurant selling alcoholic drinks and coffee

es·tate /ɪ'steɪt/ *n* **1** [C] a (large) piece of land in the country, usu. with one large house on it and one owner **2** [C] *BrE* a piece of land on which buildings (of a stated type) have all been built together in a planned way: *An industrial estate has factories on it, and a* HOUSING *estate has houses on it* **3** [U *law*] the whole of a person's property, according to the law (often in the phrs. **real estate** (=land and buildings), **personal estate** (=money and other property)) **4** [U9] *old use and fml* state, rank, or condition in life: *An Englishman reaches man's estate on his 18th birthday.|joined together in the holy estate of* MATRIMONY (=marriage) **5** [C] *old use* (esp. of France before the Revolution) social or political class: *The 3 estates of the* REALM (=country) *were the lords, the priests and the common people.|Newspapers are sometimes called the* **4th Estate**

estate a·gent /·'· ,··/ (*AmE* **real estate agent**)— *n BrE* a person whose business is to bring together people who want to sell and people who want to buy houses, property, or land, and to look after the property of others —**estate agency** *n*

estate car /·'· ·/ also **shooting brake,** *AmE* **station wagon**— *n* a private motor vehicle which carries both people and goods, with folding or removable back seats, and doors at the back which can be opened to put bags, cases, etc., inside —see picture at INTERCHANGE²

es·teem¹ /ɪ'stiːm/ *n* [U] *fml* respect; good opinion (of a person): *All David's friends held him in high esteem* —compare ESTIMATION

esteem² *v fml* **1** [T1] to respect and admire greatly (esp. a person or his character): *The old teacher was much loved and esteemed* **2** [X (*to be*) 1,7] to believe (someone or something) (to be) (esp. something good): *I did not esteem him to be worthy of trust* —compare ESTIMATE¹ (1)

es·thete /'iːsθiːt‖'es-/ *n AmE* AESTHETE —**esthetic** /iːs'θetɪk‖es-/, **esthetical** *adj* —**esthetically** *adv* [Wa4]—**esthetics** *n* [U;(P)]: see -ICS (USAGE)

es·ti·ma·ble /'estɪ̵məbəl/ *adj apprec* (of a person or his behaviour) worthy of ESTEEM¹

es·ti·mate¹ /'estɪ̵meɪt/ *v* **1** [T1 (*at*), 5a] to calculate (something which can be added or measured); form an opinion as to the degree of (something): *I estimate her age at 35.|It's impossible to estimate his abilities yet* —see also UNDER/OVERESTIMATE —compare ESTEEM² **2** [IØ] to calculate the cost of doing a job; offer to do a job for a certain price: *I asked 3 building firms to estimate for the repairs to the roof* —compare QUOTE¹ (3)

es·ti·mate² /'estɪ̵mɪ̵t/ *n* **1** [C (*of*), C5] a calculation (of something which can be added or measured, or of the degree or quality of something): *My estimate of her character was wrong* **2** [*often pl.*] an offer to do a job for a certain price: *We got 2 or 3 estimates before having the roof repaired, and accepted the lowest* —compare QUOTATION (3b) **3 at a rough estimate** not speaking exactly

es·ti·ma·tion /,estɪ̵'meɪʃən/ *n* [U] judgment or

opinion: *He has lowered himself in my estimation* —compare ESTEEM[1]

es·ti·ma·tor /ˈestᵻmeɪtəʳ/ *n* a person who ESTIMATEs[1] (2) —compare VALUER

es·trange /ɪˈstreɪndʒ/ *v* [Wv5;T1 (*from*)] to cause (esp. people in a family) to become unfriendly: *His behaviour estranged his brother|him from his brother*

es·trange·ment /ɪˈstreɪndʒmənt/ *n* [C;U: (*from, with, between*)] the state or an example of being ESTRANGED: *The quarrel led to complete estrangement (from her family)*

es·tro·gen /ˈestrədʒən, ˈiːstrə-/ *n* [U] *esp. AmE* OESTROGEN

es·trous cy·cle /ˈestrəs ˌsaɪkəl, ˈiːs-/ *n esp. AmE* OESTRUS CYCLE

es·tu·a·ry /ˈestʃʊəri/ *n* the wide lower part or mouth of a river, into which the sea enters at high TIDE

et al. /ˌet ˈæl/ *Lat humor* (of people) and the others: *Are George, Peter, et al. coming to the party?*

etc., also (*rare*) **et cet·e·ra** /ˌet ˈsetərə/ *adv* [Wa5] *Lat* and the rest; and so on: *We'd better buy tea, sugar, etc.|This nasty letter says pay at once, they've warned us before, etc., etc., etc.*

etch /etʃ/ *v* [IØ;T1: (*on*)] to draw (a picture) by cutting lines on a metal plate with a needle and then using acid to eat out the lines, so that one can print from the plate: (fig.) *This terrible event is etched for ever in my memory* —**~er** *n*

etch·ing /ˈetʃɪŋ/ *n* **1** [U] the art of ETCHing: *Mary is very keen on etching* **2** [C] a picture printed from a metal plate which has been ETCHed

e·ter·nal /ɪˈtɜːnəl‖-ɜr-/ *adj* (*sometimes cap.*) [Wa5] going on for ever; without beginning or end: *Rome has been called the Eternal City* —**-nally** *adv*

eternal tri·an·gle /·ˌ·· ˈ···/ *n* [*the*+R] the troubled state of affairs resulting from the love of 2 people, usu. of the same sex, for another person, usu. of the other sex —compare MÉNAGE À TROIS

e·ter·ni·ty /ɪˈtɜːnᵻti‖-ɜr-/ *n* **1** [U] time without end; state of time after death, which is said to last for ever: *This bomb will blow us all to eternity* (=kill us) **2** [C] a very long time which seems endless: *I was so anxious that every moment seemed an eternity*

e·ther /ˈiːθəʳ/ *n* [U] **1** a light colourless liquid made from alcohol, which burns and is easily changed into a gas. It is used in industry and as an ANAESTHETIC to put people to sleep before an operation **2** also **aether**— *poet* the upper air **3** also **aether**— a very fine substance, once believed to fill the whole of space, through which light waves were thought to travel

e·the·re·al, aethereal /ɪˈθɪərəl/ *adj* **1** of unearthly lightness and delicacy; like a spirit or fairy **2** *poet* of the ETHER (2): *the blue, ethereal sky* —**-ally** *adv*

eth·ic /ˈeθɪk/ *n* a system of moral behaviour: *the Christian ethic|a new ethic*

eth·i·cal /ˈeθɪkəl/ *adj* **1** [Wa5] of ETHICS (2): *What ought I to do? This is an ethical question* **2** [*often nonassertive*] morally good: *I oughtn't to do that; it's not ethical*

eth·i·cal·ly /ˈeθɪkəli/ *adv* **1** [Wa5] in connection with ETHICS (2): *Ethically (speaking), I disapprove of what he did, though it was certainly clever* **2** in a morally good way: *I think he has behaved quite ethically*

eth·ics /ˈeθɪks/ *n* **1** [U] the science which deals with morals **2** [P] moral rules: *What ought I to do? It's a matter of ethics* —see also -ICS (USAGE)

eth·nic /ˈeθnɪk/ also **eth·ni·cal** /-kəl/— *adj* **1** [Wa5] of or related to a racial, national, or tribal group **2** *esp. AmE* interestingly unusual because typical of such a group; EXOTIC: *This music would sound more ethnic if you played it on a tin whistle*

eth·nic·al·ly /ˈeθnɪkəli/ *adv* in connection with a racial, national, or tribal group: *Ethnically (speaking), these 2 nations are the same*

eth·nog·ra·pher /eθˈnɒgrəfəʳ‖eθˈnɑ-/ *n* a person who has studied ETHNOGRAPHY

eth·nog·ra·phy /eθˈnɒgrəfi‖eθˈnɑ-/ *n* [U] the scientific description of the different races of man —**-phic** /ˌeθnəˈgræfɪk/ *adj* [Wa5] —**-phically** *adv* [Wa4,5]

eth·nol·o·gist /eθˈnɒlədʒᵻst‖eθˈnɑ-/ *n* a person who has studied ETHNOLOGY

eth·nol·o·gy /eθˈnɒlədʒi‖eθˈnɑ-/ *n* [U] the science of the different races of man —compare ANTHROPOLOGY —**-gical** /ˌeθnəˈlɒdʒɪkəl‖-ˈlɑ-/ *adj* [Wa5] —**-gically** *adv* [Wa4,5]

e·thos /ˈiːθɒs‖ˈiːθɑs/ *n* the moral nature, set of ideas, or beliefs of a person or group

eth·yl /ˈeθəl; *tech* ˈiːθaɪl/ *n* **1** [A] *tech* of the chemical combination of 2 atoms of CARBON and 5 atoms of HYDROGEN (C_2H_5) **2** [U] any of various liquids which are added to the petrol in a car engine to reduce noise (ANTI-KNOCK[1] (5))

ethyl al·co·hol /ˌ·· ˈ···/ *n* [U] *tech* ordinary alcohol which can be drunk —compare METHYL ALCOHOL

e·ti·o·late /ˈiːtɪəleɪt/ *v* [Wv5;T1] to make (a plant) grow long stems and small pale leaves by keeping in the dark —**-lation** /ˌiːtɪəˈleɪʃən/ *n* [U]

et·i·ol·o·gy, *BrE* also **aetiology** /ˌetiˈɒlədʒi‖-ˈɑlə-/ *n* [U] *med* (the study of) the cause of disease: *What is the etiology of this condition?* (=What caused this illness?) —**-gical** /ˌetɪəˈlɒdʒɪkəl‖-ˈlɑ-/ *adj* [Wa5] —**-gically** *adv* [Wa4,5]

et·i·quette /ˈetɪket‖-kət/ *n* [U] the formal rules of proper behaviour

-ette /et/ *suffix* **1** [*n*→*n* [C]] a small kind of: KITCHENETTE|CIGARETTE **2** [*n*→*n* [C]] a female (of the stated kind): USHERETTE|SUFFRAGETTE **3** [*n*→*n* [U]] not real; IMITATION: FLANNELETTE|*chairs covered with* LEATHERETTE

et·y·mol·o·gist /ˌetᵻˈmɒlədʒᵻst‖-ˈmɑ-/ *n* a person who has studied ETYMOLOGY

et·y·mol·o·gy /ˌetᵻˈmɒlədʒi‖-ˈmɑ-/ *n* **1** [U] the scientific study of the origins, history, and changing meanings of words —compare ENTOMOLOGY **2** [C] (an account of) the history of a particular word —**-gical** /ˌetᵻməˈlɒdʒɪkəl‖-ˈlɑ-/ *adj* [Wa5] —**-gically** *adv* [Wa4,5]

eu·ca·lyp·tus /ˌjuːkəˈlɪptəs/ *n* **1** [C] any of several types of tall tree, such as the Australian GUM tree, which keep their leaves in winter, and which produce an oil used for colds **2** [U] the oil made from these trees —see picture at TREE[1]

Eu·cha·rist /ˈjuːkərᵻst/ *n* [*the*+R] (the bread and wine taken at) the Christian ceremony based on Christ's last supper on Earth: *The priest* CELEBRATED *the Eucharist* —see also MASS, COMMUNION (2) —**~ic** /ˌjuːkəˈrɪstɪk/ *adj*

eu·clid·e·an, -ian /juːˈklɪdɪən‖jʊ-/ *adj* [Wa5] (*often cap.*) of or related to the discoveries of Euclid about lines, angles, surfaces, and solids (GEOMETRY)

eu·gen·ic /juːˈdʒenɪk/ *adj* **1** [Wa5;A] connected with, or leading to, the improvement of the human race by EUGENICS **2** *apprec* that produces strong and clever children: *a eugenic marriage* —**~ally** *adv* [Wa4]

eu·gen·ics /juːˈdʒenɪks/ *n* [U;(P)] the study of ways of breeding stronger and cleverer people by choosing suitable parents —see -ICS (USAGE)

eu·lo·gist /ˈjuːlədʒᵻst/ *n* a person who EULOGIZEs

eu·lo·gis·tic /ˌjuːləˈdʒɪstɪk/ *adj* (of a speech or a piece of writing) full of EULOGY: *a eulogistic speech about the courage and goodness of the dead king* —**~ally** [Wa4]

eu·lo·gize, -gise /ˈjuːlədʒaɪz/ *v* [T1] *fml* to make a EULOGY about (usu. a person or his qualities)

eu·lo·gy /ˈjuːlədʒi/ *n* [C;U:(*on, of*)] *fml* (a speech or a piece of writing containing) high praise (usu. of a person or his qualities) —compare ELEGY

eu·nuch /ˈjuːnək/ *n* a man who has been CASTRATEd (=had part of his sex organs removed), esp. one formerly employed in the women's rooms of some Eastern courts

eu·phe·mis·m /ˈjuːfəmɪzəm/ *n* [C;U] (an example of) the use of a pleasanter, less direct name for something thought to be unpleasant: *"Fall asleep" is a euphemism for "die"* —compare EUPHUISM

eu·phe·mis·tic /ˌjuːfəˈmɪstɪk/ *adj* (of a speech or writing) containing or consisting of EUPHEMISM —**~ally** *adv* [Wa4]

eu·pho·ni·ous /juːˈfəʊnɪəs‖jʊ-/ *adj* (of language) pleasant in sound

eu·pho·ni·um /juːˈfəʊnɪəm‖jʊ-/ *n* a type of musical instrument which is a kind of TUBA, made of brass and played by blowing

eu·pho·ny /ˈjuːfəni/ *n* [U] pleasantness of sound, esp. in language —opposite **cacophony**

eu·pho·ri·a /juːˈfɔːrɪə‖jʊˈforɪə/ *n* [U] a feeling of happiness and cheerful excitement —**euphoric** /juːˈfɒrɪk‖jʊˈfɔrɪk, -ˈfɑr-/ *adj* —**-cally** *adv* [Wa4]

eu·phu·is·m /ˈjuːfjuːɪzəm/ *n* [U] a peculiar, difficult, and rather insincere style of literature which was fashionable in England in the 16th and early 17th centuries —compare EUPHEMISM

Eu·ra·sian /jʊəˈreɪʒən, -ʃən/ *adj* [Wa5] **1** of Europe and Asia **2** (of people) of mixed European and Asian birth

eu·re·ka /jʊəˈriːkə/ *interj Gk humor* (used as a cry of victory at making a discovery) I have found it!

eu·rhyth·mic, eurythmic /juːˈrɪðmɪk‖jʊ-/ *adj* [Wa5:A] of or related to EURHYTHMICS: *eurhythmic exercises*

eu·rhyth·mics, eurythmics /juːˈrɪðmɪks‖jʊ-/ *n* [U; (P)] a system of exercising the body with music —see -ICS (USAGE)

Eu·ro- /ˈjʊərəʊ/ *comb. form* **1** Europe (esp. western Europe) and: *Euro-American relations* **2** of the European money market: EURODOLLAR **3** of the EUROPEAN ECONOMIC COMMUNITY (E.E.C.): EUROCRAT

Eu·ro·crat /ˈjʊərəʊkræt/ *n* an official of the EUROPEAN ECONOMIC COMMUNITY

Eu·ro·dol·lar /ˈjʊərəʊˌdɒləʳ‖-ˌdɑ-/ *n* a US dollar which has been put into European banks to help trade and provide an international money system

Eu·ro·pe·an /ˌjʊərəˈpɪən/ *adj* [Wa5] **1** of or related to Europe **2** happening or existing all over Europe: *an actress of European fame* **3** *esp. BrE* (of people) white: *He looks European*

European Ec·o·nom·ic Com·mu·ni·ty /··ˌ·· ··ˌ·· ·ˈ···/ *n* [*the*+R] *fml* COMMON MARKET

eu·sta·chian tube /juːˌsteɪʃən ˈtjuːb‖-ˈtuːb/ *n* (*often cap.*) *med* either of the pair of tubes which join the ears to the throat —see picture at EAR[1]

eu·tha·na·si·a /ˌjuːθəˈneɪzɪə‖-ˈneɪʒə/ *n* [U] the painless killing of people who are incurably ill or very old

e·vac·u·ate /ɪˈvækjʊeɪt/ *v* [T1] **1** to take all the people away from (a place): *The village was evacuated because of floods* **2** [(*from, to*)] to move (people) out of danger **3** *fml* to empty (the bowels) —**-ation** /ɪˌvækjʊˈeɪʃən/ *n* [C;U]

e·vac·u·ee /ɪˌvækjʊˈiː/ *n* a person who has been EVACUATEd (2)

e·vade /ɪˈveɪd/ *v* **1** [T1] to get out of the way of or escape from: *evaded an enemy|The lion evaded the hunters* **2** [T1,4] *derog* to avoid, or avoid doing (something one should do): *to evade (paying) your taxes* **3** [T1] *derog* to avoid answering (a question) properly

e·val·u·ate /ɪˈvæljʊeɪt/ *v* [T1] to calculate the value or degree of: *I can't evaluate his ability* —**-ation** /ɪˌvæljʊˈeɪʃən/ *n* [C;U]

ev·a·nes·cent /ˌevəˈnesənt/ *adj fml* soon fading away, disappearing, and being forgotten —**-cence** *n* [U]

e·van·gel·ic /ˌiːvænˈdʒelɪk/ *adj* [Wa5;A] of the teachings of Christ, as recorded in the 4 books of the Bible called the GOSPELs

e·van·gel·i·cal /ˌiːvænˈdʒelɪkəl/ *adj, n* (*often cap.*) (a member) of certain PROTESTANT Christian churches which believe in the importance of religious teaching, of faith, and of studying the Bible, rather than in ceremonies and good behaviour —**~ism** *n* [U]

e·van·ge·list /ɪˈvændʒələst/ *n* a person who travels from place to place and holds EVANGELICAL religious meetings —**-lism** *n* [U] —**-listic** /ɪˌvændʒəˈlɪstɪk/ *adj*

Evangelist *n* any of the 4 writers (Matthew, Mark, Luke, and John) of the 4 books of the Bible called the GOSPELs

e·van·ge·lize, -lise /ɪˈvændʒəlaɪz/ *v* [I∅;T1] to teach the Christian religion as an EVANGELIST

e·vap·o·rate /ɪˈvæpəreɪt/ *v* [I∅;T1] to (cause to) change into steam and disappear: *The sun will evaporate the mist.*|(fig.) *My hopes are beginning to evaporate* (=to disappear) —**-ration** /ɪˌvæpəˈreɪʃən/ *n* [U]

evaporated milk /·ˌ···· ˈ·/ *n* [U] milk, usu. bought in tins, from which part of the water has been taken by evaporating (EVAPORATE)

e·va·sion /ɪˈveɪʒən/ *n* **1** [U] the act of evading (EVADE (1)): *the fox's clever evasion of the dogs* **2** [C;U] *derog* an action or lack of action which EVADEs (2): *George is in prison for tax evasion* **3** [C] *derog* a statement which EVADEs (3): *The minister's speech was full of evasions*

e·va·sive /ɪˈveɪsɪv/ *adj derog* **1** which EVADEs or tries to EVADE (2,3): *an evasive answer* **2 take evasive action** *fml* (of a ship, aircraft etc. in war) to get out of the way or try to escape —**~ly** *adv* —**~ness** *n* [U]

eve /iːv/ *n* **1** [R9 (*usu. cap.*)] the night or the whole day before a religious feast or holiday: *to go to a party on New Year's Eve* **2** [*the*+R (*of*)] the time just before an important event: *on the eve of our examination* **3** [R] *poet* evening: *bathed in eve's loveliness*

Eve *n* [R] (according to the Bible) the first woman whom God made —compare ADAM (1)

e·ven[1] /ˈiːvən/ *n* [R] *poet* evening: *"the last pale beam of even"* (Shelley)

even[2] *adj* [Wa2] **1** [(*with*)] flat, level, smooth; forming a straight line (with): *Cut the bushes even with the fence* (=not higher and not lower) **2** regular and unchanging: *an even temperature* **3** [(*with*)] (of things that can be measured and compared) equal: *He won the first game and I won the second, so now we're even/now I'm even with him* **4** [*no pass.*] **be/get even with** to do as much harm (to someone) as someone has done to oneself; to have one's REVENGE (on someone): *He cheated me, but I'll get even with him one day!* —see also BREAK EVEN —**~ly** *adv* —**evenness** *n* [U]

even[3] *adv* **1** (*used just before the surprising part of a statement, to add to its strength*) which is more than might be expected: *Even John doesn't go out in the summer* (so certainly nobody else does).|*John doesn't go out even in the summer* (so certainly not in the winter) **2** (*used for adding force to an expression*) indeed; (and) one might almost say: *He looked happy, even gay.|He looked happy, gay* *even* **3** (*used before a* COMPARATIVE) still; yet: *It was cold yesterday, but it's even colder today* **4 even as** just at the same moment as: *He fell even as I stretched out my hand to help him* **5 even if/though** though: *Even if you don't like wine* (=though you may not like wine), *try a glass of this!* (compare *If you like wine, try a glass of this!*) **6 even now/so/then** in spite of what has/had happened; though that is true: *I* (*have*) *explained everything, but even now/then she doesn't/didn't understand*

even chanc·es /ˌ·· ˈ··/ *n* [P] *infml* EVENS (often in the phr. **it's even chances that . . .**): *It's even chances that he won't come*

even-hand·ed /ˌ·· ˈ··◂/ *adj* fair and equal; equally balanced

eve·ning /ˈiːvnɪŋ/ *n* **1** [C;U] the end of the day and early part of the night, between the end of the day's work and bedtime: *a warm evening|By the time he gets home there won't be much evening left* **2** [C9] a party, performance, etc. (of the stated type), happening in the early part of the night: *Will you come to our musical evening on Thursday?*

evening dress¹ /ˈ·· ·/ also **evening gown**— *n* a dress (esp. long) worn by a woman for formal occasions in the evening

evening dress² *n* [U] the clothes worn by women, and special black clothes worn by men, for formal occasions in the evening

evening prayer /ˌ·· ˈ·/ *n* [U] EVENSONG

eve·nings /ˈiːvnɪŋz/ *adv AmE* in the EVENING repeatedly; on any evening: *I'm always at home evenings*

evening star /ˌ·· ˈ·/ also **morning star**— *n* [*the*+R] (*often cap.*) VENUS, one of the PLANETs (=worlds going round the Sun), which appears in the western sky in the evening and in the eastern sky in the morning

even num·ber /ˌ·· ˈ··/ *n* a number that can be divided exactly by 2: *2, 4, 6, 8, etc., are even numbers* —compare ODD NUMBER

even out *v adv* [IØ;T1] to (cause to) become level or equal: *Prices should even out.|We must even things out*

evens /ˈiːvənz/ also **even odds** /ˌ·· ˈ·/— *n infml* chances that are the same for and against (as when one risks £1 on a horse-race to win £1)

e·ven·song /ˈiːvənsɒŋ‖-sɔŋ/ also **evening prayer**— *n* [R] (*often cap.*) the evening service in the Church of England

e·vent /ɪˈvent/ *n* **1** a happening, usu. an important one: *the chief events of 1977* —compare FACT (1) **2** any of the races, competitions, etc., arranged as part of a day's sports: *The next event will be the 100 yards race* **3 at all events** in spite of everything; in any case: *She had a terrible accident, but at all events she wasn't killed* **4 in any event** whatever may happen (in the future): *I'll probably see you tomorrow, but in any event I'll telephone* **5 in either event** whichever happens: *I don't know whether I'm going by car or by train, but in either event I'll need money* **6 in that event** if that happens: *It may rain. In that event, we won't go* **7 in the event** *esp. BrE* as it happened; when it actually happened: *We were afraid he would be nervous on stage, but in the event he performed beautifully* **8 in the event of (something)** if (something) happens: *He asked his sister to look after his children in the event of his death* **9 in the natural/normal course of events** in the way things ordinarily happen: *Aren't you a bit worried? In the natural course of events your daughter should have been married by now* **10 (quite) an event** an important and unusual happening: *Meeting you was quite an event in her life*

even-tem·pered /ˌ·· ˈ··◂/ *adj* [Wa2] having a calm good temper; not easily made angry

e·vent·ful /ɪˈventfəl/ *adj* full of important events: *an eventful life* —**~ly** *adv* —**~ness** *n* [U]

e·ven·tide /ˈiːvəntaɪd/ *n* [R] *poet* evening: *at eventide*

e·ven·tu·al /ɪˈventʃuəl/ *adj* [Wa5;A] (of an event) happening at last as a result: *the eventual success of his efforts*

e·ven·tu·al·i·ty /ɪˌventʃuˈælɪ̈ti/ *n* a possible, esp. unpleasant, event: *We must be prepared for all eventualities/for any eventuality*

e·ven·tu·al·ly /ɪˈventʃuəli/ *adv* at last; in the end (esp. as a result): *He worked so hard that eventually he made himself ill*

e·ven·tu·ate in /ɪˈventʃueɪt/ *v prep* [T1] *fml or pomp* to result in; have as a result: *A rapid rise in prices soon eventuated in mass unemployment*

even up *v adv* [T1] to make (something, or 2 things) equal: *I'll pay for the taxi, to even things up*

ev·er /ˈevəʳ/ *adv* **1** [*nonassertive*] at any time: *Nothing ever makes him angry.|"Do you ever go to concerts?" "No, never./Yes* (*sometimes*)."*|If you're ever in Spain, come and see me.|"Have you ever been to Paris?" "No, never./Yes* (*once*)" **2** (*after* as *or* than *in comparison*) at any time (before): *as fast as ever|faster than ever* (*before*) **3** (*after* as *and before the subject in comparisons*) (used for giving force to an expression): *I did it as fast as ever I could* **4** (*after* how, what, when, where, who, why) (used for giving force to a question): *What ever are you doing?|How ever shall we get there?* **5** *old use* or in comb. always: *the ever-increasing population* **6** *AmE infml* (used for strengthening EXCLAMATIONs in the form of questions): *Is it ever big!* (=Isn't it big!) **7 ever after** always after that: *They lived happily ever after* (end of a fairy story) **8 ever and anon** *poet* from time to time **9 ever so/such** *infml esp. BrE* very: *It's ever so cold.|She's ever such a nice girl* **10 for ever** FOREVER **11 never ever** *infml* never: *"I never ever hang any washing"* (SEU S.) **12 Yours ever** also **Ever yours**— *infml* (used at the end of a letter above the signature)

USAGE **what ever? how ever?** etc., are sometimes written **whatever? however?** but this is not thought to be good English. —compare WHATEVER HOWEVER, WHENEVER, WHEREVER, WHOEVER, WHICHEVER

ev·er·green /ˈevəgriːn‖-ər-/ *adj, n* [Wa5] (a tree or bush) that does not lose its leaves in winter —opposite **deciduous** (*adj* only)

ev·er·last·ing /ˌevəˈlɑːstɪŋ◂‖ˌevərˈlæ-/ *adj* [Wa5] **1** [B;(E)] *fml* lasting for ever; without an end: *He believes in everlasting life/in life everlasting after death* **2** [B] lasting for a long time: *These tyres are advertised as being everlasting* **3** [A] *derog* lasting so long, or happening so often, that one gets tired: *I'm tired of your everlasting quarrels!*

Everlasting *n* [*the*+R] *lit* God

ev·er·last·ing·ly /ˌevəˈlɑːstɪŋli‖ˌevərˈlæ-/ *adv* in an EVERLASTING (3) manner: *He's everlastingly giving me advice I don't need*

ev·er·more /ˌevəˈmɔːʳ‖ˌevərˈmor/ *adv* **1** *lit* always (esp. in the future): *He swore to love her* (*for*) *evermore* **2** *derog* **for evermore** (*with continuous tenses using the* -ing *form*) FOREVER (2)

ev·ery /ˈevri/ *determiner* [A] **1** (*with sing. countable* [C] *noun and sing. verb*) each, counted one by one (of a number greater than 2): *Every word in this dictionary is* (=all the words are) *important.|Every action of John's shows that he's honest* —see USAGE 1 **2** [*fml*] (between a poss. and a sing. countable [C] noun): *John's every action shows that he's honest* **3** (of things which can be counted, esp. periods of time) once (in) each: *He comes to see us every day/every 3 days.|Change the oil in the car every 5,000 miles* **4** as much (hope, chance, reason,

etc.) as possible: *She made every attempt to go* **5** (of small parts of a large whole) each without exception: *I enjoyed every minute of the party* (=the whole party) **6 every other** (of things which can be counted) **a** the 1st, 3rd, 5th . . . or the 2nd, 4th, 6th . . .: *Take some medicine every other day* **b** all the others: *Every other girl in the class got a present but me!* **7 every bit as** (with adjectives and adverbs) just as: *She's every bit as clever as her sister* **8 every (single) bit of** *AmE* also **every last bit of**— all of: *Mary's eaten every bit of her dinner* **9 every now and then** also **every now and again, every so often**— from time to time; sometimes but not often: *I write to him every now and then* **10 every (single) one (of)** (people or things) all without exception (of): *Go to bed, every one of you!* —see USAGE 2 **11 every time** whenever (something happens): *John wins every time we play!* **12 in every way** from all points of view: *My new job is more fun in every way than my old job*
USAGE 1 Compare **every** and **each**: Use **every** with a singular verb, when thinking of a whole group, like **all** with a plural verb: **Every** *child knows it* (=All children know it). Use **each** when thinking of one at a time. **Every** cannot be used of only 2 people or things, or in phrs. like **each** *of the boys|the boys* **each** . . . 2 Compare **every one** and **everyone**: **everyone** or **everybody** means "each person" and is not followed by **of**; one cannot say ***everyone** *of the children*, although it is correct to say **everyone** *in the village*. **Every one** means "each person or thing" and can be followed by **of**: **every one** *of the children|of the cups.* —see EVERYBODY (USAGE)

ev·ery·bod·y /ˈevribɒdi‖-bɑdi/ also **ev·ery·one** /ˈevriwʌn/— *pron* every person: *I stayed at work when everyone else had gone home.*|(*infml*) *"Everybody decides they're a bit hungry"* (SEU S.) —compare EVERY (10) **one** —see EVERY (USAGE)
USAGE **Anybody, every**, and **everybody** are followed by a singular verb. They are sometimes followed by a plural PRONOUN: **a** *not fml* to avoid saying *he or she*, since there is no one word for this in English: **Everybody** *started waving their flags* (fml *his or her flag*).|**Anybody** *can do it if they try* (fml *if he or she tries*).|*"I saw* **every** *student before they went away"* (SEU S.) **b** in question endings like this: **Everybody** *has arrived, haven't they?* —see EVERY (USAGE)

ev·ery·day /ˈevrideɪ/ *adj* [Wa5;A] ordinary, common, and usual: *These are my everyday shoes, not my best ones*

ev·ery·thing /ˈevriθɪŋ/ *pron* **1** (*used with sing. verb*): *Everything is ready now for the party.|I've forgotten everything I learnt at school* **2** [(*to*)] (*usu. after the verb*) the most important thing or person: *Money isn't everything.|Her daughter is everything to her* **3 and everything** *infml* and so on; ETC.: *"She was very worried about her course and everything"* (SEU S.)

ev·ery·where /ˈevriweəʳ/ *AmE* also **ev·ery·place** /-pleɪs/— *adv* [Wa5] (in/at/to) every place: *I can't find it though I've looked everywhere.|Pink elephants follow him everywhere he goes.|We must clean the house—everywhere looks so dirty!|everywhere (else) but in Scotland*

every which way /ˌ·· ˈ· ·/ *adv infml AmE* (*with verbs of movement*) in every direction, without any order: *When the police arrived, the crowd started running every which way*

e·vict /ɪˈvɪkt/ *v* [T1 (*from*) *often pass.*] to take (a person) away (from a house or land) by law: *If you don't pay your rent you'll be evicted* —**~ion** /ɪˈvɪkʃən/ *n* [C;U]

eviction or·der /·ˈ·· ˌ··/ *n* an order by a court of law that someone is to be EVICTed

ev·i·dence[1] /ˈevɪ̈dəns/ *n* [U (*of, for*), U5] **1 a** (esp. in science or law) words which prove a statement, support a belief, or make a matter more clear: *Can you show me any evidence for your statement?* **b** objects which do this: *When the police arrived he had already destroyed the evidence* (=papers, films, etc.) *that showed he was guilty* **2 evidence(s) of/that** signs or proof of/that: *There are evidences that somebody has been living here* **3 bear/show evidence of** to show signs or proof of **4 in evidence** able to be seen and noticed: *Mrs Jones was much in evidence* (=very noticeable) *at the party* **5 turn Queen's/King's/** (in the US) **State's evidence** (of a criminal) to speak against another criminal in a law court

evidence[2] *v* [T1] *rare* to be or show signs or proof of (a feeling, quality, etc.): *He/His tears evidenced great sorrow for what he had done*

ev·i·dent /ˈevɪ̈dənt/ *adj* plain, esp. to the senses; clear because of EVIDENCE: *It's evident that you've been drinking.|her evident unhappiness*

ev·i·dent·ly /ˈevɪ̈dəntli/ *adv* [Wa5] it is proved by clear signs (that); it is plain (that): *He is evidently not well* —compare APPARENTLY, OBVIOUSLY

e·vil[1] /ˈiːvəl/ *adj* **-ll-** (*AmE* **-l-**) [Wa2] *fml* **1** very bad, esp. in thought or behaviour; wicked; harmful: *evil thoughts* **2 an evil tongue** a habit of saying bad things about people **3 fall on evil days** to suffer misfortune (esp. concerning money or health) **4 in an evil hour** in a time that is to bring trouble: *In an evil hour I agreed to marry him* —**evilly** /ˈiːvəl-li/ *adv*

evil[2] *n* [C;U] *fml* (a) great wickedness or misfortune: *"Deliver us from evil"* (prayer).|*"The evil that men do lives after them"* (=is remembered) (Shakespeare, *Julius Caesar*) —opposite **good**[2] (1)

e·vil·do·er /ˌiːvəlˈduːəʳ/ *n fml* a person who does evil

evil eye /ˌ·· ˈ·/ *n* [*the*+R] (*sometimes caps.*) the supposed power to harm people by looking at them

evil-mind·ed /ˌ·· ˈ··◂/ *adj* [Wa2] having bad thoughts and desires —**evil-mindedly** *adv* —**evil-mindedness** *n* [U]

evil-tem·pered /ˌ·· ˈ··◂/ *adj* having a very bad temper

e·vince /ɪˈvɪns/ *v* [T1] *fml* (of a person or his behaviour) to show clearly (a feeling, quality, etc.): *He evinced great sorrow for what he had done*

e·vis·ce·rate /ɪˈvɪsəreɪt/ *v* [T1] *fml* to cut out the bowels and other inside parts of the body from —compare CLEAN[3] (2)

e·voc·a·tive /ɪˈvɒkətɪv‖ɪˈvɑ-/ *adj* [(*of*)] that produces memories and feelings: *The taste of these cakes is evocative of my childhood*

e·voke /ɪˈvəʊk/ *v* [T1] to produce or call up (a memory, a feeling or its expression): *Her singing evoked admiration from the public* —**evocation** /ˌevəˈkeɪʃən, ˌiːvəʊ-/ *n* [C;U]

ev·o·lu·tion /ˌiːvəˈluːʃən, ˌevə-‖ˌevə-/ *n* **1** [U] (the scientific idea of) the development of the various types of plants, animals, etc., from fewer and simpler forms **2** [U] gradual change and development: *the evolution of the modern motor car* **3** [C *often pl.*] *pomp* a planned movement: *dancers/ships/groups of soldiers performing various evolutions*

ev·o·lu·tion·a·ry /ˌiːvəˈluːʃənəri, ˌevə-‖ˌevəˈluːʃəneri/ *adj* of or resulting from EVOLUTION (1,2); developing gradually

e·volve /ɪˈvɒlv‖ɪˈvɑlv/ *v* [IØ;T1] to (cause to) develop gradually: *He evolved a new system for running the factory.|The British political system has evolved over several centuries*

ewe /juː/ *n* a female sheep —compare RAM[1] (1)

ew·er /ˈjuːəʳ/ *n* **a** a large, wide-mouthed vessel with a handle, used for water, esp. for washing in a bedroom when one has no bathroom **b** the amount of water this holds

ex /eks/ *n infml* (someone's) former wife or husband, after the marriage has been ended (the people have been DIVORCEd) by law

ex- *prefix* (*used before human nouns*) former and still living: *my ex-wife|her ex-husband|an ex-minister|an ex-member of the party|an ex-child actor* —compare LATE[1] (4,5)

ex·a·cer·bate /ɪgˈzæsəbeɪt‖-ər-/ *v* [Wv5;T1] *fml* to make worse (pain, diseases, etc.): (fig.) *exacerbated relations between employers and workers* —**-bation** /ɪgˌzæsəˈbeɪʃən‖-ər-/ *n* [U;C]

ex·act[1] /ɪgˈzækt/ *v* [T1 (*from*)] *fml* **1** to demand and obtain by force, threats, etc.: *to exact payment of taxes|He exacted obedience from the children* **2** (esp. of work) to make necessary: *This difficult operation will exact all the doctor's skill*

exact[2] *adj* **1** [Wa5;A] (esp. of things that can be measured) correct and without mistakes: *The exact time is 3 minutes and 35 seconds past 2.|an exact amount/weight* **2** [B] marked by thorough consideration or careful measurement of small details of fact: *His memory is very exact; he never makes mistakes.|The* **exact sciences** *are those such as* MATHEMATICS *which depend on numbers and so can give measurable results* **3 the exact same X** *nonstandard* exactly the same X; the VERY same X: *That's the exact same man who was here last night!* —**~ness, ~itude** *n* [U]

ex·act·ing /ɪgˈzæktɪŋ/ *adj* (of a person or a piece of work) demanding much care, effort and attention: *a day of exacting and tiring work* —**~ly** *adv*

ex·ac·tion /ɪgˈzækʃən/ *n* **1** [U+*of* (*from*)] the action of EXACTing[1] (1) **2** [C] *derog* a demand, esp. for money, which is thought to be too great: *Don't pay all that rent! It's an exaction*

ex·act·ly /ɪgˈzæktli/ *adv* **1** (*used with numbers and measures, and with* what, where, who, *etc.*) with complete correctness: *Tell me exactly where she lives.|The train arrived at exactly 8 o'clock, neither earlier nor later* **2** (*used for adding force to an expression*) just; really; quite: *The doctor told him not to smoke, but he did exactly the opposite* **3** (*used as a reply to something that has been said*) Quite right! I agree!: *"We need a drink." "Exactly! Let's have one"* **4 not exactly a** not really: *We're not exactly driving fast.|She's not exactly (what you would call) stupid, but . . .* **b** (*as a reply*) That is not altogether true: *"So then you kissed her." "Not exactly. She kissed me"*

ex·ag·ge·rate /ɪgˈzædʒəreɪt/ *v* [T1;IØ] to say or believe more than the truth about (something); make (something) seem larger, better, worse, etc., than in reality: *It was a rabbit, not a lion; you're exaggerating as usual!* —**~d** *adj* —**~dly** /-tɨdli/ *adv*

ex·ag·ge·ra·tion /ɪgˌzædʒəˈreɪʃən/ *n* [C;U] (an example of) exaggerating (EXAGGERATE): *No, it was only a rabbit. To say it was a lion was an exaggeration*

ex·alt /ɪgˈzɔːlt/ *v* [T1] *fml* **1** to praise highly (esp. a person or his qualities) **2** to raise (a person) to a high rank

ex·al·ta·tion /ˌegzɔːlˈteɪʃən, ˌeksɔːl-/ *n* [U] the joy of success: *The news of the victory filled them with exaltation*

ex·alt·ed /ɪgˈzɔːltɨd/ *adj* **1** (of a person or his position) of high rank **2** (of a person or his state of mind) full of the joy of success: *The victorious students ran through the streets in an exalted state of excitement* —**~ly** *adv*

ex·am /ɪgˈzæm/ *n infml* EXAMINATION (1)

ex·am·i·na·tion /ɪgˌzæmɨˈneɪʃən/ *n* **1** [C (*in* or *on*)] a spoken or written test of knowledge **2** [C; U] (an act of) examining (EXAMINE (1)): *The doctor carried out the medical examination.|You will have to have* (UNDERGO) *a medical examination* **3** [C;U] (an act of) questioning someone in a court of law: *The examination of all the witnesses took a week* **4 under examination** being EXAMINEd (1); not yet decided

examination pa·per /···ˈ·· ˌ··/ *n fml* PAPER[1] (7)

ex·am·ine /ɪgˈzæmɨn/ *v* [T1] **1** to look at (a person or thing) closely, in order to find out something: *The doctor examined her carefully.|My bags were examined when I entered the country* **2** [(*in* or *on*)] to ask (a person) questions, in order to measure knowledge or find out something, as in a school or a court of law —compare CROSS-EXAMINE **3 need (one's) head examined** *infml* to seem foolish or slightly mad: *If she wants to go swimming in this weather she needs her head examined!* —**-iner** *n*

ex·am·ple /ɪgˈzɑːmpəl‖ɪgˈzæm-/ *n* **1** something taken from a number of things of the same kind, which shows the usual quality of the rest or shows a general rule: *Her rudeness was a typical example of her usual bad manners* **2** [(*to*)] *apprec* a person, or his behaviour, that is worthy of being copied: *Mary's courage is an example to us all* **3** [(*to*)] a piece of behaviour that may be copied by other people (often in the phrs. **set/follow a good/bad example**): *He arrived at the office early, to set an example/a good example to the others* **4** a warning: *I'm going to send you to prison for 3 weeks, and let this be an example to you!* **5 for example** here is one of the things or people just spoken of: *A lot of people here, for example, John, would rather have coffee* **6 make an example of someone** to punish someone so that others will be afraid to behave as he did

USAGE When we ourselves are an **example** to be copied, then we *set* it: *Drink your milk and set a good* **example** *to the other children!* When we invent an example to explain what we mean—*large animals, for* **example**, *elephants*—we are *giving* it.

ex·as·pe·rate /ɪgˈzɑːspəreɪt‖ɪgˈzæ-/ *v* [Wv4,5 (*at*); T1] to annoy or make angry: *I was exasperated by/at all the noise* —**-ratedly** *adv* —**-ratingly** *adv*

ex·as·pe·ra·tion /ɪgˌzɑːspəˈreɪʃən‖ɪgˌzæ-/ *n* [U] the state of being EXASPERATEd: *"Go away!" I shouted in exasperation*

ex ca·the·dra /ˌeks kəˈθiːdrə/ *adj, adv* [Wa5] *Lat* (of a statement or command) (made) by the official right of one's high office: *an ex cathedra decision*

ex·ca·vate /ˈekskəveɪt/ *v* [T1] **1** to make (a hole) by digging **2** to uncover (something under the earth) by digging: *excavated the ancient city of Troy*

ex·ca·va·tion /ˌekskəˈveɪʃən/ *n* [C;U] the work or result of excavating (EXCAVATE): *The excavation of the cave/of the buried city took a long time.|a small excavation in the river bank*

ex·ca·va·tor /ˈekskəveɪtəʳ/ *n* **1** a person who EXCAVATEs **2** *AmE usu.* **steam shovel**— a large machine that digs and moves earth in a bucket at the end of a 2-part arm —see picture at SITE[1]

ex·ceed /ɪkˈsiːd/ *v* **1** [Wv6;L1] to be greater than (something which can be measured): *The cost will not exceed £50.|The bad news exceeded* (=was worse than) *my worst fears* **2** [T1] *derog* to do more than (what is lawful, necessary, etc.): *He was punished for exceeding* (=driving faster than) *the speed limit*

ex·ceed·ing·ly /ɪkˈsiːdɪŋli/ *adv* very; to an unusual degree: *drove exceedingly fast|They were exceedingly kind*

ex·cel /ɪkˈsel/ *v* **-ll-** [Wv6;L9;T1: (*as, at, in*)] *fml* to be very good (usu. in a stated way); do or be better

than: *She excels as a teacher of dancing*
ex·cel·lence /ˈeksələns/ *n* **1** [U] the quality of being EXCELLENT: *the excellence of her cooking* **2** [C] *rare* something in which a person EXCELs: *Being a good cook is among her many excellences*
Ex·cel·len·cy /ˈeksələnsi/ *n* [C9;N9,(N)] (the word used when speaking to or of certain persons of high rank in the state or church (often in the phrs. **his/her Excellency; your Excellency (-cies); their Excellencies**)): *The King will see you now, (your) Excellency.|His Excellency will see you now, my Lord.|His Excellency the Spanish* AMBASSADOR
ex·cel·lent /ˈeksələnt/ *adj* [Wa5] very good; of very high quality: *excellent health|an excellent wife* —**~ly** *adv*
ex·cel·si·or /ɪkˈselsɪɔːʳ, -sɪəʳ‖-sɪər/ *n* [U] *AmE tdmk* small thin curled pieces of wood, used for packing breakable things like glass
ex·cept[1] /ɪkˈsept/ *v* [T1 *often neg.*] to leave out; not include: *You will all be punished; I can except no one*
except[2] also **excepting**— *prep* not including; leaving out; but not: *He answered all the questions except the last one.|I can take my holidays at any time except in August.|I know nothing about him except that he lives next door.|I know nothing about the accident except what I read in the paper.|I like her except when she's angry.|"He won't eat anything except the largest most splendid pieces of meat"* (SEU S.)—see BESIDES, BUT[2] (USAGE)
except[3] *conj* **1** apart from: *She can do everything except cook* **2** *not fml* but: *I would go, except it's too far* **3** *bibl* UNLESS
ex·cept·ed /ɪkˈseptɨd/ *adj* [Wa5;E] **1** apart from; EXCEPT FOR (1); with the EXCEPTION of: *Everyone was tired, John (always) excepted.|Everyone, John (always) excepted, was tired.|John (always) excepted, everyone was tired* **2 not excepted** included: *Everyone helped, John not excepted* (=even John helped; John helped, too)
except for /·ˈ· ·/ *prep* **1** apart from; with the EXCEPTION of: *Except for one old lady, the bus was empty.|The road was empty except for a few cars.|I know nothing about him except for the fact that* (=except that) *he lives next door.|He answered all the questions except for the last one.|Everyone was tired except for John.|Except for John, everyone was tired* **2** but for; if it were not for; without: *Except for you, I should be dead by now.|She would leave her husband except for the children* —compare BUT FOR
ex·cept·ing /ɪkˈseptɪŋ/ *prep* **1** except: *He answered all the questions excepting the last one.|They were all saved excepting the captain* **2 always excepting** except for: *Everyone was tired, always excepting John* (=John was not tired) **3 not excepting** also **without excepting**— including: *Everyone helped, not excepting John* (=John helped, too; even John helped)
ex·cep·tion /ɪkˈsepʃən/ *n* [C;U] **1** (a case of) EXCEPTing or being EXCEPTed: *You will all be punished. I can make no exceptions.|You must answer all the questions without exception.|It's been very cold this month, but today's an exception; it's warm and sunny* **2** *law* a spoken or written disagreement with something happening in a court of law: *"Exception!" shouted the lawyer, when he felt that the judge had been unfair* **3 take exception (to)** to be made angry (by): *I took the greatest exception to his rude letters* **4 with the exception of** except; apart from: *Everyone was tired with the exception of John.|Everyone, with the exception of John, was tired.|With the exception of John, everyone was tired.|I know nothing with the exception of what I read in the papers*
ex·cep·tio·na·ble /ɪkˈsepʃənəbəl/ *adj fml* that can cause someone to **take exception** (EXCEPTION (3)): *That play is quite suitable for children to see; there's nothing exceptionable in it* —opposite **unexceptionable**
ex·cep·tion·al /ɪkˈsepʃənəl/ *adj often apprec* unusual, often in a good sense: *All her children are clever, but the youngest boy is really exceptional* —**~ly** /ɪkˈsepʃənəli/ *adv*
ex·cerpt /ˈeksɜːpt‖-ɜr-/ *n* a piece taken from a book, speech, or musical work
ex·cess[1] /ɪkˈses, ˈekses/ *n* [S;U:9, esp. *of, over*] **1** the fact of EXCEEDing, or an amount by which something EXCEEDs (the stated amount): *This excess of losses over profits will ruin the business* **2** *derog* something more than is reasonable; more than the reasonable degree or amount: *an excess of anger|He praised the book to excess* **3 in excess of** more than: *He advised his son never to spend in excess of his income*
ex·cess[2] /ˈekses/ *adj* [A] additional; more than is usual, allowed, etc.: *You'll have to pay excess postal charges on this letter.|Excess profits tax is paid to the government by companies that make very high profits*
ex·cess·es /ɪkˈsesɨz/ *n* [P] *derog* actions so bad that they pass the limits expected of human behaviour: *The soldiers in the conquered town were guilty of/*COMMIT*ted the worst excesses*
ex·ces·sive /ɪkˈsesɪv/ *adj derog* too much; too great: *The prices at this hotel are excessive.|She takes an excessive interest in clothes* —**~ly** *adv*
ex·change[1] /ɪksˈtʃeɪndʒ/ *n* **1** [C;U] (a case of) the act or action of exchanging: *an exchange of shots between the 2 armies|He gave me an apple in exchange for a piece of cake* **2** [C] also **telephone exchange**— (*often cap.*) a central place where all the telephone wires are joined so that people may speak to each other **3** [C9] (*often cap.*) a place where business men meet to buy and sell (goods of the stated type): *They sell corn at the Corn Exchange, and shares in companies at the* STOCK *Exchange* —see also EMPLOYMENT EXCHANGE
exchange[2] *v* **1** [T1 (*for, with*)] (of a person or organization) to give and receive (something in return for something else): *John exchanged hats with Peter* (=each gave the other his hat).|*Where can I exchange my dollars for pounds?* —compare CHANGE[1] **2** [T1] (of 2 people or organizations) to give each other (something in return for something else): *John and Peter exchanged hats* (=each gave the other his hat).|*The 2 armies exchanged prisoners* **3 exchange contracts** (in Britain) to complete the last stages in buying or selling a house **4 exchange words/blows** to quarrel/fight: *Mary and Anne didn't actually exchange blows but they certainly exchanged words; I've never heard anything like it!* —**~able** *adj* [Wa5]
exchange rate /·ˈ· ·/ also **rate of exchange**— *n* the value of the money of one country compared to that of another country
ex·cheq·uer /ɪksˈtʃekəʳ‖ˈekstʃekər/ *n* [S] *pomp or humor* a public or private supply of money: *I can't buy a new car; the exchequer won't allow it* (=I can't afford it)
Exchequer *n* [*the*+GU] (in Britain) the Government department which collects and controls public money (often in the phr. **Chancellor of the Exchequer**=the official in charge of this department) —compare TREASURY (3)
ex·cise[1] /ˈeksaɪz/ *n* the government tax on certain goods produced and used inside a country —compare CUSTOMS (1)
ex·cise[2] /ɪkˈsaɪz/ *v* [T1] *fml* to remove by or as if by cutting out: *excised an organ from the body|part of a book* —compare AMPUTATE
ex·ci·sion /ɪkˈsɪʒən/ *n fml* **1** [U (*of*)] removal (of

something) by or as if by cutting out **2** [C] something removed as if by cutting out

ex·ci·ta·ble /ɪk'saɪtəbəl/ *adj* (of a person or animal) easily excited —**-bility** /ɪk,saɪtə'bɪl$\frac{1}{2}$ti/ *n* [U]

ex·cite /ɪk'saɪt/ *v* **1** [T1] to cause (someone) to lose calmness and to have strong feelings, often pleasant: *The story excited the little boy very much* **2** [T1;V3] to cause (someone to do something, or something to happen) by raising strong feelings: *The king's cruelty excited a rising of the people/excited the people to rise against him* **3** [T1] to raise or call out (a feeling): *The beggar's story excited my pity* **4** [T1] to make active (an organ of the body): *Strong coffee excites your nerves*

ex·cit·ed /ɪk'saɪt$\frac{1}{2}$d/ *adj* full of strong, pleasant feelings; not calm: *The excited children were opening their Christmas presents* —**~ly** *adv*

ex·cite·ment /ɪk'saɪtmənt/ *n* **1** [U] the condition of being excited: *He has a weak heart, and should avoid all excitement* **2** [C] an exciting event: *Life will seem very quiet after the excitements of our holiday*

ex·cit·ing /ɪk'saɪtɪŋ/ *adj* [B,B3] that excites one: *an exciting story/holiday* —**~ly** *adv*

ex·claim /ɪk'skleɪm/ *v* [T5,6a (*how, that*)] (mostly used with the actual words of the speaker) to say suddenly, because of strong feeling: *"Good heavens!" he exclaimed. "It's 6 o'clock."|He exclaimed how late it was* —see SAY (USAGE) —compare EXPLAIN

exclaim a·gainst *v prep* [T1] to express strongly a complaint against: *The newspapers exclaimed against the government's action*

exclaim at *v prep* [T1] to express surprise at: *She exclaimed at the beautiful view/at the child's dirty face/at the size of the bill*

ex·cla·ma·tion /,eksklə'meɪʃən/ *n* **1** [U] the act of EXCLAIMing: *She mended my socks, with much exclamation at the size of the holes* **2** [C (*of*)] the word(s) expressing a sudden strong feeling: *"Good heavens!" is an exclamation.|to* UTTER (=say) *an exclamation of anger*

exclamation mark /··'·· ·/ (*AmE* **exclamation point**)— *n BrE* a mark (!) which is written after the actual words of an EXCLAMATION (2): *"I'm hungry!" she exclaimed* (compare: *She exclaimed that she was hungry*)

ex·clam·a·to·ry /ɪk'sklæmətəri‖-tori/ *adj* (of words or noises) containing or expressing EXCLAMATION(*s*): *The letters she writes are very exclamatory* —compare EXPLANATORY

ex·clude /ɪk'sklu:d/ *v* [T1] **1** [(*from*)] to keep out (from somewhere): *excluded foreigners from (joining) the club* **2** [(*from*)] to leave out from among the rest: *You're all guilty; I can exclude no one from blame* —opposite **include** **3** to shut out from the mind (a reason or possibility): *We can exclude the possibility that it was the baby who shot the President*

ex·clud·ing /ɪks'klu:dɪŋ/ *prep* not counting; not including: *There were 30 people in the hotel, excluding the hotel workers* —opposite **including**

ex·clu·sion /ɪk'sklu:ʒən/ *n* [U (*from*)] **1** the act of excluding (EXCLUDE): *His exclusion from the tennis club hurt him very much* **2 to the exclusion of** so as to leave out (all other members of a group): *He studied history at the university, to the exclusion of all other subjects*

ex·clu·sive[1] /ɪk'sklu:sɪv/ *adj* **1** [B] **a** that EXCLUDEs socially unsuitable people and charges a lot of money **b** (of a person) not willing to make friends **2** [Wa5;A] not shared with others: *This bathroom is for the President's exclusive use* —**~ness** *n* [U]

exclusive[2] *n* **1** [C] a newspaper story at first given to or printed by only one newspaper **2** [C9] a product on sale only in the stated shop: *a Selfridges exclusive*

ex·clu·sive·ly /ɪk'sklu:sɪvli/ *adv* only; and nothing/no one else: *This room is for women exclusively/is exclusively for women.|He's exclusively employed on repairing cars*

exclusive of /·'·· ·/ *prep* not taking into account; without; EXCLUDING: *The hotel charges £6 a day, exclusive of meals* —opposite **inclusive of**

ex·co·gi·tate /eks'kɒdʒ$\frac{1}{2}$teɪt‖-'kɑ-/ *v* [T1] *fml & humor* to think out or invent (a plan, difficult idea, etc.) —**-tation** /eks,kɒdʒ$\frac{1}{2}$'teɪʃən‖-,kɑ-/ *n* [C;U]

ex·com·mu·ni·cate /,ekskə'mju:n$\frac{1}{2}$keɪt/ *v* [T1] to punish (someone) by driving out from active membership in the Christian church

ex·com·mu·ni·ca·tion /,ekskəmju:n$\frac{1}{2}$'keɪʃən/ *n* **1** [U] the act of excommunicating or state of being EXCOMMUNICATED **2** [C] (an official paper stating) a case of this

ex·co·ri·ate /ɪks'kɔ:rieɪt‖-'kor-/ *v* [T1] *fml* **1** to tear or rub the skin from: *His legs were excoriated by the prickles* **2** to express a very bad opinion of (a book, play, performance, etc.) —**-ation** /ɪks,kɔ:ri'eɪʃən‖-,kor-/ *n* [C;U]

ex·cre·ment /'ekskr$\frac{1}{2}$mənt/ *n* [U] *fml* the solid waste matter passed from the body through the bowels —compare EXCRETA

ex·cres·cence /ɪk'skresəns/ *n fml* an ugly growth on an animal or plant: *Doctor! I've got a sort of strange excrescence on my neck*

ex·cre·ta /ɪk'skri:tə/ *n* [P] *fml* the solid and liquid waste matter passed from the body, esp. through the bowels: EXCREMENT, URINE, *and* SWEAT *are all forms of human excreta*

ex·crete /ɪk'skri:t/ *v* [IØ;T1] *fml* to pass out (EXCRETA) —compare SECRETE[1]

ex·cre·tion /ɪk'skri:ʃən/ *n* [U;C: (*of*) *usu. pl.*] *fml* (the act of producing) EXCRETA: *He complains of pain during excretion*

ex·cru·ci·at·ing /ɪk'skru:ʃieɪtɪŋ/ *adj* (of pain) very bad: *an excruciating headache* —**~ly** *adv*

ex·cul·pate /'ekskʌlpeɪt/ *v* [T1 (*from*) often pass.] to free (someone) from blame; to prove that (someone) has not done something wrong; EXONERATE —**-pation** /,ekskʌl'peɪʃən/ *n* [U]

ex·cur·sion /ɪk'skɜ:ʃən‖ɪk'skɜrʒən/ *n* a short journey made for pleasure, usu. by several people together and often arranged as a business: *to go on a day excursion* (=there and back in a day) *to Blackpool*

ex·cur·sion·ist /ɪk'skɜ:ʃən$\frac{1}{2}$st‖ɪk'skɜrʒ-/ *n* a person who is on an EXCURSION: *The town is full of excursionists today*

ex·cu·sa·ble /ɪk'skju:zəbəl/ *adj* (of behaviour) that can be forgiven —opposite **inexcusable** —**-bly** /-bli/ *adv* [Wa3]

ex·cuse[1] /ɪk'skju:z/ *v* **1** [T1 (*for*), 4] to forgive (someone) for a small fault: *Please excuse my bad handwriting/my opening your letter by mistake/me for opening your letter by mistake* **2** [T1 *usu. nonassertive*] to make (bad behaviour) seem less bad, or harmless: *Nothing will excuse his cruelty to his children* **3** [T1 (*from*); *BrE* also D1 *usu. pass.*] to free (someone) from a duty: *Can I be excused from football practice today?|(BrE also) Can I be excused football practice today?* **4 Excuse me** **a** (*Polite expression used when starting to speak to a stranger, when one wants to get past a person, or when one disagrees with something he has said*) Forgive me: *Excuse me, does this bus go to the station?|He pushed his way through the crowd, saying "Excuse me."|Excuse me, but you're completely wrong* **b** *AmE* SORRY: *He said "Excuse me" when he stepped on my foot* **5 excuse oneself** **a** to offer an excuse **b** to ask permission to be absent: *He excused himself from the party* **6 May I be excused?** *euph* (*said esp. by children at school*) May I go and empty my bowels?

ex·cuse² /ɪk'skjuːs/ *n* [C;U (*for*)] **1** the reason, whether true or untrue, given when asking to be forgiven for wrong behaviour: *Have you any excuse to offer for coming so late?|Stop making excuses!* **2 in excuse of** as an excuse for: *In excuse of his failure he said he had been ill* **3 make one's/someone's excuses** to explain why one/someone is not coming USAGE When one offers an **apology** one admits that one has done wrong, says one is sorry, and perhaps gives **reasons** for what has happened: *He said by way of* **apology** *that he would have come if he had known.* If someone thinks the **reason** given is untrue or unsatisfactory, he may call it an **excuse**; thus one can say: *That's just an* **excuse**, but not **That's just a* **reason.** A **pretext** is a false **reason**: *He went home on the* **pretext** *that he was tired, but I know the real reason!* **Alibi** is often used in the meaning of an excuse made to escape from blame or punishment: *My* **alibi** *for not finishing the job was that I was ill.* Some people think this word should be used only as it is in law, to mean a proof that one could not have done a criminal action because one was not there. A **plea** means that one is asking for understanding and mercy: *He excused himself on the* **plea** *that he had to visit his mother.*

ex·di·rec·to·ry /ˌeks dɨ'rektəri/ (*AmE* **unlisted**)— *adj* [Wa5] *BrE* **1** (of a telephone number) not in the telephone book **2 go ex-directory** to have one's number removed from the telephone book

ex·e·cra·ble /'eksɨkrəbəl/ *adj* very bad: *execrable manners|She's an execrable cook* —**-bly** /-bli/ *adv* [Wa3]

ex·e·crate /'eksɨkreɪt/ *v* [T1 *often pass.*] *fml* to feel or express hatred of; curse: *Even today the memory of his evil deeds is execrated* —**-cration** /ˌeksɨ'kreɪʃən/ *n* [C;U]

ex·ec·u·tant /ɪg'zekjʊtənt‖-kjə-/ *n* [C9,(C)] a performer (of the stated type): *a clever executant on the piano*

ex·e·cute /'eksɨkjuːt/ *v* [T1] **1** to carry out; to perform or do completely (an order, plan, or piece of work): *The plan was good, but it was badly executed.|The soldier executed the captain's orders* **2** *law* to carry out the orders in (a WILL² (6)): *He asked his brother to execute his* WILL **3** *law* to make effective in law (an important written paper) by having it signed, witnessed, etc. **4** [(*for*)] to kill (someone) as a lawful punishment: *executed for murder|as a murderer|by hanging* **5** to perform (music, dance steps, etc.)

ex·e·cu·tion /ˌeksɨ'kjuːʃən/ *n* **1** [U (*of*)] the carrying out, performance or completion (of an order, plan, or piece of work): *This good idea was never put|carried into execution* **2** [U (*of*)] the act of carrying out the orders (in a WILL): *There has been some delay in the execution of my father's will* **3** [C; U] (a case of) lawful killing as a punishment: *Executions used to be held in public* **4** [U] skill in performing music: *The musician's execution was perfect, but he played without feeling*

ex·e·cu·tion·er /ˌeksɨ'kjuːʃənəʳ/ *n* the official who EXECUTE*s* (4) criminals

ex·ec·u·tive¹ /ɪg'zekjʊtɪv‖-kjə-/ *adj* [Wa5;A] **1** concerned with making and carrying out decisions, esp. in business: *a man of great executive ability* **2** having the power to carry out government decisions and laws: *The executive branch carries out the laws which have been made by the* LEGISLATURE —see also JUDICIARY

executive² *n* **1** a person in an EXECUTIVE¹ (1) position, esp. in business: *a young business executive* **2** the person or group in the EXECUTIVE¹ (2) position in a government: *The President of the US is the chief executive*

ex·ec·u·tor /ɪg'zekjʊtəʳ‖-kjə-/ *fem.* **ex·ec·u·trix** /-trɪks/— *n* the person or bank that carries out the orders in a WILL² (6): *He appointed the bank to act as his executor*

ex·e·ge·sis /ˌeksɨ'dʒiːsɨs/ *n* **-ses** /siːz/ [U;C] *tech* serious explanation after deep study (esp. of the Bible)

ex·em·pla·ry /ɪg'zempləri/ *adj* **1** [B] suitable to be copied as an example: *exemplary behaviour|courage* **2** [A] which should serve as a warning: *an exemplary punishment*

ex·em·pli·fi·ca·tion /ɪgˌzemplɨfɨ'keɪʃən/ *n* **1** [U] the act or action of EXEMPLIFYing **2** [C] something that exemplifies (EXEMPLIFY); example

ex·em·pli·fy /ɪg'zemplɨfaɪ/ *v* [T1] **1** to give an example of: *The teacher exemplified the use of the word* **2** to be an example of: *This exemplifies what I mean*

ex·empt¹ /ɪg'zempt/ *adj* [F (*from*)] freed (from a duty, service, payment, etc.): *He is exempt from military service.|Bread is exempt from taxation.|tax-exempt income*

exempt² *v* [T1 (*from*)] to make (someone or something) EXEMPT: *His bad health exempted him from military service*

ex·emp·tion /ɪg'zempʃən/ *n* **1** [C;U: (*from*)] (a case of) the act of EXEMPTing or the state of being EXEMPTed: *They were* GRANT*ed* (=given) *exemption* **2** [C] a type or amount of income EXEMPTed from taxation: *an exemption of $600 for each child*

ex·er·cise¹ /'eksəsaɪz‖-ər-/ *n* **1** [C;U] (a) use of any part of the body or mind so as to strengthen and improve it: *If you don't take|get more exercise you'll get fat.|voice exercises* **2** [C] a question or set of questions to be answered by a pupil for practice: *Copy exercise 17 into your exercise-books* **3** [U] the use of a (stated) power or right (esp. in the phr. **the exercise of**): *You can only understand this picture by the exercise of imagination* **4** [C *often pl.*] a movement made by soldiers, naval ships, etc., in time of peace, to practise fighting: *100 ships left harbour today for exercises at sea*

exercise² *v* **1** [IØ;T1] to (cause to) take exercise: *You're getting fat; you should exercise more* **2** [T1] to use (a power or right): *You should exercise patience* **3** [T1 (*by, about*) *usu. pass.*] *fml* to trouble (a person or his mind): *I've been greatly|much exercised (in mind) about what we ought to do*

ex·er·cis·es /'eksəsaɪzɨs‖-ər-/ *n* [P] *AmE* a set of events including speeches, giving of prizes, and various ceremonies (usu. in the phrs. **commencement/graduation exercises**): *We're going to see Mortimer receive his degree at the graduation exercises*

ex·ert /ɪg'zɜːt‖-ɜrt/ *v* [T1] **1** to use (strength, skill, etc.): *She couldn't open the door, even by exerting all her strength.|My wife's been exerting a lot of pressure on me to change my job* **2 exert oneself** to make an effort: *He never exerts himself to help anyone*

ex·er·tion /ɪg'zɜːʃən‖-ɜr-/ *n* [C; (*the*) U (*of*)] (a case of) EXERTing; (an) effort: *The doctor says he must avoid all exertion*

ex·e·unt /'eksiʌnt/ *v pl. of* EXIT¹

ex gra·tia /ˌeks 'greɪʃə/ *adj, adv Lat* (of a payment) (made) as a favour, not because one has a duty in law to do it

ex·ha·la·tion /ˌekshə'leɪʃən/ *n* **1** [C;U] (an act of) breathing out **2** [C] something which is sent out by or as if by breathing: *exhalations of mist on the surface of the lake*

ex·hale /eks'heɪl/ *v* [IØ;T1] to breathe out (air, gas, etc.): *Breathe deeply and then exhale slowly.|He lit his pipe and exhaled clouds of smoke* —opposite **inhale**

ex·haust[1] /ɪg'zɔːst/ *v* **1** [Wv4,5;T1] to tire out: *What an exhausting day! I'm completely exhausted* **2** [T1 *often pass.*] to use up completely: *to exhaust the supply of oxygen|My patience is exhausted* **3** [T1] to describe or deal with (a subject) completely: *We've about exhausted this subject: let's go on to the next*

exhaust[2] *n* **1** [C] also **exhaust pipe** /·'· ·/— the pipe which allows unwanted gas, steam, etc., to escape from an engine or machine —compare MUFFLER (2) **2** [U] the gas or steam which escapes through this pipe —see picture at PETROL

ex·haus·tion /ɪg'zɔːstʃən/ *n* [U] **1** the state of being tired out: *to suffer from exhaustion* **2** the act or state of EXHAUSTing[1] (2) or being EXHAUSTed[1] (2): *the exhaustion of our food supplies*

ex·haus·tive /ɪg'zɔːstɪv/ *adj* thorough; dealing completely with a subject: *to make an exhaustive study/exhaustive inquiries* —**~ly** *adv* —**~ness** *n* [U]

ex·hib·it[1] /ɪg'zɪb$\frac{1}{2}$t/ *v* **1** [IØ;T1] to show in public, as for sale, or in a competition (objects, sometimes of an understood type): *to exhibit paintings/flowers/new cars|a young painter who has not yet exhibited (his work)* **2** [T1] to show other people that one possesses (a feeling, quality, etc.): *to exhibit signs of fear/guilt*

exhibit[2] *n* **1** something that is EXHIBITed[1] (1), esp. in a MUSEUM **2** something brought into a law court to prove the truth: *Exhibit A was a knife which, the police said, belonged to the prisoner* **3** *AmE* EXHIBITION (1)

ex·hi·bi·tion /ˌeks$\frac{1}{2}$'bɪʃən/ *n* **1** a public show of objects: *an international trade exhibition* **2** [(*of*)] an act of EXHIBITing[1] (2): *an exhibition of bad temper* **3** *BrE* an amount of money given by a school or university to help a specially deserving student to study there —compare SCHOLARSHIP (1) **4 make an exhibition of oneself** to behave foolishly in public: *Get up off the floor and stop making such an exhibition of yourself!* **5 on exhibition** being shown publicly: *Some of the children's paintings are now on exhibition at the school*

ex·hi·bi·tion·is·m /ˌeks$\frac{1}{2}$'bɪʃənɪzəm/ *n* [U] **1** *often derog* the behaviour of a person who wants to be looked at and admired: *He jumped off a high rock into the lake, out of pure exhibitionism* **2** the offence of undressing in public so as to be admired sexually; INDECENT EXPOSURE: *He was charged with several acts of exhibitionism outside the girls' school* —**-ist** *n* —**-istic** /ˌeksɪbɪʃə'nɪstɪk/ *adj*

ex·hib·i·tor /ɪg'zɪb$\frac{1}{2}$təʳ/ *n* a person, firm, etc., that EXHIBITS[1] (1): *many exhibitors at the local flower show*

ex·hil·a·rate /ɪg'zɪləreɪt/ *v* [T1 *usu. pass.*] to make (someone) cheerful and excited: *I was exhilarated by/at her visit* —**-ration** /ɪgˌzɪlə'reɪʃən/ *n* [U]

ex·hil·a·rat·ing /ɪg'zɪləreɪtɪŋ/ *adj* that EXHILARATEs people: *the exhilarating air at the seaside* —**~ly** *adv*

ex·hort /ɪg'zɔːt‖-ɔrt/ *v* [T1 (*to*); V3] *fml* to urge or advise strongly (someone) to do something: *The general exhorted his men to fight well/to courage*

ex·hor·ta·tion /ˌeksɔː'teɪʃən‖-ɔr-/ *n* [C;U] (an act of) EXHORTing: *The young man acted foolishly in spite of all his father's exhortation(s)*

ex·hume /ɪg'zjuːm, eks'hjuːm‖ɪg'zuːm, ɪk'sjuːm/ *v* [T1] *fml* to take (a dead body) out of the grave —**exhumation** /ˌeksjʊ'meɪʃən/ *n* [C;U]

ex·i·gen·cy /'eks$\frac{1}{2}$dʒənsi, ɪg'zɪ-/ also **ex·i·gence** /'eks$\frac{1}{2}$dʒəns, 'egz$\frac{1}{2}$-/— *n* [*often pl.*] an urgent need; a difficult state of affairs in which one must act without delay: *After the flood, the government sent food to the people in this exigency*

ex·i·gent /'eks$\frac{1}{2}$dʒənt/ *adj fml* **1** (of a state of affairs) needing urgent attention: *Unemployment is the most exigent question facing us today* **2** *derog* (of a person) making many repeated demands and not accepting a refusal: *She is exigent in her demands for money* —**~ly** *adv*

ex·ig·u·ous /ɪg'zɪgjʊəs/ *adj fml* too small in amount; not enough: *an exiguous meal of bread and cheese* —**~ly** *adv* —**~ness** *n* [U]

ex·ile[1] /'eksaɪl, 'egzaɪl/ *n* **1** [S;U] unwanted absence from one's country, often for political reasons: *Napoleon was sent into exile.|to die in exile* **2** [C] a person who has been forced to leave his country, esp. for these reasons

exile[2] *v* [T1 (*to*)] to send (someone) into EXILE[1]: *They exiled Napoleon to the island of St Helena*

ex·ist /ɪg'zɪst/ *v* [IØ] **1** to live or be real; to have being: *Do fairies exist?|The Roman Empire existed for several centuries* **2** (of a person) to continue to live, esp. with difficulty: *They're so poor they can hardly exist.|She exists on tea and bread*

ex·ist·ence /ɪg'zɪstəns/ *n* **1** [U] the state of existing: *Harry doesn't believe in the existence of God.|a new country which came into existence in 1918/has been in existence since 1918* **2** [S] life; way of living: *I've never heard anything so silly during my whole existence!*

ex·ist·ent /ɪg'zɪstənt/ *adj* [Wa5] existing now; EXTANT: *This is the only existent copy of his last poem*

ex·is·ten·tial /ˌegzɪ'stenʃəl/ *adj* [Wa5] related to existence: *"There is no God" is an existential statement*

ex·is·ten·tial·is·m /ˌegzɪ'stenʃəlɪzəm/ *n* [U] **1** the modern belief and teaching of Kierkegaard, Sartre, Heidegger, etc., that man is alone in a meaningless world, that he is completely free to choose his actions, and that his actions determine his nature rather than the other way round **2** any of several systems of thought like this, either religious or nonreligious —**~ist** *adj, n*

ex·ist·ing /ɪg'zɪstɪŋ/ *adj* [Wa5;A] present: *Food will not get cheaper under existing conditions*

ex·it[1] /'egz$\frac{1}{2}$t, 'eks$\frac{1}{2}$t/ *v pl.* **exeunt** /'eksiʌnt/ [IØ] *Lat* (*used as a stage direction in printed copies of plays*) goes out; goes off stage: *Exit Hamlet, bearing the body of Polonius* (stage direction)

USAGE In stage directions, **exit** comes before its subject, does not take "s" in the 3rd person singular, and has only one tense

exit[2] *n* **1** (*often written over a door*) a way out, esp. from a theatre: *There's another exit at the back* **2** *AmE* (*often written on or over a door*) a way out of an enclosed place or space, esp. from a public place **3** an act of leaving, esp. of an actor leaving the stage: *Make your exit through the door at the back of the stage*

USAGE In America, the sign (NO) EXIT is much more common than in Britain, and the common British sign WAY OUT is not used.

exit[3] *v* [IØ] (of a person) to go out; leave: *exited pretty quickly after the argument*

exit vi·sa /'·· ˌ··/ *n* a mark or signature which is put on the official paper which allows one to travel (PASSPORT) giving permission to leave a particular country

ex li·bris /ˌeks 'laɪbr$\frac{1}{2}$s, -'liː-/ *prep Lat* (*used before the owner's name written inside a book*) from the books of: *"Ex libris Charles McGregor": I must remember to return the books to him*

ex·o·dus /'eksədəs/ *n* [S (*of, from*)] a going out or leaving by a great number of people: *Every fine weekend there is a general exodus of cars from the city to the country*

Exodus *n* [R] the title of the 2nd book of the Bible,

exotic birds

which tells how the Israelites left Egypt

ex of·fi·ci·o /ˌeks əˈfɪʃiəʊ/ *adj, adv* [Wa5] *Lat* because of one's position: *The president is an ex officio member of the committee* (= because he is the president)

ex·og·a·my /ekˈsɒgəmi‖ekˈsɑ-/ *n* [U] the practice of marrying outside one's own group, esp. as demanded by custom or law —**-mous** *adj* [Wa5]

ex·on·e·rate /ɪgˈzɒnəreɪt‖ɪgˈzɑ-/ *v* [T1 (*from*)] to free (someone) from blame; to decide that (someone) is not guilty: *The officer was exonerated from the charge of running away from the enemy* —**-ration** /ɪgˌzɒnəˈreɪʃən‖ɪgˌzɑ-/ *n* [U]

ex·or·bi·tant /ɪgˈzɔːbɪ̵tənt‖-ɔr-/ *adj* (of cost, demands, etc.) much greater than is reasonable: *That hotel charges exorbitant prices.|He makes exorbitant demands upon my time* —**-tance** *n* [U] —**~ly** *adv*

ex·or·cis·m /ˈeksɔːsɪzəm‖-ɔr-/ *n* [C;U] an act or the art of exorcizing (EXORCIZE)

ex·or·cist /ˈeksɔːsɪ̵st‖-ɔr-/ *n* a person who practises EXORCISM

ex·or·cize, -cise /ˈeksɔːsaɪz‖-ɔr-/ *v* [T1] **1** to drive out (an evil spirit) from a person or place, by or as if by solemn command: *It was once believed that a man could have a devil in him, and that a priest could exorcize this devil by prayer* **2** to free (a person or place) from an evil spirit in this way: *The mad girl's parents took her to the priest to be exorcized* **3** to get rid of (esp. a bad thought or feeling): *He could not exorcize the memory of his past misdeeds*

ex·ot·ic /ɪgˈzɒtɪk‖ɪgˈzɑ-/ *adj usu. apprec* strange and unusual; from or as if from a distant and often tropical country: *exotic flowers/food/smells/an exotic purple bird* —**~ally** *adv* [Wa4]

ex·pand /ɪkˈspænd/ *v* **1** [IØ;T1: (*by, into*)] to (cause to) grow larger: *Iron expands when it is heated.|He breathed deeply and expanded his chest* —opposite **contract**² (3) **2** [IØ] (of a person) to become more friendly and willing to talk: *This quiet young man expands only when he is among friends* —**~able** *adj*

expand on *v prep* [T1] to make (a story, argument, etc.) more detailed by addition: *I'm quite satisfied with your explanation, so there's no need to expand on it*

ex·panse /ɪkˈspæns/ *n* [C+*of, often pl. with sing. meaning*] a wide space (of the stated type)

ex·pan·sion /ɪkˈspænʃən/ *n* **1** [U] the action of EXPANDing (1) or state of being EXPANDED (1): *the expansion of metals when they are heated|industrial expansion* **2** [C] something which has been EXPANDED (1): *His big book is an expansion of the little book he wrote before*

ex·pan·sive /ɪkˈspænsɪv/ *adj* **1** able to EXPAND (1) or causing EXPANSION **2** (of a person) friendly and willing to talk **3** large and splendid —compare EXPENSIVE —**~ly** *adv* —**~ness** *n* [U]

ex par·te /ˌeks ˈpɑːti‖-ɑr-/ *adj, adv* [Wa5] *Lat law* from the point of view of, or in the interests of, one side only in a law case

ex·pa·ti·ate on /ɪkˈspeɪʃieɪt/ also **expatiate up·on**— *v prep* [T1] *fml* DILATE ON

ex·pat·ri·ate¹ /ekˈspætrieɪt‖ekˈspeɪ-/ *v* [T1] **1** to cause to leave the native country by force or lawful power; EXILE —compare REPATRIATE **2** to remove (oneself) from one's own country

ex·pat·ri·ate² /ekˈspætrɪət, -trieɪt‖ekˈspeɪ-/ *n* a person living in a foreign country

ex·pect /ɪkˈspekt/ *v* **1** [T3,5a,b] to think (that something will happen): *I expect (that) he'll pass the examination.|He expects to fail the examination.|"Will she come soon?" "I expect so."* **2** [T1] (*often in tenses with the* -ing *form*) to consider that (something, esp. something good) is likely to come or happen: *I'm expecting a letter* **3** [X9] to wait for (someone or something) as stated: *I expect John home at 6.0.|I'm expecting John any minute now* —see WAIT (USAGE) **4** [T1 (*from*)] to believe, hope, and think that one will receive (something considered as one's right) **5** [V3] to believe, hope, and think (that someone will do something): *The officer expected his men to do their duty in the coming battle* **6** [Wv6;T5a] *infml esp. BrE* to suppose; think (that something is true): *"Who broke that cup?" "I expect it was the cat."* **7 be expecting a baby** also *infml & euph* **be expecting** (of a woman) to be PREGNANT (= carrying a child in her body) **8 expect too much of (someone)** to think someone can do more than he can do **9 to be expected** usual; what one feels sure will happen

ex·pec·tan·cy /ɪkˈspektənsi/ also **ex·pec·tance** /-təns/— *n* [U] hope; the state of expecting: *She waited for her lover in a state of happy expectancy*

ex·pec·tant /ɪkˈspektənt/ *adj* [Wa5] **1** hopeful: *The expectant crowds in the streets waited for the queen to pass* **2 expectant mother** a PREGNANT woman; MOTHER-TO-BE —**~ly** *adv*

ex·pec·ta·tion /ˌekspekˈteɪʃən/ *n* **1** [U+*of*] the condition of expecting: *There is every/little/no expectation of a cold winter* **2 against all/contrary to (all) expectation(s)** in spite of what was expected: *We thought Mary would pass and John would fail, but contrary to expectation it was the other way round* **3 beyond (all) expectation(s)** more or better than was hoped: *We thought John would do well, but he has succeeded beyond expectation* **4 in expectation of** expecting: *They closed the windows in expectation of rain*

expectation of life /··ˌ·· · ˈ·/ also **life expectancy**— *n* [U;C] the average number of years that a person is expected to live

ex·pec·ta·tions /ˌekspekˈteɪʃənz/ *n* [P] **1** hopes: *We didn't enjoy our holiday; it fell short of/didn't come up to our expectations* **2** money that one expects to receive on someone's death

ex·pec·to·rate /ɪkˈspektəreɪt/ *v* [IØ;T1] *euph* (of a person) SPIT³ (1)

ex·pe·di·en·cy /ɪkˈspiːdɪənsi/ also **ex·pe·di·ence** /-dɪəns/— *n* [U] **1** the quality of being EXPEDIENT

2 *derog* regard only for one's own personal advantage: *He thinks only of himself, and all his actions are governed by expediency*

ex·pe·di·ent[1] /ɪk'spiːdɪənt/ *adj* [F;(B)] (of a course of action, perhaps not a correct or moral one) useful or helpful for a purpose: *She thought it expedient not to tell her mother where she had been* —opposite **inexpedient** —**~ly** *adv*

expedient[2] *n* an EXPEDIENT plan, idea or action: *As I've forgotten my key, the only expedient is to climb in through the window*

ex·pe·dite /'eksp$\frac{1}{3}$daɪt/ *v* [T1] *fml* to make (a plan or arrangement) go faster: *The builders promised to expedite the repairs to the roof*

ex·pe·di·tion /ˌeksp$\frac{1}{3}$'dɪʃən/ *n* **1** [C] (the persons, vehicles, etc., going on) a (long) journey for a certain purpose: *to form/send/take part in a small expedition to photograph wild animals in Africa* **2** [U] *fml* the quality of being EXPEDITIOUS

ex·pe·di·tion·a·ry /ˌeksp$\frac{1}{3}$'dɪʃənəri‖-neri/ *adj* [Wa5;A] of or making up an EXPEDITION (1) of war (esp. in the phr. **expeditionary force**)

ex·pe·di·tious /ˌeksp$\frac{1}{3}$'dɪʃəs/ *adj fml* (of people and their actions) quick and without delay: *The doctor was very expeditious; he arrived in 5 minutes* —**~ly** *adv*

ex·pel /ɪk'spel/ *v* **-ll-** [T1 (*from*)] **1** to force out (from the body or a container): *to expel air from one's lungs* **2** to dismiss officially (from a school, club, etc.): *The boy was expelled from school*

ex·pend /ɪk'spend/ *v* [T1 (*in, upon*)] to spend or use up (esp. time, care, etc.): *They expend all their strength in/on trying to climb out*

ex·pen·da·ble /ɪk'spendəbəl/ *adj* that may be used up for a purpose: *The officer regarded his soldiers as expendable, and was willing to see them all killed in order to gain a victory*

ex·pen·di·ture /ɪk'spendɪtʃə^r/ *n* [S;U: (*of, on*)] *fml* spending or using up: *the expenditure of time, effort, and money on a piece of work*

ex·pense /ɪk'spens/ *n* [U] **1** cost, esp. of money but also time or effort: *We won't buy a car; it's not worth the expense* —see COST (USAGE) **2 at great/little/almost no expense** costing a lot of/little/almost no money **3 at someone's expense a** with someone paying the cost: *He had his book printed at his own expense* **b** (esp. of a joke or trick) against someone, so as to make him seem silly: *He tried to be clever at my expense* **4 at the expense of** causing the loss of: *He finished the job at the expense of his health* **5 put someone/go to the expense of** to (cause someone) to pay for (doing something): *I don't want to put him to the expense of buying me dinner* **6 spare no expense** to try hard without considering cost: *spared no expense to make the party a success*

expense ac·count /·'· ·ˌ·/ *n* the record of money spent in travel, hotels, etc., in the course of one's work, which will be paid by one's employer

ex·pens·es /ɪk'spens$\frac{1}{3}$z/ *n* [P9,(P)] the money used or needed for a purpose: *If you want to go to Paris I'll pay your expenses.|travelling/holiday/funeral expenses*

ex·pen·sive /ɪk'spensɪv/ *adj* costing a lot of money; costly: *a very expensive new car|Diamonds come* (=are) *expensive* —**~ly** *adv*

ex·pe·ri·ence[1] /ɪk'spɪərɪəns/ *n* **1** [U] (the gaining of) knowledge or skill which comes from practice rather than from books: *a teacher with 5 years' experience* **2** [C] something that happens to one and has an effect on the mind and feelings: *Our journey by camel was quite an experience*

experience[2] *v* [T1] to feel, suffer, or know, as an experience: *to experience joy/difficulties/defeat|* (fig.) *Our country has experienced great changes in the last 30 years*

ex·pe·ri·enced /ɪk'spɪərɪənst/ *adj* [(*in*)] (of a person in regard to his job or OCCUPATION) having the right kind of experience: *an experienced doctor/traveller|He's very experienced in mending cars*

ex·per·i·ment[1] /ɪk'sper$\frac{1}{3}$mənt/ *n* [C;U] (a) trial made in order to learn something or prove the truth of an idea: *to make/carry out/perform an experiment|knowledge based on experiments|a scientific experiment*

experiment[2] *v* [IØ (*on, upon, with*)] to make an EXPERIMENT[1]: *experimented with new materials|experimented on animals*

ex·per·i·men·tal /ɪkˌsper$\frac{1}{3}$'mentl/ *adj* used for or connected with EXPERIMENTs[1]: *an experimental farm* —**~ly** /-təli/ *adv* [Wa4]

ex·pe·ri·men·ta·tion /ɪkˌsper$\frac{1}{3}$men'teɪʃən/ *n* [U] the making of EXPERIMENTs[1]: *After much experimentation he discovered how to split the atom*

ex·pert /'ekspɜːt‖-ɜrt/ *adj, n* [B;C: (*at, in*)] (a person) with special knowledge or training: *She's (an) expert in/at teaching small children.|an expert card-player* —**~ly** *adv* —**~ness** *n* [U]

ex·per·tise /ˌekspɜː'tiːz‖-ɜr-/ *n* **1** [U] skill in a particular field; KNOW-HOW; EXPERTness: *His expertise saved the business from failing* **2** [C] *esp. BrE* an EXPERT's report made after careful examination of something

ex·pi·ate /'ekspieɪt/ *v* [T1] to pay for or make up for (a crime or wicked action) by accepting punishment readily and by doing something to show that one is sorry: *He tried to expiate his crimes by giving money to the church* —**-ation** /ˌekspi'eɪʃən/ *n* [U]

ex·pi·ra·tion /ˌeksp$\frac{1}{3}$'reɪʃən/ also **ex·pir·y** /'eksp$\frac{1}{3}$ri, ɪk'spaɪəri/— *n* [U] the end (of a stated period of time, or of something which lasts for a period): *The President can be elected again at/on the expiration of his first 4 years in office*

ex·pire /ɪk'spaɪə^r/ *v* [IØ] **1** (of something which lasts for a period of time) to come to an end: *The trade agreement between the 2 countries will expire next year* **2** *lit* to die

ex·plain /ɪk'spleɪn/ *v* **1** [T1,5a,6a,b: (*to*); IØ] to give the meaning (of something); make (something) clear, by speaking or writing: *I don't understand this, but Paul will explain.|The lawyer explained the new law* (*to us*).|*John explained how to use the telephone.|Explain what this word means* **2** [T1,6a] to give or be the reason for; to account for: *Can you explain your stupid behaviour?|That explains why he's not here* **3 explain oneself a** to make one's meaning clear: *I don't understand what you're talking about. Would you explain yourself a little?* **b** to give reasons for one's behaviour: *Late again, Smith? I hope you can explain yourself* —**~er** *n*

explain a·way *v adv* [T1] to account, or give an excuse, for (something wrong) in order to avoid blame: *Try to explain away the false signature*

ex·pla·na·tion /ˌeksplə'neɪʃən/ *n* [C;U: (*of, for*)] **1** (an act of) explaining: *He's giving an explanation of how the machine works* **2** something that explains: *The only explanation of/for his behaviour is that he's mad.|What did he say in explanation of his lateness?*

ex·plan·a·to·ry /ɪk'splænətəri‖-tori/ *adj* (of a statement, a piece of writing, etc.) that explains: *a few explanatory words* —see also SELF-EXPLANATORY

ex·ple·tive /ɪk'spliːtɪv‖'eksplətɪv/ *n* an often meaningless word used for swearing, to express violent feeling; OATH or curse: "DAMN," "SHIT" *and* "FUCK" *are all used as expletives*

ex·pli·ca·ble /'eksplɪkəbəl‖ek'splɪ-/ *adj* [F *often nonassertive*] *fml* (of behaviour or events) that can be explained: *Her behaviour is only explicable if you* *consider her youth* —opposite **inexplicable** —**-bly** /-bli/ *adv* [Wa3]

ex·pli·cate /ˈeksplɨkeɪt/ *v* [T1] *fml* to explain in detail (esp. a work of literature)

ex·pli·cit /ɪkˈsplɪsɨt/ *adj* (of statements, rules, etc.) clear and fully expressed: *to give explicit directions* —opposite **inexplicit** —compare IMPLICIT —**~ly** *adv* —**~ness** *n* [U]

ex·plode /ɪkˈspləʊd/ *v* **1** [Wv5;IØ;T1] **a** (esp. of a bomb or other explosive) to blow up or burst **b** to cause (esp. a bomb or other explosive) to blow up or burst **2** [IØ (*in, with*)] (of a person) to show sudden violent feeling: *to explode with/in anger* **3** [IØ] (of a feeling) to burst out suddenly: *His anger exploded* **4** [Wv5;T1 *often pass.*] to destroy (a belief)

ex·plod·ed /ɪkˈspləʊdɨd/ *adj tech* (of a drawing, model, etc.) showing the parts of something separated but in correct relationship to each other

ex·ploit[1] /ˈeksplɔɪt/ *n apprec* a brave, bold, and successful deed: *He performed many daring exploits, such as crossing the Atlantic Ocean in a rowing boat*

ex·ploit[2] /ɪkˈsplɔɪt/ *v* [T1] **1** *derog* to use (esp. a person) unfairly for one's own profit: *to exploit the poor by making them work for less pay* **2** to use or develop (a thing) fully so as to get profit: *to exploit the oil under the sea* —**~ation** /ˌeksplɔɪˈteɪʃən/ *n* [U] —**~er** /ɪkˈsplɔɪtəʳ/ *n*

ex·plo·ra·tion /ˌekspləˈreɪʃən/ *n* [C;U] an act or the action of exploring (EXPLORE): *a journey of exploration into China|a full exploration of all the reasons for and against closing the railway*

ex·plo·ra·to·ry /ɪkˈsplɔːrətəri‖-tori/ also **ex·plo·ra·tive** /-tɪv/— *adj* (of an action) done in order to learn something: *The doctors carried out an exploratory operation on my stomach*

ex·plore /ɪkˈsplɔːʳ/ *v* [T1] **1** to travel into or through (a place) for the purpose of discovery **2** to examine carefully (esp. a subject or question) in order to learn more: *explored all the possibilities* —**-plorer** *n*

ex·plo·sion /ɪkˈspləʊʒən/ *n* **1** [C] (a loud noise caused by) an act of exploding: *When she lit the gas there was a loud explosion* **2** [C9] a sudden bursting out (of the stated feeling or its expression): *explosions of loud laughter* **3** [C] a sudden increase

ex·plo·sive[1] /ɪkˈspləʊsɪv/ *adj* **1** that can explode: *It's dangerous to smoke when handling explosive materials* **2 a** (of a subject or question) that can cause people to explode with strong feeling; very CONTROVERSIAL: *The question of race today is an explosive one* **b** (of a feeling) tending to strong forceful expression: *The old man has an explosive temper* —**~ly** *adv* —**~ness** *n* [U]

explosive[2] *n* **1** an explosive substance: *Gunpowder is an explosive* **2 high explosives** substances that explode with great force

Ex·po /ˈekspəʊ/ *n* [R9] a world EXPOSITION (2): *Expo 81* (=1981) *in Ruritania*

ex·po·nent /ɪkˈspəʊnənt/ *n* **1** [C9, esp. *of*] a person who expresses, supports, or is an example (of a stated belief or idea): *an exponent of the opinions of Freud* **2** [C] *tech* a sign written above and to the right of a number or letter in MATHEMATICS to show how many times that quantity is to be multiplied by itself: *In* 12^3 *the number 3 is the exponent; in* y^n *the letter n is the exponent*

ex·po·nen·tial /ˌekspəˈnenʃəl/ *adj tech* **1** produced or expressed by multiplying a set of quantities by themselves: *an exponential growth rate|The population is increasing on an exponential curve* **2** containing an EXPONENT (2): y^n *is an exponential expression*

ex·port[1] /ɪkˈspɔːt‖-ɔrt/ *v* [IØ;T1] to send (goods) out of a country for sale: *They sell to the home* MARKET (=trade within the country) *but they don't export* —compare IMPORT[1] —**~able** *adj*

ex·port[2] /ˈekspɔːt‖-ɔrt/ *n* **1** [U] (the business of) EXPORTing: *the export trade|The export of gold is forbidden* **2** [C *often pl.*] something that is EXPORTed: *Wool is one of the chief exports of Australia* —compare IMPORT[2] **3 invisible exports** money brought into a country in other ways than by the sale of goods: *Teaching English to foreigners is one of Britain's invisible exports*

ex·por·ta·tion /ˌekspɔːˈteɪʃən‖-or-/ *n* [U] the action of EXPORTing: *the exportation of corn to Asia* —compare IMPORTATION

ex·port·er /ɪkˈspɔːtəʳ‖-ɔr-/ *n* a person or country that EXPORTs: *Switzerland is a big exporter of watches* —compare IMPORTer

ex·pose /ɪkˈspəʊz/ *v* [T1] **1** [Wv5; (*to*)] to uncover, so as to leave without protection (from something): *to expose one's skin to the sun|The soldiers were warned to remain hidden and not to expose themselves.*|(fig.) *Her youth and beauty will expose her to many dangers* **2** to leave (a baby) to die of cold and hunger out of doors: *The ancient Greeks are said to have exposed their unwanted babies* **3** [(*to*)] to make known (a secretly guilty person or action): *I threatened to expose him/the plan* (*to the police*) **4** to place in view: *exposed goods for sale in the market* **5** to uncover (a film) to the light, when taking a photograph **6 expose oneself** to show one's sexual parts on purpose, in the hope of making people feel excited —compare EXHIBITIONISM (2) **7 expose (oneself or another) to** to make (oneself or another) suffer: *His fatness exposes him to a lot of joking at the office*

ex·po·sé /ekˈspəʊzeɪ‖ˌekspəˈzeɪ/ *n* [(*of*)] *Fr* a short public statement of the (esp. shameful) facts (about something)

ex·po·si·tion /ˌekspəˈzɪʃən/ *n* **1** [C;U] (an act of) explaining and making clear: *a full exposition of his political beliefs* **2** [C] an international show (EXHIBITION) of the products of industry

ex post fac·to /ˌeks pəʊst ˈfæktəʊ/ *adj, adv Lat* (done, made, or expressed) after the fact: *ex post facto approval of something that has already happened*

ex·pos·tu·late /ɪkˈspɒstʃʊleɪt‖ɪkˈspɑstʃə-/ *v* [IØ (*with* and/or *about/on*)] *fml* to complain, loudly but not with the strongest feelings (to someone, about esp. his behaviour): *She expostulated with her husband on/about his habit of smoking in bed* —**-lation** /ɪkˌspɒstʃʊˈleɪʃən‖ɪkˌspɑstʃə-/ *n* [C;U]

ex·po·sure /ɪkˈspəʊʒəʳ/ *n* **1** [U] the state of being EXPOSEd (1) to the weather: *He nearly died of exposure on the cold mountain* **2** [C;U+*to*] (a case of) being EXPOSEd (1) (to the stated influence): *much exposure to danger|a short exposure to sunlight* **3** [C;U: (*of*)] a case of exposing, or the experience of being EXPOSEd (3): *I threatened him with public exposure.|repeated exposures in the newspapers of the Government's mistakes* **4** [C] the amount of film that must be EXPOSEd (5) to take one photograph: *I have 3 exposures left on this film* **5** [C] the length of time that a film must be EXPOSEd to take a photograph: *These 2 pictures were taken with different exposures —see picture at* PHOTOGRAPHIC **6** [U] the act of exposing (EXPOSE (4)) **7** [S9] the direction in which a room or house faces: *My bedroom has a southern exposure*

ex·pound /ɪkˈspaʊnd/ *v* [T1 (*to*)] to give an EXPOSITION (1) of: *The priest expounded his religion to us*

ex·press[1] /ɪkˈspres/ *adj* [Wa5;A] **1** (of a command, wish, etc.) clearly stated; EXPLICIT: *It was her express wish that you should have her jewels after her death* **2** (of an intention or purpose) special; clearly understood: *I came here with the express* *purpose of seeing you* **3** (of a likeness) exact: *Everything the child does is an express copy of her elder sister's behaviour* **4** going or sent quickly: *an express train*|(*BrE*) *an express letter* **5** (*esp. AmE*) (of a company or its vehicles) carrying parcels quickly: *an express company*/VAN

express² *n* **1** [C] also **express train** /·ˌ· '·/— a fast train: *the 9.30 express to London* **2** [U] *BrE* a service given by the post office, railways, etc., for carrying things faster and at a higher cost than usual: *Send the letter by express*

USAGE This word is often used with a *cap.* in the name of **a** a newspaper: *The Sunday* **Express** **b** a fast train: *the Rome* **Express.**

express³ *v* **1** [T1,6a (**how**)] to show (a feeling, opinion, or fact) in words or in some other way: *She expressed her thanks.*|*The prices are expressed both in dollars and pounds* **2** [T1] *BrE* to send by EXPRESS² (2): *to express an urgent letter* **3** [T1 (*from, out of*)] to press (oil, juice, etc.) out of something: *to express poison from a wound*|*juice expressed from oranges* **4 express oneself a** to speak or write one's thoughts or feelings: *He expresses himself in good clear English* **b** to show one's feelings in any way: *The children are expressing themselves in play*

express⁴ *adv* by EXPRESS² (2): *sent the parcel express*|(*BrE*) *sent the letter express*

ex·pres·sion /ɪk'spreʃən/ *n* **1** [C;U] (an example of) the act of expressing: *They greeted him with many expressions of pleasure.*|*A government should permit the free expression of political opinion* **2** [U] the quality of showing or performing with feeling: *She has a beautiful voice, but she doesn't sing with much expression* **3** [C] a word or group of words: "FUCK *off!*" *is a very rude expression, but its meaning is different in Britain and in the US* **4** [C] a look on a person's face: *That dog has such a wise expression that he seems almost human* **5** [C] (in MATHEMATICS) a sign or group of signs that represents a quantity: x^2+4 *is an expression* **6 beyond/past expression** of a kind or to a degree that cannot be put into words: *Helen of Troy was beautiful beyond expression* **7 find expression in** (of a feeling) to be expressed in: *His anger at last found expression in loud cursing*

ex·pres·sion·is·m /ɪk'spreʃənɪzəm/ *n* [U] (*often cap.*) a movement, in art and music, to show or describe the artist's feelings rather than anything actually experienced —compare IMPRESSIONISM —**expressionist** *n, adj*

ex·pres·sion·less /ɪk'spreʃənləs/ *adj* (esp. of a voice or face) without EXPRESSION (2) —**~ly** *adv*

ex·pres·sive /ɪk'spresɪv/ *adj* [(*of*)] (esp. of words or a face) full of feeling and meaning: *A baby's cry may be expressive of hunger or pain* —**~ly** *adv* —**~ness** *n* [U]

ex·press·ly /ɪk'spresli/ *adv* **1** clearly; in an EXPRESS¹ (1) way: *I told you expressly to lock the door* **2** on purpose: *This dictionary was written expressly for you*

ex·press·way /ɪk'spresweɪ/ *n AmE* MOTORWAY

ex·pro·pri·ate /ɪk'sprəʊprieɪt/ *v* [T1] **1** to take away (something owned by another), often for public use and/or without payment: *The State expropriated his palace* **2** to take away the property of (a person) in this way: *The State expropriated the king* —**-ation** /ɪkˌsprəʊpri'eɪʃən/ *n* [U;C] —**-ator** /ɪk'sprəʊprieɪtəʳ/ *n*

ex·pul·sion /ɪk'spʌlʃən/ *n* [C;U (*from*)] (an act of) EXPELling or being EXPELled: *the expulsion of a child from school*

expulsion or·der /·'·· ˌ··/ *n* an official order for a foreigner to leave a country

ex·punge /ɪk'spʌndʒ/ *v* [T1 (*from*)] *fml* to rub out or remove (a word, name, etc.) from a list, book, etc.: (fig.) *Nothing can expunge the shame of what he did*

ex·pur·gate /'ekspəgeɪt‖-ər-/ *v* [Wv5;T1] to make (a book, play, etc.) pure by taking out anything which is considered improper —**-gation** /ˌekspə'geɪʃən‖-ər-/ *n* [C;U]

ex·qui·site /ɪk'skwɪzɪ̇t, 'ekskwɪ-/ *adj* **1** *apprec* very finely made or done; almost perfect: *exquisite manners*/*grace*/*beauty*|*an exquisite white fur coat* **2** (of pain or pleasure) very great **3** (of power to feel) sensitive and delicate —**~ly** *adv* —**~ness** *n* [U]

ex·ser·vice /ˌ· '··/ *adj* [Wa5;A] *esp. BrE* (connected with people) formerly belonging to the armed forces: *a shop selling ex-service goods*

ex·ser·vice·man /ˌ· '···/ *fem.* **ex·ser·vice·wom·an** /ˌ· '··ˌ··/— *n esp. BrE* a person who was formerly in one of the armed forces —compare VETERAN (1,3)

ex·tant /ɪk'stænt/ *adj* [Wa5;B;E] (esp. of anything written, painted, etc.) still existing

ex·tem·po·ra·ne·ous /ɪkˌstempə'reɪnɪəs/ *adj* EXTEMPORE —**~ly** *adv* —**~ness** *n* [U]

ex·tem·po·re /ɪk'stempəri/ *adj, adv* (spoken or done) in haste, without time for preparation: *to make an extempore speech*

ex·tem·po·rize, -rise /ɪk'stempəraɪz/ *v* [IØ] to perform EXTEMPORE: *The actress forgot her lines and had to extemporize* —**-rization** /ɪkˌstempəraɪ'zeɪʃən‖-pərə-/ *n* [U;C]

ex·tend /ɪk'stend/ *v* **1** [L9] (of space, land, or time) to reach, stretch, or continue: *The hot weather extended into October* **2** [T1] to make longer or greater, esp. so as to reach a desired point: *to extend one's garden*|*to extend the railway to the next town* **3** [T1] to stretch out (a part of one's body) to the limit: *a bird with its wings extended*|*He refused to take the hand I extended in friendship* **4** [D1 (*to*); T1] *fml* to give or offer (help, friendship, etc.) to someone: *to extend a warm welcome to him*|*to extend him a warm welcome*|*The bank will extend you* CREDIT (=the right to borrow money) **5** [T1 *usu. pass.*] to cause to use all possible power: *The horse won the race easily without being fully extended*

ex·ten·sion /ɪk'stenʃən/ *n* **1** [U] the act of EXTENDing or condition of being EXTENDed (2,3,4) (note the phr. **the extension of**): *the extension of our foreign trade* **2** [C (*of*)] a part which is added to make anything longer, wider, or greater: *to build an extension onto the house*|*an extension of my holiday* **3** [C] any of many telephone lines which connect the SWITCHBOARD to various rooms or offices in a large building **4** [U] *med* the unbending of a joint between the bones of a limb, finger, etc., by which the angle between the bones is increased: *Full extension has not yet returned to the broken finger* **5 University Extension** *esp. BrE* teaching and examining students who cannot attend a university all the time (esp. in the phrs. **university extension course/lecturer**) —compare EXTRAMURAL

ex·ten·sive /ɪk'stensɪv/ *adj* **1** (of an area) covering a large surface **2** large in amount; *extensive damage from the storm*|*extensive repairs to the house* —**~ly** *adv* —**~ness** *n* [U]

ex·tent /ɪk'stent/ *n* **1** [U (*of*)] the length or area to which something EXTENDs (1): *to see the full extent of the Sahara desert from the air*|(fig.) *I was surprised at the extent of the scientist's knowledge* **2** [S9;U9] (a) (stated) degree: *I agree with what you say to some extent* (=partly)/*to a certain extent*/*to a large extent* **3 to such an extent that** so much that: *The temperature rose to such an extent that the firemen had to leave the burning building*

ex·ten·u·ate /ɪk'stenjʊeɪt/ *v* [Wv4;T1] to lessen the

seriousness of, by finding excuses for (bad behaviour): *He stole the money, but there are extenuating* CIRCUMSTANCE*s* (=facts to be considered)

ex·ten·u·a·tion /ɪkˌstenjʊˈeɪʃən/ *n* **1** [C;U] (something) extenuating (EXTENUATE) **2 in extenuation (of)** as an excuse (for): *He has nothing to say in extenuation of his crime*

ex·te·ri·or¹ /ɪkˈstɪərɪəʳ/ *adj* [A;F+*to*] outer; on or from the outside (esp. of places); out-of-door: *the exterior walls of the prison|The play begins with an exterior scene in a garden* —opposite **interior**; compare EXTERNAL (1); see picture at GEOMETRY

exterior² *n* **1** the outside; the outer appearance or surface: *the exterior of the house|You mustn't judge people by their exteriors* **2** an out-door scene in a picture or play: *Some artists only paint exteriors*

ex·te·ri·o·rize, -rise /ɪkˈstɪərɪəraɪz/ *v* [T1] **1** (in PSYCHOLOGY) EXTERNALIZE **2** *med* to bring an organ out of the body for a while (as during an operation), without cutting it off —**-rization** /ɪkˌstɪərɪəraɪˈzeɪʃən/ *n* [U]

ex·ter·mi·nate /ɪkˈstɜːmɪ̀neɪt‖-ɜr-/ *v* [T1] to kill (all the creatures or people in a place, or all those of a certain kind or race) —**-nation** /ɪkˌstɜːmɪ̀ˈneɪʃən‖-ɜr-/ *n* [U]

ex·ter·nal /ɪkˈstɜːnəl‖-ɜr-/ *adj* **1** on, of, or for the outside: *an external wound|This medicine is for external use, not to drink.|An* **external student** *studies outside the university.|An* **external examination** *is arranged by people outside one's own school* **2** that can be seen but is not natural or real: *To all external appearances he was a quiet man, but he had a violent temper* **3** foreign: *This newspaper doesn't pay enough attention to external affairs* —compare EXTERIOR

external ev·i·dence /·,·· ˈ···/ *n* [U,U3,5] proof that comes from outside and not from the thing that is being examined —opposite **internal evidence**

ex·ter·nal·ize, -ise /ɪkˈstɜːnəlaɪz‖-ɜr-/ *v* [T1] **1** (in PSYCHOLOGY) to give EXTERNAL expression to (feelings) esp. by words **2** RATIONALIZE —**-ization** /ɪkˌstɜːnəlaɪˈzeɪʃən‖-ɜr-/ *n* [U;C]

ex·ter·nal·ly /ɪkˈstɜːnəli‖-ɜr-/ *adv* (on or as regards the) outside: *to study externally for a university degree* (=without being in regular attendance at a university)

ex·ter·nals /ɪkˈstɜːnlz‖-ɜr-/ *n* [P (*of*)] outward forms and appearances: *You mustn't judge people by externals*

ex·ter·ri·to·ri·al /ˌeksterɪ̀ˈtɔːrɪəl‖-ˈtor-/ *adj* EXTRATERRITORIAL

ex·tinct /ɪkˈstɪŋkt/ *adj* **1** (of a kind of animal) no longer existing: *The woolly elephant* (MAMMOTH) *has been extinct for a long time* **2** (of fire) no longer burning: *This* VOLCANO (=burning mountain) *is extinct* **3** (of non-material things) having died out: *The belief in magic is almost extinct today*

ex·tinc·tion /ɪkˈstɪŋkʃən/ *n* [(*the*) U (*of*)] **1** the act of EXTINGUISHing or making EXTINCT: *the extinction of his hopes|(fml) the extinction of a fire* **2** the state of being or becoming EXTINCT: *Is the human race threatened with complete extinction?*

ex·tin·guish /ɪkˈstɪŋgwɪʃ/ *v* [T1] *fml* to put out (a light or fire): *Smoking is forbidden. Please extinguish your cigarettes.|*(fig.) *Nothing could extinguish his faith in human nature*

ex·tin·guish·er /ɪkˈstɪŋgwɪʃəʳ/ *n* any of several types of instrument for putting out small fires by shooting liquid chemicals at them

ex·tir·pate /ˈekstɜːpeɪt‖-ɜr-/ *v* [T1] *fml* to destroy completely (something bad) by or as if by pulling up the roots: *extirpated a bad social practice* —**-pation** /ˌekstɜːˈpeɪʃən‖-ɜr-/ *n*

ex·tol /ɪkˈstəʊl/ *v* **-ll-** [T1] *fml* to praise very highly: *He keeps extolling her goodness.|The general was extolled as the man who had led the country to victory*

ex·tort from /ɪkˈstɔːt‖-ɔrt/ *v prep* [D1] to obtain (something) by force or threats (from someone): *to extort money|a promise from him*

ex·tor·tion /ɪkˈstɔːʃən‖-ɔr-/ *n* [U] the action of EXTORTing FROM someone: *a promise obtained by extortion* —**~er,** —**~ist** *n*

ex·tor·tion·ate /ɪkˈstɔːʃənɪ̀t‖-ɔr-/ *adj derog* (of a demand, price, etc.) very high; much too high; EXORBITANT —**~ly** *adv*

ex·tor·tions /ɪkˈstɔːʃənz‖-ɔr-/ *n* [P] acts of EXTORTing money FROM people: *I won't pay! I've suffered too long from your extortions*

ex·tra¹ /ˈekstrə/ *adj, adv* [Wa5] **1** [A] additional(ly); beyond what is usual or necessary: *extra money|an extra loaf of bread|to work extra hard|to arrive extra late* **2** [E;F] as well as the regular charge: *Dinner costs £3, and wine is extra.|They charge extra for wine.|£3 extra*

extra² *n* **1** something added, for which an EXTRA charge is made: *At this hotel a hot bath is an extra* **2** an actor in a cinema film who has a very small part in a crowd scene and is paid each day: *We need 1000 extras for the big scene when they cross the Red Sea* **3** a special EDITION (=one printing) of a newspaper: *Late evening extra!* (shouted by newspaper seller) **4** (*AustrE* **sundry**)— *BrE* a run in cricket which is not made off the BAT (=stick for hitting the ball)

extra- *prefix* [*adj*→*adj*] outside or beyond: EXTRAMARITAL|EXTRAJUDICIAL

ex·tract¹ /ɪkˈstrækt/ *v* [T1 (*from*)] **1** to pull or take out, often with difficulty: *to extract a tooth|Can you extract this fly from my eye?*|(fig.) *to extract information from a criminal* **2** to take out with a machine or instrument, or by chemical means (a substance which is contained in another substance): *to extract gold from the rocks|oil extracted from* COTTONSEED **3** to choose and usu. copy (words or examples from a book)

ex·tract² /ˈekstrækt/ *n* **1** [C;U (*of*)] (a) product obtained by EXTRACTing¹ (2): *meat extract|extract of meat* —compare ESSENCE² (2) **2** [C (*from*)] a passage of written or spoken matter that has been EXTRACTed¹ (3); EXCERPT: *She read me a few extracts from his letter*

ex·trac·tion /ɪkˈstrækʃən/ *n* **1** [C;U:(*from*)] the act or an example of EXTRACTing¹ (1): *the extraction of money from my father|Her teeth are so bad that she needs 5 extractions* **2** [U (*from*)] the act of EXTRACTing¹ (2): *the extraction of coal from a mine* **3** [U9] (the stated) origin (of a person's family): *an American of Russian extraction* (=his family came from Russia)

ex·tra·cur·ric·u·lar /ˌekstrəkəˈrɪkjʊləʳ‖-kjə-/ *adj* [Wa5] (esp. of activities such as sports, music or acting) outside the regular course of work (CURRICULUM) in a school or college

ex·tra·di·ta·ble /ˈekstrədaɪtəbəl/ *adj* (of a crime) for which a person can be EXTRADITED

ex·tra·dite /ˈekstrədaɪt/ *v* [T1 (*from* and/or *to*) *often pass.*] **1** to send (someone who may be guilty of a crime and who has escaped to another country) back for trial: *The English murderer was caught by the French police and extradited to Britain* **2** to obtain (such a person) for trial in this way —**-dition** /ˌekstrəˈdɪʃən/ *n* [C;U]

ex·tra·ju·di·cial /ˌekstrədʒuːˈdɪʃəl/ *adj* beyond or outside the ordinary powers of the law

ex·tra·mar·i·tal /ˌekstrəˈmærɪ̀tl/ *adj* [A] of or related to a married person's sexual relationships outside marriage: *to have extramarital relations* (*with*)

ex·tra·mu·ral /ˌekstrəˈmjʊərəl/ *adj* [Wa5;A] **1**

outside (the walls of) a town or an organization: *This hospital provides extramural care* **2** (of students, courses, etc.) connected with but outside a university: *a course run by the university extramural department* **3** *AmE* (of sports) between teams from different schools: *an extramural football game*

ex·tra·ne·ous /ɪk'streɪnɪəs/ *adj* **1** not directly connected (with the thing to which it is joined); coming from outside: *This is not part of the tree, but an extraneous growth* **2** not belonging (to the subject that is being dealt with): *extraneous events in a story* —**~ly** *adv*

extra·or·di·na·ry /ɪk'strɔːdənəri‖ɪk'strɔrdn-eri, ˌekstrə'ɔr-/ *adj* **1** [B] very strange: *What an extraordinary hat!* **2** [B] more than what is ordinary: *a girl of extraordinary beauty* **3** [Wa5;A] (of arrangements) as well as the ordinary one(s): *The committee meets regularly on Fridays, but there will be an extraordinary meeting next Wednesday* **4** [Wa5;E] *fml* (of certain officials) additional to the usual official(s); employed on a special service: *He became doctor extraordinary to the Queen*

extra·or·di·na·ri·ly /ɪk'strɔːdənərəli‖ɪkˌstrɔrdn-'erəli, ˌekstrə'ɔrdn-erəli/ *adv* **1** very strangely: *Why does he behave so extraordinarily?* **2** more than usually: *took an extraordinarily long time*

ex·trap·o·late /ɪk'stræpəleɪt/ *v* [I∅;T1] **1** (in MATHEMATICS) to work out (the value of a number which depends on measurements) by filling in the other measurements beyond those already known **2 a** to guess (something in the future) from facts already known **b** to use (facts already known) so as to form a guess about the future

ex·tra·sen·so·ry per·cep·tion /ˌekstrəˌsensəri pə'sepʃən‖-pər-/ also **E S P**— *adj* [U] knowledge or feelings about outside, past, or future things, obtained without the use of the ordinary 5 senses

ex·tra·ter·res·tri·al /ˌekstrətə'restrɪəl/ *adj* [Wa5] (coming from) outside the earth: *Does extraterrestrial life exist?*

ex·tra·ter·ri·to·ri·al /ˌekstrəterə'tɔːrɪəl‖-'tor-/ also **exterritorial**— *adj* [Wa5;A] **1** (of rights) free from control by local law: *An* AMBASSADOR (=a person of high rank who acts for his own government in another country) *has extraterritorial rights and cannot be punished for breaking the law* **2** outside the area where local law is effective: *the country's extraterritorial possessions*

ex·trav·a·gance /ɪk'strævəgəns/ *n derog* **1** [C;U] (an example of) being EXTRAVAGANT (1): *You should spend your money carefully and avoid extravagance* **2** [U] the quality of being EXTRAVAGANT (2): *the extravagance with which he praised that silly book*

ex·trav·a·gant /ɪk'strævəgənt/ *adj derog* **1 a** (of people) wasteful esp. of money: *She's an extravagant woman* **b** (of habits and behaviour) too costly: *We mustn't buy roses; it's extravagant* **2** (of ideas, behaviour, and the expression of feeling) uncontrolled; beyond what is reasonable: *He makes the most extravagant claims for his new system* —**~ly** *adv*

ex·trav·a·gan·za /ɪkˌstrævə'gænzə/ *n* **1** a play or musical work which is very free in style, and in which usually foolish things are treated solemnly or serious writers are copied to make people laugh **2** a very grand and costly show

ex·tra·vert /'ekstrəvɜːt‖-ɜrt/ *n* EXTROVERT

ex·treme¹ /ɪk'striːm/ *adj* [Wa5] **1** [A] the furthest possible; at the very beginning or very end: *the extreme end of the road|extreme old age* **2** [A] the greatest possible: *extreme heat/danger|The extreme* PENALTY (=punishment) *of the law in England used to be punishment by death* **3** [A;(B)] *often derog.* (of opinions and those who hold them) going beyond the usual limits: *to hold extreme opinions* **4 take extreme action/measures** to act in the strongest or most violent way that one's official position allows

extreme² *n* [C (*usu. pl.*)] **1** an EXTREME¹ (2) degree: *Sometimes he eats too much and sometimes he eats nothing. He goes from one extreme to the other* —compare EXTREMITY **2 go/be driven to extremes** to act too violently; to behave in an EXTREME¹ (3) way **3 in the extreme** *fml* EXTREMELY: *He has been generous in the extreme* **4 the opposite extreme** also **the other extreme**— a quality, condition, etc., which is as widely different as possible from another: *He used to be a* COMMUNIST *but now he's gone to the opposite extreme and joined the* FASCISTs

ex·treme·ly /ɪk'striːmli/ *adv* very: *I'm extremely sorry*

Extreme Unc·tion /·,· '··/ *n* [R] the ROMAN CATHOLIC ceremony (now usu. called the **Anointing of the sick**) of praying for, and putting a little oil on the head of, a person in danger of death

ex·trem·is·m /ɪk'striːmɪzəm/ *n* [U] *often derog.* (esp. in politics) the quality or state of being EXTREME¹ (3) —**extremist** *n*

ex·trem·i·ties /ɪk'streməti z/ *n* [P] *fml* **1** the human hands and feet: *His extremities were frozen* **2** cruel or violent punishments or ways of forcing someone to obey: *If she disobeys her father again he will be forced to extremities* **3 lower extremities** (human) legs **4 upper extremities** (human) arms

ex·trem·i·ty /ɪk'streməti/ *n* **1** [S;U: (*of*)] the highest degree (esp. of suffering and sorrow); (a case of) the greatest misfortune: *an extremity of pain/anger* **2 the last extremity** the greatest possible danger or misfortune

ex·tri·cate /'ekstrəkeɪt/ *v* [T1 (*from*)] to set (someone or something) free from something that it is difficult to escape from: *The wrecked car had to be lifted before the driver could be extricated.|How can we extricate the firm from this trouble?* —**-cable** /ek'strɪkəbəl/ *adj* —**-cation** /ˌekstrə'keɪʃən/ *n* [U]

ex·trin·sic /ek'strɪnsɪk/ *adj* [(*to*)] *fml* (of a value or quality) not forming a part of or not really belonging to, that with which it is connected —opposite **intrinsic**

ex·tro·vert, extravert /'ekstrəvɜːt‖-ɜrt/ *n* **1** a person who likes to spend time in activities with other people rather than in attending to his own thoughts and feelings **2** *not tech* a cheerful person who likes doing things rather than using his mind —opposite **introvert** —**-version** /ˌekstrə'vɜːʃən‖-'vɜrʒən/ *n* [U]

ex·trude /ɪk'struːd/ *v* [T1 (*from*)] **1** to push or force out by pressure: *to extrude toothpaste from the tube* **2** *tech* to shape (plastic or metal) in this way, by forcing through a DIE (=an instrument with a screw inside a tube) —**extrusion** /ɪk'struːʒən/ *n* [C;U]

ex·u·be·rance /ɪg'zjuːbərəns‖ɪg'zuː-/ *n* [U] the quality of being EXUBERANT

ex·u·be·rant /ɪg'zjuːbərənt‖ɪg'zuː-/ *adj* **1** (of people and their behaviour) overflowing with life and cheerful excitement **2** (of plants) growing strongly and plentifully: *the exuberant growth of a tropical rain forest* —**~ly** *adv*

ex·ude /ɪg'zjuːd‖ɪg'zuːd/ *v* [I∅;T1] to (cause to) flow out slowly and spread in all directions: (fig.) *She's always friendly; she simply exudes good nature*

ex·ult /ɪg'zʌlt/ *v* [I∅ (*at, in*), I3] to rejoice; to show delight (in victory, success, etc.): *The people exulted in/at the victory* —compare EXALT

ex·ul·tant /ɪg'zʌltənt/ *adj* EXULTing: *The exultant crowds were dancing in the streets* —**~ly** *adv*

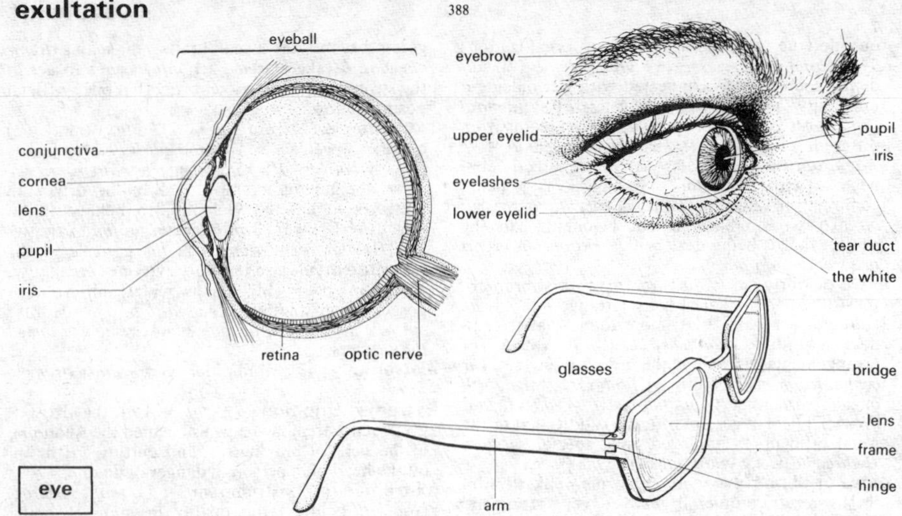

ex·ul·ta·tion /ˌegzʌlˈteɪʃən/ *n* **1** [U (*at*)] the feeling or expression of EXULTing: *The climber gave a cry of exultation when he reached the mountain top* **2** [U (*over*)] the feeling or expression of EXULTing OVER (someone)

exult o·ver *v prep* **1** [T1] to rejoice proudly over and thus usu. cause a feeling of shame to (a defeated enemy) **2** [T1,4] to EXULT at: *exulted over (winning) first prize*

-ey /i/ *suffix* [*n*→*adj* [Wa1]] (the form used for -Y, esp. after *-y*): CLAYEY *soil*

eye[1] /aɪ/ *n* **1** the organ of sight, of which there are 2 at the front of the human head: *He lost an eye in an accident, and now he has a glass eye* —see picture at HUMAN[2] **2** the front part of this organ, with the coloured parts which can be seen: *Her children have blue eyes* **3** the power of seeing: *To the painter's eye, this would be a beautiful scene.|My eye fell upon an interesting article in the newspaper* **4** the hole in a needle through which the thread passes **5** the dark spot on a potato, from which a new plant can grow —see picture at VEGETABLE[1] **6** the calm centre of a storm, esp. of a HURRICANE **7** a small ring-shaped or U-shaped piece of metal into which a hook fits for fastening: *Her dress was fastened with hooks and eyes* **8 an eye for an eye** a punishment which hurts the criminal in the same way as he hurt someone else: *If the State punishes a murderer by death it's an eye for an eye* **9 be in the public eye** to be often seen in public or on television, or mentioned in newspapers **10 catch someone's eye** *infml* **a** (of things) to be noticed: *I bought a new dress which caught my eye in the shop* **b** (of people) to draw someone's attention to oneself: *The child tried to catch the teacher's eye* **11 do someone in the eye** *BrE infml* to trick someone **12 easy on the eye(s)** *sl* (of people) attractive; pretty **13 get/keep one's eye in** *BrE* (in cricket and other ball games) to get/keep, through practice, the ability to see the ball and to judge its direction **14 give someone a black eye** also **black someone's eye**— to hit someone so that there is a discoloured area (BRUISE) round his eye **15 have an eye for** to have the ability to see, judge and understand clearly **16 have an eye on/to the main chance** to look for the best chance of personal gain **17 in one's mind's eye** in one's imagination **18 in the eye/eyes of the law** according to the law; as the law sees it **19 keep an eye on** *infml* to watch carefully: *Please keep an eye on the baby for me* **20 keep an eye out for** to try to notice and remember (someone or something); be on the LOOKOUT (6) for **21 look someone in the eye** to look straight into someone's face: *Can you look me in the eye and tell a lie?* **22 mind your eye** *BrE infml* Look out! Be careful! **23 more than meets the eye** *infml* more than actually appears or is seen: *Sewing looks quite simple, but there's more in it than meets the eye* **24 my eye!** *infml* (used for expressing a certain degree of disagreement or sometimes surprise): *A diamond, my eye! That's glass* **25 one in the eye for** *infml* a disappointment or defeat for: *If she wins the case, it'll be one in the eye for George—he hates women lawyers!* **26 see eye to eye (with)** to agree completely (with); to have the same position (as): *He and his brother always see eye to eye* **27 with/have an eye to** having/to have as one's purpose: *Since she left school, she's had an eye to marriage* **28 with half an eye** without looking closely: *You can see with half an eye that he and his wife are unhappy together* **29 with the naked eye a** without a protective covering for the eyes: *You mustn't look at the sun with the naked eye* **b** without a TELESCOPE: *Can you see that ship in the distance with the naked eye?* —see also EYES —**~less** *adj* [Wa5]

eye[2] *v* **eyeing** *or* **eying** [T1] to look at closely or with desire: *She eyed me jealously.|The child was eyeing the chocolate cake*

eye·ball /ˈaɪbɔːl/ *n* **1** the whole of the eye, including the part hidden inside the head, which forms a more or less round ball **2 eyeball to eyeball (with)** *infml, usu. humor* (esp. in an angry or dangerous state of affairs) face to face; facing each other (note the phr. **an eyeball-to-eyeball confrontation**)

eye·brow /ˈaɪbraʊ/ *n* **1** the line of hairs above each of the 2 human eyes —see picture at HUMAN[2] **2 raise one's eyebrows (at)** to express surprise, doubt, displeasure, or disapproval (at), by or as if by moving these upwards: (fig.) *There were a lot of raised eyebrows/eyebrows raised at the news of the minister's dismissal* **3 up to one's eyebrows (in)** *not fml* very busy (at): *I can't come out—I'm up to my eyebrows (in work)*

eyebrow pen·cil /ˈ·· ˌ··/ *n* [C;U] PENCIL[1] (3)

eye-catch·ing /ˈ· ˌ··/ *adj* (of a thing) so unusual that one cannot help looking at it: *an eye-catching advertisement* —**eye-catchingly** *adv*

eye·cup /ˈaɪkʌp/ *BrE* also **eye·bath** /ˈaɪbɑːθ‖-bæθ/— *n* **1** a small cup for holding liquid used for bathing the eyes **2** the amount of liquid this holds

-eyed /aɪd/ *comb. form* **1** having an eye or eyes of the stated type or number: *a one-eyed man|dark-eyed children* **2 someone's blue-eyed boy** someone's favourite: *Smith is the President's blue-eyed boy at present* **3 bug-eyed monster** any of various imaginary and terrible creatures in SCIENCE FICTION (= stories based on science)

eye·ful /ˈaɪfʊl/ *n* [S] *infml* an attractive sight worth looking at (usu. in the phrs. **have/get an eyeful**): *He got an eyeful when the ladies went swimming.|She's quite an eyeful*

eye·glass /ˈaɪglɑːs‖-glæs/ *n* **1** [C] a glass (LENS) for one eye, the sight of which is weak **2** [A] of or for EYEGLASSES: *My eyeglass frame is broken!*

eye·glass·es /ˈaɪglɑːsɪ̈z‖-glæs-/ *n* [P] GLASSES —see PAIR (USAGE)

eye·lash /ˈaɪlæʃ/ *n* any of the small hairs of which a number grow from the edge of each eyelid in humans and most hairy animals: *a child with long eyelashes*

eye·let /ˈaɪlɪ̈t/ *n* a hole with a metal ring round it, which is made in material such as leather or cloth so that a rope or cord may be passed through it

eye·lid /ˈaɪˌlɪd/ *n* **1** either of the pieces of covering skin which can move down to close each eye: *We use our eyelids to* BLINK *so as to clean our eyes* **2 hang on by one's eyelids** *infml* to continue to hold a dangerous or difficult position: *The soldiers are still holding the fort, but they're hanging on by their eyelids*

eye·lin·er /ˈaɪˌlaɪnəʳ/ *n* [U] solid paint used for giving more importance to the shape of the eyes

eye-o·pen·er /ˈ· ˌ···/ *n* [S] something surprising, which makes a person see a truth he did not formerly believe: *I knew he was strong, but it was an eye-opener to me when I saw him lift that table*

eye·piece /ˈaɪpiːs/ *n* the glass (LENS) at the eye end of an instrument such as a microscope or TELESCOPE —see picture at SCIENTIFIC

eyes /aɪz/ *n* [P] **1** *pl. of* EYE **2 a sight for sore eyes** something or someone that is dressed in an odd or funny way **3 all eyes** watching closely and attentively —compare **all** EARS[1] (5) **4 close/shut one's eyes to a** to refuse to notice: *He tried to close his eyes to the bad social conditions around him, but at last he had to act* **b** to allow to go unnoticed or unpunished: *I'll close my eyes to your mistake this time, my boy, but don't let it happen again* **5 cry one's eyes out** to weep a great deal **6 Eyes right/left/front!** (military commands) Turn your heads and look to the right/left/front! **7 (have) eyes in the back of one's head** to see everything: *How did you know I was there? You must have eyes in the back of your head* **8 in the eyes of/in someone's eyes**: in the opinion of/in someone's opinion: *The baby is beautiful in its mother's eyes/in the eyes of its mother* **9 keep one's eyes open/(***BrE* also) **skinned/(***AmE* also) **peeled** *infml* to keep a sharp look-out: *The thieves kept their eyes skinned for the police* **10 make (sheep's) eyes at (someone)** to look at (someone) with sexual love: *He makes eyes at every pretty girl he sees* **11 make someone open his eyes** to surprise someone **12 not be able to believe one's eyes** not to be able to believe that what one sees is real or true **13 (not) take one's eyes off** [*usu. neg.*] (not) to stop watching: *She never took her eyes off the baby for a moment* **14 only have eyes for** to be interested only in looking at: *He only has eyes for his beautiful wife* **15 open someone's eyes to** to make someone know or understand: *The way he deceived me opened my eyes to his true character* **16 set/clap/lay eyes on** *infml* see: *I knew he was clever, the moment I set eyes on him* **17 throw dust in someone's eyes** to deceive someone on purpose: *He tried to throw dust in my eyes, but I knew he was lying* **18 under/before one's very eyes** in front of one, usu. with no attempt to stop one from seeing: *He stole the jewels under my very eyes* **19 up to the/one's eyes in work** very busy: *The doctor is up to his eyes in work today* **20 with one's eyes open** *infml* knowing what may possibly happen: *You married him with your eyes open, so don't complain now!*

eye shad·ow /ˈ· ˌ··/ *n* [U] coloured paint used on the eyelids to give the eyes more importance

eye·shot /ˈaɪʃɒt‖-ʃɑt/ *n* [U] seeing distance: *beyond/in/out of/within eyeshot of the house* —compare EARSHOT

eye·sight /ˈaɪsaɪt/ *n* [U] the power of seeing: *He has good/poor eyesight*

eye·sore /ˈaɪsɔːʳ/ *n* something ugly to look at (esp. when many people can see it)

eye·strain /ˈaɪstreɪn/ *n* [U] a painful and tired condition of the eyes, as caused by reading very small print

eye·tooth /ˈaɪtuːθ/ *n* **-teeth** /tiːθ/ either of the 2 long pointed CANINE teeth at the 2 upper corners of the mouth

eye·wash /ˈaɪwɒʃ‖-wɔʃ, -wɑʃ/ *n* [U] **1** liquid for bathing the eyes **2** *infml* something said or done to deceive, esp. to make someone think that one is working hard or that a piece of work is good: *He seems very busy, rushing about like that, but it's all eyewash; he never does any work at all*

eye·wit·ness /ˈaɪˌwɪtnɪ̈s/ *n* [(*to, of*)] a person who himself sees an event happen, and so is able to describe it, for example in a law court: *Were there any eyewitnesses to the crime?*

eyot /eɪt, eɪət/ *n BrE* a small island in a river

ey·rie, eyry, aery, eyry /ˈɪəri, ˈeəri, ˈaɪəri/ *n* the nest of a flesh-eating bird (esp. an EAGLE) built high in rocks or cliffs: (fig.) *My friend has built himself an eyrie at the top of the mountain*

F,f

F, f /ef/ **F's, f's** *or* **Fs, fs** the 6th letter of the English alphabet

F[1] (in Western music) **a** the 4th note (*AmE* also **tone**) in the musical SCALE of C MAJOR **b** the musical KEY based on this note

F[2] *abbrev. for*: FAHRENHEIT: *Water boils at 212°F*

fa /fɑː/ *n* [C;U] the 4th note in the (SOL-FA) musical SCALE: *sing (a) fa*

Fa·bi·an[1] /ˈfeɪbɪən/ *adj* [Wa5] **1** using delay, esp. in order to wear out an opponent **2** of the FABIANs

Fabian[2] *n* a member of a SOCIALIST political group, the **Fabian society**

fa·ble /ˈfeɪbəl/ *n* **1** [C] a short story that teaches a lesson (a MORAL) or truth, esp. a story in which animals or objects speak **2** [C] a story about great people who never actually lived; LEGEND; MYTH **3** [U] such stories considered as a group **4** [C] a false story or account

fa·bled /ˈfeɪbəld/ *adj* [Wa5] spoken of or famous in FABLEs

fab·ric /ˈfæbrɪk/ *n* **1** [C;U] cloth made by threads

woven together in any of various ways **2** [U] framework, base, or system: *The whole fabric of society was changed by the war* **3** [U] the walls, roof, etc., of a building: *The cost of repairing the fabric of the church was very high*

fab·ri·cate /ˈfæbrɪkeɪt/ *v* [T1] **1** to make or invent in order to deceive: *The story was fabricated and completely untrue* **2** to make, esp. by putting parts together

fab·ri·ca·tion /ˌfæbrɪˈkeɪʃən/ *n* **1** [C] something made or invented in order to deceive, esp. a lie **2** [U] the act of making

fab·u·lous /ˈfæbjʊləs‖-jə-/ also (*infml*) **fab** /fæb/— *adj* [Wa5] **1** nearly unbelievable: *a fabulous sum of money* **2** *infml* very good or pleasant; excellent **3** existing or told about in FABLEs: *fabulous creatures*

fab·u·lous·ly /ˈfæbjʊləsli‖-jə-/ *adv* very (rich, great, etc.): *fabulously wealthy*

fa·cade, façade /fəˈsɑːd, fæ-/ *n* **1** the front of a building **2** an appearance, esp. one that is false: *a facade of honesty*

face[1] /feɪs/ *n* **1** [C] the front part of the head from the chin to the hair: *a surprised expression on one's face* **2** [C] a look or expression on the face: *a happy face* **3** [U] a position of respect (esp. in the phrs. **lose** *or* **save (one's) face**): *When he failed to beat his opponent he felt he had lost face with his friends, who all expected him to win.|After all his failures, the win saved his face/saved face for him* —see also FACE-SAVER **4** [C] the front, upper, outer, or most important surface of something: *We climbed the north face of the mountain.|The face of the building is covered with climbing plants.|They seem to have disappeared off the face of the earth* **5** [C] the surface of a rock, either on or below the ground, from which coal, gold, diamonds, etc., are dug: *The miners work at the face for 7 hours each day* **6** [C] the style or size of a letter as used by a printer: *Which face shall we print this book in?* **7** **face to face (with)** looking directly at (a person/thing/each other): *The opponents were brought face to face.|During the storm I came face to face with death* **8** **fly in the face of** to act in opposition to, on purpose: *to fly in the face of custom*/CONVENTION —see also STRAIGHT[1] (8) **9** **have the face** to be bold or rude enough to: *I don't know how you have the face to ask for such a thing* **10** **in the face of** against (something which opposes): *How could he win in the face of such united opposition?|He succeeded in the face of great danger* **11** **look (somebody) in the face** to look directly at somebody, esp. without feeling ashamed **12** **make/pull a face** also **pull faces** —to make an expression with the face to show rude amusement, disagreement, dislike, pain, etc. **13** **on the face of it** judging by what one can see; APPARENTLY **14** **pull/wear a long face** to look sad **15** **put a good/bold face on something** to behave or make it appear as if things are better than they are **16** **set one's face against** to oppose strongly **17** **show one's face** to show one's presence; appear **18** **to someone's face** in one's appearance; openly: *He wouldn't be so rude to her face* —compare BEHIND[2] (5) **someone's back**

face[2] *v* **1** [T1;L9] to have or turn the face or front towards or in a certain direction: *The house faces the park.|The building faces north/towards the north* **2** [T1] to meet or oppose firmly and not try to avoid: *He faced the difficulty with courage* **3** [T1] to need consideration or action by: *The difficulty that faces us today is one of supplying food to those in need* **4** [T1 (*with*)] to cover or partly cover (esp. the front part of) with a different material: *The front of the brick house was faced with cement* **5** **face the music** to meet an unpleasant state of affairs, a danger, or the results of one's actions: *I must face the music and accept responsibility*

face·cloth /ˈfeɪsklɒθ‖-klɔθ/ *AmE* also **washcloth**, *BrE* also **face flan·nel** /ˈ· ˌ··/— *n* a small cloth (FLANNEL) used to wash the face, hands, etc.

-faced /feɪst/ *comb. form* having a face or expression of the stated type: *red-faced; sad-faced*

face fun·gus /ˈ· ˌ··/ also **fungus**— *n* [C;U] *humor* hair growing on a man's face; beard

face·less /ˈfeɪsləs/ *adj* [Wa5] without any clear character: *Crowds of faceless people pour into the city each day*

face-lift /ˈ· ˌ·/ *n* **1** a medical operation to make the face look younger by tightening the skin: *to have had 3 face-lifts* **2** an improvement in appearance, as by repainting or restyling (RESTYLE): *to give a room a face-lift*

face out *v adv* [T1 *no pass*] to oppose or deal with bravely: *to face the matter out|to face them out*

face pack /ˈ· ·/ *n* a cream spread over the face to clean and improve the skin, and removed after a short time

face pow·der /ˈ· ˌ··/ *n* [U] a sweet-smelling powder spread on the face to make one look or smell nice

face-sav·er /ˈ· ˌ··/ *n* something, such as a type of decision (COMPROMISE), that saves someone's self-respect

face-sav·ing /ˈ· ˌ··/ *adj* [Wa5;A] which allows self-respect to be kept, trust, etc., as by making a type of decision (COMPROMISE): *a face-saving decision* —see also FACE[1] (3)

fac·et /ˈfæsɪ̈t/ *n* **1** any of the many flat sides of a cut jewel or precious stone **2** any of the many parts of a subject to be considered: *The question had many facets*

fa·ce·tious /fəˈsiːʃəs/ *adj* using or tending to use unsuitable jokes: *I became angry with the facetious boy/at his facetious remarks* —**~ly** *adv* —**~ness** *n* [U]

face-to-face /ˌ· · ˈ·◂/ *adj* [Wa5;A] being within each other's presence or sight: *They had a face-to-face argument*

face up to *v adv prep* [T1] to be brave enough to accept or deal with: *to face up to one's responsibilities|to face up to difficulties*

face val·ue /ˌ· ˈ··/ *n* **1** [C;U] the value or cost as shown on the front of something, such as a postage stamp **2** [U] the value or importance of something as it appears at first (in the phr. **at (something's) face value**): *If you take his remarks only at their face value you will not have understood his full meaning*

fa·cial[1] /ˈfeɪʃəl/ *adj* [Wa5] of or concerning the face —**~ly** *adv*

facial[2] *n* a beauty treatment in which the skin of the face is treated with various substances and may also be MASSAGEd

fa·cile /ˈfæsaɪl‖ˈfæsəl/ *adj* **1** [A] easily done or obtained: *facile success* **2** [B] too easy; not deep; meaningless: *facile remarks/answers/expression* **3** [A] moving, working, acting, or done easily: *a facile hand/writer* —**~ly** *adv* —**~ness** *n* [U]

fa·cil·i·tate /fəˈsɪlɪ̈teɪt/ *v* [T1] to make easy or easier; help: *The broken lock facilitated my entrance into the empty house* —**-tation** /fəˌsɪlɪ̈ˈteɪʃən/ *n* [U]

fa·cil·i·ties /fəˈsɪlɪ̈tiz/ *n* [P] means to do things; that which can be used: *One of the facilities our students have is a large library*

fa·cil·i·ty /fəˈsɪlɪ̈ti/ *n* **1** [C;U] (an) ability to do or perform something easily: *His facility with/in languages is surprising.|a facility in languages* **2** [U] the quality of being able to be done or performed easily: *The facility of this piece of music makes it a pleasure to play* **3** [C] an advantage; CONVENIENCE:

A free bus to the airport is a facility offered only by this hotel

fac·ing /ˈfeɪsɪŋ/ *n* [U] **1** an outer covering or surface, as of a wall, for protection, ornament, etc. **2** additional material which is put into parts near the edges of a garment when it is being made, to improve it, esp. in thickness: *to buy facing (material) to make a collar stiff*

fac·ings /ˈfeɪsɪŋz/ *n* [P] (of a garment, esp. a uniform) the collar and parts (CUFF*s*) around the wrists made in a different colour from the rest of the garment

fac·sim·i·le /fækˈsɪmɪ̆li/ *n* [C] an exact copy, as of a picture or piece of writing

fact /fækt/ *n* **1** [C,C5] something that has actual existence or an event that has actually happened or is happening; something true: *Scientists attempt to find reasons for facts.|Certain facts have become known about the materials of the moon.|It is a fact that I have written this sentence* **2** [C] information regarded as being true and as having reality: *That fire is hot is an accepted fact.|She didn't answer my letter. The fact is she didn't even read it* **3** [the+R] *law* deed; crime: *an* ACCESSORY *after the fact* **4** [U] the truth: *Is this story fact?* **5 as a matter of fact, in (actual) fact, in point of fact** really; actually: *Officially he is in charge, but in fact his secretary does all the work.|He doesn't mind. In fact, he's very pleased.|I finished it yesterday, as a matter of fact* —compare INDEED; EVENT (1)

fact find·er /ˈ· ˌ··/ *n* a person who tries to discover and make clear the facts of a state of affairs, esp. to improve difficulties between people or get information —**fact-finding** *n* [Wa5;A]: *a fact-finding committee*

fac·tion /ˈfækʃən/ *n* **1** [C] a group or party within a larger group, esp. one that makes itself noticed **2** [U] argument, disagreement, fighting, etc., within a group or party

fac·tious /ˈfækʃəs/ *adj* [Wa5] **1** acting so as to favour only a small group: *His factious arguments were disapproved of by most members* **2** caused by small groups

fac·ti·tious /fækˈtɪʃəs/ *adj* [Wa5] **1** produced by man; not natural **2** caused on purpose; unreal: *A factitious demand for sugar was caused by false stories that there would be a lack of it*

fact of life /ˌ· · ˈ·/ *n* something that exists and that must be considered: *That the rich get richer and the poor poorer is a fact of life* —see also FACTS OF LIFE

fac·tor /ˈfæktəʳ/ *n* **1** any of the forces, conditions, influences, etc., that act with others to bring about a result: *His friendly manner is a factor in his rapid success* **2** (in MATHEMATICS) a whole number which, when multiplied by one or more whole numbers, produces a given number: *2, 3, 4, and 6 are all factors of 12* **3** a person who acts or does business for another **4** *ScotE* a person who looks after the lands of another **5** *tech* a type of GENE (esp. in the phr. **genetic factor**)

fac·tor·ize, -ise /ˈfæktəraɪz/ also **factor**— *v* [T1] to divide into FACTORS (2)

fac·to·ry /ˈfæktəri/ *n* a building or group of buildings where goods are made, esp. in great quantities by machines: *factory workers*

factory farm /ˈ··· ·/ *n* an animal farm in which the animals are kept in small cages inside large buildings and made to grow or produce eggs, milk, etc., very quickly —**factory farming** /ˌ··· ˈ··/ *n*

fac·to·tum /fækˈtəʊtəm/ *n* a servant who has to perform all kinds of work

facts of life /ˌ· · ˈ·/ *n* [P] *euph* the details of sex and how babies are born: *Have you told your child about the facts of life yet?*

fac·tu·al /ˈfæktʃʊəl/ *adj* of, concerning, or based on facts: *a factual account of the war* —**~ly** *adv*

fac·ul·ty /ˈfækəlti/ *n* **1** the power or ability to do something particular: *He has the faculty to learn languages easily* —see GENIUS (USAGE) **2** a natural power or ability, esp. of the mind: *He has lost the use of his body but he is still in possession of his faculties.|the faculty of hearing* **3 a** a branch or division of learning, esp. in a university: *law/science faculty* **b** all the teachers, and sometimes all the students as well, of such a branch or division: *faculty meetings* **c** *AmE* all the teachers and other workers of a university or college

fad /fæd/ *n* a short-lived but keenly followed interest or practice: *His desire for black hats is only a passing fad* —**~dish** *adj* —**~dishly** *adv*

fade /feɪd/ *v* **1** [T1;I∅ (AWAY)] to (cause to) lose strength, colour, freshness, etc.: *Cut flowers soon fade.|The sun has faded the material* **2** [I∅ (AWAY)] to disappear or die gradually: *The shapes faded (away) into the night.|The custom is fading*

fade a·way *v adv* [I∅] (of people) to become no longer present: *When the police arrived the crowd faded away.|Old soldiers never die, they simply fade away* (song)

fade in also **fade up**— *v adv* [T1;I∅] (in film or sound mixing, as in cinema or broadcasting) to (cause to) mix slowly by increasing the sound or strength

fade out *v adv* [T1;I∅] (in film or sound mixing, as in cinema or broadcasting) to (cause to) disappear slowly by reducing the sound or strength: *to fade out the last scene* —**fadeout** /ˈfeɪdaʊt/ *n*

fae·ces, *AmE usu.* **feces** /ˈfiːsiːz/ *n* [P] *fml & tech* the solid waste material passed from the bowels —**faecal** /ˈfiːkəl/ *adj* [Wa5]

fae·ry, faerie /ˈfeəri/ *n* the world or power of fairies; the imaginary world of stories: *faerie lands*

fag¹ /fæg/ *v* **-gg- 1** [I∅ (AWAY);L9] to work hard: *We fagged at the job for hours* **2** [I∅ (*for*)] (of a student in certain English PUBLIC SCHOOL*s*) to have to do jobs for another student

fag² *n* **1** [S] an unpleasant and tiring piece of work: *Grammar lessons are a real fag* **2** [C] (in certain English PUBLIC SCHOOL*s*) a young student who has to do jobs for an older student

fag³ *n sl* CIGARETTE

fag end /ˌ· ˈ·/ *n* **1** the last, end, or remaining part of something: *the fag end of the day* **2** the last bit of a smoked cigarette

fagged /fægd/ also **fagged out** /ˌ· ˈ·/— [F] *esp. BrE sl* very tired: *I'm fagged (out) after that hard work*

fag·got, *AmE* also **fagot** /ˈfægət/— *n* **1** a bunch of small sticks for burning **2** a ball of cut-up meat mixed with bread, which is cooked and eaten **3** *AmE* also (*infml*) **fag**— HOMOSEXUAL **4** *BrE* an unpleasant person (esp. in the phr. **old faggot**)

Fah·ren·heit /ˈfærənhaɪt/ *n* [R] a scale of temperature in which water freezes at 32° and boils at 212° —see WEIGHTS & MEASURES TABLE —compare CENTIGRADE²

fai·ence /faɪˈɑːns, -ˈɒns‖feɪˈɑns/ *n* [U] a special type of clay, made into cups, dishes, etc., ornamented with bright colours, and baked hard

fail¹ /feɪl/ *v* **1** [T1;I∅,3] to be unsuccessful (in): *Why did you fail?|He failed (to pass) the test* **2** [T1] to decide that somebody has not passed an examination: *The teachers failed me on the written paper* **3** [T3;I∅] to not produce the desired result; not perform or do: *Last year the crops failed.|The car failed to climb the hill.|He failed to arrive.|We receive letters from him every week: he never fails to write* **4** [T1] to disappoint the hopes or trust of: *His friends failed him when he most needed them* **5** [T1;I∅] to be not enough; come to an end though still desired: *His courage failed him in the end.|*

words failed him **6** [I∅] to lose strength; become weak: *The sick woman is failing quickly* **7** [I∅] (of a business) to be unable to continue: *When money is in short supply many businesses fail*

fail² *n* [U] failure (only in the phr. **without fail**): *I shall bring you that book without fail*

fail·ing¹ /ˈfeɪlɪŋ/ *n* a fault, imperfection, or weakness: *That machine has one big failing*

failing² *prep* in the absence of; without: *Failing instructions I did what I thought best*

fail-safe /ˌ· ˈ·◂/ *adj* made so that a failure in any part causes the whole machine, plan, etc., to come to a stop

fail·ure /ˈfeɪljəʳ/ *n* **1** [U] lack of success; failing: *His plans ended in failure* **2** [C] a person, attempt, or thing that fails: *She had many failures before finding the right method.|As a writer, he was a failure* **3** [U] (an example of) the state of being unable to perform: (*a*) *heart failure* **4** [U;C] the nonperformance or production of something expected or desired: *crop failures|His failure to explain the noise worried us* **5** [U] loss of strength **6** [C;U] inability of a business to continue, esp. through lack of money

fain /feɪn/ *adv old use* **1** with pleasure: *I would fain stay here for ever* **2** (would) rather: *They would fain stay together, but . . .*

faint¹ /feɪnt/ *adj* **1** [F] weak and about to lose consciousness: *He felt faint for lack of food* **2** [B] performed in a weak manner; lacking strength: *faint praise* **3** [B] lacking courage or spirit; cowardly (esp in the phr. **faint heart never won fair lady**) **4** [B] lacking clearness, brightness, strength, etc.: *faint sound|The colours became more faint as the sun set* **5** [B] very small; slight: (*infml*) *I haven't the faintest idea what you're talking about* —**~ly** *adv* —**~ness** *n* [U]

faint² *v* [I∅ (AWAY)] **1** to lose consciousness, as because of loss of blood, heat, or great pain **2** *old use* to become less clear, loud, strong, etc.

faint³ *n* an act or condition of FAINTing: *She fell down in a faint*

faint-heart·ed /ˌ· ˈ··◂/ *adj* lacking courage or spirit, cowardly —**~ly** *adv* —**~ness** [U]

fair¹ /feəʳ/ *adj* **1** free from dishonesty or injustice: *a fair businessman|a fair decision* **2** that is allowed to be done, given, etc., as under the rules of a game: *It is not fair to kick another player in football* **3** fairly good, large, fine, etc.: *His knowledge of the language is fair* **4** showing by favourable conditions; likely (esp. in the phr. **in a fair way to**): *She was in a fair way to win before she fell* **5** (of the sky or weather) not stormy; fine; clear **6** having a good clear clean appearance or quality: *I have made you a fair copy of the report* **7** (esp. of the skin or hair) light in colour; not dark **8** (of a person) having pale skin and light hair **9** (of women) *esp. old use* beautiful; attractive **10** pleasing but not sincere: *fair promises* —**~ness** *n* [U]

fair² *adv* **1** in a just or honest manner or according to the rules; fairly: *You must play fair* **2** pleasantly; politely: *He speaks fair* **3** straight; directly: *I hit him fair on the nose* **4 fair and square a** honestly; justly: *He's dealt fair and square with me* **b** straight; directly: *I hit him fair and square on the nose*

fair³ *n* **1** *BrE* FUNFAIR **2** a market, esp. one held at a particular place at regular periods for selling farm produce **3** a very large show of goods, advertising, etc. as of a particular industry or country: *a book fair*

fair game /ˌ· ˈ·/ *n* [R] **1** something, such as an object or animal, that it is fair or within the rules of a game to attack or chase **2** a person, idea, etc., which can easily be shown to be lacking in power, esp. by being laughed at and CRITICIZEd: *He was fair game for our jokes.|His speech was fair game for his opponents*

fair·ground /ˈfeəgraʊnd‖ˈfeər-/ *n* an open space on which a FUNFAIR is held

fair·ly /ˈfeəli‖ˈfeərli/ *adv* **1** in a manner that is free from dishonesty, injustice, etc.: *The goods are described fairly.|He told the facts fairly* **2** in a manner that is allowed or according to certain rules: *He doesn't play the game fairly* **3** for the most part; rather; quite: *He paints fairly well* **4** completely; plainly: *It fairly destroyed the machines* —see RATHER (USAGE)

fair-mind·ed /ˌ· ˈ··◂‖ˈ· ˌ··/ *adj* fair in judgment; just

fair play /ˌ· ˈ·/ *n* [U] **1** (in sport) play that is according to the rules **2** action, treatment, punishment, etc., that is fair and just, esp. in being equal to all concerned

fair sex /ˌ· ˈ·/ *n* [*the* + GU] GENTLE SEX

fair trade /ˌ· ˈ·◂/ *n* [U] the placing of taxes on goods brought into one country from a foreign country equal to the taxes the foreign country puts on goods brought into its own land —**fair-trade** *adj* [Wa5]: *fair-trade agreements*

fair·way /ˈfeəweɪ‖-ər-/ *n* **1** a passage through a port, wide river, etc., that is clear for ships to travel along **2** that part of a GOLF COURSE in which the grass is cut short but not so short as around the holes

fair-weath·er /ˈ· ˌ··/ *adj* [A] present in times of success, absent in times of trouble (esp. in the phr. **fair-weather friend**)

fai·ry /ˈfeəri/ *n* **1** a small imaginary figure with magical powers and shaped like a human **2** *infml* a man (esp. a HOMOSEXUAL) who behaves like a woman

fai·ry·land /ˈfeərilænd/ *n* **1** the land where fairies live **2** a place of delicate and magical beauty

fairy light /ˈ·· ·/ *n* a small coloured light, esp. one of a number used to ornament a Christmas tree

fairy-tale /ˈ·· ·/ *adj* of or suitable for a FAIRY TALE; unreal, magical

fairy tale also **fairy sto·ry** /ˈ·· ˌ··/— *n* **1** a story about fairies and other small magical people **2** a story or account that is hard to believe, esp. one intended to deceive

fait ac·com·pli /ˌfeɪt əˈkɒmpli‖-ˌækɑmˈpliː (*Fr* fɛt akɔ̃pli)/ *n* **faits accomplis** /ˌfeɪt əˈkɒmpliːz‖-ˌækɑmˈpliːz (*Fr* fɛt akɔ̃pli)/ something that has already happened or has been done and that cannot be changed

faith /feɪθ/ *n* **1** [U] strong belief; trust: *He will not steal my money: I have faith in him* **2** [U] word of honour; promise: *I kept/broke faith with them* **3** [U] the condition of being sincere; loyalty (in the phrs. **good faith/bad faith**): *The unions think the government has acted in bad faith by reducing public spending* **4** [U5] belief which is not based on reason or proof: *I have faith in his ability* **5** [U] belief and trust in and loyalty to God **6** [C] something that is believed in strongly, esp. a system of religious belief; religion: *the Christian and Jewish faiths*

faith·ful /ˈfeɪθfəl/ *adj* **1** [B] full of or showing loyalty: *He is a faithful friend.|He remained faithful to his friend* **2** [B;P] believing strongly in religion: *The faithful could be seen praying* **3** [B] who or that is sure to do what has been promised or what is expected: *faithful worker* **4** [B] true to the facts or to an original: *faithful account/copy* **5** [(*to*)] loyal to one's (marriage) partner by having no sexual relationship with anyone else —compare UNFAITHFUL —see also FIDELITY —**~ness** *n* [U]

faith·ful·ly /ˈfeɪθfəli/ *adv* **1** with faith: *I promised* *you faithfully* **2** exactly: *I copied the letter faithfully* **3 yours faithfully** the usual polite way of introducing one's name at the end of a letter

faith heal·ing /ˈ· ˌ··/ *n* [U] a method of treating diseases by prayer and religious faith —**faith healer** *n*

faith·less /ˈfeɪθləs/ *adj* **1** not acting according to promises or duty; disloyal; false: *a faithless worker* **2** without belief or trust, esp. in God **3** that may not be trusted: *a faithless friend* —**~ly** *adv* —**~ness** *n* [U]

fake¹ /feɪk/ *v* **1** [T1] to make or change (esp. a work of art) so that it appears better, more valuable, etc.: *I thought the painting was old but it had been faked* **2** [L7;IØ] *infml* to pretend: *She faked illness so that she did not have to go to school.*|*I thought he was telling the truth but he was faking* **3** [T1;IØ] (in sport) to pretend to make (a certain movement) in order to deceive an opponent: *I faked a throw but kept the ball myself* —**faker** *n*

fake² *n* a person or thing that is not what he or it looks like: *The painting looked old but was a recent fake.*|*I thought he was a priest but he was a fake and robbed me*

fake³ *adj* [Wa5;A] made and intended to deceive: *fake money*

fa·kir /ˈfeɪkɪəʳ, ˈfæ-, fæˈkɪəʳ‖fəˈkɪər, fæ-/ *n* a Hindu or Muslim beggar who is regarded as a holy man

fal·con /ˈfɔːlkən‖ˈfæl-/ *n* a bird that kills and eats other animals, esp. one that has been trained by man to hunt —see picture at PREY¹

fal·con·er /ˈfɔːlkənəʳ‖ˈfæl-/ *n* a person who keeps, trains, or hunts with FALCONs

fal·con·ry /ˈfɔːlkənri‖ˈfæl-/ *n* [U] **1** the art of training FALCONs to hunt **2** the sport of hunting with FALCONs

fall¹ /fɔːl/ *v* **fell** /fel/, **fallen** /ˈfɔːlən/ **1** [IØ] to descend or go down freely, as by weight or loss of balance; drop: *The clock fell off the shelf. It fell 3 feet.*|*He fell into the lake* **2** [IØ (OVER, DOWN)] to come down from a standing position, esp. suddenly: *He fell to his knees and begged forgiveness.*|*5 trees fell over in the storm.*|*She slipped and fell (down)* **3** [IØ] to become lower in level, degree, or quantity: *The temperature fell 4°.*|*Their voices fell to a whisper* **4** [IØ (*on*)] to come or happen, as if by descending: *Night fell quickly.*|*A silence fell on the room.*|*His eyes fell on the body.*|*A light fell on the wall.*|*Christmas falls on a Friday this year.*|*The force* (ACCENT) *falls on the end of that word* **5** [L7,9] to pass into a new state or condition; become: *fall asleep*|*fall in love*|*The book was old and soon fell apart* **6** [L9] to hang loosely: *His hair falls over his shoulders/down his back* **7** [L9] to drop down wounded or dead, esp. to die in battle: *A prayer was said in memory of those who fell in the war/the fallen.*|*6 tigers fell to the hunter's gun* **8** [IØ] to be defeated or conquered: *The city fell (to the enemy)* **9** [IØ] to lose power or a high position: *The government has fallen* **10** [L9] to slope in a downward direction: *The land falls towards the river/away from the farm* **11** [Wv5;IØ] *old use* (of a woman) to do something sexually immoral: *a fallen woman* **12** [IØ] (of the face) to take on a look of sadness, disappointment, shame, etc., esp. suddenly: *Her face fell when I told her the news* **13** [L9;(IØ)] to be spoken: *I guessed what was happening by the few remarks she let fall* **14 fall flat** to fail to produce the desired effect or result: *His jokes fell flat and amused nobody* **15 fall foul of a** (of a ship) to crash (into): *The ship fell foul of the hidden rocks* **b** to quarrel, fight or get into a bad relationship (with): *I don't want to fall foul of the police* **16 fall over backwards/oneself to do something** to be very eager or too eager to do something: *They were falling over backwards to please the new minister* **17 fall short** to fail to reach a desired result, standard, etc.: *We hoped to build 100 houses this year but we have fallen short (of our aim)* —see also FALL ABOUT, FALL BACK, FALL BACK ON, FALL BEHIND, FALL DOWN, FALL FOR, FALL IN, FALL INTO, FALL IN WITH, FALL OFF, FALL ON, FALL OUT, FALL THROUGH, FALL TO, FALL UPON

fall² *n* **1** [C] the act of falling: *He suffered a fall from his horse* **2** [C] something or the quantity of something that has fallen: *A fall of rocks blocked the road.*|*a fall of snow* **3** [C] a decrease in quantity, price, demand, degree, etc.: *We have not sold our goods because of the fall in demand.*|*There was a sudden fall in temperature* **4** [S (*of*)] the distance through which anything falls **5** [C] a downward slope **6** [S (*from*)] a change to a life of sin or bad ways from a life of goodness, honesty, etc.: *a fall from grace* **7** [S (*of*)] the defeat of a city, state, etc.; surrender or capture: *the fall of Troy* **8** [R] *AmE* AUTUMN: *to visit them in the fall* —see also FALLS

fall a·bout *v adv* [IØ] *infml* to lose control of oneself (with laughter): *They fell about (laughing/with laughter) when they heard his funny voice*

fal·la·cious /fəˈleɪʃəs/ *adj* **1** likely or intended to deceive **2** containing or based on false reasoning: *a fallacious argument* —**~ly** *adv*

fal·la·cy /ˈfæləsi/ *n* **1** [C] a false idea or belief: *It is a popular fallacy that success always brings happiness* **2** [C;U] false reasoning, as in an argument

fall back *v adv* [IØ] to move or turn back, as before something attacking or moving forwards: *They forced the enemy to fall back.*|*The crowd fell back to let the policemen through*

fall back on also **fall back up·on**— *v adv prep* [T1 *no pass.*] to use when there is failure or lack of other means: *Doctors sometimes fall back on old cures.*|*We spent our wages but we had our bank account to fall back on*

fall be·hind also **get behind**— *v adv* [IØ (*with*)] to fail to produce something on time, often money: *to fall behind with the rent/one's work*

fall down *v adv* [IØ (*on*)] *infml* to fail or be lacking in power: *Where this plan falls down is on the small amount of time it allows for possible delays*

fall·en /ˈfɔːlən/ past p. of FALL

fall for *v prep* [T1] **1** to accept and be cheated by: *Don't fall for his tricks* **2** *infml* to fall in love with, esp. suddenly: *She fell for him in a big way*

fall guy /ˈ· ·/ *n AmE infml* **1** a person who is tricked into being punished for another's crime; SCAPEGOAT **2** a person who is easily cheated, tricked, or made to seem a fool

fal·li·ble /ˈfæləbəl/ *adj* able or likely to make a mistake or be wrong: *All men are fallible* —**-bility** /ˌfæləˈbɪlʒti/ *n* [U]

fall in *v adv* **1** [T1;IØ] to (cause to) form proper lines or order: *Fall in, men!*|*The captain fell the soldiers in* **2** [IØ] (of an agreement, esp. for rent) to come to an end **3** [IØ] (of a debt) to become payable

falling star /ˌ·· ˈ·/ *n* SHOOTING STAR

fall in·to *v* [T1] **1** to begin: *to fall into conversation with someone* **2** to be divided into

fall in with *v adv prep* [T1] **1** to meet by chance **2** to agree to (an idea, suggestion, etc.)

fall off *v adv* [IØ] to become less in quality, amount, etc.: *Membership of the club has fallen off this year*

fall on also **fall upon**— *v prep* [T1] **1** to attack eagerly: *The hungry children fell on the food.*|*The* *soldiers fell on the enemy* **2 fall on hard times** to become poor

fal·lo·pi·an tube /fəˌləʊpɪən ˈtjuːb‖fəˈləʊpɪən tuːb/ *n* one of the 2 tubes in a (human) female through which eggs pass to the WOMB (childbearing organ) —see also OVIDUCT

fall·out[1] /ˈfɔːlaʊt/ *n* [U] the dangerous (RADIOACTIVE) dust that is left floating in and descending through the air after an atomic (or NUCLEAR) explosion

fall-out[2] *n* [A] the number of people who give up an activity: *the fall-out rate* —compare DROP OUT

fall out *v adv* [IØ] **1** to leave proper lines or order: *Fall out, men!* **2** to happen: *It fell out that ...* **3** [(*with*)] to quarrel: *Jean and Paul have fallen out with each other over the education of their children*

fal·low /ˈfæləʊ/ *n, adj* [S;B] (land) dug (or PLOUGHed) but left unplanted to improve its quality: *He left the land fallow for a year*

fallow deer /ˈ·· ·/ *n* **-deer** [Wn3] a small deer of Europe and Asia with a light brownish-yellow coat

falls /fɔːlz/ also [C] **fall**— *n* [P] (used esp. in names) a place where the river makes a sudden drop, as over a cliff; WATERFALL: *Niagara Falls*

fall through *v adv* [IØ] to fail to be completed: *The plan fell through*

fall to[1] *v adv* [IØ] to begin to eat or attack

fall to[2] *v prep* **1** [T1,4] to begin: *I fell to thinking* **2** [T1] to be the duty of: *It falls to me to thank the speaker*

fall u·pon *v adv* FALL ON

false[1] /fɔːls/ *adj* **1** not true or correct: *false statement/ideas* **2** declaring what is untrue; deceitful; lying **3** not faithful or loyal: *a false friend* **4** not real: *false teeth/diamonds* **5** made or changed so as to deceive: *false weights* **6** (esp. in plant names) so called because it looks like the real plant of the name —**~ly** *adv* —**~ness** *n* [U]

false[2] *adv* in a false or faithless manner (only in the phr. **play somebody false** = deceive someone, esp. in love): *His wife played him false*

false a·larm /ˌ· ·ˈ·/ *n* a warning of something bad, which does not happen: *Someone shouted "Fire!" but it was a false alarm and there was no danger*

false bot·tom /ˌ· ˈ··/ *n* a piece of wood, cardboard, etc. that looks like the bottom of a box or chest but which in fact is hiding a secret space

false-heart·ed /ˌ· ˈ··◂/ *adj* disloyal; faithless

false·hood /ˈfɔːlshʊd/ *n* **1** [C] an untrue statement; lie **2** [U] the telling of lies; lying

false pre·tenc·es, *AmE* **-tenses** /ˌ· ·ˈ··‖ˌ· ˈ···/ *n* [P] acts or appearances intended to deceive: *He obtained money from her under false pretences*

false start /ˌ· ˈ·/ *n* **1** an occasion in a race when a runner leaves the starting line too soon **2** a start in some activity which fails and has to be given up

false teeth /ˌ· ˈ·/ *n* [P] *infml* DENTURES

fal·set·to /fɔːlˈsetəʊ/ *n* **-tos** **1** [U;C] (the use of) an unnaturally high voice by a man, esp. in singing **2** [C] a man with such a singing voice

fals·ies /ˈfɔːlsiz/ *n* [P] *infml* pieces of material shaped to cover the breasts and make them seem larger

fal·si·fy /ˈfɔːlsɪ̈faɪ/ *v* [T1] **1** to make false as by changing something: *falsify the receipts/facts* **2** to state or represent falsely —**-fication** /ˌfɔːlsɪ̈fɪ̈ˈkeɪʃən/ *n* [U;C]

fal·si·ty /ˈfɔːlsɪ̈ti/ *n* **1** [U] the quality of being false or untrue **2** [C] something that is untrue; lie

fal·ter /ˈfɔːltəʳ/ *v* **1** [IØ] to walk or move unsteadily, as through weakness, fear, or disrepair: *The sick man faltered a few steps then fell.|The old car faltered down the road* **2** [T1 (OUT);IØ] to speak or say (something) in a weak and broken manner **3** [IØ] to lose strength of purpose or action; HESITATE: *He faltered for a while and was unable to make a decision* **4** [IØ] to lose strength or effectiveness; weaken: *The business faltered and then failed* —**~ingly** *adv*

fame /feɪm/ *n* [U] the condition of being well known and talked about: *He hoped to find fame as a poet*

famed /feɪmd/ *adj* well known; famous: *famed for their beauty*

fa·mil·i·al /fəˈmɪlɪəl/ *adj* [Wa5;A] of, concerning, or typical of a family

fa·mil·i·ar[1] /fəˈmɪlɪəʳ/ *n* a close friend; companion

familiar[2] *adj* **1** [B (*to*)] generally known, seen, or experienced; common: *a familiar sight* **2** [F + *with*] having a thorough knowledge (of): *I am familiar with that book/too* **3** [B] without tight control; informal; easy: *He wrote in a familiar style* **4** [B] very friendly; close: *familiar friend* **5** [B] too friendly for the occasion: *The man's unpleasant familiar behaviour angered the girl*

fa·mil·i·ar·i·ty /fəˌmɪliˈærɪ̈ti/ *n* **1** [U + *with*] thorough knowledge (of): *His familiarity with many strange languages surprised us all* **2** [U] freedom of behaviour usu. only expected in the most friendly relations: *He behaved towards her with great familiarity* **3** [C *usu. pl*] an act or expression of such freedom: *His familiarities made her angry* **4** [U] absence of tight control or formality; informality: *Our letters to each other have reached a state of familiarity*

fa·mil·i·ar·ize, -ise /fəˈmɪlɪəraɪz/ *v* [T1] to make well known: *Newspapers have familiarized the cruelty of war*

familiarize with, -ise *v prep* [D1] to make (a person, often himself) informed about: *Students are familiarized with a variety of methods*

fa·mil·i·ar·ly /fəˈmɪlɪəli‖-lɪər-/ *adv* in an informal, easy, or friendly manner

fam·i·ly /ˈfæməli/ *n* **1** [GC] any group of people related by blood or marriage, esp. a group of 2 grown-ups and their children: *My family is very large.|My family are all tall* **2** [A] suitable for children as well as older people: *a family film* **3** [S; U] children: *Have you any family?|We won't have a family till we've been married a few years* **4** [GC] all those people descended from a common person (ANCESTOR): *Our family has lived in this house for over 100 years* **5** [C] a group of things related by common characteristics, esp. a group of plants, animals, or languages: *The cat family includes lions and tigers* **6** a division of an ORDER[1] (13) of living things which usu. includes several genera (GENUS): *The horse family also includes the donkey* **7 in the family way** *infml* expecting to give birth to a child; PREGNANT **8 run in a family** (of a quality) to be shared by several members of a family (and so perhaps HEREDITARY): *A gift for music runs in that family* **9 start a family** to have one's first child: *When do you hope to start a family?*

family al·low·ance /ˌ··· ·ˈ··/ *n* [S] (in Britain) a sum of money paid weekly to every family for each child

family cir·cle /ˌ··· ˈ··/ *n* the closely related members of a family

family doc·tor /ˌ··· ˈ··/ *n infml* GENERAL PRACTITIONER

family man /ˈ··· ·/ *n* **1** a man who is fond of home life with his family **2** a man with a family, esp. with a wife and children

family plan·ning /ˌ··· ˈ··/ *n* [U] the controlling of the number of children born in a family and the time of their birth by the use of any of various (CONTRACEPTIVE) methods

family tree /ˌ··· ˈ·/ *n* a map or plan of the

relationship of the members of a family, esp. one that covers a long period

fam·ine /ˈfæmən/ *n* [C;U] (a case of) very serious lack of food: *Many people die during famines every year*

fam·ish /ˈfæmɪʃ/ *v* [T1;I∅] *old use & rare* to (cause to) suffer from great hunger

fam·ished /ˈfæmɪʃt/ *adj* [F] suffering from very great hunger

fa·mous /ˈfeɪməs/ *adj.* **1** very well known: *a famous actor|He is famous for his fine acting* **2** *becoming rare* very good: *famous weather for a swim*
USAGE **Famous** is like **well-known** but much stronger. It means "known over a wide area and for a long time". **Notorious** means "famous for something bad": *the* **notorious** *murderer*. **Infamous** is a strong word meaning "wicked", but it does not necessarily mean that the wicked person or his behaviour is widely known about

fa·mous·ly /ˈfeɪməsli/ *adv* very well: *He is doing famously in his new work*

fan¹ /fæn/ *n* any of various instruments meant to make a flow of air, esp. cool air, such as an arrangement of feathers or paper in a half circle waved by hand or a series of broad blades turned by a motor —see picture at CAR

fan² *v* **-nn-** **1** [T1] to cause air, esp. cool air, to blow on (something) with or as if with a FAN¹: *She fanned her face with a newspaper* **2** [T1] to excite to activity with or as if with a FAN¹: *We fanned the fire to make it burn brighter.|His rudeness fanned her anger* **3** [T1;I∅: (OUT)] to spread like a FAN¹: *The soldiers fanned out across the hillside* **4** **fan the flame(s)** to cause excitement, anger, hatred, etc., to increase

fan³ *n* a very keen follower or supporter, as of a sport, performing art, or famous person: *football fans*

fa·nat·ic¹ /fəˈnætɪk/ also **fa·nat·i·cal** /-ɪkəl/— *adj* showing very great and often unreasoning keenness, esp. in religious or political matters —**~ally** /-ɪkli/ *adv* [Wa4]

fanatic² *n* a person who shows very great and often unreasoning keenness for something, esp. some religious or political belief: *I ignore screaming fanatics.|I am a fanatic for healthy food*

fa·nat·i·cis·m /fəˈnætəsɪzəm/ *n* [U;C] the behaviour, character, or ideas of a FANATIC²

fan belt /ˈ· ·/ *n* a continuous belt driving a FAN¹ to keep an engine cool —see picture at CAR

fan·ci·er /ˈfænsɪəʳ/ *n esp. in comb.* a person who has an active or business interest in breeding or training certain types of birds, dogs, plants, etc.: *dog-fancier*

fan·cies /ˈfænsiz/ [P] *infml* fancy cakes —see FANCY³ (4)

fan·ci·ful /ˈfænsifəl/ *adj* **1** showing imagination rather than reason and experience: *a fanciful poet* **2** unreal; imaginary **3** odd in appearance, esp. in being highly ornamented: *fanciful designs* —**~ly** *adv*

fan club /ˈ· ·/ *n* an association of admirers of a particular actor, band, sportsman, etc.

fan·cy¹ /ˈfænsi/ *n* **1** [U] imagination, esp. in a free and undirected form **2** [U] the power of creating imaginative ideas and expressions, esp. in poetry **3** [C] an image, opinion, or idea imagined and not based on fact: *I think he will come but it's only a fancy of mine* **4** [C] a liking formed without the help of reason: *I have taken a fancy to that silly hat* **5** **take/catch the fancy of** to attract or please

fancy² *v* **1** [T1;V4;X (*to be*)1] to form a picture of; imagine: *Fancy working every day!|Fancy her saying such rude things!|Fancy that!* **2** [T5a] to believe without being certain; think: *I fancy I have met you before* **3** [T1;X (*to be*) I] to have a liking for; wish for: *I fancy a swim.|I fancy that girl* **4** **fancy oneself** to have a very high opinion of oneself: *He fancies himself (as) the fastest swimmer*

fancy³ *adj* **1** [B] ornamental or brightly coloured: *fancy goods|They are too fancy for me* **2** [B] based on free imagination rather than fact: *a fancy account* **3** [A] higher than the usu. or reasonable price: *He sells poor goods and charges fancy prices* **4** [A] not ordinary; fine: *fancy cakes/fruits* **5** [A] (of birds, dogs, plants, etc.) grown or trained for particular points of beauty or quality —**fancily** *adv*

fancy dress /ˌ·· ˈ·/ *n* [U] unusual or amusing clothes worn for a special occasion: *A fancy dress ball is a dance to which people go dressed as characters from books, films, past or future periods of history, etc.*

fancy-free /ˌ·· ˈ·/ *adj* free to do anything or like anyone, esp. because not bound by love

fancy man /ˈ·· ·/ *n often humor* **1** a man with whom a woman has a social relationship which is not thought proper: *Who's your fancy man tonight?* **2** *rare* PIMP¹ (1)

fancy wom·an /ˈ·· ˌ··/ *n often humor* a woman with whom a man has a social relationship which is not thought proper: *He has a fancy woman in London as well as a wife at home*

fan·cy·work /ˈfænsiwɜːk‖-ɜrk/ *n* ornamental sewing; EMBROIDERY

fan·dan·go /fænˈdæŋgəʊ/ *n* **-gos** an active Spanish or South American dance

fan·fare /ˈfænfeəʳ/ *n* a short loud piece of usu. TRUMPET music played to introduce a person or event

fang /fæŋ/ *n* a long sharp tooth, as of a dog or a poisonous snake —see picture at REPTILE

fan·light /ˈfænlaɪt/ *n* a small window over a door, sometimes but usually not in the shape of a FAN¹

fan mail /ˈ· ·/ *n* [U] letters written to a famous person, singer, etc., by admirers

fan·ny /ˈfæni/ *n* **1** *BrE taboo sl* the outer sex organs of a woman **2** *esp. AmE sl* the part of the body on which one sits; BUTTOCKS; ARSE (1)

fan out *v adv* [I∅] (esp. of people) to spread: *The searchers fanned out to look for the missing boy*

fan·ta·si·a /fænˈteɪzɪə, ˌfæntəˈzɪə‖fænˈteɪʒə/ *n* **1** a piece of music that does not follow any regular style **2** a piece of music made up of a collection of well-known tunes

fan·tas·tic /fænˈtæstɪk/ *adj* **1** odd, strange, or wild in shape, meaning, etc.; not controlled by reason: *fantastic dream/story/fears* **2** (of an idea, plan, etc.) too unrelated to reality to be practical or reasonable **3** very great or large: *a fantastic sum of money* **4** *infml* very good; wonderful: *a fantastic play* —**~ally** *adv* [Wa4]

fan·ta·sy /ˈfæntəsi/ *n* **1** [U] imagination, esp. when freely creative **2** [C;U] a creation of such an imagination whether expressed or not: *The story is a fantasy.|He lives in a world of fantasy.|His mind is full of sexual fantasies*

far¹ /fɑːʳ/ *adv* **farther** /ˈfɑːðəʳ‖ˈfɑr-/ *or* **further** /ˈfɜːðəʳ‖ˈfɜr-/, **farthest** /ˈfɑːðəst‖ˈfɑr-/ *or* **furthest** /ˈfɜːðəst‖ˈfɜr-/ **1** [Wa1;H] at or to a great distance: *They travelled far (from home).|We didn't go (very) far.|We walked far into the woods.|They live not far beyond the hill.|How far (away) is it?* **2** [Wa1;H] (*esp. with* into) at or to a great distance in time: *He sees far into the past.|They worked far into the night.|I can't look far beyond August* **3** [Wa5] a long way; very much: *far, far too busy|far better/worse|She is far from being pleased about it; she is very angry.|The show was far from being a failure; it was a great success.|She is by far the better actress.|She is the better actress by far.|"Are you* *cold?" "Far from it!"|It's far too hot in this room; open the windows!* **4 as/so far as** to the degree or distance that: *I will help you as far as I can.|"as far as the military side is concerned . . ."* (SEU S.) **5 far and away** very much: *She is far and away the better actress* **6 far and wide** also **far and near** everywhere: *They looked far and wide for the missing dog.|People came from far and near* **7 far be it from me** I certainly would not: *Far be it from me to call him a thief* **8 go too far** to go beyond the limits of what is considered reasonable: *I think your rudeness went too far* **9 how far** to what degree or distance: *I don't know how far I should believe him* **10 in as/so far as** to the degree that: *In so far as we can believe these facts we will use them* **11 so far a** up to the present: *I have built 3 houses so far* **b** to a certain point, degree, distance, etc.: *I can only trust him so far.|When the level reaches so far we must stop the flow* **12 so far from** rather than; instead of: *So far from taking my advice, he went and did just what I warned him against* **13 So far, so good** Things are satisfactory up to this point, at least: *We're over the wall. So far, so good. Now, we must swim the river* **14 take/carry something too far:** to take something beyond the limits of what is considered reasonable: *You are taking that joke too far and becoming rude* —see also GO¹ (31) **far**, FAR-OFF, FAR-OUT, FAR-REACHING, FARSIGHTED —see FARTHER (USAGE)

USAGE The first meaning is too formal for speech, except with *too* or *so*, or in questions or NEGATIVES: *"Did you walk* **far***?" "Yes, we walked a long way/No, we didn't walk (very)* **far***/Yes, we walked much too* **far***!"*

far² *adj* **farther** *or* **further, farthest** *or* **furthest** [A] **1** [Wa1] *esp. lit or poet* distant: *a far country* **2** [Wa5] also **farther** more distant of the 2: *the far/farther side of the street* **3** [Wa1] (of a political position) very much to the LEFT or RIGHT: *a far right organization|a member of the far left* **4 a far cry** a long way: *Being religious can be a far cry from being kind*

far·a·way /ˈfɑːrəweɪ/ *adj* **1** distant: *a faraway place* **2** (of the look in a person's eyes) dreaming, as if looking at or thinking about something distant

farce /fɑːs‖fɑrs/ *n* **1** [C] a light humorous play full of silly things happening **2** [U] the branch of theatrical writing concerned with this type of play **3** [C] an occasion or set of events that is a silly and empty show: *The talks were a farce since the minister had already made the decision* —**farcical** *adj* —**farcically** *adv* [Wa4]

fare¹ /feəʳ/ *v fml & rare* **1** [L9] to get on; succeed: *I think I fared quite well in the examination* **2** [L9] to experience treatment in the stated way: *The unions will fare badly if the government's plan becomes law* **3** [*it*+L9] to turn out; happen: *It fared ill with them*

fare² *n* **1** [C] the price charged to carry a person, as by bus, train, or taxi **2** [C] a paying passenger, esp. in a taxi **3** [U] food, esp. as provided at a meal: *good/simple fare*

Far East /ˌ· ˈ·◂/ *n* [*the*+R] the countries in Asia east of India, such as China, Japan etc. —compare MIDDLE EAST, NEAR EAST, EAST (1) —**~ern** *adj*

fare·well /feəˈwel‖feər-/ *n, interj fml & old use* GOODBYE: *Farewell! I hope we meet again soon.|We shall have a farewell party before we leave*

far·fetched /ˌfɑːˈfetʃt‖ˌfɑr-/ *adj* (of an example or comparison) not easily or naturally connected; improbable or forced

far-flung /ˌ· ˈ·◂/ *adj* **1** spread over a great distance: *Our far-flung trade connections cover the world* **2** distant: *I have friends in the most far-flung cities of the world*

far-gone /ˌ· ˈ·/ *adj* [F] in an advanced state, esp. of something generally unpleasant such as madness, debt, or DRUNKENNESS: *He is far-gone in debt.|He has been going increasingly mad over the last 3 years and is now rather far-gone*

far·i·na·ceous /ˌfærǝ̇ˈneɪʃəs/ *adj* consisting of or containing much flour or STARCH: *Bread, potatoes, and grains are all farinaceous foods*

farm¹ /fɑːm‖fɑrm/ *n* **1** an area of land, together with its buildings, concerned with the growing of crops or the raising of animals: *a pig farm|We work on the farm* **2** FARMHOUSE

farm² *v* [T1;I∅] to use (land) for growing crops, raising animals, etc.: *My friend is farming in Wales*

farm·er /ˈfɑːməʳ‖ˈfɑrmər/ *n* a man who owns or plans the work on a farm: *That farmer employs many farm labourers*

farm·hand /ˈfɑːmhænd‖ˈfɑrm-/ *n* a person who works on a farm; farm labourer

farm·house /ˈfɑːmhaʊs‖ˈfɑrm-/ also **farm**— *n* **-houses** /haʊzǝ̇z/ the main house on a farm, where the farmer lives —see picture at FARMYARD

farm·ing /ˈfɑːmɪŋ‖ˈfɑrmɪŋ/ *n* [U] the practice or business of being in charge of or working on a farm

farm out *v adv* [T1] to send (work) for other people to do: *We have more work here than we can deal with and must farm some out*

farm·yard /ˈfɑːmjɑːd‖ˈfɑrmjɑrd/ *n* a yard surrounded by or connected with farm buildings

See next page for picture

far-off /ˌ· ˈ·◂/ *adj* distant in space or time

far-out /ˌ· ˈ·◂/ *adj infml* **1** very different or uncommon; strange: *far-out ideas/clothes/people* **2** very good; wonderful

far·ra·go /fəˈrɑːgəʊ, fəˈreɪ-/ *n* **-goes** a confused collection; mixture: *a farrago of useless information*

far-reach·ing /ˌ· ˈ··◂/ *adj* having a wide influence or effect

far·ri·er /ˈfærɪəʳ/ *n* a person (usu. a BLACKSMITH) who makes and fits shoes for horses

far·row¹ /ˈfærəʊ/ *v* [T1;I∅] (of a female pig) to give birth (to)

farrow² *n* a family group (LITTER) of young pigs

far·sight·ed /ˌfɑːˈsaɪtǝ̇d◂‖ˌfɑr-/ *adj* **1** also **farseeing**— able to see the future effects of present actions —opposite **shortsighted** (2) **2** *esp. AmE* LONGSIGHTED —**~ness** *n*

fart¹ /fɑːt‖fɑrt/ *v* [I∅] *taboo* to send out air from the bowels

fart² *n taboo* an escape of air from the bowels

far·ther¹ /ˈfɑːðəʳ‖ˈfɑr-/ *adv* [Wa5;H] (*compar. of* FAR) **1** at or to a greater distance or more distant point; further: *Let's not walk any farther.|They pushed the boat farther into the water.|They walked 3 miles farther (on)* **2** to a greater degree; further: *We can't go any farther (ahead) with this plan*

farther² *adj* [Wa5;A] (*compar. of* FAR) more distant; FAR² (2): *On the farther side of the street there was a large shop*

USAGE **farther**, **farthest** are used as the COMPARATIVE and SUPERLATIVE of **far** only when speaking of places, direction, and distance: **farther/further** *on/out/back*|**farther/further** *down the road|the* **farthest/furthest** *house|the* **farther** (=FAR² (2)) *side of the river.* Otherwise, use **further**, **furthest**. They are more common, and must be used to express the meaning "more; later; additional": *a college of* **further** *education*

far·thest /ˈfɑːðǝ̇st‖ˈfɑr-/ *adv, adj* [Wa5;B (*from*);H] (*superl. of* FAR) most far: *the farthest (away) from London|Who can swim farthest?* —see FARTHER (USAGE)

far·thing /ˈfɑːðɪŋ‖ˈfɑr-/ *n* (formerly) a British coin worth one quarter of a penny

fa·scia /ˈfeɪʃə/ *n* **1** a long band or board on the surface of something, esp. one over a shop bearing the shop's name **2** *BrE old use* DASHBOARD

fas·ci·nate /ˈfæsǝ̩neɪt/ *v* [T1 (*with*)] **1** to charm powerfully; be very interesting to: *I'm fascinated with/by Buddhist ceremonies* **2** to fix with the eyes so as to take away the power of movement, as a snake does with a small creature

fas·ci·nat·ing /ˈfæsǝ̩neɪtɪŋ/ *adj* that fascinates (FASCINATE (1)): *The most fascinating insect is walking across the paper.|Your ideas are fascinating to me* —**~ly** *adv*: *The Russian language is fascinatingly different from English*

fas·ci·na·tion /ˌfæsǝ̩ˈneɪʃən/ *n* **1** [U] the quality of fascinating (FASCINATE): *I used all my powers of fascination on him without success* **2** [S] something that FASCINATES (1): *Old castles have a certain strange fascination for me*

fas·cis·m /ˈfæʃɪzəm/ *n* [U] (*often cap.*) a political system in which all industrial activity is controlled by the state, no political opposition is allowed, nationalism is strongly encouraged and SOCIALISM violently opposed

fas·cist /ˈfæʃǝ̩st/ *n, adj* **1** [Wa5] (*often cap.*) (a supporter) of FASCISM: *fascist opinions|the Fascist party|to join a group of fascists* **2** [Wa5;C: (*you*) N] *derog* (a supporter) of any political movement strongly opposed to SOCIALISM: *You have no morals, you fascist pig!*

fash·ion¹ /ˈfæʃən/ *n* **1** [C;U] the way of dressing or behaving that is considered the best at a certain time: *There's a fashion for painting your nails green.|Fashions have changed since I was a girl.|Wide trousers are the latest fashion.|It's not the fashion to send children away to school now.|We must keep up with fashion/follow (the) fashion* **2** [U] changing custom, esp. in women's clothing: *to study the history of fashion* **3** [S9] *fml* a manner; way of making or doing something: *He behaves in a very strange fashion.|She does her hair after the ancient Greek fashion* **4 after a fashion** not very well: *John speaks Russian after a fashion, but Jean speaks it much better* **5 come into/be in fashion** to (start to) be considered the best and most modern: *Long hair is very much in fashion now* **6 go/be out of fashion** to stop being/no longer be considered the best and most modern **7 set a fashion** to be an example to others by doing something new **8 (someone) of fashion** *old use* someone of the upper class of society and therefore well-dressed: *The restaurant was crowded with women of fashion*

fashion² *v* [Wv5;X9] to shape or make (something into or out of something else) usually with one's hands or with only a few tools: *to fashion a hat out of leaves|to fashion some leaves into a hat*

-fashion *comb. form* [*n*→*adv*] in the way of a; like a: *to dress* SCHOOLBOY-*fashion|to eat American-fashion*

fash·ion·a·ble /ˈfæʃənəbəl/ *adj* (made, dressed, etc.) according to the latest fashion: *a fashionable hat/woman|It's fashionable to go to Bermuda for your holidays* —opposite **unfashionable** —compare OLD-FASHIONED —**-ably** /-bli/ *adv*: *fashionably dressed|to dress fashionably*

fashion de·sign·er /ˈ·· ·ˌ··/ *n* someone whose job is to plan (DESIGN) new styles in (women's) clothes

fashion plate /ˈ·· ·/ *n* a picture showing styles of fashionable dress

fast¹ /fɑːst‖fæst/ *adj* **1** [B] quick; moving quickly: *a fast car|fast music* **2** [B] firm; firmly fixed: *The colours aren't fast, so be careful when you wash this shirt* **3** [B] **a** (of a person or his behaviour) *becoming rare* wanting too much pleasure and spending too much money: *James belongs to a very fast set at college* **b** (of a woman) *old use* free in sexual matters **4** [B] (of a photographic film) suitable for being EXPOSED (=uncovered to the light) for a very short time **5** [F;E] (of a clock) showing a time that is later than the true time (often by a stated amount): *My watch is fast|is 5 minutes fast* —opposite **slow** **6** [Wa5;A] allowing quick movement: *an accident in the fast* LANE (=track) *of the* MOTORWAY —see also HARD-AND-FAST **7 fast and furious** (of games and fun) gay, noisy and active **8 make fast** to tie firmly: *Make the boat fast.|He made the rope fast to the metal ring*

fast² *adv* **1** [Wa1] quickly: *They drive very fast.|He ran faster and faster* **2** firmly; tightly: *to stick fast in the mud* **3** [H] *old use* near; close: *a house fast by the river* **4 fast asleep** sleeping deeply **5 play fast and loose** *not fml* to take advantage by telling lies: *I can't have you playing fast and loose with my daughter's* AFFECTIONs (=feelings), *young man! Are you going to marry her or not?*

fast³ *v* [I∅] to eat no food, esp. for religious reasons: *Muslims fast during Ramadan*

fast⁴ *n* an act or period of FASTing³: *Friday is a fast day.|He broke his fast by drinking some milk*

fas·ten /ˈfɑːsən‖ˈfæ-/ *v* **1** [I∅;T1: UP or TOGETHER] to make or become firmly fixed or closed: *He fastened (up) his coat.|Fasten your seat belts!* (instruction on an aircraft)|*The bag won't fasten properly.|He fastened the pages together with a pin* —opposite **unfasten** **2** [L9;X9: (*to*, ON)] to make or become firm in (a given state) or joined to (a given thing): *He fastened on his sword.|The door fastens with a hook.|*(fig.) *She fastened her eyes on him*

fasten down *v adv* [T1 (*to*)] *not fml* to make (someone) give a decision: *Can you fasten him down to a firm date?*

fas·ten·er /ˈfɑːsənəʳ‖ˈfæ-/ *n* something that fastens things together: *Please do up the fasteners on the back of my dress* —see also ZIP² (1)

fas·ten·ing /ˈfɑːsənɪŋ‖ˈfæ-/ *n* something that holds things shut, esp. doors and windows

fasten on also **fasten up·on**— *v prep* **1** [T1] to seize on; take and use: *The President fastened on the idea at once* **2** [D1] to fix (something) on: *You won't fasten the blame on me!*

fas·tid·i·ous /fæˈstɪdɪəs/ *adj* (typical of a person) who is difficult to please, disliking anything at all dirty, nasty, or rough: *Jean is too fastidious to eat with her fingers* —**~ly** *adv*: *She picked her way fastidiously through the mud* —**~ness** *n* [U]

fast·ness /ˈfɑːstnɨs‖ˈfæst-/ *n* **1** [C] a safe place which is hard to reach (esp. in the phr. **a mountain fastness**) **2** [U] the quality of being firm and fixed: *the fastness of a colour*

USAGE There is no noun formed from **fast** when it means **quick**. Use instead **speed** or **quickness**

fat¹ /fæt/ *adj* **-tt-** [Wa1] **1** (of creatures and their bodies) having (too) much fat: *fat cattle|a fat baby|You'll get even fatter if you eat all those potatoes* **2** (of meat) containing a lot of fat **3** thick and well-filled: *a fat book|*(fig.) *a fat bank account* **4** (esp. of land) producing plentiful crops: *the fat farms in the valley* **5 a fat lot of** *sl* no; not any: *A fat lot of good|of use that is!* —**~ness** *n* [U] —**~tish** *adj*

fat² *n* [U] **1** the material under the skins of animals and human beings which helps to keep them warm **2 a** this substance considered as food: *He can't eat fat.|potatoes fried in deep fat* **b** vegetable oil in a solid form used in the same way: *a packet of vegetable fat* —compare LEAN⁴ **3 chew the fat** to have a conversation or complain together **4 live on the fat of the land** to live in great comfort with plenty to eat **5 the fat is in the fire** something has been done which will make a lot of trouble

fa·tal /ˈfeɪtl/ *adj* **1** [(*to*)] causing or resulting in death: *a fatal accident/illness|*(fig.) *This piece of news was fatal to the President's political future* **2** very dangerous and unfortunate: *He took the fatal decision to marry Martha* —compare FATEFUL

fa·tal·is·m /ˈfeɪtl-ɪzəm/ *n* [U] the belief that events are decided by FATE (1) and are outside human control

fa·tal·ist /ˈfeɪtl-ɨst/ *n* someone who believes that events are decided by FATE (1) and are outside human control —**~ic** /ˌfeɪtl-ˈɪstɪk/ *adj*

fa·tal·i·ty /fəˈtælɨti/ *n fml* **1** [S] the quality of being decided by fate: *Don't you feel there's a mysterious fatality about our meeting like this, Miss Simmons?* **2** [C] a violent accidental death: *several fatalities caused by the great flood* **3** [U] the quality of being FATAL (1): *New drugs have reduced the fatality of this disease*

fa·tal·ly /ˈfeɪtəli/ *adv* **1** so as to cause death: *fatally wounded* **2** as was very unfortunate: *He decided, fatally, to go over the mountain rather than round it*

fat cat /ˌ· ˈ·/ *n AmE infml* a comfortable rich person, esp. one who gives money to a political party

fate /feɪt/ *n* **1** [R *often cap.*] the imaginary cause beyond human control that is believed to decide events: *He expected to spend his life in Italy, but fate had decided otherwise* **2** [C] an end or result, esp. death: *They met with a terrible fate/with various strange fates* **3 as sure as fate** quite unavoidably: *Whenever I'm late, as sure as fate I meet the President on the stairs!* **4 one's fate** one's future, considered to be already decided and outside one's control: *I wonder whether the examiners have decided our fate yet?* **5 (suffer) a fate worse than death a** *humor or pomp* (of a woman, esp. in former times) (to lose) one's VIRGINITY **b** (to experience) something terrible or to be feared

fat·ed /ˈfeɪtɨd/ *adj* [F3,5c] caused or fixed by FATE (1): *You and I were fated to meet.|It was fated that we should meet*

fate·ful /ˈfeɪtfəl/ *adj* (of a day, event, or decision) important (esp. in a bad way) for the future: *that fateful night when I met Miss Simmons* —compare FATAL —**~ly** *adv*

Fates /feɪts/ *n* [*the*+P] the 3 goddesses who, according to the ancient Greeks, decided the course of human life

fat·head /ˈfæthed/ *n* [C; (*you*) N] *BrE infml* a fool; stupid person: *Don't hold the bottle upside-down, (you) fathead!*

fa·ther¹ /ˈfɑːðəʳ/ *n* **1** [C;R;N] a male parent: *the fathers and mothers of the schoolchildren|I have loved her like a father should* **2 city fathers** the chief men in a town **3 our fathers** the men of the past from whom we are descended **4 The child is father to the man** One's childhood shows what one will be like when one becomes a man **5 The wish is father to the thought** If one wishes for something, one comes to believe that it is already true —**~less** *adj* [Wa5]: *a poor fatherless child* —see TABLE OF FAMILY RELATIONSHIPS

father² *v* [T1] *old use* or *humor* (of a man) to cause the birth of (one's child): (fig.) *to father a plan/an invention*

Father **1** [A;N] (a title of respect for) a priest, esp. in the ROMAN CATHOLIC Church: *Father Brown is our local priest.|Have some more tea, Father!* **2** [*our* or *the*+R] God; the 1st member of the Christian TRINITY (=3 Gods in 1): *the prayer beginning "Our Father . . ."|God the Father, God the Son, and God the Holy Spirit* **3** [C *usu. pl.*] any of those early Christian writers whose teaching is accepted as official by the Church: *the writings of the early Fathers*

Father Christ·mas /ˌ·· ˈ··/ also (*esp. AmE*) **Santa Claus**— *n* [R] *esp. BrE* an imaginary old man in red clothes with a long white beard believed by children to come down the chimney at Christmas to bring their presents

father fig·ure /ˈ·· ˌ··/ *n* an older man on whom one depends, perhaps too much, for advice and help

fa·ther·hood /ˈfɑːðəhʊd‖ˈfɑðər-/ *n* [U] the condition of being a father: *the responsibilities of fatherhood*

father-in-law /ˈ·· · ·/ *n* **-s-in-law** the father of one's wife or husband —see TABLE OF FAMILY RELATIONSHIPS

fa·ther·ly /ˈfɑːðəli‖ˈfɑðərli/ *adj* like or typical of a father: *a fatherly old doctor|He gave her a fatherly kiss* —**-liness** *n* [U]

fath·om¹ /ˈfæðəm/ *n* a measure (6 feet or 1·8 metres) of the depth of water: *The sea is 60 fathoms deep here.|The boat sank in 20 fathoms*

fathom² *v* [T1 (OUT),6a *usu. neg.*] to get at the true meaning of; come to understand: *I can't fathom your meaning|fathom what you mean.*|(*BrE*) *trying to fathom it out* —compare UNFATHOMABLE

fath·om·less /ˈfæðəmləs/ *adj* [Wa5] too deep to be measured or understood: *fathomless depths*|(fig.) *a fathomless mystery*

fa·tigue¹ /fəˈtiːg/ *n* **1** [U] great tiredness: *He was pale with fatigue after his sleepless night* **2** [U] *tech* the tendency of a metal to break as the result of repeated bending (often in the phr. **metal fatigue**) **3** [C] (in the army) a job of cleaning or cooking: *to spend Sunday doing fatigues|to be on fatigue duty* **4 on fatigue** (of a soldier) doing cleaning or cooking duties: *If you speak to an officer like that you'll be put on fatigue!*

fatigue² *v* [Wv4;T1] *fml* to make tired: *a very fatiguing job*

fatigue par·ty /·ˈ· ˌ··/ *n* [GC] a group of soldiers doing FATIGUEs¹ (3)

fa·tigues /fəˈtiːgz/ [P] **1** things that make one tired: *Have a drink after the fatigues of the day!* **2** also **fatigue uniform**—*AmE* informal army clothes

fat·less /ˈfætləs/ *adj* (of food) without fat: *a fatless* DIET (=the food to which one is limited for medical reasons)

fat·ted /ˈfætɨd/ *adj* [Wa5;A] *lit* **1** (of animals) FATTENed for eating: *fatted cattle* **2 kill the fatted calf** to welcome joyfully someone who has returned after long absence (or bad behaviour, as in the Bible story of the PRODIGAL Son)

fat·ten /ˈfætn/ *v* [T1 (*up*)] to make (a creature) fat: *Have some more cake! You need fattening up a bit*

fat·ty¹ /ˈfæti/ *adj* (of food) containing a lot of fat —**-tiness** *n* [U]

fatty² *n* [A;C;N] *infml derog* a fat person: *Fatty won't be able to get through that hole*

fa·tu·i·ty /fəˈtjuːɨti‖fəˈtuː-/ *n* [U] the quality of being FATUOUS

fat·u·ous /ˈfætʃuəs/ *adj* very silly without seeming to know it: *What a fatuous remark!* —**~ly** *adv* —**~ness** *n* [U]

fau·cet /ˈfɔːsɨt/ *n AmE* TAP¹ (1)

fault¹ /fɔːlt/ *n* **1** a mistake or imperfection: *There are several faults in that page of figures.|a small electrical fault in the motor* **2** a bad point, but not of a serious moral kind, in someone's character: *Your only fault is that you won't do what you're told.|I love her for her faults as well as for her* VIRTUEs **3** *tech* (in the science of the earth=GEOLOGY) a crack in the earth's surface, where one band of rock has slid against another **4** (in games like tennis) a mistake in a service, which may lose a point **5 at fault** in the wrong; to be rightly blamed: *Which of the 2 drivers was at fault in the car crash?|If my memory is not at fault, it was Thursday* **6 be one's fault** *not fml* to be something for which one can rightly be blamed: *Whose fault is it (that) we're late? It's not our fault* **7 find fault (with)** to complain, perhaps too much or too often, (about): *She's always finding fault with the way I do my hair* **8 to a fault** (of good qualities) too; too much: *He's generous (almost) to a fault* **9 the fault lies with . . .** . . . is to be blamed —see WRONG (USAGE)

fault² *v* **1** [T1] *nonassertive* to find a FAULT¹ (1) in: *It was impossible to fault her performance* **2** [Wv5; I0] (of rocks) to break and form a FAULT¹ (3): *ancient faulted rocks*

fault·find·ing /ˈfɔːltˌfaɪndɪŋ/ *n* [U] the (bad) habit of finding FAULT¹ (7) —**-finder** *n*

fault·less /ˈfɔːltləs/ *adj* [Wa5] without a fault; perfect: *She gave a faultless performance on the piano* —**~ly** *adv* —**~ness** *n* [U]

fault·y /ˈfɔːlti/ *adj* **-ier, -iest** (esp. of machines, apparatus, etc.) having FAULTS¹ (1): *a faulty wire in the electrical system|faulty reasoning* —**faultily** *adv*: *The wire was faultily connected*

faun /fɔːn/ *n* a type of ancient Roman god of the fields and woods. They were believed to be like a man with a goat's horns and legs.

fau·na /ˈfɔːnə/ *n* **1** [U9;C9] all the animals living wild in a particular place, or belonging to a particular age in history: *the fauna of the forest* **2** [C9] a list or description of such animals —compare FLORA

faux pas /ˌfəʊ ˈpɑː, ˈfəʊ pɑː/ *n* **faux pas** /ˌfəʊ ˈpɑːz/ *Fr* a social mistake, in words or behaviour: *My dear, I've* COMMITted *the most fearful faux pas! I offered wine to Ayoub and he's a Muslim*

fa·vour¹, *AmE* **favor** /ˈfeɪvəʳ/ *n* **1** [U] encouragement and approval; willingness to be kind: *He did all he could to win her favour.|The President will look with favour on our attempt* **2** [U] unfairly generous treatment; (too much) sympathy for one person as compared to others: *A mother shouldn't show too much favour to one of her children* **3** [C] a kind act that is not forced or necessary: *Don't try to borrow John's car—I hate asking favours of people.*|(*fml*) *We would* ESTEEM (= think) *it a great favour if you would reply at once* **4** [C] a bit of metal (BADGE) or of coloured cloth (RIBBON) worn to show that one belongs to a political party, supports a football team, etc. **5** *old use* (in business letters) a letter: *Received your favour of recent date . . .* **6 be in/out**

of someone's favour also **be in/out of favour (with someone)** to be/not be well regarded (by someone): *He worked hard to get back in the teacher's favour.|Sir Walter is out of favour at court/with the King* **7 do someone a (great) favour** also **do a (great) favour for someone** to do something (very) kind for someone: *Do me a favour by turning off that radio!* **8 find/lose favour in someone's eyes** to become/cease to be well regarded by someone **9 in favour of a** believing in or choosing; on the side of: *Are you in favour of early marriage?|He refused a job in the steel industry in favour of a university appointment* **b** (of a cheque) payable to: *a cheque made* (=written) *out in favour of the Cats' Protection Society* **10 in one's favour** to one's advantage: *The bank has made an* ERROR (=mistake) *in your favour: we owe you £100* **11 stand high in someone's favour** to be very well regarded by someone —see also CURRY¹ (2) **favour**, ILL-FAVOURED, RETURN¹ (9) **a favour, without** FEAR **or favour**¹ (11), FAVOURS

favour², *AmE* **favor** *v* [T1] **1** to believe in (a plan or idea); regard with FAVOUR¹ (1): *I favour early marriage* **2** to be unfairly fond of; treat with FAVOUR¹ (2): *A mother mustn't favour one of her children more than the others* **3** (of conditions) to make pleasant and easy: *The tax system favours early marriage* **4** (of a child) to look like (a parent); TAKE AFTER in appearance: *The baby favours his father; they both have brown eyes*

fa·vou·ra·ble, *AmE* **favorable** /ˈfeɪvərəbəl/ *adj fml* **1** (of a message, answer, etc.) saying what one wants to hear: *The doctor gave a very favourable report on my health.|I hear favourable accounts of your work* **2** [(*to*)] (of conditions) advantageous; FAVOURing² (3): *We can sail there in an hour, if the wind is favourable (to us)* —opposite **unfavourable** —**-rably** /-bli/ *adv*: *I was favourably* IMPRESSed¹ *by your work.|He speaks favourably of you* —opposite **unfavourably**; see LOVELY (USAGE)

fa·voured, *AmE* **favored** /ˈfeɪvəd‖-ərd/ *adj* **1** [B] having special advantages; favourite: *He sat in his (most) favoured corner by the fire* **2** [Wa5;F9+*with*] having advantages of the stated kind: *She is favoured with great beauty* **3 most favoured nation** the nation that pays, by agreement, the lowest DUTY (=tax) on goods brought into the country

-favoured *comb. form* [*adv→adj*] (of a person) looking; having the stated appearance (in the words **ill-favoured** (=ugly-looking) and **well-favoured** (=nice-looking)): *an* ILL-*favoured youth*

fa·vou·rite¹, *AmE* **favorite** /ˈfeɪvərɨt/ *n* **1** [C] something or someone that is loved above all others: *These books are my favourites* **2** [C] *derog* someone who receives too much FAVOUR¹ (2): *A teacher shouldn't have/make favourites in the class* **3** [*the*+C] (in horseracing) the horse in each race that is expected to win: *The favourite came in second*

favourite², *AmE* **favorite** *adj* being a favourite: *my favourite type of chocolates|his favourite son* —see LOVELY (USAGE)

favourite son /ˌ·· ˈ·/ *AmE* someone favoured by his State as a possible President of the US

fa·vou·ri·tis·m, *AmE* **favoritism** /ˈfeɪvərɨtɪzəm/ *n* [U] *derog* the practice of showing FAVOUR¹ (2): *John doesn't deserve that job—he only got it out of favouritism because he married the owner's daughter!*

fa·vours /ˈfeɪvəz‖-ərz/ *n* [P] a woman's sexual attractions, esp. when given freely for another's pleasure (usu. in the phr. **bestow one's favours**)

favour with *v prep* [D1] *fml* to give (someone, something nice): *She favoured him with a charming smile*

fawn /fɔːn/ *n* **1** [C] a young deer less than a year old: *to move with a fawnlike grace|as* TIMID *as a fawn* **2** [S;U] a light yellowish-brown colour: *a new pair of fawn trousers*

fawn on also **fawn up·on**— *v adv* **1** (of dogs) to jump on, rub against (someone) etc., as an expression of love **2** to try to gain the favour of (someone) by over-praising and being insincerely attentive: *fawning on their rich uncle*

fay /feɪ/ *n poet* FAIRY

faze /feɪz/ [T1] *AmE not fml* to surprise and shock (someone) so much as to prevent speech or action

FBI *n* [*the*+R] *abbrev* (*often used in speech*) *for*: (in the US) Federal Bureau of Investigation; the department of the police that is controlled by the central (FEDERAL) government, and is particularly concerned with matters of national SECURITY (=the protection of political secrets): *an FBI official|a member of the FBI*

fe·al·ty /ˈfiːəlti/ *n old use* (in former times) (a statement of) loyalty (to one's king or lord) (in phrs. like **swear fealty**, **take an oath of fealty**): *He swore fealty to the king for his land*

fear¹ /fɪəʳ/ *n* **1** [U] the feeling that one has when danger is near: *She learnt to swim at once—she seems totally without fear (of the water).|I couldn't move for* (=because of) *fear* **2** [S9;C5 *often pl. with sing. meaning*] the feeling that one has when a stated danger is near: *She has a great fear of fire.|I was struck with/by the fear that they might drown.|Your fear/fears that he would get lost was/were unnecessary* **3** [U5,9] danger: *There's some fear that he'll be too late.|I've not much fear of losing my way* **4** [U] *old use* great respect (in the phr. **the fear of God**) **5 for fear of** in case of; because of anxiety about: *Shut the window for fear of rain* **6 for fear (that)** LEST; because of anxiety that (something bad may happen): *Shut the window for fear (that) it may rain* **7 in fear of** (in the state of being) **a** afraid of: *I'm in daily fear of dismissal* **b** afraid for the safety of **8 in fear and trembling** very much afraid **9 No fear!** *infml* (in answer to a suggestion that one should do something) Certainly not! **10 put the fear of God into someone** to make someone very much afraid **11 without fear or favour** with justice; not showing more sympathy for one side than for the other

fear² *v fml* **1** [Wv6;T1] to be afraid of: *She has always feared mice* **2** [Wv6;IØ (*for*)] to be afraid (for the safety of someone or something): *Do not fear—I will hold your hand.|She feared for the little boy when she saw him at the top of the tree* **3** *old use* to feel great respect for (in the phr. **fear God**) **4 I fear** (*used when telling bad news*) I'm sorry that I must now say: *It's raining, I fear.|I fear we'll be late.|"Is there enough money?" "I fear not."|"Is she very ill?" "I fear so"*

fear·ful /ˈfɪəfəl‖ˈfɪər-/ *adj* **1** [B] causing fear: *a fearful storm* **2** [B] *not fml* very bad; (of bad things) very great; FRIGHTFUL: *What a fearful waste of time!* **3** [B (*of*),5c (*that*)] (typical of someone) that is afraid: *He was fearful of her anger/fearful that/*LEST *she should be angry* —opposite **fearless** —**~ly** *adv*: *a fearfully cold day* —**~ness** *n* [U]

fear·less /ˈfɪələs‖ˈfɪər-/ *adj* [(*of*)] (typical of someone) that is without fear: *fearless of what might happen* —opposite **fearful** —**~ly** *adv*: *He climbed fearlessly over the roof* —**~ness** *n* [U]

fear·some /ˈfɪəsəm‖ˈfɪər-/ *adj humor* causing fear; very unpleasant esp. in appearance: *a fearsome sight*

fea·si·ble /ˈfiːzɨbəl/ *adj* able to be carried out or done; possible: *Your plan sounds quite feasible.|It's not feasible to dismiss him* —compare PLAUSIBLE —**-sibility** /ˌfiːzəˈbɪlɨti/ *n* [U] —**-sibly** /ˈfiːzɨbli/ *adv*

feast[1] /fiːst/ *n* **1** a splendid esp. public meal; a specially good or grand meal: *The king gave/held a feast.|to invite them to a feast* **2** a day kept in memory of some happy religious event: *Christmas is an important feast for Christians* —see also MOVABLE FEAST

feast[2] *v* **1** [IØ (*on, upon*)] to eat and drink very well; have a specially good meal (of): *We feasted on chicken and coconuts* **2** [T1 (*on, upon*)] *fml* to feed (someone) specially well (on); give (someone) a feast: *The king feasted his friends (on chicken and coconuts).*|(fig.) *He feasted his eyes on the beautiful scene*

feat /fiːt/ *n* a clever esp. bodily action, showing strength, skill, or courage: *It was quite a feat to move that piano by yourself*

fea·ther[1] /ˈfeðəʳ/ *n* **1** one of the many parts of the covering which grows on a bird's body, each of which has a stiff rod-like piece in the middle, with soft hair-like material growing from it on each side —see picture at BIRD **2 a feather in one's cap** a deserved honour that one is proud of: *They want you to photograph the Queen? That'll be quite a feather in your cap!* **3 as light as a feather** with almost no weight; very light **4 birds of a feather** people of the same (often bad) kind **5 in high/good feather** (of a person) in good spirits and condition: *John seems in very high feather since his book was so successful* **6 show the white feather** to show fear; seem cowardly

feather[2] *v* [T1] **1** [(*with*)] to put feathers on (an arrow): *arrows feathered with ducks' feathers* **2** to cover with feathers (esp. in the phr. TAR **and feather**) **3** to make (the blade of an OAR) lie flat on the surface of the water **4 feather one's nest** to make oneself rich, esp. dishonestly, through a job in which one is trusted

feather bed /ˌ·· ˈ·/ *n* a MATTRESS (=large flat bag of soft material for sleeping on) that is filled with feathers: *to sleep in/on a feather bed*

fea·ther·bed /ˈfeðəbed‖-ər-/ *v* [T1] to give (a group of people) generous help in the form of money, tax advantages, working conditions, etc., as demanded by the law or by trade union agreement: *to featherbed the farmers/the fishing industry*

feather bo·a /ˌ·· ˈ··/ *n* BOA[2]

fea·ther·brained /ˈfeðəbreɪnd‖-ər-/ *adj* very silly and thoughtless: *She was too featherbrained to count the money properly.|Mildred's a featherbrained little creature*

fea·ther·weight /ˈfeðəweɪt‖-ər-/ *n, adj* **1** [C] a BOXER weighing between 118 and 126 pounds (53·5 to 57 kilos) **2** [S] someone or something **a** of very little weight **b** of very little importance

fea·ther·y /ˈfəðəri/ *adj* **1** covered with feathers **2** soft and light: *feathery pastry*

fea·ture[1] /ˈfiːtʃəʳ/ *n* **1** [C9] a (typical or noticeable) part or quality: *Wet weather is a feature of life in Scotland* **2** [C9] any of the noticeable parts of the face: *Her mouth is her worst feature* **3** [C9] a special long article in a newspaper: *a front-page feature in the "Daily Telegraph" on coalmining* **4** [C] a full-length cinema film with an invented story and professional actors: *to work as a cameraman in features* —compare DOCUMENTARY[1] (2)

feature[2] *v* **1** [T1] to include as a special FEATURE[1] (1): *a new film featuring Dustin Hoffman* **2** [T1] to advertise as a special FEATURE[1] (1): *We're featuring bedroom furniture this week* **3** [IØ] to be present as a FEATURE[1] (1): *Fish features very largely in the food of these islanders*

fea·ture·less /ˈfiːtʃələs‖-ər-/ *adj* uninteresting, because of having no noticeable FEATUREs[1] (1): *a house in the middle of a featureless plain*

fea·tures /ˈfiːtʃəz‖-ərz/ *n* [P9] the face, considered as a group of parts: *to have regular features/Chinese features*

fe·brile /ˈfiːbraɪl‖ˈfebrəl/ *adj fml & med* of or caused by fever

Feb·ru·a·ry /ˈfebrʊəri‖ˈfebjʊeri/ *n* [R;(C)] the 2nd month of the year

fe·ces /ˈfiːsiːz/ *n AmE* FAECES —**fecal** /ˈfiːkəl/ *adj*

feck·less /ˈfekləs/ *adj not fml* (typical of a person) worthless and without purpose or plans for the future —**~ly** *adv* —**~ness** *n* [U]

fec·und /ˈfekənd, ˈfiːkənd/ *adj* very FERTILE; very productive: *a fecund fruit tree*|(fig.) *Books flowed from his fecund pen* —**~ity** /fɪˈkʌndɪ̈ti/ *n* [U]

fed /fed/ *past t. and p. of* FEED —*compare* FED UP

fed·e·ral /ˈfedərəl/ *adj* [Wa5] **1** of or formed into a political FEDERATION (1): *Switzerland is a federal republic* **2** (in the US) of or relating to the central government of the FEDERATION (1) as compared with those of the States that form it: *to pay both federal taxes and state taxes*

Federal Bu·reau of In·ves·ti·ga·tion /ˌ··· ˌ·· · ···ˈ··/ *n* [*the*+R] FBI

Federal Re·serve Bank /ˌ··· ·ˈ· ·/ *n* [*the*+R] any of 12 banks set up in various parts of the US by the central banking (**Federal Reserve**) system to hold a supply (**reserve**) of money that can be lent to other banks

fed·e·ral·is·m /ˈfedərəlɪzəm/ *n* [U] the belief in political FEDERATION (2)

Federalism *n* [U] (in US politics) the beliefs of the FEDERALISTs

fed·e·ral·ist /ˈfedərəlɪ̈st/ *n, adj* [Wa5] (typical of) a believer **a** in political FEDERATION (2) in general **b** (in US politics) *often cap* in the FEDERATION (1) of the American States after the War of Independence

Federalist *n, adj* [Wa5] (in US politics) (a member) of a political party formed in 1787 that favoured a strong central government

fed·e·rate /ˈfedəreɪt/ *v* [IØ;T1] to form or become a FEDERATION (1)

fed·e·ra·tion /ˌfedəˈreɪʃən/ *n* **1** [C] a group of states united with one government which decides foreign affairs, defence, etc., but in which each state can have its own government to decide its own affairs **2** [U] the action or result of uniting in this way: *the hope of European federation* **3** [C9] a group of societies, organizations,trade unions, etc., that have come together in this way: *the Federation of British Fishing Clubs*

fed up /ˌ· ˈ·/ *adj* [F (*about, with*),F5] *infml* unhappy, tired, and discontented, esp. about something dull one has had too much of: *I won't wait any longer—I'm fed up!|I'm fed up with your complaints.|She's very fed up about it.|Mother will be a bit fed up that you didn't telephone*

fee[1] /fiː/ *n* **1** a sum of money paid for professional services to a doctor, lawyer, private school, etc. **2 in fee** in complete possession by law —see COST[2] (USAGE)

fee[2] *v* **feed,** also **fee'd** [T1] *tech & old use* to hire (someone) by payment: *He feed a lawyer to act for him*

fee·ble /ˈfiːbəl/ *adj* [Wa1,3] **1** weak; with little force: *Grandfather has been getting feebler lately* **2** (of a joke, idea, or story) silly; not well thought out: *a feeble suggestion* —**feebly** /ˈfiːbli/ *adv* —**~ness** *n* [U]

fee·ble·mind·ed /ˌfiːbəlˈmaɪndɪ̈d◂/ *adj* [Wa5] *euph* very stupid; with less than the usual INTELLIGENCE

feed[1] /fiːd/ *v* **fed** /fed/ **1** [T1 (*on, with*)] to give food to: *to feed the dog on meat|Will you feed my cat for me?|She feeds the baby with a spoon.|The baby will* *soon learn to feed himself.*|(fig.) *to feed the fire with logs*|*This medicine will feed the roots of your hair.*|*These little streams feed the lake.*|*We have to feed 120 guests after the wedding* **2** [I∅] (*infml or humor,* except of animals or babies) to eat: *What time do we feed?*|*The horses were feeding quietly in the field* **3** [X9] to put, supply, or provide, esp. continually: *to feed the wire into/through the hole*|*You feed in the money here and the coffee comes out there.*|*The information is fed back to the Government department concerned*

feed² *n* **1** [C] a meal taken by an animal or baby: *How many feeds a day does the camel get?* **2** [S] (*infml or humor* except of animals & babies) an act of FEEDing¹ (2): *Mary seems to be having a good feed over there in the corner!* **3** [U] food for animals: *a bag of hen feed* —compare CHICKENFEED **4** [C] the part of a machine through which the machine is supplied: *a blockage in the petrol feed* **5** *BrE* also *AmE* **feeder**— someone who appears on the stage with a professional funny man (COMEDIAN) to hold a conversation with him so that he can make jokes: *Was Dumont just a feed for Groucho or an actress in her own right?*

feed·back /ˈfiːdbæk/ *n* [U] information about the results of a set of actions, passed back to the person (or machine) in charge, so that changes can be made if necessary: *The company welcomes feedback from people who use the goods it produces*

feed·bag /ˈfiːdbæg/ *AmE* NOSEBAG

feed·er /ˈfiːdəʳ/ *n* **1** [C9] (*humor,* except of animals or plants) one that eats (in the stated way): *This horse is a heavy feeder* **2** [C] *BrE* a cloth or plastic shield tied under a child's chin to protect the clothes at meals —compare BIB (1) **3** [C] (*often in comb.*) a branch road, airline, railway line, etc., that joins into a main one: *a feeder road to the* MOTORWAY **4** [C] *AmE* FEED² (5)

feeding bot·tle /ˈ·· ˌ··/ *n* a bottle with a rubber cap (TEAT) shaped like the NIPPLE on a woman's breast, from which a baby can suck liquids

feed on *v adv* [T1] (of animals) to live on (a food): *Sheep feed mostly on grass*

feed to *v prep* [D1] to give (something) as food to: *You'd better feed this old bread to the hens*

feed up *v adv* [T1] to make (a creature) fat and healthy by giving it lots of good food: *That thin little boy needs feeding up*

feel¹ /fiːl/ *v* **felt** /felt/ **1** [T1,6] to get knowledge of by touching with the fingers: *Just feel the quality of the cloth!*|*I can't feel where the handle is* **2** [Wv6; T1] to experience (the touch or movement of something): *I can feel a pin sticking into me.*|*to feel one's heart beating*|*to feel the wind on one's face*|*I felt something touch(ing) my foot* **3** [L7] to experience (a condition of the mind or body); be consciously: *"Are you feeling better?" "Yes, I feel fine now."*|*Do you feel hungry yet?*|*She felt cold/cheated/happy.*|*I feel sure that's him!*|*I feel 100* (=years old) **4** [L1; Wv6] to seem to oneself to be: *I felt a fool* **5** [T1,5; V3] to believe, esp. for the moment (something that cannot be proved): *She felt that he no longer loved her* (compare *She believed the earth was flat.*).|*She felt herself to be unwanted.*|*He felt the truth of her words* **6** [L7] to give (a sensation): *Your feet feel cold.*|*How does it feel to be a lord?* **7** [Wv6;I∅] to (be able to) experience sensations: *She doesn't say much but she feels* **8** [Wv6;T1] to suffer because of (a state or event): *He feels the cold in winter* **9** [L9 (*after, for*)] to search with the fingers rather than the eyes: *She felt in her bag for a pencil* **10 feel as if/as though** to have or give the sensation that; seem to be: *I feel as if my leg were broken.*|*My leg feels as though it was broken* **11 feel free to do something** *often imper.* to be welcome to do something: *Please feel free to make suggestions* **12 feel funny** to have or give a strange sensation: *My head feels funny—may I lie down?* **13 feel in one's bones that** to be certain that **14 feel like a** to want; to be in the state for: *I don't feel like (drinking) beer tonight.*|*Do you feel like a swim?* **b** to seem like when touched: *I'm holding something that feels like a potato* **15 feel one's way a** to move carefully as in the dark: *They felt their way down the dark passage* **b** to act slowly and carefully: *He hasn't been in the job long and he's still feeling his way* **16 feel small** to feel humble or ashamed —see also **feel** BLUE¹ (2), **feel** CHEAP² (8), **feel** UP TO (3), —see SEE (USAGE)

feel² *n* [S] **1** the sensation caused by feeling something: *I like the feel of this cloth; it has a warm woolly feel* **2** an act of feeling: *Let me have a feel inside the bag* **3 get the feel of** to become used to and skilled at: *You'll soon get the feel of the new job/car*

feel a·bout also **feel a·round**— *v adv* [I∅ (*for*)] to search, or examine something, without being able to see what one is doing: *I'm feeling about for an answer to our difficulties*

feel·er /ˈfiːləʳ/ *n* **1** [*usu. pl.*] the thread-like part on the front of an insect's head, with which it touches things **2 put out feelers** *not fml* to make a suggestion as a test of what others will think or do: *I'm putting out feelers to see if he'd like to come and work for us*

feel for *v prep* [T1] to be sorry for; be unhappy about the suffering of

feel·ing¹ /ˈfiːlɪŋ/ *n* **1** [S9+*of*] a consciousness of (something felt in the mind or body): *a feeling of shame/danger/thirst/pleasure* **2** [S5] a belief or opinion, not based on reason: *I have a feeling (in my bones) that he'll come soon* **3** [U] the power to feel sensation: *He lost all feeling in his toes* **4** [U] excitement of mind, esp. in a bad sense: *His speech caused/*AROUSE*d/*PROVOKE*d a lot of (strong) feeling* **5** [U (*for*)] sympathy and understanding: *to play the piano with great feeling*|*You have no feeling for my troubles/for the beauty of nature* **6 bad/ill feeling** bitterness and anger: *The new working hours caused a lot of bad feeling at the factory*

feeling² *adj* [A] showing strong FEELINGs: *She gave him a feeling look* —**~ly** *adv*: *"I hate him," she said feelingly*

feel·ings /ˈfiːlɪŋz/ *n* [P] **1** sensations of joy, sorrow, hate, etc.; the part of a person's nature that feels, compared to the part that thinks: *She has very strong feelings on this subject* **2 hurt someone's feelings** to make someone unhappy, esp. by rudeness: *You'll hurt his feelings if you forget his birthday* **3 no hard feelings** *not fml* (said when one wishes to be friendly to a competitor) no feelings of anger: *I hope you haven't any hard feelings about my marrying Mildred?*

feel out *v adv* [T1] *no pass.* SOUND OUT

fee-pay·ing /ˈ· ˌ··/ *adj* [Wa5;A] **1** that pays FEEs: *a fee-paying student* **2** that charges FEEs: *a fee-paying school*

feet /fiːt/ *pl. of* FOOT

feign /feɪn/ *v fml* **1** [Wv5;T1,5] to pretend to have or be; put on a false air of: *He feigned death/feigned that he was dead.*|*a feigned illness* **2** [Wv5; T1] to invent (an excuse, reason, etc.)

feint¹ /feɪnt/ *n* [(*of*)] *fml* a false attack or blow, made to draw the enemy's attention away from the real danger: (fig.) *He made a feint of offering me a drink*

feint² *v* [I∅ (*at, upon, against*)] to make a FEINT, esp. by pretending to hit with one hand and then using the other: *He feinted (at me) with his left*

feld·spar /ˈfeldspɑːʳ/ also **felspar**— *n* [U] any of

several types of white or light red stone

fe·li·ci·tate /fɪˈlɪsəteɪt/ *v* [T1 (*on, upon*)] *fml* CONGRATULATE: *Allow me to felicitate you upon the birth of your daughter* —**-tations** /fɪˌlɪsəˈteɪʃənz/ *n* [P (*on, upon*)]

fe·li·ci·tous /fɪˈlɪsətəs/ *adj fml* (of words or remarks) suitable and well-chosen —**~ly** *adv*

fe·li·ci·ty /fɪˈlɪsəti/ *n fml* **1** [U] happiness: *to spend a lifetime of perfect felicity with Mildred* **2** [C;U] (an example of) the quality of FELICITOUSness: *the many felicities of his style*

fe·line /ˈfiːlaɪn/ *adj, n* [Wa5] (of or like) a member of the cat family: *Lions and tigers are felines*

fell[1] /fel/ *n fml* the skin of an animal with its fur or hair

fell[2] *v* [T1] **1** to cut down (a tree): *a felled* OAK **2** *fml* to knock down (a person): *He felled the man at a* (=with one) *blow*

fell[3] *adj* [Wa5;A] *lit* evil,dangerous and terrible: *a fell disease* —see also **at one fell** SWOOP[2] **(2)**

fell[4] *n* [C *often pl. with same meaning*] *NEngE* high wild rocky country where no crops can grow: *fell-walking races*

fell[5] *past t. of* FALL

fel·lah /ˈfelə, ˈfelɑː/ *n* **-lahin** *or* **-laheen** /ˌfeləˈhiːn/ an Egyptian worker on the land

fel·la·ti·o /fəˈleɪʃɪəʊ/ also **fel·la·tion** /-ʃən/— *n* [U] *tech, Lat* the sexual practice of sucking the male sex organ —compare CUNNILINGUS

fel·low[1] /ˈfeləʊ/ *n* **1** [C;N] *infml, esp. AmE, Ind & PakE* a man: *See if those fellows want some beer.|Poor old fellow!|A fellow* (=one) *must eat* **2** [C (*of*)] a member (of a society connected with some branch of learning): *a Fellow of the Royal Society* **3** [C (*of*)] a high-ranking member of an Oxford or Cambridge college **4** *often in comb.* someone with whom one shares a (stated) activity or spends time in a (stated) place: *She and I were schoolfellows.|to be kind to one's fellows*

fellow[2] *adj* [A] another (of 2 or more things or people like oneself): *one's fellow creatures/prisoners/students|I've met a fellow lionhunter!*

fellow feel·ing /ˌ·· ˈ··/ *n* [S;U: (*with*)] (a) feeling in common; sympathy for someone like oneself: *I have a lot of/a certain fellow feeling for her because she's black like me*

fel·low·ship /ˈfeləʊʃɪp/ *n* **1** [C] a group or society **2** [C] the position of **a** a FELLOW[1] (3) of a college: *You'll lose your fellowship if you do that!* **b** a paid RESEARCH worker at a university **3** [U] the condition of being friends through sharing or doing something together; companionship

fellow trav·el·ler /ˌ·· ˈ···/ *n* **1** someone with whom one is travelling: *telling stories to amuse his fellow travellers* **2** someone who is sympathetic to the aims of the COMMUNIST party without being actually a member

fel·on /ˈfelən/ *n* a criminal guilty of FELONY

fel·o·ny /ˈfeləni/ *n law* **1** [C] any of a group of serious crimes, such as murder or armed robbery: *Murder is a felony* —compare MISDEMEANOUR (2) **2** [U] crime of this degree: *guilty of felony* —**-nious** /fəˈləʊnɪəs/ *adj* [Wa5]

fel·spar /ˈfelspɑːʳ/ *n* [U] FELDSPAR

felt[1] /felt/ *n* [U] thick firm cloth made of wool, hair, or fur, pressed flat: *a felt hat*

felt[2] *past t. and p. of* FEEL

felt-tip pen /ˌ· · ˈ·/ also **felt-tipped pen** /ˌ·· ˈ·/, **felt tip** /ˌ· ˈ·/— *n* a pen with a small piece of FELT[1] at the end instead of a NIB, often containing a brightly-coloured ink

fe·luc·ca /fəˈlʌkə‖fəˈluːkə/ *n* a type of fast narrow sailing ship used chiefly in the Mediterranean area

fem. /fem/ *abbrev. for*: FEMININE—compare MASC.

fe·male[1] /ˈfiːmeɪl/ *n* **1** a female person or animal: *The female was sitting on the eggs while the male bird brought food* **2** *infml* a woman: *There's a young female to see you, sir!*

USAGE **Female** and **male** as adjectives tell one the sex of a creature. **Female** (*n*) is slightly rude when used of a woman. **Feminine** and **masculine** are used of the qualities that are supposed to be typical of the 2 human sexes: **feminine** CURIOSITY. Men can have **feminine** (but not **female**) qualities, and women can have **masculine** (but not **male**) ones: *her loud* **masculine** *voice.*

female[2] *adj* [Wa5] **1** of the sex that gives birth to young: *a female elephant|to employ female workers* **2** suitable to or typical of this sex, rather than the male sex: *the female form* **3** (of plants or flowers) producing fruit: *This rose is female* **4** *tech* having a hole made to receive a part that fits into it: *a female* PLUG

fem·i·nine /ˈfemənən/ *adj* **1** of or having the qualities suitable for a woman: *He has a very feminine voice* —see FEMALE[1] (USAGE) **2** *tech* (in grammar) (with the word endings) of a certain class of words: *The word for "door" is feminine in German.|"Actress" is the feminine form of "actor"*

fem·i·nin·i·ty /ˌfeməˈnɪnəti/ *n* [U] the quality of being FEMININE

fem·i·nis·m /ˈfemənɪzəm/ *n* [U] the principle that women should have the same rights and chances as men

fem·i·nist /ˈfemənəst/ *n, adj* [Wa5] (typical of) someone who believes in FEMINISM: *feminist opinions|John Stuart Mill was an early feminist*

femme fa·tale /ˌfæm fəˈtɑːl‖ˌfem-/ *n Fr* a woman who attracts men into danger by her mysterious charm

fe·mur /ˈfiːməʳ/ *n* **femurs** *or* **femora** /ˈfemərə/ *med* the long bone in the upper part of the leg: *to break one's femur* —**femoral** /ˈfemərəl/ *adj* [Wa5] —see picture at SKELETON

fen /fen/ *n* [C *often pl. with sing. meaning*] an area of low wet land esp. in the east of England: *The Fens are often windy.|The wind in Cambridge blows from the fens/fenland area*

fence[1] /fens/ *n* **1** a wall made of wood or wire, dividing 2 areas of land: *They were talking across the garden fence* **2** *not fml* someone who buys and sells stolen goods **3 come down on one side of the fence or the other** to take one side or the other in an argument **4 sit on the fence** *usu. derog* to avoid taking sides in an argument, in order to see where one's own advantage lies

fence[2] *v* **1** [IØ] to fight with a long thin pointed sword (FOIL) as a sport **2** [IØ] to avoid giving an honest answer to a question —compare HEDGE[2] (2) **3** [Wv5;T1:(AROUND)] to put a fence round: *The tree was fenced around with wire*

fence in *v adv* [T1] to surround or close in (an area) with a fence, esp. so as to protect what is inside: *We fenced in the garden to keep the sheep out*

fence off *v adv* [T1] to separate or shut out (an area) with a fence: *We fenced off the lake in case the children should fall in*

fenc·er /ˈfensəʳ/ *n* someone who FENCEs[2] (1)

fenc·ing /ˈfensɪŋ/ *n* [U] **1** the sport of fencing (FENCE[2] (1)) **2 a** material for making fences **b** all the fences in an area: *Surrounded by wire fencing/by a wire fence*

USAGE For the sport of **fencing** one wears a **mask**, and uses any of several sorts of sword: a **foil**, **épée**, or **sabre**. One SCOREs by making *hits*, and in a match the person in charge is called the *judge* or *president*.

fend /fend/ *v* **fend for oneself** to look after oneself: *I've had to fend for myself since I was 14*

fend·er /ˈfendəʳ/ *n* **1 a** a low metal wall round an

open fireplace, to stop the coal from falling out: *to sit with one's feet in the fender* **b** a higher object of this kind, to stop children from falling into the fire **2** *AmE* WING (=guard over the wheel of a car) **3** any object such as a mass of rope, an old tyre, a lump of wood, etc., that hangs over the side of a boat to protect it from damage by other boats or when coming to land

fend off *v adv* [T1] to push away; act to avoid: (fig.) *He fended off the difficult questions*

fen·nel /'fenəl/ *n* a plant with yellow flowers whose leaves and seeds are used for giving a special taste to food

feoff /fef, fi:f/ *n* FIEF

fe·ral /'fɪərəl/ *adj* [Wa5] *fml* (of an animal) wild, esp. after living with people and escaping: *Feral cats are not naturally fierce like wild cats, but in Australia they have done a lot of damage since they became wild*

fer·ment¹ /fə'ment‖fər-/ *v* [Wv5;IØ;T1] **1 a** to cause a state of FERMENTATION in: *unfermented apple juice* **b** to be in a state of FERMENTATION: *The wine is beginning to ferment* **2 a** to be in a state of political trouble and excitement **b** to cause (this state): *His speeches fermented trouble among the workers*

fer·ment² /'fɜ:ment‖'fɜr-/ *n* [U] **1** (the condition of) political trouble and excitement: *The whole country was in a state of ferment* **2 a** the period or event of FERMENTing¹ (1); FERMENTATION **b** any of the substances that cause this

fer·men·ta·tion /ˌfɜ:men'teɪʃən‖ˌfɜrmən-/ *n* [U] the period or event of increasing in size and becoming filled with gas by chemical change, caused by the action of certain living substances such as YEAST: *Leave it on the shelf during fermentation.|Milk becomes cheese by fermentation*

fern /fɜ:n‖fɜrn/ *n* [Wn1] a type of green plants with feathery shaped leaves and no flowers: *to sleep on a heap of dry fern|to plant some ferns in a pot* —**ferny** *adj*: *the ferny bank of the river* —see picture at PLANT²

fe·ro·cious /fə'rəʊʃəs/ *adj* fierce, cruel, and violent: *a ferocious lion|ferocious punishments|*(fig.) *The heat is ferocious today* —**~ly** *adv*: *Your dog attacked me ferociously* —**~ness** *n* [U]

fe·ro·ci·ty /fə'rɒsɨti‖fe'rɑ-/ *n* [U] the quality or state of being FEROCIOUS

fer·ret¹ /'ferɨt/ *n* a type of small fierce European animal of the WEASEL family, with a pointed nose. It catches rats and rabbits by going into their holes —see picture at CARNIVOROUS

ferret² *v* **1** [IØ] to hunt rats and rabbits with FERRETS: *Let's go ferreting!* **2** [L9 esp. ABOUT, AROUND] *not fml* to search by pushing things about: *I've been ferreting around among my papers for the missing letter*

ferret out *v adv* [T1] to discover (something) by searching: *to ferret out the truth*

fer·ro·con·crete /ˌferəʊ'kɒŋkri:t‖-'kɑŋ-, -kɑŋ-'kri:t/ *n* [U] REINFORCED CONCRETE

fer·rous /'ferəs/ *adj* [Wa5] *tech* related to or containing iron: *ferrous metals*

fer·rule /'ferʊl, 'ferəl‖'ferəl/ *n* a metal band or cap that is put on the end of a thin stick or tube to stop it from splitting

fer·ry¹ /'feri/ *v* [X9] to carry on or as if on a FERRYBOAT: *ferrying the children to and from school in my car*

ferry² *n* **1** [C;U] (a) FERRYBOAT: *You can cross the river by ferry* **2** [C] a place from which a FERRYBOAT leaves, or where an aircraft or HOVERCRAFT does the same sort of work: *We had to wait 3 hours at the ferry*

fer·ry·boat /'feribəʊt/ *n* a boat that goes across a river or any other narrow stretch of water, carrying people and things

fer·ry·man /'ferimən/ *n* **-men** /mən/ a man who works a FERRYBOAT

fer·tile /'fɜ:taɪl‖'fɜrtl/ *adj* **1** producing many young, fruits, or seeds: *Some fish are very fertile: they lay 1000's of eggs* —see also FRUITFUL (2) **2** (of land) which produces or can produce good crops: *fertile soil* **3** [Wa5] (of living things) able to produce young or fruit: *Are these eggs fertile?|The young of a horse and a donkey is not fertile* **4** (of a person's mind) inventive; full of suggestions, ideas, etc.: *Martha has a fertile imagination—she always thinks I'm going to be murdered* **5** [+*in*] (of a person) full (of suggestions, ideas, etc.): *George is always fertile in new plans*

fer·til·i·ty /fɜ:'tɪlɨti‖fɜr-/ *n* [U] the condition or state of being FERTILE: *the fertility of the soil/of your imagination|Margaret is taking medicine to increase her fertility*

fer·ti·lize, -ise /'fɜ:tɨlaɪz‖'fɜrtl-aɪz/ *v* [T1] **1** to start the development of young in (a female creature or plant) by sexual or other means: *Bees fertilize the flowers* **2** to put FERTILIZER on (land) —**-lization** /ˌfɜ:tɨlaɪ'zeɪʃən‖ˌfɜrtələ-/ *n* [U]: *Keep the eggs in a warm place after fertilization*

fer·ti·liz·er /'fɜ:tɨlaɪzəʳ‖'fɜrtl-aɪzər/ *n* [C;U] (any type of) chemical or natural substance that is put on the land to make crops grow better: *a bag of chemical fertilizer|Crushed bones make one of the best fertilizers*

fer·ule /'feru:l‖'ferəl/ *n* a flat ruler used for hitting schoolchildren on the hand as a punishment

fer·vent /'fɜ:vənt‖'fɜr-/ *adj* that is, feels, or shows strong and warm feelings: *a fervent desire to win|He's a fervent believer in free speech* —**-vency** *n* [U] —**~ly** *adv*: *He fervently begged us not to go*

fer·vid /'fɜ:vɨd‖'fɜr-/ *adj* that shows strong and serious feeling: *a fervid political speech* —**~ly** *adv*

fer·vour, *AmE* **-vor** /'fɜ:vəʳ‖'fɜr-/ *n* [U] the quality of being FERVENT or FERVID

fes·tal /'festl/ *adj* [Wa5] *fml* FESTIVE: *festal music|this festal occasion|festal* POMP

fes·ter /'festəʳ/ *v* [IØ] (of a cut or wound) to become infected and diseased

fes·ti·val /'festɨvəl/ *n* **1** [U] also **festivity**— public gaiety and feasting: *a week of festival in honour of the king's marriage* **2** [C] a time regularly marked out for this; a (religious) feast: *Christmas is one of the festivals of the Christian church* **3** [C9 (*often cap.*)] a time of the stated ENTERTAINMENT or at the stated place: *the Edinburgh Festival|a* POP (=popular music) *festival*

fes·tive /'festɪv/ *adj* of or suitable for (a) FESTIVAL (1, 2): *Christmas is often called the festive season.|They all sat round the festive* BOARD (=table spread with a feast)

fes·tiv·i·ty /fe'stɪvɨti/ *n* **1** [U] FESTIVAL (1) **2** [C *usu. pl. with same meaning*] a FESTIVE event: *to stay in London during the festivities*

fes·toon¹ /fe'stu:n/ *n* a chain of flowers, leaves, RIBBONS etc., hung up in a curve between 2 points as an ornament

festoon² *v* **1** [T1 (*with*)] to ornament with FESTOONS¹: *to festoon the room with flowers* **2** [X9] to hang in FESTOONS¹: *They festooned roses round the picture of their leader*

fe·tal /'fi:tl/ *adj* FOETAL

fetch /fetʃ/ *v* [T1] **1** to go and get and bring back: *Run and fetch the doctor!|Please fetch me a clean handkerchief from my bedroom* **2** *infml* to be sold for: *The house'll fetch at least £30,000* **3** to attract; cause to appear or come: *a story that fetched the tears to one's eyes|The new play is fetching large* AUDIENCES *every night* **4** to breathe (in phr. like

fetch a deep breath, fetch a sigh) **5 fetch someone a blow/kick, etc.** to hit someone in the stated way **6 fetch and carry (for)** to do the small duties of a servant (for): *You can't expect me to fetch and carry for you all day! Hang up your own uniform* —see BRING (USAGE)

fetch·ing /ˈfetʃɪŋ/ *adj not fml, becoming rare* attractive; pleasing: *You look very fetching in that cap*

fetch up *v adv* [L9] *infml* to arrive; end up, esp. without planning: *I wonder what time George will fetch up*

fete[1] /feɪt/ *n Fr* a day of public gaiety and amusement (FESTIVAL (1)) held usu. out of doors and often to collect money for a special purpose: *Our village is holding a fete to raise money for the building of the new hall*

fete[2] *v* [T1 *usu. pass.*] to show honour to (someone) with public parties and ceremonies

fet·id /ˈfiːtɨd‖ˈfetɨd/ *adj* (esp. of water) smelling bad: *the fetid breath of a wild animal*

fet·ish /ˈfetɪʃ, ˈfiː-/ *n* **1** an object that is worshipped as a god by undeveloped tribal people, and thought to have magic power **2** *tech*(in PSYCHOLOGY) an object whose presence is necessary for sexual satisfaction **3 make a fetish of** to take too seriously; admire to a foolish degree: *Martha makes a fetish of her house: she's always cleaning it*

fet·ish·is·m /ˈfetɪʃɪzəm, ˈfiː-/ *n* [U] **1** the religion of FETISH (1) worshipping **2** *tech* (in PSYCHOLOGY) the practice of having a FETISH (2)

fet·ish·ist /ˈfetɪʃɨst/ *adj, n* [Wa5;C] **1** (someone) worshipping a FETISH (1): *a tribe of fetishists|a fetishist religion* **2** *tech* (in PSYCHOLOGY) (someone) with a need for a FETISH (2)

fet·lock /ˈfetlɒk‖-lɑk/ *n* the back part of a horse's leg near the foot, that has longer hairs on it than the upper part —see picture at HORSE

fet·ter[1] /ˈfetəʳ/ *n* [*usu. pl.*] **1** a chain for the foot of a prisoner **2** anything that stops one from moving or acting: *to escape from the fetters of marriage*

fetter[2] *v* [Wv5:T1 (*to*)] to bind with or as if with FETTERs: *fettered by responsibility* —compare UNFETTERED

fet·tle /ˈfetl/ *n* [U] condition; state of body and mind (in the phr. **in fine/good fettle**)

fe·tus /ˈfiːtəs/ *n* FOETUS

feud[1] /fjuːd/ *v* [IØ] (esp. of 2 families) to keep up the memory of a quarrel by violent acts: *to spend one's time feuding with the neighbours*

feud[2] *n* a state of strong dislike and/or violence which continues over some time as a result of a quarrel, usu. between 2 people, families, or CLANs: *the feud between Romeo's family and Juliet's*

feud·al /ˈfjuːdl/ *adj* **1** [Wa5;A] *law* of or relating to the system by which people held land, and received protection, in return for giving work or military help as practised in Western Europe from about the 9th to the 15th century: *the feudal system|one's feudal lord* —see also FIEF **2** *not fml* (of behaviour or a relationship) like that which existed between lords and their servants at that time: *It seems a bit feudal to call him "sir"*

feu·dal·is·m /ˈfjuːdl-ɪzəm/ *n* [U] *law* the FEUDAL (1) system

feu·da·to·ry[1] /ˈfjuːdətəri‖-tori/ *adj* [(*to*)] owing FEUDAL (1) duties to: *He is feudatory to the King*

feudatory[2] *n* a dependant under the FEUDAL system: *He is one of the King's feudatories*

fe·ver /ˈfiːvəʳ/ *n* **1** [S;U] a medical condition caused by many illnesses, in which the sufferer suddenly develops a very high temperature: *She has a very high fever.|She has 2 degrees of fever* **2** [U;C] any of a group of (states) diseases that cause this: *yellow fever* **3** [S9+*of*] an excited state (of the stated feeling): *in a fever of impatience*

fever blis·ter /ˈ·· ˌ··/ *n AmE* COLD SORE

fe·vered /ˈfiːvəd‖-ərd/ *adj* [Wa5;A] **1** (as if) suffering from fever: *fevered cheeks* **2** too excited (often in the phr. **a fevered imagination**) **3** very strong; unnatural: *fevered haste*

fever heat /ˈ·· ·/ *n* [U] **1** the temperature of the body in fever **2** a condition of high excitement

fe·ver·ish /ˈfiːvərɪʃ/ *adj* **1** having or showing a slight fever: *in a feverish condition* **2** [Wa5] caused by fever: *a feverish dream* **3** likely to cause fever: *a feverish tropical island* **4** unnaturally fast: *feverish work*

fe·ver·ish·ly /ˈfiːvərɪʃli/ *adv* very fast and in a state of high excitement: *working feverishly to finish the job*

fever pitch /ˈ·· ·/ *n* **at/to fever pitch** at/to a high degree of excitement: *Our excitement rose to fever pitch as the great day came near*

few /fjuː/ *determiner, pron, n* **1** [Wa1;GU] (*of plurals; used, without* a *or* only, *to show the smallness of the number*) not many; not enough: *So few (people) came.|I have very few (chocolates) left.|Few of the children are tired.|There are so few that I can't give you one* (compare *There is so little . . .*).|*I have so few chances to enjoy myself* (compare *I have so little time . . .*).|*no fewer than 1000 cars|Which of you has the fewest mistakes?|"as few words as possible"* (SEU S.)|*too few machines* —compare PLENTY[2], LITTLE[3] (1) **2** [Wa5;GC] (*of plurals; used with* a) a small number, but at least some: *a few eggs and a little milk|There are only a very few left.|I'm keeping the few that remain for tomorrow.|Let's invite a few friends to come with us.|Here are a few more chocolates.|Can you stay a few days longer?|John was among the few who really understood it.|the last few years|"I may be a few minutes late"* (SEU S.) —compare LITTLE[3] (2) **3 be few** *fml* to be only a small number: *We are many and they are few* **4 few and far between** rare; not happening often: *Holidays are few and far between* **5 quite a few** also **a good few,** (*fml*) **not a few**— several; more than a few: *There were quite a few of us there.|You'll have to wait a good few weeks* **6 some few** a certain number; some (of) **7 the few** the small number of people with special needs or desires; the MINORITY: *Only the few are likely to enjoy this music*

USAGE *Only a* **few** (FEW (2)) and *only a* **little** (LITTLE[3] (2)) are commoner than FEW (1), LITTLE[3] (1) to express the idea of too small a number or amount: *Only a* **few** *of the children can read.|I understood only a* **little** *of his speech. Not much* and *not many* express the same idea. —see LESS (USAGE)

fey /feɪ/ *adj derog* (of a person or his behaviour, used esp. of women) silly in a sensitive artistic way; not practical

fez /fez/ *n* **fezzes** *or* **fezes** a kind of round red hat with a flat top and no BRIM, worn by some Muslim men

ff. *written abbrev. for*: **1** and the following (pages, VERSEs, etc.): *See pages 17ff.* **2** FOLIOs (4)

fi·an·cé /fiˈɒnseɪ‖ˌfiɑnˈseɪ/ (*fem* **fiancée** *same pronunciation*)— *n Fr* a man to whom a woman is ENGAGED (=whom she has promised to marry): *George is my fiancé.|Martha is my fiancée*

fi·as·co /fiˈæskəʊ/ *n* **-cos** (*AmE* **-coes**) [C;U] the complete failure of something planned: *The party was a total fiasco/ended in fiasco*

fi·at /ˈfaɪæt, ˈfiːæt‖-ət/ *n* [C,C5c] *Lat, fml* an order by a ruler

fib[1] /fɪb/ *n not fml* a small unimportant lie: *to tell fibs*

fib[2] *v* **-bb-** [IØ] to tell FIBs[1] —**~ber** *n* [C; *you*+N]: *You fibber!*

fi·bre, *AmE* **-ber** /ˈfaɪbəʳ/ *n* **1** [C] one of the thin thread-like parts that form many animal and plant growths such as wool, wood, or muscle. Some plant fibres are SPUN (SPIN) and woven into cloth **2** [U] a mass of these, used for making cloth, rope, etc.: *cotton fibre* **3** [C] a (type of) thread made chemically to serve the same purposes in weaving: *Nylon is a man-made fibre* **4** [U9] (of mind or morals) **a** quality: *a man of coarse fibre* **b** strength: *He lacks moral fibre*

fi·bre·board, *AmE* **-ber-** /ˈfaɪbəbɔːd‖-bərbord/ *n* [U] board made of wood FIBRE*s* pressed together

fi·bre·glass, *AmE* **-ber-** /ˈfaɪbəglɑːs‖-bərglæs/ *n* [U] material made from glass FIBRE*s*. It is used esp. for building light boats and for keeping out the cold, and its most modern use is for furnishing materials

fi·bro·si·tis /ˌfaɪbrəˈsaɪtɨs/ *n* [U] a painful RHEUMATIC disorder of the muscles

fi·brous /ˈfaɪbrəs/ *adj* like or made of FIBRE*s*: *a fruit with a fibrous shell*

fib·u·la /ˈfɪbjʊlə‖-jə-/ *n* **1** *med* the outer of the 2 bones in the lower leg —see picture at SKELETON **2** a type of ornamental pin worn by the ancient Greeks and Romans

fi·chu /ˈfiːʃuː/ *n Fr* a piece of thin cloth which women (esp. in former times) wore round the neck and over the chest

fick·le /ˈfɪkəl/ *adj* not loyal in love or friendship; often changing: *Cressida turned out to be fickle—she's left me* —**~ness** *n* [U]

fic·tion /ˈfɪkʃən/ *n* **1** [U] stories or NOVEL*s* about things that did not really happen, as compared to other sorts of literature like history or poetry: *a writer of fiction|works of light fiction|Truth is stranger than fiction* —compare NONFICTION **2** [S] an invention of the mind; an untrue story: *His account of the crime was a complete fiction* —see also LEGAL FICTION

fic·tion·al /ˈfɪkʃənəl/ *adj* [Wa5] belonging to FICTION (1); told as a story: *a fictional account of a journey to the moon* —compare FICTITIOUS —**~ly** *adv*

fic·tion·al·i·za·tion, -isation /ˌfɪkʃənəlaɪˈzeɪʃən‖-lə-/ *n* [S;U] the practice or a result of turning an account of true events into a story, by changing some details, introducing imaginary characters, etc.: *a fictionalization of the Battle of Gettysburg*

fic·ti·tious /fɪkˈtɪʃəs/ *adj* [Wa5] untrue; invented; not real: *His account of the crime was totally fictitious.|Hamlet was a fictitious character* —compare FICTIONAL —**~ly** *adv*

fid·dle¹ /ˈfɪdl/ *n* **1** *infml* a VIOLIN, or any musical instrument of that family: *Can you play the fiddle?* **2** *sl* a dishonest practice **3 a face as long as a fiddle** *humor* a very unhappy face (not used in cases of real sorrow): *George came in with a face as long as a fiddle and said it was raining again* **4 (as) fit as a fiddle** perfectly healthy **5 play second fiddle (to)** to play a less important part (than): *I'm tired of playing 2nd fiddle to George—why can't I run the business?*

fiddle² *v infml* **1** [I∅] to play the FIDDLE¹ (1) **2** [I∅] to FIDDLE WITH something: *Put down that pen and stop fiddling!* **3** [L9 (ABOUT, AROUND)] to move aimlessly rather than acting with a purpose; to delay: *Well, we'd better get started and stop fiddling about* **4** [T1] to prepare (accounts) dishonestly to one's own advantage: *to fiddle one's income tax*

fiddle-fad·dle /ˈfɪdl ˌfædl/ *n* [U] *infml* silly unimportant NONSENSE: *wasting time on useless fiddle-faddle*

fid·dler /ˈfɪdləʳ/ *n* **1** [C;N] *infml* someone who plays the FIDDLE¹ (1): *Fiddler, play us a tune!|He called for his fiddlers 3* (old song) **2** [C] *sl* someone who FIDDLE*s*² (4) or lives by FIDDLE*s*¹ (2)

fid·dle·sticks /ˈfɪdlˌstɪks/ *interj becoming rare* NONSENSE!; How silly!

fiddle with *v prep* [T1 (ABOUT, AROUND)] **1** to move (something) aimlessly in one's fingers: *Stop fiddling (around) with that gun. It might explode!* **2** to touch or move (something that is not one's own): *I don't want you fiddling with my bicycle —leave it alone!*

fid·dling /ˈfɪdlɪŋ/ *adj* [Wa5;A] unimportant and silly; too small: *I can't get this fiddling little key into the lock*

fi·del·i·ty /fɪˈdelɨti/ *n* [U] **1** [(*to*)] faithfulness; loyalty: *fidelity to one's leader* **2** [(*to*)] (in marriage) loyalty expressed by having a sexual relationship only with the marriage partner: *fidelity to one's wife* —see also FAITHFUL (5), compare INFIDELITY (2) **3** (of something copied or reported) truthfulness; closeness in sound, facts, colour, etc. to the original: *the fidelity of a translation/ of a sound recording* —see also HI-FI

fid·get¹ /ˈfɪdʒɨt/ *n* [C; *you*+N] *infml* someone, esp. a child, who FIDGET*s*² (1): *Sit still, you little fidget!*

fidget² *v not fml* **1** [I∅] to move one's body around restlessly, so as to annoy people: *children fidgeting in church* **2** [T1] to make (someone) nervous and restless: *Something seems to be fidgeting Martha* **3 begin/start to fidget** to become restless and impatient: *After listening for so long we started to fidget*

fid·gets /ˈfɪdʒɨts/ *n* [*the*+P] *infml* an attack of FIDGETing² (1) (in phrs. like **have/get the fidgets**)

fid·get·y /ˈfɪdʒɨti/ *adj infml* restless; FIDGETing² (1) or wanting to FIDGET: *feeling more and more fidgety*

fie /faɪ/ *interj* [(*on, upon*)] *old use or humor* (expressing disapproval or shock) Shame!: *Fie upon you!*

fief, feoff /fiːf/ *n* a piece of land held under the FEUDAL (1) system: *to hold one's fief from the King*

field¹ /fiːld/ *n* **1** [C] a stretch of land on a farm marked off in some way or surrounded by a fence or wall, and used for animals or crops: *fields of corn|a field full of sheep* **2** [C9] (*usu. in comb.*) any open area where **a** the stated game is played: *a football field* **b** the stated substance is MINED: *an oilfield* **c** the stated activity is practised: *an airfield|a battlefield|field of battle* **d** the surface is of the stated kind: *a snowfield|field of snow* **3** [C9] a branch of knowledge or activity: *a lawyer famous in his own field|the field of politics/art/Greek history|That's outside my field* (=not my special subject).|*Rare coins are an interesting field for/of study* **4** [*the*+R] the place where practical operations happen, as compared to places where they are planned or studied, such as offices, factories, and universities: *studying tribal languages in the field* —see also FIELD-TEST, FIELDWORK (1) **5** [C9] (in PHYSICS) the area in which the (stated) force is felt: *the moon's* GRAVITATIONal *field* **6** [*the*+GU] (in cricket or BASEBALL) the team that are FIELDing² (1) **7** [(*the*) GU] (in foxhunting) all the people taking part in a hunt: *The rest of the field was/were far behind me.|We get a large field on Saturdays* **8** [*the*+GC] (in horseracing) all the horses in the race except the FAVOURITE (=the one that is expected to win) **9** [C] the part on the surface of a coin or flag that is not the pattern: *a flag showing a red lion on a white field* **10 hold the field (against)** to remain unconquered (by) **11 take the field** to go to war

field² *v* **1** [I∅;T1] (in cricket and BASEBALL) to catch or stop (a ball that has been hit): *He fielded the ball.|OH, well fielded!* **2** [I∅] to be (a member of) the team whose turn it is to do this because they are not BATting: *We'll be fielding in the afternoon* **3** [T1] to put into operation; produce (an army, team, etc.): *The school fields 2 football teams*

field day /ˈ· ·/ *n* **1** a day of army training, on which soldiers give a public show of military skill **2** (*esp. AmE*) a sports day at a school or college **3** a time of unusually pleasant and exciting action: *The newspapers will really have a field day with this story!*

field·er /ˈfiːldəʳ/ also **fields·man** /ˈfiːldzmən/— *n* (in cricket or BASEBALL) any of the players whose business it is to FIELD[2] (2) the ball

field e·vent /ˈ· ·ˌ·/ *n* a competitive sports event, such as weight-throwing or jumping, that is not a race

field glass·es /ˈ· ˌ··/ *n* [P] large **BINOCULARS**; a hand-held instrument for looking at distant objects, usu. out of doors. It consists of 2 small TELESCOPE*s* on a single frame: *These field glasses are broken* —see PAIR (USAGE)

field gun /ˈ· ·/ *n* a light gun with wheels

field hand /ˈ· ·/ *n AmE* an outdoor farm worker

field hock·ey /ˈ· ˌ··/ also (*esp. BrE*) **hockey**— *n esp. AmE* a game played by 2 teams of 11 players each, on a field, with sticks and a ball —compare ICE HOCKEY, see HOCKEY (USAGE)

field hos·pi·tal /ˈ· ˌ···/ *n* a military hospital on or near the field of battle, that gives quick treatment to the wounded

field mar·shal /ˈ· ˌ··/ *n* [C;N] (*often cap. as part of a title*) the officer of highest rank in the British army: *Field Marshal Montgomery*

field mouse /ˈ· ·/ *n* any of various kinds of mice that live in the fields

field of·fi·cer /ˈ· ˌ···/ *n* an officer of the rank of COLONEL, LIEUTENANT COLONEL, or MAJOR

field of vi·sion /ˌ· · ˈ··/ *n* **fields of vision** the whole space within seeing distance; all that can be seen: *Our field of vision was limited by the tall buildings in front*

field-test /ˈ· ·/ *v* [T1] to try (something) out in the FIELD[1] (4): *The apparatus has all been field-tested in tropical conditions* —**field test** *n*

field·work /ˈfiːldwɜːk‖-ɜrk/ *n* **1** [U] scientific or social study done in the FIELD[1] (4), such as measuring and examining things or asking people questions: *doing fieldwork|one of our fieldworkers* **2** [C] a rough fort made quickly by soldiers

fiend /fiːnd/ *n* **1** [C] a devil or evil spirit **2** [C; *you*+N] a very wicked person: *You fiend! Have you no mercy?* **3** [C9] someone very keen on (the stated object of desire, or way of spending time): *a fresh air fiend|a drug fiend*

Fiend *n* [*the*+R] (a title given to) SATAN

fiend·ish /ˈfiːndɪʃ/ *adj* **1** fierce and cruel: *treated them with fiendish cruelty|to have a fiendish temper* **2** *not fml* **a** (of behaviour) very clever; not plain or simple: *a fiendish plan* **b** (of difficulty or cleverness) very great: *the fiendish difficulty of the job* —**~ness** *n* [U]

fiend·ish·ly /ˈfiːndɪʃli/ *adv not fml* (esp. with adjectives of difficulty or cleverness) very: *a fiendishly clever plan*

fierce /fɪəs‖fɪərs/ *adj* [Wa1] **1** angry, violent, and cruel: *a fierce dog to guard the house|He made a fierce speech, urging them to fight.|That tiger looks very fierce!* **2** (of heat, strong feelings, etc.) very great: *fierce anger|the fierce heat of the tropical sun* —**~ly** *adv* —**~ness** *n* [U]

fi·er·y /ˈfaɪəri/ *adj* [Wa1] **1** flaming and violent; looking like fire: *fiery red hair* **2** quickly moved to anger or violent action: *a fiery temper|the fiery spirits of the young soldiers*

fi·es·ta /fiˈestə/ *n Sp* (esp. in the ROMAN CATHOLIC countries of Southern Europe and South America) a religious holiday with public pleasure-making

fife /faɪf/ *n* a small musical pipe with high notes. It is played in military bands, often with drums

fif·teen /fɪfˈtiːn◂/ *determiner, n, pron* [see NUMBER TABLE 1] (the number) 15 —**~th** *determiner, n, pron, adv* [see NUMBER TABLE 3]

fifth /fɪfθ, fɪftθ/ *determiner, n, pron, adv* [see NUMBER TABLE 3] 5th

fifth col·umn /ˌ· ˈ··/ *n* a group of people who are secretly sympathetic to the enemies of the country they live in, and work to help them during a war —**~ist** *n*

fif·ty /ˈfɪfti/ *determiner, n, pron* [see NUMBER TABLE 1] (the number) 50 —**-tieth** *determiner, n, pron, adv* [see NUMBER TABLE 3]

fifty-fif·ty /ˌ·· ˈ··◂/ *adj, adv* [A;(F)] (of shares or chances) equal(ly): *Let's go fifty-fifty.|We divided it up fifty-fifty/on a fifty-fifty* BASIS.*|It's fifty-fifty that he won't succeed*

fig[1] /fɪg/ *n* **1** a soft sweet fruit with many small seeds, growing chiefly in warm countries. It is often eaten dried —see picture at BERRY **2** also **fig tree**— the broad-leaved tree that bears this fruit **3 not to care/give a fig (for)** *not fml* not to care at all (for): *I don't care a fig (for) what you think!*

fig. *written abbrev. for:* **1** FIGURE[1] (6) **2** (of an example phrase or sentence after a *def.* in this dictionary) FIGURATIVE; showing how the word that is being explained can be used, with the same meaning as in the *def.*, when speaking of ideas or events rather than solid things. The sentence *"He ploughed through the dull book to the end"* shows a fig. use of PLOUGH[2] in the meaning "to force a way or make a track".

fight[1] /faɪt/ *v* **fought** /fɔːt/ **1** [I∅ (*against, with*);T1] to use violence against (esp. others of one's kind) as in a battle: *Paul and Charles fought (on the same side in the war).|Britain fought against/with the US in the War of Independence; the Americans were fighting for/fighting to gain their freedom.|I can fight any man here!* **2** [I∅] (with pl. subject) to use violence against each other: *Paul and Charles are fighting over Mary/over who is to marry Mary.|"The lion and the* UNICORN *were fighting for the crown"* (old song) **3** [I∅, T1] to use argument against (someone, or each other): *He and his wife are always fighting* **4** [T1] to take part in (a war, battle, etc.): *to fight a* DUEL **5** to try to prevent; stand against: *to fight a fire/a disease* **6 fight one's way** to move along by fighting or pushing: *He fought his way through the crowd/the bushes* **7 fight shy of** *not fml* to avoid getting mixed up in: *I rather fought shy of telling her the truth* **8 fight to a finish** to fight until one side is completely defeated

fight[2] *n* **1** [C] a battle; an occasion of fighting: *to have a fight|to join in the fight|*(fig.) *the fight against dirt and disease* **2** [U] also **fighting spir·it** /ˌ·· ˈ··/— the power or desire to fight: *There's not much fight left in him now.|The news of the defeat took all the fight out of us* **3** [C] a BOXing match **4 put up a good/poor fight** to fight well/badly **5 show fight** to show that one is ready to fight —see also FREE FIGHT

fight back *v adv* [I∅] to defend oneself by fighting

fight·er /ˈfaɪtəʳ/ *n* **1** someone who fights, in battle or for sport; a soldier or BOXer **2** also **fighter plane** /ˈ·· ·/— a small fast aircraft that can destroy enemy aircraft in the air —compare BOMBER (1)

fighter pi·lot /ˈ·· ˌ··/ *n* someone who works the controls of a FIGHTER (2)

fighting chance /ˌ·· ˈ·/ *n* [C,C5] a small but real chance if great effort is made: *There's just a fighting chance that we'll be able to escape*

fight off *v adv* [T1] to keep (something) away with an effort: *to fight off a cold/the competition*

fight on *v adv* [I∅] to continue fighting

fight out *v adv* [T1b] to settle (a disagreement) by fighting (esp. in the phr. **fight it out**)
fig leaf /ˈ· ·/ *n* the leaf of the FIG TREE, shown as covering the sex organs in art
fig·ment /ˈfɪgmənt/ *n* something believed but not real (in the phr. **a figment of one's imagination**)
fig tree /ˈ· ·/ *n* FIG[1] (2)
fig·u·ra·tive /ˈfɪgjʊrətɪv, -gə-‖-gjə-, -gə-/ *adj* (of words) used in some way other than the ordinary meaning, to make a word picture or comparison: *"A sweet temper" is a figurative expression, but "sweet coffee" is not* —compare LITERAL[1] (3) —**~ly** *adv*
fig·ure[1] /ˈfɪgəʳ‖ˈfɪgjər/ *n* **1** [C] (the shape of) a whole human body, as shown in art or seen in reality: *a group of figures on the left of the picture* —see BODY (USAGE) **2** [C] the human shape, considered from the point of view of being attractively thin: *doing exercises to improve one's figure* **3** [C9] an important person (of the stated kind): *Mahatma Gandhi was both a political and a religious figure in Indian history* **4** [C] any of the number signs from 0 to 9: *Write the number in words and in figures* —see also -FIGURE, FIGURES (1) **5** [C9] a (stated) price: *to sell the house at a low figure* **6** [A] (used before the number of a map, drawing, etc. in a book): *Figure 10 shows the place where the body was found* **7** [C] a line drawing such as a square, circle, or DIAGRAM, used in study or for explaining something **8** [C] a division or set of movements in a dance **9 a fine figure of a man/woman** a tall, strong-looking and well-shaped person **10 cut quite a figure** also **cut a fine/good figure**— to produce a good effect; have a good appearance **11 cut a poor/sorry figure** to produce a foolish effect; have a shameful appearance
figure[2] *v* **1** [L9 (*as, in*)] to take part: *Roger figured as chief guest at the party* **2** [D1;T5a,b] *AmE not fml* to consider; believe: *I figured (that) you'd want your tea.|"Will it explode?" "John figures not"* **3** [IØ] *infml, becoming rare* to do sums: *She learnt to read and write and figure* **4 That figures!** *not fml* That seems reasonable and what I expected
-figure *comb. form* [*determiner→adj* [A]] being an amount with the stated number of DIGITs (esp. in the phrs. **3-/4-/5-/6-figure**): *a 5-figure income* (=an income of between £9,999 and £100,000) —see also FIGURES
fig·ured /ˈfɪgəd‖ˈfɪgjərd/ *adj* [Wa5;A] ornamented with a small pattern: *a dress of figured silk*
figured bass /ˌ·· ˈ·/ CONTINUO
fig·ure·head /ˈfɪgəhed‖ˈfɪgjər-/ *n* **1** an ornament formerly placed at the front of a ship, often in the shape of a person **2** someone who is the head or chief in name only
figure in *v adv* [T1] *AmE* to include (in a sum): *Have you figured in the cost of the hotel?*
figure of eight /ˌ·· · ˈ·/ also (*AmE*) **figure eight** /ˌ·· ˈ·/— *n* anything of the shape of an 8, such as a knot or stitch, or a pattern made by a moving SKATER on the ice
figure of speech /ˌ·· · ˈ·/ *n* an example of the FIGURATIVE use of words: *I didn't really mean my partner is a snake, it was just a figure of speech*
figure on *v prep* [T1,4a;V4a] *esp. AmE* to plan on; include in one's plans: *I'm figuring on (getting) a £6 pay increase.|I figured on him leaving at 6.0*
figure out *v adv* [T1,6a,b] *esp. AmE* to work out; understand by thinking: *I can't figure him out—he's a mystery!|We must figure out how to do it/what's the matter*
fig·ures /ˈfɪgəz‖ˈfɪgjərz/ *n* **1** [P9] an amount with the stated number of DIGITs (esp. in the phrs. **3/4/5/6 figures**): *She's very rich: her pay runs into 5 figures* (=she earns between £9,999 and £100,000) **2** [P] sums: *What's 4 times 17? I'm no good at figures*
fig·u·rine /ˌfɪgjʊˈriːn, ˈfɪgjʊriːn‖ˌfɪgjəˈriːn/ *n* a small ornamental human figure made of baked clay, cut stone, etc.
fil·a·ment /ˈfɪləmənt/ *n* a thin thread, such as that inside an electric light BULB: *spun glass/nylon filaments* —see picture at ELECTRICITY
fil·bert /ˈfɪlbət‖-ərt/ *n* **1** a type of small nut (the European HAZEL) that can be eaten **2** the tree on which this grows
filch /fɪltʃ/ *v* [T1] to steal secretly (something of small value)
file[1] /faɪl/ *n* a steel tool with a rough face, used for rubbing down, smoothing, or cutting through hard surfaces —see picture at TOOL[1]
file[2] *v* **1** [T1] to use a FILE[1] on: *to file one's nails* **2** [X9] to put into the stated condition by rubbing or cutting with a FILE[1]: *to file the wood smooth|to file through the bars|They file their teeth to sharp points*
file[3] *v* [T1] **1** [(*away*)] to put (papers or letters) in a FILE[4]: *Please file this letter (away), Mrs Jellaby* **2** *law* to send in or record officially: *to file an* APPLICATION
file[4] *n* **1** any of various arrangements of drawers, shelves, boxes, or cases, usu. fitted with wires or metal rods, for storing papers in an office —see FILING CABINET **2** [(*on*)] a collection of papers on one subject, stored in this way: *Here's our file on the Middle East.|to read one's own personal file* (the one that someone else keeps to record one's activities, judge one's behaviour, etc.) **3 keep/have a file on** to collect/store information about **4 on file a** stored in a file **b** recorded in this way
file[5] *n* [GC] a line of people one behind the other (often in the phr. **in single file**) —compare RANK AND FILE
file[6] *v* [L9] to march in single FILE[5]: *They filed slowly past the grave of their leader*
file down *v adv* [T1] to make shorter, lower, etc. with a FILE[1]
fil·et /ˈfɪlɨt, ˈfɪleɪ, fɪˈleɪ/ *AmE* FILLET[1] (2)
fi·li·al /ˈfɪlɪəl/ *adj* of or suitable to a son or daughter: *filial love*
filial pi·e·ty /ˌ··· ˈ···/ *n* [U] *fml* a son's or daughter's obedience to and respect for parents
fil·i·bus·ter[1] /ˈfɪlɨbʌstəʳ/ *n AmE* **1** [C] someone who starts a private war in a foreign country; esp. a North American in the 19th century who tried to persuade the people of South America to rise against their governments, without permission from his own **2** [C;U] (a case of) FILIBUSTERing[2] (2): *to hold up government business, by filibuster*
filibuster[2] *v* [IØ] *AmE* **1** to be a FILIBUSTER[1] (1) **2** to try to delay or prevent action in a parliament or other lawmaking body, by being very slow and making long speeches
fil·i·gree /ˈfɪlɨgriː/ *n* [U] delicate ornamental wire work: *silver filigree jewellery*
filing cab·i·net /ˈ·· ˌ···/ *n* a piece of office furniture with drawers, for storing papers in
filing clerk /ˈ·· ·/ *n* someone whose work is to FILE[3] (1) papers
fil·ings /ˈfaɪlɪŋz/ *n* [P] very small sharp bits that have been rubbed off a metal surface with a FILE[1]: *iron filings*
fill[1] /fɪl/ *v* **1** [IØ;T1;(D1): (*with*)] to make or become full: *to fill the bath with water|The house soon filled (with children).|Please fill (me) this cup with sugar.|(fig.) Laughter filled the room.|The thought fills me with pleasure* **2** [T1] to (cause to) enter (a position): *The office of President remained unfilled.|John's the best person to fill this* VACANCY **3** [T1] to put a FILLING into (a tooth) **4** [T1] to fulfil; meet the needs or demands of: *Can you fill*

this PRESCRIPTION, *please?* **5 fill a gap** to supply something needed **6 fill the bill** *infml* to be exactly suitable: *"I'm thirsty." "Would a glass of cold beer fill the bill?"* —see also FILL IN, FILL OUT, FILL UP

fill² *n* **1** a full supply; the quantity needed to fill something: *another fill of petrol* **2** PIPE¹ (2b) **3 one's fill a** as much as one can eat or drink: *to drink one's fill* **b** as much as one can bear: *I've had my fill of John for one evening!*

fill·er /ˈfɪləʳ/ *n* [S;U] **1** a substance that is added to another, to increase the size or weight **2** material used for filling cracks in wood before painting

fil·let¹ /ˈfɪl̥ɪt, ˈfɪleɪ, fɪˈleɪ/ *n* **1** (esp. in former times) a narrow band worn round the head, as an ornament or to keep the hair tidy **2** also *AmE* **filet**— a piece of fish or meat for eating, with the bones removed: *a fillet* STEAK|*fillets of* SOLE

fillet² *v* [T1] to remove the bones from (a piece of fish or meat); cut into FILLETS¹ (2): *filleted* SOLE

fill-in /ˈ· ·/ *n not fml* someone or something that FILLS IN (3): *I'm only here as a fill-in while Robert's away*

fill in *v adv* **1** [T1] **a** to put in (whatever is needed to complete something): *You draw the people and I'll fill in the sky.*|*Fill in your name on this cheque* **b** also (*esp. AmE*) **fill out,** (*esp. BrE nonstandard*) **fill up**— to complete (something) by putting in whatever is needed: *to fill in one's income tax* FORM¹ (9) **2** [T1(*on*)] *not fml* to supply the most recent information to: *Please fill me in on what happened at the meeting* **3** [IØ (*for*)] to take someone's place: *Can you fill in for Steve tonight as he's ill?* **4** [T1] to use up (unwanted time): *to fill in the afternoon*

fill·ing /ˈfɪlɪŋ/ *n* **1** (in DENTISTRY) **a** an act of putting material into a hole to preserve a tooth: *Mr Jones is doing some fillings* **b** (the material in) a hole in a tooth that is filled in this way: *You've got a lot of fillings* **2** a food mixture folded inside pastry, SANDWICHes, etc.

filling sta·tion /ˈ·· ˌ··/ also **service station,** (*BrE*) **petrol station,** (*AmE*) **gas station**— *n* a place (GARAGE) that sells petrol and oil and repairs motor vehicles

USAGE Some people use **filling station** for a place that supplies petrol and oil for motor vehicles, and **service station** for one that also repairs them: *They won't mend the tyre here—it's just a* **filling station**

fil·lip /ˈfɪl̥ɪp/ *n* **1** (a light blow given by) bending one's finger against one's thumb and letting it go suddenly **2** *not fml* an encouragement; something that increases attraction and interest

fill out *v adv* **1** [IØ] *not fml* to get fatter: *Her face is beginning to fill out* **2** [T1] *esp. AmE* FILL IN (1b) **3** [T1] *esp. AmE* to complete in time: *Mrs Young offered to fill out her late husband's last few months as chairman*

fill up *v adv* **1** [IØ;T1] to make or become completely full: *The room soon filled up with people* **2** [T1] *esp. BrE nonstandard* FILL IN (1b)

fil·ly /ˈfɪli/ *n* a young female horse —compare COLT

film¹ /fɪlm/ *n* **1** [S;U] a thin skin of any material: *a sheet of plastic film*|*a film of dust/oil on the surface of the water* **2** [C;U] (a roll of) the prepared substance on which one takes photographs or makes cinema pictures: *to buy a faster film for my camera* —see picture at PHOTOGRAPHIC **3** [C] *esp. BrE* a cinema picture: *to* SHOOT (=make) *a film*|*Have you seen any good films lately?*

film² *v* **1** [IØ;T1] to make a cinema picture (of): *We'll be filming all day tomorrow.*|*to film the Queen's arrival in Paris* **2** [L9] to be the subject of a cinema picture: *The Queen's arrival ought to film beautifully*

fil·ma·ble /ˈfɪlməbəl/ *adj* suitable to be FILMed² (1): *a very filmable face!*

film o·ver *v adv* [IØ] to become dull, as if covered with a FILM¹ (1)

film prem·i·ère /ˈ· ˌ···/ *n* the first performance of a new cinema film

film star /ˈ· ·/ *AmE* also **movie star**— *n* a well-known actor or actress in cinema pictures

film stock /ˈ· ·/ *n* [U] cinema FILM¹ (2) that has not yet been used

film·strip /ˈfɪlmˌstrɪp/ *n* [C;U] (a length of) photographic film by means of which photographs, drawings, etc., can be shown (PROJECTed) separately one after the other as still pictures: *a filmstrip on the life of the ant*

film test /ˈ· ·/ *n* a photographic test to find out whether someone is suitable as a cinema actor

film·y /ˈfɪlmi/ *adj* [Wa1] (esp. of cloth) so fine and thin that one can see through it: *filmy mists*|*a filmy silk dress* —**filminess** *n* [U]

fil·ter¹ /ˈfɪltəʳ/ *n* **1** an apparatus containing paper, sand, etc., through which liquids can be passed so as to make them clean: *the oil filter in a car* —see picture at LABORATORY **2** a (coloured) glass that reduces the quantity or changes the quality of the light admitted into a camera or TELESCOPE

filter² *v* **1** [T1] to send through a FILTER: *to filter the drinking water*|*to filter the light* **2** [L9] **a** (of a group) to move slowly: *People came filtering out of the cinema* **b** (of an idea) to become gradually known: *The news filtered through to everyone in the office* **3** [IØ] (of traffic in Britain) to turn left, when traffic going right or straight ahead must wait until a red light changes to green

filter out *v adv* [T1] to remove (solids or light) by means of a FILTER¹: *to filter out the dirt/the blue light*

filter tip /ˈ·· ·/ *n* **1** a FILTER¹ on the end of a cigarette **2** a cigarette made in this way: *I only smoke filter-tips* —**filter-tipped** /ˌ·· ˈ·◂/ *adj* [Wa5]: *filter-tipped cigarettes*

filth /fɪlθ/ *n* [U] **1** very nasty dirt: *Go and wash that filth off your hands* **2** words, curses, etc., that are **a** very rude: *He shouted a lot of filth at the other driver* **b** thought very unpleasant in a sexual way: *I don't know how you can read such filth*

filth·y /ˈfɪlθi/ *adj* [Wa1] **1** very dirty: covered with FILTH (1): *your filthy boots* **2** showing or containing FILTH (2) —**filthily** /ˈfɪlθl̥li/ *adv* —**filthiness** *n* [U]

filthy lu·cre /ˌ·· ˈ··/ *n* [U] *pomp* money

fin /fɪn/ *n* **1** any of the winglike parts that a fish uses in swimming —see picture at FISH¹ **2** a part shaped like this, on a man-made object such as a car, aircraft, or bomb —see picture at AIRCRAFT

fi·na·ble, fineable /ˈfaɪnəbəl/ *adj* [Wa5] (of an action) for which one must pay a FINE¹ (1): *a finable offence*

fi·nal¹ /ˈfaɪnəl/ *adj* [Wa5] **1** [A] last; coming at the end: *Z is the final letter in the alphabet.*|*a final cup of coffee before we left* **2** [B] (of a decision, offer, etc.) that cannot be changed: *I won't go, and that's final!*|*Is that your final offer?*

final² *n* **1** [*often pl.*] the last and most important in a set of matches: *the tennis finals* **2** the last EDITION of a daily newspaper: *Late Night final!* (shouted by newspaper sellers) **3** [*usu. pl.*] the last and most important examination in a college course: *When do you take your finals?*

fi·na·le /fɪˈnɑːli‖fɪˈnæli/ *n It* the last division of a piece of music

fi·nal·ist /ˈfaɪnəl-l̥st/ *n* one of the people left in the FINAL² (1), after the others have been defeated

fi·nal·i·ty /faɪˈnæll̥ti/ *n* [U] the quality of being or seeming FINAL¹ (2): *"No!" he said with finality*

fi·nal·ize, -ise /ˈfaɪnəl-aɪz/ *v* [T1] to finish (plans, arrangements, etc.); make FINAL¹ (2)

fi·nal·ly /ˈfaɪnəli/ *adv* **1** at last: *They talked about it for hours. Finally, they decided not to go.|We were finally married in the mosque* **2** so as not to allow further change: *It's not finally settled yet*

fi·nance[1] /ˈfaɪnæns, fɨ̵ˈnæns‖fɨ̵ˈnæns, ˈfaɪnæns/ *n* [U] (the science of) the control of (esp. public) money

finance[2] /faɪˈnæns, fɨ̵-‖ˈfaɪnæns, fɨ̵ˈnæns/ *v* [T1] *fml* to provide money for: *Who finances this organization?*

fi·nanc·es /ˈfaɪnænsɨ̵z, fɨ̵ˈnænsɨ̵z‖fɨ̵ˈnænsɨ̵z, ˈfaɪnænsɨ̵z/ *n* [P] the amount of money owned by esp. a government or business: *the present state of the country's finances*

fi·nan·cial /fɨ̵ˈnænʃəl, faɪ-/ *adj* [Wa5] connected with money: *The City of London is a great financial centre.|Mr Briggs is our financial advisor*

fi·nan·cial·ly /fɨ̵ˈnænʃəli, faɪ-/ *adv* as regards money: *Financially, we are doing quite well*

financial year /·,·· ˈ·/ *n* the yearly period over which accounts are calculated: *to pay one's taxes at the end of the financial year*

fi·nan·cier /fɨ̵ˈnænsɪəʳ, faɪˈnæn-‖ˌfɨ̵nənˈsɪər/ *n* someone who controls or lends large sums of money

finch /fɪntʃ/ *n* (*often in comb.*) any of many kinds of small singing birds with strong beaks, such as the CHAFFINCH, that eats seeds

find[1] /faɪnd/ *v* **found** /faʊnd/ **1** [Wv6;T1;D1 (*for*),6a;V4] to discover, esp. by searching; get (someone or something that was hidden or lost): *I can't find my boots!|They found him somewhere to live/found somewhere for him to live.|Try to find him what he wants.|They found the lost child (hiding) (in the cave.)|We've found oil under the North Sea.|They searched, but found nothing/didn't find anything.|Where were the jewels found?* **2** [T1,5a,6a,b: (OUT)] to learn or discover (a fact that was not known): *to find the answer to a question|Please find (out) what time they're coming.|I must find who to ask.|I find (that) I have plenty of time now* —compare FIND OUT (1) **3** [Wv6;X (to be)1,7,9] to discover (someone or something) to be, by chance or experience: *When we arrived, we found him in bed.|I found myself (to be) in a dark forest.|We went to her house but we found her out* (=not at home).*|I find it difficult to believe you.|He was found dead in the morning.|They found her a sensible woman* **4** [T1] (of things) to reach; arrive at: *The bullet found its mark.|The water will soon find its own level* **5** [Wv6; T1] to obtain by effort: *How ever do you find the time to make cakes?|I'm going to Bermuda if I can find the money.|At last she found the courage to tell him* **6** [Wv6;V4;X9 *usu. pass.*] to know that (something) exists or happens (in phr. like **be found, one/you find**(**s**)): *Elephants are found in Africa.|You won't find many students learning Latin now* **7** [Wv6;X7,9] *law* to decide (someone) to be: *"How do you find him?" "We find him guilty."|"Not guilty, my lord"* —compare FIND FOR **8** [Wv6;T1,5; X1] *law* to agree on and state; agree that someone or something is: *They found it murder.|They found that he had been murdered.|Have they found their* VERDICT *yet?* **9** [T1] to provide: *Do the men find their own tools, or is their employer responsible?* —compare FIND IN **10 all found** with food, shelter, etc., provided as well as wages: *The cook gets £30 a week and all found* **11 find it in one's heart/in oneself to** [*nonassertive usu. with* can *or* could] to be so cruel as to: *How can you find it in your heart to disappoint the children?* **12 find oneself** to discover one's own wishes, ability, and character: *He's been in the job a year and he's just beginning to find himself* **13 find one's tongue/voice** to be no longer afraid to speak or express an opinion **14 take (something or someone) as one finds (it or him)** to accept (something or someone) for what (it or he) is: *We always eat in the kitchen—you'll have to take us as you find us!* —see also **find** EXPRESSION[1] (7), **find** FAULT[1] (7), **find** FAVOUR[1] (8), **find** WANTING[1] (2)

find[2] *n* [C9] something good or valuable that is found: *This little restaurant is quite a find/is a real find. I didn't know it existed!*

find·er /ˈfaɪndəʳ/ *n* **1** [C9] someone who finds something: *to reward the finders of the lost jewels* **2 finders keepers** also **finding's keeping**— (said when one wishes to keep someone else's lost possession, picked up by chance)

-finder *comb. form* [*n*→*n*] **1** someone who can find the stated thing: *a* PATHFINDER **2** an instrument for finding the stated thing: *a* VIEWFINDER

fin de si·è·cle /ˌfæn də ˈsjeklə (*Fr* fɛ̃ də sjɛkl)/ *adj* [Wa5;A] *Fr* of, relating to, or typical of, the end of the 19th century

find for *v prep* [T1 *no pass.*] *law* to give judgement in favour of (someone): *The judge found for the* ACCUSED —compare FIND[1] (7)

find in *v prep* [D1] to provide (someone) with (money or other needs): *It is the employer's duty to find them in clothes* —compare FIND[1] (9)

find·ing /ˈfaɪndɪŋ/ *n* [*often pl.*] **1** *law* a decision made by a judge or JURY **2** something learnt as the result of an official enquiry: *the findings of the committee on child care*

find out *v adv* **1** [IØ;T1] to learn or discover (a fact that was hidden): *I won't tell you—you must find out for yourself!* —compare FIND[1] (2) **2** [T1] to discover (someone) in a dishonest act: *I've found you out at last, you cheat!* **3** [T1] *esp. AmE* to search for (someone): *to find out one's relatives in the US*

fine[1] /faɪn/ *n* an amount of money paid as a punishment: *to pay a £5 fine*

fine[2] *v* [D1;T1] to take money from as a punishment: *They fined him heavily.|He was fined £200*

fine[3] *adj* [Wa1] **1** [A] beautiful and of high quality; better than most of its kind: *a fine house/woman/wine/view|I've never seen a finer animal.|He's a very fine musician.|"Fine feathers don't make fine birds"* (old saying) **2** [B] **a** very thin: *fine hair/thread/silk|a pencil with a fine point* **b** in very small grains or bits: *fine sugar/dust* —opposite **coarse** **3** [B] (of weather) bright and sunny; not wet: *It's turned out fine again.|a fine summer morning* **4** [Wa5;F] *not fml* (of a person or conditions) healthy and comfortable: *"How's your wife?" "She's fine, thank you."|This flat's fine for 2 people, but not more* **5** [A] delicate; to be understood only with an effort: *I missed some of the finer points in the argument* **6** [B] (of work) delicate and careful; on a small SCALE: *fine sewing|the finest workmanship* **7** [B] (of metals) pure and unmixed: *fine gold* **8** [B] (of words) too grand and perhaps not true: *We've had enough of your fine speeches!|That's all very fine, but what about me?* **9** [B] (of behaviour) noble: *a man of the finest courage* **10** [A] *not fml* terrible: *That's a fine thing to say!|Your shoes will be in a fine state if you walk in the mud* **11 one of these fine days** *not fml* at some time or other in the future: *Martha will be getting married one of these fine days, and then where will you be?* **12 not to put too fine a point on it** to express it plainly: *Not to put too fine a point on it, I disapprove of the whole thing* —**~ness** *n* [U]

fine[4] *adv* **1** so as to be very thin or in very small bits: *Cut up the vegetables very fine* **2** *not fml* very well: *It suits me fine.|The machine works fine if you oil it* **3 cut/run it fine** *not fml* to allow only just enough time and no more: *You're cutting it a bit*

fine if you want to catch the 5.30 train!
fine- *comb. form* [*adj→adj*] **1** (pulled, spun, etc.) so as to become FINE³ (2): *fine-spun|fine-drawn* **2** (speaking) in a FINE³ (8) way: *a fine-spoken gentleman*
fi·nea·ble /ˈfaɪnəbəl/ *adj* FINABLE
fine art /ˌ· ˈ·/ *n* [U] beautiful man-made objects: *a lover of fine art*
fine arts /ˌ· ˈ·/ *n* [*the*+P] those arts such as painting, music, and SCULPTURE, that are chiefly concerned with producing beautiful rather than useful things
fine down *v adv* **1** [IØ] to reduce; become thinner **2** [T1] to make (something) purer or more exact: *The worker fined the metal down.|She fined down her choice of words*
fine·ly /ˈfaɪnli/ *adv* **1** *fml* very well, esp. in a moral sense: *I think he behaved finely* **2** closely and delicately: *These instruments are very finely set* **3** (*often in comb.*) so as to be in small grains or bits: *finely-*POWDER*ed sugar|finely cut vegetables*
fine print /ˌ· ˈ·/ *n* **1** [U] very small printing: *It says it in fine print at the bottom of the page* **2** [*the*+R] something that is on purpose made difficult to understand, such as part of an agreement or CONTRACT: *It says in the fine print that we're responsible for all the repairs*
fi·ne·ry /ˈfaɪnəri/ *n* [U] gay, beautiful clothes and ornaments, perhaps too grand for the occasion: *the guests in their wedding finery*
fines herbes /ˌfiːn ˈeəb‖-ˈeərb (*Fr* finzɛrb)/ [U] *Fr* a mixture of dried and cut plants such as PARSLEY, CHIVE*s*, and TARRAGON, which is added to food during cooking, to improve the taste
fi·nesse /fə̇ˈnes/ *n* [U] *Fr* **1** delicate skill in guiding relations between people: *Paul handled the meeting with great finesse* **2** (in card games) the holding back of one's highest card because one guesses that one will be able to win the TRICK with a lower card
fine-tooth comb /ˌ· · ˈ·, ˌ· ˈ· ·/ also **toothcomb**— *n* **1** a comb with the teeth very close together, used esp. for getting insects out of one's hair **2 go over something with a fine-tooth comb** to examine (a report, contract, etc.) very carefully
fin·ger¹ /ˈfɪŋgəʳ/ *n* **1** one of the 5 movable parts with joints, at the end of each human hand (as opposed to the toes) —see picture at HUMAN² **2** one of 8 such parts (as opposed to the thumbs) **3** a measure of alcoholic drink, equal to the width of one of these parts: *2 fingers of* GIN **4** the part of a GLOVE that is made to fit one of these parts **5 be/feel all fingers and thumbs** also **one's fingers are all thumbs** (to be/feel that) one is unable to control one's hands or hold things properly: *I feel all fingers and thumbs|My fingers are all thumbs today—I really couldn't play the piano* **6 burn one's fingers/get one's fingers burnt** to suffer after a foolish act or mistake: *George got his fingers severely burnt when that firm went out of business* **7 (have) a finger in every pie** *not fml* (to have) a part in everything that is going on **8 keep one's fingers crossed** *infml* to hope for the best: *I hope the bridge will take the weight without breaking—we must just keep our fingers crossed* **9 lay a finger on** [*nonassertive*] to harm; touch, even slightly: *It's not my fault—I never laid a finger on her!* **10 lift/raise/stir a finger** [*nonassertive*] to make any effort to help when necessary: *He was the only one who lifted a finger to save the prisoners* **11 pull one's finger out** *sl* to start working hard **12 put/lay one's finger on** *not fml* to find; show (the cause of trouble): *I can't quite put my finger on what's wrong with the engine* **13 put the finger on** *sl* to tell the police about (a criminal) **14 slip through one's fingers** *not fml* to escape; get lost: *You're not going to let a chance like that slip through your fingers, are you?* **15 twist someone round one's little finger** *not fml* to make someone do what one wishes, using charm rather than force: *She can twist her father round her little finger* **16 work one's fingers to the bone** *not fml* to work very hard
USAGE Note the word order in this fixed phr. **fingers and toes**: *My fingers and toes are cold.*
finger² *v* **1** [T1] to feel or handle with one's fingers: *She fingered the rich silk* **2** [X9] to perform (a piece of music in the stated way) with the fingers: *How do you finger this piece?* **3** [T1] to mark the numbers 1–5 on (a piece of music) so as to show the FINGERING
fin·ger·board /ˈfɪŋgəbɔːd‖-gərbord/ *n* the part of a stringed instrument against which the fingers press the strings so as to vary the note
finger bowl /ˈ·· ·/ *n* a small basin in which one person can wash his sticky fingers while sitting at a meal
-fin·gered /ˈfɪŋgəd‖-ərd/ *comb. form* [*n→adj*] having the stated number or kind of fingers: *long-fingered|5-fingered*
finger hole /ˈ·· ·/ *n* **1** any of several holes in the side of a wind instrument, which are opened or closed with the fingers to vary the note **2** any of the holes on a telephone into which one puts one's fingers when DIAL*ling*
fin·ger·ing /ˈfɪŋgərɪŋ/ *n* [U] the method of using particular fingers when playing a musical instrument: *The fingering is difficult in this piece*
fin·ger·nail /ˈfɪŋgəneɪl‖-ər-/ *n* one of the hard flat pieces at the ends of the fingers —see picture at HUMAN²
finger paint·ing /ˈ·· ˌ··/ *n* **1** [U] the art of spreading paint on wet paper with the fingers: *The children do finger painting on Tuesdays* **2** [C] a picture produced in this way, often by a small child: *This finger painting is called "Mother"*
fin·ger·plate /ˈfɪŋgəpleɪt‖-ər-/ *n* a metal or glass plate that is fastened to a door near the handle or keyhole, to keep off dirty fingermarks
fin·ger·post /ˈfɪŋgəpəʊst‖-ər-/ *n* a SIGNPOST or board that points the way
fin·ger·print¹ /ˈfɪŋgəˌprɪnt‖-ər-/ *n* **1** the mark of a finger, as used in the discovery of crime —see picture at HUMAN² **2 take someone's fingerprints** to make someone press his fingers on ink and then on paper, so that the resulting marks can be studied
fingerprint² *v* [T1] to take (someone's) FINGERPRINT*s*¹ (2)
fin·ger·stall /ˈfɪŋgəstɔːl‖-ər-/ also **stall**— *n* a cover for a hurt finger
fin·ger·tip /ˈfɪŋgəˌtɪp‖-ər-/ *n* **1** [C] the end of a finger **2** [A] near and easy to reach: *fingertip information|controls* **3 have something at one's fingertips** to have a ready knowledge of something: *You'd better ask David—he's got the whole subject at his fingertips* **4 to the/one's fingertips** completely; in all ways: *British to his fingertips*
fin·i·cky /ˈfɪnɪki/ also **fin·i·cal** /-ɪkəl/, **fi·nick·i·ty** /fə̇ˈnɪkə̇ti/— *adj* too delicate and FUSSY about details; disliking many things, esp. kinds of food: *Eat up your potatoes and don't be so finicky*
fin·is /ˈfɪnə̇s‖ˈfɪ-, ˈfaɪ-/ *n* [R] *Lat* (written at the end of a book or cinema film) The End
fin·ish¹ /ˈfɪnɪʃ/ *v* **1** [IØ;T1,4] to reach or bring to an end; reach the end of (an activity): *What time does the concert finish?|When do you finish your college course?|I haven't finished reading that book yet* **2** [Wv4;T1 (OFF)] to put the last touches or polish to (something that one has made): *I must finish (off) this dress I'm making. I'm just giving it the last finishing touches.|wood which has not been finished*

and is still rough **3** [T1 (UP, OFF)] to eat or drink the rest of: *The cat will finish (up) the fish.|Let's finish (off) the wine* **4** [L9 (UP)] to arrive or end (in the stated place or way): *We finished (up) in Paris.|The party finished with a song* **5** [T1] *infml* to take all one's powers, hopes of success, etc.: *That race finished me*

finish² *n* **1** [S] the end or last part, esp. of a race: *That was a close finish!* (=the competitors were almost level) **2** [U] the appearance or condition of having been properly finished, with paint, polish, etc.: *the beautiful finish of old French furniture*|(fig.) *Her manners lack social finish* **3 a fight to the finish** a fight until one side is completely beaten **4 be in at the finish** to be present at the end (of a race, fight, etc.)

fin·ished /ˈfɪnɪʃt/ *adj* **1** [Wa5;F] ended: *Everything is finished between us!* **2** [A] properly made and complete: *the finished product*|(fig.) *a very finished performance* —opposite **unfinished** **3** at the end of one's powers, without hope: *I'm finished; I'll never succeed in life now I've lost my job* —compare WASHED-UP

finishing school /ˈ··· ·/ *n* [C; *at*+U] a private school where rich young girls learn how to behave in social life

finish off *v adv* [T1] to kill or destroy (a creature, esp. one that is hurt or not strong): *The tiger's wounded—shall I finish him off?*

finish with *v prep* [T1] **1** to have no more use for: *I'll borrow the scissors if you've finished with them.|When you've finished with me, sir, I'll go and post the letters* **2** to have no further relationship with (someone): *I've finished with Mary after the way she's treated us*

fi·nite /ˈfaɪnaɪt/ *adj* [Wa5] **1** having an end or limit: *a finite number of possibilities|Light moves at a finite speed* —opposite **infinite** **2** (in grammar, of a verb) changing according to tense and subject: *"Am", "was", and "are" are finite forms of the verb, and "being" and "been" are* **non-finite** —**~ly** *adv*

fink /fɪŋk/ [C; *you*+N] *AmE infml* **1** someone who tells the police about fellow-criminals **2** someone who takes the place of a worker on STRIKE (=refusing to work in the hope of getting more money or better conditions)

fin·nan had·die /ˌfɪnən ˈhædi/ also **finnan had·dock** /ˌ·· ˈ··/— *n* [C;U] a kind of fish (HADDOCK) preserved in smoke and eaten as food esp. in Scotland: *a/some finnan haddie for breakfast*

Finn·ish /ˈfɪnɪʃ/ *adj* [Wa5] of or related to the language, people, or country of Finland: *the Finnish language|Finnish national dress* —see NATIONALITY TABLE

fi·ord /ˈfiːɔːd, fjɔːd‖fiːˈɔrd, fjord/ *n* FJORD

fir /fɜːʳ/ *n* **1** [C] also **firtree**— any of many kinds of straight tree that mostly keep their thin sharp leaves (NEEDLE*s*) in winter, and grow esp. in cold countries. Their seeds are formed in CONE*s* —see picture at TREE¹ **2** [U] the light soft wood of these trees, used for making houses and furniture

fire¹ /faɪəʳ/ *n* **1** [U] the condition of burning; flames and great heat: *She's afraid of fire* **2** [C] a heap of burning material, lit on purpose for cooking, heat, etc.: *tc sit round the fire|to light the kitchen fire|a cold, fi less room* **3** [C] a piece of gas, or electrical, apparatus for warming a room, with the flames or red-hot wires able to be seen —compare STOVE¹ **4** [U] destruction by fire: *insurance against fire|the danger of fire in an old wooden house* **5** [C] a case of destruction by fire: *lost during a forest fire* **6** [U] shooting by guns; firing (FIRE² (1,2)) **7** [U] strong feeling and excitement: *The boy is full of fire and courage* **8 between 2 fires** (as if) being shot at from both sides **9 blow (up) a fire** to make a fire burn more strongly by blowing air onto it **10 catch fire** to begin to burn: *First the paper caught fire and then the sticks.|Don't let your dress catch fire!* **11 fire and sword** burning and killing in war **12 hang fire** **a** (of a gun) to go off too slowly **b** (of events) to develop too slowly: *Our plans are still hanging fire till we hear from you* **13 lay a fire** to put the paper, sticks, and coal ready for lighting **14 make a fire** to put the paper, sticks, and coal ready and then light them **15 make up a fire** to add more wood, coal, etc. to a fire **16 on fire** (of something not meant to burn) burning: *The house is on fire!* **17 open/cease fire** to start/stop shooting **18 play with fire** to take great risks **19 pull (something) out of the fire** to make something successful in spite of difficulties: *We just pulled the game out of the fire* (=won it) **20 set on fire** also **fire, set fire to**— to light (something not really meant to burn): *Who set the house on fire?* **21 set the Thames on fire** [*nonassertive*] to do anything: *Jim's a nice boy but he'll never set the Thames on fire* **22 under fire** being shot at: *to show courage under fire* —see also **no** SMOKE¹ (4) **without fire** **23 would go through fire and water (for)** *not fml* would face great hardship and danger (for): *I'd go through fire and water for my dear Mildred*

USAGE If one wants something to burn, one usually **lights** it: *to* **light** *the gas/the kitchen* **fire**. One *sets* **fire** (either by accident or on purpose) *to* things that are not usually intended to burn: *Who set* **fire** *to the house?* When a thing begins to burn, it *catches* **fire**: *Her dress caught* **fire**.

fire² *v* **1** [I∅;T1: (*at*)] **a** (of a person or a gun) to shoot off bullets: *He's firing at us!* **b** (of a person) to shoot off bullets from (a gun): *She fired her gun at them* **2** [T1(*at*)] (of a person, gun, or BOW) to shoot off (bullets or arrows): *They fired poisoned arrows at us* **3** [T1] **set on** FIRE¹ (20) **4** [T1] to bake (clay pots, dishes, etc.) in a KILN: *unfired cups|to paint the plates before firing* **5** [T1] (*often in comb.*) to provide FUEL for: *an oil-fired heating system* **6** [T1] *infml* to dismiss from a job; SACK: *Get out! You're fired!* **7** [T1(*with*)] to excite or produce: *Your speech fired the crowd's admiration.|He was fired with the desire to visit China*

fire a·larm /ˈ· ·ˌ·/ *n* **1** a signal, such as a ringing bell, to warn people of fire **2** an apparatus for giving this signal

fire·arm /ˈfaɪərɑːm‖-ɑrm/ *n* [*usu. pl.*] a gun

fire a·way *v adv* [I∅ *usu. imper.*] *infml* to begin to speak or do

fire·ball /ˈfaɪəbɔːl‖-ər-/ *n* a ball of fire, such as the very hot cloud of burning dust and gases formed by an atomic explosion, a very bright METEOR, the sun, a ball-shaped flash of lightning, etc.

fire·bomb /ˈfaɪəbɒm‖ˈfaɪərbɑm/ *n* a bomb that causes fires; an INCENDIARY

fire·box /ˈfaɪəbɒks‖ˈfaɪərbɑks/ *n* **1** the place for the fire in a steam engine or boiler **2** *old use* a TINDERBOX (1)

fire·brand /ˈfaɪəbrænd‖-ər-/ *n* **1** a flaming piece of wood **2** a person who regularly causes anger and excitement among others

fire·break /ˈfaɪəbreɪk‖-ər-/ *n* a narrow piece of land cleared of trees, to prevent forest fires from spreading

fire·brick /ˈfaɪəˌbrɪk‖-ər-/ *n* a brick made of material which is not damaged by heat, used in fireplaces, chimneys, etc.

fire bri·gade /ˈ· ·ˌ·/ *AmE* **fire de·part·ment** /ˈ· ·ˌ··/— *n* [GC] *BrE* an organization for preventing and putting out fires

fire·bug /ˈfaɪəbʌg‖-ər-/ *n* a person who purposely starts fires to destroy property; ARSONist

fire·clay /ˈfaɪəklaɪ‖-ər-/ *n* the kind of clay used in making FIREBRICKs

fire con·trol /ˈ· ·ˌ·/ *n* [U] *tech* the act or system of planning, preparing, and controlling the firing of guns

fire·crack·er /ˈfaɪəˌkrækəʳ‖-ər-/ *n* a small FIREWORK that explodes loudly several times and jumps each time it explodes

fire·damp /ˈfaɪədæmp‖-ər-/ *n* [U] an explosive mixture of gases that forms in mines and becomes dangerous when mixed with air

fire·dog /ˈfaɪədɒg‖ˈfaɪərdɔg/ *n* ANDIRON

fire drill /ˈ· ·/ *n* [U;C] the set of things to be done to leave a burning building safely, practised regularly by pupils in a school, workers in a factory, etc.

fire-eat·er /ˈ· ˌ··/ *n* **1** a person who appears to put flaming material into his mouth, as a stage act **2** a quarrelsome person with violent opinions

fire en·gine /ˈ· ˌ··/ *n* a special vehicle that carries firemen (FIREMAN) and fire-fighting apparatus to a fire —see picture at INTERCHANGE²

fire es·cape /ˈ· ·ˌ·/ *n* a set of metal stairs leading down outside a building to the ground, by which people can escape in case of fire

fire ex·tin·guish·er /ˈ· ·ˌ···/ *n* a smallish metal container with water or chemicals inside for putting out a fire

fire fight·er /ˈ· ˌ··/ *n* a person who puts out fires, either as a FIREMAN or as a special helper during forest fires or in wartime

fire·fly /ˈfaɪəflaɪ‖-ər-/ *n* a type of insect with a tail that shines in the dark; GLOW-WORM

fire·guard /ˈfaɪəgɑːd‖ˈfaɪərgɑrd/ *n* a protective metal framework put round a fireplace

fire hy·drant /ˈ· ˌ··/ *AmE* **fire-plug** /ˈfaɪəplʌg‖-ər-/— *n BrE* a HYDRANT used as a water supply for fighting fires

fire i·rons /ˈ· ·/ *n* [P] the metal tools used for looking after a coal fire —see POKER¹, TONGS¹, SHOVEL¹

fire·light /ˈfaɪəlaɪt‖-ər-/ *n* [U] the soft light thrown from a fire in the fireplace: *Don't turn on the lamp; we can see in the firelight*

fire·light·er /ˈfaɪəˌlaɪtəʳ‖-ər-/ *n* [U;C] (a piece of) a substance which flames easily and helps to light a coal fire

fire·man /ˈfaɪəmən‖-ər-/ *n* **-men** /mən/ **1** a person whose job is putting out fires **2** a person who looks after the fire in a steam engine or FURNACE

fire·place /ˈfaɪəpleɪs‖-ər-/ *n* **1** the opening for a fire in the wall of a room, with a chimney above it and often an ornamental area around it **2** the HEARTH and MANTELPIECE around the fire

fire·pow·er /ˈfaɪəˌpaʊəʳ‖-ər-/ *n* [U] *tech* the ability to deliver gunfire: *The firepower of the enemy ship is far greater than ours*

fire·proof¹ /ˈfaɪəpruːf‖-ər-/ *adj* [Wa5] that is not damaged by heat —compare WATERPROOF¹

fireproof² *v* [T1] to make FIREPROOF

fire-rais·ing /ˈ· ˌ··/ *n* [U] the crime of starting fires on purpose; ARSON

fire risk /ˈ· ·/ *n* a possible cause of fire

fire·side /ˈfaɪəsaɪd‖-ər-/ *n* [(*the*) *usu. sing.*] the area around the fireplace, often thought of as representing the pleasures of home life: *to sit by the fireside|a fireside chair*

fire sta·tion /ˈ· ˌ··/ *n* a building for firemen (FIREMAN) and their fire-fighting apparatus

fire·storm /ˈfaɪəstɔːm‖ˈfaɪərstɔrm/ *n* a storm caused when a large fire draws in wind and rain to take the place of the hot rising air

fire·trap /ˈfaɪətræp‖-ər-/ *n* a building which is dangerous because it may easily catch fire and/or be difficult to escape from in case of fire

fire·walk·ing /ˈfaɪəˌwɔːkɪŋ‖-ər-/ *n* [U] the act of walking over hot stones, ASHes, etc., esp. as an act of faith in some religions —**-walker** *n*

fire·watch·er /ˈfaɪəˌwɒtʃəʳ‖ˈfaɪərˌwɑtʃər, -ˌwɔ-/ *n* a person who watches for fires, esp. those caused by enemy bombing in war —**-watching** *n* [U]

fire·wat·er /ˈfaɪəˌwɔːtəʳ‖-ər-/ *n* [U] *infml & humor* strong alcoholic drink, such as WHISKY

fire·wood /ˈfaɪəwʊd‖-ər-/ *n* [U] wood cut to be used on fires

fire·work /ˈfaɪəwɜːk‖ˈfaɪərwɜrk/ *n* a small container filled with an explosive chemical powder that burns to produce a show of light, noise, and smoke, or explodes with a loud noise

fire·works /ˈfaɪəwɜːks‖ˈfaɪərwɜrks/ *n* [P] **1** a show of FIREWORKs, esp. at a special ceremony **2** a show of anger: *I told you there'd be fireworks if you annoyed the teacher by talking in class*

firing line /ˈ·· ·/ *n* [*the*+R] **1** the position nearest to the enemy **2 be in the firing line** also (*AmE*) **be on the firing line**— to be the object of attack, blame, etc.

firing squad /ˈ·· ˌ·/ *n* a group of soldiers with the duty of putting an offender to death by shooting

fir·kin /ˈfɜːkɪn‖ˈfɜr-/ *n* **1** a small barrel (CASK) **2** a measure for liquids, about 9 GALLONs

firm¹ /fɜːm‖fɜrm/ *adj* [Wa1] **1** strong; solid; hard: *Some soft foods become firm when cold.|Do you think this jelly's firm enough to eat yet?* **2** (in business, esp. of money) not tending to become lower in value: *Prices are still firm.|The pound stayed firm against the dollar in London but fell a little in New York* **3** steady: *firm on one's feet|I don't think that chair's firm enough to stand on* **4** not changing or yielding: *a firm belief|believer in the value of cold baths* **5** strong and sure: *He kept a firm hold on her hand as he helped her over the fence* **6** unyielding: *The government must keep a firm hand on companies if its plans are to succeed* —**~ly** *adv* —**~ness** *n* [U]

firm² *v* [T1;IØ: (UP)] to (cause to) become firm: *The jelly firmed quickly.|The government must act to firm prices up*

firm³ *n* a business company

firm⁴ *adv* firmly: *Always hold firm to your beliefs*

fir·ma·ment /ˈfɜːməmənt‖ˈfɜr-/ *n* [(*the*)] *lit & old use* the sky; heavens

first¹ /fɜːst‖fɜrst/ *determiner, n, pron* **1** [see NUMBER TABLE 3] 1st; the 1st person or thing, or group of people or things (to do or be something): *He was the first who was there/the* (*very*) *first to be there.|They were the first who were there/the first to be there.|He was one of the first* (*people*) *to collect Picasso paintings.|He was among the first* (*people*) *who collected them.|"the first few battles"* (SEU S.) **2** [C] *infml* a 1st thing or act of its kind; something never done before: *famous firsts|The college* SCOREd *a first by being the 1st to give degrees to women* **3** [C] a British university examination result of the highest quality: *a very fine student who took/got a* **double first** (=*firsts* in 2 subjects) **4 at first** at the beginning: *At first I didn't like him but now I do* —compare **at** LAST¹ **(5) 5 first and last** always and most importantly: *Although he served in governments he was first and last a great soldier* **6 first come, first served** people will be dealt with as they come, without special treatment for latecomers **7 first things first** let us take things in the proper order of importance **8 from the** (**very**) **first** from the beginning; at once: *I knew I was in love, from the very first* **9 the first** [*nonassertive*] the slightest; any: *They haven't the first idea what it means; they don't know the first thing about it* —see also **in the first** INSTANCE¹ (4), **in the first** PLACE¹ (16)

first² *adv* **1** before anything else: *First*(*ly*)*, let me deal with the most important difficulty* **2** before the stated thing: *Before we go I must first change my clothes* **3** for the 1st time: *when we first met* —compare LAST² (2) **4** at the beginning: *When we first lived here there were no buses* **5** rather than do something else: *I'll never allow you to do that: I'll die first!* **6 first and foremost** most importantly; above all else: *He's written many different kinds of books, but he's first and foremost a poet* **7 first of all** in the 1st place (in time, order, etc.): *First of all let me say how glad I am to be here.|I'm interested in old coins but first of all I'm a stamp collector* **8 first off** *infml* 1st; before other things: *First off, let's see where we agree and disagree*

first aid /ˌ· ˈ·/ *n* [U] (the study and practice of) treatment to be given by an ordinary person to a person hurt in an accident or suddenly taken ill: *first aid classes|He pulled the drowning man from the water and gave him first aid*

first·born /ˈfɜːstbɔːn‖ ˈfɜrstbɔrn/ *n, adj* **firstborn** [Wa5;A;Wn3] (the) eldest among the children in a family: *the firstborn child*

first-class /ˌ· ˈ·◂/ *adj* [Wa5] of the highest or best quality: *Your work is first-class; I'm very pleased with it*

first class *n* [U] **1** a class of mail in which letters and parcels are delivered as quickly as possible: *Write "First Class" clearly on your letter* **2** the best and costliest type of seating, esp. on a train: *I always travel first class.|We have plenty of space in first class* **3** FIRST¹ (3)

first cous·in /ˌ· ˈ··/ *n* COUSIN (1)

first-de·gree /ˌ· ·ˈ·◂/ *adj* [Wa5;A] of the lowest level of seriousness: *first-degree burns|first-degree murder*

first floor /ˌ· ˈ·◂/ *n* **1** (in Britain) the 1st floor of a building above ground level **2** (in the US) the floor of a building at ground level —compare GROUND FLOOR (1)

first·fruits /ˈfɜːstfruːts‖-ɜr-/ *n* [P] **1** the first of the crops produced at HARVEST, esp. as offered to God at a special service **2** the earliest results

first·hand /ˌfɜːstˈhænd◂‖-ɜr-/ *adj, adv* [Wa5] (learnt) directly from the point of origin: *I heard her news firsthand* (=from her).|*firsthand information*

first la·dy /ˌ· ˈ··/ *n* (in the US) the wife of the President, or of the GOVERNOR of a state

first lieu·ten·ant /ˌ· ·ˈ··◂/ *n* [C;A;N] an officer of the second lowest rank in the US army, AIRFORCE, or MARINE CORPS

first·ly /ˈfɜːstli‖-ɜr-/ *adv* FIRST² (1)
USAGE Some people do not like this word, and would rather use *first* in sentences like this: *There are 3 reasons against it: First . . .*

first name /ˈ·· ·/ *n* **1** the name that stands first in one's full name: *P. G. Smith's first name is Peter; I don't know what the "G" stands for* **2** any of the names before one's SURNAME: *Smith's first names are Peter George*
USAGE Those whose SURNAMEs come before their other names, as in Chinese, Hungarian, etc., may want to use **given name** rather than **first name**

first night /ˌ· ˈ·/ *n* the evening on which the first public performance of a show, play, etc., is given

first-night·er /ˌ· ˈ··/ *n not fml* a person who attends FIRST NIGHTs *regularly*

first of·fend·er /ˌ· ·ˈ··/ *n* a person found guilty of breaking the law for the first time

first per·son /ˌ· ˈ··◂/ *n* [*the*+R] *tech* **1** (*often attrib.*) a form of verb or word standing for a noun (PRONOUN) used to show the speaker: *"I", "me", "we", and "us" are first person* PRONOUNs.|*"I am" is the first person present singular of "to be"* **2** a way of telling a story in which, esp. by frequent use of the FIRST PERSON (1) the teller shows that he took part in the story

first-rate /ˌ· ˈ·◂/ *adj* [Wa5] **1** of the best or highest quality: *to use first-rate materials* **2** *infml* very good: *How does the cake taste?—It's first-rate!*

first thing /ˌ· ˈ·/ *adv* at the first moment, esp. in the morning: *On Thursday I left the work to be done first thing in the morning|first thing on Friday*

firth /fɜːθ‖fɜrθ/ *n* (esp. in Scotland) a narrow arm of the sea, or place where a river flows out

fir·tree /ˈfɜːtriː‖ˈfɜr-/ *n* FIR (1)

fis·cal¹ /ˈfɪskəl/ *adj* [Wa5] *fml* of or related to public money, taxes, debts, etc. —**~ly** *adv*

fiscal² *n infml ScotE* PROCURATOR FISCAL

fish¹ /fɪʃ/ *n* **fish** *or* **fishes** **1** [Wn2;C] a creature whose blood changes temperature according to the temperature around it, which lives in water and uses its FINs and tail to swim: *We caught 3 little fishes|several fish* **2** [U] part of one of these, when used as food: *a piece of boiled fish* **3** [Wn2;C] *infml* any fairly large creature that lives in water, such as a WHALE **4 drink like a fish** *infml* to drink too much alcohol **5 fish and chips** pieces of fish covered with flour paste, and cooked in oil at the same time as long thin pieces of potato (CHIPs) **6 like a fish out of water** *not fml* uncomfortable because one is in a strange place among people who are very different from oneself —see also **have other fish to** FRY¹ (3)
See next page for picture

fish² *v* **1** [IØ (*for*)] to try to catch fish; to search (for something under water) as with a hook: *Let's go fishing.|to fish for* TROUT| (fig.) *Why are you fishing around in your pockets?* **2** [T1] to catch fish in (a piece of water): *This river has been fished too much* **3** [IØ;(*for*)] **a** *infml derog* to try to attract admiring words: *to fish for* COMPLIMENTs **b** to enquire indirectly: *fishing for information* **4 fish in troubled waters** to try to gain advantage out of other people's troubles

fish·cake /ˈfɪʃkeɪk/ *n* a small round flat cake made of cooked fish mixed with cooked potato

fish·er·man /ˈfɪʃəmən‖-ər-/ *n* **-men** /mən/ a man who catches fish, for sport or for his living —compare ANGLEr

fish·e·ry /ˈfɪʃəri/ *n* [*usu. pl.*] a part of the sea where the industry of catching sea fish is practised: *coastal fisheries*

fish fin·ger /ˌ· ˈ··/ also (*esp. AmE*) **fish stick** /ˈ· ·/— *n esp. BrE* a small finger-shaped piece of fish, covered with BREADCRUMBs and sold ready-cooked

fish·ing /ˈfɪʃɪŋ/ *n* [U] **1** the sport or job of catching fish: *to do some fishing in the holidays* **2** the right to practise this sport in a particular place

fishing tack·le /ˈ·· ˌ··/ *n* [U] the things needed in order to catch fish for sport, such as **fishhooks** with back-curving points (BARBs), **fishing-line**, and a long thin wooden **fishing-rod**: *I've left all my fishing tackle in the boat*

fish knife /ˈ· ·/ *n* a kind of table knife without a sharp edge, used for eating fish

fish·mon·ger /ˈfɪʃmʌŋgəʳ/ *n esp. BrE* someone who sells fish in a shop

fish out *v adv* [T1] to bring out after searching: *to fish out a coin|a handkerchief from one's pocket*

fish·plate /ˈfɪʃpleɪt/ *n* either of the pair of iron plates that fasten a RAIL to a SLEEPER on a railway track

fish slice /ˈ· ·/ *n* a flat tool with a handle, used for cutting and serving fish at meals

fish up *v adv* [T1] to pull up, as if catching a fish: *He fished up an old shoe out of the lake*

fish·wife /ˈfɪʃwaɪf/ *n* **-wives** /waɪvz/ a woman who works in a fish market: *scolding like a fishwife*

fish·y /ˈfɪʃi/ *adj* [Wa1] **1** tasting or smelling of fish

some freshwater fish
salmon
carp
roach
trout
pike
eel
some edible sea fish
flatfish
halibut
plaice
skate
sole
mullet
mouth
eye
dorsal fin
scales
nostril
gills
anus
tail fin
haddock
anchovy
cod
dogfish
mackerel
sardine
herring
other sea fish
seahorse
shark
lungfish
catfish
fish

2 seeming false; making one doubtful: *the fishiest story I've ever heard*

fis·sile /ˈfɪsaɪl‖-əl/ *n* **1** *tech & fml* tending to split along natural lines of weakness: *fissile wood* **2** able to split by atomic FISSION (2)

fis·sion /ˈfɪʃən/ *n* [U] **1** *tech* the act of splitting or dividing, esp. of one living cell into 2 or more **2** the splitting into parts of certain atoms to free their powerful forces

fis·sion·a·ble /ˈfɪʃənəbəl/ *adj* **1** (of living cells) that can split by FISSION (1) **2** able to be split by atomic FISSION (2); FISSILE (2)

fis·sure /ˈfɪʃəʳ/ *n* a deep crack in rock or earth: *grass growing in the fissures*

fist /fɪst/ *n* (the shape of) the hand with the fingers closed in tightly: *She shook her fist angrily.|The child seized a fistful of nuts*

-fist·ed /ˈfɪstɨ̣d/ *comb. form* [*n, adj→adj*] having FISTs of the stated kind: *strongfisted*|HAM-FISTED

fis·ti·cuffs /ˈfɪstɪkʌfs/ *n* [P] *old use or humor* fighting with the FISTs

fis·tu·la /ˈfɪstjʊlə‖-tʃələ/ *n* a long pipe-like ULCER (=diseased place inside the body)

fit¹ /fɪt/ *n* **1** [C9 (*of*)] the appearance of the signs of slight illness in a sudden way, for a short time: *a fit of coughing*|(fig.) *She kept them in fits* (*of laughter*) *with her jokes* **2** [C] a period of loss of consciousness with strange, uncontrolled movements of the body: *to have fits* **3** [C9+*of*] a sudden violent feeling: *He shot her in a fit of anger* **4 by/in fits and starts** *not fml* continually starting and stopping; not regularly **5 give someone/have a fit** *not fml* to (cause someone to) be greatly shocked: *Father'll have a fit when he hears!*

fit² *adj* [Wa1] **1** [B (*for*), B3] right and suitable: *a meal fit for a king*|*"All the News That's Fit to Print"* (the New York Times).|*She's not a fit person to be in charge of small children.|Go and wash! You're not fit to be seen* —opposite **unfit** **2** [F;(B)] in good health; strong in bodily condition: *He runs 3 miles every morning; that's why he's so fit.|I'm not feeling very fit this morning.|He's not a fit man: he has an unusual illness* **3 fit to burst** (as if) about to explode: *They were laughing fit to burst* **4 fit to drop** (as if) about to fall on the ground: *We worked till we were fit to drop* **5 keep fit** to preserve oneself in good bodily condition: *Martha goes to keep fit classes and does exercises every morning* **6 see/think fit to do** to decide to do (esp. something foolish): *I don't know why James saw fit to leave so suddenly* —see also **fit to hold a** CANDLE (3) **to, (as) fit as a** FIDDLE¹ (4)

fit³ *v* **-tt-** **1** [I∅;T1] to be the right size or shape (for): *This dress doesn't fit me.|The lid fits badly* **2** [T1] to make clothes the right size and shape for: *It's difficult to fit him—he's so fat* **3** [T1] to provide, and put correctly into place: *We're having new locks fitted on all the doors* —see also FITTED (2) **4** [I∅; T1] to be suitable (for): *His behaviour doesn't fit his important new position. In fact, he doesn't really fit into the organization.|His face doesn't fit* (=he's in the wrong job) —see also FIT IN (1) **5** [X9;V3] to make suitable: *His great height fitted him for team games|fitted him to play team games* **6 fit the bill** to be just what one wants: *What do you want to drink? Will beer fit the bill?* —see also **fit like a** GLOVE (5) **7 If the** (*BrE*) **cap**/(*AmE*) **shoe fits, wear it** *infml* (*usu. said to a person who is offended by what one says*) If it is true, admit it —see also FIT OUT, FIT UP

USAGE In the 1st and 4th meanings, the *AmE* past t. and past p. are **fit**: *When he left the shop, the suit fit him perfectly.*

fit⁴ *n* **1** [U] the quality of fitting well: *Fit's even more important than colour* **2** [S9] the way in which something fits: *This coat's a beautiful fit.|I'll try to climb through, but it's a tight fit*

fit·ful /ˈfɪtfəl/ *adj* restless: *to spend a fitful night* —**~ly** *adv*

fit in *v adv* **1** [T1;I∅: (*with*)] to (cause to) be suitable (to): *to fit my arrangements in with yours|to fit in with his ideas* **2** [T1] to find a time to see (someone) or do (something): *Doctor Jones can fit you in on Thursday afternoon*

fit·ment /ˈfɪtmənt/ *n* [*often pl.*] a piece of fitted furniture: *bathroom fitments*

fit·ness /ˈfɪtnɨ̣s/ *n* [U] **1** [(*for*), 3] the quality of being suitable: *his fitness for the position|his fitness to command the army* **2** the state of being fit in body: *doing exercises to improve their fitness*

fit out *v adv* [T1] to supply (esp. a person or ship) with necessary things: *The ship has been newly fitted out*

fit·ted /ˈfɪtɨ̣d/ *adj* [Wa5] **1** [F+*with*] including (a part, piece of apparatus, etc.): *Is the car fitted with a radio?* **2** [A] fixed in place: *a fitted* CARPET

fit·ter /ˈfɪtəʳ/ *n* someone whose work is either **a** putting together machines or electrical parts or **b** cutting out and fitting clothes

fit·ting¹ /ˈfɪtɪŋ/ *adj fml* right for the purpose or occasion; suitable: *It is fitting that we should remember him on his birthday* —opposite **unfitting**

fitting² *n* **1** an occasion of putting on clothes that are being made for one, to see if they fit: *I'm going for a fitting on Tuesday* **2** [*usu. pl.*] something necessary that is fixed into a building but able to be moved: *electric light fittings* —compare FIXTURE (1)

USAGE Note this fixed phr.: *fittings and fixtures|fixtures and fittings*

fit up *v adv* **1** [X9, esp. *as, with*] to arrange (esp. a place); provide (as or with): *to fit up one of the bedrooms as an office|The stage has been newly fitted up with special lighting* **2** [T1 (*with*)] *infml* FIX UP: *You haven't got a room?—I'll fix you up at home|fit you up with a bed*

five /faɪv/ *determiner, n, pron* [see NUMBER TABLE 1] (the number) 5

five-day week /ˌ· · ˈ·/ *n* [S] a working week that leaves Saturday free as well as Sunday

five o'clock shad·ow /ˌ· ·· ˈ··/ *n* [S] *not fml* a darkness on the lower part of a man's face caused by hair growing during the day after being cut closely (SHAVEd) off in the morning

fiv·er /ˈfaɪvəʳ/ *n BrE infml* £5 or a 5 pound note: *It costs a fiver.|I've only got fivers*

fives /faɪvz/ *n* [U] a British ball game in which the ball is hit with the hand or a BAT against 3 walls

fix¹ /fɪks/ *v* **1** [X9] to fasten firmly (into the stated position): *to fix the door open*|(fig.) *to fix the date in my mind* **2** [T1,3,6b: (UP)] to agree on; arrange: *We've fixed the date for the wedding* (compare *We've* FIXed ON *the 14th of April*).|*They've fixed the rent at £12.00* (compare *They've* FIXed ON *£12.00*).|*If you want to meet them, I can fix it.|We haven't fixed* (*up*) *when to leave|where to stay, yet.|Have you fixed who is to lead?|They've fixed to go to Borneo* —compare FIX ON (1) **3** [T1] to protect (colours or photographic film) from the effects of light, by chemical treatment **4** [D1 (*for*);T1] *AmE* to cook or prepare (esp. food or drink) (for someone); put in order: *She's fixing breakfast.|Let me fix you a drink!|I must fix my face* **5** [T1] to repair: *I must get the radio fixed* —compare SEE TO **6** [T1] (of things one can see) to attract (one's attention) **7** [T1] (military) to fasten (a BAYONET) into position on one's RIFLE **8** [T1] *derog* to arrange the result of: *to fix the election|the race* **9** *infml* to influence (someone) wrongly, esp. by BRIBERY: *Can they fix the judge?* **10** *sl* to deal with; get even with (someone): *Don't worry! I'll fix George*—see also FIX ON, FIX UP, FIX WITH

fix² *n* **1** [C] *infml* an awkward or difficult position: *We're in a real fix—there's nobody to look after the baby!* **2** [C (*of*)] *drug-users' sl* an INJECTION (of the stated drug) **3** [S] *infml* something FIXed¹ (8): *The election was a fix* **4** [C] a decision on one's position in space (as when on a ship) reached by looking at the stars, taking measurements, etc.

fix·a·tion /fɪk'seɪʃən/ *n* **1** [(*on*)] (in PSYCHOLOGY) **a** a strong unhealthy feeling (about) or love (for): *He has a fixation on whips|a mother fixation* **b** a stopping of the growth of the mind and character at a certain stage, so that the person remains childish **2** the act of fixing (esp. a photographic film)

fix·a·tive /'fɪksətɪv/ *n* [C;U] (a type of) chemical used for sticking things together, holding things in position (esp. hair or false teeth), or fixing colours

fixed /fɪkst/ *adj* **1** fastened; not movable: *The tables are firmly fixed to the floor.*|(fig.) *He has very fixed ideas on this subject* **2** arranged; decided on: *The date's not completely fixed yet*

fix·ed·ly /'fɪksʒdli/ *adv* unchangingly; with great attention (in phrs. like **to stare fixedly**)

fixed odds /,· '·/ *n* [P] ODDS that will be paid however many people have risked (BET) money on the result of a race

fixed star /,· '·/ *n* a star so distant that its movement can be measured only by very exact calculations over long periods, unlike that of the PLANETs

fix·i·ty /'fɪksʒti/ *n* [U] the quality of being fixed: *fixity of purpose*

fix on *v prep* **1** [T1,4,6b] to settle one's choice on; decide to have: *We've fixed on the 14th of April for the wedding.*|*We've fixed on starting tomorrow* (compare *We've fixed when to start*).|*We've fixed on George as the leader* —compare FIX¹ (2) **2** [D1] to direct (one's eyes, attention, etc.) steadily (at): *She fixed her eyes on the clock* **3 fix the blame/the crime on (someone)** to decide that someone is guilty: *You can't fix the robbery on me!*

fix·ture /'fɪkstʃə^r/ *n* **1** something necessary, such as a bath, that is fixed into a building and sold with it: *bathroom fixtures* —compare FITTING² (2) **2** a match or sports competition taking place on an agreed date

fix up *v adv* **1** [T1 (*with*)] also *infml* **fit up**— to provide (someone) with; make the arrangements for (someone): *We must fix him up with a job|with a nice girl.*|*They fixed us up in a good hotel.*|*Go with George; he'll fix you up!* **2** [IØ] *AmE* to dress carefully or formally: *Do I have to fix up to go to the Websters'?*

fix with *v prep* [D1] to look fixedly at (someone) with: *He fixed me with a glassy* STARE *and I couldn't move*

fizz¹ /fɪz/ *v* [IØ] (of a liquid, usu. a drink) to produce hollow balls (BUBBLEs) of gas, making the sound typical of this

fizz² *n* **1** [S] the sound of FIZZing¹ **2** [U] *infml* CHAMPAGNE: *a bottle of fizz*

fiz·zle /'fɪzəl/ *v* [IØ] to FIZZ¹ weakly

fizzle out *v adv* [IØ] to come to nothing after a good start; end disappointingly: *The plan fizzled out*

fiz·zy /'fɪzi/ *adj* [Wa1] that FIZZes¹: *fizzy drinks*

fizzy lem·on·ade /,·· ··'·/ *n* [U] *BrE* LEMONADE (1)

fjord, fiord /'fiːɔːd, fjɔːd‖fiː'ɔrd, fjord/ *n* a narrow arm of the sea between cliffs or steep slopes, esp. in Norway

flab·ber·gast /'flæbəgɑːst‖-ərgæst/ *v* [T1 *usu. pass.* (*at, by*)] *infml* to surprise very much; fill with shocked wonder

flab·by /'flæbi/ *adj* [Wa1] **1** having too soft flesh; (of muscles) too soft: *You're not fat but you're flabby* **2** (of character) morally weak —**-bily** *adv* —**-biness** *n* [U]

flac·cid /'flæsʒd/ *adj* not firm enough; weak and soft: *flaccid plant stems* —**~ity** /flæk'sɪdʒti/ *n* [U]

flag¹ /flæg/ *n* [Wn1] any of various types of plant with blade-like leaves, such as the wild IRIS. They grow in wet places

flag² also **flagstone**— *n* a flat square of stone for a floor or path: *an old kitchen with a flag* (or **flagged**) *floor*

flag³ *n* **1** a square or OBLONG piece of cloth, usu. with a pattern or picture on it and fastened by one edge to a pole (FLAGPOLE or FLAGSTAFF) or to a rope: *to* FLY (=have on one's pole) *the national flag of Norway|flags hanging at* HALF-MAST (=lower than the top of the pole) *as a sign of sorrow* **2** a small piece of paper like this, sold on a FLAG DAY (1) **3 keep the flag flying** *not fml* to continue to represent opinions and ideas that one believes in, and esp. to keep up practices connected with one's own country in another country: *When the country became independent and the foreign army left, only a few foreign teachers and nurses remained to keep the flag flying* **4 lower/strike one's flag** to admit defeat in an argument or difficulty **5 show the flag** *not fml* to be present at an occasion only to show others that one has attended: *We won't stay long; we'll just show the flag at dinner and then leave early* **6 show the white flag** to yield; show that one is cowardly or afraid **7 under the flag (of)** serving or protected (by): *to live under the American flag*

flag⁴ *v* **-gg-** [T1] **1** to put flags on; ornament with flags: *to flag the streets in honour of the royal wedding* **2** [(DOWN)] to cause (a car or train) to stop by waving one's arm or a flag at the driver: *to flag (down) a taxi*

flag⁵ *v* [Wv4;IØ] to be or become weak and less alive or active: *The roses were beginning to flag.*|*his flagging interest in the subject* —compare UNFLAGGING

flag day /'· ·/ *n* **1** a day on which money is collected for a good cause by selling little paper flags in the street **2** (*often cap*) (in the US) the 14th of June, kept in memory of the day in 1777 when the national flag originated

fla·gel·lant /'flædʒʒlənt, flə'dʒelənt/ *n* someone who whips himself as a religious punishment

fla·gel·late /'flædʒʒleɪt/ *v* [T1] *fml* to whip esp. as a religious punishment —**-lation** /,flædʒʒ'leɪʃən/ *n* [U]

fla·geo·let /,flædʒə'let/ *n* a small wind-instrument like a whistle, with 6 holes for the fingers

flag of con·ve·ni·ence /,· · ·'··/ *n* a flag, belonging to a nation not really their own, that is carried (FLOWN) by some ships to avoid taxation because nobody knows what country they really belong to

flag·on /'flægən/ *n* **1 a** a large container for liquids, usu. with a lid, a handle, and a lip or SPOUT for pouring **b** the amount of liquid this holds **2 a** a large bottle in which esp. wine is sold, containing about twice as much as an ordinary bottle **b** the amount of liquid this holds: *Can we drink a whole flagon?*

flag·pole /'flægpəʊl/ *n* a long pole to raise a flag on, too large to hold in the hand

fla·gran·cy /'fleɪgrənsi/ *n* [U] the quality of being FLAGRANT

fla·grant /'fleɪgrənt/ *adj* (of a bad person or action) open and shameless: *flagrant cheating|a flagrant coward* —**~ly** *adv*

flag·ship /'flæg,ʃɪp/ *n* the chief ship, on which an ADMIRAL sails, among a group of naval warships

flag·staff /'flægstɑːf‖-stæf/ *n* a FLAGPOLE, or stick

to which a flag is fastened for waving in the hand

flag·stone /ˈflægstəʊn/ *n* FLAG[2]

flag-wav·ing /ˈ· ˌ··/ *n* [U] *derog* the noisy expression of national military feeling

flail[1] /fleɪl/ *n* a wooden tool consisting of a stick swinging from the end of a long handle, used esp. in former times for beating grain to separate the seeds from the waste parts (THRESHing)

flail[2] *v* [I∅;T1] **1** to beat (grain) with a FLAIL **2** to (cause to) wave violently but aimlessly about: *He flailed his arms at me.|Her legs flailed in the water*

flair /fleəʳ/ *n* [S;U: (*for*)] (a case of) the natural ability to do some special thing: *a flair for writing|He shows little flair for this subject*

flak /flæk/ *n* [U] *Ger* the guns used for firing from the ground against enemy aircraft, and the bursting explosive SHELLs that they fire: *to avoid the flak|a sudden burst of flak*

flake[1] /fleɪk/ *n* **1** (*often in comb.*) a light leaf-like little bit (of something soft): *soap flakes|flakes of snow|of chocolate* **2** a thin flat broken-off piece (of something hard): *climbing up a flake of rock*

flake[2] *v* [I∅ (OFF)] to fall off in FLAKEs: *The paint's beginning to flake (off)*

flake out *v adv* [I∅] *infml* to faint or COLLAPSE

flak·y /ˈfleɪki/ *adj* [Wa1] made up of, tending to break into, FLAKEs: *flaky pastry* —**flakiness** *n* [U]

flam·beau /ˈflæmbəʊ/ *n* **-beaux** *or* **-beaus** /bəʊz/ *Fr* a flaming TORCH (=something that burns to give light)

flam·boy·ant /flæmˈbɔɪənt/ *adj* **1** brightly coloured and noticeable: *a flamboyant orange shirt* **2** (of a person or his behaviour) showy, gay, and bold —**~ly** *adv* —**-boyance** *n* [U]

flame[1] /fleɪm/ *n* [C;U] **1** (a tongue of) red or yellow burning gas: *The dry sticks burst into flame(s)* **2 in flames** (of something not meant to burn) burning: *The whole city was in flames* **3 old flame** *not fml* someone with whom one used to be in love: *Edward's an old flame of mine*

flame[2] *v* **1** [L9 esp. OUT, UP] to burn (more) brightly: (fig.) *The evening sky flamed with red and orange.*|(fig.) *Her anger suddenly flamed* **2** [L7] to become (red, bright, etc.) by or as if by burning: *The candles flamed brighter.|Her cheeks flamed red*

fla·men·co /fləˈmeŋkəʊ/ [U] a kind of Spanish dancing and music, very fast and exciting

flame-throw·er /ˈ· ˌ··/ *n* a gun-like instrument that throws out flames or burning liquid under pressure, used as a weapon of war or in clearing wild land

flam·ing /ˈfleɪmɪŋ/ *adj* [Wa5;A] **1** burning brightly; bright: *a flaming red sunset* **2** *sl* (used for adding force to a rude word): *You flaming fool!* —compare BLOODY[2] (1,2)

fla·min·go /fləˈmɪŋgəʊ/ *n* **-gos** *or* **-goes** a tall tropical water bird with long thin legs, pink and red feathers, and a broad beak curved downwards —see picture at WATER[1]

flam·ma·ble /ˈflæməbəl/ *adj AmE & tech* INFLAMMABLE —opposite **non-flammable**

USAGE **Flammable** and **inflammable** are not opposite in meaning. They have the same meaning, but **flammable** is used in the US and is also the *BrE tech* word, while everyone uses **inflammable** when it means "easily excited".

flan /flæn/ *n* a round flat PIE made of pastry or cake, with the filling of fruit, cheese, etc. not covered over but left open

flange /flændʒ/ *n* the flat edge that stands out from the main surface of an object such as a railway wheel, to keep it in position

flank[1] /flæŋk/ *n* **1** the side of a person or esp. of an animal, between the RIBs and the HIP **2** the side of a mountain or building **3** the side of a moving army: *The enemy attacked us on the left flank*

flank[2] *v* [T1] **1** [*often pass.* + *with, by*] to be placed beside: *a road flanked with tall trees* **2** (military) to attack from the side

flan·nel[1] /ˈflænl/ *n* **1** [U] a kind of smooth loosely-woven woollen cloth with a slightly furry surface: *flannel trousers* **2** [U] *esp. AmE* cotton cloth that looks like this **3** [C] a piece of cloth used for washing oneself —see picture at BATHROOM **4** [U] *esp. BrE infml* meaningless though attractive words: *That's just a lot of flannel—tell me the truth!*

flannel[2] *v* [L9;X9] *esp. BrE infml* to save (oneself), find (one's way) by using FLANNEL[1] (4)

flan·nel·ette /ˌflænəl-ˈet/ *n* [U] cotton cloth with a furry surface that looks like FLANNEL[1] (1)

flan·nels /ˈflænlz/ *n* [P] **1** men's FLANNEL[1] (1) trousers, esp. as worn for summer games like cricket —see PAIR (USAGE) **2** *AmE & old use* FLANNEL[1] (1) underclothes

flap[1] /flæp/ **1** [(*the*) S] the sound of FLAPping[2] (1): *the slow flap of the sails* **2** [C] a light blow given by FLAPping[2] (1): *to give him a flap on the ear with the newspaper* **3** [C] a wide flat thin part of anything that hangs down, esp. so as to cover an opening: *a cap with flaps to cover my ears|to creep under the flap of the tent|to stick down the flap of the envelope|the flaps on the wings of an aircraft* **4** [C] *infml* a state of excited anxiety: *Don't get in a flap—we'll soon find it* —see also UNFLAPPABLE

flap[2] *v* **-pp- 1** [I∅;T1] to wave (something large and soft, like wings) slowly up and down or to and fro, making a noise: *The large bird flapped its wings.|She flapped a newspaper at the insect.|She flapped at the insect with a newspaper* **2** [I∅] (of something large and soft, like wings) to move slowly up and down or to and fro, making a noise: *The sails flapped in the gentle wind* **3** [L9] (of a bird) to fly slowly (somewhere): *It flapped slowly off* **4** [I∅] *infml* to be in a FLAP[1] (4)

flap·jack /ˈflæpdʒæk/ *n* **1** a small flat cake cooked in a pan on top of the fire; a small PANCAKE **2** *BrE* a mixture of OATS and other things baked into a sweet cake

flap·per /ˈflæpəʳ/ *n sl* (in the 1920's) a young girl who showed bold freedom in behaviour and dress: *a pretty flapper on the back of Shaw's motorcycle*

flare[1] /fleəʳ/ *v* [I∅] to burn with a bright flame, but uncertainly or for a short time: *candles flaring in the wind*

flare[2] *n* **1** [S] a flaring (FLARE[1]) light: *a sudden flare as she lit the gas* **2** [C] (something that provides) a bright light out of doors, as in a street market or as a signal at an AIRFIELD **3** [U] the quality of being FLARED: *a bit more flare in the trousers*

flared /fleəd‖fleərd/ *adj* (of trousers or a skirt) shaped so as to get wider by degrees towards the bottom: *a very flared skirt*

flare path /ˈ· ·/ *n* a lit-up path for aircraft to land on

flares /fleəz‖fleərz/ *n* [P] *infml* FLARED trousers —see PAIR (USAGE)

flare up *v adv* [I∅] to show sudden increased heat, anger, or violence: *Trouble may flare up in the big cities* —**flare-up** /ˈ· ·/ *n*

flash[1] /flæʃ/ *v* **1** [Wv4;I∅] (of a light) to appear or exist for a moment: *The lightning flashed.|to watch the flashing lights of the cars* **2** [T1 (*at*)] to make a flash with; shine for a moment (at): *Why is that driver flashing his lights (at me)?|Stop flashing that light in my eyes.*|(fig.) *She flashed a sudden smile at him* **3** [X9] to send (a telegraph or radio message): *They flashed the news back to London* **4** [L9] to move very fast: *The days seem to flash by* **5** [X9 (*at*, AROUND)] to show for a moment: *to flash a message on the cinema* SCREEN|*He flashed a £1 note at the man by the door.*|(*derog*) *George certainly flashes his money around!* **6** [L9] (of an idea) to come suddenly: *It flashed into/across/through his mind that she might be married* **7** [IØ;T1] (of eyes) to shine (with excitement or feeling); express in an excited way **8** [IØ] *sl* to show the sexual parts, esp. on purpose to shock others; expose oneself (EXPOSE (7))

flash² *n* **1** [C] a sudden quick bright light: *flashes of lightning*|(fig.) *a sudden flash of merriment/of* INSPIRATION **2** [C] one movement of a light or flag in signalling **3** [C] a first short news report, received by telegraph, radio, etc.: *The latest flash from Beirut says they've been shot* **4** [C;U] (in photography) **a** the method or apparatus for taking photographs in the dark: *Did you use flash?* **b** FLASHLIGHT (2) **5** [C] the sign of a military group, worn on the shoulder of a uniform **6** [C;U] *tech* (a thin piece of) metal or plastic that gets in between 2 parts of a MOULD and is cut away from the finished article **7** [C] *drug users' sl* a sudden very pleasant feeling resulting from the INJECTION of a drug **8** [C] *sl, often humor* the sudden showing or sight of the sex organs, on purpose or by accident —see also FLASHER (2) **9** [C] FLASHLIGHT (2) **10 flash in the pan** a sudden success that offers no promise for the future, because it will not be repeated: *That wonderful book was just a flash in the pan; he'll never write another* **11 in a/like a flash** very quickly, suddenly, or soon: *I'll be back in a flash* **12 quick as a flash** (esp. of a clever remark) at once: *So I said, quick as a flash, "You're not President yet!"*

flash³ *adj* **1** [A] sudden, violent, and short (in phrs. like **flash flood, flash fire**) **2** [B] *not fml* modern, attractive, and costly-looking: *That's a very flash car—where did you get it?* —compare FLASHY

flash back *v adv* [IØ (*to*)] to return suddenly (to an earlier time), as in a FLASHBACK: *My mind flashed back to last Christmas*

flash·back /ˈflæʃbæk/ *n* [C;U] part of a cinema film that goes back in time to show what happened earlier in the story: *The events of his childhood are shown in (a) flashback*

flash·bulb /ˈflæʃbʌlb/ *n* an electric lamp in which metal wire or FOIL burns brightly for a moment, for taking a flash photograph

flash·cube /ˈflæʃkjuːb/ *n* 4 electric lamps (BULBs) packed together, for taking 4 flash photographs one after the other

flash·er /ˈflæʃəʳ/ *n* **1** something that flashes, such as a traffic signal or a light on a car **2** *sl* a man who habitually shows his sexual parts unexpectedly to strangers (EXPOSEs (6) himself); EXHIBITIONIST —see also INDECENT EXPOSURE

flash·gun /ˈflæʃgʌn/ *n* a piece of apparatus for holding a FLASHBULB, and using it at the moment when the photograph is taken —see picture at PHOTOGRAPHIC

flash·light /ˈflæʃlaɪt/ *n* **1** *esp. AmE* an electric hand-light (TORCH) **2** a piece of apparatus for taking flash photographs: *Did you bring your flashlight/your flash?* **3** a light used for signals, as in a LIGHTHOUSE

flash point /ˈ· ·/ *n* the temperature at which the gas (VAPOUR) from oil will make a small flash, but not catch fire, if a flame is put near it

flash·y /ˈflæʃi/ *adj* [Wa1] over-ornamented; unpleasantly big, bright, etc., and perhaps not of good quality: *a large flashy car*|*cheap flashy clothes* —compare FLASH³ (2) —**flashily** *adv*: *flashily dressed* —**flashiness** *n* [U]

flask /flɑːsk‖flæsk/ *n* **1 a** a narrow-necked bottle, as used by scientists in the LABORATORY **b** the amount of liquid that this contains **2 a** a narrow-necked oil or wine bottle, often covered esp. in Italy with WICKER (=twisted plant stems) **b** the amount of wine or oil that this contains: *a flask of* CHIANTI **3 a** a flat bottle for carrying alcohol or other drinks in the pocket or fastened to one's belt, SADDLE, etc. They are often made of metal or covered with leather —compare HIP FLASK **b** the amount of liquid that this contains **4** also **thermos, thermos flask, vacuum flask,** (*esp. AmE*) **thermos bottle**— **a** a bottle having 2 thin glass walls between which a VACUUM is kept, used for keeping the contents either hot or cold **b** the amount of liquid that this contains: *a flask of tea*

flat¹ /flæt/ *adj* **-tt- 1** [Wa1;B] parallel with the ground; smooth and level: *The earth is round, not flat.*|*something flat to write on* **2** [Wa5;H] spread out fully: *Lie down flat (on your back).*|*Spread the map out flat (on the floor)* **3** [Wa5;B] having a broad smooth surface and little thickness: *flat cakes*|*a flat hat* **4** [B] (of beer and other gassy drinks, or their taste) having lost the gas: *Your beer's gone flat while you were telephoning* **5** [F] dull; uninteresting: *Everything seems so flat since Robert left* **6** [F] (in music) lower than the true note: *You're flat! Sing it again* —compare SHARP³ (1) **7** [Wa5;E] (in music) half a note lower than (in the phrs. **A flat, B flat, C flat,** etc.): E *flat is a* SEMITONE *lower than* E NATURAL —compare SHARP³ (1) and see picture at NOTATION **8** [Wa5;A] complete; firm; with no more argument (in phrs. like **flat refusal, flat** DENIAL) **9** [Wa1;B] (of a tyre) without enough air in it **10** [Wa5;B] (of the feet) not having proper arches **11** [B] (of paint) not shiny **12** [A] (of colours) the same all over the surface **13** [B] (of a group of electric cells (BATTERY)) needing to be connected with a supply of electric current and CHARGEd **14** [E] *not fml* (after an expression of time, showing surprise at its shortness) exactly; and not more: *I got dressed in 3 minutes flat!* **15 fall flat** (of an idea or plan) to fail; have no effect: *The joke fell flat* **16 that's flat!** *not fml* that's my decision: *I won't go, and that's flat!* —see also **as flat as a** PANCAKE¹ (2) —**~ness** *n* [U]

flat² *n* **1** [*usu. pl.*] a low level plain, esp. near water: *mud flats* **2** [(*of*)] the flat part or side (of): *I hit him with the flat of my hand/of my sword* **3** *esp. AmE* a flat tyre: *Stop—I think we've got a flat!* **4** a movable upright piece of stage scenery **5** (the sign, ♭, for) a FLAT¹ (7) note in music: *I can't play this—there are too many flats* —compare SHARP³ (1) **6 on the flat** not on a slope; on level ground: *I can walk at 4 miles an hour on the flat*

flat³ *adv* **1** [H (*against*)] *not fml* completely: *He's flat* BROKE —compare FLATLY (2) **2** (in music) lower than the true note: *You keep singing flat* —compare SHARP³ (1)

flat⁴ also (*AmE*) **apartment**— *n* a set of rooms esp. on one floor, including a kitchen and bathroom, usu. one of many such sets in a building or block: *to divide the house into flats*|*the people in the top flat* —see picture at HOUSE¹

flat-bot·tomed /ˌ· ˈ··/ *adj* (of a boat) flat underneath, to be used where the water is not deep

flat·car /ˈflætkɑːʳ/ *n AmE* a railway goods vehicle with no raised sides or ends and no roof

flat·fish /ˈflætˌfɪʃ/ *n* [Wa2] any of several kinds of bony sea fish such as SOLE or PLAICE, with thin flat bodies —see picture at FISH¹

flat·foot /ˈflætfʊt/ *n* **-feet** *sl* a policeman

flat-foot·ed /ˌ· ˈ··/ *adj* **1** with feet whose arches are not high enough **2** *infml* (of decisions or intentions) firm; determined: *her flat-footed refusal*

flat·i·ron /ˈflætaɪən‖-ərn/ *n* IRON[1] (3)
flat·let /ˈflætl̟ɪ̟t/ *n* a very small FLAT[4]
flat·ly /ˈflætli/ *adv* **1** in a dull level way: *"It's hopeless," he said flatly* **2** completely; firmly (in phrs. like **flatly refuse**): *He is flatly opposed to the whole idea* —compare FLAT[1] (8)
flat out[1] /ˌ· ˈ·/ *adv not fml* **1** at full speed: *working flat out|The car does 100 miles an hour flat out* —compare ALL OUT **2** (of speech) directly; plainly: *Tell him flat out what you think*
flat out[2] *adj* [Wa5;F] *not fml* completely tired out: *We're all flat out after lifting that piano*
flat rac·ing /ˈ· ˌ··/ *n* [U] the sport of horseracing on flat ground with nothing to be jumped over —compare STEEPLECHASE (2)
flat rate /ˈ· ·/ *n* one charge including everything, to which nothing will be added: *You can eat as much as you like for/at a flat rate of £3*
flat spin /ˌ· ˈ·/ *n* **1** (in flying) a fast and often uncontrollable drop while spinning round and round in a level position **2 go into/be in a flat spin** *infml* to go into/be in a state of excited confusion
flat·ten /ˈflætn/ *v* **1** [(IØ);T1: (OUT)] to make or become flat: *a rabbit flattened by a passing car|I flattened myself against the wall.|The hills flatten (out) here* **2** [T1] (in music) to play or sing (a note) flat
flat·ter /ˈflætəʳ/ *v* **1** [T1 (*about, on*)] to praise (someone) too much or insincerely in order to please: *He flattered her (on/about her cooking)* **2** [Wv4;IØ;T1 *often pass.*+*at, by*] (of experiences) to give pleasure to: *She was flattered at the invitation/to be invited/that they invited her.|They made flattering remarks about her nose* **3** [Wv4;IØ;T1] (of a picture or photograph) to make (the person shown there) look too beautiful: *a flattering photograph of George|The picture certainly doesn't flatter you.|* (fig.) *Candlelight is flattering to my skin* **4 flatter oneself** to think too well of oneself: *"They're all watching me." "You flatter yourself!"* **5 flatter oneself (that)** to have the pleasant though perhaps mistaken opinion (that): *We flatter ourselves that we can do without their help* —**~er** *n* [C;*you*+N]: *You flatterer! Of course I can't sing*
flat·ter·y /ˈflætəri/ *n* **1** [U] the action of FLATTERing (1) **2** [C] a FLATTERing (1) remark
flat·top /ˈflæt-tɒp‖-tɑp/ *n AmE infml* **1** CREW CUT **2** *becoming rare* AIRCRAFT CARRIER
flat·u·lence /ˈflætjʊləns‖ˈflætʃə-/ *n* [U] (the feeling of discomfort caused by) too much gas in the stomach: *to suffer from flatulence*
flaunt /flɔːnt‖flɔnt, flɑnt/ *v* [T1] *derog* to show for public admiration (something one is proud of): *to flaunt one's new fur coat|to flaunt one's charms*
flau·tist /ˈflɔːtl̟ɪ̟st/ *AmE* usu. **flutist**— *n* someone who plays the FLUTE, esp. as a profession
fla·vour[1], *AmE* **flavor** /ˈfleɪvəʳ/ *n* **1** [C] a taste; quality that only the tongue can experience: *a strong flavour of cheese|Choose from 6 popular flavours!|*(fig.) *a story with an unpleasant flavour* **2** [U] the quality of tasting good or pleasantly strong: *This bread hasn't much flavour/has plenty of flavour* —**~less** *adj*
flavour[2], *AmE* **flavor** *v* [T1 (*with*)] to give FLAVOUR[1] to: *She flavoured the cake with chocolate*
-fla·voured, *AmE* **-flavored** /ˈfleɪvəd‖-ərd/ *comb. form* [*n*→*adj*] having the stated FLAVOUR[1]: *chocolate-flavoured cake*
fla·vour·ing, *AmE* **flavoring** /ˈfleɪvərɪŋ/ *n* [U] something added to food to give or improve the FLAVOUR[1]: *Add a spoonful of banana flavouring*
flaw[1] /flɔː/ *n* a small sign of damage, such as a mark or crack, that makes an object not perfect: *a flaw in a plate|*(fig.) *the flaws in this contract*
flaw[2] *v* [Wv5;T1] to make a FLAW in: *The* SCAR (=mark on the skin) *flawed her beauty*
flaw·less /ˈflɔːləs/ *adj* [Wa5] perfect; with no FLAW: *a flawless argument* —**~ly** *adv*
flax /flæks/ *n* [U] **1** a plant with blue flowers, that is grown for its stem and oily seeds **2** the thread made from the stems of this plant; LINEN
flax·en /ˈflæksən/ *adj* [Wa5] (of hair) pale yellow: *flaxen curls*
flay /fleɪ/ *v* [T1] **1** to remove the skin from (a creature): *to flay a dead horse* **2** *lit* to whip violently **3** to scold violently; attack severely in words
flea /fliː/ *n* **1** any of a group of small jumping insects without wings, that live on blood —see picture at INSECT **2 go/send someone off/away with a flea in his/her ear** to go/drive someone away feeling foolish because of a short severe scolding, esp. after some suggestion or attempt has been made: *He tried to kiss her, but she sent him off with a flea in his ear*
flea·bag /ˈfliːbæg/ *n sl* **1** *rare* SLEEPING BAG **2** *esp. AmE* a cheap dirty hotel **3** a dirty disliked creature: *She loves her cat, but nobody else can bear the old fleabag*
flea·bite /ˈfliːbaɪt/ *n* **1** the bite of a FLEA **2** something small and not very troublesome, though unpleasant: *I lost £5 at the races, but that's only a fleabite*
flea mar·ket /ˈ· ˌ··/ *n* a market usu. in the street, where old or used goods are sold
flea·pit /ˈfliːˌpɪt/ *n sl* a cheap dirty cinema or theatre
fleck[1] /flek/ *v* [T1 *often pass.*+*with*] to mark or cover with FLECK*s*: *The grass under the trees was flecked with sunlight*
fleck[2] *n* [C9] **1** a small mark or spot: *brown cloth with flecks of red* **2** a grain or drop (of the stated solid or liquid): *flecks of dust in the air|a fleck of milk on the baby's chin*
fledged /fledʒd/ *adj* [Wa5] (*usu. in comb.*) (of a bird) having developed wing feathers for flying: *unfledged chickens* —compare FULLY-FLEDGED (1)
fledg·ling /ˈfledʒlɪŋ/ *n* **1** a young bird that is learning to fly **2** a young person without experience: *fledgling nurses*
flee /fliː/ *v* **fled** /fled/ [IØ;(T1)] **1** to escape (from) by hurrying away: *They all fled (from) the burning ship* **2 flee the country** to go abroad for safety
fleece[1] /fliːs/ *n* a sheep's woolly coat; the amount of wool cut from one sheep at one time —compare SHEEPSKIN (1) and see picture at FARMYARD
fleece[2] *v* [T1 (*of*)] *not fml* to rob (of a lot of money) by a trick or by charging too much money: *They really fleeced us at that hotel!*
flee·cy /ˈfliːsi/ *adj* [Wa1] (seeming) woolly like a FLEECE[1]: *a coat with a warm fleecy* LINING*|little fleecy clouds*
fleet[1] /fliːt/ *n* [GC] **1** a number of ships, such as warships in the navy **2** a group of buses, aircraft, etc., under one control
fleet[2] *adj lit* fast; quick: *a fleet-footed runner* —**~ly** *adv* —**~ness** *n*
fleet ad·mi·ral /ˈ· ˌ···/ *n* [C;A;N] the officer of highest rank in the US Navy
fleet·ing /ˈfliːtɪŋ/ *adj* (of time or periods) short; passing quickly: *a fleeting look|the fleeting hours|Youth is so fleeting* —**~ly** *adv*
Fleet Street /ˈ· ·/ *n* [R] **1** the area in London where most of the important newspaper offices are **2** the influence of newspaper writing: *Fleet Street can make or break a politician*
flesh /fleʃ/ *n* **1** [U] the soft substance including fat and muscle, that covers the bones and lies under the skin **2** [U] the meat of animals used as food **3** [U] the soft part of a fruit or vegetable, which can

be eaten **4** [*the*+R] man's body as opposed to his mind or soul: *The spirit is willing but the flesh is weak* **5** [*the*+R] man's bodily desires: *the pleasures of the flesh* **6 flesh and blood a** human beings: *These sorrows are more than flesh and blood can bear* **b** relatives: *I must help them because they're my own flesh and blood* **7 go the way of all flesh** *euph* to die **8 one's pound of flesh** the exact amount of what is owed to one, esp. when this will cause the person who owes it great pain or trouble **9 in the flesh** in real life; in bodily form: *He's nicer in the flesh than in his photographs*

flesh·ings /ˈfleʃɪŋz/ *n* [P] flesh-coloured TIGHTS worn by BALLET DANCERs

flesh·ly /ˈfleʃli/ *adj* [Wa5] *lit* bodily, esp. sexual

flesh·pot /ˈfleʃpɒt‖-pɑt/ *n* [*usu. pl.*] a place supplying good food, drink, material comforts, etc.

flesh wound /ˈ· ·/ *n* a wound which does not reach the bones or the important organs of the body

flesh·y /ˈfleʃi/ *adj* [Wa1] **1** of or like flesh; consisting of a fleshlike substance **2** having much flesh; fat: *fleshy cheeks*

fleur-de-lis, fleur-de-lys /ˌflɜː de ˈliː‖ˌflɜr- (*Fr* flœr də lis)/ **fleurs-de-lis** *or* **fleurs-de-lys** /ˌflɜː də ˈliːz‖ˌflɜr-/— *n* a STYLIZED drawing of a LILY flower, formerly used on the COAT OF ARMS of the French royal family

flew /fluː/ *past t. of* FLY

flex¹ /fleks/ *v* [T1] to bend and move (one of one's limbs, muscles, etc.) so as to stretch and loosen, esp. in preparation for work: *The gardeners flexed their muscles and began to dig*

flex² *n* [C;U] *esp. BrE* (a length of) bendable electric wire enclosed in a protective covering, used for connecting an electrical apparatus to a supply —see picture at ELECTRICITY

flex·i·ble /ˈfleksəbəl/ *adj* **1** that can bend or be bent easily **2** that can change or be changed to be suitable for new needs, changed conditions, etc. —**-ibly** /-bli/ *adv* —**-ibility** /ˌfleksəˈbɪləti/ *n* [U]

flib·ber·ti·gib·bet /ˌflɪbətiˈdʒɪbət‖-bər-/ *n* a silly person, usu. a woman, who talks too much, changes her mind often, is never serious, etc. —see also FLIGHTY

flick¹ /flɪk/ *n* a short light blow, stroke, or movement as with a whip, finger, etc.: *The horses ran faster with every flick of the whip*

flick² *v* **1** [T1(D1)] to strike with a light quick blow from a whip, the finger, etc.: *The driver flicked the horse with his whip to make it go faster.*|*She flicked him a blow on the face* **2** [T2;L9] to (cause to) move with a light quick blow: *to flick the* SWITCH|*The snake's tongue flicked from side to side as it prepared to bite* **3** [X9 (*off*, OFF, AWAY)] to remove with a light quick stroke: *The cow flicked the flies away with its tail*

flick·er¹ /ˈflɪkəʳ/ *v* [Wv4;I∅] **1** to burn unsteadily; shine with an unsteady light: *The wind blew the flickering candle out.*|(fig.) *The hope still flickered within her that her husband might be alive* **2** to move backwards and forwards unsteadily: *Shadows flickered on the wall.*| *flickering eyelids*

flicker² *n* [S] a FLICKERing¹ action: (fig.) *a flicker of hope*

flick knife /ˈ· ·/ (*AmE* **switchblade**)— *n BrE* a knife with a blade inside the handle that springs into position when a button is pressed

flicks /flɪks/ *n* [*the*+P] *BrE infml* the cinema: *Would you like to go to the flicks tonight?*

fli·er, flyer /ˈflaɪəʳ/ *n* **1** someone or something that flies, esp. a pilot **2** *AmE infml* a small sheet of paper on which advertising matter is printed and given out to many people **3** *infml* FLYING START

flies /flaɪz/ *n* **1** [P] the front opening of a pair of trousers, with a band of cloth on one side to cover the fastenings —see also FLY³ (4) **2** [*the*+P] the large space above a stage from which men control and move the scenes used in a play

flight¹ /flaɪt/ *n* **1** [U;C] the act of flying: *a bird in flight*|*a bird's first flight from the nest* **2** [C] the distance covered or course followed by a flying object: *a straight flight towards home* **3** [C] a trip by plane: *Did you have a good flight?* **4** [C] the aircraft making a journey: *Flight Number 447 to Geneva is ready to leave* **5** [C] a group of birds or aircraft flying together: *a flight of* PIGEONS **6** [C] an effort that goes beyond the usual limits: *a flight of imagination* **7** [C] a set (of stairs, as between floors): *to fall down a flight of stairs* **8** [U] swift movement or passage: *the flight of time* **9 in the first flight** *esp. BrE* excellent; in a leading place; among the best

flight² *n* **1** (an example of) the act of running away or escaping (FLEEing): *Unemployment has been caused by a flight of money abroad* **2 put to flight** to cause to run away: *Our army will quickly put the enemy to flight* **3 take (to) flight** to run away

flight deck /ˈ· ·/ *n* **1** (on a ship built to carry military aircraft) the surface for taking off or landing **2** (in a plane) the room at the front from which the pilot and his helpers control the plane

flight·less /ˈflaɪtləs/ *adj* [Wa5] unable to fly: *flightless birds*

flight lieu·ten·ant /ˌ· ·ˈ··/ *n* [C;A;N] a COMMISSIONED OFFICER of low rank in the R.A.F.

flight ser·geant /ˈ· ˌ··/ *n* [C;A] a NONCOMMISSIONED OFFICER of high rank in the Royal Air Force

flight·y /ˈflaɪti/ *adj* [Wa2] (esp. of a woman or a woman's behaviour) unsteady; too influenced by sudden desires or ideas; often changing —**flightiness** *n* [U]

flim·sy¹ /ˈflɪmzi/ *adj* [Wa2] **1** (of material) light and thin: *flimsy cloth* **2** (of an object) easily broken or destroyed; lacking strength **3** weak; not carefully thought out: *a flimsy argument* —**-sily** *adv* —**-siness** *n* [U]

flimsy² *n* a very thin sheet of typing (TYPE²) paper, used esp. when several copies of something are made

flinch /flɪntʃ/ *v* [I∅ (*from*)] to move back when shocked by pain, or in fear of something unpleasant: *John didn't flinch once when the doctor was cleaning the wound.*|(fig.) *I flinched from telling her the news*

fling¹ /flɪŋ/ *v* **flung** /flʌŋ/ **1** [(T1);D1;X7,9] to throw violently or with force: *Don't fling your clothes on the floor, hang them up.*|*Every morning he flings the windows open and breathes deeply.*|*She flung her shoe at the cat* **2** [X9] to move (part of oneself) quickly or violently: *She flung back her head proudly* **3** [X9] to put suddenly, violently, or unexpectedly: *The military government flung its opponents into prison* **4** [L9] to move oneself violently, esp. in anger: *She flung around the room*|*from the house* **5 fling oneself into** to begin (an activity) with great interest or force **6 fling the past in someone's face** to blame someone for former mistakes **7 fling up one's hands in horror** to show signs of being very shocked

fling² *n* **1** an act of flinging; throw **2** a spirited Scottish dance; HIGHLAND FLING **3** a short time of satisfying one's own desires, often with no sense of responsibility; wild time (in the phr. **have one's/a fling**) **4 have a fling (at)** to make an attempt (at) **5 (at) full fling** at full speed

fling a·way *v adv* [T1] THROW AWAY

fling off *v adv* [T1] to escape from or leave: *to fling off the chains of marriage*

fling out *v adv* [T1] THROW OUT

flint /flɪnt/ *n* **1** [U] very hard fine-TEXTURED grey stone that makes very small flashes of flame when struck with steel **2** [C;U] (a piece of) this used in former times for striking fire —see also TINDERBOX **3** [C] a small piece of iron or other metal that makes a very small flash of flame when struck, used in cigarette lighters to light the petrol or gas

flint·lock /ˈflɪntlɒk‖-lɑk/ *n* a gun used in former times, in which the explosive powder was lit by a flash of flame produced by striking FLINT (2)

flint·y /ˈflɪnti/ *adj* [Wa1] **1** very hard; like FLINT (1) **2** cruel; unmerciful: *a flinty heart*

flip[1] /flɪp/ *v* **-pp- 1** [X9] to send (something) spinning, often into the air, by striking with a light quick blow **2** [T1 (OVER)] to turn over: *to flip an egg over in the pan* **3** [I∅] *sl* to become mad: *My brother really flipped after his experiences in the war* **4** [I∅] *sl* to become full of excitement and interest: *I knew you'd flip when you saw my new car* —compare FREAK OUT

flip[2] *n* **1** [C] a quick light blow, esp. one that sends something spinning into the air **2** [C;U:9] a drink made by mixing wine or a stronger alcoholic drink with sugar and egg: *egg flip*

flip[3] *adj* **-pp-** [Wa2;A] *infml* FLIPPANT: *a flip remark*

flip-flop /ˈ· ·/ *n* **1** [C *usu. pl.*] a type of open shoe (SANDAL) held on by the toes and loose at the back —see PAIR (USAGE) **2** [S] the sound of something FLAPping loosely

flip·pan·cy /ˈflɪpənsi/ *n* [U] the quality of being FLIPPANT

flip·pant /ˈflɪpənt/ *adj* disrespectful about serious subjects, esp. when trying to be amusing: *flippant remarks* —**~ly** *adv*

flip·per /ˈflɪpəʳ/ *n* a limb of certain larger sea animals that are not fish (esp. SEAL*s*), with a flat edge used for swimming

flip·ping /flɪpɪŋ/ *adj, adv BrE euph sl* BLOODY[2] (1,2): *Don't be so flipping rude!*

flip side /ˈ· ·/ *n infml* the side of a record that has the song or piece of music on that is of less interest or less popular than that on the other side

flip through *v prep* [T1] to read (a book, paper, etc.) rapidly and carelessly

flirt[1] /flɜːt‖flɜrt/ *v* [I∅ (*with*)] (esp. of a woman) to behave with a member of the opposite sex in a way that attracts interest and attention: *I don't like going to parties because my husband always flirts with every girl in the room* —see also FLIRT WITH

flirt[2] *n* a person, esp. a woman, who generally FLIRT*s*[1] with members of the opposite sex

flir·ta·tion /flɜːˈteɪʃən‖flɜr-/ *n* **1** [U] the act of FLIRTing[1] **2** [C] a short love affair which is not serious **3** [C] a passing interest in or connection with (esp. a subject of study): *a flirtation with ancient languages*|(*fig.*) *His driving became a flirtation with death* —compare FLIRT WITH

flir·ta·tious /flɜːˈteɪʃəs‖flɜr-/ *adj* **1** (esp. of a woman) that likes to FLIRT[1]; that FLIRT*s*[1] regularly: *a flirtatious young girl* **2** of or related to FLIRTing[1]: *flirtatious behaviour* —**~ly** *adv* —**~ness** *n* [U]

flirt with *v prep* [T1 *no pass.*] **1** to think about but not very seriously: *We flirted with the idea of going abroad but decided against it* **2** to deal lightly with: *to flirt with danger/death* —see also FLIRT[1]

flit[1] /flɪt/ *v* **-tt- 1** [L9] to fly or move lightly or quickly: *The birds flitted from branch to branch* **2** [I∅] *Scot & NEngE* to move house; to change from one place of living to another

flit[2] *n* **do a (moonlight) flit** *BrE infml* to move from one house to another secretly to avoid paying the rent one owes

flitch /flɪtʃ/ *n* a side of a pig preserved in salt

fliv·ver /ˈflɪvəʳ/ *n AmE* a small cheap car

float[1] /fləʊt/ *n* **1** a piece of wood or other light object that floats, used on a fishing line or to support the edge of a fishing net **2** an air-filled container used instead of wheels by planes that land on water **3** a large flat vehicle on which special shows, ornamental scenes, etc., are drawn in processions —see also MILK FLOAT **4** a sum of money collected in advance and kept for use if an unexpected need arises —compare KITTY[2] (2)

float[2] *v* **1** [I∅;T1] to (cause to) stay at the top of liquid or be held up in air without sinking: *Wood floats on water.*|*We are trying to float the sunken ship* **2** [X9] to (cause to) move easily and lightly as on moving liquid or air: *The logs float down the river to the paper factory.*|*We float them there.*|*A feather floated down on the wind* **3** [X9] (of liquid) to support and move on the surface: *The current floated the logs to shore* **4** [L9] to move aimlessly from place to place: *The old man floats from town to town with nowhere to go and nothing to do* —compare DRIFT[2] (1) **5** [T1] to establish (a business, company, etc.) by selling shares **6** [T1] to suggest: *The idea was first floated before the war* **7** [T1;I∅] **a** to allow the exchange value of (a country's money) to vary freely from day to day **b** (of a country's money) to vary freely in exchange value from day to day: *After the pound started floating other states let their monies float as well* **8** [L9, esp. ABOUT, AROUND] (*usu. in -ing form*) to be placed as stated: *Where's my pen? It must be floating about somewhere* —**~er** *n*

floa·ta·tion /fləʊˈteɪʃən/ *n* [U] FLOTATION

float·ing /ˈfləʊtɪŋ/ *adj* [Wa5] **1** not fixed or settled in a particular place: *London has a large floating population* **2 floating voters/vote** the people who do not vote for a fixed political party but change their loyalty: *He is trying to get the support of the floating voters/to win the floating vote*

floating bridge /ˌ·· ˈ·/ *n* a bridge formed by boats or floating logs

floating debt /ˌ·· ˈ·/ *n tech* a debt consisting of sums DUE within a short time, parts of which must be paid on demand or at a stated time

floating dock /ˌ·· ˈ·/ *n* a DOCK that floats and that can be lowered in the water to allow a ship to enter and then raised to bring the ship out of the water for repairs, painting etc.

floating kid·ney /ˌ·· ˈ··/ *n med* a KIDNEY that can make unusual movements in the body

floating rib /ˌ·· ˈ·/ *n* a RIB (such as one in either of the 2 lowest pairs in man) that is not connected to any other bone at the front

flock[1] /flɒk‖flɑk/ *n* [GC] **1** a group of sheep, goats, or birds **2** *infml* a crowd; large number of people **3** the group of people who regularly attend a church: *The priest warned his flock against breaking God's law*

flock[2] *v* [L9, esp. *to, into*] to gather or move in large crowds: *In the 19th century people flocked to the cities where they expected to make their fortune*

flock[3] *n* **1** [C *usu. pl.*] **a** a small mass of wool, hair, etc. **b** small pieces of any material used for filling CUSHION*s*, MATTRESSes, etc. **2** [U] soft material (on the surface of another) esp. forming ornamental patterns: *flock curtains*|**flocked** *wallpaper*

floe /fləʊ/ *n* [*often pl.*] a large mass of ice floating on the surface of the sea

flog /flɒg‖flɑg/ *v* **-gg- 1** [T1] to beat severely with a whip or stick, esp. as a punishment **2** [X9] to cause to reach the stated condition by beating: *He was flogged into accepting/acceptance* **3** [T1] *BrE sl* to (try to) sell **4 flog a dead horse a** to waste one's time with useless efforts **b** to keep repeating something already understood or accepted **5 flog**

to death *not fml* to spoil (a story, request, etc.) by repeating too often

flog·ging /ˈflɒgɪŋ‖ˈflagɪŋ/ *n* [C;U] a severe beating with a whip or stick, esp. as punishment

flood¹ /flʌd/ *n* [*often pl. with sing. meaning*] **1** the covering with water of a place that is usu. dry; great overflow of water: *The town was destroyed by the floods after the storm.*|*The water rose to flood level* **2** a large flow: *There was a flood of complaints about the bad language after the show.*|*In the 19th century a flood of settlers left Europe for America* **3** **in flood** (of a river) overflowing the banks

flood² *v* **1** [T1;IØ] to (cause to) be filled or covered with water: *Every spring the river floods the valley.*|*Our street floods whenever we have rain* **2** [IØ] to overflow: *After such a storm I'm surprised the river hasn't flooded* **3** [T1 (OUT);L9, esp. IN] to arrive (at) (a place) in such large numbers as to be difficult to deal with: *After the show complaints flooded the television company's offices.*|*Requests for information flooded in after the advertisement.*|*We were flooded out with letters* **4** [L9] to go in very large numbers: *Settlers flooded from Europe to America in the 19th century* **5** [T1;L9] to cover or spread into completely: *The room was flooded with light.*|*Toys flooded the floor.*|*His papers flooded over the desk and onto the floor* **6 flood the market** to (cause to) be offered for sale in such quantities as to bring the price down

flood·gate /ˈflʌdgeɪt/ *n* [*often pl.*] **1** a gate used for controlling the flow from a large body of water **2** **open the floodgates** to allow feelings, ideas, etc., to be suddenly shown in full after being held back: *The new law opened the floodgates of the workers' bitterness and they marched down the streets demanding justice*

flood·light¹ /ˈflʌdlaɪt/ *n* [*often pl.*] a large electric light that produces a very powerful and bright beam of light, used for lighting the outside of buildings, football grounds, etc., at night

floodlight² *v* **-lighted** *or* **-lit** /lɪt/ [Wv5;T1] to light by using FLOODLIGHTs¹: *Buckingham Palace is floodlit at night*

flood out *v adv* [T1 (*of*) *usu. pass.*] to force to leave home because of floods: *Many of the people flooded out during the storm have now returned home*

flood tide /ˈ· ·/ *n* [C;U] the flow of the TIDE inwards; rising TIDE —opposite **ebb tide**

floor¹ /flɔːʳ‖flor/ *n* **1** [C] the surface on which one stands indoors; surface nearest the ground **2** [C] (of the sea, a cave, etc.) the bottom —see LAND (USAGE) **3** [C] a level of a building; STOREY: *I live on the ground floor* (=the floor level with the street) *of a block of flats.*|*Our office is on the 6th floor* **4** [C] a lower limit of prices: *Each shop is free to set the price anywhere between a floor of 15 pence and a* CEILING *of 25 pence* —opposite **ceiling** **5** [C] the level supporting surface of any object: *the floor of a bridge* **6** [C9] a level area specially prepared for a particular purpose: *a dance floor*|*the floor of the* STOCK EXCHANGE **7** [*the*+R] the part of a parliament or council building where members sit and speak **8** [*the*+R] the right of one member to speak: *to get/have the floor* **9 take the floor** to start dancing, as at a party or in a dance hall **10 wipe the floor with** *infml* to defeat totally: *The government party wiped the floor with the opposition in the last elections*

floor² *v* [T1] **1** to provide with a floor: *floored with boards* **2** to knock down: *The soldier floored his attacker with one heavy blow* **3** *infml* to beat; defeat: *I was floored by his argument and had to admit defeat* **4** *infml* to confuse: *The news floored me*

floor·board /ˈflɔːbɔːd‖ˈflorbord/ *n* a board in a wooden floor

floor cloth /ˈ· ·/ *n* a piece of cloth used for washing or cleaning floors

floor·ing /ˈflɔːrɪŋ‖ˈflor-/ *n* [U] material used for making floors: *wooden flooring*

floor show /ˈ· ·/ *n* a number of amusing acts (such as dancing, singing, etc.) performed in a restaurant, NIGHTCLUB, etc.

floor·walk·er /ˈflɔːˌwɔːkəʳ‖ˈflor-/ *n* a person employed in a large shop to show people where to go, to look after sales, to keep watch for people stealing things, etc.

floo·zy, -sy /ˈfluːzi/ *n sl* a woman who offers sex for money; PROSTITUTE

flop¹ /flɒp‖flap/ *v* **-pp-** **1** [L9] to move or fall heavily or awkwardly: *He can't swim much; he just flops about in the water* **2** [IØ] *infml* (of a plan, a performance, etc.) to fail badly; be unsuccessful: *The new play flopped because the actors didn't know their parts properly*

flop² *n* **1** [S] the movement or noise of FLOPping¹ (1): *He fell with a flop into the water* **2** [C] *infml* a failure: *The party was a complete flop; nobody enjoyed it*

flop³ *adv* [H] with a FLOP² (1): *She fell flop on the floor unconscious*

flop·py /ˈflɒpi‖ˈflapi/ *adj* [Wa2] **1** soft and falling loosely: *This material's too floppy for a coat* **2** *infml* weak —**floppily** *adv* —**floppiness** *n* [U]

flo·ra /ˈflɔːrə‖ˈflorə/ *n* **1** [U9;(C9)] all the plants growing wild in a particular place, or belonging to a particular age in history: *the flora of chalk areas*|*stone age flora* **2** [C9] a list or description of such plants —compare FAUNA

flo·ral /ˈflɔːrəl‖ˈflorəl/ *adj* [Wa5] of flowers: *floral patterns*

floral trib·ute *n pomp* a bunch of flowers given as a TRIBUTE (2)

flo·ri·cul·ture /ˈflɔːrɪ̵ˌkʌltʃəʳ‖ˈflo-/ *n* [U] the science or business of growing flowering plants

flor·id /ˈflɒrɪ̵d‖ˈflɔ-, ˈfla-/ *adj* **1** *often derog* richly ornamented; having (too) much ornamentation: *florid language*|*That music's too florid for my taste* **2** (of a person's face) having a red skin —**~ly** *adv*

flor·in /ˈflɒrɪ̵n‖ˈflo-, ˈflɒ-/ *n* (until 1971) a silver-coloured British coin worth 2 shillings

flor·ist /ˈflɒrɪ̵st‖ˈflo-/ *n* a person who keeps a shop for selling flowers

floss /flɒs‖flas, flɔs/ *n* [U] **1** a mass of waste rough silk threads from the outer covering spun (SPIN) by a SILKWORM **2** fine silk, spun (SPIN) but not twisted, used for cleaning teeth and for sewing —see also CANDYFLOSS (1)

flo·ta·tion, floa- /fləʊˈteɪʃən/ *n* [C;U] an act or the action of getting money or other support in order to start up a business company

flo·til·la /fləˈtɪlə‖fləʊ-/ *n* a group of small warships, usu. DESTROYERs

flot·sam and jet·sam /ˌflɒtsəm ən ˈdʒetsəm‖ˌflat-/ *n* **1** [U] broken pieces of wood, plastic, and other waste materials floating about together in the sea, or washed up onto the shore **2** [U] a collection of broken unwanted things lying about in an untidy way **3** [P] people without homes or work, who move helplessly through life

flounce¹ /flaʊns/ *v* [L9 esp. OUT, *out of*] to move violently in a temper: *She refused my offers of advice and flounced out of the house*

flounce² *n* a band of cloth sewn along its top edge onto a garment, esp. a woman's skirt, as an ornament, esp. in fashions of former times

flounce³ *v* [Wv5;T1] to ornament (a garment) by sewing FLOUNCEs² on, as was fashionable in former times: *a flounced skirt*

floun·der¹ /ˈflaʊndəʳ/ *v* **1** [I∅] to move about with great difficulty, esp. making violent efforts not to sink: *The fish floundered on the river bank, struggling to breathe* **2** [L9] to move forward with great difficulty, esp. when sinking: *The horse and its rider floundered through the deep snow* **3** [I∅] to struggle or lose control when speaking or doing something: *When one of his listeners laughed rudely, he floundered and lost the place in the notes of his speech*

flounder² *n* [Wn1] a type of small flat fish, used as food

flour¹ /flaʊəʳ/ *n* [U] powder made from grain, esp. wheat, and used for making bread, pastry, cakes, etc. —see also PLAIN FLOUR, SELF-RAISING FLOUR

flour² *v* [T1] to cover with flour: *to flour the pastry board so that the mixture doesn't stick to it*

flour·ish¹ /ˈflʌrɪʃ‖ˈflɜrɪʃ/ *v* **1** [T1] to wave in the hand and so draw attention to (something): *"I've passed my examination!" shouted the boy, flourishing a letter in his mother's face* **2** [I∅] (esp. of a plant) to grow healthily: *Very few plants will flourish without water* **3** [I∅] *often humor* (of a person) to be well; be in full strength: *"How are your family?" "They're flourishing"* **4** [I∅] to be successful in business: *The bank is flourishing; it's opened 2 more branches this year* **5** [L9] to be alive or producing (good) results at a certain time in history: *Chaucer flourished at the end of the 14th century* —**~ingly** *adv*

flourish² *n* **1** a showy fancy movement or manner that draws people's attention to one: *He opened the door with a flourish* **2** a curve or ornament in writing **3** a loud showy part of a piece of music, esp. one to mark the entrance of an important person

flour·mill /ˈflaʊəˌmɪl‖-ər-/ *n* MILL¹ (1)

flour·y /ˈflaʊəri/ *adj* [Wa1] **1** covered with flour: *She was making pastry and her hands were floury* **2** soft and rather powdery: *floury potatoes*

flout /flaʊt/ *v* [T1] to treat without respect or consideration; go against: *She flouted all my offers of help and friendship.|You've flouted my orders* (=disobeyed them)

flow¹ /fləʊ/ *v* **1** [I∅] (of liquid) to run or spread smoothly; pour: *The stream flowed along rapidly.|Blood was flowing from his wound.|Her tears flowed fast* **2** [I∅] to move along smoothly without pause: *The cars flowed in a steady stream along the main road.|As the ladies drank their tea, conversation began to flow* **3** [L9] to be plentiful: *That's a rich city; money flows like water there* **4** [L9] (of hair, cloth, etc.) to fall loosely and gracefully: *Her thick wavy hair flowed over her shoulders* **5** [I∅] (of the TIDE) to rise; come in —compare EBB¹ (1); see also FLOWING

flow² *n* **1** [S (*of*)] a pouring out: *a flow of oil all over the floor|a flow of meaningless words* **2** [(*the*) U (*of*)] a smooth steady movement: *the gentle flow of the river* **3** [(*the*) U (*of*)] the rate of flowing: *The flow of the River Nile is at its fastest in the late summer* **4** [(*the*) S (*of*)] a supply of gas, electricity, etc. **5** [(*the*) U (*of*)] the rise (of the TIDE) —compare EBB¹ (1)

flow di·a·gram /ˈ· ˌ···/ also **flow·chart** /ˈfləʊtʃɑːt‖-ɑrt/— *n* a drawing in which particular shapes and connecting lines are used for showing how each particular action in a system is connected with or depends on the next or another

flow·er¹ /ˈflaʊəʳ/ *n* **1** [C] the part of a plant, often beautiful and coloured, that produces seeds or fruit **2** [C] a plant that is grown for the beauty of this part: *He grows flowers in the ornamental part of his garden, and vegetables in the kitchen garden* **3** [(*the*) U (*of*)] *lit* the best part; the most perfect (of a group): *The flower of the nation was lost in the war* **4 in flower** having the flowers open: *The roses are in flower just now*
See next page for picture

flower² *v* **1** [Wv4;I∅] (of a plant) to produce flowers: *This bush flowers in the spring.|flowering plants* **2** [L9] to develop; come to be in its best state: *His* GENIUS *as a painter flowered very early*

flow·er·bed /ˈflaʊəbed‖-ər-/ *n* a piece of ground, esp. in a garden, in which flowers are grown for ornament

flow·ered /ˈflaʊəd‖-ərd/ *adj* [A] ornamented with flower patterns: *flowered dress material*

flower gar·den /ˈ·· ˌ··/ *n* a garden in which flowers are grown, not vegetables

flower girl /ˈ·· ·/ *n* a girl or woman who sells flowers in a street or market

flow·er·ing /ˈflaʊərɪŋ/ *n* [S] a high point of development, esp. when reached for the first time: *"the flowering of New England"* (in the first half of the 19th Century)

flow·er·less /ˈflaʊələs‖-ər-/ *adj* [Wa5] not producing flowers: FERN*s are flowerless plants*

flow·er·pot /ˈflaʊəpɒt‖-ərpɑt/ *n* a pot which can be filled with earth in which a plant can be grown

flower pow·er /ˈ·· ˌ··/ *n* [U] *infml* (*sometimes caps.*) (esp. in the 1960s) the set of ideas and beliefs held by certain people (**flower children, flower people**) favouring universal love and wearing flowers, bells, etc.

flow·er·y /ˈflaʊəri/ *adj* [Wa2] **1** (of a field, hillside, etc.) full of wild flowers **2** ornamented with flowers: *a flowery pattern* **3** *usu. derog* (of speech or writing) very much ornamented; full of fanciful words

flow·ing /ˈfləʊɪŋ/ *adj* [A] moving, curving, or hanging gracefully: *The letter was written in flowing handwriting* —**~ly** *adv*

flown /fləʊn/ *past p. of* FLY

flu /fluː/ *n* [U] *infml* INFLUENZA

fluc·tu·ate /ˈflʌktʃʊeɪt/ *v* [I∅] **1** to rise and fall: *The price of vegetables fluctuates according to the weather.* **2** [Wv4 (*between*)] to change from one state to the opposite: *As a writer he experienced fluctuating fortunes; sometimes his books were laughed at, sometimes they were admired.|His feelings fluctuated between excitement and fear* —**-ation** /ˌflʌktʃʊˈeɪʃən/ *n* [U;C (*in*)]: *There's been some fluctuation in the rate of her* HEARTBEAT*s*

flue /fluː/ *n* a metal pipe or tube up which smoke or heat passes, usu. to a chimney —see picture at LIVING ROOM

flu·en·cy /ˈfluːənsi/ *n* [U (*in*)] the quality or condition of being FLUENT

flu·ent /ˈfluːənt/ *adj* **1** [(*in*)] (of a person) speaking, writing, or playing a musical instrument in an easy smooth manner: *He is fluent in 5 languages* **2** (of speech, writing, etc.) expressed readily and without pause: *She speaks fluent though not very correct English* —**~ly** *adv*

fluff¹ /flʌf/ *n* **1** [U] soft light loose waste from woollen or other materials: *The room hasn't been properly cleaned; there's fluff and dust under the furniture* **2** [U] **a** very soft fur or hair on a young animal **b** the first very fine feathers on a bird **3** [C] *infml* an awkward unsuccessful attempt, esp. at acting or at playing a stroke in a game **4 bit of fluff** *BrE sl* a young girl, esp. as considered to be sexually attractive

fluff² *v* **1** [T1 (OUT, UP)] to make (something soft) appear larger by shaking or by brushing or pushing upwards: *The bird fluffed out its feathers in the sun.|She fluffed up her hair* **2** [T1] *infml* to do (something) badly or unsuccessfully: *The actress fluffed her lines* (=forgot what she had to say).|*The*

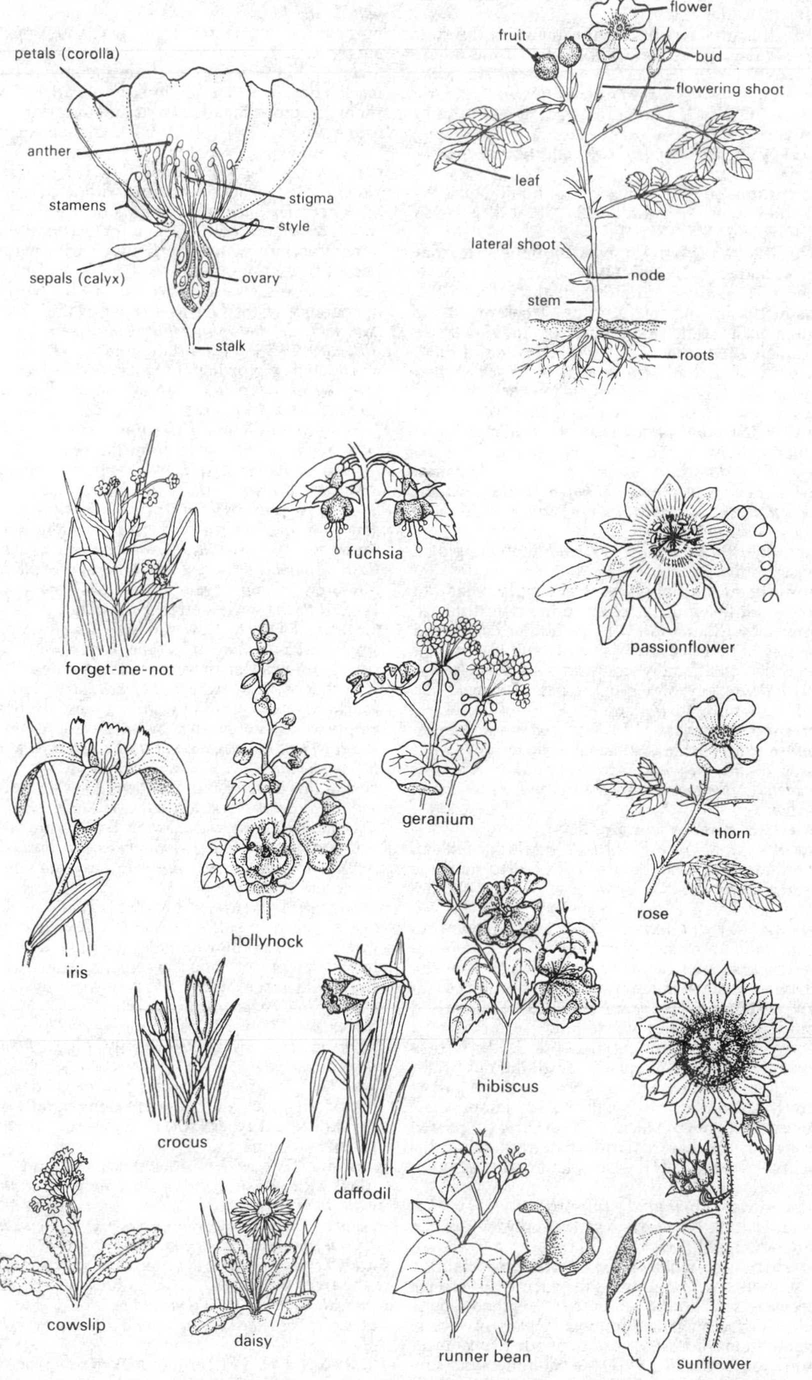
petals (corolla)
anther
stamens
stigma
style
sepals (calyx)
ovary
stalk
flower
fruit
bud
flowering shoot
leaf
lateral shoot
node
stem
roots
forget-me-not
fuchsia
passionflower
geranium
iris
hollyhock
rose
thorn
hibiscus
crocus
daffodil
cowslip
daisy
runner bean
sunflower

flowers

cricketer fluffed the catch (=dropped the ball he was trying to catch)

fluff·y /ˈflʌfi/ *adj* [Wa1] like or covered with FLUFF[1] (2)—**fluffiness** *n* [U]

flu·id[1] /ˈfluːɪ̀d/ *adj* **1** having the quality of flowing, like liquids, air, gas, etc.; not solid **2** unsettled; not fixed: *We've only just begun to plan the work, and our ideas on the subject are still fluid*

fluid[2] *n* [C;U] **1** a liquid **2** *tech* a FLUID[1] (1) substance

flu·id·i·ty /fluːˈɪdɪ̀ti/ *n* [U] the condition or quality of being FLUID[1]

fluid ounce /ˌ·· ˈ·/ *n* (a measure of liquid equal to) one 20th of a PINT or 0·0284 of a litre —see WEIGHTS & MEASURES TABLE

fluke[1] /fluːk/ *n* [Wn1] a type of flat worm that attacks and eats a sheep's LIVER

fluke[2] *n* **1** [C *often pl.*] either of the 2 broad flat ends of the instrument (ANCHOR) let down to the bottom of the sea to stop a ship from moving —see picture at FREIGHTER **2** [C *often pl.*] either of the 2 flat parts of the tail of a type of large sea animal (WHALE) **3** [C] the back-curving (BARBed) head of a fishhook or of a spear used for killing fish

fluke[3] *n* [S] *infml* **1** a piece of accidental good fortune: *He passed his examination by a fluke; he knew very little about his subject* **2** an accidental good stroke in a game: *"What a fluke," said his opponent as the ball rolled into the hole, "you've been playing badly up till now"*

fluk·y, -ey /ˈfluːki/ *adj* [Wa1] *infml* happening by a FLUKE[3]: *a fluky shot*

flume /fluːm/ *n* a sloping passage or pipe made to carry water to a mill, or for any other industrial use

flum·me·ry /ˈflʌməri/ *n* **1** [U;C *usu. pl.*] *derog* (an example of) unnecessarily unclear and showy language or intentionally confusing activity **2** [U; (C)] *old use* any of various types of sweet dish made with milk, flour, eggs, etc.

flum·mox /ˈflʌməks/ *v* [T1;Wv5] *infml esp. BrE* to confuse and make (someone) uncertain what words to use or what action to take: *She was completely flummoxed by the second examination question*

flung /flʌŋ/ *past t. & past p. of* FLING

flunk /flʌŋk/ *v infml esp. AmE* **1** [T1;I∅] to fail (an examination or study course) **2** [T1] to mark as unsatisfactory the examination answers of (someone)

flun·key, -ky /ˈflʌŋki/ *n* **1** a male servant in ceremonial dress in a wealthy house **2** *derog* a person who tries to win someone's favour by behaving with too much respect and obedience

flunk out *v adv* [I∅] *infml AmE* to be dismissed from a school or college for failure

flu·o·res·cent /flʊəˈresənt‖flʊə-, flo-/ *adj* **1** (of a substance) having the quality of giving out bright white light when electric or other waves are passed through **2** [Wa5] (of lighting, a lamp, etc.) producing light by means of electricity passed through a tube covered with material having this quality —**-cence** *n* [U]: —see picture at ELECTRICITY

flu·o·ri·date /ˈflʊərɪ̀deɪt‖ˈflʊə-, ˈflo-/ *v* [Wv5;T1] to add FLUORIDE to (a water supply) —**-dation** /ˌflʊərɪ̀ˈdeɪʃən‖ˌflʊə-, ˌflo-/ *n* [U]

flu·o·ride /ˈflʊəraɪd/ *n* **1** [U] a certain combination of FLUORINE with another substance (esp. **sodium fluoride**), said to be able to strengthen young children's teeth against decay **2** [C] any of several combinations of FLUORINE with another substance

flu·o·rine /ˈflʊəriːn/ *n* [U] a non-metallic substance, usu. in the form of a poisonous pale greenish-yellow gas

flur·ry[1] /ˈflʌri‖ˈflɜri/ *n* **1** [C] **a** a sudden sharp rush of wind or rain **b** a light fall of snow: *Snow flurries are expected this evening* **2** [S+*of*] a sudden shared feeling: *A flurry of excitement went round the hall as the king came in* **3** [S] a state of troubled hurry and excitement: *The thought of a long journey put the old lady in a flurry*

flurry[2] *v* [T1;Wv5] to confuse and make (someone) have difficulty in thinking clearly of what should be done; make nervous and uncertain

flush[1] /flʌʃ/ *v* [I∅] (of birds) to fly up suddenly —see also FLUSH FROM (1)

flush[2] *n* **1** [S (*of*)] a sudden flow (of liquid, esp. water) **2** [S] an act of cleaning with a sudden flow of water: *The pipe is blocked; give it a good flush (out)* **3** [S9] a flow of water for washing out an apparatus into which the body's waste matter is passed (a WATER CLOSET) **4** [C] a flow of blood to the face —see also HOT FLUSH **5** [S] a red appearance of the face as a result of this: *The sick boy had an unhealthy flush and breathed with difficulty* **6** [S+*of*] **a** a sudden increase, esp. as of a sudden new growing of plants: *In South India the rainy weather brings a flush of greenness to the dry land in a few hours* **b** a sudden feeling: *He felt a flush of anger* **7** [(*the*) U (*of*)] a feeling of eager excitement or success (esp. in the phr. **in the first flush of**): *In the first flush of success he ordered drinks for everybody, but later he was sorry he had done so* **8** [(*the*) U (*of*)] a sudden flow or high condition of strength (esp. in the phr **in the first flush of**): *He was killed in an accident in the first flush of manhood* (=just when he had come to his full strength and development).|*She's no longer in her first flush* (=she's no longer young)

flush[3] *v* **1** [I∅] to flow suddenly and freely: *The stream was flushing after the heavy rain* **2** [T1 (OUT)] to clean or drive out by a sudden flow of water: *The waste pipe is blocked; try flushing it (out) with hot water* **3** [T1;I∅] to (cause to) become empty of waste matter by means of a flow of water: *The* LAVATORY *won't flush; I've tried flushing it several times, but it won't work* **4** [I∅ (UP)] (of a person, his skin, or face) to turn red as a result of a sudden flow of blood to the skin: *She flushed when she couldn't answer the question* **5** [T1 *usu. pass.*] to cause to become red: *Her forehead was flushed with fever.*|*The setting sun flushed the mountain tops* —see also FLUSHED

flush[4] *adj* **1** [F (*with*);(A);Wa5] exactly on a level (with); even in surface: *These cupboards are flush with the wall* (=they do not stick out) **2** [F] *infml* having plenty of money (sometimes in the phr. **flush with money**): *He felt very flush on his first payday, and began to spend wildly*

flush[5] *adv* **1** in a FLUSH[4] (1) way: *The door fits flush into its frame* **2** *infml* exactly; fully: *He hit him flush on the jaw*

flush[6] *n* (in card games) a set of cards dealt to a person, in which all the cards belong to only one of the 4 different types (SUITS[1] (3)) —see also ROYAL FLUSH; —compare RUN[2] (9)

flushed /flʌʃt/ *adj* [F+*with*] excited and eager; filled with pleasure and pride: *The soldiers, flushed with their first success, went on to gain another victory.*|*The young parents were flushed with happiness at the birth of their first son*

flush from *v prep* [D1] **1** to drive (birds) up from (the trees or bushes), so as to be shot by hunters: *to flush the birds from their hiding places* **2** to FLUSH OUT of: *They flushed the criminals from their hiding place*

flush out *v adv* [T1 (*of*)] to make (someone) leave a hiding place: *The police flushed the criminals out; they flushed them out of their hiding place*

flus·ter[1] /ˈflʌstə[r]/ *v* [Wv5;T1] to cause (someone) to be hot, nervous, and confused: *The shouts of the crowd flustered the speaker and he forgot what he was going to say*

fluster² *n* [S] a state of being FLUSTERed¹: *She was in a fluster at the thought of receiving several unexpected guests*

flute¹ /fluːt/ *n* a pipelike wooden or metal musical instrument with finger holes, played by blowing across a hole in the side —see picture at WIND INSTRUMENT

flute² *v* [Wv5;T1] to make long thin inward curves along the whole length of (a pillar or other long narrow object) at a regular distance from each other, as an ornament: *fluted pillars*

flut·ing /ˈfluːtɪŋ/ also **flutings** [P]— *n* [U] a set of hollow curves cut on a surface as ornament: *The plates and dishes of this old dinner set are edged with fluting*

flut·ist /ˈfluːt̬ɪst/ *n AmE* FLAUTIST

flut·ter¹ /ˈflʌtəʳ/ *v* **1** [X9;IØ] (of a bird, an insect with large wings, etc.) to move (the wings) quickly and lightly without flying: *The bird on the nest fluttered her wings up and down, hoping to make the cat go away from her eggs.|I can hear a bird fluttering in the chimney* **2** [L9] to fly by doing this: *The* BUTTERFLY *fluttered from flower to flower* **3** [IØ] (of wings) to move quickly and lightly **4** [IØ; T1] **a** (of a thin light object) to wave quickly up and down or backwards and forwards: *The flag fluttered in the wind* **b** to cause (a thin light object) to do this: *She fluttered her handkerchief from the train window as a goodbye* **5** [L9] (of a thin light object) to move in the air: *The dead leaves fluttered to the ground* **6** [T1;L9] to (cause to) move in a quick irregular way: *She fluttered her eyelids at him.|He had difficulty in starting the car, but at last the engine fluttered into life* (=began to work) **7** [IØ] (of the heart) to beat quickly and irregularly: *The boy's heart fluttered with excitement*

flutter² *n* **1** [(*the*) S] a FLUTTERing¹ movement: *There was a flutter of wings among the trees* **2** [S] *infml* an excited condition; state of excited interest: *The arrival of the good-looking young man put the girls in a flutter* **3** [C *usu. sing.*] *infml esp. BrE* a chance, taken in a light way, of gaining or losing money, at cards, on the winner of a race, by buying and selling business shares, etc.: *to have a flutter on the horses* **4** [U] *tech* a shaking movement that causes a fault in the action of a machine, esp. as **a** in a machine for playing recorded sound, causing faulty high sounds —compare WOW³ (1) **b** in the wings of an aircraft **5** [C] *med* an irregular movement of the heart

flu·vi·al /ˈfluːvɪəl/ *adj* [Wa5] *tech* of, found in, or produced by rivers

flux /flʌks/ *n* **1** [U] continual change; condition of not being settled (esp. in the phr. **a state of flux**): *Our future plans are unsettled; everything's been in a state of flux since the death of our father* **2** [U] a substance added to a metal to help melting, or to help in SOLDERing 2 pieces of metal together **3** [S] a flow or flowing: *a continuous flux of unclear images*

fly¹ /flaɪ/ *v* **flew** /fluː/, **flown** /fləʊn/ **1** [IØ] to move or be moved through the air by means of wings or a machine: *Most birds and some insects fly.|A bee flew in through the open window.|The damaged aircraft was flying on only one engine.|"How did you get here?" "I flew"* (=came by aircraft).|*That businessman flies great distances every month* **2** [T1] to control and guide (an aircraft or other like vehicle) in flight: *He was the first man ever to fly that type of aircraft* **3** [T1] to carry or send (someone or something) in an aircraft: *How many passengers does this* AIRLINE *fly weekly?|He's flying his car to Europe* (=sending it in an aircraft) **4** [T1 *pass. rare*] to use (a particular AIRLINE) for travelling by: *I always fly British Airways* **5** [T1] to cross (a broad stretch of water) by means of flying: *Louis Blériot was the first man to fly the English Channel in an aircraft.|Powerful aircraft now fly the Atlantic in a few hours* **6** [L9] to be carried along by wind; spread about in the air: *Clouds were flying across the sky.|Dead leaves and bits of paper were flying about.|The sailing ship is flying before the wind* **7** [L9;(IØ)] to pass up into or through the air as a result of some directed force: *The player gave a great kick, and the football flew across the field.|Arrows were flying thick and fast from the fort.*|(fig.) *Angry words were flying as the crowd grew more and more threatening* **8** [IØ] (in sport) (of a ball) to rise from the ground (BOUNCE) more quickly and steeply than expected **9** [IØ] (of something fixed at one end) to wave or float in the air: *The national flag was flying from its pole.|The girl ran wildly, with her long hair flying about her face* **10** [T1] **a** to raise in the air on the end of a thread, rope, etc.: *You can't fly a* KITE *if there's no wind* **b** to show (a flag) ceremonially in this way: *The warship was flying the national flag* **11** [Wv4; IØ] to pass rapidly; hurry; move at speed: *Time flies.|The train flew past.|She flew up the steps.|The boy flew to the help of the baby that was made afraid by a big dog.|flying feet* **12** [IØ] *infml* to leave in a hurry (esp. in the phrs. **I/we must fly**): *I'm late; I must fly* **13** [L9] to move suddenly and with force: *The window flew open.|The head of the hammer was loose, and it flew off the handle* **14** [T1;IØ (*from*)] to escape (from); FLEE: *He was forced to fly the country.|The thief was flying from justice* **15 the bird has flown** the person needed or wanted has gone away or escaped **16 fly into a temper** to become suddenly and unexpectedly angry **17 let fly (at)** **a** to attack with blows or words **b** to shoot **18 make the dust/feathers/fur/sparks fly** to cause a quarrel or a fight: *When Derek found his bicycle damaged by Bob, it really made the feathers fly* —see also **as the** CROW **flies**¹ (2), **fly in the** FACE **of**¹ (8), FLY AT, FLYING, **fly off the** HANDLE¹ (3), **fly a** KITE

fly² *n* **1** (*often in comb.*) any of several types of small insect with 2 wings (esp. the HOUSEFLY) **2** (*in comb.*) any of several types of flying insect: *a* BUTTERFLY|*a* DRAGONFLY **3** a copy of a winged insect made of thread, feather, or silk wound round a hook used for catching fish **4 not harm/hurt a fly** to be very gentle by nature **5 there are no flies on someone** someone is not a fool and cannot be tricked —see also **a fly in the** OINTMENT (2)

fly³ *n* **1** [C] a band of strong cloth (CANVAS) over the entrance to a tent, forming a kind of door **2** [C] the end of a flag opposite to the end that is joined to the pole **3** [C] a type of light carriage used in former times for public hire, drawn by one horse **4** [A;C] (of or for) FLIES (1): *a fly button|Your fly's undone*

fly⁴ *adj infml esp. BrE* sharp and clever; not easily tricked: *He's a fly* CUSTOMER (=fellow) *and very hard to deceive*

fly at *v prep* [T1 *no pass.*] to attack suddenly and violently: *The fierce dog flew at the postman*

fly·a·way /ˈflaɪəweɪ/ *adj* [A;(F)] (of dress or esp. hair) soft and loose and easily blown out by the wind

fly·blown /ˈflaɪbləʊn/ *adj* **1** (of meat) unfit to eat because containing flies' eggs **2** covered with the small spots that are the waste matter of flies: *a dirty flyblown window* **3** *derog* **a** not pure or bright and new; in a bad condition: *our flyblown world|a few flyblown old chairs* **b** worthless because used many times before: *He always brings out the same* *flyblown old stories when he makes an after-dinner speech*

fly·by /ˈflaɪbaɪ/ *n* **-bys** *AmE* FLYPAST

fly-by-night /ˈ· · ˌ·/ *n, adj* **fly-by-nights** *derog* **1** [C; B] (a person or business) that is not firmly established, but is interested only in making quick profits, esp. by slightly dishonest methods **2** [C;B] (a debtor) who runs away

fly·catch·er /ˈflaɪˌkætʃəʳ/ *n* any of several kinds of small bird that catch flies in the air

fly·er /ˈflaɪəʳ/ *n* FLIER

fly-fish·ing /ˈ· ˌ··/ *n* [U] the practice of fishing in a river or lake with a FLY[2] (3)

fly half /ˌ· ˈ·/ also **standoff half**— *n* (in RUGBY) a fast-running player whose job is to pass the ball out to the line of players who will try to gain points with it —see picture at RUGBY

fly·ing[1] /ˈflaɪ-ɪŋ/ *adj* [Wa5;A] **1** (of a jump) made after running for a short distance: *The stream was several feet wide, but he took a flying* LEAP *and got safely across* **2** very short (esp. in the phr. **a flying visit**) **3 send/knock flying a** to knock (someone) over or backwards **b** to cause (something) to move through the air, esp. with a violent blow

flying[2] *n* [U] the action of travelling by aircraft, as a means of getting from one place to another or as a sport: *I don't like flying; it makes me feel sick.*|*a flying club*

flying boat /ˈ·· ·/ *n* an aircraft with an underside shaped like the bottom of a boat, able to land on water

flying bomb /ˈ·· ·/ *n* (in the Second World War) a small pilotless aircraft with explosives fitted at the front, that could be fired over long distances; V-1

flying but·tress /ˌ·· ˈ··/ *n* a half arch joined at the top to the outside wall of a large building (such as a church, a castle, etc.), used for supporting the weight of the wall —see picture at CHURCH[1]

flying col·ours /ˌ·· ˈ··/ *n* [P] **1** flags shown as a sign of victory **2 pass (something)/come off with flying colours** to succeed at (something) in a splendid and worthy manner

flying col·umn /ˈ·· ˌ··/ *n* a body of lightly-armed soldiers that works for a short time at a distance from its main body

flying doc·tor /ˌ·· ˈ··/ *n* (*often cap.*) (in Australia and other countries) a doctor who goes by aircraft to visit the sick in distant lonely places, in answer to radio messages

flying fish /ˌ·· ˈ·/ *n* [Wn2;C] any of several types of tropical sea fish that can jump out of the water and move forward supported by long winglike parts (FIN*s*)

flying fox /ˌ·· ˈ·/ *n* FRUIT BAT

flying of·fic·er /ˈ·· ˌ···/ *n* [C;A] (*usu. cap.*) an officer of low rank in the Royal Air Force

flying sau·cer /ˌ·· ˈ··/ *n* any of several types of usu. plateshaped spaceships which many people claim to have seen flying across the sky and believe to be piloted by creatures from another world

flying squad /ˈ·· ·/ *n* [(*the*) G;U;(C)] (*often cap.*) a group of special police cars and men who are always ready for quick action when a serious crime takes place

flying start /ˌ·· ˈ·/ *n* [S] **1 a** also (*infml*) **flier**— a start to a race in which one or more competitors begin to move the moment the starting signal is given (or just before it), and so gain an advantage over the others **b** a start to a race in which the competitors are already moving when they cross the starting line or receive the starting signal **2** a very good beginning (esp. in the phr. **get off to a flying start**): *He's got off to a flying start in his new job*

fly·leaf /ˈflaɪliːf/ *n* **-leaves** /liːvz/ a page on which there is usu. no printing, at the beginning or end of a book, fastened to the cover

fly·o·ver /ˈflaɪ-əʊvəʳ/ *n* **1** (*AmE* **overpass**)— *BrE* a place where roads or railways cross each other and where one passes high over the other by way of a kind of bridge —see picture at INTERCHANGE[2] **2** *AmE* FLYPAST

fly·pa·per /ˈflaɪˌpeɪpəʳ/ *n* [U] a length of paper covered with a sticky or poisonous substance to trap flies in a room

fly·past /ˈflaɪpɑːst‖-pæst/ (*AmE* **flyby, flyover**)— *n BrE* the actions of a group of aircraft flying in a special formation on a ceremonial occasion, esp. at a low level in front of a crowd

fly·sheet /ˈflaɪʃiːt/ *n* an additional sheet that is put over a tent for protection in rainy weather —see picture at CAMP[2]

fly·swat·ter /ˈflaɪˌswɒtəʳ‖-ˌswɑ-/ *n* an instrument for killing flies, usu. made of a flat square piece of plastic or wire net fixed to a handle

fly·trap /ˈflaɪtræp/ *n* any of several types of plant that trap and eat flies

fly·weight /ˈflaɪweɪt/ *n* a BOXER who weighs 112 pounds or less

fly·wheel /ˈflaɪwiːl/ *n* a wheel which, because of its heavy weight, keeps a machine working at an even speed —see picture at PETROL

fly·whisk /ˈflaɪˌwɪsk/ *n* a bunch of long horse hairs fastened to a handle, used for keeping flies away from the face

FM *abbrev. for:* frequency modulation; a system of broadcasting, usu. on VHF, in which the electric signal that carries the sound waves has a wave that is always of the same strength but comes at a varying number of times per second, and provides very clear words and music for the listener: *an FM radio* —compare AM

FO /ˌef ˈəʊ/ *abbrev. for:* FOREIGN OFFICE

foal[1] /fəʊl/ *n* **1** a young horse **2 in/with foal** (of a female horse) having a young horse developing inside the body

foal[2] *v* [IØ] (of a female horse) to give birth

foam[1] /fəʊm/ *n* [U] **1** a whitish mass of small balls of air or gas (BUBBLE*s*) on the surface of a liquid or on skin: *The breaking waves had edges of foam* **2** a chemical substance in this form, such as one used in controlling dangerous fires **3** *infml* FOAM RUBBER —**foamy** *adj* [Wa1]

foam[2] *v* [Wv4;L9] to produce FOAM[1] (1): *The dying animal was found foaming at the mouth.*|(fig.) *He could hardly speak; he was foaming with anger* (=was very angry)

foam rub·ber /ˌ· ˈ··◂/ *n* [U] soft rubber full of small balls of air, used for making chair seats, the soft part of beds, etc.

fob /fɒb‖fɑb/ *n* **1** also **fob chain** /ˈ· ·/— a short chain or band of cloth to which a FOB WATCH is fastened **2** an ornament on such a chain

f.o.b. /ˌef əʊ ˈbiː/ *abbrev. for:* free on board; (of goods that are to be sent by ship in large quantities) (sent to the ship and placed on it) without further cost to the buyer

fob off *v adv* **-bb-** [T1] to wave aside; take no notice of: *He took no notice of our suggestions; he fobbed them off/fobbed us off and talked of something else*

fob off on *v adv prep* [D1] to cause acceptance of (something) on (someone) by deceit: *The salesman fobbed off the faulty machine on the lady*

fob off with *v adv prep* [D1] **1** to deceive (someone) into accepting (something): *The salesman fobbed the lady off with a faulty machine* **2** to try to persuade (someone) to accept (something) as a reason for not doing what one is asked to do: *He fobbed me off with a story of his misfortunes*

fob watch /'· ·/ *n* a watch that fits into a pocket, or is pinned to a lady's dress
fo·cal /'fəʊkəl/ *adj* [Wa5;A] of or belonging to a FOCUS
focal length /ˌ·· '·/ *n* [(*the*) U (*of*)] the distance from the middle of a piece of glass (LENS) that collects light into one beam, to its FOCUS[1] (2)
focal point /'·· ·/ *n* [(*the*) U (*of*)] FOCUS[1] (4): *In winter, the fireside is the focal point of family life in many homes in Britain*
fo'c'sle /'fəʊksəl/ also (*fml*) **forecastle**— *n* the front part of a ship, where the sailors live
fo·cus¹ /'fəʊkəs/ *n* **-cuses** *or* **-ci** /kaɪ, saɪ/ **1** [C] (in MATHEMATICS) a point from which lines are drawn to any points on a curve in such a way that the lengths of these lines are related to each other by some law **2** [C] the point at which beams of light or heat, or waves of sound meet after their direction has been changed **3** [(*the*) U (*of*)] the point of distance at which the clearest picture is formed through a piece of glass (LENS) that collects light into one beam, such as on a photographic plate in a camera, or for the eye through a microscope **4** [(*the*) U (*of*)] the central point; place of greatest activity; centre of interest: *She always wants to be the focus of attention* **5 in(to)/out of focus** (not) having or giving a clear picture because the LENS is (not) correctly placed: *When a photograph isn't in focus, it isn't clear; it's out of focus*
focus² *v* **-s-** *or* **-ss-** **1** [T1 (*on*)] to bring into a FOCUS[1] (2): (fig.) *to focus one's mind on work* **2** [T1] **a** to arrange the LENS in (an instrument) so as to obtain a clear picture **b** to make (a picture) clear by doing this **3** [IØ] *infml* to think clearly: *He must be very tired today; he doesn't seem to focus at all*
focus on *v prep* **1** [T1] to come to a FOCUS[1] (2) on: *The beams of light moved across the sky and focused on the aircraft* **2** [D1] to arrange the LENS in (an instrument) so as to obtain a clear picture of (something): *The scientist focused his* TELESCOPE *on the moon* **3** [D1] to direct or cause (something) to come to a centre on (someone or something): *All eyes were focused on him.|Focus your attention on your work* **4** [T1] to direct one's attention to: *Today we're going to focus on the question of homeless people in London*
fod·der /'fɒdəʳ‖'fɑdəʳ/ *n* **1** [U] rough food for cattle or horses, gathered from the fields and stored **2** [U] *humor* food for people **3** [U9] things or people used for supplying a continuous demand: *"We are just factory fodder," complained the workers* —see also CANNON FODDER
foe /fəʊ/ *n fml* an enemy
foe·man /'fəʊmən/ *n* **-men** /mən/ *old use* a male FOE
foe·tal, fetal /'fiːtl/ *adj* [Wa5;A] of, related to, or in the stage or condition of a FOETUS
foe·tus, fetus /'fiːtəs/ *n* **1** *tech* a young creature inside the mother, esp. at a later stage when all its parts have been developed for use at birth —compare EMBRYO **2** a young human in the early stages of development inside the mother, esp. before it is recognizable as a baby or able to live separately
fog¹ /fɒg‖fɑg, fɔg/ *n* **1** [U] very thick mist **2** [C] a state or time of very thick mist: *We often have bad fogs on the south coast during winter* **3** [U;C] mistiness on a photographic plate or film, or on a print from such a film **4 in a fog** *infml* in a state of mind in which ideas or feelings are not clear, or something cannot be understood: *The boy's in a fog about his science lesson; he has no idea at all what it means*
fog² *v* **-gg-** **1** [T1;IØ: (UP)] to (cause to) become difficult to see through because of a misty covering: *The steam has fogged my glasses.|My glasses have fogged up in this steamy room* **2** [T1;IØ] to (cause to) become unclear owing to FOG[1] (3): *The light you let into the camera has fogged the film* **3** [T1 *usu. pass.*] *infml* to cause to experience difficulty in understanding: *I don't know what this sentence in French means; I'm completely fogged (by it)*
fog·bank /'fɒgbæŋk‖'fɑg-, 'fɔg-/ *n* a heavy mass of FOG[1] (1) on the surface of the sea
fog·bound /'fɒgbaʊnd‖'fɑg-, 'fɔg-/ *adj* [Wa5] prevented by FOG[1] (1) from working or travelling as usual: *We were fogbound in London and had to wait 12 hours for the air service to the north.|fogbound travellers*
fog·gy /'fɒgi‖'fɑgi, 'fɔgi/ *adj* [Wa1] **1** not clear because of FOG[1] (1); very misty: *It's unpleasant to be out on a foggy day* **2** not exact; unclear: *I didn't hear all she said; I've only a foggy idea what it was all about* **3 not have the foggiest (idea)** *infml* not to know at all: *"What are you going to do this evening?" "I haven't the foggiest"* —**foggily** *adv* —**fogginess** *n* [U]
fog·horn /'fɒghɔːn‖'fɑghɔrn, 'fɔg-/ *n* **1** a loud horn used as a warning of FOG[1] (1) by and to ships **2 have a voice like a foghorn** *derog* to have a very loud ugly voice
fog lamp /'· ·/ *n* a lamp on the front of a car or other vehicle that gives a strong beam of light to help driving during FOG[1] (1)
fo·gy, fogey /'fəʊgi/ *n* [C;*you*+N] *derog* a slow uninteresting old person who dislikes changes and does not understand modern ideas (esp. in the phr. **old fogy**)
foi·ble /'fɔɪbəl/ *n* a small rather foolish personal habit or weakness of character, which the person who has it finds rather pleasing: *My grandfather was always buying himself new suits of clothes; it was a foible of his*
foie gras /ˌfwɑː 'grɑː (*Fr* fwa grɑ)/ *n* [U] *infml* PÂTÉ DE FOIE GRAS
foil¹ /fɔɪl/ *v* [T1 (*in*) *often pass.*] to prevent (someone) from succeeding in (some plan): *The thief was foiled in his attempt to enter the house.|We foiled his attempt to escape*
foil² *n* a type of light narrow sword with a covered point, used in FENCING —see FENCING (USAGE); compare EPEE, SABRE[1] (2)
foil³ *n* **1** [U] (*often in comb.*) metal beaten or rolled into very thin paperlike sheets: *Milk bottle tops are made of tin foil* **2** [U] paper covered with this; SILVER PAPER: *Cigarettes are wrapped in foil to keep them fresh* **3** [C (*for, to*)] a person or thing of a kind that makes more noticeable the better or different quality of another: *In the play, a wicked old uncle acts as a foil to the noble young prince*
foist on /fɔɪst/ *v prep* **1** [D1] to cause (someone or something unwanted) to be borne or suffered for a time by (someone): *They didn't invite him to go out with them, but he foisted himself on them.|He foisted his company on them* **2** [D1 (OFF)] FOB OFF ON: *Don't trust that shopkeeper; he'll try to foist off damaged goods on you*
fold¹ /fəʊld/ *n* **1** [C] a sheltered corner of a field where farm animals, esp. sheep, are kept for protection, surrounded by a fence or wall —see picture at FARMYARD **2** [*the*+GU] all the people belonging to a branch of the Christian religion **3 return to the fold a** to come back home **b** to return to one's religion after having left it
fold² *v* **1** [T1 (UP)] to turn or press back one part of (something, esp. paper or cloth) and lay on the remaining part; bend into 2 or more parts: *She folded the handkerchief and put it in her pocket.|She folded up the tablecloth and put it in the cupboard.|The paper must be folded in half* **2** [X9] to bend (a limb) close to the body: *The cat sat up and folded*

its tail round its front feet **3** [T1] to press (a pair of limbs) together: *The little child folded her hands in prayer.|He folded his arms* (=crossed them over his chest).|*The insect folded its wings* **4** [X9] **a** to wrap: *Fold a piece of paper round the flowers so that they'll be easier to carry* **b** to enclose; cover: *He found some seeds folded in a little piece of paper* **5** [Wv4;IØ] to be able to be bent back; close up: *Does this table fold?|These doors are made in pieces that fold back against the wall.|This garden chair folds flat.|If you're going camping you'll need a folding bed* **6** [IØ] *infml* FOLD UP: *The business has folded*

fold³ *n* **1** a part of a thin flat material laid over another part: *Each fold in the skirt should be exactly the same width.|The curtain hung in heavy folds* **2** a mark made by folding; a CREASE: *How are we going to get the folds out of this dress that has been packed too tightly?* **3** a hollow part inside something folded: *She put her book in the fold of the newspaper to protect it from the rain* **4** **a** a bend in a valley **b** a hollow in a hill **5** *tech* a bend in the bands of rock and other material that lie one under the other beneath the surface of the earth

-fold *suffix* **1** by a stated number of times: *The value of this house has increased* FOUR*fold since we bought it* (=it is now worth 4 times as much as we paid for it) **2** of a stated number of times or kinds: *a* FOUR*fold increase in value|A window has a* TWO*fold purpose; it lets light into a room and it allows people in the room to see what is outside*

fold·a·way /ˈfəʊldəweɪ/ *adj* [Wa5;A] that can be folded up out of the way or out of sight: *a foldaway bed*

fold·er /ˈfəʊldəʳ/ *n* a folded piece of cardboard used for holding loose papers

fold in *v adv* [T1] to mix (something eatable) into a mixture that is to be cooked, by turning over gently with a spoon: *Fold in 2 eggs and then cook gently for 30 minutes*

fold in·to *v prep* [D1] to mix (something eatable) into (a mixture that is to be cooked), by turning over gently with a spoon

fold up *v adv* [IØ] (esp. of a business) to fail

fo·li·age /ˈfəʊli-ɪdʒ/ *n* [U] **1** leaves in general, esp. growing leaves **2** all the leaves on a particular plant or tree **3** gathered or arranged leaves, branches, and flowers

fo·li·o /ˈfəʊliəʊ/ *n* **-lios** **1** [C] a large sheet of paper folded once so as to give 2 sheets or 4 pages in all —compare OCTAVO, QUARTO **2** [C] a book of the largest size, made up of large sheets folded once **3** [U] the size of such a book: *This book on art has been brought out in folio* **4** [C] a single numbered sheet of paper in a book, esp. in an old book written by hand; both sides of a page **5** [C] *tech* the left- and right-hand pages facing each other in an account book, showing gains on one side and losses on the other

folk¹ /fəʊk/ *n* **1** [P9] *AmE* usu. **folks**— people: *Some folk seem unable to spend money* **2** [P9] people of one race or nation, or sharing a particular kind of life: *country folk|Most of the people on the island are fisher folk* **3** [P] *now rare* FOLKS (1)

USAGE A **state** is either a politically independent country, or one of the **States** making up a country such as the US. A **nation** is a group of people, perhaps with their own language and history, and usually but not always living in the same area: *the Jewish* **nation**|*Scotland is a* **nation** *but not a* **state**|A **race** is a group of people of the same colour and/or bodily type, descended from others of that same type since the distant past: *the white race|the European* **races**|A **tribe** is a fairly small group of people, usually not highly civilized, living together with their own customs and often under the same ruler: *a wandering* **tribe** *of hunters*|The mass of the population in a country are the **people** or (less commonly) the **folk**, according to whether one thinks of them politically or from the point of view of their ancient customs, dress, beliefs, etc.: **folk** *dancing|The* **people** *demand free speech!*

folk² *adj* [Wa5;A] of, connected with, or being music or any other art that has grown up among working and/or country people as an important part of their way of living and belongs to a particular area, trade, etc., or that has been made in modern times as a copy of this: *folk music|folk songs|a folk singer|a folk concert|folk art*

folk dance /ˈ· ˌ·/ *n* (a piece of music for) an old country dance, usu. performed by a set of dancers —**folk dancer** *n*

folk et·y·mol·o·gy /ˌ· ··ˈ···/ *n* [U;C] the changing of strange or foreign words so that they become like words that are quite common in one's own language: *Some people say* **sparrowgrass** *instead of* ASPARAGUS*; that is an example of folk etymology*

folk·lore /ˈfəʊklɔːʳ‖-lor/ *n* [U] (the scientific study of) all the knowledge, beliefs, habits, etc., of a racial or national group, still preserved by memory, or in use from earlier and simpler times

folk·lor·ist /ˈfəʊkˌlɔːrɪ̈st‖-lor-/ *n* a person who studies FOLKLORE

folks /fəʊks/ *n infml* **1** [P] **a** family; relations **b** parents: *I'd like you to meet my folks* **2** [P;N] (used esp. when addressing people in a friendly way) people: *Well, folks, shall we go out this afternoon?* **3** [P] *AmE* FOLK¹ (1)

folk·sy /ˈfəʊksi/ *adj* [Wa1] *infml* **1** simple and friendly; not formal **2** *sometimes derog* having the character of FOLK² art: *She bought herself a rather folksy little teapot*

folk·tale /ˈfəʊkteɪl/ also (*rare*) **folk sto·ry** /ˈ· ˌ··/— *n* a popular story passed on by speech over a long period of time in a simple society

folk·way /ˈfəʊkweɪ/ *n* [*usu. pl.*] a way of thinking, feeling, or acting that is common to a people or to a social group

fol·li·cle /ˈfɒlɪkəl‖ˈfɑ-/ *n* any of the small holes in a person's or animal's skin, from which hairs grow

fol·low /ˈfɒləʊ‖ˈfɑ-/ *v* **1** [T1;IØ] to come, arrive, go, or leave after; move behind in the same direction: *The boy followed his father out.|I'm sending the letter today; the packet will follow* (*later*) **2** [T1] to go in the same direction as; continue along: *The railway line follows the river for several miles.|Follow the road until you come to the hotel* **3** [T1] to go after in order to catch: *The police are following a murderer who's in hiding.|I think we're being followed* **4** [T1] to go with; attend on: *The general was followed by a large number of army officers as he walked round the camp* **5** [T1] to come next in order or on a list: *The number 5 follows the number 4* **6** [T1;IØ] to happen or take place after (something): *May follows April.|The storm was followed by a calm.|We expect even greater successes to follow* **7** [T1;IØ] to come after in some position: *King George the 6th died and then Queen Elizabeth the Second followed.|He'll be a difficult man to follow; no one understands the work as he did* **8** [T1] to carry on (a certain kind of work): *He follows the trade of baker.|You must study hard if you intend to follow the law* (=be a lawyer) **9** [T1] to keep in sight; watch: *The cat followed every movement of the mouse.|He followed her with his eyes* (=watched her movements closely) **10** [T1] to attend or listen to carefully: *He followed the speaker's words with the greatest attention* **11** [T1;IØ] to understand clearly: *I didn't follow his line of reasoning; it was too difficult for me.|I didn't quite follow; could you explain it again?*

12 [T1] to take a keen interest in: *He follows all the cricket news.|I follow Fulham* (=I'm a keen supporter of Fulham football team) —compare FOLLOWER **13** [T1] to accept and act according to: *Why didn't you follow my advice?|These orders must be followed at once.|The villagers still follow the customs of their grandfathers* **14** [T1;IØ] to copy; take (something) as a guide: *He followed the example of his friend, and went to the university.|You'll spend lots on clothes if you always follow the fashion* (=dress in the latest manner) **15** [T1;IØ] to be or happen as a necessary effect or result (of): *Disease often follows war.|Just because he's at the bottom of the class, it doesn't follow* (=you cannot reason from this) *that he has no brains; he may just be very lazy.|"As you're getting a better job, you'll be paid more." "No, that doesn't necessarily follow"* **16** **as follows** as now to be told; as given in the list below: *The results are as follows; Philip Carter 1st, Sam Cohen 2nd, Sandra Postlethwaite 3rd* **17** **follow something home/out** to reason something out to the end; get the full value or force out of something: *His argument was well put together, but he didn't follow it home* **18** **to follow** as the next dish; as the next thing to eat: *"What will you have to follow, sir?" asked the waiter.|And to follow, some fresh fruit* —see also FOLLOW ON[1,2], FOLLOW THROUGH, FOLLOW UP, **follow the** CROWD[2] (5), **follow in someone's** FOOTSTEP s (3), **follow the** HOUNDS[1] (3), **follow** SUIT[1] (7)

follow a·bout also **follow a·round, follow round**— *v adv* [T1b] to follow (a person) everywhere: *The child follows her mother about all day long*

fol·low·er /ˈfɒləʊəʳ‖ˈfɑ-/ *n* [C9] an admirer or supporter of some person, belief, or cause: *He's a faithful follower of one of the well-known football teams.|Many ancient Greeks were followers of Socrates* —see also CAMP FOLLOWER

fol·low·ing[1] /ˈfɒləʊɪŋ‖ˈfɑ-/ *adj* [Wa5] **1** [*the*+A] next: *The child was sick in the evening, but on the following day he seemed quite well again* **2** [*the*+A] that is/are to be mentioned now: *Please send me the following goods: 2 pounds of sugar, one pound of butter, and a bag of flour* **3** [A] (of wind or sea) moving in the same direction as a ship; helping: *The sailing boat made good speed thanks to a following wind*

following[2] *n* **1** [Wn3; *the*+C] the one or ones about to be mentioned: *The following have been chosen to play in tomorrow's match: Duncan Ferguson, Hugh Williams, Robin Sinclair . . .* **2** [C *usu. sing.*] a group of supporters or admirers: *This politician has quite a large following in the North*

following[3] *prep* after: *Following the speech, there will be a few minutes for questions*

follow-my-lead·er /ˌ·· · ˈ··/ *AmE* **follow-the-leader**— *n* [U] a children's game in which one of the players does actions which all the other players must copy

follow-on /ˌ·· ˈ·/ *n* [(*the*) U] the act of FOLLOWing ON[1] (2)

follow on[1] *v adv* [IØ] **1** to take place after a pause: *The second half of the concert will follow on in 20 minutes time* **2** (of a cricket team) to have a second turn at hitting the ball after the first turn in which the total of runs was much lower than that of the opposing team

follow on[2] also **follow up·on**— *v prep* [T1 *no pass.*] to result from: *Her illness followed on her mother's death*

follow-through /ˌ·· ˈ·‖ˈ·· ·/ *n* (in sports) the part of a stroke made after hitting the ball: *The tennis ball had flashed past her opponent before she'd finished her follow-through*

follow through *v adv* **1** [T1] also **follow out**— to complete; carry out exactly to the end: *to follow through a line of inquiry|to follow out the doctor's orders* **2** [IØ] (in tennis, GOLF, etc.) to complete a stroke by continuing to move the arm after hitting the ball

follow-up /ˈ·· ·/ *adj, n* [Wa5;A;S;U] (of or being) a thing done or action taken to continue or add to the effect of something done before: *follow-up visits|Our newspaper story on the sex trial was a great success; we must get someone to write a follow-up.|After an operation, follow-up is just as important as the hospital treatment*

follow up *v adv* [T1] **1** to act further on (something): *to follow up a suggestion* **2** [(*with*)] to take further action after (something) (by means of something else): *to follow up a letter with a visit*

fol·ly /ˈfɒli‖ˈfɑli/ *n* **1** [U] *fml* foolishness: *After one year at the university he gave up his studies; it was an act of the greatest folly* **2** [C *often pl.*] an unwise act, habit, etc.: *The old man smiled sadly as he remembered the follies of his youth* **3** [C] a building of strange or fanciful shape, that has no particular purpose, esp. as built only to be looked at

fo·ment /fəʊˈment/ *v* [T1] **1** to help (something evil or unpleasant) to develop **2** to put a warm cloth or liquid on (a part of the body) to lessen pain —see also POULTICE

fo·men·ta·tion /ˌfəʊmenˈteɪʃən, -mən-/ *n* **1** [U] the act of FOMENTing (1,2): *the fomentation of disorder* **2** [C] a material for FOMENTing (2)

fond /fɒnd‖fɑnd/ *adj* [Wa1] **1** [A] loving in a kind, gentle, or tender way: *He signed the letter, "With fondest love, Cyril"* **2** [A] foolishly loving; yielding weakly to loving feelings: *A fond mother may spoil her child* **3** [A] foolishly trusting or hopeful: *In spite of his bad results in the examination, he has a fond belief in his own cleverness* **4** [F+*of*] **a** having a great liking or love (for): *She has many faults, but we're all very fond of her.|I'm very fond of Elgar's music* **b** *infml* having the bad habit (of): *You're too fond of leaving the door open when you go out* —**~ness** *n* [U;C: (*for*)]

fon·dant /ˈfɒndənt‖ˈfɑn-/ *n* [C;(U)] a type of sweet made of fine sugar, that melts in the mouth

fon·dle /ˈfɒndl‖ˈfɑndl/ *v* [Wv3;T1] to touch gently and lovingly; stroke softly: *The old lady fondled her cat as it sat beside her*

fond·ly /ˈfɒndli‖ˈfɑndli/ *adv* **1** in a foolishly hopeful manner: *She fondly imagined that she could pass her examination without working* **2** in a loving way: *She greeted her old friend fondly*

fon·due, fondu /ˈfɒndjuː‖fɑnˈduː/ *n* [C;U] *Fr* **1** a dish made with melted cheese, into which pieces of bread are dipped **2** (*often in comb.*) a dish consisting of small pieces of food, such as meat or fruit, that are cooked in or dipped into a hot liquid

font /fɒnt‖fɑnt/ *n* **1** a large vessel in a church, usu. made of stone, that contains the water used for baptizing (BAPTIZE) people —see picture at CHURCH[1] **2** FOUNT[2]

food /fuːd/ *n* **1** [U] **a** something that living creatures or plants take into their bodies to give them strength and help them to develop and to live: *Milk is the natural food for young babies.|a new sort of liquid plant food* **b** something solid for eating: *We always get lots of food there, but they never give us much to drink* **2** [C] an eatable substance: *Too many sweet foods, like cakes and pastry, may increase your weight* **3** [U+*for*] subject matter (for an argument or careful thought); that which helps ideas to start working in the mind: *His father's advice gave the boy food for thought*

food poi·son·ing /ˈ· ˌ···/ *n* [U] a painful stomach disorder caused by eating food that contains harmful bacteria or poisonous substances

food·stuff /ˈfuːdstʌf/ *n* [*often pl.*] a substance used as food, esp. a simple food material that is to be cooked and/or mixed with other foods for eating

fool¹ /fuːl/ *n* **1** [C; (*you*) N] *derog* a person whom one considers to be silly; person lacking in judgment or good sense: *What fool has put that wet paintbrush on my chair?|What a fool I was to think that she really loved me* **2** [C] (in former times) a manservant at the court of a king or noble, whose duty was to amuse his master; JESTER **3** [C;U] (*usu. in comb.*) a dish made of cooked soft fruit, pressed into a liquid and beaten up with cream: GOOSEBERRY *fool* **4 A fool and his money are soon parted** A foolish person soon spends, or is deceived into spending, all his money **5 a fool to oneself** *BrE* a person whose behaviour, esp. kind behaviour to others, results in harm to himself: *Why does he go on paying for his daughter's clothes? He's a fool to himself, because they cost a lot of money and she's never grateful* **6 make a fool of oneself** to behave unwisely and lose people's respect: *We hear the old doctor has made a fool of himself with a young girl he was treating* (=has formed or tried to form a sexual relationship with her) **7 make a fool of someone** to trick someone; make someone seem stupid: *The stranger made a fool of the trusting old lady and went off with a lot of her money* **8 (the) more fool you (him, them** etc.) I think you were (he was, etc.) a fool to do, accept, expect, etc., that: *"He picked up a strange cat and it bit him." "More fool him; he should have known it would do that"* **9 no fool/nobody's fool** a person who cannot be tricked: *He tried to sell me that old car, but I'm nobody's fool; I could see it hadn't got an engine* **10 play the fool** to act in a foolish manner: *Schoolmasters don't like boys to play the fool during lessons* **11 There's no fool like an old fool** Old people can be more foolish than young people —see also APRIL FOOL

fool² *v* **1** [T1] to deceive; trick: *You can't fool him; he's much too clever for that.|She fooled the old man out of all his money* (=got it from him by a trick).| *He's fooled a lot of people into believing he's a rich man* **2** [I∅] to behave in a silly way: *Can't you be sensible for once? Can't you stop fooling?* **3** [I∅] to speak without serious intention; joke

fool³ *adj* [Wa5;A] *infml esp. AmE* stupid; foolish

fool a·bout also **fool a·round**— *v adv* [I∅] *derog* to spend the time doing nothing useful: *He never does any work; he just fools about all day long* —see also FOOL WITH

fool a·way *v adv* [T1] *derog* to waste; use senselessly

fool·e·ry /ˈfuːləri/ *n usu. derog* **1** [U] silly behaviour **2** [C *usu. pl.*] a silly action, speech, thing, etc.

fool·har·dy /ˈfuːlhɑːdi‖-ɑr-/ *adj* too bold; taking or needing useless or unwise risks: *A foolhardy general may cause the death of many of his soldiers.|He was foolhardy to try, when he knew he'd fail* —**-diness** *n* [U]

fool·ish /ˈfuːlɪʃ/ *adj derog* **1** unwise; without good sense: *It would be a foolish thing to spend money on something you can't afford* **2** showing lack of thought; stupid; laughable: *a foolish answer* —**~ly** *adv* —**~ness** *n* [U]

fool·proof /ˈfuːlpruːf/ *adj* [Wa5] **1** that cannot go wrong: *a foolproof plan|I've found a foolproof way of doing it* **2** *infml* very simple to understand, use, work, etc.: *a foolproof machine*

fools·cap /ˈfuːlskæp/ *n* [U] **1** (in Britain) a size of writing paper about 17×13½ inches **2** (in the US) a size of paper typically 16×13 inches

fool's er·rand /ˌ·ˈ··/ *n* [S] an effort that is seen in the end to be useless (esp. in the phrs. **go on/ send someone on a fool's errand**)

fool's gold /ˌ·ˈ·/ *n* [U] a substance (**iron pyrites**) that is sometimes mistaken for gold

fool's mate /ˌ·ˈ·/ *n* [U] a particular set of moves in the game of CHESS, by which a player can beat an inexperienced opponent very soon after the start of the game

fool's par·a·dise /ˌ·ˈ···/ *n* [S] a carelessly happy state, in spite of a threat of change (esp. in the phrs. **be/live in a fool's paradise**)

fool with *v prep* [T1 (ABOUT, AROUND)] to not treat seriously: *She shouldn't have fooled about with the boy's love*

foot¹ /fʊt/ *n* **feet** /fiːt/ **1** [C] the movable part of the body at the end of the leg, below the ankle, on which a man or an animal stands —see picture at HUMAN² **2** [C] (*pl. sometimes* **foot**) (a measure of length equal to) 12 inches or about ·305 metres: *3 feet make one yard.|He's 6 feet tall.|He's 5 foot 8 inches in height.|The building is 40 feet/foot high* —see WEIGHTS & MEASURES TABLE **3** [(*the*) U (*of*)] the bottom part (of); base: *A creeping plant grew along the foot of the wall.|at the foot of the page|The foot of the lamp is unsteady on the floor* **4** [(*the*) U (*of*)] the lower end (of anything) where feet lie: *the foot of the bed|She laid some flowers at the foot of her friend's grave* **5** [U9] manner of walking; step: *One old woman walked with heavy foot up the stairs.*|FLEET² *of foot* **6** [C *usu. sing.*] the part of a stocking or sock that covers the foot **7** [C] a division of a line in poetry, in which there is usu. a strong beat and one or 2 weaker ones: *In the line "The way/was long/the wind/was cold", the words between each pair of upright lines make up a foot* **8** [P] *old use, esp. BrE* soldiers who march and fight on foot; INFANTRY: *a* REGIMENT *of foot* **9 a foot in both camps** a position not completely favouring one side or the other, so that each thinks it has one's support: *His political opinions aren't very decided or courageous; he keeps a foot in both camps* **10 a foot in the door** a beginning of influence, favour, etc. **11 be on one's feet a** to be standing, walking, etc.: *It's nice to sit down after being on your feet all day* **b** to be well again after illness: *This medicine will soon have you on your feet again* **c** to be standing up, esp. in order to speak: *No sooner had the question been put than he was on his feet to reply* **12 fall on one's feet** *infml* to come out of a difficult state of affairs without harm; have good luck **13 find one's feet a** (esp. of a baby or young animal) to begin to be able to stand and walk **b** to become used to new or strange surroundings; settle in: *He's only been at the school 2 weeks, and he hasn't really found his feet yet* **14 get a foot in** *infml* to get a chance to be in: *He's joined the Sports Club in the hope of getting a foot in one of the teams* **15 get/have cold feet** to be too nervous to do something, esp. losing courage just before something: *They had cold feet at the last minute and refused to sell their house* **16 get to one's feet** to stand up **17 keep one's feet** to be able to remain standing; not fall: *He found it difficult to keep his feet on the slippery surface* **18 my foot** *infml* I don't believe it: *"She says she's too busy to speak to you." "Busy, my foot! She just doesn't want to"* **19 on foot a** (by) walking: *It takes longer to travel on foot than by car* **b** in a state of being used, made, prepared, etc.: *A plan's on foot to invite the Minister of Health to visit our hospital.|Who set that business on foot* (=started it)*?* —see also AFOOT (2) **20 put a foot wrong** [*nonassertive*] to say or do the wrong things: *He's very good at dealing with all kinds of people; he never puts a foot wrong* **21 put one's best foot forward a** to walk as fast as possible: *It's a long way to the village, but if you put your best foot forward you'll reach it before the evening* **b** to make one's best effort: *You've been so lazy in the past few months; you'll have to put your best foot forward if you want to pass that examination now* **22 put one's feet up** *infml* to rest by lying down or sitting with one's feet supported on something: *It's nice to put your feet up after a long day's work* **23 put one's foot down a** *infml* to speak and act firmly on a particular matter: *The father didn't like his son staying out at night, so he put his foot down and forbade him to do it again* **b** *BrE sl* to drive very fast **24 put one's foot in it** *infml* to say the wrong thing or make an awkward mistake **25 set foot in/on** to enter; visit: *She said she wouldn't set foot in the room until it had been properly cleaned.|No man has ever set foot on that rocky island; it's impossible to land there* —see also HAND[1] (49) **and foot, have one foot in the** GRAVE[1] (5), SWEEP[1] (14) **someone off his feet,** UNDERFOOT

foot[2] *v* [T1] **1** *infml* to pay (a bill): (fig.) *Who'll foot the bill for your stupid behaviour?* **2** to put a FOOT[1] (6) on (a sock or stocking) **3 foot it** *infml* to walk; travel on foot

foot·age /ˈfʊtɪdʒ/ *n* [U] **1** measurement or payment by the FOOT[1] (2): *"What's the footage of this wall?" "It's about 30 feet long"* **2** length of cinema film used: *some interesting old footage of the first flight across the Atlas Mountains*

foot-and-mouth dis·ease /ˌ· · ˈ· ·ˌ·/ *n* [U] a disease of cattle, sheep, and goats, in which spots appear in the mouth and on the feet, and which often causes death

foot·ball /ˈfʊtbɔːl/ *n* **1** [U] any of several games for 2 teams in which a ball is kicked and/or thrown about a field in an attempt to get GOAL*s*, esp. **a** *BrE* SOCCER **b** *BrE* RUGBY **c** *AmE* AMERICAN FOOTBALL **d** *AustrE* AUSTRALIAN RULES FOOTBALL: *football boots* **2** [C] any of several types of large ball filled with air, usu. made of leather, used in these games **3** [C9] an idea, person, etc., that people are giving all their attention to, but in a rough thoughtless way, so that the really important parts of the matter may be forgotten: *a political football* —**~er** *n*

USAGE One plays **football** with a ball that is also called a **football**, on a *field* (*BrE* also PITCH) and one SCORE*s* **goals**. In an important *match* (*AmE* usu. *game*) the person in charge is called the **referee**.

football pools /ˈ·· ·/ *n* [(*the*) P] POOLS

foot·bath /ˈfʊtbɑːθ‖-bæθ/ *n* **1** a vessel for bathing the feet: *"Wash your feet in the footbath before entering the swimming pool"* **2** an act of bathing the feet

foot·board /ˈfʊtbɔːd‖-ord/ *n* **1** a narrow board running along the outside of a railway carriage **2** a board at the FOOT[1] (4) of a bed —compare HEADBOARD **3** a sloping board against which the driver of a carriage or car can rest his feet

foot·bridge /ˈfʊtˌbrɪdʒ/ *n* a narrow bridge to be used only by people on foot, esp. for crossing railway lines at a station

-foot·ed /ˈfʊtɪ̈d/ *comb. form* **1** having a stated number of feet: *4-footed animals* **2** having feet of the stated kind: *There is a type of bird called the pink-footed* GOOSE

foot·er /ˈfʊtəʳ/ *n* [U] *infml BrE now rare* the game of football; SOCCER

-foot·er *comb. form* **1** a person who is a stated number of feet tall: *Alison's brother is a 6-footer* **2** a thing that is a stated number of feet long, high, or broad: *His first throw was an 80-footer*

foot·fall /ˈfʊtfɔːl/ *n* a sound made by setting the foot on the ground; the sound of a footstep: *strange footfalls on the stairs*

foot fault /ˈ· ·/ *n* (in tennis) an act of breaking the rules by a player, in which he steps over the back line of the court when serving (SERVE[1] (10)) the ball

foot-fault *v* [I∅] (in tennis) to be guilty of a FOOT FAULT

foot·hill /ˈfʊtˌhɪl/ *n* [C (*of*) *usu. pl.*] a low hill at the bottom of a mountain or chain of mountains: *Before the climbers could reach the high mountains, they had to cross a range of foothills.|the foothills of the Himalayas*

foot·hold /ˈfʊthəʊld/ *n* **1** [C] a space (as on a rock) where a foot can be placed to help one to continue to climb up or down: *The mountain climber couldn't find many footholds on the melting ice* **2** [C *usu. sing.*] a first introduction or entrance that may lead to success; safe position: *It isn't easy to get a foothold as a film actor*

foot·ing /ˈfʊtɪŋ/ *n* **1** [S;(U)] a firm placing of the feet; room or a surface for the feet to stand on: *She lost her footing on the muddy road, and fell.|The roof of the house sloped steeply, so the man who was doing the repairs couldn't get much of a footing on it* **2** [S] a sure position; base: *Is this business on a firm footing* (=properly planned, with enough money to support it)? **3** [S9] a special condition suited to a certain state of affairs: *In ordinary times the army is kept on a peacetime footing, but if war seems likely it is put on a wartime footing* **4** [S9] the quality of a relationship with other people: *During office hours the directors of the company work on a business footing with each other, but in private life they often meet on a friendly footing* **5** [S] an entrance into, or an accepted place in, some group, with the hope of improving one's position: *Because they're trying to gain a footing in society, they invite many famous people to visit them*

foo·tle /ˈfuːtl/ *v* [I∅ (ABOUT, AROUND)] *infml* to behave in a careless way: *She's done no work today; she's spent the time just footling about*

footle a·way *v adv* [T1] *infml* to waste in a silly careless way: *He's footled away his chances of success*

foot·lights /ˈfʊtlaɪts/ *n* [P] **1** a row of lights along the front edge of the floor of a stage at the theatre, to show up the actors —see picture at THEATRE **2** acting for the theatre: *She's always dreamt of the footlights* (=wanted to become an actress)

foot·ling /ˈfuːtlɪŋ/ *adj derog* worthless; unimportant: *Don't waste the teacher's time with such footling questions*

foot·loose /ˈfʊtluːs/ *adj* free to go wherever one pleases and do what one likes; having no family or business duties which control one's way of living (often in the phr. **footloose and fancy-free**)

foot·man /ˈfʊtmən/ *n* **-men** /mən/ a manservant who opens the front door, introduces visitors, waits at table, etc., and often is dressed in special showy clothes

foot·note[1] /ˈfʊtnəʊt/ *n* a note at the bottom of a page in a book, to explain some word or sentence, add some special remark or information, etc.

footnote[2] *v* [T1] to add FOOTNOTE*s*[1] to (a book, piece of writing, etc.)

foot·pad /ˈfʊtpæd/ *n old use* a thief who attacks travellers on the roads and takes their money —compare HIGHWAYMAN

foot·path /ˈfʊtpɑːθ‖-pæθ/ *n* a narrow path or track for people to walk on: *a footpath across the fields*

foot·plate /ˈfʊtpleɪt/ *n* a metal plate covering the floor of a railway steam engine, where the men driving the train stand

foot-pound /ˌ· ˈ·/ *n* (a measure of work equal to) the amount of force needed to lift a weight of one pound through one foot of height

foot·print /ˈfʊtˌprɪnt/ *n* **1** a footshaped mark

made up of matter from the bottom of a foot that has been pressed onto a surface: *Who left these muddy footprints on the kitchen floor?* **2** a not deep footshaped hole made by pressing a foot into a surface: *The hunter recognized the footprints of a deer near the river bank*

foot·race /ˈfʊt-reɪs/ *n* a race for runners, usu. over level ground

foot rot /ˈ· ·/ *n* [U] a disease which attacks the feet of sheep

foot rule /ˈ· ·/ *n BrE* **1** a narrow flat piece of wood or metal 12 inches long, marked off in (parts of) inches and used for measuring **2** a longer stick of this kind, marked off in lengths of a foot and used for measuring

foot·sie /ˈfʊtsi/ *n infml* **play footsie (with someone)** **a** *BrE infml* to rub one's feet on another's in a playful, sometimes exciting way: *playing footsie under the table* **b** *AmE sl* to work together (with someone), esp. in a way that is not completely honest or fair: *politicians and labour leaders playing footsie (with each other) while rail services get steadily worse*

foot·slog /ˈfʊtslɒg‖-slag/ *v* **-gg-** [IØ] *infml* to march or walk a long way in tiring conditions —**~ger** *n* —**~ging** *n* [U]

foot·sore /ˈfʊtsɔːʳ‖-sor/ *adj* having tender, painful, or swollen feet, esp. as a result of much walking: *After a long day's walk in the country, they came home hungry and footsore*

foot·step /ˈfʊtstep/ *n* **1** a mark or sound of a person's step: *Her footsteps were clearly marked in the snow.|He heard soft footsteps coming up the stairs* **2** the distance covered by one step: *The servant walked 2 or 3 footsteps behind his master* **3 follow in the footsteps of someone** to follow an example set by someone else in the past: *The boy's following in his father's footsteps and studying to be a doctor*

foot·stool /ˈfʊtstuːl/ also **stool**— *n* a low support on which a seated person can rest his feet

foot·sure /ˈfʊt-ʃʊəʳ/ also **surefooted**— *adj* able to walk firmly without slipping or falling in difficult places

foot·wear /ˈfʊtweəʳ/ *n* [U] *tech* shoes and boots: *A shopkeeper would say he sold footwear; we would say he sold shoes*

foot·work /ˈfʊtwɜːk‖-ɜrk/ *n* [U] the use of the feet, esp. skilfully in dancing, sports, etc.

fop /fɒp‖fap/ *n derog* a man who takes a womanish interest in fine clothes

fop·pish /ˈfɒpɪʃ‖ˈfa-/ *adj derog* of or like a FOP: *a foppish man|foppish clothes* —**~ness** *n* [U]

for[1] /fəʳ; *strong* fɔːʳ/ *prep* **1** that is/are intended to belong to, be given to, or used for the purpose of: *This parcel isn't for you, it's for your sister.|They've bought some new chairs for the office.|Save some of the cake for Arthur* (compare *Give some of the cake to Arthur*).*|What's this money for? It's for buying some food for dinner.|"things for measuring rainfall"* (SEU S.) **2** in order to reach: *The escaped prisoner ran for the shelter of the woods.|The children set off for school.|This train is for Brighton only* (=it doesn't stop anywhere else).*|a first-class ticket for Oxford* **3** at (the hour of); on (the day of): *We've invited our guests for 9 o'clock.|an appointment with the doctor for the 5th of March|I'm warning you for the last time.|I went there for the first time last May* **4** representing; meaning; as a sign of: *The Member of Parliament for Westford is a well-known farmer.|What's the word for "to travel" in French?|red for danger* **5** in the place of; instead of; for the good of: *"I can't do this" "Let me do it for you."|Can you give me change for a pound?|I think I speak for everybody when I say . . . .|She works for a big clothing company* **6** as being or as part of: *I took him for a fool.|We've got duck for dinner today.|He says so, and I for one believe him.|"You must say what you want for a present"* (SEU S.) —see also **for** INSTANCE[1] (3), **for** EXAMPLE[1] (5) **7** in favour of; in support of; in agreement with; in defence of: *I'm all for the young enjoying themselves.|Are you for the government or against it?|He played well for his side.|Would you die for your country?|3 cheers for the captain* **8** in order to obtain or have: *They're waiting for the bus.|For details of this post, write to Jones & CO, 25 West Street, Norton.|The demand for coal is greatest in the winter.|He's gone for a swim.|Run for your life.|"Now for a nice cool drink," he said, opening the bottle* **9** as a help to; in order to improve the condition of: *The doctor's given her some medicine for her cold.|He had an operation for a heart disease* **10** concerning; as concerns: *For one thing I don't like the colour, and for another the price is too high* —compare AS FOR **11** because of: *He was rewarded for his bravery.|We could hardly see for the thick mist.|She wept for/with joy when she heard that the child was safe.|For several reasons, I'd rather not meet him* —see also **for** FEAR[1] (5) **of, for** WANT[2] (1) **of** **12** as regards; regarding; in regard to: *I have no ear for music.|France is famous for its wines.|Are you still all right for money* (=have you enough)?*|He has a great respect for his father.|He's a great one for details* (=he always wishes all details to be correct).*|For all I know, he may be dead.|Fortunately for him, he can swim* **13** (suitable, fitting, prepared, or in need) as regards or in regard to: *The men are all ready for action.|She's the very person for the work.|It's not for the pupil to tell the teacher what to do.|used for building houses|I've sent my coat away for cleaning* **14** on the occasion of; at the time of: *He bought his son a boat for his birthday.|She's coming home for Christmas* **15** (*following a compar. adj or adv*) after; as the result of; because of: *You look all the better for your holiday.|This coat's the worse for wear* (=is badly worn) **16** (*following* too *or* enough *and an adj or adv*): *Its too early for dinner.|The hotel's quite good enough for us* **17** considering; considered as; considering that . . . is . . .: *He's heavy for a small boy.|It's cold for the time of year.|The girl's abilities are no more than average for her age* **18** in spite of (in the phr. **for all**): *For all his efforts, he didn't succeed.|"Miteff, for all his heavy appearance, is dancing there on his toes"* (SEU S.) —compare DESPITE[1], NOTWITHSTANDING **19** considering how little (in the phr. **for all**): *For all the improvement you've made in the past year, you might as well give up singing* **20** at the price of; in payment of; at the rate of: *I bought this book for 50 pence.|You can get a good room at the hotel for £4 a day.|She wouldn't go up in an aircraft for anything* (=whatever she was offered or paid).*|He wouldn't harm anybody for the world* (=on any account) **21** as the price of; as the worth of; per: *He paid 50 pence for the book.|These cigarettes are 30 pence for 20.|He got full marks for his English exercise.|a reward for finding the lost jewels* **22** to the amount of; to the number of: *She wrote a cheque for £20.|I've put my name down for 4 concert tickets.|The cricket team was all out for 342 runs* **23** (*followed by* each, every, *or a number, or by* each *or* every *and a number*) in addition to; compared with: *For every mistake you make, you'll lose half a mark.|For 14 passes in the class there was only one failure.|For every 3 who do, there are 2 who don't* **24** (*sometimes left out if it follows directly after the verb*) the length of; the distance of; over the space of: *They ran fast for a mile or 2.|The desert stretches (for) many miles* **25** (*sometimes left out if it follows directly after the verb*) during; till the end of (a period of time): *She didn't answer for* *several minutes.|I haven't seen her for (AmE also in) years.|The performance lasts (for) 3 hours.|Will you be out (for) long (=a long time)?|That's all for today* —compare SINCE[2] **26** (*followed by a noun or pron and an infin. with* to, *in such a way that the phrase so formed can be* REPLACEd *by a* CLAUSE) **a** (*as the subject of a sentence, often introduced by* it is): *For an old man to run fast is dangerous* (=that an old man should run fast).|*It isn't convenient for him to visit us next week* (=that he should visit us) **b** (*following a verb of type* [L1]): *Our plan was for one of us to travel by train with all the bags* (=that one of us should travel) **c** (*following an adj or adv, often with* too *or* enough): *It's plain for all to see* (=so that all may see it).|*He speaks too softly for her to hear* (=so softly that she cannot hear).|*Is that print clear enough for you to read* (=so clear that you can read it)? **d** (*following a noun*): *There's no need for us to argue about this* (=that we should argue) **e** (*following a verb*): *I can't bear for her to be angry with me* (=that she should be angry) **f** (*following* than): *There's nothing worse than for a person to ill-treat a child* (=than that a person should ill-treat) **g** (*used instead of an* if-CLAUSE): *His father must have allowed him to stay up very late, for him to be so tired* (=if he is/was so tired) **h** (*used instead of a* CLAUSE *of purpose, where the infin. may sometimes be left out*): *I've sent my coat away for it to be cleaned* (=in order that it may be cleaned).|*The bell rang for the lesson (to begin)* (=in order that it should begin). |*For the plants to do well they must be watered* (=in order that they should do well).|*The town was hung with flags, as if for the people to welcome a great visitor* (=as if in order that they might welcome) **27** *fml or AmE* in honour of; after: *This rare plant was named for a former governor of India* **28 be for it** *infml esp. BrE* to be likely to be punished, get into trouble, etc.: *You'll be for it if father finds out you've not been to school for 3 days* **29 for all that a** in spite of everything that has been said, done, etc.: *A man's a man, for all that* (Burns) **b** in spite of the fact that: *For all that she has a good sense of balance, she can't dance well* **30 if it weren't/if it hadn't been for** BUT FOR **31 that's . . . for you** *often derog* that's typical of . . .; that's the trouble with . . .: *When I arrived late I couldn't get a hot bath or a good meal; still, that's country hotels for you* **32 there's . . . for you** *derog* that's not what I would call . . .; that's the complete opposite of . . .: *There's* GRATITUDE *for you* —see also **for** GOOD[2] (5), **give someone** WHAT[1] (4) **for**, AS FOR, BUT FOR, EXCEPT FOR

USAGE 1 Compare **for** and **at** with prices: *I bought it* **for** *£5* (=that was what I paid).|*I bought it* **at** *£5* (=that was what it cost then, but it may be different now) 2 Compare **for** and **in** with time. After **first only**, and NEGATIVE and SUPERLATIVE forms, Americans may use **in** where the British use **for**: *the first time* **in** (*BrE* **for**) *4 years|the worst accident* **in** (*BrE* **for**) *months|He hadn't eaten a good meal* **in** (*BrE* **for**) *so long* —compare DURING (2) VERBS like **buy**, which are given the pattern [D1 (*for*)] in this dictionary, can be used without **for** only when the second object is a person or animal. Compare: *He bought his wife a new chair/a new chair* **for** *his wife.|He bought a new chair* **for** *the office* (not **He bought the office a new chair* =one to be used in the office).

for[2] *conj fml or lit* **1** (*always after the main statement*) because: *The old lady doesn't go out in the winter, for she feels the cold a great deal.|We must start early; for we have a long way to go* **2** (*introducing a statement*) it is a fact that: *For he's a* JOLLY *good fellow* (song)

for. *written abbrev. for:* foreign

for·age[1] /ˈfɒrɪdʒ‖ˈfɑ-, ˈfɔ-/ *n* **1** [U] food supplies for horses and cattle **2** [S;U] an act or the action of foraging (FORAGE[2])

forage[2] *v* **1** [L9, esp. ABOUT] *infml* to hunt about or search, turning many things over: *She foraged about in her handbag for 10 minutes, but she couldn't find her ticket* **2** [L9] to wander about looking for food or other supplies: *The campers went foraging for wood to make a fire*

forage cap /ˈ·· ·/ *n* a soft cap able to be folded flat, worn on ordinary occasions by British soldiers at about the time of the Second World War

for·as·much as /fərəzˈmʌtʃ əz‖ˈfɔrəzmʌtʃ əz/ *conj esp. bibl or law* because; as it is a fact that

for·ay[1] /ˈfɒreɪ‖ˈfɔ-, ˈfɑ-/ *v* [IØ (*into*)] to go out and attack enemy country suddenly, esp. in order to carry off food or other supplies

foray[2] *n* **1** [C] a sudden rush into enemy country, usu. by a small number of soldiers, in order to damage or seize arms, food, etc.: *The officer sent a few of his men on a foray; they brought back several prisoners for questioning* **2** [C (*into*)] a short attempt to become active in an activity that is quite different from one's usual activity: *my wife's unsuccessful foray into politics*

for·bear[1] /fɔːˈbeəʳ, fə-‖fɔr-, fər-/ *v* **-bore** /-ˈboʳ/, **-borne** /-ˈbɔːn‖-ˈborn/ [IØ (*from*), 3, 4] *fml* **1** to make no attempt to do something that one has the right to do, esp. in a generous and merciful way: *He's deserved to be punished several times, but I've forborne (from doing so).|The boy brought back the lost dog, but forbore claiming the reward* **2** to use self-control to avoid a wished-for but inconvenient action: *The wounded man could not forbear to cry out*

for·bear[2] /ˈfɔːbeəʳ‖ˈfɔr-/ *n* [C9 *usu. pl.*] FOREBEAR

for·bear·ance /fɔːˈbeərəns‖fɔr-/ *n* [U] control of one's feelings so as to show patient forgiveness: *The child doesn't understand that he's doing wrong; you must treat him with forbearance*

for·bear·ing /fɔːˈbeərɪŋ‖fɔr-/ *adj apprec* long-suffering; gentle and merciful: *He has a forbearing nature; he accepts all his troubles with a smile*

for·bid /fəˈbɪd‖fər-/ *v* **-bade** /ˈbeɪd‖ˈbæd/ *or* **-bad** /ˈbæd/, **-bidden** /ˈbɪdn/ *or* **-bid** /ˈbɪd/ **1** [V3] to command (someone or something) not to do something: *"May I use your car?" "No, I forbid you to."|I forbade my son to use my car* **2** [T1,4] to command that (something) must not be done: *Smoking is forbidden in the concert hall* **3** [D1] to refuse to allow (someone) to have, use, enter, etc., (something): *He did not like his daughter's boyfriend, and forbade him the house* **4 God forbid (that)** I very much hope it will not happen (that): *God forbid that I should ever say nasty things about you*

for·bid·den /fəˈbɪdn‖fər-/ *adj* [Wa5;A] **1** not allowed; against the teachings of religion: *There are certain nearnesses of relationship, such as brother and sister, within which marriage is not allowed; they are known as the* **forbidden degrees** **2** that may not be used, entered, or visited by ordinary people, as because of a religious law: *the forbidden city*

forbidden fruit /·ˌ·· ˈ·/ *n* [U;C] something that is wished for but is not permitted

forbidden ground /·ˌ·· ˈ·/ *n* [U] **1** any place which one may not enter **2** something which may not be talked about: *It's a rule of this club that religion and politics may not be argued about; they're forbidden ground*

for·bid·ding /fəˈbɪdɪŋ‖fər-/ *adj* having a fierce, unfriendly, or dangerous look: *Because she has a forbidding manner she's slow in making friends.|The travellers' way was blocked by a forbidding range of mountains* —**~ly** *adv*

force¹ /fɔːs‖fors/ *n* **1** [U] natural or bodily power; active strength: *The force of the explosion broke all the windows in the building.|He had to use force to get the lid off the tin* **2** [U] fierce or uncontrolled use of strength; violence: *The thief took the money from the old man by force.|The crowd broke open the locked gates by force of numbers* **3** [U;C] *tech* (measurement of) a power that changes or may produce change of movement in a body on which it acts or presses: *The force of* GRAVITY *makes things fall to earth.|What is the force of* GRAVITY *at sea level* (=how great is it)? **4** [C;(U)] a person, thing, belief, action, etc., that has a strong enough influence to cause widespread changes in a way of living, or that has uncontrollable power over living things: *That boy has been a great force for good in the school; he has set an example which has been followed by all.|Many forces have been at work in the last 50 years, that have improved the standard of living.|the forces of evil|Modern wars let loose terrible forces of destruction.|Some countries are greatly at the mercy of the forces of nature; they suffer from floods, thunderstorms, etc.|After years of world power, the Roman Empire became a* SPENT *force.|by force of* CIRCUMSTANCE*s* **5** [U] strong influence on the mind: *The force of his argument was so great that many people accepted his beliefs as true.|The mother was very neat; her daughters learnt to be neat by force of example.|I did it out of force of habit* **6** [C] a group of people banded together or trained for some kind of action, esp. military action: *Both land and sea forces were employed in the attack on the island.|The British air fighting force is called the Royal Air Force.|the police force|A small force of doctors and nurses has been rushed to the scene of the big aircraft accident* **7** [U] exact or special meaning or effect of language: *It isn't always possible, when translating a poem, to keep the complete force of the language in which it was written* **8 in force** in large numbers: *Trouble was expected at the football match, so the police had to be there in force* **9 in(to) force** (of a rule, order, law, etc.) in(to) effect, use, or operation: *Are the new charges for postage stamps in force yet?|What's the use of a government making new laws if they can't be put into force?* **10 join forces (with)** to unite (with) for a purpose: *We're joining forces with some friends to hire a hall for a big party.|Britain and America joined forces to fight for peace*

force² *v* **1** [T1;V3] to make (an unwilling person or animal) do something; drive: *The boy won't do his work if you don't force him (to).|The rider forced his horse on through the storm.|The soldiers forced their prisoners to give up their arms* **2** [T1;X7] to push using force; break: *We had to force the window open.|The thieves forced the lock of the lady's jewel case* **3** [T1] to make (a way) by using force: *I've lost the key of my house, so I'll have to force an* ENTRY.*|There was no path through the wood, and we had to force our way through the thick bushes* **4** [T1 (*into*)] to push (something) into a container that is not of the right size or shape: *It's foolish to force your foot into a shoe that's too small for you.|"I'm trying to get some more books into this box." "Don't force them; you'll break the box"* **5** [Wv5;T1] to produce by unwilling effort; produce with difficulty or against nature: *Although he was in great pain, he forced a smile.|forced laughter|The singer's voice wasn't deep enough for the song; he had to force several low notes* **6** [T1] to hasten the growth of (a plant) by the use of heat: *These plants have been forced so that they may be in flower by Christmas.|*(fig.) *It isn't wise to force a young mind* (=try to make it develop by the study of subjects that are too difficult) **7 force one's/someone's/the pace** to (cause to) take faster or too fast action: *We shan't reach the station in time for the train if we don't force our pace.|The boy's clever but very careless; perhaps the teacher has forced his pace.|Let the men decide this in their usual manner; don't force the* PACE —see also **force someone's** HAND¹ (22)

forced /fɔːst‖forst/ *adj* [Wa5;A] done or made because of a sudden happening which makes it necessary to act without delay: *The aircraft had to make a forced landing because 2 of its engines were on fire.|The soldiers had to make a forced march of 3 days to reach the safety of the city*

force-feed /ˈ· ·/ *v* **-fed** [T1] to feed (a person or animal) by forcing food or esp. liquid down the throat: *One prisoner refused to eat, so he had to be force-fed.|*(fig.) *Pupils ought not to be force-fed with Shakespeare before they can really understand it*

force from also **force out of**— *v prep* [D1] to get (something) from (an unwilling person): *She pretended that she couldn't hear, so that they would not force an answer from her*

force·ful /ˈfɔːsfəl‖ˈfors-/ *adj apprec* (of a person, words, ideas, etc.) strong; powerful: *a forceful speech|He isn't forceful enough to make a good leader* —compare FORCIBLE (2) —**~ly** *adv* —**~ness** *n* [U]

force ma·jeure /ˌfɔːs mæˈʒɜːʳ‖ˌfors mɑˈʒɜr (*Fr* fɔrs maʒœr)/ *n* [U] *Fr* force or power that cannot be acted or fought against

force·meat /ˈfɔːs-miːt‖ˈfors-/ *n* [U] meat cut up very small and mixed with strong-tasting leaves (HERB*s*), used esp. for putting inside a chicken, joint of meat, etc., that is to be cooked; type of STUFFING

force on also **force up·on**— *v prep* [D1] to cause (something) to be accepted by (an unwilling person): *He didn't want to be paid, but we forced the money on him because we knew he needed it*

for·ceps /ˈfɔːseps, -sə̇ps‖ˈfɔr-/ *n* [P] a medical instrument with 2 long thin blades joined at one end or in the middle, used for holding objects firmly: *When a baby that is being born has to have its head held and pulled by forceps, the action is called a* **forceps delivery** —see PAIR (USAGE) and see picture at MEDICAL¹

forc·es /ˈfɔːsə̇z‖ˈfor-/ *n* [(*the*) P] (*often cap.*) the army, navy, and fighting airmen of a country: *In wartime most young men are expected to join the forces.|The navy is one of the armed forces.|a Forces show on the radio* (=a show specially for soldiers, sailors, etc.)

for·ci·ble /ˈfɔːsəbəl‖ˈfor-/ *adj* [A] **1** using bodily force: *The police had to make a forcible* ENTRY *into the house where the thief was hiding* **2** (of a person, manner of speaking, etc.) having power to influence the minds of others; able to urge a case strongly: *I haven't yet heard a really forcible argument in favour of the new plan* —compare FORCEFUL

for·ci·bly /ˈfɔːsəbli‖ˈfor-/ *adv* **1** by bodily force, esp. against one's will: *He complained that he's been forcibly held by the police without good reason* **2** in a strong manner that carries belief: *Her ideas are always forcibly expressed* **3** strongly: *His manner of speaking reminded me forcibly of his father's*

ford¹ /fɔːd‖ford/ *n* a place in a river where the water is not very deep, and where it can be crossed on foot, in a car, etc., without using a bridge —**~able** *adj*

ford² *v* [T1] to cross (a river, stream, etc.) by means of a FORD¹

fore¹ /fɔːʳ‖for/ *adv* towards, in, or near the front part, esp. of a boat: *The sailor went fore to see that the sail was properly in place* —compare AFT

fore² *adj* [Wa5;A] (esp. of a part of a vehicle) front: *Your seat's in the fore part of the aircraft*

fore[3] *n* **1 come to the fore** to become well-known; come to have a leading position: *He passed his law examinations when he was very young, and soon came to the fore as a lawyer* **2 to the fore** noticeably present; ready to be of use: *She's never to the fore when there's work to be done*

fore- *comb. form* **1** earlier; before: FORESIGHT (1)| FOREARM[1] **2** happening earlier or before: *forepayment* **3** placed at the front; in front: FORESIGHT (2)|*fore*PAW|*fore*MAST **4** front part of (the stated thing): FOREARM[2]

fore and aft /ˌ‚· · ˈ·/ *adv* **1** from the front (BOW) to the back (STERN) of a boat; lengthwise: *The ship was* MAN*ned fore and aft as it sailed into harbour on a visit to a foreign port* **2** in, at, or towards both the front and back of a boat: *The captain ordered 2 flags to be placed fore and aft.*|(fig.) *His body was protected by armour fore and aft*

fore·arm[1] /ˌfɔːrˈɑːm‖ˌforˈɑrm/ *v* [T1 *usu. pass.*] **1** to prepare for an attack before the time of need **2 forewarned is forearmed** if a danger is known to be near, preparations can be made to meet it

fore·arm[2] /ˈfɔːrɑːm‖ˈforɑrm/ *n* the lower part of the arm between the hand and the elbow

fore·bear, for- /fɔːbeəʳ‖ˈfor-/ *n* [C9 *usu. pl.*] a person from whom the stated person is descended; ANCESTOR: *My forebears lived in the west of Scotland*

fore·bode /fɔːˈbəʊd‖for-/ *v* **1** [T1] to be a warning of (something unpleasant): *The teacher's angry face forebodes punishment for someone* **2** [T1,5] to feel that (something bad) is about to happen: *She's never a cheerful person; she always forebodes that the worst will happen*

fore·bod·ing /fɔːˈbəʊdɪŋ‖for-/ *n* [U;C,C5] a feeling of coming evil: *She thought of a lonely future with foreboding.*|*She had a foreboding that she'd never see him again*

fore·cast[1] /ˈfɔːkɑːst‖ˈforkæst/ *v* **-cast** *or* **-casted** [T1,5,6] to say, esp. with the help of some kind of knowledge, (what is going to happen at some future time): *forecasting the future*|*The teacher forecast that 15 of his pupils would pass the examination.*|*forecasting what the weather will be like tomorrow*

forecast[2] *n* [C,C5] a statement of future events, based on some kind of knowledge or judgment: *The weather forecast on the radio tonight tells of coming storms.*|*The newspaper's forecast that the government would only last for 6 months*

fore·castle /ˈfəʊksəl‖ˈfəʊksəl, ˈforˌkæ-/ *n* *fml* FO'C'SLE

fore·close /fɔːˈkləʊz‖for-/ *v* [T1;I∅] to repossess property because of someone's failure to repay (a MORTGAGE): *The building society will be forced to foreclose* (*this* MORTGAGE) *because regular repayments have not been made*

foreclose on *v prep* [T1] FORECLOSE

fore·clo·sure /fɔːˈkləʊʒəʳ‖for-/ *n* [U;C] (an example of) the act of foreclosing (FORECLOSURE): *If no payment is made by the borrower in the next few weeks, the bank will have to consider foreclosure*

fore·court /ˈfɔːkɔːt‖ˈforkort/ *n* **1** a courtyard in front of a large building: *He parked his car in the station forecourt* **2** (in tennis) the part of the court between service line and net

fore·doomed /fɔːˈduːmd‖for-/ *adj* [(*to*)] intended by or as if by fate to reach a usu. bad state or condition: *foredoomed to failure*

fore·fa·ther /ˈfɔːˌfɑːðəʳ‖ˈfor-/ *n* [C9 *usu. pl.*] **1** a person from whom the stated person is descended; relative in the far past; (male) ANCESTOR: *One of his forefathers was an early settler in America* **2** a person of an earlier period in the stated place or condition: *the forefathers of the village*

fore·fin·ger /ˈfɔːˌfɪŋgəʳ‖ˈfor-/ also **index finger**— *n* the finger next to the thumb, with which one points —see picture at HUMAN[2]

fore·foot /ˈfɔːfʊt‖ˈfor-/ *n* **-feet** /fiːt/ either of the 2 front feet of a 4-legged animal

fore·front /ˈfɔːfrʌnt‖ˈfor-/ *n* [*the*+R] the most forward place; leading position (esp. in the phr. **in the forefront of**): *in the forefront of the fighting*

fore·go /fɔːˈgəʊ‖for-/ *v* **-went** /ˈwent/, **-gone** /ˈgɒn‖ˈgɔn/ [T1 *past t. rare*] FORGO

fore·go·ing /ˈfɔːgəʊɪŋ‖ ˈfor-/ *adj* [(*the*) A; *the*+GU] *fml* having just been mentioned

foré·gone con·clu·sion /ˌ‥ ·ˈ‥/ *n* [S] a result that is or was certain

fore·ground /ˈfɔːgraʊnd‖ˈfor-/ *n* [*the*+R] **1** the nearest part of a scene in a view, a picture, or a photograph **2** the most important or noticeable position: *She can't bear not to be noticed; she talks a great deal in order to keep herself in the foreground* —compare BACKGROUND (3)

fore·hand /ˈfɔːhænd‖ˈfor-/ *n, adj* [Wa5;C;A] (in tennis) (a stroke) played with the inner part of the hand and arm facing forward —compare BACKHAND

fore·head /ˈfɒrɨ̍d, ˈfɔːhed‖ˈfɔrɨ̍d, ˈfɑrɨ̍d, ˈforhed/ *n* the part of the face above the eyes and below the hair —see picture at HUMAN[2]

for·eign /ˈfɒrɨ̍n‖ˈfɔ-, ˈfɑ-/ *adj* [Wa5] **1** [B] to, from, of, in, being, or concerning a country or nation that is not one's own or not the one being talked about: *foreign travel*|*These oranges are foreign produce.*|*Boys like collecting foreign stamps.*|*Have you had any foreign experience as a teacher* (=have you taught in other countries)?|*He's visited many foreign countries and has learnt several foreign languages.*|*a minister for foreign affairs* (=one who looks after the nation's relations with other countries).|*I can't understand what he says; he must be foreign* **2** [F+*to*] having no place (in); having no relation (to): *He's a very good person; unkindness is foreign to his nature* **3** [A] coming or brought in from outside; not belonging; harmful: *The swelling on her finger was caused by a* **foreign body** *in it* (=a small piece of some solid material that had entered it by accident) —compare STRANGE

foreign aid /ˌ‥ ˈ·/ *n* [U] help in the form of money, goods, etc., given to poorer countries by a richer country

for·eign·er /ˈfɒrɨ̍nəʳ‖ˈfɔ-, ˈfɑ-/ *n* a person belonging to a race or country other than one's own

Foreign Of·fice /ˈ‥ ˌ‥/ *n* [*the*+GU] the British government department which deals with foreign affairs —compare HOME OFFICE

fore·knowl·edge /fɔːˈnɒlɪdʒ‖forˈnɑl-/ *n* [U (*of*)] knowledge about something before it happens

fore·land /ˈfɔːlənd‖ˈfor-/ *n* a piece of land sticking out into the sea; CAPE

fore·leg /ˈfɔːleg‖ˈfor-/ *n* either of the 2 front legs of a 4-legged animal —see picture at DOG[1]

fore·lock /ˈfɔːlɒk‖ˈforlɑk/ *n* **1** a piece of hair growing just above and falling over a person's forehead **2 take time by the forelock** *esp. lit* to seize a chance and make good use of it **3 touch one's forelock (to someone)** (of a man esp. in former times) to greet (someone of higher social class) respectfully by putting one's hand to one's forehead, and pulling one's hair

fore·man /ˈfɔːmən‖ˈfor-/ *n* **-men** /mən/ **1** (fem. **forewoman**)— a skilled and experienced workman who is put in charge of other workers **2** (in a court of law) the leader of the 12 people (JURY) appointed to decide whether a person on trial is guilty or not

fore·most /ˈfɔːməʊst‖ˈfor-/ *adj* [Wa5; *the*+A] **1**

apprec. most important; leading: *the foremost writer in the English language* **2** furthest forward; first —see also FIRST[2] **and foremost**

fore·name /ˈfɔːneɪm‖ˈfor-/ *n fml* FIRST NAME (2)

fore·noon /fɔːnuːn‖ˈfor-/ *n fml* the time before midday; morning

fo·ren·sic /fəˈrensɪk, -zɪk/ *adj* [Wa5;A] *tech* related to or used in the law and the tracking of criminals: *The use of scientific methods by the police is known as* **forensic science**.|*A specialist in* **forensic medicine** *was called as a witness in the murder trial*

fore·or·dain /ˌfɔːrɔːˈdeɪn‖ˌforɔr-/ *v* [Wv5;T1 (*to*), 5;V3] *fml* to arrange or decide from the very beginning that, or how, (something) shall happen or be done: *Some people believe that their lives are foreordained, and others that they are given the will to choose what they do.*|*foreordained to success/to succeed*

fore·part /ˈfɔːpɑːt‖ˈforpɑrt/ *n* [C (*of*)] the front or first part

fore·play /ˈfɔːpleɪ‖ˈfor-/ *n* [U] sexual activity, such as touching the sexual organs and kissing, that is done before the sexual act

fore·run·ner /ˈfɔːˌrʌnəʳ‖ˈfo-/ *n* [+*of*] **1** a sign or warning that something is going to happen: *heavy clouds, the forerunners of a storm* **2** a person who prepares the way for, or is a sign of the coming of, a more important person: *The forerunners of the scientists of today were the men who tried to change other metals into gold*

fore·sail /ˈfɔːsəl, -seɪl‖ˈfor-/ *n* the chief and lowest square sail on the front pole (MAST) of a ship

fore·see /fɔːˈsiː‖for-/ *v* **-saw** /ˈsɔː/, **-seen** /ˈsiːn/ [T1,5,6] to form an idea or judgment about (what is going to happen in the future); expect: *He foresaw that his journey would be delayed by bad weather.*|*It's impossible to foresee whether she'll be well enough to come home from hospital next month.*|*We should have foreseen this trouble months ago*

fore·see·a·ble /fɔːˈsiːəbəl‖for-/ *adj* [Wa5] **1** that can be FORESEEN: *a foreseeable accident* **2 in the foreseeable future a** soon; within a short period of time: *We'll need some more money in the foreseeable future* **b** [*nonassertive*] as far ahead in time as one can see: *The house certainly needs a new roof, but we can't afford one in the foreseeable future*

fore·shad·ow /fɔːˈʃædəʊ‖for-/ *v* [T1] *esp. lit* to be a sign of (what is coming); represent or be like (something that is going to happen)

fore·shore /ˈfɔːʃɔːʳ‖ˈforʃor/ *n* [*the*+R] the part of the seashore which **a** is left dry when the sea goes back from its highest point to its lowest point **b** is between the edge of the sea and the part of the land that has grass, buildings, etc.

fore·short·en /fɔːˈʃɔːtn‖forˈʃortn/ *v* [Wv5;T1] **1** to draw (an object or scene) with the lines and shapes in the distance smaller, shorter, and closer together, as they appear to the human eye **2** to make (objects or scenes) seem smaller, shorter, and/or closer together than is really the case

fore·sight /ˈfɔːsaɪt‖ˈfor-/ *n* **1** [U] *usu. apprec* the ability to imagine what will probably happen, allowing one to act to help or prevent developments; care or wise planning for the future **2** [C] a small raised mark at the front end of a gun, which helps the user to shoot straight

fore·skin /ˈfɔːˌskɪn‖ˈfor-/ *n* a loose fold of skin covering the end of the male sex organ

for·est /ˈfɒrɨ̇st‖ˈfɔ-, ˈfɑ-/ *n* **1** [C;U] (a large area of land thickly covered with) trees and bushes, either growing wild or planted for some purpose: *A large part of Africa is made up of thick forest.*|*Most of the ancient forests of England have been cut down* **2** [C+*of, usu. sing.*] a large number of upright objects close together: *When the teacher asked the boys an easy question, a forest of hands shot up* **3** [C] *old use* (*sometimes cap., as part of name*) a piece of land, with or without trees, where deer and other animals were and sometimes still are kept or hunted: *the deer forests of Scotland*

fore·stall /fɔːˈstɔːl‖for-/ *v* [T1] **1** to prevent (someone) from doing (something) by doing the action first oneself: *The thieves arranged to steal the rich woman's jewels, but her servant girl forestalled them by running away with the jewels herself.*|*She forestalled their attempt* **2** to spoil (the arrangements) of (someone) by doing something earlier than expected: *I meant to meet my friend at the station, but she forestalled me by arriving on an earlier train and coming to the house.*|*She forestalled my plan*

for·est·er /ˈfɒrɨ̇stəʳ‖ˈfɔ-, ˈfɑ-/ *n* **1** an officer who is in charge of a forest and looks after trees and animals, guards against fires, etc. **2** a man who works in a forest, cuts down trees, etc.

for·est·ry /ˈfɒrɨ̇stri‖ˈfɔ-, ˈfɑ-/ *n* [U] the science of planting and caring for large areas of trees

fore·swear /fɔːˈsweəʳ‖for-/ *v* [T1] FORSWEAR

fore·taste /ˈfɔːteɪst‖ˈfor-/ *n* [S (*of*)] a small early experience (of something that will come later): *The unusually warm spring day seemed like a foretaste of summer*

fore·tell /fɔːˈtel‖for-/ *v* **-told** /ˈtəʊld/ [T1 (*to*), 5,6] to tell (what will happen in the future); PROPHESY: *The magician foretold the man's death.*|*He foretold that the man would die.*|*Who can foretell what will happen to the world in 1000 years' time?*

fore·thought /ˈfɔːθɔːt‖ˈfor-/ *n* [U] *often apprec* wise planning for future needs; consideration of what is to come: *If you'd had the forethought to bring your raincoat, you wouldn't have got wet in the storm*

for·ev·er, for ever /fəˈrevəʳ/ *adv* **1** also (*stronger*) **forever and ever**— for all time: *When her son went to fight in the war, his mother felt she'd said goodbye to him forever* **2** also (*lit*) *for* EVERMORE— (*used only with continuous tenses, esp. of annoying things*) continually: *The little boy is forever asking questions*

fore·warn /fɔːˈwɔːn‖forˈwɔrn/ *v* [T1 (*of*);D5] to warn (someone) of coming danger, unpleasantness, etc.; advise (that something will happen or be done) —see also **forewarned is** FOREARMED[1] (2)

fore·wom·an /ˈfɔːˌwʊmən‖ˈfor-/ *n* **-women** /wɪmɪn/ a female FOREMAN (1)

fore·word /ˈfɔːwɜːd‖ˈforwɜrd/ *n* a short introduction at the beginning of a book, esp. in which someone who knows the writer and his work says something about them —see PREFACE (USAGE)

for·feit[1] /ˈfɔːfɨ̇t‖ˈfɔr-/ *n* [C: *the*+U+*of*] what must be lost or FORFEITed[2] for something; price: *Some scientists who have studied dangerous substances have paid the forfeit of their lives in the cause of knowledge*

forfeit[2] *v* [T1] to have (something) taken away from one because some agreement or rule has been broken, or as a punishment, or as the result of some action: *If you don't return the article to the shop within a week, you forfeit your chance of getting your money back*

forfeit[3] *adj* [Wa5;F (*to*)] taken from one, by law, as a punishment: *If a man put his country in danger by helping the enemy, his life and possessions were forfeit to the crown*

for·fei·ture /ˈfɔːfɪtʃəʳ‖ˈfɔr-/ *n* [U (*of*)] the act of FORFEITing or condition of being FORFEITed

for·gath·er /fɔːˈgæðəʳ‖for-/ *v* [I∅] to gather together; meet, esp. in a friendly way

for·gave /fəˈgeɪv‖fər-/ *past t. of* FORGIVE

forge[1] /fɔːdʒ‖fordʒ/ *n* **1** (a building or room containing) a large apparatus with a fire inside used for heating and shaping metal objects: *Horseshoes are made in a forge* **2** (a part of a factory containing) a large apparatus that produces great heat inside itself, used for melting metal, making iron, etc.

forge² *v* **1** [T1] to form by heating and hammering: *forging the parts of a chain*|(fig.) *forging a new unity in our political party* **2** [Wv5;T1;I∅] to make a copy of (something) in order to deceive: *He got the money dishonestly, by forging his brother's signature on a cheque.|He was sent to prison for forging.|a forged* PASSPORT

forge³ *v* [L9] to move with a sudden increase of speed and power: *He forged into the lead as they came round the last bend before the end of the race*

forge a·head *v adv* [I∅] to move steadily and purposefully forward: (fig.) *He didn't do very well when he first went to school, but he's forged ahead in the last 2 years*

forg·er /ˈfɔːdʒəʳ‖ˈfor-/ *n* a person who FORGEs² (2)

for·ge·ry /ˈfɔːdʒəri‖ˈfor-/ *n* **1** [U;C] the act or an action of forging (FORGE² (2)): *He was sent to prison for forgery* **2** [C] something that has been FORGED² (2): *When he bought the picture he was told it was by Rubens, but he later found out that it was a forgery*

for·get /fəˈget‖fər-/ *v* **-got** ˈgɒt‖ˈgɑt/, **-gotten** /ˈgɒtn‖ˈgɑtn/ **1** [T1,3,4,5a,6a,b;I∅] to fail to remember or keep in the memory: *I'm sorry, I've forgotten your name.|Don't forget to bring the cases.|I'll never forget finding that rare old coin in my garden.|I'm sorry, I was forgetting (that) you don't like beans.|I forget who it was who said it.|I forget where to go.|"What's her name?" "I forget"* **2** [T1] to fail to remember to bring, buy, etc., (something): *Don't forget the cases.|I've got the meat and potatoes, but I'm afraid I forgot the bread* **3** [T1;I∅] to stop thinking about (something); put (something) out of one's mind: *They agreed to forget their disagreements and be friends again.|"I'm sorry I broke your teapot." "Forget it."|You should forgive and forget* **4** [T1] to fail to give attention to; treat with inattention: *He forgot his old friends when he became rich.|"Don't forget me" said the little boy as his aunt was giving out jelly to the other children* **5** **forget oneself** **a** to lose one's temper or self-control, or act in a way that is unsuitable or makes one look silly: *The little girl annoyed him so much that he forgot himself and hit her.|He so far forgot himself as to leave the table before everyone had finished eating* **b** to act in an unselfish way **6** **not forgetting** also including; and also: *This song has been requested for Bill, Maggie, and little Teresa, not forgetting Fido the dog*

forget a·bout *v prep* [T1,4] **1** to fail to remember (to do, bring, buy, etc.) (something) at the proper time: *"Did you lock the door when you left the house?" "No, I'm afraid I forgot (all) about it"* **2** to stop keeping the memory of (something or someone) in one's mind: *"Our former neighbours came to see us yesterday." "I'd forgotten (all) about them"*

for·get·ful /fəˈgetfəl‖fər-/ *adj* [(*of*)] having the habit of forgetting: *forgetful of one's duties|My old aunt has become rather forgetful* —**~ly** *adv* —**~ness** *n* [U]

forget-me-not /·ˈ·· ·ˌ·/ *n* a type of low-growing plant with small usu. pale blue flowers —see picture at FLOWER¹

forg·ing /ˈfɔːdʒɪŋ‖ˈfor-/ *n* a piece of FORGEd² (1) metal

for·giv·a·ble, -give- /fəˈgɪvəbəl‖fər-/ *adj* (of a thing) that can be forgiven: *a forgivable mistake* —**-bly** /-bli/ *adv* [Wa3]

for·give /fəˈgɪv‖fər-/ *v* **-gave** /ˈgeɪv/, **-given** /ˈgɪvən/ **1** [D1;T1 (*for*);I∅] to say or feel that one is no longer angry about and/or wishing to give punishment to (someone) for (something): *"Forgive me," she said; "forgive the wrongs I've done you".|He forgave her the wrongs she'd done him.|I'll never forgive you for what you said to me last night.|It's best to forgive and forget* **2** [D1] to say that (someone) need not repay (something): *I lent you that £2.50 a month ago; I'll forgive you the 50p, but I want the £2 back*

for·give·ness /fəˈgɪvnɪ̵̀s‖fər-/ *n* **1** [U (*of*)] the act of forgiving or state of being forgiven: *He asked for forgiveness of his wrong-doings* **2** [U] willingness to forgive

for·giv·ing /fəˈgɪvɪŋ‖fər-/ *adj apprec* willing or able to forgive: *a gentle forgiving nature* —**~ly** *adv*

for·go, fore- /fɔːˈgəʊ‖for-/ *v* **-went** /ˈwent/, **-gone** /ˈgɒn‖ˈgɔn, ˈgɑn/ [T1] *often humor* to give up; (be willing) not to have (esp. something pleasant): *I shall be happy to forgo (the pleasure of) his company*

fork¹ /fɔːk‖fɔrk/ *n* **1** an instrument for holding food or carrying it to the mouth, having a handle at one end with 2 or more points at the other, and usu. made of metal or plastic **2** a farm or gardening tool for breaking up the soil, lifting dried grass, etc., having a wooden handle with 2 or more metal points at one end —see picture at GARDEN¹ **3** a place where something long and narrow divides, or one of the divided parts: *We came to a fork in the road, and we couldn't decide whether to take the left fork or the right* **4** one of the 2 parallel metal points at the front of a bicycle, motorcycle, etc., between which the wheel is fixed —see picture at BICYCLE¹

fork² *v* **1** [T1] to lift, carry, move, etc., with a FORK¹ (2): *I shall have to fork over the soil in the front garden* (=turn it over with a FORK¹ (2)) **2** [I∅] (of something long and narrow) to divide, esp. into 2 parts: *There's a bird's nest in the place where the branch forks* **3** [L9] (of a person) to take the (left or right) FORK¹ (3) of a road: *Fork left at the inn*

fork³ *adj* [Wa5;A] (of a meal) having food provided at a table from which guests can go and get it, often eaten standing up: *a fork supper*

forked /fɔːkt‖fɔrkt/ *adj* [Wa5] **1** having one end divided into 2 or more points: *Snakes have forked tongues* —see picture at REPTILE **2** that divides into 2 or more parts at a point: *a forked road*

forked light·ning /ˌ· ˈ··/ *n* [U] lightning in the form of a line of wavy angles, usu. dividing into 2 or more parts near the bottom —compare SHEET LIGHTNING

fork·ful /ˈfɔːkfʊl‖ˈfɔrk-/ *n* [(*of*)] an amount that is or can be picked up on a fork: *a few forkfuls of rice*

fork·lift /ˈfɔːkˌlɪft‖ˈfɔrk-/ also **forklift truck** /ˌ·· ˈ·/— *n* a small vehicle with a movable apparatus on the front, used for lifting and lowering heavy goods

fork out *v adv* [T1;I∅: (*for* or *on*)] *infml* to pay (money) unwillingly: *I had to fork out £2,500 for that new car of mine*

fork up *v adv* [I∅ (*for*)] *infml* FORK OUT

for·lorn /fəˈlɔːn‖fərˈlɔrn/ *adj esp. lit or fml* **1** (typical of one who is) left alone and unhappy: *One little lost dog had a forlorn look on its face* —see ALONE (USAGE) **2** deserted and in poor condition: *a row of forlorn old buildings down by the port* —**~ly** *adv* —**~ness** *n* [U]

forlorn hope /·ˌ· ˈ·/ *n* [S] a plan or attempt that is very unlikely to succeed

form¹ /fɔːm‖fɔrm/ *n* **1** [C;U] shape; appearance; body; figure; image: *She has a tall graceful form.|In the early morning light we could just see the dark forms of the mountains.|Churches are often built in the form of a cross* **2** [C (*of*)] a general plan or arrangement; system; kind or sort; way something shows or expresses itself: *Different countries have different forms of government.|This disease takes the form of high fever and sickness for several days.|She dislikes any form of exercise* **3** [U] the way in which a work of art is put together: *Some writers are masters of form, but the contents of their books aren't interesting* **4** [U;C] ceremony; rule or custom; set of words and actions usual for an occasion; customary words and actions that have lost their real meaning: *When the village policeman was taking a statement from one of the villagers, he had to ask him his name as a matter of form, although he knew him very well.|They have been through a form of marriage* (=a type of marriage ceremony) **5** [U9] *infml* behaviour of the stated type in relation to what is expected in any particular society or group: *Schoolboys have their own standards of behaviour; they may think it bad form to tell a teacher of another boy's wrong-doing, but quite good form to try to waste time during a lesson* **6** [U] (esp. in sport) **a** (of a person) condition of skill: *What has this sportsman's form been like* (=how well has he been playing)? *He's been in bad form/out of form. He's been in good form/in form* **b** (of an animal) condition of health, fitness, and skill, and standard of performance: *On form this horse should win easily* (=judging from its recent standard of performance) **7** [U] spirits: *Tom was in fine form at the party last night; he amused everyone with his stories, and danced all the time* **8** [U;C] (a) way in which a word may be written or spoken as a result of VARIATIONs in spelling or pronunciation, according to some rule: *There are 2 forms of the past of "to dream"; "dreamed" and "dreamt". They are different in form but not in meaning* **9** [C] a printed paper divided by lines into separate parts, in each of which answers to questions must be written down: *If you wish to be considered for this work, you must* **fill in/fill up/fill out a form** *giving your age, name, experience, etc., and send it to the company* **10** [C] a long wooden seat, usu. without a back **11** [C] a class in a British school, and in some American schools: *Children who have just started school go into the first form; the oldest children are in the 6th form.|Some of the children's pictures are stuck up on the walls of the form room* **12** [U] *BrE sl* a record of having been found guilty of crimes: *A man who's got form finds it difficult to get a job*

form² *v* **1** [IØ] to take shape; be made; appear; develop: *Steam forms when water boils.|A plan began to form in his mind* **2** [L1] to take the shape of: *The school buildings formed a hollow square, with a playground in the middle* **3** [X9] to make (something solid): *People in far northern countries sometimes form small houses out of blocks of ice* **4** [T1] to develop as a result of thought, effort, experience, or training: *School helps to form a child's character.|form a friendship|form good habits* **5** [T1] to make according to rule: *He can't even form a correct sentence in English.|The past tense of "cook" is formed by adding "-ed"* **6** [T1] to make up; gather together; arrange: *forming a club|The new chief minister is forming his government mainly from younger men* **7** [L1] to be; be the substance of: *His courage formed an example to us all.|Flour, eggs, fat, and sugar form the main contents of a cake* **8** [T1; L9] to (cause to) stand or move in (a certain order): *The men formed a chain to pass the goods from the carts to the boats.|The teacher formed her class into 5 rows.|The soldiers formed into a line* —see also FORM UP

-form *comb. form* [n→adj] in the shape of; with the character of: UNIFORM|CRUCIFORM

form·al /ˈfɔːməl‖ˈfɔr-/ *adj* **1** ceremonial; according to accepted rules or customs: *formal dress|a formal dinner party|Business letters must always be formal, but we should write in a natural way to friends* **2** stiff in manner and behaviour; careful about correctness of behaviour: *He's very formal with everybody; he never joins in a laugh* **3** having a set or regular shape: *The bushes were cut into formal shapes of birds.|a formal garden* **4** [Wa5] unreal; belonging to appearance only: *There's only a formal likeness between the 2 brothers, for their natures are very different* **5** (in grammar) concerning rules and forms of words: *Some people study a language by means of formal grammar, others learn by practice* —compare CONVENTIONAL, TYPICAL (2) —**-ally** *adv*

for·mal·de·hyde /fɔːˈmældɪ̈haɪd‖fɔr-/ *n* [U] a type of colourless gas

for·ma·lin /ˈfɔːməlɪ̈n‖ˈfɔr-/ *n* [U] a liquid made by mixing FORMALDEHYDE with water, used for disinfecting, preventing bad smells, hardening leather, preserving dead bodies for science, making plastic, etc.

form·al·is·m /ˈfɔːməlɪzəm‖ˈfɔr-/ *n* [U] *often derog* (too great and exact an) obedience to rules and ceremonies, esp. in art and religion —**-ist** *n, adj* [C;B]

for·mal·i·ty /fɔːˈmælɪ̈ti‖fɔr-/ *n* **1** [U] careful attention to rules and accepted forms of behaviour: *There's no time for formality in much of everyday life* **2** [C] **a** an act in accordance with law or custom: *There are a few formalities to be gone through before you enter a foreign country; for example, you have to say what new goods you're bringing with you* **b** an act which has lost its real meaning: *The school has put a notice in the newspapers, to say that it needs a secretary, but this is just a formality because the headmaster has already chosen the new person*

for·mal·ize, -ise /ˈfɔːməlaɪz‖ˈfɔr-/ *v* [T1] **1** to put (an agreement, plan, etc.) into clear written form: *The agreement must be formalized before it can have the force of law* **2** to introduce FORMALITY (1) into (an occasion/event, etc.) —**-ization** /ˌfɔːməlaɪˈzeɪʃən‖ˌfɔrmələ-/ *n* [U]

for·mat /ˈfɔːmæt‖ˈfɔr-/ *n* **1** the size, shape, etc., in which something, esp. a book, is produced **2** the general plan or arrangement of something: *We're trying out a new format for this old favourite television show this year*

for·ma·tion /fɔːˈmeɪʃən‖fɔr-/ *n* **1** [U] the shaping or developing of something: *Her front teeth were irregular in formation.|School life has a great influence on the formation of a child's character* **2** [U;C] (an) arrangement of people, ships, aircraft, etc.; order: *The soldiers were drawn up in battle formation* (=in correct position to begin a battle).|*a new team of aircraft that does formation flying* (= making patterns in the sky with the aircraft) **3** [C] a thing which is formed; way in which a thing is formed: *There are several kinds of cloud formations*

for·ma·tive /ˈfɔːmətɪv‖ˈfɔr-/ *adj* [A] having influence in forming or developing: *The way in which parents treat their children has, perhaps, the greatest formative effect on their behaviour.|a child's formative years* (= the time when his character is formed) —**~ly** *adv*

form·book /ˈfɔːmbʊk‖ˈfɔrm-/ *n* [*the*+R] *infml* the way in which a person or animal can be expected to perform, esp. in a sports competition, taking into consideration his or its recent FORM¹ (6): *According to the formbook, your horse should finish last in this race*

for·mer /ˈfɔːmə^r‖ˈfɔr-/ *adj* [Wa5] *fml* **1** [A] of an earlier period: *Mr Heath, the former* PRIME MINISTER *of Britain|"Name a former* PRIME MINISTER *of Britain." "Mr Gladstone."|in former times|He made us laugh all the evening; he seemed more like* *his former self again* (=as he was before he was changed by trouble, age, illness, etc.).|*my former husband* **2** [A; *the*+GU] the first (of 2 people or things just spoken of): *Of pigs and cows, the former (animals)* (=pigs) *are less valuable.*|*Did he walk or swim? The former seems more likely* —opposite **latter**

-form·er *comb. form BrE* a pupil of the stated FORM[1] (11): *a 6th-former*

for·mer·ly /ˈfɔːməli‖ˈfɔrmərli/ *adv* in earlier times: *This famous painting was formerly owned privately, but now it belongs to the nation* —compare LATTERLY

For·mi·ca /fɔːˈmaɪkə‖fɔr-/ *n* [U] *tdmk* (*often not cap.*) a type of strong plastic made in thin sheets, used for making the top surface of tables and other articles of furniture

for·mic ac·id /ˌfɔːmɪk ˈæsɪ̣d‖ˌfɔr-/ *n* [U] a colourless fatty acid obtained from ants, and now also produced by other means, used esp. in colouring cloth and making leather

for·mi·da·ble /ˈfɔːmɪ̣dəbəl, fəˈmɪd-‖ˈfɔr-/ *adj* **1** very great and FRIGHTENing; causing fear, doubt, anxiety, etc.: *a formidable voice* **2** difficult; hard to defeat; needing much effort to succeed against: *The soldiers had to fight against a formidable enemy, strong, well-trained, and brave.*|*The examination paper contained several formidable questions* —**-bly** /-bli/ *adv* [Wa3]

form·less /ˈfɔːmləs‖ˈfɔrm-/ *adj* **1** without shape: *a strange formless creature* **2** *usu. derog* lacking order or arrangement: *The music we heard at the concert was rather formless* —**~ly** *adv* —**~ness** *n* [U]

for·mu·la[1] /ˈfɔːmjʊlə‖ˈfɔrmjələ/ *n* **-las** *or* **-lae** /liː/ **1** [C (*for*)] *tech* a general law, rule, fact, etc., expressed shortly by means of a group of letters, signs, numbers, etc.: *The chemical formula for water is H_2O.*|*There is a special formula for calculating the length of the line that encloses a circle, if the distance from the centre of the circle to the outside edge is known* **2** [C (*for*)] a list of the substances used in making something, such as a medicine, a FUEL, a drink, etc., sometimes also including a description of how they are to be mixed: *Someone has stolen the secret formula for the liquid that fires our new spaceship* **3** [C+*for*] a combination of things, events, etc., which will lead almost unavoidably (to the stated result): *Drinking alcohol and driving a car is a formula for trouble* **4** [C (*for*)] a combination of suggestions, plans, etc., that can be agreed on by both sides: *The employers and the leaders of the trade unions are trying to work out an acceptable formula for increases in workers' wages during the next year* **5** [C] **a** a set form of words or behaviour used for a particular occasion **b** an empty meaningless phrase: *Her words of thanks were just a formula; she wasn't really grateful* **6** [U] *AmE* liquid milklike food for babies

formula[2] *adj* [Wa5;A9] of, related to the use of, or being a racing car that has a size, weight, engine, etc., that is expressed, according to a set of rules, by the stated number or word: *Formula one cars are the most powerful.*|*a formula 5000 race*

for·mu·la·ic /ˌfɔːmjʊˈleɪ-ɪk‖ˌfɔrmjə-/ *adj* containing or made up of fixed expressions or set forms of words: *formulaic poetry*

for·mu·late /ˈfɔːmjʊleɪt‖ˈfɔrmjə-/ *v* [T1] **1** to express in a short clear form **2** to invent and prepare (a plan, suggestion, etc.)

for·mula·tion /ˌfɔːmjʊˈleɪʃən‖ˌfɔrmjə-/ *n* **1** [U] the act of formulating (FORMULATE) **2** [C] a FORMULATEd statement

form up *v adv* [IØ (*into*)] to make regular lines: *The children had to form up before being allowed into school*

for·ni·cate /ˈfɔːnɪ̣keɪt‖ˈfɔr-/ *v* [IØ] *esp. law or bibl* to have sexual relations with someone outside marriage

for·ni·ca·tion /ˌfɔːnɪ̣ˈkeɪʃən‖ˌfɔr-/ *n* [U] *esp. law* sexual acts between 2 people not married to each other, as when both of them are unmarried —compare ADULTERY

for·ra·der /ˈfɒrədəʳ‖ˈfɑ-/ *adv infml esp. BrE* further forward: *I've been working all the morning, but I don't seem to be much forrader* (=to have done much work)

for·sake /fəˈseɪk‖fər-/ *v* **-sook** /ˈsʊk/, **-saken** /ˈseɪkən/ [Wv5;T1] *fml* to desert; leave for ever; give up completely: *She forsook the religion of her family in favour of that of her new husband.*|*The little village had a forsaken look* —see also GODFORSAKEN

for·sooth /fəˈsuːθ‖fər-/ *adv old use* indeed; certainly; in truth

for·swear, fore- /fɔːˈsweəʳ‖for-/ *v* **-swore** /ˈswɔːʳ‖ˈswor/ **-sworn** /ˈswɔːn‖ˈsworn/ *fml* **1** [T1,4] to make a solemn promise to give up or to stop doing (something): *The priests of some religions must forswear wealth and marriage* **2 forswear oneself** PERJURE **oneself**

for·sy·thi·a /fɔːˈsaɪθɪə‖fərˈsɪ-/ *n* [U] a type of bush that bears bright yellow flowers in spring, before its leaves appear

fort /fɔːt‖fort/ *n* **1** [C] a strongly made building used for defence at some important place **2** [C;A] (*usu. cap. as part of name*) a (town containing a) fixed army camp: *In former times the British army kept lots of soldiers at Fort William in Scotland* **3 hold the fort** to look after everything while someone is away: *When the mother had to go into hospital, her eldest daughter had to hold the fort*

for·te[1] /ˈfɔːteɪ‖fort/ *n* [C9, *esp. with poss.*] a strong point in a person's character or abilities: *Games are his forte; he plays cricket and football unusually well*

for·te[2] /ˈfɔːteɪ‖ˈfɔr-/ *n, adj, adv* ((a piece of music) played) in a loud and forceful manner —see also FORTISSIMO

forth /fɔːθ‖forθ/ *adv* **1** *esp. bibl or lit* (*after a verb*) out; forward: *He went forth into the desert to pray* **2** *esp. bibl, lit, or fml* on into the future: *from this day forth* **3 and (so on and) so forth** etc.; and other like things: *She said many times that she was sorry for what she'd done, she'd never do it again, and so forth.*|"*improvement of conditions and so on and so forth*" (SEU S.) **4 back and forth** in one direction and then in the other —see also BRING FORTH

forth·com·ing /ˌfɔːθˈkʌmɪŋ◂‖ˌforθ-◂/ *adj* **1** [Wa5; B] happening or appearing in the near future: *On the noticeboard there was a list of forthcoming events at school* **2** [Wa5;F] (*often with neg.*) ready; supplied; offered when needed: *When she was asked why she was late, no answer was forthcoming* **3** [B] *infml* (*often with neg.*) ready to be helpful and friendly: *I asked several villagers the way to the river, but none of them were very forthcoming*

forth·right /ˈfɔːθraɪt‖ˈforθ-/ *adj* direct in manner and speech; expressing one's thoughts and feelings plainly: *His forthright behaviour shows that he's honest, but he seems rude to some people* —**~ness** *n* [U]

forth·with /fɔːθˈwɪð, -ˈwɪθ‖forθ-/ *adv esp. lit* at once; without delay

for·ti·eth /ˈfɔːtɪəθ‖ˈfɔr-/ *determiner, n, pron, adv* [see NUMBER TABLE 3] 40th

for·ti·fi·ca·tion /ˌfɔːtɪ̣fɪ̣ˈkeɪʃən‖ˌfɔr-/ *n* **1** [U] the act or science of FORTIFYing: *I need a little fortification; pour me out some wine* **2** [C *usu. pl.*] towers, walls, gun positions, etc., set up as a means of defence

fortified wine /ˌ··· ˈ·/ *n* [U;C] (any of several

types of) alcoholic drink made by adding a small amount of strong alcohol (such as BRANDY) to wine: SHERRY *is a fortified wine*

for·ti·fy /ˈfɔːtɪ̈faɪ‖ˈfɔr-/ *v* [Wv5;T1] **1** to build forts on; strengthen against possible attack: *a fortified city|to fortify the coastal areas* **2** to strengthen; give courage to: *After praying quietly he faced his difficulties with a fortified spirit* —**-fiable** *adj* [Wa5] —**-fier** *n*

for·tis·si·mo /fɔːˈtɪsɪ̈məʊ‖fɔr-/ *n, adj, adv* **-mos** ((a piece of music) played) in a very loud and forceful manner —see also FORTE[2]

for·ti·tude /ˈfɔːtɪ̈tjuːd‖ˈfɔrtɪ̈tuːd/ *n* [U] *apprec* firm and lasting courage in bearing trouble, pain, etc., without complaining

fort·night /ˈfɔːtnaɪt‖ˈfort-/ *n* [C *usu. sing.*] *BrE* 2 weeks: *I'm going away for a fortnight's holiday.|He's coming in a fortnight's time* (=2 weeks after today).|*Her birthday is Tuesday fortnight* (=2 weeks later than next Tuesday)

fort·night·ly /ˈfɔːtnaɪtli‖ˈfort-/ *adj, adv* [Wa5] *BrE* (happening, appearing, etc.) every FORTNIGHT or once a FORTNIGHT: *a fortnightly visit*

for·tress /ˈfɔːtrɪ̈s‖ˈfɔr-/ *n* a large fort; place strengthened for defence

for·tu·i·tous /fɔːˈtjuːɪ̈təs‖fɔrˈtuː-/ *adj* **1** happening by chance; accidental: *a fortuitous meeting* **2** *nonstandard* fortunate; lucky: *Let me wish you joy on this fortuitous occasion!* —**~ly** *adv* —**~ness** *n* [U]

for·tu·nate /ˈfɔːtʃənət‖ˈfɔr-/ *adj* having or bringing good fortune; lucky: *She's fortunate enough to have very good health.|He's fortunate in having a good wife.|It was fortunate for her that she met the doctor just when she needed him* —opposite **unfortunate**

for·tu·nate·ly /ˈfɔːtʃənətli‖ˈfɔr-/ *adv* **1** by good chance; luckily: *I was late in getting to the station, but fortunately for me, the train was late too* **2** it is/was a good thing that . . .: *Fortunately, he found the money that he'd lost* —opposite **unfortunately**

for·tune /ˈfɔːtʃən‖ˈfɔr-/ *n* **1** [U] fate; chance, esp. as an important influence on one's life; luck: *It's never been his fortune to travel far from home.|She had the good fortune to be free from illness all her life* **2** [C] whatever comes by chance, good or bad; that which will happen to a person in the future: *Through all his changing fortunes, he never lost courage.|The fortunes of war bring death to many, while others escape unharmed.|That old woman tells fortunes* (=claims to tell about a person's future by examining his hands, studying a pack of cards, a glass ball, etc.).|*I had my fortune told last week* **3** [U] success; good luck: *Fortune smiled on him* (=everything went well for him).|*Fortune favours the brave* (=brave people often succeed) **4** [C] wealth; a great amount of money, possessions, etc.: *Some men have made great fortunes by developing oil businesses.|The jewels that the rich woman was wearing last night must be worth a fortune.|He came into a fortune when his rich aunt died.* **5 a small fortune** *infml* a lot of money: *Those jewels must have cost a small fortune* **6 seek one's fortune** to leave one's home and try to find success in the world

fortune hunt·er /ˈ·· ˌ··/ *n usu. derog* a person who tries to marry for money

fortune-tell·er /ˈ·· ˌ··/ *n* a person, usu. a woman, who claims to be able to tell FORTUNEs (2)

for·ty /ˈfɔːti‖ˈfɔrti/ *determiner, n, pron* [see NUMBER TABLE 1] (the number) 40

forty-five /ˌ·· ˈ·/ *n infml* **1** also **·45**— a small gun held in the hand (PISTOL), having a barrel that is 0·45 of an inch across on the inside **2** also **45**— a record that is played by causing it to turn round 45 times every minute —compare SEVENTY-EIGHT

forty winks /ˌ·· ˈ·/ *n* [P] *infml* a short sleep in the daytime (esp. in the phr. **have forty winks**)

for·um /ˈfɔːrəm/ *n* **1** (in ancient Rome) an open place used for public business **2 a** any place where public matters may be talked over and argued about: *The letters page of this newspaper is a forum for public argument* **b** a meeting for such a purpose: *A group of schoolmasters are holding a forum on new ways of teaching history*

for·ward[1] /ˈfɔːwəd‖ˈfɔrwərd/ *adj* **1** [Wa5;A] directed towards the front or a point in front; advancing: *a forward movement* **2** [Wa5;A] near, at, or belonging to the front: *the forward part of the train* **3** [B] particularly or unusually advanced or early in development: *a forward child|a forward summer|The spring flowers are rather forward this year* **4** [B] (esp. of a young person) sure of oneself, esp. in an unpleasant way; too bold, often in sexual matters: *She's too forward for me to like her* **5** [F (*with*), F3] ready and eager: *He's always forward with help* **6** [F (*with*)] getting on fast (with work, study, plans, etc.): *We aren't very far forward with our preparations for our travels next month* —see also FORRADER **7** [B] advanced; modern: *very forward views on the way in which young children should be taught* **8** [Wa5;A] *tech* related to future business, produce, etc.: *forward prices* (=prices that will come into effect next month) —compare BACKWARD

forward[2] also **for·wards** /-wədz‖-wərdz/— *adv* **1** towards the front of a place; in advance; ahead: *The soldiers crept forward under cover of darkness.|Take 2 steps forward.|Those behind cried "Forward!"*|(fig.) *"We have gone forward with what we said we could do"* (SEU S.) **2** towards the future: *to look forward|from that day forward|a* FORWARD-LOOKING *suggestion* —see LOOK FORWARD TO **3** towards an earlier time: *We'll bring the date of the meeting forward from the 20th to the 18th* **4** into a noticeable position: *The lawyer brought forward some new reasons* —see also BACKWARDS (5) **and forwards** and compare BACKWARDS **5** also **on**— (of a clock) so as to show as later time: *to put the clock forward|The clocks go on an hour tonight* —compare BACK[2] (8)

forward[3] *n* one of the attacking players in teams of various sports (such as SOCCER, RUGBY, and HOCKEY) —compare CENTRE[1] (5), BACK[1] (8)

forward[4] *v* **1** [T1 (*to*)] to send or pass on (letters, parcels, etc.) to a new address: *When we moved house, we asked the people who took our old house to forward all our post to our new address* **2** [D1 (*to*);T1] *fml* to send: *We are forwarding you a list of the store's latest men's clothing, together with prices* **3** [T1] to help advance the development of: *forward the plans for a new school*

forward[5] /ˈfɒrəd, ˈfɔːwəd‖ˈfɔrərd, ˈfɔrwərd/ *adv naut* in or towards the front part of a ship: *"You will have to go forward of the* MAST*"* (SEU W.) —compare AFT

for·ward·ing /ˈfɔːwədɪŋ‖ˈfɔrwər-/ *n* [U;A] the act or business of FORWARDING[4] (1, 2) goods: *forwarding instructions|The man who left yesterday didn't leave a forwarding address, so I don't know where to send this letter that has come for him*

forwarding a·gent /ˈ··· ˌ··/ *n* a person who or business that FORWARDs[4] (2) goods

forward-look·ing /ˈ·· ˌ··/ *adj* [Wa5] *apprec* planning for or concerned with the future

for·ward·ly /ˈfɔːwədli‖ˈfɔrwərdli/ *adv* in a FORWARD[1] (4) manner

for·ward·ness /ˈfɔːwədnɪ̈s‖ˈfɔrwərd-/ *n* [U] the state or quality of being FORWARD[1] (3, 4)

forward pass /ˌ·· ˈ·/ *n* (esp. in RUGBY) an act of throwing the ball in the direction of one's opponents' GOAL (which is against the rules)

for·went, fore- /fɔːˈwent‖for-/ *past t. of* FORGO

fosse, foss /fɒs‖fɑs/ *n* a long hole of regular depth and with straight sides, dug round the outer walls of any defence works, esp. a fort or castle, and often filled with water; MOAT

fos·sil[1] /ˈfɒsəl‖ˈfɑ-/ *n* **1** a hardened part or print of an animal or plant of long ago, that has been preserved in rock, ice, etc. **2** *derog* an old person with unchanging ideas or habits (usu. in the phr. **old fossil**): *Mary thinks her two aunts are a pair of old fossils, because they don't like modern dance music*

fossil[2] *adj* [Wa5;A] **1** being or in the condition of a FOSSIL[1] (1): *a fossil seashell* **2** being made of substances that are living things in the distant past: *Coal is a fossil* FUEL

fos·sil·ize, -ise /ˈfɒsəlaɪz‖ˈfɑ-/ *v* [T1;IØ] **1** to (cause to) become a FOSSIL[1] (1) **2** to (cause to) cease developing and become very fixed in ideas, way of living, etc. —**-ization** /ˌfɒsəlaɪˈzeɪʃən‖ˌfɑsələ-/ *n* [U]

fos·ter /ˈfɒstəʳ‖ˈfɔ-, ˈfɑ-/ *v* [T1] **1** to help (something) to grow or develop: *The mother tried to foster her son's interest in music by taking him to concerts when he was young* **2** to keep alive in the mind; encourage: *Films and pictures about recent wars sometimes foster angry memories and feelings of hatred between nations* **3** to look after or bring up (a child or young animal) as one's own, usu. for a certain period and without taking on the full lawful responsibilities of the parent: *We fostered the young girl while her mother was in hospital* —compare ADOPT (1)

foster- *comb. form* giving or receiving parental care although not of the same family: *a foster-parent|a foster-son|a foster-home|Danny is my foster-brother* (=we have different parents, but he is being brought up with me as if belonging to my family)

fought /fɔːt/ *past t. & p. of* FIGHT[1]

foul[1] /faʊl/ *adj* **1** [Wa1;B] evil-smelling or evil-tasting; very dirty; unclean; impure: *The air in this room is foul; open the window!|a foul-tasting medicine* **2** [Wa5;A] (of a pipe, chimney, etc.) blocked with dirt or waste matter, so that liquid, smoke, etc., cannot pass freely **3** [Wa5;B] *tech, esp. naut* (of a rope, chain, etc.) twisted; knotted; mixed up in disorder: *The chain's foul; it won't wind round the wheel* **4** [Wa1;B] (of weather) rough; stormy: *It's a foul night tonight; it's pouring with rain* **5** [Wa5; A] *naut* (of wind) unfavourable **6** [Wa1;B] *derog* evil; cruel; wicked; shameful: *Murder is a foul deed.|the foul murderer|She has a foul temper; that's why she has so few friends* **7** [Wa1;B] *derog* (of language) full of curses **8** [Wa1;B] *infml* very bad; disagreeable; unpleasant: *I've had a foul morning; everything's gone wrong.|That was a foul meal to offer anybody* **9** [Wa5;A] (in sport) against the rules; unfair: *He struck his opponent a foul blow on the back of the neck* **10 by fair means or foul** somehow; in any way, good or bad: *She always gets what she wants, by fair means or foul* **11 fall foul of a** (of a ship) to run against; get caught up with: *The ship fell foul of the fishing boat* **b** to get into trouble with: *He fell foul of his employer, and lost his job.|If you steal, you'll soon fall foul of the law* (=be taken by the police and punished) —**~ly** *adv* —**~ness** *n* [U]

foul[2] *n* **1** [C] (in sport) an act that is against the rules: *The footballer was sent off the field for a foul on an opponent; he had kicked him intentionally* **2 through fair and foul** at all times; in both bad and good fortune: *He's been a good friend through fair and foul*

foul[3] *v* [T1;IØ] **1** to (cause to) become dirty, impure, or blocked with waste matter: *The dog's fouled the path.|One pipe has fouled, and the water won't go down* **2** (in sports, esp. football) to be guilty of a FOUL[2] (1) (against): *Smith ran suddenly into Jones and fouled him just as Jones was kicking the ball* **3** *naut* (of a boat) to run against (another) **4** (of a rope, chain, etc.) to get mixed up or twisted with (something)

foul-mouthed /ˌ· ˈ·◂/ *adj derog* containing or having the habit of using FOUL[1] (7) language

foul play /ˌ· ˈ·/ *n* [U] **1** (in sports) unfair play; actions that are against the rules **2** *tech* criminal violence in association with a person's death; murder: *The police aren't sure how the man died, but they think it may be a case of foul play*

foul-up /ˈ· ·/ *n infml* **1** a state of confusion caused by carelessness or lack of skill **2** a breakdown or STOPPAGE in machinery

foul up *v adv* [T1] *infml* to spoil: *Don't foul up this chance.|Don't foul things up*

found[1] /faʊnd/ *v* [T1] **1** [(*on, upon*)] to build or start building (something large): *The castle is founded on solid rock.|The Romans founded a great city on the banks of this river* **2** to begin the development of; establish: *This business company was founded in 1724* **3** to start and support by supplying money: *The rich man founded a hospital and a school in the town where he was born* —see also FOUND ON

found[2] *v* [T1] **1** to melt (metal) and pour into a hollow form (MOULD) —see also FOUNDRY **2** to make (something) of metal in this way

found[3] *past t. & p. of* FIND[1]

foun·da·tion /faʊnˈdeɪʃən/ *n* **1** [U] the act of starting the building or planning of something large, or starting some kind of organization: *The foundation of the university took place over 600 years ago* **2** [C] a building and the organization connected with it, planned for a good purpose and supported in some special way: *This school is an ancient foundation; it was started by a king who wanted boys to have the chance to learn* **3** [C] (*often cap., as part of name*) **a** an organization that gives out money for certain special purposes: *The Gulbenkian Foundation gives money to help artists* **b** the money held by such an organization **4** [U] that on which a belief, custom, way of life, etc., is based; BASIS: *The foundation on which many ancient types of society were built was the use of slaves.|The report is completely without foundation* (= is untrue) **5** [S] FOUNDATIONS (1): *A building must be laid on a firm foundation*

foundation cream /·ˈ·· ·/ *n* [U] a mixture of oils and other substances that women rub into the skin of their faces before putting on face powder

foundation gar·ment /·ˈ·· ˌ··/ *n* an undergarment worn by women, shaped so as to support and control the body

foun·da·tions /faʊnˈdeɪʃənz/ *n* [P] **1** the solid stonework, brickwork, etc., first set in holes dug deep in the earth, to support the walls of a building: *The explosion shook the building to its foundations* (=caused it to shake dangerously).| *The workmen are laying the foundations of the new hospital* **2** the base; that by which things are supported, or on which they are based: *He laid the foundations of his success by study and hard work.|The proof that the earth wasn't flat struck at the foundations of older ideas and beliefs over 400 years ago* (=destroyed the base of them)

foundation stone /·ˈ·· ·/ *n* a large block of stone, on which words are usually cut, which is laid at a public ceremony by some important person, when an important building is begun

found·er[1] /ˈfaʊndəʳ/ *n* a person who FOUNDs[1] something: *Mohammed was the founder of the*

Muslim religion.|a service in honour of the founders of the university

foun·der² *v* **1** [IØ] (of a ship) to fill with water and sink: *The ship foundered in the heavy seas* **2** [IØ] to come to nothing; fail: *The plan was a good one, but it foundered for lack of support* **3** [IØ;T1] to (cause (a horse) to) fall

founder mem·ber /ˌ·· '··/ also (*esp. AmE*) **charter member**— *n* an original member of a society or organization

founding fa·ther /ˌ·· '··/ *n* [(*of*), *often pl.*] *lit or fml* a person who begins the development (of something); FOUNDER¹: *Louis Pasteur was one of the founding fathers of modern medicine*

found·ling /'faʊndlɪŋ/ *n esp. lit, becoming rare* an unknown young child deserted by its parents and found by others, usu. in some public place

found on also **found up·on**— *v prep* [D1 *often pass.*] to base on: *a story founded on fact|The teacher founded his system of language teaching on the belief that speaking should come before reading*

foun·dry /'faʊndri/ *n* a place where metals are melted down and poured into shapes to make separate articles or parts of machinery, such as bars, wheels, etc.: *an iron foundry|foundry workers*

fount¹ /faʊnt/ *n* **1** *poet* a spring of water **2** [(*of*)] the place where something begins or comes from: *That old man is a fount of wisdom* (=is full of wise thoughts and words)

fount² /fɒnt, faʊnt‖fɑnt, faʊnt/ also **font**— *n* a complete set of letters (TYPE) of one kind and size for printing books, newspapers, etc.

foun·tain /'faʊntən/ *n* **1** (an apparatus of pipes, sometimes hidden inside beautiful stone figures or bowls set in an ornamental lake or smaller piece of water in a garden, or other open space, producing) a stream of water that shoots straight up into the air **2** [(*of*)] a flow (of liquid), esp. rising straight into the air: *A fountain of water shot up from the burst pipe* **3** [(*of*)] the place where something begins or is supplied: *The ruler was respected by his people as the fountain of honour* **4** *poet* a natural spring of water, rising out of the ground —see also DRINKING FOUNTAIN, SODA FOUNTAIN

foun·tain·head /'faʊntənhed/ *n* [(*of*), *usu. sing.*] *lit* the place from which something originates; SOURCE: *The fountainhead of this writer's poetic power is his love of Nature*

fountain pen /'·· ·/ *n* a pen with a container (BARREL) giving a continuous supply of ink as one writes with it

four /fɔːʳ‖for/ *determiner, n, pron* **1** [see NUMBER TABLE 1] (the number) 4 **2** [C] (esp. in games of cards) a set or group of 4: *Will you make up a four for a game of cards* (=complete the group of four)? **3** [C] (in cricket) 4 runs, usu. gained by hitting the ball to the edge of the field: *He hit a four* **4** [C] a rowing-boat for racing that holds 4 men **5 . . . and four** . . . and 4 horses; . . . pulled by 4 horses: *a* COACH *and four* **6 for four hands** (of a piece of music) written for 2 people to play on the piano **7 scatter (something) to the four winds** to (cause (something) to) be thrown or sent violently in all directions: *I scattered the pieces of paper to the four winds.|The pieces scattered to the four winds* **8 the four corners of the earth** the most distant parts of the earth: *He's travelled to the four corners of the earth*

four·eyes /'fɔːraɪz‖'for/ *n* [N] *infml, usu. humor* a person who wears glasses

four-foot·ed /ˌ· '··◂/ *adj* [Wa5] (of an animal) having 4 feet

four-in-hand /ˌ· · '·/ *n* **1** a carriage, used in former times, drawn by 4 horses controlled by one driver **2** *AmE* a long band of cloth worn around the neck (TIE) and tied in a knot in front letting the 2 ends hang down one behind the other: *a four-in-hand* TIE*|a four-in-hand knot* —compare **bow tie**

four-leaved clo·ver /ˌ· · '··/ also **four-leafed clover, four-leaf clover**— *n* [C;U] a CLOVER plant having a set of 4 leaves instead of the usual 3, said to bring good luck to a person who finds it

four-let·ter word /ˌ· ·· '·/ *n euph* any of several words made up of usu. 4 letters, that are not considered to be polite

four-part /'· ·/ *adj* [Wa5;A] (of music) arranged to be sung by 4 (sets of) people with 4 different kinds of voices (SOPRANO, ALTO, TENOR, and BASS), all at once

four·pen·ny /'fɔːpəni‖'forpeni/ *adj* [Wa5;A] **1** costing FOUR PENCE: *a fourpenny stamp* **2 a fourpenny one** *BrE infml* a sharp blow: *I'll give you a fourpenny one if you don't keep quiet!*

four-post·er /ˌ· '··/ also **four-poster bed** /ˌ· ·· '·/— *n* a large old kind of bed, with posts at the 4 corners to support a frame for curtains —see picture at BEDROOM

four-pound·er /ˌ· '··/ *n* a gun that fires a shot weighing 4 pounds

fours /fɔːz‖forz/ *n* **on all fours** (of a person) on the hands and knees: *The baby was creeping about on all fours*

four·square /ˌfɔː'skweəʳ‖ˌfor-/ *adj* **1** *usu. apprec* brave and unyielding **2** (esp. of a building) shaped like a square; solid and firm

four·teen /ˌfɔː'tiːn◂‖ˌfor-/ *determiner, n, pron* [see NUMBER TABLE 1] (the number) 14 —**~th** *determiner, n, pron, adv* [see NUMBER TABLE 3]

fourth /fɔːθ‖forθ/ *determiner, n, pron, adv* [see NUMBER TABLE 3] 4th

fourth di·men·sion /ˌ· ·'··/ *n* [*the*+R] time

fourth es·tate /ˌ· ·'·/ *n* [*the*+R] *lit or pomp* (*often cap.*) newspapers, their writings, and the people who write for them: *The fourth estate is a powerful force in modern society*

Fourth of Ju·ly /ˌ· · ·'·/ *n* [*the*+R] the national Independence Day of the US

four-wheel·er /ˌ· '··/ *n* a type of closed carriage, used in former times, having 4 wheels and drawn by one horse

fowl /faʊl/ *n* **fowls** *or* **fowl** **1** [Wn2;C] a farmyard bird, esp. a hen: *She keeps fowls, and sells the eggs* **2** [U] the meat of this, cooked as food **3** [Wn2;C] *old use & poet* a bird: *God made all the fowls of the air* —see also WATERFOWL, WILDFOWL

fowling piece /'·· ·/ *n* a gun for firing small shot, used for shooting certain types of bird, esp. ducks

fowl pest /'· ·/ *n* [U] a quickly-spreading disease of FOWLs (1)

fox¹ /fɒks‖fɑks/ *n* **1** [C] (fem. **vixen**)— **a** any of several types of small doglike flesh-eating wild animal with a bushy tail, esp. **b** a type of European animal with reddish fur, preserved in Britain to be hunted and often said to have a clever and deceiving nature —see picture at CARNIVOROUS **2** [U] the skin of this animal, used as fur on coats and other garments **3** [C] *infml, usu. derog* a person who deceives others by means of clever tricks: *Don't trust that man, he's a* SLY *old fox* **4 crazy like a fox** *sl, esp. AmE* clever; not easily deceived

fox² *v infml* **1** [T1] **a** to deceive cleverly; trick **b** to be too difficult for (someone) to understand: *The second question on the examination paper foxed me completely; I couldn't understand it at all* **2** [IØ] to pretend: *"Is he really ill?" "No, he's just foxing"*

fox·glove /'fɒksglʌv‖'fɑks-/ *n* a type of tall straight plant bearing pink or white bellshaped flowers all the way up its stem

fox·hole /ˈfɒkshəʊl‖ˈfɑks-/ *n* a hole in the ground from which soldiers fire at the enemy

fox·hound /ˈfɒkshaʊnd‖ˈfɑks-/ *n* a type of dog with a keen sense of smell, trained to track down and kill foxes

fox·hunt /ˈfɒkshʌnt‖ˈfɑks-/ *n* a hunt of foxes by FOXHOUNDs and people riding on horses —**~er** *n* —**~ing** *n* [U]

fox ter·ri·er /ˌ· ˈ···/ *n* a type of small dog now usu. kept as a pet, but trained in former times to drive foxes and rats from their holes

fox·trot /ˈfɒkstrɒt‖ˈfɑkstrɑt/ *n* (a piece of music for) a type of formal dance with short quick steps —**foxtrot** *v* [IØ]

fox·y /ˈfɒksi‖ˈfɑksi/ *adj* [Wa1] *derog* like a fox, in appearance or nature; not to be trusted: *The thief had a small foxy face*

foy·er /ˈfɔɪeɪ‖ˈfɔɪər/ *n* an entrance hall to a theatre or hotel, where people gather and talk

Fr *written abbrev. for:* **1** Father (as a religious title) **2** FRANC **3** France **4** French

frac·as /ˈfrækɑː‖ˈfreɪkəs/ *n* **fracas** /ˈfrækɑːz/ *AmE* **-cases** /kəsǝ̍z/ a noisy quarrel in which usu. a number of people take part, and which often ends in a fight

frac·tion /ˈfrækʃən/ *n* **1** [C (*of*)] a very small piece or amount: *She's careful with her money, and spends only a fraction of her earnings.|I'll be ready in a fraction of a second* (=a very short space of time) **2** [C] (in MATHEMATICS) a division or part of a whole number: $\frac{1}{3}$ *and* $\frac{5}{8}$ *are fractions* —see also IMPROPER FRACTION, PROPER FRACTION, VULGAR FRACTION

frac·tion·al /ˈfrækʃənəl/ *adj* [Wa5] **1** so small as to be unimportant: *The difference between his wages and yours is fractional and there's no reason to quarrel about it* **2** (in MATHEMATICS) of, related to, or being a FRACTION (2)

frac·tion·al·ly /ˈfrækʃənəli/ *adv* to a very small degree: *If calculations in planning to send a spaceship to the moon are even fractionally incorrect, there's little hope of success*

frac·tious /ˈfrækʃəs/ *adj* **1** (esp. of a child or an old or sick person) restless and complaining; bad-tempered about small things and ready to quarrel **2** (of an animal) difficult to control —**~ly** *adv* —**~ness** *n* [U]

frac·ture¹ /ˈfræktʃəʳ/ *n tech, esp. med, or fml* **1** [U (*of*)] the act or result of breaking something, esp. a bone: *Fracture of the leg can be very serious in old people* **2** [C] a crack or break, esp. in a bone or limb: *A fracture in the gas pipe allowed a lot of gas to escape.|In a* **compound fracture** *part of the broken bone pushes through the skin; in a* **simple fracture** *this doesn't happen*

fracture² *v* [T1;IØ] *tech, esp. med, or fml* to (cause to) break or crack: *He fell and fractured his upper arm.|The ice on the lake fractured under the weight of the boys playing on it*

fra·gile /ˈfrædʒaɪl‖-dʒəl/ *adj* **1** easily broken or damaged: *This old glass dish is very fragile; it's in a very fragile condition* **2** easily destroyed; not likely to last: *Their happiness was very fragile* **3 a** slight in body or weak in health: *The old lady looks very fragile* **b** *usu. humor* not in a good condition of health and spirits; weak: *"I'm feeling rather fragile this morning," he said; "I must have drunk too much beer last night"* —**-gility** /frəˈdʒɪlǝ̍ti/ *n* [U]

frag·ment¹ /ˈfrægmənt/ *n* **1** a small piece broken off: *She dropped the bowl on the floor, and it broke into fragments* **2** an incomplete part, esp. of a work of art: *This play contains the fragment of a play by a famous writer; he died without finishing it*

frag·ment² /frægˈment‖ˈfrægment/ *v* **1** [IØ] to break into FRAGMENTs¹ (1) **2** [Wv5;T1] to cause to be made up of incomplete parts, esp. not understandable: *The interruption fragmented his argument.|a fragmented account of the occasion*

frag·ment·ary /ˈfrægməntəri‖-teri/ also **frag·ment·al** /frægˈmentl/— *adj* **1** made up of pieces; not complete: *His knowledge of the subject is no more than fragmentary* **2** [Wa5] being a FRAGMENT¹ or fragments: *a few fragmentary pieces of an old dish*

frag·men·ta·tion /ˌfrægmənˈteɪʃən, -men-/ *n* [C;U] (a) separation into small pieces: *A* **fragmentation bomb** *is one that explodes into small pieces*

fra·grance /ˈfreɪgrəns/ *n* **1** [U] *apprec* the quality of being FRAGRANT: *the fragrance of the air* **2** [C] a (sweet or pleasant) smell: *This soap is made in several fragrances*

fra·grant /ˈfreɪgrənt/ *adj apprec* having a sweet or pleasant smell (esp. of flowers): *The air in the garden was warm and fragrant* —**~ly** *adv*

frail /freɪl/ *adj* [Wa1] **1** not strongly made or built: *That little chair looks too frail to take a man's weight* **2** weak in body or health: *The sick woman's frail hands could hardly hold a cup* **3** slight; weak: *There's only a very frail chance that he'll pass his examination.|What a frail excuse!*

frail·ty /ˈfreɪlti/ *n* **1** [U] the quality of being FRAIL **2** [C] a weakness of character or behaviour: *One of the frailties of human nature is laziness*

frame¹ /freɪm/ *v* **1** [T1] to surround with a solid protecting edge; put a border round: *I'm having this picture framed, so that I can hang it on the wall* **2** [T1] to act as a setting or background to: *A large hat framed the girl's pretty face* **3** [T1] to build; make: *Forts were framed for defence against land or sea forces, but are useless against an air attack* **4** [T1] to give shape to (words, sentences, ideas, etc.); express: *An examiner must frame his question clearly* **5** [T1] *infml* to cause (someone) to seem guilty of a crime by means of carefully planned but untrue statements or proofs: *He was framed by the real criminals and was sent to prison for a robbery he wasn't guilty of* **6** [L9] *becoming rare* to develop; SHAPE¹ (4): *The boy's young, but he's framing well as a cricketer*

frame² *n* **1** [C] the main supports over and around which something is stretched or built: *In some parts of the world small boats are made of skins stretched over a wooden frame* **2** [C] the hard solid parts which are fitted together to make something: *a bicycle frame|This old bed has an iron frame* —see picture at BICYCLE¹ **3** [C] (the form or shape of) a human or animal body: *a man with a powerful frame|Such hardships are more than the human frame can bear* **4** [C] a firm border or case into which something is fitted or set, or which holds something in place: *In a silver frame on the table there was a photograph of his son.|I can't close the door; it doesn't fit properly into its frame.|a window frame|The frame of her glasses needs mending; one of the pieces of glass might fall out* —see also FRAMES **5** [S] a setting; background; surroundings: *The trees make a pleasant frame to the house* **6** [C] a large wooden box set in the ground and having a sloping glass roof that can be raised or lowered, in which young plants are protected from cold or made to grow quickly **7** [C] one of a number of small photographs making up a cinema film **8** [C] a complete stage of play in the game of BOWLing (2)

frame ae·ri·al /ˈ· ˌ···/ *n* a wire fixed round a frame, instead of on a pole, to receive radio waves

frame house /ˈ· ·/ *n* a house built with a frame of wooden posts driven into the ground, joined across by boards or filled in with bricks

frame of mind /ˌ· · ˈ·/ *n* **frames of mind** [*usu. sing*] the state or condition of one's mind or feelings at a particular time

frame of ref·er·ence /ˌ·· ˈ···/ *n* **frames of reference** a set or system of facts, ideas, etc., that give a particular meaning or show how a thing is placed in relation to another thing

frames /freɪmz/ *n* [P] a FRAME[2] (4) for a pair of glasses

frame-up /ˈ· ·/ *n infml* a carefully prepared plan to make someone appear guilty of a crime; invented charge against someone —compare FRAME[1] (5)

frame·work /ˈfreɪmwɜːk‖-ɜrk/ *n* **1** a supporting frame; STRUCTURE: *In modern times most ships have a metal framework; formerly they were made of wood* **2** a plan or system: *the framework of modern government* **3** FRAME OF REFERENCE: *We usually judge others within the framework of our own experience*

franc /fræŋk/ *n* the standard coin of France, Switzerland, Belgium, and many countries that formerly belonged to France

fran·chise /ˈfræntʃaɪz/ *n* **1** [*the*+U] the right to vote in a public election, esp. one held to choose a parliament: *In England, women were given the franchise in 1918* **2** [C] *esp. AmE* a special right or freedom given by the government or by a producer of goods to one person or one group of people, esp. to carry on a type of business in a particular place or to sell the goods produced by a particular factory

Fran·cis·can /frænˈsɪskən/ *adj, n* [Wa5] (a FRIAR) belonging to the Christian religious group called the **Order of Friars Minor**, started by St Francis in 1209

Fran·co- /ˈfræŋkəʊ/ *comb. form* **1** French; of France: *a Franco*PHILE **2** French and: *Franco-American trade*

frank[1] /fræŋk/ *adj* [Wa2] *often apprec* free and direct in speech; open in manner; plain and honest; truthful: *He had a frank friendly look.|If you want my frank opinion, I don't think the plan will succeed.|Will you be quite frank with me about this matter* (=tell me the truth, without trying to hide anything)? —**~ness** *n* [U]

frank[2] *v* [T1] **1** to print a sign on (a letter) to show that the charge for posting has been paid: *Business companies that send out many letters daily save time by using a* **franking machine.**|*franked letters/envelopes* **2** *tech* to make a special mark on (an official letter or packet) showing that no charge has to be paid for posting

frank·fur·ter /ˈfræŋkfɜːtəʳ‖-ɜr-/ *n* a type of small reddish smoked SAUSAGE made of the meat of pigs (PORK) and cattle (BEEF)

frank·in·cense /ˈfræŋkɪ̈nsens/ *n* [U] a type of sticky substance obtained from certain trees which is burnt to give a sweet smell, used esp. at religious ceremonies

frank·lin /ˈfræŋklɪ̈n/ *n* (in Britain in the 14th and 15th centuries) a man who owned a small area of land and did not have any duties to do or services to give to a lord in return for it

frank·ly /ˈfræŋkli/ *adv* **1** in a FRANK[1] manner **2** speaking honestly and plainly: *Frankly, I don't think the plan will succeed*

fran·tic /ˈfræntɪk/ *adj* **1** in an uncontrolled state of feeling; wildly anxious, afraid, happy, etc.: *The mother was frantic with grief when she heard that her child was dead.|That noise is driving me frantic* (=making me mad) **2** *infml* marked by hurried and disordered activity: *I've had a frantic rush to get my work done* —**~ally** *adv* [Wa4]

frap·pé /ˈfræpeɪ‖fræˈpeɪ/ *adj* [Wa5;F] (of a drink, esp. wine) slightly cold

fra·ter·nal /frəˈtɜːnəl‖-ɜr-/ *adj* **1** [Wa5;A] of, belonging to, or like brothers: *There's a strong fraternal likeness between the 2 boys* (=it's easy to see that they're brothers, because they're so like each other) **2** [B] friendly; brotherly: *The party sent its fraternal greetings to the trade union meeting* —**~ly** *adv*

fra·ter·ni·ty /frəˈtɜːnɪ̈ti‖-ɜr-/ *n* **1** [GC] a group of men belonging to a religious organization, living together under a certain set of rules **2** [GC9] any association of people having work, interests, etc., in common: *He's a member of the medical fraternity* (= is a doctor) **3** [U] *fml* the state of being brothers; brotherly feeling **4** [C] (at some American universities) a club of men students usu. living in the same house —compare SORORITY

frat·er·nize, -ise /ˈfrætənaɪz‖-ər-/ *v* [IØ (*with*)] **1** to meet and be friendly (with someone) as equals: *Army officers may not fraternize with their men* **2** to have friendly relations (with members of an enemy nation): *While the agreement to stop firing was in force, the opposing soldiers were forbidden to fraternize* —**-nization** /ˌfrætənaɪˈzeɪʃən‖-ərnə-/ *n* [U (*with*)]

frat·ri·cide /ˈfrætrɪ̈saɪd/ *n* **1** [U] the act of murdering one's brother or sister **2** [C] *fml* a person who murders his brother or sister —**-cid·al** /ˌfrætrɪ̈ˈsaɪdl/ *adj*

Frau /fraʊ/ *n* [A] (of a German woman) Mrs

fraud /frɔːd/ *n* **1** [C;U] (an act of) deceitful behaviour for the purpose of gain, which may be punishable by law: *He carried out a number of frauds on trusting people who lent him money.|The judge found the man guilty of fraud* **2** [C] *derog* a person who pretends or claims to be what he is not: *People who offer to tell your future by means of a pack of cards are frauds* **3** [C] *derog* a thing which is not, or does not do, what is claimed for it: *This woollen dress is a fraud; it's supposed to be washable, but now I've washed it, it's too small to wear*

fraud·u·lence /ˈfrɔːdjʊləns‖-dʒə-/ *n* [U] **1** behaviour or actions intended to deceive **2** the quality of being FRAUDULENT

fraud·u·lent /ˈfrɔːdjʊlənt‖-dʒə-/ *adj* deceitful; got or done by FRAUD (1): *She got the post of science teacher by fraudulent means; she pretended she'd studied at a university* —**~ly** *adv*

fraught /frɔːt/ *adj* **1** [F+*with*] full of (something that has or gives warning of a probable unpleasant result): *The long journey through the forest was fraught with difficulties and danger* **2** [B] *infml* troubled by small anxieties

USAGE Careful writers say that **fraught** must be followed by *with*: **fraught** *with danger*. However, the word is used in rather *infml* speech to mean that someone is worried or conditions are difficult: *You're looking very* **fraught**, *Mildred! Is there anything the matter?*

frau·lein /ˈfrɔɪlaɪn/ *n* a German unmarried woman

Fraulein *n* [A] (of a German woman) Miss

fray[1] /freɪ/ *n* [*the*+R] *lit* (the state of activity or action of a person who joins in) a fight, game, argument, quarrel, etc.: *Are you ready for the fray* (=ready for action, ready to begin)?|*He rushed into the fray* (=joined boldly in the fighting)

fray[2] *v* **1** [T1;IØ] **a** to cause (rope, cloth, etc.) to become thin or worn by rubbing, so that loose threads develop: *The beggar's shirt was frayed at the neck* **b** (of rope, cloth, etc.) to become thin or worn so that loose threads develop: *The electric wire is fraying and could be dangerous to handle* **2** [IØ] (of cut cloth) to develop loose threads along the cut edge: *She found it difficult to make a nylon dress, because the material frayed so quickly when* *she cut it* **3** [T1;I∅] **a** to cause (a person's temper, nerves, etc.) to become worn out: *Her nerves were frayed by the noises in the street* **b** (of a person's temper, nerves, etc.) to become worn out: *Tempers began to fray in the hot weather*

fraz·zle /ˈfræzəl/ *n* [S] *infml* **1** a condition of being completely tired in body and mind, owing to hard work or other difficulties (esp. in the phr **worn to a frazzle**) **2** a thoroughly burnt condition (esp. in the phr **burnt to a frazzle**)

freak[1] /fri:k/ *n* **1** [C] a living creature of unnatural form: *One of the new lambs is a freak; it was born with 2 tails* **2** [C] *infml* a person with rather strange habits or ideas **3** [C] a peculiar happening: *By some strange freak, a little snow fell in Egypt a few years ago* **4** [C] a sudden strange wish or change of mind **5** [C9] *sl* a person who takes a special interest in the stated thing; FAN[3]: *a film freak*

freak[2] *adj* [Wa5;A] unnatural in degree or type; very unusual: *The country's been having freak weather; it's been very hot during the winter.|a freak storm*

freak·ish /ˈfri:kɪʃ/ *adj* unusual; unreasonable; strange: *Her behaviour's becoming so freakish that I wonder if she's mad* —**~ly** *adv* —**~ness** *n* [U]

freak of na·ture /ˌ· · ˈ··/ *n* **freaks of nature** FREAK[1] (1)

freak out *v adv* [I∅;T1] *infml* to (cause to) become greatly excited or anxious, esp. because of drugs

freak-out /ˈ· ·/ *n infml* **1** a state of mind, usu. caused by a drug, in which a person sees everything in a strange dreamlike way and feels cut off from reality **2** a person who is in this state of mind

freck·le /ˈfrekəl/ *n* [*often pl.*] a small flat brown spot on the skin —**-led** *adj*: *a freckled nose*

free[1] /fri:/ *adj* **1** [Wa1;B] moving about at will; not tied up or bound; not shut up or held in prison: *Wild animals in their natural state are free.|The prisoner wished to be free again.|He pitied the trapped bird, and set it free* **2** [Wa1;B] owing no service or duty to anyone; not in the power of anyone; independent: *Every child in England is born free.|She's not free; she has to look after her old father.|He had plenty of money, and, as he was free, he decided to travel and see the world* **3** [Wa1;B] self-governing; not controlled by the state; having a form of government that respects the rights of private people: *Britain is a free country; it has a free* PRESS (=newspapers) **4** [Wa5;B;(E)] without payment of any kind; costing nothing; given away: *Members of this music society get a free ticket for 4 concerts every year.|Anyone who buys this breakfast food gets a free gift of a small plastic toy.|"Are the drinks free?" "No, you have to pay for them."|The goods will be sent to you post free* (=with no charge added on for posting) **5** [Wa1; B] not controlled or limited in any way or not accepting any control, esp. by rule or custom: *In this poem the writer has given free play to his fancy* (=has let his imagination work as it pleases).|*He gave me free* ACCESS *to his valuable collection of scientific books* (=let me use them whenever I wanted).|*a* FREETHINKER|*a free translation* (=one in which the meaning is translated without giving an exact translation of every single word) **6** [Wa1; B] (esp. of bodily action) natural; graceful; not stiff or awkward: *free movement to music|Hit the ball with a long free swing of the arm.|The skirt hung in free folds from the waist* **7** [Wa5;B] not fixed onto anything; not set in position; loose: *The free end of the flag has been torn by the wind, while the part fastened to the pole is whole* **8** [Wa5;B] not busy; without work or duty; having time to give attention to someone or something: *He has little free time; he has a great deal to do.|She gets a free afternoon once a week.|The doctor will be free in 10 minutes' time; can you wait that long?* **9** [Wa5;B] not being used; empty; not kept for or promised to anybody: *"Is this seat free?" "Yes; no one is using it."|Can you find a free space where we can park the car?* **10** [Wa1;B] (of a way or passage) open; not blocked: *The way is free; we can make our escape now.|Ice sometimes prevents the free passage of ships in the winter* **11** [Wa1;A;F (*with*)] ready to give; generous; full in quantity: *She's very free with her money.|He's too free with his advice* (=gives advice when it isn't wanted).|*As soon as the speech was over, there was a free flow of conversation in the hall* **12** [Wa1;B] *derog* too friendly; lacking in respect; not controlled by politeness: *The boy's manner is rather free in the presence of his teachers.|After they'd been smoking and drinking their talk became a bit free* **13** [Wa1;F+*from*] without (someone or something unwanted); safe from; untroubled or unspoilt by: *The old lady is never free from pain.|Keep the table free from dirt by putting a cover over it* **14** [Wa5;F+*of*] **a** without making or asking payment of: *If your wages are very small, they'll be free of income tax.|free of charge* **b** away from; outside: *They like living in a village, free of crowds and noise.|By 7 o'clock the boat was free of the harbour and our travels had begun* **c** clear of; no longer troubled by: *She talks too much; you'll be glad when you're free of her* **15** [Wa1;F3] not prevented in any way; allowed: *When she's finished her work, she'll be free to enjoy herself.|Use my house as if it were your own; you're free to come and go as you please* **16** [Wa5;B] (in chemistry) not combined with any type of matter (ELEMENT); pure **17 for free** *infml* without payment: *I got this letter for free* **18 free and easy** lacking in too great seriousness and ceremony; cheerful and unworried: *She leads a free and easy sort of life and never troubles much about anything* **19 have one's hands free a** to have one's hands empty; be holding nothing **b** to have no duties or business to which one must give one's attention **20 make free with** to use without respect, or as if one's own: *She's made free with my cigarettes during my absence* (=has taken as many as she wanted without asking me).|*He makes too free with the girls in the office* (=treats them without proper respect) **21 make someone free of something** *fml* to give someone the right to use or have a share in something

free[2] *adv* **1** in a FREE[1] (1) manner: *Don't let the dog run free on the main road* **2** without payment: *Babies are allowed to travel free on buses* **3** in a loose position; so as to be no longer joined: *2 screws in this old wooden door have worked themselves free* (=loosened or fallen out as a result of use).|*The window had stuck, but he pushed it hard and it swung free*

free[3] *v* **freed** /fri:d/ [T1] **1** [(*from*)] to set (a person or animal) FREE[1] (1): *When will the prisoners be freed?|She freed the bird from its cage* **2** [(*from*)] to make (a slave) FREE[1] (2) **3** [(*from*)] to move or loosen (a person or thing when prevented from moving): *Part of the old wall fell on the workman, and it took half an hour to free him.|Her dress got caught on a rose bush, and she tore it when she tried to free it/herself from the prickles* **4** [(*from, of*)] to take away from (a person or animal) anything uncomfortable, inconvenient, difficult, unwelcome, etc.: *I need to go out; can you free me (from duty) for an hour?|She can't free herself of the idea that someone's watching her all the time* —see also FREE OF

-free *comb. form* **1** without: *People with certain diseases have to eat saltfree foods.*|CAREFREE **2** without payment of: *a taxfree gift of £500*

free a·gent /ˌ· ˈ··/ *n* a person who can act as he chooses: *You needn't do this if you don't want to; you're a free agent, and no one can force you*
free as·so·ci·a·tion /ˌ· ···ˈ··/ *n* [U] (in PSYCHOLOGY) a way of studying a person's secret mind by getting him to say the first word he thinks of when each of a number of words is spoken to him
free·bie, -bee /ˈfriːbiː/ *n AmE sl* something that is given or received without payment
free·board /ˈfriːbɔːd‖-ord/ *n* [U;C] the distance between the level of the water and **a** the upper edge of the side of a boat or **b** the top of a STRUCTURE that is in water
free·boot·er /ˈfriːbuːtəʳ/ *n* a person who makes war in order to grow rich by seizing all he can; PIRATE
free·born /ˌfriːˈbɔːn◂‖-ɔrn/ *adj* not born as a slave
Free Church /ˌ· ˈ·◂/ *n* [*usu. pl.*] a NONCONFORMIST church
freed·man /ˈfriːdmæn, -mən/ *fem.* **freed·wom·an** /-ˌwʊmən/— *n* **-men** /men, mən/ (esp. in Roman times) a former slave freed by his master
free·dom /ˈfriːdəm/ *n* **1** [U] the state of being free: *The master gave the slave his freedom.|During the school holidays the children enjoyed their freedom* **2** [U (*of*)] certain rights, often given as an honour: *They gave her the freedom of their house* (=gave her the right to use it as if it were her own).|*The Minister was given the freedom of the city* (=was given certain rights within the city as an honour) **3** [C;U (*of*),U3] the power to do, say, think, or write as one pleases: *2 of the 4 freedoms spoken of by President Roosevelt in 1941 are freedom of speech and freedom of religion.|the freedom to choose one's own religion|You may have complete freedom of action in dealing with this matter; do exactly what you think best.|Tight clothes don't allow enough freedom of movement* **4** [C;U (*from*)] the condition of being without something harmful or unpleasant: *One of the 4 freedoms spoken of by President Roosevelt was freedom from fear.|For the first 2 days after he broke his arm, he had little freedom from pain* —compare LIBERTY
free en·ter·prise /ˌ· ˈ···/ *n* [U] the carrying on of trade, business, etc., without much government control
free-fall /ˌ· ˈ·◂/ *n* **1** [U] the condition of moving or falling freely through air or space without being held back by anything **2** [U;C] the part of a jump or fall from an aircraft which is made before the jumper opens an apparatus for slowing him down (PARACHUTE): *a free-fall* PARACHUTIST
free fight /ˌ· ˈ·/ *n infml* a fight without any rules that breaks out suddenly and in which many people join, sometimes without knowing why they do so
free-float·ing /ˌ· ˈ··◂/ *adj* not having firm feelings of support for one side, purpose, etc., or another
free-for-all /ˌ· · ˈ·/ *n infml* **1** an argument, quarrel, etc., in which many people join and express their opinions, esp. in a noisy way **2** FREE FIGHT
free·hand /ˈfriːhænd/ *adj* [Wa5] (of drawing or a drawing) done by natural movements of the hand, without the use of a ruler or other instrument —**freehand** *adv*: *I can't draw very well freehand*
free hand /ˌ· ˈ·/ *n* [S] unlimited freedom of action; complete rights: *He's given his brother a free hand to direct his business during his absence*
free·hand·ed /ˌ· ˈ··◂/ *adj apprec* generous in giving
free·hold /ˈfriːhəʊld/ *n, adj* [Wa5;C;U;F] (with) ownership of land or buildings for an unlimited time and without any conditions: *Who has just bought the freeholds of these houses?|freehold property|They bought it freehold* —compare LEASEHOLD
free·hold·er /ˈfriːhəʊldəʳ/ *n* an owner of FREEHOLD land or property
free house /ˌ· ˈ·, ˈ· ·/ *n BrE* an inn not controlled by a particular beer-making firm, but getting and selling whatever kind of beer it chooses —compare TIED HOUSE
free kick /ˌ· ˈ·/ *n* (in football) an unopposed kick given to one team when a rule of the game is broken by the other team
free·lance[1] /ˈfriːlɑːns‖-læns/ *n, adj* [Wa5] (done by) a writer or other trained worker, esp. a newspaper writer, who earns his money without being in the regular employment of any particular organization
freelance[2] *v* [IØ] to work as a FREELANCE —**-lancer** *n*
free-liv·ing /ˌ· ˈ··◂/ *adj* living for pleasure, esp. for food and drink —**free-liver** *n*
free·load /ˈfriːləʊd/ *v* [IØ] *infml AmE* to live on money and goods given by other people, without giving anything in return; SPONGE[2] (3) —**~er** *n*
free love /ˌ· ˈ·/ *n* [U] *esp. old use* the belief in and practice of sexual love as one pleases, without marriage
free·ly /ˈfriːli/ *adv* **1** willingly; readily: *I freely admit that what I said was wrong* **2** openly; plainly; without hiding anything: *You may speak quite freely in front of me; I shan't tell anyone what you say* **3** without any limitation on movement or action: *Oil the wheel; then it will turn more freely* **4** generously: *He gives freely to many organizations that help the poor* **5** in great amounts: *The wound was bleeding freely*
free·man /ˈfriːmən/ *n* **-men** /mən/ [(*of*)] a person who, as an honour, has been given certain special rights in a city: *The famous politician was made a freeman of the City of London* —see also FREEDOM (2)
Free·ma·son /ˈfriːˌmeɪsən, ˌfriːˈmeɪsən/ also **mason**— *n* (*sometimes not cap.*) a man belonging to an ancient and widespread society (the **Free and Accepted Masons**), the members of which give help to each other and to other people, treat each other like brothers, and have certain signs and words by which they are known to each other
free·ma·son·ry /ˈfriːˌmeɪsənri, ˌfriːˈmeɪ-/ *n* [U] **1** also **masonry**— (*often cap.*) the system and practices of the FREEMASON*s* **2** the natural unspoken understanding and friendly feeling between people of the same kind, or having the same interests, beliefs, etc.: *There's a sort of freemasonry among people who race in cars*
free of *v prep* [D1] to clear (a place) of (someone or something unwanted): *He opened the window to free the room of smoke*
free on board /ˌ· · ˈ·/ *adv, adj fml* F.O.B.
free par·don /ˌ· ˈ··/ *n law* a PARDON[1] (2) allowing someone to go free as though he had never done anything wrong
free pass /ˌ· ˈ·/ *n* an official paper giving a person the right to travel without payment
free port /ˌ· ˈ·/ *n* a port where goods of all countries may be brought in or taken out without paying tax
free·post /ˈfriːpəʊst/ *n* [U] (in Britain) an arrangement by which a business firm pays the cost of letters sent to it by post
free-range /ˌ· ˈ·◂/ *adj* [Wa5] being, concerning, or produced by hens that are kept under natural conditions in a farmyard or field: *free-range hens|I like free-range eggs* —compare BATTERY (3)
free rein /ˌ· ˈ·/ *n* [U] complete freedom of action (esp. in the phr. **give free rein to**): *In this poem the writer has given free rein to his imagination*
free·si·a /ˈfriːzɪə‖-ʒə/ *n* **1** any of several types of

plant with sweet-smelling white, yellow, or red flowers **2** a flower of this plant

free speech /ˌ· ˈ·/ *n* [U] the right to express one's ideas in public, without being prevented by the government

free·stand·ing /ˌfriːˈstændɪŋ◂/ *adj* standing alone without being fixed to a wall, frame, or other support

free·stone /ˈfriːstəʊn/ *n* [U] any kind of building stone (such as SANDSTONE or LIMESTONE) that is easily cut in any direction

free·style /ˈfriːstaɪl/ *n, adj* [Wa5;U;B] **1** (of) a competition or method of swimming using the CRAWL stroke: *Which swimmer won the 100 metres freestyle?|to swim freestyle|to be good at freestyle (swimming)* **2** (in WRESTLING) (with) the use of movements according to choice, not set rules: *freestyle* WRESTLING

free·think·er /ˌfriːˈθɪŋkəʳ/ *n* a person who forms his religious opinions on reason and not on the teaching of the Christian Church —**-thinking** /ˌ· ˈ··◂/ *adj*

free thought /ˌ· ˈ·/ *n* [U] the forming of religious opinions based on reason

free trade /ˌ· ˈ·◂/ *n* [U] the system by which foreign goods are allowed to enter a country in unlimited quantities and without payment of high charges

free verse /ˌ· ˈ·/ *n* [U] poetry in a form that does not follow any regular or accepted pattern

free·way /ˈfriːweɪ/ *n* a wide high-speed road which either has no roads crossing it or has closely controlled points of entering and leaving

free·wheel /ˌfriːˈwiːl/ *v* [IØ] to ride a bicycle or drive a vehicle, esp. downhill, without providing power from the legs or the engine —compare COAST² (1)

free·wheel·ing /ˈfriːˈwiːlɪŋ◂/ *adj* not greatly worrying about rules, formal behaviour, responsibilities, or the results of actions

free·will /ˌfriːˈwɪl◂/ *adj* [Wa5;A] given or done at one's own wish (esp. in the phr. **freewill offering**)

free will /ˌ· ˈ·/ *n* [U] the belief that every person has the power to decide freely what he will do, and that his actions are not fixed in advance by God —compare PREDESTINATION (1)

freeze¹ /friːz/ *v* **froze** /frəʊz/, **frozen** /ˈfrəʊzən/ **1** [Wv4,5;T1;IØ (UP);L7;X7] to (cause (water or another liquid) to) harden into ice as a result of great cold: *Water freezes at the temperature of 0 degrees* CENTIGRADE.|*The north wind has frozen the water in the pool in the garden.|The lake has frozen up.|Periods of freezing rain are expected later.|The water has frozen solid* **2** [Wv5;T1;IØ;L7;X7] to (cause (esp. a wet mixture) to) become solid at a very low temperature: *She slipped on the frozen mud.|The cold has frozen the earth solid* **3** [T1;IØ (UP);L7;X7] to (cause (something) to) be unable to work properly as a result of ice or very low temperatures: *The engine has frozen up.|The cold has frozen the lock on the car door* **4** [Wv5;T1;IØ] to (cause (land, a solid surface, etc.) to) become covered with ice and snow: *The roads are frozen in places.|the frozen January farmland* **5** [*it*+IØ] (of weather) to be at or below the temperature at which water becomes ice: *It's freezing tonight.|It froze hard last night* **6** [Wv4;IØ] *infml* to be, feel, or become very cold: *It's freezing in this room; can't we have a fire?|The mountain climbers were lost in the snow, and nearly froze to death* (=died of cold).| (fig.) *His terrible stories made our blood freeze* (= made us cold with fear) **7** [Wv5;T1] to make very cold, stiff, or without feeling: *He looks half frozen; he needs a hot drink.|I was frozen stiff after sitting so long, and could hardly walk* **8** [T1;IØ] to (cause to) stop suddenly or become quite still or unable to show any feeling: *The race was so exciting to watch that it froze him to the spot.|The teacher froze the noisy class with a single look.|The child froze at the sight of the snake.|A wild animal will sometimes freeze in its tracks when it smells an enemy* **9** [Wv4,5;IØ] to become unfriendly in manner: *She gave me a freezing look.|After their quarrel, they sat in frozen silence* **10** [Wv5;T1] to preserve (food) by means of very low temperatures: *Meat from New Zealand is frozen and brought to England in special ships.|Frozen foods have taken the place of tinned foods in many homes.|frozen beans* **11** [L9] (of food) to be able to be preserved in this way: *Do* BLACKCURRANT*s freeze well?* **12** [T1] to fix (prices or wages) officially at a given level for a certain length of time **13** [Wv5;T1] to prevent (business shares, bank accounts, etc.) from being used, by government order

freeze² *n* [S] **1** a period of very cold icy weather: *He slipped and broke his leg during the big freeze last winter* **2** (*often in comb.*) a fixing of prices or wages at a certain level: *a wage freeze*

freeze-dry /ˌ· ˈ·/ *v* [Wv5;T1] to preserve (esp. food) by drying in a frozen state: *freeze-dried vegetables*

freeze in *v adv* [T1 *usu. pass.*] to hold (something) firm in ice: *The ship was frozen in for the winter*

freeze out *v adv* [T1] **1** *infml* to prevent (someone or something) from being included: *They froze out the competition* **2** *AmE* to prevent because of great cold: *The meeting was frozen out*

freeze o·ver *v adv* [T1;IØ] to (cause the surface of (something) to) turn into ice: *The lake has frozen over; you can walk on it, but you can see the fish swimming under the ice*

freez·er /ˈfriːzəʳ/ *n* **1** also **deep freeze** /ˌ· ˈ·/— a type of large REFRIGERATOR in which supplies of food can be stored at a very low temperature for a long time **2** also **freezing com·part·ment** /ˈ·· ·ˌ··/— an enclosed part of a REFRIGERATOR in which there is a specially low temperature for making small ice blocks, storing frozen foods, etc.

freeze up *v adv* [IØ] *infml* (of an actor) to become too nervous on stage to speak or move

freez·ing /ˈfriːzɪŋ/ *n* [R] *infml* FREEZING POINT (1): *It must be 5 degrees below freezing today*

freezing point /ˈ·· ·/ *n* **1** [R] the temperature (0 degrees CENTIGRADE) at which water becomes ice: *It's very cold today; the temperature has dropped to freezing point* **2** [(*the*) R (*of*)] the temperature at which any particular liquid freezes: *The freezing point of alcohol is much lower than that of water*

freight¹ /freɪt/ *n* [U] **1** (money paid for) the carrying of goods by some means of TRANSPORT: *This aircraft company deals with freight only; it has no travel service* **2** the goods carried in this way: *This freight must be carefully handled when loading*

freight² *v* [T1] **1** to send (something) as FREIGHT¹ (2) **2** [(*with*)] to load (esp. a ship) with goods: *The boat is freighted with coal*

freight car /ˈ· ·/ *n AmE* GOODS WAGGON

freight·er /ˈfreɪtəʳ/ *n* a ship or aircraft for carrying goods

See next page for picture

freight·lin·er /ˈfreɪtˌlaɪnəʳ/ also **linertrain**— *n* a train that carries large amounts of goods in special containers

freight train /ˈ· ·/ *n AmE* GOODS TRAIN

French¹ /frentʃ/ *adj* belonging to France, its people, etc.: *French wine*

French² *n* **1** [*the*+P] the people of France **2** [U] the language of France: *a French lesson*

French bean /ˌ· ˈ·/ *n esp. BrE* a type of bean having a narrow green case (POD), used as a

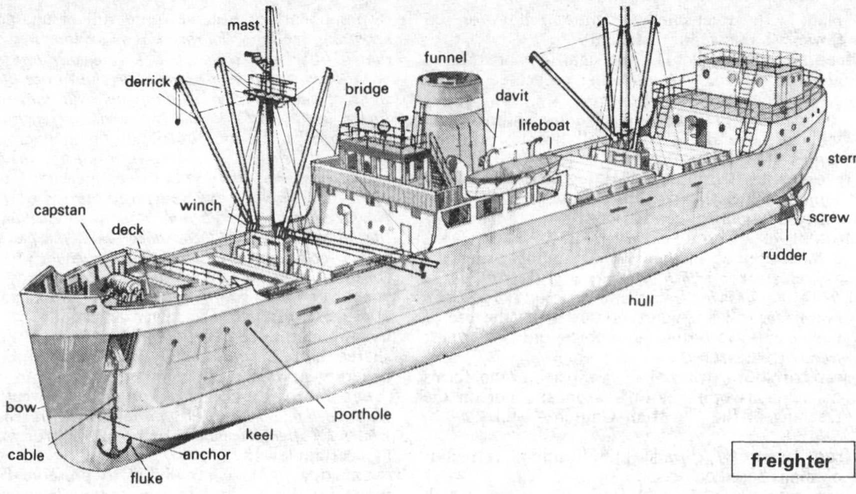

vegetable of which both the bean and the case are eaten

French bread /ˌ· ˈ·/ *n* [U] bread in the form of French loaves (FRENCH LOAF)

French chalk /ˌ· ˈ·/ *n* [U] a type of fine hard chalklike stone used for marking cloth in dress-making, and, in powder form, for making a floor smooth for dancing

French dress·ing /ˌ· ˈ··/ *n* [U] a liquid made of oil and VINEGAR, used for putting on dishes made with raw vegetables (SALADs)

French fry /ˌ· ˈ·/ *n* [*usu. pl.*] *esp. AmE* CHIP[1] (4)

French horn /ˌ· ˈ·/ *n* a type of brass musical instrument made of thin pipe wound round and round into a circular form, having a wide bell-shaped mouth, and played by blowing —see picture at WIND INSTRUMENT

French kiss /ˌ· ˈ·/ *n* a kiss made with the mouth open, and usu. with the tongues touching

French leave /ˌ· ˈ·/ *n* [U] absence from work or duty taken without permission (esp. in the phr. **take French leave**)

French letter /ˌ· ˈ··/ *n infml, not AmE* a (rubber) SHEATH (4); CONDOM

French loaf /ˌ· ˈ·/ *n* a type of long thin round loaf

French·man /ˈfrentʃmən/ *fem.* **French·wom·an** /ˌwʊmən/— *n* **-men** /mən/ a French citizen born in France or of French parent(s)

French pol·ish /ˌ· ˈ··/ *n* [U] a liquid mixture of SHELLAC and alcohol rubbed onto wooden furniture to give a hard and lasting shine

French-polish *v* [T1] to treat (furniture) with FRENCH POLISH

French win·dows /ˌ· ˈ··/ also (*esp. AmE*) **French doors** /ˌ· ˈ·/— *n* [P] a pair of light outer doors made up of squares of glass in a frame, usu. opening out onto the garden of a house —see picture at LIVING ROOM

fre·net·ic, phrenetic /frəˈnetɪk/ *adj* showing FRANTIC activity; overexcited —**~ally** *adv* [Wa4]

fren·zied /ˈfrenzid/ *adj* full of uncontrolled excitement and/or wild activity; mad; FRANTIC: *The people greeted their leader with frenzied shouts of joy* —**~ly** *adv*

fren·zy /ˈfrenzi/ *n* [S;(U)] a state of wild uncontrolled feeling, expressed with great force; sudden, but not lasting, attack of madness: *In a frenzy of hate he killed his enemy.|She worked herself up into a frenzy because she thought she'd miss her train*

fre·quen·cy /ˈfriːkwənsi/ *n* **1** [U (*of*)] the repeated or infrequent happening of something: *The frequency of accidents on that road gives the doctors a lot of work.|Accidents are happening there with increasing frequency* **2** [C] *tech* a rate at which something happens or is repeated; the number of times that something happens in a given period: *This radio signal has a frequency of 200 000* CYCLEs *per second* **3** [C] a particular number of radio waves per second at which a radio signal is broadcast: *This radio station broadcasts on 3 different frequencies* —see also FM, VHF

fre·quent[1] /ˈfriːkwənt/ *adj* common; found or happening often; repeated many times; habitual: *Sudden rainstorms are frequent on this coast.|It's a frequent practice of his to take an early morning swim* —**~ly** *adv*

fre·quent[2] /friˈkwent‖friˈkwent, ˈfriːkwənt/ *v* [T1] *fml* to be often in (a place, someone's company, etc.): *She's fond of books, and frequents the library.|This wood's frequented by all kinds of birds*

fres·co[1] /ˈfreskəʊ/ *n* **-coes** *or* **-cos 1** [U] the art of painting in water colour on a surface consisting of a fresh wet mixture of lime, water, sand, etc. (PLASTER) **2** [C] a picture painted in this way

fresco[2] *v* [Wv5;T1] to paint (something) in FRESCO[1]: *frescoed walls*

fresh /ˈfreʃ/ *adj* **1** [Wa1;B] in good natural condition because not long gathered, caught, produced, etc.; not spoilt in taste, appearance, etc., by being kept too long; new: *You can buy fresh fruit and vegetables in the market.|This fish smells; I think it's not quite fresh* **2** [Wa5;A;(F)] (of water) not salt; drinkable **3** [Wa5;A] (of food) not preserved by added salt, TINning, bottling (BOTTLE[2]), freezing, or other means: *Tinned fruit never has quite the same taste as fresh fruit.|Fresh butter has no salt added to it* **4** [Wa5;(*a*)A;F+*from*] newly prepared; newly cooked: *Let me make you a fresh pot of tea.|This bread's fresh from the* OVEN (=is newly baked) **5** [Wa5;A;F+*from*] lately arrived, happened, found, grown, or supplied; added just now: *Fresh goods appear in our shops every week.|There's been no fresh news of the fighting since yesterday.|The new teacher's fresh from university.|Can you throw any fresh light on this subject* (=add anything that will help to explain it)? **6** [Wa5;A] clean; unused: *He bathed and put on fresh clothes.|These cut flowers in the pot need fresh water.|I've spoilt this drawing; I must start again on a fresh piece of paper* **7** [Wa5;(*a*)A] (an) other and additional; RENEWed: *He's making a fresh attempt to pass his examination this year* **8** [Wa5;(*a*)A] (an) other and different: *It's time to take a fresh look at this affair.|When the thief came out of prison, he decided to make a fresh start* (=begin life again) *as an honest man* **9** [Wa1;F;(A)] not tired; young, healthy, and active; strengthened: *She always seems fresh, however much work she's done.|He said he never felt fresher.|The plants look fresh after the rain* **10** [Wa1;B] (of colour) pure; bright; clear: *The colours of the paintings on the walls of some caves in France have remained fresh for many centuries* **11** [Wa1;B] (of skin) clear and healthy: *She has dark hair and a fresh* COMPLEXION **12** [Wa5;B] (of paint) newly put on; not dry **13** [Wa1;B] *usu. apprec* (of air) pure; cool: *Open the window and let in some fresh air.|It's healthy to spend one's time in the fresh air* (=out of doors) **14** [Wa1;B] *often tech* (of wind) rather strong; gaining in force: *The winds will be fresh or strong tonight, according to the radio* **15** [Wa1;F] *infml* (of weather) cool and windy: *It's a bit fresh today* **16** [Wa5;F+*to*] (of a person) inexperienced (in): *She's quite fresh to office work; this is her first post* **17** [Wa5;F] *infml* (too) bold with someone of the opposite sex (esp. in the phrs. **get/be fresh with**): *That girl's not behaving at all well; she's trying to get fresh with my brother* **18 break fresh ground** to do something that has never been done before, or in a way that has never been tried before —see also AFRESH, **fresh as a** DAISY (2) —**~ness** *n* [U]

fresh- *comb. form* (*in combination with a past p. used as an adj*) newly: *Many people in the village sell fresh-picked fruit from their own gardens*

fresh·en /ˈfreʃən/ *v* [IØ] (of wind) to gain in force; become stronger or colder

freshen up *v adv* **1** [T1;IØ] to cause (oneself) to feel more comfortable by washing: *I must just go and freshen (myself) up before tea* **2** [T1] to cause (someone) to feel more comfortable by washing: *That bath has freshened me up* **3** [T1] to make (something) newer or more attractive; brighten: *He's freshened up the house with a new coat of paint*

fresh·er /ˈfreʃəʳ/ also **fresh·man** /-mən/— *n infml* a student in his or her first year at university

fresh·et /ˈfreʃɪ̇t/ *n poet* a small clear stream

fresh·ly /ˈfreʃli/ *adv* (*before a past p.*) just lately; just now; recently: *"This coffee smells good." "Yes, it's freshly made."|His shirts have been freshly washed and ironed*

fresh·wa·ter /ˌfreʃˈwɔːtəʳ◂‖-ˈwɔ-, -ˈwɑ-/ *adj* [Wa5;A] **1** of or living in rivers or inland lakes; not belonging to the sea: *freshwater fish|freshwater plants* **2** containing water that is not sea water: *freshwater lakes|a freshwater swimming pool*

fret[1] /fret/ *v* **-tt-** **1** [T1(AWAY);IØ (*about, at, for, over*)] to (cause to) be continually worried and anxious, dissatisfied, or bad-tempered about small or unnecessary things: *Don't fret; all will be well.|The old lady frets if she has to wait a moment for anything.|The child's fretting for his absent mother.|The continual noise fretted the woman's nerves.|It's no use fretting your life away because you can't have everything you want* **2** [T1] to wear away, damage, or make a pattern on (something) by continual rubbing or biting: *The wire round the bush is causing damage; when there's a wind, it frets the stems.|A light wind fretted the surface of the water*

fret[2] *n* [S] *infml* an anxious complaining state of mind: *She gets in a fret whenever we're late*

fret[3] *v* **-tt-** [Wv5;T1] to ornament with wood cut out in patterns

fret[4] *n* one of the raised lines on the long thin part (NECK) of a GUITAR or like musical instrument with strings, which show the player where to place his fingers to obtain the note he wants —see picture at STRINGED INSTRUMENT

fret·ful /ˈfretfəl/ *adj* complaining and anxious, esp. because of dissatisfaction or discomfort: *"Why can't I have another cake?" asked the child in a fretful voice* —**~ly** *adv* —**~ness** *n* [U]

fret·saw /ˈfretsɔː/ *n* a type of metal cutting instrument with teeth along its edge (SAW), having a thin blade fixed at each end to a frame, used for cutting out patterns in thin sheets of wood

fret·work /ˈfretwɜːk‖-ɜrk/ *n* **1** [U] the art of making ornamentally cut wooden patterns **2** [U] thin wood cut in a pattern: *The cupboard was ornamented with fretwork* **3** [U;C *usu. sing.*:(*of*)] a pattern of lines and spaces: *The ground beneath the trees was a fretwork of sunlight and shadow*

Freud·i·an /ˈfrɔɪdɪən/ *adj* **1** [Wa5] of, related to, or in accordance with the ideas and practices developed by Sigmund Freud concerning the way in which the mind works, and how it can be studied **2** *infml* concerned with or arising from ideas of sex in the mind that are not openly expressed

Freudian slip /ˌ·· ˈ·/ *n infml* an act of accidentally saying something different from what was intended, by which one seems to show one's true thoughts

Fri. *written abbrev. for:* Friday

fri·a·ble /ˈfraɪəbəl/ *adj* easily broken into small bits or into powder —**-ability** /ˌfraɪəˈbɪlɪ̇ti/ *n* [U]

fri·ar /ˈfraɪəʳ/ *n* a man belonging to any of several Christian religious groups who, esp. in former times, lived only by begging and had no possessions or fixed place in which to live, and who travelled around the country teaching the Christian religion and doing good works —compare MONK

fri·ar·y /ˈfraɪəri/ *n* a building in which FRIARs lived, after their rules of living were changed

fric·as·see[1] /ˈfrɪkəsiː, ˌfrɪkəˈsiː/ *n* [U;C] a dish made of pieces of bird or other meat, cooked and served in a thick SAUCE: *chicken fricassee*

fricassee[2] *v* [Wv5;T1] to make a FRICASSEE of: *fricasseed chicken*

fric·a·tive /ˈfrɪkətɪv/ *adj, n* [Wa5] (a consonant) made by forcing air out through a narrow opening formed by placing the tongue or lip close to but not touching another part of the mouth: /f, v, θ, ð, s, z, ʃ, ʒ, h/ *are the fricative sounds in English*

fric·tion /ˈfrɪkʃən/ *n* **1** [U] the force which tries to stop one surface sliding over another: *He pushed the box very hard down the slope, but friction gradually caused it to slow down and stop* **2** [U] the rubbing, often repeated, of 2 surfaces together, or of one against another: *Friction against the rock, combined with the weight of the climber, caused his rope to break* **3** [U;C] unfriendliness and disagreement caused by 2 opposing wills or different sets of opinion, ideas, or natures: *Mary's neat and Jane's careless; if they have to share a room there'll probably be friction*

Fri·day /ˈfraɪdi/ *n* **1** [R] the 6th day of the present week; day before next Saturday or last Saturday: *He'll arrive (on) Friday.|He'll arrive on Friday morning* (=during the morning of next Friday).|*She left early on Friday* **2** [C] the 6th day of any week, or of the week that is being spoken of: *Lots of people eat fish on Fridays.|He arrived on the Friday and left on the Sunday* (=arrived on the 6th day of the week being spoken of).|*He arrived on a Friday* (=not a Thursday, Saturday, etc.).|(*esp. AmE*) *She works Fridays* —see also GIRL FRIDAY, GOOD FRIDAY, MAN FRIDAY

fridge /frɪdʒ/ *n esp. BrE, infml* a REFRIGERATOR, esp. in the home

friend /frend/ *n* **1** [C] a person who shares the same feelings of natural liking and understanding, the same interests, etc., but is not closely related: *Bill and Ben are friends.*|*"Bill is my friend," said Ben.*|*He's a close friend of my brother.*|*Mary's an old friend of mine; we've known each other for 16 years.*|*He's no friend of mine; I don't like him at all.*|*Must you quarrel all the time? Can't you be friends?*|*The children are good friends/bad friends* (=like/dislike each other very much).|*"Are you staying at a hotel?" "No, we're staying with friends"* **2** [C (*of, to*)] a helper; supporter; adviser; person showing kindness and understanding: *That rich lady is a friend of the arts; she provides money for concerts in the town.*|*Our doctor's been a good friend to us; he's always helped us when we've needed him.*|*He says he's no friend of the government.*|*A girl's best friend is her mother.*|*He didn't get the post on his own abilities; he had a friend in high places* (=someone in a position to influence others to help him) **3** [C] someone who is not an enemy; person from whom there is nothing to fear: *"Who goes there? Friend or* FOE*?" was the question asked by the soldier on guard duty in former times.*|*The escaped prisoner met some men in the wood, but he found himself among friends, for they didn't tell the police about him* **4** [C] a companion: *Who's your friend* (=the person who is with you)?|*The dog is a faithful friend of man* —see also BOYFRIEND, GIRLFRIEND **5** [C] *fml* a useful quality, condition, or thing: *Bright light is the painter's best friend* **6** [C;N] *esp. polite* a person who is being addressed or spoken of in public: *Friends, we have met here tonight to talk over a very serious matter.*|*Our good friend Mrs Jones will now speak to us about her work in hospitals.*|*In court, lawyers speak of each other as "My* LEARNED *friend."*|*In parliament, members speak of each other as "My honourable friend"* **7** [C;N (*with poss. adj*)] **a** a person whose name one does not know, esp. one who is seen regularly or often: *What can I do for you, my friend?*|*Our friend the postman is late this morning* **b** a stranger noticed for some reason, usu. with amusement or displeasure: *Our friend with the loud voice is here again* —see also FRIENDS

Friend *n* a member of the Christian group called the **Society of Friends**; QUAKER

friend·less /ˈfrendləs/ *adj* without friends or help —**~ness** *n* [U]

friend·ly[1] /ˈfrendli/ *adj* [Wa1] **1** [B (*to*)] acting or ready to act as a friend: *A friendly dog came to meet us at the farm.*|*He's not very friendly to newcomers* **2** [F (*with*)] sharing the relationship of friends (with): *They quarrelled once, but they're quite friendly now.*|*Bill is very friendly with Ben* **3** [F+*to*] favouring; ready to accept (ideas): *This business company has never been friendly to change* **4** [B] kind; generous; supporting or protecting; ready to help: *You're always sure of a friendly welcome at this hotel.*|*We found shelter from the rain under a friendly tree.*|*That's not very friendly of you* (=You're behaving unkindly) **5** [B] not an enemy: *a friendly nation* **6** [B] not causing or containing unpleasant feelings when in competitions, arguments, etc.: *We've been having a friendly argument on politics.*|*Though she didn't like my advice, she accepted it in a friendly spirit.*|*Our 2 teams are playing a friendly game next Saturday; the season's serious competition doesn't start until next month* —opposite **unfriendly** —**-li·ness** *n* [U]

friendly[2] *n not fml* a FRIENDLY[1] (6) match; game that is not part of a serious competition: *Manchester United beat Celtic in a friendly*

friendly so·ci·e·ty /ˈ·· ·ˌ···/ *n* (*often cap.*) an association, usu. of workmen, to which the members pay small weekly sums, and which provides money when they are ill and/or in their old age

friends /frendz/ *n* **1 be friends with** to have a friendship with; be a friend/friends of: *Paul is friends with Bill* **2 make friends a** (of one or more people) to form friendships: *He has a pleasant manner, and makes friends very easily.*|*They don't know anyone in the town where they're going to live, but I'm sure they'll soon make a lot of new friends* **b** (of 2 or more people) to form a friendship: *Sammy and Joey have only just met, but they've made friends already.*|*The little boys fought over a game, and then made friends again* (=forgave each other) **3 make friends with** to form a friendship with: *Have you made friends with your new neighbours yet?*

friend·ship /ˈfrendʃɪp/ *n* **1** [U] the condition of sharing a friendly relationship; feeling and behaviour that exists between friends: *Real friendship is more valuable than money.*|*My cat and dog have lived together in friendship all their lives* **2** [C] a particular example or period of this: *His friendships never last very long*

fri·er /ˈfraɪəʳ/ *n* FRYER

frieze /friːz/ *n* **1** an ornamental border along the top of the wall of a building, sometimes above pillars **2** a patterned border along the top of wallpaper in a room

frig a·round /frɪg/ *v adv* [IØ] *infml & euph* to waste one's time doing aimless, silly, or annoying things

frig·ate /ˈfrɪgɨt/ *n* a type of small fast-moving armed naval ship, used for travelling with and protecting other ships

frig·ging /ˈfrɪgɪŋ/ *adj, adv taboo* (used for giving force to an expression) FUCKING

fright /fraɪt/ *n* **1** [U] the feeling or experience of fear: *Fright gave the old lady heart failure.*|*shaking with fright*|*I nearly died of fright at the sight of the escaped lion.*|*The horse took fright at the sound of the explosion* (=had an attack of fear) **2** [C] an experience that causes sudden fear; shock: *You gave me a fright by knocking so loudly on the door.*|*I got the fright of my life* (=the biggest fright I've ever had) *when the machine burst into flames* **3** [S] *infml* a person who or thing that looks silly, unattractive, or shocking: *She looks a fright in that old black dress*

fright·en /ˈfraɪtn/ also (*lit*) **fright**— *v* **1** [Wv4;T1] to fill with fear: *The little girl was frightened by the big dog.*|*a frightening dream* **2** [X9] to influence or drive by fear: *The bird came to the window, but I moved suddenly, and this frightened it away.*|*He frightened off his attacker by calling for the police* —**~ingly** *adv*

fright·ened /ˈfraɪtnd/ *adj not fml* **1** [B (*at, of*); F3,5] in a state of fear: *The frightened horse ran away from the fire.*|*He was frightened at the thought of his coming examination.*|*She was frightened to look down from the top of the tall building.*|*The little girl was frightened* (*that*) *her mother wouldn't come back* **2** [F+*of*,F3] habitually afraid: *Some people are frightened of thunder, others of snakes* —see also AFRAID (1)

frighten in·to *v prep* [V4b] to persuade (someone) by fear into (doing something): *He frightened the old lady into signing the paper*

frighten out of *v adv prep* **1** [D1] to cause (someone) to lose (something) through fear: *The noise nearly frightened us out of our senses/out of our skins* **2** [V4b] to prevent (someone) by fear from (doing something): *The presence of the police frightened many criminals out of attempting further crimes*

fright·ful /ˈfraɪtfəl/ *adj* **1** fearful; terrible; shocking: *The battlefield was a frightful scene* **2** *infml* very bad; unpleasant; difficult: *We're having* *frightful weather this week.|The examination questions were frightful* —**~ness** *n* [U]

fright·ful·ly /ˈfraɪtfəli/ *adv infml, becoming rare* very: *I'm afraid I'm frightfully late*

fri·gid /ˈfrɪdʒ$\frac{1}{2}$d/ *adj* **1** very cold; having a continuously low temperature: *The air on the mountaintop was frigid.|The parts of the world near the North and South* POLE*s are called the* **frigid zones** **2** cold in manner; unfriendly; lacking in warmth and life: *She smiled faintly at him; it was a frigid greeting* **3** (of a woman) having an unnatural dislike for sexual activity —**~ly** *adv* —**~ness** *n* [U]

fri·gid·i·ty /frɪˈdʒɪd$\frac{1}{2}$ti/ *n* [U] **1** coldness of temperature **2** coldness of personal or sexual feeling

frill /frɪl/ *n* **1** an ornamental edge to a dress, curtain, etc., made of a band of cloth of which one edge is gathered together and sewn down in tight folds, and the other edge is left free **2** an ornamental band of cut paper, put around something **3** a natural band of long hair, feathers, etc., on an animal, bird, or plant

frilled /frɪld/ *adj* [Wa5] **1** ornamented with FRILL*s* (1,2): *a frilled edge* **2** made into FRILL*s* (1,2): *frilled paper*

frills /frɪlz/ *n* [P] **1** things that may be thought ornamental or pleasant, but are not necessary: *Most of the fine new apparatus in this aircraft is just frills; it doesn't help the aircraft to fly better* **2** behaviour that is not natural, or that is intended to make one seem different from or better than others: *There are no frills about him; he's just a plain natural person*

frill·y /ˈfrɪli/ *adj* [Wa1] **1** having many FRILL*s* (1, 2): *The little girl wore a frilly party dress* **2** *derog* having too many FRILLS (1): *a frilly style of writing* —**frilliness** *n* [U]

fringe¹ /frɪndʒ/ *n* **1** an ornamental edge of hanging threads, sometimes twisted or knotted, on a curtain, tablecloth, garment, etc. **2** [(*of*)] a line of things which borders something: *A fringe of trees stood round the pool* **3** a short border of hair, with the lower edge usu. cut in a straight line, hanging over a person's forehead: *The girl wore her hair in a fringe* **4** a border of long hair on part of an animal, or of hairlike parts on a plant: *The dog had long ears with a silky fringe to them* **5** [(*of*)] the part farthest from the centre; edge: *It was easier to move about on the fringe of the crowd.|The woodcutter had a little house on the fringes of the forest* **6** a group which is only loosely connected with a political or other movement, and may not agree with it on all points —see also LUNATIC FRINGE

fringe² *v* [T1 (*with*)] to act as a FRINGE¹ (1,2) to: *A line of trees fringed the pool.|a pool fringed with trees*

fringe ben·e·fit /ˈ· ˌ···/ *n* [*often pl.*] added favours or services given with a job, besides wages: *One of the fringe benefits of this job is free health insurance*

frip·pe·ry /ˈfrɪpəri/ *n* **1** [U] foolish unnecessary useless ornamentation, esp. on a garment **2** [C *usu. pl.*] a cheap useless small ornament

Fris·bee /ˈfrɪzbi/ *n tdmk* (*often not cap.*) a platelike piece of plastic that people throw to each other as a game

Fri·si·an /ˈfriːzɪən‖-ʒən/ also (*esp. AmE*) **Holstein**— *n esp. BrE* a black-and-white cow of a breed that give a large quantity of milk

frisk¹ /frɪsk/ *v* **1** [IØ] (of an animal or child) to run and jump about playfully: *The new lambs are frisking in the fields* **2** [T1] *infml* to search (someone) for hidden weapons, goods, etc., by passing the hands over the body

frisk² *n* [S] a joyful active movement or game: *The 2 dogs were having a frisk on the grass*

frisk·y /ˈfrɪski/ *adj* [Wa1] overflowing with life and activity; joyfully alive: *The spring weather's making me feel quite frisky* —**-ily** *adv* —**-iness** *n* [U]

fris·son /ˈfriːsɔ̃‖friːˈsɔ̃ (*Fr* frisɔ̃)/ *n Fr* a feeling of excitement and/or pleasure, esp. caused by something dangerous of which one is afraid

frit·ter /ˈfrɪtəʳ/ *n* (*often in comb.*) a thin piece of fruit, meat, or vegetable, covered with a mixture of egg and flour (BATTER) and cooked in hot fat: *apple fritters*

fritter a·way *v adv* [T1 (*on*)] *derog* to waste (time, money, etc.): *She fritters away all her money on cheap clothes and visits to the cinema*

fri·vol·i·ty /frɪˈvɒl$\frac{1}{2}$ti‖-ˈvɑ-/ *n* **1** [U] *derog* the condition of being FRIVOLOUS: *Her frivolity of mind makes her unsuited to a position of trust* **2** [C *usu. pl.*] **a** *derog* a FRIVOLOUS act or remark: *One doesn't expect a serious political speech to be full of frivolities* **b** any form of light pleasure or amusement: *People enjoy a few frivolities during their holidays*

friv·o·lous /ˈfrɪvələs/ *adj derog* **1** not serious; silly; useless: *He failed his examination because he gave a frivolous answer to one of the chief questions.|Are you playing cards again this afternoon? What a frivolous way of spending your time!* **2** unable to take important matters seriously; liking to spend time in light useless pleasures: *a frivolous girl|He has a frivolous nature; he cares for nothing but amusement* —**~ly** *adv* —**~ness** *n* [U]

frizz¹ /frɪz/ *v* [T1 (OUT, UP)] *infml* to force (hair) into tight short wiry curls

frizz² *n* [S] *infml* a mass of short tight curls of hair: *The boy had a frizz of black hair*

friz·zle¹ /ˈfrɪzəl/ *v* [Wv3] *infml* **1** [IØ (UP)] (of hair) to curl tightly **2** [T1 (UP)] to set (the hair) in a mass of tight curls

frizzle² *v* [Wv3] *infml* **1** [IØ] (of very hot fat, or something being cooked in hot fat) to make small exploding noises: *The* SAUSAGE*s were frizzling in the pan* **2** [T1 (UP)] to cook (something) in hot fat until burnt

frizz·y /ˈfrɪzi/ *adj* [Wa1] *infml* (of hair) very curly, like wool: *Some people have naturally frizzy hair*

fro /frəʊ/ *adv* away (in the phr. **to and fro**) —see TO AND FRO

frock /frɒk‖frɑk/ *n* **1** *not fml, becoming rare* a woman's or girl's dress **2** a long loose-fitting garment worn by a Christian holy man (MONK)

frock coat /ˌ· ˈ·‖ˈ· ·/ *n* a type of long coat for men, worn in the 19th century

frog /frɒg‖frɑg, frɔg/ *n* **1** any of several types of small hairless tailless animal, usu. brownish-green, that live in water and on land, have long back legs for swimming and jumping, and make a deep rough sound (CROAK) —compare TOAD and see picture at AMPHIBIAN **2** a fastening to a coat or other garment, often ornamental, consisting of a long button and a circular band for putting it through **3** a leather holder on a belt, for supporting a sword **4** a 3-sided horny part in the middle of the bottom of a horse's foot **5** **a frog in the/one's throat** *infml* a difficulty in speaking because of roughness in the throat

Frog also **Frog·gy** /ˈfrɒgi‖ˈfrɑgi, ˈfrɔgi/— *n infml, usu. derog* a French person

frogged /frɒgd‖frɑgd, frɔgd/ *adj* [Wa5] having FROG*s* (2): *a splendid frogged uniform*

frog·man /ˈfrɒgmən‖ˈfrɑg-, ˈfrɔg-/ *n* **-men** /mən/ a skilled underwater swimmer who wears a special apparatus on head and back for breathing, and large flat shoes (FLIPPER*s*) to increase the strength of his leg movements, esp. one who works under water in this way —compare SKIN DIVEr

frog·march /ˈfrɒgmɑːtʃ‖ˈfrɑgmɑrtʃ, ˈfrɔg-/ *v* [X9] **1** to force (a person) to move forward with the arms held together firmly from behind: *They frogmarched him into the yard* **2** to carry (a person) face downwards with 4 people holding the arms and legs

frog·spawn /ˈfrɒgspɔːn‖ˈfrag-, ˈfrɔg-/ *n* [U] a nearly transparent mass of FROG's (1) eggs

frol·ic[1] /ˈfrɒlɪk‖ˈfra-/ *v* **-ck-** [I∅ (ABOUT)] to play and jump about gaily: *The young lambs were frolicking in the field*

frolic[2] *n* an active and enjoyable game of amusement; playful expression of high spirits: *The children are having a frolic before bedtime*

frol·ic·some /ˈfrɒlɪksəm‖ˈfra-/ *adj* playful; merry: *Young creatures are naturally frolicsome*

from /frəm; *strong* frɒm‖frəm; *strong* frʌm, fram/ *prep* **1** (*showing a starting point in time*) **a** (of past time) beginning at; since: *From the moment he saw her, he loved her.|We've been working from morning to night* (=without stopping) **b** (of present and future time) beginning at; after: *We hope to go on holiday a month from today.|The shop will be open from half past 8 till 5 o'clock.|It will be open from about 9 o'clock* —see also **from** TIME[1] (30) **to time**; see TO[1] (USAGE) **2** (*showing a starting point in place*) having left; beginning at (the) (often in the phr. **from** (*a* [C] *noun used as a* [U] *noun*) **to** (*a* [C] *noun used as a* [U] *noun*)): *The train starts from London.|It goes from London northwards.|It goes from London to the north.|A cool wind blew from the sea.|The boy was covered in mud from head to foot* (=all over).|*She went from shop to shop trying to find what she wanted.|These birds have come from over the sea.|Where do we go from here?* —see also **from** END[1] (15) **to end** **3** (*showing a starting point in rank, order, or position*) beginning with; beginning as (often in the phr. **from** (*a* [C] *noun used as a* [U] *noun*) **to** (*a* [C] *noun used as a* [U] *noun*)): *Boys from the Third Class took their examinations in the main hall of the school.|He rose from office boy to director of the company in 15 years* **4** (*showing a starting point in price or number*) **a** starting at; at the lower limit (of): *These coats are from 10 pounds* (=the cheapest cost 10 pounds) **b** (in the phr. **from . . . to . . .** = between . . . and . . .): *There were from 60 to 80 people present* **5** sent, given, supplied, produced, or provided by; originating in; out of: *I had a letter from her yesterday.|Eggs are obtained from hens.|Meat from New Zealand is sold in shops in England.|The boy from the baker's has just called.|A bright light shone from the room.|He took the knife from his pocket.|He gets his good looks from his mother.|Light comes from the sun.|He claims to be descended from a race of kings.|"Where are you from?" "I'm from Scotland"* (=I'm Scottish).|*Tell your brother from me that I want him to return my book.|This music is from one of Mozart's* OPERA*s* (=is part of one of them).| *Who did you borrow it from?* **6** based on; using; out of: *Bread is made from flour.|The plastic of which this dish was made, is made from chemicals.|The shape of the car was developed from that of the horse carriage.|I'm speaking from experience.|She played the music from memory.|All the characters in the book are drawn from real life* **7** (*expressing the lessening or ceasing of an unwanted state*) instead of: *He needs a rest from work.|This medicine may give you some* RELIEF *from the pain in your head* **8** (*showing the first of 2 states, where a complete change of condition is expressed*) out of; after being (esp. in the phrs. **from . . . to . . ., from . . . into . . .**): *From being a thin weak boy, he became a healthy active soldier in the army.|Her behaviour is going from bad to worse.|Translate this letter from English into French* **9** (*expressing difference*) compared with; as being unlike: *He's different from his brother in character.|I don't know anything about cars; I don't know one kind from another* **10** (*showing a point of view*) using . . . as a position: *From the top of this hill you can see the sea.|From a child's point of view, this book isn't interesting.|a picture of a car seen from below|He was looking at me from over the top of a newspaper* **11** (in a state of separation) with regard to: *His absence from class was soon noticed.|It's hard for a child to be kept apart from its mother.|He lives apart from his family* **12** distant in regard to: *The village is 5 miles (away) from the coast.|It's only a few steps from here to the post office.*|(fig.) *"Nothing was further from my mind"* (SEU W.) **13** out of; off; out of the reach of; out of the possession of: *She took the matches away from the child.|Why did you move the books from the table?|If you subtract 10 from 15, 5 remains.|The wind blew his hat from off his head* **14** (in a state of protection, prevention, or separation) with regard to: *She saved the child from the fire.|A tree gave us shelter from the rain.|Keep the bad news from the sick woman.|"Protect our town from flooding"* (SEU S.) **15** because of; as a result of; through: *She suffered from heart disease.|He wasn't ill; he stayed in bed from laziness.|From no fault of their own, they lost all their money* **16** judging by; considering: *From his appearance, you wouldn't think he was old.|From the noise they were making, they might have been fighting.|From what John tells me, they're very rich.|From a practical point of view, it's stupid*

frond /frɒnd‖frand/ *n* **1** a leaf of a FERN or of a PALM **2** a delicate feathery leaf or leaflike part

front[1] /frʌnt/ *n* **1** [(*the*) R (*of*)] the position directly before someone or something: *The teacher called the boy out to the front of the class.|A pretty girl was walking past behind them, but the officer told the soldiers to look to the front* **2** [*the*+R (*of*)] the surface or part facing forwards, outwards, or upwards: *The front of the cupboard is made of glass.|The front of the postcard shows a picture of our hotel.|This dress fastens at the front* **3** [*the*+R (*of*)] the most forward or important position: *The chief guest at the concert was led to a place at the front of the hall.|He walked along to the front of the train.*|(fig.) *This new writer is rapidly coming to the front* (=becoming important) **4** [(*the*) R (*of*);C] **a** the most important side of a building, containing the main entrance; side of a building facing the street: *The front of the school faces south.|Our house front is being repainted.|In cities, shop fronts are often partly made of glass* **b** a side of a large important building: *The west front of the church contains some fine old windows* **5** [*the*+R (*of*)] (of a book or newspaper) the beginning: *Write your name at the front of this dictionary* **6** [*the*+R;(C)] a road, often built up and having a protecting wall, by the edge of the sea, esp. in a town where people go for holidays: *The hotel is right on the sea front.|The tourists walked along the front to enjoy the air* —see also PROMENADE[1] (3) **7** [S9] the manner and appearance of a person: *Whatever his difficulties, he always presents a smiling front to the world.|She was nervous of meeting strangers, but she put on a bold front* (=acted as if she wasn't afraid) *and went to the party* **8** [C] **a** part of a garment covering the chest: *I've dropped soup down my front* **b** SHIRT-FRONT **9** [*the*+R;C9] (*often cap.*) a line along which fighting takes place in time of war, together with the part behind it concerned with supplies: *He lost his life at the front.|The Minister of Defence paid a visit to the Front, to see for himself the conditions in which the men lived.|The army has defeated the enemy, and is advancing on a wide front.*|(fig.) *The fight against disease has had some fine successes, and is making advances on all fronts* **10** [C9] a combined effort or appearance against opposing forces: *The members of the government* *didn't agree on all matters of political importance, but on foreign affairs they formed a united front against the party in opposition* **11** [*the*+R9] *often humor* a group of people making a combined effort for some purpose: *During the war, she worked on the home front* (=in her own country), *helping to produce weapons for the army.|The kitchen front's busy with preparations for your Christmas dinner* **12** [C] (*often cap.*) a widespread and active political movement: *The People's Front is gaining many supporters because it favours better conditions for workers* **13** [C] a line of separation between 2 masses of air of different temperature: *A cold front is the forward edge of a mass of moving cold air.|a warm front* **14** [C (*for*)] *infml* a person, group, or thing used for hiding the real nature of a secret or unlawful activity: *The police believe that a foreign air travel company is being used as a front for bringing dangerous drugs into the country* **15 in front a** ahead; in the position directly before someone or something: *The grandmother walked slowly, and the children ran on in front* **b** in or at the part facing forwards: *This dress fastens in front* **c** in the most forward or important position: *The driver sits in front, and the passengers sit behind* **16 in front of a** in the position directly before: *We couldn't read the notice on the board because several people were standing* (*right/directly*) *in front of it.|a car parked* (*just*) *in front of the house* (compare *a man sitting in the front of the car*) **b** in the presence of: *You shouldn't use such bad language in front of the children* **17 in the front** in FRONT¹ (15b,c) **18 in the front of** in the most forward or important position: *He's sitting in the front of the car with the driver.|In the front of the picture is the figure of a man* **19 out front** *infml* in or amongst the people watching a theatrical or other performance: *My family are out front this evening, so I shall hope to give a good performance* **20 up front** *infml* (esp. in sport) in the most forward position: *In football, the players who play up front get the most* GOALS —compare BACK¹, REAR²

front² *v* **1** [T1;L9 (esp. *on, onto*)] (of a building) to have the front towards; face; stand opposite to: *The head post office fronts the railway station.|The hotel fronts on the main road.|The hospital fronts east* **2** [T1 *often pass.*] to give a surface to the wall of (a building): *The house is fronted with brick* **3** [T1] *old use* to be matched against; oppose: *to front the enemy bravely*

front³ *adj* [Wa5;A] **1** being at, related to, or coming from the FRONT¹ (1): *From our window we had a front view of the soldiers marching past* (=a clear view, with nothing in between) **2** being at the FRONT¹ (2): *Write your name on the front cover of the exercise book* **3** being at the FRONT¹ (3): *The boy lost one of his front teeth when he rode his bicycle into the wall.|We have tickets for the front row at the concert* **4** at or connected with the FRONT¹ (4a) of a building: *the front garden|the front room* **5** *infml* being a FRONT¹ (14): *Certain rich men who wish to remain unknown are using a front organization to hide their trade in forbidden goods.|a front man* **6** (in PHONETICS, of a vowel) made by raising the tongue at the front of the mouth: */iː/ is a front vowel* —opposite **back** **7** (in GOLF) being the first 9 holes of an 18-hole course: *Nicklaus did the front 9 in 34 strokes*

front·age /ˈfrʌntɪdʒ/ *n* [C9] a part of a building or of land that stretches along a road, river, etc.: *The shop has frontages on 2 busy streets.|The boat-building company is looking for a yard with a wide river frontage*

front·al /ˈfrʌntl/ *adj* [Wa5;A] **1** of, at, or to the front: *full frontal* NUDITY (=state of being completely undressed and showing the front of the body, so that esp. the sexual organs can be seen) **2** (of an attack) direct; (as if) from the front **3** *med* belonging to the forehead: *the frontal bone* **4** of or related to a weather FRONT¹ (13): *A new frontal system is moving towards Britain from the west* —**-ally** *adv*

front·bench /ˌfrʌntˈbentʃ◂/ *n* [*the*+GU] *esp. BrE* government ministers or leading members of the opposition party, who sit on one of the front seats in Parliament: *a frontbench minister|on the frontbench* —compare BACKBENCH —**~er** *n*

front door /ˌ· ˈ·/ *n* the main entrance door to a house, usu. at the front

front for *v prep* [T1] *infml* to act as a FRONT¹ (14) for

fron·tier /ˈfrʌntɪəʳ‖frʌnˈtɪər/ *n* **1** [C] the limit or edge of the land of one country, where it meets the land of another country: *They were shot trying to cross the frontier.|Sweden has frontiers with Norway and Finland* **2** [*the*+R;C] the border between settled and wild country, esp. that in the US in the past: *Areas near the frontier in America were rough and lawless in the old days* **3** [C9, esp. *of*; *often pl.*] a border between the known and the unknown: *The frontiers of medical knowledge are being pushed farther outwards as time goes on*

fron·tiers·man /ˈfrʌntɪəzmən‖frʌnˈtɪərz-/ *n* **-men** /mən/ a man living on the FRONTIER (2); early settler

fron·tis·piece /ˈfrʌntəspiːs/ *n* a picture or photograph at the beginning of a book, on the left-hand page opposite the title page

front line /ˌ· ˈ·◂/ *n* [*the*+R] **1** the most advanced or responsible position: *These doctors in Africa are in the front line of the fight against disease* **2** FRONT¹ (9): *soldiers in the front line* —**front-line** *adj* [Wa5;A]: *front-line soldiers*

front-page /ˈ· ·/ *adj* [Wa5;A] *infml* very interesting, important, or exciting; worthy of being printed on the front page of a newspaper: *front-page news|a front-page story*

front rank /ˌ· ˈ·◂/ *n* [*the*+R] *apprec* the highest position of importance or quality: *This painter isn't quite in the front rank, but he's very skilful in using colour* —**front-rank** *adj* [Wa5;A]: *a front-rank actress*

front-run·ner /ˌ· ˈ··/ *n* a person who has the best chance of success in competing for something: *"Who do you think will get the job?" "Thomson, Murray, and Jenkinson are the 3 front-runners; one of them will probably get it"*

frost¹ /frɒst‖frɔst/ *n* **1** [U] weather at a temperature below the freezing point of water; frozen condition of the ground and/or air: *Frost has killed several of our new young plants.|The radio has given a frost and icy roads warning for car drivers tomorrow.|ground frost|air frost* **2** [C] a period or state of this: *There was a hard frost last night* (=a severe one).|*Early frosts* (=ones near the start of autumn) *spoil the last of the flowers.|The young shoots on the trees have been damaged by a late frost* (=one towards the end of spring) **3** [U] a white powdery substance formed on outside surfaces from very small drops of water when the temperature of the air is below freezing point: *The grass was covered with frost in the early morning* **4** [C] *derog* a performance or planned event that is a complete failure: *The party was a frost; no one enjoyed it at all* **5 of frost** *tech* below the freezing point of water: *There was 5 degrees of frost last night and the river's completely frozen*

frost² *v* **1** [T1;IØ:(OVER)] to (cause to) become covered with FROST¹ (3): *The cold has frosted the* *windows.*|*The fields have frosted over on this wintry morning* **2** [Wv5;T1] to make the surface of a sheet of (glass) rough so that it is not possible to see through: *Frosted glass in windows and doors lets in less light than clear glass, but keeps a room private* **3** [T1] to cover (a cake) with fine white sugar; ICE[2] (2) **4** [T1] to damage (esp. a plant) with FROST[1] (1)

frost·bite /ˈfrɒstbaɪt/ *n* [U] swelling, discoloration, and sometimes poisoning of a person's limbs, caused by a great cold: *suffering from frostbite*

frost·bit·ten /ˈfrɒst,bɪtn‖ˈfrɔst-/ *adj* **1** suffering from FROSTBITE: *frostbitten toes* **2** (of a plant) damaged or killed by FROST[1] (1)

frost·bound /ˈfrɒstbaʊnd‖ˈfrɔst-/ *adj* (of the ground) hardened by FROST[1] (1): *The garden's still frostbound; it's useless to think of planting anything*

frost·ing /ˈfrɒstɪŋ‖ˈfrɔstɪŋ/ *n* [U] **1** a non-shiny surface produced on glass or metal by FROSTing[2] (2) **2** ICING

frost·y /frɒsti‖ˈfrɔsti/ *adj* [Wa1] **1** **a** stingingly cold; cold with FROST[1] (1): *It was a cold frosty day.*| *The air was bright and frosty* **b** covered or seeming to be covered with FROST[1] (3): *The fields look frosty this morning* **2** unfriendly; cold: *She gave me a frosty greeting; it was plain that she hadn't forgiven me* —**-ily** *adv* —**-iness** *n* [U]

froth[1] /frɒθ‖frɔθ/ *n* **1** [U;S] *not fml* a white mass of small balls of air (BUBBLE*s*) formed on top of or in a liquid, or in the mouth; FOAM: *There is froth at the corners of the dog's mouth; can it be mad?* **2** [U] *derog* a light empty show of talk or ideas: *The play was amusing, but it was little more than a lot of froth*

froth[2] *v not fml* **1** [IØ] to make or throw up FROTH[1] (1): *The beer frothed as it was poured out.*|*The sea was rough, and the waves frothed round the rocks.*| *The sick animal was frothing at the mouth.*|(fig.) *Your employer isn't pleased with you; he's frothing at the mouth* (=showing signs of great excitement and anger) **2** [T1 (UP)] to produce FROTH[1] (1) on or in: *Before washing the clothes, froth up the soap mixture*

froth·y /ˈfrɒθi‖ˈfrɔθi/ *adj* [Wa1] **1** *not fml* full of or covered with FROTH[1] (1): *This glass of beer is very frothy; there's only half a glass of drink in it* **2** *sometimes derog* light and gay; without serious contents: *a frothy piece of amusement* —**-ily** *adv* —**-iness** *n* [U]

frown[1] /fraʊn/ *v* **1** [IØ] to draw the hair-covered parts above the eyes (BROW*s*) together in anger or effort, so as to show disapproval or to protect the eyes against strong light, causing lines to appear on the forehead: *She frowns when the sun gets in her eyes, or when she's putting thread into a needle.*|*The teacher frowned at the noisy class* **2** [Wv4;IØ] (of a thing) to have a dangerous or unfriendly appearance when seen from below: *The mountains frown down on the plain.*|*frowning cliffs* —**~ingly** *adv*

frown[2] *n* **1** a serious or displeased look, causing lines on the forehead; act of FROWNing[1] (1): *The schoolgirl looked at her examination paper with a frown* **2** the lines left on the forehead by this act: *You'll develop a deep frown if you don't wear your glasses for reading*

frown on also **frown up·on**— *v prep* [T1,4] to disapprove of: *Mary wanted to go to Europe by herself, but her parents frowned on the idea*

frowst[1] /fraʊst/ *n* [S] *infml, esp. BrE* unpleasantly hot air inside a room: *Open the window; there's a terrible frowst in here!* —see also FUG

frowst[2] *v* [L9] *infml, esp. BrE* to remain indoors in a hot airless room: *After frowsting in the office all day, he was glad to take a long walk*

frowst·y /ˈfraʊsti/ *adj* [Wa1] *derog, esp. BrE* (of the conditions inside a room) hot and airless

frow·zy, -sy /ˈfraʊzi/ *adj* [Wa1] *derog* **1** (of a person, clothes, etc.) not neat or clean for a long time, esp. when in an enclosed space **2** (of a house or room) uncared-for; having a closed-in heavy smell

froze /frəʊz/ *past t. of* FREEZE[1]

fro·zen /ˈfrəʊzən/ *past p. of* FREEZE[1]

FRS *abbrev. for*: FELLOW of the ROYAL SOCIETY: *Sir Christopher Wren, FRS*|*an FRS*

fruc·ti·fi·ca·tion /ˌfrʌktɪ̣fɪ̣ˈkeɪʃən/ *n* [U] *fml* **1** the producing or forming of fruit **2** the producing of successful results —compare FRUITION

fruc·ti·fy /ˈfrʌktɪ̣faɪ/ *v* [T1;IØ] *fml* **1** to (cause to) produce fruit **2** to (cause to) produce successful results

fru·gal /ˈfruːgəl/ *adj* **1** [B (*of*)] not wasteful; careful in the use of money, food, etc.: *Although he's become rich, he's kept his frugal habits.*|*She's always frugal of her money* **2** [B] small in quantity and cost: *They lived simply, and usually had a frugal supper of bread and cheese* —**~ly** *adv*

fru·gal·i·ty /fruːˈgælɪ̣ti/ *n* **1** [U] the quality or state of being FRUGAL **2** [C *usu. pl.*] an example of this

fruit[1] /fruːt/ *n* **1** [C] an object that grows on a tree or bush, contains seeds, is used for food, but is not usu. eaten with meat or with salt **2** [U] these objects in general, esp. considered as food: *All this fruit has gone bad.*|*"Would you like some more fruit?" "No thank you; I've had as much as I can eat already."*|*a fruit shop*|*a fruit tree*|*fruit-bearing bushes*|*a fruit bowl* **3** [Wn2;C] a type of this object: *Apples, oranges, and bananas are fruit.*|*The potato is a vegetable, not a fruit.*|*This dish is made from a mixture of 4 different summer fruits* **4** [C] *tech* a seed-containing part of any plant **5** [Wn1;C *often pl.*] a result, good or bad: *His failure is the fruit of laziness.*|*Their plans haven't borne fruit* (=had a successful result) **6** [N] *BrE sl becoming rare* fellow (in the phr. **old fruit**) —see also FRUITS

See next page for picture

fruit[2] *v* [IØ] (of a tree, bush, etc.) to bear fruit: *The apple trees are fruiting early this year*

fruit bat /ˈ· ·/ also **flying fox**— *n* a large type of flying animal (BAT[3] (1)) that lives in hot countries and feeds on fruit

fruit·cake /ˈfruːtkeɪk/ *n* **1** [C;U] a cake containing small dried fruits, nuts, etc. **2** **as nutty as a fruitcake** *humor* (of a person) mad; silly

fruit cock·tail /ˌ· ˈ··/ *n* [C;(U)] *esp. AmE* a mixture of small pieces of fruit served in a tall glass and eaten at the beginning or end of a meal —compare FRUIT SALAD (1)

fruit·er·er /ˈfruːtərəʳ/ *n* a person who sells fruit, esp. in a fruit shop

fruit fly /ˈ· ·/ *n* any of several types of small fly that feed on fruit or decaying vegetable matter

fruit·ful /ˈfruːtfəl/ *adj* **1** successful; useful; producing good results: *a fruitful meeting* **2** *old use* (of living things) bearing many young or much fruit —**~ly** *adv*: *He used his time in Europe fruitfully in the learning of several languages* —**~ness** *n* [U]

fru·i·tion /fruːˈɪʃən/ *n* [U] fulfilment (of plans, aims, desired results, etc.): *After much delay, the plan to build the new hospital was brought to fruition by the efforts of the new Minister of Health.*|*At last their hopes came to fruition, and they were able to stop working and travel round the world* —compare FRUCTIFICATION (2)

fruit knife /ˈ· ·/ *n* a small knife, usu. with a silver blade, used for cutting up fruit at meals

fruit·less /ˈfruːtləs/ *adj* (of an effort) useless; unsuccessful; not bringing the desired result: *So far the search for the missing boy has been fruitless* —**~ly** *adv* —**~ness** *n* [U]

fruit ma·chine /ˈ· ·ˌ·/ *n BrE* ONE-ARMED BANDIT

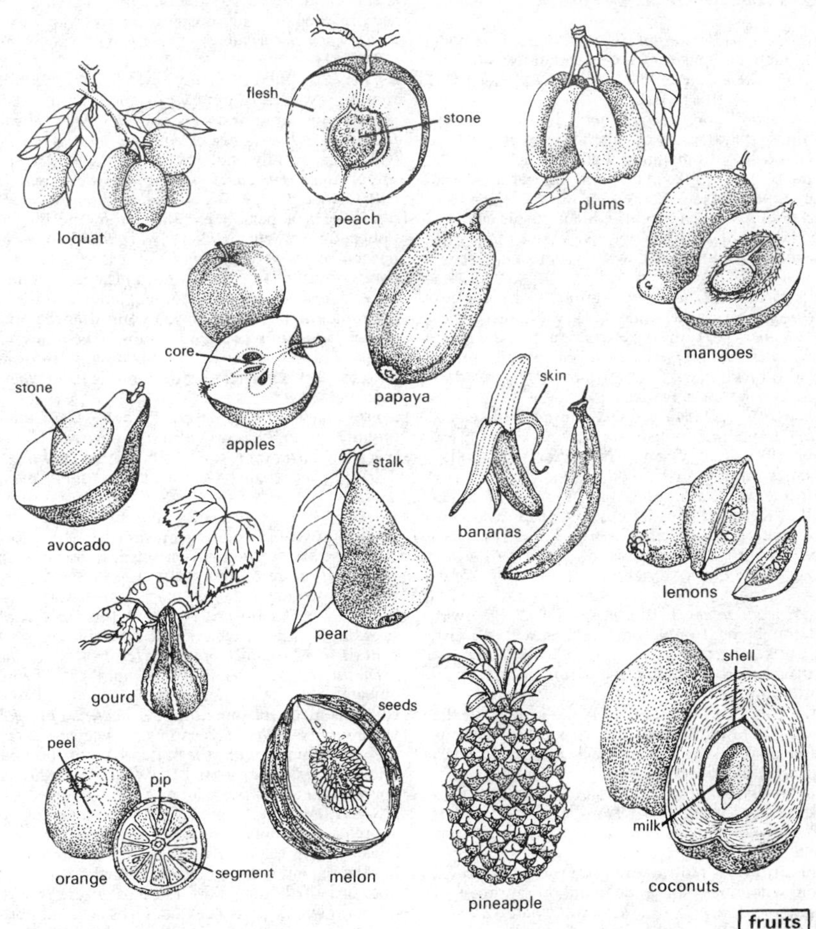

fruits /fruːts/ *n* [P9 (*of*)] **1** plants used for food or from which food can be produced, such as vegetables, corn, etc.: *the fruits of the earth* **2** rewards: *to enjoy the fruits of all one's hard work*

fruit sal·ad /ˌ· ˈ··/ *n* **1** [C;U] *esp. BrE* a dish made of several types of fruit cut up and served in a bowl at the end of a meal —compare FRUIT COCKTAIL **2** [C;U] *AmE* a dish made of pieces of fruit in a jelly **3** [U] *AmE infml* the coloured area on the left breast of a military uniform formed by the coloured squares of the MEDAL RIBBONs

fruit·y /ˈfruːti/ *adj* [Wa1] **1** *usu. apprec* like fruit; tasting or smelling of fruit: *The medicine had a fruity taste.|This red wine is soft and fruity* **2** *sl* (of talk, a remark, etc.) amusing in an improper direct way, esp. about matters of sex: *a rather fruity story* **3** *infml* (of voice) too rich and deep: *a fruity laugh*

frump /frʌmp/ *n derog* a dull old-fashioned woman (or man), esp. one who wears old-fashioned clothes —**~ish** *adj* —**~y** *adj* [Wa1]

frus·trate /frʌˈstreɪt‖ˈfrʌstreɪt/ *v* [T1] **1** [Wv5] to prevent the fulfilment of; defeat (someone or someone's effort): *The bad weather frustrated all our hopes of going out.|In his attempts to escape, the prisoner was frustrated by a watchful guard* **2** [Wv4] to cause (someone) to have feelings of annoyed disappointment: *After 2 hours' frustrating delay, our train at last arrived*

frus·tra·tion /frʌˈstreɪʃən/ *n* **1** [U] the act of frustrating or state of being FRUSTRATED: *Frustration by his father of his wish to become a doctor made the young man very unhappy.|We reached the station half a minute too late, and with a sense of frustration we saw our train disappearing round the bend* **2** [C] a particular example of this; failure of expectation; disappointment: *Life is full of frustrations for most people*

fry¹ /fraɪ/ *v* **1** [Wv5;T1;I0] to (cause to) be cooked in hot fat or oil: *Shall I fry the fish for dinner?|The eggs were frying in the pan.|fried rice* —see COOK (USAGE) **2** [I0] *infml* to have the skin burnt: *We shall fry if we stay long in this hot sun* **3 have other fish to fry** to have other affairs to attend to

fry² *n* **fry** [Wn3;C *usu. pl.*] a small fish that has just come out of its egg —see also SMALL FRY

fry·er, frier /ˈfraɪəʳ/ *n* **1** a small young chicken that is to be cooked by FRYing¹ (1) **2** (*often in comb.*) a deep pan for FRYing food: *a fish fryer*

frying pan /ˈ·· ˌ·/ *AmE* also **skillet**— *n* **1** a flat pan with a long handle, used for FRYing food esp. in the home —see picture at KITCHEN **2 out of the frying pan into the fire** out of a bad position into a worse one

fry-up /'· ·/ *n BrE infml* **1** a FRYing of various foods, such as eggs, SAUSAGE*s*, potatoes, etc., in order to make a quick meal: *to do/have a fry-up* **2** a dish cooked by this means

ft *written abbrev. for:* **1** foot **2** feet

fuch·sia[1] /'fjuːʃə/ *n* any of several types of graceful garden bush with hanging bell-like flowers in 2 colours of red, pink, bluish-red, or white —see picture at FLOWER[1]

fuchsia[2] *adj, n* (of) a bright reddish-purple colour

fuck[1] /fʌk/ *v taboo* **1** [I∅] to have sex **2** [T1] (esp. of a man) to have sex with (someone, esp. a woman)

fuck[2] *n taboo* **1** [C *usu. sing.*] an act of having sex **2** [C9 *usu. sing.*] a person, esp. a woman, considered for her part in the sexual act —compare STUD[1] (3) **3 not care/give a fuck** not to care at all

fuck[3] also **fucking hell** /,·· '·/— *interj taboo* (used as an expression of annoyance)

fuck a·bout also **fuck a·round**— *v adv* [I∅] *taboo, esp. BrE* to act in a foolish stupid way

fuck·er /'fʌkəʳ/ *n* [C; *you* + N] *taboo sl* a foolish stupid person, esp. man; fool

fuck·ing /'fʌkɪŋ/ *adj, adv* [Wa5;A] *taboo* **1** (used to give force to an expression, esp. showing annoyance): *You fucking fool!* **2** (used as an almost meaningless addition to speech): *I got my fucking foot fucking caught in the fucking chair, didn't I*

fuck off *v adv taboo* **1** [I∅ *usu. imper.*] **a** to go away **b** to stop being troublesome or annoying **2** [I∅] *AmE* FUCK ABOUT

fuck up *v adv* [T1] *taboo* to spoil; ruin —**fuck-up** /'· ·/ *n* [*usu. sing.*]

fud·dle[1] /'fʌdl/ *v* [Wv5;T1] to make (a person, the mind, etc.) slow and unable to work clearly, esp. as a result of drinking too much alcohol: *Too much strong drink will fuddle your brain*

fuddle[2] *n* [S] *infml* the condition of being unable to think clearly or quickly: *The old man's mind is weakening, and he gets in a fuddle if people talk too much to him*

fud·dy-dud·dy /'fʌdi ,dʌdi/ *n* [C; *you* + N] *derog* a person who does not understand or approve of modern ideas: *Uncle Ernest's an old fuddy-duddy; he still believes women shouldn't smoke*

fudge[1] /fʌdʒ/ *v derog* **1** [T1 (UP)] to put together roughly or dishonestly: *There's nothing new in this book; the writer has fudged up a lot of old ideas* **2** [T1;I∅ (*on*)] to avoid taking firm determined action on (something): *The government have fudged the* ISSUE *of equal rights for all races because they're afraid it would make them unpopular*

fudge[2] *n* [U] a type of soft creamy light brown sweet made of sugar, milk, butter, etc.: *Have a piece of fudge!*

fu·el[1] /fjʊəl‖fjuːəl/ *n* **1** [U] **a** material that is used for producing heat or power by burning: *Wood, coal, oil, and gas are different kinds of fuel.|The farmer cut up the old tree for his winter fuel* (= to burn in his house) **b** material that can be made to produce atomic power **2** [C] a type of this: *Petrol is no longer a cheap fuel* **3** [U] something that increases anger or any other strong active feeling: *The workers weren't satisfied with their wages, and when they were asked to work longer hours, it added fuel to the flames* (= made them more angry)

fuel[2] *v* **-ll-** (*AmE* **-l-**) **1** [I∅ (UP)] to take in FUEL[1] (1): *Aircraft sometimes fuel in midair* **2** [T1] to provide with FUEL[1] (1): *That car is being fuelled ready to try to beat the speed record*

fug /fʌg/ *n* [*usu. sing.*] a heavy unpleasant airless condition of a room or other enclosed space without open windows, caused by heat, smoke, or the presence of many people: *There's a fug in here; please open the window* —see also FROWST[1] —**~gy** *adj* [Wa2]

fu·gi·tive[1] /'fjuːdʒ½tɪv/ *adj* **1** [Wa5;A] escaping; running away **2** [B] *esp. lit or fml* **a** hard to keep present in the mind: *In the musician's mind a fugitive set of notes began slowly to form into a tune* **b** passing rapidly; not lasting, esp. in interest or importance: *The value of most newspaper writing is only fugitive*

fugitive[2] *n* a person escaping from the law, the police, danger, etc.: *He's a fugitive from justice; he's trying to avoid being caught by the police*

fugue /fjuːg/ *n* **1** [C] a piece of music in which one or 2 tunes are repeated or copied by voices or instrumental parts which begin one after the other, and continue to repeat and combine the tunes with small VARIATION*s* so as to make a well-formed pattern **2** [U] musical writing in this form: *the art of fugue*

füh·rer, fueh- /'fjʊərəʳ (*Ger.* 'fyːrər)/ *n Ger* a leader or guide; ruler who has unlimited power

-ful[1] /fəl/ *suffix* [*n, v*→*adj*] **1** full of: *an eventful day* **2** having the quality of; causing: *restful colours|Is it painful?* —**-fully** *adv*: *shouting cheerfully*

USAGE 1. It is not always possible to guess the meaning of words ending in **-ful**. BASHFUL, FRUITFUL, etc., are not regularly formed. 2. Some people do not approve of MEANINGFUL, STRESSFUL. They would rather say *full of meaning/of* STRESS.

-ful[2] /fʊl/ *suffix* [*n*→*n* [C (*of*)]] **1** the amount of a substance, liquid, etc., needed to fill the stated container: *2 cupfuls of milk|He smoked a whole packetful of cigarettes* **2** all of a number of people, objects, etc., in a space that is well filled or contains plenty of something: *A shelf-ful of books is waiting to be repaired* **3** as much as can be carried by, contained in, etc., the stated part of the body: *She was carrying an* ARMFUL *of flowers.|He drank a few* MOUTHFULS *of tea*

USAGE Words formed with **-ful** meaning the contents of a container make the plural in either of 2 ways. Both **basketfuls** and **basketsful** are correct, but the second is rather old-fashioned now.

ful·crum /'fʊlkrəm, 'fʌl-/ *n* **-crums** *or* **-cra** /krə/ the point on which a bar (LEVER) turns or is supported in lifting or moving something: *the fulcrum of a pair of* SCALES

ful·fil, *AmE* also **-fill** /fʊl'fɪl/ *v* **-ll-** [T1] **1** to do or perform (a duty, office, etc.): *A nurse has many duties to fulfil in caring for the sick.|A chimney fulfils the* FUNCTION *of taking away smoke* **2** to carry out (an order, command, conditions, etc.); obey: *The doctor's instructions must be fulfilled exactly; the sick man's life depends on it* **3** to keep or carry out faithfully (a promise, agreement, etc.): *If you make a promise you should fulfil it* **4** to supply or satisfy (a need. demand, purpose) **5** [*usu. pass.*] to make or prove to be true; cause to happen as appointed or PREDICTed: *The old belief that the world would come to an end after 1,000 years, was not fulfilled* **6** to make true; carry out (something wished for or planned, such as hopes, prayers, desires, etc.): *If he's lazy, he'll never fulfil his* AMBITION *to be a doctor* **7** to develop and express the abilities, qualities, character, etc., of (oneself) fully: *She succeeded in fulfilling herself both as an actress and as a mother*

ful·fil·ment, *AmE* also **-fill-** /fʊl'fɪlmənt/ *n* **1** [U] the act of fulfilling or condition of being fulfilled: *The help that we give her depends on her fulfilment of her promise to work harder.|After many years, his plans have come to fulfilment* **2** [U;(C)] satisfaction after successful effort: *a sense of fulfilment*

full[1] /fʊl/ *adj* **1** [Wa2;B (*of*)] (of a container) filled with liquid, powder, etc., as near to the top as is convenient in practice: *They brought us out a pot full of steaming coffee.|Do you want a full cup of tea, or half a cup?|You haven't drunk any of your tea; your cup's still full.|Why does grandmother always give you the fullest glass of orange drink?|It's rude to speak with your mouth full* (=while you are eating).|*This bag of flour is only half full* (=contains half the amount that it can hold).|(fig.) *My heart's too full for words* (=my feelings are too deep for me to express them).|*Don't fill my cup too full* **2** [Wa5;A;F (*of*) (UP (*with*))] (of a container) filled to the top; holding as much as possible: *You can't put any more liquid into a full bottle.|After the storm, the holes in the road were full of rainwater.|The bath's full up; someone forgot to turn off the water.|The drawer was full up with old clothes.*|(fig.) *When he heard of his son's wonderful success, his cup was full* (=he was contented; he had everything he could wish for) **3** [Wa2;A;F (UP)] (of a space) containing as many people, objects, etc., as possible; crowded: *The train's full (up); there are no seats left at all.|I don't like travelling on a full train.|As this page is now full, I can't write any more.|The doctor has a very full day before him* (=has work to do all the time) **4** [F+*of*] containing or having plenty (of): *The field was full of sheep feeding on the new grass.|This work's full of mistakes; I've never seen work more full of mistakes.|Her eyes were full of tears.|Every time they meet us, they're full of complaints about something* **5** [Wa1;A;F (UP)] *infml* well fed, often to the point of discomfort; satisfied: *I can't eat any more; I'm full up.|You ought not to go swimming on a full stomach* **6** [Wa1;B] complete; whole: *The full truth of the matter can never be told.|He's been working hard for a full year.|Please write down your full name and address.|She's never enjoyed a full measure of happiness* (=as much happiness as she deserved).|*This medical book is very full on* (=deals very thoroughly with) *the subject of children's diseases, but less full on how to prevent them.|She rose to her full height* (=stood up very straight and proudly).|*My foot caught in the step, and I fell full length* (=flat on the ground).|*He was lying full length on the bed* (=stretched out).|*He has led a full life* (=has had every kind of experience)*; his life has been full.|The tennis player gave the ball the full treatment* (=hit it as hard as possible) **7** [Wa5;A] the highest or greatest possible: *He drove the car at full speed through the town.|Only a very good student can obtain full marks in such a difficult examination.|Up on the hill, the full force of the wind can be felt.|The hunting dogs* (HOUNDS) *were in full cry after the fox.|The horsemen were riding over the plain at full* GALLOP (=as fast as they could) **8** [Wa5;A] possessing all the rights or qualities of the stated position: *Only full members of the club are allowed to vote at meetings* **9** [F+*of*] **a** having the mind and attention fixed only (on); thinking and talking of nothing else (except): *Some people are too full of their own troubles to care about the difficulties of others.|She's always full of herself.|She's always full of her own importance.|He's full of his coming journey to America* **b** overflowing (with a feeling, quality, etc.): *The children were full of excitement at the thought of their holiday* **10** [Wa1;B] (of a part of a garment) wide; flowing; fitting loosely: *This coat doesn't fit you well; it's too full in front.|This dress has a full skirt* **11** [Wa1;B] (of a shape, a body, or its parts) **a** *often apprec* round; rounded; fleshy: *Her face was full when she was younger; now it's much thinner.|a woman with full round breasts|The moon's full tonight* **b** *euph* fat: *This shop sells dresses for the fuller figure* **12** [Wa1;A] *apprec* (of colour, smell, sound, taste, or substance) deep, rich, and powerful: *He likes wine with a full body* (=having strength or substance).|*This fruit hasn't got a really full* FLAVOUR*; it needs more sun on it* **13** [Wa1;F+*of*] *lit* having had one's share and more: *He died in 1900, full of years and honours* (=after a long life in which he was given great honours) —see also **full of** BEANS[1] (6), **(at) full** PELT[3], **full** STEAM[1] (6) **ahead, in full** SWING[2] (8) **(at) full** TILT[2] (5)

full[2] *adv* [H] **1** straight; directly: *The ball struck him full on the chest.|The sun shone full on her face* **2** very; quite (in the phr. **full well**): *They knew full well that he wouldn't keep his promise* **3** *poet or old use* very: *Full often have we sat watching the sun set behind the hill* **4 full out** at full power; at top speed: *He was riding his motorcycle full out*

full[3] *n* **1** [R] the greatest height, degree, point, etc.: *The* TIDE*'s at the full* (=at its highest level).|*The moon's at the full* (=has its largest appearance).|*The moon's past its full* **2 in full** completely: *The debt must be paid in full* **3 to the full** to the greatest degree; very greatly: *We enjoyed our holiday to the full*

full·back /ˈfʊlbæk/ *n* (esp. in football) a defending player whose position is at the end of his own half of the field, or the farthest from the centre

full-blood·ed /ˌ· ˈ··◂/ *adj* [A] **1** [Wa5] of unmixed race: *He's a full-blooded Indian; his parents were pure Indians, and so were their parents* **2** forceful: *a full-blooded argument|a full-blooded style of writing|a full-blooded drinking song* (=very loud) **3** having all typical qualities to a great degree: *a full-blooded* SOCIALIST —**~ness** *n* [U]

full-blown /ˌ· ˈ·◂/ *adj* [Wa5] **1** *often lit* (of a flower) completely open: *a full-blown rose* **2** fully developed; possessing all the usual or necessary qualities: *We're afraid that the fighting on the border may develop into a full-blown war*

full board /ˌ· ˈ·/ *n* [U] (in lodgings, hotels, etc.) the providing of all meals

full-bod·ied /ˌ· ˈ··◂/ *adj apprec* strong; heavy and rich in taste: *This is a fine full-bodied red wine*

full cir·cle /ˌ· ˈ··/ *adv* through a set of developments that lead back to the starting point (esp. in the phr. **come full circle**): *It's January 1st; the year has come full circle*

full-dress /ˌ· ˈ·◂/ *adj* [Wa5;A] **1** formal and fully prepared: *a full-dress* DEBATE *in parliament|full-dress* BIOGRAPHY **2** being FULL DRESS: *Soldiers wear full-dress uniform on many ceremonial occasions*

full dress /ˌ· ˈ·/ *n* [U] special dress worn on ceremonial or formal occasions

ful·ler /ˈfʊləʳ/ *n* a person whose work is to clean and thicken newly made cloth

fuller's earth /ˌ·· ˈ·/ *n* [U] a type of dried clay sometimes made into a powder, used in former times for removing oil from cloth, but now used esp. in treating impure oils, to make them clearer and lighter

full-face /ˌ· ˈ·◂/ *adj, adv* [Wa5;B] showing the whole of the face: *Here's a full-face drawing of my sister.|This photograph was taken full-face* (=with the photographed person looking straight at the photographer)

full-fash·ioned /ˌ· ˈ··◂/ *adj* [Wa5] *AmE* FULLY-FASHIONED

full-fledged /ˌ· ˈ·◂/ *adj* [Wa5] *esp. AmE* FULLY-FLEDGED

full-grown /ˌ· ˈ·◂/ also (*esp. BrE*) **fully-grown**— *adj* [Wa5] (esp. of an animal, plant, or (*tech*) person) completely developed; that is not going to get any larger: *A full-grown elephant can weigh over 6,000 kilograms*

full-heart·ed /ˌ· ˈ··◂/ *adj* WHOLE-HEARTED

full house /ˌ· ˈ·/ *n* **1** (at a theatre, cinema, sports ground, etc.) as large an attendance of people as possible: *We've had 5 full houses this week; many people who wanted to see the film have been turned away* **2** (in the card game of POKER) 3 cards of one kind, and a pair of another kind

full-length /ˌ· ˈ·◂/ *adj* [Wa5] **1** (of a photograph, painting, etc.) showing a person from head to foot **2** (of a garment) reaching to the ground: *This evening dress has a full-length skirt* **3** (of a play, book, etc.) not short; not shorter than is usual: *He has written several one-act plays, but only one full-length play*

full moon /ˌ· ˈ·/ *n* **1** [*the*+R;S] the moon when seen as a circle: *A full moon shone brightly* **2** [U; (C)] the time of the month when it is seen like this: *There's a good deal of light in the sky at full moon*

full·ness, fulness /ˈfʊlnɪ̵s/ *n* [U] **1** *fml* completeness: *In the fullness of her joy, she could hardly speak* **2** the condition of being full: *She complained to the doctor that she had a feeling of fullness after eating* **3 in the fullness of time** *esp. lit or fml* when the right time comes/came: *You may have to suffer hardships now, but in the fullness of time you will have your reward*

full-page /ˌ· ˈ·◂/ *adj* [Wa5;A] covering the whole of a page, esp. in a newspaper: *It costs a lot of money to put a full-page notice in a newspaper*

full-scale /ˌ· ˈ·◂/ *adj* [Wa5] **1** [B] (of a model, drawing, copy, etc.) of the same size as the object represented: *He made a full-scale model of an elephant, but he couldn't get it out of the room* **2** [A] large; making use of all known facts, information, etc.: *He's writing a full-scale history of 19th century France* **3** [A] (of an activity) of not less than the usual kind; not shortened, lessened, etc., in any way; total: *The quarrel between the 2 countries nearly developed into a full-scale war* **4** [A] using all one's powers, forces, etc.: *a full-scale attack on an enemy position*

full stop¹ /ˌ· ˈ·/ also (*esp. AmE*) **period, point**— *n* **1** a point (.) marking the end of a sentence or a shortened form of a word **2 come to a full stop** to stop completely

full stop² *adv esp. BrE* PERIOD³

full-throat·ed /ˌ· ˈ··◂/ *adj* using the voice freely; loud: *The lion gave a full-throated* ROAR

full-time /ˌ· ˈ·◂/ *adj, adv* [Wa5] **1** working or giving regularly the proper number of hours or days in an employment, course of study, etc.: *She's a full-time student at the university.|full-time employment|He used to work full-time, but now he only works 4 days a week* —compare PART-TIME **2 a full-time job** *infml* an activity or duty that leaves one no free time: *It's a full-time job looking after 3 young children*

full time /ˌ· ˈ·/ *n* [R] (in certain types of sport, esp. football) the end of the fixed period of time during which a match is played: *At full time the 2 teams had gained an equal number of points, so they had to play another half hour to decide the match*

full toss /ˌ· ˈ·/ also **full pitch**— *n tech* (esp. in cricket) a throw in which the ball has not hit the ground (BOUNCEd) when it arrives at the place it was aimed at —**full toss** *adv*

ful·ly /ˈfʊli/ *adv* **1** [Wa5] quite; at least: *It's fully an hour since he left* **2** completely; altogether; thoroughly: *I don't fully understand his reasons for leaving.|Is she fully satisfied with the present arrangement?|a fully trained nurse*

fully-fash·ioned /ˌ·· ˈ··◂/ also (*AmE*) **full-fashioned**— *adj* [Wa5] *BrE* (of a KNITted garment) made to fit the shape of the body exactly: *fully-fashioned stockings*

fully-fledged /ˌ·· ˈ·◂/ also (*esp. AmE*) **full-fledged**— *adj* [Wa5] *esp. BrE* **1** (of a young bird) having grown all the feathers, and now able to fly **2** completely trained: *After his long time at sea in a sailing ship, he feels like a fully-fledged sailor*

fully-grown /ˌ·· ˈ·◂/ *adj* [Wa5] *esp. BrE* FULL-GROWN

ful·mar /ˈfʊlməʳ, -mɑːʳ/ *n* a type of seabird, usu. grey on the back and white below, that lives near the coasts of cold northern countries of the world

ful·mi·nate /ˈfʊlmɪ̵neɪt, ˈfʌl-/ *v* [I∅ (*against, at*)] to declare one's opposition very strongly and angrily: *My grandfather used to fulminate against the ways of the youth of his day*

ful·mi·na·tion /ˌfʊlmɪ̵ˈneɪʃən, ˌfʌl-/ *n* **1** [U] the action of fulminating (FULMINATE) **2** [C] an expression of angry opposition; fierce attack in words

ful·ness /ˈfʊlnɪ̵s/ *n* [U] FULLNESS

ful·some /ˈfʊlsəm/ *adj* giving an unnecessarily and unpleasantly large amount of praise: *I don't like such fulsome expressions of admiration.|He was too fulsome in his praise* —**~ly** *adv* —**~ness** *n* [U]

fum·ble /ˈfʌmbəl/ *v* **1** [I∅ (ABOUT, AROUND)] to move the fingers or hands awkwardly in search of something, or in an attempt to do something: *She fumbled about in her handbag for a pen.*|(fig.) *He's not a very good speaker; he often has to fumble for the right word* **2** [T1;I∅] to handle (something) without neatness or skill; mishandle: *The cricketer fumbled, and the ball dropped from his hand; he'd fumbled the catch* —**-bler** /bləʳ/ *n*

fume¹ /fjuːm/ *n* [S] *rare* an unreasonable, restless, and often useless show of anger: *She was in a fume of impatience because she had to wait for the others*

fume² *v* **1** [I∅] to show signs of great anger and restlessness (often in the phr. **fume and fret**): *She was fuming with annoyance because the books hadn't arrived.|He fumed at the delay.|"Was he angry?" "Yes, he was really fuming"* **2** [I∅] to give off FUMES; smoke: *The burnt heaps of wood were still fuming* **3** [Wv5;T1] to treat or darken (esp. wood) with chemical FUMES: *a fumed* OAK *table*

fumes /fjuːmz/ *n* [P] heavy strong-smelling air given off from smoke, gas, fresh paint, etc., that causes a pricking sensation when breathed in: *Painters sometimes suffer in health from breathing in fumes at their work.|The air in the railway carriage was thick with tobacco fumes.|Petrol fumes from car engines poison the air*

fu·mi·gate /ˈfjuːmɪ̵geɪt/ *v* [T1] to clear of disease bacteria or harmful insects by means of chemical smoke or gas: *The man was found to have an infectious disease, so all his clothes, his bed, and his room had to be fumigated* —**-gation** /ˌfjuːmɪ̵ˈgeɪʃən/ *n* [U]

fun /fʌn/ *n not fml* **1** [U] playfulness: *The little dog's full of fun* **2** [U] amusement; enjoyment; pleasure: *Children get a great deal of fun out of dressing in other people's clothes.|You're sure to have some fun at the party tonight.|There's no fun in spending the evening doing nothing.|Have fun* (=enjoy yourself)!|*What fun* (=how enjoyable)! **3** [U] a cause of enjoyment or pleasure: *Tom's good fun; we all enjoy being with him.|Swimming in the sea is great fun on holiday.|The play at the theatre was very poor fun; we hardly laughed at all* **4** [U] amusement caused by laughing at someone else: *No one takes him seriously any more; he's become just a figure of fun* **5** [A] *apprec, esp. AmE* providing pleasure, amusement, or enjoyment: *a fun party|a fun person* **6 for fun** also **for the fun of it, for the fun of the thing**— for pleasure; without serious purpose: *He's learning*

French for fun **7 fun and games** playful tricks; high-spirited behaviour of a group **8 in fun** in playfulness; without serious or harmful intention: *I'm sorry I hid your book; I only did it in fun, I didn't mean to cause trouble. It was all in fun* **9 make fun of/poke fun at** to laugh or cause others to laugh rather unkindly at: *People poke fun at her because she wears such strange hats*

func·tion¹ /ˈfʌnkʃən/ *n* **1** a special duty (of a person) or purpose (of a thing): *The function of a chairman is to lead and control meetings.|The brain performs a very important function; it controls the nervous system of the body.|The function of an adjective is to describe or add to the meaning of a noun* **2 a** a public ceremony: *The minister has to attend all kinds of official functions, such as welcoming foreign guests of the government, and opening new schools and hospitals* **b** *infml* a large or important gathering of people for pleasure or on some special occasion: *"You look as if you're dressed for some function or other." "Yes, I'm going to a friend's wedding"* **3 a** *tech* (in MATHEMATICS) a value which varies as another value varies: *In x=5y, x is a function of y* **b** a quality or fact which depends on and varies with another: *The size of the crop is a function of the quality of the soil and the amount of rainfall*

function² *v* [IØ] (esp. of a thing) to be in action; work: *The machine won't function properly if you don't oil it well*

func·tion·al /ˈfʌŋkʃənəl/ *adj* **1** made for or concerned with practical use without ornamentation: *Some people don't like the look of functional modern chairs, made on functional principles, even though they're comfortable* **2** [Wa5] made for or having a special purpose: *The workman's been taught to use that one particular machine; such functional training doesn't fit him for any other kind of work* **3** [Wa5] *med* (of a disease or disorder) having an effect only on the working of an organ, not on the organ itself —compare ORGANIC (1) —**~ly** *adv*

func·tion·al·is·m /ˈfʌŋkʃənəlɪzəm/ *n* [R] the idea and practice of making buildings and other objects for use and convenience without considering beauty or appearance, based on the belief that if an object is made to carry out its particular purpose it cannot help being beautiful

func·tion·al·ist /ˈfʌŋkʃənəlɪst/ *n, adj* (a supporter) of FUNCTIONALISM

func·tion·a·ry /ˈfʌŋkʃənəri‖-neri/ *n usu. derog* a person who has unimportant or unnecessary official duties

function as *v prep* [L1] to fulfil the duty or purpose of: *When her mother was ill, the girl had to function as both cook and nurse*

fund¹ /fʌnd/ *n* **1** [C+*of, usu. sing.*] a store or supply (of non-material things) ready for use as needed: *When explaining a new point to a class, it helps a teacher to have a fund of good examples to make his meaning clear* **2** [C] a supply or sum of money set apart for a special purpose: *Part of the school sports fund will be used to improve the condition of the football field*

fund² *v* [T1] *esp. tech* **1** to provide money for (an activity, organization, etc.): *The university scientists' search for a cure for this disease is being funded by the government* **2** to make (a debt) into a lasting debt on which a fixed yearly interest will be paid

fun·da·men·tal¹ /ˌfʌndəˈmentl/ *adj* **1** [B] (of a non-material thing) deep; being at the base, from which all else develops: *There's a fundamental difference between the 2 ministers and their aims* **2** [Wa5;A] (of a non-material thing) of the greatest importance; having a greater effect than all others: *The fundamental cause of his success was his ability to work for long hours without tiring* **3** [Wa5; F+*to*] (of a non-material thing) very necessary: *Fresh air is fundamental to good health* **4** [Wa5;A] (of a quality) belonging to a person's or thing's deep true character: *He has some rather strange ideas sometimes, but no one can doubt his fundamental good sense*

fundamental² *n* [(*of*), *often pl.*] a rule, law, etc., on which a system is based; necessary or important part: *A fundamental of good behaviour is consideration for other people.|If the boys are going to camp for 10 days, they'll need to know the fundamentals of cooking*

fun·da·men·tal·is·m /ˌfʌndəˈmentəlɪzəm/ *n* [R] the belief in and support of the older teachings of the Christian Church, esp. concerning the exact truth of the words of the Bible, as opposed to more modern Christian thought which has been influenced by scientific knowledge —**-ist** *n, adj*

fun·da·men·tal·ly /ˌfʌndəˈmentəli/ *adv* in every way that matters, is important, or is related to the true deep character of someone or something: *Although a few of your facts aren't right, your answer is fundamentally correct.|She is fundamentally unsuited to office work*

funds /fʌndz/ *n* [P] money in one's possession, ready for use: *The company's losses are being repaid out of government funds.| By the end of the week I usually get a bit short of funds* (=without much money).|*My funds are a bit low at present*

fu·ne·ral /ˈfjuːnərəl/ *n* **1** [C] a ceremony, usu. religious, of burying or burning a dead person: *Many friends attended the old lady's funeral* **2** [A] of or connected with the last ceremonies after death: *Funeral customs vary with different religions.| a funeral service* **3** [C *usu. sing.*] a procession taking a dead person to be buried or burned: *The funeral made its way slowly through the silent streets* **4** [S9] *infml* a difficulty or unpleasantness that concerns or will concern someone alone (in the phr. **it/that is your (his, their,** *etc.***) (own) funeral**): *If you choose to do it, it's your funeral; don't expect me to help you if you're caught*

funeral di·rec·tor /ˈ··· ·ˌ··/ *n fml* a person whose business is to arrange for dead people to be buried or burned; UNDERTAKER

funeral par·lour, *AmE* **-lor** /ˈ··· ˌ··/ also (*AmE*) **funeral home** /ˈ··· ·/— *n esp. AmE* a FUNERAL DIRECTOR's place of business

funeral pile /ˈ··· ·/ also **pile**— *n* a heap of wood on which a dead body is placed to be burned; PYRE

fu·ne·ra·ry /ˈfjuːnərəri‖-nəreri/ *adj* [Wa5;A] *tech* suited or used for a funeral: *The ashes of a dead person who has been ceremonially burned are sometimes put away in a large pot called a* **funerary urn**

fu·ne·re·al /fjʊˈnɪərɪəl/ *adj* heavy and sad; suitable to a funeral: *Nobody spoke for half an hour; we all sat in funereal silence.|They went along at a funereal rate* (=very slowly) —**~ly** *adv*

fun·fair /ˈfʌnfeəʳ/ *n esp. BrE* **1** a noisy brightly lit show which for small charges offers big machines to ride on, games of skill, and other amusements, esp. one that moves from town to town **2** also **amusement park**— a piece of ground out of doors where this kind of show is held

fun·gi·cide /ˈfʌndʒɪsaɪd/ *n* [C;U] a chemical substance used for preventing or destroying FUNGUS

fun·goid /ˈfʌŋgɔɪd/ *adj* [Wa5] like a FUNGUS; of the nature of a FUNGUS: *fungoid growths on young plants*

fun·gous /ˈfʌŋgəs/ *adj* [Wa5] *tech* **1** of, like, or related to FUNGUS **2** caused by a FUNGUS: *fungous plant diseases*

fun·gus /ˈfʌŋgəs/ *n* **-gi** /dʒaɪ, gaɪ/ *or* **-guses** **1** [C] any of several types of simple fast-spreading plant

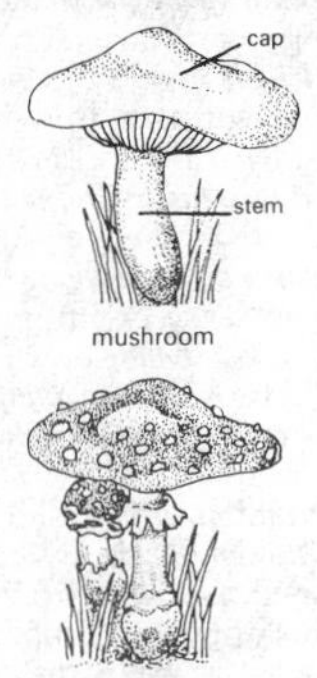

fungi

without flowers, leaves, or green colouring matter, which may be in a large form, with a fleshy stem supporting a broad rounded top (MUSHROOMs, TOADSTOOLs, etc.), or in a very small form, with a powderlike appearance (MILDEW, MOULD, etc.) **2** [U] **a** these plants in general, esp. considered as a disease: *roses suffering from fungus|Fungus can cause wooden boards to decay* **b** these plants in a large group: *The floor of the forest was covered with fungus* **3** [S;U] *derog* a disagreeable thing of sudden growth or appearance: *On the hillside a fungus of ugly little houses had sprung up and spoilt the pleasant view* **4** [C;U] *humor* FACE FUNGUS

fu·nic·u·lar /fjʊˈnɪkjʊləʳ‖-kjə-/ also **funicular rail·way** /·ˌ··· ˈ··/— *n* [C; *by*+U] a small railway up a slope or a mountain, worked by a thick metal rope, often with one carriage going up as another comes down: *to reach the top by funicular*

funk[1] /fʌŋk/ *n* **1** [S] *infml* a state of great fear; inability to face a difficulty or an unpleasant duty **2** [C] *derog, becoming rare* a coward

funk[2] *v derog* **1** [T1,4] to (try to) avoid (something or doing something) because of fear or lack of will: *We all funked telling her the truth* **2** [I∅] *becoming rare* to be afraid; show fear

funk·y /ˈfʌŋki/ *adj* [Wa1] *apprec, esp. AmE* **1** (of JAZZ or like music) having a simple coarse style and feeling, like the BLUES **2** *sl* fine; good: *a funky party*

fun·nel[1] /ˈfʌnəl/ *n* **1** a metal chimney for letting out smoke from a steam engine or steamship —see picture at FREIGHTER **2** a tubelike vessel that is large and round at the top and small at the bottom, used in pouring liquids or powders through a small hole into a vessel with a narrow neck: *He used a funnel to fill the bottle with oil* —see picture at LABORATORY

funnel[2] *v* **-ll-** (*AmE* **-l-**) **1** [X9] to pass through or as if through a FUNNEL[1] (2): *He funnelled the oil into the bottle* **2** [L9] (esp. of something large or made up of many parts) to pass through a narrow space: *The large crowd funnelled out of the gates after the football match* **3** [T1] to form into the shape of a FUNNEL[1] (2): *He funnelled his hands and whistled through them*

fun·nies /ˈfʌniz/ *n* [*the*+P] *infml, esp. AmE* the amusement pages in a newspaper, which contain jokes and funny stories told in pictures

fun·ni·ly /ˈfʌnə̩li/ *adv not fml* **1 a** in a strange or unusual way: *She's been acting rather funnily just recently* **b** in an amusing way **2 funnily enough** strange to say: *He was captain of the national cricket team, but funnily enough he was never made captain of his club team*

fun·ny /fʌni/ *adj* **1** [Wa1;B] *not fml* amusing; causing laughter: *I heard such a funny story this morning.|He's a very funny man* (=can make people laugh with amusing stories).|*I don't think that's at all funny* (=is a fit cause for laughter).|*It was the funniest thing out* (=the most amusing I've ever heard) **2** [Wa1;B] *not fml* strange; unexpected; hard to explain; unusual: *What can that funny noise be?|It's a funny thing, but she put the book on the table 5 minutes ago, and now it can't be found.|He's a funny sort of person; I don't understand him at all* **3** [Wa1;B] *infml* out of order; not quite correct; rather dishonest: *There's something funny about the telephone; it won't work this morning.|There's something funny about this affair; no one seems to know what's happened to all the money* **4** [Wa5;F] *infml* **a** slightly ill: *She always feels a bit funny if she looks down from a height* **b** *euph* slightly mad: *He went rather funny after the death of his only son* **5** [Wa1; A] *infml* (used esp. by or to children) pleasantly amusing; nice (esp. in the phr. **funny old**): *Look at that funny old dog!* **6** [Wa5;B] *infml* deceiving; using tricks; too clever: *"Don't try anything funny while my back's turned, or you'll be in trouble" he said to his prisoner.|Don't get funny with me* —**-niness** *n* [U]

funny bone /ˈ·· ·/ *n* [R;(C)] *infml* the tender part of the elbow, which hurts very much if it is knocked sharply

funny busi·ness /ˈ·· ˌ··/ *n* [U] *infml* **1** dishonest dealing **2** silly behaviour; FOOLing about

funny farm /ˈ·· ·/ *n humor, esp. AmE* a MENTAL HOSPITAL

funny ha·ha /ˌ·· ·ˈ·/ *adj* [Wa5;F] *infml* amusing; FUNNY (1) (used when comparing with FUNNY (2)) —compare FUNNY PECULIAR

funny pe·cu·li·ar /ˌ·· ·ˈ···/ *adj* [Wa5;F] *infml* strange; FUNNY (2) (used when comparing with FUNNY (1)): *"It's a funny book." "Do you mean* FUNNY HAHA *or funny peculiar?"* —compare FUNNY HAHA

fur[1] /fɜːʳ/ *v* **-rr-** [Wv5;T1;I∅] to (cause to) become covered with FUR[2] (4,5): *a furred tongue*

fur[2] *n* **1** [U] the soft thick fine hair that covers the body of some types of animal, such as bears, rabbits, cats, etc. **2** [C] a hair-covered skin of certain special types of animal, such as foxes, rabbits, MINK, BEAVERs, etc., which has been or will be treated and used for clothing: *The Canadian fur trader had a fine load of furs to sell after his hunting trip* **3** [C;A] (a garment) made of one or more of these: *She was wearing a silver fox fur across her shoulders.|a fur coat* **4** [U] a greyish covering on the tongue **5** a hard covering on the inside of pots, hot-water pipes, etc., caused by lime in heated water —see also SCALE[3] (2) **6 fur and feather** *esp. lit or fml* hair-covered animals, and birds **7 make the fur fly** to cause a quarrel: *When the woman made an unpleasant remark about another woman's child, it really made the fur fly*

fur·be·low /ˈfɜːbə̩ləʊ‖ˈfɜr-/ *n* [*usu. pl.*] *derog* a showy unnecessary ornamental part of a woman's dress (esp. in the phr. **frills and furbelows**)

fur·bish /ˈfɜːbɪʃ‖ˈfɜr-/ *v* [T1 (UP)] **1** to make (something of metal that has not been used for a long time) bright and shining: *She was furbishing an old silver ornament that she'd bought cheap* **2** to improve the appearance of (something old and worn): *We're furbishing up our house with a fresh coat of paint* **3** to put (something out of use) back into working condition: *You'll have to furbish up your French if you're going to spend the summer in France* —see also REFURBISH

fu·ri·ous /ˈfjʊəriəs/ *adj* **1** [(A);F,F3] very angry in an uncontrolled way: *He'll be furious with us if we're late.|He'll be furious at being kept waiting.|It makes* *me furious when people don't listen, and then ask silly questions.|The general was furious to hear* (=when he heard) *of the defeat* —see ANGRY (USAGE) **2** [A;(F)] powerful: *He struck his enemy a furious blow.|There was a furious knocking at the door* **3** [A;(F)] wild; uncontrolled: *He has a furious temper.|She drove the car at a fast and furious rate* —**~ness** *n* [U]

fu·ri·ous·ly /ˈfjʊərɪəsli/ *adv* **1** in a FURIOUS manner: *to shout furiously|furiously angry* **2 give someone furiously to think** to force someone to think hard and quickly: *The unexpected news gave him furiously to think*

furl /fɜːl‖fɜrl/ *v* **1** [T1] to roll or fold up and bind (a sail, flag, FAN, UMBRELLA, etc.) **2** [I∅] to be able to be rolled or folded up: *This* UMBRELLA *doesn't furl properly*

fur·long /ˈfɜːlɒŋ‖ˈfɜrlɔŋ/ *n* (a measure of length equal to) 220 yards or 201 metres —see WEIGHTS & MEASURES TABLE

fur·lough /ˈfɜːləʊ‖ˈfɜr-/ *n* [C;U] absence from duty, usu. for a length of time, esp. as permitted to government officers, soldiers, and others serving outside their own country; holiday: *9 months' furlough|He's home on furlough* —see HOLIDAY (USAGE)

fur·nace /ˈfɜːn$_{\text{ɪ}}^{\text{ə}}$s‖ˈfɜr-/ *n* **1** an apparatus in a factory, in which metals and other substances are heated to very high temperatures in an enclosed space **2** a large enclosed fire used for producing hot water or steam: *This room's like a furnace* (=it's much too hot)

fur·nish /ˈfɜːnɪʃ‖ˈfɜr-/ *v* [T1] **1** [Wv5] to put furniture in (a (part of a) building); supply with furniture: *The new hotel's finished, but it's not yet furnished.|They're renting a furnished house* (=one with furniture already in it) **2** *fml* to supply (what is necessary for a special purpose): *This shop furnishes everything that is needed for camping.|No one in the class could furnish the right answer to the question*

fur·nish·ings /ˈfɜːnɪʃɪŋz‖ˈfɜr-/ *n* [P] articles of furniture or other articles fixed in a room, such as a bath, curtains, etc.

furnish with *v prep* [D1] *fml* to supply (someone or something) with (something necessary): *He furnished himself with a pencil and paper, and began to draw*

fur·ni·ture /ˈfɜːnɪtʃəʳ‖ˈfɜr-/ *n* [U] all large or quite large movable articles that are placed in a house, room, or other area, in order to make it convenient, comfortable, and/or pleasant as a space for living in, such as beds, chairs, tables, etc.: *This old French table is a very valuable piece of furniture.|garden furniture*

fu·ro·re /fjʊˈrɔːri, ˈfjʊərɔːʳ‖ˈfjʊəror/ also (*AmE*) **fu·ror** /ˈfjʊərɔːʳ‖-ror/— *n* [S] *esp. BrE* a sudden burst of angry or excited interest among a large group of people

fur·ri·er /ˈfʌrɪəʳ‖ˈfɜr-/ *n* a person who prepares furs for use as clothing, makes fur garments, and/or sells them

fur·row[1] /ˈfʌrəʊ‖ˈfɜr-/ *n* **1** a long narrow track cut by a PLOUGH in farming land when the earth is being turned over in preparation for planting **2** any long deep cut or narrow hollow between raised edges, esp. in the earth: *The country roads were muddy and full of furrows left by farm carts* **3** a deep line or fold in the skin of the face, esp. the forehead

furrow[2] *v* [Wv5;T1] to make FURROWs in: *She looked at the examination paper with a furrowed* BROW (=a forehead with lines in it).|*The car furrowed the loose sand as it crossed the desert*

fur·ry /ˈfɜːri/ *adj* [Wa1] of, like, or covered with fur: *This furry material will make a warm coat for the winter.|a furry little rabbit*

fur seal /ˌ· ˈ·/ *n* [Wn1] any of several types of SEAL that are covered with a soft thick fur often used for making clothes or ornaments

fur·ther[1] /ˈfɜːðəʳ‖ˈfɜr-/ *adv* [Wa5] (*compar. of* FAR) **1** more; to a greater degree: *Don't try my patience any further.|We'll enquire further into this question tomorrow.|"There is nothing further we can do"* (SEU W.) **2** [(*than*)] elsewhere: *You'll have to look further than the village if you want to buy a really good radio set* **3** [H] at or to a greater distance or more distant point; FARTHER: *He's too tired to walk any further.|They live a little further along the road.|He can swim further than I can.|London is further from Glasgow than it is from Cardiff.|"much further off than is reasonable"* (SEU S.)|*to go further and further south|further back than 1960* **4** FURTHERMORE: *The house isn't big enough for us, and further, it's too far from the town* **5 go further** to give, do, or say more: *I'll give you £15 for it, but I can't afford to go any further.|We'll go further into this question tomorrow* (=make more enquiries).|*He was a very fine man; indeed I'll go (even) further, he was the most courageous man I ever knew* **6 see someone further (first)** *infml* (used when angrily refusing someone's request) will not do so: *"Bob wants you to lend him 200 pounds." "I'll see him further first"* **7 wish someone further** *infml* to wish that someone would go away, stop being troublesome, etc.: *She talked without stopping for half an hour, and I began to wish her further* —see FARTHER (USAGE)

further[2] *adj* [Wa5;A] (*compar. of* FAR) **1** later than the one spoken of: *There'll be a further performance of the play next week.|The office will be closed until further notice* (=until it is convenient to open it again) **2** more; additional: *Have you any further questions to ask?|If you have no further use for this book, I'll give it to someone else.|There being no further business, the meeting was closed.|"The money would have had to be raised by further taxation"* (SEU S.)|*It will take a further 3 days* **3** more distant; FAR[2] (2): *On the further side of the street there was a large shop* —see FARTHER (USAGE)

further[3] *v* [T1] to help (something); advance; help to succeed; give every possible advantage to: *The government wishes to further the cause of peace.|We'll do all we can to further your plans*

fur·ther·ance /ˈfɜːðərəns‖ˈfɜr-/ *n* [U (*of*)] *fml* helping forward; development; continuation: *He's gone to the university for the furtherance of his studies.|In furtherance of their aim of improving the school, the Governors are building a new set of science classrooms*

further ed·u·ca·tion /ˌ·· ··ˈ··/ also (*esp. AmE*) **adult education**— *n* [U] *BrE* education after leaving school, but not at a university —compare HIGHER EDUCATION

fur·ther·more /ˌfɜːðəˈmɔːʳ‖ˈfɜrðərmor/ *adv* (used for introducing additional matter into an argument) also; in addition; besides: *The house isn't big enough for us, and furthermore, it's too far from the town*

fur·ther·most /ˈfɜːðəməʊst‖ˈfɜrðər-/ *adj* [Wa5;A (*from*);F+*from*] most distant; farthest away: *In the furthermost corner of the room sat a tall thin man; he sat in the corner furthermost from the fire*

further to /ˈ·· ·/ *prep fml* (used esp. in business letters) in order to give additional information on the same subject as: *Further to our letter of February 5th, we are writing to say that all arrangements for your journey next month are now complete*

fur·thest /ˈfɜːð$_{\text{ɪ}}^{\text{ə}}$st‖ˈfɜr-/ *adv, adj* [Wa5;B (*from*);H] (*superl. of* FAR) FARTHEST —see FARTHER (USAGE)

fur·tive /ˈfɜːtɪv‖ˈfɜr-/ *adj* quiet, secret, and/or not direct, as expressing guilty feelings; trying or hoping to escape notice: *The man's furtive manner made the policeman watch him to see what he would do.|The thief was furtive in his movements* —**~ly** *adv* —**~ness** *n* [U]

fu·ry /ˈfjʊəri/ *n* **1** [U] very great anger: *She couldn't speak for fury* **2** [C *usu. sing.*] a state of very great anger: *It's no use trying to argue with you when you fly into a fury* (=get very angry) *for the slightest reason.|He's in one of his furies today* (=this is a thing that often happens) **3** [S9 (*of*)] a wildly excited state (of feeling): *She was in a fury of impatience to start the journey* **4** [U (*of*)] wild force or activity: *At last the fury of the storm lessened.|In the fury of battle the soldier didn't notice that he was slightly wounded* **5** [C] *infml* a fierce angry woman or girl: *Jane's a little fury if she can't get what she wants at once* **6 like fury** *infml* with great force or effort; madly: *They worked like fury to try to save some of the valuable books from the burning house*

Fury *n* [*often pl.*] one of 3 snake-haired goddesses in ancient Greek beliefs, who punished crimes: (fig.) *When the cook saw the boys stealing her newly baked cakes, she rushed on them like an avenging* (AVENGE) *Fury*

furze /fɜːz‖fɜrz/ *n* [U] GORSE

fuse¹ /fjuːz/ *n* **1** a long string treated with an explosive powder, or a narrow pipe filled with this powder, used for carrying fire to an explosive article and so causing it to blow up: *He lit the fuse and ran behind the rock before the bomb could explode* **2** an apparatus screwed into a bomb, SHELL, or other weapon, which causes it to explode when touched, thrown, etc. —see also TIME FUSE

fuse² *n* **1** [C] a (small container with a) short thin piece of wire, placed in an electric apparatus or in an electric system, which melts if too much electric power passes through it, and thus breaks the connection and prevents fires or other damage: *A fuse has blown* (=been destroyed by melting), *causing the lights to fail* —see picture at ELECTRICITY **2** [S] *infml* a failure of electric power, owing to the melting of one of these: *The lights at the end of the house have gone out. Has there been a fuse somewhere?*

fuse³ *v* **1** [T1;I∅] to (cause (metal) to) melt in great heat: *Lead will fuse at a lower temperature than some other metals* **2** [T1;I∅:(TOGETHER)] to join or become joined by melting: *Copper and* ZINC *are fused to make brass.|The aircraft came down in flames, and the heat fused most of the parts together into a solid mass* **3** [T1;I∅] to (cause to) stop working owing to a FUSE² (2): *If you connect all these apparatuses to the electricity supply at one place, you'll fuse all the lights.|The lights have fused; the whole place is in darkness* **4** [T1 (TOGETHER)] to unite; make into one

fused /fjuːzd/ *adj* [Wa5] (of a piece of electric apparatus) fitted with a FUSE² (1)

fu·se·lage /ˈfjuːzəlɑːʒ‖-səlɑʒ/ *n* the main body of an aircraft, in which travellers and goods are carried —see picture at AIRCRAFT

fuse wire /ˈ· ·/ *n* [U] special thin easily-melted wire used for making FUSEs² (1)

fu·si·lier /ˌfjuːzəˈlɪəʳ/ *n* a soldier belonging to any of several British army groups (REGIMENTs) who in former times were armed with a special type of light gun, but who now carry modern RIFLEs

fu·sil·lade /ˌfjuːzə̇ˈleɪd‖-sə̇-/ *n* a rapid continuous firing of shots: *As the soldiers marched forward, they were met by a fusillade from the fort*

fu·sion /ˈfjuːʒən/ *n* [U;C:(*of*)] **1** (a) melting or joining together by melting: *This metal is formed by the fusion of 2 other types of metal* **2** (a) uniting or mixing: *There's a great deal of variety among the people of that nation; they're the result of the fusion of several races*

fusion bomb /ˈ·· ·/ *n* HYDROGEN BOMB

fuss¹ /fʌs/ *n not fml* **1** [S;U] unnecessary, useless, or unwelcome expression of excitement, anger, impatience, etc.: *What a fuss about nothing!|Don't make so much fuss over losing a penny* **2** [S] an anxious nervous condition: *The old lady soon gets into a fuss* **3** [S] a show of annoyance probably resulting in punishment: *There's sure to be a fuss when they find the window's broken* **4** [U] unwanted or unnecessary activity; hurry: *"What's all this fuss about?" "It's because we suddenly find we must go out in half an hour"* **5 kick up a fuss** to cause trouble, esp. by complaining loudly or angrily **6 make a fuss of** to pay a lot of attention to, in order to please or to show liking for: *Aunt Mary always makes a great fuss of her sister's daughter*

fuss² *v* **1** [I∅ (ABOUT)] to act or behave in a nervous, restless, and anxious way over small matters: *Don't fuss; we're sure to catch our train* **2** [T1] to make nervous: *If you fuss him while he's adding up all those figures, he'll make a lot of mistakes* **3 not be fussed (about something)** *infml BrE* not to care greatly (about something): *"Would you like tea or coffee?" "I'm not fussed* (=I would like either)"

fuss a·bout *v prep* [T1] *usu. derog.* to be too anxious about (something): *She fusses too much about her health; she's always trying some new medicine*

fuss o·ver *v prep* [T1] to pay too much attention to (someone or something): *The old lady fusses over her little dog as if it were a sick child*

fuss·pot /ˈfʌs-pɒt‖-pɑt/ also **fuss·bud·get** /ˈfʌs-ˌbʌdʒə̇t/— *n* [C;N] *infml* a very FUSSY (1,2) person: *I know how to look after myself. Stop worrying, you old fusspot!*

fuss up *v adv* [T1;I∅] *AmE* to make too much effort to dress with care or make (something) more attractive: *The director fussed up the stage with too many people*

fuss·y /ˈfʌsi/ *adj* **1** [Wa1;B] *usu. derog* (of a person or a person's actions, character, etc.) nervous and excitable about small matters: *It's not restful to be in the company of a fussy person.|small fussy movements of her hands* **2** [Wa1;B] *usu. derog* (of a person) too much concerned about details: *He's fussy about the way his food's cooked; if it isn't cooked properly, he won't eat it* **3** [Wa5;F (*about*), F6a: *nonassertive*] *infml* (of a person) concerned; caring: *"Would you like tea or coffee?" "I'm not fussy* (=I would like either)."*|Are you fussy what time we have dinner?* **4** [Wa1;B] *derog* (of dress, furniture, etc.) having too much ornament —**fussily** *adv* —**fussiness** *n* [U]

fus·ti·an /ˈfʌstɪən‖-tʃən/ *n* [U;A] *becoming rare* **1** (made from) a type of rough heavy cotton material **2** *derog* (consisting of) empty high-sounding words

fus·ty /ˈfʌsti/ *adj* [Wa1] *derog* **1** (of a room, box, clothes, etc.) having an unpleasant smell as a result of having been shut up for a long time, esp. when not quite dry **2** not modern: *His knowledge of science is a bit fusty, as he hasn't studied it at all since he left school 30 years ago* —**-tiness** *n* [U]

fu·tile /ˈfjuːtaɪl‖-tl/ *adj* **1** *often derog* (of an action) having no effect; unsuccessful; useless: *All his attempts to unlock the door were futile, because he was using the wrong key.|Don't waste time by asking futile questions* **2** *derog* (of a person) worthless; of no importance; lacking ability to succeed: *That futile young man does nothing but waste money*

fu·til·i·ty /fjuːˈtɪlə̇ti/ *n* **1** [U] uselessness: *You don't seem to understand the futility of trying to prepare for* *such a difficult examination in only 6 months* **2** [C *often pl.*] *usu. derog* a useless action or thing: *Herbert's a very serious person and considers such things as parties, dances, and games to be complete futilities*

fu·ture /'fjuːtʃə^r/ *adj, n* [Wa5] **1** [*the*+R;A] (belonging to or happening in) the time after the present; time yet to come: *The future is always unknown to us.*|*You should save some money; it's wise to provide for the future.*|*In future years, we shall remember your visit with pleasure.*|*Keep this book for future use* (=to use at a later time).|*Many people believe in a future life* (=another form of life after death) **2** [C;A] (expected, planned, arranged, etc., for) the life in front of a person; that which will happen to someone or something: *I wish you a very happy future.*|*The future of this business company is uncertain, as it has very little money.*|*That young man has a bright future before him as a painter* (=will become successful and famous).|*my future wife* (=the woman whom I am going to marry)|*We're leaving this town; our future home will be in London* **3** [*the*+R;(C);A] (in grammar) (being) the tense of a verb that expresses what will happen at a later time: *The future (tense) of English verbs is formed with the help of "shall" and "will"* **4** [U] *infml* likelihood of success: *There's no future in trying to sell furs in a hot country* **5 in future** also (*becoming rare*) **for the future**— from now on: *In future, be more careful with your money* **6 in the future** in time yet to come: *Who can tell what will happen in the future?* **7 in the distant future** at a very much later time: *"Are you going to buy a house?" "Not now; perhaps in the distant future"* **8 in the near future** soon **9 in the not too distant future** not next week, but quite soon

fu·ture·less /'fjuːtʃələs‖-tʃər-/ *adj* having nothing to expect or hope for: *Some poor people never have a chance in life; they lead a futureless existence*

fu·tures /'fjuːtʃəz‖-ərz/ *n* [P] *tech* (agreements or contracts for) goods bought and sold in large quantities at the present price, but not produced or sent till a later time: *Cotton futures* (=cotton crops not yet grown, those of the next season or later) *are selling at high prices*

fu·tur·is·m /'fjuːtʃərɪzəm/ *n* [R *often cap.*] a style of painting, music, and literature early in the 20th century, which was quite unlike that known and accepted before, and claimed to express the violent active quality of life in this modern age of machines —**-ist** *n*

fu·tur·is·tic /ˌfjuːtʃə'rɪstɪk/ *adj* **1** *infml, often derog* of strange modern appearance; having no connection with known forms of art: *futuristic paintings*|*a table of futuristic* DESIGN **2** [Wa5] influenced by or in the style of FUTURISM —**-tically** *adv* [Wa4]

fu·tu·ri·ty /fjʊ'tʃʊərə̍ti‖-'tʊ-, -'tʃʊ-/ *n* **1** [U] future time **2** [C *often pl. with sing. meaning*] what will happen or exist in the future

fuzz[1] /fʌz/ *n infml* **1** [U] a soft light substance such as rubs off a woollen article; FLUFF **2** [U;S] a mass or light fine growth of short hair that stands up: *The girl's hair stood out in a fuzz round her head*

fuzz[2] *n* [(*the*+) GU] *sl* police

fuzz·y /'fʌzi/ *adj* [Wa1] *infml* **1** (of hair) standing up in a light short mass **2** (of something seen) not clear in shape, esp. at the edges; misty: *The television picture is rather fuzzy tonight* **3** (of cloth, a garment, etc.) having a raised soft hairy surface **4** (of a substance) like a fine soft mass of hair —**fuzzily** *adv* —**fuzziness** *n* [U]

-fy /faɪ/ also **-ify** /ə̍faɪ/— *suffix* **1** [*n, adj*→*v*] to make or become: PURIFY (=make or become pure) **2** [*n*→*v*] to fill with: TERRIFY (=fill with terror) **3** [*n*→*v* [Wv5]] *infml, often humor or derog* **a** to make (the stated thing): SPEECHIFY (=make speeches, use fine words) **b** to cause to be like or typical of: DANDIFIED

G, g

G, g /dʒiː/ **G's, g's** *or* **Gs, gs** the 7th letter of the English alphabet

G[1] (in Western music) **a** the 5th note (*AmE* also **tone**) in the row of notes which form the musical SCALE of C MAJOR **b** the musical KEY based on this note

G[2] *abbrev. for:* **1** *tech* **a** GRAVITY **b** the amount of force caused by GRAVITY on an object that is lying on the earth, used as a measure: *The people in a space vehicle have to suffer the effects of several G when it leaves the ground* **2** *AmE sl* 1,000 dollars; GRAND[2] (2): *The thieves got away with 100 G from the local bank*

gab /gæb/ *n* [U] *infml* **1** (the power of) talking well continuously **2** (**have**) **the gift of the gab** (have) the ability to speak well continuously

gab·ar·dine, -erdine /'gæbədiːn, ˌgæbə'diːn‖'gæbərdiːn/ *n* **1** [U] a strong material often used for making coats: *This coat is gabardine* **2** [C] a garment made from this material, esp. the long coat (CLOAK) worn by Jews in the Middle Ages

gab·ble[1] /'gæbəl/ *v* [IØ (AWAY, ON); T1 (OUT)] to say (words) so quickly that they cannot be heard clearly

gabble[2] *n* [U; (*the*) S] words or word-like sounds spoken so quickly that they cannot be heard clearly

ga·ble /'geɪbəl/ *n* the 3-cornered upper end of a wall where it meets the roof —see picture at ROOF[1]

ga·bled /'geɪbəld/ *adj* [Wa5] having one or more GABLES

gad·a·bout /'gædəbaʊt/ *n infml* a person who goes out for amusement often, and/or to lots of places

gad a·bout also **gad a·round**— *v prep; adv* **-dd-** [IØ; T1 *no pass.*] *infml* to travel round (somewhere) to enjoy oneself: *She gads about (Europe) a lot*

gad·fly /'gædflaɪ/ *n* **1** a fly which bites cattle **2** a person who points out faults and annoys others in an effort to improve them or their work

gad·get /'gædʒə̍t/ *n infml* a small machine or useful apparatus

gad·get·ry /'gædʒə̍tri/ *n* [U] *infml & often derog* GADGETS generally: *Her kitchen is so full of gadgetry that you can hardly move*

Gae·lic /'geɪlɪk, 'gælɪk/ *adj* [Wa5] of one of the CELTIC languages, esp. that of Scotland, or those of Ireland and the Isle of Man

gaff[1] /gæf/ *n* **1** a stick with a hook at the end, used to pull big fish out of the water **2 blow the gaff** *BrE sl* to let a secret become known

gaff[2] *v* [T1] to pull (a fish) out of water with a GAFF[1] (1)

gaffe /gæf/ *n* a remark or act which means something unpleasant to other people, though the person who makes or does it does not think so at the time

gaf·fer /'gæfə^r/ *n* [C;N] **1** (a name for) an old man, esp. in the country **2** *BrE sl* BOSS[2] (1) **3** *BrE* *sl* the man in charge of a PUB; LANDLORD (2)

gag[1] /gæg/ *v* **-gg-** **1** [T1] to put a GAG[2] into the mouth of **2** [T1] to prevent from speaking or expressing something: *The newspapers have been gagged, so nobody knows what really happened* **3** [I∅ (*on*)] *esp. AmE* to be unable to swallow and start to VOMIT: *gagged on a piece of hard bread*

gag[2] *n* **1** something put over or into the mouth to keep it still or esp. to prevent the person from talking or shouting **2** *infml* a joke or funny story

ga·ga /ˈgɑːgɑː/ *adj* having or showing a weak mind, esp. in old age: *to go gaga*

gage[1] /geɪdʒ/ *n* **1** something valuable given to a person to keep until a debt has been repaid to him or a promise fulfilled **2** GAUNTLET

gage[2] *v* [T1] to give (something) as a GAGE[1] (1)

gage[3] *n, v AmE* GAUGE

gag·gle /ˈgægəl/ *n* **1** a number of geese (GOOSE) together **2** a group of noisy people, esp. women, who talk a lot: *a gaggle of girls*

gai·e·ty /ˈgeɪəti/ *n* **1** [U] also **gayness**— the state of being gay **2** [U;C *usu. pl.*] joyful events and activities, esp. at a time of public holiday

gai·ly /ˈgeɪli/ *adv* in a GAY (1,2) manner

gain[1] /geɪn/ *n* **1** [U] the act of making a profit; increase in wealth: *He put a lot of money into the firm with the hope of gain in the future* **2** [C] a profit; increase in amount: *The baby had a gain of half a pound (in weight) last week* **3 ill-gotten gains** profits obtained dishonestly

gain[2] *v* **1** [T1] to obtain (something useful, necessary, wanted, etc.): *I'm new in the job but I'm already gaining experience* **2** [T1;I∅] to make (a profit or increase in amount): *The car gained speed as it went down the hill* **3** [I∅] (of a watch or clock) to move too fast and show a time later than the correct time; become FAST[1] (5) **4** [T1] *fml* to reach (a place), esp. with effort or difficulty: *We cut a path through the forest and gained the river next day* **5 gain ground** to make improvements or PROGRESS
USAGE The opposite of GAIN[2] (1,2,3,5) is LOSE. —see WIN (USAGE)

gain·ful /ˈgeɪnfəl/ *adj* [Wa5] *fml* which gives money; for which one is paid: *gainful employment*

gain·ful·ly /ˈgeɪnfəli/ *adv* [Wa5] *fml* in a way that gives payment: *gainfully employed*

gain on also **gain up·on**— *v prep* [T1] to reduce the distance between oneself and (a competitor)

gain·say /ˌgeɪnˈseɪ/ *v* **-said** /ˈsed/ [T1 *nonassertive*] to say that something is not so; DENY (1): *There's no gainsaying his ability. Everyone knows he's very clever*

gait /geɪt/ *n* a way or manner of walking; WALK[2] (1,2,6): *He had a strange rolling gait, like a sailor on a ship*

gai·ter /ˈgeɪtəʳ/ *n* either of a pair of cloth or leather coverings used formerly to cover the leg from knee to ankle, or just the ankle, and still sometimes worn formally by priests —compare PUTTEE —see PAIR (USAGE)

gal /gæl/ *n humor* a girl

ga·la /ˈgɑːlə‖ˈgeɪlə, ˈgælə/ *adj, n* (of) a feast-time or special public amusement: *a gala occasion*

ga·lac·tic /gəˈlæktɪk/ *adj* [Wa5] of or concerning a GALAXY

gala night /ˈ·· ·/ *n* a special evening, as of a performance at the theatre

gal·an·tine /ˈgæləntiːn/ *n* [U] a dish made of meat cut into small pieces, shaped into a loaf, cooked with SPICEs, and eaten cold

gal·ax·y /ˈgæləksi/ *n* **1** any of the large groups of stars which make up the universe **2** a splendid gathering of people, esp. those famous, beautiful, or clever

Galaxy *n* [*the* + R] the large group of stars in which our own sun and its PLANETs lie —see also MILKY WAY

gale /geɪl/ *n* **1** a weather condition in which a strong wind blows: *The old tree was blown down in a gale* **2** [*usu. pl.*] a sudden noise, esp. laughter: *As the door opened a gale of laughter came from inside*

gall[1] /gɔːl/ *n* [U] **1** *old use* a bitter liquid formed by the LIVER which allows the body to make use of fatty foods; BILE **2 a** a feeling of bitterness or hatred **b** *sl* rudeness; bad manners **3 dip the pen in gall** also **write in gall**— to write bitterly about something or somebody

gall[2] *n* **1** a painful place on an animal's skin, esp. on that of a horse, such as that formed when something has been rubbing against the skin **2** a swollen place on a tree or plant

gall[3] *v* [Wa4;T1] to hurt or be painful to (usu. the feelings): *Her unkind remarks galled me*

gal·lant[1] /ˈgælənt, gəˈlænt‖gəˈlænt, gəˈlɑnt/ *n lit* a (young) man who is particularly well-dressed and/or attentive to women

gal·lant[2] /ˈgælənt/ *adj* **1** courageous: *a gallant deed|a gallant soldier* **2** (not usu. of people) splendid; beautiful: *When that gallant ship went down there was no other like her left on the seas* —**~ly** *adv*

gal·lant[3] /gəˈlænt, ˈgælənt‖gəˈlænt, gəˈlɑnt/ *adj lit* (of men) attentive and polite to women —**~ly** *adv*

gal·lan·try /ˈgæləntri/ *n* [U;C] *lit* **1** (an act of) polite attention (paid by a man) to a woman **2** (an act of) bravery, esp. in battle

gall blad·der /ˈ· ˌ··/ *n* an organ of the body, like a small bag, in which BILE or GALL is stored —see picture at DIGESTIVE SYSTEM

gal·le·on /ˈgæliən/ *n* a large sailing ship, formerly used esp. by the Spaniards —see picture at SAIL[2]

gal·le·ry /ˈgæləri/ *n* **1** [C] a private room, hall, or building where works of art are shown and usu. offered for sale **2** [C] *AmE* usu. **museum**— a public building where paintings (and perhaps other works of art) are shown **3** [C] an upper floor built out from an inner wall of a hall, from which activities in the hall may be watched **4** [C] a covered passage, open on one side **5** [C] a long narrow room, such as one used for shooting practice **6** [C] **a** a level underground passage in a mine **b** the same sort of passage joining natural caves **7** [C] the highest upper floor in a theatre **8** [GU] the people who sit in the seats in the gallery, which are the cheapest in the theatre **9 play to the gallery** to do what will please the ordinary people, even if it is not the most sensible course of action, so as to gain popularity

gal·ley /ˈgæli/ *n* **1** (in former times) a ship which was rowed along by slaves, esp. an ancient Greek or Roman warship **2** a ship's kitchen **3 a** a long flat container used by a printer to hold the letters (TYPE) which have been arranged for the first stage of printing **b** GALLEY PROOF

galley proof /ˈ·· ·/ also **galley**— *n* [*usu. pl.*] any of the long sheets of paper on which a printer prints a book so that mistakes can be made correct before it is divided into pages

galley slave /ˈ·· ·/ *n* one of the rowers forced to work on a GALLEY (1)

Gal·lic /ˈgælɪk/ *adj* **1** [Wa5] of the ancient country of Gaul, or race of Gauls **2** French: *Gallic charm*

gal·li·cis·m /ˈgæləsɪzəm/ *n* a French word or expression, used in English or another language

gal·li·vant /ˈgæləvænt/ *v* [I∅ (ABOUT)] *infml* (*esp. in the* -ing *form*) to go around amusing oneself; GAD ABOUT: *go gallivanting*

gal·lon /ˈgælən/ *n* a measure for liquids, 8 PINTs or 4 QUARTs (in Britain 4·54, in America 3·78 LITREs) —see WEIGHTS & MEASURES TABLE

gal·lop[1] /ˈgæləp/ *n* **1** [S] the movement of a horse at its fastest speed, when all 4 feet come off the ground together: *We went at a gallop over the hills* **2** [C] a ride at this speed: *a long gallop before breakfast* **3** [S] a rush; hurry: *She went through the work at a gallop, so it can't have been done very well*

gallop[2] *v* **1** [I∅;T1: (OFF)] **a** (of a horse) to go at the fastest speed: *The horse galloped down the hill* **b** to cause (a horse) to go at the fastest speed: *They galloped off (on their horses)* **2** [I∅ (OFF)] (of a person or animal) to go very fast

gal·lop·ing /ˈgæləpɪŋ/ *adj* (of illness) getting quickly worse, until the person dies: *galloping* CONSUMPTION

gal·lows /ˈgæləʊz/ *n* **gallows** [Wn3;C *often pl. with sing. meaning*] the wooden frame on which murderers used to be killed by hanging from a rope

gallows bird /ˈ·· ·/ *n now rare* a wicked person who deserves punishment or is likely to get into serious trouble

gallows hu·mour /ˈ·· ˌ··/ *n* [U] *lit* a type of humour which makes unpleasant or dangerous people or things seem funny —compare BLACK **humour**

gall·stone /ˈgɔːlstəʊn/ *n* a hard stone or grain which forms in the GALL BLADDER

Gal·lup poll /ˈgæləp pəʊl/ *n tdmk* a special count of opinions in a country, esp. so as to guess the result of a political election, by questioning a number of people chosen to represent the whole population

ga·lore /gəˈlɔːʳ/ *adj* [E] *apprec* (in) plenty: *money galore|friends galore*

ga·losh /gəˈlɒʃ‖gəˈlɑʃ/ *n* [*usu. pl.*] OVERSHOE —see PAIR (USAGE)

ga·lumph /gəˈlʌmf/ *v* [I∅] to jump about joyfully, but also heavily and awkwardly

gal·van·ic /gælˈvænɪk/ *adj* [Wa5] **1** of or concerning the production of electricity by the action of an acid on a metal **2** (of actions and events) sudden, unnaturally strong, etc.: *The warning about the bomb had a galvanic effect, and people ran everywhere trying to find it*

gal·va·nis·m /ˈgælvənɪzəm/ *n* [U] the production of electricity by chemical means, esp. as in a BATTERY

gal·va·nize, -ise /ˈgælvənaɪz/ *v* [T1] **1** [Wv5] to put a covering of metal, esp. ZINC, over (a sheet of another metal, esp. iron), by using electricity: *galvanized iron* —compare ELECTROPLATE **2** to shock (someone) into action: *The fear of losing his life galvanized him (into fighting back)*

gam·bit /ˈgæmbɪ̵t/ *n* **1** (in CHESS) a set of opening moves in which a piece is risked so as to gain advantage later **2** an action or esp. use of language which is used to produce a future effect, esp. as part of a trick or clever plan —compare PLOY

gam·ble[1] /ˈgæmbəl/ *v* [I∅] **1** [*at*] **a** to play cards or other games for money; risk money on horse races **b** to risk one's money in business **2** [*on*] to take the risk that something will go well, or as one wishes, after doing something that depends on it: *We haven't eaten; we were gambling on the fact that they would be having dinner when we arrived, and would invite us* —**-bler** /ˈgæmbləʳ/ *n*

gamble[2] *n* [S] a risky matter or act: *The operation may not succeed; it's a gamble whether he lives or dies*

gamble a·way *v adv* [T1] to waste (esp. money) by playing cards or other games for money: *He's gambled away all his money, and now has nothing left*

gambling den /ˈ·· ·/ *n often derog* a place where people GAMBLE at cards and/or other games

gam·boge /gæmˈbəʊdʒ, -ˈbuːʒ/ *n* [U] **1** a deep yellow colour **2** the material from which artists obtain this colour

gam·bol[1] /ˈgæmbəl/ *n* [*usu. pl.*] an activity done in play, esp. jumping about

gambol[2] *v* [I∅ (*about*)] **-ll-** (*AmE* **-l-**) to jump about in play, as lambs or children do

game[1] /geɪm/ *n* **1** [C] a form of play or sport, or one example or type of this: *Football is a game which doesn't interest me.|Let's have a game of cards* —see also GAMES; see HOBBY (USAGE) **2** a set of things, usu. a board and round pieces of wood or plastic (COUNTERs) which are used to play such a game when it can be played indoors and on a table **3** [C] a single part of a set into which a match is divided, as in tennis **4** [U] wild animals, some birds and some fish, which are hunted or fished for food, esp. at certain seasons as a sport: *a game bird|game laws* —see also BIG GAME **5** a trick or secret plan: *What's your little game, then?* **6 fair game a** animals which are troublesome and can fairly be shot **b** a person who can justly be attacked in words **7 give the game away** to let a secret plan be known **8 have the game in one's hands** to be in control and sure to win **9 make game of (someone)** to laugh at; make fun of **10 off one's game** below the usual level of one's performance in a game **11 play the game** *usu. imper. or neg.* to act according to the rules, esp. by being honest and fair **12 The game's up** Your/our trick or plan has been found out and can succeed no further **13 Two can play at that game** You are not the only one that can get advantages by behaving in such a way, I can too!

game[2] *v* [I∅] *lit* GAMBLE

game[3] *adj* **1** [Wa1;B] brave and ready for action: *The little boy was shocked by the fall, but he was game enough to get up and try again* **2** [Wa5;F (*for*), F3] willing: *Who's game for a swim?* —**~ly** *adv*

game[4] also (*infml*) **gammy**— *adj* [Wa5] (of a limb, esp. a human leg) unable to be used properly because of something wrong

game·cock /ˈgeɪmkɒk‖-kɑk/ *n* a male chicken specially trained to fight other males

game·keep·er /ˈgeɪmˌkiːpəʳ/ *n* a man employed to raise and protect GAME[1] (4), esp. birds, on private land

games /geɪmz/ *n* **games** **1** [U] a school subject, including the playing of team games and other forms of bodily exercise out of doors **2** [Wn3; (*the*) GC] (in names) a particular set of games and sports competitions: *the* OLYMPIC GAMES|*the* COMMONWEALTH *Games*

games·man·ship /ˈgeɪmzmənʃɪp/ *n* [U] the art of winning by using the rules to one's own advantage without actually cheating

gaming ta·ble /ˈ·· ·/ *n* a table at which games are played for money

gam·ma /ˈgæmə/ *n* [R;(C)] the 3rd letter of the Greek alphabet(Γ, γ)

gamma glob·u·lin /ˌgæmə ˈglɒbjʊlɪ̵n‖-ˈglɑbjə-/ *n* [U] a natural substance found in the body, a form of ANTIBODY, which gives protection against certain diseases

gamma ray /ˈ·· ·/ *n* [*usu. pl.*] a beam of light of short wave length, which goes through solid objects

gam·mon /ˈgæmən/ *n esp. BrE* **1** [U] the meat from a pig (HAM), when it has been preserved by smoke or salt **2** [C] the back part and leg of a pig when used as food

gam·my /ˈgæmi/ *adj* [Wa5] *infml* GAME[4]

gamp /gæmp/ *n BrE infml & humor* an UMBRELLA, esp. a large one

gam·ut /ˈgæmət/ *n* [(*the*) S] **1** all the notes in

music from the lowest to the highest, considered together **2** the whole range of a subject, including the smallest details and the most general ideas: *He's run* (= experienced) *the whole gamut of human experience*

gam·y, gamey /ˈgeɪmi/ *adj* [Wa1] (of meat) having the strong taste of GAME[1] (4) which has been kept for some time before cooking —compare HANG[1] (3), HIGH[1] (7) —**gaminess** *n* [U]

-ga·my /gəmi/ *comb. form* [→*n*[U]] marriage (to the stated number or kind of people): BIGAMY|MONOGAMY|EXOGAMY —**-gamous** *comb. form* [→*adj*] —**-gamously** *comb. form* [→*adv*]

gan·der /ˈgændəʳ/ *n* **1** a male GOOSE **2** *infml* a look: *I had a gander at the new book but decided not to buy it*

gang /gæŋ/ *n* [GC] **1** a group of people working together, such as prisoners or building workers **2** a group of criminals **3** *often derog* a group of friends who are against other groups: *Let's ask the rest of the gang/our gang instead of going alone*

gang·er /ˈgæŋəʳ/ *n BrE* the leader (FOREMAN) of a group of workmen

gang·ling /ˈgæŋglɪŋ/ *adj* unusually tall and thin, so as to appear awkward in movement

gan·gli·on /ˈgæŋglɪən/ *n* **1** a mass of nerve cells **2** a (painful) swelling containing liquid

gang·plank /ˈgæŋplæŋk/ *n* a board of wood which is used to make a bridge to get into or out of a ship or to pass from one ship to another

gan·grene[1] /ˈgæŋgriːn/ *n* [U] (a disease which is) the decay of the flesh of part of the body because blood has stopped flowing there, usu. after a wound —**-grenous** /-grɪnəs/ *adj*

gangrene[2] *v* [T1;IØ] *med* to (cause to) have GANGRENE[1]

gang·ster /ˈgæŋstəʳ/ *n* a member of a group (GANG) of criminals, esp. those who are armed and use guns to threaten and kill their enemies

gang up *v adv* [IØ (*on, against*)] *often derog* to work together as a close group (against someone): *You've all ganged up on/against me!*

gang·way[1] /ˈgæŋweɪ/ *n* **1** an opening in the side of a ship and the movable board (GANGPLANK) which is used to make a bridge from it to the land **2** *BrE* a clear space between 2 rows of seats in a cinema, theatre, bus or train; AISLE —see picture at THEATRE

gang·way[2] /ˌgæŋˈweɪ/ *interj* Make room!; Get out of the way!

gan·net /ˈgænɨ̞t/ *n* [Wn1] any of several types of bird which live near the sea and eat fish

gan·try /ˈgæntri/ *n* a metal frame which is used to support movable heavy machinery or railway signals

gaol /dʒeɪl/ *n, v BrE* JAIL

gaol·bird /ˈdʒeɪlbɜːd‖-ɜrd/ *n BrE infml* JAILBIRD

gaol·er /ˈdʒeɪləʳ/ *n BrE* JAILER

gap /gæp/ *n* **1** an empty space between 2 objects or 2 parts of an object: *The gate was locked but we went through a gap in the fence* **2** [(*of*)] an amount of distance or difference: *There's a gap of 2 miles between us and the nearest houses* **3** [(*in*)] a lack (of something): *There are wide gaps in my knowledge of history* **4 bridge/fill/stop a gap (in)** to supply something which is lacking: *I bridged a gap in the conversation by telling a joke*

gape /geɪp/ *v* [IØ] **1** *old use* YAWN **2** [(*at*)] to look hard in surprise, esp. with the mouth open: *She gaped at the tall man, not believing that he was her younger brother* **3** [Wv4] to come apart or open (note the phr. **gape open**): *His shirt gaped open where the button had come off*

gapes /geɪps/ *n* **1** [(*the*) P; (*the*) U] a disease of birds, from which they die with their beaks open **2** [*the* + P; *the* + U] an attack of YAWNing

gap-toothed /ˌ· ˈ·ˈ‖ˈ· ·/ *adj* having or showing spaces between the teeth, esp. as when teeth are missing or when the front teeth have not grown together

gar·age[1] /ˈgærɑːʒ, -ɪdʒ‖gəˈrɑʒ/ *n* **1** a building in which motor vehicles can be kept —see picture at HOUSE[1] **2** a place where (petrol can be bought and) cars can be repaired

garage[2] *v* [T1] to put in a garage

garb[1] /gɑːb‖gɑrb/ *n* [U9] *lit or humor* clothing of a particular style, esp. clothing which shows one's type of work or is of unusual appearance: *He went to change his clothes and came back in priest's garb*

garb[2] *v* [T1 *usu. pass.*] to dress: *We garbed ourselves in black*

gar·bage /ˈgɑːbɪdʒ‖ˈgɑr-/ *n esp. AmE* **1** waste material; RUBBISH: *The street is covered with old tins and other forms of garbage* **2** *derog* stupid and worthless ideas, words, etc.

garbage can /ˈ·· ·/ *n AmE* DUSTBIN

garbage col·lec·tor /ˈ·· ·ˌ··/ *n AmE* DUSTMAN

garbage truck /ˈ·· ·/ *n AmE* DUSTCART

gar·ble /ˈgɑːbəl‖ˈgɑr-/ *v* [Wv3,5;T1] to repeat in a confused way which gives a false idea of the facts: *The newspaper gave a garbled account of the meeting*

gar·den[1] /ˈgɑːdn‖ˈgɑr-/ *n* **1** a piece of land, often near a house, on which flowers and vegetables may be grown **2** [*often pl.*] a public park with flowers, grass, paths and seats **3 lead (someone) up the garden path** to trick (someone) into believing what is not true and acting on it

See next page for picture

garden[2] *v* [IØ] to work in a garden, making plants grow —**~er** *n*

garden cit·y /ˌ·· ˈ··/ *n* a town or part of a town, such as a **garden suburb**, planned and built to have grass, trees, and open spaces, rather than factories and signs of industry —compare NEW TOWN

gar·de·ni·a /gɑːˈdiːnɪə‖gɑr-/ *n* **1** any of several types of tropical bushes with large white or yellow sweet-smelling flowers **2** the flower itself

gar·den·ing /ˈgɑːdənɪŋ‖ˈgɑr-/ *n* [U] work (done) in a garden

garden par·ty /ˈ·· ˌ··/ *n* a party held out of doors on the grass, esp. in a garden or park

gar·gan·tu·an /gɑːˈgæntʃʊən‖gɑr-/ *adj* very big: *a gargantuan meal*

gar·gle[1] /ˈgɑːgəl‖ˈgɑr-/ *v* [IØ (*with*)] to wash the throat with liquid by blowing through it at the back of the mouth

gargle[2] *n* **1** [S] an act of gargling (GARGLE) **2** [U] liquid with which one GARGLEs

gar·goyle /ˈgɑːgɔɪl‖ˈgɑr-/ *n* a hollow figure of a man or animal on a roof or wall, esp. of a church, through whose mouth rain water is carried away —see picture at CHURCH[1]

gar·ish /ˈgeərɪʃ/ *adj* unpleasantly bright: *garish colours|garish light* —**~ly** *adv* —**~ness** *n* [U]

gar·land[1] /ˈgɑːlənd‖ˈgɑr-/ *n* a circle of flowers, leaves, or both, esp. to be placed round the neck for ornament or as a sign of victory

garland[2] *v* [Wv5;T1] to put one or more GARLANDs on (someone)

gar·lic /ˈgɑːlɪk‖ˈgɑr-/ *n* [U] a plant rather like an onion, which is used in cooking to give a strong taste

gar·ment /ˈgɑːmənt‖ˈgɑr-/ *n esp. fml* (the name used, esp. by the makers, for) an article of clothing: *A new garment should be washed carefully*

gar·ner /ˈgɑːnəʳ‖ˈgɑr-/ *v* [T1] *poet* to collect or store

gar·net /ˈgɑːnɨ̞t‖ˈgɑr-/ *n* **1** [C] a type of red jewel **2** [U] a deep red colour

gar·nish[1] /ˈgɑːnɪʃ‖ˈgɑr-/ *v* [T1 (*with*)] to add to

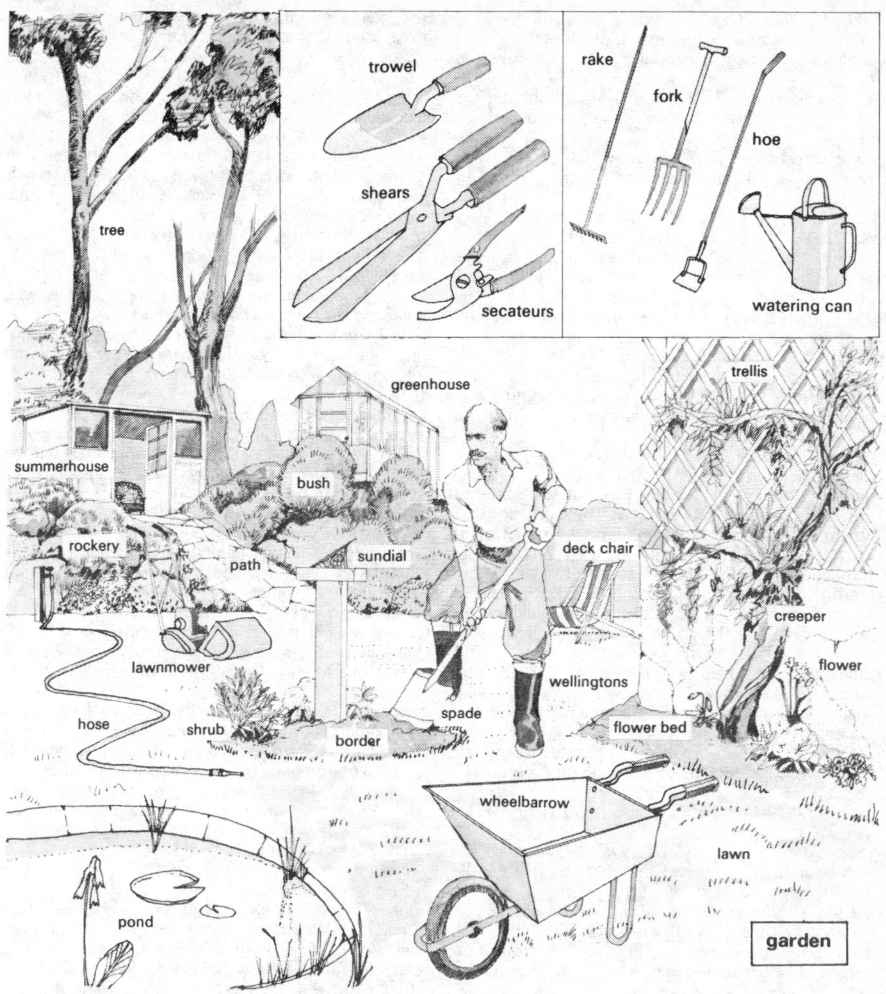

(something) as an ornament and, in the case of food, as an improvement to its taste —see DECORATE (USAGE)

garnish² *n* a SAUCE, pieces of fruit, or any of the things which are used to make food look and taste better

gar·ret /ˈgærɨ̣t/ *n* a usu. small unpleasant room at the top of a house; ATTIC

gar·ri·son¹ /ˈgærɨ̣sən/ *n* **1** [GC] a group of soldiers living in a town or fort and defending it **2** [C] a fort or camp where such soldiers live **3 garrison town** /ˌ··· ˈ·/ a town where a group of soldiers live all the time

garrison² *v* [T1] **1** to send soldiers to guard (something) in a GARRISON: *The government will garrison the coastal towns* **2** (of soldiers) to guard in a GARRISON: *The soldiers garrisoned the town*

gar·rotte¹, *AmE* also **-rote** /gəˈrɒt‖gəˈrɑt/ *n* **1** [C] a metal collar or wire which may be tightened round the neck to prevent a person from breathing and so kill him **2** [C; *the* + R] an act of putting to death by this means

garrotte², *AmE* also **-rote** *v* **-tt-** (*AmE* **-tt-** *or* **-t-**) [T1] to put to death by tightening a GARROTTE

gar·ru·li·ty /gəˈruːlɨ̣ti/ also **gar·ru·lous·ness** /ˈgærələsnɨ̣s/— *n* [U] the quality of being GARRULOUS

gar·ru·lous /ˈgærələs/ *adj* habitually talking too much, esp. about unimportant things —**~ly** *adv*

gar·ter /ˈgɑːtəʳ‖ˈgɑr-/ *n* **1** a band of elastic material worn round the leg to keep a stocking up **2** (**the Order of**) **the Garter** the highest title given in the English HONOURS (1) system

gas¹ /gæs/ *n* **gases** (*AmE* **gases** *or* **gasses**) **1** [U;C] (a type of) substance like air, which is not solid or liquid: *There are several kinds of gas in the air* **2** [U] a substance of this type which is burnt in the home to supply heat for the rooms and cooking and formerly for light **3** [U] a substance of this type which is used to poison enemies in war **4** [U] also **laughing gas**— such a substance, called **nitrous oxide** used to cause sleep while a DENTIST pulls a tooth out **5** [U] *AmE infml* GASOLINE; petrol **6** [U] *infml* unimportant talk **7** [C *usu. sing.*] *sl esp. AmE* a wildly funny or pleasant thing, or (sometimes) the opposite: *So I have to take 20 children to the cinema to watch a fairy story on film. That's sure to be a real gas* **8 step on the gas** to increase the speed (of the car)

gas² *v* **-ss-** **1** [T1] to poison (someone) with gas **2**

[L9, esp. *about*] (*esp. in tenses with the* -ing *form*) to talk a long time about unimportant things

gas·bag /ˈgæsbæg/ *n infml* a person who talks too much

gas brack·et /ˈ· ˌ··/ *n* a part of a pipe supplying gas so that a GASLIGHT can be hung from a wall or CEILING

gas cham·ber /ˈ· ˌ··/ *n* a room which can be filled with gas so that animals or people may be put to death

gas·e·ous /ˈgæsɪəs/ *adj* of or like gas

gas fit·ter /ˈ· ˌ··/ *n* a workman who puts in or repairs the pipes for gas in the home and the apparatuses worked by it, such as cookers, fires, etc.

gash[1] /gæʃ/ *v* [T1] to cut deeply, by accident or on purpose

gash[2] *n* a large deep cut or wound

gas·hold·er /ˈgæˌshəʊldəʳ/ *BrE infml* also **gas·om·e·ter** /gæˈsɒmɨ̱təʳ‖-ˈsɑ-/— *n* a very large round metal container from which gas is carried in pipes to houses and buildings

gas·i·fy /ˈgæsɨ̱faɪ/ *v* [T1;IØ] to (cause to) become gas —**-ification** /ˌgæsɨ̱fɨ̱ˈkeɪʃən/ *n* [U]

gas·ket /ˈgæskɨ̱t/ *n* **1** a flat piece of soft material which is placed between two surfaces so that steam, oil, gas, etc., cannot escape —see picture at PETROL **2** [*usu. pl.*] a small rope used for fastening a rolled-up sail to the pole or MAST[1] (1)

gas·light /ˈgæs-laɪt/ *n* **1** [U] the light produced from burning gas **2** [C] also **gaslamp**— a lamp in the house or on the street which gives light from burning gas

gas·man /ˈgæsmæn/ *n* **-men** /men/ a man who works in the gas industry, esp. an official who visits one's home to see how much gas one has used in order to calculate payment

gas mask /ˈ· ·/ *n* a breathing apparatus worn over the face to protect the wearer against poisonous gases

gas·o·line, -lene /ˈgæsəliːn/ also (*infml*) **gas**— *n* [U] *AmE* PETROL

gasp[1] /gɑːsp‖gæsp/ *v* **1** [IØ (*with, in* and/or *at*)] to catch the breath suddenly and in a way that can be heard, esp. because of surprise, shock, etc.: *I gasped with/in surprise at the unexpected news* **2** [IØ] to breathe quickly, esp. with difficulty, making a sudden noise: *I came out of the water and gasped for breath* **3** [T1 (OUT)] to say while breathing in this way: *He gasped out the message*

gasp[2] *n* **1** an act of GASPing **2 at one's last gasp** unable to do more because very tired or very near death

gas ring /ˈ· ·/ *n* a small round metal gas pipe from which gas can escape through several small holes. It is used for cooking

gas sta·tion /ˈ· ˌ··/ *n AmE* FILLING STATION

gas·sy /ˈgæsi/ *adj* [Wa1] **1** full of (a) gas **2** having the qualities of (a) gas —**gassiness** *n* [U]

gas·tric /ˈgæstrɪk/ *adj* [Wa5;A] of or belonging to the stomach: *the gastric juices* (= acids which break down food in the stomach)

gas·tri·tis /gæˈstraɪtɨ̱s/ *n* [U] an illness in which the inside of the stomach is swollen, so that a burning pain is felt

gas·tro·en·te·ri·tis /ˌgæstrəʊ-entəˈraɪtɨ̱s/ *n* [U] an illness in which the food passages including the stomach and INTESTINEs are swollen

gas·tron·o·my /gæˈstrɒnəmi‖gæˈstrɑ-/ *n* [U] the art and science of cooking and eating good food —**-nomic** /ˌgæstrəˈnɒmɪk‖-ˈnɑ-/ *adj* [Wa5] —**-nomically** *adv* [Wa4,5]

gas·works /ˈgæswɜːks‖-ɜr-/ *n* **gasworks** [Wn3;C *often pl. with sing. meaning*] a place where gas for use in the home is made from coal

gat /gæt/ *n sl* a gun

gate /geɪt/ *n* **1** a movable frame, often with bars across it, which closes an opening in a fence, wall, etc. **2** [*often pl.*] (either of) a pair of large frames such as those used for controlling the water level at LOCKs[2] (3) in a river or CANAL, or those which close the road over a railway line at a LEVEL CROSSING **3** GATEWAY **4** the number of people who go in to see a sports event, esp. a football match **5** also **gate money**— the money paid by the people who pass through the gates at a match

gâ·teau /ˈgætəʊ‖gɑˈtəʊ/ *n* **-teaux** /təʊz/ [U;C] *Fr* a specially attractive type of cream cake

gate·crash /ˈgeɪtkræʃ/ *v* [T1;IØ] CRASH[1] (6): *So many people gatecrashed that there wasn't enough food and the party was a failure* —**~er** *n*

gate·house /ˈgeɪthaʊs/ *n* **-houses** /ˌhaʊzɨ̱z/ a building placed over or beside a gate, such as the home of someone who looks after a park

gate·keep·er /ˈgeɪtˌkiːpəʳ/ *n* a person who is in charge of the opening and closing of a gate

gate·leg ta·ble /ˌgeɪtleg ˈteɪbəl/ also **gatelegged table** /ˌ·· ˈ··/— *n* a type of table whose sides can be put out to make the top larger, being supported by legs joined in pairs

gate mon·ey /ˈ· ˌ··/ *n* [U] GATE (5)

gate·post /ˈgeɪtpəʊst/ *n* **1** a post beside a gate, from which the gate is hung or to which it fastens **2 between you and me and the gatepost** *infml* BETWEEN[1] (6) **you and me**: *Between you and me and the gatepost, (I think) he's rather stupid*

gate·way /ˈgeɪt-weɪ/ *n* **1** an opening in a fence, wall, etc., across which a gate may be put **2** [(*to*)] a way of finding: (fig.) *Hard work is the gateway to success*

gath·er[1] /ˈgæðəʳ/ *v* **1** [T1;IØ: (ROUND)] to (cause to) come together: *Gather round, and I'll tell you a story.|A crowd gathered to see what had happened* **2** [T1] to obtain (information or qualities) bit by bit: *He travels about the world gathering facts about little-known countries.|As we came onto the open road we gathered speed* **3** [T1 (IN, UP)] to collect or pick (flowers, crops, several objects, etc.): *Gather your toys up.|The farmers are gathering in the corn* **4** [T1,5a,b] to understand from something said or done: *I gather she's ill, and that's why she hasn't come.|I didn't gather much from the confused story he told me* **5** [IØ] (of a swelling on the skin) to become full of yellow poisonous matter **6** [Wv5; T1] to draw (material) into small folds usu. by making small stitches with one long thread, then pulling the thread up so that the folds are pushed together: *a gathered skirt* (= at the waist) **7 be gathered to one's fathers** *fml euph* to die

gather[2] *n* something produced by GATHERing[1] (6): *She made gathers at the waist of the dress*

gath·er·ing /ˈgæðərɪŋ/ *n* a meeting

gauche /gəʊʃ/ *adj* [Wa2] *Fr* awkward (in social behaviour); doing and saying the wrong things

gau·che·rie /ˈgəʊʃəri/ *n* [U;C] *Fr* acts or words which are GAUCHE

gau·cho /ˈgaʊtʃəʊ/ *n* **-chos** *Sp* a South American COWBOY, esp. of the plains (PAMPAS) of Argentina

gau·dy /ˈgɔːdi/ *adj* [Wa1] too bright in colour and/or with too many details to ornament it —**-dily** *adv* —**-diness** *n* [U]

gauge[1], *AmE* also **gage** /geɪdʒ/ *n* **1** a standard measure of weight, size, etc., to which objects can be compared **2** the thickness of wire or certain metal objects, or the width of the barrel of a gun **3** the distance between the RAILs of a railway or between the wheels of a train or other such vehicle: *standard gauge* (4′ 8½″) —compare NARROW GAUGE **4** an instrument for measuring size, amount, etc., such as the width of wire, the amount of rain **5 take the gauge of** (something or somebody) to judge the size, value, etc.

gauge², *AmE* also **gage** *v* [T1] **1** to measure by means of a GAUGE **2** to judge the worth, meaning, etc. of (something or somebody's actions)

gaunt /gɔːnt/ *adj* [Wa1] **1** thin, as if ill or hungry —compare HAGGARD **2** (of a place) bare and unattractive: *The old house stood gaunt and empty, a complete ruin* —**~ness** *n* [U]

gaunt·let¹ /ˈgɔːntlɨt/ *n* **1** (in former times) a GLOVE (=a shaped covering for the hand) covered in metal, used as armour by soldiers **2** a long GLOVE covering the wrist, which protects the hand in certain sports, or in industry **3 throw down the gauntlet** to call someone to fight, esp. when 2 people's beliefs are opposed **4 take/pick up the gauntlet** to accept the demand to fight

gauntlet² *n* [*the*+R] (esp. in former times) a punishment, in which 2 rows of men beat a man running between them (only in the phr. **run the gauntlet** = to experience violent attack): (fig.) *He ran the gauntlet of newspaper attacks*

gauze /gɔːz/ *n* [U] material made in a fine piece which can be seen through, because it is woven like a net, sometimes used in medicine to cover wounds, or as a curtain: *wire gauze|cotton gauze* —see picture at LABORATORY —**gauzy** *adj* [Wa1]

gave /geɪv/ *past t. of* GIVE

gav·el /ˈgævəl/ *n* a small hammer used by a chairman, a judge in America, or an AUCTIONEER selling things in public, who strikes a table with it to get attention

ga·votte /gəˈvɒt‖gəˈvɑt/ *n* **1** a merry, fast dance from France, danced esp. in former times **2** a piece of music (suitable) for such a dance

gawk /gɔːk/ *v* [IØ (*at*)] to look at something in a foolish way: *Don't gawk at it, do something!*

gaw·ky /ˈgɔːki/ *adj* [Wa1] (of a person) awkward in movement —**-kiness** *n* [U]

gawp /gɔːp/ *v* [IØ (*at*)] to look at something in a foolish way, esp. with the mouth open —compare GAPE (2)

gay /geɪ/ *adj* **1** [Wa1] cheerful, merry, happy: *We were all gay at the thought of the coming holidays* **2** [Wa1] bright or attractive, so that one feels happy to see it, hear it, etc.: *The fields were gay with flowers.|We're painting the kitchen in gay colours* **3** [Wa1] not serious; only concerned with pleasure (esp. in the phr. **the gay life**) **4** [Wa5] *infml* HOMOSEXUAL

gay·ness /ˈgeɪnɨs/ *n* [U] GAIETY; quality of being gay

gaze¹ /geɪz/ *v* [L9, esp. *at*] to look steadily for a long or short period of time: *We gazed at the stranger, wondering who he was* —**gazer** *n*

gaze² *n* [S] a steady fixed look: *She turned her gaze from one person to the other*

ga·ze·bo /gəˈziːbəʊ‖-ˈzeɪ-, -ˈziː-/ *n* **-bos** a place where one can sit in the sun, such as a SUMMERHOUSE in a garden

ga·zelle /gəˈzel/ *n* [Wn1] any of a number of types of animal (ANTELOPE) like small deer, which jump in graceful movements and have beautiful large eyes

ga·zette¹ /gəˈzet/ *n* an official newspaper, esp. one from the government giving lists of people who have been employed by them, important notices, etc.

gazette² *v* [T1 *usu. pass.*] to print in a GAZETTE

gaz·et·teer /ˌgæzɨˈtɪəʳ/ *n* a list of names of places, printed as a dictionary or as a list at the end of a book of maps

ga·zump /gəˈzʌmp/ *v* [T1;(IØ)] *BrE sl* (of the owner of a house) to refuse to sell a house to (someone who thinks he has bought it) and sell instead to someone who has offered more money

GB *abbrev. for:* Great Britain

GCE *abbrev. for:* (in Britain) General Certificate of Education; an examination in one of many subjects set by various universities and taken in schools by pupils aged 15 or over

gear¹ /gɪəʳ/ *n* **1** [U] a set of things collected together, esp. when used for a particular purpose: *climbing gear* **2** [C] an apparatus or part of a machine which has a special use in controlling a vehicle: *the landing gear of an aircraft|*STEER*ing gear* **3** [C;U] any of several arrangements, esp. of toothed wheels in a machine, which allows power to be passed from one part to another so as to control the power, speed, or direction of movement: **Bottom** (or **low**) **gear** *in a car is used for starting,* **top** (or **high**) **gear** *for going fast.|"The car isn't moving!" "That's because you're not* **in gear**." = *"That's because you're* **out of gear**" —see picture at MACHINERY **4** [U] *sl esp. BrE* clothes **5 out of gear a** not connected to the GEAR¹ (3) **b** not working well

gear² *v* [T1;IØ] to supply (something) with GEAR*s*

gear·box /ˈgɪəbɒks‖ˈgɪərbɑks/ *n* a metal case containing the GEAR*s*¹ (3) of a vehicle —see picture at CAR

geared up /ˌ· ˈ·◂/ *adj* [F (*for*), F3] in a state of esp. anxious excitement and expectation about an activity: *I was all geared up to have an argument*

gear le·ver /ˈ· ˌ··/ also **gear stick** /ˈ· ·/, *AmE* usu. **gear shift** /ˈ· ·/— *n* the apparatus which controls the GEAR*s*¹ (3) of a vehicle —see picture at CAR

gear to *v prep* [D1 *often pass.*] to connect (something) closely to (something else); make (one thing) dependent (on another): *We must gear the amount of products we make to the increase in public demand.|Education should be geared to the children's needs and abilities*

geck·o /ˈgekəʊ/ *n* **-os** *or* **-oes** a type of small animal of the LIZARD family, esp. of tropical countries —see picture at REPTILE

gee /dʒiː/ also **gee whiz** /ˌ· ˈ·/— *interj esp. AmE* (an expression of surprise)

gee-gee /ˈ· ·/ *n* (*used esp. by or to children or humor sl*) a horse

geese /giːs/ *pl. of* GOOSE

Gee up /ˌ· ˈ·/ *interj* (used by a person driving a horse) Go faster!

gee·zer /ˈgiːzəʳ/ *n sl* a man, often one who is thought to be a little peculiar (often in the phr. **old geezer**)

Gei·ger count·er /ˈgaɪgə ˌkaʊntəʳ‖-gər-/ *n* an instrument for finding and measuring RADIOACTIVITY

gei·sha /ˈgeɪʃə/ also **geisha girl** /ˈ·· ·/— *n* a Japanese girl who is trained to dance, sing, and perform the various arts which amuse men

gel¹ /dʒel/ *n* [C;U] *tech* a substance in a state between solid and liquid; jelly

gel² *v* **-ll-** [IØ] **1** JELL (1) **2** *esp. BrE* JELL (2)

gel·a·tine /ˈdʒelətiːn‖-tn/ also (*esp. tech or AmE*) **gelatin** /ˈdʒelətɨn, -tn/— *n* [U] a clear substance which comes out of the bones of animals when they are boiled, used for making sweet jellies

ge·lat·i·nous /dʒɨˈlætɨnəs/ *adj esp. tech* like jelly; in a state between solid and liquid

geld /geld/ *v* [Wv5;T1] to remove the sexual organs (TESTICLES) of (certain male animals)

geld·ing /ˈgeldɪŋ/ *n* an animal, usu. a horse, that has been GELDed

gel·ig·nite /ˈdʒelɪgnaɪt/ *n* [U] a very powerful explosive

gem /dʒem/ *n* **1** a jewel; precious stone, esp. when cut into a regular shape **2** a thing or esp. person of more value than others of the type

Gem·i·ni /ˈdʒemᵻnaɪ‖-ni/ *n* **1** [R] **a** the ancient sign, 2 people born together (TWINS), representing the third division in the ZODIAC belt of stars **b** the group of stars (CONSTELLATION) formerly in this division **2** [C] a person born under the influence of this sign —see picture at PLANET

gen /dʒen/ *n* [(*the*) U (*on*)] *BrE sl* the correct or complete information: *He gave me all the gen on the new office arrangements which were made while I was away* —see also GENNED-UP

gen·darme /ˈʒɒndɑːm‖ˈʒɑndɑrm (*Fr* ʒɑ̃darm)/ *n Fr* a French soldier with the duties of a policeman

gen·der /ˈdʒendəʳ/ *n* **1** [U] (in grammar) the state of being MASCULINE, FEMININE, or NEUTER: *Differences of gender are shown between many words in German and French, but in English these differences are rare* (*except in the* PRONOUNs) **2** [C] any of these states: *German has 3 genders* **3** [C;U] *infml* the division into male or female; sex: *the female and the male genders*

gene /dʒiːn/ *n* any of several small parts of the material which makes up the centre (NUCLEUS) of a cell. Each of these parts controls the development of one or more qualities in a living thing which have been passed on (INHERITed) from its parents

ge·ne·al·o·gist /ˌdʒiːniˈælədʒᵻst/ *n* a person who studies GENEALOGY

ge·ne·al·o·gy /ˌdʒiːniˈælədʒi/ *n* **1** [U] (the study of) the history of the members of a family from the past to the present **2** [C] an account of this for one particular family, esp. when shown in a drawing with lines and names spreading like the branches of a tree **3** [U] the study of the development of any form of life or subject which changes through time, such as language —**-logical** /ˌdʒiːnɪəˈlɒdʒɪkəl‖-ˈlɑ-/ *adj* [Wa5] —**-logically** *adv* [Wa4,5]

gen·e·ra /ˈdʒenərə/ *pl. of* GENUS

gen·e·ral¹ /ˈdʒenərəl/ *adj* **1** [A;(B)] concerning or felt by everybody or most people: *The price of food is a matter of general anxiety.*|*It's not in the general* INTEREST *to close railways* (= it's not good for most people).|*the general public* (=all ordinary people)| *At first only a few people wanted to go, but now interest has become general* **2** [A;(B)] not limited to one thing, place, etc.: *a general degree* (*at a university, in several subjects*)|*general education* (=in many subjects) **3** [A;(B)] not detailed; describing the main things only: *Give me a general idea of the work* **4** [E] (*as the second part of an official title*) chief: *Postmaster-General;* MAJOR-*General* **5 general practice** /ˌ··· ˈ··/ the part of the medical service in which one doctor treats all illnesses; job of a family doctor —see also GENERAL PRACTITIONER **6 in general a** also **as a general rule**— usually; in most cases: *In general, people like her* **b** (*after a pl. noun*) most: *People in general like her* —compare GENERALLY

general² *n* **1** [C;A;N] an officer of very high rank in the army or American air force **2** [C] a person in command of an army or other fighting force

general de·liv·er·y /ˌ··· ·ˈ···/ *n* [U] *AmE* POSTE RESTANTE

general e·lec·tion /ˌ··· ·ˈ··/ *n BrE* an election in which all the voters in the country take part at the same time to choose the members of parliament

gen·e·ra·lis·si·mo /ˌdʒenərəˈlɪsᵻməʊ/ *n* **-mos** [C;A] (in some countries) a commander of the army, navy, and air force or of several armies combined together

gen·e·ral·i·ty /ˌdʒenəˈrælᵻti/ *n* **1** [U] the quality of being general **2** [P] *lit* the greater part; MAJORITY (esp. in the phr. **the generality of**): *The generality of men are neither good nor bad, but somewhere in between* **3** [C] a general statement; point for consideration which is not at all detailed: *We all know there's a lack of food in the world. But let's move on from generalities to the particular difficulties of feeding the people of this country*

gen·e·ral·i·za·tion, -isation /ˌdʒenərəlaɪˈzeɪʃən‖-lə-/ *n* **1** [U] the act of generalizing **2** [C] a general statement, principle, or opinion resulting from the consideration of particular facts

gen·e·ral·ize, -ise /ˈdʒenərəlaɪz/ *v* **1** [IØ;(T1): (*from*)] to make a general statement (about): *It's possible to generalize from all the information given to us and to make various decisions* **2** [IØ] to form or state an opinion after considering a small number of the facts: *Don't generalize; it isn't fair to say all women drivers are bad just because one knocked you down* **3** [T1] to put (a principle, statement, rule, etc.) into a more general form that covers a larger number of particular cases

gen·er·al·ly /ˈdʒenərəli/ *adv* **1** usually: *We generally go to the sea for our holidays* **2** by most people: *The plan has been generally accepted* **3** without considering details, but only the main points

general prac·ti·tion·er /ˌ··· ·ˈ···/ *n* a doctor who is trained in general medicine and whose work (**general practice** /ˌ··· ˈ··/) is to treat people in a certain local area

general staff /ˌ··· ˈ·/ *n* [(*the*) GU] (*sometimes caps.*) the officers in an army who work for the commanding officers

general strike /ˌ··· ˈ·/ *n* the stopping of work by most of the workmen in the country at the same time

gen·e·rate /ˈdʒenəreɪt/ *v* [T1] **1** *fml* to cause to exist: *Loud laughter was generated all through the crowd* **2** [Wv4] *tech* to produce (heat or electricity): *Our electricity comes from a new generating station*

gen·e·ra·tion /ˌdʒenəˈreɪʃən/ *n* **1** [U] the act or action of generating (GENERATE): *Falling water may be used for the generation of electricity* **2** [C] a period of time in which a human being can grow up and have a family, perhaps 25 or 30 years **3** [C] **a** all the members of a family of about the same age **b** all people of about the same age **4** [C] all the members of any developing class of things at a certain stage: *second generation* COMPUTERs

gen·e·ra·tive /ˈdʒenərətɪv/ *adj* [Wa5;A;(B)] having the power to produce or GENERATE

gen·e·ra·tor /ˈdʒenəreɪtəʳ/ *n* a machine which GENERATEs, usu. electricity

ge·ner·ic /dʒᵻˈnerɪk/ *adj* **1** [Wa5] of or concerning a GENUS **2** shared by or typical of a whole class of things —**~ally** *adv* [Wa4]

gen·e·ros·i·ty /ˌdʒenəˈrɒsᵻti‖-ˈrɑ-/ *n* **1** [U] the quality of being generous **2** [C *usu. pl.*] a generous act

gen·e·rous /ˈdʒenərəs/ *adj* **1** showing readiness to give money, help, kindness, etc.: *She's not very generous with the food* (= she gives small amounts) **2** in large amounts: *a generous meal* —**~ly** *adv*

gen·e·sis /ˈdʒenᵻsᵻs/ *n fml* **-ses** the beginning or origin: *The world has seen the genesis of space travel*

Genesis *n* [R] the first book of the Bible, in which the story of the beginning of the world is told

ge·net·ic /dʒᵻˈnetɪk/ *adj* [Wa5] **1** of or concerning GENEs **2** of or concerning GENETICS **3 the genetic code** the arrangement of GENEs which has an effect on the development of a living thing —**~ally** *adv* [Wa4,5]

ge·net·i·cist /dʒᵻˈnetᵻsᵻst/ *n* a person who studies GENETICS

ge·net·ics /dʒᵻˈnetɪks/ *n* [U] the study of how living things develop according to the effects of those substances passed on in the cells from the parents —see also GENE, HEREDITY

ge·ni·al /ˈdʒiːnɪəl/ *adj* **1** cheerful and kind; good-tempered **2** (of weather) gentle and good for the growth of plants —**-ally** *adv*

ge·ni·al·i·ty /ˌdʒiːniˈælɪ̌ti/ *n* **1** [U] the quality of being GENIAL **2** [C *usu. pl.*] a GENIAL act

ge·nie /ˈdʒiːni/ also **djinn**— *n* **-nies** *or* **-nii** /niaɪ/ a magical spirit in Arab fairy stories

gen·i·tal /ˈdʒenɪ̌tl/ *adj* [Wa5;A] of or concerning the sex organs —**-tally** *adv*

gen·i·tals /ˈdʒenɪ̌tlz/ also **gen·i·ta·li·a** /-ˈteɪlɪə/— *n* [P] the outer sex organs

gen·i·tive /ˈdʒenɪ̌tɪv/ *adj, n* (in grammar) (a form or a word) showing esp. possession or origin (note the phr. **genitive case**)

ge·ni·us[1] /ˈdʒiːnɪəs/ *n* **1** [U] great ability, esp. in producing works of art: *There's genius in the way this was painted* **2** [C] **a** a person of such ability **b** a person of very high INTELLIGENCE **3** [S (*for*)] a special ability, sometimes unpleasant in effect: *She has a genius for* MATHEMATICS **4** [S (of)] the typical spirit or character of a place, a group of people, etc.: *The genius of our language is its use of short words which do not change their endings* **5** [C9] a person who has strong, perhaps bad, influence over another: *My evil genius*

USAGE This is a very strong word. It is used either of a rare person or of his rare powers: *Einstein was a* **genius**.|*Goethe had* **genius. Talent** is a less strong word, and is used like **genius** for the powers with which a person is born, but not of the person himself: *She has great* **talent**.|*She has a* **talent** *for music.* **Skill** and **ability** mean the power to do something well, but unlike **talent** or **genius** they can be learnt: *She weaves with great* **skill/ability**.| *She is a very* **skilled/skilful/able** *weaver.* One may be born with a **capacity** or **aptitude** for (doing) something. Both words mean that one will easily develop **skill** if one is taught: *The child shows a great* **capacity/aptitude** *for learning languages.* **Competence** is a satisfactory but not unusual degree of **skill**: *a test of one's* **competence** *as a driver.* A **faculty** is a **skill** or **talent** in one area: *the* **faculty** *of never forgetting people's names.*

genius[2] *n* **-nii** /niaɪ/ *lit* **1** the spirit guarding a place **2** GENIE

genius lo·ci /ˌdʒiːnɪəs ˈləʊsaɪ/ *n* [*usu. sing.*] *Lat* the typical character of a place, as shown by the feelings it produces in one

genned-up /ˌ· ˈ·◂/ *adj* [F (*about, on*);(A)] *BrE sl* well-informed; KNOWLEDGEABLE; knowing a lot: *genned-up about foreign affairs* —see also GEN

gen·o·cide /ˈdʒenəsaɪd/ *n* [U] the act of killing a whole group of people, esp. a whole race

gen·re /ˈʒɒnrə‖ˈʒɑnrə (*Fr* ʒɑ̃r)/ *n Fr* a class of works of art or literature according to their type of subject

gent /dʒent/ *n nonstandard humor* a gentleman: *What are you drinking tonight, gents?* —see also GENTS

gen·teel /dʒenˈtiːl/ *adj* **1** trying to show unnaturally polite manners, esp. so as to appear socially important **2** *old use* very polite, and thus known to be of a high social class —**-teelly** /dʒenˈtiːl-li/ *adv*

gen·tian /ˈdʒenʃən/ *n* [C;U] (a HERB with) a blue flower which grows in some mountainous areas

gen·tile /ˈdʒentaɪl/ *adj, n* [(*sometimes cap.*)] (a person who is) not Jewish

gen·til·i·ty /dʒenˈtɪlɪ̌ti/ *n* [U] the quality of being GENTEEL

gen·tle /ˈdʒentl/ *adj* **1** [Wa1] kind and ready to help others: *a very gentle person, who never loses her temper* **2** [Wa1] not violent; soft in movement: *a gentle wind*|*a gentle slope* (= not steep) **3** [Wa5] *old use* **a** of the NOBILITY **b** born into a high social class —see POLITE (USAGE) —**~ness** *n* [U]

gen·tle·folk /ˈdʒentlfəʊk/ also **gentlefolks** /-fəʊks/— *n* [P] people of high social class; GENTRY

gen·tle·man /ˈdʒentlmən/ *n* **-men** /mən/ **1** a man who behaves well towards others and who can be trusted to keep his promises and always act honourably **2** *polite* a man **3** *old use* a man of good but not noble family, esp. one who served the king or nobles **4** (in former times) a man who had money (a private income) and did not need to work

USAGE When one is addressing a speech to a group of people, it is polite to begin **Ladies** *and* **Gentlemen**; but if they are only men one says **Gentlemen**, which here is the plural of *Sir*. **Gentleman** is a polite but rather old-fashioned way of speaking of a man. One may wish to use it in his presence: *Please bring this* **gentleman** *a glass of beer.* —compare LADY

gentleman-at-arms /ˌ··· · ˈ·/ *n* **gentlemen-at-arms** a man who is one of a group who guard a king or queen on important occasions

gentleman farm·er /ˌ··· ˈ··/ *n* a man of high social class who has a farm for pleasure rather than profit

gen·tle·man·ly /ˈdʒentlmənli/ *adj* fair, kind, and honourable in behaviour; being or suitable to a gentleman

gentleman's a·gree·ment /ˌ··· ·ˈ··/ *n* an unwritten agreement made between people who trust each other

gentleman's gen·tle·man /ˌ··· ˈ···/ *n* VALET

gentle sex /ˌ·· ˈ·/ also **fair sex**— *n* [*the*+GU] women considered as a group

gen·tle·wo·man /ˈdʒentlˌwʊmən/ *n* **-women** /ˌwɪmɪ̌n/ **1** *old use* a woman of high social class; lady **2** *old use* a female companion to a queen or noble lady; LADY-IN-WAITING

gent·ly /ˈdʒentli/ *adv* in a gentle way

gen·try /ˈdʒentri/ *n* [(*the*) P] people of high social class: *The* **landed gentry** *are those who own land from which they obtain their income*

Gents, Gents' /dʒents/ (*AmE* **men's room**)— *n* **Gents(')** *BrE infml* a public LAVATORY for men —see also GENT

gen·u·flect /ˈdʒenjʊflekt‖-jə-/ *v* [IØ] to bend the knee as a sign of religious respect for something or someone —**~ion** /ˌdʒenjʊˈflekʃən‖-jə-/ *n* [C;U]

gen·u·ine /ˈdʒenjʊɪ̌n/ *adj* **1** (of an object) real; really what it seems to be **2** (of feelings) real, not pretended —**~ly** *adv* —**~ness** *n* [U]

gen up *v adv* **-nn-** [IØ (*on*);T1] *BrE sl* to (cause to) learn the facts thoroughly: *We genned him up before leaving*

ge·nus /ˈdʒiːnəs/ *n* **genera** /ˈdʒenərə/ a division of a FAMILY (5) of living things, which usu. includes several closely related SPECIES (kinds of animal or plant) —see also GENERIC

ge·o- /ˈdʒiːəʊ, dʒiˈɒ‖ˈdʒiːəʊ, dʒiˈɑ/ *prefix* concerning the earth (world): GEOPHYSICS

ge·o·cen·tric /ˌdʒiːəʊˈsentrɪk/ *adj* having, or measured from, the earth (world) as the central point

ge·og·ra·pher /dʒiˈɒgrəfəʳ‖-ˈɑg-/ *n* a person who studies and knows about GEOGRAPHY

ge·og·ra·phy /dʒiˈɒgrəfi, ˈdʒɒgrəfi‖dʒiˈɑg-/ *n* **1** [U] the study of the countries of the world and of the seas, rivers, towns, etc., on the earth's surface **2 the geography of** *infml* the arrangement or positions of the parts of (a particular place): *the geography of the neighbourhood* —**-phical** /ˌdʒɪəˈgræfɪkəl/ *adj* [Wa5] —**-phically** *adv* [Wa4,5]

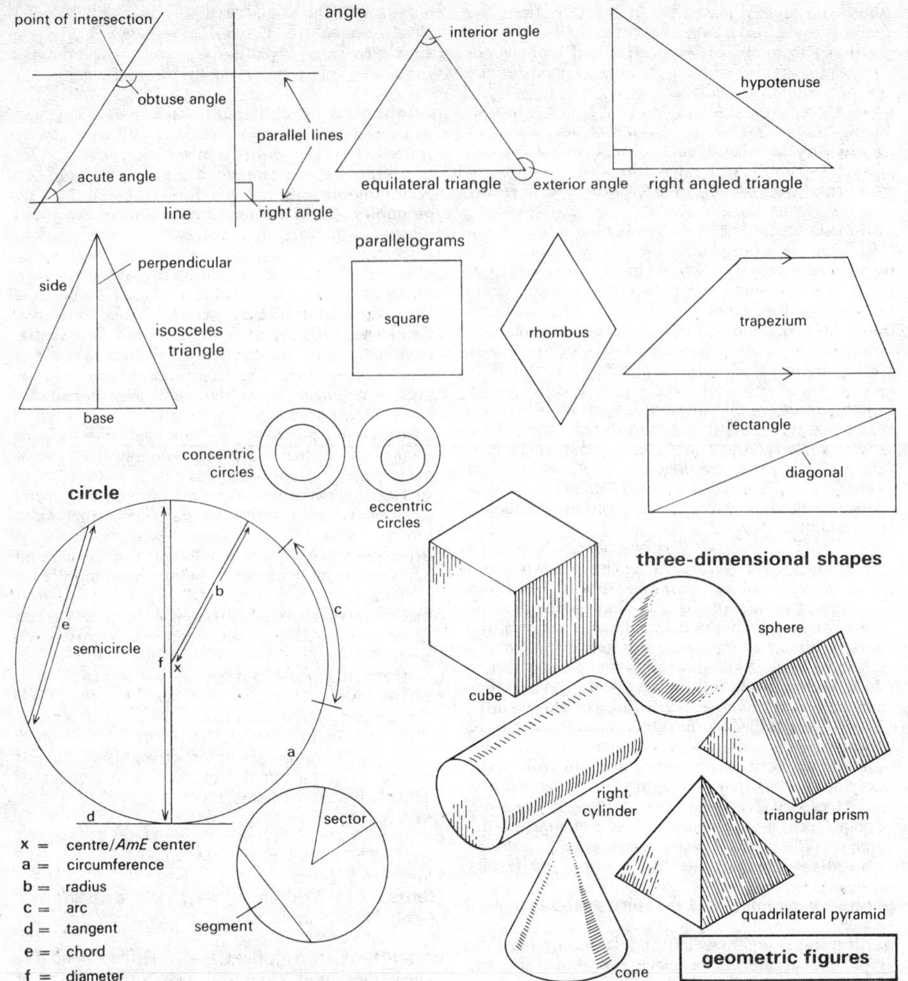

ge·ol·o·gist /dʒiˈɒlədʒɨst‖-ˈɑl-/ *n* a person who studies and knows about GEOLOGY

ge·ol·o·gy /dʒiˈɒlədʒi‖-ˈɑlə-/ *n* [U] the study of the materials (rocks, soil, etc.) which make up the earth, and their changes in the history of the world —**-gical** /ˌdʒɪəˈlɒdʒɪkəl‖-ˈlɑ-/ *adj* [Wa5] —**-gically** /-dʒɪkli/ *adv* [Wa4,5]

ge·o·met·ric /ˌdʒɪəˈmetrɪk/ also **ge·o·met·ri·cal** /-rɪkəl/— *adj* **1** [Wa5] concerning GEOMETRY **2** (esp. of straight lines and regular patterns) like the figures in GEOMETRY: *geometric patterns in Muslim art*

geometric pro·gres·sion /·ˌ·· ·ˈ··/ also **geometrical progression** /·ˌ··· ·ˈ··/— *n* a set of numbers in order in which each is multiplied by a fixed number to produce the next (as in *1, 2, 4, 8, 16, . . .*)

ge·om·e·try /dʒɪˈɒmɨtri‖-ˈɑm-/ *n* [U] the study in MATHEMATICS of the angles and shapes formed by the relationships of lines, surfaces and solids in space

ge·o·phys·ics /ˌdʒiːəʊˈfɪzɪks/ *n* [U] the study of the movements and activities of parts of the earth, including the sea bed —**-ical** /ˌdʒiːəʊˈfɪzɪkəl/ *adj* [Wa5]

ge·o·pol·i·tics /ˌdʒiːəʊˈpɒlɨtɪks‖-ˈpɑ-/ *n* [U] the study of the effect on a country's politics of its position, population, etc. —**-tical** /ˌdʒiːəʊpəˈlɪtɪkəl/ *adj* [Wa5]

georg·ette /dʒɔːˈdʒet‖dʒɔr-/ *n* [U] thin strong cloth, esp. made from silk, from which women's dresses may be made

Georg·ian /ˈdʒɔːdʒən, -dʒɪən‖ˈdʒɔrdʒən/ *adj* **1** of or concerning the area of the USSR called Georgia, in the Caucasus **2** *rare* of or concerning the state of Georgia in the US **3** of, or in the style of, the period of rule of King George the First, Second, and Third, esp. from 1714 to 1811: *Georgian* ARCHITECTURE *in Britain, Ireland, and the US* —compare COLONIAL[1] (3,4) **4** of English poetry of the time of King George the 5th, esp. from 1912 to 1922

ge·ra·ni·um /dʒəˈreɪnɪəm/ *n* any of many closely-related types of plant with red or white flowers, and leaves with rounded pieces (LOBE*s*). It is often grown in gardens or in pots in houses —see picture at FLOWER[1]

ge·ri·at·ric /ˌdʒeriˈætrɪk/ *adj* [Wa5;A] of or concerning GERIATRICS: *geriatric medicine|a geriatric hospital*

ge·ri·a·tri·cian /ˌdʒerɪəˈtrɪʃən/ *n* a doctor who specializes in GERIATRICS
ge·ri·at·rics /ˌdʒeriˈætrɪks/ *n* [U] the medical treatment and care of old people —compare GERONTOLOGY
germ /dʒɜːm‖dʒɜrm/ *n* **1** a very small living thing which cannot be seen but may live on food or dirt or in the body, so causing disease —compare BACTERIA, MICROBE **2** a beginning point, esp. of an idea (esp. in the phr. **the germ of**) **3** also **germ cell**— a small part or cell of a living thing which can grow into a new plant, animal, etc.
Ger·man /ˈdʒɜːmən‖ˈdʒɜr-/ *adj* **1** of or from Germany **2** of the language of Germany, Austria, and large parts of Switzerland
ger·mane /dʒɜːˈmeɪn‖dʒɜr-/ *adj* [(*to*)] (of ideas, remarks, etc.) suitably connected with something; RELEVANT
Ger·man·ic /dʒɜːˈmænɪk‖dʒɜr-/ *adj* **1** (of style, appearance, etc.) of or like Germany or the Germans **2** of the language family that includes German, Dutch, Swedish, English, etc.
German mea·sles /ˌ·· ˈ··/ *n* [U] an infectious disease in which red spots appear on the body for a short time. It may damage unborn children if caught by their mothers
ger·mi·cide /ˈdʒɜːmɪ̈saɪd‖ˈdʒɜr-/ *n* [C;U] a substance in liquid or powder form which kills GERM*s*
ger·mi·nal /ˈdʒɜːmɪ̈nəl‖ˈdʒɜr-/ *adj* in the earliest stage of development —see GERM (2), (3)
ger·mi·nate /ˈdʒɜːmɪ̈neɪt‖ˈdʒɜr-/ *v* [IØ;T1] **1 a** (of a seed) to start growing **b** to cause (a seed) to start growing **2 a** (of an idea, feeling, etc.) to develop **b** to cause (an idea, feeling, etc.) to develop —**-nation** *n* [U]
germ war·fare /ˌ· ˈ··/ *n* [U] BIOLOGICAL WARFARE
ger·on·tol·o·gy /ˌdʒerɒnˈtɒlədʒi‖ˌdʒerənˈtɑ-/ *n* [U] the scientific study of old age, its changes in the body, the effects of these, etc. —compare GERIATRICS
ger·ry·man·der /ˈdʒerimændəʳ, ˌdʒəriˈmændəʳ/ *n* [T1;IØ] to divide (an area) for election purposes so as to give one group or party an unfair advantage over others
ger·und /ˈdʒerənd/ *n* VERBAL NOUN
ge·stalt /gəˈʃtɑːlt/ *n Ger* a whole which is different from the sum of its parts: **Gestalt psychology** *is especially concerned with patterns of experience as wholes*
ge·sta·po /geˈstɑːpəʊ/ *n* [(*the*) GU] *Ger* (*often cap.*) secret police using cruel methods, esp. the secret police of the NAZI period in Germany in the 1930's-1940's
ges·ta·tion /dʒeˈsteɪʃən/ *n* **1** [U] the carrying of a child or young animal inside the mother's body before birth **2** [S] also **gestation period** /·ˈ·· ˌ···/— **a** the time during which this happens **b** the time of development of a thought or idea, before it is made known
ges·tic·u·late /dʒeˈstɪkjʊleɪt‖-kjə-/ *v* [IØ] to make movements of the hands and arms to express something, esp. while speaking —**-lation** /dʒeˌstɪkjʊˈleɪʃən‖-kjə-/ *n* [U;C]
ges·ture[1] /ˈdʒestʃəʳ/ *n* **1** [C] a movement, usu. of the hands, to express a certain meaning: *He made an angry gesture* **2** [U] such movements in general: *English people do not use as much gesture as Italians* **3** [C] an action which is done to show one's feelings, either friendly or unfriendly: *Some countries give rare animals to important foreign visitors as a gesture of friendship*
gesture[2] *v* [L9] to make a GESTURE[1] (1)
get /get/ *v* **got** /gɒt‖gɑt/, **got** *or* (*AmE*) **gotten** /ˈgɒtn‖ˈgɑtn/, *pres. p.* **getting** *not fml* **1** [T1 *no pass.*] to receive or experience: *I got a letter today.|I got a blow on the head* **2** [D1 (*for*);T1 *no pass.*] **a** to obtain or ACQUIRE: *We'll get the shopping tomorrow.|I'll get something to eat before I go out.|You won't get much* (=much money) *for that old piano!|"Did you get a good look at it?"* (SEU W.) **b** to take, or deal with: *I'll get* (*you*) *that book you wanted.|Don't answer the telephone. I'll get it* **3** [T4 *no pass.*] to reach the start of an activity: *Get moving!* (or **get a** MOVE[2] (5) **on**) **4** [V4] to bring (something) to a start: *I'll get the car going* **5** [L (*to be*) 1,7] to (cause oneself to) become: *The food's getting cold.|They must have got lost.|You're getting* (*to be*) *a bad influence on my children.|They've just got married.|He's getting better* (after an illness).|*I'm getting ready* **6** [L8] (*used like the* PASSIVE) to be; become: *"I wouldn't take the slightest risk of getting trapped inside"* (SEU W.) **7** [X7] to bring (into a certain state): *I'll get the children ready for school.|I can't get the car started.|Let me get this clear: is she married or not?* **8** [V3] to cause to do: *I got him to help* (*me*) *when I moved the furniture.|I can't get the car to start.|"Get the Russians to give an English broadcast"* (SEU S.) **9** [L9] to move to or arrive at: *We got there at 8.|Your books have got all over the place.|I'll get home, then.|Where's my pen got to? I can't find it* **10** [X9] to put or move into or out of the stated place: *I can't get it through the door.|Get that cat out of the house before your mother sees it!|We must get him home.|"We'll never get it into the boat by ourselves"* (SEU W.) **11** [T3 *no pass.*] to succeed in (doing): *When you get to know him you find he's quite different from how you imagined.|If I get to see him I'll ask him about it.|* (*AmE*) *At last I've gotten to go to Buckingham Palace!* **12** [T1 *pass. rare*] to prepare (a meal): *I'm in the middle of getting* (*the*) *dinner* **13** [T1 *no pass.*] to catch (an illness): *I got* FLU *twice last year* **14** [T1 *pass. rare*] *infml* to understand: *I try to make him understand, but he never gets the message.|I don't get it; why did he do that?|I don't get you; what do you mean?* **15** [T1 *no pass.*] *infml* **a** to annoy: *It really gets me when he says those stupid things* **b** to excite or cause strong feeling to: *That gets me* (*where it hurts*)*: I hate that kind of rude remark!* **16** [X9] *infml* to hit: *I got the minister on the ear with a potato.|My potato got the minister in the eye* **17** [Wv6;T1] *old use* to become the father of; BEGET —see also **get/be with** CHILD **18** [T1 *pass. rare*] to find and hear (a radio or television station): *Can you get Peking on your radio?* **19** [T1 *no pass.*] to defeat (someone) in an argument: *Now you've just said the opposite of what you said before. I've got you there!|I'll get him on that point* —see also HAVE[2] (6) **20 get done with** *infml* get finished —compare HAVE[3] (24) **done with** **21** [L;X:9] to come or bring to the stated degree of success (esp. in the phrs. **get somewhere/anywhere/nowhere**): *I feel my son has really got somewhere, in spite of his difficulties.|Work, work, work and where does it get you? It gets you exactly nowhere!|The Government won't get anywhere/very far* (*with its plans*) **22 get** (**something**) **done** **a** to cause (something) to be done; HAVE[3] (15): *to get shoes mended* **b** *esp. infml* to experience (something being done to one); HAVE[3] (17): *to get one's hand caught in the door|I got my car* SMASH*ed up in an accident/by some stupid driver* **c** *esp. infml* to do (something necessary): *I'll just get these dishes washed and then I'll come* **23 get above oneself** to have too good an opinion of oneself **24 get** (**something or someone**) **right/wrong** *infml* to understand (something or someone) correctly/wrongly: *Let me get this right—do you want to sell the house?|Don't get me wrong—I'm not complaining!* **25 have got** HAVE[2] (1,3,5,6); HAVE[4] **26 You get** *infml* There is/are: *"Within the Chinese*

language you get quite different sounds" (SEU S.)
USAGE 1 In *fml* writing it is better to avoid **get**, and to use **become**, **receive**, **obtain**, **move**, etc., according to the meaning. 2 In *BrE*, **get** and **become** can both mean "grow to be": *He's* **becoming** *an old man* = He's **getting** (*to be*) *an old man*. One should use **get** in this meaning only when there is no possibility of confusion with its other meaning of "obtain": *He's* **getting** *a new pair of shoes.*|*We're* **getting** *an old man to help in the garden.* **Become** is never used in this 2nd meaning. In *AmE*, **get** (="grow to be") is not directly followed by a noun. They say *He's* **getting** *to be an old man.* 3 Although the British often speak of **getting** to know someone, Americans use this pattern more than the British in the meaning "be allowed" or "have the chance": *She never* **gets** *to drive the car* —see GOTTEN (USAGE) —see also GET ABOUT, GET ACROSS, GET AHEAD, GET ALONG, **get a** MOVE **on**, GET AROUND, GET AROUND TO, GET AT, GET AWAY, GET AWAY WITH, GET BACK, GET BEHIND, GET BY, GET DOWN TO, GET HOME, GET IN, GET INTO, GET OFF, GET OFF WITH, GET ON, GET ONTO, GET OUT, GET OUT OF, GET OVER, GET ROUND, GET ROUND TO, GET THROUGH, GET TOGETHER, GET UP, GET UP TO

get a·bout also **get around**— *v adv* [I∅] **1** to be able to move again after an illness **2** *infml* to travel: *She gets about quite a lot, working for an international company* **3** also **get round**— (of news, etc.) to spread

get a·cross[1] also **get over**— *v adv* [T1;I∅: (*to*)] to (cause to) be understood or accepted (esp. by a large group): *Did your speech get across (to the crowd)?* —compare GET THROUGH[1] (2)

get across[2] *v prep* [T1 *no pass.*] *infml esp. BrE* to annoy (someone)

get a·head *v adv* [I∅] **1** [(*of*)] to advance (beyond someone or something): *You have to get ahead of your competitors* **2** to succeed: *"How to Get Ahead in Business"* (title)

get a·long *v adv* [I∅] **1** (of people) to move away; leave: *I must be getting along now* **2** also **get on, go along, go on**— (of people and activities) to advance; go well: *How is your work getting along?*|*It's getting along nicely, thank you* **3** also **get on**— (of people) to continue (often in spite of difficulties): *We can get along without your help* **4** [(*with*)] also **get on**— (of people) to form or have a friendly relationship (with another or each other): *Do you get along well with your aunt?* **5 Get along with you** also **Go along with you**— *infml* **a** Go away **b** I don't believe you

get a·round also **get round**— *v prep* [T1] to avoid or find a way to deal with (something) to one's advantage: *If you are clever, you can sometimes get around the tax laws*

get around to also **get round to**— *v adv prep* [T1,4] to find time, or have the time, for (something or doing something): *After a long delay, he got around to writing the letter*

get at *v prep* [T1] **1** [*pass. rare*] to reach: *Put the food where the cat can't get at it* **2** [*pass. rare*] also **come at**— *BrE* to reach and discover: *to get at the truth* **3** [*no pass.*] (*in tenses with the* -ing *form*) to mean: *What are you getting at?* **4** [*often pass.*] *infml esp. BrE* to try to BRIBE: *He's being got at* **5** *infml* (*esp. in tenses with the* -ing *form*) to say unkind things esp. repeatedly to: *Stop getting at me!*

get-at-a·ble /ˌget ˈæt əbəl/ *adj* ACCESSIBLE (1)

get·a·way /ˈgetəweɪ/ *n* [S] *infml* an escape: *As the thieves ran out of the bank the getaway car was waiting with its engine running*

get a·way *v adv* [I∅] **1** [(*with*)] to escape, esp. from the scene of a crime, or from being caught: *The thieves got away (with all our money).*|*You should have seen the fish that got away!*|*I'm sorry I'm late, I was in a meeting and couldn't get away* **2 can't get away from** to have to admit the truth of (something, esp. something unpleasant): *You can't get away from the fact that it would cost a lot of money*

get away with *v adv prep* [T1,4] to succeed in (a deceit): *How did he get away with cheating?*|*You'll never get away with it*

get back *v adv* **1** [I∅] to return, esp. to one's home: *I heard you were away. When did you get back?* **2** [I∅] to return to power after having lost it: *Will the Labour Party get back at the next election?* **3** [T1] to obtain again after loss or separation: *He got his former job back after a struggle* **4 get back at someone** also **get one's own back on someone**— *infml* to punish someone in return for a wrong done to oneself: *I'll get back at him one day!*

get be·hind also **get be·hind·hand**— *v adv* [I∅ (*with*)] FALL BEHIND

get by *v adv* [I∅] **1** to continue one's way of life: *She can't get by on such a small income* **2** to be good enough but not very good; be accepted: *Your work will get by, but try to improve it*

get down *v adv* **1** [I∅] (of children) to leave the table after a meal: *Please may I get down?* **2** [T1] to swallow with difficulty: *Try to get the medicine down* **3** [T1] to record in writing: *Get down every word she says* **4** [T1b] to make (someone) feel nervous, ill, or sad: *This continual wet weather is getting me down*

get down to *v adv prep* [T1,4] to begin to give serious attention to: *to get down to work/business* —compare **get down to** BRASS TACKS

get home also **go home**— *v adv* [I∅ (*to*)] (usu. of an unpleasant truth about the person spoken to) to be understood as intended: *Her remark about people who forget birthdays got home to her husband at last* —compare HOME[2] (2,3)

get in[1] *v adv* **1** [I∅] to arrive (inside a place): *The plane got in late* **2** [I∅] COME IN (4) **3** [T1] to collect or buy a supply of (something): *The farmers are getting the crops in* **4** [T1] to call (someone) to one's help, esp. in the house: *Get the doctor in* **5** [T1] to be able to deliver: *Did you get the paper in by the right date?* **6** [T1] to say (something), esp. by interrupting a conversation: *May I get a word in?* —see also **get a word in** EDGEWAYS **7** [I∅ (*at, on*)] to take part in (something): *to get in at the start* **8** [T1;I∅] (to cause to) be admitted to a place of education or a class, as after an examination or test: *Did your son get in?*|*I couldn't get my best pupil in* —see also **get/be in on the** ACT[2], **get/be in on the** GROUND FLOOR, **get/keep one's** HAND[1] (30) **in**

get in[2] *v adv; prep* [I∅;T1] to enter (a vehicle): *They got in and drove off* —compare GET ON[2] (2)

get in·to *v prep* **1** [T1 *no pass.*] to start (often a violent feeling): *to get into a temper*|*to get into a habit* **2** [T1 *no pass.*] to be admitted to (a school or competition): *Did your boy get into the first 3 places?* **3** GET IN[2]: *They got into the car and drove off* **4** [T1;D1] to put (oneself or someone else) into (a bad condition): *I've got (myself) into trouble.*|*I've got him into trouble* **5** [T1 *no pass.*] to learn or become accustomed to: *I'll soon get into the way of things*
USAGE *to* **get** *a woman* **into** *trouble* may mean to make her PREGNANT. Be careful with this expression! —see also **get/take it into one's** HEAD, **get/put it into someone's** HEAD, **get (something) into** SHAPE.

get off[1] *v adv* **1** [I∅] to start a journey; leave: *We must be getting off now.*|*We have to get/be off early tomorrow* **2** [T1] to send: *I'd like to get this letter off by the first post* **3** [T1;I∅: (*with*)] to (cause to) escape punishment: *The man went to prison but the 2 boys got off (with a warning)* **4** [T1;I∅] to (cause to) be able to fall asleep: *I'll come downstairs as soon as I've got the baby off (to sleep)* **5** [I∅] to stop work: *What time do you get off?|I get off at 6 o'clock* **6** [I∅] to begin; leave: *We got off to a good start* **7 tell someone where he can get off** *BrE* also **tell someone where he gets off, tell someone where to get off**— *infml* to tell someone how to behave, or esp. tell someone not to misbehave

get off² *v prep* [T1 *no pass.*] to leave (work): *When do you get off work?* —see also **get something off one's** CHEST

get off³ *v adv; prep* [I∅;T1] **1** to leave (esp. a public vehicle): *They got off the bus and walked away* **2** to stop riding (a bicycle, horse, etc.); DISMOUNT from (a bicycle, horse, etc.) —see also OFF

USAGE One would **get** *out of* a small private boat.

get off with *v adv prep* [T1] *infml esp. BrE* to start a relationship with (someone of the other sex): *She got off with him 5 minutes after the party started*

get on¹ *v adv* [I∅] **1** GET ALONG (2,3,4) **2** (*in tenses with the* -ing *form*) to become later or older: *Time is getting on* **3** [(*with*)] to continue, often after interruption: *Get on with your work!* **4** [(*with*)] to hurry: *Get on (with it), we've a train to catch* **5** [(*in*)] to succeed: *A young man has to think of getting on (in his job)*

get on² *v adv; prep* [I∅;T1] **1** to seat oneself on (a bicycle, horse, etc.): *I'll hold your horse while you get on* **2** to enter (a public vehicle) esp. as a passenger: *They got on (the plane) at Cairo* —compare GET IN²

get on for *v adv prep* [L1] *esp. BrE* (*in tenses with the* -ing *form*) to be almost reaching, in time, age, or distance; be nearly: *Grandfather is getting on for 80*

get on·to *v prep* [T1 *no pass.*] **1** *not fml* to get in touch with (someone): *I'll get onto the director and see if he can help* **2** *not fml* to learn of deceit by (someone): *He tricked people for years until the police got onto him* **3** to be elected or appointed to: *My neighbour got onto the City Council* **4** to begin to talk about or work at: *How did we get onto that subject?* **5** GET ON²: *They got onto the plane at Cairo* —compare GET IN²

get out *v adv* **1** [I∅ (*of*)] to leave: *The meeting went on late, so I got out as soon as I could* **2** [I∅;T1: (*of*)] to (cause to) escape: *Several men got out (of prison) yesterday* **3** [T1] to produce: *to get out a book|The first model of the car had some bad faults, but they've got a better one out now* **4** [T1] to speak with difficulty: *He got out a few words* **5** [I∅] LEAK OUT

get out of *v adv prep* **1** [T1,4;D1 *no pass.*] to (cause to) escape responsibility for (something or doing something): *He tried to get out of helping his mother.|You can't get her out of it* **2** [T1 *no pass.*] to be able to stop or leave: *to get out of a bad habit* **3** [D1] to force (something) from (someone): *The police got the truth out of him* **4** [D1] to gain from: *Mildred enjoys George's visits, but I don't see what he gets out of it*

get o·ver¹ *v adv* **1** [T1b (*with*)] to reach the end of (usu. something unpleasant): *You'll be glad to get your operation over|(infml) over with* **2** [T1;I∅: (*to*)] GET ACROSS

get over² *v prep* [T1] **1** to return to one's usual state of health, happiness, etc., after a bad experience of or with: *to get over an illness|She can't get over the man she was going to marry; he disappeared so unexpectedly.|Sooner or later you'll get over the shock* **2** to find a way to deal with: *How shall we get over this difficulty?* **3 I can't/couldn't get over** *not fml* I am/was very much surprised at: *I can't get over him/his having married again!*

get round¹ *v adv* **1** [I∅] GET ABOUT (2) **2** [T1] BRING AROUND (1)

get round² *v prep* [T1] **1** GET AROUND **2** to persuade (someone) to accept one's own way of thinking: *Father doesn't want to let us go, but I know I can get round him*

get round to *v adv prep* [T1,4] GET AROUND TO

get through¹ *v adv* **1** [I∅ (*to*)] to reach someone, esp. by telephone: *I tried to telephone you but I couldn't get through.|I can't get through to Paris* **2** [T1,5;I∅: (*to*)] to (cause to) be understood by (someone): *I can't get (it) through to him that he must rest.|I can't seem to get it through (to him)* —compare GET ACROSS **3** [I∅ (*with*)] to finish: *When you get through (with your work), let's go out* **4** [T1b;I∅] to (cause to) pass through a parliament: *to get the new laws through|The new law got through*

get through² *v prep* **1** [D1;T1] to (cause to) come successfully to the end of: *to get through/get someone through an examination|to get through the winter* **2** [T1] to get to the end of; finish: *to get through the work/money/food*

get to·geth·er *v adv* [I∅ (*with*)] *not fml* to have a meeting or party: *When can we get together?|It's a long time since I got together with George*

get-to·geth·er /'· ·,··/ *n* a friendly informal meeting for enjoyment: *"The old school get-together that you both went to"* (SEU W.)

get·up /'getʌp/ *n infml* **1** a set of clothes, esp. unusual clothes **2** the outer appearance

get up *v adv* **1** [T1;I∅] to (cause to) rise from bed in the morning **2** [T1;I∅] to (cause to) leave one's bed after illness **3** [I∅] (of a wind, fire, etc.) to arise and increase **4** [T1] to arrange or perform: *to get up a party/a play* **5** [T1] *BrE* to study: *to get up a subject/one's notes* **6** [X9] to ornament or change the appearance of: *She got herself up in a new dress.|She got herself up as a Roman soldier for the school play* **7** [T1] to increase the amount of: *get up steam/speed* —see also **get/put someone's** BACK¹ (17) **up**

get up to *v adv prep* [T1 *no pass.*] to reach: *What page have you got up to?*

ge·um /'dʒiːəm/ also **avens**— *n* any of several kinds of small garden plant with red or yellow flowers

gew·gaw /'gjuːgɔː/ *n* a bright attractive ornament or toy of small value

gey·ser /'giːzəʳ‖'gaɪzəʳ/ *n* **1** a natural spring of hot water which from time to time rises suddenly into the air from the earth **2** an apparatus which is used in kitchens, bathrooms, etc., for heating water by gas

ghar·ry /'gæri/ *n* (in India) a carriage drawn by one or more horses and which may be for hire

ghast·ly /'gɑːstli‖'gæstli/ *adj* [Wa2] **1** (of a person) very pale and ill-looking **2** causing great fear: *Hearing of their death was the most ghastly news* **3** *infml* very bad: *We had a ghastly time at the party, because we didn't know anybody* —**-liness** *n* [U]

ghat, ghaut /gɔːt/ *n Ind & PakE* **1** a narrow way between mountains **2** [*usu. pl.*] a mountain: *the Western Ghats* **3** a set of steps, as from a house or temple, leading down to a river or lake **4** a place where dead bodies are ceremonially burnt (esp. in the phr. **burning ghats**)

ghee, ghi /giː/ *n* [U] *Ind & PakE* melted butter, as used in India, often made from the milk of BUFFALOes

gher·kin /'gɜːkɪ̣n‖'gɜr-/ *n* a small green vegetable which is usually eaten after being PICKLEd in

VINEGAR (= kept in a sour liquid); type of CUCUMBER

ghet·to /ˈgetəʊ/ *n* **-tos** a part of a city in which a group of people live who are poor and/or are not accepted as full citizens

ghost¹ /gəʊst/ *n* **1** (the spirit of) a dead person who appears again: *Do you believe in ghosts?* (= that they exist) **2** *old use* the quality which makes one live (esp. in the phr. **give up the ghost** = die) **3** a second, fainter image, esp. on a television picture (SCREEN) **4** also **ghost writer** /ˈ· ˌ··/— a person who writes material which another person gives out as his own **5 the ghost of a** the slightest: *You haven't got the ghost of a chance of getting the job*

ghost² *v* [T1;(I∅)] to write (something) as a GHOST¹ (4): *ghosted the general's* MEMOIR*s*

ghost·ly /ˈgəʊstli/ *adj* **1** [Wa2;B] like a GHOST or spirit of the dead, esp. having a faint or uncertain colour and shape: *I saw a ghostly light ahead of me in the darkness* **2** [Wa5;A] *lit & old use* concerned with religion, as from a priest: *ghostly advice* —**-liness** *n* [U]

ghost town /ˈ· ·/ *n* an empty town, esp. one that was once busy because people came to find gold or other precious substances, and left when they were finished

ghoul /guːl/ *n* **1** a spirit which (in the stories told in Eastern countries) takes bodies from graves to eat them **2** a person who delights in (thoughts of) dead bodies and other nasty things

ghoul·ish /ˈguːlɪʃ/ *adj* very unpleasant; concerned with dead bodies and nasty behaviour: *ghoulish stories* —**~ness** *n* [U]

GHQ *abbrev. for:* General HEADQUARTERS

ghyll /gɪl/ *n NW EngE* GORGE (1) —see VALLEY (USAGE)

GI /ˌdʒiː ˈaɪ/ *n* **GI's** *or* **GIs** **1** a soldier in the US army, esp. during World War 2 **2 GI bride** a woman who married a US soldier when he was in her home country, esp. during World War 2 **3 GI Joe** a typical US soldier, esp. of World War 2

gi·ant /ˈdʒaɪənt/ *n* **1** [C] a man who is much bigger than is usual **2** [C] (in fairy stories) a very big, strong creature in the form of a man, but often unfriendly to human beings and very cruel and stupid **3** [C] a person of great ability: *Shakespeare is a giant among writers* **4** [A] very large: *The giant (size) packet gives you more for less money!*

gi·ant·ess /ˈdʒaɪəntɪ̇s/ *n rare* a female GIANT (1, 2)

giant pan.da /ˌ·· ˈ··/ also **panda**— *n* a large bearlike animal that has black and white fur and lives in China

gib·ber /ˈdʒɪbəʳ/ *v* [I∅] (of monkeys and men) to talk or appear to talk very fast (sometimes because of fear) in a way that is meaningless for the hearer

gib·ber·ish /ˈdʒɪbərɪʃ/ *n* [U] meaningless sounds, esp. talk which doesn't make sense

gib·bet /ˈdʒɪbɪ̇t/ *n* (in former times) the GALLOWS or wooden post with another piece at right angles at the top, from which criminals were hanged by the neck until dead

gib·bon /ˈgɪbən/ *n* any of several types of animal like a monkey with no tail and long arms, which lives in trees and is the smallest APE —see picture at PRIMATE²

gib·bous /ˈgɪbəs/ *adj* [Wa5;A] (of the moon) having the bright part filling more than half a circle

gibe, jibe /dʒaɪb/ *n* [(*about, at*)] a remark which makes someone look foolish, or points out someone's faults: *Don't make gibes about her behaviour until you know the reason for it*

gibe at, jibe at *v prep* [T1 (*for*)] to make a GIBE about (someone)

gib·lets /ˈdʒɪblɪ̇ts/ *n* [P] the parts, such as the heart and LIVER, of a bird which are taken out before the bird is cooked, but may themselves be cooked and eaten

gid·dy /ˈgɪdi/ *adj* [Wa1] **1** (of a person) feeling unsteady, as though everything is moving round oneself and/or as though one is falling: *The children enjoyed going round and round, but I felt giddy just watching them* **2** causing a feeling of unsteady movement and/or falling: *We looked down from a giddy height* **3** (of a person) not serious; too interested in amusement: *She's a giddy thing; you'll never get her to take life seriously* —**giddily** *adv* —**giddiness** *n* [U]

gift /gɪft/ *n* **1** [C] something which is given freely; present **2** [C (*of, for*)] a natural ability to do something: *He has the gift of speaking well.|He has a gift for music* **3** [S9] *old use* the power of giving: *The house and job are in his gift* (= he can give them to whoever he wants) **4** [C *usu. sing.*] *sl* something obtained easily, or cheap at the price: *At £2 it's a gift!* **5 a free gift** some small object given away, usu. with a certain product, to encourage people to buy that product —compare GIVEAWAY (2) **6 a gift from the Gods** a lucky chance **7 I wouldn't have it as a gift** also **I wouldn't have it if you gave it to me**— I don't want this at all, it's too bad to accept —see also **gift** HORSE

gift·ed /ˈgɪftɪ̇d/ *adj* **1** having one or more special abilities; TALENTED: *a very gifted person* **2** (esp. of a child) more INTELLIGENT than most: *the education of gifted children*

gig¹ /gɪg/ *n* **1** a small 2-wheeled carriage drawn by one horse and used esp. in former times **2** a small boat for rowing or sailing which belongs to a ship

gig² *n sl* a job, esp. a musician's job for a certain period of time: *had a few gigs playing at* JAZZ *clubs in New York*

gi·gan·tic /dʒaɪˈgæntɪk/ *adj* unusually large in amount or size —**~ally** *adv* [Wa4]

gig·gle¹ /ˈgɪgəl/ *v* [Wv3] **1** [I∅] to make GIGGLE*s*² **2** [T1] to express with GIGGLE*s*²: *She giggled her amusement*

giggle² *n* **1** a form of laughter which is repeated in an uncontrolled manner, esp. by young girls (note the phr. **have the giggles**) **2 do something for a giggle** *infml* to do something for a joke, not for serious reasons

gig·o·lo /ˈʒɪgələʊ, ˈdʒɪ-/ *n* **-los** **1** a man who is paid to dance with a woman as her partner **2** *derog* a man who is paid to be a woman's lover and companion

gild /gɪld/ *v* [T1] **1** to cover with a thin coat of gold or gold paint **2** to make bright as if with gold: *sunshine gilded the rooftops* **3 gild the lily** to try to ornament something already beautiful, so spoiling the effect **4 gild the pill** see **sugar the** PILL —**~er** *n*

gild·ed /ˈgɪldɪ̇d/ *adj* fortunate and rich (esp. in the phr. **gilded youth**)

gild·ing /ˈgɪldɪŋ/ *n* [U] any material which is used to GILD (1) things

gill¹ /dʒɪl/ *n* a measure equal to ¼ PINT or 0·142 LITRE*s* —see WEIGHTS & MEASURES TABLE

gill² /gɪl/ *n* **1** one of the organs through which a fish breathes by taking in water to pass over them —see picture at FISH¹ **2** [*usu. pl.*] *infml & humor* the area of skin around the neck and under the ears (esp. in the phrs. **go white/green about the gills** = with fear/sickness)

gil·lie, gilly /ˈgɪli/ *n* (in Scotland) a man who serves a sportsman while he is shooting or fishing

gilt /gɪlt/ *n* [U] **1** shiny material, esp. gold, used as a thin covering: *silver gilt|The plates have a gilt edge* **2 take the gilt off the gingerbread** *BrE infml* to take away the part that makes the whole attractive

gilt-edged /ˌ· ˈ··/ *adj* **gilt-edged shares/stock/securities** shares, esp. those offered for sale to the public by the Government, that are considered safe, paying a small rate of interest but unlikely to fail

gim·crack /ˈdʒɪmkræk/ *n infml* something attractive or ornamental, but badly made and worthless

gim·let /ˈgɪmlǀt/ *n* a tool which is used to make holes in wood so that screws may enter easily: (fig.) *Eyes like gimlets* (=which look very hard) —compare AWL, BRADAWL and see pictures at TOOL[1]

gim·mick /ˈgɪmɪk/ *n infml* **1** a trick object or part of an object which is used to draw attention: *The new style buttons are just a gimmick; you can't even fasten them* **2** (esp. in advertising) a special way of acting or point of appearance which is noticeable: *It's a well-known advertising gimmick to show babies or pretty girls with new goods you want to sell*

gim·mick·y /ˈgɪmɪki/ *adj infml* like or using GIMMICKs: *a gimmicky idea*

gin[1] /dʒɪn/ *n* **1** a machine, esp. one for separating cotton from its seeds **2** a trap, usu. for catching animals or birds

gin[2] *n* [U] a colourless alcoholic drink made from grain and certain berries

gin·ger[1] /ˈdʒɪndʒəʳ/ *n* [U] **1** a plant with a root which can be used in cooking to give a very hot strong taste **2** the quality of being active: *Put some ginger into your running!*

ginger[2] *adj, n* [B;U] (of) an orange-brown colour, esp. the least usual colour of human hair: *He's called "Ginger" because of his bright ginger hair*

ginger ale /ˌ·· ˈ·‖ˈ·· ·/ also **ginger beer**— *n* [U] a gassy non-alcoholic drink made with GINGER

gin·ger·bread /ˈdʒɪndʒəbred‖-dʒər-/ *n* [U] a cake or BISCUIT with GINGER in it

ginger group /ˈ·· ·/ *n* [GC] a group of people, usu. within a political party, who try to make the leaders of the party take stronger action on a particular matter

gin·ger·ly /ˈdʒɪndʒəli‖-ər-/ *adj, adv* (in a way that is) careful and controlled in movement so as not to cause harm: *He gingerly picked the delicate flower.|Gingerly I reached out to touch the snake*

ginger nut /ˈ·· ·/ also (*esp. AmE*) **gin·ger·snap** /ˈdʒɪndʒəsnæp‖-ər-/— *n esp. BrE* a hard BISCUIT with GINGER in it

ginger up *v adv* [T1] to make (something) more effective, exciting or active: *More men are needed to ginger up the police force*

ging·ham /ˈgɪŋəm/ *n* [U] a type of cotton which is usually woven with a pattern of squares (CHECKs[1] (7)) and used for making girls' dresses and tablecloths

gin·gi·vi·tis /ˌdʒɪndʒǀˈvaɪtǀs/ *n* [U] a medical condition in which the flesh out of which the teeth grow (GUMs) is red, swollen, and painful

gink·go, gingko /ˈgɪŋkəʊ/ also **maiden hair tree**— *n* **-goes** a type of tree which grows in China and Japan and has long leaves and yellow fruit

gin pal·ace /ˈ· ˌ··/ *n derog* (in former times, esp. in the last century) a shop or place for drinking cheap alcohol

gin·seng /ˈdʒɪnseŋ‖-sæŋ, -seŋ/ *n* **1** (a plant which has) a root which may be used for making a medicine used originally in China and Korea **2** the medicine itself

gip·sy, *AmE usu.* **gypsy** /ˈdʒɪpsi/ *n* **1** a member of a dark-haired race which may be of Indian origin and now travels about in covered carts (CARAVANs), earning money as horse dealers, musicians, basket makers, FORTUNE TELLERs, etc. **2** *infml & sometimes derog* a person who habitually wanders or who has the habits of someone who does not stay for long in one place

gi·raffe /dʒǀˈrɑːf‖-ˈræf/ *n* [Wn1] a type of African animal with a very long neck and legs and orangeish skin with dark spots, which eats the leaves from the branches of trees —see picture at RUMINANT

gird /gɜːd‖gɜrd/ *v* **girded** *or* **girt** /gɜːt‖gɜrt/ [D1+*round/with*] *fml & lit* to fasten (something or someone) round/with (something): *The climber girded himself with a rope.|a sea-girt island shining in the sun*

gir·der /ˈgɜːdəʳ‖ˈgɜr-/ *n* a strong beam, usu. of iron or steel, which supports the smaller beams in a floor or roof or forms the support of one part of a bridge —see picture at SITE[1]

gir·dle[1] /ˈgɜːdl‖ˈgɜr-/ *n* **1** an undergarment for women meant to hold the flesh firm; sort of light CORSET **2** a cord tied round the waist to hold loose clothes in **3** *lit* something which ENCIRCLEs something else **4** a ring round a tree which is left when a piece of the thick outer covering (BARK) is removed

girdle[2] *v* [T1] to enclose or surround

gird on *v adv* [T1] *esp. lit* to fasten (something) on, usu. to a belt: *He girded his father's sword on*

gird up *v adv* [T1] **1** *esp. lit* to roll (clothes) up to the waist: *Her long skirt was girt up above her knees* **2 gird up one's loins** also **gird one's loins**— *bibl or pomp* to get ready for action

girl /gɜːl‖gɜrl/ *n* **1** [C] **a** a young female person: *There are more girls than boys in this school* **b** a daughter: *My little girl is ill* **2** [C;N] *infml* a woman: *The men have invited the girls to play football against them* **3** [C] **a** (*usu. in comb.*) a woman worker: *the office girls|shop girls* **b** (esp. formerly) a female servant: *a girl who looks after the children* **4** [C *usu. with poss.*] GIRLFRIEND: *John's girl* **5 old girl** *esp. BrE* **a** *old use* a friendly way of speaking to a woman **b** a female former pupil of a school —compare OLD BOY

girl Friday /ˌ· ˈ··/ *n* [*usu. with poss.*] a female secretary or helper in an office who does all the useful and important jobs that the man in charge wants done

girl·friend /ˈgɜːlfrend‖ˈgɜrl-/ *n* a girl companion, esp. one with whom a boy or man spends time and shares amusements: *He seems to have a new girlfriend every week*

girl guide /ˌ· ˈ·/ (*AmE* **girl scout** /ˌ· ˈ·‖ˈ· ·/)— *n* (*often caps.*) a member of an association for girls, the **Girl Guides,** who take part in activities like camping, and learn useful skills —compare BOY SCOUT

girl·hood /ˈgɜːlhʊd‖ˈgɜrl-/ *n* [U] the state or time of being a young girl

girl·ie, girly /ˈgɜːli‖ˈgɜrli/ *adj* [Wa5;A] *infml* (usu. of magazines) showing young women with (almost) bare bodies, photographed in positions which are intended to be sexy and exciting

girl·ish /ˈgɜːlɪʃ‖ˈgɜr-/ *adj* like or suitable to a girl: *sounds of girlish laughter* —**~ly** *adv* —**~ness** *n* [U]

gi·ro /ˈdʒaɪərəʊ/ *n* (in Britain) a system of banking in which a central organization runs the accounts which are held at different branches, esp. that used by the Post Office (**National Giro**)

girt /gɜːt‖gɜrt/ *past t. and p. of* GIRD

girth /gɜːθ‖gɜrθ/ *n* **1** [U;C] the measure of thickness round something: *the girth of a tree|His girth is increasing* (= he's getting fatter) **2** [C] a band which is passed tightly round the middle of a horse, donkey, etc., to keep firm the load or SADDLE (= rider's seat) on its back

gist /dʒɪst/ *n* [*the*+R (*of*)] the general meaning, esp. of a long statement; main points (as of an argument): *I haven't time to read this report; can you give me the gist of it?*

give¹ /gɪv/ *v* **gave** /geɪv/, **given** /ˈgɪvən/ **1** [D1] to pass into someone's hands or care: *Give me the baby.|I'll give you charge of the house while we're away.|to give one's daughter in marriage (to a man)|Can you give me a job?* **2** [D1 (*to*);T1;L9] to hand (something) over as a present: *You gave him money and he wasted it.|He gives freely (to the poor)* **3** [D1 (*to*);T1 (*for*)] to pay in exchange: *She gave him a pound (£1) for his help.|What price did you give?* **4** [D1] to have (an effect) on (someone); cause to experience: *I hope my son hasn't given you a lot of trouble.|The news gave us a shock.|to give pleasure/pain* **5** [D1;T1] to produce; supply with: *cows give milk|That book has given me several ideas* **6** [D1] to allow to have: *Give him enough time to get home before you telephone.|Give me a chance to try the job.|Were you given a choice, or did you have to do it?* **7** [D1 (*to*)] to be the cause of (someone's illness): *Moving the furniture always gives me a pain in the back.|Cows can give sickness to human beings* **8** [D1 (*to*);T1] to set aside (time, thought, strength, etc.) for a purpose: *She gives all her time to her family.|Give your work more attention.|Many have given their lives in the cause of truth* **9** [D1;T1] to tell in words: *Can you give me more information?|The letter gave surprising news* **10** [D1;T1] to show (as a sign): *He gave proof of his courage when he ran back into the burning house.|The things we knew gave us a picture of a very strange man.|That clock gives the right time* **11** [D1;T1 (*for*)] to offer (a performance or amusement): *We are giving John a party for his birthday.|He gave a reading of his poetry.|Another performance will be given next week* **12** [D1] to punish with (time in) prison: *He was given 3 months* **13** [D1] to admit the truth of: *It's too late to go to the party, I give you that. But we could go somewhere else* **14** [D1] to call on (people present) to drink to the health of; ask (people) to drink a TOAST² (2) to: *Gentlemen, I give you the President* **15** [D1 *no pass.*] to allow (part of one's body) to be used by another person: *to give someone one's arm (to hold or lean on)|gave him her hand to shake|She gave me her cheek to kiss.|She gave herself (sexually)* **16** [T1;(D1)] to do an action (in such phrs. as **give a song, a beating, a cry,** etc. = to sing, beat, cry): *She gave a sudden shout of surprise.|Give me a kiss.|to give an order|to give permission|gave the door a push* **17** [V3 *often pass.*] to cause to believe because of information given: *They gave me to understand they would wait here.|You gave us to believe it would be changed.|I was given to understand that he was ill* **18** [X9 *usu. pass.*] *BrE* (in certain games) to declare (a player) to be in the stated condition: *Edrich was given* OUT¹ (8).|*Bowles was given* OFFSIDE **19** [IØ] to bend or stretch under pressure: *The leather will give when you've been wearing the shoes a few weeks* **20 give as good as one gets** to answer or fight with force equal to that of the other person **21 give it to someone (hot/straight)** *sl* to scold someone (in an angry or direct way) **22 Give me, her, etc., a/an a** I, she, at, etc. like(s) (best) a/an: *Give me a nice old house any time* **b** If you give me, her, etc., a/an: *Give her a new toy and she'll destroy it within the day* **23 give or take (a certain amount)** or (a certain amount) more or less: *It will take an hour, give or take a few minutes (either way)* **24 give (someone) what for** *infml* to scold severely, or perhaps beat, (someone) **25 give way (to) a** to yield, as in an argument **b** to break: *The floor gave way under the weight* **c** to yield when driving a car **d** to become less useful or important than: *Steam trains gave way to electric trains* **e** to allow oneself to show (esp. a feeling) **26 What gives?** *sl* (showing surprise) What's going on? Why is this strange thing happening? —see also GIVE AWAY, GIVE BACK, GIVE IN, GIVE OFF, GIVE ONTO, GIVE OUT, GIVE OVER, GIVE OVER TO, GIVE UP, GIVE UP ON —**giver** *n*

give² *n* [U] the quality of moving (esp. bending, stretching, or loosening) under pressure: *Shoes get slightly larger after wearing, because of the give in the leather.|There was too much give in the rope, and it stretched and slipped off the box it was holding*

give-and-take /ˌ· · ˈ·/ *n* [U] willingness of each person to yield to (some of) the other's wishes: *You can never say that one of you is right and the other's wrong; there has to be a bit of give-and-take on both sides*

give·a·way /ˈgɪvəweɪ/ *n* **1** [S] something unintentional that makes a secret known (note the phr. **a dead giveaway**): *She tried to hide her feelings, but the tears in her eyes were a (dead) giveaway* **2** [C] *AmE* something given in a shop with a certain product to encourage people to buy that product **3 at giveaway prices** almost free; very cheap

give a·way *v adv* **1** [T1] to make someone a present or prize of (something): *gave away all her money to the poor* **2** [T1] to deliver or officially hand over (a woman) to the husband at the wedding: *Mary was given away by her father* **3** [T1, 6b] to tell (a secret) intentionally or unintentionally (esp. in the phr. **give the game/show away**) **4** [T1b] to make known the truth about: *His way of speaking English/His clothes gave him away* **5** [T1] to show or make known (an answer): *The examiners have given away the answer* **6** [T1] to lose carelessly: *He gave away his last chance of winning the election when he said the wrong thing*

give back *v adv* **1** [D1 (*to*);T1] to return (something) to the owner or original possessor: *Give it back (to me).|I hope the holiday will give him back his good spirits* **2** [T1] to throw back (sound or light): *The cave gives back the sound of your voice*

give in *v adv* [(*to*)] **1** [IØ] to yield: *The boys fought until one gave in.|Don't give in to him/his opinion* **2** [T1] to deliver; hand in: *Give your examination papers in (to the teacher) when you've finished*

giv·en¹ /ˈgɪvən/ *adj* **1** fixed for a purpose and stated as such: *The work must be done within the given time* **2** if allowed or provided with: *(If) given the same treatment again, he is sure to get well.|I'd come and see you in Austria, (if) given the chance* **3** (at the end of official papers) written, signed, and marked with the date: *given on the 15th day of April, in the year 1543* **4 be given to** ((doing) something) to be in the habit of (doing) something: *He's given to (taking) long walks*

given² *prep* if one takes into account: *Given their inexperience, they've done a good job.|Given that they're inexperienced, they've done a good job*

given name /ˈ·· ·/ *n AmE* FIRST NAME

give off *v adv* [T1a] to send out (esp. a liquid, gas, or smell): *to give off steam|to give off a bad smell*

give on·to also **give on**— *v prep* [T1 *no pass.*] to have a view of, or lead straight to: *The window/door gives onto the garden*

give out *v adv* **1** [T1 (*to*)] to give to each of several people: *Give out the examination papers.|Give the money out to the children* **2** [IØ] also **run out**— *infml* to come to an end: *Our supply of sugar has given out.|His strength gave out* **3** [IØ] *infml* to stop working: *The engine gave out* **4** [T1] to make (something) known publicly: *The news was given out that the king had died.|The date of the election will be given out soon* **5** [L *to be* 1,7] to declare (oneself): *He gave himself out to be the real ruler of the country* **6** [T1a] to send out (esp. a noise): *The radio is giving out a strange signal*

give o·ver *v adv* **1** [T4a;I∅: *often imper.*] *BrE infml* to stop (doing something): *Give over hitting your little brother.|Do give over!* **2** [T1b (*to*)] to deliver (something) to someone's care; hand over: *The keys were given over to our neighbours during our absence* **3** [T1b (*to*)] to offer (someone) as a prisoner: *We gave him over to the police* —compare GIVE UP (8)

give over to *v adv prep* [D1;V4b] **1** to set (a time or place) apart for: *The building was given over to the youth club.|The evening was given over to singing and dancing* **2** also **give up to**— to give (oneself or something) completely to (something): *to give oneself over to one's work|to give one's life over to helping people* **3 be given over to** to be hopelessly concerned in (something bad): *He is given over to evil*

give up *v adv* **1** [T1,4] to stop having or doing (something): *The doctor told him to give up sugar and smoking.|I've given up the idea* **2** [T1] to stop working at or trying to do (something): *to give up one's studies* **3** [I∅] to stop trying to guess a joke or mystery: *I give up, tell me the end of the story* **4** [I∅] to stop attempting something: *All the girls swam the lake except 2, who gave up halfway* **5** [T1b (*for*)] to stop believing that (someone) can be saved, esp. from death: *The doctors gave my uncle up, but he lived.|The boy was given up for lost/for dead* **6** [T1] to stop having a relationship with (someone): *She gave up her lover to save her marriage.|Don't give your friends up* **7** [T1b (*to*)] to offer (someone or oneself) as a prisoner: *He gave himself up (to the police).|We gave him up to the police* —compare GIVE OVER (5) **8** [T1 (*to*)] to deliver or allow to pass (to someone else): *We had to give up the town (to the enemy).|Give your seat up to the old lady* **9** [T1b] *infml* GIVE UP ON: *I give you up: you'll never know anything about dictionaries*

give up on *v adv prep* [T1 *no pass.*] *infml* to have no further hope for: *I give up on you: you'll never know anything about dictionaries*

giz·zard /ˈgɪzəd‖-ərd/ *n* **1** the second stomach of a bird where food is broken into powder with the help of small stones it has swallowed **2 stick in one's gizzard** to be hard (to do, or think of doing): *It sticks in my gizzard to tell him his work is bad after all his efforts*

gla·cé /ˈglæseɪ‖glæˈseɪ/ *adj Fr* **1** (of fruits) covered with sugar **2** (of leather, silk, etc.) smooth and shiny

gla·cial /ˈgleɪʃəl/ *adj* [Wa5] **1** of or concerning ice or GLACIERs **2** of or concerning an ICE AGE **3** *infml* very cold

gla·ci·er /ˈglæsɪəʳ‖ˈgleɪʃər/ *n* a mass of ice which moves very slowly down a mountain valley —see picture at MOUNTAIN

glad /glæd/ *adj* **-dd- 1** [Wa1;F (*about, of*),F5a] (of people) pleased and happy about something: *I'm glad he's got the job/about his new job.|Thanks for the help; I was very glad of it* **2** [Wa1;A] causing happiness: *glad news of victory* **3** [Wa5;F3] *polite* very willing: *I'll be glad to help you repair the car if you show me what's wrong.|Yes, I'll be glad to* —**~ness** *n* [U]

glad·den /ˈglædn/ *v* [T1] to make glad or happy: *The sight of the child running about after his long illness gladdened his father's heart*

glade /gleɪd/ *n lit* an open space without trees in a wood or forest

glad eye /ˌ· ˈ·/ *n* [*the*+R] *sl* a look of sexual invitation (note the phr. **to give someone the glad eye**)

glad hand /ˌ· ˈ·, ˈ· ·/ *n* [*the*+R] a warm welcome or greeting, esp. one made in order to gain personal advantage (note the phr. **to give someone the glad hand**)

glad·i·a·tor /ˈglædieɪtəʳ/ *n* (in ancient times in Rome) an armed man who fought against men or wild animals in a public place (ARENA) —**~ial** /ˌglædɪəˈtɔːrɪəl‖-tor-/ *adj*

glad·i·o·lus /ˌglædiˈəʊləs/ *n* **-li** /laɪ/ *or* **-luses** a type of garden plant with sword-shaped leaves and tall, bright-coloured flowers

glad·ly /ˈglædli/ *adv polite* very willingly; eagerly: *I'll gladly come and help you; you should have asked me before*

glad rags /ˈ· ·/ *n* [P *often with poss.*] *infml* fine clothes; (one's) best clothes: *Put on your glad rags, and let's go out*

glam·o·rize, -ise /ˈglæməraɪz/ *v* [T1] to make (something) appear better, more attractive, etc., than in reality —**-rization** /ˌglæməraɪˈzeɪʃən‖-mərə-/ *n* [U]

glam·or·ous, -ourous /ˈglæmərəs/ *adj* having or causing GLAMOUR: *a glamorous job/girl* —**~ly** *adv*

glam·our, *AmE* **-or** /ˈglæməʳ/ *n* [U] **1** charm and beauty with a ROMANTIC[1] (1) power of attraction: *the glamour of foreign countries* **2** personal charm which excites admiration and esp. attracts men to women: *a woman with glamour*

glance[1] /glɑːns‖glæns/ *v* **1** [L9, esp. *at*] to give a rapid look: *He glanced at his watch.|I glanced round the room before I left.|She glanced down the list of names.|She glanced through the library book.|(fig.) In his book he only glances at the difficulties of the new government before passing on to the history of the country* **2** [I∅] (of bright surfaces) to flash with REFLECTed light: *The glasses glanced in the firelight* **3 glance one's eye down/over/through,** etc. to give a hurried reading or look: *He glanced his eye over the titles of the articles*

glance[2] *n* **1** [(*at*)] **a** a rapid look: *One glance at his face told me he was ill* **b** a rapid movement of the eyes: *He gave her an admiring glance* **2** a flash of light, usu. from a bright object: *A glance from one of the moving swords fell across his eyes and prevented him from seeing the blow* **3** a blow which slips to the side: *A sudden glance of the sword cut his shoulder* **4 at a glance** with one look; at once: *He saw at a glance that she'd been crying*

USAGE A **glance** is a quick look at something; to **glance** at something is to look at it quickly: *She* **glanced** *over her shoulder.|She* CAST *a quick* **glance** *at herself in the mirror.* A **glimpse** is a momentary sight of something: *She caught a sudden* **glimpse** *of herself in the mirror.* The verb to **glimpse** has the same meaning as the noun but is not common.

glance off *v adv; prep* [T1;I∅] to touch (something) with a light blow and move off at once: *The sword glanced off (the shield)*

glanc·ing /ˈglɑːnsɪŋ‖ˈglæn-/ *adj* [Wa5;A] (of a blow) which slips to one side: *He hit him a glancing blow on the chin* —**~ly** *adv*

gland /glænd/ *n* an organ of the body which produces a liquid substance, either to be poured out of the body or into the blood stream

glan·du·lar /ˈglændjʊləʳ‖-dʒə-/ *adj* concerning one or more GLANDs, or produced from a gland

glare[1] /gleəʳ/ *v* **1** [L9] to shine with a strong light and/or in a way unpleasant to the eyes: *The sun glared out of the blue sky* **2** [I∅ (*at*)] to look in an angry way: *They didn't fight, but stood there glaring at one another* **3** [T1 (*at*)] to express by doing this: *Their mother stopped the sisters fighting, but they still glared hatred at each other*

glare[2] *n* [(*the*) S] **1** a hard, unpleasant effect given by a strong light: *There was a red glare over the burning city* **2** an angry look or STARE: *I started to offer help, but the fierce glare on his face stopped me*

3 a state which continually draws the attention of the public

glar·ing /ˈgleərɪŋ/ *adj* **1 a** (of light) hard and too bright: *This glaring light hurts my eyes* **b** (of colours) too bright: *a glaring red* **2** (of mistakes) very noticeable: *The report is full of glaring faults* **3** with a GLARE[2] (2); fierce-looking; *glaring eyes* —**~ly** *adv*

glass /glɑːs‖glæs/ *n* **1** [U] a hard transparent solid material made from sand melted under great heat: *a glass bottle/window/I cut my hand on some broken glass* **2** [U] a collection of objects made of this: *glass and* CHINA **3** [C] an object made of or containing this, and shaped to make things seem larger, esp. a TELESCOPE **4** also **sandglass**— an instrument with 2 containers made of this, and set one above the other, in which a quantity of sand runs from the top one through a narrow passage to the bottom one in a fixed time, usu. an hour (for an HOURGLASS) or long enough to boil an egg (3–5 minutes) **5** [C] **a** a drinking vessel **b** also **glassful** /ˈglɑːsfʊl‖ˈglæs-/— the amount which this holds **6** [(*the*) C] an apparatus with a pointer which moves downwards when bad weather is coming; BAROMETER: *The glass is falling; it's going to be wet* **7** [C] *infml esp. BrE* LOOKING GLASS **8 have a glass too much** to get drunk **9 have a glass jaw** (of a fighter) to be easily made unconscious by a blow on the chin **10 People who live in glass houses shouldn't throw stones a** One should be careful in one's actions and remarks when one can easily be hurt in return **b** Don't blame other people for doing things that you do yourself

glass·blow·er /ˈglɑːsˌbləʊəʳ‖ˈglæs-/ *n* a person who blows into hot liquid glass in order to shape it, and who can make bottles, glass animals, etc.

glass·cut·ter /ˈglɑːsˌkʌtəʳ‖ˈglæs-/ *n* **1** a person who cuts glass into pieces or cuts patterns on glass objects **2** a tool for cutting glass

glass·es /ˈglɑːsɨz‖ˈglæ-/ also **eyeglasses**— *n* [P] 2 pieces of specially-cut glass usu. in a frame and worn in front of the eyes for improving a person's ability to see; SPECTACLES: *to lose one's glasses|some new glasses* (=*a new pair of glasses*) —see PAIR (USAGE) and SUNGLASSES; see picture at EYE[2]

glass·house /ˈglɑːshaʊs‖ˈglæs-/ *n* [*the*+R] *BrE sl* a military prison —compare BRIG (2)

glass in *v adv* [T1] to cover with or enclose in glass

glass·ware /ˈglɑːsweəʳ‖ˈglæs-/ *n* [U] glass objects generally, esp. dishes, drinking glasses, etc.

glass wool /ˌ· ˈ·/ *n* [U] a material made of very thin threads of glass, which can be used for cleaning because it is so hard, and for packing objects inside parcels —compare STEEL WOOL

glass·works /ˈglɑːswɜːks‖ˈglæswɜrks/ *n* **glassworks** [Wn3] a factory where glass is made

glass·y /ˈglɑːsi‖ˈglæsi/ *adj* [Wa1] **1** like glass, esp. (of water) smooth and shining **2** (of eyes) of a fixed expression, as if without sight or life: *After he hit his head his eyes went glassy and we knew he might be seriously hurt*

glau·co·ma /glɔːˈkəʊmə/ *n* [U] a disease which causes loss of sight, marked by increased pressure within the eyeball

glau·cous /ˈglɔːkəs/ *adj* **1** *lit* greyish green or blue in colour **2** *tech* (of parts of plants) covered with a fine whitish powdery surface (BLOOM)

glaze[1] /gleɪz/ *v* **1** [T1] to put a shiny surface on (pots and bricks) **2** [T1] to cover (esp. window frames) with glass: *The house is being double-glazed* (=2 sheets of glass are put on each window to keep in the heat) **3** [I∅ (OVER)] (of eyes) to become dull and lifeless: *His eyes glazed (over) and he fell back unconscious* **4** to cover (food) with a substance giving a shiny surface

glaze[2] *n* **1** a shiny surface, esp. one fixed on pots by heat **2** a transparent covering of oil paint spread over solid paint, esp. to change the effect of the colours **3** a jelly-like substance which may be spread over cold cooked meats or (if sweet) over fruit cooked in pastry (a FLAN)

gla·zi·er /ˈgləɪzɪəʳ‖-ʒər/ *n* a workman who fits glass into window frames

glaz·ing /ˈgleɪzɪŋ/ *n* **1** [U] the action or job of a GLAZIER **2** [U;C] the piece of glass used to fill a window (esp. in the phr. **double glazing**)

GLC *abbrev. for:* Greater London Council

gleam[1] /gliːm/ *n* **1** a shining light, esp. one making objects bright: *The red gleam of the firelight* **2** a sudden flash of light: *Gleams of sunshine came round the edges of the dark cloud* **3** a sudden showing of a feeling or quality for a short time: *A gleam of interest came into his eye*

gleam[2] *v* [I∅] **1** to give out a bright light: *The furniture gleamed after being polished* **2** (of a feeling) to be expressed with a sudden light (in the eyes): *Amusement gleamed in his eyes*

glean /gliːn/ *v* **1** [T1;I∅] to collect (grain) left behind after crops have been cut at the HARVEST **2** [T1 *often pass.*] to collect (various objects left unwanted) **3** [T1] to gather (facts or information) in small amounts and often with difficulty

glean·er /ˈgliːnəʳ/ *n* a person who GLEAN*s* in the fields

glean·ings /ˈgliːnɪŋz/ *n* [P] **1** the grain gathered in the fields after cutting the crops **2** small amounts of information or news, perhaps gathered with difficulty

glebe /gliːb/ *n* **1** *poet* the earth or soil **2** also **glebe·land** /ˈgliːblænd/— *tech* the land held by a priest to provide part of his income

glee /gliː/ *n* **1** [U] a feeling of joyful satisfaction at something which pleases one: *She danced with glee when she saw the new toys* **2** [C] a song for 3 or 4 voices together **3 glee club** a group of people who sing such songs

glee·ful /ˈgliːfəl/ *adj* showing joy and satisfaction —**-fully** *adv*

glen /glen/ *n* a narrow mountain valley, esp. in Scotland or Ireland

glen·gar·ry /glenˈgæri/ *n* a type of cap for a man with wide strings (RIBBON*s*) hanging down at the back, which is worn in the mountains of some parts of Scotland, and by some Scottish soldiers

glib /glɪb/ *adj* **-bb-** [Wa1] **1** (of a person) able to speak well and easily, whether speaking the truth or not **2** spoken too easily to be true: *a glib excuse/answer* —**~ly** *adv* —**~ness** *n* [U]

glide[1] /glaɪd/ *v* **1** [L9] to move (noiselessly) in a smooth, continuous manner, which seems easy and without effort: *The boat glided over the river.|Fish were gliding about in the lake* **2** [I∅] to use a sort of plane which has no engine but follows movements of the air currents

glide[2] *n* **1** a gliding movement (GLIDE[1]) **2** (in music) the act of passing from one note to another without a break in sound **3** *tech* (in PHONETICS) a sound made while passing from one position of the speech organs to another

glid·er /ˈglaɪdəʳ/ *n* **1** a plane without an engine —see picture at AIRCRAFT **2** a person who uses such a plane

glid·ing /ˈglaɪdɪŋ/ *n* [U] the sport of flying GLIDER*s*

glim·mer[1] /ˈglɪməʳ/ *v* [I∅] to give a very faint, unsteady light: *A faint light glimmered at the end of the passage*

glimmer[2] *n* **1** a faint unsteady light **2** a small sign: *a glimmer of hope|a glimmer of interest*

glim·mer·ings /ˈglɪmərɪŋz/ *n* [P] GLIMMER (2): *some glimmerings of interest*

glimpse¹ /glɪmps/ *v* [T1] to have a passing view of: *I glimpsed her among the crowd just before she disappeared from sight*

glimpse² *n* **1** a quick look at or incomplete view of: *I only caught a glimpse of the parcel, so I can't guess what was inside it* **2** a moment of understanding: *When I saw how worried he was, I had a glimpse of his true feelings* —see GLANCE (USAGE)

glint¹ /glɪnt/ *v* [IØ] to give out small flashes of light, as the eyes of an eager person are supposed to do: *His eyes glinted when he saw the money*

glint² *n* a flash of light, as from a shiny metal surface or a light colour against a dark background: *brown hair with golden glints|I could tell he was angry by the glint in his eye*

glis·sade¹ /glɪˈsɑːd/ *n* **1** a sliding movement over snow or ice down a mountain side, using an ice axe to slow down the speed **2** a sliding step in dancing

glissade² *v* [IØ] to make a GLISSADE¹

glis·san·do /glɪˈsændəʊ‖-ˈsɑn-/ *n, adj, adv* **-di** /daɪ/ *or* **-dos** ((a piece of music) played) by sliding the finger along the notes

glis·ten /ˈglɪsən/ *v* [Wv4;IØ (*with*)] to shine from or as if from a wet surface: *His hair glistened with oil.|I polished it till it glistened* —**~ingly** *adv*

glis·ter /ˈglɪstəʳ/ *v* [IØ] *bibl & old use* GLITTER

glit·ter¹ /ˈglɪtəʳ/ *v* [IØ (*with*)] **1** to shine brightly with flashing points of light: *The diamond glittered on her finger* **2 All that glitters is not gold** Not everything that seems good is good

glitter² *n* **1** [(*the*) S] a brightness, as of flashing points of lights: *the glitter of broken glass|with a cruel glitter in his eyes* **2** [U] attractiveness; GLAMOUR

glit·ter·ing /ˈglɪtərɪŋ/ *adj* [A] splendid: *one of the glittering stars of the modern stage/of the film industry*

gloam·ing /ˈgləʊmɪŋ/ *n* [*the*+R] *poet* (the time of) half darkness in the early evening

gloat /gləʊt/ *v* [Wv4;IØ (*over*)] to look at something or think about it with satisfaction, often in an unpleasant way: *He gloated quietly at the thought that his enemy had been trapped* —**~ingly** *adv*

glo·bal /ˈgləʊbəl/ *adj* **1** of or concerning the whole earth: *global travel|global changes* **2** of, related to, or concerning all or almost all possible considerations: *took a global view of the government's plans for dealing with unemployment* —**globally** *adv*

globe /gləʊb/ *n* **1** an object in the shape of a round ball **2** such an object on which a map of the earth or sky is painted, and which may be turned on its base **3** a cover for a lamp; LAMPSHADE **4** a round glass bowl which is filled with water for a small fish to live in

globe ar·ti·choke /ˌ· ˈ···/ *n* a type of vegetable with a round shape and leaves arranged round the sides —see also ARTICHOKE

globe·fish /ˈgləʊbˌfɪʃ/ *n* [Wn1] a type of esp. tropical fish which can swell up into a round shape when afraid

globe·trot·ter /ˈgləʊbtrɒtəʳ‖-trɑ-/ *n* a person who habitually travels round the world

glob·u·lar /ˈglɒbjʊləʳ‖ˈglɑbjə-/ *adj* **1** in the form of a GLOBULE **2** in the form of a GLOBE

glob·ule /ˈglɒbjuːl‖ˈglɑ-/ *n* a small drop of a liquid or melted solid: *Globules of wax fell from the candle*

glock·en·spiel /ˈglɒkənspiːl‖ˈglɑ-/ *n* a musical instrument with metal bars, each of which gives out a different musical note, and played by striking with 2 small hammers —see picture at PERCUSSION

gloom /gluːm/ *n* **1** [U] darkness **2** [U;C] a feeling of deep sadness: *The news of defeat filled them all with gloom*

gloom·y /ˈgluːmi/ *adj* [Wa1] **1** almost dark: *a gloomy day* **2** having or giving little hope or cheerfulness: *Our future seems gloomy* —**gloomily** *adv* —**gloominess** *n* [U]

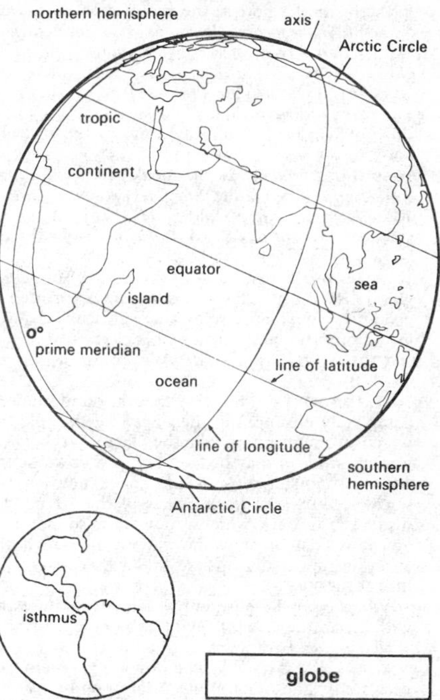

globe

Glo·ri·a /ˈglɔːrɪə‖ˈglorɪə/ *n* [*the*+R] the second part of the religious service called the MASS; esp. when sung to music

glo·ri·fi·ca·tion /ˌglɔːrɪ̵̀fɪ̵̀ˈkeɪʃən‖ˌglo-/ *n* the act of GLORIFYing or being glorified

glo·ri·fy /ˈglɔːrɪ̵̀faɪ‖ˈglo-/ *v* [T1] **1** to give praise and thanks to (God); worship (God) **2** to give glory or fame to **3** [Wv5] to cause to appear more important than in reality: *She calls it a country house, but I call it a glorified hut*

glo·ri·ous /ˈglɔːrɪəs‖ˈglo-/ *adj* **1** having, or worthy of, great fame and honour: *glorious deeds in battle* **2** beautiful; splendid: *glorious colours, a glorious day* **3** *infml* very enjoyable: *What a glorious party!* —**~ly** *adv*

glo·ry /ˈglɔːri‖ˈglori/ *n* **1** [U] great fame or success; praise and honour (esp. in the phrs. **covered in glory, crowned with glory**) **2** [U] beauty; splendid appearance: *the glory of a summer day* **3** [C *often pl.*] special beauty or cause for pride: *When that bush comes into flower it is the glory of the whole garden* **4** [U] praise offered to God: *Glory be to God* (=may God have glory) **5** [U] happiness in heaven (esp. in the (*infml*) phrs. **send to glory** (= kill), **go to glory**)

glory hole /ˈ·· ·/ *n BrE infml* a room, cupboard, or drawer where unwanted articles are left

glory in *v prep* [T1] **1** to be very happy about: *He gloried in his new freedom* **2** to enjoy in a selfish way: *He gloried in the fact that he had beaten everyone else*

gloss¹ /glɒs‖glɔs, glɑs/ *n* **1** [U] shiny brightness on a surface: *gloss photographs|gloss paint|the gloss on her hair* **2** [U;S] a pleasant but deceiving outer appearance: *They hide their hatred of each other under a surface gloss of good manners*

gloss² *n* an explanation of a piece of writing, esp.

in the form of a note at the end of a page or book: *Some of Shakespeare's language is so different from today's that I could never understand it without the gloss*

gloss³ *v* [T1] to provide a GLOSS² for

glos·sa·ry /'glɒsəri‖'glɔ-, 'glɑ-/ *n* a list of explanations of words, esp. unusual ones at the end of a book

gloss o·ver *v adv* [T1a] to speak kindly of (something bad); hide (faults): *to gloss over his failure*

gloss·y /'glɒsi‖'glɔsi, 'glɑsi/ *adj* [Wa1] shiny and smooth: *Our cat has glossy black fur* —**glossily** *adv* —**glossiness** *n* [U]

glossy mag·a·zine /ˌ·· ··'·‖ˌ·· '···/ also (*infml*) **glossy,** *AmE* usu. **slick**— *n* a magazine printed on good quality paper with a shiny surface and (usu.) lots of pictures, as of fashionable clothes

glot·tal /'glɒtl‖'glɑtl/ *adj* [Wa5] concerning the GLOTTIS

glottal stop /ˌ·· '·/ *n tech* a speech sound made by completely closing and then opening the GLOTTIS, which in English may take the place of /t/ between vowel sounds or may be used before a vowel sound

glot·tis /'glɒtɨs‖'glɑ-/ *n* the space between the VOCAL CORDS (the fleshy parts of the air passage inside the throat), which produce the sound of the voice by fast or slow movements in which this space is repeatedly opened and closed —see picture at RESPIRATORY

glove /glʌv/ *n* **1** a garment which covers the hand, with separate parts for the thumb and each finger: *Woollen gloves are warmest* **2** BOXING GLOVE —see BOXING (USAGE) **3 handle with kid gloves** to treat very gently and/or carefully **4 throw down the glove** to invite someone to fight —compare GAUNTLET **5 fit like a glove** to fit perfectly **6 the gloves were off** they were ready for a fight —see PAIR (USAGE)

glove com·part·ment /'· ·ˌ··/ *n* a sort of small space or shelf in a car in front of the passenger seat, where small articles may be kept —see picture at CAR

glove pup·pet /'· ˌ··/ *n* PUPPET (2)

glow¹ /gləʊ/ *v* [I∅ (*with*)] **1** to give out heat and/or light without flames or smoke: *The iron bar was heated till it glowed.|The cat's eyes glowed in the darkness* **2** [Wa4] to show bright strong colours: *a garden full of glowing flowers* **3** [Wa4] to show redness and heat in the face (and the body), esp. after hard work or because of strong feelings: *glowing health|I knew I had said something stupid, and my cheeks began to glow with shame*

glow² *n* [(*the*) S] **1** a light from something burning without flames or smoke: *the red glow in the sky above the factory|The oil-lamp gives a soft glow* **2** brightness of colour: *the glow of copper in the kitchen* **3** the feeling and/or signs of heat and colour in the body and face, as after exercise or because of good health: *the glow of health* **4** a strong feeling: *a glow of happiness|a glow of anger*

glow·er /'glaʊəʳ/ *v* [Wv4;I∅ (*at*)] to look with an angry expression: *Instead of answering he just glowered (at me).|a glowering look* —**~ingly** *adv*

glow·ing /'gləʊɪŋ/ *adj* which give(s) a favourable picture: *He gave a glowing description of the house, which made me want to see it for myself* —**~ly** *adv*

glow-worm /'· ·/ *n* a type of insect, the female of which has no wings and gives out a greenish light from the end of the tail

glu·cose /'glu:kəʊs/ *n* [U] a natural form of sugar found in fruit and used in the body

glue¹ /glu:/ *n* [U] a sticky substance which is obtained from animal bones or fish and used for joining things together

glue² *v* **glued,** *pres. p.* **gluing** *or* **glueing** [T1] **1** to join with GLUE¹ **2 glue oneself to** to give all one's attention to: *He glued himself to his book* **3 glued to** continually close to, directed towards: *His eyes were glued to the television.|I stayed glued to his side, because I was so afraid of getting lost*

glue·y /'glu:i/ *adj* [Wa1] **1** sticky like GLUE **2** covered with GLUE

glum /glʌm/ *adj* **-mm-** [Wa1] sad; in low spirits, esp. because of disappointment: *"You look very glum."—"I've just lost my money,"* —**~ly** *adv* —**~ness** *n* [U]

glut¹ /glʌt/ *v* **-tt-** [T1 *often pass.*] **1** to supply with too much; overfill: *The shops are glutted with fruit from abroad, because nobody will pay the high prices* **2 glut oneself (with)** to fill oneself (esp. by eating): *She glutted herself on chocolate*

glut² *n* [*usu. sing.*] **1** a larger supply than is necessary: *There was a glut of eggs (on the market) a few months ago* **2** too great a quantity: *There's a glut of old films on television these days*

glu·ten /'glu:tn/ *n* [U] the food substance, in flour made from wheat, which is a PROTEIN

glu·ti·nous /'glu:tɨnəs/ *adj* sticky: *The sugar melted into a glutinous mass*

glut·ton /'glʌtn/ *n* **1** [C; *you*+N] a person who eats too much **2** [C+*for*] *infml* a person who is always ready to do more of something hard or unpleasant (esp. in the phr. **a glutton for punishment**): *She kept coming to work even when she was ill: she's a real glutton for punishment*

glut·ton·ous /'glʌtənəs/ *adj* like a GLUTTON; GREEDY, esp. for food —**~ly** *adv*

glut·ton·y /'glʌtəni/ *n* [U] the habit of eating (and drinking) too much

gly·ce·rine, -rin /'glɪsərɪn/ *n* [U] a sweet sticky colourless liquid made from fats, which is used in making soap, medicines, and explosives

gm. *written abbrev. for:* GRAM

G-man /'dʒi: mæn/ *n* **G-men** /-men/ *AmE infml now rare* a special officer of the government police (FBI)

G.M.T. *abbrev. for:* GREENWICH MEAN TIME

gnarled /nɑ:ld‖nɑrld/ *adj* **1** (of a tree, its trunk or branches) rough and twisted, with hard lumps, esp. as a result of age **2** (of hands and fingers) twisted, with swollen joints, and rough skin, as from hard work or old age **3** (of a person) rough in appearance, as if beaten by wind and weather

gnash /næʃ/ *v* [T1] to make a noise with (one's teeth) by biting hard in anger or worry (only in the phr. **gnash one's teeth**)

gnat /næt/ *n* **1** a type of small flying insect that stings **2 strain at a gnat (and swallow a camel)** to worry about small things (though not giving attention to larger, more important ones)

gnaw /nɔ:/ *v* **1** [I∅ (AWAY, *at*);T1] **a** to keep biting (something hard), esp. until destroyed: *to gnaw a bone|*(fig.) *The fever gnawed at his strength* **b** to worry or give pain to: *Something's gnawing at my mind.|Grief gnaws my heart* **2** [X9;L9] to make (a way) by doing this: *Ants have gnawed their way into the box|through the walls* **3** [T1] to make by doing this: *Rats can gnaw holes (in wood)* **4** [X9] to destroy by doing this: *She gnawed her fingernails to pieces|gnawed them away*

gnaw·ing /'nɔ:ɪŋ/ *adj* [Wa5;A] painful and/or worrying: *gnawing hunger|gnawing anxiety*

gneiss /'naɪs/ *n* [U] a type of hard rock with light and dark bands formed from earlier rocks which were pressed together under heat

gnoc·chi /'nɒki‖'nɑki/ *n* [U;P] *It* an Italian food made of little round balls of potato and flour paste (PASTA)

gnome /nəʊm/ *n* **1** (in fairy stories) a little (old) man who lives under the ground and guards stores of gold **2** a (stone) figure representing this **3 the**

gnomes of Zurich *infml* certain powerful bankers who are said to control supplies of money to foreign governments

GNP *abbrev. for:* Gross National Product; the total worth of all the goods and services produced in a country (usu. in a single year)

gnu /nuː/ also **wildebeest**— *n* **gnu** *or* **gnus** [Wn1] a type of large animal of South Africa with a tail and curved horns; type of ANTELOPE

go¹ /gəʊ/ *v* **went** /went/, **gone** /gɒn‖gɔn/; *pres. p.* **going** **1** [I∅] to leave the place where the speaker is (so as to reach another): *I must go/be going.|When does the train go?|He went early* **2** [L9] to travel or move: *We went by bus.|It can go by post/in the post.|The car's going too fast.|We went to France for our holidays.|His hand went to his gun* **3** [Wv6;L9] to reach (as far as stated): *Which road goes to the station?|The valley goes from east to west.|The roots of the plant go deep* **4** [I∅] to start an action: *Get going* (=start) *on the work.|The signal to begin a race is "One, 2, 3, go!" or "Ready, steady, go!"* **5** [I4] **a** to do (an activity): *to go walking/shopping/swimming* **b** [*nonassertive*] *infml* to do (something undesirable): *Don't go saying that!* **6** [I∅] to be placed, esp. usually placed: *The boxes (can) go on the shelf* **7** [I∅] (of machines) to work (properly): *This clock doesn't go.|It goes by electricity.|Is it going?* **8** [L7] to become (by a natural change, or by changing on purpose): *She's going grey/Her hair's going grey.|The milk went sour.|He's gone blind/mad.|This used to be a state school, but it's gone independent.|He went white with anger* **9** [L7] to remain (in a certain state): *Her complaints went unnoticed.|After his enemy's threats he went in fear of his life.|Should a murderer go free/go unpunished?|When the crops fail, the people go hungry* **10** [I∅ (*for, to*)] to be sold: *going cheap|It went for so little.|The house went to the one who made the highest offer.|Any more offers?—Going to the man in the green hat. Going, going, gone!* **11** [L9, esp. *in, on*] to be spent or used: *Half our money goes on food and clothes for the children.|His time goes in watching television.|My money goes a long way/doesn't go far* (= buys a lot/buys little) **12** [I∅] to cease or disappear: *Summer's going.|Where's my pen? It's gone (off my desk)* **13** [I∅] (with *must, can, have to*) to be got rid of: *This car must go. We can't afford it any more* **14** [I∅] **a** to die or (sometimes) to become unconscious: *He went out like a light.|After George went, she moved into a smaller house* **b** to be damaged; to weaken or wear out: *My voice has gone because of my cold.|These shoes are going* **15** [Wv6;I∅] to (have to) be accepted or acceptable: *Anything goes* (= You can do as you like).*|That goes for all of us* (= We all agree on this).*| It goes without saying that his brother should help him* **16** [L9] to happen (in a certain way): *The hours went slowly.|How goes it?/How are things going?|The party went well.|It will go hard with him* (= be difficult for him) **17** [Wv6;L9;(L5)] **a** to be stated, said, or sung in a certain way: *The story goes that he was murdered* **b** to have or suit a certain tune: *The tune goes something like this* **18** [Wv6;I∅ (*into*)] to divide a certain sum so as to give an exact figure: *3 into 2 won't go* **19** [L9] to make the stated sound: *The mirror went crack, and fell off the wall.|The guns went "*BOOM.*"|Ducks go "*QUACK*"* **20** [L9;(I∅)] to match or fit: *It won't go in the box.|This paint doesn't go.|The belt won't go round (my waist)* —compare GO WITH, GO TOGETHER **21** [L9] to make a movement: *When he shook hands, he went like this* **22** [L9] to be sent for consideration: *Your suggestion will go before the committee.|Can this question go direct to the minister?* **23** [L9] (*only with* -ing *form,* with future meaning) to be about to, or be planning to, travel (to a place): *We were going to France, but we changed our minds* **24** [I∅] to lose one's usual powers of control (only in the phrs. **let oneself go, far gone**): *He's* PRETTY² (1) *far gone* (as in illness, when confused by feelings, or mad) **25** [L9;(T1)] (of people) to work or move, esp. with unusual effort or result (esp. in the phrs. **go (to) it, going strong**): *Her tongue goes 19 to the* DOZEN (=is very fast in talking).*|He felt ill, but tried to keep going.|If no one can help, I'll go it alone* **26** [I∅] to be on average or in general (in cost, quality, etc.) (usu. in the phr. **as things go**): *She was a good cook, as cooks go* (= compared to the average cook).*|It's cheap, as these things go* **27** to state or do up to or beyond a limit (esp. in the phr. **go as far as, go too far**): *It's quite good, as far as it goes.|You've gone too far!* —see also FAR¹ (8) **28 be going a** to be present for use or enjoyment: *Is there any food going?* **b** to be for sale —compare GO AT (3) **29 be going to (do or happen)** (*showing the future; not usu. in sentences containing a condition*) **a** (of people) to intend to: *He's going to buy her some shoes* (compare *He'll buy her some shoes if she asks him to*) **b** (of things or events that cannot be controlled) to be about to; be expected to: *Is it going to rain?|I'm going to be sick!|She's going to have a baby* **30 from the word go** from the beginning **31 go a long way** also **go far**— **a** (of money) to buy a lot **b** (of a person) to succeed **32 go and a** *not fml* to go in order to: *I'll go and bring back your boots.|He went and bought* (=he went and he bought) *another one.|It's time you went and saw your mother* —compare TRY¹ (7) **and b** *BrE infml* (expresses surprise): *She went and won first prize!|You've been/gone and done it now!* (=done something terrible) —compare BEEN (5) **33 go it alone** *not fml* to act independently **34 3, 6, etc., months gone** *infml* having been PREGNANT for 3, 6 months, etc. **35 to go** *AmE* (of cooked food sold in a shop) to be taken away and not eaten in the shop: *2 chicken dinners with corn to go!* —compare TAKE AWAY

USAGE In the meanings "to go and come back from" [L9] or, in*BrE,* in the meaning "to have arrived and left" [I∅], the past participle of **go** is **been**. Otherwise, it is **gone**. Compare: *George has* **gone** *to Paris* (so that's why he's not here).*|George has* **been** *to Paris* (so **a** he knows what it's like, or **b** that's why he wasn't here last week).*|The postman hasn't* **gone** *yet* (=he's still here).*|(BrE) The postman hasn't* **been** *yet* (=we haven't had the letters). —see BECOME (USAGE); see also GO ABOUT, GO AFTER, GO AGAINST, GO AHEAD, GO ALONG, GO AROUND, GO-AS-YOU-PLEASE, GO AT, GO AWAY, GO BACK, GO BACK ON, GO BY, GO DOWN, GO FAR, GO FOR, GO IN FOR, GOING, GOING-OVER, GOINGS-ON, GO INTO, GO OFF, GO ON, GO OUT, GO OVER, GO ROUND, GO SLOW, GO THROUGH, GO THROUGH WITH, GO TO, GO TOGETHER, GO UNDER, GO UP, GO WITH, GO WITHOUT

go² *n* **goes** **1** [U] *not fml* the quality of being full of activity: *The children are full of go. They run and play all day.|He's got plenty of (get up and) go, and is sure to do well in his job* **2** [C *usu. sing.*] *infml esp. BrE* an (awkward) state of affairs (esp. in the phr. **a rum go**) **3** [C] *not fml* an attempt to do something: *He had several goes at the examination before he passed.|He had a go at (stopping) the thief, but couldn't hold on* **4** [C *usu. sing.*] *not fml* one's turn (esp. in a game): *It's my go* **5 all systems go** (we're) ready for take-off **6 from the word go** *not fml* from the beginning: *She worked hard from the word go, and finished before anyone else* **7 it's all go** *not fml* it's very busy: *It's all go in Harlow when we're finishing a new dictionary* **8 it's no go** *not fml* it hasn't/won't happen: *It's no go. Your plan won't ever get off the ground* (= begin to succeed) **9 Have a go (at something/doing something)!** *not fml* Try (something/doing something) **10 on the go** *not fml* working all the time

go a·bout¹ *v adv* **1** [L9 (*with*)] GO AROUND (3) **2** [IØ] GET ABOUT (2) **3** [IØ] (of a ship) to turn round to face in the opposite direction

go about² *v prep* **1** [T1] to perform or do: *to go about one's business* **2** [T1,4] *not fml* also **set about**—to begin working at: *How do you go about building a boat?|Don't go about the job that way*

goad /gəʊd/ *n* **1** a sharp-pointed stick for driving cattle forward by pricking them **2** something which urges a person to action

goad in·to *v prep* [D1;V4b] to cause (someone) to (do something) by strong or continued annoyance: *He was goaded into an angry reply.|They goaded him into doing it by saying he was a coward*

goad on *v adv* [T1b] to keep (someone) active by strong or continual annoyance: *He was tired of working but the need for money goaded him on*

go af·ter *v prep* [T1 *pass. rare*] *not fml* to try to obtain or win (something or someone); chase: *to go after a job/a girl/a prize*

go a·gainst *v prep* [T1 *no pass.*] **1** to act in opposition to: *She went against her mother/her mother's wishes* **2** to be unfavourable to: *Opinion is going against us.|The case may go against you* **3** to be opposite to: *It would go against his principles to borrow money, as he thinks it wrong to be in debt*

go a·head *v adv* [IØ] **1** [(*with*)] to begin: *Go ahead, we're all listening.|The council gave us permission to go ahead with our building plans* **2** to continue going forward; advance: *The police examined the cars and allowed them to go ahead.|Work is going ahead*

go-a·head¹ /ˈ· ·ˌ·/ *n* [(*the*) S9] *not fml* permission to act: *We're all ready to start the new book, as soon as we get the go-ahead from the people concerned*

go-ahead² *adj* [A] *not fml* (of people) active in using new methods

goal /gəʊl/ *n* **1** [*usu. with poss.*] one's aim or purpose; a place or object one wishes to obtain or reach: *His goal is a place at University.|When he at last came into Rome he felt he had reached his goal.|She had always wanted to own her own house, and now she had obtained her goal* **2** (in games like football) the place where the ball, PUCK (2), etc. must go for a point to be gained —see picture at SOCCER **3** the point gained (SCOREd) when the ball is caused to do this —see FOOTBALL, HOCKEY (USAGE)

goal·keep·er /ˈgəʊlˌkiːpəʳ/ also (*infml*) **goal·ie** /ˈgəʊli/— *n* the player in a football team who is responsible for preventing the ball from getting into his team's GOAL (2) —see picture at SOCCER

goal line /ˈ· ·/ *n* a line at either end and usu. running the width of a playing area, on which a GOAL (2) or GOALPOST is placed —see picture at SOCCER

goal·mouth /ˈgəʊlmaʊθ/ *n* the space enclosed by the GOALPOSTs

go a·long *v adv* [IØ] **1** to continue (acting, moving to a place, using a plan, etc.): *I like to add up my bank account as I go along* **2** [(*with*)] *not fml* to agree with; support: *We'll go along with you/your suggestion* **3** GET ALONG (2) **4** GET ALONG (5)

goal·post /ˈgəʊlpəʊst/ *n* either of the 2 wooden posts, sometimes with a bar between them at a certain height, which mark the GOAL (2) in various games —see picture at SOCCER

go a·round also **go round**— *v adv* [IØ] *not fml* **1** (*usu. in tenses with the* -ing *form*) (of an illness) to spread: *There are a lot of colds going around* **2** GET ABOUT (2) **3** [L9 (*with*)] also **go about**— to be often out in public (with someone): *Why do you go around with such strange people?* **4** GO ROUND (4)

go-as-you-please /ˌ· · · ˈ·ˈ/ *adj not fml* cheerful, lazy, and not asking for much: *Things are very go-as-you-please here—that's why the trade figures are so bad* —compare EASY-GOING

goat /gəʊt/ *n* **1** a type of 4-legged animal related to the sheep, which also gives milk and a hairy sort of wool, which can climb steep hills and rocks and eat almost anything —see picture at FARMYARD **2** *sl* a man who is very active sexually **3 act/play the (giddy) goat** to behave wildly and foolishly **4 get someone's goat** *infml* to make someone very annoyed —see also BILLY GOAT, NANNY GOAT, KID¹ (1)

go at *v prep* **1** [T1 *no pass.*] also (*esp. when the object is a person*) **go for**— to attack: *Our dog went at the postman.*|(fig.) *He went at his breakfast as if he'd never eaten before* **2** [T1 *no pass.*] to work hard at: *The students are really going at their studies now the examinations are near* **3** [L1] also **go for**— to be sold at (a cheap price): *There were good coats going at £5!|The car went for only £100*

goa·tee /gəʊˈtiː/ *n* a little pointed beard on the bottom of the chin (like the hair on a male goat's chin)

goat·herd /ˈgəʊthɜːd‖-ɜrd/ *n* a person who looks after a group (FLOCK) of goats

goat·skin /ˈgəʊtˌskɪn/ *n* **1** [C] the skin of a goat, esp. with the hair on it **2** [U] leather made from such a skin

go a·way /ˌ· ·ˈ·/ *interj infml* Don't be silly!

gob¹ /gɒb‖gɑb/ *n sl* **1** a mass of something sticky, as of liquid from the mouth **2** [*usu. pl.*] *AmE sl* a large amount: *gobs of money*

gob² *n AmE sl* a sailor in the US navy

gob³ *n BrE sl* the mouth: *Shut your gob!*

go back *v adv* **1** [IØ] to return (to a place one has been in): *Let's go back home now* **2** [IØ] to return (in talk, thought, etc.): *Let's go back to what the chairman said earlier* **3** [L9, esp. *to*] to reach backwards in time: *My family goes back to the 18th century* **4** (of plants) to fail to grow: *Our roses went back a little in the dry weather*

go back on *v adv prep* [T1] **1** [*pass. rare*] to break or not keep (a promise, agreement, etc.): *to go back on a promise* **2** [*no pass.*] to be disloyal to (someone): *Never go back on your friends*

gob·bet /ˈgɒbɨ̣t‖ˈgɑ-/ *n infml* a lump or piece, esp. of food: (fig.) *We had to learn gobbets of poetry for the examination*

gob·ble¹ /ˈgɒbəl‖ˈgɑ-/ *v* [T1 (UP);IØ] to eat very quickly, and sometimes noisily

gobble² *v, n* (to make) the sound a TURKEY makes

gob·ble·dy·gook, -degook /ˈgɒbəldiguːk‖ˈgɑbəldigʊk, -guːk/ *n* [U] *sl* meaningless but important-sounding official language

gob·bler /ˈgɒbləʳ‖ˈgɑ-/ *n* a male TURKEY

go-be·tween /ˈ· ·ˌ·/ *n* a person who takes messages from one person or side to another, because they themselves cannot meet: *The business was arranged through a trustworthy go-between*

gob·let /ˈgɒblɨ̣t‖ˈgɑb-/ *n* a drinking vessel, usu. of glass or metal, with a base and stem but no handles, and used esp. for wine

gob·lin /ˈgɒblɨ̣n‖ˈgɑb-/ *n* a usu. unkind or evil spirit which plays tricks on people —compare HOBGOBLIN

go by¹ *v adv* [IØ] to pass (in place or time): *A car went by.|2 years went by.|He let the chance go by*

go by² *v prep* [T1 *no pass.*] **1** to act according to; be guided by: *to go by the rules/the book|Don't go by that old map* **2** to judge by: *Going by her clothes, she must be very rich.|That's nothing to go by: she's* *really very poor.|You can't go by what he says* **3 go by the name of** to be called, probably in addition to one's real name: *He goes by the name of Smith, but I don't know who he really is*

go-by /'· ·/ *n* **give someone/something the go-by** *BrE infml* to avoid or pass by without noticing: *You won't get too fat if you give sweets the go-by.|After the quarrel she gave me the go-by whenever we met*

god /gɒd‖gɑd/ *n* **1** (*fem* **god·dess** /gɒdɪ̣s‖gɑd-/) a being (one of many) which is worshipped, as one who made or rules over (a part of) the life of the world: *They spoke against the gods of their enemies* **2** a person or thing to which too great importance is given (esp. in the phr. **make a god of**): *He makes a god of his work, and forgets his family* **3 a little tin god** a person who likes to think that he is very important and should command obedience from others

God *n* [R;N] **1** the being who in the Christian, Jewish, and Muslim religions is worshipped as maker and ruler of the world **2 God forbid/grant that** May it not happen/happen that **3 God (alone) knows** *infml* It's impossible to say: *God knows where he went!|He went God knows where* **4 God willing** if all goes well **5 Oh God/My God/Good God** (expressions of surprise, fear, etc.) **6 Thank God** (an expression of gladness that trouble has passed): *Thank God you've come!*

god·child /'gɒdtʃaɪld‖'gɑd-/ *n* [*usu. with poss.*] (in the Christian religion) the child (**godson** or **god-daughter**) for whom one takes responsibility by making promises at a ceremony (BAPTISM) —compare GODPARENT

god·damn, goddam, *BrE* usu. **goddamned** /'gɒdæm‖'gɑ-/ *adj, adv* DAMN

god-fear·ing /'· ˌ··/ *adj* good and well-behaved according to the rules of the Christian religion; GODLY

god·for·sak·en /'gɒdfəseɪkən‖'gɑdfər-/ *adj* (of a place) empty, containing nothing useful or interesting, etc.

god·head /'gɒdhed‖'gɑd-/ *n* [U] the quality of being God or a god

god·less /'gɒdləs‖'gɑd-/ *adj* wicked; not showing respect to or belief in God —**~ly** *adv* —**~ness** *n* [U]

god·like /'gɒdlaɪk‖'gɑd-/ *adj* like or suitable to God or a god: *godlike beauty/calm*

god·ly /'gɒdli‖'gɑdli/ *adj* [Wa1] *fml* showing obedience to God by leading a good life; GOD-FEARING

go·down /'gəʊdaʊn/ *n* (in parts of Asia) a large building for storing goods, esp. at ports; WAREHOUSE

go down *v adv* **1** [I∅] to become lower (esp. in price): *The floods are going down.|The standard of work has gone down.|The price must go down.|Eggs are going down* **2** [I∅] (of a wind, fire, etc.) to lessen in force **3** [I∅] to sink: *3 ships went down in the storm|before the sun goes down* **4** [I∅] to become less swollen: *My ankle has gone down, so I should be able to walk soon.|This tyre is going down; I'll pump it up* **5** [I∅] to become less valuable, or reach a lower social level: *The neighbourhood is going down* **6** [L9, esp. *with*] to be accepted: *He/His speech went down well (with the crowd)* **7** [L9, esp. *in*] to be recorded: *This day will go down in history* **8** [L9, esp. *to*] also **go up**— to reach as far as **9** [I∅ (*from, to*)] *BrE* to leave a university after a period of study or a city for a less important place: *He went down without taking a degree.|going down to the country* —see DOWN¹ (USAGE) **10** [I∅ (*before*)] to be defeated or destroyed: *The city went down before the enemy*

god·pa·rent /'gɒdˌpeərənt‖'gɑd-/ *n* [*usu. with poss.*] the person (**godfather** or **godmother**) who makes promises to help a Christian newly received into the church at a special ceremony (BAPTISM) —compare GODCHILD

gods /gɒdz‖gɑdz/ *n* [*the*+GU] *infml* the seats high up at the back of a theatre

God Save the Queen /ˌ· · · '·/ *BrE infml* also **the Queen**— *n* [R] the British national song (ANTHEM) USAGE When the ruler is a king, the song is **God Save the King**.

god·send /'gɒdsend‖'gɑd-/ *n* an unexpected lucky chance or thing: *It was a godsend to have him there at the right moment*

god·speed /ˌgɒd'spiːd‖'gɑdspiːd, ˌgɑd'spiːd/ *n* **wish/bid someone godspeed** *old use* (*often cap.*) to wish someone good luck (at the beginning of an activity or journey)

go·er /'gəʊəʳ/ *n infml* a person who is always ready for new activity

-goer *comb. form* [*n*→*n*] a regular attender: *a churchgoer/theatregoer*

go far *v adv* [I∅] **1** to be successful; succeed: *The boy is clever and will go far (in his job)* **2** [*nonassertive*] to satisfy many needs: *Those potatoes won't go far when there are 10 people to feed*

go for *v prep* [T1 *no pass.*] *not fml* **1** GO AT (1) **2** to attack with words: *My wife went for me because I was late for dinner* **3** GO AFTER (something): *to go for a job/a prize* **4** to attempt (to get or do): *When you offer him sweets he goes for the biggest one* **5** to like or be attracted by: *Do you go for modern music?|I don't go for men of his type* **6** to concern or be true for (someone or something) in the same manner as for others: *I find this report badly done, and that goes for all the other work done in this office* **7** GO AT (3) (esp. in the phr. **go for a song**) —see also GO (28b), **for a** SONG (5) **8 go for nothing** to be wasted; have no result: *All my hard work went for nothing*

go-get·ter /ˌ· '··, '· ˌ··‖'· ˌ··/ *n* a person who is forceful and determined and likely to succeed in getting what he wants

gog·gle /'gɒgəl‖'gɑ-/ *v* [I∅ (*at*)] to look hard with the eyes wide open or moving around, as in surprise: *I know she was wearing a funny hat, but they all goggled, which was very rude of them.|*(fig.) *I goggled at the news*

goggle box /'·· ·/ *n sl, esp. BrE* a television

goggle-eyed /ˌ·· '·/ *adj* with the eyes standing out as if surprised

gog·gles /'gɒgəlz‖'gɑ-/ *n* (a pair of) large round glasses with an edge which fits against the skin so that dust and wind or water cannot get near the eyes —see PAIR (USAGE) and picture at LABORATORY

go-go /'· ·/ *adj* [Wa5;A] of or concerned in a form of fast dancing with excited movement, usu. performed by one or more girls in front of watchers: *go-go girls|go-go dancing*

go in for *v adv prep* **1** [T1] to take part in (a test of skill or knowledge): *I go in for the examination next year.|several people went in for the race* **2** [T1,4] to (start to) make a habit of (doing), esp. for enjoyment: *I don't go in for sports.|She goes in for (wearing) very unusual clothes*

go·ing¹ /'gəʊɪŋ/ *n* [U9] **1** [*with poss.*] the act of leaving: *Our going was delayed while the ship waited.|We were sad to hear of his going* (= death) **2** the act or speed of travel: *We climbed the mountain in 3 hours, which was better going than we expected.|slow going* **3** the condition or possibility of travel: *The mud made it rough/hard/heavy going for the car.|*(fig.) *Let's leave while the going's good*

going² *adj* [Wa5] **1** [E] in existence: *He's the biggest fool going.|That's the best car going* **2** [A] as charged at present: *the going rate for the job* **3** [A] working; in operation: *a going* CONCERN (= an active profitable business)

-going³ *comb. form* [n→n U] the activity of attendance at: *theatregoing|churchgoing*

going-o·ver /ˌ·· ˈ··/ *n* **goings-over** *not fml* **1** a (thorough) examination and/or treatment: *The car needs a proper going-over before we use it again* **2** a scolding: *His wife gave him a real going-over for coming home late*

go·ings /ˈgəʊɪŋz/ *n* see COMINGS **and goings**

goings-on /ˌ·· ˈ·/ *n* [P] *not fml* activities, usu. of an undesirable kind: *There was shouting, and loud music, and all sorts of goings-on I can't describe!*

go in·to *v prep* [T1] **1** [*no pass.*] to reach, after a journey: *to go into town/work* **2** [*no pass.*] to enter (a profession, state of life, etc.): *to go into politics/business/films* **3** to state: *Let's not go into details; just keep to the main points.|to go into an explanation* **4** to examine thoroughly: *The police are going into the murder case*

goi·tre, *AmE* **-ter** /ˈgɔɪtəʳ/ *n* [U] a medical condition in which an organ in the front of the neck (the THYROID) enlarges, sometimes because the body lacks certain chemical substances

go-kart /ˈgəʊ kɑːt‖-kɑrt/ *n BrE* a small racing vehicle made of an open framework on 4 wheels, with an engine

gold /gəʊld/ *n* [U] **1** a valuable soft yellow metal that is a simple substance (ELEMENT) used for making coins, jewellery, etc.: *He wore a gold watch.|Gold is found in rock and streams* **2** coins or objects made of this metal generally: *People used to pay in gold.|She wore so many ornaments that she seemed to be covered in gold* **3** the colour of this metal: *The sun shone on the gold of her hair.|gold paint* **4** kindness, gentleness in behaviour, etc. (esp. in the phrs. **a heart of gold, as good as gold**): *The children caused no trouble all day; they were as good as gold*

gold·beat·er /ˈgəʊldˌbiːtəʳ/ *n* a man whose work is to hammer gold into thin sheets

gold-dig·ger /ˈ· ˌ··/ *n* **1** a person who tries to find gold by digging in the earth **2** *sl now rare* a woman who tries to attract rich men so that she can get money and presents

gold dust /ˈ· ·/ *n* [U] gold in the form of a fine powder

gold·en /ˈgəʊldən/ *adj* [Wa5] **1** [B] made of gold: *a golden crown* **2** [B] of the colour of gold: *golden hair* **3** [A] very fortunate or favourable: *a golden* OPPORTUNITY

golden age /ˌ·· ˈ·/ *n* (*usu. caps.*) **1** [*the*+R] (in ancient Greek stories) a time early in history when everyone was happy **2** [C] a period of time, either real or imaginary, when art and literature were at their best

golden hand·shake /ˌ·· ˈ··/ *n* [S] a large amount of money given to someone when he leaves a firm, esp. at the end of his working life

golden ju·bi·lee /ˌ·· ˈ···/ *n* the 50th yearly return of the date of some important personal event, esp. of becoming a king and queen —compare SILVER JUBILEE, DIAMOND JUBILEE

golden mean /ˌ·· ˈ·/ *n* [(*the*) S] a sensible rule by which one never does too much or too little

golden o·ri·ole /ˌ·· ˈ···/ *n* ORIOLE (1)

golden rule /ˌ·· ˈ·/ *n* [(*the*) S] a very important rule, such as that of good behaviour towards others

golden syr·up /ˌ·· ˈ··/ *n* [U] a sweet thick liquid made from sugar. It is spread on bread and used in cooking

golden wed·ding /ˌ·· ˈ··/ also **golden wedding an·ni·ver·sa·ry** /ˌ·· ˈ·· ··ˌ···/— the 50th yearly return of the date of a wedding —compare SILVER WEDDING, DIAMOND WEDDING

gold·field /ˈgəʊldfiːld/ *n* [*often pl.*] a place where gold can be found

gold·finch /ˈgəʊldˌfɪntʃ/ *n* a type of small singing bird with some yellow feathers

gold·fish /ˈgəʊldˌfɪʃ/ *n* **goldfish** [Wn2] a small fish which is kept as a pet in glass bowls in houses, and in ornamental pools in gardens

gold leaf /ˌ· ˈ·/ *n* [U] gold which has been beaten into thin sheets for use in picture frames, ornamental letters, etc. —compare GILT

gold·mine /ˈgəʊldmaɪn/ *n* **1** a place where gold is taken (MINEd) from the rock **2** a successful business or activity which makes large profits: *He doesn't know it, but he's sitting on a goldmine* (= he possesses something very valuable)

gold plate /ˌ· ˈ·/ *n* [U] **1** articles such as dishes, made of gold **2** a covering of gold on top of another metal —**-plated** /ˌ· ˈ··◂/ *adj* [Wa5]

gold rush /ˈ· ·/ *n* the state of affairs when gold is found and many people try to get to the place in the hope of collecting large amounts of gold easily

gold·smith /ˈgəʊldˌsmɪθ/ *n* a person who makes objects out of gold

gold standard /ˈ· ˌ··/ *n* [*the*+R] the practice of using the value of gold as a standard on which to base the value of money, usu. with the purpose of keeping the value of the money from changing

golf¹ /gɒlf‖gɑlf, gɔlf/ *n* [U] a game in which people drive small hard balls into holes with special sticks (CLUBs), trying to do so with as few strokes as possible

USAGE One plays a game of **golf** on a **golf course**, using any of a set of different **clubs** to hit the (**golf**) *ball*. One wins the game by taking the fewest number of *strokes* for each *hole*, or for the total number of holes (usu. 18).

golf² *v* [I∅] (*esp. in the* -ing *form*) to play GOLF¹: *to go golfing* —**~er** *n*

golf club /ˈ· ·/ *n* **1 a** a club for GOLFers², with its own land to play on **b** the place or building where they meet **2** any of several types of long-handled wooden or metal sticks used for driving the ball in GOLF¹

golf course /ˈ· ·/ *n* an area of land with small hills, ditches, etc., across which the ball must be driven from hole to hole in GOLF —see GOLF¹ (USAGE)

golf links /ˈ· ·/ *n* **golf links** [Wn3] GOLF COURSE

go·li·ath /gəˈlaɪəθ/ *n* [*usu. sing.*] (*sometimes cap.*) a man of unusual strength or power: *He is a goliath among men*

gol·li·wog, golly- /ˈgɒliwɒg‖ˈgɑliwɑg/ also **golly**— *n* a child's toy (DOLL) made of soft material, dressed like a little man, and with a black face with big white eyes and black hair standing out round his head

gol·ly /ˈgɒli‖ˈgɑli/ *interj infml* (an expression of surprise) —compare GOSH

-gon /gən; *strong* gɒn‖gən; *strong* gɑn/ *comb. form* [→n] a figure with (the stated number of) angles: HEXAGON|POLYGON

go·nad /ˈgəʊnæd/ *n* a male or female organ in which the cells are produced from which young may be formed

gon·do·la /ˈgɒndələ‖ˈgɑn-, gɑnˈdəʊlə/ *n* **1** [C; *by*+U] a long narrow flat-bottomed boat with high points at each end, used only on the waterways (CANALs) which run between the houses in Venice in Italy —see picture at BOAT¹ **2** [C] a hanging framework for workmen to stand in when they are painting or repairing high walls and windows **3** [C] any of several types of vehicles, containers, or seats which are fixed to a framework but can swing backwards and forwards or from side to side

gon·do·lier /ˌgɒndəˈlɪəʳ‖ˌgɑn-/ *n* a man who

guides and drives a GONDOLA (1) forward by moving a long-handled OAR at the back

gone /gɒn‖gɔn/ *past p. of* GO —see GO (USAGE)

gon·er /ˈgɒnəʳ‖ˈgɔ-/ *n infml* someone who will soon die: *He's a goner. He drank poison*

gong /gɒŋ‖gɑŋ, gɔŋ/ *n* **1** a round piece of metal hanging from a frame, which when struck with a stick gives a deep ringing sound, as used in Eastern music or to call people to meals **2** *BrE sl* MEDAL

gon·na /ˈgɒnə, gənə‖ˈgɑnə, gənə/ *nonstandard* going to: *"gonna fly all over God's heaven!"* (song)

gon·or·rhe·a, -rhoea /ˌgɒnəˈrɪə‖ˌgɑ-/ *n* [U] a disease of the sex organs, passed on during sexual activity —compare SYPHILIS

goo /guː/ *n* [U] *infml* **1** sticky material **2** (words which seem to express) unnaturally sweet feelings; SENTIMENTALISM

good[1] /gʊd/ *adj* **better** /ˈbetəʳ/, **best** /best/ **1** [B] having the right qualities: *a good play|a good argument|a good friend* **2** [B] suitable; favourable: *It's a good day for a drive.|The weather's good.|a good chance of getting a job* **3** [B] morally right; in accordance with religious standards: *to do a good deed|to lead a good life* **4** [B (*to, of*)] (of people) kind; helpful: *She's always been very good to me.|It's good of you to help.|Please be good enough to close the door.|They hadn't a good word for her* (= talked unkindly about her) **5** [B] (esp. of children) well-behaved: *Be good when we visit your aunt* —see also **good as** GOLD **6** [B] suitable for its purpose: *a good idea|good advice* **7** [B] enjoyable: *a good story|a good time* **8** [B (*for*)] useful to the health or character: *Milk is good for you.|The water is not good; we must boil it before we drink it.|It isn't good* (*for you*) *to have everything you want* **9** [Wa5; B] (of food) fresh, not decayed: *The eggs are old. I hope they're still good* **10** [B] strong; in good condition; working well: *You need good shoes for walking on the hills* **11** [F (*at*)] skilful; having the ability to do something: *He's good at languages* **12** [Wa5;A] worthy of respect (usu. in polite forms of address, or when angry or in the phr. **good old . . .**): *My good man, why should I help you?|Good old John, he's always ready to help* **13** [B] of a higher standard or quality than average: *She got a good result in her examination.|This watch keeps good* (= correct) *time* **14** [Wa5;B (*for*)] effective in use (usu. over a period of time): *His cheques are not good, because he has no money.|The ticket is good for one month.|The old man's good for another 20 years* (= will live 20 years) —see also HOLD[1] (16) **good 15** [B] safe from loss of money: *a good risk|a good debt* **16** [Wa5;A] large in size, amount, etc. (in the phr. **a good . . .**): *a good while|We travelled a good distance* **17** [Wa5;A] at least or more than (in the phr. **a good . . .**): *It's a good mile away.|We wasted a good half hour* **18** [Wa5;A] (in expressions of feeling): *Good gracious!|Good God!* **19** [Wa5;A] (in greetings): *Good morning/afternoon/evening/day* —see also GOODNIGHT **20 a good deal/few** quite a lot **21** [Wa5;A] complete; thorough: *Have a good look.|a good meal|a good beating at cricket* **22 All in good time** (it will happen) at a suitable later time; be patient **23 as good as** almost (the same thing as): *He as good as refused.|We're as good as ruined* **24 Good!** I agree *or* I'm glad **25 good and . . .** *infml esp. AmE* very; completely: *He was good and angry.|I'll do it when I'm good and ready* **26 good for** likely to produce (an effect or money): *It's not a good film, but it's good for a laugh.|He's good for a few pounds* (= willing to pay) **27 Good for you!** *BrE dial* also **Good on you!**— Well done! **28 in good time** early **29 It's a good thing** It's fortunate: *It's a good thing you didn't tell me that before I went home, because I would have been too worried to sleep* **30 make good** to be successful, esp. wealthy **31 make something good a** to pay for; make up: *His loss was made good* **b** to put into effect (esp. in the phr. **make good one's escape**): *make good a promise* **c** *esp. BrE* to repair: *agreed to make good the whole area under the windows* **32 too much of a good thing** something which is usually pleasant but has gone on too long or become too great

good[2] *n* **1** [U] that which is right and useful in accordance with religious beliefs or moral standards (esp. in the phrs. **do good, for good**): *By behaving well you can be an influence for good.|He does a lot of good for the town by giving money to build new schools.|There's good in her, in spite of her bad behaviour* —compare DO-GOODER, EVIL **2** [U] that which causes gain or improvement (esp. in the phr. **for someone's (own) good/the good of something**): *I work for the good of my family.|I don't do this for* (*the good of*) *my health* (= not for fun, but because I have to).|*You have to drink the medicine, not because I want you to, but for your own good* **3** [*the*+P] good people generally; those who do what is right: *Christians believe the good go to heaven when they die* **4 do someone good** to improve someone, esp. in health or behaviour: *It will do him good to have to look after himself. Maybe he won't be so selfish in future.|Milk does you good* **5 for good (and all)** for ever: *We thought she'd come for a visit, but it seems she's staying for good* **6 in good with** *infml esp. AmE* enjoying the favour or good opinion of: *It's nice to be in good with your employer* **7 no good/not much good (doing something/to someone)** useless: *It's no good talking to him, because he never listens.|Is your new doctor any good?|A car's not much good to me. I can't drive* **8** (an amount) **to the good** with a profit of (an amount): *I sold it for more than I paid for it, so I'm £5 to the good* **9 up to no good** doing or intending to do something wrong or bad: *When I saw him climbing through the window behind the shop I knew he was up to no good* **10 What's the good of X?** also **What good is X?**— What is the use or purpose of X? X has no use or purpose: *What's the good of getting the car out when it's near enough to walk?|What good is money when you haven't any friends?*

USAGE Note the word order in this fixed phr.: **good and evil**: *How did men gain the knowledge of good and evil?*

good af·ter·noon /· ˌ··ˈ·/ *interj, n* (an expression used when meeting, or being met by, someone in the afternoon)

good book /ˌ· ˈ·‖ˈ· ·/ *n* [*the*+R] *infml* (*often caps.*) the Bible

good·bye /gʊdˈbaɪ/ *interj, n* (an expression used when leaving, or being left by, someone)

good eve·ning /· ˈ··/ *interj, n* (an expression used when meeting, or being met by, someone in the evening)

good-for-noth·ing /ˈ· · ˌ··/ *adj, n* [Wa5;A;C; *you*+N] (a person who is) worthless, who does no work, etc.

Good Fri·day /ˌ· ˈ··/ *n* [R] the Friday before EASTER

good-hu·moured, *AmE* **-humored** /ˌ· ˈ··◂/ *n* [Wa2] having or showing a cheerful, friendly state of mind: *a good-humoured smile|He was very good-humoured about repairing the clock I broke* —see also **(a) good/bad** HUMOUR[1] (3) —**~ly** *adv*: *spoke good-humouredly*

good·ish /ˈgʊdɪʃ/ *adj* [Wa5;A] **1** quite good, but not very good in quality **2** rather large, long, far, etc. (in the phr. **a goodish . . .**): *He walked a goodish distance for a sick man* (= farther than one would expect).|*It takes a goodish amount of patience to look after 4 children*

good look·er /ˌ· ˈ··/ *n* LOOKER

good-look·ing /ˌ· ˈ··◂/ *adj* [Wa1] attractive; beautiful

good looks /ˌ· ˈ·/ *n* [P] LOOKS

good·ly /ˈgʊdli/ *adj* [Wa1;A] *old use & pomp* **1** pleasant or satisfying in appearance: *The table spread with food made a goodly sight* **2** large (in amount): *a goodly supply of seeds for the garden*

good mor·ning /· ˈ··/ *interj, n* (an expression used when meeting, or being met by, someone in the morning)

good-na·tured /ˌ· ˈ··◂/ *adj* [Wa2] naturally kind; ready to help, to forgive, not to be angry, etc. —**~ly** *adv*

good·ness /ˈgʊdnɨs/ *n* [U] **1** the quality of being good **2** the best part, esp. (of food) the part which is good for the health: *All the goodness has been boiled out of the vegetables* **3** (used in expressions of surprise and annoyance): *My goodness!|Goodness me!|For goodness'* SAKE, *stop misbehaving!|I wish to goodness he'd be quiet*

good·night /gʊdˈnaɪt/ *interj, n* (an expression used when leaving, or being left by, someone at night, esp. before going to bed or to sleep)

good of·fic·es /ˌ· ˈ···/ *n* [P] power or behaviour which helps someone out of a difficulty (usu. in the phr. **through the good offices of**)

goods /gʊdz/ *n* [P] **1** possessions which can be moved, not houses, land, etc. **2** also (*esp. AmE*) **freight**— *BrE* heavy articles which can be carried by road, train, etc.: *a goods train* (=*AmE a* **freight** *train*)|*a goods wagon* (=*AmE a* **freight** *car*) **3** articles for sale: *There's a large variety of goods in the shops* **4 deliver the goods** to produce in full what is expected **5 the goods** *BrE sl* a desirable thing or person: *She thinks he's/it's the goods*

goods and chat·tels /ˌ· · ˈ··/ *n* [P] *law* personal possessions

good sense /ˌ· ˈ·/ *n* [U] the ability to judge and act wisely —compare COMMON SENSE

good·will /ˌgʊdˈwɪl/ *n* [U] **1** kind feelings towards or between people and/or willingness to act to increase the good fortune of the others: *There is goodwill between the former enemies* **2** the value of the popularity, the regular buyers, etc., of a business as part of its worth when being sold: *The shop's goodwill deserves a high price, because it is a very well-liked firm*

good·y[1] /ˈgʊdi/ *n* [*often pl.*] **1** a sweet; pleasant thing to eat **2** something particularly attractive, pleasant, good, or desirable: *all the goodies—new cars, central heating, holidays abroad—that a higher income brings*

goody[2], **goodie** *interj* (an expression of pleasure used esp. by children)

goody-good·y /ˈ·· ˌ··/ *n* **goody-goodies** a person who likes to appear faultless in behaviour so as to please others, not because he or she is really good

goo·ey /ˈguːi/ *adj* **gooier, gooiest** **1** sticky and (usu.) sweet: *gooey cakes* **2** over-sweet; SENTIMENTAL —see also GOO

goof[1] /guːf/ *n sl* **1** a foolish person **2** *esp. AmE* a silly mistake

goof[2] *v* [IØ] *sl esp. AmE* to make a GOOF (2)

go off[1] *v adv* **1** [IØ] **a** to explode **b** to ring or sound loudly: *The* ALARM *went off when the thieves got in* **2** [IØ] (of food) to go bad: *This milk has gone off* **3** [IØ] *infml* to lose skill, quality, etc.: *These classes have gone off since we had a new teacher.|The book goes off after the first 50 pages* **4** [IØ] to cease to be felt: *The pain went off after 3 treatments* **5** [L9] to succeed or fail; COME OFF (3): *"How did your plan go off?" "It went off very well, thank you"* **6** [IØ] to fall asleep or lose consciousness: *Has the baby gone off yet?* —compare GET OFF (4), DROP OFF (3) **7** [IØ] to cease operation: *The heating goes off at night.|The lights went off* **8 go off with** *not fml* to take away without permission: *She's gone off with my book!|The milkman's gone off with my wife!*

go off[2] *v prep* [T1] to lose interest in or liking for: *I've gone off coffee, give me some tea*

goof·y /ˈguːfi/ *adj* [Wa1] silly; slightly mad —**goofiness** *n* [U]

goo·gly /ˈguːgli/ *n* (in cricket) a ball BOWLed[3] (4) as if to go in one direction which in fact goes in the other direction

goon /guːn/ *n sl* **1** a silly, foolish person **2** *esp. AmE* a man employed to threaten or attack opponents

go on[1] *v adv* **1** [IØ] to take place or happen: *There's a wedding going on at the church.|What's going on here?* **2** [IØ] GET ALONG (2) **3** [IØ (*at*)] to keep complaining or scolding: *She's always going on at her husband* **4** [IØ] also **run on** *not fml*— to keep talking: *She does go on so!* **5** [IØ (*with*),3,4] to continue without stopping, or after a stop: *Go on, I'm listening.|Go on with your work* **6** [L9] to behave continually in a certain way: *If he goes on like this he'll lose his job.|To judge by the way he's going on, he's very nervous about something* **7** [IØ] (of time) to pass: *As time went on, things began to change.|As the day went on, it became hotter* **8** [L9 (*for*)] *infml esp. BrE* to support oneself (at the stated level); MANAGE (3): *How did you go on for money while you were out of work?* **9** to be put into operation: *The heating goes on later.|The lights went on* **10 go on (with you)**! I don't believe you! **11 to be going/go on with** *infml esp. BrE* (to use) for the moment: *Here's £3 to be going on with. I'll give you some more tomorrow*

go on[2] *v prep* [T1 *no pass.*] to use as a reason, proof, or base for further action: *We were just going on what you yourself had said.|A bloody handkerchief and the name "Margaret" were all the police had to go on to catch the killer*

goose[1] /guːs/ *n* **geese** /giːs/ **1** [C] (*masc.* **gander**) a type of large white bird kept on farms, which makes a HISSing noise —see picture at DOMESTIC ANIMAL **2** [U] the meat of this bird when cooked **3** any of various large wild birds of this same family **4** [C; *you*+N] a silly person, esp. female **5 cook someone's goose** *sl* to prevent someone from carrying out his plans **6 (kill) the goose that lays/laid the golden egg(s)** to spoil (by hasty action or wish for present gain) the certain chance of future gain **7 he/she can't say boo to a goose** he/she is an unusually quiet person who doesn't fight **8 all one's geese are swans** one believes everything and everyone to be much better than they are

goose[2] *v* [T1] *esp. AmE taboo* to push one finger between the BUTTOCKs of

goose·ber·ry /ˈgʊzbəri, ˈguːz-, ˈguːs-‖ˈguːsberi/ *n* **1** [C] the small, round, green fruit of a bush grown in gardens: *a gooseberry bush* —see picture at BERRY **2 I found him/her under a gooseberry bush** *humor & old use* (an expression for explaining how a baby comes to be born) **3 play gooseberry** *esp. BrE* (of a third person) to be present with a man and woman who would rather be alone

goose·flesh /ˈguːsfleʃ/ *n* [U] a condition in which the skin is raised up in small points where the hairs grow out, as when a person is cold or frightened

goose pim·ples /ˈ· ˌ··/ *n* [P] GOOSEFLESH

goose·step /ˈguːs-step/ *n* [(*the*) S] a special way of marching in which each step is taken with one leg raised high and kept stiff and straight

go out *v adv* **1** [I∅] to leave the house, esp. for amusement: *She's gone out for a walk.|We go out 3 times a week* **2** [L9 (TOGETHER, *with*)] (*usu. in the* -ing *form*) to spend time, esp. regularly (with someone of the other sex): *They've been going out together for 2 years* **3** [I∅ (*to*)] to travel (to a distant place): *My friends went out to Africa* **4** [I∅] to be made public: *Have the notices all gone out?* **5** [L9] *lit* (of time) to end: *March went out with high winds and rain* **6** [I∅] (of a fire, light, etc.) to stop burning or shining: *Without more coal, the fire will soon go out.*|(fig.) *He went out like a light* (= to sleep, or into unconsciousness) **7** [I∅] (of the sea or TIDE) to go back to its low level —compare COME IN (6) **8** [I∅] (of a government) to leave office: *This party may go out at the next election* **9** [I∅] to cease to be fashionable or customary: *Short skirts went out some time ago, but they've come back again* **10** [L9, esp. *to*] (of feelings) to be in sympathy (with): *Our thoughts go out to our friends abroad* **11** [L9] (of a woman) to leave the house for some kind of employment: *Many married women go out to work.|Country girls often used to go out as servants in rich houses*

go o·ver[1] *v prep* [T1] **1** to visit and examine: *We went over several houses, but haven't bought one yet.|We're going to go over the glass factory* **2** to look at or examine for a purpose: *We went over the list of names and chose 2* **3** to repeat: *I'll go over the explanation of how it works* **4** (of spending) to go beyond; be more than

go over[2] *v adv* **1** [L9] (of a performance) to be received (favourably): *His speech went over well* **2** [L9, esp. *from* and/or *to*] to change (one's political party, religion, etc.): *went over from the People's Party to the No-Change Party*

go·pher /ˈgəʊfəʳ/ *n* a type of ratlike animal of North and Central America which makes and lives in holes in the ground

Gor·di·an knot /ˌgɔːdɪən ˈnɒt‖ˌgɔrdɪən ˈnɑt/ *n* **cut the Gordian knot** to settle a difficulty by direct action, without thinking too much of the results

gore[1] /gɔːʳ‖gor/ *n* [U] *lit* blood, esp. that which has flowed from a wound and thickened

gore[2] *v* [T1] (of an animal) to wound by pushing the horns or TUSK*s* into

gore[3] *n* a part of a garment, usu. of a skirt, which is a piece of material widening towards the bottom —**gored** *adj* [Wa5]: *a gored skirt*

gorge /gɔːdʒ‖gɔrdʒ/ *n* **1** a narrow valley with steep sides usu. made by a stream which has run or runs through it —see VALLEY (USAGE) **2** *old use* the throat **3 my gorge rose/make my gorge rise** (an expression used when thinking of or seeing something one does not like to be connected with to mean) "I felt sick/make me feel sick"

gorge on also **gorge with**— *v prep* [D1] to fill (oneself) with (food)

gor·geous /ˈgɔːdʒəs‖ˈgɔr-/ *adj* **1** *infml* delightful; who or which gives enjoyment: *He says she is a gorgeous person.|This cake is gorgeous* **2** *infml* very beautiful: *50 gorgeous girls dancing in our show!* —**~ly** *adv* —**~ness** *n* [U]

gor·gon /ˈgɔːgən‖ˈgɔr-/ *n* **1** an ugly woman whose appearance causes fear or shows anger **2** (*usu. cap.*) any of 3 imaginary sisters in ancient Greek stories, of whom the most famous was (the) Medusa. They had snakes for hair, and anyone who looked at them would turn to stone

Gor·gon·zo·la /ˌgɔːgənˈzəʊlə‖ˌgɔr-/ *n* [U] a type of Italian cheese which is white with blue marks and has a strong taste

go·ril·la /gəˈrɪlə/ *n* **1** a type of animal like a very big monkey without a tail which is very strong and lives in Africa. It is the largest of the manlike monkeys **2** an ugly or rough man

gor·mand·ize, -ise /ˈgɔːməndaɪz‖ˈgɔr-/ *v* [I∅] to eat a lot for pleasure —compare GOURMAND

gorm·less /ˈgɔːmləs‖ˈgɔrm-/ *adj BrE infml or dial* stupid and thoughtless, as though lacking brains: *He's too gormless to remember what you asked him to do* —**~ly** *adv*

go round *v adv; prep* **1** [I∅] GET ABOUT (2) **2** [I∅] GO AROUND (1) **3** [I∅;T1] (of words, ideas, etc.) to be continuously present (in): *There's a tune going round (in) my head* **4** [I∅] also **go around**— to be enough for everyone: *If there are not enough chairs to go round, some people will have to stand*

gorse /gɔːs‖gɔrs/ also **furze**— *n* [U] a type of bush with prickles and bright yellow flowers, which grows wild

gor·y /ˈgɔːri‖ˈgori/ *adj* [Wa1] **1** *lit* covered in blood —see GORE[1] **2** full of violence: *a gory film|all the gory details*

gosh /gɒʃ‖gɑʃ/ *interj* (an expression of surprise)

gos·ling /ˈgɒzlɪŋ‖ˈgɑz-, ˈgɔz-/ *n* a young GOOSE (1)

go slow *v adv* [I∅] *BrE* to refuse to put more than the least effort into work, as a form of STRIKE

go-slow /ˌ· ˈ·/ (*AmE* **slow-down (strike)**)— *n BrE* a refusal to put more than the least effort into work, as a form of STRIKE[2] (1)

gos·pel /ˈgɒspəl‖ˈgɑs-/ *n* [(*of*)] **1** a set of instructions or teachings **2** *humor* a principle which should be followed: *He believes in the gospel of "early to bed and early to rise"*

Gospel *n* any of the 4 accounts of Christ's life in the Bible

gospel truth /ˌ·· ˈ·/ *n* [*the*+R] *infml* something which is completely true

gos·sa·mer /ˈgɒsəməʳ‖ˈgɑ-/ *n* [U] **1** light, silky thread which SPIDER*s* leave on grass and bushes, and between trees **2** a very light thin material

gos·sip[1] /ˈgɒsɪ̠p‖ˈgɑ-/ *n* **1** [U] talk about the details of other people's actions and private lives, which may not be correct or proper —compare RUMOUR **2** [C] an example of this: *2 neighbours having a nice gossip in the street* **3** [U] writing in magazines and newspapers about the lives of well-known people (esp. in the phr. **gossip column**) **4** [C] a person who likes telling about the improper details of other people's private lives

gossip[2] *v* [I∅ (*with* and/or *about*)] to talk or write GOSSIP[1] (1,2)

gos·sip·y /ˈgɒsɪ̠pi‖ˈgɑ-/ *adj* **1** (of a person) liking GOSSIP[1] (1,2) **2** full of GOSSIP

got /gɒt‖gɑt/ *past t. and p. of* GET —see GOTTEN (USAGE)

Goth·ic /ˈgɒθɪk‖ˈgɑ-/ *adj* [Wa5] **1** of or concerning a Germanic people called **Goths**, who fought against the Roman Empire **2** of a style of building common in Western Europe between the 12th and 16th centuries, with pointed arches, arched (VAULTED[1] (4)) roofs, tall thin pillars (PIER*s*), and coloured glass in the windows **3** of a type of printing with thick, pointed letters **4** of a style of writing in the 18th century which produced stories (NOVEL*s*) set in lonely fearful places

go through[1] *v adv* [I∅] to be approved officially: *Their business arrangements went through*

go through[2] *v prep* [T1] **1** to suffer or experience: *The country has gone/been through too many wars* **2** GET THROUGH[2] (2) **3** to pass through or be accepted by: *The new law has gone through Parliament.|The plan must go through several stages* **4** to perform one's part in (a ceremony): *They went through the new marriage service* **5** GO OVER[1] (2)

go through with *v adv prep* [T1] to complete (something which has been agreed or planned), often with difficulty: *He promised to marry the girl,* *but now he doesn't want to go through with it*

go to *v prep* [T1 *no pass.*] **1** to cause oneself to experience (esp. in the phr. **go to a lot of/great trouble, go to great/considerable expense**): *He went to a lot of trouble for me.|They went to great expense to educate their son* —see also **go to great/some/considerable** LENGTHs (9) **2** to start experiencing or causing (a state or action) (in phrs. like **to go to sleep, to go to war**) —see also **go to** PIECES (2)

go to·geth·er *v adv* [IØ] (of 2 things) to GO WITH (4) each other; match

got·ta /ˈgɒtə‖ˈgɑtə/ *nonstandard* have/has got to: *When you gotta go, you gotta go*

got·ten /ˈgɒtn‖ˈgɑtn/ *AmE past p. of* GET —see also ILL-GOTTEN

USAGE In *AmE*, **gotten** is more common than **got** as the past participle of **get**, except where it means 1 "possess": *I've got a new car* (=I possess one); *I've gotten a new car* (=I've obtained one). 2 "must": *I've got to go* (=I must go); *I've gotten to go* (=I've succeeded in going). But Americans often say *I have a new car*, and avoid using **got** altogether in this meaning.

gou·ache /gʊˈɑːʃ, gwɑːʃ (*Fr* gwaʃ)/ *n Fr* **1** [U] a sort of paint which contains GUM² (2) to make it thicker, and is mixed with water **2** [U] the method of using this paint in pictures **3** [C] a picture painted with this paint

Gou·da /ˈgaʊdə, ˈguːdə/ *n* [U] a type of Dutch cheese which is yellowish in colour, not very strong in taste, and often round in shape with a red covering

gouge /gaʊdʒ/ *n* a tool for cutting out hollow areas in wood

gouge out *v adv* [T1] to press or dig out with force, esp. with the thumbs: *Cornwall gouges out Gloucester's eyes in Shakespeare's play "King Lear"*

gou·lash /ˈguːlæʃ‖-lɑʃ, -læʃ/ *n* [U;C] meat and vegetables cooked together with PAPRIKA, which gives a hot taste

go un·der *v adv* [IØ] **1** (of a ship or floating object) to sink —compare GO DOWN (3) **2** (of a business or person) to fail or get into difficulties: *She has so many worries, she's sure to go under*

go up *v adv* **1** [IØ] to rise: *Prices have gone up again* **2** [IØ] to be built: *How many houses have gone up this year?* **3** [IØ] to BLOW UP (1) or be destroyed in fire: *The whole house went up in flames* —compare **go up in** SMOKE **4** [IØ (*to*)] *BrE* to travel (to a university or important place): *to go up to London* —see DOWN¹ (USAGE) **5** [L9, esp. *to*] GO DOWN (8) **6** [IØ] (of the curtain on stage) to open and start the performance: *What time does the curtain go up?*

gourd /gʊəd‖gord, gʊərd/ *n* **1** a type of fruit which is large with a hard shell, and usu. grows on the ground **2** the outer shell of such a fruit, esp. when used as a drinking vessel or dish —see picture at FRUIT¹

gour·mand /ˈgʊəmənd‖ˈgʊər- (*Fr* gurmɑ̃)/ *n Fr* a person who eats too much, esp. one who is more interested in the quantity of food than in its quality —compare GLUTTON

gour·met /ˈgʊəmeɪ‖ˈgʊər-, gʊərˈmeɪ (*Fr* gurme)/ *n Fr* a person who knows a lot about food and drink and is good at choosing what should be combined together

gout /gaʊt/ *n* [U] a disease which makes the smaller joints swell and give pain

gout·y /ˈgaʊti/ *adj* [Wa1] **1** suffering from GOUT **2** caused by GOUT

gov·ern /ˈgʌvən‖-ərn/ *v* **1** [T1;IØ] to rule (a country, city, etc. and its people): *We have a queen, but it is the* PRIME MINISTER *and* CABINET (4) *who govern* **2** [T1] to control or guide (actions and feelings): *The need for money governs all his plans.|Don't let bad temper govern your decision* **3** [T1 *often pass.*] to determine the nature of: *The rise and fall of the sea is governed by the movements of the moon* **4** [T1] (in grammar) to determine the form (CASE¹ (8) or MOOD²) of (another word)

gov·ern·ance /ˈgʌvənəns‖-ər-/ *n* [U] *esp. old use* **1** the act of governing **2** the state of being governed

gov·ern·ess /ˈgʌvən¦s‖-ər-/ *n* (esp. in former times) a female teacher who lives with a family and educates their children at home

gov·ern·ing /ˈgʌvənɪŋ‖-ər-/ *adj* [Wa5;A] having the power of governing: *the governing body* (= a group of persons) *of a university*

gov·ern·ment /ˈgʌvəmənt, ˈgʌvənmənt‖ˈgʌvərn-/ *n* **1** [U] the act or action of governing (a state): *The young prince was not suited to government, and became a bad king* **2** [U] the form or method of ruling: *The country has always had fair government* **3** [GC] (*often cap.*) the people who rule: *The Government have asked the country to decide by a vote* —**~al** /ˌgʌvənˈmentl‖ˌgʌvərn-/*adj*

gov·er·nor /ˈgʌvənəʳ/ *n* **1** [C] a person who controls any of certain types of organization: *the governor of the prison/the Bank of England* **2** [C] a member of a GOVERNING body who control a school, hospital, art GALLERY, etc. **3** [C] (esp. in former times) a person who rules a foreign country (COLONY) controlled by his own country **4** [C;A; N] a person who rules over an American state **5** a part of a machine, usu. one which controls the speed at which a gas enters it **6** [C;N] also (*sl*) **guv, guvnor**— *esp. BrE* a man who has power over the (male) speaker, usu. his father or employer: *All right, governor, I'll do what you say.|My governor won't like it* —**~ship** *n* [U]

governor-gen·e·ral /ˌ··· ˈ···/ *n* **governors-general** *or* **governor-generals** (*usu. cap.*) a person who represents the King or Queen in those COMMONWEALTH (2) countries (except Britain itself) which are not REPUBLICs

go with *v prep* [*no pass.*] **1** [T1] also **go along with**— to be in agreement with **2** [T1] to be often found with, esp. as a result of: *Happiness doesn't necessarily go with money* **3** [T1,4] to be gained with: *Responsibility goes with becoming a father* **4** [T1] to match or suit: *Mary's blue dress goes with her eyes* **5** [T1] *infml* to spend time socially (or *euph* sexually) with (someone of the other sex): *He goes with a different girl every week* **6 go with the crowd/the times/the stream** to behave or think in the same way as most people

go with·out *v prep; adv* [T1,4;IØ] **1** DO WITHOUT **2 it goes without saying** it's clear without needing to be stated

gown¹ /gaʊn/ *n* **1** *old use or AmE* a long dress, esp. one worn on formal occasions: *an evening gown* **2** a (long) loose outer garment worn for special ceremonies by judges, teachers, lawyers, and members of universities, of which the ordinary type is black **3** (*usu. in comb.*) a loose garment worn for some special purpose: *a nightgown, dressing gown,* SURGEON's *gown* (worn during operations) **4 cap and gown** the formal dress worn esp. by members of a university on special occasions **5 town and gown** the people of a town and the members of a university in the town

G P *abbrev. for:* GENERAL PRACTITIONER

GPO *abbrev. for:* General POST OFFICE

grab¹ /græb/ *v* **-bb-** [T1] **1** to seize with a sudden, rough movement, esp. for a selfish reason: *He grabbed the coin and ran off.*|(fig.) *When she was offered work in India, she eagerly grabbed the chance to travel* **2** to get quickly and perhaps unfairly: *She grabbed the seat near the fire before I could*

grab² *n* **1** a sudden attempt to seize something; SNATCH (esp. in the phr. **make a grab at**) **2 up for grabs** *infml* ready for anyone to take or win: *I tell you, George, the job is up for grabs—go in there and ask her for it!*

grab at *v prep* [T1] to try to GRAB¹ (1): *She grabbed at me, but missed, and I ran on*

grace¹ /greɪs/ *n* **1** [U] fineness in movement, form or behaviour, esp. that which seems effortless and attractive **2** [U,U3] kindness; willingness to do what is right (esp. in the phrs. **have the grace**): *She had the grace to say that he was right* **3** [U] a delay allowed as a favour, as for payment, work, etc.: *There are 3 days of grace allowed after the day for payment.|I'll give you a week's grace, but if the work is not finished then, I'll write to my lawyers* **4** [U;C] a prayer before or after meals, giving thanks to God **5** [U] (in the Christian religion) the mercy (of God): *By the grace of God the ship came safely home through the storm* **6** [U] (in the Christian religion) the state of the soul when freed from evil: *His experience changed his life and he believed that God had caused him to suffer so that he was brought into a state of grace* **7** [N;C:9] a way of speaking to or of a DUKE, DUCHESS, or ARCHBISHOP: *Your/His/Her Grace|Their Graces* **8 act of grace** something given freely, not as a right, as when someone is forgiven for a crime **9 airs and graces** a show of behaviour which is intended to charm others or make them notice, but which may not be sincere **10 fall from grace a** to/a fall out of favour **b** to/a fall back into bad old ways of behaving **11 in someone's good graces** in someone's favour **12 a saving grace** a pleasing quality for which the person's faults are forgiven him **13 with (a) good/bad grace** willingly/unwillingly: *She accepted that she was wrong with (a) bad grace* **14 year of grace** any year whose date is calculated from Christ's birth: *in the year of grace 1976*

grace² *v* [T1 *often pass.*] *fml or humor* to ornament; give pleasure to, by one's/its presence: *We were graced with the presence of our chairman.|Fine furniture graced the rooms*

grace·ful /ˈgreɪsfəl/ *adj* **1** (of shape or movement) attractive to see **2** (of speech and feeling) suitably and pleasantly expressed —see GRACIOUS (USAGE) —**-fully** *adv*

grace·less /ˈgreɪsləs/ *adj* **1** awkward in movement or form **2** lacking in good manners —**~ly** *adv* —**~ness** *n* [U]

Grac·es /ˈgreɪsɨ̇z/ *n* [*the*+P] the 3 Greek goddesses who represented various forms of beauty

gra·cious /ˈgreɪʃəs/ *adj* **1** [B] polite, kind and pleasant, esp. to those who have no claim on one's attention: *She was gracious enough to show us round her home* **2** [A] *fml* used in speaking of royal persons: *Her Gracious* MAJESTY *Queen Elizabeth* **3** [B] (of God) merciful; forgiving: *God is gracious* **4** [A] having those qualities which are made possible by the use of wealth, such as comfort, beauty, and freedom from hard work: *gracious living* —**~ly** *adv* —**~ness** *n* [U]

USAGE A person or animal is **graceful** in bodily movements: *a* **graceful** *young girl/young cat|a* **graceful** *dance|to dance* **gracefully**. The word is also used when one thanks people, says one is sorry, etc.: *He admitted* **gracefully** *that he was wrong.* When **gracious** is used of people or their manners, it suggests a very grand person being polite to someone less important: *The Queen thanked them* **graciously**.

gra·da·tion /grəˈdeɪʃən/ *n* **1** [C] a stage in a set of changes or degrees of development: *A good actor can express every gradation of feeling from joy to grief.|There are many gradations in colour between light and dark blue* **2** [U] the act of passing from one stage to another, as from one musical quality or one vowel quality to another: *vowel gradation*

grade¹ /greɪd/ *n* **1 a** a degree of rank or quality **b** the members of the group at this level: *This grade of house can be sold at a lower price* **2** *AmE* a class for the work of a particular year of a school course: *in the second/8th grade* —compare FORM¹ (11) **3** *esp. AmE* a mark for the standard of a piece of schoolwork **4** *AmE* GRADIENT **5 make the grade** to succeed; reach the necessary standard

grade² *v* [Wv5;T1] to separate into levels: *Potatoes are graded according to size and quality*

grade cross·ing /ˈ· ˌ··/ *n AmE* LEVEL CROSSING

gra·di·ent /ˈgreɪdiənt/ *n* the degree of slope, as on a road: *A gradient of 1 in 4 is a rise of one metre for every 4 metres forward*

grad·u·al /ˈgrædʒʊəl/ *adj* **1** happening slowly and by degrees; not sudden: *The change was gradual, but now it looks completely different* **2** sloping gently: *There's a gradual rise in the path* —**-ually** *adv* —**~ness** *n* [U]

grad·u·ate¹ /ˈgrædʒʊɨ̇t/ *adj, n* [Wa5;A;C] **1** (of) a person who has completed a university degree course, esp. for a first degree **2** *AmE* (*usu. in comb.*) (of) a person who has completed a course at a college, school, etc.: *a* HIGH SCHOOL *graduate* **3** POSTGRADUATE: *graduate school|a graduate student*

grad·u·ate² /ˈgrædʒʊeɪt/ *v* **1** [IØ (*from*)] to obtain a degree at a university, esp. a first degree **2** [IØ (*from*)] *AmE* to complete an educational course **3** [T1] *AmE fml* to declare that (someone) has completed such a course and passed the examinations: *The college must graduate more science students* **4** [Wv5;T1] to arrange in order of degree or quality (GRADE) **5** [Wv5;T1] *tech* to make marks showing degrees of measurement (on): *a graduated ruler*

grad·u·a·tion /ˌgrædʒʊˈeɪʃən/ *n* **1** [U] the act of graduating (GRADUATE²) **2** [C] a mark showing a measure of degree, as on a SCALE⁵ (2) **3** [C] **a** a ceremony at which one receives proof of having gained a university degree **b** *AmE* a ceremony for GRADUATE*s*¹ (2)

Grae·co- /ˈgriːkəʊ, ˈgrekəʊ/ *comb. form* GRECO-

graf·fi·ti /græˈfiːti/ *n* [U;P] drawings or writing on a wall, esp. of a rude or political nature

graft¹ /grɑːft‖græft/ *v* [T1 (*on, onto*)] **1** to make a GRAFT on a tree or body **2** to join

graft² *n* **1** [C] a piece cut from one plant and bound inside a cut in another, so that it grows there **2** [C] a piece of healthy living substance, skin or bone, placed instead of such a substance in another part of the body which has been damaged: *a skin graft on the burnt leg* **3** [U] *esp. AmE* the practice of obtaining money unlawfully or unfairly, esp. by the dishonest use of political influence (note the phr. **graft and corruption**) **4** [U] *esp. AmE* money obtained in this way

graft·er /ˈgrɑːftəʳ‖ˈgræf-/ *n* **1** a person who GRAFT*s*¹ **2** *esp. AmE* a person, esp. a politician, who practises GRAFT² (3)

Grail /greɪl/ also **Holy Grail**— *n* [*the*+R] the cup believed to have been used by Christ before his death, and in which, it is said, some of his blood was collected

grain /greɪn/ *n* **1** [C] a seed of rice, wheat, or other such food plants —see picture at CEREAL **2** [U] crops from plants which produce such seeds, esp. from wheat **3** [C] a piece of a substance which is made up of small hard pieces: *a grain of sand/salt* **4** [C] the smallest possible bit or amount: *It is a false statement with a few grains of truth in it* **5** [(*the*) U] the natural arrangement of the threads or

FIBRE*s* in wood, flesh, rock and cloth, or the pattern of lines one sees as a result of this: *It is easiest to cut meat in the direction of the grain* **6** [C] the smallest measure of weight, as used for medicines (1/7000 of a pound or ·0648 gram) —see WEIGHTS & MEASURES TABLE **7 it goes/it's against the grain** it is not what one wishes (to do, know, etc.) **8 with a grain of salt** with some doubt: *Take his words with a grain of salt: he doesn't tell lies, but sometimes he stretches the truth*

gram, gramme /græm/ *n* a measure of weight, 1/1000 of a kilogram —see WEIGHTS & MEASURES TABLE

-gram *comb. form* [→*n*] something written or drawn: TELEGRAM|DIAGRAM

gram·mar /ˈgræməʳ/ *n* **1** [U] (the study and practice of) the rules by which words change their forms and are combined into sentences **2** [U] the correct or esp. incorrect use of these rules in speech or writing: *I'm afraid my secretary sometimes has to set my grammar right* **3** [C] also **grammar book** /ˈ·· ·/— a book which teaches these rules: *This is the best Italian grammar I've seen*

gram·mar·i·an /grəˈmeərɪən/ *n* a person who studies and knows about grammar, esp. a writer of grammar books

grammar school /ˈ·· ·/ *n* [C;U] **1** (in Britain) (the educational activity of) a school for children over the age of 11, where they study languages, science, etc., for examinations which may lead to higher education **2** (in the US) (the educational activity of) a school for children under the age of 12 or 14

gram·mat·i·cal /grəˈmætɪkəl/ *adj* **1** [Wa5;A] concerning grammar **2** [B] correct according to the rules of grammar: *That is not a grammatical sentence* —**-ically** *adv* [Wa4]

gram·o·phone /ˈgræməfəʊn/ *n BrE becoming rare* RECORD PLAYER

gram·pus /ˈgræmpəs/ *n* **1** a type of sea creature which blows out air and water; kind of WHALE **2** a person who breathes noisily **3 wheeze like a grampus** to breathe noisily

gran /græn/ *n* [C;N] *BrE infml* grandmother —see TABLE OF FAMILY RELATIONSHIPS

gra·na·ry /ˈgrænəri‖ˈgreɪ-, ˈgræ-/ *n* **1** a storehouse for grain, esp. wheat **2** a place which grows a lot of wheat, esp. for other countries: *The Mid-West is the granary of the US*

grand[1] /grænd/ *adj* **1** [Wa1;B] splendid in appearance: *There's a grand view of the mountains* **2** [Wa1;B] (of people) important, or (esp.) thinking oneself so: *The king's court was full of nobles and grand ladies* **3** [Wa1;B] *infml* very pleasant; delightful: *That was a grand party* **4** [Wa5;A] complete (esp. in the phr. **the grand total**) **5** [Wa5;A] (used in certain titles): *The* **grand old man** *of British politics is old, experienced, important, and probably popular* —**~ly** *adv* —**~ness** *n* [U]

grand[2] *n* **1** *infml* a GRAND PIANO: *a concert grand* **2** [Wn3] *AmE sl* 1,000 dollars: *3 grand*

gran·dad, grand·dad /ˈgrændæd/ *n infml* **1** [C;N] a grandfather **2** [N] (a name for an old man): *Come on, grandad!* —see TABLE OF FAMILY RELATIONSHIPS

grand·child /ˈgræntʃaɪld/ *n* **grandchildren** /ˈgræn,tʃɪldrən/ the child (**grandson** or **granddaughter**) of someone's son or daughter —see TABLE OF FAMILY RELATIONSHIPS

grand·daugh·ter /ˈgræn,dɔːtəʳ/ *n* the daughter of someone's son or daughter —see TABLE OF FAMILY RELATIONSHIPS

gran·dee /grænˈdiː/ *n* **1** a Spanish or Portuguese nobleman of the highest rank **2** a man of high rank

gran·deur /ˈgrændʒəʳ/ *n* [U] great beauty or power, often combined with great size: *As he watched the storm he thought of the grandeur of nature*

grand·fa·ther /ˈgrænd,fɑːðəʳ/ *n* [A;C;N] the father of someone's father or mother —see TABLE OF FAMILY RELATIONSHIPS

grandfather clock /ˈ···· ·, ,··· ˈ·/ *n* a tall clock with a long wooden outer case and the face at the top —see picture at CLOCK[1]

gran·dil·o·quent /grænˈdɪləkwənt/ *adj often derog* (of people or speech) using long, important-sounding words —**-quence** *n* [U]

gran·di·ose /ˈgrændiəʊs/ *adj often derog* intended to have the effect of seeming important, splendid, etc.: *With a grandiose movement, he pointed out all the land that belonged to him*

Grand La·ma /,· ˈ··/ *n* [*the*+R] DALAI LAMA

grand·ma /ˈgrænmɑː/ *n* [A;C;N] *infml* grandmother —compare GRANDPA —see TABLE OF FAMILY RELATIONSHIPS

grand mal /,grɒn ˈmæl‖,grɑn- (*Fr* grɑ̃ mal)/ *n* [U] *Fr* a serious form of the disease EPILEPSY —see also PETIT MAL

grand mas·ter /,· ˈ··/ *n* **1** the top rank of CHESS player **2** (*usu. caps.*) the head of certain organizations, such as FREEMASON*s*

grand·moth·er /ˈgræn,mʌðəʳ/ *n* [A;C;N] the mother of someone's father or mother —see TABLE OF FAMILY RELATIONSHIPS

Grand Na·tion·al /,· ˈ···/ *n* [*the*+R] an English horse race with jumps (STEEPLECHASE) held yearly

grand op·e·ra /,· ˈ···/ *n* [C;U] (an) OPERA in which all the words are sung, usu. on a serious subject

grand·pa /ˈgrænpɑː/ *n* [A;C;N] *infml* grandfather —compare GRANDMA —see TABLE OF FAMILY RELATIONSHIPS

grand·par·ent /ˈgræn,peərənt/ *n* the parent (**grandfather** or **grandmother**) of someone's father or mother —see TABLE OF FAMILY RELATIONSHIPS

grand pi·an·o /,· ·ˈ··/ *n* a large piano with strings set across, level with the ground, not upright —see picture at KEYBOARD[1]

Grand Prix /,grɒn ˈpriː‖,grɑn- (*Fr* grɑ̃ pri)/ *n* **grands prix** (*same pronunciation*) *Fr* (*often caps.*) any of a set of important motorcar races held under international rules

grand slam /,· ˈ·/ *n* **1** the winning of all of a set of sports competitions **2** the winning of all the card TRICK*s*[1] (7) possible at one time, esp. the winning of 13 TRICK*s* at one time in the game of BRIDGE[3]

grand·son /ˈgrænsʌn/ *n* the son of someone's son or daughter —see TABLE OF FAMILY RELATIONSHIPS

grand·stand /ˈgrændstænd/ *n* the set of seats, arranged with each row above and behind the other and sometimes covered by a roof, from which people may watch sports matches, races, etc.

grand tour /,· ˈ·/ *n* (in former times) a tour of the chief cities of Europe, esp. as part of the education of a young English gentleman

grange /greɪndʒ/ *n* (*often cap. as part of a name*) a country house with farm buildings: *The grange has become a hospital.*|*We walked past Askham Grange*

gran·ite /ˈgrænɨt/ *n* [U] a hard type of grey rock, used for building and making roads

gran·ny, grannie /ˈgræni/ *n* [C;N] *infml* grandmother —see TABLE OF FAMILY RELATIONSHIPS

grant[1] /grɑːnt‖grænt/ *v* **1** [D1 (*to*);T1] *fml* to give, esp. what is wanted or requested: *The boys were granted a holiday for the Queen's wedding* **2** [D1,5; T1,5] to admit to (the truth of (something)): *I grant you that he wastes his money, but he always* *spends it on his friends.|I had to grant him the reasonableness of his argument* **3** [D1] *law* to give (possession of (property)) **4 granted** yes (but): *"We've been very successful this year." "Granted. But can we do it again next year?"* **5 granted that** also **granting that**— (in an argument) even though; even supposing that: *Granted that he has enough money to buy the house, it doesn't mean he's going to do so* **6 take something/someone for granted** to accept a fact or someone's presence, actions, etc., without questioning its rightness: *I take it for granted that we should build new roads*

grant² *n* **1** money given by the state, usu. for educational purposes, as to a university or to support a student during his studies: *You can get a grant to improve your house* **2** (esp. in former times) land given by a king or government

gran·u·lar /ˈgrænjʊləʳ‖-jə-/ *adj* **1** made of GRANULEs **2** with a rough surface, esp. one having small bits in it

gran·u·late /ˈgrænjʊleɪt‖-jə-/ *v* [Wv5;T1;I∅] to (cause to) form into small bits (GRAINs or GRANULEs): *granulated sugar* (=ordinary powdery sugar, not the kind in large lumps)

gran·ule /ˈgrænjuːl/ *n* a small bit like a fine grain

grape /greɪp/ *n* **1** a small round juicy fruit usu. green (called "white") or dark purple (called "black"), which grows on a VINE and is used for making wine: *a bunch of grapes* —see picture at BERRY **2 sour grapes** the act of pretending to dislike what one really desires, because it is unobtainable: *Jane said that Mary was silly to buy a new coat, and anyhow it didn't suit her; but it was just sour grapes, because Jane wanted one herself*

grape·fruit /ˈgreɪpfruːt/ *n* **grapefruit** *or* **grapefruits** [Wn2] a large round yellow fruit, with a thick skin like an orange but a more acid taste

grape·shot /ˈgreɪpʃɒt‖-ʃɑt/ *n* [U] (in former times) a mass of small iron balls fired together from a large gun (CANNON)

grape·vine /ˈgreɪpvaɪn/ *n* **1** [C] the climbing plant that bears GRAPEs **2** [*the*+R] a secret way of spreading news: *I heard it on the grapevine*

graph¹ /græf, grɑːf‖græf/ *n* a straight or curved line which is drawn between an upright line and a level line across the page to show how the 2 values represented by those lines are related to one another; for example a line which shows how quickly a child grows by marking its height each month with a point and joining the points

graph² *v* [T1] to represent on a GRAPH¹: *graphing the growth of personal income in the years 1945–52*

-graph /grɑːf‖græf/ *comb. form* **1** [→*n*] something written: *a* MONOGRAPH|*an* AUTOGRAPH **2** [→*n*] an image or message REPRODUCED in a form which can be seen or kept: *a* PHOTOGRAPH **3** [→*v*] connected with the REPRODUCTION of messages or images in a form which can be seen or kept; *to* TELEGRAPH|*to* PHOTOGRAPH **4** [→*n*] a machine or instrument that sends or records information: *sent it by* TELEGRAPH —**-grapher** /grəfəʳ/ *comb. form* [→*n* C] —**-graphic** /ˈgræfɪk/ *comb. form* [→*adj*] —**-graphically** /ˈgræfɪkəli/ *comb. form* [→*adv* Wa4] —**-graphy** /grəfi/ *comb. form* [→*n* U]: *beautiful* CALLIGRAPHY

graph·ic /ˈgræfɪk/ *adj* [A] **1** [Wa5] concerned with written signs, usu. letters or drawings **2** which gives a clear description or lifelike picture, esp. in words: *a graphic description* **3** [Wa5] by a GRAPH

graph·i·cal /ˈgræfɪkəl/ *adj* [Wa5] GRAPHIC (3); by a GRAPH

graph·i·cally /ˈgræfɪkli/ *adv* **1** in a GRAPHIC manner: *described the events so graphically that I could almost see them* **2** [Wa5] in a GRAPHIC (3) manner; by a GRAPH

graph·ite /ˈgræfaɪt/ *n* [U] a black substance (a kind of CARBON (1)) which is used in paints, oil for machines, electrical apparatus and for the writing material in the middle of pencils (usu. called "lead")

gra·phol·o·gy /græˈfɒlədʒi‖-ˈfɑ-/ *n* [U] the study of handwriting as a guide to character —**-logist** *n*

graph pa·per /ˈ· ˌ··/ *n* [U] paper with squares marked on it, on which GRAPHs can be easily measured out and drawn

grap·nel /ˈgræpnəl/ *n* an iron instrument, sometimes an ANCHOR¹ (1), with several hooks, which can be used when tied to a rope for holding a boat still, for searching for an object on the bottom of a river or lake, or (formerly) for pulling an enemy's boat close to one's own

grap·ple with /ˈgræpəl/ *v prep* [T1] **1** to seize and struggle with: *He grappled with the bank robber, but was thrown to the ground* **2** to work hard to deal with (a difficulty): *Don't interrupt John. He's grappling with the accounts*

grappling i·ron /ˈ·· ··/ also **grappling hook** /ˈ·· ·/— *n* GRAPNEL

grasp¹ /grɑːsp‖græsp/ *v* [T1] **1** to take or keep a firm hold of, esp. with the hands **2** to succeed in understanding: *I grasped the main points of the speech* **3** to try or be eager to take: *Grasp your chances while you can*

grasp² *n* [S9] **1** a firm hold: *I kept her hand in my grasp* **2** REACH² (1): *Success is within his grasp* **3** control; power: *He is in the grasp of a wicked man* **4** understanding: *This work is beyond my grasp* **5 take a grasp on oneself** to control one's feelings (of anger, worry, etc.)

grasp at *v prep* [T1] CATCH AT: *He grasped at anything that might help him*

grasp·ing /ˈgrɑːspɪŋ‖ˈgræs-/ *adj derog* eager for more, esp. money: *Don't let those grasping shopkeepers charge you too much* —**~ly** *adv*

grass¹ /grɑːs‖græs/ *n* **1** [U] various kinds of common low-growing green plants whose blades and stems are eaten by sheep, cows, etc., on hills and in fields **2** [U] land covered by grass: *Don't walk on the grass* **3** [C] any of various types of green plant with tall, straight stems and flat blades: *She arranged some attractive grasses with the flowers.|He hid behind some tall grasses* **4** [C] *BrE sl* a person (often himself a criminal) who informs the police about the people concerned in a crime, esp. habitually; INFORMER **5** [U] *sl* CANNABIS; MARIJUANA **6 let the grass grow under one's feet** [*nonassertive*] to delay action **7 out to grass/at grass a** feeding on this plant; grazing (GRAZE¹ (1)) **b** no longer working: *He's too old to work fast, so his employers have turned him out to grass*

grass² *v* **1** [T1 (OVER)] to cover (land) with grass **2** [I∅ (*on*)] *BrE sl* (esp. of a criminal) to inform the police about the action of (other) criminals: *Bill must have grassed (on us)*

grass·hop·per /ˈgrɑːsˌhɒpəʳ‖ˈgræsˌhɑ-/ *n* **1** a type of insect which can jump high and makes a sharp noise by rubbing parts of its body together **2 knee-high to a grasshopper** *infml* (of a person, esp. a child) not very tall

grass·land /ˈgrɑːslænd‖ˈgræs-/ *n* [U *often pl. with same meaning*] a stretch of land covered mainly with grass, esp. wild land used for cattle to feed on

grass roots /ˌ· ˈ·/ *n* [P] **1** the ordinary people, not the ones with power and knowledge: *grass roots opinion* **2** the basic facts: *We must go back to grass roots before we can change what has happened*

grass wid·ow /ˌ· ˈ··/ *masc.* **grass widower** /ˌ· ˈ···/— *n sometimes humor* a woman whose husband is away for a period of time

gras·sy /ˈgrɑːsi‖ˈgræsi/ *adj* [Wa1] covered with growing grass

grate¹ /greɪt/ *n* the bars and frame which hold the coal, wood, etc., in a fireplace —see picture at LIVING ROOM

grate² *v* **1** [Wv5;T1] to rub (usu. food) on a hard, rough surface so as to break into small pieces: *grated cheese* **2** [Wv4;IØ (*on*)] to make a sharp sound, unpleasant to the hearer: *The nails in his boots grated on the stones.|His whistling grated on her nerves*

grate·ful /ˈgreɪtfəl/ *adj* [F (*to* and/or *for*);A] feeling or showing thanks to another person: *I was most grateful to John for bringing the books/for his kindness*—**gratefully** *adv*—~**ness** *n* [U]

grat·er /ˈgreɪtəʳ/ *n* an instrument for grating (GRATE² (1)) things into small pieces, often one of metal with sharp, rough points

grat·i·fi·ca·tion /ˌgrætɪ̈fɪ̈ˈkeɪʃən/ *n fml* **1** [U] the act of GRATIFYing or state of being gratified: *He thinks only of the gratification of his senses.|It gave me some gratification to hear their good opinion of my son* **2** [C] **a** something which gratifies **b** *old use* a reward, esp. money

grat·i·fy /ˈgrætɪ̈faɪ/ *v* [T1] *fml* **1** [*often pass.*] to give pleasure and satisfaction to: *It gratified me to know how soon she would be well again* **2** to satisfy (a desire): *Now she has a job in France she can gratify her wish to see Europe*

grat·i·fy·ing /ˈgrætɪ̈faɪ-ɪŋ/ *adj* [B;F3] giving pleasure and satisfying: *It was gratifying to know of the success of our efforts* —~**ly** *adv*

grat·ing¹ /ˈgreɪtɪŋ/ *n* a frame or network of bars, usu. metal, to protect a hole or window: *She caught her heel in a grating at the side of the road* (= one which covers a hole connecting with a water system)

grating² *adj* (of a noise or sound) sharp, hard, and unpleasant —~**ly** *adv*

grat·is /ˈgrætɪ̈s, ˈgreɪtɪ̈s/ *adv, adj* [Wa5;F] free; (given) without payment

grat·i·tude /ˈgrætɪ̈tjuːd‖-tuːd/ *n* [U (*to* and/or *for*)] the state or feeling of gratefulness; kind feelings towards someone who has been kind: *She showed me her gratitude by inviting me to dinner*

gra·tu·i·tous /grəˈtjuːɪ̈təs‖-ˈtuː-/ *adj* **1** not deserved or necessary: *a gratuitous rude remark|Her advice was quite gratuitous; I can think for myself* **2** done freely, without reward or payment being expected —~**ly** *adv* —~**ness** *n* [U]

gra·tu·i·ty /grəˈtjuːɪ̈ti‖-ˈtuː-/ *n* **1** a gift of money for a service done; TIP⁷ **2** *esp. BrE* a gift of money to a worker or member of the armed forces when he leaves his employment

grave¹ /greɪv/ *n* **1** [C] the place in the ground where a dead person is buried **2** [*the*+R] death (esp. in the phr. **from the cradle to the grave** = from birth to death): *Is there life beyond the grave?* **3 dig one's own grave** to kill or destroy oneself by one's way of living **4 make someone turn in his grave** to do something which would anger a person now dead: *That use of English would make Shakespeare turn in his grave* **5 have/with one foot in the grave** (be) very old and near death **6 silent as the grave** not talking at all (about a secret) **7 Someone is walking over my grave** (said when one feels an unexpected coldness and fear)

grave² *adj* [Wa1] **1** serious or solemn in manner: *His face was grave as he told them about the accident* **2** important and needing attention and (often) worrying: *This is grave news.|The sick man's condition is grave* —~**ly** *adv*

grave³ /grɑːv/ *adj* [Wa5] (of a mark (ACCENT¹ (2)) put above a letter to show pronunciation) being the mark over è —compare ACUTE (7)

grav·el¹ /ˈgrævəl/ *n* [U] **1** a mixture of small stones with sand, used on the surface of roads or paths —see picture at SITE¹ **2 a** small bits of stone-like material in the BLADDER (1) **b** the disease caused by these

gravel² *v* **-ll-** (*AmE* **-l-**) [Wv5;T1 *often pass.*] **1** to cover (a road) with GRAVEL¹: *a gravelled path* **2** *BrE* to bring (someone) to a stop; confuse

grav·el·ly /ˈgrævəli/ *adj* **1** of, containing, or covered with GRAVEL¹ (1) **2** having a low sharp hard GRATING² sound: *a gravelly voice*

grave·stone /ˈgreɪvstəʊn/ *n* a stone put up over a grave bearing the name, dates of birth and death, etc., of the dead person —see picture at CHURCH¹

grave·yard /ˈgreɪvjɑːd‖-ɑrd/ *n* a piece of ground, sometimes near a church, where people are buried; CEMETERY

grav·ing dock /ˈ·· ·/ also **dry dock**— *n* a place near a harbour or river where the water can be drawn away to make it possible to clean a ship's bottom

grav·i·tate to·wards /ˈgrævɪ̈teɪt/ also **gravitate to**— *v prep* [T1] **1** (of things) to be drawn towards: *However often you mix it up in the water, the mud will gravitate towards the bottom again* **2** (of people) to be attracted and move to: *Everyone gravitated towards the corner of the room, to see what all the noise was about*

grav·i·ta·tion /ˌgrævɪ̈ˈteɪʃən/ *n* [U] **1** the act of gravitating (GRAVITATE) **2** GRAVITY (2) —~**al** *adj*

grav·i·ty /ˈgrævɪ̈ti/ *n* [U] **1 a** seriousness of manner: *Even children must behave with gravity at a funeral* **b** worrying importance: *He doesn't understand the gravity of his illness* —see GRAVE² **2** the natural force by which objects are attracted to each other, esp. that by which a large mass pulls a smaller one to it: *Anything that is dropped falls towards the centre of the earth because of the pull of gravity*

gra·vure /grəˈvjʊəʳ/ *n* [U] the method of printing from copper plates on which the picture has been marked

gra·vy /ˈgreɪvi/ *n* [U] **1 a** the juice which comes out of meat as it cooks **b** the thickened liquid made from this (with flour, etc., added) to serve with meat and vegetables **2** *sl* profit or advantage gained easily or unexpectedly **3 get on the gravy train** *sl* to take advantage of the chance of joining a profitable business or doing something that will produce a lot of money without much work

gravy boat /ˈ·· ·/ *n* a small deep long-shaped container with a handle, from which GRAVY can be poured at a meal

gray /greɪ/ *v, adj, n AmE* GREY

graze¹ /greɪz/ *v* **1** [T1;IØ] (of animals) to feed on grass (in): *The cattle are grazing (in the field)* **2** [X9] to cause (animals) to feed on grass: *We can't graze the cattle till summer* **3** [T1] to use (land) for grazing: *I shall graze the bottom field*

graze² *v* [T1;(L9)] **1** to touch (something) lightly while passing: *The wing seemed to graze the treetops as the plane climbed safely away* **2** to break the surface of (esp. the skin) by rubbing against something, by accident or on purpose: *She fell down and grazed her knee*

graze³ *n* [*usu. sing.*] a surface wound

grease¹ /griːs/ *n* [U] **1** animal fat when soft after being melted: *You will never get the grease off the plates if you don't use soap* **2** a thick, oily substance: *He puts grease on his hair to make it shiny*

grease² /griːs, griːz/ *v* [T1] **1** to put GREASE¹ on: *Grease the tin with butter before baking the cake* **2 like greased lightning** very fast —see also **grease someone's** PALM

grease gun /ˈ· ·/ *n* a hand instrument for forcing GREASE¹ (2) into machinery

grease·paint /ˈgriːs-peɪnt/ *n* [U] the type of paint used by actors and actresses on their faces and other parts of their bodies that can be seen

grease·proof /ˈgriːs-pruːf/ *adj* [A] (of paper) which does not let GREASE pass through it

greas·er /ˈgriːsəʳ, -zəʳ/ *n* **1** a person who puts GREASE on machinery to make it run smoothly **2** *AmE taboo derog* a native of Latin America, esp. Mexico

greas·y /ˈgriːsi, -zi/ *adj* [Wa1] **1** covered with GREASE or containing it: *greasy food|skin|hair* **2** slippery: *The roads are greasy after the rain* **3 greasy spoon** *AmE humor derog* a bad cheap restaurant —**greasily** *adv* —**greasiness** *n* [U]

great[1] /greɪt/ *adj* **1** [Wa1;B] of excellent quality or ability: *the great men of the past|a great king, artist, etc.* **2** [Wa1;A] important: *a great occasion* **3** [Wa1;A;(B)] large in amount or degree: *Take great care.|It was a great loss to us all.|a great deal|a great many|a great age* **4** [Wa1;A] (of people) unusually active in the stated way: *She is a great friend.|He's a great talker* **5** [Wa5;A] (*usu. before another adj. of size*) big: *That great (big) tree takes away all the light* **6** [Wa1;B] *infml* **a** splendid; very enjoyable: *What a great idea!|"I've got the use of a car." "Great! We can go to the seaside"* **b** unusually good: *He's the greatest* **7** [Wa5;A] (used in names to mark something important of its type): *the Great Wall of China|the Great Fire of London, 1666* —see also GREATER **8 great with child** *bibl* PREGNANT —**~ness** *n* [U]

great[2] *n* [*the*+P] important people): *He's always talking about his connections with the great.|She shows the same kind manner towards great and small alike*

great- *comb. form* (in a family) 3 or more stages away in direct relationship, or 2 stages indirectly —see TABLE OF FAMILY RELATIONSHIPS

Great Bear /ˌ· ˈ·/ *n* [*the*+R] PLOUGH

great be·yond /ˌ· ·ˈ·/ *n* [*the*+R] (*usu. caps.*) BEYOND[3]

great cir·cle /ˌ· ˈ··/ *n* [S] a circle on the earth's surface, with the centre of the earth as its centre: *The great circle* ROUTE *is the quickest way to fly from London to Peking*

great·coat /ˈgreɪtkəʊt/ *n* **1** a heavy military OVERCOAT **2** *becoming rare* a heavy OVERCOAT

Great Dane /ˌ· ˈ·/ *n* a type of very large tall dog with smooth hair

Great·er /ˈgreɪtəʳ/ *adj* [Wa5;A] (*in names*) **1** of a kind which is considered large, or larger than a closely-related type: *Is that bird a Greater Yellowlegs?* —opposite **Lesser** **2** including the outer areas: *Greater London|Greater New York* —compare INNER

great·ly /ˈgreɪtli/ *adv* (*with verb forms, esp. the past p.*) to a large degree; very: *greatly moved by his kindness|greatly to be feared*

Great Seal /ˌ· ˈ·/ *n* [*the*+R] an official mark put on important state papers (and, in the US, on paper money) —compare PRIVY SEAL

grebe /griːb/ *n* a type of bird without a tail which can swim under water in lakes and rivers —compare DABCHICK

Gre·cian /ˈgriːʃən/ *adj* (of style or appearance) Greek, esp. like that of ancient Greece

Gre·co-, Graeco- /ˈgriːkəʊ, ˈgrekəʊ/ *comb. form* **1** Greek; of (ancient) Greece **2** Greek and: *Greco-Roman art*

greed /griːd/ *n* [U (*for*)] *usu. derog* strong desire to obtain a lot or more than what is fair, esp. of food, money, or power: *greed for gold*

greed·y /ˈgriːdi/ *adj* [Wa1] **1** [B] *usu. derog* full of GREED for food: *The greedy little boy ate all the food at the party* **2** [F+*for*,F3] in great need (of) or with great desire (for): *The roots of the plant are greedy for water* —**greedily** *adv* —**greediness** *n* [U]

greedy-guts /ˈ·· ·/ *n* [C;N] *infml, esp. BrE* a person who likes to eat too much; GLUTTON

Greek /ˈgriːk/ *adj* [Wa5] **1** of or concerning the people, language, art, etc. of Greece —see NATIONALITY TABLE **2 It's all Greek to me** *infml* (esp. of speech or writing) It's beyond my understanding

green[1] /griːn/ *adj* [Wa1] **1** [B] of a colour between yellow and blue, which is that of leaves and grass: *a green* SALAD **2** [B] (of plants) of this colour when young or unripe: *Green apples are sour.|wood which is green* (= which is not dry enough to burn) **3** [B] *infml* young and/or inexperienced and therefore easily deceived and ready to believe anything **4** [B] unhealthily pale in the face, as though from sickness, fear, etc. **5** [B] (esp. of memories) fresh, strong, and full of life, in spite of the passing of time **6** [B] covered in fresh grass and leaves: *The country is very green in the spring* **7** [F] also **green with envy**— very jealous —**greenness** /ˈgrin-nɪ̈s/ *n* [U]

green[2] *n* **1** [U] the colour which is green: *She was dressed in green* **2** [C] a smooth stretch of grass, for a special purpose, as for playing a game or for the general use of the people of a town: *They are dancing on the village green.|a* BOWL*ing*[3] (3) *green|The* GOLF*er hit his ball onto the green in one stroke!* —see also PUTTING GREEN

green·back /ˈgriːnbæk/ *n AmE old use* an American banknote

green belt /ˈ· ·/ *n* [C;U] a stretch of land, round a town, where building is not allowed, so that fields, woods, etc., remain

green·e·ry /ˈgriːnəri/ *n* [U] green leaves and plants (FOLIAGE), esp. when used for ornament

green-eyed /ˌ· ˈ·/ *adj* [Wa5] jealous —see also **green-eyed** MONSTER (5)

green fin·gers /ˌ· ˈ··/ *n* [P] *esp. BrE* natural skill in making plants grow well —compare GREEN THUMB

green·fly /ˈgriːnflaɪ/ *n* **greenfly** *or* **greenflies** [Wn2] a very small green insect which feeds on the juice from young plants

green·gage /ˈgriːngeɪdʒ/ *n* a soft juicy greenish-yellow fruit; kind of PLUM

green·gro·cer /ˈgriːnˌgrəʊsəʳ/ *n esp. BrE* a shopkeeper who sells vegetables and fruit: *got some oranges at the greengrocer's*

green·horn /ˈgriːnhɔːn||-ɔrn/ *n* **1** a young, inexperienced person, esp. male, who is easily cheated **2** *esp. AmE* a recently-arrived IMMIGRANT, esp. male **3** a beginner, esp. male, at some kind of work or skill

green·house /ˈgriːnhaʊs/ *n* **-houses** /ˌhaʊzɪ̈z/ a building with glass roof and sides and often some form of heating, used for growing plants which need heat, light, and freedom from winds —see picture at GARDEN[1]

green·ish /ˈgriːnɪʃ/ *adj* rather (like) green

green light /ˌ· ˈ·/ *n* [*the*+R] the sign, or permission, to begin an action: *We're ready to rebuild our house. We're just waiting for the green light from the Council*

green pep·per /ˌ· ˈ··/ also **sweet pepper**— *n* a type of vegetable with a green skin, flesh and seeds, used for giving a particular hot taste to food —see picture at VEGETABLE[1]

green·room /ˈgriːnrʊm, -ruːm/ *n* [*the*+R;(C)] a room in a theatre or concert hall where actors, musicians, etc., can rest when not performing

greens /griːnz/ *n* [P] **1** green leafy vegetables that are cooked and eaten **2** *AmE* leaves and branches used for ornament, esp. at Christmas —compare GREENERY

green tea /ˌ· ˈ·/ *n* [U] tea which is made from leaves which have been heated with steam, not dried in the ordinary way

green thumb /ˌ· ˈ·/ *n* [S] *esp. AmE* GREEN FINGERS

Green·wich Mean Time /ˌgrɪnɪdʒ ˈmiːn taɪm, ˌgre-, -nɪtʃ-/ (*abbrev.* **G.M.T.**) also **Greenwich time** /ˈ·· ·/— *n* [R] the time at a place near London (Greenwich) where there is a certain point which represents the line dividing east from west. Times in the rest of the world are compared to this and said to be a number of hours earlier or later: *European time is usually one hour later than Greenwich Mean Time*

green·wood /ˈgriːnwʊd/ *n* [*the*+R] *lit* a green wood; forest: *Robin Hood and his merry men are waiting in the greenwood*

greet /griːt/ *v* **1** [T1] to welcome with words or actions: *He greeted us by shouting a friendly* "HELLO!"|*She greeted him with a loving kiss* **2** [X9] to receive with an expression of feeling: *The speech was greeted by loud cheers* **3** [T1] to come suddenly to the eyes, ears, etc.: *Inside the room complete disorder greeted us.*|*I woke up and was greeted by bird song*

greet·ing /ˈgriːtɪŋ/ *n* **1** a form of words or an action used on meeting someone: *"Good morning," I said, but she didn't return the greeting* **2** *AmE* **salutation**— the words used at the beginning of a letter: *They sent Mr. Brown a letter with the greeting "Dear Sir"* **3** [*usu. pl.*] a good wish: *We sent a card with birthday/Christmas greetings*

gre·gar·i·ous /grɪˈgeərɪəs/ *adj* **1** (of people and animals) living in groups **2** (of people) liking the society and companionship of others —**~ly** *adv* —**~ness** *n* [U]

Gre·go·ri·an cal·en·dar /grɪˌgɔːrɪən ˈkælᵊndəʳ‖ grɪˌgor-/ *n* [*the*+R] the system of arranging the days and months of the year which has been generally used since 1582, when POPE Gregory the 13th introduced it

Gregorian chant /·ˌ··· ˈ·/ *n* [C;U] a kind of church music for voices alone, according to rules that were made official by POPE Gregory the First —see also PLAINSONG

grem·lin /ˈgremlᵊn/ *n infml* a wicked little spirit, said to cause damage to aircraft engines, esp. during World War 2

gre·nade /grᵊˈneɪd/ *n* a small bomb which can be thrown by hand or fired from a gun

gren·a·dier /ˌgrenəˈdɪəʳ/ *n* **1** [C] a soldier, formerly one who threw GRENADEs **2** [C;A] a member of a special part of the British army, the **Grenadiers** or **Grenadier Guards** /ˌ··· ˈ·/

gren·a·dine /ˈgrenədiːn, ˌgrenəˈdiːn/ *n* [U] a sweet liquid made from POMEGRANATEs, and used in drinks

grew /gruː/ *past t. of* GROW

grey[1], *AmE* also **gray** /greɪ/ *adj* **1** [Wa1] of the colour like black mixed with white; the colour of lead, ashes, rain clouds, etc.: *Her hair is going grey with worry.*|*a grey coat* **2** [Wa5] having grey hair: *She's gone grey within a few weeks* **3** [Wa1] (of the skin of the face) of a pale colour because of sudden fear or illness: *His face turned grey as he heard the bad news* **4** [Wa1] dull; without light: (fig.) *Life seems grey and joyless* —**~ness** *n* [U]

grey[2], *AmE* also **gray** *n* [U;(C)] (a) grey colour: *She was dressed in grey.*|*dull greys and browns*

grey[3], *AmE* also **gray** *v* [Wa4;IØ;T1] **a** (esp. of hair) to become grey: *greying hair* **b** to cause (esp. hair) to become grey: *Sorrow has greyed his head*

grey·beard, *AmE* **gray-** /ˈgreɪbɪəd‖-bɪərd/ *n usu. lit* an old man, often one who is wise

grey·hound /ˈgreɪhaʊnd/ *n* **1** [C] a type of dog which is thin with long thin legs, and can run swiftly in hunting and racing **2** [C; *by*+U] *tdmk* (*usu. cap.*) (in the US) a type of long-distance bus

grey·ish, *AmE* **gray-** /ˈgreɪ-ɪʃ/ *adj* rather grey

grey mat·ter /ˈ· ˌ··/ *n* [U] **1** the substance of the brain and nervous system which contains cell bodies, esp. the central part of the brain **2** *infml* brain power; the power of thought

grid /grɪd/ *n* **1** a set of bars set across each other in a frame, esp. one which is set on top of a car to carry boxes and bags **2** a framework of wires inside a radio set **3** *BrE* the network of electricity supply wires connecting the power stations **4** a system of numbered squares printed on a map so that the exact position of any place on it may be stated or found **5** a system like this: *a road grid* **6** a GRIDIRON (1) for cooking **7** GRATING

grid·dle /ˈgrɪdl/ *n* a round iron plate which can be used for baking flat cakes (**griddle cakes** /ˈ·· ·/) over a fire

grid·i·ron /ˈgrɪdaɪən‖-ərn/ *n* **1** also **grid**— an open framework of metal bars for cooking meat or fish on over a very hot fire **2** *AmE* a field marked in white lines for American football

grief /griːf/ *n* **1** [U] great sorrow or feelings of suffering, esp. at the death of a loved person: *She went nearly mad with grief after the child died* **2** [C] a cause of sorrow or anxiety: *His wild behaviour was a grief to his mother* **3 come/be brought to grief** to fail, causing harm to oneself: *My plan came to grief, and I was left penniless.*|*She rode fast down the hill but came to grief and fell when she went over a stone* **4 good grief!** (an expression of surprise and some dislike)

griev·ance /ˈgriːvəns/ *n* [C] **1** a report of or cause for complaint, esp. of unjust treatment: *She has a very real grievance against the hospital, since the operation which ruined her health* **2 nurse a grievance** to keep a feeling of having been badly treated

grieve /griːv/ *v* **1** [IØ (*for*)] to suffer from grief and sadness, esp. over a loss: *She is still grieving (for her dead husband)* **2** [T1] to cause grief to; to make very unhappy: *It grieves me to see him change*

griev·ous /ˈgriːvəs/ *adj* [A] **1** very seriously harmful: *You have made a grievous mistake, which may never perhaps be put right* **2** (of wounds, pain, etc.) severe: *He received a grievous wound in battle* **3 grievous bodily harm** /ˌ·· ··· ˈ·/ *law* hurt done to a person's body in an attack, for which the attacker may be charged in a court of law —**~ly** *adv* —**~ness** *n* [U]

grif·fin, griffon, gryphon /ˈgrɪfən/ *n* an imaginary animal in stories with a lion's body and the wings and head of a bird (EAGLE)

grill[1] /grɪl/ *v* **1** [T1;IØ] to cook (something) under or over direct heat: (fig.) *He is grilling (himself) under a hot sun* —compare BROIL; see COOK (USAGE) **2** [T1] *infml* (esp. of the police) to question severely and continuously: *When the man had pointed him out as the criminal, he was grilled for 2 hours before the police would let him go*

grill[2] *n* **1** an arrangement of a metal shelf under a gas flame or electric form of heat, or of bars which can be put over a hot open fire, so that food can be cooked quickly: *Put the bread under the grill to make the* TOAST *for breakfast* —see picture at KITCHEN **2** meat cooked this way (esp. in the phr. **a mixed grill** = several types together) **3** (esp. in names of restaurants) the room or place where GRILLed foods can be ordered: *went to Murphy's* BAR[1] (10) *and Grill on 45th Street in New York*

grille /grɪl/ *n* a framework of usu. upright metal bars filling a space in a door or window, esp. in the window between a bank or post office clerk and the public or in any place where money is handled and must be protected

grim /grɪm/ *adj* **-mm-** [Wa1] **1** cruel, hard, or causing fear: *His expression was grim when he told them they were to be shot.|the grim news of his death* **2** determined in spite of fear: *a grim smile* **3** *infml* unpleasant; not cheerful: *I've had a grim day.|What a grim book, all about war and death!* **4 hold on/hang on like grim death** to keep holding or doing something with determination, in spite of difficulty —**~ly** *adv* —**~ness** *n* [U]

gri·mace[1] /grɪˈmeɪs, ˈgrɪməs‖ˈgrɪməs, grɪˈmeɪs/ *v* [IØ (*at, with*)] to make an expression of pain, annoyance, etc., which makes the face look unnaturally twisted: *She grimaced at the sight of all the work.|grimaced with pain*

grimace[2] *n* an unnatural twisting of the face, as in pain or annoyance: *a grimace of pain*

grime[1] /graɪm/ *n* [U] a surface of thick black dirt: *His face and hands were covered with grime from the coal dust*

grime[2] *v* [Wv5;T1 (*with*)] BEGRIME

grim·y /ˈgraɪmi/ *adj* [Wa1] covered with dark dirt or GRIME —**griminess** *n* [U]

grin[1] /grɪn/ *v* **-nn-** [IØ (*with, at*)] **1** to make a GRIN: *They grinned with pleasure when I gave them the sweets* —compare SMILE **2 grin and bear it** *infml* to suffer what is unpleasant without complaint **3 to grin from ear to ear/like an ape** to grin very widely/stupidly —see also CHESHIRE CAT

grin[2] *n* **1** a smile which shows the teeth; smile which seems almost to be laughing, esp. a very wide smile, which may sometimes also be an expression of suffering: *I told her to work harder and she just stood with a silly grin on her face* **2 Take/Wipe that grin off your face!** Don't laugh at me/at what I'm saying

grind[1] /graɪnd/ *v* **ground** /graʊnd/ **1** [Wv5;T1 (UP)] to crush into small pieces or a powder by pressing between hard surfaces: *Grind the eggshells up/to a powder and give it to the hens with their food.|She grinds fresh coffee beans every day* **2** [L9 (DOWN)] (of a material) to be able to be suitably crushed: *The wheat has ground down to a good white flour* **3** [T1;L9] to rub (esp. the teeth) together or against something, so as to make a crushing noise: *Some people grind their teeth during their sleep* **4** [T1] to make smooth or sharp by rubbing on a hard surface: *Your reading glasses have been spoilt and must be ground again.|A man came to grind the knives and scissors* **5** to press upon with a strong, twisting movement: *In anger, he ground his knee into the man's stomach, and hit him in the face.|The dirt was deeply ground into the floor covering* **6** [T1] to turn (esp. a BARREL ORGAN) by the handle **7** [L9, esp. AWAY, *at, for*] *infml esp. AmE* to study hard, esp. for an examination; SWOT[2]: *He's grinding away for his examination.|He's grinding away at his French* **8 grind the faces of the poor** to make poor people work very hard and give them almost nothing in return **9 grind to a halt** to come slowly and/or noisily to a stop

grind[2] *n* **1** [S] hard uninteresting work: *He finds any kind of study a real grind.|the daily grind of the housework* **2** [S] a long steady tiring effort of movement, such as a difficult race **3** [C] *AmE infml* a student who is always working; SWOT[1]

grind down *v adv* [T1] OPPRESS: *The ordinary people were ground down by lack of food and money*

grind·er /ˈgraɪndəʳ/ *n* **1** [C9] a person or machine that GRINDs: *a coffee grinder|a knife grinder* **2** [C] *infml* a large back tooth that GRINDs food in the mouth; MOLAR

grind in·to *v prep* [D1] to teach (something) with great difficulty to (someone): *He's trying to grind a lot of facts and figures into his mind*

grind out *v adv* [T1] *derog* to produce (esp. writing or music) continuously, but like a machine: *to grind out a few lines/popular stories*

grind·stone /ˈgraɪndstəʊn/ *n* **1** a round stone which is turned to sharpen tools, knives, etc. **2 one's nose to the grindstone** *infml* in a state of hard dull work: *He's got to keep his nose to the grindstone to feed his wife and 5 children*

grin·go /ˈgrɪŋgəʊ/ *n* **-s** *often derog* a foreigner in Spain or Latin America, esp. when of English or American origin

grip[1] /grɪp/ *v* **-pp-** **1** [T1;IØ] to take a very tight hold (of): *Grip harder.|She gripped my hand in fear.|He gripped the nail and pulled it out* **2** [T1] to attract and hold (someone's attention): *The strange stories gripped the hearers.|The pictures gripped my imagination*

grip[2] *n* **1** [C *usu. sing.*] a very tight forceful hold: *The policeman would not let go his grip on the thief.|He took a grip on the tooth and pulled it out* **2** [(*the*) S] control; power: *He kept a firm grip on his children.|Don't get into the grip of moneylenders.|Keep a grip on yourself* (=don't act hastily) **3** [S] power of understanding or doing: *I played badly; I seem to be losing my grip.|He has a good grip of his subject/of several modern languages* **4** [C] *AmE or old use* a bag or case for a traveller's personal belongings **5** [C] **a** (a part of) an apparatus which GRIPs: *a hair grip* **b** a handle or a part of it suitable to be GRIPped **6** [*the*+R] GRIPPE **7 come to grips (with)** to start to fight: *At last the 2 enemies came to grips* **8 come/get to grips with** to deal seriously with (something difficult): *The speaker talked a lot, but never really got to grips with the subject*

gripe[1] /graɪp/ *v* [IØ;(T1)] to cause or feel pain, esp. in the stomach: *a griping pain|I feel my stomach griping*

gripe[2] *v* [IØ (*at* and/or *about*)] *sl* to complain continually: *He's griping about his income tax again.|Mother gripes at me when I'm late for breakfast* —**~r** *n*

gripe[3] *n sl* a complaint: *My main gripe is, there's no hot water*

gripes /graɪps/ *n* [*the*+P; (*the*+U)] *sl* sudden and severe stomach pains: *He's got the gripes*

grippe, grip /grɪp, griːp‖grɪp (*Fr* grip)/ *n* [*the*+R] **1** a disease like INFLUENZA **2** *old use* INFLUENZA

grip·ping /ˈgrɪpɪŋ/ *adj* that holds the attention: *I found it a gripping film.|really gripping* —**~ly** *adv*

gris·ly /ˈgrɪzli/ *adj* [Wa2] unpleasant because of destruction, decay, or death which is shown or described: *the grisly remains of the bodies|a grisly story about people who ate human flesh* —compare GRUESOME

grist /grɪst/ *n* [U] **1** *old use* grain ready for GRINDing[1] **2 (all) grist to someone's/the mill** used for someone's profit: *Anyone else would refuse the additional work, but it's all grist to his mill, because he wants to get ahead in his job*

gris·tle /ˈgrɪsəl/ *n* [U] the material in meat which is a smooth clear substance found near the bones —compare CARTILAGE —**-tly** *adj* [Wa1]

grit[1] /grɪt/ *n* [U] **1** small pieces of a hard material, usu. stone: *Grit is spread on roads to make them less slippery in icy weather* **2** *infml* determination, lasting courage; cheerful effort made during difficulty —**gritty** *adj* [Wa1]

grit[2] *v* **-tt-** **grit one's teeth** to become determined when in a position of difficulty: *The snow was blowing in his face, but he gritted his teeth and went on*

grits /grɪts/ *n* [P;(U)] *AmE* grain which is coarsely crushed, or uncrushed but with the outer skin removed —see also HOMINY —compare GROATS

griz·zle /ˈgrɪzəl/ *v* [Wv3] *BrE infml* **1** [IØ] (esp. of young children) to cry quietly and continually as though worried **2** [I∅ (*about*),5] to complain in a self-pitying way

griz·zled /ˈgrɪzəld/ *adj* [A] greyish (-haired)

griz·zly bear /ˌ·· ˈ·‖ˈ·· ·/ also **grizzly**— *n* a type of large fierce brownish-grey bear of the Rocky Mountains of North America —see picture at CARNIVOROUS

groan[1] /grəʊn/ *v* **1** [I∅ (*with*)] to make a GROAN[2] (1,2): *The old man who had been in the accident lay groaning beside the road.*|(fig.) *The table groaned with food* **2** [T1 (OUT)] to say in a low voice like a GROAN: *He groaned out the story of how his friend had been killed* **3** [I∅ (*under*)] to suffer: *The people groaned under the load of taxes*

groan[2] *n* **1** a rather loud sound of suffering, worry, or disapproval, which is made in a deep voice: *There were loud groans when he started to sing* **2** a sound caused by the movement of wood or metal parts heavily loaded: *The old chair gave a groan when the fat woman sat down on it*

groat /grəʊt/ *n* (in England up to the middle of the 17th century) a silver coin worth a few pence

groats /grəʊts/ *n* [P] grain, esp. OATS, from which the outer shell has been removed, and which may also have been crushed

gro·cer /ˈgrəʊsəʳ/ *n* a shopkeeper who sells dry and preserved foods, like flour, coffee, sugar, rice, and other things for the home, such as matches and soap —compare GREENGROCER and see picture at STREET

gro·cer·ies /ˈgrəʊsəriz/ *n* [P] the goods sold by a GROCER: *She brought the box of groceries in from the car*

gro·cer·y /ˈgrəʊsəri/ *n* [U;C] the shop or trade of a GROCER: *We buy our flour at the nearest grocery*

grog /grɒg‖grɑg/ *n* [U] a mixture of strong drink (esp. RUM[2] (1)) and water, esp. as drunk by sailors

grog·gy /ˈgrɒgi‖ˈgrɑgi/ *adj* [Wa1;F] *infml* **1** weak because of illness, shock, etc., esp. when not able to walk steadily: *When I left my bed after my long illness I felt too groggy to stand* **2** *BrE* unsteady; not firmly joined, and likely to fall: *The table is very groggy. I think the leg's going to fall off* —**groggily** *adv*

groin /grɔɪn/ *n* **1** the hollow place where the tops of the legs meet the front of the body —see picture at HUMAN[2] **2** the curved line where 2 parts of a rounded arched roof (VAULT*s*) meet, as seen from inside **3** GROYNE

groom[1] /gruːm, grʊm/ *n* **1** a man or boy who is in charge of horses **2** BRIDEGROOM

groom[2] *v* **1** [T1] to take care of (horses), esp. by rubbing, brushing, and cleaning **2** [T1] to take care of the appearance of (oneself), by dressing neatly, keeping the hair tidy, etc. **3** [T1] (of animals) to clean the fur and skin of: *Monkeys groom each other* **4** [T1 (*for*);V3] to prepare (someone) for a special position or occasion: *grooming her for stardom* (= to play big parts in plays or films)

groove[1] /gruːv/ *n* **1** a long narrow path or track made in a surface, esp. to guide the movement of something: *The needle is stuck in the groove of the record, so it keeps repeating the same bit of music.*|*The cupboard door slides open along the groove it fits into* **2** RUT[2] (1,2) **3 in the groove** *old sl* in the best state or position: *Glenn Miller's band is really in the groove tonight! Listen to them play!*

groove[2] *v* [T1] to make GROOVE*s*[1] in: *The sand on the shore has been grooved by the waves*

groov·er /ˈgruːvəʳ/ *n sl* a GROOVY person

groov·y /ˈgruːvi/ *adj* [Wa1] *sl* attractive or interesting in the fashion of the time; modern

grope[1] /grəʊp/ *v* **1** [L9] to try to find something by feeling with the hands in a place one cannot see (properly): *He groped in his pocket for his ticket* **2** [T1] to make (one's way) by feeling with outstretched hands in or as if in the dark: *I groped my way to a seat in the dark cinema* **3** [L9, esp. *after, for*] to search with uncertainty of success for an idea or fact: *We are groping after the truth* **4** [T1] *sl* to (try to) feel over the body of (a person, usu. a woman) so as to get sexual pleasure

grope[2] *n* an act of groping (GROPE[1])

grop·ing·ly /ˈgrəʊpɪŋli/ *adv* uncertainly: *The blind man reached gropingly for the door handle*

gross[1] /grəʊs/ *adj* **1** [Wa1] unpleasantly fat **2** [Wa1] (of plants, grasses, etc.) very thick and close-growing **3** [Wa1] **a** (of food) coarse, badly prepared, etc. **b** eating or depending on such food: *Some fruit bushes are* **gross feeders**, *which live on decayed matter* **4** [Wa1] (of people's speech & habits) rough, impolite, and offensive: *She was shocked by the gross words he used* **5** [Wa1] *law* clearly wrong in law; inexcusable: *gross* NEGLIGENCE (= carelessness) **6** [Wa5] total: *The gross weight of the box of chocolates is more than the weight of the chocolates alone* —compare NET[3] (1,3) —**~ly** *adv* —**~ness** *n* [U]

gross[2] *n* [*the*+R] **1** [*fml*] the whole; the greater part **2 in gross** (*AmE* **in the gross**)— *BrE* in large amounts; WHOLESALE

gross[3] *v* [T1] to gain as total profit or earn as a total amount: *The company grossed £2,000,000 last year*

gross[4] *determiner, n* **gross** *or* **grosses** [see NUMBER TABLE 4B] a group of 144; 12 DOZEN

gro·tesque[1] /grəʊˈtesk/ *adj* **1** [B] strange and unnatural so as to cause fear or be laughable: *The child drew grotesque animals, unlike real horses, dogs, or cows* **2** [B] (of forms of art) containing figures of men, animals, plants, etc., of unusual size and shape, all mixed into one pattern **3** [*the*+U] concerning the strange and unnatural, esp. in art: *a student of the grotesque in painting* —**~ly** *adv* —**~ness** *n* [U]

grotesque[2] *n* a person or a painting showing GROTESQUE[1] qualities

grot·to /ˈgrɒtəʊ‖ˈgrɑ-/ *n* **-toes** *or* **-tos** **1** a natural cave, esp. of limestone, or a man-made one set in a garden and ornamented with shells **2** a small cave-shaped SHRINE[1] (2) for religious worship

grot·ty /ˈgrɒti‖ˈgrɑti/ *adj* [Wa1] *sl* bad, nasty, unpleasant, etc.: *She lives in a grotty little room with nowhere to cook* —**grottiness** *n* [U]

grouch[1] /graʊtʃ/ *n* **1** [C *usu. sing.*] a bad-tempered complaint: *She's always got a grouch about something; if it's not the weather, it's the rise in prices* —compare GROUSE[3] **2** [C; *you*+N] *esp. AmE* a person who keeps complaining —**~y** *adj* [Wa1] —**~iness** *n* [U]

grouch[2] *v* [I∅] to complain; GRUMBLE[1] (1)

ground[1] /graʊnd/ *n* **1** [*the* +R] the surface of the earth: *The branch broke and fell to the ground* —compare FLOOR[1] (1) **2** [U] soil; earth: *The ground is dry* —see LAND (USAGE) **3** [C9] (*usu. in comb.*) a piece of land used for a particular purpose: *a football ground*|*a playground* **4** [U] the bottom of the sea: *Our ship touched ground* **5** [C] **a** the first covering of paint: *When some of the green paint came off, we saw there was a white ground underneath* **b** the colour on which a pattern is placed; background: *The curtains have white flowers on a blue ground* **6** [U9] a base for argument, study, etc.: *The book says nothing new. It just goes over the same old ground.*|*I'm on safe ground when I talk about food, as I'm an experienced cook.*|*Don't mention politics; it's forbidden ground.*|*The mothers found themselves on common ground as they compared their children's illnesses* (=they had the same experiences **in** COMMON[2] (2)) **7 break fresh/new ground** to (start to) do something new and different, esp. to make a discovery **8 cover (the) ground a** to travel a (certain) distance **b** to study or talk about everything connected with a subject: *I'll try to cover all the ground in a short speech of half an hour* **9 cut the ground from under someone's feet** to destroy someone's chances of success by taking his ideas, or acting before him: *They cut the ground from under my feet by printing a story on the same subject the week before mine* **10 fall to the ground** (of a plan) to fail **11 gain ground a** (of an army) to advance and force the enemy back **b** to improve or have more success **12 get off the ground** to make a successful start **13 give ground a** (of an army) to be forced back **b** to yield a point in an argument, etc. **14 go to ground** (esp. of a fox or criminal) to go into hiding to escape **15 have/keep both feet/one's feet on the ground** to remain very practical and steady in one's thinking **16 hold one's ground a** to refuse to be forced back **b** to refuse to yield in argument **17 lose ground a** (esp. of an army) to be driven back **b** to be defeated on a point in argument, or become worse (in health) **18 shift one's ground** to change one's arguments **19 stand one's ground a** to refuse to be driven back **b** not to yield to attack in an argument, claim, etc. **20 suit someone down to the ground** *BrE infml* to be just what one wants or likes: *That suits him down to the ground. He's always wanted to go abroad alone* —see also GROUNDS

ground[2] *v* **1** [IØ;T1] **a**(of a boat) to strike against the bottom or the ground: *The ship grounded on a hidden sandbank* **b** to cause (a boat) to do this, by accident or on purpose: *He grounded his ship in 2 metres of water* **2** [T1] to cause (a pilot or plane) to come to or stay on the ground, instead of flying: *All aircraft have been grounded because of thick mist* **3** [X9, esp. *on, in*] to base: *I ground my argument on my own experiences* **4** [T1] *AmE* to EARTH[2] (electrical apparatus)

ground[3] *past t. and p. of* GRIND

ground bait /ˈ· ·/ *n* [U] food which is dropped to the bottom of a river, lake, etc., to attract fish to the place where one is fishing

ground bass /ˌgraʊnd ˈbeɪs/ *n* [S] a tune repeated in the BASS[3] (2) (lower than the other parts) while the notes or tunes for the higher parts change

ground cloth /ˈ· ·/ *n AmE* GROUND SHEET

ground crew /ˈ· ·/ *BrE* also **ground staff**— *n* [(*the*) GC] the team of men at an airport who do not fly aircraft but take care of them between flights

ground floor /ˌ· ˈ·◂/ *n* **1** the part of a building, often the lowest, at ground level: *I live on the ground floor* —compare FIRST FLOOR (2) **2 get/be in on the ground floor** *not fml* **a** to start a job at its lowest level **b** to be part of an activity from the time it starts

ground glass /ˌ· ˈ·◂/ *n* [U] **1** glass which has had the surface partly rubbed away so that it can spread the light which passes through it **2** glass in powder form —see also GRIND[1] (1)

ground in *v prep* [D1 *usu. pass.*] to teach (someone) the main points or rules of (something) as a base for further study: *She was well grounded by her mother in the manners used at the royal court*

ground·ing /ˈgraʊndɪŋ/ *n* [S;(U)] a complete training in the main points which will enable thorough study or work on some subject: *a good grounding in English grammar*

ground·less /ˈgraʊndləs/ *adj* (of feelings, ideas, etc.) without base or good reason —**~ly** *adv* —**~ness** *n* [U]

ground·nut /ˈgraʊndnʌt/ also **peanut**, *infml* **monkey nut**— *n esp. BrE* a kind of nut which grows in a shell under the ground, and is eaten —see picture at NUT[1]

ground plan /ˈ· ·/ *n* **1** a drawn plan of a building at ground level **2** a general plan of arrangements for a particular piece of work

ground rent /ˈ· ·/ *n* [U;C] rent paid to the owner of land which is let for building on during a certain time (in England usu. 99 years)

ground rule /ˈ· ·/ *n* [*often pl.*] *esp. AmE* **1** a sports rule which is changed slightly according to the playing field being used **2** a rule used as a base for deciding how to deal with something

grounds /graʊndz/ *n* [P] **1** small bits of solid matter which sink to the bottom of a liquid, esp. coffee: *I've just got a mouthful of coffee grounds from the bottom of this cup!* **2** a reason (esp. in the phr. **on (the) grounds**): *We have good grounds for thinking that he stole the money.|He left on (the) grounds of ill-health|on the grounds that he was ill* **3** land surrounding a large building, such as a country house or hospital, usu. made into gardens and enclosed by a wall or fence **4** a large area used for a particular purpose: *fishing grounds|hunting grounds*

ground·sel /ˈgraʊndsəl/ *n* [U] a type of wild plant with yellow flowers, which may be fed to cage birds

ground·sheet /ˈgraʊndʃiːt/ *AmE* also **ground cloth**— *n* a sheet of material through which water cannot pass (WATERPROOF), used by campers who sleep on the ground —see picture at CAMP[2]

grounds·man /ˈgraʊndzmən/ *n* **-men** /mən/ *esp. BrE* a man employed to take care of a sports field or large gardens

ground staff /ˈ· ·/ *n* [(*the*) GC] *BrE* **1** a team of men employed at a sports ground to look after the grass, the sports apparatus, etc., and sometimes to play in matches of lesser importance **2** GROUND CREW

ground swell /ˈ· ·/ *n* **1** [U;C *usu. sing.*] the strong movement of the sea which continues after a storm or troubling of the waves **2** [C *usu. sing.*] a rapid and freely-developing growth (as of political opinion)

ground·work /ˈgraʊndwɜːk‖-ɜrk/ *n* [(*the*) U] the work which forms the base for some kind of study or skill

group[1] /gruːp/ *n* **1** [C] a number of people or things placed together: *a photograph of a family group|a group of tall trees* **2** [GC] a number of people of the same interests, beliefs, age, race, etc.: *In most schools children are taught according to age groups* **3** [C] a set of things or organizations connected in a particular way: *a language group|blood group A* **4** [GC] a usu. small number of players of popular music, sometimes with a singer: *The Beatles were perhaps the most well known group of the 1960s*

group[2] *v* [T1;IØ] to form into one or more groups: *We can group animals into several types*

group cap·tain /ˌ· ˈ··◂/ *n* [C;A;N] an officer of middle rank in the Royal Air Force, equal to a captain in the Navy or COLONEL in the Army

group·ie /ˈgruːpi/ *n sl* **1** a person, esp. a young girl, who follows POP[4] (1) group players to the concerts they give, in admiration and so as to meet and know them **2** *BrE* GROUP CAPTAIN

group·ing /ˈgruːpɪŋ/ *n* [*usu. sing.*] a (way of) arrangement into a group: *The new grouping of classes means that there are larger numbers in each class*

group prac·tice /ˌ· ˈ··/ *n* [U;C] a working partnership among a number of doctors

group ther·a·py /ˌ· ˈ···/ *n* [U] a way of treating disorders of the mind by bringing sufferers together to talk about their difficulties, usu. with a doctor or specially trained leader

grouse[1] /graʊs/ *n* **grouse** [Wn3] **1** [C] any of several kinds of smallish fat birds, with feathered feet, which are shot for food and sport **2** [U] the flesh from this, used as meat

grouse[2] *v* [IØ (*about*)] *infml* to complain; GRUMBLE[1] (1)—compare GROUCH

grouse[3] *n* [*usu. sing.*] *infml* a complaint; GRUMBLE[2] (1)

grove /grəʊv/ *n* **1** (esp. of fruit trees) a group of trees, planted or natural, sometimes in a garden **2** a group of trees forming a centre of worship, esp. in former times

grov·el /ˈgrɒvəl‖ˈgrɑ-, ˈgrʌ-/ *v* **-ll-** (*AmE* **-l-**) [L9; (IØ)] *derog* **1** to lie or move flat on the ground, esp. in fear of or obedience to someone powerful: *The dog grovelled at his feet when he shouted at it.|He said he would never grovel before a conqueror* **2** [(*to*)] to be shamefully humble and eager to please: *grovelling in self-pity* —**~ler** *n*

grow /grəʊ/ *v* **grew** /gruː/, **grown** /grəʊn/ **1** [Wv4; IØ] (of (parts of) living things) to increase in size by natural development: *Grass grows after rain.|My fingernails aren't growing.|He's grown 6 inches (taller).|A lamb grows into a sheep.|She won't have her hair short, she's letting it grow.|a growing boy* **2** [IØ] (of plants) to exist and be able to develop, esp. after planting: *Cotton grows wild here.|Oranges grow in Spain* **3** [T1;X7] to cause to or allow to grow (esp. plants and crops): *He grows vegetables.|Plants grow roots.|Snakes can grow a new skin.|Cattle often grow horns.|He's grown a beard.|She's grown her hair long* **4** [Wv4;IØ] to increase in numbers, amount, etc.: *The village is growing into a town.|His influence over the children is growing as they get older* **5** [L7;I3] to become (gradually): *She's growing fat.|The noise grew louder.|The sound of the music grew less as the band marched away.|In time you will grow to like him* (= as you learn to know him you will like him).*|In time you will grow (to be) like him* (= you will become like him) —see also GROW AWAY FROM, GROW INTO, GROW ON, GROW OUT OF, GROW UP

grow a·way from *v adv prep* [T1 *no pass.*] to have a less close relationship with (esp. one's parents, husband, or wife): *I feel I don't know her any more. She's grown right away from the family*

grow·er /ˈgrəʊəʳ/ *n* [C9] **1** a person who grows plants, fruit, etc., for sale **2** a plant which grows in a certain way: *This rose is a slow grower*

growing pains /ˈ·· ·/ *n* [P] **1** aches and pains in the limbs of children who are growing up, commonly believed to be the result of growing too fast **2** difficulties at the beginning of an activity, which will not last

grow in·to *v prep* **1** [L1] to become: *He's grown into a fine young man* **2** [T1 *no pass.*] to become big enough for (clothes): *The coat is too long, but she'll grow into it* **3** [T1 *pass. rare*] to become accustomed to (work and activities): *You need time to grow into the job*

growl[1] /graʊl/ *v* **1** [Wa4;IØ] (usu. of animals) to make a deep rough sound in the throat to show anger or give warning **2** [Wv4;IØ] (of things) to make a sound like this: *growling thunder* **3** [T1 (OUT)] to express in a voice which seems like this sound: *When he came late, he growled (out) an excuse* —**growler** *n*

growl[2] *n* a deep rough sound: *the growl of the distant thunder|He answered with a growl of anger*

grown /grəʊn/ *adj* [Wa5] **1** [A] (of a person) of full size or development; ADULT: *A grown man like you shouldn't act like that* **2** [B9] (*in comb.*) (of living things) developed in a certain way: *well-grown|fully-grown*

grown-up[1] /ˌ· ˈ·◂/ *adj* fully developed, no longer (that of) a child: *She has a grown-up daughter who lives abroad*

grown-up[2] /ˈ· ·/ *n infml* a fully grown and developed person: *Go to bed now and let the grown-ups have a little time to themselves* —compare ADULT

grow on *v prep* [T1 *no pass.*] to become gradually more pleasing or more of a habit to (someone): *Modern music is difficult to listen to, but it starts to grow on you*

grow out of *v adv prep* **1** [T1] to become too big for (clothes, shoes, etc.): *My daughter has grown out of all her old clothes* **2** [T1, 4] to lose (a childish or youthful weakness) as one becomes older: *to grow out of a bad habit* **3** [T1, 4 *no pass.*] to develop as a result of: *Her sympathy grew out of understanding*

growth /grəʊθ/ *n* **1** [U] the act or rate of growing and developing: *Trees take many years to reach their full growth* **2** [U;S] increase in numbers or amount: *the growth of large companies|There has been a sudden growth in membership of the club* **3** [U] cultivation; the fact of being grown (as a crop): *oranges of Spanish growth* **4** [C *usu. sing.*] something which has grown: *Nails are thin horny growths at the ends of the fingers* **5** [C] a lump produced by an unnatural and unhealthy increase in the number of cells in a part of the body —compare TUMOUR **6 growth stocks** shares in a company which are likely to increase a lot in value

grow up *v adv* [IØ] **1** (of people) to develop from child to man or woman **2** to arise; develop into something lasting: *The custom grew up of dividing the father's land between the sons* **3 Grow up!** Stop behaving childishly

groyne, groin /grɔɪn/ *n* a low wall built out from the shore into the sea, to prevent the sea from washing away (parts of) the shore

grub[1] /grʌb/ *v* **-bb-** **1** [L9] to turn over the soil; dig: *grubbing for worms|The dog was grubbing (about) under the bush, looking for a bone* **2** [X9, esp. UP, OUT] to move or change by digging: *The old apple trees must be grubbed up and young ones planted*

grub[2] *n* **1** [C] an insect in the wormlike form it has when just out of the egg **2** [U] *infml* food

grub·by /ˈgrʌbi/ *adj* [Wa1] dirty

Grub Street /ˈ· ·/ *n* [R] the group or life-style of those who must write whatever will earn money (esp. in the phr. **a Grub-Street hack**)

grudge[1] /grʌdʒ/ also **begrudge**— *v* [D1;T4] to give or allow (something) unwillingly: *He grudged paying so much for such bad food*

grudge[2] *n* [(*against*)] **1** a cause for dislike, esp. of another person, real or imagined: *I always feel she has a grudge against me, although I don't know what wrong I've done her* **2 bear a grudge/grudges** to have feelings of anger about someone's past actions **3 owe someone a grudge** to feel that, because of a certain action, it is right to be angry with someone **4 pay off an old grudge** to punish someone for an unkind act which made one dislike him long ago —see also SCORE[1] (8)

grudg·ing /ˈgrʌdʒɪŋ/ *adj* ungenerous; unwilling (to give): *She was very grudging in her thanks* —**~ly** *adv*

gru·el /ˈgruːəl/ *n* [U] a thin liquid food, esp. for the sick, made by boiling crushed OATS (=a type of grain) in milk or water

gru·el·ling, *AmE* **grueling** /ˈgruːəlɪŋ/ *adj* very hard and tiring —**~ly** *adv*

grue·some /ˈgruːsəm/ *adj* (esp. of something connected with death or decay) terrible to the senses; shocking and sickening —~**ly** *adv* —~**ness** *n* [U]

gruff /grʌf/ *adj* [Wa1] **1** (of the human voice) deep and rough, sometimes because bad-tempered **2** (of behaviour) rough; unfriendly or impatient, esp. in one's manner of speaking: *He has a gruff manner, but a heart of gold* (=a very generous nature) —~**ly** *adv* —~**ness** *n* [U]

grum·ble¹ /ˈgrʌmbəl/ *v* **1** [Wv4;IØ (*at, over, about*)] to express discontent; complain, not loudly, but angrily; show dissatisfaction: *He has everything he needs: he has nothing to grumble about* **2** [Wv4;IØ] (of thunder and certain noises) RUMBLE **3** [T1 (OUT)] to say in a bad-tempered way: *He grumbled (out) his reasons for disliking the arrangement* —**-bler** *n*

grumble² *n* **1** [C] a complaint or expression of dissatisfaction **2** [(*the*) S] RUMBLE

grum·bling /ˈgrʌmblɪŋ/ *adj* [Wa5] *not fml* (of the human APPENDIX) unwell; causing pain or discomfort

grump·y /ˈgrʌmpi/ *adj* [Wa1] bad-tempered, esp. because of low spirits: *She's very grumpy when her tooth aches* —**grumpily** *adv* —**grumpiness** *n* [U]

Grun·dy·is·m /ˈgrʌndi-ɪzəm/ *n* [U] *esp. BrE* liking for very modest behaviour between men and women, according to social rules which allow little freedom

grunt¹ /grʌnt/ *v* **1** [Wa4;IØ] (of certain animals) to make short deep rough sounds in the throat, as if the nose were closed: *a grunting pig* **2** [IØ (*with*)] (of human beings) to make such sounds, esp. when dissatisfied or in pain **3** [T1 (OUT)] to express in a voice which seems like this sound: *"Too tired," he grunted, then fell asleep again*

grunt² *n* a short deep rough sound like that of a pig

Gru·yère /gruːˈjeəʳ (*Fr* gryjɜr)/ *n* [U] a kind of hard cheese with holes in it, from Switzerland

gryph·on /ˈgrɪfən/ *n* GRIFFIN

G-string /ˈdʒiː ˌstrɪŋ/ *n* a narrow piece of cloth worn on the lower part of the body by STRIPTEASE dancers

gua·no /ˈgwɑːnəʊ/ *n* [U] the waste droppings of seabirds, which are used to enrich soil where plants are grown

guar·an·tee¹ /ˌgærənˈtiː/ *n* **1** [C (*of*),C3,C5] a formal written declaration of good quality by the maker of an article, which is also an agreement to repair or replace it if it is found imperfect within a period of time **2** [C (*of*),C3,C5] an agreement to be responsible for the fulfilment of someone else's promise, esp. for paying a debt **3** [C (*of*),C3,C5] something of value given to someone to keep until the owner has fulfilled a promise, esp. to pay: *He gave the bank the papers which proved his ownership of the land, as a guarantee that he would repay the money provided by the bank* —compare GAGE¹ (1) **4** [C] a person who gives or receives a GUARANTEE¹ (1,2,3) **5** [C (*of*),C5] *infml* something that happens which makes something else certain, gives one a feeling of trust or faith, etc.

guarantee² *v* **1** [T1;X7] to give a promise of quality, payment, or fulfilment (a GUARANTEE¹ (1,2,3)) about (something or someone): *They guarantee the watch for 3 years.|They have guaranteed delivery* **2** [T1,3,5;D1] to promise (that something will certainly be so): *I guarantee that you'll enjoy yourself*

guar·an·tor /ˌgærənˈtɔːʳ/ *n tech or law* a person who agrees to be responsible for another person's fulfilling a promise, esp. paying a debt

guar·an·ty /ˈgærənti/ *n tech or law* a GUARANTEE (1,2,3), esp. of payment

guard¹ /gɑːd‖gɑrd/ *n* **1** [U] a state of watchful readiness to protect or defend (esp. in the phr. **on guard**): *There are soldiers on guard at the gate, to prevent anyone getting in or out.|They are keeping guard over the house* **2** [U] a position for defence, esp. in a fight: *He got in under his opponent's guard* (= struck him although he was defending himself) **3** [C] a person, esp. a soldier, policeman, or prison officer, who guards someone or something: *The camp guards are changed every night* **4** [GC *usu. sing.*] a group of people, esp. soldiers, whose duty it is to guard someone or something: *The prisoner was brought in under armed guard* **5** [C *usu. pl.*] (*usu. cap.*) a member of a group of special soldiers, originally those who guarded the king or queen, esp. in Britain: *a Horse Guard|a Guards officer* —see also GRENADIER (2) **6** [C] (*AmE* **conductor**)— *BrE* a railway official in charge of a train **7** [C] (*often in comb.*) an apparatus which covers and protects: *A fireguard prevents children getting near the fire.|A mudguard over the wheel of a bicycle* **8** [GC *usu. sing.*] guard of HONOUR¹ (9) **9 His guard was up/down a** He was/was not ready to defend himself **b** He was/was not in control of his feelings and speech **10 mount/stand guard** to take up/to be in position to watch over something **11 on/off one's guard** ready/not ready to deal with a possible sudden trick or attack: *Be on your guard against thieves*

guard² *v* [T1] **1** [(*against, from*)] to defend; keep safe, esp. by watching for danger: *The dog guarded the house (against strangers).|The wall guards the place from thieves* **2** to watch (a prisoner) in order to prevent escape: (fig.) *Guard the secret with your life: tell it to no one!* **3** to control: *You must guard your tongue carefully* (=be careful what you say)

guard a·gainst *v prep* [T1,4] to (try to) prevent by special care: *You must wash your hands when preparing food, to guard against spreading infection*

guard·ed /ˈgɑːdɪ̵d‖ˈgɑr-/ *adj* (of speech) careful; not saying too much —~**ly** *adv*

guard·house /ˈgɑːdhaʊs‖ˈgɑr-/ *n* **-houses** /ˌhaʊzɪ̵z/ [*usu. sing.*] a building for soldiers, esp. at the entrance to a camp, sometimes used for imprisonment of those who must be punished

guard·i·an /ˈgɑːdɪən‖ˈgɑr-/ *n* **1** a person or place that guards or protects: *The Bank of England is the guardian of our wealth* **2** *law* a person who has the responsibility of looking after a child not his own, esp. after the parents' death —see also WARD (3)

guardian an·gel /ˌ··· ˈ··/ *n* **1** a good spirit which protects a person or place **2** a good person who helps one a lot

guard·i·an·ship /ˈgɑːdɪənʃɪp‖ˈgɑr-/ *n* [U;S] the position of, responsibility of, or period of time as a GUARDIAN in law

guard·rail /ˈgɑrd-reɪl‖ˈgɑrd-/ *n* **1** a bar of wood or metal placed to protect people, esp. from falling from a bridge or stairs **2** also **check rail**— an additional railway line, fitted on curves to prevent the train running off the lines

guard·room /ˈgɑːd-rʊm, -ruːm‖ˈgɑrd-/ *n* a (room of a) GUARDHOUSE

guards·man /ˈgɑːdzmən‖ˈgɑr-/ *n* **-men** /mən/ (esp. in Britain) a soldier or officer in the Guards (GUARD¹ (5))

guard's van /ˈ· ·/ (*AmE* **caboose**)— *n BrE* the part of a train, usu. at the back, where the man in charge (GUARD¹ (6)) travels

gua·va /ˈgwɑːvə/ *n* **1** a type of small tropical tree bearing a round fruit with pink or white flesh and seeds in the centre **2** the fruit itself, often used to make jelly

gu·ber·na·to·ri·al /ˌguːbənəˈtɔːrɪəl‖-bərnəˈtor-/ *adj* [Wa5;A] *fml or tech* of or concerning a governor

gudg·eon /ˈgʌdʒən/ *n* **1** [Wn1] a type of small fish

which fishermen put onto their hooks (as BAIT[2] (1)) to catch other fish **2** a person who is easily cheated

guel·der rose /'geldə rəʊz‖-dər-/ *n* [*usu. sing.*] **1** a garden bush with large round masses of white flowers **2** a type of this called the **snowball tree**

guer·ril·la, guerilla /gə'rɪlə/ *n* a member of an unofficial fighting group which attacks the enemy in small groups unexpectedly

guess[1] /ges/ *v* **1** [T1,5a,6a,b;X *to be* 1,7;I∅ (*at*)] to form (a judgment) or risk giving (an opinion) without knowing or considering all the facts: *Can you guess (at) the price?|Guess how much/what it cost.|I guess her age as 35* **2** [T1] to get to know by guessing: *She guessed my thoughts.|I suppose he's late again —You've guessed it!* **3** [T5a,b] *AmE infml* to suppose; consider likely: *I guess you don't have time to go out now you have young children* **4 keep someone guessing** to keep someone uninformed and uncertain what will happen next

guess[2] *n* **1** an attempt to guess: *Have a guess at the answer.|a wild guess* (=not reasonable) **2** an opinion formed by guessing: *My guess is that he didn't come because his wife wouldn't let him* **3 at a guess** by guessing, without being certain or exact **4 it's anybody's guess** There's no way of knowing for certain (an answer/what will happen) **5 Your guess is as good as mine** I can't answer your question because I know just as little as you do

guess·work /'geswɜːk‖-ɜrk/ *n* [U] the act of guessing, or the judgment which results

guest[1] /gest/ *n* **1** [C] a person who is in someone's home by invitation, for a short time (as for a meal), or to stay (one or more nights) **2** [C] a person who is invited out and paid for at a theatre, restaurant, etc. (in the phr. **someone's guest**): *They are coming to the concert as my guests* **3** [C] a person who is lodging in a hotel, or as a **paying guest** in someone's home **4** [A] a person who is invited to perform, in a show or at a ceremony: *a guest artist* (=actor or singer)|*a guest singer* **5 be my guest!** *not fml* I would not mind if you did so; please feel free to do so: *"May I borrow your pen?" "Be my guest!"* —see CUSTOMER (USAGE)

guest[2] *v* [L9 esp. *on*;(I∅)] *esp. AmE* to take part as a GUEST[1] (4) performer: *guesting on the Bob Hope Show*

guest·house /'gesthaʊs/ *n* **-houses** /haʊzɪ̇z/ a private house where visitors may stay and have meals for payment

guest night /'· ·/ *n* a party (held in the evening) or social occasion when members of a club, college, etc., may bring in non-members

guest·room /'gest-rʊm, -ruːm/ *n* a bedroom in a private house which is kept for visitors to stay in

guf·faw[1] /gə'fɔː/ *v* [I∅] to laugh loudly, and perhaps rudely

guffaw[2] *n* a laugh which is loud and perhaps rude

guid·ance /'gaɪdəns/ *n* [U] help; advice: *I need some guidance with my studies*

guide[1] /gaɪd/ *n* **1** something or somebody that shows the way, esp. someone whose job is to show a place to tourists: *You need a guide to show you the city* **2** something which influences or controls a person's actions or behaviour: *It may not be a good thing to take your friend's experience as a guide* **3** [(*to*)] also **guide book** /'· ·/— a book which gives a description of a place, for the use of visitors **4** [(*to*)] a book which teaches the way to do something or gives the facts about something; instruction book **5** GIRL GUIDE **6** a part of a machine (often a bar) which holds the moving parts in the right places

guide[2] *v* [T1] **1** to show (someone) the way by leading: *He guided the man through the streets to the railway station|*(fig.) *The light guided them back to harbour* **2** to control (the movements of): (fig.) *The government will guide the country through the difficulties ahead* **3** [*usu. pass.*] to influence strongly: *Be guided by your feelings, and tell her the truth before it's too late* —see LEAD (USAGE)

guided mis·sile /ˌ·· '··/ *n* a MISSILE that is guided by electrical means to the thing it is aimed at, as from the ground at enemy aircraft, or from a ship at an enemy position

guide·lines /'gaɪdlaɪnz/ *n* [P] the main points about something which is to be dealt with (esp. something official)

guild /gɪld/ *n* **1** an association for businessmen or skilled workers who joined together in former times to help one another and to make rules for training new members **2** an association of people with like interests: *the Townswomen's Guild*

guil·der /'gɪldə^r/ *n* **1** GULDEN **2** (in former times) a gold or silver coin worth a GULDEN

guild·hall /ˌgɪld'hɔːl, 'gɪldhɔːl‖'gɪldhɔl/ *n* **1** [C *usu. sing.*] a building in which members of a GUILD used to meet, sometimes now the centre of local government (**town hall**) **2** [*the*+R] (*usu. cap.*) the building in which the body that governs the City of London meets, esp. for social occasions

guild so·cial·is·m /ˌ· '····/ *n* [U] (esp. in Britain before 1939) a suggested system by which industry would be owned by the state but controlled by representatives of the trade unions

guile /gaɪl/ *n* [U] deceit, esp. of a clever, indirect kind: *Don't trust her: she's full of guile* —compare CUNNING[2] —**~ful** *adj* —**~fully** *adv* —**~fulness** *n* [U]

guile·less /'gaɪl-ləs/ *adj* (appearing to be) lacking in any deceit: *She gave him a guileless look, but he knew he couldn't really trust her* —**~ly** *adv* —**~ness** *n* [U]

guil·le·mot /'gɪləmɒt‖-mɑt/ *n* any of several kinds of narrow-beaked seabird that live in northern parts of the world

guil·lo·tine[1] /'gɪlətiːn/ *n* **1** [C; *the*+R] a machine used in France for cutting off the heads of those thought guilty of great crimes, which works by means of a heavy blade sliding down between 2 posts **2** [C] a cutting instrument used by doctors in operations **3** [C] a machine used for cutting paper **4** [C; *the*+R] *BrE* the act of fixing a time to vote on a law in Parliament, so that argument about it will not go on too long

guillotine[2] *v* [T1] **1** to use a GUILLOTINE[1] (1) as punishment on: *Many members of noble families were guillotined in France in the late 18th Century* **2** *BrE* to limit (argument) in Parliament

guilt /gɪlt/ *n* [U] **1** the fact of having broken a law: *There can be no doubt about the guilt of a man who is found with stolen money in his pockets* **2** responsibility for something wrong; blame: *The children behave badly, but the guilt lies with the parents, who don't care about their behaviour* **3** the knowledge or belief that one has done wrong: *His face showed guilt, though he said he had done nothing wrong* **4** moral wickedness —**~less** *adj* —**~lessly** *adv* —**~lessness** *n* [U]

guilt·y /'gɪlti/ *adj* [Wa1] **1** [B (*of*)] having broken a law or disobeyed a moral or social rule: *guilty of murder|He was found* (=declared) *guilty* **2** [A] having or showing a feeling of guilt: *I have a guilty conscience about forgetting to post your letter* **3 not guilty a** the formal reply of a prisoner who says he is not guilty of the crime about which a judge is asking him **b** the phrase used in court for someone who has not been proved guilty of a crime, and is to be freed —**guiltily** *adv* —**guiltiness** *n* [U]

guin·ea /'gɪni/ *n* **1** a former British gold coin,

worth one pound one shilling **2** the sum of one pound one shilling (now £1·05), which was used until recently in fixing professional charges, prices of certain valuable goods (like paintings), and prizes in some horse races

guinea fowl /ˈ·· ·/ *n* **guinea fowl** [Wn2] a type of large grey bird with white spots which may be kept for its eggs and for food

guinea hen /ˈ·· ·/ *n* **1** a female GUINEA FOWL **2** GUINEA FOWL

guinea pig /ˈ·· ·/ *n* **1** also **cavy**— a small roundish furry animal with small ears, rather like a rat without a tail, which is often kept by children as a pet, and is sometimes used in scientific tests **2** a person who is the subject of some kind of test: *I must try my cooking out on someone. Will you be my guinea pig?*

gui·pure /gɪˈpjʊəʳ/ *n* [U] a sort of heavy LACE[1] (2)

guise /gaɪz/ *n* [*usu. sing.*] *fml* **1** an outer appearance (only in the phr. **in a (certain) guise**): *There is nothing new here; just the same old ideas in a different/new guise* **2** a style of dress (only in the phr. **in the guise of**): *A man appeared at the castle gate in the guise of a woodcutter* **3 under the guise of** pretending to be or have

gui·tar /gɪˈtɑːʳ/ *n* **1** a musical instrument with 6 or more strings, a long neck, and a wooden body like a VIOLIN but larger, played by striking or PLUCKing[1] (4) the strings with the fingers or a small piece of hard material (a PLECTRUM) **2** any of a number of other musical instruments like this, such as one (an **electric guitar**) with a solid body and a sound that is increased electrically —see pictures at STRINGED INSTRUMENT

gulch /gʌltʃ/ *n esp. AmE* (esp. in the western US) a narrow, stony valley with steep sides formed by a rushing stream

gul·den /ˈgʊldən‖ˈguːl-/ also **guilder**— *n* **guldens** *or* **gulden 1** the standard coin of the Netherlands **2** [Wn3] the value of this coin

gulf /gʌlf/ *n* **1** a large deep stretch of sea partly enclosed by land: *the Persian Gulf* **2** a deep hollow place in the earth's surface: *The ground trembled, and suddenly a great gulf opened before us* **3** a great area of division or difference, esp. between opinions

Gulf Stream /ˈ· ·/ *n* [*the*+R] a current of warm water which flows north eastward in the Atlantic Ocean from the Gulf of Mexico towards Europe

gull[1] /gʌl/ also (*not fml*) **seagull**— *n* any of several kinds of largish flying seabirds —see picture at WATER

gull[2] *v* [T1 (*into, of*)] to trick, cheat, or deceive: *Their claims have gulled all the money out of our pockets/gulled us into buying what we don't need/gulled us out of all our money*

gull[3] *n* a fool who is easily tricked

gul·let /ˈgʌlɨ̣t/ *n infml* the (inner) throat; foodpipe from mouth to stomach

gul·li·ble /ˈgʌləbəl/ *adj* easily tricked, esp. into a false belief —**-bility** /ˌgʌləˈbɪlɨ̣ti/ *n* [U] —**-bly** /ˈgʌlɨ̣bli/ *adv*

gul·ly, -ley /ˈgʌli/ *n* **1** a small narrow valley cut esp. into a hillside by heavy rain —see VALLEY (USAGE) and picture at MOUNTAIN **2** a deep ditch or other small waterway **3** (in cricket) a close fielding position in front of and at right angles to the BATSMAN —see picture at CRICKET[2]

gulp[1] /gʌlp/ *v* **1** [T1 (DOWN)] to swallow hastily: *Don't gulp your food* **2** [I∅] to make a sudden swallowing movement as if surprised or nervous

gulp[2] *n* **1** the action of GULPing[1]: *He ate his food in 2 gulps* **2** a large mouthful

gulp back *v adv* [T1] to prevent the expression of feeling by or as if by swallowing: *She gulped back her tears*

gum[1] /gʌm/ *n* [*usu. pl.*] either of the 2 areas of firm pink flesh in which the teeth are fixed, at the top and bottom of the mouth —see picture at TOOTH

gum[2] *n* **1** [U] any of several kinds of sticky substance obtained from the stems of some trees and bushes **2** [U] a sticky substance used for sticking things together **3** [C] also **gum tree** /ˈ· ·/— *esp. AustrE* the EUCALYPTUS tree, which produces GUM (1) **4** [U] a sticky substance which sometimes gathers in the corners of the eyes **5** [C] a hard transparent jelly-like sweet **6** [U] CHEWING GUM **7 up a gum tree** *BrE infml* in a difficult position with no means of escape

gum[3] *v* **-mm-** [X9] to stick (something somewhere) with GUM[2] (2)

gum[4] *n* **by gum** *dial or humor* by God

gum·bo /ˈgʌmbəʊ/ *n* **-bos 1** [C] OKRA **2** [U] a type of American soup with meat, vegetables, and OKRA to thicken it

gum·boil /ˈgʌmbɔɪl/ *n infml* a painful swelling on the GUM[1], usu. near a tooth which is decayed; ABSCESS

gum·boot /ˈgʌmbuːt/ *n* WELLINGTON

gum·drop /ˈgʌmdrɒp‖-drɑp/ *n esp. AmE* GUM[2] (5)

gum·my /ˈgʌmi/ *adj* [Wa1] sticky; covered with sticky GUM[2] (2) —**gumminess** *n* [U]

gump·tion /ˈgʌmpʃən/ *n* [U] *infml* common sense and ability to act bravely and successfully

gum up *v adv* [T1a] *infml* to make unworkable: *Our future plans are all gummed up by the illness of several members of the club*

gun /gʌn/ *n* **1** a weapon from which bullets or larger metal objects (SHELLs[1] (4)) are fired through a metal tube (BARREL) **2** [*usu. pl.*] *BrE* (in hunting parties) a person carrying a gun **3** a tool which forces out and spreads a substance by pressure: *a* GREASE *gun* **4 blow great guns** *infml* (of the wind) to blow very fiercely **5 bring up one's big guns** to introduce the chief reasons or people in support of one's case **6 jump the gun a** to start running in a race before the signal to start has been given **b** to start before getting permission **7 spike someone's guns** *infml* to ruin someone's plans **8 stick to one's guns** to continue to fight or argue in spite of attacks, esp. on one's beliefs —see also SON OF A GUN, CANNON

gun·boat /ˈgʌnbəʊt/ *n* a small but heavily armed naval warship for use in waters near the coast

gunboat di·plo·ma·cy /ˌ·· ·ˈ···/ *n* [U] the use of a threat or show of armed force by a country to support a claim, demand, complaint, etc., against another

gun car·riage /ˈ· ˌ··/ *n* a frame with wheels on which a heavy gun is moved from place to place

gun cot·ton /ˈ· ˌ··/ *n* [U] a type of powerful explosive

gun·dog /ˈgʌndɒg‖-dɔg/ *AmE* also **bird dog**— *n* a type of dog trained to help in the shooting of birds for sport, esp. by finding and bringing back the dead bird

gun down *v adv* [T1] to shoot, causing to fall to the ground dead or wounded

gun·fire /ˈgʌnfaɪəʳ/ *n* [U] the sound or act of firing one or more guns

gun for *v prep* **gunning for** searching for in order to attack: *Ever since I proved he'd made a mistake in the accounts he's been gunning for me, trying to get me dismissed*

gunge /gʌndʒ/ *AmE sl* **gunk** /gʌŋk/— *n* [U] *BrE sl* any unpleasant, dirty, and/or sticky substance

gun·man /ˈgʌnmən/ *n* **-men** /mən/ a criminal armed with a gun

gun·met·al /ˈgʌnˌmetl/ *n* [U] **1** a metal which is a

mixture of copper, tin, lead, and ZINC from which chains, belt fasteners, etc., are made **2** also **gunmetal grey** /ˌ··· ˈ·/— a colour which is a dark blue grey

gun·ner /ˈgʌnəʳ/ *n* [C;A] **1** a soldier in a part (REGIMENT) of the British Army which uses heavy guns (ARTILLERY) **2** a WARRANT OFFICER in the British Navy who is in charge of a group of heavy guns **3** a member of the CREW of a large bombing aircraft who protects the aircraft from attacks by enemy fighter aircraft with GUNFIRE

gun·ner·y /ˈgʌnəri/ *n* [U] the science and practice of shooting effectively with heavy guns

gun·ny·sack /ˈgʌnisæk/ *n* a large strong bag made of a loosely-woven coarse string-like material (like BURLAP) and used esp. for holding potatoes, coal, etc.

gun·point /ˈgʌnpɔɪnt/ *n* **at gunpoint** under a threat of death by shooting: *He forced them to hand over the money at gunpoint*

gun·pow·der /ˈgʌnˌpaʊdəʳ/ *n* [U] an explosive material made of various substances, in the form of a powder

gun·run·ner /ˈgʌnˌrʌnəʳ/ *n* a person who unlawfully and secretly brings guns into a country, esp. for the use of those who wish to fight against their own government —**-running** *n* [U]

gun·shot /ˈgʌnʃɒt‖-ʃɑt/ *n* **1** [U] the distance reached by a shot from a gun: *We were careful not to come within gunshot of the enemy* **2** [C] the act or sound of firing a gun **3** [C] a bullet fired from a gun

gun·shy /ˈgʌnʃaɪ/ *adj* (esp. of a GUNDOG) made afraid by the noise of a gun being fired

gun·smith /ˈgʌnˌsmɪθ/ *n* a person who makes and repairs small guns

gun·wale, gunnel /ˈgʌnl/ *n* [*usu. sing.*] *tech* the upper edge of the side of a small ship or a boat —see picture at SAIL²

gup·py /ˈgʌpi/ *n* a type of small attractive fish which bears its young alive (not as eggs), and which may be kept as a pet

gur·gle¹ /ˈgɜːgəl‖ˈgɜr-/ *v* **1** [IØ (*with*)] (esp. of babies) to make a sound like water flowing unevenly, as out of an opening or over stones, esp. in the throat **2** [L9] to flow with such a sound: *The water gurgled out of the bottle*

gurgle² *n* [(*the*) S] the sound of gurgling (GURGLE¹)

gu·ru /ˈgʊruː/ *n* **-s** **1** [C;A] an Indian priest or teacher of religious practices that produce peace of mind **2** [C] *infml, often humor* a person whose ideas are followed

gush¹ /gʌʃ/ *v* **1** [L9] (of liquids) to flow or pour out in large quantities, as from a hole or cut: *Oil gushed out from the broken pipe.|The stream gushes* FORTH *from the rock* **2** [IØ (*over*)] (often of women) to express admiration, pleasure, etc., in a great flow of words, foolishly or without true feeling

gush² *n* [S] **1** a (sudden) flow (of liquid): *There was a gush of blood as the wound re-opened* **2** a sudden rush (of words): *a gush of expressions of sorrow* **3** a sudden show (of strong feeling): *a gush of interest*/ENTHUSIASM

gush·er /ˈgʌʃəʳ/ *n* **1** a person who GUSHes (2) **2** an oilwell from which oil rushes out strongly without pumping being necessary

gush·ing /ˈgʌʃɪŋ/ *adj* **1** [A] that GUSHes (1): *a gushing spring* **2** [B] that GUSHes (2): *She's so gushing that her praises don't mean anything* —**~ly** *adv*

gush·y /ˈgʌʃi/ *adj* [Wa1] GUSHING (2) —**gushily** *adv* —**gushiness** *n* [U]

gus·set /ˈgʌsɪt/ *n* **1** a piece of cloth sewn into a larger garment, such as a 3-sided piece in the side of a skirt to make the waist wider, or an even-shaped piece forming a strengthening and widening part **2** a metal plate fixed over several beams meeting at an angle, as in a roof, to make the joint stronger

gust /gʌst/ *n* [(*of*)] **1** a sudden strong rush of air, or of rain, smoke, etc., carried by wind: *A gust of wind blew the door shut* **2** a short outflow of feeling, esp. anger: *In a gust of uncontrollable anger he broke the picture in pieces*

gus·ta·to·ry /ˈgʌstətəri‖-tori/ *adj* [Wa5] *tech or pomp* connected with tasting

gus·to /ˈgʌstəʊ/ *n* [U] eager enjoyment (in doing or having something): *He started painting with great gusto*

gust·y /ˈgʌsti/ *adj* [Wa1] (of weather, esp. over periods of time) with wind blowing in gusts

gut¹ /gʌt/ *n* **1** [U;C] the foodpipe which passes through the body: *Because of his illness, they must carry out an operation to remove part of the gut* **2** [U] a sort of strong thread made from this part of animals: *The fishing line is made of gut*

gut² *v* **-tt-** [T1] **1** to take out the inner organs (esp. GUTS) of (a dead animal) **2** [*often pass.*] to destroy completely the inside of (a building), esp. by fire

gut³ *adj* [Wa5;A] *infml* arising from or concerning one's strongest feelings and needs: *a gut feeling that the country needs the support of all its people if we are not to fail*

gut·less /ˈgʌtləs/ *adj infml* cowardly —**~ness** *n* [U]

guts /gʌts/ *n infml* **1** [P] the bowels or INTESTINEs: *He was wounded in the stomach and they had to push his guts back in* **2** [P;(U)] bravery; determination: *He has a lot of guts; he went on fighting even though he had been hurt* **3** [P;(U)] value; force: *There's no guts in his work; his reports show no sign of effort* **4** [P] the inner working parts of something, esp. of machinery: *the guts of a car*

guts·y /ˈgʌtsi/ *adj* [Wa1] *infml* brave and determined

gut·ta-per·cha /ˌgʌtə ˈpɜːtʃə‖-ɜr-/ *n* [U] a soft rubber-like material obtained from the juice (SAP) of certain Malayan trees and used for covering electric wires for protection, and also in DENTISTRY

gut·ter¹ /ˈgʌtəʳ/ *n* **1** [C] a small hollow or ditch beside a street or road, between it and the path, to collect and carry away rainwater —see picture at STREET **2** [C] an open pipe fixed at the lower edge of a roof to collect and carry away rainwater —see picture at HOUSE¹ **3** [*the*+R] the lowest poorest social conditions, as in a dirty part of a city

gutter² *v* [IØ] (of a candle) to burn unevenly, so that melted wax runs down one side

gutter press /ˌ·· ˈ·/ *n* [*the*+R] *derog* the kind of newspapers which tend to be full of shocking stories about people's personal lives

gut·ter·snipe /ˈgʌtəsnaɪp‖-ər-/ *n* [C; *you*+N] a child of the poorest part of a town, living in the worst conditions, and usu. dressed in torn dirty clothes

gut·tur·al /ˈgʌtərəl/ *adj* **1** [Wa5] of the throat **2** (of speech or a speech sound) which seems to be produced deep in the throat **3** *esp. old use* (in PHONETICS) produced by the back of the tongue against the back of the mouth; VELAR: */g/ in "goat" used to be called a guttural consonant sound*

guv /gʌv/ *n* [N;(C)] *BrE sl* GOVERNOR (6)

guv·nor, guv'nor /ˈgʌvnəʳ/ *n* [N;(C)] *BrE sl* GOVERNOR (6)

guy¹ /gaɪ/ also **guy rope** /ˈ· ·/— *n* **1** a rope, wire, or chain used to keep a load steady while it is being raised **2** a rope stretched from the top or side of a pole or from the side of a tent to the ground, to hold it in place —see picture at CAMP²

guy² *n* **1** *infml, esp. AmE* a man; fellow: *a nice guy*

2 any of the funny figures of a man burnt on November 5th, the day that Guy Fawkes tried to blow up Parliament in London in 1605 **3** *infml* a person of strange laughable appearance, esp. clothes

guy³ *v* [T1] to copy (esp. a person) in a funny way so as to make others laugh: *The politician/His speech was guyed in the next day's newspaper*

Guy Fawkes Night /ˌgaɪ ˈfɔːks naɪt/ *n* [R] November 5th, when GUYs² (2) are burnt and coloured FIREWORKs are lighted

guz·zle /ˈgʌzəl/ *v* [IØ (AWAY);T1] to eat (something) or to drink (beer) eagerly and greedily (GREEDY): *Pigs guzzle their food.|He's been guzzling beer all evening* —**guzzler** *n*

gym /dʒɪm/ *n infml* **1** [C] GYMNASIUM (1) **2** [U] PHYSICAL TRAINING: *a gym class*

gym·kha·na /dʒɪmˈkɑːnə/ *n esp. BrE* a local sports meeting, esp. horse racing, jumping, etc., and competitions for horse and carriage

gym·na·si·um /dʒɪmˈneɪzɪəm/ *n* **1** a hall with wall bars, ropes and other such things, for climbing, jumping, etc. **2** (esp. in Germany) a school for older children from which they may go on to university —compare GRAMMAR SCHOOL

gym·nast /ˈdʒɪmnæst, -nəst/ *n* a person who trains and is skilled in certain bodily exercises

gym·nas·tic /dʒɪmˈnæstɪk/ *adj* [Wa5;A] concerned with bodily exercises and training —**~ally** *adv* [Wa4,5]

gym·nas·tics /dʒɪmˈnæstɪks/ *n* [U] the art of training the body by means of certain exercises, often done in competition with others

gym·slip /ˈdʒɪmˌslɪp/ *n BrE* a garment formerly often worn by girls as part of a school uniform, and which is a sort of dress without arms

-gyn- /dʒən, gən; *strong* gaɪn/ *comb. form* woman or female: GYNAECOLOGY

gy·nae·col·o·gy, *AmE* **gynecology** /ˌgaɪnɪ̵ˈkɒlədʒi‖-ˈkɑ-/ *n* [U] the study in medicine of the workings of the female sex organs, esp. in child-bearing, and the study and treatment of their diseases —**-logical** /-kəˈlɒdʒɪkəl‖-ˈlɑ-/ *adj* [Wa5] —**-logist** /ˌgaɪnɪ̵ˈkɒlədʒɪ̵st‖-ˈkɑ-/ *n*

gyp¹ /dʒɪp/ *n* **1** (in former times) a man servant at Cambridge University who looked after students living in college rooms —compare SCOUT² (5) **2** *AmE infml* an act of cheating or esp. charging too much for something of bad quality

gyp² *v* **-pp-** [T1] *AmE infml* to cheat: *He gypped me out of $10*

gyp³ *n* [U] *sl, esp. BrE* sharp pain or punishment (only in the phr. **give someone gyp**): *My bad tooth is really giving me gyp this morning*

gyp·sum /ˈdʒɪpsəm/ *n* [U] a soft white chalklike substance, from which PLASTER OF PARIS is made, and which is used to improve the soil for growing

gyp·sy /ˈdʒɪpsi/ *n esp. AmE* (*sometimes cap.*) GIPSY

gy·rate /dʒaɪˈreɪt‖ˈdʒaɪəreɪt/ *v* [IØ] to swing round and round a fixed point, in one direction or with changes of direction: *The dancers gyrated quickly to the strong beat of the music*

gy·ra·tion /dʒaɪˈreɪʃən/ *n* **1** [U] the act of gyrating (GYRATE) **2** [C *often pl.*] a gyrating (GYRATE) movement: *the dancers' gyrations at the wild party*

gy·ro·scope /ˈdʒaɪərəskəʊp/ also (*infml*) **gy·ro** /ˈdʒaɪərəʊ/— *n* a heavy wheel which spins inside a frame, used for keeping ships and aircraft steady, and also as a children's toy —**-scopic** /ˌdʒaɪərəˈskɒpɪk‖-ˈskɑ-/ *adj*

gyves /dʒaɪvz/ *n* [P] *old use* chains or bars to be fastened to the hands or feet of a prisoner

H, h

H, h /eɪtʃ/ **H's, h's** *or* **Hs, hs** the 8th letter of the English alphabet

ha /hɑː/ *interj* a shout of surprise, interest, etc.

ha·be·as cor·pus /ˌheɪbɪəs ˈkɔːpəs‖-ˈkɔr-/ *n* [U] *law Lat* **1** a written order for someone to appear in court, so that the court can decide whether he should remain in prison (esp. in the phr. **a writ of habeas corpus**) **2** the right to demand this written order as a protection against unlimited imprisonment without charges

hab·er·dash·er /ˈhæbədæʃəʳ‖-bər-/ *n* **1** *BrE* a shopkeeper who sells pins, sewing thread, and other small things used in dressmaking **2** *AmE* a shopkeeper who sells men's clothing, esp. hats, GLOVEs, etc.

hab·er·dash·er·y /ˈhæbədæʃəri‖-bər-/ *n* **1** [C] a HABERDASHER's shop or department in a department store **2** [U] the goods that are sold in such a shop or department

ha·bil·i·ment /həˈbɪlɪ̵mənt/ *n* [*usu. pl.*] *fml* an article of clothing

hab·it /ˈhæbɪ̵t/ *n* **1** [U;C] (an example of) customary behaviour: *I smoke out of habit/by habit, not for pleasure* **2** [C] a special set of clothes, esp. that worn by MONKs and NUNs in religious ORDERs¹ (17) **3 habit of mind** /ˌ·· · ˈ·/ condition of mind (often in the phr. **a cheerful habit of mind**)

USAGE If a large group of people have been doing something for a long time it is a **custom** or (*often derog*) a **practice**: *the* **custom** *of giving presents at Christmas|the* **practice** *of eating one's enemies.* If a single person does something for a long time, it is a **practice** or a **habit**: *the bad* **habit** *of biting my nails.*

hab·i·ta·ble /ˈhæbɪ̵təbəl/ *adj* [Wa3] which can be lived in (INHABITed)

hab·i·tat /ˈhæbɪ̵tæt/ *n* the natural home of a plant or animal

hab·i·ta·tion /ˌhæbɪ̵ˈteɪʃən/ *n fml* **1** [U] the act of living in (INHABITing): *a house too old for human habitation* **2** [C] a house or place to live in

ha·bit·u·al /həˈbɪtʃʊəl/ *adj* [Wa5] **1** [A] usual; customary: *she gave her habitual greeting* **2** [A;(B)] (done) by habit: *He's a habitual thief.|His stealing is habitual* —**~ly** *adv*: *habitually late*

ha·bit·u·ate to /həˈbɪtʃʊeɪt/ *v prep* [D1;V4b] *often pass.* to accustom (oneself) to (something or doing something)

ha·bi·tu·é /həˈbɪtʃʊeɪ/ *n* [C9, esp. *of*] a regular attender: *a habitué of the theatre*

ha·ci·en·da /ˌhæsiˈendə/ *n* a large house, as found in South America, usu. considered together with the farming land (ESTATE) around it

hack¹ /hæk/ *v* [L9 (*at*, AWAY); X9] to cut (up), esp. roughly or in uneven pieces: *He hacked the tree down.|He hacked away all night.|They hacked their way through the trees*

hack² *n* [S] **1** [(*at*)] a rough cutting movement or blow: *He made a hack at the log* **2** a cut from a kick or blow in a game

hack³ *n* **1** a horse that has done too much or been ridden too much, esp. one that is old **2** a light horse for riding **3** a person who does a lot of poor quality work, esp. writing stories **4** *AmE* a taxi **5** *esp. AmE* HACKING COUGH

hack⁴ *v* [I∅] **1** to ride on horseback, for pleasure, along roads or through the country **2** *AmE* to drive a taxi

hack⁵ *n BrE* a ride on horseback, taken for pleasure, along roads or through the country

hacking cough /ˈ·· ·, ˌ··ˈ·/ *n* a cough with a rough unpleasant sound

hack·les /ˈhækəlz/ *n* [P] **1** the long feathers or hairs on the back of the neck of certain birds and animals, which stand up straight in times of danger **2 have/get one's hackles up** to be/make very angry **3 with one's hackles up** very angry; ready to fight or argue

hack·ney /ˈhækni/ *n* **1 a** a horse for riding or driving **b** a breed of horse which lifts its feet very high as it steps **2** HACKNEY CARRIAGE

hackney car·riage /ˈ·· ˌ··/ *n* **1** *fml or tech* a taxi **2** a horse-drawn carriage used for hire, esp. formerly

hack·neyed /ˈhæknid/ *adj* (of a saying) meaningless because used and repeated too often

hack·saw /ˈhæksɔː/ *n* a tool that has a fine-toothed blade which can be changed, esp. one used for cutting metal

hack·work /ˈhækwɜːk‖-wɜrk/ *n* [U] uninteresting and unoriginal work, esp. writing, done to earn money and not out of interest in it

had /d, əd, həd; *strong* hæd/ **1** *past t. and past p. of* HAVE **2 be had** *infml* to be tricked or made a fool of

had·dock /ˈhædək/ *n* **haddock** [Wn2;C;U] a common fish found in northern seas, used as food —see picture at FISH¹

Ha·des /ˈheɪdiːz/ *n* [R] the Greek land of the dead; HELL

had·ji /ˈhædʒi/ *n* HAJJI

had·n't /ˈhædnt/ *contr. of* had not —see CONTR. (USAGE)

hae·mo- /ˈhiːmə, ˈhəmə/ *comb. form BrE* HEMO-

haft /hɑːft‖hæft/ *n tech* the handle of an axe or of some long-handled weapons

hag /hæg/ *n* [C;*you*+N] an ugly or unpleasant woman, esp. one who is old and is thought to be evil

hag·gard /ˈhægəd‖-ərd/ *adj* having lines on the face and hollow places around the eyes and in the cheeks, as through tiredness or lack of sleep

hag·gis /ˈhægɨs/ *n* **-gises** *or* **-gis** [U;C] a food eaten in Scotland, made from the heart and other organs of a sheep cut up and boiled inside a skin made from the stomach

hag·gle /ˈhægəl/ *v* [I∅ (*over/about* and/or *with*)] to argue over something, esp. over fixing a price

hag·i·og·ra·phy /ˌhægiˈɒgrəfi‖-ˈɑg-/ *n* [U;C] **1** (a book giving) information about the lives of SAINT*s* or other holy people **2** (a book giving) only favourable information about the life of one or more people

hag-rid·den /ˈ· ˌ··/ *adj lit* continually worried by something as if by a bad dream

ha-ha¹ /ˌ· ˈ·/ *interj* (a shout of laughter)

ha-ha² /ˈ· ·/ *n* **ha-has** a ditch used to divide property, with or without a wall or fence in it

hai·ku /ˈhaɪkuː/ *n* **-ku** [Wn3] a type of Japanese poem with 3 lines

hail¹ /heɪl/ *n* **1** [U] frozen rain drops which fall as little hard balls **2** [S+*of*] a number of things which strike suddenly with violence, causing pain or damage: *a hail of bullets*

hail² *v* [*it*+I∅] (of HAIL) to fall: *It's hailing*

hail³ *v* **1** [T1] to call out to (someone) by name or in greeting: *An old friend hailed me from the other side of the street* **2** [X1;T1] to recognize (someone) as important by calling out (a title): *They hailed him king* **3 hail a taxi** to call out "Taxi!" and/or signal it to stop to take one somewhere **4 within hailing distance (of)** near enough to call out to someone/each other and be heard

hail as *v prep* [X1;(V4b)] to recognize (something) as (something good): *They hailed it as a work of art*

hail down *v adv; prep* [I∅ (*on*)] RAIN DOWN

hail-fel·low-well-met /ˌ· ·· · ˈ·/ *adj* [F;(B)] *sometimes derog* (of people and behaviour) very cheerful and friendly from the moment of greeting: *He's very hail-fellow-well-met with everyone*

hail from *v prep* [T1 *no pass*] *esp. AmE* to come from; have as one's home: *hails from Wales*

hail·stone /ˈheɪlstəʊn/ *n* a small ball of HAIL

hail·storm /ˈheɪlstɔːm‖-ɔrm/ *n* a storm when HAIL falls heavily, the wind blows it about in sudden movements, etc.

hair /heəʳ/ *n* **1** [C] a fine threadlike growth from the skin of a person or animal: *The cat has left her loose hairs all over my clothes* **2** [U] a mass of such growths, such as that on the head of human beings: *My hair has grown very long* —see also HEAD OF HAIR —compare FUR² and see picture at HUMAN² **3 get in (someone's) hair** *infml* to annoy (someone) **4 get/have (someone) by the short hairs** *infml* also **get (someone) by the short and curlies** *sl*—to have someone in one's power in an argument or fight **5 let one's hair down** *infml* to do as one likes; behave wildly, esp. after a period of time when one has had to be controlled in behaviour, as after a formal occasion **6 make someone's hair curl** *infml* to shock someone **7 make someone's hair stand on end** to make someone so afraid that he feels or expects to feel the movement of skin and hair which happens naturally with animals when their hair stands out from the body before a fight, making them look bigger **8 not harm a hair on someone's head** to be always gentle and kind to someone —compare **not harm a** FLY **9 not turn a hair** *infml* to show no fear or worry (when in difficulty) **10 split hairs** *derog* to concern oneself or other people with unimportant differences, esp. in arguments **11 tear one's hair** to behave wildly in sorrow or anger **12 the/a hair of the dog (that bit you)** a drink taken in the morning after one has become ill through drinking the same sort of alcohol the night before. It is supposed to cure the headache

hair·brush /ˈheəbrʌʃ‖ˈheər-/ *n* a brush used for the hair to get out dirt and to make the hair smooth —see picture at BATHROOM

hair·cut /ˈheəkʌt‖ˈheər-/ *n* **1** an occasion of having the hair cut **2** the style the hair is cut in

hair·do /ˈheəduː‖ˈheər-/ *n* **-dos 1** an occasion of a woman's having her hair shaped into a style **2** the style a woman's hair is shaped into

hair·dress·er /ˈheəˌdresəʳ‖ˈheər-/ *n* a person who shapes the hair (esp. of women) into a style by cutting, SETting¹ (14), etc., or who changes its colour —compare BARBER **—-ing** *n* [U]

-haired /heəd‖heərd/ *comb. form adj* with (a certain colour or type of) hair: *curly-haired*

hair·grip /ˈheəgrɪp‖ˈheər-/ *n* a small often ornamented pin that a woman fixes or slides into her hair to keep it in place

hair·less /ˈheələs‖ˈheər-/ *adj* [Wa5] with no hair; BALD: *His head was completely hairless*

hair·line /ˈheəlaɪn‖ˈheər-/ *n* **1** a very thin line, such as one of the lines across the area of view of some TELESCOPE*s* **2** also **hairline crack** /ˌ·· ˈ·/— a narrow crack **3** the place on the forehead where the hair starts growing

hair·net /ˈheənet‖ˈheər-/ *n* a net (worn esp. by women) which stretches over the hair to keep it in place

hair·piece /ˈheəpiːs‖ˈheər-/ *n* a piece of false hair

used to make one's own hair seem thicker

hair·pin /ˈheəˌpɪn‖ˈheər-/ also **hair·grip** /ˈheəˌgrɪp‖ˈheər-/— *n* a pin made of wire bent into a U-shape to hold the hair in position on the head

hairpin bend /ˌ·· ˈ·/ *n* a narrow U-shaped curve where a road turns back, as when going up a steep hill

hair-rais·ing /ˈ· ˌ··/ *adj* that makes one very afraid: *a hair-raising experience*

hair-re·stor·er /ˈ· ·ˌ··/ *n* [C;U] (a) substance or liquid that is supposed to make hair grow again

hair's breadth /ˈ· ·/ also **hair·breadth** /ˈheəbretθ‖ˈheərbredθ/— *n* a very short distance (esp. in the phr. **miss by a hair's breadth**): *We missed the other car by a hair's breadth and narrowly avoided an accident*

hair shirt /ˌ· ˈ·/ *n* a shirt made of rough uncomfortable cloth containing hair, worn formerly by religious people (esp. MONK*s*) to punish themselves

hair slide /ˈ· ·/ also **slide**— *n* a small fastener to keep a girl's hair in place

hair-split·ting /ˈ· ˌ··/ *n* [U] too much interest in unimportant differences and points of detail, esp. in argument

hair·spring /ˈheəˌsprɪŋ‖ˈheər-/ *n* a delicate spring inside a watch that helps to make the watch run evenly —see picture at CLOCK[1]

hair trig·ger /ˌ· ˈ··◂/ *n* a TRIGGER on a gun that needs only a very gentle pressure to fire the gun —**hair-trigger** *n* [A]

hair·y /ˈheəri/ *adj* **1** [Wa1] **a** (when used of people, not usu. describing the hair on the head) having a lot of hair: *hairy legs|a hairy chest* **b** having a rough surface like hair: *This wool is rather hairy* **2** [Wa2] *sl* exciting in a way that causes fear, or dangerous: *It was rather hairy driving down that narrow road in the darkness* —**-iness** [U]

haj·ji, hadji /ˈhædʒi/ *n* [A] the title used by a Muslim who has been to Mecca

hake /heɪk/ *n* [Wn2;C;U] any of several kinds of sea fish used as food

hal·berd /ˈhælbəd‖-ərd/ *n* a weapon used formerly, with a blade on a long handle

hal·cy·on /ˈhælsɪən/ *adj* [Wa5;A] *lit & poet* calm or peaceful (esp. in the phr. **halcyon days**)

hale /heɪl/ *adj* [Wa5] **1** *lit* healthy **2 hale and hearty** /ˌ·· ˈ··/ very healthy

half[1] /hɑːf‖hæf/ *n* **halves** /hɑːvz‖hævz/ **1** either of the 2 equal parts into which something is or could be divided; ½; 50% **2** either of 2 parts into which something is divided: *the bottom half of the history class|You've taken the bigger half of the cake!* **3** either of 2 parts into which a period of time, such as a public performance, football match, concert, etc., is divided **4** the number ½: *3 halves makes 1½* **5 by halves** in part; incompletely: *Better not (to) do it at all than do it by halves* **6 go halves (in/on something) (with someone)** *infml* to share (the cost of something) (with someone) **7 (my/your/his) better half** *humor* one's husband or wife

USAGE It is better to say *a month and a* **half** than *one and a* **half** *months*.

half[2] *n* **halfs** *or* **halves** /hɑːvz‖hævz/ **1** something which has ½ the value or quantity of something, such as a coin, ticket, or a PINT of beer: *He came over to the table with 5 halfs.|Give me a penny for 2 halfs* **2** HALFBACK

half[3] *pron* **1** either of the 2 parts of a thing or group: *Half (of it) was damaged.|Half (of them) are here.|"I haven't told you half of it yet"* (SEU W.) **2 too clever by half** *infml esp. BrE* being too sure of one's/its cleverness in a way that displeases people

half[4] *predeterminer* **1** being ½ in amount: *Half the car was damaged.|Half the boys are here.|half a minute|half my life* —see **half a** DOZEN **2 half the battle** the biggest part of the difficulty (finished): *Carrying the bags upstairs is half the battle. Then we only have to unpack them*

half[5] *adv* [Wa5] **1** partly; not completely: *half cooked|He was half under the bed, with his legs sticking out* **2 (be) not half** *BrE infml* **a** (be) very: *not half good* (=very good)|*It isn't half windy today!* (=it's very windy) **b** (in the phr. **not half bad**) not at all: *The food's not half bad* (=quite good) **3 (do) not half** *BrE infml* very much (so): *He didn't half like it!* (=He liked it very much)|*"Did you like it?" "Not half!"* (=Very much) **4 half and half** ½ one and ½ the other; 2 equal parts of 2 things: *"Is it made with milk or water?" "Half and half"* /ˌ· · ˈ·/ **5 half 7, 8, 9,** etc. *BrE* (of time) 7.30, 8.30, 9.30, etc. —see PAST[2] (1) **6 not half as** not nearly as: *"We didn't feel half as bad* (=we felt much better) *when we got there"* (SEU S.)

half[6] *comb. form* **1** being ½ in amount: *a half hour|a half pound* **2** not quite complete: *a half smile* **3 (every hour) on the half hour:** at 1.30, 2.30, 3.30, etc.

USAGE Some writers, particularly Americans, think *a* **half** *mile* is more formal and correct than **half** *a mile*.

half a crown /ˌ· · ˈ·/ also **(a) half crown**— *n* **half crowns** (in Great Britain before 1971) a rather large silver-coloured coin worth 2 shillings and 6 pence, 8 of which made £1 (a pound)

half a doz·en /ˌ· · ˈ··/ also **(a) half dozen** /ˌ· ˈ··/— *determiner, n* **half dozens** 6; a set of 6: *half a dozen eggs|I'll have 2 half dozens* (=2 groups of half a dozen)

half·back /ˈhɑːfbæk‖ˈhæf-/ also **half**— *n* (in games like football) a player or position between the centre players (FORWARD*s*[3]) and the BACK*s*[1] (8) —see picture at SOCCER

half-baked /ˌ· ˈ·◂/ *adj* (of people and ideas) stupid; not sensible; lacking planned judgment

half-breed /ˈ· ·/ *n, adj sometimes derog* (a person) with parents of different races

half-broth·er /ˈ· ˌ··/ *n* a brother related through one parent only —see TABLE OF FAMILY RELATIONSHIPS

half-caste /ˈ· ·/ *n, adj sometimes derog* HALF-BREED

half cock /ˌ· ˈ·/ **go off (at) half cock** (of a prepared event) to fail to satisfy expected standards because of poor preparation, bad luck, etc.

half-cocked /ˌ· ˈ·◂/ *adj* poorly prepared

half crown /ˌ· ˈ·◂/ *n* HALF A CROWN

half doz·en /ˌ· ˈ··/ *n* HALF A DOZEN

half-har·dy /ˌ· ˈ··◂/ *adj* [Wa5] (of plants) able to live through a cold winter but not through freezing cold

half-heart·ed /ˌ· ˈ··◂‖ˈ· ˌ··/ *adj* (of people and their acts) showing little effort and no real interest —compare WHOLE-HEARTED —**~ly** *adv* —**~ness** *n* [U]

half-hol·i·day /ˌ· ˈ···/ *n* half a day which is free from school, studies, etc.

half-length /ˌ· ˈ·◂‖ˈ· ·/ *adj* for or of the upper half of a person: *a half-length portrait* (=picture, painting)/*coat*

half-mast /ˌ· ˈ·/ *n* **1** a point near the middle of the MAST or flagpole where the flag flies to show some cause for sorrow, such as the death of an important person, or to call for help, as from a ship **2 (at) half-mast** *humor* (of full-length trousers) too short, so that the ankles can be seen

half moon /ˌ· ˈ·/ *n* **1** the shape of the moon seen when half the side facing the earth is showing **2** something of this shape

half note /ˈ· ·/ *n AmE* (in music) MINIM

half·pence /ˈheɪpəns/ *n* [P] **1** *pl. of* HALFPENNY[1,2] **2** coins of low value (esp. in the phr. **a few**

halfpence) **3 (get) more kicks than halfpence** *BrE infml* (to get) more bad treatment than good treatment —see also THREE-HALFPENCE

half·penny[1] /ˈheɪpni/ *n* **halfpennies** *or* (*BrE*) **halfpence** also (*infml*) **half p**— (in Great Britain after 1971) a very small copper and tin (BRONZE) coin, 2 of which make a (new) penny; ½p —see HALFPENNY[2] (USAGE)

halfpenny[2] *n* **halfpennies** *or* (*BrE*) **halfpence** **1** (in Great Britain, before 1971) a BRONZE coin, 2 of which made a penny; ½d **2 not have 2 halfpennies to rub together** to be very poor
USAGE *halfpennies* is used for numbers of coins, *halfpence* for amounts of money —see PENNY (USAGE)

half·penny·worth /ˈheɪpniwəθ, ˌhɑːfˈpenəθ‖ˈheɪpəniwɜrθ/ also **hap'orth**— *n* [S (*of*)] an amount of something bought for ½d

half-sis·ter /ˈ· ˌ··/ *n* a sister related through one parent only —see TABLE OF FAMILY RELATIONSHIPS

half term /ˌ· ˈ·/ *n* a short holiday, usu. 2 or 3 days, in the middle of a school TERM

half-tim·bered /ˌ· ˈ··◂/ *adj* of an old style of house building with the wood of the frame showing in the walls

half time /ˌ· ·◂‖ˈ· ·/ *n* [U] the period of time between 2 parts of a game, such as a football match

half·tone /ˌhɑːfˈtəʊn◂‖ˈhæftəʊn/ *n* **1 a** a printed picture made from a black-and-white photograph **b** the method of printing such pictures, showing varying shades by dots **2** also **half step**— *AmE* (in music) SEMITONE

half-track /ˈ· ·/ *n* a vehicle (esp. a military one) with wheels at the front but with a TRACK[1] (6) running over 2 or more back wheels on each side

half vol·ley /ˌ· ˈ··/ *n* **1** (esp. in tennis) a stroke in which the ball is hit the moment it rises (BOUNCES) from the ground **2** (in cricket) a throwing (BOWLing[3] (4)) of the ball in such a way that it can easily be hit by the BATSMAN the moment it rises from the ground

half·way /ˌhɑːfˈweɪ◂‖ˌhæf-/ *adj, adv* **1** at the midpoint between 2 things: *The halfway point was reached at 12 o'clock* **2** by a small or incomplete amount: *You can't go halfway when you're painting —once you've started you have to go on to the end* **3 meet someone halfway** to make an agreement with someone which partly satisfies the demands of both sides: *You want to pay £1 but I want £2. Meet me halfway and make it £1·50* **4 meet trouble halfway** to worry before one needs to

half-wit /ˈ· ·/ *n* [C; *you*+N] *usu. derog* a person of weak mind —**~ted** /ˌ· ˈ··◂/ *adj* —**~tedly** /ˌ· ˈ···/ *adv*

hal·i·but /ˈhælɨbət/ *n* **-but** *or* **-buts** [Wn2;C;U] a kind of very large fish used as food —see picture at FISH[1]

hal·i·to·sis /ˌhælɨˈtəʊsɨs/ *n* [U] *med* a condition when the breath from the mouth smells bad; bad breath

hall /hɔːl/ *n* **1** [C] a large room in which meetings, dances, etc., can be held **2** [C] the passage just inside the entrance of a house, from which the rooms open **3** [C; *in*+U] (in a college or university) **a** the room where all the members eat together: *to eat in hall* **b** HALL OF RESIDENCE: *I live in hall*

hal·le·lu·ja /ˌhælɨˈluːjə/ also **alleluia**— *interj, n* (a song, cry, etc., that is an expression of) praise, joy, and thanks to God

hal·liard /ˈhæljəd‖-ərd/ *n* HALYARD

hall·mark[1] /ˈhɔːlmɑːk‖-ɑrk/ *n* **1** the mark made on objects of precious metal to prove that they are silver or gold **2** [(*of*)] a typical piece of behaviour or an object which shows the nature of a person or thing: *Clear expression is the hallmark of good writing*

hallmark[2] *v* [T1] to make a HALLMARK (1) on (something)

hal·lo /həˈləʊ, he-, hæ-/ *interj, n* **-los** *BrE* HELLO

hall of res·i·dence /ˌ· · ˈ···/ also **hall**, *AmE* usu. **dormitory**— *n* a building where several students live and sleep

hal·low /ˈhæləʊ/ *v* [Wv5;T1] to make holy: (fig.) *the hallowed memories of great men*

Hal·low·e'en /ˌhæləʊˈiːn/ *n* [R] the night of October 31, when children play tricks while wearing false faces and strange clothes

hall·stand /ˈhɔːlstænd/ *n* a piece of furniture, often with a mirror, with hooks for hanging hats and coats on

hal·lu·ci·nate /həˈluːsɨneɪt/ *v* [I∅] to see things which are not there

hal·lu·ci·na·tion /həˌluːsɨˈneɪʃən/ *n* **1** [C] something that is imagined although it is not really there, often as the result of a drug or an illness of the mind **2** [U;C] the/an experience of suffering from (having) these

hal·lu·ci·na·to·ry /həˈluːsɨnətəri‖-tori/ *adj* causing, or like, a HALLUCINATION: *a hallucinatory image/experience/drugs*

hal·lu·ci·no·gen·ic /həˌluːsɨnəˈdʒenɪk/ *adj* causing HALLUCINATION

hall·way /ˈhɔːlweɪ/ *n esp. AmE* HALL (2)

hal·ma /ˈhælmə/ *n tdmk esp. BrE* an easy game for 2 or 4 players, where pieces jump over each other and move about on a board with 256 black and white squares —compare CHINESE CHEQUERS

ha·lo /ˈheɪləʊ/ *n* **-loes** *or* **-los** **1** a golden circle representing light around the heads of holy persons in religious paintings **2** a bright circle of light, as around the sun or moon in misty weather

halt[1] /hɔːlt/ *n* [*the*+P] *old use* those who are LAME (have a weakness in one or both legs which makes walking difficult)

halt[2] *v* [T1;I∅] *fml* to (cause to) stop: *The train was halted by work on the line ahead*

halt[3] *n* **1** [S] a stop or pause (esp. in the phr. **come to a halt**): *The car came to a halt just in time to prevent an accident* **2** [C] a small railway station: *a country halt* **3** [C] *fml* a bus stop

hal·ter /ˈhɔːltəʳ/ *n* **1** a rope or leather band fastened round a horse's head, esp. to lead it **2** a piece of rope for hanging criminals

hal·ter·neck /ˈhɒltənek‖ˈhɔltər-/ *adj* (of a garment, esp. a dress) that leaves the wearer's back uncovered and is held in place by a narrow band of material that passes round the neck

halt·ing /ˈhɔːltɪŋ/ *adj* stopping and starting as if uncertain: *a halting voice* —**~ly** *adv*

halve /hɑːv‖hæv/ *v* [T1] **1** to divide into halves: *Let's halve the work between the 2 of us* **2** to reduce to half

halves /hɑːvz‖hævz/ **1** *pl. of* HALF **2 go halves (in)** to share the cost (of): *Let's go halves in buying the wine.*|*Go halves with me*

hal·yard, halliard /ˈhæljəd‖-ərd/ *n tech* a rope used to raise or lower a flag or sail —see picture at SAIL[2]

ham[1] /hæm/ *n* **1** [U;C] (preserved meat from) a pig's leg considered as food **2** [C] the upper part of the leg **3** [C; *you*+N] an actor whose acting is unnatural, esp. with improbable movements and expression: *a ham actor* **4** [C] a person who receives and/or sends radio messages using his own apparatus
USAGE Note the word order in this fixed *AmE* phr. **ham and eggs**: *We had ham and eggs for breakfast.*

ham[2] *v* **-mm-** [T1 (UP); I∅] to act (a part on stage) unnaturally or wildly: *It's easier to ham the part of*

King Lear than to play it simply and sincerely

ham·a·dry·ad /ˌhæməˈdraɪəd/ *n* **1** a lesser goddess (NYMPH) living in a tree **2** a type of large BABOON of Africa **3** a type of large poisonous snake of the COBRA family

ham·burg·er /ˈhæmbɜːgəʳ‖-ɜr-/ *n* [C] a flat circular cake of very small pieces of meat, esp. this eaten in a ROLL[1] (2) of bread

ham-fist·ed /ˌ· ˈ··/ also **ham-hand·ed**— *adj* awkward in using the hands; CLUMSY

ham·let /ˈhæmlɪ̈t/ *n* a small village

ham·mer[1] /ˈhæməʳ/ *n* **1** a tool with a heavy head for driving nails into wood, or for striking things to break them or move them —see picture at TOOL[1] **2** something made to hit something else, as in a piano, or part of a gun —see picture at KEYBOARD[1] **3** a bone in the ear —see picture at EAR[1] **4 be/go at it hammer and tongs** (of 2 people) to fight or argue violently **5 come under the hammer** to be sold for the highest amount that is offered (by AUCTION) **6 throwing the hammer** a sport in which competitors throw a metal ball on the end of a wire as far as possible

hammer[2] *v* **1** [T1;IØ] to strike (something) with a hammer: *Hammer the nails in* **2** [IØ (AWAY, *at*); T1] to hit repeatedly: *I hammered away at his head* **3** [T1] *infml* to conquer (someone) by fighting, or in a game: *We hammered the other team* **4** [IØ (AWAY, *at*)] to keep working at something: *I hammered away all afternoon* **5** [T1] to declare (someone) to be no longer a member of the STOCK EXCHANGE

hammer and sick·le /ˌ·· · ˈ··/ *n* [*the*+R] the sign of a hammer crossing a SICKLE that represents COMMUNISM

hammer in *v adv* [T1] to force understanding of by repeating: *The teacher has been trying to hammer in the danger of failing the examinations*

hammer in·to *v prep* [D1] to force (someone) to understand by repeating: *The teacher has been trying to hammer into the children the danger of failing the examinations*

hammer out *v adv* [T1a] **1** to talk about in detail and come to a decision about: *The government tried to hammer out a political position that would win votes at the next election* **2** to remove by hammering: *Can you hammer out the damaged part in the side of my car?*

ham·mock /ˈhæmək/ *n* a long piece of sailcloth (CANVAS) or net which can be hung up by the ends to form a bed —see picture at BEDROOM

ham·per[1] /ˈhæmpəʳ/ *v* [T1] to cause difficulty in movement or activity: *The snow hampered my movements*

hamper[2] *n* **1** a large basket with a lid, often used for carrying food **2** *AmE* LAUNDRY BASKET

ham·ster /ˈhæmstəʳ/ *n* a type of small animal with pockets (POUCHes) in its cheeks for storing food, kept as a pet —see picture at MAMMAL

ham·string[1] /ˈhæmˌstrɪŋ/ *n* a cordlike TENDON at the back of the leg, joining a muscle to a bone

hamstring[2] *v* **-strung** /strʌŋ/ [T1] to cut the HAMSTRING, destroying the ability to walk

ham up *v adv* [T1] to act with too much expression on purpose: *Your story is very funny, but there's no need to ham it up*

hand[1] /hænd/ *n* **1** [C] the movable parts at the end of the arm, including the fingers —see picture at HUMAN[2] **2** [C] a pointer or needle on a clock or machine: *the second/minute/hour hand* **3** [S9] handwriting: *He writes a clear hand* **4** [C] a set of playing cards held by one person in a game **5** [C] a measure equal to 0.1 metres, used in measuring a horse's height at the shoulder **6** [C] a sailor on a ship: *All hands on* DECK*!* (=a call for all sailors to come up to deal with some trouble) **7** [C] (*now usu. in comb.*) a workman: *New hands needed for building work|a machine hand* **8** [C9] a performer; a practiser of a skill (esp. in the phrs. **an old hand, a good hand**): *I'm a bad hand at making pastry.|An old hand at the job is one who is very familiar with it through long experience* **9** [S] encouragement given by CLAPping the hands (in the phrs. **give a (good, big) hand to, get a (big, good) hand**) **10** [S9] quality of touch (esp. in the phrs. **have a light/heavy hand**) **11** [S] help (esp. in the phrs. **give/lend a hand to**) **12** [U] control (esp. in the phrs. **get/become out of hand**): *The meeting is getting out of hand—will everybody stop talking at once* **13 at first hand a** when known through a person who has had a direct experience: *I learnt it at first hand from my neighbour* **b** when experienced directly: *I found out at first hand by seeing it with my own eyes* **14 at hand** *fml* near in time or place: *The great day is at hand* **15 at second/third/fourth hand** when passed on through one, 2, or 3 people: *I heard it (at) second hand, when his father, who saw the fire, told my mother who told me* —see also FIRSTHAND, SECOND-HAND **16 at someone's hands** from or because of someone: *I suffered at his hands* **17 bring up by hand** to feed (an animal that has no mother) so that it can live and grow **18 by hand** by a person, not a machine or organization **19 change hands** to go from the possession of one person to that of another **20 fall/come into (someone's) hands** to come into the power or possession of: *We fell into enemy hands* **21 eat out of someone's hand** be ready to do everything someone wants: *I'll soon have him eating out of my hand!* **22 force someone's hand** to make someone act as one wishes, not as she/he wishes **23 get/keep one's hand in** to get used to an activity by practising/practice **24 give somebody a free hand** allow somebody to do things in his/her own way **25 get the upper hand (of)** to get control or power (over something/somebody difficult) **26 (tie, bind, etc., somebody) hand and foot** (tie, bind, etc.) both the hands and feet (of someone) **27 hand in glove (with)** closely connected (with someone), esp. in something bad **28 hand in hand a** holding hands, usu. of 2 people with the left hand of one in the right hand of the other **b** always happening together: *Dirt and disease go hand in hand* **29 hand over fist** very quickly and successfully: *making money hand over fist* **30 have a hand in** to share (an activity); be partly responsible for: *I had a hand in arranging the party* **31 have one's hands full** to be very busy **32 in hand** ready to be used or done: *money in hand* **33 in (someone's/good) hands** under (someone's/good) care **34 lay hands on a** to seize (someone) by force **b** (of a priest in a religious ceremony) to put the hands on the head of, as in curing an ill person, making someone else a priest, etc.: *cured by the laying-on of hands* **35 not do a hand's turn** to do no work **36 on every hand** in all directions; all around —compare RIGHT HAND, LEFT HAND **37 on hand** ready for use **38 on the one/other hand** (used for comparing different things or ideas) as one point in the argument/as an opposite point: *"I know this job of mine isn't much, but on the other hand I don't feel tied down"* (SEU W.) **39 out of hand** (esp. of decisions not to do something) at once and without any further thought: *I refused it out of hand* **40 play into (someone's) hands** to do something which gives (one's opponent) an advantage **41 (out of/off) on one's hands** (no longer) a responsibility which must be dealt with (note the phr. **Time hangs heavy on my hands**): *My children are off my hands now* **42 show one's hand** to make clear one's power **43 take/have in hand** to put/have under control: *We have the matter in hand.|The children must be taken in hand* **44 raise one's hand to/against someone** to make a movement to hit someone **45 throw in one's hand** to accept defeat **46 to hand** within reach **47 try one's hand** (**at**) to attempt (an activity): *I tried my hand at swimming, though it was the first time I'd been in the water* **48 turn one's hand to** to begin to practise (a skill) —see also SHAKE **hands,** HOLD **hands**, HANDS OFF, HANDS UP **49 wait on** (**somebody**) **hand and foot** to do every little thing for them, as if they were unable to look after themselves **50 wash one's hands of** to refuse to be concerned with or responsible for **51 win** (**a lady's**) **hand** *lit* to make (a woman) agree to marry one **52 win hands down** to win easily

hand² *v* [D1] **1** to give from one's own hand into someone else's: *Hand me that book, please* **2** (**have to**) **hand it to** (**someone**) to (have to) admit (someone's) success, esp. in something mentioned next: *You have to hand it to him, he's a good talker* —see also HAND AROUND, HAND BACK, HAND DOWN, HAND ON, HAND OUT, HAND OVER, HAND ROUND

hand a·round also **hand round**— *v adv* [T1] to pass (something, esp. food) from one person to another

hand back *v adv* [T1] to return or give back into the owner's hands

hand·bag /ˈhændbæg/ *n* a small bag for a woman to carry her money and personal things in

hand·ball /ˈhændbɔːl/ *n* **1** a game played in America, where a ball is hit against a wall by the hand **2** the ball used in playing this game

hand·bar·row /ˈhænd,bærəʊ/ *n* a small cart which can be pushed along

hand·bill /ˈhænd,bɪl/ *n* a small printed notice or advertisement to be given out by hand

hand·book /ˈhændbʊk/ *n* a short book giving all the most important information about a subject —compare MANUAL

hand·brake /ˈhændbreɪk/ *n* an apparatus (BRAKE) that stops a vehicle, worked by the driver's hand, not foot —see picture at CAR

hand·cart /ˈhændkɑːt‖-ɑrt/ *n* a small cart which can be pushed or pulled by hand

hand·clap /ˈhændklæp/ *n* a CLAPping action of the hands (esp. in the phr. **a slow handclap**, as a sign of impatience)

hand·cuff /ˈhændkʌf/ *v* [T1] to put HANDCUFFS on (someone)

hand·cuffs /ˈhændkʌfs/ also (*infml*) **cuffs**— *n* [P] metal rings joined together, for fastening the wrists of a criminal —see PAIR (USAGE)

hand down *v adv* [T1] **1** [*often pass.*] also **hand on, pass down**— to give or leave to people who are younger or come later: *This custom has been handed down since the 18th century.|This ring has been handed down in my family* **2** *AmE* to make a public statement about: *The board of directors will hand down the figures on Monday* —see also BRING DOWN (7)

-hand·ed /ˈhændɪ̵d/ *comb. form* [*adj*] using a certain (type of) hand: *right-handed|heavy-handed|a one-handed throw*

hand·ful /ˈhændfʊl/ *n* **1** [(*of*)] an amount which is as much as can be held in the hand: *I picked up a handful of letters and began to open them* **2** [(*of*)] a small number (of people): *We invited 12, but only a handful of them came* **3** a living thing which is so active that it is difficult to control: *That child is quite a handful*

hand·gun /ˈhændgʌn/ *n esp. AmE* a small gun held in one hand while firing, not raised against the shoulder; PISTOL

hand·hold /ˈhændhəʊld/ *n* an uneven place on a rock, wall, etc., which a climber can hold on to with his hand

hand·i·cap¹ /ˈhændɪkæp/ *n* **1 a** a disability: *Blindness is a great handicap* **b** a quality or event which gives one a disadvantage: *Being small is a handicap in a crowd like this* **2 a** a race or other sport or game in which the stronger competitors are given disadvantages such as carrying more weight or running further than others **b** the weight or distance, etc., added for such competitors: *He has a handicap of 100 metres* (=he starts 100 metres behind slower runners)

handicap² *v* **-pp-** [T1] **1** (of a quality or event) to cause (someone) to have a disadvantage: *Lack of money handicapped him badly* **2** [Wv5; *usu. pass.*] (of a disability of mind or body) to prevent (someone) from acting and living in the way ordinary people do: *He is handicapped by bad eyesight*|PHYSICALLY (2) *handicapped*

hand·i·craft /ˈhændɪkrɑːft‖-kræft/ *n* [*usu. pl.*] a skill needing careful use of the hands, such as sewing, weaving, etc.

hand·i·work /ˈhændɪwɜːk‖-ɜrk/ *n* **1** [U] work demanding the skilful use of the hands **2** [U9] action, usu. showing some sign of the person who has done it: *Nature is God's handiwork*

hand·ker·chief /ˈhæŋkətʃɪ̵f‖-kər-/ *n* **1** a piece of cloth or thin soft paper for drying the nose, eyes, etc. **2** *old use* a square of cloth worn round the neck (NECKERCHIEF)

han·dle¹ /ˈhændl/ *n* **1** a part of an object which is specially made for holding it or for opening it —see pictures at DOOR and CAR **2** *infml* a title (esp. in the phr. **have a handle to one's name**) **3 fly off the handle** *infml* to lose one's temper

handle² *v* [Wv3] **1** [T1] **a** to feel in the hands **b** to move by hand: *Glass—handle with care* **2** [T1] to deal with; control: *He handled a difficult argument skilfully.|I handled him carefully, because he was so angry* **3** [T1] to treat; behave towards: *Handle children kindly, if you want them to trust you* **4** [T1] to use (goods) in business, esp. for sale: *We don't handle that sort of book* **5** [L9] (of a car, boat, etc.) to obey controlling movements in the stated way —**handleable** *adj*

han·dle·bars /ˈhændlbɑːz‖-ɑrz/ *n* [P] the bar above the front wheel of a bicycle, which controls the direction it goes in

han·dler /ˈhændləʳ/ *n* a person who controls an animal

hand·loom /ˈhændluːm/ *n* a small machine for weaving by hand

hand lug·gage /ˈ· ,··/ *n* [U] a traveller's light or small bags, cases, etc., which can be carried by hand

hand·made /,hændˈmeɪd◂/ *adj* [Wa5] made by hand, not machine

hand·maid·en /ˈhænd,meɪdn/ also **hand·maid** /ˈhændmeɪd/— *n old use* a female servant

hand-me-down /ˈ· · ,·/ *n* [*usu. pl.*] REACH-ME-DOWN (2)

hand on *v adv* [T1] **1** to give from one person to another (esp. something which can be used by many people one after the other): *Please read this notice and hand it on* **2** HAND DOWN (1) **3** HAND OVER (1)

hand·out /ˈhændaʊt/ *n* **1** something given free, such as food, clothes, etc., esp. to someone poor **2** information given out, esp. a printed sheet: *Please read the handout carefully*

hand out *v adv* **1** [T1 (*to*)] to give, esp. one of (a set of things) to each member of a group of people: *Hand out the pencils* **2** [D1 (*to*); T1] to give freely: *I don't need you handing* (*me*) *out that sort of advice!*

hand o·ver *v adv* [T1 (*to*)] **1** to give control of: *The* *captain was unwilling to hand over the command of his ship* (*to a younger man*) **2** to give (something or somebody) into someone else's care: *The thief was handed over to the police*

hand·pick /ˌhænd'pɪk/ *v* [Wv5;T1] to choose carefully; choose (the best ones) out of a group

hand·rail /'hænd-reɪl/ *n* a bar of wood or metal fixed beside a place where one walks for holding onto, esp. near stairs

hand round *v adv* [T1] HAND AROUND

hand·shake /'hændʃeɪk/ *n* an act of taking each other's right hand when 2 people meet or leave each other —see also GOLDEN HANDSHAKE

hands off *interj* Don't touch!

hand·some /'hænsəm/ *adj* [Wa2] **1 a** (esp. of men) good-looking; of attractive appearance: **b** (esp. of women) strong-looking; attractive with a firm, large appearance rather than a delicate one **2** generous; plentiful **3** *AmE* clever; skilful **4 handsome is as handsome does** the people who really deserve respect are those whose actions are kind or generous —**~ly** *adv*

hand·stand /'hændstænd/ *n* a movement in which the legs are kicked into the air so that the body is upside down and supported on the hands

hands up /ˌ·· '·/ *interj* (used by gunmen) put your arms above your head!

hand-to-hand /ˌ·· · '·◂/ *adj* [Wa5;A] very close (esp. in the phr. **hand-to-hand fighting**) —**hand to hand** *adv*

hand-to-mouth /ˌ·· · '·◂/ *adj* [Wa5;A] (of a way of life) with just enough money, food, etc., to live —**hand to mouth** *adv*

hand·work /'hændwɜːk‖-ɜrk/ *n* [U] work done by hand —compare HANDIWORK

hand·writ·ing /'hændˌraɪtɪŋ/ *n* **1** [U] writing done by hand **2** [U;S] the style or appearance of such writing by a particular person: (*a*) *very clear handwriting*

hand·writ·ten /ˌhænd'rɪtn◂/ *adj* [Wa5] written by hand, not printed

hand·y /'hændi/ *adj* [Wa1] **1** useful and simple to use: *This is a handy little box* **2** clever in using the hands: *handy with her needle* **3** *infml* near; AT HAND: *The shops are quite handy* **4 come in handy** to be useful from time to time: *A few more travellers' cheques may come in handy on holiday* —**-i'ly** *adv* —**-iness** *n* [U]

hand·y·man /'hændimæn/ *n* **-men** /men/ a person who does repairs and practical jobs well, esp. in the house

hang[1] /hæŋ/ *v* **hung** /hʌŋ/ **1** [T1] to fix (something) at the top so that the lower part is free: *to hang curtains|Hang your coat* (*up*) *on the hook* **2** [L9] to be in such a position: *The curtains hang well* **3** [T1; IØ] **a** (of certain kinds of meat) to be kept in this position until ready to be eaten **b** to cause (certain kinds of meat) to be kept in this position until ready to be eaten **4** [T1 *usu. pass.*] to show (a set of paintings) publicly: *His pictures were hung in an important* GALLERY **5** [T1] **a** to fix (wallpaper) on a wall **b** to fix (a door) in position on its HINGE*s* **6** [T1] *infml* to send to the devil; DAMN[1] (5,7) (esp. in the phrs. **I'll be hanged, Hang it! Hang it all!**): *I'll be hanged if I'll do any such thing* **7 hang by a thread** to be in great danger: *His life hung by a thread* **8 hang fire** to be delayed in development; stop happening or continuing: *We are working very hard in the new house, so our plans for a holiday must hang fire for a time* **9 hang one's head** to appear ashamed **10 go hang** to go to the devil (because one doesn't care): *I'm losing my patience with him, he can go hang for all I care* **11 hang in the balance** be in an uncertain position where things may end well or badly —see also HANG ABOUT, HANG AROUND, HANG BACK, HANG ON, HANG ONTO, HANG OUT, HANG OVER, HANG TOGETHER, HANG UP

hang[2] *v* **hanged** /hæŋd/ [T1;IØ] to (cause to) die, as in punishment for a crime, by dropping with a rope around the neck: *He hanged himself in sorrow after his wife died*

hang[3] *n* [(*the*) S] **1** the shape or way something hangs: *I don't like the hang of this coat at the back* **2 get/have the hang of something** *infml* to be able to understand or use an idea or skill, or to work a machine: *Press this button when the light goes on—you'll soon get the hang of it*

hang a·bout *v adv; prep BrE infml* **1** [IØ;T1] to wait or stay near (a place) without purpose or activity: *I hung about for an hour but he didn't come* **2** [IØ] to delay or move slowly; DAWDLE: *Don't hang about, we have a train to catch!* **3** [IØ] to wait on purpose; HANG ON[1] (2): *Hang about, don't go away*

han·gar /'hæŋəʳ/ *n* a big building (SHED) where planes are kept

hang a·round *v adv; prep* [IØ;T1] to stay near (a place or person) with no clear purpose or activity: *I hung around for an hour, but he didn't come*

hang back *v adv* [IØ] to be unwilling to act or move: *The bridge looked so unsafe that we all hung back in fear*

hang·dog /'hæŋdɒg‖-dɔg/ *adj* [A] (of an expression on the face) ashamed

hang·er /'hæŋəʳ/ also **coat hanger, clothes hanger**— *n* a hook and crosspiece to fit inside the shoulders of a dress, coat, etc., to keep the shape of the garment when hung up

hanger-on /ˌ·· '·/ *n* **hangers-on** *usu. derog* a person who tries to be friendly with another person or group, esp. for his own advantage

hang glid·ing /'· ˌ··/ *n* [U] the sport of GLIDING using a large KITE (2) instead of a plane

hang·ing /'hæŋɪŋ/ *n* **1** [U] the punishment for crime in which death is caused by hanging from a rope round the neck **2** [C] a death of this type: *There have been no hangings in England for many years*

hang·ings /'hæŋɪŋz/ *n* [P] curtains and any other materials hanging over the walls, windows, doors, etc., of a house

hang·man /'hæŋmən/ *n* **-men** /mən/ the person whose work is hanging criminals

hang·nail /'hæŋneɪl/ *n* a piece of skin which has come loose near the bottom of the fingernail where it grows out from the skin

hang on[1] *v adv* [IØ] *infml* **1** [(*to*)] to keep hold of something: *Hang on* (*to the* STRAP). *The bus is starting.* **2** to wait, as on the telephone: *I finish work at 5 but I'll hang on till half past to meet you.*| *I'm afraid the line is busy, would you like to hang on?* **3** to keep doing something: *You must be tired, but try to hang on till all the work's finished*

hang on[2] also **hang up·on**— *v prep* **1** [T1] to pay close attention to: *The boy admires his teacher and hangs on his every word* **2** [T1,6a] also **hinge on**— to depend on: *The story hangs on the relationship between the 2 sisters* **3 hang on someone's lips** to listen to someone eagerly

hang on·to also **hold onto**— *v prep* [T1] **1** to try to keep: *We should hang onto the house and sell it later when prices are higher* **2** to find support or help in: *The old lady had only her religion to hang onto when her family had gone*

hang·out /'hæŋaʊt/ *n sl* a place where one lives or is often to be seen

hang out *v adv* [L9, esp. *at, in*] *infml* **1** to live or spend much time: *He hangs out at Green Street|in an old house* **2** let it **all hang out** *sl* do one's own THING (13)

hang·o·ver /ˈhæŋəʊvəʳ/ *n* **1** the feeling of headache, sickness, etc., the day after drinking too much alcohol **2** a condition or effect resulting from an earlier event or state: *His cough is a hangover from a bad illness he had*

hang o·ver[1] *v adv* [IØ (*from*)] to continue or remain: *This custom hangs over from the old days*

hang over[2] *v prep* [T1] **1** to threaten: *The danger of war hung over Europe for 21 years* **2 hang over one's head** to threaten one as a possibility, esp. of failure or unpleasantness: *The examinations are hanging over her head, that's why she can't sleep at nights*

hang to·geth·er *v adv* [IØ] **1** to remain united **2** to support the same idea in each separate part; be CONSISTENT (2): *This plan doesn't hang together, and I don't see how it can work*

hang·up /ˈhæŋʌp/ *n sl* something which a person gets unusually worried about, finds very difficult, etc.: *One of her hangups is that she's afraid to be on a railway station alone*

hang up *v adv* **1** [T1] to put (something) on a hook **2** [IØ] to finish a telephone conversation by putting the RECEIVER (2) back: *I was so angry I hung up on her* (=while she was talking) **3** [T1 *often pass.*] to delay: *The peace talks were hung up while the representatives spoke to their governments* **4** [T1] *AustrE* to tie (a horse) to a post; TETHER: *Hang up your horse and come in for a drink* **5 be hung up on/about** *sl* to be anxious or have a fixed idea about

hank /hæŋk/ *n* a length or loose ring of hair, wool, etc.

han·ker af·ter /ˈhæŋkəʳ/ *also* **hanker for**— *v prep* [T1] *infml* to have a strong wish for (usu. something one cannot have); LONG[1] for: *He's lonely and hankers for friendship*

han·ker·ing /ˈhæŋkərɪŋ/ *n* [(*for, after*)] *infml* a strong wish; LONGING: *a hankering after fame and wealth*

han·kie, -ky /ˈhæŋki/ *n infml* a handkerchief

hank·y-pank·y /ˌhæŋki ˈpæŋki/ *n* [U] deceit or improper behaviour of a not very serious kind

Han·sard /ˈhænsɑːd‖-sərd/ *n* [R] the printed report of what is said and done in the British Parliament

han·som /ˈhænsəm/ also **hansom cab** /ˈ·· ·, ˌ·· ˈ·/— *n* a 2-wheeled horse-drawn carriage used until early in the 20th century

hap[1] /hæp/ *n* [U] *old use* luck; chance

hap·haz·ard /ˌhæpˈhæzəd◂‖-ərd/ *adj* happening in an unplanned disorderly manner: *It's a haphazard timetable. Sometimes lessons happen, sometimes they don't* —**~ly** *adv*

hap·less /ˈhæpləs/ *adj poet* unlucky: *a hapless fate*

hap·ly /ˈhæpli/ *adv old use* perhaps

hap'orth /ˈheɪpəθ‖-ərθ/ *n* [S (*of*)] **1** *contr. of* HALFPENNYWORTH **2** a small amount: *You don't give me a hap'orth of help*

hap·pen[1] /ˈhæpən/ *v* **1** [IØ] to take place: *A funny thing happened* **2** [Wv6;I3] to have the good or bad luck (to): *He happens to be my friend, so don't say nasty things about him.|I happened to see him yesterday* **3** [Wv6; *it*+I5] to be true by or as if by chance (note the phrs **as it happens/happened**): *It (so) happened that I saw him yesterday* (=I saw him yesterday, as it happens)

USAGE People or things **become** something, in the meaning of passing from one state to another: *Mervyn* **became** *an engineer* (not * **became** *engineer*).|*The horse* **became/got** *thirsty.*|*This idea is* **becoming/getting** *fashionable.* Events **happen** (usually by accident) or *take* **place** (usually by arrangement): *When did the explosion* **happen**?|*When will the wedding take* **place**?

happen[2] *adv NEngE* perhaps

hap·pen·ing /ˈhæpənɪŋ/ *n* **1** something which happens; event **2** *esp. AmE* an unprepared performance or other event which catches attention

happen on also **happen upon, chance (up)on**— *v prep* [T1] *no pass.* to find or meet by chance: *I happened on an old country inn, and stopped to have a meal*

happen to *v prep* [T1] (of an event) to take place and have an effect on: *A bad accident happened to that family*

hap·pi·ly /ˈhæpɪ̣li/ *adv* **1** in a happy manner: *laughing happily* **2** fortunately: *Happily, the accident was prevented*

hap·pi·ness /ˈhæpinɪ̣s/ *n* [U] the state of being happy

hap·py /ˈhæpi/ *adj* **1** [Wa1;B] **a** (of people) feeling pleasure and contentment **b** (of relationships) giving pleasure to the people concerned **2** [Wa1;A] (of events) fortunate **3** [Wa1;B] (of behaviour, thoughts, etc.) suitable: *That was not a very happy remark* **4** [Wa5;F3,5a] *polite* pleased; not finding it difficult (to): *I'll be happy to meet him when I have free time* **5** [Wa5;A] (of wishes) joyful (esp. in phrs. like **Happy New Year**, **Happy Birthday**)

happy e·vent /ˌ·· ·ˈ·/ *n euph* the birth of a child

happy-go-luck·y /ˌ·· · ˈ··◂/ *adj usu. not derog* (of people or their acts) showing a lack of careful thought or planning; careless

happy me·di·um /ˌ·· ˈ···/ *n usu. sing.* the middle way of doing (something) when opposite ways are suggested: *I don't like to work all the time, but I wouldn't like to do nothing—I like the happy medium of working hard during the week, and enjoying myself at weekends*

har·a-ki·ri /ˌhærə ˈkɪri/ *n* [U] a Japanese way of ceremoniously killing oneself by cutting open the stomach

ha·rangue[1] /həˈræŋ/ *n* a loud or long speech, esp. one which blames those listening to it

harangue[2] *v* [T1] to attack or try to persuade with a long often loud and scolding speech

har·ass /ˈhærəs‖həˈræs, ˈhærəs/ *v* [Wv5;T1] **1** to make (somebody) worried by causing trouble, esp. on repeated occasions: (fig.) *I felt harassed by all the work at the office* **2** to make repeated attacks against: *They harassed the enemy*

har·ass·ment /ˈhærəsmənt‖həˈræs-, ˈhærəs-/ *n* [U] the act or state of being HARASSed

har·bin·ger /ˈhɑːbɪndʒəʳ‖ˈhɑr-/ *n* [(*of*)] *lit* a person or thing which lets one know that something is to happen or is on its way

har·bour[1], *AmE* **-bor** /ˈhɑːbəʳ‖ˈhɑr-/ *n* [C;U] **1** an area of water which is sheltered from rougher waters such as those of the sea, so that ships are safe inside it **2** a safe place; HAVEN

harbour[2], *AmE* **-bor** *v* [T1] **1** to give protection to, esp. by giving food and shelter to, (something/someone bad) either on purpose or without knowing: *Harbouring criminals is an offence in law* **2** to keep in the mind (thoughts or feelings): *He harbours a secret wish to be a painter* —**~er** *n*

hard[1] /hɑːd‖hɑrd/ *adj* [Wa1] **1** [B] firm and stiff; which cannot easily be broken, or pressed down, or bent, etc.: *The snow has frozen hard.|The ice is as hard as rock* —opposite **soft** **2** [B,B3] difficult (to do or understand): *There were some hard questions on the examination paper.|It's hard to know what he's really thinking* —opposite **easy** **3** [B] **a** forceful: *a hard push* **b** needing or using force of body or mind: *hard work* **4** [A] (esp. before a noun meaning a person and ending in *-er*) who puts great effort into the stated activity: *A hard worker works* HARD[2] (1).|*A hard fighter fights* HARD[2] (1).|*A hard drinker drinks* HARD[2] (2) **5** [B] full of difficulty and trouble: *a hard life|He gave me a* *hard time* (=hurt me in body or mind, as in having teeth pulled out, or being questioned closely) **6** [B (*on*)] (of people, punishments, etc.) not gentle (to); showing no kindness (to): *You're a hard woman.|She was very hard on me* (=unkind to me) **7** [B] very cold; very bad (of seasons and events in relation to weather) **8** [Wa5;B] (in English pronunciation): **a** (of the letter *c*) pronounced as k rather than s **b** (of the letter *g*) pronounced as /g/ rather than /dʒ/: *The letter "g" is hard in "get" and* SOFT *in "gentle"* **9** [B] (of water) which contains lime preventing soap from mixing properly with the water —opposite **soft** **10** [Wa5;A;(B)] (of a drug) being one on which a user can become dependent in such a way that he is ill when he does not take it —opposite **soft** **11** [A] based on or looking for facts; firm: *This difficulty demands a lot of hard thinking* **12** [B] unpleasant to the senses, esp. because too bright or too loud: *Her hard voice could be heard across the room* **13 be hard on** to wear (something) out easily or quickly: *Children are very hard on their shoes* **14 do (something) the hard way** to learn by experience, not by teaching; act alone and with difficulty **15 drive a hard bargain** to be firm in making an agreement most profitable to oneself **16 play hard to get** to pretend lack of interest in something/someone so that the person concerned will persuade one: *She refused to go to the cinema with him at first but she was only playing hard to get* **17 take (some/a few) hard knocks** to have difficulties **18 take a hard look (at)** to examine in order to make improvements (to some old thing, plan, etc.) —see also HARD UP; —see HARDEN (USAGE)

hard² *adv* **1** in a HARD¹ (4) way; with great effort: *Look hard at this picture.|Think hard and work hard* **2** strongly; heavily; in large amounts over a period of time: *It's raining harder than ever* **3 be hard hit (by)** to suffer loss because of (some event): *He was hard hit when prices went up, because he had no hope of a wage rise* **4 be hard done by** to be unfairly treated: *I was very hard done by in receiving less money than anybody else, after I had worked twice as hard* **5 be hard put (to it) to (do something)** to have great difficulty (in doing something) **6 (it) come(s) hard to** to be (an action) difficult to do: *It comes hard to live on a small amount of money when you've been rich* **7 die hard** (of habits) to be lost with difficulty: *Old habits die hard* —compare DIEHARD **8 (it) go(es) hard with** to be (an experience) difficult to accept: *It goes hard with him to be alone so often* **9 hard at it** working with all one's force in some activity **10 hard on (someone's) heels** close behind (someone); about to catch (someone) **11 take (it) hard** to suffer deeply: *She failed her examination, and she's taking it very hard* —see also HARD UPON

hard-and-fast /ˌ· · ˈ·◂/ *adj* [A] (of rules) fixed and unchangeable

hard·back /ˈhɑːdbæk‖ˈhɑrd-/ *n* a book with a strong stiff cover (BINDING) —compare PAPERBACK

hard-bit·ten /ˌ· ˈ··◂/ *adj* (of a person) very firm in argument and decision, esp. when made so by hard experience

hard·board /ˈhɑːdbɔːd‖ˈhɑrdbɔrd/ *n* [U] a sort of heavy thick strong cardboard made out of fine pieces of wood pressed into sheets and used in work where a light wood is needed

hard-boiled /ˌ· ˈ·◂/ *adj* **1** (of eggs) boiled until the yellow part is hard **2** (of people) not showing feeling, esp. when made bitter through long experience

hard·bound /ˈhɑːdbaʊnd‖ˈhɑrd-/ also **hard·cov·er** /-ˌkʌvəʳ/— *adj* [Wa5] (of books) having a firm stiff cover (BINDING)

hard by /ˌ· ˈ·/ *adj, adv* [Wa5;F] very near (to)

hard cash /ˌ· ˈ·/ *n* [U] CASH; READY MONEY: *We wanted to give him a cheque, but he demanded hard cash*

hard-core /ˌ· ˈ·◂/ *adj* [Wa5;A] *often derog* which refuses to change, yield, or improve: *hard-core opposition to the government's prices and incomes plan*

hard core /ˌ· ˈ·/ *n* **1** [U] the broken brick, stone, etc., used as a base when a road is built **2** [(*the*) GU] *often derog* the people most concerned at the centre of an activity, esp. when opposed to some other group

hard court /ˌ· ˈ·◂/ *n* a place where tennis is played, with a hard surface, not a grass one —**hard-court** *adj* [Wa5;A]

hard cur·ren·cy /ˌ· ˈ···/ *n* [U] a CURRENCY which other countries want to obtain

hard drink /ˌ· ˈ·/ also **hard liquor**— *n* [U] strong drink which contains a lot of alcohol, such as WHISKY

hard drink·er /ˌ· ˈ··/ also **heavy drinker**— *n* a person who takes strong drink, or a lot of the less alcoholic drinks such as beer

hard·en /ˈhɑːdn‖ˈhɑrdn/ *v* [T1;I∅] **1** to (cause to) become hard or firm: *The snow hardened until ice was formed* **2** (of holding movements) to (cause to) become hard or forceful: *He hardened his hold on the door* **3** to (cause to) become hard or unkind: *I hardened my heart* (=my kind feelings) *against him* **4** [*often pass.*] **a** (of water) to become HARD¹ (8): *Water hardens when lime gets into it* **b** to cause (water) to become hard: *Water is hardened by lime* **5** to (cause to) become HARD¹: *Life in the mountains hardened me until I felt no fear or weakness in mind or body.|Her mind hardened as she became used to difficulty and she became impatient of weaker people*

USAGE It is best to use *to get* **harder** about **hard** (2,4,6,12) or *to become* **hard** when the subject was certainly not at all **hard** at first. *Get* **harder** is also used for **harden** (1,3).

harden to *v prep* [D1;V4b] *usu. pass.* to make (someone) less sensitive to (something or doing something): *Dennis is becoming hardened to failure/failing*

hard feel·ings /ˌ· ˈ··/ *n* [P *usu. nonassertive*] angry memories felt for someone with whom one has quarrelled (usu. in the phr. **no hard feelings**): *No hard feelings?* (=Please don't dislike me for what I did, even though it caused you difficulty)

hard·head·ed /ˌhɑːdˈhedɪ̈d◂‖ˌhɑrd-/ *adj* practical and thorough, esp. in business

hard-heart·ed /ˌ· ˈ··◂/ *adj* [Wa2] having no kind feelings; HARD¹ (6) —**~ly** *adv* —**~ness** *n* [U]

har·di·hood /ˈhɑːdihʊd‖ˈhɑr-/ *n* [U] boldness

har·di·ness /ˈhɑːdinɪ̈s‖ˈhɑr-/ *n* [U] see HARDY

hard la·bour /ˌ· ˈ··/ *n* [U] (a punishment which consists of) hard bodily work such as digging or building

hard line /ˌ· ˈ·◂/ *n* a fixed point of view which someone keeps to in an argument or agreement (only in the phr. **take a hard line**) —**hard-line** *adj* —**hard-liner** /ˌ· ˈ··, ˈ· ˌ··/ *n*

hard luck /ˌ· ˈ·◂/ also **tough luck**, *BrE* also **hard lines**— *interj, n* [U] (sorry about your) bad luck: *You failed your examination? Hard luck!*

hard luck sto·ry /ˌ· ˈ· ˌ··, ˌ· · ˈ··/ *n infml* a speech made, usu. to a friend, which is meant to show how unlucky one has been and to encourage him to help, be sorry for one, or give one money

hard·ly /ˈhɑːdli‖ˈhɑrdli/ *adv* **1** almost not; with difficulty (in the phr. **(He) can hardly (speak, move, etc.)**): *I could hardly wait to hear the news.|I could hardly speak for tears* **2** only just; not really:

I hardly know the people I work with.|I've hardly finished, so I can't come out **3** not at all; not reasonably: *I can hardly ask him directly for more money.|This is hardly the time for buying new clothes—I've only got just enough money for food.| You can hardly blame me if you didn't like the place, as you were the one who begged me to take you there* **4** almost not: *I hardly ever go out these days* (=almost never).|*You've hardly eaten anything.| You've eaten hardly anything* (=almost nothing).| *Hardly anybody likes him* (=almost nobody) **5** only just (only in the phrs. **Hardly had** (he) . . ., (He) **had hardly** . . .): *Hardly had we arrived when she started crying to go home* (=as soon as we . . . she).|*We'd hardly arrived before we had to go back*

USAGE 1 **Hardly**, **scarcely**, and **barely** are correctly followed by *when* in sentences like these: *I had* **barely** *come in when the telephone rang.*|**Hardly** *had he arrived when she started complaining.* The use of *than* instead of *when* in such sentences is considered to be bad English, but it can be used after *no* **sooner**: *No* **sooner** *had he arrived than she started complaining.* 2 **Hardly** and **scarcely** (but not **barely** or *no* **sooner**) can be followed by *any, ever,* and *at all,* to mean "almost no", "almost never", and "almost not": **hardly/scarcely** *any money|I* **hardly/ scarcely** *ever see her.|I'm* **hardly/scarcely** *at all interested.*

hard·ness /ˈhɑːdnɪ̵s‖ˈhɑrd-/ *n* [U] the state of being HARD

hard-nosed /ˌ· ˈ·◂/ *adj infml* HARD-BITTEN; HARD-HEADED

hard nut /ˌ· ˈ·/ *n not fml* a difficult thing/person to deal with (usu. in the phr. **a hard nut to crack**)

hard of hear·ing /ˌ· · ˈ··/ *adj* **harder of hearing** [F] *euph* unable to hear properly; (rather) DEAF: *Can science help the hard of hearing to hear better?*

hard pal·ate /ˌ· ˈ··/ *n* the front part of the PALATE (1) —opposite **soft palate**

hard sell /ˌ· ˈ·◂/ *n* [(*the*) U] the method of selling by putting repeated forceful pressure on buyers; HIGH PRESSURE: *training in making the hard sell| hard-sell methods* —opposite **soft sell**

hard·ship /ˈhɑːdʃɪp‖ˈhɑrd-/ *n* [U;C] (an example of) difficult conditions of life, such as lack of money, hard work, etc.

hard shoul·der /ˌ· ˈ··/ *n* an area of ground that has been given a hard surface, beside a road, esp. a MOTORWAY, where cars may stop if in difficulty, because stopping is not allowed on the road itself —see picture at INTERCHANGE[2]

hard tack /ˈ· ·/ *n* [U] SHIP BISCUIT

hard·top /ˈhɑːdtɒp‖ˈhɑrdtɑp/ *n* a type of car with a metal roof which cannot be moved

hard up /ˌ· ˈ·◂/ *adj* [F (*for*)] in need (of); not having enough esp. money: *We were very hard up when I lost my job.|I'm hard up for clothes, but I've got lots of books*

hard up·on /ˈ· ·ˌ·/ also **hard on** /ˈ· ·/— *prep* **1** soon after **2** close behind

hard·ware /ˈhɑːdweəʳ‖ˈhɑrd-/ *n* [U] **1** goods for the home and garden, such as pans, tools, etc. —compare IRONMONGERY **2** machinery used in war **3** machinery which makes up a COMPUTER —compare SOFTWARE

hard·wear·ing /ˌhɑːdˈweərɪŋ◂‖ˌhɑrd-/ *AmE* **long-wearing**— *adj BrE* (esp. of clothes, shoes, etc.) that can be used for a long time without wearing out

hard·wood /ˈhɑːdwʊd‖ˈhɑrd-/ *n* **1** [U] strong heavy wood from trees like the OAK, used to make good furniture —opposite **softwood** **2** [C] a tree that has wood of this type

har·dy /ˈhɑːdi‖ˈhɑrdi/ *adj* [Wa1] **1** (of people or animals) strong; able to bear cold, hard work, etc. **2** *tech* (of plants) able to live through the winter above ground —**hardiness** *n* [U]

hare[1] /heəʳ/ *n* **1** [Wn1] an animal with long ears, the upper lip divided into 2 parts, a short tail and long back legs which make it able to run fast. It is usu. larger than a rabbit, and does not live in a hole **2** the person chased in the game PAPERCHASE **3 run with the hare and hunt with the hounds** to support or favour both sides in an argument; not disagree with either of 2 opposed groups **4 mad as a March hare** very wild and excitable in behaviour, like a hare in the spring **5 start a hare a** to make a hare run out of hiding so that it may be hunted **b** to bring in an idea which leads away from the main argument

hare[2], **hair** *v* [L9, esp. OFF, AWAY] *infml, esp. BrE* to run very fast: *He hared off down the road*

hare and hounds /ˌ· · ˈ·/ *n* [U] *now rare* PAPER CHASE

hare·bell /ˈheəbel‖ˈheər-/ *n* a wild plant in the form of one bell-shaped blue flower on top of a thin stem; the BLUEBELL of Scotland

hare·brained /ˈheəbreɪnd‖ˈheər-/ *adj* (of people or plans) very impractical; quite foolish

hare·lip /ˌheəˈlɪp‖ˌheər-/ *n* [U;C] (the condition of having) the top lip divided into 2 parts, because of its not developing properly before birth —**-lipped** /ˌheəˈlɪpt◂‖ˌheər-/ *adj*

har·em /ˈheərəm, hɑːˈriːm‖ˈhærəm/ *n* [GC] **1** the place in a Muslim house where the women live **2** the women who live in this

har·i·cot /ˈhærɪkəʊ/ also **haricot bean** /ˌ··· ˈ·/— *n* any of several types of small white bean

hark /hɑːk‖hɑrk/ *v* [I∅] *lit* to listen: *Hark! I can hear their voices*

hark at *v prep* [T1;V4b *imper.*] *infml esp. BrE* to listen to (someone or something that is disapproved of): *Hark at him then! Who does he think he is anyhow?*

hark back *v adv* [I∅ (*to*)] *infml* to mention or think over things which happened in the past: *You're always harking back to how things were when you were young*

har·le·quin /ˈhɑːlɪ̵kwɪ̵n‖ˈhɑr-/ *n* [C;R] (the name of) a character on the stage who wears a special type of bright clothes and plays tricks

har·le·quin·ade /ˌhɑːlɪ̵kwɪ̵ˈneɪd‖ˌhɑr-/ *n* a scene on stage in a PANTOMIME (2) in which HARLEQUIN takes part

Har·ley Street /ˈhɑːli striːt‖ˈhɑr-/ *n* [R] **1** (a street which gives its name to) an area of London where important private doctors work **2** the doctors who work in this area

har·lot /ˈhɑːlət‖ˈhɑr-/ *n* [C; *you*+N] **1** *old use* a PROSTITUTE; woman who has sex for money **2** *derog* a woman thought to behave like a PROSTITUTE —**~ry** *n* [U]

harm[1] /hɑːm‖hɑrm/ *n* [U] **1** damage; wrong (esp. in the phr. **do/be/mean no harm**): *You made a mistake, but no harm done* (=nothing's spoilt, nobody's hurt by it).|*He means no harm* (=doesn't intend to do anything hurtful) *by saying what he thinks, but people don't like it* **2 do somebody harm** to hurt them in mind or body: *I've got up early all my life, and it hasn't done me any harm.| It wouldn't do him any harm to have to work harder* (=it would be good for him) **3 out of harm's way** out of danger; safe from danger **4 come to harm/(of harm) come to someone** *usu. neg.* to be hurt/to hurt someone: *My brother's ship was caught in a storm but he came to no harm/no harm came to him* —**~ful** *adj* —**~fully** *adv* —**~fulness** *n* [U]

harm[2] *v* [T1] **1** to hurt; spoil; damage: *There was a fire in our street, but our house wasn't harmed at all.| Getting up early won't harm you!* **2 (he) wouldn't**

harm a fly (he's) very gentle by nature
harm·less /'hɑːmləs‖'hɑrm-/ *adj* that cannot cause harm: *The dog seems fierce, but he's harmless.|It was a harmless question but she took it as rudeness* —**~ly** *adv* —**~ness** *n* [U]
har·mon·ic /hɑː'mɒnɪk‖hɑr'mɑ-/ *n tech* any of a set of higher notes produced when a musical note is played; OVERTONE (1)
har·mon·i·ca /hɑː'mɒnɪkə‖hɑr'mɑ-/ *n fml or tech* MOUTHORGAN
har·mo·ni·um /hɑː'məʊnɪəm‖hɑr-/ *n* a musical instrument played like a piano but working by pumped air (as in an ORGAN (4)) —see picture at KEYBOARD[1]
har·mo·nize, -ise /'hɑːmənaɪz‖'hɑr-/ *v* **1** [T1;IØ] to add another set of notes to (something which is played or sung), either in writing music or while performing: *The singers began to harmonize the new song* **2** [T1 (*with*)] to bring into agreement with another or each other: *The two plans must be harmonized, though they seem so different* **3** [IØ (*with*)] to be in agreement, esp. in style, colour, etc., with each other or something else: *The colours don't seem to harmonize at all*
har·mo·ny /'hɑːməni‖'hɑr-/ *n* **1** [U;(C)] notes of music combined together in a pleasant sounding way —compare DISCORD **2** [U;(S)] a state of agreement (in feelings, ideas, etc.); peacefulness (esp. in the phrs. **in/out of harmony (with)**): *My cat and dog never fight—they live together in perfect harmony* —compare DISCORD **3** [U;(C)] the pleasant effect made by parts being combined into a whole: *The harmony of sea and sky make a beautiful picture* —compare CONTRAST —**-nious** /hɑː'məʊnɪəs‖hɑr-/ *adj* —**-niously** *adv* —**-niousness** *n* [U]
har·ness[1] /'hɑːnǝ̥s‖'hɑr-/ *n* [U;C *usu. sing.*] **1** the leather bands held together by metal which are used to control a horse or fasten it to a cart **2** something of this type, such as an apparatus fastened round a baby's body to support it **3 (die) in harness** (to die when) working **4 run/work in double harness** to work/live with a partner, esp. one's husband or wife, or one's business partner
harness[2] *v* [T1] **1** [(*to*)] to put a HARNESS[1] (1) on (esp. a horse) and/or fasten to a vehicle such as a cart **2** to use (a natural force) to produce useful power
harp /hɑːp‖hɑrp/ *n* a large musical instrument with strings running from top to bottom of an open 3-cornered frame, played by stroking (STROKE) or PLUCKing[1] (4) the strings with the hands —see picture at STRINGED INSTRUMENT —**~ist** *n*
harp on *v prep; adv* **1** [T1] also **harp on about**— to talk a lot about the sorrow(s) of: *My grandfather still harps on (about) the death of his youngest son* **2** [IØ] to talk a lot: *Don't keep harping on like that*
har·poon[1] /hɑː'puːn‖hɑr-/ *n* a spear with a long rope, which is used for hunting large sea animals, esp. WHALE*s*
harpoon[2] *v* [T1] to catch (a sea animal) with a HARPOON
harp·si·chord /'hɑːpsɪkɔːd‖'hɑrpsɪkɔrd/ *n* a musical instrument, used esp. formerly, like a piano except that the strings are PLUCKed rather than struck —see picture at KEYBOARD[1]
har·py /'hɑːpi‖'hɑrpi/ *n* **1** [C] a creature in old stories, half woman, half bird, very cruel and GREEDY **2** [C; *you*+N] a cruel GREEDY person
har·que·bus /'hɑːkwɪbəs‖'hɑr-/ *n esp. AmE* ARQUEBUS
har·ri·dan /'hærɪdn/ *n* [C; *you*+N] a bad-tempered, unpleasant woman; HAG
har·ri·er /'hærɪə[r]/ *n* **1** a kind of dog used for hunting HARE*s* **2** a CROSS-COUNTRY runner
Har·ris Tweed /ˌhærǝ̥s 'twiːd◂/ *n* [U] *tdmk* a type of woollen cloth woven by hand on Harris, an island off Western Scotland
har·row[1] /'hærəʊ/ *n* a farming machine with sharp metal teeth on a frame, used to break up the surface of the earth after PLOUGHing
harrow[2] *v* [T1;IØ] to draw a HARROW over (the ground)
har·row·ing /'hærəʊɪŋ/ *adj* which causes feelings of pain and worry: *To see someone killed is very harrowing|a very harrowing experience*
har·ry /'hæri/ *v* [T1] **1** to attack repeatedly: *The soldiers harried the enemy out of the country* **2** [(*for*)] to trouble continually: *We have to harry him for money, or he would never pay*
harsh /hɑːʃ‖hɑrʃ/ *adj* [Wa1] **1** unpleasant in causing pain to the senses: *a harsh light* (=too strong for the eyes)|*harsh colours|a harsh voice|This cloth is harsh to the touch* (=rough) **2** (of people, punishments, etc.) which show cruelty or lack of kindness —**~ly** *adv* —**~ness** *n* [U]
hart /hɑːt‖hɑrt/ *n esp. BrE* a full-grown male deer, esp. RED DEER, over 5 years old; STAG —compare HIND
har·tal /'hɑːtɑːl‖'hɑr-/ *n esp. Ind & PakE* a closing of shops and stopping of work (originally in India), usu. as a sign of political dissatisfaction
har·te·beest /'hɑːtǝ̥biːst‖'hɑr-/ *n* a type of large deer-like animal (ANTELOPE) of South Africa
har·um-scar·um /ˌheərəm 'skeərəm/ *adj, adv* (acting) wildly and thoughtlessly
har·vest[1] /'hɑːvǝ̥st‖'hɑr-/ *n* **1** [C;(U)] **a** the act of gathering the crops: *We all helped with the harvest* **b** the time of year when crops are picked: *The weather changed at (the) harvest* **c** the (amount of) crops gathered: *a good harvest|a large harvest* **2** [S] the results of work done (esp. in the phr. **reap the harvest of** =HARVEST[2] (2)): *All my letter writing produced a harvest of interested buyers*
harvest[2] *v* [T1] **1** to gather (a crop) —compare REAP **2** to get (the results of work or action)
har·vest·er /'hɑːvǝ̥stə[r]‖'hɑr-/ *n* **1** a person who gathers the crops **2** a machine which cuts grain and gathers it in
harvest fes·ti·val /ˌ·· '···/ *n esp. BrE* a church service where thanks is given for the crops which have been gathered —compare THANKSGIVING
harvest home /ˌ·· '·/ *n* [U;(C)] *esp. BrE* a ceremonial feast given to the workers after all the crops have been gathered
harvest moon /ˌ·· '·/ *n* the full moon in autumn
has /s, z, əz, həz; *strong* hæz/ *3rd pers. sing. pres. t. of* HAVE
has-been /'· ·/ *n* [C; *you*+N] *infml* a person or thing no longer important, useful, etc.
hash[1] /hæʃ/ *v* [T1] to cut (meat) up small
hash[2] *n* **1** [U;C] a type of meal containing meat cut up in small pieces, esp. when re-cooked **2** [S] a mixed-up affair; MESS or MUDDLE (esp. in the phr. **make a hash of it**) **3** [C] old material in a new form; REHASH **4** [U] *sl* HASHISH **5 settle (someone's) hash** *sl* to stop (someone who is causing trouble)
hash·ish /'hæʃiːʃ, -ɪʃ/ also (*sl*) **hash**— *n* [U] the most powerful form of CANNABIS (2). It is the hardened juice (RESIN) from the plant
hash out *v adv* [T1a,6a,b] *infml* to talk about or settle (a difficulty): *We must hash out the question of Mr. Brown's appointment*
hash up *v adv* [T1] *infml* MESS UP
has·n't /'hæzənt/ *v contr. of* has not —see CONTR. (USAGE)
hasp /hæsp/ *n* a metal fastener for a box, door, etc., which usu. fits over a hook and is kept in place by a PADLOCK

has·sle¹ /ˈhæsəl/ *n infml esp. AmE* **1** a difficult argument **2** a struggle of mind or body: *It's a real hassle to get this child to eat*

hassle² *v* [Wv3;I∅ (*with*)] *infml esp. AmE* to argue

has·sock /ˈhæsək/ *n* **1** a small CUSHION for kneeling on in church **2** TUSSOCK

hast /hæst/ [Wv2] **thou hast** *old use or bibl* (when talking to one person) you have

haste /heɪst/ *n* [U] **1** quick movement or action: *Make haste!* (=hurry!) **2** too quick action, which may have bad results: *More haste, less speed*

has·ten /ˈheɪsən/ *v* **1** [T1;L9] to (cause to) move or happen faster: *He hastened his steps.|He hastened home* **2** [I3] to be quick (to say), because the hearer may imagine something else has happened: *I hasten to tell you that your son is not badly hurt, although it was a serious accident*

hast·y /ˈheɪsti/ *adj* [Wa1] **1** done in a hurry: *made a hasty meal|ate a hasty meal* **2** (of people or their acts) too quick in acting or deciding, esp. with a bad result: *She's too hasty—if she would only think before speaking she wouldn't have so much trouble.|a hasty temper* —**-ily** *adv* —**-iness** *n* [U]

hat /hæt/ *n* **1** a covering placed on top of the head —compare CAP, BONNET **2 old hat** /ˌ· ˈ·/ old fashioned **3 at the drop of a hat** suddenly **4 a bad hat** *sl* a bad person **5 hang up one's hat** to stop doing a habitual activity, esp. one's work: *At the age of 60, he hung up his hat (for the last time)* **6 hat in hand** —see CAP¹ (8) **7 I'll eat my hat if** (an expression of disbelief): *I'll eat my hat if England wins tomorrow!* **8 keep (something) under one's hat** to keep (something) secret **9 my hat!** I don't believe (that): *Poor, my hat!—He's got more money than either of us* **10 pass the hat round** to collect money, esp. to give to someone who deserves it **11 take one's hat off to (someone)** to show that one admires (someone) for an action: *I take my hat off to him for the way he arranged the party* **12 talking through one's hat** *infml* saying something stupid

hat·band /ˈhætbænd/ *n* a band of cloth running round a hat

hatch¹ /hætʃ/ *n* **1** (on a ship or aircraft) **a** also **hatchway**— an opening through which people and things can pass **b** the cover used to close this —see picture at AIRCRAFT **2** an opening in a wall, esp. so that food can be passed from a kitchen to the room where people eat **3** a door which comes half-way up an opening **4 under hatches a** (on a ship) resting below DECK **b** imprisoned **5 Down the hatch!** *infml* (a phrase used before swallowing a drink)

hatch² *v* **1** [I∅;T1:(OUT)] **a** (of an egg) to break, letting the young bird out: *3 eggs have already hatched (out)* **b** to cause (an egg) to break in this way: *We hatch the eggs we find by keeping them in a warm place* **2** [I∅;T1:(OUT)] **a** (of a young bird) to break through an egg: *3 chickens have hatched (out)* **b** to cause (a young bird) to break through an egg: *She has hatched all her chickens* **3** [T1 (UP)] to make up (a plan or idea): *What is he hatching up?*

hatch·back /ˈhætʃbæk/ *n* a car having a door at the back which opens upwards —see picture at INTERCHANGE²

hatch·er·y /ˈhætʃəri/ *n* a place for HATCHing fish eggs

hatch·et /ˈhætʃɪ̈t/ *n* **1** a small axe with a short handle —see picture at TOOL¹ **2 bury the hatchet** *infml* to become friends again after a bad quarrel

hatchet man /ˈ·· ·/ *n esp. AmE* a person who is violent towards another, in word or deed, esp. when paid to destroy that person by murder, or to make his importance less by writing unpleasant things about him

hatch·ing /ˈhætʃɪŋ/ *n* [U] fine lines drawn on or cut into a surface —see CROSS-HATCHING

hatch·way /ˈhætʃweɪ/ *n* HATCH

hate¹ /heɪt/ *n* [U] **1** a strong feeling of dislike: *She looked at me with hate in her eyes* **2 (someone's) pet hate** *infml* something (or someone) greatly disliked (by someone)

hate² *v* [Wv6] **1** [T1,3,4;V3,4] to have a great dislike of: *I hate such cruelty.|He hates his little sister, because she breaks all his toys* **2** [T1,3,4;V3,4] *infml* to dislike: *She hates fish and never eats any.|He hates people asking him for money* **3** [T3,4] *infml* to be sorry: *I hate (having) to tell you, but I've damaged your car* —see LIKE (USAGE)

hate·ful /ˈheɪtfəl/ *adj* very unpleasant to experience: *You're always hateful to me, and nice to everybody else!* —**~ly** *adv* —**~ness** *n* [U]

hath /hæθ/ [Wv2] *old use or bibl* has

hat·less /ˈhætləs/ *adj* [Wa5] not wearing a hat, esp. when one should, as on a formal occasion, or in bad weather

hat·pin /ˈhætˌpɪn/ *n* a long pin used, esp. formerly, to fasten a lady's hat to her hair, which she can also use to defend herself, as it is both sharp and strong

ha·tred /ˈheɪtrɪ̈d/ *n* [U;S:(*of, for*)] the state or feeling of hating; hate: *She is full of hatred for the driver who killed her child*

hat·ter /ˈhætəʳ/ *n* a maker and/or seller of hats (esp. in the phr. **as mad as a hatter** (=completely mad))

hat trick /ˈ· ·/ *n* 3 successes of the same type coming one after the other esp. in sports, as (in cricket) when 3 men have been BOWLed³ (6) OUT by the same person or (in football) when the same player has made 3 GOAL*s* in one game

hau·berk /ˈhɔːbɜːk‖-ɜrk/ *n* (in former times) a coat of armour made up of several metal rings (CHAIN MAIL)

haugh·ty /ˈhɔːti/ *adj* [Wa1] *fml derog* (of people or their acts) appearing proud; showing that other people are thought of less importance than oneself —**-tily** *adv* —**-tiness** *n* [U]

haul¹ /hɔːl/ *v* **1** [T1 (UP);I∅ (AWAY, *at, on*)] to pull hard: *to haul logs|to haul up the fishing nets|They hauled away on the ropes* **2** [X9] to turn a ship **3** [X9 (UP)] to force to appear (before an official body); SUMMONS²: *The police have hauled Peter (up) before the court on a charge of dangerous driving* —see also HAVE UP **4 haul over the coals** to scold for something done wrong

haul² *n* **1** [S] the act of HAULing **2** [S9] the distance HAULed: (fig.) *It was a long haul home, carrying our bags up the hill* **3** [C] **a** the amount of fish caught when fishing with a net **b** *infml* the amount of something gained, esp. stolen goods

haul·age /ˈhɔːlɪdʒ/ *n* [U] **1 a** the business of carrying goods by road **b** the charge for this **2** the act of HAULing

haul down *v adv* **haul down the flag/the colours** to yield; admit defeat

haul·i·er /ˈhɔːlɪəʳ/ *AmE* **haul·er** /ˈhɔːləʳ/— *n BrE* **1** a person who runs a HAULAGE business **2** a man who HAUL*s* coal from the place where it is cut to the place where it will be raised to the surface

haulm /hɔːm/ *n* [U] the stems of crops like PEA*s*, beans, potatoes, etc., left after gathering

haul off *v adv* [I∅] *AmE sl* to raise one's arm (before striking): *He hauled off and hit Peter on the jaw*

haunch /hɔːntʃ/ *n* **1** [*usu. pl.*] (in man) the fleshy part of the body between the waist and knee **2** the back leg of an animal, esp. as food

haunt¹ /hɔːnt/ *v* [T1] **1** [Wv6] to visit (a place) regularly **2** [Wv5; *often pass.*] (of a spirit) to visit, appearing in a strange form: *A headless man haunts the castle* **3** [Wv5,6; *usu. pass.*] to be always in the thoughts of (someone): *I was haunted by his last words to me.|a haunted look*

haunt² *n* [C9, esp. *of, often pl.*] a place to go regularly, esp. as visited by those mentioned: *The inn on the seashore is a haunt of sailors.|The playground is the children's favourite haunt*

haunt·ing /ˈhɔːntɪŋ/ *adj* which remains in the thoughts —**~ly** *adv*

haut·bois, -boy /ˈəʊbɔɪ, ˈhəʊbɔɪ/ *n* **-bois** /-bɔɪz/ *or* **-boys** *old use* OBOE

hau·teur /əʊˈtɜːʳ‖hɔːˈtɜr (*Fr* otœr)/ *n* [U] *Fr fml or lit* haughtiness (HAUGHTY)

Ha·van·a /həˈvænə/ *n* a CIGAR made in Cuba

have¹ /v, əv, həv; *strong* hæv/ *v* **had** /d, əd, həd; *strong* hæd/, *3rd pers. sing. pres. t.* **has** /s, z, əz, həz; *strong* hæz/, *pres. t. neg. contr.* **haven't** /ˈhævənt/, *3rd pers. sing. pres. t. neg. contr.* **hasn't** /ˈhæzənt/, *past t. neg. contr.* **hadn't** /ˈhædnt/ [Wv2;I∅,8] **1** **a** (the AUXILIARY verb used to form perfect forms): *I've been reading.|I've written 2 letters today.|He'd been to London earlier in the day.|He'll have finished by tomorrow.|It's silly not to have gone after having accepted the invitation.|No, I haven't.|Have you finished?|Why hasn't he?|He said he had been there before* **b Had (I, he, etc.)** *lit* if (I, he, etc.) had: *Had they searched more closely, they would have found what they wanted* **2 had better/best (do/not do)** ought (not) to; should (not): *I'd better tell him before he goes home.|You'd better behave yourself!|We'd better not go until your sister arrives* **3 have had it** *infml* **a** to have had or have done all one is going to be allowed to **b** to have experienced, worked, or suffered all one can: *I've had it! Let's stop and rest.|*(fig.) *Our old car has had it! Let's get a new one*

USAGE Do not say ***I have** *seen him yesterday/last night/in 1974*. Say *I saw him yesterday/last night/in 1974*. But one may say: **having** *seen him yesterday|to* **have** *seen him last night|You should* **have** *seen him in 1974*

have² also **have got**— *v* [Wv6;(I∅);T1 *no pass.*] **1** **a** to possess; own: *Have you got a pencil?* **b** to own as a quality: *I haven't a very good temper, I'm afraid.|She hasn't got blue eyes* **c** to contain as a part of: *This coat has no pockets* (=There are no pockets in this coat) **2** **a** to experience or be experiencing: *I have bad colds every year.|I've got a bad cold now. Do you ever have colds?|You haven't got a cold now!* **b** to be supplied with: *I have free time every Saturday.|I've got time to come with you for an hour.|How often do you have free time?|Have you (got) any free time today?* **3** to keep or feel in the mind: *Have you any doubt about his guilt?|I've got no idea what to do. Do you?|Have you got any hope of finding it?* **4 have coming** also **have got coming**— to deserve (esp. something bad: *He had that defeat coming to him* **5 I have it!** also **I've got it!**— (an expression when one suddenly sees the right way to deal with something) **6 You have me there** also **You've got me there**— **a** That's a good point against me; I will have to rethink my argument, plan, etc., because of what you said **b** I don't know: *"Who won in 1928?" "I'm sorry: you have me there"*

USAGE 1 The opposite of *He* **has** *a beard* is *He* **has** *no beard* rather than ***He hasn't** *a beard*. Use **haven't/hasn't** only when another word comes between **have** and the noun: *I* **haven't** *(got) any money.|She* **hasn't** *got a chance.|I* **haven't** *(got) a very good temper.* 2 In *BrE*, **have²** is used of continuous states rather than of possession or experience at one particular moment, which is expressed by **have got**. Compare: (*esp. BrE*) "Have you got a cold now?" "Yes, I have." (*esp. AmE*) "Do you have a cold now?" "Yes, I do." (*BrE & AmE*) "Do you ever have colds?"

have³ *v* [no pass.] **1** [Wv6;T1] to gain; accept; receive; obtain (often in the phr. **There was none to be had**): *I had a letter today.|I had a win in a competition.|We gave it to him, but he wouldn't have it* **2** [Wv6;T1 *usu. imper.*] (a polite form, used esp. when displeased): *Have the kindness to answer me!* **3** [T1] to eat, drink, or smoke: *We were having breakfast.|He has 3 cigarettes each morning* **4** [X9] also **have over, have round**— to have invited as guests in the home: *We're having some people (over) tonight.|We have people here tonight* **5** [Wv6;X9] to (get to) know (esp. in the phrs. **have it from**): *He had it from John.|I have it for certain/from the horse's mouth* (=the person concerned) **6** [Wv6;T1] to say (only in the phr. **have it**): *He has it that the trains are running late.|He will have it that I was late* (=keeps saying, says loudly, etc., even if wrong).|RUMOUR *has it that the government will be defeated in Parliament tomorrow* **7** [Wv6;T1,4;V4] to permit; allow: *I only have good children in my house.|I won't have bad behaviour.|I can't have (you) running up and down all day long* **8** [T1,4;V4:*neg.*] (*in tenses with the -ing form*) to be willing to allow or permit: *I'm not having dancing in my hotel on Sundays!|I'm not having you running all over the place* **9** [Wv6;V2] *lit* (*with* will *or* would) to wish for: *Will/Would you have me go home alone?|I would have you know, sir, that the city has fallen to our army.|What would you have me say?* **10** [Wv6;T1] to keep as a pet: *I've always wanted to have a dog* **11** [T1] to give birth to: *His wife has just had a baby.|She's having a baby* **12** [Wv6;T1] *old use* to possess knowledge of: *She has a little French, but not much science* **13** [T1] *infml* (*often before* [S] *nouns with the same form as verbs*) to do (something); take: *to have a look* (=look once)|*to have a read* (=read a while)|*to have a swim/a walk/a run/a wash* —see USAGE **14** [V2,3,4] to cause (someone) to (do something): (*esp. AmE*) *I had John find me a house.|*(*esp. BrE*) *I had a man build me a house.|I had them all laughing at my jokes* **15** [V8] to cause (something) to be (done by someone) (in the phr. **have (something) done**): *to have a house built|to have one's hair cut* **16** [Wv6;X9;V8] to cause to be in the stated place or condition: *Can we have our ball back, please, sir?|I'll have your cat down from the tree in a minute, Mrs. Jones.|I had the work finished 2 days before it was needed.|Have the job done by tomorrow!* **17** [Wv6;V8] to experience (something) as having (happened): *I had my watch stolen last night* **18** [T1] to enjoy or experience, often as part of a group: *We're having a party/a meeting.|We/I had a good time* (note the fixed phrase: **a good time was had by all**) **19** [T1] also **have sex with**— to perform the act of sex with (esp. in the phr. **have a woman**) **20 have at you** *old use usu. imper.* to attack: *"Have at you!" shouted the swordsman, striking his opponent* **21 have something against someone** to dislike someone for a particular thing he or she did: *She speaks to me as if I had no right to be here—What can she have against me?* **22 have it in for (someone)** to be as unkind as possible to (someone) on purpose: *One of the teachers really has it in for that child—she shouts at him all the time* **23 have on/about one** to be carrying on one's person: *I have some money somewhere about me* **24 have done with it** to finish something and not deal with it again: *I'll do all the washing on one day, and have done with it* **25 have a down on** *BrE sl* to behave as if angry with (someone): *She seems to have a down on me: she never smiles at me* **26 have it in one (to do)** to have an unexpected (good) quality or ability: *Dear, I always knew you had it in you (to win)* **27 not having any** *infml* not accepting; not willing to listen, take an interest in, etc.: *She thinks I will go on helping her, but after the way she spoke to me, I'm not having any* **28 have it off/away with** *BrE sl* to have sex with —see also HAVE IN, HAVE OFF, HAVE ON[1,2], HAVE OUT, HAVE OVER, HAVE UP

USAGE 1 In def. 4 and def. 10 the *-ing* form can have only a future meaning. In all other cases it can be used either as a future or as a present. 2 Nouns like *a* **look**, *a* **swim**, which are formed from verbs (*to* **look**, *to* **swim**) are used with **have** or **take**; *to* **take** *a look|to* **have** *a swim*. These phrs. are less *fml* than *to* **look**, *to* **swim**.

have⁴ *v* **had** [I3] **1** also **have got**— to be forced to; must: *Do you have to go now?|Have you got to go now?|I've got to go.|I have to go.|I'll have to telephone later.|You don't have to/haven't got to do it if you don't want to* **2 have to do with** see DO WITH

USAGE 1 **Have got** is not used with *will* or the MODALs. Do not say ***I'll have got** *to telephone* or ***We may have got** *to go*. 2 When **have** and **to** come together, **have** is pronounced /hæf/: *I* **have to** /ˈhæf tə/ *go*. When **had** and **to** come together, **had** is pronounced /hæt/: *He* **had to** /ˈhæt tə/ *do it*.

have⁵ /hæv/ *n infml* a trick —see also HAVES

have in *v adv* [T1b *no pass.*] **1** [Wv6] also **have got in**— to keep a supply of (something): *Has she got enough sugar in?* **2** to call (someone) to the house to do some work: *We are having the builders in next week to improve the kitchen* **3** to invite to one's home: *We're having some friends in for coffee on Sunday evening*

ha·ven /ˈheɪvən/ *n* **1** a place of calm and safety: (fig.) *safe in the haven of his mother's arms* **2** *rare* HARBOUR (1) —see also TAX HAVEN

have-nots /ˌ· ˈ·/ *n* [(*the*) P] poor people, groups, etc. —opposite **haves**

have·n't /ˈhævənt/ [Wv2] *contr. of* have not —see CONTR. (USAGE)

have off *v adv* [T1b *no pass.*] **1** HIT OFF **2** [Wv6] also **have got off**— to have learnt, ready to speak from memory: *I have the whole poem off already* **3 have it off with** *BrE sl* see HAVE³ (28)

have on¹ *v adv* [*no pass.*] **1** [T1,5 (*in tenses with the -ing form*)] *AmE* **put on**, *BrE* also **have**— to trick (someone), usu. by pretending something not true; deceive: *He was having you on (that you were late), and you believed him.|I've been had!* —compare PUT ON¹ **2** [Wv6;T1] also **have got on**— to be wearing (something): *He had a beautiful new suit on.|We took a picture of the little boy by the sea, when he had nothing on except a hat* **3** [Wv6;T1] also **have got on**— to have (something) to do; have promised or arranged to do (something): *I don't have anything on tonight|I have nothing on (for) tonight*

have on² also **have got on**— *v prep* [Wv6;D1 *no pass.*] **1** to have (something) recorded against (someone): *You can't take me to the police station, you've got nothing on me* **2 have nothing on** *infml* to be not nearly as good as

have out *v* [T1b *no pass.*] **1** get something taken out, usu. a tooth or organ of the body: *He didn't want to have his teeth out, but he broke them and they couldn't be repaired* **2** [(*with*)] to settle a difficulty by talking freely or angrily (esp. in the phr. **have it out with (somebody)**): *Let's have the whole thing out.|I must have it out with him, and stop all this uncertainty about whether he's going to leave or not* **3** *BrE* to be allowed to finish: *Let Father have his sleep out, he's very tired*

have o·ver also **have got over**— *v prep* [Wv6;D1,5 *no pass.*] *not fml* to be better than: *He has it over me that he's been to Egypt and I haven't.|What's she got over me?* (=In what way is she better than me?)

ha·ver /ˈheɪvəʳ/ *v* [I∅] *ScotE* to talk foolishly

hav·er·sack /ˈhævəsæk‖-ər-/ *n now rare* a bag carried usu. over one shoulder when walking, esp. to hold necessary food and clothing —compare KNAPSACK, RUCKSACK

haves /hævz/ *n* [(*the*) P] rich people, groups, etc. —opposite **have-nots**

have up *v adv* [T1] to take to court: *He was had up for dangerous driving*

hav·oc /ˈhævək/ *n* [U] widespread damage or confusion (esp. in the phrs. **wreak havoc on, play havoc with, make havoc of**): *His arrival that night played havoc with* (=caused confused changes in) *my plans.|His ideas are causing havoc in the office*

haw¹ /hɔː/ *n* the red berry which is the fruit of a HAWTHORN tree

haw² *v* [I∅] see HUM³ **and haw**

haw³ *interj* (the sound made in a loud laugh)

hawk¹ /hɔːk/ *n* **1** any of many types of bird, often large, which catch other birds and small animals with their feet (CLAWs) for food, and are active during the day —see picture at PREY¹ **2** a person who believes in using force, or in increasing violence in war —opposite **dove** —**~ish** *adj* —**~ishness** *n* [U]

hawk² *v* [T1] **1** to sell (goods) on the street or at the doors of houses, esp. while moving from place to place **2** to spread around esp. by speech

hawk·er /ˈhɔːkəʳ/ *n* a person who sells goods from a light cart (BARROW) in the street

hawk-eyed /ˈ· ·/ *adj* **1** of or having sharp eyes; able to see well **2** (of a person) who watches everything and everybody closely

haw·ser /ˈhɔːzəʳ/ *n* a thick rope, or steel CABLE as used on a ship

haw·thorn /ˈhɔːθɔːn‖-ɔrn/ also **may**— *n* [U; C] a type of tree with white or red flowers (BLOSSOMs) which often grows beside country roads, and has red berries in autumn

hay /heɪ/ *n* [U] **1** grass which has been cut and dried, esp. for cattle food —see picture at FARMYARD **2 make hay a** to dry grass in the sun **b** to make use of chances: *"Make hay while the sun shines"* (=while conditions are favourable) —see also HIT¹ (12) **the hay** —**haymaking** *n* [U]

hay·cock /ˈheɪkɒk‖-kɑk/ *n* a heap of HAY, ready to be taken out of the field

hay fe·ver /ˈ· ˌ··/ *n* [U] an illness rather like a bad cold, but caused by POLLEN dust from plants which is breathed in from the air

hay·fork /ˈheɪfɔːk‖-ɔrk/ *n* a long-handled fork with 2 points (PRONGs), used for turning over HAY in the field or for gathering it

hay·mak·er /ˈheɪˌmeɪkəʳ/ *n* **1** a person who makes HAY **2** *esp. AmE* a powerful blow

hay·stack /ˈheɪstæk/ also **hay·rick** /-ˌrɪk/— *n* **1** a large pile of HAY built for storing **2 (like looking for) a needle in a haystack** (like looking for) something impossible to find among so many other things

hay·wire /ˈheɪwaɪəʳ/ *adj* [F] *sl* DISORGANIZEd and confused (esp. in the phr. **to go haywire**): *My plans are all haywire since they changed the times of our holidays*

haz·ard¹ /ˈhæzəd‖-ərd/ *n* **1** [(*to*)] a danger: *a hazard to health|a health hazard* **2** a difficult move or place in certain games or sports **3 in/at hazard** at risk; in danger

hazard² *v* [T1] **1** to risk; put in danger: *He hazarded all his money in the attempt to save the business* **2** to offer (some form of speech), when there is a risk of being wrong or unwelcome: *I hazarded a guess*

haz·ard·ous /ˈhæzədəs‖-zər-/ *adj* (of an activity)

which contains risks or danger —**~ly** *adv* —**~ness** *n* [U]

haze[1] /heɪz/ *v* [IØ;T1:(OVER)] to (cause to) become HAZY: *The sky hazed over at the end of the day*

haze[2] *n* **1** [C;U] a sort of light mist or smoke: *a haze of cigarette smoke* **2** [C] a feeling of confusion or uncertainty in the mind: *I felt a haze of tiredness come over my mind*

haze[3] *v* [T1] *AmE* **1** to worry and trouble by forcing to do unpleasant work or by saying rude things; HARASS **2** to play tricks on (a young college student) as part of the ceremony of admittance to a club or FRATERNITY (4)

ha·zel[1] /ˈheɪzəl/ *n* **1** [C] a type of tree which bears nuts which can be eaten —see picture at NUT[1] **2** [U] the wood of this tree

hazel[2] *adj* [B;U] (of) a sort of light or greenish brown colour: *She has hazel eyes*

haz·y /ˈheɪzi/ *adj* [Wa1] **1** misty; rather cloudy: *The mountains were hazy in the distance* **2** unclear; uncertain: *I'm rather hazy about the details of the arrangement* —**-ily** *adv* —**-iness** *n* [U]

H-bomb /ˈeɪtʃ bɒm‖-bɑm/ *n* HYDROGEN BOMB

h.c.f. *abbrev. for:* highest common FACTOR (2)

he[1] /i, hi; *strong* hiː/ *pron* [Wp1] (*used as the subject of a sentence*) **1** that male person or animal: *Where's John? He's gone to the cinema.|Be careful of that dog—he sometimes bites* **2** (with general meaning): *Everyone should do what he considers best* —compare THEY (2) **3 he who** the one who: *He who laughs last laughs longest* (=Never mind how long it takes you, so long as you win)

he[2] /hiː/ *n* a male animal: *Is your dog a he or a she?*

he[3] *n* [U] TAG[3]

he- *comb. form* (of an animal) male: *a he-goat* (=BILLY GOAT) —see also HE-MAN

head[1] /hed/ *n* **1 a** the part of the body which contains the eyes, ears, nose and mouth, and the brain—in animals at the front of the body, in man on top **b** (in man) the part of the head above and behind the eyes: *My head aches* **2** the end where this part rests: *at the head of the bed|the grave* **3** the mind or brain: *Can't you get these facts into your head?|Her heart* (=feelings) *rules her head.|It never entered his head to help me* **4** a ruler or leader, esp. a HEADMASTER: *the head of a firm|the family|heads of state|government|the head teacher|the head workman* **5** *infml* a headache: *I've got a bad head* **6** [*usu. pl. with sing. meaning*] the front side of a coin which often bears a picture of the ruler's head (esp. in the phr. **heads or tails?**): *"Let's* TOSS *for it"—"Heads."—"Heads it is."|Heads I win,* TAILS *you lose* (=You lose in any case) **7** a measure of height or distance: *He is half a head taller than his brother.|The horse won the race by a short head* **8** [Wn3] **a** a person (only in the phr. **so much a/per head**): *It cost £3 a head to eat there* **b** (used in counting animals, esp. cattle) an animal: *3 head of cattle* —see NUMBER TABLE **9** a part at the top of an object which is different or separate from the body: *the head of a hammer|the head of the nail* **10** the white centre of a swollen spot (BOIL or PIMPLE) on the skin when it is about to burst **11 a** the top of a page: *I put my address at the head of the letter* **b** the top or front; highest or furthest point: *I waited at the head of the line* (QUEUE) **12** the upper end, esp. of a stretch of water: *the head of the lake* **13** HEADING **14** (esp. in names) HEADLAND: *Beachy Head* **15** the top part of some plants, as when several leaves or flowers grow together there: *The heads of the flowers were blown off in the storm.|heads of* LETTUCE **16** the white FROTH on the top of drinks such as beer: *Pour the beer out so that there's a good head on it!* **17** the most important place: *the head of the table* **18 a** a body of water at a certain height, from which it may fall to produce power to work machinery **b** the pressure or force produced by such water or by a quantity of steam **19** also **magnetic head**— the part of a TAPE RECORDER which records sound **20** firmness or ability; the power to be in control of oneself, or of an activity (esp. in the phr. **a good head**): *a good head for heights|for science|for figures|She has a good head on her shoulders* **21 above someone's head** also **over someone's head**— beyond someone's understanding; too difficult **22 an old head on young shoulders** (a young person who has) the sensible behaviour of an experienced person: *He has|is an old head on young shoulders* **23 bite someone's head off** *infml* to answer severely **24 bang one's head against a brick wall** to keep making an effort without getting any result **25 a bring something to a head** to cause (an event) to reach a point where something must be done or decided **b come to a head** to reach this point **26 bury one's head in the sand** to avoid facing some difficulty **27 eat/talk/shout one's head off** *infml* to eat/talk/shout repeatedly, for a long time, or loudly **28 give someone his head** to allow someone freedom to do as he likes **29 go to someone's head a** to INTOXICATE someone **b** to over-excite someone **c** to make someone too proud, or CONCEITED **30 have a swollen head** *AmE* also **have a swelled head**— to be too proud of oneself or something one has done **31 have (something) hanging over one's head** to feel the threat of (something bad about to happen) **32 have one's head in the clouds** to be impractical; not act according to the realities of life **33 head over heels a** a turning over in the air head first **b** very much; completely: *head over heels in love* **34 keep one's head** to remain calm **35 keep one's head above water** to just be able to live on one's income **36 knock** (a plan) **on the head** *infml* to prevent (a plan) being put into action **37 lose one's head** to act wildly or without reason because afraid, angry, confused, etc. **38 not be able to make head or tail of** to be unable to understand **39 off one's head** mad **40 over someone's head a** above someone's HEAD[1] (21) **b** without first getting the permission of someone of lower rank: *He went over the captain's head to complain to the general* **41 put our/your/their heads together** to think out a plan with other people **42 put (something) into someone's head** to give someone (a new idea) **43 (do something) standing on one's head** (to do something) easily or without any trouble **44 take it into one's head (to do something)** to suddenly decide (to do something) **45 turn someone's head a** to make someone too proud (CONCEITED): *Success had not turned his head* **b** to make someone fall in love: *Her beauty had quite turned his head* —see also KNOCK **people's heads** TOGETHER, **head and** SHOULDERS[1] (6) **above**

head[2] *adj* [Wa5;A] chief: *the head cook*

head[3] *v* **1** [T1] **a** to lead; be at the front of: *The car headed the procession* **b** to be in charge of: *Who heads the government?* **2** [T1] to be at the top of; provide a HEADING for: *His address headed the letter* **3** [T1] to strike (a ball) with the head: *He headed it across the field* **4** [X9;L9] to (cause to) move in a certain direction: *We headed him towards the house.|We're heading home* —see HEAD OFF, HEAD FOR

-head *suffix* [*n*→*n*] state; quality; -HOOD: GODHEAD

head·ache /ˈhedeɪk/ *n* **1** a pain in the head: *He has headaches after reading* —see ACHE (USAGE) **2** *infml* a great difficulty: *Trying to make her eat is one big headache!* —**-achy** *adj* [Wa2]

head·band /ˈhedbænd/ *n* a band worn on the forehead, usu. to keep the hair back from the face

head·board /ˈhedbɔːd‖-bord/ *n* a board at the HEAD[1] (2) of a bed —compare FOOTBOARD (2) and see picture at BEDROOM

head·cheese /ˈhedtʃiːz/ *n* [U] *AmE* BRAWN (2)

head·dress /ˈhed-dres/ *n* an ornamental covering for the head

-head·ed /ˈhedɨd/ *comb. form adj* having a certain type of head: *curly-headed|red-headed|2-headed|empty-headed*

head·er /ˈhedəʳ/ *n* **1** a jump, as into water, with the head going down (or in) before the feet; (head first) DIVE[2] (1) **2** (in football) a striking of the ball with the head

head·first /ˌhedˈfɜːst◂‖-ɜrst/ *adj, adv* [Wa5] **1** (moving or entering) with the rest of the body following the head **2** (done) in foolish haste: *He's gone head first into trouble*

head for *v prep* [T1] **1** to move towards; go to: *'Where are you heading/headed for?"—"Manchester"* **2** to act in such a manner as to cause or fail to avoid: *You're heading for an accident if you will drive after drinking* —compare ASK FOR
USAGE *"Where are you* **heading for**?" (="Where are you **headed for**?")|*"You're* **heading for** *an accident"* (="You're **headed for** an accident").

head·gear /ˈhedgɪəʳ/ *n* [U;C *usu. sing.*] (a) covering for the head

head·hunt·er /ˈhedˌhʌntəʳ/ *n* **1** a person who cuts off his enemies' heads and keeps them **2** a person who tries to attract specially able people to other jobs by offering them better pay and more responsibility **3** *humor* a person who likes to be seen with those who are famous or important

head·ing /ˈhedɪŋ/ *n* the words written as a title at the top of a piece of writing, or at the top of each part of it

head·land /ˈhedlənd/ *n* an area of land running out from the coast into the sea

head·less /ˈhedləs/ *adj* [Wa5] **1** without a head **2** *rare or humor* without a leader

head·light /ˈhedlaɪt/ also **head·lamp** /ˈhedlæmp/— *n* [*often pl.*] a powerful light fixed at the front of a vehicle, often one of a pair —see picture at CAR

head·line[1] /ˈhedlaɪn/ *n* **1 a** the heading printed in large letters above a story in a newspaper **b** the titles of the main news stories, as shown on large notices (POSTERs) where newspapers are sold **2** [*usu. pl.*] a main point of the news, as read on radio or television —see also HIT[1] **the headlines**

headline[2] *v* [T1] to give a HEADLINE[1] (1) TO: *The newspaper headlined the changes in the government*

head·long /ˈhedlɒŋ‖-lɔŋ/ *adv, adj* [Wa5] HEADFIRST

head·man /ˈhedmən/ *n* **-men** /mən/ a chief, esp. of a tribal village

head·mas·ter /ˌhedˈmɑːstəʳ‖ˈhedˌmæstər/ *fem.* **head·mis·tress** /ˌhedˈmɪstrɨs‖ˈhedˌmɪstrɨs/— *n* the teacher in charge of a school

head off *v adv* [T1] **1** to cause to move in a different direction: *They were running towards the house, but we headed them off by calling from the field* **2** to prevent: *You will have to speak to both groups of men quickly if you want to head off a nasty disagreement*

head of hair /ˌ· · ˈ·/ *n* [C9 *usu. sing.*] a thick mass of hair on a person's head: *She has a beautiful head of hair*

head-on /ˌ· ˈ·◂/ *adv, adj* [Wa5] with the head or front parts meeting, usu. violently: *a head-on car crash*

head·phone /ˈhedfəʊn/ *n* [*usu. pl.*] either of the 2 parts (of metal, plastic, etc.) made to fit over the ears to receive radio messages and such like, which together with a piece of material joining them over the top of the head form a set or pair

head·piece /ˈhedpiːs/ *n* **1** something which fits closely over the head, such as the HELMET of a suit of armour **2** (in printing) an ornamental heading

head·quar·ters /ˈhedˌkwɔːtəz, ˌhedˈkwɔːtəz‖-ɔrtərz/ *n* **-ters** [Wn3;C *often pl. with sing. meaning*] the office or place where the people work who control a large organization, such as the police or army, or a private firm

head·rest /ˈhed-rest/ *n* something which supports the head, usu. a suitably shaped part of the back of a chair or of a front seat in some modern cars

head·room /ˈhed-rʊm, -ruːm/ *n* [U;(S)] space to move considered as height above a vehicle passing under a bridge, through a TUNNEL, etc.

head·set /ˈhedset/ *n esp. AmE* (a set of) HEADPHONEs

head·ship /ˈhedʃɪp/ *n* the position or period in office of HEADMASTER or leader of a group

head·shrink·er /ˈhedˌʃrɪŋkəʳ/ *n* **1** *humor* PSYCHIATRIST **2** a sort of HEADHUNTER who makes the heads of his enemies become smaller by removing the bones and drying the rest to preserve it

head·stall /ˈhedstɔːl/ *n* a part of a HARNESS which fits over the horse's head

head start /ˌ· ˈ·/ also **start**— *n* [(*over, on*)] an advantage, esp. in a race: (fig.) *He has a head start over his friends who are learning French, as he has already lived in France for a year*

head·stone /ˈhedstəʊn/ *n* **1** a stone which marks the top end of a grave, usu. having the buried person's name on it; GRAVESTONE **2** a stone which supports others in a building; KEYSTONE

head·strong /ˈhedstrɒŋ‖-strɒ/ *adj* (of people) determined to do what one wants against all other advice

head·way /ˈhedweɪ/ *n* [U (*against*)] forward movement against a difficulty (esp. in the phr. **make headway**)

head·wind /ˈhedˌwɪnd, ˌhedˈwɪnd/ *n* a wind blowing directly against one

head·word /ˈhedwɜːd‖-ɜrd/ *n* the word which is written at the beginning of a description of its meaning, esp. in dictionaries: *The next headword is "heady"*

head·y /ˈhedi/ *adj* [Wa1] **1** (of ideas and actions) done or formed in a foolish hurry **2** (of alcohol and its effects) tending to make drunk, GIDDY, etc. (to INTOXICATE) **3** with a feeling of lightness and excitement: *heady with success*

heal /hiːl/ *v* **1** [T1;IØ (OVER)] to (cause to) become healthy, esp. to grow new skin: *His wounds are healing (over).*|(fig.) *Their disagreements healed over with time and they became firm friends* **2** [T1 (*of*)] *fml or bibl* CURE: *He was healed of his sickness* —**~er** *n*

health /helθ/ *n* **1** [U] the state of being well, without disease: *Health is better than wealth* **2** [U] the condition of the body: *in poor health|in good health* **3** [C;U] (before drinking) (a wish for or TOAST[2] (2) to) someone's success and continued freedom from illness (esp. in the phrs. **drink someone's health, drink a health to someone, Your (good) health!**)

health·ful /ˈhelθfəl/ *adj* likely to produce good health: *the healthful air at the seaside*

health·y /ˈhelθi/ *adj* [Wa1] **1** strong, not often ill; usually in good health **2 a** HEALTHFUL **b** good for the mind or character: *That book is not healthy reading for a child* **c** natural: *He has a healthy dislike of school* **3** showing good health: *a clear healthy skin* —**healthily** *adv* —**healthiness** *n* [U]

heap[1] /hiːp/ *n* **1 a** a pile or mass of things one on top of the other: *The books lay in a heap on the floor* **b** *infml* a lot: *She's had a heap of trouble* **2 heaps of** *infml* a lot of: *We have heaps of time* **3 be struck/knocked all of a heap** *infml* to be very surprised or confused **4 heaps more/better/longer** etc. *infml* much: *I feel heaps better after my sleep*

heap² *v* **1** [D1+*on/with*; X9, esp. UP] to pile up: *He heaped the plate with food.|He heaped food on the plate* **2** [X9, esp. UP] to collect or gain in large amounts (esp. in the phr. **to heap up wealth/riches**) **3 heap praises on/upon (someone)** to give a lot of praise to (someone)

hear /hɪəʳ/ *v* **heard** /hɜːd‖hɜrd/ **1** [Wv6;T1;V2,4; I∅] to receive and understand (sounds) by using the ears: *I can't hear very well.|I heard him say so.|I can hear someone knocking* **2** [Wv6;T1,5a] to be told or informed: *I heard that he was ill* —compare HEAR ABOUT, HEAR FROM, HEAR OF, HEAR OUT **3** [T1,6a] to listen with attention (esp. to a case in court): *The judge heard the case* **4 won't/wouldn't hear of** refuse(s) to allow: *I won't hear of you coming in so late* **5 hear tell of** *infml* to get to know by being told: *I've often heard tell of the wonderful parties she gives, but I've never been invited* **6 Hear! Hear!** (a shout of agreement)

USAGE To **hear** is to experience with the ears; to **listen** is to hear with attention: *I'm* **listening** *to the music.|I'm* **listening** *for the baby* (=listening in case it cries). It is rude to say on the telephone *I'm not* **listening** when you mean *I can't* **hear**! —see SEE (USAGE)

hear a·bout *v prep* **1** [Wv6;T1,4;V4a *pass. rare*] to get to know: *Did you hear about the party?—It was a complete failure.|Have you heard about Gatsby jumping into the pool with all his clothes on?* **2** [D1] to receive (news) about (someone or something): *We've been hearing quite a lot about that young tennis player lately*

hear·er /ˈhɪərəʳ/ *n* a person who hears (a sound): *We can prove he said that—there were several hearers*

hear from *v prep* [Wv6;T1] to receive news from (someone), usu. by letter: *I heard from him last week.|I haven't heard from him since he telephoned* —compare HEAR OF

hear·ing /ˈhɪərɪŋ/ *n* **1** [U] the sense by which one hears sound: *Her hearing is getting worse* **2** [U] the distance at which one can hear; EARSHOT: *Don't talk about it in his hearing* (=so that he can hear) **3** [U;C] the act or experience of listening: *At first hearing I didn't like the music* **4** [C] a chance to be heard explaining one's position (esp. in the phr. **gain/get a hearing**): *It's a good idea, so try to get a hearing with the people in charge* **5** [C] *law* a trial of a case before a judge

hearing aid /ˈ·· ·/ *BrE infml* also **deaf-aid**— *n* a small electric machine fitted near the ear which makes sounds seem louder

hear·ken /ˈhɑːkən‖ˈhɑr-/ *v* [I∅ (*to*)] *lit* to listen

hear of *v prep* **1** [Wv6;T1,4;V4a *often nonassertive*] to know of (a fact/the existence of something or somebody): *Who's he?—We never heard of him.|I've never heard of anyone doing a thing like that* —compare HEAR FROM **2** [D1] HEAR ABOUT (2): *We've been hearing quite a lot of that young tennis player lately*

hear out *v adv* [T1 *pass. rare*] to listen till the end of (someone's) speech: *Don't interrupt, just hear me out before you start talking*

hear·say /ˈhɪəseɪ‖ˈhɪər-/ *n* [U] things which are said rather than proved

hearse /hɜːs‖hɜrs/ *n* a car which is used to carry a body in its COFFIN to the funeral before being put in the grave

heart /hɑːt‖hɑrt/ *n* **1** [C] the organ inside the chest which controls the flow of blood by pushing it through the blood vessels —see picture at RESPIRATORY **2** [C] the same organ when thought of as the centre of the feelings, esp. of kind feelings (as the brain is the centre of thought): *My heart bled* (=I was very sorry) *for him.|I felt sick at heart.|He has a kind heart.|Have a heart!* (=Don't ask me to do too much) **3** [C] something in a shape like the shape of this organ: *She sent me a birthday card with a heart on it* **4** [C] a playing-card with one or more figures of this shape printed on it in red: *the Queen of Hearts|I've only one heart left in my hand* —see CARDS (USAGE) **5** [C] the centre (of something large, and of certain leafy vegetables): *Let's get to the heart of the matter/the subject* **6** [U] courage, strength of mind (esp. in the phrs. **take heart, lose heart**): *I used to dig the garden every week, but I lost heart when the rain washed all the plants away* —compare **have the** HEART (11) **(to do)** **7 after one's own heart** just of the type one likes: *He's a man after my own heart* **8 at heart a** in reality: *He seems nice, but he's dishonest at heart* **b** in one's care: *When I say don't eat sweets, I have your health at heart* **9 break someone's/one's heart** to make/become very unhappy: *I broke my heart over his cruelty.|He broke my heart* **10 by heart** by memory: *to get/learn by heart* **11 eat one's heart out** to be very troubled; be worrying a lot **12 from the (bottom of one's) heart** with real feeling: *I pity him from the heart* **13 have the heart (to do)** to have the courage or firmness (to do): *I didn't have the heart to tell him the bad news* **14 have one's heart in (something)** also (of the heart) **be in (something)**— to be interested in: *I tried to learn music but I didn't have my heart in it/my heart wasn't in it* **15 heart and soul** with all one's feelings or agreement; completely **16 have one's heart in one's mouth/boots** to feel very afraid or worried **17 have one's heart in the right place** to be a kind person **18 in one's heart of hearts** in one's most secret feelings; in reality: *I said I loved her, but in my heart of hearts I knew it wasn't true* **19 lose one's heart to (someone)** to fall in love with (someone) **20 set one's heart on something/doing something** to want to have or do something very much and be expecting to have or do it **21 take (something) to heart** to feel the effect of something deeply (and take suitable action) **22 wear one's heart on one's sleeve** to show one's feelings (esp. to show that one is in love with a certain person) instead of hiding these feelings **23 with all one's heart** with deep feeling; completely

heart·ache /ˈhɑːteɪk‖ˈhɑrt-/ *n* [U] deep feelings of sorrow and pain

heart at·tack /ˈ· ·ˌ·/ *n* a sudden medical condition in which the heart beats irregularly and painfully, as because of a CORONARY THROMBOSIS

heart·beat /ˈhɑːtbiːt‖ˈhɑrt-/ *n* **1** [U] **a** the action of the heart as it pushes the blood **b** the sound this action makes **2** [C] one pushing movement of the heart: *We thought he was dead, but then we heard a heartbeat*

heart·break /ˈhɑːtbreɪk‖ˈhɑrt-/ *n* [U] deep sorrow; terrible disappointment which can never be put right

heart break·er /ˈ· ˌ··/ *n* [C; *you*+N] a person, usu. a woman, who hurts others' feelings deeply, esp. by letting them fall in love with her when she does not care for them

heart·break·ing /ˈhɑːtˌbreɪkɪŋ‖ˈhɑrt-/ *adj* **1** which causes great sorrow **2** (of work or activity) very tiring and producing no good result —**~ly** *adv*

heart·brok·en /ˈhɑːtˌbrəʊkən‖ˈhɑrt-/ also **broken hearted**— *adj* (of a person) deeply hurt in the feelings; full of sorrow

heart·burn /ˈhɑːtbɜːn‖ˈhɑrtbɜrn/ *n* [U] a condition in which one feels an unpleasant burning in the chest, caused by acid acting on food in the stomach; sign of INDIGESTION

heart dis·ease /ˈ· ·ˌ·/ *n* [C;U] (an) illness which prevents the heart from working properly

-heart·ed /ˈhɑːtɨ̣d‖ˈhɑr-/ *comb. form* [*adj, n→adj*] having a certain type of HEART (2,6): *kind-hearted*|*cold-hearted*|*lion-hearted*

heart·en /ˈhɑːtn‖ˈhɑr-/ *v* [T1 (UP)] to encourage: *He was heartened by her kindness*

heart·en·ing /ˈhɑːtənɪŋ‖ˈhɑr-/ *adj* strengthening; encouraging: *heartening news* —**~ly** *adv*

heart fail·ure /ˈ· ˌ··/ *n* [U] the stopping of the movement of the heart, esp. at death

heart·felt /ˈhɑːtfelt‖ˈhɑrt-/ *adj* deeply felt; sincere; true

hearth /hɑːθ‖hɑrθ/ *n* **1** the area around the fire in one's home, esp. the floor of the fireplace —see picture at LIVING ROOM **2** the home (note the phr. **hearth and home**)

hearth·rug /ˈhɑːθrʌg‖ˈhɑrθ-/ *n* a RUG (floor covering) in front of the fireplace

heart·i·ly /ˈhɑːtɨ̣li‖ˈhɑr-/ *adv* **1 a** (done) with strength, force, etc. **b** (done) in large amounts: *They ate heartily* **2** very: *I'm heartily tired/sick of your questions*

heart·less /ˈhɑːtləs‖ˈhɑrt-/ *adj* cruel; unkind; pitiless —**~ly** *adv* —**~ness** *n* [U]

heart·rend·ing /ˈhɑːtˌrendɪŋ‖ˈhɑrt-/ *adj* which causes a feeling of deep sorrow or pity; very HEARTBREAKING: *It was heartrending to hear of their death* —**~ly** *adv*

heart's blood /ˌ· ˈ·, ˈ· ·/ also **lifeblood**— *n* [U9] one's life: *I'd give my heart's blood to help him*

hearts·ease /ˈhɑːts-iːz‖ˈhɑr-/ *n* [U] *old use* PANSY

heart·sick /ˈhɑːtˌsɪk‖ˈhɑrt-/ *adj* low-spirited; feeling very unhappy

heart·strings /ˈhɑːtˌstrɪŋz‖ˈhɑr-/ *n* [P] someone's deep feelings of love and pity (esp. in the phr. **tug at someone's heartstrings**): *The sight of the small child crying tugged at my heartstrings*

heart·throb /ˈhɑːtθrɒb‖ˈhɑrtθrɑb/ *n sl* a man who is very attractive and with whom girls fall in love

heart-to-heart /ˌ· · ˈ·◂/ *adj, n* [Wa5] (a talk) done freely, mentioning personal details, without hiding anything

heart·warm·ing /ˈhɑːtˌwɔːmɪŋ‖ˈhɑrtˌwɔr-/ *adj* giving a feeling of pleasure, esp. because of a kindness done: *We don't need your help, but it was a heartwarming suggestion* —**~ly** *adv*

heart·wood /ˈhɑːtwʊd‖ˈhɑrt-/ *n* [U] the older harder wood at the centre of a tree —compare SAPWOOD

heart·y /ˈhɑːti‖ˈhɑrti/ *adj* [Wa1] **1** WARM-HEARTED and friendly: *a hearty greeting* **2** strong and healthy (esp. in the phr. **hale and hearty**) **3** (of meals) large **4** *infml, esp. BrE* (too) cheerful, esp. when noisy and trying to appear friendly **5 my hearties** *old use infml* (a friendly form of address used by and to men, esp. sailors): *Pull away, my hearties!* —**-iness** *n* [U]

heat¹ /hiːt/ *v* [T1;I∅: (UP)] to (cause to) become warm or hot: *We'll heat some milk for (the) coffee*

heat² *n* **1** [U] the quality or quantity of being warm or cold: *What is the heat of the water in the swimming pool?* **2** [U;S] **a** hotness; WARMTH: *The heat from the fire dried their clothes* **b** hot weather: *I can't walk about in this heat/in a heat of 90°!* **3** [U9] a feeling of being hot, in some medical conditions (esp. in the phr. **prickly heat**) **4** [U] a state of excitement: *In the heat of the moment/argument/battle I lost my self-control* **5** [U] a state of sexual excitement happening regularly to certain female animals, such as female dogs (BITCHes) (esp. in the phrs. (*BrE*) **on heat**/(*AmE*) **in heat**) **6** [U] *tech* the force produced by the movement of groups of atoms **7** [C] a part of a race or competition whose winners compete against other winners until there is a small enough number to decide the end result —see also DEAD HEAT

heat bar·ri·er /ˈ· ˌ···/ *n* a covering of hot air round a fast-moving aircraft

heat·ed /ˈhiːtɨ̣d/ *adj* angry —see also HEAT² (4) —**~ly**

heat·er /ˈhiːtəʳ/ *n* a machine for heating air, or water, such as those which burn gas, oil, or electricity to produce heat

heath /hiːθ/ *n* **1** [C] an open piece of wild unfarmed land where grass and other plants grow; MOOR¹ or COMMON² (1) **2** [U] any of several kinds of bushes with small flowers; HEATHER or LING

hea·then /ˈhiːðən/ *n* **1** [C] a person who does not belong to one of the large established religions: *He* CONVERT*ed*¹ (1) *the heathens to Christianity.*|*a heathen country* —compare PAGAN **2** [C; *you*+N] *infml* a wild badly behaved person —**~ish** *adj* —**~dom** *n* [U]

heath·er /ˈheðəʳ/ *n* [U] a plant which grows as a small bush on open windy land (MOOR*s*) and has flowers which are usu. pink or purple but sometimes white

heather-mix·ture /ˈ·· ˌ··/ *adj, n* [Wa5;B;U] *BrE* (a clothing material (TWEED)) of mixed colours including purple, rather like HEATHER

heat·ing /ˈhiːtɪŋ/ *n* [U] a system for keeping rooms and buildings warm

heat pump /ˈ· ·/ *n* an apparatus which controls the heat in a building by means of warm air or water, usu. sent through pipes

heat rash /ˈ· ·/ *n* **1** [C;U] PRICKLY HEAT **2** [C] also **heat spot** /ˈ· ·/— a raised red swelling which may come up on the skin during hot weather

heat shield /ˈ· ·/ *n* the part of a space vehicle which prevents the front from getting too hot as it comes back to the earth

heat·stroke /ˈhiːtstrəʊk/ *n* [U;(C)] SUNSTROKE

heat wave /ˈ· ·/ *n* a period of unusually hot weather

heave¹ /hiːv/ *v* **1** [X9] to pull and lift, esp. towards oneself: *We heaved him to his feet* **2** [I∅] to rise and fall regularly: *His chest heaved as he breathed deeply after the race* **3** [X9] *infml* to throw: *The children have just heaved a brick through my window* **4** [T1] (of a person) to give out (a sad sound) (esp. in the phrs. **heave a sigh/groan**) **5** [T1] to pull up (only in the phr. **heave the anchor**)

heave² *v* **hove** /həʊv/ [L9] **1** (of a ship) to move in the stated direction or manner: *As we came into harbour another ship hove* ALONGSIDE **2 heave in(to) sight/view** *humor* to come into one's view: *We were just about to leave when my old friend Pete hove into view*

heave³ *n* **1** [C] a pull or throw: *One more heave, boys, and it'll be in* **2** [(*the*) S] an upward movement or set of such movements at regular times: *the heave of waves upon the shore*

heave at *v prep* [T1] to try to HEAVE¹ (1): *They heaved (away) at the heavy box, but could not lift it*

heav·en /ˈhevən/ *n* **1** [U] the place where God or the gods are supposed to live; place of complete happiness where the souls of good people go after death **2** [C *usu. pl.*] the sky **3** [U;C] *infml* **a** great happiness: *I was in heaven when I heard the good news* **b** a very happy place: *This house is a little heaven* **4 move heaven and earth** to do everything possible (to cause or prevent something) —compare SKY

Heaven *n* [R *sometimes pl.*] (esp. in expressions of surprise) God: *(May) Heaven forbid!*|*Good Heavens!*

heav·en·ly /ˈhevənli/ *adj* [Wa5] **1** [A] of, from, or like heaven; in or belonging to the sky: *The sun, moon, and stars are* **heavenly bodies** **2** [B] *infml* wonderful; giving great pleasure: *What heavenly weather!*

heaven-sent /ˌ·· ˈ·◂‖ˈ·· ·/ *adj* [Wa5] happening at just the right moment (esp. in the phr. **a heaven-sent opportunity**)

heav·en·wards /ˈhevənwədz‖-ərdz/ *AmE* also **heavenward** /ˈhevənwəd‖-ərd/— *adv* towards the sky or heaven

heave on *v prep* [T1] to pull (a rope) strongly

heave to *v adv* [IØ] *tech* (of a ship) to stop moving; come to rest: *When the ship received the signal, she hove to*

heave up *v adv* [T1;IØ] BRING UP; VOMIT: *After eating that bad food he heaved up violently*

Heav·i·side lay·er /ˈhevisaɪd ˌleɪəʳ/ *n* [*the*+R] the part of the upper air (ATMOSPHERE) surrounding the earth which directs radio waves back; IONOSPHERE

heav·y¹ /ˈhevi/ *adj* [Wa1] **1** [B] of a certain weight, esp. of a weight that makes carrying, moving, or lifting difficult: *The bag is too heavy for me* **2** [B] of unusual force or amount: *heavy rain|a heavy blow|heavy fighting|a heavy punishment|heavy traffic|heavy smoking and drinking|A* **heavy smoker and drinker** *is one who smokes and drinks a lot or too much* **3** [B] **a** serious, esp. if uninteresting: *This book is heavy reading* **b** (esp. of periods of time) full of hard work: *I've had a heavy day* **4** [B] sad: *a heavy heart|heavy news* **5** [B] **a** feeling or showing difficulty or slowness in moving: *My head is heavy.|heavy movements|a heavy sleeper|* **b** difficult to do or move in: *heavy work|The soil is heavy—it makes heavy walking* **6** [B] (of food) rather solid and bad for the stomach **7** [B] (of weather) **a** still, without wind, dark, etc. **b** (at sea) stormy, with big waves **8** [F+*on*] *infml* **a** severe (towards): *a teacher who is heavy on his pupils* **b** using in large quantities: *This car is heavy on oil* **9** [B] *sl, esp. AmE* troublesome or threatening: *It's a heavy scene, man: let's leave* **10 find it heavy going** to find it very difficult **11 make heavy weather of something** to make something more difficult than it really is **12 play the heavy father** to scold someone in a very serious way —opposite **light** —**-ily** *adv*: *moving/breathing/drinking heavily* —**-iness** *n* [U]

heavy² *adv* in a troublesome or dull way (only in the phrs. **lie heavy on/hang heavy on (someone)**): *Time hung heavy on his hands*

heavy³ *n* a serious usu. male part in a play, esp. a bad character

heavy-du·ty /ˌ·· ˈ··◂/ *adj* (of clothes, tyres, machines, oil, etc.) made to be used a lot, or strong enough for rough treatment

heavy-hand·ed /ˌ·· ˈ··◂/ *adj* **1** awkward in movements of the hands; tending to break and spoil things **2** rather unkind or unfair in one's treatment of others; not careful in speech and action —**~ly** —**~ness** *n* [U]

heav·y-heart·ed /ˌheviˈhɑːtɪ̈d◂‖-ˈhɑr-/ *adj* sad

heavy hy·dro·gen /ˌ·· ˈ···/ *n* [U] a type of HYDROGEN heavier than the more common ISOTOPE

heavy in·dus·try /ˌ·· ˈ···/ *n* [U] organizations that produce goods (such as coal, steel, or chemicals) which are used in the production of other goods

heavy-lad·en /ˌ·· ˈ··◂/ *adj* **1** carrying a heavy load **2** having too many worries and troubles

heavy pet·ting /ˌhevi ˈpetɪŋ/ *n* [U] sexual play up to but not including sexual union (INTERCOURSE)

heavy-set /ˌ·· ˈ·◂/ *adj* (of people) rather broad and strong-looking in body, sometimes rather fat

heavy wa·ter /ˌ·· ˈ··/ *n* [U] water containing HEAVY HYDROGEN

heav·y·weight /ˈheviweɪt/ *n, adj* **1** (a person or thing) **a** of more than average weight **b** having great importance or influence **2** (a BOXER⁴ (1)) of the heaviest class, weighing 175 pounds or more

heb·dom·a·dal /hebˈdɒmədl‖-ˈdɑ-/ *adj* [Wa5] *fml* weekly —**~ly** *adv*

He·bra·ic /hɪˈbreɪ-ɪk/ *adj* of or concerning the HEBREW people, language, or civilization

He·brew /ˈhiːbruː/ *adj* **1** of the Jews **2** of the language used by the Jews, in ancient times and at present

hec·a·tomb /ˈhekətuːm, -təʊm/ *n* **1** *lit* the killing of great numbers of people **2** (in ancient times) the public killing of 100 oxen

heck /hek/ *interj, n euph sl* HELL¹ (3,4),²: OH, *heck! I've lost another pencil!|a heck of a lot of money*

heck·le /ˈhekəl/ *v* [Wv3;T1;IØ] to interrupt (a speaker or speech) with confusing or unfriendly remarks, esp. at a political meeting —**heckler** *n* [Wv3]

hec·tare /ˈhektɑːʳ, -teəʳ‖-teər/ *n* (a measure for the area of land which equals) 10,000 square metres —see WEIGHTS & MEASURES TABLE

hec·tic /ˈhektɪk/ *adj* full of excitement and hurried movement: *a hectic day* —**~ally** *adv* [Wa4]

hec·to- /ˈhektəʊ, -tə/ *comb. form* [→*n*] 100 (times): *hectometre|hectogram|hectolitre* —see WEIGHTS & MEASURES TABLE

hec·tor /ˈhektəʳ/ *v* [T1;IØ] to be rough in manner towards (someone); BULLY³: *The teacher hectors his students to make them work harder*

he'd /id, hid; *strong* hiːd/ [Wv2] *contr. of* (*in compound tenses*) **1** he would: *He'd go* **2** he had: *He'd gone.|He'd (got) a few minutes to spend with her* —see CONTR. (USAGE)

hedge¹ /hedʒ/ *n* **1** a row of bushes or small trees, esp. when cut level at the top, which divides one garden or field from another **2** [*against*] a protection: *Buying a house will be a hedge against the possibility of our money losing value*

hedge² *v* **1** [T1] to make a HEDGE round (a field) **2** [IØ] to refuse to answer directly: *You're hedging again—have you or haven't you got the money?* **3 hedge one's bets** to protect oneself against loss by favouring or supporting more than one side in a competition or struggle

hedge a·bout with also **hedge a·round with, hedge in with**— *v adv prep* [D1 *often pass.*] to surround with: *Building a house is hedged about with laws and difficulties*

hedge·hog /ˈhedʒhɒg‖-hɔg/ *n* a type of small insect-eating animal which comes out only at night. It has SPINES (sharp prickles) which stand out from its back to protect it when it rolls itself into a ball after being made afraid —compare PORCUPINE and see picture at MAMMAL

hedge·hop /ˈhedʒhɒp‖-hɑp/ *v* **-pp-** [IØ] to fly a plane low, rising over trees, bushes, etc. —**-hopper** *n*

hedge in *v adv* [T1] HEM IN

hedge·row /ˈhedʒrəʊ/ *n* a row of bushes, esp. along country roads, or separating fields

hedge spar·row /ˈ· ˌ··/ *n* a type of common small bird of Europe and America

he·don·is·m /ˈhiːdənɪzəm/ *n* [U] **1** the idea that pleasure is the most important thing in life **2** the living of a life of pleasure —**-ist** *n* —**istic** /ˌhiːdəˈnɪstɪk/ *adj*

hee·bie-jee·bies /ˌhiːbi ˈdʒiːbiz/ *n* [*the*+P] *infml* **1** nervous anxiety caused by fear **2** a feeling of strong dislike or annoyance

heed¹ /hiːd/ *v* [T1] *fml* to give attention to: *She didn't heed my warning*

heed² *n* [U] *fml* attention; notice (esp. in the phrs. **give/pay heed to** and **take heed of**): *For the first time he had to pay/give heed to his appearance, and in fact he became very well-dressed from then on.|Take heed of what I say, if you want to succeed* —**~ful(ly)**

adj (*adv*) —**~fulness** *n* [U] —**~less(ly)** *adj* (*adv*)

hee-haw /ˈhiː ˌhɔː/ *n* [S] **1** the sound made by a donkey **2** a loud rude laugh

heel[1] /hiːl/ *n* **1** the back part of the foot —see picture at HUMAN[2] **2** the part of a shoe, sock, etc., which covers this, esp. the raised part of a shoe underneath the foot: *There's a hole in the heel of my stocking.*|*to wear* (*high*) *heels* (=to wear shoes with high heels) **3** (in RUGBY) a backward kick with the back part of the foot **4** *sl, esp. AmE* an unpleasant person (usu. a man), esp. one who treats others badly **5 at/on one's heels** very closely behind: *He followed* (*hot*) *on my heels* **6 bring to heel** to bring under control; force to obey one **7 come to heel a** (of a dog) to follow close to its master **b** (of a person) to obey without question, or to stop disobeying **8 cool one's heels** also (*esp. BrE*) **kick one's heels**— *infml* to be made to wait for some time unwillingly: *I had to cool my heels for half an hour until he would see me* **9 down at heel a** (of a shoe) worn down at the back **b** (of a person) untidy and uncared for in appearance **10 kick up one's heels a** to jump and make kicking movements in play **b** to be free and enjoy oneself after work **11 lay (someone) by the heels** *BrE infml* to catch and put (someone) in prison **12 show a clean pair of heels (to)** to run away fast (from) **13 turn on one's heel** to turn around suddenly **14 under someone's heel** in someone's power: *Alexander the Great held the world under his heel* —see also TREAD[1] **on somebody's heels**

heel[2] *v* **1** [T1] to put a heel on (a shoe) **2** [I∅ *often imper.*] (esp. of a dog) to move along at the heels of someone **3** [T1] (in RUGBY) to send (the ball) back with the heel to another player of one's own team (esp. from the SCRUM)

heel·ball /ˈhiːlbɔːl/ *n* [U] a type of black or brown wax used by shoemakers and for rubbing patterns onto paper

heel o·ver *v adv* [I∅] to lean over at an angle, ready to fall: *The ship heeled over in the storm*

hef·ty /ˈhefti/ *adj* [Wa1] **1** big and/or strong: *a hefty man*|*plateful of meat*|*blow to the jaw* **2** (of objects) big and difficult to move —**heftily** *adv*

he·gem·o·ny /hɪˈgeməni, ˈhedʒɨməni‖hɪˈdʒeməni, ˈhedʒɨməʊni/ *n* [U] leadership of one state over a group of others

He·gi·ra, Hejira /ˈhedʒɨrə, hɪˈdʒaɪərə/ *n* [*the*+R] **1** the escape of Muhammad from Mecca to Medina in the year 622 A.D. **2** the period of time beginning then, used by Muslims in calculating dates

heif·er /ˈhefəʳ/ *n* a young cow which has not borne young (not borne a CALF)

heigh-ho /ˌheɪ ˈhəʊ, ˈheɪ həʊ/ *interj* (the sound of a SIGH, expressing tiredness, worry, etc.)

height /haɪt/ *n* **1** [U;C] the quality or degree of being tall or high: *His height makes him stand out in the crowd* **2** [C] (a point at) a fixed or measured distance above another given point: *a window at a height of 10 feet above the ground*|*During the floods the river water rose to the height of the main road beside it* **3** [C *often pl. with sing. meaning*] a high position or place: *We looked down from a great height*|*the mountain heights to see the whole town below us* **4** [(*the*) C] the main point; highest degree: *Most people take their holidays in the height of* (*the*) *summer.*|*It's the height of madness to sail when you can't swim.*|*at the height of the storm*

height·en /ˈhaɪtn/ *v* [T1;I∅] to (cause to) become greater in degree: *As she waited, her fears heightened.*|*The performance heightened my admiration for the actor*

hei·nous /ˈheɪnəs/ *adj lit* (of wicked people or acts) very shameful; very bad —**~ly** *adj* —**~ness** *n* [U]

heir /eəʳ/ *n* [(*to*)] the person who has the lawful right to receive the property or title of an older member of the family who dies: *The king's eldest son is the heir to the* THRONE (=kingdom)|*the birth of a son and heir* (=first son)

heir ap·par·ent /ˌ· ·ˈ··/ *n* **heirs apparent** the HEIR whose right to receive the family property or title cannot be taken away until he dies: (fig.) *Everyone thinks that that young minister is the heir apparent to*|*of the leader of our party*

heir·ess /ˈeərɨs, ˈeəres/ *n* a female HEIR, esp. to great wealth: *He hopes to marry an heiress and stop working*

heir·loom /ˈeəluːm‖ˈeər-/ *n* a valuable object given by older members of a family to younger ones over many years or even several centuries

heir pre·sump·tive /ˌ· ·ˈ··/ also **presumptive heir**— *n* **heirs presumptive** a person who is an HEIR (esp. to a position as a ruler) only until someone else with a stronger right is born

He·ji·ra /ˈhedʒɪrə, hɪˈdʒaɪərə/ *n* [*the*+R] HEGIRA

held /held/ *past t. and past p. of* HOLD

hel·i·cop·ter /ˈhelɨkɒptəʳ‖-kɑp-/ *n* a type of aircraft which is made to fly by a set of large fast-turning metal blades, and which can land in a small space, take off without running over the ground, and stay still in the air —see picture at AIRCRAFT

he·li·o·graph /ˈhiːlɪəgrɑːf‖-græf/ *n* an instrument which sends messages by directing flashes of sunlight with a mirror

he·li·o·trope /ˈhelɪətrəʊp, ˈhiː-‖ˈhiː-/ *n* **1** [C] a type of garden plant with purplish flowers which turn towards the sun **2** [U] the colour of this flower

hel·i·port /ˈhelɨpɔːt‖-port/ *n* a HELICOPTER airport

he·li·um /ˈhiːlɪəm/ *n* [U] a gas that is a simple substance (ELEMENT) that is lighter than air, will not burn, and is used in AIRSHIPs and some kinds of lights

hell[1] /hel/ *n* **1** [U] (esp. in the Christian and Muslim religions) a place where the souls of the wicked are said to be punished after death **2** [C] a place or state of great suffering **3** [U;E] *sl* (a swear word, used in anger or to strengthen an expression) DEVIL[1] (6,10): *I won't, you say?—By hell, I will!*|*What the hell's that thing on your head?*|*That's a hell of a good car.*|*Shut up telling me what to do—(you can) go to hell!* **4 a hell of** (used for giving force to an expression): *a hell of a nasty accident*|*a good car*|*a lot of money*|*work* **5 for the hell of it** *infml* for fun: *Then we decided to go swimming at midnight just for the hell of it* **6 give hell to** (someone) to treat or scold (someone) very roughly in anger: *My father wasn't there when I came in late, but he gave me hell in the morning* **7 hell for leather** *infml* very fast: *I was half an hour late for work, and I cycled hell for leather down the hill* **8 hell to pay** *sl* see DEVIL[1] (14) **9 like hell a** *infml* (*used after the phrase*) very much: *He worked like hell to get the house built* **b** *sl* (*used before the phrase*) not at all so: *Like hell he paid for the meal! I had to pay for it!* **10 play hell with** *infml* **a** to cause damage to (something); play the DEVIL[1] (11) with **b** *esp. BrE* to be very angry with (someone) **11 The hell you will/won't, he can/can't, etc.** *sl.* see DEVIL[1] (15) —see also **come hell or** HIGH WATER

hell[2] *BrE* also **bloody hell**— *interj sl* (an expression of strong anger or disappointment): OH, *hell! I've missed the last train.*|*Bloody hell!*

he'll /il, hil; *strong* hiːl/ [Wv2] *contr. of* **1** he will **2** he shall —see CONTR. (USAGE)

hell-bent /ˌ· ˈ·◂/ *adj* [Wa5;F+*for, on,* F3] *infml* determined (to do something) and careless of danger

hell·cat /ˈhelkæt/ *n* [C; *you*+N] a badly behaved hot-tempered woman

Hel·lene /ˈheliːn/ *n* a Greek, esp. an ancient Greek

Hel·len·ic /heˈlenɪk/ *adj* [Wa5] of or concerning the Greeks, their works of art, etc., esp. during the ancient period before Alexander the Great

Hel·le·nis·tic /ˌhel$\dot{j}$ˈnɪstɪk/ *adj* [Wa5] of or concerning the history, civilization, or art of ancient Greece and other nations conquered or influenced by Alexander the Great

hell·ish /ˈhelɪʃ/ *adj* **1** like or suitable for HELL (1, 2) **2** *infml* terrible; very unpleasant; devilish: *It's a hellish difficulty*/PROBLEM, *but we have to face it*

hell·ish·ly /ˈhelɪʃli/ *adv* very badly (so); devilishly

hel·lo /həˈləʊ, he-/ also *BrE* **hallo, hullo**— *interj, n* **-los 1 a** (the usual word of greeting): *Hello, John! How are you?* **b** (the word used for starting a telephone conversation): *Hello, is Mrs. Brown there?|Hello, who's speaking, please?* **2** *esp. BrE* (an expression of surprise): *Hello! What's happening now?|Hello! Somebody's left their hat behind* **3** (a call for attention to a distant person): *Hello! Is anybody there?* **4 Hello hello hello** *BrE humor* (supposedly said by a policeman on finding something unusual): *Hello hello hello, what's this: a knife hidden among the rose bushes?*

helm /helm/ *n* **1 a** the TILLER which guides a ship (esp. in the phr. **at the helm**) **b** the position from which things are controlled: *With our new leader at the helm things are sure to improve* **2** *old use* HELMET

hel·met /ˈhelm$\dot{j}$t/ *n* a covering to protect the head, as formerly used by men wearing armour, and now as worn by soldiers and by motorcyclists, policemen, firemen, and miners, who might hurt their heads in accidents or at work

hel·met·ed /ˈhelm$\dot{j}$t$\dot{j}$d/ *adj* wearing a helmet

helms·man /ˈhelmzmən/ *n* **-men** /mən/ a person who guides and controls, esp. when STEERing at the HELM of a boat

hel·ot /ˈhelət/ *n* **1** a slave in ancient Sparta in Greece **2** a member of any social group which is not respected

help[1] /help/ *v* **1** [T1;IØ;V3, (*esp. AmE*) 2] to do part of the work for (someone); be of use to (someone in doing something); AID; ASSIST: *Could you help me up (the stairs)?|The stick helps him (to) walk.|Your sympathy helps a lot.|Can I help (with your work)?|"Can I help you?"* (=May I show you anything?) *said the shopgirl* **2** [T1;IØ;V3, (*esp. AmE*) 2] to encourage, improve, or produce favourable conditions for (something): *Trade helps the development of industry.|Trade helps industry (to) develop* **3** [T1;IØ] to make better: *Crying won't help (you).|It won't help (you) to cry.|What have you got that will help a cold?* **4** [T1,4;V4 *neg.*] to avoid; prevent; change; have control over (only in the phr. **can/can't/couldn't help**): *I couldn't help crying.|I can't help my big feet.|She can't help herself, she doesn't mean to be so rude.|I couldn't help him saying that* **5** [T1 (*to*)] to take for (oneself), esp. dishonestly: *The money was on the table and no one was there, so he helped himself (to it).|"Can I have a drink?" "Help yourself!"* **6 it can't be helped** These things happen, we must accept it: *You've broken it now, it can't be helped* **7 I can't help it** It's not my fault, I can't stop it, etc.: *"Why are you crying?"—"I just can't help it."* **8 God helps those who help themselves** You will be successful if you try to be independent **9 more than one can help** *neg.* as little as is possible or necessary: *He never does more work than he can help* **10 so help me a** on my solemn promise: *I'll pay you back, so help me (I will)!* **b** believe it or not; although it may seem strange: *I really saw it, so help me (I did)!* **11 so help me God a** *law* (used in making solemn promises): *I swear to tell the truth, so help me God* **b** so HELP (10) me

USAGE 1 **Help** and (*fml*) **assist** have often the same meaning, but **assist** always means that the person **assisted** is able to do part of the work. One **helps** (=saves) someone who is drowning; one **helps** or **assists** someone who is moving a piano. One usually **aids** (*fml*) a group of people, esp. with money: **aid** *for developing countries.* 2 *I can't* **help** *thinking* or (*fml*) *I cannot but think* are considered better English than *I can't* **help** *but think.*

help[2] *n* **1** [U] the act of helping; AID; ASSISTANCE: *You're not (of) much help to me just sitting there.|You gave me a lot of help* **2** [C (*to*)] something or somebody that helps: *You're a good help to me.|The new fire is a great help* **3** [U *nonassertive*] a way of avoiding (esp. in the phr. **no help for it**) **4** [C] a person, esp. female, who is employed to do some of someone else's housework: *The new help left after a week* **5** [P] *esp. AmE* workers, esp. female house servants: *The help are demanding higher wages* **6 Help! a** Please bring help, I'm in danger **b** (an expression of surprise and inability to act) **7 Help Wanted** (a sign offering employment)

help·ful /ˈhelpfəl/ *adj* [(*to, in*)] willing to help; useful —**~ly** *adv* —**~ness** *n* [U]

help·ing /ˈhelpɪŋ/ *n* a serving of food; PORTION (3): *I'd like a second helping, I'm still so hungry!*

help·less /ˈhelpləs/ *adj* unable to look after oneself or to act without help: *a helpless child* —**~ly** *adv* —**~ness** *n* [U]

help·mate /ˈhelpmeɪt/ also **help·meet** /-miːt/— *n esp. bibl* a useful partner, usu. a wife

help out *v adv* [T1;IØ: (*with*)] to give help at a time of need (to some one): *My father helped me out (with money) when I lost my job*

help to *v prep* [D1] to serve (esp. oneself) with (food or drink): *He helped himself to the meat*

hel·ter-skel·ter[1] /ˌheltəʳ ˈskeltəʳ/ *adv, adj* (done) in a great hurry; disordered/disorderly: *She went helter-skelter down the stairs*

helter-skelter[2] *n esp. BrE* an amusement in a FAIRGROUND where one sits down and slides from the top of a tower to the bottom, moving round and round it

helve /helv/ *n* the handle of an axe or another such tool

hem[1] /hem/ *n* **1** the edge of a piece of cloth when turned under and sewn down, esp. the lower edge of a skirt or dress **2 take the hem up** also **take a dress/skirt up**— to make a dress or skirt shorter

hem[2] *v* **-mm-** [T1] to put a HEM[1] on

hem[3] *v* **-mm-** [IØ] *esp. AmE* HUM[3]

he-man /ˈ· ·/ *n* **-men** a strong manly man —see also HE-

hem in also **hedge in, hem a·bout, hem a·round**— *v adv* [T1] to surround tightly; enclose: *The whole army was hemmed in by the enemy with no hope of escape*

hem·i·sphere /ˈhem$\dot{j}$sfɪəʳ/ *n* **1** half a SPHERE (an object which is round like a ball) **2** a half of the earth, esp. the northern or southern above and below the EQUATOR, or the eastern or western half —see picture at GLOBE

hem·line /ˈhemlaɪn/ *n* the position of the HEM; length of a dress, skirt, etc. (esp. in the phrs. **to raise/to lower the hemline**): *When fashion changes hemlines are raised or lowered*

hem·lock /ˈhemlɒk‖-lɑk/ *n* **1** [C] a type of poisonous plant with white flowers and finely divided leaves **2** [U] the poison made from this

he·mo-, *BrE* also **haemo-** /ˈhiːmə-/ *comb. form* of the blood: *a* HEMORRHAGE

he·mo·glo·bin /ˌhiːməˈgləʊb$\dot{j}$n‖ˈhiːməˌgləʊb$\dot{j}$n/ *n*

[U] a red colouring matter in the blood which contains iron and carries oxygen

he·mo·phil·i·a /ˌhiːməˈfɪlɪə/ *n* [U] a disease which shows its effects only in males, but may be passed by INHERITANCE (2) from the mother or father to the children, and which makes the sufferer bleed for a long time after a cut or small accident

he·mo·phil·i·ac /ˌhiːməˈfɪliæk/ *n, adj* (of or being) a person suffering from HEMOPHILIA

hem·or·rhage /ˈhemərɪdʒ/ *n* [U;C] a flow of blood, esp. a long or large and unexpected one

hem·or·rhoid /ˈhemərɔɪd/ *n* [*usu. pl.*] *med or fml* a swollen blood vessel at the opening (ANUS) at the lower end of the bowel —see also PILES

hemp /hemp/ *n* [U] any of a family of plants which are used for making strong rope and a rough cloth, and some of which produce a drug called CANNABIS —see also INDIAN HEMP, MANILA **hemp**

hemp·en /ˈhempən/ *adj* [Wa5] *now rare* made of HEMP

hem·stitch /ˈhemˌstɪtʃ/ *n* [U] a special way of stitching HEM*s* in which some threads are pulled out and others sewn together to give a pattern of open places

hen /hen/ *n* **1** the female bird often kept for its eggs on farms; female chicken **2** a female bird of which the male is the COCK[1] (1,2): *The* COCK *has brighter coloured feathers than the hen.*|*a hen* PHEASANT —see MEAT (USAGE)

hen·bane /ˈhenbeɪn/ *n* **1** [C] a type of poisonous wild plant with yellow flowers **2** [U] the poison taken from this

hence /hens/ *adv* [Wa5] **1** for this reason or from this origin; therefore: *The town was built on the side of a hill: hence the name Hillside* **2** *fml or old use* from here or from now: *2 miles hence*|*3 days hence*

hence·forth /ˌhensˈfɔːθ, ˈhensfɔːθ‖-orθ/ also **hence·for·ward** /ˌhensˈfɔːwed‖-ˈforwərd/— *adv* [Wa5] (esp. of promises, decisions, and results) from this time on: *I promise never to get drunk henceforth* —compare HEREAFTER

hench·man /ˈhentʃmən/ *n* **-men** /mən/ *usu. derog* a faithful supporter, esp. of a political leader, who obeys without question and may use violent or dishonest methods

hen house /ˈ· ·/ *n* a usu. wooden hut in which hens sleep —see picture at FARMYARD

hen·na /ˈhenə/ *n* [U] **1** a type of bush grown in some Asian countries which produces a reddish-brown DYE **2** the DYE from this, which may be used to colour the hair, fingernails, etc.

hen·naed /ˈhenəd/ *adj* coloured with HENNA

hen par·ty /ˈ· ˌ··/ *n infml & humor* a PARTY (2) for women only —compare STAG **party**

hen·pecked /ˈhenpekt/ *adj* (of a man) scolded by one's wife and obedient to her

hep·a·ti·tis /ˌhepəˈtaɪtɪ̈s/ *n* [U] a disease (INFLAMMATION) of the LIVER[1] (1)

hep·ta·gon /ˈheptəgən‖-gɑn/ *n* a figure with 7 sides —**~al** /hepˈtægənəl/

her[1] /əʳ, həʳ; *strong* hɜːʳ/ [Wp1] (*poss. form of* SHE) belonging to her: *That's not Mary's skirt, it's her dress.*|*That's not my dress, it's her dress.*|*Those are her shoes, not mine*

her[2] *pron* [Wp1] (*object form of* SHE): *Where is she? Can you see her*|*give it to her?*|*He wants to marry her, and her only 15!*|*Which is the girl you know? Is that her?*|*God bless this ship and all who sail in her!* —see ME (USAGE)

her·ald[1] /ˈherəld/ *n* **1** (in former times) a person who carried messages from a ruler and gave important news to the people **2** an official person who keeps records of the COAT*s* OF ARMS of noble families **3** a messenger or sign of something about to come, happen, etc. —compare HARBINGER

herald[2] *v* [T1 (IN)] to be a sign of something coming: *The singing of the birds heralded* (*in*) *the day*

he·ral·dic /heˈrældɪk/ *adj* of or concerning HERALDRY

her·ald·ry /ˈherəldri/ *n* [U] **1** the study and use of COAT*s* OF ARMS **2** the practice of the office of HERALD[1] (2)

herb /hɜːb‖ɜrb, hɜrb/ *n* any of several kinds of plant which appear to die at the end of the growing season but grow again the next year, esp. one which is used to make medicine or to make food taste stronger (to FLAVOUR food)

her·ba·ceous /həˈbeɪʃəs‖ɜrˈbeɪ-, hɜrˈbeɪ-/ *adj* (of a plant) soft-stemmed, not woody: *We have a* **herbaceous border** (= border of herbaceous plants) *round our garden*

herb·age /ˈhɜːbɪdʒ‖ˈɜr-, ˈhɜr-/ *n* [U] **1** HERB*s* generally **2** grass generally

herb·al /ˈhɜːbəl‖ˈɜr-, ˈhɜr-/ *adj* [Wa5] (made) of HERB*s*

herb·al·ist /ˈhɜːbəlɪ̈st‖ˈɜr-, ˈhɜr-/ *n* **1** a person who grows and/or sells HERB*s*, esp. for making medicine **2** a person who treats disease with HERB*s*

her·biv·o·rous /hɜːˈbɪvərəs‖ɜr-, hɜr-/ *adj* [Wa5] (of animals) which eat grass and plants

Her·cu·le·an /ˌhɜːkjʊˈliːən, hɜːˈkjuːlɪən‖-ɜr-/ *adj* (*sometimes not cap.*) of or showing (the need for) great strength: *A herculean effort was made*

herd[1] /hɜːd‖hɜrd/ *n* **1** a group of animals of one kind which live and feed together: *a herd of elephants* **2** (*in comb.*) a boy or man who looks after a group of animals; HERDSMAN: SHEPHERD|*goatherd* **3** *derog* people generally, thought of as acting all alike with no person having his own thoughts or opinions: *the herd* INSTINCT (=common feeling which makes a group violent towards a stranger or outsider)

herd[2] *v* **1** [L9] to group together: *They herded into the corner* **2** [T1] to look after or drive (animals or people) in a HERD: *The farmer herded the cows into the field*

herds·man /ˈhɜːdzmən‖-ɜr-/ *n* **-men** /mən/ a man who looks after a HERD of animals

here[1] /hɪəʳ/ *adv* [Wa5] **1** [F] at, in, or to this place: *I live* (*right*) *here.*|*2 miles from here*|*Come here!*|*It hurts here.*|*He's here!*|*I live near here.*|*Here is where I want to stay.*|*Come over* (=across to) *here.*|*It's here* (*where*) *we met* **2** (*often at the beginning of a sentence*) at this point of time: *I came to a difficulty—Here I stopped* **3** (used for introducing something or somebody, usu. followed by the verb unless the subject, is a pron): *Here comes John. Here he comes!*|*Here's the book.*|*Here is the news . . .* **4** [E] *infml* (*used after a noun*) being present; in this place: *This book here is the most useful.*|*"It's Professor Worth's secretary here"* (=speaking on the telephone) (SEU S.) **5 Here and there** scattered about **6 Here goes!** Now I'm going to have a try (to do something, esp. something difficult): *I've never been on a horse before—well, here goes!* **7 Here's to** (said when drinking a TOAST[2] (2)): *Here's to John in his new job!* **8 here, there, and everywhere** in every place **9 here today and gone tomorrow** remaining a very short time **10 Here you are** Here's what you want **11 neither here nor there** not connected with the matter being talked about: *I know many people like the idea, but that's neither here nor there: we just can't afford it*

USAGE Note the word order in this fixed phrase: **here and now:** *Yes, I'd like a piano, but here and now we haven't enough room.*

here[2] *interj* **1** (used to call someone's attention): *Here! What are you doing?* **2 Look here** also **See here** Now give attention to my warning: *See here, I* *can't allow this bad behaviour in my house*

here·a·bouts /ˌhɪərəˈbaʊts, ˈhɪərəbaʊts/ *AmE* also **here·a·bout** /-aʊt/— *adv* [Wa5] somewhere near here

here·af·ter¹ /ˌhɪərˈɑːftəʳ‖-ˈæf-/ *adv* [Wa5] *fml* after this time; in the future: *"She should have died hereafter"* (Shakespeare, "Macbeth") —compare HENCEFORTH, THEREAFTER

hereafter² *n* [S] the life after death: *Her religion promises her happiness now and in the hereafter.|Do you believe in a hereafter?*

here·by /ˌhɪəˈbaɪ, ˈhɪəbaɪ‖-ər-/ *adv* [Wa5] *fml or law* by this means; by doing or saying this: *I hereby declare her elected* —compare THEREBY

her·e·dit·a·ment /ˌherɪ̵ˈdɪtəmənt/ *n law* land and property which can be passed on after the death of the owner to his relatives (INHERITed)

he·red·i·ta·ry /hɪ̵ˈredɪ̵təri‖-teri/ *adj* [Wa5] **1 a** (of a position, right, etc.) which can be passed down from an older to a younger person, esp. in the same family **b** (of a person) who can receive by law such a position, right, etc. **2** (of a quality or condition of mind or body) which can be or is passed down from parent to child in the cells of the body: *a hereditary disease|a hereditary ability* —**-rily** *adv*

hereditary peer /·ˌ···· ˈ·/ *n* PEER OF THE REALM

he·red·i·ty /hɪ̵ˈredɪ̵ti/ *n* [U] the fact that living things have the ability to pass on their own qualities from parent to child in the cells of the body: *Some diseases develop because of the conditions one lives in, others are present by heredity*

here·in /ˌhɪərˈɪn/ *adv* [Wa5] *fml or law* in this (piece of writing): *. . . and everything herein contained* —compare THEREIN

here·in·af·ter /ˌhɪərɪnˈɑːftəʳ‖-ˈæf-/ *adv* [Wa5] *law* later in this official paper, statement, etc.

here·of /ˌhɪərˈɒv‖-ˈʌv, -ˈɑv/ *adv* [Wa5] *law* of or belonging to this: *. . . every part hereof* —compare THEREOF

her·e·sy /ˈherɪ̵si/ *n* **1** [U] the fact of holding a belief against what is accepted, esp. in official religion **2** [C] such a belief, or an act or statement which shows it

her·e·tic /ˈherɪ̵tɪk/ *n* a person who favours HERESY or is guilty of a heresy —**~al** /hɪ̵ˈretɪkəl/ *adj* —**~ally** *adv* [Wa4]

here·to /ˌhɪəˈtuː‖ˌhɪərˈtuː/ *adv* [Wa5] *fml* to this (piece of writing)

here·to·fore /ˌhɪətʊˈfɔːʳ‖ˈhɪərtʊfor/ *adv* [Wa5] *fml or law* until now; before this time; HITHERTO: *We will continue to hold meetings on Thursdays, as heretofore*

here·un·der /ˌhɪərˈʌndəʳ/ *adv* [Wa5] *fml* below, following, or in accordance with (something written)

here·up·on /ˌhɪərəˈpɒn‖-ˈpɑn/ *adv* [Wa5] *fml* **1** about this matter: *if all are agreed hereupon* **2** at/after this point in time: *Hereupon they all began to shout* —compare THEREUPON

here·with /ˌhɪəˈwɪð‖ˌhɪər-/ *adv* [Wa5] **1** (in business) with this (letter or written material): *I send you herewith 2 copies of the contract* **2** (in business) at once; now

her·i·ta·ble /ˈherɪ̵təbəl/ *adj* **1** (of property) which can be passed on to one's descendants by law **2** (of qualities, diseases, etc.) which can or could be passed to one's descendants (INHERITed); HEREDITARY **3** who can INHERIT

her·i·tage /ˈherɪ̵tɪdʒ/ *n* [*usu. sing.*] something which is passed down over many years within a family or nation: *the country's artistic heritage* (=pictures and beautiful buildings)

her·maph·ro·dite /hɜːˈmæfrədaɪt‖hɜr-/ *n, adj* (a living thing) with the organs or appearance of both male and female —**-ditic** /hɜːˌmæfrəˈdɪtɪk‖hɜr-/ *adj*

her·met·ic /hɜːˈmetɪk‖hɜr-/ also **her·met·i·cal** /-ɪkəl/— *adj* **1** *old use* (*often cap.*) concerning magic or ALCHEMY **2** very tightly closed; AIRTIGHT: *A hermetic* SEAL² (4) *is used at the top of this glass bottle* —**~ally** *adv* [Wa4]

her·mit /ˈhɜːmɪ̵t‖ˈhɜr-/ *n* **1** (esp. in former times) a holy man who lived alone, thinking and praying **2** a person who avoids other people

her·mit·age /ˈhɜːmɪ̵tɪdʒ‖ˈhɜr-/ *n* a place where a HERMIT (1) lives or has lived

her·ni·a /ˈhɜːnɪə‖ˈhɜr-/ also **rupture**— *n* **1** [C] a part of the body where the covering wall of an organ is stretched and the organ is pushing through it, usu. when the bowel is pushed through the stomach wall **2** [U] the unhealthy condition of this part of the body

he·ro /ˈhɪərəʊ/ *fem.* **her·o·ine** /ˈherəʊɪn/— *n* **-roes** **1** a person remembered for bravery, strength, or goodness, esp. when admired for an act of courage under difficult conditions **2** the most important character in a play, poem, story, etc.

he·ro·ic /hɪˈrəʊɪk/ *adj* **1 a** showing the qualities of a HERO (1) **b** needing or showing bravery **2** large and/or grand: *heroic-sounding speeches* —**~ally** *adv* [Wa4]

heroic coup·let /·ˌ·· ˈ··/ *n* a pair of lines of a type once common in English poetry, which RHYME² (1) and are written in IAMBIC PENTAMETER (with 5 beats each)

he·ro·ics /hɪˈrəʊɪks/ *n* [P] speech or actions which are meant to appear grand, though they mean nothing

her·o·in /ˈherəʊɪn/ *n* a drug made from MORPHINE, which is used for lessening pain, and which one can become dependent on (ADDICTed to)

her·o·is·m /ˈherəʊɪzəm/ *n* [U] **1** the quality of being a HERO (1): *You don't often find soldiers with such heroism* **2** great courage: *It was an act of heroism to stop the train*

her·on /ˈherən/ *n* [Wn1] a type of bird which has long legs and lives near water, where it catches small animals to eat —see picture at WATER¹

her·on·ry /ˈherənri/ *n* a place where several HERONs have their nests

her·pes /ˈhɜːpiːz‖ˈhɜr-/ *n* [U] a skin disease in which red spots spread around the body —compare SHINGLES

Herr /heəʳ (*Ger* hɛr)/ *n* [A] (the German word for) Mr

her·ring /ˈherɪŋ/ *n* **-rings** *or* **-ring** [Wn2] **1** a type of fish used for food, which swims in large groups (SHOALs) in the sea —see picture at FISH¹ **2 red herring** a fact or point of argument which is introduced to draw attention away from the main point

her·ring·bone /ˈherɪŋbəʊn/ *n* (used esp. of an ornamental arrangement of bricks or of a sewing stitch) a pattern where 2 sides slope in opposite directions, forming a continuous line of V's

hers /hɜːz‖hɜrz/ *pron* [Wp1] (*poss. form of* SHE) that/those belonging to her: *The sheep is/are hers.|Hers is/are over there.|That fool of a brother of hers!* —see also OF (6)

her·self /əˈself, hə-; *strong* hɜː-‖ər-, hər-; *strong* hɜr-/ *pron* [Wp1] **1** (*refl. form of* SHE): *She cut herself in the kitchen.|She's sorry for herself* **2** (*strong form of* SHE): *She told me herself, so it must be true.|She herself said so.|Herself still only a girl, Victoria was called upon to become queen of a great empire* **3** *infml* (in) her usual state of mind or body (in the phr. **be herself, come to herself**): *She was very ill yesterday, but she's more herself today.|She lost her temper, but soon came to herself* (=regained control) *and said she was sorry* **4 (all) by herself** alone, without help: *The little girl wrote the letter all by herself.|She lives by herself in the country* —see YOURSELF (USAGE)

hertz /hɜːts‖hɜrts/ *n* **hertz** [Wn3] (a measure meaning) one time each second: *These radio waves are coming at 15,000* CYCLES[1] (1) *per second, that's 15* KILOHERTZ *or 15,000 hertz*

he's /iz, hiz; *strong* hiːz/ *contr. of* **1** [Wv1] he is: *He's a writer.|He's coming* **2** [Wv2] (*in compound tenses*) he has: *He's got 2 cars.|He's had a cold* —see CONTR. (USAGE)

hes·i·tan·cy /ˈhezətənsi/ also **hes·i·tance** /-təns/— *n* [U] the state or quality of being HESITANT

hes·i·tant /ˈhezətənt/ *adj* showing uncertainty or slowness about deciding to act; tending to HESITATE: *She's hesitant about making new friends* —**~ly** *adv*

hes·i·tate /ˈhezəteɪt/ *v* [I∅,3] **1 a** to pause in or before an action: *He who hesitates is lost* (=loses his chance and will never succeed) **b** to be slow in deciding: *She hesitated over the choice between the two dresses* **2** (*as a polite form*) to be unwilling; find it unpleasant: *I hesitate to ask you, but will you lend me some money?* —**-tating** *adj* —**-tatingly** *adv*

hes·i·ta·tion /ˌhezəˈteɪʃən/ *n* **1** [U] the act of hesitating (HESITATE): *Without hesitation, I would say . . .|I have no hesitation in saying . . .* **2** [C] an example of this

Hes·pe·rus /ˈhespərəs/ *n* [R] *poet* the evening star (VENUS) seen shining brightly in the western sky

hes·si·an /ˈhesiən‖ˈheʃən/ *n* **1** [U] a thick rough type of cloth made from HEMP; SACKCLOTH —compare BURLAP **2** [C *usu. pl.*] (in former times) a type of high boot

het·e·ro- /ˈhetərə, -rəʊ/ *comb. form* other; opposite; different: *heterosexual* —compare HOMO-

het·e·ro·dox /ˈhetərədɒks‖-dɑks/ *adj* (of beliefs, practices, etc.) against accepted opinion, esp. in religion; not ORTHODOX

het·e·ro·dox·y /ˈhetərədɒksi‖-dɑk-/ *n* [U] the state or quality of being HETERODOX; UNORTHODOXY

het·e·ro·ge·ne·ous /ˌhetərəʊˈdʒiːniəs/ *adj* of (many) different kinds: *a heterogeneous mass of papers* —**~ly** *adv* —**-ity** /ˌhetərəʊdʒəˈniːəti/ *n* [U]

het·e·ro·sex·u·al /ˌhetərəˈsekʃʊəl/ *adj, n* (of or being) a person attracted in the usual way by people of the other sex —**~ly** *adv* —**~ity** /ˌhetərəsekʃʊˈæləti/ *n* [U]

het up /ˌhet ˈʌp/ *adj* [F (*about*)] *infml* (of people) excited; anxious: *all het up about going*

heu·ris·tic /hjʊəˈrɪstɪk/ *adj* **1** (of education) by experience; by one's own personal discoveries **2** of practical, though perhaps unexplained, use in invention or discovery: *heuristic ideas that seem helpful although we really don't know why* —**~ally** *adv* [Wa4]

heu·ris·tics /hjʊəˈrɪstɪks/ *n* [U;P] (the study of) the use of experience and practical efforts to find answers to questions or to improve performance

hew /hjuː/ *v* **hewed, hewed** *or* **hewn** /hjuːn/ **1** [T1;I∅] to cut in(to) by striking blows with an axe or weapon; HACK: *They hewed at the door/hewed away* **2** [T1 (DOWN)] to cut down by blows: *to hew (down) trees* **3** [T1] to cut and shape out by blows from a larger mass: *Miners hew coal. They hew it out of the rock.|to hew one's way through the forest* **4** [T1 (OUT)] to cause to exist or develop by the use of one's efforts: *He hewed out an important position for himself in the company*

hew·er /ˈhjuːəʳ/ *n* **1** a person who HEWs wood, or esp. coal in the mines **2 hewers of wood and drawers of water** *lit or bibl* people with humble work; the lower classes

hex[1] /heks/ *n AmE* a magic charm, often harmful

hex[2] *v* [T1] *AmE* to put a magic charm on (someone or something)

hex·a·gon /ˈheksəgən‖-gɑn/ *n* a figure with 6 sides —**~al** /hekˈsægənəl/ *adj*

hex·a·gram /ˈheksəgræm/ *n* a 6-pointed star made up from 2 3-sided figures (TRIANGLEs)

hex·am·e·ter /hekˈsæmətəʳ/ *n* (in poetry, esp. Greek or Latin) a type of line with 6 beats

hey /heɪ/ *interj* (a shout used to call attention or to express surprise, interest, etc.): *Hey! Where are you going?*

hey·day /ˈheɪdeɪ/ *n* [S] **1** the highest point (of some desirable state): *In the heyday of housebuilding there were enough homes for everybody* **2** the best time of one's youth, when one is strong and cheerful

hey pres·to /ˌheɪ ˈprestəʊ/ *interj infml* **1** suddenly; all at once: *At one moment the street was empty, and then hey presto!, there he was standing on the corner* **2** (used by someone performing a magic trick) Here is the result of my trick!

hi /haɪ/ *interj* **1** *esp. BrE* HEY **2** *infml* HELLO

hi·a·tus /haɪˈeɪtəs/ *n* [*usu. sing.*] **1** *fml* a space or GAP where something is missing: *The end of Mr. Jones' set of talks left a hiatus to be filled in in the timetable* **2** a place where something is missing, esp. a word in old writings **3** *tech* a pause between (or lack of a sound which joins) 2 vowel sounds

hi·ber·nate /ˈhaɪbəneɪt‖-ər-/ *v* [I∅] (of animals) to be or go into a state like a long sleep during the winter: *Many animals hibernate in winter* —**-nation** /ˌhaɪbəˈneɪʃən‖-ər-/ *n* [U]

hi·bis·cus /həˈbɪskəs, haɪ-/ *n* a type of plant with large bright flowers, which grows in hot countries —compare MALLOW and see picture at FLOWER[1]

hic·cup[1], **hiccough** /ˈhɪkʌp, -kəp/ *n* [*often pl.*] **1** a movement in the chest which stops the breath and causes one to make a sudden sharp sound **2** the sound made by this movement: *In the middle of the prayer there was a loud hiccup from my son*

hiccup[2], **hiccough** *v* [I∅] **1** to be having HICCUPs: *I hiccuped all night after drinking all that wine* **2** to make a HICCUP, or a sound like one

hick /hɪk/ *n AmE sl* a foolish person from the country

hick·o·ry /ˈhɪkəri/ *n* **1** [C] a type of tree of North America which provides hard wood and bears nuts **2** [U] the wood of this tree **3** [C] a walking-stick made from this

hide[1] /haɪd/ *v* **hid** /hɪd/, **hidden** /ˈhɪdn/ **1** [T1] to put or keep out of sight; make or keep secret: *I hid the broken plate behind the table.|You're hiding some important facts.|Don't hide your feelings, say what you think* **2** [I∅] to place oneself or be placed so as to be unseen: *I'll hide behind the door.|Where's that book hiding?*

hide[2] *n* **1** an animal's skin, esp. when removed to be used for leather **2 hide or/nor hair of** *infml usu. neg.* any sign of: *I haven't seen hide or hair of them for 20 years at least!* **3 tan someone's hide** *infml* to beat someone

hide[3] *n* a place from where a person may watch animals, esp. birds, without being seen by them, and from which he may be able to take photographs of them

hide-and-seek /ˌ· · ˈ·/ *n* [U] a children's game in which some hide and others search for them

hide·a·way /ˈhaɪdəweɪ/ *n infml* a place, such as a house, where one can go to avoid people

hide·bound /ˈhaɪdbaʊnd/ *adj* (of people) having fixed, unchangeable opinions; not willing to consider new ideas; NARROW-MINDED

hid·e·ous /ˈhɪdɪəs/ *adj* having a terrible effect on the senses, esp. shocking to the eyes: *a hideous face|a hideous noise|He suffered a hideous fate when* *the enemy caught him* —**~ly** *adv* —**~ness** *n* [U]

hid·ing¹ /ˈhaɪdɪŋ/ *n infml* a beating: *I'll give you a good hiding when we get home!*

hiding² *n* [U] the state of being hidden (only in the phrs. **go into hiding, be in hiding**)

hie /haɪ/ *v* **hied, hying** *or* **hieing** [L9;X9] *old use or humor* to cause (one or oneself) to hurry or go quickly: *I will hie (me/myself) to the market*

hi·er·ar·chy /ˈhaɪərɑːki‖-ɑr-/ *n* **1** [C;(U)] the organization of a system into higher and lower ranks, esp. official ranks: (fig.) *a hierarchy of moral values|Do you believe in the principle of hierarchy?* **2** [GC] a group of ruling priests —**-chical** /haɪəˈrɑkɪkəl‖-ɑr-/ *adj* —**-chically** *adv* [Wa4]

hi·e·ro·glyph /ˈhaɪərəglɪf/ *n* a picture-like sign which represents a word, esp. in the writing system of ancient Egypt —**~ic** /ˌhaɪərəˈglɪfɪk/ *adj*

hi·e·ro·glyph·ics /ˌhaɪərəˈglɪfɪks/ *n* [P] the system of writing which uses HIEROGLYPH*s*

hi-fi /ˈhaɪ faɪ, ˌhaɪ ˈfaɪ/ *n* **hi-fis** [C;U] HIGH FIDELITY (=very sensitive) apparatus for reproducing recorded sound: *When you listen to my hi-fi (set), it's like sitting in the concert hall!*

hig·gle·dy-pig·gle·dy /ˌhɪgəldi ˈpɪgəldi/ *adj, adv infml* in disorder; mixed together without system

high¹ /haɪ/ *adj* **1** [Wa1;B;E] **a** (not usu. of living things) reaching some distance above ground, esp. a large distance: *How high is it?|It's a very high building.|a high wall|4 feet high* **b** at a point above the ground, esp. a long way above: *"How high is he now?" "He's very high up".|Those books are too high for me.|The plane is high in the sky* **2** [Wa1;B] important; chief (esp. in the phrs. **high society, high circles, high life**=those of the wealthy, noble, etc.): *high office in the government* **3** [Wa1;B] showing goodness: *high principles* **4** [Wa1;B] near the top of the set of sounds which the ear can hear: *She held a high note.|She has a very high voice* **5** [Wa1;B] above the usual level, rate of movement, etc.: *the high cost of food|The gas is kept at high pressure.|high speed* **6** [Wa5;A] (of time) at the most important or mid-point of: *It's high time we went.|They met at high* NOON, *with the sun's heat beating down on them fiercely.|high summer* **7** [Wa1;B] (of food) not fresh; spoilt by age **8** [Wa1;F] *infml* **a** drunk **b** under the effects of drugs **9 hold one's head high** to show pride and courage, esp. in difficulty —opposite usu. **low**; see also HIGHER

USAGE When we speak of a **high** building or mountain, we are thinking of distance above the ground: *a mountain 2,000 metres* **high**|*The shelf is too* **high** *for me to reach* (opposite **low**). When we are thinking of length from top to bottom we use the word **tall**. This means **high** but also narrow, and is used esp. of people, trees, or buildings of the same sort of shape: *a very* **tall** man (opposite **short**)|*The ship is too* **tall** *to go under the bridge.*

high² *adv* [Wa1] **1** [F] to or at a high level in position, movements or sound: *They climbed high.|The plane flew high above.|The bird sang high and clearly* **2** [F] to or at a high or important degree esp. of social movement (esp. in the phr. **aim high**): *He's risen high in the world.|*(fig.) *He's flying high, but he'll fall soon* **3 feelings ran high** people got excited and angry **4 high and dry** without help; deserted: *He took all the money and left me high and dry* **5 high and low** everywhere **6 high on the hog** *AmE sl* well and richly: *They've been living high on the hog since they struck oil* —opposite usu. **low**

high³ *n* **1** [U] a high place, esp. heaven (only in the phr. **on high**) **2** [C] *not fml* a high point; the highest level: *The price of food reached a new high this week* **3** [C] *infml* a state of great excitement and often happiness produced by or as if by a drug **4** [C] ANTICYCLONE (=a weather condition with a high-pressure area) **5** [U] the high GEAR¹ (3) in cars (esp. in the phr. **move into high**)

-high *comb. form* [*n→adj, (adv)*] having the stated height: *sky-high|waist-high|a 5-mile-high mountain*

high-and-might·y /ˌ· · ˈ··◂/ *adj infml* too proud: *Who do you think you are, Mr. High-and-Mighty?*

high·ball /ˈhaɪbɔːl/ *n esp. AmE* an alcoholic drink, esp. WHISKY or BRANDY with SODA (1)

high·born /ˈhaɪbɔːn‖-ɔrn/ *adj* of noble birth

high·boy /ˈhaɪbɔɪ/ *n AmE* TALLBOY

high·brow /ˈhaɪbraʊ/ *n sometimes derog* a person thought to show more than average knowledge of art and INTELLECTUAL interests —compare LOWBROW, MIDDLEBROW

high chair /ˌ· ˈ·‖ˈ· ·/ *n* a chair with long legs at which a baby or small child can sit, esp. when eating from a table or from a special TRAY joined to the chair

High Church /ˌ· ˈ·◂/ *adj* of the part of the CHURCH OF ENGLAND which places great importance on ceremony —**~man** *n*

high-class /ˌ· ˈ·◂/ *adj* [Wa2] **1** of good quality **2** of high social position

high com·mis·sion /ˌ· ·ˈ··/ *n* [GC] (*often caps.*) (the group of people who work in) the office (like an EMBASSY) of a HIGH COMMISSIONER

high com·mis·sion·er /ˌ· ·ˈ···/ *n* (*often caps.*) a person (like an AMBASSADOR) who represents one COMMONWEALTH country in another

high court /ˌ· ˈ·◂/ *n* the court which is above all the rest and which can be asked to change the decision of a lower court

high·er /ˈhaɪəʳ/ *adj* **1** see HIGH **2** [Wa5] more advanced, esp. in development, organization, or knowledge needed: *higher animals|higher nerve centres|higher* MATHEMATICS —opposite usu. **lower**

higher ed·u·ca·tion /ˌ·· ··ˈ··/ *n* [U;(C)] education at a university or college —compare FURTHER EDUCATION

higher-up /ˌ·· ˈ·◂/ *n* [*usu. pl.*] a more important official person

high ex·plo·sive /ˌ· ·ˈ··◂/ *n* [U *often pl. with same meaning*] powerful explosives

high·fa·lu·tin /ˌhaɪfəˈluːtɪ̆n◂‖-tn/ *adj infml* foolishly trying to appear grand: *a highfalutin manner*

high fi·del·i·ty /ˌ· ·ˈ···◂/ also **hi-fi**— *adj* (of TAPE RECORDER*s*, RECORD PLAYER*s*, etc.) able to give out sound which represents very closely the details of the original sound before recording

high-fli·er, -flyer /ˌ· ˈ··/ *n* a clever person who has high aims —see also HIGH² (2)

high-flown /ˌ· ˈ·◂/ *adj* (of language) grand-sounding, though lacking in meaning

high-fly·ing /ˌ· ˈ··◂/ *adj* **1** which flies high: *high-flying aircraft* **2** like a HIGH-FLIER

high-grade /ˌ· ˈ·◂/ *adj* [Wa2] of high quality: *high-grade cloth for suits*

high-hand·ed /ˌ· ˈ··◂/ *adj* [Wa2] using one's power too forcefully: *It was rather high-handed to punish the child for the accident* —**~ly** *adv* —**~ness** *n* [U]

high horse /ˈ· ·, ˌ· ˈ·/ *n* **on one's high horse** behaving, esp. talking, as if one knows best, or more than others

high jinks /ˈ· ·, ˌ· ˈ·/ *n* [P;(U)] wild fun of a harmless type

high jump /ˈ· ·/ *n* **1** a sport in which people jump over a bar which is raised higher and higher **2 be for the high jump** *BrE infml* to be about to get a bad punishment (formerly hanging) or scolding: *He'll be for the high jump when they know he's used the firm's car*

high-keyed /ˌ· ˈ·◂/ *adj* [Wa2] at a high level of sound or excitement —compare KEYed-UP

high·land /ˈhaɪlənd/ *adj, n* [Wa5] (of) a mountainous area

high·land·er /ˈhaɪləndəʳ/ *n* (*often cap.*) a person from a mountainous land, esp. in Scotland

Highland fling /ˌ·· ˈ·/ *n* a Scottish dance

High·lands /ˈhaɪləndz/ *n* [*the*+P] the mountainous area of Scotland

high-lev·el /ˌ· ˈ··◂/ *adj* [Wa2;A] **1** at a high level **2** in or at a position of high importance: *high-level peace talks*

high-life /ˈ· ·/ *n* **1** [(*the*) U] the enjoyable life of the rich and fashionable, which includes lots of amusement, good food, etc. —see also HIGH[1] (2) **2** [U] a type of music and dance popular in West Africa

high·light[1] /ˈhaɪlaɪt/ *n* [*often pl.*] **1** *tech* the area on a picture or photograph where most light appears to fall **2** an important detail which stands out from the rest: *We'll show you a film of the highlights of the competition, as there isn't time for the whole thing*

highlight[2] *v* [T1] to pick out (something) as an important part; throw attention onto

high·ly /ˈhaɪli/ *adv* **1** (*esp. before adjectives made from verbs*) to a high degree (HIGH); very: *highly pleased|highly skilled|highly interesting|highly enjoyable* **2 a** (very) well: *highly paid|He speaks very highly of the boy's behaviour* **b** very much; more so than usual: *highly* SALT*ed*

highly-strung /ˌ·· ˈ·◂/ also **high-strung**— *adj* nervous; excitable

high mass /ˌ· ˈ·/ *n* [C;U] a MASS (=type of church service) with singing and music

high-mind·ed /ˌ· ˈ··◂/ *adj* (of people) having high principles, perhaps too high —**~ly** *adv* —**~ness** *n* [U]

High·ness /ˈhaɪnɪ̈s/ *n* [C9;N9] (a title used of or to certain royal persons): *His/Her/Your Highness|His Highness Prince Leopold*

high noon /ˌ· ˈ·/ *n* [U] see HIGH[1] (6)

high-oc·tane /ˌ· ˈ··◂/ *adj* [Wa1] (of petrol) of a high OCTANE number, that shows good quality

high-pitched /ˌ· ˈ·◂/ *adj* **1** (of a sound or voice) having a high PITCH[3] (7) (sound level); not low or deep **2** (of a roof) sloping steeply

high-pow·ered /ˌ· ˈ··◂/ *adj* [Wa2] showing great force (in an activity): *high-powered selling methods| a high-powered car|high-powered politicians*

high-pres·sure[1] /ˌ· ˈ··◂/ *adj* **1** (of a machine or substance) which uses or is at high pressure **2** (of an action, job, or person) carried out or working with great speed and force: *A high-pressure salesman may make you buy something you don't want*

high-pressure[2] /ˈ· ˌ··/ *v* [T1(*into*)] *esp. AmE* to make (someone) do or buy something by HIGH-PRESSURE[1] (2) methods

high priest /ˌ· ˈ·/ *n* the chief priest, as in a temple

high-prin·ci·pled /ˌ· ˈ···◂/ *adj* honourable

high-rank·ing /ˌ· ˈ··◂/ *adj* [Wa2;A] of high rank

high re·lief /ˌ· ·ˈ·/ *n* [U;C] (an example of) a form of art in which figures are cut out of the stone or wood surface of a wall so that they stand well out from the background, which has been cut away —compare BAS-RELIEF

high-rise /ˈ· ·/ *adj* [Wa5;A] **1 a** (of buildings, esp. blocks of flats with several floors) built very high **b** concerning buildings of this type **2** higher or taller than usual, as of the HANDLEBAR*s* of a bicycle —**high rise** *n*

high·road /ˈhaɪrəʊd/ *n* **1** *esp. BrE* a main road; broad HIGH STREET: *got it at a shop in Kilburn High Road* **2** the easiest or best way: *the highroad to health* —compare HIGHWAY

high school /ˈ· ·/ *n* [C;U] *esp. AmE* (*caps. in names*) a SECONDARY school esp. for children over age 14

high seas /ˌ· ˈ·/ *n* [*the*+P] the oceans of the world which do not belong to any particular country

high sea·son /ˌ· ˈ··/ *n* [(*the*) U] the time of year when business is greatest and prices are highest: *Your ticket will cost more if you fly during (the) high season in the summer*

High Sher·iff /ˌ· ˈ··/ also **Sheriff**— *n* the royally-appointed chief officer in an area (COUNTY) of Britain with various duties in courts and in ceremonies

high-sound·ing /ˌ· ˈ··◂/ *adj* (of words, ideas, etc.) which are grand in style but have no meaning

high-speed /ˌ· ˈ·◂/ *adj* [Wa5;A;(B)] which travels, works, etc., very fast: *high-speed gas* (said to cook food quickly)

high-spir·it·ed /ˌ· ˈ···◂/ *adj* [Wa2] **1** (of a person, esp. a child or woman, or of behaviour) full of fun; adventure-loving **2** (of an animal, esp. a horse, or of animal behaviour) active, esp. nervously active, and hard to control

high spot /ˈ· ·/ *n* the most important part of an activity, esp. one remembered with pleasure

high street /ˈ· ·/ *n BrE* (*often caps, esp. when used as or in a name*) the main street of a town: *Camden High Street|"A Shop in the High Street"* (title of Czech film in Britain)

high-strung /ˌ· ˈ·◂/ *adj* [Wa2] HIGHLY-STRUNG

high ta·ble /ˌ· ˈ··/ *n* [U] (esp. in Britain) the table at which the teachers (DON*s*) at a college eat, which is at a level raised above that of the area where the students eat

high tea /ˌ· ˈ·/ *n* [U;(C)] *BrE* an early-evening meal taken in some parts of Britain instead of afternoon tea and late dinner, and at a time between the times of those meals

high-ten·sion /ˌ· ˈ··◂/ *adj* which carries a powerful electrical current: *high-tension wires*

high tide /ˌ· ˈ·/ *n* **1** [U;C] the moment when the water is highest up the sea shore because the TIDE has come in **2** [C *usu. sing.*] the point on the shore which the water reaches at this moment **3** [C *usu. sing.*] the highest point of success

high time /ˌ· ˈ·/ *n* [U] see HIGH[1] (6)

high-toned /ˌ· ˈ·◂/ *adj* concerned with great aims (of speeches, ideas, etc.)

high trea·son /ˌ· ˈ··/ *n* [U] the crime of putting one's country or its ruler in danger by giving help to their enemies, as by a plan to kill the king, or by giving important secrets to foreign powers

high wa·ter /ˌ· ˈ··/ *n* **1** [U;(C)] the moment when the water in a river is at its highest point because of the TIDE **2** [C *usu. sing.*] the point on the river bank which the water reaches at this moment **3** **come hell or high water** *BrE* (in spite of) whatever difficulties there may be

high water mark /ˌ· ˈ·· ·/ *n* **1** a mark showing the highest point reached by a body of water, such as a river **2** the highest point of success

high·way /ˈhaɪweɪ/ *n* **1** *esp. AmE* a broad main road used esp. by traffic going in 2 directions, and often leading from one town to another **2** HIGH-ROAD (2)

Highway Code /ˌ·· ˈ·/ *n* [(*the*) R;(C)] (in Britain) (a copy of) the official list of rules for the behaviour of drivers on the road

high·way·man /ˈhaɪweɪmən/ *n* **-men** /mən/ (in former times) a man who used to stop horsemen and carriages on the old roads, which were unlit and badly made, and rob them of their money

hi·jack[1] /ˈhaɪdʒæk/ *v* [T1] to take control of (a vehicle or aircraft) by force of arms, formerly for the purpose of stealing, now more often for other aims, such as political ones —**~er** *n* —**~ing** *n* [U;C]

hijack[2] *n* a case of HIJACK*ing*

hike[1] /haɪk/ *v* **1** [I∅] to go on a HIKE[2] **2** [I∅] *AmE* to travel about the country, or an area, esp. on foot or without regular use of a vehicle **3** [T1] *infml esp. AmE* to raise suddenly and steeply: *trying to hike rents* —**hiker** *n* —**hiking** *n* [U]

hike[2] *n* a long walk in the country, such as one taken by a group of people for a whole day

hike up *v adv AmE infml* **1** [T1] to raise suddenly or with one movement; HIKE[1] (3): *hiked his son up on his shoulders to see the marching soldiers* **2** [T1] HITCH UP (1): *hiked up his trousers*

hi·lar·i·ous /hɪˈleərɪəs/ *adj* **1** full of laughter: *The party got quite hilarious after they brought more wine* **2** causing wild laughter: *We thought his mistake was the most hilarious joke we'd ever heard* —**~ly** *adv* —**~ness** *n* [U]

hi·lar·i·ty /hɪˈlærɪ̣ti/ *n* [U] cheerfulness, expressed in laughter

hill /hɪl/ *n* **1** a raised part of the earth's surface, not so high as a mountain, and not usu. so bare, rocky, etc. **2** the slope of a road or path

hill·bil·ly /ˈhɪlbɪli/ *n* [C; *you*+N] *AmE often derog* a farmer or someone from a small country place

hill·ock /ˈhɪlək/ *n* **1** a little hill **2** a heap of earth shaped like a hill

hill·side /ˈhɪlsaɪd/ *n* the slope of a hill, as opposed to the top (**hill top**)

hill·y /ˈhɪli/ *adj* [Wa1] (of country or roads) full of hills

hilt /hɪlt/ *n* **1** the handle of a sword, or of a knife which is used as a weapon **2** (**up**) **to the hilt** (usu. of something bad) completely: *She's up to the hilt in trouble/in trouble up to the hilt*

him /ɪm; *strong* hɪm/ *pron* [Wp1] (*object form of* HE): *If that dog doesn't come in when I call him, I'll beat him when he does!|Which is the boy you know? Is that him?|She wants to marry him, and him at least 75 years old*

USAGE After some verbs, the object PRONOUN*s* **him, it, me, them, us, you** are always used when another verb follows: *I heard* **him** *sing/singing.|We watched* **them** *go/going.* These verbs are always marked [V] in this dictionary. After some other verbs, and after PREPOSITION*s*, there is a choice, and usually the forms **his, its, my, their, our, your** are more *fml* and considered better English: *I remember* **you**/(*fml* **your**) *telling me that.|Are you in favour of* **us**/(*fml* **our**) *joining the group?* The same rule is true of nouns: *This led to the country/*(*fml the country's*) *losing a lot of trade.* Look carefully for the [V]. —see ME (USAGE)

him·self /ɪmˈself; *strong* hɪm-/ *pron* [Wp1] **1 a** (*refl. form of* HE): *Did he hurt himself when he fell?* **b** (with general meaning): *Everyone should be able to defend himself* **2** (strong form of HE): *I want the man himself, not his secretary.|He himself did it.|He did it himself.|Himself still only a child, he had to rule over grown men* **3** *infml* (in) his usual state of mind or body (often in the phrs. **be himself, come to himself**): *He can't be well, he doesn't seem himself today.|When he saw the letter he was so angry he would have torn it up, but he came to himself* (=regained control) *in time and telephoned to say he'd already paid* —see YOURSELF (USAGE) **4** (**all**) **by himself** alone, without help: *The baby can walk by himself now.|He lives all by himself in the country*

hind[1] /haɪnd/ *n* [Wn1] a female deer, esp. of the red deer family —compare HART

hind[2] *adj* [Wa5;A] (usu. of animals' legs) belonging to the back part —see picture at DOG[1]

hin·der /ˈhɪndəʳ/ *v* [T1 (*from*)] **1** to stop (someone from doing something): *You're hindering me in my work by talking all the time* **2** to prevent (an activity from being done): *You're hindering my work*

hind·most /ˈhaɪndməʊst/ *adj old use* furthest behind

hind·quar·ters /ˈhaɪndˌkwɔːtəz‖-ˌkwɔrtərz/ also **quarters** —*n* [P] the back part of an animal including the legs —compare HAUNCHes and see picture at HORSE

hin·drance /ˈhɪndrəns/ *n* [(*to*)] **1** [U] the act of HINDERing: *This delay has caused some hindrance to my plans* **2** [C] something or somebody that HINDER*s*: *Lack of money is a real hindrance to my plans for travelling*

hind·sight /ˈhaɪndsaɪt/ *n* [U] *sometimes derog* the ability to see how and why something happened, esp. to know that it could have been prevented —compare FORESIGHT (1)

Hin·du /ˈhɪnduː, hɪnˈduː/ *adj* [Wa5] of Hinduism

Hin·du·is·m /ˈhɪnduː-ɪzəm/ *n* [U] the Hindu religion esp. as practised in India and its customs, such as its social ranks (CASTE system), the belief that one returns after death in another form, etc.

hinge[1] /hɪndʒ/ *n* **1** a metal part which joins 2 objects together and allows the first to swing around the (usu. fixed) second, such as one joining a door or gate to a post, or a lid to a box: *Oil the hinges, the gate is* CREAK*ing* (making an unpleasant noise) —see picture at DOOR **2** the point on which something else depends: *The home is the hinge on which family life turns*

hinge[2] *v* [T1 *often pass.*] to fix (something) on HINGE*s*: *The cupboard door is hinged on the right, so it opens on the left*

hinge on also **hinge up·on**— *v prep* [T1,4,6a] to depend on; HANG ON[2] (2): *Everything hinges on what we do next*

hint[1] /hɪnt/ *n* **1 a** a small or indirect suggestion **b** a suggestion (in the phr. **a broad hint**=a clear hint) **2** a small sign: *There's a hint of summer in the air, although it's only May* **3** [*often pl.*] useful advice: *helpful hints* **4 be able to take a hint** to understand what is meant and act on it: *I kept looking at my watch, but she can't take a hint, and it was midnight before she left*

hint[2] *v* [T1,5;I∅: (*to*)] to suggest indirectly: *I hinted (to him) that I was dissatisfied with his work*

hint at *v prep* [T1] to speak about in an indirect way: *The government minister hinted at an early election*

hin·ter·land /ˈhɪntəlænd‖-ər-/ *n* [C;(U)] the inner part of a country, beyond the coast or the banks of an important river

hip[1] /hɪp/ also **rose hip**— *n* [*usu. pl.*] the red fruit of the rose (esp. in the phr. **hips and** HAWS)

hip[2] *n* the fleshy part of either side of the human body above the legs: *Women have rounder hips than men* —see picture at HUMAN[2]

hip[3] *interj* **hip, hip, hooray!** (a cry or cheer)

hip[4] also (*now rare*) **hep**— *adj* **-pp-** [Wa2] *sl* of or favouring the latest fashions in behaviour, amusements, etc.; MODERN

hip·bath /ˈhɪpbɑːθ‖-bæθ/ *n* a bath in which one can sit but not lie

hip flask /ˈ· ·/ *n* a small bottle, not usu. made of glass, for carrying BRANDY or other SPIRITS, made to fit into a hip pocket

hip·pie, hippy /ˈhɪpi/ *n* a person who is, or is thought to be, against the standards of ordinary society, esp. when he shows this by dressing in unusual clothes, living in groups together, and (sometimes) taking drugs for pleasure

hip pock·et /ˌ· ˈ··/ *n* a pocket on the HIP[2] of a pair of trousers or of a skirt

Hip·po·crat·ic oath /ˌhɪpəkrætɪk ˈəʊθ/ *adj*

[*the*+R] the promise made by medical students to try to save life and to follow the standards set for the medical profession

hip·po·drome /ˈhɪpədrəʊm/ *n* **1** (in ancient Greece and Rome) an OVAL track for horse and CHARIOT races **2 a** an open place for horse-shows and shows with animals (esp. CIRCUSes) **b** (*often cap. as the name of*) a theatre

hip·po·pot·a·mus /ˌhɪpəˈpɒtəməs‖-ˈpɑ-/ also (*infml*) **hip·po** /ˈhɪpəʊ/— *n* **-muses** *or* **-mi** /maɪ/ [Wn1] a type of large animal of Africa with a large head, thick body, and thick hairless skin, which lives near water —see picture at RUMINANT

hip·ster /ˈhɪpstəʳ/ *n* **1** a person who is HIP[4] **2** [*usu. pl.*] an article of clothing which fits up to the HIP*s*[2], not the waist: *These trousers are hipsters*

hire[1] /haɪəʳ/ *n* [U] **1** the act of hiring or state of being hired: *Boats for hire.|to pay for the hire of a room* **2** payment for this: *to work for hire*

hire[2] *v* [T1] **1** to get the use of (something) for a special occasion on payment of a sum of money **2** [Wv5] to employ (someone) for a time for payment

USAGE In *BrE* one **hires** clothes or a boat for a short time, and their owner **hires** them **out**; one **rents** or **hires** a car; one **rents** a house, paying regular **rent**, and the owner **lets** it. The owner **lets out** a room or part of a building. In *AmE* one **rents** all these, and their owner **rents** them **out**. To **lease** means the same as to **rent** (a house). One **charters** a bus, ship, or aircraft. In *AmE* (and *infml BrE*) one **hires** people (*fml* **appoint** or **engage**). When they start to work they are **employed**, or (*AmE*) **hired**: *a* **hired** *hand* (=worker)|*He* **hires** (*himself*) *out as a field hand.*

hire·ling /ˈhaɪəlɪŋ‖ˈhaɪər-/ *n* [C; *you*+N] *derog* **1** a person whose services may be hired: *hireling politicians* **2** a person who cares only for the money he earns, but doesn't care about the type of work —compare MERCENARY

hire out *v adv* [T1 (*to*)] **1** to give the use of (something) for payment: *Why don't you hire out your car to your neighbours while you're away, and earn some money?* **2** to give (one's services) for payment: *Farm labourers used to hire themselves out for the summer*

hire pur·chase /ˌ· ˈ··/ also (*infml*) **the never never**, *AmE* **the instalment plan**— *n* [U] a system of payment for goods by which one pays small sums of money regularly after receiving the goods (usually paying more than the original price)

hir·sute /ˈhɜːsjuːt, hɜːˈsjuːt‖ˈhɜrsuːt, hɜrˈsuːt/ *adj* [(of a man)] **1** hairy **2** with untidy hair on the face; with the beard and hair of the head uncut

his[1] /ɪz; *strong* hɪz/ *determiner* [Wp1 (*poss. form of* HE)] **1** belonging to him: *John's away ill, not on his holidays.|That's not John's knife, it's his fork.|That's not my knife, it's his knife* **2** (with general meaning): *Everyone must do his best.|A fool and his money are soon* PART*ed* —compare THEIR

his[2] /hɪz/ *pron* [Wp1 (*poss. form of* HE)] **1** that/those belonging to him: *Which coat is John's? Is that one his?|His is/are on the table.|That fool of a sister of his!* —see also OF (6) **2** (with general meaning): *Everyone wants only what is his by right* —compare THEIRS

hiss[1] /hɪs/ *v* **1** [Wv4;I∅] to make a sound like a continuous "s": *Snakes hiss when they're angry.|The iron hissed as it pressed the wet cloth.|Gas escaped with a hissing noise from the broken pipe* **2** [T1 (*to*)] to say in a sharp whisper: *The boy hissed a warning to be quiet to the others* **3** [T1] also **hiss at**— to show disapproval and dislike of: *The crowd hissed the speaker when he said taxes should be increased*

hiss[2] *n* a HISSing sound: *The snake gave a hiss*

hiss off *v adv; prep* [T1;D1 *often pass.*] to cause (someone, esp. a performer) to leave (usu. a stage) by making a HISSing noise

hist /hɪst/ *interj old use* (a sound used for drawing attention or asking for silence) —compare PSST

his·ta·mine /ˈhɪstəmiːn/ *n* [U] a chemical compound which can increase the flow of blood, either when used as a drug or when produced as a natural substance in the body

his·tol·o·gy /hɪˈstɒlədʒi‖-ˈstɑ-/ *n* [U] the study of the cells of the body

his·to·ri·an /hɪˈstɔːrɪən‖-ˈsto-/ *n* a person who studies history and/or writes about it

his·tor·ic /hɪˈstɒrɪk‖-ˈstɔ-, -ˈstɑ-/ *adj* **1** important in history —see HISTORY (USAGE) **2** [Wa5] of the times whose history has been recorded: *happened within historic times* —compare PREHISTORIC

his·tor·i·cal /hɪˈstɒrɪkəl‖-stɔ-, -ˈstɑ-/ *adj* [Wa5] **1** connected with history as a study: *He gave all his historical papers to the library.|the historical method* (=one which goes from earlier to later times) *of studying developments* **2** which represents a fact/facts of history: *a historical play/*NOVEL —see HISTORY (USAGE) —**~ly** *adv* [Wa4,5]

historic pres·ent /·ˌ·· ˈ··/ also **historical pres·ent** /ˌ··· ˈ··/— *n* the present tense as used in many languages to tell a story which happened in the past, when the teller wants to make it sound more real

his·to·ry /ˈhɪstəri/ *n* **1** [U] (the study of) events in the past, such as those of a nation, arranged in order from the earlier to the later, esp. events concerning the rulers and government of a country, social and trade conditions, etc. **2** [U] (the study of) the development of anything in time: *There have been many changes in the history of the English language* **3** [C] **a** a (written) account of history: *a short history of the last war* **b** *old use* a historical play **4** [C] *med* CASE HISTORY: *Mr. Jones gives a history of headaches since childhood* **5** [C] **a** a set of interesting events: *The village has no known history* **b** a long story including details of many events: *She told me her life history* **6 make history** to do or be concerned in something important which will be recorded and remembered **7 past/ancient history** *not fml* something that may have been true in the past, but is no longer important

USAGE A **story** tells of a number of connected events which may or may not have really happened: *She told the children a* **story**. **History** is the real events of the past, and a **history** book is one, usually a school book, that describes these. **Historical** characters or events are those that have really existed or happened in the past, and a (long) **story** about them is a **historical novel**. A place is **historic** if it has a long **history** and an event is **historic** if it will be remembered in **history**.

his·tri·on·ic /ˌhɪstriˈɒnɪk‖-ˈɑnɪk/ *adj* **1** concerning the theatre or acting **2** done or performed in a theatrical way; not showing real feelings, but pretended ones —**~ally** *adv* [Wa4]

his·tri·on·ics /ˌhɪstriˈɒnɪks,‖-ˈɑn-/ *n* [P;(U)] **1** the art of acting **2** behaviour which is like a theatrical performance, with no real feelings behind it: *All the shouting and histrionics are just for effect, he doesn't really mean anything by it*

hit[1] /hɪt/ *v* **hit**, *pres. p.* **hitting** [T1] **1** to give a blow to; strike: *He hit the other man.|He hit the ball* (*with the* BAT) **2 a** to come against with force: *The ball hit the window.|The car hit the wall* **b** to cause to do this by accident or on purpose: *She hit her head on the table* **3** *infml* to reach: *We hit the main road 2 miles further on.|I hit a difficult point in my work, and decided it was time for a cup of tea* **4** to have a bad effect on: *The increase in food prices hits the* HOUSEWIFE*'s pocket* (=money) **5** (in cricket) SCORE² (1): *He hit 3 runs* **6 be hard hit** to suffer: *a town hard hit by a storm* **7 hit the nail on the head** to be exactly right (in saying something) **8 hit a man when he's down** to attack someone already defeated **9 hit (someone) below the belt** to attack (someone) unfairly or in an unpleasant or dishonourable way **10 hit someone where it hurts (most)** to attack someone through their weaknesses **11 hit the bottle** *infml* to (start to) drink too much alcohol **12 hit the hay** *AmE* also **hit the sack**— *sl* to go to bed **13 hit the road** *infml* **a** to start on a journey **b** *usu. imper. esp. AmE* to leave **14 hit the roof** *AmE* also **hit the ceiling**— *infml* to show or express great anger **15 hit the headlines** to get into the news, esp. by being important enough to appear in the titles (HEADLINE*s*) on the front page **16 hit (someone) for six** to defeat or surprise (someone) completely by an unexpectedly quick action

hit² *n* **1** a blow; stroke: *He made a hit at the man's face, but missed.|That was a good hit. It almost saved the game* **2** a move which brings something against another with force: *The arrow* SCORE*d*² (5) *a hit* **3** a musical or theatrical performance which is successful: *The song was a hit at once* **4** a remark which causes the desired effect, esp. if unpleasant: *That joke was a nasty hit at me* **5 make a hit (with)** to be successful (with): *She likes you. You've made a hit*

hit-and-run /ˌ· · ˈ·◂/ *adj* [Wa5;A] **1 a** (of a road accident) of a type in which the guilty driver does not stop to help **b** (of an air attack) of a type in which a plane attacks quickly and leaves as soon as possible **2** (of a person) who behaves in this way

hit at *v prep* [T1] to strike a blow at; try to hit: *He hit at me, but missed*

hitch¹ /hɪtʃ/ *v* **1** [X9] to fasten by hooking a rope or metal part over another object: *He hitched the horse's rope over the pole.|Another railway carriage has been hitched on* **2** [T1;I∅] *infml* to travel by getting (rides in a car): *He hitched across Europe.|Let's hitch a ride* **3 get/be hitched** *sl* to get/be married

hitch² *n* **1** a short, sudden push or pull (up): *He gave his sock a hitch when he felt it slipping down* **2** a type of knot used by sailors **3** a difficulty which delays something for a while: *a slight hitch|A* TECHNICAL *hitch prevented the lights from working*

hitch·hike /ˈhɪtʃhaɪk/ *v* [I∅] to go on a (long) journey by getting rides in other people's cars —**-hiker** *n*

hitch up *v adv* [T1] **1** to pull upwards into place: *John hitched up his trousers* **2** to fasten (to something) by HITCH*ing*¹: *hitched up the horses (to the cart)*

hith·er /ˈhɪðəʳ/ *adv* **1** *old use* to here; to this place **2 come-hither look** /ˌ· ˈ·· ·/ *not fml* a look which attracts, esp. sexually **3 hither and thither** in all directions

hith·er·to /ˌhɪðəˈtuː◂‖-ər-/ *adv fml* until this/that time

hit off *v adv* [T1] **1** to act or draw a good likeness of (someone): *The boy pretended to be the teacher and hit her off to perfection* **2 hit it off (with)** *infml* to have a good relationship (with): *I'm glad to see the 2 girls hitting it off so well*

hit on also **hit up·on**— *v prep* [T1,4] to find by lucky chance or have a good idea about: *I hope that after all these talks, someone will hit on a way out of our difficulty*

hit-or-miss /ˌ· · ˈ·/ *adj* which depends on chance; which is not planned carefully

hit out at *v adv prep* [T1] **1** also **hit out a·gainst**— to disagree violently with and attack in words: *The voters are hitting out at the government's latest decision* **2** HIT: *He hit out at me without thinking, and missed*

hit pa·rade /ˈ· ·ˌ·/ *n now rare* a list of popular records (of songs) in order of the number which are sold of each —compare **top of the** POP*s*⁴ (2)

hive /haɪv/ *n* **1 a** also **beehive**— a place where bees live, like a small hut or box **b** the group of bees who live together —see picture at FARMYARD **2** a crowded busy place (esp. in the phrase **a hive of industry**): *What a lot of hard workers! I've never seen such a hive of industry!*

hive off *v adv* **1** [I∅] *infml, esp. BrE* to disappear or go away without warning: *Where's Jim? I suppose he's hived off again* **2** [I∅ (*from* and/or *into*)] *esp. BrE* to separate one's activities; start a new line of work: *The salesman was so successful that in the end he hived off from the firm into his own business* **3** [T1 (*from*)] to separate: *The business was becoming so large that the directors decided to hive off some parts of the work and start new firms*

hives /haɪvz/ *n* [P;U] a skin disease which is red and painful

h'm /m, hm/ *interj* HUMPH

HMS *abbrev. for:* **1** His/Her MAJESTY's Service **2** His/Her MAJESTY's Ship

ho /həʊ/ *interj usu. lit* (a call which expresses surprise or draws attention): *Land ho!|Westward ho!*

hoard¹ /hɔːd‖hord/ *n* **1** a (secret) store, esp. of something valuable to the owner **2** [*often pl. with sing. meaning*] a large amount

hoard² *v* [T1] **1** to store secretly, esp. more than is allowed **2** [(UP)] to save in large amounts: *The* SQUIRREL *hoards up nuts for the winter* —**~er** *n*

hoard·ing /ˈhɔːdɪŋ‖ˈhor-/ *n* **1** a fence round a piece of land, esp. when building is going on **2** *AmE* **billboard**— a high fence or board on which large advertisements are stuck —see picture at STREET

hoar·frost /ˈhɔːfrɒst‖ˈhorfrɔst/ *n* [U] frozen drops of water which look white, esp. those seen on the grass after a cold night

hoarse /hɔːs‖hors/ *adj* **1** (of a voice) HARSH-sounding, as though the surface of the throat is rougher than usual, as during a cold **2** (of a person) having a voice of this type —**~ly** *adv* —**~ness** *n* [U]

hoar·y /ˈhɔːri‖ˈhori/ also (*lit*) **hoar** /hɔːʳ‖hor/— *adj* [Wa1] **1** (of hair) grey or white **2** (of people) having grey or white hair in old age —**hoariness** *n* [U]

hoax¹ /həʊks/ *n* a trick, esp. one which makes someone believe something which is not true, and take action upon that belief: *There was no bomb, as the telephone caller said. It was all a hoax*

hoax² *v* [T1] to play a trick on (someone) —**~er** *n*

hob /hɒb‖hɑb/ *n* (when coal fires were used) a metal shelf beside an open fire where food and water could be cooked or warmed

hob·ble /ˈhɒbəl‖ˈhɑ-/ *v* [Wv3] **1** [I∅] to walk in an awkward way, with difficulty: *I hurt my foot, but just succeeded in hobbling along* **2** [T1] to fasten together 2 legs (esp. of a horse): *The horse has been hobbled so that he can't run away*

hob·ble·de·hoy /ˈhɒbəldihɔɪ‖ˈhɑ-/ *n now rare* an awkward young person

hobble skirt /ˈ·· ·/ *n* a very tight skirt which makes it difficult to walk

hob·by /ˈhɒbi‖ˈhɑ-/ *n* an activity which one enjoys doing in one's free time

USAGE **Play**, **pastime** (*fml*), and **recreation** are general words for things that one does for fun and not for money. The verb **play** is used without an object to describe what children do when they are amusing themselves: *Run away and* **play**! A quiet activity like collecting stamps or playing a musical instrument is a **hobby**. A **sport** is a bodily activity such as swimming or bicycling. A **game** is usually an activity in which people compete, either with their bodies as in football or with their brains as in cards: *Tennis is a* **game**.|*to play several* **games** *of tennis*. An important public **game** (in this second meaning) of football, tennis, etc., is a **match**. An important public occasion at which people compete in many different bodily ways is called **sports** (*our school* **Sports** *Day*) or **games** (*the Olympic* **Games**).

hob·by·horse /'hɒbihɔːs‖'hɑbihɔrs/ *n* **1** a child's toy like a horse's head on a stick, which the child pretends to ride on **2** a fixed idea to which a person keeps returning in conversation

hob·gob·lin /hɒb'gɒbl$\frac{1}{2}$n, 'hɒbgɒb-‖'hɑbgɑb-/ *n* a GOBLIN which plays tricks on people

hob·nail /'hɒbneɪl‖'hɑb-/ *n* a large nail with a big head used to make heavy shoes and boots stronger underneath (esp. in the phr. **hobnail boots**) —**~ed** /ˌhɒb'neɪld◂‖ˌhɑb-/ *adj* [Wa5]

hob·nob /'hɒbnɒb‖'hɑbnɑb/ *v* **-bb-** [IØ (TOGETHER, *with*)] *sometimes derog* to have a (pleasant) social relationship, as expressed in drinking together, talking and friendly behaviour

ho·bo /'həʊbəʊ/ *n* **hoboes** *or* **hobos** *AmE sl* a wanderer who has no regular work; TRAMP² (4)

Hob·son's choice /ˌhɒbsənz 'tʃɔɪs‖ˌhɑb-/ *n* [R; (S)] lack of choice; the choice of taking or doing one thing (or nothing at all)

hock¹ /hɒk‖hɑk/ *n* **1** a joint of meat from an animal's leg, above the foot **2** (in animals) the middle joint of the back leg —see pictures at HORSE and DOG¹

hock² *n* [U;C] (any of) several kinds of German white wine

hock³ *n* **in hock** *sl* **a** PAWNed **b** in prison

hock⁴ *v* [T1] *sl* PAWN² (1)

hock·ey /'hɒki‖'hɑki/ *n* **1** *esp. BrE* FIELD HOCKEY **2** *esp. AmE* ICE HOCKEY

USAGE One plays a *game* of (**field**) **hockey** on a *field*, using a (**hockey**) *stick* to hit the *ball*, and *scoring* (SCORE² (1)) **goals**. In an important *match*, the person in charge is called the **referee**.

ho·cus-po·cus /ˌhəʊkəs 'pəʊkəs/ *n* [U] **1** TRICKERY **2** pointless activity or words, esp. when they draw one's attention from what is really happening

hod /hɒd‖hɑd/ *n* **1** a container shaped like a box with a long handle, used by builders' workmen for carrying bricks —see picture at SITE¹ **2** a box for carrying and holding coal; COALSCUTTLE

hodge·podge /'hɒdʒpɒdʒ‖'hɑdʒpɑdʒ/ *n* [S] *esp. AmE* HOTCHPOTCH

hoe¹ /həʊ/ *n* a long-handled garden tool used for breaking up the soil and removing wild plants (WEEDs) —see picture at GARDEN¹

hoe² *v* **hoed,** *pres. p.* **hoeing** **1** [IØ] to use a HOE **2** [T1] to remove or break with a HOE

hog¹ /hɒg‖hɑg, hɔg/ *n* [Wn1] **1** *AmE* a pig, esp. a fat one for eating **2** a male pig on a farm that cannot produce young (is CASTRATEd) and is kept for meat —compare BOAR, SOW **3** a dirty person who eats too much **4 go (the) whole hog** *infml* to do something thoroughly, or too well **5 road hog** a driver who endangers others on the roads by his careless behaviour

hog² *v* **-gg-** [T1] **1** *sl* to take and keep (all of something) for oneself **2 hog the road** to drive in the middle of the road

hog·gish /'hɒgɪʃ‖'hɑ-, 'hɔ-/ *adj* (of people or habits) pig-like, dirty, selfish, etc.

Hog·ma·nay /'hɒgməneɪ‖ˌhɑgmə'neɪ/ *n* [R] (in Scotland) NEW YEAR'S EVE and the parties, drinking, etc., which take place then

hogs·head /'hɒgzhed‖'hɑgz-, 'hɔgz-/ *n* **1** a barrel, esp. one which holds 52½ GALLONs (=238·5 litres) in Britain, or 63 gallons in the US **2** the amount of liquid which can be held in such a barrel

hog·wash /'hɒgwɒʃ‖'hɑgwɑʃ, 'hɔg-, -wɔʃ/ *n* [U] *esp. AmE* stupid talk; NONSENSE

hoi pol·loi /ˌhɔɪ pə'lɔɪ/ *n* [*the*+P] *derog Gk* the common people; everybody

hoist¹ /hɔɪst/ *v* [T1 (UP)] to raise up by force, esp. when using ropes on board ship: *He hoisted it over his shoulder.*|*The sailors hoisted the flag.*|*They hoisted sail*

hoist² *n* **1** an upward push **2** an apparatus for lifting heavy goods —see picture at SITE¹

hoi·ty-toi·ty /ˌhɔɪti 'tɔɪti/ *adj derog* behaving in a proud way, as though more important than other people; HAUGHTY

hold¹ /həʊld/ *v* **held** /held/ **1** [T1] to keep or support with a part of the body, esp. with the hands: *He held the flowers while she cut some more.*|*She's holding the baby (in her arms).*|*I held his hand* **2** [X9] to put or keep (a part of the body) in a certain position: *They held their heads up.*|*The dog held its tail between its legs.*|*Hold (yourself) still* **3** [T1] to keep back or control: *We held our breath in fear* **4** [Wv6;T1] to be able to contain: *How much water does the pan hold?*|*The car can hold 4.*|(fig.) *Life holds many surprises.*|*I can't hold the sum in my head* **5** [T1] (esp. of an army) to keep in control or in one's possession: *The city is held by the enemy* **6** [Wv6;T1] to possess (money, land, or position): *He holds a half share in the business.*|*He holds the rights to hunt on this land.*|*She holds the office of chairman* **7** [T1;X7] to keep (someone) in (an interested state of mind): *His speech held their attention/held them silent* **8** [X9] to keep in the stated position or condition: *She held them up/down/off/at arm's length.*|(fig.) *We held ourselves in readiness for bad news* **9** [T5;X *to be* 1,7] to express one's belief (that); consider: *I hold him to be a fool/that he's a fool/the view that he's a fool.*|*He holds some strange ideas* **10** [IØ] to be or remain in a certain state; continue: *What he said still holds* (=is true).|*Can the good weather hold?* **11** (of a ship or aircraft) to follow correctly; HOLD TO: *The plane held its course across the sky* **12** [T1 *often pass.*] (of objects) to keep in position and/or support: *Her hair was held back.*|*The roof was held up by pillars* **13** [T1 *often pass.*] to make (something) happen: *We were holding a meeting* **14 be left holding the** (*BrE*) **baby**/(*AmE*) **bag** to find oneself responsible for doing something which someone else has started and left unfinished **15 hold court** to receive admirers in a group **16 hold good** to be true: *This rule holds good at all times and places* **17 hold hands (with)** to hold the hand (of another) or the hands (of each other), esp. as a sign of love **18 Hold it!** Stay like that; don't move! **19 hold one's own** to keep one's (strong) position, even when attacked **20 hold the line** [*often imper.*] to wait (on the telephone) —compare HOLD ON (1) **21 hold the road** (of a car) to stay in position on the road while moving, esp. in spite of speed, wet weather, etc. —see also **hold a** CANDLE **to,** HOLD AGAINST, HOLD BACK, HOLD BY, HOLD DOWN, HOLD FORTH, HOLD OFF, HOLD ON, **hold one's** GROUND **hold one's** TONGUE, HOLD OUT (**for, on**), HOLD OVER, **hold the** FORT, HOLD TO, HOLD TOGETHER, HOLD UP, **hold** WATER, HOLD WITH

hold² *n* **1** [U] the act of holding; GRIP² (1) (esp. in the phrs. **take/get/catch/lay hold of, keep hold of, lose hold of**) **2** [C] something which can be held, esp. in climbing: *Can you find a hold for your hands* *so that you can pull yourself up?* —compare FOOTHOLD, HANDHOLD **3** [C] **a** the forceful closing of the hand; GRIP[2] (1): *He's got a strong hold; he can break a glass* **b** influence; control: *He's got a good hold of his subject* **4 have a hold over** to know something which gives one an influence over —compare HOLD OVER **5 get hold of** to find and make use of: *I must get hold of some more writing paper*

hold[3] *n* the part of a ship (below DECK) where goods are stored

hold a·gainst *v prep* [D1] to allow (something bad that someone has done) to influence one's feelings about (this person): *Don't hold his past behaviour against him!*

hold·all /'həʊld-ɔːl/ *n* a large bag or small case for carrying clothes and articles for travelling

hold back *v adv* **1** [T1] also **keep back**— to make (something) stay in place; control: *The men built banks of earth to hold back the rising flood waters* **2** [T1] also **hold in, keep back**— to control, esp. feelings: *Jim was able to hold back his anger and avoid a fight* **3** [T1] also **keep back**— to prevent the development of: *You could become a good musician, but your lack of practice is holding you back* **4** [I∅] also **hang back, hang behind**— to be slow or unwilling to act: *Mary is afraid of people; she always holds back when we take her to a party* —compare HOLD OFF (1) **5** [T1;I∅] to keep (something) secret: *We must have the whole story: don't hold (anything) back*

hold by *v prep* **1** HOLD TO: *During the whole struggle he held by his principles* **2** HOLD WITH: *I don't hold by some of the strange ideas you believe in*

hold down *v adv* [T1] **1** to keep (esp. a job): *Jim has not held down a job for more than a year* **2** to keep at a low level: *We must try to hold prices down* **3** to control or limit the freedom of: *You can't hold a good man down* —see also KEEP DOWN (2)

hold·er /'həʊldəʳ/ *n* a person who has control, as of a place, or possesses land, money, or titles: *The holder of the office of chairman is responsible for arranging meetings* —compare HOLD[1] (5,6)

-holder *comb. form* [n→n] **1** a person who holds property; TENANT: a LEASE-*holder* **2** something which holds or contains: *cigarette holder* **3** a cloth which helps to hold hot things —see also OFFICE-HOLDER

hold forth *v adv* [I∅ (*on*)] to speak at length

hold·ing /'həʊldɪŋ/ *n* something which is in one's possession, esp. land or SHARES[1] (2) —see also SMALLHOLDING

holding com·pa·ny /'·· ˌ···/ *n* a firm or company whose main business is to hold a controlling number of the SHARES[1] (2) of other companies

hold off *v adv* **1** [T1;I∅ (*from*)] also **keep off**— to (cause to) remain at a distance: *We must hold off the enemy's attack.|Mary tends to hold off from people who try to be friendly* —compare HOLD BACK (1,4) **2** [T1] also **put off**— to delay: *The leaders will hold off their decision until Monday* **3** [I∅] also **keep off**— to be delayed; stay away: *Will the rain hold off until after the game?*

hold on *v adv* [I∅] **1** to wait (often on the telephone); HANG ON: *Hold on there a minute: what's that you said?* —compare HOLD[1] (20) **2** to continue in spite of difficulties; HANG ON[1] (3) **3** HOLD OUT (3) **4** to continue: *The rain held on steadily all afternoon*

hold on·to *v prep* [T1] HANG ONTO (1,2)

hold out *v adv* **1** [T1a] to offer: *I don't hold out much hope that our traffic troubles will improve* **2** [I∅] to last: *I think the car will hold out till we reach London* **3** [I∅] also **hang on, hold on**— to last in spite of difficulties; ENDURE: *The town was surrounded but the people held out until help came* **4** [T1] EXTEND (3,4): *He held out his hand in friendship*

hold out for also **stick out for**— *v adv prep* [T1] to demand firmly and wait in order to get: *The men are still holding out for more pay*

hold out on *v adv prep* [T1] *infml* **1** to keep a secret from (someone): *Why didn't you tell me at once, instead of holding out on me?* **2** to refuse to support or reply to (someone): *Jim sent his request to Head Office some weeks ago but they are still holding out on him*

hold·o·ver /'həʊldˌəʊvəʳ/ *n* [(*from*)] *esp. AmE* something that has continued to exist longer than expected

hold o·ver[1] *v adv* [T1 *often pass.*] **1** to move to a later date: *The concert was held over till the following week because of the singer's illness* **2** to continue (a show) longer than originally planned: *The film will be held over for another week because it is so popular*

hold over[2] *v prep* [D1] to use (usu. knowledge of something) as a threat against (someone): *He knows I have been to prison and is holding it over me*

hold to also **hold by, keep to**— *v prep* [T1;D1] to (cause to) follow exactly or keep to: *Whatever your argument, I shall hold to my decision*

hold to·geth·er also **keep together**— *v adv* [T1] to (cause to) remain united: *used a pin to hold the 2 pages together|The needs of the children often hold a marriage together*

hold-up /'həʊld-ʌp/ *n* **1** a delay, as of traffic **2** also (*infml*) **stickup**— an attempt at robbery by threatening people with a gun

hold up *v adv* **1** [T1 *often pass.*] to delay: *The building of the new road has been held up by bad weather* **2** [T1] to stop in order to rob: *The criminals held up the train/the passengers and took all the money* **3** [T1 (*to* and/or *as*)] to show as an example: *Grandfather always held up his youngest son as a model of hard work* **4** [I∅] HOLD OUT **5** [I∅] KEEP UP (4) **6** [T1] raise; keep up: *Hold up your right hand*

hold with *v prep* [T1] to approve of; agree with: *I don't hold with some of the strange ideas you believe in*

hole[1] /həʊl/ *n* **1** an empty space within something solid: *The men have dug a hole in the road.|There's a hole in my sock* **2 a** (*often in comb.*) the home of a small animal **b** *infml* a small, unpleasant living-place **3** *infml* a position of difficulty: *Having lost my money puts me in rather a hole* **4** (in GOLF) a hollow place into which the ball must be hit **5 in holes** (of materials) having a lot of HOLEs[1] (1) **6 make a hole in** *not fml* to use up a large part of: *Going out for a meal really made a hole in the week's money for food* **7 pick holes in something** to say what is wrong with something, esp. when it is not really faulty

hole[2] *v* **1** [T1] to make a hole in **2** [I∅ (OUT); T1] to put (a ball) in a hole in GOLF: *to hole in one* (=one stroke)

hole-and-cor·ner /ˌ· · '··/ *adj* [Wa5;A] (of actions) secret or hidden, esp. because dishonest

hole up *v adv* [L9] *sl esp. AmE* to hide, as a means of escape: *After the bank robbery, the criminals holed up in a disused factory*

hol·i·day[1] /'hɒlɨdi‖'hɑlɨdeɪ/ *n* **1** a time of rest from work, a day (often originally of religious importance) or longer **2 on holiday/on one's holidays** having a holiday, esp. over a period of time USAGE In *BrE*, **holiday** is the general word for the period in the year when a person does not work. In *AmE* this is called **vacation**: *He's on* holiday/(*AmE*) on **vacation**.|*Where are you going for your* **holiday(s)**?/(*AmE*) *for your* **vacation**? **Vacation** is also used by British universities and British lawyers: *The college is closed during* (*the*) **vacation**. Soldiers and people employed by the government go on **leave**, and the word is also used in such expressions as **sick leave**, **leave** *of absence*. **Furlough** is a rarer word for military or official holidays, used when someone working abroad goes home on holiday to his own country.

holiday² *AmE* also **vacation**— *v* [I∅] to have a period of holiday: *holidaying in Majorca*

hol·i·day·mak·er /ˈhɒlɨ̈di ˌmeɪkəʳ‖ˈhɑlɨ̈deɪ-/ *n* a person on holiday —**-ing** *n* [U]

hol·i·ness /ˈhəʊlinɨ̈s/ *n* [U] the state or quality of being holy

Holiness *n* [N9;C9] (a title of the POPE): *His/Your Holiness|His Holiness* POPE *Paul|His Holiness the* POPE

hol·land /ˈhɒlənd‖ˈhɑ-/ *n* [U] a sort of rough cloth

hol·ler¹ /ˈhɒləʳ‖ˈhɑ-/ *v infml esp. AmE* **1** [T1;5: (OUT, *to*, *at*)] to shout out (a word/words): *"Let go," he hollered* **2** [I∅ (*at*)] to cry out, as to scold, to attract attention, or in pain

holler² *n infml esp. AmE* an act of HOLLERing: *let out a holler as soon as he saw me*

hol·low¹ /ˈhɒləʊ‖ˈhɑ-/ *adj* [Wa1] **1** having an empty space inside; not solid **2** (of parts of the body) lacking flesh so that the skin sinks inwards: *hollow cheeks* **3** (of sounds) having a ringing sound like the note when an empty container is struck **4** (of feelings, words, etc.) not real; empty of real meaning **5 beat (someone) hollow** *infml* to defeat (someone) completely —**~ly** *adv* —**~ness** *n* [U]

hollow² *n* **1** a space sunk into something, esp. into the ground: *The ground was covered in little hollows which could easily break the leg of anyone whose foot got caught* **2 (in) the hollow of one's hand** (in) the curved PALM² (1a,4)

hollow out *v adv* [T1] **1** to make a hollow place in (something): *to hollow out a log* **2** [(*of*)] to make by doing this: *to hollow a* CANOE *out of a log*

hol·ly /ˈhɒli‖ˈhɑli/ *n* [U;C] a type of small tree with dark green shiny prickly leaves and red berries

hol·ly·hock /ˈhɒlihɒk‖ˈhɑlihɑk/ *n* a type of garden flower which grows very tall —see picture at FLOWER¹

Hol·ly·wood /ˈhɒliwʊd‖ˈhɑ-/ *n* [R] an area in Los Angeles, California, famous because many popular films have been made there

hol·o·caust /ˈhɒləkɔːst‖ˈhɑ-/ *n* the loss of many lives, esp. by burning

hol·o·graph /ˈhɒləgrɑːf‖ˈhɑləgræf/ *n* a written paper completely hand-written by the person who signed it

Hol·stein /ˈhɒlstaɪn‖ˈhɑlstiːn, -staɪn/ *n esp. AmE* FRISIAN

hol·ster /ˈhəʊlstəʳ/ *n* a leather holder for a PISTOL (=small hand gun), esp. one that hangs on a belt around the waist

ho·ly¹ /ˈhəʊli/ *adj* **1** of God and religion: *the Holy Bible* **2** (of a person or life) in the service of God and religion, esp. when leading a pure and blameless life **3** *sl euph* very bad (esp. in the phr. **a holy terror** (=a person))

holy² *n* a most holy place (only in the phr. **holy of holies**)

Holy Com·mu·nion /ˌ·· ·ˈ··/ *n* [R] COMMUNION (2)

Holy Grail /ˌ·· ˈ·/ *n* GRAIL

Holy See /ˌ·· ˈ·/ *n* [*the*+R] *fml* the office of the POPE (chief of priests in the ROMAN CATHOLIC church); SEE² of Rome

Holy Sep·ul·chre /ˌ·· ˈ···/ *n* [*the*+R] the SEPULCHRE where Jesus' body was buried

Holy Spir·it /ˌ·· ˈ··/ also **Holy Ghost** /ˌ·· ˈ·/— *n* [*the*+R] (in the Christian religion) God in the form of a spirit

Holy Week /ˈ·· ·/ also **Passion Week**— *n* [R] (in the Christian Church) the week between PALM SUNDAY and EASTER

Holy Writ /ˌ·· ˈ·/ *n* [R] the Bible

hom·age /ˈhɒmɪdʒ‖ˈhɑ-/ *n* [U] **1** signs of great respect (esp. in the phrs. **pay/do homage to someone**) **2** a ceremony of former times in which a man recognized the power of another, esp. a king, over him

hom·burg /ˈhɒmbɜːg‖ˈhɑmbɜrg/ *n* a soft FELT hat for men, with a wide piece (BRIM) standing out round the edge

home¹ /həʊm/ *n* **1 a** the house where one lives **b** the place where one was born or habitually lives: *"Where do you live?" "Well, Nigeria is my home, but I'm living in London just now."* —see USAGE **2** the house and family one belongs to **3** a place where a living thing can be found living and growing wild, esp. in large numbers: *India is the home of elephants and tigers* **4** a place for the care of a group of people or animals of the same type, who do not live with a family: *a children's home* **5** (in some games and sports) a place which a player must aim to reach, such as the GOAL (2) or the finishing line of a race (esp. in the phr. **the home stretch/straight** (=the last part)) **6 at home a** in the house or family: *"He's left the notes of his speech at home"* (SEU W.) **b** ready to receive visitors: *If he telephones, say I'm not at home to visitors till 10* **7 be/feel at home** to be comfortable; not feel worried, esp. because one has the right skills or experience: *He's completely at home in chemistry* **8 leave home** to go away from one's family to live independently for the first time, esp. after an argument **9 make oneself at home** [*often imper.*] to behave freely, sit where one likes, smoke, etc., as if at home **10 nothing to write home about** *infml* nothing special; not as good as it might be —**~less** *adj* [Wa5] —**~lessness** *n* [U]

USAGE We use the simple tenses of *live* (not **stay*) when talking about **home**. —compare AT HOME —see HOUSE (USAGE)

home² *adv* [Wa5] **1** [F] to or at one's home: *Is he home from work?|I'm going home.|"Home, James!" I said to the driver of my car.|"I really must be getting home in a moment"* (SEU S.) **2** as far as possible and/or to the right place: *He struck the nail home.*|(fig.) *They were hard words, but they struck home* (=made the listener accept the truth).|*He drove his point home* **3 come home to (someone)/bring (something) home to (someone)** to be understood by (someone)/to make (someone) understand (something): *At last it's come home to me how much I owe to my parents* —see also **if/when one's** SHIP **comes home**

USAGE The adverb form without *to* is used when speaking of movement towards one's home, even with the verb *be*: *I'm coming* **home.**|*Henry will be* (=come) **home** *before 7.* When no movement is concerned, *at* **home** (HOME¹ (6)) is always correct: *staying at* **home**|*Is Henry at* **home**? It is also common, esp. in *infml AmE*, to say *Is Henry* **home**?|*I've been* **home** *all day.* Some people do not think this is good English.

home³ *adj* [Wa5;A] **1** of, related to, or being a home, place of origin, or base of operations: *the home office of an international firm* **2** not foreign; DOMESTIC¹ (3): *the home country|home affairs|the* HOME OFFICE **3 a** prepared, done, or intended for use in a home: *home cooking* **b** (*in comb.*) **home-**

baked /ˌ· ˈ·◂/ *bread*|HOMEMADE *products* **4** working, playing, or happening in a home area: *the home team*|*home games*

home⁴ *v* [IØ] (of birds such as PIGEONs) to find one's way back to the starting place —see also HOME IN ON, HOMING

home brew /ˌ· ˈ·/ *n* [U;C] beer made at home —**~ed** /ˌ· ˈ·◂/ *adj*

home·com·ing /ˈhəʊmˌkʌmɪŋ/ *n* an arrival home, esp. after long absence

Home Coun·ties /ˌ· ˈ··/ *n* [*the*+P] the counties (COUNTY) around London, in southeast England

home e·co·nom·ics /ˌ· ··ˈ··/ *n* [U;(P)] the study of HOUSEHOLD (1) affairs, esp. the buying of food; HOUSECRAFT

home from home /ˌ· · ˈ·/ *AmE* **home a·way from home** /ˌ· ·· · ˈ·/— *n BrE* a place as pleasant, comfortable, etc., as one's own house; place where one is as welcome as in one's own home

home front /ˌ· ˈ·/ *n* [*the*+R] (the activities of) the people working in their own country, while others are away at war

home·grown /ˌhəʊmˈgrəʊn◂/ *adj* [Wa5] (of plants for food) grown in the home country, not abroad

Home Guard /ˌ· ˈ·/ *n* [C; *the*+GU] (in the Second World War) (a member of) the citizen army formed at home to help to defend Britain in case of attack from abroad —compare TERRITORIAL ARMY

home help /ˌ· ˈ·/ *n BrE* a woman who is sent in by the medical and social services to do housework for someone who is ill or very old

home in on *v adv prep* [T1] to aim exactly towards

home·land /ˈhəʊmlænd, -lənd/ *n* one's native country

home·like /ˈhəʊmlaɪk/ *adj* pleasant, comfortable, etc., like something in one's home

home·ly /ˈhəʊmli/ *adj* [Wa2] **1** simple, not grand: *a homely meal of bread and cheese* **2** *AmE* (of people, faces, etc.) not good-looking —**-liness** *n* [U]

home·made /ˌhəʊmˈmeɪd◂/ *adj* [Wa5] *sometimes derog or apprec* (of clothes, food, etc.) made at home, not bought from a shop

ho·me·o- /ˈhəʊmɪə, ˌhəʊmiˈɒ/ *comb. form* (esp. *AmE* spelling for words beginning with) **homoeo-**: HOMEOPATH|HOMEOPATHY

Home Of·fice /ˈ· ˌ··/ *n* [*the*+GU] the British government department which deals with home affairs —compare FOREIGN OFFICE

home plate /ˌ· ˈ·◂/ *n* [R] (in BASEBALL) PLATE¹ (15)

Ho·mer·ic /həʊˈmerɪk/ *adj* **1 a** of the poet Homer **b** of the style of his poetry; EPIC; HEROIC **2** (of laughter) loud

home rule /ˌ· ˈ·/ *n* [U] self-government by a politically-dependent area

home run /ˌ· ˈ·/ also (*infml*) **hom·er** /ˈhəʊməʳ/— *n* (in BASEBALL) a hit which produces from 1 to 4 runs (points)

home·sick /ˈhəʊmˌsɪk/ *adj* feeling a great wish to be at home, when away from it —**~ness** *n* [U]

home·spun /ˈhəʊmspʌn/ *adj, n* [Wa5;U] **1** (cloth from thread) spun (SPIN¹ (1)) at home, esp. in former times **2** (something) simple and ordinary

home·stead /ˈhəʊmsted, -stɪ̈d/ *n* **1** a house and land; a farm with its buildings **2** *esp. AmE* a piece of land given by the state (esp. in former times) on condition that the owner farms it

home stretch /ˌ· ˈ·/ *n* **1** the last part of a race **2** the last part of any activity

home·town /ˌhəʊmˈtaʊn/ *n* the town where one was born and/or passed one's childhood

home truth /ˌ· ˈ·/ *n* a fact about someone which is unpleasant for him to know, but true

home·ward /ˈhəʊmwəd‖-ərd/ *adj* [Wa5] going towards home

home·wards /ˈhəʊmwədz‖-ərdz/ *AmE* usu. **home·ward** /ˈhəʊmwəd‖-ərd/— *adv* [Wa5] towards home

home·work /ˈhəʊmwɜːk‖-ɜrk/ *n* [U] **1** studies which must be done at home so as to learn and prepare for what is studied at school **2** preparation done before taking part in an important activity —compare HOUSEWORK

hom·ey, homy /ˈhəʊmi/ *adj* [Wa1] *AmE infml* pleasant, like home; HOMELIKE

hom·i·cid·al /ˌhɒmɪ̈ˈsaɪdl◂‖ˌhɑ-/ *adj* (of a person or character) likely to murder

hom·i·cide /ˈhɒmɪ̈saɪd‖ˈhɑ-/ *n fml or law* **1** [U;C] (an act of) murder **2** [C] a murderer

hom·i·let·ic /ˌhɒmɪ̈ˈletɪk‖ˌhɑ-/ *adj* of or concerning homilies (HOMILY)

hom·i·let·ics /ˌhɒmɪ̈ˈletɪks‖ˌhɑ-/ *n* [U] the art of giving SERMONs

hom·i·ly /ˈhɒmɪ̈li‖ˈhɑ-/ *n* **1** SERMON **2** *usu. derog.* a talk, esp. a long one, which gives one advice on how to behave: *another of my mother's little homilies on what not to do at parties*

hom·ing /ˈhəʊmɪŋ/ *adj, n* [Wa5;A;U] **1** (of) the ability to find one's way home, as used by PIGEONs and in animal behaviour **2** (of) the ability of some machines, esp. modern weapons of war, to guide themselves onto the place they are aimed at

homing pi·geon /ˈ·· ˌ··/ *n* **1** a PIGEON trained to return to a particular place, esp. as used in races against other pigeons **2** CARRIER PIGEON

hom·i·ny /ˈhɒmɪ̈ni‖ˈhɑ-/ *n* [U] a sort of American MAIZE corn, esp. when boiled —compare GRITS

hominy grits /ˈ··· ·/ *n* [U;P] (in the US) a treated form of HOMINY

ho·mo- /ˈhəʊməʊ, ˈhɒmə‖ˈhəʊməʊ, ˈhɑ-/ *comb. form* same; like: *homosexual*|HOMOGRAPH —compare HETERO-

ho·moe·o·path, homeo- /ˈhəʊmɪəpæθ/ *n* a person, usu. a doctor, who treats a disease by giving very small amounts of a type of drug which in larger amounts would usually produce an illness like that disease —**~ic** /ˌhəʊmɪəˈpæθɪk/ *adj* —**~ically** *adv* [Wa4]

ho·moe·op·athy, homeo- /ˌhəʊmiˈɒpəθi‖-ˈɑp-/ *n* [U] the practice of medicine in the manner of HOMOEOPATHs

ho·mo·ge·ne·ous /ˌhəʊməˈdʒiːnɪəs/ *adj* formed of parts of the same kind —**-ity** /ˌhəʊmədʒɪ̈ˈniːɪ̈ti/ *n* [U] —**~ly** /ˌhəʊməˈdʒiːnɪəsli/ *adv*

ho·mo·ge·nize, -ise /həˈmɒdʒənaɪz‖-ˈmɑ-/ *v* [Wv4;5;T1] to make (the parts of a whole, esp. a mixture) become evenly spread: *homogenized milk* (=where there is no cream, because the fat is broken up all through the liquid)

hom·o·graph /ˈhɒməgrɑːf, ˈhəʊ-‖ˈhɑməgræf, ˈhəʊ-/ *n* a word that has the same spelling as another, but is different in meaning, origin, or pronunciation: *The noun "record" and the verb "record" are homographs* (*of each other*)

hom·o·nym /ˈhɒmənɪm, ˈhəʊ-‖ˈhɑ-, ˈhəʊ-/ *n* **1** HOMOGRAPH **2** HOMOPHONE **3** a word which has both the same sound and spelling as another, though different in meaning or origin: *The noun "bear" and the verb "bear" are homonyms* (*of each other*)

hom·o·phone /ˈhɒməfəʊn, ˈhəʊ-‖ˈhɑ-, ˈhəʊ-/ *n* a word which sounds the same as another but is different in meaning, origin, or spelling: *"Knew" and "new" are homophones* (*of each other*)

Ho·mo sa·pi·ens /ˌhəʊməʊ ˈsæpɪenz‖-ˈseɪpɪənz/ *n* [R] *Lat* the form of man now alive on the earth; people generally

ho·mo·sex·u·al /ˌheʊməˈsekʃʊəl/ *adj, n* (of or

being) a person sexually attracted to members of the same sex

hom·y /ˈhəʊmi/ *adj* [Wa1] *AmE infml* HOMEY

hon. *written abbrev. for:* HONORARY: *He is the hon. chairman*

USAGE This *abbrev.* sometimes receives the very informal pronunciation /ɒn‖ɑn/.

Hon. *written abbrev. for:* HONOURABLE —see HON. (USAGE)

hone¹ /həʊn/ *n* a stone used to sharpen knives and tools; WHETSTONE

hone² *v* [Wv5;T1] to sharpen (knives, swords, etc.) with a HONE

hon·est /ˈɒnɪ̆st‖ˈɑn-/ *adj* **1** (of people) trustworthy; not likely to lie or to cheat **2** (of actions, appearance, etc.) showing such qualities: *an honest face* **3** direct; not hiding facts **4 make an honest living** to earn one's pay fairly **5 turn an honest penny** to gain money by fair means **6 make an honest woman of (her)** *often humor* to marry (a woman) after having a sexual relationship with her

hon·est·ly /ˈɒnɪ̆stli‖ˈɑn-/ *adv* **1** in an honest way **2** [Wa5] **a** really; speaking truthfully: *I can't honestly say it matters to me.|I didn't tell anyone, honestly I didn't* **b** (used for expressing strong feeling usu. mixed with disapproval): *Honestly! What a thing to do!*

honest-to-good·ness /ˌ·· · ˈ··◂/ *adj* [Wa5;A] *infml apprec* pure and simple; in its natural state; unmixed

hon·es·ty /ˈɒnɪ̆sti‖ˈɑn-/ *n* [U] **1** the quality of being honest **2** a type of European garden plant with seed-containers which look like round white leaves

hon·ey /ˈhʌni/ *n* **honeys** **1** [U] the sweet sticky soft material produced by bees, which is eaten on bread **2** [N;C] *esp. AmE* DARLING: *Go to bed now, honeys!* **3** [C] *infml, esp. AmE* something excellent: *That new car of his is a real honey!*

hon·ey·bee /ˈhʌnibiː/ *n* the bee which makes HONEY

hon·ey·comb /ˈhʌnikəʊm/ *n* **1** a container made of beeswax and consisting of 6-sided cells in which honey is stored **2** something like this in shape, as in an arrangement of bricks

hon·ey·combed /ˈhʌnikəʊmd/ *adj* [(*with*)] filled with holes, hollow passages, etc.

hon·ey·dew /ˈhʌnidjuː‖-duː/ *n* [U] **1** a sticky material found on plants in hot weather, produced by small insects **2** *poet* AMBROSIA **3** sweetened tobacco

honeydew mel·on /ˌ··· ˈ··/ *n* [C;(U)] a common type of MELON with a pale skin and flesh and a very sweet taste

hon·eyed /ˈhʌnid/ *adj* (of words) sweet and pleasing; FLATTERing

hon·ey·moon¹ /ˈhʌnimuːn/ *n* **1** the holiday taken by a man and woman who have just got married **2** a pleasant period of time

honeymoon² *v* [L9] to have one's HONEYMOON —**~er** *n*

hon·ey·suck·le /ˈhʌniˌsʌkəl/ *n* [C;U] a type of climbing plant, growing both wild and in gardens, with sweet-smelling yellow flowers

honk¹ /hɒŋk‖hɑŋk, hɔŋk/ *n* **1** the sound a wild GOOSE makes **2** the sound made by a car horn

honk² *v* [I∅ (*at*);T1] to (cause to) make a HONK: *He honked his horn as he went past.|The geese* (GOOSE) *flew honking above*

hon·kie, honky /ˈhɒŋki‖ˈhɑŋki, ˈhɔŋki/ *n* [C;N] *derog* (*used esp. by black people*) a white man

hon·ky-tonk /ˈhɒŋki tɒŋk‖ˈhɑŋki tɑŋk, ˈhɔŋki tɔŋk/ *adj* [Wa5] of or used in a merry form of piano-playing

hon·o·rar·i·um /ˌɒnəˈreəriəm‖ˌɑnə-/ *n* **-iums** *or* **-ia** /ɪə/ a sum of money offered for professional services, for which by custom the person does not ask to be paid

hon·or·ar·y /ˈɒnərəri‖ˈɑnəreri/ *adj* **1** (of a rank, a university degree, etc.) given as an HONOUR, not according to the usual rules **2** (of an office or position held) without payment for one's services: *He's the honorary chairman* —compare HONOURABLE

hon·or·if·ic /ˌɒnəˈrɪfɪk‖ˌɑnə-/ *adj, n* (a title or expression) which shows respect, esp. as used in Eastern languages —**~ally** *adv* [Wa4]

hon·our¹, *AmE* **-or** /ˈɒnəʳ‖ˈɑnər/ *n* **1** [U] great respect, often publicly expressed: *He won honour for his courage* **2** [U] high standards of character or REPUTATION: *He didn't need to state publicly that he knew nothing about the* CRIME, *but he couldn't let his honour be questioned.|to fight for/to save the honour of one's country* **3** [S (*to*)] a person who brings respect (to): *He's an honour to his parents* **4** [C9;N9] (a title of respect for a judge): *Your/His Honour* —compare **my** LORD¹ **5** [S] (a polite word): *Would you do me the honour of dancing with me?* **6** [U] *often humor* the CHASTITY of a woman (esp. in the phr. **lose one's honour**) **7 a debt of honour** money or services which must be returned in order to be seen to behave well, not because it is necessary by law **8 do honour (to) a** to show respect (to), esp. publicly: *He was a great king, and all the kings of smaller countries did him honour* **b** to bring respect (to): *Your refusal to accept the stolen money does you honour* **9 guard of honour** a group of soldiers or some other (uniformed) group who welcome an important person ceremonially **10 (in) honour bound** forced by one's standards of good behaviour: *You're (in) honour bound to lend him money when he did the same for you* **11 a point of honour** something considered important for one's self-respect **12 put someone on his honour** to trust someone to do something by making him feel that shame would come on him if he were not to do it

honour², *AmE* **-or** *v* [T1] **1** [Wv5] to respect by feelings or by an action which shows feelings: *I'm honoured that you should notice me* **2** to keep (an agreement), often by making a payment, as in giving money for a cheque or bill: *Please honour our arrangement by exchanging the damaged goods.|You must have enough money to honour your cheques before writing them*

hon·our·a·ble, *AmE* **honorable** /ˈɒnərəbəl‖ˈɑn-/ *adj* **1** worthy of honour or respect **2** showing good character —compare HONORARY —**-bly** *adv* [Wa3]

Honourable, *AmE* **Honorable** (*abbrev.* **Hon.**)— *adj* [Wa5;A9] (a title given to the children of certain British noblemen, to judges, and various official people, including Members of Parliament when talking to one another in the HOUSE OF COMMONS): *Will the Honourable member please answer the question?|As my Honourable friend has said, . . .|the Honourable Glencora Smith-Fortescue*

honourable men·tion /ˌ···· ˈ··/ *n* [U;C] a special mark of honour in a competition or show, given for work of high quality that has not won first, second, or third prizes

honour roll /ˈ·· ·/ *n AmE* ROLL OF HONOUR

hon·ours, *AmE* **honors** /ˈɒnəz‖ˈɑnərz/ *n* [P] **1** marks of respect, such as titles given in Britain to important people on the Queen's birthday and at New Year in the **honours list** **2** a specialized university UNDERGRADUATE degree, or a level gained in it: *He couldn't get honours, in fact he only just passed* **3** the highest playing cards in a game **4 (full) military honours** ceremonies at which soldiers attend to greet an important person, or to bury a great man **5 do the honours** *infml* to act as the host or hostess, as by offering drink

hooch /huːtʃ/ *n* [U] *AmE sl* alcoholic drink, esp. WHISKY

hood /hʊd/ *n* **1 a** a covering for the whole of the head and neck (except the face), usu. fastened on at the back, as to a coat, so that it can be pushed back when not needed **b** a covering for the head of a hunting bird **2** something like a hood which covers or fits over the top of something else, as over a chimney to keep the wind out or over a cooker to draw gases out of the room **3** a folding cover over a car, PRAM (=baby carriage), etc. **4** *AmE* the BONNET (3) covering the engine of a car **5** *sl* HOODLUM

-hood *suffix* [*n*→*n* [U;(C)]] the state or time of being: *childhood*

hood·ed /ˈhʊdɪ̣d/ *adj* **1** [Wa5] wearing a HOOD **2** hidden by a covering: *hooded eyes* (=half shut)

hood·lum /ˈhuːdləm/ *n sl* a violent and/or criminal person

hoo·doo¹ /ˈhuːduː/ *n* **-doos** *infml esp. AmE* **1** [C] a person or thing which brings bad luck **2** VOODOO

hoodoo² *v* **-dooed** /duːd/ [T1] *infml esp. AmE* to bring bad luck on (someone)

hood·wink /ˈhʊdˌwɪŋk/ *v* [T1] to trick or deceive

hoo·ey /ˈhuːi/ *n* [U] *AmE sl* stupid talk; NONSENSE

hoof /huːf‖hʊf/ *n* **hoofs** *or* **hooves** /huːvz‖hʊfs/ **1** the hard foot of certain animals, as of the horse —see picture at HORSE **2 on the hoof** (of a meat animal) before being killed for meat; still alive

hoo-ha /ˈhuː hɑː/ *n* [U] *infml* noisy talk about something unimportant; FUSS

hook¹ /hʊk/ *n* **1 a** a curved piece of metal, plastic, etc., for catching something on or hanging things on: *a fish hook|Hang your coat on the hook* **b** a small one used with an EYE¹ (7) to fasten clothing —see picture at TOOL¹ **2** something curved or bent like this: *Hook of Holland* **3** (*usu. in comb.*) a tool for cutting grass, branches, etc. **4 a** (in cricket, GOLF, etc.) a flight of a ball away from a course straight ahead and towards the side of the player's weaker hand —opposite **slice b** (in BOXING) a blow given with the elbow bent **c** (in RUGBY) a kick back **5** the part on which a telephone RECEIVER (2) rests or is hung **6 be on the hook** to be in a position of difficulty, esp. when it is difficult to find a way out **7 be/get off the hook** to be/get out of one's difficulties **8 by hook or by crook** by any means possible **9 hook, line and sinker** (with expressions of belief) completely: *swallowed the unlikely story hook, line and sinker* **10 sling one's hook** *BrE sl* to go away

hook² *v* **1** [T1] to catch with or as if with a HOOK¹ (1): *to hook a fish/a rich husband* **2** [X9] to hang on or fasten with or as if with a HOOK¹ (1): *Hook my dress up.|Hook it over that nail* **3** [X9] to make into the shape of a hook: *He hooked his arm round her neck and pulled her head down* **4** [IØ;T1] **a** (of a ball) to travel in a HOOK¹ (4) **b** to hit (a ball) in a HOOK¹ (4)

hook·ah /ˈhʊkə/ also **water pipe**— *n* a tobacco pipe whose smoke is drawn through water by a long tube before reaching the mouth

hooked /hʊkt/ *adj* **1** [B] shaped like a hook: *a hooked nose* **2** [Wa5;B] having one or more hooks **3** [Wa5;F] caught on or as if on a hook: *Keep still, your hair's hooked on a button* **4** [F (*on*)] *infml* **a** dependent (on drugs) **b** having a great liking for and very frequently using, doing, eating, etc. —compare ADDICTed (to)

hook·er /ˈhʊkəʳ/ *n* **1** *AmE sl* a PROSTITUTE **2** (in RUGBY) a player whose job it is to HOOK² (4b) the ball

hook-nosed /ˌ· ˈ·◂‖ˈ· ·/ *adj* having a nose curved out in the middle

hook up *v adv* [T1] to connect to a power supply or central system

hook·up /ˈhʊk-ʌp/ *n* the connection of a network of radio stations so that they can broadcast the same PROGRAMME together

hook·worm /ˈhʊkwɜːm‖-ɜrm/ *n* **1** [C] a worm which lives in the INTESTINEs of man **2** [U] the disease caused by this worm

hook·y, hookey /ˈhʊki/ *n* [U] *AmE sl* TRUANT (only in the phr. **play hooky**)

hoo·li·gan /ˈhuːlɪ̣gən/ *n* a noisy, rough person who causes trouble by fighting, breaking things, etc. —**~ism** *n* [U]

hoop¹ /huːp‖hʊp, huːp/ *n* **1 a** a circular band of wood or metal, esp. round a barrel **b** such a band used as a child's toy **2** a circular frame, as formerly used to hold women's skirts out, or for animals to jump through at the CIRCUS **3** a metal arch through which the ball is driven in CROQUET **4 put someone/go through the hoops** to cause someone to have a difficult time/to have a difficult time

hoop² *v* [T1] to put a HOOP on (a barrel) —see also COOPER

hoop-la /ˈhuːp lɑː‖ˈhuːp-, ˈhʊp-/ *n* [U] **1** a game in which prizes are won when a ring is thrown right over them **2** shouts of excitement

hoo·ray /hʊˈreɪ/ *interj, n* HURRAY

hoot¹ /huːt/ *v* [IØ (*at, with*); T1] **1** to (cause to) make a HOOT **2** [IØ] *infml* to laugh very much: *Mother will hoot when she hears!*

hoot² *n* **1** the sound an OWL makes **2** the sound made by a car or ship's horn **3** a shout of dislike, unpleasant laughter, etc. **4 not care a hoot/2 hoots** *infml* not to care at all: *He doesn't care 2 hoots whether he passes his examination or not*

hoot down *v adv* [T1] to show disapproval of by making a HOOTing noise —compare HOWL DOWN

hoot·er /ˈhuːtəʳ/ *n* **1** a SIREN (1) or whistle, esp. of the type which signals the beginning or end of work **2** *BrE sl* the nose

hoot off *v prep* [D1] to drive off by HOOTing: *The actor was hooted off the stage*

hoo·ver¹ /ˈhuːvəʳ/ *n tdmk BrE not fml* (*often cap.*) (a type of) VACUUM CLEANER

hoover² *v* [T1 (OUT); IØ] *tdmk BrE not fml* (*sometimes cap.*) VACUUM²

hooves /huːvz‖hʊfs/ *pl. of* HOOF

hop¹ /hɒp‖hɑp/ *v* **-pp- 1** [IØ] **a** (of people) to jump on one leg **b** (of small creatures) to jump: *The bird hopped onto my finger* **2** [T1] to cross by hopping: *hopped the stream* **3 Hop it!** *BrE sl* Go away! **4 hopping mad** very angry —see MAD (USAGE) **5 hop the twig** *BrE humor* **a** to die **b** to leave without paying debts —see also HEDGEHOP

hop² *n* **1** an act of HOPping; jump **2** *infml* informal dance **3** *infml* a distance travelled by a plane before landing: *It's a short hop from London to Paris* **4 catch someone on the hop** *infml* to meet someone when he is unprepared **5 keep someone on the hop** *infml* to keep someone busy or moving, esp. by worrying him **6 on the hop** *infml* busy, active —see also HOP, SKIP, AND JUMP; HOP, STEP, AND JUMP

hop³ *n* **1** a tall climbing plant with flowers **2** [*usu. pl.*] the seed-cases of this plant, esp. when dried and used for giving taste to beer

hope¹ /həʊp/ *v* [IØ (*for*); T3,5a,b] **1** to wish and expect; desire in spite of doubts: *I hope he'll come tomorrow.|We're hoping to visit France this year.|After this dry weather everyone hopes for rain* **2 hope against hope** to continue to hope when there is little chance of success **3 hope for the best** to trust that things will go well when a rather unsuccessful-

looking arrangement has been made: *You don't need to make the soup carefully; just mix everything together and hope for the best*
USAGE Compare **hope** and **wish**: If one **wishes** to do or have something, one wants it without thinking whether it is possible: *I* **wish** *to go* (=I want to go). The word is also used for impossible desires: *I* **wish** *I were French.|I* **wish** *you'd told me.* But if one **hopes** to do or have something, one wants it and believes that it is possible to do or get it: *He* **hopes** *to become a doctor* (=he has the chance to study and he thinks he can pass the examinations).|*I* **hope** *you will help me* (=I want you to and I think you can.) One cannot **hope**, or have **hopes**, about impossible things. Compare: *I have no* **wish** *to go* (=I don't want to).|*I have no* **hope** *of going* (=I want to but I know I won't).

hope² *n* [U,U5;C,C5] **1** the expectation of something happening as one wishes: *Do you have any hope that he'll come?* **2** a person or thing that seems likely to bring success: *You're my only hope/last hope. Please help me* **3 hold out hope** to give reason to expect: *He can hold out no hope of succeeding* **4 beyond/past hope** beyond the possibility of success **5 live in hope(s)** (of) *esp. BrE* to be hoping (for something to succeed): *Things seem bad, but we live in hope* **6 in the hope of** (doing) hoping (to do) **7 raise someone's hopes** to make someone hope for success, esp. when it is unlikely

hope chest /ˈ· ·/ *n AmE* **1** a collection of useful HOUSEHOLD things which a woman keeps in expectation of marriage **2** (in former times) a chest in which these things were kept —see BOTTOM DRAWER

hope·ful¹ /ˈhəʊpfəl/ *adj* **1** [B (*of*); F5] (of people) feeling hope: *I'm hopeful that he'll arrive early* **2** [B] giving cause for hope of success: *He's the most hopeful man in politics* —**~ness** *n* [U]

hopeful² *n* a person who seems likely to succeed, or who desires to succeed: *a young hopeful*

hope·ful·ly /ˈhəʊpfəli/ *adv* **1** in a hopeful way **2** [Wa5] *esp. AmE* if our hopes succeed: *Hopefully we'll be there by dinnertime*
USAGE It is considered incorrect, by many teachers and writers of *BrE*, to use **hopefully** meaning "If our hopes succeed . . .; It is to be hoped that . . ." but this is becoming very common, esp. in speech.

hope·less /ˈhəʊpləs/ *adj* **1** (not usu. of people) showing lack of hope: *hopeless tears* **2** giving no cause for hope: *Our position is hopeless, we'll never get out alive* **3** *infml* useless: *Your work is hopeless and so are you* **4** incurable: *She has a terrible illness; it's a hopeless case* —**~ly** *adv* —**~ness** *n* [U]

hopped-up /ˌ· ˈ·◂/ *adj esp. AmE* **1** *sl* (of people) excited by having taken drugs **2** *infml* (of car engines) specially increased in power; SOUPED-UP

hop·per /ˈhɒpəʳ‖ˈhɑ-/ *n* **1** a FUNNEL through which grain or coal is passed **2** (*usu. in comb.*) a creature which HOPs: *a* GRASSHOPPER **3** a boat which takes mud out to sea

hop-pick·er /ˈ· ˌ··/ *n* a person or machine used for gathering HOPs³

hop pole /ˈ· ·/ *n* a pole for HOPs³ to climb up

hop·scotch /ˈhɒpskɒtʃ‖ˈhɑpskɑtʃ/ *n* [U] a children's game in which a stone is thrown onto numbered squares and each child HOPs and jumps from one to another

hop, skip, and jump /ˌ· · · ˈ·/ *n* [S] *esp. AmE* a short distance: *just a hop, skip, and jump away*

hop, step, and jump /ˌ· · · ˈ·/ *n* [*the*+R;S] TRIPLE JUMP

horde /hɔːd‖hord/ *n* [*often pl.*] **1** [C (*of*)] a large number or crowd: *a horde of children|Hordes of children ran over the building* **2** [C9] (in history) a large wandering group of people of a certain nationality, esp. a fighting one

ho·ri·zon /həˈraɪzən/ *n* **1** [*usu. sing.*] the limit of one's view across the surface of the earth, where the sky seems to meet the earth or sea **2** [*usu. pl. with sing. meaning*] the limit of one's thoughts

hor·i·zon·tal /ˌhɒrɪ̈ˈzɒntl‖ˌhɑrɪ̈ˈzɑntl/ *adj, n* [B; *the*+R] (in) the flat position, along or parallel to the ground: *Stand the table on its legs, so that the top is horizontal!|in the horizontal* PLANE (=position)|*level with the horizontal* —compare VERTICAL —**~ly** *adv*

hor·mone /ˈhɔːməʊn‖ˈhɔr-/ *n* any of several substances directed from organs of the body into the bloodstream so as to influence growth, development, etc.

horn /hɔːn‖hɔrn/ *n* **1** [C] a hard pointed growth found in a pair on the top of the heads of cattle, sheep, and goats —see picture at FARMYARD **2** [C] something which stands out from an animal's head like these growths, as on a SNAIL **3** [U] the material that these growths are made of: *The knife has a horn handle* **4** [C] a hollow drinking vessel like these growths in shape or material **5** [C9] (*often in comb.*) something originally made of the material of these growths: *a hunting horn* **6** [C] any of a number of musical instruments consisting of a long metal tube, usu. bent several times and played by blowing: *the French horn|a hunting horn* **7** [C] a sound-making apparatus (perhaps originally horn-shaped), as in a car, which gives usu. only one note as a warning —see picture at CAR **8 draw in one's horns a** to become less active or concerned in something **b** *BrE* to spend less **9 horn of plenty** CORNUCOPIA **10 on the horns of a dilemma** having to choose between 2 unpleasant things **11 take the bull by the horns** to face a difficult thing or person rather than avoiding them —**~like** *adj* —**~less** *adj* [Wa5]

horn·beam /ˈhɔːnbiːm‖ˈhɔrn-/ *n* **1** [C] a type of small tree with hard wood, sometimes used in HEDGEs **2** [U] the wood of this tree

horn·bill /ˈhɔːnˌbɪl‖ˈhɔrn-/ *n* a type of bird with a horn-like growth on its BILL (beak)

horned /hɔːnd‖hɔrnd/ *adj* **1** (*often in comb.*) having horns: *horned cattle|4-horned sheep* **2** *old use* curved like the new moon

hor·net /ˈhɔːnɪ̈t‖ˈhɔr-/ *n* a type of large insect which can sting, related to the WASP

hornet's nest /ˌ·· ˈ·‖ˈ·· ·/ *n* a lot of trouble and anger between people (esp. in the phr. **stir up a hornet's nest**)

horn in *v adv* [I∅ (*on*)] *sl* to interrupt or join without invitation: *Nobody asked you to horn in (on our conversation)!*

horn·pipe /ˈhɔːnpaɪp‖ˈhɔrn-/ *n* **1** a type of dance, esp. performed by sailors **2** the music for this dance

horn-rimmed /ˌ· ˈ·◂/ *adj* [Wa5] (of glasses for the eyes) surrounded by an edge made of horn or a material like it

horn·y /ˈhɔːni‖ˈhɔrni/ *adj* [Wa1] **1** hard and rough: *The old gardener had horny hands* **2** *taboo sl* (of a man) sexually excited

ho·rol·o·gy /hɒˈrɒlədʒi‖həˈrɑ-/ *n* [U] the art of making clocks and watches and of measuring time

hor·o·scope /ˈhɒrəskəʊp‖ˈhɑ-, ˈhɔ-/ *n* a set of ideas about someone's character, life and future, which are gained by knowing the positions of the stars or PLANETs at the time of his birth and the effects these are said to have

hor·ren·dous /həˈrendəs‖hɑ-, hɔ-/ *adj* really terrible; causing great fear —**~ly** *adv*

hor·ri·ble /ˈhɒrəbəl‖ˈhɔ-, ˈhɑ-/ *adj* **1** causing HORROR: *a horrible accident* **2** *infml* very unkind,

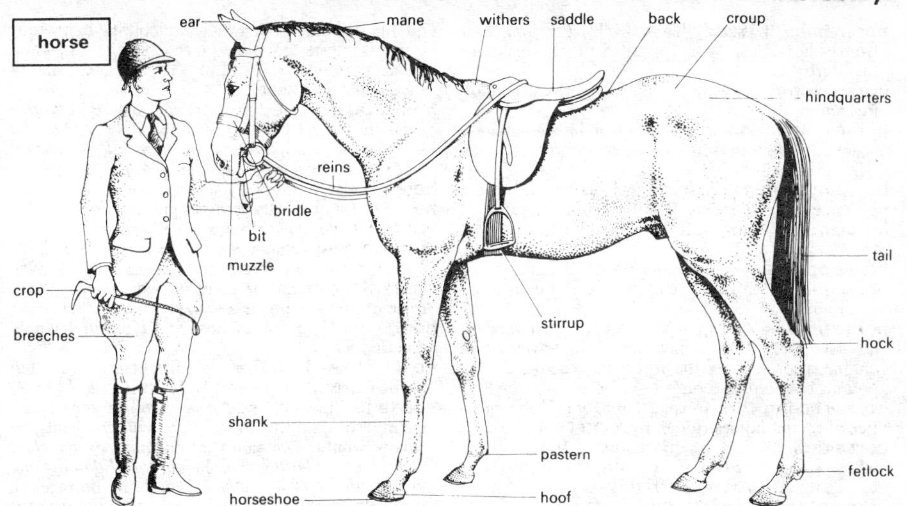

unpleasant, or ugly: *What a horrible dress!* —**-bly** *adv* [Wa3]

hor·rid /ˈhɒrɨd‖ˈhɔ-, ˈhɑ-/ *adj* [(*to*)] very unpleasant or unkind; HORRIBLE (2): *Don't be horrid (to Aunt Agatha)! You shouldn't say such unkind things!* —**~ly** *adv* —**~ness** *n* [U]

hor·rif·ic /hɒˈrɪfɪk, hə-‖hɔ-, hɑ-/ *adj* able to or meant to HORRIFY, shock, etc.: *The film showed the most horrific murder scenes* —**~ally** *adv* [Wa4]

hor·ri·fy /ˈhɒrɨfaɪ‖ˈhɔ-, ˈhɑ-/ *v* [Wv4,5;T1] to shock; fill with HORROR: *I was horrified at/by the news* —**~ingly** *adv*

hor·ror /ˈhɒrəʳ‖ˈhɔ-, ˈhɑ-/ *n* **1** [U] a feeling of great shock, fear, and dislike: *We were filled with horror at the bad news.|I cried out in horror as I saw the man killed* **2** [(*the*) U] the quality of causing this feeling: *thought about the horror of their lives|the horror of war* **3** [C] an unpleasant person: *The little horror never stops playing tricks on his parents* **4** **Chamber of Horrors** (in a place where wax figures of people are shown) the room where murderers, TORTURErs, etc., are represented in wax **5** **have a horror of** to hate, dislike very much: *I have a horror of snakes* **6** **horror film** a film of a popular type in which fearful things happen which could not happen in reality, such as dead people coming to life, people turning into animals, and men and women sucking one another's blood

hor·rors /ˈhɒrəz‖ˈhɔrərz, ˈhɑ-/ *n* [*the*+P] **1** a state of great fear, worry, or sadness: *to give someone/have the horrors* **2** DELIRIUM TREMENS **3** things, events, or actions that cause the feeling of HORROR: *the horrors of war*

horror-strick·en /ˈ·· ˌ··/ also **horror-struck** /ˈ·· ·/— *adj* [B (*at*), B3] filled with HORROR; shocked: *Her face was horror-struck at the thought*

hors de com·bat /ˌɔː də ˈkɒmbɑː‖ˌɔr də ˈkɑmbɑ (*Fr* ɔr də kɔ̃ba)/ *adj, adv* [F] *Fr* unable to fight, because wounded

hors d'oeu·vre /ˌɔː ˈdɜːv‖ˌɔr ˈdɜrv (*Fr* ɔr dœvr)/ *n* **-d'oeuvres** /dɜːv‖dɜrvz (*Fr* dœvr)/ *or* **-d'oeuvre** *Fr* any of several types of strong-tasting food offered in small amounts at the beginning of the meal

horse /hɔːs‖hɔrs/ *n* **1** [C] a type of large strong animal with MANE, tail, and hard feet (hooves (HOOF)), which men ride on and use for pulling and carrying heavy things —see BICYCLE (USAGE) **2** [C] VAULTING HORSE **3** [C] (*usu. in comb.*) a frame on which things can be hung: *a clothes horse* **4** [P] (in former times) a number of soldiers on horseback; CAVALRY **5** [U] *sl* HEROIN **6** **dark horse** a person whose abilities are hidden or unknown **7** **back the wrong horse** to favour the losing side **8** **eat like a horse** to eat a lot **9** **(straight) from the horse's mouth** *infml* (of something) told to one directly, from the person concerned **10** **flogging a dead horse** being active in something which no longer interests anyone else **11** **Hold your horses!** Don't rush hastily into an activity or decision **12** **a horse of another/a different colour** a completely different thing; something to be considered separately from the present point **13** **Don't look a gift horse in the mouth** Don't complain about a gift **14** **put the cart before the horse** to do or put things in the wrong order —compare USAGE **15** **a willing horse** a helpful person, who often gets all the work to do **16** **work like a horse** to work very hard **17** **You can lead a horse to water but you can't make it drink** Good suggestions can be made but people cannot be forced to do what they don't want to
USAGE Note the word order in this fixed phr.: **horse and cart**: *I'll go and get it with the horse and cart.*

horse-and-bug·gy /ˌ· · ˈ··/ *adj* [Wa5;A] *infml esp. AmE* **1** of times before the motor car: *horse-and-buggy days* **2** old-fashioned: *horse-and-buggy methods*

horse a·round also **horse a·bout**— *v adv* [IØ] *infml* to play roughly or waste time in rough play

horse·back /ˈhɔːsbæk‖ˈhɔrs-/ *n* **1** [A] *esp. AmE* of or on the back of a horse: *Do you like horseback riding?* **2** **on horseback** (riding) on a horse **3** **a man on horseback** a possible forceful leader or DICTATOR, esp. a military man: *The whole country was unable to act and seemed to be waiting for a man on horseback to save it*

horse·box /ˈhɔːsbɒks‖ˈhɔrsbɑks/ *n* a large vehicle in which a horse can stand and which can be carried or pulled along by another vehicle

horse chest·nut /ˌ· ˈ··‖ˈ· ˌ··/ *n* **1** a large tree with white or pink flowers **2** a nut from this tree. These nuts are not usually eaten, but children put them on strings and strike one against another in the game of CONKERs —compare CHESTNUT[1] (1,2) and see picture at TREE[1]

horse·flesh /ˈhɔːsfleʃ‖ˈhɔrs-/ *n* [U] **1** meat from a horse **2** horses generally: *a good judge of horseflesh*

horse·fly /ˈhɔːsflaɪ‖ˈhɔrs-/ *n* a type of large fly that stings horses and cattle

horse·hair /ˈhɔːsheəʳ‖ˈhɔrs-/ *n* [U] the long hair from a horse, esp. when used to fill the inside of furniture

horse·laugh /ˈhɔːs-lɑːf‖ˈhɔrs-læf/ *n* a loud (impolite) laugh

horse·man /ˈhɔːsmən‖ˈhɔrs-/ (*fem.* **horsewoman**)— *n* **-men** /mən/ a person who rides a horse, esp. one who rides well

horse·man·ship /ˈhɔːsmənʃɪp‖ˈhɔrs-/ *n* [U] **1** the practice of horse-riding **2** skill in riding horses

horse·meat /ˈhɔːs-miːt‖ˈhɔrs-/ *n* [U] HORSEFLESH (1)

horse op·e·ra /ˈ· ˌ···/ *n humor* WESTERN (2)

horse·play /ˈhɔːspleɪ‖ˈhɔrs-/ *n* [U] rough noisy behaviour

horse·pow·er /ˈhɔːsˌpaʊəʳ‖ˈhɔrs-/ (*abbrev.* **HP**)— *n* **horsepower** [Wn3] a measure of the power of an engine, representing the force needed to pull 550 pounds one foot a second

horse·rac·ing /ˈhɔːsˌreɪsɪŋ‖ˈhɔrs-/ *n* [U] the practice of racing horses ridden by JOCKEYs, for money

horse·rad·ish /ˈhɔːsˌrædɪʃ‖ˈhɔrs-/ *n* **1** [C] a plant whose root is used to make a strong-tasting SAUCE to be eaten with meat **2** [U] this SAUCE

horse sense /ˈ· ·/ *n* [U] COMMON SENSE

horse·shit /ˈhɔːsˌʃɪt‖ˈhɔrs-/ *n, interj* [U] *taboo sl esp. AmE* BULL[5] (1)

horse·shoe /ˈhɔːʃ-ʃuː, ˈhɔːs-‖ˈhɔr-/ *n* **1** also **shoe**— (the shape of) a curved piece of iron nailed on under a horse's foot —see picture at HORSE **2** something made in this shape, such as an ornamental one given at weddings to bring good luck

horse-trad·ing /ˈ· ˌ··/ *n* [U] argument about prices or about who should do what —**horse trader** *n*

horse·whip /ˈhɔːsˌwɪp‖ˈhɔrs-/ *v* **-pp-** [T1] to beat (someone) hard, as if driving a horse on

horse·wom·an /ˈhɔːsˌwʊmən‖ˈhɔrs-/ *n* **-women** /ˌwɪmɨ̣n/ a female HORSEMAN

hors·y /ˈhɔːsi‖ˈhɔrsi/ *adj* [Wa1] **1** interested in horses, fond of riding, etc. **2** of an appearance which reminds one of horses —**horsiness** *n* [U]

hor·ta·tive /ˈhɔːtətɪv‖ˈhɔr-/ also **hor·ta·to·ry** /-təri‖-tori/— *adj fml* (of advice, speech, etc.) encouraging

hor·ti·cul·ture /ˈhɔːtɨ̣ˌkʌltʃəʳ‖ˈhɔr-/ *n* [U] the science of growing fruit, flowers, and vegetables —**-tural** /ˌhɔːtɨ̣ˈkʌltʃərəl‖ˌhɔr-/ *adj* —**-turalist** *n*

ho·san·na /həʊˈzænə/ *n, interj bibl* a shout of praise to God

hose[1] /həʊz/ *n* [P] **1** (used esp. in shops) stockings or socks **2** tight-fitting leg coverings worn by men in former times

hose[2] also **hose·pipe** /ˈhəʊzpaɪp/— *n* [C;U] (a piece of) rubber or plastic tube which can be moved and bent to direct water onto fires, a garden, etc. —see picture at GARDEN[1]

hose[3] *v* [T1 (DOWN)] to use a HOSE[2] on, esp. for washing: *hosing the car down|to hose the yard out*

ho·sier /ˈhəʊzɪəʳ‖ˈhəʊʒər/ *n* a shopkeeper who sells socks and men's underclothes

ho·sier·y /ˈhəʊzɪəri‖ˈhəʊʒəri/ *n* [U] socks, stockings, underclothes, etc.

hos·pice /ˈhɒspɨ̣s‖ˈhɑ-/ *n* a house made for travellers to stay and rest in, esp. when kept by a religious group

hos·pi·ta·ble /ˈhɒspɪtəbəl, hɒˈspɪ-‖hɑˈspɪ-, ˈhɑspɪ-/ *adj* (of people or their acts) showing the wish to give attention to the needs of others, esp. by feeding them, asking them into one's home, etc. —**-bly** *adv* [Wa3]

hos·pi·tal /ˈhɒspɪtl‖ˈhɑ-/ *n* [C; (*esp. BrE*) U] a place where ill people stay and have treatment which should cure them: *The* PATIENT[2] (1) *was (BrE) in hospital|(AmE) in the hospital*

hos·pi·tal·i·ty /ˌhɒspɨ̣ˈtælɨ̣ti‖ˌhɑ-/ *n* [U] **1** the quality of being HOSPITABLE; welcoming behaviour towards guests **2** food, a place to sleep, etc., when given to a guest (esp. in the phr. **PARTAKE of someone's hospitality**)

hos·pi·tal·ize, -ise /ˈhɒspɪtəl-aɪz‖ˈhɑ-/ *v* [T1 *often pass.*] to put (a person) into hospital: *He broke a leg and was hospitalized for a month* —**-ization** /ˌhɒspɪtəl-aɪˈzeɪʃən‖ˌhɑspɪtəl-əˈzeɪ-/ *n* [U;(C)]

host[1] /həʊst/ *n* [GC (*of*)] a large number

host[2] *n* **1** a man who receives guests (note the phr. **host to**): *He acted as host to his father's friends.|* (fig.) *the* **host country** *for the Olympic Games* **2** *old use or humor* an innkeeper (note the phr. **mine host**) **3** an animal or plant on which some lower form of life is living as a PARASITE

host[3] *v* [T1] to act as host at (a party, friendly meeting, etc.)

host[4] *n* [*the*+R] (*often cap.*) the holy bread eaten in the Christian service of Holy COMMUNION (2)

hos·tage /ˈhɒstɪdʒ‖ˈhɑ-/ *n* **1** a person kept by an enemy so that the other side will do what the enemy wants: *The man with the gun took the child with him as a hostage and no one could do anything for fear the child would be killed* **2 give hostages to fortune** to accept responsibilities that may make it hard to act freely in the future: *Francis Bacon believed that a married man had given hostages to fortune because he had to consider his wife and children before taking any risks* **3 take (someone) hostage** to catch (someone) from the other side to use as a hostage

hos·tel /ˈhɒstl‖ˈhɑ-/ *n* **1** a building in which certain types of person can live and eat, as for students, young people working away from home, etc. **2** YOUTH HOSTEL

hos·tel·ler, *AmE* usu. **hos·tel·er** /ˈhɒstələʳ‖ˈhɑ-/ *n* a person travelling from one HOSTEL (2) to another

hos·tel·ry /ˈhɒstəlri‖ˈhɑ-/ *n old use* an inn

host·ess /ˈhəʊstɨ̣s/ *n* **1** [C] a female host **2** [C] *old use or humor* a female innkeeper (note the phr. **mine hostess**) **3** a young woman who acts as companion, dancing partner, etc., in a social club **4** [C;(N)] AIRHOSTESS

hos·tile /ˈhɒstaɪl‖ˈhɑstl, ˈhɑstaɪl/ *adj* **1** belonging to an enemy **2** [(*to*)] unfriendly; showing dislike

hos·til·i·ties /hɒˈstɪlɨ̣tiz‖hɑ-/ *n* [P] acts of fighting in war: *Hostilities have broken out* (BREAK OUT) *between the 2 countries*

hos·til·i·ty /hɒˈstɪlɨ̣ti‖hɑ-/ *n* [U] the state of being unfriendly

hos·tler /ˈhɒsləʳ‖ˈhɑs-/ *n esp. AmE* OSTLER

hot /hɒt‖hɑt/ *adj* **-tt-** [Wa1] **1** having a certain degree of heat, esp. a high degree: *How hot is the water?|The water isn't hot yet* **2** causing a burning taste in the mouth: *Pepper makes food hot* **3** (esp. in hunting) fresh **4** (of news) very recent; fresh **5** (not usu. of people) excitable: *a hot temper|hot feelings* —compare HEATED **6 a** *infml* (of people) (tending to be) sexually excited: *hot with* PASSION (1) **b** *infml* sexually exciting: *one of the hottest books written* **7** *sl* (of stolen goods) difficult to pass on because still known to the police, esp. soon after the crime has taken place **8** [(*on*)] *infml* (of people) clever, well-informed, and usu. very interested **9** (of JAZZ (1)) with a certain sort of strong beat **10 blow hot and cold** to be changeable in one's opinions, esp. by seeming sometimes interested and at other times uninterested in a plan **11 drop (someone) like a hot potato** to stop all signs of friendship towards (someone) suddenly **12 get hot** (in a guessing game) to get near something hidden or to guess nearly right **13 get hot under the collar** to get angry or excited and ready to argue **14 hot and bothered** worried by a feeling that things are going wrong **15 hot on**

(someone's) trail/track chasing and ready to catch (someone) **16 hot on the heels (of)** following or happening just after **17 make it (too) hot for (someone)** to drive (someone) away by unpleasant behaviour or by causing difficulties **18 not so hot** *infml* not very good; not as good as expected

hot air /ˌ· ˈ·/ *n* [U] meaningless talk or ideas

hot·bed /ˈhɒtbed‖ˈhɑt-/ *n* [C9] a place or condition where growth and development of some undesirable state or activity go on: *The city is a hotbed of crime.|This club is a hotbed of argument*

hot-blood·ed /ˌ· ˈ··◂/ *adj* [Wa2] showing strong feelings; PASSIONATE

hotch·potch /ˈhɒtʃpɒtʃ‖ˈhɑtʃpɑtʃ/ *AmE* usu. **hodgepodge**— *n* [*usu. sing.*] a number of things mixed up without any sensible order of arrangement

hot cross bun /ˌ· · ˈ·/ *n* a sort of small cake made of bread with a cross-shaped mark on top, which is eaten on Good Friday, just before EASTER

hot dog /ˌ· ˈ·‖ˈ· ·/ *n* a special sort of long red SAUSAGE in a bread ROLL¹ (2)
USAGE In *infml AmE*, the expression **Hot dog!** (/ˌ· ˈ·/) can be used for showing approval or pleased surprise: *"You mean we're really going? Hot dog!"*

ho·tel /həʊˈtel/ *n* a building where people can stay if they pay a certain amount of money each night
USAGE One BOOK*s*² (1) or RESERVE*s*¹ (2) a *double* or *single* room in a **hotel**, *with bath/without bath.*

ho·tel·i·er /həʊˈtelieɪ, -lıəʳ/ *n* a man who keeps a hotel

hot flush /ˌ· ˈ·/ *AmE* usu. **hot flash** /ˌ· ˈ·/— *n* [*usu. pl.*] a sudden feeling of heat in the skin, esp. as experienced by women at about the time (MENOPAUSE) when they cease to be able to bear children

hot·foot¹ /ˌhɒtˈfʊt◂‖ˈhɑtfʊt/ *adv infml* (of movements) fast and eagerly: *We ran hotfoot to find out the news*

hotfoot² *v* **hotfoot it** *infml* to move fast: *We hotfooted it down the street*

hot·head /ˈhɒthed‖ˈhɑt-/ *n* a person who does things in haste, without thinking —**~ed** /ˌhɒtˈhedɪ̇d◂/ *adj* [Wa2] —**~edly** /ˌhɒtˈhedɪ̇dli/ *adv*

hot·house /ˈhɒthaʊs‖ˈhɑt-/ *n* **-houses** /ˌhaʊzɪ̇z/ **1** a warm building where flowers and delicate plants can grow; GREENHOUSE **2 hothouse plant** a delicate or sensitive person who must be treated more carefully than other people

hot line /ˈ· ·/ *n* a direct, usu. telephone, line between heads of government, to be used at times of great difficulty, esp. when war is threatened

hot·ly /ˈhɒtli‖ˈhɑtli/ *adv* **1** in anger and with force **2** closely and eagerly (often in the phr. **hotly pursued**)

hot·plate /ˈhɒtpleɪt‖ˈhɑt-/ *n* a metal surface, usu. on an electric cooking STOVE, which is heated and on which food can be cooked in a pan —see picture at KITCHEN

hot·pot /ˈhɒtpɒt‖ˈhɑtpɑt/ *n* [C;U] a mixture of MUTTON (sheep meat), potatoes and onions, cooked slowly in a pot, which is eaten esp. in the North of England

hot po·ta·to /ˌ· ·ˈ··/ *n infml* something difficult or dangerous to deal with

hot rod /ˈ· ·/ *n AmE sl* an old car rebuilt for high speed rather than appearance —compare STOCK-CAR

hot seat /ˈ· ·/ *n* [*the*+R] **1** *sl* the ELECTRIC CHAIR, in which murderers are put to death in parts of the US **2** *infml* a position of difficulty from which one must make important decisions

hot spot /ˈ· ·/ *n* a place where there is likely to be much unrest and perhaps war or unsettled government

hot spring /ˌ· ˈ·/ *n* [*usu. pl.*] water which comes hot from the ground

hot stuff /ˌ· ˈ·/ *n* [U] *infml now rare* **1** something of very good quality **2** something or someone exciting or dangerous, esp. sexually

hot-tem·pered /ˌ· ˈ··◂/ *adj* [Wa2] having or showing a readiness to become angry quickly and easily; quick-tempered

Hot·ten·tot /ˈhɒtntɒt‖ˈhɑtntɑt/ *adj* **1** (of a person) of a dark-skinned race of Southern Africa **2** of the language of this race

hot up *v adv* **-tt-** [T1;I∅] to (cause to) increase in activity which is often exciting or dangerous: *Industrial troubles are hotting up in the North* —compare HEAT **up**

hot wa·ter /ˌ· ˈ··/ *n* [U] trouble (in the phrs. **get into/be in hot water**)

hot-water bot·tle /ˌ· ˈ·· ˌ··/ *n* a usu. rubber container into which hot water is put, and which is placed esp. inside a bed to warm it

hound¹ /haʊnd/ *n* **1** [C] (*often in comb.*) a hunting dog, esp. a foxhound **2** [C;*you*+N9] a person who is disliked and thought unpleasant **3 follow the hounds/ride to hounds** to go foxhunting **4 Hare and Hounds** PAPER CHASE —see also MASTER OF HOUNDS

hound² *v* [T1] to chase or worry continually: *I must finish the work so I don't have him hounding me all the time*

hound down *v adv* [T1] HUNT DOWN

hound's-tooth /ˌ· ˈ·◂/ also **hound's-tooth check** /ˌ· · ˈ·/— *n* [S;U] a pattern with squares of colour sloping slightly sideways and joined by colour at 2 corners, used esp. on cloth and clothes; broken CHECK*s*

hour /aʊəʳ/ *n* **1** the period of time, 60 minutes, of which 24 make a day **2** a time of day when a new such period starts: *He arrived on the hour* **3** a distance which one can travel in this period of time: *It's only an hour away* **4** [*often pl.*] a fixed point or period of time: *The hour has come for us to have a serious talk* **5** [*usu. pl.*] a certain period of time: *The hours I spent with you were the happiest of my life* **6** a time, esp. an important one like the present: *In my hour of need* (=when I needed help) *no one helped me.|My hour has come* (=something important or death) **7 after hours** /ˌ·· ˈ·/ later than the usual times of work or business **8 at all hours** (at any time) during the whole of a period of time **9 (at) the eleventh hour** (at) the last moment; very late **10 (every hour) on the hour** at 1.00, 2.00, 3.00, etc. **11 in an evil hour** by misfortune; by ill luck: *I lost my money in an evil hour* **12 keep late/good/bad hours** to go to bed late/early/late or at irregular times **13 out of hours** before or after the usual times **14 the small hours** also (*humor*) **the wee hours**— the hours soon after midnight (1, 2, 3 o'clock) **15 zero hour** /ˈ·· ·/ the time when something happens, after a certain period of waiting has passed

hour·glass /ˈaʊəglɑːs‖ˈaʊərglæs/ *n* a glass container made narrow in the middle like a figure 8 so that the sand inside can run slowly from the top half to the bottom, taking just one hour

hour hand /ˈ· ·/ *n* the small pointer on a clock which shows the hour nearest in time —see picture at CLOCK¹

hou·ri /ˈhʊəri/ *n* **-s** a beautiful young woman in the Muslim PARADISE

hour·ly /ˈaʊəli‖ˈaʊərli/ *adj, adv* [Wa5] **1** (happening, appearing, etc.) every hour or once an hour **2 expect somebody hourly** to expect someone at any time soon

house¹ /haʊs/ *n* **houses** /ˈhaʊzɪ̇z/ **1 a** a building for people to live in **b** the people in such a

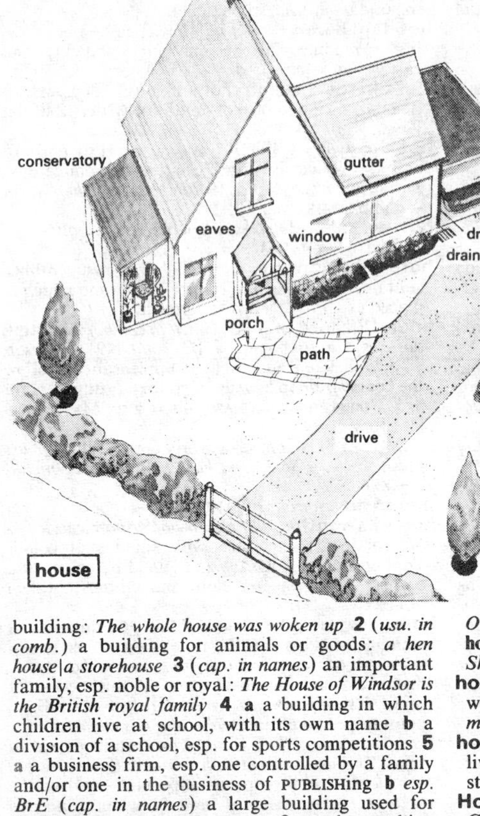

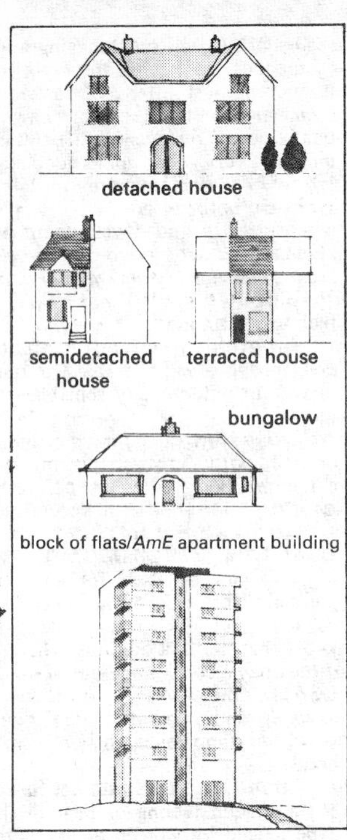

building: *The whole house was woken up* **2** (*usu. in comb.*) a building for animals or goods: *a hen house|a storehouse* **3** (*cap. in names*) an important family, esp. noble or royal: *The House of Windsor is the British royal family* **4 a** a building in which children live at school, with its own name **b** a division of a school, esp. for sports competitions **5 a** a business firm, esp. one controlled by a family and/or one in the business of PUBLISHing **b** *esp. BrE* (*cap. in names*) a large building used for business —compare BUILDING **6 a** a law-making body **b** (*cap. in names*) the building where it meets **7** [*usu. sing.*] the people voting after a DEBATE (esp. in the phr. **this house**): *This house does not support the changes made by the government* **8** [*usu. sing.*] a theatre, or the people in it: *a full house|The whole house laughed.|a thin house* (=not many people) **9** (*in comb.*) (*cap. in names*) a group of stars, with their usual names: *the House of the Lion* **10** (*only in certain phrs.*) a place where people meet for a certain purpose: *a picture house* (=cinema)|*a public house* (PUB) **11 bring the house down** (of a performance or play) to cause great admiration, usu. expressed loudly **12 eat (someone) out of house and home** to eat so much that it costs (the head of the house) too much money **13 keep house** to do or control the cleaning, cooking, and other things usu. done in a house **14 keep open house** to welcome visitors at any time **15 get on like a house on fire** to become or be very good friends very easily **16 on the house** (usu. of drinks) being paid for by the people in charge, as by the owner of a public house, by a firm, etc. **17 (as) safe as houses** *BrE* very safe **18 set one's house in order** to re-arrange one's affairs so that they are in better order, either in business or by improving one's private behaviour

USAGE British speakers think that one's **home** is the place to which one belongs and where one feels comfortable, and that it is more than just a **house**: *Our new* **house** *is beginning to look more like a real* **home**. Americans often use **home** to mean **house**: *She has a beautiful* **home**.|*"New* **Homes** *for Sale"*.

house² *adj* [Wa5;A] intended to be read by people working in a particular firm or industry: *a house magazine*

house³ /haʊz/ *v* [T1] **1** to provide with a place to live for a short or long time **2** to provide space for storing (something)

House /haʊs/ *n* [*the*+GU] **1** (in Britain and Canada) HOUSE OF COMMONS **2** (in the US) HOUSE OF REPRESENTATIVES

house a·gent /ˈ· ˌ··/ *n* a person who arranges for houses to be rented or sold —compare ESTATE AGENT

house ar·rest /ˈ· ·ˌ·/ *n* **under house arrest** forbidden to leave one's house by a government which believes one is dangerous

house·boat /ˈhaʊsbəʊt/ *n* a boat fitted with everything necessary for living there

house·bound /ˈhaʊsbaʊnd/ *adj* not able to move out of the house, or to spend much time outside it

house·boy /ˈhaʊsbɔɪ/ *n* a boy or young man who does general work about a house or hotel

house·break·er /ˈhaʊsˌbreɪkəʳ/ *n* a thief who enters a house by force, esp. during the day —compare BURGLAR

house·bro·ken /ˈhaʊsˌbrəʊkən/ *adj AmE* HOUSE-TRAINED

house·coat /ˈhaʊskəʊt/ *n* a garment worn by women at home, esp. when partly undressed just before or after their night's sleep; woman's DRESSING GOWN

house·craft /ˈhaʊs-krɑːft‖-kræft/ *n* [U] *BrE* a subject in school consisting of the study of cooking, washing, etc.; DOMESTIC SCIENCE

house·dog /ˈhaʊsdɒg‖-dɔg/ *n* a dog which guards the house when the owners are out or asleep

house·fa·ther /ˈhaʊsˌfɑːðəʳ/ (*fem.* **housemother**)— *n* a person who acts as parent to children with no

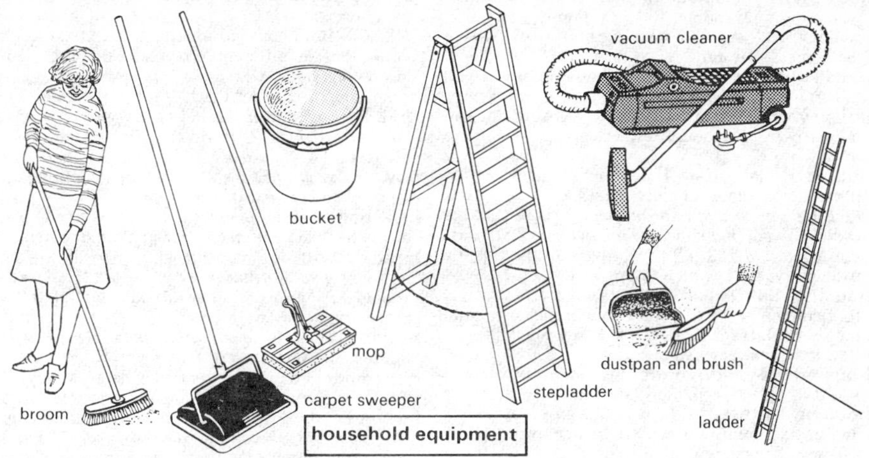

families, who live in a special home together

house·fly /ˈhaʊs-flaɪ/ *n* the most common type of fly, which comes into the house in hot weather —see picture at INSECT

house·ful /ˈhaʊs-fʊl/ *n* an amount or number which is as much as a house can hold

house·hold /ˈhaʊshəʊld/ *n* **1** [GC] all the people living together in a house **2** [A] (esp. in Britain) having the special responsibility of guarding the king or queen, or the royal palace: *household* CAVALRY

house·hold·er /ˈhaʊsˌhəʊldəʳ/ *n* a person who owns or is in charge of a house

household name /ˌ·· ˈ·/ also **household word**— *n* a thing or person known and spoken of by almost everybody, or thought to be very well known

house·keep·er /ˈhaʊsˌkiːpəʳ/ *n* a person who has charge of the running of a house —see also HOUSE[1] (13)

house·keep·ing /ˈhaʊsˌkiːpɪŋ/ *n* [U] **1** the care, cleaning, cooking, etc., of and for a house and the people who live in it **2** also **housekeeping mon·ey** /ˈ··· ˌ··/— an amount of money set aside each week or month by the husband and/or wife to pay for food and other things needed in the home

house lights /ˈ· ·/ *n* [P] the lights used in the part of a cinema or theatre where people sit (HOUSE[1] (8))

house·maid /ˈhaʊsmeɪd/ *n* a female servant who cleans the house

housemaid's knee /ˌ·· ˈ·/ *n* [U] a swelling of the knee, which may happen because of too much kneeling on the floor

house·man /ˈhaʊsmən/ *AmE* **intern**— *n* **-men** /mən/ a JUNIOR (4) doctor completing hospital training, and often (esp. in Britain) living in the hospital

house mar·tin /ˈ· ˌ··/ *n* a type of bird which sometimes makes a nest under the roof of a house

house·mas·ter /ˈhaʊsˌmɑːstəʳ‖-ˌmæ-/ *fem.* **house·mis·tress** /-ˌmɪstrɪ̌s/— *n esp. BrE* a teacher who is in charge of one house of a school (HOUSE[1] (4))

house·moth·er /ˈhaʊsˌmʌðəʳ/ *n* a female HOUSEFATHER

house of cards /ˌ· · ˈ·/ *n* **1** an arrangement of playing cards built up carefully but easily knocked over **2** a plan which is too badly arranged to succeed

House of Com·mons /ˌ· · ˈ··/ also **Commons**— *n* [*the*+GU] the lower but more powerful of the 2 parts of the British or Canadian parliament, the members of which are elected by anybody over 18 years of age who is not a member of the HOUSE OF LORDS

house of cor·rec·tion /ˌ· · · ˈ··/ *n old euph* a prison

house of God /ˌ· · ˈ·/ *n* a church

House of Lords /ˌ· · ˈ·/ also **Lords**— *n* [*the*+GU] the upper but less powerful of the 2 parts of the British parliament, the members of which are not elected but have positions because of their rank or titles of honour —compare HOUSE OF COMMONS

House of Rep·re·sen·ta·tives /ˌ· · ··ˈ···/ also **House**— *n* [*the*+GU] the lower of the 2 parts of the central law-making body in such countries as New Zealand, Australia, the US, etc. —compare SENATE

house par·ty /ˈ· ˌ··/ *n* a PARTY (2) lasting for several days, in a house, esp. a large house in the country

house phy·si·cian /ˈ· ·ˌ··/ *n* **1** the chief doctor living in a hospital **2** a HOUSEMAN who is a PHYSICIAN

house-proud /ˈ· ·/ *adj* liking to have everything in perfect order in the house and spending a lot of time on keeping it clean and tidy, perhaps too much so

house·room /ˈhaʊs-rʊm, -ruːm/ *n* **not give (something) houseroom** not to accept (something) which one finds very unpleasant: *I told him to take his old furniture away; I wouldn't give it houseroom for anything*

Houses of Par·lia·ment /ˌ·· · ˈ···/ *n* [*the*+P] the buildings in which the British parliament sits

house spar·row /ˈ· ˌ··/ *n* the most common bird of the SPARROW family

house sur·geon /ˈ· ˌ··/ *n* a HOUSEMAN who is a SURGEON

house-to-house /ˌ· · ˈ·◂/ also **door-to-door**— *adj* [Wa5;A] (done by) visiting each house in turn: *a house-to-house salesman*

house·tops /ˈhaʊs-tɒps‖-tɑps/ *n* **shout/proclaim** (something) **from the housetops** to make (something) known publicly

house-trained /ˈ· ·/ (*AmE* **housebroken**)— *adj BrE* **1** (of house pets) trained to go out of the house to empty the bowels or BLADDER **2** *humor* (of people) taught to be tidy and careful at home

house·warm·ing /ˈhaʊsˌwɔːmɪŋ‖-ˌwɔr-/ *n* a party given for friends when one has moved into a new house

house·wife /ˈhaʊs-waɪf/ *n* **-wives** /waɪvz/ a woman who works at home for her family, cleaning, cooking, etc., esp. one who does not work outside the home —**~ly** *adj*

house·wif·e·ry /ˈhaʊswɪfəri‖ˈhaʊswaɪfəri/ *n* [U] the art of taking care of a house

house·work /ˈhaʊswɜːk‖-ɜrk/ *n* [U] work done in taking care of a house, esp. cleaning —compare HOMEWORK

hous·ing /ˈhaʊzɪŋ/ *n* **1** [U] the act or action of providing a place to live: *The government feels housing is in need of improvement* **2** [U] the places provided: *Too many people are living in bad housing (conditions)* **3** [C] protective covering, as for machinery: *the engine housing*

housing as·so·ci·a·tion /ˈ·· ···ˌ··/ *n* a society formed by a group of people so that they can build houses or flats for themselves or buy the houses or flats in which they live

housing de·vel·op·ment /ˈ·· ·ˌ···/ *n esp. AmE* a HOUSING ESTATE, esp. a private one

housing es·tate /ˈ·· ·ˌ·/ *n BrE* a group of houses and/or flats built in one place by one owner, as by a Town Council, and let or sold

housing pro·ject /ˈ·· ˌ··/ *n esp. AmE* a HOUSING ESTATE, esp. a public one, usu. built with government money for low-income families

hove /həʊv/ *tech or humor past t.* (*and sometimes past p.*) *of* HEAVE[2]

hov·el /ˈhɒvəl‖ˈhʌ-, ˈhɑ-/ *n* a small, dirty place to live in

hov·er /ˈhɒvəʳ‖ˈhʌ-, ˈhɑ-/ *v* [L9 esp. *over*; (IØ)] **1** (of birds, certain aircraft, etc.) to stay in the air in one place **2** (of people) to wait around one place: (fig.) *A question hovered on his lips.*|(fig.) *He's hovering between life and death* —**hoverer** *n*

hov·er·craft /ˈhɒvəkrɑːft‖ˈhʌvərkræft, ˈhɑ-/ *n* [C; *by*+U] (*cap. as tdmk*) a sort of boat which moves over land or water with a strong force of air underneath lifting it above the ground, sea, etc. —see picture at SHIP[1]

how[1] /haʊ/ *adv* [Wa5] **1** (*in questions*) **a** in what way or by what means: *How can I get to Cambridge?*|*How is this word spelt?*|*I told her how to find me.*|*"Do you remember how he arrived?" "Yes, I do: he came by car."* **b** in what condition, of health or mind: *How is your mother?*|*How are you* (*feeling*)*?*|*I want to know how he feels about working until 8* (not . . . **how does he feel*) **c** by what amount; to what degree: *How much does this cost?*|*I don't know how long this will take.*|*I wonder how soon he'll come.*|*I don't know how old a man he is.*|*"I forget how many there are"* (SEU S.) **2** (in EXCLAMATIONs, showing a large degree): *How pleased he was to see us!*|*How nice of you to come.*|*How they shout!*| (not **How difficult books they are*) —see USAGE —compare WHAT[2] **3 And how!** *infml esp. AmE* Very much so: *"So they enjoyed themselves?" "And how!"* **4 How/However can you, he, etc.?** You, he, shouldn't: *How can you say such an unkind thing?*|*However can he drink boiling water?* **5 How come?** *infml* (*in/or as an expression of surprise*) Why is it? How can it be that . . . ?: *How come they left you alone in the dark?*|*How come I never see him any more?* **6 How do you do?** also **How d'ye do?** (the phrase used to someone just met or introduced to the speaker; this person replies with the same phrase. They usually shake hands at the same time. For its pronunciation, see HOW DO YOU DO) **7 How are you?** /ˌ· ˈ· ·/ **a** (a question about someone's health) **b** (a phrase used when meeting again a person already known. The reply is often *"Fine* (*thanks*). (*And*) **how are you** /ˌ· · ˈ·/?") **8 How's that? a** (in cricket) (a call suggesting that the BATSMAN is out) **b** Please repeat: *"I've just seen a flying elephant." "How's that* (*again*)*?"* —compare **how** ABOUT[2] (9)

USAGE Both **how** and **what** are used in EXCLAMATIONs, but in different patterns. Compare: **How** *nice!*|**What** *a nice person!*

how[2] *conj* **1** the fact that: *"Do you remember how he arrived almost at the end of the party?" "Yes, I do: that's right!"* **2** HOWEVER[1]: *In one's own home one can act how one likes*

how[3] *n* **the how and the why** the way something can be done and the reason for it

how·dah /ˈhaʊdə/ *n* a seat for a person to sit on an elephant's back, often covered and ornamented

how do you do /ˌhaʊ djə ˈduː, ˌhaʊ də jʊ ˈduː/ also **how d'ye do** /ˌhaʊ djə ˈduː/— *n* **a fine how do you do** *infml* a mixed-up or difficult state of affairs —see also HOW[1] (6)

how·dy /ˈhaʊdi/ *interj AmE infml* (*used when meeting someone*) HELLO

how·ev·er[1] /haʊˈevəʳ/ *conj* in whatever way: *In one's own home one can act however one wishes*

however[2] *adv* [Wa5] **1** to whatever degree: *However cold it is, she always goes swimming.*|*I refuse, however favourable the conditions* **2** in spite of this; NEVERTHELESS: *It's raining hard. However, I think we should go out.*|*He hasn't arrived. He may, however, come later* **3** *not fml* (showing surprise) HOW[1] (1): *However did you find it?* —see EVER (USAGE)

how·it·zer /ˈhaʊɪtsəʳ/ *n* a short heavy gun which fires SHELLs[1] (4) high over a short distance

howl[1] /haʊl/ *v* **1** [IØ (*with*)] to make HOWLs: *The dogs howled all night.*|*The wind howled in the trees.*|*We howled with laughter* **2** [T1 (OUT)] to say or express with a HOWL: *He howled* (*out*) *my name* **3** [IØ (*with*)] to weep loudly

howl[2] *n* a long loud cry, as in pain, anger, etc., esp. that made by certain animals, as wolves (WOLF) and dogs

howl down *v adv* [T1] to make a loud disapproving noise so as to prevent (someone) from being heard

howl·er /ˈhaʊləʳ/ *n infml* a very silly mistake which makes people HOWL with laughter, esp. when the wrong word is used in a piece of writing so that the meaning is changed

howl·ing /ˈhaʊlɪŋ/ *adj* [Wa5;A] **1** *infml* very great: *a howling success* **2 howling wilderness** *bibl or infml* a very wild lonely place, esp. one without comfortable places to live

how·so·ev·er /ˌhaʊsəʊˈevəʳ/ *adv lit* HOWEVER[2] (1)

hoy·den /ˈhɔɪdn/ *n* a girl who is wild and rough rather than gentle and polite —**~ish** *adj*

hp *abbrev. for:* **1** (*sometimes caps.*) HORSEPOWER **2** (*BrE*) HIRE PURCHASE: *got it on* (*the*) *hp*

HQ *abbrev. for:* HEADQUARTERS: *See you back at HQ in half an hour*

hr hrs *written abbrev. for:* hour

HRH *abbrev. for:* His/Her Royal Highness: *HRH the Prince of Wales*

ht *written abbrev. for:* height

hub /hʌb/ *n* **1** the central part of a wheel, round which it turns and to which the outside edge (RIM) is connected by SPOKEs —see picture at BICYCLE[1] **2** the centre of activity or importance

hub·ble-bub·ble /ˈhʌbəl ˌbʌbəl/ *n* a form of HOOKAH

hub·bub /ˈhʌbʌb/ *n* [S] a mixture of loud noises

hub·by /ˈhʌbi/ *n infml* a husband

hub·cap /ˈhʌbkæp/ *n* a metal covering over the centre of the wheel of a motor vehicle —see picture at CAR

hu·bris /ˈhjuːbrɨs/ *n* [U] *Gk* a feeling of pride in oneself, often resulting in rudeness to others and sometimes bringing ruin to the person who shows it

huck·a·back /ˈhʌkəbæk/ *n* [U] a rough type of cloth used for making TOWEL*s*

huck·le·ber·ry /ˈhʌkəlbəri‖-beri/ *n* a dark blue fruit, which grows in North America and is rather like the English BILBERRY

huck·ster /ˈhʌkstəʳ/ *n* **1** a person who sells small things in the street or at the doors of houses; HAWKER **2** *AmE often derog* a person who writes advertisements for radio and television

hud·dle¹ /ˈhʌdl/ *v* [X9;L9] to (cause to) crowd together, in a group or in a pile: *The boys huddled together under the rock to keep warm out of the wind.*|(*esp. BrE*) *Your clothes are all huddled up inside that bag getting spoilt.*|(*esp. BrE*) *Don't huddle all the boxes into one cupboard*

huddle² *n* **1** a crowd of people, or (*esp. BrE*) a number of things, close together and not in any ordered arrangement **2 go into a huddle** (of people) to get together away from others to have a private talk about what should be done

hue /hjuː/ *n* **1** [C] a colour: *The diamond shone with every hue under the sun* **2** [U;C] a degree of brightness in colour: *The sky darkened in hue as night drew nearer*

hue and cry /ˌ· · ˈ·/ *n* [*usu. sing.*] the expression of worry, anger, etc., by noisy behaviour either when searching for something or showing opposition to something: *They raised a (great) hue and cry against the new rule*

huff¹ /hʌf/ *v* **1** [I∅] to breathe with a noisy movement of air, as after a climb; see PUFF¹ (1) **2** [T1] (in the game of DRAUGHTS) to take (a piece belonging to (an opponent who has failed to take a piece himself))

huff² *n* [S] a state of bad temper when offended (esp. in the phr. **go into a huff**): *She's gone into a huff because my brother didn't remember her name*

huff·ish /ˈhʌfɪʃ/ *adj* HUFFY

huff·y /ˈhʌfi/ *adj* [Wa1] **1** (often) in a HUFF **2** rudely proud —**-ily** *adv* —**-iness** *n* [U]

hug¹ /hʌg/ *v* **-gg-** **1** [T1] **a** to hold (someone) tightly in the arms **b** (of bears) to hold (a person) with the front PAW*s* (=legs) **c** (esp. of children) to hold in the same way (toys which are like animals or human beings, such as DOLL*s*) **2** [X9] to hold (something) in one's arms, close to one: *hugging a pile of books against her* **3** [T1] to hold on to (an idea) with a feeling of pleasure or safety: *He smiled and hugged the thought to himself* **4** [T1] to go along while staying near: *The boat hugged the coast* **5 hug oneself** to feel very pleased with oneself

hug² *n* the act of hugging (HUG¹) —compare BEAR HUG

huge /hjuːdʒ/ *adj* [Wa1] **1** very big in size: *a huge house* **2** *infml* very big in the mind's view: *a huge success* —**~ness** *n* [U]

huge·ly /ˈhjuːdʒli/ *adv infml* very much

hug·ger-mug·ger /ˈhʌgə ˌmʌgəʳ‖ˈhʌgər-/ *n, adj, adv* [U;B] **1** (in) secrecy **2** (in) disorder

Hu·gue·not /ˈhjuːgənəʊ‖-nɑt/ *n* a French PROTESTANT in the 16th and 17th centuries

huh /hʌh/ *interj* (used for asking a question or for expressing surprise or disapproval)

hu·la /ˈhuːlə/ also **hula-hula** /ˌ·· ˈ··ˌ/— *n* a Hawaiian dance done by men and/or women

hulk /hʌlk/ *n* **1** the body of an old ship, no longer used at sea and left in disrepair **2** a heavy, awkward person or creature

hulk·ing /ˈhʌlkɪŋ/ *adj* [A;(B)] big, heavy, and awkward: *We can't move that hulking great table on our own*

hull¹ /hʌl/ *n* the main body of a ship —see pictures at SAIL² and FREIGHTER

hull² *n* the outer covering of some grain, fruit, and seeds, esp. of peas and beans

hull³ *v* [T1] to take the HULL² off; SHELL (PEA*s* and beans): *Rice is gathered, cleaned and hulled before being sold*

hul·la·ba·loo /ˈhʌləbəluː, ˌhʌləbəˈluː/ *n* **-loos** [*usu. sing.*] a lot of noise, esp. of voices

hul·lo /hʌˈləʊ/ *interj, n* **-los** *esp. BrE* HELLO

hum¹ /hʌm/ *v* **-mm-** **1** [I∅] (of bees and certain animals) to make a continuous BUZZ **2** [I∅;T1] (of people) to make a sound like a continuous **m**, esp. as a way of singing music with closed lips: *to hum a song* **3** [I∅ (*with*)] (of work being carried out) to be active; to move fast: *Things are starting to hum (with activity)*

hum² *n* [S] the sound of humming (HUM)

hum³ (*AmE* **hem**)— *v* **-mm-** *BrE* **hum and haw** to express uncertainty whether to do something

hu·man¹ /ˈhjuːmən/ *adj* **1** of or concerning man: *the human voice*|*a story with lots of* **human interest**, *which our newspaper considers more important than international politics* **2** showing the feelings, esp. those of kindness, which people are supposed to have: *He seems quite human when you know him* —opposite **inhuman** —compare HUMANE

human² also **human be·ing** /ˌ·· ˈ··/— *n* a man, woman, or child, not an animal

USAGE A **human** or (more commonly) a **human** *being* is not only a person as compared to an animal. The word is also used of a person as compared to a fairy, a god, or a GHOST (=spirit of a dead person).

See next page for picture

hu·mane /hjuːˈmeɪn/ *adj* **1** showing human kindness and the qualities of a civilized person —opposite **inhumane** —compare HUMAN **2** *rare* (of studies) concerned with the ARTS, such as literature **3 humane killer** something which can be used to kill animals without giving them pain

hu·man·is·m /ˈhjuːmənɪzəm/ *n* [U] (*often cap.*) **1** a system of beliefs and standards concerned with the needs of man, and not with religious principles **2** the study in the RENAISSANCE of the ideas of the ancient Greeks and Romans —**-ist** *n, adj* —**-istic** /ˌhjuːməˈnɪstɪk/ *adj*

hu·man·i·tar·i·an /hjuːˌmænʒˈteərɪən/ *n, adj* (a person) concerned with trying to improve life for human beings by giving them better conditions to live in and by changing laws, esp. those which punish too severely

hu·man·i·tar·i·an·is·m /hjuːˌmænʒˈteərɪənɪzəm/ *n* [U] the beliefs and practices of a HUMANITARIAN

hu·man·i·ties /hjuːˈmænʒtiz/ *n* [(*the*) P] studies such as literature, the languages of ancient Greece and Rome, history, etc.; the ARTS

hu·man·i·ty /hjuːˈmænʒti/ *n* [U] **1** the quality of being HUMANE or human **2** human beings generally

hu·man·ize, -ise /ˈhjuːmənaɪz/ *v* [T1] **1** to cause to be or seem human **2** to make HUMANE

hu·man·kind /ˌhjuːmənˈkaɪnd/ *n* [U;P] *lit* MANKIND

hu·man·ly /ˈhjuːmənli/ *adv* according to human powers: *It's not humanly possible to complete all the work*

human race /ˌ·· ˈ·/ *n* [*the*+R] HUMANITY (2); MANKIND

hum·ble¹ /ˈhʌmbəl/ *adj* [Wa2,3] **1 a** (of people) low in rank or position **b** (of positions) unimportant; not held in high regard by society **2** having a low opinion of oneself and a high opinion of others **3 eat humble pie** to be very sorry and to show it by saying so **4 your humble servant** a way of ending a

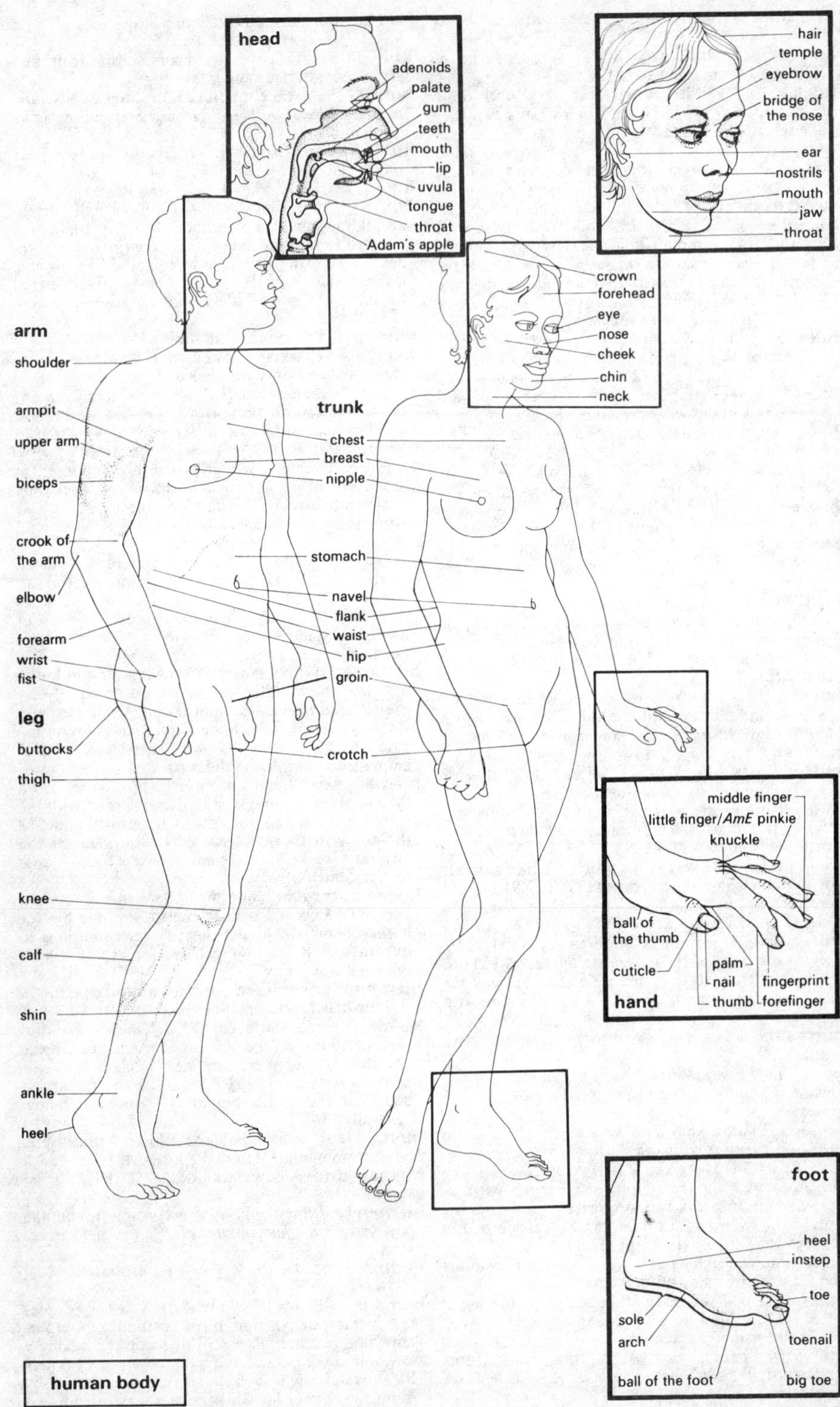
head
adenoids
palate
gum
teeth
mouth
lip
uvula
tongue
throat
Adam's apple
hair
temple
eyebrow
bridge of the nose
ear
nostrils
mouth
jaw
throat
crown
forehead
eye
nose
cheek
chin
neck
arm
shoulder
armpit
upper arm
biceps
crook of the arm
elbow
forearm
wrist
fist
leg
buttocks
thigh
knee
calf
shin
ankle
heel
trunk
chest
breast
nipple
stomach
navel
flank
waist
hip
groin
crotch
middle finger
little finger/AmE pinkie
knuckle
ball of the thumb
cuticle
palm
nail
thumb
fingerprint
forefinger
hand
foot
heel
instep
toe
sole
arch
toenail
ball of the foot
big toe
human body

letter before signing it, used esp. formerly —**-bly** *adv* [Wa3]

humble² *v* [Wv3;T1] to make (someone or oneself) humble or lower in position: *to humble one's enemy*

hum·bug¹ /ˈhʌmbʌg/ *n* **1** [C] *BrE* a sweet made of hard boiled sugar meant to be sucked, usu. tasting of MINT³, and typically white with dark lines on the outside **2** [U] deceiving acts or talk; TRICKERY: *You can't make money out of old stone; that idea's a load of humbug* **3** [U] nonsense **4** [C; *you*+N] a deceitful person who pretends to be something he is not **5** [C] a thing which is not what it seems

humbug² *v* **-gg-** [T1 (*into, out of*)] to trick

hum·ding·er /hʌmˈdɪŋəʳ/ *n infml AmE* a wonderful person or thing

hum·drum /ˈhʌmdrʌm/ *adj* too ordinary; without variety or change

hu·mer·us /ˈhjuːmərəs/ *n* the bone in the top half of the arm —see picture at SKELETON

hu·mid /ˈhjuːm$\frac{1}{2}$d/ *adj* (of air and weather) containing water; DAMP³

hu·mid·i·fy /hjuːˈmɪd$\frac{1}{2}$faɪ/ *v* [T1] to make HUMID

hu·mid·i·ty /hjuːˈmɪd$\frac{1}{2}$ti/ *n* [U] the (amount of) water contained in the air: *It's difficult to work because of the humidity*

hu·mi·dor /ˈhjuːm$\frac{1}{2}$dɔːʳ/ *n* a case usu. for CIGARs in which the air is kept from becoming too dry

hu·mil·i·ate /hjuːˈmɪlieɪt/ *v* [T1] to cause to feel humble or to lose the respect of others —**-ation** /hjuːˌmɪliˈeɪʃən/ *n* [U;C]

hu·mil·i·ty /hjuːˈmɪl$\frac{1}{2}$ti/ *n* [U] the quality of being humble

hum·ming·bird /ˈhʌmɪŋbɜːd‖-ɜrd/ *n* any of many kinds of very small birds whose wings beat very fast and make a humming noise (HUM)

hum·mock /ˈhʌmək/ *n* a small HILLOCK

hu·mor·ist /ˈhjuːmər$\frac{1}{2}$st‖ˈhjuː-, ˈjuː-/ *n* a person who makes jokes, in speech or writing

hu·mor·ous /ˈhjuːmərəs‖ˈhjuː-, ˈjuː-/ *adj* funny; that makes people laugh: *a humorous play/remark/character in a play* —**~ly** *adv*

hu·mour¹, *AmE* **humor** /ˈhjuːməʳ‖ˈhjuː-, ˈjuː-/ *n* **1** [U] the ability to be amused: *a sense of humour* **2** [U] the quality of causing amusement: *a play with no humour in it* **3** [C *usu. sing.*] *becoming rare* a state of mind; MOOD (only in certain phrs.): *in a good humour|in a bad humour* **4** [C] *old use* any of 4 liquids thought in the MIDDLE AGES to be present in the body in varying degrees, and to influence the character **5 out of humour** in a bad temper; MOODY

humour², *AmE* **humor** *v* [T1] to keep (someone) happy or calm by acceptance of (esp.) foolish wishes, behaviour, etc.

-hu·moured, *AmE* **-humored** /ˈhjuːməd‖ˈhjuːmərd, ˈjuː-/ *comb. form* [*adj*→*adj*] of the stated condition of mind: *good-humoured|ill-humoured*

hump¹ /hʌmp/ *n* **1** [C] a lump or round part which stands out noticeably **2** [C] a lump on the back, as on a camel, or on certain human beings who are mis-shaped **3** [*the*+R] *BrE infml* a feeling of bad temper or dislike of life in general: *It's giving me the hump* **4 over the hump** past the worst part of the work

hump² *v* **1** [T1;I∅] to curve into a hump **2** [X9] *BrE infml* to carry on the back: *humped it upstairs* **3** [T1] *taboo sl* to have sex with

hump·back /ˈhʌmpbæk/ *n* HUNCHBACK —**~ed** *adj*

humph, h'm /hʌmf, hmh, hm/ *interj* (a sound made mostly with the lips closed to express a feeling of doubt or dissatisfaction with something said or done)

USAGE This sound is usually spelt **humph** in writing. Some people pronounce it /hʌmf/ when they are reading aloud.

hu·mus /ˈhjuːməs/ *n* [U] rich soil made of decayed plants, leaves, etc.

Hun /hʌn/ *n* **1** a member of a race who attacked and destroyed many parts of Europe in the 4th and 5th centuries **2** *derog sl* a German

hunch¹ /hʌntʃ/ *n* [C,C5a] *not fml* **1** an idea based on feeling rather than on reason: *I have a hunch he didn't really want to go* **2 play one's hunch** to act according to a hunch or guess

hunch² *v* [T1 (UP)] to pull ((part of) the body) into a rounded shape: *She hunched her shoulders over her book*

hunch·back /ˈhʌntʃbæk/ *n* (a person with) a back mis-shaped by a round lump —see also HUMP¹ (2) —**~ed** *adj*

hun·dred /ˈhʌndr$\frac{1}{2}$d/ *determiner, n, pron* **-dred** *or* **-dreds** [see NUMBER TABLE 2] (the number) 100 —**~th** *determiner, n, pron, adv* [see NUMBER TABLE 3]

USAGE In talking roughly about large numbers, we say *2 or 3* **hundred**, *7 or 8* **million**, *5 or 6* **thousand**. It is always, for example, *2 or 3*, not **3 or 2*.

hun·dred·weight /ˈhʌndr$\frac{1}{2}$dweɪt/ (*written abbrev.* **cwt**)— *n* **-weight** [Wn3] (in Britain) 112 pounds, (in America) 100 pounds

hung /hʌŋ/ *past t. and past p. of* HANG¹

hun·ger¹ /ˈhʌŋgəʳ/ *n* **1** [U] the wish or need for food **2** [S (*for*)] a strong wish: *His hunger for excitement gets him into a lot of trouble* **3** [U] lack of food: *There is hunger in all the places where the crop was spoilt*

hunger² *v* [Wv4;I∅] *rare or bibl* to feel hunger

hunger for also **hunger af·ter**— *v prep* [T1] to want very much

hunger march /ˈ·· ·/ *n* a procession made by a large number of people together, esp. when unemployed, to make known the difficulties of those who cannot afford to eat —**~er** *n*

hunger strike /ˈ·· ·/ *n* a refusal to eat as a sign of strong dissatisfaction —**~er** *n*

hun·gry /ˈhʌŋgri/ *adj* [Wa1] **1** feeling or showing hunger **2** causing hunger (esp. in the phr. **hungry work**) **3** (of land) lacking good soil **4** [(*for*)] with a strong wish: *We're hungry for news of our brother, who lives away from home* **5 go hungry** to remain without food: *If you can't cook your own dinner, then you'll have to go hungry, because I'm not doing it* —**-grily** *adv*

hunk /hʌŋk/ *n* a thick piece, esp. of food, broken or cut off

hun·kers /ˈhʌŋkəz‖-ərz/ *n* [P] *infml* **1** the HAUNCHES **2 on one's hunkers** SQUATting

hunt¹ /hʌnt/ *v* **1** [T1;I∅] to chase in order to catch and kill (animals and birds) either for food or for sport **2** [T1;I∅] **a** to chase foxes on horseback with dogs (HOUNDs) **b** to do this in (an area): *to hunt the* COUNTY **c** to use (one's horse) for this: *to hunt one's horse* **3** [T1;I∅] to search (for) **4** [X9] to drive away: *You can't hunt the birds off the seeds. You'll have to trap them in cotton thread*

USAGE In Britain, anyone going after animals or (more often) birds with a gun says *I'm going* **shooting**; to go **hunting** means using a number of dogs (HOUNDs) to chase the animal (a fox, deer, or HARE). One usually rides after these dogs on a horse. In the US, the word **hunting** is used for both these sports.

hunt² *n* **1** (*often in comb.*) an act of hunting: *the long hunt through the fields and woods|a bear-hunt|an elephant-hunt* **2 a** the act of hunting foxes **b** the people who regularly hunt foxes together **c** the area they hunt **3** a search: *Our hunt for a house is at last at an end* **4 the hunt is on (for)/X is on the**

hunt (for) a search has begun (for)/X is searching (for)

hunt down also **hound down, hunt out**— *v adv* [T1] to succeed in finding after much effort

hunt·er /ˈhʌntəʳ/ *n* **1** a person or animal that hunts, usu. wild animals **2** a strong horse used in foxhunting **3** [(*after*)] someone who searches too eagerly (esp. for something of advantage to himself): *a fortune hunter* **4** a sort of watch with a metal cover over the front (FACE)

hunt for *v prep* [T1] HUNT[1] (3)

hunt·ing /ˈhʌntɪŋ/ *n* [U] the action of hunting, esp. (in Britain) foxhunting

hunting crop /ˈ··· ·/ *n* CROP[1] (5)

hunting ground /ˈ··· ·/ *n* **1** a place where hunting is carried on **2** a place where one may hope to find what one is searching for **3 happy hunting ground** /ˌ·· ˈ··· ·/ *humour* heaven

hunting pink /ˌ··· ˈ·/ *n, adj* [Wa5;B;U] (of) the red colour of the coats worn by people who hunt foxes together

hunt out *v adv* [T1] **1** HUNT DOWN **2** also **hunt up**— to search for with much effort

hunt·ress /ˈhʌntrɪ̈s/ *n* a woman (or sometimes a female animal) that hunts; female hunter

hunts·man /ˈhʌntsmən/ *n* **-men** /mən/ **1** a person, usu. a man, who hunts; hunter **2** the person in charge of the HOUNDs (dogs) during a fox hunt

hur·dle[1] /ˈhɜːdl‖-ɜr-/ *n* **1** a wood frame used with others for making fences **2** a frame for jumping over in a race **3** a difficulty which is to be conquered

hurdle[2] *v* [I∅] to run a HURDLE[1] (2) race —**-dler** *n*

hur·dy-gur·dy /ˈhɜːdi ˌgɜːdi‖ˌhɜdi ˈgɜrdi/ *n* a sort of small BARREL ORGAN

hurl /hɜːl‖hɜrl/ *v* [X9;(T1)] **1** to throw with force: *He hurled a brick through the window* **2** to shout out violently: *He hurled curses at the unfortunate man who had made the mistake*

hurl·ing /ˈhɜːlɪŋ‖ˈhɜr-/ *n* [U] an Irish ball game between 2 teams of 15 players each

hur·ly-bur·ly /ˈhɜːli ˌbɜːli‖ˌhɜrli ˈbɜrli/ *n* [U;S] noisy activity

hur·ray, hooray /hʊˈreɪ/ also (*becoming rare*) **hurrah** /hʊˈrɑː/— *interj, n* a shout of joy or approval (note the phr. **hip, hip, hurray**): *3 cheers for the losing team: Hip, hip, hurray!|We've done it! Hurray for us!*

hur·ri·cane /ˈhʌrɪ̈kən‖ˈhɜrɪ̈keɪn/ *n* a storm with a strong fast wind, esp. as happens in the West Indies: CYCLONE or TYPHOON —see TYPHOON (USAGE)

hurricane lamp /ˈ···· ·/ *n* a lamp which has a strong cover to protect the flame inside from a strong wind —see picture at CAMP[2]

hur·ried /ˈhʌrid‖ˈhɜrid/ *adj* done in haste: *hurried work* —**~ly** *adv*

hur·ry[1] /ˈhʌri‖ˈhɜri/ *v* **1** [T1;I∅] to (cause to) be quick in action, sometimes too quick: *Don't hurry; we're not late.|He hurried across the road in front of a car* **2** [X9] to send or bring quickly: *Doctors and nurses were hurried to the accident*

hurry[2] *n* [U] **1** haste; quick activity **2** need for haste **3 in a hurry a** hastily: *You make mistakes if you do things in a hurry* **b** eager: *You're never in a hurry to get up in the mornings* **c** *infml* (*usu. with neg.*) without difficulty or quickly: *I won't forget her kindness in a hurry* **d** *infml* (*usu. with neg.*) willingly: *I won't help her again in a hurry, when she's been so ungrateful* **4 in no hurry a** willing to wait: *I'm in no hurry to go* **b** not eager: *I'm in no hurry to go out in the rain* **c** unwilling: *I'm in no hurry to help her, after what she did*

hurry up *v adv* **1** [T1;I∅] to (cause to) move faster: *I tried to hurry him up, but he wouldn't walk any faster* **2** [T1] to do faster: *We have to hurry up this job if we want to finish by Thursday*

hurt[1] /hɜːt‖hɜrt/ *v* **hurt 1** [T1] to cause pain and/or damage (INJURY) to (esp. a part of the body): *He hurt his leg when he fell* **2** [T1;I∅] to cause (a person or other living creature) to feel pain: *My leg hurts.|Is that tight shoe hurting (you/your foot)?* **3** [T1] to cause pain to (the feelings of (a person)): *My feelings were hurt when he didn't ask me to the party* **4** [*it*+T1; *it*+I∅ *nonassertive*] *infml* to matter (to); have a bad effect (on): *It won't hurt to wait a bit longer.|It won't hurt you to miss breakfast for once* **5 (he) wouldn't hurt a fly** see HARM[2] (2)

USAGE When **hurt** is used in the sense of bodily damage (def. 1), one may be *slightly/badly/seriously* **hurt**. Do not use *badly* or *seriously* when speaking of unhappiness caused by someone's behaviour (def. 3): *I was very (much)* **hurt** *at his words.* —see WOUND (USAGE)

hurt[2] *n* **1** [U] harm; damage, esp. to feelings **2** [C *often pl.*] damage; INJURY to the body

hurt·ful /ˈhɜːtfəl‖ˈhɜrt-/ *adj* harmful; painful to the feelings: *There's no need to make such hurtful remarks* —**~ly** *adv* —**~ness** *n* [U]

hur·tle /ˈhɜːtl‖ˈhɜr-/ *v* [L9] to move or rush with great speed: *Rocks hurtled down the cliffs/through the air*

hus·band[1] /ˈhʌzbənd/ *n* **1** the man to whom a woman is married **2 husband and wife** a married pair —see TABLE OF FAMILY RELATIONSHIPS

husband[2] *v* [T1] *fml* to save carefully and/or make the best use of: *to husband one's strength*/RESOURCES (*in a time of difficulty*)

hus·band·man /ˈhʌzbəndmən/ *n* **-men** /mən/ *old use & bibl* a farmer

hus·band·ry /ˈhʌzbəndri/ *n* [U] *fml* farming: *animal husbandry*

hush[1] /hʌʃ/ *v* [T1;I∅ *often imper.*] to (cause to) be silent and/or calm —compare SHUSH

hush[2] *n* [U;C] (a) silence, esp. a peaceful one: *A hush fell over the room*

hush-hush /ˌ· ˈ·‖ˈ· ·/ *adj infml* (of plans, arrangements, etc.) hidden, or to be hidden, from other people's knowledge; secret

hush mon·ey /ˈ· ˌ··/ *n* [U] money paid secretly to prevent some shameful fact from being known publicly —compare BLACKMAIL

hush up *v adv* [T1] to keep secret by forcing silence about: *The President tried to hush up the fact that his adviser had lied* —**hush-up** /ˈ· ·/ *n* [S]

husk[1] /hʌsk/ *n* **1** the dry outer covering of some fruits and seeds: *Brown bread contains the husk of wheat* —compare HULL (2) **2** the useless outside part of something

husk[2] *v* [T1] to take the HUSKs off

hus·ky[1] /ˈhʌski/ *adj* [Wa1] **1** (of a person or voice) difficult to hear and breathy, as if the throat were dry —compare HOARSE **2** (of a person) big and strong —compare HEFTY —**-kily** *adv* —**-kiness** *n* [U]

husky[2] *n* any of several types of rather large working dogs with thick hair that live in northern Canada, Alaska, and eastern Siberia, and are used by ESKIMOes to pull SLEDGEs over the snow —see picture at DOG[1]

hus·sar /hʊˈzɑːʳ/ *n* a soldier in the part of the CAVALRY (=horse soldiers) which carries light arms

hus·sy /ˈhʌsi, ˈhʌzi/ *n* [C; *you*+N] a badly behaved girl or woman (note the phrs. **brazen/shameless hussy**)

hus·tings /ˈhʌstɪŋz/ *n* [(*the*) P] the speeches, attempts to win votes, etc., which go on before an election

hus·tle[1] /ˈhʌsəl/ *v* [Wv3] **1** [X9;I∅] to (cause to) move fast: *She hustled the children off to school and started working* **2** [X9, esp. *into*; I∅] *esp. AmE* to sell to or gain from (someone) by forceful, esp. deceitful activity **3** [I∅] *infml esp. AmE* to work as a PROSTITUTE

hustle[2] *n* [U] hurried activity (esp. in the phr. **hustle and bustle**)

hus·tler /ˈhʌsləʳ/ *n* **1** a very active person **2** *esp. AmE* a person who HUSTLEs[1] (2) **3** *infml esp. AmE* PROSTITUTE

hut /hʌt/ *n* a small building, often made of wood, esp. one used for living in or for shelter —compare SHED[2]

hutch /hʌtʃ/ *n* a small box or cage with one side made of wire netting, esp. one for keeping rabbits in

hut·ment /ˈhʌtmənt/ *n* a group of huts, esp. army huts for soldiers to camp in

huz·zah, huzza /hʊˈzɑː/ *interj, n old use* HURRAY

hy·a·cinth /ˈhaɪəsɪ̇nθ/ *n* a plant with a head of bell-shaped flowers and a sweet smell, which grows from a BULB below the ground and opens in spring

hy·ae·na /haɪˈiːnə/ *n* HYENA

hy·brid /ˈhaɪbrɪ̇d/ *n* **1** a living thing produced from parents of different breeds; CROSS[1] (11): *The hybrid from a donkey and a horse is called a* MULE **2** a word which is made of 2 parts, each from a different language

hy·brid·ize, -ise /ˈhaɪbrɪ̇daɪz/ *v* [T1;I∅] to (cause to) produce a HYBRID —**-ization** /ˌhaɪbrɪ̇daɪˈzeɪʃən‖-brɪ̇də-/ *n* [U]

hy·dra /ˈhaɪdrə/ *n* **1 a** (in ancient Greek stories) a snake with many heads which grew again when cut off **b** an evil thing which is difficult to destroy **2** a very small animal which lives in rivers and has long thread-like TENTACLEs near its mouth

hy·dran·gea /haɪˈdreɪndʒə/ *n* a plant which grows as a bush with round heads formed of several large brightly-coloured flowers

hy·drant /ˈhaɪdrənt/ *n* a water pipe in the street from which one may draw water from the public supply, as for cleaning the streets or putting out a fire

hy·drate /ˈhaɪdreɪt/ *n* [U;C] *tech* (*often in comb.*) a combination of a chemical substance with water

hy·draul·ic /haɪˈdrɒlɪk, -ˈdrɔː-/ *adj* [Wa5] concerning or moved by the pressure of water or other liquids: *Hydraulic cement hardens under water pressure* —**~ally** *adv* [Wa4,5]

hy·draul·ics /haɪˈdrɒlɪks, -ˈdrɔː-/ *n* [U] the science which studies the use of water to produce power

hy·dro- /ˈhaɪdrə, ˈhaɪdrəʊ/ *comb. form* containing or concerning water

hy·dro·car·bon /ˌhaɪdrəˈkɑːbən‖-ˈkɑr-/ *n tech* any of several chemical compounds of HYDROGEN and CARBON, such as gas or petrol

hy·dro·chlor·ic ac·id /ˌhaɪdrəˈklɒrɪk‖-ˈklɔ-/ *n* [U] an acid containing HYDROGEN and CHLORINE

hy·dro·e·lec·tric /ˌhaɪdrəʊ-ɪˈlektrɪk/ *adj* [Wa5] concerning or producing electricity by the power of falling water —**~ally** *adv* [Wa4,5]

hy·dro·foil /ˈhaɪdrəfɔɪl/ *n* [C; *by*+U] a type of large motor-boat which raises itself out of the water as it moves —see picture at SHIP[1]

hy·dro·gen /ˈhaɪdrədʒən/ *n* [U] a gas that is a simple substance (ELEMENT), without colour or smell, that is lighter than air and that burns very easily

hydrogen bomb /ˈ··· ·/ also **H-bomb, fusion bomb**— *n* a bomb using HEAVY HYDROGEN which explodes when the central parts of the atoms join together

hydrogen per·ox·ide /ˌ··· ·ˈ··/ *n* [U] *tech* PEROXIDE

hy·dro·pho·bi·a /ˌhaɪdrəˈfəʊbɪə/ *n* [U] **1** a disease in which the throat muscles tighten so that drinking is impossible; RABIES **2** fear of water

hy·dro·plane /ˈhaɪdrəpleɪn/ *n* **1** [C; *by*+U] a flat-bottomed motor-boat which can move very fast over the surface of the water **2** [C; *by*+U] *old use* a plane which can land on water; SEAPLANE **3** [C] a control apparatus which allows a SUBMARINE (=underwater ship) to rise and fall in the water

hy·dro·pon·ics /ˌhaɪdrəˈpɒnɪks‖-ˈpɑ-/ *n* [U] the science of growing plants in water with chemical substances added, rather than in soil —**hydroponic** *adj* [Wa5]

hy·dro·ther·a·py /ˌhaɪdrəʊˈθerəpi/ also (*infml*) **hy·drop·a·thy** /haɪˈdrɒpəθi‖-ˈdrɑ-/— *n* [U] the treatment of diseases by the use of water, usu. water containing special chemical substances, either for drinking or for bathing in

hy·e·na, hyaena /haɪˈiːnə/ *n* an animal of Africa and Asia, rather like a dog, which eats meat and has a wild cry like a laugh —see picture at CARNIVOROUS

hy·giene /ˈhaɪdʒiːn/ *n* [U] **1** the study and practice of how to keep good health, esp. by paying attention to cleanliness **2** cleanliness generally

hy·gien·ic /haɪˈdʒiːnɪk‖-ˈdʒe-, -ˈdʒiː-/ *adj* **1** causing or keeping good health **2** clean —**~ally** *adv* [Wa4]

hy·men /ˈhaɪmən/ *n* a fold of skin partly closing the entrance (VAGINA) to the sex organs of a woman who is a VIRGIN (that is, one who has never experienced the act of sex)

hy·me·ne·al /ˌhaɪməˈniːəl/ *adj* [Wa5;A] *poet* (from the name of the Greek god Hymen) concerning marriage

hymn[1] /hɪm/ *n* a song of praise, esp. to God, usu. the religious songs of the Christian church which all the people sing together during a service

hymn[2] *v* [T1 (*to*)] *poet* to sing (praise): *They hymned their thanks to God*

hym·nal /ˈhɪmnəl/ also **hymn book** /ˈ· ·/— *n* a book containing written HYMNs

hy·per- /ˈhaɪpəʳ/ *prefix* above (something) or too much (so): HYPERSENSITIVE (=too sensitive): *hyperactive* —opposite **hypo-**

hy·per·bo·la /haɪˈpɜːbələ‖-ɜr-/ *n* a curve which never reaches the sides (axes —see AXIS) that it curves towards

hy·per·bo·le /haɪˈpɜːbəli‖-ɜr-/ *n* [U;C] (the use of) a form of words which makes something sound big, small, loud, etc., by saying that it is like something even bigger, smaller, louder, etc.; EXAGGERATION

hy·per·bol·ic /ˌhaɪpəˈbɒlɪk‖-pərˈbɑ-/ also **-ical** /ɪkəl/— *adj* **1** of, marked by, or tending to use HYPERBOLE **2** of, related to, or being like a HYPERBOLA

hy·per·crit·i·cal /ˌhaɪpəˈkrɪtɪkəl‖-pər-/ *adj* too ready to see faults or things which are wrong, rather than noticing the good points —**~ly** *adv* [Wa4]

hy·per·mar·ket /ˈhaɪpəˌmɑːkɪ̇t‖-pərˌmɑr-/ *n* a very large shop (large SUPERMARKET) where one may buy large amounts of many types of food and other things needed in the home

hy·per·sen·si·tive /ˌhaɪpəˈsensɪ̇tɪv‖-ər-/ *adj* [(*to, about*)] unusually sensitive; too easily hurt in the feelings: *hypersensitive to cold|hypersensitive about her looks* —**-tivity** /ˌhaɪpəsensɪ̇ˈtɪvɪ̇ti‖-ər-/ *n* [U (*to, about*)]

hy·phen /ˈhaɪfən/ *n* a short written or printed line (-) which can join words or SYLLABLEs —compare DASH[2] (6)

hy·phen·ate /ˈhaɪfəneɪt/ *v* [T1;(I∅)] to join with a HYPHEN —**-ation** /ˌhaɪfəˈneɪʃən/ *n* [U]

hyp·no·sis /hɪp'nəʊsǥs/ *n* [U] (the production of) a sleep-like state in which a person's mind and actions can be controlled by the person who produced it —**-tic** /hɪp'nɒtɪk‖-'nɑ-/ *adj* —**-tically** *adv* [Wa4]

hypnotic sug·ges·tion /·,·· ·'··/ *n* [U;(C)] (a) suggestion made to someone under HYPNOSIS: *headaches cured by hypnotic suggestion*

hyp·no·tis·m /'hɪpnətɪzəm/ *n* [U] the practice of HYPNOSIS

hyp·no·tist /'hɪpnətǥst/ *n* a person who practises HYPNOTISM and can produce HYPNOSIS

hyp·no·tize, -ise /'hɪpnətaɪz/ *v* [T1] to produce HYPNOSIS in (someone)

hy·po /'haɪpeʊ/ *n* **hypos** **1** [U] hypoSULPHITE of SODA; a chemical substance used for fixing photographs **2** [C] HYPODERMIC

hypo- /'haɪpə, 'haɪpeʊ/ *prefix* below, under, too little, etc. —opposite **hyper-**

hy·po·chon·dri·a /,haɪpə'kɒndrɪə‖-'kɑn-/ *n* a state of anxiety and worry about one's health

hy·po·chon·dri·ac /,haɪpə'kɒndriæk‖-'kɑn-/ *n, adj* (of, like, or being) a person suffering from HYPOCHONDRIA

hy·poc·ri·sy /hɪ'pɒkrǥsi‖-'pɑ-/ *n* [U] the act or practice of pretending to believe, feel, or be something very different from, and usu. better than, what one actually believes, feels, or is

hyp·o·crite /'hɪpəkrɪt/ *n* [C; *you* + N] a person who says one thing and does another, usu. something worse; one who practises HYPOCRISY —**-critical** /,hɪpə'krɪtɪkəl/ *adj* —**-critically** *adv* [Wa4]

hy·po·der·mic[1] /,haɪpə'dɜːmɪk‖-ɜr-/ *adj* [Wa5] (of an instrument or means of putting drugs into the body) which is made to enter, or INJECTed beneath, the skin —**-~ally** *adv* [Wa4,5]

hypodermic[2] *n* a needle for putting drugs into the body by pricking the skin and making them go in underneath it; hypodermic SYRINGE or needle —see picture at MEDICAL[1]

hy·pot·e·nuse /haɪ'pɒtǥnjuːz‖-'pɑtənuːs, -nuːz/ *n* the longest side of a right-angled TRIANGLE (three-sided figure), which is opposite the right angle —see picture at GEOMETRY

hy·po·ther·mi·a /,haɪpəʊ'θɜːmɪə‖-ɜr-/ *n* [U] a medical condition in which the body temperature falls below the usual level, esp. as happens with old people who do not keep warm at home

hy·poth·e·sis /haɪ'pɒθǥsǥs‖-'pɑ-/ *n* **-ses** /siːz/ an idea which is thought suitable to explain the facts about something: *His new hypothesis gives a possible reason for the change in the weather*

hy·po·thet·i·cal /,haɪpə'θetɪkəl/ *adj* supposed to be so; not yet proved to be true or known to have happened —**-~ly** *adv* [Wa4]

hys·ter·ec·to·my /,hɪstə'rektəmi/ *n* [C;U] the medical operation for removing the WOMB (= the organ in women where a baby can grow before birth)

hys·te·ri·a /hɪ'stɪərɪə‖-'sterɪə/ *n* [U] **1** a condition of nervous excitement in which the sufferer laughs and cries uncontrollably and/or shows strange changes in behaviour or bodily state **2** wild excitement, as of a crowd of people —**-ric** /hɪ'sterɪk/ *n*

hys·ter·i·cal /hɪ'sterɪkəl/ *adj* **1** (of people) in a state of HYSTERIA **2** (of feelings) expressed wildly, in an uncontrolled manner —**~ly** *adv* [Wa4]

hys·ter·ics /hɪ'sterɪks/ *n* [P] attack(s) of HYSTERIA: *She always has hysterics at the sight of blood*

Hz *written abbrev. for:* HERTZ

I, i

I[1], **i** /aɪ/ **I's, i's** *or* **Is, is** **1** the 9th letter of the English alphabet —see also CROSS[2] **one's "t's" and dot one's "i's"** **2** the ROMAN NUMERAL (number) for 1

I *pron* [Wp1] (*used as the subject of a sentence*) the person speaking: *I'm your mother, aren't I? (fml) am I not?|My husband and I are glad to be here*
USAGE In speech, people often use **I** as the 2nd of 2 objects after a verb or PREPOSITION, although this is not considered good English: *He won't let you and* **I**/*my wife and* **I** *into the house.*|*People like George and* **I**|*between you and* **I**. —see ME (USAGE)

-i·al /ɪəl/ *suffix* [*n→adj*] -AL: MANORIAL

i·amb /'aɪæm‖'aɪæm, 'aɪæmb/ also **i·am·bus** /aɪ'æmbəs/— *n* **-s** /'aɪæmz/ a measure of poetry consisting of one weak (or short) beat followed by one strong (or long) beat (as in the word "alive") —**-ic** /aɪ'æmbɪk/ *adj, n* [Wa5]: *written in iambic lines*|*iambics*

-i·an /ɪən/ *suffix* [*n→adj, n*] -AN: (*a*) NEWTONIAN| *Christians*

I·be·ri·an /aɪ'bɪərɪən/ *adj* [Wa5] of Spain and Portugal

i·bex /'aɪbeks/ *n* [Wn1] a type of wild goat of the Alps and Pyrenees

ib·i·dem /'ɪbɪdem, ɪ'baɪdem/ also **ib·id** /'ɪbɪd/— *adv Lat* in the same place, usu. in a (part of a) book already mentioned

-i·bil·i·ty /ə'bɪlǥti/ *suffix* -ABILITY

i·bis /'aɪbǥs/ *n* [Wn1] a type of bird living in warm wet areas

-i·ble /əbəl/ *suffix* -ABLE

-ic /ɪk/ *suffix* [*n→adj*] connected with: *atomic science*|*an atomic bomb*|*an alcoholic drink*|*Byronic* (= of or like the poet Byron) —**-ically** *suffix* [Wa4; *n→adj*]: *alcoholically*
USAGE Compare **-ic** and **-ical**: **a** When forming an adjective from a noun ending with **-ic**, one may add *-al*: *music→musical*; or there may be 2 adjectives, one formed by adding *-al* and another for which nothing at all is added: *magic* (n)→*magic* (adj), *magical*. **b** Where there are 2 adjectives formed from the same noun, they may have different meanings: *history→histor***ic**, *histor***ical**; or they may have almost the same meaning, apart from their use in certain fixed phrases: *poet→poet***ic**, *poet***ical.**

-i·cal /ɪkəl/ *suffix* [*n→adj*] -IC: *political* —see -IC (USAGE) —**-ically** *suffix* [Wa4;*n→adv*]: *politically*

ICBM *abbrev for:* INTERCONTINENTAL BALLISTIC MISSILE

ice[1] /aɪs/ *n* **1** [U] water which has frozen to a solid: *Some wines are kept on ice.*|*ice on the lake in winter*|*Her hands were like ice*/*were as cold as ice* **2** [C] *esp. BrE* a serving of ice cream **3** [C] also **water ice**— a type or a serving of a cold sweet food like ice cream, but made with fruit juice instead of milk or cream **4 break the ice** to begin to be friendly with people one did not know before, or to begin something difficult **5 cut no ice (with someone)** to have little effect (on someone) **6 skating on thin ice** taking risks; being in a dangerous position **7 keep (something) on ice** to keep for later use

ice² *v* [Wv5;T1] **1** to make very cold by using ice: *iced drinks* **2** to cover (a cake) with a mixture of fine powdery sugar and liquid

ice age /ˈ· ·/ *n* any of several periods when ice covered many northern countries

ice axe /ˈ· ·/ *n* an axe used for cutting the ice into steps when climbing mountains

ice bag /ˈ· ·/ *n AmE* ICE PACK

ice·berg /ˈaɪsbɜːg‖-ɜrg/ *n* a large piece of ice floating in the sea, most of which is below the surface

ice·bound /ˈaɪsbaʊnd/ *adj* that cannot be reached because of the presence of ice: *an icebound port*

ice·box /ˈaɪsbɒks‖-bɑks/ *n* **1** a box where food is kept cool with blocks of ice **2** *AmE* REFRIGERATOR

ice·break·er /ˈaɪsˌbreɪkəʳ/ *n* a boat which cuts through floating ice

ice cap /ˈ· ·/ also **ice sheet**— *n* a lasting covering of ice, such as that on the north and south POLE*s*

ice-cold /ˌ· ˈ·◂/ *adj* [Wa5] very cold; as cold as ice: *ice-cold drinks/hands*

ice cream /ˌ· ˈ·◂‖ˈ· ·/ *n* [U;C] (a type or a serving of) a sweet mixture which is frozen and eaten cold, usu. containing milk products and often eggs: *chocolate ice cream*

ice-cream so·da /ˌ· · ˈ··/ also **soda**— *n* a dish made from ice cream, sweet SYRUP, and SODA WATER, usu. served in a tall glass

ice·fall /ˈaɪs-fɔːl/ *n* a stretch of water frozen as it falls from a higher to a lower place —compare WATERFALL

ice field /ˈ· ·/ *n* a very large area of ice, esp. on the sea

ice floe /ˈ· ·/ *n* a large area of floating ice

ice hock·ey /ˈ· ˌ··/ also (*esp. AmE*) **hockey**— *n* [U] a team game like FIELD HOCKEY played on ice

ice·house /ˈaɪshaʊs/ **-houses** /ˌhaʊz½z/— *n* a building, sometimes underground, where ice is stored for use in preserving food during the heat of the summer

Ice·lan·dic /aɪsˈlændɪk/ *adj* [Wa5] of Iceland, its people, or their language —see NATIONALITY TABLE

ice-lol·ly /ˌ· ˈ··/ *n BrE* a piece of ice on a stick, which tastes of fruit or other sweet tastes

ice·man /ˈaɪs-mæn/ *n* **-men** /men/ *AmE* the man who brings the ice to the home for use in ICEBOXes

ice pack /ˈ· ·/ *n* **1** an area of broken ice crushed together to cover a large stretch of the sea **2** *AmE* also **ice bag**— a bag containing ice, used to make parts of the body cool

ice pick /ˈ· ·/ *n* a tool for breaking ice —compare PICKAXE

ice skate /ˈ· ·/ *n* SKATE² (1) —see PAIR¹ (USAGE)

ice-skate /ˈ· ·/ *v* [I∅] to SKATE on ice —**ice-skater** *n* —**ice-skating** *n* [U]: *Ice-skating is my favourite winter sport*

ice up also **ice o·ver**— *v adv* [I∅] to become covered with ice

ice wa·ter /ˈ· ˌ··/ *n* [U] water made very cold, as by the use of ice, and used esp. for drinking

ichneumon fly /ɪkˈnjuːmən flaɪ‖-ˈnuː-/ *n* a type of insect which lays eggs inside the young (LARVA) of other insects

i·ci·cle /ˈaɪsɪkəl/ *n* a pointed stick of ice formed when water freezes as it runs down

ic·ing /ˈaɪsɪŋ/ also **frosting**— *n* [U] a mixture of fine powdery sugar with liquid, used to cover cakes

i·con, ikon /ˈaɪkɒn‖-kɑn/ *n* an image of a holy person, used in the worship of the Eastern branches of Christianity

i·con·o·clast /aɪˈkɒnəklæst‖-ˈkɑ-/ *n* a person who attacks widely-held beliefs or customs —**~ic** /aɪˌkɒnəˈklæstɪk‖-ˌkɑ-/ *adj*

-ics /ɪks/ *suffix* [→*n*] **1** study; knowledge; skill; practice: LINGUISTICS|ELECTRONICS **2** typical actions or activities: ACROBATICS **3** typical qualities, operations, or events: MECHANICS

USAGE Names of sciences ending in **-ics** usually take a singular verb when we speak of them as school subjects: **Physics** *is my best subject*. They usually take a plural verb when there is an adjective or descriptive phrase: *The* **physics** *of this subject are difficult.|His* **politics** *are unusual*. Other words ending in **-ics** take a plural verb.

ic·y /ˈaɪsi/ *adj* [Wa1] **1** very cold: *My hands are icy.|* (fig.) *She gave me an icy look* **2** covered with ice: *Icy roads are dangerous* —**icily** *adv* —**iciness** *n* [U]

I'd /aɪd/ [Wv2] *contr. of* (*in compound tenses*) **1** I had: *I'd gone* **2** I would: *I'd go* —see CONTR. (USAGE)

id /ɪd/ *n* (in Freudian PSYCHOLOGY) the one of the 3 parts of the mind that is completely unconscious, but has needs and desires —compare EGO (2), SUPEREGO

ID card /ˌaɪ ˈdiː kɑːd‖-kɑrd/ *n not fml* IDENTITY CARD

-ide /aɪd/ *suffix* [→*n*[U]] *tech* a chemical compound: CYANIDE|SULPHIDE

i·dea /aɪˈdɪə/ *n* **1** [C;U] a picture in the mind: *I've got a good idea of what he wants.|Have you any idea of what I'm trying to explain?* **2** [C] a plan: *I have an idea for a new book* **3** [C] an opinion: *He'll have his own ideas about that* **4** [C] a guess; feeling of probability: *I've an idea that she likes him better than anyone else* **5** [C;U] understanding (esp. in the phr. **no idea**): *You have no idea how worried I was!* **6** [C] a suggestion or sudden thought: *What a good idea!* **7 get the idea that** to come to believe (often mistakenly) **8 one's idea of** (used for expressing what one likes a lot): *Going to a film is not my idea of spending a sunny day well* **9 put ideas in someone's head** to make someone hope for things they can't have **10 The idea!** also **What an idea!**— (an expression of surprise at a strange thought or suggestion, or of disagreement with a silly thought or suggestion)

i·deal¹ /aɪˈdɪəl/ *adj* [Wa5] **1** perfect: *an ideal marriage* **2** expressing possible perfection which is unlikely to exist in the real world: *the ideal system of government* —opposite **real**

ideal² *n* **1** a perfect example: *That's my ideal of what a house should be like* **2** [*often pl.*] (a belief in) high or perfect standards

i·deal·is·m /aɪˈdɪəlɪzəm/ *n* [U] **1** the system of living according to one's IDEAL*s*² (2), or the belief that such a system is possible: *youthful idealism* **2** (in art) the principle of showing the world in a perfect form, although such perfection may not exist —opposite **realism** **3** (in PHILOSOPHY) the belief that ideas are the only real things —compare REALISM (3)

i·deal·ist /aɪˈdɪəl½st/ *n* a person who has IDEAL*s*² (2) or who believes in or practises IDEALISM: *a youthful idealist* —**~ic** /ˌaɪdɪəˈlɪstɪk/ *adj* —**~ically** *adv* [Wa4]

i·deal·ize, -ise /aɪˈdɪəlaɪz/ *v* [T1;I∅] to imagine or represent (something or someone) as perfect or as better than in reality —**-ization** /aɪˌdɪəlaɪˈzeɪʃən‖-lə-/ *n* [U;C]

i·deal·ly /aɪˈdɪəli/ *adv* **1** in an IDEAL way: *ideally beautiful* **2** in an IDEAL state of affairs: *Ideally, we should have twice as much office space as we have now*

id·em /ˈɪdem, ˈaɪdem/ *pron Lat* (of a book, writer, etc., already mentioned) the same

i·den·ti·cal /aɪˈdentɪkəl/ *adj* [Wa5] **1** the same: *It's the identical coat which was stolen from me* **2** [*with, to*] exactly alike: *I've never before met 2 sisters with*

identical voices.|*Your voice is identical to hers* —**-cally** *adv* [Wa4]
USAGE It is always correct to say **identical** *with*: *This chair is* **identical** *with mine*. Many people now say **identical** *to*, but this is not thought to be such good English.

identical twin /·ˌ··· '·/ *n* [*usu. pl.*] either of a pair of children or animals born from one egg of the mother and usu. looking alike

i·den·ti·fi·ca·tion /aɪˌdentɪ̈fɪ̈'keɪʃən/ *n* [U] **1** the act of IDENTIFYing or state of being identified: *identification of the dead body by the brother* **2** means (such as an official paper) of proving who one is

identification pa·rade /·ˌ···'·· ·ˌ·/ *n* a number of people standing in a row, one or more of whom is thought by the police to be guilty of a crime, and who are looked at by a witness to the crime, who tries to recognize the criminal(s)

i·den·ti·fy /aɪ'dentɪ̈faɪ/ *v* [T1] **1** to prove or show the IDENTITY of: *I identified the coat at once—it was my brother's.*|*I identified the criminal* **2** to show or feel to be IDENTICAL: *I'd identify the 2 tastes*

identify with *v prep* **1** [D1 *often pass.*] to cause or consider (someone) to be connected with (something): *That politician is too closely identified with the former government to become a minister in ours* **2** [D1] to consider (something) equal to (something): *Never identify opinions with facts* **3** [T1] to feel sympathy for (someone), or feel that one shares (something): *Reading this book, we can identify with the main character's struggle*
USAGE It is rather modern and American to use this verb in sentences like *She* **identified with** *foreign workers* rather than saying *She* **identified** *herself with* . . . Some people do not like it.

i·den·ti·kit /aɪ'dentɪ̈ˌkɪt/ *n* a collection of parts which can be fitted together to produce pictures of different faces, so that witnesses to a crime may choose the face that looks most like that of the criminal

i·den·ti·ty /aɪ'dentɪ̈ti/ *n* **1** [U;C] who or what a particular person or thing is: *Please prove your identity* **2** [U] sameness; exact likeness **3** [C] *infml* IDENTIFICATION (2)

identity card /·'··· ·/ also **ID card, identity cer·ti·fi·cate** /·'··· ·ˌ···/— *n* a card with one's name, photograph, signature, etc., which proves who one is

id·e·o·gram /'ɪdiəgræm/ also **id·e·o·graph** /-grɑːf‖-græf/— *n* a written sign for a word that gives more idea of the meaning of the word than of its sound, as in Chinese writing

i·de·ol·ogy /ˌaɪdi'ɒlədʒi‖-'ɑlə-/ *n* [U;C] *sometimes derog* a set of ideas, esp. if typical of a social or political group: MARXIST *ideology* —**-ogical** /ˌaɪdɪə'lɒdʒɪkəl‖-'lɑ-/ *adj* —**-ogically** *adv* [Wa4]: *Ideologically, they have many differences* —**-ogist** /ˌaɪdi'ɒlədʒɪ̈st‖-'ɑlə-/ *n*

ides /aɪdz/ *n* [P] *lit* (in the ancient Roman CALENDAR) a date or period of time around the middle of the month (esp. in the phr. **the Ides of March**, meaning March 15th, when Julius Caesar was killed)

id·i·o·cy /'ɪdiəsi/ *n* **1** [U] the state of being very foolish **2** [U] *tech* the state of being an IDIOT (2) **3** [C] an act of stupidity

id·i·om /'ɪdiəm/ *n* **1** a phrase which means something different from the meanings of the separate words: *To be "hard up" is an English idiom meaning to lack money* **2** the way of expression typical of a person or a people in their use of language: *The French and the English idioms have very different characters.*|(fig.) *the new and exciting idiom of modern popular music*

id·i·o·mat·ic /ˌɪdiə'mætɪk/ *adj* (containing phrases which are) typical of the natural speech of a native speaker of the language: *a Frenchman who speaks idiomatic English*|*"To pull a face" is an idiomatic expression* —**~ally** *adv* [Wa4]

id·i·o·syn·cra·sy /ˌɪdiə'sɪŋkrəsi/ *n* **1** a peculiarity of one person: *Liking wild flowers in his garden is his personal idiosyncrasy* **2** *infml* a peculiar act: *One of their idiosyncrasies was when they camped out in the garden*

id·i·ot /'ɪdiət/ *n* **1** [C; (*you*) N] a foolish person: *Idiot! You've dropped my book!* **2** [C] *old use or tech* a person of very weak mind usu. from birth, who cannot behave or think in the ordinary way: *born an idiot*|*her idiot son* —**~ic** /ˌɪdi'ɒtɪk‖-'ɑ-/ *adj* —**~ically** *adv* [Wa4]

i·dle[1] /'aɪdl/ *adj* [Wa1,3] **1** **a** not working: *Men are left idle when machines break down* **b** (of time) not used for doing anything: *Idle hours flew by* **2** lazy **3** of no use; not producing anything good (note the phr. **idle gossip**): *I knew what would happen, but it was idle to warn her* —**~ness** *n* [U] —**idly** *adv* [Wa3]

idle[2] *v* [Wv3;IØ] **1** to waste time doing nothing **2** (of an engine) to run slowly because it is disconnected, so that power is not used for useful work —**idler** *n*

idle a·way *v adv* [T1] to waste (time)

i·dol /'aɪdl/ *n* **1** an image worshipped as a god **2** someone or something admired or loved too much

i·dol·a·ter /aɪ'dɒlətə^r‖-'dɑ-/ (*fem* **i·dol·a·tress** /-trɪ̈s/)— *n* a worshipper of IDOLs (1), or admirer of IDOLs (2)

i·dol·a·trous /aɪ'dɒlətrəs‖-'dɑ-/ *adj* **1** worshipping IDOLs **2** like IDOLATRY: *idolatrous love of money* —**~ly** *adv*

i·dol·a·try /aɪ'dɒlətri‖-'dɑ-/ *n* [U] **1** the worship of IDOLs **2** too great admiration of someone or something

i·dol·ize, -ise /'aɪdəl-aɪz/ *v* [T1] to treat as an IDOL: *He idolizes his father*

id·yll, idyl /'ɪdl, 'aɪdl‖'aɪdl/ *n* **1** a simple, happy period of life, often in the country, or a scene from such a time: *an idyll of 2 young lovers* **2** a description of this, esp. a poem about country life —**~ic** /aɪ'dɪlɪk/ *adj*: *an idyllic scene* —**~ically** *adv* [Wa4]

-ie /i/ *suffix* [*n→n*] -Y[2] (1)

i.e. /ˌaɪ 'iː/ *abbrev. for*: (*Lat*) id est; that is to SAY[1] (13): *females, i.e. girls and women*

-i·er /iə^r/ *suffix* comp. of -Y[1]: *dirtier*

-ies /iz/ *suffix* pl. of -Y[2]: *doggies* (DOGGY)

-i·est /iɪ̈st/ *suffix* superl. of -Y[1]: *dirtiest*

if[1] /ɪf/ *conj* **1** (*not usu. followed by the future tense*) supposing that; on condition that: *We'll go* (*only*) *if it rains* (=we won't go except on the condition that it rains).|*If she telephones,*|(*fml*)*If she should telephone, let me know.*|*If she comes,* (*then*) *we'll tell her.*|*If he told you that, he was lying.*|*Go to bed. If not, I'll tell father.*|*Send the goods now, if* (*they're*) *ready.*|*If John was/were here, he would know.*|*If you'd listened*/(*fml*) *Had you listened to me, you wouldn't be in such trouble now.*|*"We can send you a map if you wish"* (SEU S.) **2** accepting that; although; in spite of the fact that: **a** (usu. with *even*) *We'll go even if it rains* (=we'll go, whether it rains or not).|*Even if you hate beer, try this!*|*If she's poor, at least she's honest* **b** (joining nouns, adjectives, or adverbs): *a pleasant if noisy child* **3** (*in reported questions, or after verbs like* know *or* wonder; *not followed directly by* or not) whether: *Do you know if/whether she's coming?*|*I wonder if/whether she isn't mistaken?* (=I think she is.)|*"Ask them if they could let you have this letter."* (SEU S.)|*"I'll see if he wants to talk to you"* (SEU S.) **4** (*used like* that *after words expressing surprise,*

sorrow, pleasure): *I'm sorry if she's annoyed.|I don't care if she is black; I love her.|Do you mind if I smoke?* (=May I smoke?) **5 if I were you** (used when giving advice): *If I were you I'd leave at once* **6 if you like** (*used when something is expressed in a strange way*) if I may say it in this/that way: *It's a duty, if you like, rather than a pleasure* **7 it isn't/it's not as if** it is not true that: *It isn't as if she weren't* (=isn't) *pretty* (=It isn't as if she were/is ugly)
USAGE 1 It is more correct to say **If** *only I were rich!*|**If** *he were older we could take him* than **If** *only I was* . . . **If** *he was* . . . . But when **if** means **whether** it must be followed by *was*: *I don't know* **if** *he was there.* 2 One can use **if** with *will/won't* only when **a** they have a human subject and mean "be willing": **If** *you won't help me* (=if you refuse) *I'll shoot myself* or **b** though the condition expressed by **if** is in the future, the whole sentence speaks of a truth in the present: **If** *it will help, I'll lend you £50* (=if it is true now that £50 will help). —see WHETHER (USAGE)

if² *n* **ifs and buts** reasons given for delay: *I don't want any ifs and buts—swallow your medicine at once*

-i·form /ɪ̵fɔːm‖ɪ̵fɔrm/ *comb. form* [*n*→*adj*] -FORM

-i·fy /ɪ̵ˌfaɪ/ *suffix* [→*v*] -FY

ig·loo /ˈɪgluː/ *n* **-loos** a house made of hard icy blocks of snow, esp. as built by Eskimos

ig·ne·ous /ˈɪgnɪəs/ *adj* [Wa5] *tech* **1** related to fire **2** (of rocks) formed from LAVA

ig·nis fat·u·us /ˌɪgnɪs ˈfætʃʊəs/ *n* **ignes fatui** /ˌɪgniːz ˈfætʃuːiː/ [*usu. sing.*] *Lat* a moving light seen over wet ground because of the burning of waste gases —see also WILL O' THE WISP

ig·nite /ɪgˈnaɪt/ *v* [T1;I∅] to (cause to) start to burn

ig·ni·tion /ɪgˈnɪʃən/ *n* **1** the act or action of igniting (IGNITE) **2** the means, or apparatus for, starting an engine by electrically firing the gases from the petrol —see picture at CAR

ig·no·ble /ɪgˈnəʊbəl/ *adj* [Wa2,3] dishonourable; which one should be ashamed of —**-bly** *adv* [Wa3]

ig·no·min·i·ous /ˌɪgnəˈmɪnɪəs/ *adj* of a type which brings strong public disapproval; shameful to one's pride: *ignominious behaviour|an ignominious defeat* —**~ly** *adv*

ig·no·mi·ny /ˈɪgnəmɪni/ *n* **1** [U] a state of shame or dishonour **2** [C] an act of shameful behaviour

ig·no·ra·mus /ˌɪgnəˈreɪməs/ *n* [C; *you*+N] an IGNORANT person

ig·no·rance /ˈɪgnərəns/ *n* [U (*of*)] lack of knowledge: *Ignorance of the law is no excuse*

ig·no·rant /ˈɪgnərənt/ *adj* [(*of*)] **1** lacking knowledge: *ignorant of even the simplest facts* —see IGNORE (USAGE) **2** *infml* rude, impolite, esp. because of lack of social training: *He's an ignorant person—he always goes through a door in front of a lady*

ig·nore /ɪgˈnɔːʳ‖ɪgˈnor/ *v* [T1] not to take notice of: *Ignore the child if he misbehaves, and he'll soon stop*
USAGE To be **ignorant** of something is not to know it. *He is quite* **ignorant** *of Latin.|She was* **ignorant** *of his presence* (=she didn't know he was there). To **ignore** something is to pretend not to know or see it: *She saw him coming but she* **ignored** *him.*

i·gua·na /ɪˈgwɑːnə/ *n* a type of large LIZARD of tropical America —see picture at REPTILE

i·kon /ˈaɪkɒn‖-kɑn/ *n* ICON

il- /ɪl/ *prefix* (*before the letter* l) IN-: *il*LOGICAL

i·lex /ˈaɪleks/ *n* **1** also **holmoak**— the EVERGREEN OAK tree **2** *tech* a family of trees including HOLLY

ilk /ɪlk/ *n* [S] kind, type, etc., or (originally) place or family (usu. in the phr. **of that ilk**)

ill¹ /ɪl/ *adj* **worse** /wɜːs‖wɜrs/, **worst** /wɜːst‖wɜrst/ **1** [F;(B)] not well in health: *She's ill, so she can't come* **2** [F9] *BrE* hurt: *One week after the fighting, 2 policemen were still seriously ill in hospital* **3** [A] bad; harmful: *ill luck|He suffers from ill health* —see SICK (USAGE)

ill² *adv* [Wa5 (*often in comb.*)] **1** badly, cruelly, or unpleasantly; with (a) bad . . .: *The child has been* ILL-TREAT*ed* **2** hardly; scarcely; not enough: *ill fed|I can ill afford the time* **3** unfavourably: *to think/speak ill of someone*

ill³ *n* [*often pl.*] a bad thing: *the ills of life*

I'll /aɪl/ [Wv2] *contr. of*: **1** I will **2** I shall —see CONTR. (USAGE)

ill-ad·vised /ˌ· ·ˈ·◂/ *adj* unwise

ill-as·sort·ed /ˌ· ·ˈ··◂/ *adj* that do not go well together: *an ill-assorted pair*

ill at ease /ˌ· · ˈ·/ *adj* [F] not comfortable because of lack of understanding or skill: *He's ill at ease at parties*

ill-bred /ˌ· ˈ·◂/ *adj* badly behaved or rude, probably as the result of being badly brought up as a child: *an ill-bred remark|He's very ill-bred*

il·le·gal /ɪˈliːgəl/ *adj* [Wa5] against the law: *It's illegal to park your car here* —compare LEGAL (1) —**~ly** *adv*

il·le·gal·i·ty /ˌɪlɪˈgælɪ̵ti/ *n* **1** [U] the state of being ILLEGAL **2** [C] an act against the law

il·le·gi·ble /ɪˈledʒəbəl/ also **unreadable**— *adj* which cannot be read —compare UNREADABLE —**-bility** /ɪˌledʒəˈbɪlɪ̵ti/ *n* [U] —**-bly** *adv*

il·le·git·i·mate /ˌɪlɪ̵ˈdʒɪtɪ̵mɪ̵t/ *adj* **1** not allowed by the rules —compare ILLEGAL **2** [Wa5] born to a mother who is not married —**~ly** *adv* —**-macy** /ˌɪlɪ̵ˈdʒɪtɪ̵məsi/ *n* [U]

ill-fat·ed /ˌ· ˈ··◂/ *adj* unlucky: *an ill-fated attempt that ended in death*

ill-fa·voured /ˌ· ˈ··◂/ *adj* (of a person) ugly, esp. in the face

ill-got·ten /ˌ· ˈ··◂/ *adj* obtained by dishonest means (usu. in the phr. **ill-gotten gains**)

il·lib·e·ral /ɪˈlɪbərəl/ *adj* **1** not supporting freedom of expression or personal behaviour; not in favour of allowing people to do as they like: *illiberal opinions* **2** ungenerous —**~ity** /ɪˌlɪbəˈrælɪ̵ti/ *n* [U] —**-rally** /ɪˈlɪbərəli/ *adv*

il·li·cit /ɪˈlɪsɪ̵t/ *adj* [Wa5] (done) against a law or a rule: *an illicit act|illicit trade in drugs* —**~ly** *adv*

il·lim·i·ta·ble /ɪˈlɪmɪ̵təbəl/ *adj* [Wa5] with no known limit; which cannot be measured: *illimitable spaces*

il·lit·e·rate /ɪˈlɪtərɪ̵t/ *adj, n* [Wa5] **1** unable to read and write: *illiterate tribes* **2** *infml* showing little skill in these activities: *He writes like an illiterate: there are mistakes on every page* —**~ly** *adv* —**-racy** /ɪˈlɪtərəsi/ *n* [U]

ill-man·nered /ˌ· ˈ··◂/ *adj* rude

ill-na·tured /ˌ· ˈ··◂/ *adj* of a bad-tempered character; unkind: *an ill-natured remark*

ill·ness /ˈɪlnɪ̵s/ *n* [U;C] (a) disease; unhealthy state of the body: *Illness makes one weak.|A bad illness like a throat infection leaves one weak afterwards* —see DISEASE (USAGE)

il·lo·gi·cal /ɪˈlɒdʒɪkəl‖ɪˈlɑ-/ *adj* (of people or ideas) **a** going against LOGIC **b** *infml* not sensible —**~ly** *adv* [Wa4]

ill-o·mened /ˌ· ˈ··◂/ *adj* ILL-FATED; not promising success

ill-starred /ˌ· ˈ·◂/ *adj lit* ILL-FATED

ill-tem·pered /ˌ· ˈ··◂/ *adj fml* bad tempered

ill-timed /ˌ· ˈ·◂/ *adj* (done) at the wrong time: *That was an ill-timed remark that hurt her feelings*

ill-treat /ˌ· ˈ·/ *v* [T1] to be cruel to: *He ill-treats his dogs* —**~ment** /ˌ· ˈ··/ *n* [U]

il·lu·mi·nate /ɪˈluːmɪ̵neɪt, ɪˈljuː-‖ɪˈluː-/ *v* [T1 (*with*)] **1** **a** to give light to **b** to ornament (buildings, streets, etc.) with lights for a special occasion **2** [Wv5] (esp. in former times) to paint with gold and bright colours: *an illuminated* MANUSCRIPT

il·lu·mi·nat·ing /ɪˈluːmɨneɪtɪŋ, ɪˈljuː-‖ɪˈluː-/ *adj* that helps to explain: *an illuminating remark, that showed her real character*

il·lu·mi·na·tion /ɪˌluːmɨˈneɪʃən, ɪˌljuː-‖ɪˌluː-/ *n* **1** [U] the act of illuminating or state of being ILLUMINATED **2** [C *usu. pl.*] (esp. in former times) a picture painted on a page of an old book **3** [U] the strength of light: *The illumination is too weak to show the detail of the painting*

il·lu·mi·na·tions /ɪˌluːmɨˈneɪʃənz, ɪˌljuː-‖ɪˌluː-/ *n* [P] the show of (coloured) lights used to make a town bright and colourful

il·lu·sion /ɪˈluːʒən/ *n* **1** [U] the condition of seeing things wrongly **2** [C] something seen wrongly, not as it really is (note the phr. **an optical illusion**): *It was an (optical) illusion caused by the weak lights that made me think I saw a man in the shadows* **3** [C] a false idea esp. about oneself **4 be under an illusion** to be wrong **5 cherish the illusion that** to believe wrongly **6 have no illusions about** to know how bad something/someone is: *I have no illusions about his ability*
USAGE An **illusion** is usually something that seems true to the senses, but is known to be false: *the* **illusion** *that the sun goes round the earth.* A **delusion** is something really believed by a person who is **deluded** or even mad: *his* **delusion** *that he is Napoleon the first.*

il·lu·sion·ist /ɪˈluːʒənɨst/ *n* a person who plays tricks on the eyes in a stage performance: *The illusionist made us believe he had really cut the lady in half*

il·lu·so·ry /ɪˈluːsəri/ also **il·lu·sive** /ɪˈluːsɪv/— *adj fml* deceiving and unreal; based on an ILLUSION: *an illusory belief*

il·lus·trate /ˈɪləstreɪt/ *v* [T1] **1** [Wv5] to add pictures to (something written): *a beautifully illustrated history of science* **2** to show the meaning of (something) by giving related examples: *The story he told about her illustrates her true generosity very clearly*

il·lus·tra·tion /ˌɪləˈstreɪʃən/ *n* **1** [U] the act of illustrating (ILLUSTRATE): *Illustration by example is better than explanations in words* **2** [C] a picture to go with the words of a book, speaker, etc. **3** [C] an example which explains the meaning of something **4 by way of illustration** as an example

il·lus·tra·tive /ˈɪləstreɪtɪv, -strət-‖ɪˈlʌstrətɪv/ *adj* used for explaining the meaning of something —compare ILLUSTRATE (2) —**~ly** *adv*

il·lus·tra·tor /ˈɪləstreɪtəʳ/ *n* a person who draws pictures esp. for a book

il·lus·tri·ous /ɪˈlʌstrɪəs/ *adj apprec* famous; known for one's great works: *the illustrious name of Shakespeare* —**~ly** *adv*

ill will /ˌ· ˈ·/ *n* [U] bad feeling; feeling of hatred or strong dislike

im- /ɪm/ *prefix* IN-: *impossible*

I'm /aɪm/ [Wv1] *contr. of:* I am —see CONTR. (USAGE)

im·age /ˈɪmɪdʒ/ *n* **1** a picture esp. in the mind: *An image of a country garden came into my mind* **2** *old use* likeness; form: *According to the Bible, man was made in the image of God* **3** a copy: *He's the (very) image of his father* **4** an object made to represent a god or person to be worshipped —compare IDOL (1) **5** a METAPHOR or SIMILE; phrase suggesting something by means of a poetical form **6** someone's appearance, esp. good or bad, as seen by other people: *The government has a very bad image because it continues with plans that nobody likes* **7** *tech* a picture formed of an object in front of a mirror or LENS, such as the picture formed on the film inside a camera, or one's REFLECTION in an ordinary mirror

im·ag·e·ry /ˈɪmɪdʒəri/ *n* [U] IMAGE*s* (5) generally, esp. as used in literature

i·ma·gi·na·ble /ɪˈmædʒənəbəl/ *adj* that can be imagined

i·ma·gi·na·ry /ɪˈmædʒənəri‖-dʒɨneri/ *adj* not real, but produced from pictures in someone's mind: *All the characters in this book are imaginary.|My little daughter has an imaginary friend* —compare IMAGINATIVE

i·ma·gi·na·tion /ɪˌmædʒɨˈneɪʃən/ *n* **1** [U;C] the act of imagining or the ability to imagine **2** [C *often with poss.*] the mind: *The difficulties are all in your imagination* **3** [U] *infml* something only imagined and not real: *Her pains are mostly imagination*

i·ma·gi·na·tive /ɪˈmædʒənətɪv/ *adj* **1** that shows use of the imagination: *imaginative writing* **2** good at inventing imaginary things or artistic forms, or at producing new ideas: *an imaginative child* —compare IMAGINARY —**~ly** *adv*

i·ma·gine /ɪˈmædʒɨn/ *v* [Wv6] **1** [T1,4;V4] to form (a picture or idea) in the mind: *I can imagine the scene clearly in my mind.|Can you imagine George cooking the dinner?* **2** [T5a,b,6a,b] to suppose or have an idea about, esp. mistakenly or without proof: *He imagines that people don't like him* **3 (just) imagine (it)!** an expression of disapproval for the plan or suggestion just mentioned, because no sensible person would imagine that it could happen

im·am /ˈɪmɑːm, ˈɪmæm/ *n* a Muslim priest and/or prince, or someone who studies Muslim law

im·bal·ance /ɪmˈbæləns/ *n* a lack of balance or proper relationship, esp. between 2 qualities or between 2 examples of one thing: *population imbalance, in which more males are born than females*

im·be·cile /ˈɪmbəsiːl‖-səl/ *n* **1** [C] a person of weak mind, but less weak than an IDIOT **2** [C; (*you*) N] a fool or stupid person —compare IDIOT

im·be·cil·i·ty /ˌɪmbɨˈsɪlɨti/ *n* **1** [U] the state of being an IMBECILE **2** [U;C] *derog* (an act of great foolishness

im·bed /ɪmˈbed/ *v* **-dd-** [D1 + *in/with usu. pass.*] EMBED

im·bibe /ɪmˈbaɪb/ *v* [T1;I∅] *fml* to drink or take in: *imbibing knowledge at his mother's knee* (= as a small child)

im·bro·gli·o /ɪmˈbrəʊliəʊ/ *n* **-glios** **1** an occasion filled with confused action **2** a misunderstanding or difficult and confusing state of affairs, esp. as part of the action of a play

im·bue with /ɪmˈbjuː/ *v prep* [D1 *usu. pass.*] to fill (usu. someone) with (something, often a strong feeling or opinion): *A President should be imbued with a sense of responsibility for the nation*

im·i·tate /ˈɪmɨteɪt/ *v* [T1] **1** to take (something/someone) as an example: *You should imitate his way of doing things* **2** to copy the behaviour, appearance, speech, etc., typical of (a person) **3** *usu. infml* to appear like something else: *It's plastic, made to imitate leather*

im·i·ta·tion /ˌɪmɨˈteɪʃən/ *n* **1** [U] the act or action of imitating (IMITATE) **2** [C] a copy of someone's behaviour, appearance, speech, etc.: *His imitation of that singer is perfect* **3** [C] a copy of the real thing: *It's an imitation of leather.|imitation jewellery*

im·i·ta·tive /ˈɪmɨtətɪv‖-teɪtɪv/ *adj* following the example of someone or something else —**~ly** *adv* —**~ness** *n* [U]

im·i·ta·tor /ˈɪmɨteɪtəʳ/ *n* someone who IMITATES

im·mac·u·late /ɪˈmækjʊlɨt‖-kjə-/ *adj* [Wa5] **1** clean and unspoilt: *immaculate white shoes* **2** pure; unmarked; without fault: *immaculate behaviour* —**~ly** *adv*

Immaculate Con·cep·tion /·ˌ··· ·'··/ *n* [*the*+R] (according to ROMAN CATHOLIC belief) the idea that Jesus Christ's mother Mary did not have the fault (ORIGINAL SIN) that all ordinary people have when they are born

im·ma·nence /'ɪmənəns/ also **im·ma·nen·cy** /-nənsi/— *n* [U] the state or condition of being IMMANENT

im·ma·nent /'ɪmənənt/ *adj fml or tech* **1** (of qualities) spreading through something: *hope, which seems immanent in human nature* —compare IMMINENT **2** (of God) present in all parts of the universe —compare TRANSCENDENT

im·ma·te·ri·al /ˌɪmə'tɪərɪəl/ *adj* **1** unimportant: *Don't tell me where it happened—that's quite immaterial* **2** without substance: *The body is material but the soul is immaterial*

im·ma·ture /ˌɪmə'tʃʊəʳ‖-'tʊər/ *adj* **1** not fully formed or developed **2** showing a lack of control and good sense in one's behaviour when one is old enough to have gained wisdom —**~ly** *adv* —**-turity** /ˌɪmə'tʃʊərɪ̈ti‖-'tʊər-/ *n* [U;(C)]

im·mea·su·ra·ble /ɪ'meʒərəbəl/ *adj* [Wa5] that cannot be measured —**-bly** *adv*

im·me·di·a·cy /ɪ'miːdɪəsi/ also **im·me·di·ate·ness** /-dɪətnɪ̈s/— *n* [U] the nearness or urgent presence of something, which causes it to be noticed and taken care of without delay: *the immediacy of the danger|Television brings a new immediacy to world difficulties*

im·me·di·ate /ɪ'miːdɪət/ *adj* [Wa5] **1** done or needed at once: *an immediate reply* **2** nearest; next: *in the immediate future|My immediate family consists of my son and my wife*

im·me·di·ate·ly¹ /ɪ'miːdɪətli/ *adv* [Wa5;H] at once: *I came immediately after I'd eaten.|Stop that, immediately!*

immediately² *conj BrE* as soon as: *I came immediately I'd eaten*

im·me·mo·ri·al /ˌɪmɪ̈'mɔːrɪəl‖-'mor-/ *adj* [Wa5] going back to ancient times (note the phr. **from/since time immemorial**): *immemorial customs*

im·mense /ɪ'mens/ *adj usu. apprec* very large: *an immense improvement/palace*

im·mense·ly /ɪ'mensli/ *adv apprec* very much: *I enjoyed it immensely*

im·men·si·ty /ɪ'mensɪ̈ti/ *n* [U *sometimes pl. with same meaning*] great size: *the immensity of space*

im·merse /ɪ'mɜːs‖-ɜrs/ *v* [T1 (*in*)] **1** to put deep under water: *He lay immersed in a hot bath* **2** to cause (oneself) to enter deeply into an activity: *I immersed myself in work so as to stop thinking about her*

im·mer·sion /ɪ'mɜːʃən, -ʒən‖-ɜr-/ *n* **1** [U] the action of immersing or state of being immersed (IMMERSE) **2** [U;C] BAPTISM by going under water

immersion heat·er /·'·· ˌ··/ *n* an electric heater which works in the water to be heated for use in a house

im·mi·grant /'ɪmɪ̈grənt/ *n* a person coming into a country from abroad to make his home there

im·mi·grate /'ɪmɪ̈greɪt/ *v* [IØ] to come into a country to make one's life and home there —see EMIGRATE (USAGE) —**-gration** /ˌɪmɪ̈'greɪʃən/ *n* [U;S]

im·mi·nence /'ɪmɪ̈nəns/ also **im·mi·nen·cy** /-nənsi/— *n* [U] the nearness of something which is going to happen

im·mi·nent /'ɪmɪ̈nənt/ *adj* [Wa5] which is going to happen very soon: *There's a storm imminent* —**~ly** *adv*

im·mo·bile /ɪ'məʊbaɪl‖-bəl/ *adj* [Wa5] unmoving: *to keep a broken leg immobile* —**-bility** /ˌɪməʊ'bɪlɪ̈ti/ *n* [U]

im·mo·bi·lize, -lise /ɪ'məʊbɪ̈laɪz/ *v* [T1] **1** to make (something or someone) unable to move: *When its engine broke down, the car was immobilized for weeks* **2** to take (money) out of the ECONOMIC system: *Capital flow was immobilized*

im·mod·e·rate /ɪ'mɒdərɪ̈t‖ɪ'mɑ-/ *adj* not (done) within sensible limits: *immoderate eating|immoderate feelings of sorrow* —**~ly** *adv* —**-racy** /ɪ'mɒdərəsi‖-'mɑ-/ *n* [U]

im·mod·est /ɪ'mɒdɪ̈st‖ɪ'mɑ-/ *adj derog* **1** telling the good things about oneself instead of hiding them **2** (usu. concerning women) showing parts of the body which should not be seen in public or behaving too freely with men —**~ly** *adv* —**~y** *n* [U]

im·mo·late /'ɪməleɪt/ *v* [T1] to kill as a SACRIFICE —**-lation** /ˌɪmə'leɪʃən/ *n* [U]

im·mor·al /ɪ'mɒrəl‖ɪ'mɔ-/ *adj* **1** not considered good or right: *Using other people for one's own profit is immoral* **2** of or concerning sexual behaviour that is not considered good or right: *A* PROSTITUTE *lives off immoral earnings* **3** offensive to society's ideas of what is good or right, esp. in sexual matters; OBSCENE: *an immoral book* —compare AMORAL —see MORAL¹ (USAGE) —**-ally** *adv*

im·mo·ral·i·ty /ˌɪmə'rælɪ̈ti/ *n* **1** [U] immoral behaviour **2** [C *usu. pl.*] an act which goes against accepted standards

im·mor·tal /ɪ'mɔːtəl‖-ɔr-/ *adj* [Wa5] that will not die; that continues for ever

im·mor·tal·i·ty /ˌɪmɔː'tælɪ̈ti‖-ɔr-/ *n* [U] **1** never-ending life **2** endless fame: *the immortality of Shakespeare's poetry*

im·mor·tal·ize, -ise /ɪ'mɔːtəlaɪz‖-ɔr-/ *v* [T1 (*in*)] to give endless life or fame to (someone): *Dickens' father was immortalized for ever as Mr. Micawber in "David Copperfield"*

im·mo·va·ble /ɪ'muːvəbəl/ *adj* [Wa5] **1** which cannot be moved —compare IRREMOVABLE **2** which cannot be changed —**-bly** *adv*

im·mune /ɪ'mjuːn/ *adj* [Wa5] **1** [(*to*)] unable to be harmed because of special powers in oneself: *immune to disease|immune to unpleasantness* **2** [(*from*)] marked by protection: *The criminal was told he would be immune from punishment if he said what he knew about the murder* —**immunity** *n* [U]

im·mu·nize, -nise /'ɪmjʊnaɪz‖'ɪmjə-/ *v* [T1] to make (someone) safe against disease by putting certain substances into the body usu. by means of a HYPODERMIC needle —see also INOCULATE —**-nization** /ˌɪmjʊnaɪ'zeɪʃən‖ˌɪmjənə-/ *n* [U;(C)]

im·mure /ɪ'mjʊəʳ/ *v* [T1] to imprison; shut (someone) away alone

im·mu·ta·ble /ɪ'mjuːtəbəl/ *adj* [Wa5] *fml* unchangeable: *immutable laws of nature* —**-bly** *adv* [Wa3,5] —**-bility** /ɪˌmjuːtə'bɪlɪ̈ti/ *n* [U]

imp /ɪmp/ *n* **1** a little devil **2** a child, esp. one who misbehaves in a not very serious way —see also IMPISH

im·pact /'ɪmpækt/ *n* **1** the force of one object hitting another **2** the force of an idea, invention, system, etc. **3 on impact** at the moment of hitting

im·pact·ed /ɪm'pæktɪ̈d/ *adj* (usu. of a WISDOM TOOTH) growing under another tooth instead of upwards into the mouth

im·pair /ɪm'peəʳ/ *v* [T1] to spoil or weaken —**~ment** *n* [U]

im·pa·la /ɪm'pɑːlə/ *n* [Wn1] a type of large brownish graceful African deerlike animal (ANTELOPE)

im·pale /ɪm'peɪl/ *v* [T1 (*on*)] to run a sharp stick or weapon through (someone's body) —**~ment** *n* [U]

im·pal·pa·ble /ɪm'pælpəbəl/ *adj* [Wa5] **1** which cannot be felt by touch **2** not easily understood: *impalpable ideas floating through his mind*

im·pan·el /ɪm'pænl/ *v* [T1] EMPANEL

im·part /ɪm'pɑːt‖-ɑrt/ *v* [T1 (*to*)] *fml* to give

(qualities, knowledge, etc.): *imparted the secret to a friend|The good teacher imparts wisdom to his pupils*
im·par·tial /ɪm'pɑːʃəl||-ɑr-/ *adj* [Wa5] fair; giving equal attention to all concerned —**-tially** *adv* —**~ity** /ɪm,pɑːʃi'æləti||-ɑr-/ *n* [U]
im·pass·a·ble /ɪm'pɑːsəbəl||ɪm'pæ-/ *adj* [Wa5] which cannot be travelled over —compare IMPOSSIBLE
im·passe /æm'pɑːs||'ɪmpæs (*Fr* ɛ̃pɑs)/ *n* [*usu. sing.*] a point where further movement is blocked
im·pas·sioned /ɪm'pæʃənd/ *adj* (usu. of speech) moved by deep feelings
im·pas·sive /ɪm'pæsɪv/ *adj sometimes derog* (of people) showing (or having) no feelings; unusually calm —**~ly** *adv* —**-sivity** /,ɪmpæ'sɪvəti/ *n* [U]
im·pa·tience /ɪm'peɪʃəns/ *n* [U] **1** (of people) inability to wait calmly or bear the weaknesses of others **2** [+*for*, U3] eagerness
im·pa·tient /ɪm'peɪʃənt/ *adj* **1** [B] not patient: *too impatient with slow learners* **2** [F+*for*, F3] eager: *impatient for his dinner/to see his wife* —**~ly** *adv*
im·peach /ɪm'piːtʃ/ *v* [T1] **1** *fml* to raise doubts about (esp. in the phr. **impeach someone's motives**) **2** *law* **a** to say that (someone) is guilty of a serious crime, esp. against the state **b** (esp. in the US) to charge (a public official) before an official body with serious misbehaviour in office
im·pec·ca·ble /ɪm'pekəbəl/ *adj* [Wa5] faultless —**-bly** *adv* [Wa3,5]
im·pe·cu·ni·ous /,ɪmpɪ'kjuːnɪəs/ *adj* [Wa5] *fml, sometimes humor or euph* having little or no money, esp. continually —**~ly** *adv* —**~ness** *n* [U]
im·ped·ance /ɪm'piːdəns/ *n* [U;S] *tech* (a measure of) the power of a piece of electrical apparatus to stop the flow of an ALTERNATING CURRENT
im·pede /ɪm'piːd/ *v* [T1] to get in the way of; make (something) difficult to do
im·ped·i·ment /ɪm'pedəmənt/ *n* **1** [(*to*)] a fact or event which makes action difficult or impossible **2** (of bodily abilities, esp. speech) a difficulty in working smoothly
im·ped·i·men·ta /ɪm,pedə'mentə/ *n* [P] bags and possessions in the form of LUGGAGE, esp. supplies carried by an army; (fig.) (*humor*) *They brought their 3 children, the cat, the dog, and the rest of their impedimenta*
im·pel /ɪm'pel/ *v* **-ll-** [T1 (*in, into*); V3] (esp. of an idea, feeling, etc.) to push (someone) forward: *Hunger impelled me to finish my work quickly*
im·pend·ing /ɪm'pendɪŋ/ *adj* [Wa5] (usu. of something unpleasant) about to happen —compare IMMINENT
im·pen·e·tra·ble /ɪm'penətrəbəl/ *adj* **1** which cannot be gone into or through: *the impenetrable forest|* (fig.) *impenetrable darkness* (=in which the eye can see nothing) **2** not able to be understood or helped: *an impenetrable difficulty* **3** not able to receive or accept, esp. ideas: *impenetrable to all requests*
im·pen·i·tent /ɪm'penətənt/ *adj fml* not sorry (for wrongdoing): *an impenitent criminal* —**-tence** *n* [U] —**-tently** *adv*
im·per·a·tive¹ /ɪm'perətɪv/ *adj* **1** [B] urgent; which must be done: *It's imperative that you (should) not be seen here* **2** [A;(B)] showing proud power: *an imperative manner* **3** [A;(B)] of, about, or using the IMPERATIVE² —**~ly** *adv*
imperative² *n* ((an example of) the form which shows) the use of the verb to express a command: *In "Come here!" the verb "come" is in the imperative*
im·per·cep·ti·ble /,ɪmpə'septəbəl||-pər-/ *adj* [Wa5] unable to be noticed because of smallness or slightness —**-bility** /,ɪmpəseptə'bɪləti||-pər-/ *n* [U] —**-bly** *adv* [Wa3,5]
im·per·fect¹ /ɪm'pɜːfɪkt||-ɜr-/ *adj* [Wa5] **1** not perfect; faulty: *an imperfect knowledge of French* **2** of or about the IMPERFECT²: *the imperfect tense* —**-fection** /,ɪmpə'fekʃən||-ər-/ *n* [U;C] —**-fectly** /ɪm'pɜːfɪktli||-ɜr-/ *adv*
imperfect² *n* (an example of) the tense of the verb which shows incomplete action in the past
im·pe·ri·al /ɪm'pɪərɪəl/ *adj* [Wa5 *often cap.*] **1** concerning an empire or its ruler **2** (of a measure) British standard: *The Imperial* GALLON *is not the same size as the US one* —see WEIGHTS & MEASURES TABLE —**-ally** *adv*
im·pe·ri·al·is·m /ɪm'pɪərɪəlɪzəm/ *n* [U] **1** the making of empires **2** the belief that it is good to make or enlarge empires, esp. the empire of one's own nation **3** *derog* the gaining of political and trade advantages over poorer nations by a powerful country which rules them or helps them with money: *"Western Imperialism" is the name given in some eastern countries to the European and American political systems* —compare COLONIALISM, CAPITALISM
im·pe·ri·al·ist /ɪm'pɪərɪələst/ *adj, n* (*sometimes cap.*) **1** *often derog* (of) a supporter of IMPERIALISM **2** (of) someone who worked in an official position in a country of the British Empire: *an old/a former Imperialist* **3** (of) a supporter of the ways of life which Englishmen had in countries of their Empire: *an Imperialist feeling about foreigners* —**~ically** /ɪm,pɪərɪə'lɪstɪkli/ *adv* [Wa4]
im·pe·ri·al·is·tic /ɪm,pɪərɪə'lɪstɪk/ *adj often derog* **1** of IMPERIALISM **2** of an IMPERIALIST (1) —**~ally** *adv* [Wa4]
im·per·il /ɪm'perəl/ *v* **-ll-** (*AmE* **-l-**) [T1] to put (something or someone) in danger
im·pe·ri·ous /ɪm'pɪərɪəs/ *adj fml* **1** (too) commanding or as if commanding: *an imperious voice* **2** urgent: *an imperious command* —**~ly** *adv* —**~ness** *n* [U]
im·per·ish·a·ble /ɪm'perɪʃəbəl/ *adj* [Wa5] which will always exist or cannot wear out: *imperishable rubber/fame*
im·per·ma·nent /ɪm'pɜːmənənt||-ɜr-/ *adj* which will change or be lost: *an impermanent arrangement* —**-nence** *n* [U]
im·per·me·a·ble /ɪm'pɜːmɪəbəl||-ɜr-/ *adj* [Wa5] which substances (esp. liquids) cannot get through
im·per·son·al /ɪm'pɜːsənəl||-ɜr-/ *adj* **1** not showing or including one's feelings in one's behaviour **2** not human (in the phr. **impersonal forces**) **3** (in grammar) having no subject, or a subject represented by meaningless or empty "it" (such as *rained* in *it rained*) —**-ally** *adv*
im·per·so·nate /ɪm'pɜːsəneɪt||-ɜr-/ *v* [T1] to pretend to be by copying the appearance, behaviour, etc., of (another person): *He impersonates all the well-known politicians exactly right* —compare IMITATE (esp. 2) —**-nation** /ɪm,pɜːsə'neɪʃən||-ɜr-/ *n* [U;C] —**-nator** /ɪm'pɜːsəneɪtə^r^||-ɜr-/ *n*
im·per·ti·nent /ɪm'pɜːtənənt||-ɜr-/ *adj* rude or not respectful, esp. to an older or more important person —**-nence** *n* [U] —**-nently** *adv*
im·per·tur·ba·ble /,ɪmpə'tɜːbəbəl||-pər'tɜr-/ *adj* that cannot be worried; that remains calm and steady in spite of difficulties or confusion —**-bility** /,ɪmpətɜːbə'bɪləti||-pərtɜr-/ *n* [U] —**-bly** /,ɪmpə'tɜːbəbli||-pər'tɜr-/ *adv* [Wa3]
im·per·vi·ous /ɪm'pɜːvɪəs||-ɜr-/ *adj* [Wa5; (*to*)] **1** not allowing anything to pass through: *impervious to gases and liquids* **2** too certain in one's opinions to be changed: *impervious to reason/threats*
im·pe·ti·go /,ɪmpə'taɪgəʊ/ *n* [U] a type of infectious skin disease
im·pet·u·ous /ɪm'petʃʊəs/ *adj* showing swift action but lack of thought —**-osity** /ɪm,petʃʊ'ɒsəti||-'ɑs-/ *n* [U] —**-ously** /ɪm'petʃʊəsli/ *adv*

im·pe·tus /ˈɪmp$\frac{1}{2}$təs/ *n* **1** [U] the force of something moving: *The car ran down the hill under its own impetus* **2** [U;C] a push forward: (fig.) *Her speech gave an impetus to my ideas*

im·pi·e·ty /ɪmˈpaɪ$\frac{1}{2}$ti/ *n* **1** [U] lack of respect, esp. for religion **2** [C *often pl.*] an act showing lack of respect

im·pinge on /ɪmˈpɪndʒ/ also **impinge up·on**— *v prep* [T1 *pass. rare*] to have an effect on: *The need to see that justice is done impinges on every decision made in the courts*

im·pi·ous /ˈɪmpɪəs/ *adj* lacking respect usu. for religion; showing IMPIETY (1) —**~ly** *adv*

imp·ish /ˈɪmpɪʃ/ *adj* like a little devil: *an impish smile|a charmingly impish child* —**~ly** *adv* —**~ness** *n* [U]

im·plac·a·ble /ɪmˈplækəbəl/ *adj* which cannot be satisfied, or whose demands cannot be reduced: *an implacable enemy|implacable dislike*

im·plant /ɪmˈplɑːnt‖ɪmˈplænt/ *v* [T1 (*in, into*)] to fix in deeply, usu. into the body or mind

im·ple·ment[1] /ˈɪmpl$\frac{1}{2}$mənt/ *n* a tool or instrument: *farming/gardening implements*

im·ple·ment[2] /ˈɪmpl$\frac{1}{2}$ment/ *v* [T1] to carry out or put into practice: *to implement one's ideas*

im·pli·cate /ˈɪmpl$\frac{1}{2}$keɪt/ *v* [T1 (*in*)] *fml* to show that (someone else) is also to blame —compare INVOLVE

im·pli·ca·tion /ˌɪmpl$\frac{1}{2}$ˈkeɪʃən/ *n fml* **1** [U] the act of implicating (IMPLICATE) **2** [U] the act of IMPLYing **3** [C] a suggestion not expressed but understood: *He smiled, with the implication that he didn't believe me*

im·pli·cit /ɪmˈplɪs$\frac{1}{2}$t/ *adj* **1** [B (*in*)] (of a statement, rule, etc.) meant though not plainly expressed: *an implicit threat|a threat implicit in the way he looked* —compare EXPLICIT **2** [A;(B)] unquestioning and complete: *implicit trust* —**~ly** *adv*: *to obey an order implicitly*

im·plore /ɪmˈplɔːʳ‖-or/ *v* [Wv4;T1;V3] to ask (someone) in a begging manner (for something or to do something): *an imploring look*

im·plo·sion /ɪmˈpləʊʒən/ *n* [U;C] bursting (of air or other substances) towards the inside —compare EXPLOSION (1)

im·ply /ɪmˈplaɪ/ *v* [T1,5] **1** to express indirectly; suggest: *His manner implies that he would like to come with us.|You do not say you were present, but your words imply that you were* —see INFER (USAGE) **2** to cause to seem likely: *Refusal to answer implies guilt* **3** to cause to be necessary: *Rights imply duties*

im·po·lite /ˌɪmpəˈlaɪt/ *adj* not polite —**~ly** *adv* —**~ness** *n* [U;C]

im·pol·i·tic /ɪmˈpɒl$\frac{1}{2}$tɪk‖ɪmˈpɑ-/ *adj* (of an action) not well-judged for one's purpose; not wise

im·pon·de·ra·ble[1] /ɪmˈpɒndərəbəl‖-ˈpɑn-/ *adj* of which the importance cannot be calculated or measured exactly

imponderable[2] *n* [*usu. pl.*] something whose effects are IMPONDERABLE[1]: *Many imponderables influence the result of an election*

im·port[1] /ɪmˈpɔːt‖-ort/ *v* [Wv5;T1 (*from*)] to bring in (something). esp. from abroad: *imported silk* —**~er** /ˈɪmpɔːtəʳ‖-or-/ *n*

im·port[2] /ˈɪmpɔːt‖-ort/ *n* **1** [C *often pl.*] something brought into a country from abroad **2** [U] IMPORTATION (1): *the import of food from abroad* **3** [(*the*) S] *fml* the meaning: *the import of the speech*

im·por·tance /ɪmˈpɔːtəns‖-ɔr-/ *n* **1** [U] the quality or state of being important **2** [U9] the reason why something or someone is important: *The importance of washing one's hands is that it prevents infection*

im·por·tant /ɪmˈpɔːtənt‖-ɔr-/ *adj* **1** which matters a lot: *It's important to learn to read* **2** (of people) powerful; having influence —**~ly** *adv*

im·por·ta·tion /ˌɪmpɔːˈteɪʃən‖-ɔr-/ *n* **1** [U] the act of IMPORTing **2** [C] something new brought in from an outside area, esp. an object or way of behaviour typical of another place: *The phrase* LAISSEZ-FAIRE *is an importation from France*

im·por·tu·nate /ɪmˈpɔːtʃʊn$\frac{1}{2}$t‖ɪmˈpɔrtʃən$\frac{1}{2}$t/ *adj* **1** always demanding things **2** urgent —**~ly** *adv* —**-nity** /ˌɪmpəˈtjuːn$\frac{1}{2}$ti‖ˌɪmpərˈtuː-/ *n* [U]

im·por·tune /ˌɪmpəˈtjuːn‖ˌɪmpərˈtuːn/ *v* [T1 (*with*); V3;I∅] *fml* to beg (someone) repeatedly for things or to do things: *My children importune me with demands for new toys*

im·pose /ɪmˈpəʊz/ *v* [(*on, upon*)] **1** [T1] to establish (an additional payment) officially: *A new tax has been imposed on wine* **2** [T1] to force the acceptance of: *She imposed herself as their leader.|The conquerors imposed difficult conditions of peace on the defeated enemy* **3** [T1] to force into unwelcome closeness with, or on the attention of, another **4** [I∅] to take unfair advantage, in a way that causes additional work and trouble: *Thank you, but I don't think I'll stay the night: I don't want to impose on you*

im·pos·ing /ɪmˈpəʊzɪŋ/ *adj* powerful in appearance; strong or large in size: *an imposing view across the valley|an imposing building* —**~ly** *adv*

im·po·si·tion /ˌɪmpəˈzɪʃən/ *n* **1** [U (*of, on, upon*)] the act of imposing (IMPOSE) **2** [C (*on, upon*)] *becoming rare* something IMPOSEd, such as a punishment at school, a tax, etc. **3** [C (*on, upon*)] an act of taking unfair advantage of someone: *It's an imposition to ask us to stay at work till 7 o'clock at night*

im·pos·si·ble /ɪmˈpɒsəbəl‖ɪmˈpɑ-/ *adj* **1** [Wa5;B,B3] not possible **2** [B] hard to bear; very unpleasant: *His bad temper makes life impossible for all the family.|You're impossible!|You're the most impossible person I've ever met!* —**-bility** /ɪmˌpɒsəˈbɪl$\frac{1}{2}$ti‖ɪmˌpɑ-/ *n* [U] —**-bly** /ɪmˈpɒsəbli‖ɪmˈpɑ-/ *adv* [Wa3,5]: (*not used with verbs*) *impossibly difficult*

im·pos·tor /ɪmˈpɒstəʳ‖ɪmˈpɑs-/ *n* [C; *you*+N] someone who deceives by pretending to be someone else

im·pos·ture /ɪmˈpɒstʃəʳ‖ɪmˈpɑs-/ *n* [C;U] (an act or example of) pretending to be someone else so as to deceive people

im·po·tent /ˈɪmpətənt/ *adj* **1** [B;F3] lacking power to do things: *a government that seems impotent in dealing with the trade unions|He wanted to do something for the people in the accident, but he was quite impotent to help* **2** [Wa5;B] (of a man) generally unable to perform the sex act —**-tence** *n* [U] —**-tently** *adv*

im·pound /ɪmˈpaʊnd/ *v* [T1] *fml* or *law* to take and shut up officially until claimed (esp. something lost or not taken care of)

im·pov·e·rish /ɪmˈpɒvərɪʃ‖ɪmˈpɑ-/ *v* [Wv5;T1 *often pass.*] **1** to make poor **2** to make worse or incomplete by the removal of something important; DEPLETE (1): *impoverished by the death of that great artist*

im·prac·ti·ca·ble /ɪmˈpræktɪkəbəl/ *adj* [Wa5] that cannot be used in practice: *The building plans are impracticable* —**-bility** /ɪmˌpræktɪkəˈbɪl$\frac{1}{2}$ti/ *n* [U] —**-bly** /ɪmˈpræktɪkəbli/ *adv* [Wa3,5]

im·prac·ti·cal /ɪmˈpræktɪkəl/ *adj* not sensible or reasonable; not practical: *an impractical person who can't even boil an egg|an impractical plan that is impossible to fulfil* —**-cally** /ɪmˈpræktɪkli/ *adv* [Wa4] —**-cality** /ɪmˌpræktɪˈkæl$\frac{1}{2}$ti/ *n* [U]

im·pre·ca·tion /ˌɪmprɪˈkeɪʃən/ *n fml* **1** [C] a curse; swear word **2** [U] the act of cursing

im·preg·na·ble /ɪmˈpregnəbəl/ *adj* which cannot

be entered or conquered by attack —**-bility** /ɪmˌpregnəˈbɪlɨti/ *n* [U] —**-bly** /ɪmˈpregnəbli/ *adv* [Wa3]

im·preg·nate /ˈɪmpregneɪt‖ɪmˈpreg-/ *v* [T1] **1** *fml* to make PREGNANT (1) **2** [(*with*)] to cause a substance to enter and spread completely through (another substance) **3** (of a substance) to enter and spread completely through (another substance)

im·pre·sa·ri·o /ˌɪmprɨˈsɑːriəʊ/ *n* **-os** **1** the business MANAGER of a theatre or concert company, or of a single famous performer —compare ENTREPRENEUR (2) **2** a person who arranges for performances of various types in various theatres, concert halls, etc.

im·press[1] /ɪmˈpres/ *v* **1** [T1 (*into, on*)] to press (something) into something else, or to make (a mark) as a result of this pressure: *a pattern impressed on the clay pots before baking* **2** [T1] to fill (someone) with admiration: *I was very impressed by/at/with his performance* **3** [D1+*on/with*] to make the importance of (something) clear to (someone): *My father impressed on me the value of hard work*

im·press[2] /ˈɪmpres/ *n fml & lit* the mark left when a SEAL[2] or other object is IMPRESSed[1] on something: (fig.) *Time has left its impress upon him*

im·press[3] /ɪmˈpres/ *v* [Wv5;T1 (*into*)] (esp. in former times) to force into naval service

im·pres·sion /ɪmˈpreʃən/ *n* **1** [U] the act of IMPRESSing[1] or state of being impressed **2** [C] a mark left by pressure: *the impression of a heel in the mud* **3** [C] the image a person or thing gives to someone's mind, esp. as regards its strength or quality: *a strong impression|a bad impression|First impressions are often wrong.|What's your impression of him?—I mean as a worker, not as a person* **4** [C,C5a *often sing.*] a feeling about the nature of something: *I had an impression of largeness, roundness, purple and red, but I couldn't understand what the picture was supposed to represent.|I got the impression (that) they'd just had an argument.|I asked him for a job* **under the impression that** *he was the head of the firm—but he wasn't* **5** [C *often sing.*] the copies or copy of something made at one printing —compare REPRINT[2], EDITION (1) **6** [C] an attempt to copy in a funny way the most interesting parts of a person's appearance or behaviour, esp. when done as a theatrical performance: *He did/gave an impression of the minister which made us all laugh*

im·pres·sio·na·ble /ɪmˈpreʃənəbəl/ *adj* (of a person) easy to influence, often with the result that one's feelings and ideas change easily and esp. that one is ready to admire other people —**-bly** /ɪmˈpreʃənəbli/ *adv* [Wa3] —**-bility** /ɪmˌpreʃənəˈbɪlɨti/ *n* [U]

im·pres·sion·is·m /ɪmˈpreʃənɪzəm/ *n* [U (*often cap.*)] **1** a style of painting (esp. in France, 1870–1900) which produces effects by light and colour rather than by details of form **2** a style of music (in France 1870–1914, and in England later) that produces feelings and images by the quality of sounds rather than by a pattern of notes —compare EXPRESSIONISM

im·pres·sion·ist[1] /ɪmˈpreʃənɨst/ *n* **1** (*often cap.*) a person who practises or favours IMPRESSIONISM in painting or music **2** a person who does IMPRESSIONs (6), esp. as a theatrical performance

impressionist[2] *adj* (*often cap.*) of or about IMPRESSIONISM: *an impressionist painter/painting*

im·pres·sion·is·tic /ɪmˌpreʃəˈnɪstɪk/ *adj* **1** based on IMPRESSIONs rather than on knowledge, fact, or detailed study **2** IMPRESSIONIST[2] —**~ally** *adv* [Wa4]

im·pres·sive /ɪmˈpresɪv/ *adj* causing admiration by giving one a feeling of size and/or importance —**~ly** *adv* —**~ness** *n* [U]

im·pri·ma·tur /ˌɪmprɨˈmeɪtəʳ, -ˈmɑː-/ *n* [(*the*) S] **1** official permission to print a book, esp. as given by the ROMAN CATHOLIC church **2** *sometimes humor* approval, esp. from an important person

im·print[1] /ɪmˈprɪnt/ *v* [T1 (*on*)] to print or press (a mark) on something: *The shape of the coin was imprinted on his hand.*|(fig.) *Every detail is imprinted on my mind*

im·print[2] /ˈɪmprɪnt/ *n* **1** a mark left on or in something **2** the name of the PUBLISHER as it appears on a book: *This dictionary is* PUBLISH*ed under the Longman imprint*

im·pris·on /ɪmˈprɪzən/ *v* [T1] to put in prison or keep in a place or state from which one cannot get out as one wishes —**~ment** *n* [U;(C)]

im·prob·a·bil·i·ty /ɪmˌprɒbəˈbɪlɨti‖-ˌprɑ-/ *n* **1** [U] being improbable: *the improbability of his not arriving in time* **2** [C] something unlikely to happen

im·prob·a·ble /ɪmˈprɒbəbəl‖-ˈprɑ-/ *adj* not likely to have happened or to be going to happen: *an improbable idea|Snow is improbable at this time of year* —**-bly** *adv* [Wa3]

im·promp·tu[1] /ɪmˈprɒmptjuː‖ɪmˈprɑmptuː/ *adj, adv* [Wa5] (said or done) at once without preparation

impromptu[2] *n* **-tus** (in music) a short piece which may have been made up without preparation, or seems so

im·prop·er /ɪmˈprɒpəʳ‖-ˈprɑ-/ *adj* **1** not suitable: *"What a terrible hat!" is an improper remark to make when the wearer is present* **2** not correct: *the improper use of a singular verb with a plural subject* **3** showing thoughts which are socially undesirable, esp. about sex (esp. in the phr. **an improper suggestion**, made by a man to a woman) —**~ly** *adv*

improper frac·tion /ˌ·ˌ·· ˈ··/ *n* a FRACTION in which the number above the line is greater than the one below it: $\frac{107}{8}$ *is an improper fraction*

im·pro·pri·e·ty /ˌɪmprəˈpraɪɨti/ *n* **1** [U] the quality or state of being improper **2** [C] a socially undesirable act

im·prove /ɪmˈpruːv/ *v* **1** [T1] to use well and/or make better: *I want to improve my abilities.|I'll improve the shape of the handle so that it's easier for you to use* **2** [Wv5;T1] to increase the value of (land or property) by farming, building, etc. **3** [IØ] to get better: *His health's improving.|He's improving in health*

im·prove·ment /ɪmˈpruːvmənt/ *n* [U;C] (a sign of) the act of improving or the state of being improved

USAGE An **improvement** *in* something means that it has got better: *There has been an* **improvement** *in the weather.* One can speak of an **improvement** *on* something, only when 2 things are compared: *Today's weather is an* **improvement** *on yesterday's.*

improve on also **improve up·on**— *v prep* [T1] to produce or be something better than; BETTER[5] (2): *Tom has never improved on his first book*

im·prov·i·dent /ɪmˈprɒvɨdənt‖-ˈprɑ-/ *adj* (esp. of someone who wastes money) not preparing for the future —**-dence** *n* [U] —**-dently** *adv*

im·pro·vise /ˈɪmprəvaɪz/ *v* [T1;IØ] **1** to do or make (something one has not prepared for) because a sudden need has arisen: *I forgot the words of my speech, so I had to improvise.|She improvised a cake although she had no sugar* **2** to make up (a piece of music) as one is playing —**-visation** /ˌɪmprəvaɪˈzeɪʃən‖-prəvə-/ *n* [U;C]

im·pru·dent /ɪmˈpruːdənt/ *adj* unwise and thoughtless (in one's actions) —**-dence** *n* [U] —**-dently** *adv*

im·pu·dent /ˈɪmpjʊdənt‖-pjə-/ *adj* shamelessly

bold, esp. to an older or more important person —**-dence** *n* [U] —**-dently** *adv*

im·pugn /ɪm'pjuːn/ *v* [T1] *fml* to raise doubts about (someone's acts, qualities, etc.)

im·pulse /'ɪmpʌls/ *n* **1** [C] a single push, or a force acting for a short time in one direction along a wire, nerve, etc.: *an electrical impulse|a nervous impulse|*(fig.) *A sudden impulse of anger arose in him* **2** [C,C3;U,U3] a sudden wish to do something: *She almost yielded to an unexpected impulse to dance in the street.|a man of impulse*

impulse buy·ing /'·· ,··/ *n* [U] the sudden urge to buy goods one does not really want. It is encouraged by shopkeepers who put suitable objects where they can easily be reached

im·pul·sion /ɪm'pʌlʃən/ *n* **1** [U] the act of IMPELling or state of being impelled **2** [C,C3] a push forward; IMPULSE: (fig.) *an impulsion to act*

im·pul·sive /ɪm'pʌlsɪv/ *adj* having or showing a tendency to act suddenly without thinking about the suitability, results, etc., of one's acts —compare IMPULSE (2) —**~ly** *adv* —**~ness** *n* [U]

im·pu·ni·ty /ɪm'pjuːnǯti/ *n* [U] certainty of not being punished (usu. in the phr. **with impunity**)

im·pure /ɪm'pjʊəʳ/ *adj* [Wa2] **1** not pure, but mixed with something else: *impure drugs* **2** morally bad; of bad sexual habits: *impure thoughts|an impure life*

im·pu·ri·ty /ɪm'pjʊərǯti/ *n* **1** [U;C] the state of not being pure, or an act showing this **2** [C] something mixed with something else so that it is not pure

im·pu·ta·tion /,ɪmpjʊ'teɪʃən‖-pjə-/ *n* **1** [U] the act of imputing something to someone (IMPUTE TO) **2** [C] a charge of crime or suggestion of something bad: *an imputation of guilt*

impute to /ɪm'pjuːt/ *v prep* [D1;V4b] to blame (something) on (something or someone): *The police impute the rise in crime to the greater freedom enjoyed by young people*

in¹ /ɪn/ *prep* **1** (so as to be) contained by (something with depth, length, and height); within; inside: *to live in the house|to keep the money in a box|to sit in a car* (compare *on a bicycle*)*|to go swimming in the sea* (compare *sailing on the sea*)*| lying in bed* (compare *lying on the bed, outside the covers*)*|"lying in 8 feet of water"* (SEU W.)*|*(*not fml*) *He came in* (=into) *the room.|Get in* (=into) *the car!|*(fig.) *I wonder what's in his mind* **2** *infml* through in an inward direction: *He came in the door* **3** surrounded by (an area); within and not beyond: *cows in a field|my face in* (=within the frame of) *the mirror|a plant in the window* (=on a shelf just inside)*|in the corner of the room* (compare *at the corner of Broadway and 42nd street*)*|wounded in the leg* **4** (with the names of countries, seas, and large towns) at; not outside: *in London|in France| an island in the Atlantic* **5** (with the name of a place connected with an activity) attending for the usual purpose: *George is in hospital with a broken leg* (compare *George works at the hospital*)*.|in prison for stealing|in church praying* **6** shown or described as the subject of: *a character in a story| the people in this photograph* **7** (showing employment): *She's in business/in politics/in insurance/in the law.|to take a university degree in history|He's in* (=works with, at) *plastics/building/furniture.|He was in conversation with a priest* **8** wearing: *dressed in silk|a girl in red/in a fur coat|a man in armour/in uniform* **9** towards (a direction): *in this direction|in the wrong direction|in all directions at once* **10** using to express oneself; with or by means of: *Write it in pencil/in ink/in French.|painted in oils|printed in red* **11** (with certain periods of time) at some time during; at the time of: *in January|in Spring|in 1976| in the 18th century|in the* (*early*) *afternoon* (compare *on Monday afternoon*)*|in the night* (compare *at night*)*|in his youth|in the 1930's|in the First World War|in the past* **12** (with lengths of time) **a** during not more than the space of: *He learnt English in 3 weeks* (=and then he knew it; compare *He learnt English for 3 weeks*) **b** after; at the end of: *It's 2 o'clock; I'll come in an hour* (=at 3 o'clock; compare *for an hour* =from 2 to 3)*|"will be finished in a month or so"* (SEU S.) —compare **in** TIME¹ (36) **c** *esp. AmE* (*with* no, not, first, only *and* SUPERLATIVES²) during; for: *He hasn't had a good meal in a week.|the first time I've seen her in 2 years* —compare WITHIN² (1) **13** (showing the way something is done or happens): *in public* (=publicly)*|in secret* (=secretly)*|in fun|in* EARNEST¹*|"the way in which we would make a living"* (SEU S.) **14** (showing division and arrangement) so as to be: *Pack them in 10's* (=10 in each parcel)*.|in rows|in groups| to stand in a circle|Cut it in 2* (=into 2 halves) **15** (showing a relation or PROPORTION) per: *a slope of 1 in 3|to pay a tax of 40p in the £* **16** (showing quantity or number): *in large numbers|They arrived in* (*their*) THOUSANDS*.|in part* (=partly) **17** as to; as regards: *weak in judgment|lacking in courage| better in every way|They're equal in distance.|10 feet in length/in depth* **18** having or so as to have (a condition): *in difficulties|in danger|in good health|in ruins|in a hurry|in doubt|in tears|to be/fall in love* **19** as a/an; by way of: *What did you give him in return?|She said nothing in reply* **20 as in** as if part of: *The beautiful scene is still before my eyes, as in a painting* **21 in all** together; as the total **22 in that** because: *"I'm in a slightly awkward position, in that he's not arriving until the 10th"* (SEU S.)

in² *adv* **1** (so as to be) contained or surrounded; away from the open air, the outside, etc.: *Open the bag and put the money in.|a cup of tea with sugar in| Let's go in there where it's warm* —compare OUT¹ (1) **2** (so as to be) present (esp. at home or under the roof of a building): *I'm afraid Mr. Jones is out, but he'll be in/he'll come in again soon.|Let's spend the evening in* (=at home) *watching television| "Come in!"* (when someone knocks at a door)*|The train isn't in yet/will be in in 5 minutes* —compare OUT¹ (2) **3** from a number of people, or from all directions to a central point: *Letters have been coming/pouring in from everybody who heard the news on the radio.|Papers/marks must be in by Monday* —compare OUT¹ (4) **4** so as to be added or included where not formerly present: *The picture is almost finished—I can paint in the sky later.* (=I can paint the sky in later.)*|I very much like your play—could you write in a part for me?* —compare OUT¹ (6) **5 a** (of one side in a game such as cricket) BATting: *Our side were in/went in to* BAT *first.|*(fig.) *The Labour party are in* (=elected) **b** (of the ball in a game such as tennis) inside the line —opposite **out** **6** (so as to be) fashionable: *Long skirts came in* (opposite **went out**) *last year; they're in* (opposite **out**) *now* **7** (of the TIDE (=sea water)) close to the coast; (so as to be) high **8 be in at** to be present at (an event) **9 be in for** *not fml* to be about to have (trouble, bad weather, etc.) **10 be/get in on** *not fml* to take part in; have/get a share in **11 be in with** *not fml* to be friendly with: *He's* (*well*) *in with the Board of Directors* **12 day in, day out, year in, year out,** etc. day after day, year after year, etc., without change **13 go/be in for** to enter/be entered on the list for (a competition) **14 have (got) it in for (someone)** *infml* to be waiting to do harm to (someone) **15 in and out (of)** sometimes inside and sometimes outside: *He's been in and out of prison for years*

in³ *adj* [Wa5] **1** [A] used for sending something to

one, from someone else: *I found the letter in my in* TRAY —opposite **out** **2** [A] *sl* fashionable: *That new restaurant is the in place to go now* **3** [A] *not fml* shared by only a few favoured people: *an in joke* **4** [F] (of a fire) lit; burning: *Is the fire still in?* —compare OUT³ (4), ON² (7)

in⁴ *n* **the ins and outs (of something)**: the various parts and difficulties to be seen when something is looked at in detail: *the ins and outs of politics*

in- also **il-**, **im-**, **ir-**— *prefix* [*adj, n→adj, n*] not; non-; un-

USAGE The usual form is **il-** before *l* (*illimitable*), **im-** before *b, m,* or *p* (*imbalance, immoral, impractical*), **ir-** before *r* (*irregular*), and **in-** before other letters (*inability, independent, insensitive*).

-in *comb form* [*v→n*[C]] (added to words describing a meeting where people act together): SIT IN,| TEACH-IN,|PHONE-IN

in·a·bil·i·ty /ˌɪnəˈbɪlɨti/ *n* [U,U3;S;S3] lack of power or skill: (*an*) *inability to work alone*

in·ac·ces·si·ble /ˌɪnəkˈsesəbəl/ *adj* [(*to*)] which cannot be reached —**-bility** /ˌɪnəksesəˈbɪlɨti/ *n* [U] —**-bly** /ˌɪnəkˈsesəbli/ *adv* [Wa3]

in·ac·cu·rate /ɪnˈækjʊrɨt‖-kjə-/ *adj* not correct; not ACCURATE —**~ly** *adv* —**-racy** /ɪˈnækjʊrəsi‖-kjə-/ *n* [U;C *often pl.*]

in·ac·tion /ɪnˈækʃən/ *n* [U] lack of action or activity; quality or state of doing nothing

in·ac·tive /ɪnˈæktɪv/ *adj* not active —**~ly** *adv* —**-tivity** /ˌɪnækˈtɪvɨti/ *n* [U]

in·ad·e·qua·cy /ɪnˈædɨkwɨsi/ *n* **1** [U; (*the*) S] the quality or state of being INADEQUATE: *a troublesome feeling of personal inadequacy|an inadequacy of water* **2** [C *often pl.*] an example of incompleteness or of unsatisfactory quality: *several inadequacies in your report*

in·ad·e·quate /ɪnˈædɨkwɨt/ *adj* **1** [(*to, for*)] not good enough in quality, ability, size, etc. (for some act): *I feel inadequate to the occasion.|The food was inadequate for 14 people* **2** (of a person) not good at looking after oneself, esp. in social life —**~ly** *adv*

in·ad·mis·si·ble /ˌɪnədˈmɪsəbəl/ *adj* [Wa5] which cannot be allowed —**-bility** /ˌɪnədmɪsəˈbɪlɨti/ *n* [U] —**-bly** /ˌɪnədˈmɪsəbli/ *adv* [Wa3,5]

in·ad·ver·tent /ˌɪnədˈvɜːtənt‖-ɜr-/ *adj* (done) without paying attention or by accident —**~ly** *adv*: *He inadvertently upset the bowl of flowers* —**-tence** *n* [U;C]

in·a·li·e·na·ble /ɪnˈeɪlɪənəbəl/ also (*now rare*) **unalienable**— *adj* [Wa5] which cannot be taken away (often in the phr. **inalienable rights**)

i·nam·o·ra·ta /ɪˌnæməˈrɑːtə/ **-tas** /təz/— *n* [*often with poss.*] *now rare* the woman whom a man loves

i·nane /ɪˈneɪn/ *adj* empty of meaning; really stupid —**~ly** *adv*

in·an·i·mate /ɪnˈænɨmɨt/ *adj* [Wa5] not living —**~ly** —**~ness** *n* [U]

in·a·ni·tion /ˌɪnəˈnɪʃən/ *n* [U] **1** *tech* weakness from lack of food and water: *died of inanition* **2** absence or loss of the ability to act effectively, esp. with regard to society, morality, or the mind

i·nan·i·ty /ɪˈnænɨti/ *n* **1** [U] the quality or state of being INANE **2** [C *often pl.*] an INANE act or remark

in·ap·pli·ca·ble /ɪnˈæplɪkəbəl/ *adj* [Wa5] which cannot be used or is unrelated to the subject —**-bility** /ɪnˌæplɪkəˈbɪlɨti/ *n* [U] —**-bly** /ɪˈnæplɪkəbli/ *adv* [Wa3,5]

in·ap·pro·pri·ate /ˌɪnəˈprəʊpriɨt/ *adj* [(*for, to*)] not suitable: *Your short dress is inappropriate for a formal party* —**~ly** *adv* —**~ness** *n* [U]

in·apt /ɪnˈæpt/ *adj* [Wa2; (*for*)] (esp. of something non-material) unsuitable —**~ly** *adv* —**~ness** *n* [U]

in·ap·ti·tude /ɪnˈæptɨtjuːd‖-tuːd/ *n* [U (*for*)] lack of ability: *His inaptitude for the job is very unfortunate*

in·ar·tic·u·late /ˌɪnɑːˈtɪkjʊlɨt‖ˌɪnɑrˈtɪkjəlɨt/ *adj* **1** (of speech) not well-formed **2** (of a person) not speaking clearly, so that the intended meaning is not expressed or is hard to hear —**~ly** *adv* —**~ness** *n* [U]

in·art·is·tic /ˌɪnɑːˈtɪstɪk‖-ɑr-/ *adj* **1** (of people) without ability or not skilful in understanding drawing and painting (also sometimes music and literature) **2** (of works of art) not showing ability and skill —**~ally** *adv* [Wa4]

in·as·much as /ˌɪnəzˈmʌtʃ əz/ *conj* **1** owing to the fact that; because: *Forgive them, inasmuch as they are young* (=Forgive all of them) **2** *now rare* to the degree that: *Forgive them, inasmuch as they are young* (=particularly the younger ones)

in·at·ten·tion /ˌɪnəˈtenʃən/ *n* [U (*to*)] lack of attention

in·at·ten·tive /ˌɪnəˈtentɪv/ *adj* [(*to*)] not giving attention: *an inattentive pupil* —**~ly** *adv* —**~ness** *n* [U]

in·au·di·ble /ɪnˈɔːdəbəl/ *adj* that is too quiet to be heard —**-bility** /ɪˌnɔːdəˈbɪlɨti/ *n* [U] —**-bly** /ɪˈnɔːdəbli/ *adv* [Wa3]

in·au·gu·ral /ɪˈnɔːgjʊrəl‖-gjə-/ *adj* [Wa5;A] concerning an inauguration (INAUGURATE): *an inaugural ceremony*

in·au·gu·rate /ɪˈnɔːgjʊreɪt‖-gjə-/ *v* [T1] **1** [*usu. pass.*] to introduce (someone important) into a new place or job by holding a special ceremony **2** to start (a public affair) with a ceremony **3** to be the beginning of (something, esp. an important period of time): *The introduction of free milk inaugurated a period of better health for children*

in·aus·pi·cious /ˌɪnɔːˈspɪʃəs/ *adj* seeming to show bad luck to come; not giving good hopes for the future —compare AUSPICIOUS —**~ly** —**~ness** *n* [U]

in·board /ˈɪnbɔːd‖-bord/ *adj* [Wa5;A;(B)] **1** inside a boat: *an inboard motor* **2** (of a boat) having the motor inside —compare OUTBOARD MOTOR

in·born /ˌɪnˈbɔːn◂‖-ɔrn/ *adj* [Wa5] present from birth; part of one's nature: *an inborn ability to do sums|an inborn love of jokes*

in·bound /ˈɪnbaʊnd/ *adj* [Wa5] *AmE* (when travelling) coming home

in·bred /ˌɪnˈbred◂/ *adj* [Wa5] **1** having become part of one's nature as a result of early training **2** (resulting from being) bred from closely related members of a family

in·breed·ing /ˈɪnbriːdɪŋ/ *n* [U] **1** breeding from (closely) related members of a family: *Inbreeding is used to get pure white animals or plants* **2** *derog* limitation of interest or activity to a small group of closely related people or ideas: *the* INTELLECTUAL *inbreeding that one feels in some university departments*

Inc /ɪŋk; *fml* ɪnˈkɔːpəreɪtɨd‖-ɔr-/ *abbrev. for*: (in the US) INCORPORATED (2): *General Motors, Inc* —compare LTD

in·cal·cu·la·ble /ɪnˈkælkjʊləbəl‖-kjə-/ *adj* [Wa5] **1** which cannot be counted or measured, esp. if very great **2** (esp. of people's qualities, feelings, etc.) changeable —**-bly** *adv* [Wa3,5]

in·can·des·cent /ˌɪnkænˈdesənt‖-kən-/ *adj* giving a bright light when heated: (fig.) *the incandescent spirit of freedom* —**-cence** *n* [U] —**-cently** *adv*

in·can·ta·tion /ˌɪnkænˈteɪʃən/ *n* [U;C] (the saying of) words used in magic

in·ca·pa·ble /ɪnˈkeɪpəbəl/ *adj* [F (*of*); (B)] **1** not able to do something: *Flowers are incapable of growing/growth in strong winds* **2** too good to do something bad: *I'm incapable of deceiving you* —**-bility** /ɪnˌkeɪpəˈbɪlɨti/ *n* [U] —**-bly** /ɪnˈkeɪpəbli/ *adv* [Wa3]

in·ca·pa·ci·tate /ˌɪnkəˈpæsɨteɪt/ *v* [T1 (*for*)] to make (someone) not able to do something

in·ca·pa·ci·ty /ˌɪnkəˈpæsɪ̇ti/ *n* [U (for), U3;S (*for*), S3] lack of ability or power (to do something): *His incapacity for kindness makes everybody dislike him.|an incapacity to laugh*

in·car·ce·rate /ɪnˈkɑːsəreɪt‖-ɑr-/ *v* [T1] *fml* to imprison —**-ration** /ɪnˌkɑːsəˈreɪʃən‖-ɑr-/ *n* [U;(C)]

in·car·nate¹ /ɪnˈkɑːnɪ̇t‖-ɑr-/ *adj* [Wa5;E;(B)] in the form of a body (not a spirit or idea): *the devil incarnate|She was happiness incarnate*

in·car·nate² /ɪnˈkɑːneɪt‖-ɑr-/ *v* [T1 (*in, as*)] **1** [*usu. pass.*] to put (an idea, spirit, etc.) into bodily form **2** [*often pass.*] EMBODY (1)

in·car·na·tion /ˌɪnkɑːˈneɪʃən‖-ɑr-/ *n* **1** [U] the act of incarnating (INCARNATE²) or state of being INCARNATE¹ **2** [C] time passed in a particular bodily form or state: *She believed that in a former incarnation she had been an Egyptian queen* **3** [C] a person or thing that is the perfect example of a quality, or that possesses the quality to an unusually great degree (esp. in the phr. **the incarnation of**): *She's the incarnation of all goodness*

Incarnation *n* [*the*+R] (in Christianity) the coming of God to earth in the body of Jesus Christ

in·cau·tious /ɪnˈkɔːʃəs/ *adj* not careful; (doing things) which will lead to trouble —**~ly** *adv* —**~ness** *n* [U]

in·cen·di·a·ris·m /ɪnˈsendɪərɪzəm/ *n* [U] INCENDIARY² action or behaviour

in·cen·di·a·ry¹ /ɪnˈsendɪəri‖-dieri/ *n* **1** also **incendiary bomb** /·ˈ···· ˌ·/— a bomb which causes fires **2** *rare* a person who burns things down (ARSONist) or causes trouble because of his violent opinions

incendiary² *adj* [Wa5;A] **1** which causes fires **2** (of a person or behaviour) causing fires or causing trouble by violent (INFLAMMATORY) means

in·cense¹ /ˈɪnsens/ *n* [U] any of several substances that give off a sweet smell when burnt, some of which may be used in religious services

in·cense² /ɪnˈsens/ *v* [Wv5 (*at*); T1 *often pass.*] to make (someone) very angry

in·cen·tive /ɪnˈsentɪv/ *n* **1** [U,U3;C;C3] an encouragement to greater activity: *His interest gave me (an) incentive and I worked twice as hard* **2** [U *usu. neg.*] the urge and ability to get things done: *He's got no/little incentive*

in·cep·tion /ɪnˈsepʃən/ *n fml* the beginning

in·cer·ti·tude /ɪnˈsɜːtɪ̇tjuːd‖ɪnˈsɜrtɪ̇tuːd/ *n* [U] *pomp* uncertainty

in·ces·sant /ɪnˈsesənt/ *adj* [Wa5] never stopping —**~ly** *adv*

in·cest /ˈɪnsest/ *n* [U] a sexual relationship between close relatives in a family, as between brother and sister

in·ces·tu·ous /ɪnˈsestʃʊəs/ *adj* **1** (of people or relationships) including or doing acts of INCEST **2** *esp. derog* (of relationships) unusually close, esp. in a way that does not include people from outside or that is thought to be unhealthy —**~ly** *adv*

inch¹ /ɪntʃ/ *n* **1** a measure of length; 1/12 of a foot (about 0·025 metres) —see WEIGHTS & MEASURES TABLE **2 inch by inch** by small degrees **3 by inches a** very closely; only just **b** gradually (esp. in the phrs. **kill/die by inches**) **4 every inch** completely; in all ways: *every inch a man* **5 Give him an inch and he'll take a yard/a mile** If you allow him a little freedom or power he'll try to get a lot more **6 within an inch of** very near: *He came within an inch of death* **7 not give/budge an inch** not to change one's opinions when other people try to make you agree to theirs: *I tried every argument, but he didn't budge an inch*

inch² *v* **1** [X9;L9] to make (one's way) slowly and with difficulty in the way stated: *I inched (my way) through the narrow space between the cars* **2** [X9] to move (something) slowly and with difficulty in the way stated

in·cho·ate /ɪnˈkəʊɪ̇t/ *adj* [Wa5] *fml* (of desires, wishes, plans, etc.) at the beginning of development; not fully formed

in·ci·dence /ˈɪnsɪ̇dəns/ *n* [(*the*) S] the rate of happening: *There's a high incidence of disease there.|Disease has a high rate of incidence*

in·ci·dent¹ /ˈɪnsɪ̇dənt/ *n* **1** an event, esp. one in a story: *That was one of the strangest incidents in my life* **2** an event that includes violence, such as fighting or explosions: *In a recent incident 2 bombs exploded*

incident² *adj* [Wa5;F (*to*)] *fml* forming a part (of); connected (with): *the duties incident to a position of responsibility|These duties are incident upon me as a teacher*

in·ci·den·tal /ˌɪnsɪ̇ˈdentəl◂/ *adj, n* [(*to*)] **1** (something) happening or appearing irregularly or as a less important part of something important which spreads over a period of time **2** (something, esp. a fact or detail which is) unimportant

incidental ex·pens·es /ˌ···· ·ˈ··/ *n* [P] additional money which must be claimed to pay for food, travel, etc., which one needs for something such as a business trip

in·ci·den·tal·ly /ˌɪnsɪ̇ˈdentəli/ *adv* [Wa5] (used for adding something to what was said before, either on the same or another subject) BY THE WAY: *I must go now. Incidentally, if you want that book I'll bring it next time*

incidental mu·sic /ˌ···· ˈ··/ *n* [U] descriptive music played during a play to give the right feeling or to go with the action

in·ci·den·tals /ˌɪnsɪ̇ˈdentəlz/ *n* [P] additional things which one needs or which appear to be necessary after the main things have been done, bought, etc.

in·cin·e·rate /ɪnˈsɪnəreɪt/ *v* [T1 *often pass.*] to destroy (unwanted things) by burning —**-ration** /ɪnˌsɪnəˈreɪʃən/ *n* [U;(C)]

in·cin·e·ra·tor /ɪnˈsɪnəreɪtəʳ/ *n* a machine for burning unwanted things

in·cip·i·ence /ɪnˈsɪpɪəns/ also **in·cip·i·en·cy** /-pɪənsi/— *n* [U] *fml or med* the state or fact of being INCIPIENT

in·cip·i·ent /ɪnˈsɪpɪənt/ *adj* [Wa5] *fml or med* at an early stage: *incipient disease*

in·cise /ɪnˈsaɪz/ *v* [T1 *often pass.*] *tech* to make a cut into (something)

in·ci·sion /ɪnˈsɪʒən/ *n* [U;C] *tech, esp. med* the act of cutting or a cut into something, done with a special tool for a special reason: *An incision was made into the diseased organ*

in·ci·sive /ɪnˈsaɪsɪv/ *adj apprec* going directly to the centre or main point of the matter that is being considered —**~ly** *adv*

in·ci·sor /ɪnˈsaɪzəʳ/ *n* any of the teeth at the front of the mouth, which have one cutting edge, 4 in each jaw in man —see picture at TOOTH

in·cite /ɪnˈsaɪt/ *v* **1** [T1 (*to*); V3] to (try to) cause or encourage (someone) to a strong feeling or action: *His words incited the soldiers (to anger).|He incited them to rise up against their officers* **2** [T1] to (try to) cause or lead to (a strong feeling or action): *His words incited anger in/among the soldiers* —**~ment** *n* [U;(C): (*to*)]: *Incitement to violence is sometimes a crime*

in·ci·vil·i·ty /ˌɪnsɪ̇ˈvɪlɪ̇ti/ *n* [U;C] *fml* (an act of) impoliteness

in·clem·ent /ɪnˈklemənt/ *adj fml* (of weather) bad, esp. cold or stormy —**-ency** *n* [U]

in·cli·na·tion /ˌɪnklɪ̇ˈneɪʃən/ *n* **1** [S] a slope; sloping position **2** [C *usu. sing.*] a movement from a higher to a lower place: *an inclination of the* *head/the hand* **3** [U;C: (*to, towards,* 3) *often pl.*] that which one likes; liking; wish for: *You always follow your own inclinations instead of thinking of our feelings.|I've no inclinations towards life as a doctor/no inclination to be a doctor* **4** [C3 *usu. sing.*] *fml* a tendency: *I've an inclination to get fat*

in·cline¹ /ɪn'klaɪn/ *v* **1** [T1;I∅] to (cause to) slope **2** [T1] to cause to move downward: *to incline one's head (in greeting)* **3** [X9, esp. *to, towards*; V3] to tend to encourage or cause (someone) to feel, think, etc.: *The news inclines me to change my mind/inclined me to anger* **4** [L9, esp. *to, towards*; I3] to tend (to); feel drawn (to): *I incline to (take) the opposite point of view* **5** [L9, esp. *to, towards*; L3] to tend (to); be likely (to show a quality): *I incline to/towards tiredness in winter* —compare INCLINED (2)

in·cline² /'ɪnklaɪn/ *n* a slope: *a steep incline*

in·clined /ɪn'klaɪnd/ *adj* [F3] **1** encouraged; feeling a wish (to): *The news makes me inclined to change my mind* **2** likely; tending (to): *I'm inclined to get tired easily*

inclined plane /·,· '·/ *n tech* a flat sloping surface that meets the horizon at an angle which is less than a right angle

in·close /ɪn'kləʊz/ *v* [Wv5;T1 (*by, in*) *often pass.*] ENCLOSE

in·clos·ure /ɪn'kləʊʒəʳ/ *n* ENCLOSURE

in·clude /ɪn'kluːd/ *v* [T1,4] **1** to have as a part; contain in addition to other parts: *The price includes postage charges* **2** to put in with something else: *I included eggs on the list of things to buy*

in·clud·ed /ɪn'kluːd$\frac{1}{2}$d/ *adj* [Wa5;E] INCLUDING: *all of us, me included*

in·clud·ing /ɪn'kluːdɪŋ/ *prep* having as a part; which includes: *6 people, including 3 women|all of us, including me*

in·clu·sion /ɪn'kluːʒən/ *n* **1** [U] the act of including or state of being included **2** [C] something that is included

in·clu·sive /ɪn'kluːsɪv/ *adj* **1** [B] containing or including everything (or many things): *an inclusive charge* **2** [Wa5;E (*of*)] (of a price or charge) including other costs that are often paid separately: *The rent is £10 inclusive of heating.|The rent is £10 inclusive (of everything)* **3** [Wa5;E] including all the numbers or dates: *Wednesday to Friday inclusive* —see USAGE **4 all-inclusive** including everything —**~ly** *adv*

USAGE An *AmE* expression for *Monday to Friday* **inclusive** is *Monday* **through** *Friday*. When British speakers say We stayed *from Monday* **to/till** *Friday*, it is not clear whether Friday was included. The phrase *Monday* **through** *to Friday* is beginning to be used in Britain but is felt to be *AmE*.

in·cog·ni·to¹ /,ɪnkɒg'niːtəʊ‖,ɪnkɑg-/ *adj, adv* [Wa5;F] hiding one's IDENTITY, esp. by taking another name when one's own is well-known

incognito² *n* **-tos** a false IDENTITY or false name

in·co·her·ent /,ɪnkəʊ'hɪərənt/ *adj* showing lack of suitable connections between ideas or words: *the incoherent words of a madman|He became quite incoherent as the disease got worse* —**-ence** *n* [U] —**-ently** *adv*

in·com·bus·ti·ble /,ɪnkəm'bʌstəbəl/ *adj* [Wa5] which cannot be burnt

in·come /'ɪŋkʌm, 'ɪn-/ *n* [U;C] money which one receives regularly for one's daily spending, usu. payment for one's work, or interest from INVESTMENTs: (*a*) *very small/low income|Low-income families need government help*

income tax /'·· ·/ *n* [U;C] tax on one's income

in·com·ing /'ɪnkʌmɪŋ/ *adj* [Wa5;A] coming towards one; about to enter or start (to be): *the incoming* TIDE|*incoming traffic*

in·com·men·su·ra·ble /,ɪnkə'menʃərəbəl/ *adj* [Wa5; (*with*)] *fml* which cannot be compared in size with (another thing/one another)

in·com·men·su·rate /,ɪnkə'menʃər$\frac{1}{2}$t/ *adj* [Wa5; F+*to*] too small in comparison to what is needed

in·com·mode /,ɪnkə'məʊd/ also **discommode**— *v* [T1] *fml or pomp* to trouble (someone)

in·com·mo·di·ous /,ɪnkə'məʊdɪəs/ *adj fml or pomp* not convenient; causing trouble —**~ly** *adv*

in·com·mu·ni·ca·ble /,ɪnkə'mjuːnɪkəbəl/ *adj* which cannot be said or made known

in·com·mu·ni·ca·do /,ɪnkəmjuːnɪ'kɑːdəʊ/ *adv, adj* [Wa5;F] (of people) kept away from people outside, and not able to give or receive messages

in·com·mu·ni·ca·tive /,ɪnkə'mjuːn$\frac{1}{2}$kətɪv‖-keɪtɪv/ *adj* UNCOMMUNICATIVE

in·com·pa·ra·ble /ɪn'kɒmpərəbəl‖-'kɑm-/ *adj* [Wa5] too great in degree to be compared with other examples of the same type: *incomparable wealth* —**-bility** /m,kɒmpərə'bɪl$\frac{1}{2}$ti‖-,kɑm-/ *n* [U] —**-bly** /ɪn'kɒmpərəbli‖-'kɑm-/ *adv* [Wa3,5]: *incomparably wealthy|incomparably the best*

in·com·pat·i·ble /,ɪnkəm'pætəbəl/ *adj* [(*with*)] not suitable to be together with (another thing or person/each other): *Their natures are incompatible.|His own plan is incompatible with my own intentions* —**-bility** /,ɪnkəmpætə'bɪl$\frac{1}{2}$ti/ *n* [U;C] —**-bly** /,ɪnkəm'pætəbli/ *adv* [Wa3]

in·com·pe·tence /ɪn'kɒmp$\frac{1}{2}$təns‖-'kɑm-/ also **in·com·pe·ten·cy** /-tənsi/— *n* [U] lack of ability and skill resulting in useless work

in·com·pe·tent /ɪn'kɒmp$\frac{1}{2}$tənt‖-'kɑm-/ *adj, n* [B; F3] (a person who is) completely unskilful (in something): *an incompetent teacher|quite incompetent to be the leader* —**~ly** *adv*

in·com·plete /,ɪnkəm'pliːt/ *adj* not complete; not perfect —**~ly** *adv* —**~ness** *n* [U]

in·com·pre·hen·si·ble /ɪn,kɒmprɪ'hensəbəl‖-,kɑm-/ *adj* [(*to*)] *sometimes derog* which cannot be understood and/or accepted —**-bility** /ɪn-,kɒmprɪhensə'bɪl$\frac{1}{2}$ti‖-,kɑm-/ *n* [U]

in·com·pre·hen·si·bly /ɪn,kɒmprɪ'hensəbli‖-,kɑm-/ *adv* **1** in an INCOMPREHENSIBLE way **2** [Wa5] it is INCOMPREHENSIBLE (that): *Incomprehensibly, my best pupil came last in the examination!*

in·com·pre·hen·sion /ɪn,kɒmprɪ'henʃən‖-,kɑm-/ *n* [U] the state of not understanding

in·con·cei·va·ble /,ɪnkən'siːvəbəl/ *adj* [(*to*)] **1** which is too strange to be thought real: *It once seemed inconceivable (to everyone) that men should travel to the moon* **2** *infml* impossible; which can't happen: *He can't go on holiday alone: it's inconceivable* —**-bility** /,ɪnkənsiːvə'bɪl$\frac{1}{2}$ti/ *n* [U] —**-bly** /,ɪnkən'siːvəbli/ *adv* [Wa3]

in·con·clu·sive /,ɪnkən'kluːsɪv/ *adj* which has not led to a decision or result; which did not decide or settle the reasons for something —**~ly** *adv* —**~ness** *n* [U]

in·con·gru·i·ty /,ɪnkən'gruː$\frac{1}{2}$ti/ *n* **1** [U] also **incongruousness**— the state of being INCONGRUOUS **2** [C] an act or event which seems out of place because of its difference from what is happening around it

in·con·gru·ous /ɪn'kɒŋgruəs‖-'kɑŋ-/ *adj* [(*with*)] comparing strangely with what surrounds it: *a modern building that looks incongruous in that old-fashioned village* —**~ly** *adv* —**~ness** *n* [U]

in·con·se·quent /ɪn'kɒns$\frac{1}{2}$kwənt‖-'kɑn-/ *adj fml* **1** not properly related to the idea, words, etc., going before **2** INCONSEQUENTIAL —**-quence** *n* [U] —**-quently** *adv*

in·con·se·quen·tial /ɪn,kɒns$\frac{1}{2}$'kwenʃəl‖-,kɑn-/ *adj* unimportant: *an inconsequential idea* —**-tiality** /ɪn-,kɒns$\frac{1}{2}$kwenʃi'æl$\frac{1}{2}$ti‖-,kɑn-/ *n* [U] —**-tially** /ɪn-,kɒns$\frac{1}{2}$'kwenʃəli‖-,kɑn-/ *adv*

in·con·sid·e·ra·ble /ˌɪnkənˈsɪdərəbəl/ *adj* of small size or worth: *£10 is an inconsiderable amount of money to a rich man*

in·con·sid·er·ate /ˌɪnkənˈsɪdərɨt/ *adj derog* not thinking of other people's feelings: *He's inconsiderate to his family because he never tells them he's working late* —**~ly** *adv* —**~ness** *n* [U]

in·con·sis·tent /ˌɪnkənˈsɪstənt/ *adj* **1** [(*with*)] (of ideas, opinions, etc.) not agreeing with something else/one another: *Those remarks are inconsistent with what you said yesterday.|The 2 remarks are inconsistent* **2** likely to change; including parts which do not agree together —**~ly** *adv* —**-tency** *n* [U;C]

in·con·so·la·ble /ˌɪnkənˈsəʊləbəl/ *adj* who cannot be comforted because of great sorrow or which is too great to be removed by comforting: *She is inconsolable for the loss of her dog.|an inconsolable misfortune* —**-bly** *adv*: *inconsolably sad*

in·con·spic·u·ous /ˌɪnkənˈspɪkjʊəs/ *adj* not easily seen; not attracting attention —**~ly** *adv* —**~ness** *n* [U]

in·con·stant /ɪnˈkɒnstənt‖-ˈkɑn-/ *adj fml* (of people and behaviour) tending to change; unfaithful in feeling: *an inconstant lover* —**-stancy** *n* [U;C *usu. pl.*]

in·con·tes·ta·ble /ˌɪnkənˈtestəbəl/ *adj* **1** which cannot be changed by argument **2** clearly true; INCONTROVERTIBLE: *incontestable proof* —**-bility** /ˌɪnkəntestəˈbɪlɨti/ *n* [U] —**-bly** /ˌɪnkənˈtestəbli/ *adv*

in·con·ti·nent /ɪnˈkɒntɨnənt‖-ˈkɑn-/ *adj* **1** unable to control the water in the BLADDER, so that it is passed from the body when one does not wish to pass it **2** *becoming rare* unable to control oneself sexually —**-nence** *n* [U]

in·con·tro·ver·ti·ble /ɪnˌkɒntrəˈvɜːtəbəl‖ɪnˌkɑntrəˈvɜr-/ *adj* which cannot be disproved; INDISPUTABLE —**-bly** *adv*

in·con·ve·ni·ence[1] /ˌɪnkənˈviːnɪəns/ *n* **1** [U] a state of difficulty when things do not suit one: *It causes a lot of inconvenience when buses don't come* **2** [C] an act, event, or fact which doesn't suit one's needs

inconvenience[2] *v* [T1] to make things difficult for (someone)

in·con·ve·ni·ent /ˌɪnkənˈviːnɪənt/ *adj* causing difficulty; not what suits one: *It's an inconvenient time to come visiting* —**~ly** *adv*

in·cor·po·rate[1] /ɪnˈkɔːpəreɪt‖-ɔr-/ *v* **1** [T1 (*in, into, with*)] to make (something) a part of a group; include: *They incorporated his new ideas into their plans.|The new plan incorporates the old one.|I incorporated the new plans with the old* **2** [IØ (*with*)] to join with one another/someone else in making a company or CORPORATION (2) —**-ration** /ɪnˌkɔːpəˈreɪʃən‖-ɔr-/ *n* [U]

in·cor·po·rate[2] /ɪnˈkɔːpərɨt‖-ɔr-/ *adj* [Wa5;B;E] *fml* joined in a group, company, etc.

in·cor·po·rat·ed /ɪnˈkɔːpəreɪtɨd‖-ɔr-/ *adj* [Wa5] **1** [B] united in one body or group **2** [B;E] (abbrev. **Inc**)— *fml esp. AmE* formed into a CORPORATION (2) according to law —compare LIMITED (2)

in·cor·po·re·al /ˌɪnkɔːˈpɔːrɪəl‖-kɔrˈpor-/ *adj* [Wa5] without a body; not made of any material substance —**-ally** *adv*

in·cor·rect /ˌɪnkəˈrekt/ *adj* not correct —**~ly** *adv* —**~ness** *n* [U]

in·cor·ri·gi·ble /ɪnˈkɒrɨdʒəbəl‖-ˈkɔ-/ *adj* (of people or behaviour) very bad and unable to be changed for the better —**-bility** /ɪnˌkɒrɨdʒəˈbɪlɨti‖-ˌkɔ-/ *n* [U] —**-bly** /ɪnˈkɒrɨdʒəbli‖-ˈkɔ-/ *adv* [Wa3]

in·cor·rup·ti·ble /ˌɪnkəˈrʌptəbəl/ *adj* **1** which cannot decay or be destroyed **2** (esp. of one who will not take money (BRIBEs)) who is too honest to be persuaded from his judgment —**-bility** /ˌɪnkərʌptəˈbɪlɨti/ *n* [U] —**-bly** /ˌɪnkəˈrʌptəbli/ *adv*

in·crease[1] /ɪnˈkriːs/ *v* [Wv4,5;T1;IØ] to make or become larger in amount or number: *The population of this town has increased.|I increased the amount of water to be added during cooking*

in·crease[2] /ˈɪŋkriːs/ *n* [U;C] **1** a rise in amount, numbers, etc. **2** **on the increase** increasing: *Crime is on the increase*

in·creas·ing·ly /ɪnˈkriːsɪŋli/ *adv* more and more all the time: *He's increasingly rude to me.|increasingly bad work*

in·cred·i·ble /ɪnˈkredəbəl/ *adj* **1** [Wa5] too strange to be believed; unbelievable: *an incredible idea/story/excuse* **2** *infml* wonderful; unbelievably good: *She has an incredible house* —**-bility** /ɪnˌkredəˈbɪlɨti/ *n* [U] —**-bly** /ɪnˈkredəbli/ *adv*

in·cre·du·li·ty /ˌɪnkrɨˈdjuːlɨti‖-ˈduː-/ *n* [U] disbelief

in·cred·u·lous /ɪnˈkredjʊləs‖-dʒə-/ *adj* showing disbelief: *an incredulous look* —**~ly** *adv*

in·cre·ment /ˈɪŋkrɨmənt/ *n* [U;C] (an) increase in money or value —**~al** /ˌɪŋkrɨˈmentl/ *adj* [Wa5] —**~ally** *adv* [Wa5]

in·crim·i·nate /ɪnˈkrɪmɨneɪt/ *v* [Wv4;T1] to cause (someone) to seem guilty of a crime or fault —**-nation** /ɪnˌkrɪmɨˈneɪʃən/ *n* [U]

in·crust /ɪnˈkrʌst/ *v* [T1] ENCRUST: *a path incrusted in ice*

in·crus·ta·tion /ˌɪnkrʌˈsteɪʃən/ *n* **1** [C] dirt or material laid down on top of something else **2** [U] a way of putting jewels, precious metals, etc., together —compare ENCRUST

in·cu·bate /ˈɪŋkjʊbeɪt‖-kjə-/ *v* **1** [T1;IØ] **a** to sit on and keep (eggs) warm until the young birds come out **b** (of eggs) to be kept warm until HATCHed —compare HATCH[2] **2** [T1] to plan or think over (something to be done) —compare HATCH **3** [T1] *med* to be holding in one's body (an infection which is going to develop into a disease)

in·cu·ba·tion /ˌɪŋkjʊˈbeɪʃən‖-kjə-/ *n* [U] **1** the act of incubating (INCUBATE) **2** **a** the time taken in keeping eggs warm before the young bird comes out **b** *med* the time taken for a disease to develop

in·cu·ba·tor /ˈɪŋkjʊbeɪtəʳ‖-kjə-/ *n* a machine for **a** keeping eggs warm until they HATCH **b** keeping alive babies that are too small to live and breathe in ordinary air

in·cu·bus /ˈɪŋkjʊbəs‖-kjə-/ *n* **-buses** *or* **-bi** /baɪ/ **1** a male devil supposed to have sex with a sleeping woman —compare SUCCUBUS **2** **a** a bad dream (NIGHTMARE) **b** a difficulty which is a general cause for anxiety: *the incubus of debt, like a weight on one's mind*

in·cul·cate /ˈɪnkʌlkeɪt‖ɪnˈkʌl-/ *v* [D1 + *with/in*; T1 (*in*)] *fml* to fix (ideas, principles, etc.) in the mind of (someone): *He inculcated the spirit to succeed in all his children.|He inculcated all his children with the spirit of success* —**-cation** /ˌɪnkʌlˈkeɪʃən/ *n* [U]

in·cul·pate /ˈɪnkʌlpeɪt‖ɪnˈkʌl-/ *v* [T1] *fml* to show or suggest that (someone) is guilty of crime; INCRIMINATE

in·cum·ben·cy /ɪnˈkʌmbənsi/ *n* **1** the quality or state of being INCUMBENT[2] **2** something that is INCUMBENT[2]; duty **3** the field of activity or period in office of an INCUMBENT[1]

in·cum·bent[1] /ɪnˈkʌmbənt/ *n* **1** a priest in the Church of England who is in charge of a church and its PARISH (BENEFICE) **2** *esp. AmE* the holder of an office, esp. a political office

incumbent[2] *adj* [Wa5] **1** [B (*on, upon*)] *fml* being the moral duty of (someone): *It's incumbent on you to give a father's advice before your son leaves home* **2** [A] holding the stated office: *the incumbent priest|(esp. AmE) the incumbent president*

in·cur /ɪn'kɜː'/ *v* **-rr-** [T1] to receive (some unpleasant thing) as a result of certain actions: *I incurred his dislike from that day on.|to incur a debt*

in·cur·a·ble /ɪn'kjʊərəbəl/ *adj* [Wa5] that cannot be cured —**-bility** /ɪnˌkjʊərə'bɪlɨti/ *n* [U] —**-bly** /ɪn'kjʊərəbli/ *adv* [Wa3,5]

in·cu·ri·ous /ɪn'kjʊərɪəs/ *adj* [Wa5] lacking natural interest; not paying attention: *incurious about the outside world*

in·cur·sion /ɪn'kɜːʃən, -ʒən‖ɪn'kɜrʒən/ *n* a sudden attack on or entrance into a place which belongs to other people

in·curved /ˌɪn'kɜːvd◂‖-ɜr-/ *adj* curving inwards: *incurved horns*

in·debt·ed /ɪn'detɨd/ *adj* [(*to*)] very grateful to (someone) for help given: *I'm indebted to all the people who worked so hard to make the party a success* —**~ness** *n* [U]

in·de·cent /ɪn'diːsənt/ *adj* **1** not DECENT (1); offensive to general standards of behaviour: *an indecent remark/joke* —compare IMMODEST (2) **2** *infml* not reasonable; not suitable (in amount or quality): *You've given us an indecent amount of work to do* (=too much) *and indecent wages* (=too little) —**~ly** *adv*: *indecently dressed* —**-cency** *n* [U;C]

indecent as·sault /·ˌ·· ·'·/ *n* [U;C] *law* an attack with blows (ASSAULT) and some form of sexual violence

indecent ex·po·sure /·ˌ·· ·'··/ *n* [U;C] the intentional showing of part of one's body (esp. the male sex organ) in a place where this is likely to be an offence against generally accepted moral standards

in·de·ci·pher·a·ble /ˌɪndɪ'saɪfərəbəl/ *adj* [Wa5] which cannot be DECIPHERed or understood —**-bility** /ˌɪndɪsaɪfərə'bɪlɨti/ *n* [U] —**-bly** /ˌɪndɪ'saɪfərəbli/ *adv* [Wa3,5]

in·de·ci·sion /ˌɪndɪ'sɪʒən/ *n* [U] uncertainty before deciding to do something, choose something, etc.

in·de·ci·sive /ˌɪndɪ'saɪsɪv/ *adj* **1** giving an uncertain result: *an indecisive answer/victory* **2** (of people) unable to make decisions —**~ly** *adv* —**~ness** *n* [U]

in·dec·o·rous /ɪn'dekərəs/ *adj fml or euph* showing bad manners —**~ly** *adv* —**~ness** *n* [U]

in·de·co·rum /ˌɪndɪ'kɔːrəm‖-'kor-/ *n* [U] lack of DECORUM

in·deed /ɪn'diːd/ *adv* [Wa5] **1** (*said in answer to a speaker who has suggested the answer*) certainly; really: *Yes, it is indeed beautiful weather.|"Did you hear the explosion?" "Indeed I did"* **2** *fml* it is even true (that): *I didn't mind. Indeed, I was pleased.|Here's Percy Maltravers, for that/such indeed is his name* **3** (*used after* very+adjective *or* adverb *to make the meaning even stronger*): *The crowds were very large indeed.|"I liked some of it very much indeed"* (SEU S.) **4** (showing surprise and often disbelief or unfavourable interest): *"He left without finishing his work." "Did he, indeed?"|"I earn $1,000 a minute." "Indeed!"*

in·de·fat·i·ga·ble /ˌɪndɪ'fætɪgəbəl/ *adj* [Wa5] that shows no sign of tiring

in·de·fen·si·ble /ˌɪndɪ'fensəbəl/ *adj* [Wa5] **1** which cannot be excused; too bad to be defended: *indefensible behaviour* **2** which cannot be defended: *We had to yield our indefensible position to the enemy*

in·de·fi·na·ble /ˌɪndɪ'faɪnəbəl/ *adj* [Wa5] which cannot be DEFINED or described —**-bly** *adv* [Wa3,5]

in·def·i·nite /ɪn'defənɨt/ *adj* **1** not clear: *indefinite opinions|indefinite responsibilities* **2** [Wa5] not fixed, esp. as to time: *at an indefinite date* —**~ness** *n* [U]

indefinite ar·ti·cle /·ˌ··· '···/ *n* **1** (in English) A or AN **2** (in other languages) a word with uses or meanings like those of the English words "a" and "an"

in·def·i·nite·ly /ɪn'defənɨtli/ *adv* **1** for a period of time without a fixed end: *You can borrow the book indefinitely* **2** in an INDEFINITE way: *expresses himself rather indefinitely*

in·del·i·ble /ɪn'deləbəl/ *adj* [Wa5] which cannot be rubbed out: *indelible ink|an indelible pencil|*(fig.) *an indelible* STAIN *on his character* —**-bly** *adv* [Wa3,5]: *an experience indelibly printed on my memory*

in·del·i·cate /ɪn'delɨkɨt/ *adj* not polite or modest; rough in manners: *an indelicate remark* —**~ly** *adv* —**-cacy** /ɪn'delɨkəsi/ *n* [U;C]

in·dem·ni·fi·ca·tion /ɪnˌdemnɨfɨ'keɪʃən/ *n* **1** [U] the action of INDEMNIFYing or condition of being indemnified **2** [C;U] money or something else received to repair the effect of a loss or hurt; INDEMNITY (2)

in·dem·ni·fy /ɪn'demnɨfaɪ/ *v* [T1] **1** [(*against, for*)] to promise to pay (someone) in case of loss, hurt, or damage **2** [(*for*)] to pay (someone) for loss, hurt, or damage **3** [(*for*)] *fml* to repay

in·dem·ni·ty /ɪn'demnɨti/ *n* **1** [U] protection against loss, esp. in the form of a promise to pay **2** [C] payment for loss or money, goods, etc.: *When a country has been defeated in war, it sometimes has to pay an indemnity to the winners*

in·dent[1] /ɪn'dent/ *v* **1** [Wv5;T1] to make a usu. toothlike mark on the surface or edge of **2** [T1;I∅] to start (a line of writing) further into the page than the others **3** [T1] to do this by (the stated amount) **4** [I∅ (*on* and/or *for*)] *esp. BrE* to order goods by INDENT[2]: *If you want all those new pencils, you'll have to indent* (*on the company*) *for them*

in·dent[2] /'ɪndent/ *n* [(*on* and/or *for*)] *esp. BrE* **1** an order for goods to be sent abroad, or for stores in the army **2** an official, usu. written, order for goods

in·den·ta·tion /ˌɪnden'teɪʃən/ *n* **1** [U] the action of INDENTing or the condition of being indented **2** [C] a space pointing inwards: *the indentations in a coastline* **3** [C] a space at the beginning of a line of writing

in·den·ture[1] /ɪn'dentʃə'/ *n* [*often pl.*] a written agreement in at least 2 copies, esp. one in former times between an APPRENTICE and his master

indenture[2] *v* [Wv5;T1 (*to, as*)] to cause to enter employment on conditions stated in INDENTURE*s*: *an indentured bricklayer*

in·de·pen·dence /ˌɪndɨ'pendəns/ *n* [U (*from*)] the quality or state of being independent; freedom: *This money gives me independence from my family.|India gained independence from Britain in 1947*

Independence Day /··'·· ·/ *n* [R] a public holiday on the day when a country declared or gained its independence from another, such as (in the US) the 4th of July

in·de·pen·dent[1] /ˌɪndɨ'pendənt◂/ *adj* **1** [(*of*)] not needing other things or people **2** [Wa5] (of money) belonging to one privately, so that one can live without working (note the phr. **independent means**) **3 a** not allowing oneself to be controlled; habitually taking decisions alone: *She went out all alone—she's very independent* **b** the result of taking one's own decisions: *independent work* **4** not governed by another country —**~ly** *adv*: *I did this work independently* (*of other people's ideas*)

Independent[2] *n* (*sometimes not cap.*) a person who does not always favour the same political party

independent clause /··ˌ·· '·/ also **main clause**— *n* a CLAUSE which can make a sentence by itself. It may have one or more DEPENDENT CLAUSE*s* as parts of it or joined to it: *"I told him" is the independent clause in the sentence "When he came in, I told him"*

in·de·scri·ba·ble /ˌɪndɪsˈkraɪbəbəl/ *adj* [Wa5] which cannot be described, usu. because beautiful beyond belief, or because description is too difficult to attempt —**-bly** *adv* [Wa3,5]

in·de·struc·ti·ble /ˌɪndɪˈstrʌktəbəl/ *adj* [Wa5] which is too strong to be destroyed —**-bility** /ˌɪndɪstrʌktəˈbɪl$\frac{1}{2}$ti/ *n* [U] —**-bly** /ˌɪndɪˈstrʌktəbli/ *adv* [Wa3,5]: *indestructibly strong*

in·de·ter·mi·na·ble /ˌɪndɪˈtɜːm$\frac{1}{2}$nəbəl‖-ɜr-/ *adj* which cannot be decided or fixed: *the indeterminable question—what is the purpose of life?* —**-bly** *adv* [Wa3]

in·de·ter·mi·nate /ˌɪndɪˈtɜːm$\frac{1}{2}$n$\frac{1}{2}$t‖-ɜr-/ *adj* not clearly seen as, or not fixed as, one thing or another: *Our holiday plans are still at an indeterminate stage* —**-nacy** *n* [U]

in·dex¹ /ˈɪndeks/ *n* **-dexes** *or* **-dices** /d$\frac{1}{2}$siːz/ **1 a** an alphabetical list at the back of a book, of names, subjects, etc., mentioned in it and the pages where they can be found **b** also **card index**— a list of the same kind, of books and writers to be found in a library, written on separate cards, for use by library borrowers **2** *rare* a pointer on a machine **3** *fml* a sign: *These new ideas in education are an index of change to come* —compare INDICATION (2) **4** *tech* also **exponent**— a number which shows how many times to multiply a number by itself, such as the number 4 in the expression $2^4 = 2 \times 2 \times 2 \times 2 = 16$ **5** the system of numbers by which prices, costs, etc., can be compared to a former level, usu. fixed at 100 (esp. in the phr. **cost of living index**)

index² *v* **1** [T1] to provide with an INDEX **2** [T1] to include in an INDEX **3** [IØ] to prepare an INDEX —**~er** *n*

Index *n* [*the*+R] the list of books which ROMAN CATHOLICs cannot read without permission

index fin·ger /ˈ·· ˌ··/ *n* FOREFINGER

In·di·an /ˈɪndɪən/ *n, adj* [Wa5] **1** (someone) belonging to or connected with India **2** also **American Indian**— (someone) belonging to or connected with any of the original peoples of North, Central, or South America except the Eskimos

Indian club /ˌ··· ˈ·‖ˈ··· ·/ *n* a usu. wooden CLUB shaped like a large bottle with a narrow neck, usu. used in a pair, one in each hand, and swung for exercise

Indian corn /ˌ··· ˈ·/ *n* [U] MAIZE

Indian file /ˌ··· ˈ·‖ˈ··· ·/ *n, adv* [U] SINGLE FILE: *walked (in) Indian file*

Indian hemp /ˌ··· ˈ·/ *n* [U] **1** a type of HEMP, used for ropes and mats, which produces a drug **2** this drug; CANNABIS (2)

Indian ink /ˌ··· ˈ·/ *n* [U] dark black ink made from natural substances, such as that used for Chinese and Japanese writing with a brush

Indian sum·mer /ˌ··· ˈ··/ *n* **1** [C;(U)] a period of warm weather in the autumn **2** [C] a time in old age when things go well, and one feels as well as in one's youth

In·di·a pa·per /ˈɪndɪə ˌpeɪpəʳ/ *n* [U] **1** thin soft paper for printing detailed pictures, maps, etc. **2** thin strong paper used for its lightness

india rub·ber /ˌ··· ˈ··◂/ *n* [U;C] *tech* (*sometimes cap.* I) rubber, esp. as used for making toys or rubbing out pencil marks: *an india-rubber ball*

in·di·cate /ˈɪnd$\frac{1}{2}$keɪt/ *v* **1** [T1] to point out: *I asked him where my sister was and he indicated the shop opposite* **2** [T1,5a,b,6a,b] to make a sign (for): *He indicated that I could leave.|His answer indicated that I could leave* **3** [T5a,b] to make clear: *I indicated that his help was not welcome* **4** [IØ; T1,5,6a,b] to show (the direction in which one is turning in a vehicle) by making signs with the hand or flashing the special coloured lights to the sides of a car at front and back: *He's indicating left* **5** [T1 *often pass.*] to show a need for; suggest: *The change in his illness indicates the use of stronger drugs*

in·di·ca·tion /ˌɪnd$\frac{1}{2}$ˈkeɪʃən/ *n* **1** [U] the action of indicating (INDICATE) **2** [C;U: (*of,* 5)] a sign or suggestion: *There are indications that the weather is changing.|There is every indication* (=strong likelihood) *of a change in the weather*

in·dic·a·tive¹ /ɪnˈdɪkətɪv/ *adj* **1** [F (*of*), F5] showing; suggesting: *His presence is indicative of his wish to help/that he wishes to help* **2** [Wa5;B] of the INDICATIVE²: *an indicative verb form* —**~ly** *adv*

indicative² *n* a verb form or set of verb forms (MOOD²) that shows an act or state as a fact

in·di·ca·tor /ˈɪnd$\frac{1}{2}$keɪtəʳ/ *n* **1** a needle or pointer on a machine showing the measure of some quality, or a substance which shows what is happening in a chemical mixture **2** any of the lights on a car which flash to show which way it is turning —see picture at CAR **3** something that gives an idea of the presence, absence, nature, quantity, or degree of something else: *Is a cold wet nose an indicator of health in dogs?|a good/bad indicator*

in·di·ces /ˈɪnd$\frac{1}{2}$siːz/ *pl. of* INDEX

in·dict /ɪnˈdaɪt/ *v* [T1 (*for*)] to charge (someone) formally with an offence in law —**~ment** *n* [U;C]

in·dict·a·ble /ɪnˈdaɪtəbəl/ *adj* [Wa5] *law* for which one can be INDICTed: *an indictable offence*

in·dif·fer·ent /ɪnˈdɪfərənt/ *adj* **1** [F (*to*); (B)] not interested in; not caring about or noticing: *I was so excited to see snow that I was indifferent to the cold* **2** [B] not very good: *good, bad, or indifferent?|I'm an indifferent cook* —see DIFFERENT (USAGE) —**~ly** *adv* —**-ence** *n* [U (*to, towards*)]: *He treats me with indifference*

in·di·ge·nous /ɪnˈdɪdʒənəs/ *adj* [(*to*)] *fml or tech* native; belonging (to a place) —**~ly** *adv*: *plants not found here indigenously, but introduced in the 17th century*

in·di·gent /ˈɪndɪdʒənt/ *adj fml* poor; lacking money and goods —**-gence** *n* [U]

in·di·ges·ti·ble /ˌɪndɪˈdʒestəbəl/ *adj* **1** (of food) which cannot be easily broken down in the stomach into substances to be used by the body **2** (of facts) which cannot be taken into the mind easily —**-bility** /ˌɪndɪdʒestəˈbɪl$\frac{1}{2}$ti/ *n* [U] —**-bly** /ˌɪndɪˈdʒestəbli/ *adv* [Wa3]

in·di·ges·tion /ˌɪndɪˈdʒestʃən/ *n* [U] illness or pain caused by the stomach being unable to deal with the food which has been eaten

in·dig·nant /ɪnˈdɪgnənt/ *adj* [(*at, over, about*)] expressing or feeling surprised anger (at something which should not be so) —**~ly** *adv*

in·dig·na·tion /ˌɪndɪgˈneɪʃən/ *n* [U (*at, over, about*)] feelings of anger (against something wrong): *I expressed my indignation at being unfairly dismissed*

in·dig·ni·ty /ɪnˈdɪgn$\frac{1}{2}$ti/ *n* **1** [U] a state which makes one feel less respected (unDIGNIFIED) or that one is on public show: *The indignity of having to say I was sorry in front of all those people* **2** [C] an act which makes one feel loss of respect (DIGNITY), self-control, etc.: *the indignities of an illness, such as being washed and dressed by someone else, as if one were a child*

in·di·go /ˈɪndɪgəʊ/ *n* [U] a colour or DYE of a dark blue-purple

in·di·rect /ˌɪnd$\frac{1}{2}$ˈrekt◂/ *adj* **1** not straight; not directly connected (to or with) **2** not paid directly but through price rises (esp. in the phr. **indirect taxation**) **3 a** meaning something which is not directly mentioned: *an indirect remark/answer* **b** happening in addition to, or instead of, what is directly meant: *the indirect result* —**~ly** *adv* —**~ness** *n* [U]

indirect ob·ject /ˌ··· ˈ··/ *n* the person (or sometimes the thing) that the DIRECT OBJECT is given to, made for, etc.: *"Him" is the indirect object in "I asked him a question"*

indirect speech /ˌ··· ˈ·/ also **reported speech**— *n* [U] the style used to tell what somebody said without repeating the actual words. "That" is used, and the 3rd person PRONOUN*s*: *"She said, 'I don't want to go'" has a form in indirect speech: "she said (that) she didn't want to go"*

in·dis·cer·ni·ble /ˌɪndɪˈsɜːnəbəl‖-ɜr-/ *adj* (often of something small or hidden by darkness) which cannot be seen: *a path almost indiscernible in the mist*

in·dis·ci·pline /ɪnˈdɪsɪ̵plɪ̵n/ *n* [U] lack of DISCIPLINE[1] (2); state of disorder because of lack of control

in·dis·creet /ˌɪndɪˈskriːt/ *adj* not acting carefully and politely, esp. in the choice of what one says and does not say —**~ly** *adv*

in·dis·cre·tion /ˌɪndɪˈskreʃən/ *n* **1** [U] the state or quality of being INDISCREET; lack of DISCRETION (1) **2** [C] **a** an act of an impolite careless nature **b** *euph* bad behaviour including small crimes and sexual experiences which are socially undesirable

in·dis·crim·i·nate /ˌɪndɪˈskrɪmɪ̵nɪ̵t/ *adj* [Wa5] not choosing or chosen carefully —**~ly** *adv*

in·di·spen·sa·ble /ˌɪndɪˈspensəbəl/ *adj* [(*to*)] that is too important to live without —**-bility** /ˌɪndɪspensəˈbɪlɪ̵ti/ *n* [U] —**-bly** /ˌɪndɪˈspensəbli/ *adv* [Wa3]

in·dis·posed /ˌɪndɪˈspəʊzd/ *adj fml* **1** [F] *often euph* not very well (in health): *It says "Speaker indisposed" on the notice, but I know very well he's too drunk to give a speech* **2** [F3] not very willing: *indisposed to do it|to help*

in·dis·po·si·tion /ɪnˌdɪspəˈzɪʃən/ *n* **1** [U;C] a slight illness **2** [U,U3;C,C3] a certain degree of unwillingness

in·dis·pu·ta·ble /ˌɪndɪˈspjuːtəbəl/ *adj* [Wa5] which is too certain to be questioned —**-bly** *adv* [Wa3,5]

in·dis·so·lu·ble /ˌɪndɪˈsɒljʊbəl‖-ˈsɑljə-/ *adj* [Wa5] *fml* which cannot be separated or broken up; lasting —compare DISSOLVE (esp. 3) —**-bility** /ˌɪndɪsɒljʊˈbɪlɪ̵ti‖-sɑljə-/ *n* [U] —**-bly** /ˌɪndɪˈsɒljʊbli‖-ˈsɑljə-/ *adv* [Wa3,5]

in·dis·tinct /ˌɪndɪˈstɪŋkt/ *adj* not clear to the eye or mind or ear: *an indistinct memory|an indistinct area in a photograph* —**~ly** *adv* —**~ness** *n* [U]

in·dis·tin·guish·a·ble /ˌɪndɪˈstɪŋgwɪʃəbəl/ *adj* [Wa5; (*from*)] which cannot be seen or known to be different from something else or each other: *All 3 sisters are indistinguishable.|The material is indistinguishable from real silk, but much cheaper* —**-bly** *adv* [Wa3,5]

in·di·vid·u·al[1] /ˌɪndɪ̵ˈvɪdʒʊəl/ *adj* **1** [Wa5;A] (*often with* each) single; particular; separate: *each individual leaf on the tree is different* **2** [Wa5;A] suitable for each person or thing only: *Individual attention must be given to every fault in the material* **3** [B] (of a manner, style, way of doing things) particular to the person, thing, etc., concerned (and different from others)

individual[2] *n* **1** a single being or member of a group, treated separately: *The rights of the individual are sometimes the most important rights in a free society* **2** *infml* a person: *What a bad-tempered individual you are!* —see PEOPLE (USAGE)

in·di·vid·u·al·is·m /ˌɪndɪ̵ˈvɪdʒʊəlɪzəm/ *n* [U] **1** the idea that the rights and freedom of the INDIVIDUAL are the most important rights in a society **2** *euph* selfishness —**-ist** /ˌɪndɪ̵ˈvɪdʒʊəlɪ̵st/ *n, adj* —**-istic** /ˌɪndɪ̵ˌvɪdʒʊəˈlɪstɪk/ *adj* —**-istically** *adv* [Wa4]

in·di·vid·u·al·i·ty /ˌɪndɪ̵ˌvɪdʒʊˈælɪ̵ti/ *n* [U;S] the character and qualities which make someone or something different from all others: *a dull woman, who lacks individuality*

in·di·vid·u·al·ize, -ise /ˌɪndɪ̵ˈvɪdʒʊəlaɪz/ *v* [Wv5; T1] to cause to change according to the special needs or character of a person or thing: *Individualized gifts for your best friends* —**-ization** /ˌɪndɪ̵ˌvɪdʒʊəlaɪˈzeɪʃən‖-lə-/ *n* [U]

in·di·vid·u·al·ly /ˌɪndɪ̵ˈvɪdʒʊəli/ *adv* **1** [Wa5] one by one; separately: *Individually, they're really quite nice, but in a group they get nasty* **2** in an INDIVIDUAL[1] (3) way

in·di·vis·i·ble /ˌɪndɪ̵ˈvɪzəbəl/ *adj* [Wa5] which cannot be divided or separated into parts —**-bility** /ˌɪndɪ̵ˌvɪzəˈbɪlɪ̵ti/ *n* [U] —**-bly** /ˌɪndɪ̵ˈvɪzəbli/ *adv* [Wa3,5]

In·do- /ˈɪndəʊ/ *comb. form* of India and (the other nation or national group mentioned): *Indo-China*| INDO-EUROPEAN

in·do·cile /ɪnˈdəʊsaɪl‖ɪnˈdɑsəl/ *adj* not DOCILE —**-cility** /ˌɪndəʊˈsɪlɪ̵ti‖ˌɪndɑ-/ *n* [U]

in·doc·tri·nate /ɪnˈdɒktrɪ̵neɪt‖ɪnˈdɑk-/ *v* [T1 (*with*)] *usu. derog* to put ideas into (someone's) mind: *They have those political opinions because they've been indoctrinated all their lives* —**-nation** /ɪnˌdɒktrɪ̵ˈneɪʃən‖ɪnˌdɑk-/ *n* [U]

Indo-Eu·ro·pe·an /ˌ·· ··ˈ··◂/ *adj* [Wa5] **1** of or concerning a group of languages that includes most of those spoken in Europe (and now spread to America and parts of Africa), Persia, and India **2** of or concerning a member of a group which speaks any of these languages

in·do·lent /ˈɪndələnt/ *adj* lazy; not liking to be active: *an indolent worker* —**~ly** *adv* —**-lence** *n* [U]

in·dom·i·ta·ble /ɪnˈdɒmɪ̵təbəl‖ɪnˈdɑ-/ *adj* that is too strong to be discouraged: *his indomitable spirit* —**-bly** *adv* [Wa3]

In·do·ne·sian /ˌɪndəˈniːʒən, ˈniːzɪən/ *adj* [Wa5] of Indonesia, its peoples, or their official national language

in·door /ˈɪndɔːʳ‖ˈɪndor/ *adj* [Wa5;A] which is (done, used, etc.) inside a building: *indoor sports|indoor clothes*

indoor re·lief /ˌ·· ·ˈ·/ *n* [U] *old use* (in Britain in former times) help given to the poor in the WORKHOUSE (=place for homeless poor people) —compare OUTDOOR RELIEF

in·doors /ˌɪnˈdɔːz◂‖-orz◂/ *adv* to(wards), in, or into the inside of a building: *We went indoors.|We stayed indoors*

in·dorse /ɪnˈdɔːs‖-ɔrs/ *v* [T1] ENDORSE

in·drawn /ˌɪnˈdrɔːn◂/ *adj* drawn into the body: *an indrawn breath*

in·du·bi·ta·ble /ɪnˈdjuːbɪ̵təbəl‖ɪnˈduː-/ *adj* [Wa5] *fml* which cannot be doubted to be so; unquestionable —**-bly** *adv* [Wa3,5]

in·duce /ɪnˈdjuːs‖ɪnˈduːs/ *v* **1** [V3] to lead (someone) (into an act) often by persuading: *I was induced to come against my will* **2** [T1 *often pass.*; (I∅)] **a** to cause (LABOUR[1] (3)) to begin by using medical drugs **b** *infml* to cause (a baby) to be born, or (a mother) to give birth, by medical means **3** [T1] to cause or produce: *Too much food induced sleepiness*

in·duce·ment /ɪnˈdjuːsmənt‖ɪnˈduːs-/ *n* [U;C,C3] (something, esp. money, which provides) encouragement to do something: *The promise of a holiday at the seaside is no great inducement to study hard, when I don't like the seaside anyhow*

in·duct /ɪnˈdʌkt/ *v* [T1 *often pass.*] **1** to introduce (someone, esp. a priest) into an official position in a special ceremony **2** *AmE* to introduce (someone) into a group or organization, esp. into the army

in·duc·tion /ɪnˈdʌkʃən/ *n* **1** [U] the act or action of INDUCTing **2** [U] the action of inducing (INDUCE) **3** [C;U] **a** a ceremony in a church when a BISHOP or important person introduces a younger priest who is to work there **b** *esp. AmE* a ceremony in which someone is made officially a member of the armed forces: *his induction into the army* **4** [C;U] (the action of causing) the birth of a child which has been hastened by the use of drugs **5** [C] also **induction course** /·'·· ·/— introduction into a new job, organization, etc. **6** [U] *tech* the production of electricity in one object by another which already has electrical (or MAGNETIC power) **7** [U;C] (the act, action, or result, or an example of) a way of reasoning using known facts to produce general laws

induction coil /·'·· ·/ *n* a sort of TRANSFORMER where a strong electric current is produced by INDUCTION from an inner to an outer COIL² (3)

in·duc·tive /ɪn'dʌktɪv/ *adj* **1** *tech* using INDUCTION (6): *inductive apparatus* **2** using or showing INDUCTION (7): *inductive reasoning* —**~ly** *adv*

in·due with /ɪn'djuː‖ɪn'duː/ *v prep AmE* ENDUE WITH

in·dulge /ɪn'dʌldʒ/ *v* **1** [T1] to yield, perhaps too much, to the desires of (someone), esp. habitually **2** [T1] to let oneself have (one's wish to do or have something, etc.): *I indulged my interest in flowers for several years by planting a large flower-garden* **3** [T1;I∅] *infml* to let (oneself) have what one wants, esp. large quantities or forbidden types of food or drink: *I wouldn't say he's a drinker but he indulges at parties*

indulge in *v prep* [T1,4;D1] to allow (oneself) to enjoy (something): *I sometimes indulge in (smoking) a cigarette*

in·dul·gence /ɪn'dʌldʒəns/ *n* **1** [U (*in*)] the (habitual) act of indulging (esp. in strong drink) or state of being INDULGEd **2** [C] an act of taking, doing, etc., something one likes, or the thing itself: *Sweets are my only indulgence* **3** [C;U] also **pardon**— (in the ROMAN CATHOLIC church) (an act or example of) freedom from the punishment for wrong-doing, given by a priest

in·dul·gent /ɪn'dʌldʒənt/ *adj* (showing that a person is) likely to INDULGE (1) or habitually too kind to other people: *They're very indulgent parents—they give their children presents all the time.|an indulgent smile* —**~ly** *adv*

in·dus·tri·al /ɪn'dʌstrɪəl/ *adj* **1** of industry and the people who work in it: *industrial unrest|disagreement* **2** having highly developed industries: *an industrial nation* —compare INDUSTRIOUS —**~ly** *adv*: *an industrially developed country*

industrial ar·chae·ol·o·gy /·,··· ··'···/ *n* [U] the study of the factories, machinery, and products of earlier stages of the INDUSTRIAL REVOLUTION

industrial es·tate /·,··· ·'·/ also **trading estate**— *n BrE* a special area of land where factories are built

in·dus·tri·al·is·m /ɪn'dʌstrɪəlɪzəm/ *n* [U] the system by which a society gains its wealth esp. through industries and machinery

in·dus·tri·al·ist /ɪn'dʌstrɪəlɪ̵st/ *n* a person who is closely concerned in the system of earning profits in industry, esp. a factory owner

in·dus·tri·al·ize, -ise /ɪn'dʌstrɪəlaɪz/ *v* [Wv5;T1;I∅] to (cause to) become industrially developed —**-ization** /ɪn,dʌstrɪəlaɪ'zeɪʃən‖-lə-/ *n* [U]

industrial rev·o·lu·tion /·,··· ··'··/ *n* (*often cap.*) a period of time when machines are invented and factories set up, and the changes which go on during this time (as in Britain around 1750–1850)

in·dus·tri·ous /ɪn'dʌstrɪəs/ *adj* hard-working —compare INDUSTRIAL —**~ly** *adv* —**~ness** *n* [U]

in·dus·try /'ɪndəstri/ *n* **1** [U] (the work of) factories and large organizations generally: *The country is supported by industry* **2** [U] the private owners and share-holders of such factories and organizations: *Does industry agree with the government?* **3** [C9,(C)] a particular sort of work, usu. employing lots of people and using machinery and/or modern methods: *the clothing industry|The tourist trade has become a real industry* **4** [U] continual hard work

-ine /aɪn/ *suffix* [*n→adj*] made of; of or concerning; like: CRYSTALLINE

i·ne·bri·ate¹ /ɪ'niːbrieɪt/ *v* [Wv5;T1] *fml* to make drunk —**-ation** /ɪ,niːbri'eɪʃən/ *n* [U]

i·ne·bri·ate² /ɪ'niːbrɪ̵t, -eɪt/ *adj, n fml* (someone who is) habitually drunk

in·ed·i·ble /ɪn'edəbəl/ *adj* not suitable for eating —**-bility** /ɪn,edə'bɪlɪ̵ti/ *n* [U] —**-bly** /ɪn'edəbli/ *adv* [Wa3]

in·ed·u·ca·ble /ɪn'edjʊkəbəl‖-djə-/ *adj* who cannot be educated, esp. because of weakness of mind —**-bility** /ɪn,edjʊkə'bɪlɪ̵ti‖-djə-/ *n* [U] —**-bly** /ɪn'edjʊkəbli‖-djə-/ *adv* [Wa3]

in·ef·fa·ble /ɪn'efəbəl/ *adj* [Wa5] **1** which is too wonderful to be described in words: *ineffable joy* **2** (esp. of the name of God in some religions) not to be spoken aloud: *the ineffable name* —**-bility** /ɪn,efə'bɪlɪ̵ti/ *n* [U] —**-bly** /ɪn'efəbli/ *adv* [Wa3,5]

in·ef·face·a·ble /,ɪnɪ̵'feɪsəbəl/ *adj* [Wa5] (of a mark, memory, etc.) which cannot be rubbed out or destroyed

in·ef·fec·tive /,ɪnɪ̵'fektɪv/ *adj* which does not produce any result or who cannot do anything well: *An ineffective person should not be chairman* —**~ly** *adv* —**~ness** *n* [U]

in·ef·fec·tu·al /,ɪnɪ̵'fektʃʊəl/ *adj* which does not give a good enough effect, or who is not able to get things done: *an ineffectual plan|an ineffectual fellow* —**~ly** *adv*

in·ef·fi·cient /,ɪnɪ̵'fɪʃənt/ *adj* that does not work well so as to produce good results quickly: *an inefficient machine|an inefficient secretary* —**~ly** *adv* —**-ciency** /,ɪnɪ̵'fɪʃənsi/ *n* [U]

in·e·las·tic /,ɪnɪ̵'læstɪk/ *adj* **1** which cannot stretch and spring back to its shape, like rubber **2** which cannot change or be changed to suit changing needs —compare INFLEXIBLE

in·el·e·gant /ɪn'elɪgənt/ *adj* **1** not showing good manners **2** awkward —**~ly** *adv* —**-gance** *n* [U]

in·el·i·gi·ble /ɪn'elɪ̵dʒəbəl/ *adj* [Wa5;B (*for*); F3] not ELIGIBLE (2): *ineligible to vote, because he didn't belong to the club* —**-bility** /ɪn,elɪ̵dʒə'bɪlɪ̵ti/ *n* [U]

in·e·luc·ta·ble /,ɪnɪ'lʌktəbəl/ *adj* [Wa5] *lit* which cannot be escaped from —**-bly** *adv* [Wa3,5]

in·ept /ɪ'nept/ *adj* **1** foolishly unsuitable: *an inept remark* **2** totally unable to do things: *He's quite inept at tennis* —**~ly** *adv*

in·ep·ti·tude /ɪ'neptɪ̵tjuːd‖-tuːd/ also **in·ept·ness** /ɪ'neptnɪ̵s/— *n* [U] the quality or state of being INEPT

in·e·qual·i·ty /,ɪnɪ'kwɒlɪ̵ti‖-'kwɑ-/ *n* **1** [U] lack of equality: *social inequality* **2** [C *usu. pl.*] a difference in size, amount, etc., esp. in justice

in·eq·ui·ta·ble /ɪn'ekwɪ̵təbəl/ *adj* unjust —**-bly** *adv* [Wa3]

in·eq·ui·ty /ɪn'ekwɪ̵ti/ *n* **1** [U] injustice; unfairness **2** [C] an example of injustice or unfairness

in·e·rad·i·ca·ble /,ɪnɪ'rædɪkəbəl/ *adj* (esp. of character) which cannot be completely removed: *an ineradicable fault*

in·ert /ɪ'nɜːt‖-ɜrt/ *adj* **1** [Wa5] lacking the power to move: *inert matter* **2** [Wa5] not acting chemically with other substances: *inert gases* **3** (of people) slow to activity; lazy —**~ly** *adv* —**~ness** *n* [U]

in·er·tia /ɪ'nɜːʃə‖-ɜr-/ *n* [U] **1** the force which prevents a thing from being moved when it is standing still, and keeps it moving (or prevents it from being stopped) when it is moving **2** the state of being powerless to move or too lazy to move: *a* *feeling of inertia on a hot summer day*

in·es·ca·pa·ble /ˌɪnɪsˈkeɪpəbəl/ *adj* [Wa5] which cannot be escaped from or avoided

in·es·sen·tial¹ /ˌɪnɨ̣ˈsenʃəl/ *adj* [Wa5; (*to*)] not at all necessary

inessential² *n* [*often pl.*] something not at all necessary

in·es·ti·ma·ble /ɪnˈestɨ̣məbəl/ *adj* too great to be calculated; very important: *of inestimable value* —**-bly** *adv* [Wa3]

in·ev·i·ta·ble /ɪˈnevɨ̣təbəl/ *adj* [Wa5] **1** [B] which cannot be prevented from happening: *An argument was inevitable because they disliked each other so much* **2** [A] *infml* which always happens, or is present with someone or something else: *wearing her inevitable large hat* —**-bility** /ɪˌnevɨ̣təˈbɪlɨ̣ti/ *n* [U] —**-bly** /ɪˈnevɨ̣təbli/ *adv* [Wa3,5]

in·ex·act /ˌɪnɪɡˈzækt/ *adj* not exact

in·ex·ac·ti·tude /ˌɪnɪɡˈzæktɨ̣tjuːd‖-tuːd/ also **in·ex·act·ness** /-ˈzæktnɨ̣s/— *n* the quality or state of being INEXACT

in·ex·cu·sa·ble /ˌɪnɪkˈskjuːzəbəl/ *adj* which is too bad to be excused: *inexcusable behaviour/lateness* —**-bly** *adv* [Wa3]

in·ex·haus·ti·ble /ˌɪnɪɡˈzɔːstəbəl/ *adj* which is in such large amounts that it can never be finished —**-bly** *adv* [Wa3]

in·ex·o·ra·ble /ɪnˈeksərəbəl/ *adj* [Wa5] whose actions or effects cannot be changed or prevented by one's efforts —**-bly** /ɪnˈeksərəbli/ *adv* [Wa3,5] —**-bility** /ɪnˌeksərəˈbɪlɨ̣ti/ *n* [U]

in·ex·pe·di·en·cy /ˌɪnɪkˈspiːdɪənsi/ also **in·ex·pe·di·ence** /-dɪəns/— *n* [U] the quality or fact of being INEXPEDIENT

in·ex·pe·di·ent /ˌɪnɪkˈspiːdɪənt/ *adj* (of acts) not EXPEDIENT; not suitable or advisable: *It would be inexpedient to set out in the rain*

in·ex·pen·sive /ˌɪnɪkˈspensɪv/ *adj* not EXPENSIVE; low in price —**~ly** *adv*

in·ex·pe·ri·ence /ˌɪnɪkˈspɪərɪəns/ *n* [U] lack of experience

in·ex·pe·ri·enced /ˌɪnɪkˈspɪərɪənst/ *adj* (of people) who lack the knowledge which one gains by experiencing some activity or life generally

in·ex·pert /ɪnˈekspɜːt‖-ɜrt/ *adj* not good at doing something: *his inexpert attempts to help/to cook* —**~ly** *adv*

in·ex·pi·a·ble /ɪnˈekspɪəbəl/ *adj* which cannot be made less bad by sorrow and attempts to make things well again: *an inexpiable crime* —**-bly** *adv* [Wa3]

in·ex·plic·a·ble /ˌɪnɪkˈsplɪkəbəl/ *adj* which is too strange to be explained or understood: *the inexplicable disappearance of the woman, who was never seen again* —**-bility** /ˌɪnɪkˌsplɪkəˈbɪlɨ̣ti/ *n* [U]

in·ex·plic·a·bly /ˌɪnɪkˈsplɪkəbli/ *adv* **1** in an INEXPLICABLE way: *He behaved inexplicably* **2** it is an INEXPLICABLE fact (that): *Inexplicably, he arrived late, although he had never done so before*

in·ex·pres·si·ble /ˌɪnɪkˈspresəbəl/ *adj* (of feelings) too great or too strong to be expressed in words —**-bly** *adv* [Wa3]

in·ex·tin·guish·a·ble /ˌɪnɪkˈstɪŋɡwɪʃəbəl/ *adj* [Wa5] (of fire and feelings) which cannot be put out or destroyed: *inextinguishable hopes*

in ex·tre·mis /ˌɪn ɪkˈstriːmɪs/ *adv* [Wa5] *Lat* at or as if at the moment of death: *The government's prices and incomes plan was saved in extremis by the new members of parliament*

in·ex·tri·ca·ble /ɪnˈekstrɪkəbəl, ˌɪnɪkˈstrɪ-/ *adj* **1** which cannot be escaped from because it is so difficult **2** which cannot be untied or separated —**-bly** *adv* [Wa3]: *Our fates are inextricably united*

in·fal·li·ble /ɪnˈfæləbəl/ *adj* **1** (of people) never making mistakes or doing anything bad **2** (of things) always having the right effect: *an infallible cure/medicine* —**-bility** /ɪnˌfæləˈbɪlɨ̣ti/ *n* [U]

in·fal·li·bly /ɪnˈfæləbli/ *adv* **1** in an INFALLIBLE way: *a memory that is infallibly exact* **2** *infml* always; without FAIL²; inevitably (INEVITABLE): *Infallibly, he arrives just when I want to go home*

in·fa·mous /ˈɪnfəməs/ *adj* **1** well known for wicked behaviour: *an infamous criminal* **2** evil; wicked: *infamous behaviour* —see FAMOUS (USAGE)

in·fa·my /ˈɪnfəmi/ *n* **1** [U] the quality of being INFAMOUS **2** [C *often pl.*] an act which is INFAMOUS

in·fan·cy /ˈɪnfənsi/ *n* [S;U] **1** early childhood: *a happy infancy* **2** a beginning or early period of existence: *Our new plan is still only in its infancy*

in·fant /ˈɪnfənt/ *n* **1** [C] a very young child **2** [C *often pl.*] the young of a creature **3** [A] intended for young children

in·fan·ti·cide /ɪnˈfæntɨ̣saɪd/ *n* **1** [U;C] the crime of killing a child. esp. an INFANT **2** [C] a person guilty of this crime

in·fan·tile /ˈɪnfəntaɪl/ *adj* **1** [B] *often derog* like (that of) a small child **2** [Wa5;A] concerning, or happening to, small children

infantile pa·ral·y·sis /ˌ··· ·ˈ···/ *n* [U] *now rare* POLIO

infant prod·i·gy /ˌ·· ˈ···/ also **child prodigy**— *n* a young child with the abilities or understanding of a clever grown-up person

in·fan·try /ˈɪnfəntri/ *n* [(*the*) GU] soldiers who fight on foot

in·fan·try·man /ˈɪnfəntrimən/ *n* **-men** /mən/ [C;A] a soldier who fights on foot

infant school /ˈ·· ·/ *n* [U;(C)] (in Britain) a school for children from about 5 to 7 years of age

in·fat·u·at·ed /ɪnˈfætʃʊeɪtɨ̣d/ *adj* [(*with*)] (of people) filled with a strong unreasonable feeling of love for (someone)

in·fat·u·a·tion /ɪnˌfætʃʊˈeɪʃən/ *n* [U;C: (*with*)] a state or period of being INFATUATED with someone

in·fect /ɪnˈfekt/ *v* [T1 (*with*)] **1** [Wv5] to put disease into the body of (someone): *The disease infected her eyes, and she became blind* **2** [Wv5] to make impure by spreading into (something) **3** to make (someone else) have feelings of the same type: *She infected the whole class with her laughter*

in·fec·tion /ɪnˈfekʃən/ *n* **1** [U] the state or result of being infected, or the action of infecting: *infection from impure water/by flies* **2** [C] an illness brought by infection: *suffering from a lung infection*

in·fec·tious /ɪnˈfekʃəs/ *adj* **1** (of a disease) which can be spread by infection, esp. in the air: *Colds are infectious* —compare CONTAGIOUS (1) **2** which produces the same feelings or actions in others: *infectious laughter* **3** *infml* CONTAGIOUS (1) —**~ly** *adv* —**~ness** *n* [U]

in·fe·li·ci·tous /ˌɪnfɨ̣ˈlɪsɨ̣təs/ *adj pomp* (of actions, words, etc.) not suitable; not acceptable: *an infelicitous remark about the size of her nose* —**-licity** /-ti/ *n* [U;C]: *infelicity of style in a writer*

in·fer /ɪnˈfɜːʳ/ *v* **-rr-** [T1,5,5b,6a,b: (*from*)] to draw the meaning from (something): *I infer from your letter that you do not wish to see us* —compare IMPLY

USAGE Correctly, it is the listener or reader who **infers** things: *I looked at his boots and* **inferred** *that he must be a policeman.* The speaker or writer **implies** things: *He said it was late,* **implying** *that we ought to go home.* People now often say **infer** for **imply**, but this is not thought to be good English.

in·fer·ence /ˈɪnfərəns/ *n* **1** [U] the act or action of INFERring **2** [C] the meaning which one draws from something done, said, etc.: *He never arrives on time, and my inference is that he feels the meetings are useless* —compare IMPLICATION

in·fer·en·tial /ˌɪnfəˈrenʃəl/ *adj* [Wa5] which can be or has been INFERred: *inferential proof* —**-tially** *adv*

in·fe·ri·or[1] /ɪnˈfɪərɪəʳ/ *adj* [Wa5; (*to*)] **1** *fml & tech* lower in position: *an inferior court of law* **2** (of people and things) not good or less good in quality or value: *His work is inferior to mine.|He's so clever, he makes me feel inferior* —**~ity** /ɪnˌfɪəriˈɒrɪ̈ti‖-ˈɑrɪ̈-/ *n* [U]

inferior[2] *n* [C9] *often derog* a person of lower rank, esp. in a job: *You mustn't be afraid of making your inferiors work harder* —compare SUPERIOR[2] (1), SUBORDINATE (1)

inferiority com·plex /···'··· ˌ··/ *n* a state of mind when one feels oneself of less value than others, sometimes resulting in one's avoiding other people, sometimes in one's trying to attract attention

in·fer·nal /ɪnˈfɜːnəl‖-ɜr-/ *adj* **1** [Wa5;B] of HELL[1] (1): *the infernal powers* **2** [A] *infml becoming rare* (used for expressing anger) very bad; terrible: *that infernal noise!* —**~ly** *adv*: *infernally noisy*

in·fer·no /ɪnˈfɜːnəʊ‖-ɜr-/ *n* **-nos** **1** a place or state that is like HELL: *the inferno of war* **2** (a place marked by) very great heat and large noisy flames: *The burning building became an inferno*

in·fer·tile /ɪnˈfɜːtaɪl‖-ɜrtəl/ *adj* **1** [Wa5] not FERTILE; not able to produce young **2** (of land) not able to grow plants —**-tility** /ˌɪnfɜːˈtɪlɪ̈ti‖-ɜr-/ *n* [U]

in·fest /ɪnˈfest/ *v* [T1 (*with*)] to cause trouble to or in, by being present in large numbers: *Mice infested the old house* —**~ation** /ˌɪnfesˈteɪʃən/ *n* [U; (C)]

in·fi·del /ˈɪnfɪ̈dl/ *n old use & derog* (used esp. in former times by Christians and Muslims of each other) someone who does not follow one's own religion; unbeliever

in·fi·del·i·ty /ˌɪnfɪ̈ˈdelɪ̈ti/ *n* [U;C] **1** (an example or act of) disloyalty **2** (an act of) sex with someone other than one's marriage partner; UNFAITHFULNESS

in·field /ˈɪnfiːld/ *n* **1** [C] (in cricket and BASEBALL) an area near the WICKET (1b) or within the DIAMOND (5a) —see picture at BASEBALL **2** [GC] the men who field the ball there —compare OUTFIELD

in·fight·ing /ˈɪnfaɪtɪŋ/ *n* [U] **1** (in sport) fighting when the bodies are close together **2** competition and disagreement, often bitter, which goes on between close members of a group, such as partners in a company or organization

in·fil·trate /ˈɪnfɪltreɪt‖ɪnˈfɪltreɪt, ˈɪnfɪl-/ *v* [T1 (*in, into*)] to (cause to) go into and among (the parts or members of something), esp. quietly and with an unfriendly purpose: *The enemy infiltrated our land.|We infiltrated men into enemy country* —**-trator** *n*

in·fil·tra·tion /ˌɪnfɪlˈtreɪʃən/ *n* **1** [U] the act of infiltrating (INFILTRATE) **2** [C *usu. sing.*] a method of attack by entering unnoticed into the enemy's land, one's opponents' area of activity, etc.

in·fi·nite /ˈɪnfɪ̈nɪ̈t/ *adj* [Wa5] **1** without limits or end **2** very large; as much as there is —**~ly** *adv*: *infinitely large/many*

in·fin·i·tes·i·mal /ˌɪnfɪnɪ̈ˈtesɪ̈məl/ *adj* [Wa5] very small —**-mally** *adv*

in·fin·i·tive /ɪnˈfɪnɪ̈tɪv/ *n, adj* (of) the form of the verb that can be used after other verbs and with *to* before it (such as *go* in *I can go, I want to go,* and *It is important to go*) —see also SPLIT[1] **an infinitive**

in·fin·i·tude /ɪnˈfɪnɪ̈tjuːd‖-tuːd/ *n* [U;S] *fml* largeness; wideness; lack of limits

in·fin·i·ty /ɪnˈfɪnɪ̈ti/ *n* [U;S] **1** limitless time or space: *the infinity of the universe* **2** a very large amount of time or space: *I seemed to wait for an infinity*

in·firm /ɪnˈfɜːm‖-ɜrm/ *adj* **1** weak in body or mind, esp. from age: *old and infirm* **2 infirm of purpose** *lit* unable to decide

in·fir·ma·ry /ɪnˈfɜːməri/ *n* **1** a hospital **2** a room or other place where the sick are lodged for care and treatment, as in a school

in·fir·mi·ty /ɪnˈfɜːmɪ̈ti/ *n fml* **1** [U] weakness of body or mind: *suffering from age and infirmity* **2** [C] a lack of a particular human ability: *The infirmities left by an illness can be worse than the illness itself*

in·flame /ɪnˈfleɪm/ *v* [T1 (*with*)] to make (someone) angry

in·flamed /ɪnˈfleɪmd/ *adj* (of a part of the body) red and swollen because hurt or diseased: *an inflamed eye*

in·flam·ma·ble /ɪnˈflæməbəl/ *adj* **1** also (*esp. AmE or tech*) **flammable**— which can be set on fire —opposite **nonflammable** **2** easily excited or made angry —compare INFLAMMATORY; see FLAMMABLE (USAGE)

in·flam·ma·tion /ˌɪnfləˈmeɪʃən/ *n* [U;C] swelling and soreness, which is often red and hot to the touch: *an inflammation of the lungs* —see also INFLAMED

in·flam·ma·to·ry /ɪnˈflæmətəri‖-tori/ *adj* likely to cause strong feelings to rise, or violence to happen —see also INFLAME; compare INFLAMMABLE

in·fla·ta·ble /ɪnˈfleɪtəbəl/ *adj* [Wa5] which must be INFLATEd for use

in·flate /ɪnˈfleɪt/ *v* [Wv5;T1;I∅] *fml* to (cause to) fill until swelled with air, gas, etc.; blow up —opposite **deflate**

in·flat·ed /ɪnˈfleɪtɪ̈d/ *adj* **1** **a** blown up (as with air): *an inflated lung* **b** *fml* (of people) PUFFed UP; filled with pride **2** (of prices) risen to a high level, usu. caused by an increase in the money supply and/or not enough goods or services **3** (of feelings, speech, etc.) giving an appearance of importance when there is no reason to do so: *an inflated opinion of himself*

in·fla·tion /ɪnˈfleɪʃən/ *n* [U] **1** the act of inflating or state of being INFLATED **2** the rise in prices thought to be caused by increases in the costs of production **(cost-push inflation)** or an increase in the money supply **(demand-pull inflation)** —compare DEFLATION, REFLATION

in·fla·tion·a·ry /ɪnˈfleɪʃənəri‖-ʃəneri/ *adj* of or likely to cause INFLATION (2)

inflationary spi·ral /·ˌ···· ˈ··/ *n* the rises in wages and prices which follow an increase in the money supply

in·flect /ɪnˈflekt/ *v* [I∅;T1] **1** [Wv5] **a** (of a word) to change in form at its end according to use: *The word "child" inflects differently in the plural to the word "boy".|an inflected verb* **b** to cause (a word) to change in form according to use: *a highly inflected language* —compare CONJUGATE[1] (1,2), DECLINE[1] (4) **2** **a** (esp. of the voice) to change, esp. in level, according to the needs of expression **b** to cause (the voice) to change in this way

in·flec·tion, *BrE* also **inflexion** /ɪnˈflekʃən/ *n* **1** [U] the act or result of INFLECTING **2** [C] **a** the part of a word which can be changed: *In "largest",* -EST *is the inflection meaning "most"* **b** a movement up or down of the voice: *A sentence that asks a question usually ends on a rising inflection* —see also INTONATION

in·flex·i·ble /ɪnˈfleksəbəl/ *adj* **1** [Wa5] which cannot be bent —compare FLEX[1], FLEXIBLE **2** **a** (of people) who cannot be turned away from their purpose **b** (of ideas, decisions, etc.) which cannot be changed —**-bility** /ɪnˌfleksəˈbɪlɪ̈ti/ *n* [U] —**-bly** /ɪnˈfleksəbli/ *adv* [Wa3]

in·flic·tion /ɪnˈflɪkʃən/ *n* **1** [U] the act of inflicting

something on someone (INFLICT ON) **2** [C] something inflicted on someone; punishment
inflict /ɪnˈflɪkt/ *v* [T1;X9] to cause (damage, suffering, etc.): *The storm inflicted heavy damage all over the country*
inflict on also **inflict up·on**— *v prep* [D1] to force (something unwanted or unpleasant) on (someone): *Don't inflict your ideas on me*
in·flow /ˈɪnfləʊ/ also **influx**— *n* [U;C] the act of flowing in or something which does so: *the inflow of money to the banks*
in·flu·ence¹ /ˈɪnflʊəns/ *n* **1** [U;C: (*over, with, on, upon*)] **a** power to gain an effect on the mind of or get results from, without asking or doing anything: *He has a strange influence over the girl.|Her influence made me a better person* **b** a person with this power: *He's an influence for good in the club* **2** [C; U: (*on, upon*)] action of power; effect: *The stars' influence on men has not been proved* **3** [U] the power to get things done, which important men have by using their wealth, position, etc.: *to use one's influence to get a job* **4 a good/bad influence** someone or something that has (the power to produce) a good/bad moral effect **5 under the influence** *humor* drunk; AFFECTed² by alcohol **6 under the influence of** in the power of; experiencing the effects of (people, things)
influence² *v* [T1;V3] to have an effect on; AFFECT²: *Don't let me influence your decision.|What influenced you to do it?*
in·flu·en·tial /ˌɪnflʊˈenʃəl/ *adj* having great influence: *an influential decision/man* —**-tially** *adv*
in·flu·en·za /ˌɪnflʊˈenzə/ also (*infml*) **flu**— *n* [U] a disease which is like a bad cold but more serious
in·flux /ˈɪnflʌks/ *n* **1** [C *usu. sing.*] the arrival, or movement inside, of large numbers/quantities: *There was a sudden influx of goods onto the market* —compare FLUX **2** [U;C] INFLOW
in·fo /ˈɪnfəʊ/ *n* [U] *infml* information
in·form /ɪnˈfɔːm‖-ɔrm/ *v* [T1 (*of, about*); D5,(6a,b)] *fml* to tell; to give information to: *I informed him (about) where to go* —see SAY (USAGE)
inform a·gainst also **inform on, inform up·on**— *v prep* [T1] to tell the police, or someone in charge, about (someone who has done something wrong)
in·for·mal /ɪnˈfɔːməl‖-ɔr-/ *adj* **1** not formal; without ceremony: *an informal meeting* **2** (of clothes and behaviour) worn or done to suit oneself, rather than according to particular rules or customs **3** *tech* not including all the details or stating all the stages in the reasoning: *an informal proof of the* THEOREM —**~ity** /ˌɪnfɔːˈmælɪ̆ti‖-ɔr-/ *n* [U] —**-mally** /ɪnˈfɔːməli‖-ɔr-/ *adv*
in·for·mant /ɪnˈfɔːmənt‖-ɔr-/ *n tech* a person who gives information, esp. someone who gives details of his language, social customs, etc., to someone who is studying it —compare INFORMER
in·for·ma·tion /ˌɪnfəˈmeɪʃən‖-ər-/ *n* [U] (something which gives) knowledge in the form of facts
USAGE One *gets* or *obtains* **information**, or *a piece/bit of* **information**.
in·for·ma·tive /ɪnˈfɔːmətɪv‖-ɔr-/ *adj* that tells one some useful things: *an informative speech* —**~ly** *adv*
in·formed /ɪnˈfɔːmd‖-ɔr-/ *adj* **1** knowing things; having all the information: *well-informed|badly informed|I read the newspapers to keep myself informed as to what is happening everywhere* **2** having and using suitable knowledge: *an informed guess*
in·form·er /ɪnˈfɔːməʳ‖-ɔr-/ *n sometimes derog* a person who INFORMs AGAINST another, esp. to the police
in·fra /ˈɪnfrə/ *adv Lat & fml* below (in a book)
infra- *prefix* below: *infrahuman creatures such as monkeys*
in·frac·tion /ɪnˈfrækʃən/ *n* [U;C] *fml* the act or an example of breaking a rule
infra dig /ˌ·· ˈ·/ *abbrev. for:* (*Lat & humor*) **infra dignitatem** (=beneath one's DIGNITY (4)); not good enough (for someone) to do: *She'd like to have a servant—it's infra dig for her to wash her own clothes*
in·fra·red /ˌɪnfrəˈred◂/ *adj* [Wa5] of the heat-giving RAYs² of light of longer wave-length than the red light which can be seen
in·fra·struc·ture /ˈɪnfrəˌstrʌktʃəʳ/ *n* the system which supports the operation of an organization
in·fre·quent /ɪnˈfriːkwənt/ *adj* not (happening) often: *infrequent visits* —**~ly** *adv*: *comes infrequently* —**-quency** /ɪnˈfriːkwənsi/ *n* [U]
in·fringe /ɪnˈfrɪndʒ/ *v* [T1] to go against or take over (the right of another) —**~ment** *n* [U;C]: *an infringement of the law*
infringe up·on also **infringe on**— *v prep* [T1] INFRINGE: *to infringe upon a nation's fishing rights at sea*
in·fu·ri·ate /ɪnˈfjʊərieɪt/ *v* [Wv4;T1] to make (someone) very angry
in·fuse /ɪnˈfjuːz/ *v* **1** [I∅;T1] **a** (of a substance such as tea) to stay in hot water so as to make a liquid of a certain taste **b** to cause (a substance such as tea) to do this **2** [D1+*with/into*] to fill (someone) with (a quality): *His speech infused the men with eagerness.|He infused eagerness into the men*
in·fu·sion /ɪnˈfjuːʒən/ *n* **1** [U] the act of infusing (INFUSE) **2** [C] a liquid made in this way, often for medical use **3** [C;U: (*into*)] (an example of) the act of mixing or filling (with something new): *an infusion of new ideas into all of us*
-ing /ɪŋ/ *suffix* **1** [*v→v,adj*] (forms the present participle of verbs. It is often used as an adjective): *They're drinking beer.|to go dancing|a dancing bear* —see USAGE **2** [*v→n* [U]] the action of: *She hates swimming.|No Parking* (on a notice) **3** [*v→n* [C]] **a** a case of: *to hold a meeting* **b** a product or result of: *to spend one's earnings|a beautiful painting* **4** [*v,n→n* [C;U]] something used for, or used for making: *a silk* LINING|*10 yards of shirting*
USAGE Verbal adjectives ending with **-ing** always mean that the noun they describe is the subject or doer: *a* **charming** *girl* (=she charms me)|*an* **interesting** *play* (=it interests me). Verbal adjectives ending with **-ed** mean that the noun they describe is the object: *an* **interested** *crowd* (=something interests them). When one hears a piece of news, one may say *I'm very (much)* **interested**, but it would be stupid to say *I'm very* **interesting!**
in·gath·er·ing /ˈɪngæðərɪŋ/ *n* [U;C] *lit* the action, or an act, of gathering in, esp. crops or people
in·ge·ni·ous /ɪnˈdʒiːnɪəs/ *adj* having or showing cleverness at making or inventing things: *an ingenious person/idea/toy* —compare INGENUOUS —**~ly** *adv*
in·ge·nue, -gé- /ˈænʒeɪnjuː‖ˈændʒənuː (*Fr* ɛ̃ʒeny)/ *n Fr* a young inexperienced girl, esp. when played by an actress
in·ge·nu·i·ty /ˌɪndʒɪ̆ˈnjuːɪ̆ti‖-ˈnuː-/ *n* [U] skill and cleverness in making or arranging things
in·gen·u·ous /ɪnˈdʒenjʊəs/ *adj* (of people and their acts) simple, direct, and inexperienced: *too ingenuous in believing what people say* —compare INGENIOUS —**~ly** *adv* —**~ness** *n* [U]
in·gest /ɪnˈdʒest/ *v* [T1] *tech* to take (food) into the stomach —**~ion** /ɪnˈdʒestʃən/ *n* [U]
in·gle·nook /ˈɪŋgəlnʊk/ *n* (a seat in) a partly enclosed space near a large open fireplace
in·glo·ri·ous /ɪnˈglɔːrɪəs‖ɪnˈglor-/ *adj lit* shameful; bringing dishonour: *an inglorious defeat* —**~ly** *adv*

in·go·ing /ˈɪngəʊɪŋ/ *adj* [Wa5;A] going in; entering, esp. taking possession of property one has just rented

in·got /ˈɪŋgət/ *n* a lump of metal in a regular shape, often brick-shaped; bar (of gold or silver)

in·graft /ɪnˈgrɑːft‖ɪnˈgræft/ *v* [T1 (*into, on, onto, upon*)] ENGRAFT

in·grained /ɪnˈgreɪnd/ *adj* fixed deep (inside) so that it is difficult to get out or destroy: *ingrained dirt|ingrained habits*

in·gra·ti·ate /ɪnˈgreɪʃieɪt/ *v* [T1 (*with*)] to make (oneself) very pleasant to someone in order to gain favour: *ingratiated himself with his employer*

in·gra·ti·at·ing /ɪnˈgreɪʃieɪtɪŋ/ *adj* (of people and their acts) showing that one wishes to gain favour: *an ingratiating smile* —**~ly** *adv*

in·grat·i·tude /ɪnˈgrætɪ̵tjuːd‖-tuːd/ *n* [U] ungratefulness

in·gre·di·ent /ɪnˈgriːdɪənt/ *n* a particular one of a mixture of things, esp. in baking: *Flour and fat are the most important ingredients.*|(fig.) *Imagination and hard work are the ingredients of success*

in·gress /ˈɪngres/ *n* [U] *fml or lit* the act of entering or the right to enter —opposite **egress**

in-group /ˈ· ·/ *n* [GC] *often derog* a group that treats members better than non-members: *There's a little in-group that seems to keep all the good jobs for itself/themselves* —opposite **out-group**; compare CLIQUE

in·grown /ˌɪnˈgrəʊn◂/ also **in·grow·ing** /ˌɪnˈgrəʊɪŋ◂/— *adj* [Wa5;A] growing inwards, esp. into the flesh: *an ingrown toenail*

in·hab·it /ɪnˈhæbɪ̵t/ *v* [Wv6;T1] to live in —see LIVE[1] (USAGE) —**~able** *adj*: *an inhabitable area*

in·hab·i·tant /ɪnˈhæbɪ̵tənt/ *n* a person (or sometimes an animal) that lives in a particular place regularly, as a general rule, or for a period of time: *inhabitants of large cities*

in·hale /ɪnˈheɪl/ *v* [T1;IØ] **1** to breathe (something) in: *He inhaled deeply* **2** to draw (smoke) into the lungs —opposite **exhale**

in·hal·er /ɪnˈheɪləʳ/ *n* an apparatus which is used for inhaling (INHALE) medicine in the form of VAPOUR, usu. to make breathing easier

in·har·mo·ni·ous /ˌɪnhɑːˈməʊnɪəs‖-ɑr-/ *adj* not suitable to something else/each other: *an inharmonious set of colours|inharmonious sounds* —**~ly** *adv* —**~ness** *n* [U]

in·here in /ɪnˈhɪəʳ/ *v prep* [T1] *fml or tech* to be a natural part of

in·her·ent /ɪnˈhɪərənt/ *adj* [(*in*)] forming a natural part (of a set of qualities, a character, etc.)

in·her·ent·ly /ɪnˈhɪərəntli/ *adv* in itself or oneself; by its or one's nature; as such; INTRINSICally

in·her·it /ɪnˈherɪ̵t/ *v* [(*from*)] **1** [T1] to receive (property, a title, etc.) left by someone who has died **2** [IØ] to be the one who receives what is left, esp. at another's death, or to take possession of what one has the right to as HEIR **3** [T1] to receive (qualities of mind or body) from one's parents, grandmother or grandfather, etc.

in·her·i·tance /ɪnˈherɪ̵təns/ *n* **1** [U] the act of INHERITING **2** [C *usu. sing.*] property, a title, and/or qualities of mind or body received by INHERITing

in·hib·it /ɪnˈhɪbɪ̵t/ *v* [T1] **1** to hold back (from something): *Thirst inhibited the desire to eat* **2** to make (someone) INHIBITED: *His presence inhibits me*

in·hib·it·ed /ɪnˈhɪbɪ̵tɪ̵d/ *adj* (of people and character) unable to express what one really feels or do what one really wants: *too inhibited to laugh freely/to talk about sex* —compare UNINHIBITED —**~ly** *adv*

inhibit from *v prep* [V4b;(D1)] to prevent from (doing something), esp. by some controlling influence: *Fear inhibits me from talking*

in·hi·bi·tion /ˌɪnhɪ̵ˈbɪʃən/ *n* [U;C] the state of being INHIBITed; feeling that something cannot be done: *She gets rid of her inhibitions when she's drunk 2 or 3 glasses of wine*

in·hos·pi·ta·ble /ˌɪnhɒˈspɪtəbəl‖-hɑ-/ *adj* **1** (of people and their acts) not showing kindness esp. not giving food and shelter in one's own home **2** (of places) not forming a shelter; not suitable to stay in —**-bly** *adv* [Wa3]

in·hu·man /ɪnˈhjuːmən/ *adj* **1** too cruel, lacking in feelings, etc., to be worthy of human behaviour **2** [Wa5] *rare* not human

in·hu·mane /ˌɪnhjuːˈmeɪn/ *adj* (of people and their acts) not showing human kindness, esp. when it should be shown —**-manely** *adv*

in·hu·man·i·ty /ˌɪnhjuːˈmænɪ̵ti/ *n* **1** [U] the quality or state of being cruel and harming other human beings **2** [C *often pl.*] an act showing this quality

in·im·i·cal /ɪˈnɪmɪkəl/ *adj* [(*to*)] *fml* being an enemy (of); very unfavourable (to): *conditions inimical to comfort*

in·im·i·ta·ble /ɪˈnɪmɪ̵təbəl/ *adj* too good for anyone else to copy with the same high quality —see IMITATE —**-bly** *adv*

in·iq·ui·tous /ɪˈnɪkwɪ̵təs/ *adj fml* very unjust or wicked —**~ly** *adv*

in·iq·ui·ty /ɪˈnɪkwɪ̵ti/ *n* [U;C] (an act of) injustice or wickedness

i·ni·tial[1] /ɪˈnɪʃəl/ *adj* [Wa5;A] which is (at) the beginning of a set: *The initial talks were the base of the later agreement*

initial[2] *n* a large letter at the beginning of a name, esp. when used alone to represent a person's first name(s) and last name

initial[3] *v* **-ll-** (*AmE* **-l-**) [T1] to sign one's name on (a piece of writing) by writing one's INITIAL*s*, usu. to show approval or agreement

i·ni·tial·ly /ɪˈnɪʃəli/ *adv* [Wa5] at the beginning; at first: *Initially, she opposed the plan, but later she changed her mind*

i·ni·ti·ate[1] /ɪˈnɪʃieɪt/ *v* [T1] **1** to start (something) working **2** [(*into*) *often pass.*] to introduce (someone) into a club, group, etc., esp. with a special ceremony **3** [(*into*) *often pass.*] to introduce to (someone) some secret or mysterious knowledge

i·ni·ti·ate[2] /ɪˈnɪʃiɪ̵t/ *n* a person who is instructed or skilled in some special field, esp. one who knows its secrets or mysteries

i·ni·ti·a·tion /ɪˌnɪʃiˈeɪʃən/ *n* [(*into*)] **1** [U;C] (an example of) the act of initiating or action of being INITIATED: *initiation into a secret society* **2** [C] a ceremony of initiating (INITIATE), esp. one through which a young man or woman is officially recognized as an ADULT in a particular society

i·ni·tia·tive /ɪˈnɪʃətɪv/ *n* **1** [C] the first movement or act which starts something happening (esp. in the phr. **take the initiative**) **2** [U] the ability to do things in a way one has worked out for oneself to be the best **3 on one's own initiative** (done) according to one's own plan and without help

in·ject /ɪnˈdʒekt/ *v* [D1+*with*/*into*; T1] to put (liquid) into (someone) with a special needle (SYRINGE[1]): *They are injecting him with new drugs.*|*They injected every possible drug into him.*|(fig.) *to inject new life, interest, etc., into something*

in·jec·tion /ɪnˈdʒekʃən/ *n* **1** [U] the act of INJECTing **2** [C] an occasion when this is done: *It's time for another injection.*|(fig.) *an injection of new money into the business* **3** [C] the liquid used for this: *a large/small injection*

in·ju·di·cious /ˌɪndʒʊˈdɪʃəs/ *adj* (of acts) not wise

or sensible to do; showing poor judgment —**~ly** *adv* —**~ness** *n* [U]

in·junc·tion /ɪnˈdʒʌŋkʃən/ *n* [C (*against*), C3,5c] **1** *fml* an order **2** *law* a command or official order to do or not to do something

in·jure /ˈɪndʒəʳ/ *v* [T1] **1** [Wv5] to hurt (a living thing): *She was injured badly in the accident.*|*The injured (people) were taken to hospital* **2** to offend: *I hope I didn't injure her (feelings)*
USAGE One can be *slightly/badly/seriously* **injured**. —see WOUND[1] (USAGE)

in·ju·ri·ous /ɪnˈdʒʊəriəs/ *adj* [(*to*)] which will cause harm: *Smoking is injurious to health* —**~ly** *adv*

in·ju·ry /ˈɪndʒəri/ *n* **1** [U] harm; damage to a living thing: *insurance against injury at work*|(fig.) *injury to one's pride* **2** [C] an act that damages or hurts: *several serious injuries to the legs and arms* **3 add insult to injury** to do or say something more against someone when one has already harmed them enough

in·jus·tice /ɪnˈdʒʌstɪ̣s/ *n* **1** [U] the fact of not being just; unfairness **2** [C] an act showing this **3 do someone an injustice** to judge someone in an unfair way and/or believe something bad about him which is untrue

ink /ɪŋk/ *n* [U] coloured liquid used for writing (or drawing)

ink·bot·tle /ˈɪŋkˌbɒtl‖-ˌbɑtl/ also **ink·pot** /ˈɪnkpɒt‖-pɑt/— *n* a container for ink

ink in *v adv* [T1] to complete with ink (something drawn in pencil or left unfilled)

ink·ling /ˈɪŋklɪŋ/ *n* [S;U: (*of, as to*)] a possible idea or a suggestion (only in the phrs. **have an/no/some/any inkling, give someone an inkling**): *His explanation gave me an inkling of the difficulties*

ink·pad /ˈɪŋkpæd/ *n* a container with ink which has been put on a thick piece of cloth or other material, for use in putting ink onto a marker that is to be pressed onto paper

ink·stand /ˈɪŋkstænd/ *n* a flat piece of hard material shaped to hold ink-bottles, pens, etc.

ink·well /ˈɪŋk-wel/ *n* an inkpot which fits into a hole in a desk

ink·y /ˈɪŋki/ *adj* [Wa1] **1** marked with ink: *inky fingers* **2** inklike; very dark black: *inky darkness* —**inkiness** *n* [U] —**inkily** *adv*

in·laid /ˌɪnˈleɪd◂/ *adj* [Wa5] **1** [(*in, into*)] set ornamentally into another substance: *gold inlaid in(to) wood*|*inlaid gold* **2** [(*with*)] having another substance set in: *wood inlaid with gold*|*inlaid wood*

in·land[1] /ˈɪnlənd/ *adj* [Wa5;A] done or placed inside a country, not near the coast or other countries: *the inland forests*|*inland trade*

in·land[2] /ɪnˈlænd/ *adv* [Wa5;F] towards or in the heart of the country: *We walked inland.*|*There are mountains inland*

Inland Rev·e·nue /ˌ·· ˈ···/ *n* (esp. in Britain) **1** [*the* +GU] the office which collects national taxes **2** [U;S] the money collected as taxes by this office

in-laws /ˈ· ·/ *n* [P] the father and mother of the person someone has married, and also (sometimes) other relatives by marriage

in·lay /ˈɪnleɪ/ *n* **1** an INLAID pattern, surface, or substance: *wood with an inlay of gold* **2** a filling of a metal or another substance used in the inside of a decayed or damaged tooth

in·let /ˈɪnlet, ˈɪnlɪ̣t/ *n* **1** a narrow stretch of water reaching from a sea, lake, etc., into the land or between islands **2** a way in (for water, liquid, etc.) —compare OUTLET

in lo·co pa·ren·tis /ɪn ˌləʊkəʊ pəˈrentɪs/ *adv Lat* having the responsibilities of a parent towards someone else's children

in·mate /ˈɪnmeɪt/ *n* a person living in the same room or building as others, esp. unwillingly as in a hospital or prison

in me·mo·ri·am /ɪn mɪ̣ˈmɔːriəm‖-ˈmor-/ *prep Lat* (used before the name marked on a stone above a grave) in memory of: *In Memoriam John Jones, 1871–1956*

in·most /ˈɪnməʊst/ also **in·ner·most** /ˈɪnəməʊst‖-ər-/— *adj* **1** farthest inside: *the inmost depths of the cave* **2** most well hidden: *inmost desires*

inn /ɪn/ *n* a small hotel or place where one can stay and/or drink alcohol, eat meals, etc., esp. one built (in the style of) many centuries ago: *an old country inn*

in·nards /ˈɪnədz‖-ər-/ *n* [P] *infml* the inner parts, usu. of the stomach

in·nate /ˌɪˈneɪt◂/ *adj* [Wa5] (of qualities) which someone was born with: *innate kindness* —**~ly** *adv*: *innately kind*

in·ner /ˈɪnəʳ/ *adj* [Wa5;A] **1** (placed) inside: *the inner ear*|*an inner room* **2** closest to the centre (and in control) of what is happening (esp. in the phr. **inner circle**) **3** secret, esp. if of the spirit: *an inner meaning*|*inner life*

inner tube /ˈ·· ·/ *n* the circular tube inside a tyre which is filled with air

in·ning /ˈɪnɪŋ/ *n* any of the usu. 9 playing periods into which a game of BASEBALL or SOFTBALL is divided

in·nings /ˈɪnɪŋz/ *n* **innings** [Wn3] **1** the period of time during which a cricket team or player BATs **2** *BrE* a time when one is active, esp. in a public position

inn·keep·er /ˈɪnˌkiːpəʳ/ *n* [C;N] *becoming rare* a person who looks after an inn —see also PUBLICAN (1)

in·no·cent[1] /ˈɪnəsənt/ *adj* **1** [Wa5; (*of*)] (of people) guiltless: *He was innocent of the crime* **2** (of things) harmless: *innocent enjoyment/pleasures* **3** (of people) simple; not able to recognize evil: *a trusting innocent young child* —**~ly** *adv* —**-cence** *n* [U]

innocent[2] *n* **1** a simple person with no knowledge of evil **2** *becoming rare* someone weak in mind —compare IDIOT (1)

in·noc·u·ous /ɪˈnɒkjʊəs‖ɪˈnɑk-/ *adj* (esp. of actions, statements, etc.) harmless; not intended to offend —**~ly** *adv* —**~ness** *n* [U]

in·no·vate /ˈɪnəveɪt/ *v* [IØ] to make changes —**-vator** *n*

in·no·va·tion /ˌɪnəˈveɪʃən/ *n* **1** [U] the introduction of something new: *the innovation of air travel during this century* **2** [C] a new idea, method, or invention: *recent innovations in printing methods*

Inns of Court /ˌ· · ˈ·/ *n* [*the*+P] the college-like law societies in London, to one of which an English BARRISTER must belong

in·nu·en·do /ˌɪnjʊˈendəʊ/ *n* **-does** *or* **-dos** **1** [U] the act of suggesting something unpleasant in words without saying it directly **2** [C] a remark of this type: *made innuendoes about her coming home at 4 o'clock in the morning*

in·nu·me·ra·ble /ɪˈnjuːmərəbəl‖ɪˈnuː-/ *adj* [Wa5] too many to be counted

i·noc·u·late /ɪˈnɒkjʊleɪt‖ɪˈnɑkjə-/ *v* [T1;(IØ): (*with* and/or *against*)] to introduce a weak form of a disease into (a living body) as a protection against the disease —compare VACCINATE, INJECT —**-lation** /ɪˌnɒkjʊˈleɪʃən‖ɪˌnɑkjə-/ *n* [U;C]

in·of·fen·sive /ˌɪnəˈfensɪv/ *adj* (of people and their acts) not causing any harm; not causing dislike in other people: *an inoffensive manner*|*a quiet inoffensive sort of woman* —**~ly** *adv* —**~ness** *n* [U]

in·op·e·ra·ble /ɪnˈɒpərəbəl‖ɪnˈɑ-/ *adj* **1** [Wa5] (of diseased growths on or in the body) that cannot be removed by operation so as to cure the person **2**

which cannot be put into practice or made to continue: *an inoperable plan*

in·op·e·ra·tive /ɪn'ɒpərətɪv‖ɪn'ɑ-/ *adj* [Wa5 (of laws, rules, etc.)] **1** not able to work as usual **2** without effect

in·op·por·tune /ɪn'ɒpətjuːn‖ˌɪnɑpər'tuːn/ *adj* **1** unsuitable for the time: *an inopportune visit/remark* **2** (usu. of time) unsuitable (for something to happen): *He called at an inopportune moment, when we were busy* —**~ly** *adv* —**-tuneness** *n* [U]

in·or·di·nate /ɪ'nɔːdənɪ̇t‖-ɔr-/ *adj fml* beyond reasonable limits: *inordinate demands for higher wages* —**~ly** *adv*: *inordinately great demands*

in·or·gan·ic /ˌɪnɔː'gænɪk◂‖-ɔr-/ *adj* [Wa5] **1** not of living material; not ORGANIC (1) **2** not showing the pattern or organization typical of natural growth —**~ally** *adv* [Wa4,5]

inorganic chem·is·try /ˌ···· '···/ *n* [U] the scientific study of INORGANIC (1) material

in-pa·tient /'· ˌ··/ *n* someone staying in a hospital for treatment —compare OUTPATIENT

in·put /'ɪnpʊt/ *n* [U;S:(*to*)] something put in for use, esp. by a machine, such as electrical current or information for a COMPUTER

in·quest /'ɪŋkwest/ *n* an official INQUIRY (3) usu. to find out the cause of death when a sudden or unexpected death has happened, and there is a possibility of crime

in·qui·e·tude /ɪn'kwaɪɪ̇tjuːd‖-tuːd/ *n* [U] anxiety; lack of peace of mind

in·quire, en- /ɪn'kwaɪə^r/ *v* **1** [T1,6a: ((*fml*) *of*)] to ask: *I inquired* ((*fml*) *of him*) *what he wanted/ whether he would come.|I inquired his reason for coming.|I inquired the answer* ((*fml*) *of him*) **2** [IØ (*about*)] to ask for information: *I'll inquire about the trains.|I don't know the times, I must inquire* **3** **inquire within** (a sign or notice saying that information can be found inside) —**~r** *n*

inquire af·ter *v prep* [T1] ASK AFTER: *She inquired after my mother's health*

inquire for *v prep* [T1 *pass. rare*] to ask to see (someone): *A man has been inquiring for you at the office*

inquire in·to *v prep* [T1 *pass. rare*] to search for information about; LOOK INTO

in·quir·ing, en- /ɪn'kwaɪərɪŋ/ *adj* [Wa5] that shows an interest in knowing about things (esp. in the phr. **an inquiring (turn of) mind**) —**~ly** *adv*: *He looked at me inquiringly*

in·quir·y, en- /ɪn'kwaɪəri‖ɪn'kwaɪəri, 'ɪŋkwəri/ *n* **1** [U] the act of inquiring (INQUIRE) **2** [C] an example of this: *My inquiry about his health was never answered* **3** [C (*into*)] actions and meetings which are arranged to find out the reason for something or how something happened

USAGE **Enquiry** and **inquiry** are almost exactly the same. **Enquiry** is more often used, especially in the plural, about requesting information (*your kind* **enquiries** *about my health*) and **inquiry** for a long serious study: *an* **inquiry** *into the diseases caused by smoking*.

in·qui·si·tion /ˌɪŋkwɪ̇'zɪʃən/ *n usu. derog* an INQUIRY (3), esp. one that is carried out with little regard for the rights of the people being questioned

Inquisition *n* [*the*+R] (in former times) the official ROMAN CATHOLIC organization for the discovery and punishment of HERESY (=incorrect and misleading religious beliefs)

in·quis·i·tive /ɪn'kwɪzɪ̇tɪv/ *adj* (of people and their acts) of a type which tries to find out (too many) details about things and people —**~ly** *adv* —**~ness** *n* [U]

in·quis·i·tor /ɪn'kwɪzɪ̇tə^r/ *n* **1** *usu. derog* a person making an INQUISITION **2** (*often cap.*) (in former times) an officer of the INQUISITION

in·quis·i·to·ri·al /ɪnˌkwɪzɪ̇'tɔːrɪəl‖-'tor-/ *adj usu. derog* like or typical of an INQUISITOR: *inquisitorial people/behaviour* —**-ally** *adv*

in-res·i·dence /ˌ· '···/ *adj* [Wa5;E,(A)] (*usu. in comb.*) being officially connected with an organization in the stated manner or position: *She was made poet-in-residence at the university, and worked with students for a year*

in·road /'ɪnrəʊd/ *n* [((*up*)*on, in*(*to*)) *usu. pl.*] **1** an attack upon or advance into a new area, esp. one in possession of the enemy: *They made inroads into enemy country* **2** an effort or activity that lessens the quantity or difficulty of what remains afterwards: *Teaching makes inroads on my free time* —compare INCURSION

in·rush /'ɪnrʌʃ/ *n* a rushing in; INFLOW; INFLUX: *an inrush of visitors*

in·sa·lu·bri·ous /ˌɪnsə'luːbrɪəs/ *adj fml* (esp. of CLIMATE or a place) not SALUBRIOUS; of a type which encourages bad health: (fig.) *an insalubrious friendship* —see HEALTHY (2a,b)

in·sane /ɪn'seɪn/ *adj* (of people and their acts) mad —**~ly** *adv*: *insanely jealous*

in·san·i·ta·ry /ɪn'sænɪ̇təri‖-teri/ *adj* which is likely to harm the health by causing disease: *insanitary conditions*

in·san·i·ty /ɪn'sænɪ̇ti/ *n* [U] **1** madness **2** foolishness: *the insanity of going out in the rain*

in·sa·tia·ble /ɪn'seɪʃəbəl/ *adj* that cannot be satisfied: *an insatiable love for music| You can't be hungry again—you're insatiable!* —**-bly** *adv* [Wa3]: *insatiably thirsty*

in·sa·ti·ate /ɪn'seɪʃiɪ̇t/ *adj lit* not satisfied by anything

in·scribe /ɪn'skraɪb/ *v* **1** [D1+*in, into, on/with*; T1] to write (something) by marking into (a surface); mark (a surface) with (something written): (fig.) *They have inscribed their names upon the pages of history.*|(fig.) *The pages of history are inscribed with their names* **2** [Wv5;T1] to write a name in (a book, esp. one given as a present on a special occasion): *an inscribed book/copy* —compare INSCRIPTION

in·scrip·tion /ɪn'skrɪpʃən/ *n* something INSCRIBEd, such as **a** a piece of writing marked into the surface of stone or something hard, such as a coin —compare LEGEND (3,4) **b** a piece of handwriting at the beginning of a book saying who gave the book to whom and giving the date, year, etc.

in·scru·ta·ble /ɪn'skruːtəbəl/ *adj* (of people and their acts) whose meaning is hidden or hard to find out; mysterious: *an inscrutable smile* —**-bility** /ɪnˌskruːtə'bɪlɪ̇ti/ *n* [U] —**-bly** /ɪn'skruːtəbli/ *adv* [Wa3]

in·sect /'ɪnsekt/ *n* **1** [C] a small creature with no bones and a hard outer covering, 6 legs, and a body divided into 3 parts, such as an ant or fly **2** [C] *infml* a very small animal that creeps along the ground, such as a SPIDER or worm **3** [C; *you*+N] *derog* a small person or one of little value

See next page for picture

in·sec·ti·cide /ɪn'sektɪ̇saɪd/ *n* [U;C] (any of various types of) chemical substance made to kill insects —**-cidal** /ɪnˌsektɪ̇'saɪdl/ *adj*

in·sec·ti·vore /ɪn'sektɪ̇vɔː^r‖-vor/ *n* an INSECTIVOROUS creature

in·sec·tiv·o·rous /ˌɪnsek'tɪvərəs/ *adj* eating insects as food: *Many birds are insectivorous*

in·se·cure /ˌɪnsɪ'kjʊə^r/ *adj* **1** **a** not safe; which cannot support people, things, etc.: *an insecure wall* **b** not safe; not supported; likely to fall: (fig.) *I'm insecure in a job where I may be told to leave any day* **2** (feeling) afraid; (feeling) unsupported: *He's a very insecure person—that's why he seems always*

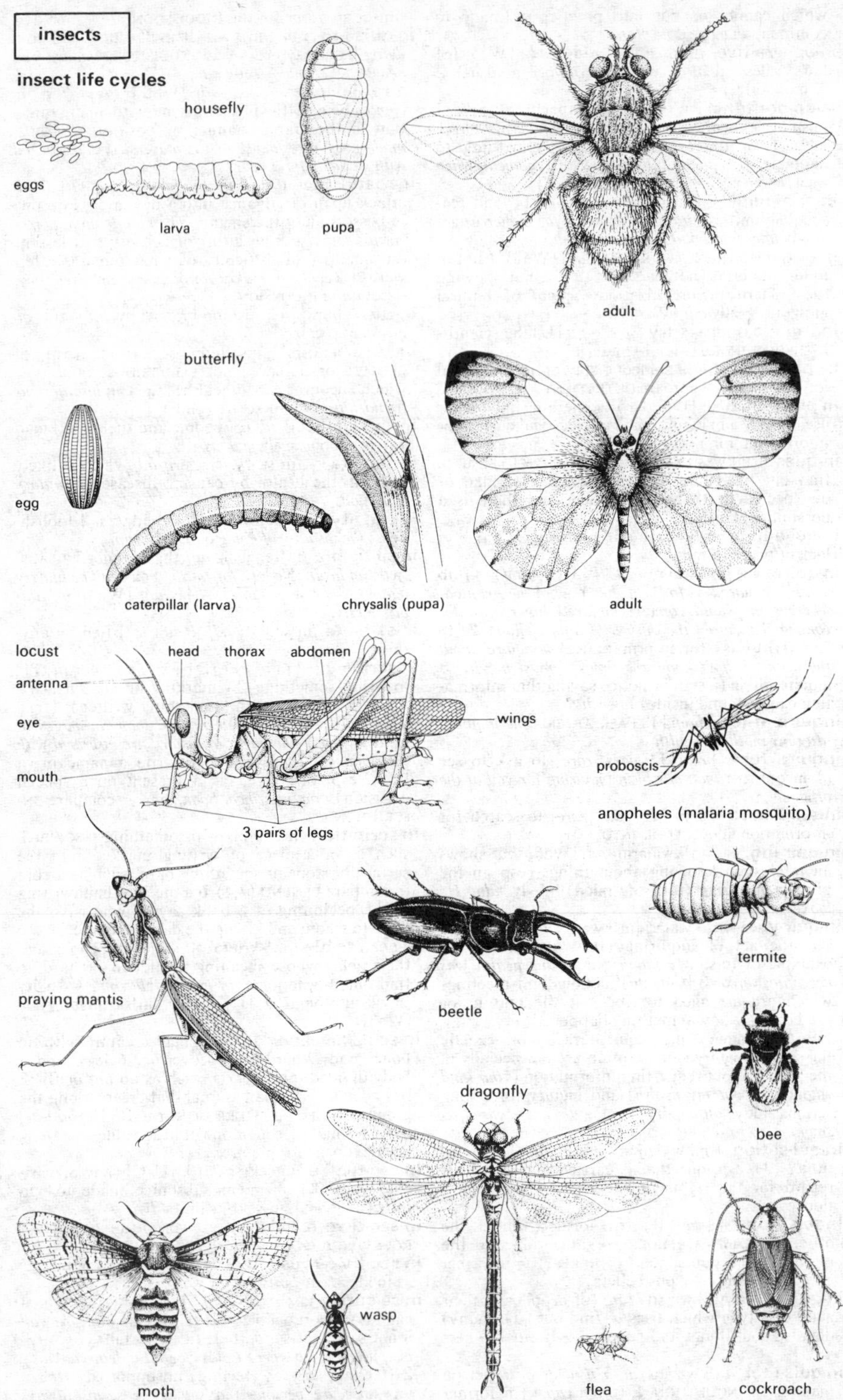
insects
insect life cycles
housefly
eggs
larva
pupa
adult
butterfly
egg
caterpillar (larva)
chrysalis (pupa)
adult
locust
head
thorax
abdomen
antenna
eye
mouth
wings
3 pairs of legs
proboscis
anopheles (malaria mosquito)
praying mantis
beetle
termite
bee
dragonfly
moth
wasp
flea
cockroach

bad-tempered —**-curity** /ˌɪnsɪˈkjʊərɪ̵ti/ *n* [U] —**~ly** /ˌɪnsɪˈkjʊəli‖-ər-/ *adv*

in·sem·i·nate /ɪnˈsemɪ̵neɪt/ *v* [T1] to put or introduce male seed into (a female), by the sexual act, by hand, or by means of an instrument

in·sem·i·na·tion /ɪnˌsemɪ̵ˈneɪʃən/ *n* [U;C] the act of putting male seed into a female —see also ARTIFICIAL INSEMINATION

in·sen·sate /ɪnˈsenseɪt/ *adj* **1** [Wa5] without the power to have feelings **2** lacking in human feelings; unreasoning: *insensate anger* —**~ly** *adv*

in·sen·si·bil·i·ty /ɪnˌsensəˈbɪlɪ̵ti/ *n fml* **1** [U;S: (*to*)] *old use* lack of ability to feel (love, sympathy, anger, etc.) or to be moved in feelings by art, music, etc. **2** [U] unconsciousness

in·sen·si·ble /ɪnˈsensəbəl/ *adj fml* **1** [F (*to*)] *old use* unable to have feelings (of) —see INSENSITIVE (1) **2** [Wa5;B] not conscious —compare SENSELESS (1) **3** [F (*of*)] UNAWARE (of); lacking knowledge of: *insensible of his danger* **4** [B] too small to be noticed: *an insensible change*
USAGE *Not* the opposite of **sensible**.

in·sen·si·tive /ɪnˈsensɪ̵tɪv/ *adj* [(*to*)] **1** not having the feeling which is usual when one meets (a certain) experience: *insensitive to pain|an insensitive mind* **2** (of people and their acts) not kind to others because one does not understand how they feel; TACTless: *an insensitive remark* —**-tivity** /ɪnˌsensɪ̵ˈtɪvɪ̵ti/ *n* [U;S] —**~ly** *adv*

in·sep·a·ra·ble /ɪnˈsepərəbəl/ *adj* [(*from*)] that cannot be separated (from something else or from one another): *inseparable friends* —**-bility** /ɪnˌsepərəˈbɪlɪ̵ti/ *n* [U] —**-bly** /ɪnˈsepərəbli/ *adv* [Wa3]

in·sert¹ /ɪnˈsɜːt‖-ɜrt/ *v* [T1 (*in*(*to*))] to put something inside (something else): *to insert a key in a lock*

in·sert² /ˈɪnsɜːt‖-ɜrt/ *n* something that is or can be INSERTed¹, esp. written or printed material put in between the pages of a book

in·ser·tion /ɪnˈsɜːʃən‖-ɜr-/ *n* **1** [U] the act or action of INSERTing¹ **2** [C] something INSERTed¹, esp. an advertisement or ANNOUNCEMENT in a newspaper

in-ser·vice /ˌ· ˈ··◂/ *adj* [Wa5;A;(B)] (taking place) during one's work (esp. in the phr. **in-service training**)

in·set¹ /ˈɪnset/ *n* something put as an addition into something else, esp. a picture or map set in one corner of the frame of a larger one, or additional pages in a book

in·set² /ɪnˈset/ *v* **-tt-; inset** *or* **insetted** [D1+*in, into/with*; T1] to put (something) in as an INSET¹; provide (something) with one or more INSETs

in·shore /ˌɪnˈʃɔːʳ◂‖-or◂/ *adv* [Wa5;F] near, towards, or to the shore —**inshore** *adj* [Wa5;A]

in·side¹ /ɪnˈsaɪd/ *n* **1** the area within (something else); the part that is nearest to the centre, or that faces away from other people or from the open air: *paint the inside of the house|This coat is fur on the inside and cloth on the outside* —opposite **outside** **2** [*usu. sing.*] the side near the buildings when one is walking on the path (PAVEMENT) beside a road: *Walk on the inside, away from the traffic* **3** [*often pl.*] *infml* the stomach: *a pain in one's insides*

in·side² /ˈɪnsaɪd/ *adj* [Wa5;A] **1** to or on the area within (something else), esp. in a house; facing the INSIDE¹ (1): *the inside pages* —opposite **outside** **2** at or from the heart or centre of the action: *our inside man* (=someone who lets us know what's happening in a secret and/or important event)|*the inside story* (=the details of something in the news esp. as reported in the newspaper)|*an inside job* (=a robbery done by somebody connected with the place, organization, etc., which has been robbed)

inside³ /ɪnˈsaɪd/ *prep* on or to the INSIDE¹ (1) of; within: *"inside a social club"* (SEU W.)|*the girl sitting inside the car*
USAGE Both **inside** and **within** express the idea of being surrounded, although **inside** is less *fml* and seems to be more often used for small things: **inside** *the box*|**within** *the castle*. **Within** is used more than **inside** to mean "not beyond": **within** *a mile*| **within** *3 weeks*.

inside⁴ /ɪnˈsaɪd/ *adv* [Wa5;F] **1** to or in the INSIDE¹ (1): *The children are playing inside because it's raining.|He opened the box and looked inside* —opposite **outside** **2** *sl esp. BrE* in prison: *inside for murder*

inside of /·ˈ·· ·/ *prep* **1** *infml* in less time than: *He'll be here inside of an hour* **2** *AmE* INSIDE³

inside out /ˌ·· ˈ·/ *adv* [Wa5;F] in or to a form with the usual inside parts on the outside: *He put his socks on inside out*

in·sid·er /ɪnˈsaɪdəʳ/ *n* someone who is in a group whose membership gives him special information and/or power

inside track /ˌ·· ˈ·/ *n* **1** (in racing) the track nearest the inside, which is shorter —see LANE (4) **2** *AmE* an advantageous position in a competition

in·sid·i·ous /ɪnˈsɪdɪəs/ *adj* unnoticed in action but causing something very bad in the end; secretly harmful: *the insidious growth of decay* —**~ly** *adv* —**~ness** *n* [U]

in·sight /ˈɪnsaɪt/ *n* [(*into*)] **1** [U] the power of using one's mind to understand something deeply, without help from outside information **2** [C] an example of this, or the understanding, which results (esp. in the phr. **have an insight**)

in·sig·ni·a /ɪnˈsɪgnɪə/ *n* [P] BADGEs or objects which represent the power of an official or important person, such as the crown of a king or the STRIPEs of an officer

in·sig·nif·i·cant /ˌɪnsɪgˈnɪfɪkənt/ *adj* not (seeming or looking) of value and/or importance —**-cance** *n* [U] —**~ly** *adv*

in·sin·cere /ˌɪnsɪnˈsɪəʳ/ *adj* not sincere —**~ly** /ˌɪnsɪnˈsɪəli‖-ɪər-/ *adv* —**-cerity** /ˌɪnsɪnˈserɪ̵ti/ *n* [U]

in·sin·u·ate /ɪnˈsɪnjʊeɪt/ *v* [Wv4;T5 (*to*)] to suggest (something unpleasant) by one's behaviour or questions: *Are you insinuating* (*to me*) *that I can't do the work here, or do you really think that I could get a better job if I left?|an insinuating remark*

insinuate in·to *v prep* [D1] to cause (oneself or something) to become part of (something): *to insinuate oneself into someone's favour*

in·sin·u·a·tion /ɪŋˌsɪnjʊˈeɪʃən/ *n* **1** [U] the act or action of insinuating (INSINUATE, INSINUATE INTO): *She blamed him, not directly but by insinuation* **2** [C] an unpleasant suggestion, not directly expressed in the words: *insinuations that he might not be quite honest* —compare IMPLICATION (3)

in·sip·id /ɪnˈsɪpɪ̵d/ *adj* lacking a strong effect esp. a taste: *insipid food|an insipid character* —**~ly** *adv* —**~ness** *n* [U] —**~ity** /ˌɪnsɪ̵ˈpɪdɪ̵ti/ *n* [U;C *often pl.*]

in·sist /ɪnˈsɪst/ *v* **1** [I∅ (*on, upon*); T5a (*to*)] to declare firmly (when opposed): *I insisted* (*to everyone*) *that he was wrong.|I insisted on my correctness* **2** [I∅ (*on, upon*); T5c (*to*)] to order (something to happen): *I insisted on him going.|I insisted that he* (*should*) *go.|You must come with us, I insist*

in·sis·tence /ɪnˈsɪstəns/ *n* **1** [U] the act of INSISTing: *I did it, but only at your insistence* **2** [C] an example of this **3** [U] the quality or state of being INSISTENT (1)

in·sis·ten·cy /ɪnˈsɪstənsi/ *n* [U] INSISTENCE (3)

in·sis·tent /ɪnˈsɪstənt/ *adj* **1** [B (*on, upon*); F5] (of people) repeatedly INSISTing or making demands:

He's very insistent that he'll finish in time.|an insistent refusal **2** [B] (of acts) needing to be done, answered, etc.; urgent: *an insistent message* —**~ly** *adv*

in si·tu /ˌɪn ˈsɪtjuː‖ˌɪn ˈsaɪtuː/ *adv* [Wa5;F] *Lat* in its original place

in so far as /ˌ· · ˈ· ·/ also **in as far as, in·so·far as** /ˌɪnsəˈfɑːr əz/— *conj* to the degree that: *I'll help you in so far as I can*

in·sole /ˈɪnsəʊl/ *n* a piece of material inside a shoe or boot, shaped to fit the bottom of the foot

in·so·lent /ˈɪnsələnt/ *adj* (of people and their acts) showing disrespectful rudeness; INSULTing (to someone else) —**~ly** *adv* —**-solence** *n* [U]

in·sol·u·ble /ɪnˈsɒljʊbəl‖ɪnˈsɑljə-/ *adj* [Wa5] **1** which cannot be made right, brought to a good result, or SOLVED **2** which cannot be DISSOLVED (esp. 1,2): *insoluble in water*

in·sol·va·ble /ɪnˈsɒlvəbəl‖ɪnˈsɑl-/ *adj* [Wa5] *AmE* INSOLUBLE (1)

in·sol·vent /ɪnˈsɒlvənt‖ɪnˈsɑl-/ *adj* [Wa5] **1** not having money to pay what one owes **2** *humor* having used up one's money, esp. one's wages —**-vency** *n* [U]

in·som·ni·a /ɪnˈsɒmnɪə‖-ˈsɑm-/ *n* [U] habitual inability to sleep

in·som·ni·ac /ɪnˈsɒmniæk‖ɪnˈsɑm-/ *n, adj* (someone) who habitually cannot sleep, or can sleep only for a short period of the night

in·so·much as /ˌɪnseʊˈmʌtʃ əz/ *conj* to the degree that; IN SO FAR AS

in·sou·ci·ance /ɪnˈsuːsɪəns/ *n* [U] the state of not caring about anything, even when one should —**-ant** *adj*

in·spect /ɪnˈspekt/ *v* [T1] **1** to examine (the details of something) **2** to make an official visit to judge the quality of (an organization, machine, etc.)

in·spec·tion /ɪnˈspekʃən/ *n* **1** [U] the act of INSPECTing or the state of being inspected: *a tour of inspection* **2** [C] an example of this: *I gave the radio a thorough inspection before I bought it.|an inspection tour* (=a tour of inspection)

in·spec·tor /ɪnˈspektəʳ/ *n* **1** [C] an official who INSPECTs: *A ticket inspector got on the train* **2** [C;A;N] a police officer of middle rank

in·spec·tor·ate /ɪnˈspektərɪ̈t/ *n* **1** a group of INSPECTORs **2** the position of INSPECTOR **3** the area covered in the INSPECTOR's work **4** the period in office of an INSPECTOR

in·spec·tor·ship /ɪnˈspektəʃɪp‖-ər-/ *n* INSPECTORATE (2,4)

in·spi·ra·tion /ˌɪnspɪ̈ˈreɪʃən/ *n* **1** [U] the act of inspiring or state of being INSPIRED (2,3) **2** [U;C] (something or someone which causes) an urge to produce good and beautiful things, such as works of art: *Dante was the inspiration for my book on Italy* **3** [C] a good idea: *I've had an inspiration—let's go to the country* —**~al** *adj*

in·spire /ɪnˈspaɪəʳ/ *v* **1** [T1 (*to*); V3] to encourage in (someone) the ability to act: *You inspire me to greater efforts.|I was inspired to work harder* **2** [T1] **a** to give unusual power to do good, as from God **b** [Wv4] to give a feeling of power, usu. to do good: *inspiring music* **3** [T1] to be the force which produces (usu. a good result): *His best music was inspired by the memory of his mother* **4** [D1+*with/in*; T1] to fill (someone) with a feeling towards the subject, or put (such a feeling towards the subject) into someone: *You inspire me with admiration.|He inspires hate/dislike in me*

in·spired /ɪnˈspaɪəd‖-ərd/ *adj* so clever as to seem to show INSPIRATION (2), esp. from God: *an inspired guess|She sang as if inspired*

inst. /ɪnst/ *obs abbrev. for*: (in business letters) of this present month: *on the 24th inst.*

in·sta·bil·i·ty /ˌɪnstəˈbɪlɪ̈ti/ *n* **1** [U] lack of STABILITY; unsteadiness **2** [U;S] (of people) a tendency to act in changeable ways; fact of having a character which is strong but changeable, not always suitable to the occasion

in·stall /ɪnˈstɔːl/ *v* [T1 (*in*)] **1** to settle (someone) in an official position, esp. with ceremony **2** to set (an apparatus) up, ready for use: *I won't have oil heating installed* **3** to settle (oneself/something) somewhere: *I installed myself in front of the fire*

in·stal·la·tion /ˌɪnstəˈleɪʃən/ *n* **1** [U] the act of INSTALLing or state of being installed **2** [C] an apparatus in a fixed state ready for use

in·stal·ment, *AmE* also **-stall-** /ɪnˈstɔːlmənt/ *n* **1** a single payment of a set which, in time, will complete full payment: *to pay the last instalment of my debt* **2** a single part of a book, play, or television show which appears in regular parts until the story is completed

instalment plan /·ˈ·· ·/ *n* [C; *the*+R] *AmE* HIRE PURCHASE

in·stance¹ /ˈɪnstəns/ *n* [(*of*)] **1** a single fact, event, etc., expressing a general idea; example; case: *an instance of bad behaviour* **2 at (someone's) instance** because of (someone's) wish **3 for instance** for example: *You can't depend on her: for instance, she arrived late for an important meeting yesterday* **4 in the first instance** first of all; as a beginning; at the beginning

instance² *v* [T1] *often fml* to give an example of

in·stant¹ /ˈɪnstənt/ *n* **1** a moment of time: *Not for an instant did I believe he had lied* **2** a point of time: (*At*) *The instant I saw him I knew he was my brother*

instant² *adj* [Wa5] **1** [B] happening at once: *instant change* **2** [A] urgent: *in instant need* **3** [A;(B)] (of food and such) which can be made up easily for use: *instant hot water with our new heating system!|instant coffee* **4** [E] INST.

in·stan·ta·ne·ous /ˌɪnstənˈteɪnɪəs/ *adj* [Wa5] happening at once —**~ly** *adv* —**~ness** *n* [U]

in·stant·ly /ˈɪnstəntli/ *adv* [Wa5] at once: *came to my help instantly*

in·stead /ɪnˈsted/ *adv* [Wa5] in place of that: *It's too wet to walk, we'll go swimming instead.|She never studies. Instead, she plays tennis all day*

instead of /·ˈ· ·/ *prep* in place of: *If I hadn't got a cold I'd be working instead of lying here in bed.|Will you go to the party instead of me, so that our host won't be too offended?*

in·step /ˈɪnstep/ *n* **1** the upper surface of the foot between the toes and the ankle —see picture at HUMAN² **2** the part of a shoe (or other thing worn on the foot) which covers this part of the foot

in·sti·gate /ˈɪnstɪ̈geɪt/ *v* **1** [T1] to start (something happening) by one's action: *He instigated the 5-year political plan* **2** [V3] to cause to act usu. wrongly, esp. by forceful speech: *She instigated the man to disobey orders* —**-gator** *n*

in·sti·ga·tion /ˌɪnstɪ̈ˈgeɪʃən/ *n* [U] **1** the act of instigating or the state of being INSTIGATED **2 at someone's instigation** by someone's act, or request for action

in·stil, *AmE* also **instill** /ɪnˈstɪl/ *v* **-ll-** [T1 (*in, into*)] to put (ideas, feelings, etc.) into someone's mind by a continuing effort: *I instilled the need for good manners into all my children* —**~lation** /ˌɪnstɪ̈ˈleɪʃən/ *n* [U]

in·stinct¹ /ˈɪnstɪŋkt/ *n* **1** [U;C,C3] the force in animals at birth which causes certain behaviour patterns, such as nest-building, which are not based on learning or thinking: *Some animals hunt by instinct.|Most animals have an instinct to protect their young* **2** [C *often pl.*] *sometimes apprec or derog* natural feeling(s) (in human beings); ways of behaviour which one would follow before thinking: *Trust your instincts*

instinct² *adj* [F+*with*] *lit* filled (with a quality, usu. a good quality)

in·stinc·tive /ɪn'stɪŋktɪv/ *adj* [Wa5] resulting from INSTINCT¹: *instinctive fear of snakes* —**~ly** *adv*: *Instinctively, I knew she was ill*

in·sti·tute¹ /'ɪnstɪ̈tjuːt‖-tuːt/ *v* [T1] to set up for the first time (a society, rules, actions in law, etc.)

institute² *n* a society formed for a special purpose: *a scientific institute*

in·sti·tu·tion /ˌɪnstɪ̈'tjuːʃən‖-'tuː-/ *n* **1** [U] the act or action of instituting (INSTITUTE¹): *the institution of a new law* **2** [C] **a** a habit, custom, etc., which has been in existence for a long time: *Marriage is an institution in many societies* **b** *humor & infml* a person who has been seen in the same place and/or doing the same thing for a long time: *The old man in the park is a regular institution* **3** [C] a large society or organization, usu. set up to do something for others: *an institution for good works* **4** [C] a large building for an organization where people are provided with help, work, medical treatment, or protection, such as a school (public or private) or a hospital (for those ill in body or mind): *became old and weak and had to be put into an institution* —**~al** *adj*

in·struct /ɪn'strʌkt/ *v* **1** [T1 (*in*), 5b;D5b,6a,b] to give knowledge or information to: *They instructed me in the best ways of doing the job.|I will instruct him whether (he needs) to come today or tomorrow.|She instructed him (in) how to do it* **2** [V3] to give orders to: *I instructed him to come to work earlier* **3** [D5,5b;V3;T1] *law* to advise or inform officially: *The judge instructed the witness that he should tell the whole truth* —see ORDER² (USAGE)

in·struc·tion /ɪn'strʌkʃən/ *n* **1** [U] the act or action of instructing; teaching: *He's not yet trained, but still under instruction* **2** [C *often pl.*] an order (to a person or machine), or advice on how to do something: *an instruction book|a book of instruction* —**~al** *adj*

in·struc·tive /ɪn'strʌktɪv/ *adj* giving useful information —**~ly** *adv*

in·struc·tor /ɪn'strʌktəʳ/ **1** a person who teaches an activity: *a driving instructor* **2** [(*in*)] a person who holds the lowest teaching rank at an American university or college: *an instructor in chemistry|a chemistry instructor* —compare LECTURER (2)

in·struc·tress /ɪn'strʌktrɪ̈s/ *n becoming rare* a female INSTRUCTOR (1)

in·stru·ment /'ɪnstrəmənt/ *n* **1** an object used to help in work: *medical instruments* **2** also **musical instrument** /ˌ··· '···/— an object which is played to give musical sounds (such as a piano, a horn, etc.) —see ORGAN (USAGE) **3** someone or something which seems to be used by an outside force to cause something to happen: *an instrument of fate*

in·stru·men·tal /ˌɪnstrə'mentəl/ *adj* **1** [(*in*)] helpful (in); (part of) the cause of: *I was instrumental in catching the criminal* **2** [Wa5] (of music) for instruments, not voices: *an instrumental work*

in·stru·men·tal·ist /ˌɪnstrə'mentəlɪ̈st/ *n* a person who plays a musical instrument, esp. in a group of people who make music, one or more of whom sing —compare VOCALIST

in·stru·men·tal·i·ty /ˌɪnstrəmen'tælɪ̈ti/ *n* **1** [U] the quality or state of being INSTRUMENTAL (1) **2** [C] a person or thing that helps to produce an effect; means

in·stru·men·ta·tion /ˌɪnstrəmen'teɪʃən/ *n* [U] the act of (re-)writing or arranging music for instruments —compare ORCHESTRATE

in·sub·or·di·nate /ˌɪnsə'bɔːdənɪ̈t‖-ɔr-/ *adj* ((of the behaviour) of a person of lower rank) disobedient; not showing willingness to take orders —**-nation** /ˌɪnsəbɔːdə'neɪʃən‖-ɔr-/ *n* [U;C *often pl.*]

in·sub·stan·tial /ˌɪnsəb'stænʃəl/ *adj* **1** [Wa5] lacking substance or material nature; without material reality **2** lacking firmness or solidity; weak or unsatisfying: *an insubstantial meal*

in·suf·fe·ra·ble /ɪn'sʌfərəbəl/ *adj* unbearable (in behaviour); too proud in manner: *insufferable rudeness|He's insufferable* —**-bly** *adv* [Wa3]

in·suf·fi·cien·cy /ˌɪnsə'fɪʃənsi/ *n* **1** [U;S: (*of*)] the quality or state of being INSUFFICIENT: *(an) insufficiency of money* **2** [C *often pl.*] something INSUFFICIENT: *Conscious of his insufficiencies, he tried to improve himself* —see SUFFICIENCY (USAGE)

in·suf·fi·cient /ˌɪnsə'fɪʃənt/ *adj* [Wa5; (*for*, (*fml*) *of*)] not enough: *insufficient help|help insufficient for the purpose|(fml) insufficient of the butter for our needs* —**~ly** *adv*

in·su·lar /'ɪnsjʊləʳ‖'ɪnsələr/ *adj* **1** [Wa5] of, concerning, or like an island **2** narrow (in mind); interested only or mainly in a small group, country, etc. —compare PAROCHIAL (2)

in·su·lar·i·ty /ˌɪnsjʊ'lærɪ̈ti‖ˌɪnsə-/ also **in·su·lar·is·m** /'ɪnsjʊlərɪzəm‖'ɪnsə-/— *n* [U] the quality or state of being INSULAR (2)

in·su·late /'ɪnsjʊleɪt‖'ɪnsə-, 'ɪnʃə-/ *v* [T1] **1** [(*from*, *against*)] to cover (something) so as to prevent the passing of unseen forces such as electricity, heat, or sound: *Many houses could be warmer if they were insulated so that the heat is not lost* **2** [(*from*)] to protect (a person) from ordinary experiences: *Don't insulate your mother from everyday difficulties even if she is old*

in·su·la·tion /ˌɪnsjʊ'leɪʃən‖ˌɪnsə-/ *n* [U] **1** the action of insulating or the state of being INSULATEd **2** material which INSULATEs

in·su·la·tor /'ɪnsjʊleɪtəʳ‖'ɪnsə-/ *n* an object or material which INSULATEs, esp. one which does not allow electricity to pass through it

in·su·lin /'ɪnsjʊlɪ̈n‖'ɪnsə-/ *n* [U] a substance produced naturally in the body which allows sugar to be used for ENERGY, esp. such a substance taken from sheep to be given to sufferers from a disease (DIABETES) which makes them lack this substance

in·sult¹ /ɪn'sʌlt/ *v* [Wv4;T1 (*by*)] to do something to offend, by speech or act: *insulted me by saying that*

in·sult² /'ɪnsʌlt/ *n* **1** [U] speech or action which INSULTs¹ **2** [C (*to*)] an example of this: *an insult to the memory of our brave soldiers* **3 add insult to injury** see INJURY

in·su·pe·ra·ble /ɪn'sjuːpərəbəl‖ɪn'suː-/ *adj* [Wa5] (of something in one's way) which is too difficult to be conquered or passed: *insuperable difficulties/BARRIERs* —**-bly** *adv* [Wa3,5]: *insuperably difficult*

in·sup·por·ta·ble /ˌɪnsə'pɔːtəbəl‖-'por-/ *adj* unbearable (because bad): *insupportable behaviour/pain/discontent*

in·sur·ance /ɪn'ʃʊərəns/ *n* **1** [U] agreement by contract to pay money esp. in case of a misfortune (such as illness, death, or accident): *life insurance|car insurance* **2** [U] the business of making this type of contract and providing such payments: *worked in insurance* **3** [U] **a** money paid (by an **insurance company**) as a result of such a contract **b** money paid (to an **insurance company**) in order to make or keep such a contract **4** [U;S: (*against*)] protection (against something): *I have one lock but I bought another as an additional insurance against thieves*

insurance pol·i·cy /·'·· ˌ···/ *n* a (written) contract of insurance

in·sure /ɪn'ʃʊəʳ/ *v* **1** [T1 (*against*)] to protect (oneself or another), esp. against loss of (money, life, goods, etc.) by INSURANCE (1): *My house is* *insured against fire.*|*I am insured* **2** [T5] *esp. AmE* ENSURE

USAGE **Assure** and **ensure** both mean "to make certain": *to* **ensure** *our victory*|*an* **assured** *success*| *You may rest* **assured** (= You may be certain). The social quality of **assurance** means that one is sure of oneself and not afraid of people: *She seems very self-***assured***!* The words for protection through money are **insure** and (sometimes) **assure**: *to* **insure** *one's life*|*fire* **insurance**. REASSURE does *not* mean "to **assure** again".

in·sured /ɪn'ʃʊəd‖-ərd/ *adj* [Wa5;B;(*the*+)GU] having insurance of any type: *If the camera is stolen the insured (person/people) receive(s) a sum of money.*|*Are you insured (against fire)?*

in·sur·er /ɪn'ʃʊərə^r/ *n* a person or company that provides insurance: *If the camera is stolen the insurer will pay a sum of money*

in·sur·gent¹ /ɪn'sɜːdʒənt‖-ɜr-/ *n* [*often pl.*] a person who is ready to fight against those people who have power

insurgent² *adj* [Wa5;A] ready to take power by or as if by force, after rising against the people who have power

in·sur·moun·ta·ble /ˌɪnsə'maʊntəbəl‖-sər-/ *adj* [Wa5] too large, difficult, etc., to be dealt with —compare INSUPERABLE

in·sur·rec·tion /ˌɪnsə'rekʃən/ *n* [U;C] the act or occasion of rising against the people who have power, such as the government —**~ist** *n*

in·tact /ɪn'tækt/ *adj* [Wa5] whole because no part has been touched or spoilt: *The delicate parcel arrived intact* —**~ness** *n* [U]

in·ta·gli·o /ɪn'tɑːliəʊ/ *n* **-glios** **1** [U] the art of making a picture, ornament, etc., by cutting a pattern deeply into the surface of a hard substance **2** [C] **a** the result of this **b** a jewel into which has been marked such a pattern

in·take /'ɪnteɪk/ *n* [S] **1** the amount or number allowed to enter, or taken in: *a large intake of food*| *the yearly intake of students* **2** the place in a tube, pipe, etc., where air, gas, or liquid is taken in **3** a narrow place in a tube

in·tan·gi·ble /ɪn'tændʒəbəl/ *adj* [Wa5] **1** which by its nature cannot be known by the senses, though it can be felt: *an intangible quality*|*an intangible presence in the room* **2** which is difficult to understand: *intangible difficulties* **3** which is hidden or not material, but known to be real: *intangible* ASSETS (=money belonging to a business) —**-bility** /ɪnˌtændʒə'bɪlɨti/ *n* [U] —**-bly** /ɪn'tændʒəbli/ *adv* [Wa3,5]

in·te·ger /'ɪntɨdʒə^r/ *n* a whole number: *6 is an integer, but 6⅔ is not*

in·te·gral /'ɪntɨgrəl/ *adj* [Wa5;A] **1** necessary (to complete something): *an integral part of the argument* **2** concerning an INTEGER

integral cal·cu·lus /ˌ··· '···/ *n* [(*the*) U] a way of measuring the distance which a moving object has covered at a particular moment; one of the 2 ways of making calculations about quantities which are continually changing —compare DIFFERENTIAL CALCULUS

in·te·grate /'ɪntɨgreɪt/ *v* [(*with, into*)] **1** [T1] to join to something else so as to form a whole: *I integrated your suggestion with my plan* **2** [IØ;T1] **a** (of members of social groups) to join in society as a whole; spend time with members of other groups and develop habits like theirs: *Do they really want to integrate (with us)?* **b** to cause (members of social groups) to do this: *to integrate a criminal into society* —**-gration** /ˌɪntɨ'greɪʃən/ *n* [U]: RACIAL *integration in the school system*

in·te·grat·ed /'ɪntɨgreɪtɨd/ *adj* [(*sometimes in comb.*)] showing a usu. pleasing mixture of qualities, groups, etc.: *an integrated school with children of different races and social classes*|*(well-)integrated characters*|*a poorly-/badly-integrated person*

in·teg·ri·ty /ɪn'tegrɨti/ *n* [U] **1** strength and firmness of character or principle; honesty that can be trusted **2** state of wholeness; completeness: *Our integrity as a nation is threatened*

in·teg·u·ment /ɪn'tegjʊmənt‖-gjə-/ *n tech or fml* an outer covering, such as a shell, the skin of a fruit, etc.

in·tel·lect /'ɪntɨlekt/ *n* [U;C] the ability to reason (rather than to feel or act) —see INTELLIGENT (USAGE)

in·tel·lec·tual¹ /ˌɪntɨ'lektʃʊəl/ *adj* **1** concerning the INTELLECT: *intellectual subjects* **2** able to use the INTELLECT well; showing unusual reasoning powers: *an intellectual argument*|*family* —see INTELLIGENT (USAGE); compare SPIRITUAL¹ (1) —**~ly** *adv*: *intellectually unsatisfying*|*Intellectually, it's unsatisfying, but it makes one feel good*

intellectual² *n* a person who works and lives by using his mind, and who is interested in activities which include thinking and understanding rather than feeling and doing

in·tel·li·gence /ɪn'telɨdʒəns/ *n* [U] **1** (good) ability to learn and understand: *an intelligence test*|*Use your intelligence!* **2** information gathered esp. about an enemy country, or the group of people who gather it: *He's in intelligence.*|*the Central Intelligence* AGENCY *of the US*

intelligence quo·tient /·'··· ˌ··/ (*abbrev.* **IQ**)— *n* a measure of INTELLIGENCE (1), with 100 representing the average

in·tel·li·gent /ɪn'telɨdʒənt/ *adj* having or showing powers of reasoning or understanding: *All human beings are much more intelligent than animals.*|*an intelligent plan*|*an intelligent dog easily trained to control sheep* —**~ly** *adv*: *Try to act intelligently*

USAGE An **intellectual**, or **intellectual** person, is one who has developed his brain and **intellect**, is highly educated, and is interested in subjects that exercise the mind. One can be very **intelligent**/have great **intelligence**, without knowing much. A small child with a clever quick mind is **intelligent** but he can hardly be an **intellectual**.

in·tel·li·gent·si·a /ɪnˌtelɨ'dʒentsɪə/ *n* [(*the*) GU] the people in society who concern themselves with ideas and new developments, as in art or politics, and who (esp. in writing) suggest new plans

in·tel·li·gi·ble /ɪn'telɨdʒəbəl/ *adj* (esp. of speech or writing) which can be understood —opposite **unintelligible**; compare ARTICULATE¹ (1,2) —**-bility** /ɪnˌtelɨdʒə'bɪlɨti/ *n* [U] —**-bly** /ɪn'telɨdʒəbli/ *adv* [Wa3]

in·tem·per·ate /ɪn'tempərɨt/ *adj* (of people and their acts) IMMODERATE esp. in eating and drinking; doing too much of an activity, never keeping to the usual average: *intemperate habits* —**-ance** *n* [U] —**-ately** *adv*

in·tend /ɪn'tend/ *v* **1** [T3,5c; V3] to plan; to mean (to do): *I've made a mistake, though I didn't intend to.*|*I intend to go.*|*I intend them to go.*|*I intend that they should go* **2** [X9, esp. *for, as*;V3 *usu. pass.*] to mean to be: *The chair was intended for you, but she took it away.*|*It was intended as a joke.*|*It was intended to be cooked slowly*

in·tend·ed /ɪn'tendɨd/ *n* [*usu. sing. with poss.*] *humor* (someone's) future wife: *Let me introduce my intended*

in·tense /ɪn'tens/ *adj* [Wa2] strong (in quality or feeling): *intense cold*|*intense sorrow*|*a very intense person who cares deeply about everything* —**~ly** *adv*

in·ten·si·fi·er /ɪn'tensɨfaɪə^r/ *n* a word which makes an adjective stronger in feeling: *"Very" is an* *intensifier, "completely" sometimes is, as in "very good" or "completely good"*

in·ten·si·fy /ɪn'tensɪ̇faɪ/ *v* [IØ;T1] to (cause to) become more INTENSE —**-fication** /ɪn,tensɪ̇fɪ'keɪʃən/ *n* [U]

in·ten·si·ty /ɪn'tensɪ̇ti/ *n* [U] **1** the quality of being INTENSE **2** an appearance showing strong feeling: *the intensity of her face as she looked at him*

in·ten·sive /ɪn'tensɪv/ *adj* **1** which gives a lot of attention or action to a small amount of something/in a small amount of time: **Intensive care** *in hospitals is given to the seriously ill* **2** very strong; INTENSE —**~ly** *adv*

in·tent¹ /ɪn'tent/ *n* **1** [U,U3] *law* intending to do something bad: *entered the building with intent to steal* **2** [U] purpose; INTENTION (2): *with good intent* **3 to all intents (and purposes)** in almost every way; very nearly

intent² *adj* [(*on*)] showing fixed attention (in doing or wishing to do): *an intent look|He's intent on his studies/on going to France* —**~ly** *adv* —**~ness** *n* [U]

in·ten·tion /ɪn'tenʃən/ *n* **1** [U] a determination to act in a certain way **2** [C] a plan which one has; purpose: *She felt offended at my remarks, but it wasn't my intention to hurt her* **3 good intentions** the wish to bring about a good result, often used when something bad has already happened

in·ten·tion·al /ɪn'tenʃənəl/ *adj* [Wa5] (done) on purpose —opposite **unintentional** —**~ly** *adv*

-in·ten·tioned /ɪn'tenʃənd/ *comb. form* [→*adj*] having or showing intentions of the stated type: *well-intentioned|ill-intentioned*

in·ten·tions /ɪn'tenʃənz/ *n* **1** a man's plans with regard to marriage: *"Just what are your intentions, young man?" asked her father* **2 have honourable intentions** *now rare or humor* (of a man) to intend to marry a girl, rather than to treat her less seriously

in·ter /ɪn'tɜːʳ/ *v* **-rr-** [T1] *fml* to bury (a dead person)

in·ter- /'ɪntəʳ/ *prefix* between; among (a group): *to* INTERMARRY|*intercity travel|international*

in·ter·act /,ɪntə'rækt/ *v* [IØ (*with*)] to have an effect on each other or something else: *The 2 ideas interact*

in·ter·ac·tion /,ɪntə'rækʃən/ *n* [(*between, with*)] the state or activity of working together (or with something else) to produce an effect on each other/the other(s)

in·ter a·li·a /,ɪntər 'eɪlɪə, -'ɑːlɪə/ *adv Lat & fml* among other things: *Our success depends, inter alia, on the number of trained people we can employ*

in·ter·breed /,ɪntə'briːd‖-ər-/ *v* **-bred** /'bred/ [T1; IØ] to (cause to) produce young from parents of different breeds, groups, etc.: *Can lions and tigers interbreed?* —compare CROSSBREED², INBREEDING

in·ter·ca·la·ry /ɪn'tɜːkələri‖ɪn'tɜrkəleri/ *adj* [Wa5;A] **1** *fml* put in between; added between **2** *tech* **a** (of a day or month) added to a year to make the year the right length **b** (of a year) having such time added

in·ter·ca·late /ɪn'tɜːkəleɪt‖-ɜr-/ *v* [T1] **1** to put (esp. a day) into a CALENDAR (1) **2** to put in between or among the already existing parts or surfaces

in·ter·cede /,ɪntə'siːd‖-ər-/ *v* [IØ (*with* and/or *for*)] to speak in favour of another, esp. in order to save him from punishment: *He interceded with the governor for me, and I was saved*

in·ter·cept /,ɪntə'sept‖-ər-/ *v* [T1] to stop and usu. seize (a person or thing moving from one place to another) —**~ion** /,ɪntə'sepʃən‖-ər-/ *n* [C;U]

in·ter·cep·tor /,ɪntə'septəʳ‖-ər-/ *n* **1** someone who INTERCEPTS **2** a light fast aircraft which fights others

in·ter·ces·sion /,ɪntə'seʃən‖-ər-/ *n* **1** [U] the act of interceding (INTERCEDE) **2** [U;C] a certain sort of prayer which asks for other people to be helped, made well, etc.

in·ter·change¹ /,ɪntə'tʃeɪndʒ‖-ər-/ *v* **1** [T1] to put each of (2 things) in the place of the other **2** [T1; IØ] to exchange

in·ter·change² /'ɪntətʃeɪndʒ‖-ər-/ *n* **1** [U;C] (an example of) the act or action of interchanging (INTERCHANGE¹); exchange: *a useful interchange of ideas* **2** [C] also **interchange sta·tion** /'··· ,··/— a place where one leaves one form of public TRANSPORT to get on another **3** [C] *esp. AmE* a point where one drives onto a road without crossing any of the roads which join there

See next page for picture

in·ter·chan·gea·ble /,ɪntə'tʃeɪndʒəbəl‖-tər-/ *adj* [Wa5; (*with*)] which can be used in place of each other/something else —**-bility** /,ɪntətʃeɪndʒə'bɪlɪ̇ti‖-tər-/ *n* [U] —**-bly** /,ɪntə'tʃeɪndʒəbli‖-tər-/ *adv* [Wa3,5]: *The 2 words are used interchangeably*

in·ter·col·le·giate /,ɪntəkə'liːdʒɪ̇t‖-tər-/ *adj* [Wa5] (done) among members of different colleges: *intercollegiate sports*

in·ter·com /'ɪntəkɒm‖'ɪntərkɑm/ also (*fml*) **intercommunication sys·tem** /,·· ···'·· ,··/— *n* a system by which one can talk through a machine to people in a near place, often to several people at once, as used by someone to call a secretary to his/her office from an outer room

in·ter·com·mu·ni·cate /,ɪntəkə'mjuːnɪ̇keɪt‖-tər-/ *v* [IØ] **1** to COMMUNICATE (=make feelings, news, etc., known) with each other **2** to COMMUNICATE (=have a door opening into another room) with each other: *All 3 rooms intercommunicate* —**-cation** /,ɪntəkə,mjuːnɪ̇'keɪʃən‖-tər-/ *n* [U]

in·ter·com·mu·ni·on /,ɪntəkə'mjuːnɪən‖-tər-/ *n* [U] a service of COMMUNION between different branches of the Christian church, such as CHURCH OF ENGLAND and METHODIST

in·ter·con·ti·nen·tal /,ɪntəkɒntɪ̇'nentəl‖-tər'kɑn-/ *adj* [Wa5] (used, done, connected with, etc.) different land masses (CONTINENTs): *intercontinental trade*

intercontinental bal·lis·tic mis·sile /,······ ·,·· '··/ (abbrev. **ICBM**)— *n* a MISSILE (1) that can be fired a very great distance

in·ter·course /'ɪntəkɔːs‖'ɪntərkors/ *n* [U] **1** an exchange of feelings, actions, etc., which make people know each other more closely **2** SEXUAL INTERCOURSE

in·ter·de·nom·i·na·tio·nal /,ɪntədɪ̇nɒmɪ̇'neɪʃənəl‖,ɪntərdɪ̇nɑ-/ *adj* [Wa5] between or among different branches of the Christian church

in·ter·de·pen·dent /,ɪntədɪ'pendənt‖-ər-/ *adj* [Wa5] depending on each other; necessary to each other —**-dence** *n* [U] —**-dently** *adv*

in·ter·dict¹ /'ɪntədɪkt‖-ər-/ *n* an order not to do something, esp. a punishment in the ROMAN CATHOLIC church preventing one from taking part in the important services —compare EXCOMMUNICATION

in·ter·dict² /,ɪntə'dɪkt‖-ər-/ *v* [T1] **1** to give an order, esp. an INTERDICT¹, not to do (something) **2** to destroy, cut, or damage (esp. an enemy line of supply) by means of a large attack

in·terest¹ /'ɪntrɪ̇st/ *n* **1** [U;C: (*in*)] a readiness to give attention: *I have no interest in politics.|He's showing an interest in music* **2** [U (*in*)] a quality of causing attention to be given: *There's no interest in going to a concert when you don't understand music* **3** [C] an activity, subject, etc., which one gives time and attention to: *Eating seems to be his only interest in life* **4** [C *often pl.*] advantage, advancement, or favour (esp. in the phr. **in the interest of (something)/in someone's interest**): *It's in your*

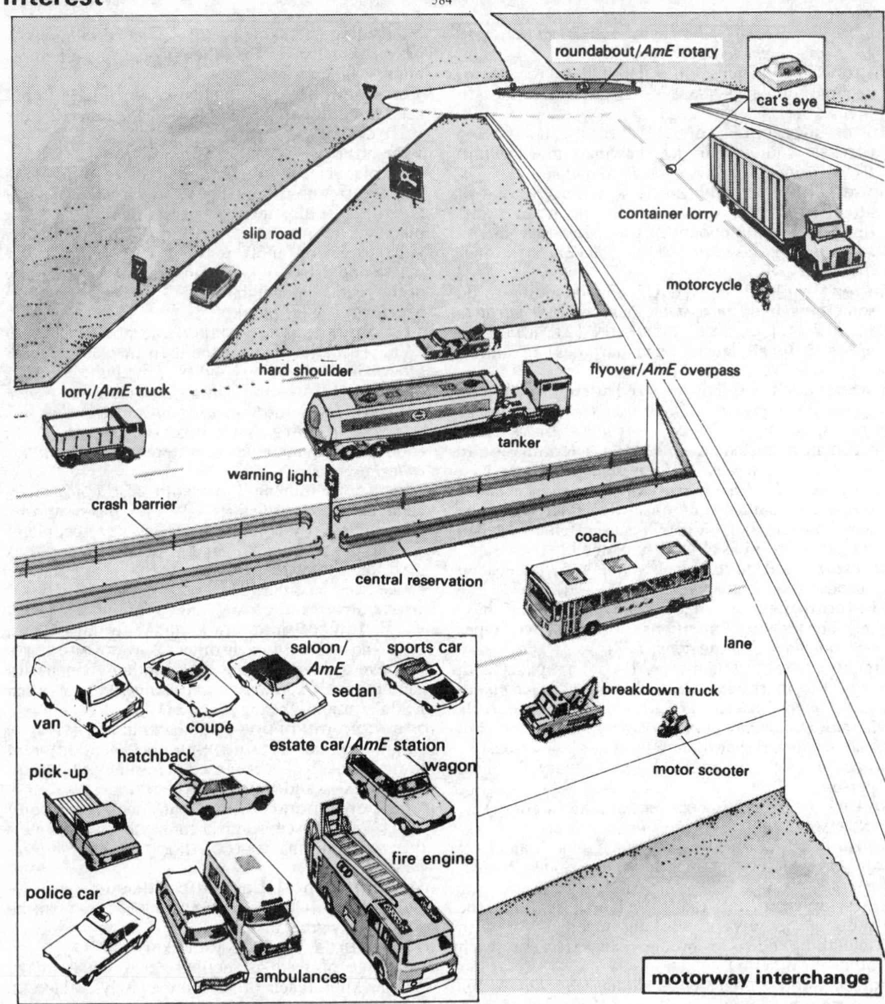

interest to put your point of view first **5** [C] a share (in a company, business, etc.) **6** [U] money paid for the use of money: *He lent me the money at 6% interest* **7 to one's interest** to one's advantage; for one's own good —compare ADVANTAGE¹ (2) **8 with interest** with additional, unexpected force, amount, etc.

interest² *v* [T1 (*in*)] **1** to cause (someone) to have a feeling of interest **2** to make (someone) want to buy, take, eat, do something, etc.: *Can I interest you in this book?*

in·terest·ed /ˈɪntrəstəd/ *adj* **1** [B (*in*); F3] concerned; having or showing interest: *I was interested in your remark.|I was interested to hear your remark.|an interested look on his face* **2** [A] personally concerned; on whom there will be an effect; who cannot make a fair judgment from the outside: *the interested* PARTY (=*tech* person) —**~ly** *adv*

in·terest·ing /ˈɪntrəstɪŋ/ *adj* **1** which takes (and keeps) one's interest: *an interesting idea* **2 in an interesting condition** *old euph* PREGNANT (1) —**~ly** *adv*

in·terests /ˈɪntrəsts/ *n* [P9] people and organizations concerned in some particular activity: *business interests*

in·ter·face /ˈɪntəfeɪs‖-ər-/ *n* a place or area where different things meet and have an effect on each other

in·ter·fere /ˌɪntəˈfɪəʳ‖-ər-/ *v* [I∅ (*with, in, between*)] **1** to get in the way of another; block the action of another **2** [Wv4] *derog* to push oneself into a matter which does not concern one: *I don't like interfering old busybodies* (BUSYBODY)

USAGE To **interfere** *in* something is to take part in it without being wanted: *I never* **interfere** *in his affairs.* To **interfere** *with* something is to prevent it from happening: *The noise* **interferes** *with my work.*

in·ter·fer·ence /ˌɪntəˈfɪərəns‖-tər-/ *n* [U] **1** [(*with*)] the act or action of interfering (INTERFERE) **2** the noises and shapes which spoil the working of electrical apparatus, esp. when a radio station is difficult to listen to because of the effect of one near to its WAVELENGTH **3** [(*with*)] the unlawful blocking of an opponent in sports

interfere with *v prep* [T1] *euph* to annoy or touch sexually

in·ter·im¹ /ˈɪntərɪm/ *n* **1** also **interim pe·ri·od** /ˈ...

ˌ···/— the time between 2 events **2 in the interim** MEANWHILE (1)

interim² *adj* [Wa5;A] (done) as a less complete part of something to be given in full later: *an interim measure* (=means) *to help those in need|the interim report of the society*

in·te·ri·or /ɪnˈtɪərɪəʳ/ *adj, n* (the part which is) inside, indoors, or farthest from the edge or outside: *interior furnishings|went into the interior* (*of the country*)

interior dec·o·ra·tor /·ˌ··· ˈ····/ also **decorator**— *n* a person who plans and chooses the colours, furnishings, etc., for the inside of a room or house (but usu. does not do the actual work of putting them in)

in·ter·ject /ˌɪntəˈdʒekt‖-ər-/ *v* [T1;IØ] to make a sudden remark between others: *"Not like that!" he interjected while explaining how to fasten the wires*

in·ter·jec·tion /ˌɪntəˈdʒekʃən‖-ər-/ *n* **1** [C] a phrase, word, or set of sounds used as a sudden remark usu. expressing feeling; EXCLAMATION (2): *interjections such as* "OH!" *or* "*Well done!*" **2** [U] the act of INTERJECTing

in·ter·lace /ˌɪntəˈleɪs‖-ər-/ *v* [T1 (*with*)] to join together or to something else by twisting over and under the other: *interlaced branches*

in·ter·lard /ˌɪntəˈlɑːd‖ˌɪntərˈlɑrd/ *v* [T1 (*with*)] LARD² (3)

in·ter·leave /ˌɪntəˈliːv‖-ər-/ also **in·ter·leaf** /ˌɪntəˈliːf‖-ər-/— *v* [T1 (*with*)] to put (sets of pages) together or (one) with another, one page from one set following one from another

in·ter·line /ˌɪntəˈlaɪn‖-ər-/ *v* [T1 (*with*)] **1** to print (different sorts of line, such as lines from different languages) together, or to print (one line) with another **2** to (cause to) be between the outer surface and the LINING of (a garment)

in·ter·lin·e·ar /ˌɪntəˈlɪnɪəʳ‖-ər-/ *adj* [Wa5] written or printed between the original lines: *an interlinear translation*

in·ter·link /ˌɪntəˈlɪŋk‖-ər-/ *v* [Wv5;T1 (*with*)] to join (things) together, or (one thing) with something else: *interlinked fates*

in·ter·lock¹ /ˌɪntəˈlɒk‖ˌɪntərˈlɑk/ *v* [Wv4,5;T1;IØ] to fasten or be fastened together, esp. in a certain order or so that movement of one part causes movement in others: *interlocking questions which cannot be answered separately*

in·ter·lock² /ˈɪntəlɒk‖ˈɪntərlɑk/ *n* [U] material in which threads are caught closely together

in·ter·loc·u·tor /ˌɪntəˈlɒkjʊtəʳ‖ˌɪntərˈlɑkjətər/ *n fml* the person who is talking to one, or to someone else: *my interlocutor|2 interlocutors*

in·ter·lop·er /ˈɪntələʊpəʳ‖-tər-/ *n* a person or creature found in a place, esp. among others, with no right to be there —compare INTRUDER

in·ter·lude /ˈɪntəluːd‖-ər-/ *n* **1** a free period of time between activities: *Holidays are such short interludes in a life of work!* **2 a** the time (INTERVAL) between parts of a play, film, concert, etc. **b** music, a short play, a talk, etc., used for filling this time

in·ter·mar·riage /ˌɪntəˈmærɪdʒ‖-ər-/ *n* [U] **1** marriage between members of different groups, families, etc. **2** marriage within a related group or family

in·ter·mar·ry /ˌɪntəˈmæri‖-ər-/ *v* [IØ (*with*)] **1** to become connected by marriage with each other or someone else (of another group, family, etc.): *The 2 families have been intermarrying for 100 years* **2** to marry each other or someone else (within the same group, family, etc.): *Members of some ancient races intermarried with their own sisters*

in·ter·me·di·a·ry /ˌɪntəˈmiːdɪəri‖ˌɪntərˈmiːdieri/ *n, adj* [Wa5] (a person) coming between 2 other things, groups, people, often so as to join them, bring them into agreement, etc. —compare INTERMEDIATE

in·ter·me·di·ate /ˌɪntəˈmiːdɪət‖-ər-/ *adj* [Wa5] (done or happening) between 2 others; halfway

in·ter·ment /ɪnˈtɜːmənt‖-ɜr-/ *n* [U;C] burial —see also INTER; compare INTERNMENT

in·ter·mez·zo /ˌɪntəˈmetsəʊ‖-ər-/ *n* **-zos** *or* **-zi** /tsi/ a short piece of music played alone, or one which connects longer pieces

in·ter·mi·na·ble /ɪnˈtɜːmɨnəbəl‖-ɜr-/ *adj* (seeming) endless —**-bly** *adv* [Wa3]

in·ter·min·gle /ˌɪntəˈmɪŋgəl‖-ər-/ also **in·ter·mix** /-ˈmɪks/— *v* [Wv3;IØ (*with*)] (usu. of groups or masses) to mix together or with something else: *The waters of the streams met and intermingled.|The green liquid intermingled with the water*

in·ter·mis·sion /ˌɪntəˈmɪʃən‖-ər-/ *n* **1** [U] *fml* the act of pausing **2** [C] *esp. AmE* INTERVAL (2)

in·ter·mit·tent /ˌɪntəˈmɪtənt‖-ər-/ *adj* happening, then stopping, then happening again, with pauses in between; not continuous —**~ly** *adv*

in·tern¹ /ɪnˈtɜːn‖-ɜrn/ *v* [T1] to put in prison or limit the freedom of movement of (someone considered dangerous), esp. in wartime or for political reasons

in·tern², -terne /ˈɪntɜːn‖-ɜrn/ *n esp. AmE* a person who has nearly or recently finished professional training (esp. in medicine or teaching) and is gaining controlled practical experience (esp. in a hospital or classroom) —compare HOUSEMAN

in·ter·nal /ɪnˈtɜːnl‖-ɜr-/ *adj* [Wa5; (*to*)] **1** of or in the inside, esp. of the body: *internal damage* **2** DOMESTIC¹ (3); not foreign: *internal trade* **3** existing or obtainable within that which is under consideration rather than from other pieces of writing, witnesses, etc. (often in the phr. **internal evidence**) —**~ly** *adv*

internal-com·bus·tion en·gine /·ˌ·· ·ˈ·· ˌ··/ *n* an engine (such as a car engine) which produces power by the burning of a substance (such as petrol) inside itself

in·ter·nal·ize, -ise /ɪnˈtɜːnəlaɪz‖-ɜr-/ *v* [T1] to make (esp. a principle or a pattern of behaviour) a conscious or unconscious part of the self as the result of learning or repeated experience in society —**-ization** /ɪnˌtɜːnəlaɪˈzeɪʃən‖ɪnˌtɜrnələ-/ *n* [U]

in·ter·na·tion·al¹ /ˌɪntəˈnæʃənəl‖-tər-/ *adj* having to do with more than one nation —**~ly** *adv*

international² *n* **1** an international sports match **2** a person who plays for his country's team in such a match

International *n* any of 4 international LEFT-WING political associations

In·ter·na·tio·nale /ˌɪntənæʃəˈnæl‖-tər-/ *n* **1** [*the*+R] the SOCIALIST song **2** [C] INTERNATIONAL

in·ter·na·tion·al·is·m /ˌɪntəˈnæʃənəlɪzəm‖-tər-/ *n* [U] the principle that nations should work together, because their differences are less important than the needs they have in common —**-ist** *n*

in·ter·na·tion·al·ize, -ise /ˌɪntəˈnæʃənəlaɪz‖-tər-/ *v* [T1] **1** to make (something) international **2** to bring under the control of several nations —**-ization** /ˌɪntənæʃənəlaɪˈzeɪʃən‖ˌɪntərnæʃənələ-/ *n* [U]

in·ter·ne·cine /ˌɪntəˈniːsaɪn‖ˌɪntərˈniːsən, -ˈnesiːn/ *adj* [Wa5] **1** having to do with bitter struggle or fighting within a group **2** (of war) which destroys both sides

in·tern·ee /ˌɪntɜːˈniː‖-ɜr-/ *n* someone who is INTERNed¹

in·tern·ment /ɪnˈtɜːnmənt‖-ɜr-/ *n* **1** [U] the act of interning or the state of being INTERNed¹ **2** [C] the period of time during which a person is INTERNed¹

in·ter·pel·late /ɪnˈtɜːpəleɪt‖ˌɪntərˈpeleɪt/ *v* [T1]

tech (in some parliaments) to interrupt (a government minister) to ask for an explanation —compare INTERPOLATE

in·ter·pen·e·trate /ˌɪntəˈpenɨtreɪt‖-ər-/ *v* [IØ;(T1)] to enter and influence (each other) —**-tration** /ˌɪntəpenɨˈtreɪʃən‖-ər-/ *n* [U]: *the interpenetration of opposite things*

in·ter·per·son·al /ˌɪntəˈpɜːsənəl‖-ɜr-/ *adj* being, related to, or concerning relations between persons: *interpersonal relations*

in·ter·plan·e·ta·ry /ˌɪntəˈplænɨtəri‖ˌɪntərˈplænɨteri/ *adj* [Wa5] (happening or done) between the PLANETS: *interplanetary travel/space*

in·ter·play /ˈɪntəpleɪ‖-ər-/ *n* [U] INTERACTION: *the interplay of the coloured lights*

In·ter·pol /ˈɪntəpɒl‖ˈɪntərpəʊl/ *n* [GU] the International Police

in·ter·po·late /ɪnˈtɜːpəleɪt‖-ɜr-/ *v* [T1] to put in (additional words): *He interpolated a phrase about the growth of profits*

in·ter·po·la·tion /ɪnˌtɜːpəˈleɪʃən‖-ɜr-/ *n* **1** [U] the act or action of interpolating (INTERPOLATE) **2** [C] something (such as a word or phrase) that is INTERPOLATEd

in·ter·pose /ˌɪntəˈpəʊz‖-ər-/ *v* [(*between, among, in*)] **1** [T1;IØ] to put or come between **2** [T1] to introduce or say between the parts of a conversation or argument

in·ter·po·si·tion /ˌɪntəpəˈzɪʃən‖-ər-/ *n* **1** [U] the act of interposing (INTERPOSE) **2** [C] something INTERPOSED

in·ter·pret /ɪnˈtɜːprɨt‖-ɜr-/ *v* **1** [T1 (*as*)] to understand the likely meaning of (something): *How can I interpret this behaviour?|I interpret his silence as dislike* **2** [T1] to show the (possible) meaning of (something), esp. in art, the theatre, etc.: *He interprets Shakespeare as no one has ever done before* **3** [T1] to put (a language) into the words of another language usu. by speech —compare TRANSLATE (1) **4** [IØ] to act as INTERPRETER

in·ter·pre·ta·tion /ɪnˌtɜːprɨˈteɪʃən‖-ɜr-/ *n* **1** [U] the act or the result of INTERPRETING; explanation **2** [C;U] (an example of) the performance of the intentions of a musician, writer, etc., by the person who performs the music or play: *a wonderful interpretation of a piece of music*

in·ter·pre·ta·tive /ɪnˈtɜːprɨtətɪv‖ɪnˈtɜrprəteɪtɪv/ also **in·ter·pre·tive** /ɪnˈtɜːprɨtɪv‖-ɜr-/— *adj* [Wa5] of or concerning INTERPRETATION

in·ter·pret·er /ɪnˈtɜːprɨtəʳ‖-ɜr-/ *n* a person who INTERPRETs, esp. one who says in another language the words of a speech that is being, or has just been, given

in·ter·ra·cial /ˌɪntəˈreɪʃəl/ *adj* [Wa5] (done, happening, etc.) between (human) races: *interracial friendship* —**~ly** *adv*

in·ter·reg·num /ˌɪntəˈregnəm/ *n* **-nums** *or* **-na** /nə/ **1** a period of time when a country has no king, because the new ruler has not yet taken up his position **2** a period of time between events, esp. when waiting for someone to take up an important position

in·ter·re·late /ˌɪntərɪˈleɪt/ [Wv5;IØ (*with*)] to be connected to each other or with something else in a way that makes one depend on the other: *Wages and prices interrelate/are interrelated*

in·ter·re·la·tion /ˌɪntərɪˈleɪʃən/ also **in·ter·re·la·tion·ship** /ˌɪntərɪˈleɪʃənʃɪp/— *n* [C;U: (*between*)] a (close) connection: *the interrelation between wages and prices*

in·ter·ro·gate /ɪnˈterəgeɪt/ *v* [T1] to question formally for a special purpose, esp. for a certain length of time —see ASK (USAGE) —**-gation** /ɪnˌterəˈgeɪʃən/ *n* [U;C] —**-gator** /ɪnˈterəgeɪtəʳ/ *n*

in·ter·rog·a·tive[1] /ˌɪntəˈrɒgətɪv‖-ˈrɑ-/ *adj* [Wa5] which asks a question —**~ly** *adv*

interrogative[2] *n* **1** an INTERROGATIVE[1] sentence, phrase, or form: *Put this statement into the interrogative* **2** a word (such as *who, what, which*) used in asking a question

in·ter·rog·a·to·ry /ˌɪntəˈrɒgətəri‖-ˈrɑgətori/ *adj* which seems to ask a question: *in an interrogatory voice*

in·ter·rupt /ˌɪntəˈrʌpt/ *v* [T1;IØ] **1** to break the flow of (something continuous) **2** to break the flow of speech of (someone) by saying something —**~ion** /ˌɪntəˈrʌpʃən/ *n* [U;C]

in·ter·sect /ˌɪntəˈsekt‖-ər-/ *v* [T1;IØ] to be in such a position as to cut across (each other or something else)

in·ter·sec·tion /ˌɪntəˈsekʃən‖-ər-/ *n* **1** [U] the act or action of INTERSECTing **2** [C] a point where roads, lines, etc., INTERSECT, esp. where 2 roads cross; CROSSROADS (1) —see picture at GEOMETRY

in·ter·sperse /ˌɪntəˈspɜːs‖ˌɪntərˈspɜrs/ *v* [X9] to set (something) here and there among other things: *small dots interspersed in the pattern*

intersperse with *v prep* [D1 *usu. pass.*] to vary or interrupt (something) with (something different): *The pattern was interspersed with small dots*

in·ter·state /ˌɪntəˈsteɪt◂‖-ər-/ *adj* [Wa5;A] done, connecting, or happening between states such as the states of the US

in·ter·stel·lar /ˌɪntəˈsteləʳ◂‖-ər-/ *adj* [Wa5;A] (placed or moving) between the stars: *interstellar gases/space*

in·ter·stice /ɪnˈtɜːstɨs‖-ɜr-/ *n* [*usu. pl.*] a small space or crack between things placed close together

in·ter·tri·bal /ˌɪntəˈtraɪbəl◂‖-ər-/ *adj* [Wa5;A] (done, happening, etc.) between tribes: *intertribal marriages*

in·ter·twine /ˌɪntəˈtwaɪn‖-ər-/ *v* [T1;IØ: (*with*)] to (cause to) twist together or with something else

in·ter·ur·ban /ˌɪntərˈɜːbən‖-ˈɜr-/ *adj* [Wa5;A] (placed or moving) between towns: *interurban road systems*

in·ter·val /ˈɪntəvəl‖-ər-/ *n* **1** a stretch of time between events: *There was a long interval before he replied* **2** (*AmE* **intermission**)— *BrE* such a stretch of time between the parts of a play, concert, etc.: *I like to eat ice cream in the interval* **3 at intervals (of)** happening regularly after equal periods of time or appearing at equal distances (of): *at 20-minute intervals|Seeds are planted at intervals of 3 inches*

in·ter·vene /ˌɪntəˈviːn‖-ər-/ *v* [IØ] **1** (of events) to happen so as to prevent or cause something **2** [(*in*)] (of people) to interrupt something, esp. to prevent a bad result: *They were about to fight when their father intervened* **3** [Wv4; (*between*)] (of time) to come between events or after an event: *in the intervening years*

in·ter·ven·tion /ˌɪntəˈvenʃən‖-ər-/ *n* [U;(C)] (an example of) the act of intervening (INTERVENE)

in·ter·view[1] /ˈɪntəvjuː‖-ər-/ *n* **1** a meeting where a person is asked questions by another or others, esp. to decide whether he can enter a university or take up a job **2 a** such a meeting between an important person and another or others who want to know about his actions, points of view, etc., sometimes broadcast on radio or television **b** an article written about this

interview[2] *v* [T1] to ask questions of (somebody) in an INTERVIEW[1] —**~er** *n*

in·ter·weave /ˌɪntəˈwiːv‖-ər-/ *v* **-wove** /ˈwəʊv/, **-woven** /ˈwəʊvən/ [T1 (*with*)] to weave together or with something else: *They interweave red and gold.|They interwove red with gold.|(fig.) Our lives are interwoven*

in·tes·tate /ɪn'testeɪt, -stɨt/ *adj* [Wa5] *esp. law* not having made a WILL[2] (6) which leaves one's property to named people (in the phr. **die intestate**)

in·tes·ti·nal /ɪn'testɨnl/ *adj* [Wa5] of or concerning the INTESTINE

in·tes·tine /ɪn'testɨn/ *n* [*usu. pl. with sing. meaning*] the tube carrying food from the stomach; bowels —see also SMALL INTESTINE, LARGE INTESTINE; compare BOWELS (1)

in·ti·ma·cy /'ɪntɨməsi/ *n* **1** [U (*with*)] the state of being INTIMATE[2] **2** [U (*with*)] close friendship **3** [U (*with*)] *euph* the act of sex **4** [C *often pl.*] speech or an action such as is permitted only between people who know each other very well: *exchanging intimacies with one's close friends* **5 on terms of intimacy** —see **on** INTIMATE[2] **terms**

in·ti·mate[1] /'ɪntɨmeɪt/ *v* [T1,5,5b] to make known indirectly; suggest: *He intimated a wish to go by saying that it was late.*|*He intimated that he wanted to go* —**-mation** /ˌɪntɨ'meɪʃən/ *n* [U;C: (*of*, 5)]

in·ti·mate[2] /'ɪntɨmɨt/ *adj* **1** [(*with*)] (concerning people who are) close in relationship or wish to seem so: *intimate friends*|*an intimate party*|*an intimate restaurant where you eat by candlelight* **2** personal; private: *one's intimate beliefs* **3** [(*with*)] concerned in a sexual relationship with someone else or each other: *They were intimate.*|*to be intimate with someone* **4** detailed; resulting from close connection with **5 on intimate terms** also **on terms of intimacy**— close in friendship or concerned in a sexual relationship —**~ly** *adv*

intimate[3] /'ɪntɨmɨt/ *n* [C9 *esp. with poss.*] a friend or person closely connected with another: *one's friends and intimates*|*an intimate of the President('s)*

in·tim·i·date /ɪn'tɪmɨdeɪt/ *v* [T1] to make (someone) fearful enough to do what one wants

in·tim·i·da·tion /ɪnˌtɪmɨ'deɪʃən/ *n* **1** [U] the act of intimidating (INTIMIDATE) **2** [C] a threat; act which makes somebody behave as one wants through fear

in·to /'ɪntə; *before consonants* 'ɪntʊ; *strong* 'ɪntuː/ *prep* **1** to the INSIDE[1] of: *"They broke into his store"* (SEU W.)|*"down some steps into the garden"* (SEU S.)|*"He's got to go into a hospital"* (SEU S.).|*"I pressed 5 shillings into her hand"* (SEU S.) **2** so as to be in: *"went into the law and then went into business"* (SEU S.)|*"getting deeper and deeper into debt"* (SEU S.)|*to fall into the water*|*to get into a temper*|*to come into office*|*"We're 8 minutes into the second half"* (SEU S.)|*It lasted well into this century* **3** so as to be: *to translate it into French*|*to join them all into one company*|*to turn the prince into a rabbit*|*to divide it into 5 parts*|*She developed into a beautiful woman* **4** (used when dividing one number by another): *3 into 6 goes twice* **5** *sl* keen on; interested in (a subject or belief): *He's given up photography now and he's into religion and modern music*

in·tol·e·ra·ble /ɪn'tɒlərəbəl‖-'tɑ-/ *adj* which is too difficult, painful, etc., to be borne; unbearable —**-bly** *adv* [Wa3]

in·tol·e·rant /ɪn'tɒlərənt‖-'tɑ-/ *adj* not by one's nature able to accept ways of thinking and behaving which are different from one's own: *intolerant of any opposition* —**~ly** *adv* —**-rance** *n* [U]

in·to·na·tion /ˌɪntə'neɪʃən/ *n* [U;C] (a pattern of) rise and fall in the level (PITCH[3]) of the voice

in·tone /ɪn'təʊn/ *v* [T1;IØ] to say (a poem, prayer) in an almost level voice; CHANT[1] (1)

in to·to /ˌɪn 'təʊtəʊ/ *adv* [Wa5] *Lat* totally; as a whole

in·tox·i·cant /ɪn'tɒksɨkənt‖ɪn'tɑk-/ *n, adj* [Wa5] (something) which INTOXICATES, esp. an alcoholic drink

in·tox·i·cate /ɪn'tɒksɨkeɪt‖ɪn'tɑk-/ *v* [T1;(IØ)] **1** (of alcohol) to cause loss of control of actions and feelings in (someone) **2** to bring out strong feelings of wild excitement in (someone): *Success intoxicated him* —**-cation** /ɪnˌtɒksɨ'keɪʃən‖ɪnˌtɑk-/ *n* [U]

in·tra- /ˌɪntrə/ *prefix* **1** inside or between: *intra*CONTINENTAL **2** during; within: *intra*NATAL **3** INTRO-: INTRAVENOUS

in·trac·ta·ble /ɪn'træktəbəl/ *adj* (of people and their acts) showing such a strong will as to be difficult to control —**-bility** /ɪnˌtræktə'bɪlɨti/ *n* [U] —**-bly** /ɪn'træktəbli/ *adv* [Wa3]

in·tra·mu·ral /ˌɪntrə'mjʊərəl/ *adj* [Wa5;A] **1** being or happening within a building or organization: *intramural courses at college* **2** (of a competition) limited to the student body of a single school, university, etc.: *intramural sports* —compare EXTRAMURAL

in·tran·si·gent /ɪn'trænsɨdʒənt/ *adj* (of people and their acts) showing strong ideas which cannot be changed by others' wishes —**-gence** *n* [U] —**-gently** *adv*

in·tran·si·tive /ɪn'trænsɨtɪv/ *n, adj* [Wa5] (a verb) which has a subject but not an object: *In this dictionary the mark* [I] *shows an intransitive* (*verb*) —**~ly** *adv*

in·tra·u·te·rine de·vice /ɪntrəˌjuːtəraɪn dɪ'vaɪs‖-tərən-/ (*abbrev.* **IUD**)— *n* the LOOP[1] (3) or COIL[2] (4); an object placed in the child-bearing organ of a woman to prevent her from having children

in·tra·ve·nous /ˌɪntrə'viːnəs/ *adj* [Wa5] (done) within a VEIN (=blood vessel taking blood back to the heart): *an intravenous* INJECTION —**~ly** *adv*

in·trench /ɪn'trentʃ/ *v* [IØ;X9] ENTRENCH

in·trep·id /ɪn'trepɨd/ *adj* (of people and their acts) showing no fear —**~ly** /ɪn'trepɨdli/ *adv* —**~ity** /ˌɪntrə'pɪdɨti/ *n* [U]

in·tri·ca·cy /'ɪntrɪkəsi/ *n* **1** [U] the quality or state of being INTRICATE **2** [C *often pl.*] something INTRICATE: *the intricacies of political behaviour*

in·tri·cate /'ɪntrɪkɨt/ *adj* containing many detailed parts and thus difficult to understand —**~ly** *adv*

in·trigue[1] /ɪn'triːg/ *v* **1** [Wv4;T1] to interest greatly **2** [IØ] to make a secret plan

in·trigue[2] /'ɪntriːg, ɪn'triːg/ *n* **1** [U] the act or practice of planning something secretly **2** [C] a secret plan or activity between 2 or more people

in·trin·sic /ɪn'trɪnsɪk, -zɪk/ *adj* [Wa5; (*to, in*)] being part of the nature or character of someone or something —**~ally** *adv* [Wa4,5]

int·ro /ˌɪntrəʊ/ *n* **-s** *infml* an introduction: *Can you arrange an intro to the chairman for me?*

in·tro-, intra- /ˌɪntrə/ *prefix* into; inside: INTROSPECTION

in·tro·duce /ˌɪntrə'djuːs‖-'duːs/ *v* [T1] **1** to make known for the first time to each other or someone else, esp. by telling 2 people each other's names: *I introduced them.*|*Let me introduce myself: my name is Simpson* **2** to bring in for the first time: *They introduced the idea that children could learn to read as babies* **3** to produce the first part of (something), esp. to suggest or explain the main part: *The first few notes introduce a new type of music*

introduce in·to *v prep* [D1] to put (something) into (something): *introduced a new idea into the conversation*|*introduced the pipe into the hole*

introduce to *v prep* [D1;V4b] to make (someone) known to (someone else) or familiar with (something such as an idea, a city, or an activity): *I introduced John to Mary, 2 years before they were married.*|*Let me introduce you to (the pleasures of) dancing*

in·tro·duc·tion /ˌɪntrə'dʌkʃən/ *n* **1** [U9, esp. *of, to, into*] the act or action of introducing or the state of being introduced **2** [C (*to*) *often pl.*] an occasion of telling people each others' names **3** [C (*to*)] **a** a written or spoken explanation at the beginning of a book or speech —see PREFACE[1] (USAGE) **b** a book which gives one a knowledge of the most important things before going on to advanced studies **4** [C] the beginning part of anything, as of a piece of music

in·tro·duc·to·ry /ˌɪntrəˈdʌktəri/ *adj* [Wa5] which INTRODUCEs (3): *a few introductory remarks before the main points*

in·troit /ˈɪntrɔɪt‖ˈɪntrəʊɨt, ˈɪntrɔɪt/ *n* [C; *the*+R] (*often cap.*) a special song at the beginning of a Christian church service

in·tro·spec·tion /ˌɪntrəˈspekʃən/ *n* [U] the habit of looking into one's own thoughts and feelings to find out their real meaning, the reasons for them, etc.

in·tro·spec·tive /ˌɪntrəˈspektɪv/ *adj* tending to think (too) deeply about oneself

in·tro·vert /ˈɪntrəvɜːt‖-ɜrt/ *n* a person of an INTROVERTED type —compare EXTROVERT

in·tro·vert·ed /ˈɪntrəvɜːtɨd‖-ɜr-/ *adj* concerning oneself with one's own thoughts, acts, personal life, etc., rather than spending much time sharing activities with others —**introversion** /ˌɪntrəˈvɜːʃən‖-ˈvɜrʒən/ *n* [U]

in·trude /ɪnˈtruːd/ *v* [(*into, on, upon*)] **1** [T1] to bring in unnecessarily: *He intruded his own ideas into the argument* **2** [IØ] to come in when not wanted: *I don't want to intrude*

in·trud·er /ɪnˈtruːdəʳ/ *n* a person who has come in unasked, esp. one intending to steal

in·tru·sion /ɪnˈtruːʒən/ *n* [(*on*)] **1** [U] the act of intruding (INTRUDE) **2** [C] an occasion when someone or something forms an interruption of work, someone else's affairs, etc.: *The meeting at 6 was an intrusion on my time, but I succeeded in finishing the work later*

in·tru·sive /ɪnˈtruːsɪv/ *adj* **1** of or concerning INTRUSION **2** [Wa5] *tech* (of a sound) which tends to or does INTRUDE, or come in unnecessarily

in·trust /ɪnˈtrʌst/ *v* ENTRUST

in·tu·it /ɪnˈtjuːɨt‖-ˈtuː-/ *v* [T1,(5);IØ] to know by INTUITION

in·tu·i·tion /ˌɪntjʊˈɪʃən‖-tʊ-/ *n* **1** [U] **a** the power to know how something happens or will happen, without reasoning **b** the (feeling of) understanding which results **2** [C,C5] an example of this, or the piece of knowledge that results: *an intuition that her friend was ill*

in·tu·i·tive /ɪnˈtjuːɨtɪv‖-ˈtuː-/ *adj* (of people and their acts) showing or formed by INTUITION —**~ly** *adv* —**~ness** *n* [U]

in·tu·mes·cence /ˌɪntjʊˈmesəns‖-tʊ-/ *n* [U;C] *med* the act or condition of swelling

in·un·date /ˈɪnəndeɪt/ *v* [T1 (*with*) *often pass.*] to flood over in large amounts esp. so as to cover: (fig.) *I was inundated with requests for money*

in·un·da·tion /ˌɪnənˈdeɪʃən/ *n* **1** [U] the act of inundating or the state of being INUNDATED **2** [C] an example of this; flood

in·ure to /ɪˈnjʊəʳ/ *v prep* [D1;V4b *usu. pass.*] to accustom (someone) by experience to (something): *The old soldier was inured to danger*

in·vade /ɪnˈveɪd/ *v* **1** [T1;IØ] to attack and spread into so as to take control of (a country, city, etc.) **2** [T1;IØ] to enter in large numbers: *Holiday makers invaded the seaside in summer months* **3** [T1] to enter into and spoil: *to invade someone's* PRIVACY —**~r** *n*

in·val·id[1] /ɪnˈvælɨd/ *adj* [Wa5] not correct or correctly expressed, esp. in law; not (any longer) suitable for use: *an invalid claim* —**~ly** /ɪnˈvælɨdli/ *adv* —**~ity** /ˌɪnvəˈlɪdɨti/ *n* [U]

in·va·lid[2] /ˈɪnvəliːd, -lɨd‖-lɨd/ *n* a person made weak by illness: *my invalid mother*

in·val·i·date /ɪnˈvælɨdeɪt/ *v* [T1] to make (something) INVALID[1]; show that (something) is not correct —**-dation** /ɪnˌvælɨˈdeɪʃən/ *n* [U]

in·va·lid·is·m /ˈɪnvəliːdɪzəm, -lɨ-‖-lɨ-/ *n* [U] **1** the condition or state of being an INVALID **2** the per cent of INVALIDs[2] in a given population during a given time

invalid out /ˈɪnvəliːd, -lɨd‖-lɨd/ *v adv* [T1 (*of*) *usu. pass.*] to allow (someone) to leave esp. a military force because of ill-health

in·val·ua·ble /ɪnˈvæljʊbəl‖-jə-/ *adj* (of qualities) too valuable for the worth to be measured: *your invaluable help* —see WORTHLESS (USAGE)

in·var·i·a·ble /ɪnˈveərɪəbəl/ *adj* [Wa5] which cannot vary or change —**-bly** /ɪnˈveərɪəbli/ *adv* [Wa3,5]: *It's invariably wet when I take my holidays* —**-bility** /ɪnˌveərɪəˈbɪlɨti/ *n* [U]

in·va·sion /ɪnˈveɪʒən/ *n* **1** an act of invading (INVADE), esp. an attack in war when the enemy spreads into and tries to control the country, a city, etc. **2** the incoming or spread of something usu. harmful

in·vec·tive /ɪnˈvektɪv/ *n* [U;(C)] forceful, attacking speech (used for blaming someone for something and often including swearing)

in·veigh a·gainst /ɪnˈveɪ/ *v prep* [T1,4] to attack (someone or something) bitterly with words

in·vei·gle in·to /ɪnˈveɪgəl, ɪnˈviː-‖ɪnˈveɪ-/ *v prep* [V4b] to trick (someone) into (doing something)

in·vent /ɪnˈvent/ *v* [T1] **1** to make up or produce for the first time (esp. a new or useful thing or idea): *Alexander Graham Bell invented the telephone in 1876* **2** to make up (something unreal or untrue): *The whole story was invented*
USAGE One **discovers** something that existed before but was not known, such as a place or a fact. One **invents** something that did not exist before, such as a machine or a method.

in·ven·tion /ɪnˈvenʃən/ *n* **1** [U] the act of inventing: *the invention of the telephone* **2** [C] something invented: *The telephone is a wonderful invention*

in·ven·tive /ɪnˈventɪv/ *adj apprec* having or showing the ability to invent or think in new and different ways —**~ly** *adv* —**~ness** *n* [U]

in·ven·tor /ɪnˈventəʳ/ *n* a person who invents something new

in·ven·tory[1] /ˈɪnvəntri‖-tori/ *n* a list, esp. one of all the goods in a place: *a detailed inventory of all the jobs to be done*

inventory[2] *v* [T1] to take or make an INVENTORY[1] of

in·verse /ˈɪnvɜːs‖-ɜrs/ *adj, n* [Wa5;A;C] **1** (that which is) opposite (in order or position): *the inverse of 4 (=4/1) is 1/4; the figure 4 is in (the) inverse position* **2 in inverse relation/proportion (to)** (of 2 things or one to another) getting bigger as the other gets smaller —**~ly** *adv*

in·ver·sion /ɪnˈvɜːʃən‖ɪnˈvɜrʒən/ *n* **1** [U] the act, action, or result of INVERTing **2** [C] an example of this

in·vert /ɪnˈvɜːt‖-ɜrt/ *v* [T1] to put in the opposite position or order, esp. upside down

in·ver·te·brate /ɪnˈvɜːtɨbrɨt, -breɪt‖-ɜr-/ *adj, n* [Wa5] *tech* (a living creature) which has no BACKBONE (3) —compare VERTEBRATE

inverted com·ma /·ˌ·· ˈ··/ *n BrE* QUOTATION MARK

in·vest /ɪnˈvest/ *v* [T1;IØ: (*in*)] **1** to use (money) to make more money out of something that will increase in value: *He invested £100 in a growing business.*|*She invested in a house/a painting by a young artist.*|(fig.) *I've invested a lot of time and effort in this plan, and I don't want it to fail.*|(*humor*) *I've decided to invest in* (=buy) *a new car* **2** *lit* to surround with soldiers or ships so as to prevent escape or entrance —see also INVEST WITH

in·ves·ti·gate /ɪn'vestɪ̈geɪt/ *v* [T1;IØ] to examine the reasons for (something), the character of (someone), etc.: *to investigate the crime|He has been investigated and found blameless* —**-gator** /ɪn'vestɪ̈geɪtə^r/ *n* —**-gation** /ɪn,vestɪ̈'geɪʃən/ *n* [U;C]

in·ves·ti·ture /ɪn'vestɪ̈tʃə^r‖-tʃʊə^r/ *n* a ceremony to accept someone into office, to give them certain powers, etc. —see also INVEST WITH

in·vest·ment /ɪn'vestmənt/ *n* **1** [U] the act or action of INVESTing (1) **2** [C] something INVESTed or in which one INVESTs (1): *an investment of £100 in a growing business|Some people say children are a good investment against loneliness when one is old*

invest with *v prep* [D1 *often pass.*] *fml or lit* to give officially to (a person) (the outward signs of rank or power, or the power itself): *invested with* AUTHORITY

in·vet·e·rate /ɪn'vetərɪ̈t/ *adj* [Wa5;A] settled in the usu. bad habits of (the type of person or quality mentioned): *an inveterate* LIAR|*inveterate hatred*

in·vid·i·ous /ɪn'vɪdɪəs/ *adj* [Wa5;A;(B)] which will make people unjustly offended or jealous of one another —**~ly** *adv* —**~ness** *n* [U]

in·vi·gi·late /ɪn'vɪdʒɪ̈leɪt/ *v* [T1;IØ] *BrE* to watch over (an examination or the people taking it) in order to prevent dishonesty —**-lator** /ɪn'vɪdʒɪ̈leɪtə^r/ *n* —**-lation** /ɪn,vɪdʒɪ̈'leɪʃən/ *n* [U]

in·vig·o·rate /ɪn'vɪgəreɪt/ *v* [Wv4;T1] to give a feeling of strength and/or power to

in·vin·ci·ble /ɪn'vɪnsəbəl/ *adj* [Wa5] too strong to be conquered —**-bility** /ɪn,vɪnsə'bɪlɪ̈ti/ *n* [U] —**-bly** /ɪn'vɪnsəbli/ *adj* [Wa3,5]

in·vi·o·la·ble /ɪn'vaɪələbəl/ *adj* [Wa5] which cannot be VIOLATEd; which is too highly respected to be attacked, changed, etc.: *inviolable rights* —**-bility** /ɪn,vaɪələ'bɪlɪ̈ti/ *n* [U]

in·vi·o·late /ɪn'vaɪəlɪ̈t/ *adj* [Wa5] *lit* not VIOLATED

in·vis·i·ble /ɪn'vɪzəbəl/ *adj* [Wa5] **1** that cannot be seen because of nature, size or position; hidden from sight **2** that is not usually recorded, esp. in statements of profit and loss: *invisible earnings*/EXPORTs —**-bility** /ɪn,vɪzə'bɪlɪ̈ti/ *n* [U] —**-bly** /ɪn'vɪzəbli/ *adv* [Wa3,5]

in·vi·ta·tion /,ɪnvɪ̈'teɪʃən/ *n* **1** [U] the act of inviting: *entrance by written invitation only* **2** [C (*to*); C3] an often written request to be present or take part **3** [C+*to*; C3] an encouragement to an action: *The king's evil deeds were an invitation to* REBELLION/*to* REBEL²

in·vite /ɪn'vaɪt/ *v* **1** [Wv5;T1 (*to*)] to ask (somebody) to or as if to a social occasion: *We invited all our relatives.|Why don't you invite me in (to the house)?|Let's invite them over (for a drink).|the invited guests* **2** [T1;V3] to ask for, esp. politely: *Questions were invited after the meeting.|I invited her to go for a walk* **3** [T1;V3] to encourage or seem to cause (an action): *Some shops invite crime by making it easy to take goods*

USAGE This word is not used when one is actually **inviting** someone. We may say *"Will you come to the party?"* and then later remark *"I invited them to the party"*.

in·vit·ing /ɪn'vaɪtɪŋ/ *adj* attractive; which encourages a suitable action: *inviting lips|inviting goods in the shop window* —**~ly** *adv*

in·vo·ca·tion /,ɪnvə'keɪʃən/ *n* **1** [U] the act of invoking (INVOKE) **2** [C] a form of words calling for help esp. from God or the gods; prayer

in·voice¹ /'ɪnvɔɪs/ *n* a bill for goods received

invoice² *v* [T1] **1** to make an INVOICE¹ for (goods) **2** to send an INVOICE¹ to (someone)

in·voke /ɪn'vəʊk/ *v* [T1] **1** to call out to (a power, esp. God) for help **2** to put into effect; call into use: *to invoke the powers of the law to prevent a crime* **3** to request or beg for: *I invoked their help|their forgiveness* **4** to call on and cause (spirits) to appear

in·vol·un·ta·ry /ɪn'vɒləntəri‖ɪn'vɑlənteri/ *adj* [Wa5] not (done) from choice or intention; unwilled —**-tarily** *adv* —**-tariness** *n* [U]

in·volve /ɪn'vɒlv‖ɪn'vɑlv/ *v* **1** [T1 (*in, with*)] to cause (someone) to become connected or concerned: *Don't involve other people in your mistakes.|We are all involved, whether we like it or not* **2** [T1,4] to have as a part or result: *Taking the job involves living abroad* —**~ment** *n* [U]

in·volved /ɪn'vɒlvd‖ɪn'vɑlvd/ *adj* **1** having related parts which are difficult to understand; COMPLICATED (2) **2** [(*with*)] (of a person) closely connected in relationships and activities with others, esp. in a personal or sexual way: *He's deeply involved (with her) and feels he must marry her because everyone expects it*

in·vul·ne·ra·ble /ɪn'vʌlnərəbəl/ *adj* [Wa5] that cannot be harmed by attack: (fig.) *an invulnerable argument* —**-bility** /ɪn,vʌlnərə'bɪlɪ̈ti/ *n* [U] —**-bly** /ɪn'vʌlnərəbli/ *adv* [Wa3,5]

in·ward /'ɪnwəd‖-ərd/ *adj* [Wa5] **1** (placed) on the inside **2** moving towards the inside **3** of the mind or spirit —**~ly** *adv*: *inwardly happy*

in·ward·ness /'ɪnwədnɪ̈s‖-ər-/ *n* [U] (in religion) the inner meaning felt in the spirit

in·wards /'ɪnwədz‖-ər-/ *AmE* also **inward**— *adv* [Wa5] towards the inside

in·wrought /,ɪn'rɔːt◂/ *adj* [Wa5;F;(B)] **1** (of a pattern) worked into the material **2** (of a material) with a pattern worked in

i·o·dine, -din /'aɪədiːn‖-daɪn/ *n* [U] a simple substance (ELEMENT (6)) that is used in photography and medicine, as on wounds to prevent infection

i·o·dize, -dise /'aɪədaɪz/ *v* [Wv5;T1] to add IODINE to (something)

i·on /'aɪən‖'aɪən, 'aɪɑn/ *n* an atom which has been given (+) or (−) NEGATIVE¹ force by the taking away or addition of an ELECTRON

-ion /ɪən/ *suffix* [*v*→*n*] (*used for forming nouns*) act, action, or state: COMPLETION

I·on·ic /aɪ'ɒnɪk‖aɪ'ɑ-/ *adj* [Wa5] of, related to, like, or typical of a slightly ornamental style of ancient Greek ARCHITECTURE (building): *an Ionic pillar* —compare DORIC; CORINTHIAN

i·on·ize, -ise /'aɪənaɪz/ *v* [Wv5;T1;IØ] to (cause to) form IONs —**-ization** /,aɪənaɪ'zeɪʃən‖-nə-/ *n* [U]

i·on·o·sphere /aɪ'ɒnəsfɪə^r‖aɪ'ɑ-/ *n* [*the*+R] a part of the ATMOSPHERE surrounding the earth which directs radio waves around the earth

i·o·ta /aɪ'əʊtə/ *n* **1** [R;(C)] the 9th letter of the Greek alphabet (I, ι) **2** [S *nonassertive*] a very small amount: *There's not an iota of truth in that*

IOU /,aɪ əʊ 'juː/ *abbrev. for*: "I owe you"; a piece of paper saying that one owes a certain amount of money to someone else, with one's signature at the bottom

IPA *abbrev. for*: International PHONETIC Alphabet or International PHONETIC Association

ip·so fac·to /,ɪpsəʊ 'fæktəʊ/ *adv Lat* (*used for showing that something else is known or proved by the known facts*) "by the fact itself"

IQ *abbrev. for*: INTELLIGENCE QUOTIENT: *a high IQ*

ir- /ɪ-/ *prefix* (*before words beginning with* r) IN-: IRREGULAR

IRA *abbrev. for*: Irish REPUBLICAN Army

I·ra·ni·an /ɪ'reɪnɪən, ɪ'rɑː-/ *adj* [Wa5] of the people, language, art, etc. of Iran

i·ras·ci·ble /ɪ'ræsəbəl/ *adj* (of a person) tending to get angry —**-bility** /ɪ,ræsə'bɪlɪ̈ti/ *n* [U] —**-bly** /ɪ'ræsəbli/ *adv* [Wa3]

zornig, wütend

i·rate /aɪˈreɪt/ *adj fml* (of people and their acts) showing (strong) anger: *an irate letter* —**~ly** *adv* —**~ness** *n* [U]

ire /aɪəʳ/ *n* [U] *lit* anger —**~ful** *adj*

ir·i·des·cent /ˌɪrəˈdesənt/ *adj* [Wa5] showing changing colours as light falls on it —**-cence** *n* [U]

i·rid·i·um /ɪˈrɪdiəm/ *n* [U] a type of hard metal which is a simple substance (ELEMENT (6))

i·ris /ˈaɪərəs/ *n* **1** a type of tall yellow or purple wild flower with large leaves, which grows near rivers; FLAG¹ **2** a type of garden flower like this —see picture at FLOWER¹ **3** the round, coloured part of the eye which surrounds the black movable opening (PUPIL) —see picture at EYE¹

I·rish /ˈaɪərɪʃ/ *adj* [Wa5] of Ireland, its people, or their language

I·rish·man /ˈaɪərɪʃmən/ (*fem.* **I·rish·wom·an** /-ˌwʊmən/)— *n* **-men** /mən/ a person from Ireland

Irish set·ter /ˌ·· ˈ··/ *n* a type of brown-haired dog which finds the birds which the hunter has shot

Irish stew /ˌ·· ˈ·/ *n* [U;C] a kind of food with meat, potatoes, and onions which have been boiled together

irk /ɜːk‖ɜrk/ *v* [T1] to annoy; make (someone) feel troubled: *It irks him to have to help his wife, but he does it even so* —see ANGRY (USAGE)

irk·some /ˈɜːksəm‖ˈɜrk-/ *adj* troublesome; annoying

lästig, ermüdend

i·ron¹ /ˈaɪən‖ˈaɪərn/ *n* **1** [U] a silver-white metal that is a simple substance (ELEMENT (6)) and is the most useful metal, being necessary to animal and plant life, and MAGNETIC **2** [U] the same metal found in natural food (eggs, vegetables), and which is used in the formation of blood **3** [C] a heavy object with a handle on top, shaped in a point at the front and flat underneath, which is heated and used for making clothing and cloth smooth **4** [A] of great strength (of character); unyielding: *an iron will* **5** [C] any of the set of 9 GOLF CLUBs (2) (numbered from 1 to 9) which have metal heads with sloping faces for driving a ball short distances: *a 6 iron* (=the one with the number 6)|*an iron shot* —compare WOOD¹ (4) **6 rule (someone) with a rod of iron** to be firm and command obedience **7 the iron hand/fist in the velvet glove** a very firm intention hidden under a gentle appearance **8 strike while the iron's hot** *usu. imper.* to make use of a favourable occasion as soon as it comes, without losing valuable time **9 have (several) irons in the fire** to have various different interests, activities, or plans at the same time **10 a man/woman of iron** a cruel, hard person

iron² *v* **1** [T1;I∅] **a** to cause (clothes) to become smooth by using an IRON¹ (3): *Your shirt is already ironed.*|*I've been (doing the) ironing all day* **b** (of clothes) to become smooth by the action of an IRON¹ (3): *You wouldn't expect a pair of socks to iron well* **2** [T1a] IRON OUT (2)

Iron Age /ˈ·· ·/ *n* [*the*+R] the time in the history of man when iron was used for tools, weapons, etc., which was a more advanced period than the BRONZE Age before it, when a softer metal was used

i·ron·clad /ˈaɪənklæd‖-ər-/ *adj, n old use* (a ship) covered in iron to protect it in war

Iron Cur·tain /ˌ·· ˈ··/ *n derog becoming rare* **1** [*the*+R] the name for the western border between the USSR (and other COMMUNIST countries) and the rest of the world, which cannot be easily crossed for purposes of trade, the exchange of information, travel, etc. (note the phr. **behind the Iron Curtain**) **2** [A] of or being a country of Eastern Europe which has signed the Warsaw PACT

iron found·ry /ˈ·· ˌ··/ *n* a factory where iron is melted and made pure

iron-grey /ˌ·· ˈ·/ *adj* of a shiny grey colour: *iron-grey hair*

iron horse /ˌ·· ˈ·/ *n* [*the*+R] *old use or poet* the railway

i·ron·ic /aɪˈrɒnɪk‖aɪˈrɑ-/ also **i·ron·i·cal** /-kəl/— *adj* expressing IRONY; of a strange and often bitterly funny quality which shows that things are not as they seem or were meant to be: *an ironic saying, such as "God sends you nuts when you've no teeth"*

i·ron·i·cal·ly /aɪˈrɒnɪkəli‖aɪˈrɑ-/ *adv* **1** in an IRONIC way: *smiled ironically* **2** it is IRONIC (that): *Ironically, he became ill on the day of his marriage*

i·ron·ing /ˈaɪənɪŋ‖-ər-/ *n* [U] things (such as clothes, tablecloths, and sheets) which are made smooth (ironed) or to be made smooth after washing

ironing board /ˈ··· ·/ *n* a sort of long narrow table on which clothes are spread to be made smooth (IRONed)

iron lung /ˌ·· ˈ·/ *n* a machine fitted over the body which helps one breathe in and out by putting repeated pressures on the chest

i·ron·mon·ger /ˈaɪənˌmʌŋgəʳ‖ˈaɪərnˌmʌŋ-, -ˌmɑŋ-/ *n BrE* a shopkeeper who sells HARDWARE (1), esp. metal goods

i·ron·mon·ger·y /ˈaɪənˌmʌŋgəri‖ˈaɪərnˌmʌŋ-, -ˌmɑŋ-/ *n* [U] *BrE* HARDWARE (1), esp. if made of metal

i·ron·mould /ˈaɪənməʊld‖-ər-/ *n* [U] a brown mark left by RUST from iron, or from ink

iron out *v adv* **1** [T1] *infml* to remove or find an answer to (something): *to iron out the difficulties* **2** [T1a] to remove by using an IRON¹ (3): *He offered to iron out the* WRINKLE*s in her dress*

iron ra·tions /ˌ·· ˈ··/ *n* [P] small amounts of substances with high food value (such as chocolate) carried by soldiers, climbers, etc., for use in time of need

i·rons /ˈaɪənz‖ˈaɪərnz/ *n* [P] **1** a chain or chains to keep a prisoner from moving **2** an iron apparatus (CALLIPER*s*) put on the leg to keep it straight after being broken or hurt

i·ron·stone /ˈaɪənstəʊn‖-ər-/ *n* [U] the impure form of iron before it is melted out of the rock

i·ron·ware /ˈaɪənweəʳ‖-ər-/ *n* [U] iron goods

i·ron·work /ˈaɪənwɜːk‖ˈaɪərnwɜrk/ *n* [U] iron shaped into an ornamental pattern and used for making gates, RAIL*s*, etc. —compare WROUGHT IRON

i·ron·works /ˈaɪənwɜːks‖ˈaɪərnwɜrks/ *n* **ironworks** [Wn3;C *often pl. with sing. meaning*] a factory for preparing iron and making it into heavy objects —compare IRON FOUNDRY

i·ron·y /ˈaɪərəni/ *n* **1** [U] use of words which are clearly opposite to one's meaning, usu. with an amusing purpose (as by saying "This is beautiful weather" when the weather is bad) **2** [U;C] a course of events or a condition which has the opposite result from what is expected, usu. a bad result: *life's little ironies*

ir·ra·di·ate /ɪˈreɪdieɪt/ *v* [T1] **1** to make bright by throwing light on: (fig.) *Their faces were irradiated by happiness* **2** to treat as with X-RAY*s*

ir·ra·tion·al /ɪˈræʃənəl/ *adj* **1** (of living things) without power to reason **2** (of people and their acts) not (done by) using reason; against reasonable behaviour —**~ity** /ɪˌræʃəˈnæləti/ *n* [U] —**~ly** /ɪˈræʃənəli/ *adv*

ir·rec·on·ci·la·ble /ɪˌrekənˈsaɪləbəl/ *adj* [*with*] (of people and their acts) which cannot be brought into agreement together or with something else —**-bly** *adv* [Wa3]

ir·re·cov·e·ra·ble /ˌɪrɪˈkʌvərəbəl/ *adj* [Wa5] which cannot be got back or recovered —**-bly** *adv* [Wa3,5]

ir·re·dee·ma·ble /ˌɪrɪˈdiːməbəl/ *adj* **1** (esp. of paper money) that cannot be exchanged for goods or gold **2** (esp. of paper promises to pay (BONDs)) that cannot be exchanged for money, though yearly interest is received on the value **3** that cannot be made good again: *an irredeemable loss* —**-bly** *adv* [Wa3]

ir·re·du·ci·ble /ˌɪrɪˈdjuːsəbəl‖-ˈduː-/ *adj* [Wa5] which cannot be made smaller or simpler —**-bly** *adv* [Wa3,5]

ir·re·fu·ta·ble /ˌɪrɪˈfjuːtəbəl/ *adj* [Wa5] that is too strong to be disproved: *an irrefutable argument* —**-bly** *adv* [Wa3,5]

ir·reg·u·lar[1] /ɪˈregjʊləʳ‖-gjə-/ *adj* **1** (of shape) having different-sized parts; uneven; not level **2** (of time) at unevenly separated points; not equal **3** not according to the usual rules, habits, etc. **4** (in grammar) not following the usual pattern: *an irregular verb* —**~ly** *adv*

irregular[2] *n* a soldier in a non-regular army, which is not part of the official army of a country

ir·reg·u·lar·i·ty /ɪˌregjʊˈlærɪ̈ti‖-gjə-/ *n* **1** [U] the state of being IRREGULAR[1] **2** [C] something irregular **3** [U;C] the/an act of wrong doing; something which goes against the rules usually followed: *Certain irregularities were found in the report, making it seem that someone had taken money for himself*

ir·rel·e·vance /ɪˈrelɪ̈vəns/ also **ir·rel·e·van·cy** /-vənsi/— *n* **1** [U] the state of being IRRELEVANT **2** [C] a remark or fact which is IRRELEVANT

ir·rel·e·vant /ɪˈrelɪ̈vənt/ *adj* not having any real connection with or relation to something else: *If he can do the job well, his age is irrelevant* (=does not matter) —**~ly** *adv*

ir·re·li·gious /ˌɪrɪˈlɪdʒəs/ *adj* (of people and their acts) **a** against religion **b** showing lack of religion or religious feeling

ir·re·me·di·a·ble /ˌɪrɪˈmiːdɪəbəl/ *adj* [Wa5] which is too bad to be put right, or made well —**-bly** *adv* [Wa3,5]

ir·re·mo·va·ble /ˌɪrɪˈmuːvəbəl/ *adj* [Wa5] *tech* that cannot be removed, esp. from an official position —compare IMMOVABLE (1)

ir·rep·a·ra·ble /ɪˈrepərəbəl/ *adj* [Wa5] which is too bad to be repaired or put right —**-bly** *adv* [Wa3]

ir·re·place·a·ble /ˌɪrɪˈpleɪsəbəl/ *adj* [Wa5] that is too special or unusual to be REPLACED (2)

ir·re·pres·si·ble /ˌɪrɪˈpresəbəl/ *adj* [Wa5] that is too strong or forceful to be held back: *irrepressible high spirits|an irrepressible talker* —**-bly** *adv* [Wa3,5]

ir·re·proa·cha·ble /ˌɪrɪˈprəʊtʃəbəl/ *adj* [Wa5] (of people and their acts) so good that not the smallest blame could be given; faultless —**-bly** *adv* [Wa3,5]

ir·re·sis·ti·ble /ˌɪrɪˈzɪstəbəl/ *adj* [Wa5] **1** (of people and their qualities) too strong not to have the intended effect; that cannot be RESISTED (3,4): *She's an irresistible child* **2** so strong or powerful as to control the actions of people or things; that cannot be RESISTED (1,2,3): *an irresistible argument/force* —**-bly** *adv* [Wa3,5]

ir·res·o·lute /ɪˈrezəluːt/ *adj* (typical of a person who is) unable to make decisions and take action; weak in character —**-lution** /ɪˌrezəˈluːʃən/ *n* [U]

ir·re·spec·tive of /ˌɪrɪˈspektɪv əv/ *prep* without regard to: *They send information every week, irrespective of whether it's useful or not*

ir·re·spon·si·ble /ˌɪrɪˈspɒnsəbəl‖-ˈspɑn-/ *adj* (of people and their acts) showing lack of ability to behave carefully, think of the effect of actions on others, etc. —**-bility** /ˌɪrɪspɒnsəˈbɪlɪ̈ti‖-spɑn-/ *n* [U] —**-bly** /ˌɪrɪˈspɒnsəbli‖-ˈspɑn-/ *adv* [Wa3]

ir·re·trie·va·ble /ˌɪrɪˈtriːvəbəl/ *adj* [Wa5] that cannot be got back or put back into the original better state —**-bly** *adv* [Wa3,5]

ir·rev·e·rent /ɪˈrevərənt/ *adj* (of people and their acts) showing lack of respect, esp. for religion —**-rence** *n* [U] —**~ly** *adv*

ir·re·ver·si·ble /ˌɪrɪˈvɜːsəbəl‖-ɜr-/ *adj* [Wa5] which cannot be turned back to bring about a former state —**-bly** *adv* [Wa3,5]

ir·rev·o·ca·ble /ɪˈrevəkəbəl/ *adj* [Wa5] that cannot be changed once started: *an irrevocable decision* —**-bly** *adv* [Wa3,5]

ir·ri·gate /ˈɪrɪ̈geɪt/ *v* [T1] **1** to supply water to (dry land) esp. by providing with man-made streams (CANALs) **2** *med* to wash (a wound) with a flow of liquid —**-gable** /ˈɪrɪgəbəl/ *adj* [Wa5] —**-gation** /ˌɪrɪˈgeɪʃən/ *n* [U]

ir·ri·ta·ble /ˈɪrɪ̈təbəl/ *adj* **1** tending to get angry at small things which are being said or done **2** *tech* able to produce action when influenced by touch, light, heat, etc. —**-bility** /ˌɪrɪ̈təˈbɪlɪ̈ti/ *n* [U] —**-bly** /ˈɪrɪ̈təbli/ *adv* [Wa3]

ir·ri·tant /ˈɪrɪ̈tənt/ *n, adj* [C;A] (a substance) which IRRITATEs (3)

ir·ri·tate /ˈɪrɪ̈teɪt/ *v* [T1] **1** [Wv4] to make angry or excite in an unpleasant way **2** *tech* to cause (something living, esp. part of a body) to act when influenced by a force **3** to make painful and sore: *Rough material irritates the skin*

ir·ri·ta·tion /ˌɪrɪ̈ˈteɪʃən/ *n* **1** [U] the act of irritating or the state of being IRRITATED **2** [C] an example of this **3** [C] a sore place or feeling: *a skin irritation*

ir·rup·tion /ɪˈrʌpʃən/ *n* [(*into*)] *fml* a sudden rush (of people or force): *a violent irruption of soldiers into the building|a strong irruption of angry feelings* —compare ERUPTION

is /s, z, əz; *strong* ɪz/ [Wv1] *3rd pers. sing. pres. of* BE

-ise /aɪz/ *suffix esp. BrE* -IZE —**-isation** /aɪˈzeɪʃən‖əˈzeɪ-/ *suffix*

-ish /ɪʃ/ *suffix* **1** [*n* [R]→*adj* [Wa5]] (esp. with names of countries and areas) belonging to: *Sweden→ Swedish|Turkey→ Turkish|Cornwall→Cornish* **2** [*n*[C]→*adj*] *often derog* having the character of: *foolish*|SNOB*bish*|SELFISH —see USAGE **3** (with ages and times) about; APPROXIMATEly: *Come for dinner at 8ish* (=at 8 o'clock or slightly later).|*He's 70ish* (=from about 68 to about 75 years old) **4** [*adj*[*esp.* Wa1]→*adj*] *esp. BrE* to some degree; SOMEWHAT (1): *reddish|latish|tallish|poorish|youngish*

USAGE When **-ish** is added to a noun it often means "having the nature of . . ., in a bad sense"; it is unkind to call someone *child***ish**, but all right to call them *childlike*.

i·sin·glass /ˈaɪzɪŋglɑːs‖-glæs/ *n* [U] **1** a sort of clear jelly taken from parts of certain fish and used for making GLUE to stick things together, for preserving eggs, and for making wine and beer **2** MICA

Is·lam /ˈɪslɑːm, ˈɪz-, ɪsˈlɑːm/ *n* [R] **1** the Muslim religion, started by Mohammed —see also PROPHET **2** the people and countries that practise this religion —**~ic** /ɪzˈlæmɪk, ɪs-/ *adj*

is·land /ˈaɪlənd/ *n* **1** a piece of land surrounded by water: *Britain is an island* —see picture at GLOBE **2** something or someone standing alone or apart from other things: *an island of pleasure among the sorrows of life* **3** also **traffic island**, *AmE* also **safety island**— a raised place in the middle of the road where people crossing the road can stand to wait for traffic to pass —see picture at STREET

is·land·er /ˈaɪləndəʳ/ *n* a person who lives on an island (which may be one of a group), usu. a small one with a simple social system: *a South Sea islander*

isle /aɪl/ *n poet* an island

is·let /ˈaɪlɪ̈t/ *n* a small island

is·m /ˈɪzəm/ *n* a set of ideas or principles, usu. held by a political or religious group, and often having a name ending in -ISM: *socialism, communism, and all the other isms of the modern world*

-ism *suffix* [*n, adj→n*] the ideas, principles, or teaching of: BUDDHISM|FANATICISM —compare -IST (1)

is·n't /ˈɪzənt/ [Wv1] *contr. of* is not —see CONTR. (USAGE)

i·so·bar /ˈaɪsəbɑːʳ/ *n* a line on a map joining places where the air pressure is the same

i·so·late /ˈaɪsəleɪt/ *v* [T1 *often pass.*] **1** to cause to be alone or separated from others: *Several villages have been isolated by the lack of buses* **2** to keep apart from other people so that a disease will not be spread **3** to separate (one substance) from others for examination alone: *They have isolated the bacterium in its pure form*

i·so·lat·ed /ˈaɪsəleɪtɨd/ *adj* standing out on its own; the only one of its type: *On one isolated occasion I saw him laugh.|an isolated farmhouse*

i·so·la·tion /ˌaɪsəˈleɪʃən/ *n* the act of isolating or the condition of being ISOLATEd, esp. for medical reasons: *in complete isolation in the country|an isolation hospital*

i·so·la·tion·is·m /ˌaɪsəˈleɪʃənɪzəm/ *n often derog* (the practice of) the principle that a country should not concern itself with the affairs of other countries, join international political organizations or (perhaps) join in trade with foreigners —**-ist** *n*

i·sos·ce·les tri·an·gle /aɪˌsɒsɨliːz ˈtraɪæŋgəl‖-ˌsɑ-/ *n* a TRIANGLE having 2 equal sides —see picture at GEOMETRY

i·so·therm /ˈaɪsəθɜːm‖-ɜrm/ *n* a line on a map joining points where the temperature is the same

i·so·tope /ˈaɪsətəʊp/ *n* any of 2 or more forms of a simple substance (ELEMENT (6)) in which the atoms are of the same chemical type but a different ATOMIC WEIGHT

Is·rae·li /ɪzˈreɪli/ *adj* [Wa5] of the modern state of Israel

Is·rael·ite /ˈɪzrəlaɪt‖ˈɪzrɪə-/ *adj* [Wa5] of the ancient kingdom of Israel

is·sue[1] /ˈɪʃuː, ˈɪsjuː‖ˈɪʃuː/ *n* **1** [U] the act of coming out: *the issue of new ideas from the pen of a well-known writer* **2** [C *usu. sing.*] **a** an example of this: *an issue of blood* **b** something which comes or is given out: *a daily issue of free milk to schoolchildren* **3** [U] the act of bringing out something in a new form: *I bought the book the day after its issue* **4** [C] something, esp. something printed, brought out again or in a new form: *There's a new issue of Christmas stamps every year.|today's issue of "The Times" (newspaper)* **5** [C] an important point: *the real issue is . . .* **6** [C] *rare* the result: *to hope for a good issue* **7** [GU] *old use and law* children (esp. in the phr. **die without issue**) **8 at issue** of importance; under consideration **9 take issue with** to disagree or begin to quarrel with

issue[2] *v* **1** [T1] to bring out (esp. something printed and/or official) for the notice of the public **2** [D1+*to*/*with*; T1 (*to*)] to supply or provide officially: *issued guns (to the soldiers)|issued the soldiers with guns*

issue forth *v adv lit* to go or come out

issue from *v prep* [T1 *no pass.*] to come or result from: *His difficulties issue from his lack of knowledge.|smoke issuing from the chimneys*

-ist /ɨst/ *suffix* **1** [*n,adj→n,adj*] (typical of) someone who believes in (the stated ideas, principles, or teaching): RACIAL*ist opinions|a group of* NATIONALIST*s*|IMPRESSIONIST —compare -ISM **2** [*n,v→n*] someone who is employed in (the stated work) or who plays (the stated musical instrument): *A* PIANIST *plays the* PIANO.|TYPIST*s are people who* TYPE[2]

isth·mus /ˈɪsməs/ *n* a narrow area of land with sea on each side, joined to a large land mass at each end —see picture at GLOBE

it[1] /ɪt/ *pron* [Wp1] (*used as subject or object*) **1 a** that thing: *"Whose coat is this?" "It's mine."|"Where's my dinner?" "The cat ate it"* **b** that plant: *There is a rosebush near the fence and it is very beautiful* **c** that person or animal whose sex is unknown or not thought to be important: *What a beautiful baby—is it a boy?* **d** that group of people or things: *The government has become very unpopular since it was/they were elected* **e** that idea, principle, practice, or other non-material thing: *Beauty is everywhere and it makes us happy* **2** (*used in* IDENTIFY*ing a person who is not well enough known*) that person: *"Who's that?" "It's me!"|"It's Harry!"|"It's the postman!"* —see THERE[2] (USAGE) **3** (used in the pattern *it+be+*a statement) **a** (about the weather): *It's raining.|It's hot.|It's a beautiful day* **b** (about time): *It's Thursday.|It'll soon be breakfast time.|"It's too early to start getting ready"* (SEU S.) **c** (about distance): *It's not far to Paris.|It's 112 miles from London to Birmingham* **4** (used in various verb patterns to represent a verb phrase, a CLAUSE, or a COMPLEMENT[1] (3)): **a** it+[L1] *verb+noun+*-ing *or* to+*infin.*: *It's fun* **being a singer**.|*It seemed a pity* **to refuse**.|*It cost £100* **to mend the roof**.|*It proved no* PROBLEM **to open the door**.|*It's no use* **worrying b** it+[L] *verb+*COMPLEMENT+-ing *or* to+*infin.*: *It's easy* **to talk**.|*It felt funny* **being called Grandmother**.|What's it like **being married**?|*Might it be possible for us* **to escape through this open window**? **c** it+[L7] *verb+adjective+*for: *It's easy* **for John to talk d** it+[L7]*verb+adjective+*of: *It was kind of you* **to wait e** it+[L]*verb+*CLAUSE: *It's true* **that he stole the jewels**.|*It's a pity* **(that) you forgot f** it+[I0]*verb+*CLAUSE: *Does it matter* **if I don't wash**? **g** it+[T1]*verb+noun+*to+*infin.*: *It surprised/annoyed me* **to hear** . . . (=I was surprised/annoyed to hear . . .) **h** it+be+*past participle*: *It was considered impossible* **(for them) to fail**.|*It's said/believed/thought* **that he's a criminal**.|*Is it known* **where they went**? **i** as object after an [X7] *verb*: *They found it exciting* **to throw stones at the priest**.|*I regard it as important* **to finish this job on time**.|*They kept it quiet* **that he was dead j** as object after a [T1] verb: *I liked it* **when she kissed me 5** (in phrs. with *seem, appear, happen*): *"She's drunk." "So it appears!"|It seems (that) she lost her way.|As it happens, I'm French.|It happened that we met* (=we happened to meet) **6** (*used like* this *or* that) what has been mentioned or what will be mentioned: *They were all shouting—it was terrible!|"I've broken the mirror." "It can't be helped"* **7** (used when expressing an idea in another way, making one part of the sentence more important) **a** (with the subject): *It was Jean who shot the President yesterday* (=I didn't shoot him!) **b** (with the object): *It was the President that Jean shot yesterday* (=she didn't shoot the king) **c** (with an ADJUNCT (2) or ADVERBIAL): *It was yesterday that Jean shot the President* **8** *usu. not fml* (used as a meaningless subject of the verb in certain phrs.): *It's my turn!|How's it* (=your life, work, etc.) *going?|It says in the newspaper that . . .* **9** *usu. infml* (used as a meaningless object of certain verbs including some verbs of movement): LEG*ged it back to camp* **10 Go it!** (used as a cry of encouragement to players or fighters) **11 if it weren't/hadn't been for** without the help or influence of; BUT FOR: *If it hadn't been for the snow, we could have climbed that mountain* **12 That's it a** That's complete; there's nothing more to come: *You can have a boiled egg and that's it* **b** That's right: *Hold the ladder for me—that's it!* **13 catch it** *infml* to get into trouble **14 have had it** *infml* to have no further hope of success: *I'm afraid we've had it: the bus left 5 minutes ago* **15 have what it takes** to have the necessary qualities of character —see HIM (USAGE)

it² *n* [U] **1** the most important person/child in a game, esp. the one who finds the others who are hiding **2** the Italian wine-based drink VERMOUTH (only in the phr. **gin and it**) **3** *sl now rare* (*often cap.*) sexiness: *Clara Bow, the It girl* **4** *sl* **a** very important person: *He thinks he's it* **b** the important point: *This is it—I'll have to make my mind up now or never* **5 with it** *sl becoming rare* **a** up-to-date in fashion, ways of behaviour, etc.; very modern **b** quick in understanding ideas; on the BALL

i.t.a. /ˌaɪ tiː ˈeɪ/ *abbrev. for*: INITIAL¹ teaching alphabet: *How different is the i.t.a. from the* IPA?

ITA *abbrev. for*: (in Britain) Independent Television Authority —compare BBC

I·tal·i·an /ɪˈtæliən/ *adj* [Wa5] of Italy, its people, or their language

i·tal·ic¹ /ɪˈtælɪk/ *adj* [Wa5;B;U] **1** of or concerning ITALICS: *This is an italic example* **2** of or concerning ITALIC²: *italic handwriting*

italic² *n* [U] **1** *tech* ITALICS **2** a style of sloping handwriting that looks like printed ITALICS: *I write italic*

i·tal·i·cize, -cise /ɪˈtæləsaɪz/ *v* [Wv5;T1;I∅] to put or print (something) in ITALICS, usu. for a stronger effect

i·tal·ics /ɪˈtælɪks/ *n* [P;U] (the style of) printing with small sloping letters: *This example is printed in italics* —compare ROMAN, CAPITALS

I·tal·o- /ɪˈtæləʊ/ *comb. form* **1** Italian; of Italy: *an Italo*PHILE **2** Italian and: *an Italo-Austrian agreement*

itch¹ /ɪtʃ/ *v* **1** [I∅] (of a person) to feel a soreness which one wants to rub or SCRATCH: *I itch all over* **2** [I∅] to cause soreness which makes one want to SCRATCH: *The wound itches all the time* **3** [T3] *infml* (*usu. in the* -ing *form*) to have a desire to do something soon: *I'm itching to go* —see also **have an itching** PALM²

itch² *n* **1** a sore feeling which makes one want to rub or SCRATCH the skin **2** [(*for*) *usu. sing.*] a strong desire

itch for *v prep* [T1;V4a] *infml* (*usu. in the* -ing *form*) to want (something) soon or very much: *He seems to be itching for a fight.|I'm itching for them to go*

itch·y /ˈɪtʃi/ *adj* [Wa1] **1** (of people or parts of the body, materials, etc.) feeling, or causing one to feel, an ITCH²: *rough itchy woollen socks* **2 itchy feet** *infml* a desire or tendency to wander —**-iness** *n* [U]

it'd /ˈɪtəd/ [Wv2] *contr. of* (*in compound tenses*) **1** it would: *It'd be all right if I had enough money* **2** it had: *It'd rained* —see CONTR. (USAGE)

-ite /aɪt/ *suffix* **1** [*n*→*n*] someone belonging to (a place or tribe): *I'm a Hampsteadite.|the* ISRAELITE*s in the Bible* **2** [*n*→*n, adj*] *sometimes derog* (someone) believing in or in favour of (a leader, a faith, etc.): *some Labourites|his Stalinite opinions* **3** [*n*→*n*] (in chemistry) (forming the name of a chemical substance): BAUXITE

i·tem¹ /ˈaɪtəm/ *adv* (*used in a list for introducing each article after the first*) and in addition; also

item² *n* **1** a single thing among a set or on a list **2** also **news item**— a piece of news on television or in a newspaper

i·tem·ize, -ise /ˈaɪtəmaɪz/ *v* [Wa5;T1] to set out all the details of (each ITEM)

it·e·rate /ˈɪtəreɪt/ *v* [Wv5;T1] *esp. tech* to say or do again, or again and again; REITERATE —**-ration** /ˌɪtəˈreɪʃən/ *n* [U]

i·tin·e·rant /aɪˈtɪnərənt/ *adj* [Wa5;A] habitually travelling from place to place, esp. to practise one's trade or profession: *an itinerant judge*

i·tin·e·ra·ry /aɪˈtɪnərəri‖-nəreri/ *n* a plan of a journey including places (to be) seen and visited

-i·tis /ˈaɪtəs/ *n* [*n*→*n* [U]] **1** (in medicine) disease or infection of: TONSILLITIS **2** *humor* **a** suffering caused by: *televisionitis* **b** too much keenness on: JAZZ*itis*

it'll /ˈɪtl/ [Wv2] *contr. of* (*in compound tenses*) **1** it will: *it'll rain* **2** it shall —see CONTR. (USAGE)

ITN *abbrev. for*: (in Britain) Independent Television News

its /ɪts/ *adj* [Wp1] (*poss. form of* IT¹) belonging to it: *The cat drank its milk and washed its ears*

it's *contr. of*: **1** [Wv1] it is: *it's raining* **2** [Wv2 (*in compound tenses*)] it has: *it's rained* —see CONTR. (USAGE)

it·self /ɪtˈself/ *pron* [Wp1] **1** (*refl. form of* IT¹): *The cat's washing itself* **2** (*strong form of* IT¹): *We won't buy new tyres when the car itself is so old.|Rome is older than London, itself an ancient city* **3 (all) by itself** alone; without help **4 in itself** without considering the rest; as such —see YOURSELF (USAGE)

it·sy-bit·sy /ˌɪtsi ˈbɪtsi◂/ *adj* **1** [A;(B)] *humor* very small; TINY **2** [B] *infml* consisting of too many small bits, which do not fit together into a satisfying whole

it·ty-bit·ty /ˌɪti ˈbɪti◂/ *adj* ITSY-BITSY (1)

ITV *abbrev. for*: (in Britain) Independent Television —compare BBC

-i·ty /əti/ *suffix* [*adj*→*n*[U;(C)]] the quality or an example of (being): REGULARITY|*another of his stupidities* (STUPIDITY)

IUD /ˌaɪ juː ˈdiː/ *abbrev. for*: INTRAUTERINE DEVICE

-ive /ɪv/ *suffix* [→*adj*,(*n*)] ((having) a tendency to do or cause an action): OFFENSIVE|EXPLOSIVE|ACTIVE

I've /aɪv/ [Wv2] *contr. of*: (*in compound tenses*) I have: *I've been here before.|I've got lots of time.|* (*esp. BrE*) *I've lots of time* —see CONTR. (USAGE)

i·vied /ˈaɪvid/ *adj* [Wa5] covered with IVY: *an ivied wall*

i·vo·ry /ˈaɪvəri/ *n* **1** [U] a hard white substance, of which elephants' TUSK*s* are made **2** [U] the colour of this substance **3** [C *often pl.*] *infml* something usu. made of this substance, esp. a piano KEY¹ **4 tickle the ivories** *humor* to play the piano

ivory tow·er /ˌ··· ˈ··/ *n* a place where one avoids the reality of ordinary life

i·vy /ˈaɪvi/ *n* [U] a type of plant which climbs over walls and has shiny 3- or 5-pointed leaves —compare POISON IVY

-ize, *BrE* also **-ise** /aɪz/ *suffix* [*n,adj*→*v*] **1** [Wv5;T1;I∅] to make of the stated type or put into the stated condition: PUBLICIZE|MODERNIZE|AMERICANIZE|UNIONIZE **2** [I∅] to become or act as: CRYSTALLIZE|PHILOSOPHIZE —**-ization** /aɪˈzeɪʃən‖əˈzeɪ-/ *suffix* [→*n*[U;C]]: (*a*) CIVILIZATION

USAGE 1 New [T1] verbs are being formed from other words all the time, using **-ize** in the meaning "to put into the stated condition": HOSPITALIZE, FINALIZE. Many of them are disliked by old-fashioned people. 2 The form **-ise** is commoner in *BrE* than in *AmE*. But after something which is not itself a word, **-ise** is usually the only spelling in *AmE* as well as *BrE*. The following verbs *must* be spelt with **-ise**: ADVERTISE, ADVISE, CHASTISE, CIRCUMCISE, COMPRISE, COMPROMISE, DESPISE, DEVISE, DISGUISE, EXCISE, EXERCISE, IMPROVISE, INCISE, MERCHANDISE, REVISE, SUPERVISE, SURMISE, SURPRISE.

J, j

J, j /dʒeɪ/ **J's, j's** *or* **Js, js** the 10th letter of the English alphabet

J *written abbrev. for*: **1** JACK (2) **2** JOULE

jab[1] /dʒæb/ *v* **-bb-** [X9;L9 esp. AWAY, *at*] to push with force (something pointed); strike quick blows from a short distance: *He jabbed his stick into my face.*|*Don't jab out my eye!*|*The fighters jabbed (away) at each other for a long time.*|*Suddenly a stick jabbed into my face*

jab[2] *n* **1** a sudden forceful push made with anything pointed **2** a quick straight blow, usu. from a short distance **3** *infml* INJECTION (2)

jab·ber[1] /ˈdʒæbəʳ/ *v* [T1 (OUT);IØ (AWAY)] to talk or say (something) quickly and not clearly: *I can't understand you if you keep jabbering (away) like that.*|*He jabbered (out) the words in what seemed a foreign language* —**~er** *n*

jabber[2] *n* [U;S] JABBERing; quick unclear speech, or noise which is like speech

jack /dʒæk/ *n* **1** an apparatus for lifting off the ground anything of heavy weight, such as a car —see also JACK UP **2** also **knave**— a playing card with a picture of a man on it and a rank between the 10 and the queen: *the jack of hearts* —see CARDS (USAGE) **3** a flag, flown at the front end of a ship **4** the small white ball at which the players aim in the game of BOWLS **5** *BrE sl* (*often cap.*) a policeman

Jack *n* **every man Jack/jack** *infml* every man

jack·al /ˈdʒækɔːl, -kəl‖-kəl/ *n* any of several types of wild animal of the dog family, often believed to eat what other animals have killed —see picture at CARNIVOROUS

jack·a·napes /ˈdʒækəneɪps/ *n* **-napes** [Wn3;C *usu. sing.*] *now rare* a child who likes to play tricks

jack·ass /ˈdʒæk-æs/ *n* **1** [C; *you*+N] *not fml* a fool **2** [C] *now rare* a male donkey (ASS)

jack·boot /ˈdʒækbuːt/ *n* **1** [C] a large high boot, esp. as worn by certain soldiers **2** [*the*+R] the rule of military men

jack·daw /ˈdʒækdɔː/ *n* a type of noisy bird of the CROW family, believed to steal small bright objects

jack·e·roo, -aroo /ˌdʒækəˈruː/ *n AustrE* a younger helper on a large sheep or cattle farm (STATION)

jack·et /ˈdʒækɪ̈t/ *n* **1** a short coat with SLEEVEs: *a brown jacket and grey trousers* **2** the skin that covers a potato: *potatoes cooked in their jackets* **3** an outer cover for certain machines or engines that get very hot **4** DUST JACKET **5** *AmE* SLEEVE (2)

Jack Frost /ˌ· ˈ·/ *n* [R] FROST considered as a person

jack in *v adv* [T1] *BrE sl* to stop; be unwilling to continue: *I'm going to jack this job in*

jack-in-the-box /ˈ· · · ˌ·/ *n* **1** a children's toy which is a box from which an amusing figure jumps when the top is opened **2** a person (or thing) that jumps up and down frequently

jack knife[1] /ˈ· ·/ *n* **jack knives** /-naɪvz/ a usu. large pocket knife, the blade of which folds into the handle

jack knife[2] also **jack-knife dive** /ˈ· · ˌ·/— *n* **jack knifes** a DIVE in which the body is bent (so that the hands touch the feet) and then straightened before entering the water

jack-knife *v* [IØ] (esp. of a vehicle made up of several parts fastened together) to bend sharply in the middle so as to look like the letter "V"

jack-of-all-trades /ˌ· · ˈ· ·/ *n sometimes derog* (*sometimes cap.*) a person who can do many different kinds of work (but who may not be good at any of them)

jack-o'-lan·tern /ˌdʒæk ə ˈlæntən‖-ərn/ *n* (*sometimes cap.*) **1** a lamp made by sticking a lighted candle into a hollow PUMPKIN with a face cut into the outside of it **2** WILL-O'-THE-WISP (1)

jack·pot /ˈdʒækpɒt‖-pɑt/ *n* **1** the biggest amount of money to be won in a game of cards or in any competition decided by chance or luck **2 hit the jackpot** *infml* **a** to win the JACKPOT **b** to have a big success

jack·rab·bit /ˈdʒækˌræbɪ̈t/ *n* a large North American HARE, like a big rabbit, with long ears

Jack Rob·in·son /ˌdʒæk ˈrɒbɪ̈nsən‖-ˈrɑ-/ *n* **before you (he, she, etc.) could/can say Jack Robinson** *infml* quickly and unexpectedly

jack tar /ˌ· ˈ·/ also **tar**— *n becoming rare* (*sometimes cap.*) a British sailor

jack up *v adv* [T1] to lift with a JACK (1): *Jack up the car.*|(fig.) *Jack up the price*

Jac·o·be·an /ˌdʒækəˈbɪən/ *adj, n* [Wa5] (a person) of the period 1603 to 1625, when James I was king of England: *Jacobean poetry/furniture*

Jac·o·bite /ˈdʒækəbaɪt/ *n, adj* [Wa5] (of or like) a person who wanted a descendant of King James II to be king of England

jade[1] /dʒeɪd/ *n* **1** a worn out old horse **2** *derog or humor* a woman

jade[2] *n* [U] **1** a precious usu. green stone from which ornaments and jewellery are made **2** its colour

ja·ded /ˈdʒeɪdɪ̈d/ *adj* tired because of having had too much of something, such as experience

jaf·fa /ˈdʒæfə/ *n tdmk, BrE* (*often cap.*) a type of large orange

jag[1] /dʒæg/ *v* **-gg-** [T1;IØ] to (cause to) cut or tear in a rough uneven way, leaving JAG*s*[2]

jag[2] *n* **1** a sharp point or edge (esp. of rock) that sticks out **2** an uneven hole (esp. torn in a garment)

jag[3] *n infml* a period of excitement and wild activity, usu. with a lot of drinking of alcohol

jag·ged /ˈdʒægɪ̈d/ also **jag·gy** /ˈdʒægi/— *adj* [Wa1] having a rough uneven edge, often with sharp points —**~ly** *adv*

jag·u·ar /ˈdʒægjʊəʳ‖ˈdʒægwɑr/ *n* a type of large spotted wild cat of Central and South America and Mexico —see picture at CAT

jail[1], *BrE* also **gaol** /dʒeɪl/ *n* [C;U] a prison or place where criminals are kept as part of their punishment

jail[2], *BrE* also **gaol** *v* [T1] to put in JAIL[1]

jail·bird, *BrE* also **gaolbird** /ˈdʒeɪlbɜːd‖-ɜrd/ *n infml* a person who has spent a lot of time in prison

jail·break /ˈdʒeɪlbreɪk/ *n* an escape from prison

jail·er, jailor, *BrE* also **gaoler** /ˈdʒeɪləʳ/ *n* a person, esp. a man, who is in charge of a prison or prisoners

ja·lop·y /dʒəˈlɒpi‖-ˈlɑpi/ *n humor* a worn-out old car

jam[1] /dʒæm/ *v* **-mm-** **1** [X9;L9: (TOGETHER)] to (cause to) be packed, pressed, or crushed tightly into a small space: *I can't jam another thing into this bag.*|*The 2 pieces of wood always jam together if I don't hold them apart.*|*The bus was so full that I was jammed in and couldn't move* **2** [T1] to crowd with people, cars, etc., so that movement is difficult or impossible: *The crowds jammed the streets, and no cars could pass* **3** [X9] to push forcefully and suddenly: *She jammed the top of the box down on my finger* **4** [IØ (UP)] **a** (of parts of machines) to get stuck **b** (esp. of machines) to become unable to work because moving parts have got stuck **5** [T1] to block (radio messages) by broadcasting noise

jam² *n* **1** a mass of people or things JAMmed so close together that movement is difficult or impossible: *a traffic jam|a log jam* **2 get into/be in a jam** *infml* to get into/be in trouble

jam³ *n* [U] **1** fruit boiled and preserved in sugar and used esp. for spreading on bread **2 money for jam** *BrE infml* something for nothing; something got very easily, without hard work

jamb /dʒæm/ *n* a side post of a door or window

jam·bo·ree /ˌdʒæmbəˈriː/ *n* **1** a noisy happy party **2** a concert of FOLK music **3** a large gathering of BOY SCOUTs

jam·my /ˈdʒæmi/ *adj* [Wa1] *BrE sl* **1** easy: *That examination was really jammy* **2** lucky, esp. in a way that makes other people annoyed: *You jammy fellow! Why can't I ever win as much money as that?*

jam on *v adv* [T1] to put sudden pressure on: *He jammed on the* BRAKEs

jam-packed /ˌ· ˈ·◂/ *adj* [(*with*)] *infml* with many people or things very close together; very CROWDED

jam ses·sion /ˈ· ˌ··/ *n* a JAZZ performance in which the music played has not been practised in advance

Jan. *written abbrev. for:* January

jan·gle /ˈdʒæŋgəl/ *v* **1** [Wv4;T1;IØ] to (cause to) make a sharp unpleasant sound, as of metal striking against metal **2** [IØ] to quarrel noisily

jan·is·sa·ry /ˈdʒænɨsəri‖-seri/ also **jan·i·za·ry** /-zəri‖-zeri/— *n* (until 1926) a member of a special group of soldiers in Turkey

jan·i·tor /ˈdʒænɨtəʳ/ *n* **1** *esp. AmE* a person who takes care of a building, keeping it clean and doing some repairs —compare CARETAKER **2** a person who guards or watches a door; DOORKEEPER —compare PORTER¹

Jan·u·a·ry /ˈdʒænjʊəri‖-jʊeri/ *n* [R;(C)] the first month of the year

ja·pan /dʒəˈpæn/ *v* **-nn-** [Wv5;T1] to cover (wood or metal) with a special kind of paint that gives a black shiny surface, as first done in Japan

Jap·a·nese lan·tern /ˌdʒæpəniːz ˈlæntən‖-ərn/ *n* CHINESE LANTERN

japan ware /·ˈ· ·/ *n* [U] dishes, plates, etc., that have been JAPANned

jape /dʒeɪp/ *n now rare* a playful trick

ja·pon·i·ca /dʒəˈpɒnɪkə‖-ˈpɑ-/ *n* a type of ornamental bush from Japan with bright red flowers

jar¹ /dʒɑːʳ/ *v* **-rr-** [Wv4] **1** [IØ (*on*)] to make an unpleasant sound **2** [T1] to give an unpleasant shock to: *The fall jarred every bone in my body* **3** [IØ (*with*)] to not go well together: *jarring opinions/colours*

jar² *n* (something that causes) an unpleasant shock

jar³ *n* **1** a vessel like a bottle with a short neck and wide mouth, which may be of glass, stone, clay, etc.: *a* JAM *jar* **2** also **jarful** /ˈdʒɑːfʊl‖-ɑr-/— the contents of a JAR³ (1): *2 jars of fish paste*

jar·gon /ˈdʒɑːgən‖-ɑr- -gɑn/ *n* [U;C] *often derog* language that is hard to understand, esp. because it is full of special words known only to the members of a certain group

jas·mine /ˈdʒæzmɨn/ *n* [C;U] any of several types of climbing plants with sweet-smelling white or yellow flowers

jas·per /ˈdʒæspəʳ/ *n* [U] a type of precious stone, not of great value, which is red, yellow, or brown

jaun·dice /ˈdʒɔːndɨs‖ˈdʒɔn-, ˈdʒɑn-/ *n* [U] a disease that causes a yellowness of the skin, the white part of the eyes, etc.

jaun·diced /ˈdʒɔːndɨst‖ˈdʒɔn-, ˈdʒɑn-/ *adj* **1** suffering or appearing to suffer from JAUNDICE **2** mistrustful; (of a person) tending to judge others unfavourably: *He looks on all these modern ideas with a rather jaundiced eye*

jaunt¹ /dʒɔːnt‖dʒɔnt, dʒɑnt/ *v* [IØ (ABOUT, AROUND)] to go on a JAUNT²

jaunt² *n* a short journey, usu. for pleasure

jaunt·ing car /ˈ·· ·/ *n* a light open carriage used in Ireland, which is drawn by horses and has 2 wheels and seats back to back along the sides

jaun·ty /ˈdʒɔːnti‖ˈdʒɔnti, ˈdʒɑnti/ *adj* [Wa1] (showing that one feels) satisfied with oneself and pleased with life: *a jaunty person/wave of the hand* —**-tily** *adv* —**-tiness** *n* [U]

jav·e·lin /ˈdʒævəlɨn/ *n* **1** [C] a light spear for throwing, now used mostly in sport **2** [*the*+R] the sport of throwing this

jaw¹ /dʒɔː/ *n* **1** [C] one of the 2 bony parts of the face in which the teeth are set: *the upper/lower jaw|*(fig.) *the jaws of death* —see picture at HUMAN² **2** [C] the appearance of the lower jaw: *A strong square jaw is a sign of firm character* **3** [C;U] *infml, sometimes derog* (a) talk

jaw² *v* [IØ (AWAY, *at*)] *infml sometimes derog* to talk

jaw·bone /ˈdʒɔːbəʊn/ *n* one of the big bones of the upper or lower jaw

jaw·break·er /ˈdʒɔːˌbreɪkəʳ/ *n infml* a word that is hard to pronounce

jaws /dʒɔːz/ *n* [P] the 2 parts of a machine or tool (esp. a VICE²) between which something may be held tightly or crushed

jay /dʒeɪ/ *n* any of several noisy brightly-coloured birds of the CROW family

jay·walk /ˈdʒeɪwɔːk/ *v* [IØ] to cross streets in a careless and dangerous way, esp. in the wrong place or without paying attention to the traffic lights —**~er** *n*

jazz /dʒæz/ *n* [U] **1** any of several types of music originated by black Americans, usu. with a strong beat and some free playing by each musician in the band **2** *sl* empty meaningless talk **3 and all that jazz** *sl* and things like that: *He spends his money on clothes, cars, women, and all that jazz*

jazz up *v adv* [T1] *infml* **1** [Wv5] *often derog* to play (music) in the style of JAZZ **2** to make (something) more active, interesting, or enjoyable **3** [Wv5] *often derog* to ornament (something), often cheaply, with bright colours

jazz·y /ˈdʒæzi/ *adj* [Wa1] *infml* **1** like JAZZ music **2** attracting attention, as with bright loud colours: *a very jazzy dress|a jazzy new car* —**-ily** *adv*

jeal·ous /ˈdʒeləs/ *adj* [(*of*)] *often derog* **1** wanting to keep what one has; POSSESSIVE: *He is jealous of his possessions/of his wife's love/of his rights.|Othello was a jealous husband* **2** wanting to get what someone else has; ENVIOUS: *He is jealous of their success* **3** shocked and angry at not being liked so well as someone else: *He was jealous when he discovered that she loved someone else* —**~ly** *adv*: *The dog jealously guarded its bone.|He jealously defended the honour of his tribe*

USAGE If one is **envious**/feels **envy** of a person, one **envies** their luck, possessions, or qualities, meaning that one wishes one had those things. If one is **jealous**/feels **jealousy** (no verb) one hates the lucky person who has received something that should have been given to oneself. It is a stronger and more unpleasant feeling.

jeal·ous·y /ˈdʒeləsi/ *n* **1** [U] JEALOUS feeling; the state of being JEALOUS **2** [C] anything done or said that shows this

jeans /dʒiːnz/ *n* [P] trousers made of a strong, usu.

blue, cotton cloth, worn for work and informally by men, women, and children —see PAIR[1] (USAGE)

jeep /dʒiːp/ *n* [C;*by*+U] a type of small car suitable for travelling over rough ground

jeer[1] /dʒɪəʳ/ *v* [Wv4;T1;I0 (*at*)] to laugh rudely (at): *The crowd jeered (at) the prisoners.|As the prisoners passed, the crowd jeered.|jeering laughter*

jeer[2] *n* a JEERing remark or noise

Je·ho·vah /dʒɪˈhəʊvə/ *n* [R] a name given to God in the first part of the Bible (the OLD TESTAMENT)

Jehovah's Wit·ness /·ˌ·· ˈ··/ *n* a member of a religious organization that believes in every word of the Bible and sends its members to people's houses to try to make them join

je·june /dʒɪˈdʒuːn/ *adj fml* **1** (esp. of writings) poor; uninteresting; unsatisfying **2** *esp. AmE* childish

jell /dʒel/ *v* [I0] **1** also **gel**— to become firmer, like JELLY **2** also (*esp. BrE*) **gel**— (of ideas, thoughts, etc.) to take a clear shape

jel·lied /ˈdʒelid/ *adj* [Wa5] prepared in jelly: *jellied fish*

jel·lo /ˈdʒeləʊ/ *n* [U] *tdmk, AmE* JELLY (1a)

jel·ly /ˈdʒeli/ *n* **1** [U;C] **a** a sweet soft food substance that shakes when moved, made with GELATINE: *an orange jelly* **b** other such substances that are not sweet **2** [U;(C)] fruit juice boiled with sugar and then made cool so as to become soft, clear, and fairly solid, used for spreading on bread: *apple jelly* —compare JAM[3] (1) **3** [U;S] any material that is between a liquid and a solid state

jel·ly·fish /ˈdʒelifɪʃ/ *n* **-fish** *or* **-fishes** [Wn2] a sea creature with a body like jelly

jem·my[1] /ˈdʒemi/ (*AmE* **jimmy**)— *n BrE* an iron bar, curved and flat at one end, used esp. by thieves to break open locked doors, windows, etc.

jemmy[2] (*AmE* **jimmy**)— *v* [T1;X7+*open*] *BrE* to open with a JEMMY[1]: *The thief jemmied (open) the window*

je ne sais quoi /ˌʒə nə seɪ ˈkwɑː (*Fr* ʒənsekwa)/ *n* [S] *Fr usu. apprec* a quality that cannot be described or expressed

jen·ny /ˈdʒeni/ *n* see SPINNING JENNY

jeop·ar·dize, -dise /ˈdʒepədaɪz‖-ər-/ *v* [T1] to endanger

jeop·ar·dy /ˈdʒepədi‖-ər-/ *n* [U] danger (esp. in the phr. **in jeopardy**): *His foolish behaviour may put his whole future in jeopardy*

jer·bo·a /dʒɜːˈbəʊə‖-ɜr-/ *n* a type of small jumping desert rat, found esp. in North Africa

jer·e·mi·ad /ˌdʒerɪ̈ˈmaɪəd/ *n lit* a long complaint, often combined with a forceful statement against wrong

jerk[1] /dʒɜːk‖dʒɜrk/ *v* **1** [T1] to give a JERK[2] to; pull suddenly: *She jerked out the knife that was stuck in the wood* **2** [I0] to move with a JERK[2] or jerks: *The old bus jerked to a stop*

jerk[2] *n* **1** [C] a short quick strong pull: *The knife was stuck but she pulled it out with a jerk* **2** [C] a short quick movement (esp. backwards, often unintentional) **3** [C; *you*+N] *AmE derog sl* (used esp. by young people) a foolish and ungraceful person

jer·kin /ˈdʒɜːkɪ̈n‖-ɜr-/ *n* a short coat, usu. SLEEVE-less

jerk off *v adv* [T1;I0] *esp. AmE taboo sl* to MASTURBATE

jerk·y /ˈdʒɜːki‖-ɜr-/ *adj* [Wa1] **1** moving by JERKs[2]; not smooth in movement **2** (of speaking) with sudden starts and stops **3** *AmE sl* (of a person or his behaviour) silly; foolish; ungraceful —**-ily** *adv* —**-iness** *n* [U]

jer·o·bo·am /ˌdʒerəˈbəʊəm/ *n* a large wine bottle that holds 4 times the amount of an ordinary wine bottle

jer·ry /ˈdʒeri/ *n infml BrE, becoming rare* CHAMBER POT

Jerry *n* [R;C] *sl, esp. BrE, now rare* (a name used esp. by soldiers for) a German

jerry-build /ˈ·· ·/ *v* [Wv5;T1;I0] *derog* to build (esp. houses) quickly, cheaply, and not well —**-builder** *n* —**-built** *adj*

jer·sey /ˈdʒɜːzi‖-ɜr-/ *n* **1** [C] a tight KNITted woollen garment for the upper part of the body **2** [U] a kind of fine usu. woollen cloth used esp. for women's dresses

Jersey *n* a type of cow with light brown hair, that produces cream and milk of very good quality

Je·ru·sa·lem ar·ti·choke /dʒəˌruːsələm ˈɑːtɪ̈tʃəʊk‖-ˈɑr-/ *n* ARTICHOKE (2)

jest[1] /dʒest/ *n* **1** *fml* something that makes people laugh; joke **2 in jest** not seriously

jest[2] *v* [I0] *fml* to speak without serious intention; joke

jest·er /ˈdʒestəʳ/ *n* a man kept in former times by a ruler to amuse him, tell jokes, etc.

jest·ing /ˈdʒestɪŋ/ *adj fml* in JEST[1]; that is able to or intended to make people laugh: *a jesting person/remark* —**~ly** *adv*

jest with *v prep* [T1] to treat (someone) without the necessary seriousness: *Don't jest with me, my young friend!*

Je·su·it /ˈdʒezjʊɪ̈t‖ˈdʒeʒʊɪ̈t, ˈdʒezʊɪ̈t/ *n* **1** a ROMAN CATHOLIC man who is a member of the Society of Jesus and lives a religious life **2** *derog* a person, esp. a man, who believes that anything is good if done for a good purpose

je·su·it·i·cal /ˌdʒezjʊˈɪtɪkəl‖ˌdʒeʒʊ-, ˌdʒezʊ-/ also **je·su·it·ic** /-ˈɪtɪk/— *adj usu. derog* (*often cap.*) of or like a JESUIT (2) —**-cally** *adv* [Wa4]

jet[1] /dʒet/ *n* [U] a hard black material that can be made to shine brightly, used for making ornaments

jet[2] *v* **-tt-** [T1 (OUT);L9] to come or send out of a small opening in a JET[3] or jets: *The water jetted out.|The flamethrower jetted (out) flames*

jet[3] *n* **1** [C] a narrow stream or streams of liquid, gas, etc., coming forcefully out of a small hole: *The firemen directed jets of water at the burning house* **2** [C] a narrow opening from which this is forced out: *Put a match to the gas jet to light the gas* **3** [C; *by*+U] any aircraft that is pushed through the air by a JET ENGINE: *travelling by jet|several jet aircraft*

jet[4] *v* **-tt-** [L9] to travel by JET[3] (3)

jet-black /ˌ· ˈ·◂/ *adj* [Wa5] of the colour of JET[1]; very dark shiny black

jet en·gine /ˌ· ˈ··/ *n* an engine that pushes out a stream of hot air and gases behind it, and is used for making aircraft fly —see picture at AIRCRAFT

jet-pro·pelled /ˌ· ·ˈ·◂/ *adj* **1** [Wa5] (of a plane) pushed through the air by a JET ENGINE **2** *infml* very fast

jet pro·pul·sion /ˌ· ·ˈ··/ *n* [U] a way of pushing a plane through the air by using JET ENGINEs

jet·sam /ˈdʒetsəm/ *n* see FLOTSAM AND JETSAM

jet set /ˈ· ·/ *n* [(*the*) GU;(GC)] (the group of) rich, successful, and mostly young people who go everywhere by JET[3] (3)

jet·ti·son /ˈdʒetɪ̈sən, -zən/ *v* [T1] to get rid of by throwing out: (fig.) *He will jettison anything—his principles or even his friends—in order to succeed in his work*

jet·ty /ˈdʒeti/ *n* a kind of wall built out into water, used either for getting on and off ships or as a protection against the force of the waves

Jew /dʒuː/ *n* a member of the race or religion of people living in the land where CHRIST was born about 2000 years ago, some of whom now live in

Israel and others in various countries, chiefly in the western world —see also HEBREW
USAGE A SLANG use of this word may sometimes be met with, but should be avoided as it is likely to give offence to Jewish people

jew·el /ˈdʒuːəl/ *n* **1** a stone that is worth a lot of money and is used as an ornament: *diamonds and other jewels* **2** an ornament for wearing that contains one or more of these **3** a person or thing considered of great value

jew·elled, *AmE* **jeweled** /ˈdʒuːəld/ *adj BrE* (of things) ornamented with, or having, jewels: *a jewelled crown*

jew·el·ler, *AmE* **jeweler** /ˈdʒuːələʳ/ *n BrE* a person who buys and sells jewels or ornaments containing jewels or who makes such ornaments

jew·el·lery, -elry /ˈdʒuːəlri/ *n* [U] JEWEL*s* (2)

Jew·ess /ˈdʒuːɪ̈s/ *n not polite* a Jewish woman

Jew·ish /ˈdʒuːɪʃ/ *adj* of the JEW*s*: *the Jewish religion*

Jew's harp /ˌ· ˈ·‖ˈ· ·/ *n* a small musical instrument held between the teeth and played by striking a piece of metal with one finger

Jez·e·bel /ˈdʒezəbəl, -bel/ *n* a shameless immoral woman

jib¹ /dʒɪb/ *n* **1** a small sail —see picture at SAIL² **2 the cut of someone's jib** *infml* someone's style or appearance: *I don't like the cut of his jib*

jib² *n* the long bar (or "arm") which stands out at an angle from a CRANE¹ (1) or DERRICK

jib³ *v* **-bb-** [IØ] (of a horse) to stop suddenly

jib at *v prep* **-bb-** [T1,4 *no pass.*] to be unwilling to do or face (something difficult or unpleasant)

jib boom /ˌ· ˈ·/ *n* the pole (or BOOM) on which the lower part of a JIB¹ (1) is fixed

jibe /dʒaɪb/ *n* GIBE

jibe at *v prep* [T1] GIBE AT

jif·fy /ˈdʒɪfi/ *n* [S] *infml* **1** a moment: *I won't be a jiffy* (=I'll be ready very soon) **2 in a jiffy** in a moment; quickly; very soon

jig¹ /dʒɪg/ *n* **1** (music for) a quick gay dance **2** a quick short movement, esp. up and down

jig² *v* **-gg- 1** [IØ] to dance a JIG¹ (1) **2** [X9;L9] to (cause to) move with quick short movements up and down

jig·ger /ˈdʒɪgəʳ/ *n* **1** also (*esp. AmE*) **chigger**— *esp. BrE* any of several types of small insect, esp. those that go in under human skin and cause discomfort **2** a measure used in mixing alcoholic drinks, often one fitted onto bottles **3** *sl, esp. AmE* any small piece of apparatus

jig·gered /ˈdʒɪgəd‖-ərd/ *adj* [F] *infml BrE* **1** very surprised: *Well, I'll be jiggered!* (=I am very surprised) **2** very tired

jig·ger·y-po·ker·y /ˌdʒɪgəri ˈpəʊkəri/ *n* [U] *infml* dishonest behaviour or tricks, to be kept secret if possible

jig·gle¹ /ˈdʒɪgəl/ *v* [T1;IØ] *infml* to (cause to) move from side to side with short quick light JERK*s* —**-gly** *adj* [Wa2]

jiggle² *n infml* one or more short light quick movements from side to side

jig·saw /ˈdʒɪgsɔː/ *n* **1** a type of SAW used for cutting out shapes in thin pieces of wood **2** JIGSAW PUZZLE

jigsaw puz·zle /ˈ·· ˌ··/ *n* a picture stuck onto wood and cut up into many small irregular pieces to be fitted together for amusement

ji·had /dʒɪˈhɑːd, dʒɪˈhæd/ *n* a holy war fought by Muslims as a religious duty

jilt /dʒɪlt/ *v* [T1] to refuse to see (a lover) any more; unexpectedly refuse to marry (someone) after having promised to do so

jim crow /ˌdʒɪm ˈkrəʊ/ *n AmE* (*often caps.*) **1** [R; A] the system of unfair treatment of black Americans: *jim crow laws* **2** [A] for black Americans only, and usu. of poor quality: *jim crow schools|buses*

jim·i·ny /ˈdʒɪmɪ̈ni/ *interj* (a not very strong expression of surprise)

jim·jams /ˈdʒɪmdʒæmz/ *n* [*the*+P] JITTERS

jim·my /ˈdʒɪmi/ *n, v AmE* JEMMY

jin·gle¹ /ˈdʒɪŋgəl/ *v* [T1;IØ] to (cause to) sound with a JINGLE²

jingle² *n* **1** a repeated sound as of small bells ringing or light metal objects striking against each other **2** a simple poem with a very regular beat, usu. of poor quality

jin·go /ˈdʒɪŋgəʊ/ *n* **by jingo!** (an expression of eagerness): *You're 100% right, by jingo!*

jin·go·is·m /ˈdʒɪŋgəʊɪzəm/ *n* [U] *derog* CHAUVINISM (1), esp. that which has a military tendency —**-ist(ic)** /ˈdʒɪŋgəʊɪ̈st, ˌdʒɪŋgəʊˈɪstɪk/ *adj*

jinks /dʒɪŋks/ *n* see HIGH JINKS

jinn /dʒɪn/ also **jin·ni** /ˈdʒɪni/— *n* GENIE

jin·riki·sha /ˌdʒɪnˈrɪkʃɔː/ *n* RICKSHAW

jinx¹ /dʒɪŋks/ *n* **1** a person or thing that brings bad luck **2** [(*on*)] a not very strong curse: *There seems to be a jinx on our team, because we always lose*

jinx² *v* [T1] *infml* to bring bad luck to; put a JINX¹ (2) on

jit·ney /ˈdʒɪtni/ *n esp. AmE* a taxi that lets people get in and out at different places on its regular journey

jit·ter·bug /ˈdʒɪtəbʌg‖-ər-/ *n* **1** a quick active popular dance of the 1940's **2** a person who did this sort of dance

jit·ters /ˈdʒɪtəz‖-ərz/ *n* [*the*+P] *infml* anxiety before an event: *I've got the jitters about that examination* —**jittery** /ˈdʒɪtəri/ *adj*

jiu·jit·su /ˌdʒuːˈdʒɪtsuː/ *n* [U] JUJITSU

jive¹ /dʒaɪv/ *n* **1** [U] (dancing performed to) a type of popular music with a strong regular beat **2** [C] a dance performed to this music **3** [U] *AmE sl* deceiving or foolish talk

jive² *v* [IØ] to dance to JIVE¹ music

Jnr *written abbrev. for*: (*BrE*) JUNIOR (1)

job /dʒɒb‖dʒɑb/ *n* **1** a piece of work that has been or must be done: *Do a better job next time.|He gets paid by the job* **2** something hard to do: *It was a (real) job to talk with all that noise* **3** *sl* a dishonest or harmful piece of work, esp. robbery or a beating: *He's in prison for a job he did in Liverpool.|John's been in hospital since Paul did that job on him* **4** regular paid employment: *He has a good job in a bank.|Job safety is important* **5** *infml* an example of a certain type: *That new Rolls of yours is a beautiful job* **6 a job of work** *BrE infml* a piece of work, usu. well done: *You can be sure my brother will do a job of work for the money you pay him* **7 on the job** (of people or, sometimes, machines) at work; working; busy **8 out of a job** unemployed **9 a good/bad job** *BrE infml* a good/bad thing: *This restaurant is not cheap, so it's a good job you've brought plenty of money.|He's gone, and a good job too!* **10 make the best of a bad job** to do as much or as well as possible in unfavourable conditions **11 give up (on) someone/something as a bad job** to decide that nothing more can be done for (someone/something) **12 jobs for the boys** employment for one's supporters **13 pull a job** *sl* to do a robbery **14 just the job** exactly the thing wanted or needed: *Thanks for that screw: it was just the job*
USAGE One is **appointed** to a **post** or **position**. These are grander and more formal words for a **job**. An **appointment** is not a **job**, but it can mean the act of **appointing** someone: *Recent government* **appointments** *include* . . . . The word **vocation** is used of certain professions such as teaching and

nursing, which people are thought to enter for serious moral reasons. People **work** in all these **jobs**, but expressions like *out of* **work**, *the* **workers**, *looking for* **work**, are used particularly of people who work with their hands —see WORK[1] (USAGE)

Job /dʒəʊb/ *n* [R] a man in the Bible who was patient in spite of many misfortunes: *You need the patience of Job to read her handwriting*

job·ber /ˈdʒɒbəʳ‖ˈdʒɑ-/ *n* a person who buys and sells on the STOCK EXCHANGE

job·ber·y /ˈdʒɒbəri‖ˈdʒɑ-/ *n* [U] *rare* dishonest use of one's power as an officer of government

job·bing /ˈdʒɒbɪŋ‖ˈdʒɑ-/ *adj* [Wa5;A] working and getting paid by the JOB (1): *We use a jobbing gardener who comes on Thursdays*

job·less /ˈdʒɒbləs‖ˈdʒɑb-/ *adj* [Wa5;B; *the*+P] without a JOB (4)

job lot /ˈ· ·, ˌ· ˈ·/ *n* a group of things of different kinds, bought or sold together

Job's com·fort·er /ˌ· ˈ···/ *n* a person who may want to make others feel better but actually makes them feel worse

jock·ey[1] /ˈdʒɒki‖ˈdʒɑki/ *n* a person who rides in horse races, esp. professionally

jockey[2] *v* [X9] **1** to get (someone to do something or into a certain position) by skilful tricks **2 jockey for position** to try by all possible means to get into a good position

Jockey Club /ˈ·· ·/ *n* [*the*+GU] the club that controls horse racing in Britain

jock·strap /ˈdʒɒkstræp‖ˈdʒɑk-/ *n infml* a tight-fitting undergarment for supporting the sex organs, worn by men taking part in sports

jo·cose /dʒəˈkəʊs, dʒəʊ-/ *adj fml or lit* (of or from a person who is or looks serious) meant or meaning to cause laughter —**~ly** *adv* —**~ness, jocosity** /dʒəˈkɒsɪ̍ti, dʒəʊ-‖-ˈkɑ-/ *n* [U]

joc·u·lar /ˈdʒɒkjʊləʳ‖ˈdʒɑkjələr/ *adj fml* meant or meaning to cause laughter, perhaps in reply to a serious question: *a jocular reply/person* —**~ly** *adv* —**~ity** /ˌdʒɒkjʊˈlærɪ̍ti‖ˌdʒɑkjə-/ *n* [U;C]

joc·und /ˈdʒɒkənd‖ˈdʒɑ-/ *adj lit & poet* merry; cheerful; ready to laugh happily: *"A poet could not but be gay, in such a jocund company"* (Wordsworth) —**~ity** /dʒəʊˈkʌndɪ̍ti, dʒə-/ *n* [U]

jodh·purs /ˈdʒɒdpəz‖ˈdʒɑdpərz/ *n* [P] trousers for horse riding that are tight from the knee to the ankle and loose above, worn by men and women —see PAIR[1] (USAGE)

jog[1] /dʒɒg‖dʒɑg/ *v* **-gg-** **1** [T1] to shake slightly (esp. causing an up and down movement); give a slight push or knock with the arm, hand, etc.: *You jogged my elbow and spoiled what I was drawing* **2** [L9] to move slowly and unsteadily: *The carriage jogged along on the rough road* **3** [L9] to move along slowly, steadily, but uneventfully: *Our lives just jog along from day to day* **4** [IØ] to run slowly and steadily **5 jog someone's memory** to make someone remember

jog[2] *n* **1** a slight shake, push, or knock **2** something that makes someone remember **3** JOG TROT

jog·gle[1] /ˈdʒɒgəl‖ˈdʒɑ-/ *v* [T1;IØ] *infml* to (cause to) shake often, but slightly

joggle[2] *n infml* a slight shake

jog trot /ˈ· ·/ *n* a slow steady run

john /dʒɒn‖dʒɑn/ *n AmE sl* **1** a man who visits a PROSTITUTE **2** LAVATORY

John Barleycorn /ˌ· ˈ···/ *n* [R] MALT LIQUOR considered as a person

John Bull /ˌ· ˈ·/ *n* **1** [R] England **2** [C] a typical Englishman

John Doe /ˌ· ˈ·/ *n* **1** [R] *law* an imaginary name used in law cases when the real name is unknown **2** [C] a typical man: *great men and plain John Does*

john·ny /ˈdʒɒni‖ˈdʒɑni/ *n infml* (*often cap.*) a fellow

joie de viv·re /ˌʒwɑː də ˈviːvrə/ *n* [U] *Fr* the joy of life

join[1] /dʒɔɪn/ *v* **1** [T1 (*to*, TOGETHER, UP)] to fasten; connect: *to join their 2 hands* (*together*)|*to join one pipe to another|to join the 2 ends of the rope together in a knot* **2** [T1] to unite: *to join 2 towns by a railway* **3** [X9 esp. *in*] to bring together: *to join people in friendship/in marriage* **4** [T1 (*in*)] to meet; be, go, or take part together with: *Will you join me in a walk/a drink/in buying a present for her?* **5** [T1] to become a member of: *to join the army/the Labour party* **6** [T1] to run into; meet: *Where does the path join the road?* **7** [IØ;T1] to become united (with each other): *Where do the 2 streams join* (*each other*)*?* **8 join forces** (**with**) to come together or unite for a common purpose **9 join hands** (**with**) **a** to hold hands (with (each other)): *Let us join hands in friendship* **b** JOIN[1] (8) forces (with) **10 join battle** to begin a battle or struggle of any kind —see also JOIN IN, JOIN UP, JOIN WITH IN

join[2] *n* a place where 2 things are joined together

join·er /ˈdʒɔɪnəʳ/ *n* **1** a woodworker who makes doors, doorframes, windowframes, etc., inside a building —compare CARPENTER **2** *infml* a person who likes to join organizations

join·er·y /ˈdʒɔɪnəri/ *n* [U] *esp. BrE* **1** the art, skill, or trade of a JOINER; woodwork in building **2** work done by a JOINER: *In this house the joinery is very good* —compare CARPENTRY

join in *v adv* [IØ (*with*)] to take part in an activity as a member of a group: *Sarah never joins in* (*with us*)*; she always plays on her own*

joint[1] /dʒɔɪnt/ *n* **1** a thing used for making a join **2** a place where things (esp. bones) join **3** (*AmE* **roast**)— *BrE* a large piece of meat for cooking **4** *derog sl* a public place, esp. one where people go for amusement —compare CLIP JOINT **5** *sl* a cigarette containing the drug CANNABIS **6 out of joint** (of a joint of the body) out of the proper position **7 put someone's nose out of joint** *infml* to make someone jealous by taking his place as the centre of attraction

joint[2] *adj* [Wa5;A] shared by 2 or more people: *our joint opinion|to take joint action|joint owners* —**~ly** *adv*

joint[3] *v* [Wv5;T1] **1** to provide with JOINTs[1] (1,2) **2** also (*fml*) **disjoint**— to separate (meat) into pieces at the JOINTs[1] (2)

joint ac·count /ˌ· ·ˈ·/ *n* a bank account owned by 2 or more people, esp. husband and wife

joint-stock com·pa·ny /ˌ· ˈ· ˌ···/ (*AmE* **stock company**)— *n* a business company owned by all the people who have bought shares in it

join up *v adv* [IØ] to offer oneself for military service

join with in *v prep prep* [D1;V4b] **1** to take part together with (someone) in (something): *Join with me in this activity.|Join with me in buying a present for her* **2** to show sympathy for (someone) because of (something): *We all join with Mr and Mrs Smith in their sorrow*

joist /dʒɔɪst/ *n* one of the beams onto which a floor is fixed

joke[1] /dʒəʊk/ *n* **1** anything said or done to cause laughter or amusement: *She told some very funny jokes* **2** a person, thing, or event that is laughed at and not taken seriously **3 be/go beyond a joke** to be/become too serious or unpleasant to laugh at **4 have a joke with someone** to share a joke with someone **5 He can't take a joke** He isn't amused when someone plays a joke on him **6 I don't see the joke** I don't understand what is funny **7 make a joke** to tell a joke **8 no joke** *infml* a serious or difficult matter: *War is no joke.|It was no joke carrying those heavy bags* **9 play a joke on someone** to do something to make other people laugh at someone **10 The joke's on someone** (an expression describing someone who was trying to make others look foolish but who became the subject of his or her own joke) —see also PRACTICAL JOKE

joke² *v* [Wv4;IØ(*with* or *about*)] to tell jokes: *I didn't think you meant that seriously: I thought you were joking.|You mustn't joke with him about religion.* —**jokingly** *adv*: *His remarks were meant jokingly*

jok·er /ˈdʒəʊkəʳ/ *n* **1** a person who likes to make jokes **2** *infml* a person who is not serious or who should not be taken seriously: *Don't trust that joker* **3** an additional playing card, which in some games may have any value

jol·li·fi·ca·tion /ˌdʒɒlǰfǰˈkeɪʃən‖ˌdʒɑ-/ *n* [U;C *often pl. with sing. meaning*] *infml pomp* harmless merry-making

jol·li·ty /ˈdʒɒlǰti‖ˈdʒɑ-/ also **jol·li·ness** /ˈdʒɒlinǰs‖ˈdʒɑ-/— *n* [U] the quality or state of being JOLLY¹ (1)

jol·ly¹ /ˈdʒɒli‖ˈdʒɑli/ *adj* [Wa1] **1** merry; happy: *a jolly person/laugh* **2** *infml euph* slightly drunk **3** nice; pleasant: *a jolly holiday* —**jollily** *adv*

jolly² *adv* [Wa5] *BrE infml* **1** very: *It was a jolly good thing I got there in time* **2 a jolly good fellow** a very nice person or companion

jolly³ *v* [X9] *infml* to make (someone) willing or eager (to do something); urge gently: *They jollied her into going with them*

jolly a·long *v adv* [T1b] to encourage (someone) through enjoyment; keep happy

jolly boat /ˈ·· ·/ *n* a small boat used by a ship's sailors for general work

Jolly Ro·ger /ˌ·· ˈ··/ *n* [*the*+R;(C)] the flag of a PIRATE of former times, showing a SKULL and bones crossed under it —compare BLACK FLAG

jolly well /ˈ·· ·/ *adv BrE infml* (used for giving force to verbs and certain other expressions) indeed; certainly: *I jolly well told him what I thought of him*

jolt¹ /dʒəʊlt/ *v* **1** [Wv4;T1;IØ (ALONG)] to (cause to) shake or be shocked: *The cart jolted (along) over the rough road, jolting every bone in his body.|Her angry words jolted him* **2** [X9] to bring into a certain state by doing this: *Her angry words jolted him out of the belief that she loved him*

jolt² *n* a sudden shake or shock

jolt·y /ˈdʒəʊlti/ *adj* [Wa1] that JOLTS¹: *a jolty bus*

Jo·nah /ˈdʒəʊnə/ *n* a person who seems to bring bad luck wherever he goes

jon·quil /ˈdʒɒŋkwǰl‖ˈdʒɑŋ-/ *n* a type of sweet-smelling spring flower of the NARCISSUS family

josh /dʒɒʃ‖dʒɑʃ/ *v AmE infml* **1** [IØ] to joke **2** [T1] to make fun of, without wanting to hurt

joss stick /ˈdʒɒs ˌstɪk‖ˈdʒɑs-/ *n* a stick of INCENSE¹

jos·tle /ˈdʒɒsəl‖ˈdʒɑ-/ *v* [T1;IØ] (of a person) to knock or push against (someone): *Don't jostle (against) me*

jot¹ /dʒɒt‖dʒɑt/ *n* [S (*of*) *usu. neg.*] a very small amount; a bit: *not a jot of truth in it*

jot² *v* **-tt-** [T1 (DOWN)] to write quickly, esp. without preparation

jot·ter /ˈdʒɒtəʳ‖ˈdʒɑ-/ *n* a number of pieces of paper joined together, used for writing rough notes on

jot·ting /ˈdʒɒtɪŋ‖ˈdʒɑ-/ *n* [*usu. pl.*] a rough note

joule /dʒuːl‖dʒuːl, dʒaʊl/ *n tech* a measure of ENERGY or work

jour·nal /ˈdʒɜːnəl‖-ɜr-/ *n* **1** a DIARY (1) **2** a PERIODICAL

jour·nal·ese /ˌdʒɜːnəlˈiːz‖-ɜr-/ *n* [U] *derog* the language of newspapers, believed to go beyond the truth and to be full of expressions which if new are unnecessary and if old are almost meaningless through continual use

jour·nal·is·m /ˈdʒɜːnəl-ɪzəm‖-ɜr-/ *n* [U] **1** the work or profession of producing, esp. writing for, JOURNALs (2), esp. newspapers **2** writing that may be all right for a newspaper, but that lacks imagination and beauty: *His writing is only journalism, not true literature* —**-istic** /ˌdʒɜːnəlˈɪstɪk‖-ɜr-/ *adj* —**-istically** *adv* [Wa4]

jour·nal·ist /ˈdʒɜːnəlǰst‖-ɜr-/ *n* a person whose profession is JOURNALISM (1)

jour·ney¹ /ˈdʒɜːni‖-ɜr-/ *n* **1** a trip of some distance, usu. by land: *a long train journey|It's (a) 3 days' journey on horseback from here to there.|He's going on/making a long journey*|(fig.) *Life is a journey from birth to death* —see TRAVEL² (USAGE) **2 break one's journey** to interrupt one's journey **3 one's journey's end** *lit* **a** the end of any journey **b** the end of one's life

journey² *v* [L9] to travel; go on a journey or journeys: *She's journeyed all over the world*

jour·ney·man /ˈdʒɜːnimən‖-ɜr-/ *n* **-men** /mən/ (*usu. in comb.*) **1** a trained workman who works for another, often paid by the day: *a journeyman printer* **2** an experienced person whose work is good, but not of the very best: *a journeyman painter, not one of the greatest*

joust /dʒaʊst/ *v* [IØ (*with*)] **1** (in former times) to fight on horseback with spears, as sport **2** (in newspaper writing) to take part in a personal struggle or competition

Jove /dʒəʊv/ *n* **by Jove!** *BrE infml now rare* (an expression of surprise, also used for giving force to other expressions)

jo·vi·al /ˈdʒəʊviəl/ *adj* (esp. of fat old men) full of good humour; friendly; loving company: *a jovial person/voice* —**~ly** *adv* —**~ity** /ˌdʒəʊviˈælǰti/ *n* [U]

jowl /dʒaʊl/ *n* [*usu. pl. with sing. meaning*] the lower part of the side of the face, esp. loose skin and flesh near the lower jaw —see also CHEEK¹ (5) **by jowl**

-jowled /dʒaʊld/ *comb. form* with JOWLs of the stated type: *a heavy-jowled man*

joy /dʒɔɪ/ *n* **1** [U] great happiness: *He was filled with joy* **2** [U] something that shows joy: *I saw the joy in her smiling face* **3** [C] a person or thing that causes joy: *My children are a great joy to me* **4** [U] *BrE infml* success: *I tried to get through to her on the telephone, but I didn't have any joy* (=I wasn't able to) **5 for joy** because of (feeling) joy **6 to the joy of someone/to someone's joy** as a cause of joy to someone: *To the joy of his mother, he won first prize*

joy·ful /ˈdʒɔɪfəl/ *adj* full of joy: *a joyful person/event* —**~ly** *adv* —**~ness** *n* [U]

joy in *v prep* [T1] *lit or poet* to be filled with happiness because of

joy·less /ˈdʒɔɪləs/ *adj* without joy; unhappy —**~ly** *adv* —**~ness** *n* [U]

joy·ous /ˈdʒɔɪəs/ *adj esp. lit* full of or causing joy: *a joyous heart/event* —**~ly** *adv* —**~ness** *n* [U]

joy·ride /ˈdʒɔɪraɪd/ *n infml* **1** a ride for pleasure in a vehicle, esp. a stolen vehicle, often marked by careless driving **2** behaviour or action like this, esp. in not considering the cost or possible results

joy·stick /ˈdʒɔɪˌstɪk/ *n* **1** a stick whose movement directs the movement of an aircraft **2** *infml* a stick whose movement controls the movement of any other machine

JP /ˌdʒeɪ ˈpiː/ also (*fml*) **justice of the peace**— *n* a person who gives judgments in small courts of law; MAGISTRATE

Jr *written abbrev. for:* JUNIOR (1)

jub·i·lant /ˈdʒuːbǰlənt/ *adj* filled with or expressing great joy: *a jubilant person/shout* —**~ly** *adv*

ju·bi·la·tion /ˌdʒuːbɨ'leɪʃən/ *n* [U] great joy; rejoicing at a success, victory, etc.

ju·bi·lee /'dʒuːbɨliː, ˌdʒuːbɨ'liː/ *n* a period of great rejoicing, esp. to mark or remember some event

Ju·da·ic /dʒuː'deɪ-ɪk/ *adj* of Jews or JUDAISM

Ju·da·is·m /'dʒuːdeɪ-ɪzəm, 'dʒuːdə-‖'dʒuːdə-, 'dʒuːdi-/ *n* [U] the religion and civilization of the Jews

Ju·das /'dʒuːdəs/ *n derog* a person who helps the enemies of his friends; TRAITOR

jud·der /'dʒʌdəʳ/ *v* [IØ] *esp. BrE* to shake violently; VIBRATE (1)

judge[1] /dʒʌdʒ/ *v* **1** [T1;IØ] to act as a judge in (a law case): *Who will judge the next case?*|(fig.) *God will judge all men* **2** [T1;IØ] to give a decision about (someone or something), esp. in a competition: *to judge horses* **3** [T1,5,6a;X (*to be*) 1, (*to be*) 7;IØ (*of*)] to form or give an opinion about (someone or something): *A man should be judged by his deeds, not his words.*|*Judge (of) its size.*|*Judge whether he's right or wrong.*|*I judge that it's bigger.*|*I judge it (to be) the biggest.*|*How can I judge?*

judge[2] *n* **1** [C;A;(N)] (*often cap.*) a public official who has the power to decide questions brought before a court of law: *a Judge of the High Court* **2** [C] a person who has the right to make a decision, esp. in a competition **3** [C (*of*)] a person who has the knowledge and experience to give valuable opinions: *I'm no judge of music, but I know what I like*

judg·ment, judgement /'dʒʌdʒmənt/ *n* **1** [C] an official decision given by a judge or a court of law **2** [C] an amount of money that must be paid as the result of a judgment in law: *a judgment of £100 against Mr Jones* **3** [C] an opinion: *to form a judgment*|*In my judgment, we should do it* **4** [U] the ability to judge correctly: *a man of good/weak judgment*|*an* ERROR (=mistake) *of judgment* **5 It's a judgment on him** It's as if God were punishing him **6 pass judgment on** to give (a) judgment on (a case in a court of law) **7 sit in judgment on** to prepare to give (a) judgment on, esp. as in a court of law

judgment day /'·· ·/ also **last judgment, day of judgment**— *n* [R] (*often cap.*) **1** the day when God will judge all men **2** a time when people will be punished for their misdeeds even if they have not been punished before

ju·di·ca·ture /'dʒuːdɨkətʃəʳ/ *n* **1** [U] the power of giving justice in a court of law **2** [GC] JUDICIARY

ju·di·cial /dʒuː'dɪʃəl/ *adj* [Wa5] **1** of, by, related to, or connected with a court of law, a judge, or his judgment: *a judicial decision* —compare JUDICIOUS **2 (bring/take) judicial proceedings** (to bring/take) action in a court of law —**~ly** *adv*

ju·di·cia·ry /dʒuː'dɪʃəri‖-ʃieri, -ʃəri/ *n* [GC] the judges (in law) considered as one group

ju·di·cious /dʒuː'dɪʃəs/ *adj* having or showing good judgment, the ability to form sensible opinions, make sensible decisions, etc. —compare JUDICIAL —**~ly** *adv* —**~ness** *n* [U]

ju·do /'dʒuːdəʊ/ *n* [U] a type of fighting from Asia based on holding and throwing the opponent, developed from JUJITSU

jug[1] /dʒʌg/ *n* **1** [C] (*AmE* **pitcher**)— *BrE* **a** a pot for liquids with a handle and a lip for pouring **b** also **jugful**— the amount such a pot will hold **2** [C] **a** a pot for liquids with a narrow opening at the top that can usu. be closed with a CORK **b** also **jugful**— the amount such a pot will hold **3** [(*the*) R] *sl* prison

jug[2] *v* **-gg-** [T1] **1** [Wv5] to boil (meat) in a closed pot or JUG[1] (2) **2** *sl* to put in prison

jug·ger·naut /'dʒʌgənɔːt‖-ər-/ *n* **1** a great force or object that destroys everything it meets **2** *infml BrE, usu. derog* a very large vehicle (LORRY) that carries loads over long distances and may be a danger to other vehicles

jug·gle /'dʒʌgəl/ *v* [T1;IØ (*with*)] **1** to keep (several objects) in the air at the same time by throwing them up quickly and catching them again —see picture at THEATRE **2** to play with (something): *He likes to juggle (with) ideas* **3** to do something tricky or dishonest with (something): *Don't juggle (with) your accounts* —**~r** *n*

jug·u·lar vein /'dʒʌgjʊlə veɪn‖-gjələr-/ also **jugular**— *n* either of 2 large bloodvessels, one on each side of the neck, that return blood from the head —see picture at RESPIRATORY

juice[1] /dʒuːs/ *n* **1** [U;C] the liquid part of fruit, vegetables, and meat: *orange juice*|*I like cooked vegetables with all the natural juices still in* **2** [U;C] the liquid in certain parts of the body, esp. the stomach, that helps people and animals to use (DIGEST) food **3** [U] *sl* anything that produces power, such as electricity, gas, petrol, etc.

juice[2] *v* [T1] to get the juice out of

juice up *v adv* [T1] *infml AmE* to give more life, spirit, fun, etc., to

juic·y /'dʒuːsi/ *adj* [Wa1] **1** having a lot of juice: *a juicy orange* **2** that will result in a lot of money: *a juicy contract that will make you rich* **3** interesting, esp. because providing information about bad or improper behaviour: *I want all the juicy details* —**-iness** *n* [U]

ju·jit·su, jiujitsu /ˌdʒuː'dʒɪtsuː/ *n* [U] a type of fighting from Japan in which you hold and throw your opponent

ju·ju /'dʒuːdʒuː/ *n* a magic charm in West Africa

ju·jube /'dʒuːdʒuːb/ *n* a small jelly-like sweet, often with throat medicine added

juke·box /'dʒuːkbɒks‖-bɑks/ *n* a machine, found in places of amusement, which plays music (or records) when a coin is put into it

Jul. *written abbrev. for:* July

ju·lep /'dʒuːlɨp/ *n* an American drink in which alcohol and sugar are mixed and poured over ice, and MINT[3] is added

Ju·li·an cal·en·dar /ˌdʒuːlɪən 'kælɨndəʳ/ *n* [*the*+R] the system of numbering, naming, and ordering days brought in by Julius Caesar in 46 B.C. and used in Europe and America until the GREGORIAN CALENDAR began to be used instead

Ju·ly /dʒʊ'laɪ/ *n* [R;(C)] the 7th month of the year

jum·ble[1] /'dʒʌmbəl/ *v* [T1 *often pass.*; IØ: (UP or TOGETHER)] to mix in disorder: *Her books/thoughts (were) all jumbled (up/together)*

jumble[2] *n* [S (*of*)] a disorderly mixture (of things or ideas)

jumble sale /'·· ·/ (*AmE* **rummage sale**)— *n BrE* a sale of used clothes and other things to get money for some good work such as helping the poor

jum·bo /'dʒʌmbəʊ/ also **jumbo-sized** /'·· ·/— *adj* [Wa5;A] larger than others of the same kind: *a jumbo-sized plate of ice cream*|*a jumbo* JET

jump[1] /dʒʌmp/ *v* **1** [IØ] to spring suddenly and quickly away from where one has been, by using the legs (or tail): *to jump up/down/over the water/out of the water*|*She jumped to her feet and ran out of the room.*|(fig.) *He keeps jumping from one subject of conversation to another* **2** [T1] to spring over: *He jumped the stream* **3** [IØ] (esp. of money or quantity) to rise suddenly and sharply: *The price of oil jumped sharply in 1973* **4** [IØ] to make any quick sudden movement as a result of strong feeling: *His heart jumped for joy.*|(fig.) *The noise made me nearly jump out of my skin!* **5** [T1] *infml* to leave (something) suddenly and without permission: *One sailor jumped ship at Gibraltar* **6** [T1] *infml* to travel unlawfully on (a train) without paying **7**

[T1] to attack suddenly **8 jump to it** *infml* to hurry: *You'll have to jump to it if you want to catch the train* **9 jump a claim** to try to claim valuable land which someone else already owns **10 jump the gun** to start something (like a race) too soon **11 jump the queue** to obtain an unfair advantage over others who have been waiting longer **12 jump down someone's throat** *sl* to begin to disagree with someone before they have finished talking

jump² *n* **1** an act of jumping **2 get the jump on** *infml* to get an advantage by starting quicker than **3 be/stay one jump ahead** *infml* to know what others are going to do and act in accordance with that knowledge —see also HIGH JUMP, LONG JUMP

jump at *v prep* [T1] to be eager to accept: *She jumped at the chance*

jumped-up /ˌ·· ˈ·/ *adj* [A] *derog* having too great an idea of one's own importance, esp. because of having just risen high socially

jump·er¹ /ˈdʒʌmpəʳ/ *n* **1** a person who jumps **2** a horse that jumps

jumper² *n* **1** *BrE* a garment for the upper half of the body, pulled on over the head, usu. made of wool and without buttons or other fasteners; SWEATER **2** *AmE* a SLEEVEless dress, usu. worn over a BLOUSE

jumping-off place /ˌ·· ˈ· ˌ·/ also **jumping-off point**— *n* a starting point or place

jump on *v prep* [T1] to scold; TELL OFF (1)

jumps /dʒʌmps/ *n* [*the*+P] *infml* a nervous excited condition in which one is unable to keep still

jump·y /ˈdʒʌmpi/ *adj* [Wa2] nervously excited —**-ily** *adv* —**-iness** *n* [U]

Jun. *written abbrev. for:* **1** June **2** JUNIOR (1)

junc·tion /ˈdʒʌŋkʃən/ *n* an example or, usu., a place of joining, meeting, or uniting: *This railway station is a busy junction for lines from all over the country*

junc·ture /ˈdʒʌŋktʃəʳ/ *n fml* a state of affairs or point in time (esp. in the phr. **at this juncture**): *At this juncture in our nation's affairs, we need firm leadership*

June /dʒuːn/ *n* [R;(C)] the 6th month of the year

jun·gle /ˈdʒʌŋgəl/ *n* **1** [C;U] a tropical forest too thick to walk through easily: *jungle animals/birds*|(fig.) *Without care, your garden will become a jungle.*|(fig.) *the jungle of business/of the big city* **2** [C] a disorderly mass of things that is hard to understand: *the jungle of tax laws*

ju·ni·or /ˈdʒuːnɪəʳ/ *n, adj* [Wa5;B (*to*); C] **1** younger: *my junior brother*|*You are still my junior* **2** of lower rank or position: *a junior officer/minister*|*He is junior to many other people who work here*

Junior *n esp. AmE* **1** [E] the younger: *John Smith Junior is the son of John Smith* **2** [R;N] a name for one's (eldest) son: *Junior always thinks he knows more than his father.*|*Come here, Junior*

ju·ni·per /ˈdʒuːnɪ̈pəʳ/ *n* a type of low bush whose leaves remain green all year and whose oil has a pleasant smell

junk¹ /dʒʌŋk/ *n* [U] **1** *infml* old useless things: *What will you pay me for all this old junk?* **2** *infml* material of poor quality: *His latest book is junk* **3** *sl* the dangerous drug HEROIN

junk² *v* [T1] *infml* to get rid of as worthless

junk³ *n* a type of Chinese sailing ship with a flat bottom and rather square sails

jun·ket /ˈdʒʌŋkɪ̈t/ *n* **1** [U;C] (a dish of) milk thickened and made solid by adding an acid, sweetened and often given a particular taste **2** [C] *infml, esp. AmE* a trip or journey, esp. one made by a government official and paid for with government money

jun·ket·ing /ˈdʒʌŋkɪ̈tɪŋ/ *n* [U;C *often pl. with sing. meaning*] *infml* (a) happy social gathering with lots of eating and drinking, esp. as provided for the amusement of an important person

junk·ie, junky /ˈdʒʌŋki/ *n sl* a person who takes JUNK¹ (3) as a habit

junk mail /ˈ· ·/ *n* [U] *AmE derog* mail, usu. for advertising, that is sent to people even if they have not asked to receive it

Ju·no·esque /ˌdʒuːnəʊˈesk/ *adj* (of a woman) tall and having a proud queenly beauty like that of the Greek goddess Juno

jun·ta /ˈdʒʌntə, ˈhʊntə/ *n* [GC] *Sp often derog* a government, esp. a military one, that has come to power by armed force rather than election

Ju·pi·ter /ˈdʒuːpɪ̈təʳ/ *n* [R] the largest PLANET of the group that includes the Earth, 5th in order from the sun —see picture at PLANET

ju·rid·i·cal /dʒʊəˈrɪdɪkəl/ *adj fml* of or related to the LAW¹ (2) or to judges —**~ly** *adv* [Wa4]

jur·is·dic·tion /ˌdʒʊərɪ̈sˈdɪkʃən/ *n* [U9] **1** the power held by an official or an official body, esp. a court of law **2** the right to use such power: *The prisoner refused to accept the jurisdiction of the court* **3** the limits of this right (esp. in the phrs. **within/outside someone's jurisdiction**)

ju·ris·pru·dence /ˌdʒʊərɪ̈sˈpruːdəns/ *n* [U] *fml* the science or knowledge of law

ju·rist /ˈdʒʊərɪ̈st/ *n fml* a person with a thorough knowledge of law

ju·ror /ˈdʒʊərəʳ/ *n* a member of a JURY

ju·ry /ˈdʒʊəri/ *n* [GC] **1** a group of usu. 12 people chosen to decide questions of fact in a court of law, and who have solemnly promised to give an honest opinion **2** a group of people chosen to judge a competition of any kind, and pick the winner: *the jury of the Miss World competition*|(fig.) *the jury of public opinion*

jury box /ˈ·· ·/ *n* the enclosed place where the JURY sit during a law case

ju·ry·man /ˈdʒʊərimən/ (*fem.* **ju·ry·wom·an** /-ˌwʊmən/)— *n* **-men** /mən/ JUROR

just¹ /dʒʌst/ *adj* **1** fair; in accordance with what is right and true: *a very just man/judge/law* **2** well-deserved: *You have received a just reward/punishment* **3** proper; fitting: *It's just that you should be rewarded for your work* **4** exact: *a just balance between the 2 of them* —**~ly** *adv* —**~ness** *n* [U]

just² /dʒəst; *strong* dʒʌst/ *adv* **1** (*not neg.*) exactly; (at) the exact time or place: *He was sitting just here.*|*He came just as I was leaving.*|*That's just what I wanted* (—compare *That's not quite what I wanted*).|*Do just as you like!*|*He looks just like his brother.*|*I can just as well use this one* **2** *infml* completely; very: *That's just perfect.*|*Isn't that just beautiful!* **3** (*not neg., often with* only) to the amount needed, but not more than; almost not; hardly: *He (only) just succeeded.*|*He lives just round the corner.*|*The skirt comes just below my knees* **4** (*usu. not with the past t.*) only a very short time ago; only at this moment and not sooner: *I've just been reading a very interesting book.*|*They've (only) just arrived.*|(*infml*) *"Buy me a drink!" "I just did"* —see USAGE **5** only a short time from now; only at this moment and not later: *I'm just coming!*|*He's just about to leave* **6** (*with adverbs, or adverb phrases, of time*) only a little; only a short time: *They left just before/just after Christmas* **7** *not fml* only; MERELy: *Just a moment!* (= Wait a moment!)|*Don't worry—that's just Aunt Fanny practising her balancing act* **8 I should just think . . .** *infml* of course; naturally: *"John's very proud of his daughter." "I should just think so!/just think he is!"* **9 just my luck** (said when something bad has happened) exactly the sort of bad luck I always have **10 just now a** at this moment: *We're having dinner just now—come back later* **b** a moment ago: *Paul*

telephoned just now—he wants the money **11 just on** *not fml* nearly; almost exactly: *just on 90 years ago* **12 just the thing a** exactly what is wanted: *"Here's a ladder." "Just the thing! We'll use that"* **b** exactly what I meant: *"But John's stopped drinking." "That's just the thing—he's nicer when he's drunk"* **13 just yet** (*with* no, not, *etc.*) quite yet: *I can't come just yet*
USAGE **Already**, **yet**, and **just** (when it is used of time) were formerly not used with the past tense. Expressions like the following are now common in *infml AmE*: *I* **already** *saw him.|The bell* **just** *rang.|Did you eat* **yet**? These are coming into *BrE*, but some teachers and examiners do not like them.

just a·bout /ˈ· ·ˌ·/ *adv* **1** almost; very nearly: *just about 500|It's just about here.|They had just about won the game when they had to stop playing* (=they didn't actually win) **2** almost not; very nearly not: *I just about won the game: I finished only one point ahead* (=I won)

jus·tice /ˈdʒʌstɨ̥s/ *n* **1** [U] the quality of being just; rightness; fairness: *He claimed—with justice, I might add—that he had not received his fair share* **2** [U] correctness: *The justice of these remarks was clear to everyone* **3** [U] the action or power of the law: *to bring a criminal to justice|a court of justice* **4** [C] *AmE* a judge (of a law court) **5 do justice to someone/do someone justice** to treat someone in a fair way; show the true value of

Justice *n* [C;A] a part of the title of a judge (of a law court): *Mr Justice Smith has been made Chief Justice*

Justice of the Peace /ˌ··· · ˈ·/ *n fml* JP

jus·ti·fi·a·ble /ˈdʒʌstɨ̥faɪəbəl/ *adj* that is or can be JUSTIFIED —**-bly** *adv*

jus·ti·fi·ca·tion /ˌdʒʌstɨ̥fɨ̥ˈkeɪʃən/ *n* [U] **1** a good reason for doing something: *There is no justification for his rude behaviour* **2 in justification** as a good reason: *What can be said in justification of his behaviour?*

jus·ti·fied /ˈdʒʌstɨ̥faɪd/ *adj* provided with a good reason: *Is he justified in his behaviour?* —**~ly** *adv*

jus·ti·fy /ˈdʒʌstɨ̥faɪ/ *v* [T1 (*to*), 4] **1** to give a good reason for: *How can you justify your rude behaviour?* **2** to be a good reason for: *Nothing can justify such rude behaviour*

jute /dʒuːt/ *n* [U] a substance used for making rope and rough cloth, from either of 2 plants grown esp. in Eastern India and Bangladesh

jut out /dʒʌt/ *v adv* **-tt-** [I∅] to be in a position further forward than its surroundings: *The wall juts out here to allow room for the chimney*

ju·ve·nile[1] /ˈdʒuːvənaɪl‖-nəl, -naɪl/ *adj* **1** of, like, by, or for young people, no longer babies but not yet fully grown: *juvenile books|a juvenile court* **2** young and foolish

juvenile[2] *n* **1** *fml or tech* a young person, no longer a baby but not yet fully grown **2** an actor or actress who plays such a person

juvenile de·lin·quen·cy /ˌ··· ·ˈ···/ *n* [U] crimes by JUVENILE*s* —**-quent** *n*: *He's too old to be treated as a juvenile delinquent*

jux·ta·pose /ˌdʒʌkstəˈpəʊz‖ˈdʒʌkstəpəʊz/ *v* [T1] to place side by side or close together

jux·ta·po·si·tion /ˌdʒʌkstəpəˈzɪʃən/ *n* [U] the act of placing, or the state of being placed, side by side or close together

K, k

K, k /keɪ/ **K's, k's** *or* **Ks, ks** the 11th letter of the English alphabet

K *written abbrev. for:* (in CHESS and cards) king

kaf·fir, kafir /ˈkæfəʳ/ *n derog esp. SAfrE* a black African

kaf·tan /ˈkæftæn‖kæfˈtæn/ *n* CAFTAN

Kai·ser /ˈkaɪzəʳ/ *n* [*the*+R;(C);A;(N)] *Ger* (the title of) the king of Germany (1871–1918)

kale, kail /keɪl/ *n* **1** [C;U] a type of vegetable (a CABBAGE), esp. one that has open curled leaves **2** [U] (in Scotland) a soup made from this

ka·lei·do·scope /kəˈlaɪdəskəʊp/ *n* **1** a tube fitted at one end with mirrors and pieces of coloured glass which shows many coloured patterns when turned **2** [(*of*) *usu. sing.*] a pattern or a scene that has many different bright colours, or that has colours often changing: *At sunset the sky became a kaleidoscope of colours*

ka·lei·do·scop·ic /kəˌlaɪdəˈskɒpɪk‖-ˈskɑ-/ *adj* (esp. of scenes and colours) changing quickly and often —**~ally** *adv* [Wa4]

kal·ends /ˈkælendz/ *n* [*the*+P] CALENDS

kam·pong /ˈkæmpɒn‖ˈkɑm-, ˈkæm-, -pɔŋ/ *n* (in Malaysia) an enclosed space such as around a house, or a village

kan·ga·roo /ˌkæŋgəˈruː◂/ *n* **-roos** [Wn1] a type of Australian animal which jumps along on its large back legs and which carries its young in a special pocket of flesh —see picture at MAMMAL

kangaroo court /ˌ··· ˈ·/ *n infml* an unofficial court established by some members of a group to try and usu. to punish other members of the same group

ka·o·lin /ˈkeɪələ̥n/ *n* [U] a kind of fine white clay used for making cups, plates, etc., and also in medicine

ka·pok /ˈkeɪpɒk‖-pɑk/ *n* [U] a very light soft cotton-like material used for filling things that people lie on when sleeping and things that help people to float

kap·pa /ˈkæpə/ *n* the 10th letter (Κ, κ) of the Greek alphabet

ka·put /kəˈpʊt/ *adj* [Wa5;F] *sl, Ger* broken; finished; no longer useful

kar·at /ˈkærət/ *n* CARAT

ka·ra·te /kəˈrɑːti/ *n* [U] any of several Asian styles of fighting without a weapon that include blows with the hands and feet

kar·ma /ˈkɑːmə‖-ɑr-/ *n* [U] (in Hinduism and Buddhism) the force produced by a person's actions in one life on earth which will influence his next life on earth

ka·ty·did /ˈkeɪtidɪd/ *n* a type of jumping insect found in the US, like a GRASSHOPPER

kay·ak /ˈkaɪæk/ *n* **1** a narrow covered boat used by Eskimos **2** any boat like this —see picture at BOAT[1]

ka·zoo /kəˈzuː/ *n* **-zoos** a type of toy musical instrument, played by blowing

K.C. /ˌkeɪ ˈsiː/ also (*fml*) **King's Counsel**— [C;E] (the title given, while a king is ruling, to) a British lawyer (BARRISTER) of high rank —compare Q.C.

ke·bab, -bob /kɨ̥ˈbæb‖kɨ̥ˈbɑb/ *n* a dish of cut up meat and usu. vegetables put on a stick and cooked

kedg·e·ree /ˈkedʒəriː/ *n* [U;(C)] a dish of rice and fish mixed together, with eggs and cream sometimes added

keel /kiːl/ *n* **1** a long bar along the bottom of a boat or ship from which the whole frame of the boat or ship is built up —see pictures at SAIL[2] and FREIGHTER **2 on an even keel** without any sudden changes; without trouble; steady; steadily; calm(ly)

keel·haul /ˈkiːlhɔːl/ *v* [T1] **1** (in former times) to drag (someone) under a ship's KEEL as a punishment **2** to scold severely

keel o·ver *v adv* [IØ] to fall over sideways: *The ship keeled over in the storm.|He keeled over with laughter when I told him the joke*

keen[1] /kiːn/ *adj* [Wa1] **1** [B] sharp; with a fine cutting edge: *Careful with that knife: it's got a keen edge!*|(fig.) *There was a keen wind blowing from the east* **2** [B] (of the mind, the feelings, the 5 senses, etc.) good, strong, quick at understanding, deeply felt, etc.: *a keen mind|a keen desire|keen sorrow|keen sight*|(fig.) *a keen eye* **3** [B] (of a game or struggle of any kind) done with eagerness and activity on both sides: *a keen football match/struggle for power|keen competition for the job* **4** [(*BrE*) B;F3; (*AmE*) A] (of a person) having a strong, active interest in something; eager or anxious to do something: *a keen student of politics*|(*BrE*) *keen to pass the examination*|(*BrE*) *Her father wants her to go to university, but she is not keen* **5** [F+*on*] *infml* having a strong liking for or a strong active interest in something or someone; eager or anxious to do something: *keen on politics/on John/on passing the examination* —**~ly** *adv*: *He feels the heat more keenly than before* —**keenness** *n* [U, (*BrE*) U3]

keen[2] *v* **1** [IØ] to sing a KEEN[3] **2** [IØ] to make sounds like a KEEN[3] **3** [IØ] to express sorrow loudly **4** [T1] to express something by means of a KEEN[3] or in a way that is like a KEEN: *to keen one's sorrow*

keen[3] *n* (in Ireland) an expression of grief for the dead that is like a loud sad song or cry

keep[1] /kiːp/ *v* **kept** /kept/ **1** [T1] to fulfil: *She kept her promise/appointment* **2** [T1] to take notice of by suitable behaviour; OBSERVE (2): *She keeps only the most important religious holidays* **3** [T1 (*from*)] to guard; protect: *May God keep you (from harm)!* **4** [T1] to take care of and provide with necessary goods and services: *She kept her sister's children.|He needs more money to keep his wife and children* **5** [T1] to own, employ, or have the use of: *to keep a house/2 cars/a gardener* **6** [T1] to own and make money from: *They keep a shop/a small hotel* **7** [T1] to own and take care of (farm animals) in order to use or make money from: *to keep hens/chickens/cows* **8** [D1;T1] to have for some time or for more time: *Please keep this for me until I come back.|He was in trouble at first, but he succeeded in keeping his job.|These old clothes are not worth keeping* **9** [T1] to have without the need of returning: *You can keep it; I don't need it.|Here's more money than you need to buy it; keep the change* **10** [X1,7,9;V4] to cause (something or someone) to continue to (be in a certain state or do something): *That kept her warm/in bed/a student/studying.|Her illness kept her in hospital 6 weeks* **11** [L7,9;T4 (ON)] to continue to be (in a certain state), move (in a certain way), or do (something) usu. as a result of some effort or activity: *She kept warm/to the left/studying* **12** [L9] to be (in the stated condition of health): *"How are you keeping?" "I'm keeping quite well, thank you"* **13** [T1] to be for some time in a state of (esp. in the phr. **keep silence**) **14** [IØ] (of food) to remain fresh and fit to eat: *This fish won't keep: we must eat it now.*|(fig.) *My news will keep until you are ready to hear it* **15** [T1] to know without telling (esp. in the phr. **to keep a secret**) **16** [T1] to delay (someone): *What kept you (so long)?|I'll only keep you for a few minutes* **17** [T1] to offer regularly for sale: *That shop keeps everything you will need* **18** [T1] to make regular written records of or in: *He keeps exact accounts of the money he spends and a* DIARY *of the events of his holidays* **19 keep your shirt** (*BrE* also **hair**) **on** *infml* keep calm!; don't worry! —see also KEEP AT, KEEP BACK, KEEP DOWN, KEEP FROM, KEEP IN, KEEP IN WITH, KEEP OFF[1,2], KEEP ON, KEEP ON AT, KEEP OUT, KEEP OUT OF, **keep** TIME, KEEP TO, KEEP UNDER, KEEP UP

keep[2] *n* **1** [C] a great tower of a castle —see picture at CASTLE[1] **2** [U] (the cost of providing) necessary goods and services (esp. in the phr. **earn one's keep**): *He doesn't do enough for us to earn his keep*

keep at *v prep* [T1 *no pass.*; D1] to (cause to) continue working at (something): *The work is tiring but he'll keep at it until he's finished*

keep back *v adv* [T1] **1** to not tell; keep silent about: *She told us most of the story, but kept back the bit about her uncle* **2** to keep (usu. some of something) in one's possession; WITHHOLD (1): *I kept a few books back and gave him the rest*

keep down *v adv* [T1] **1** to control (something); prevent from increasing: *Chemicals are used for keeping insects down* **2** to keep (people) in a state like slavery; OPPRESS (1) **3** to prevent (food or drink) from passing back from the stomach through the mouth

keep·er /ˈkiːpəʳ/ *n* **1** a person who guards, protects, or looks after: *The keeper is feeding the animals* **2** (*in comb.*) a person who is in charge of or who has special duties in relation to: *shopkeeper|doorkeeper|innkeeper* **3** *infml* **a** GOALKEEPER **b** WICKET KEEPER

keep from *v prep* **1** [D1;V4b] to prevent (someone) from (something or doing something): *I mustn't keep you from your work.|Can't you keep him from forgetting?* **2** [T4] to prevent oneself from (doing something): *I could hardly keep from laughing*

keep in *v adv* **1** [T1;IØ] to (cause to) stay indoors, esp. in school as a punishment **2** [T1] to take care of; not allow to cease: *Keep the fire in*

keep·ing /ˈkiːpɪŋ/ *n* **1** [U9] care or charge: *She left her jewellery in her sister's keeping* **2 in safe keeping** being kept, guarded, or protected carefully: *Don't worry; your jewels are in safe keeping* **3 out of/in keeping (with something)** not in/in agreement (with something); going unsuitably or suitably (with something): *His words and his actions are out of keeping (with each other)*

keep in with *v adv prep* [T1] to (try to) remain friendly with

keep off[1] *v adv* [IØ;T1] to (cause to) remain at a distance; (cause to) not come or happen: *If the rain keeps off, we shall go out.|Draw the curtain to keep the sun off* (= to stop it shining on you)

keep off[2] *v prep* [T1] to stay away from: *Keep off the grass!*

keep on *v adv* **1** [T4a] to continue (doing something): *Prices keep on increasing* **2** [T1] to continue to employ (someone): *Were you able to keep both the gardeners on?* **3** [T1] to continue to have (something): *I'll keep the flat on through the summer* **4** [IØ (*about*)] to talk continuously: *He keeps on about his operation*

keep on at *v adv prep* [T1;3] to talk to (someone) continuously or ask repeatedly: *His wife kept on at him to buy her a new coat*

keep out *v adv* [T1;IØ: (*of*)] to (cause to) not enter: *This notice should keep unwanted visitors out; it says "Keep out!"|Warm clothing will keep out the cold*

keep out of *v adv prep* [T1;D1] to (cause to) stay away from (usu. something bad): *I hope you'll keep (him) out of trouble while I'm away*

keeps /ki:ps/ *n* **for keeps** *sl* (for keeping) for ever: *She says that this marriage will be for keeps*

keep·sake /ˈki:pseɪk/ *n* something, usu. small, given to be kept in memory of the giver

keep to *v prep* **1** [T1] to move or remain in (a certain position): *Traffic in Britain keeps to the left* **2** [T1] to limit oneself to (something): *keep to the subject* **3** [T1] to stay in (something); not leave: *keep to one's room/bed* **4** [D1] to keep (something) private to (oneself): *He kept the news to himself.|Keep it to yourself* (= don't tell anyone) **5 keep oneself to oneself** to remain private; avoid meeting other people: *She doesn't go out much; she likes to keep herself to herself*

keep un·der *v adv* [T1b] **1** to control (something): *Jim kept his feelings under.|We tried to keep the fire under* **2** to control (someone); limit the freedom of: *Former rulers kept the people under*

keep up *v adv* **1** [T1] to cause (something) to remain high: *The farmers are keeping prices up.|* (fig.) *She kept up her spirits by singing* **2** [T1] to keep (something) in good condition: *How do you keep up this large house?* **3** [T1] to continue (something): *keep up the good work|Keep it up; don't stop now!* **4** [I∅] to remain the same: *Will the fine weather keep up?* **5** [T1;I∅] to (cause to) remain out of bed: *"I hope I'm not keeping you up." "No, we often keep up late"* **6** [I∅ (*with*)] to remain level: *I had to run to keep up (with the girls)* **7 keep up with the Joneses** to stay level with social changes; compete with one's neighbours socially

keg /keg/ *n* a small barrel

kelp /kelp/ *n* [U] any of several kinds of large brown SEAWEED (=plant that grows in the sea)

kel·vin /ˈkelvən/ *n* a degree in a modern international scale of temperature according to which ABSOLUTE ZERO=0°

ken¹ /ken/ *v* **-nn-** [T1,5;I∅] *ScotE* to know

ken² *n* [U9] knowledge; the limits of knowledge (esp. in the phrs. **beyond/outside/not within one's ken**): *What happens after death is beyond our ken*

ken·nel¹ /ˈkenl/ *n* **1** a usu. small house for a dog **2** *AmE* KENNELS

kennel² *v* [T1] to keep or put in a KENNEL¹ or a KENNELS

ken·nels /ˈkenlz/ *n* **kennels** [Wn3;C] a place where small animals are looked after while their owners are away: *They left their dog in a kennels when they went on holiday*

ke·pi /ˈkeɪpi:/ *n* **kepis** a cap worn by some French soldiers

kept /kept/ *past t. and past p. of* KEEP

kept wom·an /ˌ· ˈ··/ *n* a woman supplied with a place to live and money by a man who is not married to her but visits her regularly for sex

kerb, *AmE* **curb** /kɜ:b‖kɜrb/ *n* a line of raised stones (**kerbstones** /ˈkɜ:bstəʊnz‖ˈkɜrb-/) separating the footpath (for walkers) from the road (for vehicles) —see picture at STREET

ker·chief /ˈkɜ:tʃəf‖ˈkɜr-/ *n* a square piece of cloth worn (usu. by women) to cover the head, neck, etc.

ker·fuf·fle /kəˈfʌfəl‖kər-/ *n* [C;U] *infml BrE* unnecessary and/or noisy excitement (esp. in the phr. **fuss and kerfuffle**)

ker·nel /ˈkɜ:nl‖ˈkɜr-/ *n* **1** the part, usu. eatable, inside the hard shell of a nut, or inside a fruit stone —see picture at NUT¹ **2** the part of a seed contained inside its hard covering: *the kernel of a grain of corn* **3** the important or main part of something, often surrounded by unimportant or untrue matter

ker·o·sene, -sine /ˈkerəsi:n/ *n* [U] *AmE* PARAFFIN (1)

ker·sey /ˈkɜ:zi‖-ɜr-/ *n* [U] rough cloth made of wool

kes·trel /ˈkestrəl/ *n* a type of red-brown European bird (FALCON) which feeds on mice, insects, and small birds

ketch /ketʃ/ *n* a small sailing-ship with 2 upright poles for its sails (2 MASTs)

ketch·up /ˈketʃəp/ also **catsup**— *n* [U] a thick red sour liquid made from TOMATOes, used for giving pleasant taste to food

ket·tle /ˈketl/ *n* **1** a usu. metal pot with a lid, a handle, and a SPOUT (=a narrow curved mouth for pouring), used mainly for boiling or heating water **2 a pretty/fine kettle of fish!** an awkward state of affairs that may cause difficulty to a person **3 put the kettle on** to start heating a kettle so that the water in it will boil

ket·tle·drum /ˈketldrʌm/ *n* a large metal drum, used in music, with a round curved-up bottom —see picture at PERCUSSION

key¹ /ki:/ *n* **1** [C] an instrument, usu. made of metal, for locking or unlocking (a door), winding (a clock), tightening or loosening (a spring), or starting and stopping (a car engine) —see picture at DOOR **2** [C] any one of the parts in a musical instrument, or in a machine, that is pressed down to produce the desired sound or other result: *the keys of a piano/a* TYPEWRITER —see picture at WIND INSTRUMENT **3** [C (*to*)] something that explains, answers, or helps you to understand: *a key to the grammar exercises/to the secret writing|* (fig.) *Her very unhappy childhood is the key to the way she behaves now* **4** [A] someone or something that is very important; that is necessary for success: *He is a very important man with a key position in the firm.|He is a key man.|key towns* **5** [C] a set of musical notes with a certain starting or base note: *played in the key of C|a song in too high a key for the singer|*(fig.) *The book is not very exciting; it is written in a very low key from beginning to end* **6** [C] a seed of certain types of tree (such as the ASH¹ and ELM), which has winglike parts to help it float through the air **7 all in the same key** without any change of expression of voice or manner of writing

key² *v* [T1] **1** [*usu. pass.*] to tighten or loosen the strings of (a musical instrument) so that the right notes are produced: *The concert was a failure because the instruments were wrongly keyed* **2** [(*to*); *usu. pass.*] to make ready for or more suitable for: *Their factories are keyed to produce the things that their army needs/are keyed to the needs of the army* —see also KEY UP

key³, cay *n* (esp. in the W. Indies or off the coast of Florida, US) **1** a low island **2** a chain of rocks in the sea whose tops may be above or below the surface of the water

key·board¹ /ˈki:bɔ:d‖-bord/ *n* a row of KEYs¹ (2) on a musical instrument or machine: *the keyboard of a piano or a* TYPEWRITER
See next page for picture

keyboard² *v* [T1;I∅] **1** to work the KEYBOARD¹ of (a machine, esp. a calculating machine or a COMPUTER) **2** to provide a machine with (information) by working a KEYBOARD¹: *Our best workers can keyboard (the information) very quickly indeed* —**~er** *n*

key·hole /ˈki:həʊl/ *n* a hole for the key in a lock, a clock, etc. —see picture at DOOR

key·less /ˈki:ləs/ *adj* [Wa5] *becoming rare* (of a clock) not needing a key for winding

key mon·ey /ˈ· ˌ··/ *n* [U] money, additional to the rent, sometimes unlawfully demanded before a person is allowed to begin living in a flat or house

key·note¹ /ˈki:nəʊt/ *n* **1** [C] the particular note on

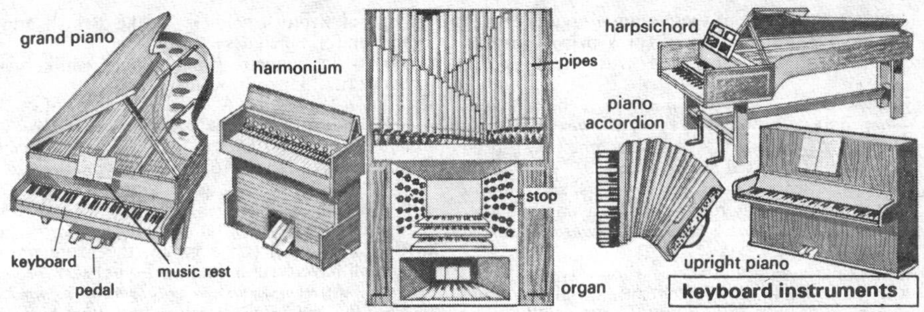

keyboard instruments

which a musical KEY[1] (5) is based **2** [A;C] (containing) a central or the most important idea: *The keynote of his speech was that we need higher wages.|a keynote speech*

keynote² *v* [T1] *infml* to give special force to certain ideas in speaking or writing so that they will be noticed or remembered: *He keynoted the need for higher wages*

key·punch /ˈkiːpʌntʃ/ *n AmE* CARDPUNCH —**~er** *n*

key ring /ˈ· ·/ *n* a ring or ring-shaped thing on which keys are kept

key sig·na·ture /ˈ· ˌ···/ *n* a mark or marks in a system of musical writing that show in which KEY[1] (5) a piece of music is —see picture at NOTATION

key·stone /ˈkiːstəʊn/ *n* [*usu. sing.*] **1** the middle stone in the top of an arch, considered the most important because it keeps the other stones in position **2** [(*of*)] something (esp. an idea, belief, etc.) on which everything else depends: *Social justice is the keystone of their political plan*

key up *v adv* [Wv5 (*about, for*);T1] to make (someone) excited or nervous: *I was keyed up about the examination*

kg. *written abbrev. for:* KILOGRAM(*s*)

kha·ki /ˈkɑːki‖ˈkæki, ˈkɑki/ *adj, n* [Wa5] **1** [B;U] a yellow-brown colour **2** [U] cloth of this colour, esp. as worn by soldiers

kha·lif /ˈkeɪlɨf, kɑːˈliːf/ *n* [C;A] CALIPH

kha·lif·ate /ˈkeɪlɨfeɪt/ *n* CALIPHATE

khan /kɑːn/ *n* (*often cap.*) (a title of) a ruler or official in Asia

kib·butz /kɪˈbʊts/ *n* **-zim** /sɪm/ *or* **-zes** a farm or settlement in Israel where many people live and work together

ki·bosh /ˈkaɪbɒʃ‖-bɑʃ/ *n* **put the kibosh on** *sl, esp. BrE* to put an end to (something, esp. a hope, plan, etc.)

kick¹ /kɪk/ *v* **1** [T1] to hit with the foot: *He's crying because she kicked him.|The horse kicked me when I tried to ride it.|Kick the ball!* **2** [X9] to move (usu. something) by doing this: *He kicked over a chair.|She kicked the sand up/away* **3** [T1] (esp. in RUGBY) to make or SCORE by doing this: *He kicked a* GOAL **4** [I∅] to move the foot or feet as if to strike a blow: *Babies kick to exercise their legs* **5** [I∅] (esp. of a gun) to move back with force: *When she fired the gun, it kicked so hard that she nearly fell backwards* **6** [I∅] (esp. of a ball) to rise from the ground more quickly and steeply than expected **7** [I∅] *infml* to complain; show anger **8 kick someone upstairs** *infml* to move someone from work that they cannot do well to a position which appears higher or more important but which really has less power —see also KICK ABOUT[1,2], KICK AGAINST, KICK AROUND, KICK OFF, KICK OUT, KICK UP

kick² *n* **1** [C] an act of kicking: *Give the door a kick to open it* **2** [C] *sl* a sharp, strong feeling of excitement, pleasure, etc.: *Driving a car at high speed gives her a kick.|She drives fast (just) for kicks* **3** [U] *infml* (of a person) power to continue making efforts, struggling, etc.: *He's a sick man, but he still has some kick in him* **4** [U] *infml* (of a thing) strength; power to produce an effect: *This wine has a lot of kick in it* —see also KICKS

kick a·bout¹ also **kick around**— *v prep* [T1 *no pass.*] *infml* **1** to travel in (a place): *He's been kicking about Africa for years* **2** to lie unnoticed in (a place): *That old thing has been kicking about the house for years*

kick about² *v adv infml* **1** [I∅] to lie unnoticed: *"Where's my cap?" "Oh, it's kicking about somewhere"* **2** [T1b] to treat (someone or something) roughly

kick a·gainst also **kick at**— *v prep* [T4] to oppose or dislike (doing something)

kick a·round *v adv infml* **1** [T1b] to give (someone) unnecessary orders **2** [I∅] KICK ABOUT[2] (1) **3** [T1b] KICK ABOUT[2] (2)

kick·back /ˈkɪkbæk/ *n* [C;U] *sl* money for services (usu. unlawful) that have helped you to make money: *a kickback of $10,000*

kick·er /ˈkɪkəʳ/ *n* a person or animal that kicks, esp. a horse with a habit of kicking

kick·off /ˈkɪk-ɒf‖-ɔf/ *n* the first kick, at the start of (the second half of) a game of football: *The kickoff is at 3 o'clock today*

kick off *v adv* [I∅] to start a game of football

kick out *v adv* [T1 (*of*)] to remove or dismiss (someone), esp. violently

kicks /kɪks/ *n* [P] *sl* cause(s) for complaint: *You're getting paid enough: you've got no real kicks*

kick-start /ˈ· ·/ *n* **1** a way of starting a machine (esp. a motorcycle) by pushing down a special part of it **2** also **kick-start·er** /ˈ· ˌ··/— the special part of the machine that is pushed down to start it

kick up *v adv* [T1] *infml* to cause or make (something troublesome or unwanted) (esp. in the phrs. **kick up a fuss/row/shindy/stink,** etc.)

kid¹ /kɪd/ *n* **1** [C] a young goat **2** [U] leather made from the skin of this **3** [C;N *usu. pl.*] *infml* a child **4** [C;N] *infml esp. AmE* a young person: *college kids* **5** [A] *AmE sl* (of a brother or sister) younger: *That girl over there is his kid sister*

kid² *v* **-dd-** *infml* **1** [T1 (ON); I∅] to pretend, esp. in a playful manner; deceive: *He's not really hurt: he's only kidding.|Don't kid me: I know you're not telling the truth* **2 You're kidding!** The things that you are saying are hard to believe —**kidder** *n*

kid·die, -dy /ˈkɪdi/ *n* [C;N *usu. pl.*] *infml* a child

kid gloves /ˌ· ˈ·/ *n* [P] gentle methods of dealing with people: *Don't treat those young criminals with kid gloves* —**kid-glove** /ˈ· ·/ *adj* [Wa5;A]

kid·nap /ˈkɪdnæp/ *v* **-pp-** (*AmE* **-p-** *or* **-pp-**) [T1] to take (someone) away unlawfully in order to demand money or something else for his safe return —**kidnapper** *n*

kid·ney /ˈkɪdni/ *n* **1** [C] one of the pair of human or animal organs in the lower back area, which separate from the blood waste liquid that will be passed from the body —see picture at DIGESTIVE

SYSTEM **2** [C] one of these animal organs cooked and eaten **3** [S] *lit or fml* (of a person) nature, character, or kind: *I wouldn't trust anyone of that kidney*

kidney bean /ˌ·· ˈ·‖ˈ·· ·/ *n* a type of bean that is shaped like a KIDNEY and eaten as a vegetable

kidney ma·chine /ˈ·· ·ˌ·/ *n* a machine that can do the work of diseased human KIDNEY*s*

kidney shaped /ˈ·· ·/ *adj* [Wa5] shaped like a KIDNEY; irregularly roundish with a small hollow: *That rich man owns a big kidney shaped swimming pool*

kike /kaɪk/ *n AmE taboo derog* a Jew

kill¹ /kɪl/ *v* **1** [T1;I∅] to cause to die: *to kill insects/one's enemies*|(fig.) *My feet are killing me!* (=hurting very much) **2** [T1] to cause (something) to finish or fail: *That mistake has killed his chances.*|*The suggested law was killed before it could be passed* **3** [T1] to destroy, weaken, or spoil the effect of (something by comparison with it or closeness to it): *Her bright red hat killed the quiet colour of her dress* **4 kill someone with kindness** to treat someone with too much kindness, so that they feel uncomfortable or, (*BrE*) if children, are spoilt **5 kill time** to make free time pass by finding something to do: *While waiting for the train he killed time by going for a walk* **6 kill two birds with one stone** to get 2 good results from one action **7 dressed (fit) to kill** *infml* dressed in one's best clothes in order to be admired —see also KILL OFF

kill² *n* **1** [S] the bird(s) or animal(s) killed in hunting: *The lion didn't leave his kill until he had satisfied his hunger* **2** [*the*+R] the act of killing, esp. hunted birds or animals **3 (be) in at the kill** (to be) actively present when something is killed or at the end of a struggle, competition, etc.

kill·er /ˈkɪləʳ/ *n infml* **1** [C] a person who kills or has killed someone; murderer **2** [C;A] an animal or thing that kills: *These animals are killers.*|*killer* SHARK*s*|*This disease is a killer.*|*killer diseases*|*killer* FOG*s*

killer whale /ˈ·· ·/ *n* a type of fierce meat-eating WHALE 20 to 30 feet long

kill·ing¹ /ˈkɪlɪŋ/ *n* **make a killing** to make a large amount of money suddenly, esp. in business

killing² *adj* **1** that kills or makes very tired: *This work is really killing* **2** *infml now rare* very funny: *a killing joke* —**~ly** *adv*

kill·joy /ˈkɪldʒɔɪ/ *n* [C;N] a person who "kills joy" by spoiling the pleasure of other people

kill off *v adv* [T1] to kill (living things) one at a time: *The trees were killed off by the severe winter*

kiln /kɪln/ *n* (*often in comb.*) a box-shaped heating apparatus for baking pots, bricks, or lime, and for drying wood

kil·ner jar /ˈkɪlnə dʒɑːʳ‖-nər-/ *n* (*often cap.* K) *tdmk* a large glass vessel with a tight-fitting lid, used for preserving fruit and vegetables

ki·lo /ˈkiːləʊ/ *n* **kilos** *infml* KILOGRAM

kil·o- /ˈkɪlə, kɪˈlɒ‖ˈkɪlə, kɪˈlɑ/ *comb. form* 1,000 —see WEIGHTS & MEASURES TABLE

kil·o·gram, -gramme /ˈkɪləgræm/ *n* 1,000 grams —see WEIGHTS & MEASURES TABLE

kil·o·hertz /ˈkɪləhɜːts‖-ɜr-/ also **kil·o·cy·cle** /ˈkɪləˌsaɪkəl/— *n* **-hertz** [Wn3] 1,000 HERTZ

kil·o·li·tre, *AmE* **-ter** /ˈkɪləˌliːtəʳ/ *n* 1,000 litres —see WEIGHTS & MEASURES TABLE

kil·o·me·tre, *AmE* **-ter** /ˈkɪləˌmiːtəʳ, kɪˈlɒmɨtəʳ‖kɪˈlɑmɨtər/ *n* 1,000 metres —see WEIGHTS & MEASURES TABLE

kil·o·watt /ˈkɪləwɒt‖-wɑt/ *n* 1,000 WATT*s*

kilt /kɪlt/ *n* a short skirt with many pressed folds, worn by Scotsmen

kilt·ed re·gi·ment /ˈ·· ˌ···/ *n* any of several official groups of Scottish soldiers in the British army whose uniform includes a KILT

ki·mo·no /kɪˈməʊnəʊ/ *n* **-nos** a long coatlike garment worn in Japan by women

kin /kɪn/ *n* [P] *old use & fml* **1** members of one's family **2 next of kin** a person's closest relative or relatives: *His next of kin were/was told of his death* **3 no kin to** not related to: *He's no kin to me* —see also KITH AND KIN

-kin also **-kins**— *suffix* [*n*→*n*] *infml* (shows smallness and often niceness): LAMBKIN|*a little babykins*

kind¹ /kaɪnd/ *n* **1** [C] a group, the members of which all have certain qualities; type; sort: *people of many different kinds*|*the only one of its kind*|*a book of that kind*|*Haven't you got any other kind?* **2** [C+*of*] a group which is part of a larger group; type; sort: *many different kinds of people*|*that kind of book*|(*nonstandard*) *that kind of a book*|(*nonstandard*) *those kind of books*|*He had a kind of feeling that he'd never had before* **3** [U] nature or type: *They are different in size but not in kind.*|*A difference in degree can become a difference in kind* **4 a kind of** an unusual kind of; weak or unclear sort of: *He had a kind of feeling that he would get a letter from his daughter today.*|(*nonstandard*) *a kind of a feeling* **5 in kind** (of payment) using goods or natural products rather than money **6 of a kind a** of the same kind: *They're all of a kind.*|*3 of a kind beats 2 of a kind in cards* **b** of a kind which is not very good: *She gave us coffee of a kind, but we couldn't drink it* **7 (be) someone's kind** (to be) of the same kind as someone: *How can they be lovers when she's not his kind at all?* —see also KIND OF

USAGE 1 It is common to say *Those* **kind/sort** *of questions are very difficult*, but teachers and examiners do not like it. When writing, you should use this form: *That* **kind/sort** *of question is very difficult*; or *Questions of that* **kind/sort** *are very difficult* 2 *What* **kind/sort** *of car is it?* means "Is it a Ford, a Volkswagen, etc.?" *What* **kind/sort** *of a car is it?* may mean "Is it any good?"

kind² *adj* [Wa1] helpful; (that shows one is) interested in the happiness or feelings of others: *a kind person/action/thought*|*Be kind to animals.*|*Would you be kind enough to do it?*|*Would you be so kind as to do it?*|*It was very kind of you to do it*

kin·der·gar·ten /ˈkɪndəgɑːtn‖-dərgɑrtn/ *n* [C;U] NURSERY SCHOOL

kind-heart·ed /ˌ· ˈ··◂‖ˈ· ˌ··/ *adj* having or showing a kind nature ("heart"): *That's very kind-hearted of you.*|*a kind-hearted person/action* —**~ly** *adv* —**~ness** *n* [U]

kin·dle /ˈkɪndl/ *v* **1** [T1;I∅] to (cause to) start to burn or become a flaming red colour: *We tried to kindle the wood but it was wet and wouldn't kindle easily* **2** [T1;I∅] **a** to cause (a feeling, usu. bad) to start: *His cruelty kindled hatred in the hearts of the people* **b** (of a feeling) to start: *Her desire for him kindled with every word* **3** [I∅ (*with*)] to show a feeling: *When she saw him her eyes kindled (with desire)*

kin·dling /ˈkɪndlɪŋ/ *n* [U] materials for lighting a fire, esp. dry wood, leaves, grass, etc.: *The campers gathered kindling in the woods*

kind·ly¹ /ˈkaɪndli/ *adj* [Wa2] pleasant; friendly, esp. to those who are younger, weaker, or humbler than oneself: *a kindly smile*|*the kindliest*|*the most kindly person I have ever met* —**-liness** *n* [U]

kindly² *adv* **1** in a kind manner: *She spoke kindly to him* **2** please: *Will you kindly put that book back?*|*Kindly put it back* **3 take kindly to** [*nonassertive*] to accept easily or willingly: *He didn't take kindly to his new responsibilities*

kind·ness /ˈkaɪndnɨs/ *n* **1** [U] the quality of being kind **2** [C] a kind action: *Please have the kindness* *to answer this letter quickly.|(BrE) Please do me the kindness to answer this letter quickly*

kind of *adv* [Wa5] *infml, esp. AmE* to a certain degree; in a certain way: *I'm feeling kind of tired.|She kind of hoped to be invited.|"All you can do is kind of nurse it"* (SEU S.)

kin·dred¹ /ˈkɪndrɨd/ *n* **1** [U] family relationship: *He claims kindred to me, but I don't know who he is* **2** [P] one's relatives or family: *Only a few of his kindred were present at his funeral* —compare KIN

kindred² *adj* [Wa5;A] **1** related; belonging to the same group: *Italian and Spanish are kindred languages with the same origin* **2 kindred spirit** a person with almost the same habits, interests, etc.: *He and I are kindred spirits: we both enjoy music and football*

kine /kaɪn/ *n* [P] *old use* cattle

ki·net·ic /kɪˈnetɪk, kaɪ-/ *adj* [Wa5] *fml and tech* of or about movement —**~ally** *adv* [Wa4]

kinetic art /·,·· ˈ·/ *n* [U] art that includes the use of moving objects

kinetic en·er·gy /·,·· ˈ···/ *n* [U] the power of something moving, such as running water

ki·net·ics /kɪˈnetɪks, kaɪ-/ *n* [U] the science that studies the action of force in producing or changing movement

kin·folk /ˈkɪnfəʊk/ *n* [P] KINSFOLK

king /kɪŋ/ *n* **1** [C (*of*); A] (*sometimes cap.*) (the title of) the male ruler of a country, usu. the son of a former ruler: *the King of Spain|King Edward* **2** [C (*of*)] a man who has more importance, ability, or power than all or most others in the same group: *a king among men* **3** [C (*of*)] the most important member of a group: *The lion is the king of the* JUNGLE **4** [C] (in certain games played on a table) **a** the most important piece **b** a very important piece **c** any of the 4 playing cards with a picture of a king —see CARDS, CHESS (USAGE) **5 uncrowned king (of)** someone who is thought by most people to be the best (in): *Joe Bloggs, the uncrowned king of British car racing*

king·cup /ˈkɪŋkʌp/ *n* any of several types of small plant with bright yellow flowers; type of large BUTTERCUP

king·dom /ˈkɪŋdəm/ *n* **1** [C] a country governed by a king (or queen) **2** [C] an area over which someone or something has complete control: *The cook's kitchen is her kingdom* **3** [C9] any of the 3 great divisions of natural objects: *the animal/vegetable/mineral kingdom* **4 the Kingdom of God** the rule of God **5 kingdom come** the state after death: *She's dead I tell you—she's gone to kingdom come!*
USAGE A **kingdom** may be ruled over by a **queen**, like Britain at present.

king·fish·er /ˈkɪŋˌfɪʃəʳ/ *n* a type of small bird with brightly-coloured feathers that feeds on fish in rivers, lakes, etc. —see picture at BIRD

King James Ver·sion /ˌkɪŋ ˈdʒeɪmz ˌvɜːʃən‖-ˌvɜrʒən/ *n* [*the*+R] AUTHORIZED VERSION

king·ly /ˈkɪŋli/ *adj* [Wa2] that belongs or is suitable to a king: *Not all kings behave in a kingly way*

king·mak·er /ˈkɪŋˌmeɪkəʳ/ *n* a person who has the power to influence appointments to very high political office

king pair /ˌ· ˈ·/ *n infml* (in cricket) a PAIR¹ (7) made by twice being dismissed in one match at one's first attempt to hit the ball

king·pin /ˈkɪŋˌpɪn/ *n* the most important person in a group, upon whom the success of the group depends

Kings /kɪŋz/ *n* [R] (the name of) either of 2 of the parts (books) of the older division of the Bible (the OLD TESTAMENT): *First Kings* (*the First Book of King's*) *tells the story*

King's Bench /ˌ· ˈ·/ also **King's Bench Di·vi·sion** /ˌ· ˈ· ·ˌ··/— *n* (the name given, while a king is ruling, to) a division of the High Court of Justice in England —compare QUEEN'S BENCH

King's Coun·sel /ˌ· ˈ··/ *n fml* K.C.

King's Eng·lish /ˌ· ˈ··/ *n* [*the*+R] see ENGLISH

king's ev·i·dence /ˌ· ˈ···/ also **queen's evidence,** (*AmE*) **state's evidence**— *n* (*often caps.*) **turn king's evidence** *BrE* (of a criminal) to give information in a court of law against other criminals in order to get less punishment

king's e·vil /ˌ· ˈ··/ *n* [*the*+R] *old use* (*sometimes caps.*) a disease once believed to be curable by a king's touch; SCROFULA

king·ship /ˈkɪŋʃɪp/ *n* **1** the condition of being a king **2** the official position of a king **3** *rare* the period of rule of a king

kink /kɪŋk/ *n* **1** a backward turn or twist in hair, a rope, chain, pipe, etc. **2** a peculiarity of the mind or character

kink·y /ˈkɪŋki/ *adj* [Wa1] **1** (esp. of hair) having a KINK or kinks **2** having or showing a strange character or way of behaving

-kins /kɪnz/ *suffix* -KIN

kins·folk /ˈkɪnzfəʊk/ also **kinfolk**— *n* [P] members of one's family: *He has no kinsfolk in America*

kin·ship /ˈkɪnʃɪp/ *n* [U;S] **1** family relationships: *The kinship system of that tribe includes many more people as relatives than we do* **2** likeness (in character, understanding, etc.): *There is a strong feeling of kinship between them even though they have only just met*

kins·man /ˈkɪnzmən/ *fem.* **kins·wo·man** /-ˌwʊmən/— *n* **-men** /mən/ *old use* a relative

ki·osk /ˈkiːɒsk‖-ɑsk/ *n* **1** a small open hut, such as one used for selling newspapers **2** *BrE fml* a public telephone box, indoors or outdoors

kip¹ /kɪp/ *n BrE* **1** [S;U] *infml* (a period of) sleep: *to have a kip|Did you get enough kip last night?* **2** [C] *sl* a place to sleep: *to find a kip for the night*

kip² *v* **-pp-** *BrE infml* **1** [I∅] to sleep **2** [L9 (DOWN)] to go to bed: *Let's kip (down) here for the night*

kip·per /ˈkɪpəʳ/ also (*fml*) **kippered her·ring** /ˌ·· ˈ··/— *n* a salted fish (HERRING) that is cut open and preserved by being treated with smoke

kirk /kɜːk‖kɜrk/ *n ScotE* a church

Kirk *n* [*the*+R] *ScotE* CHURCH OF SCOTLAND

kirsch /kɪəʃ‖kɪərʃ (*Ger* kɪrʃ)/ *n* [U] a strong alcoholic drink made from the juice of the CHERRY (=a type of fruit) and which may be served after meals

kir·tle /ˈkɜːtl‖ˈkɜrtl/ *n old use* **1** a woman's loose outer garment or skirt **2** a sort of shirt or short coat worn by men

kis·met /ˈkɪzmet, ˈkɪs-/ *n* [R] *lit* (the Turkish word for) fate

kiss¹ /kɪs/ *v* **1** [T1] to touch with the lips as a sign of love or as a greeting: *He took her in his arms and kissed her/her lips/her on the lips* **2** [D1;X9, esp. AWAY] to express or put into a given state by kissing: *He kissed his wife and children good-bye.|She kissed away his tears* **3** [T1] (in BILLIARDS) (of a ball) to hit against (another ball) **4** [I∅] to kiss each other: *They kissed when they met.|The 2 balls kissed.|They kissed good-bye when they went away* **5** [T1] (not of people) to touch gently: *The wind kissed her hair* **6 kiss hands** (in Britain) to kiss the king's or queen's hand on first taking a high position in the national government **7 kiss the book** to kiss the Bible on making a solemn promise, such as to tell the truth in a court of law **8 kiss the rod** to accept punishment without complaining, as if kissing the stick that beats you **9 kiss the dust/ground a** to show acceptance of complete defeat **b** to be completely defeated (or killed) —**~able** *adj*

kiss² *n* **1** an act of kissing **2 kiss of life** *esp. BrE* a

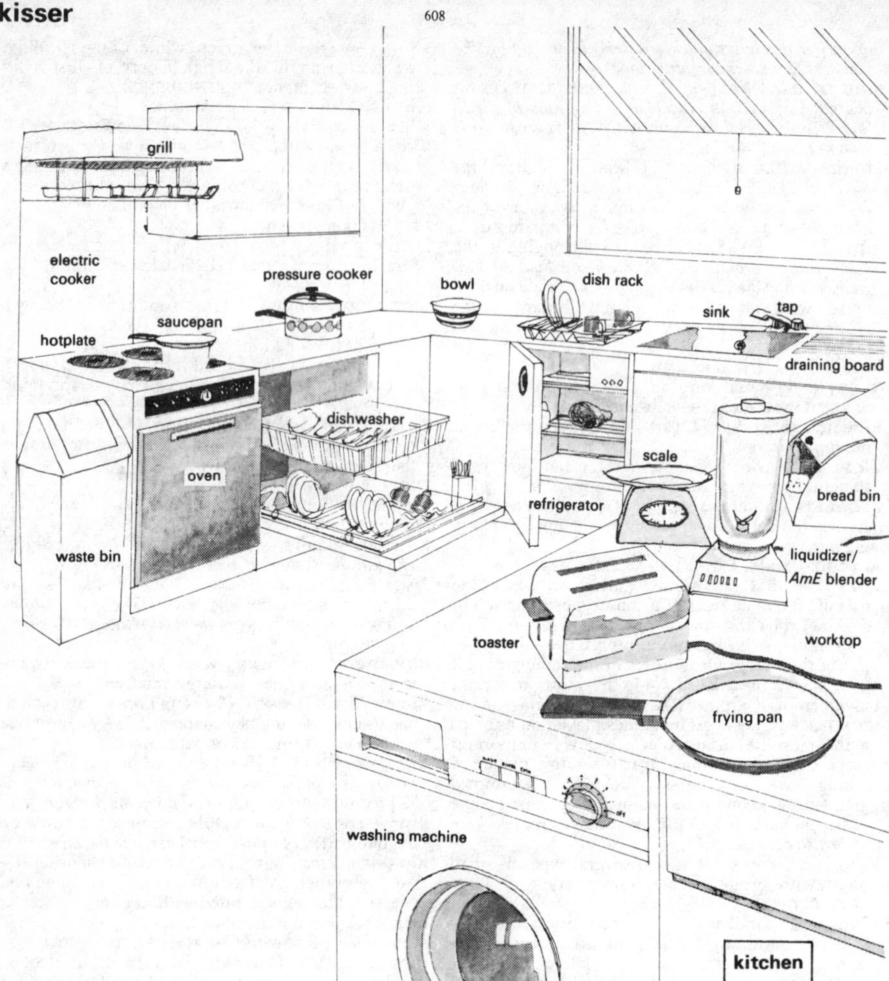

method of preventing the death of a drowning person by breathing into his mouth: (fig.) *The government gave that business the kiss of life by voting it more money* **3 kiss of death** *infml* something that makes failure certain: *Everyone hates John so much that his approval of the plan will give it the kiss of death*

kiss·er /ˈkɪsəʳ/ *n* **1** a person who kisses **2** *sl* the mouth

kit /kɪt/ *n* **1** [U] *esp. BrE* the clothes and other articles needed by a soldier, sailor, etc., or carried by a traveller: *Don't lose any of your kit.|camping kit* **2** [C] (a box for) a set of articles, esp. tools, needed for a certain kind of work, or for a particular purpose: *This toy aircraft is made from a kit* (= a set of small separate pieces) **3 the whole kit and caboodle** *AmE sl* the whole lot; everything: *Let's sell the whole kit and caboodle* —see also KIT OUT

kit bag /ˈ· ·/ *n esp. BrE* a long narrow bag used by soldiers, sailors, etc., for carrying KIT (1)

kitch·en /ˈkɪtʃɪ̣n/ *n* **1** a room used for cooking **2 everything/all but the kitchen sink** *humor* a very large amount, esp. more than is thought necessary: *He's only staying 3 days, but he arrived here with everything but the kitchen sink* (= lots of bags, cases, etc.)

USAGE A **kitchen** is a room, a **cooker** or (cooking) STOVE is a machine, and a **cook** is a person. —see also COOKING, CUISINE

kitch·en·ette /ˌkɪtʃɪ̣ˈnet/ *n* a very small kitchen, or a separate part of a larger room used for cooking

kitchen gar·den /ˌ·· ˈ··/ *n* a garden where fruit and vegetables are grown, usu. for eating at home rather than for sale

kitchen maid /ˈ·· ·/ *n* a female servant who works in a large home kitchen, helping the cook

kitchen-sink dra·ma /ˌ·· · ˈ··/ *n* [U;C] a serious play or plays about working-class home life, esp. as written in Britain in the late 1950's and the 1960's

kite /kaɪt/ *n* **1** a type of large bird (HAWK) that kills and eats small birds and animals **2** a frame of very light wood or metal covered with paper or cloth for flying in the air, often as a plaything, at the end of a long string **3 fly a kite** to say or do something to test whether other people are for or against a possible course of action **4 Go fly a kite!** *sl esp. AmE* Go away!

kith and kin /ˌkɪθ ən ˈkɪn/ *n* **1** [P9] (friends, esp. from one's own country, and) relatives: *We may* *not agree with their politics, but we must remember that they are our kith and kin* **2** [S9] one of these: *Don't quarrel with him; he's your own kith and kin*

kit out also **kit up**— *v adv* **-tt-** [T1 (*with*) *often pass.*] to supply (someone or something, such as a ship) with necessary things, esp. clothes: *all kitted out (with clothes) for the holiday*

kitsch /kɪtʃ/ *n* [U] *derog* popular ornamental objects, works of literature, etc., which pretend to be art but are considered to be silly, funny, or worthless —**~y** *adj* [Wa1]

kit·ten /ˈkɪtn/ *n* **1** a young cat **2 have kittens** *BrE infml* to be in a very nervous anxious condition

kit·ten·ish /ˈkɪtənɪʃ/ *adj* of or like a KITTEN, esp. in being playful —**~ly** *adv*

kit·ti·wake /ˈkɪtiweɪk/ *n* any of several kinds of seabird (GULL¹) with long wings

kit·ty¹ /ˈkɪti/ *n* [C;N] (*used esp. by or to children*) a cat or KITTEN: *"Here, kitty kitty," called the little girl*

kitty² *n* **1** (in some card games) a sum of money put out by all the players at the beginning and taken by the winner **2** *infml* a sum of money collected by a group of people such as the members of a family, and used for an agreed purpose

ki·wi /ˈkiːwiː/ *n* **-s 1** a type of New Zealand bird with very short wings that cannot fly **2** (*usu. cap.*) *sl* a New Zealander

klax·on /ˈklæksən/ *n* (the sound of) a very loud hard-sounding horn

Kleen·ex /ˈkliːneks/ *n* [U;C *usu. sing.*] *tdmk* (a sheet of) thin soft paper, used instead of a handkerchief

klep·to·ma·ni·a /ˌkleptəˈmeɪnɪə/ *n* [U] a disease of the mind causing an uncontrollable desire to steal

klep·to·ma·ni·ac /ˌkleptəˈmeɪniæk/ *n* a person suffering from KLEPTOMANIA

km *written abbrev. for:* kilometre(s)

knack /næk/ *n* [(*of*) *usu. sing.*] *infml* a special skill or ability (to do something successful), usu. the result of practice: *He has a/the knack of making friends wherever he goes*

knack·er /ˈnækəʳ/ *n BrE* **1** a person who kills horses that are no longer fit for work and sells various parts of them, such as their flesh as animal food **2** a person who buys and breaks up old buildings, ships, etc., in order to sell the materials in them that are still of use

knack·ered /ˈnækəd‖-ərd/ *adj* [F] *BrE sl* very tired

knacker's yard /ˌ·· ˈ·/ *n* a KNACKER's place of business

knap·sack /ˈnæpsæk/ *n becoming rare* RUCKSACK

knave /neɪv/ *n* **1** *old use* a dishonest man, whose actions are dishonourable or deceitful **2** JACK (2) —**knavish** *adj* —**knavishly** *adv* —**knavishness** *n* [U]

knav·e·ry /ˈneɪvəri/ *n* [C;U] *old use* (an example of) bad behaviour, as of a KNAVE (1)

knead /niːd/ *v* [T1;(I∅)] **1** to mix together and make a paste of (something, such as flour and water for making bread) by pressing with the hands **2** to press or make other movements on (a muscle or other part of the body) to cure pain, stiffness, etc.

knee¹ /niː/ *n* **1** the middle joint of the leg (of people, animals, and long-legged birds), where the leg bends: *to move about on one's hands and knees instead of walking* —see picture at HUMAN² **2** the part of a garment (esp. trousers) that covers the knee: *big holes in the knees of his old trousers* **3 gone at the knees** *infml* (of trousers) having the knees torn, worn, or stretched out of shape because of much use **4 learn something at one's mother's knee** to learn something from one's mother or when one was very young **5 bring someone to his knees** to defeat someone completely, and force him to admit defeat **6 bend the knee to (someone)** to admit that (someone) is master **7 go/fall on one's knees** to admit defeat and ask for mercy

knee² *v* **-d** [T1 (*in*)] to hit with the knee: *Knee him in the stomach, Johnny boy!*

knee breech·es /ˈ· ˌ··/ *n* [P] short trousers reaching to, and fitting tightly, just below the knee, esp. as worn by certain officials at court on ceremonial occasions

knee·cap¹ /ˈniːkæp/ *n* **1** the bone in front of the knee —see picture at SKELETON **2** a covering worn to protect the knee

kneecap² *v* [T1] to shoot the KNEECAPs¹ (1) off (someone)

knee-deep /ˌ· ˈ·◂/ *adj* [Wa5] **1** [B] deep enough to reach the knees: *The water is knee-deep.|knee-deep water* **2** [F+*in*] in trouble (over): *knee-deep in debt*

knee-high /ˌ· ˈ·◂/ *adj* [Wa5] high or tall enough to reach the knees: *I knew that man when he was only knee-high!* —see also **knee-high to a** GRASSHOPPER

kneel /niːl/ *v* **knelt** /nelt/ [I∅ (DOWN, *on*)] to go down or remain on the knee(s): *She went into the church, knelt (down) and began to pray*
USAGE **Knelt** is more common in *BrE* than **kneeled**, except in literature, but **kneeled** is more common in *AmE.*

knell /nel/ *n* **1** the sound of a bell rung on a sad occasion, esp. for a death or funeral **2** anything showing or warning of something sad or the end of something happy: *His failure sounds the knell of all his hopes*

knew /njuː‖nuː/ *past t. of* KNOW¹

knick·er·bock·ers /ˈnɪkəˌbɒkəz‖ˈnɪkərˌbɑkərz/ *n* [P] short loose trousers made to fit tightly round the legs just below the knees, worn esp. in former times —see PAIR¹ (USAGE); compare PLUS FOURS

knick·ers¹ /ˈnɪkəz‖-ərz/ *n* [P] **1** *BrE infml* women's UNDERPANTS **2** *esp. AmE* KNICKERBOCKERS **3 get one's knickers in a twist** *BrE often humor* to become angry and/or annoyed —see PAIR¹ (USAGE)

knickers² *interj BrE sl* (an expression of annoyance)

knick-knack, nicknack /ˈnɪk næk/ *n infml* a small object of any type used as an ornament for the house or clothing

knife¹ /naɪf/ *n* **knives** /naɪvz/ **1** a blade fixed in a handle used for cutting as a tool or weapon **2 under the knife** during a medical operation on the body: *The sick man died under the knife* **3 have/get one's knife in someone** *infml* to treat someone as an enemy and always try to harm him: *Be careful with George; he wants to get his knife in you* **4 before you can/could say "knife"** *BrE sl becoming rare* very quickly: *She ran off before you could say "knife"*
USAGE Note the word order in this fixed phr.: **knife and fork**: *Put your knife and fork down on the plate if you've finished eating.*

knife² *v* [T1 (*in*)] to strike with a knife used as a weapon: *During the fight he was knifed in the back*

knife-edge /ˈ· ·/ *n* **1** [C] a long sharp line of rocks **2** [A] (esp. of the folds (PLEATs) of a dress or trousers) with sharp folds **3 on a knife-edge a** (of a person) very anxious about the future result of something: *on a knife-edge about the examinations* **b** delicately balanced with the results extremely uncertain: *The success or failure of the plan was balanced on a knife-edge*

knight¹ /naɪt/ *n* **1** (in former times) a noble soldier on horseback serving a ruler **2** a man who has been given a certain title of honour by the king or queen of England, which title has a rank below the rank of LORD¹ (2): *Sir George (Smith) was made a knight for his service to his country* **3** (in CHESS) a piece, usu. with a horse's head, that moves 2 squares forward in a straight line and one to the side —see CHESS (USAGE)

knight² *v* [T1] to make (someone) a KNIGHT: *Sir George (Smith) has been knighted by the Queen*

knight-er·rant /ˌ· ˈ··/ *n* **knights-errant** *old use* a KNIGHT who rode in search of brave and noble deeds to perform

knight·hood /ˈnaɪthʊd/ *n* **1** [C;U] the rank, title, or state of a KNIGHT **2** [*the*+R] the set of all KNIGHTs: *The knighthood of England suffered heavy losses in the Wars of the Roses* **3** [U] the beliefs and values of KNIGHTs: *The golden age of knighthood was a long time ago*

knight·ly /ˈnaɪtli/ *adj* [Wa2] of or like (the acts of) a KNIGHT, esp. in being brave or noble

knit /nɪt/ *v* **knitted** *or* **knit** **1** [D1 (*for*); T1;I0] to make (things to wear) by uniting threads into a kind of close network by means of long needles: *She's knitting her husband a pair of socks* **2** [T1;L9] *tech* (*often used in giving instructions*) to use the commonest stitch in this activity (for a time): *Knit one,* PURL *one.|Knit to the last 10 stitches, then turn the needles and knit back* —see also PLAIN³ **3** [T1; I0: (TOGETHER)] to unite or join closely (people or things): *I hope the 2 edges of that broken bone will knit (together) smoothly* —see also **knit one's** BROWs

knit·ter /ˈnɪtəʳ/ *n* a person who makes things to wear by KNITting

knit·ting /ˈnɪtɪŋ/ *n* [U] that which is being KNITted: *She keeps her knitting in a bag*

knit up *v adv* **1** [T1] to complete by KNITting: *knit up this pattern|knit up this collar* **2** [I0] to be suitable for KNITting: *This wool knits up well*

knit·wear /ˈnɪt-weəʳ/ *n* [U] KNITted clothing: *This shop sells knitwear*

knives /naɪvz/ *pl. of* KNIFE¹

knob /nɒb‖nɑb/ *n* **1** a round lump on the surface or at the end of something: *a stick with a big knob on the end* **2** round handle or control button: *He opened the door by turning the knob (the doorknob)* **3** any small round lump: *a knob of butter*

knob·bly /ˈnɒbli‖ˈnɑbli/ (*AmE* **knob·by** /ˈnɒbi‖ˈnɑbi/)— *adj* [Wa1] *BrE* having round KNOBlike lumps: *He has very thin legs and knobbly knees*

knob·ker·rie /ˈnɒbkeri‖ˈnɑb-/ *n* a short stick with a round head formerly used as a weapon by some South African black tribes

knock¹ /nɒk‖nɑk/ *v* **1** [I0] to strike a blow, intentionally or unintentionally, usu. making a noise when doing so: *Please knock (on/at the door) before entering* **2** [X9 esp. *on*] to hit hard: *He knocked the fish on the head to kill it quickly* **3** [X7,9] to bring into a certain state by hitting hard: *She knocked him senseless/down/into a corner* **4** [T1] *sl* to express unfavourable opinions about (someone or something): *Don't knock other dictionaries just because they aren't as good as this one* **5** [I0] (of an engine) to make a noise because of something wrong with the machinery: *This old car engine has been knocking a lot recently* **6** [T1] *BrE sl* to surprise greatly; shock: *Her words really knocked me* **7 knock the bottom out of** to cause to fail: *Her refusal has knocked the bottom out of my plans.|His reasoning knocked the bottom out of my argument* **8 knock on the head** to put an end to (a hope, plan, suggestions, etc.): *Her refusal has knocked all my careful plans on the head* **9 knock spots off someone (at something)** to do or be much better than someone (at something): *He can knock spots off me at almost any game we play* **10 knock someone cold/out a** to knock someone senseless **b** also **knock someone sideways/for a loop/for six**—to surprise and usu. make unable to act in reply: *Her unexpected words knocked me cold* **11 you could have knocked me down/over with a feather** I was very surprised —see also KNOCK ABOUT¹,², KNOCK BACK, KNOCK DOWN, KNOCK INTO, KNOCK OFF, KNOCK ON, KNOCK OUT, KNOCK TOGETHER, KNOCK UP

knock² *n* **1** (the sound of) a blow: *a knock at the door* **2** (one) sound made by an engine KNOCKing¹ (5) **3** a piece of bad luck or trouble: *He's taken/had quite a few knocks lately* **4** *infml* (in cricket) a player's INNINGS

knock·a·bout /ˈnɒkəbaʊt‖ˈnɑ-/ *adj* [Wa5;A] **1** (of a theatre performance, a cinema film, or a performer) causing laughter by rough noisy acting; SLAPSTICK **2** (of clothes, cars, etc.) suitable for rough use

knock a·bout¹ also **knock a·round**— *v prep* [T1 *no pass.*] *infml* to lie unnoticed in (a place): *That old thing has been knocking about the house for years*

knock about² also **knock around**— *v adv infml* **1** [L9] to be present or active: *"Who's that man? I've not seen him before." "Oh, he's been knocking about here for years"* **2** [I0] to travel continuously: *He's knocked about in Africa for years* **3** [I0 (*with,* TOGETHER)] to be seen in public (with someone); have a relationship, often sexual, (with someone): *Sally's been knocking about with Jim for years* **4** [T1b] to treat (someone or something) roughly: *They say he knocks his wife about*

knock back *v adv infml, esp. BrE* **1** [T1a] to drink (something) quickly or in large quantities: *She knocked back 10 glasses of wine* **2** [D1 *no pass.*] to cost: *That car must have knocked her back a few pounds* **3** [T1] to surprise (someone): *The news knocked him back*

knock·down¹ /ˈnɒkdaʊn‖ˈnɑk-/ *n* a knocking-down of one fighter (BOXER⁴) by another: *The first knockdown came soon after the beginning of the match*

knockdown² *adj* [Wa5] **1** that causes a fall or an unpleasant surprise (esp. in the phr. **knockdown blow**): *The news of his failure came as a knockdown blow to him* **2** the lowest acceptable or possible (esp. in the phr. **knockdown price**): *He couldn't sell them even at the knockdown price*

knock down *v adv* **1** [T1 *often pass.*] to destroy (a building, bridge, etc.) by means of blows: *Our house is being knocked down to make way for a new road* **2** [T1 *often pass.*] also **knock over**— to strike to the ground with a vehicle: *Alec was knocked down by a bus yesterday* **3** [X9 esp. *to, at, for, often pass.*] (at an AUCTION) to sell (something), usu. at a low price: *The wine was knocked down at £30/was knocked down to Mr. Johnson for £30* **4** [T1b (*to*), *often pass.*] to (cause to) reduce (a price): *The price was knocked down to £3.|I knocked him down to £3*

knock·er /ˈnɒkəʳ‖ˈnɑkəʳ/ *n* **1** a person who knocks **2** also **doorknocker**— a metal instrument fixed to a door and used by visitors for knocking at the door —see picture at DOOR **3** *sl, usu. derog* a person who is always expressing unfavourable opinions about someone or something

knock·ers /ˈnɒkəz‖ˈnɑkərz/ *n* [P] *BrE sl* a woman's breasts

knock in·to *v prep* **1** [D1] to teach (something) by force to (someone): *Knock some sense into him/his head* **2** [T1] to meet unexpectedly; BUMP INTO **3 knock something into shape** to make something more perfect

knock-kneed /ˌ· ˈ·‖ˈ· ·/ *adj* having knees that turn inwards and knock together, or at least touch, when walking (**knock-knees**)

knock off *v adv* **1** [T1a,4;I0] *infml* to stop (work): *Let's knock off (work) early today.|knock off working* **2** [T1,4;I0: *usu. imper.*] *sl* to stop: *Knock off!|Knock it off!* **3** [T1] *infml BrE* to steal (something): *Who's knocked off my coat?* **4** [T1a] *infml* to rob: *They knocked off a bank* **5** [T1] *infml* to murder (someone) **6** [T1] to take (something) from a total payment: *I'll knock $2 off* **7** [T1] *infml* to write (words or music) quickly: *He knocked off a poem in 5 minutes* **8** [T1b] *infml* to finish: *I've a lot of work to knock off before I can take my holiday* **9** [T1a] *infml* to defeat or destroy: *knock off 3 opponents|knock off the whole cake* **10** [T1] *sl* (of a man) to have sex with (a girl or woman)

knock-on /ˌ· ˈ·/ also **knock-for·ward** /ˌ· ˈ··/— *n* (in RUGBY) an act of KNOCKing ON

knock on also **knock for·ward**— *v adv* [T1;I∅] (in RUGBY) to break the rules of the game by causing (the ball) to fall in front of one by dropping a catch

knock·out /ˈnɒk-aʊt‖ˈnɑk-/ *n* **1** also (*infml*) **KO**— a KNOCKing OUT of one fighter (BOXer[4]) by another: *He won the fight by a knockout* —see BOXING, WRESTLE (USAGE) **2** *infml* someone (or something) causing great admiration (or surprise): *You really look a knockout in your new dress*

knock out *v adv* [T1] **1** (in BOXING) to make (one's opponent) lose consciousness or be unable to rise before a count of 10 seconds **2** *infml* to surprise (someone) **3** (of a drug) to make (someone) go to sleep **4** [*often pass.*] to cause (someone) to be dismissed from a competition: *Our team was knocked out in the first part of the competition* **5** *infml* to play roughly: *He knocked out a tune on the piano* —see also **knock the** BOTTOM (15) **out of**

knock to·geth·er *v adv* [T1] **1** to make (something) roughly, without care **2 knock people's heads together** to make people see sense

knock-up /ˈ· ·/ *n BrE* (esp. in tennis) an act or period of KNOCKing UP (6)

knock up *v adv* **1** [T1] *BrE infml, usu. derog* to build in a hurry: *This house was just knocked up* **2** [T1] *BrE infml* to make (something) in a hurry: *Can you knock up a meal for us now?* **3** [T1] *BrE infml* to make (money): *Andrew knocked up over £4,000 last year* **4** [T1] *BrE infml* (in cricket) to add to the number of runs already made: *The team needs to knock up 45 more runs before tea* **5** [T1b] *BrE infml* to awaken by knocking: *Knock me up at 7.30* **6** [I∅] *BrE* (esp. in tennis) to practise before beginning a real game **7** [T1] *AmE taboo sl* to cause (a woman) to become PREGNANT: *Marty knocked up his girl friend and her family are causing trouble* **8** [T1 *usu. pass.*] *BrE infml* to tire (someone): *The long journey knocked the old lady up* **9 knock up copy** *BrE tech* to prepare writing for printing

knoll /nəʊl/ *n* a small round hill

knot[1] /nɒt‖nɑt/ *n* **1** a lumplike fastening formed by tying together the ends of a piece or pieces of string, rope, wire, etc.: *She tied her belt with a knot* **2** an ornament or sign of military rank in the shape of a knot **3** a hard mass in wood where a branch has come off a tree **4** a hard swelling or mass: *The muscles of his arms stood out in knots as he lifted the heavy box* **5** a small group of people close together: *a knot of whisperers* **6** something that unites people (esp. in the phr. **the marriage knot**) **7** a measure of the speed of a ship, about 1,853 metres (about 6,080 feet) per hour **8 get tied (up) into knots (over)** to become confused (about) **9 tie someone (up) in knots** to confuse someone —see also GORDIAN KNOT

knot[2] *v* **-tt- 1** [X9 esp. TOGETHER; (T1)] to make a knot in or join (a piece or pieces of string, rope, wire, etc.) together with a knot: *to knot the rope tightly|Knot the end of the thread before you begin sewing* **2** [T1] to fasten with knots: *to knot a parcel* **3** [I∅] to allow knots to be tied: *This wire is too stiff to knot easily*

knot·hole /ˈnɒthəʊl‖ˈnɑt-/ *n* a hole in a piece of wood where a KNOT[1] (3) used to be

knot·ty /ˈnɒti‖ˈnɑti/ *adj* [Wa2] **1** containing one or more KNOTs[1] (3) **2** full of difficulties: *a knotty question, hard to answer*

knout /naʊt/ *n* a type of whip formerly used in Russia to punish people

know[1] /nəʊ/ *v* **knew** /njuː‖nuː/, **known** /nəʊn/ [Wv6] **1** [T1,5a,(b);I∅] to have (information) in the mind: *I know (that) that is true.|I know what happened.|You can be sure that he knows (it) by now* **2** [T6a,b] to have learnt: *I know how to swim|where to go|how that should be done* **3** [X *to be* 1] to accept the fact that . . .: *I know him to be a fool* **4** [V3, (*BrE*)2: (*past and perfect tenses only*)] to have seen, heard, etc.: *I've known him to run|(BrE) run faster than that* **5** [T1] to have experienced: *He has known both grief and happiness* **6** [T1] to have met and spoken to (someone) several times: *I've known Martin for years* **7** [T1 (*by*)] to be able to recognize: *She knows a good wine when she tastes it.|You'll know him by the colour of his hair* **8** [I∅] to agree: *"He's very ill." "Yes, I know"* **9 know a thing or two/the ropes/one's onions** *infml* to have practical useful information gained from experience **10 know one's business** to be good at one's business **11 know what one's talking about** to speak from experience **12 know one's own mind** to know what one wants **13 know all the answers** *infml derog* to behave as if one knew everything **14 you know** (used for adding force to a statement): *You'll have to try harder, you know, if you want to succeed.|You know (very well) that you shouldn't do that!* **15 (well) what do you know (about that)!** *AmE infml* (used as an expression of surprise) —see also **know** APART[1] (7), **know** BACKWARDS (7), KNOW ABOUT, KNOW BETTER, KNOW FROM, KNOW OF

USAGE To **learn** is to get to know (a fact or subject, not a person): *He's* **learning** *French*/**learning** *(how) to cook.*|**learning** *all about Africa|He* **learnt** *of his son's behaviour*/**learnt** *that he was wrong*. To **know** is to be conscious of (something the speaker thinks is true) or to have complete skill in (a subject): *She* **knows** *French* (not **is* **knowing**)/**knows** *how to* cook (not ***knows** *to cook*) /**knows** *all about Africa*/**knows** *of her son's behaviour*/**knows** *(that) she's wrong*. **Know** is also the word used about people whom one has met before: *I don't* **know** *him; he's a stranger*.

know[2] *n* **in the know** well-informed; having more information (about something) than most people

know a·bout *v prep* [T1,4,6a,b] to have learnt about: *I know about that|swimming|how to do it|how it should be done*

know-all /ˈ· ·/ also **know-it-all** /ˈ· · ˌ·/— *n derog* a person who behaves as if he knew everything

know bet·ter *v adv* [I∅ (*than*)] **1** to be wise or well-trained enough (not to): *She is old enough to know better than to spend all her money on clothes* **2** *derog* to think that one knows more (than someone or anyone else): *I suppose you think you know better than your parents!*

know from *v prep* [D1 *usu. nonassertive*] **1** to be able to tell the difference between (someone or something) and (someone or something else): *He doesn't know his left from his right* **2 I don't know from nothing (about it)** *AmE nonstandard* I don't know anything (about it) **3 not know someone from Adam** *infml* not to know who someone (esp. a man) is: *I've met her several times, but she says she doesn't know me from Adam*

know-how /ˈ· ·/ *n* [U] *infml* practical ability or skill; "knowing how" to do something

know·ing[1] /ˈnəʊɪŋ/ *adj* (showing that one is) well-informed or possessing secret understanding:

a knowing person/smile|He said nothing but gave us a knowing look

knowing² *n* **there's no knowing** it's impossible to know: *There's no knowing what their next move will be/what the weather will be*

know·ing·ly /ˈnəʊɪŋli/ *adv* **1** in a KNOWING¹ manner **2** intentionally; with knowledge of the probable effect: *She would never knowingly hurt anyone*

knowl·edge /ˈnɒlɪdʒ‖ˈnɑ-/ *n* [U;S] **1** understanding: *a knowledge of/not much knowledge of the truth* **2** learning; that which is known: *Knowledge is power.|a knowledge of/not much knowledge of French* **3** familiarity (familiarness) with; information about: *He has a good knowledge of London* **4 bring to someone's knowledge** to cause someone to know: *The matter was never brought to the knowledge of the minister* **5 come to someone's knowledge** to become known to (by) someone: *The matter never came to the knowledge of the minister* **6 to the best of one's knowledge (and belief)** so far as one knows: *I am not quite sure, but to the best of my knowledge his story is true* **7 to one's knowledge** so far as one knows: *He has been there several times to my knowledge* **8 without someone's knowledge** although someone did not know: *He left home without his wife's knowledge* —compare LEARNING

knowl·edge·a·ble /ˈnɒlɪdʒəbəl‖ˈnɑ-/ *adj* (of a person) having a good deal of knowledge; well-informed: *He's very knowledgeable about wines* —**-bly** *adv*: *He speaks very knowledgeably about wines*

known¹ /nəʊn/ *adj* [Wa5] **1** [A] also **well-known**— generally recognized (as being something): *He's a known criminal* **2 known as a** generally recognised as: *She's known as a great singer* **b** also publicly called; named: *Samuel Clemens, known as Mark Twain, became a famous American writer* **3 known to** also **well-known to**— known by: *He's known to everyone as a good actor.|He's known to the police (as a criminal)* **4 make it known that . . .** *fml* to declare or cause to know that . . . : *He made it known to his friends that he did not want to enter politics* **5 make oneself known to** *fml* to introduce oneself to

known² *past p. of* KNOW¹

know of *v prep* [T1] **1** to have heard of or about (a person): *I know of him, but I can't really say that I know him* **2 Not that I know of** not so far as I know; not to my knowledge

knuck·le /ˈnʌkəl/ *n* **1** a finger joint —see picture at HUMAN² **2 (to) rap over the knuckles a** (to give) a hard blow on the knuckles, esp. as a punishment for schoolboys **b** (to make) an attack with sharp words: *He rapped the government over the knuckles for wasting public money* **3 near the knuckle** almost improper: *That joke of his was a bit near the knuckle, don't you think?*

knuckle down *v adv* [IØ (*to*)] to start working hard: *You'll really have to knuckle down if you want to pass the examination.|He knuckled down to the job/to finding the answer*

knuckle-dust·er /ˈ·· ˌ··/ *AmE* usu. **brass knuckles**— *n* a metal covering for the KNUCKLEs, worn to make more damaging a blow with the closed hand

knuckle un·der *v adv* [IØ (*to*)] to admit defeat; yield

KO¹ /ˌ· ˈ·/ *n infml* KNOCKOUT (1)

KO² *v* [T1] *infml* to KNOCK OUT (1): *Ali KO'd him right at the start of the fight*

ko·a·la /kəʊˈɑːlə/ also **koala bear** /·ˌ·· ˈ·/— *n* a type of Australian animal like a small bear with no tail, which climbs trees and is covered with fur

kohl /kəʊl/ *n* [U] a powder used in the East by women to darken the skin above the eyes

kohl·ra·bi /ˌkəʊlˈrɑːbi/ *n* [U;C] a type of CABBAGE (a vegetable) used for food

kook·a·bur·ra /ˈkʊkəbʌrə/ also **laughing jackass**— *n* a type of Australian bird with a cry like laughter

ko·peck, -pek /ˈkəʊpek/ *n* the 100th part of a ROUBLE, money used in the Soviet Union

kop·je, koppie /ˈkɒpi‖ˈkɑpi/ *n* a small low hill in South Africa

Ko·ran /kɔːˈrɑːn, kəˈrɑːn, ˈkɔːræn‖kəˈræn, -ˈrɑn, ˈkoræn/ *n* [*the*+R] the holy book of the Muslims —**~ic** *adj* [Wa5]

ko·sher /ˈkəʊʃəʳ/ *adj* **1** [Wa5] of or about food, esp. meat, which it is lawful for Jews to eat: *kosher meat|a kosher restaurant* **2** *infml* proper: *We found things going on that were not kosher*

kow·tow¹ /ˌkaʊˈtaʊ/ also **ko·tow** /ˌkəʊ-/— *n* a former Chinese ceremony of touching the ground with the head as a sign of respect, of yielding, etc.

kowtow² also **kotow**— *v* [IØ (*to*)] **1** to perform a KOWTOW¹ **2** to obey without question; be too humble (towards): *Be polite, but don't kowtow (to him)*

kraal /krɑːl/ *n* **1** a type of village built by black South Africans, with a fence around it **2** *SAfrE* an enclosed piece of ground in which cows, sheep, etc., are kept at night

Krem·lin /ˈkremlɪ̣n/ *n* **1** [*the*+R] the group of buildings in Moscow which are the centre of the government of the Soviet Union **2** [*the*+GU] the government of the Soviet Union: *How will the Kremlin answer the latest message from Washington?*

kris /kriːs/ *n* (in Malaysia or Indonesia) a knife with a wavy blade, used as a weapon

kro·na /ˈkrəʊnə/ *n* **-nor** /nɔːʳ/ the standard coin in the money system of Sweden

kro·ne /ˈkrəʊnə/ *n* **-ner** /nəʳ/ the standard coin in the money system of Denmark and Norway

Kt *written abbrev. for:* KNIGHT: *Sir John Falstaff, Kt*

ku·dos /ˈkjuːdɒs‖ˈkuːdɑs/ *n* [U] *esp. BrE* honour, praise, glory, and thanks (for something done): *He got a great deal of kudos for his work at the university*

Ku Klux Klan /ˌkuː klʌks ˈklæn/ *n* [*the*+GU] (in the US, esp. the South-East) a secret political organization whose members must be PROTESTANT white men born in the United States

kuk·ri /ˈkʊkri/ *n* a type of curved knife used as a weapon by the fighting men of Nepal

ku·mis /ˈkuːmɪs/ *n* [U] an alcoholic drink made from horse's milk by the Tartars

küm·mel /ˈkʊməl‖ˈkɪməl (*Ger* ˈkʏməl)/ *n* [U] *Ger* a strong alcoholic drink to which certain plants (HERBs) give a special taste, and which is served after dinner

kum·quat /ˈkʌmkwɒt‖-kwɑt/ *n* a type of small fruit like an orange

kung fu /ˌkʊŋ ˈfuː/ *n* [U] a Chinese style of fighting without weapons that includes blows with the hands and feet, related to KARATE

kuo·min·tang /ˌkwəʊmɪnˈtæŋ/ *n* [*the*+R] a former political party of China

ku·rus /kʊˈrʊʃ/ *n* **kurus** [Wn3] the 100th part of a LIRA¹, money used in Turkey

kvass /kvɑːs/ *n* [U] a slightly alcoholic drink made in Eastern Europe and Russia

kw *written abbrev. for:* KILOWATT(*s*)

kwash·i·or·kor /ˌkwɒʃiˈɔːkəʳ‖ˌkwɑʃiˈɔr-/ *n* [U] a tropical disease of children caused by eating food that does not contain enough PROTEIN

kwe·la /ˈkweɪlə/ *n* [U] a kind of danceable music popular among black South Africans including a type of whistle among its instruments

ky·ri·e e·lei·son /ˌkɪrɪ-i ɪˈleɪsən‖ˌkɪriːeɪ əˈleɪsɑn/ also **kyrie**— *n* [*the*+R] *Gr* (in the ROMAN CATHOLIC church) a prayer for God's mercy, which is the first part of the religious service called the MASS, esp. when performed with music

L, l

L, l /el/ **L's, l's** *or* **Ls, ls** **1** the 12th letter of the English alphabet **2** the ROMAN NUMERAL (number) for 50

l *abbrev. for:* (*often cap.*) (on a map) **1** lake **2** (in Scotland) LOCH **3** (in Ireland) LOUGH

L *abbrev. for:* (*BrE*) (on an L-PLATE) learner; a driver of a car or other motor vehicle who has not passed the official driving test —see also L-DRIVER

la /lɑː/ *n* [C;U] the 6th note in the (SOL-FA) musical scale: *sing (a) la*

laa·ger /ˈlɑːgəʳ/ *n* (esp. formerly in S Afr) a camp surrounded by a circle of carts

lab /læb/ *n infml* a LABORATORY

Lab *abbrev. for:* LABOUR PARTY

la·bel¹ /ˈleɪbəl/ *n* **1** a piece of paper or other material, fixed to something, on which is written what it is, where it is to go, who owns it, etc. **2** a word or phrase describing a group or class

label² *v* **-ll-** (*AmE* **-l-**) [T1;X1,7] **1** to fix or tie a LABEL¹ on: *The doctor labelled the bottle poison/poisonous* **2** to put into a kind or class; describe as: *His enemies labelled the boy a thief*

la·bi·al /ˈleɪbɪəl/ *n, adj* [Wa5] *tech* (a consonant) produced by a lip or the lips

la·bor·a·tory /ləˈbɒrətri‖ˈlæbrətori/ *n* a building or room in which a scientist works, with apparatus for the examination and testing of materials

la·bo·ri·ous /ləˈbɔːrɪəs‖-ˈbor-/ *adj* **1** needing great effort **2** showing signs of being done with difficulty —**~ly** *adv* —**~ness** *n* [U]

la·bour¹, *AmE* **labor** /ˈleɪbəʳ/ *n esp. BrE* **1** [U] work or effort —see WORK¹ (USAGE) **2** [U]

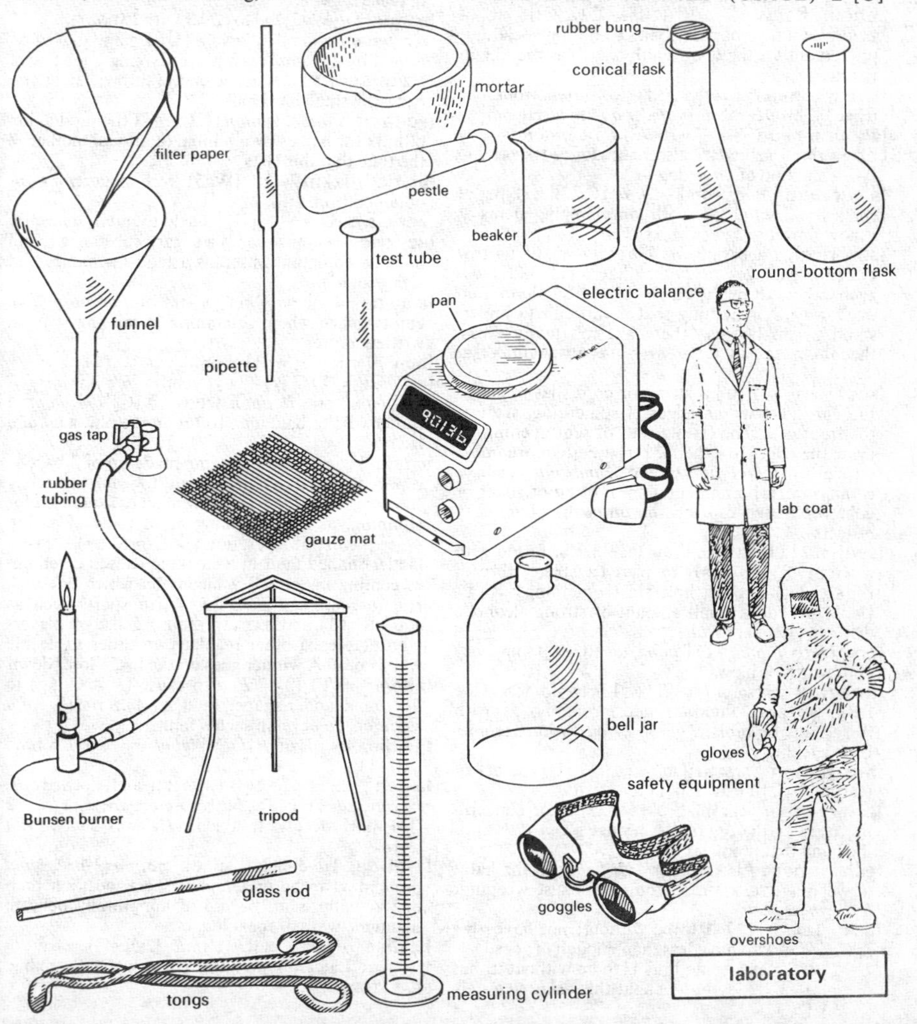

workers, esp. those who use their hands, considered as a class **3** [U;S] the act of giving birth **4** [C] a piece of work —see also HARD LABOUR

labour², *AmE* **labor** *v esp. BrE* **1** [IØ] to work, esp. hard **2** [IØ] to move or act with difficulty; struggle: *She laboured up the hill with her bags* **3** [T1] to work something out in too great detail or at unnecessary length (often in the phr. **labour the point**) **4** [IØ] (of the engine of a motor vehicle) to be working with difficulty at too low a speed

Labour *n, adj* [Wa5;B;R] (supporting or having a connection with) the LABOUR PARTY

Labour Day /'·· ·/ *n* a day when workers make a public show with marches, meetings, etc. (in North America, the first Monday in September)

la·bour·er, *AmE* **laborer** /'leɪbərəʳ/ *n esp. BrE* a worker whose job needs strength rather than skill

labour ex·change /'·· ·,·/ *n* EMPLOYMENT EXCHANGE

La·bour·ite /'leɪbəraɪt/ *n infml* a supporter of the LABOUR PARTY

labour mar·ket /'·· ,··/ *n* [*the*+R] the supply of workers who are ready or suitable for work

labour of love /,·· · '·/ *n* **labours of love** a piece of work done gladly and without thought of gain

Labour Par·ty /'·· ,··/ *n* [*the*+GU;(C)] one of several political parties trying to obtain social improvement for the less wealthy, such as the one in Britain

labour un·der *v prep* [T1] to suffer from; be troubled by: *He laboured under a misunderstanding*

labour u·ni·on /'·· ,···/ *n AmE* TRADE UNION

Lab·ra·dor /'læbrədɔːʳ/ also **Labrador re·triev·er** /,··· ·'··/— *n* a kind of large dog

la·bur·num /lə'bɜːnəm‖-ɜr-/ *n* [C;U] a type of small ornamental tree with long hanging stems of yellow flowers

lab·y·rinth /'læbərɪnθ/ *n* **1** a network of narrow twisting passages or paths that meet and cross each other, through which it is difficult to find one's way **2** something that is difficult to understand or do because there are too many ideas, thoughts, etc., in it —**~ine** /,læbə'rɪnθaɪn, -θən/ *adj* [A;(F)]

lace¹ /leɪs/ *n* **1** [C] a string or cord that is pulled through holes in the edges of something, such as the front of a shoe (SHOELACE) or tent opening, to draw the edges together **2** [U] a netlike ornamental cloth made of fine thread: *handmade lace|lace curtains* **3** [U] ornamental cord, often of silver or gold wire, used esp. on the uniforms of military officers

lace² *v* **1** [T1 (UP)] to draw together or fasten with a LACE¹ **2** [T1 (UP)] to pass (a string, thread, LACE¹, etc.) through holes in (something) **3** [T1 (*with*)] to add a small amount of strong alcoholic drink to (weaker drink)

lace in·to *v prep* [T1] *infml* to attack (someone) with words or blows

la·ce·rate /'læsəreɪt/ *v* [T1] **1** *tech* to tear (the flesh, an arm, the face, etc.) roughly, as with fingernails or broken glass **2** *fml* to hurt (somebody's feelings)

la·ce·ra·tion /,læsə'reɪʃən/ *n tech* **1** [U] the act of tearing **2** [C] a tear, esp. in the flesh

lach·ry·mal /'lækrəməl/ *adj* [Wa5] of or concerning tears or the organ (**lachrymal gland** /'··· ·/) of the body that produces them

lach·ry·mose /'lækrəməʊs/ *adj fml* **1** in the habit of weeping; TEARFUL **2** tending to cause weeping: *lachrymose poetry*

lack¹ /læk/ *v* [T1] **1** to be without; not have: *We lacked food* **2** to have less than enough of; need
USAGE To **lack** something is to be without it, but one may be quite happy about this: *He completely* **lacks** *conscience*. If one is **short** *of* something one has less than enough, and to be *in* **want** *of* it is even stronger; one needs it badly and knows this.

lack² *n* [C;U: (*of*)] absence or need: *The plants died through/for lack of water*

lack·a·dai·si·cal /,lækə'deɪzɪkəl/ *adj* lacking in interest or effort: *too lackadaisical to be a good student* —**-cally** *adv* [Wa4]

lack·ey /'læki/ *n derog* a person who behaves like a servant by obeying others without question

lack for *v prep* [T1] to lack (esp. in the phr. **lack for nothing**)

lack·ing /'lækɪŋ/ *adj* [Wa5;F] **1** not present; missing: *Help was lacking during the storm* **2** *BrE infml* having less than the usual powers of thought **3 be lacking in** to have little of; need

lack·lus·tre, *AmE* **-ter** /'læk,lʌstəʳ/ *adj BrE* (esp. of eyes) lacking brightness; dull

la·con·ic /lə'kɒnɪk‖-'kɑ-/ *adj* using few words —**~ally** *adv* [Wa4]

lac·quer¹ /'lækəʳ/ *n* [C;U] a transparent, sometimes coloured, substance (such as one obtained from SHELLAC) used for forming a hard shiny surface on metal or wood, or for making hair stay in place

lacquer² *v* [Wv5;T1] to cover with LACQUER¹

la·crosse /lə'krɒs‖lə'krɔs/ *n* [U] a game played on a field by 2 teams, each player having a long stick (CROSSE) with a net at the end to throw, catch, and carry the small hard ball

lac·ta·tion /læk'teɪʃən/ *n* [U] *tech* **1** the production of milk for babies by a human or animal mother **2** the time that this lasts

lac·tic /'læktɪk/ *adj* [Wa5] *tech* concerning or obtained from milk

lactic a·cid /,·· '··/ *n* [U] an acid found in sour milk

lac·tose /'læktəʊs/ *n* [U] a sugary substance found in milk, sometimes used as a food for babies and sick people

la·cu·na /lə'kjuːnə‖-'kuː-/ *n* **-nae** /niː/ *or* **-nas** *fml* an empty space where something is missing, esp. in written matter

lac·y /'leɪsi/ *adj* [Wa1] of or like LACE¹ (2)

lad /læd/ *n* **1** [C;N] a boy; youth: *He's just a lad* **2** [N] *infml, esp. N EngE* fellow **3** [C] *BrE infml* a rather wild or bold man (often in the phr. **a bit of a lad**)

lad·der¹ /'lædəʳ/ *n* **1** a frame made up of 2 bars or ropes of equal length joined to each other by shorter bars (RUNGs) that form steps, and used for climbing, as up a building or the side of a ship —see picture at HOUSEHOLD **2** (*AmE* **run**)— *BrE* a ladder-shaped fault in a stocking caused by stitches coming undone **3** a means by which one may rise to success, fame, etc. **4** (in sports such as SQUASH² (3) and TABLE TENNIS) a list of players who play each other regularly in order to decide who is best. A winner goes up the list, a loser down

ladder² *v* [T1;IØ] *BrE* **a** to cause (a stocking) to develop a ladder-shaped fault **b** (*AmE* **run**)— (of a stocking) to develop such a fault

lad·die, -dy /'lædi/ *n* [C;N] *infml, esp. ScotE* a boy; LAD (1)

la·den /'leɪdn/ *adj* **1** [B (*with*)] heavily loaded: *the heavily laden ship|The bushes were laden with fruit* **2** [F+*with*] deeply troubled: *He was laden with sorrow*

la-di-da, lah-di-dah /,lɑː di 'dɑː/ *adj BrE infml* pretending to be in a higher social position than one actually is in, by use of unnaturally delicate manners, ways of speaking, etc.

La·dies, -dies' /'leɪdiz/ (*AmE* **Ladies(') room** /'·· ·/)— *n* **Ladies(')** [Wn3] *BrE* a women's public LAVATORY

ladies' man, lady's man /'·· ·/ *n* a man who likes to please or be with women
la·ding /'leɪdɪŋ/ *n* see BILL OF LADING
la·dle[1] /'leɪdl/ *n* a large deep spoon with a long handle, used esp. for lifting liquids out of a container: *a soup ladle*
ladle[2] *v* [T1 (OUT, *into, out of*)] to serve (food, soup, etc.) with or as if with a LADLE[1]
ladle out *v adv* [T1] *infml* to give out freely and usu. without careful judgment: *ladle out too much information to a class of small children*
la·dy /'leɪdi/ *n* **1** [C;N *pl.*] **a** *polite* a woman, esp. a woman of good social position or of good manners or education: *Good morning, ladies!* —compare GENTLEMAN **b** a woman in a position of command or control: *the lady of the house* **2** [A] also **woman**— female: *a lady doctor* **3** [C] *old use or poet* a woman with whom a man is in love **4** [N] *sl, esp. AmE* a woman: *You dropped your handkerchief, lady!*
USAGE When one is addressing a speech to a group of people, it is polite to begin **Ladies** *and* **Gentlemen**, but if they are only women one says **Ladies**. **Lady** is a polite but rather old-fashioned way of speaking of a woman. One may wish to use it **a** in her presence: *Please bring this* **lady** *a glass of beer* **b** with **old**; it is pleasanter to call someone an *old* **lady** than an *old* **woman**. It is better to use **woman**, not **lady**, in phrases like *a* **woman** *teacher|a* **woman** *doctor*. It is rather rude to use **female** about people, but it is the only word for animals: *a* **female** *elephant*.
Lady *n* [A;C; *my*+N] a title put before the name of **a** a woman of noble rank **b** the wife or daughter of a nobleman of one of certain ranks: *Lady Wilson* **c** another title of rank or position: *Lady President*
la·dy·bird /'leɪdibɜːd‖-ɜrd/ *AmE* **la·dy·bug** /'leɪdibʌg/— *n esp. BrE* a type of small round insect (a BEETLE), often of a kind that is red with black dots
lady-in-wait·ing /ˌ··· '··/ *n* **ladies-in-waiting** a lady who attends a queen or princess
lady-kill·er /'·· ˌ··/ *n infml* a man who is believed to charm and conquer all the women he meets
la·dy·like /'leɪdilaɪk/ *adj apprec* (of a woman) looking or behaving like a lady; having good manners
la·dy·ship /'leɪdiʃɪp/ *n* [N9;C9] (*often cap.*) (the word used when speaking to or of) a woman with the title of LADY (1a,b) (in the phrs. **her ladyship**; **your ladyship(s)**; **their ladyships**)
lag[1] /læg/ *v* **-gg-** [IØ (BEHIND, *behind*)] to move, advance, or develop more slowly (than others)
lag[2] *n* TIME LAG
lag[3] *v* **-gg-** [T1 (*with*)] to cover (water pipes and containers) with a special material to prevent loss of heat
lag[4] *n sl, esp. BrE* a man who has been sent to prison for breaking the law
la·ger /'lɑːgəʳ/ *n* **1** [U] a light kind of beer **2** [C] a drink, glass, or bottle of this
lag·gard /'lægəd‖-ərd/ *n, adj* [(*in, about*)] *old use* (a person or thing) that is very slow or late
lag·ging /'lægɪŋ/ *n* [U;(C)] material used to LAG[3] a water pipe or container
la·goon /lə'guːn/ *n* a lake of sea water, partly or completely separated from the sea, as by banks of sand or rock
lah-di-dah /ˌlɑː di 'dɑː/ *adj* LA-DI-DA
laid /leɪd/ *past t. and p. of* LAY[1]
lain /leɪn/ *past p. of* LIE[1]
lair /leəʳ/ *n* the place where a wild animal hides, rests, and sleeps: (fig.) *The police tracked the thieves to their lair*
laird /leəd‖leərd/ *n* a Scottish landowner —compare SQUIRE[1] (1)
lais·sez-faire, laisser-faire /ˌleɪseɪ 'feəʳ (*Fr* lesefɛr)/ *n* [U] *Fr* (the principle of) allowing people's activities (esp. of businesses) to develop without control
la·i·ty /'leɪ̍ti/ *n* [*the*+P] **1** those members (LAYMEN) of a religious group who are without the special training of priests or other religious office-holders **2** people without a particular professional training, as compared with those who have it
lake[1] /leɪk/ *n* a large mass of water surrounded by land
lake[2] also **crimson lake**— *n* [U] a deep bluish-red colouring matter
lakh, lac /lɑːk/ *n Ind & PakE* (esp. of RUPEE*s*) 100,000
la·ma /'lɑːmə/ *n* a Buddhist priest of Tibet, Mongolia, etc. —see also DALAI LAMA
La·ma·is·m /'lɑːmə-ɪzəm/ *n* [R] the type of Buddhism found in Tibet, Mongolia, etc.
la·ma·se·ry /'lɑːməsəri‖-seri/ *n* a building or group of buildings where LAMA*s* live together
lamb[1] /læm/ *n* **1** [C] a young sheep —see picture at FARMYARD **2** [U] the meat of a young sheep —see MEAT (USAGE) **3** [C] *infml* a young gentle person
lamb[2] *v* [IØ] (of sheep) to give birth to lambs
lam·baste /'læmbeɪst/ also **lam·bast** /-bæst/— *v* [T1] *infml* to attack fiercely with words or blows
lam·bent /'læmbənt/ *adj lit* **1** (of flames) having a soft light and moving over a surface without burning it **2** (of light) softly shining **3** gently or playfully clever: *lambent humour*
lamb·like /'læmlaɪk/ *adj* **1** gentle; harmless **2** obedient
lamb·skin /'læmˌskɪn/ *n* **1** [C] the skin of a lamb, esp. with the wool on it **2** [U] leather made from such a skin
lame[1] /leɪm/ *adj* [Wa1] **1** not able to walk easily or properly as a result of some weakness in, or accident to, a leg or foot **2** not easily believed; weak: *He gave a lame excuse for being absent* **3** (of lines in a poem) unpleasantly irregular; awkward —**~ly** *adv* —**~ness** *n* [U]
lame[2] *v* [T1] to cause to become LAME[1] (1)
la·mé /'lɑːmeɪ‖lɑ'meɪ (*Fr* lame)/ *n* [U] cloth containing gold or silver threads: *gold lamé*
lame duck /ˌ· '·/ *n* **1** a person or a business that is helpless or ineffective **2** *AmE* a political official whose period in office will soon end
la·ment[1] /lə'ment/ *v* **1** [T1,4;IØ (*over*)] to feel or express grief or sorrow (for or at) **2 the late lamented** the recently dead (person)
lament[2] *n* **1** [(*for*)] a strong expression of grief or deep sorrow **2** a song or piece of music expressing sorrow, esp. for the death of somebody
lam·en·ta·ble /'læməntəbəl, lə'mentəbəl/ *adj* **1** causing one to be very dissatisfied or to wish that something had not happened **2** worthy of blame; bad in quality —**-bly** *adv*
lam·en·ta·tion /ˌlæmən'teɪʃən/ *n* [C;U] (an expression of) grief or sorrow
lam·i·nate[1] /'læm̍neɪt/ *v* **1** [T1;IØ] to break or split (something) into thin flat sheets that cover one another (LAYER*s*) **2** [T1] to make (a strong material) by firmly uniting many thin sheets of the material on top of each other **3** [T1] to cover with thin metal or plastic sheets **4** [T1] to beat or roll (metal) into thin sheets
lam·i·nate[2] /'læm̍n̍t, -neɪt/ *n* [U;C] material made by laminating (LAMINATE[1] (2)) sheets, as of plastic
lam in·to /læm/ *v prep* **-mm-** [T1] *sl* to beat or attack with words or blows

lam·ming /ˈlæmɪŋ/ *n sl* an attack with words or blows —see LAM INTO

lamp /læmp/ *n* **1** any of various types of apparatus for giving light, as from oil, gas, or electricity **2 a** any of various types of electrical apparatus used for producing health-giving forms of heat: *an* INFRARED *lamp* **b** (*in comb.*): *a* SUNLAMP —see also BLOWLAMP

lamp-black /ˈ· ·/ *n* [U] a fine black colouring material made from the black matter (SOOT) produced by the smoke of a burning lamp

lam·poon[1] /læmˈpuːn/ *n* a piece of fierce writing attacking a person, government, etc., by making them look foolish —**~ist** *n*

lampoon[2] *v* [T1] to attack by means of a LAMPOON[1]

lamp·post /ˈlæmp-pəʊst/ *n* a tall thin pillar, usu. of metal, supporting a lamp which lights a street or other public area —see picture at STREET

lam·prey /ˈlæmpri/ *n* a type of snakelike fish with a sucking mouth

lamp·shade /ˈlæmpʃeɪd/ *n* a cover, usu. ornamental, for a lamp

lance[1] /lɑːns‖læns/ *n* **1** a long spearlike weapon used by soldiers on horseback in former times **2** a spear used for catching fish

lance[2] *v* [T1] to cut (the flesh) with a medical instrument

lanc·er /ˈlɑːnsəʳ‖ˈlæn-/ *n* **1** a soldier in a military group (REGIMENT) formerly armed with LANCE*s* **2** *old use* a soldier who fought with a LANCE while riding a horse

lanc·ers /ˈlɑːnsəz‖ˈlænsərz/ *n* [*the*+U] an old dance, or the music for this dance, for groups of 4 pairs of men and women

lan·cet /ˈlɑːnsɪ̵t‖ˈlæn-/ *n* a small very sharp pointed knife with 2 cutting edges, used to LANCE[2] flesh

land[1] /lænd/ *n* **1** [U] the solid dry part of the earth's surface: *The storm blew fiercely over land and sea.|Land travel and sea travel are both pleasant* **2** [U9] **a** a part of the earth's surface all of the same natural type: *forest land* —compare LANDS **b** (*in comb.*): HIGHLAND|LOWLAND **3** [C] a part of the earth's surface forming a political whole; country; nation: *war between lands*|(fig.) *the land of the dead* **4** [U] earth; soil **5** [U] ground owned as property: *You are on my land.|Land prices have risen quickly* **6** [U] ground used for farming **7** [*the*+R] life in the country as opposed to that in towns and cities **8 make land** (of a ship, sailor, etc.) to reach the shore **9 see how the land lies** to try to discover the present state of affairs
USAGE An area considered as property is a piece of **land** or **ground**. The substance in which plants grow is also **ground**, **earth**, or **soil**. The surface on which we walk is the **ground** or, indoors, the **floor**. As compared with the sea it is the **land**, but as compared with the sky it is the **earth**.

land[2] *v* **1** [T1;I∅] to come to, bring to, or put on land or water: *The ship landed the goods at Dover.|We landed safely* **2** [I∅] (of something moving through the air) to settle, come to rest, or fall: *The bird landed on the branch.|The ball landed in the water* **3** [X9;L9 (UP)] to come, put, arrive, or cause to arrive in a condition, place, or position: *That will land him in prison* **4** [T1] to catch (a fish) **5** [T1] *infml* to obtain; gain: *He landed a valuable prize* **6** [T1;D1] *infml* to strike; hit: *I landed a blow on his nose* **7 land on one's feet a** to have good luck **b** to come successfully out of a difficulty

land a·gent /ˈ· ˌ··/ *n* one who looks after the land, cattle, farms, etc., belonging to someone else

land ar·my /ˈ· ˌ··/ *n* a force of (mainly) women who work on farms, etc., during wartime, to help with food supplies while the men are away fighting

lan·dau /ˈlændɔː‖-daʊ/ *n* a 4-wheeled horsedrawn carriage with 2 seats and a top that folds back in 2 parts

land breeze /ˈ· ·/ *n* a light wind (BREEZE) blowing from the land to the sea, esp. at night

land crab /ˈ· ·/ *n* a small creature with a shell on its back (CRAB) that lives mainly on land near the sea

land·ed /ˈlændɪ̵d/ *adj* [Wa5;A] **1** owning large amounts of land: *a landed family* **2** made up of land: *landed property*

landed in·terests /ˌ·· ˈ··/ *n* [P] the group of large landowners

land·fall /ˈlændfɔːl/ *n* the first sight of land after a journey by sea or air

land·ing /ˈlændɪŋ/ *n* **1** the level space or passage at the top of a set of stairs from which one enters rooms **2** a level space between 2 sets of stairs **3** the act of arriving or bringing to land **4** a place where people and goods are landed, esp. from a ship

landing craft /ˈ·· ·/ *n* a flat-bottomed boat that opens at one end, used for landing soldiers and army vehicles directly on enemy shores

landing field /ˈ·· ·/ also **landing strip** /ˈ·· ·/— *n* a stretch of prepared land for aircraft to take off from and land on

landing gear /ˈ·· ·/ *n* [U] the wheels and underpart of an aircraft used when landing

landing net /ˈ·· ·/ *n* a net on a long handle used for lifting out of the water a fish caught on a hook

landing stage /ˈ·· ·/ *n* a level surface, floating in or supported over the water, onto which passengers and goods are landed

land·la·dy /ˈlændˌleɪdi/ *n* **1** a woman who owns and runs a small hotel (BOARDINGHOUSE (1)): *seaside landladies* **2** a female LANDLORD

land·locked /ˈlændlɒkt‖-lɑkt/ *adj* enclosed or almost enclosed by land: *a landlocked country, that lacks a port for sea trade*

land·lord /ˈlændlɔːd‖-ɔrd/ *n* **1** [C] a person, esp. a man, from whom someone rents all or part of a building, land, etc. **2** [C;N] a person, esp. a man, who owns or is in charge of an inn, hotel, etc. —compare LANDLADY

land·lub·ber /ˈlændˌlʌbəʳ/ *n infml* a person not used to the sea and ships —**~ly** *adj*

land·mark /ˈlændmɑːk‖-ɑrk/ *n* **1** an easily recognizable object, such as a tall tree or building, by which one can tell one's position **2** something that marks an important point or change, as in a person's life or the development of knowledge **3** something marking the limits of a piece of land

land·mine /ˈlændmaɪn/ *n* an explosive apparatus, hidden in or on the ground, which blows up when a person or vehicle passes over it

land rov·er /ˈ· ˌ··/ *n tdmk* (*often cap.*) a type of car suitable for travelling over rough ground

lands /lændz/ *n* [(*the*) P9] parts of the earth's surface all of the same natural type: *the forest lands of Norway*

land·scape[1] /ˈlændskeɪp/ *n* **1** [C] a wide view of country scenery **2** [C] a picture of such a scene **3** [U] the art of representing scenery

landscape[2] *v* [T1] to make (the land around new houses, factories, etc.) more like interesting scenery

landscape gar·den·ing /ˌ·· ˈ···/ *n* [U] the art of arranging trees, paths, etc., in gardens to give a pleasing effect

land·slide /ˈlændslaɪd/ *n* **1** a sudden fall of earth or rocks down a slope, hill, cliff, etc. **2** a very large, often unexpected, success for a person, political party, etc. in an election

land·slip /ˈlændˌslɪp/ *n* a small LANDSLIDE (1)

land·ward /ˈlændwəd‖-ərd/ *adj* towards the land

land·wards /'lændwədz‖-ərdz/ (*AmE* usu. **landward**)— *adv esp. BrE* towards the land

lane /leɪn/ *n* **1** a narrow, often winding, road or way between fields, walls, houses, etc., in town or country **2** a fixed path across the sea or through the air used regularly by ships or aircraft **3** any of the parallel parts into which wide roads are divided to keep fast and slow cars apart —see picture at INTERCHANGE[2] **4** a path marked for each competitor in a race

lan·guage /'læŋgwɪdʒ/ *n* **1** [U] the system of human expression by means of words **2** [C] a particular system of words, as used by a people or nation: *He is learning 2 foreign languages* **3** [C;U] any system of signs, movements, etc., used to express meanings or feelings: *The movement of the cat's tail was clearly part of his language of anger* **4** [U] a particular style or manner of expression: *the poet's beautiful language* **5** [(*the*) C] the words and phrases of a particular group, science, profession, etc. **6** [U] words and phrases that are impolite or shocking (esp. in the phrs. **bad language, strong language**)

language la·bor·a·tory /'·· ·,···‖'·· ,····/ *n* a room in which people can learn foreign languages by means of special teaching machines, esp. TAPE RECORDERS

lan·guid /'læŋgwɪd/ *adj* lacking strength or will; slow and weak —**~ly** *adv*

lan·guish /'læŋgwɪʃ/ *v* [IØ] **1** to be or become lacking in strength or will **2** [(*in*)] to experience long suffering: *to languish in prison* **3** [(*for*)] to become weak or unhappy through desire: *She languished for his love and gave him languishing looks*

lan·guor /'læŋgəʳ/ *n esp. lit* **1** [U] tiredness of mind or body; lack of strength or will **2** [U] pleasant or heavy stillness **3** [C *often pl.*] a feeling or state of mind of tender sadness and desire —**~ous** *adj* —**~ously** *adv*

lank /læŋk/ *adj* [Wa5] **1** having very little flesh; very thin **2** hanging loosely and without strength **3** (of hair) straight and lifeless —**~ly** *adv* —**~ness** *n* [U]

lank·y /'læŋki/ *adj* [Wa1] (esp. of a person) very thin and ungracefully tall or long —**lankily** *adv* —**lankiness** *n* [U]

lan·o·lin /'lænələ̇n/ *n* [U] a fatty substance obtained from sheep's wool, used in skin creams

lan·tern /'læntən‖-ərn/ *n* **1** a container, usu. of glass and metal, that encloses and protects the flame of a light **2** *tech* the top of a building or tower (such as a LIGHTHOUSE) with windows on all sides —see also MAGIC LANTERN

lantern-jawed /,·· '·◂/ *adj* (of a person) having long narrow jaws and hollow cheeks

lan·tern·slide /'læntənslaɪd‖-ər-/ *n* an early type of SLIDE[2] (5), made of glass, as used in a MAGIC LANTERN

lan·yard /'lænjəd‖-ərd/ *n* **1** a thick string on which a knife or whistle is hung round the neck, esp. by sailors **2** a short piece of rope, used on ships for tying, binding, etc.

lap[1] /læp/ *n* **1** the front part of a seated person between the waist and the knees **2** the part of any clothes covering this **3 in the lap of luxury** having every comfort and service **4 in the lap of the gods** dependent on chance or fate

lap[2] *v* **-pp-** **1** [X9 esp. *over*] *esp. lit* to fold over or round; wrap round; surround **2** [T1] (in racing, swimming, etc.) to be the distance of at least once round the track ahead of (a competitor) **3** [L9] (esp. in racing) to race completely round the track: *James Hunt lapped in under 2 minutes*

lap[3] *n* **1** (in racing, swimming, etc.) a single journey round the track **2** one part or division of a planned action or development **3** the amount of material necessary to go round an object once

lap[4] *v* **-pp-** **1** [T1 (UP)] to drink by taking up with quick movements of the tongue **2** [IØ (*against*)] to move or hit with little waves and soft sounds —see also LAP UP

lap[5] *n* **1** [C] an act of LAPping[4] (1) a liquid with the tongue **2** [*the*+S] the sound of LAPping[4] (2), as of waves

lap·dog /'læpdɒg‖-dɔg/ *n* a small pet dog

la·pel /lə'pel/ *n* the part of the front of a coat (or JACKET) that is folded back below the neck on each side towards the shoulders

lap·i·da·ry[1] /'læpə̇dəri‖-deri/ *n* a person skilled in cutting precious stones, making them shine and cutting patterns, names, etc., in them

lapidary[2] *adj* [A;(B)] *fml apprec* (of words, phrases, etc.) cut or suitable for cutting in stone

lap·is laz·u·li /,læpə̇s 'læzjʊli‖-'læzəli/ *n* **1** [U;C *usu. sing.*] a type of bright blue stone **2** [U] the colour of this stone

lapse[1] /læps/ *n* **1** a small fault or mistake, as one of memory, esp. one that is quickly put right **2** a failure in correct behaviour, belief, duty, etc. **3** a gradual passing away, esp. of time: *after a lapse of several years* **4** a short period of time in the past **5** *law* the ending of a title, right, etc., owing to lack of use, death, or failure to claim

lapse[2] *v* [IØ] **1** [(*into*)] to sink, pass, or fall, slowly or by degrees: *to lapse into silence* **2** [(*from*)] to fail with regard to correct behaviour, belief, duty, etc. **3** (of business agreements, titles, rights, etc.) to come to an end, esp. because of lack of use, death, or failure to claim

lapsed /læpst/ *adj* [Wa5;A] **1** no longer following the practices, esp. of one's religion **2** *law* no longer in use

lapse rate /'· ·/ *n* the rate of decrease in the temperature of air according to its height above the earth

lap up *v adv* **-pp-** [T1] to listen eagerly to; accept without thought

lap·wing /'læp,wɪŋ/ also **pewit, peewit**— *n* a type of small bird with raised feathers on its head

lar·board /'lɑːbəd‖'lɑrbərd/ *n* [R] *now rare* PORT[5]

lar·ce·ny /'lɑːsəni‖'lɑr-/ *n* [U;C] *law* (an act of) stealing

larch /lɑːtʃ‖lɑrtʃ/ *n* **1** [C] a type of tall upright tree with bright green needle-like leaves and hard-skinned fruit (CONES) —see picture at TREE[1] **2** [U] the strong hard wood of this tree

lard[1] /lɑːd‖lɑrd/ *n* [U] pig fat made pure by melting, used in cookery

lard[2] *v* [T1] **1** to spread LARD[1] over **2** to put small pieces of preserved pig meat (BACON) into or on (other meat) before cooking **3** [(*with*)] to ornament (speech or writing) with noticeable phrases, esp. of some particular kind

lar·der /'lɑːdəʳ‖'lɑr-/ *n* a storeroom or cupboard for food in a house —see also PANTRY (1)

large /lɑːdʒ‖lɑrdʒ/ *adj* [Wa1] **1** more than usual in size, number, or amount **2** having much room or space **3 as large as life** unexpectedly but unmistakably the real person **4 at large a** (esp. of dangerous people or animals) free; uncontrolled **b** *becoming rare* fully; completely **c** as a whole; altogether: *The country at large is hoping for great changes* —see also BY AND LARGE —**~ness** *n* [U]

large-heart·ed /,· '··◂/ *adj* [Wa2] generous, kind, or forgiving —**~ness** *n* [U]

large in·tes·tine /,· ·'··/ *n* the lower bowel, including the COLON[1] and RECTUM where food is changed into solid waste matter —compare SMALL INTESTINE and see picture at DIGESTIVE SYSTEM

large·ly /ˈlɑːdʒli‖ˈlɑr-/ *adv* **1** [Wa5] to a great degree; chiefly: *This country is largely desert land* **2** in great quantity; much

large-mind·ed /ˌ· ˈ··◂/ *adj* [Wa2] willing to consider ideas and allow others to have ideas that are opposed to one's own —**~ness** *n* [U]

lar·gesse, *AmE* also **-gess** /lɑːˈʒes‖lɑrˈdʒes (*Fr* larʒɛs)/ *n* [U] *Fr* generosity to those in need, esp. from those in a higher position to those in a lower position

lar·go /ˈlɑːgəʊ‖-ɑr-/ *adv, adj, n* **-s** (a piece of music) in a slow or solemn manner

lar·i·at /ˈlærɪət/ *n esp. AmE* LASSO[1]

lark[1] /lɑːk‖lɑrk/ *n infml* something done for a joke or amusement; bit of fun

lark[2] *n* any of several small light brown birds with long pointed wings, esp. the SKYLARK

lark a·bout also **lark a·round**— *v adv* [IØ] *infml* to play rather wildly; have fun

lark·spur /ˈlɑːkspɜːʳ‖ˈlɑr-/ *n* DELPHINIUM

lar·rup /ˈlærəp/ *v* [T1] *infml* to hit; beat

lar·va /ˈlɑːvə‖ˈlɑrvə/ *n* **-vae** /viː/ the wormlike young of an insect between leaving the egg and changing into a winged form —see picture at INSECT —**~l** *adj* [Wa5]

la·ryn·ge·al /ˌlærɪ̵nˈdʒɪəl, ləˈrɪndʒəl/ *adj* [Wa5] *tech* of the LARYNX

lar·yn·gi·tis /ˌlærɪ̵nˈdʒaɪtɪ̵s/ *n* [U] a painful swollen condition of the LARYNX

la·ryn·go·scope /ləˈrɪŋgəskəʊp/ *n* an instrument with a mirror for examining the LARYNX

lar·ynx /ˈlærɪŋks/ also (*infml*) **voice box**— *n* the hollow boxlike part at the upper end of the throat's air passage (WINDPIPE) in which the sounds of the voice are produced by the VOCAL CORDS —see picture at RESPIRATORY

la·sa·gna /ləˈzænjə‖-ˈzɑn-/ *n* [U] (an Italian dish made with) long flat pieces of PASTA (wider than SPAGHETTI)

las·civ·i·ous /ləˈsɪvɪəs/ *adj* causing, feeling, or showing uncontrolled sexual desire —**~ly** *adv* —**~ness** *n* [U]

la·ser /ˈleɪzəʳ/ *n* an apparatus for producing a very powerful narrow beam of light; type of MASER

lash[1] /læʃ/ *v* **1** [T1] to strike with or as if with a whip **2** [T1;IØ (ABOUT)] to strike or move violently or suddenly: *The waves lashed the rocks.|The cat's tail lashed about angrily* **3** [T1] to attack violently with words **4** [T1 (*into*)] to excite to violence **5** [X9] to tie firmly, esp. with rope

lash[2] *n* **1** [C] the thin striking part of a whip **2** [C] a stroke given with a whip **3** [C] a sudden movement **4** [(*the*) S] violent beating: *the lash of the waves on the rocks* **5** [*the*+R] *old use* an official whipping given as punishment **6** [C] EYELASH

lash·ing /ˈlæʃɪŋ/ *n* **1** a beating **2** a rope used for binding

lash·ings /ˈlæʃɪŋz/ *n* [P (*of*)] *infml* a large supply, esp. of food and drink

lash out *v adv* **1** [IØ (*at, against*)] to strike or attack violently with a weapon, hand, foot, etc. **2** [IØ (*at, against*)] to attack with violent speech **3** [T1a;IØ (*on*)] *infml* to give out (esp. money) in large quantities: *He lashed out the food.|He lashed out on a new car*

lass /læs/ also **lass·ie** /ˈlæsi/— *n* [C;N] *Scot & N Eng E* **1** a young girl or woman **2** a young man's girlfriend

las·so[1] /ləˈsuː, ˈlæsəʊ/ also (*esp. AmE*) **lariat**— *n* **-s** a rope with one end that can be tightened in a circle (NOOSE) used (esp. in the US) for catching horses and cattle

lasso[2] *v* [T1] to catch with a LASSO

last[1] /lɑːst‖læst/ *determiner, pron* **1** (the one or ones) after all others; following all the rest: *the last 2 days of the week|the second last* (=next to the last) *page|He was the last to arrive.|They were* (*among*) *the last to arrive* **2** (being) the only remaining: *I'm almost out of money; this is my last £1.|to drink the last of the wine* **3** (in time) **a** the one or ones before the one mentioned or before now; most recent; PRECEDING: *Our last election was hard-fought.|He's lived here for the last few years|for the last 3 or 4 years* **b** (*without* the) the one before this: *This week's class was duller than last* (*week's*).|*Today is Sunday the 15th. Last Sunday was the 8th and last Tuesday was the 10th.|the week before last* —compare NEXT[1] (2), BEFORE[1] (2) **4** (*with* the) the least suitable or likely: *He's the last person I thought would come!* **5 at (long) last** in the end; after a long time —compare **at** FIRST[1] (4) **6 every last** *infml* every, not leaving out any: *pick up every last bit of paper from the floor* **7 breathe one's last** *pomp* to die **8 to the last** until the latest moment; till the end —compare END[1], NEXT[1]

last[2] *adv* [Wa5] **1** after all others: *What line comes last in the poem?* —compare FIRST[2] (1) **2** on the occasion nearest in the past: *when we met last|When did you last see your father?* —compare NEXT[2] (2), FIRST[2] (3) **3** LASTLY **4 last but not least** important(ly), although coming at the end

last[3] *v* **1** [L1,9] to measure in length of time; go on; continue: *Our holiday lasts 10 days.|The hot weather lasted until September* **2** [IØ] to remain of use, in good condition, or unweakened: *Her anger won't last* **3** [D1 *no pass*; L1] to be enough for: *This food will last* (*them*) (*for*) *3 days*

last[4] *n* a piece of wood or metal shaped like a human foot, used by shoemakers and shoe repairers

last-ditch /ˌ· ˈ·◂/ *adj* [Wa5;A] done as one last effort before yielding

last·ing /ˈlɑːstɪŋ‖ˈlæs-/ *adj* [A;(F)] continuing for a long time; unending: *a lasting sorrow*

last judg·ment /ˌ· ˈ··/ *n* [*the*+R] (*often cap.*) JUDGMENT DAY

last·ly /ˈlɑːstli‖ˈlæst-/ *adv* after everything else; in the end: . . . *Lastly, let me mention the great support I've had from my wife*

last straw /ˌ· ˈ·/ *n* [*the*+R] the difficulty, trouble, etc., that makes the total unbearable when it is added to one's present difficulties or troubles

last word /ˌ· ˈ·/ *n* [*the*+R] **1** the word or phrase that ends an argument **2** [(*in*)] *infml* the most modern example: *That's the last word in cars*

lat *written abbrev. for:* LATITUDE (1)

latch[1] /lætʃ/ *n* **1** a simple fastening for a door, gate, window, etc., worked by dropping a bar into a U-shaped space —see picture at WINDOW **2** a spring lock for a house door that can be opened from the outside with a key—see picture at DOOR **3 off the latch** not fully closed; slightly open **4 on the latch** fastened only with the latch; not locked

latch[2] *v* [T1;IØ] to fasten or be able to be fastened with a LATCH[1]

latch·key /ˈlætʃkiː/ *n* a key for opening a lock on an outside door of a house or flat

latchkey child /ˈ·· ·/ *n* a child who must let himself in and out of his house because his parents are working

latch on *v adv* [IØ (*to*)] *infml* to understand; CATCH ON (2)

latch on·to *v prep infml* **1** [T1,6a,b] to understand **2** [T1] **a** to refuse to allow (someone) to go **b** to refuse to leave (someone)

late[1] /leɪt/ *adj* **1** [Wa1;B;E] arriving, developing, happening, etc., after the usual, arranged, or expected time: *The train was 10 minutes late* —compare EARLY[2] (1) **2** [Wa1;B] happening towards the end of the day, life, a period, etc.: *She*

returned in the late afternoon —compare EARLY² (2) **3** [Wa1;A] happening a short time ago: *the late changes in the government* **4** [Wa5;A] existing in the recent past; former: *the late government* **5** [Wa5;A] who has died recently: *her late husband* **6** [Wa5;A] just arrived; new; fresh: *Some late news of the war has just come in* —**~ness** *n* [U]
USAGE One can speak of *a* **late**/*an* **early** *hour* or *the* **late/early** *afternoon*, but not of **a* **late**/*an* **early** *minute* or **a* **late**/*an* **early** *time*. —see also LATEST

late² *adv* [Wa5] **1** after the usual, arranged, or expected time: *The bus arrived 5 minutes late* —compare EARLY¹ (1) **2** towards the end of a period: *The bush was planted late in the season* —compare EARLY¹ (2) **3** until or at a late time of the night: *We went to bed late* **4 of late** recently

late·com·er /ˈleɪtˌkʌməʳ/ *n* someone who arrives late

la·teen sail /ləˈtiːn seɪl/ *n* a large 3-sided sail for a boat

late·ly /ˈleɪtli/ *adv* in the recent past

la·tent /ˈleɪtənt/ *adj* existing but not yet noticeable, active, or fully developed: *a latent infection* —**-tency** *n* [U]: *A* **latency period** *is the length of time between catching a disease and showing signs of having caught it*

latent heat /ˌ·· ˈ·/ *n* [U] the additional heat necessary to change a solid (at its MELTING POINT) into a liquid, or a liquid (at its BOILING POINT) into a gas

lat·e·ral¹ /ˈlætərəl/ *adj* [A] of, at, from, or towards the side —**-rally** *adv*

lateral² *n tech* something, such as a branch, which is at or from the side

lat·est /ˈleɪtɨst/ *n* [*the*+U] **1** the most recent news, fashion, or example: *Have you heard the latest about the war?|She is wearing the latest in hats* **2 at the latest** and no later: *Please be here tomorrow at the latest*

la·tex /ˈleɪteks/ *n* [U] a thick whitish liquid produced by certain plants, esp. the rubber tree

lath /lɑːθ‖læθ/ *n* **laths** /lɑːðz, lɑːθs‖læðz, læθs/ **1** one of many long flat narrow pieces of wood used in building to support wall-covering material (PLASTER) or roof-covering material (TILE*s* or SLATE*s*) **2** any other long narrow piece of material

lathe /leɪð/ *n* a machine that turns a piece of wood or metal round and round against a sharp tool that gives it shape

la·ther¹ /ˈlɑːðəʳ‖ˈlæ-/ *n* [U;S] **1 a** a white mass produced by shaking a mixture of soap and water **b** a mass like this, formed in the liquid (SWEAT) produced from the hot skin of a horse that has been ridden too fast **2 in a lather** worried because hurried —**~y** *adj*

lather² *v* **1** [I∅] (esp. of soap) to produce a LATHER¹ **2** [T1(UP)] to cover with LATHER¹ **3** [T1] *infml* to attack violently with blows

Lat·in /ˈlætɪn/ *n, adj* **1** [U;B] (of) the language of the ancient Romans **2** [C;B] (a member) of any nation that speaks a language that comes from LATIN (1), such as Spanish, Portuguese, Italian, or French

Latin A·mer·i·can /ˌ·· ·ˈ···ˈ/ *adj* [Wa5] of the Spanish- or Portuguese-speaking countries of South and Central America

lat·in·ize, -ise /ˈlætɨnaɪz/ *v* [T1] (*sometimes cap.*) **1** to translate into the LATIN (1) language **2** [Wv5] to use LATIN (1) words and phrases, as in poetry: *a Latinized style* —**-ization** /ˌlætɨnaɪˈzeɪʃən‖-tɨnə-/ *n* [C;U]

lat·i·tude /ˈlætɨtjuːd‖-tuːd/ *n* [U;S] **1** the distance north or south of the EQUATOR (the imaginary line from east to west round the earth at its widest point) measured in degrees: *The latitude of the ship is 20 degrees south* —compare LONGITUDE; see picture at GLOBE **2** freedom in action, opinion, expression, etc.

lat·i·tudes /ˈlætɨtjuːdz‖-tuːdz/ *n* [P] an area at a certain LATITUDE: **High latitudes** *are those areas a long way north or south of the* EQUATOR

lat·i·tu·di·nal /ˌlætɨˈtjuːdɨnəl‖-ˈtuː-/ *adj* [Wa5;A] of LATITUDE (1)

lat·i·tu·di·nar·i·an /ˌlætɨtjuːdənˈeəriən‖-tɨtuː-/ *n, adj fml* (a person) allowing freedom of opinion and action, esp. in matters of religion —compare LATITUDE (2) —**~ism** *n* [U]

la·trine /ləˈtriːn/ *n* (esp. in camps) a hole in the ground into which people may empty their bowels

-la·try /ˌlətri/ also **-olatry**— *comb. form* worship: IDOLATRY

lat·ter /ˈlætəʳ/ *adj* [Wa5] *fml* **1** [A] (*after* the, this, *or* these) nearer to the end; later: *the latter years of his life* **2** [A; *the*+GU] the second (of 2 people or things just spoken of): *Of the pig and the cow, the latter (animal) is more valuable.|Of pigs and cows, the latter* (=cows) *are more valuable.|Did he walk or swim? The latter seems unlikely* —opposite **former**

latter-day /ˈ·· ·/ *adj* [Wa5;A] *old use* modern; recent

lat·ter·ly /ˈlætəli‖-ər-/ *adv* recently; lately —compare FORMERLY

lat·tice /ˈlætɨs/ *n* **1** a framework of flat wooden or metal lengths crossed over each other with open spaces between, esp. as used as a fence, a support for climbing plants, etc. **2** also **lattice win·dow** /ˌ·· ˈ··/— an old kind of window with many small pieces of glass held together by narrow bands of lead —see picture at WINDOW

laud /lɔːd/ *v* [T1] *old use or pomp* to praise

lau·da·ble /ˈlɔːdəbəl/ *adj* (esp. of behaviour, actions, etc.) deserving praise —compare LAUDATORY —**-bility** /ˌlɔːdəˈbɪlɨti/ *n* [U] —**-bly** /ˈlɔːdəbli/ *adv*

lau·da·num /ˈlɔːdənəm/ *n* [U] a substance containing the drug OPIUM in alcohol, used (esp. formerly) as a medicine to lessen pain and for its pleasant effects

lau·da·to·ry /ˈlɔːdətəri‖-tori/ *adj* [Wa5;A] expressing praise or admiration —compare LAUDABLE

laugh¹ /lɑːf‖læf/ *v* **1** [I∅] to express amusement, happiness, careless disrespect, etc., by making explosive sounds with the voice, usu. while smiling **2** [L9] to experience the feeling for which this is the expression: *He laughed silently to himself* **3** [X9] to bring, put, drive, etc., with laughing: *They laughed her out of the house* **4** [X7] to cause (oneself) to become by laughing: *He laughed himself sick* **5** [T1] to express with a laugh: *She laughed her disrespect* **6 laugh in/up one's sleeve** to laugh secretly **7 laugh in somebody's face** to show clear disrespect or disobedience towards somebody **8 laugh on the wrong side** (*or* **the other side**) **of one's face** to experience disappointment, sorrow, failure, etc., after expecting success or joy **9 no laughing matter** serious

laugh² *n* **1** the act or sound of laughing **2** an expression of amusement, happiness, careless disrespect, etc., through laughing **3** *infml* something done for a joke or amusement **4 have the last laugh** to win after earlier defeats **5 have the laugh on** to make a fool of someone who was trying to make others look foolish

laugh·a·ble /ˈlɑːfəbəl‖ˈlæ-/ *adj* **1** causing laughter; funny **2** fit only to be laughed at; foolish —**-bly** *adv*

laugh at *v prep* [T1] **1** to treat as foolish, worthless, or an object of fun **2** to take no notice of; be careless of

laugh down *v adv* [T1] to make (someone) silent by laughing loudly

laugh·ing gas /ˈ·· ·/ *n* [U] a gas which may cause laughter when breathed in, used for producing unconsciousness, esp. during short operations for removing teeth

laughing jack·ass /ˌ·· ˈ··/ *n* KOOKABURRA

laugh·ing·stock /ˈlɑːfɪŋstɒk‖ˈlæfɪŋstɑk/ *n* somebody or something that is regarded as foolish and causes unkind laughter

laugh off also **laugh a·way**— *v adv* [T1] to cause, by laughing, to seem less or unimportant: *He bravely laughed off his pain*

laugh·ter /ˈlɑːftəʳ‖ˈlæf-/ *n* [U] **1** the act of or sound of laughing **2** the experience of which laughing is the expression: *He was filled with silent laughter*

launch[1] /lɔːntʃ/ *v* [T1] **1** to set (a boat, esp. one that has just been built) into the water **2** to send (a modern weapon or instrument) into the sky or space by means of scientific explosive apparatus **3** [(*at*)] to throw with great force **4** to cause (an activity, plan, way of life, etc.) to begin

launch[2] *n* [(*the*) S] the act of LAUNCHing[1]

launch[3] *n* a large usu. motor-driven boat used for carrying people on rivers, lakes, harbours, etc.

launch·ing pad /ˈ·· ·/ also **launching site**— *n* a base from which a modern weapon (MISSILE) or space vehicle is sent off into the sky

launch in·to *v prep* [T1] to begin with eagerness, strength of will, force, etc.

launch out *v adv* [L9] to begin something new, such as a large plan or action or way of life: *He left his father's shop and launched out into business for himself*

laun·der /ˈlɔːndəʳ/ *v* **1** [T1] to wash (or wash and iron) (clothes, sheets, etc.) **2** [IØ] (of clothes, sheets, etc.) to be able to be washed (or washed and ironed)

laun·derette /lɔːnˈdret/ also (*esp. AmE*) **laun·dro·mat** /ˈlɔːndrəmæt/— *n* a place where the public may wash their clothes in machines that work when coins are put in them

laun·dress /ˈlɔːndrɨs/ *n* a woman whose work it is to wash and iron clothes

laun·dry /ˈlɔːndri/ *n* **1** [C] a place or business where clothes, etc., are washed and ironed **2** [U] clothes, sheets, etc., needing washing or that have just been washed (or washed and ironed)

laundry bas·ket /ˈ·· ˌ··/ also **linen basket,** *AmE* **hamper**— *n* a large basket with a lid, in which dirty clothing, sheets, TOWEL*s*, etc., are put ready for washing

laur·e·ate /ˈlɔːriɨt/ *adj* see POET LAUREATE

laur·el /ˈlɒrəl‖ˈlɔ-, ˈlɑ-/ *n* **1** a kind of small tree with smooth shiny leaves that do not fall in winter **2** a circle of leaves of this tree regarded as a sign of honour, esp. when given by the ancient Greeks or Romans to the winner of races, fights, etc.

laur·els /ˈlɒrəlz‖ˈlɔ-, ˈlɑ-/ *n* [P] **1** honour gained for something done **2 rest on one's laurels** to be satisfied with what one has done already, and therefore not do any more —see also LOOK TO **one's laurels**

la·va /ˈlɑːvə/ *n* [U] **1** rock in a very hot liquid state flowing from an exploding mountain (VOLCANO) **2** this material when it has become cool and turned into a grey solid with many small air holes

lav·a·to·ry /ˈlævətəri‖-tori/ also (*infml*) **lav** /læv/— *n* **1** a large seatlike bowl fixed to the floor and connected to a pipe (DRAIN), used for getting rid of the body's waste matter **2** a room containing this **3** a small building containing a number of lavatories (LAVATORY (2))

lave /leɪv/ *v* [T1] *poet* **1** to wash or bathe **2** to flow softly along or against

lav·en·der[1] /ˈlævɨndəʳ/ *n* [U] **1** a type of plant with stems of small strongly-smelling pale purple flowers **2** the dried flowers and stems of this plant used for giving stored clothes, sheets, etc., a pleasant smell **3** a pale purple colour

lavender[2] *adj* [Wa5] of the colour LAVENDER[1]: *lavender (blue) walls*

lav·ish /ˈlævɪʃ/ *adj* **1** very free, generous, or wasteful in giving or using: *a lavish spender|lavish with help|lavish of time* **2** given, spent, or produced in great quantity: *lavish praise|a lavish feast* —**~ly** *adv* —**~ness** *n* [U]

lavish on *v prep* [D1] to give or spend freely, generously, or wastefully: *He lavished money/kindness on his friends*

law /lɔː/ *n* **1** [C] a rule that is supported by the power of government and that governs the behaviour of members of a society **2** [(*the*) U] the whole body of such rules in a country: *The law forbids stealing* **3** [U] the condition of society when such a body of rules is generally respected and obeyed (esp. in the phr. **law and order**) **4** [U] the whole body of these rules and the way in which they work: *to study law* **5** [*the*+U] the body of people who have studied these rules and whose job it is to see that they are put into effect properly **6** [U] the operation of these rules in court, as in punishing criminals and deciding claims: *It's a question of law, not a question of fact* **7** [U] the body of these rules concerned with a particular subject: *business law* **8** [C] a generally accepted rule of behaviour **9** [C] a rule of action in a sport, art, business, etc.: *the laws of cricket* **10** [C] a statement expressing what has been seen always to happen in certain conditions: *Boyle's law is a scientific principle* **11** [*the*+GU] *infml* the police or a policeman: *The law was/were there in force* **12 be a law unto oneself** to take no notice of the law and other rules of behaviour and do what one wishes **13 go to law** to begin a case in law on a matter that concerns one **14 lay down the law** to give an opinion or an order in an unpleasant commanding manner **15 the long arm of the law** *humor* the police, considered as a force that will certainly catch criminals, no matter how hard they try to escape **16 take the law into one's own hands** to take no notice of society's rules and act alone, usu. by force

law-a·bid·ing /ˈ· ·ˌ··/ *adj* obeying the law

law-break·er /ˈ· ˌ··/ *n* a person who breaks the law; criminal

law·ful /ˈlɔːfəl/ *adj* [Wa5] **1** allowed by law **2** recognized by law: *a lawful marriage* **3** obeying the law —see LEGAL (USAGE) —**~ly** *adv* —**~ness** *n* [U]

law·less /ˈlɔːləs/ *adj* **1** (of a country or place) not governed by laws **2** uncontrolled; wild —**~ly** *adv* —**~ness** *n* [U]

lawn[1] /lɔːn/ *n* a stretch of usu. flat ground, esp. next to a house, covered with closely cut grass

lawn[2] *n* [U] a type of fine smooth material, as used in summer dresses, handkerchiefs, and shirts

lawn ten·nis /ˌ· ˈ··/ *n* [U] tennis, esp. when played on a grass surface

law·suit /ˈlɔːsjuːt‖-suːt/ also **suit**— *n* a noncriminal case in a court of law

law·yer /ˈlɔːjəʳ/ *n* a person (esp. a SOLICITOR) whose business it is to advise people about laws and to represent them in court

lax /læks/ *adj* [Wa2] **1** not giving attention to details or to what is correct or necessary **2** careless or lazy **3** lacking in control **4** (of muscles, knots, etc.) not firm; loose **5** *med* (of bowels) emptying too easily —**~ly** *adv* —**~ness** *n* [U]

lax·a·tive /ˈlæksətɪv/ *n, adj* (a medicine or something that is eaten) that causes the bowels to empty easily

lax·i·ty /ˈlæksɪ̈ti/ also **lax·ness** /ˈlæksnɪ̈s/— *n* **1** [U] the condition of being LAX **2** [C] a careless lack of exactness

lay[1] /leɪ/ *v* **laid** /leɪd/ **1** [X9, esp. DOWN] to place; put: *Lay it down.|Lay it on the table* **2** [T1] to set in proper order or position: *This workman is able to lay bricks very quickly* **3** [T1] to place knives, forks, etc., on, ready for a meal (esp. in the phr. **lay the table**) **4** [T1] to cause to lie flat, settle, disappear, or cease to be active: *The rain quickly laid the dust.|Her fears were soon laid (to rest)* **5** [T1;IØ] (of birds, insects, etc.) to produce (an egg or eggs): *The hens aren't laying* **6** [T1 (*on*)] to risk (esp. money) on the result of some happening, such as a race; BET[2] **7** [X9] to put into a particular condition, esp. of weakness, helplessness, obedience, etc.: *The country was laid in ruins* —see also LAY FLAT, LAY LOW, LAY WASTE **8** [X9] to make (a statement, claim, charge, etc.) in a serious, official, or public way: *Your employer has laid a serious charge against you* **9** [D1 + *with/on*; T1 (*on*)] to cover or spread over: *He laid the floor with mats.|He laid mats on the floor* **10** [T1] *taboo sl* (esp. of a man) to have sex with **11 lay claim to** to claim **12 lay hold of** to catch and hold firmly —see also LAY ABOUT, LAY ASIDE, LAY AT, LAY DOWN, LAY FLAT, LAY IN, LAY INTO, LAY LOW, LAY OFF, LAY ON, LAY OPEN, LAY OUT, LAY OVER, LAY TO, LAY UP, LAY WASTE

USAGE Do not confuse **lay** [T1] (**laid, laid**) with **lie** [IØ] (**lay, lain**). A bird **lays** an egg. A person **lays** (also, *esp. AmE,* **sets**) the table with knives, plates, etc. A person or thing **lies** in bed, on the floor, etc. A 3rd verb **lie** [IØ] (**lied, lied**) means "to tell a **lie**".

lay[2] *n* **1** [(*the*) U] the manner or position in which something lies or is laid **2** [C] *taboo sl* **a** a woman considered for her part in the sexual act **b** the sexual act **3 lay of the land** *esp. AmE* LIE[2] (2) of the land

lay[3] *adj* [Wa5;A] **1** of, to, or performed by people who are not in official positions within a religion **2** not trained in or having knowledge of a particular profession or branch of learning, such as law or medicine

lay[4] *n* **1** a short poem that tells a story and is meant to be sung, esp. one written in earlier times **2** *poet* a song

lay[5] *past t. of* LIE[1]

lay·a·bout /ˈleɪəbaʊt/ *n BrE infml* a lazy person who avoids working

lay a·bout *v prep* [T1] to attack; strike wildly with words or blows

lay a·side also **lay by**— *v adv* [T1] **1** to store for future use **2** to stop using or practising; give up

lay at *v prep* **lay something at someone's door** to say that someone is responsible for something

lay bro·ther /ˌ· ˈ··/ (*fem.* **lay sister**)— *n* a man (or *fem.* woman) who has made the promises of obedience that are usual in a religious group, but who is employed mostly in humble work in the kitchen or garden of a religious house

lay-by /ˈ· ·/ *n* **-bys** *BrE* a space next to a road where vehicles may park out of the way of traffic

lay down *v adv* [T1] **1** to put down (tools, arms, etc.) as a sign that one will not use them **2** [(*for*)] to give up in order to help a cause (esp. in the phr. **lay down one's life**) **3** to plan or begin building **4** [*often pass.*] to declare or state firmly **5** to store (esp. wine) for future use

lay·er[1] /ˈleɪəʳ/ *n* **1** a thickness of some material (often one of many) laid over a surface: *These seeds must be covered with a layer of earth* **2** (*usu. in comb.*) a person or thing that lays something: *a bricklayer* **3** a bird, esp. a hen, that lays eggs: *a good layer|a bad layer* **4** a plant stem that has been fastened partly under the ground, in order to grow roots and so become a separate plant

layer[2] *v* **1** [T1] to make a LAYER[1] (1) of; put down in LAYERs[1] (1) **2** [T1;IØ] **a** to fasten (a stem) down and cover with earth **b** (of a plant) to form roots where a stem meets the soil

lay·ette /leɪˈet/ *n* a complete set of clothes and other things needed for a newborn baby

lay fig·ure /ˌ· ˈ··/ *n* a figure of the human body, usu. wooden, with movable limbs, used by artists

lay flat *v adv* [T1] to knock down to the ground

lay in *v adv* [T1] to obtain and store a supply of

lay in·to *v prep* [T1] to attack with words or blows

lay low *v adv* [T1b *often pass.*] **1** to knock or bring down, esp. in a way that destroys or makes hopeless **2** to make (someone) ill

lay·man /ˈleɪmən/ *n* **-men** /mən/ **1** a person who is not a priest in a religion **2** a person who is not trained in a particular subject or type of work, esp. as compared with those who are

lay off *v adv; prep* **1** [T1;D1] to stop employing (a worker), esp. for a period in which there is little work: *They laid us off (work) for 3 months* **2** [T1,4a;IØ] *infml* to stop: *Lay off work for a few months.|Lay off, will you! Lay off hitting me!*

lay-off /ˈ· ·/ *n* **1** the stopping by a business of a worker's employment at a time when there is little work **2** the period during which workers are unemployed for this reason, or when any person has not been doing his usual activity

lay on *v adv* **1** [T1 (*to, for*)] to supply or provide **2** [D1] also **lay up·on**— to put (some serious charge or responsibility) upon (someone) **3 lay it on a** to tell something in a way that goes beyond the truth **b** to praise or admire too greatly, esp. in order to please

lay o·pen *v adv* [T1] **1** to uncover or make known **2** to cut; wound: *The blow laid his head open* **3 lay oneself open to** to put oneself in the position of receiving (attack, blame, etc.)

lay·out /ˈleɪaʊt/ *n* **1** the planned arrangement of a town, garden, etc. **2** a drawing or plan of a building **3** the way in which printed matter is set out on paper

lay out *v adv* [T1a,(b)] **1** to spread out or arrange **2** to plan (a building, town, garden, etc.) **3** to arrange (a dead body) for burial **4** to knock or strike (a person) down **5** *infml* to spend (money, esp. a large amount)

lay o·ver *v adv* [IØ] *AmE* STOP OVER

lay read·er /ˌ· ˈ··/ *n* a person who is not a priest and who reads part of certain religious services

lay sis·ter /ˌ· ˈ··/ *n* see LAY BROTHER

lay to *v adv* [T1;IØ] **a** (of a ship) to stop **b** to stop (a ship)

lay up *v adv* [T1] **1** to collect and store for future use **2** [*usu. pass.*] to cause to be kept indoors or in bed with an illness **3** [*usu. pass.*] to put (a boat) out of service, esp. for repairs

lay waste *v adv* [T1] to make (a place) bare, esp. by violence; destroy, as in war

laze[1] /leɪz/ *v* [L9] to rest lazily

laze[2] *n* [S] a short period of restful and lazy inactivity

laze a·bout also **laze a·round**— *v adv* [IØ] to waste time enjoyably, with little effort

laze a·way *v adv* [T1] to spend (time) lazily

la·zy /ˈleɪzi/ *adj* [Wa1] **1** disliking and avoiding activity or work **2** (esp. of periods of time) encouraging inactivity: *a lazy afternoon* **3** moving slowly: *lazy river* —**-zily** *adv* —**-ziness** *n* [U]

lb *written abbrev. for:* pound (weight)

lbw *abbrev. for:* LEG[1] (23) before wicket
LCM *abbrev. for:* least/lowest common MULTIPLE[2] (2): *20 is the LCM of 4 and 5*
L-Do·pa /ˌel ˈdəʊpə/ also (*esp. BrE*) **levodopa**— *n* [U] a drug used in the treatment of a disease of the nervous system (PARKINSON'S DISEASE)
L-driv·er /ˈ· ˌ··/ *n BrE* a person who is learning to drive
lea /liː/ *n poet* an open piece of grassy land
leach /liːtʃ/ *v tech* **1** [T1 (OUT, AWAY);IØ] **a** to separate certain substances from (a material, such as soil) by passing water through it **b** (of a material, such as soil) to lose certain substances, by the passage of water through it **2** [IØ (AWAY, *out of*)] (of certain substances in a material) to disappear by the action of water
lead¹ /liːd/ *v* **led** /led/ **1** [T1 (ALONG); IØ (ON)] to show (somebody) the way; go before or with (somebody) **2** [V3;T1 (*to, into*)] to guide in opinion or action; persuade; influence: *What led you to believe I was ill?|Her careless spending led her into debt* **3** [X9;L9] to be the means of (something) reaching a place, going through an area, etc.: *This path leads to the village* **4** [X9] to take or bring with, or as if with, force: *The horses were led into the yard* **5** [T1;IØ] to direct, control, or govern (an army, a movement, a meeting, etc.) **6** [T1;IØ] to be ahead in sports or games **7** [T1;IØ (*with*)] to start or open in (a match or game, esp. of cards, a dance, etc.) **8** [T1] to start or open a game, esp. of cards, with: *She led her highest card* **9** [T1] to experience or cause to experience (a kind of life): *He led a hard life* —see also LEAD ASTRAY, LEAD OFF, LEAD ON, LEAD TO, LEAD UP TO
USAGE To **lead** is to show someone the way by going first: *to* **lead** *an army|You* **lead** *and we'll follow*. To **guide** is to show the way and explain things: *to* **guide** *a party round the Taj Mahal*. To **drive** is either to control a moving vehicle, or to make animals move forward by going behind them: **driving** *the cattle to market*. To **steer** is to control the direction of a moving vehicle or boat. —see RIDE[1] (USAGE)
lead² *n* **1** [S] the act of leading **2** [C] a guiding suggestion or example **3** [C] information that may lead to a discovery or something being settled; CLUE **4** [*the*+U] the first or front place in a race, competition, etc. **5** [S (*of, over*)] the distance, number of points, etc., by which a person or thing is in advance of another person or thing: *Our product still has a good lead over that of our competitor* **6** [(*the*) S] (in card games) **a** the right to play the first or opening card **b** the first card player **7** [(*the*) C] **a** the chief acting part in a play or film **b** the person who plays it **8** [C] the main or opening part of a piece of newspaper writing **9** [A] being the main and most important article in a newspaper **10** [C] also (*fml or tech*) **leash**— *esp. BrE* a length of rope, leather, chain, etc., tied to a dog to control it —see picture at DOG[1] **11** [C] an electric wire for taking the power from the supply point to an instrument or apparatus —see picture at CAR **12 take the lead** to start an action; take the controlling most active part
lead³ /led/ *n* **1** [U] a soft heavy easily melted greyish-blue metal, used for waterpipes, to cover roofs, etc. **2** [C] a thin rope with a mass of lead fastened to one end which is lowered from a ship to measure the depth of water **3** [U;C] GRAPHITE, esp. a thin stick of it used in pencils: *I need a soft lead pencil* **4** [C] a thin piece of metal that separates lines of print on a printing machine **5 swing the lead** *BrE sl* to avoid one's work or duty, as by pretending to be ill —see also RED LEAD, WHITE LEAD
lead a·stray /liːd/ *v adv* [T1] to cause (someone) to behave wrongly
lead·en /ˈledn/ *adj* **1** [Wa5] made of lead **2** [Wa5] of the colour of lead; dull grey: *a leaden sky* **3** dull; heavy; sad: *a leaden heart*
lead·er /ˈliːdəʳ/ *n* **1** a person or thing that leads or is in advance of others **2** a person who guides or directs a group, movement, etc. **3** something produced by a business and sold very cheaply to interest buyers in other goods **4** (*AmE* **concertmaster**)— *BrE* the first VIOLIN player of an ORCHESTRA, who by custom helps the CONDUCTOR (1) **5** *AmE* the musician (CONDUCTOR) who directs the playing of a group (ORCHESTRA), usu. by regular movements of the hands **6** the chief lawyer for each side in a law case **7** the strongest stem or branch of a tree **8** *BrE* EDITORIAL[2]: *the "Times" leader writers*
lead·er·ship /ˈliːdəʃɪp‖-ər-/ *n* **1** [U] the position of leader **2** [U] the qualities necessary in a leader **3** [U] control or power over a group **4** [GC] a group of people who lead: *The leadership of the movement is/are divided*
lead-in /ˈliːd ɪn/ *n* **1** a wire connecting a radio receiver with the part (AERIAL[2]) that picks up the radio waves **2** remarks made by someone while introducing a radio show
lead·ing¹ /ˈliːdɪŋ/ *adj* [Wa5;A] **1** most important; chief; main **2** guiding, directing, or controlling **3** having the main part (esp. in the phr. **leading actor** or **actress**)
lead·ing² /ˈledɪŋ/ *n* [U] lead used for covering roofs, for window frames, etc.
leading ar·ti·cle /ˌliːdɪŋ ˈɑːtɪkəl‖-ˈɑr-/ *n BrE* EDITORIAL[2]
leading light /ˌliːdɪŋ ˈlaɪt/ *n* [(*in, of*)] a person of importance or influence
leading ques·tion /ˌliːdɪŋ ˈkwestʃən/ *n* a question formed in such a way that it suggests the desired answer
leading reins /ˈliːdɪŋ reɪnz/ also **reins**— *n* [P] bands of leather or rope that support a baby by the shoulders while learning to walk
leading strings /ˈliːdɪŋ strɪŋz/ *n* [P] **1** *BrE* continuous control and guidance (esp. in the phr. **keep in leading strings**) **2** *rare* LEADING REINS
lead off /liːd/ *v adv* [IØ (*with*); (T1 (*with*))] to make a start; begin: *She led off (the show) with a song*
lead on /liːd/ *v adv* **1** [T1b;V3] to cause to believe something that is not true **2** [T1b (*into*)] to influence (somebody) into doing something not in his best interests **3** [T1b] LEAD[1] (1)
leads /ledz/ *n* [P] **1** sheets of lead used for covering a roof **2** narrow bands of lead used for holding small pieces of glass together to form a certain type of window (LATTICE (2))
lead to /liːd/ *v prep* [T1,4] to have as a result; cause
lead up to /liːd/ *v adv prep* [T1] to be an introduction to or preparation for: *My kind words led up to a request for money*
leaf¹ /liːf/ *n* **leaves** /liːvz/ **1** [C] one of the usu. flat and green parts of a plant that are joined to its stem or branch —see picture at FLOWER[1] **2** [C] a thin sheet of paper, esp. one in a book on which 2 pages are printed **3** [U] metal, esp. gold or silver, in a very thin sheet: *gold leaf* **4** [C] part of a tabletop, door, etc., that may be slid, folded, or taken into or out of use —see picture at LIVING ROOM **5 in(to) leaf** having or starting to have leaves **6 take a leaf out of somebody's book** to follow somebody's example **7 turn over a new leaf** to begin a new course of improved behaviour, habits, etc.
leaf² *v* [IØ (OUT)] to grow or develop leaves
leaf·age /ˈliːfɪdʒ/ *n* [U] leaves in general; FOLIAGE

leafed /liːft/ *adj* LEAVED
leaf·let /ˈliːflǝ̇t/ *n* **1** a small sheet, often folded, of printed matter, usu. given free to the public **2** a small young leaf **3** one of the parts of a leaf made up of several separate parts
leaf mould, *AmE* **leaf mold** /ˈ· ·/ *n* [U] *esp. BrE* dead decaying leaves which form a rich top surface to soil
leaf out *v adv* [I∅] *AmE* (of a plant) to come into leaf
leaf through *v prep; adv* [T1;I∅] to turn the pages of (a book, magazine, etc.) quickly without reading much
leaf·y /ˈliːfi/ *adj* [Wa1] covered with, belonging to, or having many leaves
league¹ /liːg/ *n obs* a measure of distance of about 3 miles or 5 kilometres
league² *n* [GC] **1** a group of people, countries, etc., who have joined together to protect or improve their position, or to work for some aim **2** the agreement made between such people, countries, etc. **3** a group of sports clubs or players that play matches amongst themselves: *Is this game a league match?* **4** *infml* a level of quality: *They're not in the same league* **5 in league (with)** working together, often secretly or for a bad purpose
league³ *v* [T1;I∅:(TOGETHER)] to unite in or join a LEAGUE² (1)
leak¹ /liːk/ *v* **1** [T1;I∅] to let (a liquid, gas, etc.) in or out of a LEAK² (1): *The bottle leaks* **2** [I∅] (of a liquid, gas, etc.) to pass through a LEAK² (1) **3** [T1 (OUT, *to*)] to make known (news, facts, etc., that ought to be secret)
leak² *n* **1** [C] a small accidental hole or crack through which something flows in or out **2** [C] the liquid, gas, etc., that escapes through such a hole: *I can smell a gas leak* **3** [C *usu. sing.*] the amount that escapes or is lost **4** [C] an accidental or unintentional spreading of news, facts, etc., that ought to be secret **5** [C] an escape of electricity, esp. through a badly covered (INSULATED) wire **6** [S] *sl* an act of passing water from the body
leak·age /ˈliːkɪdʒ/ *n* **1** [U] the act of LEAKing¹ (2) **2** [C] that which LEAKs in or out **3** [C] the amount of such a LEAK² (2)
leak out *v adv* [I∅] (of news, facts, etc., that ought to be secret) to become known
leak·y /ˈliːki/ *adj* [Wa1] letting liquid LEAK¹ (2) in or out: *a leaky bucket* —**-ily** *adv* —**-iness** *n* [U]
lean¹ /liːn/ *v* **leant** /lent/ *or* **leaned** **1** [I∅] to be in a position that is not upright; slope **2** [L9] to bend (from the waist): *He leaned forward/down/over to hear what she said* **3** [L9] to support or rest oneself in a bent or sloping position: *She leaned against his shoulder* **4** [X9] to rest (something) somewhere: *Lean it on/against the wall* **5 lean over backwards (to)** to make every possible effort (to)
USAGE **Leaned** and **leant** are both used in *BrE*, but **leaned** is the main form in *AmE*.
lean² *n* [S (*of*)] the act or amount of leaning: *a lean of 90°*
lean³ *adj* [Wa1] **1** (of people and animals) very thin **2** (of meat) without much fat **3** producing or having little value —**~ness** *n* [U]
lean⁴ *n* [(*the*) U] the part of cooked meat that is not fat
lean·ing /ˈliːnɪŋ/ *n* [(*towards*)] a feeling or opinion (in favour of)
lean on *v prep* [T1] **1** also **lean up·on**— to depend on **2** *infml* to influence (someone) by threats
lean-to /ˈ· ·/ *n* **-tos** a small building with a roof that rests on the side of a larger building
lean to·wards (*AmE* **lean to·ward**)— *v prep* [T1] *esp. BrE* to favour (an opinion, idea, etc.)
leap¹ /liːp/ *v* **leapt** /lept/ *or* **leaped** /lept‖liːpt/ **1** [L9; I∅] to spring through the air, often landing in a different place: *They leaped for joy.|They leaped over the stream* **2** [T1] to jump over **3** [L9] to act, pass, rise, etc., rapidly, as if with a jump: *The idea leaped into his mind*
USAGE **Leapt** is more common in *BrE* than **leaped**, except in literature, but **leaped** is more common in *AmE*.
leap² *n* **1** a sudden jump, spring, or movement **2** the distance crossed by LEAPing¹ **3** a sudden increase in number, amount, quantity, etc. **4 by leaps and bounds** very quickly **5 a leap in the dark** an action or risk taken without knowing what will happen
leap at *v prep* [T1] to accept (a chance, offer, etc.) eagerly
leap·frog /ˈliːpfrɒg‖-frɔg, -frɑg/ *n* [U] a game in which one person bends down and another jumps over him from behind
leap out *v adv* [I∅ (*at*)] to be noticeable: *His name leapt out at me from the newspaper*
leap year /ˈ· ·/ *n* [C;U] a year, every 4th year, in which February has 29 days instead of 28 days
learn /lɜːn‖lɜrn/ *v* **learned** *or* **learnt** /lɜːnt‖lɜrnt/ **1** [I∅;T1,3,6b] to gain knowledge (of) or skill (in): *The child is learning quickly.|I'm trying to learn French.|She is learning to be a dancer.|He is learning how to play the drums* **2** [T1] to fix in the memory; MEMORIZE: *You should learn this list of words by tomorrow* **3** [T1,5a,b,6a,b;I∅ (*of* or *about*)] to become informed (of): *His mother learnt of her son's success in the newspapers* **4** [T1] *often humor* to punish (someone) by scolding, beating, etc. **5 learn one's lesson** to suffer so much from doing something that one will not do it again
USAGE The past tense and past participle are usually **learned** in *AmE*; but in *BrE* **learnt** is equally common, particularly in the past participle, and it may be better to use this form, to avoid confusion with the adjective **learned** (="wise"). —see KNOW¹
learn·ed /ˈlɜːnǝ̇d‖ˈlɜr-/ *adj* **1** [B] having much knowledge as the result of study and reading **2** [Wa5;A] of, for, or concerning advanced study: *a learned work* —**~ly** *adv*
learn·er /ˈlɜːnǝʳ‖ˈlɜr-/ *n* a person who is learning, esp. a person (**learner driver** /ˌ·· ˈ··/) who is learning to drive a car: *She's a rather slow learner* (=is slow at learning)
learn·ing /ˈlɜːnɪŋ‖ˈlɜr-/ *n* [U] deep and wide knowledge gained through reading and study —compare KNOWLEDGE
lease¹ /liːs/ *n* **1** a written agreement, made according to law, by which the use of a building or piece of land is given (LET³ (5)) by its owner to somebody for a certain time in return for rent **2** the length of time such an agreement is to last **3 a new lease of** (*AmE* **on**) **life** *BrE* new strength or desire to be happy, successful, etc.
lease² *v* [T1 (OUT)] to give or take the use of (land or buildings) on a LEASE¹ (1)
lease·hold /ˈliːshǝʊld/ *n, adj* [Wa5;U;B] (land or buildings) held on a LEASE¹ (1) —compare FREEHOLD —**~er** *n*
leash /liːʃ/ *n fml or tech* LEAD² (10)
least¹ /liːst/ *adj* (*superl. of* LITTLE) [Wa5] **1** [B] smallest in size, amount, degree, measure, etc.: *He has least money of us all* —opposite **most** **2** [A *nonassertive*] slightest: *I haven't the least idea*
least² *n* **1** [*the*+U] the smallest thing, amount, degree, etc.: *Giving him food was the least we could do* —compare LITTLE³, LESS¹; opposite **the most** **2 at least** if nothing else: *The food wasn't good, but at least it was cheap* **3 at (the) least** not less than: *It costs at least 5 pounds.|At the least, it costs 5 pounds*

—opposite **at (the) most** **4 in the least** *nonassertive* at all: *"Nobody would worry in the least"* (SEU S.) **5 to say the least (of it)** I will not say more than that

least³ *adv* (*superl. of* LITTLE) **1** in the smallest amount, degree, etc.: *It happened just when we least expected it.|one of the least known of the modern poets* —opposite **most** **2 least of all** especially not **3 not least** partly; quite importantly: *Trade has been bad, not least because of the increased cost of rubber*

least·ways /ˈliːstweɪz/ also **least·wise** /ˈliːstwaɪz/— *adv* [Wa5] *rare* at LEAST² (2)

leath·er¹ /ˈleðəʳ/ *n* [U] animal skin that has been treated (TANned) to preserve it, used for making shoes, bags, etc.: *a leather coat*

leather² *v* [T1] **1** [(*with*)] *infml* to beat, esp. with a leather belt **2** *rare* to cover with leather

leath·er·ette /ˌleðəˈret/ *n* [U] a cheap material made to look like leather

leath·er·y /ˈleðəri/ *adj* like leather; hard and stiff: *leathery meat*

leave¹ /liːv/ *v* **left** /left/ **1** [T1;I∅ (*for*)] to go away (from): *The car left the road and hit a tree.|We must leave early.|When shall we leave for the party?* **2** [T1;I∅] to cease to remain (in or with); stop working for (a business): *I am leaving England.|He left his wife 3 months ago* **3** [X1,7,9: *often pass.*] to let stay; cause to be: *We left the work in the office.|The window was left open* **4** [D1 (*for*); T1] to allow or cause to remain after going away: *The postman left a letter for us* **5** [T1] to allow to remain untaken, unused, unchanged, uneaten, etc.: *You've left your food* **6** [T1] to allow to remain undone, perhaps until a later time: *Let's leave that for another day* **7** [T1 (*with, to*), 4] to give into the care or charge of someone: *He left his cat with us.|I'll leave it to you to buy the tickets.|I'll leave buying the tickets to you* **8** [T1] to have remaining after death: *He leaves a wife and 2 children* **9** [D1 (*to*); T1] to give (through a WILL² (6)) after the death of the giver **10** [D1 *no pass.*; L1] to have left over: *2 from 8 leaves (you) 6* **11** [T1] LEAVE BEHIND: *Don't leave your coat!* **12 leave someone/something alone** to LET³ (7) someone/something alone **13 leave someone/something be** to allow someone/something to remain untouched, unused, not put out of position or order, etc.: *"The baby's crying!" "Leave him be; he'll soon stop"* **14 leave go/hold of** to stop holding; let go **15 leave it at that** to do or say no more **16 leave one cold** to fail to excite or interest one **17 leave (people) to (them)selves/to (their) own devices** not to control the activities of (people) **18 leave well alone** (*AmE* **leave well enough alone**)— *BrE* to LET³ (22) well alone

leave² *n* **1** [U,U3] permission **2** [U] permission to be absent from work or duty, esp. in government or army service **3** [C] time spent in such an absence **4** [C *usu. sing.*] a holiday —see HOLIDAY¹ (USAGE) **5 take leave (of)** to say goodbye (to); go away (from) —see also FRENCH LEAVE, SICK LEAVE

leave be·hind *v adv* [T1] to fail to take or bring, esp. by accident

leaved /liːvd/ also **leafed**— *adj* [A;(B)] having leaves, esp. leaves of the stated type or number: *a narrow-leaved plant*

leav·en¹ /ˈlevən/ *n* **1** [U] a substance (esp. YEAST) that is added to flour and water to make it swell and produce bread **2** [C;U] an influence that causes a gradual change in character

leaven² *v* [T1] **1** to add LEAVEN¹ to (a cooking mixture, esp. flour and water) **2** to influence; change

leav·en·ing /ˈlevənɪŋ/ *n* [C;(U)] LEAVEN¹ (esp. 2)

leave of ab·sence /ˌ·· ˈ··/ *n* **leaves of absence** [U;C *usu. sing.*] LEAVE² (2, 3)

leave off *v adv* **1** [T1] to wear no longer (esp. an article of clothing) **2** [T1a,4a;I∅] to stop (doing something); give up: *He has left off working*

leave out *v adv* [T1 (*of*)] **1** to fail to put in or include: *I left out the important point.|England have left Amiss out (of their cricket team)* **2** to fail to consider; forget: *Nobody speaks to him; he's always left out*

leave o·ver *v adv* [T1] to delay doing, considering, etc., till a later time

leaves /liːvz/ *pl. of* LEAF

leave tak·ing /ˈ· ˌ··/ *n fml* the act of saying goodbye and going away

leav·ings /ˈliːvɪŋz/ *n* [(*the*) P] things that are left or unwanted, esp. food after a meal

lech¹ /letʃ/ *v* [I∅] *sl* to look continually for sexual pleasure

lech² *n* [*usu. sing.*] *sl* a LECHEROUS desire or act

lech·er /ˈletʃəʳ/ *n* a man who continually looks for sexual pleasure

lech·er·ous /ˈletʃərəs/ *adj* (of a man) having a desire for continual sexual pleasure —see EROTIC (USAGE) —**~ly** *adv* —**~ness** *n* [U]

lech·er·y /ˈletʃəri/ *n* **1** [U] continual searching for sexual pleasure **2** [C] an act resulting from this search

lec·tern /ˈlektən‖-ərn/ *n* a sloping table for holding a book, esp. the Bible in a church —see picture at CHURCH¹

lec·ture¹ /ˈlektʃəʳ/ *n* [(*on, about*)] **1** a speech spoken or read before a group of people, esp. as a method of teaching at universities **2** a long solemn scolding or warning

lecture² *v* [T1;I∅ (*to*): (*on, about*)] **1** to give a LECTURE¹ (1) (to) **2** to scold solemnly and at length

lec·tur·er /ˈlektʃərəʳ/ *n* **1** a person who gives LECTURE*s*, esp. at a university or college **2** a person who holds the lowest teaching rank at a British university or college

lec·ture·ship /ˈlektʃəʃɪp‖-ər-/ *n* the position of a LECTURER (2) at a British university or college

lecture the·at·re /ˈ·· ˌ···/ also **theatre**— *n* a hall or room with seats in rows rising one behind the other for talks, LECTURE*s*, etc.

led /led/ *past t. & p. of* LEAD¹

ledge /ledʒ/ *n* **1** a narrow flat shelf or surface, esp. one on the edge of an upright object **2** a flat shelf of rock, esp. one that stretches a long way below the sea

led·ger /ˈledʒəʳ/ *n* **1** an account book recording the gains and money spent of a business, bank, etc. **2** also **ledger line** /ˈ·· ·/, **leger, leger line**— a short line added above or below the usu. 5 lines (STAFF¹ (3)) on which music is written, for notes that are too high or too low to be recorded on the STAFF

lee /liː/ *n* [*the*+R] **1** shelter, esp. from rough weather or wind **2** the side, esp. of a ship, that is away from the wind —see also LEE SHORE, LEE TIDE

leech /liːtʃ/ *n* **1** any of several types of small wormlike creature living in wet places that pricks the skin of animals and drinks their blood, formerly used for lowering the blood pressure of sick people **2** a person who continually makes profit out of another **3** *old use or humor* a doctor **4 cling like a leech (to)** to be unwilling to be separated (from)

leek /liːk/ *n* a type of vegetable like the onion but with a long white fleshy stem —see picture at VEGETABLE¹

leer¹ /lɪəʳ/ *v* [I∅ (*at*)] to look with a LEER² —**~ingly** *adv*

leer² *n* an unpleasant smile or sideways look

expressing cruel enjoyment, rudeness, or thoughts of sex

leer·y /ˈlɪəri/ *adj* [Wa2;F (*of*)] *sl* watchful and not trusting: *I'm very leery of him*

lees /liːz/ *n* [(*the*) P] the bitter undrinkable thick matter (SEDIMENT) at the bottom of a wine bottle, barrel, etc.

lee shore /ˌ· ˈ·/ *n* a shore onto which the wind blows from the sea

lee tide /ˌ· ˈ·/ *n* a rise of the sea (TIDE) moving in the same direction as the wind, and therefore greater than the usual rise

lee·ward[1] /ˈliːwəd, *tech* ˈluːəd‖-ərd/ *adj* [Wa5] with or in the direction of the wind; away from the wind —compare WINDWARD

leeward[2] *n* [U] the side or direction towards which the wind blows

lee·way /ˈliːweɪ/ *n* **1** [U] the sideways movement of a ship or aircraft with the wind **2** [C] the amount a ship or aircraft is blown off its intended course by the wind **3** [C;U] *BrE* loss of time or advance **4** [C;U] additional time, space, money, etc., that allows a chance to succeed in doing something: *10 minutes should be* (*a big*) *enough leeway to allow for delays*

left[1] /left/ *adj* **1** [Wa5;A] on or belonging to the side of the body that usu. contains the heart: *one's left arm/eye* **2** [Wa5;A] on, by, or in the direction of one's left side: *the left bank of the stream* **3** [Wa2;B] belonging to, connected with, or favouring the LEFT[2] (3) in politics: *He's very left.|He votes left* —opposite **right**

left[2] *n* **1** [*the*+U] the left side or direction: *Keep to the left* **2** [C] the left hand **3** [*the*+GU] political parties or groups (such as those for SOCIALISM and COMMUNISM) that favour the equal division of wealth and property and generally support the workers rather than the employers

left[3] *adv* [Wa5] towards the left

left[4] *past t. and p. of* LEAVE[1]

left-hand /ˌ· ˈ·◂/ *adj* [Wa5;A] **1** on or to the left side: *the left-hand page* **2** of, for, with, or done by the left hand: *a left-hand stroke* **3** turning or going to the left: *They drove too fast round the left-hand bend*

left-hand·ed /ˌ· ˈ··◂/ *adj* [Wa5] **1** using the left hand for most actions rather than the right **2** made for use by a left-handed person: *left-handed scissors* **3** unskilful, awkward, or unsuccessful **4** **left-handed compliment** a remark that might cause either pleasure or displeasure —**~ly** *adv* [Wa5] —**~ness** *n* [U]

left-hand·er /ˌ· ˈ··/ *n* **1** a person who usu. uses his left hand **2** a blow or stroke given with the left hand

left·ist /ˈleftɪ̈st/ *n, adj* (a supporter) of the LEFT[2] (3) in politics

left lug·gage of·fice /ˌ· ˈ·· ˌ··/ (*AmE* **baggage room**)— *n BrE* a place, esp. in a station, where one can leave one's bags for a certain period, to be collected later

left·o·vers /ˈleftˌəʊvəz‖-ərz/ *n* [P] food remaining uneaten after a meal, esp. when served at a later meal

left·ward /ˈleftwəd‖-ərd/ *adj* [Wa5] on or towards the left

left·wards /ˈleftwədz‖-ərdz/ (*AmE* **leftward**)— *adv* [Wa5] *esp. BrE* on or towards the left

left wing /ˌ· ˈ·◂/ *adj, n* **1** [B; *the*+GU] (the group of members) of a political party (esp. a SOCIALIST or COMMUNIST party) or group that favour greater political changes **2** [B; *the*+GU] (of) the political party or group itself; LEFT[1,2] (3): *left-wing ideas* **3** [B;C; *the*+R] ((of) the player in certain sports, such as football, whose position is on) the edge of the left of the field —**left-winger** /ˌ· ˈ··/ *n*

leg[1] /leg/ *n* **1** [C] a limb on which an animal walks and which supports its body **2** [C] that part of this limb above the foot **3** [C;U] the leg of a fleshy animal as food **4** [C] the part of a garment that covers the leg **5** [C] one of the long thin supports on which a piece of furniture stands —see picture at LIVING ROOM **6** [C] something like a leg in use or appearance **7** [C] one part or stage, esp. of a journey or competition **8** [U] that part of a cricket field behind and to the left of the (right-handed) player who strikes the ball (BATSMAN) as he faces the man who throws it —see picture at CRICKET[2] **9** [C] (*in combs.*) a fielder placed in this part of the field: *The ball was fielded by short leg* **10 be/get (up) on one's (hind) legs** to stand up in order to say or argue something, esp. in public **11 on one's/it's last legs a** very tired **b** nearly worn out or failed **c** close to death **12 be (up) on one's legs a** to be standing or walking about, esp. for a long time **b** (after an illness) to be able to get up and walk about **13 get somebody back on his legs a** to bring someone back into good health **b** help someone to a condition in which he can support himself in money matters **14 give a leg up a** to help someone to climb or get on something **b** to help someone in trouble **15 have no leg to stand on** to have no good reason or excuse **16 have the legs of someone** *infml* to (be able to) run faster than someone **17 pull someone's leg** to make fun of a person in a playful way, as by laughing at some weakness or by making him believe something that is not true —see also LEG-PULL **18 shake a leg** *sl* (*usu. imper.*) to act fast; hurry **19 show a leg** *infml* to get out of bed **20 stand on one's own legs/feet** not to depend on others or need their help **21 stretch one's legs** to take a short walk, esp. when feeling stiff after sitting for a long time **22 take to one's legs/heels** to run away —see also LEG[2] **23 leg before wicket** a way in which a cricketer's turn to strike the ball can be ended by his (usu. accidental) stopping with his leg a ball which would otherwise have hit the 3 posts of his WICKET

leg[2] *v* **-gg- leg it** *infml* to walk or run fast, esp. to run away

leg·a·cy /ˈlegəsi/ *n* **1** money or personal possessions that pass to someone on the death of the owner according to his official written wish (WILL[2] (6)) **2** something passed on or left behind by someone else **3** a lasting result: *These ruined buildings are a legacy of the war*

le·gal /ˈliːgəl/ *adj* [Wa5] **1** [B] allowed or made by law; lawful: *a legal claim* —compare ILLEGAL **2** [A] of, concerning, or using the law: *legal action* —**~ly** *adv*

USAGE **Legal** and **lawful** both mean "allowed according to the law": *Children can't buy alcohol: it's not* **legal/lawful**. **Legal** also means "connected with the law"; *the* **legal** *profession*|**legal** *formalities*. **Lawful** is particularly used in the meaning "allowed or appointed according to moral and religious law": *your* **lawful** *king*.

legal aid /ˌ·· ˈ·/ *n* [U] the services of a lawyer in a court case provided free to people too poor to pay for them

legal fic·tion /ˌ·· ˈ··/ *n* something that one pretends is true for convenience, although it may be false

le·gal·i·ty /lɪˈgælɪ̈ti/ *n* [U] the condition of being lawful; lawfulness

le·gal·ize, -ise /ˈliːgəlaɪz/ *v* [T1] to make lawful —**-ization** /ˌliːgəlaɪˈzeɪʃən‖-gələ-/ *n* [U]

legal ten·der /ˌ·· ˈ··/ *n* [U] money which by law must be accepted when offered in payment

leg·ate /ˈlegɪ̈t/ *n* **1** a priest of high rank, appointed by the POPE as his representative **2** *tech* a member of a LEGATION (1)

leg·a·tee /ˌlegəˈtiː/ *n* a person who receives some of the possessions of another person on that person's death

le·ga·tion /lɪˈgeɪʃən/ *n* [GC] **1** a group of government servants working under a minister (of the highest rank below AMBASSADOR) who represent their government in a foreign country **2** the official home of the minister in charge of the group **3** the offices of the group

le·ga·to /lɪˈgɑːtəʊ/ *adj, adv* (of music) (played or to be played) smoothly, with the notes sliding smoothly into each other —compare STACCATO

leg bye /ˌ· ˈ·/ *n* a run in cricket made after the ball has touched a leg or any part of the body except the hands of the player (BATSMAN) who tried to hit it

le·gend /ˈledʒənd/ *n* **1** [C] an old story about great deeds and men of ancient times having slight possible base in truth **2** [U] such stories collectively: *a character in legend* **3** [C] the words or phrase on a coin **4** [C] the words that explain a picture, map, table, etc., in a book **5** [C] a famous person or act, esp. in a particular area of activity: *He is a legend in his own lifetime for his scientific discoveries*

le·gen·da·ry /ˈledʒəndəri‖-deri/ *adj* **1** of, like, or told in a LEGEND (1) **2** famous

le·ger /ˈledʒəʳ/ also **leger line** /ˈ·· ·/— *n* LEDGER (2)

le·ger·de·main /ˌledʒədəˈmeɪn‖-dʒər-/ *n* [U] **1** quick skilful use of the hands in performing tricks **2** clever but rather deceitful use of argument

leg·ged /legd, ˈlegɪ̈d/ *adj* [Wa5] having legs, esp. of a stated number or kind: *4-legged|cross-legged*

leg·gings /ˈlegɪŋz/ *n* [P] an outer covering of strong cloth, or leather, worn to protect the legs, esp. from foot to knee

leg·gy /ˈlegi/ *adj* [Wa1] (esp. of children and women, and young animals) having long legs, esp. by comparison with the rest of the body —**-giness** *n* [U]

le·gi·ble /ˈledʒəbəl/ *adj* (of handwriting or print) that can be read, esp. easily —opposite **illegible** —**-bility** /ˌledʒəˈbɪlɪ̈ti/ *n* [U] —**-bly** /ˈledʒəbli/ *adv*

le·gion[1] /ˈliːdʒən/ *n* [GC] **1** (in ancient Rome) a division of the army containing between 3000 and 6000 foot soldiers **2** a group of present or former soldiers or other armed men **3** a large group of people: *a legion of admirers*

legion[2] *adj* [Wa5;F] *fml* very many

le·gion·a·ry /ˌliːdʒənəri‖-neri/ *n* a member of a LEGION

le·gis·late /ˈledʒɪ̈sleɪt/ *v* [IØ (*for, against*)] to make laws

legislate a·gainst *v prep* [T1;V4a] *fml* to (tend to) prevent (something, or someone doing something): *The higher travel costs legislate against government officers travelling abroad so often*

legislate for *v prep fml* [T1;(V4a)] to make plans with; make ALLOWANCES (4) for

le·gis·la·tion /ˌledʒɪ̈sˈleɪʃən/ *n* [U] **1** the act of making laws **2** a body of laws

le·gis·la·tive /ˈledʒɪ̈slətɪv‖-leɪtɪv/ *adj* [Wa5;A] **1** of or concerning the making of laws **2** having the power and duty to make laws **3** ordered by or in accordance with a body of laws —**~ly** *adv* [Wa5]

le·gis·la·tor /ˈledʒɪ̈sleɪtəʳ/ *n* a maker of laws or a member of a lawmaking body

le·gis·la·ture /ˈledʒɪ̈sleɪtʃəʳ, -lətʃəʳ/ *n* the body of people who have the power to make and change laws

le·git /lɪˈdʒɪt/ *adj sl* LEGITIMATE (1)

le·git·i·mate /lɪˈdʒɪtɪ̈mɪ̈t/ *adj* **1** according to law or another body of rules or standards; lawful or correct **2** [Wa5] born of parents who are lawfully married to each other **3** reasonable; sensible: *The accident that delayed our bus gave us a legitimate reason for being late* —opposite **illegitimate** —**~ly** *adv* —**-macy** *n* [U]

le·git·i·ma·tize, -tise /lɪˈdʒɪtɪ̈mətaɪz/ also **le·git·i·mize, -mise** /lɪˈdʒɪtɪ̈maɪz/— *v* [T1] **1** to make lawful **2** to make (a child) LEGITIMATE (2), esp. by the marriage of the parents

leg-pull /ˈ· ·/ *n infml* a playful attempt to make a fool of someone —compare **pull someone's** LEG[1] (17)

leg·room /ˈlegrʊm, -ruːm/ *n* [U] room enough to stretch out one's legs comfortably

leg·ume /ˈlegjuːm, lɪˈgjuːm/ *n* **1** any plant of the bean family that bears its seeds in a thin case (POD) which breaks in 2 along its length, esp. such a plant eaten as a vegetable **2** the seed case of such a plant **3** such a plant used as food for horses and cattle

le·gu·mi·nous /lɪˈgjuːmɪ̈nəs/ *adj* [Wa5] **1** of or like LEGUMEs **2** bearing seed cases of LEGUMEs

lei /leɪ/ *n* (esp. in Hawaii) a circular bunch of flowers placed round one's neck as a greeting

lei·sure /ˈleʒəʳ‖ˈliː-/ *n* **1** [U] time when one is free from employment or duties of any kind; free time **2 at leisure a** not working or busy; free **b** without hurry **3 at one's leisure** at a convenient free time; when one pleases

lei·sured /ˈleʒəd‖ˈliːʒərd/ *adj* **1** having no regular business but plenty of free time **2** LEISURELY[1]

lei·sure·ly[1] /ˈleʒəli‖ˈliːʒərli/ *adj* (moving, acting, or done) without haste: *a leisurely walk* —**-liness** *n* [U]

leisurely[2] *adv rare* in a LEISURELY[1] way

leit·mo·tive, -tif /ˈlaɪtməʊˌtiːf/ *n Ger* **1** a musical phrase that is played at various times during an OPERA (or like musical work) to suggest or go along with particular characters or ideas **2** something in a person's character, speech, or work of art that keeps appearing and which is seen to be a controlling influence or important interest

lem·ming /ˈlemɪŋ/ *n* a type of small ratlike animal living in very cold parts of the world, esp. northern Europe, which sometimes travels long distances in large groups without regard to possible danger

lem·on /ˈlemən/ *n* **1** [C;U] a type of fruit like an orange but with a light yellow skin and sour juice: *a lemon drink* —see picture at FRUIT[1] **2** [C] also **lemon tree** /ˈ·· ·/— the tree bearing this fruit **3** [U] a drink made from this fruit **4** [U] light bright yellow: *lemon yellow* **5** [C] *BrE sl* a foolish or ugly person **6** [C] *sl* something unpleasant, unsatisfactory, or worthless, esp. a failure

lem·on·ade /ˌleməˈneɪd/ *n* [U] **1** also **fizzy lemonade**— *BrE* **a** (*AmE* **lemon so·da** /ˈ·· ˌ··/)— a yellow drink tasting of LEMONs, containing small balls of gas, to which water is not added before drinking **b** (*AmE* **lemon-lime** /ˈ·· ·/)— a bitter-sweet tasting transparent drink, containing small balls of gas **2** *AmE* a drink made from fresh LEMONs with sugar and water added **3** *BrE* LEMON SQUASH

lemon curd /ˌ·· ˈ·/ also **lemon cheese**— *n* [U] a cooked mixture of eggs, butter, and LEMON juice, eaten on bread

lemon sole /ˌ·· ˈ·/ *n* [Wn2;C;U] (meat of) a kind of flat fish

lemon squash /ˌ·· ˈ·/ *n* [U] *esp. BrE* a drink made from LEMON juice and sugar, to which water is added before it is drunk

le·mur /ˈliːməʳ/ *n* any of several kinds of monkey-like forest animals that are active at night, found in Madagascar

lend /lend/ *v* **lent** /lent/ **1** [D1 (*to*); (T1)] to give (someone) the possession or use of (something, such as money or a car) for a limited time: *Can you* *lend me £10?* **2** [D1 (*to*); (T1)] to supply (someone) with (something) on condition that it or something like it will be returned later: *As the shops are shut I'll lend you some bread* **3** [D1 (*to*); T1] to give out (money) for profit, esp. as a business **4** [T1 (*to*); (D1)] to add or give: *The many flags lent colour to the streets* **5 lend oneself/one's name to** to let oneself agree to be part of (an unworthy action) **6 lend itself/themselves to** (of things) to be suitable for **7 lend a hand (with)** to give help (with) **8 lend an ear** *old use* to listen —compare BORROW; see LOAN² (USAGE) —**~er** *n*

lending li·bra·ry /'·· ,···/ *n* a library which lends books, music, etc.

length /leŋθ/ *n* **1** [U] the measurement from one end to the other or of the longest side of something: *the length of the table/room* **2** [*the*+R (*of*)] the distance from one end to the other (of something stated): *We walked the length of the street* **3** [C] the measure from one end to the other of a horse, boat, etc., used in stating distances in races: *The horse won by 3 lengths* **4** [C (*of*)] a piece of something, esp. of a certain length or for a particular purpose: *a length of string* **5** [(*the*) C] the amount of time from the beginning to the present or to the end: *the length of a holiday* **6** [U] the quality or condition of being long: *A book is not judged only on its length* **7** [(*the*) C] amount of spoken, written, or printed words: *The student complained about the length of the examination paper* **8 at length a** after a long time; at last **b** for a long time; in many words **c** in great detail; thoroughly **9 go to any length(s)/great/some/considerable lengths** to be prepared to do anything, however dangerous, unpleasant, or wicked **10 keep at arm's length a** to keep at a distance **b** to prevent someone becoming too friendly with one, esp. by severe behaviour **11 measure one's length (on)** *BrE* to fall over suddenly (onto)

length·en /'leŋθən/ *v* [T1;IØ] to make or become longer

length·ways /'leŋθweɪz/ also **length·wise** /-waɪz/— *adv* [Wa5] in the direction of length; along the length

length·y /'leŋθi/ *adj* **1** [Wa1] very long **2** [Wa5] (esp. of speeches and writings) of too great a length —**-ily** *adv* —**-iness** *n* [U]

le·ni·ence /'liːnɪəns/ also **le·ni·en·cy** /-si/— *n* [U] the quality of being LENIENT

le·ni·ent /'liːnɪənt/ *adj* **1** merciful in judgment; gentle: *a lenient punishment* **2** allowing less than the highest standards of work, behaviour, etc. —**~ly** *adv*

len·i·ty /'lenɪ̇ti/ *n* [U] *fml* mercy; gentleness

lens /lenz/ *n* **1** a piece of glass or other transparent material, curved on one or both sides, which makes a beam of light passing through it bend, spread out, become narrower, change direction, etc., used in glasses for the eyes, cameras, microscopes, etc. —see picture at OPTICS **2** such an instrument made of natural animal material in the eye behind the black opening (PUPIL) in front of the eye —see picture at EYE¹

lent /lent/ *past t. and p. of* LEND

Lent *n* [R] the 40 days before EASTER, during which many Christians do not allow themselves all their usual pleasures and eat less food

len·til /'lentl/ *n* the small round seed of a beanlike plant, dried and used for food —see picture at VEGETABLE¹

len·to /'lentəʊ/ *adj, adv* (of music) played slowly

Lent term /'· ·/ *n* [R] the British university TERM during which LENT takes place

Le·o /'liːəʊ/ *n* **1** [R] **a** the ancient sign, a lion, representing the 5th division of the ZODIAC belt of stars **b** the group of stars (CONSTELLATION) formerly in this division **2** [C] a person born under the influence of this sign —see picture at PLANET

le·o·nine /'liːənaɪn/ *adj fml* belonging to or like a lion: *a noble leonine head*

leop·ard /'lepəd‖-ərd/ *fem.* **leop·ard·ess** /'lepədes‖-ər-/— *n* [Wn1] a type of large fierce meat-eating catlike animal, yellowish with black spots, found in Africa and Southern Asia —see picture at CAT

le·o·tard /'liːətɑːd‖-ɑrd/ *n* a single close-fitting garment that covers the body, worn esp. by dancers

lep·er /'lepəʳ/ *n* **1** a person who has the disease LEPROSY and who is usu. avoided by healthy people: *leper hospital* **2** a person who is avoided by other people

lep·re·chaun /'leprəkɔːn‖-kɑn, -kɔn/ *n* (in old Irish stories) a kind of fairy in the form of a little man

lep·ro·sy /'leprəsi/ *n* [U] a disease in which the skin becomes rough and thick with small round hard whitish pieces (SCALEs), the flesh and nerves are slowly destroyed, and fingers, toes, etc., drop off —**-rous** /rəs/ *adj*

les·bi·an /'lezbɪən/ *adj, n* (of or concerning) a woman who is sexually attracted to other women rather than to men —**~ism** *n* [U]

lese-ma·jes·ty /,liːz 'mædʒɪ̇sti/ also **lèse-ma·jes·té** /,liːz 'mædʒɪ̇sti (*Fr* lɛz maʒəste)/— *n* [U] *Fr* **1** criminal action against a ruling king or government **2** *infml* behaviour that makes a more important person feel offended

le·sion /'liːʒən/ *n* **1** a wound **2** a dangerous change in the form or working of a part of the body, esp. after an operation or accident

less¹ /les/ *determiner, pron* (*compar. of* LITTLE) [(*of, than*)] **1** (*with* [U] *nouns and sing.* [C] *nouns*) a smaller amount (than); not so much (of): *They buy less beer and fewer cigarettes now.|I don't want all that cake—give me rather less (of it).|Can we have a bit less noise/less of that noise?|She gives them less to eat in summer.|(not fml) She's less of a fool than I thought.|He's eating (even) less than usual* —opposite **more 2** *not fml* (*with pl.* [C] *nouns*) a smaller number (than); not so many (of); fewer: *If only there were less holes in the roof!* —see USAGE **3** [+*than*] (*with numbers*) a lower number (than); not so much (as): *less than 5 minutes|(even) less than £5|14 is less than 17* **4 any the less** *nonassertive* to at all a lower degree: *Margaret doesn't seem any the less healthy in spite of/for all her drinking!* **5 less and less** (an amount) that continues to become smaller: *Margaret eats less and less/does less and less work/is less and less able to get out of bed* —opposite **more and more 6 Less of it/of that** *imper.* Stop it! **7 less than no time** a very short time **8 no less (than) a** (expressing surprise at a large number or amount): *No less than 1000 people came* **b** (expressing surprise at a very important person or thing): *Good heavens! It's the President himself, no less!* **9 no less a person/a thing than** that very important person/thing: *no less an event than a world war* **10 none the less** but all the same; in spite of everything; NEVERTHELESS: *I can't swim. None the less, I'll try to cross the river.|She's no use but I love her none the less* **11 nothing less than** nothing under; not below (a stated large amount) **12 nothing (more or) less than** just the same as; no better than (something bad): *It's nothing more or less than murder to send that poor boy down the Falls Road without a gun* **13 not less (than)** not fewer (than); as much or as many (as) and perhaps more **14 the less** (used with a comparison) according to the amount, degree, etc.: *The less he eats the thinner he gets* **15 think (all) the less of** to have a (much) lower opinion of —opposite **think (all) the more of**

USAGE It is considered better English to use **fewer** rather than **less** with pl. [C] nouns, as in def. 2.

less² *adv* [Wa5; (*than*)] **1** (*with adjectives and adverbs*) not so; to a smaller degree (than): *Jane's less beautiful than Susan* (more usu. *not so beautiful as*).|*Would you mind speaking less quickly?* (more usu. *more slowly*) **2** (*with verbs*) not so much: *Try to shout less.*|*He works less than he used to.*|*One of the less known modern poets* —compare MORE² (1) and -ER¹ **3 less and less** —see LESS¹ (5) **4 much/still less** (*with* no, not, *etc.*) certainly not: *The baby can't even walk, much less run*

less³ *prep* not counting; but we subtract; MINUS¹: *She gave me £100, less £5 for her own costs* (=she gave me £95)

-less /l$\frac{1}{2}$s/ *suffix* **1** [*n→adj*] lacking: *childless*|*rainless* **2** [*n→adj*] free from: PAINLESS|HARMLESS **3** [*n→adj*] without: *hatless*|ENDLESS **4** [*n→adj*] beyond: SPEECHLESS **5** [*v→adj*] that never ...s or that cannot be ...ed: CEASELESS|TIRELESS

les·see /le'siː/ *n tech* a person who by written agreement is given the use of a house, building, or land for a certain time in return for a fixed regular payment to the owner (the LESSOR)

less·en /'lesən/ *v* **1** [T1;IØ] to make or become less **2** [T1] to make less in size, worth, importance, appearance, etc.

less·er /'lesəʳ/ *adj, adv* [Wa5;A] *fml* (*not used with* than) not so great or so much as the other (of 2) in worth, degree, size, etc.: *the lesser of 2 evils*|*one of the lesser-known modern poets*

les·son /'lesən/ *n* **1** the period of time a pupil or class studies a subject, esp. as one of many such periods: *Each history lesson lasts 40 minutes* **2** something taught to or learned by a pupil, esp. in school: *lessons in drawing* **3** the part of a subject taught or studied at one time: *a French lesson on irregular verbs* **4** something, such as a warning example or experience, from which one should learn: *His car accident has been a lesson to him to stop driving too fast* **5** a piece of wisdom learnt from such an example or experience: *That accident taught me a lesson; I shan't drive too fast again* **6** a short piece read from the Bible during religious services

les·sor /le'sɔːʳ/ *n tech* a person who lets a house, building, or land by a written agreement (LEASE) to someone else (the LESSEE) for a certain time, in return for a fixed regular payment

lest /lest/ *conj fml* **1** in order that . . . not; in case: *I obeyed her lest she should be angry.*|*I'll be kind to her lest she decide to leave me* **2** (with words expressing fear) for fear that: *I was afraid lest she should be angry.*|*I fear lest she decide to leave me*

let¹ /let/ *v* **-tt-** [T1 (*from*)] *old use* to prevent

let² *n* **1** [U] *esp. law* anything that prevents something from being done; prevention (in the phr. **without let or hindrance**) **2** [C] (in tennis and other like games) a stroke that does not count and must be played again, esp., in tennis, one in which a ball that has been served hits the top of the net on its way over

let³ *v* **let**; *pres. p.* **letting** **1** [V2 *usu. not pass.*] to allow (to do or happen): *She lets her children play in the street.*|*Please let us buy you a drink!*|*I don't smoke because my wife won't let me* (*smoke*).|*He's letting his beard grow.*|*He let a week go by before answering the letter.*|*The grass has been let* (*to*) *grow* **2** [V2 *imper.*] (the named person) must, should, may, is to: *Let each man decide for himself.*|*Let the enemy come!*|*Let him do what he likes; I don't care.*|*Let there be no mistake about it.*|*Don't let me have to speak to you again.*|*Let me see—what are 4 17's?* **3** [V2 *imper.*] (*before* us) **a** (*never abbrev. to* let's) allow us to: *Please let us buy you a drink!* **b** (*used when suggesting a plan; often abbrev. to* let's) we must/should; why not . . .: *Let's have a party, shall we?*|(*fml*) *Let us pray* (said by the priest in church).|*Let's face it, we're going to be late* **4** [V2 *imper.*] (with an object in the 3rd pers. that is to be made, or supposed for the purpose of argument): *Let the line AB be equal in length to the line XY* **5** [T1 (*to,* OUT)] to give the use of (a room, a building, land, etc.) in return for regular payments: *We're hoping to let this field* (*to a farmer*).|*This room is let* (*out*) *to a student.*|*"To Let"* (sign on a house) —compare LET OUT (5); see HIRE² (USAGE) **6 let alone** not to mention; even less: *The baby can't even walk, let alone run* —compare EVEN³ (1) **7 let/leave someone/something alone** to stop worrying or touching someone/something **8 let someone/something be** to leave someone/something unworried; not scold or INTERFERE: *Let him be, he's doing no harm* **9 let blood** *med* to purposely draw blood from a bloodvessel, so as to cure someone **10 let drop/fall** to make (a remark, suggestion, etc.) known, as if by accident but really on purpose **11 let fly (at)** to aim (a blow or attack in words) (at): *"Curry . . . lets fly with the left foot"* (SEU S., account of a football match) **12 let go (of)** to stop holding: *Don't let go* (*of*) *the handle. Hold it tight and don't let go.*|*Let go! You're hurting my arm* **13 let someone go** to set someone free; allow to escape **14 let oneself go a** to behave more freely and naturally than usual: **b** to take less care of one's appearance than usual: *Buy some new clothes and get your hair cut, my dear—you mustn't let yourself go like this* **15 let it go at that** *not fml* to stop taking any more trouble; to agree not to say any more **16 let something go hang** *infml* to stop caring completely about something **17 let someone know** to tell someone; inform: *"If he wants to see me before* EASTER *perhaps he'll let me know"* (SEU S.) **18 let pass** to leave (a wrong statement, mistake, etc.) without putting it right: *He said Shakespeare was an American and I couldn't let that pass* **19 let something ride** *not fml* to allow something to take its natural course **20 let something rip** *infml* to free something from control, esp. of speed **21 let slip a** to allow (a fact) to be known, accidentally **b** to miss (a chance) **22 let well alone** (*AmE* **let well enough alone**)— *BrE* to allow existing conditions to remain as they are, for fear of making things worse **23 live and let live** to accept other people's ideas and customs and not to try to force one's opinions upon them —see also LET DOWN, LET IN, LET IN FOR, LET IN ON, LET INTO, LET LOOSE, LET OFF, LET ON, LET OUT, LET THROUGH, LET UP, LET UP ON

USAGE 1 **Let** *us* is only shortened to **Let's** when it includes the person addressed, as a suggestion: *Come on Mary,* **let's** *dance!* Otherwise it must be **let** *us*: *Please, sir,* **let** *us go now.* 2 The neg. of **Let's** is **Let's** *not,* in both *BrE* and *AmE*. *BrE* also *Don't* **let's,** *AmE* also sometimes **Let's** *don't*.

let⁴ *n BrE* **1** an act of renting a house or flat to (or from) someone **2** a house or flat that is (to be) rented **3** *infml* a person who rents, or is willing to rent, a house or flat from one: *They can't find a let for their flat*

-let /l$\frac{1}{2}$t/ *suffix* [*n→n*] **1** a small kind of: BOOKLET|STARLET **2** an article worn on (the stated part of the body): ARMLET

let·down /'letdaʊn/ *n infml* a disappointment: *We were going out today, but now it's raining so we can't; what a letdown!*

let down *v adv* **1** [T1] to make (clothes) longer **2** [T1b] to cause (someone) to be disappointed in one's loyalty; fail to keep a promise to (someone)

3 let one's hair down *infml* to behave informally; enjoy oneself freely

le·thal /ˈliːθəl/ *adj* able or certain to kill

leth·ar·gy /ˈleθədʒi‖-ər-/ *n* [U] state of being sleepy or unnaturally tired; lazy state of mind

let in *v adv* [T1] to admit: *let in the possibility of doubt*

let in for *v adv prep* [D1] to cause (someone or oneself) to have (something unwanted): *let oneself in for trouble|for a lot of work*

let in on *v adv prep* [D1] to allow (someone) to share (a secret or something secret)

let in·to *v prep* [D1] **1** to allow (someone) to join **2** to cause (something) to be sunk into the surface of (something) **3** LET IN ON

let loose *v adv* [T1] **1** to free (something or someone): *children let loose from school* **2 be let loose on** to be free to cause trouble for, make changes in (something or someone), etc.

let off¹ *v prep* [D1;V4b] **1** to excuse (someone) from (punishment, duty, etc.): *She let the boy off (doing) his music practice* **2 let someone off the hook** to free someone from difficulty, responsibility for decisions, etc.

let off² *v adv* [T1] **1** to cause (something) to explode or be fired **2** to excuse (someone) from punishment **3** to allow (someone) to leave a vehicle **4 let off steam a** (of a railway engine) to allow unwanted steam to escape **b** to behave actively, using up strength

let on *v adv* [I∅ (*about*); T5,6a,b] *infml* to tell a secret: *Don't let on that I told you.|Don't let on about the meeting*

let out *v adv* **1** [T1] to make (clothes) wider **2** [T1,5] to allow (a secret) to be known: *He accidentally let out that he hadn't been home for 3 weeks* **3** [T1 (*of*)] to give freedom to (someone) **4** [T1] to express: *He let out a cry of pain* **5** [T1] *esp. BrE* to allow people to use (vehicles, horses, etc.) for a certain period, in return for payment —compare LET³ (5); see HIRE² (USAGE) **6** [I∅ (*at*)] to attack with blows or words **7** [I∅] *AmE* to close for the day **8 let the cat out (of the bag)** *infml* to tell a secret

Let·ra·set /ˈletrəset/ *n* [U] *tdmk* letters sold on a special sheet which can be put onto other surfaces by the use of pressure

let·ter¹ /ˈletəʳ/ *n* **1** [C] a written or printed message sent usu. in an envelope **2** [C] one of the signs in writing or printing that represents a speech sound **3** [(*the*) S] the words of an agreement, law, rule, etc., rather than its real, intended, or general meaning: *be bound by the letter of the law* —opposite **spirit 4 to the letter a** with close attention to the written details of an agreement, law, etc. **b** to the fullest degree —compare LETTERS

letter² *v* [T1] to mark with LETTERs¹ (2)

let·ter·box /ˈletəbɒks‖ˈletərbɑks/ *AmE* usu. **mailbox**— *n esp. BrE* **1** a box in a post office, street, etc., in which letters may be posted —see picture at STREET **2** a hole or box in the front of or by the entrance to a building for receiving letters from the post —see picture at DOOR

let·tered /ˈletəd‖-ərd/ *adj fml* educated —opposite **unlettered**

let·ter·head /ˈletəhed‖-ər-/ *n* **1** [C] the name and address of a person or business printed at the top of the owner's writing paper **2** [U] writing paper with this printed on it

let·ter·ing /ˈletərɪŋ/ *n* [U] **1** the act of writing, drawing, etc., letters or words **2** the letters or words written or drawn, esp. with regard to their style

letter-per·fect /ˌ·· ˈ··◂/ *adj* [F] *AmE* WORD-PERFECT

let·ter·press /ˈletəpres‖-ər-/ *n* **1** [U] a method of printing in which words, pictures, etc., to be printed stand as a raised area on the printing machine **2** [C] the printed words of a book, as opposed to the pictures

let·ters /ˈletəz‖-ərz/ *n* **1** [GU] literature in general **2 man of letters** a person who writes works respected for expressions of thought and imagination

letters pa·tent /ˌ·· ˈ··/ *n* [P] **1** an official letter from a government or ruler giving a noble title, special right, etc. **2** *law* PATENT² (1)

let through *v adv* [T1] to allow (something or someone) to pass

let·ting /ˈletɪŋ/ *n tech, esp. BrE* a house or flat that is (to be) let: *unfurnished lettings*

let·tuce /ˈletʃs/ *n* **1** [C] a type of common garden plant with large tender pale green leaves folded round each other **2** [U] the leaves of this, used in SALADs —see picture at VEGETABLE¹

let·up /ˈletʌp/ *n* [C;U] (a) stopping or lessening of activity

let up *v adv* [I∅] **1** to lessen; gradually cease: *When will this rain let up?* **2** to stop working: *The doctor has been working for 50 hours without letting up*

let up on *v adv prep* [T1 *no pass.*] *infml* to treat (someone) less severely

leu·co·cyte, leuko- /ˈluːkəsaɪt/ *n* one of the many white cells in the blood which fight disease

leu·cot·o·my /luːˈkɒtəmi‖-ˈkɑ-/ (*AmE* **lobotomy**)— *n BrE* **1** [U] the cutting away of part of the brain to calm the behaviour of people with particularly violent characters **2** [C] an operation for this —**-mize, -mise** *v* [T1]

leu·ke·mia, *BrE* also **-kae-** /luːˈkiːmɪə/ *n* [U] a disease in which the blood contains too many white cells

lev·ee¹ /ˈlevi/ *n old use* a meeting in which a ruler received visits from men only

levee² *n* **1** a raised bank of mud added to a river each time it overflows **2** a bank built to stop a river overflowing

lev·el¹ /ˈlevəl/ *n* **1** [C] a smooth flat surface, esp. a wide area of flat ground **2** [C (*of*)] a position of height: *The garden is arranged on 2 levels* **3** [C (*of*)] general standard, quality, or degree **4** [C (*of*)] amount, size, or number: *The workmen have been told to increase the level of their production* **5** [U] position, esp. in society, power, or learning: *This government difficulty is being considered at ministerial level* **6** [C] an instrument used while preparing an area for building, which measures differences in height **7** [C] *esp. AmE* SPIRIT LEVEL **8 on the level** *infml* honest(ly); truthful(ly)

level² *v* **-ll-** (*AmE* **-l-**) **1** [T1;I∅: (OUT, OFF)] to make or become flat and even **2** [T1 (UP or DOWN)] to raise or lower to the same height everywhere or to the height of something else **3** [T1] to knock or pull down to the ground **4** [T1; I∅: (OUT, OFF)] to make or become equal in position, rank, strength, etc.

level³ *adj* **1** having a surface which is the same height above the ground all over: *A table top must be level* **2** flat; smooth: *A football field needs to be level* **3** [Wa5] equal in position or standard: *The child's head is level with his father's knee* **4** steady and unvarying: *He gave me a level look* **5** also **level-head·ed** /ˌ·· ˈ··◂/— calm and sensible in judgment **6 one's level best** *infml* one's best effort; all that one can

level⁴ *adv* so as to be level

level at *v prep* [D1] **1** to aim (a weapon) at **2** [*often pass.*] also **level a·gainst**— to bring (a charge) against (someone): *A serious charge was levelled at the minister*

level cross·ing /ˌ·· ˈ··/ (*AmE* **grade crossing**)— *n BrE* a place where a road and a railway cross each other, usu. protected by gates that shut off the road while a train passes

lev·el·ler, *AmE* **-eler** /ˈlevələʳ/ *n BrE derog* a person who wishes to get rid of all social differences

level off also **level out**— *v adv* [IØ] (of an aircraft, ROCKET, etc.) to stop climbing higher and continue at a fixed height

level with *v prep* [T1] *infml* to speak freely and truthfully to; not hide facts from

le·ver¹ /ˈliːvəʳ‖ˈle-, ˈliː-/ *n* **1** a bar or other strong tool used for lifting or moving something heavy or stiff. One end is placed under or against the object, the other end is pushed down with force, and the bar turns on a fixed point (FULCRUM) **2** any part of a machine working in the same way **3** something which may be used for influencing

lever² *v* [X9] to move (something) with a LEVER¹: *They levered it into position.*|(fig.) *They're trying to lever him out of his job as head of the firm*

le·ver·age /ˈliːvərɪdʒ‖ˈle-, ˈliː-/ *n* [U] **1** the action or use of a LEVER¹ **2** the power of a LEVER¹ **3** power, influence, or other means of obtaining a result

lev·e·ret /ˈlevərɨ̣t/ *n* a young HARE

le·vi·a·than /lɪˈvaɪəθən/ *n* **1** (in the Bible) a sea animal of very great size **2** something very large and strong, esp. a large ship or a large sea animal (WHALE)

Le·vi's /ˈliːvaɪz/ *n* [P] *tdmk* JEANS

lev·i·tate /ˈlevɨ̣teɪt/ *v* [T1;IØ] to (cause to) rise and float in the air as if by magic —**-tation** /ˌlevɨ̣ˈteɪʃən/ *n* [U]

lev·i·ty /ˈlevɨ̣ti/ *n* [U] *fml or pomp* lack of respect for serious matters; lack of seriousness

lev·o·do·pa /ˌlevəˈdəʊpə/ *n* [U] *esp. BrE* L-DOPA

lev·y¹ /ˈlevi/ *n* **1** an official demand for a tax or for people to become soldiers **2** the collection of such a tax, people, etc. **3** the money, soldiers, etc., collected **4 capital levy** the taking by the state of a share of the wealth owned by all the people in a country, group, etc.

levy² *v* [T1] **1** [(*on, upon*)] to demand and collect officially: *levy a tax on tobacco* **2** to gather (men to join an army) often by force **3** [(*on, upon, against*)] *esp. fml or lit* to declare and make (war)

levy on *v prep* [T1] *law* to obtain (payment that is owing) by seizing the debtor's possessions officially

lewd /luːd/ *adj* [Wa2] **1** wanting or thinking about sex, esp. in a manner that is not socially acceptable **2** impure; rude; dirty; OBSCENE: *lewd songs* —**~ly** *adv* —**~ness** *n* [U]

lex·i·cal /ˈleksɪkəl/ *adj* [Wa5] *tech* of or concerning words —**-cally** *adv* [Wa4]

lex·i·cog·ra·pher /ˌleksɪˈkɒgrəfəʳ‖-ˈkɑ-/ *n* a person who writes the meanings of words in a dictionary

lex·i·cog·ra·phy /ˌleksɪˈkɒgrəfi‖-ˈkɑ-/ *n* [U] the writing and making of dictionaries

lex·i·con /ˈleksɪkən‖-kɒn, -kən/ *n* a dictionary, esp. of an ancient language

lex·is /ˈleksɨ̣s/ *n* **-es** /ˈleksiːz/ *tech* all the words in a particular language, or that a person knows, or that belong to a particular subject, etc.

li·a·bil·i·ty /ˌlaɪəˈbɪlɨ̣ti/ *n* **1** [U] the condition of being LIABLE **2** [C] something for which one is responsible, esp. by law **3** [C *usu. pl. with sing. meaning*] amount of debt that must be paid —opposite **asset** **4** [C] *infml* something that limits one's activities or freedom; disadvantage: *This old car's a real liability; I can't use it but I have to pay for somewhere to keep it*

li·a·ble /ˈlaɪəbəl/ *adj* **1** [F+*to*] often suffering from: *She is liable to bad colds* **2** [F3] likely to, esp. from habit or tendency: *He's liable to shout when angry* **3** [F (*for*), F3] responsible, esp. in law, for paying for something: *He declared that he was not liable for his wife's debts* **4** [Wa5;F+*to*] likely to suffer in law: *People who walk on the grass are liable to a* FINE *of £5*

li·aise /liˈeɪz/ *v* [IØ (*with*)] *tech or pomp* (esp. in the army or in business) to make or keep a connection and act together: *We must liaise closely about this*

li·ai·son /liˈeɪzən‖ˈlɪəzɑn, liˈeɪ-/ *n* [(*with, between*)] **1** a working association or connection **2** a sexual relationship between a man and a woman not married to each other

li·a·na /liˈɑːnə, liˈænə/ also **li·ane** /liˈɑːn, liˈæn/— *n* (a long climbing stem of) any of several types of woody plant that climb round trees, up walls, etc., in tropical countries

li·ar /ˈlaɪəʳ/ *n* a person who tells lies

lib /lɪb/ *n* [U9] *infml* LIBERATION (esp. in the phrs. **women's lib, gay lib** (see GAY (4))) —**~ber** /ˈlɪbəʳ/ *n*: *The women's libbers are trying to get into this men's club*

Lib *abbrev. for*: LIBERAL PARTY

li·ba·tion /laɪˈbeɪʃən/ *n* **1** an offering of wine to a god, esp. in ancient Greece and Rome **2** *pomp* a drink of wine or other alcohol

li·bel¹ /ˈlaɪbəl/ *n* **1** [C] *law* a printed or written statement, picture, etc., that unfairly damages the good opinion held about a person by others **2** [U] the printing of such a statement, picture, etc. —compare SLANDER¹ **3** [C] *infml* an unfair or untrue remark, description, etc., of somebody

libel² *v* **-ll-** (*AmE* **-l-**) [T1] **1** to print a LIBEL¹ (1) against **2** *infml* to make an unfair or untrue remark about or description of

li·bel·lous, *AmE* **-belous** /ˈlaɪbələs/ *adj BrE* **1** being or containing a LIBEL¹ (1) **2** in the habit of writing LIBEL*s* —**~ly** *adv*

lib·e·ral¹ /ˈlɪbərəl/ *adj* **1** willing to understand and respect the ideas and feelings of others: *a liberal mind/thinker* **2** favouring some change, as in political or religious affairs **3** favouring a wide general knowledge, the broadening of the mind, and wide possibilities for self-expression: *a liberal education* **4** giving freely and generously: *a liberal supporter of the hospital* **5** given freely; large: *a liberal supply of drinks* **6** neither close nor very exact: *a liberal reading of a rule*

liberal² *n* a person with wide understanding, who is in favour of change

Liberal *n, adj* [Wa5] (a person) supporting or connected with the LIBERAL PARTY

liberal art /ˌ··· ˈ·/ *n* [*usu. pl.*] *tech* any university subject except science and MATHEMATICS

lib·e·ral·is·m /ˈlɪbərəlɪzəm/ *n* [U] wide understanding and advanced opinions

Liberalism *n* [R] the aims and beliefs of the LIBERAL PARTY

lib·e·ral·i·ty /ˌlɪbəˈrælɨ̣ti/ *n* **1** [U] also **lib·e·ral·ness** /ˈlɪbərəlnɨ̣s/— **a** generosity **b** broadness of mind **2** [C] *fml* a gift given generously

lib·e·ral·ize, -ise /ˈlɪbərəlaɪz/ *v* [T1;IØ] to make or become LIBERAL —**-ization** /ˌlɪbərəlaɪˈzeɪʃən‖-rələ-/ *n* [U]

lib·e·ral·ly /ˈlɪbərəli/ *adv* **1** generously; freely **2** in great amount; in large quantities

Liberal Par·ty /ˈ··· ˌ··/ *n* [*the*+GU] a British political party whose aims are social and industrial improvement

lib·e·rate /ˈlɪbəreɪt/ *v* [T1] **1** [(*from*)] to set free (from control, prison, anxiety, duty, etc.) **2** *tech* to cause or allow (gas) to escape from a chemical substance —**-rator** *n*

lib·e·rat·ed /ˈlɪbəreɪtɨ̣d/ *adj* having or showing freedom of action in social and sexual matters

lib·e·ra·tion /ˌlɪbəˈreɪʃən/ *n* [U] setting free or being set free

lib·er·tar·i·an /ˌlɪbəˈteərɪən‖-bər-/ *n* **1** a person who stands for freedom in matters of thought, religion, etc. **2** *old use* a person who believes that man is free to make choices

lib·er·ties /ˈlɪbətiz‖-ər-/ *n* [P] **1** rights given by a king or any powerful ruling body **2 take liberties (with) a** to act in a rude, too friendly way (towards) **b** to make changes (in) (a piece of writing, history, etc.)

lib·er·tine /ˈlɪbətiːn‖-ər-/ *n* a man who continually looks for sexual pleasure and shows little respect for women

lib·er·ty /ˈlɪbəti‖-ər-/ *n* **1** [U] freedom from too hard (OPPRESSIVE) a government or from foreign rule **2** [U] freedom from control, service, being shut up, etc. **3** [U] chance or permission to do or use something **4** [S] freedom of speech or behaviour taken without permission and which is sometimes regarded as rude: *"I allowed myself the liberty of reading your letters." "What a liberty!"* —see also **take** LIBERTIES **5 at liberty a** free from prison, control, etc. **b** not busy; free **c** not in use **d** having permission or the right (to do something) —compare FREEDOM

li·bid·i·nous /lɪˈbɪdɪnəs/ *adj fml or tech* having or showing strong sexual desires all the time —**~ly** *adv* —**~ness** *n* [U]

li·bi·do /lɪˈbiːdəʊ/ *n* **-dos** *tech* (esp. in FREUDIAN PSYCHOLOGY) **1** the strong force of life in a person **2** the sexual urge

Li·bra /ˈliːbrə/ *n* **1** [R] **a** the ancient sign, a pair of scales, representing the 7th division of the ZODIAC belt of stars **b** the group of stars (CONSTELLATION) formerly in this division **2** [C] a person born under the influence of this sign —see picture at PLANET

li·brar·i·an /laɪˈbreərɪən/ *n* a person who is in charge of or helps to run a library —**~ship** *n* [U]

li·bra·ry /ˈlaɪbrəri‖-breri/ *n* **1** a building or part of a building which contains books that may be borrowed by the public (**public library**) or by members of a special group **2** a collection of books **3** a room or other place where books are kept and may be looked at, usu. with tables at which to study **4** a set of books looking alike, usu. on related subjects —see also RECORD LIBRARY

li·bret·tist /lɪˈbretɪ̥st/ *n* the writer of a LIBRETTO

li·bret·to /lɪˈbretəʊ/ *n* **-tos** the words of a musical play (such as an OPERA OR ORATORIO)

lice /laɪs/ *pl. of* LOUSE

li·cence, *AmE* usu. **-cense** /ˈlaɪsəns/ *n esp. BrE* **1** [C] an official paper, card, etc., showing that permission has been given to do something, usu. in return for a fixed payment: *a dog licence* **2** [U] permission given, esp. officially, to do something **3** [U] freedom of action, speech, thought, etc. **4** [U] misuse of freedom, esp. in causing harm or damage; uncontrolled behaviour **5** [U] the freedom claimed by an artist to disobey the rules of his art or to change the facts in order to improve a work of art —see also POETIC LICENCE

li·cense, -cence /ˈlaɪsəns/ *v* [T1] to give official permission to or for

li·censed, -cenced /ˈlaɪsənst/ *adj* [Wa5;B;F3] having official permission, esp. to sell alcoholic drinks

licensed vict·ual·ler /ˌ·· ˈ···/ *n tech* a keeper of a shop or inn who is permitted to sell alcoholic drink

li·cen·see /ˌlaɪsənˈsiː/ *n* a person to whom official permission is given, esp. to sell alcoholic drinks or tobacco

license plate /ˈ·· ·/ *n AmE* NUMBERPLATE

licensing laws /ˈ··· ·/ *n* [*the*+P] the laws in Britain that limit the sales of alcoholic drinks to certain times and places

li·cen·ti·ate /laɪˈsenʃɪət/ *n* **1** a person given official permission, esp. by a university, to practise a special art or profession: *a licentiate of the Royal College of Music* **2** a (written) declaration that this permission has been given

li·cen·tious /laɪˈsenʃəs/ *adj fml* behaving in a sexually uncontrolled manner —**~ly** *adv* —**~ness** *n* [U]

li·chen /ˈlaɪkən, ˈlɪtʃən/ *n* [U] a dry-looking greyish, greenish, or yellowish flat spreading plant that covers the surfaces of stones and trees —see picture at PLANT[2]

li·cit /ˈlɪsɪ̥t/ *adj fml & rare* not forbidden; lawful —opposite **illicit** —**~ly** *adv*

lick¹ /lɪk/ *v* **1** [T1] to move the tongue across (a surface) in order to taste, clean, make wet, etc.: *to lick a postage stamp* **2** [T1 (UP, OUT, OFF, etc.)] to take into the mouth with the tongue: *The cat licked up the drops of milk from the floor* **3** [T1;I0] (esp. of flames or waves) to pass lightly or with rapid movements over or against (a surface) **4** [T1] *infml* to beat with blows, esp. as a punishment **5** [T1] *infml* to defeat in a game, race, fight, etc. **6** [T1] *infml BrE* to cause (somebody) to be unable to understand something: *It licks me how you were able to get there first* **7 lick into shape a** to train (someone), esp. in good manners or a skill needing self-control **b** make (something) clean, ready, or perfect; give a finished form to **8 lick/bite the dust** to be knocked down, defeated, or killed **9 lick someone's boots** to obey someone like a slave, through fear, admiration, or desire for favour

lick² *n* **1** [C] the act of LICKing¹ **2** [C (*of*)] a small amount (of cleaning, paint, etc.): *This door needs a lick of paint.|Before we go out I'll just give the room a quick lick* **3** [C9] a place where animals go to lick salt in the ground: *a salt lick* **4** [S] *infml* speed: *running down the hill at a great lick* **5 a lick and a promise** *infml BrE* a quick careless wash

lick·ing /ˈlɪkɪŋ/ *n* **1** the act of one who or that which LICKS **2** *infml* a beating **3** *infml* a defeat

lic·o·rice /ˈlɪkərɪs, -rɪʃ/ *n* [U] LIQUORICE

lid /lɪd/ *n* **1** the piece that covers the open top of a vessel, box, or other container and that lifts up or can be removed **2** *sl* a hat, cap, etc. **3** an eyelid **4 take/lift/blow the lid off** to make known the truth about (something) **5 put the lid on a** to be the last and worst misfortune of (a set) **b** to put an end to

li·do /ˈliːdəʊ/ *n* **-dos 1** a public swimming bath open to the air **2** a special part of a BEACH or of the edge of a lake used for swimming and lying in the sun

lie¹ /laɪ/ *v* **lay** /leɪ/, **lain** /leɪn/, *pres. p.* **lying** /ˈlaɪ-ɪŋ/ **1** [L9 esp. DOWN] (of a person) to be in a flat resting position, as on the ground or a bed: *The wounded man was lying on the battlefield* **2** [Wv6; L9 esp. DOWN] to put the body into such a position: *I'm tired; I must lie down* **3** [L7,9] to be or remain in a flat position on a surface: *the book that is lying on the table* **4** [L9] to be in a described place, position, or direction: *The town lies to the east of us.*|(fig.) *The truth lies somewhere between the statements of the 2 men* **5** [L9] to be, remain, or be kept in a described condition or position: *The man lay in prison for 7 years.|The wine is at present lying in London* **6** [L9] to have an unpleasant effect; cause continual anxiety, discomfort, etc.: *A curse has always lain over that family* **7** [L9] to be the responsibility of; be: *The decision lies with you* **8** [L7,9] to remain unused, unwanted, unknown, etc.: *money lying in the bank* **9** [L7,9] (of a dead body) to be buried **10** [I0] *tech* (of a point or claim in a law court) to be successfully argued or proved **11** [L9] *old use* to stay, as with friends or at a hotel **12 lie in state** (of a dead body) to be placed in a public place so that people may honour it **13 lie low** to be in hiding or avoid being noticed —see also LIE ABOUT, LIE BEHIND, LIE DOWN, LIE IN, LIE OFF, LIE OVER, LIE TO, LIE UP, LIE WITH; see LAY¹ (USAGE)

lie² *n* [*usu. sing.*] **1** the way or position in which something lies, esp., in GOLF, the position in which the ball lies on the grass: *a good/bad lie* **2 the lie** (*AmE* **lay**) **of the land**— *BrE* **a** the appearance, slope, etc., of a piece of land **b** the state of affairs

lie³ *v* **1** [IØ] to tell a lie **2** [IØ] to have a false appearance **3** [X9] to get, bring, put, etc., (oneself) into, out of a certain condition by telling lies: *He lied himself out of trouble.|She lied her way out of trouble*

lie⁴ *n* **1** an untrue statement purposely made to deceive: *to tell lies* **2** a false appearance intended to deceive **3 give the lie (to) a** to charge directly with telling a lie **b** to show that (something) is untrue —see also WHITE LIE

lie a·bout *v adv* [IØ] to be lazy; do nothing

lie be·hind *v prep* [T1 *no pass.*] to be the reason for (something)

lied·er /ˈliːdəʳ/ *n* [P] *Ger* (*often cap.*) German songs, esp. those which are part of serious 19th-century music: *sang several Schubert lieder*

lie de·tec·tor /ˈ· ·ˌ··/ *n* an instrument that is supposed to show when a person is telling lies

lie down *v adv* [IØ (*under*)] to suffer without complaint or attempt at opposition: *We'll not take your rudeness lying down*

lie-down /ˌ· ˈ·/ *n infml* a short rest, usu. on a bed

lief /liːf/ *adv old use & lit* willingly; gladly (esp. in the phr. **as lief**)

liege /liːdʒ/ *n old use* **1** also **liege lord** /ˌ· ˈ·/— a lord or ruler to whom others must give loyalty and service **2** also **liege man** /ˈ· ·/— a man or servant who must give loyalty and service to his lord

lie in *v adv* [IØ] **1** *BrE* to stay in bed late in the morning **2** *becoming rare* (of a woman) to remain in bed for the birth of a child

lie-in /ˈ· ·, ˌ· ˈ·/ *n BrE infml* a stay in bed later than usual in the morning

lien /lɪən/ *n tech* the right by law to keep possession of something belonging to a person in debt until that debt has been paid

lie off *v adv* [IØ] (of a ship) to keep a short way from the shore or another ship

lie o·ver *v adv* [IØ] (of work or matters needing consideration) to wait or be delayed for another time

lie to *v adv* [IØ] (of a ship) to be still or almost still while facing the wind

lieu /luː/ *n* **in lieu (of)** instead (of)

lie up *v adv* [IØ] **1** to stay in bed, esp. for a long period **2** to stay in hiding or avoid being noticed

lieu·ten·ant /lefˈtenənt‖luː-/ *n* **1** a person who acts for, or in place of, someone in a higher position; DEPUTY (1) **2** an officer of low rank in the navy, British army, American police, etc. **3** (*in comb.*) an officer with the rank next below the one named (as in **lieutenant colonel**)

lie with *v prep* [T1] *old use* to have sex with

life /laɪf/ *n* **lives** /laɪvz/ **1** [U] the active force that makes those forms of matter (animals and plants) that grow through feeding and produce new young forms like themselves, different from all other matter (stones, machines, objects, etc.): *The life* PROCESS*es continue until death* **2** [U] matter having this active force: *There is no life on the moon* **3** [C] the state or period in which animals and plants are alive **4** [U] the condition of existence, esp. of a human being: *Life isn't all fun* **5** [C] **a** the period between birth and death **b** the period between birth and a certain point in somebody's life, or between a certain point in somebody's life and their death: *I had been a coward all my life.|a life member* **6** [C] the period for which a machine, organization, etc., will work or last **7** [C] a person: *Several lives were lost* **8** [U] living things in general: *plant life* **9** [C] a manner or kind of existence: *a full life|a holy life* **10** [U] existence as a collection of widely different experiences: *You'll never see life if you stay at home for ever* **11** [U] existence as social life and relationships: *This book about the life of bees describes how they help each other find food* **12** [U] activity; movement: *There were signs of life in the forest as the sun rose* **13** [U] spirit; strength; force; cheerfulness: *He was tired, and spoke without much life* **14** [U] the cause of interest, pleasure, or happiness in living: *His study of wild birds is his life* **15** [*the*+R+*of*] a person who or thing that is the cause of enjoyment or activity in a group: *He was the life of the party* **16** [U] also **life im·pris·on·ment** /· ·ˈ···/— the punishment of being put in prison for a (long) length of time which is not fixed **17** [C] also **life sto·ry** /ˈ· ··/— a written, filmed, or other account of a person's existence; BIOGRAPHY (1) **18** [C;U] existence in some form after the death of the body (esp. in the phrs. **after life, eternal life, life everlasting, future life**) **19** [U] using a living person as the subject of painting, drawing, etc.: *life classes|painted from life* **20 as large as life** not able to be mistaken; real **21 change of life** MENOPAUSE **22 come to life a** to regain one's senses after fainting **b** to show or develop interest, excitement, etc. **23 for dear life** with the greatest effort **24 not on your life!** certainly not! **25 take one's (own) life** to kill oneself **26 take one's life in one's (own) hands** *infml* to be in continual danger of death **27 take someone's life** to kill someone **28 to the life** copying or copied exactly

life as·sur·ance /ˈ· ·ˌ··/ also **life in·sur·ance**— *n* [U] an agreement between a company and a person (the ASSURED) by which in return for regular monthly or yearly payments (PREMIUM*s*), either that person will receive a sum of money on reaching a certain age or, if he dies, another (named) person will receive it

life belt /ˈ· ·/ *n* a belt made of a material that will float, used for preventing a person from sinking after falling into water

life·blood /ˈlaɪfblʌd/ *n* [U] **1** blood regarded as the life-giving power **2** something that gives continuing strength and force: *Trade is the lifeblood of most modern states*

life·boat /ˈlaɪfbəʊt/ *n* **1** a strong boat kept on shore and used for saving people in danger at sea **2** one of the small boats carried by a ship for escape in case of wreck, fire, etc. —see picture at FREIGHTER

life buoy /ˈ· ·/ also **buoy**— *n* a circle, usu. made of CORK, thrown to somebody who has fallen into water to prevent them from sinking

life cy·cle /ˈ· ˌ··/ *n* the regular development or changes in form of a SPECIES of living matter in the course of its life, such as that of insects from egg to wormlike form and then to winged form

life·guard /ˈlaɪfgɑːd‖-ɑrd/ *n* **1** a swimmer employed, as on a shore or at a swimming bath, to help swimmers in danger **2** a personal guard of men protecting a person from attack

life his·to·ry /ˌ· ˈ···/ *n* the regular development or changes in form of a particular animal or plant in the course of its life

life jack·et /ˈ· ˌ··/ *n* an air-filled garment that is worn round the chest to support a person in water

life·less /ˈlaɪfləs/ *adj* **1** [Wa5] having no life **2**

[Wa5] dead **3** lacking strength, spirit, interest, or activity —**~ly** *adv* —**~ness** *n* [U]

life·like /ˈlaɪflaɪk/ *adj* very much like real life or a real person: *a lifelike photograph*

life·line /ˈlaɪflaɪn/ *n* **1** a rope used for saving life, esp. at sea **2** a rope fastened to a swimmer who goes down to great depths (DIVER) by which he can send signals **3** something on which one's life depends, such as an only means of CONTACT

life·long /ˈlaɪflɒŋ‖-lɔŋ/ *adj* [Wa5;A] lasting all one's life: *my lifelong friend*

life peer /ˌ· ˈ·/ *n* a person given the rank of PEER[1] (3), but who is not allowed to pass it on to his eldest son when he dies —compare PEER OF THE REALM

life pre·serv·er /ˈ· ·ˌ··/ *n esp. AmE* a life-saving apparatus (such as a LIFE BELT or LIFE JACKET)

lif·er /ˈlaɪfəʳ/ *n sl* a person who has been sent to prison for life

life-size /ˌ· ˈ·◂/ also **life-sized** /ˌ· ˈ·◂/— *adj* [Wa5] (of a work of art) of the same size as that which it represents

life·time /ˈlaɪftaɪm/ *n* the time during which a person is alive

life work /ˌ· ˈ·/ also **life's work** /ˌ· ˈ·/— *n* [U] work that lasts, or to which a person gives, the whole of a life

lift[1] /lɪft/ *v* **1** [T1 (UP)] to raise from one level and hold or move to another level: *Lift (up) the stone.|The baby was lifted onto the bed* **2** [T1 (UP)] to raise to a higher level, condition, or quality **3** [IØ] (of movable parts) to move or go upwards or outwards: *The top of this box won't lift (off)* **4** [T1 (UP)] to raise or move upwards or to an upright position: *The dog lifted (up) its ears* **5** [X9 esp. *to*] to carry by air **6** [IØ] (esp. of clouds, mist, etc.) to move upwards, melt, or disappear **7** [T1] to bring to an end; remove: *The unpopular tax was soon lifted* **8** [T1] (in some games) to cause (a ball) to rise, often unintentionally **9** [IØ] (in cricket) (of a ball) to BOUNCE higher than expected **10** [T1] *infml* to steal (esp. small articles) **11** [T1] to take and use (other people's ideas, writings, etc.) as one's own without stating that one has done so **12** [T1] *tech* to dig up (root crops, or plants), esp. carefully **13** [T1 (UP)] to make (the voice) loud, as in singing

lift[2] *n* **1** [C] the act of lifting, rising, or raising **2** [C] the distance or height something is raised **3** [U;C] a lifting force, such as an upward pressure of air on the wings of an aircraft **4** [C] (*AmE* **elevator**)— *BrE* an apparatus in a building for taking people and goods from one floor to another **5** [C] any of various pieces of apparatus for lifting **6** [C] a free ride in a vehicle, esp. one given to a traveller **7** [C *usu. sing.*] a helping upwards or onwards **8** [C] an upward movement: *the proud lift of his head* **9** [S] *infml* a feeling of increased strength, higher spirits, etc.

lift·boy /ˈlɪftbɔɪ/ also **lift·man** /ˈlɪftmæn/— *n* **-men** /men/— a boy or man who is in charge of a LIFT[2] (4) between the floors of a hotel or large shop

lift off *v adv* [IØ] (of an aircraft or space vehicle) to take off

lift-off /ˈ· ·/ also **blast-off**— *n* the start of the flight of a space vehicle

lig·a·ment /ˈlɪgəmənt/ *n* one of the strong bands that join bones or hold some part of the body in position

lig·a·ture /ˈlɪgətʃəʳ/ *n* **1** something used for binding or tying, esp. a thread used for tying a blood vessel to prevent loss of blood **2** 2 or more letters joined in their printed form

light[1] /laɪt/ *n* **1** [U] the natural force that is produced by or redirected from objects and other things, so that we see them: *sunlight|gaslight|firelight* **2** [C] something that produces such force and causes other things to be seen, such as a lamp or TORCH **3** [U] a supply of light, esp. in regard to its strength, quality, or kind: *powerful light|green light|poor light* **4** [U] the light of the sun or the time it lasts: *I must finish this painting while the light lasts* **5** [C] something that will set something else, esp. a cigarette, burning, such as a match or cigarette LIGHTER: *Can you give me a light, please?* **6** [C] a window, one of many pieces of glass in a window, or an opening in a roof or wall that allows light into a room **7** [U] a supply of light that reaches a person or thing: *I can't read while you're standing in my light* **8** [U;S] brightness, as in the eyes, showing happiness or excitement **9** [C *usu. sing.*] the bright part of a painting: *light and shade* **10** [U] the condition of being or becoming seen or known or of being made known, as to the public (esp. in the phrs. **come/bring to light**) **11** [C] the way (ASPECT) in which something or someone appears or is regarded: *The workers and the employers look at difficulties in quite a different light* **12** [U] knowledge, understanding, or explanation **13 in a good/bad light** in a favourable/unfavourable way **14 in the light of** taking into account; considering **15 see the light a** to be born or come to exist **b** to be made public **c** to understand or accept an idea or the truth of something **d** to understand or accept a religious belief; have a SPIRITUAL experience which changes one's beliefs **16 throw/shed light on** to make clear; explain —see also LIGHTS[1], LEADING LIGHT

light[2] *adj* [Wa1] **1** having light; not dark; bright: *a light room* **2** not deep or dark in colour; pale

light[3] *v* **lit** /lɪt/ *or* **lighted** **1** [T1 (UP); IØ] to (cause to) start to burn: *He lit (up) a cigarette* **2** [T1] to cause to give light; give light to: *We lit the candle and the candle lit the room* **3** [T1 (UP); L9 esp. UP] to (cause to) become bright with pleasure or excitement: *Suddenly a smile lit (up) her face.|Her face lit up when she saw he was coming* **4** [X9] to show the way with a light: *He lit him up the stairs to bed with a candle* —see also LIGHT UP

USAGE Use **lit** as the past participle of **light**, except when it stands as an adjective before the noun: *He's* **lit** *a match.|The match is* **lit**.|*a* **lighted** *match.*

light[4] *adj* **1** [Wa1;B] of little weight; not heavy: *as light as air* **2** [Wa1;B] of little weight as compared with size: *as light as a feather* **3** [Wa1;B;E] of less than the correct weight or value **4** [Wa1;B] small in amount; less than average or expected: *a light crop of wheat* **5** [Wa1;B] easy to bear or do; not difficult or tiring: *light punishment|light duties* **6** [Wa5;A] not intended for heavy or rough use or work: *light weapons* **7** [Wa1;B] not serious; unimportant: *light reading* **8** [Wa1;B] soft; gentle: *A light hand is needed in playing quiet music.|light wind* **9** [Wa1;B] (of movements or the person making them) quick and graceful; skilful: *a light dancer* **10** [Wa1;B] (of sleep) from which one wakes easily; not deep: *A light sleeper is a person whose sleep is easily ended, as by a soft noise* **11** [Wa1;B] (of meals) small in amount **12** [Wa1;B] (of food) easily taken into the stomach (DIGESTED) **13** [Wa1;B] (of wine and other alcoholic drinks) not very strong **14** [Wa1;B] (of behaviour or a character) not steady or serious **15** [Wa1;B] happy; cheerful; gay **16** [Wa1;B] free of care; untroubled (esp. in the phr. **light (of) heart**) **17** [Wa1;B] (of the head) having an unsteady feeling, as when in a feverish condition or after drinking alcohol; DIZZY[1] (1); GIDDY (1) **18** [Wa1;B] (of books, music, plays, actors, etc.) having the intention of amusing only; not deep in meaning **19** [Wa1;B] not carrying much: *a light army|a light boat* **20** [Wa1;B] (of soil) easily broken up; loose; sandy **21** [Wa1;B] (of cake, bread, etc.) full of air; well risen; not heavy **22 make light of** to treat as of little importance

light⁵ *adv* [Wa1] without many travelling cases or possessions (LUGGAGE): *I travel light*

light⁶ *v* **lit** *or* **lighted** [L9 esp. *on, upon*] *old use* to come down from flight and settle; ALIGHT¹ —see also LIGHT OUT, LIGHT UPON

light air·craft /ˌ· ˈ··/ *n* [Wn3] a small aircraft typically driven by a PROPELLER —see picture at AIRCRAFT

light ale /ˌ· ˈ·/ *n* [U] a type of rather weak pale beer, usu. bottled

light bulb /ˈ· ·/ *n* a BULB (2) that produces electric light —see picture at ELECTRICITY

light·en¹ /ˈlaɪtn/ *v* **1** [T1;I∅] to make or become brighter or less dark **2** [I∅] to brighten or light up with excitement, happiness, etc. **3** [*it*+I∅] to flash with lightning

lighten² *v* [T1;I∅] **1** to make or become less heavy, forceful, etc. **2** to make or become more cheerful or less troubled

light·er¹ /ˈlaɪtəʳ/ *n* a large open flat-bottomed boat used for loading and unloading ships

lighter² *n* **1** that which lights or sets on fire **2** also **cigarette lighter**— an instrument that produces a small flame for lighting cigarettes, pipes, or CIGAR*s*

ligh·ter·age /ˈlaɪtərɪdʒ/ *n* [U] the money paid for the loading and unloading of ships

light-fin·gered /ˌ· ˈ··◂/ *adj* **1** having fingers that move easily and quickly, as in playing an instrument **2** *infml* having the habit of stealing small things

light-head·ed /ˌ· ˈ··◂/ *adj* **1** unable to think clearly or move steadily as during fever or after drinking alcohol; DELIRIOUS (2); GIDDY (1) **2** not being sensible or serious; foolish; thoughtless —**~ly** *adv* —**~ness** *n* [U]

light-heart·ed /ˌ· ˈ··◂/ *adj* cheerful; happy; gay

light heav·y·weight /ˌ· ˈ···/ *n, adj* [Wa5] (a BOXer) weighing between 160 and 170 pounds

light·house /ˈlaɪthaʊs/ *n* **-houses** /ˌhaʊzɨz/ a tower or other building with a powerful flashing light that guides ships or warns them of dangerous rocks

light·ing /ˈlaɪtɪŋ/ *n* [U] **1** the act of making something give light or start burning **2** the system, arrangement, or apparatus that lights a room, building, street, etc., or the quality of the light produced

light·ly /ˈlaɪtli/ *adv* **1** with little weight or force; gently **2** to a slight or little degree: *lightly cooked|lightly armed* **3** with little effort; easily **4** without careful thought or reasoning **5** without proper respect

light-mind·ed /ˌ· ˈ··◂/ *adj* not sensible or serious —**~ly** *adv* —**~ness** *n* [U]

light·ness /ˈlaɪtnɨs/ *n* [U] the quality or condition of being LIGHT⁴

light·ning /ˈlaɪtnɪŋ/ *n* **1** [U] a powerful flash of light in the sky passing from one cloud to another or to the earth, usu. followed by thunder —see also FORKED LIGHTNING, SHEET LIGHTNING **2** [A] very quick, short, or sudden: *a lightning visit*

lightning con·duc·tor /ˈ·· ·ˌ··/ *n* a metal wire or bar leading from the highest point of a building to the ground to protect the building from damage by lightning

lightning strike /ˌ·· ˈ·/ *n* a sudden stopping of work (STRIKE) by dissatisfied workers without the usu. warning of intention

light out *v adv* [I∅ (*for*)] *AmE infml* to leave: *The fox lit out for the forest*

lights¹ /laɪts/ *n* [P] **1** FOOTLIGHTS (1) **2 according to one's lights** in regard to or depending on one's knowledge, powers of judgment, ideas, and other personal abilities

lights² *n* [P] the lungs of sheep, pigs, etc., used as food

light·ship /ˈlaɪtˌʃɪp/ *n* a small ship fixed (ANCHORed) near a dangerous place that warns and guides other ships by means of a powerful flashing light

lights-out /ˌ· ˈ·, ˈ· ·/ *n* [U] the time when a group of people in beds (in a school, the army, etc.) must put the lights out and go to sleep: *No talking after lights-out!*

light up *v adv* **1** [T1;I∅] to give light to; make or become bright with light or colour: *The candles on the Christmas tree lit up the room* **2** [Wv4;I∅] to cause (electric) lamps to begin shining, giving light: *Lighting-up time is 6.50 tonight* **3** [I∅] *infml* to begin to smoke a cigarette or pipe

light up·on also **light on**— *v prep* [T1] to discover or find (esp. something or someone pleasant) by chance

light·weight /ˈlaɪt-weɪt/ *n, adj* **1** (a person or thing) **a** of less than average weight **b** *derog* lacking in strength of character or in ability to think deeply **2** (a BOXer) weighing between 126 and 135 pounds

light year /ˈ· ·/ *n* **1** (a measure of length equal to) the distance that light travels in one year (about 6,000,000,000,000 miles), used for measuring distances between stars **2** [*usu. pl. with sing. meaning*] *infml* a very long time: *It seems light years since we were in Sorrento, but it was only 1976*

lig·ne·ous /ˈlɪgnɪəs/ *adj* [Wa5] *tech* like wood

lig·nite /ˈlɪgnaɪt/ *n* [U] a soft material like coal, used for burning

lig·num vi·tae /ˌlɪgnəm ˈvaɪti/ *n* **1** [C] a type of South American tree with very hard wood **2** [U] the wood of this tree

li·ka·ble, likeable /ˈlaɪkəbəl/ *adj* (of a person) pleasant; attractive

like¹ /laɪk/ *v* [Wv6] **1** [T1,3,4;(V3,4)] to be fond of; find pleasant: *I've never tasted it, but I'm sure I'd like it.|I like walking.|I like to visit her as often as possible.|I don't like him to be unhappy.|I don't like it when he's unhappy* **2** [T3,4: *neg.*] to be willing (to): *I know she could help, but I don't like to ask her when she's so busy.|I don't like asking for money except when I have to* **3** [T3;V3] (*with* should, would) to wish: *I'd like to see you.|I'd like him to come* **4** [T1] to choose to have **a** *polite* (*with* should, would): *I'd like the red one, please* **b** habitually: *When do you like your breakfast?|What do you like for tea?* **5** [T1 *neg.*] *infml* (of a food) to be able to be eaten without giving pain, sickness, etc.: *Bananas don't like me!* **6 How do you like . . . ? a** What's your judgment on . . . ?: *How do you like the idea?|my dress?* **b** Do you/would you like . . . ?: *How does she like the work?|How would you like a holiday?* **7 I'd like to** (as a threat, or in disbelief) I'd be surprised to: *I'd like to see him do better, even if he does think he's so clever.|I'd like to know what he means by that* **8 I like that!** What an annoying thing! **9 if you like** if you do not want something else: *We can go out if you like.|"Shall we go?" "(Yes.) If you like"*

USAGE If you want something, say *I would* (*fml should*) **like** . . . when asking for it: *I'd* **like** *a bath.|We'd* **like** *to go home now.* If you want to offer something, say *Would you* **like** . . . ?: *Would you* **like** *a bath?|Would you* **like** *to go home now?* Use **like** alone for questions and statements about what one enjoys or is fond of: *I* **like** *driving* (*AmE* also *I*

like *to drive) fast cars.|Do you* **like** *driving (AmE* also *Do you* **like** *to drive) fast cars?* The verbs **love** and **hate** are used in the same way: *I'd* **love** *a swim.| I* **love** *swimming.|I'd* **hate** *to catch a cold.|I* **hate** *catching colds.*

like² *adj* **1** [F] the same in many ways; ALIKE¹: *Jimmy and his brother are very like* **2** [Wa5;A] with the same qualities: *Like thinking produces like ideas* **3** [Wa5;A] of the same type: *running, swimming, and like sports* **4** [F3] *becoming rare* likely: *He's like to ask what you think of his plan, so have an answer ready* **5 as like as two peas (in a pod)** the same in all ways

like³ *prep* **1** in the same way as: *to die in the street like a dog|You must do it like this* **2** with the same qualities as: *He was like a son to me.|When the car's painted it will look like new.|Jimmy's brother is (very much) like him* **3** typical of: *It was (just) like him to think of helping her.|You seem like* (=seem to be) *a sensible man* **4** *not fml* for example: *There are several people interested, like Mrs. Jones and Dr. Simpson* **5** very violently/very much so (in phrs. like **like hell, like mad,** etc.): *She was shouting like mad.|They love her like anything* —see also HELL¹ (9) **6 feel like** to wish to have: *I feel like a drink.|I feel like telling him what I think of him.|"Do you feel like a swim?"* (SEU W.) **7 look like** to seem probable: *It looks like a good time for a change.|It looks like snow/snowing* **8 something like** about; more or less: *It'll cost something like £100*

USAGE Note the difference between these uses of **like** and **as**: *Let me speak to you* **as** *a father* (=I am your father and I am speaking in that character).| *Let me speak to you* **like** *a father* (=I am not your father but I am speaking in the way your father might).

like⁴ *n* **1** [*(the)* R9 *usu. nonassertive*] something of equal (high) value (to something else): *I've never seen its like.|You'll never see her like again* **2** [*the*+R] something of the same kind: *running, swimming, and the like* **3 I've never seen/heard the like** I'm shocked at such behaviour —see also LIKES

like⁵ *adv* **1** *sl or nonstandard* (added esp. at the end of a sentence) so to say: *He's an old fellow, like, and he can't, like, walk very far on his own, like* **2** *old use* in the same way (in the phr. **like as**) **3 as like as not** *infml* probably **4 like enough** *infml* probably

like⁶ *conj* **1** *infml* as; in the same way as: *Do it like I tell you.|Do you make bread like you make cakes?* **2** *nonstandard* as if: *He acts like he's a king*

-like *comb. form* of the same form in many ways: *a hairlike thread*

like·li·hood /ˈlaɪklihʊd/ *n* [U (*of*)] the fact or degree of being likely

like·ly¹ /ˈlaɪkli/ *adj* [Wa2] **1** [F,F3] probable; expected: *Are we likely to arrive in time?|"Is it likely that he'll arrive so late?" "No, it's not very likely."* —opposite **unlikely** **2** [B] suitable to give results: *a likely plan|He's the most likely/the likeliest of the people who've asked for the job* **3 a likely story!** (said when showing that one disbelieves what someone has said)

likely² *adv* **1** probably (esp. in the phrs. **most likely, very likely**): *They'll very likely come by car* **2 as likely as not** probably

like-mind·ed /ˌ· ˈ··◂/ *adj* [Wa5] having the same ideas, interests, etc. —**~ness** *n* [U]

like·ness /ˈlaɪknɪ̌s/ *n* **1** [U;C] sameness in form: *a family likeness* **2** [C] *old use* a photograph or painting of a person; PORTRAIT (1)

lik·en to /ˈlaɪkən/ *v prep* [D1 *often pass.*] to compare with

likes /laɪks/ *n* [P] **1** things that one likes (usu. in the phr. **likes and dislikes**) —see also LIKING **2 the likes of** *infml* people or things of the stated type: *High class restaurants aren't for the likes of us*

like·wise /ˈlaɪk-waɪz/ *adv fml* **1** in the same way; the same: *"Go and do likewise"* **2** also; in addition: *You must pack plenty of food for the journey. Likewise, you'll need warm clothes, so pack them too*

lik·ing /ˈlaɪkɪŋ/ *n* **1** [S+*for*] fondness: *to have a liking for sweets* **2** [S9] what one likes: *It's not my liking to go walking on a cold day* **3 to one's liking** which suits one's ideas or expectations

li·lac /ˈlaɪlək/ *n* **1** [C] a type of tree with pinkish purple or white flowers giving a sweet smell **2** [U] the flowers of this tree **3** [U] a colour like the purple colour of these flowers

lil·li·pu·tian /ˌlɪlɪ̌ˈpjuːʃən/ *adj* [Wa5] very small

li·lo /ˈlaɪləʊ/ *n* **-los** *BrE* a sort of bed made of a large plastic bag that can be filled with air, used for lying on by the sea

lilt¹ /lɪlt/ *v* [Wv4;IØ] to have a regular pattern of usu. pleasant sound: *a lilting voice|a lilting tune*

lilt² *n* **1** [S] a regular pattern of rising and falling sound: *He speaks with a Welsh lilt* **2** [S;(U)] this quality in a song **3** [C] a song with this quality

lil·y /ˈlɪli/ *n* any of several types of plant with large flowers of various colours, but esp. the one with clear white flowers

lily-liv·ered /ˌ·· ˈ··◂/ *adj* cowardly

lily of the val·ley /ˌ·· · · ˈ··/ *n* **lilies of the valley** a type of plant with 2 green leaves and several small bell-shaped flowers with a sweet smell

lily-white /ˌ·· ˈ·◂/ *adj* pure white

li·ma bean /ˈliːmə biːn/ *n* a type of bean with flat seeds which can be eaten

limb /lɪm/ *n* **1** a leg, arm, or wing of an animal **2** a (large) branch of a tree **3** *now rare* a badly-behaved child **4 out on a limb** alone without support, esp. in opinions or argument **5 tear limb from limb** to tear apart —see also **sound in** WIND¹ (16) **and limb** —**~less** *adj* [Wa5]

-limbed /lɪmd/ *comb. form* having the stated number or type of limbs

lim·ber¹ /ˈlɪmbəʳ/ *n tech* the front part of a movable gun, with the wheels, which can be removed

limber² *adj becoming rare* loose (in muscle); moving and bending easily; SUPPLE (1)

limber³ *v* [T1;IØ: (UP)] *tech* to fasten the movable part with wheels to (a gun)

limber up *v adv* [IØ] to make the muscles stretch easily by exercise, esp. before violent exercise such as a race

lim·bo¹ /ˈlɪmbəʊ/ *n* **-bos** [U;(C)] **1** (*often cap.*) (in the Christian religion) a place neither heaven nor hell where the souls of those who have not done evil may go even though they were not Christians during their life **2** a state of uncertainty: *I'm in limbo, waiting for something to happen, ever since I heard that I might have won the competition*

limbo² *n* **-bos** a West Indian dance in which a dancer passes under a rope or bar which is moved nearer and nearer to the floor

lime¹ /laɪm/ *n* [U] **1** also **quicklime**— a white substance obtained by burning LIMESTONE, used in making cement **2** the substance made by adding water to this; SLAKED lime **3** BIRDLIME

lime² *v* [T1] to add lime to (fields, land, etc.) in order to control acid substances

lime³ also **lime tree** /ˈ· ·/, **linden**— *n* a type of tree with yellow sweet-smelling flowers

lime⁴ *n* **1** a type of tree which bears a small juicy green fruit with a sour taste **2** the fruit of this tree

lime·ade /laɪmˈeɪd/ *n* [U] a type of green drink made of the juice of LIMEs⁴ or something like it, with sugar added and sometimes gas —compare LEMONADE

lime·juice /ˈlaɪmdʒuːs/ *n* [U] the juice of the LIME⁴,

which has a bitter taste and may be mixed in other drinks

lime·kiln /ˈlaɪm,kɪln/ *n* an enclosed place (KILN) in which LIMESTONE is burnt

lime·light /ˈlaɪmlaɪt/ *n* **1** [U] a bright white light produced by heating lime in a strong flame, which was formerly used in theatres to light the stage **2** [*the*+R] a lot of attention from the public

lim·e·rick /ˈlɪmərɪk/ *n* a type of short poem with 5 lines, usu. humorous

lime·stone /ˈlaɪmstəʊn/ *n* [U] a type of rock containing material from bones, a combination of CALCIUM with other substances —see also LIME[1]

li·mey /ˈlaɪmi/ *n* **-meys** *infml, esp. AmE* **1** an Englishman **2** a British sailor

lim·it[1] /ˈlɪm$\frac{1}{2}$t/ *n* **1** [C (*of*) *often pl. with sing. meaning*] the farthest point or edge (of something): *the limit of one's patience|to set a limit to the amount| I can't walk 10 miles; I know my own limits* **2** [*the*+R] *infml* someone or something too bad to bear: *You're the limit! Can't you make your mind up!* **3 off limits (to)** *AmE* where one is not allowed to go; out of BOUNDS (2) (to) **4 within limits** up to a reasonable point (amount, time, etc.)

limit[2] *v* [T1 (*to*)] to keep below or at a certain point or amount: *We must limit our spending.|We must limit ourselves to an hour/to one cake each*

lim·i·ta·tion /,lɪm$\frac{1}{2}$ˈteɪʃən/ *n* **1** [U] the fact or conditions of limiting or being limited **2** [C *often pl.*] a fact which limits or reduces the power of something or someone **3** [C *usu. pl.*] a weakness of body or character which limits one's actions: *A wise man knows his own limitations*

lim·it·ed /ˈlɪm$\frac{1}{2}$t$\frac{1}{2}$d/ *adj* **1** [B] small in amount, power, etc., and not able to increase: *He is not very clever and his ability to improve his work is very limited* **2** [Wa5;A;E] (of a company) having a LIMITED LIABILITY: *Longman Group Limited*

limited li·a·bil·i·ty /,··· ··ˈ···/ *n* [(U);C] *tech* the NECESSITY of paying back debts only up to a limit which is the same as the amount held (by the company): *a limited liability company*

lim·it·ing /ˈlɪm$\frac{1}{2}$tɪŋ/ *adj* which prevents improvement, increase, etc.: *a limiting* FACTOR

lim·it·less /ˈlɪm$\frac{1}{2}$tləs/ *adj* [Wa5] without limit or end —**~ly** *adv* —**~ness** *n* [U]

limn /lɪm/ *v* [T1] **1** *fml* to describe **2** *old use* to paint or draw

lim·ou·sine /ˈlɪməziːn, ,lɪməˈziːn/ *n* a car with the driver's seat separated from the back by a sheet of glass

limp[1] /lɪmp/ *v* [IØ] **1** to walk with an uneven step, one foot or leg moving less well than the other **2** [Wv4] (of speech, music, poetry, etc.) to have an uneven pattern

limp[2] *n* [S] a way of walking with one foot dragging unevenly; the condition of LIMPing[1]: *He walks with a limp*

limp[3] *adj* lacking strength or stiffness: *The heat was too much for her; she went limp and fell to the ground* —**~ly** *adv* —**~ness** *n* [U]

lim·pet /ˈlɪmp$\frac{1}{2}$t/ *n* **1** a type of very small sea animal with a shell, which holds on tightly to the rock where it lives —see picture at MOLLUSC **2 hold on/hang on/cling like a limpet (to)** to hold on very tightly (to)

lim·pid /ˈlɪmp$\frac{1}{2}$d/ *adj esp. lit* (esp. of liquid) clear; transparent: *eyes like limpid pools* —**~ly** *adv* —**~ity** /lɪmˈpɪd$\frac{1}{2}$ti/ *n* [U]

lim·y /ˈlaɪmi/ *adj* [Wa1] **1** covered in or containing LIME[1]: *limy soil* **2** tasting like a LIME[4] (2)

linch·pin /ˈlɪntʃ,pɪn/ *n* **1** a piece of iron passed through an AXLE, which keeps the wheel on **2** [(*of*)] an important part or member which keeps the rest together

Lin·coln green /,lɪŋkən ˈgriːn/ *n* [U] a bright green colour, esp. of a cloth

linc·tus /ˈlɪŋktəs/ *n* [U] *BrE* liquid medicine to cure coughing

lin·den /ˈlɪndən/ *n* LIME[3]

line[1] /laɪn/ *v* [T1 (*with*) *often pass.*] **1** to cover the inside of with material (as a coat with light cloth or a box with paper or something soft): *Some skirts are lined so that they keep their shape better* **2** to be an inner covering for: *the soft slippery substance that lines the stomach* **3 line one's pocket(s)/purse** to make money for oneself

line[2] *n* **1** [C] a piece of string or thin cord: *a clothes line or washing line* **2** [C;(U)] a thin mark with length but no width, which can be drawn on a surface: *to draw a straight line|a line drawing* —see picture at GEOMETRY **3** [C] a telephone connection or wire: *Hold the line* (=don't disconnect).|*The lines have crossed* (=there's a wrong connection).| *The lines went down in the storm* —see also HOT LINE, PARTY LINE, HOLD[1] **the line** **4** [C] a cord with a hook at the end, usu. fastened on a rod, used for fishing **5** [C] a limit marked by a drawn line: *They thought he would win the race, but he was the last to cross the line* **6** [C] a border or edge: *the line between East and West Germany*|(fig.) *There's a very fine line between punishment and cruelty* **7** [C] OUTLINE **8** [C] a WRINKLE or mark (of age) in the skin **9** [C] a row: *a line of coats behind the door* **10** [C; *in*+U] a row of people side by side or a QUEUE standing one behind the other **11** [C] a set of people following one another in time, esp. a family: *Christ was born of David's line.|a line of kings* —see also LINEAGE **12** [C] a row of words on a printed page: *There are 12 words on a line/to a line* **13** [C] a row of words in a poem: *Each line has 5 beats* **14** [S] *infml* a short letter: *I must drop a line* (=write a short message) *to John, asking him to come* **15** [C *sometimes pl.*] a row of military defence works, esp. that nearest the enemy: *the front line* **16** [C] a row of tents in a military camp **17** [*the*+R] **a** (in the British army) the regular foot soldiers of the army (not the Guards): *a line* REGIMENT **b** (in the US army) all the regular fighting forces **18** [C] also **line of battle**— the arrangement of soldiers, ships, etc., side by side: *a ship of the line* (=a large warship) **19** [C *sometimes pl. with sing. meaning*] a railway track: *Passengers are not allowed to cross the lines.|the main line from London to Leeds* **20** [C] (*usu. in comb.*) a system for travelling by or moving goods by road, railway, sea or air; TRANSPORT system: *an airline|a shipping line* **21** [*the*+R] *tech* EQUATOR **22** [(*the*) S9, esp. *of*] a direction followed: *line of march|the line of fire* (=firing of guns) **23** [C *often pl.*] a course of action: *You haven't got the right answer but you're on the right lines* (=following the right method) **24** [C] an official POLICY (esp. in the phr. **to take a strong line**): *to follow the party line* (esp. in politics) **25** [C] a business, profession, trade, etc.: *My line is selling.|in the bakery line* **26** [S9] an area of interest (esp. in the phr. **in one's line**) —compare **up one's** STREET **27** [C] a type of goods: *a new line in hats* **28 all along the line** in every part: *I accept that all along the line* **29 bring/come into line (with)** to (cause to) agree (with) or do the same (as) **30 draw the line at** to refuse to do or accept **31 get a line on** *infml* to find out something about **32 hard lines!** (an expression of sympathy) What bad luck you had! **33 in line for** about to get: *in line for the job* **34 in line with** straight or level compared with: (fig.) *That isn't in line with my ideas at all* **35 on the line** (of paintings) hung at the level where the eye can look straight at them, and so, most favourably placed in a show **36 (reach) the end of the line** (to reach) the last stages, esp. the point of failure **37 read between the lines** to find hidden meanings **38 shoot a line** *sl* to BOAST[2] (1) **39 toe the line** to keep to accepted ideas; obey what one has been told —see also LINES, **line of least** RESISTANCE, STEP[2] **out of line**

line[3] *v* [T1] **1** [Wv5] to draw lines on: *lined paper* **2** [Wv5] to mark with lines or WRINKLES*s*: *Signs of worry lined his face* **3** to form rows along: *The crowds lined the streets* —see also LINE UP

line a·breast /ˌ· ·ˈ·/ *n* [(*in*) U] (a set of ships) lined up side by side —compare LINE ASTERN

lin·e·age /ˈlɪni·ɪdʒ/ *n* [U] the line of descent from one person to another in a family

lin·e·al /ˈlɪnɪəl/ *adj* [Wa5] in direct descending line, esp. from father to son —**~ly** *adv*

lin·e·a·ment /ˈlɪnɪəmənt/ *n* [*usu. pl.*] *fml* **1** a FEATURE of the face **2** a typical quality

lin·e·ar /ˈlɪnɪəʳ/ *adj* [Wa5] **1** of or in lines **2** (in art) using OUTLINE*s* (2) to show form **3** of length: *linear measurements*

linear mo·tor /ˌ··· ˈ··/ *n* a motor that produces power without the use of GEAR*s*

line a·stern /ˌ· ·ˈ·/ *n* [(*in*) U] (a set of ships) lined up one behind the other —compare LINE ABREAST

line draw·ing /ˈ· ˌ··/ *n* a drawing done with a pen or pencil

line·man /ˈlaɪnmən/ *n* **-men** /mən/ **1** also **lines·man**— a man whose job is to take care of railway lines or telephone wires **2** *AmE* a football player in the attacking (FORWARD[3]) line

lin·en /ˈlɪnɨn/ *n* [U] **1** a type of cloth made from the plant FLAX **2** underclothes, esp. white: *to change one's linen* **3** [*sometimes pl. with sing. meaning*] sheets and bedclothes, tablecloths, etc.: *to buy bed linen|on the third floor they sell linens* **4 wash one's dirty linen (in public)** to make private arguments known when others are present

linen bas·ket /ˈ·· ˌ··/ *n esp. BrE* LAUNDRY BASKET

line of bat·tle /ˌ· · ˈ··/ *n* **lines of battle** LINE[2] (18)

line of sight /ˌ· · ˈ·/ *n* **lines of sight** the straight line along which one looks towards an object

line·out /ˈlaɪnaʊt/ *n* (in RUGBY) 2 parallel lines of players to whom the ball is thrown after it has been kicked off the field of play

line print·er /ˈ· ˌ··/ *n* a machine which prints information from a COMPUTER at a very high speed —**-ing** *n* [U]

lin·er /ˈlaɪnəʳ/ *n* **1** [C] a large passenger ship of a steamship company (LINE[2] (20)) —see picture at SHIP[1] **2** [C;U] a pencil, brush, or material used around the eyes to give a usu. dark line (OUTLINE); EYELINER **3** [C] a piece of material used inside another to protect it: *a* NAPPY *liner*

lin·er·train /ˈlaɪnətreɪn‖-ər-/ *n* FREIGHTLINER

lines /laɪnz/ *n* [P] **1** a set of written lines to be copied by a pupil a certain number of times, as a punishment **2** the words learnt by an actor to be said in a play **3** *lit* a poem: *"Lines on the death of Nelson"* —see also MARRIAGE LINES

line·shoot·er /ˈlaɪnˌʃuːtəʳ/ *n sl* a person who shoots a LINE[2] (38); BOASTer —**-ing** *n* [U]

lines·man /ˈlaɪnzmən/ *n* **-men** /mən/ **1** (in sport) an official who stays near the lines marking the side of the playing area and decides which team has gone outside the limits, done something wrong, etc. —see picture at SOCCER **2** LINEMAN (1)

line-up /ˈlaɪn-ʌp/ *n* [*usu. sing.*] **1** an arrangement of people, esp. in a line looking forward **2** the arrangement of players or competitors side by side at the beginning of a race or game: *There are 7 horses in the lineup* **3** a set of events, following one after the other

line up *v adv* [T1;IØ] to (cause to) move into a row, side by side or one behind the other: *He lined up behind the others to wait his turn.|Line up the glasses and I'll fill them.|Everybody line up, facing the front*

line up be·hind *v adv prep* [T1] *infml* to support (someone), esp. in political affairs

ling[1] /lɪŋ/ *n* **ling** *or* **lings** [Wn2] a type of seafish which can be eaten

ling[2] *n* [U] a type of plant very like HEATHER, with bell-shaped pink flowers —see also HEATH (2)

-ling *suffix* small or unimportant: *a duckling|a* HIRELING

lin·ger /ˈlɪŋgəʳ/ *v* [L9 (ON)] **1** to wait for a time instead of going; delay going: *She should have gone out but lingered over her meal till it was too late* **2** to live on the point of death for some time, esp. when suffering from a disease **3** to be slow to disappear: *The pain lingered on for weeks* —**~er** *n*

lin·ge·rie /ˈlænʒəriː‖ˌlɑnʒəˈreɪ, ˈlænʒəriː/ *n* [U] *fml & tech* underclothes for women, esp. for sale in shops

lin·ger·ing /ˈlɪŋgərɪŋ/ *adj* [Wa5] slow to end or disappear: *a lingering death|a lingering fear of cars, after an accident* —**~ly** *adv*

lin·go /ˈlɪŋgəʊ/ *n* **-goes** *sl* **1** a language, usu. foreign **2** a type of speech full of expressions one cannot understand —compare JARGON

lin·gua fran·ca /ˌlɪŋgwə ˈfræŋkə/ *n* **lingua francas** a language used between peoples whose native languages are different. It may originally be made up of parts of several languages

lin·gual /ˈlɪŋgwəl/ *adj* [Wa5] *tech* **1** of or concerning the tongue **2** (of a sound) made by the movement of the tongue —see also BILINGUAL

lin·guist /ˈlɪŋgwɨst/ *n* **1** a person who studies and is good at foreign languages **2** a person who studies the science of language (LINGUISTICS)

lin·guis·tic /lɪŋˈgwɪstɪk/ *adj* [Wa5;A] **1** concerning one or more languages: *great linguistic knowledge* **2** concerning words and patterns of words: *linguistic development|change* **3** concerning LINGUISTICS —**~ally** *adv* [Wa4]

lin·guis·tics /lɪŋˈgwɪstɪks/ *n* [U] the study of language in general and of particular languages, of the patterns of their grammar, sounds, etc., their history, origins, and use

lin·i·ment /ˈlɪnɨmənt/ *n* [C;U] a liquid substance containing oil, to be rubbed on the skin, esp. to help soreness and stiffness of the joints

lin·ing /ˈlaɪnɪŋ/ *n* **1** [C] a piece of material covering the inner surface of a garment, box, etc. **2** [U] cloth of a type used for lining (LINE[1]) coats

link[1] /lɪŋk/ *n* **1** something which connects 2 other parts: *Is there a link between smoking and lung diseases?* **2** one ring of a chain **3** *now rare* (a measure of length equal to) 7·92 inches or about 20 centimetres **4** [*usu. pl.*] CUFF LINK —see also MISSING LINK

link[2] *v* **1** [T1 (TOGETHER)] to join or connect: *The road links all the new towns.|They walked with linked arms* **2** [IØ (TOGETHER, UP)] to be joined: *These pieces of information link up to suggest who the thief was*

link[3] *n old use* a TORCH (2) carried to light one's way in the streets

link·age /ˈlɪŋkɪdʒ/ *n* **1** [C] a set of LINK*s*[1] **2** [U;S] the fact or way of being connected

link·man[1] /ˈlɪŋkmən/ also **link·boy** /ˈlɪŋkbɔɪ/— *n* **-men** /mən/ (in former times) a man (or boy) whose job was to light the streets with his TORCH for those going home late

linkman[2] /ˈlɪŋkmæn/ *n* **-men** /men/ a man whose job is to introduce all the separate parts of a television or radio broadcast

links /lɪŋks/ *n* **links** **1** [Wn3;C *often pl. with sing. meaning*] a piece of ground on which GOLF is played **2** [P] sandy ground near the sea

link·up /ˈlɪŋk-ʌp/ *n* a point of joining or connection: *a road linkup|a television linkup*
lin·net /ˈlɪnɨ̍t/ *n* a type of small brown singing bird
li·no·cut /ˈlaɪnəʊkʌt/ *n* **1** [U] the art of cutting a pattern on a block of LINOLEUM **2** [C] a print made from such a block
li·no·le·um /lɨ̍ˈnəʊlɪəm/ also (*infml, esp. BrE*) **li·no** /ˈlaɪnəʊ/, (*BrE*) **oilcloth**— *n* [U] a material used (esp.) as a floor-covering, made up of strong cloth combined with a thickness of material made from LINSEED OIL and other substances
li·no·type /ˈlaɪnəʊtaɪp/ *n tdmk* a machine which makes a line of letters for printing (TYPE) together on one bar of metal
lin·seed /ˈlɪnsiːd/ *n* [U] the seed of FLAX —see also LINEN (1)
linseed oil /ˌ·· ˈ·/ *n* [U] the oil from LINSEED, used in LINOLEUM, in some paints, inks, etc., and for rubbing onto cricket BATs
lint /lɪnt/ *n* [U] soft material used for protecting wounds
lin·tel /ˈlɪntl/ *n* a piece of stone or wood across the top of a window or door, forming part of the frame —see pictures at DOOR and WINDOW
li·on /ˈlaɪən/ *fem.* **li·on·ess** /ˈlaɪənes, -nɨ̍s/— *n* **1** [Wn1] a type of large yellow 4-footed animal of the cat family which hunts and eats meat, and lives mainly in Africa, the male having a thick growth of hair over the head and shoulders —see picture at CAT **2** a famous and important person **3 the lion's share (of)** the greatest part (of); most (of)
lion-heart·ed /ˌ·· ˈ··◂/ *adj* [Wa5] very brave
li·on·ize /ˈlaɪənaɪz/ *v* [T1] to treat (a person) as important; cause to be famous —**-ization** /ˌlaɪənaɪˈzeɪʃən‖-nə-/ *n* [U]
lip /lɪp/ *n* **1** [C] one of the 2 edges of the mouth where the skin is delicate and rather red: *He kissed her on the lips* **2** [C] this area with the ordinary skin around there, esp. around the top below the nose: *Hair grows on the top lip of many men* —see picture at HUMAN² **3** [C (*of*) *usu. sing.*] the edge (of a hollow vessel or opening): *the lip of the cup* **4** [U] *sl* rude or arguing talk **5 hang on the lips of** to listen to with great attention **6 open one's lips** to speak **7 a stiff upper lip** a lack of expression of feeling —see also BITE¹ (9)
lip·id /ˈlɪpɨ̍d/ *n* any of a class of fatty substances in living things, such as fat, oil, or wax
-lipped /lɪpt/ *comb. form* having lips of the stated type: *full-lipped|red-lipped*
lip-read /ˈlɪp riːd/ *v* [IØ] (usu. of people who cannot hear) to watch people's lip movements so as to understand what they are saying —**~ing** *n* [U]
lip ser·vice /ˈ· ˌ··/ *n* [U] **pay lip service to** to support in words, but not in fact; give loyalty, interest, etc., in speech, while thinking the opposite
lip·stick /ˈlɪpˌstɪk/ *n* [C;U] (a stick-shaped mass of) material for brightening the colour of the lips
liq·ue·fac·tion /ˌlɪkwɨ̍ˈfækʃən/ *n* [U] *tech* the act of making or becoming liquid
liq·ue·fy /ˈlɪkwɨ̍faɪ/ *v* [T1;IØ] to (cause to) become liquid: *Butter liquefies in heat*
li·ques·cent /lɪˈkwesənt/ *adj* [Wa5] *tech* **1** in the state of becoming liquid **2** able or likely to become liquid
li·queur /lɪˈkjʊəʳ‖lɪˈkɜr/ *n* any of several types of very strong alcoholic drink, each of which has a special, rather sweet taste, usu. drunk in small quantities after a meal
liq·uid¹ /ˈlɪkwɨ̍d/ *adj* [Wa5] **1** (esp. of something which is usu. solid or gas) in the form of a liquid: *liquid gold|liquid oxygen* **2** clear, as if covered in clean water: *liquid colours* **3** (esp. of food) soft and watery **4** (of money in banks, not coin) which can be obtained as coin (esp. in the phr. **liquid assets**) **5** (of sounds) clear and flowing, with pure notes
liquid² *n* **1** [C;U] (a type of) substance not solid or gas, which flows and has no fixed shape: *Water is a liquid* **2** [C] *tech* either of the consonants r and l
liquid air /ˌ·· ˈ·/ *n* [U] air which has become a liquid at a very low temperature
liq·ui·date /ˈlɪkwɨ̍deɪt/ *v* **1** [T1] to get rid of; destroy **2** [T1] *infml* to kill **3** [T1] to arrange the end of business for (a company), esp. when it has too many debts **4** [IØ] (of a company) to bring business to an end in this way, esp. becoming BANKRUPT **5** [T1] *tech* to pay (a debt)
liq·ui·da·tion /ˌlɪkwɨ̍ˈdeɪʃən/ *n* [U] **1** the fact or state of stopping trade in order to pay debts, esp. being made BANKRUPT (usu. in the phr. **go into liquidation**) **2** *infml* being destroyed or killed
liq·ui·da·tor /ˈlɪkwɨ̍deɪtəʳ/ *n* an official who ends the trade of a particular business, esp. to pay its debts
liq·uid·i·ty /lɪˈkwɪdɨ̍ti/ *n* [U] **1** *tech* the state of having money in one's possession, or goods that can easily be sold for money **2** *rare* the state of being liquid
liq·uid·ize /ˈlɪkwɨ̍daɪz/ *v* [T1] to crush (esp. fruit or vegetables) into a liquid-like form or juice
liq·uid·iz·er /ˈlɪkwɨ̍daɪzəʳ/ *BrE & AmE* also **blend·er**— *n BrE* a small electric machine, for use in the kitchen, that can be used for making solid foods into liquid-like forms, such as soups or juices —see picture at KITCHEN
liquid par·af·fin /ˌ·· ˈ···/ *n* [U] a form of PARAFFIN (1) without smell or taste, drunk (as a LAXATIVE) to clear out solid waste matter from the body
liq·uor /lɪkəʳ/ *n* [U] **1** *BrE fml or tech* alcoholic drink **2** *AmE* strong alcoholic drink, such as WHISKY **3** the liquid produced from a boiled food, such as the juice from meat
liq·uo·rice, licorice /ˈlɪkərɪs, -rɪʃ/ *n* [U] **1** a type of plant from which a sweet black substance is produced **2** the substance produced from this, as used in medicine and sweets
lir·a¹ /ˈlɪərə/ *n* an amount of money used as a standard in Turkey or Syria; Turkish or Syrian POUND¹ (3a)
lira² *n* **-e** /ˈlɪəreɪ/ *or* **-as** an amount of money used as a standard for Italian coins
lisle /laɪl/ *n* [U] a type of cotton material, used esp. formerly for GLOVEs and stockings
lisp¹ /lɪsp/ *v* [IØ;T1 (OUT)] to speak or say with /s/ sounds which are not clear, esp. when the tongue is placed on the teeth, making the /s/ seem like /θ/ —**~ingly** *adv*
lisp² *n* [S] the fault in speech of LISPing¹: *She speaks with a lisp*
lis·som, lissome /ˈlɪsəm/ *adj* (of a person or the body) graceful in shape and movement —**~ly** *adv* —**~ness** *n* [U]
list¹ /lɪst/ *v* [IØ] *old use* to wish; desire
list² *v* [IØ (*to*)] *old use* to listen
list³ *n* a set of names of things written one after the other, so as to remember them or keep them in order so that they can be found: *a list of things to buy|a shopping list*
list⁴ *v* [T1] *esp. fml* to write in a list
list⁵ *v* [IØ] (esp. of a ship) to lean or slope to one side
list⁶ *n* [S] a leaning position, esp. of a ship
lis·ten¹ /ˈlɪsən/ *v* [IØ (*to*)] **1** to give attention in hearing: *Are you listening or are you just pretending?|Listen to the music; don't make a noise* **2 Don't listen to someone** Don't believe or do what someone says —see HEAR (USAGE)
listen² *n* [S] *infml* an act of listening: *Have a listen*
lis·ten·a·ble /ˈlɪsənəbəl/ *adj* [(TO)] *infml* which is

pleasant to hear: *The music is quite listenable.|Is it listenable to?*

lis·ten·er /ˈlɪsənəʳ/ *n* [C;N *usu. pl.*] a person who listens or is listening, esp. to the radio: *Good morning, listeners!*

listen for *v prep* [T1] to pay attention so as to be sure of hearing: *Listen for the moment when the music changes*

listen in *v adv* [IØ] **1** [(*to*)] to listen to (a broadcast on) the radio: *to listen in at news time|to listen in to the news* —see also TUNE IN **2** [(*on, to*)] to listen to (the conversation of) other people, esp. when one should not, as to someone else's telephone message: *to listen in on a false telephone connection|to listen in to a conversation* —compare EAVESDROP

listen out *v adv* [IØ (*for*) *usu. imper.*] *infml* to listen carefully, esp. for an expected sound: *Listen out in case she calls.|Listen out for your name to be called*

list·less /ˈlɪstləs/ *adj* (of a person who is) lacking power of movement, activity, etc.: *Heat makes some people listless* —**~ly** *adv* —**~ness** *n* [U]

list price /ˈ· ·/ *n* a price which is suggested for an article by the people who make it, but which the shopkeeper does not necessarily have to charge

lists /lɪsts/ *n* [*the*+P] **1** (in former times) **a** the fences enclosing a piece of ground for fighting on horseback as a sport **b** the ground itself —see JOUST (1) **2 enter the lists** to (start to) take part in a competition, argument, etc.

lit¹ /lɪt/ *past t. & p. of* LIGHT[3,6]

lit² *abbrev. for:* **1** literature **2** LITERALLY (3) **3** litre

lit·a·ny /ˈlɪtəni/ *n* a form of prayer in the Christian church in which the priest calls out and the people reply, always in the same words

li·tchi /ˈlaɪtʃiː/ *n* LYCHEE

li·ter /ˈliːtəʳ/ *n AmE* LITRE

lit·e·ra·cy /ˈlɪtərəsi/ *n* [U] the state or condition of being able to read and/or write (being LITERATE)

lit·e·ral¹ /ˈlɪtərəl/ *adj* **1** exact: *a literal account of a conversation* **2** giving one word for each word (as in a foreign language): *A literal translation is not always the closest to the original meaning* **3** following the usual meaning of the words, without any additional meanings: *The literal meaning of the word "cat" is an animal not a girl* —opposite **figurative** **4** not showing much imagination: *a literal* APPROACH *to a subject* **5** [Wa5] *tech* (in printing) concerning letters of the alphabet: *a literal mistake* —**~ness** *n* [U]

literal² *n tech* a mistake in printing

lit·e·ral·ly /ˈlɪtərəli/ *adv* **1** [Wa5] exactly: *to do literally nothing at all* **2** word by word: *to translate literally* **3** according to the words and not the intention: *I took what he said literally, but afterwards it became clear that he really meant something else* **4** [Wa5] (used for giving force to an adjective): *literally blue with cold*

lit·e·ra·ry /ˈlɪtərəri‖ˈlɪtəreri/ *adj* **1** [B] of or concerning literature **2** [Wa5;A] **a** producing literature; being a writer: *a literary man* **b** studying literature: *a literary course* **3** [B] more typical of literature and poetry, esp. that of former times, than of ordinary speech or writing

lit·e·rate¹ /ˈlɪtərɨt/ *adj* **1** [Wa5] able to read and write **2** well-educated —opposite **illiterate** —**~ly** *adv* —**~ness** *n* [U]

literate² *n* a person who can read and write

lit·e·ra·ti /ˌlɪtəˈrɑːti/ *n* [P] *fml* people with great knowledge of books and skills of the mind, esp. forming a fairly small group in a society

lit·e·ra·ture /ˈlɪtərətʃəʳ‖-tʃʊər/ *n* **1** [U] **a** written works which are of artistic value: *English literature* **b** these books as a subject for study **2** [U] written works which are not scientific **3** [U9] a set of works written in a certain country or at a certain time, esp. as a subject for study: *the literature of Asia|modern literature* **4** [C9;U9] a set of works on a particular subject: *a developing literature of social work* **5** [U] *infml* printed material, esp. giving information

lithe /laɪð/ *adj* able to bend and move easily —**~ly** *adv*

lith·i·um /ˈlɪθɪəm/ *n* [U] a soft silver-white simple substance (ELEMENT (6)) that is the lightest known metal

lith·o·graph¹ /ˈlɪθəgrɑːf‖-græf/ *v* [T1;IØ] to print (something) by LITHOGRAPHY

lithograph² *n* a picture, print, etc., made by LITHOGRAPHY

lith·o·graph·ic /ˌlɪθəˈgræfɪk/ *adj* [Wa5] by or of LITHOGRAPHY —**~ally** *adv* [Wa4]

li·thog·ra·phy /lɪˈθɒgrəfi‖lɪˈθɑ-/ *n* [U] a way of printing patterns, pictures, etc., from a piece of stone or metal

lit·i·gant /ˈlɪtɨgənt/ *n tech* a person concerned in a certain action of a court of law

lit·i·gate /ˈlɪtɨgeɪt/ *v tech* **1** [IØ] to bring a case in a court of law **2** [T1] to defend or DENY (a case) in law

lit·i·ga·tion /ˌlɪtɨˈgeɪʃən/ *n* [U] *tech* action in law, as in making and defending claims in court

li·ti·gious /lɪˈtɪdʒəs/ *adj* **1** *fml, often derog* habitually liking to make a case in law: *a litigious person* **2** [Wa5] *tech* which can be defended or denied (DENY) in law: *a litigious argument* —**~ness** *n* [U]

lit·mus /ˈlɪtməs/ *n* [U] a colouring material which turns red when touched by an acid substance and blue when touched by an ALKALI

litmus pa·per /ˈ·· ˌ··/ *n* [U] a type of paper containing LITMUS, used in chemical tests to find out if a substance is acid or ALKALI

li·to·tes /ˈlaɪtətiːz, -təʊ-/ *n* [U] *tech* a way of expressing a thought by its opposite, esp. with "not"

li·tre, *AmE* **-ter** /ˈliːtəʳ/ *n BrE* (a measure of liquid equal to) about 1¾ PINT*s* —see WEIGHTS & MEASURES TABLE

lit·ter¹ /ˈlɪtəʳ/ *n* **1** [U] things (to be) thrown away, esp. paper scattered untidily **2** [U] STRAW used as an animal's bed **3** [U] STRAW used for protecting plants from freezing cold (FROST) **4** [C] a bed or seat with handles, on which a person may be carried, esp. because wounded or (in former times) as a sign of riches and importance **5** [GC] a group of young animals born at the same time to one mother, as of KITTEN*s* (=baby cats)

litter² *v* **1** [T1 (*with*)] to cover untidily: *to litter the room with papers|papers littering the room* **2** [X9] to scatter; spread: *to litter papers round the room|littering papers all over the place*

lit·te·ra·teur /ˌlɪtərəˈtɜːʳ/ *n* a person who writes works of literature

lit·ter·bin /ˈlɪtəˌbɪn‖-ər-/ *AmE* **lit·ter·bag** /-bæg/— *n BrE* a container for objects to be thrown away, esp. in a public place

lit·ter·lout /ˈlɪtəlaʊt‖-ər/ *esp. AmE* **lit·ter·bug** /-bʌg/— *n BrE* a person who leaves on public ground things which should be thrown away at home or in a special place

lit·tle¹ /ˈlɪtl/ *adj* **1** [Wa1;A;(B)] small: *a little door|2 little insects* **2** [Wa5;A] short: *a little time* **3** [Wa5;B] young: *my little girl* (=daughter)|*She's too little to ride a bicycle* **4** [Wa1;B] not important: *the little things of life*

little² *adv* **less, least** [Wa1] **1** to only a small degree: *a little known fact* **2** (*with verbs of feeling and knowing*) not at all: *They little thought that the truth would be discovered.|He little cares.|Little does he care whether we live or die* **3** rarely (esp. in the

phr. **very little**): *I go there very little*
USAGE **little** (1) is rare as an adv. alone. People usually use **not much** instead: *She eats very little* or *She doesn't eat much* are more acceptable than *She eats little*.

little³ *determiner, pron, n* **less, least** **1** [Wa1;U] (*of* [U] *nouns; used without* a *or* only, *to show the smallness of the amount*) not much; not enough: *The little I have is not worth giving* (compare *The few I have are not . . .*).|*I have very little* (*money*) *left.*|*I understood little of his speech.*|*I have so little time to enjoy myself* (compare *I have so few chances . . .*).|*no less than a mile*|*the one that costs the least* (*money*) —compare PLENTY², FEW (1) **2** [Wa5;S] a small amount, but at least some: *a few eggs and a little milk*|*There's only a very little left.*|*Give me a little of that wine.*|*I'd like some cake; just a little* (*more*).|*I had a little difficulty in finding the house.*|*She speaks a little French* —compare FEW (2) **3** [Wa5;S] a short time: *He came back after a little.*|*Can't you stay a little longer?*|*a little over 60 years*|*Let's walk* (*for*) *a little* **4 a little** also (*infml*) **a little bit**— to some degree; rather: *I was a little annoyed.*|*"He thinks it's all a little bit stupid"* (SEU S.) **5 in little** *fml* in the same form but smaller **6 little by little** gradually **7 make little of a** to treat as unimportant **b** to understand little —compare **make** NOTHING¹, MUCH¹ **of**; see FEW (USAGE)

little broth·er /ˌ·· ˈ··/ *n* one's younger brother

little fin·ger /ˌ·· ˈ··/ *n* the smallest finger on the hand

little peo·ple /ˈ·· ˌ··/ also **little folk** /ˈ·· ·/— *n* [*the*+P] *esp. IrE* fairies

little sister /ˌ·· ˈ··/ *n* one's younger sister

little toe /ˌ·· ˈ·/ *n* the smallest toe on the foot

little wom·an /ˌ·· ˈ··/ *n* [*the*+R] *sometimes derog* (an expression for mentioning) one's wife

lit·to·ral /ˈlɪtərəl/ *n, adj* [Wa5] *fml & tech* (land) near the coast

li·tur·gi·cal /lɪˈtɜːdʒɪkəl‖-ɜr-/ *adj* [Wa5] like or used in a LITURGY —**~ly** *adv* [Wa4]

lit·ur·gy /ˈlɪtədʒi‖-ər-/ *n* **1** [C] a form of worship in the Christian church, using prayers, songs, etc., according to fixed patterns in religious services **2** [*the*+R] (*sometimes cap.*) the written form of these services

liv·a·ble, liveable /ˈlɪvəbəl/ *adj* [Wa5] **1** worth living; acceptable to experience: *a livable life*|*The pain is bad, but it's livable* **2** suitable to live in: *The house is not livable* **3 livable with** acceptable to live with: *Such behaviour is not livable with*

live¹ /lɪv/ *v* **1** [IØ] *fml* to be alive; have life: *The rich live while the poor die* **2** [L9;(IØ)] to continue to be alive: *If he goes on driving like a madman he won't live long.*|*His illness is so serious, he is unlikely to live.*|*A writer's words live beyond his death* **3** [L9] to have one's home; DWELL: *Where do you live?* **4** [X9] to pass (a certain sort of life): *to live one's life alone* **5** [IØ] to lead an interesting varied life: *to live, not just to exist* **6** [IØ] (of characters in books, plays, etc.) to seem real **7** [IØ] to afford what one needs: *to earn enough to live* **8 live and learn** to have learnt something surprising: *Do Americans really have a higher temperature than Europeans?! Well, you live and learn* **9 live and let live** to accept others' behaviour; be TOLERANT **10 live by/on one's wits** to get money by clever tricks rather than by a trade, esp. dishonestly **11 live it up** *infml* to enjoy a full exciting social life or social occasion —see also LIVE BY, LIVE DOWN, LIVE FOR, LIVE IN, LIVE OFF, LIVE ON¹·², LIVE OUT, LIVE THROUGH, LIVE TOGETHER, LIVE UP TO, LIVE WITH
USAGE **Dwell** (*lit* or *fml*) and **reside** (*fml* or *pomp*) are both used like **live** when one is speaking of a place: *to* **live** *in China*|*to* **dwell** *among the mountains*|*to* **reside** *at the castle*. **Inhabit** means "to **live** in", and is used esp. of tribes and races: *They* **inhabit** *the tropical forests*. **Live** is the only one of those words that can mean "not to be dead": *Will he* **live**, *doctor?* or can be used in expressions about food or money: *She* **lives** *on fish*|**lives** *on a small income*.

live² /laɪv/ *adj* [Wa5] **1** [A] alive; living: *The cat was playing with a live mouse* —opposite **dead** (1) **2** [B] (of lighted coal or wood) still burning **3** [B] having power which can be used in an explosion and flames when it hits something hard: *a live bomb* **4** [B] carrying free electricity which can shock anyone who touches it **5** [B] (of broadcasting) seen and/or heard as it happens: *It wasn't a recorded show, it was live* **6 a real live . . .** *infml* (used for giving force to a noun, esp. when something unexpected is seen): *Look! A real live elephant!*

live birth /ˌlaɪv ˈbɜːθ‖-ɜrθ/ *n tech* a baby born alive

live by /lɪv/ *v prep* **1** [T1 *no pass.*, 4] to make an income from **2** [T1 *no pass.*] to behave according to the rules of

-lived /lɪvd/ *comb. form* lasting the stated length of time: *a short-lived interest*

live down /lɪv/ *v adv* [T1] to cause (a bad action) to be forgotten, esp. by future good behaviour

live for /lɪv/ *v prep* [T1 *no pass.*] **1** to give most attention to: *He lives for his car* **2** to wish for (something in the future) very much (esp. in the phr. **live for the day when . . .**)

live in /lɪv/ *v adv* [IØ] to sleep and eat in a house where one is employed —compare LIVE OUT (1)

live·li·hood /ˈlaɪvlihʊd/ *n* the way by which one earns enough to pay for what is necessary

live·long /ˈlɪvlɒŋ‖-lɔŋ/ *adj* [Wa5;A] *esp. poet* (of the day or night) whole: *the livelong day*

live·ly /ˈlaɪvli/ *adj* [Wa1] **1** gay; full of quick movement, thought, etc.: *a lively mind*|*a lively song* **2** lifelike; as if real; VIVID (2): *a lively description* **3** (in sport, esp. cricket) which has or causes quick movement (of the ball): *a lively* PITCH³ (4) **4 look lively** to act fast; start doing or moving **5 make it lively for someone** to cause trouble for someone —**-liness** *n* [U]

liv·en up /ˈlaɪvən/ *v adv* [T1;IØ] to (cause to) become LIVELY (1)

live off /lɪv/ *v prep* [T1] **1** to produce one's food or income from **2** *usu. derog* to get money for one's needs from: *to live off one's parents*

live on¹ /lɪv/ *v prep* [T1] to have as one's only food or income: *to live on fruit*|*to live on the rent from one's property*

live on² *v adv* [IØ] to continue in life or use

live out /lɪv/ *v adv* **1** [IØ] to live in a place away from one's place of work —compare LIVE IN **2** [T1] to live till the end of: *Will the old man live out the month?*

liv·er¹ /ˈlɪvəʳ/ *n* **1** [C] a large organ in the body which produces BILE and cleans the blood —see picture at DIGESTIVE SYSTEM **2** [C;U] this organ from an animal's body, used as food

liver² *n* [C9] a person who lives in the stated way: *a clean liver*|*an evil liver*

liv·e·ried /ˈlɪvərid/ *adj* [Wa5] wearing LIVERY¹ (1,2)

liv·er·ish /ˈlɪvərɪʃ/ *adj infml* suffering from sickness and slight illness, esp. after eating and/or drinking too much

liver saus·age /ˈ·· ˌ··/ *AmE* also **liv·er·wurst** /ˈlɪvəwɜːst‖ˈlɪvərwɜrst/— *n* [U] a type of cooked SAUSAGE made mainly of LIVER¹, and eaten on bread

liv·e·ry¹ /ˈlɪvəri/ *n* **1** [(*in*) U;C] uniform of a special type for servants employed by the same person **2** [(*in*) U;C] uniform worn at ceremonies

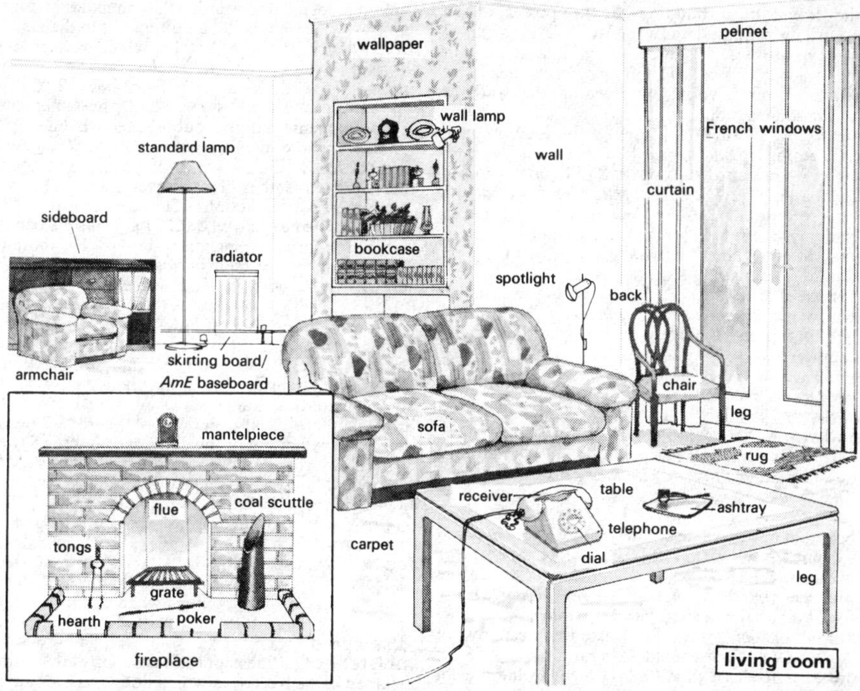

by members of certain trade associations (GUILDs) in London **3** [U] *poet* dress; covering

liv·er·y² *adj* LIVERISH

livery com·pa·ny /ˈ··· ˌ···/ *n* one of several trade associations (GUILDs) in London with a special uniform

liv·e·ry·man /ˈlɪvərimən/ *n* **-men** /mən/ a member of a LIVERY COMPANY

livery sta·ble /ˈ··· ˌ··/ *n* [*often pl. with sing. meaning*] a place where owners may pay to have horses kept, fed, etc., or where horses may be hired for use

lives /laɪvz/ *pl. of* LIFE

live·stock /ˈlaɪvstɒk‖-stɑk/ *n* [GU] **1** animals kept on a farm **2** *infml* small unwanted biting insects and other creatures, such as FLEAs and LICE: *This bed's full of livestock!*

live through /lɪv/ *v prep* [T1] to remain alive during and in spite of (difficulty)

live to·geth·er /lɪv/ *v adv* [IØ] *euph* (of 2 people of different sexes) to LIVE WITH (1) each other

live up to /lɪv/ *v adv prep* [T1] to keep to the high standards of

live wire /ˌlaɪv ˈwaɪəʳ/ *n infml* a very active person

live with /lɪv/ *v prep* [T1] **1** *euph* to live in the same house as (someone of the opposite sex), like a married person **2** to accept (an unpleasant thing): *I don't enjoy the pain, but I can live with it*

liv·id /ˈlɪvɪ̈d/ *adj* **1** blue-grey, as of marks on the skin (BRUISEs) after being hit **2** (of the face) very pale **3** *infml* very angry —**~ly** *adv*

liv·ing¹ /ˈlɪvɪŋ/ *adj* [Wa5] **1** [B; *the*+P] alive now: *a living person|The living are more important to us than the dead* **2** [B] existing in use: *a living language* **3** [A;(B)] exact in likeness (esp. in the phr. **the living image of**) **4** [A;(B)] (of feelings, ideas, etc.) full of power and force: *in living colour*

living² *n* **1** [C] the gain of earnings with which one buys what is necessary to life: *to make a living in industry* **2** [C] wages; income: *I make £100 on what I sell, and that's my living* **3** [C] a trade or profession **4** [U] (*usu. in comb.*) a standard one reaches in food, drink, etc.: *the cost of living|high living* **5** [C] BENEFICE

living day·lights /ˌ·· ˈ··/ *n infml* **1 knock the living daylights out of** to strike or beat very severely **2 scare the living daylights out of** to shock very greatly

living death /ˌ·· ˈ·/ *n* [S] **1** a life so unpleasant it is worse than death **2** burial when still alive

living fos·sil /ˌ·· ˈ··/ *n* **1** an animal of a very ancient type, which lives now although it seemed to have ceased to exist in the past **2** *infml* a very old-fashioned person

living room /ˈ·· ·/ also (*esp. BrE*) **sitting room**— *n* the main room in a house where people can do things together, (usu.) apart from eating

living space /ˈ·· ·/ *n* [U] **1** land claimed (and sometimes conquered) by a nation as necessary for the growth of its population **2** the area taken up by the floors in a house, esp. by the kitchen and LIVING ROOM

living stan·dard /ˈ·· ˌ··/ *n* STANDARD OF LIVING

living wage /ˌ·· ˈ·/ *n* [S] a wage which is enough to buy the necessary things in daily life

liz·ard /ˈlɪzəd‖-ərd/ *n* any of several types of (usu.) small creatures which are REPTILEs, with a rough skin, 4 legs, and a long tail —see picture at REPTILE

ll *written abbrev. for:* lines: *see ll 104–201*

-'ll /əl, l/ [Wv2] *contr. of:* **1** will **2** shall —see CONTR. (USAGE)

lla·ma /ˈlɑːmə/ *n* a type of animal of South America with thick woolly hair, sometimes used for carrying goods

lo /ləʊ/ *interj old use* look —see also LO AND BEHOLD

load¹ /ləʊd/ *n* **1** an amount being carried, or to be carried, esp. heavy: *a load of furniture*|(fig.) *Her grief is a heavy load to bear* **2** (*in comb.*) the amount which a certain vehicle can carry: *a car load* **3** the work done by a moving part such as a motor or engine **4** the amount of weight borne by the frame of a building **5** the power of an electricity supply **6** the CHARGE² (7) in a gun **7** **loads of** also (*sl*) **a load of**— *infml* a large amount of; a lot of **8** **a load off someone's mind** the removing of a worry, by learning the truth or taking some action

load² *v* **1** [T1;IØ: (UP)] to put a full load on or in (something): *Load the car.|Have you finished loading up?* —see also LOAD WITH **2** [T1 (*into, onto*)] to place a load of: *Load the furniture onto the back* **3** [T1] to put a CHARGE² (7) or film into (a gun or camera) **4** [Wv5;T1] *tech* to add weight to

load down *v adv* [T1 (*with*)] to load with a great weight —compare WEIGH DOWN

load·ed /ˈləʊdɪ̆d/ *adj* **1** [B] giving an unfair advantage: *The argument was loaded in his favour* **2** [B] containing a hidden trap; suggesting or encouraging something, esp. bad: *a loaded question/statement* **3** [F] *infml* having lots of money: *Let him pay; he's loaded*

load·star /ˈləʊdstɑːʳ/ *n* LODESTAR

load·stone /ˈləʊdstəʊn/ *n* LODESTONE

load with *v prep* [D1] to put a load of (something) on: *They loaded the car with their possessions.*|(fig.) *They loaded me with gifts*

loaf¹ /ləʊf/ *n* **loaves** /ləʊvz/ **1** [C] bread shaped and baked in one piece, usu. fairly large: *a loaf of bread* —compare ROLL¹ (2) **2** [C] a CONE-shaped piece of sugar **3** [C] *sl* the head and mind (esp. in the phr. **use your loaf**) **4** [C;U] (*usu. in comb.*) any food prepared in a solid piece: *meat loaf*

loaf² *v* [IØ (*about*)] *infml* to waste time, esp. by not working when one should —**~er** *n*

loaf·sug·ar /ˈləʊfˌʃʊgəʳ/ *n* [U] sugar in lumps, not grains

loam /ləʊm/ *n* [C;U] good soil made of sand, clay, and decayed plant material —**~y** *adj* [Wa1]

loan¹ /ləʊn/ *n* **1** something which is lent: *The book is a loan, not a gift* **2** an amount of money lent: *a £1,000 loan* **3** the act of lending: *the loan of a book* **4** **on loan** being borrowed, as a book is from a library

loan² *v* [D1 (*to*)] *esp. AmE* to give (someone) the use of; lend
USAGE It is perfectly good *AmE* to use **loan** in the meaning of **lend**: *He* **loaned** *me $10.* The word is often used in *BrE*, esp. in the meaning "to lend formally for a long period": *He* **loaned** *his collection of pictures to the public* GALLERY but many people do not like it to be used simply in the meaning of **lend** in *BrE*.

loan col·lec·tion /ˈ· ·ˌ··/ *n* a number of pictures, precious objects, artistic works given by the owner for the public to see

lo and be·hold /ˌ· · ·ˈ·/ *interj infml* (an expression of surprise at something unexpected): *She had looked everywhere for her key when lo and behold there it was in her bag!*

loan·word /ˈləʊnwɜːd‖-ɜrd/ *n* a word originally from a foreign language, now used as a member of the language

loath, loth /ləʊθ/ *adj* **1** [F3] unwilling: *loath to lend money* **2** **nothing loath** quite willing

loathe /ləʊð/ *v* [T1,4] to feel hatred or great dislike for

loath·ing /ˈləʊðɪŋ/ *n* [U;C] hatred; a feeling of DISGUST¹

loath·some /ˈləʊðsəm/ *adj* which causes great dislike; very unpleasant: *the loathsome smell of burning flesh* —**~ly** *adv* —**~ness** *n* [U]

loaves /ləʊvz/ *pl. of* LOAF¹

lob¹ /lɒb‖lɑb/ *v* **-bb-** **1** [T1] to send (a ball) in a LOB² **2** [L9] (of a ball) to move in a high gentle curve

lob² *n* **1** (in cricket) a ball thrown by the hand moving forward towards the shoulder (UNDERARM¹) **2** (in tennis) a ball hit high into the air

lob·by¹ /ˈlɒbi‖ˈlɑbi/ *n* **1** [C] a hall or passage, not a room, which leads from the entrance to the rooms inside a building: *the hotel lobby* **2** [C] (in the HOUSE OF COMMONS) **a** a hall where members of parliament and the public meet **b** one of 2 passages where members go to vote for or against something **3** [GC] a group of people who try to persuade a member of parliament, SENATOR, etc., to support certain actions: *The minister was met by a lobby of industrialists* **4** [GC] a group of people who unite for or against an action, so that those in power will change their minds: *The clean air lobby are against the plans for the new factory*

lobby² *v* **1** [T1;L9] to meet (a member of parliament) in order to persuade him/her to support one's actions and needs, esp. by suggesting a new law **2** [L9] to be active in making public actions, plans, etc., which should be changed, so as to bring about this change

lobe /ləʊb/ *n* **1** also **earlobe**— the round fleshy piece at the bottom of the ear —see picture at EAR¹ **2** *tech* any rounded division of an organ, esp. the brain and lungs —see picture at RESPIRATORY

lobed /ləʊbd/ *adj* [Wa5] having LOBE*s*

lo·bot·o·my /ləʊˈbɒtəmi, lə-‖-ˈbɑ-/ *n* [C;U] *AmE* LEUCOTOMY

lob·ster /ˈlɒbstəʳ‖ˈlɑb-/ *n* **1** [C] a type of large 8-legged sea animal with a shell, the flesh of which may be eaten after boiling, when it turns bright red —see picture at CRUSTACEAN **2** [U] the flesh of this as food

lob·ster·pot /ˈlɒbstəpɒt‖ˈlɑbstərpɑt/ *n* a trap shaped like a basket, in which LOBSTER*s* are caught

lo·cal¹ /ˈləʊkəl/ *adj* [Wa5] **1** of or in a certain place, esp. the place one lives in: *the/our local doctor|local news* **2** *tech* concerning a particular part, esp. of the body: *a local infection*

local² *n infml* **1** [*often pl.*] a person who lives in the place he is in: *I asked one of the locals which way to go* **2** a PUB (=inn) near where one lives, esp. which one often drinks at

local col·our /ˌ·· ˈ··/ *n* [U] details in a story or picture which are true to the time or place being represented, making it seem real

lo·cale /ləʊˈkɑːl/ *n lit or fml* a place where something particular happens or happened

lo·cal·is·m /ˈləʊkəlɪzəm/ *n* **1** [U] closeness to the interests and activities of the area one lives in, esp. with inability to accept different ways of thinking and behaving **2** [C] a way of speaking typical of a local area, not of the country as a whole

lo·cal·i·ty /ləʊˈkælɪ̆ti/ *n* a place or area, esp. in which something happens or has happened

lo·cal·ize, -ise /ˈləʊkəlaɪz/ *v* [T1] **1** to set in, or as if in, a particular place, time, etc. **2** to keep within a small area: *to localize the pain* —**-ization** /ˌləʊkəlaɪˈzeɪʃən‖-kələ-/ *n* [U]

lo·cal·ly /ˈləʊkəli/ *adv* [Wa5] **1** in a local area **2** near by: *We have no shops locally*

local op·tion /ˌ·· ˈ··/ *n* [U] the right which a part of a country may have to decide whether alcohol should be sold in that area

local time /ˈ·· ·/ *n* [U] (according to) the time system in that part of the world: *10 o'clock local time*

lo·cate /ləʊˈkeɪt‖ˈləʊkeɪt/ *v* **1** [T1] to find or learn the position of **2** [X9] to fix or set in a certain place: *to locate one's home in the country* **3** [L9] *AmE* to settle (down) in a place

lo·cat·ed /ləʊˈkeɪtɪ̆d‖ˈləʊkeɪ-/ *adj* [Wa5;F9] positioned: *The house is located next to the river*

lo·ca·tion /ləʊˈkeɪʃən/ *n* **1** [C] a place or position: *a suitable location for a camp* **2** [C] a place away

from a film STUDIO, where one or more scenes are made for a cinema picture **3** [U] *rare* the act of locating or state of being LOCATEd **4 on location** in a town, country, etc., to make (parts of) a film
loch /lɒx, lɒk‖lɑk, lɑx/ *n ScotE* **1** a lake **2** a part of the sea enclosed by land, except at the mouth
lo·ci /ˈləʊsaɪ/ *pl. of* LOCUS
lock[1] /lɒk‖lɑk/ *n* a small piece of hair: *a curly lock*
lock[2] *n* **1** [C] an apparatus for closing and fastening something by means of a key —see picture at DOOR **2** [C] the part of a gun which fires it **3** [C] a stretch of water closed off by gates, esp. on a CANAL, so that the level can be raised or lowered to move boats up or down a slope **4** [C] a hold which some fighters may use, esp. wrestlers (WRESTLE), to prevent the opponent from moving **5** [C] something which stops a wheel moving **6** [U] (in a machine) the state of being stopped or blocked: *in the lock position* **7** [C;U] the degree to which a STEERING WHEEL can be turned **8 lock, stock, and barrel** completely **9 under lock and key** **a** safely hidden and fastened in **b** imprisoned
lock[3] *v* **1** [T1;I∅] to fasten with a lock: *Lock the door.|The door won't lock* **2** [X9] to put in a place and lock the entrance: *to lock one's jewels in the cupboard* **3** [I∅] to become fixed or blocked: *I can't control the car; the wheels have locked* —see also LOCK AWAY, LOCK IN, LOCK ONTO, LOCK OUT, LOCK UP —**~able** *adj* [Wa5]
lock a·way *v adv* [T1] **1** to keep (something) safe or secret, (as) by putting in a locked place **2** LOCK UP (4)
lock·er /ˈlɒkəʳ‖ˈlɑ-/ *n* **1** a small cupboard for keeping things in, esp. at a school where there is one for each pupil or in a sports building where clothes may be left after changing **2 Davy Jones's locker** *humor* the bottom of the sea, meaning death by drowning
locker room /ˈ·· ·/ *n* a place where lots of LOCKERs are kept, esp. in a sports building for leaving clothes in
lock·et /ˈlɒkɨt‖ˈlɑ-/ *n* a small ornament for the neck, a metal case usu. on a chain in which small pictures or pieces of hair can be kept
lock gate /ˈ· ·/ *n* one of the gates which close a LOCK[2] (3) on a river or CANAL
lock in *v adv* [T1] to put (esp. a person or animal) inside a place and lock the doors
lock·jaw /ˈlɒkdʒɔː‖ˈlɑk-/ *n* [U] TETANUS
lock keep·er /ˈ· ˌ··/ *n* a person whose job is to open and close the LOCK GATEs on a river or CANAL
lock·nut /ˈlɒknʌt‖ˈlɑk-/ *n* a NUT[1] (2) which keeps another one firm
lock on·to *v prep* [T1] (of a modern moving weapon) to find and follow (the object to be attacked)
lock·out /ˈlɒk-aʊt‖ˈlɑk-/ *n* the employers' action of not allowing men to go back to work, esp. in a factory, until they accept an agreement
lock out *v adv* [T1] **1** to prevent (workmen) from entering a place of work until a disagreement is settled as the employers want it **2** [(*of*)] to keep out of a place by locking the entrance
locks /lɒks‖lɑks/ *n* [P] *poet* the hair of the head
lock·smith /ˈlɒkˌsmɪθ‖ˈlɑk-/ *n* a person who makes and repairs locks
lock·stitch /ˈlɒkˌstɪtʃ‖ˈlɑk-/ *n* the usual type stitch of a sewing machine in which a thread from above the material and one from below fasten together at small distances apart
lock·up /ˈlɒk-ʌp‖ˈlɑk-/ *n* **1** a small prison or prison-like room where a wrongdoer may be kept for a short time, as in a village or small town **2** *infml* a prison
lock up *v adv* **1** [T1;I∅] to make (a building) safe by locking the doors, esp. for the night **2** [T1] to hide in a place of safety and lock the entrance: *to lock up one's possessions|Lock up your daughters when the soldiers are in town* **3** [T1] to put (money) where it cannot easily be moved: *All his money is locked up in foreign companies* **4** [T1] **a** to put in prison **b** to put in a special hospital, because mad
lo·co /ˈləʊkəʊ/ *adj sl, esp. AmE* mad
lo·co·mo·tion /ˌləʊkəˈməʊʃən/ *n* [U] *tech* movement; ability to move
lo·co·mo·tive[1] /ˌləʊkəˈməʊtɪv/ *adj* [Wa5] *tech* concerning or causing movement: *locomotive powers*
locomotive[2] *n fml* a railway engine
lo·cum /ˈləʊkəm/ also (*fml*) **locum ten·ens** /ˌləʊkəm ˈtenenz/— *n* a doctor or priest doing the work of another who is away
lo·cus /ˈləʊkəs/ *n* **-ci** /ˈləʊsaɪ/ *tech* a position or point
locus clas·si·cus /ˌləʊkəs ˈklæsɪkəs/ *n* **-ci classici** /ˌləʊsaɪ ˈklæsɨsaɪ/ *Lat, fml* a passage from a written work which has become the standard explanation of a word or subject
lo·cust /ˈləʊkəst/ *n* **1** a type of insect of Asia and Africa which flies from place to place in large groups, often destroying almost all crops —see picture at INSECT **2** **a** also **locust tree** /ˈ·· ·/— CAROB (1) **b** also **locust bean** /ˈ·· ·/— CAROB (2)
lo·cu·tion /ləʊˈkjuːʃən/ *n* **1** [C;(U)] *tech* a way of speaking **2** [C] *fml* a phrase, esp. one used locally or within a special group of people
lode /ləʊd/ *n tech* an amount of metal in its natural form (ORE)
lode·star, loadstar /ˈləʊdstɑːʳ/ *n* **1** *esp. lit* the POLE STAR, used as a guide by sailors **2** a guide or example to follow
lode·stone, loadstone /ˈləʊdstəʊn/ *n* [C;U] (a piece of) iron which acts as a MAGNET
lodge[1] /lɒdʒ‖lɑdʒ/ *v* **1** [L9] to stay, usu. for a short time and paying rent: *to lodge at a friend's house/ with friends* **2** [I∅] to live in lodgings **3** [T1] to give or find (someone) a home for a time, sometimes for payment: *to lodge students* **4** [L9] to settle firmly in a position: *A small chicken bone lodged in his throat, and had to be removed by a doctor* **5** [T1] to fix in place: *He lodged the wood in the hole* **6** [X9] to put into a safe place **7** [T1] to make (a statement) officially: *to lodge a complaint*
lodge[2] *n* **1** [C] a small house near the entrance to a (house and) park **2** [C] a small house for hunters, sportsmen, etc., to stay in while crossing wild country or mountains —compare CHALET (2) **3** [C] a room for a person who is responsible for seeing who enters a building (a PORTER[1]), as in a block of flats or a college **4** [C] (esp. in Cambridge) the house where the head of a university college lives **5** [GC] a local branch of FREEMASONs **6** [C] the building where they meet **7** [C] *tech* a BEAVER's home **8** [C] *AmE* WIGWAM
lodg·er /ˈlɒdʒəʳ‖ˈlɑ-/ *n* a person who pays rent to stay in somebody's house
lodg·ing /ˈlɒdʒɪŋ‖ˈlɑ-/ *n* [S;U] a place to stay: *a lodging for the night|to find lodging* —compare BOARD[1] (6)
lodging house /ˈ·· ·/ *n* a building where rooms may be rented for days or weeks
lodg·ings /ˈlɒdʒɪŋz‖ˈlɑ-/ *n* [P] **1** the room(s) one pays rent for in a private house: *My lodgings are only 2 rooms* **2** a house where rooms are rented out: *to stay in lodgings*
lodg·ment, lodgement /ˈlɒdʒmənt‖ˈlɑdʒ-/ *n* **1** [U] the act of lodging (LODGE[1] (7)) a statement **2** [C] **a** the growth of a mass of material which settles firmly in place, esp. blocking something **b** the

material itself **3** [C] *tech* strong position gained by fighting or effort

lo·ess /ˈləʊes, -ɪ̈s‖les, lɜrs, ˈləʊɪ̈s/ *n* [U] a type of soil like a yellowish powder, common in China and parts of Europe and N America

loft[1] /lɒft‖lɔft/ *n* **1** a room under the roof of a building; ATTIC —see picture at ROOF **2** a room over a STABLE, where HAY is kept **3** *tech* a GALLERY (3) in a church

loft[2] *v* [T1] (esp. in cricket and GOLF) to hit (a ball) high

loft·ed /ˈlɒftɪ̈d‖ˈlɔf-/ *adj* **1** (of a hit, esp. in cricket and GOLF) made high into the air **2** (of a GOLF CLUB (2)) having a shaped end that makes it possible to hit the ball high into the air

loft·y /ˈlɒfti‖ˈlɔfti/ *adj* [Wa1] **1 a** of unusually high quality of thinking, feeling, desires, etc.: *lofty aims* **b** as if of personal importance; showing belief of being better than other people: *a lofty smile* **2** *poet* high: *the lofty walls of the city* —**-ily** *adv* —**-iness** *n* [U]

log[1] /lɒg‖lɔg, lɑg/ *n* **1** a thick piece of wood from a tree **2** an official written record of a journey, as in a ship, plane, or car **3** an apparatus which measures the speed of a ship **4 sleep like a log** to sleep deeply without moving

log[2] *v* **-gg-** [T1] to record in a LOG (2)

-log *comb. form AmE* -LOGUE

lo·gan·ber·ry /ˈləʊgənbəri‖-beri/ *n* a type of red fruit grown from a plant which is half BLACKBERRY and half RASPBERRY

log·a·rith·m /ˈlɒgərɪðəm‖ˈlɔ-, ˈlɑ-/ also (*infml*) **log**— *n* a number which represents a value of another number, and which can be used for additions instead of multiplying the original number; number equal to the POWER[1] (12) of a fixed number (usu. 10) which would equal a stated number: *The logarithm of 100 is 2 because* $10^2 = 100$

log·a·rith·mic /ˌlɒgəˈrɪðmɪk‖ˌlɔ-, ˌlɑ-/ *adj* [Wa5] **1** of or concerning LOGARITHM*s* **2** increasing by MULTIPLICATION —**~ally** *adv* [Wa4]

log·book /ˈlɒgbʊk‖ˈlɔg-, ˈlɑg-/ *n* REGISTRATION BOOK

log cab·in /ˌ· ˈ··/ *n* a (small) house made of logs of wood

log·ger /ˈlɒgəʳ‖ˈlɔ-, ˈlɑ-/ *n* a person whose job is to cut down trees

log·ger·heads /ˈlɒgəhedz‖ˈlɔgər-, ˈlɑ-/ *n* **at loggerheads (with)** always disagreeing (with)

log·gi·a /ˈlɒdʒɪə‖ˈləʊdʒɪə, ˈlɔ-/ *n* **1** a part of a house with a side and roof and the other side open **2** GALLERY (4)

lo·gic /ˈlɒdʒɪk‖ˈlɑ-/ *n* [U] **1** the science of reasoning by formal methods **2** a way of reasoning **3** *infml* reasonable thinking: *There's no logic in spending money on useless things*

lo·gic·al /ˈlɒdʒɪkəl‖ˈlɑ-/ *adj* **1** [Wa5] according to the rules of LOGIC or reason **2** having or showing good reasoning; sensible

USAGE Both **logical** and **reasonable** can mean "in accordance with reason"; but **logical** is used when we speak of the rules and science of **logic**, and **reasonable** when we mean ordinary sensible clear thinking, not confused by feelings: *a* **logical** *argument*/CONCLUSION|*a* **reasonable** *man*|*no* **reasonable** *doubt*|*It's* **reasonable** *to suppose* . . .. A person may be said to have *a* **logical** *mind*, but we do not usually speak of **a* **logical** *person*.

lo·gic·al·ly /ˈlɒdʒɪkəli‖ˈlɑ-/ *adv* **1** in a LOGICAL way **2** [Wa5] according to what is reasonable or LOGICAL: *Logically, one should become wiser with experience, but some people never do!*

lo·gi·cian /ləˈdʒɪʃən‖ləʊ-/ *n* a person who studies and knows a lot about LOGIC

-lo·gist /lədʒɪ̈st/ *comb. form* a student of or specialist in the stated branch of science: BIOLOGIST

lo·gis·tic /ləˈdʒɪstɪk‖ləʊ-/ *adj* [Wa5] of LOGISTICS —**~ally** *adv* [Wa4]

lo·gis·tics /ləˈdʒɪstɪks‖ləʊ-/ *n* **1** [U] the study or skill of moving soldiers, supplying them with food, etc. **2** [(*the*) P (*of*)] the ways in which the details of a particular military operation are or may be handled

log·jam /ˈlɒgdʒæm‖ˈlɔg-, ˈlɑg-/ *n* **1** a tightly-mixed mass of floating logs on a river **2** *esp. AmE* a difficulty that prevents one from continuing; IMPASSE

log·roll·ing /ˈlɒgˌrəʊlɪŋ‖ˈlɔg-, ˈlɑg-/ *n* [U] *AmE* the practice of giving praise or help to someone's work in return for receiving the same

-logue, *AmE* also **-log** /lɒg‖lɔg, lɑg/ *comb. form* [→*n*] **1** talk; something spoken: DIALOGUE|TRAVELOGUE **2** *rare* -LOGIST*: an ideologue*

-lo·gy /lədʒi/ also **-ology**— *comb. form* [→*n*[U]] (forming the name of a branch of science, used) **a** generally: PHYSIOLOGY/GEOLOGY *is an interesting subject* **b** in relation to the stated field, part, area, or group: *the* PHYSIOLOGY *of the nervous system/of large muscles*|*The* GEOLOGY *of north Devon is interesting*

loin /lɔɪn/ *n* [C;U] (a piece of) meat from the lower part of an animal —see also SIRLOIN

loin·cloth /ˈlɔɪnklɒθ‖-klɔθ/ *n* a loose covering for the lower part of the body above the legs, usu. for men, worn in hot countries esp. by poor people

loins /lɔɪnz/ *n* [P] **1** the lower part of the body below the waist and above the legs on both sides **2** *bibl* the male line of DESCENT in a family **3 gird up one's loins** to prepare for action

loi·ter /ˈlɔɪtəʳ/ *v* [IØ] to move on or move about with frequent stops —**~er** *n*

loll /lɒl‖lɑl/ *v* **1** [L9, esp. ABOUT, AROUND] to be in a lazy loose position: *She was lolling in a chair, with nothing to do* **2** [T1;IØ: (OUT)] to (allow to) hang down loosely: *The dog's tongue lolled out*

lol·li·pop /ˈlɒlipɒp‖ˈlɑlipɑp/ *n* **1** a type of hard sweet made of boiled sugar, to be eaten from a stick on which it is set **2** anything like this, esp. frozen juice on a stick

lollipop man /ˈ··· ·/ *fem.* **lollipop wom·an** /ˈ··· ˌ··/— *n BrE* a person whose job is to stop traffic (so that school children can cross) by turning towards the cars a stick with a notice on top telling them to stop

lol·lop /ˈlɒləp‖ˈlɑ-/ *v* [L9] *infml* to move with long ungraceful steps: *He lolloped away into the distance*

lol·ly /ˈlɒli‖ˈlɑli/ *n BrE* **1** [U] *sl* money **2** [C] *infml* LOLLIPOP

lone /ləʊn/ *adj* [Wa5;A] without (other) people: *a lone rider* —see ALONE (USAGE)

lone·ly /ˈləʊnli/ *adj* [Wa1] **1** alone: *a lonely life in the country* **2** unhappy because of being alone or without friends **3** (of places) without people; unvisited —see ALONE (USAGE) —**-liness** *n* [U]

lonely hearts /ˌ·· ˈ·/ *adj* [Wa5;A] for people who wish to find a lover: *a lonely hearts club*

lon·er /ˈləʊnəʳ/ *n* a person who spends a lot of time alone, not in groups of people

lone·some /ˈləʊnsəm/ *adj infml* **1** feeling lonely: *She is lonesome without the children* **2** which makes one feel lonely: *a lonesome place* —see ALONE (USAGE)

lone wolf /ˌ· ˈ·/ *n* a person who spends much of his time alone, esp. from choice

long[1] /lɒŋ‖lɔŋ/ *adj* [Wa1] **1** [B] **a** measuring a good deal from one end to the other: *long hair*|*a long dress* **b** covering a great distance or time: *He's taking a long time to get here* —opposite **short** **2** [B; E] covering a certain distance or time: *How long is* *the speech?|It's a foot long.|an hour long* **3** [B] which seems to last more than is wished: *It was a long day waiting for the news* **4** [B] (of memory) able to remember things far back in time **5** [B] (of a vowel) longer lasting than a short vowel in the same position **6 be long about something/doing something** to take a long time to do something **7 by a long** (*BrE*) **chalk**/(*AmE*) **shot** *infml* **a** (*neg.*) at all; nearly: *"Is he ready yet?" "No, not by a long chalk"* **b** *rare* by far; much: *X is better than Y by a long chalk* —see also **in the long** RUN[2], **in the long** TERM[1], **take the long** VIEW[1]

long² *adv* **1** [Wa1] (for) a long time: *I can't wait much longer.|Will you be long?* (= will it take you a long time to come, to finish what you are doing, etc.?)|*He hasn't long been back* (= he has only just returned) **2** [Wa5;H] at a distant time: *long ago|not long after that* (= a short time after) **3 as/so long as** if; on condition that: *You can go out, as long as you promise to be back before 11 o'clock.|"So long as other . . . costs do not increase"* (SEU W.) **4 no longer** (*neg.*)/**any longer** (*nonassertive*) (not) any more; (formerly but not) now: *"Does he live here any longer?" "No, he no longer lives here|he doesn't live here any longer"* **5 so long** *infml* goodbye for now

long³ *n* **1 before long** after a short period of time; soon **2 for long** *nonassertive* for a long time: *Were you there for long?|I can't stay for long* **3 take long (to do something)** *usu. nonassertive* to need a long time for completion: *He always takes so long to eat his breakfast!* **4 the long and (the) short of it** the general state of affairs

long⁴ *v* [I3] to want very much: *longing to go* —see also LONG FOR

long·boat /ˈlɒŋbəʊt‖ˈlɔŋ-/ *n* the largest type of boat carried by a sailing vessel

long·bow /ˈlɒŋbəʊ‖ˈlɔŋ-/ *n* a large powerful BOW[3] made of a single long thin curved piece of wood, for use with arrows —compare CROSSBOW

long-dis·tance¹ /ˌ· ˈ··◂/ *adj* [Wa5;A] from one point to a distant point: *a long-distance runner|a long-distance telephone call*

long-distance² *adv* to or from a distant point: *to telephone long-distance*

long-distance call /ˌ· ·· ˈ·/ *n AmE* TRUNK CALL

long di·vi·sion /ˌ· ·ˈ··/ *n* [U] the method of dividing large numbers by others, in which each stage is written out

long doz·en /ˌ· ˈ··/ *n* 13

long-drawn-out /ˌ· · ˈ·◂/ *adj* lasting too long

long drink /ˈ· ·/ *n* a large drink of something which usu. contains a little alcohol in a large amount of liquid, such as beer or fruit juice —compare SHORT[3] (2)

lon·gev·i·ty /lɒnˈdʒevəti‖lɑn-, lɔn-/ *n* [U] great length of life

long face /ˌ· ˈ·/ *n* an unhappy expression

long for *v prep* [T1;V3] to want very much: *to long for freedom|longing for something to happen*

long·haired /ˌlɒŋˈheəd◂‖ˌlɔŋˈheərd◂/ *adj* [Wa5] **1** having long hair **2** *usu. derog* of or being a person (esp. a man) **a** who is concerned only with art, music, literature, and other things of the mind: *longhaired* INTELLECTUALs **b** who is young and leads a socially unacceptable life, takes drugs, supports the LEFT[2] (3) in politics, etc.: *These longhaired fellows are ruining our universities.|long-haired views*

long·hand /ˈlɒŋhænd‖ˈlɔŋ-/ *n* [U] full writing by hand, not in any shortened or machine-produced form —compare SHORTHAND

long haul /ˌ· ˈ·/ *n* [S] an activity which has taken a long time and some difficulty, esp. a journey or part of a life

long·head·ed /ˌlɒŋˈhedəd◂‖ˌlɔŋ-/ *adj* clever; wise

long·hop /ˈlɒŋhɒp‖ˈlɔŋhɑp/ *n* (in cricket) a ball that strikes the ground a long way in front of the hitter, so that it can easily be hit

long·ing¹ /ˈlɒŋɪŋ‖ˈlɔŋɪŋ/ *n* [U;C (*for*)] a feeling of wanting something; strong wish: *a longing for fame|secret longings*

longing² *adj* [Wa5;A] showing a strong wish —**~ly** *adv*

long·ish /ˈlɒŋɪʃ‖ˈlɔŋɪʃ/ *adj* quite long

lon·gi·tude /ˈlɒndʒətjuːd‖ˈlɑndʒətuːd/ *n* [U;C] the position on the earth east or west of a MERIDIAN, usu. measured, in degrees, from Greenwich —compare LATITUDE (1) and see picture at GLOBE

lon·gi·tu·di·nal /ˌlɒndʒəˈtjuːdənəl‖ˌlɑndʒəˈtuː-/ *adj* [Wa5] **1** of or concerning LONGITUDE **2** in length; going from end to end, not across —**~ly** *adv*

long johns /ˌ· ˈ·/ *n* [P] *infml* underclothes with long legs, esp. like long trousers, for men

long jump /ˈ· ·/ *n* [*the*+R;C] a sport in which people jump as far as possible in distance along the ground

long-lived /ˌlɒŋ ˈlɪvd◂‖ˌlɔŋ-/ *adj* [Wa2] living or lasting a long time: *a long-lived breed|a long-lived friendship*

long mea·sure /ˈ· ˌ··/ *n* [U] the system of measurements of length

long odds /ˌ· ˈ·/ *n* [P (*on, against*)] the probability in BETting in which one of 2 results is very likely or unlikely; a far from even chance: *There are long odds against his winning*

long-play·ing rec·ord /ˌ· ·· ˈ··/ also **album**, (*not fml*) **LP**— *n* a larger type of record, with recorded music, speech, etc., which turns fairly slowly and plays for a long time (perhaps ½ an hour each side) rather than a few minutes

long-range /ˌ· ˈ·◂/ *adj* [Wa2;A;(B)] concerning or covering a long distance or time: *long-range guided weapons*

long run /ˈ· ·/ *n* **in the long run** after time has passed by; EVENTUALLY: *It's difficult to save money now, but it's worth it in the long run*

long·ship /ˈlɒŋˌʃɪp‖ˈlɔŋ-/ *n* a type of long narrow open warship once used by the VIKINGs, with OARs and a small square sail

long·shore·man /ˈlɒŋʃɔːmən‖ˈlɔŋʃor-/ *n* **-men** /mən/ *esp. AmE* a man employed to unload goods from ships, as at DOCKs[3]

long shot /ˈ· ·/ *n* [S] an attempt which may be unlikely to succeed, but which one risks making

long·sight·ed /ˌlɒŋˈsaɪtəd◂‖ˌlɔŋ-/ also (*esp. AmE*) **farsighted**— *adj esp. BrE* able to see objects clearly or read things only when they are far from the eyes —opposite **shortsighted**

long·stand·ing /ˌlɒŋˈstændɪŋ◂‖ˌlɔŋ-/ *adj* [Wa5] which has existed in the same form for some time: *a longstanding complaint about the heating*

long·stop /ˈlɒŋstɒp‖ˈlɔŋstɑp/ *n* (in cricket) (esp. in former times) a player who fields near the edge of the playing area and stops balls which the WICKET KEEPER fails to catch —see picture at CRICKET[2]

long·suf·fer·ing /ˌlɒŋˈsʌfərɪŋ◂‖ˌlɔŋ-/ *adj* patient under continued difficulty, esp. trouble from another person

long suit /ˌ· ˈ·/ *n* [S9] one's best quality or the thing one does best

long-term /ˌ· ˈ·◂/ *adj* [Wa2] for or in the distant future: *a long-term plan|No one knows what the long-term effects of new drugs will be*

long ton /ˌ· ˈ·/ *n tech* (a measure of weight equal to) 2,240 pounds

lon·gueur /lɒŋˈgɜːʳ‖lɔŋ-/ *n* [*usu. pl. with sing. meaning*] *lit* a very dull part or period

long va·ca·tion /ˌ· ·ˈ··/ also (*infml*) **long vac** /ˌ·

ˈ·/— *n BrE* the period of 3 months in the summer when universities are closed

long wave /ˌ· ˈ·ˈ/ *n* [U] radio broadcasting or receiving on waves of 1,000 metres or more in length

long·ways /ˈlɒŋweɪz‖ˈlɔŋ-/ *adv* [Wa5] LENGTHWAYS

long·wear·ing /ˌlɒŋˈweərɪŋˈ‖ˌlɔŋ-/ *adj AmE* HARDWEARING

long·wind·ed /ˌlɒŋˈwɪndʒdˈ‖ˌlɔŋ-/ *adj* [Wa5] (of a person or a way of speaking) saying too much without stopping, esp. slowly and dully —**~ly** *adv* —**~ness** *n* [U]

long·wise /ˈlɒŋwaɪz‖ˈlɔŋ-/ *adv* [Wa5] LENGTHWAYS

loo /luː/ *n* **loos** *infml, esp. BrE* LAVATORY

loo·fah, loofa /ˈluːfə/ *n* the long thin dried framework of a plant, used in washing the body

look¹ /lʊk/ *v* **1** [IØ (*at*)] to give attention in seeing; use the eyes: *to look at the baby in her bed|We looked at him jumping.|You could see it if you'd only look* **2** [L9] to turn the eyes and see in a certain direction: *look round the corner/over the wall|to look under the covers at the baby* **3** [L (*to be*) 1, (*to be*) 7] to seem by expression or appearance: *to look well/ill/tired/happy|Judging by her letter, she looks to be the best person for the job* **4** [T1] to express with the eyes: *She said nothing but looked all interest* **5 Look alive/lively!** Act or work fast! **6 look down one's nose at** to (seem to) dislike (someone thought less socially important) —compare LOOK DOWN ON **7 look good a** to seem favourable or attractive **b** to give the right effect: *Make the idea look good, even if it isn't* **8 look someone in the eye/face** to look directly and boldly at someone who is near **9 look oneself** to have one's usual appearance of strength of mind or body **10 Look sharp!** Hurry up! **11 look small** to (be made to) appear unimportant or silly **12 look well** to give a favourable effect —see also LOOK ABOUT, LOOK AFTER, LOOK AHEAD, LOOK AROUND, LOOK AT, LOOK BACK, LOOK DOWN ON, LOOK FOR, LOOK FORWARD TO, LOOK IN, LOOK INTO, LOOK ON[1,2], LOOK ONTO, LOOK OUT, LOOK OUT ON, LOOK OVER, LOOK ROUND[1,2], LOOK THROUGH[1,2], LOOK TO, LOOK UP, LOOK UP AND DOWN, LOOK UP TO, **look** LIKE³ (7) —see SEE¹ (USAGE)

look² *n* **1** [C (*at*) *usu. sing.*] an act of looking: *Have a look at that* **2** [C] a (short) period of giving attention with the eyes; GLANCE² (1): *She gave me a strange look* **3** [C *usu. sing.*] an expression, esp. in the eyes: *I knew she didn't like it by the look on her face* **4** [(*the*) S] an appearance: *He has the look of a winner.|This year's fashion introduces a new look in skirts* **5 by the look(s) of it, him, etc.** probably; judging from the way it, he, etc., appears or seems: *By the looks of it we shan't have much rain this year* **6 I don't like the look of it/the looks of this** This (state of affairs, place, etc.) suggests something bad to me —see also LOOKS

look³ also **look here** /ˌ· ˈ·/— *interj* (an expression, often angry, used for drawing attention before making a statement): *Look, I don't mind you borrowing my car, but you ought to ask me first.|Now look here, you can't say things like that to me!*

look a·bout *v prep* [T1] to examine the place or state of affairs of (one): *Look about you and decide if you like your position*

look af·ter *v prep* [T1] to take care of (someone or something): *Who will look after the baby while they're out?|I can look after myself* (=be independent and not let other people take advantage of me).|*Are you being well looked after?*

look a·head *v adv* [IØ] to plan for the future

look-a·like /ˈ· ·ˌ·/ *n esp. AmE* something of the same appearance as something else; DOUBLE² (3)

look a·round also **look round,** (*rare*) **look about**— *v adv* [IØ (*for*)] to search

look at *v prep* **1** [T1;V4a, (*AmE*) 2] to watch: *looking at television|Look at him jumping!* —see SEE¹ (USAGE) **2** [X9] to regard; judge: *He looks at work in a different way now he's in charge* **3** [T1 *nonassertive*] to consider: *I wouldn't look at such a small offer* **4** [T1] to examine: *He is looking at a new idea for selling dictionaries.|You must have your bad tooth looked at* **5** [T1 *usu. imper.*] to notice or remember and learn from: *Look at Mrs Jones; drugs didn't help her, she's dead!* **6 not much to look at** unpleasant in appearance

look back *v adv* [IØ] **1** [(*to, on*)] to remember **2** to fail to advance (in the phr. **never look back**): *After he got the advantage at the beginning of the competition he never looked back* (= he won)

look down on *v adv prep* [T1] to have or show a low opinion of (esp. someone thought less socially important)

look·er /ˈlʊkəʳ/ also **good looker**— *n infml* a person, usu. a woman, of attractive appearance: *The little girl is growing up to be a real looker*

look for *v prep* [T1] **1** to try to find **2** *infml* to be likely to produce, by bad behaviour: *You're looking for a fight if you say things like that to me* **3** *esp. old use* to expect

look for·ward to *v adv prep* [T1,4] to expect to feel pleasure in (something about to happen) USAGE This is always followed by a noun or the *-ing* form of a verb. Never say **I* **look forward to** *see you.*

look-in /ˈ· ·/ *n* [S] *infml* **1 a** the chance to take part: *I never got a look-in, with everybody else talking at once* **b** the chance to succeed: *I don't get a look-in, because you know so much more than me about the game* **2 a** a quick look **b** a short visit

look in *v adv* [IØ] *infml* **1** [(*on*)] to pay a short visit: *to look in on the party* **2** [(*at*)] to watch television

look·ing glass /ˈ·· ·/ also (*infml*) **glass**— *n becoming rare* a mirror

look in·to *v prep* [T1] to examine the meaning or causes of

look on¹ *v adv* [IØ] **1** to watch while others take part —see also ONLOOKER **2** [(*with*)] *fml, now rare* to read music, a book, etc., with someone else

look on² also **look up·on**— *v prep* [X9 esp. *as, with*] to consider; regard: *to look on him as a friend|I look on him with dislike*

look on·to *v prep* [T1] to have a view of: *Our office looks onto the park*

look·out /ˈlʊk-aʊt/ *n* **1** [S] a future possibility: *It's not a good lookout for his family if he's going to work abroad* **2** [S] the act of keeping watch **3** [C] a place to watch from **4** [C] a person who keeps watch **5 one's own lookout** a state of affairs one must take care of for oneself, without others' help: *If you want to go into that lion's cage, it's your own lookout* **6 on the lookout for** searching for

look out *v adv* **1** [IØ *usu. imper.*] to take care: *Look out! You could fall off the edge here!* **2** [IØ (*for*)] to keep watching (for): *Look out for your aunt at the station* **3** [T1] to choose from one's possessions: *to look out a dress for a party*

look out on also **look out o·ver**— *v adv prep* [T1] to have a view of outside: *Our house looks out on the park*

look-o·ver /ˈ· ˌ··/ *n* [S] *infml* a (short) examination

look o·ver *v adv* [T1] to examine, esp. quickly —compare OVERLOOK

look round¹ *v adv* [IØ] **1** to look at everything that is interesting, without taking any other action, esp. before buying **2** [(*for*)] LOOK AROUND

look round² *v prep* [T1] to examine the parts of: *Do we have to pay to look round the gardens?*

looks /lʊks/ also **good looks**— *n* [P] an attractive appearance: *She kept her looks even in old age* —compare LOOKER
look through¹ *v adv* [T1] to examine, esp. for points to be noted
look through² *v prep* [T1] to look at without seeming to notice (a person), on purpose or because of deep thought
look to *v prep* **1** [T1] *fml* to be careful about (esp.) improving (something): *We must each look to our own work* **2** [T1;V3] to depend on the action of: *We look to you for help/to help us* **3 Look to it that** Make sure that **4 look to one's laurels** to guard against competition; make sure one does one's best
look up *v adv* **1** [IØ] to get better, esp. after being bad: *Trade should look up later in the year* **2** [T1] to find (information) in a book: *Look up the word in the dictionary* **3** [T1] to find and visit (someone) when in the same place
look up and down *v adv* [T1b] to examine (a person) in appearance, as if in dislike or interest
look up to *v adv prep* [T1] to respect (someone)
loom¹ /luːm/ *n* a frame or machine on which thread is woven into cloth
loom² *v* **1** [L9 esp. UP] to come into sight without a clear form, esp. in a way that appears very large and unfriendly, causing fear: *A figure loomed (up) out of the mist.*|(fig.) *The examinations are looming up* **2** [L7] to appear great and very worrying in the mind (esp. in the phr. **loom large**)
loon¹ /luːn/ *n now rare* a foolish or lazy person
loon² *n* any of various types of large bird that catch fish beneath the surface of the sea
loon·y /ˈluːni/ *n, adj* [Wa1] *sl* (a person who is) mad or foolish; LUNATIC
loony bin /ˈ·· ·/ *n sl, often humor* MENTAL HOSPITAL
loop¹ /luːp/ *n* **1** the shape made by a piece of string, wire, rope, etc., when curved back on itself to produce a closed or slightly open curve **2** something, such as a piece of string, wire, rope, etc., having this shape, esp. one used as a handle or fastening: *Carry the parcel by this loop of string* **3** a piece of metal or plastic put inside a woman to prevent her having more children; INTRAUTERINE DEVICE **4** also **loop line** /ˈ· ·/— a railway line that leaves the main track and then joins it again a little further on **5** a circle made by an aircraft while flying along, up, back, down, and then along again
loop² *v* **1** [T1;IØ] to make, make into, or form a LOOP¹ or LOOPs **2** [T1] to pass through a LOOP¹, esp. in order to fasten: *Loop that end of the rope through this and make a knot with it* **3** [T1] to fasten with a LOOP¹ of string, rope, etc. **4** [IØ;(T1)] (of an aircraft) to fly a LOOP¹ (5) (often in the phr. **loop the loop**)
loop·hole /ˈluːphəʊl/ *n* **1** a small or narrow opening in a wall, esp. one from which arrows may be shot in a castle **2** a way of escaping or avoiding something, esp. one provided by a rule or agreement written without enough care: *a loophole in the law*
loose¹ /luːs/ *adj* **1** [Wa5;F] not fastened, tied up, shut up, etc.; free from control: *The animals broke loose and left the field.*|*I have one hand loose but the other is tied* **2** [Wa5;B] not bound together, as with string or in a box: *I bought these sweets loose* **3** [Wa1;B] not firmly fixed; not tight; not strong: *This pole is coming loose and will soon fall over.*|*a loose button* **4** [Wa1;B] (of clothes) not fitting tightly, esp. because too big **5** [Wa1;B] made of parts that are not tight together: *a loose weave/soil* **6** [Wa1;B] not exact: *That word has many loose meanings.*|*He is a loose thinker* **7** [Wa1;B] having many sexual adventures: *a loose woman|loose living* **8** [Wa1;B] not well controlled: *She has a loose tongue and will tell everybody* **9** [Wa1;B] careless, awkward, or not exact: *Loose play lost them the match* **10** [Wa1;B] (of the bowels) allowing waste matter to flow naturally, or more than is natural **11** [Wa5;A] not given a fixed purpose: *loose money|loose change* **12 at a loose end** having nothing to do **13 cut loose a** to break away from a group or condition **b** to start to take violent action: *After losing the first game, Ashe really cut loose and won the match easily* —see also FAST² **and loose** —**~ly** *adv* —**~ness** *n* [U]
loose² *v* [T1] **1** to let loose; untie; make free **2 a** to cause (an arrow) to fly **b** to fire (a gun, weapon, etc.) **3** to free from control: *The wine loosed his tongue* —compare LOOSEN
loose³ *adv* [Wa1] in a loose manner; loosely
loose⁴ *n* **on the loose** free, esp. having freedom from the control of law and order or freedom to enjoy oneself in wild excitement
loose·box /ˈluːsbɒks‖-bɑks/ *n* a space inside a horse's STABLE where it need not be tied up
loose-leaf /ˌ· ˈ·◂/ *adj* [Wa5] (of a book) able to have pages put in and taken out
loos·en /ˈluːsən/ *v* **1** [T1;IØ] to make or become less firm, fixed, tight, etc. **2** [T1;IØ] to make or become less controlled or more easy and free in movement: *a medicine that loosens the bowels* **3** [T1] to set free; unfasten: *He loosened his coat (=undid the buttons/belt) but didn't take it off* —compare LOOSE²
loosen up *v adv* [T1;IØ] to (cause to) become ready for action by exercising the muscles: *The runners are just loosening up before the race*
loot¹ /luːt/ *n* [U] goods, esp. valuable objects, taken away unlawfully, as by soldiers after defeating an enemy or by thieves
loot² *v* [T1;IØ] to take LOOT¹ (from): *Anyone found looting the bombed houses and shops will be shot* —**~er** *n*
lop¹ /lɒp‖lɑp/ *v* **-pp- 1** [T1] to cut branches off from (a tree) **2** [T1 (AWAY, OFF, *off*)] to cut (branches) off from a tree **3** [T1 (AWAY, OFF, *off*)] to remove or stop because unnecessary, unprofitable, etc.: *Some train services have been lopped off this line*
lop² *v* **-pp-** [IØ (DOWN)] (esp. of an animal's ears) to hang downwards loosely
lope¹ /ləʊp/ *n* [S] an easy fairly fast movement with long springing steps
lope² *v* [L9] (esp. of animals) to move easily and fairly fast with springing steps: *The deer loped down the hill*
lop-eared /ˌ· ˈ·◂/ *adj* [Wa5] having ears that hang down loosely: *a lop-eared rabbit*
lop·pings /ˈlɒpɪŋz‖ˈlɑ-/ *n* [P] branches cut from a tree
lop-sid·ed /ˌ· ˈ··◂/ *adj* having one side heavier or lower than the other; not balanced
loq·ua·cious /ləʊˈkweɪʃəs/ *adj fml* liking to talk a great deal —**~ly** *adv* —**-city** /-ˈkwæsɨti/ *n* [U]
loq·uat /ˈləʊkwɒt‖-kwɑt/ *n* **1** a type of attractive tree, grown mostly in China and Japan, that bears small yellowish fruit **2** the fruit of this tree —see picture at FRUIT¹
lord¹ /lɔːd‖lɔrd/ *n* **1** [C; *my*+N] a man who rules people; ruler; master **2** [C; *my*+N] a nobleman of high rank **3** [C] a powerful person in a particular industry **4 (as) drunk as a lord** very drunk **5 live like a lord** to live splendidly, having the best of everything **6 one's lord and master** *old use or humor* one's husband
lord² *v* **lord it (over someone)** to behave like a lord (to someone), esp. in having the manner of a powerful person or in giving orders

Lord[1] *n* **1** [*the*+R] God **2** [C;A] (part of the title of certain official people): *the Lord* MAYOR *of London* **3 Lord (only) knows** no one knows: *Lord knows where I left my bag*
Lord[2] *interj* a term of surprise, wonder, fear, etc. (in such phrs. as **Oh Lord!, Good Lord!**)
lord·ly /ˈlɔːdli‖-ɔr-/ *adj* [Wa1] **1** suitable for a lord; grand **2** behaving like a lord, esp. in giving orders —**-liness** *n* [U]
Lords /lɔːdz‖lɔrdz/ *n* **1** [*the*+P] the members of the HOUSE OF LORDS as a group **2** [*the*+R] HOUSE OF LORDS
lord·ship /ˈlɔːdʃɪp‖-ɔr-/ *n* **1** [U (*over*)] the power or rule of a lord **2** [C9;N9] (*often cap.*) (the title used when speaking to or of) a judge or certain noblemen (in the phrs. **his lordship, your lordship(s), their lordships**): *I've written to his Lordship*
Lord's Prayer /ˌ· ˈ·/ also **Our Father**— [*the*+R] the commonest prayer in the Christian church, beginning with the words "Our Father, which ART[1] in heaven, . . ."
lore /lɔːʳ‖lor/ *n* [U] knowledge or wisdom, esp. of an unscientific kind, about a certain subject or possessed by a certain group of people: *bird lore|a countryman's weather lore*
lor·gnette /lɔːˈnjet‖-ɔr-/ *n* a pair of glasses held in front of the eyes by a long handle
lorn /lɔːn‖lɔrn/ *adj* [Wa5] *poet* sad and lonely
lor·ry /ˈlɒri‖ˈlɔri, ˈlɑri/ (*AmE* **truck**)— *n BrE* a large motor vehicle for carrying big goods —see picture at INTERCHANGE[2]
lose /luːz/ *v* **lost** /lɒst‖lɔst/ **1** [T1] to come to be without, as through carelessness; fail to find: *I have lost my book.|He lost his way in the mist* **2** [T1; IØ: (*by, to*)] to fail to win, gain, or obtain: *He lost the argument.|England lost to Australia* (= were beaten by them) **3** [D1] to cause the loss of: *His foolish behaviour lost him the job* **4** [T1;IØ: (*by, on*); D1] to (cause to) come to be without (money): *We lost £200 on that job.|We lost on that job.|That job lost us £200* **5** [T1] to have less of: *The aircraft began to lose height* **6** [T1] to have taken away or cease to possess, as through death, destruction, ruin, or time: *She lost her parents while she was very young.|He lost an eye in the accident.|They lost all their money when the business failed* **7** [T1] to free oneself from: *It took her many years to lose her fear of water* **8** [T1] to fail to hear, see, or understand: *His voice was soft and I lost some of his words* **9** [T1] to fail to use; waste: *The doctor lost no time in getting the sick man to hospital* **10** [T1] to fail to keep: *I've lost interest in that subject* **11** [T1] to be too late for; miss: *We just lost the train* **12** [T1 (*in*)] to give all (one's) attention to something so as not to notice anything else: *He lost himself in the book* **13** [T1;IØ] (of a watch or clock) to work too slowly by (an amount of time): *This watch loses (50 minutes a day)* **14** [T1] to cause (oneself) to miss the way **15 lose one's head** to lose self-control, as in a sudden anger or terror **16 lose one's temper** to become very angry —see also LOST
lose out *v adv* [IØ (*on*)] **1** to make a loss (often large) (from something): *The firm lost out on the deal* **2** to be defeated, esp. in an unlucky way: *Dicky came second again; he always loses out*
los·er /ˈluːzəʳ/ *n* a person who has been defeated: *A good loser is somebody who doesn't become annoyed or angry when defeated.|I'm a born loser* (=I'm always defeated)
loss /lɒs‖lɔs/ *n* **1** [U] the act or fact of losing possession: *Did you report the loss of your jewellery to the police?* **2** [U] the harm, pain, damage, etc., caused by losing something: *He was unable to hide his great loss from his family* **3** [C *usu. sing.*] a failure to keep or use: *The vehicle developed a loss of power* **4** [C] a failure to win or obtain **5** [C] a person, thing, or amount that is destroyed or taken away: *He's given up work; it's a great loss to our firm* **6** [C] a failure to make a profit: *We made a loss on those shoes* **7** [C] the amount by which the cost of an article is greater than the selling price: *The shop made a loss of £2 on those shoes* **8 at a loss a** at a price lower than the original cost **b** unable or uncertain what to do, think, or say; confused **9 be a dead loss** *infml* to have no worth or use
loss lead·er /ˈ· ˌ··/ *n* an article sold at a low price in order to attract people into a shop
lost /lɒst‖lɔst/ *adj* [Wa5] **1** [B] no longer possessed: *It's no use thinking about one's lost youth* **2** [B] that cannot be found: *a lost dog|lost keys* **3** [F] unable to find the way: *lost in the mists* **4** [B] not used, obtained, or won: *a lost chance* **5** [F] destroyed, ruined, killed, drowned, etc.: *The boat and all its men were lost in the storm* **6** [B] *now rare* not behaving in a way acceptable to society or a religion **7** [F+*to*] **a** no longer belonging to: *My son was lost to me when he married* **b** no longer possible for (somebody) **c** not noticing: *He was reading his book, completely lost to the world* **8** [F+(*up*)*on*] having no influence on: *Good advice is lost on him*
lost cause /ˌ· ˈ·/ *n* an effort or action which has been or will now certainly be defeated
lost prop·er·ty /ˌ· ˈ···/ *n* [U] articles found in public places which are collected and kept in a special place (**lost property office**) to which people who have lost anything can go in the hope of getting it back
lot[1] /lɒt‖lɑt/ *n not fml* **1** [C (*of*) *often pl. with sing. meaning*] a great quantity, number, or amount: *He has (quite) a lot of friends.|He has lots (and lots) of friends.|I want lots (of food).|She gave the boys lots to eat* —compare PLENTY[2] **2** [*the*+GU (*of*)] the whole quantity, number, or amount: *Give me the lot.|The whole lot of you|All the lot of you are mad!* **3** [C9] a group of people or things of the same type; amount of a substance or material: *Another lot of students are arriving soon.|This wine's no good but I hope the next lot will be better* **4 a lot/lots** *not fml* (esp. in comparisons) much; a great deal: *This is a lot better.|He's lots older than I am* **5 a (fat) lot I/you/etc. care!** *infml* I/you/etc. don't care at all **6 What a lot!** What a great number or amount!
lot[2] *n* **1** [C] an article or a number of articles sold together, as in an AUCTION sale: *Lot 49, a fine old silver cigarette case* **2** [C] *esp. AmE* an area of land, esp. one for a particular purpose such as for building or parking cars on **3** [C] a building in which films are made and the ground surrounding it **4** [C] *infml* person; character (esp. in the phr. **a bad lot**) **5** [C] one of several objects used for coming to a decision by chance **6** [U] the use of such objects to make a choice or decision: *decide by lot* **7** [(*the*) S] the decision or choice made in this way: *The lot fell to/on me* **8** [C] share: *They divided the money and each went away with his lot* **9** [S9] one's way of life; fortune; fate **10 draw/cast lots** make a choice or decision by the use of several objects of different sizes or with different marks
loth /ləʊθ/ *adj* [F3] LOATH
lo·tion /ˈləʊʃən/ *n* [C;U] a liquid mixture, used on the skin or hair to make it clean and healthy
lot·te·ry /ˈlɒtəri‖ˈlɑ-/ *n* **1** [C] an arrangement in which many numbered tickets are sold to people and then a few are picked by chance, as out of a hat, and prizes given to those who bought them **2** [S] something whose result or worth is uncertain or risky: *Life is a lottery*
lot·to /ˈlɒtəʊ‖ˈlɑ-/ *n* [U] *now rare* BINGO (1)
lo·tus /ˈləʊtəs/ *n* **1** a white or pink flower found,

esp. in Asia, on the surface of lakes that are not deep **2** the shape of this flower used formally in ornamental patterns, esp. in ancient Egyptian art **3** (in ancient Greek stories) a fruit which, when eaten, caused the eater to feel contented, dreamy, and unwilling to be active

lotus-eat·er /ˈ·· ˌ··/ *n* a person who leads a contented dreamy life and is not concerned with the business of the world

loud[1] /laʊd/ *adj* [Wa1] **1** being or producing great strength of sound; not quiet; noisy: *loud music|a loud radio* **2** attracting attention by being unpleasantly noisy or colourful: *loud behaviour|a loud pattern* —**~ly** *adv* —**~ness** *n* [U]

loud[2] *adv* [Wa1] loudly; in a loud way: *Try to sing louder*

loud·hail·er /ˌlaʊdˈheɪləʳ/ *n* MEGAPHONE

loud·mouth /ˈlaʊdmaʊθ/ *n* a person who talks too much and in an offensive manner —**~ed** *adj*

loud·speak·er /ˌlaʊdˈspiːkəʳ, ˈlaʊdˌspiːkəʳ/ also **speaker**— *n* that part of a radio or record player that turns electrical current into sound —see picture at SOUND[3]

lough /lɒk, lɒx‖lɑk, lɑx/ *n* (in Ireland) a lake or a part of the sea almost surrounded by land

lounge[1] /laʊndʒ/ *v* **1** [IØ] to stand or sit in a leaning lazy manner **2** [IØ (ABOUT, AROUND); X9 esp. AWAY] to pass (time) in a lazy manner, doing nothing

lounge[2] *n* **1** [S] an act or period of lounging (LOUNGE[1]) **2** [C] a comfortable room for sitting in, as in a house, hotel, or inn

lounge bar /ˈ· ·/ *n BrE* SALOON BAR

loung·er /ˈlaʊndʒəʳ/ *n* a lazy person who does no work

lounge suit /ˈ· ·/ *n* a man's informal suit, as worn during the day

lour, *AmE* usu. **lower** /ˈlaʊəʳ/ *v* [IØ] **1** [(*at,* (*up*)*on*)] to look in a dissatisfied bad-tempered manner; FROWN[1] (1) **2** [Wv4] (of the sky or weather) to be dark and threatening

louse /laʊs/ *n* **lice** /laɪs/ **1** any of several types of small insect that live on the skin and in the hair of people and animals, esp. when they are dirty **2** *sl* a worthless person deserving no respect

louse up *v adv* [T1] *AmE infml* to deal unsuccessfully with; MESS UP

lou·sy /ˈlaʊzi/ *adj* [Wa1] **1** [F;(B)] covered with LICE **2** [B] *infml* very bad, unpleasant, useless, etc. **3** [F+*with*] *infml* **a** filled with **b** having plenty of (esp. money)

lout /laʊt/ *n* a rough awkward man or boy with bad manners —**~ish** *adj*

lou·vre, *AmE* **-ver** /ˈluːvəʳ/ *n esp. BrE* an arrangement of narrow sloping bands of wood, plastic, metal, etc., fixed in a frame that swings across a window to allow some light in but keep rain or strong sun out

lov·a·ble, loveable /ˈlʌvəbəl/ *adj* **1** deserving, causing, or worthy of love **2** pleasant; attractive

love[1] /lʌv/ *n* **1** [U] a strong feeling of fondness for another person, esp. between members of a family or between people of the opposite sex: *a mother's love for her child|The young pair are in love* (*with each other*) **2** [U (*of, for*)] warm interest and enjoyment and attraction (to): *love of music|learning* **3** [C (*of*)] the object of such interest and attraction: *Music was one of the great loves of his life* **4** [C9; *my*+N] a person who is loved **5** [N] also (*nonstandard or humor*) **luv**— *BrE* (a friendly word of address): HELLO *love!* **6** [C] *infml* a person or thing that one loves or likes very much: *Look at that little dog! Isn't he a love!* **7** [U] (in tennis) the state of having no points: *Connors leads 15-love* **8 give/send somebody one's love** to send friendly greetings to **9 no love lost between** no friendship between **10 not for love nor money** not by any means; impossible to get or do —see also MAKE[1] **love** (**to**)

love[2] *v* [Wv6] **1** [T1;IØ] to feel love, desire, or strong friendship (for) **2** [T1,3,4;V3] to have a strong liking for; take pleasure in: *He loves playing the piano.|I love to hear you sing.|I love beer.|I'd love you to come and see us.|She loves Beethoven* **3** [T1] to have sex with —see LIKE[1] (USAGE)

love af·fair /ˈ· ·ˌ·/ *n* **1** an experience of love between 2 people, esp. between a man and a woman **2** a sexual relationship, esp. between a man and a woman

love·bird /ˈlʌvbɜːd‖-ɜrd/ *n* **1** any of various types of a particular bird (PARROT) that stand in pairs **2** [*usu. pl.*] *infml* a person who is showing love for a person of the opposite sex

love·child /ˈlʌvtʃaɪld/ *n* **-children** /ˌtʃɪldrən/ *old use or euph* BASTARD[1] (1)

love·less /ˈlʌvləs/ *adj* **1** not giving or able to give love; cold **2** not receiving love **3** without love: *a loveless marriage*

love·lorn /ˈlʌvlɔːn‖-ɔrn/ *adj* [B; *the*+P] sad because one's love is not returned

love·ly[1] /ˈlʌvli/ *adj* [Wa1] **1** beautiful, attractive, etc., esp. to both the heart and the eye **2** *infml* very pleasant: *a lovely meal* —**-liness** *n* [U]

USAGE A person or thing that one loves is **beloved**: *My* **beloved** *husband!|Come here,* **beloved***!* The one that one likes or loves best is one's **favourite**: *my* **favourite** *dance|her* **favourite** *child|John's a great* **favourite** *with his grandmother.* **Lovely** is a strong word of praise for anything beautiful or nice: *a* **lovely** *woman/dinner/day.* Things are **favourable** when they are helpful, and people if they approve or agree: *a very* **favourable** *answer to my letter|If the weather's* **favourable** *we'll have dinner in the garden.*

lovely[2] *n* [C; *my*+N] *infml* a beautiful woman: *Come here, my lovely!*

love·mak·ing /ˈlʌvˌmeɪkɪŋ/ *n* [U] **1** words or actions expressing love or sexual desire **2** the act of having sex

lov·er /ˈlʌvəʳ/ *n* **1** [C] a man in love with or having a sexual relationship with a woman outside of marriage: *He is her lover; she is his* MISTRESS.*|She has had many lovers* **2** [C9] a person who is very keen on something: *a lover of art|art lovers*

lov·ers /ˈlʌvəz‖-ərz/ *n* [P] 2 people in love with and/or having a sexual relationship with each other: *Yes, I admit it; we are lovers*

love·sick /ˈlʌvˌsɪk/ *adj* **1** sad or sick because of unreturned love **2** expressing such sadness: *a lovesick poem*

lov·ey /ˈlʌvi/ *n* [N] *BrE sl* (a term of address for a person): *Come here, lovey!*

lov·ing /ˈlʌvɪŋ/ *adj* showing or expressing love; fond: *a loving look* —**~ly** *adv*

loving cup /ˈ·· ·/ *n* a large drinking vessel, usu. with more than 2 handles, that is sometimes passed round at a ceremonial feast, to be drunk out of by everybody

loving-kind·ness /ˌ·· ˈ··/ *n* [U] *lit* gentle and tender care, friendship, or love

low[1] /ləʊ/ *v* [IØ] *esp. lit* MOO[1]

low[2] *adj* [Wa1] **1** [B] not measuring much from the base to the top; not high: *a low wall* **2** [B] being not far above the ground, floor, base, or bottom: *a low shelf|That comes low on the list of jobs to be done* **3** [B] being or lying below the general level of height: *a low bridge|low ground|The river is getting low and will soon dry up* **4** [B] being near or at the bottom of a supply or measure: *The coal's* *getting low; we must order some more.|a low temperature* **5** [F] on the ground, as after a blow, or dead: *I laid him low with my gun* **6** [F] lacking in strength; weak: *He is low with an illness* **7** [F] also **low-spirited**— lacking spirit; unhappy; DEPRESSED (1) **8** [B] small in size, degree, amount, worth, etc.: *a low figure* **9** [A] having only a small amount of a particular substance, quality, etc.: *low-fat milk* **10** [A] regarding something as of little worth; unfavourable: *I have a low opinion of that book* **11** [B] near the bottom in position or rank: *a man of low birth* **12** [B] not worthy, respectable, good, etc.: *low behaviour|low language* **13** [B] cheap: *a low price* **14** [B] for a slow or slowest speed: *Use a low* GEAR *when driving slowly* **15** [F] hidden; unnoticed (esp. in the phr. **lie low**) **16** [B] not greatly developed; simple: *low plant life* **17** [B] (of a musical note) deep **18** [B] not loud; soft **19** **bring low** to make low in health, position, wealth, etc. —opposite **high** —**~ness** *n* [U]

low³ *adv* [Wa1] **1** in or to a low position, point, degree, manner, etc.: *shoot low|bent low over a book* **2** near the ground, floor, base, etc.; not high **3** (in music) in or with deep notes **4** quietly; softly **5** **run low** to become less than enough —compare **run** SHORT²

low⁴ *n* **1** [C] a point, price, degree, etc., that is low: *Profits have reached a new low this month* **2** [C] an area of low force (PRESSURE) in the air **3** [U] the part of the machine (GEAR) used to make a vehicle move slowly

low·born /ˌləʊˈbɔːn◂‖-ɔrn◂/ *adj lit* born to parents of low social rank

low·bred /ˌləʊˈbred◂/ *adj* not respectable; rude

low·brow /ˈləʊbraʊ/ *n* [C;A] *usu. derog* a person who likes and is satisfied with simple music, painting, poetry, etc. —compare HIGHBROW, MIDDLEBROW

low com·e·dy /ˌ· ˈ···/ *n* [U;C] a type of funny play similar to FARCE

low·down /ˈləʊdaʊn/ *n* [*the*+R (*on*)] *sl* the plain facts or truth, esp. when not generally known

low-down /ˈ· ·/ *adj* [A] worthless; dishonourable: *a low-down trick*

low·er¹ /ˈlaʊəʳ/ *v* [IØ] *esp. AmE* LOUR

low·er² /ˈləʊəʳ/ *adj* [Wa5;A] in or being the bottom part: *He was wounded in the lower leg* (= the bottom part of the leg) —opposite **upper**

lower³ /ˈləʊəʳ/ *v* **1** [T1;IØ] to make or become smaller in amount, price, degree, strength, etc.: *Lower the price|your voice* **2** [T1;IØ] to move or let down in height: *Lower your aim before you shoot* **3** [T1;V3 *usu. nonassertive*] to bring (someone, esp. oneself) down in rank, worth, or opinion, as by doing something not worthy or wrong; DISGRACE¹ (1): *I wouldn't lower myself to speak to him*

lower a·way *v adv* [IØ *often imper.*] to lower a boat or sail

lower case /ˌ·· ˈ·◂/ *n, adj* [Wa5;U;B] (a type of letter) written or printed in its usual small form (such as *a, b, c*) rather than in its large (CAPITAL) form (such as *A, B, C*)

lower class /ˌ·· ˈ·◂/ *n* [*the*+R, *often pl. with sing. meaning*] a social class generally regarded as being of the lowest rank; WORKING CLASS: *The lower classes are always with us.|lower-class morals*

lower deck /ˌ·· ˈ·/ *n* **1** [C] the floor (DECK) of a boat below the main one **2** [*the*+GU] all sailors who are not officers, as a group

Lower House /ˌ·· ˈ·/ also **Lower Cham·ber** /ˌ·· ˈ··/— *n* [*the*+R] one of the 2 branches of a law-making body, esp. the one that is larger, more representative, and more powerful

low·er·most /ˈləʊəməʊst‖ˈləʊər-/ *adj* [Wa5] lowest, as in height, size, or price

low-key /ˌ· ˈ·◂/ also **low-keyed**— *adj* **1** controlled in style or quality; not loud or bright **2** *infml* not important; weak

low·land /ˈləʊlənd/ *n, adj* [Wa5;U *often pl. with sing. meaning*; B] (*often cap. as part of a name*) (an area of land) that is lower than the land surrounding it: *areas of lowland|lowland areas|the Lowlands of Scotland*

low·land·er /ˈləʊləndəʳ/ *n* (*sometimes cap.*) a person who lives in a LOWLAND area

low·ly¹ /ˈləʊli/ *adv* **1** in a low position, manner, or degree: *lowly paid workers* **2** in a manner that is not proud

lowly² *adj* [Wa1] **1** low in rank, position, or degree **2** not grand or proud; simple; humble —**-liness** *n* [U]

low-ly·ing /ˌ· ˈ··◂/ *adj* **1** (of land) not much above the level of the sea; not high **2** below the usual level: *low-lying clouds*

low-mind·ed /ˌ· ˈ··◂/ *adj* [Wa2] *derog* having or expressing a rude, unpleasant, or dishonest mind

low-necked /ˌ· ˈ·◂/ *adj* (of a garment) cut so as to leave the neck and shoulders uncovered

low-pitched /ˌ· ˈ·◂/ *adj* [Wa2] **1** (of a musical note) deep **2** (of a roof) not high or steep

low pro·file /ˌ· ˈ··/ *n* [*usu. sing.*] the state of not drawing attention to oneself or one's actions (esp. in the phr. **keep a low profile**)

low sea·son /ˈ· ˌ··/ *n* [(*the*) U] the time of year when business is least and prices are lowest: *Winter is (the) low season at seaside hotels* —compare HIGH SEASON

low-spir·it·ed /ˌ· ˈ···◂/ *adj* LOW² (7)

low tide /ˌ· ˈ·/ *n* **1** [C] the moment when the water is at its lowest point on the sea shore because of the TIDE **2** [U] the point on the shore to which the water reaches at this moment

low wa·ter /ˌ· ˈ··/ *n* [U] **1** the moment when the water in a river is at its lowest point because of the TIDE **2** this point on the river bank

loy·al /ˈlɔɪəl/ *adj* true to one's friends, group, country, etc.; faithful —**~ly** *adv*

loy·al·ist /ˈlɔɪəlɪ̈st/ *n* a person who remains faithful to an existing ruler or government during fighting between those who want to change and those who want to keep the existing ruler or government

loy·al·ty /ˈlɔɪəlti/ *n* **1** [U] the quality of being loyal **2** [C *usu. pl.*] a connection which binds a person to someone or something to which he is loyal: *He had divided loyalties; he wanted to be loyal to his firm, but he also wanted to be loyal to his family*

loz·enge /ˈlɒzɪ̈ndʒ‖ˈlɑ-/ *n* **1** a small flat sweet, esp. one containing medicine and that melts slowly in the mouth: *a cough lozenge* **2** a figure having 4 straight and equal sides and 2 sharp angles opposite each other and 2 wide angles **3** something made in this shape, such as a piece of a window

LP /ˌel ˈpiː/ *n not fml* LONG-PLAYING RECORD

L-plate /ˈel pleɪt/ *n BrE* one of 2 flat squares, marked with a letter L, that are fixed to the front and back of a vehicle, to show that the driver is a learner

LSD /ˌel es ˈdiː/ also (*sl*) **acid**— *n* [U] a tasteless drug causing one to see life and the world as much more beautiful, strange, cruel, etc., than usu., and to see things that do not exist

Lsd, £sd /ˌel es ˈdiː/ *n* [U] *BrE infml* (a word used, esp. before decimal money was introduced in Britain, for) money

Ltd *written abbrev.* (*used after the name of a* LIMITED LIABILITY *company*) *for*: LIMITED (2): *M.Y. Dixon and Son, Ltd, Booksellers*

lub·ber /ˈlʌbəʳ/ *n* a big awkward person —see also LANDLUBBER —**~ly** *adj* [A;(B)]: *a great lubberly fellow*

lu·bri·cant /ˈluːbrɪkənt/ *n* [C;U] a substance, esp. oil, able to make parts that move next to each other, as in a machine, move more easily
lu·bri·cate /ˈluːbrɪkeɪt/ *v* [T1] **1** to put oil or an oily substance into (the moving parts of a machine) to make them work more easily: (fig.) *We lubricated his tongue with wine* **2** to make smooth and able to move or be moved easily: *This oil lubricates the machine* —**-cation** /ˌluːbrɪˈkeɪʃən/ *n* [U]
lu·bri·ca·tor /ˈluːbrɪkeɪtəʳ/ *n* a person or instrument that puts oil on, as to the parts of a machine
lu·bri·cious /luːˈbrɪʃəs/ *adj fml* having or showing too great an interest in sex, esp. in a way that is unpleasant or socially unacceptable
lu·cerne /luːˈsɜːn‖-ɜrn/ (*AmE* **alfalfa**)— *n* [U] *BrE* a type of plant whose leaves grow in groups of 3 and which is used for feeding farm animals
lu·cid /ˈluːsɪ̈d/ *adj* **1** easy to understand; clear: *a lucid explanation* **2** when able to understand: *The old man's confused most of the time but he does have lucid moments* **3** *old use* bright; transparent —**~ly** *adv* —**~ity** /luːˈsɪdɪ̈ti/ *n* [U]
luck /lʌk/ *n* [U] **1** that which happens, either good or bad, to a person in the course of events by, or as if by, chance; fate; fortune: *Luck was with us and we won easily.|I've had bad luck all week* **2** success as a result of chance; good fortune: *I wish you luck.|What luck I met you!* **3 be down on one's luck** to have bad luck, esp. to be without money **4 be in/out of luck** to have/not have good fortune **5 for luck** to bring good fortune: *I'll put in 3 drops of oil—and one more for luck* **6 worse luck** unfortunately: *He reached the food before I did, worse luck!*
luck·less /ˈlʌkləs/ *adj* **1** without good fortune: *a luckless man* **2** ending in failure: *a luckless attempt*
luck out *v adv* [IØ] *AmE infml* to be lucky
luck·y /ˈlʌki/ *adj* [Wa1] having, resulting from, or bringing good luck: *a lucky man/discovery/flower* —**-ily** *adv*: *Luckily, she was in when I called* —**-iness** *n* [U]
lucky dip /ˌ·· ˈ·/ *n BrE* **1** [C] a barrel filled with wrapped objects of various values, into which a person may put his hand and pick out one, for a payment **2** [S] something whose result depends on chance; LOTTERY (2)
lu·cra·tive /ˈluːkrətɪv/ *adj* bringing in plenty of money; profitable —**~ly** *adv*
lu·cre /ˈluːkəʳ/ *n* [U] *derog or humor* money; profit (esp. in the phr. **filthy lucre**)
lu·di·crous /ˈluːdɪ̈krəs/ *adj* causing disrespectful laughter; very foolish; RIDICULOUS —**~ly** *adv* —**~ness** *n* [U]
lu·do /ˈluːdəʊ/ *n* [U] a children's game played with little flat objects (COUNTER*s*²) on a board
luff /lʌf/ *v naut* **1** [IØ (UP)] to bring the front of a sailing boat closer to or directly facing the wind **2** [T1] to position one's boat between the wind and (an opponent's boat)
lug¹ /lʌg/ *v* **-gg-** [X9;(T1)] *infml* to pull or carry with great effort and difficulty
lug² *n* [*usu. sing.*] *infml* a heavy or difficult pull
lug³ *n* a little piece that sticks out from something, such as a handle of a cooking pot
lug·gage /ˈlʌgɪdʒ/ *n* [U] the cases, bags, boxes, etc., of a traveller
luggage rack /ˈ·· ·/ *n* a shelf in a train, bus, etc., for putting one's bags and cases on
luggage van /ˈ·· ·/ *n BrE* the part of a train in which only boxes, cases, etc., are carried
lug·ger /ˈlʌgəʳ/ *n* a type of small boat with one or more LUGSAIL*s*
lug·hole /ˈlʌghəʊl, ˈlʌgəʊl/ also **lug**— *n BrE sl* an ear
lug·sail /ˈlʌgseɪl, -səl/ also **lug**— *n* a 4-sided sail supported on a bar that hangs sloping from the main upright pole (MAST) of a boat
lu·gu·bri·ous /luːˈguːbrɪəs/ *adj* doing and feeling little because unhappy; too sorrowful, esp. in a way that draws attention to one —**~ly** *adv* —**~ness** *n* [U]
lug·worm /ˈlʌgwɜːm‖-ɜrm/ also **lug**— *n* a type of small worm that lives in the sand by the sea and is used by fishermen to catch fish
luke·warm /ˌluːkˈwɔːm◂‖-ɔrm◂/ *adj* [Wa5] **1** (esp. of liquid) not much hotter than cold **2** showing hardly any interest; not eager
lull¹ /lʌl/ *v* **1** [T1] to cause to sleep or rest **2** [T1;IØ] to come or bring to an end; make or become less active: *We lulled her fears*
lull² *n* [S (*in*)] a period in which activity is less
lul·la·by /ˈlʌləbaɪ/ *n* a pleasant song used for causing children to sleep
lum·ba·go /lʌmˈbeɪgəʊ/ *n* [U] pain in the lower back
lum·bar /ˈlʌmbəʳ/ *adj* [Wa5] *med* of or belonging to the lower part of the back
lum·ber¹ /ˈlʌmbəʳ/ *v* [L9] to move in a heavy awkward manner
lumber² *n* **1** [U] *esp. BrE* useless or unwanted articles, such as furniture, stored away somewhere **2** [U] *esp. AmE* TIMBER¹ (1) **3** [S] *BrE infml* someone or something that causes difficulty, esp. by giving unwanted responsibility
lumber³ *v* **1** [T1 (*with*), *often pass.*] *BrE infml* to cause difficulty to (someone), esp. by giving unwanted responsibility: *I'm really lumbered now; I've been left with 60 cases of wine I can't sell.|The suppliers have lumbered me with 60 cases of wine I didn't want* **2** [IØ] *AmE* to cut trees or wood into TIMBER¹ (1)
lum·ber·jack /ˈlʌmbədʒæk‖-ər-/ *n* (esp. in the US and Canada) a man who cuts down trees for wood
lum·ber·man /ˈlʌmbəmən‖-bər-/ *n* **-men** /mən/ *AmE* a man whose business is the cutting down of trees and the selling of wood
lumber-room /ˈ·· ·/ *n esp. BrE* a room in which useless or unwanted furniture, broken machines, etc., are stored
lum·ber·yard /ˈlʌmbəjɑːd‖-bərjɑrd/ *n* a yard where building wood, boards, etc., are kept for sale
lu·mi·na·ry /ˈluːmɪ̈nəri‖-neri/ *n* **1** a person whose mind, learning, or actions are famous and respected by others: *the luminaries of the stage* (= famous actors) **2** *lit* something that gives light, esp. a star
lu·mi·nous /ˈluːmɪ̈nəs/ *adj* **1** giving light; bright **2** easily understood; clear: *a luminous speaker/speech* —**~ly** *adv* —**-nosity** /ˌluːmɪ̈ˈnɒsɪ̈ti‖-ˈnɑ-/ *n* [U]
luminous paint /ˌ··· ˈ·/ *n* [U] a paint containing a special substance that causes it to give off light after light has been shone on it
lum·me, -my /ˈlʌmi/ *interj infml, esp. BrE* (an expression of surprise)
lum·mox /ˈlʌməks/ *n esp. dial* an awkward ungraceful person
lump¹ /lʌmp/ *n* **1** [C (*of*)] a mass of something solid without a special size or shape: *a lump of lead* **2** [C] a hard swelling on the body: *She was afraid when she felt a lump in her left breast* **3** [*you*+N; (C)] *infml* a heavy mindless awkward person **4** [C (*of*)] a small square-sided block (of sugar), as for use in tea: *Do you take one lump or 2?* **5** [*the*+R] *BrE infml* the group of workers in the building industry who are not employed on a continuous contract, but only as and when they are needed **6 lump in the throat** a tight sensation in the throat caused by unexpressed pity, sorrow, etc.
lump² *v* [IØ] to form into lumps
lump³ *adj* [Wa5] **1** [A] not divided into parts; all together: *Instead of giving you 5 small sums of*

money I'll give you one lump sum **2** [A;(B)] being in the form of lumps: *lump sugar*

lump⁴ *v* **lump it** *infml* to accept unchangeable bad conditions without complaint (often in the phr. **like it or lump it**): *"I don't want you playing your piano in here all day." "Well, I'm not going to stop; you'll just have to like it or lump it!"*

lump·ish /ˈlʌmpɪʃ/ *adj infml* awkward or stupid

lump to·geth·er *v adv* [T1] to consider as a unity: *The cost of these 2 trips can be lumped together for tax purposes*

lump·y /ˈlʌmpi/ *adj* [Wa1] **1** filled or covered with lumps: *lumpy soup* **2** stupid or awkward **3** (of a large area of water) rough; full of small waves

lu·na·cy /ˈluːnəsi/ *n* **1** [U] the condition of being sick in the mind; madness **2** [U] foolish or wild behaviour **3** [C *usu. pl.*] an act of foolish or wild behaviour

lu·nar /ˈluːnəʳ/ *adj* [Wa5] **1** of or concerning the moon **2** made for use on or around the moon: *lunar vehicles*

lunar month /ˌ·· ˈ·/ *n* a period of 28 days, being the time it takes for the moon to circle the earth, counted from full moon to full moon

lu·nate /ˈluːneɪt/ *adj tech* shaped like a new moon

lu·na·tic¹ /ˈluːnətɪk/ *n* **1** *old use or derog* a person who is suffering from an illness of the mind **2** a wildly foolish person

lunatic² *adj* wildly foolish: *lunatic behaviour*

lunatic a·sy·lum /ˈ··· ·ˌ··/ *n now taboo* a hospital for people who are suffering from illness of the mind; MENTAL HOSPITAL

lunatic fringe /ˌ··· ˈ·/ *n* [(*the*) GC] the wildest people, or people with the strangest ideas, beliefs, etc., in a group

lunch¹ /lʌntʃ/ also (*fml*) **lun·cheon** /ˈlʌntʃən/— *n* [C;U] a meal eaten at about the middle of the day

lunch² *v* **1** [I∅] to eat LUNCH¹: *We're lunching with the Forsyths today* **2** [T1] to provide with or take out to LUNCH¹

luncheon meat /ˈ·· ·/ *n* [U] *BrE* a mixture of meat (usu. PORK) and other substances, pressed together in loaflike form

lunch·time /ˈlʌntʃtaɪm/ *n* [U] the time at or during which LUNCH¹ is eaten

lung /lʌŋ/ *n* either of the 2 breathing organs in the chest of man or certain other animals —see also IRON LUNG

lunge¹ /lʌndʒ/ *v* [I∅ (OUT)] to make a sudden forceful forward movement, esp. with the arm

lunge² *n* a sudden forceful forward movement, as of the body or a knife

lung·fish /ˈlʌŋˌfɪʃ/ *n* **-fish** [Wn2] any of several types of fish that breathe partly by means of a lunglike organ —see picture at FISH¹

lung·pow·er /ˈlʌŋˌpaʊəʳ/ *n* [U] strength of voice

lu·pin /ˈluːpɪ̈n/ *n* a type of garden plant with a tall stem covered in many flowers

lurch¹ /lɜːtʃ‖lɜrtʃ/ *n* **leave someone in the lurch** *infml* to leave someone alone and without help in a place or time of difficulty; desert someone

lurch² *n* a sudden movement forward or sideways: *The boat gave a lurch towards the rocks*

lurch³ *v* [I∅] to move with irregular sudden movements: *The wounded man lurched across the field*

lure¹ /lʊəʳ, ljʊəʳ‖lʊəʳ/ *n* **1** [C] something that attracts by promising pleasure: *the lures of a woman* **2** [*the*+R (*of*)] attraction; promise: *He was attracted by the lure of large profits* **3** [C] an apparatus, such as a plastic bird or fish, to attract animals into a place where they can be caught **4** [C] a group of bright feathers fastened together, used for attracting a hunting bird back to its master while it is being trained

lure² *v* [T1 (ON)] to attract or TEMPT, esp. away from what one should do into something one should not

lur·gy /ˈlɜːgi‖-ɜr-/ *n BrE humor* an illness or disease

lu·rid /ˈlʊərɪ̈d, ˈljʊərɪ̈d‖ˈlʊərɪ̈d/ *adj* **1** unnaturally bright; strongly coloured: *a lurid sunset* **2** shocking, esp. because violent; unpleasant: *The papers gave the lurid details of the murder* —**~ly** *adv* —**~ness** *n* [U]

lurk /lɜːk‖lɜrk/ *v* [L9] **1** to wait in hiding, esp. for an evil purpose: *The murderer lurked behind a tree for the minister* **2** to move quietly as if having done wrong and not wanting to be seen **3** to exist unseen: *Danger lurks in that quiet river*

lus·cious /ˈlʌʃəs/ *adj* **1** having a very pleasant taste or smell; sweet: *luscious fruit/wine* **2** very attractive; beautiful: *a luscious girl* **3** ripe and healthy: *luscious red apples hanging on the trees* —**~ly** *adv* —**~ness** *n* [U]

lush¹ /lʌʃ/ *adj* [Wa1] **1** (of plants, esp. grass) growing very well, thickly, and healthily **2** *infml* comfortable, esp. as provided by wealth

lush² *n AmE sl* a person who is drunk

lust /lʌst/ *n* **1** [U] strong sexual desire, esp. when uncontrolled or considered wrong **2** [U (*for*);C (*of*)] strong usu. evil desire; eagerness to possess: *lust for power* —see DESIRE² (USAGE)

lust for also **lust af·ter**— *v prep* [T1] to desire eagerly, esp. sexually

lust·ful /ˈlʌstfəl/ *adj* full of strong, esp. sexual, desire —**~ly** *adv* —**~ness** *n* [U]

lus·tre, *AmE* **-ter** /ˈlʌstəʳ/ *n BrE* **1** [U;S] brightness as of light thrown back (REFLECTed) from a shiny surface: *He polished the metal until it had a fine lustre* **2** [U] glory; fame

lus·trous /ˈlʌstrəs/ *adj esp. lit* shining; BRILLIANT¹ (1): *lustrous black hair* —**~ly** *adv*

lust·y /ˈlʌsti/ *adj* [Wa1] **1** full of strength, power, health, etc.: *lusty singing* **2** full of sexual desire: *lusty young men* —**~ily** *adv* —**~iness** *n* [U]

lu·ta·nist, -tenist /ˈluːtənɪ̈st/ *n* a person who plays a LUTE¹

lute¹ /luːt/ *n* a type of musical instrument with strings, having a long neck and a body shaped like a PEAR, played with the fingers and used esp. in former times

lute² *n* [U] *tech* a substance, esp. clay or cement, used for filling cracks, holes, etc.

lute³ *v* [T1] *tech* to fill, cover, or fix with clay, cement, etc.

luv /lʌv/ *n* [N] *BrE, nonstandard or humor* LOVE¹ (5)

lux·u·ri·ant /lʌgˈzjʊərɪənt, ləgˈʒʊərɪənt‖ləgˈʒʊərɪənt/ *adj* **1** growing well, esp. in health and number: *Luxuriant forests covered the hills* **2** very productive **3** very highly ornamented **4** having or showing the comforts of wealth —compare LUXURIOUS —**~ly** *adv* —**-ance** *n* [U]

lux·u·ri·ate in /lʌgˈzjʊərieɪt, ləgˈʒʊəri-‖ləgˈʒʊəri-/ *v prep* [T1] *fml* to enjoy oneself lazily in: *She sits there luxuriating in the sun/in a big chair, while her husband does all the work*

lux·u·ri·ous /lʌgˈzjʊərɪəs, ləgˈʒʊərɪəs‖ləgˈʒʊərɪəs/ *adj* **1** very fine and costly: *a luxurious meal* **2** providing the greatest comfort: *a luxurious hotel* **3** fond of comfort and of satisfying the senses: *He had luxurious habits* —compare LUXURIANT —**~ly** *adv*

lux·u·ry /ˈlʌkʃəri/ *n* **1** [U] great comfort, as provided without worry about the cost: *They led a life of luxury.|a luxury flat* **2** [C] something that is not necessary and not often had or done but which is very pleasant: *Sleeping in a warm bed was a luxury for the poor man*

-ly /li/ *suffix* **1** [*n*→*adj*] like in manner, nature, or appearance: QUEENLY|MOTHERLY|ORDERLY¹ **2** [*n*→*adj* [Wa5]] happening at regular periods of:

HOURLY|YEARLY **3** [*adj→adv*] in the stated manner: *quickly|slowly* **4** [*adj→adv* [Wa5]] from the stated point of view: *Musically (speaking), he's the cleverest member of his family*

ly·cée /ˈliːseɪ||liːˈseɪ/ *n* a French school for older pupils, either in France or for (esp.) French children abroad

ly·chee, litchi /ˈlaɪtʃiː/ *n* **1** a type of fruit with a hard rough nutlike shell and a sweet white flesh that contains a single seed **2** the tree, growing in southeast Asia, that bears this fruit —see picture at BERRY

lych·gate /ˈlɪtʃgeɪt/ *n* a gate with a roof leading into the grounds of a church —see picture at CHURCH[1]

lye /laɪ/ *n* [U] a liquid produced by passing water through the ashes of wood, used in washing and in making soap

ly·ing[1] /ˈlaɪ-ɪŋ/ *pres. p. of* LIE[1]

lying[2] *pres. p. of* LIE[3]

lying-in /ˌ·· ˈ·/ *n* **lyings-in, lying-ins** [*usu. sing.*] CONFINEMENT (1)

lymph /lɪmf/ *n* [U] a clear watery liquid formed in the body of animals which passes into the blood system

lym·phat·ic /lɪmˈfætɪk/ *adj* [Wa5] of, connected with, producing, or containing LYMPH

lynch /lɪntʃ/ *v* [T1] (esp. of a crowd of people) to attack and put to death, esp. by hanging, (a person thought to be guilty of a crime), without a lawful trial

lynch law /ˈ· ·/ *n* [U] the punishment of a supposed criminal, usu. by death, without a lawful trial

lynx /lɪŋks/ *n* [Wn1] a type of large strong wild animal of the cat family with long legs and a short tail —see picture at CAT

lynx-eyed /ˌ· ˈ··/ *adj* having very keen sight or noticing everything

lyre /laɪəʳ/ a type of ancient Greek musical instrument with strings stretched on a U-shaped frame

lyre·bird /ˈlaɪəbɜːd||ˈlaɪərbɜrd/ *n* a type of Australian bird, the male having a long tail shaped like a LYRE

lyr·ic[1] /ˈlɪrɪk/ *adj* [A] **1** [Wa5] of or intended for singing **2** [Wa5] expressing strong personal feelings, usu. in songlike form: *lyric poet/poetry* **3** joyful: *a lyric passage of music*

lyric[2] *n* **1** a short poem suitable for singing **2** a poem or other form of expression about strong personal feelings

lyr·i·cal /ˈlɪrɪkəl/ *adj* **1** full of admiration, pleasure, eagerness, etc.: *She became quite lyrical about his gift* **2** LYRIC[1] —**~ly** *adv* [Wa4]

lyr·i·cis·m /ˈlɪrᵻsɪzəm/ *n* **1** [U] LYRIC[1] style or quality, esp. in poetry **2** [C] an expression of strong personal feeling

lyr·i·cist /ˈlɪrᵻsᵻst/ *n* **1** a LYRIC[1] (2) poet **2** a writer of LYRICS; songwriter

lyr·ics /ˈlɪrɪks/ *n* [P] the words of a song, esp. a modern popular song

M, m

M, m /em/ **M's, m's** *or* **Ms, ms** **1** the 13th letter of the English alphabet **2** the ROMAN NUMERAL (number) for 1000

m *abbrev. for:* METRE

M *abbrev. for:* MOTORWAY

-'m /m/ [Wv1] *contr. of:* am: *I'm ready.|"Are you French?" "Yes, I am./No, I'm not"* —see CONTR., 's (USAGE)

ma /mɑː/ *n infml* (*usu. cap.*) **1** [N] (a name for mother, not considered polite): *Ma, give me some milk* **2** [N;A] (a name for an (old) woman, not considered polite): *You've dropped your bag, Ma!| Old Ma Harris was taken to hospital yesterday*

MA /ˌem ˈeɪ/ *abbrev. for:* Master of Arts; (a title for someone who has) a university degree which can be taken one or 2 years after a BA (=first degree): *Mary Jones, MA|an MA*

ma'am /mæm, mɑːm, məm||mæm/ *n* [N] *polite* **1** (a short form for MADAM, used for addressing the Queen and (in former times) (noble) ladies) **2** *AmE* (a respectful word used for addressing a woman): *Yes, ma'am, I will*

mac[1] /mæk/ *n BrE infml* MACKINTOSH

mac[2] *n* [N] *AmE sl* (*usu. cap.*) (used for addressing a man whose name is not known) fellow

ma·ca·bre /məˈkɑːbrə, -bəʳ/ *adj* causing fear, esp. because connected with death and the dead —compare GRUESOME

ma·cad·am /məˈkædəm/ *n* [U] a material which is made of small broken stones, often mixed with a substance (TAR) which holds them together, and which is rolled on roads to make a smooth hard surface

ma·cad·am·ize, -ise /məˈkædəmaɪz/ *v* [T1 *often pass.*] to cover (a road surface) with MACADAM

mac·a·ro·ni /ˌmækəˈrəʊni/ *n* [U] a food made from flour paste (PASTA) in the form of thin pipes which have been dried and are made soft again for eating by boiling in water —compare SPAGHETTI, VERMICELLI

mac·a·roon /ˌmækəˈruːn/ *n* a small flat cake made mainly of sugar and egg, with ALMOND*s* (a sort of nut)

ma·caw /məˈkɔː/ *n* a type of large brightly-coloured bird with a long tail (PARROT) of Central and South America

mace[1] /meɪs/ *n* **1** an ornamental rod, often made of or covered with precious metals, which is carried or placed before an official in certain ceremonies as a sign of power **2** a short heavy stick (CLUB) used as a weapon in former times, usu. of metal with sharp points sticking out around the head

mace[2] *n* [U] a powder made from the dried shell of a NUTMEG and used as a SPICE in cooking (=to give food a special taste)

mace-bear·er /ˈ· ˌ··/ *n* a person who carries a MACE[1] (1) before an official in (the procession before) a ceremony

ma·cer·ate /ˈmæsəreɪt/ *v* [T1;I∅] to (cause to) become soft by putting or being left in water: *Paper can be made from wood in powder form which has been macerated* —**-ation** /ˌmæsəˈreɪʃən/ *n* [U]

Mach /mæk||mɑk/ *n* [R9] the speed of an aircraft in relation to the speed of sound: *If a plane is flying at Mach 2, it is flying at twice the speed of sound*

ma·chet·e /məˈtʃeɪti||məˈʃeti, məˈtʃeti/ also **machet** /məˈtʃet, ˈmætʃᵻt/— *n* a knife with a broad heavy blade, which is used as a cutting tool and weapon in South America and elsewhere

Mach·i·a·vel·li·an /ˌmækɪəˈvelɪən/ *adj* (of people and actions) having or showing skill in using evil means to gain one's own aims, esp. in politics; dishonest

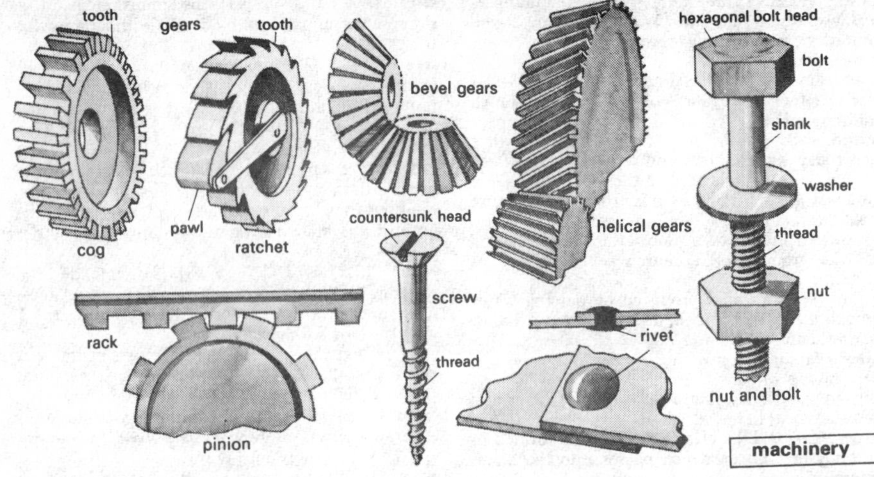

mach·i·na·tion /ˌmækǝ̇ˈneɪʃǝn/ *n* [*usu. pl.*] a plan for doing harm

ma·chine[1] /mǝˈʃiːn/ *n* **1** [C] a man-made instrument or apparatus which uses power (such as electricity) to perform work: *a sewing machine* **2** [C] a person who acts according to order or habit, without seeming to have feelings or thoughts **3** [C] a group of people that controls and plans the activities of a political party: *the party machine* **4** [C] a system or organization which influences people so that their behaviour becomes typical of the group **5** [A] produced by machining (MACHINE[2] (2)): *a machine edge*
USAGE An instrument for doing work, such as a hammer or spade, is a **tool**. They are simpler and usually smaller than **machines**, but this is a matter of degree. Some **tools**, like **machines**, run on electricity, oil, etc. The **engine** of a **machine** is the part that provides this power.

machine[2] *v* [T1] **1** to make or produce by machine, esp. in sewing and printing **2** [(DOWN)] to produce according to exact measurements: *The edge must be machined down to 0·03* MILLIMETREs

ma·chine·gun /mǝˈʃiːngʌn/ *n* a quick-firing gun, often supported on legs, which fires continuously as long as the TRIGGER is pressed

ma·chin·e·ry /mǝˈʃiːnǝri/ *n* [U] **1** machines in general **2** the working parts of an apparatus **3** a system or organization by which action is controlled: *The machinery of the law works slowly*

machine tool /·ˈ· ˌ·/ *n* a power-driven tool for cutting and shaping wood, metal, etc.

ma·chin·ist /mǝˈʃiːnǝ̇st/ *n* **1** a person who makes machines **2** a person who uses a machine at work, esp. for sewing

mack·e·rel /ˈmækǝrǝl/ *n* [Wn2;C;U] **1** a type of sea fish which can be eaten, having oily strong-tasting flesh. It has bands of blue-green colour across the top of its body —see picture at FISH[1] **2 a mackerel sky** a sky with bands of high white cloud

mack·in·tosh /ˈmækǝ̇ntɒʃ‖-tɑʃ/ also (*infml*) **mack** /mæk/, **mac**— *n esp. BrE* a coat made to keep out the rain, (esp.) formerly one treated with rubber, now often one of plastic or of material treated with a chemical substance

ma·cra·mé /mǝˈkrɑːmi‖ˌmækrǝˈmeɪ/ *n* [U] the art or practice of knotting string together in ornamental patterns

mac·ro- /ˈmækrǝʊ/ *prefix* long, large, or great —compare MICRO-

mac·ro·bi·ot·ic /ˌmækrǝʊbaɪˈɒtɪk‖-ˈɑtɪk/ *adj* [Wa5] concerning a type of food or eating habits which are thought to produce good health, esp. because of the presence of whole grains in flour products and the use of vegetable foods grown without chemicals

mac·ro·cos·m /ˈmækrǝʊkɒzǝm‖-kɑ-/ *n* **1** [*the*+R] the world as a whole; universe **2** [C] any large system containing smaller systems

mad /mæd/ *adj* **-dd-** [Wa1] **1** [B (*with*)] showing that one suffers from a disease of the brain or disorder of the mind: *She went mad after the death of her son* **2** [B] (of a dog) suffering from a disease which causes wild and dangerous behaviour; RABID **3** [B] very foolish and careless of danger: *You mad girl, to go out with no coat on a cold day!* **4** [F (*about, for*)] filled with strong feeling, interest, etc.: *He's mad about football* **5** [F (*with, at*), F5] *infml* angry: *Mother gets mad with me for coming home late* **6 drive someone mad** to worry or annoy someone enough to make him go mad **7 like mad** *infml* very hard, fast, loud, etc.: *They ran like mad to catch the moving bus* —see also **mad as a March** HARE, **mad as a** HATTER
USAGE There are different ways of making this word stronger. When it means "angry" one can say (*infml*) *He was* **hopping mad**. When it means "ill in the mind" one can say *He was* **raving mad**. —see ANGRY (USAGE).

mad·am /ˈmædǝm/ *n* **1** [N] (*often cap.*) (a respectful way of addressing a woman, esp. a customer in a shop when being served) **2** [C9 *usu. sing.*; (N)] a (young) female who likes to give orders: *She's a little madam, she won't do anything I suggest* **3** [C] a woman who is in charge of a house of PROSTITUTEs, taking from them some of the money they are paid by the men who use them sexually

Madam *n* **Mesdames** /ˈmeɪdæm‖meɪˈdɑːm (*Fr* madam)/ **1** [N9] (a word of address used at the beginning of a business letter to a woman, after the word *Dear*): *Dear Madam . . .* —compare SIR **2** [A] (a word for addressing a woman official, followed by the name of her office): *Madam President, may I ask a question?*

Ma·dame /ˈmædɑːm, mǝˈdɑːm‖mǝˈdæm (*Fr* madam)/ *n* **Mesdames** [A] *Fr* (the French word for Mrs, used as a title for certain married foreign women, usu. French ones)

mad·cap /ˈmædkæp/ *adj* [Wa5;A] wild and thoughtless: *your madcap plans to go mountain* *climbing in the middle of winter* —**madcap** *n*

mad·den /ˈmædn/ *v* [T1 *often pass.*] to make wild or angry

mad·den·ing /ˈmædənɪŋ/ *adj* **1** causing much pain or worry: *The pain was maddening and she couldn't sleep* **2** *infml* very annoying —**~ly** *adv*

mad·der /ˈmædəʳ/ *n* [U] **1** a plant from whose roots a red colouring matter (DYE) is obtained **2** the red colouring matter so obtained

made[1] /meɪd/ *past t. & p. of* MAKE

made[2] *adj* [Wa5] **1** [F] *not fml* sure of success: *When you find gold you're made (for life)* **2** [F+*for*] *not fml* completely suited: *a night made for love* **3** [F+(UP) *of*] formed: *Clouds are made of water/made up of little drops of water* **4 a made man** a man certain of success, because of luck or help

Ma·dei·ra /məˈdɪərə/ *n* [U] a type of strong usu. sweet wine produced in the island of Madeira

Madeira cake /·ˈ·· ·/ (*AmE* **pound cake**)— *n* [U] *BrE* a type of yellow cake of the lightest sort (SPONGE CAKE), but made heavier by the addition of fat to the mixture

mad·e·moi·selle /ˌmædəmwəˈzel (*Fr* madmwazɛl)/*n* **mesdemoiselles**/ˌmeɪdəmwəˈzel(*Fr* medmwazel)/ [N] (the French word for Miss, used as a way of addressing a (young) French girl): *How are you, mademoiselle?*

Mademoiselle *n* [A] *Fr* (the French word for Miss, used as a title for a young unmarried French girl)

made-to-mea·sure /ˌ·· ˈ··/ *adj* [Wa5] BESPOKE

mad·house /ˈmædhaʊs/ *n* **-houses** /ˌhaʊzɨz/ **1** (in former times) a hospital for those with disordered minds; MENTAL HOSPITAL **2** [*usu. sing.*] *infml* a place where there is a noisy and/or disorderly crowd of people

mad·ly /ˈmædli/ *adv* **1** in a wild way as if mad: *He rushed madly out of the room, knowing that he couldn't control his temper if she continued being so rude* **2** *infml* very (much): *It's madly exciting*

mad·man /ˈmædmən/ (*fem.* **mad·wom·an** /ˌwʊmən/)— *n* **-men** /mən/ a person who is mad: (fig.) *He drives like a madman. I'm sure he'll have an accident one day*

mad·ness /ˈmædnɨs/ *n* [U] **1** the state of being mad **2** behaviour that appears mad

Ma·don·na /məˈdɒnə‖məˈdɑ-/ *n* **1** [*the*+R] Mary, the mother of Christ in the Christian religion **2** [C] a picture or figure of Mary

Madonna lil·y /·ˌ·· ˈ··‖·ˈ·· ˌ··/ *n* a type of white flower (LILY) sometimes shown in the MADONNA's hand in pictures

ma·dras /məˈdræs, məˈdrɑːs‖ˈmædrəs/ *n* [U] a type of roughly-woven cotton

mad·ri·gal /ˈmædrɪgəl/ *n* **1** a song for several singers without using music from instruments **2** a short love poem, esp. one which may be sung

mael·strom /ˈmeɪlstrəm/ *n esp. lit* **1** a stretch of water moving round in a strong circular movement, which can suck objects down; violent WHIRLPOOL **2** [*usu. sing.*] the violent force of events which may lead to destruction

mae·nad /ˈmiːnæd/ *n* **1** (in former times) a female follower or priestess of the god of wine in ancient Greece or Rome **2** a woman behaving wildly, as if influenced by drinking wine

maes·tro /ˈmaɪstrəʊ/ *n* **-tros** *or* **-tri** /triː/ [C;N;(A)] a great or famous musician, esp. one who directs the playing of music (a CONDUCTOR)

maf·i·a /ˈmæfɪə‖ˈmɑ-, ˈmæ-/ *n* [(*the*) GC] (*often cap.*) an organization of criminals who control many activities by threats of violence, esp. those existing for many years in the west of Sicily and more recently in the US

mag /mæg/ *n infml* MAGAZINE (1)

mag·a·zine /ˌmægəˈziːn‖ˈmægəziːn/ *n* **1** a sort of book with a paper cover and usu. large-sized pages, which contains writing, photographs, and advertisements, usu. on a special subject or for a certain group of people, and which is printed and sold every week or month **2** a storehouse or room for arms, explosives, bullets, etc. **3** the part of a gun, or weapon of that type, in which bullets (CARTRIDGEs) are placed before firing **4** the place where the (roll or CARTRIDGE of) film is kept away from the light in a camera or in an apparatus for showing pictures

ma·gen·ta /məˈdʒentə/ *n, adj* [U;B] (of) the colour or colouring matter which is a dark purplish red

mag·got /ˈmægət/ *n* a small wormlike creature, the young of a fly or certain other insects, found on flesh and food where flies have laid their eggs

mag·got·y /ˈmægəti/ *adj not fml* full of MAGGOTs

ma·gi /ˈmeɪdʒaɪ/ *pl. of* MAGUS

Magi *n* [*the*+P] (in the Christian religion) the three wise men who visited and brought gifts for the baby Jesus

ma·gic[1] /ˈmædʒɪk/ *n* [U] **1** the system of trying to control events by calling on spirits, secret forces, etc. **2** *tech* the system of thought which imagines that images or parts of objects have a power over the objects themselves: *People who believe in magic think that pricking a figure of a man will wound the man himself* **3** the art employed by a theatrical performer (CONJURER) who produces unexpected objects and results by tricks **4 a** a strange influence or power **b** a charming and/or mysterious quality **5 as if by magic/like magic** so suddenly or well as seems unreasonable or unexplainable

magic[2] *adj* [A;(F)] caused by or used in magic: *She has a magic touch. She puts everything right*

ma·gic·al /ˈmædʒɪkəl/ *adj* of strange power, mystery, or charm: *a magical evening beneath the bright stars* —**~ly** *adv* [Wa4]

magic eye /ˌ·· ˈ·/ *n infml* an apparatus which notices or shows the presence of something by means of light waves; PHOTOELECTRIC CELL —see picture at SOUND[3]

ma·gi·cian /məˈdʒɪʃən/ *n* **1** (in stories) a person who can make strange things happen by magic **2** a person who does magic tricks; CONJURER

magic lan·tern /ˌ·· ˈ··/ *n* an apparatus for throwing images of pictures from glass plates onto a white sheet; early type of PROJECTOR

ma·gis·te·ri·al /ˌmædʒɨˈstɪərɪəl/ *adj* **1** [B] having or showing the power of a master; like (that of) someone who is in complete control of an action, subject, etc.: *a magisterial judgment on a historical event* **2** [Wa5;A] of or done by a MAGISTRATE —**~ly** *adv*

ma·gis·tra·cy /ˈmædʒɨstrəsi/ *n* **1** [U] the office of MAGISTRATE **2** [GU] a group of (the) MAGISTRATEs considered together

ma·gis·trate /ˈmædʒɨstreɪt, -strɨt/ *n* an official who has the power to judge cases in the lowest courts of law, esp. a police court; JUSTICE OF THE PEACE

mag·ma /ˈmægmə/ *n* [U] hot melted rock found below the solid surface of the earth

mag·na·nim·i·ty /ˌmægnəˈnɪmɨti/ *n* [U] the quality of being generous, esp. by helping others more than they deserve, or more than is usual

mag·nan·i·mous /mægˈnænɨməs/ *adj* having or showing unusually generous qualities towards others —**~ly** *adv*

mag·nate /ˈmægneɪt, -nɨt/ *n sometimes derog* a man of wealth, who has a leading position and power in business or industry, or who owns land

mag·ne·sia /mægˈniːʃə, -ʒə/ *n* [U] a light white powder used as a stomach medicine

mag·ne·si·um /mæg'niːzɪəm/ *n* [U] a silver-white metal that is a simple substance (ELEMENT (6)), is common in nature, burns with a bright white light, and is used in making FIREWORK*s* and mixtures of metals

mag·net /'mægnɨ̣t/ *n* **1** any object, esp. a piece of iron, which can draw other objects, esp. of iron, towards it either naturally or because of an electric current being passed through it **2** a person or thing which draws or attracts (people)

mag·net·ic /mæg'netɪk/ *adj* having the qualities of a MAGNET: *The iron has lost its magnetic force.|a magnetic person* —**~ally** *adv* [Wa4]

magnetic field /·,·· '·/ *n* the space in which a MAGNETIC force is effective round an object which has MAGNETIC power

magnetic pole /·,·· '·/ *n* one of 2 unfixed points near the NORTH POLE and the SOUTH POLE of the earth towards which the compass needle points

magnetic tape /·,·· '·/ *n* a TAPE[1] (3) on which sound or other information can be recorded

mag·net·is·m /'mægnɨ̣tɪzəm/ *n* [U] **1** (the science dealing with) the qualities of MAGNET*s* (1) **2** the quality of strong personal charm, the power to attract, etc.

mag·net·ize, -ise /'mægnɨ̣taɪz/ *v* [T1] **1** to give the qualities of a MAGNET to (esp. a piece of iron): *The iron was magnetized by passing electricity through wire wound round it* **2** to attract or draw by MAGNETISM: *His speech magnetized the listeners*

mag·ne·to /mæg'niːtəʊ/ *n* **-tos** an apparatus containing one or more MAGNET*s* (1), able to produce electricity esp. in a car —compare GENERATOR, DYNAMO

Mag·nif·i·cat /mæg'nɪfɪkæt/ *n* [*the*+R] the song of Mary, the mother of Jesus Christ, which praises God for his favour to her, and the words of which are sung as a prayer in services of the CHURCH OF ENGLAND

mag·ni·fi·ca·tion /,mægnɨ̣fɨ̣'keɪʃən/ *n* **1** [U] the act of MAGNIFYing **2** [C] the power of MAGNIFYing to a stated number of times bigger than in reality: *The apparatus has a magnification of 8*

mag·nif·i·cent /mæg'nɪfɨ̣sənt/ *adj* great, grand, generous, etc.: *The queen was wearing a magnificent silver dress* —**-cence** *n* [U] —**~ly** *adv* —compare HANDSOME

mag·ni·fi·er /'mægnɨ̣faɪə^r/ *n* something, such as an instrument, which magnifies (MAGNIFY)

mag·ni·fy /'mægnɨ̣faɪ/ *v* [T1] **1** to make (something) appear larger than in reality **2** *old use & bibl* to praise (God) highly —see also MAGNIFICAT

magnifying glass /'···· ·/ *n* a piece of glass (LENS), usu. curved on one or both sides with a frame and handle, which makes what is seen through it look bigger —see picture at OPTICS

mag·nil·o·quent /mæg'nɪləkwənt/ *adj fml* grand-sounding (in speech) —**-quence** *n* [U] —**~ly** *adv*

mag·ni·tude /'mægnɨ̣tjuːd‖-tuːd/ *n* **1** [U] greatness of size or importance: *The book was a work of such magnitude that it took 10 years to write* **2** [C] the degree of brightness of a star

mag·no·li·a /mæg'nəʊlɪə/ *n* a type of tree with large sweet-smelling flowers —see picture at PLANT[2]

mag·num /'mægnəm/ *n* (a large bottle containing) a measure of about 1.5 litres, esp. for wine

mag·num o·pus /,mægnəm 'əʊpəs/ *n fml, Lat* a great work of art, often a book, considered the best piece of work of the person who produced it; MASTERPIECE

mag·pie /'mægpaɪ/ *n* **1** a type of noisy bird with black and white feathers, which often picks up and takes to its nest small bright objects **2** *infml* **a** a person who likes collecting objects **b** a person who talks a lot

ma·gus /'meɪgəs/ *n* **magi** /'meɪdʒaɪ/ **1** a priest of ancient Persia **2** *fml* a magician

ma·ha·ra·ja, -jah /,mɑːhə'rɑːdʒə/ *n* (*often cap.*) (the title of) an Indian prince

ma·ha·ra·ni, -nee /,mɑːhə'rɑːniː/ *n* (*often cap.*) (the title of) the wife of a MAHARAJA

ma·hat·ma /mə'hætmə‖mə'hɑt-/ *n* [A;(C)] (*usu. cap.*) (a title given to) a wise and holy man in India, a religious leader, etc.: *Mahatma Gandhi*

mah-jong, -jongg /,mɑː 'dʒɒŋ‖-'ʒɑŋ/ *n* [U] a type of Chinese game, for 4 players, played with small painted pieces of wood, bone, etc.

mahl·stick /'mɔːl,stɪk/ *n* MAULSTICK

ma·hog·a·ny /mə'hɒgəni‖mə'hɑ-/ *n* **1** [C] a type of tree from which a dark reddish wood is obtained **2** [U] the wood from this tree, used for making good furniture **3** [U;A] a reddish-brown colour

ma·hout /mə'haʊt, mɑː'huːt‖mə'haʊt/ *n* (in India) a person who drives an elephant, and keeps and trains elephants

maid /meɪd/ *n* **1** (*often in comb.*) a female servant: *a housemaid|a kitchenmaid* —see also NURSEMAID, MILKMAID, OLD MAID **2** *lit & old use* a girl or (young) woman who is not married

maid·en[1] /'meɪdn/ *n* **1** *lit* a girl who is not married **2** *tech* a horse which has not won a race **3** also **maiden o·ver** /,·· '··/— (in cricket) an OVER in which no runs are made

maiden[2] *adj* [Wa5;A] **1** fresh; not used before: *maiden land* **2** first; not done before: *The aircraft makes its maiden flight tomorrow* **3** (of a woman) unmarried: *a maiden aunt|a maiden lady*

mai·den·hair /'meɪdnheə^r/ *n* [U] a kind of FERN —see also GINGKO

maid·en·head /'meɪdnhed/ *n esp. old use* **1** [U] (for a woman) the state of being a VIRGIN; fact of not having had sexual experience **2** [C] HYMEN

maid·en·hood /'meɪdnhʊd/ *n* [U] *esp. lit* the condition or time of being a young unmarried girl

maid·en·ly /'meɪdnli/ *adj esp. lit* like or suitable to a MAIDEN[1] (1); sweet, gentle, etc.

maiden name /'·· ·/ *n* the family name a woman has or had before marriage

maid of hon·our /,· · '··/ *n* **1** an unmarried lady who serves a queen or princess **2** a kind of small cake

maid·ser·vant /'meɪd sɜːvənt‖-ɜr-/ *n* a female servant

mail[1] /meɪl/ *n* **1** [(*BrE*)U9; (*AmE*)U] the postal system directed and worked by the government: *Air mail is quicker than sea mail.|(AmE) It came in the mail* **2** [U *sometimes pl. with sing. meaning*] letters and anything else sent or received by post, esp. those travelling or arriving together: *There are special trains to take the mails* **3** [C] also **mail train** /'· ·/— (esp. in names) a train which carries mail
USAGE This word is often used with a *cap.* in the name of **a** a newspaper: *The Daily* **Mail** **b** a train or boat service: *the Irish* **Mail.**

mail[2] *v* [D1 (*to*); T1] *esp. AmE* to POST

mail[3] *n* [U] armour made of metal plates or rings, worn by soldiers in past times —compare CHAIN MAIL

mail·bag /'meɪlbæg/ *n* **1** a bag made of strong cloth for carrying mail in trains, ships, etc. **2** *AmE* a postman's bag for carrying mail to be delivered

mail·box /'meɪlbɒks‖-bɑks/ *n AmE* **1** a place for collecting mail; POSTBOX (1) **2** a place where one's mail is left near the house; LETTERBOX (2) separate from the door
USAGE In America there are no PILLAR-BOXes standing in the streets.

mailing list /ˈ·· ·/ *n* a list of names and addresses kept by an organization, to which it sends information in the post

mail or·der /ˌ· ˈ··/ *n* [U] a method of selling goods in which the buyer chooses them at home, often from a book (CATALOGUE) which lists them, and what is ordered is sent to him by post

maim /meɪm/ *v* [T1] to harm in a part of the body so that it can not be used; *After the car accident she was maimed for life*

main[1] /meɪn/ *n* **1** [C *usu. pl.*] **a** a chief pipe supplying water or gas, or a chief wire carrying electricity, from outside into a building: *Water is supplied from the mains* —see also MAINS **b** a chief SEWER pipe taking waste, water, etc., out from a building: *The main of this house needs repairing* **2** [*the*+R] *poet* the sea **3 in the main** on the whole; usually; mostly —see also **by/with** MIGHT **and main**

main[2] *adj* [Wa5;A] **1** chief; first in importance or size: *a busy main road|Our main meal is in the evening.|Note down the main points of the speech.|soldiers guarded the main gates* **2 by main force** *esp. lit* by all the strength of the body

main chance /ˌ· ˈ·/ *n* [*the*+R] *not fml* the possibility of making money or other personal gain: *He always had an eye to* (=had as his purpose) *the main chance*

main clause /ˌ· ˈ·/ *n* a CLAUSE which can stand by itself to make a sentence —compare DEPENDENT CLAUSE

main deck /ˌ· ˈ·‖ˈ· ·/ *n* [*the*+R;(C)] the upper level on a ship

main drag /ˌ· ˈ·/ *n* [(*the*) C] *AmE sl* HIGH STREET

main·land /ˈmeɪnlənd/ *n* [*the*+R] a land mass, considered without its islands

main·line /ˈmeɪnlaɪn/ *v* [I∅] *sl* to put (INJECT) a drug into one of the chief blood vessels (VEINs) of the body, for pleasure or need, not for medical reasons

main line /ˌ· ˈ·/ *n* one of the chief railway lines

main·ly /ˈmeɪnli/ *adv* [Wa5] chiefly: *I don't know what his interests are, because we talk mainly about work when we meet.|His money comes mainly from business interests*

main·mast /ˈmeɪnmɑːst, -məst‖-mæst, -məst/ *n* the chief of the poles (MASTs) which hold up the sails on a ship

mains /meɪnz/ *n* [A] supplied from a MAIN[1] (1a): *mains electricity|a mains radio*

main·sail /ˈmeɪnsəl, *not tech* -seɪl/ *n* the chief sail on a ship, usu. that on the MAINMAST —see picture at SAIL[2]

main·spring /ˈmeɪnˌsprɪŋ/ *n* **1** the chief spring in a watch —see picture at CLOCK[1] **2** [(*of*) *usu. sing.*] the chief force or reason that makes something happen: *His belief in freedom was the mainspring of his fight against slavery*

main·stay /ˈmeɪnsteɪ/ *n* [*usu. sing.*] **1** [(*of*)] someone or something which provides the chief means of support: *After the father's death the son became the mainstay of the family* **2** a rope stretching from the top of the MAINMAST to the bottom of a shorter pole in front

main·stream /ˈmeɪnstriːm/ *n* [*the*+R] the main or usual way of thinking or acting in a subject

main·tain /meɪnˈteɪn, mən-/ *v* **1** [T1] to continue to have, do, etc., as before: *He took the lead, and maintained it till the end of the race.|to maintain an increase|maintaining the attack* **2** [T1] to support with money: *He is too poor to maintain his family* **3** [T1] to keep in existence: *It isn't easy to maintain life in the desert.|to maintain one's health* **4** [T1] to keep in good condition, by making repairs to, and taking care of: *to maintain a house|a car|a railway line* **5** [T1,5a,b;X *to be* 7] to state as true; argue for (an opinion): *to maintain one's opinion|He maintained that he was not to blame.|He maintained his right to enter the building when he wished* —**~able** *adj*

main·te·nance /ˈmeɪntənəns/ *n* [U] **1** the act of MAINTAINing (esp. 4) **2** money given to wives and/or children by a husband who does not live with them

maintenance or·der /ˈ··· ˌ··/ *n* an order made by a law court that a person shall pay for the support of others, esp. a man for his wife and children

mai·son·ette, maisonnette /ˌmeɪzəˈnet/ *n* a small flat or house, often part of a larger house, arranged as a separate living place

maize /meɪz/ *n* [U] *esp. BrE* CORN[1] (2) —see picture at CEREAL

ma·jes·tic /məˈdʒestɪk/ *adj* having or showing MAJESTY; STATELY —**~ally** *adv* [Wa4]

ma·jes·ty /ˈmædʒɪ̈sti/ *n* [U] greatness; a show of power, as of a king or queen: *the snow-covered mountains in their majesty*

Majesty *n* [N9;C9] (a title for addressing or speaking of a king or queen (in the phr. **His/Her Majesty; Your Majesty/-ies; Their Majesties**)): *Their Majesties will open the new bridge today*

ma·jol·i·ca /məˈdʒɒlɪkə‖məˈdʒɑ-/ *n* [U] an Italian style of pots, cups, plates, etc.

ma·jor[1] /ˈmeɪdʒəʳ/ *adj* [Wa5] **1** [A;(B)] greater when compared with others, in size, number, or importance: *The car needs major repairs.|The play is a major success* **2** [E] *old public school BrE* being the elder of 2 boys of the stated name (esp. in the same school): *Brown major* —opposite **minor** **3** [A; E;(B)] (in music) greater than MINOR by a half TONE (3) **4** [A;(B)] (of an operation) more than usually risky

USAGE Although it means "larger" or "of greater importance", **major** is not used in comparison with *than*: * *He is* **major** *than I am.* —compare SENIOR

major[2] *n* **1** [C;A;N] (*often cap.*) an officer of middle rank in the army or American airforce **2** [C] *fml & law* a person who has, in law, reached the grown-up state, in Britain the age of 18 years —compare MINOR[2] **3** [C] *AmE* a chief or special subject taken by a student at a university

ma·jor·do·mo /ˌmeɪdʒəˈdəʊməʊ‖-ər-/ *n* **-mos** (esp. in former times) a person in charge of the servants in a large house, esp. in Spain or Italy

ma·jor·ette /ˌmeɪdʒəˈret/ *n* DRUM MAJORETTE

major gen·e·ral /ˌ·· ˈ···/ *n* [C;A] (*often caps.*) an officer of high rank in the army or American airforce

major in *v prep* [T1] *AmE* to study as the chief subject(s) when completing one's degree: *He majored in French last year*

ma·jor·i·ty[1] /məˈdʒɒrɪ̈ti‖məˈdʒɑ-/ *n* **1** [(*the*) GS (*of*)] the greater number or amount (esp. of people); most: *The majority of doctors believe smoking is harmful to health.|A majority voted for the new party* **2** [C *usu. sing.*] the difference in number between a large and smaller group: *He won by a large majority|a majority of 900 votes* **3** [C *usu. sing.*] *law* the age when one becomes grown-up (a MAJOR[2] (2)): *She can't get married without her parents' permission, as she hasn't reached her majority* **4** [C *usu. sing.*] *tech* the rank of MAJOR[2] (1) **5 in the majority** (one of) the greater number of people or things: *People who can read and write are not in the majority in some countries*

majority[2] *adj* [Wa5;A] reached by agreement of most, but not all, of the members of a group

major prem·ise /ˌ·· ˈ··/ *n* (in LOGIC) the first statement of a set of reasoned ideas (SYLLOGISM)

major scale /ˌ·· ˈ·/ *n* the system of musical notes in

which there are 4 half TONEs (3) between the first and third notes

major suit /ˌ·· ˈ·/ *n* (in BRIDGE[3]) either of the SUITs[1] (4), HEARTs (4) or SPADEs[3] (1), which have a higher value than the MINOR SUITs

make[1] /meɪk/ *v* **made** /meɪd/ **1** [D1 (*for*); T1] to produce by work or action: *to make a cake|to make oneself/someone a cup of coffee|The children are making a lot of noise* **2** [T1] to tidy (a bed that has just been slept in) by straightening the sheets, pulling over the cover, etc. **3** [X1,7;V8] to put into a certain state, position, etc.: *Too much food made him ill.|The king married her and made her his queen.|He made himself heard across the room* **4** [T1] to earn, gain, or win (money or success): *He makes a lot (of money) in his job.|He makes a living* (=earns enough to live) **5** [V2;(V3 *pass.*)] to force or cause (a person to do something/a thing to happen): *The pain made him cry out.|She was made to wait for over an hour.|Some people say if you step on a worm it makes it rain* **6** [V2;(V3 *pass.*);X1,7] to represent as being, doing, happening, etc.; cause to appear as: *In the film, the battle is made to take place in the winter.|This photograph makes her (look) very young* **7** [T1;X1, (*to be*) 9,(7)] to calculate (and get as a result): *He added up the figures and made a different answer from the one I got.|I make it nearly 3 years since I saw him.|What time do you make it?|Is that the right time? I make it later* **8** [L1] to add up to; come to (an amount) as a result: *2 and 2 make 4* **9** [L1] to be counted as (first, second, etc.): *This makes our third party this month.|That makes 4 who want to go* **10** [L1;D1 (*for*)] to have the qualities of (esp. something good): *No one could have made him a better wife.|This story makes good reading.|The hall would make a good theatre* **11** [T1] *not fml* to travel (a distance) or at (a speed): *He made a few more yards before he fell to the ground.|The train was making 70 miles an hour* **12** [T1] to arrive at or on: *We made the station in time to catch the train.|We just made the train* (=almost missed it).*|We at last made the party* **13** [T1 (*of*); X1] to form (into or from): *Experience has made him a man.|The navy has made a man of him* —see also **make a** FOOL **of** **14** [X9 esp. *into, out of*] to change or produce (to or from): *Working in the kitchen made the boy into a good cook/made a good cook out of the boy.|We made the material into a skirt/made a skirt out of the material* **15** [T1] to establish (a law) **16** [T1] (in cricket) to get (a certain number of runs); SCORE: *England have made 342 for 7* **17** [D1 (*to*); T1] to put forward for consideration or acceptance (a suggestion of payment or a gift): *I'll make you an offer of £100.|Let me make you a present of it* **18** [T3] *fml* to be about (to): *He made to speak, but I stopped him* **19** [T1] *sl* to obtain (a) sexual experience with: *He's been pretending that he made her when they went camping* **20** [T1] *infml* to give the particular qualities of; complete: *It's the bright paint which really makes the room* **21** [T1] *old use* to eat (in the phr. **make a good/hearty meal**) **22** [T1] (used with a noun instead of a verb alone): *to make a promise* (=to promise)*|to make no answer* (=not to answer)*|making a search|We made an early start.|She made a good choice.|He's made his decision.|An important discovery has been made* —see also **make** CERTAIN, **make** GOOD, **make** SURE **23 make as if to** to be about to: *He made as if to speak, but I stopped him* **24 make believe** to pretend: *The children are making believe that they're princes and princesses* **25 make it a** to arrive in time **b** *infml* to succeed **26 make love (to) a** to have sex (with): *They made love.|He made love to her* **b** *esp. old use* to show that one is in love (with) by always being with, kissing, etc. **27 make one's way** to go: *I made my way home/to the house/towards the trees/along the road/up the stairs* **28 make or mar/break** which will cause success or complete failure: *a make or break decision/plan* **29 make things/it warm/hot for someone** *sl* to cause someone to experience pain, shame, or difficulty: *Let's make it hot for the enemy, boys!*

USAGE 1 Compare **do** and **make**: They are each used in many expressions about which there is no rule, such as **make** *war*, **do** *a favour*; but very often one **makes** something that was not there before: *to* **make** *a cake/a noise/a fire*; and one **does** an action: *to* **do** *the shopping/one's exercises.|"What are you* **making**?" *"A shirt."|"What are you* **doing**?" *"Playing football."* 2 Compare: *The table is* **made** *of wood.|Bread is* **made** *from corn.* We use *from* when the result no longer looks like the original material, and *of* when something shorter and simpler has been done. —see also MADE, **make** DO[2] (21), **make** LITTLE/MUCH/NOTHING/SOMETHING **of,** MAKE AFTER, MAKE AWAY WITH, MAKE FOR, MAKE OF, MAKE OFF, MAKE OFF WITH, MAKE OUT, MAKE OVER, MAKE TOWARDS, MAKE UP, MAKE UP FOR, MAKE UP TO, MAKE WITH

make[2] *n* **1** the type to which a set of (man-made) objects belongs, esp. the name of the makers: *This watch has gone wrong; I wish I'd bought a better make* **2 on the make** *sl* **a** searching for personal profit or gain **b** trying to obtain a sexual experience with someone

make af·ter *v prep* [T1] *esp. old use* to chase; run after: *He threw the ball, and the dog made after it*

make a·way with *v adv prep* [T1] *infml, becoming rare* **1** also **make off with**— to steal **2** to kill; DO AWAY WITH: *Father's made away with himself!*

make-be·lieve /ˌ· ·ˈ·/ *n* [U] a state of pretending or the things which are pretended: *She lives in a world of make-believe/a make-believe world if she thinks she can succeed without working hard* —see also MAKE[1] (24)

make for *v prep* [T1 *no pass.*] **1** to move in the direction of (usu. quickly or purposefully): *It started raining, so she made for the nearest shelter* **2** also **make at**— to move to attack: *As the thief opened the door, the dog made for him* **3** to result in: *The large print makes for easier reading*

make of *v prep* [D1 *no pass., usu. nonassertive*] to understand (partly or at all) by: *I don't know what to make of his behaviour* (=I can't understand it)

make off *v adv* [I∅] to escape in a hurry

make off with *v adv prep* [T1] MAKE AWAY WITH

make out *v adv* **1** [T1,6] to see or understand with difficulty: *I can just make out the writing.|Can you make out what he's trying to say?* **2** [T1] to write in complete form: *to make out a bill/a list* **3** [I∅] *infml* to succeed (in business or life generally): *The firm is not making out as well as was hoped.|How did he make out while his wife was away?* **4** [I∅ (*with*)] to have a (esp. friendly) relationship: *How did you make out with your new employer?|He seems to be making out (with the girl)* **5** [T5a;X *to be* 7] *infml* to claim or pretend (that someone or something is so), usu. falsely: *He makes out he's younger than me.|He makes himself out to be very important.|He's not so bad as they make out he is/as they make him out to be* **6** [T1 (*for*)] to argue as proof (esp. in the phr. **make out a case** (=to give good reasons)): *I'm sure we can make out a case for allowing you another holiday in place of the one you missed*

make o·ver *v adv* [T1] **1** [(*into*)] to change: *The garage has been made over into a play room.|He has been made over into a new man* (=a completely different person) —compare MAKE (13) **2** [(*to*)] to pass over possession of, esp. in law: *His wealth was* *made over to his children.|He made over his house for use as a hospital in the war*

mak·er /ˈmeɪkəʳ/ *n* **1** [C *often pl.*] (*often in comb.*) one of the people (esp. a firm) who make something: *My watch has gone wrong; I'm sending it back to the makers.|a watchmaker|a dressmaker* **2** [R] (*usu. cap.*) God (esp. in the phr. **meet one's maker** (=to die))

make·shift /ˈmeɪkˌʃɪft/ *adj* [A;(B)] used at the time because there is nothing better: *This is just a makeshift arrangement of the furniture; I'll change it all when the floor's been cleaned* —see also **make** SHIFT

make to·wards also **make to·ward**— *v prep* [T1 *no pass.*] *fml* to move in the direction of; MAKE FOR: *traffic making towards the city in the morning*

make-up /ˈ· ·/ *n* **1** [C *usu. sing.*] the combination of qualities (in a person's character): *The make-up of his character can't be changed at his age* **2** [C *usu. sing.*] the way in which the print, pictures, etc., in a newspaper or on a page are arranged **3** [U;C *usu. sing.*] **a** powder, paint, etc., worn on the face: *Too much make-up looks unnatural* **b** an appearance produced by the use of this: *She changed his make-up of an old man for that of a Chinese*

make up *v adv* **1** [T1 (*with*); I∅] to become friends again after (a quarrel): *You don't really hate each other, so why don't you kiss and make up?|It's time you made up your quarrel/made it up with your sister* **2** [T1;I∅:(*as*)] to use special paint and powder on the face of (someone or oneself) so as to change or improve the appearance: *She makes herself up/makes up her face in 20 minutes in the morning.|You have 10 minutes in which to make up* **3** [T1] to invent (a story, poem, etc.), esp. in order to deceive **4** [T1] to prepare (a drug), esp. according to a doctor's note: *He made up the doctor's* PRESCRIPTION/ *another bottle of medicine* **5** [T1 (*to*)] to make (an amount or number) complete: *They made up a 4 at tennis.|to make up the money* (*to the right amount*) **6** [T1] to repay or give (an amount) in return: *You must make up what you owe before the end of the month* **7** [T1 (*into*); L9 esp. *into*] **a** to produce (something) from (material) by cutting and sewing: *I've made up the curtains/the dress* **b** to be produced by cutting and sewing: *It will make up well/into a beautiful dress* **8** [T1] to collect together: *to make up parcels* **9** [T1] to arrange for printing: *to make up the page/a book* **10** [T1 *often pass.*] to form as a whole: *The tea is made up from a mixture of several different types* **11** [T1] to arrange ready for use: *Bring the sheets and make up the bed.|I'll make up a bed on the floor*

make up for *v adv prep* [T1,4] **1** to repay or COMPENSATE for (what was bad before) with something good: *This beautiful autumn makes up for/is making up for the wet summer* **2 make up for lost time** to work fast, because of time lost earlier

make up to *v adv prep* [T1] **1** to try to gain the favour of (someone) by appearing friendly, pleasant, and full of praise: *Many people make up to him only because of his wealth* **2 make it up to someone/make (it) up to someone for something** to repay someone with good things in return for something good done or something bad experienced by him: *You've been so kind. I'll make it all up to you one day.|How can we make (it) up to them for all the worry we've caused them?*

make with *v prep* [T1] *sl, esp. AmE* to produce; bring: *I'm hungry; make with the dinner*

mak·ing /ˈmeɪkɪŋ/ *n* **1** [*the*+R+*of*] the cause of great improvement: *Hard work will be the making of him* —compare UNDOING **2 in the making** **a** while being made: *It was spoilt in the making* **b** ready to be produced: *There's a fortune in the making for anyone willing to work hard*

-making *comb. form* [*adj*→*adj*] *infml* which causes one to feel: *sick-making*

mak·ings /ˈmeɪkɪŋz/ *n* [*the*+P *of*] the possibility of developing (into): *He has the makings of a good doctor*

mal- /mæl/ *comb. form* bad(ly): MALFORMED|MALPRACTICE|MALTREAT

ma·lac·ca cane /məˌlækə ˈkeɪn/ *n* a walking stick made of a kind of wood (PALM) which comes from Malaya

mal·a·chite /ˈmæləkaɪt/ *n* [U] a type of green stone used for ornaments

mal·ad·just·ed /ˌmæləˈdʒʌstɨ̈d/ *adj* (of a person) of a character which had developed unsuitably, so that the person can not be happy or behave well in his surroundings —**-ment** *n* [U]

mal·ad·min·i·stra·tion /ˌmælədˌmɪnɨ̈ˈstreɪʃən/ *n* [U] carelessness and lack of ability in carrying out duties, usu. by someone in an official position

mal·a·droit /ˌmæləˈdrɔɪt/ *n fml* not skilful in action or behaviour; awkward —**~ly** *adv* —**~ness** *n* [U]

mal·a·dy /ˈmælədi/ *n fml & lit* **1** something that is wrong with a system or organization **2** *esp. old use* an illness

ma·laise /məˈleɪz/ *n* **1** [U] a feeling of illness without any particular pain or appearance of disease **2** [C *usu. sing.*; U] a lack of wellbeing, esp. shown in lack of activity: *The general social malaise is causing the country to produce less goods every year*

mal·a·prop·is·m /ˈmæləprɒpɪzəm‖-prɑ-/ *n* a wrong use of a word, in which a word is used which sounds like the correct word, but means something quite different (as in *I couldn't understand the difficulty when she said the handbag fell off the door, but then I saw she meant the handle*)

mal·ap·ro·pos /ˌmælæprəˈpəʊ/ *adj, adv fml & pomp* unsuitable or unsuitably for the occasion

ma·lar·i·a /məˈleərɪə/ *n* [U] a disease of hot countries, caused by a small living thing which enters the blood when the person is bitten by certain types of mosquito

ma·lar·i·al /məˈleərɪəl/ *adj* [Wa5;A;(B)] **1** suffering from MALARIA **2** (of a place) in which MALARIA is common

Ma·lay /məˈleɪ‖məˈleɪ, ˈmeɪleɪ/ also **Ma·lay·an** /-ən/— *adj* [Wa5] of the people or language of Malaysia —see NATIONALITY TABLE

mal·con·tent /ˈmælkəntent‖ˌmælkənˈtent/ *n* a person dissatisfied with a state of affairs, esp. with politics, and usu. likely to take action against this state

mal·con·tent·ed /ˌmælkənˈtentɨ̈d/ also (*rare*) **malcontent**— *adj* dissatisfied; being a MALCONTENT

male¹ /meɪl/ *adj* [Wa5] **1** [B] of the sex that does not give birth to young: *a male monkey* **2** [B] suitable to or typical of this sex, rather than the female sex: *a male voice* **3** [A] (of a part of a machine) made to fit into a hollow part —see FEMALE (USAGE)

male² *n* a male person or animal: *In most birds the male is bigger and more brightly coloured than the female*

mal·e·dic·tion /ˌmælɨ̈ˈdɪkʃən/ *n esp. fml or lit* a curse; prayer that harm may come (esp. to someone) —compare BENEDICTION

mal·e·fac·tor /ˈmælɨ̈fæktəʳ/ *n esp. fml or lit* a person who does evil things, esp. a criminal —compare BENEFACTOR

ma·lef·i·cent /məˈlefɨ̈sənt/ *adj* [A;(B)] *fml or lit* able to do, or doing, evil —compare BENEFICENT —**-cence** *n* [U]

ma·lev·o·lent /məˈlevələnt/ *adj esp. lit* having or

expressing a wish to do evil to others —**-lence** *n* [U] —**~ly** *adv*

mal·feas·ance /mæl'fiːzəns/ *n law* **1** [U] wrongdoing **2** [C] an unlawful act, esp. of an official in government

mal·for·ma·tion /ˌmælfɔː'meɪʃən‖-ɔr-/ *n* **1** [U] the condition of being formed or shaped wrongly **2** [C] **a** a wrong shape, esp. of a part of the body **b** a badly shaped part, esp. of material used to make something

mal·formed /ˌmæl'fɔːmd◂‖-ɔr-/ *adj* [Wa5] made or shaped badly —compare DEFORM (1)

mal·func·tion /mæl'fʌŋkʃən/ *n fml* a fault in operation: *The sheets came back torn because there was a malfunction in the washing machine*

mal·ice /'mælǝ̣s/ *n* [U] **1** the wish, desire, or intention to hurt one or more others **2 bear malice** to feel dislike for someone because of their behaviour **3 with malice aforethought** *law* (of a criminal act) planned before it was done; done on purpose

ma·li·cious /mə'lɪʃəs/ *adj* feeling or expressing MALICE —**~ly** *adv*

ma·lign¹ /mə'laɪn/ *adj* [A] *often lit* (of things) harmful; causing evil

malign² *v* [T1] to express evil of, esp. wrongly: *He felt the charge of stealing maligned his character*

ma·lig·nan·cy /mə'lɪgnənsi/ *n* **1** [U] the state or quality of being MALIGNANT **2** [C] a dangerous growth of cells; TUMOUR of a MALIGNANT kind

ma·lig·nant /mə'lɪgnənt/ *adj* **1** full of hate and a strong wish to hurt: *a malignant nature|a malignant look* **2** (of a disease or condition) serious enough to cause death if not prevented —**~ly** *adv*

ma·lig·ni·ty /mə'lɪgnǝ̣ti/ *n* **1** [U] the state or quality of being MALIGN **2** [C] an example of this **3** [U] also **malignancy**— MALIGNANT (2) quality (of a disease)

ma·lin·ger /mə'lɪŋgəʳ/ *v* [IØ] to avoid work by pretending to be (still) sick —**~er** *n*

mall /mɔːl, mæl‖mɔl/ *n AmE* an area of streets where one can walk to and around shops

mal·lard /'mæləd‖-ərd/ *n* [Wn1] a type of wild duck —see picture at WATER¹

mal·le·a·ble /'mælɪəbəl/ *adj* **1** (of metals) that can be beaten, pressed, rolled, etc., into a new shape **2** (of people, character, nature, etc.) easily formed, changed, or trained —**-bility** /ˌmælɪə'bɪlǝ̣ti/ *n* [U]

mal·let /'mælǝ̣t/ *n* **1** a wooden hammer —see picture at TOOL¹ **2** a wooden hammer with a long handle, used in games (CROQUET and POLO)

mal·low /'mæləʊ/ *n* a type of wild and garden plant with pink or purple flowers and fine hairs on its stem and leaves —see also MARSHMALLOW

malm·sey /'mɑːmzi/ *n* [U] a sweet dark type of MADEIRA

mal·nu·tri·tion /ˌmælnjʊ'trɪʃən‖-nʊ-/ *n* [U] **1** bad feeding with food that is the wrong sort and/or too small in amount **2** the poor condition of health resulting from this

mal·o·dor·ous /ˌmæl'əʊdərəs/ *adj fml or pomp* **1** having a bad smell **2** improper; not lawfully or socially acceptable

mal·prac·tice /ˌmæl'præktǝ̣s/ *n* **1** [U] unlawful activity, usu. for personal advantage, by a person in a position of trust or responsibility, esp. a lawyer or minister **2** [U] *law* bad treatment by a doctor **3** [C] an example of such behaviour

malt¹ /mɔːlt/ *n* [U] grain, usu. BARLEY, which has been kept in water for a while, then dried, and is used for preparing drinks, like beer

malt² *v* **1** [T1] to make (grain) into MALT **2** [IØ] (of grain) to become MALT **3** [T1] to make or treat with MALT

malted milk /ˌ·· '·/ *n* [U;C] (a drink made from) milk treated with MALT

Mal·tese /ˌmɔːl'tiːz◂/ *adj* [Wa5] of the people or language of the island of Malta —see NATIONALITIES TABLE

Maltese cross /ˌ·· '·/ *n* a cross with 2 points at the end of each of the 4 arms

Mal·thu·si·an /mæl'θjuːzɪən‖-'θuːʒən/ *adj* [Wa5] connected with, esp. supporting, the writings of Thomas Malthus (1776–1834), which say that the population of the world would grow faster than its food supply if not controlled, either by disease and wars or by planning

mal·treat /mæl'triːt/ *v* [T1] *sometimes fml* to treat roughly and/or cruelly —compare ILL-TREAT —**~ment** *n* [U]

malt·ster /'mɔːltstəʳ/ *n* a person whose job is to MALT grain

ma·ma¹, mamma /mə'mɑː/ *n* [C;N] *BrE fml, now rare* (a name for) mother

ma·ma², mamma /'mɑːmə/ also (*infml*) **momma**— *n* [C;N] *AmE becoming rare* (a name for) mother —see also MAMMY

mam·ba /'mæmbə‖'mɑmbə, 'mæmbə/ *n* a type of large very poisonous black or green African tree snake

mam·bo /'mæmbəʊ‖'mɑmbəʊ/ *n* **-bos** a type of West Indian dance like the RUMBA

mam·mal /'mæməl/ *n* an animal of the type which is fed when young on milk from the mother's body See next page for picture

mam·ma·ry /'mæməri/ *adj* [Wa5] *tech* of or concerned with the breast

mam·mon /'mæmən/ *n* [R] (*often cap.*) wealth, esp. when considered as attracting too much respect and admiration

mam·moth /'mæməθ/ *n* **1** [C] a kind of elephant which lived on earth during the early stages of human development, larger than the modern one, and covered with hair —see picture at PREHISTORIC **2** [A] very large

mam·my /'mæmi/ *n* **1** [N;(C)] *esp. IrE & AmE* (*used esp. by or to children*) mother **2** [C] *AmE, usu. derog* a black woman who cares for white children

man¹ /mæn/ *n* **men** /men/ **1** [C] a fully-grown human male **2** [C] a human being: *All men must die* **3** [R] **a** men in general: *Man is taller than woman* **b** the human race: *Man must change in a changing world* **4** [C9] **a** a husband (in the phr. **man and wife**): *They can't stay in the same room if they're not man and wife* (=married) **b** *infml* a husband, lover, or other fully-grown male with whom a woman lives: *waiting for her man to come out of prison* **5** [C] (*often in comb.*) a fully-grown male in employment or a soldier of low rank: *He's in charge of a small factory and has several men under him.|The general made a speech to the men.|officers and men|a postman* **6** [C] a male member of a team: *Lloyd led his men onto the field* **7** [C] a male person with courage, firmness, etc.: *The army will make a man of you.|The boy tried to be a man, but tears came to his eyes because of the pain* **8** [C9 *usu. sing.*] the right male person: *You want a good cricketer? Well, here's the* VERY *man/your man/the man for the job* **9** [C9] a present or former male student at a university (esp. in such phrs. as **an Oxford man, a Harvard man**) **10** [N] (used for addressing a fully-grown male, esp. when the speaker is excited, angry, etc.): *Wake up, man, you can't sleep all day!* **11** [N] *sl, esp. Am & CarE* (used for addressing someone, esp. a fully-grown male): *This party's really great, man!* **12** [C] any of the objects moved by each player in a board game: CHESS *men* **13 as one man** with the agreement of everyone **14 man about town** a (rich) man who does not work but spends time at social gatherings,

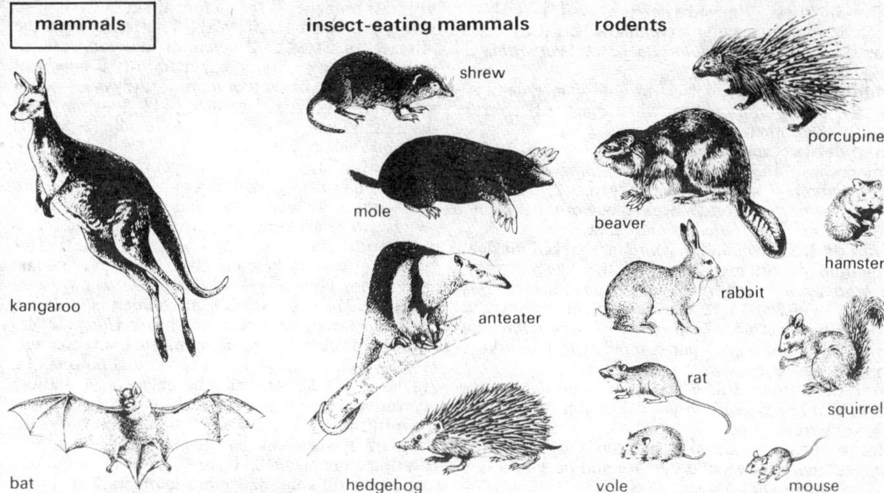

in clubs, theatres, etc. **15 man and boy** all one's life: *He was born in the village and worked on the farm man and boy* **16 the man in the street** (the idea of) the average person, who represents general opinion **17 man of God** a priest **18 man of my/your/his word** a keeper of promises: *He said he'd help, and he's a man of his word, so we know he will* **19 man of the world** an experienced man who knows how people behave **20 one's own man** independent in action, esp. work **21 to a man** every person: *They agreed to a man* **22 to the last man** until none was left —**~like** *adj* —see also OLD MAN, GENTLEMAN, PEOPLE (USAGE)

USAGE Note the word order in this fixed phr.: **men and women.**

man² *v* **-nn-** [T1] to provide with men for operation: *Man the guns.|The buses are under-manned* (=there are too few workers to drive and take money)

man³ *interj AmE infml* (used for expressing strong feelings, as of excitement, surprise, etc.)

-man /mən/ (*fem.* **-woman** /ˈwʊmən/)— *suffix* **-(wo)men** /mən; ˈwɪmɪn/ **1** [*n, adj→n*] a person who lives in: *a Frenchman|2 of my countrywomen* **2** [*n→n*] a person who works at: *a* BUSINESSMAN|*a* POSTMAN

man·a·cle¹ /ˈmænəkəl/ *n* one of a pair of iron rings joined by a chain, for fastening the hands or feet of a prisoner

manacle² *v* [T1] to put MANACLEs on

man·age /ˈmænɪdʒ/ *v* **1** [T1] **a** to control (esp. a business): *to manage a hotel|a house|He couldn't manage his horse, and it threw him to the ground* **b** to deal with or guide, esp. by using skill: *She manages the money very well.|She knows how to manage him when he's angry* **2** [T1,3;IØ] (*often used with* can, could) to succeed in dealing with (a difficult movement or action): *It's heavy, but I can manage/can manage (to carry) it* **3** [IØ] to succeed in living, esp. on a small amount of money: *We have very little, but we manage* **4** [T1] *infml* (*used with* can, could) to succeed in taking or using: *I can't manage another mouthful.|I could manage another holiday soon, I'm so tired.|I couldn't manage 2 weeks' holiday this year, only one* —see COULD (USAGE)

man·age·a·ble /ˈmænɪdʒəbəl/ *adj* easy to control or deal with: *A book as big as that is not a manageable size* —**-bility** /ˌmænɪdʒəˈbɪlɪ̈ti/ *n* [U]

man·age·ment /ˈmænɪdʒmənt/ *n* **1** [U] the act of managing (MANAGE), esp. a business or money **2** [U] skill in dealing with (usu.) a person (esp. in the phr. **more by luck than management**): *He didn't do very well in the test, but he got the job more by luck than management* **3** [GC] the people who are in charge of a firm, industry, etc., considered as one body: *The workers are having talks with the management*

man·ag·er /ˈmænɪdʒəʳ/ *n* **1** a man who controls a business **2** a person who makes arrangements, esp. for the use of money to live on: *She must be a very good manager to feed her children so well on so little money*

man·ag·er·ess /ˌmænɪdʒəˈres‖ˈmænɪdʒərɪ̈s/ *n* a woman who controls a business, esp. a shop or restaurant; female MANAGER (1)

man·a·ge·ri·al /ˌmænɪ̈ˈdʒɪəriəl/ *adj* [Wa5;A] of or concerning a MANAGER or MANAGEMENT: *a managerial position|managerial talks*

man-at-arms /ˌ· · ˈ·/ *n* a soldier of former times, esp. one with a horse and heavy armour and weapons

man·a·tee /ˌmænəˈtiː/ *n* a type of large sea creature which is a MAMMAL, related to the SEA COW but with a rounded tail —see picture at SEA

man·da·rin /ˈmændərɪn/ *n* **1** [C] a government official of high rank in China's former empire **2** [C] *not fml* **a** a person who holds an important official position **b** an official who keeps to the old ways and/or will not change detailed and difficult methods of doing things **3** [U] (*usu. cap.*) the official form of the Chinese language; language of Peking and the north and of educated Chinese generally **4** [C] also **mandarin or·ange** /ˌ··· ˈ··/— a small kind of orange with a special taste and skin which comes off easily

mandarin duck /ˌ··· ˈ·/ *n* an attractive type of small duck with clearly marked areas of coloured feathers, esp. round the head and eyes, originally from Asia, but now kept in parks in all parts of the world

man·date¹ /ˈmændeɪt/ *n* **1** a formal command to act in a certain way, given by a higher to a lower official **2** [*usu. sing.*] the right and power given to a government, or any body of people chosen to represent others, to act according to the wishes of those who voted for it **3** the power given to a country by the LEAGUE of Nations after the First World War to govern (part of) another country

mandate² *v* [Wv5;T1 (*to*)] to put (a place) under a MANDATE¹ (3): *a mandated* TERRITORY

man·da·to·ry[1] /ˈmændətəri‖-tori/ *adj* [Wa5] **1** containing or carrying a command **2** which must be done/so: *It's mandatory to pay a debt within a certain period of time*

mandatory[2] /ˈmændətəri‖-tori/ also **man·da·ta·ry** /-təri‖-teri/— *n* a country which has a MANDATE[1] (3) over another

man·di·ble /ˈmændəbəl/ *n tech* **1** a jaw which moves, usu. the lower jaw of an animal or fish, or its jawbone —see picture at REPTILE **2** the upper or lower part of a bird's beak **3** one of the 2 biting or holding parts in insects and CRABs

man·do·lin /ˌmændəˈlɪn/ *n* a round-backed musical instrument with metal strings, rather like a LUTE

man·drake /ˈmændreɪk/ also **man·drag·o·ra** [U] /mænˈdrægərə/— *n* [C] a type of plant from which drugs may be made, esp. those causing sleep, the root of which is in 2 parts, thought to look like a man's legs

man·drill /ˈmændrɪl/ *n* a kind of large BABOON (a sort of monkey) with bright colours on its face and lower parts behind

mane /meɪn/ *n* the long hair on the back of a horse's neck, or around the face and neck of a lion —see picture at HORSE

man-eat·er /ˈ· ˌ··/ *n* a living thing which eats human flesh, usu. an animal but sometimes a CANNIBAL (1) —**man-eating** *adj* [Wa5;A]

ma·neu·ver /məˈnuːvəʳ/ *n, v AmE* MANOEUVRE

ma·neu·ve·ra·ble /məˈnuːvərəbəl/ *adj AmE* MANOEUVRABLE

man Fri·day /ˌ· ˈ··/ *n* a male general helper who can be trusted —compare GIRL FRIDAY

man·ful /ˈmænfəl/ *adj* brave; determined: *He made manful efforts to move the heavy furniture* —**~ly** *adv*

man·ga·nese /ˈmæŋgəniːz/ *n* [U] a greyish white metal that is a simple substance (ELEMENT (6)) used in making glass, steel, etc.

mange /meɪndʒ/ *n* [U] a skin disease of animals, esp. dogs and cats, caused by the bite of a very small insect and leading to the loss of areas of hair or fur and a poor condition of health

man·gel-wur·zel /ˈmæŋgəl ˌwɜːzəl‖-ɜr-/ *n* one of certain kinds of vegetable with a large round root which can be eaten, often grown on farms as cattle food

man·ger /ˈmeɪndʒəʳ/ *n* **1** a long container, open at the top, in which food is placed for horses and cattle —see picture at FARMYARD **2 dog in the manger** a person who does not wish others to enjoy what he cannot use for his own enjoyment

man·gle[1] /ˈmæŋgəl/ *v* [T1 *often pass.*] to tear or cut to pieces; crush: *After the accident they tried to find out who the people were, but the bodies were too badly mangled to be recognized*

mangle[2] *n* **1** a machine with rollers turned by a handle between which water is pressed from clothes, sheets, etc., being passed through. It is usually separate from a washing machine, and was used esp. before modern electric washing machines were invented —compare WRINGER **2** *rare* a WRINGER on a washing machine

mangle[3] *v* [T1] to put (wet clothes, sheets, etc.) through a MANGLE or WRINGER

man·go /ˈmæŋgəʊ/ *n* **-goes** *or* **-gos 1** a type of tree of tropical countries which bears a fruit with sweet yellow-coloured flesh and a long hard seed (STONE) **2** the fruit of this tree —see picture at FRUIT[1]

man·go·steen /ˈmæŋgəstiːn/ *n* **1** a type of tree of East Asia which bears a fruit with a thick skin and large seeds covered with a sweet white fleshy substance **2** the fruit of this tree

man·grove /ˈmæŋgrəʊv/ *n* a type of tree of tropical countries which grows on muddy land (a SWAMP) and near water and puts down new roots from its branches —see picture at TREE[1]

mang·y /ˈmeɪndʒi/ *adj* [Wa1] **1** suffering from the disease of MANGE **2** *infml* of bad appearance because of loss of hair, as in MANGE **3** *infml* not satisfactory in amount or quality —**-ily** *adv*

man·han·dle /ˈmænhændl/ *v* [T1] **1** to move by using the force of the body **2** to handle (a person) roughly, using force

man·hole /ˈmænhəʊl/ *n* an opening, usu. with a cover, on or near a road, through which a man can go down to a place where underground pipes and wires can be examined, repaired, etc.

man·hood /ˈmænhʊd/ *n* **1** [U] the condition or period of time of being a man: *Members of certain races must perform special tests when they come to manhood.|Throughout his manhood and into old age he remained the strongest man of the village* **2** [U] the good qualities of a man, such as courage, strong will, etc. **3** [U] *euph* the sexual powers of a man **4** [GU] *rare* all the men of a nation, considered together as one body

man-hour /ˈmæn-aʊəʳ/ *n* (a measure of) the amount of work done by one man in one hour

ma·ni·a /ˈmeɪnɪə/ *n* **1** [U] disorder of the mind of a very forceful kind, dangerous to others **2** [C (*for*)] *not fml* a desire so strong that it seems mad: *She has a mania for (driving) fast cars* **3** [U9] *not fml or* (*in comb.*) *tech* strong unreasonable desire or keenness: *He's got car mania.*|KLEPTOMANIA|MEGALOMANIA

ma·ni·ac /ˈmeɪniæk/ *n* **1** (*often tech in comb.*) a person (thought to be) suffering from MANIA (1,3) of some kind: *a dangerous maniac|a car maniac* **2** a wild thoughtless person: *He drives like a maniac; I'm sure he'll cause an accident*

ma·ni·a·cal /məˈnaɪəkəl/ *adj* [Wa5] of or like a MANIAC —**~ly** *adv* [Wa4]

man·ic /ˈmænɪk/ *adj* [Wa5] *tech* of or suffering from MANIA (1)

manic-de·pres·sive /ˌ·· ·ˈ··/ *adj, n* [Wa5] (a person) with continual changes of feeling, states of great joyful excitement being followed by sad hopelessness, although the mind may be clear in the time between the 2 states

man·i·cure[1] /ˈmænəkjʊəʳ/ *n* [U;C] (a) treatment for the hands and (esp.) the fingernails, including cleaning, cutting, etc.

manicure[2] *v* [T1] to give a MANICURE to (the hands)

man·i·cur·ist /ˈmænəkjʊərəst/ *n* a person, often a woman, whose job is to MANICURE hands

man·i·fest[1] /ˈmænəfest/ *adj* [Wa5] *fml* plain to see or clear to the mind: *Fear was manifest on his face* —**~ly** *adv*

manifest[2] *v* [T1] *fml* to show (something or itself) plainly: *He doesn't manifest much interest in his studies.|The speech manifested the truth of the story*

manifest[3] *n tech* a list of goods carried, esp. on a ship

man·i·fes·ta·tion /ˌmænəfeˈsteɪʃən‖-fə-/ *n* **1** [U] *fml* the act of showing or making clear and plain **2** [C] *fml* anything said or done which shows clearly (a feeling, belief, truth, etc.) **3** [C] an appearance, or other sign of presence, of a spirit

man·i·fes·to /ˌmænəˈfestəʊ/ *n* **-tos** *or* **-toes** a (written) statement making public the intentions, opinions, etc., of a ruler or group of people, esp. of a political party: *the* LABOUR *party manifesto*

man·i·fold[1] /ˈmænəfəʊld/ *adj* [Wa5] *fml* many in number and/or kind: *His interests are manifold*

manifold[2] *n tech* a pipe with holes connecting it to a number of smaller pipes, to allow gases to enter or escape from an engine, such as that of a car —see picture at CAR

man·i·kin, manni- /ˈmænɪkən/ *n* **1** a man of much

smaller size than is usual; DWARF **2 a** a figure of the human body for use by artists **b** such a figure for use by medical students **3** MANNEQUIN

ma·nil·a, -nilla /mə'nɪlə/ *n* **1** [A] (*often cap.*) (of paper) of a strong brown kind **2** [U] also **manila hemp** /·ˌ·· '·/— (*usu. cap.*) a material obtained from a plant grown in the Philippine Islands, used in making rope

ma·nip·u·late /mə'nɪpjʊleɪt‖-pjə-/ *v* [T1] **1** to handle or control (esp. a machine), usu. skilfully: *to manipulate the controls* **2** to use (someone) for one's own purpose by skilfully controlling and influencing, often in an unfair or dishonest manner —**-lative** /mə'nɪpjʊlətɪv‖-pjəleɪ-/ *adj* [Wa5]

ma·nip·u·la·tion /məˌnɪpjʊ'leɪʃən‖-pjə-/ *n* **1** [U] the act of manipulating or condition of being MANIPULATEd: *Some people can put back a twisted joint, like the shoulder, by careful manipulation* **2** [C] an example of this

man jack /ˌ· '·/ *n* [S] a man, considered as a single person (in the phr. **every man jack**): *We can succeed only if every man jack of us tries his hardest*

man·kind /ˌmæn'kaɪnd/ *n* [GU] **1** the human race, both men and women —see SOCIETY (USAGE) **2** *rare* men (not women) considered together as one body

man·ly /'mænli/ *adj* [Wa1] having the qualities suitable to a man: *A manly man would not have run away.|The boy walked with a manly* STRIDE (=large step) —**-liness** *n* [U]

man-made /ˌ· '·◂/ *adj* [Wa5] **1** produced by the work of men; not found in nature: *The lake is man-made; there used to be a valley here until they changed the course of the river* **2** (of materials) not made from natural substances, like wool or cotton, but from combinations of chemicals; SYNTHETIC: *Nylon is a man-made* FIBRE

man·na /'mænə/ *n* [U] **1** the food which in the Bible was provided by God for the Israelites in the desert after their flight from Egypt **2** anything which comes unexpectedly to help one, when one is in need: *Her kind words were manna to his troubled mind*

manned /mænd/ *adj* [Wa5] (of machines, esp. in space) having men on board: *the development of manned from unmanned spacecraft*

man·ne·quin, manikin /'mænɪkɪ̈n/ *n* **1** *becoming rare* a person, usu. a woman, who is employed to wear new clothes and show them to possible buyers **2** a figure of the human body used for showing clothes in shop windows; MODEL or TAILOR'*s* DUMMY

man·ner /'mænəʳ/ *n* **1** [C (*of*) *usu. sing.*] *fml* the way in which anything is done or happens: *The sheets are usually folded in this manner.|He spoke in such a manner as to offend them|in such a manner that they were offended* **2** [S] a personal way of acting or behaving towards other people: *I don't like to talk to him; he has a very rude manner.|a pleasant manner* **3** [C9 *usu. sing.*] a way or style of writing, painting, building, etc., which is typical of one or more persons, of a country, or of a time in history: *in the French manner* **4** [S+*of*] *old use* kind or sort (of person or thing) (esp. in the phr. **What manner of?**): *What manner of son can treat his mother so badly?* **5 all manner of** every sort of **6** (**as**) **to the manner born** in a natural way as if accustomed from birth, esp. to a position: *She played the queen as to the manner born* **7 in a manner** *fml* considered in a certain way; to a certain amount: *He blames me, and in a manner, he's right* **8 in a manner of speaking** (used for making something seem less forceful than the words appear) if one may express it this way **9 not by any manner of means** not at all; not to any degree

man·nered /'mænəd‖-ərd/ *adj* having or showing an unnatural way of acting: *a mannered way of speaking*

-mannered *comb. form* [*adv, adj→adj*] having or showing the stated sort of MANNERS: *good/well-mannered|bad/*ILL-*mannered*

man·ner·is·m /'mænərɪzəm/ *n* **1** [C] a peculiar way of behaving, speaking, etc., that has become a habit **2** [U] the repeated use of a trick of style in the arts, such as writing or painting

man·ner·ly /'mænəli‖-ər-/ *adj rare* of good social manners; polite —compare UNMANNERLY

man·ners /'mænəz‖-ərz/ *n* [P] **1** (polite) social practices or habits: *Remember your manners; thank your friend when you leave the party* **2** social behaviour; ways of living (esp. of a nation or group of people): *She has written a book on the manners and customs of the ancient Egyptians*

man·nish /'mænɪʃ/ *adj derog* (of a woman) like a man in character, behaviour, appearance, etc. —**~ly** *adv* —**~ness** *n* [U]

ma·noeu·vra·ble, *AmE* **maneuverable** /mə'nuːvərəbəl/ *adj* that can be moved or directed easily, esp. turned: *a very manoeuvrable car* —**-bility** /məˌnuːvərə'bɪlɪ̈ti/ *n* [U]

ma·noeu·vre[1], *AmE* **maneuver** /mə'nuːvəʳ/ *n* **1** [*often pl.*] the moving of (part of) an army or of warships, planned for a certain purpose; a set of such moves being done for training purposes **2** a skilful move or clever trick, intended to deceive, to gain something, to free oneself from a difficult position, etc.

manoeuvre[2], *AmE* **maneuver** *v* **1** [T1;I∅] **a** to cause (a soldier or ship) to perform one or more MANOEUVRE*s* **b** (of a soldier or ship) to perform one or more MANOEUVRE*s* **2** [X9] to move (to a position) esp. skilfully: *It was difficult to manoeuvre the furniture through the door* —**-vrer** /mə'nuːvərəʳ/ *n*

man-of-war /ˌ· · '·/ also **man-o'-war** /ˌmæn ə 'wɔːʳ/— *n old use* a warship in the navy

ma·nom·e·ter /mə'nɒmɪ̈təʳ‖-'nɑ-/ *n* an instrument for measuring the pressure of gases —**-tric** /ˌmænə'metrɪk/ *adj* —**-trical** /ˌmænə'metrɪkəl/ *adj* —**-trically** *adv* [Wa4]

man·or /'mænəʳ/ *n* **1** the land belonging to a nobleman (the **lord of the manor**) under the FEUDAL system, some of which he kept for his own use, the rest being rented to farmers who paid by giving services, esp. labour, and part of the crops they grew **2** a large house with land **3** *BrE sl* a police DISTRICT

manor house /'·· ·/ *n* the house in which the owner of a MANOR lives

ma·no·ri·al /mə'nɔːrɪəl‖mə'nor-/ *adj* [Wa5;A] of or belonging to a MANOR

man·pow·er /'mænˌpaʊəʳ/ *n* [U] **1** the number of workmen needed for a certain type of work, as in industry, the army, or police: *The movement of young men from the country to the cities leaves the farms short of manpower* **2** the workpower supplied by men rather than machines **3** a measure of the power of one man at work, usu. 1/10 HORSEPOWER

man·qué /'mɒŋkeɪ‖mɑŋ'keɪ/ *adj* [Wa5;E] *Fr* who could have been but failed to be; unsuccessful: *He paints beautiful pictures; he's an artist manqué*

man·sard /'mænsɑːd‖-ɑrd/ also **mansard roof** /'·· ·/— *n* a roof with a lower and upper part, the lower having a steeper slope —see picture at ROOF[1]

manse /mæns/ *n* the house of a PRESBYTERIAN minister, esp. in the CHURCH OF SCOTLAND

man·ser·vant /'mænˌsɜːvənt‖-ɜr-/ *n* a male servant

-man·ship /mən'ʃɪp/ *suffix* [*n→n* [U]] the art or skill of a man or woman of the stated type: SEAMANSHIP|STATESMAN*ship*|*the* HORSEMANSHIP *of Princess Anne* —compare -SHIP —see also ONE-UPMANSHIP

man·sion /'mænʃən/ *n* a large house, usu. belonging to a wealthy person

man·sions /'mænʃənz/ *n* [P9] (*usu. cap.*) (in names of buildings) a building containing flats —see VILLA (USAGE)

man-sized /'· ·/ also **man-size**— *adj* [Wa5;A;(B)] *infml* (esp. used in advertising) large enough for a man

man·slaugh·ter /'mænˌslɔːtəʳ/ *n* [U] *law* the crime of killing a person, unlawfully but not intentionally

man·tel·piece /'mæntlpiːs/ also (*esp. old use*) **man·tel** /'mæntl/— *n* a frame above and at the sides of a fireplace, esp. the part on top which can be used as a small shelf, esp. for ornaments —see picture at LIVING ROOM

man·tel·shelf /'mæntlʃelf/ *n* **-shelves** /ʃelvz/ the top part of a MANTELPIECE, forming a shelf

man·til·la /mæn'tɪlə/ *n* an ornamental piece of thin material worn by Spanish women, covering the head and falling onto the shoulders; sort of VEIL or SHAWL

man·tis /'mænt¹₃s/ *n* PRAYING MANTIS

man·tle¹ /'mæntl/ *n* **1** *old use* a loose outer garment without SLEEVE*s*, shoulders, or arms; sort of CLOAK: (fig.) *a mantle of snow on the trees* **2** a cover made of netlike material, which is put over a gas flame in a lamp and becomes very hot and bright

mantle² *v* [T1] *lit* to cover: *Snow mantled the trees*

man-to-man /ˌ· · '·/ *adj* [Wa5;A] *infml* open; without unnecessary politeness

man·trap /'mæntræp/ *n* a trap used formerly to catch people unlawfully on private land, usu. when hunting animals

man·u·al¹ /'mænjʊəl/ *adj* [Wa5] of or using the hands: *Manual workers often earn more than office workers* —**~ly** *adv*

manual² *n* a (small) book of teaching information about something —compare HANDBOOK

man·u·fac·ture¹ /ˌmænjʊ'fæktʃəʳ‖-jə-/ *n* **1** [U] the act of manufacturing (MANUFACTURE) **2** [U] the method of doing this **3** [C *usu. pl.*] something which has been MANUFACTURE*d*

manufacture² *v* [T1] **1** to make or produce by machinery, esp. in large quantities: *Many countries sell manufactured goods abroad* **2** to invent (an untrue story, reason, etc.)

man·u·fac·tur·er /ˌmænjʊ'fæktʃərəʳ‖-jə-/ *n* [*often pl.*] a person or firm responsible for manufacturing (MANUFACTURE) goods

man·u·mit /ˌmænjʊ'mɪt‖-jə-/ *v* **-tt-** [T1] *law* (in former times) to free (someone) from slavery —**-mission** /'mɪʃən/ *n* [U]

ma·nure¹ /mə'njʊəʳ‖mə'nʊər/ *n* [U] waste matter from animals which is put on the land to make it produce better crops —compare FERTILIZER

manure² *v* [T1] to put MANURE on

man·u·script /'mænjʊskrɪpt‖-jə-/ *n* **1** [C; *in*+U] the first or only copy of a book or piece of writing, esp. written by hand **2** [C] a handwritten book, of the time before printing was invented

Manx /mæŋks/ *adj* [Wa5] of the Isle of Man, its people, or the CELTIC language originally spoken there

Manx cat /ˌ· '·/ *n* a kind of cat which has no tail —see picture at CAT

man·y /'meni/ *determiner, pron, n* —see MORE /mɔːʳ‖mor/, MOST /məʊst/ [P] **1** (*of plurals; used without* a *or* only, *usu. nonassertive, to show the large size of the number*) a great number (of): *How many letters are there in the alphabet?*|*Were there many people at the play?*|*There are so many that I can't choose.*|*He ate 3 and said he could eat as many again* (=3 more).|*You have* (*far*) *too many books on the shelf.*|*Many people* (*fml* for *A lot of people*) *would like to take holidays abroad.*|*He invited all his many friends to the party.*|*Not many of us will pass the examination.*|*There are many, many reasons against it.*|*a many-coloured pattern* (=with many colours)|*many more cars than usual* **2 a good/great many** *not fml* a large number of: *"a very low standard of life . . . amongst a great many people"* (SEU S.) **3 in so many words** in actual words; in exactly those words: *He didn't invite us in so many words, he just asked whether we were coming* **4 many a man, hour, etc.** many men, hours, etc. **5 many's the time, day, etc.,** (**that**) there have been many times, days, etc., (that): *Many's the time I've wondered what he meant* **6 one too many for** (**someone**) clever enough to beat (someone) **7 one, two, three, etc., too many** one, 2, 3, etc., more than is needed **8 the many** (compared to **the few**) the large number of people who **a** possess little or **b** have ordinary needs or desires

many-sid·ed /ˌ·· '··◂/ *adj* [Wa5] **1** with many sides **2** with many meanings **3** having many different qualities —**~ness** *n* [U]

Mao·is·m /'maʊɪzəm/ *n* [U] belief in and practice of the principles of Mao Tse Tung, the first leader of modern COMMUNIST China —**-ist** *adj, n*

Mao·ri /'maʊri/ *adj* [Wa5] of the language or customs of the original peoples of New Zealand

map¹ /mæp/ *n* **1** a representation of the earth's surface, as if seen from above, showing the shape of countries, the position of towns, the height of land, the rivers, etc. **2** a plan of the stars in the sky **3** a representation showing the position or state of anything **4 off the map a** (of a place) far away and unreachable **b** *infml* not in existence **5** (**put something**) **on the map** *infml* (to cause something to be) considered important: *This big new hotel certainly put our town on the map*

map² *v* **-pp-** [T1] **1** to make a map of **2** [(*onto*)] *tech* to represent the pattern of (something) on something else

ma·ple /'meɪpəl/ *n* **1** [C] a type of tree with many-pointed leaves which grows in the northern half of the world, and one kind of which yields a sugary liquid —see picture at TREE¹ **2** [U] the wood of this tree

maple sug·ar /ˌ·· '··/ *n* [U] the sugar produced from **maple syrup,** the juice (SAP) of the MAPLE

map out *v adv* [T1,6a,b] to plan (time, an event, etc., esp. in the future): *She has every advantage; her future is all mapped out for her*

map·ping /'mæpɪŋ/ *n tech* an act of representing one thing by another, or fitting one onto another

map-read·er /'· ˌ··/ *n* [C9] a person who can understand (READ) maps

ma·quis /mæ'kiː, 'mækiː‖mæ'kiː, mɑ'kiː (*Fr* mɑki)/ *n Fr* **1** [U] the thick growth of bushes covering large stretches of land in parts of France and the surrounding countries **2** [*the*+P] (*often cap.*) (in the Second World War) the secret groups of armed people who fought the Germans in France

mar /mɑːʳ/ *v* **-rr-** [T1] *esp. lit* to spoil: *The noise marred the peace of the night* —see also MAKE **or mar**

mar·a·bou, -bout /'mærəbuː/ *n* **1** [C] a type of large African STORK (=a long-legged bird) **2** [U] the feathers of this bird used for ornament **3** [C] an ornament made from these feathers, esp. a neck covering

mar·a·schi·no /ˌmærəˈskiːnəʊ, -ˈʃiː-/ *n* **-nos** (*sometimes cap.*) **1** [U] a type of sweet alcoholic drink (LIQUEUR) made from a kind of black CHERRY (a small fruit) **2** [C] a type of sugar-covered CHERRY which has been kept in this or a like drink, used for ornamenting sweet cakes and dishes

mar·a·thon /ˈmærəθən‖-θɑn/ *n* **1** [C] **a** (*often cap*) a running race of about 26 miles, esp. at the OLYMPIC GAMES **b** any activity that tests one's power over a long time **2** [A] *not fml* very long: *a marathon speech of 6 hours*

ma·raud /məˈrɔːd/ *v* [Wv4;IØ] (of people or animals) to move around in search of something to steal, burn, or destroy: *They went in fear of attack by marauding bands* —**~er** *n*

mar·ble /ˈmɑːbəl‖ˈmɑr-/ *n* **1** [U] a hard sort of LIMESTONE used for building, SCULPTURE, gravestones, etc., when cut and polished, and usu. showing an irregular pattern of colours **2** [A;(U)] *lit* **a** (of) a smooth and white quality: *In spite of her age there were no lines on her marble forehead* **b** (of) a hard and cold quality: *He has a marble heart/a heart of marble* **3** [C] a small hard ball of usu. coloured glass used by children to play the game of MARBLES

mar·bled /ˈmɑːbəld‖ˈmɑr-/ *adj* [Wa5] marked with irregular colours and lines like a kind of MARBLE (1)

mar·bles /ˈmɑːbəlz‖ˈmɑr-/ *n* **1** [U] a game in which small hard glass balls are rolled along the ground towards each other **2** [P] a set of SCULPTURE*s* made of MARBLE **3 lose one's marbles** *BrE humor sl* to become mad

marc /mɑːk‖mɑrk/ *n* [U] (a strong alcoholic drink made from) the material left after the juice has been pressed from esp. GRAPE*s* or apples

mar·ca·site /ˈmɑːkəsaɪt‖ˈmɑr-/ *n* [U] a natural substance which can be used for making a shiny sort of cheap jewellery

march¹ /mɑːtʃ‖mɑrtʃ/ *n* [*usu. pl. with sing. meaning*] (*often cap. as part of a name*) a border area, as between Scotland or Wales and England, where there was often disagreement and/or fighting over who owned the land: *the Welsh Marches*

march² *v* **1** [IØ] to walk with a regular, esp. forceful, step like a soldier: *They watched the soldiers marching.|She was very angry and marched out (of the shop).|*(fig.) *Time marches on* **2** [X9] to force to walk (away): *The little boy behaved badly, so she marched him up to bed* —see also FROGMARCH **3 Quick march!** (a command to soldiers to start marching) —**~er** *n*

march³ *n* **1** [*the*+U] the act of marching: *The soldiers went past at the march* (=marching) **2** [C] the distance covered while marching in a certain period of time: *It was a short/a day's march from the city to the camp* **3** [*the*+S (*of*)] regular movement forward: *the march of time* **4** [C] a piece of music played in regular time, as of the movements in marching **5** [C] marching by a large number of people from one place to another to make ideas or dissatisfactions public: *a hunger march* **6 line of march** *tech* the place or direction in which marchers move **7 on the march a** moving forward: *The army were on the march at 6 o'clock* **b** moving ahead and improving: *Science is on the march* **8 steal a march on (someone)** *not fml* to secretly or unexpectedly gain advantage over (someone) by acting quickly —see also FORCED **march**

March *n* [R;(C)] the third month of the year

marching or·ders /ˈ·· ˌ··/ *n* **1** [P] orders given to soldiers to move from one place to another **2** [P9] (*AmE* **walking papers**)— *BrE infml* official notice that one's services are no longer needed

mar·chio·ness /ˌmɑːʃəˈnes‖ˈmɑrʃənɨ̣s/ *n* the wife of a MARQUIS, or the title of a noblewoman of the same rank

march-past /ˈ· ·/ *n* a ceremonial march of soldiers past a person or place of importance

march with *v prep* [T1] *old use* (of a country, piece of land, etc.) to have a common border with

Mar·di gras /ˌmɑːdi ˈgrɑː‖ˈmɑrdi grɑ/ *n* [C;R] *Fr* (a feast held in some countries on) the last day before the beginning of LENT, the time when Christians eat only simple food for a few weeks; SHROVE TUESDAY

mare¹ /meəʳ/ *n* a female horse or donkey

ma·re² /ˈmɑːreɪ/ *n* **-ri·a** /rɪə/ *Lat* (*usu. cap. as part of a name*) any of several large dark areas on the surface of the moon or Mars, which look like seas

mare's nest /ˈ· ·/ *n* a discovery which proves to be untrue or valueless

mar·ga·rine /ˌmɑːdʒəˈriːn, ˌmɑːgə-‖ˈmɑrdʒərɨ̣n/ also (*infml*) **marge** /mɑːdʒ‖mɑrdʒ/— *n* [U] a food prepared from animal or vegetable fats or both, used instead of butter

mar·gin /ˈmɑːdʒɨ̣n‖ˈmɑr-/ *n* **1** one or both sides of a page near the edge, where there is no writing or printing: *to make notes in the margin of a book* **2** the area on the outside edge of a larger area: *the margin of the stream* **3** an amount above what is necessary, esp. for success: *He left home early and caught the train by a comfortable margin* **4** (in business) the difference between the buying and selling price

mar·gin·al /ˈmɑːdʒɨ̣nl‖ˈmɑr-/ *adj* **1** [Wa5;A] (printed or written) on or in a MARGIN (1) **2** [B] of small, rather than central, importance, or of small amount: *The new law will have only a marginal effect on the lives of most people* **3** [B] (of a place (SEAT) in parliament) which may be lost or won by a small number of votes, and so is quite likely to pass from the control of one political party to that of another **4** [Wa5;B] (of land) too poor to produce many crops, and farmed only when there is a special need for additional crops **5** [B] (of life, existence, etc.) led by people who have only just enough to eat and so to continue living —**~ly** *adv*

mar·gue·rite /ˌmɑːgəˈriːt‖ˌmɑr-/ *n* a type of large white flower with a yellow centre; kind of DAISY

mar·i·gold /ˈmærɨ̣gəʊld/ *n* any of several types of flower with a golden-yellow head

mar·i·jua·na, -huana /ˌmærɨ̣ˈwɑːnə, -ˈhwɑːnə/ *n* [U] the common form of the drug CANNABIS sometimes used in western countries, which is usually not very powerful in its effect. It is the dried flowers, stems, and leaves of the INDIAN HEMP plant

ma·rim·ba /məˈrɪmbə/ *n* a kind of musical instrument like a XYLOPHONE

ma·ri·na /məˈriːnə/ *n* an area near the sea where small boats can come into harbour, people can stay in hotels, etc.

mar·i·nade /ˌmærɨ̣ˈneɪd/ *n* **1** [U;C] a mixture of wine and/or VINEGAR, oil, SPICE*s*, etc., in which meat or fish can be kept and cooked, which preserves the food and gives it a special taste and softens it **2** [C] a meat or fish dish prepared in this

mar·i·nate /ˈmærɨ̣neɪt/ also **marinade** /ˈmærɨ̣neɪd/— *v* [Wv5;T1] to keep (meat or fish) in a MARINADE before cooking

ma·rine¹ /məˈriːn/ *adj* [Wa5;A] **1** of, near, living in, found in, or obtained from the sea: *The rocks are covered by marine plants* **2** of ships and their goods and trade at sea, esp. concerning the navy: *marine insurance|marine stores*

marine² *n* **1** [R9] the ships of a country which carry goods or travellers (only in the phr. **merchant/mercantile marine**) **2** [C] a soldier who serves on a naval ship **3** [C;A] a member of the Royal Marines or MARINE CORPS **4 Tell that/it to the marines!** *infml* (an expression of complete disbelief in what is said)

Marine Corps /ˌ·ˈ· ·/ *n* [*the*+GU] (in the US) a small army-like force connected to the navy

mar·i·ner /ˈmærɨnəʳ/ *n tech or poet* a sailor or seaman —see also MASTER MARINER

mar·i·o·nette /ˌmærɪəˈnet/ *n* a small figure of a person, animal, etc., moved by strings or wires at a performance in a theatre; sort of PUPPET —see picture at THEATRE

mar·i·tal /ˈmærɨtl/ *adj* [Wa5] of or concerning (the duties of) marriage —**~ly** *adv*

mar·i·time /ˈmærɨtaɪm/ *adj* [Wa5;A] **1** concerning ships or the sea **2** living or existing near the sea

mar·jo·ram /ˈmɑːdʒərəm‖ˈmɑr/ *n* [U] a plant (HERB) with sweet-smelling leaves and flowers, used in cooking to give a special taste and in the preparation of medicine

mark[1] /mɑːk‖mɑrk/ *n* **1** [C] a spot, line, or cut that spoils the natural colour or appearance of something: *His feet left (dirty) marks all over the floor* **2** [C] an object or sign serving as a guide: *We followed the marks that the car had left in the grass* —see also BOOKMARK, LANDMARK **3** [C] an action or sign showing a feeling, quality, or condition: *They stood as a mark of respect when he entered the room.|The years in prison have left their mark (on him/his character)* **4** [C] a spot on the face or body by which a person or animal can be recognized: *There were no marks on the dead body to show who it was* —see also BIRTHMARK **5** [C9] a figure or printed or written sign which shows something: *Every garment in the shop has a price mark sewn on it.|Put a question/*PUNCTUATION *mark at the end of that sentence* —see also LAUNDRY MARK, POSTMARK, TRADEMARK **6** [C] a figure, letter, or sign which represents a judgment of quality in another's piece of work, behaviour, performance in a competition, etc.: *The highest mark in the test was 9 out of 10* **7** [C] the object or place one aims at: *He fired but missed the mark/his mark* **8** [U] *fml* success (only in certain phrs.): *a man of mark* **9** [*the*+S] the suitable level of quality (in the phrs. **up to/below the mark**) **10** [(*the*) R;(C)] the starting place, esp. for a race: (fig.) *She didn't understand what to do; she's not very quick off the mark* (=not clever) **11** [C] **a** a sign, usu. in the form of a cross, made by a person who cannot write his name: *It was signed "Joan Smith, X, her mark"* **b** *humor* a signature **12** [C9] (*often cap.*) (esp. with numbers) a particular type of a machine: *The Mark 4 gun is stronger than the old Mark 3.|a new mark* **13 (give someone) full marks (for (doing) something)** to admire (an action or quality): *He went into that burning house to save the dog; I'll give him full marks for courage, if not for good sense* **14 (fall) wide of the mark a** (to be) far from the subject **b** (to be) far from being correct **15 make one's mark (on)** to gain success, fame, etc., (in) by showing one's best qualities **16 not (quite) up to the mark** not (very) well (in health) **17 On your marks, get set, go!** (used for starting a race) READY, STEADY, GO!

mark[2] *v* **1** [T1] to make a mark on, esp. one that spoils the appearance: *The hot cups have marked the table badly* **2** [IØ] to receive an unwanted mark, causing a spoiled appearance: *This table marks very easily; don't put the hot cup on it* **3** [T1] to show (by position): *The heap of stones marks the grave of a traveller* **4** [T1 (*with*) *usu. pass.*] to cover with marks, esp. on the body: *The disease marked her face for life.|*(fig.) *marked with suffering* **5** [X7] **a** to give a mark of quality: *He marked the work 10 out of 10* **b** to record the presence, absence, etc., of: *Each morning the teacher marks the pupils present, absent, or late* **6** [T1] to show (the qualities of): *She has the qualities that mark a good nurse* —see also MARKED (3) **7** [T1,6a] to pay attention to (esp. in the phr. **Mark my words**) **8** [T1] to be a sign of: *Today's ceremony marks 100 years of trade between our countries* **9 mark time a** to make the movements of marching while remaining in the same place **b** to spend time on work, business, etc., without advancing —see also MARK DOWN, MARK OFF, MARK OUT, MARK UP

mark[3] *n* a German coin

mark·down /ˈmɑːkdaʊn‖ˈmɑrk-/ *n* the amount by which a price is made lower: *The markdown price is 10 pounds less.|a markdown of £10*

mark down *v adv* [T1] **1** to note in writing **2** to reduce (goods) in price **3** to give a lower MARK[1] (6) to

marked /mɑːkt‖mɑrkt/ *adj* **1** [Wa5;B] having marks by which to be recognized: *Marked money can be recognized after being stolen* **2** [B] noticeable: *He showed a marked lack of interest.|a marked increase* **3** [Wa5;F+*by*] (typically) having: *This writer's plays are marked by a gentle humour* **4 a marked man** a man who is being watched by an enemy, and therefore likely to come to harm —**~ly** /ˈmɑːkɨdli‖ˈmɑr-/ *adv*

mark·er /ˈmɑːkəʳ‖ˈmɑr-/ *n* **1** a tool for making marks **2** an object which marks a place **3** a person or instrument marking the SCORE in a game

mar·ket[1] /ˈmɑːkɨt‖ˈmɑr-/ *n* **1** [C] a building, square, or open place where people meet to buy and sell goods, esp. food, or sometimes animals: *a cattle market|the market square* **2** [U;C] a gathering of people to buy and sell on certain days at such a place: *There's no market this week.|market day* **3** [C9] an area, country, or countries, where there is a demand for goods: *They sell to foreign markets/the home market.|They have a world market* **4** [U;C (*for*)] demand for goods: *There's no market for such goods.|*(fig.) *He can't find a market for his skills* **5** [C] (the state of) trade in certain goods, esp. the rate of buying and selling: *We'll lose money by selling on a falling market* (=when prices are falling).*|There's great activity in the tea market* **6 in the market (for)** ready to buy **7 on the market** (of goods) for sale **8 play the market** to buy and sell business shares to try to make a profit

market[2] *v* **1** [IØ] *esp. AmE* to do shopping (esp. in the phr. **go marketing**) **2** [T1] to offer for sale: *The firm markets many types of goods* —**~able** *adj* —**~ability** /ˌmɑːkɨtəˈbɪlɨti‖ˌmɑr-/ *n* [U]

mar·ket·eer /ˌmɑːkɨˈtɪəʳ‖ˌmɑr-/ *n* [C9] *not fml* a person who supports a certain sort of MARKET[1] (3,5)

mar·ket·er /ˈmɑːkɨtəʳ‖ˈmɑr-/ *n* a person or firm that sells a product

market gar·den /ˌ·· ˈ··/ (*AmE* **truck farm**)— *n BrE* a large area for growing vegetables and fruit for sale —**~er** *n* —**~ing** *n* [U]

mar·ket·ing /ˈmɑːkɨtɪŋ‖ˈmɑr-/ *n* [U] **1** the various activities by which goods are supplied, advertised, and sold **2** *esp. AmE* shopping

mar·ket·place /ˈmɑːkɨtpleɪs‖ˈmɑr-/ *n* **1** [C] an open area where a market is held, esp. a square **2** [*the*+R] the place where goods are sold to the public (as opposed to where they are made, sent out, etc.)

market price /ˌ·· ˈ·/ *n* the price which a range of buyers will pay for something

market re·search /ˌ·· ·ˈ·‖ˌ·· ˈ··/ *n* [U] the activity which studies what people buy and why, usu. done by firms so that they can find ways of increasing sales

market town /ˈ·· ·/ *n* a town where a market is

held, esp. one for buying and selling sheep, cattle, etc.

mark·ing /ˈmɑːkɪŋ‖ˈmɑr-/ *n* [C *usu. pl.*; (U)] (one of a set of) coloured marks on an animal's skin, fur, or feathers

marking ink /ˈ·· ·/ *n* [U] special ink for marking names on cloth, which does not wash off easily

mark off *v adv* [T1] **1** to make into a separate area by drawing lines **2** to note (something) as being done, esp. on a list

mark out *v adv* [T1] **1** to draw (an area) with lines: *They marked out the tennis court with white paint* **2** [(*for*)] to show or choose (someone) as suitable to have, get, etc. (usu. future advance, esp. in work): *His courage and determination mark him out for high rank at an early age*

marks·man /ˈmɑːksmən‖ˈmɑrks-/ (*fem.* **marks·wom·an** /-ˌwʊmən/)— *n* **-men** /mən/ a person who can hit the right mark easily, usu. with a gun

marks·man·ship /ˈmɑːksmənʃɪp‖ˈmɑrks-/ *n* [U] the quality or ability of a MARKSMAN; skill in shooting

mark·up /ˈmɑːk-ʌp‖ˈmɑrk-/ *n* the amount by which a price is raised: *a markup of 20 pence*

mark up *v adv* [T1] to raise (goods) in price

marl /mɑːl‖mɑrl/ *n* [U] a type of soil formed of clay and lime

mar·line·spike /ˈmɑːlənspaɪk‖ˈmɑr-/ *n* a pointed iron rod which seamen use for separating the twisted threads of a rope so that it can be joined to another

mar·ma·lade /ˈmɑːməleɪd‖ˈmɑr-/ *n* [U] a type of sticky sweet food (JAM) which is spread on bread, made from oranges or like fruits

mar·mo·re·al /mɑːˈmɔːrɪəl‖mɑrˈmor-/ *adj* [Wa5] *lit* of or like MARBLE, esp. as being white and/or cool

mar·mo·set /ˈmɑːməzet‖ˈmɑrməset, -zet/ *n* any of several types of very small monkey from Central and South America, with a lot of hair and large eyes —see picture at PRIMATE[2]

mar·mot /ˈmɑːmət‖ˈmɑr-/ *n* a type of small animal related to the SQUIRREL

ma·ro·cain /ˌmærəˈkeɪn‖ˈmærəkeɪn/ *n* [U] a material for making dresses, with a pattern of lines on the surface

ma·roon[1] /məˈruːn/ *n* (in former times) a slave of black West Indian origin, who has run away from his master

maroon[2] *v* [T1] **1** to put (someone) off a ship in a place where no one lives **2** [*usu. pass.*] to leave (one or more people) alone, with no means of getting away

maroon[3] *n, adj* [U;B] (of) a very dark red-brown colour

maroon[4] *n* a small ROCKET that explodes high in the air, used as a signal, esp. at sea

mar·quee /mɑːˈkiː‖mɑr-/ *n* a large tent, esp. for public performances or showing flowers, animals, etc., in competitions, or for eating and drinking at outdoor public events

mar·quet·ry /ˈmɑːkətri‖ˈmɑr-/ *n* [U] (the art of making) a type of pattern in wood, in which different coloured pieces are fitted together, esp. on the surface of furniture

mar·quis, marquess /ˈmɑːkwəs‖ˈmɑr-/ *n* (the title of) a nobleman of high rank: *the Marquis of Bath* —see also MARCHIONESS

mar·ram grass /ˈmærəm grɑːs‖-græs/ *n* [U] a type of tall grass that grows by the sea

mar·riage /ˈmærɪdʒ/ *n* [C;U] **1** the union of a man and woman by a ceremony in law: *Marriage by a priest is lawful in England without another ceremony* **2** the state of being so united: *Marriage is for life* (=it should last all one's life)/*a serious business*

mar·ria·gea·ble /ˈmærɪdʒəbəl/ *adj* [Wa5] *fml* (esp. of girls) suitable (in age, character, appearance, etc.) for marriage —**-bility** /ˌmærɪdʒəˈbɪləti/ *n* [U]

marriage lines /ˈ·· ·/ *n* [P] *not fml* the official paper (CERTIFICATE) which proves that a marriage has taken place

mar·ried /ˈmærid/ *adj* [Wa5] **1** [B] having a husband or wife —compare UNMARRIED **2** [F+*to*] having as a husband/wife: (fig.) *He's married to his work* (=gives it all his attention) **3** [A] of the state of marriage: *married life*

mar·row /ˈmærəʊ/ *n* **1** [U] the soft fatty substance in the hollow centre of bones: *It was so cold that he felt frozen to the marrow* (=as if the cold had entered his bones) **2** [*the*+R (*of*)] the most important and necessary part **3** [C] also **vegetable marrow**, (*AmE*) **squash**— a type of dark green vegetable which can grow very big along the ground —see picture at VEGETABLE[1]

mar·row·bone /ˈmærəʊbəʊn/ *n* a bone containing (a lot of) MARROW which can be used in cooking

mar·row·fat /ˈmærəʊfæt/ also **marrowfat pea** /ˌ··· ˈ·/— *n* a large kind of PEA

mar·ry /ˈmæri/ *v* **1** [T1;IØ] to take (a person) in marriage: *He married late in life/never married.*| (fig.) *She married money* (=a rich man) **2** [T1] (of a priest or official) to perform the ceremony of marriage for (2 people): *An old friend married them* **3** [T1 (*to*)] to cause to take in marriage: *She wants to marry her daughter to a rich man*

marry off *v adv* [T1 (*to*)] *not fml* to find a partner in marriage for (esp. a daughter)

Mars /mɑːz‖mɑrz/ *n* [R] the PLANET 4th in order from the sun, and next to the earth —see picture at PLANET

Mar·sa·la /mɑːˈsɑːlə‖mɑrˈsɑlə/ *n* [U] a type of sweet strong wine from Marsala in the island of Sicily

Mar·seil·laise /ˌmɑːsəˈleɪz‖ˌmɑr- (*Fr* marsɛjɛz)/ *n* [*the*+R] *Fr* the national song (ANTHEM) of France

marsh /mɑːʃ‖mɑrʃ/ *n* [C;U] (a piece of) land that is all or partly soft and wet, because of its low position

mar·shal[1] /ˈmɑːʃəl‖ˈmɑr-/ *n* **1** [C;A;N] an officer of the highest rank in certain armies and airforces **2** [C] an official appointed by a king or queen, who is in charge of making arrangements for an important public ceremony or event **3** [C] an official of the law courts, either one in charge of prisoners, or one in attendance on a judge **4** [C;A;N] (in the US) **a** an official who carries out the judgments given in a court of law; one who has the duties of a SHERIFF **b** a chief officer of a police or fire-fighting force

marshal[2] *v* **-ll-** (*AmE* **-l-**) [T1] **1** to arrange (esp. facts) in good or correct order: *He gave a good speech, in which he marshalled clearly the reasons for changing the law* **2** to lead (a person) to the correct place, esp. on a ceremonial or important occasion

marshalling yard /ˈ··· ·/ *n* a railway yard in which the parts of a train, esp. a goods train, are put together in preparation for a journey

marsh gas /ˈ· ·/ *n* [U] gas formed by dead vegetable matter under the surface of water in a MARSH; METHANE

marsh·mal·low /ˌmɑːʃˈmæləʊ‖ˈmɑrʃmeləʊ/ *n* **1** a type of plant with leaves and pink flowers, growing near MARSHes **2** a type of soft round sweet

marsh·y /ˈmɑːʃi‖ˈmɑr-/ *adj* [Wa1] **1** of or like a MARSH **2** (of a place) having many MARSHES

mar·su·pi·al /mɑːˈsjuːpɪəl‖mɑrˈsuː-/ *adj, n* [Wa5] (one) of the type of animal which is born only partly developed and is carried until grown in a pocket of skin (POUCH) on the mother's body

mart /mɑːt‖mart/ *n* (*sometimes in comb.*) a market; place of trade, esp. a busy one
mar·ten /ˈmɑːtǩn, -tn‖ˈmartn/ *n* **1** [C] any of several types of small flesh-eating animal, kept or hunted for their fur **2** [U] the fur of these animals
mar·tial /ˈmɑːʃəl‖ˈmar-/ *adj* [A;(B)] **1** of or concerning war, soldiers, etc. **2** *fml or pomp* ready to fight —**~ly** *adv*
martial law /ˌ·· ˈ·/ *n* [U] government under special laws by the army, esp. when there has been fighting against the established government
Mar·tian /ˈmɑːʃən‖ˈmar-/ *adj, n* [Wa5] (a person) of the PLANET MARS, usu. in imaginary stories
mar·tin /ˈmɑːtǩn‖ˈmartn/ *n* either of 2 sorts of bird (HOUSE MARTIN and **sand martin**) of the SWALLOW family
mar·ti·net /ˌmɑːtǩˈnet‖ˌmar-/ *n* a person who demands total obedience to rules and orders
mar·ti·ni /mɑːˈtiːni‖mar-/ *n* an alcoholic drink (COCKTAIL) made by mixing GIN, VERMOUTH, and BITTERS
Mar·tin·mas /ˈmɑːtǩnməs‖ˈmar-/ *n* [R] the feast of SAINT Martin on 11th November
mar·tyr[1] /ˈmɑːtəʳ‖ˈmar-/ *n* **1** a person who by his death or sufferings proves the strength of his beliefs **2** [(*to*)] *not fml* a person who suffers, or appears to suffer, because of something he must do or experience **3** *not fml* a person who gives up his own wishes or chance of gain or who accepts something unpleasant, in order to please others, and sometimes in the hope of being praised (esp. in the phr. **make a martyr of oneself**)
martyr[2] *v* [Wv5;T1] to put to death, or cause to suffer greatly, for a belief
mar·tyr·dom /ˈmɑːtədəm‖ˈmartər-/ *n* [U] **1** the state of being a MARTYR[1] (1) **2** the death or suffering of a MARTYR[1] (1) **3** (a time of) great suffering
mar·vel[1] /ˈmɑːvəl‖ˈmar-/ *n* **1** [(*of*)] a wonder; wonderful thing or example: *The operation was a marvel of medical skill.|the marvels of nature|How he got there is a marvel to me* **2** *infml* a person or thing that causes surprise for some reason: *You're a marvel; how can you work so hard at your age?* **3** **work/do marvels** to succeed in doing something wonderful, or in producing wonderful results
marvel[2] *v* **-ll-** (*AmE* **-l-**) [I∅ (*at*);T5a,6a] to wonder; feel great surprise: *We marvelled at their skill*
mar·vel·lous, *AmE* **-velous** /ˈmɑːvələs‖ˈmar-/ *adj* wonderful, esp. because surprisingly good: *What marvellous weather* —**~ly** *adv*
Marx·is·m /ˈmɑːksɪzəm/ *n* [U] the teaching of Karl Marx on which COMMUNISM is based, which explains the changes in history according to the struggle between social classes —**-ist** *n, adj*
Marxism-Len·in·is·m /ˌmɑːksɪzəm ˈlenǩnɪzəm/ *n* [U] MARXISM as explained, added to, and practised by Lenin —**Marxist-Leninist** *n, adj*
mar·zi·pan /ˈmɑːzǩpæn‖ˈmartsǩ-, ˈmarzǩ-/ *n* **1** [U] a very sweet paste, used for making some sweets and for putting on top of cakes, in which ALMOND nuts in powder form, sugar, and egg are mixed **2** [C] a small sweet or cake made from this
masc. *written abbrev. for:* MASCULINE —compare FEM.
mas·ca·ra /mæˈskɑːrə‖mæˈskærə/ *n* [U] a dark coloured substance for painting and thickening the EYELASHes
mas·cot /ˈmæskət‖ˈmæskɑt/ *n* an object, an animal, or a person thought to bring good fortune
mas·cu·line[1] /ˈmæskjʊlǩn‖-kjə-/ *adj* **1** of or having the qualities suitable for a man —see FEMALE (USAGE) **2** [Wa5] (in the grammar of many languages) in or related to a class (GENDER) of words that are not FEMININE or NEUTER
masculine[2] *n* **1** a MASCULINE[1] (2) word or word form **2** the class of such words
mas·cu·lin·i·ty /ˌmæskjʊˈlɪnǩti‖-kjə-/ *n* [U] the quality or state of being MASCULINE[1] (1)
ma·ser /ˈmeɪzəʳ/ *n* an apparatus for producing very powerful electric force —compare LASER
mash[1] /mæʃ/ *n* **1** [C;U] a mixture of grain, BRAN, etc., with water forming a soft mass, used as food for animals **2** [U] a mixture of MALT with hot water, used in making beer **3** [U] *not fml* MASHed[2] potatoes
mash[2] *v* [Wv5;T1] to crush into a soft substance: *mashed potatoes* (=crushed after cooking in boiling water)
mash·ie /ˈmæʃi/ *n becoming rare* a CLUB[1] (4) with an iron head, used in the game of GOLF for hitting the ball so that it rises high in the air before hitting the ground
mask[1] /mɑːsk‖mæsk/ *n* **1** a covering for the face, or for the upper or lower part of it, which hides or protects it, esp. so as to avoid being recognized, to protect the wearer from dangerous substances, or to protect others from infection —see also GAS MASK, FENCING (USAGE) **2** a covering like a face, often of paper, as worn by some actors, by children in play, and in some tribal religious and magical ceremonies —see also DEATH MASK **3** [(*of*)] an appearance which hides the truth or reality; any form of pretending: *He hid his hatred for his master under a mask of loyalty* **4** *tech* (in hunting) a fox's face
mask[2] *v* [T1] **1** to cover with a MASK **2** to hide (esp. feelings): *His smile masked his anger*
masked /mɑːskt‖mæskt/ *adj* [Wa5] (with people) wearing MASKs: *masked men|a masked* BALL
masking tape /ˈ·· ·/ *n* [U] sticky material in a long narrow band, which can be used for covering the edge of an area one wishes to leave unpainted when one is painting a surface
mas·o·chis·m /ˈmæsəkɪzəm/ *n* [U] the wish to be hurt so as to gain (sexual) pleasure —compare SADISM —**-chist** *n* —**-chistic** /ˌmæsəˈkɪstɪk/ *adj*
ma·son /ˈmeɪsən/ *n* **1** STONEMASON **2** (*usu. cap.*) FREEMASON
Mason-Dix·on line /ˌmeɪsən ˈdɪksən laɪn/ *n* [*the*+R] the southern edge of Pennsylvania, dividing the southern states of the US from the north
ma·son·ic[1] /məˈsɒnɪk‖məˈsɑ-/ *adj* [Wa5] (*often cap.*) of or connected with FREEMASONs, their beliefs, practices, etc.
masonic[2] *n* a social gathering of FREEMASONs at which singers, actors, etc., perform
ma·son·ry /ˈmeɪsənri/ *n* [U] **1** the skill of preparing and fixing stones in building **2** a stone (part of a) building: *A fall of masonry crushed the man in the old house* **3** (*often cap.*) FREEMASONRY (1)
masque /mɑːsk‖mæsk/ *n* a form of theatrical play often performed in the 16th & 17th centuries for kings, queens, or noblemen, written in poetry and with music, dancing, and songs
mas·que·rade[1] /ˌmæskəˈreɪd/ *n* **1** a MASKED BALL **2** something pretended; hiding of the truth
masquerade[2] *v* [I∅ (*as*)] to pretend (to be): *He got a free ticket to the play by masquerading as a friend of the actors* —**-rader** *n*
mass[1] /mæs/ *n* a piece of music written specially for all the main parts of the MASS (=a Christian religious service)
mass[2] *n* **1** [C (*of*)] a quantity or heap (of matter): *The ship cut its way slowly through masses of ice.|a solid mass of earth* **2** [C (*of*), *often pl. with sing. meaning*] *not fml* a large number (of people or things): *Her garden is a mass of flowers.|There are masses of people in here* **3** [U] (in science) the amount of matter in a body, measured by the

power used in changing its movement **4 in the mass** considered as a whole

mass[3] *v* [T1;I∅] to gather together in large numbers: *Crowds massed along the road where the queen would pass.|Dark clouds massed, and we expected rain*

mass[4] *adj* [Wa5:A] of or for a mass, esp. of people: *a mass murderer* (=one who has killed lots of people)|*a mass meeting*

Mass *n* [(*the*) C;U] (used in the CATHOLIC and ORTHODOX churches) the EUCHARIST

mas·sa·cre[1] /'mæsəkəʳ/ *n* **1** a merciless killing of large numbers, usu. of people who cannot defend themselves properly **2** *infml* a severe defeat

massacre[2] *v* [T1] **1** to kill (a number of people) without mercy: (fig.) *He made a powerful speech, massacring his opponents* **2** *infml* to defeat severely

mas·sage[1] /'mæsɑːʒ‖mə'sɑːʒ/ *n* **1** [U] the system of treating a person's body by pressing and rubbing one's hands (or feet) on it to take away pain or stiffness from the muscles and joints **2** [C] an example of this

massage[2] *v* [T1] to give a MASSAGE to (someone or a part of the body)

mass·es /'mæsɨz/ *n* [*the*+P] the lower classes of society: *He spent his life trying to improve the living conditions of the masses*

mas·seur /mæ'sɜːʳ, mə-/ (*fem.* **mas·seuse** /mæ'sɜːz, mə-/)— *n* a man who gives MASSAGE*s*

mas·sif /'mæsiːf‖mæ'siːf/ *n tech* a group of mountains forming one mass

mas·sive /'mæsɪv/ *adj* **1** of great size; strong and heavy **2** (esp. of the head) large and solid-seeming **3** (of qualities and actions) great; powerful: *We must make massive efforts to improve things* —**~ly** *adv* —**~ness** *n* [U]

mass me·di·a /ˌ· '···/ *n* [*the*+GU] the modern means of giving news and opinions to large numbers of people, esp. radio and television —see MEDIA (USAGE)

mass-pro·duce /ˌ· ·'·/ *v* [Wv5;T1] to produce (goods) in large numbers to the same pattern: *Mass-produced furniture is cheaper than furniture made one piece at a time by hand*

mass pro·duc·tion /ˌ· ·'··/ *n* [U] the making of large numbers of the same article by a fixed method

mass·y /'mæsi/ *adj* [Wa1] *tech or lit and poet* heavy; of great MASS[2] (3)

mast[1] /mɑːst‖mæst/ *n* **1** a long upright pole of wood or metal for carrying flags or sails on a ship —see pictures at SAIL[2] and FREIGHTER **2** a flagpole anywhere —see also HALF-MAST **3** an upright metal framework for radio and television AERIAL*s*

mast[2] *n* [U] nuts from forest trees such as the OAK, which pigs eat from the ground

mas·tec·to·my /mæ'stektəmi/ *n* **1** an operation for the removal of a breast **2** the state resulting from this

mas·ter[1] /'mɑːstəʳ‖'mæ-/ *n* **1** [C (*of*)] a man in control of people, animals, or things: *After hard fighting, the defenders were still masters of the city* —compare RINGMASTER **2** [C] (*fem.* **mistress**)— a man who is the head of a house and family **3** [C] a man who commands, or has the right to command, a ship carrying goods or people, or a large fishing boat; MASTER MARINER **4** [C9] (*fem.* **mistress**)— *esp. fml and old use* a male teacher **5** [C9] (*fem* **mistress**)— a man who owns an animal **6** [C] a man who employs workmen or servants —see also MAN[1] (5) **7** [A] a skilled workman with his own business: *a master builder* **8** [C] a man of great skill in art or work with the hands: *a master* CRAFTSMAN| *The painting is the work of a master/ done by a master hand* —see also OLD MASTER, GRAND MASTER **9** [C;N] (*usu. cap.*) the title of a head of certain male university colleges **10 one's own master** independent in work or action

master[2] *adj* [Wa5;A] chief; most important: *the large master bedroom*

master[3] *v* [T1] **1** to gain control over: *The horse tried to run away, but Paul succeeded in mastering it* **2** to gain as a skill: *He never mastered the art of public speaking*

Master *n* [A] *becoming rare* (a title for addressing) a young boy (as on the address of a letter): *Master John Smith, 4 New Road*

master-at-arms /ˌ·· · '·/ *n* **masters-at-arms** an officer with police duties in a ship, either naval or one carrying passengers

master card /'·· ·/ *n* **1** a playing card that cannot be beaten by another in the game **2** a specially good reason, piece of knowledge, etc., which will have more effect than anything else

mas·ter·ful /'mɑːstəfəl‖'mæstər-/ *adj* having or showing an ability or wish to control others: *He spoke in a masterful manner* —compare MASTERLY —**~ly** *adv*

master key /ˌ·· '·/ *n* a key that will open several different locks

mas·ter·ly /'mɑːstəli‖'mæstərli/ *adj* showing great skill: *a masterly speech* —compare MASTERFUL —**-liness** *n* [U]

master mar·i·ner /ˌ·· '···/ *n* (the official title for) a seaman in command of, or having the right to command, a ship carrying goods or travellers

mas·ter·mind[1] /'mɑːstəmaɪnd‖'mæstər-/ *n not fml* a very clever person

mastermind[2] *v* [T1] *infml* to plan (a course of action), usu. in detail and cleverly: *to mastermind a crime*

Master of Arts /ˌ·· · '·/ *n* MA

master of ce·re·mo·nies /ˌ·· · '····/ *n* (*often caps.*) a person whose duty is to see that ceremonies are carried out properly at a public social occasion

Master of Hounds /ˌ·· · '·/ *n* a man in charge of a group who go foxhunting

Master of Science /ˌ·· · '··/ *n* MSC

mas·ter·piece /'mɑːstəpiːs‖'mæstər-/ also **mas·ter·work** /-wɜːk‖-wɜrk/— *n* a piece of work, esp. art, which is the best of its type or the best a person has done

mas·ter's /'mɑːstəz‖'mæstərs/ *n* **master's** [Wn3] *infml esp. AmE* (*often cap.*) a degree of MASTER OF ARTS, MASTER OF SCIENCE, etc.

mas·ter·ship /'mɑːstəʃɪp‖'mæstər-/ *n* **1** [U] the state of having command or control **2** [C] *fml & old use* the position, duties, etc., of a schoolmaster

mas·ter·stroke /'mɑːstəstrəʊk‖'mæstər-/ *n* an action done with great skill which results in complete success

mas·ter·y /'mɑːstəri‖'mæ-/ *n* [U (*over, of*)] control (over) or skill (in): *The enemy had complete mastery of the seas and no ships could get through*

mast·head /'mɑːsthed‖'mæst-/ *n* the top of a (ship's) MAST

mas·tic /'mæstɪk/ *n* [U] **1** a substance from the juice (RESIN) of a tree which is used to make colourless shiny paint (VARNISH) **2** a substance used for preventing liquid from entering or escaping, as from the points where pipes are joined

mas·ti·cate /'mæstɨkeɪt/ *v* [I∅;T1] *fml* to bite on and through (food); CHEW —**-cation** /ˌmæstɨ'keɪʃən/ *n* [U]

mas·tiff /'mæstɨf/ *n* a type of large powerful dog, which can be used for guarding houses

mas·ti·tis /mæs'taɪtɨs/ *n* [U] swelling (INFLAMMATION) of the breast or the part of the female body that produces milk

mas·to·don /'mæstədɒn‖-dɑn/ *n* a type of large

animal like an elephant, which lived 1,000s of years ago —compare MAMMOTH

mas·toid /'mæstɔɪd/ *n* **1** [(*the*)] also **mastoid bone** /'·· ·/— a small round point of bone behind the ear **2** *infml* a case of MASTOIDITIS

mas·toid·i·tis /ˌmæstɔɪ'daɪtɨ̣s/ *n* [U] pain and swelling (INFLAMMATION) behind the ear

mas·tur·bate /'mæstəbeɪt‖-ər-/ *v* [IØ;T1] to excite the sex organs (of) by handling, rubbing, etc. —**-bation** /ˌmæstə'beɪʃən‖-ər-/ *n* [U] —**-batory** /ˌmæstə'beɪtəri‖'mæstərbətori/ *adj* [Wa5]

mat¹ /mæt/ *n* **1** a piece of rough strong material, such as rope or rubber, used for covering part of a floor —see also DOORMAT **2** a very small RUG or piece of CARPET **3** a small piece of material, either strong or delicate, used for putting under objects on a table or other wooden surface: *Put the hot dish down on the mat, so you don't spoil the table* —see also TABLEMAT **4** [(*of*), *usu. sing.*] a twisted mass, esp. of hair **5 on the mat** *infml* punished by the person in charge —compare **on the** CARPET

mat² *v* **-tt-** [Wv5;IØ;T1] to (cause to) become twisted in a thick mass: *matted hair*

mat³, matt, *AmE* **matte** *adj* [Wa5] of a dull, not shiny, surface: *These photographs have a mat* FINISH

mat·a·dor /'mætədɔːʳ/ *n* the man who kills the BULL in the sport of BULLFIGHTING

match¹ /mætʃ/ *n* **1** [S (*for*)] a person who is equal in strength, ability, etc., (to another): *I'm good at tennis and I'm a match for any player/but I'm no match for an international player* **2** [S] **a** something like or suitable to something else: *We can't find a match for this ornament* **b** a number of things suitable together: *The hat and shoes are a perfect match* **3** [C9 *usu. sing.*] *esp. old use* **a** a person considered as a possible husband or wife **b** a marriage (esp. in the phr. **make a match**): *Both her daughters made good matches* **4** [C] a game or sports event where teams or people compete —see HOBBY (USAGE) **5 find/meet one's match a** to meet a person of equal skill, strength, etc., whom it is difficult to beat **b** to meet something very difficult to do, for which one's skill may not be enough **6 make a match of it** (of 2 people) to get married

match² *v* **1** [T1 (*in, for*)] **a** to be equal to (a person) (in a quality): *You can't match him in knowledge of wild plants/his knowledge of wild plants* **b** to find an equal for: *This hotel can't be matched for good service and food* **2** [IØ (UP); T1] to be like or suitable for use with (something else): *The curtains don't match the paint* **3** [T1 (UP)] to find something like or suitable for use with: *I need some yellow wool like this; can you match it, please?* **4** [T1 (*against*)] to cause to compete (with): *He matched his dog against his neighbour's in a race* **5** [T1 (*with*)] *esp. old use* to arrange a marriage for (someone) **6 well-/ill-matched a** suitable/not suitable to be with each other **b** like/not like each other in strength, skill, etc., so as to be able/not to be able to compete well together

match³ *n* a short thin stick, usu. of wood, with a head covered by chemicals which flame when rubbed or struck against a rough surface and cause the stick to burn

match·box /'mætʃbɒks‖-bɑks/ *n* a small box in which matches are sold, with rough material along one or both sides on which to strike them

match·ing /'mætʃɪŋ/ *adj* [Wa5;A] (esp. of colours and appearance) which are the same or suited

match·less /'mætʃləs/ *adj* [Wa5] which has or could have no equal in quality —**~ly** *adv*

match·lock /'mætʃlɒk‖-lɑk/ *n* a kind of gun, used esp. formerly, which was fired by lighting a FUSE

match·mak·er /'mætʃˌmeɪkəʳ/ *n* a person who likes to and tries to encourage people (who she/he thinks suitable) to marry each other —**-making** *n* [U]

match point /ˌ· '·‖'· ·/ *n* [R:(C)] the position in a game, esp. tennis, when the player who is leading wins the match if he gains the next point

match·stick /'mætʃˌstɪk/ *n* a single match, esp. a used one

match up to *v adv prep* [T1] to be of as high a quality as (something expected): *It wasn't a bad holiday, but the weather didn't match up to our hopes*

match·wood /'mætʃwʊd/ *n* [U] **1** wood suitable for making matches **2** wood split into small thin pieces

mate¹ /meɪt/ *n, v* [C;U;T1] CHECKMATE[1,2] (1)

mate² *n* **1** [C] (*often in comb.*) a fellow workman or friend: *His mates/workmates/schoolmates waited for him by the gate* **2** [N] *BrE infml* (a way of addressing a man): *"What time is it, mate?" he shouted to the man passing by* **3** [C] (not in the navy) a ship's officer in command after the captain: *first mate|second mate* **4** [C9] a helper to a skilled workman: *a builder's mate* **5** [C] one of a male–female pair, usu. of animals

mate³ *v* [IØ;T1:(*with*)] to form (into) a couple, esp. of animals, for sexual union and the production of young: *Birds mate in the spring, the* **mating season**.| *They mated a horse with a donkey*

ma·té /'mɑːteɪ/ *n* [U] a kind of tea made from the leaves and stems of a South American plant

ma·te·ri·al¹ /mə'tɪərɪəl/ *adj* **1** [Wa5] **a** of or concerning matter or substance, not spirit: *The storm did a great deal of material damage* (=to buildings and such) **b** of the body, rather than the mind or soul: *She's too poor to satisfy her family's material needs* (=food, clothing, etc.) **2** [(*to*)] important and necessary: *We must make a material change in our plans* **3** *law* concerning information necessary for a just decision: *material* EVIDENCE|*a material witness* —**~ly** *adv*

material² *n* **1** [U;C] anything from which something is or may be made: *Rubber is a widely used material.*|*When building materials cost more, the price of houses increases* **2** [U;C] cotton or other woven cloth from which clothes may be made: *dress material|a light material* **3** [U (*for*)] knowledge of facts from which action may be taken or a (written) work may be produced: *collecting material for a book|We have material against him since we found out about the crime* **4** [U (*for*)] people considered for what they may become after training or development: *There is officer material among these new soldiers* (=some are good enough to become officers) —see also RAW MATERIAL, WRITING MATERIALS

ma·te·ri·al·is·m /mə'tɪərɪəlɪzəm/ *n* [U] **1** the belief that only matter exists, and that there is no world of the spirit **2** a state of mind or way of life which enjoys the pleasures of the world, objects which can be bought, etc., and not activities of the mind or spirit, in art and religion —**-istic** /məˌtɪərɪə'lɪstɪk/ *adj* —**-istically** *adv* [Wa4]

ma·te·ri·al·ist /mə'tɪərɪəlɨ̣st/ *adj, n* **1** (a person) who believes in MATERIALISM **2** (a person) who believes that human actions are governed by the wish to gain things for oneself

ma·te·ri·al·ize, -ise /mə'tɪərɪəlaɪz/ *v* **1** [IØ;T1] to (cause to) take on bodily form: *The shape of a man materialized out of the shadows* **2** [IØ] to become real: *He always wanted a large family, but his hopes never materialized* —**-ization** /məˌtɪərɪəlaɪ'zeɪʃən‖-lə-/ *n* [U]

ma·ter·nal /mə'tɜːnəl‖-ɜr-/ *adj* **1** [B] of, like, or natural to a mother **2** [Wa5;A;(B)] related through the mother's side of the family —**~ly** *adv*

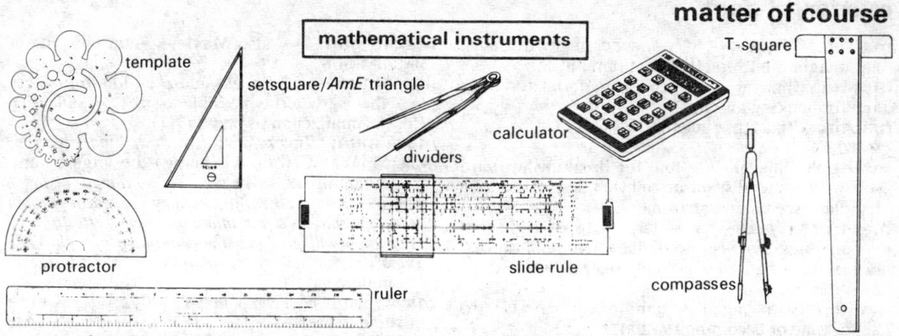

ma·ter·ni·ty /mə'tɜːnɪ̈ti‖-ɜr-/ *n* **1** [U] motherhood **2** [A] of the bodily condition of becoming a mother; for PREGNANCY and giving birth: *a maternity dress|a maternity hospital/*WARD

mat·ey /'meɪti/ *adj* [Wa1] *infml* friendly

math·e·mat·i·cal /ˌmæθə'mætɪkəl/ *adj* **1** [Wa5] of or concerning MATHEMATICS **2** (of numbers, reasoning, etc.) exactly correct —**~ly** *adv* [Wa4]

math·e·ma·ti·cian /ˌmæθəmə'tɪʃən/ *n* a person who studies and understands MATHEMATICS

math·e·mat·ics /ˌmæθə'mætɪks/ also (*BrE infml*) **maths** /mæθs/, (*AmE infml*) **math** /mæθ/— *n* [U] the study or science of numbers

mat·i·née /'mætɪ̈neɪ‖ˌmætɪ̈'neɪ/ *n* a performance of a play, music, etc., given in the afternoon

matinée coat /'··· ·/ *n* a small, usu. woollen, coat for a young baby

mat·ins, mattins /'mætɪ̈nz‖'mætnz/ *n* [GU] (*often cap.*) a service in the CHURCH OF ENGLAND, held in the morning

mat·ri- /'meɪtri, 'mætrɪ̈/ *prefix* mother: MATRICIDE| MATRIARCHY —compare PATRI-

ma·tri·arch /'meɪtriɑːk‖-ɑrk/ *n* **1** a woman who rules a family or people **2** one of the older women in a family, such as a mother or grandmother, who influences the family strongly —**~al** /ˌmeɪtri'ɑːkəl‖-'ɑr-/ *adj*

ma·tri·ar·chy /'meɪtriɑːki‖-ɑr-/ *n* [U;C] (an example of) a social system in which the (oldest) woman is head of the family, and passes possessions, powers of control, etc., on to her daughters

mat·ri·cide /'mætrɪ̈saɪd/ *n* **1** [U;C] the crime of killing one's mother **2** [C] *tech* a person who kills his/her mother

ma·tric·u·late /mə'trɪkjʊleɪt‖-kjə-/ *v* **1** [T1;I∅] to (allow to) become a member of a university, esp. after an examination or test **2** [I∅] (formerly in Britain) to take an examination which gave one the right to go to university after passing. Its place was taken by the GCE —**-lation** /məˌtrɪkjʊ'leɪʃən‖-kjə-/ *n* [U;C]

mat·ri·mo·ny /'mætrɪ̈məni‖-məʊni/ *n* [U] *fml* the state of marriage (esp. in the phr. **holy matrimony**) —**-monial** /ˌmætrɪ̈'məʊnɪəl/ *adj* [Wa5]

ma·trix /'meɪtrɪks/ *n* **matrices** /-trɪ̈siːz/ *or* **matrixes** **1** a hollow container (MOULD) into which melted metal or other suitable material is poured so that it may be formed into the right shape, such as letters for printing, RECORDS, etc. **2** the rock or stone in which hard stones or jewels have been formed **3** (in MATHEMATICS, science, etc.) an arrangement of numbers, figures, or signs in a square made up of rows **4** a living part in which something is formed or developed, such as the part below the fingernail **5** *old use* the WOMB

ma·tron /'meɪtrən/ *n* **1** [C;N] (the title of) a woman in charge of a hospital who has control over the work of all the nurses and others who work there, but not over doctors (in Britain now officially called a **senior nursing officer**) **2** [C;N] (the title of) a woman who is in charge of arrangements for children to live in a school, esp. for medical care, repair of clothes, providing sheets, etc. **3** [C] *esp. lit or old use* an older married woman, esp. one of quiet careful behaviour

ma·tron·ly /'meɪtrənli/ *adj* **1** fatter than a young girl should be **2** (of a woman) DIGNIFIED like a MATRON (3)

matt, matte /mæt/ *adj* [Wa5] MAT[3]

mat·ter[1] /'mætə^r/ *n* **1** [U] the material which makes up the world and everything in space which can be seen or touched, as opposed to thought or mind **2** [U] a subject itself as opposed to the form in which it is spoken or written about (esp. in the phr. **subject matter**) **3** [C] a (business) affair; subject to which one gives attention: *I don't talk to my employer about private matters* **4** [*the*+S] a trouble or cause of pain, illness, etc. (only in the phrs. **What's/something/nothing the matter**): *What's the matter; why are you crying?|There's nothing the matter|Nothing's the matter with me* (=nothing's wrong) **5** [U] (of) importance (only in the phr. (**make**) **no matter**): *It made no matter to him that his brother lost all his money* **6** [U] written material (esp. in the phrs. **reading matter, printed matter**) **7** [U] a yellow poisonous material from a wound or skin infection; PUS **8 a matter of** an amount (of time, distance, money, etc.) which is: *Don't worry; it's only a matter of hours till the doctor arrives* **9 a matter of life or death** something so serious that failure to do it may result in death **10 a matter of opinion** a subject on which different persons may think differently **11 as a matter of fact** really; in fact: *"I thought you wouldn't mind." "Well, as a matter of fact I do"* compare MATTER-OF-FACT **12 for that matter** also (*becoming rare*) **for the matter of that**— as further concerns the thing mentioned: *This new book will be of interest to policemen and prison officers; and, for that matter, to anyone who has to deal with criminals* **13 in the matter of** *fml* concerning (a particular thing): *The children have everything they need in the matter of clothes, but very few toys* **14 let the matter drop/rest** to take no (further) action to deal with something **15 make matters worse** to make a state of affairs more serious, more difficult to deal with, etc. **16 no laughing matter** something to be treated seriously **17 no matter (how, where, etc.)** it makes no difference **18 (a victory of) mind over matter** (an action gained by) a strong will conquering bodily weakness

matter[2] *v* [I∅] **1** [(*to*)] to be important: *It doesn't matter if I miss my train, because there's another later.|I don't think anybody matters to her apart from herself* **2** *tech* to form and give out MATTER[1] (7) or PUS: *The cut got dirty and after a few days began to matter*

matter of course /ˌ··· '·/ *n* [S] a natural or usual event: *When I go out of the house I lock the door as a matter of course* —**matter-of-course** *adj*

matter-of-fact /ˌ·· · ˈ·ˈ/ *adj* concerned with facts, not imagination; practical, not fanciful
mat·ting /ˈmætɪŋ/ *n* [U] rough material for mats and for packing goods
mat·tins /ˈmætənz‖ˈmætnz/ *n* [GU] (*often cap.*) MATINS
mat·tock /ˈmætək/ *n* a tool for breaking up hard soil with a metal head at right angles to the long handle —see picture at TOOL[1]
mat·tress /ˈmætrəs/ *n* a large bag of solid but yielding material, usu. wool, hair, feathers, rubber, or metal springs, on which one sleeps —see picture at BEDROOM
ma·tu·ra·tion /ˌmætʃʊˈreɪʃən‖ˌmætʃə-/ *n* [U] the act or time of becoming MATURE
ma·ture[1] /məˈtʃʊəʳ/ *adj* [Wa1] **1 a** fully grown and developed: *A monkey is mature at a few years old, but a human being isn't mature till at least 16* **b** typical of a fully developed mind, controlled feelings, etc.; sensible: *You mustn't be jealous when your sister gets presents; you must learn to behave in a more mature way* **2** (of cheese, wine, etc.) ready to be eaten or drunk; ripe **3** carefully decided, after a time of thought **4** *tech* (of a bill) ready to be paid —**~ly** *adv*
mature[2] also (*rare*) **mat·u·rate** /ˈmætʃʊreɪt‖ˈmætʃə-/— *v* [T1;I0] to (cause to) become MATURE: *After 6 years in bottle, the wine will have (been) fully matured*
ma·tu·ri·ty /məˈtʃʊərəti/ *n* [U] the state or time of being MATURE
maud·lin /ˈmɔːdlɪn/ *adj* showing foolish sadness in a pitiful way, esp. because of drinking alcohol, and not for good reasons
maul /mɔːl/ *v* [T1 (ABOUT)] **1** (esp. of animals) to hurt by tearing the flesh: *The hunter was mauled by a lion and badly hurt* **2** to handle roughly or in an unwelcome way: (fig.) *The minister's speech sounded quite different when the newspapers had mauled it about*
maul·stick, mahl- /ˈmɔːlˌstɪk/ *n* a stick held by a painter to support the hand which holds the brush
maun·der /ˈmɔːndəʳ/ *v* **1** [L9 (ON)] to talk in an unclear and usu. complaining way **2** [L9 esp. ABOUT] to walk or act in a tired slow unhappy way
Maun·dy Thurs·day /ˌmɔːndi ˈθɜːzdi‖-ɜr-/ *n* [R] the Thursday before EASTER when in England by an old custom the King or Queen gives **Maundy money** /ˈ·· ˌ··/ to certain poor people
mau·so·le·um /ˌmɔːsəˈlɪəm/ *n* a fine stone building (TOMB) raised over a grave, esp. that of a famous or important person
mauve /məʊv/ *adj, n* [Wa5;B;U] (of) a pale purple colour
mav·e·rick /ˈmævərɪk/ *n* **1** *AmE* a young cow without its owner's mark **2** a person who acts independently because he thinks differently from the rest of the group, esp. among politicians
maw /mɔː/ *n* **1** a bird's CROP **2** an animal's stomach, esp. the 4th stomach of a cow **3** an event which seems to draw things in and destroy them: *The war swallowed up many young men into its maw*
mawk·ish /ˈmɔːkɪʃ/ *adj* having or expressing feelings, of love, admiration, etc., in a silly way —**~ly** *adv* —**~ness** *n* [U]
max·i /ˈmæksi/ *n, adj* [Wa5;C;A] *infml* (*often in comb.*) (any woman's garment) of full length reaching to the feet
max·im /ˈmæksəm/ *n* a rule for good and sensible behaviour, esp. when expressed in a short well-known saying
max·i·mal /ˈmæksəməl/ *adj* [Wa5] as great as possible: *to make maximal use of something* —compare MINIMAL —**~ly** *adv*
Maxim gun /ˈ·· ·/ also **Maxim**— *n* an old type of MACHINEGUN
max·i·mize, -mise /ˈmæksəmaɪz/ *v* [T1] to increase to the greatest possible size —**-mization** /ˌmæksəmaɪˈzeɪʃən‖-səmə-/ *n* [U]
max·i·mum /ˈmæksəməm/ *n, adj* **-ma** /mə/ *or* **-mums** [Wa5;C (*of*); A] (being) the largest number, amount, etc.: *What's the maximum distance you've ever walked?|maximum speed|maximum depth|He smokes a maximum of 10 cigarettes a day.|This lamp will give you the maximum of light.|The sound has reached its maximum* (=is at its loudest) —compare MINIMUM
may[1] /meɪ/ *v neg. contr.* **mayn't** [Wv2;I0,2] **1** to be in some degree likely to: *He may come or he may not.|This news is so strange that you may not believe it.|"Why hasn't he come?" "He may have been hurt."* (=we still don't know whether he has or not)|"*. . . use whatever reasonable degree of force may be necessary*" (SEU W.) —compare MIGHT[1] (1) **2** to have permission to; be allowed to: *May I leave this with you?|"May I come in?" "Yes, you may."|I may say I find your questions rather rude* (=it is my opinion that they are rude) —compare MIGHT[1] (2) **3** (*usu. with the subject following the verb*) I/we hope very much that: *May there never be another world war!* **4** also **might**— (*followed by* but) although perhaps: *You may think you're very clever, but that doesn't give you the right to order me about* (=although you think you're clever, that doesn't . . .) **5** (*in* CLAUSES) **a** (*expressing purpose*) can: *Sit here, so that I may see your face more clearly* **b** (*with words expressing hope, wish, or fear*) will: *The doctor fears that she may not live much longer* —compare MIGHT[1] (3) **6** *becoming rare* MIGHT[1] **7 may well** to be very likely to: *His appearance has changed so much that you may well not recognize him.|The team may well have won the football match, but I don't know because I wasn't there* —compare MIGHT **well 8 may/might (just) as well** to have no strong reason not to: *There's nothing to do, so I may as well go to bed* —see CAN (USAGE)
may[2] *n* [U] HAWTHORN flowers
May *n* [R;(C)] the 5th month of the year
may·be /ˈmeɪbi/ *adv* [Wa5] perhaps: *"Will they come?" "Maybe not."|"Maybe it's my imagination"* (SEU S.)
may·bee·tle /ˈmeɪˌbiːtl/ also **may·bug** /ˈmeɪbʌg/— *n* a type of insect which eats young plants; COCKCHAFER
may·day /ˈmeɪdeɪ/ *n* (*sometimes cap.*) a radio signal used as a call for help from a ship or plane
May Day /ˈ· ·/ *n* [R] the 1st of May, when dances, games, etc., are held to welcome spring, and when political parties of the LEFT hold processions and public meetings
may·fly /ˈmeɪflaɪ/ *n* a type of small fly which has a short life, and is used for fishing with
may·hem /ˈmeɪhem/ *n* [U] **1** *AmE & law* serious bodily wounding, esp. that which causes a limb to be useless **2** *infml* disorder and confusion
may·n't /meɪnt/ [Wv2] *contr. of* may not: *They mayn't have arrived yet, if the traffic's been bad.|Father, mayn't I come?* —see CONTR. (USAGE)
may·on·naise /ˌmeɪəˈneɪz‖ˈmeɪəneɪz/ *n* **1** [U] a thick yellowish SAUCE with eggs, oil, milk, etc., in it, which may be poured over cold foods **2** [C; U:9] a dish which contains solid food in such a SAUCE: *egg mayonnaise*
mayor /meəʳ‖ˈmeɪər/ *n* a man or woman elected each year by a town council to be head of that city or town —**~al** *adj* [Wa5]
mayor·al·ty /ˈmeərəlti‖ˈmeɪərəlti/ *n* [U;(C)] the office of MAYOR or time during which it is held

may·or·ess /ˈmeərɨ̇s‖ˈmeɪərɨ̇s/ *n* the wife or chosen companion of a MAYOR who is a man, or a lady who is a companion to a woman MAYOR and is present with her at ceremonial occasions
may·pole /ˈmeɪpəʊl/ *n* a pole which can be ornamented with flowers and round which people dance on May 1st, esp. formerly in villages
May Queen /ˈ· ·/ *n* a girl who is queen of the dances, games, etc., on May 1st, and is crowned with flowers
mayst /meɪst/ [Wv2] **thou mayst** *old use or bibl* (when talking to one person) you may
maze /meɪz/ *n* **1** an arrangement in lines with a central point reached by twists and turns, some of them blocked, so that it is difficult to get into the centre and out again, such as a printed pattern in which one follows the lines or a garden where one follows the paths: *She was lost in the maze for several hours.|a maze of narrow winding streets|a maze of railway lines* —compare LABYRINTH **2 in a maze** in a wondering state of mind, not knowing what is going on
mazed /meɪzd/ *adj rare* wondering and unable to think clearly
ma·zur·ka /məˈzɜːkə‖-ɜr-/ *n* **1** a Polish dance to quick gay music **2** a piece of music for this
MC *abbrev. for:* MASTER OF CEREMONIES
Mc·Car·thy·is·m /məˈkɑːθi-ɪzəm‖-ɑr-/ *n* [U] (esp. formerly in America) a political plan for getting rid of any publicly known person who might be connected with COMMUNISM and (esp.) various unpleasant and unacceptable methods of finding and dealing with such people
MD *abbrev. for:* **1** Doctor of Medicine: *John Snow, MD* **2** MENTAL(ly) DEFECTIVE
me /mi; *strong* miː/ *pron* [Wp1] (*object form of* I): *He bought me a drink.|He bought a drink for me.|He wants to marry me, and me only 15!|That's me on the left of the photograph*
USAGE After *as, than,* and *be,* the object PRONOUNs **him, her, me, us, them** are used in speech, but the subject PRONOUNs **he, she, I, we, they** should be used in *fml* writing: *I'm fatter than* **him**/(*fml*) *than* **he**.|*I'm not as pretty as* **her**/(*fml*) *as* **she**.|*It's* **me**!/(*fml*) *It is* **I**. When a verb follows, one must say . . . *than* **he** *is*|. . . *as* **she** *is*, but even then there is a choice after **be**: *It was* **I** *who did it*/(*infml*) *It was* **me** *that did it.|It's* **me** *he loves*/(*fml*) *It is* **I** *whom he loves.* —see I (USAGE)
mead /miːd/ *n* [U] **1** an alcoholic drink made from HONEY and water, drunk esp. formerly in England **2** *poet* MEADOW
mead·ow /ˈmedəʊ/ *n* **1** [U] grassland on which cattle, sheep, etc., may feed **2** [C] a field of grass for animals to eat, esp. grass which is cut and dried to make HAY
mead·ow·sweet /ˈmedəʊswiːt/ *n* [U] a common type of wild flower with large heads of many little white flowers and a strong sweet smell
mea·gre, *AmE* **-ger** /ˈmiːgəʳ/ *adj* **1** (of a (part of the) body) thin; having little flesh: *He was so weak from hunger he could hardly raise his meagre arms* **2** not enough in quantity, quality, strength, etc.: *He cannot exist on his meagre income* —**~ly** *adv* —**~ness** *n* [U]
meal[1] /miːl/ *n* **1** an amount of food eaten at one time: *She cooks a hot meal in the evenings.|The dog has one meal a day* **2** the occasion of eating a meal: *The whole family meets at meals*
meal[2] *n* [U] grain which has been crushed into a powder, esp. for flour
mea·lie /ˈmiːli/ *n* [*often pl.*] *SAfrE* an ear of MAIZE
meal·time /ˈmiːltaɪm/ *n* [*usu. pl.*] the time of day for having a particular meal
meal·y /ˈmiːli/ *adj* [Wa1] **1** like or containing MEAL **2** pale in colour and/or powdery in form: *mealy potatoes* —see also FLOURY
meal·y·bug /ˈmiːlibʌg/ *n* a type of small insect which eats plants kept in hot places, esp. in a GREENHOUSE
mealy-mouthed /ˌ·· ˈ·ˈ/ *adj* of a type of person who tends to express things not freely or directly, using words which are not plain in meaning, esp. when something unpleasant must be said
mean[1] /miːn/ *adj* [Wa1] **1** [B] ungenerous; unwilling to share or help **2** [B] unkind; of unpleasant behaviour which others dislike: *Let me go out; don't be so mean to me.|I felt mean for not letting her go* (=like a mean person) **3** [A] (esp. of abilities) poor; bad (often in the phr. **no mean something**): *a man of the meanest abilities|He's no mean cook* (=he's a very good cook) **4** [B] *AmE* bad-tempered; liking to hurt: *That's a mean dog; be careful it doesn't bite you* **5** [B] *rare* poor or poor-looking, as of a building: *They could only afford the meanest of rooms in a poor area* **6** [A;(B)] *old use & rare* of low social position: *a man of mean birth* —**~ly** *adv* —**~ness** *n* [U]
mean[2] *v* **meant** /ment/ [Wv6] **1** [T1,5a] to represent (a meaning): *What does this French word mean?|The red light means "stop".|The sign means that cars cannot enter.|It doesn't mean what you thought (it meant)* **2** [T1,3,5a;V3;D1] to intend (to say); have in mind as or for a purpose: *She said Tuesday, but she meant Thursday.|I mean to go tomorrow.|He means that he wants your help.|Although he seems angry with his son, he means him nothing but good/means (him) no harm.|He is very angry and he means trouble* (=his purpose is to cause trouble) **3** [T1] to be determined about/to act on: *I mean what I say.|I said I would change things, and I meant it* **4** [T1 (*for*); V3: *usu. pass.*] to intend (to be) because of abilities, fate, etc.: *He is not meant for a soldier and will always be unhappy in the army.|His parents meant him for a priest.|He believes he is meant to be a great man* **5** [T1,4,5a] to be a sign of: *The dark clouds mean rain.|That expression means that he's angry.|His expression means trouble.|Missing the train means waiting for an hour* (=one will have to wait) **6** [T1 (*to*)] to be of importance by (a stated amount): *Does success in examinations really mean anything when considering ability for a job?|It doesn't mean a thing to her that we are all waiting because she's late.|His work means a lot/means everything to him* **7 be meant to** *esp. BrE* to have to; be supposed to: *You're meant to take your shoes off when you enter a Hindu temple* **8 mean business** *not fml* to intend seriously to act **9 mean mischief** to have evil intentions **10 mean well** to do or say what is intended to help, but often doesn't **11 mean well by someone** to intend to do what is best for someone
mean[3] *n* **1** an average amount, figure, or value: *The mean of 7, 9, and 14 is found by adding them together and dividing by 3* **2** a state or way of behaviour or course of action which is not too strong or weak, too much or too little, but in between, in the middle position (esp. in the phr. **the golden mean**) —see also HAPPY MEDIUM
mean[4] *adj* [Wa5;A] average: *The mean yearly rainfall is 20 inches* —see also GREENWICH MEAN TIME
me·an·der /miˈændəʳ/ *v* [L9;(I∅)] **1** (of rivers and streams) to flow slowly, turning here and there **2** (of people or talk) to speak or move on in a slow aimless way —**~ingly** *adv*
me·an·der·ings /miˈændərɪŋz/ *n* [P] a wandering course or movement
mean·ing[1] /ˈmiːnɪŋ/ *n* [U;C] **1** the idea which is intended to be understood: *Explain the meanings of*

these foreign words . . .|What's the meaning of this? (=explain this to me) *Why have you left all your clothes untidily on the floor?* **2** importance or value: *He says his life has lost its meaning (for him) since his wife died*

meaning² *adj* **1** [A] which gives an effect of important (hidden) meaning or thought: *When she asked if she had passed the examination the teacher said he couldn't tell her, but gave her a meaning smile* **2** [B9] (*in comb.*) with the stated intentions: *well-meaning|*ILL*-meaning*

mean·ing·ful /ˈmiːnɪŋfəl/ *adj* of important meaning; containing information —**~ly** *adv* —**~ness** *n* [U]

mean·ing·less /ˈmiːnɪŋləs/ *adj* without meaning or purpose —**~ly** *adv* —**~ness** *n* [U]

means /miːnz/ *n* **means** **1** [Wn3;C (*of*) *often pl. with sing. meaning*] a method or way (of doing): *The quickest means of travel is by plane* **2** [P] money, income, or wealth, esp. large enough for comfort: *Have you the means to support a wife?|a man of means|private means* (=income not worked for, but from rent, one's family, etc.) **3 by all means** certainly; please do **4 by fair means or foul** by using any methods, good or bad, to have a certain success **5 by means of** by using: *She could not speak, but made her wishes known by means of signs* **6 a by no means** not at all: *I am by no means pleased with this behaviour* **b by no manner of means** in no way: *I can by no manner of means pretend to be pleased with this behaviour* **7 live within/beyond one's means** to spend not more than/more than one can afford **8 a means to an end** a way, good or bad, of getting a certain result **9 the end(s) justifies/justify the means** a bad action is allowable if the result is good **10 ways and means** various methods, as of collecting money to do (government) work: *The ways and means committee raised £200 for a new sports building* —see also WAYS AND MEANS

USAGE When it means "a way to an end" this word is used with either a sing. or a pl. verb according to the words before it: *Every/One* **means** *has not been tried.|This is a dangerous* **means**.|*All/Such* **means** *are unpleasant.* When it means "money or material possessions", **means** is always pl.: *Her* **means** *are small.*

means test /ˈ· ·/ *n often derog, esp. BrE* an inquiry into the amount of money a person has, when he needs money from the state

meant /ment/ *past t. and p. of* MEAN

-meant *comb. form* (of actions, words, etc.) showing a good/bad intention: *well-meant|*ILL*-meant*

mean·time /ˈmiːntaɪm/ *n* [*the*+R] the time between (2 events) (esp. in the phr. **in the meantime**)

mean time /ˌ· ˈ·ˈ/ *n* see GREENWICH MEAN TIME

mean·while /ˈmiːnwaɪl/ also (*infml*) **meantime**— *adv* [Wa5] **1** in the MEANTIME: *They'll be here in 10 minutes. Meanwhile, we'll have some coffee* **2** during the same period of time: *Eve was cutting the grass, and Adam was meanwhile planting roses*

mea·sles /ˈmiːzəlz/ *n* [(*the*) U] an infectious disease in which the sufferer has a fever and small red spots on the face and body

meas·ly /ˈmiːzli/ *adj* [Wa1] *infml* of small value, size, etc. —**-liness** *n* [U]

mea·su·ra·ble /ˈmeʒərəbəl/ *adj* [Wa5] which is large enough or not too large to be reasonably measured —**-bly** *adv* [Wa3,5]

mea·sure¹ /ˈmeʒəʳ/ *n* **1** [U] a system for calculating amount, size, weight, etc.: *An* OUNCE *in liquid measure is different from an* OUNCE *in dry measure* **2** [C] an amount in such a system: *An hour is a measure of time* **3** [C9] an instrument or apparatus used for calculating amount, length, weight, etc., esp. a stick or container: *The glass is a litre measure.|The ruler is a foot measure* —see also TAPE MEASURE **4** [U;S:+*of*] a certain amount: *He has not become rich in business, but he has had a certain measure of success/some measure of success* **5** [U] true amount or quality: *There are no words to express the full measure of my gratitude* **6** [C *often pl.*] an action taken to gain a certain end: *This medicine may not help him, but it is the only measure I can take before the doctor comes.|If he refuses to pay I shall take measures against him* **7** [C] a law suggested in Parliament **8** [C] a musical BAR or poetic pattern of sounds which are repeated (METRE) **9 beyond measure** great without limit **10 for good measure** in addition **11 full/short measure** the right/less than the right amount **12 hard/strong measures** firm actions which cause some suffering **13 in some/a great (large) measure** to a certain/a great degree **14 take someone's measure/get the measure of someone** to judge what someone is like, esp. by comparing his abilities or character with one's own **15 tread a measure** *old use* to dance —see also MADE-TO-MEASURE

measure² *v* **1** [IØ;T1] to find the size, length, amount, degree, etc., (of) in standard measurements **2** [T1] to consider carefully (the effect of): *She works hard and doesn't measure the cost* (=harm) *to her health* **3** [L1] to be of a certain size: *He measures more round the waist than he used to* **4 measure one's length** *not fml* to fall flat on the ground **5 measure one's strength (with someone)** to fight or struggle (against someone) **6 measure swords (with someone)** to fight (against someone) **7 measure one's wits (against someone)** to struggle to find if one is cleverer (than someone)

measure a·gainst *v prep* [D1] to see if the size of (something) is right by comparing with (something else): *I measured the coat against her and found it was too long*

mea·sured /ˈmeʒəd‖-ərd/ *adj* careful; exact; steady: *He spoke in measured words*

mea·sure·less /ˈmeʒələs‖-ər-/ *adj esp. lit* limitless; too great to be measured

mea·sure·ment /ˈmeʒəmənt‖-ər-/ *n* **1** [U] the act of measuring **2** [C *usu. pl.*] a length, height, etc., found by measuring: *Which measurement shall I take first—along the room or across it?*

measure off *v adv* [T1] to mark (the limit of length): *He measured off 6 yards of material*

measure out *v adv* [T1] to give (a certain quantity): *She measured out the flour, butter, and sugar and started to mix a cake*

measure up *v adv* [IØ (*to*)] to show good enough qualities (for): *He didn't measure up to the job*

meat /miːt/ *n* [U] **1** the flesh of animals, apart from fish and birds, which is eaten **2** the flesh of animals, including birds but not fish, as opposed to their bones: *There's not much meat on that bone/chicken* **3** *old use* food (esp. in the phr. **meat and drink**) **4** valuable matter, ideas, etc.: *It was a clever speech, but there was no real meat in it* **5 cold meats** also **cooked meats, sliced meats**— meat foods like SALAMI and HAM which are cooked or prepared in a large piece but cut into thin pieces and eaten cold —compare COLD CUTS **6 be meat and drink to** to be something which gives great enjoyment to

USAGE There is often a special word for the flesh of a creature considered as food, which is different from the name of that creature when it is alive: **Chicken** is the only one of these words that is also used of the creature when it is alive: *to feed the* **hens**/*the* **chickens**. **Lamb** is the word both for a young sheep and for its meat: *some dear little* **lambs**/*a piece of* **lamb.**

meat·ball /ˈmiːtbɔːl/ *n* a small round ball made out

of finely cut-up meat, several of which may be eaten together at a meal

meat·y /ˈmiːti/ *adj* [Wa1] **1** full of meat **2** full of valuable ideas —**meatiness** *n* [U]

mec·ca /ˈmekə/ *n* [C9, esp. *of*] (*often cap.*) a place that many people wish to reach: *Lord's (cricket ground) is the cricketer's mecca*

me·chan·ic /mɪˈkænɪk/ *n* a person who is skilled in using, repairing, etc., machinery

me·chan·i·cal /mɪˈkænɪkəl/ *adj* **1** [Wa5] of, connected with, moved, worked, or produced by machinery **2** (of people or their acts) as if moved by machinery; by habit, not will: *He was asked the same question so many times that the answer became mechanical* —**~ly** *adv* [Wa4]

me·chan·ics /mɪˈkænɪks/ *n* **1** [U] the science of the action of forces on objects **2** [U] the science of making machines **3** [(*the*) P (*of*)] the ways of producing or doing: *she has natural ability, but has yet to learn the mechanics of her chosen work* —compare TECHNIQUE

mech·a·nis·m /ˈmekənɪzəm/ *n* **1** [C] the different parts of a machine arranged together, and the action they have: *The clock doesn't go; there's something wrong with the mechanism* **2** [C] the arrangement and action which parts have in a whole: *the mechanism of the brain* **3** [U] the belief that living things are controlled only by chemical and other material forces

mech·a·nis·tic /ˌmekəˈnɪstɪk/ *adj* **1** [Wa5] of or like machinery or MECHANISMs **2** of the belief that all actions of living things can be explained by forces and results, as in machines —**~ally** *adv* [Wa4]

mech·a·nize, -nise /ˈmekənaɪz/ *v* [T1] to supply machines to, instead of using the effort of human beings or animals for work on —**-nization** /ˌmekənaɪˈzeɪʃən‖-nə-/ *n* [U]

med·al /ˈmedl/ *n* a round flat piece of metal, or a cross, with a picture and/or words marked on it, which is usu. given to a person as an honour for an act of bravery or strength, or which is made in memory of something important

me·dal·li·on /mə̇ˈdæliən/ *n* a round MEDAL like a large coin, or a pattern like this, used for ornament

med·al·list, *AmE* **medalist** /ˈmedələ̇st/ *n* a person who has won a (certain sort of) MEDAL, esp. in sport

med·dle /ˈmedl/ *v* [IØ (*in, with*)] to interest oneself or take action (in affairs or with what belongs to someone else) when it is not one's concern; INTERFERE —**-dler** *n*

med·dle·some /ˈmedlsəm/ *adj* in the habit of meddling (MEDDLE) —**~ness** *n* [U]

me·di·a /ˈmiːdɪə/ *n* [(*the*) GU] the newspapers, television, and radio; MASS MEDIA

USAGE **Media** and **mass media** are now beginning to be used with a sing. verb, but many people still think this is bad English.

med·i·ae·val /ˌmediˈiːvəl‖ˌmiː-/ *adj* [Wa5] MEDIEVAL

me·di·al /ˈmiːdɪəl/ *adj* [Wa5;A;(B)] **1** in the middle position: *a medial consonant* (=between 2 vowels) **2** average —**~ly** *adv*

me·di·an¹ /ˈmiːdɪən/ *n tech* a line passing from a point of a 3-sided figure (TRIANGLE) to the centre of the opposite side

median² *adj* [Wa5;A] *tech* in or passing through the middle

me·di·ate /ˈmiːdieɪt/ *v* [IØ (*between*); T1] to act as a peacemaker coming between opposing sides to bring about (peace, agreement, etc.): *The government mediated between the workers and the employers.|The army leaders have mediated peace|a* CEASE-FIRE|*a settlement* —**-ation** /ˌmiːdiˈeɪʃən/ *n* [U] —**-ator** /ˈmiːdieɪtəʳ/ *n*

med·ic /ˈmedɪk/ *n infml* **1** a medical student **2** *esp. AmE* a soldier with medical duties —compare MEDICO

med·i·cal¹ /ˈmedɪkəl/ *adj* [Wa5] **1** of or concerning medicine and treating the sick: *a medical student|a medical examination* (=of the body by a doctor) **2** of the treatment of disease by methods other than operation —compare SURGICAL —**~ly** *adv* [Wa4]

See next page for picture

medical² *n infml* a medical examination (of the body)

me·dic·a·ment /mɪˈdɪkəmənt, ˈmedɪ-/ *n fml or tech* a substance used on or in the body to treat a disease

med·i·care /ˈmedɪkeəʳ/ *n* [R] (*often cap.*) (in America) a system of government medical care, esp. for the old

med·i·cate /ˈmedə̇keɪt/ *v* [Wv5;T1] to cover, fill, or mix with a medical substance: *medicated* SHAMPOO

med·i·ca·tion /ˌmedə̇ˈkeɪʃən/ *n* **1** [U] the act of medicating (MEDICATE) **2** [U;(C)] *fml* a medical substance, esp. a drug: *It is better to sleep naturally, without taking medication*

me·di·ci·nal /mə̇ˈdɪsənəl/ *adj* [Wa5] **1** used for medicine **2** having the effect of curing, like medicine —**~ly** *adv*

medi·cine /ˈmedsən‖ˈmedə̇sən/ *n* **1** [C;U] a substance used for treating disease: *Put the bottle of medicine away.|She has taken a lot of different medicines, but none has cured the disease* **2** [U] the science of treating and understanding disease **3** [U] (something having) magical power —see also MEDICINE MAN **4 give someone a taste/dose of his own medicine** *not fml* to treat someone as (badly as) he has treated others, as a punishment **5 take one's medicine (like a man)** to accept punishment or unpleasantness

medicine ball /ˈ·· ·‖ˈ··· ·/ *n* a large heavy ball thrown and caught as an exercise for strengthening the muscles

medicine chest /ˈ·· ·‖ˈ··· ·/ *n* a small cupboard or box where medicines are kept, esp. in the home

medicine man /ˈ·· ·‖ˈ··· ·/ *n* (in societies that still believe in magic, because they have not developed modern ways of thinking) a man believed to have magical powers over people and nature —see also WITCHDOCTOR

med·i·co /ˈmedɪkəʊ/ *n* **-s** *infml* a medical doctor —compare MEDIC

med·i·e·val, mediaeval /ˌmediˈiːvəl‖ˌmiː-/ *adj* **1** [Wa5] of the period in history between about 1100 and 1500 (the MIDDLE AGES) **2** *derog not fml* very old or old-fashioned

me·di·o·cre /ˌmiːdiˈəʊkəʳ/ *adj* of not very good or bad quality or ability, usu. not good enough

me·di·oc·ri·ty /ˌmiːdiˈɒkrə̇ti‖-ˈɑk-/ *n* **1** [U] the state or quality of being MEDIOCRE **2** [C] a person who shows no very good qualities or abilities

med·i·tate /ˈmedə̇teɪt/ *v* **1** [IØ (*on, upon*)] to think seriously or deeply: *He meditated for 2 days before giving his answer* **2** [IØ] to fix and keep the attention on one matter, having cleared the mind of thoughts, esp. for religious reasons and/or to gain peace of mind **3** [T1] to plan or consider carefully: *They are meditating a change in the office arrangements*

med·i·ta·tion /ˌmedə̇ˈteɪʃən/ *n* **1** [U] the act or time of meditating (MEDITATE) **2** [U] the practice of deep religious thought **3** [C *often pl.*] an example of deep thought on a subject, as expressed in a piece of speech or writing

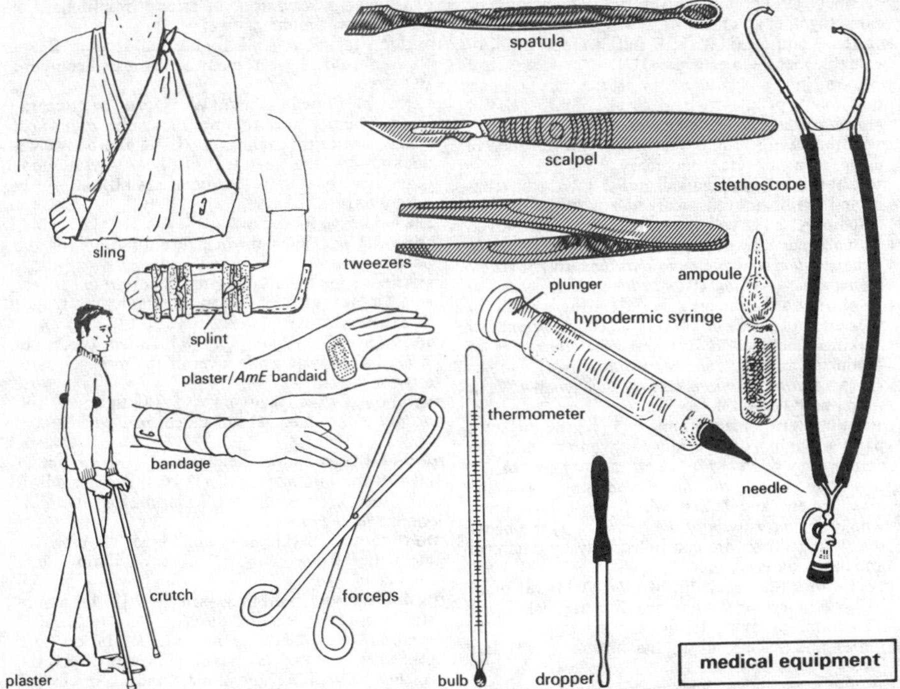

med·i·ta·tive /ˈmedʒtətɪv‖-teɪtɪv/ *adj* thoughtful; showing deep thought —**~ly** *adv*

Med·i·ter·ra·ne·an /ˌmedʒtəˈreɪnɪən/ *adj* [Wa5;A;(B)] of or near the Mediterranean sea or the countries around it

me·di·um¹ /ˈmiːdɪəm/ *n* **-dia** /dɪə/ *or* **-diums** **1** a method for giving information; form of art: *He writes stories, but the theatre is his favourite medium.|His best work was in the medium of oil paints.|Television can be a medium for giving information and opinions, for amusing people, and for teaching them foreign languages and other subjects* —see also MASS MEDIA, MEDIA **2** a substance in which objects or living things exist, or through which a force travels; surroundings in which one lives: *A fish in water is in its natural medium.|Sound travels through the medium of air* **3** a middle position (esp. in the phr. **the happy medium**): *There's a happy medium between eating all the time and not eating at all* —see also **golden** MEAN

medium² *n* **-diums** a person who claims to have power to receive messages from the spirits of the dead

medium³ *adj* [Wa5;A;(B)] of middle size, amount, quality, value, etc.; not great or small

medium wave /ˌ··· ˈ·/ *n* [U] radio broadcasting or receiving on waves of medium length (between about 150 and 550 metres): *a medium-wave broadcast* (=a broadcast on medium wave)

med·lar /ˈmedləʳ/ *n* **1** a type of small tree with a fruit like a wild apple **2** the fruit of this tree, eaten when partly decayed

med·ley /ˈmedli/ *n* **1** [(*of*)] a mass or crowd (of different types) mixed together: *a medley of moving people|a medley of different ideas* **2** a piece of music made up of parts of other musical works

meed /miːd/ *n* [*usu. sing.*] *poet* that which one deserves

meek /miːk/ *adj* [Wa1] **1** gentle in nature; yielding to others' actions and opinions **2 meek and mild** **a** gentle; uncomplaining **b** *derog* lacking courage and will to complain —**~ly** *adv* —**~ness** *n* [U]

meer·schaum /ˈmɪəʃəm‖ˈmɪər-/ *n* **1** [U] a type of hard white clay used for making pipes for smoking **2** [C] a pipe made of this substance

meet¹ /miːt/ *v* **met** /met/ **1** [T1;IØ] to come together (with), by chance or arrangement: *Let's meet for dinner.|I met him in the street* —compare MEET WITH **2** [T1] to find or experience; MEET WITH: *I met a lot of difficulties in the work* **3** [IØ] to come together or close: *The cars almost met* HEAD-ON (=one front against the other), *but drew away and drove on* **4** [T1;IØ] to get to know or be introduced (to) for the first time: *Come to the party and meet some interesting people.|We met at Ann's party, didn't we, but I don't remember your name* **5** [IØ] to join at a fastening point: *My skirt won't meet round my middle* **6** [IØ] to gather together: *The whole school met to hear the speech* **7** [T1;IØ] to touch, (as if) naturally: *Their lips met (in a kiss).|Her hand met his face in a violent blow* **8** [T1 (*with*)] to answer, esp. in opposition: *His charges were met with cries of anger.|Angry cries met his speech* **9** [T1] to be there at the arrival of: *I'll meet you off the train.|The taxi will meet the train/will meet you off the train* **10** [T1] to pay: *Can you meet this amount?* **11** [T1] to satisfy: *Does this meet your hopes?|This new road meets a long-felt need* **12 make ends meet** to use one's (small amount of) money carefully so as to afford what one needs **13 meet someone's eye** also **look someone in the eye**— to look directly or steadily at someone **14 more (in/to something) than meets the eye** hidden facts or reasons (in or for something) —see also **meet** HALFWAY

meet² *n* **1** *esp. BrE* a gathering of men on horses with hunting dogs (HOUNDs) to hunt foxes **2** *AmE* a meeting of people, esp. for sports events

meet³ *adj* [(*for*)] *old use & bibl* suitable; right

meet·ing /ˈmiːtɪŋ/ *n* **1** [C *usu. sing.*] the coming together of 2 or more people, by chance or arrangement: *Our meeting in Tokyo was later than I expected.|chance meetings* **2** [C] a gathering of people, esp. for a purpose **3** [*the*+GU] the people in such a gathering: *Is this the opinion of the meeting?*

meet·ing·house /ˈmiːtɪŋhaʊs/ *n* **-houses** /ˌhaʊzɪ̵z/ a place for religious meetings, esp. of NONCONFORMISTs

meet up *v adv* [IØ (*with*)] *infml* to meet, esp. not by a formal arrangement: *Let's meet up after the play.|I met up with a strange fellow*

meet with *v prep* [T1] **1** to experience or find by chance: *I met with some difficulties when I tried to enter the country.|They met with an accident on their way back* **2** *AmE* to have a meeting with: *Our representatives met with several heads of state in an effort to reach agreement over the price of oil*

meg·a- /ˈmegə/ *comb. form* one MILLION; 1,000,000

meg·a·death /ˈmegədeθ/ *n* the death of 1,000,000 people, as in a NUCLEAR war

meg·a·hertz /ˈmegəhɜːts‖-ɜr-/ also **meg·a·cy·cle** /ˈmegəˌsaɪkəl/— *n* **-hertz** [Wn3] 1,000,000 HERTZ

meg·a·lith /ˈmegəlɪθ/ *n* a large stone which has usu. been standing since before historical times, perhaps raised as a religious or other type of sign

meg·a·lith·ic /ˌmegəˈlɪθɪk/ *adj* [Wa5] **1** of or using MEGALITHs: *a megalithic circle* (usu. called a **stone circle**) **2** of the time when such stones were raised, before the time of recorded history

meg·a·lo·ma·ni·a /ˌmegələʊˈmeɪnɪə/ *n* [U] **1** the belief that one is more important, powerful, etc., than one really is **2** *tech* the condition in which a mad person holds a strong belief of this kind

meg·a·lo·ma·ni·ac /ˌmegələˈmeɪniæk/ *n* **1** a person who acts as if he is very powerful and important **2** *tech* a mad person with MEGALOMANIA (2)

meg·a·phone /ˈmegəfəʊn/ also **loudhailer**— *n* an instrument shaped like a horn which makes the voice louder when spoken through it, so that it can be heard over a distance, as at large meetings out of doors

meg·a·ton /ˈmegətʌn/ *n* (a measure of force of an explosion equal to that of) 1,000,000 TONs (about 1,016,000,000 kilograms) of a type of powerful explosive called TNT: *a 5-megaton bomb*

me·grim /ˈmiːgrɪ̵m/ *n* [C;(U)] *old use* MIGRAINE

mei·o·sis /maɪˈəʊsɪ̵s/ *n* [U] **1** the division of a cell into 2 new cells, in such a way that each of the resulting cells has only a half set of character-bearing parts (CHROMOSOMEs) —compare MITOSIS **2** *tech* UNDERSTATEMENT —compare LITOTES

mel·an·cho·li·a /ˌmelənˈkeʊlɪə/ *n* [U] *becoming rare* a condition in which one feels generally sad and DEPRESSED; DEPRESSION

mel·an·chol·ic /ˌmelənˈkɒlɪk‖-ˈkɑ-/ *adj* sad; DEPRESSED

mel·an·chol·y[1] /ˈmelənkəli‖-kɑli/ *n* [U] sadness, esp. over a period of time and not for any particular reason

melancholy[2] *adj* **1** sad: *alone and feeling melancholy* **2** causing DEPRESSION (4): *melancholy news*

mé·lange /meɪˈlɑːnʒ (*Fr* melɑ̃ʒ)/ *n* [(*of*) *usu. sing.*] *Fr* a mixture of many types

meld[1] /meld/ *v* [T1;IØ] (in certain card games) to put on the table (a combination of cards) for which one wins points

meld[2] *n* a combination of cards that is MELDed

mel·ee /ˈmeleɪ‖ˈmeɪleɪ/ *n* [*usu. sing.*] a struggling or disorderly crowd

me·li·o·rate /ˈmiːlɪəreɪt/ *v* [T1;IØ] *fml & rare* AMELIORATE —**-ration** /ˌmiːlɪəˈreɪʃən/ *n* [U]

me·li·o·ris·m /ˈmiːlɪərɪzəm/ *n* [U] *tech* the belief that man can improve his world by effort —**-rist** *adj, n* [Wa5]

mel·li·flu·ous /mɪ̵ˈlɪfluəs/ *adj* (of words, music, or a voice) with a sweet smooth flowing sound

mel·low[1] /ˈmeləʊ/ *adj* [Wa1] **1** (of fruit and wine) sweet and ripe or MATURE, esp. after being kept for a long time **2** (of colours and surfaces) soft, warm, and smooth, esp. worn so by time **3** wise and gentle through age or experience **4** *not fml, sometimes euph* pleasant to be with, esp. because rather drunk —**~ly** *adv* —**~ness** *n* [U]

mellow[2] *v* [T1;IØ] to (cause to) become (more) MELLOW with the passing of time: *A few more years will mellow the wine.|The colours mellowed as the sun went down.|The years have mellowed him*

me·lod·ic /mɪ̵ˈlɒdɪk‖mɪ̵ˈlɑ-/ *adj* **1** [Wa5] of or having a MELODY **2** MELODIOUS

me·lo·di·ous /mɪ̵ˈleʊdɪəs/ *adj* sweet-sounding; tuneful —**~ly** *adv* —**~ness** *n* [U]

mel·o·dra·ma /ˈmelədrɑːmə/ *n* **1** [C;U] a (type of) play which is too exciting to be believed, with sudden changes and events which are meant to have a strong effect **2** [C] a very exciting event which causes strong feelings or interest

mel·o·dra·mat·ic /ˌmelədrəˈmætɪk/ *adj* exciting in effect, often too much so to be thought real: *That's a very melodramatic statement. You know you wouldn't really do that!* —**~ally** *adv* [Wa4]

mel·o·dy /ˈmelədi/ *n* **1** [U] the arrangement of music in a pleasant way **2** [C] a song or tune **3** [C] the part which forms a clearly recognizable tune in a larger arrangement of notes

mel·on /ˈmelən/ *n* **1** [C] any of a few kinds of fruit which are large and rounded, with very juicy flesh inside a firm skin **2** [U] the flesh of this —see also WATERMELON, CANTALOUP, HONEYDEW MELON and see picture at FRUIT[1]

melt /melt/ *v* **1** [T1;IØ] **a** to cause (a solid) to become liquid: *The sun melted the snow* **b** (of a solid) to become liquid: *The ice is melting* **2** [T1;IØ] to (cause to) become gentle, sympathetic, etc.: *He scolded the child, but his heart was melting with joy because she was safe* **3** [T1;IØ] to (cause to) disappear: *Her anger melted* **4** [L9, esp. *into*] (of a colour, sound, or sensation) to become lost (in another) by moving gently into or across: *The notes melted into the next song* **5 melt in the mouth** *apprec* (of solid food) to be soft or tender when eaten, or to become liquid quickly

USAGE The adjective **molten** means **melted** (in former times, it was the *past p.* of **melt**), but it is only used of things that melt at a very high temperature: **molten** *rock/metal*|**melted** *chocolate/ice*.

melt a·way *v adv* [IØ] to disappear easily: *The opposition melted away*

melt down *v adv* [T1] to make (a metal object) liquid by heating, esp. so as to use the metal again

melt·ing /ˈmeltɪŋ/ *adj* [Wa5] (esp. of a voice) gentle, soft, and pleasant —**~ly** *adv*

melting point /ˈ·· ·/ *n* the temperature at which a solid melts

melting pot /ˈ·· ·/ *n* **1** a container in which metals can be melted **2** a place where there is a mixing of different types of people, ideas, etc. **3 in the melting pot** not fixed; likely to be changed

mem·ber /ˈmembəʳ/ *n* **1** [(*of*)] a person belonging to a club, group, etc.: *a member of the family|a member of a political party|a member of the committee* **2 a** *fml* a part of the body, such as an organ or limb **b** *euph* the male sexual organ: *the male member*

Member of Par·lia·ment /ˌ··· ˈ···/ *n* MP

mem·ber·ship /ˈmembəʃɪp‖-ər-/ *n* **1** [U] the state of being a member of a club, society, etc. **2** [GC] all the members of a club, society, etc.

mem·brane /'membreɪn/ *n* [C;U] soft thin skin in the body, covering or connecting parts of it

mem·bra·nous /'membrənəs/ *adj* [Wa5] of or like MEMBRANE

me·men·to /mɪ̇'mentəʊ/ *n* **-tos** a small object which reminds one, esp. of a holiday, a friend, etc.

mem·o /'meməʊ/ *n* **memos** **1** a note of something to be remembered **2** a note from one person or office to another within a firm or organization; MEMORANDUM

mem·oir /'memwɑːʳ/ *n fml* **1** a story of someone's life, esp. a personal one, as by a friend **2** a short piece of writing on a subject the writer has studied

mem·oirs /'memwɑːz‖-ɑrz/ *n* [P] the story of one's own life

mem·o·ra·bil·i·a /ˌmemərə'bɪlɪə/ *n* [P] *Lat* things that are very interesting and worth remembering, esp. in connection with a famous person or event: *a valuable collection of Shelley memorabilia, including several love letters and a piece of his hair*

mem·o·ra·ble /'memərəbəl/ *adj* **1** which is worth remembering: *memorable for its strange colours* (=remembered because of) **2** noticeable; special: *memorable beauty* —**-bly** *adv* [Wa3]

mem·o·ran·dum /ˌmemə'rændəm/ *n* **-da** /də/ *or* **-dums** **1** a short agreement in writing, to sell, to form a company, etc. **2** *fml* MEMO

me·mo·ri·al /mɪ̇'mɔːrɪəl‖mɪ̇'mor-/ *n* **1** **a** an object, such as a stone MONUMENT, in a public place in memory of a person, event, etc. **b** a custom which serves the same purpose: *The service is a memorial to those killed in the war* **2** [*usu. pl.*] a historical record: *memorials of a past age* **3** *law & rare* PETITION

Memorial Day /·'··· ˌ·/ *n* [R] (in the US) a day of holiday at the end of May, when soldiers killed in war are remembered —compare REMEMBRANCE DAY

mem·o·rize, -rise /'meməraɪz/ *v* [T1] to learn and remember, on purpose

mem·o·ry /'meməri/ *n* **1** [C;U] (an) ability to remember events and experience **2** [C (*of*)] an example of remembering: *one of my earliest memories* **3** [(*the*) S9] the time during which things happened which can be remembered: *There have been 2 wars within his memory/within the memory of my grandfather* **4** [C] the opinion held of someone after his death: *to praise his memory* **5** **commit something to memory** *fml* to learn and remember on purpose; MEMORIZE **6** **in memory of** as a way of remembering or being reminded of **7** **to the best of my memory/my remembrance/my recollection** as well as I can remember; if I remember right **8** **within living memory** in the time which can be remembered by people now alive

mem·sahib /'memˌsɑːb‖-ˌsɑhɪb, -ˌsɑb/ *n* [C;N] *Ind & Pak E* a European woman, or an Indian woman of high social class

men /men/ *pl. of* MAN

USAGE Note the word order in this fixed phr.: **men and women.**

men·ace[1] /'menɪ̇s/ *n* **1** [C (*to*); U] something which suggests a threat or brings danger: *He spoke with menace in his voice.|The road outside the school is a menace to the children's safety* **2** [C] *infml* a troublesome person or thing: *Your toys are a menace. I'm always falling over them*

menace[2] *v* [Wv4;T1] *esp. fml* to threaten: *2 men menaced him with weapons and forced him to give up his money* —**-acingly** *adv*

mé·nage /meɪ'nɑːʒ, mə-/ *n* a house and the people who live in it; HOUSEHOLD

ménage à trois /ˌmeɪnɑːʒ ɑː 'trwɑː‖məˌnɑʒ- (*Fr* menaʒ a trwɑ)/ *n* [S] *Fr* a relationship in which 3 people, such as a married pair and a lover of one of the pair, live together

me·na·ge·rie /mɪ̇'nædʒəri/ *n* **1** a collection of wild animals kept privately or for the public to see; zoo **2** the place where they are kept, usu. in cages

mend[1] /mend/ *v* **1** [T1] to repair (a hole, break, fault, etc.) in (something) **2** [T1;IØ] to repair by sewing: *I'll mend that shirt* **3** [T1] to improve (esp. in the phr. **mend one's ways**) **4** [IØ] *not fml* to regain one's health: *He's mending nicely* **5** [T1] *infml esp. dial* to build up (a low fire) —**~er** *n*

mend[2] *n* **1** a part mended after breaking or wearing **2** a fault closed or covered on material; PATCH OR DARN **3** **on the mend** *not fml* getting better after illness

men·da·cious /men'deɪʃəs/ *adj fml* (esp. of a statement) not truthful; lying —**~ly** *adv*

men·da·ci·ty /men'dæsɪ̇ti/ *n* [U] *fml* (habitual) untruthfulness

Men·de·li·an /men'diːlɪən/ *adj* [Wa5] of the ideas of G. Mendel (1822–1884), who showed that qualities are passed on from parent to young according to rules

men·di·cant /'mendɪ̇kənt/ *adj, n* [Wa5] (a person) living as a beggar

mend·ing /'mendɪŋ/ *n* [U] **1** sewing to repair material **2** clothes to be mended

men·folk /'menfəʊk/ *n* [P] **1** *infml* men **2** male relatives

me·ni·al[1] /'miːnɪəl/ *adj* **1** not interesting or important-seeming: *the menial work concerned in running a house* **2** *old use* of or suitable for a servant —**~ly** *adv*

menial[2] *n often derog* a servant in a house, esp. one who must do all the hardest work

men·in·gi·tis /ˌmenɪ̇n'dʒaɪtɪ̇s/ *n* [U] an illness in which the outer part of the brain may be swollen (INFLAMEd)

me·nis·cus /mɪ̇'nɪskəs/ *n tech* the curved surface of liquid in a tube

men·o·pause /'menəpɔːz/ also **change of life**— *n* [*the*+R] the time when a woman's PERIODs[1] (5) stop, usu. in middle age

men·ses /'mensiːz/ *n* [(*the*) P] *fml or tech* the material mixed with blood that is lost from a woman's WOMB about once a month; MENSTRUAL flow —see also PERIOD[1] (5), MENSTRUATE

men's room /'· ·/ *n AmE* GENTS

men·stru·al /'menstrʊəl/ *adj* [Wa5] concerning the changes in a woman's body during a month, esp. with loss of the MENSES

menstrual pe·ri·od /ˌ··· '···/ *n* [*often pl.*] *fml* PERIOD[1] (5)

men·stru·ate /'menstrʊeɪt/ *v* [IØ] to have a natural flow of blood from the WOMB; lose the MENSES —**-ation** /ˌmenstrʊ'eɪʃən/ *n* [U;C]

men·su·ra·ble /'menʃərəbəl‖-sərə-/ *adj* [Wa5] *fml* which can be measured

men·su·ra·tion /ˌmenʃə'reɪʃən‖-sə'reɪ-/ *n* **1** *fml* the act of measuring **2** *tech* the study and practice of measuring length, area, and VOLUME (3)

-ment /mənt/ *suffix* [*v*→*n* [C;U]] the cause, means, or result of (an action): *an* ENTERTAINMENT|DEVELOPMENT —**~al** /'mentl/ *suffix* [→*adj*]: DEVELOPMENT*al* —**~ally** /'mentəli/ *suffix* [→*adv*]: DEVELOPMENT*ally*

men·tal /'mentl/ *adj* [Wa5] **1** [B] of the mind: *mental powers* **2** [A] done only in or with the mind, esp. without the help of writing **3** [A] concerning disorders or illness of the mind: *a* MENTAL HOSPITAL|*mental treatment* **4** [F;(B)] *nonstandard* mad: *Don't listen to him; he's mental* —see NATURAL (USAGE) —**~ly** *adv*

mental age /ˌ·· '·/ *n* a measure of a person's ability and development of mind, according to the usual age at which such ability would be found: *The children are aged from 7 to 13, but they all have a mental age of less than 5*

mental de·fec·tive /ˌ·· ·ˈ··/ *n* a person who cannot learn or be independent because of **mental deficiency** (=lack of power of the mind)

mental hos·pi·tal /ˌ·· ˈ···‖ˈ·· ˌ···/ also **mental home** /ˈ·· ·/— *n* a hospital or other building where people whose minds are ill are treated and looked after

mental ill·ness /ˌ·· ˈ··/ *n* [U;C] (a) disorder of the thoughts, feelings, and usual powers of the mind

men·tal·i·ty /menˈtælɪ̈ti/ *n* **1** [U] the abilities and powers of the mind: *of weak mentality* **2** [C] character; habits of thought: *I can't understand the mentality of anyone who would do a terrible thing like that!*

mental pa·tient /ˈ·· ˌ··/ *n* a person being treated for MENTAL ILLNESS, esp. in a hospital

men·thol /ˈmenθɒl‖-θɔl, -θɑl/ *n* [U] a white substance with a MINTY[3] taste

men·tho·lat·ed /ˈmenθəleɪtɪ̈d/ *adj* [Wa5] containing added MENTHOL

men·tion[1] /ˈmenʃən/ *n* **1** [U] the act of mentioning: *He made no mention of her wishes* **2** [C *usu. sing.*] a short remark about something **3** [C *usu. sing.*] *not fml* a naming of someone, esp. to honour them: *He was given a mention in the list of helpers*

mention[2] *v* **1** [T1,5] to tell about in a few words, spoken or written: *He mentioned their interest in flowers* **2** [T1] to say the name of: *He mentioned a useful book.|Soon after going abroad with the army he was mentioned in* DESPATCH*es* (=given special honour for bravery) **3 Don't mention it** *polite* There's no need for thanks; I'm glad to help: *"Thanks very much." "Don't mention it"* **4 not to mention (something/the fact that)** and in addition there's . . .: *They have 3 dogs to find a home for, not to mention the cat and the bird*

-men·tioned /ˈmenʃənd/ *comb. form* which was mentioned earlier or later in a piece of writing: *the above-mentioned book*

men·tor /ˈmentɔʳ/ *n* a person who habitually advises and helps another who knows less than him

men·u /ˈmenjuː/ *n* a list of dishes in a meal or to be ordered as separate meals, esp. in a restaurant

me·ow /miˈaʊ/ *n, v* [C;IØ] *AmE* MIAOW

Me·phis·toph·e·les /ˌmefɪ̈ˈstɒfɪ̈liːz‖-ˈstɑ-/ *n* [R;N] (a name for) the devil, in his most wicked form —**-lean** /-stəˈfiːlɪən/ *adj*

mer·can·tile /ˈmɜːkəntaɪl‖ˈmɜrkəntiːl, -taɪl/ *adj* [Wa5] **1** of or concerning MERCHANT*s* (=people whose business is trade) **2** of trade and COMMERCE: *mercantile law*

Mer·ca·tor pro·jec·tion /məˌkeɪtə prəˈdʒekʃən‖mərˌkeɪtər-/ also **Mercator's projection**— *n* a way of drawing a map so that it can be divided into regular squares (instead of getting thinner at the northern and southern part of the earth)

mer·ce·na·ry[1] /ˈmɜːsənəri‖ˈmɜrsəneri/ *n* a soldier who fights for the country that pays him, not for his own country

mercenary[2] *adj* influenced by the wish to gain money or other reward

mer·cer /ˈmɜːsəʳ‖ˈmɜr-/ *n esp. old use* DRAPER

mer·cer·ize, -ise /ˈmɜːsəraɪz‖ˈmɜr-/ *v* [Wv5;T1] to make (cotton thread) smooth by special treatment

mer·chan·dise[1] /ˈmɜːtʃəndaɪz, -daɪs‖ˈmɜr-/ *n* [U] things for sale; goods for trade

merchandise[2] *v* [T1] to try to persuade people to buy (goods): *If this product is properly merchandised, it should sell very well*

mer·chant /ˈmɜːtʃənt‖ˈmɜr-/ *n* a person who buys and sells goods, esp. in large amounts in foreign countries

mer·chant·man /ˈmɜːtʃəntmən‖ˈmɜr-/ also **merchant ship** /ˈ·· ·/— *n* **-men** /mən/ a ship carrying goods for trade

merchant na·vy /ˌ·· ˈ··/ also (*esp. AmE*) **merchant ma·rine** /ˌ·· ·ˈ·/, (*esp. BrE*) **mercantile marine** /ˌ··· ·ˈ·/— *n* **1** those ships of a nation which are used in trade **2** the people who work on these ships

mer·ci·ful /ˈmɜːsɪfəl‖ˈmɜr-/ *adj* **1** [(*to*)] showing mercy; willing to forgive instead of punishing: *The merciful king saved him from death* **2** by the kindness of God or fortune: *a merciful death* (=it was fortunate to die, rather than suffer) —**~ly** *adv* [Wa4] —**~ness** *n* [U]

mer·ci·less /ˈmɜːsɪləs‖ˈmɜr-/ *adj* [Wa5; (*to*)] showing no mercy; willing to punish rather than forgive —**~ly** *adv* —**~ness** *n* [U]

mer·cu·ri·al /mɜːˈkjʊərɪəl‖mɜr-/ *adj* **1** [Wa5] *tech* of or containing MERCURY **2** changeable: *a mercurial temper* **3** quick; active: *her mercurial mind* —compare QUICKSILVER —**~ly** *adv*

mer·cu·ry /ˈmɜːkjʊri‖ˈmɜrkjəri/ also **quicksilver**— *n* [U] a heavy silver-white metal that is a simple substance (ELEMENT (6)), which is liquid at ordinary temperatures and is used esp. in scientific instruments such as THERMOMETER*s* and BAROMETER*s*

Mercury *n* [R] the PLANET nearest to the sun —see picture at PLANET

mer·cy /ˈmɜːsi‖ˈmɜrsi/ *n* **1** [U] willingness to forgive, not to punish: *He showed mercy to his enemies and let them live* **2** [U *sometimes pl. with sing. meaning*] kindness or pity towards those who suffer or are weak: *God's mercy has/mercies have no limits* **3** [S] *not fml* a fortunate event: *It's a mercy we didn't know of her illness till afterwards, as we would have been so worried* **4 at the mercy of** powerless against: *They were lost at sea, at the mercy of wind and weather* **5 leave to someone's (tender) mercies** to give in to the (cruel) control of: *You will be more tired than you ever were in your life before if they leave you to the tender mercies of the mountain-climbing instructor*

mercy kill·ing /ˈ·· ˌ··/ *n* [U] EUTHANASIA

mere[1] /mɪəʳ/ *n* **1** *poet* a small lake **2** (*usu. in comb., as part of a name*) a lake: (*Lake*) *Windermere in Cumbria*

mere[2] *adj* **1** [Wa5;A] nothing more than (a): *A mere 2 miles isn't too far to walk* **2 the merest** as small or unimportant as possible: *The merest little thing makes him nervous*

mere·ly /ˈmɪəli‖-ər-/ *adv* [Wa5] only . . . and nothing else: *He merely wants to know the truth*

mer·e·tri·cious /ˌmerɪ̈ˈtrɪʃəs/ *adj fml* attractive on the surface, but of no value or importance —**~ly** *adv* —**~ness** *n* [U]

merge /mɜːdʒ‖mɜrdʒ/ *v* **1** [IØ (*into*)] to become lost in or part of something else/each other: *One colour merged into the other.|the place where the roads merge* **2** [IØ;T1: (*with*)] **a** (of firms or companies) to combine **b** to cause (firms or companies) to combine

merg·er /ˈmɜːdʒəʳ‖ˈmɜr-/ *n* a joining of 2 or more companies or firms

me·rid·i·an /məˈrɪdɪən/ *n* **1** [C] an imaginary line drawn from the top point of the earth (NORTH POLE) to the bottom over the surface of the earth, one of several used on maps to show position —see picture at GLOBE **2** [(*the*) R;(C)] *tech* the highest point, esp. of a star —compare ZENITH **3** [(*the*) R;(C)] *tech* midday, when the sun reaches its highest point

me·rid·i·o·nal /məˈrɪdɪənəl/ *adj* [Wa5] *tech* of the south, esp. in European countries

me·ringue /məˈræŋ/ *n* **1** [C] a sort of light round cake made of sugar and the white part of eggs, beaten together **2** [U] the same mixture, sometimes used as part of a sweet dish

me·ri·no /məˈriːnəʊ/ *n* **-nos** **1** [C] a type of sheep with soft wool **2** [U] material made from this wool

mer·it[1] /ˈmerɨt/ *n* **1** [U] the quality of deserving praise, reward, etc.; personal worth: *There's little merit in telling us now it's too late.|men of merit* **2 on its/his, etc., merits** by or for its/his, etc., own qualities, good or bad, not by one's own opinions

merit[2] *v* [T1,4] *usu. fml* to deserve; have a right to: *He merited all the praise they gave him*

mer·i·toc·ra·cy /ˌmerɨˈtɒkrəsi‖-ˈtɑ-/ *n* **1** [C] a social system which gives the highest positions to those with the most ability **2** [(*the*) GU] the people who rule in such a system

mer·i·to·ri·ous /ˌmerɨˈtɔːrɪəs‖-ˈtor-/ *adj fml* deserving reward or praise —**~ly** *adv*

mer·maid /ˈmɜːmeɪd‖ˈmɜr-/ *n* (in stories) a young and usu. attractive woman with the bottom half of her body like a fish's tail

mer·man /ˈmɜːmæn‖ˈmɜr-/ *n* **-men** /men/ (in stories) a man with the bottom half of his body like a fish's tail; male MERMAID

mer·ri·ment /ˈmerɪmənt/ *n* [U] laughter and sounds of enjoyment

mer·ry /ˈmeri/ *adj* [Wa1] **1 a** cheerful, esp. laughing: *a merry smile* **b** habitually fond of laughter, fun, etc.: *a merry fellow* **2** causing laughter and fun: *a merry joke* **3** *infml* rather drunk: *grew merry on wine* **4 make merry** *infml lit* to have fun, esp. eating and drinking for enjoyment **5 Merry Christmas!** Have a happy time at Christmas —**-rily** *adv* —**-riness** *n* [U]

merry-go-round /ˈ·· · ˌ·/ *AmE* also **carousel**— *n* ROUNDABOUT[1] (1)

mer·ry·mak·ing /ˈmeriˌmeɪkɪŋ/ *n* [U] *infml lit* fun and enjoyment, esp. eating, drinking, and games: *There was joy and merrymaking in the whole country when the king's son was born* —**-maker** *n*

me·sa /ˈmeɪsə/ *n* **-s** a flat-topped formation with steep rocky walls, to be found in dry areas

mes·ca·lin, -line /ˈmeskəliːn, -lɨn/ *n* [U] a drug which is obtained from a type of CACTUS plant and causes dreams that seem real

Mes·dames /ˈmeɪdæm‖meɪˈdɑːm (*Fr* medam)/ *pl. of* MADAM, MADAME

mes·de·moi·selles /ˌmeɪdəmwəˈzel (*Fr* medmwazɛl)/ *pl. of* MADEMOISELLE

me·seems /mɪˈsiːmz/ **-seemed** /siːmd/ *old use* it seems to me that —see also METHINKS

mesh[1] /meʃ/ *n* **1** [C;U] (a piece of) material woven in a fine network with small holes between the threads: *We put some/a fine wire mesh over the windows so that the birds couldn't get out* **2** [C *usu. sing.*] the spaces of a certain size within such a network: MICROMESH *stockings* **3** [C *usu. pl.*] the threads in such a network: *The fish were caught in the meshes of the net* **4** [C] a trap: *caught in a mesh of lies* **5 in mesh** held together, as the teeth of GEARS

mesh[2] *v* **1** [T1] to catch (fish) in a net **2** [I∅ (*with*)] to connect; be held (together): *The wheels meshed* **3** [I∅] (of qualities, ideas, etc.) to fit together suitably: *Their characters just don't mesh*

mes·mer·ic /mezˈmerɪk/ *adj* [Wa5] that MESMERIZES

mes·mer·is·m /ˈmezmərɪzəm/ *n* [U] *old use* HYPNOTISM

mes·mer·ist /ˈmezmərɨst/ *n old use* a HYPNOTIST, esp. (formerly) one who performs publicly on the stage

mes·mer·ize, -ise /ˈmezməraɪz/ *v* [T1] **1** to surprise very much, esp. so as to make speechless and unable to move: *The country girl stood by the road, mesmerized at the speed of the cars racing past* **2** *esp. old use* HYPNOTIZE

mess[1] /mes/ *n* **1** [U;S] a state of disorder or untidiness (esp. in the phr. **in a mess**): *I'll have to clear up all the mess in this room.|This room's in a mess* **2** [C *usu. sing.*] *infml* a person whose appearance, behaviour, or thinking is in a disordered state: *You're a mess, you'll have to change* **3** [U;S] dirty material, esp. passed from an animal's body: *Now you've dropped the food you can clear up the mess* **4** [S] *infml* trouble (esp. in the phr. **in a mess**): *You're in a nice mess now you've been caught stealing!* **5** [C] a place to eat, esp. for soldiers or other members of the armed forces **6** [GC] the people who eat together in such a place **7** [U;C] the food eaten in such a place **8 make a mess of** *infml* to disorder, spoil, ruin, etc.: *This illness makes a mess of my holiday plans* —see also MESS UP

mess[2] *v* [L9, esp. *with*, TOGETHER] to have meals (with someone/together) in a group

mess a·bout also **mess a·round**— *v adv* **1** [I∅] to be lazy: *He spent all day Sunday just messing about* **2** [I∅] to act or speak stupidly: *Stop messing about and tell me clearly what happened!* **3** [I∅ (*with*)] to work without speed or plan: (*humor esp. BrE*) *I'm not much of a sailor, but I like to mess about in my little boat on the river* **4** [T1] to treat badly or carelessly: *Don't mess me about; I want the money you promised me*

mes·sage /ˈmesɪdʒ/ *n* **1** [C,C3,5] a spoken or written piece of information passed from one person to another **2** [*the*+R,R5] the important or central idea: *the message of this book* **3** [*the*+R,R5] teachings of moral or social value: *Christ brought the message that God loved the world* **4 get the message** *sl* to understand what is wanted or meant

mes·sen·ger /ˈmesəndʒəʳ/ *n* a person who brings one or more messages

mess hall /ˈ· ·/ *n AmE* MESS[1] (5)

mes·si·ah /mɨˈsaɪə/ *n* [*usu. sing.*] **1** (*often cap.*) a new leader in a (new) religion, esp. one whom PROPHETs told of, and esp. (*cap.*) Christ in the Christian religion or the man still expected by the Jews **2** *infml* a person who brings new ways and saves people from difficulty

mes·si·an·ic /ˌmesiˈænɪk/ *adj* [Wa5] of or like a MESSIAH

Mes·sieurs /meɪˈsjɜːz‖-ɜrz (*Fr* mesjø)/ *pl. of* MONSIEUR

mess·mate /ˈmes-meɪt/ *n* [C;(N)] *now rare or lit* a person in the same MESS[1] (6) as oneself, as in the Navy

Mes·srs /ˈmesəz‖-ərz/ *n* [A] (used chiefly in writing as the *pl.* of MR, esp. in the names of firms): *Messrs Ford and Dobson, piano repairers*

mes·suage /ˈmeswɪdʒ/ *n law* a house with other buildings and land around it

mess up *v adv* [T1] *infml* to disorder, spoil, etc.: *Her late arrival messes up our plans* —**mess-up** /ˈ· ·/ *n*

mess with *v prep* [T1 *usu. neg. imper.*] *infml* to cause trouble to: *Don't mess with me, or you'll be sorry!*

mess·y /ˈmesi/ *adj* [Wa1] **1** untidy **2** dirty **3** causing the body to become dirty: *It's a messy business having a tooth taken out* —**messily** *adv* —**messiness** *n* [U]

mes·ti·zo /meˈstiːzəʊ/ *n* **-zos** a person with one Spanish parent and one American Indian parent

met /met/ *past t. and p. of* MEET

met·a- /ˌmetə/ *prefix* above, higher than, or beyond: *meta*PSYCHOLOGY|*a meta*GALAXY

met·a·bol·ic /ˌmetəˈbɒlɪk‖-ˈbɑ-/ *adj* [Wa5] concerning METABOLISM

me·tab·o·lis·m /mɨ̆'tæbəlɪzəm/ *n* the chemical activities in a living thing by which it gains power (ENERGY), esp. from food: *In some diseases the metabolism is slowed down, and the person cannot move or think quickly*
me·tab·o·lize, -lise /mɨ̆'tæbəlaɪz/ *v* [T1] to use for the METABOLISM
met·a·car·pal /ˌmetə'kɑːpəl‖-ɑr-/ *adj, n* [Wa5] (of) one of the small bones in the hand —see picture at SKELETON
met·al¹ /'metl/ *n* **1** [C;U] any usu. solid shiny mineral substance of a group which can all be shaped by pressure and used for passing an electric current, and which share other properties: *Copper and silver are both metals.|a metal box* **2** [U] *BrE* broken stone for making the surface of roads **3** [U] *tech* glass in its liquid form before it becomes cool
metal² *v* **-ll-** (*AmE* **-l-**) [Wv5;T1] *BrE* to cover (a road) with a surface of broken stones
met·a·lan·guage /'metəˌlæŋgwɪdʒ/ *n* [C;U] expressions and phrases used for talking about language; the language of LINGUISTICS
me·tal·lic /mɨ̆'tælɪk/ *adj* **1** [Wa5] **a** of or like metal: *metallic colours|metallic coins* **b** partly of metal: *a metallic mixture* **2** with a ringing quality (of sound): *a sharp metallic note*
me·tal·lur·gist /mɨ̆'tælədʒɨ̆st‖-lər-/ *n* a person who studies and knows about metals and their use
met·al·lur·gy /'metəlɜːdʒi‖-ɜr-/ *n* [U] the study and practice of removing metals from rocks, melting them, and using them —**-gical** /ˌmetə'lɜːdʒɪkəl‖-ɜr-/ *adj* [Wa5]
met·al·work /'metlwɜːk‖-ɜrk/ *n* [U] **1** objects shaped in metal **2** the study and practice of making metal objects, esp. as a school subject —**~er** *n*
met·a·mor·phose /ˌmetə'mɔːfəʊz‖-ɔr-/ *v* [T1;IØ: (*into*)] *rare* to change into another form
met·a·mor·pho·sis /ˌmetə'mɔːfəsɨ̆s‖-ɔr-/ *n* **-ses** /siːz/ [C;U] (a) complete change from one form to another, esp. in the life of an insect: *A* BUTTERFLY *is produced by metamorphosis from a* CATERPILLAR
met·a·phor /'metəfəʳ, -fɔːʳ‖-fɔr/ *n* [C;U] (the use of) a phrase which describes one thing by stating another thing with which it can be compared (as in *the roses in her cheeks*) without using the words "as" or "like" —compare SIMILE
met·a·phor·i·cal /ˌmetə'fɒrɪkəl‖-'fɔ-, -'fɑ-/ *adj* **1** using or concerning the use of METAPHOR **2** not meant to be understood in the ordinary meaning of the words: *It was a metaphorical phrase; we didn't really mean that he has green fingers, only that he is good at gardening* —**~ly** *adv* [Wa4]
met·a·phys·i·cal /ˌmetə'fɪzɪkəl/ *adj* **1** [Wa5] of or concerning METAPHYSICS **2** [Wa5] based on reasoning **3** [Wa5] (of poetry) concerning a 17th century style of poetry which combined strong feelings with clever arrangements of words **4** (of ideas or thinking) at a high level and difficult to understand —**~ly** *adv* [Wa4]
met·a·phys·ics /ˌmetə'fɪzɪks/ *n* [U] **1** a branch of the study of thought (PHILOSOPHY) concerned with the science of being and knowing **2** any type of thinking at a high level, which is hard to understand
met·a·tar·sal /ˌmetə'tɑːsəl‖-ɑr-/ *adj, n* [Wa5] (of) one of the small bones in the foot —see picture at SKELETON
me·tem·psy·cho·sis /mɨ̆ˌtemsaɪ'kəʊsɨ̆s‖-sɨ̆'kəʊ-/ *n* [U] *tech* the passing of a soul into another body after death; TRANSMIGRATION
me·te·or /'miːtɪəʳ/ *n* **1** any of various small pieces of matter floating in space that form a short-lived line of light if they fall into the earth's air (ATMOSPHERE) **2** the line of light produced by this
me·te·or·ic /ˌmiːti'ɒrɪk‖-'ɔrɪk, -'ɑrɪk/ *adj* **1** [Wa5] of or concerning a METEOR **2** [Wa5] *tech* of or concerning the earth's air (ATMOSPHERE) **3** like a METEOR, esp. in being very fast or in being bright and short-lived: *a meteoric rise to fame* —**~ally** *adv*
me·te·o·rite /'miːtɪəraɪt/ *n* a small piece of matter from space (METEOR) that has landed on the earth without being totally burnt up
me·te·o·roid /'miːtɪərɔɪd/ *n* **1** a small piece of matter in space (METEOR) that travels around the sun **2** a METEOR considered without relation to the light it produces when entering the earth's air (ATMOSPHERE)
me·te·o·rol·o·gist /ˌmiːtɪə'rɒlədʒɨ̆st‖-'rɑ-/ *n* a person who studies and knows about the weather
me·te·o·rol·o·gy /ˌmiːtɪə'rɒlədʒi‖-'rɑ-/ *n* [U] the study of weather conditions and the activities and changes around the earth (=in its ATMOSPHERE) that cause such conditions —see also MET OFFICE —**-gical** /ˌmiːtɪərə'lɒdʒɪkəl‖-'lɑ-/ *adj* [Wa5]
mete out /miːt/ *v adv* [T1 (*to*)] *fml & lit* to give carefully as if in measured amounts
me·ter¹ /'miːtəʳ/ *n* (*often in comb.*) a machine which measures the amount used: *a gas meter|a* PARKING METER
meter² *n AmE* METRE
-me·ter /ˌmiːtəʳ, mɨ̆təʳ/ *comb. form* [→n] **1** *AmE* -METRE **2** used for showing the number of beats (feet) in each line of a poem: PENTAMETER **3** forming the names of instruments used for measuring: ALTIMETER|BAROMETER
me·thane /'miːθeɪn‖'me-/ *n* [U] a natural gas which is formed from decaying matter and burns easily, sometimes causing explosions in mines —see also WILL-O'-THE-WISP
me·thinks /mɪ'θɪŋks/ **-thought** /θɔːt/ *old use or humor* it seems to me that —see also MESEEMS
meth·od /'meθəd/ *n* **1** [C] a way or manner (of doing): *That's not a good method for making people like you* **2** [C;U] (the use of) an orderly system or arrangement: *to use method rather than luck* **3** **method in one's madness** a hidden system behind disordered actions
me·thod·i·cal /mɨ̆'θɒdɪkəl‖mɨ̆'θɑ-/ *adj* careful; using an ordered system —**~ly** *adv* [Wa4]
Meth·o·dis·m /'meθədɪzəm/ *n* [U] a Christian group which follows the teachings of John Wesley —**-dist** *adj, n* [Wa5]
meth·o·dol·o·gy /ˌmeθə'dɒlədʒi‖-'dɑ-/ *n* [C;U] *tech* the set of methods used for study or action in a particular subject, as in science or education: *a new methodology* —**-gical** /ˌmeθədə'lɒdʒɪkəl‖-'lɑ-/ *adj* [Wa5] —**-gically** *adv* [Wa5]
meths /meθs/ *n* [U] *BrE infml* METHYLATED SPIRITS
me·thu·se·lah /mɨ̆'θjuːzɨ̆lə‖mɨ̆'θuː-/ *n* a very large wine bottle that holds just over 9 litres, used esp. for CHAMPAGNE
Methuselah *n often humor* a person who has lived many years, or who is unusually old-fashioned, named after the man in the Bible who was said to have lived for 969 years
meth·yl al·co·hol /ˌmeθɨ̆l 'ælkəhɒl, *tech* ˌmiːθaɪl-‖-hɔl/ also **meth·a·nol** /'meθənɒl, *tech* 'miː-‖-nɔl/, **wood alcohol**— *n* [U] a type of poisonous alcohol found in some natural substances, such as wood
meth·yl·at·ed spir·its /ˌmeθɨ̆leɪtɨ̆d 'spɪrɨ̆ts/ *n* [U] *BrE* alcohol for burning, in lamps, heaters, etc.
me·tic·u·lous /mɨ̆'tɪkjʊləs‖-kjə-/ *adj* very careful, with attention to detail: *meticulous drawings|a meticulous worker* —**~ly** *adv* —**~ness** *n* [U]
mé·ti·er /'metieɪ, 'meɪ-‖me'tjeɪ, 'metjeɪ/ *n* one's trade, profession, or type of work
Met Of·fice /'met ˌɒfɨ̆s‖-ˌɔfɨ̆s, -ˌɑf-/ *n* [(*the*) GU]

infml the group of people who study and give reports on the weather

me·tre¹, *AmE* **meter** /ˈmiːtəʳ/ *n* [C;U] (any type of) arrangement of notes or esp. words (as in poetry) into strong and weak beats —see also RHYTHM

metre², *AmE* **meter** *n* (a measure of length equal to) 39·37 inches —see WEIGHTS & MEASURES TABLE

-me·tre, *AmE* usu. **-meter** /ˌmiːtəʳ, m½təʳ/ *comb. form* [→*n*] a (stated) part of a metre: MILLIMETRE

met·ric /ˈmetrɪk/ *adj* [Wa5] concerning the system of measurement based on the metre and kilogram

met·ri·cal /ˈmetrɪkəl/ also **metric**— *adj* [Wa5] (of poetry) arranged in regular beats —**~ly** *adv* [Wa4]

met·ri·ca·tion /ˌmetrɪˈkeɪʃən/ *n* [U] the change from standards of measurement that had been used before (as, in Britain, the foot and the pound) to metres, grams, etc.

met·ri·cize, -cise /ˈmetr½saɪz/ *v* [T1;IØ] to change to the METRIC SYSTEM

metric sys·tem /ˈ·· ˌ··/ *n* [*the*+R] a system of weights and measures, now common through all the world, which works by divisions of 10, the standard measures being the kilogram for weight and the metre for length

metric ton /ˌ·· ˈ·/ *n* TON (2)

met·ro /ˈmetrəʊ/ *n* **-ros** [*the*+R;C; *by*+U] (*often cap.*) an underground railway system in cities in France or various other countries: *the Leningrad Metro* —compare UNDERGROUND

met·ro·nome /ˈmetrənəʊm/ *n* an instrument with a moving arm that can be fixed to move from side to side with a sharp sound a particular number of times per minute, and so give the speed at which a piece of music should be played

me·trop·o·lis /m½ˈtrɒpəl½s‖m½ˈtrɑ-/ *n* **1** [C; *the*+R] *fml* a chief city or the capital city of a country **2** [*the*+R] *BrE fml or humor* (*often cap.*) London **3** [*the*+R] a city or country which is in control of a system of foreign colonies (COLONY)

met·ro·pol·i·tan¹ /ˌmetrəˈpɒl½tn‖-ˈpɑ-/ *n* **1** [C;A: (*of*)] (*often cap.*) the chief priest of high rank (BISHOP) of an area in which there are BISHOPs of lower rank, esp. in the Russian ORTHODOX CHURCH **2** [C] a citizen of a METROPOLIS

metropolitan² *adj* of a METROPOLIS: *The Greater London police force is known as the Metropolitan Police.*|*She left the small island of Saint Pierre and became famous in metropolitan France*

metropolitan bish·op /··,··· ˈ··/ *n* (*often caps.*) METROPOLITAN¹ (1)

met·tle /ˈmetl/ *n* [U] **1** *fml* **a** the quality of courage **b** *often apprec* the will to continue struggling: *The runner fell and hurt his knee, but he showed his mettle by continuing in the race* **2 be on one's mettle/put someone on his mettle** to be/put someone in a position in which one/he must make the best possible effort in order to be successful

met·tle·some /ˈmetlsəm/ *adj esp. lit, usu. apprec* high-spirited

mew /mjuː/ *n, v* [C;IØ] **1** (to make) the noise that GULLs make **2** MIAOW

mews /mjuːz/ *n* **mews** [Wn3] **1** (esp. in former times) a street, square, or yard in which there are places for lodging and feeding horses **2** such a street, square, etc., that has been partly rebuilt so that people can live there, cars can be stored there, etc.

mez·za·nine /ˈmezəniːn, ˈmetsə-‖ˈmezə-/ *n* **1** also **entresol**— a floor that comes between 2 other floors of a building, esp. between the bottom floor and the next floor up, and usu. does not stretch all the way from one wall to the other **2** *AmE* (the first few rows of seats in) the lowest BALCONY in a theatre

mez·zo¹ /ˈmetsəʊ/ *adv tech* (in music) quite; not too (esp. in the phrs. **mezzo forte** and **mezzo piano**): *You shouldn't sing as loud as that; the direction in the music only says mezzo* FORTE

mezzo² *n* **mezzos** *infml* MEZZO-SOPRANO (2)

mezzo-so·pra·no /ˌ·· ·ˈ··/ *n* **1** [U] (a part in singing for) a woman's voice that is not so high as a SOPRANO*'s* nor so low as a CONTRALTO*'s* **2** [C] a woman singer with this voice

mez·zo·tint /ˈmetsəʊˌtɪnt, ˈmedzəʊ-/ *n* **1** [U] a way of printing pictures from a metal plate which has a rough surface that is polished in places to produce areas of light and shade **2** [C] a picture printed in this way

mg *written abbrev. for:* MILLIGRAM

mi /miː/ *n* [C;U] the third note in the (SOL-FA) musical SCALE: *sang (a) mi*

mi·aow, *AmE* **me·ow** /miˈaʊ/ also **mew**— *n, v* [C; IØ] (to make) the crying sound a cat makes

mi·as·ma /miˈæzmə, maɪ-/ *n* **1 a** a thick poisonous mist, believed in former times to be the cause of fevers **b** any thick unpleasant mistlike cloud **2** an evil or unpleasant influence or state that tends to weaken: *the miasma of hopelessness* —**~l** *adj*

mi·ca /ˈmaɪkə/ *n* [U] a glasslike substance that can be easily divided into very thin sheets, and is much used in making electrical instruments

mice /maɪs/ *pl. of* MOUSE

Mich·ael·mas /ˈmɪkəlməs/ *n* [R;(C)] 29th September, the feast day in honour of SAINT Michael

Michaelmas dai·sy /ˌ··· ˈ··/ *n* a type of tall garden plant that bears flat bluish-red or pink flowers at the beginning of autumn

mick /mɪk/ *n derog sl* (*often cap.*) an Irishman

mick·ey /ˈmɪki/ *n* **1** *sl* (*often cap.*) an alcoholic drink to which a drug has been secretly added that will cause the drinker to become unconscious **2 take the mickey (out of someone)** *infml* to cause someone to feel foolish by laughing at (teasing (TEASE)) him

mickey finn /ˌ·· ˈ·/ *n sl* (*often caps.*) MICKEY (1)

mi·cro- /ˈmaɪkrəʊ/ *prefix* (esp. with scientific words) little; very small: *A micro*SWITCH *is a very small electric* SWITCH —compare MACRO-

mi·crobe /ˈmaɪkrəʊb/ *n* a living creature that is so small that it cannot be seen without a microscope, and that may cause disease; bacterium

mi·cro·bi·ol·o·gist /ˌmaɪkrəʊbaɪˈɒlədʒ½st‖-ˈɑl-/ *n* a person who is trained in and works at MICROBIOLOGY

mi·cro·bi·ol·o·gy /ˌmaɪkrəʊbaɪˈɒlədʒi‖-ˈɑl-/ *n* [U] the scientific study of very small living creatures, such as bacteria —**-gical** /-baɪəˈlɒdʒɪkəl‖-ˈlɑ-/ *adj* [Wa5]

mi·cro·cos·m /ˈmaɪkrəkɒzəm‖-kɑ-/ *n* **1** [(*of*)] a small system or group of people regarded as a little self-contained world that represents all the qualities, activities, etc., of something larger **2** man, regarded (esp. by ancient thinkers) as representing the whole world or universe —compare MACROCOSM

mi·cro·e·lec·tron·ics /ˌmaɪkrəʊ-ɪˌlekˈtrɒnɪks‖-ˈtrɑ-/ *n* [U] the making of electrical apparatuses using very small parts

mi·cro·fiche /ˈmaɪkrəfiːʃ/ *n* **-fiche** *or* **-fiches** [Wn2;C;U] a sheet or piece of MICROFILM

mi·cro·film¹ /ˈmaɪkrəˌfɪlm/ *n* [C;U] (a length of) film for photographing a page, a letter, etc., in a very small size in such a way that it can be made larger by means of a machine when one wants to read it

microfilm² *v* [T1] to photograph (something) using MICROFILM

mi·cro·mesh /ˈmaɪkrəʊmeʃ/ *n* [U] a very fine net material used esp. for making stockings

mi·crom·e·ter /maɪˈkrɒmɪ̀tə‖-ˈkrɑ-/ *n* an instrument for measuring very small objects —see picture at SCIENTIFIC

mi·cron /ˈmaɪkrɒn‖-krɑn/ *n* one 1,000,000th of a metre

mi·cro·or·gan·is·m /ˌmaɪkrəʊˈɔːgənɪzəm‖-ˈɔr-/ *n* a living creature too small to be seen without a microscope

mi·cro·phone /ˈmaɪkrəfəʊn/ also (*infml*) **mike**— *n* an instrument for receiving sound waves and changing them into electrical waves, used in carrying or recording sound (as in radio, telephones, etc.) or in making sounds louder —see picture at SOUND³

mi·cro·scope /ˈmaɪkrəskəʊp/ *n* **1** an instrument that makes very small near objects seem larger, and so can be used for examining them —see picture at SCIENTIFIC **2 put someone/something under the microscope** to examine very carefully the nature of something or the behaviour, character, words, actions, etc., of someone

mi·cro·scop·ic /ˌmaɪkrəˈskɒpɪk‖-ˈskɑ-/ *adj* **1 a** of or by means of a microscope: *The scientist made a microscopic examination of the dust collected from the prisoner's clothes* **b** as if by means of a microscope: *She made a microscopic examination of her home to see that it was completely clean* **c** like a microscope: *Her house is completely clean; she has a microscopic eye for dirt* **2** *often infml* very small: *It's impossible to read his microscopic handwriting* —**~ally** *adv* [Wa4]

mi·cro·sec·ond /ˌmaɪkrəʊˈsekənd/ *n* one 1,000,000th of a second

mi·cro·wave /ˈmaɪkrəweɪv/ *n* an electric wave of very short length, used esp. in sending messages by radio, in RADAR, and in cooking food

mid /mɪd/ *prep poet* among; in the middle of

mid- *comb. form* middle; in the middle of: *She's in her mid-20s* (=is about 25 years old).|*He starts his summer holiday in mid-July.*|*It was a cold midwinter night*

mid·air /ˌmɪdˈeəʳ◂/ *n* [U] a point quite high up in the sky

mid·course /ˌmɪdˈkɔːs◂‖-ˈkors◂/ *adj* [Wa5;A; *in*+U] for or during the middle part of the course of an aircraft, space vehicle, etc.

mid·day /ˌmɪdˈdeɪ◂‖ˈmɪd-deɪ/ *n* [U] the middle of the day; 12 o'clock NOON

mid·den /ˈmɪdn/ *n* a large heap of waste matter, esp. from animals

mid·dle¹ /ˈmɪdl/ *adj* [Wa5;A] in or nearly in the centre; at the same distance from 2 or more points, or from the beginning and end of something

middle² *n* [(*the*) U;S] **1** the central part, point or position: *He planted rose trees in the middle of the garden.*|*This bill must be paid not later than the middle of the month* **2** *infml* the waist or the part below the waist: *As a man grows older, he often becomes fatter round the middle* **3 in the middle of something/doing something** in the course of or busy with something/doing something
USAGE **Centre** is close in meaning to **middle**, but **a** it gives the idea of a particular point: *the* **centre** *of the circle*|*the* **middle** *of the forest* **b** it cannot be used of long narrow things: *the* **middle** (not **the* **centre**) *of the street.*

middle³ *v* [T1] (esp. in cricket) to succeed in hitting (a ball, stroke, etc.) with the middle of a striking instrument (esp. a BAT)

Middle *adj* [Wa5;A] (of a language) of a form that developed from an earlier stage, and into a later stage: *Middle English was spoken from about* AD *1100 to 1450* —compare OLD

middle age /ˌ·· ˈ··◂/ *n* [U] the years between youth and old age: *He's nearly 60, but he still considers himself to be in middle age* —**middle-aged** *adj*

Middle Ag·es /ˌ·· ˈ··/ *n* [*the*+P] the period in European history between about AD 1100 and 1500 (or sometimes, in a wider sense, between AD 500 and 1500)

middle age spread /ˌ·· · ˈ·/ also **middle-aged spread**— *n* [U] *often humor* the increase of flesh round the waist which happens to many people when they reach MIDDLE AGE —compare SPARE TYRE

mid·dle·brow /ˈmɪdlbraʊ/ *n sometimes derog* a person who likes and is satisfied with music, painting, poetry, etc., that is of average good quality but is not very difficult to understand —compare HIGHBROW, LOWBROW

middle class /ˌ·· ˈ·◂/ *adj, n* [B; (*the*) GC *often pl. with sing. meaning*] (of) the social class to which people belong who are neither very noble, wealthy, etc., nor workers with their hands —compare LOWER CLASS, UPPER CLASS, WORKING CLASS

middle course /ˈ·· ·/ *n* [(*the*) S] a course of action which is between 2 very different ones (esp. in the phrs. **follow/take a/the middle course**)

middle-dis·tance /ˌ·· ˈ··◂/ *adj* [Wa5;A] (in sport) being or taking part in running competitions over neither very short nor very long distances

middle distance *n* [*the*+R] **1** *tech* the part of a picture or view between what is or appears to be close to the looker (FOREGROUND) and what is farthest away (background) **2** a position neither very near to nor very far from one who is looking

middle ear /ˌ·· ˈ·◂/ *n* [(*the*) S] the middle of the 3 parts of the ear, which contains 3 small bones that carry to the inner ear movements caused by sounds —see picture at EAR¹

Middle East /ˌ·· ˈ·◂/ *n* [*the*+R] the countries in Asia west of India, such as Iran, Iraq, Syria, etc., —compare FAR EAST, NEAR EAST —**Middle Eastern** *adj* [Wa5]

middle fin·ger /ˌ·· ˈ··/ *n* the longest finger, in the middle between the thumb and the shortest finger —see picture at HUMAN²

Middle King·dom /ˌ·· ˈ··/ *n* [*the*+R] *lit* China

mid·dle·man /ˈmɪdlmæn/ *n* **-men** /men/ a person who buys goods from a producer, and sells (at a gain) to a shopkeeper or directly to a user

middle name /ˌ·· ˈ·/ *n* **1** [C] a name coming between the FIRST NAME and the SURNAME: *His name is James Michael Parks; Michael is his middle name* **2** [R9] *infml* something for which a person is well known, or which is a main part of someone's character

middle-of-the-road /ˌ·· · · ˈ·◂/ *adj* [A;(F)] favouring ideas, esp. political ideas, that most people would agree with; not EXTREME or wholly in favour of one side or another

middle school /ˈ·· ·/ *n* **1** [U;C] (in certain countries) a school for children between the ages of 9 and 13 **2** [*the*+R] (in Britain) a part of a SECONDARY school for children of about 14 and 15

middle-sized /ˈ·· ·/ *adj* [Wa5] neither very large nor very small

mid·dle·weight /ˈmɪdlweɪt/ *adj, n* [Wa5] **1** (a person or thing) of average weight **2** (a BOXER) who weighs more than 147 but not more than 160 pounds

Middle West /ˌ·· ˈ·/ also **Midwest**— *n* [*the*+R] that part of the US through which flow the Mississippi river and the other smaller rivers that come into it, as far south as Kansas, Missouri, and the Ohio river —**Middle Western** *adj* [Wa5]

mid·dling¹ /ˈmɪdəlɪŋ/ *adj* [Wa5] *infml* **1** [B] that is between large and small in size, degree, etc.; that is neither good nor bad in quality, kind, etc.; average **2** [F] *esp. dial* neither very well nor ill:

"How are you today, George?" "Fair to middling"

middling² *adv infml, esp. dial* fairly; quite: *This pupil behaves middling well in class*

midge /mɪdʒ/ *n* a type of very small flying insect, like a mosquito

midg·et /ˈmɪdʒɪ̈t/ *n* **1** [C] a very, or unusually, small person **2** [A] very small, compared with others of the same kind: *midget cars|midget cameras*

mid·i /ˈmɪdi/ *n* **1** [C] a dress, skirt, etc., that reaches to about halfway between the knee and the ankle **2** [A] (of a dress, skirt, etc.) having this length

mid·land /ˈmɪdlənd/ *adj* [Wa5;A] of the middle or central part of a country

Mid·lands /ˈmɪdləndz/ *n* [*the*+P] the central parts of England

mid·most /ˈmɪdməʊst/ *adj* [Wa5;A] *esp. lit* that is in the exact middle: *There stood a wooden hut in the midmost part of the forest*

mid·night /ˈmɪdnaɪt/ *n* **1** [U] 12 o'clock at night **2** [A] in the middle of the night: *The doctor received a midnight call* **3 burn the midnight oil** to stay up late at night working, esp. studying

midnight sun /ˌ·· ˈ·/ *n* [*the*+R] the sun that can be seen at midnight in the very far north or south of the world

mid-off /ˌ· ˈ·/ *n* **1** [U] (in cricket) the position on the field behind and just to the left of the person who throws (BOWLs) the ball **2** [C] a person who fields or is fielding in this position —see picture at CRICKET²

mid-on /ˌ· ˈ·/ *n* **1** [U] (in cricket) the position on the field behind and just to the right of the person who throws (BOWLs) the ball **2** [C] a person who fields or is fielding in this position —see picture at CRICKET²

mid·point /ˈmɪdpɔɪnt/ *n* [*usu. sing.*] a point at or near the centre or middle: *We are now at the midpoint of this government's period of office*

mid·riff /ˈmɪdrɪf/ *n* **1** *infml* the part of the human body between the chest and the waist **2** *med* the muscle that separates the chest from the lower part of the body; DIAPHRAGM

mid·ship·man /ˈmɪdʃɪpmən/ *n* **-men** /mən/ [C;A] a boy or young man who is being trained to become a naval officer

mid·ships /ˈmɪdʃɪps/ *adv tech* AMIDSHIPS

midst¹ /mɪdst/ *n* [U9] *lit or old use* the middle part or position: *The soldier's courage was such that he was always in the midst of the fight.|the enemy in our midst* (=among us)

midst² *prep old use* in the middle of; among

mid·sum·mer /ˈmɪdˌsʌməʳ/ *n* [R] **1** the middle of summer **2** the summer SOLSTICE (22nd June)

Midsummer Day /ˌ··· ˈ·/ *n* [R] 24th June

midsummer mad·ness /ˌ··· ˈ··/ *n* [U] the highest degree of madness or of foolish behaviour

mid·way /ˌmɪdˈweɪ◂‖ˈmɪdweɪ/ *adj, adv* [Wa5] (that is) halfway or in a middle position (esp. in the phr. **midway between**): *There's a small village midway between these 2 towns*

mid·week /ˌmɪdˈwiːk◂‖ˈmɪdwiːk/ *n, adj* [Wa5; B;U] (happening during) the middle days of the week; Tuesday, Thursday, and/or esp. Wednesday

Mid·west /ˌmɪdˈwest/ *n* [*the*+R] MIDDLE WEST —**Midwestern** *adj*

mid·wick·et /ˌmɪdˈwɪkɪ̈t/ *n* **1** [U] (in cricket) the position on the field in front and to the right of the person who throws (BOWLs) the ball, and about halfway to the edge of the field **2** [C] a person who fields or is fielding in this position

mid·wife /ˈmɪdwaɪf/ *n* **-wives** /waɪvz/ a woman, usu. a nurse, who has received special training to help other women when they are giving birth to children

mid·wif·e·ry /ˈmɪdˌwɪfəri‖-ˌwaɪfəri/ *n* [U] the skill of, or the work done by, a MIDWIFE

mien /miːn/ *n* [C9] *esp. lit* a person's appearance, manner, or expression of face, as showing a feeling: *The judge looked at the prisoner with a thoughtful and solemn mien*

miffed /mɪft/ *adj* [F;(B)] *infml* slightly angry

might¹ /maɪt/ *v neg. contr.* **mightn't** [Wv2;I∅,2] **1 a** to be in some small degree likely to: *He might come or he might not* **b** to have been in some degree likely to: *Did you see that car nearly hit me? I might have been killed* (=but I wasn't) —compare MAY (1) **2** *polite* (in questions) to have permission to; be allowed to: *"Might I come in?" "Yes, you may"* —compare MAY (2) **3** (in CLAUSEs) **a** (expressing purpose) could: *I wrote down his telephone number, so that I might remember it* **b** (with words expressing hope, wish, or fear) would: *The prisoner had hopes that he might be set free* —compare MAY (5) **4** (suggesting that a person should do something, behave in a certain way, etc.) should: *You might at least say "thank you" when someone helps you* —compare COULD (4) **5** could have been expected to (in the phr. **might have**+*past p.*): *You might have known she'd refuse.|I might have known he'd do something silly; he's been acting strangely all week* **6** (in reported speech) MAY (1,2,3,5): *He told us that he might come, but he might not.|He asked whether he might leave it with her.|He said he feared that she might not live much longer.*|(fml) *He said I might go if I wished* **7** also (*becoming rare*) **may**— *pomp or humor* (in questions) do/does: *And what might this mean?* (=what does this mean?)|*Who might you be?* (=who are you?) —see CAN (USAGE) **8** *becoming rare past t. of* MAY (1,2): *In former times the king might do nothing without asking the permission of parliament* (=was not allowed to do anything) **9** MAY (4): *You might think you're very clever, but that doesn't give you the right to order me about!* **10 might well** to be likely to: *We lost the football match, but we might well have won if one of our players hadn't been hurt* —compare MAY **well 11 might (just) as well** MAY (just) as well: *No one will eat this food; it might just as well be thrown away*

might² *n* [U] **1** power; strength; force: *The army fought bravely, but it was crushed by the might of its powerful enemy.|He tried with all his might to move the heavy rock from the road* **2 (by/with) might and main** (by using) all one's power and strength; (by making) the greatest possible efforts

might-have-beens /ˈ·· ˌ·/ *n* [*the*+P] *infml* desirable things that could have happened in the past, but did not: *The old lady would sit for hours, thinking sadly of all the might-have-beens*

might·i·ly /ˈmaɪtɪ̈li/ *adv* **1** with power or strength; greatly: *He swore mightily* **2** *infml, becoming rare* very: *I was mightily amused by the story my friend told me*

might·n't /ˈmaɪtənt/ [Wv2] *contr. of* might not —see CONTR. (USAGE)

might·y¹ /ˈmaɪti/ *adj* [Wa1] **1** *often lit or bibl* having great power or strength; very great: *He raised the heavy hammer and struck the rock a mighty blow.|Even the mightiest of empires come to an end.|These ancient ruins are the only memory left of a mighty king* **2** *lit* appearing strong and powerful because of great size: *The mountains and the oceans are among the mighty works of God* **3 high and mighty a** *derog* considering oneself important; showing pride and a feeling of one's own importance: *Ever since she was appointed to the club committee she's been acting in a very high and mighty way* **b** of high rank and great power

mighty² *adv infml* very: *It was a mighty good meal, and everyone enjoyed it*

mi·gnon·ette /ˌmɪnjəˈnet/ *n* [U;C] a type of garden plant bearing small sweet-smelling light green flowers

mi·graine /ˈmiːgreɪn, ˈmaɪ-‖ˈmaɪ-/ *n* [C;U] a severe and repeated headache, usu. with pain on only one side of the head or face, and typically with disorder of the eyesight

mi·grant /ˈmaɪgrənt/ *n* a person or animal or esp. bird that MIGRATEs or is migrating: *Migrant workers move from country to country in search of well-paid work*

mi·grate /maɪˈgreɪt‖ˈmaɪgreɪt/ *v* [IØ (*from, to*)] **1** to move from one place to another; change one's place of living, esp. for a limited period: *Wealthy people often migrate in winter to warmer sunnier countries* **2** (of birds and fish) to travel regularly from one part of the world to another, according to the seasons of the year —see EMIGRATE (USAGE)

mi·gra·tion /maɪˈgreɪʃən/ *n* **1** [U] the act of migrating (MIGRATE): *Scientists have studied the migration of fish from one part of the ocean to another over long distances* **2** [C] a movement of many people, birds, etc., in a body from one part of the world to another: *Wars always cause great migrations of people who have been taken prisoner or taken away to work*

mi·gra·to·ry /ˈmaɪgrətəri‖-tori/ *adj* having or showing the habit of migrating (MIGRATE)

mi·ka·do /məˈkɑːdəʊ/ *n* **-dos** [*the*+R;C] (*often cap.*) (a title given by foreigners in former times to) the ruler of Japan

mike /maɪk/ *n infml* MICROPHONE

mi·la·dy /mɪˈleɪdi/ *n* [N;(A)] (*sometimes cap.*) (a form of address or title given in former times to) an English lady of high social rank —compare MILORD

milch cow /ˈmɪltʃ kaʊ/ *n* **1** a cow giving milk, or kept for milking **2** a person from whom it is easy to get money or other profit

mild¹ /maɪld/ *adj* [Wa1] **1** *usu. apprec* (of a person, his nature, temper, etc.) gentle; soft: *He has too mild a nature to get angry, even if he has good cause* —see also MEEK **and mild** **2** not hard or causing much discomfort or suffering; slight: *The thief was given a milder punishment than he deserved.*|*It's been a mild winter this year* (=not a cold winter).|*only a mild fever* **3** (of food, drink, etc.) not strong or bitter in taste: *This is a very mild cheese; it has a delicate taste and hardly any smell* —**~ness** *n* [U]

mild² *n* [U] *BrE infml* a type of beer that has a MILD¹ (3) taste: *a glass of mild and bitter* (=a mixture of mild and bitter beer)

mil·dew¹ /ˈmɪldjuː‖-duː/ *n* [U] **1** a plant disease in which plants become covered with a soft usu. whitish growth **2** a soft usu. whitish growth that forms on food, leather, etc., that has been kept for a long time in warm and slightly wet conditions —**~y** *adj*

mildew² *v* [Wv5;IØ;T1] to (cause to) become attacked by or covered with MILDEW

mild·ly /ˈmaɪldli/ *adv* **1** in a MILD manner: *She complained loudly to the shopkeeper, who answered her mildly* **2** slightly: *I was only mildly interested in the story I read in the newspaper* **3 to put it mildly** describing something as gently as possible, without making it appear as bad, serious, etc., as it may in fact be: *The minister didn't act very sensibly, to put it mildly*

mile /maɪl/ *n* **1** [C] (a measure of length or distance equal to) 1,609 metres or 1,760 yards: *He has a 10-mile drive*|*a 10 miles' drive each day to and from his work.*|*They walked for miles* (=a very long way) *without seeing a house* —see WEIGHTS & MEASURES TABLE **2** [*the*+R] a race over this distance **3** [C *usu. pl.*] *infml* a very long way; a great deal: *He was miles out in his calculations* (=they were completely wrong).|*There's no one within miles of him*|*within a mile of him as a cricketer* (=he is the best one) —see also NAUTICAL MILE

mile·age /ˈmaɪlɪdʒ/ *n* **1** [C *usu. sing.*; U] the distance that is travelled, measured in miles: *When one buys an old car, one usually asks what mileage it has done* **2** [C *usu. sing.*; U] also **mileage al·low·ance** /ˈ·· ·ˌ··/— a fixed amount of money paid for each mile that is travelled: *He uses his own car for business purposes, and is paid a generous mileage* **3** [U] *infml* an amount of use; period of usefulness: *Cecil has got a lot of mileage out of that joke I told him last year; I'm always hearing him retell it in afterdinner speeches*

mile·om·e·ter, milometer /maɪˈlɒmətəʳ‖-ˈlɑ-/ *n* an instrument fitted in a car or other vehicle to record the number of miles it travels

mil·er /ˈmaɪləʳ/ *n infml* a person/horse that runs in one-mile races

mile·stone /ˈmaɪlstəʊn/ *n* **1** a stone at the side of a road, on which is marked the number of miles to the next town **2** an (important) date, time, or event in a person's life, or in history: *The invention of the wheel was a milestone in the history of man*

mi·lieu /ˈmiːljɜː‖miːˈljɜː, -ˈjuː/ *n* **-s** *or* **-x** [*usu. sing.*] surroundings, esp. a person's social surroundings

mil·i·tan·cy /ˈmɪlətənsi/ *n* [U] *usu. derog or apprec* the state or quality of being MILITANT

mil·i·tant¹ /ˈmɪlətənt/ *adj usu. derog or apprec* having or expressing a readiness to fight or use force; taking an active part in war, a fight, or a struggle: *A few militant members of the crowd started throwing stones at the police.*|*a militant speech* —compare MILITARY —**~ly** *adv*

militant² *n usu. derog or apprec* a MILITANT person: *They say these student disorders have been caused by a few militants*

mil·i·ta·ris·m /ˈmɪlətərɪzəm/ *n* [U] *usu. derog* belief in war or the use of armed force in the directing of a nation's affairs at home and abroad —**-rist** *n* —**-ristic** /ˌmɪlətəˈrɪstɪk/ *adj* —**-ristically** *adv* [Wa4]

mil·i·ta·rize, -rise /ˈmɪlətəraɪz/ *v* [T1] **1** to supply (a country, area, etc.) with military forces and defences **2** [Wv5] to give a military character to (something): *militarizing the police force* **3** to change (something) for military use

mil·i·ta·ry¹ /ˈmɪlətəri‖-teri/ *adj* [A;(B)] of, for, by, or connected with soldiers, armies, or war fought by armies: *In some countries every healthy young man must do a year's military service* (=be a soldier for a year) *when he becomes of military age* (=old enough).|*combined naval and military operations*|*His bearing was very military* (=he looked and acted like a soldier).|*a military hospital*|*He's of a military family* (=his father, grandfather, etc., were soldiers) —compare MILITANT

military² *n* [*the*+P; (*AmE* usu. S9)] soldiers; the army: *As the police were no longer able to keep order in the city, the military were asked to help them*

military po·lice /ˌ···· ·ˈ·/ *n* [*the*+P] (*often cap.*) a special police force formed of soldiers, and dealing only with soldiers, such as those who break army rules

military po·lice·man /ˌ···· ·ˈ··/ *n* (*often cap.*) a member of the MILITARY POLICE

mil·i·tate a·gainst /ˈmɪləteɪt/ *v prep* [T1,4] to act, serve, or have importance as a reason against: *The fact that he'd been in prison militated against his chances of getting fresh employment*

mi·li·tia /məˈlɪʃə/ *n* [(*the*) GC] a body of men not belonging to a regular army, but trained as soldiers to serve only in their home country, in time of need or war —compare HOME GUARD, NATIONAL GUARD

mi·li·tia·man /mə̇ˈlɪʃəmən/ *n* **-men** /mən/ a man serving in the MILITIA

milk[1] /mɪlk/ *n* [U] **1** a white liquid produced by human or animal females for the feeding of their young, and (of certain animals, such as the cow and goat) drunk by human beings or made into butter and cheese **2** a whitish liquid or juice obtained from certain plants and trees: COCONUT *milk* —see picture at FRUIT[1] **3 come home with the milk** *BrE humor* to come home very early in the morning after being at a party all night **4 cry over spilt milk** to waste time being sorry about something bad that cannot be repaired or changed for the better **5 in milk** (esp. of a cow) in a condition to be able to produce milk **6 the milk of human kindness** the kindness and pity for the sufferings of others that are or should be natural to human beings —see also CONDENSED MILK

milk[2] *v* **1** [T1;I∅] to take milk from (a cow, goat, or other animal): *The farmer whistled as he milked* **2** [L9;(I∅)] (of a cow, goat, etc.) to give milk: *There's something wrong with this cow; she isn't milking very well* **3** [T1] to take away the poison from (a snake) **4** [T1] *infml* to get money, knowledge of a secret, etc., from (someone or something) by clever or dishonest means: *The minister was too experienced to be milked by newspaper men* (= he refused to give them any news)

milk bar /ˈ· ·/ *n* (esp. in Britain) a shop where milk, drinks made with milk, ice cream, etc., are sold and drunk or eaten

milk choc·o·late /ˌ· ˈ···/ *n* [U] chocolate for eating, made with the addition of milk and sugar —compare PLAIN CHOCOLATE

milk churn /ˈ· ·/ *n* CHURN

milk·er /ˈmɪlkəʳ/ *n* **1** [C] a person who MILKs **2** [C9] a cow that gives milk in a stated way or amount: *The farmer pointed to one of his cows, and said that it was his best milker*

milk float /ˈ· ·/ *n BrE* a vehicle used by a MILKMAN for delivering milk, now usu. driven by electricity

milking ma·chine /ˈ·· ·ˌ·/ *n* a machine for MILKing cows

milk jel·ly /ˌ· ˈ··/ *n* [C;U] (a) fruit jelly made with the addition of milk

milk loaf /ˈ· ·/ *n* a loaf of specially sweetened white bread

milk·maid /ˈmɪlkmeɪd/ *n* (esp. in former times) a woman who milks cows; DAIRYMAID

milk·man /ˈmɪlkmən/ *n* **-men** /mən/ a man who sells milk, esp. one who goes from house to house each day to deliver it

milk of mag·ne·si·a /ˌ·· · ·ˈ···/ *n* [U] a type of liquid medicine that has the colour of milk, used esp. for making the bowels move

milk pow·der /ˈ· ˌ··/ also **dried milk**— *n* [U] a powder made by taking away all the water from milk

milk pud·ding /ˌ· ˈ··/ *n* [U;C] a sweet food made with rice or a like substance, baked with milk

milk round /ˈ· ·/ *n* the journey made by a milkman when he delivers milk at houses

milk run /ˈ· ·/ *n infml* a familiar and frequently travelled journey or course

milk shake /ˌ· ˈ·‖ˈ· ·/ *n* a drink of milk and usu. ice cream shaken up together and given the taste of fruit, chocolate, etc.

milk·sop /ˈmɪlksɒp‖-sɑp/ *n derog* a boy or man who has too soft and gentle a nature, and is afraid or unwilling to do anything dangerous

milk tooth /ˈ· ·/ also (*esp. AmE*) **baby tooth**— *n* a tooth belonging to the first set of teeth of young children and animals, which come before the main set

milk·weed /ˈmɪlk-wiːd/ *n* any of several types of plant with a milklike juice

milk·y /ˈmɪlki/ *adj* [Wa1] **1** made of, containing, or like milk: *I like my coffee milky* (=made with a lot of milk) **2** (of water or other liquids) not clear; cloudy; having a milklike appearance —**milkiness** *n* [U]

Milky Way /ˌ·· ˈ·/ *n* [*the*+R] the pale white band of stars and clouds of gas that can be seen across the sky at night

mill[1] /mɪl/ *n* **1** [C] also **flourmill**— (a building containing) a machine for crushing corn or grain into flour —see also WATERMILL, WINDMILL **2** [C] a factory or WORKSHOP, esp. in the cotton industry: *Cotton cloth is made in a cotton mill.|Paper is made in a paper mill* **3** [C9] a small machine in which a stated material can be crushed into powder: *a coffee mill|a pepper mill* **4 put someone/go through the mill** to (cause someone to) pass through (a time of) hard training, hard experience, or suffering —see also RUN-OF-THE-MILL

mill[2] *v* [T1] **1 a** to crush (grain) in a mill **b** to produce (flour) by this means **2** to press or roll (a metal) in a machine **3** to cut (steel) into bars in a machine **4** [Wv5] to mark (the edge of something made of metal, esp. a coin) with regularly placed lines

mill a·bout also **mill a·round**— *v adv* [I∅] *infml* to move without purpose in large numbers: *The crowd/The cattle were milling about in the streets*

mill·board /ˈmɪlbɔːd‖-bord/ *n* [U] a type of material like cardboard but much stronger, used in making the stiff covers of books

mill·dam /ˈmɪldæm/ *n* a bank or wall of stone built across a stream so as to form a MILLPOND

mil·le·nar·i·an /ˌmɪlə̇ˈneərɪən/ *n* a person who believes that the MILLENNIUM (2) will come

mil·lenn·i·um /mɪˈlenɪəm/ *n* **-nia** /nɪə/ **1** [C] a period of 1,000 years **2** [*the* + R] a future age in which all people will be happy, contented, and living in good conditions

mil·le·pede /ˈmɪlə̇piːd/ *n* MILLIPEDE

mill·er /ˈmɪləʳ/ *n* a man who owns or works a mill that produces flour, esp. a WINDMILL or a WATERMILL

mil·let /ˈmɪlə̇t/ *n* [U] **1** the small seeds of certain grasslike plants used as food: *millet cakes|a bag of millet* **2** a plant producing such seeds —see picture at CEREAL

mil·li- /ˈmɪlə̇/ *prefix* [*n*→*n*] a 1,000th part of (a standard measure in the metric system): *a* MILLIGRAM|*a* MILLIMETRE —see WEIGHTS & MEASURES TABLE

mil·li·bar /ˈmɪlə̇bɑːʳ/ *n* a standard amount used in measuring the pressure of the air (ATMOSPHERE)

mil·li·gram, -gramme /ˈmɪlə̇græm/ *n* 1,000th of a gram —see WEIGHTS & MEASURES TABLE

mil·li·li·tre, *AmE* **-ter** /ˈmɪlə̇ˌliːtəʳ/ *n* 1,000th of a litre —see WEIGHTS & MEASURES TABLE

mil·li·me·tre, *AmE* **-ter** /ˈmɪlə̇ˌmiːtəʳ/ *n* 1,000th of a metre —see WEIGHTS & MEASURES TABLE

mil·li·ner /ˈmɪlə̇nəʳ/ *n* a person who makes and/or sells women's hats and ornamental additions to them

mil·li·ne·ry /ˈmɪlə̇nəri‖-neri/ *n* [U] **1** the articles made or sold by a MILLINER **2** the work of a MILLINER

mil·lion /ˈmɪljən/ *determiner, n, pron* **million** *or* **millions** [see NUMBER TABLE 2] **1** (the number) 1,000,000; 10^6 —see HUNDRED (USAGE) **2 in a million** of the highest quality, character, etc; of whom or which it would be difficult to find the

equal: *She thinks her husband is a man in a million* **3 a/one chance in a million** very little chance —**~th** *determiner, n, pron, adv* [see NUMBER TABLE 3]
mil·lion·aire /ˌmɪljəˈneəʳ/ *n* a person who has 1,000,000 pounds or dollars; very wealthy man
mil·li·pede, millepede /ˈmɪlåpiːd/ *n* a type of small creature rather like a worm, with a body formed of many joints, most of which have 2 pairs of legs
mill·pond /ˈmɪlpɒnd‖-pɑnd/ *n* **1** a stretch of water kept in place by a bank built across a stream, used for driving the wheel of a WATERMILL **2 like a millpond** also **as calm as a millpond**— (of the sea) very calm
mill·race /ˈmɪlreɪs/ *n* the fast-flowing current of water that turns the wheel of a WATERMILL
mill·stone /ˈmɪlstəʊn/ *n* **1** one of the 2 circular stones between which corn is crushed into flour in a mill **2** a person who or thing that gives someone great trouble, anxiety, etc.: *His lazy son, who refuses to do any work, is a millstone round his neck*
mill·wheel /ˈmɪlwiːl/ *n* a large wheel, esp. one turned by water, used for driving a mill
mill·wright /ˈmɪlraɪt/ *n* a skilled workman who makes and repairs WINDMILL*s* and WATERMILL*s*
mil·om·e·ter /maɪˈlɒmåtəʳ‖-ˈlɑ-/ *n* MILEOMETER
mi·lord /mɪˈlɔːd‖-ɔrd/ *n* [N;C;(A)] (*sometimes cap.*) (a name, form of address, or title given by the French in former times to) a wealthy Englishman, who might or might not be a lord —compare MILADY
milt /mɪlt/ *n* [U] (the organ of a male fish containing) seeds that cause the eggs of female fish to grow
mime¹ /maɪm/ *n* **1** [C;U] an act or the practice of using actions to show meaning, as for amusement or when one cannot speak a language: *I couldn't speak Chinese, but I showed in mime that I wanted a drink.*|*the art of mime* **2** [C] (in ancient Greece and Rome) a type of simple theatrical play in which the actors made fun of real people and real events **3** [C] an actor who performs without using words
mime² *v* **1** [I∅] to act in MIME **2** [T1] to act (something) out in the manner of a MIME: *The actor was miming the movements of a bird* **3** [T1] to copy the appearance, behaviour, manners, etc., of (someone) in an amusing way
mim·e·o·graph¹ /ˈmɪmiəgrɑːf‖-græf/ *n AmE* DUPLICATOR
mimeograph² *v* [Wv5;T1] *AmE* DUPLICATE: *a mimeographed copy*
mi·met·ic /måˈmetɪk/ *adj usu. tech* having or showing the ability, habit, or quality of copying
mim·ic¹ /ˈmɪmɪk/ *n* **1** a person who copies, or who is good at copying another's manners, speech, etc., esp. in a way that causes laughter **2 a** an animal that copies the actions of people **b** a bird that can copy the human voice
mimic² *adj* [Wa5;A] **1** not real; pretended: *The children formed themselves into 2 groups, and fought a mimic battle* **2** giving protection by being like something else: *The mimic colouring of tigers protects them when they are among trees*
mimic³ *v* **-ck-** [T1] **1** to copy (someone or something), esp. in order to make people laugh: *The boy made all his friends laugh by mimicking the teacher's slow and solemn way of talking* **2** to appear so like (something else) as to deceive people into thinking it is the real thing: *She cut and painted pieces of paper that mimicked flowers so well that some people thought they were real*
mim·ic·ry /ˈmɪmɪkri/ *n* [U] **1** the act of MIMICking³ (1) **2** (of animals, birds, plants, etc.) a likeness, in colour, patterns, etc., to the natural surroundings, that gives protection against enemies
mi·mo·sa /mɪˈməʊzə, -sə‖-sə/ *n* **1** [C;U] any of several types of plant or small tree, esp. one that bears small sweet-smelling flowers in round yellow balls **2** [U] the flowers of this plant
min *written abbrev. for:* **1** MINIMUM **2** minute(s)
min·a·ret /ˌmɪnəˈret, ˈmɪnəret/ *n* a tall thin tower, one or more of which form part of a mosque, from which Muslims are called to prayer
min·a·to·ry /ˈmɪnətəri‖-tori/ *adj fml* showing an intention to punish or to hurt; threatening
mince¹ /mɪns/ *v* **1** [Wv5;T1] to cut (esp. meat) into very small pieces **2** [Wv4;T1;I∅] *derog* to pronounce (words) too nicely, showing, or pretending to show, a fineness of mind or nature and an absence of roughness **3** [Wv4;L9] *derog* to walk in an unnatural way, taking little short steps, esp. (of a man) in a womanlike way **4 mince matters/one's words** (*usu. neg.*) to speak of something bad or unpleasant using soft language, and avoiding plain direct words
mince² *n* [U] **1** *BrE* MINCEd meat **2** *AmE* MINCEMEAT
mince·meat /ˈmɪns-miːt/ *n* [U] **1** a mixture of CURRANT*s*, dried fruit, dried orange skin, and other things, but no meat, all cut into very small pieces, that is used as a sweet filling to put inside pastry and is eaten esp. at Christmas **2 make mincemeat of** *infml* **a** to defeat (a person) completely **b** to destroy (a belief, an opinion, an argument, etc.) by the use of better arguments
mince pie /ˌ· ˈ·/ *n* a small round covered piece of pastry filled with MINCEMEAT
minc·er /ˈmɪnsəʳ/ also **mincing ma·chine** /ˈ·· ·ˌ·/— *n* a machine containing blades, used for cutting food, esp. meat, into very small pieces
minc·ing·ly /ˈmɪnsɪŋli/ *adv* in a mincing (MINCE¹ (2,3)) way
mind¹ /maɪnd/ *n* **1** [C] thoughts; a person's way of thinking or feeling: *Her mind is filled with dreams of becoming a great actress* **2** [C *usu. sing.*] the quality which gives the ability to think or feel; INTELLECT: *He has a very sharp mind* (=he thinks and understands quickly) **3** [C] a person who thinks, esp. one with a good brain and the ability to lead, to control, etc.: *The best minds* (=the cleverest people) *in the country are trying to find a way out of its difficulties* **4** [C *usu. sing.*] intentions: *Nothing was further from my mind* (=that was not at all what I intended) **5 be in two minds (about something)** to have different opposing thoughts (about something), and so be unable, or find it difficult, to reach a decision **6 be of one mind** (of 2 or more people) to agree; have the same opinion: *There was no disagreement among the ministers; they were all of one mind* (*on/about this subject*) **7 be of the same mind a** (of one person) to have the same unchanged opinion, intention, etc.: *A year ago he formed an unfavourable opinion of her character, and he's of the same mind today* **b** (of 2 or more people) to agree; have the same opinion: *He and his wife are of the same mind; they both want their daughter to go to university* **8 call/bring to mind** to remember **9 change one's mind** to form a new and different intention, opinion, or desire **10 come to mind** to be thought about; present itself to the thoughts **11 from time out of mind** from a time that goes back further than human memory **12 go out of someone's mind** to be forgotten: *She should have answered the letter yesterday, but it went right out of her mind* (=she completely forgot to answer it) **13 have a good mind to** *infml* to have a strong wish to; be very near a decision to: *He's not grateful for all the help I've given him, so I've a good mind not to help him any more* **14 have half a mind to** to have a desire or intention that is not firmly formed; be in a state between making and not making a decision

to **15 in one's right mind** *usu. nonassertive* not mad; able to think rightly: *He'd never have done such a terrible thing if he'd been in his right mind* —compare **out of one's** MIND **16 keep/bear something in mind** not to forget something; include something in one's considerations: *He promised to keep my wishes in mind* **17 keep one's mind on something** to continue to think about or pay attention to something, without letting one's thoughts or attention wander to another subject **18 know one's own mind** to know and be sure about the things one wants, or intends to do **19 make up one's mind** to reach a decision **20 make up one's mind to something/to doing something** to accept something (considered to be) bad, unpleasant, etc., that cannot be avoided or changed: *If he accepts the position in the firm, he must make up his mind to living in a very lonely place* **21 mind over matter** *sometimes humor* control of events or material objects by the power of the mind **22 on one's mind** troubling one's thoughts; causing anxiety, unhappiness, etc. **23 out of one's mind** not able to think correctly; mad: *His sufferings in prison sent him out of his mind* —compare **in one's right** MIND **24 out of sight, out of mind** it is easy to forget someone or something not seen regularly **25 put someone in mind of someone or something** to remind someone of someone or something; cause someone to remember, esp. because of a likeness in appearance, character, manners, etc. **26 put one's mind to something** also **give one's mind to something**— to give all, or much of, one's thoughts or attention to a particular subject **27 set one's mind on something/on doing something** to have a firm unchangeable desire for something; be strongly determined **28 speak one's mind** to express plainly one's thoughts and opinions, even if unpleasant to hear **29 take one's/someone's mind off something** to turn one's/someone's thoughts or attention from an unpleasant to a more pleasant subject: *She found that hard work was the best way to take her mind off her sorrow* **30 to one's mind a** in one's opinion; according to the way in which one thinks: *Most people agree with him, but to my mind he's quite wrong* **b** *becoming rare* to one's liking: *The arrangements he made were very much to my mind; I was quite happy with them* **31 turn one's mind to something** to direct one's thoughts to some new matter —see also ABSENCE OF MIND, PRESENCE OF MIND, ONE-TRACK MIND, CROSS **someone's mind, give someone a** PIECE **of one's mind**

mind² *v* **1** [T1,5a,6a;I∅(OUT): *imper. or infin.*] *esp. BrE* to be careful (of); pay close attention (to): *He said to the little boy "Mind! Don't go too near the edge of the cliff."*|*When you drive through the village, mind the holes in the road.*|*The workmen on the roof shouted to the people in the street below "Mind your heads"* (= something is falling, and might fall on your heads).|*Mind your backs!* (= please get out of the way, as I want to come through).|*Just get on with your work; don't mind me* (=don't pay any attention to my presence).|*"Don't mind me!" he said, as the rude man pushed past him* (=I am annoyed that you have been rude and thoughtless to me).|*Don't mind me; I'll be all right* (=don't trouble yourself about me).|*Mind you read the examination questions very carefully before you begin to answer them* (=be sure to read them; take care to read them) **2** [Wv6;T1,4,5,6a;V4;X7;I∅] (*esp. in neg. sentences, sentences with* would, *questions, and answers saying* yes) to have a reason against or be opposed to (a particular thing); be troubled by or dislike: *He asked me if he could go home early, and I said I didn't mind* (=I agreed to it).|*He asked me which one I'd like, and I said I didn't mind* (=I would be pleased with either).|*"What do you think of the new teacher?" "I don't mind him"* (=I quite like him, but not very much).|*I wouldn't mind a cup of tea* (=I'd rather like one).|*"Do you mind the window (being) open?" "Yes, I do mind; it's much too cold."*|*"Do you mind waiting for an hour or 2?" "Yes, I mind very much."*|*I don't mind how you do it, as long as you get it finished quickly.*|*"Have some more beer" "I don't mind if I do"* (=thank you, I would like some) **3** [T1] to take care or charge of; look after: *He stayed at home and minded the baby while his wife was out.*|*I asked a stranger if he'd mind my bags while I went to make a telephone call* **4** [T1,5a,6a] *dial, esp. ScotE* to remember: *I mind the time when we were in Edinburgh together* **5 mind one's own business** (*usu. imper.*) to pay attention to one's own affairs, and not to those of another or others: *"What has John sent you in that little parcel?" "Mind your own business"* (=I won't tell you) **6 mind you** also **mind— a** take this fact into account: *"Roger has been very bad-tempered this week" "Yes, but mind you, he's been rather ill just recently"* **b** do not think that what I am saying is not true: *He's a very nice fellow, mind you, but I wouldn't want to marry him* (=he's very nice, but even so, I wouldn't want to) **7 never mind a** do not feel sorry, sad, or troubled: *When she lost her watch, her father said "Never mind; I'll buy you another one"* **b** it does not matter (about); it is not important: *"Never mind your damaged gate; what about the front of my car!" said the angry driver after he had crashed into the gate* **8 never you mind** *infml* it is not your business, and you are not to be told: *She told her daughter "Never you mind what your father and I were talking about; we're not going to tell you"* **9 would you mind** also **do you mind— a** *polite* please: *Would you mind making a little less noise?* **b** I am offended or annoyed: *"Here, do you mind!" he said when she knocked over his drink* —see also **mind one's** P's **and q's**

mind-bend·ing /ˈ· ˌ··/ *adj infml* **1** (of a drug) causing one to imagine strange things in the mind, have strange feelings, etc. **2** difficult beyond understanding

mind-blow·ing /ˈ· ˌ··/ *adj infml* **1** very exciting; very shocking **2** (of a drug) causing one to see strange things in the mind, have strange feelings, etc. —compare BLOW **someone's/one's mind**

mind-bog·gling /ˈ· ˌ··/ *adj infml* causing very great surprise and wonder; ASTOUNDing

mind·ed /ˈmaɪndɨd/ *adj* [F3,9] having in some degree the will or desire: *He has enough money to travel all over the world, if he were so minded*

-minded *comb. form* **1** [*adj→adj*] possessing the kind of mind described: *You shouldn't take any notice of what these evil-minded men say about you.*|*It needs a strong-minded man to deal with this difficult state of affairs* —see also ABSENT-MINDED, BLOODY-MINDED, BROADMINDED, HIGH-MINDED, NARROW-MINDED, SINGLE-MINDED **2** [*n→adj*] having a mind that is interested in or sees the value or importance of the thing stated: *There'd be fewer accidents if all roadusers were more safety-minded*

-mind·er /ˈmaɪndəʳ/ *comb. form* a person whose job is to look after the thing stated: *a child-minder*|*a machine-minder*

mind-ex·pand·ing /ˈ· ·ˌ··/ *adj infml* (of a drug) causing all one's senses and feelings to become stronger and deeper than usual

mind·ful /ˈmaɪndfəl/ *adj* [F+*of*] *fml* giving thought or careful attention (to); not forgetful (of): *He said he was mindful of his promises, and intended to keep them* —**~ness** *n* [U+*of*]

mind·less /ˈmaɪndləs/ *adj* **1** [B] *derog* not having, needing, or using the power of thinking; stupid: *It's tiring and mindless work.*|*mindless cruelty* **2**

[F+*of*] not giving thought or attention (to); regardless or forgetful (of): *The fireman rushed into the burning house, mindless of the danger* **3** [B] *esp. lit* having no mind; not controlled by the mind of man: *Man has always been in fear of the mindless forces of nature* (=thunder, lightning, etc.) —**~ly** *adv* —**~ness** *n* [U]

mind read·er /ˈ· ˌ··/ *n often humor* a person who is thought to, or claims to, be able to know what another person is thinking without being told —**mind reading** *n* [U]

mind's eye /ˌ· ˈ·/ *n* [U] the imagination; the memory (esp. in the phr. **in one's mind's eye**): *The old lady can still see in her mind's eye every piece of furniture in the house where she lived as a child*

mine¹ /maɪn/ *determiner old use, bibl, or poet* (before a vowel sound or *h*, or after a noun) my: *Mine eyes have seen the glory of the coming of the Lord.|mine host*

mine² *pron* [Wp1] (*poss. form of* I) that/those belonging to me: *That bag's mine; it has my name on it.|That's a particular favourite of mine* (=one of my particular favourite things).|*This isn't my own car; mine is being repaired* —see also OF (6)

mine³ *n* **1** [C] (*often in comb.*) a deep hole or network of holes under the ground from which coal, gold, tin, and other mineral substances are dug: *a tinmine|Many men were buried where they worked when there was an accident at the mine* —see also COALMINE, GOLDMINE, and compare QUARRY **2** [S+*of*] a person from whom or thing from which one can obtain a great deal (of something, esp. information or knowledge): *The old man had lived in the village all his life, and he's a mine of information about its history* **3** [C] a metal case containing explosives, that is placed just below the ground and is exploded electrically from far away or when stepped on or passed over **4** [C] a metal case containing explosives, that is placed on or below the surface of the sea and is exploded when touched by a ship or, electrically, when a ship passes over it —compare DEPTH CHARGE **5** [C] (a passage dug underground beneath an enemy position, containing) an explosive **6** [C] a type of FIREWORK made from a case containing several small explosives that are thrown into the air by an explosion, and themselves explode with a loud noise and often with coloured flames

mine⁴ *v* **1** [T1;I∅ (*for*)] to dig or work a MINE³ (1) in (the earth): *These men work underground for 6 hours at a time, mining for coal* **2** [T1] to obtain by digging from a MINE³ (1): *A great deal of tin used to be mined in the south-western part of England* **3** [T1 *often pass.*] to lay MINE*s*³ (3,4) in or under: *All the roads leading to the city had been mined* **4** [T1 *usu. pass.*] to destroy by MINE*s*³ (3,4): *Many seamen lost their lives when their ship was mined* **5** [T1] to dig a MINE³ (5) under: *Parties of soldiers worked day and night until they had mined the walls of the castle* —compare UNDERMINE

mine de·tec·tor /ˈ· ·ˌ··/ *n* an instrument used for discovering the presence of a MINE³ (3,4)

mine dis·pos·al /ˌ· ·ˈ··/ *n* [U] the action of making MINE*s*³ (3,4) harmless, as by taking out the part (FUSE) that sets off the explosion

mine·field /ˈmaɪnfiːld/ *n* **1** a stretch of land or water in which MINE*s*³ (3,4) have been placed **2** something that is full of hidden dangers

mine·lay·er /ˈmaɪnˌleɪəʳ/ *n* a ship or aircraft used for putting MINE*s*³ (4) into the sea —**-laying** *n* [U]

mine out *v adv* [T1 *usu. pass.*] to take all the minerals from (a place) by mining (MINE⁴ (1)): *The whole area has been mined out*

min·er /ˈmaɪnəʳ/ *n* **1** (*often in comb.*) a worker in a MINE³ (1) **2** a soldier who digs or lays MINE*s*³ (5) —compare MINOR²

min·e·ral¹ /ˈmɪnərəl/ *n* **1** any of various esp. solid substances that are formed naturally in the earth (such as stone, coal, salt, etc.), esp. as obtained from the ground for man's use **2** [*usu. pl.*] *BrE* MINERAL WATER (3): *This shop sells minerals*

mineral² *adj* [Wa5] of, connected with, containing, or having the nature of minerals; belonging to the class of minerals: *Salt is a mineral substance.|Many African countries have great mineral wealth*

mineral king·dom /ˈ··· ˌ··/ *n* [*the*+R] one of the 3 divisions into which the world is generally divided; all matter except animals and plants —compare ANIMAL KINGDOM, VEGETABLE KINGDOM

min·e·ral·o·gist /ˌmɪnəˈrælədʒɪ̈st‖-ˈrɑ-, -ˈræ-/ *n* a person who has studied and has knowledge of MINERALOGY

min·e·ral·o·gy /ˌmɪnəˈrælədʒi‖-ˈrɑ-, -ˈræ-/ *n* [U] the scientific study of minerals

mineral oil /ˈ··· ·/ *n* [C;U] any type of oil that is obtained from the ground

mineral wa·ter /ˈ··· ˌ··/ *n* **1** [C *usu. pl.*; U] water that comes from a natural spring and contains minerals, often drunk for health reasons **2** [U] water to which gas has been added, mostly sold in bottles as a drink **3** [U] *BrE* a nonalcoholic drink containing gas, sweetened and given a particular taste (as of orange), mostly sold in bottles

min·e·stro·ne /ˌmɪnɪ̈ˈstrəʊni/ *n* [U] a type of soup (of Italian origin) containing vegetables, small pieces of soft pastry (PASTA), and meat juices

mine·sweep·er /ˈmaɪnˌswiːpəʳ/ *n* a naval ship fitted with special apparatus for taking MINE*s*³ (4) from the sea —**-sweeping** *n* [U]

min·gle /ˈmɪŋgəl/ *v esp. lit* **1** [I∅ (*with*, TOGETHER)] to mix (with another thing or with people); come together to form an undivided whole: *The king often left his palace at night, and mingled unknown with the people in the streets.|The wounded soldier fell back in the river, and his blood mingled with its waters* **2** [T1 (*with*, TOGETHER) *often pass.*] to mix (different things) together: *a speech that contained praise mingled with blame*

min·gy /ˈmɪndʒi/ *adj* [Wa1] *infml* not generous, with money or in quantity; STINGY: *He's so mingy that he hates spending even a penny*

min·i /ˈmɪni/ *n infml* anything that is smaller than others of its kind usually are, esp. **a** (*usu. cap., as tdmk*) a type of small car **b** a MINIskirt

mini- *comb. form* [*n*→*n*] *infml* very small or short compared with others of its kind: *a mini*CAB|*a minidress|a miniskirt*

min·i·a·ture /ˈmɪnɪətʃəʳ, ˈmɪnɪ̈tʃəʳ‖ˈmɪnɪətʃʊər/ *n* **1** [C] a very small painting of a person **2** [U] *tech* the art of painting such pictures **3** [C (*of*)] a very small copy or representation of anything **4** [A] (esp. of something copied or represented) very small: *The child was playing on the floor with his collection of miniature farm animals* **5 in miniature** very like the stated thing or person, but much smaller

min·i·a·tur·ist /ˈmɪnɪətʃərɪ̈st, ˈmɪnɪ̈tʃə-‖ˈmɪnɪə-tʃʊ-/ *n* an artist who paints MINIATURE*s*

min·i·bus /ˈmɪnibʌs/ *n* [C; *by*+U] a large VAN² (1) fitted with seats so that between 6 and 12 people can travel in it

min·im /ˈmɪnɪ̈m/ *AmE* usu. **half note**— *n* a musical note that is sounded only half as long as a whole note (SEMIBREVE) —see picture at NOTATION

min·i·mal /ˈmɪnɪ̈məl/ *adj* [Wa5] of the smallest possible amount, degree, or size: *Fortunately, the storm only did minimal damage to the farmer's crops.|Her clothing was minimal* —**~ly** *adv*

min·i·mize, -mise /ˈmɪnɪ̈maɪz/ *v* [T1] **1** to lessen to the smallest possible amount or degree: *You can minimize the dangers of driving, by taking care to obey all the rules of the road* **2** to put the value, importance, effect, etc., of (something) at the lowest possible amount; consider, judge, or treat (something) not seriously: *He'd made a serious mistake, and it was no use trying to minimize its seriousness*

min·i·mum /ˈmɪnɨməm/ *n* **-ma** /mə/ *or* **-mums** **1** [C *usu. sing.*] the least, or the smallest possible, quantity, number, or degree: *This price is his minimum; he refuses to lower it any further.|The temperatures recorded were the minima for the area* **2** [A] smallest, or smallest possible (in amount, degree, etc.): *The minimum pass mark in this examination is 40 out of 100.|He couldn't join the police, because he was below the minimum height allowed by the rules* —opposite **maximum**

minimum wage /ˌ··· ˈ·/ *n* [*usu. sing.*] the lowest wage permitted by law, by a rule, or by agreement, for certain work

min·ing /ˈmaɪnɪŋ/ *n* [U] (*often in comb.*) the action or industry of getting minerals out of the earth by digging: *coalmining|a mining company*

min·i·on /ˈmɪnɪən/ *n* [C9 *often pl.*] *derog, esp. lit* a person who, in order to please, is full of praise for his important or powerful master, behaves towards him like a slave, and receives special favours from him

minion of the law /ˌ··· · · ˈ·/ *n* **minions of the law** [*often pl.*] *derog, often humor* a policeman, prison officer, or other person whose duty it is to see that laws are obeyed

min·is·ter /ˈmɪnɨstəʳ/ *n* [C;N] **1** a person in charge of a particular department of the government **2** a person of lower rank than an AMBASSADOR, who represents his government in a foreign country **3** a Christian leader in charge of a single group of PRESBYTERIAN or NONCONFORMIST worshippers, and their church. He does work much like that of a priest but is not given that name

min·is·ter·i·al /ˌmɪnɨˈstɪərɪəl/ *adj* [Wa5] **1** of a MINISTER (1,2): *As a part of his ministerial duties, he often had to call on the president of the country* **2** of the body of MINISTER*s* (1,2) that form a government: *It's believed in the country that ministerial changes will be made in the near future* (=that some ministers will be dismissed, and new ones appointed) —**~ly** *adv*

ministering an·gel /ˌ···· ˈ··/ *n apprec, esp. lit* a person, usu. a woman, who helps and serves, with love and kindness, those who are sick or in trouble

minister to also **administer to**— *v prep* [D1;T1] *esp. lit* to serve; perform duties to help (someone or something): *ministering to the sick*

min·is·trant /ˈmɪnɨstrənt/ *n esp. lit* a person who gives good careful service to others, or supplies them with things that are needed

min·is·tra·tion /ˌmɪnɨˈstreɪʃən/ *n* [U;C *usu. pl. with sing. meaning*] (a) giving of help and service, esp. to the sick or to those in need of, or desiring, the services of a priest: *All the ministrations of the doctors and nurses couldn't save the sick child's life.| Before the murderer was hanged, he was given the ministrations of a priest*

min·is·try /ˈmɪnɨstri/ *n* (*often cap.*) **1** [C (*of*)] **a** a government department led by a MINISTER (1): *The army, navy, and airforce are all controlled by the Ministry of Defence* **b** the building(s) in which such a department works **2** [C9 *usu. sing.*] the office or position of a MINISTER (1,2), or the length of time during which this is held **3** [C *usu. sing.*] the body of MINISTER*s* (1) forming a government **4** [*the*+GU] priests, considered as a body **5** [*the*+R] the priests' profession: *Our son wants to ente the ministry*

min·i·ver /ˈmɪnɨvəʳ/ *n* [U] *tech* a type of white fu used esp. for ornamenting noblemen's ceremonia clothes

mink /mɪŋk/ *n* **1** [Wn1;C] a type of small WEASEL like animal —see picture at CARNIVOROUS **2** [U the valuable brown fur of this animal, often use for making ladies' coats

min·now /ˈmɪnəʊ/ *n* any of several types of ver small FRESHWATER fish

mi·nor[1] /ˈmaɪnəʳ/ *adj* [Wa5] **1** [B] lesser or smalle in degree, size, etc.: *He left most of his money to hi sons; his daughter received only a minor share of hi wealth* **2** [B] of lesser importance or seriousness *The young actress was given a minor part in the ne play* **3** [B] *med* not dangerous to life: *a mino illness|a minor operation* **4** [E] *old public school Br* being the younger of 2 boys (usu. brothers) of th stated name (esp. in the same school): *Simkin minor* **5** [E] (in music) being the stated MINO KEY: *a* SYMPHONY *in F minor* —compare MAJOR

USAGE Although it means "smaller" or "of lesse importance", **minor** is not used in comparison with *than*: **He is* **minor** *than I am.* Compar JUNIOR.

minor[2] *n law* a person below the age (now 18 i Britain) at which he is fully responsible in law fo his actions —compare MINER

mi·nor·i·ty /maɪˈnɒrɨti‖mɨˈnɔ-, mɨˈnɑ-/ *n* **1** [G *usu. sing.*] the smaller number or part; a number c part that is less than half: *The nation wants peace only a minority want the war to continue.|As all th members of the committee except the chairman wer in favour of the suggestion, he was in a minority o one* **2** [C] a small part of a population which i different from the rest in race, religion, etc.: *Law were passed to protect religious minorities* **3** [A] of c supported by a small, or the smaller, number c people: *Cricket is a minority interest in the US.| members of the committee disagreed with the ma report, so they produced a minority report* **4** [U9] *la* the state or time of being a MINOR: *The cou ordered the boy to be looked after in a special hom during his minority* —compare MAJORITY

minority gov·ern·ment /·ˌ··· ˈ···/ *n* a governmen which has fewer seats in a parliament than th combined opposition parties have

minor key /ˌ·· ˈ·/ *n* **1** (in music) a set of note (KEY) in which there is a MINOR THIRD, whic gives the music a sad sound **2 in a minor key** (c speech or writing) quietly; not causing excitement sadly

minor plan·et /ˌ·· ˈ··/ *n* ASTEROID

minor suit /ˌ·· ˈ·/ *n* (in BRIDGE[3]) either of th SUIT*s*[1] (3) CLUB*s*[1] (5) or DIAMOND*s* (4), which hav a lower value than the MAJOR SUIT*s*

minor third /ˌ·· ˈ·/ *n* (in music) a degree c difference (INTERVAL) of 3 SEMITONE*s* between notes

Min·o·taur /ˈmɪnətɔːʳ, ˈmaɪ-/ *n* [*the*+R] a creatur which had the body of a man and the head of BULL, and which lived, according to the ancien Greek stories, in the LABYRINTH (1) of Crete

min·ster /ˈmɪnstəʳ/ *n* (now usu. part of a name (*often cap.*) a great or important church, esp. on that formed part of a SETTLED COMMUNITY of hol men (ABBEY): *Westminster|York Minster*

min·strel /ˈmɪnstrəl/ *n* **1** (in the MIDDLE AGES) musician who travelled about the country singin songs and poems written by himself or others one of a company of performers who travel abou and give light amusing shows to people on holida by the sea, at FAIR*s*, etc.

min·strel·sy /ˈmɪnstrəlsi/ *n* [U] **1** the art of

MINSTREL **2** the songs and music of a MINSTREL

mint¹ /mɪnt/ *n* **1** [C] a place, esp. a government building, in which official coins are made **2** [S] *infml* a large amount (of money) **3** [A] (of a coin or postage stamp) in perfect condition, as if new and unused **4 in mint condition** (of any objects which people collect for pleasure, such as books, postage stamps, coins, etc.) in perfect condition, as if new and unused

mint² *v* [T1] **1** to make (a coin) **2** to invent (a new word, phrase, etc.): *The poet minted several words that can't be found in any dictionary*

mint³ *n* **1** [U] any of several types of small plant, all of which have leaves with a particular smell and taste, used in preparing drinks, in making CHEWING GUM and other types of sweet, etc.: *mint tea|Many people put mint leaves in the water when they boil potatoes* **2** [C] *infml* PEPPERMINT: *Have one of these mints!*

mint ju·lep /ˌ· ˈ··/ *n* JULEP

mint sauce /ˌ· ˈ·/ *n* [U] a type of green liquid made of MINT leaves, cut into very small pieces and mixed with VINEGAR and sugar, served in Britain with lamb

min·u·et /ˌmɪnjʊˈet/ *n* (a piece of music for) a type of slow graceful dance first performed in France about 300 years ago

mi·nus¹ /ˈmaɪnəs/ *prep* **1** made less by (the stated figure or quantity): *17 minus 5 leaves 12* **2** being the stated number of degrees below the freezing point of water: *The temperature was minus 10 degrees* **3** *infml* without: *He won the fight, but when it ended he was minus 2 front teeth* —opposite **plus**

minus² *n* **1** also **minus sign** /ˈ·· ·/— a sign (−) used for showing **a** that the stated number is less than zero **b** that the second number is to be taken away from the first **2** a quantity that is less than zero: *He calculated his gains and losses of money, and the result was a minus*

minus³ *adj* [Wa5;A] (of a number or quantity) less than zero

min·us·cule /ˈmɪnəskjuːl/ *adj* very small

min·ute¹ /ˈmɪnɪ̵t/ *n* **1** [C] one of the 60 parts into which an hour is divided: *The train arrived at exactly 4 minutes past 8.|It's only a few minutes' walk from here to the station* (=a walk taking a very short time) **2** [S] *infml* a very short space of time: *I'll be ready in a minute* (=very soon).|*"Are you ready yet?" "No, but I won't be a minute"* (=I'll be ready very soon) **3** [C] one of the 60 parts into which a degree of angle is divided: *The exact measurement of this angle is 80 degrees 30 minutes, which can be written as 80° 30′* —see WEIGHTS & MEASURES TABLE **4** [C] a short note of an official nature, such as on a report prepared by someone else, asking for certain action to be taken, expressing an opinion, etc.: *The minister read the report very carefully, and at the end wrote a minute expressing his complete agreement* —see also MINUTES **5 the minute (that)** as soon as: *Although we hadn't met for 25 years, I recognized him the minute (that) I saw him* **6 to the minute** (of the stated time) exactly: *He wakes up every morning at 7 o'clock to the minute* —see also UP TO THE MINUTE

minute² /ˈmɪnɪ̵t/ *v* [T1] to make a note of (something) in the MINUTES of a meeting

mi·nute³ /maɪˈnjuːt‖-ˈnuːt/ *adj* [Wa1] **1** very small, in size or degree: *His writing's so minute that it's difficult to read.|a minute improvement* **2** giving attention to the smallest points; very careful and exact —**~ness** *n* [U]

minute book /ˈmɪnɪ̵t bʊk/ *n* a book in which the MINUTES of a meeting are written

minute gun /ˈmɪnɪ̵t gʌn/ *n* a gun fired every minute, as a sign of sorrow at the death or funeral of a king or other great person, or (in the days before radio) by a ship in danger of being wrecked

minute hand /ˈmɪnɪ̵t hænd/ *n* the longer of the 2 hands on a watch or clock, that shows the minutes —see picture at CLOCK¹

mi·nute·ly /maɪˈnjuːtli/ *adv* **1** to a very small degree: *The 2 men's accounts of the accident varied only minutely* **2** very carefully and exactly: *He examined the jewel minutely before saying how much it was worth* **3** into very small pieces: *Cut the bread up minutely*

min·ute·man /ˈmɪnɪ̵tmæn/ *n* **-men** /men/ an American citizen who was ready, if given a minute's warning, to serve as a soldier in the war of independence against Great Britain

min·utes /ˈmɪnɪ̵ts/ *n* [(*the*) P (*of*)] a written record of business done, suggestions made, decisions taken, etc., at a meeting: *Before the committee started its work, the minutes of the last meeting were read out.|to take* (=write) *minutes*

minute steak /ˈmɪnɪ̵t steɪk/ *n* a small thin piece of fine meat (STEAK) that can be quickly cooked

mi·nu·ti·a /maɪˈnjuːʃɪə, mɪ̵-‖mɪ̵ˈnuː-/ *n* **-tiae** /ʃi-iː/ [(*of*) *usu. pl.*] a very small point, that often does not seem worth considering; small exact detail: *A high court official planned all the minutiae of the ceremony of crowning the queen*

minx /mɪŋks/ *n* [C; *you*+N] *derog, often humor* a young girl who does not show, or behave with, proper respect towards those older than her

mir·a·cle /ˈmɪrəkəl/ *n* **1** [C] an act or happening (usu. having a good result), that cannot be explained by the laws of nature, esp. one done by a holy person: *According to the Bible, Christ worked many miracles; one of these miracles was the turning of water into wine.|Doctors do their best to treat the sick, but they can't perform miracles* **2** [C] a wonderful surprising unexpected event: *The teacher told the lazy careless pupil that it'd be a miracle if he passed the examination* **3** [C+*of*] a wonderful example (of a quality, ability, etc.): *The doctors performed a heart operation that was a miracle of medical skill*

miracle play /ˈ··· ·/ also **mystery play**— *n* a type of theatrical play, often performed in the MIDDLE AGES, based on stories from the Bible, on the life of Christ, or on the lives of holy men and women —compare MORALITY PLAY

mi·rac·u·lous /mɪ̵ˈrækjʊləs‖-kjə-/ *adj* very wonderful; caused, or seeming to be caused, by powers beyond those of nature: *The army won a miraculous victory over a much stronger enemy* —**~ly** *adv*: *It was a terrible explosion but, miraculously, no one was killed*

mi·rage /ˈmɪrɑːʒ‖mɪ̵ˈrɑʒ/ *n* **1** a strange effect of hot air conditions in a desert, in which distant objects seem near, or in which objects appear which are not really there: *The travellers in the desert saw in the distance a lake and trees growing beside it, but it was only a mirage* **2** something, such as a dream, a hope, or a wish, that cannot come true

mire¹ /maɪəʳ/ *n* [U] *esp. lit* **1** deep mud, such as that on soft ground after heavy rain **2 drag someone/someone's name through the mire** to bring shame or dishonour on a person, by making public something bad, unpleasant, etc. **3 in the mire** in difficulties, esp. such as bring shame or dishonour on a person

mire² *v esp. lit, becoming rare* **1** [T1;I∅: (*in*)] to (cause to) sink and become fixed in deep mud **2** [T1] to cover or make dirty with mud **3** [T1 (*in*)] to cause (a person) to be caught up in difficulties

mir·ror¹ /ˈmɪrəʳ/ *n* **1** (*often in comb.*) a piece of glass, or other shiny or polished surface, that throws back (REFLECTs) images that fall on it: *A woman usually carries a small mirror in her bag.|The motorist saw in his driving mirror that a police car was following him* **2** [(*of*)] a true faithful representation (of something): *This newspaper claims to be the mirror of public opinion* (=claims to express what the people are really thinking)

mirror² *v* [T1] to show, as in a MIRROR: *The table top was so highly polished that it mirrored the ornaments placed on it*

mirror im·age /'·· ,··/ *n* [(*of*)] an image or representation of something in which the right side of the original appears on the left, and the left side on the right

mirth /mɜːθ‖mɜrθ/ *n* [U] *esp. lit* merriness and gaiety expressed by laughter: *Christmas is a time of mirth, especially for children* —**~ful** *adj* —**~fully** *adv* —**~less** *adj*

mir·y /'maɪəri/ *adj* [Wa1] *esp. lit* muddy; covered or made dirty with MIRE

mis- /mɪs/ *prefix* **1** bad(ly): MISFORTUNE|MISBEHAVE **2** wrong(ly): MISCALCULATION|MISUNDERSTAND **3** (shows the opposite of, or lack of, something): MISTRUST

mis·ad·ven·ture /,mɪsəd'ventʃəʳ/ *n* [C;U] **1** *esp. lit* (an accident; event caused by) bad luck: *He worked hard, and his lack of success was the result of misadventure* **2 death by misadventure** *law* the death or killing of a person by accident

mis·ad·vise /,mɪsəd'vaɪz/ *v* [Wv5;T1 *usu. pass.*] to give (a person) wrong advice

mis·al·li·ance /,mɪsə'laɪəns/ *n* a uniting of people that is wrong or unsuitable, esp. a marriage with a person of a different social class

mis·an·thrope /'mɪsənθrəʊp/ also **mis·an·thro·pist** /mɪs'ænθrəpɪ̈st/— *n* a person who hates everybody, trusts no one, and avoids being in the company of others —compare MISOGYNIST, PHILANTHROPIST —**-thropic** /,mɪsən'θrɒpɪk‖-'θrɑ-/ *adj* —**-thropically** *adv* [Wa4]

mis·an·thro·py /mɪs'ænθrəpi/ *n* [U] hatred or distrust of everyone

mis·ap·pli·ca·tion /,mɪsæplɪ̈'keɪʃən/ *n* [C;U: (*of*)] (a) wrong or bad use (of something): *He was wrongly made to pay a fine, owing to a misapplication of the law*

mis·ap·ply /,mɪsə'plaɪ/ *v* [Wv5;T1] to put to a wrong use; use wrongly or for a wrong purpose

mis·ap·pre·hend /,mɪsæprɪ'hend/ *v* [T1] *fml* to understand (something) in a mistaken way: *The accident was caused by one motorist completely misapprehending the intentions of the other/misapprehending what the other intended*

mis·ap·pre·hen·sion /,mɪsæprɪ'henʃən/ *n* [C,C5] *often fml* **1** a mistaken understanding or failure to take the correct meaning **2 (labour) under a misapprehension** (to be) in a state of understanding incorrectly or of being mistaken: *I thought there was a fast train every hour, but I was (labouring) under a misapprehension*

mis·ap·pro·pri·ate /,mɪsə'prəʊprieɪt/ *v* [Wv5;T1] *fml or tech* to take dishonestly and put to a wrong use, esp. one's own use: *The lawyer was sent to prison for misappropriating a large amount of money placed in his care* —**-ation** /-prəʊpri'eɪʃən/ *n* [U;C: (*of*)]

mis·be·got·ten /,mɪsbɪ'gɒtn◂‖-'gɑ-/ *n* **1** [A] *derog or humor* (of a person) worthless; CONTEMPTIBLE **2** [A] *derog or humor* (of an idea, plan, opinion, etc.) badly produced or formed **3** [B] *lit* **a** born to an unmarried mother **b** born unlucky

mis·be·have /,mɪsbɪ'heɪv/ *v* [T1;I∅] to behave (oneself) badly or improperly: *The pupil was punished, not for bad work, but for misbehaving (himself) in class*

mis·be·haved /,mɪsbɪ'heɪvd◂/ *adj* behaving badly: *a misbehaved child*

mis·be·ha·viour, *AmE* **-vior** /,mɪsbɪ'heɪvɪəʳ/ *n* [U] bad improper behaviour

mis·cal·cu·late /,mɪs'kælkjʊleɪt‖-kjə-/ *v* [T1;I∅] to calculate (figures, time, etc.) wrongly; form a wrong judgment of (something): *I missed the train; I'd miscalculated the time it'd take me to reach the station* —**-lation** /mɪs,kælkjʊ'leɪʃən‖-kjə-/ *n* [C;U]

mis·call /,mɪs'kɔːl/ *v* [T1;X1 *usu. pass.*] to call (someone or something) by a name that is wrong, untrue, or not deserved: *This is a town, although it's often miscalled a city*

mis·car·riage /,mɪs'kærɪdʒ, 'mɪskærɪdʒ/ *n* **1** [C] an act or case of producing lifeless young, esp. early in their development, before the proper time of birth —compare ABORTION, STILLBIRTH **2** [C;U] *fml* (an example of) **a** failure to act on an intention, arrangement, plan, etc. **b** failure to reach an intended result or place, or to reach that place at the intended time

miscarriage of jus·tice /,··· · '··/ *n* [C;U] *law* (a) failure by the law courts to do justice; wrong judgment or decision by a law court, as when a person who is not guilty is sent to prison

mis·car·ry /mɪs'kæri/ *v* [I∅] **1** (of a woman) to give birth too early for life to be possible; have a MISCARRIAGE **2** (of an intention, plan, etc.) to be unsuccessful; fail to have the intended or desired result

mis·cast /,mɪs'kɑːst‖-'kæst/ *v* **miscast** [T1 *usu. pass.*] **1** to give (an actor or actress) an unsuitable part in a play, film, etc. **2** to provide (a part in a play, film, etc.) with an unsuitable actor or actress **3** to provide (a play, film, etc.) with actors and actresses who are given unsuitable parts

mis·ce·ge·na·tion /,mɪsɪ̈dʒɪ̈'neɪʃən‖-sedʒ-/ *n* [U] the production of young by a sexual union of people belonging to different races

mis·cel·la·ne·ous /,mɪsə'leɪnɪəs/ *adj* of several kinds or different kinds; having a variety of sorts, qualities, etc. —**~ly** *adv* —**~ness** *n* [U]

mis·cel·la·ny /mɪ'seləni‖'mɪsɪ̈leɪni/ *n* [(*of*)] **1** a mixture of various kinds: *The minister's speech was a miscellany of wise and foolish arguments* **2** a collection of writings on different subjects, often by different writers: *a miscellany of American short stories*

mis·chance /,mɪs'tʃɑːns‖-'tʃæns/ *n* [C;U] *fml* (an example of) bad luck: *Only a serious mischance will prevent him from arriving tomorrow*

mis·chief /'mɪstʃɪ̈f/ *n* **1** [U] bad, but not seriously bad, behaviour or actions, as of children, probably causing trouble, and possibly damage or harm: *If his mother leaves him alone for 5 minutes, the little boy gets into mischief.|She knew the children were up to some mischief* (=doing or planning something wrong), *and she found them in the garden digging up the flowers* **2** [U] troublesome playfulness, or an expression, such as a smile or a look, of a desire to behave in this way: *She gave her father a smile that was full of mischief, and he wondered what trick she planned to play on him* **3** [C] *infml* a person, esp. a child, who is often troublesomely playful: *Before long, the baby will be as big a mischief as his 3-year-old brother* **4** [U] damage, harm, or hurt done by a person, animal, or thing; wrong-doing: *The monkey did a lot of mischief before it was caught and put back in its cage; it broke a number of things.|He's sorry for having told lies, but the mischief* (=the harm caused by his lies) *has been done and can't be undone* **5 do someone/oneself a mischief** *usu. humor esp. BrE* to hurt someone/oneself: *If you try to lift a heavy weight like that you'll do yourself a mischief* **6 to make mischief (between people)** to speak so as to cause trouble, disagreement, quarrels, unfriendly feelings, etc. (between people)

mis·chie·vous /ˈmɪstʃ$\frac{1}{2}$vəs/ *adj* **1** *sometimes apprec* having or showing a liking for playfulness, esp. of a rather troublesome kind: *One expects healthy children to be mischievous at times* **2** *derog* causing harm, often with intention: *Someone's spreading mischievous stories about the minister's private life* (=is saying that it is bad) —**~ly** *adv* —**~ness** *n* [U]

mis·con·ceive /ˌmɪskənˈsiːv/ *v* [T1] **1** [Wv5] to think (something) out badly and without proper consideration for what is suitable: *The government's plan for the railways is wholly misconceived; it is quite unsuitable for a modern travel system* **2** *fml* to be mistaken in one's understanding of (something); MISCONSTRUE: *He completely misconceived my meaning*

mis·con·cep·tion /ˌmɪskənˈsepʃən/ *n* [C;U] (an example of) understanding wrongly; state of being mistaken in one's understanding

mis·con·duct[1] /ˌmɪsˈkɒndʌkt‖-kɑn-/ *n* [U] *fml* **1** [(*with*)] bad behaviour, esp. improper sexual behaviour: *found guilty of misconduct with his neighbour's wife* **2** [(*of*)] bad control, as of a business company

mis·con·duct[2] /ˌmɪskənˈdʌkt/ *v* [T1] *fml* **1** to behave (oneself) badly or improperly, esp. with a person of the opposite sex: *It was proved that his wife had misconducted herself with several men* **2** to control (something, such as a business or business affairs) badly; deal badly with: *He has so misconducted his affairs that he's deep in debt*

mis·con·struc·tion /ˌmɪskənˈstrʌkʃən/ *n* **1** [U] mistaken understanding: *His actions were perfectly honest and open, and there's no possibility of misconstruction* **2** [C] an example of this; untrue meaning placed on something said or done: *A law must be stated in the clearest language, so that there may be no misconstructions of it* **3 open to misconstruction** that may be understood wrongly

mis·con·strue /ˌmɪskənˈstruː/ *v* [Wv5;T1] to place a wrong meaning on (something said or done)

mis·count[1] /ˌmɪsˈkaʊnt/ *v* [T1;IØ] to count wrongly: *The teacher miscounted the number of boys who were present*

miscount[2] *n* an example or case of miscounting

mis·cre·ant /ˈmɪskrɪənt/ *n* [C; *you*+N] *old use* a person of evil character and deeds, deserving to be hated

mis·cue /ˌmɪsˈkjuː/ *v* **1** [IØ] (in BILLIARDS) to make a faulty stroke with the CUE (=a long wooden stick) **2** [Wv5;T1;IØ] (in cricket) to hit (the ball) not with the centre of the BAT, and in a direction different from the one intended

mis·date /ˌmɪsˈdeɪt/ *v* [Wv5;T1] **1** to put a wrong date on (a letter, cheque, etc.) **2** to give a wrong date to (something, such as an historical event)

mis·deal[1] /ˌmɪsˈdiːl/ *v* **-dealt** /ˈdelt/ [Wv5;T1;IØ] to DEAL wrongly, as when giving cards to players: *He's so awkward with his hands that he always misdeals the cards.*|*the misdealt cards*

misdeal[2] *n* [*usu. sing.*] a mistake in DEALing cards, such as one resulting in a player receiving more or fewer cards than he should have

mis·deed /ˌmɪsˈdiːd/ *n esp. fml or lit* a wrong or wicked deed; act deserving punishment: *He deserved long imprisonment for his many misdeeds*

mis·de·mea·nour, *AmE* **-nor** /ˌmɪsdɪˈmiːnəʳ/ *n* **1** a bad or improper act that is not very serious **2** *law* a crime that is less serious than, for example, stealing or murder

mis·di·rect /ˌmɪsd$\frac{1}{2}$ˈrekt/ *v* [T1] **1** to direct (someone) wrongly: *I asked a boy the way to the station, but he misdirected me* **2** [Wv5] to address (a letter, parcel, etc.) wrongly **3** [Wv5] to use (one's strength, abilities, etc.) in the wrong way, or for a wrong purpose: *The work isn't worth doing, and he misdirects his efforts by spending so much time on it* **4** (of a judge) to guide (a JURY) incorrectly on the law with the result that a wrong decision is, or may be, given —**~ion** /-ˈrekʃən/ *n* [U (*of*)]

mis·do·ing /ˌmɪsˈduːɪŋ/ *n* [*usu. pl.*] *esp. lit or fml* a bad act; MISDEED: *God will punish him for his misdoings*

mise-en-scène /ˌmiːz ɒn ˈsen, -ˈseɪn‖-ɑn- (*Fr* mizɑ̃sɛn)/ *n* **mise-en-scènes** (*same pronunciation*) *Fr* **1** *tech* (the arranging of) the furniture, scenery, and other objects used on the stage in the performance of a play **2** *lit* the surroundings in which an event takes place: *I listened on the radio to a description of the splendid mise-en-scène during the ceremony of crowning the queen*

mi·ser /ˈmaɪzəʳ/ *n* [C; *you*+N] *derog* a person who loves money and hates spending it, and who becomes wealthy by storing it

mis·e·ra·ble /ˈmɪzərəbəl/ *adj* **1** [B] very unhappy: *The child is cold, hungry, and tired, so of course he's feeling miserable* **2** [B] causing unhappiness, discomfort, etc.: *They started their holiday on a miserable day; it was cold, and the rain never stopped.*|*miserable conditions* **3** [A] very poor (in quality) or very small or low (in degree or amount), and thus often not worthy of consideration or respect: *That man would sell his honour for a few miserable pounds.*|*a miserable failure*

mis·e·ra·bly /ˈmɪzərəbli/ *adv* **1** in a way that causes great discomfort, unhappiness, etc.: *It was a miserably cold morning when he left the house* **2** in or to a very bad or low degree: *She failed miserably.*|*Soldiers so miserably armed* (=with weapons of poor quality) *can't be expected to fight well*

mi·ser·ly /ˈmaɪzəli‖-ər-/ *adj derog* having or showing the nature of a MISER —**-liness** *n* [U]

mis·e·ry /ˈmɪzəri/ *n* **1** [U *often pl. with sing. meaning*] great unhappiness or great pain and suffering (of body or of mind): *There are poor people without homes, who sleep in the streets, and live in misery.*|*Her baby died and, to add to her misery, her husband deserted her* **2** [C;(N)] *derog infml, esp. BrE* a person who is always unhappy and complaining, esp. one who does not like others to enjoy themselves

mis·fire[1] /ˌmɪsˈfaɪəʳ/ *v* [IØ] **1** (of a gun) to fail to send out the bullet when fired **2** (of a car engine) to produce irregularly, or to fail to produce, the flash that explodes the petrol mixture **3** (of a plan, joke, etc.) to fail to have the desired or intended result

misfire[2] *n* **1** an act of misfiring (MISFIRE) **2** something that MISFIREs

mis·fit /ˈmɪsˌfɪt/ *n* **1** a person who does not fit well and happily into his social surroundings, or who is not suitable for the position he holds **2** *tech* a garment that fits badly the person for whom it is made

mis·for·tune /mɪsˈfɔːtʃən‖-ɔr-/ *n* **1** [U] bad luck, often of a serious nature: *His failure in business was due not to misfortune, but to his own mistakes* **2** [C] a very unfortunate condition, accident, or event: *She believed that the greatest of her misfortunes was that she'd never had any children*

mis·giv·ing /ˌmɪsˈgɪvɪŋ/ *n* **1** [U *often pl. with sing. meaning*] feelings of doubt, fear (of the future), and/or distrust: *He looked with misgiving at the food on his plate. It was the first time Mary had cooked him a meal.*|*She hoped her new servant could be trusted, but she had some misgivings* **2** [C] a particular feeling of doubt, fear, etc.: *I like your* *plan in principle; my only misgiving is that it may take too long to carry out*

mis·gov·ern /ˌmɪsˈgʌvən‖-ərn/ *v* [Wv5;T1] to govern (a country) badly or unjustly —**~ment** *n* [U]

mis·guide /mɪsˈgaɪd/ *v* [T1 *usu. pass.*] to lead or influence (someone) into a wrong or foolish course of action, or into forming an incorrect opinion

mis·guid·ed /mɪsˈgaɪdɨd/ *adj* **1** (of a person) led by oneself or by others to act or think wrongly or foolishly **2** (of behaviour, an action, etc.) directed to wrong or foolish results; badly judged: *The child deserved punishment, and it was misguided kindness not to punish him* —**~ly** *adv*

mis·han·dle /ˌmɪsˈhændl/ *v* [Wv5;T1] to handle or treat (something or someone) roughly, without skill, or insensitively: *This scientific instrument will break very easily if it's mishandled.|Our company lost an important order because the whole affair was badly mishandled by the directors*

mis·hap /ˈmɪshæp/ *n* **1** [U] unfortunate or unwanted happenings, usu. not of a serious nature: *The little girl travelled alone; fortunately, the long journey passed without mishap* **2** [C] an unfortunate, often slight, accident; unfortunate happening: *He hurt his knee during the football match, but this mishap didn't stop him playing*

mis·hear /ˌmɪsˈhɪəʳ/ *v* **-d** /-ˈhɜːd‖-ˈhɜrd/ [Wv5;T1; IØ] to hear (someone or something) wrongly or mistakenly

mis·hit¹ /ˌmɪsˈhɪt/ *v* **-hit**; *pres. p.* **-hitting** [T1;IØ] (in cricket, GOLF, etc.) to hit (the ball) in a faulty way

mishit² *n* (in cricket, GOLF, etc.) a faulty stroke

mish·mash /ˈmɪʃmæʃ/ *n* [S (*of*); U] *infml* an untidy, disorderly mixture: *This new book is a strange mishmash of ideas* —compare HOTCHPOTCH

mis·in·form /ˌmɪsɪnˈfɔːm‖-ɔrm/ *v* [Wv5;T1 (*about*)] to tell (someone) something that is incorrect or untrue, either on purpose or by accident: *He charged the government with misinforming the nation about the cost of its plans*

mis·in·ter·pret /ˌmɪsɪnˈtɜːprɨt‖-ɜr-/ *v* [Wv5;T1] to put a wrong meaning on (something said, done, etc.); explain wrongly: *The driver misinterpreted the policeman's signal and turned in the wrong direction* —**~ation** /ˌmɪsɪntɜːprɨˈteɪʃən‖-ɜr-/ *n* [U;C]

mis·judge /ˌmɪsˈdʒʌdʒ/ *v* [Wv5;T1] to judge (a person, action, time, distance, etc.) wrongly; form a wrong opinion of: *He's honest, and you misjudge him if you think he isn't*

mis·judg·ment, -judgement /mɪsˈdʒʌdʒmənt/ *n* [C; U: (*of*)] an act or the action or fact of forming a wrong opinion (about something or someone)

mis·lay /mɪsˈleɪ/ *v* **-laid** /ˈleɪd/ [Wv5;T1] to put (something) in a place and forget where; lose (something) in this way, often only for a short time

mis·lead /mɪsˈliːd/ *v* **-led** /ˈled/ [Wv4,5;T1 (*into*)] to cause (someone) to think or act wrongly or mistakenly; guide wrongly, sometimes with the intention to deceive: *Her appearance misled him; he thought she was young, but she wasn't.|Don't let his friendly words mislead you into trusting him.|a misleading description|a poor misled young girl* —**~ingly** *adv*

mis·man·age /ˌmɪsˈmænɪdʒ/ *v* [Wv5;T1] to control or deal with (private, public, or business affairs) badly or wrongly —**~ment** *n* [U (*of*)]

mis·match¹ /ˌmɪsˈmætʃ/ *v* [Wv5;T1 *often pass.*] to match wrongly or unsuitably: *These 2 football teams have been mismatched; one is much stronger than the other, and is certain to win.|mismatched socks*

mis·match² /ˈmɪs-mætʃ/ *n* an act, case, or result of mismatching

mis·name /ˌmɪsˈneɪm/ *v* [Wv5;T1 *often pass.*] to call (someone or something) by a wrong or unsuitable name

mis·no·mer /mɪsˈnəʊməʳ/ *n* a wrong or unsuitable name given to someone or something: *To call him a landowner is a misnomer; he rents the land that he farms*

mi·so·gy·nist /mɨˈsɒdʒɨnɨst‖mɨˈsɑ-/ *n* a person who hates women

mi·so·gy·ny /mɨˈsɒdʒɨni‖mɨˈsɑ-/ *n* [U] hatred of women

mis·place /ˌmɪsˈpleɪs/ *v* [T1 *often pass.*] **1** to put in an unsuitable or wrong place or position: *Among all this old furniture that modern chair looks misplaced* **2** [Wv5] to have (good feelings) for an undeserving person or thing: *Your trust in that man is misplaced; he'll deceive you if he gets the chance* **3** [Wv5] MISLAY: *I've misplaced my glasses again* —**~ment** *n* [U (*of*)]

mis·print¹ /ˌmɪsˈprɪnt/ *v* [Wv5;T1] to make a mistake in printing (a word, letter, etc.): *The word "battle" was misprinted in the newspaper as "bottle"*

mis·print² /ˈmɪs-prɪnt/ *n* a mistake in printing

mis·pro·nounce /ˌmɪs-prəˈnaʊns/ *v* [Wv5;T1] to pronounce (a word, letter, etc.) incorrectly

mis·pro·nun·ci·a·tion /ˌmɪs-prənʌnsiˈeɪʃən/ *n* [C; U: (*of*)] (an example of) incorrect pronunciation

mis·quote /ˌmɪsˈkwəʊt/ *v* [Wv5;T1] to make a mistake or mistakes in reporting (words) spoken or written by (a person): *The minister complained that several newspapers had misquoted him/had misquoted his speech/had misquoted what he said* —**-quotation** /ˌmɪskwəʊˈteɪʃən/ *n* [U;C]

mis·read /ˌmɪsˈriːd/ *v* **-read** /ˈred/ [T1] **1** [Wv5] to read (something) wrongly: *He misread the date on the letter; it was October 15th, not 16th* **2** to make a mistake in understanding (something read or thought about): *The general misread the enemy's intentions, and didn't expect an attack*

mis·re·port /ˌmɪsrɪˈpɔːt‖-ˈport/ *v* [Wv5;T1 *often pass.*] to give an incorrect or untrue account of (something), or of (words) spoken by (someone), often on purpose: *The story in the newspaper isn't completely true; some of the facts have been misreported*

mis·rep·re·sent /ˌmɪsreprɪˈzent/ *v* [T1] to give an untrue account, explanation, or description of (someone, or someone's words or actions), in such a way that unfavourable ideas may be spread: *You misrepresent his refusal to fight when you say it was because he was afraid* —**~ation** /ˌmɪs-reprɪzenˈteɪʃən/ *n* [U;C: (*of*)]

mis·rule¹ /ˌmɪsˈruːl/ *v* [Wv5;T1] MISGOVERN

misrule² *n* [U] **1** government that is bad, or that lacks order: *The people suffered under the misrule of the young and inexperienced governor* **2** *esp. lit* disorder; lawlessness

miss¹ /mɪs/ *v* **1** [T1,4;IØ] to fail to hit, catch, find, meet, touch, hear, see, etc. (something or someone): *The falling rock just missed my head.|The fielder missed an important catch, and the cricket match was lost.|He arrived too late and missed the train.|She went to the station to meet her husband, but missed* (=failed to meet) *him in the crowd.|Please be quiet; I don't want to miss a word of the news on the radio.|We arrived late at the theatre, and missed* (=failed to see and hear) *the first act of the play.|If I don't miss my guess* (=if I'm not guessing wrongly), *that's old Frank over there.|I don't want to miss seeing that singer on television tonight* **2** [T1,4] to avoid or escape from (something unpleasant) by such a failure: *I was lucky to miss the traffic accident; most days I'd have been driving along that* *road at that time.|He narrowly missed being seriously hurt, if not killed, by the explosion* **3** [T1] to discover the absence or loss of (someone or something): *She thought her little boy was standing behind her in the shop; she didn't miss him till she looked round* **4** [T1] to feel or suffer from the lack of (something): *Give the beggar a coin; you won't miss it* **5** [T1,4] to feel sorry or unhappy at the absence or loss of (someone or something): *The old man sometimes told his children that they'd miss him when he was dead.|He missed the sunshine when he returned to England after 4 years in a hot country* **6 miss the boat** also **miss the bus**— *infml* to lose a good chance, esp. by being too slow: *You should have bought those shares a month ago; now you've missed the boat* **7 miss the/one's mark** to fail to reach the/one's intended or desired aim or result: *Some people think the book very amusing, but I think it misses the mark* (=it fails to amuse me) —see also HIT-OR-MISS, MISSING, MISS OUT

miss² *n* **1** a failure to hit, catch, hold, etc., that which is aimed at: *The hunter's first shot was a miss, but his second killed the lion.|The fielder dropped an easy catch; it was a bad miss* —see also NEAR MISS **2** *infml* MISCARRIAGE (1) **3 a miss is as good as a mile** an escape from danger, defeat, etc., that is only just successful is as good as one that is easily obtained **4 give something a miss** *infml, esp. BrE* to avoid something; not take, do, etc., something

miss³ *n* (*sometimes cap.*) **1** [N] (a form of address used) **a** *esp. BrE* (by pupils to) a woman teacher **b** (esp. by shopkeepers, servants, etc., to) an unmarried woman **c** (by anyone to) a waitress, girl working in a shop, etc. **2** [N;C] *often humor or derog* a girl or young woman, esp. one who is playful or has the faults expected of a schoolgirl **3** [C *usu. pl.*] *tech* a girl whose size (for the purpose of buying garments) is between that of a child and a woman

Miss *n* [A] **1** (a title placed before the name of) an unmarried woman or a girl: *Miss Brown|The Miss Browns|the Misses Brown are sisters.|the Misses Brown and White* **2** (a title placed before) the name of a place or a type of activity which a young unmarried woman has been chosen to represent, usu. for reasons of beauty: *Miss England 1978|Miss Industry 1971*

mis·sal /ˈmɪsəl/ *n* (*often cap.*) a book containing the complete religious service during the year for MASS (1) in the ROMAN CATHOLIC church

mis·shap·en /ˌmɪsˈʃeɪpən, mɪˈʃeɪ-/ *adj* (esp. of the body or a part of it) badly or wrongly shaped or formed

mis·sile /ˈmɪsaɪl‖ˈmɪsəl/ *n* **1** [C] an explosive weapon which can fly under its own power (ROCKET), and which can be aimed at a distant object —see also GUIDED MISSILE, INTERCONTINENTAL BALLISTIC MISSILE **2** [A] of, for, or related to such weapons: *The missile* BASE *was closely guarded* **3** [C] *fml, often pomp* an object or a weapon thrown by hand or shot from a gun or other instrument: *The angry crowd at the football match threw bottles and other missiles at the players*

miss·ing /ˈmɪsɪŋ/ *adj* [Wa5] **1** [B] not to be found; not in the proper or expected place; lost: *One of the duties of the police is to try to find missing persons.|I noticed that he had a finger missing from his left hand* **2** [F; *the*+P] (of a soldier, fighting vehicle, etc.) not found after a battle, and therefore considered killed, wounded, destroyed, etc.: *7 of our planes are missing.|wept for the missing and the dead*

missing link /ˌ·· ˈ·/ *n* **1** [C] a fact that must be found in order to complete an argument, an act of reasoning, a proof of something, etc. **2** [*the*+R; (C)] **a** a form of creature, supposed but not proved to have existed, mid-way in the development of man from monkey-like creatures **b** *humor* an ugly man who looks rather like a monkey

mis·sion /ˈmɪʃən/ *n* **1** a group of people, esp. people acting for their country (DELEGATES), who are sent abroad for a special reason: *a medical mission of doctors and nurses|a British trade mission to Russia* **2** the duty or purpose for which these people are sent: *A party of soldiers was landed secretly at night on the enemy coast; their mission was to blow up the radio station.|When they had landed on the moon, they sent a radio message back to mission control* (=the people who were controlling the space flight) *on earth* **3** (*often cap.*) **a** a building or an office or offices where the work of these people is planned or carried out **b** a building or group of buildings in an area, at home or abroad, in which a particular form of religion is taught, medical services are given, poor people are helped, etc.: *They come to the mission from many miles around to see a doctor or a priest* **4** the particular work for which one believes oneself to have been sent into the world; that which one believes oneself to have been chosen by God to do: *He believed that it was his mission to carry the word of God to those who'd never heard it.|She's always helping people in trouble; that seems to be her mission in life* **5 mission accomplished** *infml* (said when someone has been ordered to go somewhere to do something and has done it successfully)

mis·sion·a·ry /ˈmɪʃənəri‖-neri/ *n* a person who is sent usu. to a foreign country, to teach and spread his religion there

mis·sive /ˈmɪsɪv/ *n esp. humor or pomp* a letter, esp. one of great, or too great length

miss out *v adv* **1** [T1] to leave out; fail to put in, add, read, etc.: *His account of the accident misses out 1 or 2 important facts.|When the teacher was giving the children sweets, she missed me out* **2** [IØ (*on*)] to lose a chance to gain advantage or enjoyment: *When sweets are being given out she always misses out, because she's never there.|When he couldn't come to the office party he thought he was missing out on something, but he wasn't really, because it wasn't very enjoyable*

mis·spell /ˌmɪsˈspel/ *v* **-spelt** /ˈspelt/ *or* **-spelled** [Wv5;T1] to spell wrongly —**~ing** *n* [C;U]

mis·spend /ˌmɪsˈspend/ *v* **-spent** /ˈspent◂/ [Wv5; T1] to spend (time, money, etc.) wrongly or unwisely; waste

mis·state /ˌmɪsˈsteɪt/ *v* [Wv5;T1] to state (a fact, argument, etc.) wrongly or falsely

mis·state·ment /ˌmɪsˈsteɪtmənt/ *n* [C;(U)] a wrong or untrue statement: *The minister's speech contained several misstatements about the cost of the new aircraft.|a misstatement of fact*

mis·sus, missis /ˈmɪsɨz/ *n* [*the*+R,R9] *infml* **1** *nonstandard* the wife of the man speaking, spoken to, or spoken about: *The missus* (=my wife) *will be angry if I'm home late.|How's the missus?* (=your wife) **2** *now rare* (used esp. among servants) the woman who is the head, or wife of the head, of a house or family: *The postman asked the servant girl who opened the door, "Can I have a word with your missus?"*

miss·y /ˈmɪsi/ *n* [N;A] *infml now rare* (*used as a friendly form of address or title*) a young girl

mist¹ /mɪst/ *n* **1** [C;U] (a period or area of) cloudlike bodies made up of very small drops of water floating in the air, near or reaching to the ground; thin FOG: *The mountaintop was covered in mist.|John Keats, a famous English poet, wrote that autumn was the season of mists* —see also MISTS, SCOTCH MIST **2** [U; (*the*) S] a film, esp. one formed of small drops of water, through which it is hard to see clearly: *She could hardly recognize her son through the mist of tears that filled her eyes* **3** [(*the*) S] something that darkens or confuses the mind, making understanding or good judgment difficult —see also MISTS

mist² *v* [T1 (OVER, UP)] to cover with MIST¹ (2): *The railway carriage became so hot that the air misted (up) the windows* —see also MIST OVER

mis·take¹ /mə̇'steɪk/ *v* **-took** /mə̇'stʊk/, **-taken** /mə̇'steɪkən/ [T1] **1** to have a wrong idea about (someone or something); understand wrongly: *Don't mistake him; if he says he'll punish you, he'll do so.|She doesn't speak very clearly, so I mistook what she said.|He'd mistaken the address, and gone to the wrong house* **2** to not recognize (someone or something): *You can't mistake his car in the busiest of streets; he's painted it bright red and yellow* **3** **there's no mistaking** it is not possible to fail to recognize or understand

mistake² *n* **1** a wrong thought, act, etc.; something done, said, believed, etc., as a result of wrong thinking or understanding, lack of knowledge or skill, etc.: *The teacher found several spelling mistakes in the pupils' written answers. "You've made too many mistakes," he said. "You'll have to do the exercise again."|There must be some mistake in this bill; please add up the figures again* —see ERROR (USAGE) **2 and no mistake** *infml* (used for giving force to an expression) without the slightest doubt: *That apple's a big one and no mistake!* **3 by mistake** as a result of being careless, forgetful, etc.: *She put salt into her cup of tea by mistake* **4 Make no mistake** Do not have the slightest doubt; Be quite sure: *If you don't improve your behaviour, you'll be punished; make no mistake about it* **5 there's no mistake about it** it is quite certain; there can be no doubt about it: *There's no mistake about it, he's the biggest fool I've met*

mistake for *v prep* [X1] to think wrongly that (someone or something) is (someone or something else): *They mistook him for his brother.|I mistook the house for a hotel*

mis·tak·en /mə̇'steɪkən/ *adj* **1** [Wa5;F (*about*)] (of a person) wrong; having understood incorrectly: *If you thought she intended to be rude, you were mistaken* **2** [Wa5;F] (of a statement, idea, etc.) misunderstood: *The minister doesn't use simple plain language, and what he says is often mistaken* **3** [B] (of an action, idea, etc.) incorrect; not well-judged; based on wrong thinking, lack of knowledge, etc.: *The teacher has a mistaken opinion of this pupil; he's much cleverer than she thinks.|She trusted the servant, in the mistaken belief that he was honest* —**~ly** *adv*

mis·ter /'mɪstəʳ/ *n* **1** [N] *nonstandard* sir: *A little boy stopped me in the street and asked, "What's the time, mister?"* **2** [C *usu. sing.*] *infml* a man who has not got a title of rank or profession that he can add to his name: *At the moment I'm only a mister, but when I get my higher degree I'll be a doctor*

Mister *n* [A] (*sometimes used in writing*) MR

mis·time /ˌmɪs'taɪm/ *v* [Wv5] **1** [T1] to do or say (something) at a wrong or unsuitable time: *The general mistimed his attack; it should have been made at the beginning, not at the end of summer.|He made a mistimed remark about his wife's cooking* (=saying that it was bad) *in front of all the guests* **2** [T1;I∅] (in sport) to fail to hit (the ball, a stroke, etc.) at the most effective moment

mis·tle·toe /'mɪsəltəʊ/ *n* [U] a type of plant that grows on trees, has pale green leaves that do not fall off in winter, and small white berries, and is often hung in rooms at Christmas time

mist o·ver *v adv* [I∅] **1** to become covered with MIST: *The sun set behind the hills, and slowly the valley misted over* **2** also **mist up**— to become covered with MIST¹ (2): *The windows began to mist up*

mis·tral /'mɪstrəl/ *n* [*the*+R;C] a strong cold dry wind that blows from the north down the Rhone valley in southern France

mis·trans·late /ˌmɪstræns'leɪt, -trɑːnz-‖-trænz-, -træns-/ *v* [T1;I∅] to translate (something) incorrectly —**-lation** /-træns-, -trɑːnz-‖-trænz-, -træns-/ *n* [U;C]

mis·tress /'mɪstrə̇s/ *n* **1** [C (*of*)] a female MASTER¹ (2,4,5): *She felt she was no longer mistress in her own house when her husband's mother came to stay.|England is no longer mistress of the seas.|*(*esp. BrE*) *All the girls like their new English mistress* (=teacher of English).|(*esp. BrE*) *schoolmistresses* **2** [C] a woman with whom a man has a sexual relationship, usu. not a socially acceptable one: *After his wife left him he began seeing another woman, who soon became his mistress* (=began to have sex with him) **3** [C9] *poet* a woman loved by a man who hopes she will love him: *He addressed many poems to his mistress, praising her beauty, and begging her at least to smile on him*

Mistress *n* [A] *old use or ScotE* (a title placed before the name of) any woman or girl: *Mistress Quickly is a character in Shakespeare's plays*

mis·tri·al /ˌmɪs'traɪəl/ *n law* a trial during which some mistake in law is made, with the result that no judgment from it would be lawful or could be acted on

mis·trust¹ /mɪs'trʌst/ *n* [U;S: (*of*)] lack of trust; distrust: *He keeps his money at home because he has a great mistrust of banks*

mistrust² *v* [T1] not to trust; distrust —see DISTRUST (USAGE)

mis·trust·ful /mɪs'trʌstfəl/ *adj* [(*of*)] having or showing MISTRUST; distrustful: *You seem mistrustful even of your friends* —**-fully** *adv* —**-fulness** *n* [U]

mists /mɪsts/ *n* [*the*+P (*of*)] *esp. lit* the unrecorded ages (of past time), about which little or nothing is known: *There are secrets hidden in the mists of history/of the far distant past that will never be uncovered*

mist·y /'mɪsti/ *adj* [Wa1] **1** full of, covered with, or hidden by MIST: *It was a misty morning, but it soon became clear when the sun began to shine.|the misty mountains|eyes misty with tears* **2** not clear to the mind; VAGUE: *The old man has only the mistiest memories of his childhood* —**-ily** *adv* —**-iness** *n* [U]

mis·un·der·stand /ˌmɪsʌndə'stænd‖-ər-/ *v* **-stood** /'stʊd/ **1** [T1;I∅] to understand wrongly; put a wrong meaning on (something said, done, etc.) or on something said by (someone) **2** [Wv5;T1] to fail to see or understand the true character or qualities of (someone): *He complains that his wife misunderstands him*

mis·un·der·stand·ing /ˌmɪsʌndə'stændɪŋ‖-ər-/ *n* **1** [U (*of*)] the act or action of putting a wrong meaning (on something); failure to give the correct or intended meaning (of something): *He's made his intentions very clear, and he hopes there'll be no misunderstanding of them* **2** [C (*of*)] an example of this: *She knows very little French; this often leads to misunderstandings when she visits France* **3** [C] *often euph* a disagreement less serious than a quarrel

mis·use¹ /ˌmɪs'juːz/ *v* [T1] **1** to use (something) in a wrong way or for a wrong purpose **2** to treat (something) badly: *This watch will last you a lifetime if you don't misuse it*

mis·use² /ˌmɪs'juːs/ *n* [C;U: (*of*)] (an example of) bad, wrong, or unsuitable use: (*an*) *unforgivable misuse of the power his office gave him*

mite /maɪt/ *n* **1** [C] a small child, esp. for whom one feels sorry **2** [S (*of*)] a very small amount or part (of anything): *He told his wife he'd had enough and couldn't eat a mite more* **3** [C] any of several types of very small insect-like creature, often found in food —see picture at ARACHNID **4** [C *usu. sing.*] *esp. lit* a very small offering, esp. of money, from someone who cannot afford more: *She's a poor old woman, but she gives her mite to every beggar she passes on the street* **5** [C] *esp. bibl* (in former times) a coin of very small value

mit·i·gate /ˈmɪtəgeɪt/ *v* [T1] *fml* **1** to lessen the seriousness of (wrong or harmful action): *The judge said that nothing could mitigate the cruelty with which the mother had treated her child* **2** to lessen (the evil, harm, etc., caused by some action): *The minister, in his second speech, tried to mitigate the harm he'd done when he made his first* **3** to make (suffering of any kind) easier to bear: *The doctor did his best to mitigate the sufferings of the dying woman* —**-gation** /ˌmɪtəˈgeɪʃən/ *n* [(*in*) U (*of*)]

mit·i·gat·ing cir·cum·stanc·es /ˌ···· ˈ····/ *n* [P] *often law* conditions that make a crime, mistake, etc., less serious, and that may lessen the punishment

mi·to·sis /maɪˈtəʊsəs/ *n* [U] *tech* the division of a cell into 2 new cells, in such a way that each of the resulting cells has a complete set of character-bearing parts (CHROMOSOME*s*) —compare MEIOSIS

mi·tre, *AmE* usu. **miter** /ˈmaɪtəʳ/ *n* **1** a type of tall pointed hat worn by priests of high rank (BISHOP*s* and ARCHBISHOP*s*) on ceremonial occasions **2** also **mitre joint** /ˈ·· ·/— a joint between 2 pieces of wood, in which each piece is cut at an angle of 45 degrees to its side, forming a right angle between the joined pieces, as in the corners of a picture frame

mitre box /ˈ·· ·/ *n* a piece of wood with cuts made in it at special angles, used for guiding a cutting tool (SAW) when making a MITRE (2)

mitt /mɪt/ *n* **1** (*usu. in comb.*) a special type of hand covering (GLOVE) used for giving protection for special purposes: *She put on an* OVEN *mitt to take the hot dishes out of the* OVEN **2** a specially strong hand covering (GLOVE) worn by a BASEBALL player **3** *sl, often humor* a hand: *Those are my cigarettes; get your mitts off them* **4** MITTEN

mit·ten /ˈmɪtn/ *n* **1** a type of garment for the hand (GLOVE) in which all 4 fingers are covered by one large baglike part **2** a covering for the hand and wrist, but not for the fingers, worn, esp. in former times, by women in the house in cold weather —see PAIR (USAGE)

mix[1] /mɪks/ *v* **1** [T1 (UP); IØ (*with*)] to (cause to) be combined so as to form a whole, of which the parts have no longer a separate shape, appearance, etc., or cannot easily be separated one from another: *You can't mix oil and water.|You can't mix oil with water.|Oil and water don't mix.|Oil doesn't mix with water.|She put the flour, eggs, etc., into a bowl and mixed them together; she mixed them up well.|The artist mixed blue with yellow paint, to produce the green colour he wanted* **2** [D1 (*for*); T1] to prepare (such a combination of different substances): *His wife mixed him a hot drink of milk, sugar, and chocolate* **3** [IØ (*with*)] (of a person) to be, be put, or enjoy being in the company of others: *He's such a friendly person that he mixes well in any company* **4 mix it** *infml* to fight in a rough way —see also MIX IN, MIX UP

mix[2] *n* **1** [U;C] (*usu. in comb.*) a combination of different substances, prepared to be ready, or nearly ready, for (the stated) use: *She's too lazy to make cakes by mixing all the separate substances; she always buys cake mix from the shops* **2** [S (*of*)] a group of different things, people, etc.; mixture: *There was rather a strange mix of people at the party: doctors, postmen, lawyers, farmers, etc.*

mixed /mɪkst/ *adj* **1** of different kinds: *His feelings about his daughter's marriage are rather mixed* (=he's pleased in some ways, but displeased in others) **2** [Wa5] of or for both sexes: *a mixed school|mixed bathing|This joke isn't suitable to be told in mixed company* (=isn't suitable for women to hear) **3** combining people of 2 or more races or religions: *a mixed marriage*

mixed bag /ˌ· ˈ·/ *n* [S] *infml* a collection or group of things of many different kinds, and usu. of different qualities

mixed doub·les /ˌ· ˈ··/ *n* **mixed doubles** [Wn3] (esp. in tennis) a match, or competition made up of matches, in which a man and a woman play against another man and woman

mixed farm·ing /ˌ· ˈ··/ *n* [U] work on a farm which includes 2 or more different kinds of farming, such as cattle raising and corn growing

mixed grill /ˌ· ˈ·/ *n* a food dish of various kinds of meat cooked (GRILLed) together

mixed met·a·phor /ˌ· ˈ···/ *n* a use of 2 different METAPHOR*s* together in a way that produces a foolish or funny effect: *"The great arch of heaven was filled with 1,000 stars" is a mixed metaphor*

mixed up /ˌ· ˈ·◂/ *adj* **1** [F+*in*] connected (with something bad): *I'm afraid he's mixed up in some dishonest business.|Don't get mixed up in the quarrels of other people* **2** [F+*with*] connected (with someone undesirable): *He got mixed up with an older man who had a bad influence on him* **3** [B] troubled in mind, and unable to think clearly and see the right course to follow: *He listened to so many political arguments that he got all mixed up, and had no idea which was right and which was wrong*

mix·er /ˈmɪksəʳ/ *n* **1** [C] (*often in comb.*) an apparatus, usu. a machine, by or in which substances are mixed **2** [C9] a person who MIXes[1] (3) well or badly with other people: *She's such a bad mixer; she never talks to people at parties* **3** [C] *tech* a person who balances and controls the words, music, and sounds that are recorded for or with a cinema or television film

mix in *v adv* [T1] to combine (a substance) thoroughly with other substances, esp. when making food or drink: *Add the milk to the flour, and then mix in 3 eggs*

mix·ture /ˈmɪkstʃəʳ/ *n* **1** [C (*of*); U] (esp. of chemicals in a liquid) a set of substances mixed together, which keep their separate qualities while combined in one mass: *This tobacco is a mixture of 3 different sorts.|You need some cough mixture* (=medicine for preventing coughing) **2** [S (*of*)] a combination (of things or people of different types or qualities): *His new play is a strange mixture of sadness and humour.|His father was French and his mother Chinese; he's a bit of a mixture* **3** [U] *fml* the action of mixing or state of being mixed **4 the mixture as before** *infml, usu. derog* the same treatment or set of actions as formerly

mix-up /ˈ· ·/ *n infml* a state of disorder, as caused by bad planning, faulty arrangements, etc.: *There was a mix-up at the station; some members of the party got into one train, some into another, and a few were left behind*

mix up *v adv* **1** [T1 (*with*)] to confuse (someone) or mistake (something): *It's easy to mix him up with his brother; they're so very like each other* **2** [T1] to put into disorder: *If you mix up those papers we shan't find the one we need quickly*

miz·zen, mizen /ˈmɪzən/ *n* **1** the lowest square sail on a MIZZENMAST **2** MIZZENMAST

miz·zen·mast /ˈmɪzənmɑːst‖-mæst/ *n* the tall pole (MAST) nearest the back end (STERN) of a ship with 3 MAST*s*

miz·zle /ˈmɪzəl/ *v* [*it*+IØ] *infml or dial* to rain in very small drops

mm *written abbrev. for*: MILLIMETRE*s*

mne·mon·ic /nɪˈmɒnɪk‖nɪˈmɑ-/ *adj, n* (something, esp. a few lines of VERSE) used for helping the ability to remember: *The spelling guide "i before e except after c" is a mnemonic* —**~ally** *adv* [Wa4]

mne·mon·ics /nɪˈmɒnɪks‖nɪˈmɑ-/ *n* [U] *fml or tech* the art of, or means of, increasing the ability to remember, or the ways, rules, poems, etc., used in doing this

mo /məʊ/ *n* [S] *BrE infml* **1** a very short space of time: *Wait a mo; I shan't be long* **2 half a mo a** a very short space of time: *Wait there on the corner while I go into the shop; I shan't be half a mo* **b** wait, I have just had a thought: *That's a very nice girl Richard's with—here, half a mo, isn't she the girl you went out with last week?*

MO /ˌem ˈəʊ/ *abbrev. for*: (*infml*) **1** an army doctor; medical officer **2** MODUS OPERANDI

-mo /məʊ/ *suffix tech* (used for showing that the stated number of pages have been made by folding a large sheet of paper): *16mo*

mo·a /ˈməʊə/ *n* [Wn1] any of several types of very large bird that lived in former times in New Zealand, and could not fly —compare DODO

moan¹ /məʊn/ *n* **1** [C] a low sound of pain, grief, or suffering: *From time to time, during the night, there was a moan* (*of pain*) *from the sick man* **2** [(*the*) S (*of*)] sounds that give the idea of sadness or suffering: *the moan of the wind through the lonely trees* **3** [C] *usu. derog* a complaint, expressed in a voice that has a suffering or discontented sound: *She's never satisfied; she always has some moan or another*

moan² *v* **1** [IØ] to make the sound of a MOAN or moans: *The sick child moaned a little, and then fell asleep.|The wind moaned round the house all night; it wasn't a cheerful sound* **2** [T1,5: (OUT)] to express with MOAN*s*: *The prisoner moaned* (*out*) *a prayer for mercy* **3** [IØ (*about*); T5] *derog* to complain; speak in a complaining voice: *Stop moaning; you really have nothing to complain about* —**~er** *n*

moat /məʊt/ *n* a long deep hole that in former times was dug for defence round a castle, fort, etc., and was usually filled with water —see picture at CASTLE¹

moat·ed /ˈməʊtɪ̣d/ *adj* [Wa5;A;(B)] provided with or protected by a MOAT

mob¹ /mɒb‖mɑb/ *n* **1** [C] *often derog* a large noisy crowd, esp. one which is violent: *There was such a mob at the station that I couldn't find the friend I'd gone to meet.|The police carried shields, to protect themselves against the stones thrown by the mob* **2** [*the*+R] *derog* the common people, considered as being people whose opinions, feelings, etc., change from moment to moment, and whose actions are not the result of thought or reason **3** [A] *derog* of, by, or for the common people, considered in this way: *mob rule|mob law|mob violence|a mob* ORATOR (=a RABBLE-ROUSER) **4** [C] a group of thieves or other lawbreakers

mob² *v* **-bb-** [T1] **1** (of a group of people or birds) to attack: *The angry crowd mobbed the football team as it left the ground, because it had played so badly.|The large bird was being mobbed by all the smaller birds* **2** (of a group of people) to crowd around (someone) because of interest or admiration: *When he left the hall after making a speech, the party leader was mobbed by his supporters*

mo·bile¹ /ˈməʊbaɪl‖-bəl, -biːl/ *adj* **1** movable; able to move, or be moved, quickly and easily; not fixed in one position: *Many workmen aren't mobile; if they move to new employment they have difficulties in moving their families.|She's much more mobile* (=able to move from place to place) *now that she's bought a car.|mobile weapons* **2** [Wa5] contained, and driven from place to place, in a vehicle: *a mobile shop|a mobile library|*(*esp. AmE*) *a mobile home* **3** changing quickly, as of a person's face that quickly shows changes in his feelings or thoughts: *He has a mobile face, like an actor's*

mo·bile² /ˈməʊbaɪl‖-biːl/ *n* an ornament or work of art made of small models, cards, etc., tied to wires or string and hung up so that they are moved by currents of air

mo·bil·i·ty /məʊˈbɪlɪ̣ti/ *n* [U] the state or quality of being MOBILE¹ (1,3): *The army's in need of many more vehicles to increase its mobility.|the mobility of her face*

mo·bil·i·za·tion, -sation /ˌməʊbɪ̣laɪˈzeɪʃən‖-lə-/ *n* [U;C] the action or an act of mobilizing, or the state of being MOBILIZED: *The mobilization of the army was completed in 48 hours*

mo·bil·ize, -ise /ˈməʊbɪ̣laɪz/ *v* **1** [T1] to gather together (people or things) for a particular service or use: *Our country's in great danger; we must mobilize the army.|He's trying to mobilize all the support/supporters he can obtain for the political party he's formed.|to mobilize one's* ENERGY/RESOURCE*s* **2** [IØ] (of armed forces) to become ready for service in war: *The fear of war grew when the people learned that the army was mobilizing*

mob·ster /ˈmɒbstəʳ‖ˈmɑb-/ *n* a member of a MOB¹ (4); GANGSTER

moc·ca·sin /ˈmɒkəsɪn‖ˈmɑ-/ *n* a type of simple shoe made of soft leather, as first worn by North American Indians

moch·a /ˈmɒkə, ˈməʊkə‖ˈməʊkə/ also **mocha cof·fee** /ˌ·· ˈ··/— *n* [U] (*sometimes cap.*) a type of coffee of fine quality, first brought from the Red Sea port of Mocha

mock¹ /mɒk‖mɑk/ *v* **1** [Wv4;T1;IØ (*at*)] to laugh at (someone or something) when it is wrong to do so; speak or act with regard to (someone or something) as if one is not serious, esp. when one should be: *He had no religious beliefs, and he went to church only to mock.|The pupil did his best, and the teacher was wrong to mock at his efforts, although they were bad.|What made him angry wasn't losing the game, but the mocking laughter of the man who'd beaten him* **2** [T1] to copy (something) in such a way that the person or thing copied is laughed at: *He made all the other boys laugh by mocking the way the teacher spoke and walked* **3** [T1] *fml* to cause (the efforts, skill, strength, etc., of other people) to be useless or have no effect, success, etc.: *For 5 years this small country has mocked the strength of the powerful nation with which it is at war* —**~er** *n* —**~ingly** *adv*

mock² *n* **1 make a mock of** make a MOCKERY of **2 make mock of** *lit* to cause to appear foolish or silly; make fun of

mock³ *adj* [Wa5;A] *sometimes derog* not real or true; like (in appearance, taste, etc.) something real: *The army training exercises ended with a mock battle*

mock- *comb. form* only pretendingly: *He spoke to her in a mock-serious manner*

mock·ers /ˈmɒkəz‖ˈmɑkərz/ *n BrE sl* **put the mockers on something** to spoil something: *Those 2 defeats last week have put the mockers on our team's chances of winning this year's competition*

mock·e·ry /ˈmɒkəri‖ˈmɑ-/ *n* **1** [U] the act or action of laughing at something that should not be laughed at or of treating something serious as if it is not: *He finished his speech, in spite of the noisy* *mockery of many of his listeners* **2** [C *usu. sing.*] a person or thing that is foolish, shameful, and/or deserving to be laughed at: *The teacher's so foolish, and does his work so badly, that he's become a mockery to the whole school* **3** [S] something untrue or pretended, that is not worthy of any respect or serious consideration: *The medical examination was a mockery; the doctor hardly looked at the child* **4** [C *often pl.*] an act of MOCKing **5 hold someone or something up to mockery** to cause or attempt to cause someone or something to appear foolish **6 make a mockery of a** to cause to be done without useful result: *His failure made a mockery of the teacher's great efforts to help him* **b** to prove to be untrue or pretended: *His evil life makes a mockery of his claims to be a holy man*

mock·ing·bird /ˈmɒkɪŋbɜːd‖ˈmɑkɪŋbɜrd/ *n* a type of American bird that copies the songs of other birds

mock tur·tle soup /ˌ· ·· ˈ·/ also (*infml*) **mock turtle** /ˌ· ˈ··/— *n* [U] soup made from meat, but tasting as if made from TURTLE

mock-up /ˈ· ·/ *n* a representation or model, often full-size, of something planned to be made or built

mo·dal /ˈməʊdl/ *adj tech* **1** [Wa5;A] of or concerning the MOOD of a verb **2** [Wa5;A] of or concerning musical MODE*s* **3** [B] (of music) written in one or more of the MODE*s*: *Much early music is modal* —**~ly** *adv*

modal aux·il·i·a·ry /ˌ·· ·ˈ····/ also (*infml*) **modal**— *n* any of the verb forms *can, could, may, might, shall, should, will, would, must, ought to, used to,* NEED, and DARE

mod con /ˌmɒd ˈkɒn‖ˌmɑd ˈkɑn/ *n* [*often pl.*] *BrE infml* (used esp. in newspaper advertisements of houses for sale) a modern convenience; something that makes living easier and more comfortable, such as hot water at all times, central heating, etc.

mode¹ /məʊd/ *n* **1** [(*of*)] a way or manner of acting, behaving, speaking, writing, living, etc.: *He suddenly became wealthy, which changed his whole mode of life.|Do you know the correct mode of address when speaking to a princess?* **2** *tech* a way, arrangement, or condition in which something is done or happens: *This is a fever which will return from time to time, if it follows its usual mode.|As the space vehicle came closer to the earth, it was put into its re-entering mode* **3** *tech* either of the 2 systems (MAJOR and MINOR) of arranging notes in modern Western music **4** *tech* any of the 6 systems (such as **Dorian** and **Phrygian**) of arranging notes in music of ancient times, much used also in the music of the common people since then, and in written music of the 20th century

mode² *n* **1** [*the*+R;(C)] the style of dressing (esp. by women), or of doing something, favoured by most people at a certain moment: *Are very long skirts the present mode?|Giving students much greater freedom is all the mode today* **2** [C *usu. pl.*] *tech or pomp, becoming rare* a fashionable type of woman's garment: *Marguerite's Modes* (name of a shop) —see also À LA MODE

mod·el¹ /ˈmɒdl‖ˈmɑdl/ *n* **1** [C (*of*)] a small representation or copy (of something): *On this table you can see a model of the new theatre that's going to be built in this town.|The little boy enjoys making models.|a plastic model of an aircraft* **2** [C+*of, usu. sing.*] *BrE* a person or thing exactly, or almost exactly, like another, but not always of the same size: *She's a perfect model of her aunt* **3** [C (*of*)] *apprec* a person or thing that can serve as a perfect example or pattern, worthy to be followed or copied: *This young man is a model of all that a good army officer should be.|This pupil's written work is a model of care and neatness* **4** [C] (*masc.* **male model** /ˌ· ˈ··/)— a person, esp. a young woman, employed to wear articles of clothing, and to show them to possible buyers (as in a shop, by being photographed, etc.) **5** [C] a person employed to stand or sit while an artist, such as a painter or photographer, makes a picture or other representation of him or her **6** [C9] an article which is one of a number of articles (such as clothes, cars, weapons, machines, or instruments of any kind) of a standard pattern or standard manner of making: *The car industry's always producing new models.|This heavy gun's an old model, but it's still a very useful weapon* **7** [C] *BrE* an article of clothing, esp. of woman's clothing, worn by a MODEL¹ (4) or shown in a shop, and described as the only one, or one of a very few, of its kind: *You won't see any other dresses like this, miss; it's a model*

model² *v* **-ll-** (*AmE* **-l-**) **1** [T1] **a** to form or shape (something) in a soft substance: *In ancient times, people modelled cooking pots in clay by hand* **b** to make a model or copy of: *The little boy spent the afternoon modelling a ship out of bits of wood* **2** [I∅] to act or work as a MODEL¹ (4,5): *She'd like to be a film actress, but at present she's modelling* **3** [T1] to show (an article of clothing) as a MODEL¹ (4): *A very pretty girl was chosen to model a silk evening dress at the dress show*

model³ *adj* [Wa5;A] **1** being a small representation or copy: *The little boy has a very large collection of model cars* **2** *apprec* perfect; having all the necessary good qualities; deserving to be copied: *She's a model mother; no woman could take better care of her children*

model on also **model up·on**— *v prep* [D1] **1** to form (something) as a copy of (something): *The railway system was modelled on the successful plan used in other countries* **2** to form the character, qualities, etc., of (oneself) as a copy of (someone else): *She modelled herself on her mother*

mod·e·rate¹ /ˈmɒdərɪ̈t‖ˈmɑ-/ *adj* **1** [Wa5] of middle degree, power, or rate; neither large nor small, high nor low, fast nor slow, etc.: *It's a large house, but the garden is of moderate size.|At the time of the accident, the train was travelling at a moderate speed* **2** (done or kept) within sensible limits: *The workers' demands are moderate; they're asking for only a small increase in their wages* **3** [Wa5] *often euph* of average or less than average quality or amount: *The teacher thinks that his pupil has only moderate ability* **4** not favouring political or social ideas that are very different from those of most people; not EXTREME: *He holds moderate political opinions; he doesn't want to keep conditions just as they are, but nor does he wish for violent changes*

mod·e·rate² /ˈmɒdəreɪt‖ˈmɑ-/ *v* [Wv4;T1;I∅] to make or become less in force, degree, rate, etc.; reduce: *There'll be no agreement between the workers and the employers if the workers don't moderate their demands.|He should moderate his language when children are present* (=shouldn't use words not fit for them to hear).|*The wind was strong all day, but it moderated after sunset*

mod·e·rate³ /ˈmɒdərɪ̈t‖ˈmɑ-/ *n* a person whose opinions are MODERATE¹ (4) —compare EXTREMIST

mod·e·rate·ly /ˈmɒdərɪ̈tli‖ˈmɑ-/ *adv* [Wa5] to a MODERATE¹ (1,3) degree; not very: *The examination questions were moderately difficult*

mod·e·ra·tion /ˌmɒdəˈreɪʃən‖ˌmɑ-/ *n* [U (*in*)] **1** reduction in force, degree, rate, etc.: *Even after sunset there was little moderation in the temperature* **2** the ability or quality of keeping one's desires within reasonable limits, of controlling one's habits, etc.; self-control: *He showed great moderation in answering so gently the attacks made on his character* **3 in moderation** within sensible limits: *Some people* *say that smoking in moderation isn't harmful to health*

mod·e·ra·tions /ˌmɒdəˈreɪʃənz‖ˌmɑ-/ also (*infml*) **mods** /mɒdz‖mɑdz/— *n* [P] (*often cap.*) the first public examination in some subjects for the degree of BACHELOR OF ARTS at Oxford University

mod·e·ra·to /ˌmɒdəˈrɑːtəʊ‖ˌmɑ-/ *n, adj, adv* **-s** [C;B] ((a piece of music) played) at an average even speed

mod·e·ra·tor /ˈmɒdəreɪtəʳ‖ˈmɑ-/ *n* **1** a person who tries to help people or sides who disagree to reach an agreement **2** (*often cap.*) a president or chairman of a church court, esp. in the PRESBYTERIAN Church **3** *tech* a substance (such as GRAPHITE or water) used for slowing down the action of NEUTRONs in an atomic REACTOR **4** an examiner who makes sure that an examination paper arranged by someone else is fair, and also that the marks given by other examiners are of the right standard

mod·ern¹ /ˈmɒdn‖ˈmɑdərn/ *adj* **1** [Wa5] of the present time, or of the not far distant past; not ancient: *The modern history of Italy dates from 1860, when the country became united under one government.|In this part of the city, you can see ancient and modern buildings next to each other* **2** *often apprec* new and different from the past: *He has modern ideas, in spite of his great age* **3** [Wa5] (*often cap.*) (of a language) in use today; not ancient: *It's more useful for a boy to learn modern languages (such as French and German) at school than Latin* —compare CONTEMPORARY —see also SECONDARY MODERN

modern² *n* [*usu. pl.*] **1** [C] a person living in modern (as compared with ancient) times **2** [C9] a person with modern ideas

mod·ern·is·m /ˈmɒdənɪzəm‖ˈmɑdər-/ *n* **1** [U] the spirit, thought, or character of modern times **2** [U] (*often cap.*) the principles and practices of modern art, esp. a self-conscious change of direction from the past and a search for new forms of expression **3** [C] a modern use, such as of a word: *You'll find very few modernisms in this writer's books* —**-ist** *adj, n* [B;C]

mod·ern·ist·ic /ˌmɒdəˈnɪstɪk‖ˌmɑdər-/ *adj* **1** favouring modern ideas, systems, etc. **2** very noticeably or unusually new and modern —**~ally** *adv* [Wa4]

mo·der·ni·ty /mɒˈdɜːnǝ̇ti‖məˈdɜr-/ *n* [U (*of*)] the state or quality of being modern: *The modernity of this writer's thoughts is surprising, when one remembers that he wrote the book 500 years ago*

mod·ern·ize, -ise /ˈmɒdənaɪz‖ˈmɑdər-/ *v* **1** [T1] to make (something) suitable for modern use, or for the needs of the present time: *He bought an old house, and spent a lot of money modernizing it; he's put in electricity, had a bathroom built, etc.* **2** [IØ] to become modern in ways of thinking, doing things, etc.: *Every business is in danger of losing money if it can't modernize* —**-ization** /ˌmɒdənaɪˈzeɪʃən‖ˌmɑdərnə-/ *n* [U;C]

mod·est /ˈmɒdǝ̇st‖ˈmɑ-/ *adj* **1** *apprec* having or expressing a lower opinion than is probably deserved, of one's own ability, knowledge, skill, successes, etc.; hiding one's good qualities: *The young actress is very modest about her success; she says it's as much the result of good luck as of her own abilities.|After the war, the general wrote a very modest book about the part he'd played in winning it* **2 a** not large in quantity, size, value, etc.: *Please accept this modest gift; it's all I can afford* **b** not having or showing a desire for much or for too much: *The servant girl was very modest in her demands, and asked for only a small increase in wages* **3** *apprec* (esp. of a woman or something concerning a woman) avoiding or not showing anything that is improper or impure —**~ly** *adv*

mod·es·ty /ˈmɒdǝ̇sti‖ˈmɑ-/ *n* [U] *often apprec* **1** the quality, state, or fact of being MODEST: *His natural modesty saved him from being spoilt by fame and success* **2 in all modesty** *often euph* without wishing to seem to praise oneself too much: *I think I can say, in all modesty, that there's no more successful man in the whole town than me*

mod·i·cum /ˈmɒdɪkəm‖ˈmɑ-/ *n* [S (*of*)] a small amount (of anything): *If he had a modicum of sense, he wouldn't do such a foolish thing*

mod·i·fi·ca·tion /ˌmɒdǝ̇fǝ̇ˈkeɪʃən‖ˌmɑ-/ *n* **1** [U] the act of MODIFYing or state of being modified: *The law, in its present form, is unjust; it needs modification* **2** [C (*to*)] a change made in something: *A few simple modifications to this plan would greatly improve it*

mod·i·fi·er /ˈmɒdǝ̇faɪəʳ‖ˈmɑ-/ *n* (in grammar) a word that modifies (MODIFY (3)) another word: *Adjectives and adverbs are modifiers*

mod·i·fy /ˈmɒdǝ̇faɪ‖ˈmɑ-/ *v* [T1] **1** to change (something, such as a plan, an opinion, a condition, or the form or quality of something), esp. slightly: *These plans must be modified if they're to be used successfully* **2** to make (something, such as a claim or condition) less hard to accept or bear: *The 2 governments will never reach an agreement if one or the other does not modify its demands* **3** (in grammar) (of a word, esp. an adjective or adverb) to describe or limit the meaning of (another word): *An adverb modifies the verb in the phrase "to talk quietly"*

mod·ish /ˈməʊdɪʃ/ *adj* fashionable: *It used to be modish for women to have their hair cut short* —**~ly** *adv*

mods /mɒdz‖mɑdz/ *n* [P] *infml* (*often cap.*) MODERATIONS

mod·u·lar /ˈmɒdjʊləʳ‖ˈmɑdʒə-/ *adj* [Wa5] *tech* **1** of, related to, or based on a MODULE **2** built or made using MODULEs (2): *modular furniture*

mod·u·late /ˈmɒdjʊleɪt‖ˈmɑdʒə-/ *v* **1** [T1] to vary the strength, nature, etc., of (a sound): *Some people are able to modulate their voices according to the size of the room in which they speak* **2** [L9, esp. *from* and/or *to*] to pass by regular steps from one musical KEY to another: *At this point the music modulates|the players have to modulate from* E *to* G **3** [T1] *tech* to vary the size or rate of (a radio wave or signal)

mod·u·la·tion /ˌmɒdjʊˈleɪʃən‖ˌmɑdʒə-/ *n tech* **1** [U] the action of modulating or state of being MODULATED **2** [C] a change resulting from this, esp. a change of musical KEY: *a modulation from* F *to* B

mod·ule /ˈmɒdjuːl‖ˈmɑdʒuːl/ *n tech* **1** a standard of measurement, esp. as used in building **2** a part having a standard shape and size, used in building, making furniture, etc. **3** a part of a space vehicle that can be used independently of the other parts: *While one of the space travellers went round the moon in the* **command module**, *the other 2 went down to the surface in the* **lunar module**

mo·dus op·e·ran·di /ˌməʊdəs ˌɒpəˈrændi‖-ˌɑpə-/ also (*infml*) **MO**— *n* [S *often with poss.*] *Lat* a particular way of doing something or in which something is done, esp. a particular criminal's usual way of carrying out crimes

modus vi·ven·di /ˌməʊdəs vɪˈvendi/ *n* [S *often with poss.*] *Lat* **1** an arrangement between people of different opinions, habits, etc., to live or work together without quarrelling **2** a way of living

mog·gy /ˈmɒgi‖ˈmɑgi, ˈmɔgi/ *n BrE infml, usu. humor* a cat

mo·gul /ˈməʊgəl/ *n* a person of very great power,

molluscs/*AmE* mollusks

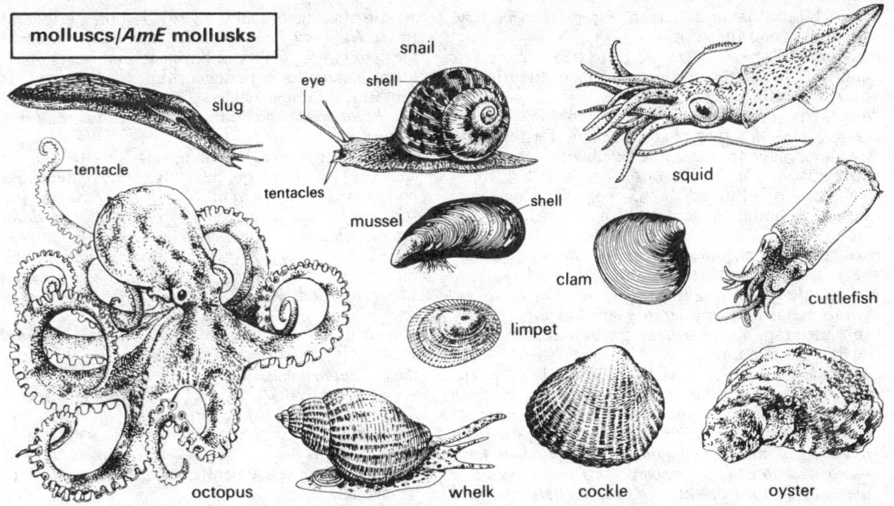

influence, wealth, and/or importance: *the moguls of the film industry*

MOH *abbrev. for:* Medical Officer of Health; (in Britain) an official doctor who is responsible for public health in a particular area, such as a town

mo·hair /ˈməʊheəʳ/ *n* [U] (cloth made from) the long fine silky hair of the ANGORA goat

Mo·ham·me·dan /məʊˈhæmʒ̇dn, mə-/ also **Muhammadan**— *adj, n* [Wa5] (a) Muslim

Mo·ham·me·dan·is·m /məʊˈhæmʒ̇dənɪzəm, mə-/ also **Muhammadanism**— *n* [U] the Muslim religion —see also PROPHET²

moi·e·ty /ˈmɔɪʒ̇ti/ *n* [(*of*) *usu. sing.*] *law or lit* a half share or division (of something): *The judge ordered that the dead man's 2 children should each receive a moiety of his possessions*

moi·ré /ˈmwɑːreɪ‖mɔˈreɪ, mwɑ- (*Fr* mware)/ also **watered silk**— *n* [U] *Fr* a type of silk material, the surface of which has the appearance of being covered with shiny waves, like the surface of water

moist /mɔɪst/ *adj* [Wa1] **1** slightly wet: *The thick steam in the room had made the walls moist.|The story was so sad that at the end my eyes were moist with tears* **2** (of air, wind, etc.) containing some water; DAMP: *The air became moister as we descended the hill towards the river bank* **3** (esp. of food) not unpleasantly dry: *moist brown sugar|This cake's nice and moist* —**~ly** *adv* —**~ness** *n* [U]

moist·en /ˈmɔɪsən/ *v* [T1;I∅] to make or become slightly wet: *Her eyes moistened as she listened to the sad story*

mois·ture /ˈmɔɪstʃəʳ/ *n* [U] water, or other liquids, in small quantities or in the form of steam or mist: *The desert air's so dry that it contains hardly any moisture.|The hot sun drew up the moisture from the earth*

mois·tur·ize, -ise /ˈmɔɪstʃəraɪz/ *v* [Wv4;T1] to cause to contain MOISTURE; remove the dryness from: *Her hands get so dry that she has to use moisturizing cream on them*

moke /məʊk/ *n BrE infml, esp. humor* a donkey

mo·lar /ˈməʊləʳ/ *n, adj* [Wa5] (any) of the large teeth at the back of the mouth with rounded or flattened surfaces used for breaking up food —see picture at TOOTH

mo·las·ses /məˈlæsʒ̇z/ *n* [U] **1** a thick dark sweet liquid produced from newly cut sugar plants **2** *AmE* TREACLE

mold /məʊld/ *n, v AmE* MOULD

mol·der /ˈməʊldəʳ/ *v* [I∅ (AWAY)] *AmE* MOULDER

mold·ing /ˈməʊldɪŋ/ *n* [U;C] *AmE* MOULDING

mold·y /ˈməʊldi/ *adj* [Wa1] *AmE* MOULDY —**moldiness** *n* [U]

mole¹ /məʊl/ *n* a small, dark brown, slightly raised mark on a person's skin, usu. there since birth

mole² *n* **1** a small furry almost blind animal that digs passages underground to live in —see picture at MAMMAL **2** *BrE infml* a person who gives secret information to an enemy about an organization or company in which he/she is employed —compare SPY¹

mole³ *n* a stone wall of great strength built out into the sea from the land as a defence against the force of the waves, or to act as a road (as from the shore to an island)

mo·lec·u·lar /məˈlekjʊləʳ‖-kjə-/ *adj* of, connected with, or produced by one or more MOLECULE*s*

mol·e·cule /ˈmɒlɪkjuːl‖ˈmɑ-/ *n* the smallest part of any substance that can be separated from the substance without losing its own chemical form and qualities, and consists of one or more atoms —see picture at ATOM

mole·hill /ˈməʊlˌhɪl/ *n* **1** a small heap of earth thrown up on the surface by a MOLE when it is digging underground **2 make a mountain/mountains out of a molehill/molehills** to make a small difficulty, or an unimportant matter, appear greater or more important than it is

mole·skin /ˈməʊlˌskɪn/ *n* [U] the fur of a MOLE, or a type of strong cotton cloth looking rather like this, used, esp. in former times, for making garments and hats

mo·lest /məˈlest/ *v* [T1] **1** to trouble or annoy (a person or animal) intentionally, esp. by attacking: *A dog has been molesting the sheep* **2** *sometimes euph* to attack or annoy (a person, esp. a woman or a child) sexually —**~ation** /ˌməʊleˈsteɪʃən/ *n* [U]

moll /mɒl‖mɑl/ *n sl* a woman companion of a criminal

mol·li·fy /ˈmɒlʒ̇faɪ‖ˈmɑ-/ *v* [T1] to make (a person or a person's feelings) calmer, less angry, etc.: *He bought his angry wife a gift, but she refused to be mollified* —**-fication** /ˌmɒlʒ̇fʒ̇ˈkeɪʃən‖ˌmɑ-/ *n* [U]

mol·lusc, *AmE* also **mollusk** /ˈmɒləsk‖ˈmɑ-/ *n* any of a class of animals which have soft bodies without a backbone or limbs and are usu. covered with a shell: *LIMPETs, SNAILs, SLUGs, and OCTOPUSes are molluscs*

mol·ly·cod·dle¹ /ˈmɒliˌkɒdl‖ˈmɑliˌkɑdl/ *n* [C;

you+N] *usu. derog* a person, esp. a man or boy, who has been MOLLYCODDLEd

mollycoddle² *v* [T1] *usu. derog* to treat (oneself or another) too softly, paying too much attention to health, comfort, etc.

Mol·o·tov cock·tail /ˌmɒlətɒf ˈkɒkteɪl‖ˌmalətɔf ˈkak-, ˌmɔl-/ *n* a type of simple bomb for throwing by hand, made from a bottle filled with petrol

molt /məʊlt/ *v, n AmE* MOULT

mol·ten /ˈməʊltn/ *adj* [Wa5] (of metal or rock) turned to liquid by very great heat; melted —see MELT (USAGE)

mol·to /ˈmɒltəʊ‖ˈməʊl-, ˈmɔl-/ *adv* (in music) very: *molto* ALLEGRO (=very quickly)

mo·lyb·de·num /məˈlɪbdənəm/ *n* [U] a silver-white metal that is a simple substance (ELEMENT (6)) used esp. in strengthening and hardening steel

mom /mɒm‖mam/ *n* [C;N] *AmE* MUM³ —see TABLE OF FAMILY RELATIONSHIPS

mo·ment /ˈməʊmənt/ *n* **1** [C] a period of time considered too short to measure; point of time: *At that moment, something unexpected happened.|I'd like to speak to you for a moment.|I had to think for a moment before I remembered his name.|Wait a moment!|Just a moment: she's coming.|He said he'd written the book at odd moments* (=short periods of time when he had nothing else to do) **2** [C (*for*), C3 *usu. sing.*] the time for doing something; occasion: *The nation's at war; this isn't the moment to quarrel among ourselves.|Choose your moment well if you want to ask your employer for higher wages* **3** [*of*+U] *fml* importance: *The president will speak to the nation tonight on a matter of the greatest moment* **4** [C (*of*) *usu. sing.*] *tech* (a measure of) the turning power of a force: *The moment of a force is the strength or weight of the force multiplied by its distance at a right angle from the point against which it is used* **5 at any moment** at an unknown time only a little after a time in the present or past **6 at every moment** continually; ceaselessly: *At every moment I am reminded of the great difficulties we have still to face* **7 at the last moment** only just in time; just before the start of an activity: *He's never late for school, but he often comes into the classroom at the last moment* **8 at the moment** at the present time; now **9 at this moment in time** *pomp esp. BrE* at this MOMENT (1) **10 in a moment** only a little later; very soon: *I'll be/She came back in a moment* **11 not for a moment** at no time; not at all: *I wasn't for a moment deceived by his friendly words* **12 the moment (that)** just as soon as; at exactly the time when: *We hadn't met for 20 years, but I recognized him the moment (that) I saw him* **13 this moment** at the present point of time: *I've only (just) this moment* (=just now) *remembered that I have to see the doctor this evening* —see also MAN OF THE MOMENT, **on the** SPUR **of the moment**

mo·men·tar·i·ly /ˈməʊməntərɨli‖ˌməʊmənˈterɨli/ *adv* [Wa5] for just a very short period of time: *He was so surprised that he was momentarily unable to speak*

mo·men·ta·ry /ˈməʊməntəri‖-teri/ *adj* [Wa5] **1** [B] lasting for a very short time: *Her feeling of fear was only momentary; it soon passed* **2** [A] *fml and becoming rare* at every moment: *The escaped prisoner passed his days in momentary fear of being caught and sent back to prison* —compare MOMENTOUS

moment of truth /ˌ·· · ˈ·/ *n* [*the*+R;(C)] a moment when something very important, dangerous, etc., will happen or be done, on the result of which a very great deal depends

mo·men·tous /məʊˈmentəs, mə-/ *adj* of very great importance or seriousness: *We listened on the radio to the momentous news that war had begun* —compare MOMENTARY

mo·ments /ˈməʊmənts/ *n* [P9] **1** short periods of time: *He spent many pleasant moments looking at the books in the library* **2 have one's moments** *infml, often humor* to experience times when one is important, famous, successful, happy, etc.: *I may not be of much importance now, but I've had my moments*

mo·men·tum /məʊˈmentəm, mə-/ *n* **-ta** /tə/ *or* **-tums 1** [U;C] *tech* the quantity of movement in a body, measured by multiplying its mass by the speed at which it moves: *As the rock rolled down the mountainside, it gathered momentum* (=moved faster and faster) **2** [U] the force gained by the movement or development of events: *The national struggle for independence is gaining momentum every day*

mom·ma /ˈmɒmə‖ˈmamə/ *n AmE* **1** [C;N] *infml* MAMA **2** [C9] *sl* a woman: *Sophie Tucker, the last of the red-hot mommas*

mom·my /ˈmɒmi‖ˈmami/ *n* [C;N] *AmE* MUMMY

Mon. *written abbrev. for:* Monday

mon·arch /ˈmɒnək‖ˈmanərk, -ark/ *n* a ruler of a state (such as a king, queen, etc.) who has a right by birth to the office or title, and does not have to be elected

mo·nar·chic /məˈnɑːkɪk‖məˈnar-/ also **mo·nar·chi·cal** /-kɪkəl/— *adj* [Wa5] of, by, or related to a MONARCH or a MONARCHY: *monarchic rule*

mon·arch·is·m /ˈmɒnəkɪzəm‖ˈmanər-/ *n* [U] MONARCHIC government or principles

mon·arch·ist /ˈmɒnəkɨst‖ˈmanər-/ *n, adj* [C;A] (a person in favour) of the idea that kings, queens, etc., should rule, rather than elected leaders

mon·ar·chy /ˈmɒnəki‖ˈmanərki/ *n* **1** [U] rule by a king or queen **2** [C] a state ruled by a king or queen

mon·as·tery /ˈmɒnəstri‖ˈmanəsteri/ *n* a building in which MONKs live according to the religious rules that they have promised to obey

mo·nas·tic /məˈnæstɪk/ *adj* [Wa5] of monasteries (MONASTERY) or MONKs —**~ally** *adv* [Wa4,5]

mo·nas·ti·cis·m /məˈnæstɨsɪzəm/ *n* [U] the life, or way of life, of MONKs in a MONASTERY

mon·au·ral /ˌmɒnˈɔːrəl‖ˌman-/ *adj* [Wa5] **1** *tech* having, using, or for, one ear only **2** *fml* MONO

Mon·day /ˈmʌndi/ *n* **1** [R] the second day of the present week; day before next Tuesday or last Tuesday: *He'll arrive on Monday evening* (=during the evening of next Monday) **2** [C] the second day of any week, or of the week that is being spoken of: *Many people do their week's washing on Mondays.|He arrived on the Monday and left on the Wednesday* (=arrived on the second day of the week being spoken of).*|He arrived on a Monday* (=not a Sunday, Tuesday, etc.).|(*esp. AmE*) *She works Mondays*

mon·e·ta·ry /ˈmʌnɨtəri‖ˈmanɨteri/ *adj* [Wa5] *esp. tech* of or connected with money: *The monetary system of certain countries used to be based on gold*

mon·ey /ˈmʌni/ *n* [U] **1** pieces of metal made into coins, or paper notes with their value printed on them, given and taken in buying and selling: *He doesn't usually carry much money on him* (=in his pockets) **2** wealth: *Money doesn't always bring happiness.|He made his money* (=became rich) *buying and selling land for house building* **3 any money** *infml* as much money as you are willing to risk; as much as you ask: *I'll* BET *you any money that your team won't win* **4 in the money** *infml* in a state where one can gain a great deal of wealth: *If this old picture of ours really is by a famous artist, we're in the money* **5 marry money** to marry someone who is wealthy **6 one's money's worth** full value for the money one has spent: *We enjoyed the film so much that we felt we'd got our money's worth*

7 pay good money (for something) *infml* to pay a high price (for something): *Look after that watch your father gave you; he paid good money for it* **8 put money into (a business)** to lend money to people starting or controlling (a business), in the hope of getting good interest **9 raise money on (something)** to get money by selling or PAWNing (something) **10 throw one's money about/around** to spend money foolishly, often so as to show one's wealth —see also COIN **money (in)**, **money for** JAM, **money for old** ROPE, PIN MONEY, POCKET MONEY —**~less** *adj* [Wa5]

mon·ey·bags /'mʌnibægz/ *n* **moneybags** [Wn3;C; *you*+N9] *infml* a very wealthy person

mon·ey·box /'mʌnibɒks‖-bɑks/ *n* a box for collecting or saving money, usu. with an opening into which coins can be put

mon·ey·chang·er /'mʌni,tʃeɪndʒəʳ/ *n* a person whose business is exchanging the money of one country for that of another

mon·eyed /'mʌnid/ *adj* [A;(B)] *esp. fml or pomp* having much money; rich: *He isn't poor, but he certainly doesn't belong to the moneyed classes*

money-grub·ber /'·· ,··/ *n derog* a person so interested in money, and so eager to become rich, that he will do anything, even the lowest kind of work, that will help him reach his purpose —**money-grubbing** *adj*

mon·ey·lend·er /'mʌni,lendəʳ/ *n* **1** a person who lends money, and charges interest on it **2** *derog* USURER: *fell into the hands of moneylenders*

mon·ey·mak·er /'mʌni,meɪkəʳ/ *n* **1** a person who has the ability always to gain money **2** *usu. apprec* something that brings gain in money —**moneymaking** *adj, n* [Wa5;A;U]

money or·der /'·· ,··/ *n* an official paper of a certain value (higher than that of a POSTAL ORDER), which can be bought (as from a post office) by one person and sent to another person, who can then take it (as to another post office) and be given the amount of money the first person paid for it

mon·eys, monies /'mʌniz/ *n* [P] *law or old use* amounts of money: *The moneys placed in the lawyer's trust couldn't be given to the young man until he had reached the age of 18*

money-spin·ner /'·· ,··/ *n infml, esp. BrE* something that brings in much money: *This seaside hotel's a real money-spinner, especially in the summer months*

mon·ger /'mʌŋgəʳ‖'mɑŋ-, 'mʌŋ-/ *n* (*usu. in comb.*) **1** a tradesman; person dealing in the stated articles, esp. one who has a small business: *a* COSTERMONGER|*a* FISHMONGER|*an* IRONMONGER **2** *usu. derog* a person who likes to spread, or encourage the spread of, the stated unpleasant thing: *a* GOSSIP *monger*|*a* WARMONGER

mon·gol /'mɒŋgəl‖'mɑŋ-/ *n* a person born with a weakness of the mind and a broad flattened head and face and sloping eyes

mon·gol·is·m /'mɒŋgəlɪzəm‖'mɑŋ-/ *n* [U] the condition of mind and body from which a MONGOL suffers

mon·goose /'mɒŋguːs‖'mɑŋ-/ *n* **-gooses** a type of small furry animal, common in India and other eastern countries, that is very good at killing snakes and rats —see picture at CARNIVOROUS

mon·grel /'mʌŋgrəl‖'mɑŋ-, 'mʌŋ-/ *n* **1** an animal, esp. a dog, which is of no particular breed but whose parents were of mixed breeds or different breeds **2** *often derog* a person of mixed race or origin **3** *infml* something, such as a plant or a word, that is mixed in its making: *Some English words are mongrels; they are formed from a mixture of different languages* (*such as* tele (*Greek*) -vision (*Latin*))

mon·i·tor¹ /'mɒnɪ̆təʳ‖'mɑ-/ *n* **1** a pupil chosen to help the teacher in various ways: *Little Jimmy has been made dinner money monitor* (=he collects the money paid by the children for their school meals) **2** also **monitor screen** /'··· ·/— a television set used by people working in a television STUDIO, to make sure that the picture and sound are clear, and to choose that which is the best or most suitable to be broadcast **3** an apparatus for finding out whether or not there is a fault in the sending or receiving of news, messages, etc., by radio or other electrical means **4** a person whose work is to listen to radio news, messages, etc., from foreign stations and report their contents **5** an instrument that can discover the presence of RADIOACTIVITY **6** any of several types of large LIZARD that live in Africa, Asia, and Australia

monitor² *v* [T1] to listen to (a radio broadcast, esp. one from a foreign country) and take careful note of what is said in order to gain information

monk /mʌŋk/ *n* a member of an all-male group united by a solemn promise to give their lives to the service of a religion and living together in a special building (MONASTERY) —compare FRIAR, NUN —**~ish** *adj*

mon·key /'mʌŋki/ *n* **1** any of several types of long-tailed active tree-climbing animals, belonging to that class of animals most like man —see picture at PRIMATE² **2** *infml* a child who is full of annoying playfulness and tricks **3** *BrE sl* 500 pounds or dollars: *He won a monkey at the horse races* **4** *BrE sl* a large lump (HUMP) on a person's back **5 get one's monkey up** *BrE infml* to become angry **6 have a monkey on one's back** *sl* **a** to be a person who cannot stop himself from taking dangerous drugs **b** to have a continual feeling of dislike for someone because of what he has done to one **7 make a monkey (out) of someone** *infml* to make someone appear foolish **8 put someone's monkey up** *BrE infml* to make someone angry

monkey a·bout also **monkey a·round**— *v adv* [I∅] *infml* to play in a foolish way: *The boys were monkeying about in the playground, and one of them was knocked down and hurt his head* —see also MONKEY WITH

monkey busi·ness /'·· ,··/ *n* [U] *infml* behaviour which causes trouble or is intended to deceive, or is full of tricks: *I put £7 in this box, and now there's only £5 there; I think there's been some monkey business by someone* (=someone has taken some of the money)

monkey nut /'·· ·/ *n BrE becoming rare* PEANUT

monkey-puz·zle /'·· ,··/ also **monkey-puzzle tree** /'·· ·· ,·/— *n* a type of tree with dark green prickly leaves growing very close together on long branches —see picture at TREE¹

monkey tricks /'·· ·/ *n* [P] *infml* MONKEY BUSINESS

monkey with *v prep* [T1] *infml* to touch, use, or examine (esp. something that is not one's concern) without skill and so possibly causing damage (often in the phrs. **monkey about/around with**): *You'll break that radio set if you don't stop monkeying about with it*

monkey wrench /'·· ·/ *n* a tool that can be ADJUSTed for holding or turning things of different widths

mon·o¹ /'mɒnəʊ‖'mɑ-/ also (*fml*) **monaural**, (*fml*) **monophonic**— *adj* [Wa5] using a system of sound recording, broadcasting, or receiving in which the sound appears to come from one direction only when played back: *a mono record/record player/radio/radio broadcast/recorder* —compare STEREO

mono² *n* **monos** *infml* **1** [U] MONO sound production **2** [C] a MONO record

mono- *comb. form* one; single: *mono*COTYLEDON|MONOPLANE

mon·o·chrome¹ /ˈmɒnəkrəʊm‖ˈmɑ-/ *n* **1** [U] (the use of) only one colour, or different degrees of brightness of the same colour, in painting, photography, etc. **2** [C] a MONOCHROME painting, photograph, etc.

monochrome² *adj* [Wa5] having, using, or showing one colour only: *a monochrome television set* (=one showing black and white pictures, not coloured ones)

mon·o·cle /ˈmɒnəkəl‖ˈmɑ-/ *n* an apparatus like glasses, but for one eye only

mo·nog·a·mous /məˈnɒgəməs‖məˈnɑ-/ *adj* [Wa5] having only one wife or husband at a time —**~ly** *adv*

mo·nog·a·my /məˈnɒgəmi‖məˈnɑ-/ *n* [U] the custom or practice of having only one wife or husband at one time

mon·o·gram /ˈmɒnəgræm‖ˈmɑ-/ *n* a figure formed of 2 or more letters, esp. the first letters of a person's names, joined together by placing parts of one letter over or under parts of another, often printed on writing paper, sewn on handkerchiefs, etc. —**~med** *adj*

mon·o·graph /ˈmɒnəgrɑːf‖ˈmɑnəgræf/ *n* an article or short book on one particular subject or branch of a subject (scientific, medical, etc.) that the writer has studied deeply

mon·o·lith /ˈmɒnəlɪθ‖ˈmɑ-/ *n* a large pillar made from one piece or mass of stone and standing by itself

mon·o·lith·ic /ˌmɒnəˈlɪθɪk‖ˌmɑ-/ *adj* **1** [Wa5] of or related to a MONOLITH **2** forming a very large tall whole, separate from all others, and showing great solidity, weight, and force: *the monolithic buildings of a great city* **3** *often derog* forming a large unchanging whole, in which all the parts must behave in the same way as each other and very little freedom of activity is allowed: *People aren't free to express opinions against the government in a monolithic state* —**~ally** *adv* [Wa4]

mon·o·logue, *AmE* also **monolog** /ˈmɒnəlɒg‖ˈmɑnəlɔg, -lɑg/ *n* **1** a spoken part in a play or film, for a single performer, usu. acting alone **2** a poem or other piece of writing intended to be spoken on stage by one person only **3** *infml* a rather long speech by one person, which prevents others from taking part in the conversation

mon·o·ma·ni·a /ˌmɒnəʊˈmeɪnɪə‖ˌmɑ-/ *n* **1** [U] a condition of the mind in which a person is interested in nothing except one particular subject, or can think of nothing except one particular idea **2** [C *usu. sing.*] an example of this

mon·o·ma·ni·ac /ˌmɒnəʊˈmeɪniæk‖ˌmɑ-/ *n* a person suffering from MONOMANIA

mon·o·nu·cle·o·sis /ˌmɒnəʊnjuːkliˈəʊsɪ̍s‖ˌmɑnəʊnuː-/ *n* [U] *esp. AmE* GLANDULAR fever

mon·o·phon·ic /ˌmɒnəˈfɒnɪk‖ˌmɑnəˈfɑ-/ *adj* [Wa5] *fml* MONO

mon·oph·thong /ˈmɒnəfθɒŋ‖ˈmɑnəfθɔŋ/ *n* a single vowel sound produced with the organs of speech remaining in the same position —compare DIPHTHONG

mon·o·plane /ˈmɒnəpleɪn‖ˈmɑ-/ *n* an aircraft having a single wing on each side of it —compare BIPLANE

mo·nop·o·list /məˈnɒpəlɪ̍st‖məˈnɑ-/ *n* a person who has a MONOPOLY —**~ic** /məˌnɒpəˈlɪstɪk‖məˌnɑ-/ *adj* —**~ically** *adv* [Wa4]

mo·nop·o·lize, -lise /məˈnɒpəlaɪz‖məˈnɑ-/ *v* [T1] **1** to have or obtain a MONOPOLY of; have or get complete unshared control of: *These 2 firms are so big and powerful that they monopolize between them the production and sale of cigarettes in this country* **2** to take wholly to or for oneself, not allowing another or others to share —**-lization** /məˌnɒpəlaɪˈzeɪʃən‖məˌnɑpələ-/ *n* [U (*of*)]

mo·nop·o·ly /məˈnɒpəli‖məˈnɑ-/ *n* **1** [C (*of*); C3] a right or power of one person or one group, and no other, to provide a service, trade in anything, produce something, etc. **2** [(*the*) S+*of*] possession of, or control over, something, which is not shared by another or others: *He seems to think he has a monopoly of brains* (=that he alone is clever).|*A university education shouldn't be the monopoly of those whose parents are rich* **3** [C] something of which one person or one group has complete unshared control: *The postal services weren't always a government monopoly; in the past they were sometimes provided by private companies* **4** [U] *tdmk* (*often cap.*) a type of game in which the winner obtains all the pretended money, property, etc.

mon·o·rail /ˈmɒnəʊreɪl, -nə-‖ˈmɑ-/ *n* [C; *by*+U] (a train or other vehicle travelling on) a railway with a single rail

mon·o·syl·lab·ic /ˌmɒnəsɪˈlæbɪk‖ˌmɑ-/ *adj* **1** [Wa5] (of a word) having one SYLLABLE **2** (of speech, a remark, etc.) formed of words with one SYLLABLE; short, esp. in a rather rude way: *All I could get from him were monosyllabic replies, such as "yes" and "no"* —**~ally** *adv* [Wa4]

mon·o·syl·la·ble /ˈmɒnəˌsɪləbəl‖ˈmɑ-/ *n* a word of one SYLLABLE: *"Can, hot, neck" are monosyllables*

mon·o·the·is·m /ˈmɒnəʊθiːɪzəm, -nə-‖ˈmɑ-/ *n* [U] the belief or teaching that there is only one God —compare POLYTHEISM —**-t** *n*

mon·o·tone /ˈmɒnətəʊn‖ˈmɑ-/ *n* [S] a manner of speaking or singing in which the voice neither rises nor falls, but continues on one and the same note

mo·not·o·nous /məˈnɒtənəs‖məˈnɑ-/ *adj* having a tiring uninteresting sameness or lack of variety: *He spoilt the poem by reading it aloud in a monotonous voice.|Some workmen lead a monotonous life, doing exactly the same things day after day* —**~ly** *adv*

mo·not·o·ny /məˈnɒtəni‖məˈnɑ-/ also **mo·not·o·nous·ness** /məˈnɒtənəsnɪ̍s‖məˈnɑ-/— *n* [U (*of*)] sameness or lack of variety that is tiring or uninteresting: *the monotony of his voice*

mon·o·type /ˈmɒnətaɪp‖ˈmɑ-/ *n* [U;C] *tdmk* (*often cap.*) (a method of printing using) a machine that prepares the letters one by one —compare LINOTYPE

mo·nox·ide /məˈnɒksaɪd‖məˈnɑk-/ *n* [C;U] *tech* (*usu. in comb.*) (an) OXIDE containing one atom of oxygen in the MOLECULE

Mon·sieur /məˈsjɜːʳ (*Fr* məsjø)/ *n* **Messieurs** /meɪˈsjɜːz‖-ɜrz (*Fr* mesjø)/ [A] *Fr* the title of a French(-speaking) man: *Monsieur Legrand|Messieurs Duval and Lalande*

mon·si·gnor /mɒnˈsiːnjəʳ‖mɑn-/ *n* [C;A;N] (*usu. cap.*) (a title given to) any of various priests of high rank in the ROMAN CATHOLIC church

mon·soon /mɒnˈsuːn‖mɑn-/ *n* **1** [*the*+R;(C)] **a** (the period or season of) heavy rains which fall in India and other countries near it from about April to October **b** *tech* the wind that blows from the Indian Ocean, bringing these rains **2** [C] *infml* a very heavy fall of rain

mon·ster /ˈmɒnstəʳ‖ˈmɑn-/ *n* **1** [C] an animal, plant, or thing of unusually great size or strange form: *That dog's a real monster; I've never seen such a big one.|Some modern aircraft are monsters compared with those of 50 years ago* **2** [C] a creature, imaginary or real, that is unnatural in shape, size, or qualities, and usu. with an appearance so ugly as to cause fear: *a sea monster|She dreamt that terrible monsters with flaming eyes and sharp teeth were chasing her through the wood* **3** [C (*of*); *you*+N] a person whose evil qualities or actions are such as to raise strong feelings of dislike, hatred, fear, etc.: *The judge told the murderer that he was a monster, not fit to be called a human being* **4** [A] unusually large (in size or number): *Have you ever seen such monster vegetables as those growing here?* **5 the green-eyed monster** *pomp* jealousy

mon·strance /ˈmɒnstrəns‖ˈmɑn-/ *n* a glass vessel, usu. ornamented with gold or silver, raised by the priest during a service in a ROMAN CATHOLIC church, so that the people may see the HOST that it contains

mon·stros·i·ty /mɒnˈstrɒsɪ̆ti‖mɑnˈstrɑ-/ *n* **1** a person, animal, plant, or object of unnatural shape or unusual size: *A dog with 2 heads would be a monstrosity* **2** something made or built in such a way that it is, or is considered, very ugly: *The palace is a monstrosity; I've never seen such a strange, ugly building*

mon·strous /ˈmɒnstrəs‖ˈmɑn-/ *adj* **1** not following the usual course of nature; of unnaturally large size, strange shape, etc.: *The tree planted by the magician quickly grew to a monstrous height* **2** so bad as to cause strong feelings of disagreement, opposition, dislike, hatred, etc.: *He treated his own son with monstrous cruelty* **3** completely opposed to reason; shocking; DISGRACEFUL: *It's monstrous that he should be ungrateful for all the help his friends have given him* —**~ly** *adv*

mons ven·e·ris /ˌmɒnz ˈvenərɪ̆s‖ˌmɑnz-/ *n* [*usu. sing.*] *Lat* a raised rounded area of flesh at the bottom of the front part of a woman's body, between the tops of the legs and just above the sex organs

mon·tage /ˈmɒntɑːʒ‖mɑnˈtɑʒ/ *n Fr* **1** [C] **a** a picture made by combining several separate pictures together **b** a piece of writing or music, or another work of art, made from separate parts combined together **2** [U] the action of making such a picture or other work of art **3** [U] the choosing, cutting, and combining together of separate photographic material, so as to make a connected film

month /mʌnθ/ *n* **1** one of the 12 named divisions of the year **2** a period of about 4 weeks, esp. from a particular date to the same date about 4 weeks later: *The baby was born on 23 September, so he'll be exactly 6 months old tomorrow* (*23 March*) **3 a month of Sundays** *infml* a very long time —see also LUNAR MONTH, CALENDAR MONTH

month·ly[1] /ˈmʌnθli/ *adj, adv* [Wa5] (happening, appearing, etc.) every month or once a month: *a monthly meeting*

monthly[2] *n* a magazine appearing once a month

monthly pe·ri·od /ˌ·· ˈ···/ *n* [*often pl.*] PERIOD[1] (5)

mon·u·ment /ˈmɒnjʊmənt‖ˈmɑnjə-/ *n* **1** a building, pillar, GRAVESTONE, STATUE, or something that preserves, or is intended to preserve, the memory of a person or event: *This great church is its builder's monument* (=that by which he is remembered) **2** a building or place of great age, or that which remains of it, considered worthy of preservation for its historic interest or beauty: *The ruins of the castle are an ancient monument, which the government pays money to preserve* **3** a work, esp. a book, worthy of lasting fame: *His history of the ancient Roman Empire is a monument of learning and deep study* —see also NATIONAL MONUMENT **4** [+*to*] an outstanding example (of): *His actions are a monument to foolishness*

mon·u·ment·al /ˌmɒnjʊˈmentl◂‖ˌmɑnjə-/ *adj* **1** [Wa5;A] of, intended for, or having the nature of a MONUMENT (1): *This monumental pillar was built in memory of a great naval victory* **2** [B] very large, needing much work, and of great and lasting worth: *The artist spent years on his monumental painting, which covered the whole roof of the church* **3** [B] very great in degree: *The army was defeated, in spite of its monumental efforts to hold the city*

mon·u·ment·al·ly /ˌmɒnjʊˈmentəli‖ˌmɑnjə-/ *adv* to a very great degree: *How could anyone have done such a monumentally stupid thing?*

moo[1] /muː/ *v* [I∅] to make the noise that a cow makes —see also LOW[1]

moo[2] *n* **-s** **1** the sound that a cow makes **2** *BrE derog sl* a stupid or worthless woman

mooch /muːtʃ/ *v* [T1] *AmE sl* to get by asking for: *He tried to mooch a drink off me, but I said no*

mooch a·bout also **mooch a·round**— *v adv* [I∅] *infml* to wander about slowly, without aim or activity: *He had nothing to do and nowhere to go, and spent the morning mooching about, his hands in his pockets and his eyes on the ground*

moo·cow /ˈmuːkaʊ/ *n* [C;N] (*a child's word for*) a cow

mood[1] /muːd/ *n* **1** [C] a state of the feelings at a particular time: *The beautiful sunny morning put him in a happy mood.|His moods change very quickly; one moment he's cheerful, and the next complaining about his life.|She's not going to ask her husband to buy her a new dress while he's in such a bad mood* (=in a bad temper) **2** [C] a state of feeling in which one is bad-tempered, silently angry or displeased, etc.: *Don't ask him to lend you money when he's in one of his moods* (=in a bad temper, as he often is) **3** [(*the*) R (*for*), R3] the right state of mind (for a particular activity, thing, etc.): *She was very tired, and in no mood for dancing*

mood[2] *n tech* any of 3 groups of forms of a verb, expressing **a** a fact (INDICATIVE) **b** a command or request (IMPERATIVE) **c** a condition, doubt, etc. (SUBJUNCTIVE)

mood·y /ˈmuːdi/ *adj* [Wa2] *usu. derog* **1** having MOODS[1] (1) that change often and quickly: *I'd never marry that girl; she's so moody. You never know whether she's going to be happy or bad-tempered* **2** bad-tempered, angry, displeased, or unhappy, esp. when such feelings, or the reasons for them, are not expressed: *He became rather moody while he was waiting to hear the result of the examination* —**moodily** *adv* —**moodiness** *n* [U]

moon /muːn/ *n* **1** [*the*+R] the body which moves round the earth once every 28 days, and can be seen shining palely in the sky at night —see picture at PLANET **2** [S] this body as it appears at a particular time: *On the night of the attack, there was a moon that gave more help to the defenders than to the attacking army.|Last night there was a full moon* (=appearing as a full circle, that is, with its whole front part lit up, when opposite the sun) **3** [C] a body that turns round a PLANET other than the earth: *Saturn has several moons* **4** [C *usu. pl.*] *esp. poet* a month: *many moons ago* **5 cry for the moon** to desire strongly something that cannot be gained **6 once in a blue moon** *infml* once in a very long time; very rarely; almost never **7 over the moon** very happy: *She's over the moon about her new baby* **8 promise someone the moon** to promise to give someone something that is beyond one's means or power to give —see also MAN IN THE MOON —**~less** *adj* [Wa5]

moon a·bout also **moon a·round**— *v adv* [I∅] *infml* to wander about or behave in an aimless unhappy way

moon a·way *v adv* [T1] *infml* to pass (time) in an aimless way

moon·beam /ˈmuːnbiːm/ *n* a beam of light from the moon
moon·calf /ˈmuːnkɑːf‖-kæf/ *n* **1** MONSTER (2) **2** a foolish person of weak mind or memory
moon·light[1] /ˈmuːnlaɪt/ *n* [U] the light of the moon: *The moonlight on the calm sea added to the beauty of the scene*
moonlight[2] *v* **~ed** [IØ] *infml* to have a second job in addition to a regular one —**~er** *n*
moon·lit /ˈmuːnˌlɪt/ *adj* [Wa5;A] given light by the moon: *He painted a picture of a moonlit valley*
moon o·ver *v prep* [T1] *infml* to spend time in a dreamlike state caused by unsatisfied desire for (esp. a person): *mooning over a popular actor*
moon·shine /ˈmuːnʃaɪn/ *n* [U] *infml* **1** talk, opinions, etc., that are not based on reality **2** *esp. AmE* strong alcoholic drink produced unlawfully
moon·stone /ˈmuːnstəʊn/ *n* a milky-white stone, not of great value, used in making cheap jewels
moon·struck /ˈmuːnstrʌk/ *adj infml* suffering from a slight form of madness, supposed to be caused by the influence of the moon on a person's mind
moon·y /ˈmuːni/ *adj* [Wa1] *infml* in the habit of acting in a dreamy aimless way
moor[1] /mʊəʳ/ *n* [*often pl. with sing. meaning*] *esp. BrE* a wide, open, often raised area of land, covered with rough grass or low bushes, that is not farmed because of its bad soil, and, in Britain, is often used as a place where birds are kept, to be shot for sport at a certain season of the year
moor[2] *v* [T1 (*to*); IØ] to fasten (a ship, boat, etc.) to land, the bed of the sea, etc. by means of ropes, chains, an ANCHOR, etc.
moor·hen /ˈmʊəhen‖ˈmʊər-/ also **water hen**— *n* [Wn1] a type of black bird with a bright red or orange mark above its beak, that lives beside streams and lakes —see picture at WATER[1]
moor·ings /ˈmʊərɪŋz/ *n* [P] **1** a place where a ship or boat is MOORed: *He lowered his sails as he came near his moorings* **2** the ropes, chains, etc., used for MOORing[2]: *The moorings broke during the storm, and the boat was blown onto the rocks* **3** moral principles used as a guide for behaviour (esp. in the phr. **lose one's moorings**)
Moor·ish /ˈmʊərɪʃ/ *adj* of or related to the Muslim peoples of mixed Arab race (**Moors**) who conquered Spain and held power there in the years from 711 to 1492
Moorish arch /ˌ·· ˈ·/ also **Saracenic arch**— *n* a type of pointed arch in which the rounded part at the top is wider than the sides
moor·land /ˈmʊələnd‖ˈmʊər-/ *n* [U *often pl. with same meaning*] open country that is a MOOR
moose /muːs/ *n* **moose** [Wn3] a type of large deer, with very large flat horns, that lives in the northern parts of America (and in some northern countries of Europe, where it is called an ELK)
moot /muːt/ *v* [T1 *usu. pass.*] to state (a question, matter, etc.) so that consideration and argument can take place and, if possible, a decision can be made: *The question of changing the entrance rules was mooted at the last meeting of the club committee*
moot point /ˌ· ˈ·/ also **moot ques·tion** /ˌ· ˈ··/— *n* [C *usu. sing.*; S6] an undecided point; point on which there is disagreement, doubt, more than one opinion, etc.
mop[1] /mɒp‖mɑp/ *n* **1** a tool for washing floors, made up of a long stick with either a number of threads of rope or thick string, or a piece of SPONGE, fastened to one end —see picture at HOUSEHOLD **2** a tool for washing dishes, made up of a short stick with a number of threads of thick string fastened to one end **3** [(*of*) *usu. sing.*] *infml* a thick mass (of hair), standing up from the head, and looking as if it is not brushed
mop[2] *v* **-pp-** **1** [T1] to clean with, or as if with, a MOP[1] (1): *She has to mop the kitchen floor at least once a day* **2** [T1] to make dry by rubbing with something dry: *It was such a hot day that he kept mopping his face with his handkerchief* **3** [X9] to remove (unwanted liquid, dirt, etc.) by touching with cloth or other soft material: *The nurse gently mopped the blood from the wound with a soft cloth* —see also MOP UP **4 mop the floor with someone** *infml* to defeat someone completely, and often easily (in a game, fight, argument, etc.)
mope[1] /məʊp/ *v* [IØ] to be in low spirits, often without trying to become more cheerful
mope[2] *n* [S] *infml* an act of moping (MOPE): *She's always complaining; there's nothing she enjoys better than (having) a good mope*
mope a·bout also **mope a·round**— *v adv* [IØ] to wander about, feeling sad or low-spirited
mo·ped /ˈməʊped/ *n* a bicycle which has a small engine, to help the rider esp. when going uphill: *She goes to work on a moped*
mop·pet /ˈmɒpɨt‖ˈmɑ-/ *n infml, usu. apprec* a child, esp. a girl
mop-up /ˈ· ·/ *n infml* an action taken to finish something, so that nothing is left
mop up *v adv* **1** [T1] to remove (unwanted liquid, dirt, etc.) with, or as if with, a MOP[1] (1): *It was you who dropped the milk; you'll have to mop it up* **2** [T1a] *infml* to finish dealing with: *I must just mop up the last of the work.|The battle was won, except for mopping up a few small groups of enemy soldiers who continued to fight*
mo·quette /mɒˈket‖məʊ-/ *n* [U] a type of thick material used for making floor coverings, furniture coverings, etc.
mo·raine /məˈreɪn/ *n* a mass of earth, pieces of rock, etc., carried by a GLACIER on its downward path, and left in the form of a line at its edge or end
mor·al[1] /ˈmɒrəl‖ˈmɔ-/ *adj* **1** [Wa5;A] concerning character, behaviour, or actions, considered or judged as being good or evil, right or wrong; ETHICAL: *The closing of the school may save money, but the Council's action is wrong by moral standards, as it will do harm to the children* **2** [Wa5;A] based on the idea of what is right (compared with what is lawful); having, or being directed towards, right: *He refused to join the army, believing that he had no moral right to kill.|a man of great moral courage|A judge must base his decisions on the law of the land, and not on the moral law.|I can't help you with money, but I'll give you* **moral support** *in your struggle against your employer* **3** [B] good (in character, behaviour, etc.); pure, esp. in matters of sex: *He didn't lead a moral life before his marriage.|My grandfather was a very moral man; he'd never allow cursing* —opposite **immoral** **4** [Wa5;B] of or related to pureness and goodness, esp. in matters of sex: *A young girl living alone in a big city faces moral dangers* **5** [Wa5;A] able to recognize the difference between right and wrong, good and evil: *A baby isn't born with a moral sense* —compare AMORAL **6** [B] teaching, showing, or intended to show that which is good or right in human behaviour: *The film was not only amusing, but it also gave a valuable moral lesson.|This is a very moral book*
USAGE Although **immoral** means "morally bad", it is not always the opposite of **moral**, which often means "in connection with good or bad" in phrs. like **moral** *principles*|**moral** *standards*. There is the same difference between **immorality**, a strong word for bad behaviour, and **morality**: *the* **immorality** *of his sexual practices|to lead a life of perfect* **morality** (=good behaviour)|*an act of doubtful* **morality**

(=behaviour). One's **morals** are one's **moral** beliefs and principles, which can also be good or bad.

moral² *n* a good lesson (in behaviour, in the ways of leading one's life, etc.) that can be learnt from a story or happening: *The moral of this story for children is that brothers and sisters shouldn't quarrel*

moral cer·tain·ty /ˌ·· ˈ···/ *n* [*usu. sing.*] *fml* a probability so great that one feels sure, without having certain proof: *The teacher told his student that it was a moral certainty that he'd pass the examination*

mo·rale /məˈrɑːl‖məˈræl/ *n* [U] the state of mind (of a person or group of people, often an army) with regard to pride, faith in the rightness of one's actions, determination not to yield, strength of spirit, etc.: *Trapped in the cave by a fall of rock, the men kept up their morale by singing together* —compare MORALS

mor·al·ist /ˈmɒrəlᵻst‖ˈmɔ-/ *n* **1** a person who teaches, studies, writes about, etc., MORAL principles **2** *usu. derog* a person who concerns himself with trying to control the MORALS of other people

mor·al·ist·ic /ˌmɒrəˈlɪstɪk‖ˌmɔ-/ *adj derog* having or showing very firm unyielding narrow ideas about right and wrong behaviour —**~ally** *adv* [Wa4]

mo·ral·i·ty /məˈrælᵻti/ *n* **1** [U] rightness or pureness of behaviour, of an action, etc.: *His ways of doing business are certainly successful, but we're doubtful about their morality.|One sometimes wonders if there's any morality in politics* **2** [C] MORALITY PLAY

morality play /·ˈ··· ·/ *n* an old form of theatrical play (often performed in the years 1400–1600), in which good and bad human qualities were represented as people by the actors —compare MIRACLE PLAY

mor·al·ize, -ise /ˈmɒrəlaɪz‖ˈmɔ-/ *v* [Wv4;IØ (*about, on, upon*)] *usu. derog* to express one's thoughts (often not welcome to the listener or reader) on the rightness or, more usually, the wrongness of behaviour, actions, etc. —**~r** *n*

mor·al·ly /ˈmɒrəli‖ˈmɔ-/ *adv* **1** *apprec* in a MORAL¹ (3) manner —opposite **immorally** **2** with regard to right or good behaviour: *It isn't unlawful to leave one's children alone in the house at night, but it's morally wrong; they might have an accident* **3** *fml* most probably; almost certainly: *It's morally certain that he'll be the next minister of education*

Moral Re-Ar·ma·ment /ˌ·· ·ˈ···/ *n* [R] OXFORD GROUP

mor·als /ˈmɒrəlz‖ˈmɔ-/ *n* [P] rules of behaviour, or behaviour itself, esp. in matters of sex; standards on which behaviour is based: *She's a woman of loose morals* (=of bad sexual behaviour).|*In his business affairs he has no morals* (=he'll lie, act dishonestly, etc.) —see MORAL (USAGE)

mo·rass /məˈræs/ *n* **1** [C] a stretch of low ground that is soft and wet to a great depth, so that it is dangerous for walking **2** [(*the*) S (*of*)] a difficult position or an evil state of living, from which it is almost impossible to free oneself

mor·a·to·ri·um /ˌmɒrəˈtɔːrɪəm‖ˌmɔrəˈto-/ *n* **-ria** /rɪə/ **1** [(*on*)] a declaration, esp. by a government, that a particular activity or action (such as the production of weapons or the payment of a debt) will be stopped or delayed for a certain period of time **2** the length of such a delay

mor·bid /ˈmɔːbᵻd‖ˈmɔr-/ *adj* **1** *derog* having or showing an unhealthy unnatural interest in or liking for unpleasant subjects, esp. concerning death **2** [Wa5] *med* diseased; connected with or caused by disease (of body or mind) —**~ly** *adv*

mor·bid·i·ty /mɔːˈbɪdᵻti‖mɔr-/ *n* **1** [U] also **morbidness** /ˈmɔːbɪdnᵻs‖ˈmɔr-/— *derog or med* the state of being MORBID **2** [U;S] *med* the amount of sickness, or of a particular sickness, in a particular area

mor·dant /ˈmɔːdnt‖ˈmɔr-/ *adj* (esp. of the manner of expressing thoughts) biting or cutting, and thus able to hurt: *His political opponents feared his mordant tongue, and even more his mordant pen* (=the ways in which he spoke and wrote against them) —**~ly** *adv*

more¹ /mɔːʳ‖mor/ *determiner, pron, n* (*compar. of* **many, much**) [GU (*of, than*)] **1** a greater number, quantity, or part (of): *There are more cars on the roads in summer than in winter.|50 is more than 40.|The weather was bad last summer, but this summer there's been even more rain.|Many people support the government, but (many) more are against it.|"How many rooms are there in this house?" "More than in mine."|As he grows older, he spends more of his time in bed.|It's no/not more than a mile to the sea.|More than one school has closed.|"It costs more than making your own beer"* (SEU S.) —opposite **less, fewer** **2** an additional or further number, amount, or quantity (of): *I've given you all you asked for; what more d'you want?|I have to write 2 more letters this morning* (=in addition to those already written).|*Have you got any more work to do today?|Can I have more time to answer your questions?|They have one child, and would like a few more.|A lot of new houses are being built, but many more are needed.|If you stay at that hotel, you'll have to pay a little more.|He'd like to know more about the young man his daughter wants to marry.|"Have you had enough to eat, or would you like some more?" "Yes, give me a bit more of that cake."|Tell me more!* (=I'm interested in what you say) **3 more and more** increasingly; (an amount) that continues to become larger: *As time went on, he found it more and more difficult to support his family* **4 more or less a** almost; nearly: *The work's more or less finished* **b** about; not exactly: *The repairs to the car will cost £50, more or less* **5 more than meets the eye** something additional but not easy to see, which makes the matter less simple than it appears: *There's more in her refusal than meets the eye; I think she's trying to hide something* **6 see more of someone** to meet someone again, or more often: *He liked the girl, and thought he'd like to see more of her* **7 the more** the greater; in a greater degree (the stated thing): *The more fool you, if you accepted such a low price* **8 the more . . ., the more/less, etc.** by the amount that . . ., by a greater/less amount: *The more he gives his children, the more they want.|The more I see of him, the less I like him*

USAGE *A few*, (*a good/great*) *many*, and the numbers are only used with **more** when it stands for or is followed by a pl.: *many* **more** *friends|3* **more** *eggs|I've eaten those—give me a few* **more***!* When there is no pl. one can use *much, rather, a little, a bit, a good/great deal*: *a bit* **more** *time|rather* **more** *quickly|a great deal* **more** *useful|much* **more** *to say*. In both cases one can use *far, some, any, no*, and (*infml*) *lots/a lot*: *lots* **more** *friends/money|far* **more** *eggs|a lot* **more** *useful*.

more² *adv* [Wa5 (*than*)] **1** (used for forming the COMPARATIVE of most adjectives and adverbs that have more than 2 SYLLABLES, and of many that have only 2): *His illness was (much) more serious than the doctor first thought.|I asked him if he could explain the matter (rather) more simply.|The first question is more difficult than the second.|(fml) John is the more stupid boy of the 2* **2** to or in a greater degree; for a longer space of time: *He'll never be a good games player if he doesn't practise more.|He seems to care (far/much) more for his dogs than for his children.|Surprisingly her face had more the* *appearance of anger than pleasure.|The king, more than parliament, was responsible.|It's her voice I dislike, more than what she says* **3** again (in the phrs. **any more, once more, no more**): *The old man stays in his village now; he doesn't travel any more* (=any longer).|*The teacher said he'd repeat the question once more.|"Once more, are you going to tell me the truth?" he threatened.|The ship sank below the waves, and was seen no more* (=no longer, never again) **4 and what is more** also, and more importantly, seriously, etc.: *You've come late for school, and what's more you've lost your books* **5 more and more** —see MORE[1] (3) **6 more than . . .** *fml* . . . to a degree at which ". . ." is no longer a strong enough or suitable word: *We were more than happy to hear of your escape!* **7 more than a little** *pomp or fml* very: *If you tell your father what you've done, he'll be more than a little angry* **8 more . . . than . . .** It is more true to say . . . than . . .: *He's more mad* (not **madder*) *than stupid* **9 no more** neither: *He can't afford a new car, and no more can I* **10 no more . . . than** in no greater degree . . . than: *He's no more fit to be a minister than a schoolboy would be* **11 the more . . ., the more/less . . .** to the degree that . . ., to an equal/less degree . . .: *The more angry he became, the more she laughed at him.|The more difficult the questions are, the less likely I am to be able to answer them*

mo·rel·lo /mə'reləʊ/ also **morello cher·ry** /·,·· '··/— *n* **-los** a type of bitter dark red CHERRY used esp. in cooking and in making a type of alcoholic drink

more·o·ver /mɔː'rəʊvə^r^‖mo-/ *adv* [Wa5] in addition (to that which has been stated); also; besides: *The price is too high, and moreover, the house isn't in a suitable position*

mo·res /'mɔːreɪz‖'mo-/ *n* [P] *fml or tech* the fixed moral customs and standards of a particular group

Mo·resque /mɔː'resk/ *adj tech* having all the usual qualities of the MOORISH style of art or building

mor·ga·nat·ic /,mɔːgə'nætɪk‖,mɔr-/ *adj* [Wa5] *tech* of a marriage between a member of a royal or noble family and someone of lower rank, in which neither the person of lower rank, nor the children of the marriage, are allowed to take royal or noble titles —**~ally** *adv* [Wa4,5]

morgue /mɔːg‖mɔrg/ *n* **1** *AmE* a building in which dead bodies of unknown people are kept until it is discovered who they were —compare MORTUARY **2** *derog* a comfortless lifeless sad place **3** *infml tech* a collection of past copies of a newspaper, kept in the offices of the newspaper to provide background information when necessary

mor·i·bund /'mɒrɪ̈bʌnd‖'mɔ-, 'mɑ-/ *adj* **1** (of a thing) near to the end of existence: *The club's moribund; it has very few members left, and no new members are joining* **2** [Wa5] (of a person or a person's condition) being near to death

Mor·mon /'mɔːmən‖'mɔr-/ *n* a member of a religious body, formed in 1830 by Joseph Smith in the US, and calling itself **The Church of Jesus Christ of Latter-Day Saints**, in which, until 1890, it was considered lawful for the men to have more than one wife

Mor·mon·is·m /'mɔːmənɪzəm‖'mɔr-/ *n* [U] the beliefs or organization of the MORMON*s*

morn /mɔːn‖mɔrn/ *n poet* a morning

morn·ing /'mɔːnɪŋ‖'mɔr-/ *n* **1** [C;(U)] the first part of the day, from the time when the sun rises, usually until the time when the midday meal is eaten: *She goes shopping on Tuesday and Friday mornings.|I must go to the shops some time during the morning.|I don't want to telephone him so late at night; can't it wait until morning?|The people next door play their radio from morning till night.|in the morning|on the morning of the first of June* **2** [A] of, in, or taking place in this part of the day: *The servant came into the bedroom with an early morning cup of tea.|a morning concert|the morning newspapers* **3** [C;(U)] the part of the day from midnight until midday: *He didn't get home until 2 o'clock in the morning* **4** [*the*+R+*of*] *lit, often apprec* the early part (of anything): *She's only 12, still in the morning of her life* **5 in the morning** tomorrow morning: *I haven't got what you want now, but I can get it for you in the morning* —see also GOOD MORNING

morning coat /'·· ·/ *n* a type of coat that comes down to the waist in front, and slopes down to the level of the knees at the back, worn as part of MORNING DRESS

morning dress /'·· ·/ *n* [U] formal clothes worn by a man at official or social ceremonies in the morning, or, sometimes, in the afternoon

morning glo·ry /,·· '··‖'·· ,··/ *n* [C;U] a type of climbing plant having blue flowers that show their brightest colours in the morning

Morning Prayer /,·· '·/ *n* [R] a service in the CHURCH OF ENGLAND, that takes place in the morning

morning room /'·· ·/ *n* a room used for sitting in during the morning (esp. in a large house, where a rich family lives)

morn·ings /'mɔːnɪŋs‖'mɔr-/ *adv esp. AmE* in or during early morning, or most mornings: *Mornings I usually go for a walk by the river*

morning sick·ness /'·· ,··/ *n* [U] (a feeling of) sickness in the early morning, suffered by women who are going to give birth to a child a few months later

morning star /,·· '·/ *n* [*the*+R] a bright heavenly body (PLANET), esp. Venus, seen when it rises before the sun —see also EVENING STAR

mo·roc·co /mə'rɒkəʊ‖mə'rɑ-/ *n* [U] a type of fine soft leather made esp. from the skin of goats, used esp. for covering books

mo·ron /'mɔːrɒn‖'morɑn/ *n* **1** [C;*you*+N] *derog* a very foolish person **2** [C] *tech* a person born with a weakness of mind, whose powers of understanding, even when grown up, remain at the level of those of a child between the ages of 8 and 12

mo·ron·ic /mə'rɒnɪk‖mə'rɑ-/ *adj derog* very stupid —**~ally** *adv* [Wa4]

mo·rose /mə'rəʊs/ *adj* having no sweetness of temper or nature; not cheerful; looking as if angry or unhappy: *He came home tired and morose after a long and unsuccessful day's work* —**~ly** *adv* —**~ness** *n* [U]

mor·pheme /'mɔːfiːm‖'mɔr-/ *n tech* a meaningful word or part of a word, which contains no smaller meaningful parts: *"Gun" is one morpheme; "gun-s" contains 2 morphemes; "gun-fight-er" contains 3 morphemes*

mor·phe·mics /mɔː'fiːmɪks‖mɔr-/ *n* [U] *tech esp. AmE* MORPHOLOGY (1)

Mor·phe·us /'mɔːfɪəs, -fjuːs‖'mɔr-/ *n* **in the arms of Morpheus** *lit or pomp* asleep

mor·phine /'mɔːfiːn‖'mɔr-/ also (*rare*) **mor·phi·a** /-fɪə/— *n* [U] a substance (in liquid or powder form) having a strong effect on the nerves and used for stopping pain

mor·phol·o·gy /mɔː'fɒlədʒi‖mɔr'fɑ-/ *n* [U] *tech* **1** the study of the MORPHEME*s* of a language, and of the way in which they are joined together to make words **2** the scientific study of the formation of animals, plants, and their parts —**-gical** /,mɔːfə'lɒdʒɪkəl‖,mɔrfə'lɑ-/ *adj* [Wa5]

mor·ris dance /'mɒrɪ̈s dɑːns‖'mɔrɪ̈s dæns, 'mɑ-/ *n* an old English country dance for a group of men, who, when performing, wear special clothes to which small bells are often fixed

mor·row /'mɒrəʊ‖'mɑ-/ *n* **1** [*the*+R] *lit* **a** the day following today, or any particular day in the past: *Let's hope that the morrow will bring better news* **b** the time closely following an event: *The war was at an end, and the nation was full of hopes for the morrow* **2** [U9] *old use* (esp. in greetings) morning: *Good morrow, sir!*

Morse code /ˌmɔːs ˈkəʊd‖ˌmɔrs-/ also (*infml*) **Morse**— *n* [U] a system of sending messages by telegraph, radio, a lamp, etc., in which each letter is represented by a sign made up of one or more short signals (dots) and long signals (DASHes) in sound or light

mor·sel /ˈmɔːsəl‖ˈmɔr-/ *n* **1** [C (*of*)] a very small piece (of food) **2** [C] a specially nice small piece of food: (fig.) *That new secretary's a tasty morsel* **3** [C+*of, usu. nonassertive*] a very small piece or quantity (of anything): *He wouldn't do such silly things if he had a morsel of sense*

mor·tal[1] /ˈmɔːtl‖ˈmɔrtl/ *adj* [Wa5] **1** [B] that must die; not living for ever —opposite **immortal** **2** [A] human; of human beings: *It's beyond mortal power to bring a dead man back to life* **3** [B] causing death: *He received a mortal wound soon after the battle began* **4** [A] (of an enemy) having a lasting hatred, that can never be changed into friendship **5** [A] (of a fight, struggle, etc.) continuing until, or ending in, death or the complete defeat of one side: *mortal* COMBAT **6** [A] (of danger, fear, etc.) so great as to cause, or fill the mind with thoughts of, death **7** [A] *infml* **a** very great (in degree): *It's a mortal shame that she's paid so little; she deserves much higher wages* **b** (of time) tiringly long: *He had to wait a mortal time before the doctor could see him* **8** [A] *infml* (used for adding force to *every*) possible: *She does every mortal thing to please her husband, but he's still not satisfied*

mortal[2] *n* **1** [C *usu. pl.*] *esp. lit* a human being (as compared with a god, a spirit, etc.): *We're all mortals, with our human faults and weaknesses* **2** [C9] *BrE infml* a person of the stated kind: *I've never known such a lazy mortal as you*

mor·tal·i·ty /mɔːˈtælɨ̣ti‖mɔr-/ *n* **1** [U;S] the number of deaths from a certain cause: *If this disease spreads in the country, the doctors fear that there'll be a high mortality* **2** [U;S] the rate at which deaths take place, as among a certain number or a certain type of people: *There's naturally a higher mortality among old people in winter than in summer* **3** [U] the condition of being MORTAL[1] (1) —opposite **immortality**

mortality ta·ble /·ˈ··· ˌ··/ *n tech* a list showing how long people of various ages may be expected to live, used in calculating how much money they will have to pay for insurance

mor·tal·ly /ˈmɔːtəli‖ˈmɔr-/ *adv* **1** in a manner that causes death: *The young soldier fell to the ground, mortally wounded* **2** very greatly; deeply: *She's mortally afraid of walking home alone on a dark night*

mortal sin /ˌ·· ˈ·/ *n* [C;U] (in the CATHOLIC religion) (an act of) wrongdoing so great that it will bring everlasting punishment to the soul after death if it is not forgiven —compare VENIAL **sin**, DEADLY **sin**

mor·tar[1] /ˈmɔːtəʳ‖ˈmɔr-/ *n* **1** a type of heavy gun with a short barrel, firing an explosive that falls from a great height **2** a bowl made from a hard material, in which substances are crushed with a PESTLE into very small pieces or powder —see picture at LABORATORY

mortar[2] *n* [U] a mixture of lime, sand, and water, used in building to hold bricks, stones, etc., together —see picture at SITE[1]

mortar[3] *v* [T1] to join or cover (bricks, stones, etc.) with MORTAR

mor·tar·board /ˈmɔːtəbɔːd‖ˈmɔrtərbord/ *n* a type of cap with a flat square piece on top, usu. black, worn by members of a university, by students at the ceremony of receiving their university degrees, by teachers, etc.

mort·gage[1] /ˈmɔːgɪdʒ‖ˈmɔr-/ *n* **1** an agreement to have money lent, esp. so as to buy a house, with the house or land belonging to the lender until the money is repaid **2** the amount lent on a mortgage

mortgage[2] *v* [T1] to give the right or the claim to the ownership of (a house, land, etc.) in return for money lent for a certain period

mort·gag·ee /ˌmɔːgəˈdʒiː‖ˌmɔr-/ *n* a person who lends money for a certain period in return for the right to ownership of the borrower's property

mort·ga·gor /ˈmɔːgɪdʒəʳ‖ˈmɔr-/ *n* a person who borrows money from a MORTGAGEE

mor·ti·cian /mɔːˈtɪʃən‖mɔr-/ *n AmE* a person whose work is to make all the arrangements for funerals; UNDERTAKER

mor·ti·fi·ca·tion /ˌmɔːtɨ̣fɨ̣ˈkeɪʃən‖ˌmɔr-/ *n* [U] **1** the condition of being mortified (MORTIFY (1)): *He discovered, to his mortification, that his young son knew much more about the subject than he did* **2** the act of MORTIFYing (2) (esp. in the phr. **mortification of the flesh**) **3** *med* decay (of flesh)

mor·ti·fy /ˈmɔːtɨ̣faɪ‖ˈmɔr-/ *v* **1** [Wv4,5;T1] to hurt (a person's) feelings, causing shame, anger, and loss of self-respect: *The teacher was mortified by his own inability to answer such a simple question* **2** [T1] to conquer natural human desires of (oneself or the body) by self-punishment, refusing all the comforts of life, etc. (esp. in the phr. **mortify the flesh**) **3** [I0] *med* (of flesh) to decay: *The doctor had to cut away some of the flesh round the wound, as it had mortified*

mor·tise[1], **-tice** /ˈmɔːtɨ̣s‖ˈmɔr-/ *n tech* a hole cut in a piece of wood or stone to receive the specially shaped end (TENON) of another piece, and thus form a joint

mortise[2], **-tice** *v tech* **1** [X9] to join or fasten by means of a MORTISE and TENON **2** [T1] to cut or make a MORTISE in (wood, stone, etc.)

mortise lock /ˈ·· ·/ *n* a type of lock that fits into a hole cut in the edge of a door —see picture at DOOR

mor·tu·a·ry /ˈmɔːtʃʊəri‖ˈmɔrtʃʊeri/ *n* **1** [C] a place, such as a special room in a hospital or a special building, where a dead body is kept until the time of the funeral **2** [A] *fml* of or connected with death or funerals

mo·sa·ic /məʊˈzeɪ-ɪk/ *n* **1** [C;U] (a piece of ornamental work produced by) the fitting together of small pieces of coloured stone, glass, etc., on a base to which they are fixed, so as to form a pattern or picture **2** [C (*of*) *usu. sing.*] something that has the appearance of such a piece of work, or that is made by putting together a number of different things: *The sky this morning is a mosaic of blue and white*

Mosaic *adj* [Wa5] of or connected with Moses, the great leader of the Jewish people in ancient times

mo·selle /məʊˈzel/ *n* [U] (*often cap.*) a type of white wine produced esp. in the valley of the River Mosel in Germany

mo·sey /ˈməʊzi/ *v* [L9, esp. ALONG] *AmE infml* to walk in an unhurried manner; SAUNTER

Mos·lem /ˈmɒzlɨ̣m‖ˈmɑz-/ *n, adj* [Wa5] Muslim

mosque /mɒsk‖mɑsk/ *n* a building in which Muslims worship

mos·qui·to /məˈskiːtəʊ/ *n* **-toes** any of several types of small flying insect that prick the skin and then drink blood, one of which can cause the disease of MALARIA —see picture at INSECT

mosquito net /·ˈ·· ·/ *n* a cotton net placed over a bed as a protection against mosquitoes

moss /mɒs‖mɔs/ *n* [U;C] **1** (any of several types of) a small flat green or yellow flowerless plant that grows in a thick furry mass on wet soil, or on a wet surface —see picture at PLANT² **2 a rolling stone gathers no moss** a person who is always changing his work, or place of work, does not succeed, become rich, etc. —see also ROLLING STONE

moss-grown /ˈ· ·/ *adj* covered with MOSS: *This very old house has a moss-grown roof*

moss·y /ˈmɒsi‖ˈmɔsi/ *adj* [Wa1] **1** covered with MOSS: *He sat down and rested on a mossy bank in the woods* **2** like MOSS: *The colour of her coat was a mixture of mossy yellow and green*

most¹ /məʊst/ *determiner, pron* (*superl. of* MANY, MUCH) **1** [(*the*)] greatest in number, quantity, or degree: *The money should be shared among those who have* (*the*) *most need of it.*|*The youngest of his children takes* (*the*) *most interest in the toys.*|*The storm did most damage to the houses on the edge of the cliff* (=those houses were damaged more than others).|*Which is most—10, 20, or 30?* **2** nearly all: *He's visited most* (*of the*) *countries in Europe.*|*Most English words form their plural by adding s.*|*A few people were killed in the fire, but most were saved.*|*Most of his time is spent travelling.*|*"Most people had worked harder than me"* (SEU S.) **3 for the most part** nearly completely; mainly; in almost all cases or with regard to almost everything: *Summers in the south of France are for the most part dry and sunny.*|*I agree for the most part with what you say*

most² *adv* [Wa5] **1** [(*the*)] (forming the superl. of the greater number of adjectives and adverbs with more than one SYLLABLE): *Which do you think is the most comfortable hotel in this town?*|*All the questions were difficult, but which did you think was most difficult?*|*"It's one of the most beautiful drinks I've ever made!"* (SEU S.) **2** in the greatest or highest degree; more than anything else: *What people like most about the doctor is his kindness.*|*I like all kinds of books, but most of all I like books about history.*|*You can help me most by preparing the vegetables for dinner* **3** (used for giving force) **a** (to an adjective) very: *"It really is most annoying!"* (SEU S.)|*It's most kind* (not ***kindest**) *of you!*|*He thanked his host for a most enjoyable party.*|*It's most dangerous to play with explosives* **b** (to an adverb) quite; very: *Whatever happens, I shall most certainly attend the meeting.*|*He'll most probably sell the house and go and live with his daughter* **4** *dial or AmE infml* almost: *He plays cards most every evening.*|*Most everyone in this small town owns a car*
USAGE **Most** can mean "very" only before adjectives or adverbs that are coloured by feeling and opinion (are SUBJECTIVE): **most** *beautiful*|**most** *certainly*|but not ***most** *tall*, ***most** *quickly*.

most³ *n* [*the*+R] **1** the greatest amount: *We tried to stop the house burning down, but the most we could do was to save some of the pictures and furniture* **2 at (the) most/at the very most** not more than (the stated amount): *She's at most 25 years old.*|*The repairs to your car will cost £35, at the most* **3 make the most of** to get the best use or greatest gain from: *He doesn't do well because he doesn't make the most of his ability*

-most *suffix* **1** [*prep* or *adj→superl. adj*] most; to the highest possible degree: INMOST|MIDMOST|NORTH(ERN)MOST **2** [*n→superl. adj*] most towards: *headmost*|*the bottommost house in a steep street*

most·ly /ˈməʊstli/ *adv* [Wa5] mainly; in the greatest number of cases: *She uses her car mostly for going to the shops.*|*He enjoys a cigarette sometimes, but mostly he smokes a pipe*

M.o.T. /ˌəm əʊ ˈtiː/ *n infml* (in Britain) **1** a regular official examination of cars more than 3 years old, carried out to make sure that they are fit to be driven **2** (a piece of paper proving) the fact of having passed this examination

mote /məʊt/ *n* a very small piece or grain, esp. of dust: *He watched the motes* (*of dust*) *dancing in the sunlight that shone through the window*

mo·tel /məʊˈtel/ *n* a hotel specially built for travelling motorists, made up of separate rooms or small houses, each with space for a car

mo·tet /məʊˈtet/ *n* a piece of church music, usu. for voices only

moth /mɒθ‖mɔθ/ *n* **1** [C] any of several types of quite large winged insects, related to the BUTTERFLY but not (so) brightly coloured, which fly mainly at night and are attracted by flames or lights —see picture at INSECT **2** [*the*+R] *esp. BrE* an infection of clothes by the young of certain types of this insect, which eat wool, fur, etc.: *Most of the clothes in the cupboard have got the moth in them; they'll have to be thrown away*

moth·ball /ˈmɒθbɔːl‖ˈmɔθ-/ *n* [*usu. pl.*] a small ball made of a strong-smelling substance (esp. NAPHTHALENE), usu. white, used for keeping away the MOTH

moth·balls /ˈmɒθbɔːlz‖ˈmɔθ-/ *n* [P] **1** the state of being stored, or kept in existence, but not used: *He keeps his car in mothballs during the winter months* **2** the state of having been put aside, as of no further use: *We shall have to put this idea in mothballs*

moth-eat·en /ˈ· ˌ··/ *adj* **1** (of a garment) destroyed, or partly destroyed, by the MOTH (2) **2** *derog* very worn out and/or untidy; SCRUFFY: *moth-eaten old chairs* **3** *derog* no longer in modern use, or suitable for modern ways of thinking: *At every committee meeting for the last 30 years, he's made the same moth-eaten suggestion*

moth·er¹ /ˈmʌðəʳ/ *n* **1** [C] a female parent —see TABLE OF FAMILY RELATIONSHIPS **2** [C; R;N] one's own female parent **3** [C] a female head of a religious society of women (NUNs) living together —see also MOTHER SUPERIOR **4** [*the*+R+*of*] that which is the cause of anything happening, being produced, etc.: *Hunger is often the mother of crime* **5 become a mother** to give birth to a child **6 every mother's son** every man with none left out —**~less** *adj* [Wa5]

mother² *v* [T1] **1** (esp of a woman) to care for (someone) like a mother **2** (of a woman or female animal) to give birth to **3** *derog* to treat (someone, esp. a child) with too great protectiveness and care

Mother *n* **1** [A;N] a title of respect for a MOTHER¹ (3): *Mother Teresa* —see also MOTHER SUPERIOR **2** [A] *infml* a title given to an old woman: *Old Mother Williams next door has lost her cat again* **3** [N] *infml* (*used esp. by a man*) an old woman: *Come along now, Mother, get into the* AMBULANCE

mother car·ey's chick·en /ˌmʌðə ˌkeərɪz ˈtʃɪkɪ̣n‖ˌmʌðər-/ *n* [*usu. pl.*] (*usu. cap* M *and 1st* C) STORMY PETREL (1)

mother coun·try /ˈ·· ˌ··/ *n* [(*the*) R;(C)] **1** the country of one's birth; one's native land **2** the country of origin of a group of settlers in another part of the world which is usu. also mentioned or understood: *Most Australians regard Britain as the/their mother country*

Mother Goose rhyme /ˌ·· ˈ· ·/ *n AmE* NURSERY RHYME

moth·er·hood /ˈmʌðəhʊd‖-ər-/ *n* [U] the state of being a mother: *Motherhood doesn't suit her; she shouldn't have had children*

mother-in-law /ˈ·· · ·/ *n* **mothers-in-law** the mother of a person's husband or wife —see TABLE OF FAMILY RELATIONSHIPS

moth·er·ly /ˈmʌðəli‖-ər-/ *adj apprec* having or

showing the love, kindness, etc., of, or natural to, a mother —**-liness** *n* [U]

Mother Na·ture /ˌ·· ˈ··/ *n* [R] *often humor* NATURE (4): *Cats are Mother Nature's way of limiting the number of mice*

mother-of-pearl /ˌ·· · ˈ·/ *n* [U] a hard smooth shiny variously coloured substance on the inside of the shell of certain shellfish, used for making ornamental articles

mother ship /ˈ·· ·/ *n* a ship that supplies other ships with their needs, at sea or in harbour

mother su·pe·ri·or /ˌ·· ·ˈ···/ *n* [C;N] (*usu. caps.*) the female head of a CONVENT

mother-to-be /ˌ·· · ˈ·/ *n* **mothers-to-be** a future mother; PREGNANT woman

mother tongue /ˌ·· ˈ·/ *n* a person's native language

mother wit /ˈ·· ·/ *n* [U] *becoming rare* a person's native or natural sense (not obtained from education)

moth·proof[1] /ˈmɒθpruːf‖ˈmɔθ-/ *adj* (of cloth, floor coverings, etc.) made safe, by being chemically treated, against damage or destruction by the MOTH (2)

mothproof[2] *v* [T1] to make (something) MOTHPROOF

mo·tif /məʊˈtiːf/ also **motive**— *n* **1** a subject, pattern, idea, etc., forming the main base on which something, esp. a work of art, is made, or from which it is developed, and which is often given a special meaning **2** a single or repeated pattern or colour: *a cat motif on the side of the pot* **3** an arrangement of notes, forming a main part of a musical work that is developed around this arrangement

mo·tion[1] /ˈməʊʃən/ *n* **1** [U] the act, manner, or state of moving: *The gentle rolling motion of the ship made me feel sleepy.|The train was already in motion when he jumped on.|Parts of the film were shown again in slow motion* (=making the movements appear slower than in real life) **2** [C] a single or particular movement or way of moving: *He made a motion with his hand, as if to tell me to keep back.|the dancer's graceful motions* **3** [C,C3,5,5c] a suggestion formally put before a meeting, which is the subject of arguments for and against, and that is accepted or refused according to the number of those who express agreement or disagreement: *At the last committee meeting, the motion that the club (should) remain open until midnight was defeated.|a motion to make the sale of alcohol lawful* **4** [C] *esp. BrE* an act of emptying the bowels; MOVEMENT: *The doctor asked the mother if the child's motions were regular* **5 put/set something in motion** to start something moving, being active, or working: *Pull this handle towards you to set the machine in motion.|He warned the government that if it declared war, it would set in motion something that might spread to the rest of the world*

motion[2] *v* **1** [L9] to signal by means of a movement, usu. with the hand: *She motioned to the waiter, and he came over and asked what she wanted* —see also MOTION TO **2** [X9;V3] to direct (someone) by means of a movement, usu. with the hand: *The policeman motioned the people away from the area of the accident.|He opened the door and motioned me into the room*

mo·tion·less /ˈməʊʃənləs/ *adj* without any movement; quite still: *The cat remained motionless, waiting for the mouse to come out of its hole* —**~ly** *adv* —**~ness** *n* [U]

motion pic·ture /ˌ·· ˈ··◂/ *n AmE* PICTURE[1] (7)

mo·tions /ˈməʊʃənz/ *n* **go through the motions** *not fml* to do something, do a piece of work, etc., without care or interest, only because one has to or is expected to: *The doctor was sure the man wasn't really ill, but he went through the motions of examining him*

motion to also **motion at**— *v prep* [V3] to request (someone) to do something by means of a signal or movement, usu. with the hand

mo·ti·vate /ˈməʊtɪ̈veɪt/ *v* **1** [T1;V3] to provide (someone) with a (very strong) reason or cause for doing something, taking some action, etc.: *He was motivated only by his wish to help me, and expected nothing in return.|These children just sit around all day doing nothing; they need something to motivate them* **2** [T1 *often pass.*] to be the reason why (something) is or was done: *This murder was motivated by hatred*

mo·ti·va·tion /ˌməʊtɪ̈ˈveɪʃən/ *n* [U,U3;(C,C3)] the act or state of being MOTIVATED; need or purpose: *The stronger the motivation, the more quickly a person will learn a foreign language*

mo·tive[1] /ˈməʊtɪv/ *n* **1** a cause of or reason for action; that which urges a person to act in a certain way: *In a case of murder, the police question everyone who might have a motive.|His love of money is the only motive that drives him to work so hard* **2** MOTIF —**~less** *adj* [Wa5]

motive[2] *adj* [Wa5;A] *tech* (of power, force, etc.) causing movement: *The wind provides the motive power that turns this wheel*

mot juste /ˌməʊ ˈʒuːst (*Fr* mo ʒyst)/ *n* **mots justes** (*same pronunciation*) *Fr* the exactly right word or phrase

mot·ley[1] /ˈmɒtli‖ˈmɑtli/ *adj* **1** [B] *often derog* of different kinds, esp. having a mixture of good and bad, of higher and lower worth, class, etc.: *There's a motley collection of books on the shelf* **2** [Wa5;A] *lit* (esp. of a garment) of different mixed unconnected colours, like the clothes worn by a JESTER in former times

motley[2] *n* [U] *lit or tech* **1** the clothes worn by a JESTER **2 put on/wear the motley a** to dress as a JESTER **b** to act the part of a fool

mo·to·cross /ˈməʊtəʊkrɒs‖-krɔs/ *n* [U] a form of racing for motorcycles in which the competitors race over a rough country track including steep hills, mud, grass, streams, etc.

mo·tor[1] /ˈməʊtəʳ/ *n* **1** [C] a machine that changes power, esp. electrical power, into movement: *This grass-cutting machine is driven by a small electric motor* **2** [C; *by*+U] *BrE becoming rare* a car

motor[2] *adj* [Wa5;A] **1** driven by an engine: *a motor vessel|a* MOTOR SCOOTER*|a motor* MOWER **2** of, for, or concerning vehicles driven by an engine, esp. those used on roads: *the motor industry/trade|Motor insurance costs more if a car is used in a big city.|motor sports|motor racing|a motor magazine* **3** *tech* of, related to, or being a nerve that causes a muscle or muscles to move

motor[3] *v* [IØ] *becoming rare* to travel by car, esp. by one that is privately owned; drive: *We spent all day by the sea, and motored home in the evening*

mo·tor·bike /ˈməʊtəbaɪk‖-tər-/ *n* [C; *by*+U] **1** *BrE infml* a motorcycle **2** *AmE* a small light motorcycle —see BICYCLE (USAGE)

mo·tor·boat /ˈməʊtəbəʊt‖-tər-/ *n* [C; *by*+U] a boat or small ship driven by an engine or electric motor, esp. such a boat made to travel fast —see picture at BOAT[1]

mo·tor·cade /ˈməʊtəkeɪd‖-tər-/ *n* a procession of cars

mo·tor·car /ˈməʊtəkɑːʳ‖-tər-/ *n* [C; *by*+U] *fml* a car

mo·tor·cy·cle /ˈməʊtəˌsaɪkəl‖-tər-/ *n* [C; *by*+U] a large heavy bicycle driven by an engine —see picture at INTERCHANGE[2]

mo·tor·cy·clist /ˈməʊtəˌsaɪklɪ̈st‖-tər-/ *n* a person

who rides, and usu. owns, a motorcycle

mo·tor·ing /ˈməʊtərɪŋ/ *n* [U] driving, or travelling in, a car, often for pleasure: *Motoring isn't as pleasant as it used to be, when there were not so many cars on the roads*

mo·tor·ist /ˈməʊtərɨst/ *n* a person who drives, and usu. owns, a car

mo·tor·ize, -ise /ˈməʊtəraɪz/ *v* [Wv5;T1] to provide (soldiers, an army, etc.) with motor vehicles: (*humor*) *At last we've got a car, and now that we're motorized, we can get to work more easily*

mo·tor·man /ˈməʊtəmæn‖-tər-/ *n* **-men** /men/ a man who controls the operation of a vehicle driven by a motor, esp. an electric train or TRAM

motor scoot·er /ˈ·· ˌ··/ *n* a low bicycle-like vehicle driven by an engine, rather like a child's SCOOTER, having 2 small wheels and usu. a wide curved part at the front to protect the legs —see picture at INTERCHANGE²

mo·tor·way /ˈməʊtəweɪ‖-tər-/ *n BrE* a very wide road built esp. for fast vehicles travelling long distances, and on which one may come to a stop only if one's car breaks down

mot·tled /ˈmɒtld‖ˈmɑ-/ *adj* marked irregularly with variously coloured spots or parts: *The underside of this snake is all yellow, but its back is mottled*

mot·to /ˈmɒtəʊ‖ˈmɑ-/ *n* **-tos** (*AmE* **-toes** *or* **-tos**) **1** a short sentence or a few words taken as the guiding principle of a person and the way he behaves, of a noble family, of a school, etc.: *Don't lose hope; remember the motto "Never say die".|The ancient motto of this noble family is cut in stone above the gates of the castle* —compare SLOGAN **2** *esp. BrE* an amusing or clever short saying, printed on a piece of paper that is put round a sweet, in a CHRISTMAS CRACKER, etc. **3** a few words, a sentence or sentences, or a short musical phrase, placed at the beginning of a book or CHAPTER, or of a piece of music, giving some idea of, or considered suitable to, the contents

mould¹, *AmE* usu. **mold** /məʊld/ *n* [U] (*often in comb.*) loose earth that is easily broken into small pieces, esp. good soft soil that is rich in (the stated) decayed vegetable substances: *He planted the seeds of the flowers in a wooden box filled with* LEAF MOULD

mould², *AmE* usu. **mold** *n* **1** [C] a hollow vessel of metal, stone, glass, etc., having a particular shape, into which melted metal or some soft substance is poured, so that when the substance becomes cool or hard, it takes this shape **2** [C *usu. sing.*; U] *esp. lit* (a person's) character, nature, etc., considered as having been shaped by family type, education, training, experience, etc.: *He'll never give up fighting against unjust treatment, if he's made in his father's mould* (=if he has the same character as his father)

mould³, *AmE* usu. **mold** *v* [T1] **1** to shape or form (something solid): *a figure of a man moulded out of/in clay|He moulded little pieces of soft bread into balls* **2** to shape or form (character, behaviour, etc.): *His character has been moulded more by his experiences in life than by the education he got at school*

mould⁴, *AmE* usu. **mold** *n* [U;(C)] a soft woolly growth (often greenish in colour) on bread, cheese, etc., that has been kept too long, or on other substances or objects (such as leather, wood, a book, etc.) which have been left for a long time in warm wet air

moul·der, *AmE* usu. **molder** /ˈməʊldəʳ/ *v* [Wv4;IØ (AWAY)] *often lit* to decay slowly: *The walls of this ancient ruin are mouldering away.|mouldering walls*

mould·ing, *AmE* usu. **molding** /ˈməʊldɪŋ/ *n* **1** [U] the act, work, or way of giving shape to something, esp. to a soft substance **2** [C] **a** an ornamental edge or band of stone, wood, etc., that stands out from a wall or other surface **b** an ornamental piece of wood used like this, as by being stuck or fastened in some way to the edge of a piece of furniture **3** [C] an object, such as a piece of plastic, produced from a MOULD² (1)

mould·y, *AmE* usu. **moldy** /ˈməʊldi/ *adj* [Wa1] *derog* **1** covered with MOULD⁴: *mouldy cheese* **2** like MOULD⁴ in appearance, smell, etc.: *When one opens this old cupboard in a dark corner of the room, there's a very mouldy smell* **3** *infml* spoiled or made worse by lack of use; not modern: *He hasn't used his brains for years, and they're getting rather mouldy* **4** *BrE sl* bad in quality, value, etc.: *What a mouldy meal we were given at that hotel!* **5** *BrE* (*used esp. by children*) (of a person) showing an unwillingness to allow others to have pleasures; nasty: *Our mouldy old uncle won't ever let us play in his garden* **6** *BrE* (*used esp. by children*) (of an amount) resulting from an unwillingness to give freely to others; small; STINGY: *What! Only a mouldy 5 pence for all the work we've done for you?* —**mouldiness** *n* [U]

moult¹, *AmE* usu. **molt** /məʊlt/ *v* [T1;IØ] **1** (of a bird) to lose or throw off (feathers) at the season when new feathers grow **2** (of an animal, esp. a dog or cat) to lose or throw off (hair or fur)

moult², *AmE* usu. **molt** *n* **1** the act, condition, or time of MOULTing: *When do the young of this bird have their first moult?* **2 in moult** MOULTing: *Our dog's in moult; there are hairs all over the mat*

mound /maʊnd/ *n* [(*of*)] **1** a heap (of earth, stones, etc.), esp. one built in ancient times as a defence, or over a grave; small hill **2** a large pile or amount (of anything): *I've still got a mound of letters to answer*

mount¹ /maʊnt/ *n* [A;(C)] *lit or old use, or (cap.) as part of a name* a mountain: *The highest mountain in the world is Mount Everest*

mount² *v* **1** [IØ (UP); T1] to get on (a horse, a bicycle, etc.): *He mounted the bicycle and rode away.|The soldiers stood beside their horses, waiting for the order to mount (up)* **2** [IØ (*to*); T1] to go up; climb: *The old lady can mount the stairs only with difficulty* **3** [Wv5;T1 (*on*)] to provide (someone) with a horse or other animal, a bicycle, etc., to ride on: *The soldiers were mounted on fine black horses.|the mounted police* **4** [T1 (*on*)] to put (someone) on horseback, on a bicycle, etc.: *He lifted up his little son, and mounted him on the donkey* **5** [Wv4;IØ (UP)] to rise in level or increase in amount: *The level of the water mounted until it reached my waist.|The temperature mounted into the 90s.|In spite of all his efforts, his debts continued to mount up* **6** [T1] to fix on a support or in a surrounding substance; put in a position so as to be ready for use or to be shown: *He mounted the photograph on stiff paper, and then put it in a frame.|The dead insect was mounted on a card by means of a pin* **7** [T1] to prepare or begin (an attack): *The opposing political party is getting ready to mount a powerful attack on the government* **8** [T1] to prepare and produce (a play) for the stage: *It'll cost a great deal of money to mount this play* **9** [T1] *tech* (of a male animal, esp. a large one) to get up on (a female animal) in order to breed **10 mount guard (at/over)** to be on guard duty: *The dog mounted guard over his master's bicycle* **11 mount the throne** to become king, queen, etc.

mount³ *n* **1** an animal on which one rides: *This old donkey is a good quiet mount for a child* **2** something on which or in which a thing is fixed, as a support, for ornamental purposes, etc.: *The winner*

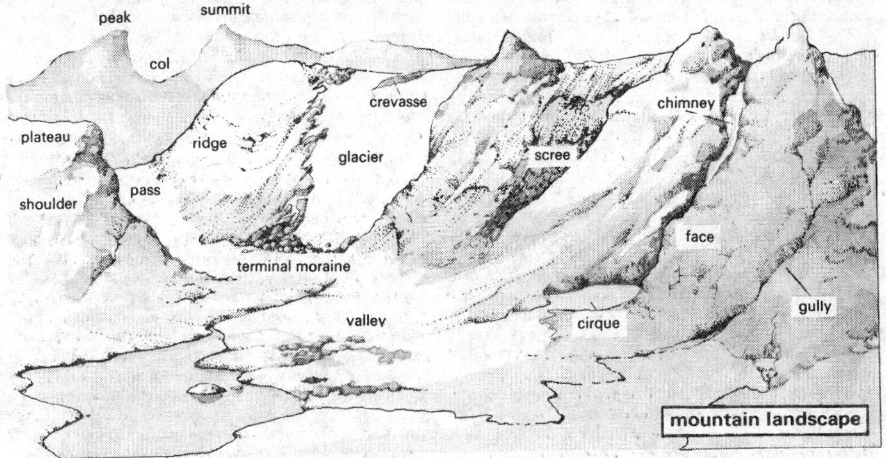

mountain landscape

of the competition was given a silver cup, on a wooden mount

moun·tain /ˈmaʊntɨn/ *n* **1** [C] a very high hill, usu. of bare or snow-covered rock: *He looked down from the top of the mountain to the valley far below.|mountain paths|mountain goats* **2** [C+*of, often pl. with sing. meaning*] a very large amount, mass, etc.: *She has a mountain of dirty clothes to wash*

mountain ash /ˌ·· ˈ·/ *n* ROWAN

mountain chain /ˈ·· ·/ *n* MOUNTAIN RANGE

moun·tain·eer /ˌmaʊntɨˈnɪəʳ/ *n* a person who climbs mountains as a sport or profession

moun·tain·eer·ing /ˌmaʊntɨˈnɪərɪŋ/ *n* [U] the sport or profession of climbing mountains

mountain li·on /ˈ·· ˌ··/ *n* [Wn1] COUGAR

moun·tain·ous /ˈmaʊntɨnəs/ *adj* **1** full of or containing mountains: *Because of the mountainous nature of the country, the army couldn't advance quickly* **2** very large or high: *mountainous waves*

mountain range /ˈ·· ·/ *n* a group of mountains, esp. in a row

moun·tain·side /ˈmaʊntɨnsaɪd/ *n* [*usu. sing.*] the side or slope of a mountain: *The great rocks rolled down the mountainside*

moun·tain·top /ˈmaʊntɨntɒp‖-tɑp/ *n* the top, PEAK, or SUMMIT of a mountain

moun·te·bank /ˈmaʊntɪbæŋk/ *n lit & derog, now rare* a man who, by clever talk, deceives, or tries to deceive, people into buying something of no use or worth, or into believing worthless promises, etc.

Mount·ie /ˈmaʊnti/ *n infml* a member of a special Canadian police force (the **Royal Canadian Mounted Police**) who often work on horseback

mourn /mɔːn‖morn/ *v* **1** [IØ (*for, over*)] to feel and/or show grief, esp. for the death of someone; be sorrowful: *The old woman still mourns for her son, 30 years after his death.|He sat alone after the battle, mourning over the loss of his best friend* **2** [T1] to grieve for (the death, loss, etc., of someone): *The whole nation mourned the death of a much-loved king*

mourn·er /ˈmɔːnəʳ‖ˈmor-/ *n* a person who attends a funeral, esp. a relative or friend of the one who is dead

mourn·ful /ˈmɔːnfəl‖ˈmorn-/ *adj sometimes derog* sad; causing, feeling, expressing, or seeming to express sorrow or grief —**-fully** *adv* —**-fulness** *n* [U]

mourn·ing /ˈmɔːnɪŋ‖ˈmor-/ *n* [U] **1** (the expression of) grief, esp. for a death: *All the theatres and cinemas were closed, as a sign of mourning for the dead president* **2** the clothes, black in some countries, worn by people who wish to show grief at the death of someone **3 go into mourning a** to start wearing MOURNING, after someone has died **b** to begin to show or feel MOURNING **4 in (deep) mourning a** dressed (completely) in MOURNING **b** showing or feeling (strong or deep) MOURNING

mouse /maʊs/ *n* **mice** /maɪs/ **1** (*often in comb.*) any of several types of small furry animal with a long tail, rather like a small rat, that lives in houses and in fields: *a house mouse|a field mouse* —see picture at MAMMAL **2** a person, esp. a woman, who is quiet and easily made afraid **3 as poor as a church mouse** very poor **4 play cat and mouse with someone** to treat someone cruelly, as a cat does a mouse by letting it escape for a moment and then pulling it back

mous·er /ˈmaʊsəʳ/ *n* a cat that catches mice: *Our pet cat's a good mouser* (=is clever at catching mice)

mouse·trap /ˈmaʊs-træp/ *n* **1** [C] a trap for catching mice, worked by a spring, and usu. supplied with a small piece of cheese for attracting the mice **2** [U] also **mousetrap cheese** /ˌ·· ˈ·/— *derog, often humor, esp. BrE* cheese that is old and hard, or of bad quality

mous·sa·ka /muːˈsɑːkə/ *n* [U] a Greek dish made from meat and AUBERGINE*s*, often with cheese on top

mousse /muːs/ *n* [C;U] (*often in comb.*) (a sweet dish made from) cream, eggs, and other substances to give it a particular taste, mixed together and then frozen

mous·tache, *AmE* usu. **mustache** /məˈstɑːʃ‖ˈmʌstæʃ/ *n* hair growing on the upper lip

mous·y /ˈmaʊsi/ *adj* [Wa1] **1** *infml* of, like, or related to mice **2** *often derog* (of hair) having a dull brownish-grey colour **3** *derog* (of a person, esp. a woman) unattractively plain and quiet; DRAB —**mousiness** *n* [U]

mouth¹ /maʊθ/ *n* **mouths** /maʊðz/ **1** [C; *by*+U] the opening on the face through which an animal or human being may take food into the body, and by which sounds are made: *medicine to be taken by mouth* —see picture at HUMAN² **2** [C (*of*) *usu. sing.*] an opening, entrance, or way out: *A fall of rock blocked the mouth of the cave* **3 by word of mouth** by speaking and not by writing **4 down in the mouth** not cheerful; in low spirits **5 keep one's**

mouth shut *infml* to avoid saying or speaking about something, esp. something secret; keep silent: *You can tell him a secret; he knows how to keep his mouth shut* **6 put the mouth on someone** *BrE & AustrE sl* to (seem to) make someone's actions or attempts unsuccessful by saying that he is doing very well **7 put words in(to) someone's mouth a** to tell someone what to say **b** *derog* to suggest or claim, falsely, that someone has said a particular thing **8 shut one's mouth** *infml* **a** *usu. imper.* to stop talking; be silent: *Shut your mouth, you stupid fool!* **b Well, shut my mouth!** *Southern AmE* (an expression of surprise) **9 stop someone's mouth** *fml* to make someone keep silent: *He's determined to tell the truth, even if it is unpleasant, and nothing will stop his mouth* **10 take the words out of someone's mouth** to say something that someone else was going to say, before he has had time or a chance to speak —see also **look a** GIFT HORSE **in the mouth**, SHOOT **one's mouth** OFF

mouth² /maʊð/ *v* [T1;I∅] to speak or say (something), esp. repeatedly without understanding or sincerity, or in some other way that is displeasing: *He crept into the corner, mouthing curses*

-mouthed /maʊðd, maʊθt/ *comb. form* [*adj*,(*n*)→*adj*] **1** having the stated type of mouth: *a small-mouthed woman* **2** *usu. derog* having the stated way of speaking: *loud-mouthed*|FOUL-MOUTHED

mouth·ful /ˈmaʊθfʊl/ *n* **1** [C (*of*)] as much (food or drink) as fills the mouth; small quantity taken in the mouth: *He'd had enough, and couldn't eat another mouthful (of dinner)* **2** [S] *infml, usu. humor* a big long word that one finds difficulty in saying or pronouncing **3** [S] *infml, often humor or derog* a statement that is important, or that is long and tries to sound important

mouth·or·gan /ˈmaʊθˌɔːgən‖-ˌɔr-/ *n* a type of small musical instrument, played by being held to the mouth, passed backwards and forwards across the lips, and blown into or sucked through; HARMONICA —see picture at WIND INSTRUMENT

mouth·piece /ˈmaʊθpiːs/ *n* **1** the part of anything (such as a musical instrument, a tobacco pipe, a telephone, an apparatus for breathing through, etc.) that is held in or near the mouth —see picture at WIND INSTRUMENT **2** [(*of*) *usu. sing.*] *often derog* a person, newspaper, etc. that expresses the opinions of others: *This newspaper is the mouthpiece of the government* **3** *AmE sl* a lawyer who defends people charged with crimes

mouth-to-mouth /ˌ· · ˈ·◂/ *adj* [Wa5 A;(B)] of, related to, or being a method of RESUSCITATION (helping a person who is not breathing to breathe again) in which one places one's mouth tightly against the mouth of the person who is not breathing and blows in order to get air into his lungs

mouth·wash /ˈmaʊθwɒʃ‖-wɔʃ, -wɑʃ/ *n* [C;U] any of several liquids used in the mouth, for making it feel fresh, helping to cure infected parts, etc.

mouth-wa·ter·ing /ˈ· ˌ···/ *adj* (of food) that makes one want to eat; very good

mo·va·ble¹, moveable /ˈmuːvəbəl/ *adj* **1** that can be moved; not fixed in one place or position: *toy soldiers with movable arms and legs* **2** [Wa5] *law* (of property) that can be taken from place to place —opposite **real**

movable², moveable *n* [*usu. pl.*] *law* a personal possession, such as a piece of furniture, that can be moved, as from one house to another —opposite **fixture**

movable feast /ˌ··· ˈ·/ *n* a religious day, such as EASTER, the date of which varies from year to year

move¹ /muːv/ *v* **1** [T1;I∅] to (cause to) change place or bodily position: *The prisoner was tied so tightly that he couldn't move hand or foot.*|*The child moved just as his father was taking a photograph of him.*|*The baby hasn't moved since he was put to bed: is everything all right?* **2** [T1;I∅] to take or go from one place to another: *Please move your car; it's blocking my way out.*|*The sick woman's bed was moved downstairs.*|*He stood in the doorway, and wouldn't move out of my way.*|*The talks have been moved from Paris to London* **3** [I∅] to be in movement; go, walk, run, etc., esp. in a particular way: *The guard blew his whistle, and the train began to move.*|*Have you ever seen a dancer move more gracefully?* **4** [X9;L9] to (cause to) change: *Attempts were made to move the talks from a consideration of principles to more practical ideas.*|*The government's opinions on this matter haven't moved; they're still favourable* **5** [I∅] *infml* to travel, run, etc., very fast: *That car was really moving; it must have been doing 90 miles an hour* **6** [T1;I∅] (in games such as CHESS) to change the position of (a piece) from one square to another **7** [I∅] to change one's place of living or working: *Their present house is too small, so they've decided to move* —see also MOVE IN, MOVE OUT **8** [Wv4;T1] **a** to take (furniture and other articles) from one house, office, etc., to another: *a moving* VAN **b** *infml* to take (a person's) furniture and other articles from one house, office, etc., to another: *We're being moved by Richardson and Company* **9** [T1 (*to*)] to cause (a person) to have or show feelings, as of pity, sadness, anger, admiration, etc.: *The sick child's suffering moved his father to tears* —see also MOVING **10** [I∅ (*on*)] (esp. in newspaper articles) to take action (with regard to something): *When will the government move on this important matter?* **11** [T1;V3] to cause (a person) to act, change an opinion, etc.: *This artist can paint only when the spirit moves him* (=when he feels the desire to paint).|*I felt moved to speak* **12** [I∅] (of work, events, etc.) to advance; go forward; get nearer to an end: *His business affairs aren't moving, and his debts are increasing.*|*Work on the new building is moving more quickly than was expected.*|*Let's get things moving* (=let's take effective action) **13** [L9, esp. *among, in*] to lead one's life or pass one's time (esp. with or among people of a certain class): *She's a very wealthy woman, and moves in the highest circles of society* (=among people of high rank) **14** [T1,5b,c] to put forward, at a meeting (a suggestion on which arguments for and against are heard, and a decision taken, esp. by voting): *I wish to move an* AMENDMENT *to this law.*|*The oldest member of the committee moved that the meeting (should) be continued after dinner* —compare MOTION (3) **15** [T1;I∅] **a** to cause (the bowels) to empty **b** (of the bowels) to empty **16 move heaven and earth (to do something)** to make all possible efforts (to do something); do everything in one's power **17 move house** *BrE* to take one's furniture and other property to a new home **18 move with the times** to change one's ways of thinking, living, etc., in accordance with the changes produced by the passing of time; give up ways that are not modern —see also MOVE ABOUT, MOVE ALONG, MOVE AWAY, MOVE DOWN, MOVE FOR, MOVE IN, MOVE OFF, MOVE ON, MOVE OUT, MOVE OVER, MOVE UP

move² *n* **1** [S] an act of moving; movement: *With one move he was by her side* **2** [C] an act of going to a new home, office, etc.: *They're now living in the city; their next move will be to a house in the country* **3** [C] (in games such as CHESS) **a** an act of taking a piece from one square and putting it on another: *My opponent made a very clever move* **b** a way in which this may be done, according to the rules: *The first lesson in* CHESS *is to learn all the different moves* **c** a player's turn to do this: *It's your move* **4** [C] a (step in a) course of action (towards a particular result): *None of the moves to stop the war has been successful* **5 get a move on** *infml* (*often imper.*) to hurry up: *He'll never finish the work if he doesn't get a move on* **6 make a move a** to (start to) leave, go, etc.: *It's getting late; we must be making a move* **b** to begin to take action: *Neither side is willing to make a move, so there's nothing that can be done*

move a·bout also **move a·round**— *v adv* **1** [T1;IØ] to (cause to) move continually; fail to keep still: *I can hear somebody moving about upstairs* **2** [IØ] to change one's home, place of work, etc., continually

move a·long *v adv* **1** [IØ] to move further towards the front or back: *The people standing in the bus moved along, to make room for others* **2** [T1;IØ] MOVE ON (2)

move a·way *v adv* [IØ] to go to a new home in a different area: *"Do the Simpsons still live here?" "No, they've moved away"*

move down *v adv* [T1;IØ] to (cause to) go to a lower level or rank than before: *We had to move that student down to an easier class* —opposite **move up**

move for *v prep* [T1] (in Parliament) to make a formal request for (something)

move in *v adv* [IØ] **1** to take possession of a new home: *We've bought the house, but we can't move in until next month* **2** [(*on*)] to (prepare to) take control, attack, etc.: *Our competitors have gone out of business, so now our company can move in*

move·ment /ˈmuːvmənt/ *n* **1** [U] the act of moving or condition of being moved; activity: *Movement's painful when your back hurts.|There's little movement after sunset, in the streets of this quiet village.|the movement of goods by road* **2** [C] a particular act of changing position or place: *He's very old, and his movements are getting slower and slower* **3** [GC] a group of people who make united efforts for a particular purpose: *The aim of the trade union movement was, and is, to obtain higher wages and better conditions for workers* **4** [C] a way of thinking, acting, etc., not directed by any particular person or group, towards something new, or away from something that exists: *The old man thinks that the movement towards greater freedom for women has brought them too much freedom* **5** [C] a main division of a musical work, esp. of a SYMPHONY **6** [C] the moving parts of a piece of machinery, esp. the wheels of a clock or watch **7** [C] (the amount of waste matter produced during) an act of emptying the bowels

move·ments /ˈmuːvmənts/ *n* [P9, *esp. with poss.*] the whole of the activities of a person, esp. when he is at a distance: *The police think this man may be the thief they're looking for, so they're watching his movements carefully*

move off *v adv* [IØ] to leave; DEPART: *The guard blew his whistle, and the train moved off*

move on *v adv* **1** [IØ (*to*)] to change (to something new): *I think we've talked enough about that subject; let's move on* **2** [T1;IØ] to (order to) go away to another place or position: *The man was drunk and was annoying people, so the policeman moved him on.|"Come on, sir, move on," said the policeman*

move out *v adv* [IØ (*of*)] to leave and cease to live in a home

move o·ver *v adv* **1** [T1;IØ] to (cause to) change position in order to make room for someone or something else: *Move over and let your grandmother sit down* **2** [IØ] to yield: *Uncle left his position on the board of directors, as he felt he should move over in favour of a younger man*

mov·er /ˈmuːvəʳ/ *n* [C9] **1** a person who moves, esp. in the stated way: *She's a beautiful mover* (=moves very gracefully) **2** a person who MOVES¹ (14) a suggestion —see also PRIME MOVER

move up *v adv* [T1;IØ] to (cause to) go to a higher level or rank than before: *She's learnt so fast that we can now move her up to a more advanced class* —opposite **move down**

mov·ie /ˈmuːvi/ *n esp. AmE, not fml* FILM¹ (3): *to see a good movie*

mov·ies /ˈmuːviz/ *n* [*the*+P] *not fml, esp. AmE* PICTURES: *We're going to the movies*

movie star /ˈ·· ·/ *n AmE* FILM STAR

mov·ing /ˈmuːvɪŋ/ *adj* **1** [B] having a strong effect on the feelings; causing strong feelings, esp. of pity: *The beggar told her such a moving story that she almost wept* **2** [Wa5;A] that moves; not fixed; changing position: *Oil the moving parts of this machine regularly* —**~ly** *adv*

moving pic·ture /ˌ·· ˈ··/ *n fml, esp. AmE* FILM¹ (3)

moving stair·case /ˌ·· ˈ··/ *n* ESCALATOR

moving van /ˈ·· ˌ·/ *n* REMOVAL VAN

mow /məʊ/ *v* **mown** /məʊn/ *or* **mowed** [T1;IØ] to cut (grass, corn, etc.), or cut that which grows in (a field or other area), with a MOWER or a SCYTHE

mow down *v adv* [T1] to kill, destroy, or knock down, esp. in great numbers: *The soldiers were mown down by fire from the enemy's guns*

mow·er /ˈməʊəʳ/ *n* **1** a machine for MOWing, esp. (a **lawnmower**) one for cutting grass in gardens, having blades that turn round as it moves —see picture at GARDEN¹ **2** a person who MOWS

MP *abbrev. for:* **1** Member of Parliament; a person who has been elected to represent the people in a parliament, esp. (in Britain) in the HOUSE OF COMMONS: *Sir Harold Wilson, MP|an MP* **2** (*infml*) MILITARY POLICEMAN

mpg *abbrev. for:* miles per GALLON (esp. of petrol): *a car that does 35 mpg*

mph *abbrev. for:* miles per hour: *driving along at 60 mph*

Mr, also (*rare*) **Mister** /ˈmɪstəʳ/ *n* [A] **1** a title for a man who has no other title: *Mr Smith|Mr John Smith* —compare MESSRS **2** a title for certain people in official positions/officials: *Mr Chairman|*(in the US) *Mr President* **3** used before the name of a place, sport, profession, etc., to form a title for a man who is recognized as representing that thing: *Mr America|Mr* BASEBALL

MRA /ˌem ɑːr ˈeɪ/ *abbrev. for:* (*esp. AmE*) MORAL RE-ARMAMENT

Mrs /ˈmɪsɨz/ *n* [A] **1** a title for a married woman who has no other title: *Mrs Jones|Mrs John Jones* **2** used before the name of a place, sport, profession, etc., to form a title for a married woman who is recognized as representing that thing: *Mrs 1978 in her modern kitchen*

Ms /mɪz, məz/ *n* [A] a title for a woman who does not wish to call herself either "Mrs" or "Miss"

MS , *pl* **MSS** *abbrev. for:* MANUSCRIPT

MSc *AmE* also **MS**— *abbrev. for:* Master of Science; (a title for someone who has) a university degree in science at the first level above the BSc: *John Smith, MSc|an MSc*

Mt *written abbrev. for:* MOUNT¹: *Mt Everest*

mu /mjuː/ *n* [R;(C)] the 12th letter of the Greek alphabet (Μ, μ), used for representing a measure in science; a MICRON

much¹ /mʌtʃ/ *determiner, pron, n* —see MORE, MOST [U] **1** (*of mass nouns, usu. nonassertive, except with* so, too) a large quantity, amount, or part (of): *I haven't got much interest in cooking.|not (very) much time|I've got (far) too much (work) to do.|How much* *time have we got?*|(*fml*) *Much of the night I read.*|*Some was lost, but much was saved.*|*We haven't seen much of you* (=you haven't visited us) *recently.*|*I borrowed the book, but I haven't read very much* (*of it*) *yet.*|*How much does it cost?*|*You eat too much.*|*When you've cooked meat, there's never as much as when you bought it.*|*"It's not going to make much sense"* (SEU S.).|*I have much pleasure in giving you this prize* **2 as much again** twice as much **3 as much as one can do** the most possible **4 I thought as much** I expected that (esp. something bad): *So they found out he's been cheating. I thought as much* **5 make much of a** to treat as important **b** to gain or understand a lot: *I couldn't make much of that new book of his* **c** to treat (people) with a show of fondness —compare **make** LITTLE, NOTHING, SOMETHING **of 6 not much of a** not a very good: *It's not much of a day for a walk* (=bad weather) **7 not up to much** not very good or well: *The film's not up to much, although the actors are good* **8 (not) think (too) much of** to have a low/high opinion of: *I don't think much of his ideas* **9 so much for** that is the end of: *Now it's started raining; so much for my idea of taking a walk* **10 this/that much** the particular amount or words: *I'll say this much, he's a good worker* (*although I don't like him personally*) **11 too much for** having too many difficulties; too hard for: *Climbing the smallest hill is too much for her since her illness*

much² *adv* **1** [*usu. nonassertive*] **a** frequently: *I don't read much because I don't have the time* **b** to a great degree: *I don't much like that idea.*|*I don't like that idea much.*|(*esp. fml*) *I'm much surprised to hear that.*|*Much to my surprise/displeasure she forgot our meeting* (=surprising/displeasing me greatly by that) **2** (in all types of sentences in the phrs. **how much?, too much, so much, very much**): *How much do you like him?*|*I like him very much.*|*I've been walking too much in the hot sun.*|*He would so much like to go.*|*She talks* (*a great deal*) *too much.*|*However much you hate them, you must eat them up.*|*Thanks very much!* **3** by a large degree **a** (*with* COMPARATIVE): *It was much worse than I thought.*|*He's getting much fatter these days.*|*He's much the fatter of the 2* **b** (*with* the+*superl.*): *much the quickest worker*|*much the most interesting story* **c** (*with* too, more, rather): *It's much too cold.*|*I'd much rather not* **4** nearly; in most ways: *much the same as usual*|*Today was much like yesterday* **5 much as I** although I greatly: *Much as she hated cruelty, she couldn't help watching the fight* **6 much more/less** and even more/less so (to): *I can hardly bear to walk, much less run* **7 not/nothing much** hardly anything: *There's nothing much we can do* **8 not much good at** not very good at **9 So much the worse/better (for)** it is to that degree worse/better (for): *"It's dark." "So much the better* (*for us*)*! They won't see us climbing the wall"* **10 so much . . . as** (not)—but rather: *I don't so much dislike him as hate him!*

USAGE 1 Use **much** with PASSIVE*s* and verbal [F] adjectives, in the same way as **very** is used with ordinary adjectives: *This table is* **much** *admired.*|*I wasn't* **much** *amused* (compare *This table is very beautiful.*|*I wasn't very happy*). 2 Do not use **much** between a verb and its object, unless the object is a very long one: *We very* **much** *enjoyed that party.*|*We enjoyed that party very* **much**.|*We enjoyed very* **much** *that party we went to at your house.*|not **We enjoyed very* **much** *that party.*

much·ness /ˈmʌtʃnɪ̈s/ *n* **much of a muchness** all or both the same in most ways

mu·ci·lage /ˈmjuːsɪ̈lɪdʒ/ *n* [U] any of various kinds of sticky liquid obtained from plants and used esp. as GLUE

muck¹ /mʌk/ *n* [U] *infml & dial* **1** dirt **2 a** the waste matter dropped from animals' bodies **b** this matter when used for spreading on the land; MANURE **3** a useless thing or material **4 make a muck of a** to make dirty **b** to spoil (arrangements) or do (something) wrong

muck² *v* [T1] *infml* to spread MANURE (=animal waste matter) on: *to muck the fields*

muck a·bout also **muck a·round**— *v adv* [IØ] *esp. BrE, not fml* **1** to behave in a silly way for fun: *Stop mucking about and listen to what I'm saying* **2** to be lazy: *not working, just mucking about*

muck·heap /ˈmʌkhiːp/ *n* a heap of MANURE (=animal waste matter), esp. outside a farm

muck in *v adv* [IØ (*with*)] *infml* to join in work or activity (with others): *If we all muck in we'll soon finish the work*

muck out *v adv* [IØ;T1] **1** to clean (STABLE*s* or other places where animals live) **2** to do this for (an animal): *to muck out the horses*

muck·rake /ˈmʌk-reɪk/ *v* [Wv4;IØ] to search out and tell unpleasant stories, true or otherwise, about well-known people: *a nasty muckraking newspaper article about me and Lady Jones* —**-raker** *n* —**-raking** *n* [U]

muck up *v adv* [T1] *esp. BrE infml* **1** to dirty: *He fell down and came home with his clothes all mucked up* **2 a** to spoil (an arrangement): *The change in the weather has mucked up our sports timetable* **b** to do (something) wrong: *to muck up an examination*

muck·y /ˈmʌki/ *adj* [Wa1] *infml & dial* **1** dirty **2** (of weather) bad; stormy

mu·cous /ˈmjuːkəs/ *adj* [Wa5] *tech* of or producing MUCUS

mucous mem·brane /ˌ·· ˈ··/ *n* [U] the type of skin on delicate parts of the body which is kept wet and smooth by producing MUCUS

mu·cus /ˈmjuːkəs/ *n* [U] a slippery liquid produced in certain parts of the body, and by SNAIL*s* to help them move along: *When one has a cold the nose produces too much mucus*

mud /mʌd/ *n* [U] **1** very wet earth in a sticky mass **2 one's name is mud** one is spoken badly of after causing trouble **3 throw mud at** to speak badly of, esp. so as to spoil someone's good name unnecessarily

mud bath /ˈ· ·/ *n* a beauty or health treatment in which (usu.) warm mud is put on the face and/or body

mud·dle¹ /ˈmʌdl/ *n* [S;(C)] **1** a state of confusion and disorder **2** confusion of the mind; BEWILDERment: *I was all in a muddle and didn't even know what day it was*

muddle² *v* [T1 (UP)] **1** to put into disorder: *You're muddling up the papers* **2** to confuse, esp. in the mind: *I get muddled when they give so many orders so quickly* —**-dler** *n* [C; *you*+N]

muddle a·long *v adv* [IØ] to continue in a confused manner, without a plan

muddle-head·ed /ˌ·· ˈ··◂/ *adj* having or showing a confused, uncontrolled mind —**~ness** *n* [U]

muddle through *v adv* [IØ] *apprec* to have successful results without the best methods of reaching them: *The government are in trouble, but I expect the country will muddle through*

mud·dy¹ /ˈmʌdi/ *adj* [Wa1] **1** covered with or containing mud: *the muddy waters of the river* **2** (of colours) like mud: *a muddy brown* **3** not clear: *muddy thinking* **4** of a dull unhealthy colour: *a muddy* COMPLEXION —**-diness** *n* [U]

muddy² *v* [T1] to make dirty with mud: *Your dog's muddying my dress*

mud·flat /ˈmʌdflæt/ *n* [*often pl.*] a stretch of muddy land, covered by the sea when it comes up and uncovered when it goes down

mud·guard /ˈmʌdgɑːd‖-ɑrd/ *AmE* also **fender**— *n* a metal cover over the wheel of a vehicle to keep the mud from flying up —see picture at BICYCLE[1]

mud·pack /ˈmʌdpæk/ *n* a MUD BATH for the face

mud·sling·er /ˈmʌdˌslɪŋəʳ/ *n* a person who says damaging things about others —see also SLING **mud at** —**-ing** *n* [U]

mues·li /ˈmjuːzli/ *n* [U] grain, nuts, dried fruits, etc., mixed together with milk and eaten as a breakfast dish

mu·ez·zin /muːˈezɪn, ˈmwezɪn/ *n* a man who calls Muslims to prayer from the tower (MINARET) of a mosque

muff[1] /mʌf/ *n* a short open-ended tube of thick soft cloth or fur, into which one can put one's hands to keep them warm

muff[2] *n* **1** a failure, esp. to catch the ball in a game **2** *becoming rare* a person who does things wrong, esp. in sports

muff[3] *v* [T1] **1** to fail to catch; miss: *to muff a* CATCH **2** *not fml* to do (a bit of work) less well than one might; let (a chance) go (usu. in the phr. **muff it**): *I hate making speeches in public—I'm always afraid of muffing it*

muf·fin /ˈmʌfɪn/ *n* **1** *BrE* a thick round cake tasting rather like bread, usu. eaten hot with butter **2** *AmE* any of various types of small ROLL (which may be eaten with butter) or sweet CUP CAKE (without ICING)

muf·fle /ˈmʌfəl/ *v* [*usu. pass.*] **1** [T1] to make (a sound) less easily heard, esp. with a material: *The sound of the bell was muffled by the curtains behind the door.|muffled drums at a soldier's funeral* **2** [X9 (UP)] to cover thickly and warmly: *He went into the snow muffled in 2 woollen coats* —compare WRAP UP

muf·fler /ˈmʌfləʳ/ *n* **1** *esp. old use* a sort of SCARF worn to keep one's neck warm **2** *AmE* SILENCER (b)

muf·ti[1] /ˈmʌfti/ *n* a person who officially explains Muslim law

mufti[2] *n* **in mufti** wearing ordinary clothes, not a uniform (as of the armed forces) which one has been wearing

mug[1] /mʌg/ *n* **1** [C] a round drinking vessel with a flat bottom, straight sides, and handle, not usu. with a SAUCER **2** [C] also **mug·ful** /ˈmʌgfʊl/— the contents of this: *to make a mug of coffee* **3** [C] *sl* the face **4** [C; *you*+N] *BrE infml* a foolish person who is easily deceived —see also MUG'S GAME

mug[2] *v* **-gg-** [T1] to rob with violence, as in a dark street —**mugging** *n* [U;C]

mug·ger /ˈmʌgəʳ/ *n* a person who MUGs or has mugged one or more people

mug·gins /ˈmʌgɪnz/ *n* [C;N] *BrE sl* a fool

mug·gy /ˈmʌgi/ *adj* [Wa1] *not fml* (of weather) unpleasantly warm but not dry —**-giness** *n* [U]

mug's game /ˈ· ˌ·/ *n* [S] *BrE infml* an action that is unlikely to be rewarding or profitable: *Writing's a mug's game—I think I'll get a job in a shop!* —see also MUG[1] (4)

mug up *v adv* [T1] *infml* to study and get to know closely: *to mug up the law on this subject*

mug·wump /ˈmʌg-wʌmp/ *n AmE derog* a person who tries to be independent of the leaders in politics and believes his ideas are better than theirs

Mu·ham·ma·dan /mʊˈhæmədn, mə-/ *adj* MOHAMMEDAN

Mu·ham·ma·dan·is·m /mʊˈhæmədənɪzəm, mə-/ *n* MOHAMMEDANISM

mu·lat·to /mjuːˈlætəʊ‖mʊ-/ *n* **-tos** (*AmE* **-toes**) a person with one parent of the NEGRO race and one of a white race

mul·ber·ry /ˈmʌlbəri‖-beri/ *n* **1** also **mulberry tree** /ˈ··· ·/— a tree with a dark purple fruit which can be eaten, and whose leaves are the food of SILKWORM*s* **2** the fruit of this tree

mulch[1] /mʌltʃ/ *n* [S;U] a covering of material, often made from decaying plants, which is put over the soil and over the roots of plants to protect and improve them —compare HUMUS

mulch[2] *v* [T1] to cover with a MULCH

mulct /mʌlkt/ *v* [T1 (*of*); D1] *fml* **1** to punish by taking away (money); to FINE: *They mulcted him (of) £50 for driving when he was drunk* **2** to cheat by taking away (money): *Look at this hotel bill! They've really mulcted us*

mule[1] /mjuːl/ *n* **1** the animal which is the young of a donkey and a horse **2** a sort of SPINNing-machine **3 as stubborn as a mule** very STUBBORN; refusing to do anything except what one wants, not what others want

mule[2] *n* [*usu. pl.*] a type of shoe or SLIPPER with no back, but only a piece of material across the toes to hold it on

mu·le·teer /ˌmjuːlɪˈtɪəʳ/ *n* a man who drives one or more MULE*s*[1] (1)

mul·ish /ˈmjuːlɪʃ/ *adj* STUBBORN —**~ly** *adv* —**~ness** *n* [U]

mull[1] /mʌl/ *v* [Wv5;T1] to heat (wine or beer) with sugar, SPICE*s*, and other things to improve the taste

mull[2] *n ScotE* an area of land standing out into the sea; PROMONTORY

mul·lah /ˈmʌlə, ˈmʊlə/ *n* a Muslim teacher of law and religion

mul·let /ˈmʌlɪt/ *n* [Wn2] any of several types of sea fish which can be eaten —see picture at FISH[1]

mul·li·ga·taw·ny /ˌmʌlɪgəˈtɔːni‖-ˈtɔni, -ˈtɑni/ *n* [U] a soup with a strong hot taste, containing SPICE*s*

mul·li·on /ˈmʌlɪən/ *n* the wood, metal, or esp. stone part running up and down between the glass parts of a window—see picture at CHURCH[1]

mul·li·oned /ˈmʌlɪənd/ *adj* [Wa5] having (thick) MULLIONS

mull o·ver *v adv; prep* [T1] to think over; consider for a time: *I haven't decided what to do; I'm mulling over it*

mul·ti- /ˈmʌltɪ/ *comb. form* **1** (of) many: MULTIRACIAL|*a multinational company* **2** many times over: *a* MULTIMILLIONAIRE

mul·ti·far·i·ous /ˌmʌltɪˈfeərɪəs/ *adj* [Wa5] of many different types: *In spite of his multifarious activities he likes to stay at home more than anything else* —**~ly** *adv* —**~ness** *n* [U]

mul·ti·form /ˈmʌltɪfɔːm‖-ɔrm/ *adj* [Wa5] having several different shapes or ways of seeming

mul·ti·lat·e·ral /ˌmʌltɪˈlætərəl/ *adj* [Wa5] concerning or including more than 2 (usu. political) groups of people, esp. who have different interests and needs but come together in an agreement: *a multilateral agreement|multilateral trade* —compare BILATERAL —**-rally** *adv*

mul·ti·lin·gual /ˌmʌltɪˈlɪŋgwəl/ *adj* [Wa5] **1** containing or expressed in many different languages **2** able to speak many different languages; POLYGLOT

mul·ti·mil·lio·naire /ˌmʌltɪˌmɪljəˈneəʳ/ *n* a person who has several MILLION pounds or dollars

mul·ti·ple[1] /ˈmʌltɪpəl/ *adj* [Wa5] including many different parts, types, etc.: *multiple injuries* (INJURY) *to my leg*

multiple[2] *n* [(*of*)] **1** a number which contains a smaller number an exact number of times: *3×4=12; so 12 is a multiple of 3* **2 common multiple** a number which contains 2 or more smaller numbers an exact number of times: *12 is the (lowest) common multiple of 3 and 4* —see also LCM

multiple scle·ro·sis /ˌ··· ··ˈ··/ *n* [U] a disease with an unknown cause, in which an important covering around the nerves is reduced over a period of time, causing more and more difficulties in movement and control of bodily actions

multiple store /ˌ··· ˈ·/ also (*infml*) **multiple**— *n* CHAIN STORE: *one of the big multiples|The multiple stores still make large profits*

mul·ti·plex /ˈmʌltɨpleks/ *adj tech* having many parts: *the multiplex eye of the fly*

mul·ti·pli·ca·tion /ˌmʌltɨplɨˈkeɪʃən/ *n* **1** [U] the method of combining 2 numbers by adding one of them to itself as many times as the other states: *2×4=8 is an example of multiplication* **2** [U] the act of increasing in number: *The multiplication of numbers has made our club building too small* **3** [S] an example of such acts

multiplication ta·ble /ˌ···ˈ·· ˌ··/ TABLE¹ (7)

mul·ti·pli·ci·ty /ˌmʌltɨˈplɪsɨti/ *n* **1** [S] a large number: *the multiplicity of births in the world each day* **2** [S] a great variety: *a multiplicity of ideas* **3** [U] the state of being many: *the stars in all their multiplicity*

mul·ti·ply¹ /ˈmʌltɨplaɪ/ *v* **1** [T1 (*by*, TOGETHER)] to combine by MULTIPLICATION: *to multiply 2 by 3|2 multiplied by 3 (2×3)=2+2+2|to multiply 2 numbers together|to multiply 3 and 7 together* **2** [IØ] to have or practise this skill: *Can you multiply?|You added when you should have multiplied* **3** [T1;IØ] to increase: *to multiply one's chances of success|Our chances multiplied* **4** [IØ] to breed: *When animals have more food, they generally multiply faster*

mul·ti·ply² /ˈmʌltɨpli/ *adv* [Wa5] **1** in a MULTIPLE way **2** in several ways: *multiply useful objects*

mul·ti·ra·cial /ˌmʌltɪˈreɪʃəl◂/ *adj* [Wa5] consisting of or involving several races of people

mul·ti·sto·rey /ˌmʌltɪˈstɔːri◂‖-ˈstori◂/ *adj* [Wa5] (of a building, esp. a very high one) having several levels or floors

mul·ti·tude /ˈmʌltɨtjuːd‖-tuːd/ *n* **1** [C (*of*)] a large number: *a multitude of thoughts filled her mind* **2** [C] *old use & bibl* a large crowd **3** [*the*+R *often pl. with sing. meaning*] ordinary people, esp. considered as not well educated: *The multitude may laugh at his music, but we know better* **4 cover a multitude of sins** to be a common (and useful) excuse: *I won't say I slept late and forgot the meeting. I'll say I was late. That covers a multitude of sins*

mul·ti·tu·di·nous /ˌmʌltɨˈtjuːdɨnəs‖-ˈtuː-/ *adj* very large in number: *all my wife's multitudinous relatives* —**~ly** *adv* —**~ness** *n* [U]

mum¹ /mʌm/ *adj* [Wa5;F] not saying or telling anything; silent (esp. in the phr. **keep mum**)

mum² *interj* **Mum's the word** Silence must/will be kept about this; This won't be talked about: *Remember it's a secret. Mum's the word.*

mum³ (*AmE* **mom**)— *n* [C;R;N] *BrE infml* mother —see TABLE OF FAMILY RELATIONSHIPS

mum·ble /ˈmʌmbəl/ *v* **1** [T1,5;IØ] to speak (words) unclearly: *The old woman mumbled a prayer.|He mumbled that he was tired.* **2** [T1] to bite (food) slowly as if without teeth: *an old dog mumbling a bone*

mum·bo jum·bo /ˌmʌmbəʊ ˈdʒʌmbəʊ/ *n* [U] *not fml* **1** mysterious talk which means nothing **2** religious activity which to some people seems meaningless, esp. repeating sounds

mum·mer /ˈmʌməʳ/ *n* (esp. in Britain in former times) a member of a group of actors who went MUMMING

mum·mer·y /ˈmʌməri/ *n* **1** [U] acting by MUMMERS **2** [U;(C)] *derog* a performance or pretended and unnecessary ceremony, esp. religious

mum·mi·fy /ˈmʌmɪfaɪ/ *v* [Wv5;T1] to preserve (a dead body) as a MUMMY¹; dry up —**-fication** /ˌmʌmɪfɨˈkeɪʃən/ *n* [U]

mum·ming /ˈmʌmɪŋ/ *n* **go mumming** (esp. formerly in Britain) to visit people at Christmas wearing special clothes and a MASK, esp. to give a performance in a group, according to custom

mum·my¹ /ˈmʌmi/ *n* a dead body preserved from decay by treatment with special substances

mummy² (*AmE* **mommy, momma, mama**)— *n* [C;R;N] *BrE* (*used esp. by or to children*) (a word for) mother —see TABLE OF FAMILY RELATIONSHIPS

mumps /mʌmps/ *n* [(*the*): P;U] an infectious illness in which the GLANDs (=organs which send substances into the bloodstream) swell, particularly those around the neck and mouth

munch /mʌntʃ/ *v* **1** [T1] to eat with a strong movement of the jaw, esp. making a noise: *munching an apple* **2** [L9 (AWAY *at*)] to eat something in this way: *muching away (at some chocolate)*

mun·dane /mʌnˈdeɪn/ *adj* **1** of the world, esp. of ordinary daily life when compared with that of religion and the Spirit **2** ordinary, with nothing new in it —**~ly** *adv*

mu·ni·ci·pal /mjuːˈnɪsɨpəl‖mjʊ-/ *adj* [Wa5] concerning (the parts of) a town, city, etc., under its own government: *municipal affairs/buildings* —**~ly** *adv* [Wa4]

mu·ni·ci·pal·i·ty /mjuːˌnɪsɨˈpælɨti‖mjʊ-/ *n* **1** [C] a town, city, or other small area having its own government for local affairs **2** [GC] the body of people who govern the town

mu·nif·i·cence /mjuːˈnɪfɨsəns‖mjʊ-/ *n* [(S);U] *fml* generosity

mu·nif·i·cent /mjuːˈnɪfɨsənt‖mjʊ-/ *adj fml* **1** very generous **2** showing great generosity: *a munificent gift* —**~ly** *adv*

mu·ni·ments /ˈmjuːnɨmənts/ *n* [P] *fml & law* papers in law which prove that one has the right to (own) something, such as a house —**muniment** *n* [A]

mu·ni·tion /mjuːˈnɪʃən‖mjʊ-/ *n* [A] *BrE* concerned with MUNITIONS: *munition workers*

mu·ni·tions /mjuːˈnɪʃənz‖mjʊ-/ *n* [P] large arms for war, such as bombs, guns, etc.

mu·ral¹ /ˈmjʊərəl/ *adj* [Wa5;A] *fml* of, like, or on a wall

mural² *n* a painting which is painted on a wall —see also FRESCO

mur·der¹ /ˈmɜːdəʳ‖ˈmɜr-/ *n* **1** [C;U] the crime of killing a man unlawfully **2** [U] pointless death, esp. caused by carelessness: *the murder of little children by those who delayed sending food* **3** [U] *infml* a very difficult or tiring experience: *At last I repaired the clock, but it was murder getting the pieces back in* **4 blue murder** loudly and violently (in PROTEST): *The child SCREAMed blue murder, but his mother didn't change her mind*

murder² *v* **1** [Wv5;T1] to kill unlawfully, esp. on purpose: *a murdered man* **2** to ruin (language, music, etc.) by a bad performance —**~er** *n* [C; *you*+N] —**~ess** *n* [C; *you*+N]

mur·der·ous /ˈmɜːdərəs‖ˈmɜr-/ *adj* **1** likely to cause death: *murderous violence* **2** violent (in appearance): *a murderous expression on his face* **3** of or like murder: *a murderous plan|murderous intentions* —**~ly** *adv* —**~ness** *n* [U]

murk /mɜːk‖mɜrk/ *n* [U] *lit* darkness

murk·y /ˈmɜːki‖ˈmɜr-/ *adj* [Wa1] *lit* **1 a** dark and unpleasant: *a murky night* **b** thick: *murky* FOG **2** shameful: *a murky secret|a criminal with a murky past* —**murkily** *adv*

mur·mur¹ /ˈmɜːməʳ‖ˈmɜr-/ *n* **1** [C] a soft low sound: *the murmur of the stream* **2** [C] MURMURed² (1) speech: *a murmur of voices* **3** [C;U] a sound made by the heart, which may show illness or disease of this organ **4** [S] a case of MURMURing²

(2); complaint: *He obeyed me without a murmur*

murmur² *v* **1** [IØ;T1,5] to make a sound, esp. to speak or say in a quiet voice: *a child murmuring in her sleep* **2** [IØ (*at, against*)] *becoming rare* to complain, not officially but in private: *the people murmuring against the government* —**~ing** *n* [C;U]

mur·phy /ˈmɜːfi‖ˈmɜr-/ *n* **-phies** *sl* a potato

mur·rain /ˈmʌrɨn‖ˈmɜr-/ *n* [U] **1** a disease of cattle **2** *old use* PLAGUE (esp. in the phr. **A murrain on you!** = Curse you!)

mus·ca·tel /ˌmʌskəˈtel/ *n* **1** [U] a sweet light-coloured wine made from a fruit (GRAPE) of the same name **2** [C] the GRAPE from which this wine is made

mus·cle /ˈmʌsəl/ *n* **1** [U;C] (one of) the pieces of elastic material in the body which can tighten to produce movement, esp. bending of the joints: *to develop one's arm muscles by playing tennis* **2** [U] strength: *Put some muscle into your work* **3 not move a muscle** to stay quite still

muscle-bound /ˈ·· ·/ *adj* having large too-developed muscles after too much bodily exercise

mus·cled /ˈmʌsəld/ *adj* [Wa5] (*usu. in comb.*) having muscles of a certain type or quality: *a well-muscled body|tight-muscled*

muscle in *v adv* [IØ (*on*)] *sl* to force one's way into (esp.) a group activity, usu. so as to gain a share in what is produced

mus·cle·man /ˈmʌsəlmæn/ *n* **-men** /men/ a man who has developed big muscles by special exercises

Mus·co·vite /ˈmʌskəvaɪt/ *n rare* a Russian, esp. one from Moscow

mus·cu·lar /ˈmʌskjʊləʳ‖-kjə-/ *adj* **1** [Wa5] of, concerning, or done by muscles: *a muscular disease| the muscular system* **2** having big muscles: *a muscular body* **3** strong-looking: *He's big and muscular* —**~ly** *adv*

muscular dys·tro·phy /ˌmʌskjʊlə ˈdɪstrəfi‖-kjələr-/ *n* [U] a disease of unknown cause in which the muscles become weaker over a period of time

muse¹ /mjuːz/ *v* [IØ (*over,* (*up*)*on*)] to think deeply, forgetting about the world around one: *She sat musing for hours* —**musingly** *adv*

muse² *n* **1** [C] (*sometimes cap.*) an ancient Greek goddess, one of 9, who each represented an art or science **2** [C9] the force which seems to cause someone to write, paint, etc., esp. with unusually good results: *a musician whose muse has left him* (=who can no longer write music well) **3** [C9] *pomp* a person who acts as this force: *I'd like you to meet Martha—she's my muse!* —compare INSPIRATION, INSPIRE

mu·se·um /mjuːˈzɪəm‖mjʊ-/ *n* a building where objects are kept and usu. shown to the public because of their scientific, historical, and artistic interest

museum piece /·ˈ·· ·/ *n* **1** an object interesting enough to keep in a MUSEUM **2** *humor* an old-fashioned person or thing

mush¹ /mʌʃ/ *n* [U] **1** a soft mass of half-liquid, half-solid material, esp. food **2** *AmE* boiled corn (MAIZE) in a sort of PORRIDGE **3** *infml* words, writing, etc., which seem to express feelings thought too sweet, too sad, etc., to be acceptable; SENTIMENTALITY

mush² /mʊʃ/ *n BrE sl* **1** [C *usu. sing.*] a face **2** [N] fellow: *Come here, mush!*

mush·room¹ /ˈmʌʃruːm, -rʊm/ *n* **1** any of several types of plant (FUNGUS), some of which can be eaten, which grow and develop very quickly —see picture at FUNGUS **2** also **mush·room·ing** /ˈmʌʃruːmɪŋ, -rʊm-/— anything which grows and develops fast: *the mushroom* (*development*) *of new housing* **3** the shape of the cloud above and after a NUCLEAR explosion

mushroom² *v* **1** [L9] to form and spread in the shape of a MUSHROOM: *The smoke mushroomed into the sky* **2** [IØ] to grow and develop fast: *Since the opening of the first shop new branches have mushroomed all over the country* **3** [IØ] to gather MUSHROOMs: (*to go*) *mushrooming in the woods*

mush·y /ˈmʌʃi/ *adj* [Wa1] **1** like MUSH (1): *mushy potatoes|mushy* PEAs **2** (of writing, plays, etc.) too sweet, sad, etc.; SENTIMENTAL

mu·sic /ˈmjuːzɪk/ *n* [U] **1** the arrangement of sounds in pleasant patterns and tunes: (fig.) *Her voice was music to my ears* **2** the art of doing this: *to study music|a music student* **3** an example of such an arrangement: *This music is Beethoven's 5th* SYMPHONY **4** a written or printed set of notes: *Give me my music and I'll play it for you.|a sheet of music* **5 face the music** to admit to blame, responsibility, etc., and accept the results, esp. punishment or difficulty

mu·sic·al¹ /ˈmjuːzɪkəl/ *adj* **1** [Wa5;A] of, like, or producing music: *musical instruments|to join a musical society* **2** skilled in and/or fond of music: *a very musical child* **3** pleasant to hear **4** performed to music

musical² also (*becoming rare*) **musical com·e·dy** /ˌ··· ˈ···/— *n* a musical play or film with spoken words, songs, and often dances

musical box /ˈ··· ·/ also (*esp. AmE*) **music box** /ˈ·· ·/— *n esp. BrE* a box containing a clockwork apparatus which plays music when the lid is lifted

musical chairs /ˌ··· ˈ·/ *n* [U] a game sometimes played at parties in which, when the music stops, each person tries to find a chair to sit on, although there is one chair too few

mu·sic·al·ly /ˈmjuːzɪkəli/ *adv* **1** in a musical way: *She laughed musically* **2** [Wa5] with regard to music: *Musically it's a good song, but I don't like the words*

music hall /ˈ·· ·/ *n BrE* **1** [U] a type of theatre show with songs, humour and special acts **2** [C] a theatre used for such performances —compare VAUDEVILLE

mu·si·cian /mjuːˈzɪʃən‖mjʊ-/ *n* **1** a person who performs on a musical instrument, or who writes music —compare COMPOSER **2** a person who studies and knows a lot about music

mu·si·cian·ship /mjuːˈzɪʃənʃɪp‖mjʊ-/ *n* [U] skill in performing or judging music

music stand /ˈ·· ·/ *n* a movable apparatus which holds sheet-music

musk /mʌsk/ *n* [U] a strong smelling material produced by the male of a type of deer, used in making sweet-smelling PERFUMEs

musk deer /ˈ· ·/ *n* a type of small Asian deer with no horns

mus·ket /ˈmʌskɨt/ *n* an early type of gun used before the invention of the RIFLE

mus·ket·eer /ˌmʌskɨˈtɪəʳ/ *n* (in former times) a soldier armed with a MUSKET

mus·ket·ry /ˈmʌskɨtri/ *n* [U] the skill or practice of using (small) guns

musk·mel·on /ˈmʌskˌmelən/ *n* a very sweet type of fruit (MELON)

musk·rat /ˈmʌsk-ræt/ *n* **1** [Wn1;C] a North American water rat, whose fur is valuable **2** [U] the fur of this animal; MUSQUASH

musk rose /ˈ· ·/ *n* a climbing rose with a strong sweet smell

musk·y /ˈmʌski/ *adj* [Wa1] like MUSK (in smell): *a musky smell* —**muskiness** *n* [U]

Mus·lim /ˈmʌzlɨm, ˈmʊz-, ˈmʊs-/ also **Moslem**— *n, adj* (a person) of the religion started by Mohammed —see also ISLAM, MOHAMMEDAN

mus·lin /ˈmʌzlɨn/ *n* [U] a very fine thin cotton material, used (esp. formerly) for light dresses

must¹—USAGE

Must I means that I want you to, while **have to** means that it is necessary for some outside reason. Compare: **a** *You must stay for dinner* (= because I want you to) **b** *I'm sorry you have to stay for dinner* (= there's nowhere else to go). **Be to** is like **must I**, but would not be used in this way for an invitation. It is often used for official commands, instructions, and arrangements: *Officers* **must**/*are to wear their uniforms at all times* (military order); *We are to arrive at 6 o'clock* (arrangement). But as **must** has no past tense, we speak of necessity in the past with **have to** or **be to,** except in reported speech: *I said he* **must**/*was to go* is different from *I was sorry he had to go*, just as it would be in the present.

Some (*esp. AmE*) speakers also use **have to** for **must II**: *You have to be joking!* For the relation between **need** and **must,** see the table.

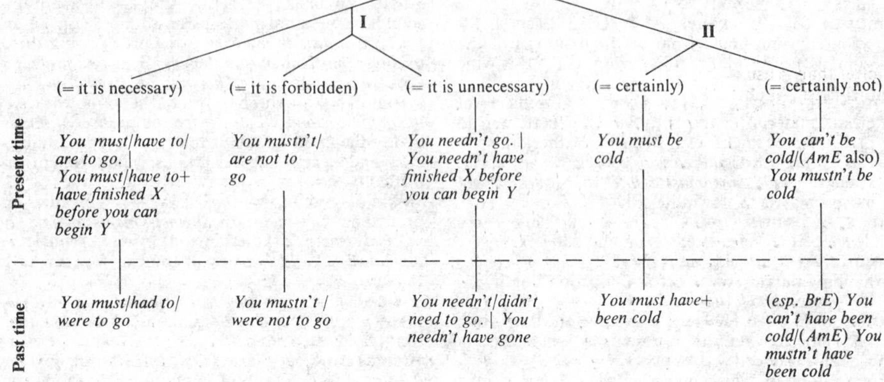

mus·quash /ˈmʌskwɒʃ‖-wɑʃ, -wɔʃ/ *n* [U] the fur of the MUSKRAT

muss¹ /mʌs/ *n* [U;C] *AmE* (a state of) disorder; MESS

muss² *v* [T1 (UP)] *esp. AmE infml* to disorder or make a MESS of (esp. the hair)

mus·sel /ˈmʌsəl/ *n* a type of small sea animal (a MOLLUSC) living inside a black shell made of 2 parts, whose soft body can be eaten as food —see picture at MOLLUSC

must¹ /mʌst/ *v. 3rd pers. sing.* **must,** *neg. contr.* **mustn't** [Wv2;I2] **1** to have to (*past* usu. **had to**): *I must leave at 6* (compare *I had to leave at 6 yesterday*).|*I said I must leave but I stayed.*|*The teacher says they mustn't talk during lessons.*|*Old people used to say "Children must be seen and not heard".*|*Must I drink this nasty soup?*|*I must admit I don't like her* **2** to be, do, etc., very probably or certainly (*past* **must have**): *I think they must have left early.*|*You must know the reason.*|*You must live near my friend, if you live in New Street.*|*I must look funny in this hat!*|*There must be some more tea in the pot* —compare CANNOT (2) **3** to be necessary: *The house must be clean if there are guests* **4** to do, in spite of being unwise or unwanted: *Must you shout so loudly!*|*Of course, after I gave her my advice, she must go and do the opposite* **5** should or ought to: *We must think about this very seriously.*|*You must recognize that we can't allow such behaviour* **6 must have** *old use* (*in a sentence with* if) would have certainly: *If he had told me I must have helped him*

must² *n* [S] *not fml* something which it is necessary or very important to have or experience: *Warm clothes are a must in the mountains*

must³ *n* [U] the liquid from which wine is made; GRAPE-juice

mus·tache /məˈstɑːʃ‖ˈmʌstæʃ/ *n AmE* MOUSTACHE

mus·ta·chi·o /məˈstɑːʃiəʊ‖məˈstæ-/ *n* **-chios** [*usu. pl.*] a type of large hairy MOUSTACHE

mus·tang /ˈmʌstæŋ/ *n* a small American horse which lives wild on the plains; BRONCO

mus·tard /ˈmʌstəd‖-ərd/ *n* [U] **1** a yellow-flowered plant with seeds from which a hot-tasting powder can be made **2 a** this powder, which has a hot taste **b** a thick mixture of this powder with water, eaten in small quantities with meat **3 as keen as mustard** very interested

mustard gas /ˈ·· ·/ *n* [U] a poisonous gas, which burns the skin, sometimes used in the First World War

mustard plas·ter /ˈ·· ˌ··/ *n* a POULTICE containing MUSTARD

mus·ter¹ /ˈmʌstəʳ/ *v* **1** [T1 (UP)] to gather or collect: *to muster one's courage* **2** [IØ] to come together: *The* TROOPS *mustered on the hill*

muster² *n* **1** a gathering of people, esp. of soldiers to march or be INSPECTED (=examined) **2** the number or names of these soldiers: *to call the muster* **3 pass muster** to be satisfactory

must·n't /ˈmʌsənt/ [Wv2] *contr. of* must not: *We must meet again, mustn't we*/(*fml*) *must we not?*|*"Mustn't there be endless stories about this"* (SEU S.) —see CONTR. (USAGE)

must·y /ˈmʌsti/ *adj* [Wa1] with an unpleasant smell as if old: *musty old books* —**mustiness** *n* [U]

mu·ta·ble /ˈmjuːtəbəl/ *adj* which is able or likely to change —**-bility** /ˌmjuːtəˈbɪl$\frac{1}{2}$ti/ *n* [U]

mu·tant /ˈmjuːtənt/ *n* a living thing which has a quality not the same as any of its parents' qualities but produced by a change in the material of all its cells (a MUTATION)

mu·ta·tion /mjuːˈteɪʃən/ *n* **1** [U] the action of change in the cells of a living thing producing a new quality in the material or parts of the body, sometimes causing illness **2** [C] **a** an example of this: *Pet animals often have fur of a colour not found in the wild, which is caused by a mutation* **b** a type of animal or plant showing such a change: *If a black rose really exists, it must be a mutation* **3** [U] *tech* (in PHONETICS) change of the quality of a vowel because of the influence of the next vowel (in the next SYLLABLE): *Vowel mutation has caused the vowel in "man" to be different from that in "men", because "men" used to have a plural ending, as it still does in German* —see also UMLAUT

mu·ta·tis mu·tan·dis /muːˌtɑːt$\frac{1}{2}$s muːˈtænd$\frac{1}{2}$s‖-ˈtɑnd$\frac{1}{2}$s/ *adv* [Wa5] *Lat* with or including necessary changes; taking into consideration differences in details

mute¹ /mjuːt/ *adj* [Wa1] **1** silent; without speech

2 not pronounced: *The word "debt" contains a mute letter* —**~ly** *adv* —**~ness** *n* [U]

mute² *n* **1** a person who cannot speak **2** *tech* an object which makes a musical instrument give a softer sound when placed against the strings or in the stream of air —see picture at WIND INSTRUMENT

mute³ *v* [T1] to reduce the sound of: *to mute a musical instrument*

mute⁴ *v* [I0] *tech* (of a bird) to pass waste matter from the body

mut·ed /ˈmjuːtᵻd/ *adj* [Wa5] (of a sound) made softer than is usual

mu·ti·late /ˈmjuːtᵻleɪt/ *v* [Wv5;T1 *often pass.*] **1 a** to damage by removing a part of: *She was mutilated in the accident and now has only one leg* **b** to destroy the use or form of: to MAIM: *Her arm was mutilated in the accident* **2** to spoil: *You've mutilated the story by making such big changes*

mu·ti·la·tion /ˌmjuːtᵻˈleɪʃən/ *n* **1** [U] the act of mutilating (MUTILATE) **2** [C] the condition resulting from this

mu·ti·neer /ˌmjuːtᵻˈnɪəʳ, -tən-/ *n* a person who is taking part or has taken part in a MUTINY

mu·ti·nous /ˈmjuːtᵻnəs, -tən-/ *adj* **1** [Wa5] **a** taking part in a MUTINY **b** guilty of MUTINY **2** having or showing a wish to act against someone in power —**~ly** *adv*

mu·ti·ny¹ /ˈmjuːtᵻni, -təni/ *n* **1** [C;U] (an example of) the act of taking power from the person in charge, esp. from a captain on a ship: *A mutiny has taken place off the coast of South America* **2** [U] a state of feelings or set of actions against someone's power: *He's started his own private mutiny against that teacher, and won't do any work for him*

mutiny² *v* [I0] to take part in a MUTINY

mutt /mʌt/ *n* [C; *you*+N] *infml* a fool

mut·ter¹ /ˈmʌtəʳ/ *v* [I0;T1,5] to speak (usu. angry or complaining words) in a low voice, not easily heard: *He muttered a threat.|She's muttering to herself* —**~er** *n*

mutter² *n* [S] a sound of MUTTERing

mut·ton /ˈmʌtn/ *n* [U] **1** the meat from a sheep —see MEAT (USAGE) **2 as dead as mutton** completely dead **3 mutton dressed as lamb** an older woman trying to look like a young one

mut·ton·chops /ˌmʌtnˈtʃɒps◂‖ˈmʌtntʃɑps/ also **muttonchop whis·kers** /ˌ··· ˈ··/— *n* [P] a growth of beard on the sides of the cheeks, but not on the chin

mu·tu·al /ˈmjuːtʃʊəl/ *adj* [Wa5] **1** equally shared by each one: *mutual interests|a mutual love of flowers* **2** equally so, one towards the other: *Stalin and Trotsky were mutual enemies* —**~ly** *adv*

USAGE People often use **mutual** of things shared between 2 or more: *a* **mutual** *friend|our* **mutual** *interests.* Others believe strongly that the right word here is **common**, and that **mutual** should be kept only for what each feels or does towards the other: *our* **mutual** *admiration* (=I admire you and you admire me).

mutual fund /ˈ··· ·/ *n AmE* UNIT TRUST

mu·tu·al·i·ty /ˌmjuːtʃʊˈælᵻti/ *n* [U] the condition of being MUTUAL

mu·zak /ˈmjuːzæk/ *n* [U] *tdmk, often derog* (*often cap.*) recorded music played continuously though usu. not loudly in some restaurants, places of work, etc.

muz·zle¹ /ˈmʌzəl/ *n* **1** the front part of an animal's face, with the nose and mouth —see picture at DOG¹ **2** the front end of a gun barrel **3** a covering round an animal's mouth, to prevent it from biting

muzzle² *v* [T1] **1** to put a MUZZLE¹ (3) on **2** to force to keep silent; prevent from telling something: *Those who know the truth have been muzzled by those in power*

muzzle-load·er /ˈ·· ˌ··/ *n* a gun which is loaded through the MUZZLE, as in earlier times, instead of at the BREECH (=the back end of the barrel)

muzzle ve·lo·ci·ty /ˈ·· ·ˌ···/ *n* the speed at which a shot leaves a gun when fired

muz·zy /ˈmʌzi/ *adj* [Wa1] **1** not clear: *The television picture's muzzy* **2** not thinking clearly, as because of illness or alcohol —**-zily** *adv* —**-ziness** *n* [U]

my /maɪ/ *determiner* [Wp1] (*poss. form of* I) **1** belonging to me: *my car|my mother* **2** a cry of surprise, pleasure, etc.: *My (my)! What a clever boy you are* **3 my dear** *polite or humor* (a form of address): *My dear sir, I'm so sorry.|Come in, my dear*

my·col·o·gy /maɪˈkɒlədʒi‖-ˈkɑ-/ *n* [U] the study of fungi (FUNGUS)

my·e·li·tis /ˌmaɪəˈlaɪtᵻs/ *n* [U] any form of disease causing swelling and damage to the nerves of the SPINAL CORD

my·nah, myna /ˈmaɪnə/ also **mynah bird** /ˈ·· ·/— *n* any of several types of bird from Asia which are large and dark in colour and can learn to talk —see picture at EXOTIC

my·o·pi·a /maɪˈəʊpɪə/ *n* [U] *fml* inability to see clearly objects which are not close; SHORT-SIGHTEDNESS —**-pic** /maɪˈɒpɪk‖-ˈɑpɪk/ *adj*: (*fig.*) *myopic minds* —**-pically** *adv* [Wa3]

myr·i·ad /ˈmɪrɪəd/ *adj, n, pron* **1** *lit* (of) a great and varied number: *A myriad of thoughts passed through her mind* **2** *old use* 10,000

myrrh /mɜːʳ/ *n* [U] a sticky substance (GUM) obtained from trees, which has a bitter taste, and is used in making sweet-smelling products such as PERFUME and INCENSE

myr·tle /ˈmɜːtl‖ˈmɜr-/ *n* a small tree with shiny green leaves and sweet-smelling white flowers

my·self /maɪˈself/ *pron* [Wp1] **1** (*refl. form of* I): *I cut myself in the kitchen* **2** (*strong form of* I): *I'll do it myself, if you won't.|Myself a Muslim, I understood what he meant* **3** *infml* (in) my usual state of mind or body (often in the phrs. **be myself, come to myself**): *I feel more myself today* (=not so ill as before) **4 (all) by myself** alone, without help: *I carried it all by myself.|I live by myself* —see YOURSELF (USAGE)

mys·te·ri·ous /mɪˈstɪərɪəs/ *adj* **1** not easily understood: *a mysterious explanation* **2** secret: *the mysterious plan which nobody has been told* **3** suggesting mystery: *a mysterious look* —**~ly** *adv* —**~ness** *n* [U]

mys·te·ry /ˈmɪstəri/ *n* **1** [C] something which cannot be explained or understood: *Her death is a mystery* **2** [U] a strange secret nature or quality: *stories full of mystery* **3** [C *usu. pl.*] a religious teaching or belief that is beyond human understanding or that is kept secret

mystery play /ˈ··· ·/ *n* MIRACLE PLAY

mys·tic¹ /ˈmɪstɪk/ *adj* **1** representing or like a religious mystery: *a mystic* SYMBOL *of God* (=object which is a sign of his presence) **2** concerning the power of religion or magic: *mystic ceremonies|mystic words* **3** mysterious **4** MYSTICAL

mystic² *n* a person who practises MYSTICISM

mys·tic·al /ˈmɪstɪkəl/ *adj* **1** concerning MYSTICISM **2** of hidden religious power and importance —**~ly** *adv* [Wa4]

mys·ti·cis·m /ˈmɪstᵻsɪzəm/ *n* [U] the attempt to gain, or practice of gaining, a knowledge of real truth and union with God by prayer and MEDITATION

mys·ti·fi·ca·tion /ˌmɪstᵻfᵻˈkeɪʃən/ *n* **1** [U] the act of MYSTIFYing or state of being mystified **2** [C] something that mystifies (MYSTIFY)

mys·ti·fy /ˈmɪstɪ̈faɪ/ *v* [Wv5;T1] to make (someone) wonder; completely BEWILDER: *I'm quite mystified about what happened.|She laughed at his mystified expression*

mys·tique /mɪˈstiːk/ *n* [*usu. sing.*] *Fr* **1** a feeling of mystery or separateness which something has, esp. because of the way it is admired: *the mystique of the fashion industry* **2** a secret skill that cannot be taught

myth /mɪθ/ *n* **1** [C] an ancient story, usu. containing religious or magical ideas, which may explain natural or historical events **2** [U] such stories generally: *an idea common in myth* **3** [C,C5] a false story or idea: *the myth that elephants never forget* **4** [C] something or someone invented, not real: *Her wealth is a myth*

myth·i·cal /ˈmɪθɪkəl/ *adj* [Wa5] **1** of or in a MYTH (1) **2** not real; imagined or invented

myth·o·lo·gi·cal /ˌmɪθəˈlɒdʒɪkəl‖-ˈlɑ-/ *adj* [Wa5] **1** concerning the study of MYTH*s* (1) **2** MYTHICAL (1)

my·thol·o·gist /mɪˈθɒlədʒɪ̈st‖-ˈθɑ-/ *n* a person who studies and knows a lot about MYTH*s* (1)

my·thol·o·gy /mɪˈθɒlədʒi‖-ˈθɑ-/ *n* **1** [U;C] a system of beliefs contained in MYTH*s* (1): *He studies Greek and Roman mythology* **2** [U] the study of MYTH*s* (1)

myx·o·ma·to·sis /ˌmɪksəməˈtəʊsɪ̈s/ *n* [U] a disease which infects rabbits, usu. killing them

N, n

N, n /en/ **N's, n's** *or* **Ns, ns**— the 14th letter of the English alphabet

n *abbrev. for:* **1** noun **2** note

N **1** the chemical sign for NITROGEN **2** *abbrev. for*: North(ern)

Naaf·i, NAAFI /ˈnæfi/ *n* **-s** **1** [*the*+R] the organization which runs shops and eating places in British military establishments **2** [C] one of these shops or eating places —compare PX

nab /næb/ *v* **-bb-** [T1] *infml* **1** [(*for*)] to seize (as a thief); ARREST: *He was nabbed before he could escape with the money.|They nabbed him for stealing the money* **2** to get for oneself, seize, or catch quickly: *Can I nab a cup of coffee before we go?|Run with this letter and nab the postman*

na·bob /ˈneɪbɒb‖-bɑb/ *n* **1** (in the 18th and 19th centuries) a man who became rich in the East and returned to Europe **2** *derog* a rich or powerful man **3** a governor of any of the parts of India during the Mogul Empire

na·celle /næˈsel, nə-/ *n tech* an enclosure containing one of the engines on an aircraft —see picture at AIRCRAFT

na·cre /ˈneɪkəʳ/ *n* [U] MOTHER-OF-PEARL

na·dir /ˈneɪdɪəʳ‖-dər/ *n* **1** [*the*+R] the point in the heavens directly below a person looking from earth —opposite **zenith** **2** [C *usu. sing.*] the lowest point, as of hope or fortune: *After he lost the election, his spirits sank to their nadir*

nag¹ /næg/ *n* **1** *not fml* a horse that is old or in bad condition **2** *infml, esp. derog* a horse, esp. one which races

nag² *v* **-gg-** **1** [T1 (*for*),3;IØ (*at, for*);V3] to try to persuade (someone) by continuous complaining: *His wife nags (at him) all day.|She kept nagging (her husband) for a new car/to go* **2** [Wv4;T1;IØ (*at*)] to worry or annoy continuously: *a nagging headache* —**~ger** *n*

nag³ *n infml* a person who has the habit of NAGging² (1)

nag in·to *v prep* [D1] to cause (someone to do something) by NAGging: *She nagged her son into leaving the house.|He was at last nagged into obedience*

nai·ad /ˈnaɪæd‖ˈneɪæd, ˈnaɪ-, -əd/ *n* **-ads** *or* **-ades** /ədiːz/ (in ancient Greek literature) any of the young female water spirits (NYMPH*s*) living in and having power over lakes, springs, rivers, etc.

nail¹ /neɪl/ *n* **1** a thin piece of metal with a point at one end and a flat head at the other for hammering into a piece of wood, usu. to fasten the wood to something else **2** **a** FINGERNAIL **b** *rare* TOENAIL **3** **hard as nails** *infml* **a** without any tender feelings **b** also **tough as nails**— having a body in very good condition **4** **hit the nail on the head** *infml* to do or say something exactly right; find the right answer **5** **(pay cash) on the nail** *infml* (to pay for something) at once —see also **nail in someone's** COFFIN

nail² *v* [T1] **1** [(*to, on*)] to fasten (as) with a nail or nails: *nail a sign to/on the post* **2** *sl* to hit, esp. with something one throws or shoots: *He nailed a rabbit with his first shot*

nail·brush /ˈneɪlbrʌʃ/ *n* a small stiff brush for cleaning hands, and esp. FINGERNAIL*s* —see picture at BATHROOM

nail down *v adv* [T1] **1** to fasten down, with a nail or nails: *nail down a loose board in the floor* **2** *not fml* be sure about; establish; settle: *nail down an agreement* **3** [(*to*)] *not fml* to force (someone) to tell plans or wishes clearly: *What does she want? I can never nail her down (to anything)*

nail file /ˈ· ·/ *n* a small instrument with a rough surface for shaping FINGERNAIL*s*

nail scis·sors /ˈ· ˌ··/ *n* [P] a small pair of scissors for cutting FINGERNAIL*s* or TOENAIL*s*

nail up *v adv* [T1] **1** to fasten (something, such as a picture, sign, etc.) with a nail or nails to a wall, post, etc. **2** to fasten (something, such as a disused door or window) shut with nails: *The empty house was all nailed up*

nail var·nish /ˈ· ˌ··/ (*AmE* **nail pol·ish** /ˈ· ˌ··/)— *n* [U] *BrE* coloured or transparent liquid which dries to give a hard shiny surface, used by women to make their fingernails and toenails more attractive

na·ive, naïve /naɪˈiːv‖nɑˈiːv/ *adj* **1** having or showing no experience (as of social rules or behaviour), esp. because one is young: *The youngest boy was laughed at for his naive remarks* **2** believing what anyone says or what is most favourable: *It's naive (of you) to believe he'll do what he says* **3** *tech* having almost no knowledge or experience of a particular subject: *We need naive people* (=who have not studied the subject before) *to take this test* —**~ly** *adv*

na·ive·ty, naïvety, -eté /naɪˈiːvti‖nɑˌiːvəˈteɪ/ *n* **1** [U] the state of being NAIVE (1) **2** [C *usu. pl.*] a NAIVE action or statement

na·ked /ˈneɪkɪ̈d/ *adj* **1** [Wa5;B] (of (a part of) a person's body) not covered by clothes: *He was naked to the waist* (=wore nothing above his waist) **2** [B] not covered by the usual covering: *a naked hillside* (=without trees)|*a naked light* (=without glass over it) **3** [A] not hidden, esp. by false statements; plain to see; STARK¹ (1): *the* *naked truth* **4** [Wa5;A] (of the eye) without any instrument to help one see: *too small/too far away to see with the naked eye* —**~ly** *adv* —**~ness** *n* [U]: *nakedness and hunger in the poor village*

name[1] /neɪm/ *n* **1** [C] the word(s) that someone or something is called or known by: *Her name is Mary (Wilson)* **2** [C] a usu. offensive title for someone arising from his character: *to call someone names* (=say bad or rude things about someone)| *He will always have the name "thief" in this town* **3** [C *usu. sing.* (*for*)] fame; recognition by others; REPUTATION: *He has a good name in the business. You can trust him.|Its slow service gave the restaurant a bad name.|She made a name for herself/made her name* (=became famous) *as a painter.|The school has a name for good science teaching* **4** [A] *sl, esp. AmE* famous; well-known: *A (big-)name band will play at their wedding* **5** [C] *sl* a well-known person (esp. in the phrs. **big name, famous name,** etc.): *There were several (big) names* (=famous people) *at the party* **6** [(*the*) S] *bibl* (of God) his own self: *Praise the name of the Lord! Praise his holy name* **7 by name** using or by means of one or more NAMES[1] (1): *He calls all his students by name.| Can you list the kings of England by name?|I only know him by name* (=I know his name but have not met him) —see NAMELY (USAGE) **8 by the name of** *not fml* having the NAME (1): *a boy by the name of David* **9 in name only** in appearance or by title but not in fact: *He is a doctor in name only; he paints pictures all day* **10 in the name of** by the right or power of: *Open the door, in the name of the law!* **11 the name of the game** *sl* the quality or object which is most necessary or important: *In fishing, patience is the name of the game* **12 to one's name** *infml* (*esp. with "no", "not", etc.*) (esp. of money) as one's property: *He hasn't a penny to his name* **13 under the name (of)** using (a NAME) different from one's own: *H. H. Munro wrote under the name (of) Saki* —see also **take someone's name in** VAIN

name[2] *v* **1** [T1;X1] to give a name to (someone or something): *They didn't name their baby for a week, and then they named him John.|He was named after* (=given the same name as) *his father* **2** [T1] to tell the name(s) of; IDENTIFY: *Can you name all the plants in the garden?* **3** [T1 (*as, for*);V3;X (*to be*) 1] to choose or appoint; SPECIFY: *The President named him (as/to be) Secretary of State.|We've named August 23rd for our wedding day.|Name a price for your car; I'd like to buy it*

USAGE In *BrE* one **names** a baby *after* its father, but Americans may also say *We* **named** *him for his father*, or *The college is* **named** *for George Washington.*

name day /ˈ· ·/ *n old use* [C9] the date each year when the Church honours the holy person (SAINT) that one is named after

name·drop /ˈneɪmdrɒp‖-drɑp/ *v* **-pp-** [I∅] *derog & infml* to mention famous people's names to make it seem that one knows them or their work well: *He hasn't any real knowledge of the subject. He's just namedropping* —**~per** *n* —**~ping** *n* [U]

name·less /ˈneɪmləs/ *adj* [Wa5] **1 a** not known by name: ANONYMOUS (1): *the work of a nameless 13th century poet|a nameless town in ancient Britain* **b** not to be known by name: *a certain person who must/shall be nameless* (=whose name I will not tell) **2** having no name; never given a name: *He discovered some new and nameless kinds of plants* **3** not marked by a name; without the name of the owner, maker, giver, etc., stated: *a nameless grave| a nameless gift to the college* **4** (esp. of feelings) not clear enough to describe: *nameless fears* **5** too terrible to describe or name: *guilty of nameless crimes*

name·ly /ˈneɪmli/ *adv* (and) that is (to say): *Only one person can do the job, namely you.|Arabic is written in the opposite direction to English, namely from right to left* —compare I.E.; VIZ.

USAGE As **namely** means "that is to say" it can be followed by a name or a fact. *By* **name** means "with the name" or "called", so it must introduce a name that we have not heard before. Compare: *the youngest boy,* **namely** *Peter* (=that's the one I mean)|*the youngest boy, Peter by* **name** (=and that's what he's called).

name·plate /ˈneɪmpleɪt/ *n* a plate, usu. fastened to something, showing the name of the owner or maker, or the person who lives or works within

name·sake /ˈneɪmseɪk/ *n* **1** [C] one of 2 or more people with the same name: *I often get letters belonging to my namesake John Smith down the street; it's confusing that we're namesakes* **2** [C9] a person named after a stated person: *He is his grandfather's namesake*

nan·ny /ˈnæni/ *n* [C;N] (in Britain, esp. formerly in rich families) a woman employed to take care of children: *Some American parents want a British nanny for their children*

nanny goat /ˈ·· ·/ *n* a female goat —compare BILLY GOAT

nap[1] /næp/ *v* **-pp-** [I∅] **1** to sleep for a short time, esp. during the day; DOZE **2 catch someone napping** *infml* to find, or take advantage of, someone off guard or not doing his duty

nap[2] *n not fml* a short sleep, esp. during the day: *Father always takes/has a nap in the afternoon*

nap[3] *n* [*usu. sing.*] the soft surface on some cloth and leather, made by brushing the short fine threads or hairs usu. in one direction: *against the nap* (=in the opposite direction to this brushing) —compare PILE[4]

nap[4] *n* [U] a type of card game

nap[5] *v* [T1] *BrE infml* (esp.of a newspaper writer) to say that one thinks (a certain horse) will win its race

na·palm /ˈneɪpɑːm‖-pɑm, -pɑlm/ *n* [U] a jelly made from petrol, which burns fiercely and is used in bombs

nape /neɪp/ *n* [*usu. sing*] the back (of the neck), near the head: *the nape of the neck*

naph·tha /ˈnæfθə/ *n* [U] any of the various liquid chemicals (HYDROCARBON*s*) used esp. for starting fires, removing spots of dirt from clothes, and weakening other chemicals

naph·tha·lene /ˈnæfθəliːn/ *n* [U] a white strong-smelling solid substance used (in MOTHBALL*s*) for protecting clothes and in making chemicals that change the colours of things (DYE*s*)

nap·kin /ˈnæpkɨn/ *n* **1** a usu. square piece of cloth or paper used for protecting one's clothes and for cleaning one's hands and lips during a meal **2** (*AmE* **diaper**)— *BrE fml* NAPPY

napkin ring /ˈ·· ˌ·/ *n* a small ring of wood, silver, etc., in which a cloth NAPKIN is rolled and kept for the use of one particular person

nap·py /ˈnæpi/ (*AmE* **diaper**)— *n BrE not fml* a piece of soft cloth or paper fastened and worn between the legs and around the waist of a baby

nar·cis·sis·m /ˈnɑːsɨsɪzəm‖ˈnɑr-/ *n* [U] **1** *med* the condition of mind in which someone's own body is an object of sexual pleasure **2** too great love for one's own abilities or esp. appearance —**-sist** *n* —**-sistic** /ˌnɑːsɨˈsɪstɪk‖ˌnɑr-/ *adj* —**-sistically** *adv* [Wa4]

nar·cis·sus /nɑːˈsɪsəs‖nɑr-/ *n* **-suses** *or* **-si** /saɪ/ any of several types of white or yellow flowers of early spring, such as the DAFFODIL

nar·cot·ic[1] /nɑːˈkɒtɪk‖nɑrˈkɑ-/ *n* [*often pl.*] a drug which in small amounts causes sleep or takes away pain, and in large amounts is harmful and habit-forming: *He was sent to prison on a narcotics charge* (=an offence concerning selling or using these drugs)

narcotic[2] *adj* **1** [B] taking away pain or esp. causing sleep: *a narcotic drink* **2** [Wa5;A] of or related to NARCOTICs (drugs): *narcotic* ADDICTION (=dependence on drugs)

nark[1] /nɑːk‖nɑrk/ (*AmE* **stoolpigeon**)— *n BrE derog sl becoming rare* a person who mixes with criminals and reports on them to the police

nark[2], **narc** *n AmE sl* a police officer (**narcotics agent**) who deals with crimes concerning unlawful drugs

nark[3] *v BrE sl* **1** [T1] to annoy; make angry: *He was narked at/by her words* **2** [I∅] to complain: *Stop narking and get back to work!*

nark·y /ˈnɑːki‖ˈnɑr-/ *adj* [Wa1] *BrE sl* bad-tempered: *She gets a bit narky when I play my records too loud*

nar·rate /nəˈreɪt‖ˈnæreɪt, næˈreɪt, nə-/ *v* **1** [T1] *fml* to tell (a story); describe (an event or events) in order: *Shall I narrate a strange experience of mine?* **2** [I∅] to be the person (NARRATOR) in a play, broadcast, etc., who tells the story: *In the new play, who is going to narrate?*

nar·ra·tion /nəˈreɪʃən‖næ-, nə-/ *n* **1** [U] the act of narrating (NARRATE) **2** [C;U] NARRATIVE[1]

nar·ra·tive[1] /ˈnærətɪv/ *n* **1** [C;U] that which is NARRATEd; a story: *a narrative of last week's events|Narrative makes up most of the book* **2** [U] the act or practice of narrating (NARRATE): *The writer had great skill in narrative*

narrative[2] *adj* [Wa5] **1** telling a story or having the form of a story: *a narrative poem* **2** of or concerning storytelling: *the narrative art*

nar·ra·tor /nəˈreɪtəʳ‖ˈnæreɪ-, næˈreɪtəʳ, nə-/ *n* **1** a person in some books, television shows, plays, music, etc., who tells the story or explains what is happening **2** a person who NARRATEs a story

nar·row[1] /ˈnærəʊ/ *adj* [Wa1] **1** small from one side to the other, esp. in comparison with length or with what is usual: *a narrow river|The gate is too narrow for a car; we'll have to walk through* **2** limited; small; RESTRICTED (4): *The secret is known only to a narrow group of people.|in the narrow meaning of the word* **3** almost not enough or only just successful: *to win by a narrow* MAJORITY*|a narrow escape* —compare CLOSE[4] (6); opposite **wide, broad** **4** *fml* careful and thorough: *a narrow examination of the facts* —**~ness** *n* [U]

narrow[2] *v* **1** [I∅;T1] to (cause to) decrease in width: *The river narrows at this point.|In the bright sunlight she had to narrow her eyes* (=partly close them) **2** [T1 (DOWN)] to reduce in size; limit; RESTRICT: *Let's narrow (down) what we mean by "justice"*

narrow boat /ˈ·· ˌ·/ *n* a long narrow boat for use on CANALs

narrow gauge /ˌ·· ˈ·/ *n* a size of railway track which is less than 4 feet 8½ inches wide: *a narrow-gauge railway|narrow-gauge track* —see also GAUGE[1] (3)

nar·row·ly /ˈnærəʊli/ *adv* **1** hardly; only just: *One car went too fast and narrowly missed hitting the other one* **2** in a narrow way or form or within narrow limits: *moving narrowly between 2 limits that are close together* **3** in a thorough and usu. doubting way: *The teacher questioned the boy narrowly about why he was late* **4** *derog* exactly or too exactly; STRICTly (2a): *a narrowly religious person*

narrow-mind·ed /ˌ·· ˈ··‖ˈ·· ˌ··/ *adj derog* considering only part of a question or favouring only one opinion; PREJUDICED: *The narrow-minded articles in this newspaper make me angry* —opposite **broad-minded** —**~ness** *n* [U]

nar·rows /ˈnærəʊz/ *n* [P] (*cap. as part of name*) a narrow course or passage between 2 larger stretches of water: *the Narrows of New York harbour*

nar·whal /ˈnɑːwəl‖ˈnɑrwɑl, -wəl/ *n* [Wn1] a type of large animal (WHALE) of the northern ocean, valuable for its oil and the long horn (TUSK) of the male

na·sal[1] /ˈneɪzəl/ *n, adj tech* (any of the sounds of a language) made through the nose: *The English consonant sounds /m/, /n/, and /ŋ/ are nasals*

nasal[2] *adj* **1** [Wa5;A] of or related to the nose: *breathe through the nasal passage* **2** marked by NASAL[1] sounds: *His nasal voice is hard to listen to.|The horn made a nasal sound* —**~ity** /neɪˈzælɪ̈ti/ *n* [U] —**~ly** /ˈneɪzəli/ *adv*

na·sal·ize, -ise /ˈneɪzəlaɪz/ *v* [I∅;T1] to speak or pronounce through the nose: *In French there are nasalized vowel sounds* —compare VELARIZE, PALATALIZE —**-ization** /ˌneɪzəlaɪˈzeɪʃən‖-zələ-/ *n* [U]

nas·cent /ˈnæsənt/ *adj fml* beginning to be; starting to grow or develop: *nascent feelings of dislike|nascent ability in music*

nas·tur·tium /nəˈstɜːʃəm‖-ɜr-/ *n* **1** a type of common garden plant with orange, yellow, or red flowers and circular leaves **2** a flower of this plant

nas·ty /ˈnɑːsti‖ˈnæsti/ *adj* [Wa1] *not fml* **1** very ugly or unpleasant to see, taste, smell, etc.: *cheap and nasty furniture|nasty weather* **2** morally bad or improper; OBSCENE: *It's a nasty book, the work of a nasty mind* **3** harmful; painful; severe: *a nasty accident with one person killed|a nasty cut on the head|The hotel bill was a nasty shock* **4** causing difficulty or danger: *a nasty calculation|a nasty place to cross a main road|a nasty storm at sea* **5** angry or threatening: *a nasty temper|He turned nasty* (= started to threaten me) *when I said I couldn't pay him* —**-tily** *adv* —**-tiness** *n* [U]

na·tal /ˈneɪtl/ *adj* [A] *pomp* of or connected with someone's birth: *her natal day* (=birthday)

na·tion /ˈneɪʃən/ *n* **1** a large group of people living in one area and usu. having an independent government: *The President spoke on radio to the nation.|newly independent nations* —compare COUNTRY[1] (1) **2** a large group of people with the same race and language: *the Indian nations in the western United States* —see FOLK (USAGE)

na·tion·al[1] /ˈnæʃənəl/ *adj* [Wa5] **1** of, being, or concerning a nation, esp. as opposed to **a** any of its parts: *a national newspaper* (=one read everywhere in the country)*|a national holiday* (=a holiday everywhere in the country) **b** another nation or other nations: *The national news comes after the international news* **2** owned or controlled by the central government of a country: *a national bank* —**~ly** *adv*

national[2] *n* [C9] a person, esp. someone abroad, who belongs to another, usu. stated, country: *American nationals in England|Foreign nationals were asked to leave the country* —compare CITIZEN, ALIEN

national an·them /ˌ··· ˈ··/ *n* the official song of a nation, to be sung or played on certain formal occasions: *"The Marseillaise" is the national anthem of France*

national as·sist·ance /ˌ··· ·ˈ··/ *n* [U] *BrE old use* SOCIAL SECURITY

national debt /ˌ··· ˈ·/ *n* [(*the*) S] the total amount of money owed by the government of a country: *Parliament has power to increase the national debt.|a national debt of £200,000,000*

national gov·ern·ment /ˌ··· ˈ···/ *n tech* a government formed by most or all of the political parties in a country: *In the last war, Britain had a national government*

national guard /ˌ··· ˈ·/ *n* [(*the*) GU] (*usu. caps.*) (in the US) a body of part-time soldiers called to deal with public violence (RIOT*s*) and for strengthening the army

National Health Ser·vice /ˌ··· ˈ· ˌ··/ *n* **1** (in Britain) the system of medical treatment for everyone paid for by taxes **2 on the National Health Service** also (*not fml*) **on the National Health**— free or cheap because paid for by this system: *Can you get your glasses on the National Health or must you pay for them privately?*

National In·sur·ance /ˌ··· ·ˈ··/ *n* [U] (in Britain) (a system of) insurance run by the government, into which workers and employers make regular payments, and which provides money for people who are unemployed, old, or ill

na·tion·al·is·m /ˈnæʃənəlɪzəm/ *n* [U] **1** (too great) love of and pride in a country shown by its people **2** desire by a racial group (NATIONALITY) to form an independent country: *Scottish nationalism*

na·tion·al·ist[1] /ˈnæʃənəl}st/ *adj* of or believing in NATIONALISM (2): *the nationalist party in Wales*

nationalist[2] *n* a person who wants political independence for his racial group (NATIONALITY): *a Scottish nationalist*

na·tion·al·is·tic /ˌnæʃənəˈlɪstɪk/ *adj often derog* of or showing (too) great love of a country: *a nationalistic election speech* —**~ally** *adv* [Wa4]

na·tion·al·i·ty /ˌnæʃəˈnæl}ti/ *n* **1** [U;C] membership of a country by a person, esp. when abroad: *She lives in France but has British nationality.|people of the same nationality* —compare CITIZENSHIP **2** [C] a large group of people with the same race, origin, language, etc.: *the different nationalities of the USSR*

na·tion·al·ize, -ise /ˈnæʃənəlaɪz/ *v* [T1] (of a central government) to buy or take control of (a business, industry, etc.): *The British government nationalized the railways in 1948* —**-ization** /ˌnæʃənəlaɪˈzeɪʃən‖-nələ-/ *n* [U]

national mon·u·ment /ˌ··· ˈ···/ *n esp. AmE* a beautiful or interesting place (such as a mountain or old building) which is kept open by the central government for people to visit

national park /ˌ··· ˈ·/ *n* also **park**— a usu. large piece of land which is kept in its natural state by the government of a country for people to visit and for native plants and animals to live in

national ser·vice /ˌ··· ˈ··/ *n BrE* (*often caps.*) **1** [R] *AmE* **draft, selective service**— the system of making all men serve in the armed forces for a limited period; CONSCRIPTION: *Britain no longer has national service* **2** [U] military duty in this system: *I did my national service in the navy*

National So·cial·is·m /ˌ··· ˈ····/ *n* [R] *tech* NAZISM

National Trust /ˌ··· ˈ·/ *n* [*the*+R] a British organization which takes care of beautiful places and buildings

nation state /ˌ·· ˈ·/ *n* a people (a nation) living together as one politically independent state (country): *The modern European nation states began to develop in the 13th Century*

na·tion·wide /ˌneɪʃənˈwaɪd◂/ *adj* [Wa5] (used esp. in newspapers, on the radio, etc.) happening, existing, etc., over a whole country; NATIONAL[1] (1a): *a nationwide search for the criminals|a nationwide broadcast* (=heard everywhere in the country)

na·tive[1] /ˈneɪtɪv/ *adj* **1** [A] belonging to or being the place of one's birth: *her native language|He was never popular in his native Australia* **2** [A] (of a person) belonging to a country from birth: *a native(-born) Englishman|native speakers of English* (=those who learn English as their first language, esp. in Britain, America, Australia, etc.) **3** [B (*to*)] growing, living, produced, found, etc., in a place; not brought in from another place: *a plant native to the eastern US|a native bird|a house built of native stone|native farm products* **4** [B (*to*)] (as of a quality) belonging to someone from birth; not learned; INNATE: *native ability|a beauty native to her family* **5** [A] *often derog and becoming rare* of or concerning the original people, esp. the non-Europeans, of a place: *native customs|a native village|native doctors* **6 go native** *infml* (as of tourists) to live in the manner of the people who usually live in a place: *In Japan we wanted to go native and not stay in a European hotel*

native[2] *n* **1** [C9, esp. *of*] someone who was born (in a place): *A native of New York City, Mr Thompson lived mostly in California* **2** [C] someone who lives in a place all the time or has lived in a place a long time: *Are you a native here, or just a visitor?* **3** [C *often pl.*] *often derog and becoming rare* someone who belongs to an earlier or original people, esp. the non-Europeans, living in a place: *The government of the island treated the natives badly* **4** [C9, esp. *of*] a plant or animal living naturally (in a place): *The bear was once a native of Britain*

na·tiv·i·ty /nəˈtɪv}ti/ *n pomp & fml* birth: *I have just visited the place of my nativity*

Nativity *n* **1** [*the*+R] the birth of Christ **2** [C] a painting or other picture showing some part of the Bible story of Christ's birth **3** [C+*of, usu. sing.*] the day each year on which the Church honours the birth (of a holy person (SAINT)): *September 8th is the Nativity of Mary the mother of Jesus*

nativity play /·ˈ··· ·/ *n* (*often cap.* N) a play telling the story of the NATIVITY —compare PASSION PLAY

NATO /ˈneɪtəʊ/ *n* [R] the North Atlantic Treaty Organization; a group of countries including Britain, the US, Canada, Turkey, etc., agreeing (in a TREATY) to give military help to each other

nat·ter[1] /ˈnætə^r/ *v* [I∅ (AWAY, ON)] *BrE infml* to talk continuously about unimportant things; CHATTER: *They nattered (away) all afternoon and never did any work*

natter[2] *n* [S] *BrE infml* an informal conversation, esp. about unimportant things

nat·ty /ˈnæti/ *adj* [Wa1] *infml* neat in appearance; SMART[2] (3): *He's a very natty dresser but of course he's got lots of money* —**-tily** *adv*

nat·u·ral[1] /ˈnætʃərəl/ *adj* **1** [Wa5;B] of, concerning, or being what is or happens ordinarily in the world, esp. **a** not caused, made, or controlled by people: *the natural mineral wealth of a country|death from natural causes* —compare MAN-MADE, ARTIFICIAL (1,2) **b** of or concerning forces which can be explained: *a natural explanation for the strange event* **2** [B] expected from experience or from the character of someone or something; usual; ordinary: *It's natural to shake hands with someone you've just met* **3** [B] not looking or sounding different from usual; UNAFFECTED (1): *Try to look natural for your photograph* **4** [B (*to*)] belonging to someone from birth; not learned: *natural charm|the charm that is natural to him|natural musicianship* **5** [A] (of a person) not needing to be taught; having a skill or quality already in oneself: *a natural musician* **6** [Wa5;A] (of a family member) actually having the stated relation even if not in law: *John was* ADOPT*ed as a baby: he never knew his natural parents and grew up in another town far away* **7** [Wa5;A] *euph now rare* ILLEGITIMATE (2): *She claimed to be the natural*

child of the king **8** [Wa5;E] (of a note in music) not raised or lowered (not SHARP or FLAT), or changed back from being raised or lowered: *Don't sing C* SHARP, *sing C natural!*
USAGE When **natural** means "ordinary", or "what is to be expected", the opposite is **unnatural** or **abnormal:** *It's quite* **natural**/*not at all* **abnormal** *to be tired after such a long walk.* **Supernatural** is the opposite of **natural** when one is thinking of gods, fairies, or spirits. **Physical** can mean "concerning the body" as compared with **mental** "concerning the mind".

natural[2] *n* **1** [*usu. sing.*] *infml* someone or something well suited (to a job, part in a play, etc.) or certain to succeed: *The horse is a natural to win the next race* **2** (in music) **a** a note which is not raised or lowered (by a SHARP or FLAT); a white note on the piano: *a piece of music played only on the naturals* **b** also **natural sign** /ˈ··· ·/— the sign showing that a note is not raised or lowered: *Should there be a natural in front of this G?* —see picture at NOTATION **3** *old use and euph* a person with a weak mind; IDIOT

natural gas /ˌ··· ˈ·/ *n* [U] gas which is taken from under the earth (or under the bottom of the sea) and mainly used for burning to cook and heat

natural his·to·ry /ˌ··· ˈ···/ *n* [U] the study of plants, animals, and rocks, esp. as a subject of general interest

nat·u·ral·is·m /ˈnætʃərəlɪzəm/ *n* [U] **1 a** the idea that art and literature should show the world and people scientifically and exactly as they are **b** the quality of such art and writing **2** (the system of) thought which tries to explain everything by natural causes and laws

nat·u·ral·ist /ˈnætʃərəlǫst/ *n* **1** a person who studies plants or animals, esp. outdoors (not in a LABORATORY) **2** a person who believes in or practises NATURALISM in art or literature

nat·u·ral·is·tic /ˌnætʃərəˈlɪstɪk/ also **naturalist**— *adj* related to, showing, or practising NATURALISM: *a naturalistic writer/painting* —**~ally** *adv* [Wa4]

nat·u·ral·ize, -ise /ˈnætʃərəlaɪz/ *v* [T1 *often pass.*] **1** to make (a person born elsewhere) a citizen of a country: *He was naturalized after living in Britain for 10 years* **2** to bring (a plant or animal) into a new place to live like a native: *Some European birds have become naturalized in America* **3** to accept (a foreign word or phrase) as part of a language: *"*APROPOS*" is a French phrase now naturalized into/in English* —**-ization** /ˌnætʃərəlaɪˈzeɪʃən‖-lə-/ *n* [U]

natural law /ˌ··· ˈ·/ *n* [C;U] **1** (a) moral law regarded as fixed by the nature of the world and not dependent on the control of people **2** (a) scientific law about the behaviour of objects: *the natural law that gases become hot under pressure*

nat·u·ral·ly /ˈnætʃərəli‖-tʃərəli, -tʃərli/ *adv* **1** according to the nature of someone or something: *Her cheeks are naturally red* **2** without trying to look or sound different from usual: *Speak naturally when talking on the telephone* **3** in a manner to be expected; as a natural result: *The new safety laws naturally led to higher car prices* **4** of course; as one could have expected: *"Did you win the game?" "Naturally."|Naturally you will want to have a bath* **5 come naturally to** also (*infml*) **come natural to** —to be easy for or be easily learned by (someone): *She's a good player; the game seems to come naturally to her*

nat·u·ral·ness /ˈnætʃərəlnǫs/ *n* [U] the state or quality of being NATURAL[1] (1,2,3,4,5)

natural phi·los·o·phy /ˌ··· ·ˈ···/ *n* [U] *old use* science, esp. PHYSICS

natural re·sourc·es /ˌ··· ·ˈ··/ *n* [P] the land, forests, mineral wealth, etc., that a country possesses

natural sci·ence /ˌ··· ˈ··/ *n* **1** [U] BIOLOGY, chemistry, and PHYSICS **2** [C *usu. pl.*] any of these: *the natural sciences*

natural se·lec·tion /ˌ··· ·ˈ··/ also **survival of the fittest**— *n* [U] *tech* the course of events by which plants and animals best suited to the conditions around them live while those not suited to these conditions die

na·ture /ˈneɪtʃəʳ/ *n* **1** [U;C] **a** the qualities which make someone or something different from others; character: *What is the nature of the new chemical?| It's not in her nature to do anything rude; she's polite by nature* (=she has a polite nature) **b** (*usu. with* to+*verb*) one of these qualities: *It's his nature to be generous.|It's only human nature to like money* (=everyone likes money) **2** [S] type; kind; sort: *ceremonies of a solemn nature* **3** [U] (*often cap.*) the whole world, esp. as something lasting and not changed by people: *so quiet that all Nature seemed asleep|the beauties of nature* (=scenery)|*Some ancient peoples had nature gods* (=worshipped nature) **4** [U] also (*humor*) **Mother Nature**— the force which controls the world independently of people: *Cats are nature's/Mother Nature's way of limiting the number of mice.|Growing crops on this land is a struggle against nature* **5 call of nature** *euph* a need to pass water or waste matter from the body **6 let nature take its course** *infml* to allow events to happen, esp. to allow 2 people to fall in love, without help from anyone **7 state of nature a** the supposed unspoiled condition of people before civilization **b** *humor* NAKEDness —see also SECOND NATURE

na·tur·is·m /ˈneɪtʃərɪzəm/ *n* [U] NUDISM —**-ist** *n*

na·tu·ro·path /ˈneɪtʃərepæθ/ *n* a person who treats illness by such means as changing the food that people eat, and tries to help the body to cure itself without the use of dangerous drugs —**~ic** /ˌneɪtʃərəˈpæθɪk/ *adj* —**~ically** *adv* [Wa4] —**~y** /ˌneɪtʃəˈrɒpəθi‖-ˈrɑ-/ *n* [U]

naught /nɔːt‖nɔt, nɑt/ *n* **1** [C;U] NOUGHT (1) **2** [U] *old use & poet* nothing: *to care naught for it* (=to dislike or not to care about it) **3 come to naught** also **go for naught**— *lit* (as of a plan) to fail; bring no good result: *All his work came to naught when the fire destroyed the house he was building* **4 set at naught** *lit & old use* not care about or not fear

naugh·ty /ˈnɔːti‖ˈnɔti, ˈnɑti/ *adj* [Wa1] **1** bad in behaviour; not obeying a parent, teacher, etc.: **a** (of children or their actions): *You naughty boy! I told you not to play in the road.|It's naughty to pull your sister's hair* **b** *humor* (of grown-up people): *It was naughty of Father to stay out so late.|*(*esp. BrE*) *It was rather naughty of that scientist to mention only the people who agree with his ideas* **2** *euph* (esp. in newspapers) morally, esp. sexually, improper: *an amusing and naughty book* **3** *obs* bad; wicked —see WICKED (USAGE) —**-tily** *adv* —**-tiness** *n* [U]

nau·se·a /ˈnɔːzɪə, -sɪə‖-zɪə, -ʃə/ *n* [U] a feeling of sickness and desire to VOMIT (to cough up or throw up the contents of the stomach)

nau·se·ate /ˈnɔːzieɪt, -si-‖-zi, -ʒi-/ *v* [Wv4;T1] **1** to cause to feel NAUSEA: *a nauseating smell|He was nauseated by the movement of the ship* **2** to be hateful or very displeasing to (someone); SICKEN (1): *It's nauseating to see how he treats his children*

nau·se·ous /ˈnɔːzɪəs, -sɪəs‖-zɪəs, -ʃəs/ *adj* **1** causing NAUSEA: *a nauseous smell* **2** *AmE nonstandard* feeling NAUSEA or great distaste; NAUSEATEd: *Seeing violence always makes him nauseous* —**~ly** *adv* —**~ness** *n* [U]

nautch /nɔːtʃ/ *n* a show performed by trained dancing girls (**nautch girls**) in India

nau·ti·cal /ˈnɔːtɪkəl/ *adj* [Wa5] of or concerning sailors, ships, or the practice of sailing —**~ly** *adv* [Wa4]
nautical mile /ˌ··· ˈ·/ *n* a measure of distance, used at sea, equal to 1,852 metres
nau·ti·lus /ˈnɔːtləs/ also **chambered nautilus**— *n* **-luses** *or* **-li** /laɪ/ a type of small animal (MOLLUSC) of the South Pacific and Indian Oceans which lives in a growing SPIRAL-shaped shell
na·val /ˈneɪvəl/ *adj* [Wa5] of, concerning, or belonging to a navy or ships of war: *naval officer|naval battles|naval powers* (=countries with large navies)
nave /neɪv/ *n* the long central part of a church usu. between 2 AISLE*s* —see picture of CHURCH[1]
na·vel /ˈneɪvəl/ *n* [C] a small mark or sunken place in the middle of the stomach, left when the connection to the mother (the UMBILICAL CORD) was cut at birth —see picture at HUMAN[2]
navel or·ange /ˌ·· ˈ··/ *n* a type of large seedless orange, grown mostly in California, with a sunken place at the top that looks like a NAVEL
nav·i·ga·ble /ˈnævɪgəbəl/ *adj* **1** (of a river or other body of water) deep and wide enough to allow ships to travel: *The St Lawrence River is navigable from the Great Lakes to the sea* **2** *fml* (of a ship, vehicle, etc.) able to be guided in the direction desired; STEERable[2] (1): *With its engine broken down, the great ship wasn't navigable* —**-gability** /ˌnævɪgəˈbɪlɪti/ *n* [U]
nav·i·gate /ˈnævɪgeɪt/ *v* **1** [IØ;T1] to direct the course of (a ship, plane, etc.): *to navigate by the stars* (=using the positions of stars for a guide)| *Can that big ship be easy to navigate?*|(fig.) *Get in the car: I'll drive if you hold the map and navigate* **2** [T1] to go by sea, air, etc. from one side or end to the other of (a place): *the first man/machine to navigate the Atlantic by air|navigate a narrow sea passage*| (fig.) *When you walk down, be careful how you navigate the stairs!*
nav·i·ga·tion /ˌnævɪˈgeɪʃən/ *n* [U] **1** the act or practice of sailing, or of piloting an aircraft: *Navigation is difficult on this river because of the rocks* **2** the science of planning and keeping on a course on water or in the air from one place to another: *The compass is an instrument of navigation* **3** movement or traffic of ships or aircraft: *a passage open to navigation*
nav·i·ga·tor /ˈnævɪgeɪtəʳ/ *n* the officer on a ship or aircraft who has the job of recording and controlling its course
nav·vy /ˈnævi/ *n BrE* a labourer doing a heavy unskilled job in digging or building
na·vy /ˈneɪvi/ *n* **1** [(*the*) (G)C] (*sometimes cap.*) the organization, including ships, people, buildings, etc., which makes up the power of a country for war at sea: *The Navy wants/want more money for ships this year* **2** the ships of war belonging to a country: *a small navy of 10 ships*
navy blue /ˌ·· ˈ·◂/ also **navy**— *adj, n* [B;U] very dark blue (colour)
nay[1] /neɪ/ *adv* **1** *obs* no —opposite **yea** or **aye** **2** *lit* not only that but also (used for adding something stronger or more exact to what has been said): *a bright, nay (a) blinding light* **3 say someone nay** *lit* to forbid someone: *If he wants to smoke in his own house, who can say him nay?*
nay[2] *n* **1** a vote or voter against an idea, plan, law, etc.: *It took a long time to count the nays* **2 The nays have it!** (said in Parliament to declare that more people have voted no than yes) —opposite **aye**
Na·zi /ˈnɑːtsi, ˈnæ-/ *n* **Nazis** **1** a person belonging to the political party of Adolf Hitler which controlled Germany from 1933 to 1945 **2** *often derog* (*sometimes not cap.*) a person considered to be like a member of this party in beliefs or actions —**Nazi** *adj*: *a Nazi officer|the Nazi party|Nazi politics|a* NEO-*Nazi*
Naz·is·m /ˈnɑːtsɪzəm, ˈnæ-/ also **Na·zi·is·m** /ˈnɑːtsi-ɪzəm, ˈnæ-/— *n* [U] the political beliefs and methods of Hitler and the NAZI party
N B, n b *fml* (*used esp. in writing to begin a note*) nota bene; take notice; note well
NCO /ˌen siː ˈəʊ/ *n infml* NONCOMMISSIONED OFFICER: *He became an NCO at 18*
-nd *written suffix* (forms ORDINAL numbers with 2): *the 2nd* (=second) *of March|her 22nd birthday*
NE *written abbrev. for:* northeast(ern)
Ne·an·der·thal /niˈændətɑːl‖-dərəl, -tɑl/ *n infml & humor* a strong, heavy, hairy, and not clever man (as NEANDERTHAL MAN is regarded): *Tell that Neanderthal brother of yours to get his hair cut!*
Neanderthal man /·ˈ··· ·/ *n* [R;(C)] a type of early human creature who lived in Europe during the early STONE AGE
ne·a·pol·i·tan /nɪəˈpɒlɪtn‖-ˈpɑ-/ *adj* [Wa5] (of ice cream) in the shape of a brick with 3 or 4 bands of different colours and tastes
neap tide /ˈ· ·/ also **neap** /niːp/— *n* a very small rise and fall (TIDE) of the sea at or soon following the time of the first and third quarters of the moon —compare SPRING TIDE
near[1] /nɪəʳ/ *adj, adv, prep* [Wa1 (*to*)] (*the word* to *may be used with* nearer *and* nearest, *but not usu. with* near) not far from in distance, time, degree, quality, etc.; close (to): *the near future|an object in the near distance|Pick an apple from the nearest tree, the one nearest (to) the house.|a building near the station|How near is the station to here* (=from here)*?|His opinion is very near my own; it's nearer (to) my own than any other.|an attendance near 15,000 at the cricket match|a time (somewhere) near midnight|Don't go too near the edge of the cliff; just near enough to see over it.|Was your answer very near the right one?|She came near to tears* (=almost cried).|*Call me again nearer (to) the time of the meeting.|Nobody was near*
USAGE **near** and **close** are almost the same in meaning; but there are certain phrases in which each of these words is used before a particular noun and cannot be changed for the other. Notice *the near future|the near distance* (not **close**); *a close friend|a close* CONTACT (not **near**).
near[2] *adv* **nowhere near** also **not anywhere near**— *infml* not nearly: *The bus is nowhere near as dear as the train* (=it's much cheaper) —compare NOTHING **like**, NIGH (2)
near[3] *adj* [Wa1] **1** [B] in a close relation or association: *All my near relatives live abroad.|2 ideas in near relation* **2** [A] (of one of 2 things) **a** *esp. BrE* left-hand: *the near front wheel of a car* —opposite **off** **b** closer: *Can we fish from the near bank of the river, or must we cross over?* —opposite **far** **3 nearest and dearest** **a** (of a relative or friend) best-loved: *my nearest and dearest friend* **b** *pomp & humor* one's family: *Our nearest and dearest* (=our families) *need our care, don't they?* —**~ness** *n* [U (*to*)]
near[4] *v* [T1;IØ] to come closer in distance or time (to); APPROACH[1] (1,2): *He got more and more nervous as the day neared.|We could see the tall buildings as we neared New York*
near[5] *comb. form* **1** almost: *a near-perfect performance|music near-perfectly performed|a near-white colour* **2** closely: *2 near-related ideas* **3** something almost the stated thing: *a near-war* (=violence almost as bad as a war)
near·by[1] /nɪəˈbaɪ‖nɪər-/ *adv, prep* [Wa5;F] near; close by; a short distance away (from): *a football match being played nearby*

near·by² /ˈnɪəbaɪ‖ˈnɪər-/ *adj* [Wa5;A] near; within a short distance: *a nearby post-box*

Near East /ˌ· ˈ·/ *n* [*the*+R] **1** the countries around the eastern Mediterranean Sea, esp. Turkey **2** the ARABIC-speaking countries of North Africa —compare FAR EAST, MIDDLE EAST —**~ern** *adj*

near·ly /ˈnɪəli‖ˈnɪərli/ *adv* **1** almost; not quite or not yet completely: *He* (*very*) *nearly died.*|*2 nearly equal amounts*|*"Is the job nearly finished?"*|*"The train was nearly full"* (SEU S.) **2** *rare* closely: *nearly related types of flowers*|*a question which concerns me nearly* **3 not nearly** *not fml* by no means; far from: *There are not nearly enough people here to do the job!* —see ALMOST (USAGE)

near miss /ˌ· ˈ·/ *n* **1** a bomb, shot, etc., which does not hit exactly the right spot but comes close to it **2** *not fml* something which fails but almost succeeds, or which fails to be completely successful: *He thought his idea was the best, but it was a near miss: it only won second prize*

near·side /ˈnɪəsaɪd‖ˈnɪər-/ *adj* [A] *esp. BrE* being on the left-hand side, esp. of an animal or of a car, road, etc.: *the nearside back light of a car* —opposite **offside**

near·sight·ed /ˌnɪəˈsaɪtɪ̵d◂‖ˈnɪərsaɪtɪ̵d/ *adj esp. AmE* SHORTSIGHTED —**~ly** *adv* —**~ness** *n* [U]

near thing /ˌ· ˈ·/ also **close thing**— *n* [*usu. sing.*] *infml* a game, election, risk taken, attack, etc., which is almost not won or not successful: *What a near thing that was! My enemies nearly got me!* —compare CLOSE **run** THING, CLOSE CALL

neat /niːt/ *adj* [Wa1] **1** in good order; arranged well; showing care in appearance; tidy: *neat handwriting*|*He keeps his office neat* **2** liking order and good arrangement; orderly: *Cats are neat animals* **3** simple and exact; ELEGANT (3): *a neat description* **4** clever and effective: *a neat trick* **5** *AmE infml* very good; very pleasant; fine: *a neat bicycle*|*It was a really neat party: I enjoyed myself* **6** [Wa5] *infml* (*AmE* usu. **straight**) (of alcoholic drinks) without ice or water or other liquid: *I like my* WHISKY *neat* —**~ly** *adv* —**~ness** *n* [U]

'neath /niːθ/ *prep poet* beneath

neb·u·la /ˈnebjʊlə‖-bjə-/ *n* **-lae** /liː/ *or* **-las** **1** a mass of gas and dust in space among the stars, appearing often as a bright cloud at night **2** a mass of stars (GALAXY) which has this appearance

neb·u·lar /ˈnebjʊləʳ‖-bjə-/ *adj* of, related to, or like a NEBULA

neb·u·lous /ˈnebjʊləs‖-bjə-/ *adj* **1** not clear, esp. in meaning or expression: VAGUE (1,2); not DISTINCT (2): *nebulous political ideas* **2** like a cloud; cloudy: *a nebulous liquid* —**-losity** /ˌnebjʊˈlɒsɪ̵ti‖-bjəˈlɑ-/ *n* [U]: *the nebulosity of his ideas* —**~ly** /ˈnebjʊləsli‖ˈnebjə-/ *adv* —**~ness** *n* [U]: *the nebulousness of his ideas*

ne·ces·sa·ries /ˈnesɪ̵səriz‖-seriz/ *n* [P] things which are needed: *enough money for the necessaries* (*of life*)*: food, clothing, and shelter*

USAGE Things that one needs are **necessaries**; things that one would die if one did not have are **necessities**, a much stronger word: *a few* **necessaries** *for the journey, like socks and a hairbrush*|*Water is a* **necessity** *of life.*

ne·ces·sar·i·ly /ˈnesɪ̵sərɪ̵li, ˌnesɪ̵ˈserɪ̵li‖ˌnesɪ̵ˈserɪ̵li/ *adv* in a way that must be so; unavoidably: *Good-looking food doesn't necessarily taste good* (=it might sometimes taste bad)

ne·ces·sa·ry /ˈnesɪ̵səri‖-seri/ *adj* **1** [(*to, for*)] that must be had or obtained; needed: *Food is necessary for life.*|*the power necessary to a government*|*to make the necessary laws*|*It's necessary for him to go* **2** [Wa5] that must be; that cannot be different or avoided; determined or fixed by the nature of things: *Death is the necessary end of life* **3 necessary evil** *not fml* something bad or unpleasant which, however, produces good results that could not be obtained in any other way: *I don't like working such long hours, but it's a necessary evil until we've saved enough for a car*

ne·ces·si·tate /nɪ̵ˈsesɪ̵teɪt/ *v* [T1,4] *fml* to cause a need for; make necessary: *Your remarks may necessitate my thinking about the question again.*|*A smaller car is necessitated by the high price of petrol*

ne·ces·si·tous /nɪ̵ˈsesɪ̵təs/ *adj pomp & euph* **1** poor; NEEDY: *a necessitous family* **2** *fml* necessary and urgent: *no money except for the most necessitous reasons* —**~ly** *adv*

ne·ces·si·ty /nɪ̵ˈsesɪ̵ti/ *n* **1** [S;U: (*of, for,* 3)] the condition of being necessary, needed, or unavoidable; need: *Is there any necessity for another election?*|*He'll never learn German until the necessity arises* (=until he needs to learn it).|*We're faced with the necessity of buying* (=we have to buy) *a new car.*|*You must understand the necessity of*/*the necessity to get a good education.*|*There's a necessity for hard work in this office!*|*There is no necessity for rudeness: you can be polite even if you disagree* **2** [C] something that is necessary: *Food and clothing are necessities of life* **3** [U] the condition of being poor or in need: *He was forced by necessity to steal a loaf of bread* **4 make a virtue of necessity a** to act as if something that has to be done is done by one's own choice **b** to try to get some good results from an unpleasant but unavoidable state of affairs: *Since we have to spend some time in Foulchester anyhow, let's make a virtue of necessity by visiting the 11th-Century castle* **5 of/by necessity** unavoidably; necessarily

neck¹ /nek/ *n* **1** [C] the part of the body between the head and shoulders —see picture at HUMAN² **2** [U;C] this part of the body of an animal, used as food: *neck of lamb*|*best end of neck* **3** [C] the part of a garment for this part of the human body: *the neck of a shirt* **4** [C] the part of something which is shaped like this part of the body: *the neck of a bottle*|*the neck of a* VIOLIN **5** [C] a narrow piece of land or water: *a neck of land coming out from the coast* (=CAPE) **6 break one's neck** *infml* to work very hard: *Don't break your neck on this job: it's not urgent* **7 breathe down someone's neck** *sl* **a** to get very close to someone **b** to watch or control someone too closely **8 by a neck** *infml* (to win, lose, etc.) by a little or at only a short distance from another **9 get it in the neck** *infml* to be severely scolded or punished: *You'll get it in the neck if you wreck your father's car* **10 neck and crop** completely (esp. (in cricket) in the phr. **bowl someone neck and crop**) **11 neck and neck** *infml* (of 2 horses, people, etc., in competition) equal so far; with an equal chance of winning **12 neck of the woods** *sl, esp. AmE* area or part of the country: *People don't do that sort of thing in my neck of the woods!* **13 risk one's neck** to endanger one's life **14 save one's neck** *infml* to save one's head from being cut off; save oneself from any punishment **15 stick one's neck out** *infml* to take a risk; say or do something which may fail, be wrong, or hurt one: *A politician supporting an unpopular law is sticking his neck out: he may lose the next election* **16 up to one's neck** (**in**) also **up to one's ears** (**in**)— *infml* busy (with), deeply concerned (with or by): *I'm up to my neck in debt* (=I owe a lot of money)

neck² *v* [IØ] *infml* to kiss, CARESS, etc., but without having full sexual relations: *a boy and girl necking in the back of a car*|*She likes necking, but she won't go all the way*

neck·band /ˈnekbænd/ *n* (on a piece of clothing) a narrow piece which fits around the neck

-necked /nekt/ *comb. form* (of a piece of clothing) having a neck in the stated shape or condition: *a V-necked dress|an open-necked shirt* (=with the collar unbuttoned)|*She wore a low-necked dress that showed more than her neck*

neck·er·chief /ˈnekətʃɪ̵f‖-ər-/ *n* a square of cloth which is folded and worn around the neck

neck·lace /ˈnek-lɪ̵s/ *n* a string of jewels, BEADS, PEARLS, etc., or a chain of gold, silver, etc., worn around the neck as an ornament esp. by women

neck·let /ˈnek-lɪ̵t/ *n* a short NECKLACE

neck·line /ˈnek-laɪn/ *n* the line made by the neck opening of a piece of women's clothing

neck·tie /ˈnektaɪ/ *n esp. AmE* TIE

neck·wear /ˈnek-weəʳ/ *n* [U] (*used in shops*) pieces of clothing (esp. TIES) worn around the neck: *You'll find it in our neckwear department on the 5th floor*

nec·ro·man·cer /ˈnekrəmænsəʳ/ *n lit* a person who practises NECROMANCY

nec·ro·man·cy /ˈnekrəmænsi/ *n* [U] *lit* **1** the practice which claims to learn about the future by talking with the dead **2** magic, esp. evil magic

nec·ro·phil·i·a /ˌnekrəʊˈfɪlɪə, -rə-/ also **ne·croph·i·lis·m** /nɪ̵ˈkrɒfɪ̵lɪzəm‖-ˈkrɑ-/— *n* [U] *tech* (too) great interest in the dead, esp. sexual attraction felt by someone towards dead bodies

nec·ro·phil·i·ac /ˌnekrəʊˈfɪliæk, -rə-/ *n tech* a person who suffers from NECROPHILIA

ne·crop·o·lis /nɪ̵ˈkrɒpəlɪ̵s‖-ˈkrɑ-/ *n lit* a large burial ground (CEMETERY), esp. that of an ancient city

nec·tar /ˈnektəʳ/ *n* [U] **1** (in ancient Greek and Roman literature) the drink of the gods —compare AMBROSIA **2** a sweet and good-tasting drink: (fig.) *taste the nectar of success* (=enjoy one's success) **3** the sweet liquid collected by bees from flowers

nec·ta·rine /ˈnektəriːn‖ˌnektəˈriːn/ *n* a kind of small and hard PEACH (a sweet fruit) with a smooth skin

née /neɪ/ *adv Fr* (*used after a married woman's name and before her original family name*) formerly named; at first having the name; born with the name: *Mrs Robert Cook née Carol Williams|Mrs Carol Cook née Williams*

need¹ /niːd/ *n* **1** [S;U:(*of, for*)] a/the condition of lacking or wanting something necessary or very useful: *children's need for milk|no need for such a new law|people in need of help|help in time of need|a need for good government* **2** [U;S: (*for,* 3)] (a) necessary duty; what must be done; OBLIGATION: *a/the need for taxes to pay for public spending|No need to go yet: it's still early* **3** [C *usu. pl.*] *esp. fml* something necessary to have: *supply all our needs* (=*our every need*) **4** [U] *fml & euph* the state of not having enough food or money; POVERTY (1): *illness, need, and other troubles of the world* **5 a friend in need** *not fml* a true friend, who comes to help one in trouble **6 have need of** *fml* to need **7 if need be** if it's necessary; if I, we, etc., must: *I must finish this job! I'll work all night if need be* **8 when/as/if the need arises** at any time when it is necessary or when something is needed: *take money from the bank as the need arises*

need² *v* [Wv6;T1,3,4;V3,8, (*N Eng E*) 4] to have a need for; want for some useful purpose; lack; REQUIRE: *Children need milk.|This soup needs salt.|My coat needs mending/needs to be mended.|You need to learn the value of money.|I need my coat mended*=(*N Eng E*) *I need my coat mending.|This job needs a lot of care, attention, and time.|I need you to work for me, young man!|She likes to feel needed.|*(fig.) *That young thief needs* (*a good*) *beating!|No one under 18 needs to come for the job; they can write a letter.|Do you think I need to go to the meeting? It's so far away!|You didn't need to tell him the news; it just made him sad.|I'll need to work very hard tonight*

need³ *v, neg. contr.* **needn't** [Wv2,6;I∅,2 *non-assertive*] to have to: *We needn't go yet; the show doesn't start for an hour* (=we don't have to go yet).|*Need you go so soon?|I dressed very warmly for the trip, but I needn't have* (*done so*)*; the weather was hot.|No one under 18 need come for the job* (=it's for someone older).|*You needn't talk so loud* (=you don't have to talk so loud=you shouldn't talk so loud).|*Do you think I need go to the meeting? It's so far away!|You needn't have told him the news; he knew it already.|"Need I go?" "No, you needn't"*
USAGE 1 Books often tell one to say *I didn't* **need** *to go* (=so I didn't go) and *I* **needn't** *have gone* (=but I did go). In fact, when someone says *I didn't* **need** *to go* one does not know whether he went or not, although if he says *I* **needn't** *have gone*, one knows that he went. 2 In neg. and question sentences there is a choice between the 2 verb patterns with **need**: **Need** *he study?*=*Does he* **need** *to study?|He* **needn't** *study*=*He doesn't* **need** *to study*. There is only one way to make a POSITIVE statement with **need**: *He* **needs** *to study*. —see MUSTN'T (USAGE)

need·ful /ˈniːdfəl/ *adj now rare* necessary; needed: *the instruments needful for his work* —**~ly** *adv*

nee·dle¹ /ˈniːdl/ *n* **1** a long metal pin used in sewing for pulling thread, with a sharp point at one end and a hole in the other end for the thread **2** a thin pointed object that seems to look like this: *a* PINE *needle* (=a thin leaf of this tree)|*an* ACUPUNCTURE *needle* —see picture at TREE¹ **3** any of various thin rods with points or hooks used in working with long threadlike pieces of wool or other cloth: KNIT*ting needles* **4** (in a RECORD PLAYER) the very small pointed jewel or piece of metal which touches a record as it turns and picks up the sound recorded on it; STYLUS **5** a very thin hollow pointed tube (at the end of a HYPODERMIC **syringe**) which is pushed into someone's skin to put a liquid (esp. medicine) into the body **6** a long thin pointer fixed to the centre of a usu. circular surface: *The needle of the compass shows that we're facing north* **7 needle in a haystack** *infml* something very small which is hard to find in a big place

needle² *v infml* **1** [T1;I∅] to push through (something) with or as if with a needle: *She needled the wool rapidly through the sock she was mending* **2** [T1 (*about, into*)] to annoy (someone) by repeated unkind remarks, jokes, etc., esp. in order to influence; PROVOKE (1); TEASE (1): *The boys always needled Jim about being fat, but they never could needle him into eating less* **3** [T1] to push (one's way) through a small space or small spaces; thread: *They needled their way through the crowd*

need·less /ˈniːdləs/ *adj* **1** not needed; unnecessary: *Your worries are needless: I'll be all right.|needless trouble preparing for guests who didn't come* **2 needless to say** *not fml* of course; as was to be expected: *Needless to say, it rained when I left my car windows open*

need·less·ly /ˈniːdləsli/ *adv* without a reason; unnecessarily: *She was needlessly rude: I had said nothing to annoy her.|Let's not argue needlessly: the question is already settled*

nee·dle·wom·an /ˈniːdlˌwʊmən/ *n* **-women** /ˌwɪmɪ̵n/ a woman who sews (skilfully): *She's a good cook, but not a needlewoman* (=does not sew well)

nee·dle·work /ˈniːdlwɜːk‖-wɜrk/ *n* [U] **1** sewing and EMBROIDERY; work, esp. fancy work, done with needle and thread: *tired eyes from doing fine* *needlework* **2** examples of this work: *chairs covered with needlework*

need·n't /ˈniːdnt/ *contr. of* NEED[3] not: *You needn't do it if you don't want to.|You needn't have told him the news: he knew it already* —see CONTR. (USAGE)

needs /niːdz/ *adv old use or humor* necessarily (in the phrs. **must needs** or **needs must**): *Your fool of a brother must needs telephone just as we were going out!*

need·y /ˈniːdi/ *adj* [Wa1;B;*the*+P] poor in money; in need of food, clothing, etc.; not having enough to live on: *a needy family|those who are poor and needy|money to help the needy* —**neediness** *n* [U]

ne'er /neəʳ/ *adv poet* never: *Will he ne'er come home again?*

ne'er-do-well /ˈneə duː ˌwel‖ˈneər-/ *n* **-wells** *derog* a useless or lazy person who never does any good work

ne·far·i·ous /nɪˈfeərɪəs/ *adj fml* against laws or moral principles; wicked; evil: *a nefarious plan to cheat his own company|a nefarious criminal* —**~ly** *adv* —**~ness** *n* [U]

neg. /neg/ *abbrev. for:* NEGATIVE

ne·gate /nɪˈgeɪt/ *v* [T1] **1** to cause to have no effect or force; NEUTRALIZE: *to negate the effect of the cold by wearing 2 pairs of socks* **2** to disprove the truth or fact of; DENY (1) —**-gation** /nɪˈgeɪʃən/ *n* [U;C]

neg·a·tive[1] /ˈnegətɪv/ *adj* **1 a** refusing, doubting, or disapproving; saying or meaning "no": *a negative answer to my request|(fml) I have a negative opinion of/on the value of this idea* (=I don't think it's good) **b** containing one of the words "no", "not", "nothing", "never", etc.: *negative expressions like "not at all"* —opposite **affirmative** **2** without any active, useful, or helpful qualities: *negative advice that only tells you what not to do* **3** showing the lack of what was looked for, hoped for, or expected: *I'm looking for an honest man, but with negative results so far* (=I haven't found one).|*(med) The test for bacteria was negative* (=none were found) **4** (of or in electricity) of the type that is based on ELECTRONs and is produced by rubbing RESIN with wool **5** (of a photograph or film) showing dark places in nature as light and light places as dark **6 a** (of a number or quantity) less than zero: *a negative profit* (=a loss)|*If* x *is* POSITIVE *then* −x *is negative* **b** of or concerning such a quantity: *the negative sign* (=the sign −) **7** *med* having no RHESUS FACTOR (in the blood): *The baby's mother was negative, but I'm not sure about the father* —opposite **positive** —**~ly** *adv*

negative[2] *n* **1** a statement saying or meaning "no"; a refusal or DENIAL: *The answer to my request was a strong negative* —opposite **affirmative** **2** one of the words and expressions "no", "not", "nothing", "never", "not at all", etc.: *A short sentence should usually have no more than one negative in it* **3** a NEGATIVE[1] (5) photograph or film **4 in the negative a** against a question to be decided: *The vote was in the negative* **b** with the answer "no": *The answer to my request was in the negative* **5 in(to) the negative** (so as to be) containing a NEGATIVE[2] (2): *Please put that statement in(to) the negative*

negative[3] *v* [T1] *infml* **1** [*often pass.*] to decide or vote against; refuse to accept: *The plan was negatived by (vote of) the committee* **2** NEGATE

negative pole /ˌ··· ˈ·/ *n* **1** (of a MAGNET) the end which naturally turns away from the earth **2** CATHODE

ne·glect[1] /nɪˈglekt/ *v* **1** [T1,4] to give no or too little attention or care to: *a neglected poet whose poems are not often read|The government has neglected socializing industry* **2** [T3,4] to fail (to do something), esp. because of carelessness or forgetfulness: *Don't neglect to lock the door /locking the door when you leave*

neglect[2] *n* [U] **1** the action of NEGLECTing: *the owner's neglect of repairs to his house* **2** the condition or fact of being NEGLECTed: *an old person living in unhappy neglect*

ne·glect·ful /nɪˈglektfəl/ *adj* in the habit of NEGLECTing things; forgetful or careless: *a mother who is neglectful of her children* —**~ly** *adv* —**~ness** *n* [U]

neg·li·gee /ˈneglɪ̆ʒeɪ‖ˌneglɪ̆ˈʒeɪ/ *n* a woman's light and usu. fancy NIGHTDRESS

neg·li·gence /ˈneglɪdʒəns/ *n* [U] **1** the quality of being NEGLIGENT; carelessness **2** *law* the offence of not taking necessary or expected care: *guilty of criminal* (=punishable) *negligence*

neg·li·gent /ˈneglɪdʒənt/ *adj* **1** not taking or showing enough care; NEGLECTFUL: *He's been negligent in not locking the doors as he was told to do.|a negligent way of doing business* **2** needing or showing little or no effort; careless in a usu. pleasant way: *to dress with negligent grace* —**~ly** *adv*

neg·li·gi·ble /ˈneglɪdʒəbəl/ *adj* too slight or unimportant to make any difference or to be worth any attention: *a negligible amount of rain* (=not enough to measure)|*The damage to my car is negligible* —**-bly** *adv*

ne·go·ti·a·ble /nɪˈgəʊʃɪəbəl, -ʃə-/ *adj* **1** open to being settled or changed by being NEGOTIATED: *a negotiable contract|He says his claim is not negotiable* **2** *infml* that can be passed through, along, etc., or dealt with: *a steep, hardly negotiable hill* **3** (of a cheque or order to pay money) that can be exchanged for money **4 negotiable instrument** *tech* BILL OF EXCHANGE

ne·go·ti·ate /nɪˈgəʊʃieɪt/ *v* **1** [IØ (*on, over, with, for*),3] to talk with another person or group in order to settle a question or disagreement; try to come to an agreement: *The government has had to negotiate with the opposition party on/over the new law.|The trade union is negotiating with the employers to get a better contract* **2** [T1 (*with*)] to produce (an agreement) or settle (a piece of business) in this way: *The trade union negotiated a new contract with the owner* **3** [T1] *infml* **a** to go safely over, through, along, etc.: *Will this small car negotiate that steep hill?* **b** to deal with; have success with: *a player negotiating a hard piece of music* **4** [T1] *tech* to get or give money for (an order to pay money such as a cheque): *I'm sorry: our bank doesn't negotiate foreign cheques* —**-ator** *n*

ne·go·ti·a·tion /nɪˌgəʊʃiˈeɪʃən/ *n* **1** [U;C *often pl. with sing. meaning*] an act or the action of negotiating (NEGOTIATE (2)): *The agreement was the result of long negotiation=a long negotiation=long negotiations.|the negotiation of a new contract|The contract is under negotiation* (=now being settled) **2** [U9] the successful completion of a usu. difficult trip or other activity: *Negotiation of the wet road was not easy* **3** [U] *tech* an exchange for money: *the negotiation of a cheque*

Ne·gress /ˈniːgrɪ̆s/ *n tech or not polite* a NEGRO woman

Ne·gro /ˈniːgrəʊ/ *n* **-es** *tech or not polite* a person who has black or dark skin by race; BLACK person

ne·gus /ˈniːgəs/ *n* [U] a type of drink made from hot water and wine, sugar, and SPICE

neigh /neɪ/ *v, n* [IØ;C] (to make) the loud and long cry that a horse makes

neigh·bour, *AmE* **-bor** /ˈneɪbəʳ/ *n* one of 2 or more people that are near one another: *my next-door* *neighbour* (= living in the house next to mine)

neigh·bour·hood, *AmE* **-borhood** /ˈneɪbəhʊd‖-ər-/ *n* **1** [GC] a group of people and their homes forming a small area within a larger place such as a town: *a quiet neighbourhood with good shops|a neighbourhood school* **2** [(*the*) S] the area around a point or place (esp. in the phr. **in the neighbourhood (of)**): *You'll find it somewhere in the neighbourhood (of the station).*|(fig.) *He paid in the neighbourhood of £500 for the car*

neigh·bour·ing, *AmE* **-boring** /ˈneɪbərɪŋ/ *adj* [Wa5;A] (as of places) near or close by: *a bus service between the town and the neighbouring villages*

neigh·bour·ly, *AmE* **-borly** /ˈneɪbəli‖-ər-/ *adj* **1** friendly; like (that of) a good neighbour: *to speak in a neighbourly way* **2** of, among, or concerning neighbours: *a neighbourly duty to keep one's house looking neat* —**-liness** *n* [U]

neighbour on, *AmE* **-bor on** *v prep* [T1 *no pass.*] (of a piece of land or a place) to be near or esp. next to: *Our farm neighbours on a large stretch of woods*

nei·ther[1] /ˈnaɪðəʳ‖ˈniː-/ *pron* (*sometimes used after a* PRONOUN) not one and not the other of 2: *"Which of the books did you like?" "Neither (of them)! They were both dull."|2 books that are neither of them very good* (= neither is good)|(*They*) *neither of them wanted to go.|"There was no meeting of minds because neither could get the wave-length of the other"* (SEU W.)

neither[2] *conj* (used before the first of 2 or more choices which are expressed by like noun phrases, verb phrases, etc., separated by "nor") not either: *neither by day nor by night* (= never)|*He neither ate, drank, nor smoked; he liked neither the meal nor the cigarettes.|Neither my father nor I were there* —compare EITHER . . . OR

neither[3] *determiner* not one and not the other of 2: *Neither road out of town is very good, but this one is better than the other one.|"Neither man spoke"* (SEU W.) —compare EITHER[1] (1), NONE[1] (2)

neither[4] *adv* (*used in answer to or in addition to an expression or sentence with* no, not, never, *etc.*) nor; no more; also not: *"I can't swim!" "Neither can I!"* = (*infml*) *"Me neither!"* (= I can't, either)|*Just as I haven't good eyes, so neither has my son, neither have my children*

USAGE Notice the word order of *Neither/Nor can I,* which is the same as that of a question. Also *Never have I heard. . . .|Nowhere have I found . . .* —see EITHER (USAGE).

nel·son /ˈnelsən/ *n* (in WRESTLING) a way of holding an opponent by putting one arm (a **half nelson**) or both arms (a **full nelson**) under the opponent's arm(s) and pressing the back of his neck with the hand(s)

nem con /ˌnem ˈkɒn‖-ˈkɑn/ *adv Lat & law* without any opposition; UNANIMOUSly: *The suggestion was accepted nem con by the committee*

nem·e·sis /ˈneməsəs/ *n* **-ses** /siːz/ *lit* **1** [U] (*sometimes cap.*) just and esp. unavoidable punishment, often considered as a goddess or an active force **2** [C9] **a** a person who carries out such punishment **b** a powerful enemy or opponent

ne·o- /ˈniːəʊ, ˈniːə/ *prefix* (*used before nouns, adjectives, and sometimes adverbs*) new; a new, recent, or later, and different kind of (an older language, idea, or system): *Neo-Latin* (= Latin used in modern speech or writing)|*neo*-FASCISM (= since 1945)|NEOCLASSICAL

ne·o·clas·sic·al /ˌniːəʊˈklæsɪkəl/ *adj tech* done more recently, but in the (CLASSICAL) style of a particular former time considered to have set a standard of artistic purity, esp. **a** (of building, painting, and literature) in the style of ancient Greece and Rome: *Palladio's wonderful 16th-century neoclassical buildings* **b** (of music) in the style of the 18th century: *Stravinsky's 20th-century music for "Pulcinella," based on the earlier music of Pergolesi, is neoclassical*

ne·o·co·lo·ni·al·is·m /ˌniːəʊkəˈləʊnɪəlɪzəm/ *n* [U] **1** in powerful countries, an act or the idea of controlling the new countries of Asia, Africa, and South America (former colonies (COLONY)) by trade or other means which are not political or military **2** the trading and political practices by which a powerful country indirectly keeps or enlarges its control over esp. recently independent countries, without the need of military force

ne·o·lith·ic /ˌniːəˈlɪθɪk/ *adj* [Wa5] *tech* of, being, or concerning the latest period of the STONE AGE, when people began to settle in villages, grow crops, keep animals, polish stone for tools, and use the wheel: *neolithic villages*

ne·ol·o·gis·m /niːˈɒlədʒɪzəm‖-ˈɑl-/ *n* **1** [C] a new word or expression: *In the 17th century, "gas" was a scientific neologism* **2** [C] a new meaning for a word: *The use of "gay" to mean* HOMOSEXUAL *is a neologism* **3** [U] the use of such new words or meanings: *Try to avoid neologism in formal writing*

ne·on /ˈniːɒn‖-ɑn/ *n* [U] a chemically inactive gas that is a simple substance (ELEMENT) found in small amounts in the air

ne·o·nate /ˈniːəneɪt/ *n med* a baby that has just been born

neon light /ˈ·· ·/ also **neon lamp**— *n* a glass tube filled with NEON which lights when an electric current goes through it, often twisted to form shapes in a sign (a **neon sign**)

ne·o·phyte /ˈnɪəfaɪt/ *n* **1** a student of an art, skill, trade, etc., with no experience; BEGINNER; NOVICE **2 a** a new member of a religious group; PROSELYTE **b** a new priest or MONK in the ROMAN CATHOLIC Church

ne·o·plas·m /ˈniːəʊplæzəm, ˈnɪə-/ *n* [C;(U)] a growth of flesh having no purpose in the body; TUMOUR

neph·ew /ˈnevjuː, ˈnef-‖ˈnef-/ *n* **1** the son of one's brother or sister **2** the son of one's wife's or husband's brother or sister —compare NIECE; see TABLE OF FAMILY RELATIONSHIPS

ne·phri·tis /nɪˈfraɪtəs/ *n* [U] *med* a type of disease of the KIDNEYs

ne plus ul·tra /ˌniː plʌs ˈʌltrə, ˌneɪ-/ *n* [U9, esp. *of;* (S)] *Lat & lit* **1** the point of highest quality that can be reached: *Bach's work is perhaps the ne plus ultra of church music* **2** the best or greatest degree (of a quality): *suffer the ne plus ultra of shame*

nep·o·tis·m /ˈnepətɪzəm/ *n* [U] the practice of favouring one's relatives when one has power or a high office, esp. by giving them good jobs

Nep·tune /ˈneptjuːn‖-tuːn/ *n* [R] the PLANET 8th in order from the sun —see picture at PLANET

Ner·e·id /ˈnɪəri-ɪd/ *n* (in ancient Greek literature) a young nature goddess (NYMPH) living in the sea

nerve[1] /nɜːv‖nɜrv/ *n* **1** [C] any of the threadlike parts of the body which form a system to carry feelings and messages to and from the brain **2** [U] strength or control of mind; courage: *a man of nerve|a test of nerve* **3** [U;S] *derog* boldness, esp. boldness which is rude or disrespectful; EFFRONTERY (1): *He's the worst-dressed man I know, and he has the nerve to tell me my shoes need a shine! The nerve of him!|What a nerve!|Some nerve!* **4** [C] a sore or sensitive subject (esp. in such phrs. as **hit/touch a nerve**): *I'm afraid I hit a nerve when I mentioned her dead mother, and she began to cry* **5** [C] any of the stiff lines on a leaf or an insect's wing; VEIN **6 lose one's nerve** *infml* to become afraid or lose the courage to do something: *I wanted to write an angry letter but I lost my nerve when I sat down to do it* **7 strain every nerve** *not fml* to try as hard as possible

nerve² *v* [T1] to give courage to (someone, esp. oneself): *He nerved himself for battle by thinking about past victories*

nerve cell /ˈ· ·/ *n* any of the cells that form part of the NERVOUS SYSTEM, usu. including long threadlike branches which come out from them and carry messages to and from the body of the cell

nerve cen·tre /ˈ· ˌ··/ *n* **1** *not fml* the place from which a system, organization, etc., is controlled **2** a group of NERVE CELL*s* with the same purpose; GANGLION

nerve·less /ˈnɜːvləs‖ˈnɜr-/ *adj infml* **1** weak or without courage or power **2** not becoming nervous; COOL¹ (3) —**~ly** *adv* —**~ness** *n* [U]

nerve-rack·ing, -wracking /ˈ· ˌ··/ *adj infml* difficult to do or bear calmly because annoying and tiring to the mind, or dangerous: *a nerve-racking journey through the high mountains*

nerves /nɜːvz‖nɜrvz/ *n* [P] *infml* **1** self-control, patience, or balance of mind: *Have you the nerves for this delicate and dangerous work?* **2** a condition of great nervousness: *He is/has a bad case of nerves* (=he's very nervous).|*She gets nerves before every examination* **3 get on someone's nerves** to make someone annoyed or bad-tempered: *I can't study with that loud music getting on my nerves* **4 My nerves will crack** I shall be unable to continue to behave calmly: *My nerves will crack if the baby cries much longer* **5 war of nerves** a test of the opponent's strength of will or purpose

ner·vous /ˈnɜːvəs‖ˈnɜr-/ *adj* **1** [(*about*)] **a** excited and anxious; worried: *Don't be nervous! The doctor wants to help you* **b** of or resulting from this kind of condition: *a nervous movement* (=shaking) *of the hands*|*nervous* ENERGY|*a nervous smile* **c** (of a person) easily excited and worried: *He's too nervous a person to talk in front of a large group of people* **2** of or related to the NERVOUS SYSTEM of the body, or to the feelings: *a nervous disease* **3** [(*of*)] *BrE* slightly afraid; TIMID: *nervous of going too near the wild animals* **4 make someone nervous a** to annoy someone: *You're making me nervous with your continual singing* **b** to make someone worried: *You're making me nervous with your stories of how hard the examination is* —**~ly** *adv* —**~ness** *n* [U]

USAGE Compare **nervous**, **anxious**, and **upset**: *The child was* **nervous** *of the big dog.*|*I'm always* **nervous** *when I have to make a speech.*|*Your mother will be* **anxious** *until she hears you're safe.*|*I was very* **upset** *when the dog died.* One is **nervous** (=rather afraid) while something is happening, **anxious** (=worried) when one fears what might happen, and **upset** (=rather unhappy and displeased) because of something that has happened. Do not use **upset** about great sorrows; it is a dog that has died, not a child.

nervous break·down /ˌ·· ˈ··/ *n not fml* an unnatural condition of deep worrying, anxiety, weeping, and tiredness which stops one from doing one's ordinary work: *She had a nervous breakdown a few months ago, but she's looking much healthier now*

nervous sys·tem /ˈ·· ˌ··/ *n* (in animals) the system (=the brain, SPINAL CORD, NERVE*s*, and NERVE CENTRE*s*) which receives and passes on feelings, messages, and other such information from inside and outside the body

nerv·y /ˈnɜːvi‖ˈnɜr-/ *adj* [Wa1] *sl* **1** *BrE* nervous and anxious **2** *AmE* boldly rude; having NERVE¹ (3); BRASH

ness /nes/ *n* (usu. in names of places) a point of land stretching out into a body of water; PROMONTORY: *Dungeness in Kent*

-ness /nǝ̀s/ *suffix* [*adj*[esp. Wa1,2]→*n*[U;(C)]] the stated condition, quality or degree: *not so much loudness*|*health and illness*|*a great sadness*|*bigness*|KIND-HEARTED*ness*|COLD-BLOODED*ness*

nest¹ /nest/ *n* **1** a hollow place built or found by a bird for a home and a place to hold its eggs **2** the settled and protected home of any of certain other animals or insects: *an ants' nest*|(fig.) *The husband and wife built themselves a comfortable nest* **3** a protected place for hiding or evil activity: *The palace was a nest of crime* **4** a group of like objects which fit closely into or inside one another: *a nest of tables/boxes/spoons* **5** a protected position for one or more weapons (esp. in the phrase **machine-gun nest**)

nest² *v* **1** [IØ] to build or use a nest: *Most birds nest in trees* **2** [Wv5;T1;IØ] to (cause to) fit closely inside another thing or each other: *nested cooking pots*

nest egg /ˈ· ·/ *n not fml* an amount of money saved for future use: *a holiday nest egg* (=money to spend on a holiday) *of £100*

nest·ing /ˈnestɪŋ/ *n* [U] *BrE* searching for birds' nests, esp. in order to take eggs from them (esp. in the phr. **go nesting**)

nes·tle /ˈnesəl/ *v* [Wv3] **1** [L9, esp. DOWN] to settle into a warm, close, or comfortable position: *She nestled down* (*into the big chair*) *and began to read* **2** [L9] to lie or rest warmly, closely, or comfortably: *villages nestling among the mountains* **3** [Wv5;X9] to shelter, put, or press in a close comfortable position; CRADLE: *She nestled her head on/against his shoulder.*|*villages nestled among the mountains*

nestle up *v adv* [Wv3;IØ (*to, against*)] to settle in a close or warm position: *Nestle up* (*to me*), *children, and I'll tell you a story*

nest·ling /ˈnestlɪŋ, ˈneslɪŋ/ *n* a young bird who has not left the nest

Nes·tor /ˈnestɔːʳ, ˈnestəʳ/ *n* [*usu. sing.*] *lit* a wise old adviser: *He no longer wrote, but was a Nestor to young writers*

net¹ /net/ *n* **1** [U;C] a material of strings, wires, threads, etc. twisted, tied, or woven together with regular equal spaces between them —compare MESH **2** [C] any of various objects made from this, as **a** a large piece or surface spread out under water to catch fish **b** a carrier for heavy goods (**cargo net**) **c** a length dividing the 2 sides of the court in tennis, BADMINTON, etc. **d** an enclosure (the GOAL) in football, HOCKEY, etc.—see picture at TENNIS **3** [C] **a** a trap made from this: *a* BUTTERFLY *net* **b** anything like a trap that catches and holds: *caught in the net of fate* **4** [C] a network (esp. in the phrs. **radio net, communication(s) net**) **5** [C] a piece of material in a frame, used (as by firemen) for catching someone falling or jumping **6** [C *usu. sing.*] (in cricket) an act or period of practising in the NETS: *"I played very badly today," said the cricketer; "I must have a long net tomorrow"* **7** [A] (in cricket) of or done in the NETS: *net practice*

net² *v* **-tt- 1** [D1 (*for*);T1] to catch in or as if in a net: *netted no fish large enough to keep*|*She's netted* (*herself*) *a rich husband*|*netted a rich husband for herself* **2** [T1] to cover with a net: *Net the fruit trees to protect them from birds*

net³ *adj* [Wa5] **1** [A] (of an amount) when nothing further is to be subtracted: *net profit* (=after tax, rent, etc. are paid)|*net weight* (=of an object without its packet) —opposite **gross** **2** [A] when everything has been considered; FINAL (esp. in the phr. **net result**): *The net result of the tax changes was to make the rich even richer* **3** [B;E] (of a price) not allowed to be made lower: *The price of the book is £3 net: no bookshop will sell it for less*

net[4] *v* **-tt-** [D1 (*for*);T1] to gain as a profit: *The sale netted* (*the company*) *a fat profit/netted a fat profit for the company*

net[5] *n tech* a NET[3] amount, price, etc.: *The bill says "Net 30 days"* (=it must be paid in full within a month)

net·ball /ˈnetbɔːl/ *n* [U] a women's game in which teams make points by making a ball fall through one of the 2 high rings at the opposite ends of a court (related to BASKETBALL but not common in the USA)

neth·er /ˈneðəʳ/ *adj* [A] *lit or humor* **1** in the lower place; lower; under: *Her nether lip trembled* **2 the nether regions/world** (esp. in ancient literature) the home of the dead down inside the earth

neth·er·most /ˈneðəməʊst‖-ðər-/ *adj* [A] *lit* lowest: *The bottom of Africa is the nethermost point on this map*

nets /nets/ *n* [(*the*) P] (in cricket) one or more WICKETs surrounded by a net, in which people can practise BATting

nett /net/ *adj* [Wa5;B;E] *BrE* NET[3] (1, 3)

net·ting /ˈnetɪŋ/ *n* [U] string, wire, etc., made into a net: *a fence of wire netting*

net·tle[1] /ˈnetl/ *n* **1** any of various wild plants having leaves with hairs which may sting and make red marks on the skin: *a painful fall into a* BED (=group) *of nettles* **2 grasp the nettle** to deal boldly with an unpleasant job or subject

nettle[2] *v* [T1] to annoy (someone); make (someone) angry or impatient: *to nettle a speaker with rude questions*

nettle rash /ˈ·· ·/ *n* [C;U] an area of red spots on one's skin (a RASH) being or looking like the result of the stinging of a NETTLE: *I sometimes get* (*a*) *nettle rash from eating fish*

net·work /ˈnetwɜːk‖-wɜrk/ *n* **1** a large system of lines, tubes, wires, etc., that cross or meet one another: *Britain's railway network|a plant with a large network of roots|the network of bloodvessels in the body* **2** a group or system whose members are connected in some way: *a network of friends in different cities* **3 a** a group of radio or television stations in different places using many of the same broadcasts **b** a large company producing material for broadcasting by such a group: *a contract with one of the 3 big American networks*

neu·ral /ˈnjʊərəl‖ˈnʊərəl/ *adj med* of or related to the NERVOUS SYSTEM

neu·ral·gia /njʊˈrældʒə‖nʊ-/ *n* [U] *med* sharp pain along the length of one or more nerves, usu. in the head —**-gic** *adj*: *neuralgic pain*

neu·ras·the·ni·a /ˌnjʊərəsˈθiːnɪə‖ˌnʊərəs-/ *n* [U] *med, old use* a condition of tiredness of the nerves, marked by worry, DEPRESSION, and any of various other feelings of illness —compare NERVOUS BREAKDOWN

neu·ras·then·ic[1] /ˌnjʊərəsˈθenɪk‖ˌnʊərəs-/ *adj med, old use* of, related to, or suffering from NEURASTHENIA

neurasthenic[2] *n med, old use* a person with NEURASTHENIA

neu·ri·tis /njʊˈraɪtɪ̈s‖nʊ-/ *n* [U] *med* a type of disease of a nerve or its outer covering

neu·ro- /ˈnjʊərə‖ˈnʊərə/ also **neur-** /njʊər‖nʊər/— *prefix* of the nerves: *a* NEUROLOGIST|NEURALGIA

neu·rol·o·gist /njʊˈrɒlədʒɪ̈st‖nʊˈrɑ-/ *n* a doctor who treats or studies diseases of the NERVOUS SYSTEM

neu·rol·o·gy /njʊˈrɒlədʒi‖nʊˈrɑ-/ *n* [U] the scientific study of the NERVOUS SYSTEM, esp. of its diseases and their treatment

neu·ro·sis /njʊˈrəʊsɪ̈s‖nʊ-/ *n* **-ses** /siːz/ [U;C] *med* a disorder of the mind marked by strong unreasonable fears and ideas about the outside world, troubled relations with other people, and often by various feelings of illness in the body: *an anxiety neurosis*

neu·rot·ic[1] /njʊˈrɒtɪk‖nʊˈrɑ-/ *adj* marked by or related to NEUROSIS: *neurotic fears*

neurotic[2] *n* a person who is unbalanced in mind; someone with a NEUROSIS

neu·ter[1] /ˈnjuːtəʳ‖ˈnuː-/ *adj* **1** (in the grammar of many languages) in or related to a class (GENDER) of words (esp. nouns, PRONOUNs, and adjectives) not connected to male or female qualities: *a neuter noun/ending* **2** (of plants or animals) with no or undeveloped sexual organs: *Worker bees are neuter*

neuter[2] *n* **1 a** a NEUTER word or word form **b** the class of such words and forms: *Has Hebrew a neuter?|To put this adjective into the neuter, you must change its ending* **2** *rare* a NEUTER plant or animal

neuter[3] *v* [Wv5;T1 *usu. pass.*] *euph esp. BrE* to remove part of the sex organs of (an animal) by an operation —compare CASTRATE, SPAY, ALTER (2)

neu·tral[1] /ˈnjuːtrəl‖ˈnuː-/ *adj* **1** neither or none of 2 or more particular things; in a position in between opposite or different choices; with no qualities of the stated kind, as of something **a** very weak or colourless: *trousers of a neutral colour that look good with any colour of socks* **b** (in chemistry) neither acid nor BASE **c** with no electrical charge **2** being or belonging to a country which is not fighting or helping either side in a war: *a neutral country|neutral waters* **3** without any feelings on either side of a question: *I'm neutral in this argument: I don't care who wins* **4** (in a car or other machine) of or concerning the position of the GEARs in which no power is carried from the engine to the wheels —**~ly** *adv*

neutral[2] *n* **1** [U] the NEUTRAL[1] (4) position of the GEARs in a car or other machine (esp. in the phr. **in neutral**): *When you start the engine, be sure the car is in neutral* **2** [C] a NEUTRAL[1] (2) country

neu·tral·i·ty /njuːˈtrælɪ̈ti‖nuː-/ *n* [U] **1** the condition of a country which takes no part in a war: *Keeping its neutrality, Ireland didn't allow English ships to use its ports* **2** (in general) the condition or quality of being NEUTRAL[1]

neu·tral·ize, -ise /ˈnjuːtrəlaɪz‖ˈnuː-/ *v* [T1] **1** to cause to have no effect; destroy the qualities, force, or activity of: *to neutralize an acid with a* BASE|(*fig.*) *The airforce quickly neutralized the enemy's small navy.*|(fig.) *High taxes will neutralize increased wages* —compare NEGATE, COUNTERACT **2** to prevent (a country) by an international agreement from being used by or helping either side in a war —**-ization** /ˌnjuːtrəlaɪˈzeɪʃən‖ˌnuːtrələ-/ *n* [U]

neu·tral·iz·er /ˈnjuːtrəlaɪzəʳ‖ˈnuː-/ *n* a person, object, or chemical that NEUTRALIZEs (1) the effect of another

neu·tron /ˈnjuːtrɒn‖ˈnuːtrɑn/ *n* a very small piece of matter (like a PROTON) that is part of the centre of an atom and carries no electricity —see picture at ATOM

nev·er /ˈnevəʳ/ *adv* **1** not ever; not at any time: *I've never met him and I hope I never will meet him.|He never gets up early in the morning.|Never forget to lock the door at night.|Never* (*before*) *have I met such a strange person.|"Have you been to Paris?" "Never!"* **2** not (esp. in such phrs. as **never so much as** and **never do,** and in commands): *Never fear!* (=don't worry)|*He never so much as said "Thanks"* (= didn't even thank me).|*This dirty shirt will never do* (=isn't good enough to wear) **3 Never mind** *infml* **a** Don't worry: *"I forgot to bring your book." "Never mind* (*about*) *that. I'll get it myself* *tomorrow"* **b** Don't pay any attention to what has just been said: *"Where's my book? Never mind; I've found it"* **4 Well, I never!** I've never seen/heard anything like this!: *"You mean he actually did it? Well, I never!"* —see NEITHER (USAGE)

nev·er·more /ˌnevəˈmɔːʳ◂‖ˌnevərˈmor◂/ *adv poet* never again; at no time after this or after that

never-never /ˌ·· ˈ··/ *n* **on the never-never** *BrE humor sl* by HIRE PURCHASE: *I can't pay for it all at once, so I suppose I'll have to get it on the never-never*

never-never land /ˌ·· ˈ·· ·/ *n* [C;R] *not fml* (*sometimes caps.*) an imaginary wonderful place: *to dream of a never-never land where everyone is rich*

nev·er·the·less /ˌnevəðəˈles‖-vər-/ *adv* in spite of that; yet: *What you said was true but (it was) nevertheless unkind.|I can't follow your advice. Nevertheless, thank you for giving it.|Although he's a fool, I like him nevertheless.*|WHILE² (2a) *it's not surprising, it's nevertheless disappointing*

new¹ /njuː‖nuː/ *adj* **1** [Wa1;B] having begun or been made only a short time ago or before: *a new government|new fashions|new wine|newer fashions* **2** [Wa5;B] not used by anyone before: *We sell new and used furniture.|a used car, but good as new* (=as if it had never been used) **3** [Wa1;A] **a** being found or becoming known only now or recently in the past: *the discovery of a new star* **b** being in the stated position only a short time: *a new member of the club|the new nations of Africa|a college producing new teachers* **4** [Wa5;A] different from the earlier thing(s) done, known about, etc., or people known (about), for a longer time; (an)other: *to learn a new language|Our teacher got a new job, so our class had to get a new teacher* (=another teacher) **5** [Wa5;A] (of things of the same kind in an ordered set) just beginning or to be begun, used, etc.; fresh; (an)other: *a new day* (=another day) **6** [Wa5;A;(B)] taken from the ground early in the season; first picked of a crop: *small and good-tasting new potatoes* **7 new to a** just beginning to know about or do; still unfamiliar with: *a young lady new to the job* **b** unfamiliar to: *It's not a new idea but it's new to me: I hadn't heard it before* —**~ness** *n* [U]

new- *comb. form often poet* newly; freshly; recently: *a new-laid egg|". . . my America, my new-found land!"* (John Donne)

new·born /ˈnjuːbɔːn‖ˈnuːbɔrn/ *adj* [Wa5;A] (of a baby) recently or just born: *The newborn baby was lying in its mother's arms*

new·com·er /ˈnjuːkʌməʳ‖ˈnuː-/ *n* [(*to*)] one who has recently come, or has begun coming: *a newcomer to the city* (=visiting or living there for the first time)|*Our club welcomes newcomers.|The team is a newcomer to the competition* (=hasn't been in it before or often).|*She's a newcomer to chemistry but she's already made some important discoveries*

new deal /ˌ· ˈ·/ *n* **1** [*the*+R] (*usu. caps.*) a system of government laws and actions in the US in the 1930s to provide jobs for people and improve social and business conditions **2** [C] *pomp* a strong plan of action by a government in favour of an unfairly treated group of people: *a new deal for farmers with higher meat and milk prices*

new·el /ˈnjuːəl‖ˈnuːəl/ also **newel post** /ˈ·· ·/— *n* **1** a post (supporting the HANDRAIL) at the top or bottom or at a turn in a set of stairs **2** the pillar at the centre of a circular set of stairs

new·fan·gled /ˌnjuːˈfæŋgəld◂‖ˌnuː-/ *adj* [Wa2;A] *derog or humor* (of ideas, inventions, etc.) new and unnecessary or of no value: *We need better teachers, not newfangled ideas of education!|No newfangled machine can wash my clothes as well as I can by hand* —**~ness** *n* [U]

New·found·land /njuːˈfaʊndlənd, ˈnjuːfəndlənd‖ˈnuːfəndlənd/ *n* a type of very large strong usu. black dog

New Left /ˌ· ˈ·/ *n* [*the*+GU] (since the 1960s) an active group of mostly young people supporting sharp changes in political and social practices

new·ly /ˈnjuːli‖ˈnuːli/ *adv* (*used before a past participle*) **1** recently; freshly: *a newly built house* **2** in a new way: *an old idea newly expressed*

new·ly·wed /ˈnjuːliwed‖ˈnuː-/ *n not fml* a man or usu. woman recently married: *Mr and Mrs Smith are newlyweds/are a newlywed* COUPLE

new·mar·ket /ˈnjuːmɑːkɪ̆t‖ˈnuːmɑr-/ *n* [U] (*often cap.*) a type of card game

new moon /ˌ· ˈ·/ *n* **1** the time (about once a month) when the moon's dark side is turned towards the earth: *a table showing the times of new moons/of the new moon* **2** the bright thin edge of the moon seen in the sky a few days after this: *to see the new moon tonight*

new pen·ny /ˌ· ˈ··/ *n* **-pence** or **-pennies** PENNY (1)

news /njuːz‖nuːz/ *n* **1** [U] what is reported, esp. about a recent event or events; new information: *news of the election results|nothing but bad news in the newspaper today|Our latest news of* (=about) *our son was a letter a month ago.|to listen to the 7 o'clock news broadcast* **2** [*the*+U] any of the regular reports of recent events broadcast on radio and television: *to listen to the 7 o'clock news on radio* **3 break the news (to someone)** *infml* to be the first to inform (someone) of something, usu. something unpleasant: *You'd better break the news to her gently that her daughter has left home* **4 news to someone** *infml* something, esp. concerning oneself, which one has not heard about before: *There's no class tomorrow? That's news to me: no one told me*

USAGE This word is often used with a *cap.* in the name of a newspaper: *The Evening* **News.**

news a·gen·cy /ˈ· ˌ···/ *n* a company or organization supplying news and information to newspapers, radio, and television

news·a·gent /ˈnjuːzˌeɪdʒənt‖ˈnuːz-/ *AmE* **news deal·er** /ˈ· ˌ··/— *n BrE* a person in charge of a shop selling newspapers and magazines: *You can get that paper at your local newsagent's (shop)* —see picture at STREET

news·boy /ˈnjuːzbɔɪ‖ˈnuːz-/ also (*esp. AmE*) **paperboy**— *n* a boy or man who sells or delivers newspapers

news·cast /ˈnjuːzkɑːst‖ˈnuːzkæst/ *n* a radio or television broadcast of news

news·cast·er /ˈnjuːzkɑːstəʳ‖ˈnuːzkæ-/ *BrE* also **news·read·er** /-ˌriːdəʳ/— *n* a person who broadcasts news on radio or television

news con·fer·ence /ˈ· ˌ···/ *n* PRESS CONFERENCE

news·let·ter /ˈnjuːzˌletəʳ‖ˈnuːz-/ *n* a small sheet of news sent weekly or monthly to a particular group of people

news me·di·a /ˈ· ˌ···/ *n* [(*the*) P] the organizations which make news public, esp. newspapers, radio, and television —compare MASS MEDIA, MEDIA

news·mon·ger /ˈnjuːzˌmʌŋgəʳ‖ˈnuːzˌmʌŋ-, ˈnuːzˌmɑŋ-/ *n often derog* someone who spreads news, esp. by GOSSIP (talking, esp. about the faults of others)

news·pa·per /ˈnjuːsˌpeɪpəʳ‖ˈnuːz-/ *n* **1** [C] also (*not fml*) **paper**—a paper printed and sold to the public usu. daily or weekly, with news, notices, advertisements, etc.: *a daily newspaper* (=printed at least 5 days a week) **2** [C] a company which produces one or more of these papers: *One of our oldest newspapers had to go out of business because of low sales* **3** [U] paper on which these have been printed: *a piece of newspaper* —compare NEWSPRINT

news·print /ˈnjuːzˌprɪnt‖ˈnuːz-/ *n* [U] *tech* a cheap kind of paper used mostly for newspapers

news·reel /ˈnjuːzriːl‖ˈnuːz-/ *n* a short cinema film of news

news·room /ˈnjuːzrʊm, -ruːm‖ˈnuːz-/ *n* the office in a newspaper or broadcasting station where news is received and rewritten for broadcasting to the public

news·sheet /ˈnjuːzʃiːt‖ˈnuːz-/ *n* a small newspaper, usu. of one or 2 pages

news·stand /ˈnjuːzstænd‖ˈnuːz-/ *n* a table, often inside a shelter outdoors, from which newspapers and sometimes magazines and books are sold

news·ven·dor /ˈnjuːzˌvendəʳ‖ˈnuːz-/ *n* a person who sells newspapers

news·wor·thy /ˈnjuːzˌwɜːði‖ˈnuːzˌwɜrði/ *adj* important and interesting enough to be reported as news

news·y /ˈnjuːzi‖ˈnuːzi/ *adj* [Wa1] *not fml* filled with news of a not very serious kind: *a newsy letter* —**newsiness** *n* [U]

newt /njuːt‖nuːt/ also **eft**— *n* a type of small 4-legged animal (SALAMANDER) living partly on land and partly in water —see picture at AMPHIBIAN

New Tes·ta·ment /ˌ· ˈ···/ *n* [*the*+R] the second half of the Bible, containing the earliest Christian writings —compare OLD TESTAMENT

New·to·ni·an /njuːˈtəʊnɪən‖nuː-/ *adj* [Wa5;A;(B)] of or related to the ordinary understanding of forces and of the movements of objects (MECHANICS, esp. as developed by Sir Isaac Newton), esp. objects which are not very small and not moving at very fast speeds —compare QUANTUM, RELATIVISTIC

new town /ˌ· ˈ·/ *n* any of several towns built in Britain since 1946, each planned and built as a whole with factories, houses, shops, etc.: *Harlow New Town*

New World /ˌ· ˈ·/ *n* [*the*+R] North, Central, and South America; the Western HEMISPHERE; the Americas —compare OLD WORLD

new year /ˌ· ˈ·/ *n* [C;*the*+R] (*often caps.*) **1** the year which has just begun or will soon begin: *hope for better business in the new year than in this past year|Happy New Year!* (=a greeting spoken around the beginning of the year) **2** *BrE* the beginning of the year: *Last year business got better just after the new year*

New-Year /ˌ· ˈ·◂/ *AmE* usu. **New Year's**— *adj* [A] of or related to the first day or beginning of the year: *a New-Year party*

New Year's Day /ˌ·· ˈ·/ *n* [R] the first day of the year; (in Western countries) January 1st: *Is New Year's Day a holiday in your country?*

New Year's Eve /ˌ·· ˈ·/ *n* [R] (the evening of) the last day of the year (in Western countries, December 31st): *Are you having a party on New Year's Eve?*

next[1] /nekst/ *adj* [Wa5] **1** without anything coming before or between; nearest: *The next house to ours is a mile away.|the next left turn past the school=the left turn next after the school|not this turn but the next|The best way is by air; the next best (way) is by train.|If I miss the next train I'll catch the next after that.|"It's the next on the left"* (SEU W.) **2** (in time) **a** the one after the one mentioned or after now; following: *In 1855 he was 46: the next year, 1856, he was 47.|Where will you be during the next few weeks?|"before or after the next election"* (SEU S.)|*Will you be at our next meeting?* **b** (*without* the) the one after this: *This week's class was dull but next week's should be interesting.|Today is Sunday the 5th. Next Sunday is the 12th. This Tuesday is the 7th and next is the 14th.|The week after next* —compare LAST[1] (3) **3 (the) next day** the day after —compare **the** OTHER **day** **4 Next!** Will the next person waiting please come forward?

next[2] *adv* **1** in the order, place, etc., or at the time following nearest; just afterwards: *What line comes next in the poem?|What will you do next?|I like riding best of all sports, and swimming next.|My turn comes next after yours.|First, we add water; next, we boil* **2** at the first time after this or that: *when we next meet/met* —compare LAST[2] (2)

next-door /ˌ· ˈ·◂/ *adj* [A] in or being the next building, esp. in a row: *next-door neighbours*

next door /ˌ· ˈ·/ *adv* [F(*to*)] in or being the next building: *the neighbours next door* (=the people living next door)|(*infml*) *"next door's back garden"* (SEU S.)

next of kin /ˌ· · ˈ·/ *n* **next of kin** [Wn3] the person most closely related to someone

next to[1] /ˈ· ·/ *prep* **1** also (*old use*) **next**— in the closest place to: *the table next to the door|I don't like wool next to my skin.|We live in the next-to-the-last house in the road* (=*BrE* also *"in the second-last house in the road"*) **2** closest in order, degree, etc. to: *Next to riding, I like swimming best* **3** *infml* in a close relation to; in a position to know (about): *I could never get next to him to find out what he was really like*

next to[2] *adv not fml* almost: *The speech said next to nothing.|It's next to impossible to drive in this traffic*

nex·us /ˈneksəs/ *n* a connection or network of connections between objects, ideas, etc.

NHS *abbrev. for:* (in Britain) National Health Service: *free medicine on the NHS|NHS hospitals*

Ni /ˌen ˈaɪ/ the chemical sign for NICKEL

ni·a·cin /ˈnaɪəsən/ *n* [U] an important chemical (a type of VITAMIN B) found in foods like milk and eggs

nib /nɪb/ *n* the pointed usu. metal piece fitting on the end of a pen, with a crack for ink to flow to the point

nib·ble[1] /ˈnɪbəl/ *v* [Wv3] **1** [I∅ (AWAY, *at, on*);T1] to take small bites (out of something); eat (something) with small bites: *Aren't you hungry? You're only nibbling (at) your food.|He didn't answer, but just continued to nibble (away) (at his food).|to nibble (on) a piece of cake|*(fig.) *Food and rent nibbled (away) at the money they had saved* **2** [X9, esp. AWAY, OFF] to remove in this way: *The mice have nibbled away a part of the cheese.|*(fig.) *Food and rent nibbled away the money they had saved* **3** [X9;(T1)] to make in this way: *The mice have nibbled a hole in the cheese.|The mice nibbled their way through the wooden door* **4** [I∅ (*at*)] to show interest (in something); show signs of accepting (something): *She's nibbling (at the offer of a job in the new company)*

nibble[2] *n not fml* **1** [(*at*)] an act of nibbling (NIBBLE) (at) something: *Mice had had a nibble at the cheese.|I haven't sold my car yet but I've had some nibbles* (=some people have been interested in buying it) **2** a very small amount of food: *Is that all you want for dinner? It's only a nibble*

nib·lick /ˈnɪblɪk/ *n now rare* a GOLF CLUB (2) with a heavy metal head for driving a ball high and for a short distance; a number 8 IRON

nibs /nɪbz/ *n* **his nibs** *sl* a man who acts as if he were important but usu. is not, esp. one in charge of a group of people: *His nibs has wine with his meal, but we workers have to be content with water*

nice /naɪs/ *adj* [Wa1] **1** [B,B3] good, esp. **a** kind: *It's hard to be nice to someone you don't like.|How nice of you to do that!* **b** well done or made: *a nice shot|a nice piece of work* **c** pleasant; pleasing: *nice-looking clothes|a nice day* (=with good weather)|*This soup tastes very nice.|How nice to see you!* (=a greeting to a guest) **2** [B] showing or needing careful understanding or decision; fine; delicate: *a nice point of law|a nice difference between 2 meanings* **3** [B] *becoming rare, sometimes derog* having or showing (too) high standards, as of moral or social behaviour; PROPER[1] (3): *nice society|Nice girls don't do that!* **4** [B] *derog & infml* bad; wrong: *I need £5 and I've left all my money at home: this is a nice state of affairs!|You're a nice friend: you won't even lend me £5!* **5 nice and** *not fml* (used before adjectives and adverbs to give a favourable meaning): *nice and warm sitting by the fire|I didn't like the speech, but at least it was nice and short.|We flew nice and low* —**~ness** *n* [U]

USAGE In *fml* writing it is better to avoid **nice**, and to use **amusing**, **beautiful**, **interesting**, etc., according to the meaning.

nice·ly /ˈnaɪsli/ *adv* **1** well; in a good, pleasant, kind, or skilful way: *a job nicely carried out|Try to behave nicely.|The man is doing nicely* (=his condition is all right) *in hospital after his accident* **2** in an exact, fine, or delicate way: *a difference expressed nicely*

ni·ce·ty /ˈnaɪsəti/ *n* **1** [C9 esp. *of, usu. pl.*] a pleasant or enjoyable thing: *the niceties of city life* **2** [U9] the quality of needing or showing exactness or delicateness: *a man with great nicety of judgment|a question of some nicety* **3** [C *usu. pl.*] a fine or delicate point; detail: *Let's answer the question in general: we haven't time to consider all the niceties*

niche /nɪtʃ/ *n* **1** a hollow place in a wall, usu. made to hold a piece of art (like a BUST or STATUE) **2** a suitable place, job, position, etc.: *He's found a niche* (*for himself*) *doing the job he always wanted to do*

nick[1] /nɪk/ *n* **1** [C] a small cut, often made accidentally, in a surface or edge: *not badly hurt, only nicks and cuts* **2** [*the*+R;(C)] *BrE infml* prison (esp. in the phr. **in the nick**): *10 years in the nick* **3 in the nick of time** *not fml* just in time; at the necessary moment: *caught the baby in the nick of time before he fell down the stairs*

nick[2] *v* **1** [T1] to make or cut a NICK in: *He nicked the wall in moving the table.|A bullet nicked the soldier's leg* **2** [T1] *infml esp. BrE* to steal: *He nicked my bicycle and rode away* **3** [T1] *BrE sl* ARREST: *The police nicked him before he'd gone far on the stolen bicycle* **4** [D1;X9, esp. *for*] *infml esp. AmE* to charge (someone) (a usu. high price): *They nicked me* (*for*) *£1 just to have my hair cut!*

nick[3] *n* [U] *BrE sl* bodily condition; SHAPE[2] (3) (esp. in such phrs. as **in good/bad nick**): *The doctor says my heart is still in good nick.|A well-kept house in excellent nick* (=in very good repair)

nick·el[1] /ˈnɪkəl/ *n* **1** [U] a hard silver-white metal that is a simple substance (ELEMENT) and is used in the production of other metals **2** [C] **a** the coin of the US and Canada worth 5 cents: *Can you give me a* DIME *for 2 nickels?* **b** a small amount of money: *not worth a nickel*

nickel[2] also **nickel-plate** /ˌ·· ˈ·/— *v* **-ll-** (*AmE* **-l-**) [Wv5;T1] to put a thin surface (PLATE) of NICKEL[1] (1) over: *nickelled/nickel-plated steel*

nick·er /ˈnɪkəʳ/ *n* **nicker** [Wn3] *BrE sl* a pound; £1: *It cost me 50 nicker*

nick·nack /ˈnɪknæk/ *n infml* KNICK-KNACK

nick·name[1] /ˈnɪkneɪm/ *n not fml* a name used informally instead of (some)one's own name, usu. given because of one's character or as a short form of the actual name (the **real name**): *He got the nickname "Happy" because he never smiles*

nickname[2] *v* [X1] *not fml* to give (someone) a NICKNAME: *They nicknamed him "Fats" because of his weight*

nic·o·tine /ˈnɪkətiːn/ *n* [U] **1** a chemical which is poisonous alone and which provides the taste and effect of tobacco **2 nicotine fit** *usu. humor* a great desire, marked by nervousness, to smoke a cigarette: *to have a bad nicotine fit*

niece /niːs/ *n* **1** the daughter of one's brother or sister **2** the daughter of one's wife's or husband's brother or sister —compare NEPHEW; see TABLE OF FAMILY RELATIONSHIPS

niff /nɪf/ *n* [S] *BrE infml* a bad smell —**niffy** *adj* [Wa1]: *The fish is niffy: it isn't fresh*

nif·ty /ˈnɪfti/ *adj* [Wa1] *infml* very good, attractive, or effective, esp. well or cleverly done or made: *a nifty little machine|hit hard by a nifty blow on the jaw*

nig·gard /ˈnɪgəd‖-ərd/ *n derog* a person not willing to spend money; STINGY person

nig·gard·ly /ˈnɪgədli‖-ər-/ *adj derog* **1** (of a person) not willing to spend money, time, etc.; STINGY: *a niggardly husband who never gave her enough money for food* **2** (as if) spent or given unwillingly; small or limited; MEAN[1] (1): *a niggardly offer for such a good bicycle|niggardly praise* —**-liness** *n* [U]

nig·ger /ˈnɪgəʳ/ *n* [C;N] *taboo sl* a BLACK person; NEGRO

nig·gle /ˈnɪgəl/ *v* [Wv3;I∅] **1** [(*about, over*)] to pay too much attention to small details, esp. to find fault: *She niggled* (*over everything*) *until my patience was worn out* **2** [(*at*)] to annoy someone in a slight but continual way: *a doubt which niggled at his brain* —**~r** *n*

nig·gling /ˈnɪgəlɪŋ/ *adj* [A] **1** annoying **a** in a slight way; PETTY[1] (1): *niggling remarks* **b** slightly and continually: *a niggling doubt* **2** (of a piece of work) showing or needing too much attention to detail: *the niggling job of mending all the small holes in the socks*

nigh /naɪ/ *adv, prep* **1** *poet & old use* near: *The time has drawn nigh* (=it has nearly come) **2 well nigh** also **nigh on/onto/unto**—*usu. dial or old use* almost: *served the king well nigh 50 years*

night /naɪt/ *n* **1** [C;U] the dark part of each day when the sun cannot be seen: *last night|tomorrow night|Sunday night|higher pay for work at night|The moon gives light by/at night.|Night begins to fall* (=it starts to get dark).|*a few nights ago*|(*esp. not fml AmE*) *Mary works nights* —compare DAY, DAYLIGHT, DAYTIME **2** [C;U] any of various parts of this period, such as **a** the evening: *This evening is my night off* (=I don't have to work this evening) **b** the period after bedtime: *sleep well all night* **c** the period before midnight: (*on*) *the night of May 5th* **3** [C] an evening, considered as an occasion: *We saw the show on its first night* (=at its first performance, in the evening).|*Saturday is our cinema night* (=We go to the cinema on Saturday evenings) **4** [C9 *usu. sing.*] the evening or dark period following a holiday or church feast day: *Christmas night* —compare EVE (2) **5** [C9 esp. *of*] *lit* a period or experience without bright qualities like glory, hope, knowledge, etc.: *through the night of doubt and sorrow* **6 all night** (**long**) right through the night without stopping: *I lay awake all night wondering about it* **7 at night** **a** during the night: *keep a light on at night* **b** at the end of the day: *come home from work at night* **8 by night** *esp. lit* during the night (esp. when compared with **by day**): *He works in an office by day and drives a taxi by night.|What do you think of Paris by night?* **9 have a good/bad night** to sleep well/badly —see also GOODNIGHT **10 in the night** at some time during the night: *I woke up twice in the night* **11 make a night of it** *infml* to spend all or most of night in enjoyment **12 night after night** *infml* regularly every night: *He goes out drinking night after night* **13 night and day** also **day and night**— *infml* all the

time: *I think about Irene night and day*
night bird /ˈ· ·/ *n* **1** *infml* NIGHTHAWK **2** any of various birds which are seen or active at night
night blind·ness /ˈ· ˌ··/ *n* [U] inability to see things at night or in weak light
night·cap /ˈnaɪtkæp/ *n* **1** a soft cloth cap worn in bed esp. in former times **2** a usu. alcoholic drink taken before going to bed
night·clothes /ˈnaɪtkləʊðz, -kləʊz/ *n* [P] garments worn in bed
night·club /ˈnaɪtklʌb/ *n* a restaurant open late at night where people may drink, dance, and see a show
night·dress /ˈnaɪtdres/ also (*infml*) **nightie** /ˈnaɪti/, (*esp. AmE*) **night·gown** /-gaʊn/— *n* a piece of women's clothing like a loose dress, made to be worn in bed.
night·fall /ˈnaɪtfɔːl/ *n* [U] the beginning of night; DUSK (esp. in the phr. **at nightfall**): *We gave up searching for the lost key at nightfall*
night·hawk /ˈnaɪthɔːk/ also **night owl** /ˈ· ·/, **night bird**— *n infml* a person with the habit of staying up and doing things at night, or one who thinks or works best at night
nigh·tin·gale /ˈnaɪtɪŋgeɪl/ *n* any of several European THRUSHes (= a type of bird) known for the beautiful song of the male heard at night in the spring
night·jar /ˈnaɪtdʒɑːʳ/ *n* a type of brown bird of Europe with a long tail and wings that is active at night
night·life /ˈnaɪtlaɪf/ *n* [U] the activity of people who go out to enjoy themselves at night (as in BAR*s*, NIGHTCLUB*s*, etc.)
night·light /ˈnaɪtlaɪt/ *n* a low light which is left on, or a small candle which is kept burning, through the night: *Little Johnny won't sleep without a nightlight*
night·line /ˈnaɪtlaɪn/ *n* a fishing line left in the water to catch fish at night
night·long /ˈnaɪtlɒŋ‖-lɔŋ/ *adj, adv* (lasting) through the whole night: *a nightlong job|working nightlong to finish the job*
night·ly /ˈnaɪtli/ *adj, adv* [Wa5] (happening, done, used, etc.) every night: *a play performed nightly|a nightly news broadcast*
night·mare /ˈnaɪtmeəʳ/ *n* **1** an unpleasant and terrible dream: *I woke cold and shaking from the nightmare* **2** a bad, fearful, or terrible experience or event **a** thought to be possible in the future: *the nightmare of an atomic war* **b** in the past: *Driving on that ice was a nightmare* —**-marish** *adj* —**-marishly** *adv* —**-marishness** *n* [U9]
night por·ter /ˈ· ˌ··/ *n* a person who is on duty through the night at the front desk of a hotel
nights /naɪts/ *adv* [Wa5] *esp. AmE* at night repeatedly; during any night: *I lie awake nights and wonder . . .*
night safe /ˈ· ·/ *n* a locked box (SAFE² (1)) in the outside wall of a bank, into which people may put money when the bank is closed
night school /ˈ· ·/ *n* [U;(C)] a school or set of classes meeting in the evening, esp. for people who have jobs during the day: *learn French at/*(*AmE*) *in night school*
night·shade /ˈnaɪt-ʃeɪd/ *n* [U;C] (any of) a family of plants with flowers, related to the potato and including some poisonous plants such as DEADLY NIGHTSHADE
night shift /ˈ· ·/ *n* **1** [C] a period of time, usu. between 10 o'clock at night and 8 o'clock in the morning, worked regularly by a group of people, as in a factory: *work (on) the night shift|a night-shift worker* **2** [(*the*) GU] this group of workers: *one of the night shift*
night·shirt /ˈnaɪt-ʃɜːt‖-ʃɜrt/ *n* a piece of men's clothing like a long loose shirt, made to be worn in bed
night soil /ˈ· ·/ *n* [U] *euph* waste matter from the human bowels which is collected from places not connected to SEWERS and used for making the soil better for crops to grow (used as FERTILIZER)
night·stick /ˈnaɪtˌstɪk/ *n AmE* a short thick stick often carried by policemen in America; TRUNCHEON
night·time /ˈnaɪt-taɪm/ *n* [U] the time each day when it is dark —opposite **daytime**
night watch·man /ˌ· ˈ··/ *n* a man with the job of guarding against thieves, fires, etc., at a building at night
ni·hil·is·m /ˈnaɪə̇lɪzəm/ *n* [U] **1** the belief that nothing has meaning or value **2** the belief that social and political organization should be destroyed, even if nothing better can take its place —**-ist** *n* —**-istic** /ˌnaɪə̇ˈlɪstɪk/ *adj*
-nik /nɪk/ *suffix* [*n, adj→n*] *not fml* a person who is connected with (a thing) or has (a quality): BEATNIK|COMPUTER*nik*
nil /nɪl/ *n* [R] **1** nothing; zero: *The new machine reduced labour costs to almost nil* **2** *BrE* (in a sport) a total of no points: *a victory in the match by 4 points to nil = a 4–nil* (usu. written "4–0") *victory*
Ni·lot·ic /naɪˈlɒtɪk‖-ˈlɑ-/ *adj tech* of or related to the River Nile, the black African peoples living around it, or their languages
nim·ble /ˈnɪmbəl/ *adj* [Wa2,3] *apprec* **1** quick, light, and neat in movement; AGILE: *a nimble climber|a piano player with nimble fingers* **2** quick in thinking or understanding: *a nimble imagination|nimble in his answer to the hard question* —**~ness** *n* [U] —**-bly** *adv*
nim·bus /ˈnɪmbəs/ *n* **-buses** *or* **-bi** /baɪ/ **1** a dark spreading cloud that may bring rain or snow **2** a shining cloud or ring often shown in pictures around the heads of gods, ANGEL*s*, and holy people —compare HALO
Nim·rod /ˈnɪmrɒd‖-rɑd/ *n lit* (*sometimes not cap.*) a great hunter
nin·com·poop /ˈnɪŋkəmpuːp/ *n infml* a stupid person; fool
nine /naɪn/ *determiner, n, pron* **1** [see NUMBER TABLE 1] (the number) 9 **2** [C *usu. sing.*] (in the game of GOLF) the first or last half of a COURSE (playing area) of 18 holes: *He played better on the* **front nine** (= the first 9 holes) *than on the* **back nine** (= the last 9 holes) **3 nine times out of ten** *infml* almost always: *Even before I open my mouth, my wife seems to know what I'm going to say nine times out of ten* —see also NINES
nine days' won·der /ˌ· · ˈ··/ *n not fml* a thing or event that causes excitement for a short time and then is forgotten
nine·pin /ˈnaɪnˌpɪn/ *n* **1** [A] of or for the game of NINEPINS **2** [C] any of the 9 bottle-shaped objects (**pins**) set up to be knocked down in the game of NINEPINS
nine·pins /ˈnaɪnˌpɪnz/ *n* [U] an early form of the game of BOWLING using 9 instead of 10 bottle-shaped objects
nines /naɪnz/ *n* **dressed (up) to the nines** *BrE infml* wearing one's best and most formal clothes
nine·teen /ˌnaɪnˈtiːn◂/ *determiner, n, pron* [see NUMBER TABLE 1] **1** (the number) 19 **2 talk nineteen to the dozen** *infml* see DOZEN —**~th** *determiner, adv, n, pron* [see NUMBER TABLE 3]
nine·ty /ˈnaɪnti/ *determiner, n, pron* [see NUMBER TABLE 1] (the number) 90 —**-tieth** /ˈnaɪntiə̇θ/ *determiner, n, adv, pron* [see NUMBER TABLE 3]
ninety-nine /ˌ·· ˈ·◂/ *determiner, n, pron* **1** (the number) 99 **2 ninety-nine times out of a hundred**

not fml very nearly every time; almost always —**ninety-ninth** *determiner, n, pron, adv* [see NUMBER TABLE 3]

nin·ny /ˈnɪni/ *n* [C;*you*+N] *infml & derog* a silly foolish person: *You ninny! That's the telephone ringing, not the doorbell!*

ninth /naɪnθ/ *determiner, adv, n, pron* [see NUMBER TABLE 3] 9th

nip¹ /nɪp/ *v* **-pp- 1** [T1;I∅] to catch (something or someone) in a tight sharp hold between 2 points or surfaces: *The dog nipped the postman on the leg.|a piece of wood held nipped in the* VICE|*I nipped my finger in the* VICE *and had to go to the doctor.|Don't go too near that dog; he nips (people)* **2** [T1 (OFF)] to cut off by this means: *to nip off the corner of the page with scissors|to nip (off) some of the flowers in early spring to help the plant later on* **3** [T1] *rare* to do harm to, esp. so as to keep from growing: *The cold weather has nipped the fruit trees* **4** [L9, esp. OFF, IN, OUT, UP, DOWN] *infml esp. BrE* to go quickly; hurry: *I'll nip out and buy a newspaper.|to nip in for a quick cup of tea* **5 nip in the bud** *not fml* to do harm to (something), esp. so as to keep from succeeding: *If we attack quickly, we can nip the enemy's plans in the bud*

nip² *n* [S] **1** a coldness or cold wind: *There's a nip in the air today: winter's coming* **2** *AmE* a strong taste: *old cheese with a nip in it* **3** the act or result of NIPping¹ (1): *Give the wire a nip/Make a nip in the wire to hold it fast* **4** *infml esp. BrE* the act or result of NIPping¹ (4): *to have a quick nip out to buy a newspaper*

nip³ *n* [*usu. sing.*] *infml* a small amount of an alcoholic drink other than beer or wine: *a little nip of* WHISKY *now and then*

nip and tuck /ˌ·· ˈ·/ *adj, adv* (of a race) so evenly matched that the leader is now one person, horse, etc., and now another: *The race stayed nip and tuck until the last minute: it was a nip-and-tuck battle between the 2 horses*

nip at *v prep* [T1 (AWAY)] to be or follow next to and (try to) bite sharply: *The postman ran away with the dog nipping (away) at his heels.*|(fig.) *The cold wind nipped at her face*

nip in *v adv* **1** [I∅] *infml esp. BrE* to move quickly sideways in traffic or in a race: *I had to stop when another car nipped in in front of me* **2** [T1] to make (esp. clothing) narrow: *I had to nip this dress in at the waist to make it fit*

nip·per /ˈnɪpəʳ/ *n* [C9] *infml* a child, esp. a boy: *a clever little nipper|a nipper of 9 years old*

nip·pers /ˈnɪpəz‖-ərz/ *n* [P] any of various tools like PLIERS which are used for NIPping: *These nippers are too small to fit round the wire* —see PAIR (USAGE)

nip·ping /ˈnɪpɪŋ/ *adj* [A] sharp or cold; HARSH: *a nipping wind|very nipping remarks*

nip·ple /ˈnɪpəl/ *n* **1** one of the areas of darker skin which stand out from the breasts and through which a baby may suck milk from a woman —compare TEAT and see picture at HUMAN² **2** *esp. AmE* the piece of rubber shaped like this on the end of a baby's bottle; TEAT **3** a small opening shaped like this on a machine, for oil or GREASE **4** a short tube used for connecting the ends of 2 pipes

nip·py /ˈnɪpi/ *adj* [Wa1] **1** quick in movement: *You'll have to be nippy if you don't want to be late* **2** having a NIP (in coldness or taste): *a nippy winter morning|(AmE) nippy cheese* —**-piness** *n* [U]

nir·va·na /nɪəˈvɑːnə, nɜː-‖nɪər-, nɜr-/ *n* **1** [R] (*usu. cap.*) (in Buddhism and Hinduism) the state of rest and freedom from desire gained through self-control, and leading to union with the spirit of the universe **2** [C;U] (*sometimes cap.*) peace and happiness of mind: *a strange nirvana produced by drugs*

ni·si /ˈnaɪsaɪ/ see DECREE NISI

Nis·sen hut /ˈnɪsən hʌt/ *n BrE* a shelter with a cement floor and a roof and main walls in one round piece made of iron sheets —compare QUONSET HUT

nit¹ /nɪt/ *n* an egg of an insect (usu. a LOUSE) that is sometimes found in people's hair

nit² *n* [C;*you*+N] *BrE derog infml* NITWIT

nit·pick /ˈnɪtˌpɪk/ *v* [I∅ (*at*)] to practise NITPICKING; CARP: *Our rules can't deal with every little detail, so stop nitpicking (at them) and get back to work!* —**~er** *n*

nit·pick·ing /ˈnɪtˌpɪkɪŋ/ *adj, n* [U;B] *derog infml* complaining, arguing, reasoning, etc., by noticing small and unimportant differences; TRIVIAL(ity): *a dull nitpicking speech|a dull speech that contained nothing but nitpicking*

ni·trate /ˈnaɪtreɪt, -trɨ̣t/ *n* [U9;C] any of several chemicals (containing NITROGEN and oxygen in the group NO_3) used mainly (as FERTILIZER) in improving soil for growing crops: *farmers buying nitrates from foreign* SOURCE*s*|SODIUM *nitrate*

ni·tre, *AmE* **niter** /ˈnaɪtəʳ/ *n* [U] any of certain NITRATE*s*, including SALTPETRE, esp. as substances found in nature

ni·tric /ˈnaɪtrɪk/ *adj* [Wa5;A] *tech* (of a chemical compound) containing NITROGEN: *nitric* OXIDE —see also NITROUS

nitric ac·id /ˌ·· ˈ··/ *n* [U] a powerful acid (HNO_3) which eats away (CORRODE*s*) other materials and is used in explosives and other chemical products

ni·tro·chalk /ˈnaɪtrəʊtʃɔːk/ *n* [U] *BrE* a type of chemical (a FERTILIZER) used to make grass grow

ni·tro·gen /ˈnaɪtrədʒən/ *n* [U] a gas that is a simple substance (ELEMENT), without colour or smell, that forms most of the earth's air, and that is found in all living things

ni·tro·gly·ce·rine, -rin /ˌnaɪtrəʊˈglɪsərɨ̣n, -trə-, -riːn‖-rɨ̣n/ *n* [U] a type of powerful liquid explosive —see also DYNAMITE; compare TNT

ni·trous /ˈnaɪtrəs/ *adj* [Wa5;A] (of a chemical compound) containing NITROGEN (esp. with a lower VALENCY than in NITRIC compounds): *nitrous acid*

nitrous ox·ide /ˌ·· ˈ··/ *n* [U] *tech* LAUGHING GAS

nit·ty-grit·ty /ˌnɪti ˈgrɪti/ *n* **get down to/come to the nitty-gritty** *sl* to deal with the difficult and practical part of a matter, esp. a question or a decision: *You say we need £100, but now let's get down to the nitty-gritty: How are we going to get it?*

nit·wit /ˈnɪtˌwɪt/ *n* [C;*you*+N] *infml* a silly foolish person

nix¹ /nɪks/ *adv AmE sl* (*as a decision or answer*) no: *"Will you give me a ride home?" "Nix, man! I'm not going that way."|Father said nix to our plan, so we couldn't go*

nix² *v* [T1] *AmE infml* (used esp. by newspapers) to answer no to; not allow; not approve: *The city nixed the plan to build a theatre with public money*

no¹ /nəʊ/ *adv* **1** (in an answer to a statement, question, request, etc., expressing refusal or disagreement): *"Is it raining?" "No, it's snowing."|"Will you post this letter for me?" "No, I don't want to go out in the snow."|"Hasn't it stopped snowing?" "No, it hasn't."|"Please post the letter." "No! Do it yourself."|"Is(n't) he here?" "Yes, he is." "No, he isn't"* **2** (used for expressing great surprise): *"I bought this bicycle for £5." "No! Could it really have been so cheap?"* —see also NO WAY² **3** *often pomp* (used before an adjective to give the opposite meaning to the phrase containing the adjective): *had no small part* (=had a large part) *in its success|*

a question of no great importance (=of little importance)|*But this is no unimportant question, my dear Holmes!* (=it is really an important question)|*We wanted good weather for our holiday, but* (*we had*) *no such luck; it rained the whole time* **4** (*before a* COMPARATIVE *adjective*) not (any): *I'm feeling no worse* (=feeling the same or better) *than yesterday.*|*There were no fewer than 150 people at the party last night.* (=There were really as many people as that at the party)|*No more than 3 people came to my class, unfortunately* —compare NOT (1) **5** (*after* or) not (esp. in the phr. **whether or no**): *You may not like it, but you'll have to do it, whether or no.* (=whether or not you like it)|*Like it or no, you'll have to do it*

no² *determiner* **1** not a; not one; not any: *no sugar in the bowl*|*no telephone in our house*|*no buses in this part of town*|*You can't lie to me; I'm no fool!*|*"This is no particular* CONCERN *of yours"* (SEU S.) **2** (in formal commands, warnings, road signs, etc., expressing what is not allowed): *No smoking*|*No parking*|*No bare feet*|*No bicycles against this wall* **3** *infml* very little; hardly any: *We're almost home; we'll be there in no time* (=very soon).|*It's no distance at all to the school, only a short walk* **4** *infml* **there's no knowing/saying/telling**, etc. it's not possible to know/say/tell, etc.: *He's such a strange person: there's no knowing what he'll do next*

USAGE Compare **no** and **not**. Besides being the opposite of **yes**, **no** means "not any", and can be used with nouns, with verbs used like nouns, or with adjectives, wherever **any** could also be used: **no** (=not any) *time*|**no** (=not any) *friends*|**no** (=not any) *telephone*|"**No** (=Not any) *Smoking*"|*I've* **no** (=I haven't any) *thick shoes.*|*He's* **no** (=He isn't any) *better.*|*It's* **no** (=It isn't any) *different.* One could not use **any** before words like **a, the, all, both, every** (DETERMINER*s* and PREDETERMINER*s*) so here one must use **not** instead of **no**: **not** *a chance*|**not** *the least*|**not** *all of us*|**not** *everyone*|**not** *enough.* For the same reason, use **not** with names, adverbs, PREPOSITION*s*, and most adjectives where no noun follows: *me*, **not** *George*|**not** *wisely*|**not** *on Sundays*|*They're* **not** *thick.* The main purpose of **not** is to change verbs to their opposite meaning: *I'm* **not** *coming.* **No** is never used like this.

no³ *n* **noes** **1** [*usu. sing.*] an answer or decision of no: *a clear no to my request for money* **2** [*usu. pl.*] a vote or voter against a question to be decided: *The noes won and the idea was dropped* —opposite **aye** **3** **The noes have it!** (said when more people have voted against something than in favour of it)

no. nos. *written abbrev. for:* NUMBER¹ (2)

No. 10 *written abbrev. for:* (*not fml*) NUMBER TEN

no-ac·count /ˈ· ·ˌ·/ *n, adj* [C;*you*+N;A] *infml AmE* (a person who is) worthless or unable to do anything good: *Tell your no-account friend to go jump in the lake!*

No·ah's ark /ˌnəʊəz ˈɑːk‖-ˈɑrk/ see ARK

nob¹ /nɒb‖nɑb/ *n BrE sl* the head: *hit on the nob by a cricket ball*

nob² *n infml & derog or humor* a person with money and a high social position: *We don't see them any more: they've become nobs and live in the big house on the hill*

no ball /ˌ· ˈ·/ *n* (in cricket) an act of throwing (BOWLing) the ball in a way that is not allowed by the laws of the game, such as with one's arm bent at the elbow

nob·ble /ˈnɒbəl‖ˈnɑ-/ *v* [T1] *BrE sl* **1** to get the attention of (someone), esp. in order to persuade or gain a favour: *Well, I nobbled him at the party and I said, "I've got a nice little property that's just right for you"* **2** to win, catch, or get dishonestly: *nobbled first prize before he was caught* **3** to prevent (a racehorse) from winning, esp. by the unlawful use of drugs

No·bel prize /nəʊˌbel ˈpraɪz, ˌnəʊbel-/ *n* any of several prizes given in Sweden each year for important work in science and literature, and work towards world peace: *winner of a Nobel prize in medicine*|*a Nobel Peace prize*

no·bil·i·ty /nəʊˈbɪlᵻti, nə-/ *n* **1** [(*the*) GU] (in certain countries) the group of people of the highest social class, family, or rank, who have titles **2** [U] the quality or condition of being NOBLE¹ (3) in social rank **3** [U] also **no·ble·ness** /ˌnəʊbəlnᵻs/— the quality or condition of being NOBLE¹ (1,2) in character or appearance: *He acted with great nobility of purpose*

no·ble¹ /ˈnəʊbəl/ *adj* **1** [Wa1,3] of high quality, esp. morally; deserving praise; worthy; unselfish: *a woman of noble mind*|*noble and generous feelings*|*The attempt to save the child's life was very noble* **2** [Wa1,3] admirable in appearance; grand: *a building of noble size*|*a noble-looking horse* **3** [Wa1,3] of or belonging to a high social rank with a title: *a noble family*|*a man of noble birth* **4** [Wa5] (of metals like gold and silver) not chemically changed by air —compare **BASE** **5 the noble art** *pomp* BOXING

noble² *n* [*usu. pl.*] (esp. in FEUDAL times) a man of the highest and most powerful social class

no·ble·man /ˈnəʊbəlmən/ (*fem.* **noblewoman** /-ˌwʊmən/)— *n* **-men** /mən/ a person belonging to the class of the NOBILITY; PEER¹ (2,3)

noble-mind·ed /ˌ·· ˈ··/ *adj* [Wa2] having or showing high moral quality; noble in mind —**~ly** *adv* —**~ness** *n* [U]

no·blesse o·blige /nəʊˌbles əˈbliːʒ/ *Fr* (a French sentence which means) "People with high rank, money, good education, etc., must use these things for the good of everyone": *I don't really like giving money to beggars, but* (*it's a case of*) *noblesse oblige, don't you know?*

no·bly /ˈnəʊbli/ *adv* **1** in a noble way, esp. in a way that is unselfish and deserving of praise: *She nobly did my work as well as hers while I was ill* **2** with a noble rank (in the phr. **nobly born**)

no·bod·y¹ /ˈnəʊbədi‖-ˌbɑdi, -bədi/ also **no one**— *pron* not anybody; no person: *She likes nobody and nobody likes her.*|*Can you help me? Nobody else* (=no other person) *can.*|*He said he loved nobody but me* (=only me).|*"Nobody ever eats the Christmas tea"* (SEU S.).|*"There's nobody in the library"* (SEU S.) —see also **nobody's** FOOL; **like nobody's** BUSINESS

nobody² *n* [*usu. sing.*] a person of no importance: *I want to be famous! I'm tired of being a nobody*

noc·tur·nal /nɒkˈtɜːnl‖nɑkˈtɜr-/ *adj* [Wa5] *fml or tech* of, done or happening, or active at night: *a nocturnal visit*|*a nocturnal bird* —**~ly** *adv*

noc·turne /ˈnɒktɜːn‖ˈnɑktɜrn/ *n* a piece of art related to the night, esp. a dreamy piece of music for the piano: *Play us another of your charming nocturnes,* MONSIEUR *Chopin*

nod¹ /nɒd‖nɑd/ *v* **-dd-** **1** [IØ;T1] to bend (one's head) forward and down, esp. to show agreement or give a greeting or sign: *She nodded* (*her head*) *when she passed me in the street.*|*The president nodded and everyone sat down around the table.*|*He nodded as if to say yes* **2** [T1] to show in this way: *They nodded their agreement* **3** [IØ (OFF)] to let one's head drop in falling asleep while sitting down: *I nodded off in the meeting and didn't hear what was said* **4** [IØ] *rare* to be careless for a moment; make a small mistake: *Even the great Greek poet Homer nods now and then* **5** [IØ] to bend downward or forward: *flowers nodding in the wind*

nod² *n* [*usu. sing.*] **1** an act of NODDing: *He greeted* *us with a nod* (*of the head*) **2 get the nod** *infml* to be the one chosen from among a number of others **3 on the nod** *BrE infml* **a** on CREDIT **b** by quick agreement without any formal consideration

no·dal /ˈnəʊdl/ *adj* of, near, or related to one or more NODE*s*

nod·ding ac·quaint·ance /ˌ·· ·ˈ··/ *n* [S] *not fml* **1** [(*with*)] **a** a relation between people who know each other only slightly: *She and I have a nodding acquaintance.*|*I have a nodding acquaintance with her* **b** a very slight familiarity (with a subject): *a nodding acquaintance with chemistry* **2** a person whom one hardly knows, or knows only slightly: *She's not really a friend, only a nodding acquaintance.*|*She and I are not really friends, only nodding acquaintances*

nod·dle /ˈnɒdl‖ˈnɑdl/ *n sl* the head: *Think! Use your noddle!*

node /nəʊd/ *n* **1** a swelling or roundish lump, as on a tree trunk or a person's body **2** a place where branches meet or join, as on a plant or in any treelike pattern or network —see picture at PLANT[2] **3** *tech* (in a system, body, etc., moving in waves) a point which remains still

no doubt /ˌ· ˈ·/ *adv* **1** (almost) certainly or very probably: *No doubt he was just trying to help, but he's spoiled our work.*|*The court will no doubt deal severely with the criminals.*|*"John will probably be late, won't he?" "No doubt"* **2** (*used often in expressions expecting an answer, esp. one of agreement*) I'm sure; I suppose: *No doubt you would like a drink* (=You'd like one, wouldn't you?)|*You no doubt know what's happened* (=I suppose you know it.)|*You're new around here, no doubt* —see DOUBT (USAGE)

nod·u·lar /ˈnɒdjʊləʳ‖ˈnɑdʒə-/ *adj* **1** of, related to, or marked by NODULE*s* **2** found in NODULE*s*: *nodular minerals*

nod·ule /ˈnɒdjuːl‖ˈnɑdʒuːl/ *n* a small round mass or lump as of a mineral, or esp. a small round swelling on a plant or a person's body

No·el /nəʊˈel/ *n* [R] *poet* (the season of) Christmas: *a happy Noel*

noes /nəʊz/ *pl. of* NO[3]

nog /nɒg‖nɑg/ *n* [U] any drink, usu. alcoholic, containing eggs

nog·gin /ˈnɒgɪ̵n‖ˈnɑ-/ *n* [*usu. sing.*] **1** *sl* a person's head: *Hit him right on the noggin!*|*Think! Use your noggin!* **2** a small amount (usu. a GILL) of an alcoholic drink

no-go ar·e·a /ˌ· ˈ· ˌ···/ *n infml* (in a city with 2 opposed groups of people) an area controlled by one group and dangerous for anyone in the other group to enter

no·how /ˈnəʊhaʊ/ *adv nonstandard or humor* in no way: *We couldn't get that cow out of the ditch nohow*

noise /nɔɪz/ *n* **1** [U;C] (an) unwanted or unpleasant sound: *Try not to make any noise when you go into the bedroom.*|*a holiday away from city noises* **2** [U] confused meaningless and continuing sound, esp. **a** the sound heard in any public place: *There's so much noise in this restaurant I can hardly hear you talking* **b** unwanted sound which keeps wanted sounds on radio, telephones, etc., from being heard clearly; STATIC[2] **3** [C] an unmusical sound that is difficult to describe or strange: *What's wrong with my car? The engine makes funny noises.*|*Make a noise like a train* **4 big noise** *derog* an important person: *He likes to think he's a big noise* **5 make a/some noise about** *infml* to complain about: *The bus was late again today! Let's make a noise to the company about it* **6 make noises** *not fml* to express feelings or intentions of the stated kind: *My teacher made encouraging noises when I said I wanted to go to university* —**~less** *adj* —**~lessly** *adv* —**~lessness** *n* [U]

USAGE A **sound** is anything that one hears: *the* **sound** *of voices/of music/of breaking plates.* A **voice** is the sound that a person makes when speaking or singing: *to have a loud/high/charming* **voice**|*a song for 4 male* **voices**|*That sounds like Mary's* **voice**! A **noise** is usually a loud unpleasant **sound**: *Stop making such a* **noise**/*so much* **noise**; but the word can be used of small and/or pleasant **sounds**: *the* **noise** *of children singing/of a cat drinking milk.* **Noisy** always means "loud".

noise a·bout also **noise a·broad, noise a·round**— *v adv* [T1,5 *often pass.*] *not fml* to make (a report, RUMOUR, or news) public: *It's being noised around that the factory is going to close*

noi·some /ˈnɔɪsəm/ *adj lit* very unpleasant and annoying: *rude and noisome people/behaviour*

nois·y /ˈnɔɪzi/ *adj* [Wa1] making or marked by a lot of noise: *a noisy car*|*It's very noisy in this office=This is a very noisy office* —**noisily** *adv*: *walked noisily downstairs/walked downstairs noisily* —**noisiness** *n* [U]

nom. *written abbrev. for:* NOMINATIVE

no·mad /ˈnəʊmæd/ *n* **1** [*often pl.*] a member of a tribe which travels about, esp. to find grass for its animals: *the nomads of the desert* **2** a person who travels with no fixed aim: *He wandered about Europe for 3 months, but in the end he got tired of being a nomad*

no·mad·ic /nəʊˈmædɪk/ *adj* **1** of, like, or concerning a tribe of NOMAD*s*: *nomadic tribes/habits* **2** not living in one place for long; wandering: *a nomadic young man with no home* —compare VAGRANT —**~ally** *adv* [Wa4]

no-man's-land /ˈ· · ˌ·/ *n* **1** [R] (*sometimes caps.*) the belt of land between 2 opposing armies **2** [S] an area of bare, unclaimed, or waste land: *a no-man's-land where there was once a great city* **3** [S] a dangerous or not well understood state, field of ideas, condition, etc., usu. between 2 other states, ideas, etc.: *a scientific no-man's-land of untested ideas*

nom de plume /ˌnɒm də ˈpluːm‖ˌnɑm-/ *n* **noms de plume** (*same pronunciation*) *Fr* PEN NAME

no·men·cla·ture /nəʊˈmenklətʃəʳ, ˈnəʊmənkleɪ-‖ˈnəʊmənkleɪ-/ *n* **1** [U;C] a system of naming things, esp. in a branch of science: *medical nomenclature*|*the nomenclature of chemical compounds* —compare TERMINOLOGY **2** [U] a set of names or acts of naming: *The nomenclature of towns in England is interesting*

nom·i·nal /ˈnɒmɪ̵nl‖ˈnɑ-/ *adj* **1** in name or form but usu. not in reality: *nominal Christianity*|*The old man is only the nominal head of the business: his son makes the decisions* **2** of, related to, or used as a noun: *a nominal phrase*|*nominal endings like* -NESS, -ATION, *etc.* **3** (of an amount of money) very small; NEGLIGIBLE: *sold at* (*a*) *nominal price* (=a price far below the value of the object) **4** *tech* (of the price of something which is not often bought and sold) based on present opinion but not on what has been paid in the past —**~ly** *adv*

nom·i·nate /ˈnɒmɪ̵neɪt‖ˈnɑ-/ *v* **1** [T1 (*for*)] to suggest or name (someone) officially for election to a position, office, honour, etc.: *I wish to nominate Jane Morrison for president of the club* **2** [T1 (*as*);X (*to be*) 1] to appoint (someone) to such a position, office, etc.: *The president nominated me* (*as/to be*) *his representative at the meeting* **3** [T1 (*for, as*)] *infml & humor* to suggest informally, as being worthy of some honour or title: *I nominate that as the worst joke I've ever heard!* **4** [T1 (*for, as*);V3] to suggest or name (someone) for some usu. stated purpose: *I nominate John* (*for the job*).|*I* *nominate John to be present at the meeting|to go to the meeting*

nom·i·na·tion /ˌnɒmǝ̇ˈneɪʃən‖ˌnɑ-/ *n* [U;C] **1** (an example of) the act, action, or result of nominating or being nominated (NOMINATE): *The committee has the power of nomination to the jobs* (=they can suggest or appoint people for them).|*The club agreed to all the committee's nominations.|Who will get the nomination for president?* **2 place someone's name in nomination** *fml* to NOMINATE someone: *I would be happy to place your name in nomination for the office of president*

nom·i·na·tive¹ /ˈnɒmǝ̇nətɪv, ˈnɒmnə-‖ˈnɑ-/ *adj* [Wa5] showing esp. that a word is the subject of a verb, usu. by special endings or other forms: *nominative endings|Put this noun in(to) the nominative* CASE.|*"We" is a nominative* PRONOUN

nominative² *n* **1** [*usu. sing.*] (esp. in such languages as Latin, Greek, German, etc.) the CASE (set of forms) showing esp. that a word is the subject of a verb: *Put this noun in(to) the nominative* **2** a word in this CASE: *How many nominatives are there on this page?*

nom·i·nee /ˌnɒmǝ̇ˈniː‖ˌnɑ-/ *n* a person who has been NOMINATED

non- /nɒn‖nɑn/ *prefix* [(*used with nouns, adjectives, and adverbs*)] **1** not; the lack of; the opposite of: *nonalphabetical|non-naval|non-English* —see UN- (USAGE) **2** *infml* so bad as not to deserve the name: *It was really a bad book—a non-story with non-characters*

no·nage /ˈnəʊnɪdʒ‖ˈnɑ-, ˈnəʊ-/ *n* [U] *esp. law* the time or condition of being under the age (now 18 in Britain, the US, and elsewhere) fixed by law for full responsibility; MINORITY (4)

no·na·ge·nar·i·an /ˌnəʊnədʒǝ̇ˈneərɪən/ *adj, n* (a person who is) 90 or more and less than 100 years old

non·ag·gres·sion /ˌnɒn-əˈgreʃən‖ˌnɑn-/ *n* [A] not attacking: *a nonaggression agreement* (=each side promising not to attack the other)

non·a·ligned /ˌnɒn-əˈlaɪnd‖ˌnɑn-/ *adj* (of a country) not usually supporting the actions of any particular powerful country or group of countries —compare THIRD WORLD

non·a·lign·ment /ˌnɒn-əˈlaɪnmənt‖ˌnɑn-/ *n* [U] the condition of being NONALIGNED

non·as·sert·ive /ˌnɒn-əˈsɜːtɪv‖ˌnɑn-əˈsɜr-/ *adj* [Wa5] *tech* **1** (of a sentence or CLAUSE) not a simple POSITIVE statement: *The following are all nonassertive*: **a** *"Is he coming?"* **b** *"He isn't coming"* and **c** *"if he's coming"* in *"I wonder if he's coming"* **2** (of a word or phrase) not used in simple POSITIVE statements (such as *ever* in *Is he ever late?*) —**~ly** *adv*

nonce¹ /nɒns‖nɑns/ *n* **for the nonce** *not fml* for the present time; for the TIME being: *Just for the nonce let's plan to go by air: then we can change our minds if it costs too much*

nonce² *adj* [Wa5;A] (esp. of a word, form, etc., in a language) invented for a particular occasion only

non·cha·lance /ˈnɒnʃələns‖ˌnɑnʃəˈlɑns/ *n* [S;U] the state of being NONCHALANT: *He showed a surprising nonchalance the first time he flew a plane*

non·cha·lant /ˈnɒnʃələnt‖ˌnɑnʃəˈlɑnt/ *adj* marked by or showing unforced calmness, and often lack of interest; COOL (3): *a nonchalant carelessness|He appeared nonchalant in court even when the judge spoke to him* —**~ly** *adv*

non·com·ba·tant /ˌnɒnˈkɒmbətənt‖ˌnɑnkəmˈbætənt/ *n* a person, esp. a member of the army or other military force (such as a CHAPLAIN, MEDIC, etc.), not part of or used in actual fighting: *military duty as a noncombatant=noncombatant duty*

non·com·mis·sioned of·fi·cer /ˌnɒnkəˌmɪʃənd ˈɒfɪsəʳ‖ˌnɑn-; -ˈɔf-, -ˈɑf-/ *n* a member of the army, navy, etc., who is lower in rank than a COMMISSIONED OFFICER but has some responsibility to command others; an ENLISTED MAN of higher rank (such as CORPORAL, SERGEANT, or PETTY OFFICER)

non·com·mit·tal /ˌnɒnkəˈmɪtl‖ˌnɑn-/ *adj* not expressing a clear opinion or a clear intention or promise to do something: *I asked him to vote for me but he was noncommittal* —**~ly** *adv*: *answered noncommittally*

non com·pos men·tis /ˌnɒn ˌkɒmpəs ˈmentǝ̇s‖ˌnɑn ˌkɑm-/ *adj* [F] *Lat* lacking the ability to think clearly and esp. to be responsible for one's actions: *The court judged him to have been non compos mentis when he did the murder* —opposite **compos mentis**

non·con·duc·tor /ˌnɒnkənˈdʌktəʳ‖ˌnɑn-/ *n* a material which allows little or no sound, heat, or esp. electricity to pass through it —compare INSULATOR

non·con·form·ist /ˌnɒnkənˈfɔːmǝ̇st‖ˌnɑnkənˈfɔr-/ *adj, n* (of, concerning, or being) a person who does not follow some customary way(s) of living, acting, thinking, etc.: *a political nonconformist|nonconformist habits of dressing*

Nonconformist¹ *n* a member of a NONCONFORMIST Christian religious group: *They're Nonconformists and go to a different church from my family's*

Nonconformist² *adj* [Wa5] of, being, or concerning any of several Christian religious groups which have separated from the CHURCH OF ENGLAND: *Nonconformist churches in England|Their religious opinions are Nonconformist*

non·con·for·mi·ty /ˌnɒnkənˈfɔːmǝ̇ti‖ˌnɑnkənˈfɔr-/ also **non·con·form·is·m** /ˌnɒnkənˈfɔːmɪzəm‖ˌnɑnkənˈfɔr-/— *n* [U] the refusal to follow some customary practice(s): *nonconformity to the usual ways of dressing*

Nonconformity *n* **1** [U] the ideas and practices of NONCONFORMIST groups **2** [R] the whole group of NONCONFORMIST people and organizations

non·con·trib·u·to·ry /ˌnɒnkənˈtrɪbjʊtəri‖ˌnɑnkənˈtrɪbjətori/ *adj* [A;(B)] (of a PENSION plan) paid for by the employer only and not by the person who will receive the money (the EMPLOYEE) —compare CONTRIBUTORY

non·de·script /ˈnɒndǝ̇ˌskrɪpt‖ˌnɑndǝ̇ˈskrɪpt/ *adj* without any strong or interesting qualities; very ordinary-looking; dull: *Her clothes were so nondescript I can't remember what she was wearing*

none¹ /nʌn/ *pron* **1** not any; no amount or part: *"Got any money?" "(I've got) none at all|none whatever. None of that money on the table is mine."|She had none of her mother's beauty.|None of your foolishness, please!* (=Stop being/don't be foolish)| *"None of us wants to be killed young"* (SEU S.) **2** not any; not one (usu. of a group of more than 2): *None of my friends ever come(s) to see me.|None of the telephones is/are working.|If you need a repairman, there's none better than my brother* —compare NEITHER **3** *usu. lit* not any such thing or person: *Once I had a lover but now I have none* **4 have none of** *fml* to take no part in, not allow, or not accept: *I'll have none of your stupid ideas!|He was offered a job but he said he'd have none of it* **5 none but** *often lit* not any thing or person except: *None but the best coffee is good enough.|None but a strong man could have lifted it* **6 none other (than)** (*used for expressing surprise*) no one else (but): *"It's none other than Tom! We thought you were in Africa! Can it really be you?" "None other!"* (=it's really me) —see also NONETHELESS; see EITHER (USAGE)

none² *adv* **1 none the** (*before a* COMPARATIVE *word* +*usu.* for) not; in no way: *He spent 2 weeks in hospital but he's none the better for it.|My car is none the worse for* WEAR (=Use has done it no harm) **2**

none the wiser not knowing about or not discovering a fact, secret, trick, etc.; UNAWARE: *If we take only one piece of cake, mother will be none the wiser* **3 none too** (before an adjective or adverb) not very or not at all: *The service in this restaurant is none too fast.|He gave a none-too-believable excuse for his absence*

non·en·ti·ty /nɒ'nentɨti‖nɑ-/ *n* **1** [C] a person without much ability, character, or importance: *a weak government, full of political nonentities* **2** [U] the condition of being such a person or of being unimportant: *came to office after years of political nonentity*

none·such /'nʌnsʌtʃ/ *n* [*usu. sing.*] *lit* a person without equal: *skills which made him a nonesuch in the world of music* —compare NONPAREIL

none·the·less /ˌnʌnðə'les◂/ *adv* NEVERTHELESS

non-e·vent /ˌ··'·/ *n infml* a happening that is much less important, interesting, etc., than expected or planned: *The election was a non-event/the non-event of the year: the same old people got back in office*

non·fic·tion /ˌnɒn'fɪkʃən‖ˌnɑn-/ *n* [U] writing that is about facts rather than imagined things; not poetry, plays, stories, and NOVELS

non·flam·ma·ble /ˌnɒn'flæməbəl‖ˌnɑn-/ also **non·in·flam·ma·ble** /ˌnɒn-ɪn'flæməbəl‖ˌnɑn-/— *adj* difficult or impossible to set on fire —opposite **inflammable**

non·in·ter·ven·tion /ˌnɒnˌɪntə'venʃən‖ˌnɑnˌɪntər-/ also **non·in·ter·fer·ence** /ˌnɒnˌɪntə'fɪərəns‖ˌnɑnˌɪntər-/— *n* **1** the practice by a government of taking no part in the affairs of another country or in disagreements between other countries **2** (in general) the practice of not trying to influence the decisions of others

non-i·ron /ˌ· '··◂/ *adj* [Wa5] (of a garment) that does not need to be ironed after washing

non·ob·serv·ance /ˌnɒn-əb'zɜːvəns‖ˌnɑn-əb'zɜr-/ *n* [U] failure to keep a rule or practise a custom: *Nonobservance of the rules could get you into trouble*

non·pa·reil /'nɒnpərəl, -pəreɪl‖ˌnɑnpə'rel/ *adj, n lit* (a person) so excellent as to have no equal; PARAGON(-like): *an object of nonpareil beauty*

non·pay·ment /ˌnɒn'peɪmənt‖ˌnɑn-/ *n* [U (*of*)] failure to pay (bills, tax, etc.): *in trouble for nonpayment of his last year's tax*

non·plus /ˌnɒn'plʌs‖ˌnɑn-/ *v* **-ss-** [Wv5;T1 *usu. pass.*] to cause (someone) to be surprised and not know what to think or do: *The speaker looked very nonplussed. The angry remarks from his listeners had nonplussed him*

non-prof·it-mak·ing /ˌ· '·· ˌ··/ *adj* **1** not successful in making a profit: *The business turned out to be non-profit-making and soon closed down* **2** (*AmE* **non-profit** /ˌ· '··/)— *BrE* not run in order to make a profit: *a non-profit-making service supported by government money*

non·pro·lif·e·ra·tion /ˌnɒnprəˌlɪfə'reɪʃən‖ˌnɑn-/ *n* [U] **1** the result of keeping atomic weapons in only the same amounts and the same countries as at the (present) time: *a nonproliferation agreement* **2** (in general) the principle of preventing the spreading of something regarded as undesirable

non·res·i·dent /ˌnɒn'rezɨdənt‖ˌnɑn-/ *adj, n* (a person) not living in a certain place, such as **a** a country: *May I drive a car here as a nonresident?* **b** a university building: *a nonresident student* **c** a hotel: *The hotel restaurant is open to nonresidents*

non·re·stric·tive /ˌnɒnrɨs'trɪktɪv‖ˌnɑn-/ *adj* [Wa5] (in grammar) not limiting, but giving more information: *In "My brother, who collects stamps", the words "who collects stamps" are a nonrestrictive* CLAUSE, *because they do not tell us which brother is meant but tell us something else about him* —compare RESTRICTIVE

non·sense /'nɒnsəns‖'nɑnsens/ *n* **1** [U;(*BrE* also S)] speech or writing with no meaning: *She left out 3 words when she copied the sentence and the result was (a) nonsense* **2** [U] speech, writing, thinking, etc., that goes against good sense; RUBBISH[1] (2): *A lot of the government's new ideas are nonsense.|"I can't go out dressed like this." "Nonsense!/What nonsense! You look fine."* **3** [U] foolish behaviour: *Stop that nonsense, children! Behave yourselves.|a* STRICT *teacher who would stand no nonsense* **4** [U] humorous and fanciful poetry usu. telling a rather meaningless story: *Edward Lear's wonderful nonsense (poetry)* **5 make nonsense of** *BrE* also **make a nonsense of**— to spoil or make of no effect: *Your foolish anger made nonsense of our plans for peace with the enemy!*

non·sen·si·cal /nɒn'sensɨkəl‖nɑn-/ *adj* being, marked by, or full of NONSENSE; foolish or ABSURD: *nonsensical opinions/sounds* —**~ly** *adv* [Wa4]

non seq·ui·tur /ˌnɒn 'sekwɨtə'‖ˌnɑn-/ *n* **non sequiturs** *fml & Lat* a statement which does not follow from the facts or arguments which are given; an incorrect piece of reasoning

non·skid /ˌnɒn'skɪd‖ˌnɑn-/ *adj* [Wa5;A;(B)] (of a tyre) built so as not to slip (SKID) easily on the road

non·smok·er /ˌnɒn'sməʊkə'‖ˌnɑn-/ *n* **1** a person who does not smoke tobacco **2** *BrE* a (part of a) railway carriage where smoking is not allowed

non·stan·dard /ˌnɒn'stændəd◂‖ˌnɑn'stændərd◂/ *adj* **1** (of words, expressions, pronunciations, etc.) not usually used by educated careful native speakers of a language **2** (in general) not standard —compare SUBSTANDARD (2)

non·start·er /ˌnɒn'stɑːtə'‖ˌnɑn'stɑr-/ *n* [*usu. sing.*] *BrE infml* a person or idea without any chance of success: *We wanted to buy a house, but that was a nonstarter: we hadn't nearly enough money*

non·stick /ˌnɒn'stɪk◂‖ˌnɑn-/ *adj* [Wa5;A;(B)] (as of a cooking pan) having a specially treated smooth inside surface that food will not stick to

non·stop /ˌnɒn'stɒp◂‖ˌnɑn'stɑp◂/ *adv* [Wa5;F] **1** (of a trip, esp. a flight) without stopping before the end: *Fly nonstop to New York!* **2** *not fml* without a pause or interruption: *music playing nonstop all night* —**nonstop** *adj* [Wa5]

non-U /ˌnɒn 'juː◂‖ˌnɑn-/ *adj humor, esp. BrE* (esp. of words or behaviour) not of the UPPER CLASS: *Calling the midday meal "dinner" is often considered non-U* —opposite **U**

non·u·ni·on /ˌnɒn-'juːnɪən◂‖ˌnɑn-/ *n* [Wa5] **1** not belonging to a trade union: *nonunion workmen* **2** not favouring trade union members or giving official recognition to a trade union: *a nonunion business*

non·ver·bal /ˌnɒn'vɜːbəl◂‖ˌnɑn'vɜr-/ *adj* not carried out or marked by the use of words: *nonverbal means of expression|nonverbal* COMMUNICATION —**~ly** *adv*

non·vi·o·lence /ˌnɒn'vaɪələns‖ˌnɑn-/ also **nonviolent re·sist·ance** /·ˌ··· ·'··/, (*now rare*) **passive resistance**— *n* [U] opposition without using force or violence for fighting, shown esp. by not obeying laws or orders

non·vi·o·lent /ˌnɒn'vaɪələnt◂‖ˌnɑn-/ *adj* not using violence, esp. because of a belief that violence should not be used for a political purpose: *nonviolent action in the form of a march through the streets of London* —**~ly** *adv*

non·white /ˌnɒn'waɪt◂‖ˌnɑn-/ *adj, n* [Wa5] (a person) not WHITE by race

noo·dle /'nuːdl/ *n* [*usu. pl.*] a usu. long thin piece of a paste made from flour, water, and eggs. The pieces are boiled until soft and eaten in soups, with meat, etc.

nook /nʊk/ *n* **1** *humor or lit* a small space in a corner of a room: *sitting in the chimney nook* (=the space in a corner beside the chimney) **2** *humor or lit* a sheltered and private place: *resting in a shady nook in the garden* **3 nooks and crannies** *not fml* hidden or little-known places: *search every nook and cranny* (=look everywhere)

noon /nuːn/ *n* [R] the middle of the day; 12 o'clock in the daytime; MIDDAY: *leave home at noon|eat the noon meal|Noon is the earliest time I can come.|sleep until noon*

noon·day /ˈnuːndeɪ/ *n lit* MIDDAY: *the noonday sun*

no one /ˈ· ·/ *pron* NOBODY[1]

noose /nuːs/ *n* **1** [C] a ring formed by the end of a cord, rope, etc., which closes more tightly as it is pulled **2** [*the*+R] a rope with such a ring in it, used to hang a person; death by hanging: *How did he escape the* (HANGMAN'*s*) *noose for so many years?|*(*infml*) *This time you've really put your head in the noose* (=You've let yourself be caught and punished)

nope /nəʊp/ *adv infml* NO[1] (1): *"Want anything to eat?" "Nope. I'm not hungry"*

no place /ˈ· ·/ *adv, n not fml, esp. AmE* nowhere

nor /nɔːʳ/ *conj* **1** (used between the 2 or more choices after *neither*): *just warm, neither cold nor hot* —see NEITHER[2] **2** (*used before the 2nd, 3rd, etc., choices after* not) and/or not: *The job cannot be done by you nor* (*by*) *me nor* (*by*) *anyone else* **3** (*used at the beginning of an expression just before a verb*) and also +not: *I don't want to go, nor will I* (=and I won't).*|We have many enemies; nor can we be sure of all our friends* (*BrE* also *and nor can we be sure . . .*)*.|The meal didn't cost much, nor was it very good* (*BrE* also *but/and nor was it very good*)
USAGE *BrE* can use *and* and *but* before NOR (3), *AmE* cannot. Both *BrE* and *AmE* can use *and* and *but* before NEITHER[4]: *. . . but/and* **neither** *was it very good.* —see NEITHER (USAGE).

nor'- *prefix* (used by seamen) north: *nor'east|nor'west*

Nor·dic /ˈnɔːdɪk‖ˈnɔr-/ *adj* **1** of or related to the Germanic peoples of northern Europe **2** of or related to Norway, Sweden, Denmark, Iceland, and Finland

Nor·folk jack·et /ˌnɔːfək ˈdʒækɪ̠t‖ˌnɔr-/ *n* a man's short coat with a belt and with flat folds (PLEATs) down the right and left sides in front and at the back

norm /nɔːm‖nɔrm/ *n* **1** [*often pl.*] a standard of proper behaviour or principle of right and wrong; rule: *social norms* **2** a usual or expected number, amount, pattern of action or behaviour, etc.: average: *The national norm in this examination is 70 out of 100*

nor·mal /ˈnɔːməl‖ˈnɔr-/ *adj* **1** according to what is expected, usual, or average: *normal working hours from 9 to 5|normal temperatures during November|It's perfectly normal to get angry with your mother sometimes.|Rainfall has been above/below normal this July* **2** (of a person) developing in the expected way; without any disorder in mind or body: *a normal child in every way* **3** [(*to*)] *tech* at right angles; PERPENDICULAR[1] (1,2) **4** *tech* (of a chemical SOLUTION) of the strength of 1 gram per litre

nor·mal·i·ty /nɔːˈmælɪ̠ti‖nɔr-/ *AmE* also **nor·mal·cy** /ˈnɔːməlsi‖ˈnɔr-/— *n* [U] the quality or fact of being NORMAL

nor·mal·ize, -ise /ˈnɔːməlaɪz‖ˈnɔr-/ *v* **1** [IØ;T1] to (cause to) become NORMAL **2** [IØ;T1] **a** (esp. of relations between countries) to come back to a good or friendly state: *Relations were slow to normalize after the war* **b** to cause (esp. relations between countries) to come back to a good or friendly state: *The enemies were slow to normalize their relations after the war* **3** [T1] to make (a piece of writing) follow only one set of rules for spelling, ABBREVIATION, etc. —**-ization** /ˌnɔːməlaɪˈzeɪʃən‖ˌnɔrmələ-/ *n* [U]

nor·mal·ly /ˈnɔːməli‖ˈnɔr-/ *adv* **1** in a NORMAL way or to a NORMAL degree: *behaving normally in spite of anxiety|a normally active child* **2** in the usual conditions; ordinarily: *I normally go to bed early, but I stayed up late last night*

normal school /ˈ·· ·/ *n* [C;U] *AmE now rare* (a) college for training school teachers

Nor·man /ˈnɔːmən‖ˈnɔr-/ *adj* Wa5 **1** of or concerning the northern French people who conquered England in the 11th century: *the Norman Conquest* **2** (of buildings in Britain) built in or related to a style of building (**Norman architecture**) in this period; in the ROMANESQUE style: *a Norman church|a Norman arch*

nor·ma·tive /ˈnɔːmətɪv‖ˈnɔr-/ *adj fml* **1** explaining, stating, or urging obedience to a rule; PRESCRIPTIVE: *normative judgments about how people should act* **2** *rare* according to a NORM: *a strange idea not part of normative Christian belief*

north[1] /nɔːθ‖nɔrθ/ *adv* [Wa5] (*often cap.*) **1** towards the NORTH[2] (1): *to travel* (*further*) *north|The room faces North, so it's always rather cold.|Edinburgh is* (*a long way*) (*to the*) *north of London* **2 up north** *infml* to or in the NORTH[2] (1): *to travel/live up north*

north[2] *n* (*often cap.*) **1** [(*the*) R] (the direction of) one of the 4 main points of the compass, which is on the left of a person facing the rising sun: *I'm lost: which direction is north?|a window facing the north|the north wall of a building* —compare MAGNETIC **north** POLE **2** [*the*+R;(A)] (of a wind) (coming from) this direction: *a cold north wind|The wind's in the north* —compare NORTHERLY
USAGE Note the word order in this fixed phr.: **north and south**: *People came from north and south to see the performance.*

North *n* [*the*+R] **1** (*sometimes not cap.*) the part of a country which is further north than the rest **2** (in England) the northern part of England, usu. including Manchester, Hull, and areas beyond **3** (in the US) the eastern states generally north of Washington, D.C., esp. in talking about politics or history: *The North defeated the* SOUTH *in 1865*
USAGE Clear divisions of the earth's surface, esp. political ones, are usually called **North**, **South**, **East**, or **West**. More uncertain ones are usually **Northern**, **Southern**, **Eastern**, or **Western**. Compare: **South** *Africa*|**Southern** *England|the* **North** POLE|**Northern** *Europe*|**East** *Germany*|**Eastern** *countries*. But these words are often part of a name, and there is no clear rule about which form will be chosen.

north·bound /ˈnɔːθbaʊnd‖ˈnɔrθ-/ *adj* [Wa5] travelling towards the north: *northbound traffic*

north·east[1] /ˌnɔːθˈiːst◂‖ˌnɔrθ-/ *adv* [Wa5] (*often cap.*) towards the NORTHEAST[2] (1): *to sail northeast|Burma is* (*a long way*) (*to the*) *northeast of Ceylon*

northeast[2] *n* (*often cap.*) **1** [(*the*) R] (the direction of) the point of the compass which is half-way between north and east **2** [*the*+R;(A)] (of a wind) (coming from) this direction: *a northeast wind|The wind's in the northeast* —compare NORTHEASTERLY

north·east·er /ˌnɔːθˈiːstəʳ‖ˌnɔrθ-/ *n* a strong wind or storm coming from the NORTHEAST[2] (1)

north·east·er·ly /ˌnɔːθˈiːstəli◂‖ˌnɔrθˈiːstərli◂/ *adj* **1** towards or in the NORTHEAST[2] (1) **2** [Wa5] (of a wind) coming from the NORTHEAST[2] (1)

north·east·ern /ˌnɔːθˈiːstən◂‖ˌnɔrθˈiːstərn◂/ *adj* (*often cap.*) of or belonging to the NORTHEAST[2] (1) part of anything, esp. of a country

north·east·ward /ˌnɔːθˈiːstwəd◂‖ˌnɔrθˈiːstwərd◂/ *adj* going towards the NORTHEAST² (1): *in a northeastward direction* —compare NORTHEASTERLY

north·east·wards /ˌnɔːθˈiːstwədz‖ˌnɔrθˈiːstwərdz/ *AmE* also **northeastward**— *adv* [Wa5] towards the NORTHEAST² (1); NORTHEAST¹

nor·ther·ly /ˈnɔːðəli‖ˈnɔrðərli/ *adj* **1** towards or in the north: *the northerly shore of the lake|a northerly direction* **2** [Wa5] (of a wind) coming from the north: *a cold northerly wind*

nor·thern /ˈnɔːðən‖ˈnɔrðərn/ *adj* (*often cap.*) of or belonging to the north part of anything, esp. of the world or of a country: *The northern half of the Earth is called the Northern* HEMISPHERE.|*the northern wall of a building*

Nor·thern·er /ˈnɔːðənəʳ‖ˈnɔrðər-/ *n* a person living in or coming from the northern part of a country

northern lights /ˌ·· ˈ·/ *n* [*the*+P] see AURORA

nor·thern·most /ˈnɔːðənməʊst‖ˈnɔrðərn-/ *adj* [Wa5] *fml* furthest north: *the northernmost parts of Scotland*

north pole /ˌ· ˈ·/ *n* **1** [*the*+R;C] (*usu. caps.*) (the lands around) the most northern point on the surface of the earth, or of another chief heavenly body (PLANET) **2** [*the*+R] the point in the sky to the north, around which stars seem to turn

north·ward /ˈnɔːθwəd‖ˈnɔrθwərd/ *adj* going towards the north: *in a northward direction* —compare NORTHERLY

north·wards /ˈnɔːθwədz‖ˈnɔrθwərdz/ *AmE* also **northward**— *adv* towards the north; north: *They travelled northwards*

north·west¹ /ˌnɔːθˈwest◂‖ˌnɔrθ-/ *adv* [Wa5] (*often cap.*) towards the NORTHWEST² (1): *to travel northwest|London is (a long way) (to the) northwest of Rome*

northwest² *n* (*often cap.*) **1** [(*the*) R] (the direction of) the point of the compass which is half-way between north and west **2** [*the*+R;(A)] (of a wind) (coming from) this direction: *a northwest wind|The wind's in the northwest* —compare NORTHWESTERLY

north·west·er /ˌnɔːθˈwestəʳ‖ˌnɔrθ-/ *n* a strong wind or storm from the NORTHWEST² (1)

north·west·er·ly /ˌnɔːθˈwestəli◂‖ˌnɔrθˈwestərli◂/ *adj* **1** towards or in the NORTHWEST² (1) **2** [Wa5] (of a wind) coming from the NORTHWEST

north·west·ern /ˌnɔːθˈwestən◂‖ˌnɔrθˈwestərn◂/ *adj* (*often cap.*) of or belonging to the NORTHWEST² (1) part of anything, esp. of a country

north·west·ward /ˌnɔːθˈwestwəd◂‖ˌnɔrθˈwestwərd◂/ *adj* going towards the NORTHWEST² (1): *in a northwestward direction* —compare NORTHWESTERLY

north·west·wards /ˌnɔːθˈwestwədz‖ˌnɔrθˈwestwərdz/ *AmE* also **northwestward**— *adv* [Wa5] towards the NORTHWEST² (1); NORTHWEST

nos *written abbrev. for:* numbers

nose¹ /nəʊz/ *n* **1** [C] the part of the face above the mouth, which in human beings stands out from the face, through which air is drawn in to be breathed, and which is the organ of smell —see picture at HUMAN² **2** [C] *infml* this organ regarded as representing too great interest in things which do not concern one: *a troublesome woman with her nose in/into everything|Keep your (big) nose out of my affairs!* **3** [S] **a** the sense of smell: *a dog with a good nose* **b** the ability to find (out) or recognize things: *Follow your nose on this job, and see what information you can find out* **4** [C] the front end of something, such as a car, plane, tool, or gun: *pointed the nose of the car towards home* (=drove towards home) —see picture at AIRCRAFT **5 cut off one's nose to spite one's face** to do something to one's own disadvantage because one is angry **6 lead (someone) by the nose** *infml* to control (someone) completely **7 pay through the nose (for)** *infml* to pay a great deal too much money (for) **8 put someone's nose out of joint** *infml, esp. BrE* to offend and hurt someone's feelings by taking his place in the love or admiration of others **9 rub someone's nose in (the dirt)** *infml* to punish someone, esp. by reminding him of (the bad results of his own actions): *All right; I know I'm wrong! You don't need to rub my nose in it/in the dirt!* **10 turn up one's nose (at)** *infml* to consider (something) not good enough to eat, take part in, etc.: *I wish my children wouldn't turn up their noses at vegetables/at doing their schoolwork* **11 under someone's (very) nose** *infml* in a way or place that might be easily found (out) by someone: *The pen I thought I'd lost was on my desk, right under my nose.|They made their secret plans under the enemy's (very) nose(s)!*

nose² *v* **1** [X9] to push with the nose: *The dog nosed the door open* **2** [L9;X9: (OUT)] to move or push (oneself, a vehicle, etc.) ahead slowly or carefully: *a ship nosing its way through the narrow passage|I nosed the car (out)/The car nosed (out) into the traffic*

nose a·bout *AmE* also **nose a·round**— *v adv; prep* [T1;IØ (*for*)] *infml* to search (for): *The old lady was nosing about (the house) (looking) for dust on the tables*

nose·bag /ˈnəʊzbæg/ *AmE* usu. **feedbag**— *n* a bag hung around a horse's head to hold the food it eats

nose·bleed /ˈnəʊzbliːd/ *n* a case of bleeding from the nose: *I got/had a nosebleed earlier today*

nose·cone /ˈnəʊzkəʊn/ *n* (on a space vehicle or MISSILE) the CONE-shaped front part which may separate from the rest

-nosed /nəʊzd/ *comb. form* with a nose of the stated kind or shape: *long-nosed*|SNUB-NOSED

nose·dive¹ /ˈnəʊzdaɪv/ *n* **1** a drop by an aircraft with its nose pointing straight down **2** *not fml* a sudden large drop, as in prices

nosedive² *v* [IØ] **1** (of an aircraft) to drop suddenly with the nose pointing straight down **2** *not fml* to fall or drop suddenly and by a great deal

nose flute /ˈ· ·/ *n* a musical instrument played with air from the nose

nose·gay /ˈnəʊzgeɪ/ *n lit* a small bunch of flowers, usu. to be worn on a dress or other garment —compare CORSAGE (2)

nose in·to *v prep* [T1] *infml* to show too great interest in (other people's affairs); PRY into: *guests who nose into everything in the house*

nose out *v adv* [T1] *infml* **1** to discover by close searching: *My study has nosed out some interesting facts* **2** *AmE* to win against (someone) in a race, competition, etc., by only a small amount: *He was nosed out in the election by a younger man*

nosh¹ /nɒʃ‖nɑʃ/ *v* [IØ] *esp. BrE sl* to eat: *Stop noshing and help me wash up!* —**~er** *n*

nosh² *n sl* **1** [U] *BrE* food: *It's an evil-looking restaurant but their nosh is good* **2** [S] *esp. BrE* an act of eating: *Let's have a quick nosh before the film starts*

nosh-up /ˈ· ·/ *n* [S] *BrE sl* a usu. good or big meal: *What a nosh-up we had on my birthday!*

nos·tal·gia /nɒˈstældʒə‖nɑ-/ *n* [U] fondness for something formerly known or for some period in the past: *nostalgia for the clothes of the 1920s|filled with nostalgia by hearing my old favourite song* —**-gic** *adj* —**-gically** *adv* [Wa4]

nos·tril /ˈnɒstrəl‖ˈnɑ-/ *n* **1** either of the 2 openings at the end of the nose, through which air is drawn —see picture at HUMAN² **2** either of the fleshy coverings of these openings: *The Indian princess wore a diamond in her right nostril*

nos·trum /ˈnɒstrəm‖ˈnɑ-/ *n derog* a medicine of

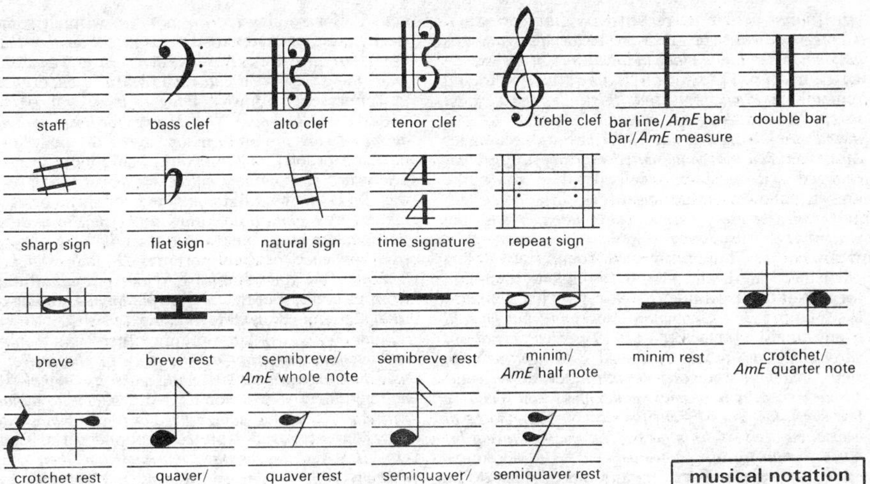

doubtful value and unknown contents, (falsely) claimed to be effective: (fig.) *There is no simple nostrum for political and social evils* —compare PANACEA

nos·y, nosey /ˈnəʊzi/ *adj* [Wa1] *derog & not fml* interested in things that do not concern one; PRYing: *Don't be so nosy! You'll find out my plans when I'm ready to tell you* —**nosiness** *n* [U]

nosy park·er /ˌ·· ˈ··/ *n* [C;*you*+N] *BrE derog & infml* a NOSY person

not /nɒt‖nɑt/ *adv* **1** (used for changing a word or expression to one with the opposite meaning): **a** (with verbs): *"You shall not kill."*—The Bible|*I will not pay!*|*I've not seen him this week.*|*"He's not arriving until the 10th"* (SEU S.).|*If you didn't like it you were wrong not to say so.*|*Not saying anything was a bad idea* —see USAGE **b** (with other words and expressions): *Not everyone likes this book* (=some people don't like it).| *It's a cat, not a dog.*|*The murder was quick, but not carefully planned.*|*The question is important and not (at all) easy to answer.* (compare *no easier than* . . .)|*"Do you want to go?" "Not me!"* (=I don't, though others may want to)|*Not all his work is successful* (=some is unsuccessful).|*Not all his work could save him* (=all his work, taken together, was not enough to save him) **2** (used in place of a whole expression, often after verbs marked [5b]): *Will he be here, or not?*|*"Will it rain today?" "I hope not"* (=I hope it won't rain).|*"Have you got £5 to lend me?" "I'm afraid not."*|*Drop that gun! If not, you'll be sorry* —opposite **so 3** *esp. pomp* (used with NEGATIVE words, esp. those beginning with *un-* and words meaning *small, slow,* etc., to give force to the opposite meaning): *a not unwelcome guest* (=a very welcome one)|*not slow to complain, and not without good reason*|*drank not a little* (=drank a lot) *of the good wine*|*He had many enemies, but found he was not without friends as well* **4 not a** (*used before a noun*) no: *Not a (single) man was killed and only 3 wounded.*|*"How much did this cost?" "Not a penny!"* (=nothing) **5 Not at all** (an answer to polite praise or thanks): *"Thanks for your trouble." "Not at all: I enjoyed it"* **6 not . . . but** (to show one choice instead of another): *Shakespeare was not a musician but a writer.*|*Othello said he loved not wisely but too well* **7 not only . . . but (also)** (to show a second choice in addition to the first one): *Shakespeare was not only a writer but (also) an actor* **8 not but what** *nonstandard* although: *He's never walked that far—not but what he could do it if he tried* **9 not half** see HALF[5] (2,6) **10 not that** *not fml* I don't mean that; although . . . not: *Not that it matters, but how did you spend the money I gave you?*|*Who were you with last night? Not that I care, of course* **11 not to say** *not fml* and almost; or perhaps even: *He sounded impolite, not to say rude.*|*It would be foolish, not to say mad, to sell your car*

USAGE **Not** can be shortened to **n't** when changing the following verbs to their opposite meaning: *is, are, was, were, has, have, had, do, does, did, can, could, would, should, must, ought, need,* (*BrE*) *may, might, dare, used*. *Shall* **not** and *will* **not** can be shortened to *shan't, won't*. Otherwise **not** is not shortened. One cannot say **I hopen't*. —see NO (USAGE)

no·ta·bil·i·ty /ˌnəʊtəˈbɪlᵻti/ *n* **1** [U] the quality of being NOTABLE[1] **2** [C *usu. pl.*] *rare* NOTABLE[2]

no·ta·ble[1] /ˈnəʊtəbəl/ *adj* [(*for*)] worthy of notice; REMARKABLE, important, or excellent; OUTSTANDING: *notable events*|*a notable lawyer*|*a horse notable for its strength*

notable[2] *n* [*usu. pl.*] a person of high rank, fame, or importance

no·ta·bly /ˈnəʊtəbli/ *adv* **1** noticeably, REMARKABLY, or in a way which might attract attention: *notably higher sales*|*many members notably absent from the meeting* **2** especially; particularly: *Many members were absent, notably the vice-chairman*

no·ta·rize, -rise /ˈnəʊtəraɪz/ *v* [Wv5;T1 *often pass.*] *fml* to make (a written statement) official as a NOTARY: *Please have your statement notarized and return it to this office*

no·ta·ry /ˈnəʊtəri/ also **notary pub·lic** /ˌ··· ˈ··/— *n* a person (in Britain usu. a SOLICITOR) with the power in law to witness the signing of written statements and make them official

no·ta·tion /nəʊˈteɪʃən/ *n* [C9 *usu. sing.*;U9] (writing that uses) a/the usu. accepted set of written signs to describe the stated kinds of things: *a page covered with musical notation*|*The 2 scientists use different notations for the same objects.*|EXPONENTIAL *notation saves space in writing large numbers*

notch[1] /nɒtʃ‖nɑtʃ/ *n* **1** a V-shaped cut in a surface or edge: *a notch in the stick, cut by a sharp knife* **2** *not fml* a degree; STEP[1] (6): *a good book, several notches above anything else by this writer* **3** *AmE* a narrow passage between mountains

notch[2] *v* **1** [T1] to make a notch in: *They fitted the logs together by notching the ends* **2** [D1 (*for*);T1:

(UP)] *infml* to win or record (a victory or gain): *The team notched (up) their 3rd victory in a row.|His action notched him a place in the history of the war*

note¹ /nəʊt/ *v* **1** [T1,5,6a,b] to pay attention to and remember: *Please note that this bill must be paid within 10 days.|Note my new name and how to spell it/and how I spell it* **2** [T1,5,6a] to recognize; OBSERVE: *You may have noted that my address has changed* **3** [T1,5,6a] to call attention to; make known; show: *In his speech he first noted the importance of the occasion.|The newspaper does not note what happened next*

note² *n* **1** [C] **a** a musical sound, usu. of a particular length and PITCH³ (7) **b** a written sign for any of these sounds **2** [S9, esp. *of*] **a** a quality of voice: *There was a note of anger in what he said* **b** any quality; ELEMENT (1): *There was a note of carelessness in the way she acted* **3** [C *usu. pl. with sing. meaning*] a record or reminder in writing: *Make notes/a note of how much money you spend on the trip.|She takes* (=writes down) *good notes of everything that's said in class.|The speaker forgot his notes so had to talk from memory* **4** [C] a remark added to a piece of writing and placed outside the main part of the writing (as at the side or bottom of a page, or at the end): *I've written notes in my copy of his book* —compare FOOTNOTE **5** [C] **a** a short usu. informal letter: *a note to say thank you for a gift* **b** a formal letter between governments: *a* DIPLOMATIC *note* **6** [C] (*AmE* usu. **bill**)— a piece of paper money: *a pound note* (=for £1)|*a £5 note| How much of the money is in notes and how much in coin?* —compare BANK NOTE **7** [C] PROMISSORY NOTE **8 compare notes** *not fml* **a** (*with*) to tell one's experiences and opinions of something (to) **b** (of 2 people) to tell these to one another: *Mary and I have been comparing notes on our trips to India: I've been comparing notes with Mary* **9 mental note** something fixed in the mind or to be remembered: *I must make a mental note to buy coffee—and a mental note of the address of the new shop* **10 of note a** of fame or importance: *a musician of note|writers of lesser note* **b** of public knowledge: *His religious opinions are a matter of (some) note* (=something known (rather widely)) **11 strike a note (of)** *not fml* to express the stated feeling or message: *Let me strike a note of hopefulness/a hopeful note: this job will not be as hard as you think* **12 take note of** to pay attention to: *Take (careful) note of what I say and please don't forget it*

note·book /ˈnəʊtbʊk/ *n* a book of plain paper in which NOTEs² (3) are or may be written: *I kept a notebook on my trip abroad* (=recorded my experiences in a book).|*buy a notebook to use in classes*

note·case /ˈnəʊtkeɪs/ *n becoming rare* WALLET (1)

not·ed /ˈnəʊtɪ̵d/ *adj* [(*for*)] well-known; famous: *a noted performer|a town noted for its cheeses*

note·pa·per /ˈnəʊtˌpeɪpəʳ/ *n* [U] paper suitable for writing letters and NOTEs² (5a)

note·wor·thy /ˈnəʊtˌwɜːðiǁ-ɜr-/ *adj* (esp. of things and events) worthy of attention; NOTABLE¹: *wrote a noteworthy book on the subject*

noth·ing¹ /ˈnʌθɪŋ/ *pron* **1** not any thing; no thing: *There's nothing in this box: it's empty.|I've got nothing at all/nothing whatever to do.|Nothing ever happens in this town.|If you have nothing to do, come with me.|This hotel leaves nothing to be desired* (=it has everything).|*There's nothing unusual about my leaving the office early* (=I do it often) **2 care nothing for** *lit* to dislike or not care about: *I don't love you and I care nothing for your money or your title!* **3 for nothing a** for no money; free: *I got this bicycle for nothing: a friend just gave it to me* **b** for no purpose; with no good result: *All our preparation for nothing! No one's even come to the party* **4 not . . . for nothing** *not fml* not . . . without some (usu. stated or understood) reason: *"You shot that bear 100 yards away!" "I wasn't born in Tennessee for nothing!"* (=You can really learn to shoot well in Tennessee!) **5 have nothing on** *infml* **a** to be no better than: (*humor*) *Now Henry Ford has nothing on me: I have my own car too!* **b** (of the police) to have no proof that (someone) has done a crime: *The police have nothing on us: we hid the body very well* **6 (in) nothing flat** *infml* (in) very little or very fast time: *I could do a little job like that in nothing flat* **7 make nothing of a** also **think nothing of**— to treat as easy or unimportant: *He thinks/makes nothing of walking 15 miles* **b** to understand nothing from (a book, speech, etc.): *I could make nothing of what he said* **8 next to nothing** see NEXT TO² **9 nothing (. . .) but** nothing other than; only: *nothing for supper but a little piece of cheese|Don't have him for a friend: he's nothing but a criminal* **10 nothing doing** *sl* **a** I won't!; No!: *"Come to a film with me." "Nothing doing: I've got to stay home and work"* **b** no result, interest, action, permission, etc.: *I asked to see the chairman, but there was nothing doing* (=I wasn't allowed) **11 nothing for it** no other way: *With the bridge destroyed, there was nothing for it; we had to swim* **12 nothing if not** much or very; EXTREMELY: *He was nothing if not clever* (=he was very clever) **13 nothing like** *infml* **a** nothing better than: *There's nothing like a holiday to make one feel rested* **b** see NOTHING² **14 nothing much** *infml* not much; very little: *"Anything interesting happening?" "No, nothing much"* **15 nothing of** *fml* no part or quality of: *There was nothing of the lady in her behaviour* (=she didn't act like a lady).|*nothing of gentleness in his voice* **16 nothing of the kind** (used in a polite or forceful answer of no): *"I'm sorry to cause you trouble." "My dear friend, it's nothing of the kind"* (=no trouble).|*"I'm going out." "You'll do nothing of the kind! You must stay at home"* **17 nothing to a** (of a person) not an object of love to (someone): *John likes Mary very much, but I'm afraid he is nothing to her* **b** also **nothing in**—no truth in (a report, story, etc.): *There is nothing in/to the stories you hear: he's really very nice* **c** no work or trouble in (doing something): *There's nothing to driving a car: you just need practice* **18 nothing to do with** (something of) no relation or concern to or with: *That idea (esp. BrE) is/ (esp. AmE) has nothing to do with me.| I want nothing to do with him or his ideas!* **19 think nothing of it** (a polite answer to thanks) you're WELCOME³ (4); NOT (5) at all **20 to say nothing of** without even considering; not to MENTION² (4): *3 people badly hurt, to say nothing of damage to the building*

nothing² *adv infml* in no way; not (esp. in the phrs. **nothing like, nothing near**): *"Is it £3 for a taxi to the airport?" "No, nothing like/near (as much as that)"* (=it's much cheaper)

nothing³ *n* **1** [*usu. sing.*] a thing or person with no value or importance: *She's an interesting person but her husband is a real nothing* **2 sweet nothings** *infml, now rare or humor* words of love: *sitting in a dark corner saying sweet nothings to one another*

noth·ing·ness /ˈnʌθɪŋnɪ̵s/ *n* [U] **1** the state of being nothing; not being: *Is there only nothingness after death?* **2** emptiness or worthlessness: *Her husband's death left a feeling of nothingness in her heart*

no·tice¹ /ˈnəʊtɪ̵s/ *n* **1** [U] **a** a warning or information about something to happen: (*fml*) *These rules are* SUBJECT *to* (=may) *change without notice.|Can you be ready at 10 minutes' notice/at short notice?* (=if I tell you only 10 minutes/a short time before) **b** formal warning that a person may no longer live or work in a place: *The company gave notice to 10 workers/gave 10 workers their notice.|I gave the company/the owner of the flat my notice* (=said I planned to leave).|*They wanted 3 weeks' notice before I left* **2** [U] attention: *His writings brought him into public notice.|local events beneath the notice of the largest newspapers|Don't take any notice of* (=pay any attention to) *what he says.|Take particular notice of* (=pay close attention to) *the road signs* **3** [C] a usu. short written statement of information or directions to the public: *sold the car by putting a notice in the newspaper|The notice on the wall says "No smoking"* **4** [C *often pl.*] a statement of opinion, as in a newspaper, about a new book, play, etc.; REVIEW[1] (3b): *The new play got mixed notices* (=some good, some bad) *after its first night* **5 sit up and take notice** *infml* to pay attention or show respect: *My new book will make the world sit up and take notice!* **6 until further notice** *fml* from now until another change is made: *This office will close at 5 o'clock from May 1 until further notice*

notice[2] *v* [Wv6;IØ;T1,5,5b,6a,b;V2,4] to pay attention (to) with the eyes, other senses, or mind: *She was wearing a new dress, but he didn't even notice (it).|Did you notice me leave/leaving the house? Did you notice whether I locked the door?|It's good to notice that the price has gone down.|Yes, so I've noticed*

no·tice·a·ble /ˈnəʊtɨsəbəl/ *adj* that can be noticed; worth noticing: *water with a noticeable, but not bad taste|a noticeable drop in the amount of crime* —**-ably** *adv*: *noticeably less rain than last year|Crime has decreased noticeably*

notice board /ˈ·· ˌ·/ (*AmE* **bulletin board**)— *n esp. BrE* a board on a wall which notices may be fixed to

no·ti·fi·a·ble /ˈnəʊtɨfaɪəbəl/ *adj tech, esp. BrE* (esp. of certain diseases) needing by law to be reported to an office of public health

no·ti·fi·ca·tion /ˌnəʊtɨfɨˈkeɪʃən/ *n* **1** [U;C *usu. sing.*] the action or an act of NOTIFYing **2** [C *usu. sing.*] something in writing which gives notice

no·ti·fy /ˈnəʊtɨfaɪ/ *v* [T1 (*of*);D5;V3] to tell (someone), esp. formally: *to notify the police of a crime|When my guest arrives, please notify me (that he's come).|Please notify me of when you may arrive, so that I'll be ready.|I'll notify my lawyer to write out the agreement*

no·tion /ˈnəʊʃən/ *n* **1** [C (*of*),C5,6] an idea, belief, or opinion (in someone's mind); CONCEPTION (2): *the old notion that the sun moved round the earth|I haven't the faintest notion (of) what you're talking about* **2** [C,C3,5] a desire or liking, esp. an unreal or sudden one: *a head full of silly notions*

no·tion·al /ˈnəʊʃənəl/ *adj* **1** existing (only) in the mind; ABSTRACT or THEORETICAL: *to give the object a notional price just for use in this calculation* **2** *tech* (of a word) having an actual meaning in a sentence: *"Have" in "I have an apple" is notional: it means "possess"* —compare RELATIONAL

no·tions /ˈnəʊʃənz/ *n* [P] *esp. AmE* small articles (like things used in sewing, small pieces of women's clothing, etc.) sold in one part of a large shop —compare DRY GOODS, HABERDASHERY

no·to·ri·e·ty /ˌnəʊtəˈraɪəti/ *n* [U] the state or quality of being NOTORIOUS: (*derog*) *gained notoriety before being caught and sent to prison*|(*rare*) *A fact of such notoriety hardly needs proof*

no·to·ri·ous /nəʊˈtɔːrɪəs, nə-‖-ˈto-/ *adj derog* widely and unfavourably known **a** as the stated kind of bad thing or person: *a notorious thief/prison* **b** for some bad quality, thing, etc.: *an area notorious for crime|His noisy parties made him notorious in the town* —see FAMOUS (USAGE) —**~ly** *adv*: *a notoriously bad year for wine* —**~ness** *n* [U]

not·with·stand·ing[1] /ˌnɒtwɪθˈstændɪŋ, -wɪð-‖ˌnɑt-/ *prep fml* (*sometimes following its object*) in spite of: *The law will go into force, any other agreements notwithstanding.*=*Notwithstanding any other agreements, the law will go into force*

notwithstanding[2] *adv fml* however; NEVERTHELESS: *He tried to prevent the marriage but it took place notwithstanding*

notwithstanding[3] *conj nonstandard* although: *He was unknown to most people, notwithstanding he had lived there a long time*

nou·gat /ˈnuːgɑː‖-gət/ *n* [U] sweet paste made of sugar, bits of fruit, nuts, etc.: *eating a piece of nougat*

nought /nɔːt/ *n* **1** *BrE* (the figure) 0; zero: *0·6 is usually read "nought point* SIX*", and ·06 is usually read "point nought* SIX*"* **2** *esp. old use & poet* nothing; NAUGHT (2,3,4)

noughts and cross·es /ˌ· · ˈ··/ (*AmE* **tick-tack-toe**)— *n* [R] *BrE* a game played by 2 people writing the marks O and X in turn on a pattern of 9 squares, with the purpose of writing 3 such marks in a row

noun /naʊn/ *n* a word that is the name of a person, place, thing, quality, action, etc., and can be used as the subject or object of a verb or the object of a PREPOSITION. Nouns are marked *n* in this dictionary —compare PRONOUN

nour·ish /ˈnʌrɪʃ‖ˈnɜrɪʃ, ˈnʌ-/ *v* [Wv4,5;T1] **1** to cause to stay alive or grow by giving food, water, etc.: *nourishing food|a well-nourished baby* **2** (of a person) to keep (a feeling, plan, etc.) alive; ENTERTAIN (3): *to nourish the hope of a trip abroad|to nourish a strong dislike for another person*

nour·ish·ment /ˈnʌrɪʃmənt‖ˈnɜrɪʃ-, ˈnʌ-/ *n* [U] **1** something that NOURISHes; food: *took no nourishment all day until dinner* **2** the condition of NOURISHing or being NOURISHed

nous /naʊs‖nuːs/ *n* [U] *BrE infml* common sense: *a clever girl with lots of nous*

nou·veau riche /ˌnuːvəʊ ˈriːʃ (*Fr* nuvo riʃ)/ *n* **nouveaux riches** (*same pronunciation*) [*usu. pl.*] *Fr usu. derog* a person with new wealth, esp. one who is not modest in spending it: *the house of some nouveaux riches, with costly but ugly furniture*

Nov. *written abbrev. for*: November

no·va /ˈnəʊvə/ *n* **~s** *or* **-vae** /ˈnəʊviː/ a star which suddenly becomes much brighter and then becomes gradually fainter

nov·el[1] /ˈnɒvəl‖ˈnɑ-/ *adj* not like something known before, esp. in being clever or strange; new: *a novel suggestion, something we hadn't tried before*

novel[2] *n* a long written story, usu. in PROSE and printed as a book, dealing with invented people and events: *"War and Peace", the great novel by Leo Tolstoy*

nov·el·ette /ˌnɒvəˈlet‖ˌnɑ-/ *n often derog* a short NOVEL or long SHORT STORY, often of a light kind and usu. about love: *girls reading silly novelettes*

nov·el·et·tish /ˌnɒvəˈletɪʃ‖ˌnɑ-/ *adj often derog* typical of a NOVELETTE, esp. in showing feelings of love, sorrow, etc., as simpler or stronger than they really are; SENTIMENTAL —**~ly** *adv*

nov·el·ist /ˈnɒvəlɨst‖ˈnɑ-/ *n* a writer of NOVELs

no·vel·la /nəʊˈvelə/ *n* **novellas** *or* **novelle** /nəʊˈveliː/ **1** *old use* a short story about one event **2** a story between the length of a NOVEL and a short story

nov·el·ty /ˈnɒvəlti‖ˈnɑ-/ *n* **1** [U] the state or quality of being NOVEL: *always looking for novelty in what she wears* **2** [C] something new and unusual: *Hard work was no novelty to a person from a poor family like him* **3** [C *usu. pl.*] an unusual cheap, usu. not very useful, small object: *shops full* *of Christmas novelties in December|a novelty toy*

No·vem·ber /nəʊˈvembəʳ, nə-/ *n* [R;(C)] the 11th month of the year

nov·ice /ˈnɒvɪ̣s‖ˈnɑ-/ *n* **1** [(*at*)] a person without training or experience in a skill or subject; BEGINNER: *a novice swimmer|a novice at swimming* **2** a person who has recently joined a religious group to become a MONK or NUN

no·vi·ti·ate, noviciate /nəʊˈvɪʃiɪ̣t, nə-, -ʃieɪt‖-ˈvɪʃɪ̣t/ *n* **1** [U9] the period or state of being a NOVICE, esp. in a religious group: *a long novitiate* **2** [C] the house of a religious group, where NOVICE*s* are trained

no·vo·caine /ˈnəʊvəkeɪn/ *n* [U] *tdmk* a drug used for stopping pain in a part of the body during a small operation, esp. on the teeth

now¹ /naʊ/ *adv* **1 a** at this time; under these conditions; at present: *Spring is here and the country is now beautiful.|We used to live in Bristol but now we live in Bath* **b** (*usu. in stories*) at this time (in the past): *He left school in 1830; now he was able to go and live in London* **2** at the time just following the present; without delay; at once: *The work must be done now; tomorrow will be too late.|We've had dinner; now let's have some coffee* **3** (used with weakened meaning to attract attention or to express a warning, command, etc., often in the phrs. **There now**; **Now then**; **Now, now**): *There, now, I've at last got the engine started.|Now then, what's happened?|Be careful, now!|Now the question I've been talking about seems important, because . . .|Now, now, child, stop crying!* **4** (*after an expression of time*) calculating from or up to the present: *Many years ago now I lived abroad.|It hasn't been that way for years now.|It's now 27 years since he died* **5 (every) now and then/again** at times; from time to time; OCCASIONALly: *I don't think about my old home very much, only (every) now and again* **6 just now** see JUST² (10) **7 now for** and now we will have, see, etc.: *That matter is settled. Now for the next question* **8 now . . . now/then** sometimes . . . and sometimes: *With prices now rising, now falling, who knows what it will cost next year?* —see HERE¹ (USAGE)

now² *n* [R] the present time or moment: *Now's the time for action.|The time for action is now!|Goodbye for now!|From now on* (=starting now) *I will try to do better.|Up to now/Until now, the work has been easy.|I hope you've understood by now* (=at or before this point) *what I mean*

now·a·days /ˈnaʊədeɪz/ *adv not fml* (esp. in comparisons with the past) at the present time; in these (modern) times; now: *We used to drive our car a lot, but nowadays petrol costs too much.|". . . most young people nowadays are . . . much more open . . . about the whole sex question than we were"* (SEU S.)|*". . . he said nobody nowadays reads Lawrence"* (SEU W.)

no way¹ /ˈ· ·/ *adv fml* in no way: *is no way to blame for what happened*

no way² /ˌ· ˈ·/ *adv sl esp. AmE* (*as an answer*) no; certainly not: *"Please do this for me." "No way, man: do it yourself!"*

no·where /ˈnəʊweəʳ/ *adv* **1** (*AmE infml* also **no place**)— not anywhere; (in/at/to) no place: *The book was nowhere to be found.|The horse finished nowhere* (=not in 1st, 2nd, or 3rd place) *in the race.|The old lady went nowhere, just stayed at home* **2** (*AmE infml* also **no place**)—(to/at) no purpose or result: *That kind of talk will get you nowhere* (=will not do you any good).|*In a costly place like this, £5 goes nowhere* (=will hardly buy anything).|*Where does this argument lead us? Exactly nowhere; we still don't know the answer* **3 from (out of) nowhere** also **out of nowhere**— *not fml* **a** from a little-known place or from being unknown: *He came from out of nowhere into national fame* **b** from somewhere not noticed: *A man came up from nowhere and hit him on the head* **4 miles from nowhere** *infml* (far) away from any town: *a lonely island, 1000 miles from nowhere|I wouldn't want to live in Foulthorpe—it's miles from nowhere!* **5 nowhere near** see NEAR² (1) —see NEITHER (USAGE)

no·wise /ˈnəʊwaɪz/ *adv lit & old use* (in) no way; not

now that /ˈ· ·/ also **now**— *conj* as a result of the fact that; CONSIDERING that (now); since: *Now (that) I've heard the music I understand why you like it*

nox·ious /ˈnɒkʃəs‖ˈnɑk-/ *adj fml* **1** harmful to people, plants, or animals: *noxious chemicals in the river water* **2** (esp. of ideas) having a harmful effect: *a noxious book* —**~ly** *adv* —**~ness** *n* [U]

noz·zle /ˈnɒzəl‖ˈnɑ-/ *n* a short tube fitted to the end of a HOSE, pipe, BELLOWS, etc., to direct and control the stream of liquid or gas coming out

-n't /ənt/ *contr. of:* not: *hadn't|didn't|wouldn't|isn't* —see CONTR., NOT (USAGE)

nth /enθ/ *adj* **the nth degree/power** *not fml* the highest, greatest, furthest, etc., degree or form: *dull and uninteresting to the nth degree|the nth power of anger*

USAGE The letter *n* is usu. printed in ITALIC.

nu·ance¹ /ˈnjuːɑːns‖ˈnuː-/ *n* a slight delicate quality or difference in colour, meaning, etc.: *nuances of taste which are hard to describe|a nuance of greater uncertainty in "I might do it" than in "I may do it"*

nuance² *v* [T1 *usu. pass.*] *lit* to give NUANCE*s* to, esp. in a delicate expression or performance

nub /nʌb/ *n* **1** a small part which remains when a large part has been worn away; STUB; STUMP **2** a lump: *a nub of coal* **3** [*usu. sing.*] the point of real importance in an argument, story, etc.; CRUX; GIST (esp. in the phr. **the nub of**): *the nub of the argument*

nu·bile /ˈnjuːbaɪl‖ˈnuːbəl/ *adj fml or humor* (of a girl) of good age and appearance for marriage; young and sexually attractive

nu·cle·ar /ˈnjuːklɪəʳ‖ˈnuː-/ *adj* [Wa5] **1** of, concerning, or being a NUCLEUS **2** of, concerning, or using the NUCLEUS of an atom, ATOMIC ENERGY, or the ATOM BOMB: *a nuclear power station|nuclear war|nuclear* PHYSICS|*a nuclear scientist*

nuclear dis·ar·ma·ment /ˌ··· ·ˈ···/ *n* [U] the giving up of atomic weapons by agreement between nations

nuclear re·ac·tor /ˌ··· ·ˈ··/ also **reactor, atomic pile**— *n* a large machine for the controlled production of ATOMIC ENERGY

nu·cle·ic ac·id /njuːˌkliːɪk ˈæsɪ̣d, -ˌkleɪ-‖nuː-/ *n* [U] see DNA, RNA

nu·cle·us /ˈnjuːklɪəs‖ˈnuː-/ *n* **-clei** /kliaɪ/ **1** an original or central point, part, or group inside a larger thing, group, organization, etc.: *100 books as the nucleus of a new school library|a nucleus of fact in the ancient stories of the Trojan War* **2** the central part of an atom, made up of NEUTRON*s* and PROTON*s* —see picture at ATOM **3** the central part of almost all cells of living matter

nude¹ /njuːd‖nuːd/ *adj* **1** [Wa1;B] not covered by clothes; NAKED **2** [Wa5;A] of, for, by, etc., people not wearing clothes: *a nude party|a nude* BEACH|*nude swimming*

nude² *n* **1** [C] a usu. female person not wearing any clothes, esp. one appearing in a photograph or piece of art **2** [C] a piece of art showing a person, usu. a woman, without clothes **3** [U] the state of being NUDE (in the phr. **in the nude**): *went swimming in the nude*

nudge¹ /nʌdʒ/ *v* **1** [T1] to touch or push gently, esp. with one's elbow, esp. in order to call a person's attention or give a signal: *nudged his friend to let him know it was time to leave* **2** [L9;X9] to move by gently or slowly pushing (things or people) to the side: *nudged through the crowd|nudged me out of the way|a ship nudging (its way) through the ice*

nudge² *n* an act of nudging (NUDGE); a slight push (as with the elbow): *gave his friend, who had fallen asleep, a nudge|felt a sharp nudge in his side*

nud·is·m /ˈnjuːdɪzəm‖ˈnuː-/ *n* [U] the practice of living, esp. in a group, without clothes —**-ist** *adj, n*: *a nudist camp* (=a place where nudists live on holiday)

nu·di·ty /ˈnjuːdɪ̵ti‖ˈnuː-/ *n* [U] the quality or state of being NUDE: *a lot of nudity in recent films*

nu·ga·to·ry /ˈnjuːgətəri‖ˈnuːgətori/ *adj fml* without force or value; TRIFLING

nug·get /ˈnʌgɪ̵t/ *n* a small rough piece or lump of a precious metal, found in the earth: *a gold nugget|* (fig.) *nuggets of information/wisdom*

nui·sance /ˈnjuːsəns‖ˈnuː-/ *n* **1** a person or animal that annoys or causes trouble; PEST: *Don't make a nuisance of yourself: sit down and be quiet!* **2** an action or state of affairs which causes trouble, offence, or unpleasantness: *What a nuisance! I've forgotten my ticket* **3** **Commit no nuisance** (as a notice in a public place) Do not use this place as **a** a LAVATORY **b** a TIP⁴

nuisance val·ue /ˈ·· ˌ··/ *n* [(*the*)S;U] the quality of being valuable as a cause of trouble or annoyance to one's enemies or opponents: *A small political group may not be able to defeat the government, but it may still have a certain nuisance value*

null /nʌl/ *adj* [Wa5;A] *tech* of, being, or concerning zero: *a null result* (=one giving the answer 0)

nul·lah /ˈnʌlə/ *n Ind & Pak E* **1** a usu. narrow steep valley cut by running water **2** a watercourse

null and void /ˌ· · ˈ·/ *adj* [Wa5;F;(B)] *fml & law* without force or effect in law: *The court ruled that the claim was null and void*

nul·li·fy /ˈnʌlɪ̵faɪ/ *v* [T1] **1** to cause or declare to have no effect in law: *a claim nullified by the court* **2** to cause to have no effect; NEGATE: *a rise in prices nullifying a rise in wages* —**-ification** /ˌnʌlɪ̵fɪ̵ˈkeɪʃən/ *n* [U]

nul·li·ty /ˈnʌlɪ̵ti/ *n* **1** [U] (esp. of a marriage) the state of being NULL AND VOID in law: *a* DECREE *of nullity* —compare ANNULment **2** [U] nothingness; lack of force, interest, etc.: *a feeling of the nullity of life* **3** [C] a person or thing of no depth or interest: *All the characters in the book seem (like) nullities*

null set /ˌ· ˈ·/ also **empty set**— *n tech* a SET with no members, usu. written {}

numb¹ /nʌm/ *adj* [Wa1;F;(B) (*with*)] (of (part of) the body) unable to feel anything, esp. as a result of cold: *My hands are numb after an hour outside on such a cold day.|*(fig.) *The sight of the lion made him numb with fear* —**~ness** *n* [U]

numb² *v* [Wv5 (*with*),4;T1 *often pass.*] **1** to cause to feel nothing or no pain; make NUMB: *fingers numbed with cold|the numbing effect of the drug* **2** to lessen (pain): *medicine to numb the pain* —**numbingly** *adv*

num·ber¹ /ˈnʌmbəʳ/ *n* **1** [C] **a** a member of the system used in counting and measuring: *Let* x *be a number from 1 to 10.|imaginary numbers|odd/even numbers|a wrong number* (=a wrong telephone number) **b** a written sign (SYMBOL) for one of these: *page numbers in the right-hand corners* **c** 1, 2, 3, . . ., 9, 0; DIGIT: *able to print numbers as well as letters* **2** [A] (*before one of these, usu. written* No., no., *or* (*AmE*) #) (having) the stated size, place in order, etc.: *a number 9* (=size 9) (*shoe*)*|My room is no. 6.|Do you know Church Street? We live at no. 107* (=our house has the number 107).|(*AmE*) *question #1 on the examination paper* —see also NUMBER ONE **3** [U;C *often pl. with sing. meaning*] (a) quantity or amount: *The number of chairs in the room is 10.|Members are few in number.|a small number of/small numbers of visitors|grains of sand beyond number* (=too many to count) **4** [C *often pl. with sing. meaning*] a group: *a member of our group, one of our number|Their numbers were increased by new members* **5** [C] a (copy of a) magazine printed at a particular time; ISSUE¹ (4): *the latest number of "Vogue" magazine|back* (=past) *numbers of "Punch"* **6** [C] a piece of music, usu. a short part of a longer performance: *sang several numbers from the* OPERA*|For my next number, I will sing . . .* **7** [C *usu. sing.*] *infml* a piece of clothing, esp. a dress, for sale: *a pretty number that will show off your figure* **8** [C *usu. sing.*] *sl* a girl: *a good looking number in a blue dress* **9** [U;C] change in the form of words, esp. (in English) nouns and verbs, depending on whether one or more than one thing is talked about: *"Horses"/"Horse" is plural/singular in number* **10** **a number of** some: *A number of people came to the meeting.|Many people came to the meeting, of whom a number left early* **11** **any number of** *infml* a large quantity of; many: *I've told you any number of times to keep the door shut!* **12** **numbers of** rather many; quite a few: *Numbers of people came to the meeting, from all over the country* **13** **by number** in a way that uses NUMBER*s*¹ (1): *He knows all the rooms in the building by number: he'll tell you who is in room 106* **14** **by numbers** (*AmE* **by the numbers**)— (esp. of the movements or actions of groups of soldiers in training) done as an ordered set of smaller actions, each carried out on a separate command **15** **have someone's number** *infml* to have knowledge useful in annoying or defeating someone: *Our team couldn't seem to do anything right: the opposing team had their number* **16** **opposite number** *not fml, esp. BrE* a person with the same position in another organization, government, etc.; COUNTERPART: *an international meeting between each minister and his opposite number* **17** **someone's number is/has come up** *infml* it is someone's turn, esp. to suffer, be punished, etc. **18** **to the number of** *fml* as many as: *persons to the number of 100* (=as many as 100 people)

USAGE The letters will generally tell you whether to use a sing. or pl. verb after the nouns in this dictionary. The matter is explained further under **each**, **either**, **everybody**, and **-ics**. Usually [P] and [C] nouns with a number greater than 1 take a pl. verb: *143 dogs/people are coming.* But when speaking of the size of the number itself, one uses a sing. verb: *143 is a large number.* This happens even when a noun follows the number: *143 years is a long time.|$143 is too much to pay.* —see AMOUNT (USAGE)

number² *v* **1** [L1,9] to reach as a total; be . . . in number: *people numbering in the* THOUSANDS*|The books in the library number 5,065/number in the* THOUSANDS **2** [L9;X9: (esp. *among, as, with*)] to include or be included; count: *He numbers/is numbered among the best writers in the US.|I'm glad to number him with my friends and not my enemies* **3** [Wv4,5;T1;X1,9 *often pass.*] to give a number to: *Number the questions (from) 1 to 10.|a numbered road* (=with an official number)*|What numbering system shall we use?|There are 2 pages numbered 16 in this book: that's a mistake!* **4** [T1] *poet* to find the number of; count: *Who can number the stars?* **5** **someone's days are numbered** someone cannot continue or live much longer: *When cars were invented,* *the* BLACKSMITH*'s days were numbered*

num·ber·less /ˈnʌmbələs‖-bər-/ *adj* [Wa5] *esp. lit* too many to count: *numberless possibilities*

number off (*AmE* **count off**)— *v adv* [IØ] *BrE* (in military use) to call out one's number when one's turn comes: *The soldiers numbered off from left to right*

number one /ˌ·· ˈ·/ *n* **1** [R] *infml* oneself and no one else: *Don't always think of number one* (=yourself) **2** [R] the chief person in an organization: *George is number one around here and I'm his* **number two** (=second in command) **3** [A;E] (the) highest in importance: *our number one difficulty|public enemy number one*

num·ber·plate /ˈnʌmbəpleɪt‖-ər-/ (*AmE* **license plate**)— *n BrE* either of the signs (usu. at the front and back ends) on a vehicle showing its official number —see picture at CAR

num·bers /ˈnʌmbəz‖-ərz/ *n* **1** [P;U] ARITHMETIC (esp. in the phr. **good/bad at numbers**) **2** [P] the state of having more supporters, soldiers, etc., than an opponent (esp. in the phr. **win by sheer force/weight of numbers**) **3** [*the*+R] (in the US) a type of usu. unlawful game in which people BET (=risk) small amounts of money on the appearance of a combination of numbers in some group of numbers appearing in a newspaper: *to play the numbers|the numbers game* **4** [P] *old use or poet* lines of poetry with a regular beat: *The poet Alexander Pope said that even as a child he spoke in numbers*

Numbers *n* [R] the 4th book of the Bible: *When was Numbers written?*

Number Ten, No. 10 /ˌ·· ˈ·/ *n* [R] *not fml* No. 10 Downing Street; the address of the home of the British PRIME MINISTER, regarded esp. as the place where he considers political questions, makes decisions, etc.: *This suggestion won't be welcomed at No. 10: the* PRIME MINISTER *will never approve it*

numb·ly /ˈnʌmli/ *adv* as though NUMB; in a way marked by no feeling: *walked around numbly after hearing the terrible news|His arm hung down numbly*

nu·me·ra·cy /ˈnjuːmərəsi‖ˈnuː-/ *n* [U] *esp. BrE* (usu. used in comparison with LITERACY) the state or condition of being NUMERATE

nu·me·ral /ˈnjuːmərəl‖ˈnuː-/ *adj, n* (any of the system of signs) used for representing a number or numbers; (of) NUMBER[1] (1b,c) —compare ROMAN NUMERALs, ARABIC NUMERALs

nu·me·rate /ˈnjuːmərɪ̈t‖ˈnuː-/ *adj esp. BrE* (usu. used in comparison with LITERATE) having a general understanding of MATHEMATICS or calculations with numbers

nu·me·ra·tion /ˌnjuːməˈreɪʃən‖ˌnuː-/ *n* [C;U] *tech* a system or the action of counting —compare ENUMERATION

nu·me·ra·tor /ˈnjuːməreɪtəʳ‖ˈnuː-/ *n* the number above the line in a FRACTION; DIVIDEND (3): *5 is the numerator in* $\frac{5}{6}$ *and* $\frac{5}{(x+y)}$

nu·mer·i·cal /njuːˈmerɪkəl‖nuː-/ *adj* [Wa5] of, concerning, showing, or shown by a number or numbers: *numerical ability* (=skill with numbers)|*numerical order* —**~ly** *adv*: *numerically greater* (=greater in number(s))

nu·me·rol·o·gy /ˌnjuːməˈrɒlədʒi‖ˌnuːməˈrɑ-/ *n* [U] the study of the magic meaning of numbers

nu·me·rous /ˈnjuːmərəs‖ˈnuː-/ *adj* **1** [B] many: *happening numerous times a day|more numerous books than I'd ever seen before* **2** [F] made up of or existing in the form of a large number of people or things: *That* (*kind of*) *bird has become more numerous around here lately* —**~ly** *adv* —**~ness** *n* [U]

nu·mi·nous /ˈnjuːmɪ̈nəs‖ˈnuː-/ *adj tech or lit* causing or marked by a sense of the presence of God; holy —**~ness** *n* [U]

nu·mis·mat·ic /ˌnjuːmɪ̈zˈmætɪk‖ˌnuː-/ *adj* [A;(B)] *tech or fml* of or related to NUMISMATICS: *an old penny of great numismatic value*

nu·mis·mat·ics /ˌnjuːmɪ̈zˈmætɪks‖ˌnuː-/ *n* [U] *tech or fml* the study or collection of coins, other kinds of money, and MEDALs; coin-collecting —**-ist** /njuːˈmɪzmətɪ̈st‖nuː-/ *n*: *a keen numismatist*

num·skull, numbskull /ˈnʌmskʌl/ *n* [C;*you*+N] *infml* a stupid person: *Only a numskull like you could ask such a question!*

nun /nʌn/ *n* a woman member of an esp. Christian religious group (ORDER) who swears to serve God by living (usu. with others in a CONVENT) a life of service, obedience, prayer, owning nothing, and not marrying —compare MONK

nun·ci·o /ˈnʌnsiəʊ/ *n* **-cios** a representative of the POPE in a foreign country

nun·ne·ry /ˈnʌnəri/ *n* a building in which NUNs live together; CONVENT —compare MONASTERY

nup·tial /ˈnʌpʃəl/ *adj* [Wa5;A] *pomp or tech* of or concerning marriage or the marriage ceremony: *the nuptial day|a nuptial* MASS

nup·tials /ˈnʌpʃəlz/ *n* [P] *pomp* wedding: *The nuptials were performed by the local priest*

nurse¹ /nɜːs‖nɜrs/ *n* [C;A;R;N] **1** a person, typically a woman, who is trained to take care of sick, hurt, or old people, esp. as directed by a doctor in a hospital: *a student nurse* (=a girl learning to be a nurse)|*hospital nurses|a male nurse|a private nurse visiting him once a week at home* **2** a woman employed to take care of a young child —compare NANNY **3** WET NURSE

nurse² *v* **1** [Wv4;IØ;T1: (*at*)] **a** (of a baby) to suck milk from a woman's breast: *nursing at its mother's breast|a nursing baby* **b** (of a woman) to give (a baby) milk from the breast: *a nursing mother* **2** [IØ] to act as or be a professional nurse: *She spent some time nursing during the war in a military hospital* **3** [T1 (*through*)] to take care of as or like a nurse: *He nursed her back to health.|All her time goes into nursing her old father.|*(fig.) *She nursed her brother through his university examinations* **4** [T1] to take care of someone suffering from: *This disease is very hard to nurse.|stayed in bed and nursed my cold* **5** [T1] *rare* to cause to develop; PROMOTE; FOSTER: *a government which nurses art and science* **6** [T1 (ALONG)] *infml* to use or handle carefully so as to preserve, keep going, etc.: *nursed a drink all evening* (=kept it without drinking much of it) **7** [T1] to hold (esp. a bad feeling) in the mind; NOURISH (2): *nursed a* GRUDGE (=angry feeling) *against her old enemy*

nurse·maid /ˈnɜːsmeɪd‖ˈnɜrs-/ *n* NURSE[1] (2)

nur·se·ry /ˈnɜːsəri‖ˈnɜr-/ *n* **1** *esp. pomp or old use* a small child's bedroom or playroom in a house **2** a place where small children are taken care of while their parents are at work, shopping, etc. —compare PLAYGROUP, CRÈCHE, DAY NURSERY **3** an area where plants and trees are grown to be sold or planted in other places

nur·se·ry·man /ˈnɜːsərimən‖ˈnɜr-/ *n* **-men** /mən/ a person (esp. a man) who grows plants in a NURSERY (3)

nursery rhyme /ˈ··· ·/ *AmE* also **Mother Goose rhyme**— *n* a short usu. old and well-known song or poem for small children

nursery school /ˈ··· ·/ *n* [C;U] a school for young children of 2–5 years of age, in which they learn mainly by playing: *going to nursery school* —compare KINDERGARTEN

nurs·ing /ˈnɜːsɪŋ‖ˈnɜr-/ *n* [U] the job of a NURSE[1] (1): *If you like helping sick people, why not go into nursing* (=become a nurse)*?*

nursing home /ˈ·· ·/ *n* **1** a usu. private establishment where people (esp. old people) who cannot take care of themselves live and are cared for by nurses **2** *BrE* a small private hospital

nurs·ling, nurseling /ˈnɜːslɪŋ‖ˈnɜr-/ *n* **1** [C] a baby who is being NURSED² (1), or taken care of by a NURSE¹ (2) **2** [C9, esp. *of*] *not fml* a thing or person trained, developed, etc.: *the chairman's favourite plan, his own nursling*

nur·ture¹ /ˈnɜːtʃəʳ‖ˈnɜr-/ *n* [U] *lit* education, training, or development

nurture² *v* [T1 *often pass.*] *lit* **1** to give care and food to: *nurtured by loving parents* **2** to train, educate, or develop: *Nurture your mind with good reading.|scientists nurtured in the university*

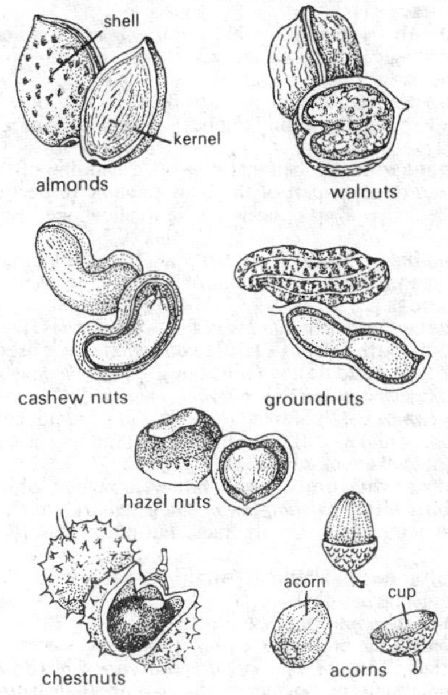

nuts

nut¹ /nʌt/ *n* **1 a** a dry fruit with a seed (KERNEL) surrounded by a hard shell consisting of usu. 2 parts **b** this seed, which is eaten **2** a small usu. 4- or 6-sided piece of metal with a THREADed hole through it for screwing onto a BOLT —see picture at MACHINERY **3** (on a musical instrument with strings) the raised bar over which the strings pass at their upper end **4** *infml* a person who is or seems to be unbalanced in mind; mad person: *What a nut he is: he always holds a book upside down to read it* **5** [C9] *infml* a person with a very strong interest of the stated kind; FREAK¹ (5): *She's a Clark Gable nut: she's seen all his films* —compare BUFF³ **6** *infml* one's head (esp. in the phr. **off one's nut**): *You must be off your nut* (=mad)! **7** *taboo sl, esp. AmE* TESTICLE **8** [*usu. pl.*] *BrE* a small lump of coal: *a load of best nuts* **9 a hard/tough nut to crack** *infml* a difficult question, person, etc., to deal with: *I asked him for the money, but he was a tough nut to crack and I went away without it* **10 do one's nut** *sl* to be very worried and/or angry **11 for nuts** *infml BrE* (*esp. after* can't) at all: *She sings well but she can't dance for nuts!* **12 nuts and bolts** *not fml* **a** the simple facts, skills, duties, etc., of a subject or job: *First learn the nuts and bolts of cooking; then you can try your own ideas* **b** the working or moving parts of a machine: *I can drive a car, but I don't know anything about the nuts and bolts of the engine*

nut² *v* **-tt- go nutting** to go out to gather nuts

nut-brown /ˈ· ·/ *adj* [Wa5] *lit* having a colour like that of ripe brown nuts, usu. thought to be warm and pleasant: *nut-brown* ALE

nut·case /ˈnʌtkeɪs/ *n infml & humor* a mad person; NUT¹ (4)

nut·crack·er /ˈnʌtˌkrækəʳ/ *n* [*often pl. with sing. meaning*] a tool for cracking the shell of a nut, usu. made of 2 metal bars in a V shape closed by hand over the nut: *Have we got a nutcracker/a pair of nutcrackers/any nutcrackers in the house?* —see PAIR (USAGE)

nut·house /ˈnʌthaʊs/ *n* **-houses** /ˌhaʊzɨ̯z/ *sl* MENTAL HOSPITAL

nut·meg /ˈnʌtmeg/ *n* **1** [C] a small hard seed of a type of tree grown on some South Pacific islands, which is usu. made into a powder used (as a SPICE) to give a particular taste to food **2** [U] this powder

nu·tri·a /ˈnjuːtrɪə‖ˈnuː-/ *n* [U] (esp. in shops and advertisements) the fur of the COYPU: *a nutria coat*

nu·tri·ent /ˈnjuːtrɪənt‖ˈnuː-/ *adj, n tech* (a chemical or food) providing for life and growth

nu·tri·ment /ˈnjuːtrɨ̯mənt‖ˈnuː-/ *n* [U;C] a substance providing for life and growth; food; NOURISHMENT

nu·tri·tion /njuːˈtrɪʃən‖nuː-/ *n* [U] **1** the action of providing or state of being provided with food; NOURISHMENT: *Good nutrition is important for good health* **2** the scientific study of how food is used by the body

nu·tri·tious /njuːˈtrɪʃəs‖nuː-/ *adj* valuable to the body as food; NOURISHing: *Eat lots of good nutritious food* —**~ly** *adv*

nu·tri·tive /ˈnjuːtrɨ̯tɪv‖ˈnuː-/ *adj* **1** *fml or tech* of or concerning NUTRITION (1): *What is the nutritive value of this food?* **2** *fml* NUTRITIOUS

nuts¹ /nʌts/ *adj* [F] *infml* **1** (seeming) unbalanced in mind; mad; CRAZY (1): *I'll go nuts if I have to wait much longer!* **2 nuts about/over a** interested and eager about; ENTHUSIASTIC over: *nuts about flying* **b** very much in love with: *nuts about/over the boy next door*

nuts² *interj sl esp. AmE* **1** (a strong expression of annoyance and anger; slightly weaker than HELL² (1)): *Nuts to you and your friends! I never want to see you again!* **2** (a strong expression of fearless refusal): *When they told him to stop fighting, he said, "Nuts!" and kept on until he won*

nut·shell /ˈnʌt-ʃel/ *n* **1** the hard outer covering of a nut **2** *infml* a short description, explanation, etc. (esp. in the phr. **in a nutshell**): *There's a lot I could say about the show, but to put it in a nutshell: it was bad*

nut·ty /ˈnʌti/ *adj* [Wa1] **1 a** tasting like nuts: *wine with a nutty taste* **b** filled with nuts: *a nutty cake* **2** *sl* mad; CRAZY: *wrote a nutty letter and signed it "Napoleon"* —see also **as nutty as a** FRUITCAKE (2) —**-tiness** *n* [U]

nuz·zle /ˈnʌzəl/ *v* **1** [L9 (UP), esp. *against*;T1] (esp. of an animal) to rub, touch, or push with the nose: *The horse nuzzled (up) against me.|The dog nuzzled the sleeping child* **2** [X9, esp. *against*] to press close, usu. with repeated short movements: *She nuzzled her head against his shoulder*

NW *written abbrev. for:* northwest(ern)

ny·lon /ˈnaɪlɒn‖-lɑn/ *n* [U] a strong elastic material made from coal, water, and air and made into cloths, cords, and plastics: *nylon thread/thread made of nylon*

ny·lons /ˈnaɪlɒnz‖-lɑnz/ *n* [P] women's nylon stockings: *a pair of nylons* —see PAIR (USAGE)

nymph /nɪmf/ *n* **1** (in Greek and Roman literature) any of the less important goddesses of nature, represented as young girls living in trees, streams, mountains, etc. **2** *lit* a girl

nym·phet /nɪm'fet, 'nɪmf$\frac{1}{2}$t‖nɪm'fet/ *n humor* a young girl of about 10–14 years old, regarded as sexually desirable

nym·pho·ma·ni·a /ˌnɪmfə'meɪnɪə/ *n* [U] unhealthily strong sexual desire in a woman

nym·pho·ma·ni·ac /ˌnɪmfə'meɪniæk/ also (*sl*) **nym·pho** /'nɪmfəʊ/— *n, adj* (of, being, or concerning) a woman with NYMPHOMANIA

O, o

O, o /əʊ/ **O's, o's** *or* **Os, os** **1** the 15th letter of the English alphabet **2** (in speech) a zero

o /əʊ/ *interj esp. poet* (*usu. cap.*) OH

o' /ə/ *prep* **1** of (esp. in the phr. **o'clock**) **2** *lit & old use* on

oaf /əʊf/ *n* [C;*you*+N] a stupid ungraceful person (esp. male) —**~ish** *adj* —**~ishly** *adv* —**~ishness** *n* [U]

oak /əʊk/ *n* **1** [C] also **oak tree** /'· ·/— any of several types of large tree with hard wood, common in northern countries —see picture at TREE[1] **2** [U] the wood of this: *an oak door*

oak ap·ple /'· ˌ··/ *n* a small round brown growth that forms on OAK trees round the eggs laid by a type of insect (WASP)

oak·en /'əʊkən/ *adj* [Wa5;A;(B)] *esp. lit & poet* made of OAK (2)

oa·kum /'əʊkəm/ *n* [U] small pieces taken from old rope and used for filling up small holes in the sides of wooden ships

OAP *abbrev. for:* OLD AGE PENSIONer

oar /ɔːʳ‖or/ *n* **1** a long pole with a wide flat blade, used for rowing a boat —see picture at BOAT[1] **2** **put/shove/stick one's oar in** *sl* to give opinions about other people's affairs without being asked to —see also BUTT IN

oar·lock /'ɔːlɒk‖'orlɑk/ *n AmE* ROWLOCK

oars·man /'ɔːzmən‖'orz-/ *fem.* **oars·wo·man** /-ˌwʊmən/— *n* **-men** /mən/ a man (or woman) who rows a boat, esp. in races

oars·man·ship /'ɔːzmənʃɪp‖'orz-/ *n* [U] skill in rowing a boat, esp. in races

o·a·sis /əʊ'eɪs$\frac{1}{2}$s/ *n* **-ses** /siːz/ **1** a place with trees and water in a desert **2** **an oasis in the desert** a welcome change from something dull

oast house /'əʊst haʊs/ *n* a building with a pointed top, for drying HOPs (=the plant used in making beer)

oat /əʊt/ *n* **1** [A] made of OATS **2** [C] *rare* a sort of grass that produces grain: *the wild oat*

oat·cake /'əʊtkeɪk/ *n* a flat cake made of OATMEAL

oath /əʊθ/ *n* **oaths** /əʊðz/ **1** a solemn promise **2** the form of words used in making this **3** an expression of strong feeling using religious or sexual words improperly **4** **swear/take an oath** to make a solemn promise **5** **be on/under oath** *law* to have made a solemn promise to tell the truth

oat·meal /'əʊtmiːl/ *n* [U] crushed OAT grains used for making cakes and breakfast food

oats /əʊts/ *n* [P] **1** a sort of grain that provides food for people and animals —see picture at CEREAL **2** OATMEAL **3** **be off one's oats** *infml* to have lost the wish to eat **4** **feel one's oats** *infml* to feel full of life and ready for action **5** **sow one's wild oats** to chase pleasure foolishly while still young

ob·bli·ga·to /ˌɒbl$\frac{1}{2}$'gɑːtəʊ‖ˌɑb-/ *n* **-tos** *or* (*esp. tech*) **-ti** /tiː/ a tune played on a single musical instrument at the same time as other music to form a complete work (often in the phr. **with . . . obbligato**): *a song with piano obbligato*

ob·du·rate /'ɒbdʒʊr$\frac{1}{2}$t‖'ɑbdə-/ *adj fml* unchangeable in beliefs or feelings; STUBBORN —**~ly** *adv* —**-racy** *n* [U]

o·be·ah /'əʊbɪə/ also **o·bi** /'əʊbi/— *n* [R] a system of magical religious beliefs in the British West Indies

o·be·di·ent /ə'biːdɪənt/ *adj* doing what one is ordered to do; willing to obey —**~ly** *adv* —**-ence** *n* [U]

o·bei·sance /əʊ'beɪsəns/ *n fml* **1** a bending of the head or other part of the body to show respect or obedience **2** **make obeisance to** to show obedience to

ob·e·lisk /'ɒbəlɪsk‖'ɑ-, 'əʊ-/ *n* **1** a tall pointed stone pillar usu. in honour of a person or event **2** DAGGER (2)

o·bese /əʊ'biːs/ *adj fml* very fat —**obesity** *n* [U]

o·bey /əʊ'beɪ, ə-/ *v* [T1;IØ] to do (what one is asked or ordered to do) by (someone): *Obey* (*the law/orders/your teachers*) *or you will be punished*

ob·fus·cate /'ɒbfəskeɪt‖'ɑb-/ *v* [T1] *fml* to confuse; make difficult to understand —**-cation** /ˌɒbfəs'keɪʃən‖ˌɑb-/ *n* [U]

o·bi·ter dic·tum /ˌɒbɪtə 'dɪktəm‖ˌɑbɪtər-, ˌəʊb-/ *n* **obiter dicta** /-tə/ *Lat, law or fml* a remark which is related to the main argument but not necessary to it

o·bit·u·a·ry /ə'bɪtʃʊəri‖-tʃʊeri/ *n* a notice that someone has died

ob·ject[1] /'ɒbdʒɪkt‖'ɑb-/ *n* **1** a thing **2** [+*of*] something or someone that produces interest or other effect: *an object of interest/of fear* **3** *infml BrE* something or someone unusual or that causes laughter **4** purpose; aim **5** (in grammar) word(s) saying with whom or with what a PREPOSITION is most directly related (**object of a preposition**), who is concerned in the results of an action (**indirect object of a verb**), or to whom or to what something has been done (**direct object of a verb**), as shown, in that order, as follows: *In* **Rome** *John gave* **Mary** *a* **book** **6** **no object** not a difficulty: *I want the best man for the job and will pay the best wages; money is no object*

ob·ject[2] /əb'dʒekt/ *v* [IØ (*to*); T5a] to be against something or someone: *Do you object to smoking?*

object glass /'·· ·/ also **object lens** /'·· ·/— *n tech* OBJECTIVE[2] (2)

ob·jec·tion /əb'dʒekʃən/ *n* [(*to*)] **1** a statement or feeling of dislike, disapproval, or opposition **2** a reason or argument against

ob·jec·tio·na·ble /əb'dʒekʃənəbəl/ *adj* [Wa3] unpleasant —**-bly** *adv*

ob·jec·tive[1] /əb'dʒektɪv/ *adj* **1** [Wa5] existing outside the mind; real **2** not influenced by personal feelings; fair **3** [Wa5] (in grammar) of the object —**~ly** *adv*: *Objectively* (*speaking*), *he can't possibly succeed* —**-tivity** /ˌɒbdʒek'tɪv$\frac{1}{2}$ti‖ˌɑb-/ *n* [U]

objective[2] *n* **1** an object to be won; purpose of a plan **2** *tech* the glass part (LENS) of a microscope or TELESCOPE which is closest to the object being looked at

object les·son /'·· ˌ··/ *n* [(*in*)] an event or story

from which one can learn how or how not to behave

object of vir·tu /ˌ·· · ˈ··/ *n* **objects of virtu** [*usu. pl.*] *tech* a small article that is of a certain interest or value as art, because it is well made, rare, very old, etc.

ob·jec·tor /əbˈdʒektəʳ/ *n* someone who OBJECTs[2]

ob·jet d'art /ˌɒbʒeɪ ˈdɑːʳ‖ˌɑb-/ *n* **objets d'art** (*same pronunciation*) *Fr* an object, usu. small, having or claimed to have some artistic value

ob·late sphere /ˌɒbleɪt ˈsfɪəʳ‖ˌɑb-/ *n tech* a ball which, like the earth, is not quite round but slightly flattened at the top and bottom

ob·la·tion /əˈbleɪʃən/ *n* [*often pl.*] *fml or tech* a religious offering

ob·li·gate /ˈɒblᵌgeɪt‖ˈɑb-/ *v fml* **1** [V3 *usu. pass.*] to make (someone) feel it necessary (to do something); OBLIGE (1): *He felt obligated to visit his parents* **2** [T1 (*to*) *usu. pass*] to make someone feel thankful: *He felt obligated to them for their kindness towards him*

ob·li·ga·tion /ˌɒblᵌˈgeɪʃən‖ˌɑb-/ *n* **1** a duty **2** **be/place under an obligation (to)**: to be/make OBLIGATED to

ob·lig·a·to·ry /əˈblɪgətəri‖-tori/ *adj* [Wa5] necessary; which must be done

o·blige /əˈblaɪdʒ/ *v* **1** [V3 *usu. pass.*] to make (someone) feel it is necessary (to do something): *I feel obliged to say "No"* **2** [T1] *polite* to do (someone) a favour: *Could you oblige me by opening the window?|Could you oblige me with a match?* (=please give me a match) **3** **(I'm) much obliged (to you)** *polite* (I'm) very grateful (to you)

o·blig·ing /əˈblaɪdʒɪŋ/ *adj* kind and eager to help —**~ly** *adv*

o·blique[1] /əˈbliːk/ *adj* **1** indirect **2** [Wa5] in a sideways direction; sloping **3** [Wa5] (of an angle) more or less than 90°

oblique[2] also **oblique stroke** /·ˈ· ·/, **slash (mark)**, **solidus**— *n* [C;U] a mark (/) used for writing FRACTIONs, to mean *per*, for separating numbers next to one another, etc. In this dictionary it is used for separating 2 or more possible choices of words, and in pairs for enclosing pronunciations

o·blit·er·ate /əˈblɪtəreɪt/ *v* [T1] to remove all signs of; destroy —**-ation** /əˌblɪtəˈreɪʃən/ *n* [U]

o·bliv·i·on /əˈblɪvɪən/ *n* [U] **1** the state of having forgotten; unconsciousness; OBLIVIOUSness **2** the state of being forgotten

o·bliv·i·ous /əˈblɪvɪəs/ *adj* [(*to, of*)] not noticing —**~ly** *adv* —**~ness** *n* [U]

ob·long /ˈɒblɒŋ‖ˈɑblɔŋ/ *adj, n* [Wa5] (a figure) with 4 straight sides, forming 4 right angles, which is longer than it is wide

ob·lo·quy /ˈɒbləkwi‖ˈɑb-/ *n* [U] *fml* **1** strong words spoken against someone **2** loss of respect and honour

ob·nox·ious /əbˈnɒkʃəs‖-ˈnɑk-/ *adj fml* unpleasant; nasty —**~ly** *adv* —**~ness** *n* [U]

o·boe /ˈəʊbəʊ/ *n* a type of musical instrument, made of wood and played by blowing through a double REED —see picture at WIND INSTRUMENT

o·bo·ist /ˈəʊbəʊᵌst/ *n* an OBOE player

ob·scene /əbˈsiːn/ *adj* (esp. of ideas, books, etc., usu. about sex) nasty; dirty —**~ly** *adv*

ob·scen·i·ty /əbˈsenᵌti/ *n* **1** [U] the state of being OBSCENE **2** [C] something which is OBSCENE

ob·scu·ran·tis·m /ˌɒbskjʊˈræntɪzəm‖ˌɑbskjə-/ *n* [U] intentionally keeping ideas and facts OBSCURE, esp. so as to hide the truth

ob·scure[1] /əbˈskjʊəʳ/ *adj* **1** hard to understand; not clear **2** not well known —**~ly** *adv*

obscure[2] *v* [T1] to hide; make difficult to see

ob·scu·ri·ty /əbˈskjʊərᵌti/ *n* **1** [U] the state of being OBSCURE **2** [C] something which is OBSCURE

ob·se·quies /ˈɒbsᵌkwiz‖ˈɑb-/ *n* [P] *fml* funeral ceremonies

ob·se·qui·ous /əbˈsiːkwɪəs/ *adj* too eager to obey or serve; too humble

ob·ser·va·ble /əbˈzɜːvəbəl‖-ɜr-/ *adj* [Wa5] that can be seen or noticed —**-bly** *adv*

ob·ser·vance /əbˈzɜːvəns‖-ɜr-/ *n* **1** [U] acting in accordance with a law, ceremony, or custom: *the observance of the speed limit/of Christmas* **2** [C *often pl.*] an action performed as part of a religious ceremony

ob·ser·vant /əbˈzɜːvənt‖-ɜr-/ *adj* **1** quick at noticing things **2** [Wa5; (*of*)] acting in accordance with law or custom (esp. religious)

ob·ser·va·tion /ˌɒbzəˈveɪʃən‖ˌɑbzər-/ *n* **1** [U;C] action of noticing **2** [U] ability to notice things **3** [C] a remark —compare OBSERVATIONS **4** [U] OBSERVANCE **5** **under observation** being carefully watched during some period of time **6** **escape observation** to pass without being noticed

observation car /ˌ··ˈ·· ·/ *n* a special carriage in a railway train for watching the passing scenery

observation post /ˌ··ˈ·· ·/ *n* a position from which the movements of the enemy can be watched

ob·ser·va·tions /ˌɒbzəˈveɪʃənz‖ˌɑbzər-/ *n* [P] sayings or writings about things noticed; report

ob·ser·va·to·ry /əbˈzɜːvətəri‖əbˈzɜrvətori/ *n* a place from which scientists watch the stars and other heavenly bodies

ob·serve /əbˈzɜːv‖-ɜrv/ *v* **1** [T1,5a,6a,b;V2,4;X *to be* 1, *to be* 7;(L9)] to see and notice; watch carefully: *She has observed the stars all her life.|They were observed entering the bank* **2** [T1] to act in accordance with (law or custom (esp. religious)) **3** [T5a (*to*)] to make a remark; say

ob·serv·er /əbˈzɜːvəʳ‖-ɜr-/ *n* **1** one who OBSERVEs (1,2) **2** one who attends meetings, classes, etc., to OBSERVE (1) only, not to speak

ob·serv·ing /əbˈzɜːvɪŋ‖-ɜr-/ *adj* OBSERVANT (1)

ob·sess /əbˈses/ *v* **1** [T1 *often pass.*] to fill (someone's) mind continuously: *She's obsessed by the thought of another war/the desire to become a great scientist* **2** [IØ (*about*)] *infml, esp. AmE* to worry continuously and unnecessarily

ob·ses·sion /əbˈseʃən/ *n* [(*about*)] a fixed idea from which the mind cannot be freed

ob·ses·sion·al[1] /əbˈseʃənəl/ *adj* **1** [B] (of a person) having OBSESSIONs **2** [B] (of an idea) causing OBSESSIONs **3** [B] (of an illness) typically with OBSESSIONs

obsessional[2] *n* a person having OBSESSIONs

ob·ses·sive[1] /əbˈsesɪv/ *adj* of or like an OBSESSION

obsessive[2] *n* a person who has OBSESSIONs

ob·sid·i·an /əbˈsɪdɪən/ *n* [U] a type of dark glass-like rock

ob·so·les·cent /ˌɒbsəˈlesənt‖ˌɑb-/ *adj* [Wa5] becoming OBSOLETE —**-cence** *n* [U]

ob·so·lete /ˈɒbsəliːt‖ˌɑbsəˈliːt/ *adj* [Wa5] no longer used; out of date

ob·sta·cle /ˈɒbstəkəl‖ˈɑb-/ *n* [(*to*)] something which stands in the way and prevents action, movement, or success

ob·ste·tri·cian /ˌɒbstᵌˈtrɪʃən‖ˌɑb-/ *n* a doctor who is a specialist in OBSTETRICS

ob·stet·rics /əbˈstetrɪks/ *n* [U] the branch of medicine concerned with the birth of children —**-ric(al)** *adj*

ob·sti·nate /ˈɒbstᵌnᵌt‖ˈɑb-/ *adj* **1** not easy to change by argument **2** not willing to obey **3** not easy to defeat —**~ly** *adv* —**-nacy** *n* [U]

ob·strep·e·rous /əbˈstrepərəs/ *adj* (esp. of children) noisy and uncontrollable —**~ly** *adv* —**~ness** *n* [U]

ob·struct /əbˈstrʌkt/ *v* [T1] **1** to block up: *obstruct* *a road* **2** to put difficulties in the way of: *obstruct a plan*

ob·struc·tion /əb'strʌkʃən/ *n* **1** [U] the act or state of OBSTRUCTing **2** [C] something that OBSTRUCTs: *an obstruction in the road*

ob·struc·tion·is·m /əb'strʌkʃənɪzəm/ *n* [U] the act or practice of intentionally OBSTRUCTing (2) —**-ist** *n*

ob·struc·tive /əb'strʌktɪv/ *adj* intentionally OBSTRUCTing (2) —**~ly** *adv* —**~ness** *n* [U]

ob·tain /əb'teɪn/ *v* **1** [D1 (*for*);T1] to get: *I haven't been able to obtain that record anywhere; can you obtain it for me?* **2** [L9] *fml* to exist: *That custom has obtained for many years*

ob·tai·na·ble /əb'teɪnəbəl/ *adj* that can be obtained

ob·trude /əb'truːd/ *v* [T1;IØ] *fml* **1** to (cause to) stick out **2** [(*on, upon*)] to (cause to) be noticed, esp. when unwanted: *An old song kept obtruding (itself) upon my consciousness*

ob·tru·sive /əb'truːsɪv/ *adj* displeasingly noticeable or active —**~ly** *adv* —**~ness** *n* [U]

ob·tuse /əb'tjuːs‖-'tuːs/ *adj* **1** *fml* stupid **2** [Wa5] (of an angle) being between 90° and 180° —see picture at GEOMETRY **3** [Wa5] *rare* not pointed —**~ly** *adv* —**~ness** *n*

ob·verse /'ɒbvɜːs‖'ɑbvɜrs/ *n* [*the*+R] **1** *tech* the front side of a coin or coinlike object (MEDAL) —opposite **reverse 2** [(*of*)] *fml* the side (of something), part, or thing that is most noticeable or intended to be shown

ob·vi·ate /'ɒbvieɪt‖'ɑb-/ *v* [T1] to clear away (a difficulty)

ob·vi·ous /'ɒbvɪəs‖'ɑb-/ *adj* easy to understand; clear; which must be recognized —**~ness** *n* [U]

ob·vi·ous·ly /'ɒbvɪəsli‖'ɑb-/ *adv* [Wa5] it can be easily seen (that); plainly: *Obviously, you didn't read it.*|*"Is she sorry?" "Obviously not! Look at her"* —compare APPARENTly, EVIDENTLY

oc·a·ri·na /ˌɒkə'riːnə‖ˌɑ-/ *n* a type of small musical instrument played by blowing

oc·ca·sion[1] /ə'keɪʒən/ *n* **1** a time when something happens: *On that occasion I was not at home* **2** a proper time for something to happen: *A birthday is no occasion for tears* **3** a special event or ceremony **4** an event that leads to other events; direct cause **5 have (no) occasion to** to have (no) need or reason to **6 on occasion** from time to time; occasionally **7 on the occasion of** at the time of (a certain event) **8 rise to the occasion** to do well what has to be done at a given time **9 sense of occasion a** a feeling for what is the right social behaviour at any particular event **b** an ability to recognize the special qualities that make any particular event different from or better than another **10 take this/that occasion to** to use this/that chance to —see CHANCE (USAGE)

occasion[2] *v* [D1;T1] *fml* to cause; be the OCCASION[1] (4) of: *Your behaviour has occasioned (us) a lot of trouble*

oc·ca·sion·al /ə'keɪʒənəl/ *adj* [Wa5] **1** [A;(B)] happening from time to time; not regular: *We get the occasional visitor here* (=visitors come occasionally) **2** [A] *fml or tech* written or intended for a special event, purpose, etc. —**~ly** *adv*

Oc·ci·dent /'ɒksɪ̈dənt‖'ɑksɪ̈dənt, -dent/ *n* [*the*+R] *esp. fml or lit* the area of the world most directly influenced by the ancient civilizations of Greece and Rome, usu. thought of as "the West"; esp. Europe and the Americas —compare ORIENT

oc·ci·den·tal /ˌɒksɪ̈'dentəl‖ˌɑk-/ *n, adj* [Wa5] *esp. fml or lit* (*sometimes cap.*) (a person) from the OCCIDENT —compare ORIENTAL

oc·cult /'ɒkʌlt, ə'kʌlt‖ə'kʌlt, 'ɑ-/ *adj* **1** [B] secret; hidden from ordinary people **2** [B;*the*+U] magical and mysterious

oc·cu·pan·cy /'ɒkjʊpənsi‖'ɑkjə-/ *n* [U] (period of) actually living in a building or on a piece of land

oc·cu·pant /'ɒkjʊpənt‖'ɑkjə-/ *n* [(*of*)] a person who is in a certain place at a particular period of time

oc·cu·pa·tion /ˌɒkjʊ'peɪʃən‖ˌɑkjə-/ *n* **1** [U (*of*)] taking possession of; having in one's possession **2** [C] a job; employment **3** [C] a way of spending time

oc·cu·pa·tion·al /ˌɒkjʊ'peɪʃənəl‖ˌɑkjə-/ *adj* [Wa5] of or about an OCCUPATION (2) —**~ly** *adv*

occupational haz·ard /··ˌ··· '··/ *n* a risk or danger connected with a particular type of work

occupational ther·a·py /··ˌ··· '···/ *n* [U] the treatment of illness as of the body or mind through productive employment —**-pist** *n*

oc·cu·pi·er /'ɒkjʊpaɪəʳ‖'ɑkjə-/ *n* **1** a person who takes or has possession of **2** an OCCUPANT, esp. of a house —see also OWNER-OCCUPIER

oc·cu·py /'ɒkjʊpaɪ‖'ɑkjə-/ *v* **1** [T1] to take and hold possession of **2** [T1] to hold (an enemy's country, town, etc.) **3** [T1] to be in (a certain place) during a particular period of time: *occupy a house/a bed/a railway carriage* **4** [T1] to fill (a certain position, space, or time): *His books occupy a lot of space* **5** [X9] to cause to spend time (doing something): *He occupied himself in/with collecting stamps* **6 be occupied in** to be (doing something): *He was occupied in writing letters* —see BUSY (USAGE)

oc·cur /ə'kɜːʳ/ *v* **-rr-** **1** [IØ] (esp. of unplanned events) to happen; take place **2** [L9;(IØ): *often neg.*] (esp. of something not alive) to exist: *That sound doesn't occur in his language so it's difficult for him to pronounce*

oc·cur·rence /ə'kʌrəns‖ə'kɜ-/ *n* **1** an event; happening **2 of . . . occurrence** happening to the stated degree: *an event of rare occurrence*

occur to *v prep* [T1 *no pass.*] (of an idea) to come to (someone's) mind: *It occurred to me that we should go there more often*

o·cean /'əʊʃən/ *n* **1** [(*the*) U] the great mass of salt water that covers most of the earth **2** [C] (*often cap. as part of a name*) any of the great seas into which this mass is divided —see picture at GLOBE **3 oceans of** *infml* lots of —**~ic** /ˌəʊʃi'ænɪk/ *adj* [Wa5]

o·cean·go·ing /'əʊʃənˌgəʊɪŋ/ also **seagoing**— *adj* [Wa5] (esp. of a ship) built to travel on the sea rather than on rivers or in harbours

o·cean·og·ra·phy /ˌəʊʃən'ɒgrəfi‖-'ɑg-/ *n* [U] the scientific study of the ocean —**-pher** *n*

oc·e·lot /'ɒsɪ̈lɒt‖'ɑsɪ̈lɑt, 'əʊ-/ *n* a type of American wild animal, like a very large cat

o·chre[1], *AmE* usu. **ocher** /'əʊkəʳ/ —*n* [U] yellow earth used as a colouring matter, for example in paints

ochre[2], *AmE* usu. **ocher**— *adj, n* [Wa5;B;U] (of) the colour of OCHRE[1]

o'clock /ə'klɒk‖ə'klɑk/ *adv* (used with the numbers from 1 to 12 in telling time) exactly the hour stated according to the clock: *"What time is it?" "It's 9 o'clock"*

USAGE In modern English, **o'clock** is used only in mentioning the exact hour, not the hour and a particular number of minutes: *9 o'clock*, but *5 past 9, half past 9*, etc.

-oc·ra·cy /'ɒkrəsi‖'ɑ-/ *suffix* **-ocracies** [→*n*] -CRACY

-o·crat /ə'kræt/ *suffix* [→*n*] -CRAT —**-ocratic** *suffix* [→*adj*] —**-ocratically** *suffix* [→*adj* [Wa4]]

oc·ta-, octo- /'ɒktə‖'ɑktə/ also **oct-** /ɒkt‖ɑkt/— *comb. form* 8

oc·ta·gon /'ɒktəgən‖'ɑktəgɑn/ *n* **1** *tech* a flat figure with 8 sides and 8 angles **2** anything in the shape of this, for example, an 8-sided room —**~al** /ɒk'tægənəl/ *adj* [Wa5]

oc·tane /ˈɒkteɪn‖ˈɑk-/ *n* [A9] a number which shows the power and quality of petrol, the higher the better: *100-octane petrol is very good for a motorcar engine*
oc·tave /ˈɒktɨv, -teɪv‖ˈɑk-/ *n* **1** a space of 8 degrees between musical notes **2** a musical note 8 degrees away from another **3** a musical note and the note 8 degrees away, played together **4** a musical note and the note 8 degrees away, played together with the 6 other notes in between **5** a group of 8 lines of poetry, esp. the first 8 of a poem of 14 lines (SONNET)
oc·ta·vo /ɒkˈteɪvəʊ‖ɑk-/ *abbrev.* **8vo**— *n* **-vos** the (size of) paper produced by folding a sheet of paper 3 times so as to give 8 sheets
oc·tet /ɒkˈtet‖ɑk-/ *n* **1** (a piece of music written for) a group of 8 people playing instruments or singing together **2** OCTAVE (5)
Oc·to·ber /ɒkˈtəʊbəʳ‖ɑk-/ *n* [R;(C)] the 10th month of the year
oc·to·ge·nar·i·an /ˌɒktəʊdʒɨˈneərɪən, -tə-‖ˌɑk-/ *n* a person who is between 80 and 89 years old
oc·to·pus /ˈɒktəpəs‖ˈɑk-/ *n* **-puses** a type of deep-sea creature with 8 arms (TENTACLE*s*) —see picture at MOLLUSC
oc·to·syl·lab·ic /ˌɒktəʊsɨˈlæbɪk, -tə-‖ˌɑk-/ *adj* [Wa5] (of a line of poetry) having 8 SYLLABLE*s*
oc·u·lar /ˈɒkjʊləʳ‖ˈɑkjə-/ *adj* [Wa5] **1** *fml or tech* of the eyes **2** *becoming rare* that can be seen: *ocular proof*
oc·u·list /ˈɒkjʊlɨst‖ˈɑkjə-/ *n* an eye-doctor
o·da·lisque /ˈəʊdəlɪsk/ *n lit* an Eastern female slave in former times, esp. one used for sexual purposes
odd /ɒd‖ɑd/ *adj* **1** [Wa1;B] strange; unusual **2** [Wa5;A] not part of a pair or set: *an odd shoe* **3** [Wa5;A] not regular; OCCASIONAL: *odd job|odd moments|(esp. BrE) Life would be very dull without the odd adventure now and then* **4** [Wa5;E] *infml* (after numbers) with rather more: *20-odd years|5 pounds odd* **5** [Wa5;B] (of a number) that cannot be divided exactly by 2: *1, 3, 5, 7, etc., are odd*—opposite **even**
odd·ball /ˈɒdbɔːl‖ˈɑd-/ *n infml, esp. AmE* a person who behaves in a strange or unusual way
odd·i·ty /ˈɒdɨti‖ˈɑ-/ *n* **1** [U;C: (*of*)] strangeness **2** [C] a strange person, thing, etc.
odd-job man /·ˈ··/ *n* a man who does ODD JOBS for pay
odd jobs /ˌ·ˈ·/ *n* [P] various pieces of work that have no real connection with each other
odd·ly /ˈɒdli‖ˈɑdli/ *adv* strangely: *He spoke oddly.|Oddly enough, he didn't seem to remember his own birthday*
odd man out /ˌ··ˈ·/ *n* **odd men out** **1** a person or thing left when all the others have been put into groups **2** *infml* someone who does not mix easily with others
odd·ment /ˈɒdmənt‖ˈɑd-/ *n* [*often pl.*] *infml* something left over or remaining
odds /ɒdz‖ɑdz/ *n* [P] **1** the probability that something will or will not happen: *The odds are 10 to 1 that her horse will not win the race.|They are fighting against heavy odds* **2 at odds (with)** in disagreement (with) **3 give/receive odds** to give/receive an advantage at the beginning of a game so that it will be harder for the better player to win **4 it/that makes no odds** *BrE* it/that makes no difference; has no importance **5 lay (someone) odds (of)** to offer (someone) ODDS (of) **6 long odds** ODDS that are strongly against (for example, 100 to 1) **7 short odds** ODDS that are not strongly against (for example, 2 to 1)
odds and ends /ˌ··ˈ·/ also (*BrE sl*) **odds and sods** /ˌ··ˈ·/— *n* [P] small articles without much value that do not all belong to the same group
odds-on /·ˈ·/ *adj* [Wa5] very likely (to win) (esp. in the phr. **odds-on favourite**): *The odds-on favourite* (=horse) *came in last, to everyone's surprise.|It's odds-on that she won't come*
ode /əʊd/ *n* a type of usu. long poem
o·di·ous /ˈəʊdɪəs/ *adj* hateful; very unpleasant —**~ly** *adv*
o·di·um /ˈəʊdɪəm/ *n* [U] *fml* widespread hatred
o·do·rif·er·ous /ˌəʊdəˈrɪfərəs/ *adj fml* having a smell, esp. a pleasant smell
o·do·rous /ˈəʊdərəs/ *adj lit & poet* having a smell
o·dour, *AmE* **-dor** /ˈəʊdəʳ/ *n esp. BrE* **1** a smell, esp. an unpleasant one **2 in bad odour with** *fml* badly thought of by —**~less** *adj* [Wa5]
od·ys·sey /ˈɒdɨsi‖ˈɑ-/ *n esp. lit* a long adventurous journey
oe·cu·men·i·cal /ˌiːkjʊˈmenɪkəl‖ˌekjə-/ *adj* ECUMENICAL
Oe·di·pus com·plex /ˈiːdɨpəs ˌkɒmpleks‖ˈe-, -ˌkɑm-/ *n* (in FREUDIAN PSYCHOLOGY) **1** (of a young boy) an unconscious sexual desire for one's mother combined with hatred of one's father **2** ELECTRA COMPLEX
o'er /əʊəʳ/ *adv, prep poet* over
oe·soph·a·gus, esophagus /ɪˈsɒfəgəs‖ɪˈsɑ-/ *n med* the food tube leading from the back of the mouth (PHARYNX) down into the stomach —see picture at DIGESTIVE SYSTEM
oes·tro·gen, estrogen /ˈiːstrədʒən‖ˈes-/ *n* [C;U] a substance produced in the part of a female's body where eggs are formed (OVARY), which causes certain changes in the body in preparation for the production of young
oes·trus cy·cle, estrus cycle /ˈiːstrəs ˌsaɪkəl‖ˈestrəs-/ *n* the set of changes which take place regularly over a fixed time in the parts of a female animal's body concerned with sex and giving birth to young, in which the body gradually goes into, reaches, and then leaves the state in which it can produce young
of /əv, ə; *strong* ɒv‖əv, ə; *strong* ɑv/ *prep* **1** (of qualities, possessions, etc.) belonging to X; that X has: *the colour of her dress|the roots of your hair|the size of the wings* **2** made from: *a dress of silk* **3** containing: *a bag of potatoes* **4** (that is) part in relation to (a whole or all) **a** (*after expressions of quantity*): *2 pounds of sugar|2 miles of bad road|much of the night|"How many hours a day of actual lessons?"* (SEU S.) **b** (*with dates*): *the 27th of February* **c** (*before mass nouns*): *lots of sugar|a blade of grass* **5** (*used for picking out in a group*) from among **a** (*after nouns and numbers*): *members of the team|one of his last poems|2 of us|the 2 of us|both of us* **b** (*after* the+COMPARATIVE *or* SUPERLATIVE): *the older of the 2|the most important of all* **c** (*after* type, sort, kind+*sing. noun*): *"any sort of flying accident"* (SEU W.) **6** (*before possessive forms*) that is/are: *those blue eyes of hers|a friend of mine* **7** (*before a phr. that is like a subject in grammar*) by: *the love of God (for men)|the shooting of the hunters* **8** (*before a phr. that is like an object in grammar*) directed towards *or* done to: *the love of God (by men)|the shooting of the animals* **9** that is (equal to): *the City of New York|the art of painting|at the age of 8* **10** (*showing origin*) from (a): *a girl of good family|a man of the (common) people* **11** (*showing cause*) by; through: (*do something*) *of one's own free will|It didn't happen of itself* **12** connected with: *the king of England|the results of the meeting|a teacher of English|the time of arrival* **13** (of works of art or literature) **a** by: *the plays of Shakespeare* **b** about; having as a subject: *stories of adventure|a picture of John* **14** in relation to: *east of Suez|slow of speech* **15** with; that has as a typical

quality: *an area of hills|a woman of ability* **16** (*before expressions of time*) **a** *AmE* (*before the numbers from 1 to 12 in telling time, without the word* o'clock) before: *5* (*minutes*) *of 2* (=5 to 2) **b** *becoming rare* during: *They always like to go there of an evening* **17** (*after nouns related to verbs*): *a lover of good music* (=someone who loves . . .) **18** (*before nouns related to adjectives*): *a woman of no importance* (=a woman who is not important) **19** (*after certain verbs*): **a** *die of hunger|ask a question of someone* **b** (*often showing separation or removal*): *cure someone of a disease|rob someone of his money* **20** (*after certain adjectives and participles*): **a** *fond of good music* **b** *old use* by: BELOVED (=loved) *of all who knew him* **21** (*in the pattern* adj (expressing a value judgment) +of+X (*meaning a person or organization*)) on X's part; for X to do . . .: *How kind of John* (*to buy the tickets*).|*It's very annoying of the Government to have raised the tax on beer* —see also **of** COURSE, **of** LATE, **of** OLD **22 of a** (*after expressions of strong feeling*) -like: *that palace of a house* (=that palace-like or PALATIAL house)|*some fool of a man* (=some fool-like or foolish man) **23 within . . . of . . .** not more than . . . from, after, or before: *within a mile of here* **24 a fine figure of a man/a woman** a man/a woman with a fine appearance

USAGE In meanings 1, 7, and 13 one could also say *Shakespeare's plays, the hunters' shooting*, but not usually **England's king, *your hair's roots*. Use **'s** for **a** the *poss.* form of anything that is alive: *John's leg|the dog's leg*. Otherwise use **of**: *the leg* **of** *the table* **b** periods of time: *a day's work|I'll see you in an hour's time*. It is also used **c** in newspapers to save space: *London's Traffic*. In meanings 7 and 13 one can use either **of** or **'s**, but *John's picture* may mean "a picture by John" or "a picture showing John as its subject."

off¹ /ɒf‖ɔf/ *adv* [Wa5] **1 a** from or no longer in a place or position; away: *drive off|Get off at the next stop.|Off you go!|"Off!" he shouted.|Goodbye, I'm off now* **b** aside: *He turned off into a side road* **2** in or into a state of being disconnected or removed; away: *The handle came off.|with his shoes off* —compare ON² (4) **3** (esp. of electrical apparatus) so as not to be lit, in use, or connected to the electricity supply: *Turn the light/*TAPs *off* —opposite **on**; compare IN³ (4), OUT³ (4) **4** to or at a (stated) distance away in time or space; away: *2 miles off|several years off* **5** so as to separate: *block an area off|He cut his ear off* **6** to, into, or resulting in a state of nonexistence, completion, or discontinuance: *kill the animals off* **7** away or free from regular work: *have Monday off* **8 better/worse off** in a better/worse condition: *You'd be better off with a bicycle rather than that old car* **9 off and on** ON² (9) **and off 10 right**/(*esp. BrE*) **straight off** *not fml* at once **11 well/badly off** rich/poor: *helping the less well off|He's very badly off.|They're better off than we are* —see BADLY-OFF, WELL-OFF **12** (**well/badly**) **off for** (well/badly) provided with; having/not having a lot of: *How well off are you|How are you off for socks?* **13 voices off** the voices of actors not on the stage but heard in the theatre

off² *prep* **1** not on; away from (a surface that is touched or rested on): *Get off my foot!|Keep off the grass.|He jumped off the horse* **2** from (something that supports or holds up): *Take the curtains off their hooks.|to eat off golden plates* **3** away from, as when subtracting: *cut a piece off the loaf|*(*infml*) *He borrowed a pound off me* **4** to or at a (stated) distance away from in time or space: *The ship was blown off* (*her*) *course.|We're going* (*right*) *off the subject.|*(fig.) *We're a long way off understanding this yet* **5** (esp. of a road) turning off (a larger one): *a narrow street off the High Street|He lives/drove/stayed* (*2 miles*) *off the main road* **6** in the sea near: *The ship sank* (*a mile*) *off Langness.|an island off the coast of France* **7** (of a person) **a** no longer keen on or fond of: *I've gone/I'm right off love stories for some reason.|He's off his food* **b** no longer taking (esp. medicine): *Bill's off drugs now* —opposite **on** —see also COME OFF **it, off** COLOUR, **off** DUTY, **off the** RECORD, **off the** MAP, **off one's** HEAD, **off the** POINT

off³ *adj* **1** [F] (of food) no longer good to eat or drink **2** [Wa5;F] (of dishes in a restaurant) no longer being served **3** [F] (of behaviour) not what one has a right to expect; rather unkind, dishonest, etc.: *I thought it was a bit off, not even answering my letter!* **4** [Wa5;A] *tech, esp. BrE* (of part of a horse or vehicle) being the right-hand one of a pair of things —opposite **near** **5** [Wa5;F] (of something that has been arranged) not going to happen after all: *I'm afraid the party's off because my wife's ill* —compare ON³ (2) **6** [Wa5;F] (of the runners in a race) started **7** [Wa5;F] (esp. of electrical apparatus) not connected to the electrical supply; not lit; not in use —compare IN³ (4), OUT³ (4) **8** [Wa5;A] (of a time) **a** unfortunate; not as good as usual: *I'm afraid this is one of his off days—he usually plays better* **b** quiet and dull: *Tickets are cheaper during the off season* **9** [Wa5;A;*the*+U] being that part of a cricket field in front and to the right of the (right-handed) player who strikes the ball (BATSMAN) as he faces the man who BOWLs it —opposites **on, leg** **10 be/get off to a good/bad start** to start well/badly **11** (**Be**) **off with you** go away! **12 on the off chance** *infml* just in case; with the unlikely chance

off- *prefix* **1** [*n, v→adj, adv, v*] away from; not on: OFFSHORE|OFF-STREET|*to* OFF-LOAD **2** [*n, adj→n, adj*] (*before colours*) not quite: OFF-WHITE

of·fal /ˈɒfəl‖ˈɔ-, ˈɑ-/ *n* [U] **1** *esp. BrE* parts of an animal which are not considered as good as the flesh for food (the heart, head, brains, etc.) **2** waste matter

off·beat /ˌɒfˈbiːt◂‖ˌɔf-/ *adj infml* unusual

off col·our /ˌ· ˈ··◂/ *adj* **1** not well **2** sexually improper

of·fence, *AmE* **-fense** /əˈfens/ *n esp. BrE* **1** [C (*against*)] a wrong; crime **2** [C (*to*)] something unpleasant: *That dirty old house is an offence to everyone who lives in the street* **3** [U] cause for hurt feelings: *give/cause offence to someone|take offence at something* **4** [U] attack **5 a first offence** the first crime of which someone has been found guilty

of·fend /əˈfend/ *v* **1** [I∅ (*against*)] to do wrong **2** [T1] to cause displeasure to **3** [T1] to hurt the feelings of: *Her words offended me*

of·fend·er /əˈfendəʳ/ *n* **1 a** a person who offends **b** *euph* a criminal **2 first offender** someone found guilty (of a crime) for the first time

of·fen·sive¹ /əˈfensɪv/ *adj* **1** causing offence; unpleasant **2** of or about attacking —opposite **defensive** —**~ly** *adv* —**~ness** *n* [U]

offensive² *n* **1** a continued attack, usu. with large military forces **2 take the offensive** to begin to attack

of·fer¹ /ˈɒfəʳ‖ˈɔ-, ˈɑ-/ *v* **1** [D1 (*to*);T1: (*for*)] to hold out (to a person) for acceptance or refusal: *She offered me £10,000 for that book* **2** [D1 (*to*);T1 (UP)] to give (to God): *He offered* (*up*) *a prayer for the return of his health* **3** [T3;I∅] to express willingness (to do something): *offer to go* **4 offer itself/themselves** to be present: *Act when the right moment offers itself*

offer² *n* **1** [C (*of*), C3] a statement offering (to do) something **2** [C (*of*)] that which is offered: *an offer of £5* —compare OFFERING **3 under offer** *BrE* (of a house that is for sale) already having a possible buyer who has offered money

of·fer·ing /ˈɒfərɪŋ‖ˈɔ-, ˈɑ-/ *n* something offered, esp. to God

of·fer·to·ry /ˈɒfətəri‖ˈɔfətori, ˈɑ-/ *n* **1** a certain part of a religious service (MASS) **2** the time during a religious service when money is collected: *Put your money in the offertory box*

off·hand /ˌɒfˈhænd◂‖ˌɔf-/ *adv, adj* **1** [B] careless; disrespectful **2** [Wa5;A] at once, without time to consider: *I can't give an answer offhand* —**~edly** *adv* —**~edness** *n* [U]

of·fice /ˈɒfɪ̵s‖ˈɔ-, ˈɑ-/ *n* **1** [C] a place where business is done **2** [C] a place where a service is provided: *a ticket office* **3** [C] a place where written work is done in connection with a business: *office work* **4** [C] (*usu. caps.*) a government department: *the Foreign Office* **5** [C] employment and special duties: *the office of president* **6** [U;C] a position of some importance, esp. in government: *hold/enter/leave office|in/out of office*

office block /ˈ·· ·/ *n* a usu. large building divided into offices

office boy /ˈ·· ·/ (*fem.* **office girl**)— *n* a boy employed to do some of the less important work in an office

of·fice·hold·er /ˈɒfɪ̵sˌhəʊldəʳ‖ˈɔ-, ˈɑ-/ also **office bear·er** /ˈ·· ˌ··/— *n* one who fills an office or holds a position, esp. in government

of·fi·cer /ˈɒfɪ̵səʳ‖ˈɔ-, ˈɑ-/ *n* **1** [C] a person in a position of command in the armed forces **2** [C] a person who holds a position of some importance, esp. in government, a business, or a group **3** [C; N] a policeman

USAGE Anyone paid to do a regular job is an **employee**. An **officer** is usually a uniformed member of the armed forces, though one may speak of a *police* **officer**. Other people who work for the Government are called **civil servants** or **officials**: *a Post Office* **official**. A **clerk** works behind a desk, and is not very high up in his organization. If he works for the Government or in a bank, rather than private industry, he too can be called an **official**. Someone who serves people in a shop is a **shop assistant**, not an **official** or an **officer**. But both **clerk** and **officer** are the titles of people in certain special jobs, esp. in the law, and these must be learnt.

of·fic·es /ˈɒfɪ̵sɪ̵z‖ˈɔ-, ˈɑ-/ *n* [P] help (in the phr. **good offices**)

of·fi·cial¹ /əˈfɪʃəl/ *n* a person who works in government, esp. one whose job is less important than that of a government OFFICER —see OFFICER (USAGE)

official² *adj* of or about a position of trust, power, and responsibility: *an official position|an official occasion|an official manner of speaking* —opposite **unofficial**; compare OFFICIOUS

of·fi·cial·dom /əˈfɪʃəldəm/ *n* [U] *often derog* OFFICIAL*s* as a group —compare RED TAPE

of·fi·cial·ese /əˌfɪʃəlˈiːz/ *n* [U] *derog* the language of government OFFICIAL*s*, considered unnecessarily hard to understand —compare JOURNALESE

of·fi·cial·ly /əˈfɪʃəli/ *adv* **1** in an official manner **2** [Wa5] as (believed to have been) stated by officials: *Officially, he's on holiday; actually, he's in hospital* —opposite **unofficially**

official re·ceiv·er /ˌ·ˌ·· ·ˈ··/ *n* [*the*+R] (*often caps.*) RECEIVER (4)

of·fi·ci·ate /əˈfɪʃieɪt/ *v* [I∅ (*at*)] to act officially

of·fi·cious /əˈfɪʃəs/ *adj derog* too eager to give orders or to offer advice —**~ly** *adv* —**~ness** *n* —compare OFFICIAL²

off·ing /ˈɒfɪŋ‖ˈɔ-, ˈɑ-/ *n* **in the offing** coming soon

off·ish /ˈɒfɪʃ‖ˈɔ-/ *adj infml rare* tending to keep apart from other people —compare STANDOFFISH

off-li·cence /ˈ· ··/ *n BrE* a shop where alcohol is sold to be taken away

off-load /ˌ· ˈ·/ *v* [T1 (*on*(*to*))] *BrE* to get rid of (something unwanted)

off-peak /ˌ· ˈ·◂/ *adj* [Wa5;A] **1** less busy: *Prices are lower during off-peak periods* **2** that exists during less busy periods: *off-peak prices*

off·print /ˈɒfprɪnt‖ˈɔf-/ *n* a separately printed copy of a piece of writing that was originally part of a book, magazine, etc.

off-put·ting /ˈ· ˌ··/ *adj esp. BrE* unpleasantly surprising and/or causing dislike —see PUT OFF

off·set¹ /ˈɒfset‖ˈɔf-/ *n* a method of printing in which paper is printed from a rubber roller which has first had the ink put onto it from a metal plate

offset² /ˈɒfset, ˌɒfˈset‖ˈɔfset, ˌɔfˈset/ *v* **-tt-** [T1] to make up for; balance

off·shoot /ˈɒfʃuːt‖ˈɔf-/ *n* a new stem or branch: (fig.) *an offshoot of a large organization*

off·shore /ˌɒfˈʃɔːʳ◂‖ˌɔfˈʃor◂/ *adv, adj* [Wa5] **1** [B] coming or moving from or off the shore: *an offshore wind* **2** [B;E] at a distance from the shore in the water: *offshore fishing|2 miles offshore*

off·side /ˌɒfˈsaɪd◂‖ˌɔf-/ *adj, adv* **1** [B;E] (in certain sports) in a position in which play is not allowed, esp. by being on the opponents' side of the ball: *2 yards offside* —opposite **onside** **2** [Wa5; A] of or about such a position: *the offside rule* **3** [Wa5;A] *esp. BrE* being on the right-hand side, esp. of an animal or of a car, road, etc. —opposite **nearside**

off·spring /ˈɒfˌsprɪŋ‖ˈɔf-/ *n* **offspring** [Wn3;C9] (*not with "an"*) a child or children; the young of an animal

off·stage /ˌɒfˈsteɪdʒ◂‖ˌɔf-/ *adv, adj* [Wa5] not on the open stage; out of sight of those watching a play

off-street /ˈ· ·/ *adj* [Wa5;A] away from the main street(s) (often in the phr. **off-street parking**)

off-the-rec·ord /ˌ· · ˈ··◂/ *adj, adv* [Wa5] (so as) not to be written down in the notes of the meeting

off-white /ˌ· ˈ·◂/ *n, adj* [U;B] a colour that is not a pure white but has some grey or yellow in it

oft /ɒft‖ɔft/ *adv poet* (*usu. in comb.*) often: *oft-repeated advice*

of·ten /ˈɒfən, ˈɒftən‖ˈɔ-/ *adv* [Wa2] **1** (at) many times: *"How often do you go there?" "Once a month."|often-repeated advice|"How often have you been there?" "Twice"* **2** in many cases: *American girls are often very pretty* **3 as often as . . .** as many times as . . .; each time that . . .: *As often as he's tried to go there, he's always failed* **4 as often as not** as many times one way as the other; at least 50% of the time **5 every so often** now and then; from time to time **6 more often than not** more times one way then the other; more than 50% of the time **7 often as** although . . . often: *Often as I ask him to, he never helps his father*

o·gle¹ /ˈəʊgəl/ *v* [Wv3;T1;I∅ (*at*)] to look (at) with great interest, esp. sexual interest

ogle² *n* [*usu. sing.*] a look of great interest, esp. sexual interest

o·gre /ˈəʊgəʳ/ *n fem.* **ogress** /ˈəʊgrɪ̵s/— **1** (in fairy stories) a fierce creature like a very large man **2** a person who makes others afraid —**ogreish** /ˈəʊgərɪʃ/ *adj* —**ogreishly** *adv*

oh /əʊ/ *interj* **1** (expressing surprise, fear, etc.) **2** (used before a name when calling someone) —see also O

ohm /əʊm/ *n* a measure of electrical RESISTANCE

o·ho /əʊˈhəʊ/ *interj lit & old use* (expressing surprise or joy at success)

-oid /ɔɪd/ *suffix* [*n*→*adj*] **1** like; in the form of: *metalloid* (=like a metal) **2** *derog* like but not having the best qualities of: *humanoid*

oil¹ /ɔɪl/ *n* [U] **1** any of several types of fatty liquid (from animals, plants, or under the ground) used for burning, for making machines run easily, also for cooking **2 burn the midnight oil** to stay up late at night to read or study **3 pour oil on troubled waters** to bring peace when people are quarrelling **4 strike oil a** to find oil underground **b** to make a valuable discovery

oil² *v* [T1] **1** to put oil on or to make parts work or run more easily **2** to rub oil on or into **3 oil the wheels** *infml* to do or say something to make things go more smoothly **4 oil someone's palm** *infml* to grease someone's PALM² (2)

oil-bear·ing /ˈ· ˌ··/ *adj* (esp. of areas under ground) containing oil

oil·cake /ˈɔɪlkeɪk/ *n* [U] food for cattle made from seeds after oil has been pressed out

oil·can /ˈɔɪlkæn/ *n* an oil container (esp. one with a long thin neck) used for oiling machinery

oil·cloth /ˈɔɪlklɒθ‖-klɔθ/ *n* [U] **1** cloth treated with oil so that water will not go through it, used for covering tables, shelves, and other surfaces **2** *BrE* LINOLEUM

oil col·ours, *AmE* **-colors** /ˈ· ˌ··/ *n* [P] OILS

oiled /ɔɪld/ *adj* see WELL-OILED

oil·field /ˈɔɪlfiːld/ *n* an area under which there is oil

oil-fired /ˈ· ·/ *adj* [Wa5] oil-burning (esp. in the phr. **oil-fired central heating**)

oil·man /ˈɔɪlmæn/ *n* **-men** /men/ *infml* a man who produces or sells oil

oil of vit·ri·ol /ˌ·· ˈ···/ *n* [U] VITRIOL (2a)

oil paint /ˈ· ·/ *n* [U;C] OILS

oil paint·ing /ˈ· ˌ··/ *n* **1** [U] the art of painting in OILS **2** [C] a picture painted in OILS **3 he's/she's/it's no oil painting** *infml often humor* he/she/it is not beautiful

oil·rig /ˈɔɪlˌrɪg/ *n* an apparatus for getting oil from underground, esp. from land that is under the sea

oils /ɔɪlz/ *n* [P] **1** paints (esp. for pictures) containing oil —compare WATERCOLOUR **2 in oils** using these paints: *She paints very well in oils*

oil·skin /ˈɔɪlˌskɪn/ *n* [C;U] (a garment made of) cloth treated with oil so that water will not pass through it

oil·skins /ˈɔɪlˌskɪnz/ *n* [P] a complete suit made of OILSKIN

oil slick /ˈ· ·/ also **slick**— *n* a thin sheet of oil floating on water

oil tank·er /ˈ· ˌ··/ *n* a ship with large containers for carrying oil

oil well /ˈ· ·/ *n* a hole made in the ground to get oil out

oil·y /ˈɔɪli/ *adj* [Wa1] **1** of, about, or like oil: *an oily liquid* **2** covered with or containing oil: *dirty oily clothes|oily Spanish food* **3** (of skin) producing a more than average amount of an oil-like substance; not dry **4** *derog* too polite

oink /ɔɪŋk/ *v, n* [I∅;C] *infml* (to make) the sound that a pig makes

oint·ment /ˈɔɪntmənt/ *n* [U;C] **1** a substance (often medicinal) containing oil or fat, to be rubbed on the skin **2 a/the fly in the ointment** one small unwanted thing that spoils the pleasure, happiness, perfection, etc., of an occasion

o·ka·pi /əʊˈkɑːpi/ *n* [Wn1] a type of rare African animal that looks rather like a horse with a long neck, and has black and white lines on its legs

o·kay¹, OK /əʊˈkeɪ/ *adv infml* **1** all right; satisfactorily: *That car goes okay now* **2** all right; agreed; yes **a** (asking for agreement, esp. to a suggestion): *Let's go there, okay?* **b** (expressing agreement): *"Shall we go there?" "Okay"* **c** (giving permission): *"Can I use your car?" "Okay"*

okay², OK *adj* [F;(B)] *infml* all right: *She seems okay now*

okay³, OK *v* **okayed, OKed; okaying, OKing** [T1] *infml* to approve

okay⁴, OK *n* **okays, OK's** *infml* approval; permission

o·kra /ˈəʊkrə/ *n* [U] a type of green vegetable from southern countries —see picture at VEGETABLE¹

-ol·a·try /ˈɒlətri‖ˈɑ-/ *comb. form* -LATRY

old /əʊld/ *adj* **1** [Wa1;B;E] advanced in age; of age: *How old are you?|You're old enough to dress yourself, child!|He is as old as John.|She is 16 years old.|She is a 16-year-old girl* **2** [Wa1;B: *the*+P; *the*+U] having lived or existed for a long time or long enough to show signs of age: *old and young people|old and new books|The old and the young do not always understand each other.|The old is sometimes more attractive than the new* **3** [Wa1;B] having been in use for a long time or long enough to show signs of use: *old shoes|an old car* **4** [Wa5;A] (*before nouns showing a relationship of equality*) having continued in the relationship for a long time: *old and new friends|old enemies* **5** [Wa5;A] former: *He got his old job back* **6** [Wa5;A] known for a long time: *Don't tell me the same old story again!|Good old John!* **7** [Wa5;A] (used for making a phrase stronger): *Come any old time.|I can use any old thing* **8 as old as the hills** very old **9 of old a** long ago; in the past: *days of old* **b** *rare* for a long time

USAGE 1 Note that **old**, not **young**, is used when measuring age: *"How* **old** *is the baby?" "He's 3 weeks* **old***."* 2 The opposite of **old** is **young** (people or animals) or **new** (things). **Ancient** is used for very old things, periods, or civilizations: *an* **ancient** *Greek bowl.* When used informally of a person or thing it means "very old"; *an* **ancient** *lady/car/dress.* **Antique** means "valuable" as well as "old": *an* **antique** *French writing desk.* When we use **venerable** of someone we mean that we should respect him because he is old: *a* **venerable** *white-haired priest.* **Archaic** is sometimes used of very old works of art, but when used of words or ideas it means that they are no longer used or believed in. **Antiquated** is also used of things or ideas that are no longer suitable or useful. **Old-fashioned** has the same meaning, but it can also be used of people, and is less *derog*: *I may be* **old-fashioned**, *but I think a baby needs a father.* —compare ELDER (2,3)

Old *adj* [Wa5;A] (of a language) of an early period in the history of the language: *Old English|Old Irish* —compare MIDDLE

old age /ˌ· ˈ·◂/ *n* [U] the part of one's life when one is old

old age pen·sion /ˌ·· ˈ··/ also **retirement pension**— *n* [U; *the*+R] money paid regularly by the State to old people —**~er** *n* —compare SENIOR CITIZEN

old boy /ˌ· ˈ·/ (*fem.* **old girl**)— *n BrE* **1** [C] a former pupil of a school **2** [N] *infml* a fellow; friend **3** [C] *infml* an old person

old-boy net·work /ˌ· ˈ· ˌ··/ *n BrE, often derog* **1** [*the*+R] the tendency of former pupils of the same school to favour each other in later life **2** [*the*+GU] the former members of the PUBLIC SCHOOLs in England, esp. those in positions of importance

old coun·try /ˈ· ˌ··/ *n* [*the*+R] the country of origin of someone who now lives in the US, Australia, etc.

old·en /ˈəʊldən/ *adj* [Wa5;A] *lit & old use* past; long ago (esp. in the phrs. **in olden days**; **in olden times**)

ol·de worl·de /ˌəʊldi ˈwɜːldi◂‖-ɜr-/ *adj infml BrE, sometimes derog* of a perhaps too consciously old-fashioned style

old-fash·ioned¹ /ˌ· ˈ··◂/ *adj* **1** (of a type that is) no longer common: *old-fashioned ideas|an old-fashioned house* —see OLD (USAGE) **2 an old-fashioned look** *infml BrE* a look that suggests disapproval

old-fashioned² /ˌ· ˈ··/ *n* (*often caps.*) a glass of a type of mixed alcoholic drink of American origin, made with WHISKY

old fo·gy, -gey /ˌ· ˈ··/ *n infml derog* a person (esp. a man) whose ideas and life-style are very old-fashioned

old guard /ˌ· ˈ·/ *n* [*the*+GU] the group of people whose ideas are very old-fashioned and who are against change

old hand /ˌ· ˈ·/ *n* [(*at*)] a very experienced person: *an old hand at fishing*

old hat /ˌ· ˈ·/ *adj* [F] *infml derog* old-fashioned

old·ish /ˈəʊldɪʃ/ *adj* [Wa5] rather old

old la·dy /ˌ· ˈ··/ *n* [*the*+R;C9 *usu. sing.*] *sl* **1** one's wife: *Have you met the/my old lady?* **2** one's mother

old maid /ˌ· ˈ·/ *n derog* **1** an unmarried woman who is no longer young **2** a person (man or woman) who is very careful and difficult to please —compare OLD WOMAN (3)

old maid·ish /ˌ· ˈ··◂/ *adj derog* of or like an OLD MAID (2)

old man /ˌ· ˈ·/ *n* **1** [*the*+R;C9 *usu. sing.*] *sl* one's husband **2** [*the*+R;C9 *usu. sing.*] *sl* one's father —compare OLD WOMAN (2) **3** [N] *infml BrE* OLD BOY (2)

old mas·ter /ˌ· ˈ··/ *n* **1** an important painter of an earlier period, esp. the 15th to 18th century **2** a picture by such a painter

Old Nick /ˌ· ˈ·/ also **Old Har·ry** /ˌəʊld ˈhæri/— *n* [R] *infml humor* the devil

old school /ˈ· ·/ *n* **of the old school** old-fashioned; like those that used to be

old school tie /ˌ·· ˈ·/ *n esp. BrE* **1** [C] a special TIE that is worn to show that someone has been a pupil at a certain school, esp. a PUBLIC SCHOOL **2** [*the*+R] the feeling that former pupils of the same school should help each other in later life

old-stag·er /ˌ· ˈ··/ *n infml BrE* a person who has had long experience in a particular activity

old·ster /ˈəʊldstəʳ/ *n infml often humor, esp. AmE* an old person —compare YOUNGSTER

Old Tes·ta·ment /ˌ· ˈ···◂/ *n* [*the*+R] the first half of the Bible, containing ancient Hebrew writings about events before the birth of Christ —compare NEW TESTAMENT

old-tim·er /ˌ· ˈ··/ *n* **1** [C] a person who has been somewhere or done something for a long time **2** [C;N] *esp. AmE* an old man

old wives' tale /ˌ· ˈ· ·/ *n* an ancient idea or belief, esp. of the sort held by old women

old wom·an /ˌ· ˈ··/ *n sl* **1** [*the*+R;C9 *usu. sing.*] one's wife **2** [*the*+R;C9 *usu. sing.*] one's mother —compare OLD LADY, OLD MAN (1,2) **3** [C] *derog* a person (usu. a man) who is difficult to please and often afraid —compare OLD MAID (2)

old-wom·an·ish /ˌ· ˈ···/ *adj derog* of or like an OLD WOMAN (3)

old-world /ˈ· ·/ *adj* [Wa5;A] *apprec* typical of CONTINENTAL Europe: *old-world charm*

Old World /ˌ· ˈ·◂/ *n* [(*the*) R] **1** Europe, Asia, and Africa (the Eastern HEMISPHERE): *Old World animals* —compare NEW WORLD **2** *esp. AmE* CONTINENTAL Europe

o·le·ag·i·nous /ˌəʊliˈædʒɨnəs/ *adj tech* oily; fatty

o·le·an·der /ˌəʊliˈændəʳ/ *n* a type of green bush from the Mediterranean area with flowers that are white, red, and pink

o·le·o·graph /ˈəʊlɪəgrɑːf‖-græf/ *n* a picture printed in OILS to look like an OIL PAINTING

O lev·el /ˈ· ˌ··/ *n* ordinary level; the lower of the 2 standards of examination (in the GCE) usu. taken at most British schools —see also A LEVEL

ol·fac·to·ry /ɒlˈfæktəri‖ɑl-, əʊl-/ *adj* [Wa5] *med* of or about the sense of smell

ol·i·garch /ˈɒlɨgɑːk‖ˈɑlɨgɑrk, ˈəʊ-/ *n* a member of an OLIGARCHY (3)

ol·i·gar·chy /ˈɒlɨgɑːki‖ˈɑlɨgɑrki, ˈəʊ-/ *n* **1** [U] government or rule by a few, (often) for their own interests **2** [C] a state governed by a few **3** [C] the group who govern such a state

ol·ive /ˈɒlɨv‖ˈɑ-/ *n* **1** [C] also **olive tree** /ˈ·· ·/— a type of tree grown in the Mediterranean countries, which has a small egg-shaped fruit **2** [C] the fruit of this tree, used for food and also for its oil (**olive oil**) —see picture at BERRY **3** [U] also **olive green** /ˌ·· ˈ·◂/— light green

olive branch /ˈ·· ·/ *n* [(*the*) S] a sign of peace (esp. in the phr. **hold out an/the olive branch** = to make a sign of peace)

olive drab /ˌ·· ˈ·/ *n, adj* [U;B] *esp. AmE* a greyish-green colour, used esp. for military uniforms

-ol·o·gist /ˈɒlədʒɨst‖ˈɑ-/ *comb. form* -LOGIST

-ol·o·gy /ˈɒlədʒi‖ˈɑ-/ *comb. form* -LOGY

O·lym·pi·ad /əˈlɪmpi-æd/ *n fml* the modern OLYMPIC GAMES, held once every 4 years: *The 14th Olympiad was held in London*

O·lym·pi·an /əˈlɪmpɪən/ *n, adj* **1** [Wa5] (like or connected with) any of the more important ancient Greek gods **2** (a person) like a god, esp. in being calm and untroubled by ordinary affairs

O·lym·pic /əˈlɪmpɪk/ *adj* [Wa5;A] of or connected with the OLYMPIC GAMES: *an Olympic runner*

Olympic Games /·ˌ·· ˈ·/ also **O·lym·pics** /əˈlɪmpɪks/— *n* **Olympic Games** [Wn3;(*the*) GC] **1** modern international sports events held once every 4 years in different countries **2** sports events held in ancient Greece once every 4 years

om·buds·man /ˈɒmbʊdzmən‖ˈɑm-/ *n* **-men** /mən/ a person appointed by a government to receive and report on any complaints made by ordinary people against the government or the public service

o·me·ga /ˈəʊmɨgə‖əʊˈmegə, -ˈmiː-, -ˈmeɪ-/ *n* [R; (C)] the last letter of the Greek alphabet (Ω, ω) —see also ALPHA AND OMEGA

ome·let, -lette /ˈɒmlɨt‖ˈɑm-/ *n* **1** eggs beaten together, often with a filling or mixture of some other food, and cooked in hot fat (by FRYing): *a cheese omelet* **2 you can't make an omelet without breaking eggs** you can't reach a good result without some loss or waste

o·men /ˈəʊmən/ *n* [(*of*)] a sign that something is going to happen in the future: *a good/bad omen*

om·i·nous /ˈɒmɨnəs‖ˈɑ-/ *adj* being an OMEN, esp. of something bad: *ominous black clouds* —**~ly** *adv*

o·mis·sion /əʊˈmɪʃən, ə-/ *n* **1** [U] the act of OMITting **2** [C] something OMITted

o·mit /əʊˈmɪt, ə-/ *v* **-tt- 1** [T1] to leave out; not include, by mistake or on purpose **2** [T4;(*BrE*) 3] to leave undone; not do: *Please don't omit locking/to lock the door when you leave*

om·ni- /ˈɒmnɪ‖ˈɑm-/ *prefix* all; universally: OMNIVOROUS

om·ni·bus /ˈɒmnɪbəs, -ˌbʌs‖ˈɑm-/ *n* **1** [C] a book containing several works, esp. by one writer, which have already been printed separately: *a Dickens omnibus* —compare ANTHOLOGY **2** [C; *by*+U] *fml & old use* BUS

om·nip·o·tent /ɒmˈnɪpətənt‖ɑm-/ *adj* [Wa5] all-powerful; having power over all things without end or limit —**-tence** *n* [U]

om·ni·pres·ent /ˌɒmnɪˈprezənt‖ˌɑm-/ *adj* [Wa5] *fml* present everywhere —**-ence** *n* [U]

om·nis·ci·ent /ɒmˈnɪʃənt, -ˈnɪsɪənt‖ɑmˈnɪʃənt/ *adj*

[Wa5] all-knowing; knowing everything —**-niscience** *n* [U]

om·niv·o·rous /ɒmˈnɪvərəs‖ɑm-/ *adj* [Wa5] **1** (esp. of animals) eating everything, esp. eating both plant and animal food —compare HERBIVOROUS, CARNIVOROUS **2** interested in everything, esp. in all books: *an omnivorous reader*

on[1] /ɒn‖ɔn, ɑn/ *prep* **1** (so as to be) touching (a surface): **a** also (*fml*) **upon**— *something on the table/the wall|a ring on my finger|He jumped on/onto the horse.|a blow on the head* (not *his head*) **b** (fig.) *on page 23* **2** also (*fml*) **upon**— supported by, hanging from, or fastened to: *jump on one foot|a ball on a string|the wheels on my car* **3** also (*fml*) **upon**— to; towards; in the direction of: *to march on Rome|make an attack on the enemy|on my right* **4** also (*fml*) **upon**— **a** very near: *a town* (*right*) *on the river/the border* **b** along (esp. a long or flat surface): *trees on both sides of the street|*(fig.) *I'm on my way to college* **5** during; at the time of: **a** *They arrive on Tuesday* (*AmE* also *They arrive Tuesday*).|*on July 1st|on time* (=not late or early)| *on the hour* (=exactly at 2, 3, etc.) **b** also (*fml*) **upon**— *on his arrival|on the morning of July 1st* (compare *in the morning*) **6** also (*fml*) **upon**— (*before the -*ing *form of verbs*) on the occasion of or directly after: *On thinking about the idea, I decided against it* **7** also (*fml*) **upon**— about: *a book on India|a poem called "On the Morning of Christmas Day"* —compare (5) and (6), see USAGE **8** (*before certain means of travelling, esp. large vehicles*) by means of and/or in: **a** *on foot/horseback* **b** also (*fml*) **upon**— *on a ship|on the 9 o'clock train* (compare *in a car, by ship, by train*) **9** by means of: **a** *They live on potatoes.|A car runs on petrol* **b** (certain machines or processes) *hear it on the radio|speak on the telephone* (compare *by telephone*) **c** *He cut his foot on a piece of glass* **10** also (*fml*) **upon**— because of; as a result of; through: *act on a lawyer's advice* **11** with the support of (money): *He went round the world on the money his aunt gave him* **12** in a state of: **a** (*before a noun or* the) *on fire|on* STRIKE*|on sale|on holiday|on the run| on the cheap|on offer|on purpose* (compare *by accident*) **b** also (*fml*) **upon**— (*before expressions of travelling*) *on a journey|I'd better be on my way* **13** also (*fml*) **upon**— as a member of: *serve on a committee* **14** working for; belonging to: *She's on the Times newspaper.|Which side was he on in the game?* **15** also (*fml*) **upon**— (*after expressions of money or effort, showing the effect*): *a tax on income* **16** also (*fml*) **upon**— (*between repeated words meaning unpleasant things*) added to; after: *suffer defeat on defeat* **17** *infml* (*before personal* PRONOUNs) with: *Have you got any money on you?* **18** (*often with alcoholic drinks*) *infml* with . . . paying: *Have a drink on me!* **19 have/get something on** (**somebody**) *sl* to have/get information that can be used against (somebody) —see also **on one's** OWN, **on the** CONTRARY, **on the other** HAND

USAGE A book **on** *rabbits* is more scientific than one **about** *rabbits*, which might be a children's story.

on[2] *adv* **1** continuously, instead of stopping: *He worked on* (*and on*) *all night* **2** further: *If you walk on you'll come to the church* **3** forward: *If any letters come while you're away, shall I send them on?* **4** in or into a state of being connected or in place: *with his coat on|He had nothing* (=no clothes) *on* —compare OFF[1] (2) **5** (with the stated part) forward: *The 2 cars crashed head on* **6** (of a clock) FORWARD[2] (5) **7** (esp. of electrical apparatus) so as to be connected to the electrical supply, lit, or in use: *Turn the light/the gas on.|*(fig.) *Her songs really turn me on* —opposite **off**; compare IN[3] (4), OUT[1] (14) **8 and so on** and other things of that kind; etc. **9 be on about** *infml & usu. derog* to be talking (esp. in a dull way and for too long) about **10 be on at** (**someone**) *infml* to be trying to persuade someone in a complaining way (to do something) **11 later on** later: some time afterwards **12 not on** *infml* impossible to do: *You can't refuse now—it's just not on!* **13 on and off** also **off and on**— from time to time; OCCASIONALly **14 on and on** without stopping

on[3] *adj* [Wa5] **1** [F] (esp. of electrical apparatus) connected to the electrical supply; lit; in use: *Is the radio on?* —opposite **off**; compare IN[3] (4), OUT[3] (4) **2** [F] (of something that has been arranged) happening or going to happen: *There's a new film on at the cinema, but it's coming off on Sunday.|I've got nothing on tonight, so let's go out* —compare OFF[3] (5) **3** [F] (of an actor, dancer, etc., in a theatre) actually performing: *You're on in 2 minutes!* **4** [A; *the*+U] being that part of a cricket field behind and to the left of the (right-handed) player who strikes the ball (BATSMAN) as he faces the man who throws it; LEG[1] (8): *the on side* —opposite **off**

on- *prefix* **1** [*v→adj, n*] (before words formed from verbs that, as verbs, can be followed by *on*): ONCOMING (COME ON)|ONLOOKER (LOOK ON)|ONRUSH (rush on) **2** [*n→adv, adj*] towards: ONSHORE

on-a·gain, off-a·gain /ˌ· ·· ˈ· ··/ *adj* [A] *esp. AmE* **1** starting and stopping without warning; undependable **2** being supposed to start and then not starting: *on-again, off-again plans*

once[1] /wʌns/ *adv* **1** one time; on one occasion: *I've done it once.|once a week* **2** some time ago; formerly: *He once knew her, but they are no longer friends.|No one remembers that once-popular singer* **3 all at once** suddenly **4 at once a** now; without delay: *Do it at once!* **b** at the same time; together: *Don't all speak at once!* **5** (**just**) **for once** for this one occasion only: *For once he was telling the truth* **6 once** (**and**) **for all** for the last time; now but never again: *John's back home once and for all; he won't go away again.|Once for all, did you take the money?* **7 once in a while** from time to time; now and then **8 once more a** one more time **b** also **once again**— now again as before: *John's back home once more* **9 once or twice** several times; a few times: *I've been there once or twice* **10 once upon a time** (*beginning a story for children*) some time ago; formerly

once[2] *n* [*this/the*+S] one time; on one occasion: *Do it just this once.|She did it just the once*

once[3] *conj* from the moment that: *Once you show any fear, he will attack you.|Once printed, this dictionary will be very popular!*

once-o·ver /ˈ· ˌ··/ *n* [*usu. sing.*] *infml* a quick look or examination

on·com·ing /ˈɒnˌkʌmɪŋ‖ˈɔn-, ˈɑn-/ *adj* [Wa5;A] **1** coming closer: *He was afraid of oncoming old age* **2** coming towards one: *oncoming cars*

one[1] /wʌn/ *determiner, n* **1** [see NUMBER TABLE I] (the number) 1: **a** *Only one person came.|* TWENTY-*one|one o'clock|page one|one pound 50| combine 2 substances into one substance|There were 3 kings and one was black* **b** a: *one/a* THOUSAND (=1,000)*|one/a third* (=$\frac{1}{3}$)*|one/a litre of wine* **c** (in the phr. **one of**): *one of your friends* (=a friend of yours)*|One of the boys has shot himself* —see USAGE **2** a certain, esp. **a** (before times): *one Sunday* (=on a certain Sunday)*|I saw her one day* (not **on one day*) *in June* **b** *fml* (before names): *One John Smith came to see you* **3** (esp. before past or future times) some: *Come again one day soon* (=some day soon) **4** [(*with*)] the same: *They all ran in one direction.|They are of one mind* (=of the same opinion).*|I am one with you/of one mind with you on this* **5** (the) only necessary and desirable:

She's the one person for this particular job —see also **one and** ONLY **6** (*as opposed to* another, the other, *etc.*) a particular example or type (of): *He can't tell one tree from another.|One (of them) went North, the other went South.|We can't take all these children! One or other is sure to be sick in the bus* **7** *AmE infml* indeed a(n); an unusually: *I tell you, she was one wonderful girl!* **8 a one** *infml* (expressing shocked admiration) a bold amusing person: *Oh, you are a one, telling that joke in front of the priest!* **9 a right one** *infml* a fool: *You're a right one, losing the tickets again!* **10 as one (man)** all together; as if they were one man **11 at one (with)** in agreement (with) **12 be all one (to)** to make no difference (to): *I don't mind which we do; it's all one (to me)* **13 be one up (on someone)** to have the advantage (over someone) —see also ONE-UPMANSHIP **14 for one** as one (person, reason, etc.) of perhaps several: *I for one think he's nice.|For one thing, he always smiles at me* **15 in one a** also **all in one**— combined; together: *She's President and Chief Minister in one* **b** *infml* in only one attempt: *Done it in one!* **16 in/by ones and twos** a few at a time **17 one after another** singly **18 one and all** every one **19 one and the same** the very same **20 one day/afternoon/evening/night** on a certain day/afternoon/evening/night —compare **the** OTHER **day** **21** [*no pl.*] **one of (a group)** a member of (a group): *Our dog is like one of the family*

USAGE We usually say *a pound and a half of sugar* rather than **one** *and a half pounds*, and *a* MILLION *and a quarter* rather than **one** *and a quarter* MILLION.

one[2] *pron* **1** (*used instead of a noun phr. that means a* (not *the*) *single thing or person*): *Have you any books on farming? I want to borrow one* (=a book on farming) (compare *I want to borrow some*=some books on farming; *Is that a book on farming? I want to borrow it*=the book on farming).|*This question is one* (=a question) *of great importance* **2** (*pl.* **ones**) (*used instead of a noun that means a single thing or person, but not immediately after* own *or possessives*): *Are those your books? I want to borrow a good one/some good ones on farming.|There were only hard chocolates left; we've eaten all the soft ones.|This is my house and that's Robert's* (not *Robert's one*).|*They don't like our country; they want to go back to their own* (not *their own one*)—see USAGE 1 **3** (*with* the; *pl.* the **ones**) **a** the person: *The officer is the one who gives the orders* **b** (of things, in phrs. like **the one in which . . ., the ones that . . .**) *not fml* that (in which . . .); those (that . . .): *They've eaten all the ones you gave them* (=all those that you gave them) **4** (+*sing. verb, and usu. the subject of the sentence*) any person, including the speaker: *One should do one's duty* (compare (*infml*) *You should do your duty*).|*"It does sort of make one slightly nervous"* (SEU S.) —see USAGE 2 **5 like one dead/possessed** like a man who is dead/is mad **6 one who/that/to, etc.** the sort of person who/that/to, etc.: *I'm not usually one to complain, but . . .* **7 the/one's little/young ones** *pomp or humor* the/one's children **8 the one about** *infml* the joke about: *Have you heard the one about the travelling salesman and the farmer's daughter?*

USAGE 1 In formal writing, avoid the use of **one[2]** (2) either **a** when 2 adjectives are used for comparison: *He buys German rather than British cars* (compare . . . *German cars rather than British* **ones**) **b** immediately after **these** or **those**: *Do you want these trousers or those?* It must be used to show the difference between sing. and pl.: *What nice shirts! Which* **one/ones** *shall we buy?* 2 In *BrE* **one[2]** (4) is usually followed by **one's** and **oneself**: **One** *should wash* **oneself**/*wash* **one's** *hair regularly.* In *AmE* it is also correct to say **One** *should wash himself/wash his hair regularly if he can*, and **One** *can't be too careful, can you?* —see also ONE ANOTHER

one- *comb. form* [*n→n, adj*] having only one: ONE-EYED

one an·oth·er /ˌ· ·ˈ··/ *pron* each other: *They hit one another.|They often stay in one another's houses*

one-armed /ˌ· ˈ·◂/ *adj* [Wa5] having only one arm

one-armed ban·dit /ˌ· · ˈ··/ also (*BrE*) **fruit machine,** (*AmE*) **slot machine**— *n sl* a machine with one long handle, into which people put money to try to win more money

one-eyed /ˌ· ˈ·◂/ *adj* [Wa5] having only one eye

one-horse /ˌ· ˈ·◂/ *adj* [Wa5;A] **1** pulled by only one horse **2** *infml* small and uninteresting: *It's only a one-horse town*

one-leg·ged /ˌ· ˈ··◂, ˌ· ˈ·◂/ *adj* [Wa5] having only one leg

one-man /ˌ· ˈ·◂/ *adj* [Wa5;A] with or worked by only one man: *a one-man boat*

one-man band /ˌ· · ˈ·/ *n* **1** a street musician who carries many different types of instrument on his body and plays them all himself at one time, with his hands, mouth, knees, feet, etc. **2** an activity which someone does all on his own, without accepting help from other people

one-night stand /ˌ· · ˈ·/ *n* a performance (as of music or a play) given only once in each of a number of places by a performer or group of performers

one-piece /ˌ· ˈ·◂/ *adj* [Wa5;A] (esp. of a BATHING SUIT) made in one piece only; having no separate parts

o·ner·ous /ˈɒnərəs, ˈəʊ-‖ˈɑ-, ˈəʊ-/ (of nonmaterial things) heavy; troublesome: *an onerous duty* —**~ly** *adv* —**~ness** *n* [U]

one·self /wʌnˈself/ *pron* **1** (REFLEXIVE pronoun of ONE[2] (4)): *One can't enjoy oneself if one/(AmE) if he is too tired* **2** (EMPHATIC pronoun, strong form of ONE[2] (4)): *To do something oneself is often easier than getting someone else to do it* **3 to oneself** for one's own private use; not to be shared —see ONE, YOURSELF (USAGE)

one-sid·ed /ˌ· ˈ··◂/ *adj* **1** seeing only one side (of a question); unfair **2** with one side much stronger than the other —**~ly** *adv* —**~ness** *n* [U]

one·time /ˈwʌntaɪm/ *adj* [Wa5;A] former

one-track mind /ˌ· · ˈ·/ *n* a mind that is limited and thinks of only one thing at a time

one-up·man·ship /wʌnˈʌpmənʃɪp/ *n* [U] *humor* the art of getting an advantage over others by means which are almost but not quite unlawful

one-way /ˌ· ˈ·◂/ *adj* [Wa5;A;(B)] **1** moving or allowing movement in only one direction: *one-way traffic|a one-way street|a one-way trip* **2** *AmE* SINGLE[1] (6) **3 a one-way ticket to** *humor* a sure cause of (something allowing no escape)

on·go·ing /ˈɒnˌgəʊɪŋ‖ˈɑn-/ *adj* continuing; that GO(es) ON

on·ion /ˈʌnjən/ *n* **1** [C] a type of round white vegetable made up of one skin within another, strong smelling, much used in cooking —see picture at VEGETABLE **2** [U] this vegetable as food **3 know one's onions** *infml* to have knowledge based on experience

on·look·er /ˈɒnˌlʊkəʳ‖ˈɔn-, ˈɑn-/ *n* a person who sees something happening without taking part in it

on·ly[1] /ˈəʊnli/ *adj* [Wa5;A] **1** having no others **a** in the same group: *the only people in the room|the only person who wants the job* **b** of the same quality; the best: *Long skirts were the only thing to wear in those days.|She is the only person for the job* **2 one and only** (a stronger form of *only*): **a** *my one and* *only friend* **b** (esp. in presenting actors, singers, etc.): *And now, the one and only Jack Johnson!* **3 an only child/daughter/son** one having no brothers or sisters/sisters/brothers

only² *adv* **1** and nothing more; and no one else: *only 5 minutes more|Ladies only!|something known only to me|He only spoke to her* (several meanings are possible according to the INTONATION).|*He saw only 5 men.|Only 5 men/5 of the men did he see.|made from fresh fruit only|not only he but the whole family|I saw him only yesterday* (=and no longer ago).|*Only a doctor can do that* **2 if only** (expressing a strong wish or desire): *If only she would come!|If she would only come!* **3 only just a** a moment before: *They've/They had only just (now) arrived* **b** almost not: *I've only just enough money* **4 only too** very: *only too happy to come*

USAGE 1 Notice the word order of a sentence beginning with **only**, which is that of a question: **Only** *5 men did he see.*|**Only** *in Paris can you buy shoes like that.* 2 **Only** can be directly followed by the numbers, including **half**, and by some DETERMINERs: **only** *a/the/my*, etc./*this*, etc. *child*|**only** *these*, etc./*some/enough/17 people*|**only** *half a/one minute*. It cannot be followed by **each**, **either**, or **neither**, or by the PREDETERMINERs **all** and **both**. 3 In writing, put **only** directly before the part of the sentence that it concerns: **Only** *John saw the lion* (=no one else saw it).|*John* **only** *saw the lion* (=he didn't shoot it).|*John saw* **only** *the lion* (=not the tiger). In speech, the commonest place to put **only** is before the verb, and the way the sentence is said (the INTONATION) makes it clear what is meant.

only³ *conj infml* but, esp. **a** (before limiting conditions): *You may go, only come back early* **b** (before unfortunate events): *He wants to go, only he can't* **c** also (*BrE*) **only that** /'·· ·/— (before a reason): *He'd succeed, only he's rather lazy*

on·o·mat·o·poe·ia /ˌɒnəmætə'piːə‖ˌɑ-/ *n* [U] the formation of words that are like natural sounds (as when the word CUCKOO is used to name the bird that makes that sound) —**-poeic** *adj*

on·rush /'ɒnrʌʃ‖'ɔn-, 'ɑn-/ *n* [*usu. sing*] a strong movement forward —**~ing** *adj* [Wa5;A]

on·set /'ɒnset‖'ɔn-, 'ɑn-/ *n* [*the*+R (*of*)] the first attack or beginning (of something bad)

on·shore /ˌɒn'ʃɔː'◂‖ˌɔn'ʃor, ˌɑn-/ *adv, adj* **1** [Wa5] coming or moving towards the shore: *The wind was blowing onshore* **2** on(to) or near the shore: *onshore fishing*

on·side /ˌɒn'saɪd◂‖ˌɔn-, ˌɑn-/ *adj, adv* [Wa5;B;E] not OFFSIDE (1)

on·slaught /'ɒnslɔːt‖'ɔn-, 'ɑn-/ *n* [(*on*)] a fierce attack (on)

on·to /'ɒntʊ, -tə‖'ɔn-, 'ɑn-/ *prep* **1** to a position or point on: *He jumped onto/on the horse* **2 be onto a good thing** *infml* to be in a good position **3 be onto someone** *infml* to have found out about someone's wrong or unlawful activities

on·tol·o·gy /ɒn'tɒlədʒi‖ɑn'tɑ-/ *n* [U] the branch of PHILOSOPHY concerned with the nature of existence and the relations between things —**-gical** /ˌɒntə'lɒdʒɪkəl‖ˌɑntə'lɑ-/ *adj* —**-gically** *adv* [Wa4]

o·nus /'əʊnəs/ *n* [*the*+R (*of*)] **1** duty; responsibility: *The onus of proof lies with you* **2** blame: *He tried to put the onus onto me*

on·ward /'ɒnwəd‖'ɔnwərd, 'ɑn-/ *adj* [Wa5;A] directed or moving forward: *the onward march of events*

on·wards /'ɒnwədz‖'ɔnwərdz, 'ɑn-/ also (esp. *AmE & fml*) **onward**— *adv* forward in time or space: *"from breakfast onwards"* (SEU W.)

on·yx /'ɒnɪks‖'ɑ-/ *n* [U;C *usu. sing.*] a (type of) precious stone having bands of various colours in it

oo·dles /'uːdlz/ *n* [P;(U): (*of*)] *sl* lots: *oodles of cream*

oof /uːf/ *interj, n often humor* **1** (a word that is supposed to be like the sound that people make when hit in the stomach) **2** [U] *old BrE sl* money

oomph /ʊmf/ *n* [U] *sl* the power of forceful activity; ENERGY

oops /ʊps/ *interj infml* (a word said when someone has made an ungraceful mistake): *Oops! I nearly dropped my cup of tea!*

oops-a-dai·sy /'·· ˌ··/ *interj infml* **1** (an expression used when helping someone to climb over or onto something) **2** *humor* (an expression used when someone falls down)

ooze¹ /uːz/ *n* [U] mud or thick liquid, as at the bottom of a river —**oozy** *adj* [Wa1]

ooze² *v* [L9;T1] **a** (of liquid) to pass or flow slowly: (fig.) *Their courage oozed away* **b** to allow (liquid) to pass slowly through: *The meat just oozed fat.*|(fig.) *"a body oozing life"* (=bleeding to death; from a song)

op¹ /ɒp‖ɑp/ *n BrE infml* OPERATION (6) —see also OPS

op² [A] *written abbrev for:* (*usu. cap.*) OPUS (1): *Beethoven's Op 106*

o·pac·i·ty /əʊ'pæsǝ̇ti/ *n* [U] **1** the quality of not allowing light to pass through **2** the quality of being hard to understand

o·pal /'əʊpəl/ *n* [C;U] a (type of) precious stone which looks like milky water with colours in it

o·pa·les·cent /ˌəʊpəl'esənt/ *adj* like an OPAL; marked by softly-shining swiftly-changing colours —**-cence** *n* [U]

o·paque /əʊ'peɪk/ *adj* **1** not allowing light to pass through **2** hard to understand —**~ly** *adv* —**~ness** *n* [U]

op art /'· ·/ *n* [U] a form of modern art (OPTICAL art) that does not show real objects but uses patterns that play tricks on your eyes

ope /əʊp/ *v* [T1;I∅] *poet* OPEN²

o·pen¹ /'əʊpən/ *adj* **1** [B] not shut: *to push the door open|with open eyes* **2** [A;(B)] not enclosed: *the open country|open fields* **3** [A;(B)] not blocked: *An open river is one without ice* **4** [Wa5;A] not covered: *an open boat|the open air* **5** [B] not fastened: *an open shirt* **6** [B] not finally decided or answered: *an open question* **7** [B] not closed to new ideas or experiences: *an open mind* **8** [Wa5;F] not filled: *The job is still open* **9** [B] not hidden: *open hatred* **10** [F;(B)] not hiding anything; honest: *Let's be open with each other* **11** [Wa5;F;(B)] ready for business: *The bank isn't open yet* **12** [Wa5;B] ready for use: *She kept her bank account open* **13** [B] that anyone can enter: *an open competition* **14** [B] spread out; unfolded: *The flowers are open* **15** [B] (in PHONETICS, of a vowel) made with the tongue low in the mouth —opposite **close** **16** [Wa5;B] (of a cheque) payable in actual money to the person whose name is written on it; not CROSSed **17 keep open house** to encourage visitors to come at any time **18 open to a** not safe from: *This book is open to misunderstanding* **b** willing to receive **c** not closed to

open² *v* **1** [T1;I∅] to (cause to) become open **2** [T1;I∅ (UP): (OUT)] to (cause to) spread out or unfold: *to open a book*|(fig.) *The country opens out to the west.*|(fig.) *A new life was opening (up/out) before her* **3** [T1;I∅] to (cause to) start: *The story opens with a snowstorm* **4** [T1;I∅] (of the usual activities in a place) to (cause to) start: *to open Parliament/a new hospital|The shop opens at 10* **5** [T1] to make or make usable (a passage) by removing the things that are blocking it **6 open fire (at/on)** to start shooting (at) —see also OPEN OUT, OPEN UP

USAGE One **opens** or **shuts** (*fml* **closes**) doors, windows, or boxes. One **turns** water or gas TAPs *on* or *off*. One **turns** or **switches** electrical things *on* or *off*.

open[3] *n* [*the*+U] **1** the outdoors: *life in the open* **2 in(to) the open** (of opinions, secrets, etc.) in(to) general knowledge

open-air /ˌ·· ˈ·/ *adj* [Wa5;A] of or in the outdoors: *an open-air theatre*

open-and-shut /ˌ·· · ˈ·/ *adj* easy to settle: *There's no mystery about this—it's an open-and-shut case of murder*

o·pen·cast /ˈəʊpənkɑːst‖-kæst/ *adj* [Wa5] of a coalmine where coal is dug from an open hole in the ground and not from a passage dug deep underground

open-door pol·i·cy /ˌ·· ˈ· ˌ···/ *n* [*the*+R] the idea of allowing traders from all countries to trade freely in a certain country

open-end·ed /ˌ·· ˈ··/ *adj* without any definite end, aim, or time limit set in advance

o·pen·er /ˈəʊpənəʳ/ *n* **1** (*usu. in comb.*) a person or thing that opens something: *a bottle opener* **2** also **opening bats·man** /ˌ··· ˈ··/— either of the 2 cricket players who take the first turn to strike the ball in their team's INNINGS

open-eyed /ˌ·· ˈ·/ *adj, adv* **1** with one's eyes wide open **a** to see clearly **b** as an expression of surprise **2** with full knowledge: *You made that agreement open-eyed, and now you must do what you promised*

open-hand·ed /ˌ·· ˈ··/ *adj* **1** [Wa5] with one's hand open **2** generous —opposite **closefisted**

open-hand·ed·ly /ˌ·· ˈ···/ *adv* generously —**-edness** *n* [U]

open-heart /ˌ·· ˈ·/ *adj* [Wa5;A] *med* of, for, or done to a heart that has been caused to stop pumping blood for a time, and cut open to be medically examined and treated (esp. in the phr. **open-heart surgery**)

o·pen·heart·ed /ˌəʊpənˈhɑːtɪ̈d‖-ɑr-/ *adj* generous and freely given —**~ly** *adv* —**~ness** *n* [U]

open-hearth /ˌ·· ˈ·/ *adj* [Wa5;A] of a way of making steel in an open fireplace or in one in which the heat is not direct but comes from a surface which has been heated

o·pen·ing[1] /ˈəʊpənɪŋ/ *n* **1** the act or an act of becoming or causing to become open **2** [(*in*)] a hole or clear space **3** [(*for*)] a favourable set of conditions (for): *good openings for business* **4** [(*at, in*)] an unfilled position in a business organization: *no openings at the bank*

opening[2] *adj* [Wa5;A] first: *her opening words*

opening night /ˈ·· ·/ *n* [C;U] the first public performance of a play (at night)

opening time /ˈ·· ·/ *n* [C;U] the time a business, library, etc., opens, esp. the time a PUB opens for business

open let·ter /ˌ·· ˈ··/ *n* a letter addressed to a particular person but meant for the general public to see

o·pen·ly /ˈəʊpənli/ *adv* **1** not secretly **2** in a way that suggests a willingness to try new ideas and experiences —**-ness** *n* [U]

open-mind·ed /ˌ·· ˈ··/ *adj* having an open mind; willing to consider new arguments, ideas, opinions, etc. —**~ly** *adv* —**~ness** *n* [U]

open-mouthed /ˌ·· ˈ·/ *adj, adv* with one's mouth wide open, esp. in great surprise

open out *v adv* [IØ] to speak more freely

open ques·tion /ˌ·· ˈ··/ *n* a question or matter that has not been settled

open sand·wich /ˌ·· ˈ··/ *n* a single piece of bread with any of various foods placed on top of it (such as are used for filling a SANDWICH)

open sea·son /ˈ·· ˌ··/ *n* the period of each year when certain animals or fish may be lawfully killed for sport —opposite **close season**

open se·cret /ˌ·· ˈ··/ *n* something supposed to be a secret but in fact known to everyone

open ses·a·me /ˌ·· ˈ···/ *n, interj often humor* (*sometimes caps.*) (a word or words with a supposed magical force used for gaining easy entrance to something that is usually difficult or impossible to enter, meaning) "open!"

open shop /ˌ·· ˈ·/ *n* a place of work where it is not necessary to belong to a trade union —opposite **closed shop**

Open U·ni·ver·si·ty /ˌ·· ··ˈ···/ *n* [*the*+R] a British university that is open to students who need not satisfy the usual conditions for being admitted to a university, and which uses a great deal of radio and television in teaching

open up *v adv* **1** [T1 (*to*)] to make possible the development of (something); start: *They opened the country up (to trade)* **2** [IØ *often imper.*] *infml* to open a door **3** [IØ] OPEN OUT

open ver·dict /ˌ·· ˈ··/ *n* (in a CORONER's court) a JURY's decision in which the fact and cause of a death are stated, but not whether it was natural, accidental, murder, etc.

open vow·el /ˌ·· ˈ··/ *n* a vowel sound made with the jaws rather wide apart and the tongue rather far down in the mouth, such as /æ, ɑː, ɒ/

o·pen·work /ˈəʊpənˌwɜːk‖-ɜrk/ *n* [U] a pattern with spaces in between thread or other material: *openwork stockings*

op·e·ra /ˈɒpərə‖ˈɑ-/ *n* **1** [C] a musical play in which many or all of the words are sung **2** [U] such musical plays as a form of art, a business, etc. —**~tic** /ˌɒpəˈrætɪk‖ˌɑ-/ *adj* —**~tically** *adv* [Wa4]

op·e·ra·ble /ˈɒpərəbəl‖ˈɑ-/ *adj med* that is able to be treated by means of an operation —**-bly** *adv*

opera glass·es /ˈ··· ˌ··/ *n* [P] glasses (small BINOCULARS) used in a theatre to see the actors or singers as if nearer

opera hat /ˈ··· ·/ *n* a TOP HAT that can be folded flat

opera house /ˈ··· ·/ *n* a theatre built especially for OPERAs

op·e·rate /ˈɒpəreɪt‖ˈɑ-/ *v* **1** [T1;IØ] to (cause to) work: *to operate a machine/a factory* **2** [L9;I3] to produce effects: *The new law doesn't operate in our favour* **3** [L9] to be in action: *That business operates in several countries* **4** [IØ (*on, for*)] *med* to cut the body in order to set right or remove a diseased part

operating the·at·re /ˈ···· ˌ···/ also (*infml*) **theatre**— *n* a special room in a hospital, where operations are done

op·e·ra·tion /ˌɒpəˈreɪʃən‖ˌɑ-/ *n* **1** [U] (a state of) working; the way a thing works: *The operation of a big new machine can be hard to learn* **2** [U] a state in which effects can be produced: *When does the law come into operation?* **3** [C *usu. pl.*] an (esp. military) action; movement: *the army's operations in Northern Ireland* —see also OPS **4** [R9] (*usu. cap.*) a large-scale planned military movement having the stated CODE name: *Operation Sunshine* **5** [C *often pl.*] a thing (to be) done; an activity: *begin operations|a difficult operation* **6** [C (*on, for*)] also (*BrE infml*) **op**— *med* the cutting of the body in order to set right or remove a diseased part: *He will perform an operation on her for a diseased lung* **7** [C] *tech* the use of a rule to get one MATHEMATICAL expression or figure from others

op·e·ra·tion·al /ˌɒpəˈreɪʃənəl‖ˌɑ-/ *adj* [Wa5] **1** [A] of or about operations: *operational costs* **2** [F;(B)] (of things) in operation; ready for use: *The new machines are not yet operational* —compare OPERATIVE[1] (1) —**~ly** *adv*

operational re·search /··ˌ··· ·ˈ·/ also **operations research** /··ˌ·· ·ˈ·/— *n* [U] *tech* the study of how best to build and use machines or plan organizations

op·e·ra·tive[1] /ˈɒpərətɪv‖ˈɑpərə-, ˈɑpəreɪ-/ *adj* [Wa5] **1** [F;(B)] (of plans, laws, etc.) in operation; producing effects **2** [A] most important (esp. in the phr. **operative word(s)**)

operative[2] *n often euph* a factory worker

op·e·ra·tor /ˈɒpəreɪtəʳ‖ˈɑ-/ *n* **1** [C] a person who works a machine, apparatus, etc. **2** [C;N] a person who works a telephone SWITCHBOARD **3** [C9] *infml & often derog* a person whose operations (in business, love, etc.) are successful but perhaps unfair: *a clever/smooth operator*

op·e·ret·ta /ˌɒpəˈretə‖ˌɑ-/ *n* a musical play in which many of the words are spoken, usu. one with a happy ending

oph·thal·mi·a /ɒfˈθælmɪə‖ɑf-/ *n* [U] *med* a disease of the eyes, with redness and swelling

oph·thal·mic /ɒfˈθælmɪk‖ɑf-/ *adj* [Wa5] *med* of the medical study and treatment of the eyes

oph·thal·mol·o·gy /ˌɒfθælˈmɒlədʒi‖ˌɑfθælˈmɑ-/ *n* [U] *med* the study of the eyes and their diseases —**-ogist** *n*

oph·thal·mo·scope /ɒfˈθælməskəʊp‖ɑf-/ *n med* a tool for examining the eyes, having a long handle and a mirror with a hole in the centre

o·pi·ate /ˈəʊpiɪ̈t, -eɪt/ *n* a sleep-producing drug

o·pine /əʊˈpaɪn/ *v* [T5(*to*)] *pomp* to express an opinion

o·pin·ion /əˈpɪnjən/ *n* **1** [C] that which a person thinks about something: *His opinions are usually based on facts.|In my opinion you're wrong* **2** [U] that which people in general think about something: *(Public) opinion has changed in favour of that group* **3** [C] professional judgment or advice: *You should get a second opinion* (= from another doctor) *before you decide to have an operation* **4 be of the opinion that . . .** to think or believe that **5 have a good/bad/high/low opinion of** to think well/badly of

o·pin·ion·at·ed /əˈpɪnjəneɪtɪ̈d/ also (*fml*) **o·pin·ion·a·tive** /-njənətɪv, -neɪ-/— *adj derog* very sure of the rightness of one's opinions

opinion poll /·ˈ·· ·/ *n* POLL[1] (4)

o·pi·um /ˈəʊpɪəm/ *n* [U] a sleep-producing drug made from the seeds of a flower (the white POPPY)

o·pos·sum /əˈpɒsəm‖-ˈpɑ-, ˈpɑsəm/ also (*infml AmE*) **possum**— *n* [Wn1] a type of small American tree-climbing animal that carries its babies in a special pocket and pretends to be dead when it is caught

op·po·nent /əˈpəʊnənt/ *n* a person who takes the opposite side, esp. in playing or fighting

op·por·tune /ˈɒpətjuːn‖ˌɑpərˈtuːn/ *adj* **1** (of times) right for a purpose: *an opportune moment* **2** coming at the right time: *an opportune remark* —**~ly** *adv*

op·por·tun·is·m /ˈɒpətjuːnɪzəm‖ˌɑpərˈtuː-/ *n* [U] *derog* the taking advantage of every chance for success now, without regard for what will happen later —**-ist** *n*

op·por·tu·ni·ty /ˌɒpəˈtjuːnɪ̈ti‖ˌɑpərˈtuː-/ *n* [C (*for, of*), C3;U] a favourable (OPPORTUNE) moment or occasion (for doing something): *a wonderful opportunity|Opportunity knocks (at the door) only once* —see CHANCE (USAGE)

op·pose /əˈpəʊz/ *v* [T1] **1** to be or act against **2** [(*to*)] to set in action (against) **3 be opposed to** to oppose: *I am opposed to that plan* —see also AS OPPOSED TO

op·po·site[1] /ˈɒpəzɪ̈t‖ˈɑ-/ *n* [C;*the*+U: (*of*)] a person or thing that is as different as possible (from another): *Black and white are opposites.|You are nice; he is just the opposite*

opposite[2] *adj* [Wa5] **1** [B (*to*)] as different as possible from: *the opposite direction|*(fig.) *the opposite sex|His political position is opposite to ours* **2** [F; E: (*to*)] facing: *the houses opposite|He sits opposite*

opposite[3] also **opposite to** /ˈ··· ·/— *prep* facing: *the houses opposite (to) ours*

opposite num·ber /ˌ··· ˈ··/ *n* a person in the same job elsewhere; COUNTERPART

op·po·si·tion /ˌɒpəˈzɪʃən‖ˌɑ-/ *n* **1** [U (*to*)] act or state of being opposed to or fighting against **2** [(*the*) GC *usu. sing.*] (*often cap.*) the political parties opposed to the government of the day, esp. the most important such party

op·press /əˈpres/ *v* [T1] **1** to rule in a hard and cruel way **2** [*usu. pass.* (*with* or *by*)] to cause to feel ill or sad: *I feel oppressed by/with worry/the heat*

op·pres·sion /əˈpreʃən/ *n* [U] the condition of oppressing or being OPPRESSED (esp. 1)

op·pres·sive /əˈpresɪv/ *adj* **1** cruel; unjust **2** causing feelings of illness or sadness —**~ly** *adv* —**~ness** *n* [U]

op·pres·sor /əˈpresəʳ/ *n* a person (or group) that OPPRESSES (1)

op·pro·bri·ous /əˈprəʊbrɪəs/ *adj fml* (esp. of words) rude; showing disrespect —**~ly** *adv*

op·pro·bri·um /əˈprəʊbrɪəm/ *n* [U] *fml* public shame or hatred

ops /ɒps‖ɑps/ *n* [P] *infml, esp. BrE* military OPERATIONS

op·ta·tive /ˈɒptətɪv‖ˈɑp-/ *adj, n* [Wa5] *tech* (of) the special way in which the form of a verb changes to express wishes or desires

opt for /ɒpt‖ɑpt/ *v prep* [T1] to choose (a particular thing) rather than any others —see also OPT OUT

op·tic /ˈɒptɪk‖ˈɑp-/ *adj* [Wa5;A] of or belonging to the eyes or the sense of sight

op·ti·cal /ˈɒptɪkəl‖ˈɑp-/ *adj* [Wa5;A] of or about the sense of sight —**-cally** *adv* [Wa4]

optical il·lu·sion /ˌ··· ·ˈ··/ *n* something that deceives the eye, such as a particular pattern of lines

op·ti·cian /ɒpˈtɪʃən‖ɑp-/ *n* a person who makes and sells glasses (for the eyes)

op·tics /ˈɒptɪks‖ˈɑp-/ *n* [U] the scientific study of light

See next page for picture

op·ti·mis·m /ˈɒptɪ̈mɪzəm‖ˈɑp-/ *n* [U] the belief that good will win over evil, that things will end well; hopeful happy feeling about life —**-mist** /ˈɒptɪ̈mɪ̈st‖ˈɑp-/ *n* —**-mistic** /ˌɒptɪ̈ˈmɪstɪk‖ˌɑp-/ *adj* —**-mistically** *adv* [Wa4]

op·ti·mum /ˈɒptɪ̈məm‖ˈɑp-/ *adj* [Wa5;A] best or most favourable

op·tion /ˈɒpʃən‖ˈɑp-/ *n* **1** [(*the*) U] the freedom to choose: *You must do it; you have no option* **2** [C] something chosen or offered for choice **3** [C (*on*)] the right to buy or sell something at a stated time in the future: *Jones has taken an option on that house* **4 keep/leave one's options open** to stay free to choose; not choose too soon

op·tion·al /ˈɒpʃənəl‖ˈɑp-/ *adj* [Wa5] which may be freely chosen—or not chosen: *optional subjects at school|You don't have to have this radio in your new car; it's an optional* EXTRA —opposites **compulsory, obligatory** —**~ly** *adv*

opt out *v adv* [IØ (*of*)] *infml* to choose not to take part (in something) —see also OPT FOR

op·u·lence /ˈɒpjʊləns‖ˈɑpjə-/ *n* [U] (a state of) very great, splendid, and showy wealth

op·u·lent /ˈɒpjʊlənt‖ˈɑpjə-/ *adj* **1** showing OPULENCE; very wealthy **2** *fml* in good supply; PLENTIFUL: *an opulent beard* **3** (too) richly ornamented with words, colours, jewels, etc. —**~ly** *adv*

o·pus /ˈəʊpəs/ *n* **opuses** or **opera** /ˈɒpərə/ [*usu. sing.*] **1** (*often cap.*) a work of music considered as coming earlier or later than other works by the same person: *Beethoven's Opus 106* **2** *often pomp or derog* any work of art —see also MAGNUM OPUS

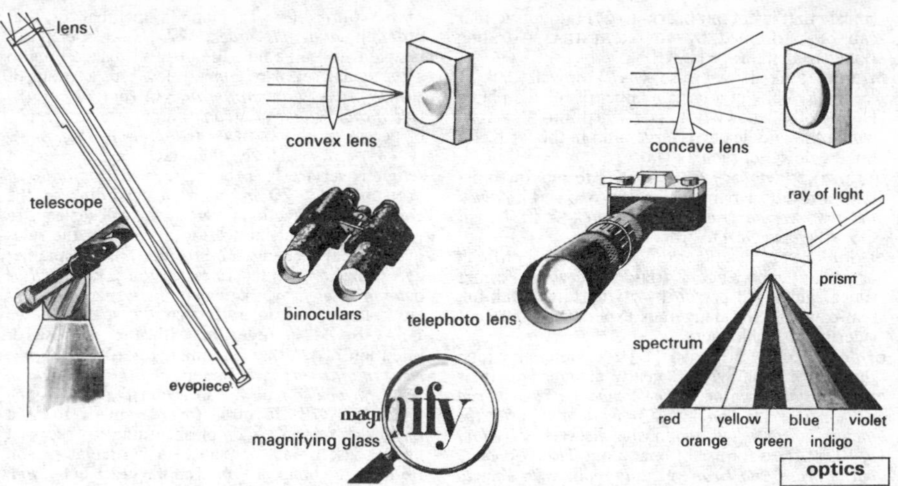

or /ər; *strong* ɔːr/ *conj* **1** (*after a neg.*) and not: *He never smokes or drinks* **2** (often with *either*; used before the last of a set of possibilities): *Which one is it, X or Y?|I don't care whether I get it or not.|Did you or didn't you?|Either say you're sorry or get out!* —see EITHER³ (USAGE) **3** (used before the second and later of several suggestions): *"a place such as Venice or Florence or somewhere like that"* (SEU S.) **4** if not; otherwise: *Wear your coat or (else) you'll be cold.|He can't be ill or he wouldn't have come* **5** (*used when giving a second name for something*) that is; that means; it would be better to say: *This medicine, or (rather) drug, has a violent effect* **6 or else** *infml* (used as a threat) or something terrible will happen: *You clean it properly, or else!* **7 or so** about; at least; or more: *a minute/3 minutes or so* **8 or two** (*after sing. nouns*) about; at least; or more: *a minute or two|a dollar or two*

-or¹ /ər/ *suffix* [v→n] (makes personal nouns from verbs): *An actor is a person who acts; an inventor is a person who invents*

-or² /ər/ *suffix* [→n] **1** [→n [U]] state; quality; condition; activity: ERROR|TERROR **2** [→n [C]] a type or example of any of these: *an* ERROR

-or³ /ər/ *suffix AmE* -OUR: COLOR|HONOR|LABOR

or·a·cle /ˈɒrəkəl‖ˈɔ-, ˈɑ-/ *n* **1** (in ancient Greece) a place where a god was believed to answer human questions, often in words hard to understand correctly or that could be understood in more than one way **2** (in ancient Greece) the person through whom a god answered human questions **3** *sometimes derog* a person who is thought to be, or believes himself to be, very wise and able to give the best advice **4 work the oracle** *infml* to succeed, or make success possible, in doing something difficult

o·rac·u·lar /ɒˈrækjʊlər, ə-‖ɔˈrækjələr, ə-/ *adj* **1** of or like an ORACLE **2** having a meaning that is hard to understand correctly or that may be understood in more than one way

o·ral /ˈɔːrəl‖ˈo-/ *adj* [Wa5] **1** spoken, not written: *an oral examination* **2** *esp. med* of, about, or using the mouth —**~ly** *adv*

or·ange¹ /ˈɒrɪ̈ndʒ‖ˈɔ-, ˈɑ-/ *n* a type of very common round bitter-sweet fruit from hot areas with a reddish-yellow outside and divided into parts inside —see picture at FRUIT¹

orange² *adj, n* [Wa5;B;U] (of) the colour of an orange

or·ange·ade /ˌɒrɪ̈nˈdʒeɪd‖ˌɔ-, ˌɑ-/ *n* [U] a drink containing orange juice or something like it

Or·ange·man /ˈɒrɪ̈ndʒmən‖ˈɔ-, ˈɑ-/ *n* **-men** /mən/ a member of a PROTESTANT political organization in Northern Ireland (Ulster)

o·rang·u·tang /ɔːˌræŋuːˈtæŋ, -ˈtæn‖əˈræŋətæŋ/ also **-tan** /tæn/— *n* a type of large manlike monkey with reddish hair and no tail, from Indonesia

o·ra·tion /əˈreɪʃən, ɔː-/ *n* a formal and solemn public speech

or·a·tor /ˈɒrətər‖ˈɔ-, ˈɑ-/ *n* **1** a person who delivers (makes) an ORATION **2** a good public speaker

or·a·tor·i·cal /ˌɒrəˈtɒrɪkəl‖ˌɔrəˈtɔ-, ˌɑrəˈtɑ-/ *adj* **1** of or like an ORATOR **2** *sometimes derog* of or like the speaking style of ORATORs; highly ornamental with long or formal words —**~ly** *adv* [Wa5]

or·a·to·ri·o /ˌɒrəˈtɔːriəʊ‖ˌɔrəˈto-, ˌɑ-/ *n* **-ios** a long musical work with singing but without acting, usu. telling a story from the Bible or about a religious subject

or·a·to·ry¹ /ˈɒrətri‖ˈɔrətori, ˈɑ-/ *n* a type of church or building used for religious purposes, usu. ROMAN CATHOLIC

oratory² *n* [U] **1** the art of making good speeches **2** *sometimes derog* language highly ornamented with long or formal words

orb /ɔːb‖ɔrb/ *n* **1** a ball standing for the sun or another heavenly body, esp. one carried by a king or queen on formal occasions **2** [*usu. pl.*] *poet* an eye, esp. the eye of a beautiful lady

or·bit¹ /ˈɔːbɪ̈t‖ˈɔr-/ *n* **1 a** the path of one heavenly body round another **b** the path of a man-made object round the earth or another heavenly body **c** the path of an ELECTRON around the central part of an atom —see picture at ATOM **2** the area within which one person or thing can have an effect upon others —**~al** /ˈɔːbɪtəl‖ˈɔr-/ *adj* [Wa5]

orbit² *v* [Wv4;T1;I∅] to move in an ORBIT¹ (1) round (something)

or·chard /ˈɔːtʃəd‖ˈɔrtʃərd/ *n* a field or part of a garden where fruit trees grow

or·ches·tra /ˈɔːkɪ̈strə‖ˈɔr-/ *n* [GC] a large group of people who play music together, esp. on stringed instruments (and usu. also other sorts of instrument)

or·ches·tral /ɔːˈkestrəl‖ɔr-/ *adj* **1** [Wa5;A;(B)] of or by an ORCHESTRA: *an orchestral player* **2** [B] for an ORCHESTRA: *orchestral music*

orchestra pit /ˈ··· ·/ *n* PIT¹ (12)

or·ches·trate /ˈɔːkɪ̈streɪt‖ˈɔr-/ *v* [T1] to change

(music that is not ORCHESTRAL (2)) into music that can be performed by an ORCHESTRA —**-tration** /ˌɔːtəˈstreɪʃən‖ˌɔr-/ *n* [U;C]

or·chid /ˈɔːkɨ̣d‖ˈɔr-/ also (*tech*) **or·chis** /ˈɔːkɨ̣s‖ˈɔr-/— *n* **1** any of a large number of related plants having often showy flowers divided into 3 parts of which the middle one is larger and in the form of a lip **2** a flower of such a plant

or·dain /ɔːˈdeɪn‖ɔr-/ *v* **1** [T1;X1] to make (someone) a priest or religious leader: *She was ordained the first woman priest of her church* **2** [T5b] (of God, the law, etc.) to order

or·deal /ɔːˈdɪːl, ˈɔːdiːl‖ɔrˈdiːl, ˈɔrdiːl/ *n* **1** a difficult or painful experience **2 trial by ordeal** (in former times) judging a person by giving him a painful, fear-causing, and dangerous experience, and considering his behaviour

or·der[1] /ˈɔːdəʳ‖ˈɔr-/ *n* **1** [U] the state in which things are carefully and neatly arranged in their proper place; neatness: *The company has employed a man to try to bring some order into the way the factory is controlled* —opposite **disorder** **2** [*in/out of*+U] fitness for use of operation: *The telephone's out of order, and I can't get any reply when I try to speak to anyone* **3** [U] the special way in which a group of people, objects, etc., are arranged in connection with each other: *alphabetical order|in order of importance* **4** [U] the condition in which laws and rules are obeyed by most of the people and the government or the person(s) in charge can keep control: *That young teacher can't keep order in her classroom* —opposite **disorder**; see also LAW (3) **5** [C,C3,5 *often pl. with sing. meaning*] a command or direction or something to be done, given by a person who has the right or power to command: *A soldier who doesn't obey orders will be in serious trouble.|Father's orders are that you must be home by 10 o'clock* (=father has ordered this).|*My orders are to let no one into the building* (=I have been ordered to do this).|*an order to seize their property|Take your medicine: it's* **doctor's orders** **6** [C (*for*)] a request (as to a tradesman) to supply goods: *an order for 3 bottles of milk to be sent to us each day* **7** [C] the goods supplied in accordance with such a request: *a letter from the shop saying we could come and collect our order at once* **8** [C] a written or printed paper which allows the holder to do something such as to be paid money, to see a house that is for sale, etc. —see also MONEY ORDER, ORDER TO VIEW, POSTAL ORDER **9** [U9] the arrangement of men, ships, aircraft, etc., of an army, navy, or airforce: *The aircraft flew in close/open order* (=with little/much space between them) **10** [U9] the kind of clothing worn and material carried on the stated duties by soldiers: *in marching order|in fighting order* **11** [C *usu. sing.*] *fml* the way things in general usually happen or are happening at a particular time in history **12** [C] *fml* kind; sort: *something of a completely different order* **13** [C] (in BIOLOGY) a division, used in putting animals, plants, etc., in groups according to relationship, which has a rank below the CLASS and above the FAMILY **14** [C] *tech* a division of any group of things, used for expressing relationships within the group: *Greek pillars of the* DORIC *and* IONIC *orders* **15** [C *often pl. with sing. meaning*] a special group, social class, or rank in a society: *the military order|*(*now rare or humor*) *the lower orders* (=workers, servants, etc.) **16** [(*the*) C (*of*)] (*often cap. as part of a name*) **a** a group of people who have all received any of several special honours given by a king, queen, etc., for service, bravery, etc.: *the Royal Victorian Order* **b** an ornamental piece of metal, silk, etc., worn as a sign that one is a member of such a group: *He was given the Order of the Garter* (=was made a member of that order).|*wearing his orders* **17** [C] a society of people who lead a holy life of service according to a particular set of religious rules, esp. a group of MONKs, FRIARs, or NUNs **18** [C (*of*) *usu. sing.*] (*often cap. as part of a name*) any of several ranks of people in holy ORDERS: *the Order of Priests* **19** [C (*of*) *usu. sing.*] *tech* the exact way in which a religious service is to be performed: *the order of* CONFIRMATION **20 by order of** according to the command or direction given by **21 call someone to order** to ask someone to stop disobeying the rules of a formal meeting **22 in order** *fml* acceptable; according to accepted rules, customs, etc.: *It'll be quite in order for you to make this suggestion at our next meeting* **23 in order that** *fml* so that —see USAGE **24 in order to** with the purpose or intention of; so that one may; to: *He stood on a chair in order to reach the top shelf.|I came early in order for you to read my speech before the meeting* —see USAGE **25 made to order** made to fit a particular person's body or according to the exact needs, description, or plan of a particular person **26 of/in the order of** (*AmE* **on the order of**)— *BrE* about; about as much or as many as: *His income is of the order of £4,000 a year* **27 on order** asked for from the maker or supplier; asked to be made or sent, but not yet supplied **28 Order! (Order!)** *tech* (spoken or shouted at a formal meeting in order to show that someone has broken the rules) **29 orders are orders** *infml* orders must be obeyed **30 out of order** not following or not in accordance with the rules of a formal meeting —see also ORDER (3) **31 put/set/leave one's affairs in order** *sometimes euph* to make sure all one's personal and business affairs are properly settled before one dies **32 under orders** having received orders: *My brother, who's in the navy, is under orders to sail to Australia next week* **33 under the orders of** commanded by

USAGE **In order to** has the same meaning as **so as to**, but is more formal: *She shut the window* **in order to/so as to**/*to keep the insects out.* **In order that** is usually followed by **may** or **might**: *They're going to London* **in order that** *they may see the Queen.* It sounds strange before **can**, **could**, **will**, or **would**. —see also MARCHING ORDERS, POINT OF ORDER, TALL ORDER

order[2] *v* **1** [T5c,(b);V3] to give an order; command: *The officer ordered that the men* (*should*) *fire the guns/that the guns* (*should*) *be fired.|He ordered the men to fire the guns* **2** [T1] to give an order that (something) should be done or made: *order an attack* **3** [X9] to command (someone or something) to go (to or from the stated place): *If you make any more noise I shall order you out of the hall!* **4** [D1 (*for*);(T1)] (of a doctor) to advise (something) as necessary: *The doctor's ordered her a month's rest in bed* **5** [D1 (*for*);T1;I∅] to ask for (something) to be brought, made, etc., in return for payment: *He ordered himself 3 new suits.|Don't forget to order a taxi* **6** [X9;T5] to arrange, direct: *We must order our affairs better*

USAGE An army officer may **command** or **order**, a doctor **orders**; these are both people with an official position. When one **charges** someone to do something, one gives an **order** which is also a moral duty: *She* **charged** *him not to forget the children.* **Enjoin**, **direct**, and **instruct** are not so strong as **command** or **order**. Note that in *AmE* **enjoin** can mean "forbid": *He was* **enjoined** *from driving the car.*

order a·bout also **order a·round**— *v adv* [T1] to annoy (someone) by giving many orders, esp. unpleasantly

order book /ˈ·· ·/ *n* a book in which people who work for a business organization write down the orders they receive for what the business sells

or·dered /ˈɔːdəd‖ˈɔrdərd/ *adj* **1** [B] arranged in good order; tidy; regular: *an ordered life* **2** [B9] arranged: *a well/badly ordered existence*

or·der·ly¹ /ˈɔːdəli‖ˈɔrdərli/ *adj* **1** well-arranged **2** loving good arrangement; of a tidy nature and habits **3** peace-loving and well-behaved —**-liness** *n* [U]

orderly² *n* **1** a soldier who attends an officer **2** an attendant in a hospital, usu. without special professional training

order of the day /ˌ·· · · ˈ·/ *n* **1** [C] a list of what is to be talked about, decided upon, etc., at a meeting **2** [*the*+R] that which is of the greatest general interest at a particular time: *At election time politics become(s) the order of the day*

order pa·per /ˈ·· ·/ *n* a written or printed list of what is to be talked about, esp. in parliament

or·ders /ˈɔːdəz‖ˈɔrdərz/ *n* [P] *tech* the state of being a priest or other person permitted to perform Christian services and duties (esp. in the phr. **holy orders**)

order to view /ˌ·· · ˈ·/ *n* **orders to view** *BrE* a written official permission for someone to enter and examine a person's house that is for sale, before deciding whether to buy it

or·di·nal¹ /ˈɔːdɪ̈nəl‖ˈɔr-/ *adj* [Wa5] showing position or order in a set of numbers

ordinal² also **ordinal num·ber** /ˌ··· ˈ··/— *n* a number showing position or order in a set: *1st, 2nd, and 3rd are all ordinals* —compare CARDINAL³ (3)

or·di·nance /ˈɔːdɪ̈nəns‖ˈɔrdənəns/ *n* an order given by a ruler or governing body: *an ordinance of the council*

or·di·nand /ˈɔːdɪ̈nænd‖ˈɔr-/ *n* a person training to become a priest

or·di·na·ri·ly /ˈɔːdənərɪ̈li‖ˌɔrdənˈerɪ̈li/ *adv* **1** in an ordinary way **2** usually: *Ordinarily, he's back by 5*

or·di·nary /ˈɔːdənri‖ˈɔrdəneri/ *adj* **1** not unusual; common **2 in the ordinary way** if nothing unusual happens **3 out of the ordinary** unusual; uncommon —**-iness** *n* [U]

ordinary sea·man /ˌ··· ˈ··/ *n* [C;U] (a sailor with) the lowest rank on a ship

or·di·nate /ˈɔːdɪ̈nɪ̈t‖ˈɔrdənɪ̈t, -neɪt/ *n tech* the upward measurement on a GRAPH (a drawing showing the relation between 2 quantities)

or·di·na·tion /ˌɔːdɪ̈ˈneɪʃən‖ˌɔr-/ *n* [U;C] the act or ceremony of ORDAINing a religious leader (such as a priest)

ord·nance /ˈɔːdnəns‖ˈɔr-/ *n* [U] **1** big guns on wheels; ARTILLERY (1) **2** military supplies, such as weapons, explosives, and vehicles used in fighting

Ordnance Sur·vey /ˌ·· ˈ··/ *n* [*the*+R] (in Britain and Ireland) an organization which makes very detailed and correct maps of the country

or·dure /ˈɔːdjʊəʳ‖ˈɔrdʒər/ *n* [U] **1** *euph* waste matter from animal or human bowels **2** *fml* dirt

ore /ɔːʳ‖or/ *n* [U;(C)] rock, earth, etc., from which metal can be obtained

o·reg·a·no /əˈregənəʊ/ *n* [U] a type of plant related to MARJORAM and used in cooking

or·gan /ˈɔːgən‖ˈɔr-/ *n* **1** a part of an animal or plant that has a special purpose: *Leaves are organs and so is the heart* **2** an organization, usu. official, that has a special purpose **3** [*often pl.*] newspapers, radio, etc., considered as able to have an effect on what people think (esp. in the phr. **organs of public opinion**) **4** any of several musical instruments whose sound is like the largest and oldest of them, which is made of many pipes of different lengths through which air is forced, played rather like a piano and often found in churches —see picture at KEYBOARD¹ **5** any of certain other instruments using air to produce music, such as a mouth organ (HARMONICA) —see also BARREL ORGAN **6** *taboo or* (in the phr. **male organ**) *euph* PENIS

USAGE An **instrument** is a man-made tool used in science or art. A microscope, a compass, and a telephone are all **instruments**, and so is a piano or a VIOLIN. In one of its meanings, **organ** is the name of the large musical **instrument** with many pipes that is played in churches. In its other meaning, "part of an animal or plant", an **organ** is not an **instrument**, as it is not man-made but natural.

or·gan·die, *AmE* also **-dy** /ˈɔːgəndi‖ˈɔr-/ *n* [U] very fine rather stiff cotton material used esp. for women's dresses

organ grind·er /ˈ·· ˌ··/ *n* a street musician who plays a BARREL ORGAN

or·gan·ic /ɔːˈgænɪk‖ɔr-/ *adj* **1** [Wa5;A] of living things or the substances related to them: *organic life/chemistry/diseases* —compare FUNCTIONAL (3) **2** [A] made of parts with specialized purposes: *an organic whole/system* **3** [B] being one of those specialized parts; necessary: *an organic part* —**~ally** *adv* [Wa4]

or·gan·is·m /ˈɔːgənɪzəm‖ˈɔr-/ *n* **1** a living being **2** a whole made of specialized parts each of which is necessary

or·gan·ist /ˈɔːgənɪ̈st‖ˈɔr-/ *n* a musician who plays an ORGAN (4)

or·gan·i·za·tion, -sation /ˌɔːgənaɪˈzeɪʃən‖ˌɔrgənə-/ *n* **1** [U;(C)] the arrangement of parts so as to form an effective whole **2** [C] a group of people with a special purpose, such as a club or business —**~al** *adj* —**~ally** *adv*

or·gan·ize, -ise /ˈɔːgənaɪz‖ˈɔr-/ *v* **1** [T1 (*into*);V3] to form (parts) into a whole **2** [Wv5;T1;IØ] UNIONIZE —**-izer** *n*

or·gan·ized, -ised /ˈɔːgənaɪzd‖ˈɔr-/ *adj* made of specialized parts that are all necessary

organ loft /ˈ·· ·/ *n* a place for an ORGAN (4) high up in a church

or·gas·m /ˈɔːgæzəm‖ˈɔr-/ *n* [C;U] the highest point of sexual pleasure —**-mic** /ɔːˈgæzmɪk‖ɔr-/ *adj*

or·gi·as·tic /ˌɔːdʒiˈæstɪk‖ˌɔr-/ *adj* **1** of or like an ORGY (1) **2** full of excitement or wild activity

or·gy /ˈɔːdʒi‖ˈɔr-/ *n* **1** a wild party, usu. with alcohol, often with sex **2** [(*of*)] *infml* a set (of pleasant but perhaps tiring activities), usu. close together in time

o·ri·el win·dow /ˈɔːriəl ˌwɪndəʊ‖ˈoriəl-/ *n tech* a large upper window built out from the wall

o·ri·ent /ˈɔːriənt, ˈɒri-‖ˈo-/ *adj* [Wa5;A] *poet* **1** eastern **2** (of the sun) rising

Orient *n* [*the*+R] *esp. fml or lit* Asia; the (Far) East —compare OCCIDENT

o·ri·en·tal /ˌɔːriˈentl, ˌɒ-‖ˌo-/ *adj* (*sometimes cap.*) of or about the ORIENT —compare OCCIDENTAL

Oriental *n esp. fml or lit* a person from the ORIENT

o·ri·en·tal·ist /ˌɔːriˈentəlɪ̈st, ˌɒ-‖ˌo-/ *n* a specialist in the languages, civilizations, etc., of the countries of the ORIENT

o·ri·en·tate /ˈɔːriənteɪt, ˈɒ-‖ˈo-/ also (*esp. AmE*) **orient**— *v* [T1] *esp. BrE* to give direction or guidance to

o·ri·en·ta·tion /ˌɔːriənˈteɪʃən, ˌɒ-‖ˌo-/ *n* [C;U] a position or direction: (fig.) *a new orientation in life*

or·i·fice /ˈɒrɪ̈fɪ̈s‖ˈɔ-, ˈɑ-/ *n fml* **1** an opening **2** a small mouth of a large hole

or·i·gin /ˈɒrɪ̈dʒɪ̈n‖ˈɔ-, ˈɑ-/ *n* **1** [C] a starting point: *the origin of a river/of a belief* **2** [U *often pl. with sing. meaning*] parents and conditions of early life: *a woman of noble origin(s)*

o·rig·i·nal¹ /əˈrɪdʒɪ̈nəl, -dʒənəl/ *adj* **1** [Wa5;A] first; earliest **2** [B] *often apprec* new; of a new type; unlike others of the same type: *an original* *idea/invention* **3** [B] *often apprec* able to be new or different from others in ideas or behaviour: *an original thinker* **4** [Wa5;A;(B)] not copied: *an original painting*

original² *n* **1** [C] (usu. of paintings) that from which copies can be made **2** [*the*+R] the language in which something was originally written: *They are studying English in order to read Shakespeare in the original* **3** [C] *infml sometimes humor or derog* a person whose behaviour, clothing, etc., are unusual

o·rig·i·nal·i·ty /əˌrɪdʒəˈnæləti/ *n* [U] *often apprec* the quality of being of a new type or different from others of the same type

o·rig·i·nal·ly /əˈrɪdʒənəli, -dʒənəli/ *adv* **1** [Wa5] in the beginning; formerly **2** in a new or different way

original sin /·ˌ··· ˈ·/ *n* [U] (esp. in various branches of Christianity) man's first disobedience to God, which marks everyone from birth on

o·rig·i·nate /əˈrɪdʒəneɪt/ *v* [T1;L9] to (cause to) begin: *Her book originated in/from a short story* —**-nator** *n*

o·ri·ole /ˈɔːriəʊl‖ˈo-/ *n* **1** also **golden oriole**— a type of European bird with black and yellow feathers **2** any of several North American birds with black and yellow feathers

or·i·son /ˈɒrəzən‖ˈɔ-, ˈɑ-/ *n old use* a prayer

Or·lon /ˈɔːlɒn‖ˈɔrlɑn/ *n* [U] *tdmk* a type of man-made material, from which cloth is made

or·mo·lu /ˈɔːməluː‖ˈɔr-/ *n* [U] a gold-coloured mixture of metals (an ALLOY) that does not contain real gold: *an ormolu clock*

or·na·ment¹ /ˈɔːnəmənt‖ˈɔr-/ *n* **1** [U] that which is added to make something richer in style or more beautiful **2** [C] an object possessed because it is (thought to be) beautiful rather than because it is useful **3** [C (*to*)] a thing or (usu.) a person that adds honour, importance, or beauty to something: *She is an ornament to her profession*

or·na·ment² /ˈɔːnəment‖ˈɔr-/ *v* [Wv5;T1 (*with*)] to add ornament to —see DECORATE (USAGE)

or·na·men·tal /ˌɔːnəˈmentəl‖ˌɔr-/ *adj* **1** adding ornament; providing or serving as ornament **2** *often derog* perhaps beautiful, but not really necessary —**~ly** *adv*

or·na·men·ta·tion /ˌɔːnəmenˈteɪʃən‖ˌɔr-/ *n* [U] the quality of having or adding ornament

or·nate /ɔːˈneɪt‖ɔr-/ *adj sometimes derog* having a great deal of ornament; not simple: *an ornate style* —**~ly** *adv* —**~ness** *n* [U]

or·ne·ry /ˈɔːnəri‖ˈɔr-/ *adj* [Wa2] *humor esp. AmE* (of a person) difficult to deal with

or·ni·thol·o·gy /ˌɔːnəˈθɒlədʒi‖ˌɔrnəˈθɑ-/ *n* [U] the scientific study of birds —**-gist** *n* —**-gical** /ˌɔːnəθəˈlɒdʒɪkəl‖ˌɔrnəθəˈlɑ-/ *adj* [Wa5]

o·ro·tund /ˈɒrəʊtʌnd‖ˈɔrə-/ *adj fml* **1** with a calm and grand manner **2** foolishly solemn: *an orotund style*

or·phan¹ /ˈɔːfən‖ˈɔr-/ *n* a person (esp. a child) lacking one or both parents

orphan² *v* [T1] to cause to be an ORPHAN¹

or·phan·age /ˈɔːfənɪdʒ‖ˈɔr-/ *n* a place where ORPHAN¹ children live

or·re·ry /ˈɒrəri‖ˈɔ-, ˈɑ-/ *n* an apparatus made up of small movable balls, used for showing the positions and movements of bodies in the SOLAR SYSTEM

or·ris·root /ˈɒrəsruːt‖ˈɔ-, ˈɑ-/ *n* [U] the sweet-smelling root of a type of plant, used for making sweet-smelling liquid (PERFUME) and in medicine

or·tho- /ɔːθə‖ˈɔr/ also **orth-** /ɔːθ‖ɔrθ/— *comb. form* right; straight

or·tho·don·tic /ˌɔːθəˈdɒntɪk‖ˌɔrθəˈdɑn-/ *adj* [Wa5] of, concerning, or used in ORTHODONTICS

or·tho·don·tics /ˌɔːθəˈdɒntɪks‖ˌɔrθəˈdɑn-/ *n* [U] *tech* **1** the putting straight of teeth that are not growing correctly, or the prevention of incorrect growth **2** the branch of dentistry that deals with this

or·tho·dox /ˈɔːθədɒks‖ˈɔrθədɑks/ *adj* **1** generally or officially accepted: *orthodox ideas* **2** holding accepted opinions: *orthodox believers*

Orthodox Church /ˌ··· ˈ·/ *n* [*the*+R] any of several Christian churches with many members esp. in eastern Europe and the NEAR EAST

or·tho·dox·y /ˈɔːθədɒksi‖ˈɔrθədɑksi/ *n* [U] the state or quality of being ORTHODOX

or·thog·ra·phy /ɔːˈθɒgrəfi‖ɔrˈθɑ-/ *n* [U] **1** spelling in general **2** correct or standard spelling —**-phic(al)** /ˌɔːθəˈgræfɪk(əl)‖ˌɔr-/ *adj* [Wa5] —**-phically** *adv* [Wa4,5]

or·tho·pae·dic, -pedic /ˌɔːθəˈpiːdɪk◂‖ˌɔr-/ *adj* [Wa5;A] *med* of, concerning, or used in ORTHOPAEDICS

or·tho·pae·dics, -pedics /ˌɔːθəˈpiːdɪks‖ˌɔr-/ *n* [U] *med* **1** the putting straight or prevention of unnaturally shaped bones, esp. in children **2** the branch of medicine that deals with this

or·to·lan /ˈɔːtələn‖ˈɔr-/ *n* [Wn1;C;U] (the meat of) a type of small wild European bird considered very good to eat

-o·ry /əri‖ori, əri/ *suffix* **1** [→*adj*] with the purpose or effect of: INHIBIT*ory*|SATISFACTORY **2** [→*n* [C]] a place or thing to be used for: DORMITORY|DIRECTORY

or·yx /ˈɒrɪks‖ˈo-, ˈɑ-/ *n* [Wn1] a type of deerlike animal (ANTELOPE) of African deserts, with long straight horns

Os·car /ˈɒskəʳ‖ˈɑs-/ *n* an American cinema prize

os·cil·late /ˈɒsəleɪt‖ˈɑ-/ *v* **1** [IØ;(T1)] *tech* to keep moving from side to side **2** [IØ (*between*)] to keep moving between 2 limits **3** [IØ (*between*)] to keep moving between 2 choices; VACILLATE

oscillating cur·rent /ˈ···· ˌ··/ *n* [U] electrical current that changes direction very many times a second

os·cil·la·tion /ˌɒsəˈleɪʃən‖ˌɑ-/ *n* **1** [U] the action of oscillating or being OSCILLATEd **2** [C] a single movement of something that is oscillating (OSCILLATE)

os·cil·la·tor /ˈɒsəleɪtəʳ‖ˈɑ-/ *n* **1** a person or thing that OSCILLATEs **2** *tech* a machine that produces electrical OSCILLATIONs

os·cil·lo·graph /əˈsɪləgrɑːf‖-græf/ *n tech* a machine that records electrical OSCILLATIONs

os·cil·lo·scope /əˈsɪləskəʊp/ *n tech* a machine that shows electrical OSCILLATIONs as wavy lines on a glass surface (a SCREEN) —see picture at SCIENTIFIC

os·cu·la·tion /ˌɒskjʊˈleɪʃən‖ˌɑskjə-/ *n* [U] *pomp & humor* the act or action of kissing

o·si·er /ˈəʊzɪəʳ‖ˈəʊʒəʳ/ *n* a tree (a type of WILLOW) whose smaller branches are used for making baskets

-o·sis /ˈəʊsəs/ *suffix* **-oses** /ˈəʊsiːz/ [→*n* [U;(C)]] **1** a condition or change: HYPNOSIS **2** (forming the name of a disease): SILICOSIS|*Many neuroses* (NEUROSIS) *can be cured* —**-otic** /ˈɒtɪk‖ˈɑtɪk/ *suffix* [→*adj*]: HYPNOTIC|NEUROTIC —**-otically** /ˈɒtɪkəli‖ˈɑ-/ *suffix* [→*adv* [Wa4]]

os·mo·sis /ɒzˈməʊsəs‖ɑz-/ *n* [U] *tech* the passing of liquid from one side to the other side of a skinlike wall (a MEMBRANE)

os·prey /ˈɒspri, -preɪ‖ˈɑ-/ *n* a type of large fish-eating bird

os·se·ous /ˈɒsɪəs‖ˈɑ-/ *adj med* bony

os·si·f·i·ca·tion /ˌɒsəfəˈkeɪʃən‖ˌɑ-/ *n* **1** [U] the action of OSSIFYing or becoming ossified **2** [C] *med* a mass or piece of bony material

os·si·fy /ˈɒsəfaɪ‖ˈɑ-/ *v* [T1;IØ] **1** to (cause to) become hard and bonelike **2** to (cause to) become unchanging in one's ideas or unfeeling for others

os·ten·si·ble /ɒˈstensəbəl‖ɑ-/ *adj* [Wa4;A(B)] seeming or pretended, but perhaps not really true (esp. in the phr. **ostensible reason**) —**-bly** *adv*: *He did it ostensibly for love, but really for money*

os·ten·ta·tion /ˌɒstənˈteɪʃən, -ten-‖ˌɑ-/ *n* [U] *derog* unnecessary show of wealth, knowledge, etc. —**-tious** *adj* —**-tiously** *adv*

os·te·o- /ˈɒstiəʊ‖ˈɑ-/ also **os·te-** /ˈɒsti‖ˈɑ-/— *comb. form med* bone

os·te·o·ar·thri·tis /ˌɒstiəʊɑːˈθraɪtəs‖ˌɑstiəʊɑr-/ *n* [U] *med* a disease of the joints, usu. with pain and swelling

os·te·o·path /ˈɒstɪəpæθ‖ˈɑ-/ *n* a person who practises OSTEOPATHY

os·te·op·a·thy /ˌɒstiˈɒpəθi‖ˌɑstiˈɑ-/ *n* [U] (a system of) treating diseases by moving and pressing muscles and bones

os·tler /ˈɒslə[r]‖ˈɑ-/ also (*esp. AmE*) **hostler**— *n* (in former times) a man who took care of guests' horses at an inn

os·tra·cize, -cise /ˈɒstrəsaɪz‖ˈɑ-/ *v* [T1] to refuse to have social dealings with —**~cism** *n* [U]

os·trich /ˈɒstrɪtʃ‖ˈɔ-, ˈɑ-/ *n* **1** a type of very large African bird with long legs, a long neck, and beautiful feathers (PLUMEs), which runs very quickly but cannot fly —see picture at EXOTIC **2** *infml* a person who hides away from and refuses to accept unpleasant reality **3 the digestion of an ostrich** *usu. humor* the ability to eat anything

oth·er /ˈʌðə[r]/ *determiner, pron* **1** (with *the, one's both, all, every*) the remaining (one or ones) of a set; what is/are left as well as that/those mentioned: *holding the wheel with one hand and waving with the other* (*one*)|*She's cleverer than* (*any of*) *the others/than the other girls in her class.*|*Why are you alone? Where are all the others/the 5 other boys/the other 5 boys/the rest?*|*These trousers are wet—I'll change into my others/my other ones* (=I have only 2 pairs) **2** (with *than*) additional (person or thing); more as well: *You can't go by car, but there are plenty of other ways of getting there.*|*John and some other boys went swimming* (compare *John and some girls*).|*Some of them are red: others are brown* (compare *the others are brown* (=all the rest)).|*You'll have to use this chair; there's no other* (*than this*) **3** (with *than*) not the same; not this, not oneself, not one's own, etc.: *He enjoys spending other people's money* (=not his own).|*Others may laugh at her but I think she's sweet.*|*He isn't here for the beer—he came for quite other reasons* (*than that*) **4 each other** one another: *Paul and Charles bit each other* (=Paul bit Charles and Charles bit Paul) **5 every other a** all the others; all that remain **b** every 2nd: *They go to the US every other year; they went in 1974 and 1976 and they're going again in 1978* **6 one after the other/after another** not together, but first one, then next, etc. **7 some . . . or other/or another** (showing that one is not certain): *We'll do it some time or* (*an*)*other* **8 the other day/afternoon/evening/night** (on) on a recent day/afternoon/evening/night —compare ONE **day 9 the other end/side** the far or opposite of 2 ends/sides from this one: *a voice at the other end of the telephone* **10 this, that, and the other** *infml* all sorts of things

USAGE **Other** is not used after **an**: the word is then **another**. Compare *Show me* **another**/*some* **others**/*some more.*|*Would you like* **another**/*any* **others**/*any more?* But we can say *I have only one* **other** *sister besides Margaret.*

other than /ˈ·· ·/ *prep* [*nonassertive*] **1** except: *There's nobody here other than me* **2** not; anything but: *She can hardly be other than grateful* **3** otherwise than; in any other way than: *You can't get there other than by swimming*

oth·er·wise /ˈʌðəwaɪz‖ˈʌðər-/ *adv* [Wa5] **1** differently; in an/the other way: *I hate him and I won't pretend otherwise* (=pretend I don't).|*He is guilty until proved otherwise* (=proved not to be).|*"people using the hospital otherwise than as private* PATIENTs*"* (changed from SEU W.) **2** apart from that; in other ways: *"Daddy still has a bit of his cold, but otherwise all are well"* (SEU W.).|*"an otherwise excellent move"* (SEU W.) **3** if not; in different conditions: *Do it now. Otherwise, it will be too late* **4 or otherwise a** or in some other way: *We'll get there somehow, by train or otherwise* **b** or not: *mothers, whether married or otherwise*

oth·er·world·ly /ˌʌðəˈwɜːldli‖ˌʌðərˈwɜr-/ *adj sometimes derog* more concerned with things of the spirit or mind than with the material things of this world

-ot·ic /ˈɒtɪk‖ˈɑtɪk/ *suffix* [→*adj*] see -OSIS —**-otically** /ˈɒtɪkəli‖ˈɑ-/ *suffix* [→*adv* [Wa4]]

o·ti·ose /ˈəʊʃiəʊs, ˈəʊti-/ *adj fml* (of ideas, words, etc.) unnecessary

ot·ter /ˈɒtə[r]‖ˈɑ-/ *n* **1** [C] any of several types of fish-eating animal that can swim and have beautiful brown fur, found in many areas —see picture at CARNIVOROUS **2** [U] its fur

ot·to·man /ˈɒtəmən‖ˈɑ-/ *n* **ottomans** a long soft seat without back or arms, sometimes hollow and used for storing things

ou·bli·ette /ˌuːbliˈet/ *n* (esp. in former times) a small usu. secret underground room where prisoners could be kept until everyone forgot about them

ouch /aʊtʃ/ *interj* (an expression of sudden pain or discomfort)

ought /ɔːt/ *v pres. t. neg. contr.* **oughtn't** /ˈɔːtənt/ [Wv2;I∅,3] **1** (of people) to have the moral duty (to do something); should: *She ought to look after her children better.*|*You ought to be ashamed of yourself.*|*"Ought I to leave tomorrow?" "No, you needn't leave till Thursday."*|*I wonder whether I oughtn't to speak to him.*|*He ought to be punished, oughtn't he?* (=someone should punish him).|*He oughtn't to have said that* (*but he did*).|*She told him he ought not to do it* (*so perhaps he didn't*).|*She told him he ought not to have done it* (*but he had done it*) **2** (*also used with the* PASSIVE *to say that some action would be right or suitable*) would be wise (to do something): *You ought to be more careful, you know.*|*Oughtn't he*/(*fml*) *ought he not to see a doctor?*|*We really ought to buy a new car, oughtn't we?*|*This old coat ought to have been thrown away years ago* **3** will probably; can be naturally expected (to do something): *Prices ought to come down soon.*|*You ought to be hungry by now* **4 You ought to** (*used when describing something exciting, funny, or beautiful*) I wish you could: *You ought to hear the way she plays the piano!*

USAGE 1 **Ought** and **should**, when used about past time (**ought** *to have*, **should** *have*) mean that something right has not been done or something wrong has been done, and it is now too late to change it: *"We have left undone those things which we* **ought** *to have done, and we have done those things which we* **ought** *not to have done"* (church service). But they can also mean that something must be done before a certain time in the future: *Students who wish to attend the second part of the course* **should** *first have completed the first part.* 2 **Needn't** is used as the opposite of **ought**, **should**, and **must**, to mean that an action is unnecessary: *We* **ought to/should/must** *wash the dishes, but we* **needn't** *dry them because they will dry themselves.* But **needn't** means only that an action is unnecessary, so it is not the same as **oughtn't**, which means that the action is wrong. —see also table at MUST

oui·ja board /ˈwiːdʒə bɔːd‖-bord/ *n* (*often cap.* O) a board with letters and other signs on it, which people try to use for receiving messages from the dead

ounce¹ /aʊns/ *written abbrev.* **oz**— *n* **1** [C] 1/16 of a pound AVOIRDUPOIS **2** [C] 1/12 of a pound TROY WEIGHT —see WEIGHTS & MEASURES TABLE **3** [S+*of*] (even) a small amount: *You wouldn't do that if you had an ounce of sense*

ounce² *n lit* SNOW LEOPARD

our /aʊəʳ/ *determiner* [Wp1] (*poss. form of* WE) belonging to us: *"as soon as we've made our minds up"* (SEU S.)|*She's our daughter, not yours*

-our, *AmE* **-or** /əʳ/ *suffix* (forms nouns and verbs related to a quality, condition, or activity): COLOUR|HONOUR|LABOUR

Our Fa·ther /ˌ· ˈ··/ *n* [*the*+R;(C)] LORD'S PRAYER

Our La·dy /ˌ· ˈ··/ *n* [R] Mary, the mother of CHRIST

ours /aʊəz‖aʊərz/ *pron.* [Wp1] (*poss. form of* WE) that/those belonging to us: *Ours is/are on the table.*|*"a friend of ours"* (SEU S.)|*That fool of a sister of ours!*—see also OF (6)

our·selves /aʊəˈselvz‖aʊər-/ *pron* [Wp1] **1** (*refl. form of* WE): *"We must ask ourselves a personal question"* (SEU S.) **2** (*strong form of* WE): *We built the house ourselves.*|*Ourselves a religious family, we were shaken at their behaviour* **3** *infml* (in) our usual state of mind or body (often in the phrs. **be ourselves, come to ourselves**) **4** (**all**) **by ourselves** alone, without help —see YOURSELF (USAGE)

-ous /əs/ *suffix* [*n*→*adj*] causing or having the nature of: *ceremonious*|*dangerous* —**-ously** *adv*

ou·sel /ˈuːzəl/ *n* OUZEL

oust /aʊst/ *v* [T1 (*from*)] (of a living being) force (a living being) out (of): *to oust the president*

out¹ /aʊt/ *adv* **1** away (from the inside); in or to the open air, the outside, etc.: *Open the bag and take the money out.*|*It's not in my pocket—it must have fallen out.*|*Shut the door to keep the wind out.*|*He put his tongue out* —compare IN² (1) **2** away (from home or from a building), so as to be absent: *I'm afraid Mr Jones is out/has gone out; he'll be back soon.*|*Let's have an evening out at the theatre.*|*Let's sleep out (in the garden).*|*She stays out late at nights* —compare IN² (2) **3** away (from land, a town, or one's own country): *to go out to Africa*|*They live right out in the country* **4** to a number of people or in all directions: *give out all the tickets*|*spread out the cloth* —compare IN² (3) **5** completely; to the end; so as to be finished: *clean out the room*|*I'm tired out.*|*He'll be back before the month is out* (=is ended) **6** so as not to be there or not to exist: *to wash out the dirty marks* —compare IN² (4) **7** in a loud voice; aloud: *Sing/Cry/Shout/Call out.*|*Read out the names* **8 a** (of a player in a game such as cricket) so as to be no longer allowed to take part according to the rules: *Sussex all out for 351*|*"How's that?" "Out!"*|(fig.) *The Labour Party are out* (=of power) **b** (of the ball in a game such as tennis) outside the line —opposite **in** **9** so as to be clearly seen, shown, understood, etc.: *Think/Plan it out properly.*|*The secret/The sun came out/is out.*|*The black trees stood out against the snow* **10** so as to be no longer fashionable: *Short skirts went out* (—opposite **came in**) *last year; they're out* (—opposite **in**) *this year* **11** (of a flower) so as to be fully open and ripe **12** (esp. in former times) (of a young girl) so as to be old enough to take part in social life, esp. of a court **13** *not fml* (*after a* SUPERLATIVE) ever; existing: *He's the stupidest man out* —compare OUT **and away** **14** (of a fire or light) so as to be no longer lit: *The fire's gone out* —compare IN³ (4), OFF¹ (3), ON² (7) **15** away **a** from a surface: *I tore my stocking on a nail that was sticking out from that wooden box* **b** from a set of things: *Pick out the best of the apples* **16** so as to be no longer working because one is on STRIKE: *The fishermen came out/are out in sympathy with the sailors* **17** (of the TIDE=flow of sea water) away from the coast; so as to be low **18 be out for** to be trying to get: *Don't trust him—he's only out for your money* **19 be out to** to be trying to: *Be careful: he's out to get* (=harm) *you* **20 out and about** (of someone who has been ill) able to get up and leave the house —compare UP² **and about** **21 out and away** (before a SUPERLATIVE) by far; much: *He's out and away the stupidest man I know* —compare OUT¹ (13) **22 Out with it!** *imper.* Say it! **23 Out you go!** *imper.* Go out! —see OUTSIDE (USAGE)

out² *v* [IØ] *becoming rare* to become publicly known (in the phr. **will out**): *The truth will always out*

out³ *adj* [Wa5] **1** [A] used for sending something away from one, to someone else: *Put the letter in the out* TRAY —opposite **in** **2** [F] impossible; out of the QUESTION (7): *I'm sorry, but that's completely out; it can't be done* **3** [F] (of a guess or sum, or the person responsible for it) incorrect: *He's badly out in his calculations* **4** [Wa5;F] (of a fire or light) no longer lit or burning: *The fire's been out for hours* —compare IN³ (4), ON³ (1), OFF³ (7) **5 out and out** complete; total: *an out-and-out believer in free trade*

out⁴ *prep infml* (used for showing an outward movement) out of: *He went out the door*

out⁵ *n* [S] *infml* **1** an excuse for leaving an activity or for avoiding blame **2 the ins and outs** see IN⁴

out- *prefix* **1** [*v*→*n*] (*before verbs that, as verbs, can be followed by* out): **a** OUTLET (LET OUT)|OUTLOOK (LOOK OUT) **b** (*often shows the beginning of an* ACTION): OUTBREAK (BREAK OUT)|OUTBURST (BURST OUT) **2** [*v*→*adj*] (*before the present or past p. of verbs that, as verbs, can be followed by* out): **a** OUTSPOKEN (SPEAK OUT)|OUTSTANDING (STAND OUT) **b** fully; completely: OUTSPREAD (spread out)|OUTSTRETCHED (stretch out) **3** [*n*→*n*] outside: OUTHOUSE|OUTBUILDING|OUTLAW **4** [*v*→*v*] beyond: OUTRUN|OUTGROW **5** [*v*→*v*] longer: OUTLIVE|OUTLAST **6** [*v*→*v*] more than or to a greater degree than (an opponent): *outargue*|OUTDO **7** [*n, adj, adv*→*n, adj, adv*] far (away): OUTLYING

out·back /ˈaʊtbæk/ *n* [*the*+R] **1** (esp. in Australia) the part of a country far away from cities **2** *derog* an area that is not worth going to

out·bal·ance /aʊtˈbæləns/ *v* [T1] **1** to be of greater weight than **2** to be of greater importance than

out·bid /aʊtˈbɪd/ *v* **-bid,** *pres. p.* **-bidding** [T1] to offer more than (someone else)

out·board mo·tor /ˌaʊtbɔːd ˈməʊtəʳ‖-bord-/ *n* a motor fixed to the back end of a small boat —see picture at BOAT¹

out·bound /ˈaʊtbaʊnd/ *adj* (going) far away, esp. to another country

out·brave /aʊtˈbreɪv/ *v* [T1] to fight bravely and strongly against, usu. with success

out·break /ˈaʊtbreɪk/ *n* [(*of*)] **1** a sudden appearance or beginning of something bad: *an outbreak of disease/of insects/of fighting* **2** a rising by people against someone or something considered unjust

out·build·ing /ˈaʊtˌbɪldɪŋ/ (*BrE* also **outhouse**)— *n* a smaller building forming part of a group with a larger main building

out·burst /ˈaʊtbɜːst‖-ɜr-/ *n* [(*of*)] a sudden powerful expression of feeling or activity: *outbursts of weeping/laughter/gunfire*

out·cast /ˈaʊtkɑːst‖-kæst/ *n, adj* (a person) forced from his home or without friends

out·caste /ˈaʊtkɑːst‖-kæst/ *n, adj* [Wa5] (a person) not, or no longer, a member of a fixed social class (CASTE) in India

out·class /aʊt'klɑːs‖-'klæs/ *v* [T1] to be very much better than

out·come /'aʊtkʌm/ *n* [(*of*) *usu. sing.*] an effect or result

out·crop /'aʊtkrɒp‖-krɑp/ *n* an amount of rock which stands up out of the ground

out·cry /'aʊtkraɪ/ *n* a public show of anger

out·dat·ed /ˌaʊt'deɪtɪ̈d◂/ also **out-of-date**— *adj* no longer in general use

out·dis·tance /aʊt'dɪstəns/ *v* [T1] to go further or faster than: (fig.) *This book has outdistanced all others in sales*

out·do /aʊt'duː/ *v* **-did** /'dɪd/, **-done** /'dʌn/, *3rd pers. sing. pres. t.* **-does** /'dʌz/ [T1] to do or be better than (usu. someone): *Not to be outdone, he sang even louder*

out·door /ˌaʊt'dɔːʳ◂‖-'dor/ also **out-of-door**— *adj* [Wa5;A] existing, happening, done, or used in the open air: *outdoor shoes|outdoor life*

outdoor re·lief /ˌ·· ·'·/ *n* [U] (in Britain in former times) help and money given to the poor in their own homes —compare INDOOR RELIEF

out·doors¹ /ˌaʊt'dɔːz‖-orz/ also **out of doors**— *adv* [Wa5] in the open air

outdoors² *n* [*the*+R] the open air

out·er /'aʊtəʳ/ *adj* [Wa5;A] **1** on the outside; at a greater distance from the middle: *the outer walls| outer islands* —opposite **inner** **2 the outer man a** the way a man seems to be but may not really be **b** the way a man looks or dresses

out·er·most /'aʊtəməʊst‖-ər-/ also **outmost**— *adj* [Wa5;A] furthest outside or furthest from the middle: *the outermost stars* —opposite **innermost**

outer space /ˌ·· '·/ *n* [U] the area where the stars and other distant heavenly bodies are

out·face /aʊt'feɪs/ *v* [T1] **1** to meet and deal with bravely **2** to cause to look away by looking at steadily

out·fall /'aʊtfɔːl/ *n* a place where water flows away from a large body of water

out·field /'aʊtfiːld/ *n* **1** [*the*+R] (in the games of cricket and BASEBALL) the part of the playing field furthest from the player who is to hit the ball —see picture at BASEBALL **2** [*the*+GU] the players in this part of the field —**~er** *n*

out·fight /aʊt'faɪt/ *v* **-fought** /'fɔːt/ [T1] (in a match or battle) to fight better than

out·fit¹ /'aʊtˌfɪt/ *n* **1** [C] all the things, esp. clothes, needed for a particular purpose **2** [GC] *infml* a group of people, esp. if working together

outfit² *v* **-tt-** [T1 (*with*)] to provide with an OUTFIT¹ (1), esp. of clothes —**~ter** *n*

out·flank /aʊt'flæŋk/ *v* [T1] **1** to go round the side of (an enemy) and attack from behind **2** to gain an advantage over (someone) by doing something unexpected

out·flow /'aʊtfləʊ/ *n* [(*of*)] a flowing out

out·fox /aʊt'fɒks‖-'fɑks/ *v* [T1] to gain an advantage over (someone) by being cleverer; OUTSMART

out·gen·e·ral /aʊt'dʒenərəl/ *v* **-ll-** (*AmE* **-l-**) [T1] **1** to defeat (an enemy) by being a better general **2** to defeat (an opponent) by better planning

out·go·ing /ˌaʊt'gəʊɪŋ◂/ *adj* **1** [Wa5;A] that is going out or leaving **2** [Wa5;A] who is finishing a period in office, esp. in political office **3** [B] having or showing eagerness to mix socially with others; friendly —compare FORTHCOMING (3)

out·go·ings /'aʊtˌgəʊɪŋz/ *n* [P] amounts of money that are spent

out·grow /aʊt'grəʊ/ *v* **-grew** /'gruː/, **-grown** /'grəʊn/ [T1] **1** to grow more than: *to outgrow one's brothers* **2** to grow too much for: *to outgrow one's clothes|one's earlier interests*

out·growth /'aʊtgrəʊθ/ *n* **1** a natural result **2** something that grows out

out-Her·od /ˌaʊt 'herəd/ *v* **out-Herod Herod** *often derog* to go further than anyone else in anything, esp. in being cruel, violent, etc.

out·house /'aʊthaʊs/ *n* **-houses** /ˌhaʊzɪ̈z/ **1** *AmE* an enclosed outside LAVATORY **2** *BrE* OUTBUILDING

out·ing /'aʊtɪŋ/ *n not fml* a short pleasure trip

out·land·ish /aʊt'lændɪʃ/ *adj usu. infml* strange and unpleasing —**~ly** *adv* —**~ness** *n* [U]

out·last /aʊt'lɑːst‖-'læst/ *v* [T1] to last longer than

out·law¹ /'aʊtlɔː/ *n* a criminal, esp. (in former times) one who was not protected by law and/or who tried to escape to another place

outlaw² *v* [T1] **1** to declare (someone) a criminal **2** to declare (something) unlawful

out·lay¹ /'aʊtleɪ/ *n* [C *usu. sing.*; (U): (*on, for*)] money spent for a purpose

outlay² *v* **-laid** /leɪd/ [T1 (*on, for*)] *esp. AmE* to spend (money) for a purpose; LAY OUT (5)

out·let /'aʊtlet, -lɪ̈t/ *n* [(*for*)] **1** a way through which something (usu. a liquid or a gas) may go out **2** a good chance to use one's powers or express one's feelings: *an outlet for his feelings*

out·line¹ /'aʊtlaɪn/ *n* [(*of*)] **1** the shape (of something): *the outline of her face in the light of the candle* **2** a line or flat figure showing the shape of something: *an outline map of Europe* **3** the main ideas or facts (of something): *an outline of history/ of the main points of the talk*

outline² *v* [T1] to make an OUTLINE¹ of

out·live /aʊt'lɪv/ *v* [T1] to live longer than (the memory of): *to outlive one's wife|to outlive one's usefulness|to outlive a crime*

out·look /'aʊtlʊk/ *n* [*usu. sing.*] **1** a view on which one looks out **2** future probabilities **3** [(*on*)] one's general point of view —see VIEW (USAGE)

out·ly·ing /'aʊtˌlaɪ-ɪŋ/ *adj* [A] far from the centre

out·ma·noeu·vre, *AmE* **-neuver** /ˌaʊtmə'nuːvəʳ/ *v* [T1] to make more effective movements than (an opponent); put in a position of disadvantage

out·march /aʊt'mɑːtʃ‖-ɑr-/ *v* [T1] to march better, faster, or longer than

out·match /aʊt'mætʃ/ *v* [T1 *often pass.*] to arrange a match on conditions unfavourable to: *Unfortunately, he was outmatched in the competition*

out·mod·ed /aʊt'məʊdɪ̈d/ *adj* no longer in fashion

out·most /'aʊtməʊst/ *adj* [Wa5;A] OUTERMOST

out·num·ber /aʊt'nʌmbəʳ/ *v* [T1] to be larger in numbers than

out of /'· ·/ *prep* **1** from inside; away from: *"Michael is moving out of Addison Gardens"* (SEU S.) **2** from a state of: *Wake up out of a deep sleep* **3** beyond the limits of: *out of sight* (=to where a thing cannot be seen) **4** from among: *3 out of 4 people choose "Silver Fox" soap!* **5** in or into a state of loss or not having; without; lacking: *We're out of water!* —compare **out of** STOCK **6** because of: *I came out of real interest, not just to have a good time!* **7** from or with (a material): *made out of wood* **8** *tech* born to (the stated female animal, esp. a horse): *Golden Trumpet, by Golden Rain out of Silver Trumpet* —compare BY (16) **9 out of one's head/mind** *infml* mad **10 be/feel out of it (all)** to be/feel (unhappy or lonely because) separated from the main centre of activity —see also **out of the** QUESTION¹ (7), **out of** SIGHT¹ (18), **out of** CONTROL² (9), **out of** DANGER

out-of-date /ˌ·· '·◂/ *adj* OUTDATED

out-of-door /ˌ·· '·◂/ *adj* [Wa5;A] OUTDOOR

out-of-doors /ˌ·· '·/ *adv* [Wa5] OUTDOORS

out-of-pock·et ex·pens·es /ˌ· · ·· ·'··/ *n* [P] that which one has to pay with ready money of one's own (not on CREDIT), usu. in small amounts for small additional things bought or for travel costs —see also **out of** POCKET¹ (13)

out-of-the-way /ˌ··· '·◂/ *adj* **1** distant; far away

from people and places **2** not known by ordinary people

out·pa·tient /ˈaʊtˌpeɪʃənt/ *n* a sick person who goes to a hospital for treatment while continuing to live at home

out·play /aʊtˈpleɪ/ *v* [T1] to play better than (an opponent)

out·point /aʊtˈpɔɪnt/ *v* [T1] (esp. in BOXING) to defeat (an opponent) by gaining more points

out·post /ˈaʊtpəʊst/ *n* [(*of*)] a group of people or settlement at some distance from the main group or settlement

out·pour·ings /ˈaʊtˌpɔːrɪŋz‖-ˌpo-/ *n* [P (*of*)] continuous strong expressions of feelings

out·put /ˈaʊtpʊt/ *n* [U;C *usu. sing.*] production: *an output of 10,000 tins a year*

out·rage[1] /ˈaʊtreɪdʒ/ *n* [C;(U)] **1** a very wrong or cruel act which causes great anger **2** an act that has a bad effect upon public opinion

outrage[2] *v* [Wv5;T1] to offend greatly

out·ra·geous /aʊtˈreɪdʒəs/ *adj* **1** very offensive **2** unexpected and probably offensive: *her outrageous jokes* —**~ly** *adv*

out·range /aʊtˈreɪndʒ/ *v* [T1] to go further or cover a greater distance than (an opponent)

out·rank /aʊtˈræŋk/ *v* [T1] to have a higher rank than (usu. a member of the same group)

ou·tré /ˈuːtreɪ‖uːˈtreɪ/ *adj Fr, usu. derog* (of ideas, behaviour, etc.) very peculiar or unusual

out·ride /aʊtˈraɪd/ *v* **-rode** /ˈrəʊd/, **-ridden** /ˈrɪdn/ [T1] to ride better, faster, or further than (esp. an opponent)

out·rid·er /ˈaʊtˌraɪdəʳ/ *n* a policeman riding on a motorcycle (or, in former times, a servant riding on a horse) at the side of, or in front of a vehicle, as a guard or attendant

out·rig·ger /ˈaʊtˌrɪgəʳ/ *n* **1** a piece of wood shaped like a small narrow boat, that is fixed to the side of a boat (esp. a CANOE) with 2 long poles, to prevent it from turning over in the water —see picture at BOAT[1] **2** a type of boat to which this is fixed, used esp. in the South Pacific **3** a small framework built out from the side of a racing boat, to which the OARs are fixed

out·right[1] /aʊtˈraɪt/ *adv* [Wa5] **1** completely: *He's been paying for that house for years; now he owns it outright* **2** completely and clearly: *She won outright* **3** completely and without delay: *be killed outright* **4** (completely and) openly: *Tell him outright just what you think*

outright[2] /ˈaʊtraɪt/ *adj* [Wa5;A] **1** complete: *an outright loss* **2** complete and clear: *the outright winner* **3** complete and open

out·ri·val /aʊtˈraɪvəl/ *v* **-ll-** (*AmE* **-l-**) [T1] to do better than (someone else) in or as if in a competition

out·run /aʊtˈrʌn/ *v* **-ran** /ˈræn/, **-run** /ˈrʌn/, *pres. p.* **-running** [T1] **1** to run better, faster, or further than (someone) (in a competition) **2** to go beyond

out·sell /aʊtˈsel/ *v* [T1] **1** to sell more or faster than **2** to be sold in larger quantities than

out·set /ˈaʊtset/ *n* [*the*+R] the beginning (esp. in the phrs. **at/from the outset**)

out·shine /aʊtˈʃaɪn/ *v* **-shone** /-ˈʃɒn‖-ˈʃəʊn/ [T1] to shine more brightly than: (fig.) *She outshines* (=is much better than) *all the other competitors*

out·side[1] /aʊtˈsaɪd, ˈaʊtsaɪd/ *n* [(*the*) S] **1** the outer part of a solid object; the part that is furthest from the centre, or that faces away towards other people or towards the open air: *paint the outside of the house|This coat is fur on the inside and cloth on the outside* —opposite **inside** **2 at the (very) outside** at the most; and not more —compare OUTSIDE[2] (5)

outside[2] /ˈaʊtsaɪd/ *adj* [Wa5;A] **1** facing the OUTSIDE[1] (1): *an outside covering|wrapping* —opposite **inside** **2** in the open air: *Outside workers need warm clothes in winter* **3** coming from or happening elsewhere: *We can't do it ourselves—we must get outside help.|an outside broadcast* (=not from the STUDIO) **4** (of a chance or possibility) slight; unlikely; distant **5** (of things that can be measured) greatest; most that can be allowed or accepted: *an outside figure of £100* —compare **at the** OUTSIDE[1] (2)

outside[3] /aʊtˈsaɪd/ *adv* [Wa5] to or on the OUTSIDE[1] (1): *children playing outside in the street|It's quite dark outside—there's no moon* —opposite **inside**

USAGE When leaving the inside of a place one goes **out**, or **outside**, but **out** is usually further. Compare: *to go* **out** *for a drive|to go* **outside** *for a smoke.*

outside[4] /aʊtˈsaɪd, ˈaʊtsaɪd/ *prep* **1** on or to the OUTSIDE[1] (1) of: *"everybody sort of waiting outside the door"* (SEU S.)|*"outside the West Gate of Ch'iung-Lai city"* (SEU W.) **2** beyond the limits of; not in: *"staying somewhere outside New York"* (SEU S.)|(fig.) *It's quite outside my experience* —opposite **within** **3** more than (something that can be measured): *anything outside £100* —opposite **within**

outside of /·ˈ· ·/ *prep infml* **1** *AmE* outside: *Passengers are asked not to ride outside of their part of the train* **2** *esp. AmE* except for: *Outside of John, there's no one for the job*

out·sid·er /aʊtˈsaɪdəʳ/ *n* **1** a person who is not accepted as a member of a particular social group **2** a person or animal not considered to have a good chance to win

out·size /ˈaʊtsaɪz/ *adj* [Wa5;A] (esp. of clothing) larger than the standard sizes

out·skirts /ˈaʊtskɜːts‖-ɜr-/ *n* [P (*of*)] **1** (esp. of a town) the outer areas (esp. in the phr. **in the outskirts**) **2** the outer limits (esp. in the phr. **on the outskirts**)

out·smart /aʊtˈsmɑːt‖-ɑr-/ *v* [T1] *infml* **1** to win by acting more cleverly than —compare OUTWIT **2 outsmart oneself** to lose by acting too cleverly

out·spo·ken /aʊtˈspəʊkən/ *adj not derog* expressing openly what is thought or felt —**~ly** *adv* —**~ness** *n* [U]

out·spread /ˌaʊtˈspred◂/ *adj* [Wa5] spread out flat or to full width: *with arms outspread*

out·stand·ing /aʊtˈstændɪŋ/ *adj* **1** better than others; very good **2** easily seen; important **3** [Wa5] not yet done: *some work still outstanding* **4** [Wa5] not yet paid: *some debts still outstanding* —**~ly** *adv*

out·stay /aʊtˈsteɪ/ *v* [T1] **1** to stay longer than (other people at the same event) **2 outstay one's welcome** to stay so long (as a guest) that one is no longer welcome

out·stretched /ˌaʊtˈstretʃt◂/ *adj* [Wa5] stretched out to full length

out·strip /aʊtˈstrɪp/ *v* **-pp-** [T1] **1** to pass in running **2** to do better than

out·talk /aʊtˈtɔːk/ *v* [T1] to talk better or longer than

out·vote /aʊtˈvəʊt/ *v* [T1] to vote in larger numbers than

out·ward /ˈaʊtwəd‖-ərd/ *adj* [Wa5;A] **1** away: *the outward voyage* **2** towards the outside: *an outward look from inside the car* **3** of the outside; appearing to be true but perhaps not really true: *Outward calm can hide inward sadness.|"the outward forms of Christianity"* (SEU W.) **4 the outward man** the OUTER (2) man **5 to all outward appearances** as things seem, but may not really be **6 outward bound** going away (esp. from the shore)

out·ward·ly /ˈaʊtwədli‖-ər-/ *adv* according to the appearance of things, which may not be the same as their reality

out·wards /ˈaʊtwədz‖-ər-/ also (*esp. AmE & fml*) **outward**— *adv* **1** away (from the centre): *The branch is growing straight outwards* **2** away (from being concerned only with oneself): *Look outwards and interest yourself in other people*

out·wear /aʊtˈweəʳ/ *v* **-wore** /ˈwɔːʳ‖ˈwor/, **-worn** /ˈwɔːn‖ˈworn/ [T1] to stay usable longer than: *Good shoes will always outwear cheap ones*

out·weigh /aʊtˈweɪ/ *v* [T1] **1** to be more important than: *My love for her outweighs everything else* **2** to weigh more than

out·wit /aʊtˈwɪt/ *v* **-tt-** [T1] to win by being cleverer or behaving more cleverly than

out·work /ˈaʊtwɜːk‖-ɜr-/ *n* **1** [C *usu. pl.*] a militarily strong position at some distance from a larger one **2** [U] work for a business that is done outside the usual place of business —**~er** *n*

out·worn /aʊtˈwɔːn‖-ˈworn/ *adj* (of an idea, custom, etc.) that is no longer useful or used —compare WORN-OUT

ou·zel, -sel /ˈuːzəl/ *n* any of several types of small singing birds

ou·zo /ˈuːzəʊ/ *n* [U] a type of Greek alcoholic drink, drunk with water

o·va /ˈəʊvə/ *tech pl. of* OVUM

o·val /ˈəʊvəl/ *n, adj* (anything which is) egg-shaped

o·var·i·an /əʊˈveərɪən/ *adj* [Wa5;A;(B)] of or related to an OVARY

o·va·ry /ˈəʊvəri/ *n* **1** the part of a female animal, bird, etc., that produces eggs **2** the part of a female plant that produces seeds —see picture at FLOWER¹

o·va·tion /əʊˈveɪʃən/ *n* a joyful expression of public welcome or approval

ov·en /ˈʌvən/ *n* **1** any of several types of enclosed boxlike spaces used for cooking, baking clay, etc. —see COOK (USAGE) —see picture at KITCHEN **2 like an oven** uncomfortably hot: *It's like an oven in here; open the window*

ov·en·ware /ˈʌvənweəʳ/ *n* [U] cooking pots, dishes, etc., that can be put in a hot OVEN without cracking

o·ver¹ /ˈəʊvəʳ/ *adv* **1** downwards from an upright position: *He pushed me and I fell over* **2** up, out, and downwards across an edge: *The milk's boiling over!* **3** so that another side is shown: *Turn the page over.|dogs rolling over (and over) on the grass* **4** right through; completely from beginning to end: *You'd better think/talk it over carefully* **5** across a distance or open space, either towards or away from the speaker: *to go over to the US|"He's seen me! He's coming over".* (SEU W.)|*"We must ask some amusing people over to cheer her up"* (SEU W.) **6** (showing that something is repeated): *She's asked me several times over to buy her a fur coat* **7** remaining; not used when part has been taken: *Was there any money over?|3 into 7 goes twice and one over* **8** so as to be in each other's positions or be exchanged: *Let's change these 2 pictures over and hang this one up there* **9** from one (person or group) to another: *He signed over the money to his son* **10** *esp. AmE* during or beyond a certain period: *Don't leave now; why not stay/stop over till Monday?* **11** (*before an adjective or adverb*) too; more than is good: *Don't be over anxious about it.|I'm not over keen on it.|He didn't do it over well* (=he did it badly) **12** so as to be covered and not seen: *Let's paint it over in green.|Cover her over with a sheet* **13** *AmE* again: *My sums were wrong and I had to do them over* **14 (all) over again** again; once more **15 and/or (a bit/a little) over** (of things that can be measured) and/or more; and/or upwards: *children of 14 and over* **16 Over!** also **Over to you!**—(in radio signalling) You speak now! **17 over against a** opposite to: *to live over against the church* **b** compared to: *the quality of this product over against that one* **18 over and over (again)** repeatedly; again and again **19 over here** on or to this side: *Let's sit over here by this window* **20 over there** on or to that side: *Let's sit over there by that window* —see also ONCE-OVER

over² *prep* **1** (so as to be or pass) directly above; higher than, but not touching: *The lamp hung over/above the table* (compare *The lamp stood on the table*).|*The doctor leaned over the body* —opposite **under 2** (so as to be) completely or partly covering; resting on top of: *"I kept my hand over the top" (of the bottle)* (SEU S.) —opposite **under 3** to the other side of, esp. by going up and then down again: *to jump over the wall/the ditch* (compare *across the ditch*, but not *across the wall*)|*If we can't go over the mountain we must go round it* **4** from side to side of: *a bridge over/across the river|The ball rolled over/across the grass.|"the window that looks out over the* GREEN*"* (SEU S.)|*The car ran over a dog and killed it* **5** on the far side of: *They live (just) over the street.*|(fig.) *We're over* (=past) *the worst of our troubles now* **6** down across the edge of: *to fall over a log/over the cliff* **7** in, on, or through many or all parts of: *They travelled (all) over Europe* **8** (showing command or control): *He ruled over a large kingdom* **9** higher in rank than; commanding: *I don't want anyone over me telling me what to do* —opposite **under 10** more than (something that can be measured): *over 30 books|just over £5.00|"over 8 years ago"* (SEU W.) **11** during; in the course of (an event or period): *"1 or 2 informal meetings over dinner"* (SEU W.)|*Over the years he's become more and more patient* **12** till the end of; through (an event or period): *Are you staying in London over Christmas?* **13** (heard or said) by means of or using: *I don't want to say it over the telephone* **14** in connection with; on the subject of: *difficulties over his income tax|"taking rather a long time over it"* (SEU S.) **15 over and above** as well as; besides —compare ABOVE²

over³ *adj* [F (*with*)] (of an event or period of time) finished; ended: *Let's do it now and get it over (with).|It's all over with us now* (=we are ruined; we have nothing to hope for)

over⁴ *n* (in cricket) (the period of) the act of delivering (BOWLing) the ball at the hitter (BATSMAN) a particular number of times by one player in the other team from one end of the WICKET: *In England there are 6 balls in an over, but in Australia there are 8*

over- *prefix* **1** [*n→n*] outer or upper: OVERCOAT|OVERSHOE **2** [*n→n;v→v*] above; beyond; across: OVERLORD|OVERARCH|OVERHANG **3** [*n→n*] more than; additional: OVERTIME **4** [*n→n;v→v;adj→adj*] too (much): *to overcook|overactive|overactivity*

o·ver·act /ˌəʊvərˈækt/ *v* [T1;I∅] to act (a part) in a way that goes beyond what is necessary to seem natural

o·ver·age /ˌəʊvərˈeɪdʒ◂/ *adj* [Wa5] too old for some purpose: *The army wouldn't have him because he was overage*

o·ver·all¹ /ˌəʊvərˈɔːl◂/ *adj, adv* [Wa5;A;E] **1** including everything: *the overall measurements of the room|The fish measured 5 feet 3 inches overall* **2** on the whole; generally: *Overall, prices are still rising* **3 dressed overall** *tech* (of a ship) having all flags flying for a ceremonial occasion

o·ver·all² /ˈəʊvərɔːl/ *n* **1** [C] *esp. BrE* a loose-fitting coatlike garment worn by women workers over other clothes **2** [A] of or for OVERALLS

o·ver·alls /ˈəʊvərɔːlz/ *n* [P] loose trousers often

fastened over the shoulders by means of STRAPs and worn esp. by men workers over other clothes

o·ver·arch /ˌəʊvərˈɑːtʃ‖-ˈɑr-/ *v* [Wv4;T1;IØ] *esp. lit* to form (part of) an arch over

o·ver·arm /ˈəʊvərɑːm‖-ˌɑr-/ also **overhand**— *adj, adv* (in sport) with the arm moving above the shoulder: *He threw it overarm.|an overarm throw*

o·ver·awe /ˌəʊvərˈɔː/ *v* [T1] to fill with respect and fear

o·ver·bal·ance /ˌəʊvəˈbæləns‖-vər-/ *v* [IØ;(T1)] to (cause to) become unbalanced and perhaps fall over

o·ver·bear /ˌəʊvəˈbeəʳ‖-vər-/ *v* **-bore** /ˈbɔːʳ‖ˈbor/, **-borne** /ˈbɔːn‖ˈborn/ [T1 *usu. pass.*] *fml* to defeat or force into agreement

o·ver·bear·ing /ˌəʊvəˈbeərɪŋ‖-vər-/ *adj* trying to make other people obey without regard for their ideas or feelings —**~ly** *adv*

o·ver·bid¹ /ˌəʊvəˈbɪd‖-vər-/ *v* **-bid,** *pres. p.* **-bidding** **1** [IØ(*for*); T1] (esp. in an AUCTION) to offer too high a price for (something) **2** [T1] (esp. in an AUCTION) to OUTBID **3** [T1;IØ] (in the game of BRIDGE) to say that (one's cards) are better than (another player's) or better than they really are

o·ver·bid² /ˈəʊvəˌbɪd‖-ər-/ *n* an act of OVERBIDding

o·ver·blown /ˌəʊvəˈbləʊn◂‖-vər-/ *adj* using too many words and movements of the hands

o·ver·board /ˈəʊvəbɔːd‖ˈəʊvərbord/ *adv* **1** over the side of a ship or boat into the water **2** **go overboard for/about** *infml* to become very attracted to **3** **throw overboard** *infml* to get rid of

o·ver·bur·den /ˌəʊvəˈbɜːdn‖ˌəʊvərˈbɜrdn/ [T1 (*with*)] **1** to make (someone or something) carry or do too much **2** [*usu. pass.*] to trouble (someone) greatly

o·ver·call /ˌəʊvəˈkɔːl‖-vər-/ *v* [T1;IØ] OVERBID¹ (3) —**overcall** *n*

o·ver·cap·i·tal·ize, -ise /ˌəʊvəˈkæpɪ̵tələɪz‖-vər-/ *v* [T1;IØ] **1** to collect or supply more money for (a business) than is needed **2** to put a value on (a business) higher than it is actually worth —**-ization** /ˌəʊvəkæpɪ̵təlaɪˈzeɪʃən‖-vərkæpɪ̵tələ-/ *n* [U;(C)]

o·ver·cast¹ /ˌəʊvəˈkɑːst◂‖ˌəʊvərˈkæst◂/ *adj* **1** dark with clouds: *an overcast sky/day* **2** [(*with*)] covered (with sadness): *Her face was overcast with sadness*

o·ver·cast² /ˈəʊvəkɑːst‖ˈəʊvərkæst/ *n* [U] clouds completely covering the sky

o·ver·charge¹ /ˌəʊvəˈtʃɑːdʒ‖ˌəʊvərˈtʃɑrdʒ/ *v* **1** [T1;IØ:(*by*);D1] to charge (someone) too much (by a stated amount): *They overcharged me* (*by*) *25p for the food* **2** [T1(*with*)] to fill or load too much: *overcharge the electrical apparatus*|(fig.) *overcharged with feeling*

o·ver·charge² /ˈəʊvətʃɑːdʒ‖ˈəʊvərtʃɑrdʒ/ *n* [*usu. sing.*] **1** the amount (of money) OVERCHARGED¹ **2** an act of overcharging (OVERCHARGE¹)

o·ver·cloud /ˌəʊvəˈklaʊd‖-vər-/ *v* [T1] **1** [*usu. pass.*] to cover with clouds (or shadows) **2** to make sad or less happy: *The fear of illness overclouded their holiday* **3** [*usu. pass.*] to make appear sad: *His face was overclouded with sadness* —see also CLOUD² (1)

o·ver·coat /ˈəʊvəkəʊt‖-vər-/ *n* a long warm coat worn over other clothes by men and women when going out esp. in cold weather

o·ver·come /ˌəʊvəˈkʌm‖-vər-/ *v* **-came** /ˈkeɪm/, **-come** /ˈkʌm/ **1** [T1;IØ] to fight successfully against; defeat: *overcome the enemy/a bad habit* **2** [T1] (usu. of feelings) to take control and influence the behaviour of (someone) **3** [T1 *usu. pass.*] to make (someone) weak or ill

o·ver·com·pen·sate /ˌəʊvəˈkɒmpənseɪt, -pen-‖-vərˈkɑmpən-, -pen-/ *v* [IØ (*for*)] to try to correct some weaknesses by taking too strong an action in the opposite direction —**-sation** /ˌəʊvəkɒmpənˈseɪʃən, -pen-‖-vərˌkɑmpən-, -pen-/ *n* [U]

o·ver·crop /ˌəʊvəˈkrɒp‖ˌəʊvərˈkrɑp/ *v* **-pp-** [T1] *tech* to reduce the quality of (farmland) by making it produce too many crops

o·ver·crowd /ˌəʊvəˈkraʊd‖-vər-/ *v* [Wv5;T1 (*with*)] to put or allow too many people or things in (one place)

o·ver·de·vel·op /ˌəʊvədɪˈveləp‖-vər-/ *v* [Wv5;T1] to develop too much: *an overdeveloped sense of his own importance*

o·ver·do /ˌəʊvəˈduː‖-vər-/ *v* **-did** /ˈdɪd/, **-done** /ˈdʌn/ [T1] **1** [*often pass.*] to do, ornament, perform, etc., too much: *The love scenes in the play were a bit overdone, don't you think?* **2** to show too much (feeling) **3** to use too much: *Don't overdo the salt in your cooking* **4** **overdo it** to work, practise a sport, etc., too much: *I've been rather overdoing it lately; I need a holiday*

o·ver·done /ˌəʊvəˈdʌn‖-vər-/ *adj* cooked too much —opposite **underdone**

o·ver·dose /ˈəʊvədəʊs‖-vər-/ *n* too much of a drug: *Every time I try to leave her, she threatens to take an overdose*

o·ver·draft /ˈəʊvədrɑːft‖ˈəʊvərdræft/ *n* a sum lent to a person by a bank of more money than he has in the bank

o·ver·draw /ˌəʊvəˈdrɔː‖-vər-/ *v* **-drew** /ˈdruː/, **-drawn** /ˈdrɔːn/ [T1;IØ] to get a bank to pay one more money than one has in (one's account)

o·ver·drawn /ˌəʊvəˈdrɔːn‖-vər-/ *adj* **1** [(*by*)] **a** (of a person) having OVERDRAWn **b** (of a bank account) having been OVERDRAWN **2** made to appear greater, worse, etc., than in reality; EXAGGERATEd

o·ver·dress /ˌəʊvəˈdres‖-vər-/ *v* [T1;IØ] to (cause to) dress in clothes that attract attention to themselves rather than to the wearer

o·ver·drive /ˈəʊvədraɪv‖-vər-/ *n* [U;(C)] an apparatus that allows a car to keep going at a given speed while its engine produces the least power necessary for that speed

o·ver·due /ˌəʊvəˈdjuː◂‖ˌəʊvərˈduː◂/ *adj* [B;E] **1** left unpaid too long **2** later than expected: *The train is 15 minutes overdue*

o·ver·es·ti·mate /ˌəʊvərˈestɪ̵meɪt/ *v* **1** [T1] to have too high an opinion of the degree or number of **2** [T1;IØ] to give too high a value for (an amount): *We overestimated the distance, so we still have some time left after our walk* —see also ESTIMATE

o·ver·ex·pose /ˌəʊvərɪkˈspəʊz/ *v* [T1] to give too much light to (a film or photograph), usu. spoiling the picture —see also EXPOSE (5)

o·ver·flow¹ /ˌəʊvəˈfləʊ‖-vər-/ *v* **1** [T1;IØ] to flow over the edges (of): *The river overflowed* (*its banks*) **2** [T1;IØ: (*into*)] to go beyond the limits (of): *The crowd overflowed the theatre into the street* **3** [IØ] to be so full that the contents flow over the edges: *The bath is overflowing; who left the water running?* **4** [IØ (*with*)] to be very full (of): *His heart is overflowing with kindness*

o·ver·flow² /ˈəʊvəfləʊ‖-vər-/ *n* **1** an act of OVERFLOWing **2** that which OVERFLOWs: *Bring a pot to catch the overflow from this pipe.|So many people came that we had to have a special overflow meeting* **3** a pipe or CHANNEL for carrying away water that is more than is needed

o·ver·fly /ˌəʊvəˈflaɪ‖-vər-/ *v* **-flew** /ˈfluː/, **-flown** /ˈfləʊn/ [T1] (of a pilot or aircraft) to fly over (a place), esp. in a group on a ceremonial occasion

o·ver·grown /ˌəʊvəˈgrəʊn◂‖-vər-/ *adj* **1** [B (*with*)] covered (esp. with plants growing uncontrolled) **2** [Wa5;A] that has grown too much or too fast

o·ver·growth /ˈəʊvəgrəʊθ‖-vər-/ *n* **1** [U] growth that is too much or too fast **2** [S (*of*)] that which grows in an uncontrolled way

o·ver·hand /ˈəʊvəhænd‖-vər-/ *adj, adv* OVERARM

o·ver·hang[1] /ˌəʊvəˈhæŋ‖-vər-/ *v* **-hung** /ˈhʌŋ/ **1** [Wv4;T1;I∅] to hang over (something) or stand out over (something): *overhanging cliffs* **2** [T1] (of something bad) to threaten to happen to (someone)

o·ver·hang[2] /ˈəʊvəhæŋ‖-vər-/ *n* that which OVERHANGS: *an overhang of 5 feet* —compare HANGOVER

o·ver·haul[1] /ˌəʊvəˈhɔːl‖-vər-/ *v* [T1] **1** to examine thoroughly and perhaps repair if necessary: *overhaul a car* **2** to come up to from behind and pass (something moving): *The new ship overhauled the old one rapidly*

o·ver·haul[2] /ˈəʊvəhɔːl‖-vər-/ *n* a thorough examination and repair if necessary

o·ver·head[1] /ˌəʊvəˈhed‖-vər-/ *adv, adj* [Wa5] above one's head

o·ver·head[2] /ˈəʊvəhed‖-vər-/ *n* **1** [A] of OVERHEADS: *Overhead costs include lighting and heating* **2** [C] *AmE* OVERHEADS

o·ver·heads /ˈəʊvəhedz‖-vər-/ *n* [P] *esp. BrE* money spent regularly to keep a business running

o·ver·hear /ˌəʊvəˈhɪəʳ‖-vər-/ *v* **-heard** /ˈhɜːd‖ˈhɜrd/ [T1;V2,4] to hear (what others are saying) without their knowledge

o·ver·joyed /ˌəʊvəˈdʒɔɪd‖-vər-/ *adj* [F,F3,5;(B)] very pleased; full of joy

o·ver·kill /ˈəʊvəkɪl‖-vər-/ *n* [U] **1** more than enough weapons (esp. atomic weapons) to kill every man, woman, and child in an enemy country **2** something that causes harm by going beyond the desirable or safe limits

o·ver·land /ˌəʊvəˈlænd◂‖-vər-/ *adv, adj* [Wa5] across or by land and not by sea or air

o·ver·lap[1] /ˌəʊvəˈlæp‖-vər-/ *v* **-pp-** [T1;I∅] to cover (something) partly and go beyond it: *Roofs are made with overlapping flat stonelike squares.*|(fig.) *History and politics overlap and should be studied together*

o·ver·lap[2] /ˈəʊvəlæp‖-vər-/ *n* [C;U] the amount by which 2 or more things OVERLAP[1] each other

o·ver·lay[1] /ˌəʊvəˈleɪ‖-vər-/ *v* **-laid** /ˈleɪd/ [T1 (*with*) *usu. pass.*] to cover usu. thinly

o·ver·lay[2] /ˈəʊvəleɪ‖-vər-/ *n* something laid over something else: (fig.) *He writes stories of deep sadness with an overlay of humour*

o·ver·leaf /ˌəʊvəˈliːf‖ˈəʊvərliːf/ *adv* [Wa5] on the other side of the page

o·ver·leap /ˌəʊvəˈliːp‖-vər-/ *v* **-leapt** /ˈlept/ *or* **-leaped** /ˈlept‖ˈliːpt/ [T1] **1** to jump over **2** OVERREACH

o·ver·load[1] /ˌəʊvəˈləʊd‖-vər-/ *v* **-loaded** *or* **-laden** /ˈleɪdən/ [T1] **1** to load too heavily **2** to cause to produce too much electricity: *Don't overload the electrical system by using too many machines at once*

o·ver·load[2] /ˈəʊvələʊd‖-vər-/ *n* [*usu. sing.*] the fact or amount of OVERLOADING[1] (2)

o·ver·long /ˌəʊvəˈlɒŋ‖-vərˈlɔŋ/ *adv, adj* [Wa5] too long (in space or time)

o·ver·look /ˌəʊvəˈlʊk‖-vər-/ *v* [T1] **1** to have or give a view of (something or someone) from above: *Our room/We overlooked the sea.*|*We're overlooked here* (=the neighbours can see into our house) **2** to look at but not see; not notice; miss **3** to pretend not to see; forgive

o·ver·lord /ˈəʊvəlɔːd‖ˈəʊvərlɔrd/ *n* a person (esp. a lord) in a higher position in relation to people in a lower position

o·ver·ly /ˈəʊvəli‖-vər-/ *adv* [Wa5] **1** too (much): *Food should not be overly cooked* **2** very: *I'm not overly interested in music*

o·ver·man /ˌəʊvəˈmæn‖-vər-/ *v* **-nn-** [T1;I∅] to provide too many workers for (a job, factory, industry, etc.) —**~ning** *n* [U]

o·ver·mas·ter /ˌəʊvəˈmɑːstəʳ‖-vərˈmæstər/ *v* [Wv4;T1] *fml* to conquer (a feeling or a person) by greater power: *an overmastering desire*

o·ver·much /ˌəʊvəˈmʌtʃ◂‖-vər-/ *adv, determiner, pron* **1** too much: *to work overmuch|to do overmuch|overmuch work* **2** [*neg.*] very much: *He doesn't like to work overmuch*

o·ver·night /ˌəʊvəˈnaɪt◂‖-vər-/ *adv, adj* [Wa5] **1** for or during the night: *an overnight journey|an overnight bag* **2** suddenly: *Byron became famous overnight*

o·ver·pass /ˈəʊvəpɑːs‖ˈəʊvərpæs/ *n AmE* FLYOVER

o·ver·pay /ˌəʊvəˈpeɪ‖-vər-/ *v* **-paid** /ˈpeɪd/ [T1 (*for*)] to pay (someone) too much or too highly: *Mozart said that he was overpaid for what he did, but not paid enough for what he could do*

o·ver·play /ˌəʊvəˈpleɪ‖-vər-/ *v* [T1] **1** to make (something) appear larger or more important than it really is **2 overplay one's hand** to promise or try to do more than one really can do

o·ver·pop·u·lat·ed /ˌəʊvəˈpɒpjʊleɪtɪ̣d‖ˌəʊvərˈpɑpjə-/ *adj* having too many people

o·ver·pop·u·la·tion /ˌəʊvəpɒpjʊˈleɪʃən‖ˌəʊvərpɑpjə-/ *n* [U] (the state of having) too many people

o·ver·pow·er /ˌəʊvəˈpaʊəʳ‖-vər-/ *v* [T1] **1** to conquer (someone) by greater power **2** OVERCOME (1,2)

o·ver·pow·er·ing /ˌəʊvəˈpaʊərɪŋ‖-vər-/ *adj* **1** very or too strong: *an overpowering desire* **2** (of a person) having a too forceful character —**~ly** *adv*

o·ver·print /ˌəʊvəˈprɪnt‖-vər-/ *v* [T1;(I∅)] to print more on top of and partly covering (what has already been printed)

o·ver·rate /ˌəʊvəˈreɪt/ *v* [Wv5;T1] to put too great or high a value on (something or somebody)

o·ver·reach /ˌəʊvəˈriːtʃ/ also **overleap**— *v* [T1] to defeat (oneself) by trying to do too much —compare OVERPLAY **one's hand**

o·ver·ride /ˌəʊvəˈraɪd/ *v* **-rode** /ˈrəʊd/ **-ridden** /ˈrɪdn/ [T1] to take no notice of (another person's orders, claims, etc.); do the opposite of (that which another person wants)

o·ver·rid·ing /ˌəʊvəˈraɪdɪŋ◂/ *adj* more important than anything else: *It is of overriding importance to find an answer to this question*

o·ver·rule /ˌəʊvəˈruːl/ *v* [T1] (of someone in a higher position) to decide against (someone in a lower position, or something)

o·ver·run[1] /ˌəʊvəˈrʌn/ *v* **-ran** /ˈræn/, **-run** /ˈrʌn/ [T1] **1** to spread over and usu. harm: *The enemy overran the conquered country* **2** to continue beyond (a time limit or an appointed stopping place)

o·ver·run[2] /ˈəʊvərʌn/ *n* **1** the fact of continuing beyond a time limit **2** [*usu. sing.*] the amount of this: *an overrun of 15 minutes*

o·ver·seas /ˌəʊvəˈsiːz◂‖-vər-/ *adv, adj* [Wa5] to, at, or in somewhere across the sea; foreign: *They've gone to live overseas*

USAGE **Overseas** *students* have come to one's own country from abroad in order to study; the same idea is expressed by *students from* **overseas.** But *students* **overseas** are people studying in other countries.

o·ver·see /ˌəʊvəˈsiː‖-vər-/ *v* **-saw** /ˈsɔː/, **-seen** /ˈsiːn/ [T1;(I∅)] to watch to see that work is properly done: *oversee the work|the workers*

o·ver·seer /ˈəʊvəsɪəʳ‖-vər-/ *n* a person who OVERSEES

o·ver·sell /ˌəʊvəˈsel‖-vər-/ *v* **-sold** /ˈsəʊld/ [T1] *infml* to praise too much

o·ver·sexed /ˌəʊvəˈsekst‖-vər-/ *adj* having too much sexual desire —compare UNDERSEXED

o·ver·shad·ow /ˌəʊvəˈʃædəʊ‖-vər-/ *v* [T1] **1** to

throw a shadow over **2** to make appear less important: *Her new book will overshadow all her earlier ones*

o·ver·shoe /ˈəʊvəʃuː‖-vər-/ also **galosh**— *n* a rubber shoe worn over an ordinary shoe when it rains or snows

o·ver·shoot /ˌəʊvəˈʃuːt‖-vər-/ *v* **-shot** /ˈʃɒt‖ˈʃɑt/ [T1;(I∅)] **1** to shoot over or beyond (something aimed at) **2** to go too far or beyond at a fast speed and miss **3 overshoot the mark** to do or say more than what is considered right

o·ver·side /ˌəʊvəˈsaɪd◂‖-vər-/ *adv* [Wa5] *AmE* over the side (esp. of a ship which is not at a landing place)

o·ver·sight /ˈəʊvəsaɪt‖-vər-/ *n* **1** [C;U] (an) unintended failure to notice or do something: *I didn't mean to do it; the mistake was the result of (an) oversight* **2** [S;U] *fml* general and careful watchfulness; SUPERVISION

o·ver·sim·pli·fy /ˌəʊvəˈsɪmplɪ̵faɪ‖-vər-/ *v* [Wv5; T1;I∅] to express (something) so simply that the true meaning is changed or lost —**-fication** /ˌəʊvəˌsɪmplɪ̵fɪ̵ˈkeɪʃən‖-vər-/ *n* [C;(U)]

o·ver·sleep /ˌəʊvəˈsliːp‖-vər-/ *v* **-slept** /ˈslept/ [I∅] to sleep too long or too late

o·ver·spill /ˈəʊvəˌspɪl‖-vər-/ *n* [*usu. sing.*] *esp. BrE* people who leave a city because too many people live there, and settle on the edges or beyond: *A new town was built for London's overspill.|overspill towns*

o·ver·state /ˌəʊvəˈsteɪt‖-vər-/ *v* [T1] to state too strongly, making things appear better, worse, or more important than they really are (esp. in the phrs. **overstate one's case**)

o·ver·state·ment /ˌəʊvəˈsteɪtmənt‖-vər-/ *n* **1** [U] overstating (OVERSTATE) **2** [C] something OVERSTATED

o·ver·stay /ˌəʊvəˈsteɪ‖-vər-/ *v* [T1] **1** to stay beyond the end of (a certain period of time) **2 overstay one's welcome** to stay too long as a guest

o·ver·steer /ˌəʊvəˈstɪəʳ‖-vər-/ *v* [I∅] (of a car or other vehicle) to tend to turn too sharply when one turns the STEERING WHEEL

o·ver·step /ˌəʊvəˈstep‖-vər-/ *v* **-pp-** [T1] to go beyond (a limit of what is wise or proper) (often in the phr. **overstep the mark**)

o·ver·stock /ˌəʊvəˈstɒk‖ˌəʊvərˈstɑk/ *v* [T1;I∅: (*with*)] to keep more than enough in (a place): *We overstocked (the shop) with copies of a book that nobody wanted*

o·ver·strung /ˌəʊvəˈstrʌŋ‖-vər-/ *adj* too sensitive and nervous

o·ver·stuffed /ˌəʊvəˈstʌft‖-vər-/ *adj* (of furniture for sitting on) **1** filled with too much soft thick material for comfort **2** [Wa5] *tech* well filled round the frame with soft material to provide a deep and comfortable seat

o·ver·sub·scribed /ˌəʊvəsəbˈskraɪbd‖-vər-/ *adj* (esp. of new business SHARE*s*) with more wanted than are on sale: *This play is very popular; seats in the theatre are oversubscribed*

o·vert /ˈəʊvɜːt, əʊˈvɜːt‖-ɜrt/ *adj fml* public; not secret —**~ly** *adv*

o·ver·take /ˌəʊvəˈteɪk‖-vər-/ *v* **-took** /ˈtʊk/, **-taken** /ˈteɪkən/ **1** [T1;I∅] to come up level with from behind (and usu. pass): *A car overtook me although I was going very fast* **2** [T1] (of something unpleasant) to reach suddenly and unexpectedly: *We have been overtaken by events* (=new (and unpleasant) events have happened that have destroyed our plans)

o·ver·tax /ˌəʊvəˈtæks‖-vər-/ *v* [T1] **1** to put too great a tax on **2** to demand too great a tax from **3** to force beyond a limit: *Don't overtax your strength/yourself!*

o·ver·throw[1] /ˌəʊvəˈθrəʊ‖-vər-/ *v* **-threw** /ˈθruː/, **-thrown** /ˈθrəʊn/ [T1] to defeat; remove from official power: *to overthrow the government*

o·ver·throw[2] /ˈəʊvəθrəʊ‖-vər-/ *n* **1** [(*the*) *usu. sing.*] defeat; removal from official power **2** (in cricket) a run made after a fielder has thrown the ball accidentally past the WICKET

o·ver·time /ˈəʊvətaɪm‖-vər-/ *n, adv* [U] **1** (time) beyond the usual time, esp. working time: *They're working overtime to finish the job.|He's late because he's on overtime tonight* **2** payment for working beyond the usual time **3 work overtime to do something** *infml* to use much effort to do something

o·ver·tone /ˈəʊvətəʊn‖-vər-/ *n tech* **1** a musical note higher than a main note and sounding together with it to produce the effect of a single note **2** a colour that you think you can see when looking at another colour

o·ver·tones /ˈəʊvətəʊnz‖-vər-/ *n* [P (*of*)] things that are suggested but not shown or stated clearly: *His words were polite, but there were overtones of anger in his voice*

o·ver·top /ˌəʊvəˈtɒp‖ˌəʊvərˈtɑp/ *v* **-pp-** [T1] **1** to be higher than **2** *fml* to be better or more successful than

o·ver·trump /ˌəʊvəˈtrʌmp‖-vər-/ *v* [T1;I∅] (in some games of cards) to play a higher TRUMP than

o·ver·ture /ˈəʊvətjʊəʳ, -tʃʊəʳ, -tʃəʳ‖-vər-/ *n* **1** a musical introduction to a large musical piece, esp. an OPERA: *the overture to Mozart's "Don Giovanni"* **2** a shortish musical piece meant to be played by itself esp. at the beginning of a concert: *Elgar's concert overture "In the South"*

o·ver·tures /ˈəʊvətjʊəz, -tʃʊəz, -tʃəz‖ˈəʊvərtjʊərz, -tʃʊərz, -tʃərz/ *n* [P] an offer to begin to deal with someone in the hope of reaching an agreement or becoming friendly

o·ver·turn /ˌəʊvəˈtɜːn‖ˌəʊvərˈtɜrn/ *v* **1** [T1;I∅] to (cause to) turn over: *They overturned the boat/the lamp.|The boat/The lamp overturned* **2** [T1] to bring (esp. a government) to an end suddenly

o·ver·ween·ing /ˌəʊvəˈwiːnɪŋ‖-vər-/ *adj fml & derog* (of people who are) too proud and too sure of themselves: *overweening pride* —**~ly** *adv*

o·ver·weight[1] /ˈəʊvəweɪt‖-vər-/ *n* [U] too great weight: *Overweight* (=being too fat) *is bad for health.|I asked for 3 kilos of apples and got 4; they gave me overweight*

o·ver·weight[2] /ˌəʊvəˈweɪt‖-vər-/ *v* [T1] **1** [Wv5] to put too much weight esp. on one side of (something), so as to make proper balance difficult **2** [*usu. pass.*] to cause (a statement, argument, plan, etc.) to favour one side or course of action unfairly

o·ver·weight[3] /ˌəʊvəˈweɪt◂‖-vər-/ *adj* [B;E] weighing too much: *This parcel/person is overweight by 2 kilos/is 2 kilos overweight.|an overweight person* —compare UNDERWEIGHT

o·ver·whelm /ˌəʊvəˈwelm‖-vər-/ *v* [T1] **1** (of water) to cover completely and usu. suddenly **2** to defeat or make powerless (usu. a group of people) by much greater force of numbers **3** (of feelings) to OVERCOME (2) completely and usu. suddenly

o·ver·whelm·ing /ˌəʊvəˈwelmɪŋ‖-vər-/ *adj* **1** very large or great; too large or great to oppose **2 overwhelming majority** by far the greater number —**~ly** *adv*

o·ver·work[1] /ˌəʊvəˈwɜːk‖ˌəʊvərˈwɜrk/ *v* **1** [T1; I∅] to (cause to) work too much **2** [Wv5;T1] to use (a word, expression, etc.) too much

overwork[2] *n* [U] too much work; working too hard

o·ver·wrought /ˌəʊvəˈrɔːt◂/ *adj* too nervous and excited

o·vi·duct /ˈəʊvɪ̵dʌkt/ *n tech* **1** also **Fallopian tube**—(in MAMMAL*s*) either one of the 2 tubes through which eggs pass into the WOMB (=the place in the body where they can develop until ready for birth) **2** (in birds) the tube through which eggs pass to be laid

o·vip·a·rous /əʊˈvɪpərəs/ *adj* [Wa5] *tech* egg-laying

o·void /ˈəʊvɔɪd/ *adj, n fml or tech* (an object that is) egg-shaped

ov·u·late /ˈɒvjʊleɪt‖ˈɑvjə-/ *v* [IØ] to produce eggs from the OVARY

o·vum /ˈəʊvəm/ *n* **ova** /ˈəʊvə/ *tech* an egg, esp. an egg that develops inside the mother's body until ready for birth

ow /aʊ/ *interj* (a sound used for expressing sudden slight pain)

owe /əʊ/ *v* **1** [D1 (*to*);T1: (*for*)] to have to pay: *He owes* (*me*) (*£20*) (*for my work*) **2** [T1 (*to*); (D1)] to have to give: *We owe loyalty to our country* **3** [D1 (*to*)] to feel grateful (to) (for): *We owe our parents a lot*

owe to *v prep* [D1] to admit as the cause, discoverer, or point of origin of: *She owes her wealth to hard work and good luck*

ow·ing /ˈəʊɪŋ/ *adj* [Wa5;F] still to be paid: *How much is owing to you?|There is still £5 owing*

owing to /ˈ·· ·/ *prep* because of: *We were late, owing to the snow* —see DUE TO (USAGE)

owl /aʊl/ *n* any of several types of night bird with large eyes, supposed to be very wise —see picture at PREY[1]

owl·et /ˈaʊlɪ̈t/ *n* a young OWL

owl·ish /ˈaʊlɪʃ/ *adj* (of a person) having a round face and large eyes, usu. with glasses —**~ly** *adv*

own[1] /əʊn/ *determiner, pron* **1** (adding force to the idea of possession) that belongs to (oneself) and to nobody else; that is (one's): *I only borrowed it; it's not my own.|They treated the child as if she were their own.|The country has its own oil and doesn't need to buy any from abroad.|Get on with your own job and let me get on with mine!|"Your life is your own affair".* (SEU W.)|*She would rather have a room of her* (*very*) *own than sleep with her sister.|"The 5 children . . . grew up and had families of their own"* (SEU S.) **2 come into one's own** to begin to be properly respected for one's qualities **3 for one's very own** (of something given, esp. to a child) to have for oneself; not to be shared **4 have/get one's own back (on someone)** to succeed in doing harm (to someone) in return for harm done to oneself **5 hold one's own (against)** to avoid defeat (by) **6 on one's own a** alone **b** without help: *I can't carry it on my own; it's too heavy*

own[2] *v* **1** [T1] to possess (something), esp. by lawful right: *Who owns this house/this dog?* **2** [T5a,(1)] to admit: *He owns he was wrong* **3** [X1,7] to describe (esp. oneself) as: *He owned himself defeated*

own·er /ˈəʊnəʳ/ *n* a person who owns something, esp. one who possesses something by lawful right

owner-driv·er /ˌ·· ˈ··/ *n esp. BrE* a person who drives a car which he owns

owner-oc·cu·pi·er /ˌ·· ˈ····/ *n esp. BrE* a person who owns the house or flat in which he lives —compare TENANT —**-pied** /ˌ·· ˈ···/ *adj* [Wa5]: *owner-occupied flats*

own·er·ship /ˈəʊnəʃɪp‖-nər-/ *n* [U] the owning of something, esp. by lawful right

own to *v prep* [T1,4] *fml* to admit: *I must own to a feeling of anxiety.|I must own to feeling rather anxious*

own up *v adv* [IØ (*to*)] to admit a fault or crime: *If no one will own up* (*to this misbehaviour/to misbehaving*)*, all pupils will be kept in after school*

ox /ɒks‖ɑks/ *n* **ox·en** /ˈɒksən‖ˈɑk-/ **1** a male cow which has been made unable to breed, used for pulling vehicles and for heavy work on farms **2** any of several kinds of large animal of the cattle type, wild or used by man

Ox·bridge /ˈɒksˌbrɪdʒ‖ˈɑks-/ *n* [R] the universities of Oxford and/or Cambridge rather than the other, esp. the newer, British universities —compare REDBRICK

ox·cart /ˈɒkskɑːt‖ˈɑkskɑrt/ *n* a cart pulled by one or more oxen

ox·eye /ˈɒksaɪ‖ˈɑk-/ *n* any of several kinds of flower

Ox·ford Group /ˈɒksfəd gruːp‖ˈɑksfərd-/ also **Moral Re-Armament**— *n* [*the*+R] a religious movement started by Frank Buchman, in favour of publicly admitting moral faults, whose members are often active in political and social fields

Oxford move·ment /ˈ·· ˌ··/ *n* [*the*+R] (*often cap.* M) a 19th-century English religious movement in favour of drawing together the CHURCH OF ENGLAND and the ROMAN CATHOLIC church

ox·ide /ˈɒksaɪd‖ˈɑk-/ *n* [C;U] a chemical substance in which something else is combined with oxygen: *iron oxide*

ox·i·dize, -dise /ˈɒksɪ̈daɪz‖ˈɑk-/ *v* [T1;IØ] to (cause to) combine with oxygen, so as to produce a new chemical substance, esp. in such a way as to make or become RUSTY —**-dization** /ˌɒksɪ̈daɪˈzeɪʃən‖-də-/ *n* [U]

Ox·on /ˈɒksɒn‖ˈɑksɑn/ *abbrev.* (used esp. after the title of a degree) of Oxford University: *David Trustram,* B.A. *Oxon*

Ox·o·ni·an /ɒkˈsəʊnɪən‖ɑk-/ *n, adj* [Wa5] *fml* (of) a past or present member (student or teacher) of Oxford University

ox·tail /ˈɒksteɪl‖ˈɑks-/ *n* [U;(C)] the tail of an ox, esp. when used as food: *oxtail soup*

ox·y·a·cet·y·lene /ˌɒksɪəˈsetɪ̈liːn‖ˌɑk-/ *n* [U] *tech* a mixture of oxygen and another gas (ACETYLENE) which produces a very hot white flame when burning

ox·y·gen /ˈɒksɪdʒən‖ˈɑk-/ *n* [U] a gas present in the air, without colour, taste, or smell, but necessary for all forms of life on earth

ox·y·gen·ate /ˈɒksɪdʒəneɪt, ɒkˈsɪ-‖ˈɑksɪ-, ɑkˈsɪ-/ also **ox·y·gen·ize, -ise** /ɒkˈsɪdʒənaɪz, ˈɒksɪ-‖ɑkˈsɪ-, ˈɑksɪ-/— *v* [T1] to add oxygen to, without producing a new chemical substance

oxygen mask /ˈ··· ·/ *n* an apparatus placed over the nose and mouth to supply oxygen, esp. to people who are ill or are in aircraft flying very high

oxygen tent /ˈ··· ·/ *n* a tentlike apparatus within which oxygen can be supplied to people who are ill

o·yez /əʊˈjez‖ˈəʊjez/ *interj* (a word used in some law courts at the beginning of business, and, esp. in former times, by official people (TOWN CRIER*s*) giving news in the streets, for the purpose of getting people's attention, meaning) listen!

oy·ster /ˈɔɪstəʳ/ *n* **1** a type of flat shellfish, eaten cooked or raw, which can produce a jewel called a PEARL —see picture at MOLLUSC **2 the world is one's/someone's oyster** there are no limits on where one/someone can go, what one/someone can do, etc.

oyster bar /ˈ·· ·/ *n* an eating place where OYSTER*s* are served raw

oyster bed /ˈ·· ·/ also **oyster bank**— *n* an area at the bottom of the sea where there are large numbers of OYSTER*s*, esp. where they are bred and kept to be caught and eaten

oy·ster·catch·er /ˈɔɪstəˌkætʃəʳ‖-ər-/ *n* a type of seabird that WADE*s* (=walks in water that is not too deep) and catches and eats shellfish

oz *written abbrev. for:* OUNCE[1]

o·zone /ˈəʊzəʊn/ *n* [U] **1** *infml* air that is pleasant to breathe, esp. near the sea or running water **2** *tech* a type of oxygen

P, p

P, p /piː/ **P's, p's** *or* **Ps, ps** **1** the 16th letter of the English alphabet **2 mind one's p's and q's** to be careful in what one says so as to avoid displeasing others

p[1] *abbrev for*: (*BrE infml*) (new) penny/pence: *This newspaper costs 8p* —see PENNY (1) (USAGE)

p[2] *written abbrev for*: **1** page —see also PP (2) **2** participle **3** population **4** PIANO[1] —see also PP (1)

P *abbrev for*: PARKING

pa /pɑː/ *n* [N] *infml & becoming rare* a name for father

PA /ˌpiː ˈeɪ/ *n* **1** PERSONAL ASSISTANT: *She's his PA* **2** PUBLIC-ADDRESS SYSTEM: *loud and clear over the PA*

pab·u·lum /ˈpæbjʊləm‖-bjə-/ *n* [U] **1** *rare* food **2** *fml* food for thought; something to think about or to consider (esp. in the phr. **mental pabulum**)

pace[1] /peɪs/ *n* **1** [S] rate or speed in walking, marching, or running, or of development, advance of a plan, etc.: *The old man can walk only at a very slow pace.|The plans are being prepared at quite a good pace* **2** [C] a single step in running or walking, or the distance moved in one such step: *If you advance one pace, I will shoot you.|The fence is 10 paces from the house* **3** [C *usu. sing.*] (esp. of a horse) manner or pattern of walking or running: *The natural paces of the horse include the walk, the* TROT, *and the* GALLOP **4 go the pace** *infml & becoming rare* **a** to move at a fast speed **b** to spend money wildly, esp. on foolish, wasteful, or harmful things **5 keep pace with** to go forward at the same rate as: *This horse is too weak to keep pace with the others.|You're thinking much too fast for me; I can't keep pace with you* **6 put somebody through his paces** to make somebody do something in order to show his abilities, qualities, etc.: *The director of the film spent the morning in putting the new actor through his paces* **7 set the pace** to fix the speed for others to copy: *If we let the fastest runner set the pace the others will be left behind* **8 show one's paces** to show one's abilities, qualities, etc.

pace[2] /peɪs/ *v* **1** [L9] to walk with slow, regular, steady steps, esp. backwards and forwards: *The people waiting for the train paced up and down, trying to keep warm* **2** [T1] to move across or from one side of (a room, space, etc.) to the other and back again: *The lion paced the floor of his cage* **3** [T1 (OFF, OUT)] to measure by taking steps of an equal and known length: *I think the hall is 80 metres long: I'll pace it* **4** [T1] to set the speed or rate of movement for: *Driving slowly in a car, Jones paced the runners at 15 miles an hour*

pa·ce[3] /ˈpeɪsiː, ˈpɑːkeɪ/ *prep Lat* giving proper respect to, but in a polite way disagreeing with (somebody)

pace bowl·er /ˈ· ˌ··/ also **pace man** /ˈ· ·/— *n* (in cricket) a person who throws (BOWL*s*) the ball at a high speed

pace·mak·er /ˈpeɪsˌmeɪkəʳ/ *n* **1 a** a person or animal that sets a speed that others in a race try to keep up with **b** a person who sets an example for others **2** a machine used to make weak or irregular heartbeats regular

pace·set·ter /ˈpeɪsˌsetəʳ/ *n esp. AmE* PACEMAKER (1)

pach·y·derm /ˈpækɪdɜːm‖-ɜrm/ *n tech* any of several types of thick-skinned animal, such as the elephant and the RHINOCEROS

pa·cif·ic /pəˈsɪfɪk/ *adj fml* **1** helping to cause peace **2** having or showing calmness; peace-loving —**~ally** *adv* [Wa4]

pac·i·fi·er /ˈpæsəfaɪəʳ/ *n* **1** a person who pacifies (PACIFY) **2** *AmE* DUMMY (3)

pac·i·fis·m /ˈpæsəfɪzəm/ *n* [U] the belief that all wars are wrong

pac·i·fist /ˈpæsəfəst/ *n* an active believer in PACIFISM; person who refuses to fight in a war because of such a belief

pac·i·fy /ˈpæsəfaɪ/ *v* [T1] **1** to make calm, quiet, and satisfied: *Try to pacify the baby; he's been crying for hours* **2** to bring a state of peace to; end war in (a country, area, etc.) —**-fication** /ˌpæsəfəˈkeɪʃən/ *n* [U]

pack[1] /pæk/ *n* **1** [C] a number of things wrapped or tied together, or put in a case, esp. for carrying on the back by a person or animal: *The climber carried some food in a pack on his back* **2** [C] **a** a group of wild animals (esp. the WOLF) that hunt together, or a group of dogs trained together for hunting: *Foxes hunt alone, never in packs* **b** a group of fighting machines that fight together as one force, esp. used of SUBMARINE*s* and aircraft **c** (in RUGBY football) the group of players (FORWARD*s*[3]) whose job is to get possession of the ball for their side: *The pack played well* **d** a group of CUB*s* of the BOY SCOUT*s* or BROWNIE*s* of the GIRL GUIDE*s* **3** [C9, esp. *of*] *derog* a collection, group, etc. (esp. in the phrs. **pack of thieves, pack of lies**) **4** [C] a complete set of cards used in playing a game **5** [C] *AmE* a packet: *a pack of cigarettes* **6** [C] a wet cloth, sometimes containing ice or medicine, used in treating wounds or body conditions; COMPRESS **7** [C] a paste of various materials used on the face (esp. by a woman) as a beauty treatment **8** [U;C] PACK ICE **9 "No names, no pack drill"** *BrE infml* "If I tell you no names, then there will be no blame or punishment"

pack[2] *v* **1** [Wv5;D1 (*for*);T1;I∅] to put (things, esp. one's belongings) into (cases, boxes, etc.) for travelling or storing: *a packed meal|She packed her husband some bread and cheese for his dinner.|We leave tomorrow but I haven't begun to pack yet!* **2** [Wv5;X9;L9: esp. DOWN, IN, TOGETHER] to fit, crush, push (people, things) into a space: *If you pack those things down we can get a little more in the box.|The moment the door was opened, people began to pack into the hall* **3** [X9;I∅] to settle or be driven closely together or into a mass: *The wind packed the snow against the side of the house* **4** [L9] to be suitable for fitting easily into cases, boxes, etc. **5** [T1] to prepare and put (food) into tins or other containers for preserving or selling in shops **6** [T1] to cover, fill, or surround closely with a protective material: *Pack some paper round the dishes in the box so that they will not break* **7** [T1] *derog* to choose members of (a committee or a JURY) favourable to one's own purpose or ideas **8** [T1] *AmE infml* to carry regularly: *to pack a gun* **9 pack a (hard) punch** *infml* **a** (of a fighter or somebody fighting) to be able to give a strong hard blow **b** to use very forceful direct language, as in argument **10 send somebody packing** *infml* to cause somebody undesirable to leave quickly

pack·age[1] /ˈpækɪdʒ/ *n* **1** an amount or a number of things packed together: *He carried a large package of books under his arm* **2** the container of these things: *The package got torn on the way to the station*

package² *v* [T1] **1** [(UP)] to make into or tie up as a PACKAGE: *She packaged up the old clothes and put them in the cupboard* **2** [Wv5] to place (food) in a special PACKAGE before selling to the public

package deal /ˈ·· ·/ also **package of·fer** /ˈ·· ˌ··/— *n infml* an offer or agreement that includes a number of things all of which must be accepted together

package tour /ˈ·· ·/ *n* a completely planned holiday at a fixed price arranged by a company, so that one does not have to buy tickets, find hotels, etc., for oneself

pack an·i·mal /ˈ· ˌ···/ *n* an animal, such as a horse (**packhorse**), used for carrying parcels (PACK*s*[1] (1))

packed /pækt/ *adj* (of a room, building, etc.) full of people; CROWDED

packed-out /ˌ· ˈ·◂/ *adj* [F] *infml, esp. BrE* (of a room, building, etc.) completely full of people

pack·er /ˈpækəʳ/ *n* a person or thing that PACK*s*[2] (1,2), such as **a** a person who works where food is prepared and put into tins, etc., for preserving **b** a person employed to tie up or put in boxes the furniture, clothing, etc., of people moving from one house or city to another

pack·et /ˈpækɨ̣t/ *n* **1** a small PACKAGE; a number of small things tied or put together into a small box, case, or bag: *She bought a packet of envelopes at the shop* **2** also **packet boat** /ˈ·· ˌ·/— a boat that carries mail, and usu. people also, at regular times between 2 or more places **3** *sl* a large amount of money, esp. won or lost in a game of chance or in an act of buying or selling: *That car cost me a pretty packet* (= quite a large sum of money) **4 catch/cop/get/stop a packet** *BrE sl* **a** to get into serious trouble **b** to be hurt badly **c** to receive a heavy blow or punishment

pack ice /ˈ· ·/ *n* [(*the*) U] a large mass of ice floating on the sea, formed from broken pieces that have been crushed together into a whole

pack in *v adv* [T1] *infml* **1** to attract in large numbers: *The new music group is packing the crowds in* **2 pack it in** to cease an activity: *I'm tired of this game, let's pack it in*

pack·ing /ˈpækɪŋ/ *n* [U] material used in PACKing[2] (6)

packing case /ˈ·· ·/ *n* a large strong roughly made wooden box in which heavy articles are packed to be stored or sent elsewhere

pack off *v adv* [T1 (*to*)] *infml* BUNDLE OFF: *She packed her son off to school and then went out herself*

pack·sad·dle /ˈpækˌsædl/ *n* a supporting frame (usu. of leather) on the back of a horse, donkey, etc., used for carrying a load of goods

pack up *v adv* [IØ] **1** *infml* to finish work **2** *infml esp. BrE* (of a machine) to stop working **3** *sl* (esp. in giving or reporting an order) SHUT UP

pact /pækt/ *n* a solemn agreement: *There is some hope that a peace pact will soon be signed between the 2 nations*

pad¹ /pæd/ *n* **1** anything made or filled with a soft material used to protect something or make it more comfortable, or to fill out a shape: *A* BATSMAN *at cricket always wears pads on his legs to protect them when they are hit by the ball.|Put a clean pad of cotton over the wound* —see picture at CRICKET[2] **2** also **inkpad, inking pad**— a piece of material which is made thoroughly wet with ink, so that pieces of wood, rubber, etc., on which words or patterns are cut (STAMP*s*) can be pressed on to it and then pressed on to paper to print the word or pattern **3** a number of sheets of paper fastened together along one edge, used for writing letters, drawing pictures, etc.: *a writing pad* **4 a** the usu. thick-skinned fleshy underpart of the foot of some 4-footed animals **b** the mark of such an animal's foot in the ground **5** *tech* the large floating leaf of certain plants which grow in water, such as the WATER LILY **6** LAUNCHING PAD **7** *sl* the room, house, etc., where one lives: *My pad is on the other side of town*

pad² *v* **-dd-** [T1] **1** [Wv5] to protect, shape, or make more comfortable by covering or filling with soft material **2** [(OUT)] to make (a sentence, speech, story, etc.) longer by adding unnecessary words or sentences

pad³ *v* **-dd-** [L9, esp. ALONG, *along*] to walk steadily and usu. softly, with the foot flat on the ground: *John rode his bicycle slowly, and his dog padded along beside him*

pad·ded cell /ˌ·· ˈ·/ *n* a small room with PADded[2] (1) walls where certain kinds of mad people are kept who might hurt themselves on hard walls

pad·ding /ˈpædɪŋ/ *n* [U] **1** the act of PADding[2] **2** soft material used to PAD[2] (1) something **3** unnecessary words or sentences used to PAD[2] (2) a sentence, speech, etc.

pad·dle¹ /ˈpædl/ *n* **1** [C] a short pole with a wide flat blade at one end or (if a **double paddle**) at both ends, used for pushing and guiding a small boat (esp. a CANOE) in water. It is used freely and not held in position on the side of the boat —compare OAR; —see CANOE (USAGE) and picture at BOAT[1] **2** [S] an act or period of pushing a small boat through water with or as if with this **3** [C] anything shaped like this, such as **a** a tool like a flat spoon, used for mixing food **b** the foot of a duck **c** the object used for hitting the ball as in TABLE TENNIS

paddle² *v* [Wv3] **1** [T1;IØ] to move (a small light boat, esp. a CANOE) through water, using one or more PADDLE*s* (1); row gently **2** [IØ] to move about in water as a dog or duck does, not as in proper swimming **3** [T1] *infml* to strike with the open hand in punishing **4 paddle one's own canoe** *infml* to depend on oneself and no one else; act or speak for oneself

paddle³ *v* [Wv3;IØ] **1** *esp. BrE* to walk about in water only a few inches deep —compare WADE **2** to move the hands or feet in water: *She lay at the side of the pool and paddled in the water with her fingers*

paddle steam·er /ˈ·· ˌ··/ *n* [C;*by* +U] a steamship which is pushed forward by a pair of PADDLE WHEEL*s*

paddle wheel /ˈ·· ·/ *n* either of a pair of large wheels fixed to the sides or back of a ship, and turned by a steam-engine to make the ship move forward through the water

paddling pool /ˈ·· ·/ (*AmE* **wading pool**)— *n* a small stretch of water (as in a public garden) only a few inches deep, where children PADDLE[3] (1)

pad·dock /ˈpædək/ *n* **1** a small, usu. enclosed, field of grass, near a house or STABLE*s* where horses are kept or exercised **2** an enclosed, usu. grassy, space at a place where horses run races, where the horses are brought together before a race so that people may see them **3** *AustrE* an enclosed field

pad·dy¹ /ˈpædi/ also **rice paddy, paddy field** /ˈ·· ·/— *n* a field where rice is grown in water

paddy² *n* [S] *BrE infml* a state of or show of bad temper; great anger

Paddy *n* [C;N;(R)] *infml & usu. humor* an Irishman

paddy wag·on /ˈ·· ˌ··/ *n AmE sl* BLACK MARIA

pad·lock¹ /ˈpædlɒk‖-lɑk/ *n* a lock that can be put on and taken away, having a movable metal ring that can be passed through a U-shaped metal bar and fixed by a key in the lock

padlock² *v* [T1;IØ] **1** to fasten or lock by means of a PADLOCK **2** [(TOGETHER)] to join or lock together by means of a PADLOCK

pa·dre /'pɑːdri, -reɪ/ *n* [C;N] *infml* (*often cap.*) **1** a priest in the Armed Forces; CHAPLAIN **2** any Christian priest, esp. when spoken to

pae·an /'piːən/ *n lit* a joyous song of praise, of giving thanks, or of victory

paed·e·rast /'pedəræst/ *n* PEDERAST

paed·e·ras·ty /'pedəræsti/ *n* [U] PEDERASTY

pae·di·a·tri·cian /ˌpiːdɪə'trɪʃən/ *n* PEDIATRICIAN

pae·di·at·rics /ˌpiːdi'ætrɪks/ *n* [U] PEDIATRICS

pa·el·la /paɪ'elə‖pɑ- (*Sp* pa'eʎa)/ *n* [U] rice cooked with pieces of meat, fish, and vegetables in, esp. in Spain

pae·o·ny /'piːəni/ *n* PEONY

pa·gan¹ /'peɪgən/ *n* **1** a person who is not a believer **a** in any of the chief religions of the world **b** *old use* in Christianity **2** (used esp. of the ancient Greeks and Romans) a person who believes in many gods

pagan² *adj* of or connected with PAGAN*s* or PAGANISM

pa·gan·is·m /'peɪgənɪzəm/ *n* [U] **1** the state of being a PAGAN **2** the beliefs and practices of a PAGAN

page¹ /peɪdʒ/ *n* **1** also **page boy** /'· ·/— **a** a boy servant in a hotel, club, firm, etc., usu. uniformed **b** (at a wedding) a boy attendant on the BRIDE (woman getting married) **2** *old use* a boy of noble birth who was in training to be a KNIGHT (noble soldier) **3 a** *now rare* a boy in service to a person of high rank **b** the title of various officers at a palace: *page of honour*

page² *v* [T1] (in a hotel, club, etc.) to call aloud for (someone who is wanted for some reason)

page³ *n* **1 a** one side of a sheet of paper in a book, newspaper, etc., usu. numbered: *There is a picture of a ship on page 44* **b** the whole sheet (both sides): *Someone has torn a page out of this book* **2** *lit* something which might be written about in a book, etc., such as an important event or period: *These years will be remembered as some of the finest pages in our country's history*

page⁴ *v* [T1] to number the pages of (a book, newspaper, etc.)

pag·eant /'pædʒənt/ *n* **1** [C] **a** a splendid usu. public show or ceremony, esp. one in which there is a procession of people in rich dress **b** a steady continuous movement of things developing or passing by as if in a procession: *the pageant of history* **2** [C] a kind of play or show, usu. out of doors, in which scenes from the history of a town are acted **3** [U] also **pageantry**— splendid show that looks grand but has no meaning or shows no real power

pag·eant·ry /'pædʒəntri/ *n* [U] **1** splendid show of ceremonial grandness with people in fine dress **2** PAGEANT (3)

pag·i·na·tion /ˌpædʒə̀'neɪʃən/ *n* **1** [U] the act of numbering the pages of a book; the state of being PAGEd⁴ **2** [U;S] the arrangement of pages in a book **3** [U;S] numbers or other signs used in paging (PAGE⁴) a book

pa·go·da /pə'gəʊdə/ *n* a temple (esp. Buddhist or Hindu) built on several floors or levels, often with an ornamental roof at each level

paid /peɪd/ *past t. and p. of* PAY

paid-up /ˌ· '·◂/ *adj* having paid in full (esp. so as to continue being a member)

pail /peɪl/ *n* **1** a usu. round open vessel of metal or wood, with handles, used for carrying liquids; bucket: *a pail for milk* **2** also **pail·ful** /'peɪlfʊl/— the amount (of liquid) a pail will hold: *a pailful of milk*

pail·lasse /pæliæs‖ˌpæli'æs/ *n* PALLIASSE

pain¹ /peɪn/ *n* **1** [U] suffering; great discomfort of the body or mind: *The boy was in pain/crying with pain after he broke his arm.|His unkind behaviour caused his parents a great deal of pain* **2** [C] a feeling of suffering or discomfort in a particular part of the body —compare ACHE **3** [S;(C)] also **pain in the neck** /ˌ· · · '·/— *sl* **a** a feeling of annoyance or displeasure: *You give me a pain!* **b** a person, thing, or happening that makes one angry and tired, but is difficult to avoid; NUISANCE: *She's a real pain* **4 on/under pain of** *fml* at the risk of suffering (some punishment) if something is not done —see also PAINS

pain² *v* [T1] **1** [*no pass.*] (of a part of the body) to cause pain to; hurt **2** to cause to feel pain in the mind; hurt: *It pains me to have to disobey you, but I must*

pained /peɪnd/ *adj* **1** [F] displeased **2** [F (*at*)] hurt in one's feelings; offended: *She was pained when you refused her invitation* **3** [B] showing that one is displeased or hurt in one's feelings: *After they had quarrelled there was a pained silence between them*

pain·ful /'peɪnfəl/ *adj* [B, B3] causing pain: *He had a painful cut on his thumb.|He speaks with painful slowness* —**~ly** *adv*: *It is painfully clear that Tom has no chance of passing his examination* —**~ness** *n* [U]

pain·kill·er /'peɪnˌkɪlə'/ *n* a medicine which lessens or destroys pain

pain·less /'peɪnləs/ *adj* **1** causing no bodily pain **2** *infml* needing no effort or hard work: *This is quite a painless way of learning a foreign language* —**~ly** *adv*

pains /peɪnz/ *n* [P] **1** also **labour pains**— the sufferings and effort of giving birth to a child **2** trouble; effort: *He has tried very hard, so we must give him something for his pains* **3 be at pains to do something a** to take great trouble to do something **b** to be particularly anxious and careful to do something: *He was at pains to point out my mistake* **4 go to any/great/any great,** etc. **pains** also **take (any/great/any great,** etc.) **pains**— to make an effort: *Mary took great pains with her English lesson and got high marks*

pains·tak·ing /'peɪnzˌteɪkɪŋ/ *adj* **1** careful and thorough: *painstaking care* **2** hard-working and thorough: *She is not very clever but she is painstaking* —**~ly** *adv*

paint¹ /peɪnt/ *v* **1** [T1;X7,(1);I0] to put paint on (a surface): *He painted the door blue/a bright colour* —see also IN² (4), OUT¹ (6) **2** [T1;I0] to make (a picture or pictures of) (somebody or something) using paint: *Who painted this picture?|He has a splendid strong face and I would very much like to paint him* —see also IN² (4), OUT¹ (6) **3** [Wv5;T1] *often derog* (of a woman) to cover (the lips, face, or cheeks) with special colouring matter, for beauty **4** [T1] to describe in clear well-chosen words, with lifelike effect (often in the phr. **paint a picture**): *His letters paint a wonderful picture of his life in Burma* **5** [T1] to put medicine on (parts of the body, esp. inside the throat) with a brush **6 not as/so black as one is painted** not so bad as people say one is **7 paint in oils/in water colours** to paint pictures or a picture (of somebody or something) using oil paint or WATERCOLOUR paint **8 paint the town red,** *AmE* also **paint the town**— *infml* to have a good time, esp. by visiting PUBLIC HOUSE*s* and drinking alcohol, usu. when celebrating (CELEBRATE) something

paint² *n* [U] **1** liquid colouring matter which can be put or spread on a surface to make it a certain colour: *Where are those tins of green paint?* **2** *often derog* colouring matter used to give colour to the face (used esp. by women) **3 as fresh as paint** *infml* clean and bright (as if just painted) **4 Wet Paint** (a warning sign placed near a part of a building that has just been painted and is not yet dry)

paint·brush /ˈpeɪntbrʌʃ/ *n* a brush for spreading paint on a surface, or for making a picture using PAINTS —see picture at TOOL[1]

paint·er[1] /ˈpeɪntəʳ/ *n* **1** a person whose job is painting houses, rooms, etc. **2** a person who paints pictures; artist: *a* PORTRAIT *painter*

painter[2] *n* **1** *tech* a rope fastened to the front end of a small boat for tying it to a ship, a post on land, etc. **2 cut the painter a** to cut this rope so that the boat floats free without control **b** *becoming rare* to separate oneself on purpose and for ever from one's family, country, etc.

paint·ing /ˈpeɪntɪŋ/ *n* **1** [U] the act or action of painting houses, rooms, etc. **2** [U] the art or practice of painting pictures **3** [C] a picture made in this way

paints /peɪnts/ *n* [P] a usu. complete set of small tubes or cakes of paint of different colours, usu. in a box (**paint box**), as used by an artist: *She bought a new set of oil paints.|I have left my paints at home*

paint·work /ˈpeɪntwɜːk‖-wɜrk/ *n* [U] a painted surface, esp. of a movable object such as a car: *The paintwork was damaged when my car knocked into the gate*

pair[1] /peəʳ/ *n* **pairs** *or* **pair** [Wn2] **1** [C9, esp. *of*] something made up of 2 parts that are alike and which are joined and used together: *a pair of trousers|a pair of scissors* —compare COUPLE[2] **2** [C9, esp. *of*] **a** 2 things that are alike or of the same kind, and are usu. used together: *a pair of shoes|a beautiful pair of legs* —compare COUPLE[2] **b** 2 playing cards of the same value but of different SUITS[1] (3): *a pair of kings* **3** [GC] **a** 2 people closely connected: *a pair of dancers* **b** COUPLE[2] (2) (esp. in the phr. **the happy pair**) **c** *sl* 2 people closely connected who cause annoyance or displeasure: *You're a fine pair coming as late as this!* **4** [GC] 2 animals (male and female) that stay together for a certain length of time or for life **5** [GC] 2 horses fastened side by side to a cart, carriage, etc., to pull it **6** [C] (either of) 2 members of parliament belonging to opposite political parties who agree not to vote on a particular matter **7** [C] also **pair of spec·ta·cles** /ˌ· · ˈ···/— *infml* (in cricket) 2 turns (INNINGS) at striking the ball in one match in which the striker (BATSMAN) fails to make a run (esp. in the phr. **bag/get/make a pair**) **8 I have only one pair of hands** *infml* (*complaint said when one is asked to do too much work*) I can only do as much as my 2 hands will allow me to **9 in pairs** in 2s; 2 by 2: *The children came in in pairs*

USAGE Some words for 2 things joined together, like **trousers** and **scissors**, are used like pl. nouns: *These* **trousers** *are dirty*; but they are not thought of as having a number, so one cannot say *2 **trousers**, **both* **trousers**. *My other|some more|these* **trousers** may mean one garment or more than one, though *all my* **trousers** clearly means more than one. The [C] noun **pair** is often used with these words: *another* **pair** *of* **trousers**|*2 more* **pairs** *of* **trousers**. **Pair** is also used for things like **shoes**, which are not joined together, so that one can say *one* **shoe**, *both* **shoes**, as well as *a* **pair** *of* **shoes**. Any word in this dictionary which is followed by the note "see PAIR (USAGE)" can be used in the expression *a* **pair** *of X*. —compare BRACE, COUPLE

pair[2] *v* [T1;I∅] **1** [(OFF, UP)] to (cause to) form into one or more PAIRS[1] (2,3a,4,5): *The cupboard filled with shoes fell over and it took half an hour to pair them (up) again.|Birds often pair for life* **2** to make, or join with somebody to make a PAIR[1] (3)

pair off *v adv* [T1;I∅] to (cause to) form into pairs, usu. male and female: *Their parents have tried for years to pair the 2 young people off*

pair up *v adv* [T1;I∅: (*with*)] to (cause to) join in pairs for purposes of work or sport

pais·ley /ˈpeɪzli/ *n* [U] (*sometimes cap.*) a soft woollen cloth with curved coloured patterns

pa·ja·ma /pəˈdʒɑːmə‖-ˈdʒɑ-, -ˈdʒæ-/ *n* [A] *esp. AmE* PYJAMA

pa·ja·mas /pəˈdʒɑːməz‖-ˈdʒɑ-, -ˈdʒæ-/ *n* [P] *esp. AmE* PYJAMAS —see PAIR (USAGE)

Pak·i·sta·ni /ˌpækɪˈstɑːni‖-ˈstæni/ *adj* [Wa5] of Pakistan

pal /pæl/ *n infml* (*used esp. by, to, and of males*) **1** [C] a close friend: *an old pal of mine|We've been pals for years!* —see also PAL UP **2** [N] *esp. AmE* (often unfriendly) fellow: *Listen, pal, I don't want you talking to my sister any more, see?*

pal·ace /ˈpælɪ̵s/ *n* **1** [C] a large grand house **a** where a ruling king or queen officially lives **b** *esp. BrE* where an ARCHBISHOP or a BISHOP lives **2** [C] (esp. on the mainland of Europe) a large and splendid house: *The nobles of Florence built splendid palaces.*|(fig.) *His home is a palace compared to our poor little house* —compare STATELY HOME **3** [C] a large, often showy building used for public amusement, dancing, eating, etc.: *Some cinemas used to be called Picture Palaces* —compare PALAIS **4** [*the* +R] the important influential people who live in such a house, esp. the king or queen

palace rev·o·lu·tion /ˌ·· ··ˈ··/ *n* the removal from office of somebody in a position of great power, such as a king or president, usu. by those just beneath him in rank

pal·a·din /ˈpælədɪn/ *n* **1** any of 12 men of high rank holding power under Charlemagne (742–814) **2** *lit* a man who is strongly in favour of something, esp. in politics

pal·ae·o- /ˈpæliəʊ, -liˈɒ-‖ˈpeɪliəʊ, -liˈɑ-/ *comb. form tech* PALEO-

pal·ais /ˈpæleɪ, *infml* ˈpæli‖pæˈleɪ/ also **palais de danse** /ˌpæleɪ də ˈdɑːns‖pæˌleɪ də ˈdæns/— *n* **palais** /ˈpæleɪz‖pæˈleɪz/ *BrE* (*often cap.*) a large hall used usu. for dancing, or for other public amusement —compare PALACE (3)

pal·an·quin, -keen /ˌpælənˈkiːn/ *n* [C; *by*+U] a wheelless boxlike vehicle with a seat or bed inside it for one person, carried on poles, formerly used in India and other countries to the east of India —compare LITTER[1] (4)

pal·a·ta·ble /ˈpælətəbəl/ *adj* **1** pleasant to taste **2** agreeable or acceptable to the mind; pleasant —**-bly** *adv*

pal·a·tal /ˈpælətl/ *n, adj* **1** [A] of the PALATE (1) **2** [C;B] (a consonant) produced by placing the tongue against or near the HARD PALATE

pal·a·tal·ize /ˈpælətəlaɪz/ *v* [Wv5;T1;I∅] to pronounce (a consonant) as or change (a consonant) into a PALATAL (2) —compare NASALIZE, VELARIZE

pal·ate /ˈpælɪ̵t/ *n* **1** [C] the top part (ROOF[1] (6)) of the inside of the mouth —see picture at HUMAN[2] **2** [C;U: (*for*)] a liking (for something) according to **a** one's sense of taste **b** one's feelings for what is beautiful **3** [C *usu. sing.* (*for*)] the ability to judge good food or wine —see also CLEFT PALATE, HARD PALATE, SOFT PALATE

pa·la·tial /pəˈleɪʃəl/ *adj* (usu. of buildings) like a palace; grand and splendid: *a palatial hotel* —**~ly** *adv*

pa·lat·i·nate /pəˈlætɪ̵nɪ̵t/ *n old use* (*often cap.*) an area formerly ruled over by a man of high rank (**Palatine, Count Palatine**) who was the representative of a higher ruler and was given noble titles and rights: *the Rhine Palatinate*

pa·la·ver¹ /pəˈlɑːvəʳ‖-ˈlæ-/ *n* **1** [U] *infml* continuous foolish meaningless talk about unimportant things **2** [U] *infml* talk (believed or not) meant to please people, or that praises too much **3** [U] *infml* BOTHER² (1); FUSS¹ (1) **4** [C] *becoming rare* long talks dealing with a matter of importance, esp. between people of different societies, levels of education, etc.

palaver² *v* [IØ (ON)] *infml* to talk foolishly and continuously about unimportant things

pale¹ /peɪl/ *adj* [Wa1] **1** (of a person's face) having less than the usual amount of colour; rather white **2** (of colours) not having much colouring matter; weak; not bright; *pale blue* **3** (of light) not bright —**~ly** /ˈpeɪl-li/ *adv* —**~ness** *n* [U]

pale² *v* **1** [T1;IØ] to make or become pale **2** [IØ (*before, beside*)] to seem less important, clever, beautiful, etc., when compared with: *All other anxieties paled beside the terrible fact of the fire coming close to the village*

pale³ *n* **1** a pointed piece of wood used with others in making a fence **2** **beyond/outside the pale** beyond the limit of what is considered proper behaviour in society

pale ale /ˌ· ˈ·/ *n* a light-coloured beer usu. sold in bottles

pale·face /ˈpeɪlfeɪs/ *n* [C;N] *derog & humor* (the name said to have been used formerly by Indians of North America for) a white person

pal·e·o-, palaeo- /ˈpæliəʊ, -liˈɒ-‖ˈpeɪliəʊ, -liˈɑ-/ *comb. form tech* ancient; old: *paleo*BOTANY

pal·e·og·ra·phy /ˌpæliˈɒgrəfi‖ˌpeɪliˈɑ-/ *n* [U] the study of ancient writing —**-pher** *n* —**-phic** /ˌpæliəʊˈgræfɪk‖ˌpeɪ-/ *adj* —**-phically** *adv* [Wa5]

pal·e·o·lith·ic /ˌpæliəʊˈlɪθɪk‖ˌpeɪ-/ *adj* (*often cap.*) of the earliest known time (**Old Stone Age**) when man made and used weapons and tools of stone: *a paleolithic axe* —compare NEOLITHIC

pal·e·on·tol·o·gy /ˌpæliɒnˈtɒlədʒi‖ˌpeɪliɑn-/ *n* [U] the science that deals with life on earth in earlier times, as known from the study of FOSSIL*s* —**-gist** *n*

pal·ette /ˈpælɨ̥t/ *n* **1** a board with a curved edge and a hole through it, for holding with the thumb, on which an artist mixes his colours **2** the colours used by a particular artist or for a particular picture

palette knife /ˈ·· ·/ *n* a thin bendable knife with a rounded end used **a** by artists to mix colours, and sometimes to spread paint on a picture **b** in cookery

pal·frey /ˈpɔːlfri/ *n old use & poet* a horse trained for riding, esp. for use by a woman

pal·imp·sest /ˈpælɨ̥mpsest/ *n* an ancient piece of writing material on which the original writing has been rubbed out (not always completely) so that it can be used again

pal·in·drome /ˈpælɨ̥ndrəʊm/ *n* a word, phrase, etc., that reads the same backwards as it does forwards: *The words "deed" and "level" are palindromes*

pal·ing /ˈpeɪlɪŋ/ *n* **1** [C] PALE³ **2** [U] PALE*s*³

pal·ings /ˈpeɪlɪŋz/ *n* [P] a fence made out of PALE*s*³: *He jumped over the palings*

pal·i·sade¹ /ˌpælɨ̥ˈseɪd/ *n* **1** a fence made of strong pointed iron or wooden poles, usu. used for defence **2** [*usu. pl.*] *esp. AmE* a line of high straight cliffs, esp. along a river

palisade² *v* [T1] to enclose or protect with a PALISADE¹ (1)

pal·ish /ˈpeɪlɪʃ/ *adj* pale to some degree —see also PALLID, PALLOR

pall¹ /pɔːl/ *n* **1** [C] a large piece of ornamental cloth spread over a COFFIN (a box in which a dead body is carried) **2** [C] *AmE* a COFFIN with a body inside **3** [S] something heavy or dark which covers or seems to cover: *a pall of darkness|A pall of smoke hung over the burning city*

pall² *v* [IØ (*on, upon*)] to become uninteresting or dull, esp. through being done, used, heard, etc., too often or for too long: *His talk began to pall on us all*

Pal·la·di·an /pəˈleɪdɪən/ *adj tech* **1** of or related to an Italian 16th-century style of building **2** of or related to an English early 17th-century CLASSICAL (1) style of building

pall·bear·er /ˈpɔːlˌbeərəʳ/ *n* **1** a person **a** who walks beside a COFFIN at a funeral and **b** *now rare* holds one corner of the PALL¹ (1) **2** *AmE* a person who helps to carry a COFFIN

pal·let¹ /ˈpælɨ̥t/ *n* a cloth case filled usu. with rough dry stems of crops, put on the floor for sleeping on; hard narrow uncomfortable bed

pallet² *n* **1** a flat wooden tool with a handle, used esp. by POTTER*s* **2** a large metal plate for lifting heavy goods, used with a FORKLIFT and having a hole into which the fork can be fixed

pal·li·asse, paillasse /ˈpæliæs‖ˌpæliˈæs/ *n* a long cloth case filled with dry stems of crops for sleeping on; PALLET

pal·li·ate /ˈpælieɪt/ *v* [T1] *fml* **1** to lessen the unpleasant effects of (some kind of suffering) without removing the cause **2** to make (something) seem less wrong by giving excuses

pal·li·a·tion /ˌpæliˈeɪʃən/ *n fml* **1** [U] the act of palliating (PALLIATE) **2** [C] PALLIATIVE

pal·li·a·tive /ˈpælɪətɪv/ *n, adj* **1** [C] something which PALLIATE*s*: ASPIRIN *is a commonly used palliative for headaches* **2** [B] which PALLIATE*s*

pal·lid /ˈpælɨ̥d/ *adj* **1** (of the face, skin, etc.) unusually or unhealthily pale; WAN: *He had a pallid look, as if he had been shut up without air for a long time* **2** (of coloured objects) unusually pale or lacking in deep colour —**~ly** *adv* —**~ness** *n* [U]

pal·lor /ˈpæləʳ/ *n* [U;S] unhealthy paleness of skin or face

pal·ly /ˈpæli/ *adj* [Wa1;F (*with*)] *infml* sharing the relationship of friends (with); FRIENDLY (2): *They are very pally.|John is very pally with Fred*

palm¹ /pɑːm‖pɑm, pɑlm/ *n* **1** also **palm tree** /ˈ· ·/— any of a large family of trees which grow mainly in the tropics, and which are usu. very tall with branchless stems and a mass of large leaves at the top —see also COCONUT, DATE and picture at TREE¹ **2** the leaf of this tree used as a sign of victory, success, or honour **3** **bear/carry off the palm** *fml* to win a personal victory; be judged to be the best of all (esp. in some kind of sport, study, or skill) **4** **yield the palm (to somebody)** *fml & becoming rare* to agree that somebody has defeated one or is better than oneself at some form of skill

palm² *n* **1** **a** the inner surface of the hand between the base of the fingers and the wrist **b** the part of a GLOVE that covers the inside of the hand —see picture at HUMAN² **2** **grease/oil somebody's palm (with)** *infml* to BRIBE (1) somebody (with) **3** **have an itching/itchy palm** to want money so greatly that one is willing to take it (secretly) as a payment for doing unjust favours **4** **hold/have somebody in the palm of one's hand** to have complete power over somebody —see also CROSS **someone's palm with silver**

palm³ *v* [T1] **1** to hide in one's PALM² (1), esp. when performing a trick: *The magician palmed the coin and suddenly produced it from a boy's ear* **2** *euph* to steal by picking up and hiding in one's PALM² (1) **3** [(*on, onto*)] PALM OFF³ (3)

palm·er /ˈpɑːməʳ‖ˈpɑmər, ˈpɑlmər/ *n* (in former times) a Christian who had travelled to the Holy Land (Israel) and returned wearing 2 crossed PALM¹ (1) leaves as a sign of his holy journey (PILGRIMAGE)

pal·met·to /pæl'metəʊ/ *n* **-tos** *or* **-toes** any of several sorts of small PALM[1] (1) with deeply cut leaves, found esp. in the south-eastern US
palm·ist /'pɑːmǰst‖'pɑm-, 'pɑlm-/ *n* a person who claims to be able to tell what someone is like, or what his future is, by examining the lines on his PALM[2] (1a) —compare FORTUNE-TELLER
palm·ist·ry /'pɑːmǰstri‖'pɑm-, 'pɑlm-/ *n* [U] the art or practice of being a PALMIST
palm off *v adv infml* **1** [X9, esp. *on, onto, as*] to deceitfully gain acceptance for: *The fruit seller palmed off some bad oranges onto the old lady.*|*He tried to palm the painting off as a real Renoir* —compare PASS OFF **2** [X9, esp. *with*] to deceive or cause to be satisfied by means of (lying or some other deception): *He palmed his brother off with some story or other* —compare FOB OFF WITH
palm oil /'· ·/ *n* [U] oil obtained from the nut of an African PALM[1] (1)
Palm Sun·day /,· '··/ *n* [R] the Sunday before EASTER
palm·y /'pɑːmi‖'pɑmi, 'pɑlmi/ *adj* [Wa1] **1** (esp. of past events or periods) successful, active, best **2** **(in) one's palmy days** (in) the time of one's greatest strength, beauty, success, or activity
pal·o·mi·no /,pælə'miːnəʊ/ *n* **-nos** (*sometimes cap.*) a horse of a golden or cream colour, with a white MANE and tail
pal·pa·ble /'pælpəbəl/ *adj* **1** easily and clearly known by the senses or the mind; OBVIOUS: *a palpable lie* **2** *now rare* that can be touched or felt: *"A hit, a very palpable hit"* (Shakespeare, *Hamlet* v.ii.292) —**~bly** *adv*: *What you say is palpably false*
pal·pate /'pælpeɪt/ *v* [T1] *med* to examine by touching —**-pation** /pæl'peɪʃən/ *n* [U;C]
pal·pi·tate /'pælpǰteɪt/ *v* [I∅] **1** *med* (of the heart) to beat fast and irregularly **2** [(*with*)] *fml* (of a person or the body) to tremble
pal·pi·ta·tion /,pælpǰ'teɪʃən/ *n* [U;C *often pl.*] *med* a beating of the heart that is irregular or too fast, caused by illness, too much effort, etc.
pal·sied /'pɔːlzid/ *adj old use* **1** [B] suffering from PALSY (1,2) **2** [F +*with*] made helpless or unable to control the muscles by some feeling
pal·sy /'pɔːlzi/ *n* [U] **1** *old use & med* PARALYSIS **2** a disease causing trembling of limbs
pal·sy-wal·sy /,pælzi 'wælzi/ *adj* [Wa2;B (*with*)] *sl* seeming to be very friendly with another or each other; PALLY
pal·ter with /'pɔːltə[r]/ *v prep* [T1] **1** to treat (someone or something) in a not very serious manner **2** to speak about (something) so as to deceive
pal·try /'pɔːltri/ *adj* [Wa1] **1** worthless; unimportant; worthlessly small: *He sold his paintings for a paltry sum of money* **2** *rare* having or showing a nasty or small mind or spirit; PETTY (2)
pal up *v adv* **-ll-** [I∅ (*with*)] *infml* to become friends
pam·pas /'pæmpəz, -pəs/ (*AmE* also **pam·pa** /'pæmpə/ [(*the*) S])— *n* [(*the*) S;(*the*) P] the large wide treeless plains in parts of South America
pampas grass /'·· ·/ *n* [U] tall ornamental grass with sharp-edged blades and feathery silver-white flowers
pam·per /'pæmpə[r]/ *v* [T1] to show too much attention to making (somebody) comfortable and contented; treat too kindly
pam·phlet /'pæmflǰt/ *n* a small book with paper covers which deals usu. with some matter of public interest
pam·phle·teer /,pæmflǰ'tɪə[r]/ *n* a person who writes (usu. political) PAMPHLETs
pan[1] /pæn/ *n* **1** [C] any of various kinds of container usu. with one long handle, used esp. in cooking. They are often wide, not very deep, made of metal, and often without a cover: *Usually cooking pots have 2 small handles but pans have one long handle* —see also BEDPAN, DUSTPAN, FRYING PAN, SAUCEPAN, WARMING PAN **2** [C] the bowl of a WATER CLOSET **3** [C] either of the 2 dishes on a small weighing machine —see picture at LABORATORY **4** [C] a container with holes or a wire net in the bottom used for separating precious metals, such as gold, from other materials by washing them in water **5** [C] a part of an old gun that held the explosive powder **6** [C] a piece of thin flat ice floating on the ocean **7** **a flash in the pan** something that is quickly over; effort that soon ends in failure **8** **(go) down the pan** *sl* (to become) no longer worth using or keeping —compare DRAIN[2] (5); see also BRAINPAN
pan[2] *v* **-nn-** **1** [T1 (OFF, OUT);I∅ (*for*)] to wash (soil or GRAVEL) in a PAN[1] (4) looking for or trying to separate a precious metal **2** [T1 (OFF, OUT)] to get or separate (a precious metal) by washing with a PAN[1] (4) **3** [T1] *infml* to pass a very severe judgment on; CRITICIZE very severely —see also PAN OUT
pan[3] *v* **-nn-** [(OVER, *over*, ROUND, *round, to*)] **1** [T1; I∅] to move (a camera taking moving pictures) from side to side, up and down, etc., following action which is being recorded on film or television **2** [I∅] (of a camera) to be moved in this way
pan- *prefix* (*sometimes cap.*) all-: *pan-African unity*| *Pan-Arabism* (= political union of all Arabs)
pan·a·ce·a /,pænə'sɪə/ *n often derog* **1** something that will put right all troubles **2** a medicine or other treatment that is supposed to cure any illness
pa·nache /pə'næʃ, pæ-/ *n* [U] *Fr* a manner of doing things that is showy and splendid, and without any seeming difficulty
pan·a·ma /,pænə'mɑː◂/ also **panama hat** /,··· '·/— *n* (*often cap.*) a lightweight hat for men made from the dried undeveloped leaves of a South American PALM[1] (1)
pan·a·tel·a, -tella /,pænə'telə/ *n* a long thin CIGAR
pan·cake[1] /'pæŋkeɪk/ *n* **1** a thin soft flat cake made of flour, milk, eggs, etc. (BATTER), cooked usu. in a PAN[1] (1), and usu. eaten hot **2** **as flat as a pancake** *infml* very flat, without any high places
pancake[2] *v* [I∅ (DOWN);T1] **a** (of an aircraft) to make a PANCAKE LANDING **b** to cause (an aircraft) to make a PANCAKE LANDING
Pancake Day /'·· ·/ also **Pancake Tues·day** /,·· '··/— *n* [R] *infml* SHROVE TUESDAY (on which, according to custom, PANCAKE*s*[1] are eaten)
pancake land·ing /,·· '··/ *n* a landing in which an aircraft drops flat to the ground, made usu. because it is in some trouble
pancake roll /,·· '·/ *n BrE* SPRING ROLL
pan·chro·mat·ic /,pæŋkrəʊ'mætɪk/ *adj* (of photographic film) equally sensitive to all colours and able to REPRODUCE them equally
pan·cre·as /'pæŋkrɪəs/ *n med* a part (GLAND) inside the body, near the stomach, which produces INSULIN and a liquid (**pancreatic juice** /,pæŋkriætɪk 'dʒuːs/) that helps in changing food chemically for use by the body —see also SWEETBREAD and picture at DIGESTIVE SYSTEM
pan·da /'pændə/ *n* [Wn1] **1** GIANT PANDA **2** a small bearlike animal with red-brown fur and a long tail, found chiefly in the south-eastern Himalayas
Panda car /'·· ·/ *n* [C;*by* +U] *BrE* a police car that is driven continuously along the streets of a town so that the driver and another policeman may look out for crimes, offences, etc.
Panda cross·ing /,·· '··/ *n BrE* a place to cross a busy town road, marked with broad white lines, where the walker can control traffic lights to stop

the traffic —compare ZEBRA CROSSING
pan·dem·ic /pæn'demɪk/ *adj, n med* (of) a disease which is widespread over a large area or among a population —compare ENDEMIC, EPIDEMIC
pan·de·mo·ni·um /ˌpændə̇'məʊnɪəm/ *n* **1** [U] a state of wild and noisy disorder **2** [C] a scene, place, or example of this
pan·der[1] /'pændəʳ/ *n old use* **1** PIMP[1] (1a) **2** a person (usu. a man) who uses the weaknesses and evil desires of others for his own purposes
pander[2] *v old use* **1** [I∅] PROCURE (2) **2** [T1] to act as a PANDER[1] (2) to
pander to *v prep* [T1] **1** to provide something that satisfies (the low or undesirable wishes of (somebody)): *The newspapers here pander to people's liking for stories about crime.|Don't pander to such people!* **2** to use (the weaknesses of (somebody)) for one's own purposes: *He hopes to gain her favour by pandering to her desire for continuous praise.|Don't pander to her!* **3** *old use* to act as a PANDER[1] (1) to
pan·dit /'pʌndə̇t, 'pæn-/ *n* [C;A;N] (*sometimes cap.*) (in India) a wise man: *Pandit Nehru* —compare PUNDIT
pane /peɪn/ *n* a single sheet of glass for use in a frame, esp. of a window —see picture at WINDOW
pan·e·gyr·ic /ˌpænə̇'dʒɪrɪk/ *n fml* **1** [C (*on, upon*)] a speech or piece of writing praising somebody or something **2** [U] high praise
pan·el[1] /'pænl/ *n* **1** [C] a separate usu. 4-sided division of the surface of a door, wall, etc., which is different in some way to the surface round it **2** [C] a piece of cloth of a different colour or material, set in a dress **3** [C] a board on which controls or instruments of various kinds are fastened **4** [C] a thin board with a picture painted on it **5** [C] a size of photograph that is long and narrow **6** [GC] a group of speakers who answer questions to inform or amuse the public, usu. on a radio or television show: *a panel game* —see also PANELLIST **7** [C] a list of names of people chosen to form a JURY **8** [GC] the group of people on this list (often in the phr. **serve on a panel**) **9** [C] (in Great Britain) a list of doctors who treat sick people in a particular area under the NATIONAL HEALTH SERVICE
panel[2] *v* **-ll-** (*AmE* **-l-**) [Wv5;T1 (*in, with*)] to divide into or ornament with PANEL*s*[1] (1,2)
pan·el·ling, *AmE* **paneling** /'pænəlɪŋ/ *n* [U] PANEL*s*[1] (1)
pan·el·list, *AmE* **panelist** /'pænələ̇st/ *n* a member of a PANEL[1] (6)
pang /pæŋ/ *n* a sudden sharp feeling of pain **a** of the body: *pangs of hunger* **b** of the mind: *She left her children with a pang of sadness*
pan·han·dle[1] /'pænˌhændl/ *n esp. AmE* a thin stretch of land joined to a larger area like the handle of a PAN[1] (1)
panhandle[2] *v* [I∅] *AmE sl* to beg, esp. in the streets —**~r** *n*
pan·ic[1] /'pænɪk/ *n* **1** [C;U] (a state of) sudden uncontrollable quickly-spreading fear or terror (often in the phr. **be in/get into a panic (about)**): *the likelihood of (a) panic if a fire should start in the building|panic fear* **2** [C] a sudden very severe business DEPRESSION (5) (=fall in business activity and the value of shares) **3** [S] *AmE sl* a very funny thing; SCREAM[2] (2) **4 be at panic stations (over something) a** to have to do (something) in a great hurry **b** to be in a state of confused anxiety because of this **5 push the panic button** *infml* to act quickly, without thinking, and usu. violently, as the result of a sudden unexpected and possibly dangerous state of affairs
panic[2] *v* **-ck-** **1** [I∅ (*at*);T1] to (cause to) feel PANIC[1] (1): *The crowd panicked at the sound of the guns.|The thunder panicked the horses* **2** [T1] *AmE sl* to cause to be very amused
pan·ic·ky /'pænɪki/ *adj infml* (resulting from) feeling sudden great fear
panic-strick·en /'·· ˌ··/ *adj* filled with wild terror
Pan·ja·bi /pʌn'dʒɑːbi/ *adj, n* PUNJABI
pan·jan·drum /pæn'dʒændrəm/ *n humor* a powerful person of high rank, esp. one who is very serious about his own importance
pan·ni·er /'pænɪəʳ/ *n* a basket, esp. **a** either of a pair carried by a horse or donkey, on a bicycle, etc. **b** one used to carry a load on a person's back —see picture at BICYCLE[1]
pan·ni·kin /'pænɪkə̇n/ *n Br & Austr E* **1** a small metal drinking cup **2** the amount of liquid this holds
pan·o·plied /'pænəplid/ *adj* in PANOPLY
pan·o·ply /'pænəpli/ *n* [U] splendid ceremonial show or dress
pan·o·ra·ma /ˌpænə'rɑːmə‖-'ræmə/ *n* [(*of*)] **1** a complete view of a wide stretch of land **2** a continuously changing view or scene **3** a thorough representation in words or pictures: *This book gives a panorama of life in England 400 years ago* —**-mic** /-'ræmɪk/ *adj* —**-mically** *adv* [Wa4]
pan out *v adv* [I∅] **1** [*usu. nonassertive*] to succeed: *I thought it was a good idea, but now I don't think it will pan out* **2** *tech* to yield gold
pan·pipes /'pænpaɪps/ *n* [P] a simple musical instrument made of a number of shortish pipes and played by blowing across their open ends
pan·sy /'pænzi/ *n* **1** also (*now rare*) **heart's ease**— a small plant with wide flat flowers **2** *infml* **a** a woman-like or girlish young man **b** a male HOMOSEXUAL
pant[1] /pænt/ *v* **1** [I∅] to breathe quickly, taking short breaths, esp. after great effort or in great heat **2** [I∅ (ALONG)] to move or run while breathing in this way **3** [T1 (OUT)] to say while breathing in this way **4** [I∅ (*after, for*);I3] (*now only in* -ing *forms*) to desire strongly and eagerly: *She was panting to dance, but no one asked her* —**~ingly** *adv*
pant[2] *n* a short quick breath
pant[3] *n* [A] of or for PANTS: *a pant leg*
pan·ta·loon /ˌpæntə'luːn/ *n* **1** [A] of or for a pair of PANTALOONS **2** [C;R;N] (*sometimes cap.*) (in old funny plays) a funny old man on whom others play tricks
pan·ta·loons /ˌpæntə'luːnz/ *n* [P] **1** any of several different kinds of men's close-fitting trousers, worn esp. in former times **2** *humor* TROUSERS —see PAIR (USAGE)
pan·tech·ni·con /pæn'teknɪkən‖-kɑn/ (*AmE* **moving van**)— *n* [C; *by*+U] *BrE & becoming rare* REMOVAL VAN
pan·the·is·m /'pænθi-ɪzəm/ *n* [U] **1** the religious idea that God and the universe are the same thing **2** belief in and worship of all gods known to a society —**-ist** *n* —**-istic** /ˌpænθi'ɪstɪk/ *adj* [Wa5]
pan·the·on /'pænθɪən, pæn'θiːən‖'pænθiɑn/ *n* **1** a temple built in honour of all gods, whether known or unknown **2** a building in which the famous dead of a nation are buried and/or given honour **3** all the gods of a society or nation thought of together
pan·ther /'pænθəʳ/ *n* [Wn1] **1** a LEOPARD, esp. a black one **2** *AmE* COUGAR
pan·ties /'pæntiz/ *n* [P] **1** also (*esp. BrE*) **pants**— an undergarment worn below the waist and which does not cover the upper part of the leg, worn by women and girls —compare PANTS (1) **2** *infml* children's UNDERPANTS —see PAIR (USAGE)
pan·tile /'pæntaɪl/ *n* [*usu. pl.*] a piece of baked clay

(TILE) shaped as a double curve, used in making roofs

pan·to /ˈpæntəʊ/ *n* -s [C;U] *BrE infml* PANTOMIME (2)

pan·to·graph /ˈpæntəgrɑːf‖-græf/ *n* an instrument used to make a smaller or larger exact copy of a drawing, plan, etc.

pan·to·mime /ˈpæntəmaɪm/ *n* **1** [U] MIME¹ **2** [C;U] also (*infml*) **panto**— (an example of) a kind of British play for children, usu. produced at Christmas, based on a fairy story, with music, humorous songs, etc.

pan·try /ˈpæntri/ *n* **1** a small room with shelves in a house, where food is kept; LARDER **2** a room in a big house, hotel, ship, etc. **a** where glasses, dishes, spoons, etc., used for eating, are kept **b** where cold food is prepared

pants /pænts/ *n* [P] **1** *esp. BrE* UNDERPANTS **2** *esp. BrE* PANTIES **3** *AmE* men's trousers **4** women's trousers; SLACKS **5 with one's pants down** *sl* awkwardly unprepared **6 by the seat of one's pants** *not fml* guided by one's experience rather than by a formal plan, help from others, machines, etc. **7 in long/short pants** *not fml, esp. AmE* (of a person) fully/not fully grown; MATURE/IMMATURE —see PAIR (USAGE)

pan·ty /ˈpænti/ *n* [A] of or like PANTIES: *a panty leg*

panty hose /ˈ·· ·/ *n* [P] *esp. AmE* TIGHTS (1)

pan·zer /ˈpænzəʳ/ *n* [A] *Ger* (*sometimes cap.*) of a (usu. German) TANK¹ (2) or other such armoured vehicle

pap /pæp/ *n* **1** [U] soft or liquid-like food for babies or sick people **2** [U;C] a wet mixture, more watery than a paste —compare MUSH¹ (1) **3** [U] *esp. AmE* reading matter which is only amusing, and does not instruct **4** [C] a woman's NIPPLE (1)

pa·pa¹ /pəˈpɑː/ *n* [C;N] *BrE fml* (a name for father, used formerly) —see also POP³ (1)

pap·a² /ˈpɑpə/ *AmE infml* also **pappy, poppa**— *n AmE* (a name for father)

pa·pa·cy /ˈpeɪpəsi/ *n* **1** [*the* +R] the power and office of the POPE **2** [C] the time during which a particular POPE holds office **3** [U] (*often cap.*) the system of having a POPE at the head of the (ROMAN CATHOLIC) church

pap·a·dum /ˈpæpədəm‖ˈpɑ-/ also **popadum, -dam**— *n* a type of thin flat Indian cake often eaten with CURRY

pa·pal /ˈpeɪpəl/ *adj* [Wa5;A] of the POPE or of the PAPACY (1) —see also LEGATE (1)

pa·pa·ya /pəˈpaɪə/ also (*esp. BrE & CarE*) **pawpaw**— *n* **1** [C] a tall tree grown in tropical countries, with large yellow-green fruit that are good to eat **2** [C;U] the fruit of this tree —see picture at FRUIT¹

pa·per¹ /ˈpeɪpəʳ/ *n* **1** [U] material made in the form of sheets from very thin threads of wood or cloth, used for writing or printing on, covering parcels or walls, etc.: *a sheet of paper|a paper bag* **2** [U] this material used for making things which are to be thrown away after use: *a paper handkerchief/plate|These plates are paper* **3** [C] *infml* a newspaper: *Have you seen today's paper?* **4** [U;C] WALLPAPER **5** [A] unreal: *paper profits|paper promises* —compare **paper** TIGER **6** also (*fml*) **examination paper**— **a** a set of printed questions used as an examination in a particular subject: *The teacher set us a history paper* **b** the written answers to those questions: *The teacher is reading John's history paper* **7** [C] a piece of writing for specialists, often read aloud (often in the phrs. **deliver/read a paper**) **8** [C] a piece of writing from an official group —see also WHITE PAPER **9 commit to paper** *pomp* to write down **10 not worth the paper it is/they are printed/written on** not worth anything at all **11 on paper** as written down or printed, but not yet tested by experience; unreal: *These plans seem good on paper, but we cannot be sure they will work* **12 put pen to paper** *pomp* to begin writing

paper² *v* **1** [T1 (*in, with*);X7,(1)] to cover (a wall or a room's walls) with WALLPAPER: *She papered the room green/in green/with green paper/a pretty colour* **2** [T1 (OVER, UP)] to cover with paper in order to protect or hide

pa·per·back /ˈpeɪpəbæk‖-ər-/ *n* **1** [C] a book bound with a thin cardboard cover **2** [A;(U)] the form of such a book (often in the phr. **in paperback**)

pa·per·boy /ˈpeɪpəbɔɪ‖-ər-/ *n* a boy who delivers newspapers to people's houses

paper chase /ˈ·· ·/ *n* a race across open country in which one or 2 runners drop pieces of paper which others, running some distance behind, follow

paper clip /ˈ·· ·/ *n* a small piece of curved wire used for holding sheets of paper together

pa·per·hang·er /ˈpeɪpəˌhæŋəʳ‖-ər-/ *n* a person whose job it is to stick ornamental paper (WALLPAPER) on the inside walls of a room

paper knife /ˈ·· ·/ *n* a knife that is only slightly sharp, used usu. for opening envelopes

paper mon·ey /ˈ·· ˌ··/ *n* [U] money in the form of small sheets of paper (NOTEs² (6))

paper o·ver *v adv* [T1] **1** also **plaster over**— to hide or make a show of improving (a fault in an organization) **2 paper over the cracks** to hide a fault instead of dealing with it properly

pa·pers /ˈpeɪpəz‖-ərz/ *n* [P] **1** pieces of paper with writing on them: *I think I've left my papers on the table* **2** pieces of paper with writing on them, used for official purposes **3 send in one's papers** *BrE* (of an officer) to ask to be allowed to leave the Armed Forces

pa·per·weight /ˈpeɪpəweɪt‖-ər-/ *n* a heavy object placed on top of loose papers to keep them from being scattered

pa·per·work /ˈpeɪpəwɜːk‖-pərwɜrk/ *n* [U] regular work of writing reports, letters, keeping records, lists, etc., esp. as a less important part of a job

pa·per·y /ˈpeɪpəri/ *adj* thin or stiff like paper: *a dry papery skin*

pa·pi·er-mâ·ché /ˌpæpieɪ ˈmæʃeɪ, ˌpeɪpə-‖ˌpeɪpər məˈʃeɪ/ *n* [U] *Fr* paper boiled into a soft mass, mixed with a stiffening material, and used for making boxes, ornamental figures, etc.

pa·pist /ˈpeɪpɪst/ *n derog* a member of the ROMAN CATHOLIC Church

pa·poose /pəˈpuːs‖pæ-/ *n* **1** a young child of North American Indian parents **2** a sort of bag fixed to a frame, used for carrying a baby on a person's back

pap·py /ˈpæpi/ *n* [C;N] *AmE infml & esp. dial* (*sometimes cap.*) PAPA

pap·ri·ka /ˈpæprɪkə‖pəˈpriːkə/ *n* **1** [C] a type of SWEET PEPPER **2** [U] a red powder (PEPPER) made from this and used in cooking to give a special hot taste to food

pa·py·rus /pəˈpaɪərəs/ *n* **-ruses** *or* **-ri** /raɪ/ **1** [U] a grasslike water plant formerly common in Egypt, used in ancient times esp. for making paper **2** [U] a type of paper made from this plant **3** [C] a piece of ancient writing on this paper

par¹ /pɑːʳ/ *n* **1** [R] also **par value**— the original value, written on a share of ownership in a business (STOCK (10)): *selling above/below par value* **2** [R] also **par value**— PAR OF EXCHANGE **3** [R] (in the game of GOLF) the number of strokes the average player should take to hit the ball into a hole or all of the holes **4** [S] a level which is equal or almost the same; PARITY (esp. in the phrs. **on/to a par (with)**): *These 2 things are on a par (with each* *other*) **5 above/at par** at a price higher than/the same as the PAR (1) value **6 below par a** at a price lower than the PAR (1) value **b** also **under par**—*infml* not in the usual or average condition (of health, activity, etc.) **7 (not) up to par** *infml* (not) in the usual or average condition (of health, activity, etc.)

par² *v* **-rr-** [T1] (in the game of GOLF) to play the number of strokes for (a hole or all the holes) which is equal to PAR¹ (3)

par³ also **para** /ˈpærə/— *abbrev. for:* PARAGRAPH

par·a- /ˈpærə/ also (*before a vowel or* "h") **par-**—*prefix tech* **1** at the side of: PARATHYROID **2** beyond: *para*NORMAL **3** being very like; almost: PARAMILITARY (2)|PARATYPHOID **4** connected with and helping: *paramedical*|PARAMILITARY (1)

par·a·ble /ˈpærəbəl/ *n* **1** a short simple story which teaches a moral or religious lesson **2 speak in parables** *pomp & lit* to make a statement that has a hidden meaning —**-bolical** /ˌpærəˈbɒlɪkəl‖-ˈbɑ-/ *adj* —**-bolically** *adv* [Wa4]

pa·rab·o·la /pəˈræbələ/ *n* a curve which is like the line made by a ball when it is thrown in the air and falls to the ground —**-lic** /ˌpærəˈbɒlɪk‖-ˈbɑ-/ *adj* —**-lically** *adv* [Wa4]

par·a·chute¹ /ˈpærəʃuːt/ *n* an apparatus which looks like a large UMBRELLA (1), fastened to persons or objects dropped from aircraft in order to make them fall slowly: *a parachute jump*

parachute² *v* **1** [X9] to cause to drop from an aircraft by means of a PARACHUTE¹ **2** [L9] (of a person) to drop from an aircraft by means of a PARACHUTE

par·a·chut·ist /ˈpærəʃuːtǫst/ *n* a person who drops from an aircraft using a PARACHUTE¹

Par·a·clete /ˈpærəkliːt/ *n* [*the*+R] the HOLY SPIRIT

pa·rade¹ /pəˈreɪd/ *n* **1** [C;U] (esp. of soldiers) (an example of) a gathering together in ceremonial order, for the purpose of being officially looked at, or for a march (esp. in the phr. **on parade**): *The soldiers are on parade.*|*a parade of players before the football match* **2** [C] a number of people standing in a row or walking in an informal procession, for the purpose of being looked at or heard: *a parade of witnesses* —see also IDENTIFICATION PARADE **3** [C] *often derog* an act of showing oneself (one's appearance, skill, possessions, etc.) with the intention of making others look and admire (esp. in the phr. **made a parade of**) **4** [C] also **parade ground** /·ˈ· ·/— a large flat area where soldiers PARADE² (1) **5** [C] a wide public path or street, usu. beside the seashore

parade² *v* **1** [T1;I∅] **a** (esp. of soldiers) to gather together in ceremonial order, for the purpose of being officially looked at, or for a march **b** to cause (esp. soldiers) to gather together in this way **2** [T1;L9, esp. *as*] *often derog* to walk showily about in (a room, space, area, etc.) in order to gain admiration: *She is parading (the room) in her new dress.*|(fig.) *old ideas parading as the latest information* **3** [T1] *often derog* to show in order to gain admiration: *He is always parading his knowledge/his wealth*

par·a·digm /ˈpærədaɪm/ *n* **1** an example or pattern of a word, showing all its forms in grammar: *"Child, child's, children, children's" is a paradigm* **2** a very clear or typical example of something

par·a·dig·mat·ic /ˌpærədɪgˈmætɪk/ *adj* of, like, or related to a PARADIGM —**~ally** *adv* [Wa4]

par·a·dise /ˈpærədaɪs/ *n* **1** [R] (*usu. cap.*) Heaven **2** [R] (*usu. cap.*) (in the Bible) the Garden of Eden, home of Adam and Eve **3** [S] a place of perfect happiness **4** [S9] *infml* a favourite place in which there is everything needed for a certain activity: *These forests are a hunter's paradise* **5** [U] a state or condition of perfect happiness **6 (live in) a fool's paradise** (to be in) a state of great contentment for which there is no real reason and which is unlikely to last

par·a·di·si·a·cal /ˌpærədǫˈsaɪəkəl/ also (*lit*) **par·a·di·si·ac** /-ˈsaɪək/— *adj* of or like PARADISE

par·a·dox /ˈpærədɒks‖-dɑks/ *n* **1** [C] a statement which seems to be foolish or impossible, but which has some truth in it: *"More haste, less speed" is a paradox* **2** [U] the use of such statements in speaking or writing **3** [C] an improbable combination of opposing qualities, ideas, etc.: *It is a paradox that in such a rich country there should be so many poor people* **4** [C] *now rare* a statement, idea, or fact that is opposite to what is generally believed to be true —**~ical** /ˌpærəˈdɒksɪkəl‖-ˈdɑk-/ *adj* —**~ically** *adv* [Wa4]: *Paradoxically (enough), the faster he tried to finish, the longer it seemed to take him*

par·af·fin /ˈpærəfǫn/ *n* [U] **1** also **paffin oil** /ˌ··· ˈ·/, (*AmE* **kerosene**)— *BrE* an oil made from PETROLEUM, coal, etc., burnt for heat and in lamps for light **2** also **paraffin wax** /ˌ··· ˈ·/— a waxy substance got from PETROLEUM, coal, etc., used esp. in making candles

par·a·gon /ˈpærəgən‖-gɑn/ *n* [(*of*)] a person or thing that is or seems to be a perfect model to copy (often in the phr. **a paragon of virtue**)

par·a·graph¹ /ˈpærəgrɑːf‖-græf/ *n* **1** a division of a written or printed piece made up of 1 or more sentences, of which the first word is set a little inwards to the right of a new line **2** a sign (¶) used **a** to show the beginning of such a division (esp. to a printer) **b** to call the reader's attention to a note at the foot of a page **3** a short piece of news in a newspaper

paragraph² *v* [T1] to divide into PARAGRAPHS¹ (1)

par·a·keet /ˈpærəkiːt/ *n* any of several kinds of small PARROT, usu. with a long tail, found in tropical countries

par·al·lel¹ /ˈpærəlel/ *adj* [Wa5] **1** (of 2 or more lines or rows) running side by side but never getting nearer to or further away from each other —see picture at GEOMETRY **2** [(*to, with*)] (of 1 line or row) running side by side with (another line or lines) but never getting nearer to or further away from (it or them) **3** [(*to*)] comparable (to): *My feelings in this matter are parallel to yours*

parallel² *n* **1** [C (*to, with*)] a parallel line or line of things, or surface (often in the phr. **on a parallel with**) **2** [C (*to, with*) *usu. nonassertive*] a comparable person or thing (often in the phr. **without (a) parallel**) **3** [C] a comparison that shows likeness (often in the phr. **draw a parallel (between)**) **4** [*in* +U;A] an electrical arrangement in which a number of electrical apparatuses are connected in such a way that each may receive full electrical power whether or not the others are being used —compare SERIES (5) **5** [C] also **parallel of lat·i·tude** /ˌ··· · ˈ···/— any of a number of lines on a map drawn parallel to the EQUATOR

parallel³ *v* **-l-** *or* (*BrE*) **-ll-** [T1] **1** to equal; match: *No one has paralleled his success in business* **2** [(*with*)] to compare **3** to be PARALLEL¹ (2,3) to: (fig.) *Your experience parallels my own*

parallel bars /ˌ··· ˈ·/ *n* [(*the*) P] a pair of parallel bars on 4 posts, used for exercising the body

par·al·lel·is·m /ˈpærəlelɪzəm/ *n* **1** [U] the state or quality of being PARALLEL¹ (1,3) **2** [C] PARALLEL² (3) (often in the phr. **find a parallelism (between)**)

par·al·lel·o·gram /ˌpærəˈleləgræm/ *n tech* a flat 4-sided figure with opposite sides equal and parallel

par·a·lyse, *AmE* **-lyze** /ˈpærəlaɪz/ *v* [T1] **1** to cause (some or all of the body muscles) to become uncontrollable or stiff **2** to make ineffective; cause to stop working: *The electricity failure paralysed the train service*

pa·ral·y·sis /pəˈrælᵻsᵻs/ *n* **-ses** /siːz/ [U;C] **1** (a) loss of feeling in and control of all or some of the body muscles: *paralysis of the arm* **2** (a) loss or lack of ability to move, act, think, etc.

par·a·lyt·ic /ˌpærəˈlɪtɪk/ *n, adj* **1** [C;B] (a person) suffering from PARALYSIS **2** [B] causing PARALYSIS: *a paralytic* STROKE[2] (3)|(fig.) *paralytic laughter* **3** [C;B] *infml* (a person who is) very drunk —**~ally** *adv* [Wa4]

pa·ram·eter /pəˈræmɪtə/ *n* a limit within which something must be done or someone must work

par·a·mil·i·tary /ˌpærəˈmɪlᵻtri‖-teri/ *adj* **1** [Wa5] connected with and helping a regular military force: *In some countries the police have paramilitary duties* **2** being like a regular military force, or intended for use as an irregular military force: *the paramilitary organizations of Northern Ireland*

par·a·mount /ˈpærəmaʊnt/ *adj* [Wa5] **1** *fml* great above all others; highest in power or importance: *of paramount importance* **2** (of a ruler, esp. in Africa) highest in rank (esp. in the phr. **paramount chief**)

par·a·mount·cy /ˈpærəmaʊntsi/ *n* [U (*of*)] *usu. fml* the state or condition of being PARAMOUNT

par·a·mour /ˈpærəmʊəʳ/ *n lit & old use* an unlawful lover of a married man or woman

par·a·noi·a /ˌpærəˈnɔɪə/ *n* [U] a lasting disease of the mind in which the sufferer believes that others are purposely mistreating and hating him, or that he is a person of high rank or importance

par·a·noi·ac /ˌpærəˈnɔɪæk/ *adj, n* (of or being) a person suffering from PARANOIA —**~ally** *adv* [Wa4]

par·a·noid /ˈpærənɔɪd/ *adj, n* (of or being) a person like a PARANOIAC: *Don't be so paranoid (about her)!*

par·a·pet /ˈpærəpᵻt, -pet/ *n* **1** a low wall at the edge of a roof, bridge, etc. —see picture at CASTLE[1] **2** a protective wall of earth or stone built in front of the holes (TRENCHes) used by soldiers in war

par·a·pher·na·li·a /ˌpærəfəˈneɪlɪə‖-fər-/ *n* [U;(P)] **1** a number of small articles of various kinds, esp. personal belongings or those needed for some skill or work: *I keep all my photographic paraphernalia in that cupboard* **2** *infml* unnecessary articles: *Why did you bring all that paraphernalia?*

par·a·phrase[1] /ˈpærəfreɪz/ *n* [(*of*)] a re-expression of (something written or said) in different words, esp. words that are easier to understand

paraphrase[2] *v* [T1;(I∅)] to make or give a PARAPHRASE[1] of (something written or said)

par·a·ple·gi·a /ˌpærəˈpliːdʒɪə, -dʒə/ *n* [U] PARALYSIS of the lower part of the body, including both legs

par·a·ple·gic /ˌpærəˈpliːdʒɪk/ *adj, n* (of or being) a person suffering from PARAPLEGIA —**~ally** *adv* [Wa4]

par·a·quat /ˈpærəkwɒt‖-kwɑt/ *n* [U] *tdmk* a type of very powerful liquid used to kill unwanted plants

par·as /ˈpærəz/ *n* [P] *infml* PARATROOPS

par·a·site /ˈpærəsaɪt/ *n* **1** a plant or animal that lives on or in another and gets food from it **2** a useless person who is supported by the wealth or efforts of others

par·a·sit·ic /ˌpærəˈsɪtɪk/ also **par·a·sit·i·cal** /-kəl/—*adj* **1** being, of, or like a PARASITE (1,2): *a parasitic plant* **2** caused by a PARASITE (1): *a parasitic disease* —**~ally** *adv* [Wa4]

par·a·sol /ˈpærəsɒl‖-sɔl, -sɑl/ *n becoming rare* SUNSHADE (1)

par·a·thy·roid /ˌpærəˈθaɪrɔɪd/ also **parathyroid gland** /ˌ··ˌ·· ˈ·/— *n med* any of 4 small bodily parts (GLANDs) in the throat which control the use of 2 chemicals (CALCIUM and PHOSPHORUS) by the body

par·a·troop·er /ˈpærəˌtruːpəʳ/ *n* a soldier trained to drop from an aircraft using a PARACHUTE

par·a·troops /ˈpærətruːps/ *n* [P] a number of PARATROOPERs, esp. as formed into a group to fight together

par·a·ty·phoid /ˌpærəˈtaɪfɔɪd/ *n* [U] *med* a disease that attacks the bowels, and is very like, but less serious than, TYPHOID

par·boil /ˈpɑːbɔɪl‖ˈpɑr-/ *v* [T1] **1** to boil until partly cooked **2** [Wv5] *humor & now rare* (of warm conditions) to cause to feel unpleasantly hot

par·cel /ˈpɑːsəl‖ˈpɑr-/ *n* **1** [C (*of*)] also (*esp. AmE*) **package**— *esp. BrE* a thing or things wrapped in paper and tied or fastened in some other way for easy carrying, posting, etc.: *I'm just going to take this parcel to the post office.|a parcel of clothes* **2** [C (*of*)] *esp. law & AmE* a piece of land, esp. part of a larger piece that has been divided **3** [S +*of*] *derog* a set; group (of people or things) —compare PACK[1] (3) **4 part and parcel of** a most important part that cannot be separated from the whole of

parcel out *v adv* **-ll-** (*AmE* **-l-**) [T1] to divide into parts or shares

parcel post /ˈ·· ·/ *n* [U] the system or method of sending or carrying PARCELs (1) by post

parcel up *v adv* **-ll-** (*AmE* **-l-**) [T1] to make into a PARCEL (1)

parch /pɑːtʃ‖pɑrtʃ/ *v* **1** [Wv5;T1] (of the sun or thirst) to cause to become hot and dry **2** [I∅] to become hot and dry **3** [T1] to dry by heating, esp. to cook in this way

parch·ment /ˈpɑːtʃmənt‖ˈpɑr-/ *n* **1** [U] a writing material used esp. in ancient times, made from the skin of a sheep or goat —compare VELLUM (1) **2** [C] an ancient piece of writing on this material **3** [U] any of various types of paper of good quality that look like this material **4** [C] an official piece of writing on such paper

pard /pɑːd‖pɑrd/ also **pard·ner** /ˈpɑːdnəʳ‖ˈpɑrd-/—*n* [N] *AmE dial sl* PARTNER[1] (1)

par·don[1] /ˈpɑːdn‖ˈpɑrdn/ *n* **1** [U;C: (*for*)] **a** forgiveness **b** an act or example of forgiveness **2** [C] *law* **a** an action of a court or ruler forgiving a person for an unlawful act, or forgiving the act itself **b** (a paper giving) a freedom from punishment for an unlawful act —see also FREE PARDON **3** [C] *tech* INDULGENCE (3) **4 I beg your pardon** also **pardon me**— *polite* **a** "Please excuse me for having accidentally touched/pushed you" **b** "Please get out of my way as I wish to pass" **c** also (*infml*) **beg pardon, pardon**— (*said with the voice rising at the end*) "I did not hear/understand what you said and would like you to repeat it" **d** "I'm afraid I disagree with what you have just said" **e** (*said in a firm unfriendly voice*) I'm afraid I think that what you have just said is not true/proper —compare EXCUSE **me**

pardon[2] *v* **1** [D1 (*for*);T1] to forgive; excuse: *We must pardon him his little faults* **2** [T1] to give an official PARDON[1] (2) to or for **3 pardon me** *polite* see PARDON[1] (4)

par·don·a·ble /ˈpɑːdənəbəl‖ˈpɑr-/ *adj* that can be pardoned: *a pardonable mistake* —opposite **unpardonable**

par·don·a·bly /ˈpɑːdənəbli‖ˈpɑr-/ *adv fml* in a way that, or such as, can be pardoned —opposite **unpardonably**

par·don·er /ˈpɑːdənəʳ‖ˈpɑr-/ *n* (800 to 500 years ago) a person who went about the country selling official religious INDULGENCEs (3)

pare /peəʳ/ *v* **1** [T1 (DOWN)] to cut away the thin outer covering, edge, or skin of (something), usu. with a sharp knife: *to pare one's fingernails* **2** [X9, esp. AWAY, OFF] to cut away (the thin outer covering, edge, or skin of something), usu. with a sharp knife **3** [T1 (AWAY)] PARE DOWN

pare down *v adv* [T1] to reduce (something, esp. a cost)

par·ent /ˈpeərənt/ *n* [(*of*)] **1** [*often pl.*] the father or mother of a person: *John and Mary have become parents* (= They have become the father and mother of a child) —compare RELATION, RELATIVE **2** [*usu. attrib.*] any living thing that produces another: *the parent tree* **3 a** *pomp or lit* the cause or beginning: *Pride is the parent of all evils* **b** [*usu. attrib.*] that which starts something else: *Our club is the parent association, and there are now 4 others like it* —see also PARENT COMPANY **4** [*usu. pl.*] *lit & now rare* a person from whom one is descended; ANCESTOR —see TABLE OF FAMILY RELATIONSHIPS

par·ent·age /ˈpeərəntɪdʒ/ *n* **1** [U] the state or fact of being a parent **2** [U9] origin; birth: *a child of unknown parentage*

pa·ren·tal /pəˈrentl/ *adj* [A;(B)] **1** [Wa5] of a parent **2** like a parent —**-tally** *adv*

parent com·pa·ny /ˌ·· ˈ···/ *n* a business company that controls one or more others

pa·ren·the·sis /pəˈrenθɨsɨs/ *n* **-theses** /θɨsiːz/ **1** one or more words introduced as an added explanation or thought, and in writing usu. enclosed at both ends by a COMMA, a DASH[2] (6), or a curved line as described below **2** [*usu. pl.*] (*BrE* also **round bracket,** *infml* **bracket**)— *BrE fml & AmE* either of a pair of small curved lines ( ), used together to enclose added information **3** a different and less important period of time between 2 other periods

par·en·thet·ic /ˌpærənˈθetɪk/ also **par·en·thet·i·cal** /-kəl/— *adj* **1** [Wa5;A] of a PARENTHESIS (1) **2** [B] used or said as a PARENTHESIS (1): *Parenthetic remarks should be short* —**~ally** *adv* [Wa4]

par·ent·hood /ˈpeərənthʊd/ *n* [U] the state or condition of being a parent

parent-teach·er as·so·ci·a·tion /ˌ·· ˈ·· ···ˌ··/ *n esp. AmE* an organization of teachers and the parents of their pupils that works for the improvement of the school or schools, and for the good of the pupils

par·er /ˈpeərəʳ/ *n* an instrument like a knife for removing the skin from vegetables, fruit, etc.: *a cheese-parer*

par ex·cel·lence /ˌpɑːr ˈeksəlɑːns‖-eksəˈlɑns (*Fr* par ɛksɛlɑ̃s)/ *adj* [Wa5;E] *Fr* without equal, as the best and/or most typical of its kind

par·he·li·on /pɑːˈhiːlɪən‖pɑr-/ *n* **-lia** /lɪə/ *tech* an image of the sun sometimes seen at the side of the sun at sunset

pa·ri·ah /pəˈraɪə/ *n* **1** *Ind E* a member of a low Hindu social class (CASTE) or of no such social class **2** a person not accepted by society

par·i·mu·tu·el /ˌpæri ˈmjuːtjʊəl‖-tʃʊəl/ *n* [A] *Fr* of or for a system or risking money (BETting), esp. on a horse race, in which the money risked by the losers is taken and divided up among the winners

par·ing /ˈpeərɪŋ/ *n* [*usu. pl.*] something thin that has been PARED (2) off: *They feed the pig with the vegetable parings*

par·ish /ˈpærɪʃ/ *n* **1** [C] an area in the care of a single priest and served by one main church: *a parish church|a parish priest* **2** [C] also **civil parish**— (in England) a small area, esp. a village, having its own local government (esp. in the phr. **parish council**) **3** [GC] the people living in either of these types of area: *The parish will not agree to have this new road* **4** [C] *infml esp. BrE* **a** a usu. small area in which someone, such as a policeman or a taxi driver, always works and which he knows very well —compare PATCH[1] (8) **b** an area of knowledge or work with which someone is very familiar or which is his special responsibility: *Don't worry about the printing—that's my parish* **5** **go on the parish** *old use* (of poor people) to receive help, esp. money, from a special body set up in a PARISH (2) to give such help

parish clerk /ˌ·· ˈ·/ *n* a church official in a PARISH (1) who performs various duties in/for the church

pa·rish·io·ner /pəˈrɪʃənəʳ/ *n* a person living in a particular PARISH (1,(2)), esp. one who regularly attends the PARISH church

parish-pump /ˌ·· ˈ·/ *n* [A] of local interest only (often in the phr. **parish-pump politics**)

Pa·ris·i·an /pəˈrɪzɪən‖pəˈrɪʒən, -ˈriː-/ *n, adj* (a person) of or from Paris

par·i·ty /ˈpærɨti/ *n* [U] **1** the state or quality of being equal **2** the same or equal level, position, rate, etc.

parity of ex·change /ˌ··· · ·ˈ·/ *n* [U] the rate at which the money of one country can be exchanged for that of another, as officially fixed by governments

park[1] /pɑːk‖pɑrk/ *n* **1** a large usu. grassy enclosed piece of land, or public garden, in a town, used by the public for pleasure and rest **2** *BrE* a large enclosed stretch of land with grass, trees, etc., round a large country house —compare PARKLAND **3** a space in an army camp for storing large guns on wheels and other supplies **4** NATIONAL PARK **5** [(*the*) *usu. sing.*] *BrE infml* a field on which (esp. professional) SOCCER is played —see also CAR PARK, COACH PARK

park[2] *v* **1** [T1;IØ] to put or place (a car or other vehicle) for a time: *Don't park the car in this street.| I'm parked over there* (=My car is parked over there) **2** [X9] *infml* to leave (something) in a place for a certain time: *Don't park your books on top of my papers!* **3** [X9] *infml* to settle (oneself) in a place with the intention of staying for some time —see PARKING (USAGE)

par·ka /ˈpɑːkə‖ˈpɑrkə/ *n* **1** a short coat with a protective cover (HOOD (1)) for the head, made usu. of fur **2** *esp. AmE* ANORAK

par·kin /ˈpɑːkɨn‖ˈpɑr-/ *n* [U] *esp. Scot & N Eng E* a type of cake made with and tasting of GINGER[1] (1)

park·ing /ˈpɑːkɪŋ‖ˈpɑr-/ *n* [U] **1** the leaving (parking) of a car or other vehicle in a particular place for a time **2** space in which vehicles may be so left: *There is plenty of parking behind the cinema*
USAGE One **parks** (one's car) in a **carpark** or **parking** place. When it is standing there, it is **parked**. The signs *Parking, No Parking* mean "Permission/No Permission to **park**". They are not the name of a place, so one cannot ask **Where is the* **parking**?

parking lot /ˈ·· ·/ *n esp. AmE* CAR PARK

parking me·ter /ˈ·· ˌ··/ *n* an apparatus at the side of a street, into which one puts a coin to pay for parking a car beside it for a certain time —see picture at STREET

parking or·bit /ˈ·· ˌ··/ *n* a path round the earth followed by a space vehicle for a limited time before it goes further out into space

Par·kin·son's dis·ease /ˈpɑːkɨnsənz dɪˌziːz‖ˈpɑr-/ *n* [U] a kind of PARALYSIS, esp. of old people, in which the muscles become stiff and the limbs continually shake

Parkinson's law /ˈ··· ·/ *n* [R] *esp. humor* the idea that work spreads to fill the time allowed for it

park keep·er /ˈ· ˌ··/ also (*sl*) **parky**— *n BrE* a person in charge of or who helps to look after a park

park·land /ˈpɑːk-lænd‖ˈpɑrk-/ *n* [U] **1** *BrE* grassy land surrounding a large country house, covering a large area and having trees growing in it —compare PARK[1] (2) **2** land used as or fit for use as a park

par·ky /ˈpɑːki‖ˈpɑrki/ *adj* [Wa2] *BrE infml* (of the air, weather, etc.) rather cold

par·lance /ˈpɑːləns‖ˈpɑr-/ *n* [U9] *fml* a particular manner of speech or use of words: *In naval parlance, a floor is a* "DECK"

par·ley[1] /ˈpɑːli‖ˈpɑrli/ *v* [IØ (*with*)] to talk (with an enemy or other opponent) in order to make peace

parley[2] *n* a talk held esp. between leaders of opposing forces, in order to make peace

par·lia·ment /ˈpɑːləmənt‖ˈpɑr-/ *n* (*usu. cap.*) **1** [C] a body of people (MEMBERS OF PARLIAMENT) wholly or partly elected by the people of a country to make laws **2** [R] (in the United Kingdom) the main law-making body, made up of the King or Queen, the Lords, and the elected representatives of the people: *Parliament sits at Westminster* **3** [C] this body as it exists for the time between its ceremonial opening and its official closing **4 open parliament** (of the King or Queen) to declare, with ceremony, that a new parliament has begun

par·lia·men·tar·i·an /ˌpɑːləmənˈteəriən‖ˌpɑr-/ *n* **1** a person who is a skilled and experienced member of a parliament **2** [*often pl.*] (*usu. cap.*) ROUNDHEAD

par·lia·men·ta·ry /ˌpɑːləˈmentəri‖ˌpɑr-/ *adj* of or concerning a parliament

par·lour, *AmE* **parlor** /ˈpɑːləʳ‖ˈpɑr-/ *n* **1** *now rare* a room in a private house used by the family for receiving guests, reading, and other amusements **2** *esp. AmE* (*in comb.*) a shop furnished like a room, for some kind of personal service or for selling a particular type of article: *an ice-cream parlour* **3** *becoming rare* BAR PARLOUR **4** *becoming rare* a room in certain public buildings where guests are received

parlour car /ˈ·· ·/ *n AmE* PULLMAN

parlour game /ˈ·· ·/ *n* a game which can be played indoors, usu. sitting down, such as a guessing game or a word game

parlour maid /ˈ·· ·/ *n BrE* a woman who serves at the table during meals

par·lous /ˈpɑːləs‖ˈpɑr-/ *adj* [A;(B)] **1** having or showing uncertainty and danger as important qualities: *the parlous state of international relations* **2** *old use or humor* difficult; dangerous; risky

Par·me·san /ˌpɑːmɪ̈ˈzæn◂‖ˈpɑrmɪ̈zɑn, -zæn/ also **Parmesan cheese** /ˌ··· ˈ·/— *n* [U] a kind of hard strong-tasting cheese made at Parma and elsewhere in North Italy

pa·ro·chi·al /pəˈrəʊkiəl/ *adj* **1** [Wa5] (in religious matters) **a** of a PARISH (1) **b** *esp. AmE* supported by a religious body **2** (of the mind, one's interests, opinions, etc.) limited; narrow —**~ly** *adv* —**~ism** *n* [U]

par·o·dist /ˈpærədɪ̈st/ *n* a person who writes or makes parodies (PARODY[1] (1))

par·o·dy[1] /ˈpærədi/ *n* **1** [C;U: (*of, on*)] (a piece of) writing or music intended to amuse, which recognizably copies the manner of a known writer or musician **2** [C (*of, on*)] a weak and unsuccessful copy of somebody or something, not intended to amuse: *a parody of a restaurant, where no one should ever eat!*

parody[2] *v* [T1] to make a PARODY[1] (1) of

par of ex·change /ˌ· · ·ˈ·/ *n* [R;(S)] also **par, par value**— the accepted value of the money of one country stated or shown in the money of another country

pa·role[1] /pəˈrəʊl/ *n* **1** [U] the letting out of a person from prison, conditional upon good behaviour (esp. in the phr. **on parole**) **a** before the end of the official period of imprisonment **b** for a particular time within that period **2** [S] this letting out, or the length of time it lasts **3 break one's parole** to fail to return to prison after being out on PAROLE (1b)

parole[2] *v* [T1] to set free on PAROLE[1] (1)

par·ox·ys·m /ˈpærəksɪzəm/ *n* [(*of*)] **1** a sudden uncontrollable explosive expression: *paroxysms of anger* **2** (of a sharp pain or a disease that comes regularly) a sudden but passing attack: *paroxysms of pain/of coughing*

par·quet /ˈpɑːkeɪ, ˈpɑːki‖pɑrˈkeɪ/ *n* [A;(U)] *Fr* (of) small flat blocks of hard wood fitted together in a pattern and stuck onto the floor of a room: *a parquet floor*

parr /pɑːʳ/ *n* **parr** [Wn2] a young SALMON

par·ri·cide /ˈpærɪ̈saɪd/ *n* **1** [U] the murder of one's own parent (esp. father) or other near relative **2** [C] a person guilty of this

par·rot[1] /ˈpærət/ *n* **1** any of a large group of birds, usu. native to tropical countries, having a curved beak and usu. brightly coloured feathers. Some kinds of these birds can be taught to copy human speech —see picture at EXOTIC **2** *usu. derog* a person who repeats, often without understanding, the words or actions of another

parrot[2] *v* [T1] *usu. derog* to repeat (the words or actions of another) without thinking or understanding

parrot-cry /ˈ·· ·/ *n derog* a meaningless phrase used repeatedly for a time by many people, as in expressing some opinion, supporting or opposing some course of action, etc.

parrot fash·ion /ˈ·· ˌ··/ *adv often derog* by means of continuous repeating, but usu. without real understanding

parrot fe·ver /ˈ·· ˌ··/ *n* [U] PSITTACOSIS

par·ry[1] /ˈpæri/ *v* [T1] to turn aside or keep away (an attacking blow or a weapon): (fig.) *He parried the unwelcome question skilfully*

parry[2] *n* an act of PARRYing[1]; movement of defence in some sports, esp. fencing (FENCE[2] (1))

parse /pɑːz‖pɑrs/ *v* [T1;IØ] (in grammar) **1** to give the PART OF SPEECH, the particular form (INFLECTION), and the use in a given sentence of (a word) **2** to give this information about all the words in (a sentence)

Par·see, Parsi /pɑːˈsiː‖ˈpɑrsiː/ *adj* [Wa5] of an ancient Persian religious group in India

par·si·mo·ni·ous /ˌpɑːsɪ̈ˈməʊniəs‖ˌpɑr-/ *adj fml* too careful with money; unwilling to spend; ungenerous —**~ly** *adv* —**~ness** *n* [U]

par·si·mo·ny /ˈpɑːsɪ̈məni‖ˈpɑrsɪ̈məʊni/ *n* [U] **1** *fml* too careful use of money; ungenerousness **2** *tech* careful use of anything not material, using only exactly what is needed and no more

pars·ley /ˈpɑːsli‖ˈpɑr-/ *n* [U] a small plant (HERB) with curly strong-tasting leaves, grown in gardens and used in cooking or on uncooked foods

pars·nip /ˈpɑːsnɪp‖ˈpɑr-/ *n* **1** [C] a plant grown in gardens, with a thick white or yellowish root that is used as a vegetable **2** [C;U] the root of this plant cooked and eaten as food

par·son /ˈpɑːsən‖ˈpɑr-/ *n* [C;A] **1** a priest of the CHURCH OF ENGLAND who is in charge of a PARISH (1) **2** *infml* any priest

par·son·age /ˈpɑːsənɪdʒ‖ˈpɑr-/ *n* the house where a PARSON (1) lives

parson's nose /ˌ·· ˈ·/ *n infml humor euph, esp. BrE* the piece of flesh at the tail end of a cooked bird, such as a chicken

part[1] /pɑːt‖pɑrt/ *n* **1** [C (*of*)] any of the pieces that make up a whole: *"What part of his leg is broken?" "The knee"* **2** [C;U: (*of*)] any of the divisions into which something is or may be considered as being divided (whether separated from a whole or connected with it) and which is therefore less than the whole: *This piece of glass seems to be (a) part of a lamp.|Parts of this town are beautiful.|the greater part of his life* **3** [C (*of*)] any of several equal divisions which make up a whole: *This mixture is 3 parts wine and 2 parts water* **4** [C] a division of **a** a book (usu. marked in some way) **b** a set of books produced regularly one after another (**part work**) **c** a story or other work which appears on radio or television, in a newspaper, etc. **5** [C] **a** a necessary or important piece of a machine or other apparatus **b** SPARE PART **6** [S;U] a share or duty in some activity (often in the phr. **take part in**): *Did you have any part in this fighting?|Did you take part in the fighting?|He was the host, so it wasn't my part to tell him what to do at the party* **7** [U] a side or position **a** in an argument: *Tom took my part/took part with me in the disagreement* (= supported my side) **b** *law* in an agreement: *an agreement between Tom Jones of the first/of one part and John Smith of the second/of the other part* **8** [C] **a** a character acted by an actor in a play (often in the phrs. **play/take a part**) **b** the words and actions of an actor in a play **c** a written copy of these words: *I've left my part on the stage* **9** [C] (in music) **a** one of the tunes, esp. for a particular voice or instrument, which when put together make up a piece of music: **b** a written copy of this **10** [C] *AmE* PARTING[1] (2) **11 for my part** as far as I am concerned; speaking for myself **12 for the most part a** mostly: *This orange drink is for the most part water* **b** most of the time; in most cases: *She is for the most part a well-behaved child* **13 in part** in some degree; partly **14 on the part of (somebody) /on (somebody's) part a** of (somebody): *It was a mistake on the part of Jones to sign the agreement without reading it* **b** by (somebody): *The agreement has been kept on my part but not on his* **15 play a part** to pretend a feeling, belief, etc. **16 play a part in** to have an influence on: *Explain the part that weather plays in our country's trade* **17 take in good part** not be offended by: *I hope you will take this unpleasant advice from me in good part*

part² *v* **1** [T1 (*from*);IØ (*from, as*);L1,7] to (cause to) separate or no longer be together: *The war parted many men from their families.|I hope we can part (as) friends* **2** [T1;IØ] to (cause to) separate into parts or spread apart: *The clouds parted and the sun shone* **3** [T1;IØ] to (cause to) separate, break, or move apart: *He tried to part the 2 angry dogs* **4** [T1] to separate (hair on the head) along a line with a comb **5 part company (with) a** to end a relationship (with) **b** no longer be together (with): *I'm getting off the train here, so we must part company* **c** to disagree (with) —see also PART WITH

part³ *adv* PARTLY (esp. in the phr. **part x, part y**): *A* CENTAUR *is part man, part horse*

part⁴ *adj* [Wa5;A] not complete; PARTIAL (1): *I will give you a pound in part payment*

par·take /pɑː'teɪk‖pɑr-/ *v* **partook** /pɑː'tʊk‖pɑr-/, **partaken** /pɑː'teɪkən‖pɑr-/ [IØ (*of*)] *old use or humor* to eat or drink, esp. something offered: *We have a lot of wine here—will you partake?|Will you do us the great favour of partaking of our humble wine?*

par·terre /pɑː'teəʳ‖pɑr- (*Fr* partɛr)/ *n Fr* **1** a level space in a garden, with an area of grass and ornamental areas of flowers **2** the rows of seats at the front or at the back of the ground floor of a theatre

par·the·no·gen·e·sis /ˌpɑːθɪ̵nəʊ'dʒenɪ̵sɪ̵s‖ˌpɑr-/ *n* [U] *tech* the production of a new plant or animal from a female without sexual union with a male

par·tial /'pɑːʃəl‖'pɑr-/ *adj* **1** [Wa5;B] not complete: *The play was only a partial success* **2** [B] favouring one person, side, etc., more than another, esp. in a way that is unfair —opposite **impartial** **3** [F +*to*] having a strong liking for: *I'm very partial to sweet foods*

par·ti·al·i·ty /ˌpɑːʃi'ælɪ̵ti‖ˌpɑr-/ *n* **1** [U] the quality or fact of being PARTIAL (2); BIAS[1] (2) —opposite **impartiality** **2** [S9, esp. *for*] a special liking

par·tial·ly /'pɑːʃəli‖'pɑr-/ *adv* **1** not completely; PARTLY: *I am partially to blame for the accident* **2** in a PARTIAL (2) way

par·tic·i·pant /pɑː'tɪsɪ̵pənt‖pɑr-/ *n* [(*in*)] a person who takes part or has a share in an activity or event

par·tic·i·pate /pɑː'tɪsɪ̵peɪt‖pɑr-/ *v* [IØ (*in* and/or *with*)] to take part or have a share in an activity or event

par·tic·i·pa·tion /pɑːˌtɪsɪ̵'peɪʃən‖pɑr-/ *n* [U (*in*)] the act of taking part or having a share in an activity or event

par·ti·cip·i·al /ˌpɑːtɪ̵'sɪpɪəl‖ˌpɑr-/ *adj* [Wa5] (in grammar) being or using a PARTICIPLE: *"Singing" in "a singing bird" is a participial adjective* —**~ly** *adv*

par·ti·ci·ple /'pɑːtɪ̵sɪpəl‖'pɑr-/ *n* (in English grammar) either of 2 forms of a verb (PAST PARTICIPLE and PRESENT PARTICIPLE) which may be used in compound forms of the verb or as adjectives

par·ti·cle /'pɑːtɪkəl‖'pɑr-/ *n* **1 a** a piece (of something that is made up of very small pieces): *dust particles floating in the sunlight* **b** *tech* a piece of matter smaller than, and part of, an atom **c** a very small, or the smallest, quantity (of something): *particles of food|*(fig.) *There wasn't a particle of truth in what he said* **2** (in grammar) **a** any of several usu. short words that are not as important in a sentence as the subject, verb, etc.: PREPOSITIONs *and* CONJUNCTIONs *are particles* **b** AFFIX

par·ti-col·oured, party- /ˌpɑːti 'kʌləd◂‖ˌpɑrti 'kʌlərd◂/ *adj* [Wa5] having different colours in different parts

par·tic·u·lar¹ /pə'tɪkjʊləʳ‖pər'tɪkjələr/ *adj* **1** [Wa5; A] worthy of notice; special; unusual: *There was nothing in the letter of particular importance* **2** [Wa5;A;(B)] single and different from others; of a certain sort: *I don't like this particular hat, but the others are quite nice* **3** [B (*about, over*)] **a** showing (too) much care or interest in small matters: *He is very particular about having his breakfast at exactly 8 o'clock* **b** hard to please: *He is very particular about his food* **4** [A;(B)] careful and exact: *Give me a full and particular description of what happened* **5 in particular** especially: *I noticed his eyes in particular, because they were very large*

particular² *n* **1** a small single part of a whole; detail: *This work must be correct in every particular/in all particulars* **2 go into particulars** to give all the details —see also PARTICULARS

par·tic·u·lar·i·ty /pəˌtɪkjʊ'lærɪ̵ti‖pərˌtɪkjə-/ *n rare* **1** [U] exactness; attention to detail **2** [C] PARTICULAR **3** [C] PECULIARITY

par·tic·u·lar·ize, -ise /pə'tɪkjʊləraɪz‖pər'tɪkjə-/ *v* [T1;IØ] to give the details of (something) one by one —**-ization** /pəˌtɪkjʊləraɪ'zeɪʃən‖pərˌtɪkjələrə-/ *n* [U;(C)]

par·tic·u·lar·ly /pə'tɪkjʊləli‖pər'tɪkjələrli/ *adv* especially; in a way that is special and different from others: *He isn't particularly clever.|Watch that horse particularly—it bites!*

par·tic·u·lars /pə'tɪkjʊləz‖pər'tɪkjələrz/ *n* [P (*of*)] the facts (esp. about an event)

part·ing¹ /'pɑːtɪŋ‖'pɑr-/ *n* **1** [U;C] (an example of) the action of PARTing² (1, 2, and 3) **2** [C] *AmE*

part— the line on the head where the hair is PARTed[2] (4)
parting[2] *adj* [Wa5;A] done or given at the time of PARTing[2] (1): *a parting kiss*
parting shot /ˌ·· ˈ·/ *n* a last remark, special look, or action made at the moment of leaving, esp. as the last reply in an argument
par·ti·san, -zan /ˌpɑːtɨˈzæn‖ˈpɑrtɨzən, -sən/ *n* **1** a strong, esp. unreasoning, supporter of a party, group, plan, etc.: *a partisan speech* **2** a member of an armed group that fights in secret against an enemy that has conquered its country —**~ship** *n* [U]
par·ti·ta /pɑːˈtiːtə‖pɑr-/ *n* a piece of European instrumental music, esp. of former times, which is usu. either a SUITE (3) or a set of VARIATIONS (3)
par·ti·tion[1] /pɑːˈtɪʃən‖pər-, pɑr-/ *n* **1** [U] division into 2 or more parts (esp. of a country) **2** [C] a part formed by dividing **3** [C] something that divides, esp. a thin wall inside a house
partition[2] *v* [T1 (*into*)] to divide into 2 or more parts
partition off *v adv* [T1] to make (esp. a part of a room) separate by means of a PARTITION[1] (3)
par·ti·tive /ˈpɑːtɨtɪv‖ˈpɑr-/ *n, adj* [Wa5] *tech* (a word) which expresses a part of a whole: *"Some" is a partitive word, as in the phrase "some cake"* —**~ly** *adv*
part·ly /ˈpɑːtli‖ˈpɑr-/ *adv* **1** not completely: *I have partly finished it* **2** in some degree: *I admit that what you say is partly true*
part·ner[1] /ˈpɑːtnəʳ‖ˈpɑr-/ *n* **1** [C (*with* and/or *in*)] a person who shares (in the same activity): *They have been partners for a long time, so they know each other very well* **2** [C (*in*)] any of the owners of a business, who share the profits and losses esp. equally —see also SLEEPING PARTNER **3** [C] either of 2 people **a** dancing together **b** playing against each other, or playing together against 2 others, in any of several games, such as tennis or BRIDGE[3] **c** married to each other **d** who go to a dinner together and sit together **4** [N;(C)] *infml esp. AmE* (*used esp. by and of males*) a male friend **5 be partners with** to be a partner of, esp. in a game: *"I want to be partners with Jane," said the little boy*
partner[2] *v* [T1] **1** to act as partner to **2** [(*with*)] PARTNER UP
part·ner·ship /ˈpɑːtnəʃɪp‖ˈpɑrtnər-/ *n* **1** [U] the state of being a partner, esp. in business **2** [C] a business owned by 2 or more partners
partner up *v adv* [T1;IØ: (*with*)] to (cause to) be a partner or partners: *She partnered up the 2 young people.|Please don't partner me up with Mr. Jones for dinner!|John and Mary have partnered up for the dance.|John has partnered up with Mary*
part of speech /ˌ· · ˈ·/ *n* (in grammar) any of the classes into which words are divided according to their use: *"Noun," "verb," and "adjective" are parts of speech*
par·took /pɑːˈtʊk‖pɑr-/ *past t. of* PARTAKE
part own·er /ˌ· ˈ··/ *n* a person who shares the ownership (of the same article): *They are part owners of the bicycle*
par·tridge /ˈpɑːtrɪdʒ‖ˈpɑr-/ *n* [Wn1] **1** [C] any of various middle-size birds, with a round body and short tail, shot for sport and food **2** [U] the meat of this bird as food
parts /pɑːts‖pɑrts/ *n* [P9] **1** a general area or division of a country, without fixed limits: *We never have bad weather in these parts* **2 of parts** *lit or pomp* of many different abilities (usu. in the phr. **a man/woman of parts**)
part-song /ˈ· ·/ *n* a song which is made up of 3 or more PARTS[1] (9a) —**part-singing** /ˈ· ˌ··/ *n* [U]
part-time /ˌ· ˈ·◂/ *adj, adv* [Wa5] (working or giving work) during only a part of the regular working time —compare FULL-TIME
par·tu·ri·tion /ˌpɑːtjʊˈrɪʃən‖ˌpɑrtə-, -tʃə-/ *n* [U] *tech* the act of giving birth
part with *v prep* [T1] to give up: *It's not easy to part with one's favourite possessions*
par·ty /ˈpɑːti‖ˈpɑrti/ *n* **1** [C] a group of people **a** doing something together: *A party of schoolchildren is going to France* **b** given a special duty together: *a search party looking for the lost child* **2** [C] a gathering of people, usu. by invitation, for food and amusement: *She likes parties, because she enjoys meeting people.|a tea party|a party dress* —see also GARDEN PARTY, HEN PARTY, HOUSE PARTY **3** [C] an association of people having the same political aims, esp. as formed to try to win elections **4** [U] the needs and aims of such an association **5** [A;(U)] the system of government based on political parties: *the party system|I am tired of party politics* **6** [C] *law* one of the people or sides in an agreement or argument **7** [C] *esp. fml* a person who is concerned in some action or activity: *We know he is the guilty party, as we saw him take the money* **8** [C] *infml & humor* a person: *She is a sweet old party, though she talks too much* **9 be (a) party to** *often derog* to take part in, know about, or support (some action or activity) **10 (follow) the party line (on)** (to act according to) the official opinion of a political party (about)
party-col·oured /ˌ·· ˈ··◂/ *adj* [Wa5] PARTI-COLOURED
party line /ˈ·· ·/ *n* a telephone line connected to 2 or more telephones belonging to different people (SUBSCRIBERS) —compare **follow the** PARTY (10) **line**
party spir·it /ˌ·· ˈ··/ *n* [U] eager interest in and loyalty to a group, esp. a political party —**~ed** *adj*
party wall /ˌ·· ˈ·/ *n* a dividing wall between 2 houses, belonging to the owners of both houses
par val·ue /ˌ· ˈ··/ *n* [R] **1** PAR[1] (1) **2** also **par**— PAR OF EXCHANGE
par·ve·nu /ˈpɑːvənjuː‖ˈpɑrvənuː/ *n Fr & often derog* a person of a low social position who suddenly gains power or wealth
pas·chal /ˈpæskəl/ *adj* [Wa5;A] (*often cap.*) **1** of the Jewish holiday of PASSOVER **2** *lit & old use* of EASTER: *the Paschal lamb*
pash·a /ˈpæʃə, ˈpɑːʃə/ *n* [C;E;(U)] (the title of) an army or government officer of high rank in Turkey or Egypt in former times: *Glubb Pasha trained the soldiers*
pass[1] /pɑːs‖pæs/ *v* **1** [IØ] to go forward; advance: *Because of the large crowd in the street the carriage was unable to pass* **2** [T1;IØ] **a** to reach and move beyond (a person or place): *I have been standing here for an hour but no one has passed (me)* **b** (of a car or motorist) to reach and move beyond (another car); OVERTAKE (1) **3** [T1;IØ] to get or go through, across, over, or between: *No one is allowed to pass the gates of the camp* **4** [X9;L9] to move, place, or be placed (in or for a short space of time): *We can pass a rope round this dead tree.|A cloud passed across the sun* **5** [D1 (*to*);T1] to give (esp. by hand): *Please pass the bread—I can't quite reach it.|He passed him the bread* **6** [L9] to be given (and received): *The news/wine passed round the hall* **7** [T1;IØ;(D1) :(*to*)] (in various sports) to kick, throw, hit, etc. (esp. a ball) to a member of one's own side **8** [T1] to send out from the bowels or KIDNEYS: *You must tell the doctor that you are passing blood* **9** [IØ;T1] **a** (of time) to go by **b** to cause (time) to go by, esp. in a way that does not seem too long or dull: *She passed the time by picking flowers* **10** [L9, esp. *between*] to be said or done; happen: *Angry words passed between them*

11 [I∅] *fml or bibl* to happen (esp. in the phrs. **bring something to pass, come to pass**) **12** [L9, esp. *from* and *to, into*] to change: *In summer butter often passes from a solid to an oily state* **13** [I∅;T1;D1] **a** (of money) to be accepted as lawful **b** to cause (money) to be accepted as lawful, esp. by dishonest means: *Somebody passed me a lead shilling!* **14** [T1] to say; speak (esp. in the phrs. **pass a comment, pass a remark**) **15** [I∅;T1] **a** (of a suggested law or other formal suggestion) to be given official acceptance **b** to give official acceptance to (a suggested law or other formal suggestion) **16** [T1;I∅] to succeed in (an examination): *"Do you think you've passed the test?" "No, I haven't passed"* —opposite **fail** **17** [T1 (*as*);(X7)] to accept (someone or something) after examination: *I can't pass this bad piece of work!|The doctor wouldn't pass him (as) fit/ready for work* **18** [I∅] (of feelings, thoughts, etc.) to come to an end **19** [T1] (of actions, ideas, etc.) to go beyond; be beyond the limits of: *It passes my understanding how he can do so many things so well* **20** [L9, esp. *as, under*] to be generally, but wrongly, known: *He may pass as an actor here, but he wouldn't in London* —see also PASS FOR **21** [T1 (*on, upon*)] to give (a judgment, opinion, etc.) **22** [I∅] to go unnoticed, unchanged, unpunished, etc. (esp. in the phr. **let something pass**) **23** [L9, esp. *to, into*] to go from the control or possession of one to that of another: *On his death, the farm will pass to his son/into the hands of the state* **24** [I∅] (in card games) to let one's turn go by without playing a card, putting down money, or making a BID³ (3) **25 pass in review** to (cause to) go by for or as if for official military examination (INSPECTION): (fig.) *The events of his past life passed in review before his eyes* **26 pass remarks** *euph* to say, esp. in the presence of the person concerned, something that is of too personal a nature to be polite **27 pass the hat (round)** *infml* to take a collection of money from a group of people **28 pass the time of day (with)** to give a greeting (to), and/or have a short conversation (with) **29 pass water** *euph* URINATE —see also PASS AWAY, PASS BY, PASS DOWN, PASS FOR, PASSING, PASS OFF, PASS ON, PASS OUT, PASS OVER, PASS THROUGH, PASS UP; see PAST (USAGE)

pass² *n* **1** a way by which one may PASS¹ (3), esp. over a range of mountains **2 sell the pass** *lit or pomp* to give up a defended position; be disloyal to an agreed purpose or aim

pass³ *n* **1** [C] an act of moving something (made esp. by the human hand or by an aircraft) over or in front of something else: *The magician made a few passes over the hat, and then produced a rabbit from it* **2** [C] (in various sports) an act of PASSing¹ (7) a ball (to a member of one's own side) **3** [C] (in FENCING (1)) a forward movement with a sword (usu. in the phr. **make a pass**) **4** [C] (in card games) an act of PASSing¹ (24) **5** [C] a piece of paper with printing, which shows that one is permitted to do a certain thing (such as travel on a railway, leave an army camp for a short time, etc.), esp. without paying **6** [C] **a** a successful result in an examination **b** (esp. in Britain) the completing of a university course with an examination standard that is acceptable but not good enough for HONOURS (2) (usu. in the phr. **a pass degree**) **7** [S] *infml* a difficult state or condition (esp. in the phrs. **come to/reach a pretty/fine/sad pass**) **8 make a pass at** *sl* (esp. of men) to try to make (a member of the opposite sex) sexually interested in one

pass. *abbrev. for:* PASSIVE¹ (4) —compare POSS.

pass·able /ˈpɑːsəbəl‖ˈpæ-/ *adj* [Wa5] **1** (just) good enough to be accepted; not bad **2 a** (of a road) fit to be used **b** (of a river) fit to be crossed (on foot or horseback) —opposite **impassable**; compare IMPOSSIBLE (1)

pas·sage /ˈpæsɪdʒ/ *n* **1** [U (*of*)] the action of going across, by, over, through, etc., in space: *The old bridge is not strong enough to allow the passage of heavy vehicles* **2** [U (*of*)] (of time) course; onward flow **3** [U (*from, to*)] *lit & old use* the change from one condition or state to another **4** [S;U: (*from, to*)] (the cost of) a long journey by ship (or aircraft): *"A Passage to India"* (E.M. Forster)|*He is too poor to afford the passage, and so he will have to work his passage by doing jobs on the ship* **5** [C] a usu. narrow way through; opening: *He forced a passage through the crowd* **6** [U] the right or permission to go through or across something **7** [C] PASSAGEWAY **8** [U (*of*)] (the time taken for) the action of passing a BILL (=suggested law) **9** [C] a usu. short part of a speech or a piece of writing or music, considered by itself **10 bird of passage a** a bird that regularly flies away to a distant country when the seasons change **b** a person who moves about from one place to another, and does not stay in one place for long **11 rough passage a** a stormy sea or air journey **b** a difficult time, in which people act in an unpleasant way towards one

passage of arms /ˌ·· · ˈ·/ also **passage at arms**— *n old use* a fight between 2 people of rank

pas·sage·way /ˈpæsɪdʒweɪ/ also **passage**— *n* a usu. long narrow connecting way, esp. inside a building —compare CORRIDOR (1)

pass a·way *v adv* [I∅] **1** also **pass on, pass over**— *euph* (esp. of a person) to die **2** to move away **3** PASS OFF (1)

pass·book /ˈpɑːsbʊk‖ˈpæs-/ *n* **1** BANKBOOK **2** (in S. Africa) a small book carried by non-white people allowing them to be in a certain area

pass by *v adv* **1** [T1] also **pass over**— to pay no attention to; disregard: *The voters passed him by.|Life has passed me by* **2** [I∅] to go past

pass down also **pass on**— *v adv* [T1 *often pass.*] HAND DOWN (1)

pas·sé /ˈpɑːseɪ, ˈpæseɪ‖pæˈseɪ/ *adj* [F;(B)] *Fr & derog* no longer considered modern; not now favoured as formerly; old-fashioned

pas·sen·ger /ˈpæsəndʒəʳ, -sən-/ *n* **1** a person going from one place to another in a public or private vehicle **2** *BrE infml* a member of a team or other group who does not do his share of the work of the group

passe-par·tout /ˌpæs pɑːˈtuː‖-pərˈtuː, -pɑr-/ *n Fr* **1** [U] a sort of sticky material in the form of a long narrow band, used esp. to form the frame of a small picture **2** [C] a key which opens all the doors in a hotel, office, etc.; PASSKEY

pass·er-by /ˌpɑːsəˈbaɪ‖ˌpæsər-/ *n* **passersby** /-səz-‖-sərz-/ a person who happens (by chance) to pass by a place

pass for *v prep* [L1] to gain (usu. false) recognition as: *He passes for a skilled doctor.|She could pass for a much younger woman*

pas·sim /ˈpæsɪm/ *adv Lat & tech* (of a phrase, idea, etc., that appears in a book, a writer's work, etc.) frequently; in many places

pass·ing¹ /ˈpɑːsɪŋ‖ˈpæ-/ *n* [U9] **1** the act of going by: *the passing of the years* **2** ending; disappearance: *I do not like to see the passing of all these old customs* **3** *euph* death: *His passing grieved us all* **4 in passing** in the course of a statement (esp. a statement about a different matter): *He was talking about his holiday in Spain, and he mentioned in passing that you were thinking of going there next year*

passing² *adj* [Wa5;A] **1** moving or going by: *He*

watched the passing crowd **2** not lasting very long: *She did not give the matter even a passing thought* **3** quick; not thorough: *He took a passing look at the political news, then turned to the sports page*

passing³ *adv* [Wa5] *old use* very: *passing strange*

passing bell /ˈ·· ·/ *n* [(*the*) R] a bell rung before and during a funeral service in some Christian churches

pas·sion /ˈpæʃən/ *n* **1** [U;(C)] strong, deep, often uncontrollable feeling, esp. of sexual love, hatred, or anger: *The poet expressed his burning passion for the woman he loved.|Can't we talk about this with a little less passion?* **2** [S] a sudden show of anger or bad temper **3** [S +*for*] *infml* a strong liking —**~less** *adj* —**~lessly** *adv*

Passion *n* [*the* +R] the suffering and death of Christ

pas·sion·ate /ˈpæʃənǰt/ *adj* **1** able to feel strongly with PASSION (1): *a passionate woman* **2** showing or filled with PASSION (1): *a passionate speech* **3** very eager; very strong: *a passionate interest in sports*

pas·sion·ate·ly /ˈpæʃənǰtli/ *adv* **1** fiercely; deeply; in a PASSIONATE (1,2) way **2** very (much); strongly; in a PASSIONATE (3) way

pas·sion·flow·er /ˈpæʃənˌflaʊəʳ/ *n* any of various usu. climbing plants, usu. growing in warm countries, with large flowers and egg-shaped fruit (**passionfruit**) which is good to eat —see picture at FLOWER¹

passion play /ˈ·· ·/ *n* (*often cap. first* P) a play telling the story of the PASSION

Passion Sun·day /ˌ·· ˈ··/ *n* [R] (in the Christian Church) the 5th Sunday in LENT; the Sunday before PALM SUNDAY

Passion Week /ˈ·· ·/ *n* [R] (in the Christian Church) **1** HOLY WEEK **2** the week between PASSION SUNDAY and PALM SUNDAY

pas·sive¹ /ˈpæsɪv/ *adj* **1** *esp. derog* not active; influenced by outside forces but without doing anything in return **2** (esp. of animals) *often apprec* quiet; not likely to be dangerous **3** suffering but not opposing **4** [Wa5] *tech* (of verbs or sentences) expressing an action which is done to the subject of a sentence: *"Was thrown" is a passive verb phrase in "The boy was thrown from his horse"* —compare ACTIVE (3) —**~ly** *adv*

passive² *n* (in grammar) **1** [(*the*) S] also **passive voice** /ˌ·· ˈ·/— the PASSIVE¹ (4) part or forms of a verb **2** [C] an example of this

passive re·sis·tance /ˌ·· ·ˈ··/ *n* [U] NONVIOLENCE

pas·siv·i·ty /pæˈsɪvǰti/ also **pas·sive·ness** /ˈpæsɪvnǰs/— *n* [U] the state or quality of being PASSIVE¹ (esp. 1,2,3)

pas·siv·ize /ˈpæsɪvaɪz/ *v* [I∅;(T1)] *tech* (in grammar) to (cause to) become PASSIVE¹ (4) —**-ization** /ˌpæsɪvaɪˈzeɪʃən‖-və-/ *n* [U]

pass·key /ˈpɑːs-kiː‖ˈpæs-/ *n* **1** a key made to open a particular door or gate, and given only to those few people allowed to use the door, etc. **2** a key that will open a number of different locks, all of which have keys of their own —compare MASTER KEY

pass off *v adv* **1** [I∅] also **pass away**— to stop: *The storm/the rain passed off* **2** [L9] to take place successfully: *The meeting passed off well* **3** [X9, esp. *as*] to present falsely: *She passed herself off as an experienced actress* **4** [T1] to direct attention away from (something): *He passed off the difficult question*

pass on *v adv* **1** [I∅] *euph* PASS AWAY (1) **2** [T1] HAND DOWN (1) **3** [I∅] to move on: *Let us now pass on to the next subject*

pass out *v adv* **1** [I∅] to faint **2** [I∅] *esp. BrE* (esp. at a military school) GRADUATE **3** [T1] *AmE* HAND OUT; DISTRIBUTE (3)

pass o·ver¹ *v adv* **1** [I∅] *euph now rare* PASS AWAY (1) **2** [T1] PASS BY (1)

pass over² *v prep* [T1] also **slide over, slur over**— to fail to deal with; try not to mention (something): *Let us pass over his rude remarks in silence*

Pass·o·ver /ˈpɑːsəʊvəʳ‖ˈpæs-/ *n* [R] (in the Jewish religion) a holiday in memory of the freeing of the Jews from Egypt, as told in the Bible

pass·port /ˈpɑːspɔːt‖ˈpæsport/ *n* [C] **1** a small official book, obtained from a government by one of its citizens, to be shown esp. when entering a foreign country or returning home **2** [(*to*) *usu. sing.*] something (a quality, connection, name, etc.) that permits a person easily to do or get something else: *He thought that money was a passport to happiness*

pass through *v prep* [T1] GO THROUGH

pass up *v adv* [T1,(4a)] to let slip; miss: *Never pass up a chance to improve your English.|Don't pass up going there: it'll be wonderful*

pass·word /ˈpɑːswɜːd‖ˈpæswɜrd/ *n* a secret word or phrase which one has to know in order to be allowed to enter a building, camp, etc.

past¹ /pɑːst‖pæst/ *adj* **1** [A;E] (of time) much earlier than the present: *In years past/past years they never would have done that* **2** [A;E] (*with the perfect tenses*) (of time) a little earlier than the present; up until now or until the time of speaking: *I've not been feeling very well for the past few days.|"This had been a war* ZONE (2) *for some time past"* (SEU W.) **3** [B] finished; ended: *Winter is past and spring has come* **4** [A] former: *my past successes|John Smith is a past president of our club* **5** [A] (of a verb form) expressing an action or event that took place before the present moment: *the past tense*

USAGE The past participle of **pass** is **passed**, but it is not used as an adjective. Instead, use **past**, which has the same sound. Compare: *The week has* **passed**.|*The week is* **past**.|*the* **past** *week*

past² *prep* **1** after; beyond in time: *The time is half past 3.|She is a woman far past her youth.|The trains leave at 10 past (the hour)* **2 a** farther than: *The hospital is about a mile past the school* **b** up to and beyond: *The boys rushed past us* **3** beyond the possibility of: *The sick man's condition is past hope* **4 past it** *infml* no longer able to do the things one could formerly do **5 would put it past somebody (to do something)** *infml nonassertive* to consider it unlikely for someone (to do something improper, unusual, etc.): *I wouldn't put it past him to cheat at cards!*

past³ *n* **1** [(*the*) S] time before the present: *In the past I have had many jobs* **2** [(*the*) S] what happened in time (long) before the present: *If only one could change the past, how different things might be* **3** [S] **a** (of a country) history: *Our country has a glorious past* **b** (of a person) life, actions, etc., before the present time, esp. when these contain wrong-doing of some kind: *Stories were told that she was a woman with a past* **4** [(*the*) S] the past tense

past⁴ *adv* by; to and beyond a point in time or space: *Children came running past.|Days went past without any news*

pas·ta /ˈpæstə‖ˈpɑ-/ *n* [U] nonsweet food made, in various different shapes, from flour paste. It is often covered with SAUCE and/or cheese

paste¹ /peɪst/ *n* [U;C] **1 a** a thin mixture of flour and water used for sticking paper together, or onto other surfaces **b** other sorts of mixture used for this **2** any soft wet mixture of powder and liquid that is easily shaped or spread: *This is where they mix the paste for toothpaste* **3** a mixture of flour, fat, and a small amount of liquid, for making pastry **4** a food made by crushing solid foods into a smooth soft mass, used for spreading on bread: *meat paste|fish paste* —compare PÂTÉ **5** a shining material made of lead and glass, used to copy the appearance of real jewels

paste² *v* **1** [X9] to stick or fasten (paper) with paste: *Please paste these sheets of paper together* **2** [T1] *infml & becoming rare* to strike; give a beating to —see also PASTING

paste·board /ˈpeɪstbɔːd‖-bord/ *n* **1** [U] flat stiff cardboard made by pasting (PASTE² (1)) sheets of paper together **2** [A] **a** made of this **b** lacking strength, value, or reality; cardboard; SHAM¹ (3)

paste down *v adv* [T1] to stick or fasten down (paper) using paste

pas·tel /ˈpæstl‖pæˈstel/ *n* **1** [U] (the art or practice of drawing using) a solid chalklike substance made of powdery colouring matter **2** [C] a small stick made of this substance, for easy holding **3** [C] a picture drawn using this substance **4** [A;(C)] any soft light colour (often in the phr. **pastel shade(s)**)

pas·tern /ˈpæstɜːn‖-ɜrn/ *n* the narrow upper part of a horse's foot, above the horny part (HOOF) —see picture at HORSE

paste-up /ˈ· ·/ *n* a group of small pieces of paper stuck on a larger sheet, so that the result will look like a page of a book that is to be printed, in order to judge its size, appearance, etc.

paste up *v adv* **1** [T1] to stick or fasten (paper) to a surface using paste **2** [T1] also **paste o·ver**— to cover with paper, stuck on using paste: *The windows that were pasted up did not break during the explosion* **3** [I∅] to stick small pieces of paper on larger sheets, so that the result will look like a page of a book that is to be printed

pas·teur·ize, -ise /ˈpæstʃəraɪz, -stə-/ *v* [Wv5;T1] to heat (a liquid, esp. milk) in a certain way in order to destroy bacteria —**-ization** /ˌpæstʃəraɪˈzeɪʃən, -stə-‖-rə-/ *n* [U]

pas·tiche /pæˈstiːʃ/ *n* **1** [C] a work of art (such as a piece of writing or music) that is purposely made in the manner of a different artist **2** [C] a work of art made up of pieces of various other works put together **3** [U] the style or practice of making works of art in either of these ways

pas·tille /pæˈstiːl/ *n* a small round hard sweet, esp. one containing a medicine for the throat

pas·time /ˈpɑːstaɪm‖ˈpæs-/ *n* something done to pass one's time in a pleasant way; RECREATION —see HOBBY (USAGE)

past·ing /ˈpeɪstɪŋ/ *n infml* **1** a hard beating **2** (in sport or other sorts of competition) a severe defeat

past mas·ter /ˌ· ˈ··/ *n* [(*at, in, of*)] a person who is very clever or skilled (in a particular subject or action)

pas·tor /ˈpɑːstəʳ‖ˈpæ-/ *n* [C;N] a Christian religious leader in charge of a church and its members (esp. of a Church other than the CATHOLIC Church, the CHURCH OF ENGLAND, or the CHURCH OF SCOTLAND)

pas·tor·al¹ /ˈpɑːstərəl‖ˈpæ-/ *adj* **1** *esp. lit* concerning simple peaceful country life, esp. as lived by SHEPHERDS: *a pastoral scene of cows drinking from a stream|pastoral poetry* **2** (of land) grassy; suitable for feeding sheep and cattle **3** *tech* of or concerning Christian priests, esp. BISHOPS **4** *tech* of or concerning the members of a religious group, or its leader's duties towards them: *The priest*/RABBI *makes pastoral visits every Tuesday*

pastoral² *n* **1** a PASTORAL¹ (1) poem, piece of music, picture, etc. **2** also **pastoral let·ter** /ˌ··· ˈ··/— *tech* an official letter sent by a BISHOP to the church members in his area

pastoral care /ˌ··· ˈ·/ *n* [U] nonmaterial help, esp. advice, offered esp. **a** by a religious leader to the members of his religious group or church **b** by a teacher or educational official to students

pas·to·rale /ˌpæstəˈrɑːli, -ˈrɑːl/ *n* a piece of music written in PASTORAL¹ (1) style

pas·tor·ate /ˈpɑːstərɪ̇t‖ˈpæ-/ *n* **1** **a** the office of a PASTOR **b** the length of time in office of a PASTOR **2** a body or company of PASTORS

past par·ti·ci·ple /ˌ· ˈ····/ also **perfect participle**— *n* (in grammar) a form of a verb which may be used in compound forms of the verb to express actions done or happening in the past, or sometimes as an adjective: *"Done" and "seen" are the past participles of "do" and "see"*

past per·fect /ˌ· ˈ··/ *n* PLUPERFECT

pas·tra·mi /pəˈstrɑːmi/ *n* [U] (esp. in the US) very strong-tasting meat of the cow (BEEF) usu. cut from the shoulder, and dried in smoke

pas·try /ˈpeɪstri/ *n* **1** [U] paste made of flour, fat, and milk or water, eaten when baked, used esp. to enclose other foods **2** [C] an article of food (esp. a small sweet cake) made wholly or partly of this **3** [U] these articles in general

pas·tur·age /ˈpɑːstʃərɪdʒ‖ˈpæs-/ *n* [U] **1** the right to use land for feeding one's cattle, horses, etc. **2** grass for feeding cattle, horses, etc. **3** also **pas·ture·land** /ˈpɑːstʃəlænd‖ˈpæstʃər-/— (natural) grassland suitable for feeding cattle on

pas·ture¹ /ˈpɑːstʃəʳ‖ˈpæs-/ *n* **1** [U] **a** grass considered or used as food for cattle **b** land where this is grown and where cattle feed on it **2** [C] a piece of land where this is grown **3 put out to pasture** *infml* to allow to stop working, esp. because of age: (fig.) *It's about time to put our old car out to pasture and get a new one*

pasture² *v* **1** [T1] (of people) **a** to put (farm animals) in a PASTURE¹ (2) **b** to feed (farm animals) on PASTURE¹ (1a) **2** [T1;L9] (of cattle, sheep, etc.) to feed on (an area of growing grass), esp. in a PASTURE¹ (2); GRAZE¹ (1) **3** [T1] *tech* to use (land) as PASTURE¹ (1b)

pas·ty¹ /ˈpæsti/ *n* (esp. in Britain) a folded piece of pastry baked with meat in it, usu. enough for one person to eat —see also CORNISH PASTY

past·y² /ˈpeɪsti/ *adj* [Wa1] (of the skin of the face) white and unhealthy-looking

pasty-faced /ˈpeɪsti feɪst/ *adj usu. derog* having a white and unhealthy looking face

pat¹ /pæt/ *n* **1** [C] a light friendly stroke with the flat hand, not intended to hurt: *He gave the dog a pat as he walked past* **2** [S;(C)] a sound made by hitting something lightly with a flat object **3** [C] a small shaped mass esp. of butter, made by or as if by PATting² (2) **4 a pat on the back** *infml* an expression of praise or satisfaction for something done

pat² *v* **-tt-** **1** [T1] to touch or strike gently and repeatedly with a flat object, esp. the flat hand (often to show kindness, pity, etc.): *She patted her hair to be sure that it was neat* **2** [L9] to touch or strike something gently and repeatedly **3 pat somebody/oneself on the back** *infml* to praise somebody/oneself for doing something well

pat³ *adv* [Wa5] **1** *often derog* at once; without delay: *The answer came pat* **2 have/know something (off) pat** *sometimes derog* to know something thoroughly and have it ready in one's mind so that one can speak or write it without delay **3 stand pat** **a** (in POKER) to play with the cards one has and not take new cards **b** to refuse to change one's decision

pat⁴ *adj* [Wa5] *often derog* (of words or events) coming (too) easily or readily, as if prepared before

pat-ball /ˈ· ·/ *n* [U] *infml* tennis or cricket badly played

patch[1] /pætʃ/ *n* **1** a (usu. small) piece of material used to cover a hole or a damaged place **2** an (often irregularly shaped) part of a surface or space that is different (esp. in colour) from the surface or space round it: *Wet patches on the wall* **3** a (usu. small) piece of ground, esp. as used for growing vegetables: *a potato patch* **4** *infml* a short part of a piece of work, esp. of writing or music, that is different from the rest **5** a protective piece of material worn over an eye that has been hurt **6** *now rare* STICKING PLASTER **7** also **beauty patch, beauty spot**— (in the 17th and 18th century) a small round usu. black piece of silk or other material worn by women on the face, to show up the beauty of the skin **8** *BrE infml* a usu. small area in which someone, esp. a policeman, always works and which he knows very well —compare PARISH (4) **9 be in/hit/strike/a bad patch** *esp. BrE* to experience a time of trouble or misfortune **10 in patches** in parts; here and there: *This poem is good in patches, but I don't like all of it* **11 not a patch on** *infml* not nearly as good as

patch[2] *v* [T1] **1** to cover (a hole) with a PATCH[1] (1) **2** to put a PATCH[1] (1) on a hole, worn place, etc. in (esp. some part of a garment): *The elbows on your coat have worn thin, so I must patch them* **3** (of a material) to serve as a PATCH[1] (1) for **4** to make from PATCHWORK (1)

pa·tchou·li /pəˈtʃuːli, ˈpætʃʊli/ *n* [U] **1** a bushy strong-smelling Indian plant **2** a sweet-smelling liquid (PERFUME) made from this

patch pock·et /ˌ· ˈ··/ *n* a pocket made by sewing a square piece of material onto the outside of a garment

patch up *v adv* [T1] **1** MAKE UP (1) **2** to mend with PATCHes (1): *to patch up an old coat*|(fig.) *The doctors patched up the wounded soldier and sent him back to fight again*

patch·work /ˈpætʃwɜːk‖-ɜrk/ *n* **1** [A;(U;C)] sewn work made by joining together a number of pieces of cloth of different colours, patterns, and shapes: *a patchwork bed cover*|(fig.) *From the aircraft he could see a patchwork of fields of different shapes and colours* **2** [S] *derog* something made up of a number of different bits and pieces

patch·y /ˈpætʃi/ *adj* [Wa1] **1** having a number of, or made up of, PATCHes[1] (2): *The sun has faded the curtains and their colour is now patchy* **2** (of certain types of weather) appearing in PATCHes[1] (2): *patchy mist* **3** *usu. derog* **a** incomplete: *Her knowledge of science is patchy* **b** only good in parts: *The concert was patchy* —**-ily** *adv* —**-iness** *n* [U]

pate /peɪt/ *n old use or humor* the top of the head (esp. in the phr. **bald pate**)

pât·é /ˈpæteɪ‖pɑˈteɪ, pæ-/ *n* **1** [U;(C)] a food made by crushing solid foods (esp. LIVER[1] (2)) into a smooth soft mass —compare PASTE[1] (4) and see also PÂTÉ DE FOIE GRAS **2** [C] *now rare* a PIE or PATTY

pâté de foie gras /ˌpæteɪ də ˌfwɑː ˈgrɑː‖pɑˌteɪ-, pæ- (*Fr* pɑte də fwa grɑ)/ also (*infml*) **foie gras**— *n* [U] *Fr* PÂTÉ made from the LIVER of a GOOSE

pa·tel·la /pəˈtelə/ *n med* KNEECAP (1)

pa·tent[1] /ˈpeɪtnt, ˈpæ-‖ˈpæ-/ *adj* **1** [B] (esp. of things that are not material) easy and plain to see; OBVIOUS **2** [Wa5;A] protected, by a PATENT[2] (1), from being copied or sold by those who do not have a right to do so: *a patent lock* **3** [Wa5;A] concerned with PATENTs[2] (1): *patent law* **4** [Wa5; A] *infml* (of some act of skill invented by a particular person) clever; rather new or different

patent[2] *n* **1** a piece of writing from a government office (**Patent** /ˈpætnt/ **Office**) giving someone the right to make or sell a new invention for a certain number of years **2** the right given in such a piece of writing: *The patent runs out in 2 years' time* **3** something protected by a PATENT[2] (1) **4** *infml* someone's own clever way of doing something

patent[3] *v* [T1] to obtain a PATENT[2] (1) for —compare PATENT[1] (2)

pa·tent·ee /ˌpeɪtnˈtiː‖ˌpæ-/ *n esp. law* a person to whom a PATENT[2] (1) is given

patent leath·er /ˌpeɪtnt ˈleðəʳ‖ˌpæ-/ *n* [U] fine thin very shiny leather, usu. black: *patent-leather shoes*

pa·tent·ly /ˈpeɪtntli‖ˈpæ-/ *adv derog* clearly and plainly: *He was patently lying.*|*a patently false statement*

patent medi·cine /ˌ·· ˈ···/ *n* [U;C] **1** *usu. derog* (a) medicine made of a secret mixture and claiming to produce a wonderful effect on the health **2** (a) medicine officially permitted to be made by only one firm

pa·ter /ˈpeɪtəʳ/ *n* [N;(C9)] *BrE old public school sl* (*sometimes cap.*) father

pa·ter·fa·mil·i·as /ˌpeɪtəfəˈmɪliæs‖-tər-/ *n* **patresfa·milias** /ˌpɑːtreɪs-, ˌpeɪtriːs-/ [*usu. sing.*] *humor* the father or male head of a (usu. large) family

pa·ter·nal /pəˈtɜːnl‖-ɜr-/ *adj* **1** [Wa5] of, like, or received from a father: *paternal love* —compare MATERNAL **2 a** fatherly; protecting **b** *derog* too kindly; that protects people but does not allow them any freedom **3** related to a person through the father's side of the family —**-nally** *adv*

pa·ter·nal·is·m /pəˈtɜːnəl-ɪzəm‖-ɜr-/ *n* [U] *derog* the PATERNAL (2b) way of controlling an association or ruling a country —**-t** *n* —**-tic** /pəˌtɜːnəˈlɪstɪk‖-ɜr-/ *adj* —**-tically** *adv* [Wa4]

pa·ter·ni·ty /pəˈtɜːnəti‖-ɜr-/ *n* **1** [U] fatherhood **2** [U] *esp. law* origin from the male parent **3** [U9] *fml* the beginnings from which an idea, plan, etc., has developed

pa·ter·nos·ter /ˌpætəˈnɒstəʳ‖-tərˈnɑ-/ *n* (*usu. cap.*) (an act of saying) the LORD'S PRAYER, esp. in the LATIN (1) language

path /pɑːθ‖pæθ/ *n* **1** [C] also **pathway**— a track or way made by people walking over the ground: *Grass has grown over the path through the woods now that people no longer use it* **2** [C] FOOTPATH **3** [C (*through*)] an open space made to allow forward movement: *They used axes to clear a path through the forest* **4** [C] a line along which something moves: *The path of an arrow is a curve* **5** [(*the*) C] (of action, thought, living, etc.) a way: *Hard work is the path to success* **6 beat a path a** to make a PATH (3) (as through a forest) by beating down plants and bushes that are in the way **b** to come rushing: *"If you build a better mousetrap, people will beat a path to your door"* (Emerson) (= cleverness brings success) **7 cross somebody's path** to meet somebody by accident **8 stand in somebody's path** to prevent somebody from doing what he wants to do —**~less** *adj*

Pa·than /pəˈtɑːn/ *adj* of a group of people living esp. in Afghanistan

pa·thet·ic /pəˈθetɪk/ *adj* **1** causing a feeling of pity or sorrow: *the little dog's pathetic cries* **2** *derog* worthless; hopelessly unsuccessful: *pathetic attempts to learn French* —**-ically** *adv* [Wa4]

pathetic fal·la·cy /·ˌ·· ˈ···/ *n* [*the* +R;(C)] *tech* (esp. in a work of literature) the use of the mistake of saying that objects without life have human qualities, feelings, etc.; ANTHROPOMORPHISM

path·find·er /ˈpɑːθˌfaɪndəʳ‖ˈpæθ-/ *n* **1 a** a person who goes on ahead of a group and finds the best way through unknown land **b** a person who discovers new ways of doing things —compare PIONEER **2** *tech* an aircraft, or the person in it, that guides other aircraft over a place they are going to bomb

path·o·log·i·cal /ˌpæθəˈlɒdʒɪkəl‖-ˈlɑ-/ *adj* **1** [Wa5;A] *med* of or concerning PATHOLOGY **2** [Wa5;B] *med* caused by disease, esp. of the mind **3** [B] *infml* unreasonable; unnatural; caused by the imagination only: *a pathological fear of the dark* —**-cally** *adv* [Wa5]: *pathologically jealous*

pa·thol·o·gist /pəˈθɒlədʒɪst‖-ˈθɑ-/ *n med* a person (esp. a doctor) who is a specialist in PATHOLOGY (esp. one who examines a dead body to find out how the person has died)

pa·thol·o·gy /pəˈθɒlədʒi‖-ˈθɑ-/ *n* [U] *med* the study of disease

pa·thos /ˈpeɪθɒs‖-θɑs/ *n* [U] *esp. lit* the quality in speech, writing, etc., that causes a feeling of pity and sorrow

path·way /ˈpɑːθweɪ‖ˈpæθ-/ *n* PATH (1)

pa·tience /ˈpeɪʃəns/ *n* [U] **1** the ability **a** to wait for something calmly for a long time: *You need to have patience if you want to get served in this shop* **b** to control oneself when angered, esp. at foolishness or slowness: *If you don't stop making that noise I'm going to lose my patience* **2** the power of bearing pain or other unpleasant things without complaining **3** (the power of showing) care and close attention to work that is difficult or tiring: *I wouldn't have the patience to sit mending watches all day* **4** *AmE* **solitaire**— any of a number of card games, usu. for one player

pa·tient¹ /ˈpeɪʃənt/ *adj* having or showing patience —**~ly** *adv*

patient² *n* **1** a person receiving medical treatment from a doctor and/or in a hospital **2** any of the group of people who go to a particular doctor when they need medical treatment —see CUSTOMER (USAGE)

pat·i·na /ˈpætɪnə/ *n* **1** [U;S] a usu. green surface covering formed on all copper or BRONZE (1) **2** [U;S] a smooth shiny surface on wood, walls, etc. **3** [S] an appearance (esp. in a person) that comes from long experience of something: *the patina of wealth*

pat·i·o /ˈpætiəʊ/ *n* **-tios** **1** an open space between a house and garden, with a stone floor, used for sitting on in fine weather **2** an inner roofless courtyard of a Spanish or Spanish-American house

pa·tis·se·rie /pəˈtiːsəri (*Fr* pɑtisri)/ *n Fr* a shop that sells French-style pastry or cakes

pa·tois /ˈpætwɑː/ *n* **-tois** /twɑːz/ [C;U] *Fr & often derog* a form of spoken language used by the people of a small area, which is different from the national language, esp. if felt to be nonstandard —compare DIALECT

pat·ri- /ˈpeɪtrɪ, ˈpætrɪ/ *prefix* father: PATRICIDE| PATRIARCHY —compare MATRI-

pa·tri·al /ˈpeɪtrɪəl, ˈpætrɪəl/ *n esp. BrE* a person who for special reasons (esp. because one of his parents or his grandfather or grandmother was born in the United Kingdom) has a lawful right to settle in the United Kingdom

pa·tri·arch /ˈpeɪtriɑːk‖-ɑrk/ *n* **1** **a** a priest of high rank (BISHOP) in the early Christian Church **b** (*usu. cap.*) one of the chief BISHOPs of the Eastern Churches: *the Patriarch of Jerusalem* **c** (*usu. cap.*) a BISHOP of the ROMAN CATHOLIC Church, in rank just below the POPE **2** an old and much-respected man **3** *esp. bibl* the male head of a family or tribe

pa·tri·arch·al /ˌpeɪtriˈɑːkəl‖-ɑr-/ *adj* **1** of or like a PATRIARCH **2** ruled or controlled only by men: *a patriarchal society*

pa·tri·arch·ate /ˈpeɪtriɑːkɪt‖-ɑr-/ *n* the rank, length of rule, area, or home of a religious PATRIARCH (1)

pa·tri·arch·y /ˈpeɪtriɑːki‖-ɑr-/ *n* [U;C] a social group or system ruled or controlled only by men

pa·tri·cian¹ /pəˈtrɪʃən/ *n* **1** a member of the governing classes in ancient Rome —compare PLEBEIAN **2** *derog or apprec* a nobleman; ARISTOCRAT

patrician² *adj* **1** belonging to the governing classes in ancient Rome **2** *derog or apprec* of or like a PATRICIAN¹ (2)

pat·ri·cide /ˈpætrɪsaɪd/ *n* **1** [U] the murder of one's own father **2** [C] a person guilty of this —compare PARRICIDE

pat·ri·mo·ny /ˈpætrɪməni‖-məʊni/ *n* [U;S;(C)] **1** property received by right of birth (INHERITed) from one's father, grandfather, etc. **2** *tech* land, money, etc., given to and belonging to a church —**-nial** /ˌpætrɪˈməʊnɪəl/ *adj*

pat·ri·ot /ˈpætrɪət, -triɒt, ˈpeɪ-‖ˈpeɪtrɪət, -triɑt/ *n usu. apprec* a person who loves and is willing to defend his country

pat·ri·ot·ic /ˌpætriˈɒtɪk, ˌpeɪ-‖ˌpeɪtriˈɑtɪk/ *adj usu. apprec* having or expressing the qualities of a PATRIOT: *patriotic songs* —**-ically** *adv* [Wa4]

pat·ri·ot·is·m /ˈpætrɪətɪzəm, ˈpeɪ-‖ˈpeɪ-/ *n* [U] *usu. apprec* love for and loyalty to one's country

pa·trol¹ /pəˈtrəʊl/ *n* **1** [U] **a** the act of PATROLling² (1) (esp. in the phr. **on patrol**) **b** the time of PATROLling² (1): *All was quiet during his patrol* **2** [C] (esp. in military use) a small group of people, vehicles, etc., sent out from a place to search for the enemy, or to protect that place from the enemy **3** [C] a small body of BOY SCOUTs or GIRL GUIDEs

patrol² *v* **-ll-** **1** [T1;L9] to go at regular times round (an area, building, etc.) to see that there is no trouble, that no one is trying to get in or out unlawfully, etc. **2** [T1] *often derog* to walk along (an area), esp. in a group: *Bands of youths patrol the streets on Saturday nights*

patrol car /·ˈ· ·/ *n* a car used by the police for PATROLling² (1) roads

pa·trol·man /pəˈtrəʊlmən/ *n* **-men** /mən/ **1** *BrE* a person working for a car-owners' association who drives along certain roads to give help to motorists who need it **2** *esp. AmE* a policeman who regularly PATROLs² (1) a particular area

patrol wag·on /·ˈ· ˌ··/ *n AmE* a vehicle used to carry people who have been caught (ARRESTed) by the police; BLACK MARIA

pa·tron /ˈpeɪtrən/ *n* **1** [(*of*)] a person or group that supports and gives money to a person, a group of people, or some worthy purpose **2** [(*of*)] a person (esp. one of importance) who takes an interest in and allows his or her name to be used in connection with some group **3** *now rare* PATRON SAINT **4** a person who uses a particular shop, hotel, etc., esp. regularly: *a special offer for our regular patrons* —compare CUSTOMER

pat·ron·age /ˈpætrənɪdʒ/ *n* **1** [U] the support given by a PATRON (1,2) **2** [U] the trade and support received from a PATRON (4) **3** [S] all the PATRONs (4) of a shop, hotel, etc., as a group: *This shop has a large patronage* —compare CLIENTELE **4** [U] *sometimes derog* the right to appoint or act of appointing people to important positions, esp. without regard to their ability **5** [U] *usu. derog* the showing of favour or kind treatment in a patronizing (PATRONIZE (2)) way

pa·tron·ess /ˈpeɪtrənɪs/ *n* a female PATRON (1,3)

pat·ron·ize, -ise /ˈpætrənaɪz‖ˈpeɪ-, ˈpæ-/ *v* [T1] **1** to be a PATRON (4) of **2** [Wv4] to act towards as if better or more important than: *Some people cannot speak to children, even kindly, without patronizing them* **3** to act as a PATRON (1) towards

patron saint /ˌ·· ˈ·/ *n* [(*of*)] a Christian holy man or woman of former times (SAINT), regarded as giving special protection to a particular place, activity, etc.: SAINT *Christopher is the patron saint of travellers*

pat·ro·nym·ic /ˌpætrəˈnɪmɪk/ *adj, n* [Wa5] (a name) formed from the name of a father, grandfather, etc.

pat·ten /ˈpætn/ *n* a wooden shoe (CLOG), with pieces of iron on the bottom to keep the feet above the mud

pat·ter¹ /ˈpætəʳ/ *v* [L9;(T1)] to say (words, prayers, or meaningless things) quickly and without thought

patter² *n* **1** [U;(S)] very fast continuous amusing talk, esp. as used by a magician while doing tricks or by a man telling jokes **2** [U] the words of a fast amusing song (often in the phr. **patter song**) **3** [U;(S)] words quickly spoken between the lines of a song **4** [U] the language, words, etc., used by a particular class of people: *thieves' patter*

patter³ *v* **1** [L9;I∅] to make a number of light quickly repeated noises: *the falling leaves pattering against the windows* **2** [L9] to run with short quick-sounding steps, making light noises: *The dog pattered down the stairs*

patter⁴ *n* [S (*of*)] the sound of something striking a hard surface lightly, quickly, and repeatedly

pat·tern¹ /ˈpætn‖ˈpætərn/ *n* **1** a regularly repeated arrangement (esp. of lines, shapes, or colours on a surface, with ornamental effect, or of sounds, words, etc.): *The cloth has a pattern of red and white squares* **2** the way in which something happens or develops: *The illness is not following its usual pattern* **3** a small piece of cloth that shows what a large piece (of usual size) will look like; SAMPLE **4** a shape used as a guide for making something, esp. **a** a piece of paper used to show the shape of a part of a garment **b** a piece of wood used to set the shape of metal parts of machinery, made by a man (**patternmaker**) in a special room (**pattern shop**) in a factory **5** [(*of*) *usu. sing.*] a person or thing that is an excellent example to copy: *This company is a pattern of what a good company should be* —compare MODEL¹ (3)

pattern² *v* **1** [L9, esp. *after, on, upon*] to make according to a PATTERN¹ (4,5); copy exactly: *patterning himself upon a man he admired* **2** [T1 (*with*)] to make an ornamental PATTERN¹ (1) on

pat·ty /ˈpæti/ *n* **1** a small PIE or PASTY **2** *AmE* food cut into very small pieces, formed into small flat shapes and cooked

pau·ci·ty /ˈpɔːsəti/ *n* [S;(U): (*of*)] *fml* a number or quantity (of something) that is small and esp. less than what is needed; DEARTH

paunch /pɔːntʃ/ *n derog or humor* a fat stomach, esp. a man's —see also POT (13), POTBELLY (1)

paunch·y /ˈpɔːntʃi/ *adj* [Wa2] *derog or humor* (esp. of a man) having a fat stomach —**-iness** *n* [U]

pau·per /ˈpɔːpəʳ/ *n* **1** *esp. old use* a person who is too poor to be able to look after himself, and therefore receives official help **2** a person who is very poor

pau·per·is·m /ˈpɔːpərɪzəm/ *n* [U] the quality or state of being a PAUPER

pau·per·ize, -ise /ˈpɔːpəraɪz/ *v* [T1] to cause to become a PAUPER —**-ization** /ˌpɔːpəraɪˈzeɪʃən‖-rə-/ *n* [U]

pause¹ /pɔːz/ *n* **1** [(*in*)] a short but noticeable break (in activity, or speech): *a pause in the conversation* **2** (in music) a mark (𝄐) over a note, showing that the note is to be played or sung longer than usual **3 give somebody pause** to cause somebody to stop and consider carefully what he is doing

pause² *v* [I∅] to make a pause; stop for a short time: *"Why did you pause? Go on."*|*pausing to pick up a stone*

pause on also **pause up·on**— *v prep* [T1] to make the sound of (a word or musical note) longer than usual

pa·vane, pavan /pəˈvæn, ˈpævən‖pəˈvɑn, pəˈvæn/ *n* (the music for) a formal COURTLY dance of the 16th and 17th centuries

pave /peɪv/ *v* [T1 (*with*)] **1** to cover (a path, area, etc.) with a hard level surface (esp. of PAVING STONE*s*) **2 pave the way for somebody** to go before somebody and make easier some action that he had to do **3 pave the way for/to (something)** to make (something) easier, or possible: *The agreement paves the way for a lasting peace*

paved /peɪvd/ *adj* [Wa5] **1** [B] (of a path, area, etc.) covered with a hard level surface (esp. of PAVING STONE*s*) **2** [F +*with*] made easy (by); full (of): *His way through life was paved with success*

pave·ment /ˈpeɪvmənt/ *n* **1** *AmE* **sidewalk**— a PAVED surface or path at the side of a street for people to walk on **2** *AmE* the PAVED surface of a street **3** a PAVED surface of any sort; PAVING (2)

pavement art·ist /ˈ·· ˌ··/ (*AmE* **sidewalk artist**)— *n* a person who draws pictures on a PAVEMENT (1) with coloured chalk, hoping that people passing will give him money

pa·vil·ion /pəˈvɪljən/ *n* **1** *esp. BrE* a building beside a sports (esp. cricket) field, for the use of the players and those watching the game **2** a large lightly made usu. ornamental building used for public amusements or EXHIBITION*s* (1), esp. one intended to be used only for a short time **3** a large tent, esp. one used for summer shows of flowers, farm goods, etc. —compare MARQUEE

pav·ing /ˈpeɪvɪŋ/ *n* **1** [U] material used to PAVE (1) a surface **2** [U] a PAVED surface of any sort; PAVEMENT (3) **3** [C *usu. pl.*] PAVING STONE —see also CRAZY PAVING

paving stone /ˈ·· ·/ also **paving**— *n* a piece of flat stone, fitted close to other such stones to form a PAVEMENT —see picture at STREET

paw¹ /pɔː/ *n* **1** an animal's foot that has nails or CLAW*s* —compare HOOF and see picture at CAT **2** *infml & esp. humor* a human hand: *Go and wash your dirty paws!*

paw² *v* **1** [T1] also **paw at**— (of an animal) to touch or make a strike at with a PAW¹ (1): *The dog pawed (at) the bone* **2** [T1;I∅ (*at*)] (of an animal) to strike at (the ground) with the HOOF in anger, fear, impatience, etc. **3** [T1 (ABOUT);I∅ (*at*)] *infml* (of a person) to feel or touch with the hands, esp. in a rude, rough, or sexually improper manner: *She wanted to watch the film, but he kept pawing her (about)*

paw·ky /ˈpɔːki/ *adj* [Wa1] *esp. BrE* amusing in an odd clever way, so that one cannot tell whether the thing said was meant to be funny or serious (esp. in the phr. **pawky humour**) —**-kily** *adv* —**-kiness** *n* [U]

pawl /pɔːl/ *n* a short piece of metal that fits between the teeth of a toothed wheel or bar (RATCHET) so as to allow movement in one direction but not in the other

pawn¹ /pɔːn/ *n* [U] *fml* the state of being PAWNed² (1) (esp. in the phr. **in pawn**)

pawn² *v* [T1] **1** to leave (something of value) with a PAWNBROKER as a promise that one will repay the money he has lent one **2** to give up (one's life, word, etc.) in return for something

pawn³ *n* **1** (in CHESS) one of the 8 smallest and least valuable of a player's pieces —see CHESS (USAGE) **2** an unimportant person used by somebody else for his own advantage

pawn·bro·ker /ˈpɔːnˌbrəʊkəʳ/ *n* a person to whom people bring valuable articles so that he will lend them money, and who has the right to sell the articles if the money is not repaid within a certain time

pawn·shop /ˈpɔːnʃɒp‖-ʃɑp/ also *BrE sl* **popshop**— *n* a PAWNBROKER'*s* place of business

paw·paw /ˈpɔːpɔː/ *n* [C;U] *esp. BrE and CarE* PAPAYA

pay[1] /peɪ/ *v* **paid** **1** [D1 (*to*);T1 (*for*);V3;I∅ (*for*); I3] to give (money) for goods bought, work done, etc.: *I paid (2 pounds) for that book|to have my radio mended.|I'll pay you 2 pounds for it.|I don't mind paying to have my door painted.|I'm afraid I can't pay (you) (anything) (for it).|He paid them (£5) to take it away.|He paid to see the show* **2** [T1] to settle (a bill, debt, etc.) **3** [X9, esp. *into*] to put ((a form of) money) into (a bank, an account, etc.) to be kept safe **4** [T1;I∅] to be profitable; be worth the trouble or cost (to somebody): *It doesn't pay (you) to argue with him.|We must make this farm pay* **5** [Wv5;L9] (of work, something done, etc.) to bring or give one money or something of value in return: *a badly paid job* **6** [D1 (*to*)] to make or say (esp. in the phrs. **pay a visit, pay a call, pay a compliment, pay one's respects**): *I'll pay you a visit next week* **7** [T1 (*to*)] to give willingly or as is considered proper (esp. in the phrs. **pay attention/heed (to)**) **8** [I∅ (*for*)] to suffer for some bad action: *He thinks he can get away with cheating me, but I'll make him pay* —see also PAY BACK, PAY FOR **9** **pay one's way** to pay money for things as one buys them so as not to get into debt —see also PAY BACK, PAY FOR, PAY IN, PAY INTO, PAY OFF, PAY OUT, PAY OVER, PAY UP

pay[2] *n* [U] **1** money received for work **2** **in the pay of** *esp. derog* employed by: *This man is in the pay of the enemy*
USAGE This is the most general word for the money one receives for work. **Remuneration** is a very formal word for **pay**. Another formal word, **emoluments**, means **pay** and may include, for example, money to pay for the use of a car. **Wages** and **salary** are **pay** received at regular times, but a **salary** is usually paid monthly straight into a bank by one's employer, and suggests a rather grander job than **wages**, which are handed over weekly in an envelope.

pay·a·ble /ˈpeɪəbəl/ *adj* **1** [F] (of a bill, debt, etc.) **a** that must be paid: *This bill is payable next Tuesday* **b** that may be paid: *This bill is payable at any time up to next Tuesday* **2** [F +*to*] (of a cheque) having written on it the name of (a particular person) to whom the stated amount of money will be paid

pay back *v adv* **1** [T1 (*for*)] also (*infml*) **pay off** *BrE* also **pay out, serve out**— to return punishment to (someone who has done something wrong to oneself) **2** [D1 (*to*);T1: (*for*)] to return what is owing: *Have I paid (you) back the £10 you lent me for those books?*

pay·day /ˈpeɪdeɪ/ *n* [R;C] the day on which wages are (to be) paid

pay dirt /ˈ· ·/ *n* [U] *AmE* **1** earth found to contain valuable minerals, such as gold **2** a valuable or useful discovery

P A Y E /ˌpiː eɪ waɪ ˈiː/ *abbrev. for:* (*BrE*) pay as you earn; a system by which income tax is taken away from wages before the wages are paid

pay·ee /peɪˈiː/ *n tech* a person to whom money is or should be paid

pay en·ve·lope /ˈ· ˌ···/ *n AmE* PAY PACKET (1)

pay·er /ˈpeɪəʳ/ *n often tech* a person who pays or is supposed to pay for something

pay for *v prep* [T1,(4)] to receive punishment or suffering for (something): *You'll have to pay for your crime.|We are paying for the fine summer with a wet winter*

pay in *v adv* [T1] to pay (money) into a bank account

pay in·to *v prep* [D1] to pay (money) into (a bank account)

pay·load /ˈpeɪləʊd/ *n* **1** (the weight of) the part of a load of a load-carrying vehicle for which payment is received **2** the amount of explosive in the head of a MISSILE (1)

pay·mas·ter /ˈpeɪˌmɑːstəʳ‖-ˌmæ-/ *n* **1** an official in a factory, the Armed Forces, etc., who pays wages to people **2** [*often pl.*] *derog* a person who pays somebody to do something for him, and who therefore has control over the other person's actions

paymaster gen·e·ral /ˌ··· ˈ···/ *n* **paymasters general** *or* **paymaster generals** [C;(A)] (*often caps.*) a minister in the British government who may be given any duty in the government (but usu. one connected with the TREASURY)

pay·ment /ˈpeɪmənt/ *n* **1** [U] the act of PAYing[1] (1,3) **2** [C] an amount of money (to be) paid **3** [U;(S)] something done, said, or given in return for something done or as a result of one's action —compare REWARD[2] (1)

pay·nim /ˈpeɪnɪ̆m/ *n old use & usu. derog* (*sometimes cap.*) (esp. as used of Muslims by Christians during the time of the CRUSADE*s* (1)) HEATHEN (1)

pay·off /ˈpeɪɒf‖-ɔf/ *n* [(*the*) S] *infml* **1** **a** the act or time of paying wages, debts, money won at cards, etc. **b** payment of someone whom one has employed to do something unlawful, immoral, etc. **2** the end of a number of connected acts (esp. the end of a story someone has been telling, when everything is explained) —compare PUNCH LINE **3** punishment of someone for his (repeatedly) doing wrong; RETRIBUTION

pay off *v adv* **1** [T1] to pay the whole of (a debt) **2** [T1] *infml* PAY BACK (1) **3** [T1] to pay and dismiss (someone) **4** [T1] to pay (someone) to keep silent about a wrong act **5** [I∅] to be successful: *Did your plan pay off?*

pay·o·la /peɪˈəʊlə/ *n sl* **1** [U;S] a secret or not direct payment made in return for a business favour (as to a radio broadcaster, so that he will often play (PLUG (2)) a particular record on the radio) **2** [U] the practice of making such payments

pay out *v adv* [T1] **1** to pay (money) in small amounts **2** also **run out**— to allow (esp. a rope) to be made or pulled gradually longer **3** *BrE* PAY BACK (1)

pay o·ver *v adv* [T1 (*to*)] to make formal payment of (money)

pay pack·et /ˈ· ˌ··/ *n BrE* **1** *AmE* **pay envelope**— an envelope containing wages and a piece of paper (**pay slip**) showing the amount of wages given to an employed person each week **2** the amount of wages a person earns

pay phone /ˈ· ·/ also **pay tel·e·phone** /ˈ· ˌ···/— *n* a public telephone which one can use only after putting a coin into a special machine

pay·roll /ˈpeɪrəʊl/ *n* **1** [C] a list of workers employed by a company and the amount of wages each person is to be paid **2** [S] the total amount of wages paid to all the workers in a particular company

pay sta·tion /ˈ· ˌ··/ *n AmE* PAY PHONE

pay up *v adv* [I∅] to pay a debt in full, often unwillingly —compare PAID-UP

P.C. *abbrev. for:* (*BrE*) Police Constable; a male member of the police force having the lowest rank: *P.C. Johnson|2 P.C.'s were attacked*

P E /ˌpiː ˈiː/ *n* [U] *infml* PHYSICAL education; PHYSICAL TRAINING

pea /piː/ *n* **1** a large round green seed which is used for food **2** any of various climbing plants which produce long vessels (PODs) containing these seeds —see picture at VEGETABLE[1] **3 as like as two peas (in a pod)** exactly the same in appearance

peace /piːs/ *n* **1** [U;S] **a** a condition in which there is no war between 2 or more nations **b** a period in which there is no war **2** [*the* +R] a state of freedom from disorder within a country, with the citizens living according to the law (esp. in the phrs. **keep the peace, a breach of the peace, the King's/Queen's peace**) **3** [U] a state of agreement or friendliness among people living or working together **4** [U] calmness; quietness: *Please let me get on with my work in peace* (often in the phr. **peace and quiet**) **5** [U] freedom from anxiety or troubling thoughts: *peace of mind* **6 be at peace** *euph* to be dead **7 hold one's peace** to remain silent although one has something to say **8 make one's peace with (somebody)** to settle a quarrel with (somebody)

peace·a·ble /ˈpiːsəbəl/ *adj* **1** disliking argument or quarrelling **2** calm; free from disorder or fighting: *a peaceable agreement* —**-bly** *adv*

Peace Corps /ˈ· ·/ *n* [*the* +GU] a body of trained people, esp. young people, who are sent abroad from the US to help developing countries

peace·ful /ˈpiːsfəl/ *adj* **1** quiet; untroubled: *How peaceful it is in the country now!* **2** loving peace: *peaceful nations* —**~ly** *adv* —**~ness** *n* [U]

peace·mak·er /ˈpiːsˌmeɪkəʳ/ *n* **1** a person who causes nations or people to stop fighting or quarrelling with each other **2** *esp. humor & AmE* REVOLVER

peace of·fer·ing /ˈ· ˌ···/ *n* something offered to show that one wants to be friendly (esp. with someone whom one has annoyed)

peace pipe /ˈ· ·/ also **pipe of peace**— *n* [S;(C)] an ornamental ceremonial tobacco pipe smoked by North American Indians as a sign that peace had been made with an enemy (esp. in the phr. **smoke the peace pipe**)

peace·time /ˈpiːstaɪm/ *n* [U;(S)] a time when a nation is not at war —opposite **wartime**

peach[1] /piːtʃ/ *n* **1** [C] a round fruit with soft yellowish-red skin and sweet juicy flesh, and having a large rough seed in its centre —see picture at FRUIT[1] **2** [U] the colour of the skin of this fruit; yellowish-red **3** [C] also **peach tree** /ˈ· ·/— the small tree on which this grows **4** [S;(C)] *infml* a person (esp. a pretty young girl) or thing that is greatly admired: *She has bought herself a peach of a new hat*

peach[2] *v* [I∅ (*against, on*)] *sl* (*used esp. by schoolboys*) to give information about somebody who has done wrong, esp. somebody who has reason to trust one

pea·chick /ˈpiːˌtʃɪk/ *n* a young PEAFOWL

Peach Mel·ba /ˌpiːtʃ ˈmelbə/ *n* **Peach Melbas** [C;(U)] half a PEACH[1] (1) served with ice cream and RASPBERRY juice

pea·cock /ˈpiːkɒk‖-kɑk/ *n* **1** the male PEAFOWL, famous for its long tail feathers which can be spread out showing beautiful colours and patterns **2** also **peacock but·ter·fly** /ˌ·· ˈ···/— an insect (BUTTERFLY) with large wings which have patterns on them like those on the tail of this bird **3** PEAFOWL: *a female peacock*

peacock blue /ˌ·· ˈ·◂/ *n, adj* [Wa5;B;U] (a colour that is) bright shiny blue

pea·fowl /ˈpiːfaʊl/ *n* **peafowl** *or* **peafowls** [Wn2] a type of large bird now often kept in parks for ornamental purposes

pea green /ˌ· ˈ·◂/ *n, adj* [Wa5;B;U] (a colour that is) light bright green like the colour of PEAs (1)

pea·hen /ˈpiːhen/ *n* a large brownish bird, the female PEAFOWL

peak[1] /piːk/ *v old use* **peak and pine** to become thin as a result of grief

peak[2] *n* **1 a** a sharply pointed mountain top: *The (mountain) peaks are covered with snow all the year* **b** a whole mountain with a sharp top: *Here the high peaks begin to rise from the plain* —see picture at MOUNTAIN **2** a part that curves to a point above a surface: *The wind blew the waves into great peaks* **3** the flat curved part of a cap which sticks out in front above the eyes **4** hair growing or shaped to a point **5** *tech* the narrow part of the inside of a ship, either at the front or back, where goods are stored **6** the highest point, level, etc., esp. of a varying amount, development, etc.: *Sales have reached a new peak.|The roads are full of traffic at peak hours* —compare OFF-PEAK

peak[3] *v* [I∅] to reach a PEAK[2] (6): *Sales have now peaked, and we expect them to decrease soon*

peaked[1] /piːkt/ *adj* [Wa5;A;(B)] having a PEAK[2] (3,1)

peaked[2] /piːkt‖ˈpiːk½d/ *adj* PEAKY (1)

pea·ky /ˈpiːki/ *adj* [Wa1] **1** also **peaked**— thin, weak, and sick-looking, with the bones showing sharply **2** *infml* slightly ill: *I'm feeling a bit peaky this morning*

peal[1] /piːl/ *n* **1** the sound of the loud ringing of bells **2** *tech* a musical pattern made by the ringing of a number of bells one after another **3** *tech* a set of bells on which these patterns can be played **4** a loud long sound or number of sounds one after the other: *a peal of thunder|peals of laughter*

peal[2] *v* **1** [I∅ (OUT)] (esp. of bells) to ring out or sound loudly (and continually) **2** [T1] to cause (bells) to ring out

pea·nut /ˈpiːnʌt/ also (*becoming rare*) **monkey-nut,** *AmE dial* also **goober**— *n* **1** *esp. BrE* a GROUNDNUT as used for eating **2** *esp. AmE* GROUNDNUT

peanut but·ter /ˈ·· ˌ··/ *n* [U] a soft substance made of crushed PEANUTs (1), usu. eaten on bread

pea·nuts /ˈpiːnʌts/ *n* [P] *sl esp. AmE* a sum of money so small that it is not worth considering

pear /peəʳ/ *n* a sweet juicy fruit, narrow at the stem end and wide at the other

pear drop /ˈpeədrɒp‖ˈpeərdrɑp/ *n* a sweet shaped liked a small PEAR

pearl[1] /pɜːl‖pɜrl/ *n* **1** [C] **a** a hard round small silvery-white mass formed inside the shell of shell fish, esp. OYSTERs, very valuable as a jewel **b** a man-made copy of this **2** [C] something which has the shape or colour of this **3** [A;(U)] MOTHER-OF-PEARL **4** [C] something or somebody very precious, esp. a woman **5 cast pearls before swine** to offer something valuable to someone who cannot understand how valuable it is

pearl[2] *v* [I∅] to search in water for shells containing PEARLs[1] (1a) (esp. in the phr. **go pearling**)

pearl bar·ley /ˌ· ˈ··/ *n* [U] the grain of BARLEY after the outside covering has been taken off, rolled until it is small and round

pearl div·er /ˈ· ˌ··/ also (*now rare*) **pearl fish·er** /ˈ· ˌ··/— *n* a person who swims under water at sea, looking for shells containing PEARLs[1] (1a)

pearl fish·er·y /ˈ· ˌ···/ *n* a part of the seabed where shells containing PEARLs[1] (1a) are gathered

pearl·y /ˈpɜːli‖ˈpɜrli/ *adj* [Wa1] like or ornamented with PEARLs[1] (1) or PEARL[1] (2): *pearly teeth|a pale pearly grey* —**-iness** *n* [U]

pear·main /ˈpeəmeɪn‖ˈpeər-/ *n* (*usu. in comb.*) a type of apple

peas·ant /ˈpezənt/ *n* **1** [C] (now used esp. of developing countries or former times) a person who works on the land, esp. one who owns and lives on a small piece of land **2** [C;N] *derog* a person without education or manners

peas·ant·ry /ˈpezəntri/ *n* [(*the*) GU] all the PEASANTs (1) of a particular country

pease pud·ding /ˌpiːz ˈpʊdɪŋ/ *n* [U;(C)] a dish made of dried PEAs (1), boiled to a soft brown mass

pea·shoot·er /ˈpiːˌʃuːtəʳ/ *n* a small tube used by children for blowing small objects (esp. dried PEAs (1)) at people or things

pea soup·er /ˌ· ˈ··/ *n infml* a thick heavy yellow FOG

peat /piːt/ *n* **1** [U] partly decayed vegetable matter which takes the place of ordinary soil in a certain area (**peat bog**), and is used for burning instead of coal or for making plants grow better **2** [C] a piece of this cut out to be used for making fires —**~y** *adj* [Wa1]

peb·ble /ˈpebəl/ *n* **1** [C] a small roundish smooth stone found esp. on the seashore or on a riverbed **2** [U] a hard glasslike kind of stone, sometimes formerly used for making the LENSes of glasses **3** [C] a LENS of a pair of glasses, esp. one made of this stone **4 not the only pebble on the beach** not the only person who has to be considered; only one out of many others who deserve attention

peb·ble·dash /ˈpebəldæʃ/ *n* [U] CEMENT[1] (1) with lots of small PEBBLEs (1) set in it used for covering the outside walls of a house

peb·bly /ˈpebli/ *adj* [Wa1] covered with PEBBLEs (1)

pe·can /pɪˈkæn‖pɪˈkɑn, pɪˈkæn/ *n* **1** a type of large HICKORY tree of the south central US **2** a nut produced by this tree, grown for eating

pec·ca·dil·lo /ˌpekəˈdɪləʊ/ *n* **-loes** *or* **-los** an unimportant fault

pec·ca·ry /ˈpekəri/ *n* [Wn1] either of 2 kinds of wild hairy piglike animal found esp. in Central and South America

peck[1] /pek/ *n* **1** [C] a measure (= about 9 litres) used formerly esp. for grain **2** [S] *infml* a large amount (esp. in the phr. **a peck of trouble(s)**)

peck[2] *v* **1** [IØ (AWAY, *at*);T1] (of birds) to (try to) strike (at something) with the beak: *That bird tried to peck me.*|*birds pecking* (*away*) *at the apples*|(fig.) *You're only pecking at your food: what's wrong?* **2** [X9] (of birds) to make by striking with the beak: *The bird pecked a hole in the tree* **3** [X9, esp. OFF, AWAY] (of birds) to remove or destroy by striking with the beak **4** [T1 (UP);IØ] (of birds) to pick up and eat (food) with the beak: *The hens are pecking the corn* **5** [T1] *infml* to kiss in a hurry or without much feeling

peck[3] *n* **1** a stroke made by PECKing[2] (1) **2** a mark or wound made by PECKing[2] (1) **3** *infml* a hurried kiss

peck·er /ˈpekəʳ/ *n* **1** *AmE taboo sl* PENIS **2 keep one's pecker up** *BrE infml* to remain cheerful even when it is difficult to do so

pecking or·der /ˈ·· ˌ··/ *n often humor* the social order of a particular body of people, by means of which each person knows who is more important and who is less important than himself

peck·ish /ˈpekɪʃ/ *adj* [F;(B)] *infml esp. BrE* hungry

pec·tic /ˈpektɪk/ *adj* [Wa5;A] *tech* of, from, or concerning PECTIN

pec·tin /ˈpektɪn/ *n* [U] *tech* a sugar-like chemical compound substance found in certain fruits

pec·to·ral /ˈpektərəl/ *adj* [Wa5;A] **1** *tech* of or connected with the chest: *pectoral muscles* **2** *med* used for treating chest diseases

pectoral cross /ˌ··· ˈ·/ *n tech* an ornamental cross worn on the chest by priests of high rank (BISHOPs)

pec·u·late /ˈpekjʊleɪt‖-kjə-/ *v* [T1;IØ] *fml & esp. pomp* to take and use for one's own purposes (money put into one's care) —compare EMBEZZLE —**-lation** /ˌpekjʊˈleɪʃən‖-kjə-/ *n* [U;C]

pe·cu·li·ar /pɪˈkjuːlɪəʳ/ *adj* **1** [F +*to*;(B)] belonging only (to a particular person, place, time, etc.): *That way of speaking is peculiar to people in this small part of the country* **2** [B] strange; unusual (esp. in a troubling or displeasing way): *What a peculiar thing to say!*|*This food has a peculiar taste* **3** [B] rather mad; ECCENTRIC (1) **4** [F] *infml* rather ill: *I'm feeling rather peculiar—I think I'll go and lie down* **5** [A;(B)] special; particular

pe·cu·li·ar·i·ty /pɪˌkjuːliˈærɪ̈ti/ *n* **1** [U] the quality of being PECULIAR **2** [C] something which is PECULIAR (1): *Bad driving is wrongly said to be a peculiarity of women* **3** [C] something strange or unusual

pe·cu·li·ar·ly /pɪˈkjuːlɪəli‖-ər-/ *adv* **1** especially; more than usually: *This question is peculiarly difficult* **2** strangely

pe·cu·ni·a·ry /pɪˈkjuːnɪəri‖-nieri/ *adj fml & esp. pomp* connected with or consisting of money —**-rily** *adv*

ped·a·gogue /ˈpedəgɒg‖-gɑg/ *n* **1** a teacher who is too much concerned with rules **2** *old use or humor* a teacher

ped·a·go·gy /ˈpedəgɒdʒi‖-gəʊ-/ also **ped·a·gog·ics** /ˌpedəˈgɒdʒɪks‖-ˈgɑ-, -ˈgəʊ-/— *n* [U] the study of ways of teaching —**-gic** /ˌpedəˈgɒdʒɪk‖-ˈgɑ-, -ˈgəʊ-/ *adj* [Wa5] —**-gical** *adj* [Wa5] —**-gically** *adv* [Wa4,5]

ped·al[1] /ˈpedl/ *n* **1** [C] a barlike part of a machine which can be pressed with the foot in order to control the working of or drive the machine: *One of the pedals has come off my bicycle* —see pictures at BICYCLE[1] and CAR **2** [A] worked by means of one or more of such instruments: *a pedal boat*

ped·al[2] /ˈpedl, ˈpiːdl/ *adj* [Wa5;A] *tech* of the foot (esp. of an animal)

pedal[3] /ˈpedl/ *v* **-ll-** (*AmE* **-l-**) **1** [IØ] to work the PEDALs[1] (1) of a machine **2** [T1] to work (a machine) by using PEDALs[1] (1) **3** [X9;L9] to move (a bicycle) along by using PEDALs[1] (1): *He pedalled the bicycle up the hill.*|*I was just pedalling along*

ped·ant /ˈpednt/ *n* [C;N] *derog* a person whose attention to detail is too great (or is greater than one's own)

pe·dan·tic /pɪˈdæntɪk/ *adj derog* of or like a PEDANT —**~ally** *adv* [Wa4]

ped·ant·ry /ˈpedntri/ *n derog* **1** [U] **a** the quality of being a PEDANT **b** the nature or manner of a PEDANT **2** [C] a PEDANTIC expression or action

ped·dle /ˈpedl/ *v* **1** [IØ] to go from place to place trying to sell small goods **2** [T1] **a** to try to sell (small goods) by going from place to place: *He's the one who's peddling the drugs unlawfully* **b** *derog* to try to make people accept (ideas, plans, etc.) **c** *derog* to spread about (esp. harmful stories about other people)

ped·dler /ˈpedləʳ/ *n* **1** *AmE* PEDLAR **2** a person who PEDDLEs (2a) dangerous or unlawful drugs —compare PUSHER (2)

ped·e·rast, paederast /ˈpedəræst/ *n tech or euph* a man who practises PEDERASTY

ped·e·ras·ty, paederasty /ˈpedəræsti/ *n* [U] *tech or euph* (of men) the practice of having sex with boys

ped·es·tal /ˈpedɪ̈stl/ *n* **1** the base on which a pillar or STATUE stands **2** either of 2 supports, usu. with drawers, on either side of a certain type of desk (**pedestal desk**) **3 knock somebody off his pedestal** to show or prove that somebody has been too well thought of by others **4 put/set somebody on a pedestal** to consider somebody better, nobler, etc., than oneself or others

pe·des·tri·an[1] /pɪ̈ˈdestrɪən/ *adj* **1** [Wa5;A] connected with walking; done on foot **2** [B] **a** in no way unusual; lacking in imagination: *She was* *rather a pedestrian student* **b** (of writing, talking, etc.) dull; uninteresting

pedestrian² *n* a person walking (esp. in a street or other place used by cars) —compare MOTORIST and see picture at STREET

pedestrian cross·ing /·,··· '··/ *n* a special place for PEDESTRIANs to cross the road

pedestrian pre·cinct /·,··· '··/ *n* an area of streets in the centre of a town where motor traffic is not allowed

pe·di·a·tri·cian, paediatrician /ˌpiːdɪəˈtrɪʃən/ *n* a doctor who specializes in PEDIATRICS

pe·di·at·rics, paediatrics /ˌpiːdiˈætrɪks/ *n* [U] the branch of medicine concerned with children and their diseases

ped·i·cab /ˈpedɪkæb/ *n* (in parts of South Asia) a small 3-wheeled bicycle-like passenger vehicle with a box at the front or back where 2 people can sit

ped·i·cel /ˈpedɪ̈sel/ also **ped·i·cle** /-kəl/— *n tech* **1** a stem of a single small flower that is one of a group of flowers on a large stem **2** a stemlike part of an insect or sea-creature

ped·i·cure /ˈpedɪkjʊəʳ/ *n* a treatment of the feet and toenails, to make them more comfortable or more beautiful —**-curist** *n*

ped·i·gree /ˈpedɪ̈griː/ *n* **1** [C] a list or drawing showing the families from which one is descended; FAMILY TREE **2** [U;C] **a** (a set of) people from whom or animals from which a person, family, or animal is descended; ANCESTRY: *a dog of unknown pedigree* **b** *apprec* the ancient set of people from whom a person or family is descended: *She comes from a family of pedigree* **3** [A] (of animals) descended from a long and recorded (and usu. specially chosen) family of animals, and therefore of high quality —compare PUREBRED, THOROUGHBRED

ped·i·ment /ˈpedɪ̈mənt/ *n* a 3-sided piece of stone or other material placed above the entrance to a building (found esp. in the buildings of ancient Greece)

ped·lar, *AmE* also **peddler** /ˈpedləʳ/ *n* a person who goes from place to place trying to sell small articles

pe·dom·e·ter /pɪˈdɒmɪ̈təʳ‖-ˈdɑ-/ *n* an instrument that records the distance travelled by a walker

pee¹ /piː/ *v* [IØ] *sl* URINATE

pee² *n sl* **1** [S] an act of urinating (URINATE) (esp. in the phrs. **go for/have a pee**) **2** [U] URINE

peek¹ /piːk/ *v* [IØ (*at*)] *infml* to look (at something) quickly, esp. when one should not: *They caught him peeking through the hole at what was going on in the room* —compare PEEP³, PEER

peek² *n* [S] *infml* an act of PEEKing

peek·a·boo /ˌpiːkəˈbuː/ *BrE* also **peepbo**— *n, interj* [U] (a cry in) a game played to amuse babies: *He put his hand in front of his face, then took it away again, and went "Peekaboo!"*

peel¹ /piːl/ *v* **1** [T1] to remove the outer covering from (a fruit, vegetable, etc.): *a machine that peels potatoes* **2** [X9, esp. OFF, *off*] to remove (the outer covering) from something: *peeled the skin off* (*the potato*)|*They peeled off their clothes and jumped into the water* **3** [IØ] to lose an outer covering or surface: *The walls were quite wet and were peeling* **4** [IØ] (of an outer covering or surface) to come off, esp. in small pieces: *My skin always peels when I've been in the sun* **5 keep one's eyes peeled** *infml* to keep careful watch for anything dangerous or unusual which may happen

peel² *n* [U;C] the outer covering, esp. of those fruits and vegetables which one usu. PEELs¹ (1) before eating: *One speaks of orange peel, and apple peel, but of* TOMATO *skin* —compare RIND and see picture at FRUIT¹

peel·er¹ /ˈpiːləʳ/ *n* (*usu. in comb.*) a tool or machine for PEELing¹ (1) fruit or vegetables

peeler² *n BrE old sl* a policeman

peel·ings /ˈpiːlɪŋz/ *n* [P] parts PEELed¹ (1) off (esp. from potatoes)

peel off *v adv* **1** [T1] PEEL¹ (2) **2** [IØ] to remove all one's clothes: *They peeled off and jumped into the water* **3** [IØ] (of an aircraft) to turn and move away from other aircraft in the air

peep¹ /piːp/ *v* [IØ] to make a PEEP² (1)

peep² *n* **1** [C] a short weak high sound as made by a young bird or a mouse **2** [S] *infml* **a** a sound, esp. something spoken: *I don't want to hear a peep out of you until dinnertime* **b** news: *I haven't had a peep out of Smith for a month* **3** [C] *infml* (*used esp. by or to children*) the sound of a car's horn

peep³ *v* **1** [IØ (*at*)] to look (at something) quickly and secretly: *It's rude to peep* (*at other people's work*) **2** [L9] to look through a hole or other opening: *peeping through the curtains* **3** [L9] to begin slowly to appear; come partly into view: *The flowers are beginning to peep through the soil* —compare PEEK, PEER

peep⁴ *n* **1** [S (*at*)] **a** a short incomplete look: *I got a quick peep at him through the crowd* **b** a hurried or secret look: *He took a peep at the back of the book to find out the answers to the questions* **2 peep of day** *lit* the first appearance of daylight

peep·er /ˈpiːpəʳ/ *n* **1** [*usu. pl.*] *sl* eye **2** *often derog* a person who PEEPs³ (1,2)

peep·hole /ˈpiːphəʊl/ *n* a small hole esp. in a door or wall through which one can PEEP³ (1, 2) at something

peeping Tom /ˌ·· ˈ·/ *n* (*often cap.* P) a person who secretly looks at others who think they are not being watched, esp. when they are undressing —see also VOYEUR

peep show /ˈ· ·/ *n* a lighted box containing small pictures, which one looks at through a hole fitted with a glass that makes them look larger

pee·pul /ˈpiːpəl/ *n* PIPAL

peer¹ /pɪəʳ/ *n* **1** an equal in rank, quality, or worth: *Older boys and girls form groups of their peers/peer groups* **2** (in Britain) a member of any of 5 noble ranks (BARON, VISCOUNT, EARL, MARQUIS, and DUKE) **3** (in Britain) a person who has the right to sit in the HOUSE OF LORDS —see also PEERESS

peer² *v* [L9, esp. *at*;(IØ)] to look very carefully or hard, esp. as if not able to see well: *She peered through the mist, trying to find the right path.*|*He peered at me over the top of his glasses* —compare PEEK, PEEP³

peer·age /ˈpɪərɪdʒ/ *n* **1** [U] **a** the whole body of PEERs¹ (2,3) **b** the rank of a PEER¹ (2,3) **2** [C] a book containing a list of PEERs¹ (2,3) and the families from which they are descended

peer·ess /ˈpɪərɪ̈s/ *n* **1** a female PEER¹ (3) **2** the wife of a PEER¹ (3)

peer·less /ˈpɪələs‖ˈpɪər-/ *adj* [Wa5] without an equal; better than any other

peer of the realm /ˌ· · · ˈ·/ also **hereditary peer**— *n* a PEER¹ (2,3) who received this rank from his parents, and who passes it to his eldest son when he dies —compare LIFE PEER

peeve /piːv/ *v* [Wv5;T1] *infml* to annoy

peev·ish /ˈpiːvɪʃ/ *adj* bad-tempered; easily annoyed by unimportant things —**~ly** *adv* —**~ness** *n* [U]

pee·wit /ˈpiːwɪt/ *n* PEWIT

peg¹ /peg/ *n* **1** a rather short piece of wood, metal, etc., usu. thinner at one end than at the other, esp. **a** used for sticking through a hole to hold esp. wooden surfaces together **b** fixed to a wall for hanging coats and hats on: *a hat peg* **c** also **tent peg**— hammered into the ground and used to hold the ropes supporting a tent —see picture at CAMP²

d hammered into the ground to mark the limits of a piece of land **e** placed in the hole (VENT² (1)) in the side of a barrel **f** used for keeping a record of points made in the game of CRIBBAGE **g** *sl esp. Br & Austr E* STUMP¹ (4) **2** *BrE* CLOTHES PEG **3** also **pin**— a wooden screw used to tighten or loosen the strings of certain musical instruments —see picture at STRINGED INSTRUMENT **4** *BrE becoming rare* a measured drink, esp. of WHISKY or BRANDY with SODA WATER in it **5 a** PEG LEG (1) **b** *humor* a leg **6** a subject, reason, or pretended reason used as a base for a talk or argument: *He will use anything as a peg to hang an argument on* **7 (buy something) off the peg** (to buy clothes) not specially made to fit a particular person's measurements: *Off-the-peg clothes are usually cheaper* **8 a square peg in a round hole** a person who is not suited to the position or group in which he finds himself **9 take somebody down a peg (or two)** *infml* to show somebody that he is not as important as he thought he was

peg² *v* **-gg-** [T1] **1** to fasten with a PEG¹ (1a,c) **2** [(OUT, UP)] *BrE* to fasten (clothes) to a rope with a PEG¹ (2) **3** to fix or hold (prices, wages, etc.) at a certain level

peg a·way at also **plug away at**— *v adv prep* [T1 *no pass.*] *infml* to work hard and steadily at

peg down *v adv* [T1] NAIL DOWN

peg leg /'· ·/ *n infml* **1** [C] also **peg**— a wooden leg **2** [C;N] a person with a wooden leg

peg out *v adv* **1** [IØ] *infml esp. BrE* to die **2** [T1] to mark (a piece of ground) with wooden sticks

pe·jo·ra·tive /pɪ'dʒɒrətɪv‖-'dʒɔ-, -'dʒɑ-/ *n, adj fml* (a word, phrase, etc.) that suggests that somebody or something is bad or worthless —**~ly** *adv*

pe·kin·ese, pekingese /ˌpiːkɨ'niːz/ also (*infml*) **peke** /piːk/— *n* **pekinese** *or* **pekineses** [Wn2] (*often cap.*) a type of small dog with a short flat nose and long silky hair —see picture at DOG¹

pe·koe /'piːkəʊ/ *n* [U] (*sometimes cap.*) a kind of black tea considered of high quality

pe·lag·ic /pɨ'lædʒɪk/ *adj* [Wa5] *fml or tech* done on or living in the deep sea far from the shore: *pelagic fishing|pelagic fish*

pelf /pelf/ *n* [U] *lit or derog* money; wealth

pel·i·can /'pelɪkən/ *n* [Wn1] a type of large water bird which catches fish for food and stores them in a long baglike part under its beak —see picture at WATER¹

pel·lag·ra /pɨ'lægrə/ *n* [U] a disease caused by not eating enough health-giving foods, and which produces great tiredness, and disorder of the skin and central nervous system

pel·let /'pelɨt/ *n* **1** a small ball of any soft material made by or as if by rolling between the fingers **2** a small ball of metal made to be fired from a gun **3** *tech* a small mass of feathers, small bones, etc., thrown up from the stomach by certain meat-eating birds **4** *esp. BrE* a small round hard mass of medicinal paste; PILL (1)

pell-mell /ˌpel 'mel◂/ *adv becoming rare* in disorderly haste —**pell-mell** *adj* [A]

pel·lu·cid /pɨ'luːsɨd/ *adj* [Wa5] *lit* very clear: *a pellucid stream* —**~ly** *adv*

pel·met /'pelmɨt/ also (*esp. AmE*) **valance**— *n esp. BrE* a narrow piece of wood or cloth above a window that hides the rod on which curtains hang —see picture at LIVING ROOM

pe·lot·a /pə'lɒtə‖-'ləʊ-/ *n* [U] a kind of ball game played esp. in Spain, Spanish America, and the Philippines, in which a long basket tied to the wrist is used to hit the ball against a wall

pelt¹ /pelt/ *n* **1** the skin of a dead animal **a** with the fur or hair still on it **b** with the fur or hair removed and ready to be prepared as leather **2** the fur or hair of a living animal

pelt² *v* **1** [T1 (*with*)] to attack by throwing things at: *He picked up some stones and began to pelt us.*| (fig.) *The children pelted him with questions about his journey* **2** [IØ (DOWN)] (of rain) to fall heavily and continuously: *I'm not going out there—it's really pelting (down)!*|(*esp. BrE*) *It always pelts with rain when I'm here* **3** [L9;(IØ)] to run very fast: *The boys came pelting down the hill*

pelt³ *n* **(at) full pelt** as fast as possible

pel·vic /'pelvɪk/ *adj* [Wa5;A] *med* of or near the PELVIS: *a pelvic bone*

pel·vis /'pelvɨs/ *n* **-vises** *or* **-ves** /viːz/ the bowl-shaped frame of bones at the base of the backbone (SPINE (1)) —see picture at SKELETON

pem·mi·can, pemican /'pemɪkən/ *n* [U] dried meat beaten into small pieces and pressed into flat round shapes, used by travellers in far places where food cannot be got

pen¹ /pen/ *n* **1** (*often in comb.*) a small piece of land enclosed by a fence, used esp. for keeping animals in **2** PLAYPEN **3** SUBMARINE PEN **4** *CarE* a farm

pen² *v* **-nn-** [T1 (UP, *in,* IN)] **1** to shut (animals) in a PEN¹ (1) **2** to shut (people) in a small space

pen³ *n* **1** an instrument for writing or drawing with ink, esp. **a** a thin short piece of wood, with a thin pointed piece of metal (NIB) at one end which is dipped into the ink **b** FOUNTAIN PEN **c** BALLPOINT **d** QUILL (2) —see also FELT-TIP PEN **2** [*usu. sing.*] the action of writing stories, books, etc.: *He lives by his pen* (=earns money by writing) **3** [*usu. sing.*] *lit* a writer: *a poem by an unknown pen* **4 put/set pen to paper** also **take up one's pen**— *pomp* to start to write

pen⁴ *v* **-nn-** [T1 (*to*)] *pomp* to write with a pen

pe·nal /'piːnl/ *adj* **1** [Wa5] of punishment (by law): *penal laws* **2** [Wa5] for which one may be punished by law: *a penal offence* **3** very severe; severely unpleasant: *a new and penal tax* —**penally** /'piːnəli/ *adv*

pe·nal·ize, -ise /'piːnəl-aɪz‖'piːnəl-, 'penəl-/ *v* [T1] **1** to put (someone) in a very unfavourable or unfair position or condition **2** [(*for*)] (in sports) to punish (a team, a player, or a player's action) by giving an advantage to the other team (esp. by giving the other team a PENALTY (4b)) **3** to make punishable by law —**-ization** /ˌpiːnəl-aɪ'zeɪʃən‖-nəl-ə-/ *n* [U;(C)]

penal ser·vi·tude /ˌ·· '···/ *n* [U] punishment by being sent to prison and made to do especially hard work (HARD LABOUR)

penal set·tle·ment /'·· ˌ···/ also **penal col·o·ny**— *n* an area, usu. far from big cities, to which people found guilty of a crime (CONVICTS) are sent as a punishment, and where they live in a group

pen·al·ty /'penlti/ *n* **1** punishment for breaking a law, rule, or agreement in law (often in the phr. **pay the penalty**) **2** something (such as a number of years in prison or an amount of money to be paid) that is ordered as a punishment: *Fishing in this river is forbidden—penalty £5* **3** suffering or loss that is the result of one's unwise action or of one's condition or state (often in the phr. **pay the penalty**): *One of the penalties of fame is that people point at you in the street* **4** (in sports) **a** a disadvantage given to a player or team for breaking a rule: *If you pick up the ball with your hand in* GOLF, *you suffer a penalty* **b** an advantage given to a team because the other team have broken a rule (esp. a **penalty kick** at the GOAL in football) **c** (in football) also **penalty goal** /'··· ·/— a GOAL scored by this means **5** (in sports) an unfavourable condition (HANDICAP) placed on a player or team known to be very good in order to give the opponent a better chance of winning

penalty ar·e·a /'··· ,···/ *n* (in football) a space in front of the GOAL where the breaking of a rule means that the opposing team gets a PENALTY (4b) —see picture at SOCCER

penalty clause /'··· ·/ *n tech* part of a contract which states how much money must be paid by any person breaking the agreement

pen·ance /'penəns/ *n* **1** [U] self-punishment suffered willingly to show that one is sorry for having done wrong (often in the phr. **do penance for**) **2** [U] (esp. in the ROMAN CATHOLIC and ORTHODOX churches) an effort to obtain forgiveness for wrongdoing, esp. by means of an action advised by a priest **3** [C] something that one must do, but which one greatly dislikes **4 do penance for** *humor* to suffer for (something foolish that one has done)

pen-and-ink /,· · '·◂/ *adj* [Wa5;A] drawn with a pen and ink

pence /pens/ *esp. BrE pl. of* PENNY —see also TWOPENCE, THREEPENCE, SIXPENCE; see PENNY (USAGE)

pen·chant /'pɒnʃɒn, 'pentʃənt‖'pentʃənt (*Fr* pɑ̃ʃɑ̃)/ *n* [(*for*) *usu. sing.*] *Fr* a strong liking: *a penchant for pretty girls*

pen·cil¹ /'pensəl/ **1** [C] a narrow pointed wooden (or metal) instrument containing a thin stick of a black substance (GRAPHITE) or coloured material, used for writing or drawing **2** [U] the black (or coloured) material in this instrument, as used in writing or drawing: *Should I sign this paper in pencil or ink?* **3** [C] also **eyebrow pencil**— a stick of coloured material in a holder, used for darkening the EYEBROWS **4** [C] a narrow beam (of light) beginning from or ending in a small point

pencil² *v* **-ll-** (*AmE* **-l-**) [T1] to draw, write, or mark with a PENCIL¹ (1,2)

pen·dant, -dent /'pendənt/ *n* **1** a hanging ornament, esp. a chain worn round the neck with a small ornamental object hanging from it **2** PENNANT

pen·dent /'pendənt/ *adj* [Wa5] **1** hanging supported from above: *a pendent lamp* **2** *fml* hanging over; sticking out beyond a surface: *pendent rocks* **3** *fml* PENDING² (2)

pend·ing¹ /'pendɪŋ/ *prep* **1** *fml* until: *This matter must wait pending his return from Europe* **2** *becoming rare* during and till the end of

pending² *adj* [Wa5;F;(B)] **1** happening in the near future **2** waiting to be decided or settled

pen·du·lous /'pendjʊləs‖-dʒə-/ *adj esp. fml* hanging down loosely so as to swing freely: *pendulous breasts* —**~ly** *adv*

pen·du·lum /'pendjʊləm‖-dʒə-/ *n* **1** a weight hanging from a fixed point so as to swing freely **2** a rod with a weight at the bottom, used to control the working of a clock —see picture at CLOCK¹ **3 (the) swing of the pendulum** the change of public opinion from one belief to the opposite

pen·e·trate /'penȷ̊treɪt/ *v* **1** [I∅ (*into, through*);T1] to enter, pass, cut, or force a way (into or through something): *The knife penetrated his stomach.|Rain has penetrated right through this coat* **2** [I∅] (of sound) to be easily heard at a distance **3** [T1] to see into or through **4** [T1] to understand: *penetrate the mystery of the atom* **5** [I∅] *infml* to come to be understood: *I heard what you said, but it didn't penetrate* **6** [Wv5 (*with*);T1] to fill: *The whole country is penetrated with fear* **7** [T1] to come to understand the truth behind (something false) (esp. in the phr. **penetrate someone's disguise**) —**-trable** /trəbəl/ *adj* —**-trability** /,penȷ̊trə'bɪlȷ̊ti/ *n* [U]

pen·e·trat·ing /'penȷ̊treɪtɪŋ/ *adj* **1** (of the eye, sight, questions, etc.) sharp and searching **2** (of a person, the mind, etc.) able to understand clearly and deeply **3** (of sounds) sharp and loud **4** spreading and reaching everywhere: *The cold is very penetrating today* —**~ly** *adv*

pen·e·tra·tion /,penȷ̊'treɪʃən/ *n* **1** [U;(C)] the act or action of penetrating (PENETRATE) **2** [U9] the ability to understand quickly and clearly: *The penetration of that woman's mind is really wonderful!*

pen·e·tra·tive /'penȷ̊trətɪv‖-treɪtɪv/ *adj* **1** able to PENETRATE (1) easily **2** (of the mind, products of the mind, etc.) keen; INTELLIGENT —**~ly** *adv*

pen friend /'· ·/ *AmE* **pen pal**— *n* a person, esp. in a foreign country, whom one has come to know by the friendly exchange of letters, but whom one has usu. never met

pen·guin /'peŋgwȷ̊n/ *n* any of several types of often large black-and-white flightless seabirds of esp. the ANTARCTIC, which use their wings for swimming —see picture at WATER¹

pen·i·cil·lin /,penȷ̊'sɪlȷ̊n/ *n* [U] a substance used as a medicine to destroy certain bacteria in people and animals

pe·nin·su·la /pȷ̊'nɪnsjʊlə‖-sələ/ *n* a piece of land almost completely surrounded by water but joined to a larger mass of land: *Italy is a peninsula* —**-lar** *adj* [Wa5]

pe·nis /'piːnȷ̊s/ *n* the outer sex organ of male animals that is the instrument of COPULATION and URINATION

pen·i·tent¹ /'penȷ̊tənt/ *adj* feeling or showing sorrow for having done wrong, with the intention not to do so again —**~ly** *adv* —**-tence** *n* [U (*for*)]

penitent² *n* **1** a person who has done wrong and is now PENITENT **2** (in the ROMAN CATHOLIC and ORTHODOX churches) a person who is doing or suffering PENANCE

pen·i·ten·tial /,penȷ̊'tenʃəl/ *adj* **1** of or expressing the quality of being PENITENT¹ **2** of PENANCE (2) —**~ly** *adv*

pen·i·ten·tia·ry /,penȷ̊'tenʃəri/ *n* a prison, esp. a state or national prison in the US

pen·knife /'pen-naɪf/ *n* **-knives** /naɪvz/ a small knife with usu. 2 folding blades, usu. carried in the pocket —compare JACK KNIFE

pen·man·ship /'penmənʃɪp/ *n* [U] art of or skill in writing by hand

pen name /'· ·/ *n* a name used by a writer instead of his real name —see also PSEUDONYM

pen·nant /'penənt/ *n* **1** also **pendant**— a long narrow pointed flag, esp. as used on ships for signalling **2** also **pendant, pennon**— a flag, esp. a long narrow one, esp. as used by schools, sports teams, etc.

pen·ni·less /'penɪləs/ *adj* having no money

pen·non /'penən/ *n* **1** a long narrow pointed flag, esp. as carried on the end of a spear (LANCE) by soldiers on horseback **2** PENNANT (2)

pen·n'orth /'penəθ‖-ərθ/ also (*fml*) **pen·ny·worth** /'penɪwəθ‖-wərθ/— *n* **penn'orth** *or* **penn'orths** [(*of*)] *becoming rare* as much as can be bought for a penny: *a penn'orth of sweets|6 penn'orth of apples*

pen·ny /'peni/ *n* **pennies** *or* (*BrE*) **pence** *or* (*BrE infml*) **p 1** [C] also (*infml*) **copper**, (*becoming rare*) **new penny**, (*infml*) **p**— (in Great Britain after 1971) a small copper and tin (BRONZE) coin, 100 of which make a pound **2** [C] also (*infml*) **copper**— (in Great Britain before 1971) a BRONZE coin, 12 of which made a shilling; 1d **3** [C] (in the US and Canada) (a coin worth) a cent **4** [S *nonassertive*] a small amount of money: *The journey won't cost you a penny if you come in my car* **5 a pretty penny** *infml* a rather large amount of money **6 be two/ten a penny** to be very cheap and easy to obtain, and therefore of little value **7 in for a penny, in for a pound** if something has been begun it should be finished whatever the cost may be **8 spend a penny**

euph URINATE **9 the penny dropped/has dropped** *BrE infml* the meaning (of something said) was at last understood **10 turn an honest penny** to earn a little money by doing some work

USAGE In Britain, the US, and Canada, the pl. **pennies** is used when speaking or writing of the coins themselves, not as an amount of money: *He had a number of coins in his pocket, but no* **pennies**. In Britain the pl. **pence** or **p** is used when speaking or writing about an amount of money: *It will only cost a few* **pence**, and esp. when combined with a number to name a particular amount of money that is more than one **penny**: *6* **pence** /(ˌ· ˈ·)/; *10* **p** /(ˌ· ˈ·)/. Some people think it is bad English to pronounce *5p* as it is written, and would rather say *5* **pence**. *1p* is often called a **penny** in speech, and **penny** is always used when speaking of the money of the past, or in phrs. like *spend a* PENNY.

-pen·ny /pəni; *strong* ˈpeni/ *comb. form* [*adj→adj* [A]] costing (the stated number of) pence: *a* FOUR*penny stamp*

penny-far·thing /ˌ·· ˈ··/ *n BrE* (esp. in the late 19th century) a type of bicycle with a very large front wheel and a very small back wheel

penny-half·penny /ˌ·· ˈ··/ *n* THREE-HALFPENCE

penny pinch·er /ˈ·· ˌ··/ also **pinchpenny**— *n infml* a person who is unwilling to spend or give money; MISER —**penny-pinching** *adj, n* [B;U]

pen·ny·weight /ˈpeniweɪt/ *n* (in the TROY WEIGHT system) a weight equal to 24 GRAIN*s* or a 20th of an OUNCE —see WEIGHTS & MEASURES TABLE

pen·ny·wort /ˈpeniwɜːt‖-wɜrt/ *n* any of various kinds of small round-leaved plants

pe·nol·o·gy /piːˈnɒlədʒi‖-ˈnɑl-/ *n* [U] the study of matters concerned with the punishment of criminals and the operation of prisons

pen pal /ˈ· ·/ *n AmE* PEN FRIEND

pen push·er /ˈ· ˌ··/ *n derog* a clerk

pen·sion¹ /ˈpenʃən/ *n* an amount of money paid regularly (esp. by a government or a company) to someone who can no longer earn (enough) money by working, esp. because of old age or illness —see also OLD AGE PENSION

pen·si·on² /ˈpɒnsiɒn‖ˌpɑnsiˈəʊn (*Fr* pɑ̃sjɔ̃)/ *n Fr* (not in English-speaking countries) a house where for a fixed amount of money per week or month one is provided with a room and food; BOARDING-HOUSE

pen·sion·a·ble /ˈpenʃənəbəl/ *adj* [Wa5] giving one the right to receive a PENSION¹

pen·sion·er /ˈpenʃənəʳ/ *n* a person who is receiving a PENSION¹ —see also CHELSEA PENSIONER

pension off *v adv* [T1] to dismiss from work but continue to pay a PENSION¹ to

pen·sive /ˈpensɪv/ *adj* **1** deeply or dreamily thoughtful: *The woman in this painting has a pensive smile* **2** sadly thoughtful: *You've been looking pensive all day—is anything wrong?* —**~ly** *adv* —**~ness** *n* [U]

pen·ta- /ˈpentə, penˈtæ/ also **pent-** /pent/— *comb. form* containing or made up of 5 parts or things

pen·ta·gon /ˈpentəgən‖-gɑn/ *n* a flat shape with 5 sides and 5 angles —**~al** /penˈtægənl/ *adj* [Wa5]

Pentagon *n* [*the*+R] **1** the building in Washington from which the armed forces of the US are directed **2** the leading officers of high rank who work in this building and direct the armed forces of the US

pen·ta·gram /ˈpentəgræm/ *n* a 5-pointed star, used as a magic sign

pen·tam·e·ter /penˈtæmᵻtəʳ/ *n* a line of poetry with 5 main beats

Pen·ta·teuch /ˈpentətjuːk‖-tuːk/ *n* [*the*+R] the first 5 books of the Bible

pen·tath·lon /penˈtæθlən/ *n* a type of sports event in which those taking part have to compete against each other in 5 different sports (running, swimming, riding, shooting, and FENCING)

Pen·te·cost /ˈpentɪkɒst‖-kɔst, -kɑst/ *n* [R] **1** (in the Jewish religion) a holiday 50 days after PASSOVER **2** *esp. AmE* (in the Christian religion) the 7th Sunday after EASTER; WHITSUNDAY

pent·house /ˈpenthaʊs/ *n* **-houses** /ˌhaʊzᵻz/ **1** a small house or set of rooms built on top of a tall building, often considered very desirable to live in **2** *becoming rare* **a** a sloping roof fixed to the wall of a building **b** a shelter formed by this

pent up /ˌ· ˈ·◂/ *adj* [F] shut up within narrow limits: *I don't like being pent up in the house all the time.*|(fig.) *Her feelings were pent up inside her* —**pent-up** *adj* [A]: *pent-up feelings*

pe·nul·ti·mate /pᵻˈnʌltᵻmᵻt/ *adj* [Wa5;A;(B)] next to the last: *November is the penultimate month of the year*

pe·num·bra /pᵻˈnʌmbrə/ *n* a slightly dark area between full shadow or darkness and full light

pen up *v adv* **-nn-** [T1] to shut (usu. an animal) in an enclosed space: *penned-up animals* —compare PENT UP

pe·nu·ri·ous /pᵻˈnjʊəriəs/ *adj fml* very poor —**~ly** *adv*

pen·u·ry /ˈpenjʊri‖-jə-/ *n* [U] *fml* the state of being very poor; POVERTY

pe·on /ˈpiːən/ *n* **1** (in Spanish America) a farm worker who does not own his own land **2** (in India) a person employed to carry messages

pe·o·ny, paeony /ˈpiːəni/ *n* a type of garden plant with large round white, pink, or esp. dark red flowers

peo·ple¹ /ˈpiːpəl/ *n* **1** [P] persons in general; persons other than oneself: *Were there many people at the meeting?*|*If you do that, people will start to talk* (*about your behaviour*) **2** [P9] the persons belonging to a particular place, class, trade, group, etc.: *People who live in the south of England speak in a different way from people who live in the north.*|*I like theatre people* **3** [*the*+P] all the persons forming a State: *Abraham Lincoln spoke of "government of the people, by the people, for the people"* **4** [*the*+P] the persons in a society who do not have special rank or position: *Many politicians like to be thought of as a man of the* (*common*) *people* **5** [C] a race; nation: *The Chinese are a hard-working people.*|*the peoples of Africa* **6** [P9] **a** the persons from whom one is descended and to whom one is related: *His people have lived in this valley for over 200 years* **b** *infml & becoming rare* one's close relatives, esp. parents: *One day I'll take you home to meet my people* **7 go to the people** (of a political leader) to hold an election or REFERENDUM in order to gain the approval of the PEOPLE¹ (3) for a government or a plan

USAGE The usual plural of **person** is **people**; **persons** is *fml*, and is used when they are considered more as numbers than as human beings: *He was murdered by a* **person** *or* **persons** *unknown*. An **individual** is one **person**, as opposed to a group: *We can't change the rules for a single* **individual**. Do not use **men** when you mean **people**, as it suggests males only, but one can use **man** for the whole human race, including women: *Is* **man** *descended from monkeys?* A **people** is a national group: *The British are a funny* **people**. —see FOLK (USAGE)

people² *v* [Wv3;T1] **1** to fill with PEOPLE¹ (1) **2** to live in (a place): *His race has peopled this island through all recorded history*

pep /pep/ *n* [U] *infml* keen activity and forcefulness; VIGOUR

pep·per¹ /ˈpepəʳ/ *n* **1** [U] **a** a hot-tasting greyish or pale yellowish powder made from the crushed seeds (PEPPERCORNs) of certain plants, used for making food taste better —see also BLACK PEPPER, WHITE PEPPER **b** a powder like this, made from certain other plants —see PAPRIKA (2) **2** [C] also (*tech*) **capsicum**— (any of various plants with) a large round or long narrow red or green fruit used esp. as a vegetable, with a special, sometimes hot taste —see also GREEN PEPPER, SWEET PEPPER

pepper² /ˈpepəʳ/ *v* [T1] **1** to add or give the taste of PEPPER¹ (1) to (food) **2** [(*with*)] to hit repeatedly (esp. with shots or with small but annoying things)

pepper-and-salt /ˌ·· · ˈ·◂/ *adj* [Wa5;A;(B)] having small spots of black and white mixed together to give a greyish appearance

pep·per·corn /ˈpepəkɔːn‖ˈpepərkɔrn/ *n* **1** the seedlike fruit of certain plants, which is dried and crushed to make PEPPER¹ (1a) **2** also **peppercorn rent** /ˌ··· ˈ·/— a very small amount of money paid as rent

pep·per·mint /ˈpepəˌmɪnt‖-ər-/ *n* **1** [U] **a** a type of MINT³ (1) plant with a special strong taste, used esp. in making sweets and medicine **b** the taste of this plant **2** [C] also (*infml*) **mint**— a sweet with this taste

pepper pot /ˈ·· ·/ *AmE* also **pep·per·box** /ˈpepəbɒks‖ˈpepərbɑks/— *n* a small container with small holes in the top, used for shaking PEPPER¹ (1a) onto food

pep·per·y /ˈpepəri/ *adj* **1** (of food) like or tasting of PEPPER¹ (1) **2** (of a person) having a quick temper; easily angered: *the peppery old general*

pep pill /ˈ· ·/ *n* [*usu. pl.*] *infml* a small ball of solid medicine (PILL) taken to make one quicker in thought and action or happier, for a short time

pep·sin /ˈpepsɪ̇n/ *n* [U] a liquid in the stomach that changes food into a form that can be used by the body

pep talk /ˈ· ·/ *n infml* a talk intended to fill the listener(s) with an urge to complete something well, to win, etc.

pep·tic /ˈpeptɪk/ *adj* [Wa5;A] **1** of, producing, or caused by PEPSIN (esp. in the phr. **peptic ulcer**) **2** of or concerned with the body action of changing food in the stomach (DIGESTION)

pep up *v adv* **-pp-** [T1] *infml* to make (something or someone) more active, or happier: *pepped up the drink|pepped up the party|A holiday will pep you up*

per /pəʳ; *strong* pɜːʳ/ *prep* **1** (esp. of amounts, prices, etc.) for each: *apples costing 10 pence per pound* **2** (of time) during each: *How many of these can you do per day/a day?* **3** *tech* by means of **4** according to (esp. in the phr. **as per**): *The work has been done as per instructions* **5 as per usual** *infml* as usual

per·ad·ven·ture /ˌperədˈventʃəʳ/ *adv* **1** *old use* perhaps **2** *old use or pomp* (*after* if *or* LEST) by chance

per·am·bu·late /pəˈræmbjʊleɪt‖-bjə-/ *v* [T1;L9;(I∅)] *fml* to walk about, round, or up and down (a place) without hurry —**-lation** /pəˌræmbjʊˈleɪʃən‖-bjə-/ *n* [C;U]

per·am·bu·la·tor /pəˈræmbjʊleɪtəʳ‖-bjə-/ *n fml* PRAM

per an·num /pər ˈænəm/ *adv esp. tech* for or in each year

per cap·i·ta /pə ˈkæpɪ̇tə‖ˌpər-/ *adv fml or tech* for or by each person —**per capita** *adj* [A]: *What is the average per capita wage in this country?*

per·ceive /pəˈsiːv‖pər-/ *v* [T1,5a,b,6a,b;V(2),4;X *to be* 1,7] *fml* to have or come to have knowledge of (something) through one of the senses (esp. sight) or through the mind; see: *I can't perceive any difference between these coins.|We perceived that we were unwelcome and left* —**-ceivable** *adj*

USAGE One **perceives** (=notices, becomes conscious of) something that already exists. One **conceives** (=forms in the mind) a completely new idea: *I* **perceived** *that she was drunk.|I* **perceived** *an ant in my beer.|He* **conceived** *a bold plan of escape.*

per cent¹ /· ˈ·/ *adv* in or for each 100; %: *I am 100 per cent in agreement with you* (= totally in agreement)

per cent² *n* **per cent** [Wn3] one part in or for each 100: *This company can only supply 30 per cent* (= 30% = 30/100 = 3/10) *of what we need*

per·cen·tage /pəˈsentɪdʒ‖pər-/ *n* **1** [C (*of*) *usu. sing.*] an amount stated as if it is part of a whole which is 100; PROPORTION (3): *What percentage of babies die of this disease every year?* **2** [A] (of a sport) played in a calm steady manner so that one will probably succeed quite well, rather than trying very hard to win and so risking defeat: *percentage tennis* **3 no percentage** no advantage or profit **4 play the percentages** to try to calculate what is most likely to happen and act in accordance

per·cen·tile /pəˈsentaɪl‖pər-/ *n tech* a value on a scale of 100 that shows the per cent of a group that is equal to or below it

per·cep·ti·ble /pəˈseptəbəl‖pər-/ also (*rare*) **per·cei·va·ble**— *adj fml* that can be PERCEIVEd; noticeable —**-bly** *adv* —**-bility** /pəˌseptəˈbɪlɪ̇ti‖pər-/ *n* [U]

per·cep·tion /pəˈsepʃən‖pər-/ *n* **1** [U] also **perceptiveness, perceptivity**— the ability to PERCEIVE; keen natural understanding **2** [C] a result of perceiving (PERCEIVE); something noticed and understood

per·cep·tive /pəˈseptɪv‖pər-/ *adj* quick to notice and understand —compare SENSITIVE —**~ly** *adv* —**~ness** *n* [U] —**-tivity** /pəˌsepˈtɪvɪ̇ti‖pər-/ *n* [U]

perch¹ /pɜːtʃ‖pɜrtʃ/ *n* **1** a branch, rod, etc., where a bird rests (often specially provided for the purpose) **2** a high position in which a person or building is placed: *From our perch up there on top of the cliff we can see the whole town.*|(fig.) *He has a perch in his father's bank for as long as he wants it* **3** *humor* a seat **4** ROD —see WEIGHTS & MEASURES TABLE **5 knock somebody off his perch** to show or prove that somebody has been too well thought of by others

perch² *v* [(esp. *on, upon*)] **1** [L9] (of a bird) to come to rest from flying **2** [X9;L9] to (cause to) go into or be in the stated position (esp. unsafely, or on something narrow or high): *He perched a funny little hat on his head.|She perched* (*herself*) *on a tall chair*

perch³ *n* **perch** *or* **perches** [Wn2] any of several types of lake and river fish with prickly FINs, used as food

per·chance /pəˈtʃɑːns‖pərˈtʃæns/ *adv old use or lit* **1** perhaps **2** (*after* if *or* LEST) by chance

per·cip·i·ent /pəˈsɪpɪənt‖pər-/ *adj fml* quick to notice and understand; PERCEPTIVE —**-ence** *n* [U]

per·co·late /ˈpɜːkəleɪt‖ˈpɜr-/ *v* **1** [I∅ (*through*)] to pass slowly (through a material having small holes or GAPs (1) in it) **2** [I∅;T1] also (*infml*) **perk**— **a** (of coffee) to be made in a special pot by the slow passing of hot water through crushed coffee beans **b** to make (coffee) by this method **3** [I∅ (*through*)] (of ideas, feelings, etc.) to become felt, experienced, thought, etc., all through (a group of people) —**-lation** /ˌpɜːkəˈleɪʃən‖ˌpɜr-/ *n* [U;C]

per·co·la·tor /ˈpɜːkəleɪtəʳ‖ˈpɜr-/ *n* a pot in which coffee is PERCOLATEd (2b)

per·cus·sion /pəˈkʌʃən‖pər-/ *n* **1** [U] **a** the forceful striking together of 2 (usu. hard) objects **b** the effect or sound produced by this **2** [GU] musical instruments that are played by being struck, esp. as a division of a band (**percussion section**): *The*

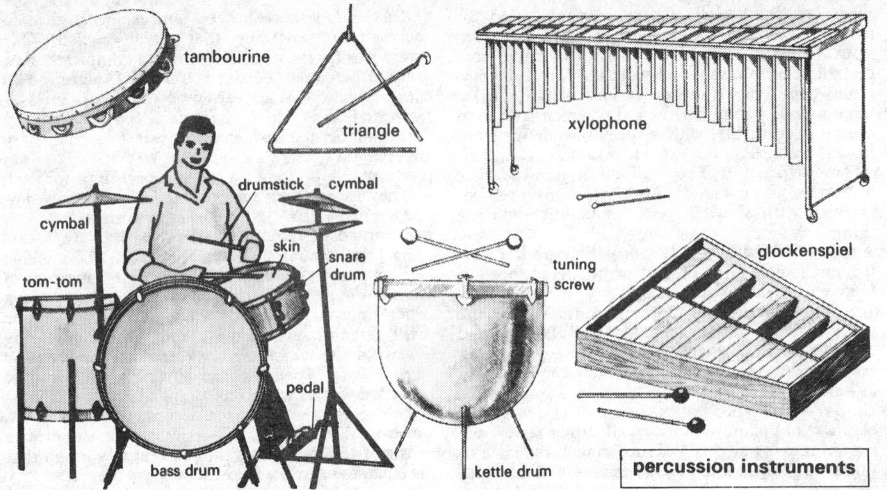

drum is a percussion instrument.|The percussion is/are too loud —**-sive** /pəˈkʌsɪv‖pər-/ *adj*

percussion cap /·ˈ·· ·/ *n* **1** a small container holding an explosive, used formerly in firing guns **2** *fml* CAP (6)

per·cus·sion·ist /pəˈkʌʃənɨst‖pər-/ *n* a person who plays PERCUSSION (2) instruments

per di·em /pə ˈdɪem, -ˈdaɪem‖pər ˈdɪəm/ *adv, adj fml or tech* for each day

per·di·tion /pəˈdɪʃən‖pər-/ *n* [U] *fml* **1** everlasting punishment after death **2** complete destruction

per·e·gri·na·tion /ˌperɨgrɨˈneɪʃən/ *n* [*often pl.*] *lit or humor* a long and wandering journey, esp. in foreign countries

per·e·grine fal·con /ˌperɨgrɨn ˈfɔːlkən‖-ˈfɔl-, -ˈfɑl-/ also **peregrine** /ˈ···/— *n* a type of large black and white hunting bird

pe·remp·to·ry /pəˈremptəri/ *adj* **1** (of a person, his manner, etc.) **a** *fml* showing an expectation of being obeyed at once and without question **b** *derog* impolitely quick and unfriendly **2** *fml* (of commands) that must be obeyed —**-rily** *adv*

peremptory writ /·ˌ··· ˈ·/ *n BrE law* a written order to appear in court

pe·ren·ni·al[1] /pəˈrenɪəl/ *adj* [Wa5] **1** lasting through the whole year **2** lasting forever or for a long time; CONSTANT: *Politics provide a perennial subject of argument* **3** (of a plant) that lives for more than 2 years —**~ly** *adv*

perennial[2] *n* a PERENNIAL[1] (3) plant

per·fect[1] /ˈpɜːfɪkt‖ˈpɜr-/ *adj* [Wa5] **1** [B] of the very best possible kind, degree, or standard: *The weather during our holiday was perfect.*|(fig.) *a perfect crime* (= one in which the criminal is never discovered) **2** [B] agreeing in every way with an example accepted as correct: *He's only been studying for a year, but already his English is almost perfect* **3** [B] complete, with nothing missing, spoilt, etc.: *She still has a perfect set of teeth* **4** [B (*for*)] suitable and satisfying in every way: *This big house is perfect for our large family* **5** [A] *often infml* complete; thorough; UTTER: *a perfect stranger*|*It's perfect nonsense to say you're 200 years old* **6** [B] skilled to the highest degree; thoroughly and completely trained (esp. in the phr. **Practice makes perfect**) **7** [A;(B)] *tech* (of verb forms, tenses, etc.) concerning a period of time up to and including the present (**present perfect**), past (**past perfect**), or future (**future perfect**) (as in "He *has gone*", "He *had gone*", "He *will have gone*"): *the perfect tense*
USAGE It is usually thought bad English to say that something is ****very* **perfect** or ****more* **perfect**; but the US CONSTITUTION speaks of *a more* **perfect** union.

per·fect[2] /pəˈfekt‖pər-/ *v* [T1] to make perfect: *He went to Italy to perfect his singing voice*

perfect[3] /ˈpɜːfɪkt‖ˈpɜr-/ also (*fml*) **perfect tense** /ˌ·· ˈ·/, **present perfect (tense)**— *n tech* **1** [*usu. sing.*] the tense of a verb that shows a period of time up to and including the present, and in English is usu. formed with *have* and a past p. **2** a verb phrase in this tense —see also PAST PERFECT, PLUPERFECT

per·fec·ti·ble /pəˈfektəbəl‖pər-/ *adj* [Wa5] that can be made perfect —**-bility** /pəˌfektəˈbɪlɨti‖pər-/ *n* [U]

per·fec·tion /pəˈfekʃən‖pər-/ *n* [U] **1** the state or quality of being perfect (often in the phr. **bring something to perfection**): *The meat was cooked to perfection* **2** [(*of*)] the act of developing completely or making perfect **3** [(*of*)] the perfect example: *As an actress, she is perfection itself.*|*the perfection of beauty*

per·fec·tion·ist /pəˈfekʃənɨst‖pər-/ *n* **1 a** a person who is not satisfied with anything other than PERFECTION (1) **b** *derog* a person who values correctness in small things too much **2** *tech* a person who believes that man is morally or religiously PERFECTIBLE —**-ism** *n* [U]

per·fect·ly /ˈpɜːfɪktli‖ˈpɜr-/ *adv* **1** in a perfect way: *He speaks French perfectly* **2** completely; very well: *The colours match perfectly* **3** *often infml* very; completely; UTTERLY: *The walls must be perfectly clean before you paint them*

perfect par·ti·ci·ple /ˌ·· ˈ····/ *n* PAST PARTICIPLE

per·fid·i·ous /pəˈfɪdɪəs‖pər-/ *adj fml & esp. lit* disloyal; TREACHEROUS (1) —**~ly** *adv* —**~ness** *n* [C;U]

per·fi·dy /ˈpɜːfɨdi‖ˈpɜr-/ *n fml & esp. lit* **1** [U] also **perfidiousness**— disloyalty; TREACHERY **2** [C] an example of this

per·fo·rate /ˈpɜːfəreɪt‖ˈpɜr-/ *v* [Wv5] **1** [T1; I∅: (*through*)] to make a hole or holes through (something): *They sent the dog in a perforated box so that it could breathe* **2** [T1] to make a line of small holes in (paper), so that a part may be torn off: *This machine perforates the sheets of stamps.*|*perforated edges* **3** [T1] to make (a hole or holes) through something

per·fo·ra·tion /ˌpɜːfəˈreɪʃən‖ˌpɜr-/ *n* **1** [U;(C)] **a** the action or an act of perforating (PERFORATE) **b** the state of being PERFORATED **2** [C *often pl.*] a small hole or line of holes made by perforating (PERFORATE (2,1)) something: *the perforations in a sheet of stamps*

per·force /pəˈfɔːs‖pərˈfors/ *adv old use & lit* because it is necessary

per·form /pəˈfɔːm‖pərˈfɔrm/ *v* **1** [T1] **a** to do; carry out (a piece of work): *The doctor performed the operation.|to perform a scientific* EXPERIMENT **b** to fulfil (a promise, order, etc.) **2** [T1;I∅] to give, act, or show (a play, a part (ROLE) in a play, a piece of music, tricks, etc.) esp. before the public: *What play will be performed tonight?|a magician performing tricks|He will be performing on the horn/at the piano.|a performing bear* **3** [T1] to direct or go through the form and actions of (a ceremony) **4** [L9] **a** (of machines) to work (in the proper or intended way): *This car performs well on hills* **b** *infml* (of people) to carry out a particular activity, esp. well and with great skill: *Our team performed very well in the match yesterday.|She can really perform (in bed)* (= sexually)

per·form·ance /pəˈfɔːməns‖pərˈfɔr-/ *n* **1** [U (*of*)] the action of PERFORMing (1,3) something: *Our football team's performance has been excellent during the whole year* **2** [C (*of*)] the action or an act of PERFORMing (2) a (character in a) play, a piece of music, tricks, etc., esp. before the public: *His performance of/as Othello was very good* **3** [C] an action PERFORMed (1), esp. very well **4** [U] (of people or machines) the ability to do something, esp. needing skill **5** [S] **a** *infml* a (troublesome) set of preparations or activities: *I enjoy this dish, but it's too much of a performance to cook it often* **b** *derog* an example of bad behaviour (esp. in the phr. **What a performance!**)

per·form·er /pəˈfɔːmər‖pərˈfɔr-/ *n* **1** [C] a person (or thing) that PERFORMs (2), esp. an actor, musician, etc. **2** [C9] a person or thing that PERFORMs (4): *He is a good performer on the cricket field* (=plays well)

per·fume[1] /ˈpɜːfjuːm‖ˈpɜr-/ also (*esp. BrE*) **scent**— *n* [U;C] **1** a sweet or pleasant smell, as of flowers **2** (any of the many kinds of) sweet-smelling liquid, often made from flowers, for use esp. on the face, wrists, and upper part of the body of a woman —compare AFTER-SHAVE

per·fume[2] /pəˈfjuːm‖pər-/ *v* [Wv5 (*with*);T1] **1** *fml or poet* to fill with PERFUME[1] (1) **2** to put PERFUME[1] (2) on: *a perfumed handkerchief*

per·fum·i·er /pəˈfjuːmɪər‖pər-/ also (*becoming rare*) **per·fum·er** /pəˈfjuːmər‖pər-/— *n BrE* a maker or seller of PERFUME[1] (2)

per·func·to·ry /pəˈfʌŋktəri‖pər-/ *adj* **1** (of an action) done hastily and without thought, interest, or care **2** (of a person) acting in this manner —**-rily** *adv* —**-riness** *n* [U]

per·go·la /ˈpɜːgələ‖ˈpɜr-/ *n* an arrangement of posts built in a garden (usu. over a path) over which climbing plants can grow

per·haps /pəˈhæps‖pər-/ *adv* **1** it may be; possibly: *Perhaps I am wrong, but I think he is 41 years old.|"driving what is considered to be perhaps the most important carriage in the morning's procession"* (SEU S.)|*"Will he come?" "Perhaps not"* **2** (in making polite requests): *Perhaps you would be good enough to read this* (= would you be . . .?)

per head /· ˈ·/ *adv* **1** PER CAPITA **2** each: *How much beer will they drink per head?*

per·i·gee /ˈperɨdʒiː/ *n* [*usu. sing.*] the point where the path (ORBIT) of an object through space is closest to the earth —compare APOGEE (1)

per·i·he·li·on /ˌperɨˈhiːlɪən/ *n* [*usu. sing.*] the point where the path (ORBIT) of an object through space is closest to the sun

per·il[1] /ˈperɨl/ *n* **1** [U] (great) danger, esp. of being harmed or killed **2** [C] something that causes danger **3 at one's peril** (used when advising someone not to do something) with the near certainty of meeting great danger

per·il·ous /ˈperɨləs/ *adj* dangerous; risky —**~ly** *adv* —**~ness** *n* [U]

pe·rim·e·ter /pəˈrɪmɨtər/ *n* **1** the border round any closed flat figure or special area of ground, esp. a camp or airfield: *The perimeter of the airfield is protected by guard-dogs.|a perimeter fence* **2** the length of this: *What is the perimeter of this square?*

pe·ri·od[1] /ˈpɪərɪəd/ *n* **1** a stretch of time with a beginning and an end, but not always of measured length: *There were long periods when we had no news of him* **2 a** a particular stretch of time in the development of a person, a civilization, the earth, an illness, etc.: *The Victorian period of English history is the time when Victoria was queen* **b** the same stretch of time as stated or suggested before: *lords and ladies of ancient times dressed in clothes of the period* **3** a complete and repeated stretch of time fixed by the forces of nature: *the rainy period in India* **4** a division of a school day; lesson: *a history period* **5** [*often pl.*] also (*fml*) **menstrual period**— a monthly flow of blood from the body of a woman —see also MENSTRUATE **6 a** *esp. AmE* FULL STOP[1] **b** *now rare* a pause made at the end of a sentence when speaking **7** (in grammar) a complete sentence, esp. one that is a combination of several smaller sentences **8 put a period to** to bring to an end; stop —compare PERIODS

period[2] *adj* [Wa5;A;(B)] (of furniture, dress, buildings, etc.) belonging to or copying the special qualities of a stated or suggested earlier PERIOD[1] (2) in history

period[3] also (*esp. BrE*) **full stop**— *adv infml esp. AmE* (*used at the end of a sentence, expressing strong feeling*) and that is all I am going to say on the subject; and that is what I have firmly decided

pe·ri·od·ic /ˌpɪəriˈɒdɪk‖-ˈɑ-/ also **periodical**— *adj* [Wa5] happening repeatedly, usu. at regular times: *periodic attacks of fever* —**~ally** *adv* [Wa4]

pe·ri·od·i·cal /ˌpɪəriˈɒdɪkəl‖-ˈɑ-/ *n* a PERIODICAL magazine

periodic ta·ble /ˌ···· ˈ··/ *n* a list of simple chemical substances (ELEMENTs (6)) arranged according to their atomic weights

period piece /ˈ··· ·/ *n* **1** a fine example of a piece of furniture, ornament, etc., of a certain PERIOD[1] (2) in history **2** *infml & esp. humor* an old-fashioned person or thing

per·i·ods /ˈpɪərɪədz/ *n* [P] *fml & esp. lit* carefully built-up language intended to have a grand effect, often full of ornamental or unnecessary phrases

per·i·pa·tet·ic /ˌperɨpəˈtetɪk/ *adj fml or tech* travelling about; going from place to place —**~ally** *adv* [Wv4]

pe·riph·e·ral /pəˈrɪfərəl/ *adj* **1** of slight importance by comparison; not central: *matters of peripheral interest* **2** of or connected with a PERIPHERY (1,3) —**-rally** *adv*

pe·riph·e·ry /pəˈrɪfəri/ *n* **1** [*usu. sing.*] a line or area enclosing something; outside edge: *a factory built on the periphery of the town* **2** [(*the*) *usu. sing.*] the part of a social or political group which is not near the centre of power, and is therefore of slight importance in comparison with the main group **3** *med* the places where the nerves end, as in fingers or toes

pe·riph·ra·sis /pəˈrɪfrəsɨs/ *n* **-ses** /siːz/ **1** [U] *sometimes derog* the use of long words or phrases, or of unclear expressions, when short simple ones are all that is needed **2** [U] (in grammar) the use of AUXILIARY words instead of INFLECTed forms **3** [C] an example of either of these practices

per·i·phras·tic /ˌperɪ̇ˈfræstɪk/ *adj sometimes derog* using or expressed in PERIPHRASIS (1,2) —**~ally** *adv* [Wa4]

per·i·scope /ˈperɪ̇skəʊp/ *n* a long tube with mirrors placed in it so that people who are lower down (esp. in underwater boats (SUBMARINE*s*)) can see what is above them

per·ish /ˈperɪʃ/ *v* **1** [T1] (in writing, and esp. in newspapers) to die, esp. in a terrible or sudden way; be completely destroyed **2** [T1;IØ] *esp. BrE* to (cause to) decay or lose natural qualities: *Continuous washing has perished the rubber in this garment* **3 Perish the thought!** (*said as an answer to an unwelcome suggestion*) I hope that this will not happen

per·ish·a·ble /ˈperɪʃəbəl/ *adj* (of food) that quickly decays if not properly cared for —**perishables** *n* [P]

per·ish·er /ˈperɪʃəʳ/ *n* [C;*you*+N9] *sl & often humor, esp. BrE* a troublesome person, esp. a child: *Come out of there, you little perisher!*

per·ish·ing[1] /ˈperɪʃɪŋ/ *adj infml esp. BrE* **1** [F (*with*)] also **perished**— (of people) feeling very cold: *Let's get indoors—I'm perishing/perished* (*with cold*) **2** [F] (of weather) very cold: *It's really perishing this morning!* **3** [A] (*used for giving force to a noun expressing something bad*) cursed: *It's a perishing shame* **4 perishing cold** very unpleasant and severe coldness; cold that causes suffering: *I hate this perishing cold!*

perishing[2] also **per·ish·ing·ly** /ˈperɪʃɪŋli/— *adv infml* (*used for giving force to an expression of something bad*) very: *It's perishing cold this morning.*|*There's no need to be so perishing rude*

per·i·style /ˈperɪ̇staɪl/ *n* **1** a row of pillars round a temple, courtyard, etc. **2** the space surrounded by this

per·i·to·ni·tis /ˌperɪ̇təˈnaɪtɪ̇s/ *n* [U] *med* a poisoned and sore condition (INFLAMMATION) of the inside wall of the lower part of the body (ABDOMEN)

per·i·wig /ˈperɪwɪg/ also **peruke**— *n* a white ornamental head-covering usu. made of hair (WIG), with rolls of curls at the sides, now worn esp. by lawyers

per·i·win·kle[1] /ˈperɪwɪŋkəl/ *n* a type of small plant with light blue or white flowers, that grows along the ground

periwinkle[2] *n* WINKLE

per·jure /ˈpɜːdʒəʳ‖ˈpɜr-/ *v* **perjure oneself** to tell a lie on purpose after promising solemnly to tell the truth (esp. in a court of law)

per·jur·er /ˈpɜːdʒərəʳ‖ˈpɜr-/ *n* a person who PERJURE*s* himself

per·ju·ry /ˈpɜːdʒəri‖ˈpɜr-/ *n* **1** [U] the act of perjuring oneself (PERJURE) **2** [C] a lie told on purpose, esp. in a court of law

perk[1] /pɜːk‖pɜrk/ also (*fml*) **perquisite**— *n* [*usu. pl.*] *infml* **1** money or goods that one gets regularly and lawfully from one's work apart from pay **2** a material or non-material advantage gained from one's employment: *One of the perks of this job is that you don't have to work on Tuesday afternoons*

perk[2] *v* [T1;IØ] *infml* PERCOLATE (2)

perk up *v adv* [T1;IØ] to (cause to) become more cheerful, show interest, etc.

perk·y /ˈpɜːki‖ˈpɜrki/ *adj* [Wa1] **1** boldly cheerful; full of life and interest **2** *often derog* (of people) having a bold, almost disrespectful manner —**-ily** *adv* —**-iness** *n* [U]

perm[1] /pɜːm‖pɜrm/ *n* also (*fml*) **permanent wave** /ˌ··· ˈ·/ (*AmE infml* also **permanent**)— *infml esp. BrE* the putting of waves or curls into straight hair by chemical treatment so that they will last for several months

perm[2] *v BrE infml* **1** [T1] to give a PERM[1] to **2** [L9; (IØ)] (of hair) to show the effect of a PERM[1]

perm[3] *n BrE infml* (in FOOTBALL POOLS) any of the possible combinations of the names of football teams which one chooses in the hope of winning a large amount of money

perm[4] *v* [T1 (*from*)] *BrE infml* (in FOOTBALL POOLS) to pick out and combine (the names of football teams) in a particular order: *Perm any 2 from 3*

per·ma·frost /ˈpɜːməfrɒst‖ˈpɜrməfrɔst/ *n* [U] a thickness of soil, esp. below the earth's surface, that is frozen all the time

per·ma·nence /ˈpɜːmənəns‖ˈpɜr-/ *n* [U (*of*)] the state of being PERMANENT

per·ma·nen·cy /ˈpɜːmənənsi‖ˈpɜr-/ *n* **1** [C] a person who or thing that is PERMANENT **2** [U (*of*)] PERMANENCE

per·ma·nent /ˈpɜːmənənt‖ˈpɜr-/ *adj* lasting or intended to last for a long time or for ever: *a coat giving permanent protection against heavy rain* —compare TEMPORARY —**~ly** *adv*

permanent way /ˌ··· ˈ·/ *n BrE* a railway track and the stones and beams on which it is laid

per·man·ga·nate /pəˈmæŋgənɪ̇t‖pərˈmæŋgəneɪt/ also **permanganate of pot·ash** /·ˌ··· · ˈ··/— *n* [U] a dark purple chemical compound used for disinfecting

per·me·a·ble /ˈpɜːmɪəbəl‖ˈpɜr-/ *adj* [(*by*)] that can be PERMEATEd, esp. by water —**-bility** /ˌpɜːmɪəˈbɪlɪ̇ti‖ˌpɜr-/ *n* [U]

per·me·ate /ˈpɜːmieɪt‖ˈpɜr-/ *v* [L9, esp. *through*; T1;(IØ)] to spread or pass through or into every part of (something): *Water permeated through the cracks in the wall.*|*A strong desire for political change permeated the country* —**-ation** /ˌpɜːmiˈeɪʃən‖ˌpɜr-/ *n* [U]

per·mis·si·ble /pəˈmɪsəbəl‖pər-/ *adj* [(*to*)] allowed; that is permitted —**-bly** *adv*

per·mis·sion /pəˈmɪʃən‖pər-/ *n* [U,U3] an act of PERMITing[1]; agreement; CONSENT: *With your permission I'll leave now.*|*Did he give you permission to take that?*

per·mis·sive /pəˈmɪsɪv‖pər-/ *adj* **1** *often derog* allowing a great deal of, or too much, freedom, esp. in sexual matters (often in the phr. **the permissive society**) **2** (esp. of laws) allowing something but not ordering it —**~ly** *adv* —**~ness** *n* [U]

per·mit[1] /pəˈmɪt‖pər-/ *v* **-tt-** **1** [T1,4;V3] to allow: *I cannot permit such cruelty.*|*I have too much to do to permit my coming yet.*|*Permit me to inform you . . .* **2** [IØ] to make it possible (for a stated thing to happen): *I will come in June if my health permits.*|*weather permitting* (= if the weather is good enough to allow it) **3** [X9] to allow to be or to come: *She won't permit dogs in the house* **4** [T1] to allow as possible; admit: *The facts permit no other explanation*

per·mit[2] /ˈpɜːmɪt‖ˈpɜr-/ *n* an official written statement giving one the right to do something

permit of /pəˈmɪt‖pər-/ *v prep* [T1 *no pass.*] *fml* PERMIT[1] (4)

per·mu·ta·tion /ˌpɜːmjʊˈteɪʃən‖ˌpɜr-/ *n* **1** [U;C] (esp. in MATHEMATICS) (the act of) changing the order of a set of things arranged in a group: *The 6 possible permutations of ABC are, ABC, ACB, BCA, BAC, CAB, and CBA* **2** [C] a complete change; TRANSFORMATION

per·mute /pəˈmjuːt‖pər-/ *v* [T1] *tech* to rearrange in a different order

per·ni·cious /pəˈnɪʃəs‖pər-/ *adj* very harmful; having an evil effect —**~ly** *adv* —**~ness** *n* [U]

pernicious a·nae·mi·a /·,·· ·'···/ *n* [U] *med* ANAEMIA that will kill the sick person if it is not treated

per·nick·e·ty /pə'nɪkɪ̈ti‖pər-/ *adj infml & often derog* worrying (too much) about small things; FUSSY —compare PERSNICKETY

Per·nod /'pɜːnəʊ‖per'nəʊ (*Fr* pɛrno)/ *n* [U] *tdmk* a strong alcoholic French drink tasting of ANISEED

per·o·ra·tion /,perə'reɪʃən/ *n* **1** the last part of a speech, esp. the part in which the main points are repeated in a shorter form **2** *often derog* a grand, lengthy, but meaningless speech

per·ox·ide /pə'rɒksaɪd‖-'rɑk-/ also (*fml*) **hydrogen peroxide**— *n* [U] *infml* a chemical liquid used to take the colour out of dark hair and to kill bacteria

peroxide blonde /·,·· '·/ *n derog* a woman who has made her naturally dark hair very light yellowish, esp. by using PEROXIDE —compare PLATINUM BLONDE

per·pen·dic·u·lar[1] /,pɜːpən'dɪkjʊləʳ‖,pɜrpən'dɪkjələr/ *adj* **1** exactly upright; not leaning to one side or the other **2** [(*to*)] (of a line or surface) at an angle of 90 degrees to a line or surface —see picture at GEOMETRY **3** (*often cap.*) of the style of 14th and 15th century English buildings, esp. churches, in which there was ornamentation by the use of PERPENDICULAR[1] (1) lines —**~ly** *adv*

perpendicular[2] *n* **1** [(*the*) U] a PERPENDICULAR[1] (1,2) position **2** [C] a PERPENDICULAR[1] (2) line

per·pe·trate /'pɜːpɪ̈treɪt‖'pɜr-/ *v* [T1] *fml or humor* to be guilty of; do; COMMIT (1) (something wrong or criminal or something very foolish or amusing): *Who perpetrated the murder?|Did you perpetrate this terrible poem?* —**-tration** /,pɜːpɪ̈'treɪʃən‖,pɜr-/ *n* [U9, esp. *of*] —**-trator** /'pɜːpɪ̈treɪtəʳ‖'pɜr-/ *n*

per·pet·u·al /pə'petʃʊəl‖pər-/ *adj* [Wa5] **1** lasting for ever or for a long time: *the perpetual snows of the mountaintops* **2** *often derog* **a** uninterrupted: *the perpetual noise of the machines* **b** happening often: *I'm tired of your perpetual complaints* —**~ly** *adv*

perpetual mo·tion /·,··· '··/ *n* [U] the movement of an imagined machine which would continue to run for ever by means of its own power

per·pet·u·ate /pə'petʃʊeɪt‖pər-/ *v* [T1] to preserve; cause to be continued or remembered —**-ation** /pə,petʃʊ'eɪʃən‖pər-/ *n* [U9, esp. *of*]

per·pe·tu·i·ty /,pɜːpɪ̈'tjuːɪ̈ti‖,pɜrpɪ̈'tuː-/ *n* [U] the state of being PERPETUAL (1); time without end: *The land was given to them in perpetuity* (= for ever)

per·plex /pə'pleks‖pər-/ *v* [T1] to cause to feel confused and troubled by being difficult to understand or answer

per·plexed /pə'plekst‖pər-/ *adj* **1** being or showing that one is confused and troubled (esp. from lack of understanding) **2** difficult to understand and deal with —**~ly** /-'pleksɪ̈dli, -stli/ *adv*

per·plex·i·ty /pə'pleksɪ̈ti‖pər-/ *n* **1** [U] the state of being PERPLEXED (esp. 1) **2** [C] something that PERPLEXes

per·qui·site /'pɜːkwɪ̈zɪt‖'pɜr-/ *n* [*often pl.*] *fml* PERK[1]

per·ry /'peri/ *n* [U] an alcoholic drink made from PEARS

pers. *written abbrev. for:* person

per se /,pɜː 'seɪ‖,pɜr 'siː, ,pɜr 'seɪ, ,peər 'seɪ/ *adv Lat* considered alone and not in connection with other things

per·se·cute /'pɜːsɪkjuːt‖'pɜr-/ *v* **1** [T1] to treat cruelly; cause to suffer (esp. for religious or political beliefs) **2** [X9;(T1)] to trouble continually; annoy —compare PROSECUTE —**-cutor** *n*

per·se·cu·tion /,pɜːsɪ'kjuːʃən‖,pɜr-/ *n* **1** [U] the act of persecuting (PERSECUTE) **2** [U] the state of being PERSECUTED **3** [C] a case or example of this

per·se·ver·ance /,pɜːsɪ̈'vɪərəns‖,pɜr-/ *n* [U] continual steady effort made to fulfil some aim

per·se·vere /,pɜːsɪ̈'vɪəʳ‖,pɜr-/ *v* [IØ (*at, in, with*)] to continue firmly in spite of difficulties

per·se·ver·ing /,pɜːsɪ̈'vɪərɪŋ‖,pɜr-/ *adj* showing PERSEVERANCE: *hard persevering work*

Per·sian /'pɜːʃən, -ʒən‖'pɜrʒən/ *adj* **1** of the people, language, art, etc. of Persia (now called Iran) **2** of a kind of cat with long silky hair —see picture at CAT

per·si·flage /'pɜːsɪflɑːʒ‖'pɜr-/ *n* [U] *fml* light amusing talk, esp. concerned with laughing at the small weaknesses of others

per·sim·mon /pə'sɪmən‖pər-/ *n* **1** a type of orange-coloured soft fruit **2** a type of tree on which this grows

per·sist /pə'sɪst‖pər-/ *v* **1** [IØ (*in, with*)] to continue firmly (and perhaps unreasonably) in spite of opposition or warning: *If you persist in breaking the law you will go to prison* **2** [L9;IØ] to continue to exist: *The bad weather will persist all over the country*

per·sis·tence /pə'sɪstəns‖pər-/ *n* [U] **1** the act or fact of PERSISTing (2) **2** the quality of being PERSISTENT (1)

per·sis·tent /pə'sɪstənt‖pər-/ *adj often derog* **1 a** continuing in a habit or course of action, esp. in spite of opposition or warning: *a persistent thief* **b** showing this quality: *your persistent attempts to annoy me* **2** continuing to exist, happen, or appear for a long time, esp. for longer than is usual or desirable: *a persistent cough* —**~ly** *adv*

per·snick·e·ty /pə'snɪkɪ̈ti‖pər-/ *adj infml, esp. AmE* **1** SNOBbish (1) **2** PERNICKETY

per·son /'pɜːsən‖'pɜr-/ *n* **1** [C] a human being considered as having a character of his or her own, or as being different from all others: *Would you call a week-old baby a person?|You're just the person I wanted to see* —see PEOPLE (USAGE) **2** [C] *sometimes derog* (often in official writings) a human being in general; somebody unknown or not named or not considered worthy of respect: *No person may enter the hall without permission.|murder by a person or persons unknown|Some person or other has torn my newspaper* **3** [C *usu. sing.*] a living human body or its outward appearance: *He put his person between the little girl and the mad dog.|She was small and neat of person* **4** [*the*+R] a human being in one of the many parts or activities of his life (esp. in the phr. **in the person of**): *The club has a faithful supporter in the person of Jim Brown* **5** [U] bodily presence (in the phr. **in person**): *I can't attend the meeting in person* (= myself; personally), *but I'm sending someone to speak for me* **6** [C] (*sometimes cap.*) any of the 3 types of the existence of God in the TRINITY **7** [C9;U] (in grammar) any of the 3 special forms of verbs or PRONOUNs that show the speaker (**first person**), the one spoken to (**second person**), or the human being or thing spoken about (**third person**) **8 on/about one's person** carried about with one, as in one's pocket

per·so·na /pə'səʊnə‖pər-/ *n* (in PSYCHOLOGY) the outward character a person takes on in order to persuade other people (and himself) that he is a particular type of person

per·son·a·ble /'pɜːsənəbəl‖'pɜr-/ *adj* (esp. of men) attractive in appearance or character —**-bly** *adv*

per·son·age /'pɜːsənɪdʒ‖'pɜr-/ *n* **1** *fml or pomp* a famous or important person **2** a character in a play

per·son·al /'pɜːsənəl‖'pɜr-/ *adj* **1** [Wa5] concerning, belonging to, or for the use of a particular person; private: *father's personal chair|a letter marked "Personal"* **2** [Wa5] done or made directly by a particular person, not by a representative:

The minister made a personal visit to the scene of the fighting **3** [Wa5] of the body or appearance: *Personal cleanliness is important for health* **4** **a** (of things said) directed against (the appearance or character of) a particular person; rude **b** (of people) (in the habit of) directing such remarks; rude **5** [Wa5] *law* concerning all possessions of a person except land —see PERSONAL PROPERTY **6** [Wa5] (in grammar) showing the PERSON (7) —see PERSONAL PRONOUN

personal as·sis·tant /ˌ··· ·ˈ··/ *n* a secretary employed to look after the affairs of just one person

personal col·umn /ˈ··· ˌ··/ *n* a usu. regular part of a newspaper that gives or asks for messages, news, etc., about particular persons

per·son·al·i·ties /ˌpɜːsəˈnælɪ̈tiz‖ˌpɜr-/ *n* [P] unkind or rude remarks directed against someone's appearance, character, etc.

per·son·al·i·ty /ˌpɜːsəˈnælɪ̈ti‖ˌpɜr-/ *n* **1** [U;C] the state of existing as a particular person: *Can a man who has lost his mind and gone mad be said to have a personality?* **2** [U;C] the whole nature or character of a particular person: *He has a weak personality.|Forceful personality is needed for this job* **3** [U] unusual, strong, exciting character: *People with a great deal of personality often have admiring friends and bitter enemies* **4** [C] a person who is well known to the public or to people connected with some particular activity: *a new television personality*

personality cult /··ˈ··· ·/ *n usu. derog* the practice of giving too great admiration, praise, love, etc., to a particular person, esp. a political leader

per·son·al·ize, -ise /ˈpɜːsənəlaɪz‖ˈpɜr-/ *v* **1** [T1; (I∅)] *often derog* to change so as to be concerned with personal matters or relationships rather than with facts: *Let's not personalize (this argument)* **2** [Wv5;T1] to make PERSONAL (1), esp. by adding one's address or (the first letter(s) (INITIAL(s)) of) one's name: *personalized handkerchiefs* **3** [T1] PERSONIFY (2) —**-ization** /ˌpɜːsənəlaɪˈzeɪʃən‖ˌpɜrsənələ-/ *n* [U;C]

per·son·al·ly /ˈpɜːsənəli‖ˈpɜr-/ *adv* **1** directly and not through somebody acting for one: *He is personally in charge of all the arrangements* **2** speaking for oneself only; as far as oneself is concerned: *She said she didn't like it, but personally I thought it was very good* **3** as a person; not considered for any qualities that are not PERSONAL (1): *Personally she may be very charming, but will she be a good secretary?* **4** in a private way: *May I speak to you personally about this difficult matter?* **5** as directed against oneself in a PERSONAL (4) way: *You must not take my remarks about your plan personally*

personal pro·noun /ˌ··· ˈ··/ *n* a word standing for a noun (PRONOUN) and used for showing the speaker, the one spoken to, or the one spoken of: *"I", "you", and "they" are personal pronouns*

personal prop·er·ty /ˌ··· ˈ···/ also **personal es·tate** /ˌ··· ·ˈ·/, **per·son·al·ty** /ˈpɜːsənəlti‖ˈpɜr-/— *n* [U] *law* all the things owned by somebody except land and buildings

persona non gra·ta /pəˌsəʊnə nɒn ˈgrɑːtə‖pərˌsəʊnə nɑn ˈgrætə/ *n* [U] *Lat* a person who is not acceptable or welcome, esp. in someone's house or to a government

per·son·i·fi·ca·tion /pəˌsɒnɪ̈fɪ̈ˈkeɪʃən‖pərˌsɑ-/ *n* **1** [C] a person or thing considered as a perfect example (of some quality) (usu. in the phr. **the personification of**): *He's so brave that he's the personification of courage* **2** [C;U] (an example of) the act of PERSONIFYing (2) something that is without life

per·son·i·fy /pəˈsɒnɪ̈faɪ‖pərˈsɑ-/ *v* [T1] **1** to be a (perfect) example of; be the living form of (some quality) **2** to think of or represent (something that is without life) as a human being or as having human qualities: *A ship is often personified as "she"*

per·son·nel /ˌpɜːsəˈnel‖ˌpɜr-/ *n* **1** [P] all the people employed by a company, in the armed forces, etc.: *army personnel|The personnel are unhappy about these changes, sir* **2** [U] the department in a company that deals with (the complaints and difficulties of) these people

per·spec·tive /pəˈspektɪv‖pər-/ *n* **1** [U] **a** the art of drawing solid objects on a flat surface so that they give a natural effect of depth, distance, and solidity **b** the rules governing this art (esp. in the phrs. **in perspective, out of perspective**) **2** [U;(C)] the way in which a matter is judged, so that (proper) consideration and importance is given to each part (esp. in the phrs. **see/look at (something) in perspective, in its right/wrong perspective**) **3** [C (*of*)] a view, esp. one stretching far into the distance: (fig.) *a perspective of our country's history*

per·spex /ˈpɜːspeks‖ˈpɜr-/ *n* [U] *tdmk* (*sometimes cap.*) a type of strong plastic material that can be seen through and is used instead of glass

per·spi·ca·cious /ˌpɜːspɪˈkeɪʃəs‖ˌpɜr-/ *adj fml* having or showing keen judgment and understanding —**~ly** *adv* —**-city** /-ˈkæsɪ̈ti/ *n* [U]

per·spi·ra·tion /ˌpɜːspəˈreɪʃən‖ˌpɜr-/ *n* [U] **1** the act or action of SWEATing[1] (1) **2** SWEAT[2] (1)

per·spire /pəˈspaɪəʳ‖pər-/ *v* [I∅] *euph* SWEAT[1]

per·suade /pəˈsweɪd‖pər-/ *v* **1** [T1 (*of*);D5] to cause to feel certain; CONVINCE: *She was not persuaded of the truth of his statement* **2** [T1 (*into, out of*);V3] to cause to do something by reasoning, arguing, begging, etc.: *Try to persuade him to let us go with him.|Nothing would persuade him.|*(fig.) *He persuaded the piece of wood into the little crack* (= made it go gradually into)

per·sua·sion /pəˈsweɪʒən‖pər-/ *n* **1** [U] **a** the act of persuading (PERSUADE) **b** the state of being PERSUADEd **2** [U] the ability to influence others **3** [S9] a strongly held belief or opinion **4** [C] (a group holding) a particular (often religious) belief: *People of many different (religious) persuasions* **5** [C *usu. sing.*] kind; sort: *an artist of the modern persuasion*

per·sua·sive /pəˈsweɪsɪv‖pər-/ *adj* having the power to influence others into believing or doing what one wishes —**~ly** *adv* —**~ness** *n* [U]

pert /pɜːt‖pɜrt/ *adj* **1** (esp. of girls and young women) slightly disrespectful in a bold and rather amusing way **2** gay; full of life: *She wore a pert little hat* —**~ly** *adv* —**~ness** *n* [U]

per·tain to /pəˈteɪn‖pər-/ *v prep* [T1, 4] *fml* to belong to or have a connection with (something)

per·ti·na·cious /ˌpɜːtɪ̈ˈneɪʃəs‖ˌpɜr-/ *adj fml & often derog* holding to an opinion, course of action, etc., in a very determined way; STUBBORN —**~ly** *adv* —**-city** /-ˈnæsɪ̈ti/ *n* [U]

per·ti·nent /ˈpɜːtɪ̈nənt‖ˈpɜr-/ *adj* [(*to*)] *fml* connected directly (with something that is being considered); RELEVANT: *several pertinent questions* —opposite **irrelevant**, not **impertinent** —**~ly** *adv* —**-nence** *n* [U]

per·turb /pəˈtɜːb‖pərˈtɜrb/ *v* [T1] *fml* to cause to worry; put into a state of disorder

per·tur·ba·tion /ˌpɜːtəˈbeɪʃən‖ˌpɜrtər-/ *n* **1** [U] *fml* the state of being PERTURBed; great anxiety or disorder **2** [U;C] *fml* the action or an act of PERTURBing **3** [C] *tech* an irregular movement of a body (PLANET) that goes round the sun, caused by the special pulling (GRAVITATIONal) force of other such bodies

pe·ruke /pəˈruːk/ *n* PERIWIG

pe·ruse /pəˈruːz/ *v* [T1] **1** *fml* to read through

carefully **2** *infml & often humor* to read —**perusal** /pə'ru:zəl/ *n* [U;C]

Pe·ru·vi·an /pə'ru:vɪən/ *adj* of the people, language, art, etc., of Peru —see NATIONALITY TABLE

per·vade /pə'veɪd‖pər-/ *v* [T1] (of smells and of ideas, feelings, etc.) to spread through every part of

per·va·sive /pə'veɪsɪv‖pər-/ *adj sometimes derog* of a kind that will probably or easily PERVADE; widespread: *the pervasive influence of television* —**~ly** *adv* —**~ness** *n* [U]

per·verse /pə'vɜːs‖pər'vɜrs/ *adj* **1** (of people, actions, etc.) purposely continuing in what is wrong or unreasonable: *Even the most perverse person must agree that this is wrong* **2** (of people or events) unreasonably opposed to the wishes of (other) people; awkward and annoying: *We all wanted to go tomorrow, but she had to be perverse, and chose to go today* **3** (of behaviour) different or turned away from what is right or reasonable —**~ly** *adv* —**~ness** *n*

per·ver·sion /pə'vɜːʃən, -ʒən‖pər'vɜrʒən/ *n* **1** [U] **a** the action of PERVERTing[1] **b** the state of being PERVERTed[1] **2** [C] **a** a PERVERTed[1] form (of what is true, reasonable, etc.): *a newspaper story full of perversions of the truth* **b** a form of sexual behaviour that is considered to be unnatural

per·ver·si·ty /pə'vɜːsɨ̞ti‖pər'vɜr-/ *n* **1** [U] also **perverse·ness**— the quality or state of being PERVERSE **2** [C] a PERVERSE act

per·vert[1] /pə'vɜːt‖pər'vɜrt/ *v* [T1] **1** [Wv5] **a** to turn away from what is (considered) right and natural **b** to influence (esp. a young person) in the direction of (what are considered) unnatural sexual habits **2** [Wv5] to use for a bad purpose: *scientific knowledge perverted to help cause destruction and war|To* **pervert the course of justice** *is to prevent justice being done* **3** to change or twist (the meaning of words)

per·vert[2] /'pɜːvɜːt‖'pɜrvɜrt/ *n derog* a person whose sexual behaviour is different from (what is considered) natural

pe·se·ta /pə'seɪtə (*Sp* pe'seta)/ *n* a Spanish coin, on which the Spanish money system is based —see MONEY TABLE

pes·ky /'peski/ *adj* [Wa1;A;(B)] *AmE infml* annoying and causing trouble

pe·so /'peɪsəʊ (*Sp* 'peso)/ *n* **pesos** a small coin on which the money systems of many Spanish American countries are based —see MONEY TABLE

pes·sa·ry /'pesəri/ *n* **1** a medicine in solid form put into the female sex organ (VAGINA) **2** an instrument put into the VAGINA to hold the organ of childbirth (WOMB) up in place, or as a means of birth control

pes·si·mis·m /'pesɨ̞mɪzəm/ *n* [U] **1** the habit of thinking that whatever happens will be bad **2** the belief that evil is more powerful than good in the world

pes·si·mist /'pesɨ̞mɨ̞st/ *n* a person who thinks that whatever happens will be bad —**-mistic** /ˌpesɨ̞'mɪstɪk/ *adj* —**-mistically** *adv* [Wa4]

pest /pest/ *n* **1** a usu. small animal or insect that harms or destroys food supplies **2** [*usu. sing.*] *infml* an annoying person or thing: *That child is a real pest, continually asking questions*

pes·ter /'pestə^r/ *v* [T1 (*for, with*);V3;I∅] to annoy (somebody) continually, esp. with demands: *The poor children pestered the travellers for money.|My daughter has been pestering me to take her with me*

pes·ti·cide /'pestɨ̞saɪd/ *n* [U;C] a chemical substance used to kill PESTs (1)

pes·tif·e·rous /pe'stɪfərəs/ *adj humor* very annoying

pes·ti·lence /'pestɨ̞ləns/ *n* [C;U] *esp. old use* a disease that causes death and spreads quickly to large numbers of people (esp. BUBONIC PLAGUE)

pes·ti·lent /'pestɨ̞lənt/ also **pes·ti·len·tial** /ˌpestɨ̞'lenʃəl/— *adj* **1** *esp. old use* concerning or causing PESTILENCE; destroying or harmful to life **2** *esp. old use* having an evil influence **3** *often humor* continually annoying and unpleasant: *a pestilent cold*

pes·tle[1] /'pesəl, 'pestl/ *n* an instrument with a heavy rounded end, used for crushing substances in a special bowl (MORTAR) —see picture at LABORATORY

pestle[2] *v* [T1] to crush with a PESTLE

pet[1] /pet/ *n* **1** [C] an animal kept by a person in the home as a companion: *a pet dog|He keeps a monkey as a pet* **2** [C] a person (esp. a child) or thing specially favoured above others: *She is the teacher's pet.|Politicians are my pet hate* **3** [C *usu. sing.*;N] a person who is specially loved or lovable **4** [S] *infml* (*used esp. in* EXCLAMATIONs *by women*) an admired object: *What a perfect pet of a dress!*

pet[2] *v* **-tt-** **1** [T1] to touch kindly with the hands, showing love **2** [T1] to show special kindness and care for the comfort of **3** [T1;I∅] *infml* to kiss and touch (another or each other) in sexual play

pet[3] *n* a condition of sudden childish bad temper (esp. in the phr. **in a pet**)

pet·al /'petl/ *n* any of the (usu. coloured) leaflike divisions of a flower —see picture at FLOWER[1]

pet·alled, *AmE* also **petaled** /'petld/ *adj* having PETALs (esp. of a stated number or kind)

pe·tard /pɨ̞'tɑːd‖-ɑrd/ *n* **hoist with one's own petard** made to suffer by some evil plan with which one had intended to harm others

Pe·ter /'piːtə^r/ *n* **rob Peter to pay Paul** to take or get something from one person in order to pay another

pe·ter·man /'piːtəmən‖-tər-/ *n* **-men** /mən/ *BrE sl now rare* SAFEBREAKER

peter out *v adv* [I∅] to come gradually to an end

pet·it bour·geois /pəˌtiː 'bʊəʒwɑː, ˌpeti-‖-'bʊər-/ also **petty bourgeois**— *n, adj Fr* **1** (a person, such as a small shopkeeper or skilled worker) of the lower middle class **2** *usu. derog* BOURGEOIS

pe·tite /pə'tiːt/ *adj apprec* (of a woman, her appearance, etc.) small and neat

petit four /ˌpeti 'fʊə^r, -'fɔː^r/ *n Fr* any of various kinds of small sweet cakes or BISCUITs (1)

pe·ti·tion[1] /pɨ̞'tɪʃən/ *n* **1** (a piece or pieces of paper containing) a (respectful) request or demand made to a government or other body, usu. signed by many people **2** a proper official letter to a court of law, asking for consideration of one's case **3** a solemn prayer to God

petition[2] *v* **1** [T1 (*for*), 5c;V3;D5c] to make a (written) PETITION[1] (1) to: *They petitioned the government to reconsider its decision* **2** [I∅ (*for*), 3] to ask or beg some official body: *The people petitioned to be allowed to return to their island*

pe·ti·tion·er /pɨ̞'tɪʃənə^r/ *n* **1** a person who makes or signs a PETITION[1] **2** *law* a person asking for the ending of his or her marriage

petit mal /ˌpeti 'mæl/ *n* [U] *Fr* a slight form of the disease of EPILEPSY —see also GRAND MAL

pet name /ˌ· '·/ *n* a name given to someone whom one specially likes or loves, used instead of that person's real name

pet·rel /'petrəl/ *n* any of various types of smallish black and white seabirds —see also STORMY PETREL

pet·ri·fac·tion /ˌpetrɨ̞'fækʃən/ *n* **1** [U] shocked inability to move or think **2** [U] turning or being turned into stone **3** [C] something that has been turned into stone

pet·ri·fy /'petrɨ̞faɪ/ *v* [Wv5] **1** [T1] to put into a state of shock or fear so that the power of thought

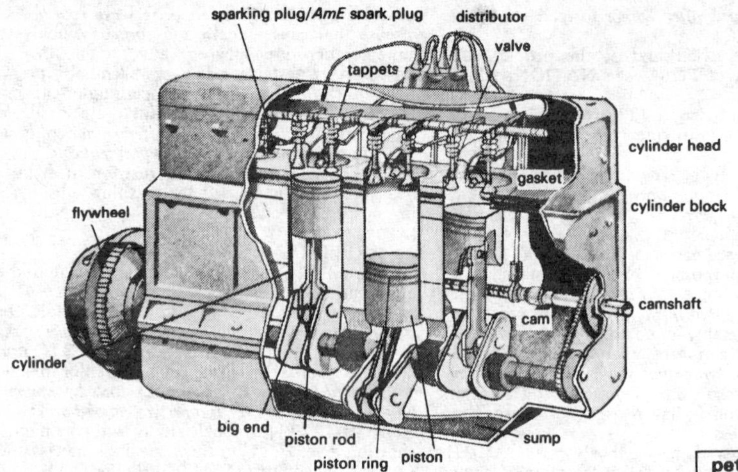

petrol engine

and action is lost **2** [T1;I∅] to turn into stone: *the Petrified Forest in Arizona*

pet·ro·chem·i·cal /ˌpetrəʊˈkemɪkəl/ *n* a chemical substance obtained from PETROLEUM or natural gas: *the petrochemical industry*

pet·rol /ˈpetrəl/ (*AmE* **gas, gasoline**)— *n* [U] *BrE* a liquid obtained esp. from PETROLEUM, used esp. for producing power in the engines of cars, aircraft, etc.: *We can fill (the car) up with petrol at the petrol station*

pe·tro·le·um /pə̀ˈtrəʊlɪəm/ *n* [U] a mineral oil obtained from below the surface of the earth, and used to produce PETROL, PARAFFIN, and various chemical substances

petroleum jel·ly /·ˌ··· ˈ··/ *AmE* usu. **pet·ro·la·tum** /ˌpetrəˈleɪtəm/— *n* [U] a solid substance made from PETROLEUM, used as a medicine for the skin and to make parts of machines work more smoothly

pe·trol·o·gy /pə̀ˈtrɒlədʒi‖-ˈtrɑ-/ *n* [U] the scientific study of rocks —**-gist** *n*

petrol sta·tion /ˈ·· ˌ··/ *n BrE* FILLING STATION

pet·ti·coat /ˈpetikəʊt/ *n* **1** [C] a type of skirt worn by women as an undergarment **2** [A] *usu. derog or humor* of or by women: *The phrase* **"petticoat government"** *means control of men by women*

pet·ti·fog·ging /ˈpetiˌfɒgɪŋ‖-ˌfɑ-, -ˌfɔ-/ *adj derog* **1** needlessly concerned with small unimportant things **2** (of things) too small to be worth considering **3** (of people, esp. bad lawyers) using small indirectly dishonest tricks to gain one's purpose

pet·tish /ˈpetɪʃ/ *adj derog* **1** (of people) impatiently angry; showing childish bad temper, esp. over something unimportant **2** (of remarks, acts) said or done in a bad temper —**~ly** *adv* —**~ness** *n* [U;C]

pet·ty /ˈpeti/ *adj* **1** [Wa1] (by comparison) unimportant: *Our difficulties seem petty when compared to those of people who never get enough to eat* **2** [Wa1] *derog* having or showing a mind that is limited, narrow, and ungenerous: *petty acts of unkindness* **3** [Wa5] of second rank or importance —**-tily** *adv* —**-tiness** *n* [U;C]

petty bour·geois /ˌ·· ˈ··/ *n* PETIT BOURGEOIS

petty cash /ˌ·· ˈ·/ *n* [(*the*) U] an amount of money kept ready in an office for making small payments

petty lar·ce·ny /ˌ·· ˈ···/ *n* [U;(C)] *law* the stealing of articles of little value

petty of·fi·cer /ˌ·· ˈ···/ *n* [C;A] a NONCOMMISSIONED OFFICER in the navy

pet·u·lant /ˈpetʃʊlənt‖-tʃə-/ *adj* showing childish bad temper over unimportant things, or for no reason at all: *petulant behaviour* —**~ly** *adv* —**-lance** *n* [U (*at*)]

pe·tu·ni·a /pə̀ˈtjuːnɪə‖pə̀ˈtuː-/ *n* [C] a type of garden plant with esp. white or bluish-red flowers shaped like a widening tube

pew /pjuː/ *n* **1** a long seat (BENCH (1)) with a back to it, for people to sit on in church —see picture at CHURCH[1] **2** *humor* a seat (esp. in the phr. **take a pew**)

pe·wit, pee- /ˈpiːwɪt/ *n* LAPWING

pew·ter /ˈpjuːtəʳ/ *n* [U] **1** a type of greyish metal made by mixing lead and tin **2** also **pewter ware** /ˈ·· ˌ·/— dishes and vessels made from this

pey·o·te /peɪˈəʊti/ *n* [U] a type of drug related to MESCALIN

pfen·nig /ˈfenɪg (*Ger* ˈpfɛnɪç)/ *n* a small German coin worth 100th of a MARK[3]

PG /piː dʒiː/ *n, adj* [Wa5;C;A] (in Britain) (a film) which has SCENE*s* which may be unsuitable for children

phag·o·cyte /ˈfægəsaɪt/ *n med* a type of blood cell (such as a LEUCOCYTE) which protects the body by destroying ("eating") foreign bodies such as bacteria

pha·lanx /ˈfælæŋks‖ˈfeɪ-/ *n* **-lanxes** *or* **-langes** /fəˈlændʒiːz/ **1** (esp. in ancient Greece) a group of soldiers packed closely together for better protection **2 a** any group of men or animals packed closely together for attack or defence **b** a group of people that is fiercely active in support of some (political) purpose **3** *med* a bone in a finger or toe —see picture at SKELETON

phal·a·rope /ˈfælərəʊp/ *n* [Wn1] any of various types of shore bird that swim in the sea, in lakes, etc.

phal·lic /ˈfælɪk/ *adj* of or like a PHALLUS (often in the phr. **phallic symbol**)

phal·lus /ˈfæləs/ *n* an image of the male sex organ (PENIS), esp. as used in some simple forms of religion as a sign of the power of man to produce children

phan·tas·ma·go·ri·a /fænˌtæzməˈgɔːrɪə, ˌfæntæz-‖-ˈgo-/ *n* a confused dreamlike changing scene of different things, real and/or imagined —**phantasmagoric** /-ˈgɒrɪk‖-ˈgɑ-, -ˈgo-/ *adj* —**phantasmagorical** *adj*

phan·tas·mal /fænˈtæzməl/ also **phan·tas·mic** /-mɪk/— *adj esp. lit* of or like a PHANTOM

phan·ta·sy /ˈfæntəsi/ *n* [U;C] *esp. BrE* FANTASY

phan·tom /ˈfæntəm/ *n* **1** a shadowy likeness of a dead person that seems to appear on earth; GHOST: *phantom riders passing by in the night* **2** something that exists only in one's imagination: *the phantoms that troubled his dreams*

pha·raoh /ˈfeərəʊ/ *n* [C;A;(R)] (*often cap.*) (the title of) the ruler of ancient Egypt

phar·i·sa·ic /ˌfærɨ̇ˈseɪ-ɪk/ also **phar·i·sa·i·cal** /-ɪkəl/— *adj* **1** *derog* making a show of being good and religious **2** (*often cap.*) of or like a PHARISEE —**-ism** /ˈfærɨ̇seɪ-ɪzəm/ *n* [U]

phar·i·see /ˈfærɨ̇siː/ *n derog* a person who in a self-satisfied way values too highly the outward form of something (esp. a religion) compared with its true meaning

Pharisee *n* a member of an ancient group of Jews who were very careful and serious in obeying religious laws, and considered themselves very holy because of this

phar·ma·ceu·ti·cal /ˌfɑːməˈsjuːtɪkəl‖ˌfɑrməˈsuː-/ *adj* [Wa5;A;(B)] connected with (the making of) medicine —**-cally** *adv* [Wa4,5]

phar·ma·cist /ˈfɑːməsɨ̇st‖ˈfɑr-/ *n* **1** a person skilled in the making of medicine **2** *fml* a person who sells medicine; CHEMIST (3)

phar·ma·col·o·gy /ˌfɑːməˈkɒlədʒi‖ˌfɑrməˈkɑ-/ *n* [U] the scientific study of medicines and drugs —**-gist** *n*

phar·ma·co·poe·ia /ˌfɑːməkəˈpiːə‖ˌfɑr-/ *n* **1** an official book describing medicines, what they contain, the amount to be given to a sick person, etc. (esp. of one particular country) **2** all the medicines that are (officially permitted to be) used in a particular country

phar·ma·cy /ˈfɑːməsi‖ˈfɑr-/ *n* **1** [U] the making and/or giving out of medicine **2** [C] a (part of a) shop where medicines are given out or sold; CHEMIST'*s* (3) (shop)

phar·yn·gi·tis /ˌfærɪnˈdʒaɪtɨ̇s/ *n* [U] *med* sore throat

phar·ynx /ˈfærɪŋks/ *n med* the tube at the back of the mouth that leads from the back of the nose to the point where the air-passage and food-passage divide —see picture at RESPIRATORY

phase[1] /feɪz/ *n* **1 a** a stage of development: *a new and dangerous phase in the relations between the 2 nations* **b** the time during which this lasts: *the most productive phase in this artist's life* **2** any of a fixed number of changes in the appearance of the moon or a body (PLANET) moving round the sun as seen from the earth at different times during their movement through space: *the phases of the moon* **3 out of/in phase (with)** not working/working or going together (with another or each other)

phase[2] *v* [Wv5;T1] to plan or arrange in separate PHASE*s*[1] (1)

phase in *v adv* [T1] to introduce (something) in stages or gradually

phase out *v adv* [T1] to stop or remove (something) in stages or gradually —**phase-out** /ˈ· ·/ *n*

PhD /ˌpiː eɪtʃ ˈdiː/ also **D Phil**— *abbrev. for:* (the university degree of) a DOCTOR OF PHILOSOPHY

pheas·ant /ˈfezənt/ *n* **pheasant** *or* **pheasants** **1** [Wn2;C] any of various large long-tailed birds hunted for food, the male of which is usu. brightly coloured —see picture at BIRD **2** [U] the meat of this as food

phe·no·bar·bi·tone /ˌfiːnəʊˈbɑːbɨ̇təʊn‖-ˈbɑr-/ (*AmE* **phe·no·bar·bi·tal** /-bɨ̇tl‖-bɨ̇təl)/— *n* [U] a calming drug that helps a person to sleep

phe·nol /ˈfiːnɒl‖-nol/ *n* [U] *tech* CARBOLIC ACID

phe·nom·e·nal /fɪˈnɒmɨ̇nəl‖-ˈnɑ-/ *adj* **1** very unusual; scarcely able to be believed when compared with what is usual: *phenomenal strength* **2** *fml* known through the senses: *a phenomenal experience* **3** *fml* concerned with phenomena (PHENOMENON (1)): *the phenomenal sciences*

phe·nom·e·nal·ly /fɪˈnɒmɨ̇nəli‖-ˈnɑ-/ *adv* **1** very; almost too much to be believed **2** *fml* as a PHENOMENON (1)

phe·nom·e·non /fɪˈnɒmɨ̇nən‖fɪˈnɑmɨ̇nɑn, -nən/ *n* **-na** /nə/ **1** a fact or event in nature (or society) as it appears or is experienced by the senses, esp. one that is unusual and/or of scientific interest: *the phenomena of nature|Snow in Egypt is an almost unknown phenomenon.|Unmarried mothers should not be regarded simply as a social phenomenon* **2** a very unusual person, thing, event, etc.: *A child who can play the piano at the age of 2 would be called a phenomenon*

phew, **whew** *interj* (the sound of) a quick short whistling breath, either in or out, meaning **a** I am glad that that uncomfortable and/or worrying experience is over! **b** I am tired and/or out of breath **c** I am shocked and/or very surprised
USAGE This sound is usually spelt either **phew** or **whew** in writing. Some people pronounce **phew** as /fjuː/ and **whew** as /hjuː/ when they are reading aloud.

phi /faɪ/ *n* [R;C] a Greek letter (Φ, φ), represented in English spelling by *ph* /f/

phi·al /ˈfaɪəl/ *n* **1** a small bottle, esp. one of liquid medicines **2** the amount that this will hold

phi·lan·der /fɨ̇ˈlændəʳ/ *n* [I∅] (of a man) to amuse oneself by making love to women, with no serious intentions —**-derer** *n*

phil·an·throp·ic /ˌfɪlənˈθrɒpɪk‖-ˈθrɑ-/ *adj* of or showing PHILANTHROPY; kind and helpful —**~ally** *adv* [Wa4]

phi·lan·thro·pist /fɨ̇ˈlænθrəpɨ̇st/ *n* a person who is kind and helpful to those who are poor or in trouble, esp. by making generous gifts of money

phi·lan·thro·py /fɨ̇ˈlænθrəpi/ *n* [U] a feeling of kindness and love for all people, esp. as shown in an active way by giving help to people who are poor or in trouble

phi·lat·e·list /fɨ̇ˈlætəlɨ̇st/ *n tech* a stamp-collector

phi·lat·e·ly /fɨ̇ˈlætəli/ *n* [U] *tech* (the practice of) stamp-collecting —**-lic** /ˌfɪləˈtelɪk/ *adj* [Wa5]

-phile /faɪl/ also **-phil**— *comb. form* [→*n* [C]] a person who likes or has a tendency towards; person showing -PHILIA (1): *a life-long* ANGLOPHILE|ANGLOPHILE *tendencies* —opposite **-phobe** —compare -PHILIAC

phil·har·mon·ic /ˌfɪləˈmɒnɪk, ˌfɪlhɑː-‖ˌfɪlərˈmɑ-, ˌfɪlhɑr-/ *adj* [Wa5;A] (*usu. cap. and in names*) musical; of or for musical concerts: *the Royal Philharmonic Society*

phil·hel·lene /fɪlˈheliːn/ *n, adj* (a person) friendly to or admiring the Greek people, civilization, etc. —**-lenic** /ˌfɪlheˈliːnɪk‖-ˈlen-/ *adj*

-phil·i·a /ˈfɪlɪə/ *comb. form* [→*n* [U]] **1** a tendency towards or liking for: ANGLOPHILIA —opposite **-phobia**; see also -PHILE **2** *med* a diseased or unhealthy tendency towards or liking for: NECROPHILIA —see also -PHILIAC

-phil·i·ac /ˈfɪliæk/ *comb. form* [→*n, adj*] *med* (of or being) a person suffering from -PHILIA (2): *a* NECROPHILIAC|NECROPHILIAC *tendencies* —compare -PHILE, -IAC

phi·lip·pic /fɨ̇ˈlɪpɪk/ *n lit or fml* a bitter angry speech attacking somebody in public

phil·is·tine /ˈfɪlɨ̇staɪn‖-stiːn/ *n* [C;*you*+N] *derog* a person who does not understand and actively dislikes art, music, beautiful things, etc., and is proud or content to remain in this condition —**-tinism** /-stɪnɪzəm/ *n* [U]

Philistine *adj* [Wa5;A;(B)] of a nation of Palestine in biblical times, against whom the ISRAELITE*s* fought

phil·o·log·i·cal /ˌfɪlə'lɒdʒɪkəl‖-'lɑ-/ *adj* of or dealing with PHILOLOGY —**-cally** *adv* [Wa4]

phi·lol·o·gist /fɪ̈'lɒlədʒɪ̈st‖-'lɑ-/ *n* a person who studies and knows a lot about PHILOLOGY

phi·lol·o·gy /fɪ̈'lɒlədʒi‖-'lɑ-/ *n* [U] the science of the nature and growth of words, language, or a particular language

phi·los·o·pher /fɪ̈'lɒsəfəʳ‖-'lɑ-/ *n* **1** a person who studies and has much knowledge of (and usu. teaches) PHILOSOPHY (1) **2** a person who has formed a PHILOSOPHY (2) **3 a** a person who is governed by reason and calmness, esp. in times of difficulty **b** *infml* a person who thinks deeply about things: *You're quite a philosopher*

philosopher's stone /·ˌ··· '·/ *n* an imaginary substance thought in former times to have the power to change any other metal into gold

phil·o·soph·i·cal /ˌfɪlə'sɒfɪkəl‖-'sɑ-/ also **phil·o·soph·ic** /ˌfɪlə'sɒfɪk‖-'sɑ-/— *adj* **1** accepting (esp. difficulty or unhappiness) with calmness and quiet courage **2** [Wa5] of or concerning PHILOSOPHY (1) —**-cally** *adv* [Wa4]

phi·los·o·phize, -phise /fɪ̈'lɒsəfaɪz‖-'lɑ-/ *v* [IØ (*about*)] to think, talk, or write like a PHILOSOPHER

phi·los·o·phy /fɪ̈'lɒsəfi‖-'lɑ-/ *n* **1** [U] the study of the nature and meaning of existence, reality, knowledge, goodness, etc. **2** [C] any of various systems of thought having this as its base: *the philosophy of Aristotle* **3** [C] a rule or set of rules for living one's life, esp. based on one's own beliefs and experiences: *Eat, drink, and be merry—that's my philosophy* **4** [U] calmness and quiet courage, esp. in spite of difficulty or unhappiness

phil·tre, *AmE* also **-ter** /'fɪltəʳ/ *n* a magic drink intended to make a person fall in love

phiz·og /'fɪzɒg‖-zɑg/ also **phiz** /fɪz/— *n* [*usu. sing.*] *humor esp. BrE* (expression of the) face

phle·bi·tis /flɪ'baɪtɪ̈s/ *n* [U] a swollen condition (INFLAMMATION) of the blood vessels (VEIN*s* (1))

phle·bot·o·my /flɪ'bɒtəmi‖-'bɑ-/ *n* [U;C] (esp. in former times) the medical operation of drawing out some of a sick person's blood

phlegm /flem/ *n* [U] **1** the thick jelly-like substance produced in the nose and throat (esp. when one has a cold) **2** *sometimes apprec* slowness in showing feeling, interest, or activity; calmness

phleg·mat·ic /fleg'mætɪk/ *adj* having PHLEGM (2); calm and unexcitable —**-ically** *adv* [Wv4]

phlox /flɒks‖flɑks/ *n* **phlox** *or* **phloxes** [Wn2] any of several types of tall garden plant which bear groups of brightly coloured flowers

-phobe /fəʊb/ *comb. form* [→*n*] a person whose state of mind shows the presence of -PHOBIA (1): *an* ANGLOPHOBE|*a* XENOPHOBE|ANGLOPHOBE *tendencies* —opposite **-phile**

pho·bi·a /'fəʊbɪə/ *n* a strong, unnatural and usu. unreasonable fear and dislike: *She has a phobia about water and won't learn to swim* —**phobic** *n, adj*: *phobic behaviour*|*became* (*a*) *phobic*

-pho·bi·a *comb. form* [→*n*[U]] **1** (forms the names of states of mind which take the form of PHOBIA*s*): ANGLOPHOBIA|XENOPHOBIA —opposite **-philia 2** *med* (forms the names of diseases which take the form of PHOBIA*s*): AGORAPHOBIA|CLAUSTROPHOBIA

-pho·bic /'fəʊbɪk/ *comb. form* [→*adj, n*] *med* (of or being) a person suffering from -PHOBIA (2): *became* (*a*) CLAUSTROPHOBIC —**-phobically** *comb. form* [→*adv* [Wa4]]

Phoe·ni·cian /fɪ'nɪʃən, -'niː-/ *adj* of a race of people who lived on the eastern coasts of the Mediterranean in ancient times

phoe·nix /'fiːnɪks/ *n* an imaginary (LEGENDARY (1)) bird of ancient times, believed to live for 500 years and then burn itself and be born again from the ashes

phon- /fən; *strong* fɒn‖fɑn/ also **phono-**— *comb. form* voice; speech: PHONETICS|PHONOGRAPH

phone[1] /fəʊn/ *n infml* a telephone

phone[2] *v* [T1 (UP);D1,5a;IØ (UP), 3;(V3)] *infml* to telephone: *I phoned him up last night.*|*He phoned (me) to say he couldn't come.*|*I'll phone you the news*

phone[3] *n tech* a single sound made in speaking

-phone *suffix* [*n, adj* → *n*] an instrument or machine connected with sound and/or hearing: EARPHONE|SAXOPHONE|TELEPHONE

phone-in /'· ·/ *AmE* **call-in**— *n BrE* a period of time (PROGRAMME (2)) on radio or television during which telephoned questions, statements, etc., from the public are broadcast

pho·neme /'fəʊniːm/ *n tech* the smallest part (UNIT (1)) of speech that can be used to make a word different from another that is the same in every other way: *In English, the "b" in "big" and the "p" in "pig" represent 2 different phonemes*

pho·ne·mic /fə'niːmɪk/ *adj* [Wa5] *tech* **1** (of a system of writing down speech sounds (TRANSCRIPTION)) using only one sign for each PHONEME —compare PHONETIC (2) **2** of or connected with PHONEME*s* **3** (of speech sounds) that are (different) PHONEME*s* —**~ally** *adv* [Wa4,5]

pho·ne·mics /fə'niːmɪks/ *n tech* **1** [U] the study and description of the PHONEMIC (2) systems of languages **2** [U;P] the PHONEMIC (2) system of one or more particular languages

pho·net·ic /fə'netɪk/ *adj* **1** [Wa5] of or concerning the sounds of human speech **2** [Wa5] (of a system of writing down speech sounds (TRANSCRIPTION)) having the possibility of using more than one sign for each PHONEME, depending on its actual sound quality **3** (of a language) with all the words spelled very much as they sound —**~ally** *adv* [Wa4]

pho·ne·ti·cian /ˌfəʊnɪ̈'tɪʃən/ *n* a person who has special knowledge of PHONETICS

pho·net·ics /fə'netɪks/ *n* **1** [U] the study and science of speech sounds **2** [P] *not tech* the speech sounds of a particular language

pho·ney[1]**, phony** /'fəʊni/ *adj* [Wa1] *sl usu. derog* pretended; false; unreal —**-niness** *n* [U]

pho·ney[2]**, phony** *n* [C;*you*+N] *sl usu. derog* a PHONEY person

phon·ic /'fɒnɪk, 'fəʊ-‖'fɑ-/ *adj* [Wa5] *tech* **1** of sound **2** of speech sounds

phon·ics /'fɒnɪks, 'fəʊ-‖'fɑ-/ *n* [U] *tech* **1** ACOUSTICS (1) **2** a way of teaching reading through understanding the pronunciation of letters and groups of letters

pho·no- /'fɒnə, -nəʊ‖'fɑ-/ *comb. form* PHON-

pho·no·graph /'fəʊnəgrɑːf‖-græf/ *n AmE* a RECORD PLAYER

pho·nol·o·gy /fə'nɒlədʒi‖-'nɑ-/ *n* [U] *tech* **1** the study of speech sounds, esp. the history of their changes in a particular language and the laws governing these **2** PHONETICS and PHONEMICS **3** the system of speech sounds in a particular language at a particular time in history: *Old English phonology* —**-gical** /ˌfɒnə'lɒdʒɪkəl‖ˌfɑnə'lɑ-/ *adj* [Wa5] —**-gically** *adv* [Wa4, 5] —**-gist** /fə'nɒlədʒɪ̈st‖-'nɑ-/ *n*

phoo·ey /'fuːi/ *interj infml* **1** "I don't believe what you have said" **2** "I am very disappointed"

phos·phate /'fɒsfeɪt‖'fɑs-/ *n* **1** [C;U] any of various forms of a salt of PHOSPHORIC acid, widely used in industry **2** [C *usu. pl.*;U] a material containing these salts, used as a plant food (FERTILIZER)

phos·pho·res·cence /ˌfɒsfə'resəns‖ˌfɑs-/ *n* [U] **1**

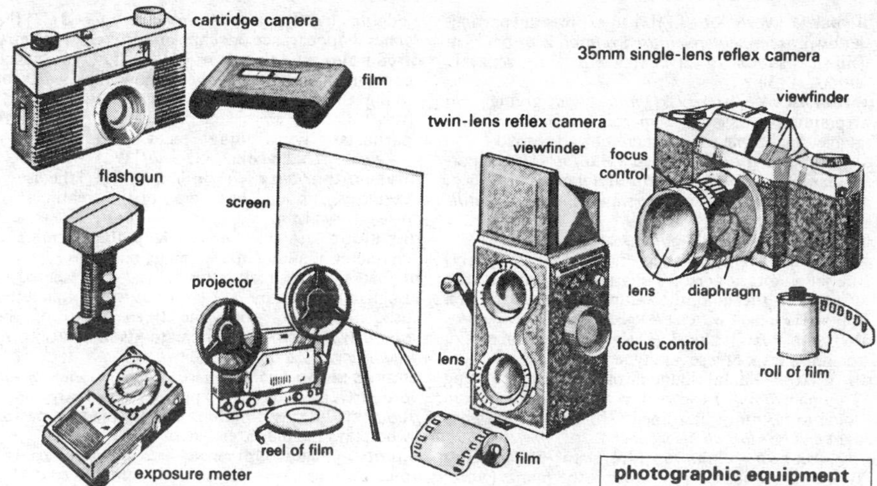

photographic equipment

the giving out of light with little or no heat **2** the giving out of faint light, only noticeable in the dark, as by some insects and sea creatures

phos·pho·res·cent /ˌfɒsfəˈresənt‖ˌfɑs-/ *adj* having the quality of PHOSPHORESCENCE: *the strange phosphorescent light seen at night on tropical seas* —**~ly** *adv*

phos·phor·ic /fɒsˈfɒrɪk‖fɑsˈfɔ-, fɑsˈfɑ-, ˈfɑsfərɪk/ *adj* of or containing PHOSPHORUS: *phosphoric acid*

phos·pho·rus /ˈfɒsfərəs‖ˈfɑs-/ *n* [U] a poisonous yellowish waxlike simple substance (ELEMENT (6)) that shines faintly in the dark and starts to burn when brought out into the air

pho·to /ˈfəʊtəʊ/ *n* **-tos** *infml* a photograph

photo- /ˈfəʊtəʊ, fəˈtɒ‖ˈfəʊtəʊ, fəˈtɑ/ *comb. form* **1** also **-photo**— of or concerning light; PHOTOSENSITIZE|TELEPHOTO **2** of or concerning photography: PHOTO FINISH|PHOTOGENIC

pho·to·cop·i·er /ˈfəʊtəʊˌkɒpɪəʳ‖-təˌkɑ-/ *n* a machine that makes photocopies (PHOTOCOPY)

pho·to·cop·y¹ /ˈfəʊtəʊˌkɒpi‖-təˌkɑpi/ *n* a photographic copy of an official letter, a drawing, etc. —compare PHOTOSTAT, XEROX

photocopy² *v* [T1] to make a PHOTOCOPY of —compare PHOTOSTAT, XEROX

pho·to·e·lec·tric /ˌfəʊtəʊ-ɪˈlektrɪk◂/ *adj* [Wa5] of, concerning, or using an electrical effect which is controlled by light

photoelectric cell /ˌ····· ˈ·/ *n* **1** an instrument that changes light into electricity **2** also (*infml*) **electric/magic eye**— an instrument by which light is made to start an electrical apparatus working

photo fin·ish /ˌ·· ˈ··/ *n* **1** the end of a race, esp. a horse or dog race, in which the leaders finish so close together that a photograph has to be taken to show which is the winner **2** a close finish in any competition

pho·to·gen·ic /ˌfəʊtəʊˈdʒenɪk, ˌfəʊtə-/ *adj* (esp. of people) having an appearance that looks pleasing or effective when photographed

pho·to·graph¹ /ˈfəʊtəgrɑːf‖-græf/ also (*infml*) **photo, picture, snap**— *n* **1** a picture obtained by using a camera and film sensitive to light: *Have you seen John's photograph in the newspaper?* (= a photograph of John) **2 take a photograph** to use a camera to obtain this

photograph² *v* **1** [T1] also (*infml*) **snap**— to take a photograph of **2** [L9] to produce an effect, likeness, or picture (of the stated kind) when used as the subject of a photograph

pho·tog·ra·pher /fəˈtɒgrəfəʳ‖-ˈtɑ-/ *n* a person who takes photographs, esp. as a business or an art

pho·to·graph·ic /ˌfəʊtəˈgræfɪk/ *adj* [Wa5;A;(B)] **1** concerning, got by, or used in producing photographs **2** able to remember things with very great exactness (esp. in the phr. **a photographic memory**) —**-ically** *adv* [Wa4]

pho·tog·ra·phy /fəˈtɒgrəfi‖-ˈtɑ-/ *n* [U] the art, system, or business of producing photographs

pho·to·sen·si·tive /ˌfəʊtəʊˈsensɪ̇tɪv‖-təˈsen-/ *adj* changing under the action of light

pho·to·sen·si·tize, -tise /ˌfəʊtəʊˈsensɪ̇taɪz‖-təˈsen-/ *v* [Wv5;T1] to make PHOTOSENSITIVE —**-tization** /ˌfəʊtəʊsensɪ̇taɪˈzeɪʃən‖-təˈzeɪ-/ *n* [U;(C)]

Pho·to·stat /ˈfəʊtəstæt/ *n tdmk* (*usu. not cap.*) **1** also **Photostat cop·y** /ˌ··· ˈ··/— a type of photographic copy of an official letter, a drawing, etc. —compare PHOTOCOPY **2** a machine used for making this —**~ic** /ˌfəʊtəˈstætɪk/ *adj* [Wa5]

photostat *v* **-tt-** [T1] *tdmk* to make a PHOTOSTAT (1) of

pho·to·syn·the·sis /ˌfəʊtəʊˈsɪnθɪ̇sɪ̇s‖-təˈsɪn-/ *n* [U] the production of special sugar-based substances that keep plants alive, caused by the action of sunlight on the green matter (CHLOROPHYLL) in leaves; the way green plants make their own food

phr. phrs. *written abbrev. for:* phrase

phras·al /ˈfreɪzəl/ *adj* [Wa5] made up of or connected with a PHRASE¹ (1b) or phrases

phrasal verb /ˌ·· ˈ·/ also **phrasal**— *n* a group of words that acts like a verb and consists usu. of a verb with an adverb and/or a PREPOSITION: *"Get by" and "use up" are phrasal verbs*

phrase¹ /freɪz/ *n* **1 a** a small group of words **b** (in grammar) a group of words without a FINITE verb, esp. as forming part of a sentence: *"Walking along the road" and "a packet of cigarettes" are phrases* **2** a short expression, esp. one that is clever and very suited to what is meant **3** a short independent passage of music that is part of a longer piece **4 a coin a phrase** to invent a PHRASE¹ (2) (where there was no suitable common one before) **b to coin a phrase** *humor* "What I have just said is a very well-known and ordinary PHRASE¹ (2), and I wish to be excused for using it": *Many hands make light work, to coin a phrase* **5 a turn of phrase** a (usu. stated) way of combining words; manner of expression **6 turn a phrase** to say a clever thing neatly

phrase² *v* [Wv5;X9;(T1)] **1** to express in (particular) words: *a politely-phrased refusal* **2** to perform (music) so as to give full effect to separate PHRASE*s*¹ (3)
phrase·book /ˈfreɪzbʊk/ *n* a book giving and explaining phrases of a particular (foreign) language, for people to use when they go abroad
phra·se·ol·o·gy /ˌfreɪziˈɒlədʒi‖-ˈɑ-/ *n* [U] the (particular) way in which words are chosen, arranged, and/or used: *I don't understand all this scientific phraseology*
phre·net·ic /frɪˈnetɪk/ *adj* FRENETIC
phre·nol·o·gy /frɪˈnɒlədʒi‖-ˈnɑ-/ *n* [U] (formerly) the judging of a person's character, mind, etc., by examining the natural swellings (BUMP*s*² (2)) on top of the head (SKULL) —**-gist** *n*
phthi·sis /ˈθaɪsɨ̇s, ˈtaɪ-/ *n* [U] *med* TUBERCULOSIS of the lungs, esp. of a severe type
phut /fʌt/ *n* **1** a dull sound as of something bursting **2 go phut** *infml* **a** to break down completely **b** to come to nothing; be ruined: *His business has gone phut and he's lost all his money*
phyl·lox·e·ra /fɪˈlɒksərə, ˌfɪlɒkˈsɪərə‖-ɑk-/ *n* [U] a type of small insect that destroys the plants (VINE*s* (1)) whose fruit is used to make wine
phy·lum /ˈfaɪləm/ *n* **phyla** /ˈfaɪlə/ a main division of the animals or plants on the earth: *The* MOLLUSC*s form a phylum* —see also CLASS¹ (4), ORDER¹ (13), FAMILY (5), GENUS, SPECIES
phys·i- /ˈfɪzɪ/ also **physio-**— *comb. form* connected with nature and living bodies: PHYSICAL|PHYSICS
phys·ic¹ /ˈfɪzɪk/ *n* [U;C] *old use or humor* (a) medicine (esp. in the phr. **a dose of physic**)
physic² *v* **-ck-** [T1] *esp. old use or humor* to treat with medicine
phys·i·cal /ˈfɪzɪkəl/ *adj* **1** [B] of or concerning matter or material things (as opposed to things of the mind, spirit, etc.): *the physical world* —see NATURAL (USAGE) **2** [A] concerning the natural formation of the earth's surface **3** [B] of or according to the laws of nature: *Is there a physical explanation for these strange happenings?* **4** [B] of or concerning the body: *physical exercise* **5** [A] (of certain sciences) of the branch that is connected with PHYSICS: *physical chemistry*
physical an·thro·pol·o·gy /ˌ··· ··ˈ···/ *n* [U] the study of man's form, race, and nature, compared with those of animals —compare SOCIAL ANTHROPOLOGY
physical ge·og·ra·phy /ˌ··· ·ˈ···/ *n* [U] the study of man's natural surroundings in different parts of the world
physical jerks /ˌ··· ˈ·/ *n* [P] *humor* bodily exercises
phys·i·cally /ˈfɪzɪkli/ *adv* **1 a** according to the laws of nature **b** *infml* completely (esp. in the phr. **physically impossible**) **2** with regard to the body: *physically fit*
physical train·ing /ˌ··· ˈ··/ also (*infml*) **PT, physical ed·u·ca·tion** /ˌ··· ··ˈ··/, (*infml*) **PE**— *n* [U] development of the body by games, exercises, etc., esp. in schools
phy·si·cian /fɨ̇ˈzɪʃən/ *n* a doctor, esp. one who treats diseases with medicines (as opposed to a SURGEON, who performs operations)
phys·i·cist /ˈfɪzɨ̇sɨ̇st/ *n* a person who makes a special study of PHYSICS
phys·ics /ˈfɪzɪks/ *n* [U] a science concerned with the study of matter and natural forces (such as light, heat, movement, etc.)
phys·i·o /ˈfɪziəʊ/ *n* **-s** *infml* physiotherapist (PHYSIOTHERAPY)
physio- *comb. form* PHYSI-
phys·i·og·no·my /ˌfɪziˈɒnəmi‖-ˈɑ-, -ˈɑg-/ *n* **1** [C] the general appearance of the face, esp. as showing the character and the mind **2** [U] the art of judging character by examining the face **3** [U] the general appearance or shape of a stretch of country
phys·i·ol·o·gy /ˌfɪziˈɒlədʒi‖-ˈɑ-/ *n* **1** [U] a science concerned with the study of how the bodies of living things, and their various parts, work **2** [(*the*) C *usu. sing.*] the system by which any particular living thing keeps alive —**-gist** *n* —**-gical** /ˌfɪzɪəˈlɒdʒɪkəl‖-ˈlɑ-/ *adj* [Wa5]
phys·i·o·ther·a·py /ˌfɪziəʊˈθerəpi/ *n* [U] the use of exercises, rubbing, heat, etc., in the treatment of disease —**-pist** *n*
phy·sique /fɨ̇ˈziːk/ *n* [C;(U)] the form and character of a human, esp. male, body
pi /paɪ/ *n* **1** a Greek letter (Π, π), represented in English spelling by *p* **2** (in GEOMETRY) this letter used for representing the fixed RATIO of the CIRCUMFERENCE of a circle to its DIAMETER: *Pi equals about 22/7 or 3·14159*
pi·a·nis·si·mo /pɪəˈnɪsɨ̇məʊ/ *adv, adj, n* **-mos** *or* **-mi** /miː/ ((a piece of music) played) very softly
pi·a·nist /ˈpɪənɨ̇st, ˈpjɑː-‖piˈænɨ̇st, ˈpɪə-/ *n* a person who plays the piano, esp. with skill
pia·no¹ /ˈpjɑːnəʊ‖piˈænəʊ/ *adv, adj, n* **-nos** ((a piece of music) played) softly —compare FORTE²
pi·an·o² /piˈænəʊ/ also (*fml*) **pi·an·o·for·te** /piˌænəʊˈfɔːtɪ‖-fort/— *n* **-os** a large musical instrument, played by pressing narrow black or white bars (KEY*s*) which cause small hammers to hit wire strings
piano ac·cor·di·on /·ˌ·· ·ˈ···/ *n* an ACCORDION played by means of narrow bars (KEY*s*) like those of a piano
Pi·a·no·la /pɪəˈnəʊlə/ *n tdmk* (*often not cap.*) a type of PLAYER PIANO
pi·as·tre, -ter /piˈæstəʳ/ *n* a small coin or banknote in Turkey (=the KURUS), Egypt, Syria, the Lebanon, and the Sudan. It is 1/100th part of the amounts on which their money systems are based
pi·az·za /piˈætsə/ *n* a public square or marketplace, esp. in Italy
pi·broch /ˈpiːbrɒk, -brɒx‖-brɑ-/ *n* a piece of Scottish music, to be played on BAGPIPES
pic·a·dor /ˈpɪkədɔːʳ/ *n* (in a BULLFIGHT) a man on horseback who annoys and weakens the BULL¹ (1) by sticking a long spearlike weapon (LANCE) into it
pic·a·resque /ˌpɪkəˈresk/ *adj* (of a story or type of story) dealing with the adventures and travels of a character of whom one rather disapproves but who is usu. not really wicked
pic·ca·lil·li /ˌpɪkəˈlɪli/ *n* [U] a type of hot-tasting food made with cut-up vegetables, usu. eaten with meat
pic·ca·nin·ny, pick·a- /ˌpɪkəˈnɪni, ˈpɪkənɪni/ *n not polite* a small child of a black-skinned race
pic·co·lo /ˈpɪkələʊ/ *n* **-los** a small musical instrument that looks like a FLUTE but plays higher notes —see picture at WIND INSTRUMENT
pick¹ /pɪk/ *v* **1** [T1;V3] to choose: *I don't know which of the 3 dresses to pick—I like them all* **2** [D1 (*for*);T1] to pull or break off (part of a plant) by the stem from a tree or plant; gather: *He picked her a rose.|They've gone (fruit) picking today* **3** [T1 (*from*)] to take up or remove, usu. with the fingers or a pointed instrument, esp. separately or bit by bit: *The little birds were picking the grain.|picking the meat from a bone* **4** [T1] to remove unwanted pieces from, esp. with a finger or a pointed instrument: *Don't pick your nose!* **5** [X9, esp. *in*; (T1)] to make with or as with a pointed instrument (usu. in the phr. **pick a hole/holes in**) **6** [X9; (T1)] to pull apart: *As this skirt fits badly, I shall pick it to pieces and remake it* **7** [T1] *AmE* PLUCK¹ (4) **8** [T1 (*with*)] to bring about intentionally (usu. in the phr. **pick a fight/quarrel with someone**) **9** [T1] to steal or take from, esp. in small amounts:

It's easy to have your pocket picked in a big crowd.| *He's good at picking people's brains* (= getting people to say what their ideas are, esp. so that he can use them for himself) **10** [T1] to unlock (a lock) with any instrument other than a key, esp. secretly and for a bad purpose **11 pick and choose** to choose very carefully, considering each choice for a long time **12 pick a winner** *infml* to make a very good choice **13 pick clean** to remove everything from: *The dog picked the bone clean* **14 pick holes in** *usu. derog* to find fault with; find the weak points in **15 pick one's way/steps** to walk carefully choosing the place to put one's foot down **16 pick to pieces** *infml* to examine the nature of (a person or thing) closely in order to find fault —see also PICK AT, PICK OFF, PICK ON, PICK OUT, PICK OVER, PICK UP

pick² *n* [U9] **1** choice (often in the phr. **take your pick**): *Which of the books is your pick?*| *Which one do you want—take your pick!* **2** the best (of many) (esp. in the phr. **the pick of**)

pick³ *n* **1** (*usu. in comb.*) a sharp pointed, usu. small instrument: *an ice pick*|*a* TOOTHPICK **2** *infml* PICKAXE **3** *infml* PLECTRUM

pick·a·back /ˈpɪkəbæk/ also **piggyback**— *adj, adv, n* [A;C] ((a ride given to a child who is) carried) high on the back across the shoulders

pick at *v prep* [T1] **1** to perform or deal with (something) with little effort or interest **2** PICK ON (2)

pick·axe, *AmE* **-ax** /ˈpɪk-æks/ *n* a large tool with a wooden handle fitted into a curved iron bar with 2 sharp points, used for breaking up roads, rock, etc. —see picture at TOOL¹

picked /pɪkt/ *adj* [Wa5;A] *often apprec* chosen as very suitable for a special purpose: *a picked band of climbers*

pick·er /ˈpɪkəʳ/ *n* (*usu. in comb.*) a person or instrument that gathers: *The cotton pickers want more money*

pick·er·el /ˈpɪkərəl/ *n* **pickerel** *or* **pickerels** [Wn2] **1** *esp. BrE* a young PIKE **2** *AmE* (*usu. in comb.*) any of several types of small fish

pick·et¹ /ˈpɪk$\frac{1}{2}$t/ *n* **1** [C] a soldier with the special job of guarding a camp **2** [GC] a small group of such soldiers **3** [C] a man placed, esp. by a trade union, at the entrance to a factory, shop, etc., to prevent anyone (esp. other workers) from going in until a quarrel with the employers is over **4** [C] *infml* PICKET LINE **5** [C *often pl.*] a strong pointed stick fixed into the ground, esp. used with others to make a fence (**picket fence**)

picket² *v* **1** [IØ] to act as PICKETs¹ (1,2) **2** [T1] to surround with or as PICKETs¹ (3) and stop the work or activity of: *The men picketed the factory/picketed all the people who wanted to go inside to work* **3** [T1] to enclose with PICKETs¹ (3) **4** [X9] to place (men) in position as guards —~**er** *n*

picket line /ˈ·· ·/ *n* a group or line of PICKETs¹ (3)

pick·ings /ˈpɪkɪŋz/ *n* [P9;(P)] *infml* **1** small bits and pieces left over from which some gain may be obtained **2** small additional means of gain (usu. of a stated kind) taken dishonestly or considered as a right: *There are some easy pickings to be made in this job*

pick·le¹ /ˈpɪkəl/ *n* **1** [U] a type of liquid (esp. VINEGAR or salt water) used to preserve meat or esp. vegetables **2** [C *usu. pl.*;U] a (piece or pieces of) vegetable preserved in this **3** [C;(U)] **a** *BrE* (an) onion preserved in this **b** *AmE* (a) CUCUMBER or GHERKIN preserved in this **4** [S] *infml* a dirty, difficult, or esp. disordered condition (esp. in the phr. **in a pickle**) **5** [C;(N)] *infml BrE* a child who playfully does small slightly harmful things **6 have a rod in pickle for someone** *becoming rare* to have a punishment or something else unpleasant planned for someone

pickle² *v* [T1] to preserve (food) in PICKLE¹ (1)

pick·led /ˈpɪkəld/ *adj* **1** [Wa5;B] (of food) which has been PICKLEd² **2** [F] *infml* drunk

pick-me-up /ˈ·· ˌ·/ *n infml* something, esp. a drink or a medicine, that makes one feel stronger and more cheerful

pick off *v adv* [T1] to shoot (people or animals) one by one, by taking careful aim

pick on *v prep* **1** [T1;V3] to choose (something or someone): *The examiners can pick on any student to answer questions* **2** [T1] to choose (someone) for punishment or blame: *Why pick on me?*

pick out *v adv* [T1] **1** to choose **2** to see (someone or something) clearly among others: *Can you pick out your sister in this crowd?* **3** to understand by careful study **4** to find (a tune) by ear on a musical instrument **5** [*often pass.*] to make (something) clear to see: *The houses in the painting were picked out in white*

pick o·ver *v adv* [T1] *infml* **1** to examine (too) carefully in order to choose the best or remove the unwanted **2** to keep talking or thinking about (esp. something unpleasant): *Don't keep picking over our old quarrels: let's be friends again*

pick·pock·et /ˈpɪkˌpɒk$\frac{1}{2}$t‖-ˌpɑk-/ *n* a person who steals things from people's pockets, esp. in a crowd

pick up *v adv* **1** [T1] to take hold of and lift up **2** [T1] to gather together; collect: *picked up all the pieces*|(fig.) *After our political defeat, we must pick up the pieces and start again* **3** [IØ] to improve: *Trade is picking up again* **4** [IØ] to improve in health **5** [T1] to gain; get: *Where did you pick up that book/your excellent English/the habit/such ideas?* **6** [T1] to cause to increase: *to pick up speed* **7** [T1;IØ] to (cause to) start again: *to pick up where we left off*|*to pick up the conversation after an interruption* **8** [T1] to collect (something); arrange to go and get (someone): *Pick me up at the hotel* **9** [T1] to give (someone) a ride in a vehicle **10** [T1] *infml* (esp. of a man) to become friendly with (someone, esp. a woman) after a short meeting, usu. with sexual intentions **11** [T1] to catch (a criminal) **12** [T1] to earn (an income, usu. small) **13** [T1] to be able to hear or receive: *We picked up signals for help from the burning plane.*|*My radio can pick up France very clearly* **14** [IØ (*after*)] to tidy a room: *I won't pick up after you children* **15** [T1] to raise (oneself) after a fall or failure **16** [T1] to be prepared to pay: *The government should pick up the bill for the damaged ship* **17** [T1] *tech* to break (hard soil) with a PICKAXE **18** [T1] to save (someone or something) from danger **19** [T1] to make (someone) feel better **20** [T1] (in KNITting) (1,2)) to form again: *pick up a dropped stitch* **21 pick up and leave** *infml* to collect one's belongings and leave suddenly

pick-up /ˈ· ·/ *n* **1** an act of PICKing UP **2** *infml* a person, esp. a woman, who is PICKed UP (8) **3** the part of a record-player which receives and plays the sound from a record (esp. the needle and arm) **4** a type of light VAN having an open body with low sides —see picture at INTERCHANGE²

pick·y /ˈpɪki/ *adj* [Wa1] *derog esp. AmE* CHOOSY —**pickiness** *n* [U]

pic·nic¹ /ˈpɪknɪk/ *n* **1 a** a pleasure trip in which (cold) food is taken to be eaten somewhere in the country: *They went on/for a picnic with their friends* **b** *BrE* the meal itself **2** [*usu. sing.*] *infml* something especially easy or pleasant to do: *It's no picnic having to look after 6 small children all day*

picnic² *v* **-ck-** [L9;(IØ)] to go on or have a PICNIC¹ (1)

pic·nick·er /ˈpɪknɪkəʳ/ *n* a person who is PICNICKing[2]
pic·ric ac·id /ˌpɪkrɪk ˈæsɪ̇d/ *n* [U] a yellow acid used in medicine and in making explosives and colouring-matter
pic·to·ri·al[1] /pɪkˈtɔːrɪəl‖-ˈto-/ *adj* having, or expressed in, PICTURES[1] (1) —**-ally** *adv*
pictorial[2] *n* a newspaper or magazine made up mainly of photographs
pic·ture[1] /ˈpɪktʃəʳ/ *n* **1** [C] a painting or drawing: *Draw a picture of that tree* **2** [C] a photograph **3** [C] a representation of somebody or something made by painting, drawing, or photography: *Will you let me paint/take your picture?* (=a picture of you) **4** [S] a person or thing that is beautiful to look at: *This garden is a picture in the summer* **5** [S] **a** the perfect example (esp. in the phr. **the picture of**): *That baby is the picture of health* **b** the exact likeness or copy: *She's the picture of her mother* **6** [C *usu. sing.*] what is seen on a television set or at the cinema: *You can't get a clear picture on this set* **7** [C] a cinema film: *There's a good picture being shown this week* **8** [C (*of*) *usu. sing.*] an image in the mind, esp. an exact one produced by a skilful description: *This book gives a good picture of life in England 200 years ago* **9** [S] a state of affairs: *The present political picture gives much cause for anxiety* **10 get the picture** *infml* to understand: *You come in 5 minutes after me—get the picture?* **11 in/out of the picture** *infml* **a** in/not in the position of knowing all the facts: *I've been away for a few weeks so I'm rather out of the picture* **b** receiving/not receiving one's share of attention: *She always wants to be in the picture* **12 (as) pretty as a picture** very pretty
picture[2] *v* **1** [X9] to paint or draw so as to give an idea of: *The artist has pictured him as a young man in riding dress* **2** [T1,6a] to imagine: *I can't quite picture myself as a father* **3** [T1] to describe
picture book /ˈ·· ·/ *n* a book for young children, made up mostly of pictures
picture card /ˈ·· ·/ *n* a playing card with a picture of a king, queen, or JACK on it
picture post·card /ˌ·· ˈ··/ *n* **1** [C] *fml* POSTCARD (2) **2** [A] very pretty; PICTURESQUE (1): *a picture-postcard village*
pic·tures /ˈpɪktʃəz‖-ərz/ also (*esp. AmE*) **movies**— *n esp. BrE* **1** [*the*+P] the cinema: *Are you going to the pictures tonight?* **2** [P] the business of producing or acting in cinema films
pic·tur·esque /ˌpɪktʃəˈresk/ *adj* **1** charming or interesting enough to be made into a picture **2** (of people, their manner, dress, etc.) rather strange and unusual: *He was a picturesque figure with his long beard and strange old clothes* **3** (of language) unusually clear, strong, and descriptive —**~ly** *adv* —**~ness** *n* [U]
pid·dle /ˈpɪdl/ *v* [IØ] *infml* URINATE —**piddle** *n* [U]
pid·dling /ˈpɪdlɪŋ/ *adj derog* small and unimportant
pid·gin /ˈpɪdʒɪ̇n/ *n* **1** [U;C] a type of language which is a mixture of 2 or more other languages, esp. as used between people who do not speak each other's language **2** [S9] *becoming rare* PIGEON (2)
pie /paɪ/ *n* [C;U] **1** (*often in comb.*) an often round pastry case filled with meat or fruit, baked usu. in a deep dish (**pie dish**): *an apple pie|a meat pie|Have some more pie* **2 as easy as pie** *infml* very easy **3 have a finger in the/every pie** to concern oneself with or be connected with the matter/many matters, esp. in an unwelcome way **4 mud/sand pie** a little heap of wet mud/sand made by children at play, who press it into a small bucket and then turn it out while preserving the shape **5 pie in the sky** *infml* a hopeful plan or suggestion that has not been, or has little chance of being, put into effect

USAGE For a *BrE* speaker, a **pie** must be covered with pastry. If the top is left open, and except if it contains meat or fish, it is a **tart**: *apple/cheese* **tarts**. The word **tart** is rarer in *AmE*, and used only of small sweet ones. It does not matter to an *AmE* speaker whether the top is covered with pastry or left open.

pie·bald /ˈpaɪbɔːld/ *adj, n* [Wa5] (a horse) coloured with large black and white shapes (PATCHes) —compare SKEWBALD
piece[1] /piːs/ *n* **1** [C (*of*)] a bit, such as: **a** a part (of anything solid) which is separated, broken, or marked off from a larger or whole body: *a piece of land|He tore off a small piece of paper* **b** a single object that is an example of a kind or class, or that forms part of a set: *a piece of paper* (= a whole sheet)|*a piece of furniture* **2** [C] **a** any of many parts made to be fitted together: *I bought this table in pieces, but one piece is missing* **b** (*usu. in comb.*) an object or person forming part of a set: *an 80-piece band* (= one with 80 players or instruments) **3** [C] one of a set of small round objects or figures used in playing certain board games, esp. CHESS **4** [C] a standard size or weight in which something is made or sold **5** [C (*of*) *usu. sing.*] a small amount: *Let me give you a piece of advice* **6** [C9, (C): (*of*) *usu. sing.*] an example of something made or done, esp. of a stated quality: *This watch is a fine piece of work* **7** [C (*of*) *often sing.*] **a** something whole and complete made by an artist: *This piece (of music) should be played with great feeling* **b** a short amount that is part of this **8** [(*the*) S] an amount of work (to be) done: *We pay our workers by the piece here, not by the time they take to do the work* —see PIECEWORK **9** [C *usu. sing.*] a short written statement in a newspaper, magazine, etc.: *Did you see the piece in the paper about Mrs. Smith's accident?* **10** [C] *BrE* a coin: *a 50-penny piece|30 pieces of silver* —see also PIECE OF EIGHT **11** [C9 *usu. sing.*] also **piece of work/goods**— *infml* **a** a person, esp. a man, who is disapproved of in the stated way: *He's a nasty piece (of work), I warn you* **b** a woman, esp. regarded as a sexual object: *That girl you were with last night was a nice piece* **12** [C] *now rare* (*usu. in comb.*) a gun **13 a piece of cake** *infml* something very easy to do **14 give somebody a piece of one's mind** to tell somebody angrily what one thinks of him; scold somebody severely **15 in one piece** *infml* **a** (of a thing) undamaged; still whole **b** (of a person) unharmed, esp. after an accident **16 of a piece a** like each other in character **b** in agreement: *His action is of a piece with what he has been saying he will do for the past few months* **17 piece by piece** one by one; one part at a time **18 say one's piece** to say what one wants to or has planned to say, esp. in a way that is annoying or unwelcome to others
piece[2] *v* [Wv5;T1] to make (something sewn) by joining pieces together
pi·èce de ré·sis·tance /piːˌes də reziːˈstɑːns (*Fr* pjɛs də rezistɑ̃s)/ *n* **pièces de résistance** (*same pronunciation*) *Fr* **1** the main part of a meal **2** the main thing or event, among a number
piece·meal /ˈpiːsmiːl/ *adj, adv* (done, made, etc.) bit by bit; only one part at a time: *He does his work piecemeal*
piece of eight /ˌ· · ˈ·/ *n* [*usu. pl.*] (esp. in stories) a type of silver coin formerly used in Spain
piec·es /ˈpiːsɪ̇z/ *n* **1 come to pieces** to be able to be separated into parts for easy storing or moving **2 go (all) to pieces** to lose the ability to think or act clearly because of fear, sorrow, etc. **3 in pieces** broken; destroyed **4 pull to pieces a** to show to be ineffective: *He pulled their argument to pieces* **b** to find fault with **5 take to pieces** to (cause to)

separate into parts: *Take this engine to pieces and see what's wrong with it. Does it take to pieces?* **6 to pieces** into (small) bits: *This coat is so old that it's dropping to pieces*

piece to·geth·er *v adv* [T1] **1** also **piece out**— to make (something, as a story) complete by adding part to part: *The policeman tried to piece together the facts* **2** to make (something non-material) out of separate parts, often not well suited to each other; put together

piece·work /ˈpiːswɜːk‖-wɜrk/ *n* [U] work paid for by the amount done rather than by the hours worked

pie·crust /ˈpaɪ-krʌst/ *n* [C;U] the baked pastry on top of a PIE

pied /paɪd/ *adj* [A;(B)] (esp. of certain types of bird) irregularly coloured with 2 or more colours

pi·ed-à-terre /ˌpjeɪd æ ˈteəʳ‖piˌed ə ˈteər (*Fr* pjet a tɛr)/ *n* **pieds-à-terre** (*same pronunciation*) *Fr* a small second home or set of rooms which one keeps for use when needed

pie-eyed /ˌpaɪ ˈaɪd◂/ *adj sl* drunk

pier /pɪəʳ/ *n* **1** an ornamental bridgelike framework of wood, metal, etc., built out into the sea at places where people go for holidays, with small buildings on it where people can eat and amuse themselves **2** a bridgelike framework built out into the sea at which boats can stop to take in or land their passengers or goods **3** a pillar of stone, wood, metal, etc., esp. as used to support a bridge, or the roof of a high building

pierce /pɪəs‖pɪərs/ *v* **1** [T1;I0̸] to make a hole in or through (something) with a point: *The needle pierced her finger.|He pierced the rubber ball with a knife* **2** [X9;(T1)] to make (a hole) using a pointed instrument **3** [T1;I0̸: (*into, through*)] to force or make (a way) into or through (something): *We pierced our way through the thick forest.|He couldn't pierce her unfriendly manner* **4** [T1;L9;(I0̸)] (of light, sound, pain, etc.) to be suddenly seen, heard, or felt in or through (someone or something): *A cry of fear pierced the silence.|No light has ever pierced down here*

pierc·ing /ˈpɪəsɪŋ‖ˈpɪər-/ *adj* **1** (of wind) very strong and cold **2** (of sound) very sharp and clear, esp. in an unpleasant way **3** going to the centre or the main point; searching: *a piercing look* —**~ly** *adv*

Pier·rot /ˈpɪərəʊ (*Fr* pjɛro)/ *n Fr* **1** [C] (*often not cap.*) (esp. formerly) a member of a group of singers with whitened faces and wearing loose white clothes who perform esp. at holiday places **2** [R;(C)] a character in French plays (PANTOMIME) with an appearance like this

pi·e·tà /ˌpieˈtɑː‖ˌpieɪˈtɑ (*It* pjeˈta)/ *n It* a representation in painting or stone of the Virgin Mary holding the dead body of Christ

pi·e·ty /ˈpaɪəti/ *n* **1** [U] the showing and feeling of deep respect for God and religion **2** [C] an act that shows this —see also FILIAL PIETY

pie·zo·e·lec·tric /ˌpiːzəʊ-ɪˈlektrɪk, ˌpiːtsəʊ-‖piː-ˌeɪzəʊ-/ *adj* [Wa5] worked by electricity produced by pressure on a small piece of a certain type of stone (CRYSTAL): *a piezoelectric cigarette lighter*

pif·fle /ˈpɪfəl/ *n* [U] *infml* nonsense

pif·fling /ˈpɪflɪŋ/ *adj infml* **1** useless; meaningless **2** small and unimportant

pig[1] /pɪg/ *n* **1** [C] *AmE* also **hog**— any of various fat short-legged animals with a usu. curly tail and thick skin with short stiff hairs, esp. as kept on farms for food —see MEAT (USAGE) and picture at FARMYARD **2** [C;*you*+N] *derog* a person who eats too much, is dirty or ugly in manners, or refuses to consider others **3** [C;U] (a long block or mass of) PIG IRON **4** [C] *derog sl* a policeman **5** **make a pig of oneself** *infml* to eat (or drink) too much **6 pigs might fly** *esp. humor* what you have just said is not possible —see also (**buy**) **a pig in a** POKE[1]

pig[2] *v* **-gg- pig it** *becoming rare* (of people) to live close together in dirty conditions

pi·geon /ˈpɪdʒɪ̇n/ *n* **1** [Wn1;C;U] (the meat of) any of various quite large light grey short-legged birds —see picture at BIRD **2** [S9] also (*becoming rare*) **pidgin**— *infml* responsibility; affair: *It's not my pigeon—someone else can deal with it* **3** [C] CLAY PIGEON **4 set/put the cat among the pigeons** *infml* to cause sudden trouble and confusion, esp. by making known a fact that ought to have been kept secret

pigeon-chest·ed /ˌ·· ˈ··◂‖ˈ·· ˌ··/ *adj* (of a person) having a chest that is narrow and sticks out unnaturally

pi·geon·hole[1] /ˈpɪdʒɪ̇nhəʊl/ *n* one of a set of boxlike divisions in a frame (as on a wall or on top of a desk) for putting esp. papers in

pigeonhole[2] *v* [T1] **1** to keep carefully for possible future use **a** by putting into a PIGEONHOLE[1] **b** by remembering **2** to put aside and intentionally do nothing about **3** to put into the proper class or group: *It's the sort of job you can't pigeonhole—he seems to do different things every week*

pigeon-toed /ˈ·· ·/ *adj* (of a person) having the feet pointing inwards

pig·ge·ry /ˈpɪgəri/ *n* **1** a pig farm **2** PIGSTY

pig·gish /ˈpɪgɪʃ/ *adj derog* (of a person) like a pig, esp. in being dirty or eating too much —**~ly** *adv* —**~ness** *n* [U]

pig·gy[1] /ˈpɪgi/ *n* [C;N] *infml* (*used esp. by or to children*) a (little) pig

piggy[2] *adj* [Wa1] *infml* (esp. of a child) always wanting more, esp. to eat

pig·gy·back /ˈpɪgibæk/ *adj, adv, n* [A;C] PICKA-BACK

pig·gy·bank /ˈpɪgibæŋk/ *n* a small container, usu. in the shape of a pig, used by children for saving coins

pig·head·ed /ˌpɪgˈhedɪ̇d◂/ *adj derog* determinedly holding to an opinion or course of action in spite of argument, reason, etc.; STUBBORN —**~ly** *adv* —**~ness** *n* [U]

pig i·ron /ˈ· ˌ··/ *n* [U] an impure form of iron obtained directly from a BLAST FURNACE

pig·let /ˈpɪglɪ̇t/ *n* a young pig

pig·ment /ˈpɪgmənt/ *n* **1** [C;U] (any of various types of) dry coloured powder that is mixed with oil, water, etc., to make paint **2** [U] natural colouring matter of plants and animals, as in leaves, hair, skin, etc.

pig·men·ta·tion /ˌpɪgmənˈteɪʃən/ *n* [U] **1** the spreading of colouring matter in parts of living things **2** the colouring of living things

pig·my /ˈpɪgmi/ *n* PYGMY

pig·nut /ˈpɪgnʌt/ *n* EARTHNUT

pig·skin /ˈpɪgˌskɪn/ *n* [U] leather made from pig's skin: *a pigskin bag*

pig·stick·ing /ˈpɪgˌstɪkɪŋ/ *n* [U] the sport of hunting wild pigs with spears on horseback; sport of STICKing[2] (2) pigs

pig·sty /ˈpɪgstaɪ/ also (*esp. AmE*) **pig·pen** /ˈpɪgpen/— *n* **1** also **sty**— an enclosure with a small building in it, where pigs are kept —see picture at FARMYARD **2** a very dirty room or house, esp. one also in bad repair

pig·swill /ˈpɪgˌswɪl/ also **pig·wash** /ˈpɪgwɒʃ‖-wɔʃ, -wɑʃ/— *n* [U] **1** waste food, such as vegetable skins, given to pigs **2** tasteless or bad-tasting food, esp. in liquid form —compare HOGWASH

pig·tail /ˈpɪgteɪl/ *n* (worn esp. by young girls) a length of hair that has been twisted together

(PLAITed) and hangs down the back of the neck and shoulders —compare PONYTAIL —**~ed** *adj*: *pigtailed young girls*

pike¹ /paɪk/ *n* (*usu. cap. as part of placenames in Northern England*) a hill, esp. formerly the pointed top of this

pike² *n* **pike** *or* **pikes** [Wn2] a type of large fish-eating fish that lives in rivers and lakes —see picture at FISH¹

pike³ *n* a type of long-handled spear formerly used by soldiers fighting on foot

pike⁴ *v* [T1] to kill or wound with a PIKE³

pike·staff /ˈpaɪkstɑːf‖-stæf/ *n* the long wooden handle of a PIKE³ —see also **as** PLAIN² (7) **as a pikestaff**

pi·las·ter /pǝ̸ˈlæstǝʳ/ *n* a square pillar only part of which sticks out beyond the wall of a building, esp. one that is only ornamental

pi·lau /pɪˈlaʊ, ˈpiːlaʊ/ also **pi·laf, pi·laff** /ˈpɪlæf, ˈpiːlæf‖pɪˈlɑf/— *n* [U;(C)] (*often in comb.*) a type of hot-tasting dish made from rice and sometimes vegetables, and often served with meat: *chicken pilau*

pil·chard /ˈpɪltʃǝd‖-ǝrd/ *n* any of various small sea fish like the HERRING, often preserved in tins as food

pile¹ /paɪl/ *n* a heavy wooden, metal, or stonelike (CONCRETE) post hammered upright into the ground as a support for a building, a bridge, etc. —see picture at SITE¹

pile² *n* **1** a tidy heap, esp. as made of a number of things of the same kind placed on top of each other: *The cupboard was full of piles of old books* **2** [*usu. pl. with sing. meaning*] *infml* a lot: *I've got piles of work to do today* **3** [*usu. sing.*] *infml* a very large amount of money; fortune **4** *pomp* a large tall building or group of buildings: *an ancient pile* **5** a type of apparatus for producing electricity (BATTERY) **6** ATOMIC PILE **7 make one's pile** *infml* to gain enough money to have no more need to work

pile³ *v* **1** [X9;(T1)] to make a PILE² (1) of: *He piled the boxes one on top of the other.*|*Help us pile these books* **2** [T1 (*with*)] to load, fill, or cover: *The cart was piled high with fruit and vegetables* **3** [L9, esp. IN, *into*, OUT, *out of*] (of people) to come or go in a (disorderly) crowd: *He opened the doors and they all piled in*

pile⁴ *n* [U;C] the soft surface of short threads on some cloths (esp. VELVET) and floor coverings (CARPETs)

pile driv·er /ˈ· ˌ··/ *n* **1** a machine for hammering PILEs¹ into the ground **2** *infml* a very hard blow (PUNCH), esp. in BOXING

pile on *v adv infml* **1 pile it on** to stretch the truth; EXAGGERATE **2 pile on the agony** to enjoy making something seem worse

piles /paɪlz/ *n* [P;(U)] HEMORRHOIDs

pile·up /ˈpaɪlʌp/ *n infml* a traffic accident in which a number of vehicles crash into each other

pile up *v adv* **1** [T1;IØ] to (cause to) form into a mass or large quantity: *piled up the boxes*|*My work is piling up.*|*The clouds are piling up* **2** [IØ] (of a number of vehicles) to crash into each other

pil·fer /ˈpɪlfǝʳ/ *v* [T1;IØ] to steal (something small or a lot of small things) from (a place): *a boy found pilfering from other children's desks*|*My desk's been pilfered* —**pilferer** *n*

pil·fer·age /ˈpɪlfǝrɪdʒ/ *n* **1** [U;C] the act of PILFERing **2** [U] loss by PILFERing

pil·grim /ˈpɪlgrǝ̸m/ *n* a person who travels (esp. a long way) to a holy place as an act of religious love and respect

pil·grim·age /ˈpɪlgrǝ̸mɪdʒ/ *n* **1** [C;U] (a) journey made by a PILGRIM (often in the phrs. **go on (a) pilgrimage, go in pilgrimage**) **2** [C] a journey made to visit a place with which one has personal associations, or in which one has a particular respectful interest

Pilgrim Fa·thers /ˌ·· ˈ··/ also **Pilgrims**— *n* [*the* + P] the group of English settlers who arrived on the ship "the Mayflower" at Plymouth, Massachusetts, in 1620

pill /pɪl/ *n* **1** [C] a small ball of solid medicine, made to be swallowed whole **2** [*the*+R] (*often cap.*) *not fml* a PILL (1) taken regularly by women as a means of birth control **3** [C *usu. sing.*] *infml* an unpleasant person **4** [C] *infml & esp. humor* (esp. in some sports) a ball **5 a bitter pill (to swallow)** something very unpleasant that one has to accept **6 go/be on the pill** *infml* to start/be taking the PILL (2) regularly **7 sugar/sugarcoat/sweeten the pill** to make something unpleasant (seem) less so

pil·lage¹ /ˈpɪlɪdʒ/ *n* [U] the act of pillaging (PILLAGE²); PLUNDER

pillage² *v* [T1] to steal things violently from (a place taken in war); PLUNDER —**~r** *n*

pil·lar /ˈpɪlǝʳ/ *n* **1** a tall upright usu. round post made usu. of stone **a** used as an (ornamental) support for a roof **b** standing alone, as in a square, in memory of some person or event **2** [(*of*)] something tall and upright that looks like this: *a pillar of smoke*|*Lot's wife was turned into a pillar of salt* **3** [(*of*)] an important member and active supporter: *She has been a pillar of the church all her life* **4 (be driven) from pillar to post** (to be chased or hunted) from one place or difficulty to another

pillar-box /ˈ·· ·/ also **postbox,** (*AmE* **mailbox**)— *n BrE* a round hollow pillar-shaped iron box about 5 feet high standing in the street, with a hole in it for people to post letters

pill·box /ˈpɪlbɒks‖-bɑks/ *n* **1** a small round box for holding PILLs (1) **2** a hat shaped rather like a large box of this sort **3** a small usu. circular shelter made of a hard stonelike material (CONCRETE), having a gun inside it, built as a defence esp. along a shore

pil·li·on /ˈpɪlɪǝn/ *n* **1** a seat for a second person on a motorcycle, placed behind the driver: *a pillion passenger* **2 ride pillion** to ride on this

pil·lock /ˈpɪlǝk/ *n BrE infml* a foolish worthless person

pil·lo·ry¹ /ˈpɪlǝri/ *n* a wooden post with a bar at the top into which in former times the neck and wrists of wrongdoers were locked as a punishment

pillory² *v* [T1] **1** to punish by putting in a PILLORY¹ **2** to attack with words, esp. so as to cause to be treated with disrespect by the public

pil·low¹ /ˈpɪlǝʊ/ *n* **1** a cloth bag longer than it is wide, filled with soft material, used for supporting the head in bed **2** an object used for supporting the head, esp. while sleeping

pillow² *v* **1** [X9, esp. *on*;(T1)] to rest (esp. one's head) on a PILLOW¹ (esp. 2), esp. in order to go to sleep **2** [T1] to serve as a PILLOW¹ (esp. 2) for (the head)

pil·low·case /ˈpɪlǝʊkeɪs/ also **pillow slip** /ˈ·· ·/— *n* a washable baglike cloth covering for a PILLOW¹ (1)

pi·lot¹ /ˈpaɪlǝt/ *n* **1** a person who flies an aircraft **2** a person with a special knowledge of a particular stretch of water, esp. the entrance to a harbour, and who is trained and specially employed to go on board and guide ships that use it **3** a person who directs, advises, or guides through difficulties **4** a part of a machine that guides the movement of another part

pilot² *v* **1** [T1] to act as PILOT¹ (1,2) of (an aircraft or ship) **2** [X9] to help and guide: *He piloted the old lady through the crowd to her seat* **3** [X9, esp. *through*;(T1)] to guide carefully to a successful result: *This politician has piloted several suggested laws* (BILLS) *through Parliament*

pilot³ *adj* [Wa5;A] serving as a trial for something: *We're doing a pilot study to see if this product will sell well, and if it does we shall go into full production*

pilot fish /ˈ·· ·/ *n* **-fish** *or* **-fishes** [Wn2] a type of small fish that follows ships and swims along with larger fish, esp. with a SHARK

pilot light /ˈ·· ·/ *n* **1** a small electric light on a piece of electrical apparatus that shows when it is turned on **2** also **pilot burn·er** /ˈ·· ˌ··/— a small gas flame kept burning all the time, used for lighting larger gas burners when the gas in them is turned on

pilot of·fi·cer /ˈ·· ˌ···/ *n* [C;A;N] an officer of the lowest officer rank in an Air Force (as in the British Royal Air Force)

pi·men·to /pʒ̍ˈmentəʊ/ *n* **-tos** *or* **-to** **1** [U] the seeds of a West Indian tree, or a powder made from these, used to give a hot taste to food **2** [C] a type of tree that produces these

pimp¹ /pɪmp/ *n* **1** **a** a man who provides a woman (PROSTITUTE) for the satisfying of someone's sexual desires **b** a man who controls and makes a profit from the activities of such women **2** *AustrE* a person who secretly tells the police about the activities of criminals

pimp² *v* [I∅ (*for*)] to act as a PIMP¹ (1a)

pim·per·nel /ˈpɪmpənel‖-ər-/ *n* a type of small low-growing wild plant with flowers that are blue, white, or esp. red (SCARLET PIMPERNEL)

pim·ple /ˈpɪmpəl/ *n* **1** a small raised diseased spot on the skin **2** *humor* something small, esp. something that looks funny when compared with something big: *The little hat looked like a pimple on top of the fat man's head* —**-ply** *adj* [Wa1,3]: *pimply skin* —**-pled** *adj*

pin /pɪn/ *n* **1** a short thin stiff piece of metal that looks like a small nail, used for fastening together pieces of cloth, paper, etc. **2** a quite short thin piece of metal, pointed at one end and with an ornament at the other, used esp. as a form of jewellery **3** a short piece of wood or metal used as a support, for fastening things together, etc.; PEG **4** (in GOLF) a stick with a flag on it that is put into the hole **5** PEG¹ (3) **6 bright/clean/neat as a new pin** very bright/clean/neat **7 for two pins** *infml* without needing to be persuaded very hard: *He's just stepped on my clean floor—for two pins I'd hit him!* **8 not to care two pins** *infml* not to care at all

pin² *v* **-nn-** [X9] **1** to fasten or join with a pin or pins **2** to keep in one position: *In the accident he was pinned under the car* —see also PIN BACK, PIN DOWN, PIN ON

pin·a·fore /ˈpɪnəfɔːʳ‖-for/ *n* **1** also (*infml*) **pinny**— a loose garment that does not cover the arms or usu. the back, worn over a dress to keep it clean **2** also **pinafore dress** /ˈ··· ·/— a type of dress that does not cover the arms, and under which a BLOUSE (1) or other garment is worn

pin back *v adv* **pin back your ears** *infml esp. BrE* (*used esp. in giving or reporting orders*) to listen carefully

pin·ball ma·chine /ˈpɪnbɔːl məˌʃiːn/ *n esp. AmE* PINTABLE

pince-nez /ˌpæns ˈneɪ, pɪns- (*Fr* pɛ̃s ne)/ *n* **pince-nez** /-ˈneɪz/ [C;(P)] *Fr* (esp. formerly) glasses that are held in position on the nose by a spring (instead of by pieces fitting round the ears) —see PAIR (USAGE)

pin·cer /ˈpɪnsəʳ/ *n* [*usu. pl.*] either of the pair of footlike parts, made up of 2 pieces of pointed horny material, at the end of the legs of certain shellfish, used for seizing food —see picture at CRUSTACEAN

pincer move·ment /ˈ·· ˌ··/ *n* an attack by 2 groups of soldiers advancing from opposite directions to trap the enemy between them

pin·cers /ˈpɪnsəz‖-ərz/ *n* [P] a tool made of 2 crossed pieces of metal with curved parts at one end, used for holding tightly and pulling small things, such as a nail from wood —compare PLIERS; see PAIR (USAGE) and picture at TOOL¹

pinch¹ /pɪntʃ/ *v* **1** [T1;I∅] to press (esp. a person's flesh) tightly (and painfully) between 2 hard surfaces, or between the thumb and a finger, accidentally or on purpose: *He pinched his fingers in the car door.*|*The car door pinched his fingers.*|*He pinched her bottom.*|*Stop pinching!* **2** [I∅] to give pain by being too tight: *Don't buy the shoes if they pinch* **3** [X9] to cause to be in (the stated condition or position) by pressing tightly between 2 hard surfaces, or between the thumb and a finger: *He pinched the paper into a number of folds* **4** [Wv5 (*with*);T1 *usu. pass.*] **a** to cause pain to: *They came in pinched with cold and hunger* **b** to make (the face) thin or tired-looking: *Her face was pinched with anxiety for her lost child* **5** [I∅] to spend only what is necessary (or even less) (esp. in the phr. **pinch and save, pinch and scrape**) **6** [T1] to cause to be careful in the spending of money; cause to suffer lack of money **7** [T1] *infml* to take without permission; steal **8** [T1 *often pass.*] *infml* (of the police) to take to a police station and charge with a crime; ARREST (1): NAB (1)

pinch² *n* **1** [C] an act of PINCHing¹ (1) **2** [C (*of*)] an amount that can be picked up between the thumb and a finger: *a pinch of salt* **3** [*the*+R] suffering caused by lack of necessary things, esp. money (esp. in the phr. **feel the pinch**) **4 at a pinch** (*AmE* **in a pinch**)— if necessary

pinch·beck /ˈpɪntʃbek/ *n* [U] a mixed metal (ALLOY) made from copper and ZINC and looking rather like gold

pinched /pɪntʃt/ *adj* [F (*for*)] without enough; SHORT¹ (3): *We're rather pinched* (*for money*) *these days*

pinch·pen·ny /ˈpɪntʃˌpeni/ *n* PENNY PINCHER

pin·cush·ion /ˈpɪnˌkʊʃən/ *n* a filled bag like a small CUSHION into which PINs¹ (1) are stuck until they are needed, used esp. by dressmakers

pin down *v adv* [T1] **1** to fasten down; prevent from moving **2** *not fml* to make (someone) give details or be clear; NAIL DOWN

pine¹ /paɪn/ *v* **1** [L9 (AWAY)] to become thin and lose activity, strength, and health slowly, through disease or esp. grief **2** [I∅] (esp. of animals) to grieve **3** [I∅ (*for*), 3] to have a strong but esp. unfulfillable desire

pine² *n* **1** [C] also **pinetree** /ˈpaɪntriː/— any of several types of tall tree with thin sharp leaves (**pine needles**) that do not drop off in winter, found esp. in colder parts of the world —see picture at TREE¹ **2** [U] the white or yellowish soft wood of this tree

pin·e·al /ˈpɪnɪəl‖ˈpaɪnɪəl/ *adj* [Wa5;A;(B)] of or concerning a small PINECONE-shaped growth (**pineal body** *or* **pineal gland**) in the brain, the exact purpose of which is not known, but which may be sensitive to light in some way

pine·ap·ple /ˈpaɪnæpəl/ *n* **1** [C] **a** a type of large dark yellow tropical fruit with a mass of thin stiff leaves on top **b** the plant on which this grows **2** [U] the sweet juicy yellow flesh of this fruit, used as food —see picture at FRUIT¹

pine·cone /ˈpaɪnkəʊn/ *n* the woody fruit or seed-case of a PINE² (1) —see picture at TREE¹

pine mar·ten /ˈ· ˌ··/ *n* [Wn1] a type of small European meat-eating animal that lives in forests

pine·wood /ˈpaɪnwʊd/ *n* **1** [C *often pl. with sing.*

meaning] a PINE² (1) forest **2** [U] PINE² (2)

pin·ey /ˈpaɪni/ *adj* [Wa1] PINY

ping¹ /pɪŋ/ *n* [S;(C)] a short sharp ringing sound, as made by hitting a glass with something hard

ping² *v* **1** [L9;(I∅)] to make the sound of a PING¹ **2** [I∅] *AmE* PINK⁵

ping-pong /ˈ· ·/ *n* [U] *infml* TABLE TENNIS

pin·head /ˈpɪnhed/ *n* **1** [C] the head of a pin **2** [C] something very small **3** [C;N] a rather stupid person

pin·ion¹ /ˈpɪnɪən/ *n* **1** the joint or part of a bird's wing furthest away from the body **2** any of the stiff feathers that support a bird when flying **3** *poet* a bird's wing

pinion² *v* [T1] **1** to hold or tie up (the limbs) in order to prevent movement **2** [(*to*)] to prevent the movement of (a person or animal) by holding or tying up the limbs **3** *tech* to cut off the PINIONs¹ (1,2) from (a bird or bird's wing) in order to prevent flight

pinion³ *n* a small wheel, with teeth on its outer edge, that fits into a larger wheel and turns it or is turned by it —compare COGWHEEL, RACK² (4) and see picture at MACHINERY

pink¹ /pɪŋk/ *v* [T1] **1** to wound slightly with or as if with the point of a sword or a shot from a gun **2** [(OUT)] to ornament (cloth or leather) with a number of small holes **3** to cut (cloth) with PINKING SHEARS

pink² *n* a type of garden plant with sweet-smelling pink, white, or red flowers

pink³ *n, adj* [Wa1;B;U] **1** (a colour that is) pale red **2 in the pink (of condition/health)** *usu. humor* in perfect health; very well

pink⁴ *adj* [Wa1] *often derog* giving some slight support to SOCIALIST political parties and ideas

pink⁵ *v* (*AmE* **ping**)— [I∅] *BrE* (of a car engine) to make high knocking sounds as a result of not working properly

pink el·e·phant /ˌ· ˈ···/ *n* [*often pl.*] *humor* an imaginary thing supposed to be seen by someone who is drunk

pink·eye /ˈpɪŋkaɪ/ *n* [U] a diseased condition of the outside skin of the eyeball; CONJUNCTIVITIS

pink gin /ˌ· ˈ·/ *n* **1** [U] a kind of alcoholic drink made of GIN, with ANGOSTURA added to give it a pink colour and a slightly bitter taste **2** [C] a single glass or drink of this

pink·ie, -y /ˈpɪŋki/ *n ScotE, AmE* the last and smallest finger of the human hand —see picture at HUMAN²

pink·ing shears /ˈ·· ·/ also **pinking scis·sors** /ˈ·· ˌ··/— *n* [P] a special type of scissors with blades that have V-shaped teeth, used to cut cloth in such a way that the threads along the cut edge will not come out easily —see PAIR (USAGE)

pink·ish /ˈpɪŋkɪʃ/ *adj* slightly PINK³

pink·o /ˈpɪŋkəʊ/ *n* **-oes, -os** *derog infml* a person who gives some slight support to SOCIALIST political parties and ideas

pin mon·ey /ˈ· ˌ··/ *n* [U] *infml* a small amount of (additional) money that is earned by a woman esp. by doing small jobs, and that she can spend on herself

pin·nace /ˈpɪnɨs/ *n* a type of small boat used for taking people (and goods) to and from a ship —compare LIGHTER

pin·na·cle /ˈpɪnəkəl/ *n* **1** a pointed stone ornament like a small tower, built on a roof esp. in old churches and castles —see picture at CHURCH¹ **2** a thin tall pointed rock or rocky mountain top **3** [(*of*) *usu. sing.*] the highest point or degree

pin·nate /ˈpɪneɪt/ *adj* [Wa5] *tech* (of a leaf) made of little leaves arranged opposite each other in 2 rows along a stem

pin·ny /ˈpɪni/ *n infml* PINAFORE (1)

pin on *v prep* [D1] **1** FASTEN ON (2) **2 pin one's hopes on someone** to depend on someone for help, a favour, etc.

pin·point¹ /ˈpɪnpɔɪnt/ *v* [T1] **1** to find or describe the exact nature or cause of **2** to show the exact position of

pinpoint² *n* [(*of*)] **1** the point of a pin **2** a very small area or point: *a pinpoint of light at the end of the long tube*

pinpoint³ *adj* [Wa5;A] **1** (of a thing (TARGET) to be hit by gunfire, bombs, etc.) very small (esp. as seen from a distance) and needing great care and exactness of aim **2** very exact

pin·prick /ˈpɪnˌprɪk/ *n* **1** a small mark or hole made by or as if by a pin **2** something that causes one to be slightly annoyed

pins and nee·dles /ˌ· · ˈ··/ *n* [P] *infml* slight continuous pricking pains in a part of the body (esp. a limb) to which the supply of blood is returning after having been stopped by pressure

pin·stripe /ˈpɪnstraɪp/ *n* **1** any of a number of thin (usu. white) lines repeated at regular spaces along (usu. dark) cloth to form a pattern **2** also **pinstripe suit** /ˌ·· ˈ·/— a suit made of cloth having a pattern of these —**~d** *adj*

pint /paɪnt/ *n* **1** a measure for liquids (and some dry goods), equal to about 0.57 of a litre; half a QUART —see WEIGHTS & MEASURES TABLE **2** an amount of liquid equal to this **3** *infml* a drink of beer of this amount

pint·a /ˈpaɪntə/ *n BrE infml* a PINT of milk

pin·ta·ble /ˈpɪnˌteɪbəl/ also (*esp. AmE*) **pinball machine**— *n BrE* a machine with a sloping board down which a rolling ball is guided by various means, often used to risk money on

pint-size /ˈpaɪntsaɪz/ also **pint-sized** /ˈpaɪntsaɪzd/— *adj* small and unimportant

pin-up /ˈpɪnʌp/ *n* **1** a picture of an admired member of the opposite sex (esp. female), such as a popular singer, a woman wearing no clothes, etc., esp. as stuck up on a wall by the admirer **2** the person in such a picture

pin·wheel /ˈpɪnwiːl/ *n* **1** a small CATHERINE WHEEL **2** *AmE* WINDMILL (2)

pin·y, piney /ˈpaɪni/ *adj* [Wa1] like or containing PINE² (1) trees: *a piny smell|piny mountain slopes*

pi·o·neer¹ /ˌpaɪəˈnɪəʳ/ *n* **1** one of the first settlers in a new or unknown land, who is later followed by others **2** [(*of*)] a person who does something first and so prepares the way for others: *a pioneer of operations on the human heart|a pioneer plan* **3** a member of a special group of soldiers who go forward to prepare the way for an army's advance, by clearing roads, building bridges, etc.

pioneer² *v* **1** [T1] to begin or help in the early development of **2** [L9;(I∅)] to act as a PIONEER¹ (esp. 1,2)

pi·ous /ˈpaɪəs/ *adj* **1** [B] showing and feeling deep respect for God and religion **2** [B] *derog* pretending to have such respect and to do one's duty **3** [A] unlikely to be fulfilled (esp. in the phr. **a pious hope**) —**~ly** *adv*

pi·ous·ness /ˈpaɪəsnɨs/ *n* [U] PIETY

pip¹ /pɪp/ *n* **1** [*the*+R] *infml esp. BrE* a feeling of annoyance or low spirits (esp. in the phr. **give someone the pip**) **2** [*the*+R;U] a disease of hens and other birds

pip² *n infml* **1** each of the small marks on playing cards, DICE, and DOMINOes **2** *BrE* each of the stars on the shoulders of the coats of army officers of certain ranks

pip³ *n* a small fruit seed, esp. of an apple, orange, etc. —see picture at FRUIT¹

pip⁴ *n* a short high-sounding note, esp. as given on

the radio to show the exact time, or as used in the operation of telephones: *3 short pips*

pip[5] *v* **-pp-** [T1] *BrE infml* **1** to beat in a race, competition, etc.; defeat **2** to (cause to) fail (an examination): *She pipped her examination.|Her bad grammar pipped her* **3** to hit with something fired from a gun **4 pipped at the post** just beaten at the end of some struggle

pi·pal, peepul /ˈpiːpəl/ *n* a type of large Indian tree

pipe[1] /paɪp/ *n* **1** [C] (*often in comb.*) a tube used for carrying liquids and gas, often underground: *a gas pipe* **2** [C] **a** a small tube with a bowl-like container at one end, used for smoking tobacco **b** also **fill, pipe·ful** /ˈpaɪpfʊl/— the amount of tobacco the bowl of this will hold **c** the tobacco in the bowl of this: *He lit his pipe* **d** the smoking of a bowlful of tobacco: *He sat down before the fire to enjoy a pipe* **3** [C] **a** a simple tubelike musical instrument, played by blowing **b** any of the tubelike metal parts through which air is forced in an ORGAN (4) —see picture at KEYBOARD[1] **4** [C] *tech* **a** a whistle used by a BOATSWAIN **b** the sounding of this **5** [C] **a** a barrel for wine, holding about 480 litres **b** the amount of wine in one of these **6** [(*the*) S] PIPING[1] (4) **7 Put that in your pipe and smoke it** *infml* (of something just said that the listener does not want to believe or accept) You'll have to accept that, whether you like it or not

pipe[2] *v* **1** [T1 (*into, to*) *often pass.*] to carry (esp. liquid or gas) through PIPE*s*[1] (1) **2** [T1;IØ] to play (music) on a PIPE[1] (3a) or BAGPIPES **3** [X9] to put into or in the stated condition by playing on a PIPE[1] (3a): *Can rats and snakes be piped out of their holes?* **4** [T1;IØ] **a** (of a bird) to sing (a high note or notes) **b** (of a person) to speak (words) or sing (a song) in a high childish voice **5** [X9] *tech* **a** to call or give orders to (seamen) by blowing a PIPE[1] (4a) **b** to welcome onto a ship by blowing a pipe **6** [X9;(T1) :(*with*)] to ornament (a dress, cake, etc.) with PIPING (3) —see also PIPE DOWN, PIPE UP

pipe clay /ˈ· ·/ *n* [U] a fine white clay used (esp. formerly) in making simple PIPE*s*[1] (2a), and by soldiers for cleaning or whitening leather

pipe clean·er /ˈ· ˌ··/ *n* a length of wire covered with thread, used to unblock the stem of a PIPE[1] (2a)

piped mu·sic /ˌ· ˈ··/ also **canned music**— *n* [U] *derog* quiet recorded music played continuously in a public place, such as a shop or restaurant

pipe down *v adv* [IØ] *infml* SHUT UP (1)

pipe dream /ˈ· ·/ *n* an impossible hope, plan, idea, etc.

pipe·line /ˈpaɪp-laɪn/ *n* **1** a line of PIPE*s*[1] (1) connected end to end, often underground, esp. for carrying liquids or gas a long distance from a central supply **2** *AmE* a direct means of receiving important news or facts **3 in the pipeline** on the way

pipe of peace /ˌ· · ˈ·/ *n* PEACE PIPE

pipe o·pen·er /ˈ· ˌ···/ *n* a practice game or trial before the main activity starts

pip·er /ˈpaɪpə[r]/ *n* **1** a musician who plays on a PIPE[1] (3a), or esp. on BAGPIPES **2 He who pays the piper calls the tune** The person who pays has the right to decide how the money is spent **3 pay the piper** to bear the cost

pipe rack /ˈ· ·/ *n* a small frame for holding several PIPE*s*[1] (2a)

pipes /paɪps/ *n* [P] *infml* BAGPIPES

pi·pette /pɪˈpet‖paɪ-/ *n* a thin glass tube used in chemistry, into which small measured amounts of liquid can be sucked, to be taken from one place to another —see picture at LABORATORY

pipe up *v adv* [IØ;(T1)] to begin to speak or sing, esp. in a high voice

pip·ing[1] /ˈpaɪpɪŋ/ *n* **1** [U] a number or system of PIPE*s*[1] (1); pipes in general: *The piping outside the house needs painting.|I fell over a length of piping in the yard* **2** [U] the act or art of playing on a PIPE[1] (3a) or BAGPIPES, or the music produced by this **3** [U] **a** a narrow band of cloth, often enclosing a length of twisted threads like thick string, used for ornamenting the edges of some garments, furniture, etc. **b** thin lines of special sugar (ICING) used for ornamenting cakes **4** [(*the*) S;(U)] **a** a high song or note of a bird **b** the sound of high voices

piping[2] *adj* [A] (esp. of a voice) high-sounding

piping[3] *adv* **piping hot** (esp. of liquids or food) very hot

pip·it /ˈpɪpɪt/ *n* (*usu. in comb.*) any of several types of small bird

pip·pin /ˈpɪpɪn/ *n* (*often cap. as part of name*) any of various kinds of sweet apple

pip·squeak /ˈpɪpskwiːk/ *n* [C;(*you*) N] *derog* a person who is not worth one's attention or respect (but usu. thinks that he is)

pi·quant /ˈpiːkənt/ *adj* **1** having a pleasant sharp taste that increases the desire to eat **2** pleasantly interesting and exciting to the mind: *Her face wasn't beautiful, but it had a piquant charm* —**~ly** *adv* —**-quancy** *n* [U]

pique[1] /piːk/ *n* **1** [U] a feeling of displeasure, esp. caused by the hurting of one's pride (often in the phr. **in a fit of pique**) **2** [C] a sudden show of this

pique[2] *v* [T1] **1** [*often pass.*] to make angry by hurting the pride **2** to excite (a person or a person's interest)

pi·quet /pɪˈket/ *n* a card game for 2 players, played with 32 cards

pi·ra·cy /ˈpaɪərəsi/ *n* **1** [U] robbery by PIRATE*s*[1] (1a) **2** [U] the action of pirating (PIRATE) **3** [C] an example of either of these

pi·ra·nha /pə̇ˈrɑːnjə, -nə/ *n* a type of fierce South American meat-eating river fish

pi·rate[1] /ˈpaɪərət/ *n* **1** (esp. formerly) **a** a person who sails the seas stopping and robbing ships **b** a ship used by such a person or persons **2** a person who takes and uses the work of other people without official permission, such as one who prints and sells a book when the right to do so (COPYRIGHT) is held by someone else, or one who works a private radio station and plays records without paying to do so —**-ratical** /paɪˈrætɪkəl, pə̇-/ *adj* —**-ratically** *adv* [Wa4]

pirate[2] *v* [Wv5;T1] to make and sell (a book, newly invented article, etc.) without permission or payment, when the right to do so belongs to someone else

pir·ou·ette[1] /ˌpɪrʊˈet/ *n* a very fast turn made on one toe or the front part of one foot, esp. as by a BALLET dancer

pirouette[2] *v* [L9;(IØ)] to dance one or more PIROUETTE*s*[1]; move along in this way

pis·ca·to·ri·al /ˌpɪskəˈtɔːrɪəl‖-ˈto-/ also **pis·ca·to·ry** /ˈpɪskətəri‖-tori/— *adj* of or connected with fishing or fishermen

Pis·ces /ˈpaɪsiːz/ *n* **-ces** [Wn3] **1** [R] **a** the ancient sign, 2 fish, representing the 12th division of the ZODIAC belt of stars **b** the group of stars (CONSTELLATION) formerly in this division **2** [C] a person born under the influence of this sign —see picture at PLANET

pish /pɪʃ/ *interj now rare* (used to express feelings of not very strong anger or impatience)

piss[1] /pɪs/ *v taboo* **1** [IØ] URINATE **2** [T1] **a** to make wet in doing this: *He's pissed his trousers* **b** to cause to come out of the body in doing this: *pissing blood*

3 [*it*+I∅ (DOWN)] *sl* to rain heavily **4 piss oneself** to laugh uncontrollably

piss[2] *n* [U] *taboo* **1** URINE **2 take the piss out of** to make fun of

piss a·bout also **piss a·round**— *v adv* [I∅] *taboo sl* to act in a foolish irresponsible way; waste time

pissed /pɪst/ *adj* [F] *taboo sl* **1** drunk **2 pissed as a newt, pissed out of one's head/mind** very drunk

piss off *v adv taboo sl* **1** [I∅] (*used in giving or reporting orders*) to go away **2** [Wv5 (*with*);T1 *usu. pass.*] to tire (someone); make (someone) lose interest

pis·ta·chi·o /pə̇ˈstɑːʃiəʊ‖pə̇ˈstæ-/ *n* **-chios** **1** [C] **a** a type of small pleasant-tasting green nut: *pistachio ice cream* **b** a tree on which this grows **2** [U] also **pistachio green** /·ˌ··· ˈ·/— the light green colour of this nut

pis·til /ˈpɪstl/ *n tech* the female seed-producing part of a flower

pis·tol /ˈpɪstl/ *n* **1** a type of small gun held and fired in one hand **2 hold a pistol to someone's head** to try to force someone to do what one wants by using threats

pis·ton /ˈpɪstn/ *n* a round metal plate or a short solid pipe-shaped piece of metal that fits tightly into a tube (CYLINDER (3)) in which it is moved up and down by pressure or explosion, used in pumps and in engines to give movement to other parts of a machine by means of a connecting rod (**piston rod**) —see picture at PETROL

piston ring /ˈ·· ·/ *n* a circular metal spring used to stop gas or liquid escaping from between a PISTON and its CYLINDER (3) —see picture at PETROL

pit[1] /pɪt/ *n* **1** [C] a natural hole in the ground **2** [C] (*usu. in comb.*) a deep hole dug in the ground to get materials out **3** [(*the*) C *often sing.*] **a** a coal mine: *worked all his life down the pit* **b** the workers, machinery, etc., connected with a coal mine **4** [C] a hole dug in the ground and covered over, used to trap animals **5** [(*the*) C *usu. pl.*] (in motor racing) a place beside a track where cars can come during a race to be quickly examined and repaired **6** [C] a hole in the floor of a garage from which the underside of cars can be examined **7** [C] (*usu. in comb.*) an enclosed place or hole where fierce animals are safely kept in a ZOO, or are made to fight each other **8** [C] (*usu. in comb.*) a hole made in the ground or a floor for any of several special purposes, esp. industrial, such as **a** one containing some particular material: *a sand pit* **b** one used for standing and working in: *a* SAW *pit* **9** [C] a natural hollow in the surface of a living thing (esp· in the phr. **pit of the stomach** = the hollow place just below the bones of the chest, esp. thought of as being the place where fear is felt) —see also ARMPIT **10** [C *often pl.*] a small hollow mark or place in the surface of something, esp. as left on the face after certain diseases, esp. SMALLPOX **11** [(*the*) C *usu. sing.*] *BrE* **a** the seats at the back of the ground floor of a theatre, behind the STALL*s* **b** the people sitting in these **12** [C] also **orchestra pit**— the space below and in front of a theatre stage where musicians sit and play during a (musical) play —see picture at THEATRE **13** [(*the*) C] *AmE* (*usu. in comb.*) that part of a central place of business (EXCHANGE) where arrangements are made for buying and selling a particular article of trade **14** [*the*+R] *esp. bibl* HELL[1] (1) **15** [C *usu. sing.*] *BrE humor* a (particular person's) bed: *in my pit* **16 dig a pit for someone** to try to trap someone in any way

pit[2] *v* **-tt-** [T1] to mark with PIT*s*[1] (10)

pit[3] *n AmE* the hard central part of certain types of fruit; STONE[1] (3) —compare PIP[3]

pit[4] *v* **-tt-** [T1] *AmE* to remove the PIT[3] from (a fruit); STONE[2] (2)

pit a·gainst *v prep* [D1] to match or set against, in a fight, competition, struggle, etc.: *pitting his strength against that of a man twice his size*

pit-a-pat /ˈ· · ˌ·/ also **pitter-patter**— *adv, adj, n* [(*the*) S] *infml* (making or having) the sound or movement of a number of quick light beats or steps

pitch[1] /pɪtʃ/ *n* [U] **1** any of various black substances that are melted into a sticky material used for making hard protective coverings or for putting between cracks (esp. in a ship) to stop water coming through **2 as black/dark as pitch** very dark; difficult to see in

pitch[2] *v* **1** [T1;L9] to set up (a tent, camp, etc.) in position on open ground, esp. for a certain time only —opposite **strike** **2** [T1;L9] (of a cricketer) to make (a ball) hit the ground (in a stated place) when BOWLing: *If you pitch too short the ball can be hit very easily* **3** [I∅] (of a ball in cricket or GOLF) to hit the ground **4** [T1;I∅] (in the game of BASEBALL) **a** to aim and throw (a ball) **b** to be a PITCHER **5** [X9] to throw, esp. in a way that shows dislike or annoyance: *We pitched those noisy people out* (*of our club*) **6** [X9] to set the degree or highness or lowness of (a sound, music, etc.) **7** [X9] to give a particular feeling or expression to (something said or written): *He pitched his speech at a very simple level so that even the children could understand* **8** [X9;L9] to (cause to) fall heavily or suddenly forwards or outwards: *His foot caught in a rock and he pitched forwards* **9** [I∅] (of a ship or aircraft) to move backwards and forwards with the movement of the waves or air; move along with the back and front going up and down independently —compare ROLL (6) **10** [X9;L9] to (cause to) slope downwards: *The roof of this house pitches sharply* **11 pitch wickets** (in cricket) to fix in place the upright pieces of wood (STUMP*s*) at which the ball is aimed

pitch[3] *n* **1** [C] a place in some public area, such as a street or market, where somebody regularly tries to gain money from people who are passing, as by performing, selling small articles, etc. **2** [C] *AmE* **field**— (in sport) a special marked-out area of ground on which football, HOCKEY, NETBALL, etc., are played **3** [*the*+R (*of*)] the place where the ball hits the ground after being thrown (BOWLed (4)) **4** [C] WICKET —see CRICKET (USAGE) **5** [C] also **pitch shot** /ˈ· ·/— (in GOLF) the hitting of a ball in such a way that it rolls only a very short distance when it lands **6** [C] (in BASEBALL) the way or act of PITCHing[2] (3a) a ball **7** [C] the degree of highness or lowness of a musical note or speaking voice **8** [S9 (*of*)] degree; level: *The children were at a high pitch of excitement before the holiday* **9** [U;S;(C) :(*of*)] (esp. in building) amount or degree of slope **10** [(*the*) S] (of a ship or aircraft) a backward and forward movement; the action of PITCHing[2] (9) —compare ROLL (6) **11** [C] *infml* a salesman's special way of talking about the goods he is trying to sell: *He has a very clever* **sales pitch**

pitch-and-toss /ˌ· · ˈ·/ *n* [U] a game played for money in which coins are thrown at a particular mark or spot

pitch-black /ˌ· ˈ·/ also **pitch-dark**— *adj* [Wa5] very dark; difficult to see in —**~ness** *n* [U]

pitch·blende /ˈpɪtʃblend/ *n* [U] a dark shiny substance dug from the earth, from which URANIUM and RADIUM are obtained

pitched bat·tle /ˌ· ˈ··/ *n* **1** a fierce and usu. long quarrel or argument **2** (in former times) a battle on a chosen ground between complete forces or armies with positions already prepared —compare SKIRMISH

pitch·er¹ /ˈpɪtʃəʳ/ *n* **1** a large container for holding and pouring liquids, usu. made of clay and having 2 ear-shaped handles **2** *AmE* JUG **3** also **pitch·er·ful** /ˈpɪtʃəfʊl‖-ər-/— the amount that either of these will hold

pitcher² *n* (in BASEBALL) a player who throws the ball towards the BATTER —see picture at BASEBALL

pitch·fork¹ /ˈpɪtʃfɔːk‖-fɔrk/ *n* a long-handled farm tool with 2 long curved metal points at one end, used esp. in lifting and throwing dried cut grass (HAY)

pitchfork² [T1] **1** to lift or throw with or as if with a PITCHFORK¹ **2** [(*into*)] to force suddenly and without preparation or willingness

pitch in *v adv* [IØ] *infml* to start to work or eat eagerly

pitch in·to *v prep* [T1] **1** to make an eager start on (work or food) **2** to attack; LASH at

pitch pine /ˈ· ·/ *n* **1** [C] any of various types of PINE² tree which produce PITCH¹ as a form of RESIN **2** [U] the wood of this tree, used in building

pit·e·ous /ˈpɪtɪəs/ also **pitiful**— *adj* **1** causing or intended to cause pity: *The dog in the empty house gave a piteous cry* **2** feeling or showing pity —see PITY¹ (USAGE) —**~ly** *adv* —**~ness** *n* [U]

pit·fall /ˈpɪtfɔːl/ *n* an unexpected danger or difficulty; mistake that may easily be made: *There are many pitfalls in English spelling for foreign students*

pith /pɪθ/ *n* [U] **1** a soft white springy substance that fills the stems of certain plants and trees **2** a white material just under the coloured outside skin of oranges and other fruit of the same type **3** force, esp. of mind **4 the pith of** the main or central part of

pit·head /ˈpɪt-hed/ *n* the entrance to a coal mine

pith hel·met /ˈ· ,··/ also **topee**— *n* a large light hat made of dried PITH (1), worn in the tropics, esp. in former times, to protect the head from the sun

pith·y /ˈpɪθi/ *adj* [Wa1] **1** of, like, or having much PITH (1,2) **2** (of something said or written) strongly stated without wasting any words —**-ily** *adv* —**-iness** *n* [U]

pit·i·a·ble /ˈpɪtɪəbəl/ *adj* **1** worthy of pity **2** *derog* worthless; weak —see PITY¹ (USAGE) —**-bly** *adv* [Wa3]

pit·i·ful /ˈpɪtɪfəl/ *adj* **1** causing or deserving pity **2** *derog* not worthy or deserving respect **3** *old use* feeling or showing pity —see PITY¹ (USAGE) —**-fully** *adv* [Wa4] —**~ness** *n* [U]

pit·i·less /ˈpɪtɪləs/ *adj* **1** merciless; showing no pity: *a pitiless king who made all his people suffer* **2** unbearably severe: *the pitiless north wind*|(fig.) *the cold and pitiless light of reason* —**~ly** *adv* —**~ness** *n* [U]

pit·man /ˈpɪtmən/ *n* **-men** /mən/ a coal miner

pi·ton /ˈpiːtɒn‖ˈpiːtɑn (*Fr* pitɔ̃)/ *n Fr* a short pointed metal rod that can be hammered into rock, having a hole at one end to pass a rope through, used as a hold in mountain climbing

pi·tot tube /ˈpiːtəʊ tjuːb‖-tuːb/ *n* (*sometimes cap.* P) an instrument used in measuring the speed of an aircraft

pit po·ny /ˈ· ,··/ *n* a small horse used esp. formerly for moving coal in a coal mine

pit prop /ˈ· ·/ *n* a support for the roof of a coal mine

pit·tance /ˈpɪtəns/ *n* [*usu. sing.*] a very small ungenerous amount of pay or money given regularly as support

pit·ter-pat·ter /ˈpɪtəʳ ,pætəʳ/ *adv, adj, n* [(*the*) S] PIT-A-PAT

pi·tu·i·ta·ry /pɪ̇ˈtjuːɪ̇təri‖pɪ̇ˈtuːɪ̇teri/ also **pituitary gland** /·ˈ,···· ·/— *n* a small roundish organ at the base of the brain which produces various special substances (HORMONE*s*) which influence the growth and development of the body

pit·y¹ /ˈpɪti/ *n* **1** [U] sensitiveness to and sorrow for the suffering or unhappiness of others: *Don't help me* **out of pity**, *but only if you think I deserve it* **2** [S] a sad, unfortunate, or inconvenient state of affairs: *It's a pity it's too cold to go swimming today.*|*What a pity you won't be back before I leave!* **3 for pity's sake** (used to add force to a request) please: *For pity's sake be quiet and let me get on with my work* **4 have/take pity on (someone)** to help (someone) as a result of feeling PITY¹ (1) **5 it's a thousand pities** it is very unfortunate **6 more's the pity** *infml* unfortunately: *"I hear you won't be able to come this evening." "No, more's the pity"*

USAGE It is probably best to use **piteous** to mean "feeling **pity**", **pitiable** to mean "causing **pity**," and **pitiful** to mean "shameful; causing a low opinion"; but they can each express more than one of these meanings: *She looked at the poor old man with a* **piteous/pitiful** *face.*|*The poor old man was a* **pitiable/pitiful** *sight.*|*Her performance on the piano was* **pitiful/pitiable**.

pity² *v* [T1] **1** [Wv4] to feel PITY¹ (1) for **2** *derog* to consider to be PITIABLE (2); have a low opinion of: *I pity you if you can't answer such a simple question!*

piv·ot¹ /ˈpɪvət/ *n* **1** a fixed central point or pin on which something turns **2** the action of turning on a point **3** a person on whom or thing on which an important action, event, etc., depends: *The mother is often the pivot of family life/on which family life turns*

pivot² *v* **1** [L9;(IØ)] to turn round on or as if on a PIVOT¹ (1) **2** [T1] to provide with or fix by means of a PIVOT¹ (1): *The light was pivoted on a bar so that it could be turned round*

piv·ot·al /ˈpɪvətl/ *adj* **1** [Wa5] of or being a PIVOT¹ (1) **2** of central importance and influence

pivot on *v prep* [T1 *no pass.*] to turn or depend on: *The whole war pivoted on a single battle*

pix·ie, pixy /ˈpɪksi/ *n* a type of small fairy believed to like playing tricks on people

pix·i·lat·ed /ˈpɪksɪ̇leɪtɪ̇d/ *adj humor infml esp. AmE* **1** slightly mad **2** drunk

piz·za /ˈpiːtsə/ *n* [C;U] a plate-shaped piece of bread DOUGH or pastry baked with a mixture of cheese, TOMATOes, etc., on top

piz·zi·ca·to /,pɪtsɪˈkɑːtəʊ/ *adj, adv, n* **-tos** ((a piece or passage of music) played) by means of picking the strings (of a VIOLIN, CELLO, etc.) with a finger instead of using a BOW³ (2)

pl. *written abbrev. for:* plural

plac·ard¹ /ˈplækɑːd‖-ərd/ *n* a large printed or written notice or advertisement, put up in a public place or sometimes carried about

plac·ard² /ˈplækɑːd‖-ɑrd/ *v* [X9;(T1):] **1** to stick PLACARD*s*¹ on **2** to give public notice of, by means of PLACARD*s*¹

pla·cate /pləˈkeɪt‖ˈpleɪkeɪt/ *v* [T1] **1** to cause to stop feeling angry **2** to cause (esp. a feeling of anger) to stop or grow less —**-catory** /pləˈkeɪtəri, ˈplækə-‖ˈpleɪkətori/ *adj*: *His placatory words had little effect on the angry travellers*

place¹ /pleɪs/ *n* **1** [C] a particular part of space or position in space: *This is the place where the accident happened* **2** [C] an empty space: *We must find a place for this new picture* **3** [C *usu. sing.*] a position which one considers to be of value or importance: *Sports never had a place in his life* **4** [C] a particular part of the earth's surface, stretch of land, town, etc.: *Moscow is a very cold place in winter* **5** [C] a particular spot or area on a surface: *a sore place on her hand* **6** [C (*of*)] a room, building, or piece of land used for a particular

stated purpose: *The town has many places of amusement such as theatres and cinemas* **7** [C] **a** a usual or proper position: *Put it back in its place.|Which is your place at the table?* **b** a proper or suitable occasion or moment: *A public dinner isn't the place at which to talk about one's private affairs* **8** [C] a person's position in a line of waiting people (QUEUE) **9** [C] **a** a particular part of a piece of writing: *This is the place in the story where the child dies* **b** the particular part (of a book, story, etc.) that one is reading (esp. in the phr. **find/lose one's place**): *I put a piece of paper in the book to keep my place* **10** [C *usu. sing.*] a position of respect or greatness: *The famous general is sure of a place in history* **11** [C *usu. sing.*] a (numbered) position in the result of a competition, race, etc.: *John took first place in the history examination* **12** [C *usu. sing.*] any of the first 3 positions in the result of a horse race **13** [C *usu. sing.*] a position of employment, in a team, etc.: *He has won a place at the university* **14** [C] social position; rank: *one's place in society|This has been talked about in high places* (= by people of high rank and influence) **15** [S9] duty; what one has to do: *It's not your place to tell me what to do* **16** [S9] a (numbered) point in an argument, explanation, etc.: *In the first place I don't want to, and in the second place I can't afford to* **17** [C] a seat: *There were several empty places in church last Sunday* **18** [S9;(S)] *infml* a house; home: *They've bought a charming place in the country.|Come over to my place* **19** [C] the position of a figure in a row of figures, to the right of a decimal point: *If you divide 11 by 9 and calculate the division to 4 decimal places, the answer is 1.2222* **20 all over the place** *infml* **a** everywhere **b** in disorder: *She's left her books spread all over the place* **21 change places (with someone)** to exchange positions so that each goes where the other one was: *If we change places you'll be able to see better.|Would you mind changing places with me, as I'm too hot here* **22 give place to** to give way to; be followed by: *It's time he gave place to a younger man* **23 go places** *infml* (*usu. in tenses formed with* -ing *and/or* will) to be increasingly successful **24 in/out of place a** in/not in the proper or usual position **b** suitable/unsuitable; proper/improper (for one's surroundings): *I think an expression of thanks to our host would be in place.|I felt out of place among the foreigners* **25 in place of** instead of **26 know one's place** (formerly, of a servant) to consider oneself as of low rank and behave respectfully to gentlemen and ladies **27 lay/set a place for** to put the knives, forks, spoons, etc., in position for (one person) at a meal table **28 make place for** *now rare* make room for **29 put somebody in his place** to show somebody that one has a low opinion of him **30 take one's place a** to go to one's special position for some activity: *Take your places for the next dance* **b** to be considered as being: *This new work will take its place among the most important paintings of this century* **31 take place** to happen: *When did this conversation take place?* **32 take/have pride of place** to be considered the best **33 take somebody's** *or* **something's place** to act or be used instead of (REPLACE) somebody or something: *Electric trains have now taken the place of steam trains in England*
USAGE **Room** [U] and **place** [C] both mean free space that can be used for a purpose; but a **place** is a position, a particular part of space that is taken by or chosen for one person or thing, while the word **room** is more likely to be used when one is looking for a large enough **place**. Compare: *"Is there* **room** *(for me) in the boat?" "Yes, that* **place** (not **that* **room**) *in the corner is empty."|Which will be the best* **place** (not **the best* **room**) *to put the piano?|There's no/not much/enough/lots of* **room** *to play cricket.|This is the* **place** (not **the* **room**) *where we play cricket* —see HAPPEN (USAGE)

place² *v* **1** [X9] to put or arrange in a certain position: *Isn't that picture placed too high on the wall?*|(fig.) *You place me in a very difficult position* **2** [X9;(T1)] to find employment, a home, etc., for: *I'm placing you in charge.|Can you place these 2 homeless children?* **3** [T1] to pass to a person, firm, etc., who can do the needed action: *I placed an order with them for 500 pairs of shoes* **4** [X9;(T1)] to make a judgment of the worth, social rank, etc., of: *How high would you place her among the singers of this country?* **5** [T1] to remember fully all the details of, and where and when one last saw, heard, etc. **6** [X9] to fix; put (with certainty): *The teacher places a great deal of importance on correct grammar* **7** [X7, 9 *usu. pass.*] to state the position of (a runner) at the end of a race: *He was originally placed first, but after a complaint he was placed second* **8** [X9] to put (money) for the purpose of earning interest **9** [IØ] *AmE* to finish second in a horse or dog race —compare PLACED

Place *n* [R9] **1** a large house in the country with land around it: *Penshurst Place is a large house in Kent, England* **2** a short street, square, etc., in a town: *Hyde Park Place*

place bet /ˈ· ·/ *n* **1** *BrE* a risking of money (BET) on the chance that a particular horse will be first, second, or third in a race **2** *AmE* a risking of money (BET) on the chance that a particular horse will be first or second in a race

pla·ce·bo /pləˈsiːbəʊ/ *n* **-bos** *or* **-boes** a substance given instead of real medicine, as to a person who only imagines that he is ill

place card /ˈ· ·/ *n* a small card with a person's name on it put on a table to show where he is to sit at a formal dinner

placed /pleɪst/ *adj esp. BrE* **be placed** (esp. of a horse) to be one of the first 3 to finish a race —compare PLACE² (9)

place·kick /ˈpleɪsˌkɪk/ *n* (in RUGBY and American football) a kick made at a ball that has first been placed in position on the ground —compare DROP-KICK

place·ment /ˈpleɪsmənt/ *n* **1** [(*the*) S] the action of putting something in a position **2** [C] an act of finding a suitable position, job, etc. for someone **3** [C] (in tennis) an act of skilfully hitting the ball into a place from which one's opponent cannot return it

pla·cen·ta /pləˈsentə/ *n* **-tas** *or* **-tae** /tiː/ a thick mass on the inside of the child-bearing organ (WOMB) which joins the unborn child to the mother

place set·ting /ˈ· ˌ··/ *n* a set or arrangement of articles to be used by one person for eating

plac·id /ˈplæsɪ̇d/ *adj* **1** (of people or animals) quiet; not easily angered or excited **2** (of things) calm; peaceful: *the placid surface of the lake* —**~ly** *adv* —**~ity** /pləˈsɪdɪ̇ti/ *n* [U]

plack·et /ˈplækɪ̇t/ *n* a straight opening in the back or side of a dress or skirt, for easy putting on, or to lead to a pocket

pla·gia·ris·m /ˈpleɪdʒərɪzəm/ *n* **1** [U] the action of plagiarizing (PLAGIARIZE) **2** [C] an idea, story, etc., that is PLAGIARIZED —**plagiarist** *n*: *Those ideas aren't his own: everyone knows he's a plagiarist*

pla·gia·rize, -rise /ˈpleɪdʒəraɪz/ *v* [T1;IØ] **1** to take (words, ideas, etc.) from someone else's work and use as one's own without admitting one has done so **2** to take someone else's words from (written work)

plague¹ /pleɪg/ *n* **1** [C] any disease causing death and spreading quickly to a large number of people

2 [U;*the*+R] a quick-spreading quick-killing disease that produces high fever and swellings on the body **3** [C] a widespread, uncontrollable, and harmful mass or number: *a plague of rats* **4** [C *usu. sing.*] *infml* a continually troublesome person or thing **5 a plague on (someone or something)** *lit* (used as a curse) may (someone or something) suffer **6 avoid (someone or something) like the plague** to make every effort not to go near (someone or something), as in dislike or fear

plague² *v* [T1] **1** to cause continual discomfort, suffering, or trouble to **2** [(*with*)] to make rather angry, esp. by some repeated action: *You've been plaguing me with silly questions all day!*

plague·y /ˈpleɪgi/ *adj* [Wa1] *old use infml* annoying; troublesome

plaice /pleɪs/ *n* **plaice** [Wn2;C;U] a type of esp. European flat fish used for food —see picture at FISH¹

plaid /plæd/ *n* **1** [C] a long piece of woollen cloth, often with a special coloured pattern (TARTAN), worn over the shoulder by Scotsmen, esp. in former times **2** [U;(C)] cloth (esp. as used to make this) having a pattern of squares formed by (brightly) coloured crossing bands

plain¹ /pleɪn/ *n* [*often pl. with sing. meaning*] a large stretch of flat land: *the Great Plains of the US*

plain² *adj* **1** [Wa1;B] clear; easy to see, hear, or understand: *It's quite plain that you haven't been paying attention.|Explain it in plain language* **2** [Wa1;B] simple; without ornament or pattern: *plain food* **3** [Wa5;B] (of paper) without lines **4** [Wa1;B] *euph* (esp. of a woman) not pretty or good-looking; rather ugly **5** [Wa1;B] (of a person, words, actions, etc.) showing clearly, honestly, and exactly what is thought or felt, often in an impolite or unkind way **6** [Wa5;A] complete; undoubted: *It's just plain foolishness to spend all your money on amusements!* **7 as plain as day/as a pikestaff/as the nose on your face** *infml* very noticeable; clearly understandable; OBVIOUS —**~ness** *n* [U]

plain³ *n, adj* [Wa5;B;U] *tech* the base stitch in KNITting in which the needle is put into the front of a stitch and the new stitch made there, leaving a raised pattern on the front —compare PURL; see also KNIT

plain choc·olate /ˌ· ˈ··/ *n* [U] dark chocolate for eating, made without milk and with little sugar —compare MILK CHOCOLATE

plain-clothes /ˌ· ˈ·◂/ *adj* [Wa5;A] (esp. of a policeman) wearing ordinary clothes while on duty, rather than a uniform

plain deal·ing /ˌ· ˈ··/ *n* [U] truthfulness and honesty, esp. in business

plain flour /ˌ· ˈ·/ *n* [U] flour that contains no BAKING POWDER —compare SELF-RAISING FLOUR

plain·ly /ˈpleɪnli/ *adv* **1** in a PLAIN² (1,2) manner **2** it is clear that: *The door's locked, so plainly they must be out*

plain sail·ing /ˌ· ˈ··/ *n* [U] **1** a course of action that is simple and free from trouble **2** *tech* PLANE SAILING

plains·man /ˈpleɪnzmən/ (*fem.* **plainswoman** /-ˌwʊmən/)— *n* **-men** /mən/ a person who lives and works in a land of great PLAINS¹

plain·song /ˈpleɪnsɒŋ‖-sɔŋ/ also **plain·chant** /ˈpleɪntʃɑːnt‖-tʃænt/— *n* [U] a type of old Christian church music for voices that sounds more like sung speech than like ordinary music

plain·spo·ken /ˌpleɪnˈspəʊkən◂/ *adj* direct in the use of words, often in a rude way —compare OUTSPOKEN

plaint /pleɪnt/ *n* **1** *law* a charge brought against somebody in court **2** *poet* an expression of great sorrow

plain·tiff /ˈpleɪntɪ̇f/ *n law* a person who brings a charge against somebody (DEFENDANT) in court

plain·tive /ˈpleɪntɪv/ *adj* **1** expressing suffering and a desire for pity: *the plaintive cries of the child locked in the cupboard* **2** expressing gentle sadness: *a plaintive old song* —**~ly** *adv* —**~ness** *n* [U]

plait¹ /plæt‖pleɪt/ also (*esp. AmE*) **braid**— *n* [*often pl.*] a length of something, esp. hair, made by PLAITing²

plait² *v* [Wv5;T1] **1** also (*esp. AmE*) **braid**— to pass or twist 3 or more lengths of (hair, dried stems of grass, etc.) over and under each other to form one ropelike length **2** to make (an article) by doing this: *The children learnt to plait little baskets*

plan¹ /plæn/ *n* **1** a (carefully considered) arrangement for carrying out some future activity: *The police worked out a plan to catch the thief.|If you have no plans for tomorrow night, perhaps you would like to come out with me?* **2 a** an arrangement of the parts of a group or of a system: *Have you decided on the seating plan at the table for your guests at dinner?* **b** a maplike drawing showing this **3** a line drawing of a building or room as it might be seen from above, showing the shape, measurements, position of the walls, etc. **4** [*usu. pl.*] a set of drawings, with measurements, showing the parts of a machine **5 go according to plan** to happen as planned, without any difficulties

plan² *v* **-nn-** **1** [Wv5;T1 (OUT), 3;IØ (*for, on,* AHEAD)] to make a plan for (something): *We've been planning this visit for months. It's all planned out.|She never plans (ahead)—she just does things suddenly.|She hadn't planned for/on so many guests.|She'd planned on doing some work today.|She'd planned to do some work this afternoon.|Where do you plan to spend your holiday?* **2** [T1] to make drawings, models, or other representations of (something to be built or made)

plan·chette /plɑːnˈʃet‖plænˈʃet (*Fr* plɑ̃ʃɛt)/ *n Fr* a small board with 2 small wheels and a pencil. Some people believe that it writes down messages from the spirits of the dead

plane¹ /pleɪn/ *v* **1** [T1;IØ] to use a PLANE³ on (something) **2** [X7] to cut or make (into a certain condition) with a PLANE³: *Plane the table smooth* **3** [X9, esp. AWAY, DOWN, OFF] to remove or make less with a PLANE³: *Try to plane away that high spot in the wood*

plane² *n* PLANE TREE

plane³ *n* a tool with a blade that takes very thin pieces off wooden surfaces to make them smooth —see picture at TOOL¹

plane⁴ *n* **1 a** a completely flat surface **b** (in GEOMETRY) a surface such that a straight line joining any 2 points lies only on that surface **2** level; standard: *Let's keep the conversation on a friendly plane* **3** *infml* AEROPLANE —see TRAIN (USAGE)

plane⁵ *adj* [Wa5;A] **1** completely flat and smooth: *a plane surface* **2** being or concerning lines and figures with only length and width; 2-DIMENSIONAL: **Plane geometry** *is the study of plane figures, angles, measurements, etc.* —compare SOLID **geometry**

plane⁶ *v* [IØ (DOWN)] (of an aircraft) to fly, esp. using no engine

plane sail·ing /ˌ· ˈ··/ also **plain sailing**— *n* [U] *tech* the calculation of a ship's position as though the ship were on a PLANE⁴ (1) instead of the curved surface of the earth

plan·et /ˈplænɪ̇t/ *n* a large body in space that moves round a star, esp. round the sun: *The Earth is a planet*

See next page for picture

plan·e·tar·i·um /ˌplænɪ̇ˈteərɪəm/ *n* **-riums** *or* **-ria**

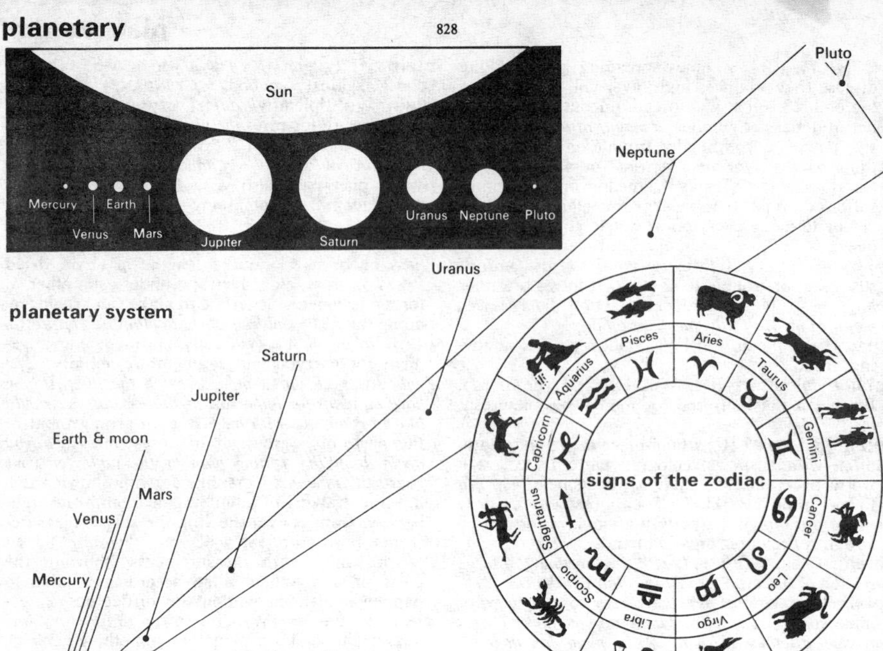

planets and stars

/rɪə/ **1** a building containing an apparatus that throws spots of light onto the inside of a curved roof to show the movements of planets and stars **2** *tech* the apparatus itself

plan·e·ta·ry /ˈplænᵻtəri‖-teri/ *adj* [Wa5;A;(B)] of or like a PLANET: *planetary movements*

plane tree /ˈ· ·/ also **plane**— *n* any of various broad-leaved wide-spreading trees that commonly grow in towns —see picture at TREE[1]

plan·gent /ˈplændʒənt/ *adj lit* (of sounds) having an expressive and sorrowful quality —**~ly** *adv* —**-gency** *n* [U]

plank[1] /plæŋk/ *n* **1** a long usu. heavy piece of board, esp. one that is 2 to 6 inches thick and at least 8 inches wide —see picture at SITE[1] **2** a main principle of a political party's stated group of aims: *They intend to fight the next election on the plank of developing the country's trade* **3 walk the plank** to be forced by PIRATE*s* (1), esp. in former times, to walk along a board laid over the side of a ship until one fell off into the sea

plank[2] *v* [T1 (*with*)] to cover with PLANK*s*[1] (1)

plank down *v adv* [T1] *sl* to put down heavily or with force

plank·ing /ˈplæŋkɪŋ/ *n* [U] PLANK*s*[1] (1), esp. put down as a floor

plank·ton /ˈplæŋktən/ *n* [U] the very small forms of plant and animal life that live in water (esp. the sea) and form the food of many fish

planned ob·so·les·cence /ˌ· ··ˈ··/ *n* [U] the principle of making products that will soon become out of date, so that people will have to keep on buying new ones

plan·ner /ˈplænəʳ/ *n* (*often in comb.*) a person who plans, esp. who plans the way in which towns are to develop: *a town planner*

plan·ning per·mis·sion /ˈ·· ·ˌ··/ *n* [U] *esp. BrE* official permission that one must obtain before a building may be put up or changed

plant[1] /plɑːnt‖plænt/ *v* **1** [T1;IØ] to put (plants or seeds) in the ground to grow: *Plant the flowers further apart.|April is the time to plant* **2** [T1 (*with*)] to supply (a place) with seeds or growing plants: *We're planting a small garden.|The hillside was planted with trees* **3** [X9] to put (an idea, belief, etc.) in the mind: *His evil talk planted the seeds of hatred in their hearts* **4** [X9] to fix or place firmly or with force: *He planted a knife in her back.|He planted himself in a chair by the fire.|(fig.) He planted a kick on the door* **5** [X9] *now rare* **a** to form (a centre of living) in an empty area of land by bringing in people **b** to settle (people) in a place **6** [T1 (*on*)] *infml* to hide (esp. stolen goods) on a person so that he will seem guilty **7** [X9;(T1)] *infml* to put (a person) secretly in a group: *His supporters had been planted in the crowd, and began shouting as soon as his enemy appeared* **8** [X9, esp. *on*] *infml* to leave (someone or something unwanted) somewhere or with someone: *She planted her noisy children on us while she went shopping*

plant[2] *n* **1** [C] a living thing that has leaves and roots, and grows usu. in earth, esp. the kind smaller than trees: *All plants need water and light.|the plant life of the area|a potato plant* **2** [C] **a** a machine; apparatus: *our own small power plant for electricity* **b** (*often in comb.*) a factory: *They've just built a new chemical plant* **3** [U] machinery: *We're getting some new plant for our factory* **4** [C *usu. sing.*] *infml* **a** a person who is placed in a group of people thought to be criminals in order to discover facts about them **b** a thing, esp. stolen goods, hidden on a person so that he will seem guilty
See next page for picture

plan·tain[1] /ˈplæntɪn‖-tn/ *n* a type of common wild plant with wide leaves growing close to the ground and small green flowers

plantain[2] *n* **1** [C] a treelike tropical plant with yellowish-green fruit that are like BANANA*s* **2** [C; U] the fruit of this plant used for food, esp. cooked

plan·ta·tion /plænˈteɪʃən, plɑːn-‖plæn-/ *n* **1** (*often*

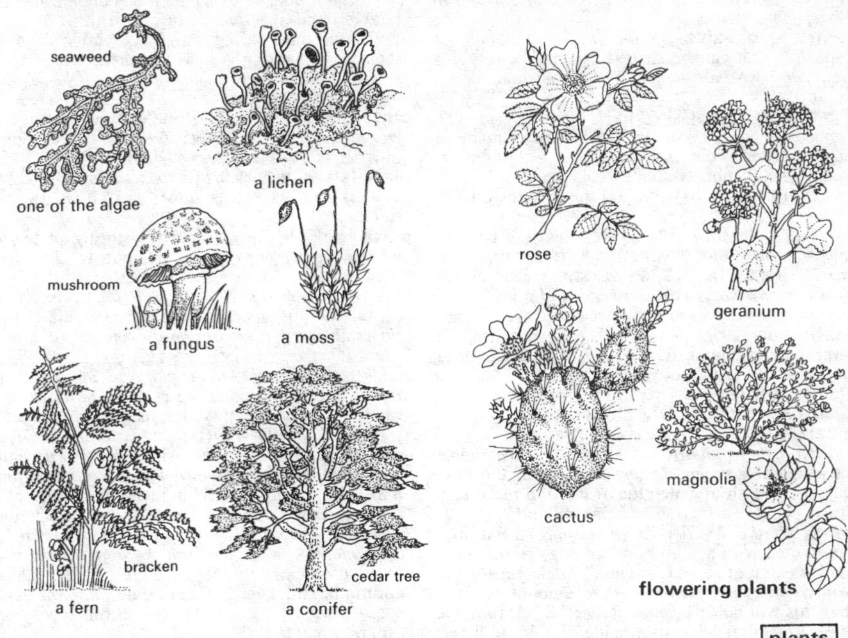

in comb.) a large piece of land, esp. in hot countries, on which crops such as tea, cotton, sugar, and rubber are grown: *a rubber plantation* **2** a large group of growing trees planted esp. to produce wood

plant·er /ˈplɑːntəʳ‖ˈplæn-/ *n* **1** (*often in comb.*) a person who owns or is in charge of a PLANTATION (1): *a tea planter* **2** (*usu. in comb.*) a machine for planting: *a corn planter* **3** *AmE* a container in which plants are grown or placed for ornamental purposes

plant out *v adv* [T1] to place (plants) in enough room for growth

plaque /plæk/ *n* **1** [C] a flat metal or stone plate, usu. with writing on it, fixed to a wall in memory of a person or event, or as an ornament **2** [U] *med* a substance that forms on teeth in the mouth, and in which bacteria can live and breed —compare TARTAR

plash[1] /plæʃ/ *n* [(*the*) S] *esp. lit* the sound of water lightly striking something solid, or of water being lightly struck: *the plash of the birds' wings in the water*

plash[2] *v esp. lit* **1** [L9] (of water) to make a PLASH[1] when striking something **2** [T1;L9] to strike (water), making a PLASH[1]

plas·ma /ˈplæzmə/ also **blood plasma**— *n* [U] the yellowish liquid in which the blood cells are held; liquid part of blood

plas·ter[1] /ˈplɑːstəʳ‖ˈplæ-/ *n* **1** [U] a pastelike mixture of lime, water, sand, etc., which hardens when dry and is used, esp. on walls, to give a smooth surface **2** [C] a piece of medically treated cloth put on a part of the body to produce heat, protect a wound, etc. **3** [C;U] STICKING PLASTER **4 in plaster** in a PLASTER CAST (2)

plaster[2] *v* [T1] **1** [(OVER)] to put wet PLASTER[1] (1) on; cover with plaster: *These rough places on the wall could be plastered over.*|(fig.) *They plastered over the difficulties with fine words* **2** [D1+*with*/*on*; T1] to spread (something) like PLASTER[1] (1), perhaps too thickly, on (something or someone): *They plastered the wall with signs.*|*They plastered signs on the wall*/*all over the wall* **3** to put a PLASTER[1] (3,2) on; cover with a plaster **4** *infml* to defeat heavily: *I'm afraid our football team really got plastered last week*

plas·ter·board /ˈplɑːstəbɔːd‖ˈplæstərbord/ *n* [U] board made of large sheets of cardboard held together with PLASTER[1] (1), used instead of plaster to cover walls and CEILINGs

plaster cast /ˌ·· ˈ·, ˈ·· ·/ *n* **1** a copy of a stone or metal figure (STATUE) made from PLASTER OF PARIS **2** a case made from PLASTER OF PARIS, placed round a part of the body to protect or support a bone that is broken or out of place

plas·tered /ˈplɑːstəd‖ˈplæstərd/ *adj* [F] *humor* drunk

plas·ter·er /ˈplɑːstərəʳ‖ˈplæ-/ *n* a man whose job is to PLASTER[2] (1) esp. walls

plas·ter·ing /ˈplɑːstərɪŋ‖ˈplæ-/ *n* **1** a covering of or as if of PLASTER[1] (1) **2** *infml* a severe defeat

plaster of par·is /ˌplɑːstər əv ˈpærɪ̈s‖ˌplæ-/ *n* [U] (*often cap. 2nd* P) a quick-drying whitish paste made of a chalklike powder (GYPSUM) mixed with water, used for PLASTER CASTs, in ornamental building work, etc.

plas·tic[1] /ˈplæstɪk/ *adj* **1** [B] (of a substance) easily formed into various shapes by pressing, and able to keep the new shape **2** [Wa5;A] connected with the art of shaping forms in clay, stone, wood, etc. (esp. in the phr. **the plastic arts**) **3** [B] *derog* having or connected with a state that is man-made rather than natural: *I don't like this new plastic milk you can buy in tins* **4** [B] *now rare* easily changed or influenced —**~ally** *adv* [Wa4]

plastic[2] *n* [C;U] any of various light man-made materials produced chemically from oil or coal, which can be made into different shapes when soft and keep their shape when hard: *a plastic spoon|The spoon is plastic*

plastic ex·plo·sive /ˌ·· ·ˈ··/ *n* **1** [U] a type of explosive that can be shaped by hand **2** [C] also (*esp. AmE*) **plastic bomb** /ˌ·· ˈ·/— a small bomb made of this

plas·ti·cine /ˈplæstǝsiːn/ *n* [U] *tdmk, esp. BrE* (*sometimes cap.*) a soft claylike substance made in many different colours, used by young children for making small models, shapes, etc.

plas·tic·i·ty /plæsˈtɪsǝti/ *n* [U] the state or quality of being PLASTIC[1] (1)

plas·tics /ˈplæstɪks/ *n* **1** [U] the science of producing PLASTIC[2] materials: *Plastics is an important branch of chemistry* **2** [P] PLASTIC[2]: *Plastics are used in many modern articles instead of wood, metal, etc.|The plastics industry is growing fast*

plastic sur·ge·ry /ˌ·· ˈ···/ *n* [U] the repairing or improving of damaged, diseased, or unsatisfactorily shaped parts of the body with pieces of skin or bone taken from other parts of the body

plas·tron /ˈplæstrǝn/ *n* a protective covering for the chest, esp. used in the sport of FENCING

plat du jour /ˌplɑː dʊ ˈʒʊǝʳ (*Fr* pla dy ʒur)/ *n* **plats du jour** (*same pronunciation*) *Fr* plate of the day; the special dish to which the owner of a restaurant draws people's attention on a particular day

plate[1] /pleɪt/ *n* **1** [C] **a** (*often in comb.*) a flat, usu. round dish with a slightly raised edge from which food is eaten or served: *a dinner plate|a paper plate* **b** also **plate·ful** /ˈpleɪtfʊl/— the amount of food that this will hold: *2 plates of meat* **2** [U] (*often in comb.*) metal articles, usu. made of gold or silver, as used at meals or in services at church: *All the church plate has been locked up* **3** [U] (*usu. in comb.*) common metal with a thin covering of gold or silver: *gold plate|It's only plate so it's not very valuable* **4** [*the*+R] **a** a round metal or wooden dish used to collect money **b** a collection of money taken in church: *The plate was more than £10* **5** [*the*+R9] (*usu. cap. as part of a name*) **a** a cup of gold or silver given to the winner of a horse race **b** the race itself **6** [C] (*often in comb.*) a flat, thin, usu. large piece of metal, glass, etc., for use in building, in parts of machinery, as a protection, etc. **7** [C] a thin sheet of glass used in photography, having on one surface chemicals that are sensitive to light **8** [C *usu. sing.*] **a** also **dental plate**— a thin piece of pink plastic shaped to fit inside a person's mouth, into which false teeth are fixed **b** also (*fml*) **denture**— a set of false teeth fixed into this **9** [C] a sheet of metal treated so that words or a picture can be printed from its surface **10** [C] a picture in a book, printed on different paper from the written part and often coloured **11** [C] a small sheet of metal, usu. brass, fixed to the entrance to an office, bearing the name of the person who works there, or of a firm **12** [C] any of the thin wide pieces of bone or horn forming a protective surface to an animal's body **13** [C] any of the very large movable parts into which the earth's surface (CRUST) is divided **14** [C *usu. pl.*] *BrE humor* a (particular person's) foot **15** [*the*+R] (in BASEBALL) HOME PLATE **16 hand/give somebody something on a plate** *infml* to hand/give somebody something desirable, too willingly and easily **17 have (a lot/too much**, *etc.*) **on one's plate** *infml* to have (a lot of/too much, etc. work or things to do) to deal with at a certain moment

plate[2] *v* [T1 (*with*)] **1** [Wv5] to cover (a metal article) thinly with another metal, esp. gold, silver, or tin: *The ring was only plated (with gold).|a silver-plated spoon* **2** to cover (esp. a ship) with metal PLATEs[1] (6)

plat·eau /ˈplætǝʊ‖plæˈtǝʊ/ *n* **-teaus** *or* **-teaux** /tǝʊ/ **1** a large stretch of level land much higher than the land around it —see picture at MOUNTAIN **2** a period of time during which the active development of something is not continued: *Business has now reached a plateau, but we hope it will begin to increase again soon*

plate glass /ˌ· ˈ·/ *n* [U] fine clear glass made in large, quite thick sheets for use in windows, mirrors, etc. —**plate-glass** *adj* [Wa5;A]

plate·lay·er /ˈpleɪtˌleɪǝʳ/ (*AmE* **tracklayer**)— *n BrE* a workman who puts down or repairs railway tracks

plate rack /ˈ· ·/ *n* a frame for storing plates, or where plates, cups, etc., are put to dry after washing

plat·form /ˈplætfɔːm‖-fɔrm/ *n* **1** [C] a raised floor of boards for speakers, performers, etc.: *That singer always gets nervous on the concert platform* **2** [*the*+R] the speakers seated on this: *Please address your remarks to the platform* **3** [C] a raised flat surface built along the side of the track at a railway station for travellers getting on or off a train **4** [*the*+R;(C)] (esp. in Britain) the open part at the end of a bus, where passengers enter and leave: *Passengers may not travel on the platform* **5** [C *usu. sing.*] the main ideas and aims of a political party, esp. as stated before an election: *Since the election, the winning party has not acted in accordance with its platform* **6** [A] (of shoes or parts of shoes) unusually high because of an additional thickness of material: *platform heels/*SOLE*s/shoes* **7** [C *usu. pl.*] a shoe of this type, worn esp. by women

plat·ing /ˈpleɪtɪŋ/ *n* [U] **1** a thin covering of metal put on by plating (PLATE[2] (1)) **2** a covering of metal PLATE*s*[1] (6) on a ship, vehicle, etc.

plat·i·num /ˈplætǝnǝm/ *n* [U] greyish-white metal that is a simple substance (ELEMENT (6)) that does not become dirty or impure and is used esp. in very valuable jewellery and in chemical industries: *a platinum ring|This ring is (of) platinum*

platinum blonde /ˌ··· ˈ·/ *n infml* a young woman having light silver-grey hair, often not natural but coloured with chemicals

plat·i·tude /ˈplætǝtjuːd‖-tuːd/ *n derog* a statement that is true but not new, made by someone who thinks it is both —compare CLICHÉ, COMMONPLACE, TRUISM —**-tudinous** /ˌplætǝˈtjuːdǝnǝs‖-ˈtuː-/ *adj*

pla·ton·ic /plǝˈtɒnɪk‖-ˈtɑ-/ *adj* (of love or friendship between a man and woman) only of the mind and spirit; not sexual —**-ically** *adv* [Wa4]

pla·toon /plǝˈtuːn/ *n* a small body of soldiers which is part of a COMPANY and is commanded by a LIEUTENANT

plat·ter /ˈplætǝʳ/ *n* **1** *AmE* a large flat dish used for serving food, esp. meat **2** *old use* a flat dish, usu. made of wood **3** *infml esp. AmE* a GRAMOPHONE record

plat·y·pus /ˈplætǝpǝs/ also **duck-billed platypus**— *n* a type of small furry Australian animal that lays eggs and has a beak like a duck's, but gives milk to its young

plau·dit /ˈplɔːdǝt/ *n* [*usu. pl.*] a show of pleased approval: *"Minister's Forceful Speech Wins Plaudits of Public"* (possible title of newspaper story)

plau·si·ble /ˈplɔːzǝbǝl/ *adj* **1** (of a statement, argument, etc.) seeming to be true or reasonable: *Your explanation sounds plausible, but I'm not sure I believe it* —compare FEASIBLE **2** (of a person) skilled in producing (seemingly) reasonable statements which may not be true: *a plausible cheat* —**-bly** *adv* —**-bility** /ˌplɔːzǝˈbɪlǝti/ *n* [U]

play[1] /pleɪ/ *n* **1** [U] activity for amusement only, esp. among the young: *young lambs at play in the* *field* **2** [U] the action or manner in a sport: *an interesting day's play in the cricket match* **3** [C] **a** a piece of writing to be performed in a theatre: *He has written a new play* **b** a performance of this: *We've been to several plays this month* **c** a printed copy of this: *She's bought the plays of Shakespeare* **4** [S9] light, quick, not lasting movement: *the play of sunshine and shadow among the trees* **5** [U] **a** freedom of movement given by slight looseness: *Give the rope some play—don't keep it so tight* **b** freedom of activity; freedom from control: *He gave full play to his feelings and began to shout angrily* **6** [S9] (somebody's) turn in a game at a table, as in cards **7** [S9;U] risking money on games of chance: *He won £1000 in last night's play* **8** [U9;(U)] (*often in comb.*) directed movement in the use of a weapon or instrument: *sword play* **9** [S] *esp. AmE* a calculated move towards a result (esp. in the phr. **make a play for**): *made a big play for the girl* **10 be in full play/come into play** to begin to be used or have an effect **11 bring into play** to (start to) use **12 in play a** (of the ball in cricket, football, etc.) in a position where the rules of the game permit it to be played **b** without serious or harmful intentions **13 out of play** (of the ball in cricket, football, etc.) in a position where the rules of the game do not permit it to be played —see HOBBY (USAGE)

play² *v* **1** [IØ (*with*)] (esp. of the young) to do things that pass the time pleasantly, esp. including running and jumping; have fun: *Can Bob come out to play (with me)?|a cat playing with a piece of string* **2** [T1] (of children) to amuse oneself at (a game): *The children were playing ball (with each other)* **3** [L1;T4] (of children) to amuse oneself by pretending to be or do (something): *Let's play doctors and nurses.|Let's play going to work by train* **4** [T1 (*on*); (D1)] to plan and perform or carry out for one's own amusement or gain: *They played a joke on me.|He played her a nasty trick by taking all the money* **5** [L9] to (seem to) move quickly, lightly, irregularly, or continuously: *Lightning played across the sky as the storm began* **6** [L9] to be aimed, directed, or fired, esp. continuously: *The warning lights played above the town* **7** [X9] to aim, direct, or fire, esp. continuously: *The firemen played water on the buildings* **8** [T1] to allow (a fish caught on a line) to become tired by pulling against the line **9** [T1;L9] (of an actor or theatre group) to perform: *Othello was played by Olivier.|Olivier is playing in "Othello" at the National Theatre.|You should not play the trial scene too slowly* **10** [T1 *no pass.*] (of an actor or theatre group) to perform in (a certain town, theatre, etc.) **11** [IØ] (of a PLAY¹ (3) or film) to be performed or shown **12** [L9] (of something written for acting) to be able to be performed (in a certain stated way): *This scene doesn't play as well as it reads* **13** [L1,7] to pretend (in real life) to be: *She likes to play the great lady.|He played dead* **14** [IØ] (of a musical instrument or apparatus) to produce sound: *The radio was playing too loudly* **15** [T1;IØ] to perform on (a musical instrument): *John plays the piano.|At the concert, Charles sang and Paul played* **16** [D1 (*for, to*); T1: (*on*)] **a** to perform (a piece of music): *They're playing a march.|Play us something happy* **b** to perform the music of (a particular writer of music): *She plays Mozart well.|Play some more Mozart for/to us* **17** [D1 (*for, to*); T1: (*on*)] to reproduce (sounds, esp. music) on an apparatus: *She plays her radio all day long.|Play us your favourite record* **18** [T1;IØ] to take part in (a sport or game): *In many countries people play football at all times of the year.|I don't feel well enough to play.|Shall we play cards?* **19** [IØ (*against*); T1: (*at*)] to be set against (another or each other) in a match: *Smith is playing Newcombe in the big tennis match.|When are England playing Australia (at cricket)?|Smith and Newcombe are playing (each other) in the big tennis match.|Smith and Newcombe are playing (against) Ashe and Connors* **20** [T1 (*in*)] to include as a member of a team: *We can't decide whether to play Smith or Jones in the cricket match* **21** [T1 (*as, at*)] to use as a particular player in a team: *The captain has decided to play Smith at* FULLBACK **22** [L1,7;IØ (*as, at*)] to have a particular position and duty in a team: *Smith will play* FULLBACK.*|Thomson will play as our third fast* BOWLER **23** [T1;IØ] to have the ability or knowledge needed for (a particular game): *He plays (cricket) very well.|We were going to ask you to have a game of cards with us but someone told us you don't play* **24** [X9;(T1)] to strike and send (a ball), esp. in a stated way: *She played the ball just over the net* **25** [T1] to place (one of one's playing cards) face upwards on the table **26** [X9] to use (one's group of playing cards) in the stated way: *She played her hand of cards cleverly* **27** [T1] (in CHESS) to move (a piece or figure) on the board **28** [L9] (of ground used for ball games) to be in a stated condition for use: *The* PITCH³ (2) *is playing rather fast today* **29** [IØ (*for*); T1] to risk (money) in a game of skill or chance: *He played his last dollar.|He won't have a game of cards with us because he knows we only play for pennies* **30 play a waiting game** to wait to see what happens before taking action **31 play both ends against the middle** to set 2 opposing sides against each other in a way that will be to one's own advantage **32 play for safety** (esp. in a game) to do something that is safe rather than something that is more advantageous but more risky **33 play for time** to cause delay, hoping to avoid defeat **34 play it cool** *infml* to remain calm in some difficult or dangerous condition **35 play (it) safe** *infml* to act in such a way that one has the best chance of avoiding a misfortune: *I don't think it will rain today, but I'd better play (it) safe and take a raincoat* **36 play it one's (own) way** to do something in the way that one thinks best **37 play one's cards close to one's chest** to do something without letting anyone else know about it; keep one's doings secret **38 play one's cards right** to use well whatever chances, conditions, facts, etc., one has **39 play the field** *infml esp. AmE* to go out socially with more than one member of the opposite sex **40 play the fool** to act foolishly **41 play the game a** to obey the rules of a game **b** to be fair, honest, and honourable **42 play the horses** *infml* to risk money on horse races **43 play the man** *lit* to act bravely **44 play the market** to buy and sell business shares in order to try to make money **45 play tricks on** (esp. of ears, eyes, or the mind) to deceive —see also PLAY ABOUT, PLAY ALONG, PLAY AT, PLAY BACK, PLAY DOWN, PLAY IN, PLAY OFF, PLAY ON, PLAY OUT, PLAY UP, PLAY UP TO, PLAY WITH —see HOBBY (USAGE)

play·a·ble /ˈpleɪəbəl/ *adj* **1** (of a (piece of) ground used for sports) fit to be played on **2** (of a ball thrown (BOWLed) in cricket) possible to hit

play a·bout also **play a·round**— *v adv* **1** [IØ] (of a person or animal) to spend time having fun **2** [IØ (*with*)] MESS ABOUT (2)

play-act /ˈ· ·/ *v* [IØ] to pretend; behave with an unreal show of feeling —**~ing** *n* [U]

play a·long *v adv* **1** [T1] to keep (someone) waiting for an answer or decision **2** [IØ (*with*)] to pretend to agree (with someone or someone's ideas)

play at *v prep* **1** [T4;(L1)] PLAY² (3) **2** [T1,(4)] to do in a way that is not very serious: *I don't play* *tennis very well: let's just say I play* **at** *tennis.|What do you think you're playing at—you can't change a wheel that way!*

play·back /ˈpleɪbæk/ also **replay**— *n* **1** a recording of something heard or seen (as on television) that is played at once after it is made, so that one can study it carefully **2** the control button that one presses, as on a TAPE RECORDER, to PLAY something BACK —see picture at SOUND[3]

play back *v adv* [T1;(I∅)] to go through and listen to (something that has just been recorded on a machine)

play·bill /ˈpleɪˌbɪl/ *n* a large or small piece of paper giving notice of the performance of a play at a certain place and time in the future

play·boy /ˈpleɪbɔɪ/ *n* a wealthy young man who lives mainly for pleasure

play down *v adv* [T1] to cause (something) to seem less important —opposite **play up**

played out /ˌ· ˈ·ˈ/ *adj* [F;(B)] **1** tired **2** of no further use; old-fashioned

play·er /ˈpleɪəʳ/ *n* **1** a person taking part in a game or sport **2** *esp. old use or pomp* an actor **3 a** a person playing a musical instrument **b** (*usu. in comb.*) an apparatus for (re-)producing (musical) sounds: *a record player*

player pi·an·o /ˌ·· ·ˈ··/ *n* a piano that is played by machinery, the music being controlled by a piece of paper (**piano roll**) with holes cut into it for the notes

play·ful /ˈpleɪfəl/ *adj* **1** gaily active; full of fun: *a playful little dog* **2** not intended seriously: *a playful kiss on the cheek* —**-fully** *adv* —**~ness** *n* [U]

play·go·er /ˈpleɪˌgəʊəʳ/ *n* a person who goes to see plays, esp. regularly

play·ground /ˈpleɪgraʊnd/ *n* **1** a piece of ground kept for children to play on, esp. at a school **2** [(*of*)] an area favoured for amusement: *The south of France is the playground of the rich*

play·group /ˈpleɪgruːp/ *n* a kind of informal school for very young children (esp. of 3 to 5) at which they learn to play with other children and learn other things mainly through play

play·house /ˈpleɪhaʊs/ *n* **-houses** /ˌhaʊzəz/ **1** (*often cap. as part of a name*) a theatre: *the Provincetown Playhouse* **2** a hut built to look like a small house, for children to play in

play in *v adv* [T1] **1** to play music during the entrance of: *The band played in the minister and his wife* **2** to accustom (oneself) to playing, esp. a sport or team game: *I need a few more minutes to play myself in*

playing card /ˈ·· ·/ *n fml* CARD[3] (1)

playing field /ˈ·· ·/ *n* a large area of ground for playing such games as football and cricket

play·mate /ˈpleɪmeɪt/ also **play·fel·low** /ˈpleɪˌfeləʊ/— *n* a companion who shares in children's games and play: *The little boy's chief playmate was his dog.|They are playmates* (=they play with each other)

play off *v adv* [T1] **1** to finish playing (a set of games): *All the matches must be played off by the end of the month* **2** [(*against*)] to set (people or things) in opposition, esp. for one's own advantage: *She played one friend off against the other.|She played her 2 friends off* (*against each other*)

play-off /ˈ· ·/ *n* a second match played to decide a winner, when the first has not done so

play on[1] *v adv tech* **1** [T1;I∅] (in cricket) (of a BATSMAN) to hit (the ball) accidentally onto the 3 wooden sticks (WICKET) and so end one's turn at playing **2** [T1] (in football) to cause (a player) to be ONSIDE

play on[2] also **play up·on**— *v prep* [T1] to try to increase or strengthen (esp. the feelings of others) for one's own advantage

play on words /ˌ· · ˈ·/ *n* **plays on words** [*usu. sing.*] PUN

play out *v* [T1] **1** to finish (a game or struggle) **2** to play until the end **3** to play music during the leaving of **4** ACT OUT

play·pen /ˈpleɪpen/ *n* a frame enclosed by bars or a net and placed on the floor for a small child to play safely in

play·room /ˈpleɪrʊm, -ruːm/ *n* a room set aside for children's play

play·suit /ˈpleɪsuːt/ *n* a loose covering garment worn by young children at play

play·thing /ˈpleɪˌθɪŋ/ *n* **1** a toy **2** [(*of*)] a person who is treated lightly and without consideration by another: *He was her plaything.|Are we the playthings of the gods?*

play through *v adv* [I∅] (in GOLF) to continue playing while other players in front wait

play·time /ˈpleɪtaɪm/ *n* a (short) period of time, esp. at a school, when children can go out to play

play up *v adv* **1** [I∅] *becoming rare* to play a game actively **2** [T1] to cause (something) to seem more important —opposite **play down** **3** [T1;I∅] to cause trouble or suffering to (someone): *My bad leg has been playing* (*me*) *up again.|The class played the new teacher up* **4** [I∅] ACT UP

play up to *v adv prep* [T1] to act so as to win the favour of (someone)

play with *v prep* [T1] **1** TOY WITH: *playing with the idea of starting her own business* —compare PLAY[2] (1) **2 play with oneself** *euph* MASTURBATE

play·wright /ˈpleɪraɪt/ *n* a writer of plays

pla·za /ˈplɑːzə‖ˈplæzə/ *n* a public square or marketplace, esp. in towns in Spanish-speaking areas USAGE This word is often used with a *cap.* as the name of a cinema: *the new film at the* **Plaza**.

plea /pliː/ *n* **1** [C (*for*)] *fml* an eager or serious request: *his plea for forgiveness* **2** [(*the*) S] an excuse given for doing or not doing something: *He refused the invitation to dinner on the plea of being too busy* —see EXCUSE[2] (USAGE) **3** [C (*of*) *usu. sing.*] *law* a statement by a person in a court of law, saying whether or not he is guilty of a charge

pleach /pliːtʃ/ *v* [Wv5;T1] to form or repair (a HEDGE) by twisting branches together

plead /pliːd/ *v* **pleaded** *or* **plead** (*esp. ScotE & AmE* **pled** /pled/) **1** [Wv4;I∅ (*for*)] to make continual and deeply felt requests: *She wept and pleaded until he agreed to do as she wished* **2** [T1] to give as an excuse for an action: *I'm sorry I didn't answer your letter—I can only plead forgetfulness* **3** [T1] to speak or argue in support of: *pleading the rights of the unemployed* **4** [I∅] *law* to answer a charge in court: *The girl charged with murder was said to be mad and unfit to plead* **5** [L7;T1] *law* to declare in official language that one is (in a state of): *She pleaded guilty/not guilty.|They made him plead madness*

plead for *v prep* [T1] *law* ACT[1] (5) for

plead·ing /ˈpliːdɪŋ/ *n* [U;C] the action or an act of one who PLEADS

plead·ings /ˈpliːdɪŋz/ *n* [P] *law* the official (usu. written) set of statements by each side in a law case, including answers made by each to the charges of the other

plead with *v prep* [T1 (*for*); V3] to make continual and deeply felt requests to: *He pleaded with them to give him more time to pay*

pleas·ant /ˈplezənt/ *adj* **1** pleasing to the senses, feelings, or mind; enjoyable: *What a pleasant surprise!|a flower with a pleasant smell* **2** (esp. of people) likeable; friendly: *She seems a pleasant woman.|Make an effort to be pleasant at the party.|a* *pleasant smile* **3** (of weather) fine; favourable: *It's quite pleasant today, though the wind is rather cool* —**~ly** *adv*

pleas·ant·ry /ˈplezəntri/ *n* a light amusing remark; pleasant joke

please[1] /pliːz/ *v* **1** [T1;I∅] to make (someone) happy; give satisfaction (to): *He's very hard to please.|The girl in the shop is always eager to please (everybody)* **2** [L9] (*not as the main verb of a sentence*) to choose; like: *Come and stay as long as you please* **3 if you please a** *fml* (used to give force after a request) PLEASE² (1): *Come this way, if you please* **b** can you believe this?: *He's broken my bicycle, and now, if you please, he wants me to get it mended so that he can use it again* **4 please God** *fml* I hope **5 please yourself** *infml* do as you wish, it doesn't matter to me

USAGE When **please** means "choose" or "like" one can say *She does as/what she* **pleases**, or *She will come if/when she* **pleases**, but not **She* **pleases** *it*.

please[2] *interj* **1** (used to make a request polite): *A cup of tea, please.|Please be quiet* **2** (used to give force to or make polite a request for attention): *Please, sir, I don't understand* **3** also **yes, please**— Yes I accept and am grateful: *"Would you like a cup of coffee?" "Please"* **4** (used for turning a question into a request): *Can you go now, please?* (Compare *Can you go now?* = is it possible?)

pleased /ˈpliːzd/ *adj* [(*with*)] **1** feeling or showing satisfaction or happiness: *I always feel pleased when I've finished a piece of work.|I'm very pleased you've decided to come.|She had a pleased look on her face.|I'm pleased with your work* **2 be pleased to (do something) a** *polite* to be very willing to; be glad to **b** *fml* (of a ruler) to decide (as an act of favour) to **3 pleased with oneself** (too) satisfied with what one has done

USAGE Some *AmE* speakers think that *very* **pleased** is bad English and would rather say *very much* **pleased**. British speakers do not mind about this.

pleas·ing /ˈpliːzɪŋ/ *adj* [(*to*)] **1** likeable; giving delight: *a pleasing young man with pleasing manners* **2** giving satisfaction: *a pleasing result to our talks* —**~ly** *adv*

plea·sur·a·ble /ˈpləʒərəbəl/ *adj fml* enjoyable —**-bly** *adv* [Wa3]

plea·sure /ˈpleʒəʳ/ *n* **1** [U] the state or feeling of happiness or satisfaction resulting from an experience that one likes: *He listened with pleasure to the beautiful music.|It gives me no pleasure to have to tell you this* **2** [U] enjoyment; RECREATION (esp. in the phr. **for pleasure**): *"Are you here on business?" "No, for pleasure—this is my holiday"* **3** [U] the enjoyment of the body, food, comfort, etc.: *He'll soon tire of the life of pleasure and want to start working again* **4** [C] a cause of happiness, enjoyment, or satisfaction: *It's been a pleasure to talk to you.|His work was his only pleasure.|Some old people have very few pleasures in life* **5** [S9] *polite* enjoyment gained by doing or having (something or some activity) (esp. in the phr. **the pleasure of**): *May I have the pleasure of the next dance with you?* **6** [S9] *polite* something that is not inconvenient and that one is pleased to do (esp in the phrs. **a/my/our pleasure**): *"Thank you for helping me." "My pleasure. It was a pleasure"* **7** [S,S5c] *fml or polite* desire; wish: *Is it your pleasure that I sign the report of the last meeting as correct?|These arrangements can be changed at your pleasure* (= as you wish or decide) **8 be detained during** (*a ruler's*) **pleasure** *BrE law* (of a person found guilty of a crime) to be kept in a place of control for as long as (a ruler or ruler's adviser) considers necessary **9 take (great, no, *etc.*) pleasure in** *often fml* to get enjoyment or satisfaction (of the stated kind) from: *My husband and I take great pleasure in opening this new school.|I take little pleasure in such things* **10 with pleasure** *polite* willingly: *"Would you take this along to the office for me?" "With pleasure"*

pleasure ground /ˈ·· ·/ *n* a piece of ground or garden, usu. public, used for rest, play, sport, etc.

pleat[1] /pliːt/ *v* [Wv5;T1] to make PLEATs² in

pleat[2] *n* a flattened narrow fold in cloth

pleb /pleb/ *n* [*often pl.*] *derog* a member of the lower social classes —**~by** *adj*

ple·be·ian /plɪˈbiːən/ *n, adj* **1** (in ancient Rome) (a member) of the common people **2** *derog* (a member) of the lower social classes: *plebeian habits*

pleb·is·cite /ˈplebɪ̣sɪ̣t‖-saɪt/ *n* [C; *by*+U] a direct vote of the people of a nation on a matter of national importance, esp. on a choice of government or ruler —compare REFERENDUM

plec·trum /ˈplektrəm/ also (*infml*) **pick** *n* —a small thin piece of wood, metal, etc., sometimes fastened to a finger, used for playing certain stringed instruments (such as the GUITAR) by picking at the strings —see picture at STRINGED INSTRUMENT

pled /pled/ *esp. ScotE & AmE a past t. and p. of* PLEAD

pledge[1] /pledʒ/ *n* **1** [C;(U)] a solemn promise or agreement: *It was told me under pledge of secrecy* **2** [C (*of*)] something given or received as a sign of faithful love or friendship: *Take this ring as a pledge of our friendship* **3** [C] **a** something valuable left with someone else as proof that one will fulfil an agreement **b** an object of value given, in return for money, into the possession of a PAWNBROKER until the money is repaid **4** [U] the state of being kept for this purpose (esp. in the phr. **in pledge**) **5** [C] *old use* TOAST² (2) **6 sign/take the pledge** *now humor* to promise or decide firmly no longer to drink alcoholic drinks

pledge[2] *v* **1** [T3,5] to make a solemn promise or agreement: *He pledged never to come back until he had found her.|They have pledged that they will always remain faithful* **2** [T1 (*to*); V3] to bind (someone) with a solemn promise: *He was pledged to secrecy.|They pledged themselves never to tell the secret* **3** [T1] to give (esp. one's word) at the risk of losing one's honour: *I pledged my word (of honour) that I would never again get into debt* **4** [T1 (*for*)] to leave (something) with someone as a PLEDGE¹ (3) **5** [T1] *fml* to express a wish for the health, success, etc., of, by taking alcoholic drink: *Everyone at the table stood up and pledged the success of the new company*

pleis·to·cene /ˈplaɪstəsiːn/ *adj* of the period in the world's history which started about 1,000,000 years ago and lasted about 800,000 years, when much of the earth was covered with ice

ple·na·ry /ˈpliːnəri/ *adj* [Wa5] **1** (of power of government) complete; without limit **2** (of a meeting) attended by all who have the lawful right to attend (esp. in the phr. **plenary session**)

plen·i·po·ten·tia·ry[1] /ˌplenɪ̣pəˈtenʃəri‖-ʃieri/ *adj* of or as a PLENIPOTENTIARY²: *The minister was given plenipotentiary powers to make a peace agreement with the enemy*

plenipotentiary[2] *n* a person having full power to act in all matters, as a representative of his government, esp. in a foreign country

plen·i·tude /ˈplenɪ̣tjuːd‖-tuːd/ *n* [U (*of*)] *pomp* **1** completeness; fullness **2** plenty; a great amount

plen·te·ous /ˈplentɪəs/ *adj esp. poet* PLENTIFUL —**~ly** *adv* —**~ness** *n* [U]

plen·ti·ful /ˈplentɪfəl/ *adj* existing in quantities or numbers that are (more than) enough: *The camp* *has a plentiful supply of food* —**-fully** *adv*: *The farms are plentifully supplied with grain*

plen·ty¹ /ˈplenti/ *n* [U] **1** the state of having a large supply of, esp. of the needs of life: *in years of plenty, when everyone has enough to eat* **2 in plenty a** in large supply: *The farms have water in plenty to last through the dry season* **b** lacking nothing (in life): *Some people live in plenty, while others haven't enough to eat*

plenty² *pron often apprec* a large quantity or number, esp. as much as or more than is/are needed or wanted; enough: *"Do you need any more money?" "No, we have plenty (of money). We have £100 and that's plenty."|If you want some chairs, there are plenty (more) in here.|Plenty of the men are/Plenty of the sugar is already here.|She gave the boys plenty to eat* —compare LOT¹

plenty³ *adv infml* **1** quite (in the phr. **plenty . . . enough**): *There's no need to add any more—it's plenty big enough already* **2** *AmE* to quite a large degree; very

ple·o·nas·m /ˈplɪənæzəm/ *n* **1** [U] the use of more words than are needed to express an idea, with the effect of repeating **2** [C] an example of this, which is usu. a phrase rather than a complete sentence: *The phrases "an apple divided into 2 halves" and "a native born in the country" are pleonasms* —see also TAUTOLOGY —**pleonastic** /ˌplɪəˈnæstɪk/ *adj*

pleth·o·ra /ˈpleθərə/ *n* [S (*of*)] *fml* an amount or supply much greater than is needed or than one can deal with

pleu·ri·sy /ˈplʊərɪ̈si/ *n* [U] a serious disease of the thin inner covering of the chest that surrounds the lungs, causing pain in the chest and sides

plex·us /ˈpleksəs/ *n med* a network of nerves or blood vessels —see also SOLAR PLEXUS

pli·a·ble /ˈplaɪəbəl/ *adj* **1** easily bent without breaking **2** able and willing to change or to accept new ways and ideas; FLEXIBLE (2) **3** PLIANT (1) —**-bility** /ˌplaɪəˈbɪlɪ̈ti/ *n* [U]

pli·ant /ˈplaɪənt/ *adj* **1** easily influenced; yielding to the wishes or commands of others **2** PLIABLE (1,2) —**~ly** *adv* —**-ancy** *n* [U]

pli·ers /ˈplaɪəz‖-ərz/ *n* [P] a type of small tool made of 2 crossed pieces of metal with long flat jaws at one end, used to hold small things or to bend and cut wire —compare PINCERS; see PAIR (USAGE) and picture at TOOL¹

plight¹ /plaɪt/ *v* [T1] *old use* **1** to give, at the risk of losing one's honour; PLEDGE² (1) **2 plight one's troth** to make a promise of marriage

plight² *n* [*usu. sing.*] a (bad, serious, or sorrowful) condition or state: *He was in a terrible plight, trapped at the back of the cave.|the plight of these poor homeless children*

plight to *v prep* [D1] *old use* to bind (oneself) by a solemn promise of marriage to (someone)

plim·soll /ˈplɪmsəl, -səʊl/ (*AmE* **sneaker**)— *n* [*usu. pl.*] *BrE* a type of light shoe with a top made of heavy cloth and a flat rubber bottom, used esp. for games and sports —see PAIR (USAGE)

Plimsoll line /ˈ·· ·/ also **Plimsoll mark** /ˈ·· ·/— *n* [(*the*) *usu. sing.*] a line painted on the outside of a ship showing the depth to which it may be allowed to settle in the water when loaded

plinth /plɪnθ/ *n* a square block, usu. of stone, serving as the base of a pillar or STATUE

pli·o·cene /ˈplaɪəsiːn/ *adj* of the period in the world's history which started about 13,000,000 years ago and lasted about 12,000,000 years

plod /plɒd‖plɑd/ *v* **-dd-** **1** [T1;L9, esp. ALONG, ON] to continue to walk slowly along (a road, path, etc.), esp. with difficulty and great effort: *He plodded the streets all day looking for work.|The old man plods along, hardly able to lift each foot* **2** [X9] to make (one's way) in this manner **3** [L9, esp. AWAY, ALONG, *at, through*] to work steadily, esp. at something uninteresting: *The boy plodded away (at the work) all night but couldn't finish it*

plod·der /ˈplɒdəʳ‖ˈplɑ-/ *n* a slow, not very clever, but steady worker who often succeeds in the end

plonk¹ /plɒŋk‖plɑŋk, plɔŋk/ also **plunk**— *n* [S] *infml* a hollow sound as of something dropping or falling onto or into a metal object: *the plonk of water falling drop by drop on metal*

plonk² also **plunk**— *adv* [H] *infml* just exactly in the place described, and with or as if with a PLONK¹: *The book fell plonk on the floor!*

plonk³ also **plunk**— *v infml* **1** [L9] to fall with a PLONK¹: *A large drop of water plonked into the bath* **2** [X9] to put down heavily or with force: *She plonked herself in the chair and refused to move* **3** [T1 (OUT)] to play (different notes) on a piano or a stringed musical instrument that is played with the fingers **4** [L9, esp. AWAY; (T1)] to play informally (a piano or a stringed instrument that is played with the fingers)

plonk⁴ *n* [U] *infml esp. BrE & Austr E* cheap wine

plonk down *v adv* PLANK DOWN

plop¹ /plɒp‖plɑp/ *n, adv* [S;H] *infml* (with a) a sound as of something dropping smoothly into liquid: *There was a loud plop as he opened the bottle of wine.|The soap fell plop into the bath*

plop² *v* **-pp-** *infml* **1** [L9, esp. *into*] to fall with or make a PLOP¹: *The stone plopped into the stream.|Did you hear it plop as it went in?* **2** [L9, esp. DOWN] (of a person) to fall or drop heavily

plo·sive /ˈpləʊsɪv/ *n, adj tech* (a consonant sound) made by stopping the air completely and then letting it quickly out of the mouth: *The sound /b/ in "bottle" is (a) plosive*

plot¹ /plɒt‖plɑt/ *n* **1** [C9,(C)] a small marked or measured piece of ground for building or growing things: *a building plot|I grow potatoes on my little plot of land* **2** *AmE* a map of a field, a farm, or the ground covered by a building **3** the set of connected events on which a story, play, film, etc., is based **4** a secret plan to do something usu. against a person, needing combined action by several people

plot² *v* **-tt-** **1** [T1] to mark (the position of a moving aircraft or ship) on a map **2** [T1] to express or represent by means of pictures or a map **3** [T1] to make (a line or curve showing certain stated facts) by marking on paper marked with small squares **4** [T1 (OUT)] to divide (land) into PLOTs¹ (1) **5** [T1,3,6a,b;I∅ (TOGETHER)] to plan together secretly: *They're plotting against him.|They're plotting to kill him/plotting his murder/plotting how to murder him* **6** [T1 (OUT)] to make a PLOT¹ (3) for (a story) —**~ter** *n* [*usu. pl.*]

plough¹, *AmE* also **plow** /plaʊ/ *n* **1** [C] a farming tool with a heavy cutting blade drawn by a motor vehicle or animal(s). It breaks up and turns over the earth in fields, esp. before seeds are planted —see picture at FARMYARD **2** [C] (*often in comb.*) any tool or machine that works like this —see also SNOWPLOUGH **3** [U] *tech* land that has been PLOUGHed² (1) **4 be under the plough** (of farmland) to be used for growing grain rather than for feeding animals **5 put/set one's hand to the plough** *esp. lit or bibl* to begin a serious or difficult piece of work with will to complete it

plough², *AmE* also **plow** *v* **1** [T1 (UP); I∅] to break up or turn over (land) with a PLOUGH¹ (1): *Farmers plough (their fields) in autumn or spring* **2** [I∅] (of land) to be fit to be cut by a PLOUGH¹ (1) **3** [T1 (UP); L9] to force a way or make a track (through or across): *The great ship ploughed (across) the ocean.*|(fig.) *He ploughed through the* *dull book to the end* **4** [X9, esp. *through*] to make (a way) in this manner: *He ploughed his way through (the crowd)* **5 plough a lonely furrow** to work or act alone without support

Plough *AmE* usu. **Big Dipper**— *n* [*the*+R] a group of 7 bright stars seen only from the northern part of the world

plough back *v adv* [T1] to put (money earned) back into a business so as to build up the business

plough·boy, *AmE* also **plowboy** /ˈplaʊbɔɪ/ *n* (esp. in former times) a boy who leads a horse or horses pulling a PLOUGH¹ (1)

plough·man, *AmE* also **plowman** /ˈplaʊmən/ *n* **-men** /mən/ a man whose job is to guide a PLOUGH¹ (1), esp. of the type pulled by animals

plough·man's lunch /ˌ·· ˈ·/ also (*infml*) **plough-man's**— *n BrE* a simple lunch eaten in an inn, usu. bread and cheese, with beer

plough·share, *AmE* also **plowshare** /ˈplaʊʃeəʳ/ also **share**— *n* the broad metal blade of a PLOUGH¹ (1) —see picture at FARMYARD

plough un·der *v adv* [T1] to cover and destroy (esp. a crop) by PLOUGHing² (1)

plov·er /ˈplʌvəʳ/ *n* [Wn1] any of several types of land bird that live usu. near the sea, of which the LAPWING is one

plow /plaʊ/ *n AmE* PLOUGH

ploy /plɔɪ/ *n infml* a way of behaving in order to gain some advantage: *Her usual ploy is to pretend to be ill, so that people will take pity on her*

pluck¹ /plʌk/ *v* **1** [T1] to pull the feathers off (a dead hen, duck, etc., being prepared for cooking) **2** [T1 (OUT, UP, *from, off*)] to pull (esp. something unwanted) sharply; pick: *He plucked the burning cigarette up from the mat* **3** [D1 (*for*); T1] *esp. poet* to pick (a flower, fruit, or leaf): *He plucked her a rose* **4** [T1; I0 (*at*)] also (*AmE*) **pick**— to play a stringed musical instrument by quickly pulling (the strings)

pluck² *n* **1** [U] courage and will: *Mountain climbers need a lot of pluck* **2** [S (*at*)] an act of PLUCKing¹ (4) or PLUCKing AT **3** [*the*+R] the heart, lungs, etc., of an animal when removed —compare GIBLETS, OFFAL

pluck at *v prep* [T1] to pull quickly and repeatedly with the fingers

pluck up also **muster up, summon up**— *v adv* **pluck up (one's) courage** to show bravery in spite of (one's) fears: *He could not pluck up enough courage to ask her to marry him*

pluck·y /ˈplʌki/ *adj* [Wa1] brave and determined, esp. in an unexpected way —**-ily** *adv* —**-iness** *n* [U]

plug¹ /plʌg/ *n* **1** a small, usu. round piece of rubber, wood, metal, etc., used for blocking a hole, esp. in a pipe: *She pulled the plug out of the bath and the dirty water ran away.|Some swimmers wear rubber plugs in their ears* —see picture at KITCHEN **2** a small plastic object with 2 or 3 metal pins. The pins are pushed into an electric power point (SOCKET) to obtain power for a movable apparatus —see picture at ELECTRICITY **3** *nonstandard* SOCKET **4** *infml* a publicly stated favourable opinion (as given on radio or television) about a record, a product, a book, etc., meant to make people want to hear, buy, read, etc., the thing spoken of **5 a** a stick or flat cake of tobacco **b** a piece cut from this for CHEWing **6** *infml* SPARKING PLUG

plug² *v* **-gg-** [T1] **1** [(UP)] to block, close, or fill up with a PLUG¹ (1): *Use this to plug (the hole in) your tooth* **2** *infml* to advertise (something) by continually or repeatedly mentioning: *He's been plugging his new book on the radio* **3** *AmE sl* to shoot (someone) with a gun

plug a·way at *v adv prep* [T1 *no pass.*] *infml* to work with the will to complete (a difficult job)

plug·hole /ˈplʌghəʊl/ *n BrE* a hole into which a PLUG¹ (1) is fitted, esp. where water flows away

plug in *v adv* [T1; (I0)] to connect to a supply of electricity

plug-ug·ly /ˈ· ˌ··/ *n AmE old sl* a rude rough man, esp. one employed to threaten others; THUG

plum /plʌm/ *n* **1** [C] a type of roundish sweet smooth-skinned fleshy fruit, usu. dark red, with a single hard nutlike seed (STONE) —see picture at FRUIT¹ **2** [C] also **plum tree**— the tree on which this fruit grows **3** [U] a dark reddish-blue colour **4** [A; (C)] *infml* something very desirable or the best of its kind, esp. comfortable well-paid employment: *This new job that he's got is a real plum.|a plum job*

plum·age /ˈpluːmɪdʒ/ *n* [U; S; (C)] a bird's covering of feathers

plumb¹ /plʌm/ also **plummet, plumb bob** /ˈ· ·/— *n* a mass of lead tied to the end of a string (**plumb line**), used to measure the depth of water or to find out whether a wall is built exactly upright

plumb² *adv infml* **1** [H] exactly: *The house is plumb in the middle of the island* **2** *esp. AmE dial* quite; completely: *He's plumb stupid*

plumb³ *v* [T1] **1** to (try to) find out the meaning of: *plumbing the deep mysteries of man's mind* **2** to measure the depth of (water) with a PLUMB¹ **3** to find out whether (something) is exactly upright by using a PLUMB¹ **4 plumb the depths (of)** *usu. derog* to reach the lowest point (of): *This new play really plumbs the depths of unpleasantness*

plumb⁴ *adj* [F; (B)] **1** exactly upright or level **2 out of plumb** not exactly upright

plum·ba·go¹ /plʌmˈbeɪgəʊ/ *n* **-gos** a type of mainly tropical plant with showy grey-blue flowers

plumbago² also **black lead**— *n* [U] a kind of mineral; GRAPHITE

plumb·er /ˈplʌməʳ/ *n* a man whose job is to fit and repair water pipes, bathroom articles, etc.

plumber's help·er /ˌ·· ˈ··/ also **plumber's friend** /ˌ·· ˈ·/— *n AmE infml* PLUNGER (1)

plumb·ing /ˈplʌmɪŋ/ *n* **1** [U] the work of a PLUMBER **2** [U9] all the pipes, containers for storing water, etc., in a building: *an old house with noisy plumbing*

plum cake /ˈ· ·/ *n* [C; U] *esp. BrE becoming rare* a type of large cake containing dried fruit, such as RAISINs and CURRANTs

plum duff /ˌ· ˈ·/ *n* [U; C] *esp. BrE becoming rare* a type of pale boiled sweet dish containing flour, dried fruit, and SUET, and rather like a CHRISTMAS PUDDING

plume¹ /pluːm/ *n* **1** [*usu. pl.*] a feather, esp. a large or showy one **2** [*often pl.*] a large feather or group of feathers worn as a (ceremonial) ornament **3** [(*of*)] something that rises into the air in a shape rather like that of a feather: *a plume of smoke* **4 dressed in borrowed plumes** *lit* in fine or beautiful clothes that are not one's own

plume² *v* [T1] (of a bird) to clean or make smooth (itself or its feathers)

plumed /pluːmd/ *adj* [Wa5; A] (*often in comb.*) having or ornamented with PLUMEs¹ (1,2)

plume up·on also **plume on**— *v prep* [D1; V4b] *lit* to be proud of (oneself) because of

plum·met¹ /ˈplʌmɪ̆t/ *n* **a** PLUMB¹ **b** a line with a PLUMB¹ tied to it

plummet² *v* [I0 (DOWN)] to fall steeply or suddenly: *The damaged aircraft plummeted down to earth.|Prices have plummeted*

plum·my /ˈplʌmi/ *adj* [Wa1] **1** *infml* desirable; very good: *a plummy part in the play* **2** *usu. derog* (of a voice) (unattractively) full-sounding and rich

plump¹ /plʌmp/ *n* [S] *infml* (the sound of) a sudden heavy fall

plump² *adj* [Wa1] **1** *apprec or euph* (of people)

rather fat: *I'm too plump to fit into this dress* **2** *apprec* (of parts of the body) nicely rounded: *a baby with plump little arms and legs* **3** (of animals as food) well covered with flesh: *a nice plump chicken* —**~ness** *n* [U]

plump down *v adv* [T1;I∅: (*on*)] *infml* to (cause to) fall suddenly, heavily, or carelessly

plump for *v prep* [T1,(4)] *infml* **1** to favour strongly **2** to decide in favour of: *At last we plumped for the new house rather than the old one*

plum pud·ding /ˌ· ˈ··/ *n* [C;U] CHRISTMAS PUDDING

plump up *v adv* [T1] to make (esp. bed coverings) rounded and soft by shaking

plum tree /ˈ· ·/ *n* PLUM (2)

plun·der[1] /ˈplʌndəʳ/ *v* [D1+(*from*)/*of*; T1;I∅ (*from*)] to seize (goods) unlawfully or by force from (people or a place), esp. in time of war or disorder: *They plundered the helpless villagers/plundered all the valuable things they could find.|crowds plundering the shops of their goods* —**plunderer** *n*

plunder[2] *n* [U] **1** goods seized by PLUNDERing[1] **2** stolen goods: *The thieves hid their plunder in the cave* **3** the act of PLUNDERing[1]

plunge[1] /plʌndʒ/ *v* **1** [X9;I∅ (DOWN, FORWARD(s), *through*)] to (cause to) move or be thrown suddenly forwards and/or downwards: *The sudden stopping of the car plunged him forwards.|The car suddenly stopped and he plunged forward.*|(fig.) *Prices have plunged* (=become suddenly lower).| *The road plunges here* **2** [I∅] (of a ship) to move with the forward end going violently up and down **3** [Wv4;I∅] (of the neck of a woman's garment) to have a low curve or V-shape that shows a quite large area of the chest: *a plunging* NECKLINE **4** [L9] *infml* to risk (a lot of) money carelessly on a game of chance, in a business, etc.

plunge[2] *n* [S] **1** an act of plunging (PLUNGE[1]), esp. head first into water **2 take the plunge** to decide upon and perform an act determinedly, after having delayed through anxiety or nervousness

plunge in *v adv* **1** [T1;I∅] to push, jump, or rush suddenly or violently into the depths or thickness of something, often with the head, point, etc., downward and/or forward: *He ran to the edge of the lake and plunged in.|He picked up the knife and plunged it in* **2** [I∅] to begin an activity suddenly or hastily

plunge in·to *v prep* **1** [D1;T1] to push (something), jump or rush suddenly or violently into the depths or thickness of (something), often with the head, point, etc., downward and/or forward: *He plunged into the water.|The elephant plunged into the forest* **2** [D1] to cause (someone or something) to feel or be in a state of (something): *The room was plunged into darkness* **3** [T1] to begin (something) suddenly or hastily: *She plunged at once into a description of her latest illness* **4** [T1] to enter (a room, building, etc.) suddenly or unexpectedly

plung·er /ˈplʌndʒəʳ/ *n* **1** a rubber cup on the end of a handle, used for unblocking kitchen pipes by means of SUCTION **2** a part of a machine that moves up and down —see picture at MEDICAL[1] **3** *infml* a person who risks a lot of money carelessly on a game of chance, in a business, etc.

plunk /plʌŋk/ *n, adv, v* PLONK[1,2,3]

plunk down *v* [T1] *infml* PLANK DOWN

plu·per·fect /pluːˈpɜːfɪkt‖-ɜr-/ also **past perfect**— *adj, n* (a tense, or a word or group of words in a tense) that expresses an action completed before a particular time in the past (stated or understood), and is formed in English with *had* and a *past p.*

plu·ral /ˈplʊərəl/ *adj, n* (a form, or a word in a form) that expresses more than one: *"Dogs" is a plural noun.|"Dogs" is the plural of "dog."|Is there a plural in Chinese?* —**~ly** *adv*: *a word used plurally*

plu·ral·is·m /ˈplʊərəlɪzəm/ *n* [U] **1** *usu. derog* the holding of more than one office at a time, esp. in the Church **2** *often apprec* the principle that people of different races, religions, and political beliefs can live together peacefully in the same society —**-ist** *n, adj* —**-istic** /ˌplʊərəˈlɪstɪk/ *adj*

plu·ral·i·ty /plʊəˈrælɪ̈ti/ *n* **1** [U] (in grammar) the state of being plural **2** [C] *tech, esp. AmE* the largest number of votes in an election, esp. when less than a MAJORITY (2) **3** [C;U] *usu. derog* (an office held by) PLURALISM (1)

plus[1] /plʌs/ *prep* **1** with the addition of: *3 plus 6 is 9* (3+6=9).|*The cost is a pound plus 10 pence for postage* **2** *infml* and also: *This work needs experience plus care*

plus[2] *n* **1** also **plus sign** /ˈ· ·/— a sign (+) showing that 2 or more numbers are to be added together, or that a number is greater than zero **2** *infml* a welcome or favourable addition: *We knew she was clever, but it's quite a plus that she's beautiful as well*

plus[3] *adj* [Wa5] **1** [A] greater than zero: *3 is a plus quantity* **2** [A] electrically POSITIVE **3** [A] *infml* additional and welcome (often in the phr. **a plus factor**) **4** [E] **a** (esp. of age) and above (a stated number): *All the children here are 12 plus* (=are 12 or more years old) **b** (of a mark given for work done) and slightly more (than the stated mark): *B plus* (B+) *is a better mark than B* **5** [E] *infml* (of a quality) with something else: *She's got beauty plus*

plus fours /ˌ· ˈ·/ *n* [P] a type of trousers with loose wide legs drawn in to fit closely just below the knee, used esp. in former times in playing GOLF —see PAIR (USAGE)

plush[1] /plʌʃ/ *n* [U] a type of silk or cotton cloth with a surface like short fur —compare SATIN, VELVET

plush[2] *adj* [Wa1;A] *infml* looking very splendid and costly: *the town's plush new cinema*

plush·y /ˈplʌʃi/ *adj* [Wa1] *infml* PLUSH[2]

Plu·to /ˈpluːtəʊ/ *n* [R] the PLANET 9th in order from the sun, the most distant of the group that includes the Earth —see picture at PLANET

plu·toc·ra·cy /pluːˈtɒkrəsi‖-ˈtɑk-/ *n* **1** [C] a ruling class of wealthy people **2** [U] government by the rich

plu·to·crat /ˈpluːtəkræt/ *n* **1** a person who has power because of his wealth **2** *infml & often derog* a very rich person —**~ic** /ˌpluːtəˈkrætɪk/ *adj*

plu·to·ni·um /pluːˈtəʊniəm/ *n* [U] a man-made simple substance (ELEMENT) that is used esp. in the production of atomic power

ply[1] /plaɪ/ *v* **1** [L9] (of a taxi driver, boatman, etc.) to wait, or travel backwards and forwards regularly at a particular place looking for passengers (esp. in the phr. **ply for hire**) **2** [L9, esp. *between*; T1] (of taxis, buses, and esp. boats) to travel regularly (in or on): *This ship plies between London and Australia.|a small boat plying across the mouth of the great river|small boats plying the Thames* **3** [T1] **a** *esp. lit* to work (regularly) at (a trade): *The newspaper-seller plies his trade in the streets* **b** *lit or old use* to use or work steadily with (a tool): *She sat plying her needle* (=sewing)

ply[2] *n* [U9 (*usu. in comb.*)] **1** a measure of the thickness of woollen thread, rope, etc., according to the number of single threads or lengths of material it is made from: *What ply is this wool? 2-ply.|This is 4-ply wool* **2** a measure of the thickness of PLYWOOD, according to the number of single thin sheets of wood it is made from: *3-ply wood*

ply with *v prep* [D1] to keep supplying (someone) with (esp. food, drink, or questions)

ply·wood /ˈplaɪwʊd/ *n* [U] a material made of

several thin sheets of wood stuck together to form a strong board

p.m. /ˌpiː ˈem/ *adv* [E] (*often caps.*) (*used after numbers expressing time*) post meridiem; after midday: *Today the sun sets at 5.49 p.m.|caught the 8 p.m. (train) to London* —opposite **a.m.**

P M *abbrev. for*: (*infml esp. BrE*) PRIME MINISTER

pneu·mat·ic /njuːˈmætɪk‖nʊ-/ *adj* [Wa5] **1** worked by air pressure: *a pneumatic* DRILL (1) **2** containing air: *a pneumatic tyre* —**~ally** *adv* [Wa4]

pneu·mo·co·ni·o·sis /ˌnjuːməʊkəʊniˈəʊsɨs‖ˌnuː-/ *n* [U] a disease of the lungs caused by dust, powder, etc., breathed in —compare SILICOSIS

pneu·mo·ni·a /njuːˈməʊnɪə‖nʊ-/ *n* [U] a serious disease of the lungs with INFLAMMATION and difficulty in breathing

po /pəʊ/ *n* **pos** *BrE infml humor* CHAMBER POT

P O /ˌpiː ˈəʊ/ *abbrev. for*: **1** POSTAL ORDER **2** PETTY OFFICER **3** POST OFFICE

poach[1] /pəʊtʃ/ *v* [Wv5;T1] to cook (esp. eggs or fish) in gently boiling water or other liquid, sometimes in a special pan

poach[2] *v* **1** [IØ (*for, on*); T1] to catch or shoot (animals, birds, or fish) without permission on private land: *a man caught poaching rabbits|Don't let me catch you poaching (on my land) again* **2** [IØ (*on*); T1] to take or use unfairly (a position or idea belonging to or claimed by someone else): *You're poaching on my preserve(s) by taking my girlfriend out*

poach·er /ˈpəʊtʃəʳ/ *n* **1** a person who POACHes[2] (1) **2** a pan for POACHing[1] eggs

P O Box /ˌpi əʊ ˈbɒks◂‖-ˈbɑks/ also (*fml*) **Post Office Box**— *n* a numbered box in a post office, to which a person's mail can be sent and from which he can collect it: *For further details, write to (PO) Box 179*

pock /pɒk‖pɑk/ *n* **1** a raised spot on the skin filled with diseased matter, caused by certain diseases **2** POCKMARK —see also POX (2)

pocked /pɒkt‖pɑkt/ *adj* POCKMARKED

pock·et[1] /ˈpɒkɨt‖ˈpɑkɨt/ *n* **1** [C] a small flat cloth bag sewn into or onto a garment, for keeping small articles in: *My keys are in my coat pocket* **2** [C *usu. sing.*] (a supply of) money; income: *My pocket can't stand all the new demands being made on it* **3** [C] a container for small or thin articles made by fitting a piece of cloth, net, etc., into the inside of a case or a car door, onto the back of an aircraft seat, etc. **4** [C] an enclosed fold in a book cover, for keeping loose pieces of paper in **5** [C] any of the 6 small net bags round a BILLIARD table, into which a ball may go when hit: *He hit the red ball into the top pocket* —see BILLIARDS (USAGE) **6** [C (*of*)] **a** a hole in the ground containing (valuable) metal, oil, etc. **b** an amount of (valuable) metal, oil, etc., as found in this **7** [C (*of*)] a small area or group that exists separated from others like it: *Pockets of mist could be seen down by the river| pockets of unemployment in the industrial areas* —see also AIRPOCKET **8** [A] **a** small enough to be carried in the pocket: *a pocket camera* **b** smaller than the usual size: *a pocket* BATTLESHIP **9 be/live in each other's pockets** *infml* (of 2 people) to be always together **10 have someone in one's pocket** to have complete influence over someone **11 have something in one's pocket** to be (almost) certain of gaining something or of being successful in something **12 line one's pockets** to become rich or make much money, esp. in a dishonourable way **13 out of pocket** *BrE* having paid a certain amount, usu. without good results: *I bought a new cigarette lighter and it broke; now I'm £10 out of pocket* —see also OUT-OF-POCKET EXPENSES **14 put one's hand in one's pocket** to spend or give money willingly **15 put one's pride in one's pocket** to act in spite of a feeling of hurt pride

pocket[2] *v* [T1] **1** to put into one's POCKET[1] (1) **2** to take (money or something small) for one's own use, esp. dishonestly: *He spent some of the money as we asked, but he pocketed most of it* **3** *infml* to gain (money) **4** to hit (a BILLIARD ball) into a POCKET[1] (5)

pock·et·book /ˈpɒkɨtbʊk‖ˈpɑ-/ *n* **1** a small notebook **2** *AmE* a small, usu. PAPERBACK book that can be carried in the pocket **3** *AmE* a woman's HANDBAG or PURSE[1] (1,4), esp. one without a shoulder STRAP **4** *becoming rare* a WALLET for money and personal papers

pock·et·ful /ˈpɒkɨtfʊl‖ˈpɑ-/ *n* [(*of*)] **1** the amount that a pocket will hold **2** *infml* a lot: *I've got pocketfuls of small coins, but no notes*

pocket-hand·ker·chief /ˌ·· ˈ···/ *n* **1** [C] a handkerchief **2** [A] *sometimes derog* square and very small: *a pocket-handkerchief garden*

pock·et·knife /ˈpɒkɨtnaɪf‖ˈpɑ-/ *n* **-knives** /naɪvz/ a small knife with one or more blades that fold into the handle

pocket mon·ey /ˈ·· ˌ··/ *n* [U] **1** also **spending money**— money for small personal needs **2** *esp. BrE* money given weekly to a child —compare (*AmE*) ALLOWANCE (1)

pock·mark /ˈpɒkmɑːk‖ˈpɑkmɑrk/ also **pock**— *n* **1** a hollow mark left on the skin where a POCK (1) has been **2** a hollow mark on a surface

pock·marked /ˈpɒkmɑːkt‖ˈpɑkmɑrkt/ also **pocked** /pɒkt‖pɑkt/— *adj* [(*with*)] covered with POCKMARK*s*: *a pockmarked face|The surface was pockmarked with little holes*

pod[1] /pɒd‖pɑd/ *n* **1** a long narrow seed vessel of various plants, esp. beans and PEA*s*: *a* PEA *pod* —see picture at VEGETABLE[1] **2** a long narrow container for petrol or other material, esp. as carried under an aircraft wing **3** a part of a space vehicle that can be separated from the main part

pod[2] *v* **-dd- 1** [T1] to take (beans, PEA*s*, etc.) from the POD[1] (1) before cooking **2** [IØ (UP)] (of bean plants, PEA plants, etc.) to produce POD*s*[1] (1)

podg·y /ˈpɒdʒi‖ˈpɑ-/ also **pudgy**— *adj* [Wa1] *infml* (of a person or part of the body) short and fat —**-iness** *n* [U]

po·di·a·try /pəˈdaɪətri/ *n* [U] *AmE* CHIROPODY —**-trist** *n*

po·di·um /ˈpəʊdɪəm/ *n* **-diums** *or* **-dia** /dɪə/ a raised part of a floor, or a large movable block, for a performer, speaker, musical CONDUCTOR, etc., to stand on

po·em /ˈpəʊɨm/ *n* a piece of writing, arranged in patterns of lines and of sounds, expressing in IMAGINATIVE language some deep thought, feeling, or human experience

po·e·sy /ˈpəʊɨzi‖-si/ *n* [U] *old use or poet* poetry

po·et /ˈpəʊɨt/ *n* **1** a person who writes (good or serious) poems **2** *apprec* an artist, musician, etc., who shows great feeling and imagination in his or her work

po·et·as·ter /ˌpəʊɨˈtæstəʳ/ *n derog, esp. lit* a writer of dull unimportant poems

po·et·ess /ˌpəʊɨˈtess◂‖ˈpəʊɨtɨs/ *n now rare* a female poet

po·et·ic /pəʊˈetɪk/ *adj* **1** of, like, or connected with poets or poetry: *poetic language|Shakespeare's plays are written in poetic form* **2** *apprec* beautiful and using imagination; expressing great feeling: *The dancer moved with poetic grace* —**~ally** *adv* [Wa4]

po·et·i·cal /pəʊˈetɪkəl/ *adj* **1** [Wa5;A] written in the form of poems: *the complete poetical works of Wordsworth* **2** [B] POETIC

poetic jus·tice /·ˌ·· ˈ··/ *n* [U] perfect justice, by which wrong-doers are punished or made to suffer in a way that seems particularly suitable or right

poetic li·cence /·ˌ·· ˈ··/ *n* [U] the freedom allowed by custom in the writing of poetry to change facts, not to obey the usual rules of grammar, etc.

poet laur·e·ate /ˌ·· ˈ··/ *n* **poets laureate** *or* **poet laureates** [C; *the*+R] (*often caps.*) a poet appointed to the British royal court, who writes poems on state occasions

po·et·ry /ˈpəʊɜ̇tri/ *n* **1** [U] the art of a poet: *Poetry is a difficult art* **2** [U] poems in general: *a book of poetry|the poetry of Dryden* **3** [U;S] *apprec* a quality of beauty, grace, and deep feeling: *This dancer has poetry in her movements*

po-faced /ˌpəʊ ˈfeɪst◂/ *adj BrE derog infml* having a silly solemn expression on the face

po·go stick /ˈpəʊgəʊ stɪk/ *n* a pole with a spring and a bar on which to place the feet at the bottom, on which a person, esp. a child, can stand and jump about

pog·rom /ˈpɒgrəm‖pəˈgrɑm/ *n* a planned killing of helpless people (esp. Jews) carried out for reasons of race or religion

poi·gnan·cy /ˈpɔɪnjənsi/ *n* [U] the quality or state of being POIGNANT

poi·gnant /ˈpɔɪnjənt/ *adj* **1** producing a sharp feeling of sadness or pity: *poignant memories of my old life in another country* **2** (of sorrow, grief, etc.) keenly and deeply felt —**~ly** *adv*

poin·set·ti·a /pɔɪnˈsetɪə/ *n* a type of tropical plant with flowerlike groups of large bright red leaves

point[1] /pɔɪnt/ *n* **1** [C (*of*)] a sharp end: *She pricked herself with/on the point of a needle* **2** [C (*of*)] the end (of a part of the body that is narrowly rounded): *the point of the jaw* **3** [C;R9] (*often cap., as part of name*) a piece of land with a sharp end that stretches out into the sea: *The ship sailed round the point.|Point Danger is in Australia* **4** [C] **a** also **decimal point**— a sign (·) used for separating a whole number from any following decimals: *When we read out 4·23 we say "4 point 2 3"* **b** FULL STOP (1) **5** [C (*of*)] a very small area or spot (often in the phr. **a point of light**) **6** [C] (in GEOMETRY) an imaginary spot or place that has position but no size **7** [C] a place; particular real or imaginary place exactly stated: *The bus stops at 4 or 5 points along this road.*|(fig.) *The only point of* CONTACT[1] (2) *between them was their love of fishing* **8** [U] an exact moment; particular time or state: *It was at that point that I saw him leave the building.|I've come to the point where I can't stand her arguing any longer* **9** [C] also **cardinal point, compass point, point of the compass**— **a** any of the 32 marks on a compass, showing direction **b** any of the equal divisions (each of 11° 15′) between any 2 of these **10** [C] a degree of temperature, or a mark representing this on a measuring instrument: *the melting point of gold* **11** [C] a measure of increase or decrease in cost, value, etc., according to some accepted standard: *The price of corn has fallen a few points this week* **12** [C] a single quantity used in deciding who is the winner in various sports and games: *We won the* RUGBY *game by 12 points to 3* **13** [U9;(C9)] (*usu. in comb., after a number*) a measurement used for the size of metal letters in printing **14** [C *usu. sing.*; (U)] the idea contained in something said or done, which gives meaning to the whole: *I didn't see the point of his last remark.|I missed the point. What did he mean?|I take your point* (=I quite understand your suggestion).| *That's not the point* (=not really important to or connected with the main thing being talked about) **15** [C] a single particular idea, fact, or part of an argument or statement: *There are 2 or 3 points in your speech that I didn't understand.|You've got a point there* (=What you have said may well be right) **16** [C9, esp. *of*] a (personal) rule of behaviour or way of thinking: *It's a point of honour with me to keep my promises* **17** [C] a noticeable quality or ability of someone or something: *Work isn't her strong point. She's rather lazy* **18** [U] purpose; use: *Begin your work now. There's no point in wasting time* **19** [U] effectiveness; forcefulness: *His speech was quite amusing, but its argument lacked point* **20** [C] also **power point**— *esp. BrE* a small plastic or metal container, usu. fixed in a wall, into which a PLUG (2) can be fitted so as to connect an electrical apparatus to the supply of electricity; SOCKET **21** [C] the end of an electrical instrument or wire across which or from which a small amount of electricity (a SPARK) is sent **22** [U9] the dangerous end of a weapon, considered as a means of having power or influence over someone (in the phrs. **at the point of, at . . . point**): *He forced his prisoner at gun point to stand against the wall* **23** [U] (in cricket) a fielding position directly facing the hitter (BATSMAN) and about ¼ of the way to the edge of the playing area —see also COVER POINT and picture at CRICKET[2] **24** [C] (in cricket) the player in this position **25** [C] (of a kind of dog) an act of standing still to show where a hunted animal is hidden (esp. in the phr. **make/come to a point**) —see POINTER (3) **26 at all points** completely; in every part **27 at the point of** just before: *at the point of death* **28 away from the point** off the POINT[1] (39) **29 carry/gain one's point** to succeed in making others agree **30 come to/get to the point** to speak about the most important or urgent part of a subject or matter: *I'm in a hurry, so come to the point* —see also POINT[1] (44) **31 give someone points** also **give points to someone**— **a** to give a weaker opponent a certain number of points before a game begins, so that he has some chance of winning **b** to be a better player (in a game or sport) than someone **32 in point** which proves or is an example of the subject under consideration (esp. in the phrs. **a case in point, an example in point**) **33 in point of** *fml* with regard to: *In point of cost, the first plan is the better* **34 in point of fact** actually; in reality: *He told you he'd seen it, but in point of fact he wasn't really there* **35 make a point of** to take particular care to: *He always makes a point of being where he should be at the exact time arranged* **36 make one's point** to prove (effectively) the truth of one's statement, by argument or in some other way **37 not to put too fine a point on it** if I may speak the plain (unpleasant) truth: *Not to put too fine a point on it, I didn't think your performance was very good* **38 on the point of** just starting to; just about to **39 off the point** away from what one should be talking or writing about; IRRELEVANT(ly) —opposite **to the point**; see also BESIDE **the point** **40 score points/a point off someone** also **score a point over someone**— to defeat someone in an argument, esp. by making a clever reply/replies to something said **41 stretch a point** to allow a little freedom from a rule, esp. on a special occasion: *As it's your birthday, we'll stretch a point and let you go to bed late* **42 to the point** (in a way that is) right for the purpose or the occasion: *Your advice was very much to the point* —opposite **off the point** **43 to the point of** to a degree that can be described as: *Her manner of speaking is direct to the point of rudeness* **44 when it comes/came to the point** when the moment for action or decision comes/came **45 win/lose/be beaten on points** (in BOXING) to win/lose a match by the number of points won, no KNOCKOUT having taken place

point[2] *v* **1** [IØ (*at, to*)] to hold out a finger, a stick, etc., towards someone or something in order to cause someone to look, or to show direction or position: *She pointed to the house on the corner and said, "That's where I live."|It's rude to point* **2** [X9, esp. *at, towards*; (T1)] to aim, direct, or turn: *You should never point a gun if you don't mean to fire it.|He pointed his car at the hole in the wall and drove as fast as possible* **3** [T1] to give added force to; STRESS² (2): *This road accident points the need for more careful driving* —see also POINT UP **4** [T1] to fill in and make smooth the spaces between the bricks of (a wall, house, etc.) with MORTAR or cement **5** [T1;I∅] (of a dog) to show where (a hunted animal or bird) is by standing very still and directing the nose at the hiding place —see POINTER (3) **6** [T1] to sharpen the end of: *an instrument for pointing pencils* **7** [T1] to bring (the toes) to a point by bending the ankles forward and stretching out the feet **8 point the finger (of scorn) (at)** to hold (someone) up to public blame; ACCUSE

point-blank /ˌ· ˈ·◂/ *adj, adv* **1** (with aim) directed at an object from a close position on a level with the object: *a point-blank shot at his head|He fired at his enemy point-blank* **2** (in a way that is) forceful and direct: *a point-blank refusal|I told him point-blank what I thought of his bad behaviour*

point du·ty /ˈ· ˌ··/ *n* [U] *BrE* the controlling of traffic by a policeman standing usu. at a point where 2 roads cross each other (esp. in the phr. **on point duty**)

point·ed /ˈpɔɪntɨd/ *adj* **1** shaped to a point at one end: *long pointed fingernails* **2** (of something said or done) directed, in a noticeable and often unfriendly way, at a particular person or group: *She looked in a pointed manner at the clock and I understood that it was time to leave* **3** sharply expressed or shown (esp. in the phr. **pointed wit**) —**~ly** *adv*

point·er /ˈpɔɪntəʳ/ *n* **1** a stick used by someone to point at things on a large map, board, etc. **2** a small needlelike piece of metal that moves and points to the numbers on a measuring apparatus **3** a type of hunting dog that stops with its nose pointed towards a hunted animal or bird that it has smelt **4** a useful suggestion or piece of advice

poin·til·lis·m /ˈpɔɪntɪlɪzəm (*Fr* pwɛ̃tijizm)/ *n* [U] *Fr* a style of painting which uses dots of colour to obtain its effect —**-list** *n, adj*: *the 19th-century French pointillist Seurat*

point·less /ˈpɔɪntləs/ *adj* **1** *often derog* meaningless **2** useless; unnecessary **3** (of a match) in which neither team gains any points; finishing 0–0 —**~ly** *adv* —**~ness** *n* [U]

point of no re·turn /ˌ· · · ·ˈ·/ *n* [(*the*) S] **1** the point on a long journey, esp. by aircraft, at which there are no longer enough supplies, petrol, etc., left to return to the starting point, so that the journey has to be continued **2** a point in something that one is doing at which one has to decide whether one will stop or go on, because if one continues any further one will not be able to stop

point of or·der /ˌ· · ˈ··/ *n* a matter connected with the organization of an official meeting (esp. in the phr. **on a point of order**)

point of view /ˌ· · ˈ·/ also **viewpoint**— *n* a way of considering or judging a thing, person, event, etc.: *We need someone with a fresh point of view to suggest changes.|From my point of view it would be better if you could come tomorrow, but you may not want to*

point out *v adv* [T1 (*to*), 5,6a,(b)] to draw attention to (something or someone): *He pointed her out to me.|May I point out that if we don't leave now we shall miss the bus*

points /pɔɪnts/ *n* [P] **1** (*AmE* **switches**)— *BrE* a pair of short RAILs that can be moved to allow a train to cross over from one track to another **2** the ends of the toes, as used to dance on in BALLET (esp. in the phr. **on points**) **3** a horse's feet, tail, and hair along the neck, esp. when of a different colour from the rest of the animal **4** the special bodily qualities considered in judging the worth of an animal in a show

points·man /ˈpɔɪntsmən/ (*AmE* **switchman**)— *n* **-men** /mən/ *BrE* a railway worker in charge of the moving of POINTS (1)

point to also **point to·wards**— *v prep* [T1] to suggest the strong possibility of; be a sign of

point-to-point /ˌ· · ˈ·/ *n* **point-to-points** a horse-race across country from one place to another, usu. with points along the way marked esp. with flags

point up *v adv* [T1] to add to, show the qualities of, or make clearer

poise¹ /pɔɪz/ *v* **1** [X9] to hold or place lightly in a position in which it is difficult to remain steady: *He poised the glass on the edge of the shelf* **2** [T1] *rare* to hold in the hand ready for use

poise² *n* [U] **1** good judgment and self-control in one's actions, combined with a quiet belief in one's abilities: *He has a great deal of poise for a boy of only 17* **2** the way of holding one's head or body: *We admired the graceful poise of the dancer*

poised /pɔɪzd/ *adj* **1** [Wa5;F+*between*] in a condition of (dangerous) uncertainty: *The sick man is poised between life and death* **2** [B] *apprec* having POISE² (1) **3** [Wa5;F9] still, as if hanging, in the air: *The bee hung poised above the flower* **4** [Wa5; F9] lightly seated: *She sat poised on the edge of a chair as if ready to go* **5** [Wa5;F (*for*), F3] in a state of readiness to act or move: *The army was poised for action*

poi·son¹ /ˈpɔɪzən/ *n* **1** [C;U] (a) substance that harms or kills if a living animal or plant takes it in: *He took poison by mistake for a medicine, and it nearly killed him* **2** [C;U] (an) evil or unwanted influence on the mind, society, etc. **3** [U] *humor sl* alcoholic drink (esp. in the phr. **what's your poison?** (=what would you like to drink?))

poison² *v* [T1] **1** to give poison to; harm or kill with poison: *Someone tried to poison our dog* **2** [Wv5] to put poison into or onto (something): *Someone tried to poison our dog's food.|a poisoned arrow* **3** [Wv5] *esp. BrE* to infect (esp. parts of the body): *a poisoned foot* **4** to make dangerously impure: *Gases from cars are poisoning the air of our cities* **5** to influence (someone's behaviour, character, mind, etc.) in a harmful or evil way: *She tried to poison her husband's mind against his sister* —**~er** *n*

poison gas /ˌ·· ˈ·/ *n* [U] gas used in war to kill or harm the enemy

poison i·vy /ˌ·· ˈ··/ *n* [U] a type of North American climbing plant that causes painful spots on the skin when touched

poi·son·ous /ˈpɔɪzənəs/ *adj* **1** containing poison in itself: *poisonous snakes|Some plants have poisonous roots or fruit* **2** having the effects of poison: *This medicine is poisonous if taken in large quantities* **3** harmful to the mind; having an evil effect on others: *poisonous ideas* **4** nasty; very unpleasant: *a poisonous green colour*|(fig.) *What a poisonous meal!* —**~ly** *adv*

poison-pen let·ter /ˌ·· ˈ· ˌ··/ *n* a usu. unsigned letter making charges of misbehaviour, or saying bad things about someone

poke¹ /pəʊk/ *n* **(buy) a pig in a poke** *infml* (to buy) something that one has not seen or examined, and that one may afterwards find to be worthless

poke² *v* **1** [X9;L9] to push sharply out of or through an opening: *His elbow was poking through his torn shirt* SLEEVE.|*She poked her head round the corner* **2** [T1 (*with*); I∅] to push (a pointed thing) into (someone or something): *You nearly poked me* *in the eye with your pencil.*|*Stop poking (me)!* **3** [T1] to move (the wood or coal) in (a fire) about with a POKER[1] or other such object **4** [X9, esp. *in, through*] to make (a hole) by pushing, forcing, etc.: *His large key had poked a hole in his pocket* **5** [X9; (T1)] *infml* to hit with the hand closed **6 poke fun at** to make jokes against **7 poke one's nose into something** *infml* to enquire into something that does not properly concern one

poke³ *n* **1** an act of poking (POKE[2] (2,3)) with something pointed **2** *infml* a blow with the closed hand (often in the phr. **take a poke at**)

poke a·bout *AmE* usu. **poke a·round**— *v adv* [IØ] *infml* **1** to search: *She poked about in her bag for her ticket* **2** to be active without much result, as when doing small unimportant jobs: *She's been poking about in the kitchen all morning, moving tins and boxes.*|*The* BATSMAN *has been poking about for 2 hours, hardly making any runs*

poke at *v prep* [T1] **1** to make a weak uncertain stroke at: *From the way she just poked at the food, we could see she wasn't hungry* **2** to try to POKE[2] (2,3,5)

pok·er¹ /ˈpəʊkəʳ/ *n* a thin, usu. ornamented metal bar used to POKE[2] (3) a fire in order to make it burn better —see picture at LIVING ROOM

po·ker² *n* [U] a type of card game usu. played for money

poker face /ˈ·· ·/ *n* a face that shows nothing of what a person is thinking or feeling —**poker-faced** /ˈ·· ·/ *adj*

po·ker·work /ˈpəʊkəwɜːk‖-kərwɜrk/ *n* [U] **1** the art of making pictures or ornamentation on wood or leather by burning the surface with hot instruments **2** ornamentation produced by this method

pok·y /ˈpəʊki/ *adj* [Wa1] *infml* (of a place) uncomfortably small and unattractive (often in the phr. **poky little . . .**): *a poky little house with a poky little garden in front* —**pokiness** *n* [U]

Po·lack /ˈpəʊlæk/ *n derog sl* a person, esp. a man, of Polish origin

po·lar /ˈpəʊləʳ/ *adj* [Wa5;A] **1** of, near, like, or coming from lands near the North or South POLE*s* **2** *fml* exactly opposite in kind, quality, etc. (often in the phr. **polar opposites**)

polar bear /ˌ·· ˈ·/ *n* [Wn1] a type of large white bear that lives near the North POLE —see picture at CARNIVOROUS

po·lar·i·ty /pəˈlærɨti/ *n* [U;C] **1** the state of having or developing 2 opposite qualities: *a growing polarity between the opinions of the government and those of the trade unions* **2 a** the state of having 2 opposite POLE*s*[3] (1,2,3) **b** either of the 2 states of electricity possessed by POLE*s*[3] (3) (in the phrs. **negative polarity, positive polarity**)

po·lar·i·za·tion, -isation /ˌpəʊləraɪˈzeɪʃən‖-rə-/ *n* **1** [C] an act of polarizing (POLARIZE) **2** [U;C] the state of being POLARIZED: *the polarization of society into 2 classes*

po·lar·ize, -ise /ˈpəʊləraɪz/ *v* **1** [T1;IØ] to (cause to) gather about 2 opposite points: *The new danger seems to have polarized society into 2 classes.*|*Society has polarized into 2 classes* **2** [T1 (*towards*)] to direct or cause to have a tendency; ORIENTATE: *a society polarized towards gaining money* **3** [T1] to give POLARITY (2) to **4** [Wv5;T1] to cause (light waves) to move up and down (VIBRATE) in a single particular pattern

Po·lar·oid /ˈpəʊlərɔɪd/ *n tdmk* **1** [U] a material with which glass is treated in order to make light shine less brightly through it, used in making SUNGLASSES, car windows, etc. **2** [C] also (*fml*) **Polaroid cam·e·ra** /ˌ··· ˈ···/— a type of camera that produces a finished photograph only seconds after the picture has been taken

Po·lar·oids /ˈpəʊlərɔɪdz/ *n* [P] *tdmk infml* a type of glasses used for protecting the eyes from bright light (SUNGLASSES), treated with POLAROID (1) —see PAIR (USAGE)

pol·der /ˈpəʊldəʳ/ *n* (esp. in the Netherlands) a piece of land, formerly covered by the sea, which has been made dry and can be used for farming

pole¹ /pəʊl/ *n* **1** (*often in comb.*) a long straight round stick or post, usu. quite thin, used as a support, to guide a flat-bottomed boat, to join 2 animals to a cart or carriage, etc.: *a flagpole*|*The hut was made of poles covered with grass mats* **2** ROD —see WEIGHTS & MEASURES TABLE **3 up the pole** *infml, esp. BrE* **a** slightly mad **b** in difficulty; not knowing what to do

pole² *v* **1** [X9;L9] to cause (a boat) to move along by pushing a pole against the bed of the river, lake, etc. **2** [L9;(IØ)] to use SKI poles or sticks to give oneself more speed in sliding over snow **3** [X9] to make (one's way) by causing (oneself) to move in either of these ways

pole³ *n* **1** either end of an imaginary straight line (AXIS) around which a solid round mass turns, esp. **a** (the lands around) the most northern and southern points on the surface of the earth or of another chief heavenly body (PLANET) **b** the 2 points in the sky to the north and south around which stars seem to turn —see also MAGNETIC POLE, NORTH POLE, SOUTH POLE **2** either of the points at the ends of a MAGNET where its power of pulling iron towards itself is greatest **3** either of the 2 points at which wires may be fixed onto an electricity-storing apparatus (BATTERY) in order to use that electricity (often in the phrs. **negative pole, positive pole**) **4** either of 2 completely different qualities, opinions, etc.: *Our opinions on this subject are at opposite poles* **5 poles apart** widely separated; having no shared quality, idea, etc.

Pole *n* a native of Poland

pole·axe¹, *AmE* usu. **-ax** /ˈpəʊlæks/ *n* **1** a type of long-handled heavy axe used in killing cattle **2** (in former times) a large axe used for fighting

poleaxe², *AmE* usu. **-ax** *v* [T1] **1** to make senseless with, or as if with, a heavy blow on the head **2** to strike or kill with a POLEAXE[1]

pole·cat /ˈpəʊlkæt/ *n* **1** a type of small fierce dark brown animal that lives in northern Europe and has a very unpleasant smell **2** *AmE infml* SKUNK

po·lem·ic /pəˈlemɪk/ *n* **1** [C] *fml* a fierce argument, esp. an attack on, or defence of, an opinion **2** [U] POLEMICS (1)

po·lem·i·cal /pəˈlemɪkəl/ also **polemic** /pəˈlemɪk/— *adj* **1** of POLEMICS **2** causing fierce argument **3** (of a person) in the habit of arguing, attacking or defending opinions, ideas, etc. —**-cally** *adv* [Wa4]

po·lem·ics /pəˈlemɪks/ *n* [U] **1** the art or practice of arguing, attacking or defending opinions, ideas, etc. **2** the branch of Christian learning (THEOLOGY) that deals with pointing out and disproving mistaken ideas in Christian writings

pole star /ˈ· ·/ also **North Star** /ˌ· ˈ·/— *n* [*the*+R] (*often cap.*) the rather bright star that at any time is nearest to the centre of the heavens (NORTH POLE (2)) in the northern part of the world

pole vault /ˈ· ·/ *n* **1** [C] a jump made over a high raised bar, the jumper using a long pole to lift himself **2** [*the*+R] the sport of doing this —**pole-vault** *v* [IØ]: *He pole-vaulted 18 feet 3 inches* —**pole-vaulter** *n*

po·lice¹ /pəˈliːs/ *n* [(*the*)P] an official body of men (and women) whose duty is to protect people and property, to make everyone obey the law, to catch criminals, etc.: *The police have caught the murderer.*|*Most police wear uniforms.*|*the police force*|*a police car*

police² *v* [T1] **1** to control (a place) by or as if using police: *Dangerous areas have to be carefully policed on Saturday nights.|The army policed the conquered city* **2** to control; keep a watch on: *a new body set up to police pay agreements*

police con·sta·ble /·ˌ· ˈ···/ *n* [C;A] *BrE fml* P.C.

police court /·ˈ· ·/ *n* a lawcourt in which the less serious cases of law-breaking (such as traffic offences) are tried

po·lice·man /pəˈliːsmən/ also **police officer** /·ˈ· ˌ···/— *n* **-men** /mən/ a member of a police force

police state /·ˈ· ·/ *n derog* a country in which most activities of the citizens are controlled by (secret) political police

police sta·tion /·ˈ· ˌ··/ *n* the local office of the police in a town, part of a city, etc.

po·lice·wom·an /pəˈliːsˌwʊmən/ *n* **-women** /ˌwɪmɨn/ [C;A] **1** a female policeman **2** a female P.C.

pol·i·cy¹ /ˈpɒlɨsi/ *n* **1** [C] a plan or course of action in directing affairs, as chosen by a political party, government, business company, etc.: *One of the new government's policies is to control public spending* **2** [U] sensible behaviour that is to one's own advantage: *It's bad policy to smoke too much; it may harm your health*

policy² *n* a written statement of the details of an agreement with an insurance company —see also INSURANCE POLICY

po·li·o /ˈpəʊliəʊ/ also (*tech*) **po·li·o·my·e·li·tis** /ˌpəʊliəʊmaɪəˈlaɪtɨs/— *n* [U] a serious infectious disease of the nerves in the backbone (SPINE), often resulting in a lasting inability to move certain muscles (PARALYSIS)

pol·ish¹ /ˈpɒlɪʃ‖ˈpɑ-/ *v* **1** [T1 (UP); X7;L9, esp. UP;(I∅)] to make or become smooth and shiny by continual rubbing: *Polish your shoes with a brush.|Silver polishes easily with this special cloth.|He polished up the old copper coins* **2** [Wv5;T1] to make (a person, his behaviour, speech, etc.) less rough, more graceful **3** [Wv5;T1] to make (a speech, piece of writing, artistic performance, etc.) as perfect as possible: *The musicians gave a very polished performance*

polish² *n* **1** [U;C] a liquid, powder, paste, etc., used in polishing a surface: *a tin of brown shoe polish|metal polish|I keep my polishes in this cupboard* **2** [S9] a smooth shiny surface produced by rubbing: *A hot plate will spoil the polish on this table/will spoil its polish.|a high polish* (=a very shiny surface) **3** [S] an act of polishing **4** [U] *apprec* fine quality or perfection (of manners, education, writing, etc.): *The village boy is rather rough. He lacks polish*

Pol·ish /ˈpəʊlɪʃ/ *adj* of Poland, its people, or their language —see NATIONALITY TABLE

pol·ish·er /ˈpɒlɪʃəʳ‖ˈpɑ-/ *n* **1** a skilled worker who polishes metal or wood **2** (*often in comb.*) an electric machine, a cloth, etc., used for polishing: *a floor polisher*

polish off *v adv* [T1] **1** to finish (something, such as food, work, etc.) **2** *sl* to kill (someone)

polish up *v adv* [T1a] BRUSH UP

po·lit·bu·ro /pəˈlɪtbjʊərəʊ, ˈpɒlɨt-‖ˈpɑlɨt-, pəˈlɪt-/ *n* **-ros** [(*the*)] (*often cap.*) the chief decision-making committee of a political party, esp. a COMMUNIST party

po·lite /pəˈlaɪt/ *adj* [Wa2] **1** having or showing good manners, consideration for others, and/or correct social behaviour: *What polite well-behaved children!|It's not considered polite to put food into your mouth with a knife* **2** *pomp* having or showing (or pretending to have or show) fineness of feeling, high development in the arts, manners, etc.; REFINED: *polite society|polite literature* —**~ly** *adv* —**~ness** *n* [U;C]

USAGE A **polite** person has good manners. It is **polite** to say "Thank you" and to open doors for people. Quiet, soft, kind behaviour is **gentle**: *her* **gentle** *voice|Wash the baby's eyes very* **gently** *so you won't hurt him.* A **noble** action is one that is admired for its great bravery and unselfishness; this is a very strong word: *It was* **noble** *of him to die for his friends.*

pol·i·tic /ˈpɒlɨtɪk‖ˈpɑ-/ *adj* [F;(B)] *usu. lit* **1** (of behaviour or actions) well-judged with regard to one's own advantage **2** (of a person) skilful in acting to obtain a desired result or one's own advantage —see also BODY POLITIC

po·lit·i·cal /pəˈlɪtɪkəl/ *adj* **1** [Wa5] of or concerning public affairs and/or the government of a country: *the loss of political freedoms|He left his own country for political reasons* **2** [Wa5] of or concerned with (party) politics: *a political party|He has very strong political opinions* **3** [Wa5] concerning or charged with acts harmful to a government: *a political prisoner|a political offence* **4** very interested in, concerned with, or active in politics: *The students in this university are very political.|I'm not really a political person; I only entered parliament to try and help people* **5** *usu. derog* connected with, influenced by, or done for reasons of personal, group, or governmental advantage rather than for the official reasons publicly reported: *We all know he is good enough to play in the team, so he must have been dropped for political reasons* —**~ly** *adv* [Wa4]

political a·sy·lum /·ˌ··· ·ˈ··/ *n* [U] protection given by a government to someone who leaves his own country for political reasons

political e·con·o·my /·ˌ··· ·ˈ···/ *n* [U] **1** the scientific study of the way in which the political practices of a government direct or influence the production and use of wealth by a nation **2** *old use* ECONOMICS —**-mist** *n*

political ge·og·ra·phy /·ˌ··· ·ˈ···/ *n* [U] the study of the earth's surface as it is divided among states, not as marked by rivers, mountain ranges, etc.

po·lit·i·cal·ize, -ise /pəˈlɪtɪkəlaɪz/ *v* [T1;I∅] POLITICIZE —**-ization** /pəˌlɪtɪkəlaɪˈzeɪʃən‖-ləˈzeɪ-/ *n* [U]

political sci·ence /·ˌ··· ˈ··/ *n* [U] the scientific study of politics and government —**political scientist** *n*

pol·i·ti·cian /ˌpɒlɨˈtɪʃən‖ˌpɑ-/ *n* **1** a person whose business is politics, esp. one who is a member of a parliament **2** *derog* a person concerned with party politics for his own personal selfish purpose or gain

po·lit·i·cize, -ise /pəˈlɪtɨsaɪz/ *v often derog* **1** [T1] to give a political character to **2** [T1;I∅] to (cause to) become interested in politics —**-cization** /pəˌlɪtɨsaɪˈzeɪʃən‖-səˈzeɪ-/ *n* [U]

pol·i·tick·ing /ˈpɒlɨtɪkɪŋ‖ˈpɑ-/ *n* [U;(C)] *often derog* an act or the action of taking part in political activity or talk, esp. for personal advantage

po·lit·i·co /pəˈlɪtɪkəʊ/ *n* **-cos** *or* **-coes** *often derog* a politician

politico- *comb. form* political and: *politico-scientific*

pol·i·tics /ˈpɒlɨtɪks‖ˈpɑ-/ *n* **1** [U;P] the art or science of government: *Tom is studying politics at university* **2** [U;P] political affairs, esp. considered as a profession and/or as a means of winning and keeping governmental control: *Is politics an honourable profession?|Politics have never interested me.|local politics|student politics* **3** [P] political opinions; the political ideas or party that one favours: *What are your politics? I support the* LIBERAL *party* **4 play politics** *derog* to speak or act in such a way as to make people argue amongst themselves, distrust each other, have doubts about the safety of their positions, etc., in order to gain an advantage for oneself

pol·i·ty /ˈpɒlȝti‖ˈpɑ-/ *n fml* **1** [U] political or governmental organization **2** [C] a particular form of this **3** [GU;(GC)] citizens as forming a state under a government

pol·ka /ˈpɒlkə, ˈpəʊlkə/ *n* **1** a type of very quick simple dance for people dancing in pairs **2** a piece of music to which this is danced

polka dot /ˈ·· ·/ *n* [*usu. pl.*] any of a number of large regularly-placed circular spots forming a pattern, used esp. on dress material: *a polka-dot skirt*

poll¹ /pəʊl/ *n* **1** [U9] the giving of votes in writing at an election: *The result of the poll won't be known until midnight* **2** [S] the number of votes recorded at an election: *They expected a heavy poll* (=expected that a large number of people would vote) **3** [C] an official list of electors: *to make sure his name was on the poll* **4** [C] also **opinion poll**— **a** a questioning of a number of people chosen by chance to find out the general opinion about something or someone **b** a record of the result of this: *the polls in today's newspapers* **5 declare the poll** to make known officially in public the result of an election

poll² *v* **1** [T1] to receive (a stated number of votes) at an election **2** [I∅] to vote at an election **3** [T1 *usu. pass.*] to take or record the votes of electors in (an electoral area) **4** [T1] to question (people) in making a POLL¹ (4) **5** [Wv5;T1] to cut off or cut short the horns of (cattle) **6** [T1] POLLARD²

Poll /pɒl‖pɑl/ *n* [R;N] (the name of a PARROT (1), used in stories)

pol·lard¹ /ˈpɒləd‖ˈpɑlərd/ *n* **1** a tree of which the top has been cut off in order to make the branches below the cut place grow more strongly **2** a hornless kind of sheep, goat, etc.

pollard² *v* [T1] to cut the top off (a tree)

pol·len /ˈpɒlən‖ˈpɑ-/ *n* [U] fine yellow dust on the male part of a flower that causes other flowers to produce seeds when it is carried to them

pollen count /ˈ·· ·/ *n* a measure of the amount of POLLEN floating in the air, esp. as a guide for people who are made ill by it

pol·li·nate /ˈpɒlȝneɪt‖ˈpɑ-/ *v* [T1] to cause (a flower or plant) to be able to produce seeds by adding or bringing POLLEN —**-nation** /ˌpɒlȝˈneɪʃən‖ˌpɑ-/ *n* [U]

poll·ing /ˈpəʊlɪŋ/ *n* [U] the giving of votes at an election; voting: *Polling was quite heavy* (=lots of people voted)

polling booth /ˈ·· ·/ *n esp. BrE* a partly enclosed place inside a POLLING STATION where a person records his vote secretly

polling sta·tion /ˈ·· ˌ··/ *n esp. BrE* a building or other place where people go to vote at an election: *Our local library is used as a polling station during elections*

poll·ster /ˈpəʊlstəʳ/ *n infml* a person who carries out POLLS¹ (4), or who explains the meaning of the results of these

poll tax /ˈ· ·/ *n* a tax of a fixed amount collected from every citizen, esp. before he can vote

pol·lut·ant /pəˈluːtənt/ *n* [C;U] a substance or thing that POLLUTEs

pol·lute /pəˈluːt/ *v* [T1] **1** to make (air, water, soil, etc.) dangerously impure or unfit for use **2** *derog* to destroy the purity of (the mind) **3** to make (esp. a holy place) ceremonially unclean

pol·lu·tion /pəˈluːʃən/ *n* [U] **1** the action of polluting (POLLUTE) **2** the state of being POLLUTED **3** (an area or mass of) a substance or other thing that POLLUTEs: *The men were clearing all the pollution off the shore*

Pol·ly /ˈpɒli‖ˈpɑli/ *n* [R;N] POLL

Pol·ly·an·na /ˌpɒliˈænə‖ˌpɑ-/ *n derog, esp. AmE* a person who habitually refuses, in an annoying way, to believe that anything bad can happen —**~ish** *adj*

po·lo /ˈpəʊləʊ/ *n* [U] a game played between 2 teams of players on horseback, who try to get GOALs by hitting a ball with long-handled wooden hammers

pol·o·naise /ˌpɒləˈneɪz‖ˌpɑ-/ *n* **1** a piece of music of a rather grand slow ceremonial kind, esp. written for the piano **2** a national dance of Poland

polo neck /ˈ·· ·/ (*AmE* **turtleneck**)— *n* a round rolled collar, usu. woollen: *a polo-neck* SWEATER

po·lo·ny /pəˈləʊni/ *n BrE* **1** [U] partly-cooked pig meat cut up small and put into a red tubelike skin to make a SAUSAGE **2** [C] a length of this

pol·ter·geist /ˈpɒltəgaɪst‖ˈpəʊltər-/ *n* a type of spirit that is said to make noises, throw objects about a room, etc.

pol·troon /pɒlˈtruːn‖pɑl-/ *n* [C; *you*+N] *derog & old use* a coward —**~ery** *n* [U]

pol·y /ˈpɒli‖ˈpɑli/ *n* **polys** *infml esp. BrE* POLYTECHNIC

poly- *comb. form* many: *polyatomic* (=having many atoms)|POLYGAMY

pol·y·an·drous /ˌpɒliˈændrəs‖ˌpɑ-/ *adj* **1** of or practising POLYANDRY **2** *tech* (of a plant) having many male parts (STAMENs)

pol·y·an·dry /ˌpɒliˈændri, ˈpɒliændri‖-pɑ-/ *n* [U] the custom or practice of having more than one husband at the same time

pol·y·an·thus /ˌpɒliˈænθəs‖ˌpɑ-/ *n* [U;(C)] a type of small garden plant with a group of round brightly-coloured flowers at the top of each stem

pol·y·es·ter /ˈpɒliestəʳ, ˌpɒliˈestəʳ‖ˈpɑliestər-/ *n* [U] a type of man-made material used esp. (mixed with wool or cotton) to make cloth for garments

pol·y·eth·y·lene /ˌpɒliˈeθəliːn‖ˌpɑ-/ *n* [U] *AmE* POLYTHENE

po·lyg·a·mist /pəˈlɪgəmȝst/ *n* a man who has more than one wife

po·lyg·a·mous /pəˈlɪgəməs/ *adj* of or practising POLYGAMY: *a polygamous society|polygamous marriages*

po·lyg·a·my /pəˈlɪgəmi/ *n* [U] the custom or practice of having more than one wife at the same time

pol·y·glot /ˈpɒlɪglɒt‖ˈpɑlɪglɑt/ *n, adj* **1** [C;A;(B)] (a group or a person) speaking or knowing many languages **2** [Wa5;A;(C)] (a book, esp. a bible) written in many languages

pol·y·gon /ˈpɒlɪgən‖ˈpɑlɪgɑn/ *n* (in GEOMETRY) a figure on a flat surface having 5 or more straight sides

pol·y·math /ˈpɒlɪmæθ‖ˈpɑ-/ *n* a person with great skill in many branches of knowledge

pol·y·mer /ˈpɒlɪməʳ‖ˈpɑ-/ *n* a compound chemical part (MOLECULE) built up from a number of simple ones of the same kind

pol·y·mor·phous /ˌpɒlɪˈmɔːfəs‖ˌpɑlɪˈmɔr-/ also **pol·y·mor·phic** /-fɪk/— *adj fml or tech* having or passing through many stages of growth, development, etc.

pol·yp /ˈpɒlȝp‖ˈpɑ-/ *n* **1** a very simple type of small water animal, having the form of a tubelike bag **2** a type of small diseased unnatural growth in the body (esp. in the nose) —**~ous** *adj*

po·lyph·o·ny /pəˈlɪfəni/ *n* [U;(S)] a form of musical writing in which a number of different patterns of notes are sung or played together, fitting in with each other musically, according to certain rules; COUNTERPOINT —**-nic** /ˌpɒlɪˈfɒnɪk‖ˌpɑlɪˈfɑnɪk/ *adj*

pol·y·pus /ˈpɒlȝpəs‖ˈpɑ-/ *n esp. BrE* POLYP (2)

pol·y·sty·rene /ˌpɒlɪˈstaɪəriːn‖ˌpɑ-/ *n* [U] a type of light plastic material that prevents the escape of heat, used esp. for making containers

polystyrene ce·ment /ˈ··ˌ·· ·ˈ·/ *n* [U] a type of sticky material (GLUE) used esp. for sticking plastic

pol·y·syl·la·ble /ˈpɒlɪˌsɪləbəl‖ˈpɑ-/ *n* a word that must be pronounced in more than 3 separate parts (SYLLABLES): *"Unnecessary" is a polysyllable* —**-bic** /ˌpɒlɪsəˈlæbɪk‖ˌpɑ-/ *adj* [Wa5] —**-bically** *adv* [Wa4,5]

pol·y·tech·nic /ˌpɒlɪˈteknɪk‖ˌpɑ-/ also (*infml*) **poly**— *n* (esp. in Britain) a place of higher education providing training and often university degrees in many arts and esp. trades connected with skills and machines

pol·y·the·is·m /ˈpɒlɪθiːɪzəm‖ˈpɑ-/ *n* [U] belief in the existence of more than one god —**-tic** /ˌpɒlɪθiːˈɪstɪk‖ˌpɑ-/ *adj*

pol·y·thene /ˈpɒləθiːn‖ˈpɑ-/ *AmE* also **polyethylene**— *n* [U] a type of plastic not easily damaged by water or certain chemicals, used esp. as a protective covering, for making household articles, etc.: *a polythene bag*

pol·y·u·re·thane /ˌpɒlɪˈjʊərəθeɪn‖ˌpɑ-/ *n* [U] a type of plastic material used esp. in making paints and VARNISHES[1] (1)

po·made[1] /pəˈmɑːd, pəˈmeɪd‖pəʊˈmeɪd/ *n* [U] a type of sweet-smelling oily paste rubbed on men's hair to make it smooth

pomade[2] *v* [Wv5;T1] to put POMADE[1] on (men's hair)

po·man·der /pəʊˈmændəʳ, pəˈmæn-‖ˈpəʊmændər/ *n* a box or ball-shaped container holding sweet-smelling substances, HERBS, etc., used for giving a room or cupboard a pleasant smell

pom·e·gran·ate /ˈpɒməgrænət‖ˈpʌmgrænət, ˈpɑm-/ *n* **1** a type of round thick-skinned reddish fruit containing a mass of small seeds in a red juicy flesh **2** a tree on which this grows

Pom·e·ra·ni·an /ˌpɒməˈreɪnɪən‖ˌpɑ-/ *adj, n* (*often not cap.*) (of) a type of small long-haired dog

pom·mel[1] /ˈpʌməl/ *n* **1** the rounded part of a horse rider's leather seat (SADDLE) that sticks up at the front **2** the ball-shaped end of a sword handle (HILT)

pommel[2] *v* **-ll-** (*AmE* **-l-**) [T1] PUMMEL

pommel horse /ˈ·· ·/ (*AmE* **side horse**)— *n* a VAULTING HORSE with handles

pom·my /ˈpɒmi‖ˈpɑ-/ also **pom** /pɒm‖pɑm/— *n* *Austr & NZE sl often derog* (*often cap.*) an Englishman, esp. one who has recently come to live in Australia or New Zealand

pomp /pɒmp‖pɑmp/ *n* [U] **1** grand solemn ceremonial show, esp. on some public or official occasion **2** unnecessary show: *getting away from the empty pomp and show of the city*

pom·pom /ˈpɒmpɒm‖ˈpɑmpɑm/ also (*becoming rare*) **pom·pon** /-pɒn‖-pɑn/— a small ball made of bits of wool worn as an ornament on garments, esp. hats: *French sailors wear a pompom on their caps*

pom·pos·i·ty /pɒmˈpɒsəti‖pɑmˈpɑ-/ *n derog* **1** [U] also **pom·pous·ness** /ˈpɒmpəsnəs‖ˈpɑm-/— the quality of being POMPOUS **2** [C] an example of this

pom·pous /ˈpɒmpəs‖ˈpɑm-/ *adj derog* foolishly solemn and self-important: *pompous language|The railway guard was a pompous little official, who thought he controlled the whole railway system himself* —**~ly** *adv*

ponce /pɒns‖pɑns/ *n BrE* **1** a man who lives with, and on the money earned by, a PROSTITUTE; PIMP **2** *derog sl* a man who acts in a showy way and/or esp. a womanish (EFFEMINATE) way

ponce a·bout also **ponce a·round**— *v adv* [IØ] *BrE sl* **1** *derog* (of a man) to act like a PONCE (2) **2** (usu. of a man) to act in a way that annoys someone else, esp. as by doing small unimportant things so that more important things are delayed

pon·cho /ˈpɒntʃəʊ‖ˈpɑn-/ *n* **-chos** *Sp* **1** a garment for the top half of the body consisting of a single long wide piece of usu. thick woollen cloth with a hole in the middle for the head **2** a garment like this but with a head covering, worn as a protection against rain

ponc·y /ˈpɒnsi‖ˈpɑ-/ *adj* [Wa1] *BrE derog sl* like a PONCE[1] (2)

pond /pɒnd‖pɑnd/ *n* **1** [C] an area of still water smaller than a lake: *Most farms have a pond from which cattle can drink.|a duck pond* **2** [*the*+R] *BrE humor* the Atlantic ocean

pon·der /ˈpɒndəʳ‖ˈpɑn-/ *v* [T1,6a,b;IØ (*on, over*)] to spend time in considering (a fact, difficulty, etc.): *When I asked her advice, she pondered (the matter) and then told me not to go.|The prisoner pondered how to escape*

pon·der·ous /ˈpɒndərəs‖ˈpɑn-/ *adj* **1** *sometimes derog* large and heavy **2** slow and awkward because of size and weight **3** *derog* dull and solemn; lacking lightness or gaiety —**~ly** *adv* —**~ness** *n* [U]

pone /pəʊn/ also **corn pone**— *n* [U] a kind of bread made from CORN, esp. by North American Indians

pong[1] /pɒŋ‖pɑŋ/ *v* [IØ] *BrE sl* to have or make a PONG[2]

pong[2] *n BrE sl* an unpleasant smell —**~y** *adj* [Wa1]

pon·iard /ˈpɒnjəd‖ˈpɑnjərd/ *n* a type of small pointed knife used in former times as a weapon

pon·tiff /ˈpɒntəf‖ˈpɑn-/ *n* **1** [*the*+R] (*usu. cap.*) the POPE **2** [C] a POPE **3** [C] *old use* a ROMAN CATHOLIC priest of high rank **4** [C] (in former times) a Roman or Jewish chief priest

pon·tif·i·cal /pɒnˈtɪfɪkəl‖pɑn-/ *adj* **1** *derog* **a** (of a person) (in the habit of) making statements that one expects others to accept as the only truth or law **b** (of actions or statements) showing this quality **2** [Wa5] of or concerning a POPE: *a pontifical letter* —**-cally** *adv* [Wa4]

pon·tif·i·cals /pɒnˈtɪfɪkəlz‖pɑn-/ *n* [P] the official dress of a priest of high rank

pon·tif·i·cate[1] /pɒnˈtɪfɪkət‖pɑn-/ *n* **1** the position or office of a PONTIFF (esp. 2) **2** the length of time that this lasts

pon·tif·i·cate[2] /pɒnˈtɪfəkeɪt‖pɑn-/ *v* [IØ (*about, on*)] *usu. derog* to speak or write as if one's own judgment is the only correct one

pon·toon[1] /pɒnˈtuːn‖pɑn-/ *n* **1** any of a number of floating hollow metal containers or flat-bottomed boats fastened together side by side in a line to support a floating bridge (**pontoon bridge**) put quickly across a river **2** either of 2 boat-shaped supports put onto an aircraft to allow it to land on and take off from water **3** a type of low flat-bottomed boat

pontoon[2] (*AmE* **twenty-one**)— *n* **1** [U] a type of card game, usu. played for money **2** [U;(C)] (in this game) a winning combination of 2 cards that is worth 21 points

po·ny /ˈpəʊni/ *n* **1** a small horse **2** *esp. humor* a horse used for racing (esp. in the phr. **bet on the ponies**) **3** *BrE sl* £25 **4** *AmE sl* CRIB (5)

po·ny·tail /ˈpəʊniteɪl/ *n* a girl's hair tied high at the back of the head and falling like a horse's tail

pony-trek·king /ˈ·· ˌ··/ *n* [U] *BrE* a holiday activity or sport in which people ride across the country on ponies (PONY (1))

pooch /puːtʃ/ *n* [C;N] *sl usu. humor* a dog

poo·dle /ˈpuːdl/ *n* a type of dog with thick curling hair, usu. cut in special shapes —see picture at DOG[1]

poof /puːf, pʊf/ also **poof·ter** /ˈpuːftəʳ, ˈpʊf-/, **poove, pouf**— *n* [C; *you*+N] *BrE derog sl* **1** a male HOMOSEXUAL **2** *often also humor* a man whose behaviour or actions are weak, ineffective, or lacking in courage —**~y** *adj* [Wa1]

pooh /puː/ *interj* **1** "That is a very unpleasant smell" **2** "That is a statement, idea, suggestion, etc., for which I have no respect or which I do not approve of"

pooh-pooh /ˌ·ˈ·/ *v* [T1,(4)] *infml* to treat as not worthy of consideration

pool¹ /puːl/ *n* **1** a small area of still water in a hollow place, usu. naturally formed: *After the rain, there were little pools of water in the garden* **2** [(*of*)] a small amount of any liquid poured or dropped on a surface: *The wounded man was lying in a pool of blood* **3** a large container filled with water and built into the ground, used for swimming, growing water plants, etc.: *a swimming pool|"Where's Sarah?" "She's in the pool"* **4** a deeper part of a stream where the water hardly moves: *Fish hide in the depths of pools*

pool² *n* **1** [C9] a common supply of money, goods, workers, etc., which may be used by a number of people: *Our firm have a car pool, so if I need a car there's always one there* —see also TYPING POOL **2** [C] **a** the combined amount of money collected from and played for by all players in certain card games **b** a container holding this money **3** [U] any of various American BILLIARD games played usu. with 15 numbered balls on a table that has 6 pockets: *Are you ready to shoot pool?* (=to play pool) —compare SNOOKER **4** [C] a combination of business companies, esp. in order to fix prices of goods and remove competition

pool³ *v* [T1] to combine; share: *If we pool our ideas, we may be able to produce a really good plan.|None of us can afford it separately, so let's pool our money*

pool·room /ˈpuːlrʊm, -ruːm/ *n* a usu. public room in America, where POOL² (3) and games of chance are played for money

pools /puːlz/ also (*fml*) **football pools**— *n* [*the* + P] an arrangement (esp. in Britain) by which people risk (BET) small amounts of money on the results of certain football matches, and those who guess the results correctly (or nearly correctly) win large shares of the combined money

poop /puːp/ *n* **1** *tech* the back end of a ship **2** also **poop deck** /ˈ· ·/— the raised floor level at this end

pooped /puːpt/ also **pooped out** /ˌ· ˈ·/— *adj* [F] *AmE sl* very tired

poor /pʊəʳ/ *adj* **1** [Wa1;B; *the*+P] having very little money and therefore a low standard of living: *He was too poor to buy shoes for his family.|The poor are always with us.|This is a poor neighbourhood, where many people cannot get work* **2** [Wa1;B] less than is needed or expected; small in size or quantity: *We had a poor crop of beans this year* **3** [Wa1;B] *derog* much below the usual standard; low in quality: *The weather has been very poor this summer; we've had little sun* **4** [Wa1;B] (of the bodily system or its parts and their working) weak; not good: *He's still in poor health after his illness* **5** [Wa1;B] *derog* (of a person or his behaviour) not noble or generous: *He gets angry when he loses a game. He's a poor loser* **6** [Wa5;A] deserving or causing pity; unlucky: *The poor old man had lost both his sons in the war* **7** [Wa5;A] remembered with sadness because dead: *My poor father was a very clever man* **8** [Wa5;A] *usu. derog* not respected, because of lack of ability or character: *The poor fool has got himself into debt again* **9** [Wa5;A] *usu. polite or humor* of little worth; not good enough for others; humble: *In my poor opinion you're making a great mistake*

poor box /ˈ· ·/ *n* a box, esp. in a church, into which money to help (local) poor people can be put

poor·house /ˈpʊəhaʊs‖ˈpʊər-/ *n* **-houses** /ˌhaʊzɪ̈z/ **1** (in former times) a building provided by public money where poor people could live and be fed —compare WORKHOUSE **2 in the poorhouse** very poor

poor law /ˈ· ·/ *n* **1** [*the*+R] (in Britain in former times) a group of laws concerning help for poor people **2** [C] any of these laws

poor·ly¹ /ˈpʊəli‖ˈpʊərli/ *adv* **1** in a poor manner or condition; without enough money: *They lived poorly* **2** badly; not well: *poorly dressed|poorly paid|They did poorly in the examination* **3 think poorly of** to have a bad or low opinion of

poorly² *adj* [F] *esp. BrE* ill: *I'm feeling rather poorly today*

poorly off /ˌ·· ˈ·/ *adj* [F] **1** having very little money **2** [(*for*)] not well supplied (with): *We're poorly off for coal at the moment; we must order some more* —opposite **well-off**

poor·ness /ˈpʊənɪ̈s‖ˈpʊər-/ *n* [U9, esp. *of*] a low standard; lack of a desired quality: *the poorness of the quality of the materials* —compare POVERTY

poor re·la·tion /ˌ· ·ˈ··/ *n* a person or thing that is regarded as the lowest or least important one among comparable people or things: *Theatre musicians often consider themselves the poor relations of the musical profession*

poor-spir·it·ed /ˌ· ˈ···/ *adj derog* not brave; not daring to do anything —**~ly** *adv*

poor white /ˌ· ˈ·/ *n often derog* (esp. in the southern US) a white-skinned person who lives in very poor conditions among a society of mainly dark-skinned people

poove /puːv/ *n* [C; *you*+N] *BrE derog sl* POOF

pop¹ /pɒp‖pɑp/ *v* **-pp- 1** [T1;I∅] to (cause to) make a short sharp explosive sound: *The bottle stopper* (CORK) *popped when he pulled it out.|He blew the bag up and then popped it between his hands* **2** [T∅ (OFF, *at*); L9, esp. *at*] *infml* to fire: *He's popping at the rabbits in the field* **3** [L9] *infml* to spring (esp. in the phrs. **pop open/out**): *The child's eyes almost popped out of her head with excitement* **4** [L9] *infml* to move, go, come, enter, etc., suddenly, lightly, or unexpectedly: *I've just popped in to return your book.|I'm afraid she's just popped out for a few minutes.|Pop down to the shops and get a bottle of milk.|She's always popping in and out* **5** [X9] *infml* to put quickly and lightly: *He popped his head round the door.|He popped his coat on* **6** [T1 (*at*)] *infml* to ask (a question or questions) suddenly and directly **7** [X9, esp. *on*] *infml* to hit: *He popped him on the jaw* **8** [I∅ (UP)] (in cricket) (of a thrown (BOWLed) ball) to rise sharply and awkwardly from the ground **9** [I∅] *infml* (esp. in tenses with the *-ing* form) (of events) to be excitingly active **10** [T1] *BrE old infml* PAWN² (1) **11 pop the question (to)** *infml* to make an offer of marriage (**to**); PROPOSE (4) (to) —see also POP OFF, POP UP

pop² *n* **1** [C] a sound like that of a slight explosion: *When he opened the bottle it went pop* **2** [U] a sweet drink containing a harmless gas, usu. made to taste of a particular fruit or of GINGER **3** [U] *BrE old infml* a state of PAWN¹ (esp. in the phr. **in pop**)

pop³ *n AmE infml* **1** [C9;N] a (particular person's) father **2** [N] an old man

pop⁴ *n* [U] **1** modern popular music of a simple kind with a strong beat and not of lasting interest, esp. as favoured for a short time by younger people: *He likes pop; he doesn't care for older music.|a pop singer|pop music|a pop group* (=a group of people who sing and play pop music)|*a pop concert* **2 top of the pops** (being) the record of this type of music that is selling the most copies at a particular time —compare ROCK²

pop⁵ *abbrev. for:* **1** popularly **2** population

pop·a·dam, popadum /ˈpɒpədəm‖ˈpɑ-/ *n* PAPADUM

pop art /ˌ· ˈ·/ *n* [U] a type of modern painting or other art in which objects from everyday life, such as advertisements, household articles, popular newspapers, etc., are represented, rather than those subjects that are usually treated in art

pop·corn /ˈpɒpkɔːn‖ˈpɑpkɔrn/ *n* [U] grains of corn that have been swollen and burst by heat, usu. eaten warm with salt and butter

pope /pəʊp/ *n* [C;A] (*often cap.*) the head of the ROMAN CATHOLIC church: *the popes of the 12th century|the new Pope|Pope John*

pop·e·ry /ˈpəʊpəri/ *n* [U] *derog* the teachings and forms of worship of the ROMAN CATHOLIC church

pop-eyed /ˌ· ˈ·/ *adj infml* having the eyes wide open, as with surprise, excitement, etc.

pop·gun /ˈpɒpgʌn‖ˈpɑp-/ *n* a toy gun that fires small objects (esp. CORK*s* (2)) with a loud noise

pop·in·jay /ˈpɒpɨ̣ndʒeɪ‖ˈpɑ-/ *n* [C; *you*+N] *derog old use* a showily-dressed young man who is full of self-admiration

pop·ish /ˈpəʊpɪʃ/ *adj derog* ROMAN CATHOLIC —**~ly** *adv* —**~ness** *n* [U]

pop·lar /ˈpɒpləʳ‖ˈpɑp-/ *n* **1** [C] any of several types of very tall straight thin tree **2** [U] the wood of this, which is a kind of SOFTWOOD

pop·lin /ˈpɒplɨ̣n‖ˈpɑp-/ *n* [U] a type of strong shiny cotton cloth used esp. for making shirts: *a poplin shirt*

pop off *v adv* [I∅] *infml* **1** to go away suddenly **2** to die

pop·pa /ˈpɒpə‖ˈpɑpə/ *n* [C9;N] *AmE infml* PAPA

pop·per /ˈpɒpəʳ‖ˈpɑ-/ *n esp. BrE* either of 2 small, usu. round pieces of metal or plastic that can be pressed together, used for fastening garments —compare PRESS-STUD

pop·pet /ˈpɒpɨ̣t‖ˈpɑ-/ *n* [C;N] *BrE infml* a child or animal that one loves, or that pleases one: *Where's little Jean? Come here, poppet.|Look at that little dog. Isn't he a poppet!*

pop·ping crease /ˈ·· ·/ also **batting crease**— *n* (in cricket) a line drawn on the ground, on which the hitter (BATSMAN) stands ready to hit the ball

pop·py /ˈpɒpi‖ˈpɑpi/ *n* any of several types of plant that have a milky juice in the stems and showy flowers in bright colours, esp. red

pop·py·cock /ˈpɒpikɒk‖ˈpɑpikɑk/ *n* [U] foolish nonsense

pop·shop /ˈpɒpʃɒp‖ˈpɑpʃɑp/ *n BrE sl* PAWNshop

pop·sy /ˈpɒpsi‖ˈpɑ-/ *n* [C9;(N)] *sl often derog* a (particular person's) girl friend

pop·u·lace /ˈpɒpjʊləs‖ˈpɑpjə-/ *n* [*the*+GU] *fml* all the common people of a country, esp. as being without social position, wealth, deep political understanding, etc.

pop·u·lar /ˈpɒpjʊləʳ‖ˈpɑpjə-/ *adj* **1** [B] favoured by many people: *a popular song|Beards are popular among young men* **2** [B] generally admired by great numbers of people: *He's a good politician but he isn't popular* **3** [B (*with*)] well liked, esp. by people one meets in daily life: *Tom is popular with girls. He's so amusing* **4** [B] general; common; widespread: *"Mary" is a very popular name for a girl* **5** [A] *sometimes derog* suited to the understanding, liking, or needs of the general public: *popular science|Some popular newspapers give too much attention to unimportant matters* **6** [Wa5;A] *fml* of or for the general public: *popular opinion|the popular vote* **7** [A;(B)] *euph* (of prices) cheap

pop·u·lar·i·ty /ˌpɒpjʊˈlærɨ̣ti‖ˌpɑpjə-/ *n* [U] the quality or state of being well liked, favoured, or admired

pop·u·lar·ize, -ise /ˈpɒpjʊləraɪz‖ˈpɑpjə-/ *v* [T1] **1** to make (something difficult) easily understandable to ordinary people by a simple explanation **2** to make (something new) generally known and used: *The company are trying to popularize their new soap powder* **3** to cause to be well liked —**-ization** /ˌpɒpjʊləraɪˈzeɪʃən‖ˌpɑpjələrə-/ *n* [U;C]

pop·u·lar·ly /ˈpɒpjʊləli‖ˈpɑpjələrli/ *adv* **1** generally; by most people: *His name is Robert, but he's popularly known as Bob* **2** *euph* cheaply: *a popularly-*PRICE*d car*

pop·u·late /ˈpɒpjʊleɪt‖ˈpɑpjə-/ *v* [T1] **1** [Wv5; *often pass.*] (of a group) to live in (a particular area): *This side of the island is populated mainly by fishermen.|Large numbers of snakes populate these woods.|a thickly-populated area* **2** to settle in and fill up (an area), esp. with people: *The new land was quickly populated by the new settlers from abroad* **3** to put people to settle in (an area): *It may be possible to populate stretches of desert land*

pop·u·la·tion /ˌpɒpjʊˈleɪʃən‖ˌpɑpjə-/ *n* **1** [U;(C): (*of*)] the number of people (or animals) living in a particular area, country, etc.: *What was the population of Europe in 1900?* **2** [GU] the people living in an area: *The population in these villages has to get its water from wells* **3** [S9;(C9)] a particular described group or kind of people (or animals) living in a particular place: *the elephant population of Kenya*

pop·u·lis·m /ˈpɒpjʊlɪzəm‖ˈpɑpjə-/ *n* [U] the beliefs of POPULIST*s*

pop·u·list /ˈpɒpjʊlɨ̣st‖ˈpɑpjə-/ *n* **1** (*often cap.*) (esp. in the US) a member of a political party that claims to represent ordinary people **2** *esp. AmE* a person who believes in the good qualities of ordinary people, esp. in political matters

pop·u·lous /ˈpɒpjʊləs‖ˈpɑpjə-/ *adj* (of a place) having a large population, esp. when compared with size —**~ness** *n* [U]

pop up *v adv* [I∅] to happen suddenly; arise; CROP UP (1)

porce·lain /ˈpɔːslɨ̣n‖ˈporsəlɨ̣n/ *n* [U] **1** thin shiny material of very fine quality, of which cups, dishes, etc., may be made, and which is produced by baking a clay mixture **2** articles made of this, considered as a group

porch /pɔːtʃ‖portʃ/ *n* **1** a built-out roofed entrance to a house or church —see picture at CHURCH[1] **2** *AmE* VERANDA

por·cine /ˈpɔːsaɪn‖ˈpor-/ *adj tech or derog* of or like a pig or pigs

por·cu·pine /ˈpɔːkjʊpaɪn‖ˈporkjə-/ *n* a type of quite small short-legged animal that has very long stiff prickles (QUILL*s*) all over its back and sides. It is larger than a HEDGEHOG —see picture at MAMMAL

pore /pɔːʳ‖por/ *n* a very small opening (esp. in the skin) through which liquids (esp. SWEAT[2] (1)) may pass

pore o·ver *v prep* [T1] to study or give close attention to (usu. something written or printed)

pork /pɔːk‖pork/ *n* [U] meat from pigs —compare BACON, HAM; see MEAT (USAGE)

pork butch·er /ˈ· ˌ··/ *n BrE* a dealer in meat who sells (only) PORK or products made from it, such as SAUSAGE*s*

pork·er /ˈpɔːkəʳ‖ˈpor-/ *n* **1** a young pig, made specially fat for food **2** *humor* a pig

pork pie /ˌ· ˈ·/ *n* [C;(U)] (esp. in Britain) a small usu. round baked pastry case containing small pieces of PORK mixed with other substances

pork·pie hat /ˌ·· ˈ·/ *n* a type of man's hat with a flat round top

pork·y /ˈpɔːki‖ˈporki/ *adj* [Wa1] *BrE infml* (esp. of a person) fat

porn /ˈpɔːn‖ˈporn/ *n* [U] *infml esp. BrE* PORNOGRAPHY

por·nog·ra·phy /pɔːˈnɒgrəfi‖porˈnɑg-/ *n* [U] **1** the treatment of sexual subjects in pictures or writing in a way that is meant to cause sexual excitement

2 books, photographs, films, etc., containing this —**-pher** *n* —**-phic** /ˌpɔːnəˈɡræfɪk‖ˌpɔr-/ *adj* —**-phically** /ˌpɔːnəˈɡræfɪkəli‖ˌpɔr-/ *adv* [Wa4]

po·ros·i·ty /pɔːˈrɒsəti‖poˈrɑ-, pə-/ *n* [U;(S)] *fml or tech* POROUSness

po·rous /ˈpɔːrəs‖ˈpo-/ *adj* **1** allowing liquid to pass slowly through: *porous soil|This clay pot is porous* **2** *tech* having or full of PORE*s*: *porous skin* —**~ness** *n* [U]

por·phy·ry /ˈpɔːfəri‖ˈpɔr-/ *n* [U] a hard bluish-red type of rock with large red and white pieces (CRYSTAL*s*) set in it, often polished and made into ornaments

por·poise /ˈpɔːpəs‖ˈpɔr-/ *n* a type of large fishlike sea animal that swims about in groups —compare DOLPHIN and see picture at SEA

por·ridge /ˈpɒrɪdʒ‖ˈpɑ-, ˈpɔ-/ *n* [U] **1** a type of soft breakfast food made by boiling crushed grain (OATMEAL) in milk or water **2** *BrE sl* a period of time spent in prison (esp. in the phr. **do porridge**)

por·rin·ger /ˈpɒrəndʒəʳ‖ˈpɑ-, ˈpɔ-/ *n* a type of small wide bowl (esp. for a child) from which soft food (such as PORRIDGE) is eaten

port¹ /pɔːt‖port/ *n* **1** [C;U] (a) harbour: *There is only one port along this rocky coast.|We must reach port by evening* **2** [C] (*sometimes cap. as part of name*) a town with a harbour, on a sea or river coast: *The holiday ship will call at several ports.|Port Said* **3 Any port in a storm** Any means of escape from trouble must be accepted —see also AIRPORT, FREE PORT, PORT OF CALL

port² *n* **1** an opening in the side of a ship for loading and unloading goods **2** a small opening in an armoured vehicle, or (in former times) in the wall of a fort, through which a gun may be pointed **3** PORTHOLE (1)

port³ *n* **at the port** (of a long gun (RIFLE)) held in a sloping position across the body

port⁴ *v* **port arms** (*usu. imper.*) (of a soldier) to hold a long gun (RIFLE) in a sloping position across the body, with the barrel towards the left shoulder, ready to be looked at for cleanness by an officer

port⁵ *n* [R] the left side of a ship or aircraft as one faces forward: *The damaged ship was leaning over to port.|Our seats in the aircraft were on the port side* —compare STARBOARD

port⁶ *n* [U] strong usu. sweet often dark red Portuguese wine usu. drunk after a meal —compare SHERRY

por·ta·ble /ˈpɔːtəbəl‖ˈpor-/ *adj* that can be (easily) carried or moved; quite small and light: *a portable television* —**-bility** /ˌpɔːtəˈbɪləti‖ˌpor-/ *n* [U]

port·age /ˈpɔːtɪdʒ‖ˈpor-/ *n* **1** [C;U] an act or the action of carrying goods, esp. across a stretch of land from one river or lake to another **2** [C] a place where this is done **3** [S;U] the cost of doing this

por·tal /ˈpɔːtl‖ˈportl/ *n* a (very grand) door or entrance to a building

por·tals /ˈpɔːtlz‖ˈportlz/ *n* [P9, esp. *of*] *fml or lit* **1** a very grand entrance to a building, esp. considered as representing the organization, company, etc., that uses that building: *No one can pass through the portals of the National Art Collection without becoming a more educated person* **2** a beginning; THRESHOLD (2): *On the day of his marriage he felt he was standing at the portals of happiness*

port·cul·lis /pɔːtˈkʌləs‖port-/ *n* (in old castles, forts, etc.) a strong gatelike framework of bars with points at the bottom, hung above an entrance and lowered as a protection against attack —see picture at CASTLE¹

porte co·chere /ˌpɔːt kɒˈʃeəʳ‖ˌport kəʊ- (*Fr* pɔrt kɔʃɛr)/ *n* **portes cocheres** (*same pronunciation*) *Fr* a covered entrance to a house from a road, which gives people shelter when they are moving between a vehicle and the building

por·tend /pɔːˈtend‖por-/ *v* [T1] *esp. fml* to be a sign or warning of (a future undesirable event)

por·tent /ˈpɔːtent‖ˈpor-/ *n* **1** [C (*of*)] a (wonderful or terrible) sign or warning, esp. of something strange or undesirable: *Dark clouds are gathering, portents of war* **2** [U] *lit* meaning, esp. with regard to the future: *of good portent* —compare OMEN

por·ten·tous /pɔːˈtentəs‖por-/ *adj* **1** that warns or FORETELL*s* (of evil happenings); threatening —compare OMINOUS **2** causing respect and fear by one's importance **3** *derog* solemnly self-important **4** most unusual; hardly able to be believed —**~ly** *adv*

por·ter¹ /ˈpɔːtəʳ‖ˈpor-/ *n esp. BrE* a man in charge of the entrance to a hotel, school, hospital, etc. —compare DOORMAN

porter² *n* **1** a person employed to carry travellers' bags at railway stations, airports, etc. **2** a person employed to carry loads at markets **3** *AmE* an attendant employed in a sleeping-carriage in a train

porter³ *n* [U] (esp. in former times) a type of dark brown bitter beer

por·ter·age /ˈpɔːtərɪdʒ‖ˈpor-/ *n* **1** [U] the work of a PORTER² (1,2) **2** [S;U] the charge made for this

por·ter·house /ˈpɔːtəhaʊs‖ˈportər-/ also **porterhouse steak** /ˌ··· ˈ·/— *n* [C;U] a large thick piece of meat from the best part of the flesh of cattle (BEEF), enough for one person

porter's lodge /ˌ·· ˈ·/ *n esp. BrE* a small room for the PORTER¹ at the entrance to a school, hospital, etc.

port·fo·li·o /pɔːtˈfəʊliəʊ‖port-/ *n* **-lios** **1** a large flat case like a very large book cover, for carrying drawings, business papers, etc. **2** a collection of drawings or other papers (such as would be) contained in this **3** the office and duties of a (particular) minister of state: *the portfolio of foreign affairs* **4** the list of shares in businesses owned by a person or a company

port·hole /ˈpɔːthəʊl‖ˈport-/ *n* **1** also **port**— a small usu. circular window or opening in a ship for light or air —see picture at FREIGHTER **2** any of the row of fixed windows along the side of an aircraft

por·ti·co /ˈpɔːtɪkəʊ‖ˈpor-/ *n* **-coes** *or* **-cos** a grand entrance to a building, consisting of a roof supported by one or 2 rows of pillars

por·tion /ˈpɔːʃən‖ˈpor-/ *n* **1** [C (*of*)] a part separated or cut off: *passengers travelling in the front portion of the train* **2** [C (*of*)] a share of something that is divided among 2 or more people: *A portion of the blame for the accident must be borne by the driver* **3** [C (*of*)] a quantity of food for one person as served in a restaurant: *He was hungry and ordered 2 portions of fish* **4** [S9, esp. *of*] *fml & esp. lit* a person's fate; LOT² (9)

portion out *v adv* [T1 (*among, between*)] to share (something)

port·land ce·ment /ˌpɔːtlənd səˈment‖ˌport-/ *n* [U] (*usu. cap.* P) a type of yellowish cement much used as a building material

portland stone /ˌ·· ˈ·/ *n* [U] (*usu. cap.* P) a type of yellowish-white stone (LIMESTONE) used in building

port·ly /ˈpɔːtli‖ˈpor-/ *adj* [Wa2] *euph or humor* (of a grown-up person, often rather old) round and fat: *the portly old general* —**-liness** *n* [U]

port·man·teau /pɔːtˈmæntəʊ‖port-/ *n* **-teaus** *or* **-teaux** /təʊz/ a type of large travelling case for clothes, esp. one that opens out in the middle into 2 equal parts

portmanteau word /ˌ·ˈ·· ˌ·/ *n* an invented word

that combines the meaning and sound of 2 words; BLEND: MOTEL *is a portmanteau word, made up from "motor" and "hotel"*

port of call /ˌ· · ˈ·/ *n* **1** a port where a ship stops (regularly) for travellers, supplies, repairs, etc. **2** *infml* **a** a place where one stops during a journey **b** a place one habitually visits

por·trait /ˈpɔːtrɨt‖ˈpor-/ *n* [(*of*)] **1** a painting, drawing, or photograph of a real person (or animal) **2** a lifelike description in words: *He called his book about modern Europe "A Portrait of Europe"*

por·trait·ist /ˈpɔːtrɨtɨst‖ˈpor-/ *n* a person who makes PORTRAITs (esp. 1)

por·trai·ture /ˈpɔːtrɨtʃəʳ‖ˈpor-/ *n* [U] **1** the art of making PORTRAITs (esp. 1) **2** PORTRAITs (1)

por·tray /pɔːˈtreɪ‖por-/ *v* **1** [T1] to be or make a representation of (someone or something) in painting, drawing, etc. **2** [X9] to represent (someone or something) in painting, in a book, etc., according to one's own ideas or so as to produce a certain effect: *In his book, the writer portrays the king as a cruel man* **3** [T1] to describe in words in a lifelike way **4** [T1] to act the part of (a particular character) in a play

por·tray·al /pɔːˈtreɪəl‖por-/ *n* **1** [U (*of*)] the act of PORTRAYing **2** [C (*of*)] a representation or description

Por·tu·guese /ˌpɔːtʃʊˈgiːz‖ˌportʃə-/ *adj* **1** of Portugal or its people: *Portuguese food* **2** of the language of Portugal, Brazil, etc.: *Portuguese tenses*

Portuguese man-of-war /ˌ··· · · ˈ·/ *n* a type of large poisonous sea animal (JELLYFISH) with long beautiful threadlike parts that hang beneath it

pose¹ /pəʊz/ *v* **1** [IØ (*for*); T1] to (cause to) sit or stand in a particular effective position, esp. for a photograph, painting, etc.: *She was employed by the art school to pose for student artists* **2** [D1 (*to*); T1] to state; offer for consideration: *You've posed us an awkward question* **3** [D1 (*for*); T1] to set; bring into being (esp. in the phr. **pose a problem/problems**) **4** [IØ] *derog* to behave or speak unnaturally in an effort to make people notice or admire one

pose² *n* **1** a position of the body, esp. as taken up to produce an effect in art: *They found the dead man seated in a strange pose* **2** *derog* a way of behaving which is pretended in order to produce an effect

pose as *v prep* [L1;(7)] to pretend to be

pos·er /ˈpəʊzəʳ/ *n infml* **1** a hard or awkward question **2** a matter that is awkward to deal with **3** a person who POSEs¹ (1) for a painter or photographer; artist's MODEL **4** POSEUR

po·seur /pəʊˈzɜːʳ/ *n Fr derog* a person who behaves unnaturally in order to produce an effect —compare POSE² (2)

posh /pɒʃ‖pɑʃ/ *adj* [Wa2] *infml* **1** *usu. apprec* very fine; splendid: *a posh new car|We stayed at a posh hotel.|You're looking very posh in your new coat* **2** *sometimes derog* fashionable; for people of high social rank: *a posh address|They live in a posh part of town*

pos·it /ˈpɒzɨt‖ˈpɑ-/ *v* [T1,5] *fml* to lay down for the purpose of argument; POSTULATE

po·si·tion¹ /pəˈzɪʃən/ *n* **1** [C] the place where someone or something is or stands, esp. in relation to other objects, places, etc.: *The house's position on the hill gives it a wonderful view of the coast.|Can you find our position on this map?|We will attack the enemy's positions* (=places where they have placed soldiers and guns) **2** [U] **a** the place where someone or something is (in the phr. **in position**): *Let's leave the* CHESS *pieces in position and finish the game tomorrow* **b** the place where someone or something is supposed to be; the proper place (in the phrs. **out of/in(to) position**): *One of the chairs is out of position. Put it back in position* **3** [U] the place of advantage in a struggle (in the phrs. **manoeuvre/jockey for position**) **4** [C] the way or manner in which someone or something is placed or moves, stands, sits, etc.: *He was working in a most uncomfortable position under the car* **5** [C *usu. sing.*] a condition or state, esp. in relation to that of someone or something else: *By telling her that, you've put me in a very difficult position.|I'd like to help you, but I'm afraid I'm not in a position to do so* (=am not able to do so) **6** [C (*in*)] a particular place or rank in a group: *top position in the class* **7** [U] high rank in society, government, or business **8** [C] a job; employment: *He's got a good position with an oil company* —see JOB (USAGE) **9** [C] an opinion or judgment on a matter: *He takes the position that what his sister does is no concern of his*

position² *v* **1** [X9;(T1)] to put in the proper POSITION¹ (2b): *Please position the chairs for the committee meeting* **2** [X9] to put in the stated POSITION¹ (1): *He positioned the cup carefully on the edge of the shelf*

po·si·tion·al /pəˈzɪʃənəl/ *adj* [Wa5] **1** [B] dependent on POSITION¹ (1) **2** [A;(B)] (in sports) of or concerning the position that a player takes up on the field in relation to the other players and to the way the game is being played: *good positional play|He has fine positional sense*

pos·i·tive¹ /ˈpɒzɨtɪv‖ˈpɑ-/ *adj* **1** [B] (of a statement) direct: *a positive refusal* **2** [B] certain; beyond any doubt: *They had to examine the dead fish before they had a positive answer as to what killed them* **3** [F (*of*), F5a] (of people) sure; having no doubt about something: *I'm positive that that's the man I saw yesterday. I'm positive of it.|"Are you sure?" "Positive"* (=yes, I am sure) **4** [Wa5;A] *infml* (*used for giving force to a noun*) complete; thorough; real: *It was a positive delight to hear her sing so beautifully* **5** [B] (of people or their behaviour) boldly certain of oneself and one's opinions **6** [Wa5;A] actual; actively noticeable: *The doctor told the nurse to call him if there was a positive change for the worse* (=not if the sick person simply remains in the same condition) **7** [B] (of medical tests) showing signs of disease **8** [B] *often apprec* effective; actually helpful: *It's no use just telling me to do it; give me positive advice as to how to do it.|positive thinking* **9** [Wa5;A] real; concerned only with facts rather than being something formed in the mind **10** [Wa5;B] (in grammar) of the simple form of an adjective or adverb, which expresses no COMPARISON: *"Good" is the positive form of the adjective; "better" and "best" are not* —compare COMPARATIVE, SUPERLATIVE **11** [Wa5;B] (in MATHEMATICS) **a** (of a number or quantity) greater than zero: *12 is a positive amount* **b** concerning such a quantity: *The positive sign is +* **12** [Wa5;B] (of or in electricity) of the type that is based on PROTONs and is produced by rubbing glass with silk **13** [Wa5;B] (of a photograph) having light and shadow as they are in nature, not the other way around; DEVELOPed (3) **14** [Wa5;B] *med* (of blood) having the RH FACTOR **15 proof positive** proof which is certain beyond any doubt —compare NEGATIVE

positive² *n* **1** (in grammar) the POSITIVE¹ (10) degree or form of an adjective or adverb: *The positive of "prettiest" is "pretty"* **2** a POSITIVE¹ (13) photograph **3** (in MATHEMATICS) a quantity greater than zero **4** *fml* something that is clearly true or offers proof that something is true —compare NEGATIVE

pos·i·tive·ly /ˈpɒzɨtɪvli‖ˈpɑ-/ *adv* **1** in a POSITIVE

(2,3,5) way, esp. with or as if with certainty: *He said quite positively that he would come, and we were all surprised when he didn't* **2** *infml* (used for adding force to an expression) really; indeed: *This food is positively uneatable/wonderful!|He ran—he positively raced—up the stairs* —compare POSITIVE[1] (4) **3** *AmE* (*as an answer*) Yes, indeed!: *"Can you really do it?" "Positively!"* **4** in a POSITIVE[1] (12) way (esp. in the phr. **positively charged**)

pos·i·tive·ness /ˈpɒzətɪvnəs‖ˈpɑ-/ *n* [U] certainty; CONFIDENCE (2)

positive pole /ˌ··· ˈ·/ *n* **1** (of a MAGNET) the end which turns naturally towards the earth **2** ANODE

pos·i·tiv·is·m /ˈpɒzətɪvɪzəm‖ˈpɑ-/ *n* [U] the system of thought (PHILOSOPHY (1)) based on real facts that can be experienced rather than on ideas formed in the mind —**-ist** *n*

pos·i·tron /ˈpɒzətrɒn‖ˈpɑzətrɑn/ *n* a very small piece (PARTICLE) of electricity that is like an ELECTRON but is POSITIVELY (4) charged

poss. /pɒs‖pɑs/ **1** *abbrev. for:* (*BrE infml*) possible (in the phr. **if poss.**): *Do it by Monday if poss.* **2** *written abbrev. for:* POSSESSIVE —compare PASS.

pos·se /ˈpɒsi‖ˈpɑsi/ *n* [(*of*)] **1** (in the US) a group of men gathered together by a local law officer (SHERIFF) to help find a criminal, keep order, etc. **2** *infml* a (large) group of people, often with a common purpose

pos·sess /pəˈzes/ *v* [Wv6;T1] **1** to own; have (as belonging to one, or as a quality): *He possesses 2 cars.|He never possessed much money, but he always possessed good health* **2** [*often pass.*] (of a feeling or idea) to influence (someone) so completely as to control or direct actions: *Fear possessed him and prevented him from moving.|What possessed you to act so strangely?* (=caused you . . .) **3** [*often pass.*] (of an evil spirit or the devil) to enter into and become master of (someone)

pos·sessed /pəˈzest/ *adj* **1** [B] wildly mad, (as if) controlled by an evil spirit: *She must have been possessed, to attack her own mother* **2** [Wa5;F+*of*] *fml or lit* (in a state of) having: *The family is possessed of a large fortune* —see also SELF-POSSESSED

pos·ses·sion /pəˈzeʃən/ *n* **1** [U (*of*)] ownership: *Does the possession of wealth bring happiness?|When his father died, he came into possession of a number of local farms* **2** [U (*of*)] *esp. law* actual control and use: *We've bought the house, but we can't get possession of it before July* **3** [C *often pl.*] a piece of personal property: *The child's favourite possession was a little wooden dog* **4** [C] a (foreign) country controlled or governed by another **5** [U] the condition of being under or as if under the control of an evil spirit **6 in possession a** having or controlling a place or thing, esp. so that someone else is prevented from doing so: *Wales can't get any points while the England players are in possession* (=have the ball) **b** *often fml* having, controlling, keeping, or living in (something): *He was found in possession of dangerous drugs* **7 in someone's possession/in the possession of someone** owned, held, kept, or controlled by someone: *stolen goods found in his possession|according to the facts in my possession* **8 take possession (of)** also (*fml*) **enter into possession (of) a** to begin to have the (lawful) use of (esp. a house) **b** to seize (something): *The soldiers took possession of the enemy's fort* —see also IN POSSESSION **9 Possession is nine tenths** (*BrE* also **nine points**) **of the law** A person who actually possesses a thing is in a better position to keep it than someone else who may have a more just claim to own it

pos·ses·sive[1] /pəˈzesɪv/ *adj* **1** *derog* **a** unwilling to share one's own things with other people **b** showing a strong desire to receive and control the full attention of someone else **2** [Wa5] (in grammar) of or being a (form of a) word that shows ownership or connection: *"My" and "its" are possessive adjectives* —compare GENITIVE —**~ly** *adv* —**~ness** *n* [U]

possessive[2] *n* **1** a POSSESSIVE[1] (2) word or form: *"Hers" is a possessive. It is the possessive of "she"* **2** the CASE[1] (8) that includes all these words

pos·ses·sor /pəˈzesəʳ/ *n* [(*the*) *usu. sing.*] an owner: *He is the possessor of a fine singing voice*

pos·set /ˈpɒsət‖ˈpɑ-/ *n* a type of drink made from warm milk mixed with wine or beer, taken in former times to cure colds

pos·si·bil·i·ty /ˌpɒsəˈbɪləti‖ˌpɑ-/ *n* **1** [U (*of*)] the state or fact of being possible: *The possibility of man's travelling to the moon has now been proved* **2** [U;S:(5, *of*)] a (degree of) likelihood: *Is there any possibility that you'll be able to come tomorrow?* **3** [C] something that is possible: *The general would not accept that defeat was a possibility* **4** [C *often pl.*] power of developing, growing, or being used or useful in the future: *The house is in bad condition, but it has possibilities if it's properly repaired* **5** [C] *infml* a suitable person or thing: *Is Jane a possibility as a wife for Richard?*

pos·si·ble[1] /ˈpɒsəbəl‖ˈpɑ-/ *adj* **1** that can exist, happen, or be done: *It isn't possible to divide a 5-inch stick into 3 parts each 2 inches long.|I'll do everything possible to help you. I'll help you if possible* (=if it is possible).*|Be as kind to her as possible* **2** that may or may not be, happen, or be expected: *It is possible but not probable that I shall go there next week* **3** acceptable; suitable: *one of many possible answers*

possible[2] *n* **1** [*the*+U] that which can be or can be done: *Politics has been called the art of the possible* **2** [C] a person who or thing that might be suitable —compare PROBABLE

pos·si·bly /ˈpɒsəbli‖ˈpɑ-/ *adv* **1** in accordance with what is POSSIBLE[1] (1): *I'll do all I possibly can.|You can't possibly walk 20 miles in an hour* **2** perhaps: *He's possibly the most selfish man in town.|"Will you come with us tomorrow?" "Possibly"*

pos·sum /ˈpɒsəm‖ˈpɑ-/ *n* [Wn1] **1** *AmE* OPOSSUM **2 play possum** *infml* to pretend to be asleep or inattentive in order to avoid notice or deceive someone

post[1] /pəʊst/ *n* **1** [C] (*often in comb.*) a strong thick upright pole or bar made of wood, metal, etc., fixed into the ground or some other base esp. as a support: *The fence was made of posts driven into the ground.|a gatepost|a signpost* **2** [*the*+R] the starting or finishing place in a race, esp. a horse race (often in the phrs. **finishing post**, **starting post**, **winning post**): *John won the race; he was first past the post.|My horse got beaten at the post* **3** [C] *infml* GOALPOST

post[2] *v* **1** [T1 (UP)] to make public or show by fixing to a wall, board, post, etc.: *The names of the members of the team will be posted up today* **2** [T1 (OVER)] to cover (a wall, board, etc.) with public notices **3** [T1 (*as*); X7 *usu. pass.*] to make known (as being) by putting up a notice: *The ship was posted missing*

post[3] *n* **1** [U] *AmE* usu. **mail**— the official system for carrying letters, parcels, etc., from the sender to the receiver: *He sent the parcel by post* **2** [(*the*) S] *AmE* usu. **mail**— a single official collection or delivery of letters, parcels, etc., by this means: *Has the morning post arrived?* **3** [S9] *AmE* usu. **mail**— all the letters, parcels, etc., dealt with by this means: *There's always a very large post at Christmas* **4** [U] also (*esp. AmE*) **mail**— letters, parcels, etc.:

Has any post come for me this morning? **5** [*the*+R] *esp. BrE* an official place, box, etc., where stamped letters are left for sending: *I've just taken her birthday card down to the post* —compare PILLAR-BOX, POSTBOX, POST OFFICE **6** [C] (in former times) any of a number of regular stopping places along a main road where travellers or messengers could rest, change horses, etc., and where letters could be passed to a fresh rider **7 by return of post** (*AmE* **by return mail**)— *BrE* by the next POST[3] (2) back

post[4] *v* **1** [T1 (OFF)] *AmE* usu. **mail**— to take (a letter, parcel, etc.) to a post office or put into a collection box for sending: *I must post off all my Christmas cards this week.|Please post this letter for me* **2** [D1 (*to*); T1] *AmE* usu. **mail**— to send (a letter, parcel, etc.) by post: *Did you post John the book?* **3** [L9] (in former times) to travel using changes of horses at POSTS[3] (6) along the road **4 keep someone posted** to continue to give someone all the latest news about something

post[5] *n* **1** [C] a small distant fort, camp, etc., esp. on a border or in a desert, at which a body of soldiers is kept **2** [C] also **trading post**— a small place for buying and selling things, started by settlers in a wild lonely part of a country, or in a foreign land **3** [C] a special place of duty, esp. on guard or on watch: *All workers must be at their posts by half past 8* **4** [C] a job: *She has a post as a cook* —see JOB (USAGE) **5** [C9] either of 2 sets of notes played at sunset on a hornlike instrument (BUGLE), esp. to call soldiers to their camp (in the phrs. **first post, last post**) —compare TAPS
USAGE This word is often used with a *cap.* in the name of a newspaper: *The Morning* **Post**.

post[6] *v* **1** [X9;(T1)] to place (soldiers or other men) on duty in a special place, esp. as a guard: *Policemen were posted all round the house.|Has the guard been posted?* **2** [X9, esp. *to*; (T1): *usu. pass.*] *esp. BrE* to send or appoint (someone) to a particular army group, a place or duty with a firm, etc.: *Smith has been posted to Hong Kong*

post- /ˈpəʊst, ˈpɒst‖ˈpəʊst, ˈpɑst/ *prefix* later than; after: POSTWAR

post·age /ˈpəʊstɪdʒ/ *n* [U;(S)] the charge for carrying a letter, parcel, etc., by post

postage stamp /ˈ·· ·/ *n* **1** STAMP **2** *infml* a very small area: *She's such a good pilot that she can land her plane on a postage stamp!*

post·al /ˈpəʊstl/ *adj* [Wa5;A] **1** connected with the public letter service: *Postal charges have increased again* **2** sent by post: *a postal vote*

postal or·der /ˈ·· ˌ··/ (*AmE* **money order**)— *n BrE* a small piece of paper that can be bought from a post office, and is sent by post to someone who can take it to a post office and exchange it for a stated amount of money

post·bag /ˈpəʊstbæg/ *n esp. BrE* **1** [S] *infml* all the letters received by someone at one particular time —compare POST[3] (3) **2** [C] a postman's bag for carrying letters; MAILBAG

post·box /ˈpəʊstbɒks‖-bɑks/ *n esp. BrE* **1** an official metal box, often set into a wall, into which letters are put for sending by post **2** PILLAR-BOX —compare MAILBOX, **mail** DROP[1] (5)

post·card /ˈpəʊstkɑːd‖-kɑrd/ *n* **1** a card of a fixed size on which a message may be written and sent by post **2** also (*fml*) **picture postcard**— a card like this with a picture or photograph on one side

post chaise /ˌ· ˈ·/ *n* (in former times) a carriage and horses hired at a POST[3] (6) or inn

post·code /ˈpəʊstkəʊd/ (*AmE* **zip code**)— *n BrE* a group of letters and numbers (in Britain) or numbers only (in the US) that means a particular part of a town and can be added to the address on letters or parcels so that they may be delivered more quickly

post·date /ˌpəʊstˈdeɪt/ *v* [T1] **1** [Wv5] to write on (a letter, cheque, etc.) a date later than the date of writing **2** to give a later date to (an event) than the actual date of happening

post·er /ˈpəʊstəʳ/ *n* a large printed notice or (coloured) drawing put up in a public place

poste res·tante /ˌpəʊst ˈrestɒnt‖-resˈtɑːnt/ (*AmE* **general delivery**)— *n* [U] *BrE* a post office department to which letters for a traveller may be sent and where they will be kept until the person collects them

pos·te·ri·or[1] /pɒˈstɪərɪəʳ‖pɑ-/ *adj* [Wa5] **1** [A] *fml* later in time or order —opposite **prior** **2** [F+*to*] *fml* later (than); after **3** [A] (in BIOLOGY) placed behind or at the back —opposite **anterior**

posterior[2] *n humor* the part of the body a person sits on; BUTTOCKS

pos·ter·i·ty /pɒˈsterəti‖pɑ-/ *n* **1** [U] people who will be born and live after one's own time **2** [GU9] *lit* a person's descendants

pos·tern /ˈpɒstən‖ˈpəʊstərn/ *n lit* a small or private gate or door, usu. at the back

poster paint /ˈ·· ·/ also **poster col·our** /ˈ·· ˌ··/— *n* [U;C] a type of artist's paint, usu. in very bright colours

post-free /ˌ· ˈ·◂/ also (*esp. AmE*) **postpaid**— *adj, adv esp. BrE* without any (further) charge to the sender for posting: *You can have it for £5, or £6 post-free*

post·grad·u·ate /ˌpəʊstˈgrædjʊət‖-ˈgrædʒʊət/ also (*esp. AmE*) **graduate** —*n, adj* [Wa5] (a person doing studies that are) done at a university after one has received one's first degree

post·haste /ˌpəʊstˈheɪst/ *adv lit* at very great speed; in a great hurry

post horn /ˈ· ·/ *n* (in former times) a horn blown by a servant in a carriage as a signal or warning

post·hu·mous /ˈpɒstjʊməs‖ˈpɑstʃə-/ *adj* [Wa5] **1** coming (soon) after one's death: *posthumous fame* **2** (of a book, musical work, etc.) printed and made public after the death of the writer **3** (of a child) born after the death of its father —**~ly** *adv*

pos·til·ion, -till- /pəˈstɪlɪən/ *n* a servant who rides on one of the horses pulling a carriage when there is no driver on or in the carriage

post·ing /ˈpəʊstɪŋ/ *n esp. BrE* an appointment to a POST[5] (4), esp. in the armed forces

post·man /ˈpəʊstmən/ (*AmE* usu. **mailman**)— *n* **-men** /mən/ a man employed to collect and deliver letters, parcels, etc.

post·mark[1] /ˈpəʊstmɑːk‖-mɑrk/ *n* an official mark made on letters, parcels, etc., usu. over the stamp, showing when and from where they are sent

postmark[2] *v* [T1;X1 *usu. pass.*] to mark (a letter, parcel, etc.) with a POSTMARK[1]: *The parcel was postmarked Brighton*

post·mas·ter /ˈpəʊstˌmɑːstəʳ‖-ˌmæ-/ (*fem.* **post·mis·tress** /-ˌmɪstrəs/)— *n* a person officially in charge of a post office

Postmaster Gen·e·ral /ˌ··· ˈ···/ *n* **Postmasters General** a person who is in charge of a national postal system

post me·rid·i·em /ˌpəʊst məˈrɪdɪəm/ *adv fml & rare* P.M.

post·mor·tem /ˌpəʊstˈmɔːtəm‖-ˈmɔr-/ *n Lat* **1** also (*fml*) **postmortem ex·am·i·na·tion** /·ˌ·· ···ˈ··/— an examination of a dead body to discover the cause of death; AUTOPSY **2** an examination of a plan or event that failed in order to discover the cause of failure: *held a postmortem on the company's poor sales results*

post of·fice /ˈ· ˌ··/ *n* a building, office, shop, etc., which deals with the post and certain other government business for a particular area, such as (in Britain) telephone bills

post office box /ˈ· ·· ˌ·/ *n fml* P O Box

post·paid /ˌpəʊstˈpeɪd◂/ *adv, adj esp. AmE* POST-FREE

post·pone /pəʊsˈpəʊn/ *v* [T1,4 (*until, to*)] to delay; move to some later time: *We're postponing our holiday until August* —**~ment** *n* [U;C]

post·pran·di·al /ˌpəʊstˈprændɪəl/ *adj* [Wa5;A; (B)] *usu. humor or fml* happening just after dinner

post·script /ˈpəʊstˌskrɪpt/ *n* **1** also (*infml*) **P.S.**— a short addition to a letter, below the place where one has signed one's name **2** a part added to a finished book, statement, etc., giving new facts, explanations, etc.: *I'd just like to add a postscript to what I said*

pos·tu·lant /ˈpɒstjʊlənt‖ˈpɑstʃə-/ *n* a person who is preparing to enter a religious ORDER (17)

pos·tu·late¹ /ˈpɒstjʊleɪt‖ˈpɑstʃə-/ *v* [T1,5,5b] to accept (something that has not been proved) as true, as a base for reasoning

pos·tu·late² /ˈpɒstjʊlɪ̆t‖ˈpɑstʃə-/ *n* something supposed or known (but not proved) to be true, on which an argument or piece of scientific reasoning is based

pos·ture¹ /ˈpɒstʃəʳ‖ˈpɑs-/ *n* **1** [U] the general way of holding the body, esp. the back, shoulders, and head: *Upright posture is natural only to man* **2** [C] a fixed bodily position **3** [C *usu. sing.*] a manner of behaving or thinking on some occasion; ATTITUDE (2): *The government's posture on this new trade agreement seems very unhelpful*

posture² *v* **1** [IØ] *often derog* to place oneself in a fixed bodily position or positions, esp. in order to make other people admire one **2** [Wv4;IØ (*as*)] *derog* to pretend to be something that one is not: *posturing as a music lover*

post·war /ˌpəʊstˈwɔːʳ◂/ *adj* [Wa5;A;(B)] belonging to the time after a war

po·sy /ˈpəʊzi/ *n* a small bunch of flowers

pot¹ /pɒt‖pɑt/ *n* **1** [C] (*often in comb.*) any of several kinds of round vessel of baked clay, metal, glass, etc., with or without a handle, cover, etc., made to contain liquids or solids, esp. for cooking: *a pot of paint|a teapot|These chickens will soon be ready for the pot* (=for cooking and eating) **2** [C] **a** POTTY² **b** CHAMBER POT **3** [C] *infml* an ornamental dish, bowl, or other vessel made by hand out of clay **4** [C] *old use* a metal drinking vessel for beer **5** [C (*of*)] also **pot·ful** /ˈpɒtfʊl‖ˈpɑt-/— the amount that any of these will hold: *A pot of tea for 2, please* **6** [C] *infml* a silver cup given as a prize in a sports competition —see also POTHUNTER (1) **7** [C (*of*) *often pl.*] *infml* a large amount (of money): *They're very rich; they've got pots of money* **8** [(*the*) S] *esp. AmE* all the money risked on one card game (esp. POKER) and taken by the winner **9** [(*the*) S] *AmE* all the money put together by a number of people for some common purpose (such as for their weekly food supply) **10** [C] *BrE* **a** any of the 6 small bags at the edge of the table into which the ball is struck in the game of BILLIARDS **b** a stroke which sends the correct ball into one of these **11** [C] *infml esp. BrE* an important person (esp. in the phr. **big pot**) **12** [U] *sl* **a** CANNABIS **b** MARIJUANA **13** [C] *usu. derog* POTBELLY (1) **14** [C] *infml* POTSHOT **15 go to pot** *infml* to pass into a state of worthlessness, esp. from lack of care **16 keep the pot boiling a** to earn enough money to live, esp. by doing work of a lower quality than one would like —see also POTBOILER **b** to make the activity of a group continue at a fast rate **17 pots and pans** kitchen cooking vessels in general **18 the pot calling the kettle black** one person blaming another for having a fault which he himself has

pot² *v* **-tt-** [T1] **1** to shoot and kill, esp. for food or sport **2** [(UP)] to set (a young plant) in a pot filled with earth **3** *infml* to sit (a young child) on a POTTY² **4** *BrE* (in BILLIARDS) to hit (a ball) into one of the 6 bags at the edge of the table —see also POTTED

po·ta·ble /ˈpəʊtəbəl/ *adj fml or humor* (of liquids, esp. water) fit for drinking; drinkable

pot·ash /ˈpɒtæʃ‖ˈpɑ-/ *n* [U] any of various salts of POTASSIUM, used esp. in farming to feed the soil, and in making soap, strong glass, and various chemical compounds

po·tas·si·um /pəˈtæsɪəm/ *n* [U] a silver-white soft easily melted metal that is a simple substance (ELEMENT (6)). It is found in nature in large quantities, but only in combination with other substances (such as in plants and rocks), and is necessary to the existence of all living things

pot at *v prep* [T1] to shoot carelessly at

po·ta·tion /pəʊˈteɪʃən/ *n fml or humor* **1** [*usu. pl.*] an act of drinking a great deal, esp. of alcoholic drink: *under the influence of their potations* **2** an (alcoholic) drink: *his favourite potation*

po·ta·to /pəˈteɪtəʊ/ *n* **-toes** **1** [C;U] a type of roundish root vegetable with a thin brown or yellowish skin, that is cooked and served in many different ways: *baked potatoes|Would you like some more potatoes?|Is there any potato left?* —see also CHIP¹ (4) **2** [C] also **potato plant** /·ˈ·· ·/— a plant which has these growing on its roots —see picture at VEGETABLE¹ **3 small potatoes** *AmE infml* something of little value —see also HOT POTATO, SWEET POTATO

potato bee·tle /·ˈ·· ˌ··/ also **Colorado beetle**— *n* a type of small harmful insect that feeds on the leaves of potato plants

potato chip /·ˈ·· ·/ also **chip**— *n AmE & AustrE* CRISP³

pot a·way *v adv* [IØ (*at*)] to shoot carelessly but repeatedly

pot·bel·lied /ˈpɒtˌbelid‖ˈpɑt-/ *adj* **1** *often derog or humor* (of a person) having a POTBELLY (1) **2** (of a vessel for liquids) having a full outward curve below the middle **3** (of a STOVE) having a rounded middle part in which coal or wood is burnt

pot·bel·ly /ˈpɒtˌbeli‖ˈpɑt-/ *n often derog or humor* **1** also **pot**— a large rounded noticeable stomach **2** a person who has this

pot·boil·er /ˈpɑtˌbɔɪləʳ‖ˈpɑt-/ *n derog* a work of art or literature produced quickly in order to obtain money

pot·bound /ˈpɒtbaʊnd‖ˈpɑt-/ *adj* [F;(B)] (of a plant growing in a pot) having roots that have grown to fill the pot, and therefore unable to grow any further

po·teen /pɒˈtiːn‖pə-/ also **po·theen** /pɒˈtʃiːn‖pə-/— *n* [U] Irish alcoholic drink made from grain (WHISKEY), and made secretly to avoid paying government tax

po·ten·cy /ˈpəʊtənsi/ *n* [U] the quality or state of being POTENT; power: *sexual potency*

po·tent /ˈpəʊtənt/ *adj* **1** (of medicines, drugs, drinks, etc.) having a strong and/or rapid effect on the body or mind **2** *fml* (of arguments, reasoning, etc.) strongly effective; causing one to agree **3** (of a male) able to have sexual relations —compare IMPOTENT **4** *lit or fml* having great power, esp. politically —**~ly** *adv*

po·ten·tate /ˈpeʊtənteɪt/ *n* **1** (esp. in former times) a ruler with direct power over his people, not limited by a law-making body **2** (*esp. in newspaper style*) a person who possesses great power and influence in a particular area of activity: *the potentates of the film industry*

o·ten·tial[1] /pəˈtenʃəl/ *adj* [Wa5] existing in possibility; not at present active or developed, but able to become so: *Every seed is a potential plant.|He is seen as a potential leader of our political party* —**~ly** *adv*

otential[2] *n* [U;S] **1** (the degree of) possibility for developing or being developed: *a new invention with a big sales potential|The boy has acting potential, but he needs training* **2** the degree of electricity or electrical force (usu. measured in VOLTs)

o·ten·ti·al·i·ty /pəˌtenʃiˈælǰti/ *n* **1** [U] the quality or condition of being POTENTIAL[1] **2** [C *usu. pl.*] **a** a hidden unused power of mind or character: *Such a forceful person may have great potentialities for either good or evil* **b** a possible future development

ot·head /ˈpɒthed‖ˈpat-/ *n sl* a person who habitually smokes POT[1] (12)

oth·er /ˈpɒðəʳ‖ˈpa-/ *n infml* **1** [S] a state of worry or anxiety arising from slight cause **2** [U] noisy unnecessary activity, often expressed in excited speech

ot·herb /ˈpɒthɜːb‖ˈpatɜrb/ *n* any of the many strong-tasting plants of which a few (dried) leaves or stems are added to food being cooked

ot·hole /ˈpɒthəʊl‖ˈpat-/ *n* **1** **a** a deep round hole in the surface of rock by which water enters and flows underground, often through a cave **b** the cave itself **2** a hole in the surface of a road caused by traffic or bad weather

ot·hol·ing /ˈpɒtˌhəʊlɪŋ‖ˈpat-/ *n* [U] the sport of climbing down and looking at POTHOLEs (1) —**potholer** *n*

ot·house /ˈpɒthaʊs‖ˈpat-/ *n* **-houses** /ˌhaʊzǰz/ *derog old use* a small inn of a rough kind

ot·hun·ter /ˈpɒtˌhʌntəʳ‖ˈpat-/ *n derog* **1** a person who competes in races or sports only in order to win the prizes **2** a hunter who shoots animals only so that he can make a show of how many he has shot **3** a person who collects objects of ARCHAEOLOGICAL value without taking care to record or preserve the place where he finds them

o·tion /ˈpəʊʃən/ *n esp. lit* a single drink of a liquid mixture, intended as medicine, poison, or a magic charm: *a sleeping potion|a love potion*

ot·luck /ˌpatˈlʌk‖ˌpat-/ *n* **take potluck** **a** to choose without enough information: *There are so many to choose from; I think I'd better take potluck and have—it doesn't matter, really—this one* **b** (esp. of an unexpected guest) to have the same meal as everyone else: *Come home with us and have supper, if you don't mind taking potluck*

ot·pour·ri /pəʊˈpʊəri‖-pʊˈri (*Fr* popuri)/ *n Fr* **1** a mixture of dried pieces of sweet-smelling flowers and leaves, kept in a bowl to give a pleasant smell to a room **2** a mixed collection, esp. of pieces of music or writing of a popular sort

ot roast /ˈ· ·/ *n* [C;U] **1** (a piece of) BEEF cooked slowly with a little water, after having been made brown by cooking in hot fat **2** (a piece of) BEEF sold to be cooked in this way

ot-roast *v* [T1] to cook (BEEF) as a POT ROAST

ot·sherd /ˈpɒt-ʃɜːd‖ˈpat-ʃɜrd/ *n* (in ARCHAEOLOGY) a broken piece of a pot

ot·shot /ˈpɒt-ʃɒt‖ˈpat-ʃat/ *n infml* a carelessly aimed shot

ot·tage /ˈpɒtɪdʒ‖ˈpa-/ *n* [U;C] *old use* thick soup

ot·ted /ˈpɒtǰd‖ˈpa-/ *adj* [Wa5;A] **1** (of meat, fish, or chicken) made into a paste and preserved in a pot, for eating when spread on bread **2** (of a plant) grown in a pot **3** *sometimes derog* (of a (well-known) book) produced in a short(er) simple(r) form: *potted Shakespeare|a potted history of the kings of England*

ot·ter[1] /ˈpɒtəʳ‖ˈpa-/ *n* a person who makes pots, dishes, etc., out of baked clay, esp. by hand

potter[2] *n* [S] *BrE infml* an act of moving slowly about, sometimes stopping to look at or do something

potter a·bout[1] *AmE* usu. **putter around**— *v adv* [IØ] *infml* to spend time in activities that demand little effort

potter about[2] *AmE* usu. **putter around**— *v prep* [T1 *no pass.*] *infml* to move about (a place) slowly, doing small unimportant jobs: *Grandmother is too old now to do hard work; she just potters about the house*

potter a·way *AmE* usu. **putter away**— *v adv* [T1] *infml* to spend or waste (time) in an unplanned way, doing unimportant things

Pot·ter·ies /ˈpɒtəriz‖ˈpa-/ *n* [*the*+P] an area in north Staffordshire, England, where the making of fine POTTERY (2) is the main industry —compare BLACK COUNTRY

potter's wheel /ˌ·· ˈ·/ *n* a round flat spinning plate fixed parallel to the ground, on which wet clay is placed to be shaped into a pot

pot·ter·y /ˈpɒtəri‖ˈpa-/ *n* **1** [U] the work of a POTTER **2** [U] pots and other objects made out of baked clay: *Modern pottery is usually ornamental* **3** [U] baked clay (EARTHENWARE), considered as the material of which pots are made: *Is pottery more breakable than glass?|a pottery dish* **4** [C] a POTTER's workroom or factory

pot·ting shed /ˈ·· ·/ *n* a small building by a garden, ALLOTMENT (3), etc., put up esp. to hold garden tools, seeds, etc.

pot·ty[1] /ˈpɒti‖ˈpati/ *adj* [Wa1] **1** [B] *infml, esp. BrE* **a** (of a person) silly; slightly mad: *That noise is driving me potty* **b** (of ideas or actions) foolish; unreasonable **2** [A] *BrE derog* small and unimportant; worthless (usu. in the phr. **potty little**): *This potty little village hasn't even got a post office* **3** [F+*about*] *BrE infml* having a strong uncontrolled interest in or admiration for (someone or something): *The girls are potty about the new television singer* —**pottiness** *n* [U]

potty[2] *n* a CHAMBER POT for children, now usu. made of plastic

potty-trained /ˈ·· ·/ *adj* (of a child) trained to use a POTTY[2]

pouch /paʊtʃ/ *n* **1** a small soft leather bag to hold tobacco, carried in the pocket **2** a leather bag to hold containers of gunpowder, fastened to a soldier's or hunter's belt **3** a baglike fold of skin inside each cheek, in which certain animals carry and store food **4** a kind of pocket of skin in the lower half of the body, in which certain animals (MARSUPIALs) carry their young **5** a soft baglike fold of loose skin that hangs down, esp. under the eye as a result of illness, old age, etc.

pouf, pouffe /puːf/ *n* **1** a low soft drum-shaped object, used as a seat or for resting the feet while sitting in a chair **2** *BrE derog sl* POOF

poul·ter·er /ˈpəʊltərəʳ/ *n* a person who sells POULTRY

poul·tice /ˈpəʊltǰs/ *n* a soft heated wet mass of any of various substances, spread on a thin cloth and laid against the skin to lessen pain, swelling, etc.: *a bread poultice*

poul·try /ˈpəʊltri/ *n* **1** [P] farmyard birds of any kind, such as hens, ducks, etc., kept for supplying eggs and meat: *Our poultry are kept at the bottom of the garden* **2** [U] hens, ducks, etc., considered as meat: *Poultry is rather cheap now*

pounce[1] /paʊns/ *v* **1** [IØ (*at, on, upon*)] to fly down or spring suddenly in order to seize something, esp. for food: *The bird pounced on the worm and swallowed it* **2** [IØ (*on, upon*)] to make a sudden attack, usu. from a hidden place: *Policemen were hiding in the bank, ready to pounce on the thieves*

pounce² *n* [*usu. sing.*] an attack made by pouncing (POUNCE¹)

pounce on also **pounce up·on**— *v prep* [T1] **1** to seize or accept eagerly **2** to notice at once and point sharply to (someone or something): *If you make a single mistake, Clive will pounce on it/you and say you're a fool*

pound¹ /paʊnd/ *n* **1** [C] **a** a standard measure of weight equal to ·454 kilograms: *Sugar is sold by the pound.|This weighs 7 pounds* (=7 lbs) **b** an amount that weighs this: *2 pounds of apples|I lost several pounds last month* (=became lighter by that amount) —see WEIGHTS & MEASURES TABLE **2** [C] **a** a measure of weight for gold and silver, equal to 0·373 kilograms **b** an amount that weighs this **3** [C] **a** the standard of money in several countries: *the Egyptian pound* **b** also (*fml or tech*) **pound sterling** /ˌ· ˈ··/— (in Britain) the standard of money, now divided into 100 pence: *5 pounds can also be written £5* **4** [*the*+R] the British money system; value at any particular time of British money at international exchange rates: *The Bank of England had to support the pound*

pound² *v* **1** [T1 (UP)] to crush into a soft mass or powder by striking repeatedly with a heavy object: *Pound the meat into a paste* **2** [T1 (AWAY, *against, at, on*)] to strike repeatedly, heavily, and noisily: *He pounded the table angrily.|The stormy waves pounded against the rocks* **3** [I∅ (AWAY, *at*); T1] to attack (an enemy position) with heavy gunfire **4** [I∅ (*with*)] to sound with unusually strong loud beats: *His heart pounded with excitement* **5** [L9] to move with heavy quick steps that make a dull sound: *The excited cattle pounded down the hill*

pound³ *n* **1** a place where lost dogs and cats, and cars that have been unlawfully parked, are kept by the police until claimed by the owner **2** (in former times) an enclosure in which wandering animals were officially kept until claimed and paid for by the owner

pound·age /ˈpaʊndɪdʒ/ *n* [U] **1** a payment of a stated amount charged for every pound in weight (as for parcels sent by post) **2** a charge made or a share paid in some business agreements, consisting of a stated amount per British £1

pound cake /ˈ· ·/ *n* [U] *AmE* MADEIRA CAKE

-pound·er /ˈpaʊndəʳ/ *comb. form* [*determiner*→*n*[C]] **1** something (esp. a fish) that weighs a stated number of pounds: *I caught a 5-pounder today* **2** a big gun that fires a shot weighing a stated number of pounds: *a 32-pounder*

pound·ing /ˈpaʊndɪŋ/ *n* [U;C] **1** the act or sound of someone or something that POUNDs² (2,4,5) **2** *infml* a severe beating: *Our football team took a real pounding from Brazil last night*

pound note /ˌ· ˈ·/ *n* (*also in comb.*) a printed official piece of paper with which one can buy things to the value of a pound (or of a stated number of pounds): *a 10-pound note*

pound out *v adv* [T1] to produce by or as if by hard striking on an instrument

pour /pɔːr‖por/ *v* **1** [L9] to flow steadily and rapidly: *Blood poured from the wound.|Smoke was pouring from the window.|*(fig.) *Curses poured from his lips* **2** [L9] (of people) to rush together in large numbers: *At 5 o'clock workers poured out of the factories* **3** [X9, esp. AWAY, IN, OUT] to cause (liquid or something that flows like liquid) to flow: *Pour away the dirty water.|Pour out some salt.|The chimney was pouring out black smoke* **4** [X9, esp. AWAY, IN, OUT] to give or send as in a flow: *He's been pouring money into the firm for 2 years but it's still in trouble* **5** [Wv4;I∅ (DOWN)] **a** to rain hard and steadily: *It's pouring this morning.|*(*BrE* also) *It is pouring with rain this morning* **b** (of rain) to fall hard and steadily: *The rain is really pouring down!|She spoilt her new shoes in the pouring rain.|It was a pouring wet day* **6** [I∅] *infml* to fill cups of tea, coffee, etc., and serve them to others at table: *Shall I pour or will you?* **7** [D1 (*for*); T1: (OUT)] to supply (someone) with a drink from a vessel: *Will you pour me out a cup of tea?* **8** [L9] (of a vessel) to be suited to pouring out a liquid or other substance

pour on¹ *v prep* **1 pour cold water on** *not fml* to discourage: *Don't pour cold water on the idea: it may be just what we need* **2 pour oil on the flames** *not fml* to make matters worse **3 pour oil on troubled waters** *not fml* to try to stop trouble or violence by making calmer the people who are causing it **4 pour scorn on** to speak with unkind disrespect of

pour on² *v adv* **pour it on** *infml* to praise or admire too greatly, esp. in order to please

pour out *v adv* [T1;I∅] **a** to tell (a story, news, one's troubles, etc.) freely and with feeling **b** (of a story, news, one's troubles, etc.) to be told freely and with feeling

pout¹ /paʊt/ *v* [T1 (OUT); I∅] to show childish or womanish bad temper and displeasure by pushing (the lips or the lower lip) forward

pout² *n* an act of POUTing¹

pov·er·ty /ˈpɒvəti‖ˈpɑvərti/ *n* **1** [U] the state of being very poor: *Poverty prevented the boy from continuing his education* **2** [U;S (*of*)] *fml & derog* (a) lack: *His later stories are not interesting because of their poverty of imagination*

poverty-strick·en /ˈ··· ˌ··/ *adj* very poor indeed

P O W /ˌpiː əʊ ˈdʌbəljuː/ *abbrev. for:* (*infml*) PRISONER OF WAR: *a POW camp|the POWs*

pow·der¹ /ˈpaʊdəʳ/ *n* **1** [U;C] (*often in comb.*) (a kind of) substance in the form of very fine dry grains: *He stepped on the piece of chalk and crushed it to powder* **2** [U] (*often in comb.*) a pleasant-smelling, often flesh-coloured substance in this form, for use on the skin: *face powder|There's too much powder on your nose, Mary* **3** [U;C] (*usu. in comb.*) (a small measured amount of a) medicine in this form: *headache powder|He took a stomach powder* **4** [U] explosive material in this form, esp. gunpowder **5 keep one's powder dry** to be carefully prepared for battle, or for dealing with an opponent

powder² *v* **1** [T1] to put POWDER¹ (2) on: *She powdered the baby after its bath* **2** [T1;I∅] to (cause to) break into POWDER¹ (1)

pow·dered /ˈpaʊdəd‖-ərd/ *adj* **1** covered with powder: *powdered hair* **2** [Wa5] produced or dried in the form of powder: *powdered milk*

powder horn /ˈ·· ·/ also **powder flask**— *n* a narrow-necked container used in former times for carrying gunpowder

powder keg /ˈ·· ·/ *n* **1** something dangerous that might explode: *Escaping gas has filled the building and turned it into a real powder keg.|*(fig.) *The degree of political dissatisfaction in that country is now so high that its neighbours look upon it as a powder keg* **2** (in former times) a small metal barrel for holding gunpowder

powder mag·a·zine /ˈ·· ··ˌ·‖ˈ·· ˌ···/ *n* a place for storing gunpowder and explosives, esp. on a warship

powder puff /ˈ·· ·/ *n* **1** a small thick piece, or ball, of soft material for spreading POWDER¹ (2) on the face or body **2** *sl* a weak person

powder room /ˈ·· ·/ *n euph* women's public LAVATORY (2,3) in a theatre, hotel, restaurant, big shop, etc.

pow·der·y /ˈpaʊdəri/ *adj* **1** like or easily broken into powder: *powdery snow* **2** covered with powder

pow·er¹ /ˈpaʊəʳ/ *n* **1** [(*the*): U (*of*), U3] a sense or ability that forms part of the nature of body or mind: *Man is the only animal that has the power of speech.|Some animals have the power to see in the dark* —compare POWERS **2** [(*the*): U (*of*), U3] the ability to do something or produce a certain effect: *She claims to have the power to see the future.|He did everything in his power to comfort her* (=did all he could) —compare POWERS **3** [U] force; strength: *You can really feel the power of the sun sitting out here.*|(fig.) *a story of great power* **4** [U] (*usu. in comb.*) strength and effectiveness of armed forces: *Formerly, sea power gave big nations influence over others* **5** [U] control over others; influence: *The power of the church in national affairs has lessened.|Power should be used wisely* **6** [U] right to govern, to give orders, or to be obeyed: *Which political party is in power now?* (=which one is the government party?) **7** [C,C3] right to act, given by law, rule, or official position: *Only certain directors in the company have the power to sign company cheques.|The police and the army have been given special powers to deal with this state of affairs* **8** [C] (*sometimes cap.*) a person, group, nation, etc., that has influence or control: *Davis is a power in this firm; it would be unwise to quarrel with him.|There is to be a meeting of the Great Powers* (=the largest and strongest states in the world).|(fig.) *No power on earth can make me do what I don't want to do* **9** [C *usu. pl.*] a good or evil spirit; unearthly force believed to be able to influence men's fate: *the powers of darkness* (=the forces of the devil) **10** [U] (*often in comb.*) force that may be used for doing work, driving a machine, or producing electricity: *Mills used to depend on wind power or water power.|The damaged ship was able to reach port under her own power* —see also HORSEPOWER, MANPOWER **11** [U] the degree of this force produced by something: *What is the power of this engine?* **12** [C] (in MATHEMATICS) **a** the number of times that an amount is to be multiplied by itself: *The amount 2 to the power of 3 is written* 2^3, *and means* $2\times2\times2$ **b** the result of this multiplying: *The 3rd power of 2 is 8* **13** [U] (of instruments containing a special shape of glass (LENS)) a measure of the strength of the ability to make objects appear larger **14** [S+*of*] *infml* a large amount; great deal: *Your visit did me a power of good* **15** [A] (of an apparatus or vehicle usu. worked by hand) provided with or worked by a motor: *a power* MOWER|POWER STEERING **16 More power to your elbow!** *infml* May your efforts succeed! **17 power behind the throne** a person who, though he has no official right or position, has great influence in private over a ruler or leader

power² *v* [T1 *usu. pass.*] to supply power to (esp. a moving machine)

pow·er·boat /ˈpaʊəbəʊt‖ˈpaʊər-/ *n* MOTORBOAT

power brakes /ˈ·· ·/ *n* [P] BRAKES for a vehicle that are helped to work by power from the vehicle's own engine

power dive /ˈ·· ·/ *n* a steep downward movement of an aircraft with the engines working —**power-dive** *v* [T1;IØ]

-pow·ered /ˈpaʊəd‖-ərd/ *comb. form* [→*adj*] **1** supplied with or producing working force in the stated way or of the stated degree: *a low-powered engine|The house has an oil-powered central heating system* **2** (of a LENS or an instrument containing one) able to make objects look larger to the stated degree —see also HIGH-POWERED

pow·er·ful /ˈpaʊəfəl‖-ər-/ *adj* **1** very strong; full of force: *Tom is a very powerful swimmer; he has powerful arms and legs* **2** of great ability; easily producing ideas: *Her imagination is too powerful* **3** strong or great in degree: *Onions have a powerful smell.|Electric current is often powerful enough to kill.|powerful glasses* **4** having a strong effect: *The minister made a powerful political speech.|This wine is very powerful* **5** having much control and influence: *Powerful nations sometimes try to control weaker ones* **6** having or using great electrical or other working power —**~ly** *adv*: *He's very powerfully built* (=has a big strong body)

pow·er·house /ˈpaʊəhaʊs‖-ər-/ *n* **-houses** /ˌhaʊzɨz/ **1** *usu. apprec* a person with great strength and keenness of body and/or mind **2** POWER STATION

pow·er·less /ˈpaʊələs‖ˈpaʊər-/ *adj* [B;F3] lacking power or strength; weak; unable: *The car went out of control, and the driver was powerless to stop it* —**~ly** *adv* —**~ness** *n* [U]

power of at·tor·ney /ˌ·· · ·ˈ··/ *n law* **1** [U] the written right given to a person to act for someone else in business or law **2** [C] a signed official paper giving this right

power plant /ˈ·· ·/ *n* **1** an engine and other parts which supply power to a factory, an aircraft, a car, etc. **2** *AmE* POWER STATION

power point /ˈ·· ·/ *n BrE* POINT¹ (20)

power pol·i·tics /ˌ·· ˈ···/ *n* [U;P] *often derog* the system of gaining an advantage for one's country in international politics by the use or show of armed force instead of by peaceful argument

pow·ers /ˈpaʊəz‖-ərz/ *n* **1** [P] general natural abilities: *She is 80 years old and very ill, and her powers are failing* (=are weakening) **2** [P9] a special combination of natural abilities of a stated type: *When he wrote this book, John was at the height of his powers as a writer* **3 the powers that be** *often humor* the people in high official positions who make decisions concerning one's life in general, or a particular matter

power sta·tion /ˈ·· ˌ··/ (*AmE* also **power plant**)— *n* a large building in which electricity is made

power steer·ing /ˌ··ˈ··/ *n* [U] a system or apparatus for STEERing a vehicle, which system is helped to work by power from the vehicle's own engine

pow·wow¹ /ˈpaʊˌwaʊ/ *n* **1** a meeting or council of North American Indians **2** *humor & becoming rare* a long talk to decide some matter

powwow² *v* [IØ] *humor & becoming rare* to hold a POWWOW¹

pox /pɒks‖pɑks/ *n* **1** [*the*+R] *infml* the disease SYPHILIS **2** [U] *old use* the disease SMALLPOX **3 A pox on (someone/something)!** *old use* May something very bad happen to (someone/something)! —see also CHICKEN POX, COWPOX, SMALLPOX

pp *abbrev. for:* **1** PIANISSIMO —see also P² (4) **2** pages: *see pp 15–37* —see also P² (1)

PPS *abbrev. for:* (in Britain) Parliamentary Private Secretary

PR *abbrev. for:* **1** PROPORTIONAL REPRESENTATION **2** PUBLIC RELATIONS

prac·ti·ca·ble /ˈpræktɪkəbəl/ *adj* **1** that can be successfully used or acted upon (though not yet tried): *Is it practicable to try to grow crops in deserts?* **2** [(*for*)] (of roads and other means of travel) able to be used —**-bly** *adv* —**-bility** /ˌpræktɪkəˈbɪlɨti/ *n* [U;C]

USAGE People are beginning to use **practical** with the same meaning as **practicable**; a **practical/practicable** plan or suggestion is one that will work. **Practicable** is not used of people.

prac·ti·cal¹ /ˈpræktɪkəl/ *adj* **1** [A;(B)] concerned with action, practice, or actual conditions and results, rather than with ideas: *Now that you're going to live in France, you'll be able to make practical use of your knowledge of French* **2** [B] effective or convenient in actual use; suited to actual conditions: *a very practical little table that* *folds up out of the way when not needed* **3** [B] **a** *often apprec* sensible; clever at doing things and dealing with difficulties; concerned with facts rather than feelings or fancies: *We've got to be practical and buy only what we can afford* **b** *derog* insensitive and lacking imagination: *As a man with a practical mind, he can't understand his son's desire to be a poet* **4** [Wa5;A] taught by actual experience or practice, not by studying books: *She's never been to cooking classes, but she's a good practical cook* **5** **for all practical purposes** actually; in reality: *He does so little work in the office that for all practical purposes it would make no difference if he didn't come* —see PRACTICABLE (USAGE)

practical² *n infml* a PRACTICAL¹ (1) lesson, test, or examination, as in science

prac·ti·cal·i·ty /ˌpræktɪˈkælǝ̇ti/ *n* **1** [U] the quality of being PRACTICAL¹ **2** [C] something that is PRACTICAL¹ (1,2)

practical joke /ˌ··· ˈ·/ *n* a trick played upon one person to give amusement to others

prac·ti·cal·ly /ˈpræktɪkəli/ *adv* **1** usefully; suitably **2** very nearly (but not quite); almost: *The holidays are practically over; there's only one day left.*|*She's practically always late for work* —see ALMOST (USAGE)

practical pol·i·tics /ˌ··· ˈ···/ *n* [U] *esp. BrE* ideas, plans, etc., that may be used at once and that will show successful results

prac·tice, *AmE* also **-tise** /ˈpræktǝ̇s/ *n* **1** [U] actual use or performance as compared with the idea, intention, rules, etc., on which the action is based: *It's claimed that this tin-opener is a very good invention, but in practice it's not easy to use.*|*We've made our plans, and now we must put them into practice* **2** [U] experience; knowledge of a skill as gained by this: *Have you had any practice in nursing the sick?*|*The student teachers are now doing their teaching practice* **3** [C;U] (a) (regularly) repeated performance or exercise in order to gain skill in some art, game, etc.: *It takes a great deal of practice to be really good at this sport.*|*We have 3* CHOIR *practices a week.*|*He used to be good at cricket, but now he's out of practice* (=unable to perform with skill because of lack of practice).|*a practice lesson* **4** [U] a standard course of action that is accepted as correct or desirable: *It is the practice in English law to consider a person as not guilty until he has been proved guilty* **5** [C *usu. sing.*] *often fml* a firmly fixed custom or regular habit: *It's not the usual practice for shops to stay open after 6 o'clock.*|*I'll lend you the money this time, but I don't intend to make a practice of it* —see HABIT (USAGE) **6** [C *usu. pl.*] *often derog* an act that is often repeated, esp. secretly, in a fixed manner or with ceremony: *The Christian church had a great struggle to stop magical practices among its people* **7** [U] regular work of a doctor or lawyer: *Is Doctor Jones still in practice here?* **8** [C] **a** the business of a doctor or lawyer, esp. as having a money value because of his trusted connection with the people he serves: *How many lawyers' practices are there in town?* **b** the place where this business is done: *Where was his practice? In the High Street* **c** the kind or number of people using his services: *Did he have a large practice? No, it was a small but wealthy practice* **9** **sharp practice** *derog* behaviour or a trick in business or work that is dishonest but not quite unlawful

prac·tise, *AmE* also **-tice** /ˈpræktǝ̇s/ *v* **1** [Wv4;T1] to act in accordance with (the ideas of one's religion or other firm belief): *Do most Christians practise their religion?*|*a practising Jew* **2** [T1] *fml* to (force oneself to) show or use (some necessary quality in behaviour): *In dealing with sick old people nurses must practise great patience* **3** [T1] *fml* to make a habit or practice of: *Our income has decreased and now we have to practise* ECONOMY (=have to avoid spending money) **4** [T1,4;I∅] to do (an action) repeatedly or do exercises regularly (esp. on a musical instrument) in order to gain skill: *She's been practising the same tune on the piano for nearly an hour.*|*You mustn't practise the drums while the baby is sleeping.*|*They're practising singing the new song.*|*You'll never learn to ride a bicycle if you don't practise* **5** [T1,4] to do (something needing special knowledge) according to rule: *Some people practise magic, or calling up the spirits of the dead* **6** [Wv4;I∅ (*as*); T1] to do (the work of) or work regularly as (a doctor, lawyer, etc.): *He's passed his law examinations and is now practising (as a lawyer).*|*One brother practises medicine and the other practises law.*|*a practising doctor* **7** [T1 (*on, upon*)] *fml* to make unfair use of (a trick) for one's own advantage **8** **practise what one preaches** to do oneself what one is always telling others to do

prac·tised, *AmE* also **-ticed** /ˈpræktǝ̇st/ *adj* **1** [B (*in*)] (of a person) skilled through practice: *a practised cheat*|*She is thoroughly practised in all the skills of her art* **2** [A] *apprec* gained by practice: *The dancer moved with practised grace* **3** [B] *derog* gained only by practice; not natural: *My hostess welcomed me with a practised smile*

prac·ti·tion·er /prækˈtɪʃənəʳ/ *n* **1** a person who works in a profession, esp. a doctor or lawyer: *medical practitioners* **2** *sometimes derog* a person who practises a skill or art —see also GENERAL PRACTITIONER

prae·sid·i·um /prɪˈsɪdɪəm, -ˈzɪ-/ *n* **-iums** *or* **-ia** /-dɪə/ PRESIDIUM

prae·tor, pretor /ˈpriːtəʳ/ *n* (in ancient Rome) a state officer of the rank below the heads of state, who held office for one year and had duties concerning the army and law

prae·to·ri·an, pre- /prɪˈtɔːrɪən‖-ˈto-/ *adj* [Wa5;A] **1** of or concerning a PRAETOR **2** (*often cap.*) of or like the guards of Roman rulers: *the praetorian guards*

prag·mat·ic /prægˈmætɪk/ *adj* dealing with matters in the way that seems best under the actual conditions, rather than following a general principle; practical —**~ally** *adv* [Wa4]

prag·ma·tis·m /ˈprægmətɪzəm/ *n* [U] **1** PRAGMATIC thinking or way of considering things **2** a system of PHILOSOPHY (1) based on the principle that the truth of an idea can be judged only by its practical results —**-tist** *n*

prai·rie /ˈpreəri/ *n* [*often pl.*] (esp. in North America) a wide treeless grassy plain

prairie dog /ˈ·· ·/ *n* a type of small furry North American animal that lives underground

praise¹ /preɪz/ *v* [T1 (*for*)] **1** to speak favourably and with admiration of **2** *fml or lit* to offer thanks and honour to (God), esp. in song in a church service

praise² *n* **1** [U (*of*)] expression of admiration (often in the phr. **in praise of**): *a book in praise of country life*|*The new film received high praise from everyone* **2** [U] *fml or lit* glory; worship: *Let us give praise to God* **3** **praise be** thank God: *At last I've found you, praise be!*

prais·es /ˈpreɪzǝ̇z/ *n* [P (*of*)] **1** words that praise someone or something: *Tom is loud in his praises of his new car* **2** *fml or lit* words that praise God (esp. in song) **3** **sing one's own praises** *often derog* to praise oneself **4** **sing the praises of** to praise very eagerly

praise·wor·thy /ˈpreɪzwɜːðɪ‖-ɜr-/ *adj apprec* deserving praise (esp. even though not successful) —**-thily** *adv* —**-thiness** *n* [U]

pra·line /ˈprɑːliːn/ *n* a type of sweet made of nuts cooked brown in boiling sugar

pram /præm/ also (*fml*) **perambulator**, (*AmE* **baby carriage**)— *n esp. BrE* a 4-wheeled carriage, pushed by hand, in which a baby can sleep or be taken about

prance¹ /prɑːns‖præns/ *v* [Wv4;L9;(IØ)] **1** (of a horse) to jump high or move quickly by raising the front legs and springing forwards on the back legs **2** to move quickly, gaily, or proudly, with a springing or dancing step: *Jane pranced into the room wearing her new clothes*

prance² *n* [S] a prancing (PRANCE) movement

prank /præŋk/ *n* a playful but foolish trick, not intended to harm: *Children like to play pranks on people.|a schoolboy prank*

prank·ster /ˈpræŋkstəʳ/ *n infml* a person who plays PRANK*s*

prat /præt/ *n BrE derog sl* a worthless stupid person

prate a·bout /preɪt/ *v prep* [T1,(4)] *derog* to talk foolishly about

prat·fall /ˈprætfɔːl/ *n not fml* an experience that lowers someone's self-respect, but is also funny

prat·tle¹ /ˈprætl/ *v* [Wv3,4;IØ (ON, *about*)] **1** *infml* to talk meaninglessly or lightly and continually in a simple way, or like a child: *The girls prattled on about their clothes* **2** *derog* to talk too readily (about the affairs of others); GOSSIP (1) —**-tler** *n*

prattle² *n* [U] *infml often derog* childish, unimportant, or careless talk

prawn¹ /prɔːn/ *n* [C;(U)] *esp. BrE* any of various types of small 10-legged sea animals, good for food, including esp. large SHRIMP*s* —see picture at CRUSTACEAN

prawn² *v* [IØ] to fish for PRAWN*s*¹ (often in the phr. **go prawning**)

prawn cock·tail /ˌ· ˈ··/ also (*esp. AmE*) **shrimp cocktail**— *n* [C;(U)] a dish made from cold cooked PRAWN*s*¹ mixed with pieces of LETTUCE in a special hot-tasting pink liquid

prax·is /ˈpræksɪs/ *n* [U] *fml* **1** customary practice **2** the exercise or practice of an art, science, or skill **3** practical reality

pray¹ /preɪ/ *v* **1** [T1,3,5,5b,c;IØ (*for, to*)] to speak, often silently, to God (or gods), privately or with others, showing love, giving thanks, or asking for (something): *They went to the mosque to pray.|I will pray to God for your safety.|We pray God's forgiveness.|He prayed to be given patience to finish the work* **2** [T5,5b,(c);IØ (*for*)] *infml* to wish or hope very strongly: *We're praying for a fine day* **3** [T1; V3,(2)] *lit or old use* to ask or beg seriously and with strong feeling for (something): *I pray you to be careful* **4 past praying for** in a hopeless condition (of illness, wickedness, etc.)

pray² *adv fml or lit* (*used for giving force to a request*) please: *Pray be quiet!*

prayer¹ /preəʳ/ *n* **1** [U] the act or regular habit of praying to God or gods: *They believed that the boy was made well through prayer* **2** [U] (*often cap.*) a fixed form of church service mainly concerned with praying: *Evening Prayer* **3** [C *usu. pl.*] a quite informal daily religious service among a special group of people, mainly concerned with praying: *school prayers|family prayers* **4** [C] a fixed form of words used (regularly) in praying: *He said his prayers every night before he went to bed* **5** [C] a solemn request made to God or gods, or to someone in a position of power: *Her prayer was answered and her husband came home safely*

pray·er² /ˈpreɪəʳ/ *n* a person who prays or is praying

prayer book /ˈ· ·/ *n* a book containing prayers for use in church

prayer meet·ing /ˈ· ˌ··/ *n* a public PROTESTANT meeting at which people offer personal prayers to God

prayer rug /ˈ· ·/ also **prayer mat**— *n* a small mat of a fixed pattern, knelt on by Muslims when they are praying

prayer wheel /ˈ· ·/ *n* a drum-shaped piece of wood or metal that turns round on a pole, and on which prayers are written, used by Buddhists in Tibet

pray·ing man·tis /ˌ·· ˈ··/ also **mantis**— *n* a type of large powerful insect that presses its front legs together as if praying. It feeds on other insects —see picture at INSECT

pre- /priː, ˈpre/ *prefix* **1** before: PREWAR **2** in advance PREARRANGE **3** *esp. med or tech* **a** in front of: *pre*MOLAR **b** front: *pre*ABDOMEN

preach /priːtʃ/ *v* **1** [T1,5;D1 (*to*); IØ] to make known (a particular religion and/or its teachings) by speaking in public: *Christ preached to large crowds.|He preached them the word of God* **2** [T1,5; D1 (*to*); IØ] (esp. of a priest) to give (a religious talk (SERMON)) as part of a service in church: *The priest preached that God would soon destroy the evil world* **3** [T1] to advise or urge others to accept (a thing or course of behaviour that one believes in, oneself): *She's always preaching the value of fresh air and cold baths* **4** [D1 (*to*); T1;IØ (*at*)] *derog* to offer (unwanted advice on matters of right and wrong (SERMON*s* (2))) in a way that tires and angers the listener: *My sister has been preaching at me again about my lack of neatness* —**~er** *n*

preach·i·fy /ˈpriːtʃɪfaɪ/ *v* [IØ] to PREACH (2,4) in a dull or ineffective way

pre·am·ble /ˈpriːæmbəl/ *n fml or derog* a statement at the beginning of a speech or piece of writing, giving its reason and purpose

pre·ar·range /ˌpriːəˈreɪndʒ/ *v* [Wv5;T1] to arrange in advance: *at a prearranged signal* —**~ment** *n* [U]

preb·end /ˈprebənd/ *n* a small regular payment made to a priest of quite high rank for services connected with a CATHEDRAL or special church

preb·en·da·ry /ˈprebəndəri‖-deri/ *n* a priest who receives a PREBEND

pre·car·i·ous /prɪˈkeərɪəs/ *adj* **1** unsafe; not firm or steady; full of danger: *The climber had only a precarious hold on the slippery rock.|An artist's life would be too precarious for me* **2** doubtful; not based firmly on facts: *precarious reasoning* —**~ly** *adv* —**~ness** *n* [U]

pre·cast /ˌpriːˈkɑːst◂‖-ˈkæst◂/ *adj* [Wa5] (of CONCRETE) formed into blocks ready for use in building

pre·cau·tion /prɪˈkɔːʃən/ *n* **1** [C] an action done in order to avoid possible known danger, discomfort, etc. (often in the phr. **take precautions**): *We have taken all the precautions we can against the painting being stolen* **2** [U] care taken for this reason —**~ary** *adj*

pre·cede /prɪˈsiːd/ *v* **1** [T1;IØ] to come or go (just) in front (of): *He came into the room preceded by a small dog.|Now that you've read that sentence, reread the one that precedes* **2** [T1] to be higher in rank or importance than: *The eldest prince precedes all men except the king* **3** [T1] to be earlier than: *Are you certain the minister's statement preceded that of the president?* **4** [X9, esp. *with*] to introduce (an activity) in the stated way: *He preceded his speech with a warning against inattention* —compare PROCEED

pre·ce·dence /ˈpresɪdəns/ *n* [U] **1** the manner in which things happen one after another (esp. in the phr. **in order of precedence**) **2** greater importance (esp. in the phr. **have/take precedence (over)**): *Some say Shakespeare takes precedence over all other writers* **3** the right to a particular place before others, esp. on social or ceremonial occasions (esp. in the phrs. **give precedence (to), have/take precedence (over/(*fml*)of), in order of precedence**): *The ruler has precedence over all others in the country*

pre·ce·dent /ˈpresədənt/ *n* **1** [U] use of former customs or decisions as a guide to present actions: *The Queen has broken with precedent by sending her children to ordinary schools* **2** [C] a former action or case that may be used as an example or rule for present or future action: *If you allow him to disobey you once without punishment, he'll use it as a precedent for disobeying you again* **3 without precedent** never known to have happened before

pre·ced·ing /prɪˈsiːdɪŋ/ *adj* [Wa5;A;(E)] that came just before in time or place: *I remember the war but nothing of the preceding years.|the years|the page preceding*

pre·cen·tor /prɪˈsentəʳ/ *n* (in some English CATHEDRALs) an official who deals with the musical arrangements for the services, and sometimes directs or leads the trained singers —compare PRESENTER

pre·cept /ˈpriːsept/ *n* **1** [C] a guiding rule on which behaviour, a way of thought or action, etc., is based: *Love of all people is a main precept of our religion* **2** [U] use of such rules

pre·cep·tor /prɪˈseptəʳ/ *n fml* a teacher

pre·ces·sion /prɪˈseʃən/ *n* [C;U] **1** also **precession of the eq·ui·nox·es** /·ˌ·· · · ˈ····/— a slow westward change in the slope at which the earth turns round daily, which causes the times of the year at which day and night are both exactly 12 hours long to be slightly earlier each year **2** *tech* a sideways or circular movement of the slope of a spinning object —**~al** *adj* [Wa5]

pre·cinct /ˈpriːsɪŋkt/ *n* **1** [C (*of*) *usu. pl.*] the space, often enclosed by walls, that surrounds an important building, group of buildings, or (holy) place: *it's quiet within the precincts of the old college* **2** [C9] a part of a town planned for, or limited to, a special use: *a new shopping precinct* (=an area containing only shops) —see also PEDESTRIAN PRECINCT **3** [C] *AmE* a division of a town or city for election or police purposes **4** [C (*of*) *usu. pl.*] a line that marks the limit of a place; BOUNDARY (1)

pre·cincts /ˈpriːsɪŋkts/ *n* [P (*of*)] **1** neighbourhood; area around (a town or other place): *The precincts of the port are full of seamen when the ships are in* **2** the inside (of a building or place), considered as representing the organization that uses it: *Women aren't allowed within the precincts of this men's club*

pre·ci·os·i·ty /ˌpreʃiˈɒsəti‖-ˈɑ-/ *n derog* **1** [U] unnatural perfection of detail, esp. in speech or pronunciation **2** [C *often pl.*] an example of this

pre·cious¹ /ˈpreʃəs/ *adj* **1** [B] of great value and beauty: *That beautiful piece of glass is very precious* **2** [F;(B)] of great value; that must not be wasted: *My time is precious; I can only give you a few minutes* **3** [B] greatly loved or very valuable as being dear to one: *Your friendship is most precious to me* **4** [B] (of an art, use of words, manners, etc.) unnaturally fine or perfect; too much concerned with unimportant details **5** [Wa5;A] *infml* (used for giving force to an expression): *"Give me my ball. You can't play with it." "Take your precious (=worthless) ball!"* —**~ly** *adv* —**~ness** *n* [U]

precious² *adv infml* very (esp. in the phrs. **precious little/few**)

precious³ *n* [N] *infml* dear one; a much loved person or animal

precious met·al /ˌ·· ˈ··/ *n* [C;U] a rare and valuable metal often used in ornaments, such as gold or silver —opposite **base metal**

precious stone /ˌ·· ˈ·/ also **stone**— *n* a rare and valuable jewel, such as a diamond, EMERALD, etc. —compare SEMIPRECIOUS

pre·ci·pice /ˈpresəpəs/ *n* **1** a steep or almost upright side of a high rock, mountain, or cliff **2 stand on the edge of a precipice** to be in very great danger

pre·cip·i·tate¹ /prəˈsɪpəteɪt/ *v* **1** [T1] to hasten the coming of (an unwanted event) **2** [T1 (*into*)] **a** *fml* to throw with great force forwards or downwards **b** to force (into a condition or state of affairs) **3** [I∅;T1] (in chemistry) **a** (of solid matter) to separate from a liquid because of chemical action **b** to cause (solid matter) to separate from a liquid by chemical action **4** [T1 (*as*); L9, esp. *as*] to (cause to) change from a mistlike form into liquid or frozen drops: *Clouds usually precipitate as rain or snow*

pre·cip·i·tate² /prəˈsɪpətət/ *n* [C;U] (in chemistry) (a) solid substance that has been separated from a liquid by chemical action —compare PRECIPITATION (3)

precipitate³ /prəˈsɪpətət/ *adj fml* wildly hasty; acting or done without care or thought —compare PRECIPITOUS —**~ly** *adv*

pre·cip·i·ta·tion /prəˌsɪpəˈteɪʃən/ *n* **1** [U] *fml* unwise haste; PRECIPITATE³ action **2** [U] *tech* (amount of) rain, snow, etc. **3** [C;U] (in chemistry) matter that has PRECIPITATED¹ (3) naturally —compare PRECIPITATE² **4** [U] (in chemistry) the act or action of precipitating (PRECIPITATE¹ (3)) **5** [U] (in chemistry) the state of being PRECIPITATED¹ (3)

pre·cip·i·tous /prəˈsɪpətəs/ *adj* **1** dangerously steep **2** like (the edge of) a PRECIPICE; frighteningly high above the ground: *They looked down from the precipitous height of the church tower* **3** *nonstandard* PRECIPITATE³: *precipitous haste* —**~ly** *adv* —**~ness** *n* [U]

pré·cis¹ /ˈpreɪsiː‖preɪˈsiː/ *n* **précis** /ˈpreɪsiːz‖preɪˈsiːz/ *Fr* **1** [C] a shortened form of a speech or piece of writing, giving only the main points **2** [U] the art or practice of writing such shortened forms, used esp. as an educational exercise

précis² *v* **précised** /ˈpreɪsiːd‖preɪˈsiːd/, *pres. p.* **précising** /ˈpreɪsiː-ɪŋ‖preɪˈsiːɪŋ/ [T1] to make a PRÉCIS¹ of

pre·cise /prɪˈsaɪs/ *adj* **1** [B] exact in form, detail, measurements, time, etc.: *very precise calculations* **2** [Wa5;A] particular; exact; VERY¹ (1): *At the precise moment that I put my foot on the step, the bus started* **3** [B] sharply clear: *A lawyer needs a precise mind* **4** [B] (too) careful and correct in regard to the smallest details: *A scientist must be precise in making tests.|a very precise old lady|precise manners* —**~ness** *n* [U]

pre·cise·ly /prɪˈsaɪsli/ *adv* **1** in a PRECISE way **2** exactly: *The train leaves at 10 o'clock precisely* **3** yes, that is correct; you are right: *"So you think we ought to wait until autumn?" "Precisely"*

pre·ci·sion /prɪˈsɪʒən/ *n* **1** [U;S] also **preciseness**— exactness: *She doesn't express her thoughts with precision, so people often misunderstand what she says* **2** [A] **a** made or done with great exactness: *a precision landing* **b** used for producing very exact results: *Precision instruments are used to help pilots in guiding their aircraft*

precision-made /·ˌ·· ˈ·◂/ *adj* (of an article) made with special care for exactness

pre·clude /prɪˈkluːd/ *v* [T1,4] *usu. fml* to prevent: *Let us be exact in what we say so as to preclude any possibility of misunderstanding* —**-clusion** /ˈkluːʒən/ *n* [U]

preclude from *v prep* [V4b] *usu. fml* to prevent

from: *The bad weather precluded me from attending the meeting*

pre·co·cious /prɪˈkəʊʃəs/ *adj* **1** (of a young person) **a** showing unusually early development of mind or body: *He was a precocious child who talked well at the age of one* **b** *derog* having qualities that are more suited to an older person: *Precocious children annoy me* **2** (of knowledge or qualities of character) developing at an unusually early age —**~ly** *adv* —**~ness** *n* [U] —**-city** /prɪˈkɒsɪ̵ti‖-ˈkɑ-/ *n* [U]

pre·cog·ni·tion /ˌpriːkɒgˈnɪʃən‖-kɑg-/ *n* [U;C] *fml* knowledge of something that will happen in the future, esp. as received in the form of a direct unexplainable message to the mind

pre·con·ceived /ˌpriːkənˈsiːvd/ *adj* (of an idea, opinion, etc.) formed in advance, without (enough) knowledge or experience

pre·con·cep·tion /ˌpriːkənˈsepʃən/ *n* an opinion formed in advance without actual knowledge

pre·con·di·tion /ˌpriːkənˈdɪʃən/ *n* PREREQUISITE

pre·cook /ˌpriːˈkʊk/ *v* [Wv5;T1] to cook (food) for eating later

pre·cur·sor /prɪˈkɜːsəʳ‖-ˈkɜr-/ *n* [C9, esp. *of*] a person or thing that comes before and is a sign or earlier type of one that is to follow: *The precursor of the modern car was a horseless carriage with a petrol engine in front*

pred·a·tor /ˈpredətəʳ/ *n* a PREDATORY (1) animal

pred·a·to·ry /ˈpredətəri‖-tori/ *adj* **1** also (*fml*) **pre·da·ceous, pre·da·cious** /prɪˈdeɪʃəs/— (esp. of a wild animal) living by killing and eating other animals **2** concerned with or living by or as if by robbery and seizing the property of others: *predatory tribes*|*a predatory attack*|(fig.) *This town is full of predatory hotel keepers who charge very high prices* **3** *derog or humor* (of a person) having the habit of using others for one's own gain or sexual pleasure: *Watch out for that predatory female; she's had 4 men this month already*

pre·de·cease /ˌpriːdɪˈsiːs/ *v* [T1] *law* to die before (someone)

pre·de·ces·sor /ˈpriːdɪ̵sesəʳ‖ˈpre-/ *n* [C9, esp. *of*] **1** a person who held an (official) position before someone else: *Our new doctor is much younger than his predecessor* **2** something formerly used, but which has now been changed for something else: *This is the 5th plan we've made and it's no better than any of its predecessors*

pre·des·ti·nate /prɪˈdestɪ̵neɪt/ *v* [T1 (*to*); V3 *usu. pass.*] *fml or lit* PREDESTINE

pre·des·ti·na·tion /prɪˌdestɪ̵ˈneɪʃən, ˌpriːdes-/ *n* [U] **1** the belief that God has decided everything that will happen, and that no human effort can change things —compare FREE WILL **2** the belief that by God's wish some souls will be saved and go to heaven, and others lost and go to HELL[1] (1)

pre·des·tine /prɪˈdestɪ̵n/ *v* [Wv5 (*for*); T1 (*to*); V3 *often pass.*] to fix, as if by fate, the future of: *He thought that whatever happened was predestined and nothing he did could have changed the result.*|*He felt that he was predestined to lead his country to freedom*

pre·de·ter·mine /ˌpriːdɪˈtɜːmɪ̵n‖-ɜr-/ *v* **1** [T1;V3 *usu. pass.*] to fix unchangeably from the beginning: *The colour of a person's eyes is predetermined by that of his parents* **2** [T1] to calculate (the amount or cost of something not yet produced): *Owing to the possibility of rises in prices and wages, it's not easy to predetermine the cost of producing this article in our factory* **3** [X9;V3] PREDISPOSE —**-mination** /ˌpriːdɪtɜːmɪ̵ˈneɪʃən‖-ɜr-/ *n* [U;C]

pre·de·ter·min·er /ˌpridɪˈtɜːmɪ̵nəʳ‖-ɜr-/ *n tech* a word that can be used before *a* or *the* (such as *all* in *all the boys* or *such* in *such a nice day*)

pre·dic·a·ment /prɪˈdɪkəmənt/ *n* a difficult or unpleasant state of affairs in which one does not know what to do, or must make a difficult choice

pred·i·cate[1] /ˈpredɪkɪ̵t/ *n* the part of a sentence which makes a statement about the subject: *In "Fishes swim" and "She is an artist", "swim" and "is an artist" are predicates*

pred·i·cate[2] /ˈpredɪ̵keɪt/ *v fml* **1** [T1 (*of*), 5;V3] to state the existence of (a quality) as belonging to (someone or something): *predicating reason of man*|*predicating man to be a reasoning creature* **2** [T1 (*on*) *often pass.*] to base: *The company's latest moves were predicated on great changes in the condition of the world market for their product*

pre·dic·a·tive[1] /prɪˈdɪkətɪv‖ˈpredɪ̵keɪ-/ *adj* **1** (of an adjective, noun, or phrase) coming after the noun being described or after the verb of which the noun is the subject: *In "He is alive", "alive" is a predicative adjective* —compare ATTRIBUTIVE **2** (of (the position of) an adjective, adverb, noun, or phrase) following an [L] verb like *be* or following the object of an [X] verb like *find* or *make* —compare ATTRIBUTIVE —**~ly** *adv*

predicative[2] *n* an adjective, noun, or phrase that is PREDICATIVE[1]

pre·dict /prɪˈdɪkt/ *v* [T1,5a,b,6a] to see or describe (a future happening) in advance as a result of knowledge, experience, reason, etc.: *The weather scientists predicted a fine summer.*|*She predicted that he would marry a doctor*

pre·dic·ta·ble /prɪˈdɪktəbəl/ *adj* **1** that can be PREDICTed **2** *derog* not being or doing anything unexpected or showing imagination: *I hate predictable men* —**-bility** /prɪˌdɪktəˈbɪlɪ̵ti/ *n* [U] —**-bly** /prɪˈdɪktəbli/ *adv*: *Predictably, he came late as he always does*

pre·dic·tion /prɪˈdɪkʃən/ *n* **1** [C,C5] something that is PREDICTed **2** [U] the act of PREDICTing —**-tive** *adj* —**-tively** *adv*

pre·di·gest /ˌpriːdaɪˈdʒest, ˌpriːdɪ̵-/ *v* [Wv5;T1] **1** to make (food) easier for sick people or babies to take, as by means of chemical treatment **2** *sometimes derog* to make (esp. a book) simpler, for easy use

pre·di·lec·tion /ˌpriːdɪˈlekʃən‖ˌpredlˈek-/ *n* [C9, esp. *for*] a special liking that has become a habit: *Many young people have a predilection for dangerous sports.*|*Charles has a predilection for red-haired women*

pre·dis·pose /ˌpriːdɪsˈpəʊz/ *v* [X9;V3] *fml* to influence (someone) in the stated way: *I have heard nothing that predisposes me in her favour* (=that influences me to favour her).|*nothing that predisposes me to like her*

predispose to *v prep* [D1 *often pass.*] to cause (someone) to tend towards (something): *His weak chest predisposes him to winter illnesses*

pre·dis·po·si·tion /ˌpriːdɪspəˈzɪʃən/ *n* [(*to*)] a state of body or mind that is favourable (to something, often something bad)

pre·dom·i·nance /prɪˈdɒmɪ̵nəns‖-ˈdɑ-/ *n* [S;(U)] the state or quality of predominating (PREDOMINATE): *There is a predominance of apple trees in this area*

pre·dom·i·nant /prɪˈdɒmɪ̵nənt‖-ˈdɑ-/ *adj* [(*over*)] most powerful, noticeable, or important: *The predominant member of the government is the chief minister.*|*Bright red was the predominant colour in the room*

pre·dom·i·nant·ly /prɪˈdɒmɪ̵nəntli‖-ˈdɑ-/ *adv* mostly; mainly: *The votes were predominantly in favour of the government*

pre·dom·i·nate /prɪˈdɒmɪ̵neɪt‖-ˈdɑ-/ *v* [IØ (*over*)] **1** to have the main power or influence: *In his mind a wish to become rich has always predominated* **2** to be greater or greatest in numbers, force, etc.; be most noticeable

pre·em·i·nent /priː'emɨnənt/ *adj usu. apprec* above all others in the possession of some (usu. good) quality, ability, or main activity —**-nence** *n* [U]

pre·em·i·nent·ly /priː'emɨnəntli/ *adv* above everything else; chiefly: *She is a musician who plays several instruments, but she is preeminently a* PIANIST

pre·empt /priː'empt/ *v* [T1] **1** to buy or get by PREEMPTION (1,2,3) **2** to cause to have no influence or force by means of taking action in advance: *The council found that their traffic plans had been preempted by a government decision* **3** *fml* to take the place of: *We were looking forward to watching our favourite television show, but it had been preempted by a political talk* **4** to seize upon or take for one's own use: *The political movement had been preempted by a group of evil men* —**~or** *n*

pre·emp·tion /priː'empʃən/ *n* [U] **1** the act or right of buying before others have a chance to buy **2 a** the right of a country at war to seize and buy at a fixed price goods such as guns which a country not at war is trying to send to an enemy of the first country **b** the act of using this right **3** *AmE* **a** the right given by the government to someone settling on publicly owned land to buy that land before others are given the chance to do so **b** the buying of land by this right **4** the act of PREEMPTing (2,3,4) someone or something **5** (in the card game of BRIDGE) the act of making a PREEMPTIVE (3) statement of the number of tricks one will try to win

pre·emp·tive /priː'emptɪv/ *adj* [Wa5] **1** of or concerning PREEMPTION (1,2,3): *preemptive buying*| *the preemptive right to buy the land* **2** done before other people have a chance to act, and in order to prevent them from doing so: *several preemptive attacks on the enemy's airforce bases* **3** (of a BID in the card game of BRIDGE) made higher than necessary on purpose in order to stop others from making further BIDs —**~ly** *adv*

preen /priːn/ *v* **1** [T1] (of a bird) to clean or smooth (itself or its feathers) with the beak **2** [T1; I0] (of a person) to make (oneself) neat

preen on also **preen up·on**— *v prep* [D1;V4b] PRIDE ON

pre·ex·ist /ˌpriːɪg'zɪst/ *v* [I0] **1** (of a person) to exist in another life before the present one **2** (of the soul) to exist before uniting with the body

pre·ex·is·tence /ˌpriːɪg'zɪstəns/ *n* [U] former existence in another state, esp. the existence of one's soul before one's birth —**-tent** *adj* [Wa5]

pre·fab /'priːfæb‖ˌpriː'fæb/ *n infml* a small house built from parts made in a factory (esp. of the type put up in Britain and elsewhere after World War 2)

pre·fab·ri·cate /priː'fæbrɪkeɪt/ *v* [T1] to make (the parts of a building, ship, etc.) in a factory in large numbers and to standard measurements ready for fitting together in any place chosen for building —see picture at SITE[1] —**-cation** /priːˌfæbrɪ'keɪʃən/ *n* [U]

pre·fab·ri·cat·ed /priː'fæbrɪkeɪtɨd/ *adj* [Wa5] (of a building, ship, etc.) built out of PREFABRICATED parts

pref·ace[1] /'prefɨs/ *n* [(*to*)] **1** an introduction to a book or speech **2** *infml* an action that is intended to introduce something else more important

USAGE A **preface**, an **introduction**, and a **foreword** all come in the first pages of a book before the main contents; an **introduction** is usually longer than a **preface**, and a **foreword** is less formal. The **beginning** of the book is the early part of the actual contents, after the **preface**

preface[2] *v* **1** [T1] to serve as a PREFACE[1] to: *Several pages of closely reasoned argument preface her account of the war* **2** [X9, esp. *with, by*] to provide with a PREFACE[1] as stated: *"How did he preface his speech?" "He prefaced his speech with an amusing story"*

pref·a·to·ry /'prefətəri‖-tori/ *adj* [Wa5] acting as a PREFACE[1] or introduction: *I must just make a few prefatory remarks before Mr. Green begins his speech*

pre·fect /'priːfekt/ *n* **1** [C] (in some British schools) an older pupil given certain powers and duties with regard to keeping order over other pupils **2** (*sometimes cap.*) (in ancient Rome and certain countries today) any of various public officers or judges with duties in government, the police, or the army: *the Prefect of Police of Paris*

pre·fec·ture /'priːfektʃʊəʳ‖-tʃər/ *n* **1** a governmental division or area of certain countries, such as France and Japan **2** (in France) the (official) home or place of work of a PREFECT (2) **3** the office or period of time in office of a PREFECT (2): *during the prefecture of Maximus* —**-tural** /prɪ'fektʃərəl/ *adj*

pre·fer /prɪ'fɜːʳ/ *v* **-rr-** **1** [Wv6;T1 (*to*), 3, 4 (*to*), (5),5c; V3] to choose (one thing or action) rather than another; like better: *"Would you like meat or fish?" "I'd prefer meat, please."*|*I prefer dogs to cats.*|*"May I wash the dishes?" "I'd prefer you to dry them."*|*Would you prefer that I come on Monday instead of on Tuesday?* **2** [T1 (*to*)] *fml or tech* to appoint (someone) (to a higher position, esp. in the church) **3** [T1 (*against*)] *law* to put forward for official consideration or action according to law (esp. in the phr. **prefer charges/a charge**)

pref·e·ra·ble /'prefərəbəl/ *adj* [Wa5 (*to*)] better (esp. because more suitable); to be PREFERred: *A dark suit is preferable to a light one for evening wear.*| *Anything is preferable to having her with us for the whole week!* —**-bly** *adv* [Wa3,5]

pref·e·rence /'prefərəns/ *n* **1** [C *usu. sing.*; U: (*for, to*)] (a) desire or liking (for one thing rather than another): *He has never liked meat, and has always had a preference for vegetables and fruit.*|*"Would you like tea or coffee?" "Either; I've no strong preference."*|*I'd choose the small car in preference to the larger one* (=rather than the larger one) **2** [C] choice; that which is liked better or best: *Tea or coffee? Which is your preference?* **3** [U] special favour or consideration shown to a person, group, etc. (esp. in business matters): *In considering men for jobs in our firm, we give preference to those with some experience.*|*Sometimes it's difficult for a teacher not to show preference to an especially clever child* **4** [C] an example of this: *special trade preferences*

preference stock /'··· ·/ (*AmE* **preferred stock**)— *n* [U] *BrE* (*often caps.*) business shares that give the owners the right to be paid interest before any money is paid to owners of ordinary shares

pref·e·ren·tial /ˌprefə'renʃəl/ *adj* [A;(B)] of, giving, receiving, or showing PREFERENCE (3): *This hotel gives preferential treatment to people who stay in it regularly* —**-tially** *adv*: *demanded to be treated preferentially*

pre·fer·ment /prɪ'fɜːmənt‖-ɜr-/ *n* [U;(C)] appointment to a higher rank or position, esp. in the church

pre·fig·ure /ˌpriː'fɪgəʳ‖-gjər/ *v* [T1] to represent or be a sign of (something that will come later)

pre·fix[1] /'priːfɪks/ *v* [T1] **1** to add a PREFIX[2] to (a word or name) **2** to add to the beginning: *We prefixed a few pages to the article on animals*

prefix[2] *n* **1** (in grammar) an AFFIX that is placed at the beginning of a word or base: *"Re-" (meaning "again") is a prefix in "refill"* —compare SUFFIX **2** a title used before a person's name: *"Mr." and "Dr." can be prefixes*

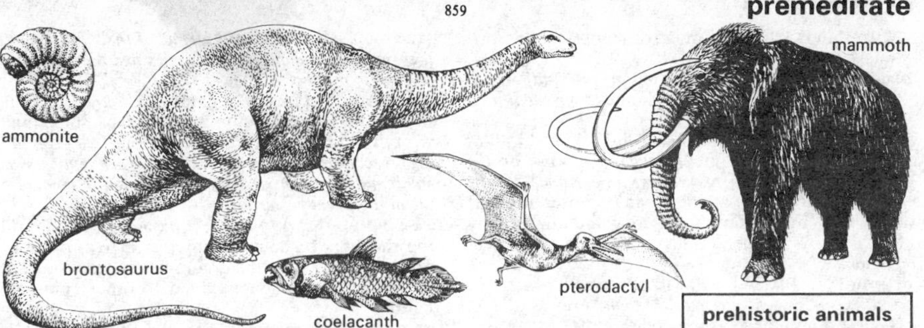

prehistoric animals

preg·nan·cy /ˈpregnənsi/ *n* **1** [U] **a** the condition of being PREGNANT (1) **b** the time of this **2** [C] an example of this: *This was her third pregnancy* **3** [U] *lit* deep meaning; importance (for the future)

pregnancy test /ˈ··· ·/ *n* a scientific test made to discover whether a woman has just become PREGNANT (1)

preg·nant /ˈpregnənt/ *adj* **1** [Wa5;B;E] (of a woman or female animal) having an unborn child or unborn young in the body: *She has been pregnant for 5 months.|She is 5 months pregnant* **2** [A] full of important but unexpressed or hidden meaning: *His words were followed by a pregnant pause* **3** [F+*with*] filled (with something not yet fully known, understood, or developed); giving signs or warnings (of some future development): *Every phrase in this poem is pregnant with meaning* **4** [A;(B)] *lit* clever; inventive: *the artist's pregnant imagination* **5 fall pregnant** *BrE* (of a woman) to become PREGNANT (1) —**~ly** *adv*

pre·heat /ˌpriːˈhiːt/ *v* [T1;IØ] to heat up (a cooking apparatus (OVEN)) to a particular temperature before use for cooking

pre·hen·sile /prɪˈhensaɪl‖-səl/ *adj* (of a part of the body) able to curl round, seize, and hold things: *a monkey hanging from the branch of a tree by its prehensile tail*

pre·his·tor·ic /ˌpriːhɪˈstɒrɪk‖-ˈstɔ-, -ˈstɑ-/ also (*fml*) **pre·his·tor·i·cal** /-kəl/— *adj* **1** of or belonging to a time before recorded history: *prehistoric man|prehistoric burial grounds* **2** *derog or humor* very old-fashioned; long used or known: *Is Simon's prehistoric car still working?|His ideas on morals are really prehistoric* —**~ally** *adv* [Wa4]

pre·his·to·ry /priːˈhɪstəri/ *n* **1** [U] the time in human history before there were any (written) records **2** [U] the study of this time, esp. by digging up ancient remains **3** [S (*of*)] the history of the earlier stages of some developing condition

pre·judge /ˌpriːˈdʒʌdʒ/ *v* [T1] to form an (unfavourable) opinion about (someone or something) before knowing or examining all the facts —**-judgment, -judgement** *n* [U;C]

prej·u·dice¹ /ˈpredʒədɨs/ *n* **1** [U] unfair and often unfavourable feeling or opinion not based on reason or enough knowledge, and sometimes resulting from fear or distrust of ideas different from one's own: *A judge must be free from prejudice.|a new law to discourage racial prejudice* (=prejudice against members of other races) **2** [C] an example of this: *He has a prejudice against lending money, because he's afraid he may not be repaid* **3** [U] **a** damage or harm caused to something or someone by the action or judgment of another (esp. in the phr. **to the prejudice of**): *He had to leave the university, to the prejudice of his own future as a scientist* **b** harm to one's own right or claim in law (esp. in the phr. **without prejudice (to)**): *He asked for higher wages, without prejudice to any increase all the other workmen might be given later*

prejudice² *v* [T1] **1** [(*against, in favour of*)] to cause (someone or someone's mind) to have a PREJUDICE¹ (2); influence: *His pleasant voice prejudices me in his favour* **2** to weaken; harm (someone's case, expectations, etc.)

prej·u·diced /ˈpredʒədɨst/ *adj usu. derog* feeling or showing PREJUDICE¹ (1); unfair

prej·u·di·cial /ˌpredʒʊˈdɪʃəl, -dʒə-/ *adj fml* **1** [F+*to*] harmful: *Too much smoking is prejudicial to health* **2** [B] leading to judgment that is too quick or opinion that is without reason or proof —**~ly** *adv*

prel·a·cy /ˈpreləsi/ *n* **1** [C] the office or rank of a PRELATE **2** [(*the*) GU] the whole body of PRELATEs

prel·ate /ˈprelɨt/ *n* a priest of high rank, esp. a BISHOP or someone with a higher rank

pre·lim /ˈpriːlɪm, prɪˈlɪm/ also (*fml*) **preliminary ex·am·i·na·tion** /·ˌ···· ···ˈ··/— *n* [*usu. pl.*] *infml* (esp. in some British universities) an examination, the result of which decides whether one may go on further with one's studies

pre·lim·i·na·ry¹ /prɪˈlɪmɨnəri‖-neri/ *n* [*usu. pl.*] a preparation; PRELIMINARY² (1) act or arrangement: *There are a lot of preliminaries to be gone through before you can visit some foreign countries*

preliminary² *adj* **1** [A;(B (*to*))] coming before and introducing or preparing for something more important: *The chairman made a preliminary statement before beginning the main business of the meeting* **2** [A] (of a part of a sports competition) being the first part, in which the weaker people lose and the winners are left to compete for the prizes in the main competition

preliminary to /·ˈ···· ·/ *prep* before; as a preparation for; PRIOR TO: *He packed his bags preliminary to leaving for the station*

pre·lims /ˈpriːlɪmz, prɪˈlɪmz/ *n* [(*the*) P] *infml esp. BrE* the material (such as the title, PREFACE, etc.) which comes before the main part of a book

pre·lit·e·rate /ˌpriːˈlɪtərɨt/ *adj* not leaving or keeping written records: *preliterate societies whose past is hard to study* —compare ILLITERATE

prel·ude /ˈpreljuːd/ *n* **1** [C+*to, usu. sing.*] something that comes before and acts as an introduction to something more important: *I fear that the widespread fighting in the streets is a prelude to more serious trouble* **2** [C] **a** a short piece of music that introduces a large musical work **b** a short separate piece of piano or ORGAN music: *Chopin's Preludes*

pre·mar·i·tal /priːˈmærɨtəl/ *adj* [Wa5] happening or existing before marriage —**-tally** *adv*

pre·ma·ture /ˈprematʃəʳ, -tʃʊəʳ, ˌpreməˈtʃʊəʳ‖ˌpriːməˈtʊər/ *adj* **1** developing, happening, ripening, or coming before the natural or proper time: *His premature death at the age of 32 is a great loss* **2** (of a human or animal baby, or a birth) born, or happening, after less than the usual period of time inside the mother's body **3** done too early or too soon; hasty —**~ly** *adv*

pre·med·i·tate /priːˈmedɨteɪt‖prɪ-/ *v* [T1] to plan

(something) carefully in advance —**-tation** /prɪˌmedʒ̇ˈteɪʃən/ *n* [U]

pre·med·i·tat·ed /priːˈmedʒ̇teɪtʒ̇d‖prɪ-/ *adj* intentional; done on purpose; planned: *premeditated rudeness*

prem·i·er[1] /ˈpremɪəʳ‖prɪˈmɪər/ *adj* [Wa5;A] **1** *lit* first (in position or importance): *His work on the cause of diseases is of premier importance to the whole world* **2** (of a nobleman) whose title has been held by his family for longer than has any like title by another family: *the premier* DUKE *of England*

premier[2] *n* **1** [C;A] the head of the government in certain countries: *Premier Mendès-France* **2** [A; (C)] (esp. in newspaper style) PRIME MINISTER: *"Premier Wilson* RESIGNS*"* (title of news story) —**~ship** *n*

prem·i·ere[1], **-ère** /ˈpremɪeəʳ‖prɪˈmɪər/ *n* the first public performance of a play or a cinema film

premiere[2], **-ère** *v* [T1 *often pass.*; I∅] **a** to give a PREMIERE[1] of (a play or a cinema film) **b** (of a play or a cinema film) to have a PREMIERE[1]

prem·ise[1], *BrE* also **-iss** /ˈpremʒ̇s/ *n* [C,C5] **1** a statement or idea on which reasoning is based: *He based his holiday plans on the premise that Wendy was coming with us, but she didn't in fact do so* **2** (in the science of reasoning) either of 2 statements (**major premise** and **minor premise**) from which a third statement may be proved to be true

premise[2] /ˈpremʒ̇s, prɪˈmaɪz/ *v* [T1,5] *fml* to state as a PREMISE[1]

prem·is·es /ˈpremʒ̇sʒ̇z/ *n* **1** [P] a house or other building with any surrounding land, considered as a particular piece of property: *"These are private premises. Keep off my premises!" shouted the owner.*|*Food bought in this shop may not be eaten on the premises* (=must be taken away before being eaten) **2** [*the*+P] *law* the first part of a written agreement in law, esp. one concerned with property

pre·mi·um /ˈpriːmɪəm/ *n* **1** a sum of money paid (regularly) to an insurance company to protect oneself against some risk of loss or damage **2** an additional payment, esp. to a worker, made as a reward for special effort **3** an additional charge made for something: *There's a premium of 10 dollars for a seat on this special fast train* **4 at a premium a** (of a business share) at a rate above the usual value **b** rare or difficult to obtain, and therefore worth more than usual: *During the holiday months of July and August hotel rooms are at a premium* **5 put a premium on** to cause (a quality or action) to be an advantage: *Work paid according to the amount done puts a premium on speed and not on quality*

premium bond /ˈ··· ·/ *n* (*often caps.*) (in Britain) a numbered piece of paper that can be bought from the government, and that gives the buyer the chance of a monthly prize of a small or large sum of money. No interest is paid to the holder of the piece of paper

pre·mo·ni·tion /ˌpreməˈnɪʃən, ˌpriː-/ *n* [C (*of*), C5] a feeling that something (esp. something unpleasant) is going to happen or will be found to have happened; forewarning

pre·mon·i·to·ry /prɪˈmɒnʒ̇təri‖-ˈmɑnʒ̇tori/ *adj fml* giving a warning

pre·na·tal /ˌpriːˈneɪtl/ *adj* [Wa5] *med esp. AmE* ANTENATAL —**-tally** *adv*

pren·tice /ˈprentʒ̇s/ *adj* [A] *esp. old use* of or like a learner of a trade (an APPRENTICE); inexperienced; imperfect

pre·oc·cu·pa·tion /priːˌɒkjʊˈpeɪʃən‖-ˌɑkjə-/ *n* **1** [U] the state of being PREOCCUPIED and not noticing what is happening **2** [C] a matter which takes up all one's attention: *Ethel has many preoccupations about family affairs just now, and has no time to visit her friends*

pre·oc·cu·pied /priːˈɒkjʊpaɪd‖-ˌɑkjə-/ *adj* with the mind fixed on something else (esp. something worrying); inattentive to present matters: *He had a preoccupied look on his face, as if something was troubling him.*|*You were too preoccupied to recognize me in the street yesterday*

pre·oc·cu·py /priːˈɒkjʊpaɪ‖-ˈɑkjə-/ *v* [T1] to fill the thoughts or hold the interest of (someone or someone's mind) almost completely, esp. so that not enough attention is given to other (present) matters

pre·or·dain /ˌpriːɔːˈdeɪn‖-ɔr-/ *v* [T1,5,5b,6a;V3] (esp. of God or fate) to fix, decide, or order before or from the beginning: *Some people believe that fate has preordained whether they will be happy or unhappy* —**-dination** /ˌpriːɔːdʒ̇ˈneɪʃən‖-ɔr-/ *n* [C;U] —**~ment** /ˌpriːɔːˈdeɪnmənt‖-ɔr-/ *n* [C;U]

prep /prep/ *n* [U] *infml BrE* **1** school work that is done at home; HOMEWORK **2** also (*fml*) **preparation**— (at schools in which the pupils live as well as study) **a** studying and getting ready for lessons **b** the time during which this is done

pre·pack /ˌpriːˈpæk/ also **pre·pack·age** /-ˈpækɪdʒ/— *v* [Wv5;T1] to wrap up (food or other articles) in a factory or other place before sending to a shop

prep·a·ra·tion /ˌprepəˈreɪʃən/ *n* **1** [U;S: (*of*)] the act or action of preparing: *She was late and only had time for a hurried preparation of dinner.*|*He did too little preparation for his examination* **2** [U] the state or course of being prepared: *Plans for selling the new product are now in preparation* **3** [C (*for*) *usu. pl.*] an arrangement (for a future event): *She is making preparations for her marriage* **4** [C] something that is made ready for use by mixing a number of (chemical) substances: *The firm is selling a new preparation for cleaning metal* **5** [U] *BrE fml* PREP (2)

pre·par·a·to·ry /prɪˈpærətəri‖-tori/ also (*fml*) **pre·par·a·tive** /-rətɪv/— *adj* [Wa5;A;(B)] done in order to get ready for something

preparatory school /·ˈ···· ·/ also (*infml*) **prep school**— *n* [C;U] **1** (esp. in Britain) (a) private school for pupils up to the age of 14, where they are made ready to attend a higher school (esp. a PUBLIC SCHOOL) **2** (in the US) (a) private school that makes pupils ready for college. It may be like (a) PUBLIC SCHOOL in Britain

preparatory to /·ˈ···· ·/ *prep* before; as a preparation for: *I have a few letters to write preparatory to beginning the day's work*

pre·pare /prɪˈpeəʳ/ *v* **1** [T1 (*for*); V3] to put (something) in a condition ready for use or for a purpose: *Please prepare the table for dinner* (=put a cloth, dishes, etc., on it).|*The nurse is preparing the child to go to the hospital* (=getting together its clothes and other articles) **2** [D1 (*for*); T1] to put together or make by treating in some special way (such as by mixing or heating substances): *This special medicine must be freshly prepared each time.*|*Mother is preparing us a meal* **3** [T1 (*for*), 3] to get or make ready by collecting supplies, making necessary arrangements, planning, studying, etc.: *Who prepared these building plans?*|*He's preparing his speech for the meeting tomorrow.*|*They are busy preparing to go on holiday* —see also PREPARE FOR (1) **4** [T1 (*for*), 3;V3] to accustom (someone or someone's mind) to some (new) idea, event, or condition: *Prepare yourself for a shock.*|*Prepare to meet your fate.*|*He prepared himself to accept defeat* —see also PREPARE FOR (2) **5** [V3] to make (someone) fit for something by special training:

This college prepares boys to enter the army as officers —see also PREPARE FOR (3)

pre·pared /prɪ'peəd‖-ərd/ *adj* [Wa5] **1** [B] got ready in advance: *The chairman read out a prepared statement* **2** [F3] willing: *I'm not prepared to listen to all your weak excuses*

pre·pared·ness /prɪ'peədnɪ̵s, -'peərɪ̵d-/ *n* [U] (the state of) being ready for something, esp. war

prepare for *v prep* **1** [T1,(4)] to get ready for: *Will you help me prepare for the party?* **2** [T1] to accustom one's mind to: *We must prepare for the worst* **3** [D1;V4b] to make (someone) fit for something by special training

pre·pay /ˌpriː'peɪ/ *v* **-paid** /'peɪd/ [Wv5;T1] to pay for (something) before the usual time

pre·pon·de·rance /prɪ'pɒndərəns‖-'pan-/ *n* [S;(U): (*of*)] the quality or state of being greater in amount, number, etc.: *There is a preponderance of tigers in the forest, and only a small number of monkeys and elephants*

pre·pon·de·rant /prɪ'pɒndərənt‖-'pan-/ *adj* [(*over*)] greater in amount, number, importance, influence, etc., than something else; main; most noticeable: *Yellow was the preponderant colour in the room* —**~ly** *adv*

pre·pon·de·rate /prɪ'pɒndəreɪt‖-'pan-/ *v* [IØ (*over*)] *fml* to be greater in quantity, importance, influence, etc.

prep·o·si·tion /ˌprepə'zɪʃən/ *n* a word used with a noun, PRONOUN, or *-ing* form to show its connection with another word: *In "a house made of wood" and "a man like my brother", "of" and "like" are prepositions, and so is "by" in "she succeeded by working hard"*

prep·o·si·tion·al /ˌprepə'zɪʃənəl◂/ *adj* as, or having the nature of, a PREPOSITION —**-ally** *adv*

prepositional phrase /ˌ····· '·/ *n tech* a phrase consisting of a PREPOSITION and the noun following it: *"In bed" and "on top" are prepositional phrases, as are "in his bed" and "on the top"*

pre·pos·sessed /ˌpriːpə'zest/ *adj* [F+*by*] *fml* **1** favourably influenced or IMPRESSED[1] (2,3) **2** PREOCCUPIED

pre·pos·sess·ing /ˌpriːpə'zesɪŋ/ *adj* (of a person or a quality of his character) very pleasing; charming; producing a favourable effect at once

pre·pos·ses·sion /ˌpriːpə'zeʃən/ *n fml* **1** [C (*against, for*)] a liking or a dislike not based on personal experience **2** [U;C] PREOCCUPATION

pre·pos·ter·ous /prɪ'pɒstərəs‖-'pas-/ *adj* **1** completely unreasonable or improbable; ABSURD **2** laughably foolish in manner or appearance: *Look at that preposterous old woman with her hair hanging down in long curls like a girl's!* —**~ly** *adv*

prep school /'· ·/ *n* [U;C] *infml* PREPARATORY SCHOOL

pre·puce /'priːpjuːs/ *n med* a fold of skin covering the end of the male sex organ; FORESKIN

Pre-Raph·ael·ite /ˌpriː 'ræfəlaɪt‖-fɪəlaɪt/ *n, adj* (in England in the second half of the 19th century) (a person) belonging to the group of artists (**Pre-Raphaelite brotherhood**) who based their work on principles and practices believed to have been those of Italian art before the painter Raphael

pre·re·cord /ˌpriːrɪ'kɔːd‖-'kɔrd/ *v* [Wv5;T1] to record (music, a play, a speech, etc.) on a machine for later use

pre·req·ui·site /priː'rekwɪ̵zɪ̵t/ *n, adj* [C (*of, for, to*); B (*for, to*)] (something) that is necessary before something else can happen or be done: *There are certain prerequisite conditions to the completion of the sale of the property*

pre·rog·a·tive /prɪ'rɒgətɪv‖-'ra-/ *n* [*usu. sing.*] a special right belonging to someone by rank, position, or nature: *A ruler may use his prerogative of mercy towards a criminal.|It's a woman's prerogative to change her mind* —see also ROYAL PREROGATIVE

pres. *written abbrev. for:* **1** present **2** (*usu. cap.*) president: *"Pres. Carter To Visit Britain"*

pres·age[1] /'presɪdʒ/ *n* [(*of*)] *lit* a warning feeling or sign that something (esp. something bad) will happen

pres·age[2] /'presɪdʒ, prɪ̵'seɪdʒ/ *v* [Wv6;T1] *lit* to be a warning of; FORETELL: *Some people say that the appearance of a black cat presages good luck*

pres·by·ter /'prezbɪ̵tə^r/ *n* **1** (in PRESBYTERIAN churches) an official person elected to serve on the governing body of a church **2** (in EPISCOPAL churches) a priest below a BISHOP in rank **3** (in the early Christian church) a leading member of a local church who helped to direct its affairs

Pres·by·te·ri·an /ˌprezbɪ̵'tɪərɪən/ *n, adj* (a member) of a PROTESTANT church governed by a body of official people all of equal rank, as in Scotland —**~ism** *n* [U]

pres·by·ter·y /'prezbɪ̵təri/ *n* **1** the eastern part of a church, behind the place where the trained singers (CHOIR) sit **2** (in the PRESBYTERIAN church) **a** a type of local court or ruling body **b** the area controlled by this court **3** (in the ROMAN CATHOLIC church) the house in which a local priest lives

pre·school /ˌpriː'skuːl◂/ *adj* [Wa5;A] of or concerning the time in a child's life before it goes to school

pre·sci·ent /'preʃɪənt/ *adj lit or fml* able to imagine or guess what will probably happen —**-ence** *n* [U]

pre·scribe /prɪ'skraɪb/ *v* **1** [T1;D1 (*for*); IØ] to order or give (something) as a medicine or treatment for a sick person: *The doctor prescribed a new medicine for the pain in my joints* **2** [T1,6a,b;IØ] (of a person or body that has the right to do so) to state (what must happen or be done in certain conditions): *What punishment does the law prescribe for this crime?|Someone who behaves as foolishly as you has no right to prescribe how others should behave*

pre·scribed /prɪ'skraɪbd/ *adj* [Wa5;A] fixed as correct or necessary: *Government schools must work for a prescribed number of days each year*

pre·script /'priːˌskrɪpt/ *n* [U;(C)] *fml* an order or rule that is PRESCRIBED (2)

pre·scrip·tion /prɪ'skrɪpʃən/ *n* **1** [U] the act of prescribing (PRESCRIBE) **2** [C] that which is PRESCRIBED: (fig.) *What's your prescription for a happy marriage?* **3** [C] **a** a particular medicine or treatment ordered by a doctor for a person's illness **b** a written order describing (the preparation and use of) this: *Take this prescription to your local* CHEMIST'S **4** [U] *law* (the getting or having of) a right connected with property, claimed by custom and long use

prescription charge /·'·· ·/ *n* [*usu. pl.*] (in Britain) a sum of money that has to be paid when obtaining medicine under the NATIONAL HEALTH SERVICE

pre·scrip·tive /prɪ'skrɪptɪv/ *adj* **1** [Wa5] *law* agreed, used, or existing by law or by a custom followed for so long that it almost has the force of law **2** *sometimes derog* giving orders about how a language ought to be used, rather than simply describing how it is used: *prescriptive grammar* —compare DESCRIPTIVE —**-tivism** *n* [U] —**-tivist** *n* —**~ly** *adv*

pres·ence /'prezəns/ *n* **1** [U] the fact or state of being present: *She was so quiet that her presence was hardly noticed* **2** [U] attendance: *Your presence is requested at the club meeting on Thursday* **3** [U] personal appearance and manner, as having a strong effect on others **4** [C *usu. sing.*] a spirit or an influence that cannot be seen but is felt to be near **5 in the presence of someone** also **in someone's presence**— close enough to be seen or heard by someone **6 make one's presence felt** to make people feel one's importance

presence of mind /ˌ·· · ˈ·/ *n* [U] *apprec* the ability to act calmly, quickly, and wisely in conditions of sudden danger or surprise: *When the fire started in the kitchen, John had the presence of mind to turn off the gas* —compare ABSENCE OF MIND

pres·ent¹ /ˈprezənt/ *n* **1** a gift: *They unwrapped their Christmas presents* **2 make someone a present of something a** to give someone something as a gift **b** *infml* to give something away to someone carelessly: *made the other team a present of a* GOAL *by careless play*

pre·sent² /prɪˈzent/ *v* **1** [D1+*to/with*; T1] to give (something) away, esp. at a ceremonial occasion: *Now that the sports competitions are over, Lady de Vere will present the prizes.|When Mr. Brown left the firm, he was given a silver teapot: the director presented it to him.|He presented her with a bunch of flowers.|We were presented with a much larger bill than we had expected* **2** [X9] to offer or bring (something) to someone's notice directly; put forward for consideration or acceptance: *This report ought to be presented in greater detail and in clearer language* **3** [T1 (*to*)] *polite* to offer (esp. in the phrs. **present one's apologies, present one's compliments, present one's respects,** etc.) **4** [T1 (*to*)] *fml* to introduce (someone) esp. to someone of higher rank: *He had the honour of being presented to the Governor.|May I present Mr. Jobbings?* **5** [T1] **a** to give a public performance of **b** to give the public a chance to see and hear (a (new) singer, actor, etc.): *The theatre company is presenting Eric Williamson as Hamlet next year.|presenting, for the very first time on an English stage, Fanny la Motte* **6** [T1] to introduce and take part in (a television or radio show) **7** [T1 (*to*)] to show; offer to the sight: *Although he may be troubled, he always presents a calm smiling face* **8** [T1 (*to*)] (of non-material things) to offer; be the cause of: *He's clever at scientific studies; they present no difficulty to him* **9 present arms** (*used esp. in giving or reporting an order*) (of a soldier) to hold a weapon upright in front of the body as a ceremonial greeting to an officer or person of high rank **10 present itself a** (of a thought) to arrive in the mind **b** (of something possible) to happen: *If the chance to buy this farm presents itself, buy it* **11 present oneself** *fml* (of a person) to attend; arrive; be present

present³ /prɪˈzent/ *n* **at the present** (of a soldier's gun) held upright in front of the body as a ceremonial greeting to an officer or person of high rank

pres·ent⁴ /ˈprezənt/ *adj* [Wa5] **1** [F] (of a person) being in the place talked of or understood: *How many people were present at the meeting?* **2** [A] existing or in course of action now: *I'm not going to buy a house at the present high prices; I'm going to wait until they get cheaper* **3** [A] being considered, talked about, written about, etc., now: *It's usually best to wait, but in the present case* (=in this case) *I'd advise you to act without delay* **4** [F (*in, to*)] *esp. fml or lit* felt or remembered as if actually there: *The terrible events of 5 years ago are still present to our minds* **5** [A;(B)] *tech* (of a tense or a form of a verb) expressing an existing state or action: *"He wants" and "they are coming" are examples of verbs in present tenses* **6** [A] *old use* ready and quick in action **7 present company** everyone now here in this place **8 "present company (always) excepted"** *polite* "but the people here are not included in the unfavourable remarks I am making"

present⁵ /ˈprezənt/ *n* **1** [*the*+R] the PRESENT⁴ (2) time: *We learn from the past, experience the present, and hope for success in the future* **2** [(*the*) C] *tech* the PRESENT⁴ (5) tense **3 at present a** *BrE and fml AmE* now; at this time; at this moment: *She's busy at present and can't speak to you* **b** during this period of time: *At present he's Professor of Chemistry at Oxford* —see PRESENTLY (USAGE) **4 for the present** for now; for the time being: *Let's leave things as they are for the present, even though we may have to change later on* **5 live in the present** to experience life as it comes, not thinking about the past or the future **6 (there is) no time like the present** if you must do something, it is best to do it now

pre·sen·ta·ble /prɪˈzentəbəl/ *adj* **1** fit to be shown, heard, etc., in public; fit to be seen and judged **2 make oneself presentable** to tidy up one's appearance ready for the company of others —**-bly** *adv* [Wa3]

pre·sen·ta·tion /ˌprezənˈteɪʃən‖ˌpriːzen-, -zən-/ *n* **1** [U;(C): (*of*)] the act or action of PRESENTing² something: *There are 2 presentations of the musical show each night* **2** [U (*of*)] the way in which something is said, offered, shown, explained, etc., to others: *This soap is like all other soaps but women buy it because of the prettiness of its presentation* (=its colour, smell, and wrapping paper) **3** [C;U] *med* the position in which a baby is lying in the mother's body just before birth

presentation cop·y /··ˈ·· ˌ··/ *n* a book given away free, esp. by the writer

pres·ent-day /ˌprezənt ˈdeɪ◂/ *adj* [Wa5;A] modern; existing now

pre·sent·er /prɪˈzentəʳ/ *n* a person who PRESENTs² (6) a television or radio show

pre·sen·ti·ment /prɪˈzentɪ̣mənt/ *n* [C (*of*), C5] an unexplained uncomfortable feeling that something (esp. something bad) is going to happen; PREMONITION

pres·ent·ly /ˈprezəntli/ *adv* **1** soon: *The doctor will be here presently* **2** *esp. AmE and ScotE* at present; in the present period; CURRENTly: *The doctor is presently writing a book*

USAGE British speakers are beginning to use **presently** to mean "now", as the Americans do, rather than "soon". *At* **present** always means "now". None of these expressions should be confused with **actual, actually**, which have nothing to do with time.

present par·ti·ci·ple /ˌ·· ˈ····/ *n* (in grammar) a form of a verb which ends in *-ing* and may be used in compound forms of the verb to express actions done or happening in the past, present, or future, or sometimes as an adjective

present per·fect /ˌ·· ˈ··/ also **present perfect tense** /ˌ·· ˌ·· ˈ·/— *n fml & tech* PERFECT³

pres·ents /ˈprezənts/ *n* **by these presents** *law* by the words in this paper written according to law

pre·ser·va·ble /prɪˈzɜːvəbəl‖-ɜr-/ *adj* (esp. of foods and other substances) that can be PRESERVED

pres·er·va·tion /ˌprezəˈveɪʃən‖-zər-/ *n* [U] **1** [(*of*)] the act or action of preserving (PRESERVE) **2** the state of being or remaining in (a stated) condition after a long time: *The old building is in a good state of preservation except for the wooden floors*

preservation or·der /··ˈ·· ˌ··/ *n esp. BrE* an official order that something (esp. a historical building) must be preserved and not destroyed

pre·ser·va·tive /prɪˈzɜːvətɪv‖-ɜr-/ *n, adj* [C;U;B] (a usu. chemical substance) that can be used to PRESERVE¹ (5) foods

pre·serve¹ /prɪˈzɜːv‖-ɜrv/ *v* [T1] **1** [(*from*)] *esp. fml or lit* to keep (someone) safe or alive; protect: *I pray that fate may preserve you from all harm* **2** to keep or save (an article) carefully from destruction for a long time **3** to cause (a condition) to last; keep unchanged: *In times of danger he always preserves his calmness* **4** [(*from*)] to keep (a substance) in good condition or from decay by some means: *Ancient Egyptians knew of means to preserve dead bodies from decay* **5** [Wv5] to prepare (foods) for being kept for a long time by some special treatment: *preserved fruit* **6** to keep and protect (a place and the animals in it) for private hunting and fishing **7** [(*from*)] to keep (a (rare) animal or plant) in existence **8 "Saints preserve us!"** "What has happened or is just happening is very fearful or unpleasantly surprising!" —see also WELL-PRESERVED

preserve² *n* **1** [C *usu. pl.*; U] (*often in comb.*) a substance made from fruit boiled in sugar, used esp. for spreading on bread; JAM **2** [C] a stretch of land or water kept for private hunting or fishing **3** [C9] something considered to belong to or be for the use of only a certain person or limited number of people: *She considers the arranging of flowers in the church to be her own preserve*

pre·serv·er /prɪˈzɜːvəʳ‖-ɜr-/ *n* someone or something that preserves life

pre·set /ˌpriːˈset/ *v* **preset,** *pres. p.* **presetting** [Wv5; T1] to set in advance: *At mid-day he preset the cooker to go on at 5 o'clock, so that dinner would be ready when he got home*

pre·shrunk /ˌpriːˈʃrʌŋk◂/ *adj* [Wa5] (of cloth used for making garments) shrunk (SHRINK) before being offered for sale in order to prevent SHRINKing after use

pre·side /prɪˈzaɪd/ *v* [Wv4;I∅ (*at*)] to be in charge; lead: *the presiding officer*

pres·i·den·cy /ˈprezədənsi/ *n* **1** [(*of*)] the office of president: *Roosevelt was elected 4 times to the presidency of the US* **2** the length of time a person is president

pres·i·dent /ˈprezədənt/ *n* **1** [C;A] (*often cap.*) the head of government in many modern states that do not have a king or queen: *the President of France*| *President Carter* **2** [C] (*often cap.*) the head of some councils or government departments: *the President of the Board of Trade* **3** [C] (*sometimes cap.*) the head of various societies concerned with art, science, sport, etc.: *the president of the Yorkshire Cricket Club* **4** [C;A] (*often cap.*) the head of some British university colleges, and of some American universities **5** [C] *AmE* (*sometimes cap.*) the head of a business company, firm, bank, etc. **6** [C;A] *AmE* a chairman

pres·i·den·tial /ˌprezəˈdenʃəl/ *adj* [Wa5;A;(B)] **1** of or concerning a president: *a presidential election* **2 presidential year** (esp. in the US) a year in which an election is held to choose a president

preside o·ver *v prep* [T1] **1** to direct (a committee or other formal group of people) **2** *lit* to control

pre·sid·i·um, praes- /prɪˈsɪdiəm, -ˈzɪ-/ *n* **~s** *or* **-ia** /-dɪə/ (esp. in COMMUNIST countries) a fixed committee chosen to represent and act for a larger body, esp. a political body

press¹ /pres/ *n* **1** [S;(C)] an act of pushing steadily against something **2** [C] (*often in comb.*) any of various apparatuses or machines used for pressing: *a* TROUSER PRESS|*She keeps her tennis* RACKET *in a press to stop it from getting out of shape* **3** [C] *infml* an act of smoothing a garment with a hot iron **4** [(*the*) S] newspapers and magazines in general (often including the news-gathering services of radio and television): *The power of the press is very great.*|*a press photographer* **5** [(*the*) GU] newspaper writers in general: *The minister invited the press to a meeting to explain his actions* **6** [S9] treatment (of the stated kind) given by newspapers in general when reporting about a person or event: *The play had a good press, but people didn't buy tickets to go and see it* **7** [C] (*usu. cap.*) a business for printing (and sometimes also for selling) books, magazines, etc.: *the University Press* **8** [C] PRINTING PRESS: *Stop the presses! A piece of late news has come in* **9** [(*the*) U] printing: *Can you have your report ready for the press by next week?* **10** [U9, esp. *of*] *fml* a crowd or closely gathered condition; close mass of moving people **11** [U9, esp. *of*] the continual hurry and effort needed for (too) much activity **12** [C] (*usu. in comb.*) an old-fashioned cupboard or set of shelves, usu. built into a wall, for holding clothes, books, etc. **13 correct the press** *tech* to correct printing mistakes **14 freedom of the press** the freedom or right to print news or fair opinion on matters of public interest without fear of being stopped or harmed by a government or other official group **15 go to press** (of a newspaper for any particular day) to start being printed **16 in the press** (*AmE* also **in press**)— being printed **17 press of sail** also **press of canvas**— *tech* as many sails as can be used on a ship with safety

press² *v* **1** [T1;I∅] to push firmly and steadily against (something): *My toe presses against the shoe.*|*The shoe is pressing my toe.*|*I don't like shoes that press* **2** [T1;I∅] to cause (something) to move by doing this, in order to make a machine, apparatus, etc., work: *Press this button to start the engine.*|*Press To Start* (a notice under a button) **3** [X9] to put or place (something) in the stated position by pushing: *He pressed a coin into the little girl's hand.*|*The little boy pressed his nose against the shop window* **4** [T1] to hold firmly as a sign of friendship, love, pity, etc.: *He pressed my hand warmly when we met* **5** [L9;T1] **a** (of clothes) to get and keep smoothness or a sharp fold (CREASE), through the use of a hot iron: *This dress presses easily* **b** to cause (clothes) to be or become smooth or sharply folded in this way **6** [T1;X7] to direct weight or force on (something) in order to crush, flatten, shape, pack tightly, or get liquid out: *She pressed the flower by putting it between the pages of an old book.*|*Before cooking, pastry is pressed flat and thin* **7** [X9;L9] to push, move, or make (one's way) strongly, esp. in a mass: *He pressed his way through the crowd.*|*So many people pressed round the famous actress that she couldn't get to her car* **8** [T1; I∅] to continue to force (an attack, hurried action, etc.) on (someone): *I don't understand why you press that particular point which seems to me unimportant.*|*He was so determined to win the game that he pressed too hard and made some silly mistakes* **9** [T1;V3] to demand or ask for, continually; urge strongly: *He didn't press his claim to the land; he allowed his brother to keep it.*|*She pressed her guest to stay a little longer* —see also PRESS FOR **10** [I∅] *infml* to need quick action or attention: *Work presses, so I can't stop to talk* —see also PRESSING **11** [T1] *tech* to make a copy of (a GRAMOPHONE record) from a MATRIX **12 time presses** there is not much time to do what must be done —see also PRESS ON¹

press³ *v* [T1] **1** (in former times) to seize and force (a man) into naval (or army) service **2 press someone/something into service** to use (someone or something that may not be completely suitable) for some purpose in a time of need, for lack of someone or something better

press a·gen·cy /ˈ· ˌ···/ *n* the office or business of a PRESS AGENT

press a·gent /ˈ· ˌ··/ *n* a person in charge of keeping an actor, musician, theatre, etc., in favourable public notice by supplying photographs, interesting facts, details of coming performances, etc., to newspapers

press bar·on /ˈ· ˌ··/ also **press lord**— *n infml sometimes derog* a person who owns and controls one or more powerful national newspapers

press box /ˈ· ·/ *n* an (enclosed) space at some outdoor events that is kept for the use of newspaper reporters, as at a football match

press con·fer·ence /ˈ· ˌ···/ also **news conference**— *n* a meeting arranged by an important person to which news reporters are invited to listen to a statement or to ask questions

press cut·ting /ˈ· ˌ··/ also **clipping**— *n* [*usu. pl.*] a short notice, picture, etc., esp. concerning one's own life or work, cut out of a newspaper or magazine

pressed /prest/ *adj* **1** [Wa5;B] (of food) given a firm shape by being packed into a tin so as to be easily cut for eating cold: *pressed duck* **2** [F+*for*] having hardly enough (of): *I'm pressed for time this morning so I can't come and see you*

press for *v prep* [D1;T1] to demand urgently (from someone): *I don't know whether to accept this new job, and the firm is pressing (me) for a decision*

press gal·le·ry /ˈ· ˌ···/ *n* (esp. in the British parliament) a raised narrow shelflike floor above or at the back of one side of the main level of a hall, kept for the use of news reporters

press·gang[1] /ˈpresgæŋ/ *n* (in former times, esp. in the 18th century) a band of sailors under an officer, employed to seize men for service in the navy

pressgang[2] *v* [T1 (*into*)] *infml* to force (someone) to do something unwillingly

press home *v adv* [T1] **1** to push (something) firmly into place **2** to get the greatest possible effect from (an advantage) **3** to continue forcefully and get a successful result from (an attack) **4** to make clear the truth or importance of (an argument, point, etc.)

press·ing[1] /ˈpresɪŋ/ *n* any of many copies of a GRAMOPHONE record made from the same form (MATRIX)

pressing[2] *adj* **1** demanding or needing attention, action, etc., now: *Pressing business matters prevented him from taking a holiday* **2** asking for something with strong urging: *My friends gave me a pressing invitation. They were so pressing that I couldn't refuse them* —**~ly** *adv*

press lord /ˈ· ·/ *n infml sometimes derog* PRESS BARON

press·man /ˈpresmæn/ *n* **-men** /men/ *BrE infml* a newspaper reporter

press·mark /ˈpresmɑːk‖-mɑrk/ *n esp. BrE* a number or mark written in a book to show its place on a shelf in a library

press on[1] also (*fml*) **press for·ward**— *v adv* [IØ (*with*)] to continue; advance with courage or without delay: *Let's press on with our work*

press on[2] also (*fml*) **press up·on**— *v prep* **1** [T1 *no pass.*] also **weigh on**— to cause worry to (someone) **2** [D1] to force acceptance of (something) by (someone)

press re·lease /ˈ· ·ˌ·/ *n* a prepared statement given out to news services and newspapers

press-stud /ˈ· ·/ also (*infml*) **popper**, *AmE* **snap fastener**— *n* a small metal fastener for a garment, in which one part is pressed into a hollow in another

press-up /ˈ· ·/ also (*esp. AmE*) **push-up**— *n esp. BrE* a form of exercise in which a person lies face down on the ground and pushes his body up with his arms

pres·sure[1] /ˈpreʃəʳ/ *n* **1** [U (*of*)] the action of pressing with force or weight: *Food is broken up in the mouth by the pressure of the teeth* **2** [U;C] the strength of this force: *These air containers will burst at high pressures.|a pressure of 10 pounds to the square inch* **3** [U] discomfort caused by a sensation of or as if of pressing: *The sick man complained of a feeling of pressure in his chest* **4** [U;C] also **atmospheric pressure**— the (force of the) weight of the air: *Low pressure often brings rain* **5** [C;U: (*of*)] (a) trouble that causes anxiety and difficulty: *the pressure of family anxieties* **6** [U] forcible influence (used for obtaining a desired action) (esp. in the phrs. **bring pressure (to bear) on someone (to do something), put pressure on someone (to do something)**) **7** [U (*of*)] high rate of speed and activity: *Villagers are unaccustomed to the pressure of modern city life* **8 under pressure a** not of one's own free will: *He says that he made his statement to the police under pressure, and that the statement is false* **b** in or into a condition of being persuaded or influenced forcibly (esp. in the phrs. **be/come under pressure (to do something)**) **c** in a condition of being forced or hurried: *He works best under pressure* —see also BLOOD PRESSURE, HIGH-PRESSURE

pressure[2] *v* [T1 (*into*); V3] *esp. AmE* PRESSURIZE (1)

pressure cab·in /ˈ·· ˌ··/ *n* a PRESSURIZED (2) inside part of a large modern aircraft, where passengers sit

pressure cook·er /ˈ·· ˌ··/ *n* [C; *by*+U] a tightly covered metal cooking pot in which food can be cooked very quickly by the pressure of hot steam —see picture at KITCHEN

pressure gauge /ˈ·· ·/ *n* an instrument for measuring the pressure of a liquid, gas, steam, etc.

pressure group /ˈ·· ·/ *n* a group of people that actively tries to influence public opinion and government action for its own advantage

pres·sur·ize, -ise /ˈpreʃəraɪz/ *v* **1** [T1 (*into*); V3] also (*esp. AmE*) **pressure**— *esp. BrE* to (try to) make (someone) do something by means of forceful demands or influence: *They have pressurized him into freeing the prisoners* **2** [Wv5;T1] to control the air pressure inside (a (part of a) high-flying aircraft) so that the pressure does not become much lower than that on earth: *a pressurized* CABIN —**-ization** /ˌpreʃəraɪˈzeɪʃən‖-rəˈzeɪ-/ *n* [U]

pres·ti·di·gi·ta·tion /ˌprestɪ̣ˌdɪdʒɪ̣ˈteɪʃən/ *n* [U] *humor or fml* the performing of tricks by quick clever use of the hands; conjuring (CONJURE)

pres·tige /preˈstiːʒ/ *n* **1** [U] general respect or admiration felt in men's minds for someone or something by reason of having, or being connected with, rank, proved high quality, etc.: *He enjoys the prestige of having such a famous man as a brother* **2** [A] *usu. apprec or derog* causing admiration as an outward sign of wealth or success: *Some people say the country should spend its money on really important things, not on prestige developments like new airports*

pres·ti·gious /preˈstɪdʒəs‖-ˈstiː-, -ˈstɪ-/ *adj usu. apprec* having or bringing PRESTIGE (1): *He has a very prestigious address; he lives in the best part of town*

pres·tis·si·mo /preˈstɪsɪ̣məʊ/ *adj, adv* (in music) (played or to be played) as quickly as possible

pres·to /ˈprestəʊ/ *n, adj, adv* **-tos** (in music) ((music) played or to be played) very quickly

pre·stressed /ˌpriːˈstrest◂/ *adj* [Wa5] (of a type of hard modern building material (CONCRETE)) strengthened by having stretched wires set inside

pre·su·ma·ble /prɪˈzjuːməbəl‖-ˈzuː-/ *adj* that may reasonably be supposed to be true; probable —**-bly** *adv* [Wa3]: *Presumably there's a good reason for* *her absence, as she doesn't usually stay away from work*

pre·sume /prɪ'zjuːm‖-'zuːm/ *v* **1** [T1,5a,b;X *to be* 1,7;I∅] to take (something) as true or as a fact without direct proof but with some feeling of being certain; suppose: *John didn't say when he would return, but I presume he'll be back for dinner.*|*From the way they talked I presumed them to be married* **2** [T1,5,5b;X (*to be*) 1,7] to accept as true until proved untrue (as a matter of law, justice, etc.): *If a person is missing for 7 years in this country, he is presumed dead* **3** [T1,5a] to be a reasonable sign or proof of: *An answer, by its nature, presumes a question* **4** [I∅,3] to behave without enough respect or politeness; dare to do something which one has no right to do: *A servant ought not to presume.*|*He presumed to tell his employer how the work ought to be done*

presume up·on also **presume on**— *v prep* [T1] *fml* to take improper advantage of (someone's good nature or connection with oneself)

pre·sump·tion /prɪ'zʌmpʃən/ *n* **1** [C,C5] **a** an act of supposing: *Your presumption that I would want to share a flat with you is false* **b** *law* an act of supposing that is reasonable and sensible **2** [U] improper boldness that shows too high an opinion of oneself

pre·sump·tive /prɪ'zʌmptɪv/ *adj* [Wa5;A;(B)] *fml, esp. law* based on a reasonable belief; probable: *presumptive proof* —**~ly** *adv*

presumptive heir /·,·· '·/ *n* HEIR PRESUMPTIVE

pre·sump·tu·ous /prɪ'zʌmptʃʊəs/ also (*fml*) **pre·sum·ing** /prɪ'zjuːmɪŋ‖-'zuː-/— *adj* showing too much boldness towards others as a result of having too high an opinion of oneself —**~ly** *adv*

pre·sup·pose /,priːsə'pəʊz/ *v* [T1,5] **1** to suppose or take to be true without trying to find out: *A scientist never presupposes the truth of an unproved fact* **2** to be necessary as something that comes before (something else) according to reason: *A child presupposes a mother.*|*An honour given to a person presupposes that he has earned it*

pre·sup·po·si·tion /,priːsʌpə'zɪʃən/ *n* **1** [U] the action of presupposing (PRESUPPOSE) **2** [C,C5] something that is PRESUPPOSEd: *Your judgment of the facts is based on the presupposition that they are true; such presuppositions are unwise*

pre·tence, *AmE* also **-tense** /prɪ'tens‖'priːtens/ *n* **1** [S;U] a false appearance, reason, or show intended to deceive or as a game: *He didn't like the food, but he made a pretence of eating some of it as he was a guest.*|*She isn't really ill; it's only pretence* **2** [U (*to*) *usu. nonassertive*] a claim to possess (some desirable quality): *a simple countryman with little pretence to education* **3** [U] too much outward show of importance, greatness, etc., intended to gain the admiration and respect of others **4 false pretences** *law* acts intended to deceive (esp. in the phrs. **by/under false pretences**)

pre·tend¹ /prɪ'tend/ *v* **1** [T1,3,5a;I∅] to give an appearance of (something that is not true), with the intention of deceiving: *He pretended sleep when his mother called him.*|*He pretended to be reading.*|*She wasn't really crying; she was only pretending* **2** [T3,5a;I∅] (usu. of a child) to imagine as a game: *Let's pretend we're father and mother* **3** [T1] to claim falsely that one has (some condition), in order to avoid difficulty or punishment **4** [T3 *nonassertive*] *infml* to attempt; dare: *I won't pretend to tell you how this machine works, because you understand it much better than I*

pretend² *adj* [Wa5] (*used esp. by children*) imagined; imaginary: *That is my pretend friend*

pre·tend·ed /prɪ'tendɪ̵d/ *adj often derog* false or unreal in spite of appearances

pre·tend·er /prɪ'tendəʳ/ *n* [(*to*)] a person who makes a (doubtful or unproved) claim to some high position, such as to be the rightful king

pretend to *v prep* [T1] to claim to possess (some desirable quality)

pre·ten·sion /prɪ'tenʃən/ *n* **1** [C (*to*) *often pl.*] a claim to possess skill, qualities, etc.: *I make no pretensions to skill as an artist, but I enjoy painting* **2** [U] *fml* PRETENTIOUSNESS

pre·ten·tious /prɪ'tenʃəs/ *adj* claiming (in an unpleasing way) importance or social rank that one does not possess —**~ly** *adv*

pre·ten·tious·ness /prɪ'tenʃəsnɪ̵s/ also (*fml*) **pretension**— *n* [U] the quality of being PRETENTIOUS

pret·er·ite, -it /'pretərɪ̵t/ *n, adj* [Wa5] *tech* (a tense or verb form) that expresses a past action or condition: *"Sang" is the preterite (form) of "sing"*

pre·ter·nat·u·ral /,priːtə'nætʃərəl‖-tər-/ *adj fml* **1** beyond what is usual: *a fighter of preternatural strength* **2** strange; beyond what is natural or can be explained naturally: *In former times people believed that thunder and lightning were signs of preternatural forces* —**~ly** *adv*: *preternaturally strong*

pre·text /'priːtekst/ *n* a reason given for an action in order to hide the real intention; excuse: *He came to the house under/on the pretext of seeing Mr Smith, but he really wanted to see Smith's daughter* —see EXCUSE (USAGE)

pre·tor /'priːtəʳ/ *n* PRAETOR

pret·ti·fy /'prɪtɪfaɪ/ *v* [T1] *usu. derog* to make pretty without serious intention or effect

pret·ti·ly /'prɪtɪ̵li/ *adv* in a pleasing or charming way

pret·ty¹ /'prɪti/ *adj* **1** [Wa1;B] (esp. of a woman, a child, or a small fine thing) pleasing or nice to look at, listen to, etc.; charming but not beautiful or grand: *She looks much prettier with long hair than with short hair.*|*What a pretty little garden!* —compare BEAUTIFUL, HANDSOME **2** [Wa1;B] *derog* (of a boy) charming and graceful but rather girlish **3** [Wa1;B] *apprec* (esp. of an action) causing admiration for neatness, cleverness, or skill: *He writes with a pretty turn of phrase* (=expresses himself in a delightful way) **4** [Wa5;A] *derog* not nice; displeasing: *It's a pretty state of affairs when I come home from work and you haven't even cooked my dinner!* **5** [Wa5;A] *infml* (of an amount of money) quite large: *He made a pretty fortune by selling all his land for building* —see also **a pretty** PASS³, **a pretty** PENNY (5) **6 sitting pretty** (of a person) in a favourable position or condition (without much effort) —**-tiness** *n* [U]

pretty² *adv infml* **1** in some degree; rather; quite though not completely: *"How are you today?" "Pretty well, thank you."*|*"I'm pretty sure that he'll say yes"* (SEU S.) **2** very: *This work of yours is a pretty poor effort. You'd better do it again* **3 pretty much** very nearly; very much: *"How is the sick man today?" "Pretty much as he was yesterday"* **4 pretty nearly** almost: *"told him pretty nearly all the secrets of her married life"* (SEU S.) **5 pretty well** very nearly; almost: *It's pretty well impossible to travel over these mountains in winter*

pretty³ *n* [N9] *infml becoming rare* a dear or pretty child or girl: *Come here, my pretty!*

pretty-pret·ty /'·· ,··/ *adj derog* (esp. of something supposed to be a work of art) pretty in a silly weak way

pret·zel /'pretsəl/ *n* a type of hard salty cake (BISCUIT) baked in the shape of a stick or a loose knot

pre·vail /prɪ'veɪl/ *v* [I∅] *fml* **1** [(*against, over*)] to gain control or victory; win a fight: *Justice has prevailed; the guilty man has been punished* **2**

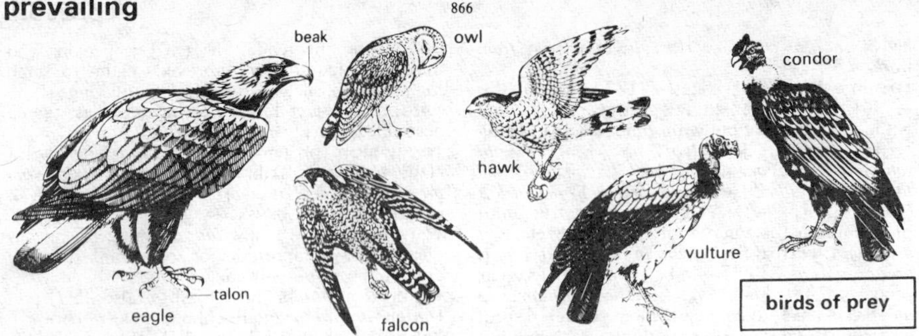

[(*among, in*)] to (continue to) exist or be widespread: *A belief in magic still prevails among some tribes*

pre·vail·ing /prɪˈveɪlɪŋ/ *adj* [Wa5;A] **1** (of a wind) that blows over an area most of the time **2** most common or general (in some place or at some time): *He wore his hair in the prevailing fashion* —**~ly** *adv*

prevail up·on also **prevail on**— *v prep* [V3] *fml* to persuade (someone): *Can I prevail upon you to stay a little longer?*

prev·a·lent /ˈprevələnt/ *adj* [(*among, in*)] *usu. fml* existing commonly, generally, or widely (in some place or at some time): *The habit of travelling by aircraft is becoming more prevalent each year.*|*Eye diseases are prevalent in some tropical countries* —**~ly** *adv* —**-lence** *n* [U (*of*)]

pre·var·i·cate /prɪˈværɨkeɪt/ *v* [IØ] **1** *fml* to try to hide the truth by not answering questions clearly or completely truthfully **2** *euph* to tell lies —**-cation** /prɪˌværɨˈkeɪʃən/ *n* [U;C] —**-cator** /prɪˈværɨkeɪtəʳ/ *n*

pre·vent /prɪˈvent/ *v* [T1; (*esp. BrE*) V4] **1** to keep (something) from happening or existing: *These rules are intended to prevent accidents.*|(*esp. BrE*) *What can we do to prevent this disease spreading?* **2** to stop or hold back (someone): *I intend to go and nothing you do can prevent me!* —**~able** *adj*

prevent from *v prep* [V4b] PREVENT: *You can't prevent me from going there!*

pre·ven·tion /prɪˈvenʃən/ *n* [U (*of*)] the act or action of PREVENTING (esp. 1): *the prevention of crime*

pre·ven·tive /prɪˈventɪv/ also **pre·ven·ta·tive** /-tətɪv/— *n, adj* (something that is) intended to or serving to PREVENT (1) something, esp. illness —**~ly** *adv*

preventive de·ten·tion /·ˌ·· ·ˈ··/ *n* [U] DETENTION (1) without trial, esp. for political reasons

pre·view¹ /ˈpriːvjuː/ *v* [T1] **1** to give a PREVIEW² (1) of (a play, cinema film, etc.) **2** to see a PREVIEW² (1) of

preview² *n* [(*of*)] **1** a private showing of paintings, a cinema film, etc., before they are shown to the general public **2** an example of what something may be like; foretaste

pre·vi·ous /ˈpriːvɪəs/ *adj* [Wa5] **1** [A] happening, coming, or being earlier in time or order: *Have you had any previous experience, or is this kind of work new to you?* **2** [F] *infml* too hasty; acting too soon: *You're a little previous in thanking me for something I haven't given you yet* —**~ly** *adv*: *I hadn't seen him previously*

previous con·vic·tion /ˌ··· ·ˈ··/ *n* [*often pl.*] an earlier CONVICTION (2) for a crime, which a judge will consider when deciding on the punishment for another crime (of the same kind)

previous to /ˈ··· ·/ *prep* before; PRIOR TO: *I know nothing about the accident; it happened previous to my arrival here*

pre·vi·sion /ˌpriːˈvɪʒən/ *n* [(*of*)] *fml* **1** [U] knowledge of something before it happens **2** [C] an example or case of this —compare PROVISION

pre·war /ˌpriːˈwɔːʳ◂/ *adj* [Wa5;A] (happening or existing) (just) before a war (esp. the First or Second World War): *conditions in prewar Europe*

prey¹ /preɪ/ *n* **1** [U] an animal that is hunted and eaten by another animal: *The lion seized its prey and ate it* **2** [U] habit or way of life based on killing and eating other animals (in the phrs. **beast/bird of prey**): *A tiger is a beast of prey* **3** [S9] a person who is helpless and suffers (easily or often) from harm: *He trusts people too much; he's an easy prey and almost anyone can trick him out of money* **4 be/become/fall a prey to** also (*esp. AmE*) **be/become/fall prey to**— **a** (of an animal) to be caught and eaten by (another animal) **b** (of a person) to be greatly troubled by (something): *Some people with disordered minds become a prey to fears of being murdered*

prey² *v* [L9] to hunt and catch living things for food: *Cats prey at night*

prey on also **prey up·on**— *v prep* [T1] **1** (of an animal) to hunt and eat as PREY (1): *Cats prey on birds and mice* **2** (of a person) to live by getting money from (someone who is weak, trusting, helpless, etc.) by influence, deceit, etc.: *He's very charming and preys on older women* **3** *often lit* (esp. of a group of people) to attack suddenly and rob **4** (of sorrow. troubles, etc.) to trouble greatly

price¹ /praɪs/ *n* **1** [C] an amount of money for which a thing is offered, sold, or bought: *What price did you pay for the house?*|*What is the price of this suit?*|*Eggs are selling at a high price* **2** [S] that which one must lose or suffer in order to do or get something one wants: *Loss of health is too high a price to pay for taking dangerous drugs* **3** [C] (in risking money, as on a horse in a race) the difference in amount between the money asked and the sum of the money one will get if one wins; ODDS: *"What price are you offering on 'Lucky Shot'?" "7 to 4"* —see also STARTING PRICE **4 above/beyond/without price** so valuable that no one could afford to buy it **5 a price on one's/someone's head** a reward for one's/someone's CAPTURE (esp. in the phrs. **have a price on one's head, put a price on someone's head**) **6 at a price** at a high price: *"Can I get any good oranges in the town?" "Yes, at a price; they're rather dear at this season"* **7 have one's price** to be willing to accept money in return for doing something (wrong), if the amount offered is large enough to satisfy one **8 not at any price** not in any condition, even if favourable **9 of a price** costing (about) the same amount of money: *These 2 coats are of a price* **10 put a price on something** to set a value on something: *You can't put a price on friendship* **11 put a price to something** to guess or remember the amount of money something costs: *I saw a beautiful coat advertised the other day, but I wouldn't like to put a price to it*

12 quote a price to state the price which one will pay, or wants to be paid, for an article **13 what price . . .?** *esp. BrE* **a** *derog* what is/was the use of . . .?; don't you think . . . is/was worthless?: *"What price Mary's singing at the concert last night?" "Wasn't it terrible!"* **b** *becoming rare* what chance is there of . . .?; what do you think of the idea of . . .?: *What price a ride on your bicycle?|What price going to the cinema tonight?* —see COST (USAGE) —see also ASKING PRICE, CLOSING PRICE, COST PRICE, LIST PRICE

price² *v* **1** [X7,9 *often pass.*] to fix the price of (something for sale): *The clothes in this shop are priced high* **2** [T1 *usu. pass.*] to mark (goods in a shop) with a price: *These dresses have only just arrived in the shop, and haven't yet been priced* **3** [T1 *pass. rare*] *infml* to ask the price of: *Before buying the coat, why not price it in a number of shops, as the prices vary for the same coat?*

price·less /ˈpraɪsləs/ *adj* **1** [Wa5] of very great value; of worth too great to be described or calculated: *Only a very rich man could afford to buy these priceless paintings* **2** *infml* very funny or laughably foolish: *You look priceless in those tight trousers!* —see WORTHLESS (USAGE)

price out of *v adv prep* [D1] to cause (oneself, one's goods, one's services) to cost too much for (people's ability to pay): *The photographer priced himself out of the market and had to change jobs*

price tag /ˈ· ·/ *n* **1** a small ticket put onto an article, showing the price at which it is being offered for sale **2** (esp. in newspaper style) a (fixed or stated) price: *The government was asked to put a price tag on its new building plans*

pric·ey, pricy /ˈpraɪsi/ *adj* **pricier, priciest** [Wa1;F;(B)] *infml, esp. BrE* dear in price; costly: *These new cars are a bit pricey.|That shop is too pricey for me; I can't afford to buy there* —**pricily** *adv* —**priciness** *n* [U]

prick¹ /prɪk/ *n* **1** a small mark or hole made by pricking: *There were pricks at the top of the papers where they had been pinned together* **2** an act of pricking **3** a small sharp pain: *He felt a sharp prick when he stepped on an upturned nail.|*(fig.) *the pricks of conscience* (=discomfort of the mind after wrongdoing) **4** *taboo* the male sex organ; PENIS **5** *taboo sl* a foolish worthless man **6** PRICKLE¹ (1) **7 kick against the pricks** *fml or lit* to complain uselessly about something that cannot be changed

prick² *v* **1** [T1 (*with, on*)] to make a very small hole or holes in the skin or surface of (something or oneself) with a sharp-pointed object: *When she was sewing she pricked her finger and made it bleed.|She pricked herself on a needle* **2** [T1 (OFF, OUT, *in*)] to make (a small hole or other mark) in a surface by using a pointed tool: *Prick a few holes in the centre of the pastry* **3** [T1;IØ] to (cause to) feel a sensation of light sharp pain on the skin: *The leaves of this plant prick if you touch them.|My skin pricks sometimes if I get too hot.|The pepper in the food pricked the back of his throat.|*(fig.) *Her conscience pricked her*

prick·le¹ /ˈprɪkəl/ *n* **1** [C] any of a number of small sharp-pointed growths on the skin of some plants or animals **2** [(*the*) S] a pricking sensation on the skin

prickle² *v* [T1;IØ] to give or feel a pricking sensation: *When a wound begins to prickle, it often means that it's getting better*

prick·ly /ˈprɪkli/ *adj* [Wa1] **1** covered with prickles: *prickly bushes* **2** that has or gives a pricking sensation: *prickly woollen underclothes* **3** *infml* (of a person) easily made angry —**-liness** *n* [U]

prickly heat /ˌ·· ˈ·/ *n* [U] an uncomfortable hot PRICKLY (1) condition of the skin with painful red spots, common in tropical countries

prickly pear /ˌ·· ˈ·/ *n* **1** a type of desert plant (CACTUS) that has yellow flowers, prickles, and roundish fruit that can be eaten **2** its fruit

prick out also **prick off**— *v adv* [T1] to place (a young plant) in a hole specially made in the earth

prick up *v adv* **1 prick up its ears** (of an animal) to raise the ears so as to listen attentively **2 prick up one's ears** (of a person) to listen carefully; be ready to learn information

pride /praɪd/ *n* **1** [U (*in*)] *derog* too high an opinion of oneself because of one's rank, wealth, abilities, etc.: *He was so full of pride that he didn't know that people usually laughed at him* **2** [U] reasonable self-respect; proper high opinion of oneself: *She wanted to beg him to stay but her pride wouldn't let her* **3** [U;S] (a feeling of) satisfaction, delight, and pleasure in what one can do or has done, or in someone or something connected with oneself: *Why can't you take a little more pride in your appearance? You never look neat* **4** [S9] the most valuable person or thing: *This fine picture is the pride of my collection* **5** [S9] *lit* the highest or finest point or part (esp. in the phr. **in the pride of**): *She was still young and in the pride of her beauty* **6** [C (*of*) *usu. sing.*] a group (of lions) **7 false pride** a mistaken feeling of pride; VANITY (1) **8 pride and joy** a person or possession that one values very greatly **9 swallow one's pride** to make an effort to forget one's PRIDE (2) for some good reason —see also **take/have pride of** PLACE (2)

pride on also **pride up·on, pique on, preen on**— *v prep* [D1,V4b] to be pleased and satisfied with (oneself) about (something): *She prided herself on her ability to speak 8 languages/on knowing 8 languages*

prie-dieu /ˌpriː ˈdjɜː (*Fr* pri djœ)/ *n* **prie-dieux** (*same pronunciation*) *Fr* a small piece of furniture, usu. in a church, used for kneeling on when praying

priest /priːst/ *n* **1** (in the Christian church, and esp. in the ROMAN CATHOLIC church) a person, esp. a man, specially trained for various religious duties (such as performing certain holy ceremonies and services) and for helping other people **2** (*fem.* **priest·ess**)— a specially-trained person with related duties and responsibilities in certain non-Christian religions

priest·hood /ˈpriːsthʊd/ *n* **1** [(*the*) U] the office, position, or rank of a priest: *He entered the priesthood* (=became a priest) **2** [(*the*) GU] the whole body of priests, usu. of a particular religion or country: *the French priesthood*

priest·ly /ˈpriːstli/ *adj* [Wa5] of or like a priest —**-liness** *n* [U]

priest-rid·den /ˈ· ˌ··/ *adj derog* (of a ruler or nation) too much under the control of a priest or priests

priest's hole /ˈ· ·/ *n* (in England in former times) a secret hiding-place (usu. inside a building) in which ROMAN CATHOLIC priests could escape from people who were trying to catch and harm them

prig /prɪg/ *n derog* a person who believes himself morally better than others and who shows unnaturally eager obedience to the details of rules, correct behaviour, etc.

prig·gish /ˈprɪgɪʃ/ *adj* of or like a PRIG —**~ly** *adv* —**~ness** *n* [U]

prim /prɪm/ *adj* **-mm-** [Wa1] **1** *usu. derog* **a** (esp. of a woman) behaving in a stiff self-controlled manner; easily shocked by anything improper or rude (often in the phr. **prim and proper**): *She's much too prim and proper to enjoy such a rude joke* **b** showing this quality **2** neat: *prim little dresses* —**~ly** *adv* —**~ness** *n* [U]

pri·ma bal·le·ri·na /ˌpriːmə bæləˈriːnə/ *n* the leading woman dancer in (a) BALLET

pri·ma·cy /ˈpraɪməsi/ *n* **1** [U (*of*)] *fml* the state, quality, or position of being first in rank, importance, position, etc. **2** [U9;S9] the position of a PRIMATE¹ (1)

prima don·na /ˌpriːmə ˈdɒnə‖-ˈdɑnə/ *n* **1** the leading woman singer in (an) OPERA **2** *derog* an excitable self-important person (esp. a woman) who is always changing her mind and expects everyone to do as she wishes: *He is a bit of a prima donna, which makes him hard to live with*

pri·mae·val /praɪˈmiːvəl/ *adj* PRIMEVAL

pri·ma fa·cie /ˌpraɪmə ˈfeɪʃi‖-ʃə/ *adj, adv* [Wa5;A] *Lat esp. law* (based) on what, on first consideration, seems to be true

pri·mal /ˈpraɪməl/ *adj fml* **1** [A;(B)] belonging to, or as if belonging to, the earliest time in the world; original: *its primal glories, which will never return* **2** [B] first in importance: *a primal need* —compare PRIMORDIAL, PRISTINE

pri·ma·ri·ly /ˈpraɪmərəli‖praɪˈmerəli/ *adv* mainly; chiefly: *We do deal with paintings here, but this is primarily a furniture shop*

pri·ma·ry¹ /ˈpraɪməri‖-meri/ *adj* **1** [Wa5;A;(B)] earliest in time or order of development: *The primary infection of a cold lasts 3 days.|The primary meaning of this word isn't used now, but you can look it up in a big dictionary* **2** [B] chief; main: *A primary cause of Tom's failure is his laziness* **3** [Wa5;A] (of education or a school) for children between 5 and 11 years old —compare SECONDARY (3), ELEMENTARY (2) **4** [Wa5;A] *tech* which produces or passes on a flow of electricity: *a primary* COIL

primary² *n* (esp. in the US) an election at which the members of a political party in a particular area vote for the person that they would like to see as their party's choice (CANDIDATE) for a political office

primary col·our /ˌ··· ˈ··/ *n* any of 3 colours (red, yellow, and blue) from which all other colours can be made by mixing

primary stress /ˌ··· ˈ·/ also **primary ac·cent** /ˌ··· ˈ··/— *n* [U;C] *tech* the strongest force (STRESS) given in speech to part of a compound or long word, and shown in this dictionary by the mark ˈ

pri·mate¹ /ˈpraɪmɪ̣t/ *n* (*often cap.*) **1** (in the CHURCH OF ENGLAND) a priest of the highest rank; ARCHBISHOP: *The* ARCHBISHOP *of Canterbury is called the Primate of All England* **2** (in the ROMAN CATHOLIC Church) a priest of the highest rank who controls other priests of like rank in a large area

pri·mate² /ˈpraɪmeɪt/ *n* a member of the most highly developed group of breast-feeding animals (MAMMAL*s*), which includes men, monkeys, and related animals

prime¹ /praɪm/ *n* **1** [(*the*) S] the state or time of (someone's or something's) greatest perfection, strength, or activity: *He was 40 years old, and still in the prime of life.|Stella is still good-looking, but she's past her prime.|Many young soldiers have been cut off in their prime* (=killed in battle while still young) **2** [R] (*often cap.*) the second church service of the day, held at sunrise or 6 o'clock in the morning **3** [(*the*) S] *lit* the earliest freshest time; beginning **4** [C] *tech* PRIME NUMBER

prime² *adj* [Wa5;A] **1** first in time, rank, or importance; chief: *a prime reason|a matter of prime importance* **2** of the very best quality or kind: *"This meat is very dear." "Yes, but it's a prime joint of* BEEF.*"|The broadcast went out on television at* **prime time**, *when everyone was watching*

prime³ *v* [T1] **1** [(*with*)] to prepare (a machine) for working by filling with water, oil, etc. **2** to put gunpowder into (a gun of the old-fashioned type) **3** [(*with*)] to instruct in advance, esp. in how to ask or answer difficult questions: *It was a difficult case, but the man on trial had been carefully primed by his lawyer* **4** to cover (a surface) with a first spreading of paint, oil, or other preparation, as a base for the main painting **5** [(*with*)] *infml often humor* to fill (someone) with food or esp. drink **6 prime the pump** to encourage the growth of an inactive business or industry by putting money into it

prime cost /ˌ· ˈ·/ *n* [U] the actual cost of producing an article, as opposed to money spent on selling it, the amount of profit, etc.

prime me·rid·i·an /ˌ· ·ˈ···/ *n* [*the*+R] the imaginary line drawn from north to south on the earth, which passes through Greenwich, England, and from which east and west are measured on a map in degrees —see picture at GLOBE

prime min·is·ter /ˌ· ˈ···/ also (*infml*) **P M**— *n* [C; (N)] (*often caps.*) the chief minister and leader of the government in Britain and many other countries —**~ship** *n*

prime mov·er /ˌ· ˈ··/ *n* **1** a natural force (such as wind or moving water) which can be used directly or to produce a more useful form of power **2** a person or thing that has great influence in starting the development of something important

prime num·ber /ˌ· ˈ··/ *n tech* a number that can be divided exactly only by itself and the number one: *23 is a prime number*

prim·er¹ /ˈpraɪməʳ‖ˈprɪmər/ *n* a simple beginner's book in any school subject

primer² /ˈpraɪməʳ/ *n* **1** [U;C] a type of paint or other substance spread over the bare surface of wood before the main painting **2** [C] a tube containing explosive, used for firing the gunpowder in a bomb, gun, etc.

pri·me·val, -mae- /praɪˈmiːvəl/ *adj* **1** [Wa5] of the earliest period of the earth's existence: *primeval oceans that have now disappeared* **2** very ancient; having been in existence for a very long time: *primeval forests*

prim·ing /ˈpraɪmɪŋ/ *n* [U] gunpowder used to fire the explosive in a bomb, gun, etc.

prim·i·tive¹ /ˈprɪmǝ̇tɪv/ *adj* **1** [A;(B)] of or belonging to the earliest stage of development, esp. of life or of man: *Primitive man made himself primitive tools from sharp stones and animal bones.|the primitive form of a language|primitive art* **2** [B] simple; roughly made or done; not greatly developed or improved: *Small seashells have sometimes been used as a primitive kind of money* **3** [B] old-fashioned and inconvenient: *Life in this village is too primitive for me; if you want any water you have to pump it up from a well* —**~ly** *adv* —**~ness** *n* [U]

primitive² *n* **1 a** a painter or other artist of the time before the RENAISSANCE: *an Italian primitive* **b** a modern artist who paints simple and rather flat-looking pictures **2** a work by such an artist **3** a member of a PRIMITIVE¹ (1) race or tribe

pri·mo·gen·i·ture /ˌpraɪməʊˈdʒenǝ̇tʃəʳ/ *n* [U] **1** also **right of primogeniture**— the system according to which property owned by a father goes after his death to the eldest son **2** the state or fact of being the eldest child of parents

pri·mor·di·al /praɪˈmɔːdɪəl‖-ˈmɔr-/ *adj* [Wa5] existing from or at the beginning (of time): *Scientists used to believe that all the stars developed from a primordial mass of gases* —**-ally** *adv*

primp /prɪmp/ *v* [T1;IØ] (esp. of a woman) to arrange or tidy (oneself, one's hair, etc.) in a (too) careful way (often in the phr. **primp and preen**)

prim·rose /ˈprɪmrəʊz/ *n* **1** [C] **a** a type of common wild plant that produces light yellow flowers in the spring **b** a flower of this plant **2** [U] also **primrose yel·low** /ˌ·· ˈ··/— a light yellow colour: *primrose curtains* **3 the primrose path** also **the primrose way**— the gay life of pleasure that may lead to ruin

prim·u·la /ˈprɪmjʊlə‖-jələ/ *n* any of various types of plant (including the PRIMROSE), many of which are grown in gardens and have brightly coloured flowers

pri·mus /ˈpraɪməs/ also **primus stove** /ˈ·· ·/— *n tdmk* a type of metal apparatus for cooking, heating water, etc., that can be easily carried about

primus in·ter pa·res /ˌpraɪməs ɪntə ˈpɑːriːz‖-ɪntər ˈpæ-/ *n* [(*the*) R] *Lat fml & apprec* first among equals; the best, most worthy, or most important person or thing among many that are equal or alike

prince /prɪns/ *n* **1** [C;A;(N)] (*often cap.*) a son or other near male relation of a king or queen: *Prince Charles will be the next king of England* **2** [C;A;(N)] (*often cap.*) a ruler, usu. of a small country or of a state protected by a bigger country: *Prince Rainier of Monaco|In former times parts of India were ruled by princes* **3** [C (*among, of*) *usu. sing.*] *lit or pomp* a very great, successful, or powerful man of some stated kind: *Shakespeare, the prince of poets* **4 live like princes/a prince** to have good food and conditions of living (often when not accustomed to them)

Prince Charm·ing /ˌ· ˈ··/ *n* [S;R;N] a man who as a lover fulfils the dreams of a young girl

prince con·sort /ˌ· ˈ··/ *n* **princes consort** /ˌ·· ˈ··/ [C; *the*+R] (*often caps.*) a special title sometimes given to the husband of a ruling queen (esp. to Prince Albert, the husband of Queen Victoria of England)

prince·dom /ˈprɪnsdəm/ *n fml* a country ruled by a PRINCE (2); PRINCIPALITY

prince·ly /ˈprɪnsli/ *adj* [Wa1] **1** of or belonging to a PRINCE (1,2): *the princely courts of Europe* **2** fine; splendid; generous: *a princely gift*

prin·cess /ˌprɪnˈses◂‖ˈprɪnsəs/ *n* [C;A;(N)] **1** (*often cap.*) a daughter or other near female relation of a king or queen **2** (*often cap.*) the wife of a PRINCE (1,2)

prin·ci·pal¹ /ˈprɪnsǝ̇pəl/ *adj* [Wa5;A] chief; main; most important; of highest rank: *The Nile is one of the principal rivers of Africa* —compare PRINCIPLE

principal² *n* **1** [(*the*) C] (*often cap.*) the head of some universities, colleges, and schools **2** [S] a sum of money lent, put into a business, etc., and on which interest is paid **3** [C *often pl.*] a leading performer in a play, group of musicians, etc. **4** [(*the*) C *often pl.*] *fml* the person for whom someone else acts as a representative in a business or other important action, event, etc. **5** [C] *law* a person who is directly concerned in the breaking of a law (as opposed to someone who helps him break it) **6** [C] *law* a person who owes money or something else and must pay it back or return it (as opposed to someone else who promises to pay it back if the debtor fails to do so) **7** [C] *tech* a main supporting beam or framework of a roof —compare PRINCIPLE

principal boy /ˌ··· ˈ·/ *n* (in Britain) **1** [(*the*) *usu. sing.*] the chief male character in a PANTOMIME, usu. played by an actress **2** an actress who (habitually) plays this character

prin·ci·pal·i·ty /ˌprɪnsǝ̇ˈpælǝ̇ti/ *n* a country that a PRINCE (2) rules, or which gives him his title

Principality *n* [*the*+R] Wales

prin·ci·pally /ˈprɪnsǝ̇pli/ *adv* chiefly; mostly: *Although he's a lawyer, he's principally employed in controlling a large business*

principal parts /ˌ··· ˈ·/ *n* [(*the*) P] *tech* the parts of a verb from which other parts are formed or can be guessed (in English usu. the *infin., past tense, pres. p.*, and *past p.*): *The principal parts of the verb "sing" are "sing," "sang," "singing," and "sung"*

prin·ci·ple /ˈprɪnsǝ̇pəl/ *n* **1** [C (*of*), C5] a general truth or belief that is used as a base for reasoning or action, or for the development of further ideas: *the principle of freedom of speech|One of the principles of this dictionary is that explanations should be in simple language* **2** [C (*of*), C5] **a** *tech* a law of nature as scientifically discovered and stated: *the principle of Archimedes* **b** such a law as governing the making or working of a machine, apparatus, etc.: *A bicycle and a motorcycle are built on the same principle, though the force that moves them is different* **3** [C (*of*), C5] a rule used by a person as a guide for action; habit based on some fixed belief: *She acts on the principle that it's pleasanter to make others wait than to be early and wait for them* —compare PRINCIPLES (2) **4** [U] strong belief in, and practice of, honourable behaviour: *a man of principle* **5** [C (*of*)] *fml* a force of the mind which influences or directs one's activities: *The desire to know is an active principle of human nature* **6 in principle a** (only) in regard to the main idea: *They agreed to the plan in principle, but there were several* *details they didn't like* **b** according to what is supposed or reasoned to be true (though not proved): *There's no reason in principle why man shouldn't one day travel to the most distant stars* **c** according to rule (but not actually): *In principle work in the office stops at 5 o'clock, but I often have to stay later* **7 on principle** from or because of settled fixed beliefs **8 stick to/live up to one's principles** to continue to act according to one's PRINCIPLE*s* (3), esp. when it is difficult to do so —compare PRINCIPAL[1,2]

prin·ci·pled /ˈprɪnsəpəld/ *adj* (*usu. in comb.*) having or based upon PRINCIPLE*s* (2,3) of the stated kind or having PRINCIPLES (3)): *a high-principled man* —see also UNPRINCIPLED

prin·ci·ples /ˈprɪnsəpəlz/ *n* [P] **1** the general rules on which a skill, science, etc., is based, and which a beginner must understand: *This course teaches the principles of cooking* **2** high personal standards of what is right and wrong, used as a guide to behaviour: *He has no principles; he'll do anything, however bad, if it will bring him money* —compare PRINCIPLE (3) **3 first principles** the most simple PRINCIPLE*s* (1), which are a base from which all others have been or can be developed

prink /prɪŋk/ *v* [T1;IØ: (UP)] (esp. of a woman) PRIMP

print[1] /prɪnt/ *n* **1** [C] (*often in comb.*) a mark made on a surface showing the shape, pattern, etc., of the thing pressed into it: *a* FOOTPRINT|*a* THUMB*print*|*The deep marks in the wet ground look like the prints of a bicycle tyre* **2** [C *usu. sing.*] *fml* a mark showing the effect of something on a person: *Sorrow had left its print on her face* **3** [C *usu. pl.*] *infml* FINGERPRINT **4** [U] letters, words, or language in printed form: *I can't read small print without my glasses* **5** [C] a picture printed from a small sheet of metal: *a set of rare old Chinese prints* **6** [C;U] (a) cloth (usu. cotton) on which a coloured pattern has been printed: *print dresses* **7** [C] a (copy of a) photograph printed from a treated photographic film **8 in print** printed in a book, newspaper, etc.: *I shan't believe the minister made such a foolish remark until I see it in print* **9 in/out of print** (of a book) that can still/no longer be obtained from the printer: *His books haven't been in print for 20 years* **10 rush into print** (of a writer or a firm that produces books) to have (a work) printed for public sale as soon as possible **11 small print** a part of an agreement in law that is printed in very small letters and which, as people often do not take the trouble to read it, may have disadvantageous details included in it

print[2] *v* **1** [T1] to press (a mark) onto a soft surface: *The mark of a man's shoe is clearly printed in this mud* **2** [T1;IØ] to press letters or pictures onto (paper) by using shapes covered with ink: *This machine can print 60 pages in a minute* **3** [T1] to press (letters or pictures) onto paper by using shapes covered with ink: *The bottom line on this page hasn't been properly printed* **4** [T1;IØ] to make (a book, magazine, etc.) by means of pressing letters or pictures onto paper: *This firm prints a lot of educational books* **5** [T1] to cause (something) to appear in or be produced as a book, newspaper, etc.: *All today's newspapers have printed the minister's speech in full* **6** [Wv5 (*with*); T1] to ornament (cloth or wallpaper) with a coloured pattern pressed or rubbed on the surface: *printed wallpaper* **7** [T1 (OFF, OUT)] to make or copy (a photograph) on paper sensitive to light, from a specially treated sheet of photographic film **8** [IØ] to produce a copy by PRINTing[2] (3,7): *The metal plate is too worn to print* **9** [L9] to be produced as a copy by PRINTing[2] (2,3,7): *The photograph didn't print well* **10** [T1;IØ] to write (something) without joining the letters: *Please print the address clearly in capital letters* **11 print money** *often derog* (esp. of a government) to produce a large supply of money so that people can afford to pay for goods whose cost has increased **12 the printed word** what is stated in a newspaper, book, etc. —see also PRINT OUT

prin·ta·ble /ˈprɪntəbəl/ *adj* **1** fit to be printed; suitable for reading by anyone —compare UNPRINTABLE **2** that can be printed or printed from

printed cir·cuit /ˌ·· ˈ··/ *n* a set of connections between points in an electrical apparatus in the form of a continuous line of a substance that will carry (CONDUCT) electricity

printed mat·ter /ˈ·· ˌ··/ *n* [U] printed articles (such as official advertisements) that can be sent by post at a special cheap rate

printed pa·pers /ˌ·· ˈ··/ *n* [P] *esp. BrE* PRINTED MATTER —**printed-paper** /ˌ·· ˈ··/ *n* [A]: *the printed-paper rate*

print·er /ˈprɪntəʳ/ *n* **1** a person employed in the trade of printing **2** an owner of a printing business **3** a machine for making copies, esp. one for making photographs

printer's dev·il /ˌ·· ˈ··/ *n* a young boy who works in a printer's office doing small jobs or learning the trade of printing

print·ing /ˈprɪntɪŋ/ *n* **1** [U] the act or action of PRINTing[2] (esp. 2): *There are a few mistakes in the printing* **2** [U] the art of PRINTing[2] (esp. 2): *The invention of printing made it possible for many people to be educated* **3** [C] an act of PRINTing[2] (4) a number of copies of a book; IMPRESSION: *This is the third printing of the book* **4** [U] letters PRINTed[2] (10) by hand

printing ink /ˈ·· ·/ also **printer's ink**— *n* [U;(C)] any of several kinds of quick-drying ink used in printing books, newspapers, etc.

printing of·fice /ˈ·· ˌ··/ also **printing house** /ˈ·· ·/, **printing shop**— *n* a place where printing is done

printing press /ˈ·· ·/ also **press, printing ma·chine** /ˈ·· ·ˌ·/— *n* a machine that prints books, newspapers, etc.

print·out /ˈprɪntˌaʊt/ *n* [C;(U)] a printed record produced by an electric calculating machine (COMPUTER)

print out *v adv* [T1] (of a COMPUTER) to produce (a printed record of information)

print shop /ˈ· ·/ *n* a shop where PRINT*s*[1] (5) are sold

pri·or[1] /ˈpraɪəʳ/ *n* [C;A;(N)] (*often cap.*) **1** (*fem.* **pri·or·ess** /ˈpraɪərəs/)— the head of a PRIORY **2** the priest next in rank below the head of a large religious house (ABBEY)

prior[2] *adj* [Wa5;A;(B)] **1** earlier; coming or planned before (often in the phr. **a prior engagement**) **2** more important; coming first in importance: *a prior claim on my time and attention*

pri·or·i·ty /praɪˈɒrəti‖-ˈɔr-/ *n* **1** [U] the state, quality, position, or right of being first in position or earlier in time: *The badly wounded take priority for medical attention over those only slightly hurt* **2** [C] something that needs attention, consideration, service, etc., before others: *The arranging of this business agreement is a* **top priority**.|*You must learn to get your priorities right* (=to understand what is most important and should be dealt with first) **3** [U] the right of a vehicle to go forward while others must wait

prior to /ˈ·· ·/ *prep fml* before

pri·o·ry /ˈpraɪəri/ *n* (*often cap.*) a Christian religious house or group of men (MONK*s*) or women (NUN*s*) living together, which is smaller and less important than an ABBEY

prise /praɪz/ *v* [X9,(7)] *esp. BrE* PRIZE[5]

prise out *v adv* [T1 (*of*)] *esp. BrE* PRIZE OUT

pris·m /ˈprɪzəm/ *n* **1** (in GEOMETRY) a solid figure with a flat base and parallel upright edges —see picture at GEOMETRY **2** a transparent 3-sided block, usu. made of glass, that breaks up white light into different colours —see picture at OPTICS

pris·mat·ic /prɪzˈmætɪk/ *adj* **1** using a PRISM (2): *a prismatic compass* **2** like, concerning, or in the shape of a PRISM **3** (of colours) very bright, clear, and varied

pris·on /ˈprɪzən/ *n* **1** [C;U] a large (government) building where criminals are kept locked up as a punishment for as long as the law has decided: *The thief was sent to prison for a year.|The criminal's wife went to the prison to visit her husband* **2** [U] the state or condition of being kept in such a place; IMPRISONment: *Many people believe that prison isn't a cure for crime* **3** [C;U] a place or condition in which one is shut up or feels a loss of freedom: *Tom hates school; it's a prison to him*

prison-break·ing /ˈ·· ˌ··/ *n* [U] the unlawful action of escaping from a prison (often by force)

prison camp /ˈ·· ·/ *n* a guarded camp, usu. surrounded by a wire fence, for prisoners of war

pris·on·er /ˈprɪzənəʳ/ *n* **1** a person kept in a prison for some crime or while waiting to be tried **2** a person or animal (seized and) held with limited freedom of movement

prisoner of war /ˌ··· · ˈ·/ also (*infml*) **POW** /ˌpiː əʊˈdʌbəlyuː/— *n* a member of the armed forces caught by the enemy during a war and kept as a prisoner, often in a camp

prison vis·i·tor /ˌ·· ˈ···/ *n* a person who visits prisoners in order to help them with their difficulties or complaints, to keep their spirits up, etc.

pris·sy /ˈprɪsi/ *adj* [Wa1] annoyingly exact or proper in behaviour —**prissily** *adv* —**prissiness** *n* [U]

pris·tine /ˈprɪstiːn/ *adj* [Wa5;A;(B)] *fml or lit* **1** of the earliest time; unchanged from the first condition **2** pure; undamaged; fresh and clean: *When the snow began to melt, it lost its pristine whiteness*

prith·ee /ˈprɪði/ also **I prithee**— *interj old use* please

priv·a·cy /ˈprɪvəsi, ˈpraɪ-‖ˈpraɪ-/ *n* [U] **1** the state of being away from the presence, notice, or activities of others: *Most people like privacy when they're dressing or undressing* **2** secrecy; avoidance of public notice: *The greatest privacy is desirable in this unfortunate affair*

pri·vate¹ /ˈpraɪvɨ̧t/ *adj* **1** [Wa5;A] personal; one's own; not shared with others: *It's wrong to read people's private letters without permission* **2** [Wa5;B] not intended for everyone, but for a particular person or chosen group; not public: *A well-known singer gave a private performance at the party* **3** [Wa5;A;(B)] independent; not connected with government, public service, etc.: *Treatment in government hospitals is free, but if you go to a private hospital you must pay* **4** [Wa5;A;(B)] unofficial; not connected with one's business, work, rank, etc., or with one's public life: *The minister has gone on a private visit to America to see his sister.|He has* RETIREd *into private life* (=he has ceased to be a public official) **5** [Wa5;A] without rank or official position: *Private citizens aren't allowed to attend some of the meetings of the town council* **6** [B] quiet; hidden from view; sheltered: *Is there some private corner in the club where we can sit and talk by ourselves?* **7** [B] (of a person) (liking to be) away from the society of others: *She's a very private person* **8** [B] secret; not generally (made) known or intended to be talked about: *Don't repeat what I've told you to anyone; it's private* **9 in private** secretly; away from public notice; away from others: *Cecil can be very rude in private, though in public he's usually polite* —**~ly** *adv*: *May I see you privately?*

private² *n* [C;A] (*often cap.*) a soldier of the lowest rank

private de·tec·tive /ˌ·· ·ˈ··/ also **private in·ves·ti·ga·tor** /ˌ·· ·ˈ····/— *n* a person who does some kind of police work (such as following people and reporting on their actions and movements) but is not in police service, esp. one who hires out his services to people

private en·ter·prise /ˌ·· ˈ···/ *n* [U] CAPITALISM

pri·va·teer /ˌpraɪvəˈtɪəʳ/ *n* **1** (in former times) an armed ship, owned and commanded by private people, that had government permission to attack and seize enemy ships carrying goods **2** the commander of, or any of the sailors on, a ship of this type

private eye /ˌ·· ˈ·/ *n infml* PRIVATE DETECTIVE

private house /ˌ·· ˈ·/ *n* a house that is built to be the home of a person or a family

private mem·ber /ˌ·· ˈ··/ *n* (esp. in Britain) a member of a parliament who is not a minister in the government

private parts /ˌ·· ˈ·/ also (*sl*) **pri·vates** /ˈpraɪvɨ̧ts/— *n* [P] *euph* the outer sexual organs

private school /ˌ·· ˈ·/ *n* a school owned and directed by a person or group, not supported by government money, where education must be paid for —compare PUBLIC SCHOOL

private sol·dier /ˌ·· ˈ··/ *n fml* PRIVATE²

pri·va·tion /praɪˈveɪʃən/ *n* **1** [C;U] (a) lack of the necessary things or the main comforts of life: *Everyone suffered privations during the war, when there wasn't enough food in the country* **2** [C *usu. sing.*] a loss of something of great importance to one's way of living: *It was a great privation to her when the doctor forbade her to eat sugar*

priv·et /ˈprɪvɨ̧t/ *n* [U] a type of bush with small white flowers and leaves that stay green all the year, often grown in gardens to form a kind of fence (HEDGE)

priv·i·lege /ˈprɪvɨ̧lɪdʒ/ *n* **1** [C] a special right or advantage limited to one person or a few (fortunate) people of a particular kind: *In countries where there are still not many schools, education is a privilege* **2** [U] *usu. derog* advantage possessed by a person or group by reason of wealth, high birth, etc.: *In modern times there is less privilege and more of an equal chance in life for everyone* **3** [C *usu. sing.*] a fault or weakness which is allowed or forgiven by common agreement: *It's a woman's privilege to change her mind* **4** [(*the*) S] a special favour; advantage that gives one great pleasure: *He gave his friend the privilege of using his private library.|He's a fine musician; it's a privilege to hear him play* **5** [C;U] (a) right to do or say things without risk of punishment, esp. in a parliament: *A member of parliament mustn't hit a fellow member; that would be* **a breach of privilege** (=a breaking of the rules about what a member may do or say)

priv·i·leged /ˈprɪvɨ̧lɪdʒd/ *adj* **1** having a PRIVILEGE (1,4) or privileges: *We are privileged tonight to have as our main speaker the Foreign Minister of France* **2** *usu. derog* having PRIVILEGE (2) **3** that must be respected by the law as secret

priv·i·ly /ˈprɪvɨ̧li/ *adv old use* secretly; privately

priv·y¹ /ˈprɪvi/ *adj* **1** [F+*to*] *fml* sharing secret knowledge (of) **2** [A] *old use* secret; private

privy² *n old use* a LAVATORY, esp. one without a water supply for carrying away waste matter

Privy Coun·cil /ˌ·· ˈ··/ *n* [(*the*) GU] (in Britain) a body of people of high rank in politics and public life who may advise the king or queen on certain State affairs. Membership of this body is now chiefly a mark of honour —**-cillor** *n*

Privy Purse /ˌ·· ˈ·/ *n* [*the*+R] (*sometimes not cap.*) (in Britain) money given by law from public money to a king or queen for personal use

Privy Seal /ˌ·· ˈ·/ *n* [*the*+R] (in Britain before 1885) a royal mark put on state papers of rather small importance —compare GREAT SEAL

prize[1] /praɪz/ *n* **1** something of value given to someone who is successful in a game, race, competition, game of chance, etc., or given for some deed that is admired: *Her beautiful roses gained* **first prize** *at the flower show* **2** a reward given to a student at school or college for especially good work **3** something of value that is gained after a struggle; a precious possession: *To some men wealth is the greatest prize in life, and to others, fame*

prize[2] *adj* [Wa5;A] **1** that has gained a PRIZE[1] (1) in a show or competition: *prize cattle|a prize rose* **2** *infml & often humor* that is worthy of a PRIZE[1] (1) for quality, size, etc.: *That hen has produced a prize egg, bigger than any I've ever seen.|She always does something silly; she's a prize fool* **3** given as a PRIZE[1] (1,2): *prize money*

prize[3] *v* [Wv5;T1] to value highly: *The boy's bicycle was his most prized possession*

prize[4] *n* **1** (esp. in former times) an enemy ship seized and taken possession of at sea, or the goods that it contains **2** anything valuable seized and taken away

prize[5], **prise** *v* [X9,(7)] PRY[2]: *With a long iron bar we prized the top off the box*

prize day /ˈ· ·/ *n* (*often cap.*) (in a school) a yearly giving of prizes for the best work done during the year

prize·fight /ˈpraɪzfaɪt/ *n* **1** (in former times) a public BOXING match for a money prize, in which the 2 men fought with bare hands **2** *infml & becoming rare* a public BOXING match for a money prize —**~er** *n* —**~ing** *n* [U]

prize·man /ˈpraɪzmən/ *n* **-men** /mən/ (*usu. in comb.*) (esp. in Britain) a person who wins a (particular) university PRIZE[1] (2)

prize out, prise out *v adv* [T1 (*of*)] to force (information) (from someone); PRY OUT

prize ring /ˈ· ·/ *n* a space enclosed by ropes in which PRIZEFIGHTs take place

pro[1] /prəʊ/ *n* **pros** [*usu. pl.*] **1** an argument or reason in favour (of something) (esp. in the phr. **pros and cons**) **2** a person or vote in favour (of a suggestion) (esp. in the phr. **pros and cons**)

pro[2] *adv* (of arguing) for or in favour of (something) (esp. in the phr. **pro and con**): *We must be fair and consider the reasons pro and* CON

pro[3] *n* **pros** *infml* **1** PROFESSIONAL: *a football pro|a pro footballer|I'm taking lessons from our* (GOLF) *pro.|That actor's a real pro, and always gives a good performance!* **2** *BrE* PROSTITUTE

pro- *prefix* **1** in favour of; supporting: *pro-American ideas|He's very pro-American* **2** acting in the place of someone or something: *A pro*CATHEDRAL *is a building used as a* CATHEDRAL *until the proper one is built*

P R O /ˌpiː ɑːr ˈəʊ/ *n infml* PUBLIC RELATIONS OFFICER

pro-am /ˌprəʊ ˈæm/ *n, adj* [Wa5;C;A] (a GOLF competition) in which those taking part include both people who play for money and those who just play for pleasure

prob·a·bil·i·ty /ˌprɒbəˈbɪlɪ̈ti‖ˌprɑ-/ *n* **1** [U] the state or quality of being probable **2** [U (*of*);U5] likelihood: *There's little probability of reaching London tonight.|There's little probability that he will reach London tonight* **3** [C (*of*);C5] a probable event or result: *War is a serious probability in the present state of affairs* **4** [C (*of*);C5] (in MATHEMATICS) the chance of an event happening, expressed as a calculation based on known numbers **5** [U] the branch of MATHEMATICS concerned with such calculations **6 in all probability** almost (but not quite) certainly

prob·a·ble[1] /ˈprɒbəbəl‖ˈprɑ-/ *adj* that may be expected to happen; that has a good chance of being true or correct; likely: *It's possible that it will rain if the wind changes, but with such a cloudless sky it doesn't seem probable.|a probable result*

probable[2] *n infml* a probable choice, winner, etc.: *Before Saturday's football team is chosen, there will be a match between the probables and the possibles*

prob·a·bly /ˈprɒbəbli‖ˈprɑ-/ *adv* almost (but not quite) certainly: *John probably told his father all about the matter; he usually tells him everything.|"Will you be able to come tomorrow?" "Probably"*

pro·bate[1] /ˈprəʊbeɪt, -bɪ̈t‖-beɪt/ *n law* **1** [U] the official act of proving, after a person's death, that his WILL (a statement expressing his wishes with regard to who shall receive his possessions) has been written and signed according to law (often in the phrs. **apply for probate, grant probate**) **2** [C] also **probate cop·y** /ˌ·· ˈ··/— a copy of a WILL[2] (6) with a signed statement showing that it has been proved to be lawful

probate[2] *v* [T1] *AmE law* to examine and prove (a WILL[2] (6)) to be lawful

pro·ba·tion /prəˈbeɪʃən‖prəʊ-/ *n* [U] **1 a** the testing, usu. over a fixed length of time, of a person's character, behaviour, abilities, etc., esp. in order to decide whether he is fit to be accepted in some position, as a member of some society, etc. (esp. in the phr. **on probation**) **b** the time of this testing **2** *law* the system of giving a law-breaker a chance to live honestly, by allowing him to go free and unpunished if he will promise to behave well (esp. in the phr. **on probation**) —**~ary** *adj*

pro·ba·tion·er /prəˈbeɪʃənəʳ‖prəʊ-/ *n* **1** a person who is being tested for membership of a church or a religious society **2** a young hospital nurse during the early part of her training **3** a law-breaker who has been freed on PROBATION (2)

probation of·fi·cer /·ˈ·· ˌ···/ *n* a person whose job is to watch, advise, and help law-breakers who are put on PROBATION (2)

probe[1] /prəʊb/ *n* **1** a long thin metal instrument, usu. with a rounded end, used by doctors to search the inside of a wound, a hole in a tooth, etc. **2** an instrument of a like shape, used to feel inside a hollow or a deep place **3** also **space probe**— **a** an apparatus sent into the sky to examine conditions in outer space **b** an act of sending such an apparatus into the sky **4** (esp. in newspapers) a careful and thorough inquiry or examination **5** an act of probing (PROBE[2])

probe[2] *v* [I∅ (*into*);T1] **1** to search with a PROBE[1] (1,2): *He probed the mud with a stick, looking for the ring he had dropped* **2** to examine (something) thoroughly; search (into): *She tried to probe my mind and discover what I was thinking.|Stop probing* (=trying to get information by repeatedly asking questions)! —**probing** *adj* —**probingly** *adv*

pro·bi·ty /ˈprəʊbɪ̈ti/ *n* [U] *fml* honesty of the highest standard; the quality of being completely honourable and trustworthy

prob·lem /ˈprɒbləm‖ˈprɑ-/ *n* **1** [C] a (serious) difficulty that needs attention and thought: *"I've left my money at home." "That's no problem. I can lend you what you need."|The unemployment problem in this area is getting worse* **2** [C] a question (esp. connected with numbers, facts, etc.) for consideration or for which an answer is needed: *The little boy can already do simple problems in addition and* *subtraction* **3** [C *usu. sing.*] *infml* a person who causes (some special) difficulty: *As a dinner guest Celia is a problem; there are many kinds of food she doesn't eat* **4** [A] dealing with a social difficulty or a matter of right and wrong: *problem plays* **5** [A] having a meaning that is not clear: *a problem picture*

prob·lem·at·ic /ˌprɒblə'mætɪk‖ˌprɑ-/ also **prob·lem·at·i·cal** /-kəl/— *adj* doubtful; not settled —**-ically** *adv* [Wa4]

problem child /'·· ·/ *n* a child who is difficult to deal with, esp. because his character is not understood

pro·bos·cis /prə'bɒsɨs‖-'bɑ-/ *n* **1** the long movable nose of certain animals, esp. the elephant: *The* **proboscis monkey** *is so called because it has a long nose* **2** a long tubelike part of the mouth of some insects (esp. the BUTTERFLY) and worms, used for drawing in liquid, making holes, etc. —see picture at INSECT **3** *humor* a human nose, esp. a long one

pro·ce·du·ral /prə'siːdʒərəl/ *adj* [Wa5] of PROCEDURE, esp. in a court of law: *procedural difficulties*

pro·ce·dure /prə'siːdʒə^r/ *n* **1** [U;C] the (proper) way or order of directing business in an official meeting, a law case, etc.: *So much time was spent on settling procedure that little actual business was finished at the party political meeting.*|PARLIAMENTARY *procedure* **2** [C] an action or set of actions necessary for doing something: *Writing a cheque is quite a simple procedure.*|*We have worked out a new set of procedures for using this machine* —compare PROCESS¹

pro·ceed /prə'siːd/ *v* **1** [IØ (*with*), 3] to begin and continue (some course of action): *Now that our plans are settled let us proceed.*|*Tell us your name and then proceed with your story.*|*As soon as he came in he proceeded to tell us all his troubles* **2** [IØ (*with*)] *often fml* to continue (after stopping): *You needn't stop speaking when someone enters the court room; please proceed.*|*Don't let me stop you; proceed with your work* **3** [L9] *fml* to advance; move forward; move along a course: *Do not proceed across a main road until you have first looked to the right and the left*

proceed a·gainst *v prep* [T1 *pass. rare*] *fml* to take an action in law against (someone)

proceed from *v prep* [T1 *no pass.*] to arise from; result from

pro·ceed·ing /prə'siːdɪŋ/ *n* **1** [U] (course of) action or behaviour **2** [C *usu. pl.*] an act (of business): *The necessary proceedings have been begun for the combining of the 2 firms*

pro·ceed·ings /prə'siːdɪŋz/ *n* [P] **1** (undesirable or unlawful) happenings: *He'd drunk so much alcohol that afterwards he lost all memory of the evening's wild proceedings* **2** an action taken in law (esp. in the phrs. **start/take (legal) proceedings (against someone)**) **3** (*often cap.*) the (printed) records of business, activities, etc., at the meetings of an association or club: *the Proceedings of the London Historical Society*

pro·ceeds /'prəʊsiːdz/ *n* [P] money gained from the sale of something, or as the result of some activity for getting money: *We gave the proceeds from the sale of old books to the school*

proceed to *v prep* [T1] *fml* **1** to pass from one matter to (another); go on to **2 a** to work towards (a degree) in a university: *Persons proceeding to the degree of B.A. must be present for examination on Thursday morning* **b** to advance from a lower university degree to (a higher one): *He will proceed to the degree of M.A. this year*

pro·cess¹ /'prəʊses‖'prɑ-/ *n* **1** [C] any continued set of natural actions connected with (the continuation, development, and change of) life or matter, over which man has little control: *the process of breathing*|*Coal was formed out of dead forests by chemical processes* **2** [C] *tech* a small part that sticks out, esp. any part of a plant or animal that grows standing out and is easily seen: *2 bony processes on each side of the mouth* **3** [C] a continued set of actions performed intentionally in order to reach some result: *the process of learning to read* **4** [U] course; time during which something is still being done (esp. in the phr. **in (the) process of**): *The firm is now in the process of moving the machines to a new factory* **5** [C] a particular system or treatment of materials used esp. in producing goods **6** [C] **a** an action in law in all its stages **b** an official written order to appear before a judge in a court —compare PROCEDURE

process² /'prəʊses‖'prɑ-/ *v* [T1] **1** [Wv5] to treat and preserve (a substance, esp. a food) by a particular PROCESS¹ (5): *processed cheese* **2** to print a picture from (a photographic film) **3** to put (facts, numbers, etc.) into a COMPUTER for examination **4** to prepare and examine in detail: *The plans are now being processed*

pro·cess³ /prə'ses/ *v* [L9] to walk in, or as if in, procession

pro·ces·sion /prə'seʃən/ *n* **1** [C] a line of people, vehicles, etc., moving forward in an orderly, often ceremonial, way **2** [U] a continuous onward movement of people or things: *The workers marched in procession to the minister's office.*|*Ideas passed in quick procession through his mind* **3** [C] *BrE infml* (in sports, esp. cricket) a very easy defeat of one's opponents; act of losing quickly and without seeming to try very hard

pro·ces·sion·al¹ /prə'seʃənəl/ *n* **1** a PROCESSIONAL² song (HYMN), piece of music, or prayer **2** a book containing these

processional² *adj* [Wa5;A;(B)] connected with or used in a solemn religious procession: *a processional march*

pro·claim /prə'kleɪm‖prəʊ-/ *v* [T1,5;X (*to be*) 1,7] **1** *fml* to make (esp. something of national importance) known publicly; declare officially: *The ringing bells proclaimed the news of the birth of the prince.*|*Peace was proclaimed.*|*The boy was proclaimed king* **2** *lit* to show clearly; be an outward sign of: *His pronunciation proclaimed that he was an American*

proc·la·ma·tion /ˌprɒklə'meɪʃən‖ˌprɑ-/ *n* **1** [C] an official public statement: *a royal proclamation* **2** [U] the action of PROCLAIMing

pro·cliv·i·ty /prə'klɪvɨti‖prəʊ-/ *n* [C (*to, towards*), C3] *fml* a strong natural liking or tendency (esp. towards something bad)

pro·con·sul /prəʊ'kɒnsəl‖-'kɑn-/ *n* **1** (in ancient Rome) a governor of a part of the Roman Empire **2** *fml or pomp* a governor of a state which is under the control of another state —**~ar** /prəʊ'kɒnsjʊlə^r‖-'kɑnsələr/ *adj* [Wa5;A;(B)]

pro·con·su·late /prəʊ'kɒnsjʊlɨt‖-'kɑnsəl-/ also **pro·con·sul·ship** /prəʊ'kɒnsəlʃɪp‖-'kɑn-/— *n* **1** the office or position of a PROCONSUL **2** the time during which a PROCONSUL is in office

pro·cras·ti·nate /prə'kræstɨneɪt/ *v* [IØ] *fml* to delay (repeatedly and without good reason) in doing some necessary act —**-nation** /prəˌkræstɨ'neɪʃən/ *n* [U]

pro·cre·ate /'prəʊkrieɪt/ *v* [T1;IØ] *esp. fml or tech* to produce or give life to (the young of one's own type of animal): *Animals have the power to procreate (their* SPECIES*)* —**-ation** /ˌprəʊkri'eɪʃən/ *n* [U]

proc·tor /'prɒktə^r‖'prɑk-/ *n* **1** (esp. at Oxford and

Cambridge) one of 2 university officers appointed yearly, whose duties include making students keep university rules **2** *AmE* a person appointed to take charge of students in an examination, esp. to make sure they do not cheat

Proctor *n* [R9] (in Britain) a law officer who watches certain kinds of cases (such as DIVORCE) in a court and has the right to stop a case if facts are being kept from the court or if a secret agreement has been made for a dishonest purpose (in the phrs. **King's Proctor/Queen's Proctor**)

pro·cu·ra·tor fis·cal /ˌprɒkjʊreɪtə ˈfɪskəl‖ˌprɑkjəreɪtər/ also (*infml ScotE*) **fiscal**— *n* (in Scotland) PUBLIC PROSECUTOR

pro·cure /prəˈkjʊəʳ‖prəʊ-/ *v* **1** [D1 (*for*);T1] *fml* to obtain, esp. by effort or careful attention: *Can you procure that rare old book for me?* **2** [T1 (*for*); I∅] to provide (a woman) for someone else's sexual satisfaction **3** [T1] *old use* to cause: *to procure someone's death* —**-curable** *adj* [Wa5] —**~ment** *n* [U]

pro·cur·er /prəˈkjʊərəʳ/ *fem.* **pro·cur·ess** /-rɪ̈s/— *n* a person who PROCUREs (esp. 2)

prod[1] /prɒd‖prɑd/ *v* **-dd- 1** [T1 (*with*);I∅ (*at*)] to push or press (something or someone) with a finger or other pointed object; POKE (2): *He prodded the snake with his toe but it didn't move* **2** [T1 (*into*)] to urge sharply into action or thought: *Cyril is lazy; he won't do any work if he's not prodded into it*

prod[2] *n* **1** an act of PRODding[1] (1) with something pointed **2** an instrument used for PRODding[1] (1) **3** something that PRODs[1] (2): *She'll certainly forget, so you'd better give her memory a prod*

prod·i·gal[1] /ˈprɒdɪgəl‖ˈprɑ-/ *adj* **1** [B] *derog* carelessly and greatly wasteful, esp. of money **2** [F+*of*] *fml & apprec* giving or producing (something) freely or generously in large amounts: *He has a mind prodigal of ideas* —**~ity** /ˌprɒdɪˈgælɪ̈ti‖ˌprɑ-/ *n* [U] —**~ly** *adv* [Wa4]

prodigal[2] *n infml, often humor* a person who leads a life of careless wasteful spending and perhaps immoral pleasure (esp. in the phr. **the prodigal has returned**)

pro·di·gious /prəˈdɪdʒəs/ *adj* wonderful, esp. because of size, amount, or quality; very great: *He never forgets anything; his memory is prodigious* —**~ly** *adv*: *What a prodigiously fat woman!*

prod·i·gy /ˈprɒdɪdʒi‖ˈprɑ-/ *n* **1** a wonder in nature: *This apple is a prodigy; it's 5 times the usual size!* **2** a person who has unusual and very noticeable abilities **3** [(*of*)] an unusual and wonderful example: *An ant's nest is a prodigy of activity* **4** an unusually clever child (often in the phrs. **child prodigy, infant prodigy**)

pro·duce[1] /prəˈdjuːs‖-ˈduːs/ *v* **1** [T1] to show, bring out, or offer for examination or consideration: *The magician produced a rabbit from a hat.*|*"Can you produce any proof that you weren't near the bank at the time of the robbery?"* **2** [T1] to bear (crops) or supply (metal or other substances) from the ground: *Good soil will produce fine crops.*|(fig.) *the finest writer our country has ever produced* **3** [T1] to give birth to (esp. young animals): *Female sheep produce 1 or 2 lambs at a time.*|(*humor*) *Mrs. Dobson has produced 2 fine sons* **4** [T1;I∅] to lay (an egg) **5** [T1] to grow or supply from something grown, or from animals, esp. in large quantities for use or sale: *Canada produces wheat and furs* **6** [T1; I∅] to make (something, esp. goods) from materials: *Gas can be produced from coal.*|*I'm bringing some friends home; can you produce dinner for 6 people?*|*The factory hasn't begun to produce yet* **7** [T1;I∅] to make (a work of art) with skill and imagination **8** [T1] to cause; have as a result or effect: *Gordon's jokes produced a great deal of laughter* **9** [T1] to prepare in all details and bring before the public: *The book was carefully produced* **10** [T1] (in GEOMETRY) to lengthen or continue (a line) to a point —see PRODUCTION (USAGE)

prod·uce[2] /ˈprɒdjuːs‖ˈprɑduːs/ *n* [U] something that has been produced, esp. by growing or farming: *The wine bottle was marked "Produce of Spain"* —see PRODUCTION (USAGE)

pro·duc·er /prəˈdjuːsəʳ‖-ˈduː-/ *n* **1** a person or company that produces goods, foods, or materials (as opposed to a person who then buys and uses them (CONSUMER)) **2** a person who has general control esp. of the money for a play, film, or broadcast, but who does not direct the actors —compare DIRECTOR, IMPRESARIO; see PRODUCTION (USAGE)

prod·uct /ˈprɒdʌkt‖ˈprɑ-/ *n* **1** something (useful) produced by growth or from the ground, or made in a factory: *Important products of South Africa are fruit and gold* **2** something that is produced as a result of thought, will, planning, conditions, etc.: *Criminals are sometimes the product of bad homes* **3** (in MATHEMATICS) the number got by multiplying 2 or more numbers: *The product of 3 multiplied by 2 multiplied by 6 is 36* **4** a new chemical compound produced by chemical action —see PRODUCTION (USAGE)

pro·duc·tion /prəˈdʌkʃən/ *n* **1** [U (*of*)] the act of showing (something), esp. to an official person: *Entrance is permitted only on production of a ticket* **2** [U] the action of producing or making products: *the production of cloth by hand* **3** [U] the amount produced: *Production has increased in the last few weeks* **4** [U (*of*)] the bringing of some natural force into being by skilled means: *the production of fire by rubbing 2 sticks together* **5** [U] the act of producing a play, film, or broadcast **6** [C] a play, film, or broadcast that is produced: *This new theatre is becoming known for its clever productions* **7** [C] something produced by the mind; work of art: *This book on political history is the writer's latest production* —see also MASS PRODUCTION

USAGE Things **produced** on a farm, such as milk, potatoes, and wool, are **produce**; things **produced** by industry are **products**. **Production** is the action of **producing** or the amount **produced**: *to increase our* **production** *of eggs*|*the* **production** *of nylon socks.* Someone who **produces** is a **producer**, and this is also the word for the person in charge of **production** in the theatre or cinema: *a new* **production** *of "Hamlet"*.

production line /·ˈ·· ·/ *n* (esp. in a factory) an arrangement of the various stages in the production of an article so that the stages follow each other in order; ASSEMBLY LINE

pro·duc·tive /prəˈdʌktɪv/ *adj* **1** [B] that produces well or much: *a very productive writer*|*a very productive meeting* **2** [F+*of*] causing or producing (a result): *It was a very long meeting, but it wasn't productive of any important decisions* **3** [B] that makes things that satisfy needs or produce wealth: *Much office work is not directly productive, even if it is necessary* —**~ly** *adv* —**~ness** *n* [U]

pro·duc·tiv·i·ty /ˌprɒdʌkˈtɪvɪ̈ti, -dək-‖ˌprɑ-/ *n* [U] the (measured) ability to grow things or the (calculated) rate of making goods

pro·em /ˈprəʊem/ *n tech* a short introduction, as to a book

prof /prɒf‖prɑf/ *n* [N;(C)] *sl* PROFESSOR (1,2)

Prof. *written abbrev. for:* PROFESSOR (1,2): *Prof. Wayland Smith, University College London*

pro·fa·na·tion /ˌprɒfəˈneɪʃən‖ˌprɑ-/ *n fml* **1** [U (*of*)] the act of profaning (PROFANE[1]): *the profanation of the temple* **2** [C] an example of this

pro·fane[1] /prəˈfeɪn/ *v* [T1] **1** to treat (something holy) disrespectfully **2** *fml or humor* to dishonour or use in a disrespectful way (something that deserves respect): *They have profaned the country's flag.|This is a men's club, which no woman is allowed to profane by her presence*

profane[2] *adj* **1** having or showing disrespect for God or for holy things: *To smoke in a church or mosque would be a profane act* —compare BLASPHEMOUS **2** (esp. of language) socially shocking or impolite, esp. because of improper use of religious words or the name of God —compare OBSCENE **3** *fml* not religious or holy; concerned with man's life in this world: *profane art* —opposite **sacred** —**~ly** *adv*

pro·fan·i·ty /prəˈfænə̇ti/ *n* **1** [U] PROFANEness[2] (1) —compare BLASPHEMY **2** [U;C] (an example of) PROFANEness[2] (2): *The men were rough and their conversation was full of profanities* —compare OBSCENITY

pro·fess /prəˈfes/ *v* **1** [T1] *fml* to declare plainly as a fact that one has (some personal feeling, belief, state, etc.): *She professed a belief in spirits* **2** [T1,3] to claim (often falsely) that one has (some knowledge, skill, or personal feeling): *I don't profess to know anything about poetry* **3** [X (*to be*) 1,7] *often fml* to declare or call (oneself), truly or falsely: *He professed himself unhappy with the price he'd got for his boat, though secretly he was very satisfied* **4** [T1] *fml* to give an appearance of having: *Her manner professed a gaiety that she did not feel* **5** [T1] *fml* to have as one's religion: *They profess no religion, but they live honourable lives* **6** [IØ] *rare fml* to make plain declaration of one's religious faith **7** [T1] *rare fml* to work in (the stated profession): *My uncle professes law* **8** [T1] *rare fml* to teach (the stated subject) as a PROFESSOR at a university: *Smithers professes English*

pro·fessed /prəˈfest/ *adj* [Wa5] **1** [A] plainly self-declared: *a professed Muslim|She is a professed man-hater* **2** [B] pretended: *a professed sorrow* **3** [A] *tech* (of a person) having been accepted, after training and tests, as a member of a religious group

pro·fess·ed·ly /prəˈfesə̇dli/ *adv fml* according to what one has declared concerning oneself, whether true or not: *She is professedly of noble birth*

pro·fes·sion /prəˈfeʃən/ *n* **1** [C; *by*+U] a form of employment, esp. one that is respected in society as honourable and is possible only for an educated person and after training in some special branch of knowledge (such as law, medicine, and the Church): *In the last century there was a great social difference between business and the professions.|He is a lawyer by profession* **2** [*the*+GU] the whole body of people in a particular profession: *The teaching profession claim(s) to be badly paid* **3** [C (*of*)] *fml* a declaration (of one's belief, opinion, or feeling)

pro·fes·sion·al[1] /prəˈfeʃənəl/ *adj* **1** [Wa5;A] working in one of the (higher) professions: *A doctor is a professional man* **2** [B] *usu. apprec* showing or using the qualities of training of a member of a profession: *The magician performed his tricks with professional skill.|professional standards|professional advice|Don't wrap up the present in that careless way; try to be a bit more professional about it* **3** [Wa5;B] doing for money what others do for enjoyment: *a professional painter|a professional gardener* **4** [Wa5;B] done by, played by, or made up of people who are paid: *professional football|professional tennis* **5** [Wa5;A] *usu. derog* skilled in (and often paid for) forcing something into public notice and causing public difficulty: *professional trouble-makers|She's a professional complainer* **6** [Wa5;A] *euph* (esp. in sports) (of a breaking of rules) intentional: *If a footballer handles the ball to stop another player getting it, it is often called a professional offence* —**~ly** *adv*

professional[2] *n* **1** a person who lives on the money he earns by practising a particular skill or sport —compare AMATEUR **2** also (*infml*) **pro**— (*often in comb.*) a person employed by a private club to play for it and to teach his sporting skills to its members, esp. in GOLF, tennis, and cricket **3** *apprec* a person who has great experience and high professional standards: *a real professional* **4 turn professional** (of a sportsman) to become a professional player

pro·fes·sion·al·is·m /prəˈfeʃənəlɪzəm/ *n* [U] **1** the behaviour, skill, or qualities shown by a PROFESSIONAL[1] (1) person **2** *apprec* the quality of being a PROFESSIONAL[2] (3) **3** (in sports) the practice of using professional players **4** *euph* (in sports) the use of small offences in order to obtain an advantage

pro·fes·sor /prəˈfesəʳ/ *n* **1** [C;A;N;(U)] *BrE* (the title of) a teacher of the highest rank in a university department: *My new history professor is Professor Ward. He is Professor of History at my university.|Professor of Chemistry in the University of Durham|the rank of professor* **2** [A;N;(C)] *AmE* a teacher at a university or college **3** [A;N;C9] a title taken by those who teach or claim various skills (often to add an undeserved importance to the position): MADAME *Chores, professor of dancing, gives lessons daily* **4** [C9, esp. *of*] *fml and rare* a person who shows his religious faith or moral beliefs

pro·fes·so·ri·al /ˌprɒfəˈsɔːrɪəl‖ˌprɑfəˈsor-/ *adj* [Wa5] of, like, or fitting for a university PROFESSOR (1,2) —**-ally** *adv*

pro·fes·sor·ship /prəˈfesəʃɪp‖-sər-/ *n* the position of a university PROFESSOR (1,2)

prof·fer[1] /ˈprɒfəʳ‖ˈprɑ-/ *v* [Wv5;D1 (*to*);T1] *usu. fml* to offer, esp. by holding out in the hands for acceptance: *He refused the proffered drink*

proffer[2] *n fml* an offer

pro·fi·cient /prəˈfɪʃənt/ *adj* [(*at, in*)] thoroughly skilled; well practised in an art, science, skill, or branch of study —**~ly** *adv* —**-ciency** *n* [U (*at, in*)]

pro·file[1] /ˈprəʊfaɪl/ *n* **1** [C; *in*+U] a side view, esp. of someone's head: *He drew her profile* **2** [C; *in*+U] an edge or shape of something seen against a background **3** [C] a short description, esp. of a person's life and character, as given on television or in a newspaper: *a profile of modern Britain* —see also LOW PROFILE

profile[2] *v* [T1] **1** to draw or write a PROFILE[1] (1,3) of **2** [*usu. pass.*] to show (something) in PROFILE[1] (2): *The old trees were profiled against the pale sky*

prof·it[1] /ˈprɒfə̇t‖ˈprɑ-/ *n* **1** [C;U] money gain; money gained by a business or a piece of business: *He sold his house at a profit* (=sold it for more than it had cost him); *he made a profit of £1000 on the sale.|There's very little profit in selling land at present* **2** [U] *fml* advantage gained from some action: *reading for profit and pleasure* —**~less** *adj*: *It would be profitless to do such a foolish thing* —**~lessly** *adv*

profit[2] *v* [T1;D1] *fml or old use* (of a thing) to be of service, use, or advantage to (someone or something): *It will profit you nothing to do that*

prof·i·ta·ble /ˈprɒfə̇təbəl‖ˈprɑ-/ *adj* **1** useful; resulting in advantage: *She spent a profitable day cleaning the house thoroughly* **2** resulting in money gain —**-bly** *adv*

profit by also **profit from**— *v prep* [T1,4] to learn or gain advantage from (something or doing something): *You can profit by my mistakes and avoid them yourself*

prof·i·teer¹ /ˌprɒfəˈtɪəʳ‖ˌprɑ-/ *n derog* a person who PROFITEERS²
profiteer² *v* [IØ] *derog* to make unfairly large profits, esp. by selling things at very high prices in time of trouble or when much-needed goods are difficult to get
profit mar·gin /ˈ·· ˌ··/ *n* the difference between the cost of production and the selling price
profit shar·ing /ˈ·· ˌ··/ *n* [U] a system according to which the owner of a factory, shop, etc., shares the profits from his business with his workers
prof·li·ga·cy /ˈprɒfləgəsi‖ˈprɑ-/ *n* [U] *fml* **1** the state or quality of being PROFLIGATE¹ **2** PROFLIGATE¹ behaviour
prof·li·gate¹ /ˈprɒfləgət‖ˈprɑ-/ *adj* **1** [(*of*)] (of a person or spending of money) carelessly and boldly wasteful (esp. of money) **2** *fml* (of a person, behaviour, an act) wicked; shamelessly immoral
profligate² *n fml* a PROFLIGATE¹ liver or spender
pro·found /prəˈfaʊnd/ *adj* **1** [B] (of a state or quality) deep; complete; very strongly felt: *There was a profound silence in the empty church.|Motherhood is a profound experience* **2** [A] *lit or fml* deep; far below the surface: *Strange creatures live in the profound depths of the ocean* **3** [B] *often apprec* having, showing, or using thorough knowledge and deep understanding: *He is a profound thinker; he has a profound mind* **4** [B] needing much study; difficult to understand or explain **5** [B] *old use* very low: *a profound* BOW² (1) —**~ly** *adv*: *I am profoundly grateful*
pro·fun·di·ty /prəˈfʌndəti/ *n* **1** [U] depth or thoroughness, esp. of mind or feeling **2** [C *usu. pl.*] *fml or humor* something PROFOUND (1,2,3,4): *No one knows how many stars move through the profundities of space.|An after-dinner speech is not an occasion for profundities* (=deep thoughts)
pro·fuse /prəˈfjuːs/ *adj* **1** [B] in plenty; freely produced or poured out: *Her head was covered with a profuse mass of curls.|profuse tears|profuse thanks* **2** [F (*in, of*)] (of a person) (too) eager, free, or generous in giving —**~ly** *adv* —**~ness** *n* [U (*of*)]
pro·fu·sion /prəˈfjuːʒən/ *n* [S9, esp *of*;(U)] great plenty; great or too great amount (often in the phr. **in profusion**): *There is a profusion of flowers in the garden in summer; flowers grow there in profusion.|The room was spoilt by a profusion of ugly little ornaments*
pro·gen·i·tor /prəʊˈdʒenətəʳ/ *n* [(*of*)] **1** *usu. tech* a person, animal, or plant of the distant past, from which a living being is descended **2** *fml* a person who starts a new idea or form in politics, an art, or a system of thought, from which a full development comes later: *Schoenberg was a progenitor of modern music*
prog·e·ny /ˈprɒdʒəni‖ˈprɑ-/ *n* [GU (*of*)] *tech or lit* **1** descendants (of some person, animal, or plant form) **2** *sometimes humor* children (of a person) or the young (of an animal): *He pitied Mrs Rogers, with her* NUMEROUS *progeny* (=large family)
pro·ges·ter·one /prəʊˈdʒestərəʊn/ *n* [U] a substance in the female organs that prepares the child-bearing part (UTERUS) for its work
prog·na·thous /prɒgˈneɪθəs‖prɑg-/ *adj tech* **1** (of a jaw) sticking out **2** having a jaw that sticks out
prog·no·sis /prɒgˈnəʊsəs‖prɑg-/ *n* **-ses** /siːz/ **1** *med* a doctor's opinion, based on medical experience, of what course a disease will probably take —compare DIAGNOSIS **2** a description of the future; judgment concerning the course and result of a set of events already begun
prog·nos·tic /prɒgˈnɒstɪk‖prɑgˈnɑ-/ *n, adj* [(*of*)] *fml* (a sign) that shows the future, warns, or gives hope
prog·nos·ti·cate /prɒgˈnɒstəkeɪt‖prɑgˈnɑ-/ *v* [T1, 5;IØ] *fml or humor* to give a sign or forewarn of (a event or condition) as the result of (suppose knowledge or experience —**-cator** *n*
prog·nos·ti·ca·tion /prɒgˌnɒstəˈkeɪʃən‖prɑgˌnɑ *n* [(*of*)] *fml or humor* **1** [U] the act of prognostica ing (PROGNOSTICATE) **2** [C] something that PRO NOSTICATES or is prognosticated
pro·gram¹ /ˈprəʊgræm/ *n* **1** a plan of the oper tions to be performed by a kind of electr calculator (COMPUTER) when dealing with a set facts **2** *esp. AmE* PROGRAMME¹
program² *v* **-mm-** *or* **-m-** [T1;V3] **1** to supply COMPUTER) with a plan of the operations to performed **2** *esp. AmE* PROGRAMME²
pro·gramme¹, *AmE* usu. **-gram** /ˈprəʊgræm/ *n* **1** (printed) list of performers or things to be pe formed at a concert, a theatre, a sports compe tion, etc. **2** a complete show or performance, es one made up of several different acts: *What is yo favourite television programme?|The band is giving programme of modern music* **3** a fixed plan of course of action; list of duties, activities, etc.: *T hospital building programme has been delayed by la of money.|What's on the programme today?* (=Wh are we going to do today?) **4** a statement by political party of the improvements it intends make in government, offered esp. at a time of national election
programme², *AmE* usu. **-gram** *v* **-mm-** [T1;V3] plan or arrange: *The central heating system of t building is programmed to start working at 6 o'clo each morning*
programmed course /ˌ·· ˈ·/ *n* an education course in which the material to be learnt is give (in books or by a machine) in small amounts, eac of which must be thoroughly learnt before passi on to the next
programmed learn·ing /ˌ·· ˈ··/ *n* [U] an educ tional system in which the learner teaches hims by means of a PROGRAMMED COURSE
programme mu·sic /ˈ·· ˌ··/ *n* [U] descripti music, using sound to suggest a story, picture, etc.
programme note /ˈ·· ·/ *n* [*often pl.*] a sho account of a piece of music, a performer, et given in a printed PROGRAMME¹ (1)
pro·gram·mer, programer /ˈprəʊgræməʳ/ *n* person who prepares a PROGRAM¹ for a COMPUTER
pro·gress¹ /ˈprəʊgres‖ˈprɑ-/ *n* **1** [U] advance journey onward; forward movement in space: *T ship made slow progress through the rough sea* **2** [U continual improvement or development: *Jane still sick in hospital, but she's making progress* (= slowly getting better) **3** [U] (natural) course; t state of continuing or being done (often in the ph **in progress**) **4** [C] *old use* an official and oft ceremonial journey, esp. of a king or queen
pro·gress² /prəˈgres/ *v* [IØ] **1** to advance: *The ye is progressing. It will soon be autumn* **2** to improv develop (favourably): *Mary is progressing in the a of cooking; her meals are becoming more eatable*
pro·gres·sion /prəˈgreʃən/ *n* **1** [U;(S)] (the actio of) PROGRESSING², esp. by stages **2** [U] (in MATH MATICS) the way in which each number in a set numbers varies from the one before it **3** [C] (i MATHEMATICS) a set of numbers that vary in particular way —see also ARITHMETIC PROGRE SION, GEOMETRIC PROGRESSION
pro·gres·sive¹ /prəˈgresɪv/ *adj* **1** [Wa5] movin forward continuously or by stages **2** [Wa5] **a** th becomes increasingly worse in its later stage *There is often a progressive loss of sight in old ag* **b** (of a tax) that is higher on larger amounts money **3** improving or changing in accordan with new ideas: *This is a progressive firm that use the most modern systems of operation in its busines*

4 *usu. apprec* that favours or is eager for change, esp. in politics or education: *He is a young man full of progressive ideas; he is a progressive thinker* **5** modern (esp. in the phr. **progressive jazz**) —**~ly** *adv*: *It got progressively worse/better* —**~ness** *n* [U]

progressive[2] *n* a person with PROGRESSIVE[1] (4) ideas, esp. about social change

pro·hib·it /prəˈhɪbɨt‖prəʊ-/ *v* [T1 (*from*),4] *fml* **1** to forbid by law or rule: *Smoking in this railway carriage is prohibited* **2** to prevent; make impossible: *His small size prohibits his becoming a policeman*

pro·hi·bi·tion /ˌprəʊhɨˈbɪʃən/ *n* **1** [U (*of*)] the act of PROHIBITing (1) **2** [U] (*often cap.*) the forbidding by law of the making or sale of alcoholic drinks **3** [U] (*usu. cap.*) (in the US) the time (from 1920 to 1933) during which a national law of this type was in effect **4** [C (*against*)] *fml* an order forbidding something

pro·hi·bi·tion·ist /ˌprəʊhɨˈbɪʃənɨst/ *n* a person who supports PROHIBITION (2, 3)

pro·hib·i·tive /prəˈhɪbɨtɪv‖prəʊ-/ *adj* **1** intended to prevent, or resulting in preventing, the use or misuse of something: *The government has put a prohibitive tax on foreign goods* **2** (of price) so high that few people can pay it —**~ly** *adv*: *prohibitively costly*

pro·hib·i·to·ry /prəˈhɪbɨtəri‖prəʊˈhɪbɨtori/ *adj fml* intended to PROHIBIT (1) something: *a prohibitory rule against dogs entering the public gardens*

proj·ect[1] /ˈprɒdʒekt‖ˈprɑ-/ *n* **1** (a plan for) work or activity of any kind: *This student is doing a special project; he's building a small electrical machine for his science class.|The government has begun a project at the port to increase the size of the harbour* **2** *AmE* HOUSING PROJECT

pro·ject[2] /prəˈdʒekt/ *v* **1** [Wv4;T1;I∅] to (cause to) stand out beyond an edge or surface: *Some creatures project their tongue to catch flies and other insects.|His ears project noticeably; he has projecting ears* **2** [T1] to (aim and) throw through the air with force **3** [T1 (*into, onto*)] to cause (heat, sound, light, or shadow) to be directed into space or onto a surface: *A singer must learn to project his voice so as to be heard in a large hall* **4** [T1] **a** to make a picture of (a solid, esp. curved, object) on a flat surface **b** to make (a map) by this means **5** [T1] to express or represent (oneself or one's nature, qualities, feelings, beliefs, etc.) outwardly, esp. in a way that has a favourable effect on others: *A politician must project himself if he wants to win an election* **6** [Wv5;T1] to consider as a possible course of action; plan: *our projected visit to Australia* **7** [T1 (*into*)] to direct (oneself or one's thoughts or imagination) so as to pass into some other time or condition: *Try to project your mind into the future and imagine what life will be like in 1000 years* **8** [T1 (*on, onto*);I∅] to imagine (one's own esp. bad feelings or thoughts) as being experienced by others: *You're projecting again: I'm not angry with you, it's you who are angry with me*

pro·jec·tile[1] /prəˈdʒektaɪl‖-tl/ *n* an object or weapon that is shot forward, esp. from a gun, or that shoots itself forward

projectile[2] *adj* [Wa5;A] *fml* **1** able to PROJECT[2] (2) things **2** suitable for being PROJECTed[2] (2)

pro·jec·tion /prəˈdʒekʃən/ *n* **1** [U (*of*)] the act of PROJECTing[2] **2** [U;C] (an example of) the PROJECTing[2] (8) of one's own feelings onto others **3** [C (*of*)] something planned, esp. a guess of future possibilities made on the base of experience and the general direction of events at a given time: *the council's projection of the town's increase in population over the next 10 years* **4** [C (*of*)] an image, light, sound, etc., that has been PROJECTed[2] (3) **5** [C] something that stands out from a surface **6** [C] **a** a figure that has been PROJECTed[2] (4); PROJECTed map **b** a framework of squares upon which a map is drawn

pro·jec·tion·ist /prəˈdʒekʃənɨst/ *n* a person who works a PROJECTOR, esp. in a cinema

projection room /·ˈ·· ·/ *n* a small room in a cinema from which films are PROJECTed[2] (3) onto a surface

pro·jec·tor /prəˈdʒektəʳ/ *n* an apparatus for PROJECTing[2] (3) films or pictures onto a surface —see picture at PHOTOGRAPHIC

pro·lapse[1] /ˈprəʊlæps‖prəʊˈlæps/ *n med* an act of prolapsing (PROLAPSE[2])

pro·lapse[2] /prəʊˈlæps/ *v* [Wv5;I∅] *med* (of an inner body organ, such as the bowel) to slip or fall down out of the proper place: *a prolapsed* UTERUS

prole /prəʊl/ *n derog* a member of the PROLETARIAT (1)

pro·le·gom·e·na /ˌprəʊlɨˈgɒmɨnə‖-ˈgɑ-/ also **pro·le·gom·e·non** /-mɨnən‖-nɑn/— *n* **-e·na** /ɨnə/ *fml* a written introduction to a book on a serious subject

pro·le·tar·i·an /ˌprəʊlɨˈteəriən/ *n, adj often derog* (a member) of the PROLETARIAT (1)

pro·le·tar·i·at /ˌprəʊlɨˈteəriət/ *n* [(*the*) GU] **1** the class of (esp. unskilled) workers who own little or no property and have to work for wages —compare BOURGEOISIE **2** (in ancient Rome) the lowest class of society

pro·lif·e·rate /prəˈlɪfəreɪt/ *v* [I∅] **1** to increase rapidly in numbers **2** *tech* (of simple forms of living matter) to grow or REPRODUCE rapidly by producing new parts, separating into pieces, etc.

pro·lif·e·ra·tion /prəˌlɪfəˈreɪʃən/ *n* **1** [S (*of*)] a rapid increase or spreading: *a proliferation of atomic weapons* **2** [U (*of*)] (in BIOLOGY) growth by active division of cells; production of a new part **3** [C (*of*)] (in BIOLOGY) a part formed by this means

pro·lif·ic /prəˈlɪfɪk/ *adj* **1** [B] producing many young: *Rats are very prolific* **2** [B] (of a tree, plant, crop, etc.) fruitful; growing in plenty **3** [B] *usu. apprec* (of a person or a person's mind, life, etc.) producing many works: *During his most prolific years, this painter was producing a new work nearly every month* **4** [F (*in, of*)] having or producing in large numbers —**~ally** *adv* [Wa4]

pro·lix /ˈprəʊlɪks‖prəʊˈlɪks/ *adj* (of a speech, story, speaker, writer, etc.) tiringly and uninterestingly long and using too many words; wordy —**~ity** /prəˈlɪksɨti‖prəʊ-/ *n* [U]

pro·logue, *AmE* **prolog** /ˈprəʊlɒg‖-lɔg, -lɑg/ *n* [(*to*)] **1** (*sometimes cap.*) an introduction to a play, long poem, etc. **2** an act or event that leads up to, introduces, or causes another more important event or set of events

pro·long /prəˈlɒŋ‖-ˈlɔŋ/ *v* [T1] to make longer; LENGTHEN: *Some people have tried to find a means of prolonging life*

pro·lon·ga·tion /ˌprəʊlɒŋˈgeɪʃən‖-lɔŋ-/ *n* **1** [U (*of*)] **a** the action of PROLONGing **b** the state of being PROLONGED **2** [C (*of*)] something added that PROLONGs something —compare EXTENSION (2)

pro·longed /prəˈlɒŋd‖-ˈlɔŋd/ *adj* continuing for a long time: *a prolonged absence*

prom /prɒm‖prɑm/ *n* **1** *BrE infml* (*often cap.*) PROMENADE CONCERT **2** *BrE infml* PROMENADE[1] (3): *sitting on the prom, smelling the fresh sea air* **3** *AmE* a formal dance party given for students by a HIGH SCHOOL or college class

prom·e·nade[1] /ˌprɒməˈnɑːd◂, ˈprɒmənɑːd‖ˌprɑməˈneɪd/ *n* **1** *fml* an unhurried walk, ride, or drive for pleasure or exercise **2** *becoming rare* a place for this, such as an entrance hall or other space in a theatre where people walk between acts of a play

3 a wide path beside a road along the coast in a holiday town

promenade² *v fml* **1** [T1;I∅] to walk slowly to and fro along (a place, street, etc.) **2** [T1] *sometimes derog* to take (someone or something) on a PROMENADE¹ (1), esp. for show

promenade con·cert /ˌ··· ˈ··/ *n* (*sometimes caps.*) (esp. in Britain) a concert at which parts of the hall have no seats and are used by listeners who stand

promenade deck /··ˈ· ·/ *n* a (wide) upper DECK of a passenger ship, usu. open at the sides, where people may walk

prom·e·nad·er /ˌprɒməˈnɑːdəʳ‖ˌprɑməˈneɪdər/ *n BrE infml* a person who regularly attends PROMENADE CONCERTs

prom·i·nence /ˈprɒmɨnəns‖ˈprɑ-/ *n* **1** [U] the quality, fact, or state of being PROMINENT; notice; importance (often in the phrs. **bring something/come into prominence**): *This young artist is coming into prominence* **2** [C] a thing or place that is PROMINENT (1): *There was a low prominence in the middle of the desert, too small to be called a hill*

prom·i·nent /ˈprɒmɨnənt‖ˈprɑ-/ *adj* **1** standing or stretching far out (beyond a surface): *her prominent teeth* **2** noticeable or most easily seen: *Our house is the most prominent one in the street; it's painted red* **3** of great ability, fame, etc. **4** [(*in*)] important and usu. widely known: *a politician prominent in matters concerning trade* —**~ly** *adv*

pro·mis·cu·i·ty /ˌprɒmɨˈskjuːɨti‖ˌprɑ-/ also **pro·mis·cu·ous·ness** /prəˈmɪskjʊəsnɨs/— *n* [U] *usu. derog* the state or quality of being PROMISCUOUS (esp. 1)

pro·mis·cu·ous /prəˈmɪskjʊəs/ *adj* **1** *derog* not limited to one sexual partner: *She's rather a promiscuous girl.|He leads a promiscuous life* **2** *derog* showing a lack of consideration of the qualities or worth of one thing compared with another **3** *fml* being of many sorts mixed together in a disorderly way —**~ly** *adv*

prom·ise¹ /ˈprɒmɨs‖ˈprɑ-/ *n* **1** [C (*of*),C3,5; *under*+U] a statement, which someone else has a right to believe and depend on, that one will or will not do something, give something, etc.: *If you make a promise you should keep it; you ought not to break a promise.|I don't trust his promise to come for a visit* **2** [U9;S9: esp. *of*] expectation or hope (esp. of success or of something good or desired): *The news of the war brings little promise of peace* **3** [U] *apprec* signs or reasons for such expectation or hope: *The boy is showing great promise as a cricketer*

promise² *v* **1** [T1,3,5a,b;V3;D1,5a;I∅] to make a promise to do or give (something) or that (something) shall be done: *Do you promise secrecy?|I promise to return your bicycle in good condition.|She promised him never to lie to him again.|They promised that the work would all be finished next week.|"She's not coming tonight." "But she promised!"|I can't give you the book; I've promised it to Susan.|I've promised Susan the book by Monday* **2** [T1; D1,5a] *infml* to say that (something) is certain; warn (someone) of (something): *He promised his son a beating if he disobeyed him* **3** [T1,3;L9] to cause usu. the speaker to expect or hope for (something); to give PROMISE¹ (2): *The clear sky promises fine weather. It promises to be a fine day.|John promises well as an actor* **4 I promise you** you can be sure of it; I warn you: *The work won't be easy, I promise you*

Promised Land /ˌ·· ˈ·/ *n* **1** [*the*+R] (in the Bible) the land of Canaan promised by God to Abraham and his people **2** [(*the*) S] a place or condition not yet experienced which one hopes or believes will bring happiness or success

prom·is·ing /ˈprɒmɨsɪŋ‖ˈprɑ-/ *adj apprec* full of PROMISE¹ (3); showing signs of advance towards success —**~ly** *adv*

prom·is·so·ry note /ˈprɒmɨsəri nəʊt‖ˈprɑmɨsori-/ *n* a written and signed promise to pay a stated amount of money to a particular person when demanded, or at a particular time

prom·on·to·ry /ˈprɒməntəri‖ˈprɑməntori/ *n* a high point of land stretching out into the sea from the coast

pro·mote /prəˈməʊt/ *v* **1** [T1 (*to*);(*esp. BrE*) X1] to advance (someone) in position or rank: *The young army officer was promoted captain/promoted to the rank of captain* **2** [T1] to help actively in forming or arranging (a business, concert, play, etc.): *Who is promoting this* BOXING *match?* **3** [T1] to bring (goods) to public notice in order to increase (sales): *The company are promoting their new sort of toothbrush on television.|How can we promote the sales of this product?* **4** [T1] to support; help in the growth of: *Milk promotes health* **5** [T1] to bring forward, introduce, and support (a suggested law (BILL³ (1))) in parliament

pro·mot·er /prəˈməʊtəʳ/ *n* **1** a person who PROMOTEs (2,3,5) activities or people **2** [(*of*) *usu. sing.*] *fml* something that PROMOTEs (4)

pro·mo·tion /prəˈməʊʃən/ *n* **1** [U;C] (an) advancement in rank or position: *There are good chances of promotion in this firm* **2** [U (*of*)] the act of promoting (PROMOTE (1)) **3** [U (*of*);C] (an) action to help something develop or succeed (esp. publicly): *This year's sales promotions haven't been very successful* **4** [C] a product that is being PROMOTEd (3): *Do you like this electric toothbrush? It's our latest promotion* —**~al** *adj* [Wa5]

prompt¹ /prɒmpt‖prɑmpt/ *v* **1** [T1;V3] to cause or urge (someone) to do something: *Hunger prompted him to steal* **2** [T1] to be the cause of (a thought, action, or feeling): *The sight of the ships prompted thoughts of his distant home* **3** [T1;I∅] to remind (an actor) of the next words in a speech when they have been forgotten **4** [T1] to help (a speaker who pauses) by suggesting how to continue: *It is forbidden to prompt a witness in court*

prompt² *adj* **1** [B] (of an action) done or given quickly, at once, or at the right time: *Prompt payment of bills greatly helps the accounts in shops* **2** [F] (of a person) acting quickly and willingly when something has to be done: *This worker is always prompt in his duties* —**~ly** *adv*: *When he called me a thief I promptly hit him.|The performance will begin promptly at 9 o'clock*

prompt³ *n* words spoken in PROMPTing¹ (3) an actor

prompt⁴ *adv infml* exactly (in regard to time): *The performance will start at 7 o'clock prompt*

prompt box /ˈ· ·/ *n* a hidden place beside or in front of a stage where a PROMPTER sits

prompt cop·y /ˈ· ˌ··/ *n* a copy of a play used by a PROMPTER

prompt·er /ˈprɒmptəʳ‖ˈprɑmp-/ *n* a person who PROMPTs¹ (3) actors who forget their lines

prompt·ness /ˈprɒmptnɨs‖ˈprɑmp-/ also (*fml*) **promp·ti·tude** /ˈprɒmptɨtjuːd‖ˈprɑmptɨtuːd/— *n* [U] readiness to act; quickness

prom·ul·gate /ˈprɒməlgeɪt‖ˈprɑ-/ *v* [T1] *fml* **1** to cause (a law or a rule of religious teaching) to be brought into effect by means of official public declaration **2** to spread (a belief, idea, etc.) widely among large numbers of people —**-gation** /ˌprɒməlˈgeɪʃən‖ˌprɑ-/ *n* [U (*of*)] —**-gator** /ˈprɒməlgeɪtəʳ‖ˈprɑ-/ *n*

pron *written abbrev. for*: PRONOUN

prone /prəʊn/ *adj* **1** [Wa5;B] (of a person or position) stretched out flat on a surface with the face and front of the body downwards —compare SUPINE **2** [Wa2;F+*to*, F3] having the probability of (usu. something undesirable): *One is more prone to make mistakes when one is tired.|He is prone to colds, especially in winter* —**~ness** *n* [U (*to*),U3]

-prone *comb. form* [*n*→*adj*] having a tendency towards (usu. something undesirable): *Mary is always falling over; she's accident-prone.|*STRIKE-*prone*[2] (1) *industries*

prong[1] /prɒŋ‖prɔŋ/ *n* **1** any one of the thin sharp-pointed parts of a fork **2** any sharp-pointed thin piece or part, such as one of the branched horns of a deer

prong[2] *v* **1** [T1] to push a fork or other such tool into **2** [X9] to lift or turn over with a fork: *The farm worker pronged the dried grass into the cart*

-pronged /prɒŋd‖prɔŋd/ *comb. form* **1** having the stated number of PRONGS[1]: *a 4-pronged fork* **2** (of an attack) made by a stated number of separate military forces, usu. coming from different directions: *a 2-pronged attack*

pro·nom·i·nal /prəʊ'nɒmɨnəl‖-'nɑ-/ *adj* (in grammar) of or like a PRONOUN —**~ly** *adv*: *a word used pronominally*

pro·noun /'prəʊnaʊn/ *n* (in grammar) a word that is used in place of a noun or a noun phrase: *Instead of saying "the man came" you can use a pronoun and say "he came"*

pro·nounce /prə'naʊns/ *v* **1** [T1;X1;L9] to make the sound of (a letter, a word, etc.) (in a particular way): *In the word "knew", the "k" is not pronounced; the word is pronounced without the "k"* **2** [T5;X (*to be*) 1,7] to declare, esp. after consideration: *Everyone pronounced the dinner to be very good.|The doctor pronounced the man dead* **3** [T5;X (*to be*) 1,7] *fml* to state or declare officially or with ceremony: *At the end of the marriage ceremony, the priest said: "I now pronounce you man and wife"* **4** [L9, esp. *for, against, on, upon*] *esp. law* to give judgment: *The court pronounced against my claim to the land.|*(fig.) *She's too ready to pronounce on/upon matters of which she really knows very little*

pro·nounce·a·ble /prə'naʊnsəbəl/ *adj* (of a sound, a word, etc.) that can be pronounced —opposite **unpronounceable**

pro·nounced /prə'naʊnst/ *adj* **1** very strong or marked: *You won't easily make him change his opinion; he has very pronounced ideas on everything* **2** very noticeable: *a pronounced* LIMP —**~ly** /prə'naʊnsɨdli/ *adv*

pro·nounce·ment /prə'naʊnsmənt/ *n* [C (*on, upon*), C5] a (solemn or official) declaration or statement

pron·to /'prɒntəʊ‖'prɑn-/ *adv* [Wa5] *infml* at once; very quickly

pro·nun·ci·a·men·to /prəˌnʌnsɪə'mentəʊ/ *n* **-tos** a public declaration, esp. in countries where the language of Spain is spoken, concerning the purposes, plans of action, etc., of a political party which is trying to cause the fall of a government in power

pro·nun·ci·a·tion /prəˌnʌnsi'eɪʃən/ *n* **1** [U] the way in which (a particular) language is pronounced **2** [U;S] a particular person's way of pronouncing a language, or the words of a language **3** [C] the way in which a word is usually pronounced

proof[1] /pruːf/ *n* **1** [U;C:(5, *of*)] (a) way of showing that something is true: *I believe what you say; I don't want any proof.|I wouldn't demand proof of honesty from a friend.|Have you any proof that you weren't there at 9 o'clock last night?* **2** [C] a test or trial to find out whether someone or something has a (necessary) quality, standard of strength, etc.: *A soldier's courage is put to the proof in battle* **3** [C] (in MATHEMATICS) a test made of the correctness of a calculation **4** [C] (in GEOMETRY) the reasoning that shows a statement (THEOREM) to be true **5** [C *often pl.*;*in*+U] a test copy made of a piece of printed matter (such as a picture, piece of writing, etc.) so that mistakes can be put right before the proper printing is done **6** [U;E] the standard of strength of some kinds of alcoholic drink (compared with that of PROOF SPIRIT): *This* GIN *is 15 per cent under proof* —see PROVE **7** **capable of proof** such as can be shown to be true or a fact

proof[2] *adj* **1** [F+*against*] **a** (of a material) of a quality or kind that gives protection against something harmful: *This tent material is proof against water* **b** unyielding; uninfluenced by: *His courage is proof against the greatest pain* **2** [Wa5;B] (of certain types of alcoholic drink (SPIRITs)) of standard strength; containing the standard amount of alcohol **3** [Wa5;E] (of certain types of alcoholic drink (SPIRITs)) of the stated alcoholic strength in comparison with some standard: *In the US,* WHISKEY *of 90 proof is 45% alcohol*

proof[3] *v* [T1] **1** [(*against*)] to treat (something, esp. cloth) in order to give protection against something unwanted, esp. water **2** *AmE* PROOFREAD

-proof *comb. form* [*n*→*adj*] treated or made so as not to be harmed by, or to give protection against, something undesirable: *a waterproof coat|a bulletproof car|a soundproof room*

proof·read /'pruːfˌriːd/ *v* [T1;I∅] to read and correct the printer's PROOFs[1] (5) of (a book, magazine, etc.) —**~er** *n*

proof sheet /'· ·/ *n* [*often pl.*] a printed sheet of paper in PROOF[1]

proof spir·it /ˌ· '··/ *n* [U] a standard mixture of alcohol and water with which the strength of certain alcoholic drinks (SPIRITs) is compared for the purposes of taxation

prop[1] /prɒp‖prɑp/ *n* **1** a support placed to hold up something heavy that is leaning or pressing down: *She uses a clothes prop to prevent the washing on her clothes line from touching the ground* **2** also **prop and stay** /ˌ· · '·/— a person on whom someone or something depends for support, strength, courage, etc.

prop[2] *v* **-pp-** [X9, esp. UP] **1** to support or keep in position by placing something under or against: *She propped up the baby's head by putting her hand behind its neck.|Prop the gate open with a brick* **2** to put in a leaning or resting position: *He propped his bicycle against the fence* —see also PROP UP

prop[3] *n infml* an aircraft's PROPELLER

prop[4] also (*fml*) **property**— *n* [*usu. pl.*] any small article (such as a weapon, piece of furniture, etc.) that is used on the stage in the acting of a play

prop·a·gan·da /ˌprɒpə'gændə‖ˌprɑ-/ *n* [U] *often derog* (action taken, esp. by a government, to influence public opinion on some matter by spreading) true or false beliefs, ideas, news, etc.: *There has been a good deal of propaganda about the dangers of smoking.|The propaganda of a political party is planned to gain votes, and isn't always the exact truth*

prop·a·gan·dist /ˌprɒpə'gændɨst‖ˌprɑ-/ *n usu. derog* a person who plans, directs, or spreads (esp. political) PROPAGANDA

prop·a·gan·dize, -ise /ˌprɒpə'gændaɪz‖ˌprɑ-/ *v* [T1 (*with, about*);L9;(I∅)] *often derog* to spread PROPAGANDA in (a place) or to (a person or group)

prop·a·gate /'prɒpəgeɪt‖'prɑ-/ *v* **1** [I∅] (of living things) to increase in number by producing young:

Most plants propagate by seed **2** [T1] to cause to have descendants: *Insects propagate themselves by means of eggs* **3** [T1] to cause (a quality) to pass to descendants: *The farmer was hoping to propagate the best qualities of both types of sheep* **4** [T1] to cause to spread or to reach and influence a great number of people: *The political party started the newspaper to propagate its ideas* **5** [T1] *tech* to cause or allow to pass through space or a substance: *Water easily propagates sound* —**-gator** *n*

prop·a·ga·tion /ˌprɒpəˈgeɪʃən‖ˌprɑ-/ *n* [U (*of*)] the act of propagating or being PROPAGATED: *The sun sometimes spoils the propagation of radio waves*

pro·pane /ˈprəʊpeɪn/ *n* [U] a type of colourless gas used for cooking and heating

pro·pel /prəˈpel/ *v* **-ll-** [T1] to move, drive, or push (steadily) forward: *One has to depend on the wind to propel a sailing boat*

pro·pel·lant[1], **-lent** /prəˈpelənt/ *adj* able to PROPEL: *a propellant chemical mixture*

propellant[2], **-lent** *n* [C;U] **1** (an) explosive used for firing a bullet from a gun **2** (an) explosive used for firing a ROCKET out into space **3** (a) gas pressed into a small space in a bottle, which drives out the contents of the bottle when the pressure is taken away

pro·pel·ler /prəˈpeləʳ/ *n* 2 or more blades fixed to a central bar that is turned at high speed by an engine, used for driving a ship or aircraft —see picture at AIRCRAFT

pro·pel·ling pen·cil /·ˌ·· ˈ··/ *n* a plastic or metal pencil in which the stick of writing material (LEAD[3] (3)) is pushed forward by a screwing apparatus inside

pro·pen·si·ty /prəˈpensǝ̀ti/ *n* [C (*for, to, towards*), C3] *fml* a natural tendency of the mind or character towards a particular (usu. undesirable) kind of behaviour: *that dog's biting propensities|a propensity for complaining|a propensity to sudden anger|a propensity to spend money*

prop·er[1] /ˈprɒpəʳ‖ˈprɑ-/ *adj* **1** [Wa5;A] right; suitable; correct: *The child is too ill to be nursed at home; she needs proper medical attention at a hospital* **2** [Wa5;A] correct (for a purpose): *These pages aren't in their proper order; page 22 comes after page 26* **3** [B] *sometimes derog* paying great attention to what is considered correct in society (sometimes in the phr. **prim and proper**): *I don't consider that short dress is proper for going to church in.|His mother has trained him to be a very proper young man* **4** [Wa5;A] *apprec* fine; splendid; good-looking: *You've made a proper job of that* (=have done it well).|*He's a proper man* (=one whom women are willing to like) **5** [Wa5;A] *esp. BrE* (*often before bad or unpleasant words*) thorough; complete: *"I've come out without the key of the house." "You're a proper fool"* **6** [Wa5;A] *infml* real; actual: *The little boy wanted a proper dog as a pet; he didn't want a toy dog* **7** [Wa5;A] exact: *Does this clock keep proper time?* **8** [F+*to*] *fml* belonging only or especially to; natural to **9** [Wa5; E] itself; in its actual, most limited meaning, not including additional things: *Many people call themselves Londoners though they live in areas that aren't part of the city proper* **10** [Wa5;E] (in HERALDRY) (of a part of the sign on a shield) shown in its natural colours

proper[2] *adv sl, esp. nonstandard dial* very; completely: *I was proper annoyed!*

proper frac·tion /ˌ·· ˈ··/ *n* a FRACTION in which the number above the line is smaller than the number below the line: *¼ and ⅛ are proper fractions*

prop·er·ly /ˈprɒpəli‖ˈprɑpərli/ *adv* **1** suitably; correctly; sensibly: *I'm learning German, but I still can't speak it properly.|She'd only just got out of bed, and wasn't properly dressed* **2** really; actually; exactly: *I'm not, properly speaking, a nurse, as I haven't been trained, but I've had a lot of experience looking after sick people* **3** *esp. BrE, usu. infml* completely; thoroughly: *You've properly ruined your chances with Jane; she saw you yesterday taking Helen out in your car*

proper mo·tion /ˌ·· ˈ··/ *n* [U] *tech* the actual movement of a star through space, not as it appears from the earth

proper noun /ˌ·· ˈ·/ also **proper name**— *n* (in grammar) a name used for a single particular thing or person, and spelt with a CAPITAL letter: *"James", "London", and "China" are proper nouns* —opposite **common noun**

prop·er·tied /ˈprɒpətid‖ˈprɑpər-/ *adj* [Wa5;A; (B)] owning a lot of property, esp. land

prop·er·ty /ˈprɒpəti‖ˈprɑpərti/ *n* **1** [U] that which is owned (and has some value); possession(s): *That car is my property; you can't use it without my permission.|The police found some stolen property hidden in the thief's house* **2** [U] land, buildings, or both together: *The city is growing and property in the centre is becoming more valuable* **3** [C] a building, piece of land, or both together: *Several properties in this street are to be let* **4** [U;S] ownership, with its rights and duties according to the law: *Most forms of human society have accepted the idea of property as necessary when living with others* **5** [C9, esp. *of*;(C)] a quality, power, or effect that belongs naturally to something: *Many plants have medicinal properties* **6** [C *usu. pl.*] *fml* PROP[4] **7 common property a** an article that is shared or used by all **b** also **public property**— something that is known to everyone **8 man of property** *fml* a wealthy man —see also LOST PROPERTY, PERSONAL PROPERTY, REAL PROPERTY

property man /ˈ··· ·/ *n* a man in charge of the PROPS[4] for a play or film, who keeps them in order and ready for each scene

proph·e·cy /ˈprɒfǝ̀si‖ˈprɑ-/ *n* **1** [U] (the power of) foreseeing and foretelling future events **2** [C,C5] a statement telling something that is to happen in the future: *The teacher's prophecy that the boy would become a great national leader was later fulfilled*

proph·e·sy /ˈprɒfǝ̀saɪ‖ˈprɑ-/ *v* [T1,5,5b,6a;I0: (*to*)] **1** to give (a warning, statement about some future event, etc.) as a result of a religious experience directed by God or a god **2** to say in advance: *I wouldn't dare to try to prophesy who will win the election*

proph·et /ˈprɒfǝ̀t‖ˈprɑ-/ *n* **1** (in the Christian, Jewish, and Muslim religions) a man who believes that he is directed by God to make known and explain God's will and/or to lead or teach a (new) religion **2** a thinker, poet, etc., who introduces and teaches some new idea which he thinks will make people's lives better: *Mary Wollstonecraft was a prophet of women's rights at the end of the 18th century* **3** a person who tells, or claims to be able to tell, the nature or course of future events: *Farmers and sailors are usually good weather prophets* **4 prophet of doom** *derog* a person who is always foretelling ruin, destruction, misfortune, etc.

Prophet *n* [*the*+R] **1** Mohammed, who formed the Muslim religion —see also ISLAM, MUSLIM **2 a follower of the Prophet** a Muslim

proph·et·ess /ˈprɒfǝ̀tes‖ˈprɑfǝ̀təs/ *n* a female PROPHET (2)

pro·phet·ic /prəˈfetɪk/ also **pro·phet·i·cal** /-kəl/— *adj* **1** of or like a PROPHET (2) **2** [(*of*)] correctly telling of things that will happen in the future —**-ically** *adv* [Wa5]: *Prophetically, the future ruler was photographed outside the palace as a child*

Proph·ets /ˈprɒfǝ̀ts‖ˈprɑ-/ *n* [*the*+P] **1** the Jewish holy men whose writings form part of the Bible **2** the writings themselves, which together with certain other writings form the second and last part of the OLD TESTAMENT **3 the Law and the Prophets** everything worth knowing or worth obeying

pro·phy·lac·tic[1] /ˌprɒfə̇ˈlæktɪk‖ˌprɑ-/ *adj med* that is intended to prevent disease —**~ally** *adv* [Wa4]

prophylactic[2] *n* something PROPHYLACTIC, esp. a CONDOM sold supposedly for the prevention of disease

pro·phy·lax·is /ˌprɒfə̇ˈlæksə̇s‖ˌprɑ-/ *n* **-lax·es** /ˈlæksiːz/ [U;C] *tech* (a) treatment for preventing disease

pro·pin·qui·ty /prəˈpɪŋkwə̇ti/ *n* [U (*of, to*)] *fml* nearness (in space, neighbourhood, or relationship)

pro·pi·ti·ate /prəˈpɪʃieɪt/ *v* [T1] *fml* to win the favour of (someone who is angry or unfriendly) by some pleasing act —**-ation** /prəˌpɪʃiˈeɪʃən/ *n* [U (*for, of*)]

pro·pi·ti·a·to·ry /prəˈpɪʃɪətəri‖-tori/ *adj fml* intended to PROPITIATE: *The day after their quarrel, Dick sent Alice a propitiatory gift of flowers*

pro·pi·tious /prəˈpɪʃəs/ *adj* **1** [B (*for, to*)] lucky; advantageous; giving a favourable chance of success: *Some people believe that the appearance of a black cat is a propitious sign; others believe that black cats are unlucky* **2** [A;F (*to, towards*)] (of gods or fate) favourable; friendly; helpful —**~ly** *adv*

prop·jet /ˈprɒpdʒet‖ˈprɑp-/ *n infml* (an aircraft that is driven by) a TURBOPROP engine

pro·po·nent /prəˈpəʊnənt/ *n* [C9, esp. *of*] a person who supports or argues in favour of (something)

pro·por·tion[1] /prəˈpɔːʃən‖-ˈpor-/ *n* **1** [U] the correct relationship between the size, position, and shape of the different parts of a whole, esp. as producing a beautiful effect: *The drawings of young children usually lack proportion; they make arms and legs look like sticks* **2** [U;C: (*of*)] compared relationship between 2 things in regard to size, amount, force, importance, etc.: *The proportion of men to women in the population has changed so that there are now fewer women and more men* **3** [C (*of*)] a part or share (as measured in amount and compared with the whole): *"What proportion of your wages do you spend on rent?" "About a quarter"* **4** [U] (in MATHEMATICS) equalness of relationship between 2 sets of numbers (often in the phr. **in proportion**): *The statement "as 6 is to 4, so is 24 to 16" is a statement of proportion* **5 in proportion as** *rare* ACCORDING AS **6 in proportion to a** according to; at the rate of: *Are you paid in proportion to the number of hours you work?* **b** as compared with (what is expected) in size, amount, etc.: *Her legs are quite long in proportion to the rest of her body* **7 in/out of proportion** (not) according to real importance; (not) sensibly: *When one is angry one often does not see things in proportion; the wrongs done to one seem much worse than they are* **8 in the proportion of** in the measure of: *The paint should be mixed in the proportion of one part of paint to 2 parts of water* **9 out of (all) proportion to** (much) too great as compared with: *The price of this article is out of all proportion to its value* **10 sense of proportion** ability to judge what matters and what does not, without being influenced by personal feeling

proportion[2] *v* [Wv5;T1 (*to*)] to make in or put into correct or suitable PROPORTION[1] (1,2)

pro·por·tion·al /prəˈpɔːʃənəl‖-ˈpor-/ *adj* **1** concerning PROPORTION[1] (2) **2** [(*to*)] in (correct) PROPORTION[1] (2): *The payment that the motorist will have to make will be proportional to the amount of damage he has done to the other person's car* —**~ly** *adv*: *She seems to earn a lot, but, proportionally, she's not really very rich*

proportional rep·re·sen·ta·tion /·ˌ··· ···ˈ··/ *n* [U] a system of voting in elections by which all political parties, small as well as large, are represented in parliament in PROPORTION[1] (6) to the number of votes they receive

pro·por·tion·ate /prəˈpɔːʃənə̇t‖-ˈpor-/ *adj* [F (*to*); B] in right PROPORTION[1] (1,2) —**~ly** *adv*

pro·por·tions /prəˈpɔːʃənz‖-ˈpor-/ *n* [P] **1** size and shape that, when considered together, produce a (pleasing) effect: *This church is a building of fine proportions, both inside and outside* **2** *sometimes humor* (great) size or measurements: *Mary is getting very fat; will she be able to fit her* AMPLE *proportions into the back seat of the car?*

pro·pos·al /prəˈpəʊzəl/ *n* **1** [U (*of*), U3,5c] the act of proposing (PROPOSE): *Everyone stood politely during the proposal of the President's health.|the proposal that we should rest for a while* **2** [C (*for*), C3,5c *often pl.*] a plan or suggestion offered: *peace proposals* **3** [C (*of*)] an offer of marriage —compare PROPOSITION[1] (4)

pro·pose /prəˈpəʊz/ *v* **1** [Wv5;T1,4,5c] to suggest; put forward for consideration: *I propose a short rest before we continue the work.|I propose resting for half an hour.|I propose that we have half an hour's rest* **2** [Wv5;T1,3,4;(I∅)] to form (as) (a plan or intention); intend: *He proposes an early holiday in the spring.|I propose to go to London on Tuesday* **3** [T1 (*as, for*), 5c;(X *to be* 1)] *fml* to put forward to be voted on by people who are meeting as a committee, a club, etc. (often in the phr. **propose a motion**): *I wish to propose Charles Robson for membership of the club.|It was proposed that this matter be considered at the next meeting* **4** [T1;I∅: (*to*)] (usu. of a man) to make an offer of (marriage) (to someone) **5** [T1] *fml* to ask a social gathering to offer (a wish for success, happiness, etc.) to someone, while raising a glass of wine which is afterwards drunk (usu. in the phrs. **propose a toast/propose someone's health**) —**-poser** *n*

prop·o·si·tion[1] /ˌprɒpəˈzɪʃən‖ˌprɑ-/ *n* **1** [C,C5] an unproved statement in which an opinion or judgment is expressed **2** [C] a suggested (business) offer, arrangement, or settlement (often in the phr. **make someone a proposition**) **3** [S9] *infml* a person who or thing that must be dealt with, considered with regard to the difficulty or chance of success, etc.: *Be careful in dealing with Murray; he's a nasty proposition, who always tries to gain an advantage by some clever trick* **4** [C] *euph* a suggested offer to have sex with someone, esp. with a girl (esp. in the phr. **make someone a proposition**) **5** [C] (in GEOMETRY) a truth that must be proved, or a question to which the answer must be found —compare PROPOSAL —**~al** *adj*

proposition[2] *v* [T1] *sl* to make (someone) a PROPOSITION[1] (esp. 4)

pro·pound /prəˈpaʊnd/ *v* [T1] *fml* to put forward as a question or matter for which an answer is needed

pro·pri·e·ta·ry /prəˈpraɪətəri‖-teri/ *adj* [A;(B)] **1** [Wa5] belonging to the PROPRIETOR; privately owned or controlled **2** of or like an owner: *Jane has rather a proprietary manner with John; she treats him as if he were her own property*

proprietary med·i·cine /·ˌ···· ˈ···/ *n* [U;C] (a) medicine that only one person or company has the right to produce and sell

proprietary name /·ˌ···· ˈ·/ *n* a trade name for goods which is protected by law and may be used only by the person or company with the right to do so

pro·pri·e·ties /prəˈpraɪətiz/ *n* [*the*+P] *fml* details of the rules of proper social behaviour

pro·pri·e·tor /prəˈpraɪətəʳ/ *n esp. fml* an owner (esp. of a business, an invention, etc.): *wealthy newspaper proprietors* (=people who own the businesses that produce newspapers)|*I wasn't satisfied with our treatment at that hotel, so I shall write and complain to the proprietor*

pro·pri·e·tress /prəˈpraɪətrɪ̈s/ *n esp. fml* a female PROPRIETOR

pro·pri·e·ty /prəˈpraɪəti/ *n* [U] *fml* **1** rightness of social or moral behaviour (esp. between men and women or between people of different positions, age, etc.): *When her skirt fell down he behaved with perfect propriety and looked the other way!* **2** fitness; rightness; SUITABILITY: *I doubt the propriety of making a public statement on prison conditions before we have studied the official reports*

pro·pul·sion /prəˈpʌlʃən/ *n* [U] *tech* force that drives (PROPELs) something, esp. a vehicle, forward: *This aircraft works by* JET *propulsion* (=it has JET engines)

pro·pul·sive /prəˈpʌlsɪv/ *adj* [A;(B)] *tech* that drives something, esp. a vehicle, forward; PROPELLING: *propulsive action*

prop up *v adv* [T1] to support with money, advice, strength of mind, etc.

pro·pyl·ene /ˈprəʊpɪ̈liːn/ *n* [U] a type of colourless gas used esp. in making compound chemicals

pro ra·ta /ˌprəʊ ˈrɑːtə‖-ˈreɪtə/ *adv, adj tech Lat* (that is calculated) according to the rate, fair share, etc., of each

pro·ro·ga·tion /ˌprəʊrəˈgeɪʃən‖ˌprəʊrəʊ-/ *n* [U;C] *tech* the action or an act of proroguing (PROROGUE)

pro·rogue /prəʊˈrəʊg, prə-/ *v* [T1] *tech* to bring to an end a regular set of meetings (SESSION) of (a parliament) until the members return on a stated day to continue unfinished business

pro·sa·ic /prəʊˈzeɪ-ɪk, prə-/ *adj* **1** dull; uninteresting: *I've got a very prosaic job, so I like to travel to interesting places on my holidays* **2** lacking the finer qualities of feeling and imagination —**~ally** *adv* [Wa4]

pro·sce·ni·um /prəˈsiːnɪəm, prəʊ-/ *n* [(*the*)] **1** also **proscenium arch** /·ˌ··· ˈ·/— the front arch of a theatre stage (where a curtain may be lowered between scenes) **2** the part of a stage that comes forward beyond this —see picture at THEATRE

pro·scribe /prəʊˈskraɪb/ *v* [T1] **1** *fml* to forbid (something, esp. something dangerous or harmful), esp. by law **2** *old use* to state publicly that (a citizen) is an enemy of the state and has been put outside the protection of the law

pro·scrip·tion /prəʊˈskrɪpʃən, prə-/ *n fml or old use* **1** [U] the act of proscribing or the state of being PROSCRIBED **2** [C] an example of this

prose /prəʊz/ *n* **1** [U;(S)] written language in its usual form (as different from poetry): *Newspapers are written in prose.*|*He isn't a poet; he's a prose writer.*|*He writes a very clear simple prose* **2** [C] *BrE* a pupil's or student's exercise in translating into a foreign language: *I've got 2 French proses to do before tomorrow morning*

pros·e·cute /ˈprɒsɪkjuːt‖ˈprɑ-/ *v* **1** [T1;I∅;(*for*)] to bring a criminal charge against (someone) in a court of law: *He was prosecuted for stealing* **2** [I∅] (of a lawyer) to represent in court the person who is bringing a criminal charge against someone **3** [T1] *fml* to continue steadily (esp. something that needs effort) —compare PERSECUTE

pros·e·cu·tion /ˌprɒsɪˈkjuːʃən‖ˌprɑ-/ *n* **1** [U] the action of prosecuting or state of being PROSECUTED (1) by law **2** [C] an example of this **3** [(*the*) GU] **a** the group of people who are concerned in bringing a criminal charge against someone in court: *A famous lawyer has been asked to appear fo[r] the prosecution* **b** one or more lawyers who repre[-]sent this group: *The prosecution will try to show tha[t] the prisoner was seen near the place where the crim[e] happened* —compare DEFENCE **4** [U] *fml* (steady continuation of something to be done (often in th[e] phr. **in the prosecution of**): *He has to travel a grea[t] deal in the prosecution of his duties*

pros·e·cu·tor /ˈprɒsɪkjuːtəʳ‖ˈprɑ-/ *n* the perso[n] (often a lawyer) who PROSECUTEs (1) anothe[r] —see also PUBLIC PROSECUTOR

pros·e·lyte /ˈprɒsɪ̈laɪt‖ˈprɑ-/ *n* a person who ha[s] just been persuaded to join a religious group[,] political party, etc., different from the one t[o] which he formerly belonged; CONVERT

pros·e·lyt·ize, -ise /ˈprɒsələtaɪz‖ˈprɑ-/ *v* **1** [I∅] t[o] (try to) persuade people to become PROSELYTEs esp. of another religion **2** [T1] *fml* to (try to) persuade (someone) to become a PROSELYTE, esp[.] of another religion —**-izer** *n*

prose po·em /ˈ· ˌ··/ *n* a work in PROSE that ha[s] some of the qualities of a poem

pros·o·dy /ˈprɒsədi‖ˈprɑ-/ *n* [U] the science of th[e] writing of poetry, and the study of the laws tha[t] govern the ways in which its regular patterns o[f] sounds and beats are arranged —**-dic** /prəˈsɒdɪk -ˈsɑ-/ *adj* [Wa5A]—**-dically** *adv* [Wa4]

pros·pect[1] /ˈprɒspekt‖ˈprɑ-/ *n* **1** [U9, esp. *of*] reasonable hope (of something happening)[:] *There's not much prospect of my being able to come t[o] see you before next month* **2** [U9;S9: esp. *of*] something which is expected or considered proba[-]ble (soon), and of which the idea remains in th[e] mind: *She doesn't like the prospect of having to liv[e] alone* —see also PROSPECTS **3** [C9 *usu. sing.*] a wid[e] or distant view (esp. from a high place): *From th[e] top of the hill there's a beautiful prospect over th[e] valley.*|(fig.) *The prospect before us is one of har[d] work until victory is ours!* —see VIEW (USAGE) **4** [C9;(C)] a person who it seems probable might b[e] offered or might accept or win a position, office etc. **5** [C9;(C)] *infml* a person from whom on[e] may gain some advantage **6** [C9;(C)] *AmE* [a] person whom one hopes to have as a buyer of one'[s] goods **7 in prospect** expected to happen soon

pros·pect[2] /prəˈspekt‖ˈprɑspekt/ *v* [I∅;(T1) (*for*)] to examine (land, an area, etc.) in order t[o] find something, esp. gold, silver, oil, etc.

pro·spec·tive /prəˈspektɪv/ *adj* [Wa5] **1** not yet i[n] effect; coming into operation at some future tim[e] **2** expected; probable; intended: *The prospectiv[e] Member of Parliament for our town will be intro[-]duced to the local party tonight*

pro·spec·tor /prəˈspektəʳ‖ˈprɑspektər/ *n* a perso[n] who PROSPECTs[2] for gold, oil, etc.

pros·pects /ˈprɒspekts‖ˈprɑ-/ *n* [P] **1** chances (o[f] success): *The prospects of finishing the work soo[n] aren't very hopeful* **2** *fml & now rare* expectations o[f] wealth, social position, etc., in the future: *"Sir, [I] wish to marry your daughter." "And what are you[r] prospects, young man?"*

pro·spec·tus /prəˈspektəs/ *n* a printed statemen[t] describing the advantages of something (such as [a] privately owned school, a new business, etc.) sen[t] to people who, it is thought, might give thei[r] support

pros·per /ˈprɒspəʳ‖ˈprɑ-/ *v* **1** [I∅] to becom[e] successful and rich **2** [I∅] to develop favourably[;] grow well **3** [T1] *old use* (of God, Heaven, etc.) t[o] cause to succeed

pro·sper·i·ty /prɒˈsperɪ̈ti‖prɑ-/ *n* [U] (the state o[f] having) good fortune and success, esp. in mone[y] matters

pros·per·ous /ˈprɒspərəs‖ˈprɑ-/ *adj* successful; wealthy; very favourable —**~ly** *adv*

pros·tate /ˈprɒsteɪt‖ˈprɑ-/ also **prostate gland** /ˈ·· ·/— *n* an organ in the body of male animals that produces a liquid in which seeds (SPERMATOZOA) are carried out of the body

pros·the·sis /prɒsˈθiːsǝs‖prɑs-/ *n* [U] *tech* the supplying of man-made (ARTIFICIAL) limbs, teeth, or other parts for the body to take the place of missing ones

pros·ti·tute¹ /ˈprɒstǝtjuːt‖ˈprɑstǝtuːt/ *v* [T1] *fml* **1** (esp. of a woman) to hire (oneself) as a PROSTITUTE² **2** to put to a dishonourable or wrong use, esp. in order to gain money

prostitute² (*masc.* **male prostitute**)— *n* a person, esp. a woman, who earns money by having sex with anyone who will pay for it

pros·ti·tu·tion /ˌprɒstǝˈtjuːʃən‖ˌprɑstǝˈtuːʃən/ *n* [U] **1** the act, practice, condition, or trade of being a PROSTITUTE² **2** [(*of*)] *fml* dishonourable or shameful misuse, esp. for gain

pros·trate¹ /ˈprɒstreɪt‖ˈprɑ-/ *adj* **1** [Wa5] lying in a flat position or stretched out flat, with the face to the ground —compare PRONE (1) **2** *fml* (of a nation, country, etc.) conquered and powerless **3** in a state of such bodily weakness that one can hardly move **4** having lost all strength, courage, and ability to act, as a result of some experience: *She was prostrate with grief*

pros·trate² /prɒˈstreɪt‖ˈprɑstreɪt/ *v* **1** [T1] to put (someone, esp. oneself, or something) in a PROSTRATE¹ (1) position **2** [T1] *fml* to conquer and destroy the pride of (a nation, country, etc.) **3** [Wv4;T1 *usu. pass.*] to cause to be PROSTRATE¹ (3,4): *a prostrating illness*

pros·tra·tion /prɒˈstreɪʃən‖prɑ-/ *n* **1** [U] the condition of being PROSTRATE¹ (3) **2** [U;C] (a) (ceremonial) action of putting oneself in a PROSTRATE¹ (1) position: *Prostration of the body in the direction of Mecca is part of the ceremony of Muslim prayer* **3** [U] the state of being PROSTRATE¹ (1,2)

pros·y /ˈprəʊzi/ *adj* [Wa1] saying too much in a dull, tiring, uninteresting manner —**-ily** *adv* —**-iness** *n* [U]

prot- /prəʊt/ *comb. form* PROTO-

pro·tag·o·nist /prəʊˈtægənǝst/ *n* **1** [C9, esp. *of*] a noticeable supporter or defender of some (new) idea or purpose: *Mrs Pankhurst was one of the chief protagonists of women's rights* **2** [C9, esp. *of*] the chief person or leader in some kind of struggle or affair: *Mrs Pankhurst, the protagonist of women's rights* **3** [(*the*) C] the chief character in a play or story

pro·te·an /ˈprəʊtiən, prəʊˈtiːən/ *adj lit* continually changing; able to appear in various forms or characters

pro·tect /prəˈtekt/ *v* [T1] **1** [(*against, from*)] to keep safe (from harm, loss, etc.), esp. by guarding or covering: *The hard shell of a nut protects the seed inside it.|A line of forts was built along the border, to protect the country against attack.|He raised his arm to protect his face from the blow* **2** [(*against, from*)] to prevent (something) from being dangerous by separating, covering, etc.: *These electric wires are protected by a rubber covering* **3** to help (local industry or the sale of goods produced in one's own country) by taxing foreign goods of the same kind and so making them dear to buy **4** [(*against*)] to guard (someone or something) against possible future loss, damage, etc., by means of insurance

pro·tec·tion /prəˈtekʃən/ *n* **1** [U] the act of protecting or state of being protected: *Such a thin coat gives little protection against the cold* **2** [S] a person who or thing that protects: *Shoes are a protection for the feet* **3** [U] the condition of having an agreement with an insurance company to save oneself from having to pay for accidents, loss, etc. **4** [U] also **protection mon·ey** /·ˈ·· ˌ··/— *euph sl* money paid to people who run a PROTECTION RACKET

pro·tec·tion·is·m /prəˈtekʃənɪzəm/ *n* [U] *often derog* the system of protecting one's own country's trade, esp. by TARIFFs —**-ist** *n*

protection rack·et /·ˈ·· ˌ··/ *n sl* an organization or system by which criminals demand money from the owners of shops, restaurants, etc., for protection against damage that would be caused by the criminals themselves

pro·tec·tive /prəˈtektɪv/ *adj* **1** [A;(B)] that gives protection: *protective clothing* **2** [B (*towards*)] having or showing a wish to protect: *As a mother she's too protective towards her daughter; she should let her see more of the world* —**~ly** *adv* —**~ness** *n* [U]

protective col·our·ing /·ˌ·· ˈ···/ also **protective col·or·a·tion** /·ˌ·· ··ˈ··/— *n* [U] (arrangement of) colours on an animal's or insect's body that make it difficult for enemies to see

protective cus·to·dy /·ˌ·· ˈ···/ *n* [U] the state of being kept safe, esp. by the police

protective tar·iff /·ˌ·· ˈ··/ *n* a fixed charge put on goods brought in from a foreign country

pro·tec·tor /prəˈtektəʳ/ *n* **1** a person who protects **2** (*often in comb.*) any article that protects: *a chest protector* **3** (*usu. cap.*) (in former times) a prince or nobleman appointed to act as governor of England during the childhood or illness of the king

Protector *n* [*the*+R] the official title of Oliver Cromwell and Richard Cromwell when they ruled Britain (1653–1659) —see PROTECTORATE

pro·tec·tor·ate /prəˈtektərǝt/ *n* **1** [C] a country controlled and/or protected by a more powerful nation that takes charge esp. of its defence and foreign affairs **2** [S;(C)] also **pro·tec·tor·ship** /prəˈtektəʃɪp‖-tektər-/— the time during which a PROTECTOR (3) serves

Protectorate *n* [*the*+R] the time (1653–1659) during which Oliver and Richard Cromwell ruled Britain

prot·é·gé /ˈprɒtǝʒeɪ‖ˈprəʊ-/ (*fem.* **protégée** (*same pronunciation*))— *n* [C9] *Fr* a person who is guided and helped, esp. in his life's work, by someone of influence or power: *This young politician is the minister's protégé*

pro·tein /ˈprəʊtiːn/ *n* [C;U] any of many substances (present in such foods as meat and eggs) that help to build up the body and keep it healthy

pro tem /ˌprəʊ ˈtem/ also (*fml*) **pro tem·po·re** /ˌprəʊ ˈtempəri/— *adv* [Wa5] now but only for a short time; for the present only

pro·test¹ /ˈprəʊtest/ *n* **1** [C] a (written or official) complaint or a spoken expression of dissatisfaction, disagreement, opposition, etc. (often in the phrs. **enter/lodge a protest (against something)**) **2** [U] unwillingness, opposition, dissatisfaction, etc., as shown or expressed in some manner: *If everyone refused to buy meat in protest, the shops would have to bring their meat prices down* **3 under protest** unwillingly and with a feeling that something is not just **4 without protest** not opposing; calmly and quietly

pro·test² /prəˈtest/ *v* **1** [I∅ (*about, against, at*)] to express one's disagreement, feeling of unfairness, annoyance, etc.: *They protested about the bad food at the hotel; they protested to the owner.|There was a large crowd in the square, protesting against the war* **2** [T1] *AmE* to make a PROTEST¹ (1) against: *There was a large crowd in the square, protesting the war* **3** [T1,5] to declare solemnly, esp. against disbelief; declare in complaint or opposition: *We urged her* *to come to the party with us, but she protested that she was too tired* —**~er** *n*

Prot·es·tant /ˈprɒtɜ̇stənt‖ˈprɑ-/ *n, adj* (a member) of any of several branches of the part of the Christian church that separated from the ROMAN CATHOLIC Church in the 16th century —**~ism** *n* [U]

prot·es·ta·tion /ˌprɒtɜ̇ˈsteɪʃən ˌprəʊ-‖ˌprɑ- prəʊ-/ *n fml* **1** [C (*of*);C5] a (solemn) declaration, esp. against opposition: *The meeting ended with protestations of friendship from all sides* **2** [U (*against*)] the act of PROTESTING² (1)

pro·to- /ˈprəʊtəʊ, -tə/ also **prot-**— *comb. form* **1** first in time or order and/or causing others to come after: PROTOTYPE|*proto*MARTYR **2** (*usu. cap.*) being or related to the recorded or supposed language from which another language or group of languages has developed: *Proto*-INDO-EUROPEAN

pro·to·col /ˈprəʊtəkɒl‖-kɔl/ *n* **1** [U] the ceremonial system of fixed rules and accepted behaviour that governs the means of talking and acting between rulers or representatives of the governments of different countries, between people on official occasions, etc. **2** [C] *tech* a note or first written form of an agreement that is being considered between nations, signed by their representatives

pro·ton /ˈprəʊtɒn‖-tɑn/ *n* a very small piece of matter that helps to form the central part of an atom and carries a standard amount of POSITIVE¹ (12) electricity —see picture at ATOM

pro·to·plas·m /ˈprəʊtəplæzəm/ *n* [U] the colourless jellylike living substance from which all plants and creatures are formed

pro·to·type /ˈprəʊtətaɪp/ *n* [(*of*)] the first form of anything, from which all later forms develop, sometimes with improvements

Pro·to·zo·a /ˌprəʊtəˈzəʊə/ *n* [*the*+P] the division of animal life made up of protozoa (PROTOZOON)

pro·to·zo·an /ˌprəʊtəˈzəʊən/ *n, adj* (a single member) of the PROTOZOA

pro·to·zo·on /ˌprəʊtəˈzəʊən/ *n* **-zo·a** /ˈzəʊə/ a very small living thing of the simplest kind that lives mainly in water, is made of a single piece of living matter, and can be seen only under a microscope

pro·tract /prəˈtrækt‖prəʊ-/ *v* [Wv5;T1] to increase the time during which (something) happens or lasts; make longer: *Let's not protract this argument; there's nothing else useful to be said.*|*a protracted stay in hospital*

pro·trac·tion /prəˈtrækʃən‖prəʊ-/ *n* [U;(C): (*of*)] the action or an act of making longer in time

pro·trac·tor /prəˈtræktəʳ‖prəʊ-/ *n* an instrument usu. in the form of a half-circle, used for measuring and drawing angles —see picture at MATHEMATICAL

pro·trude /prəˈtruːd‖prəʊ-/ *v* [Wv4;I∅;(T1)] to (cause to) stick out or stretch outwards from a place or through a surface: *The policeman stopped the man when he saw a gun was protruding from his pocket.*|*protruding teeth*

pro·tru·sion /prəˈtruːʒən‖prəʊ-/ *n* **1** [U (*of*)] the act of protruding or state of being PROTRUDED **2** [C] something that PROTRUDES

pro·tru·sive /prəˈtruːsɪv‖prəʊ-/ *adj fml* that PROTRUDES; sticking out —**~ly** *adv* —**~ness** *n* [U]

pro·tu·ber·ance /prəˈtjuːbərəns‖prəʊˈtuː-/ *n* **1** [C] a swelling: *Small protuberances on a stem will often show the places where a leaf will develop* **2** [U (*of*)] the quality or state of being PROTUBERANT

pro·tu·ber·ant /prəˈtjuːbərənt‖prəʊˈtuː-/ *adj* swelling or curving outwards from the surrounding surface: *protuberant ankles* —**~ly** *adv*

proud¹ /praʊd/ *adj* **1** [Wa1;B] *apprec* having the quality of self-respect and showing this in one's standards of behaviour: *They're poor but proud; they never borrow money or ask for help* **2** [Wa1;B] *derog* having too high an opinion of oneself or a false idea of one's own importance: *He's too proud to be seen in public with his poorly-dressed mother* **3** [Wa1;B;F(3,5 *of*)] having or expressing a proper personal feeling of satisfaction and pleasure in something connected with oneself: *Tom is very proud of his new car.*|*Our football team feels proud that it has won every match this year* **4** [(Wa1);A] splendid; noble; grand; glorious: *This proud and great university has produced many famous men* **5** [B] *esp. BrE* (esp. of a part of something made by joining pieces together) sticking out above a surface —see PRIDE —**~ly** *adv*

proud² *adv infml* **1** *esp. BrE* in a PROUD¹ (5) manner **2 do someone proud** to treat someone, esp. a guest, splendidly

proud flesh /ˌ· ˈ·/ *n* [U] unhealthy growth of flesh in or round the edges of a wound

pro·va·ble /ˈpruːvəbəl/ *adj* that can be proved —**-bly** *adv*

prove /pruːv/ *v* **proved** /pruːvd/, **proved** or (*esp. AmE*) **proven** /ˈpruːvən/ **1** [T1 (*to*), 5a,6a;X (*to be*) 1,7] to give proof of; show to be true or give cause for belief in: *He has proved his courage in battle.*|*"I wasn't in London on May 3rd." "Can you prove that to the court?"*|*The marks of his fingers on the gun proved that the prisoner had held the gun; they proved him to be the guilty man.*|*Can you prove where you were on May 3rd?* **2** [T1] to test (a quality or the quality of something): *In order to prove the servant's honesty she left a bag containing money on the table* **3** [L (*to be*) 1,7;X (*to be*) 1,7] to show (oneself or itself) afterwards, in the course of time or experience, etc., to be of the quality stated: *On the long journey he proved himself to be an amusing companion.*|*As it happened, my advice proved to be wrong.*|*Perhaps this book will prove (to be) of some use to you in your studies* **4** [I∅] *tech* (of a loaf or cake that is being baked) to rise to the proper degree of lightness **5** [T1] *law* to show that (a written statement left by a dead person concerning what shall be done with his possessions (a WILL)) has been made according to law —see PROOF

prov·en /ˈpruːvən; *Scot* ˈprəʊvən/ *adj* **1** [A] also **proved**— *apprec* that has been tested and shown to be true: *a man of proven ability* **2 not proven** (in the law of Scotland) a decision in a criminal trial that, as the facts neither prove nor disprove the prisoner to be guilty, he must be set free

prov·e·nance /ˈprɒvənəns‖ˈprɑ-/ *n* [U9] *fml or tech* (place of) origin: *Gunpowder is now considered to be of Chinese provenance*

Prov·en·çal /ˌprɒvɒnˈsɑːl‖ˌprɑvənˈsɑl (*Fr* prɔvɑ̃sal)/ *adj* [Wa5] *Fr* of Provence in southern France

prov·en·der /ˈprɒvɜ̇ndəʳ‖ˈprɑ-/ *n* [U] **1** dry food for horses and cattle **2** *infml, often humor* food for human beings

prov·erb /ˈprɒvɜːb‖ˈprɑvɜrb/ *n* a short well-known saying usu. in popular language: *"A cat has 9 lives" is a proverb*

pro·ver·bi·al /prəˈvɜːbɪəl‖-ɜr-/ *adj* **1** [B] of, concerning, or like a PROVERB: *In country areas a piece of knowledge about local weather is often expressed in proverbial form* **2** [Wa5;A] *infml* spoken of in a popular saying or comparison: *"He takes a lot of risks and has escaped many dangers." "Yes, he seems to have 9 lives, like the proverbial cat"* **3** [B] very widely known and spoken of; undoubted: *His generosity is proverbial*

pro·ver·bi·al·ly /prəˈvɜːbɪəli‖-ɜr-/ *adv* **1** by means of a PROVERB or proverbs **2** as is widely and generally known: *He's proverbially late; no one ever expects him to come at the right time*

Prov·erbs /ˈprɒvɜːbz‖ˈprɑvɜrbz/ *n* [R] one of the

books in the older half of the Bible (OLD TESTAMENT), which contains wise thoughts intended as rules for behaviour

pro·vide /prəˈvaɪd/ *v* **1** [T1;D1+*for*/*with*] to supply (something needed or useful): *That hotel provides good meals.*|*Can your shop provide tents for 20 campers?*|*a new shop to provide campers with tents and cooking apparatus* **2** [T5] (of a law, rule, agreement, etc.) to state a special arrangement that must be fulfilled: *The law provides that valuable ancient buildings must be preserved by the government*

provide a·gainst *v prep* [T1] **1** to take action or guard against (a danger or time of danger) **2** (of a law, rule, etc.) to forbid

pro·vid·ed /prəˈvaɪdɪ̈d/ also **provided that** /·ˈ·· ·/— *conj* if and only if; on condition that: *I will go, (always) provided (that) you go too.*|*Provided (that) there is no opposition* (=only if there is no opposition), *we shall hold the meeting here*

provide for *v prep* **1** [T1] to support; supply with the necessary things of life: *He has 5 children and a wife to provide for* **2** [T1,4] to make the necessary arrangements for (someone or something) in the future: *When cutting the cloth for my suit, leave enough at the edges to provide for my getting fatter* **3** [T1,4] (of a law, rule, etc.) to allow; make possible

prov·i·dence /ˈprɒvɪ̈dəns‖ˈprɑ-/ *n* **1** [U;S] a special act showing God's care or the kindness of fate (often in the phr. **divine providence**): *It seemed like providence that the doctor happened to be passing just at the time of the accident* **2** [U] *old use* good sense shown in making arrangements (esp. by saving money) for future needs

Providence *n* [R] God and his wise care and direction of the affairs of all living creatures; fate as a kindly influence

prov·i·dent /ˈprɒvɪ̈dənt‖ˈprɑ-/ *adj* (careful in) providing for future needs, esp. by saving or storing —**~ly** *adv*

prov·i·den·tial /ˌprɒvɪ̈ˈdenʃəl‖ˌprɑ-/ *adj* happening just when needed; lucky —**-tially** *adv*

pro·vid·er /prəˈvaɪdəʳ/ *n* a person who provides, esp. one who supports a family

pro·vid·ing /prəˈvaɪdɪŋ/ also **providing that** /·ˈ·· ·/— *conj* PROVIDED: *Providing (that) there is no opposition, we shall hold the meeting here*

prov·ince /ˈprɒvɪ̈ns‖ˈprɑ-/ *n* **1** [C] one of the main divisions of some countries (and formerly of some empires) that forms a separate whole for purposes of government control **2** [C] an area under the charge of a priest of very high rank (ARCHBISHOP) **3** [U9] a division of land in connection with the special plants and animals that are native to it: *Australia is the province of the* KANGAROO **4** [U9] a branch of thought, knowledge, or study considered as having fixed limits: *I know nothing about Persian art; that's quite outside my province. My province is European art* **5** [U9] *infml* a person's proper or particular duty, business, or activity

Province *n* [*the*+R] Ulster; Northern Ireland

prov·inc·es /ˈprɒvɪ̈nsɪ̈z‖ˈprɑ-/ *n* [*the*+P] the parts of a country that are distant from the main city and centre of government: *I saw the new film in London; it's not yet being shown in the provinces*

pro·vin·cial[1] /prəˈvɪnʃəl/ *n* **1** a PROVINCIAL[2] (esp. 3) person **2** the head of a PROVINCE (2)

provincial[2] *adj* **1** [Wa5;A] of a PROVINCE (1) **2** [Wa5;A] of the PROVINCES **3** [B] *often derog* having or showing the manners, speech, opinions, rather limited or old-fashioned customs, etc., regarded (esp. in former times) as typical of people of the PROVINCES —**~ism** *n* [U;C]: *provincialism(s) of dress and manner* —**~ly** *adv*

prov·ing ground /ˈpruːvɪŋ graʊnd/ *n* **1** a place for scientific testing, esp. of vehicles **2** a place where something new is tried out: *They were hoping for a small war which would be a proving ground for their new weapons*

pro·vi·sion[1] /prəˈvɪʒən/ *n* **1** [U+*of*] the act of providing: *The provision of a new and larger library has been of great educational advantage to the students* **2** [U+*against* or *for*] preparation (against future risks or for future needs): *They spend all their money and make no provision for the future* **3** [C+*of*] a (measured) supply **4** [C; (*the*) S5,5c] a condition in an agreement or law; PROVISO: *According to the provisions of the agreement the money must be paid back in monthly amounts.*|*The doctor agreed to go to Africa for one year with the provision that he could take his family with him* **5** [A] that sells PROVISIONS: *a provision business*

provision[2] *v* [T1 (*for*)] to provide with food and other supplies in large quantities for a long time

pro·vi·sion·al /prəˈvɪʒənəl/ *adj* [Wa5] for the present time only, with the strong probability of being changed —**~ly** *adv*: *Provisionally, let's arrange the meeting for next Tuesday, even though we may have to change it*

pro·vi·sions /prəˈvɪʒənz/ *n* [P] food supplies

pro·vi·so /prəˈvaɪzəʊ/ *n* **-sos** [C; (*the*) S5,5c] something added that limits the conditions in which an agreement will be accepted, esp. in business matters: *I've agreed to do the work, with the proviso that I'm paid before I do it*

prov·o·ca·tion /ˌprɒvəˈkeɪʃən‖ˌprɑ-/ *n* **1** [U] the act of provoking or state of being PROVOKEd: *It's true that John hit Billy first, but Billy is guilty of provocation, because he called John a coward* **2** [U] reason for provoking or being PROVOKEd: *After giving him such provocation, how can you be surprised that he's angry?* **3** [C] something that tests one's powers of self-control: *the provocations of teaching a class of badly-behaved children*

pro·voc·a·tive /prəˈvɒkətɪv‖-ˈvɑ-/ *adj* causing or intended to cause interest (often of a sexual kind), argument, anger, etc.: *Amanda is looking very provocative in that short skirt.*|*He made a provocative speech that caused a great deal of argument* —**~ly** *adv*

pro·voke /prəˈvəʊk/ *v* **1** [T1] to make (a person or animal) angry or bad-tempered: *That dog is very dangerous when provoked* —see ANGRY (USAGE) **2** [V3] to cause or force: *Her rudeness provoked me to strike her* **3** [T1] to be the sudden cause of (a favourable or unfavourable feeling or action): *Don't throw one bone to 2 dogs; you'll only provoke a fight* **4** [T1] (of a woman) to try purposely to attract the attention, interest, or sexual feeling of (a man)

provoke in·to *v prep* [D1;V4b] to cause or force (someone) into (an action or doing something)

pro·vok·ing /prəˈvəʊkɪŋ/ *adj usu. fml* annoying —**~ly** *adv*

prov·ost /ˈprɒvəst‖ˈprəʊ-, ˈprɑ-/ *n* [C;N] (*usu. cap.*) **1** (the title of) the head of certain colleges, esp. in the universities of Oxford and Cambridge **2** (in Scotland) the head of a town council

pro·vost mar·shal /prəˌvəʊ ˈmɑːʃəl‖ˌprəʊvəʊ ˈmɑrʃəl/ *n* an officer in command of a body of military police in a camp, town, etc.

prow /praʊ/ *n esp. lit* the pointed front part of a ship or boat; BOW

prow·ess /ˈpraʊɪ̈s/ *n usu. fml or lit* **1** [U9] great personal bravery: *The tribesmen sang a song of victory, describing their prowess in battle* **2** [U9, esp. *as, at, in*] unusual ability or skill: *His prowess as a footballer makes it certain that he'll be chosen for the team*

prowl¹ /praʊl/ *v* **1** [IØ] (esp. of an animal looking for food, or of a thief) to move about in a quiet way trying not to be seen or heard: *I woke in the middle of the night and heard someone prowling about in the garden* **2** [L9] *infml* to wander about looking and examining: *She likes to prowl round the shops* **3** [T1] to move silently and secretly through (a place): *Some rather rough-looking men prowl the streets in this area after dark*

prowl² *n infml* **1** [S9] an act of PROWLing¹ (1,2): *I'm going for a prowl round the bookshops to see what I can find* **2 on the prowl** PROWLing¹ (esp. 1): *A lion on the prowl is a hungry lion*

prowl car /'· ·/ *n AmE* a police car that is driven round the streets of a city looking for crime

prowl·er /'praʊləʳ/ *n* **1** [C] a person who PROWLs¹ (1) around houses and streets, usu. at night, probably with the intention of stealing **2** [C9] a person or animal that PROWLs¹ (1,2) for any reason

prox /prɒks‖praks/ *abbrev. for:* PROXIMO

prox·i·mal /'prɒksɪ̇məl‖'pra-/ *adj* [(*to*)] *med* nearest or next to the point of joining or origin, to a central point, or to the point of view; lying towards the centre of the body —opposite **distal** —**~ly** *adv* [(*to*)]

prox·i·mate /'prɒksɪ̇mɪ̇t‖'prak-/ *adj* [Wa5] *fml* **1** [B (*to*)] nearest; just before or after in time, position, order, or family relationship **2** [A] (of a cause) direct —**~ly** *adv*

prox·im·i·ty /prɒk'sɪmɪ̇ti‖prak-/ *n* [U (*to*)] *usu. fml* **1** nearness **2 in the proximity of** *pomp* near

prox·i·mo /'prɒksɪ̇məʊ‖'prak-/ *adj* [E] *tech or pomp* of next month: *The meeting will be held on the 13th proximo*

prox·y /'prɒksi‖'praksi/ *n* **1** [U] the right given to a person to let someone else act for or represent him on a single occasion, esp. as a voter at an election **2** [C] an official paper giving this right **3** [C] a person whom one chooses to act for or represent one, esp. as a voter: *I can't come to the meeting so I'm sending a proxy to vote for me*

prude /pruːd/ *n derog* a person who makes a show of being easily shocked and takes great care not to do, say, hear, etc., anything supposed to be impure, esp. of a sexual nature

pru·dence /'pruːdəns/ *n* [U] the state or quality of being PRUDENT; wise thought before acting: *Prudence prevented Oscar from disobeying his father, who had a fierce temper*

pru·dent /'pruːdənt/ *adj* sensible and wise; careful to consider one's advantage, esp. by avoiding risks, unpleasantness, difficulties, etc.: *It's prudent to wear a thick coat when the weather is cold* —**~ly** *adv*

pru·den·tial /pruː'denʃəl/ *adj fml* resulting from or showing PRUDENCE, esp. in business matters: *prudential habits|They wanted to call themselves "The Prudential Insurance Company", but someone else had already taken that name* —**~ly** *adv*

prud·er·y /'pruːdəri/ *n derog* **1** [U] the manners of or quality of being a PRUDE **2** [C *usu. pl.*] a PRUDISH act or remark

prud·ish /'pruːdɪʃ/ *adj derog* being or like a PRUDE —**~ly** *adv* —**~ness** *n* [U]

prune¹ /pruːn/ *n* **1** a type of dried fruit (a dried PLUM) usu. gently boiled to become soft and swollen before eating **2** *infml* a dull or foolish person

prune² *v* [T1] **1** [(BACK)] to cut off or shorten some of the branches of (a tree or bush) in order to improve the shape, growth, production of flowers or fruit **2** [(AWAY or BACK)] to remove (branches, stems, etc.) in this way **3** [(AWAY or DOWN)] to take out anything useless from (something); lessen in amount by careful choice: *You should prune the speech down; it's too long*

prun·ing /'pruːnɪŋ/ *n* [A] (of a kind of tool) especially made for use in pruning (PRUNE² (1)) trees or bushes: *a pruning hook|a pruning knife|pruning scissors*

pru·ri·ence /'prʊərɪəns/ also **pru·ri·en·cy** /-ənsi/— *n* [U] *fml* the quality or state of being PRURIENT

pru·ri·ent /'prʊərɪənt/ *adj* having or showing an unpleasantly great and unhealthy interest in sexual matters —compare PURULENT —**~ly** *adv*

pru·ri·tus /prʊ'raɪtəs‖pruː-/ *n* [U;C *usu. sing.*] *med* a feeling (an ITCH² (1)) on the skin that makes one want to rub it, esp. near the opening through which waste matter leaves the body (ANUS)

Prus·sian /'prʌʃən/ *adj* of Prussia in Germany

Prussian blue /ˌ·· '·/ *n, adj* [U;B] a deep blue colour or colouring matter

prus·sic ac·id /ˌprʌsɪk 'æsɪ̇d/ *n* [U] a type of powerful poisonous acid that quickly causes death

pry¹ /praɪ/ *v* [Wv4;IØ] to (try to) look secretly at or find out about someone else's private possessions or affairs: *I don't wish to pry in any way, but may I ask if it's true that you've sold your house?|prying newspaper reporters*

pry² also **prize**— *v* [X9] to raise, move, lift, or break with a tool or metal bar: *I couldn't pry the cover off this wooden box without breaking it*

pry in·to *v prep* [T1] to inquire with too much interest into (other people's business)

pry out also **prize out**— *v adv* [T1 (*of*)] to force someone to give or tell one (something), by using skill or patience in one's demands

P.S.¹ /ˌpiː 'es/ *n abbrev. for:* **1** *infml* POSTSCRIPT (1): *He had written a P.S. at the end of the letter* **2** (written before a POSTSCRIPT (1) in a letter): *. . . Yours sincerely, J. Smithers. P.S. I shan't be able to come before Thursday*

P.S.² /'piː es/ *n* [A] *abbrev. for:* (*AmE*) Public School; a school for children from 6 to 12, supported by the state: *went to P.S. 89 in New York City* —see also PUBLIC SCHOOL

psalm /sɑːm‖sam, salm/ *n* a song or poem in praise of God, esp. one of the PSALMS

psalm·ist /'sɑːmɪ̇st‖'sam-, 'salm-/ *n* a writer of PSALMs

psalm·o·dy /'sɑːmədi, 'sæl-‖'sam-, 'salm-/ *n* **1** [U] the art or practice of singing PSALMs, esp. in public worship **2** [C] a collection of PSALMs with the music to which they are meant to be sung

Psalms /sɑːmz‖samz, salmz/ *n* **1** [*the*+P] the collection of PSALMs in the Bible, used in forming part of some church services, and sung in a special way **2** [R] the book of the Bible containing this collection

psal·ter /'sɔːltəʳ/ *n* a book containing a collection of (some of) the PSALMS with music, for use in church services

Psalter *n* [*the*+R] the Book of PSALMS of the Bible, esp. when printed separately

psal·ter·y /'sɔːltəri/ also **psal·try** /-tri/— *n* a type of ancient musical instrument having strings stretched over a flat board, played by pulling at (PLUCKing) the strings with the fingers —compare ZITHER

pse·phol·o·gy /se'fɒlədʒi‖siː'fa-/ *n* [U] the scientific study of the way people vote at elections —**-gist** *n*

pseud /sjuːd‖suːd/ *n infml, esp. BrE* a person who acts as though he is better than others in knowledge, social position, etc., but is seen not to be

pseu·do- /'sjuːdəʊ‖'suː-/ also **pseud-** /sjuːd‖suːd/— *comb. form* not real; pretended; false: *John considers that the study of the stars as an influence on man's fate is only a pseudoscience*

pseu·do·nym /ˈsjuːdənɪm‖ˈsuːdənɪm/ *n* an invented name used (esp. by a writer of books) in place of the real name: *Harry Macdonald writes accounts of football matches in the evening newspaper, under the pseudonym of "Sportsman"*

pseu·don·y·mous /sjuːˈdɒnɪ̈məs‖suːˈdɑ-/ *adj* [Wa5] **1** written or printed using a PSEUDONYM: *pseudonymous literature* **2** writing under a PSEUDONYM: *the pseudonymous writer of this work*

pshaw /ʃɔː, pʃɔː/ *interj lit now rare* (used for expressing disapproval or disbelief)

psit·ta·co·sis /ˌsɪtəˈkəʊsɪ̈s/ also **parrot fever**— *n* [U] a serious disease of certain types of bird, that can be caught by people, in whom it produces high fever

pso·ri·a·sis /səˈraɪəsɪ̈s/ *n* [U] a diseased condition of the skin in which red sore marks appear and little pieces of skin come off

psst /ps/ *interj* (the sound of) a short SPITting[3] (2) HISS, used for drawing attention while asking for secrecy: *Psst! Put your shoes on before he comes in!* —compare HIST

psych- /saɪk/ *comb. form* PSYCHO-

psy·che /ˈsaɪki/ *n* [C9 *usu. sing.*] **1** *tech* the human mind at all its levels, as being a person's self **2** *fml or lit* the human soul or spirit

psy·che·del·ic[1] /ˌsaɪkɪ̈ˈdelɪk/ *adj* **1** (of a mind-influencing drug) having the effect of making the senses seem keener than in reality; causing strange excited sensations of power, happiness, hopelessness, etc. **2** (of a form of art) producing an effect on the brain by means of strong patterns of noise, colour, lines, moving lights, etc. —**~ally** *adv* [Wa4]

psychedelic[2] *n* a PSYCHEDELIC drug

psyche out *v adv* [T1] *sl, esp. AmE* PSYCH OUT

psy·chi·at·ric /ˌsaɪkiˈætrɪk/ *adj* [Wa5] of, concerning, or by PSYCHIATRY: *A person who suddenly begins to steal may be in need of psychiatric treatment* —**~ally** *adv* [Wa4]

psy·chi·a·trist /saɪˈkaɪətrɪ̈st‖sə-/ *n* a doctor trained in PSYCHIATRY

psy·chi·a·try /saɪˈkaɪətri‖sə-/ *n* [U] the study and treatment of diseases of the mind, esp. when considered as a branch of medicine

psy·chic[1] /ˈsaɪkɪk/ also **psy·chi·cal** /-kɪkəl/— *adj* **1** [Wa5] concerning the soul; connected with the spirits of the dead **2** (of a person) having powers unexplained by scientists and not experienced by most people, such the ability to see into the future **3** [Wa5] (of an illness) of the mind as opposed to the body: *psychic disorders* —**~ally** *adv* [Wa4]

psychic[2] *n* **1** a PSYCHIC[1] (2) person **2** a person who acts or claims to be able to act as one through whom others can receive messages from the dead; MEDIUM

psychical re·search /ˌ··· ·ˈ·/ *n* [U] scientific study and searching into the truth of cases of strange unexplained happenings connected with the spirits of the dead, the seeing of the future, etc.

psy·cho /ˈsaɪkəʊ/ *n* **psychos** *sl* a person who has a severe illness of the mind

psycho- /ˈsaɪkəʊ, saɪˈkəʊ/ *comb. form* of or concerning the mind, as opposed to the body: PSYCHOANALYTIC|*psycho*NEUROSIS

psy·cho·an·a·lyse, *AmE* also **-lyze** /ˌsaɪkəʊˈænəlaɪz/ *v* [T1] to treat by PSYCHOANALYSIS (1)

psy·cho·a·nal·y·sis /ˌsaɪkəʊ-əˈnælɪ̈sɪ̈s/ *n* [U] **1** a way of treating certain nervous disorders of the mind by examination of all that the sufferer can be made to remember of his past life, dreams, etc., in an effort to find hidden forgotten anxieties, desires, or past experiences that may be causing the illness **2** the scientific study (based on what has been discovered by this treatment) of the hidden parts of the mind which influence one's behaviour without one's knowing it. It was developed by Sigmund Freud

psy·cho·an·a·lyst /ˌsaɪkəʊˈænəlɪ̈st/ *AmE* also **analyst**— *n* a person who is trained to give PSYCHOANALYTIC treatment

psy·cho·an·a·lyt·ic /ˌsaɪkəʊ-ænəˈlɪtɪk/ also **psy·cho·an·a·lyt·i·cal** /-kəl/— *adj* [Wa5] of, concerning, or by PSYCHOANALYSIS (esp. 1) —**~ally** *adv* [Wa4]

psy·cho·ki·ne·sis /ˌsaɪkəʊkaɪˈniːsɪ̈s‖-kɪ̈ˈniː-/ *n* [U] the moving of solid objects by the power of the mind —**-tic** /-ˈnetɪk/ *adj* —**-tically** *adv* [Wa4]

psy·cho·log·i·cal /ˌsaɪkəˈlɒdʒɪkəl‖-ˈlɑ-/ *adj* **1** [B] of, concerned with, or connected with the way that the mind works: *a psychological play about the power that a mother had over her children's minds|There must be some psychological explanation for his bad temper, as he's usually so gentle* **2** [A] using PSYCHOLOGY: *Psychological tests may be used to find out a person's character* **3 at the psychological moment** *infml* just at the right time to save one from something unpleasant or dangerous: *Lenny appeared at the psychological moment to prevent me from being bitten by the dog* **4 the psychological moment** the moment or occasion when conditions are the most favourable for an action: *"I must ask Paul to lend me some money." "You'd better choose the psychological moment, when he's just had a good dinner"* —**-cally** *adv* [Wa4]

psychological war·fare /··ˌ··· ˈ··/ *n* [U] action taken to lessen enemy courage and loyalty by spreading fear, anxiety, different political beliefs, etc., esp. by radio

psy·chol·o·gist /saɪˈkɒlədʒɪ̈st‖-ˈkɑ-/ *n* **1** a person who has studied or is skilled in PSYCHOLOGY **2** *infml* a person who understands people's characters and what influences their behaviour

psy·chol·o·gy /saɪˈkɒlədʒi‖-ˈkɑ-/ *n* **1** [U] the study or science of the mind and the way it works, and of behaviour as an expression of the mind **2** [U9] a branch of this study that deals with a particular group or division of human activity: *educational psychology|criminal psychology* **3** [U9; (C9)] *infml* the mind and behaviour patterns of a particular person or group; a person's character: *I can't understand that man's psychology* **4** [U] *infml* cleverness in understanding people

psy·cho·path /ˈsaɪkəpæθ/ *n* a person who has a continual or incurable disorder of character, arising from continual changes of feelings, that prevents him from fitting well into society (with the result that he may become a criminal, a wanderer, etc.) —**~ic** /ˌsaɪkəˈpæθɪk/ *adj* —**~ically** *adv* [Wa4]

psy·cho·sis /saɪˈkəʊsɪ̈s/ *n* **-ses** /siːz/ [C;U] any of several types of serious disorders of the mind that may produce character changes, and are marked by a loss of touch with reality

psy·cho·so·mat·ic /ˌsaɪkəʊsəˈmætɪk‖-kəse-/ *n* **1** (of an illness) caused by a hidden fear or anxiety in the mind as well as, or rather than, by a bodily disorder **2** concerning the relationship between the mind and the body in illness: *psychosomatic medicine* —**~ally** *adv* [Wa4]

psy·cho·ther·a·py /ˌsaɪkəʊˈθerəpi/ *n* [U] treatment of disorders of the mind by means of action on the mind itself, using PSYCHOLOGY rather than drugs, operations, etc. —**-pist** *n*

psy·chot·ic /saɪˈkɒtɪk‖-ˈkɑ-/ *n, adj* (of or being) a person suffering from a PSYCHOSIS: *psychotic behaviour|He became (a) psychotic* —**~ally** *adv* [Wa4]

psych out, psyche out /saɪk/ *v adv* [T1] *sl, esp. AmE* to understand by INTUITION: *I psyched him out at once, and knew I could not trust him.|trying to psych out her intentions*

pt *written abbrev. for:* **1** part **2** payment **3** PINT(*s*) **4** point **5** (*often cap.*) port: *Pt Moresby*

P T *abbrev. for:* (*infml*) PHYSICAL TRAINING
PTA *abbrev. for:* Parent-Teacher Association
ptar·mi·gan /ˈtɑːmɪgən‖ˈtɑr-/ *n* [Wn1] a type of bird of far northern lands, with grey or black feathers that turn white in winter
P T boat /ˌpiː ˈtiː bəʊt/ *n now rare* a type of light fast fighting boat used esp. during World War 2
pter·o·dac·tyl /ˌterəˈdæktɪl‖-tl, -tɪl/ *n* a type of flying animal that lived many MILLIONS of years ago —see picture at PREHISTORIC
pto /ˌpiː tiː ˈəʊ/ *abbrev. for:* (*BrE*) (*usu. cap.*) (written at the bottom of a page) please turn over; look at the next page —compare OVER
Ptol·e·ma·ic sys·tem /ˌtɒlɪ̇ˈmeɪ-ɪk ˌsɪstɪ̇m‖ˌtɑl-/ *n* [*the*+R] the system according to which, in former times, the earth was believed to be at the centre of the universe, with the sun, stars, and chief heavenly bodies (PLANETS) travelling round it —compare COPERNICAN SYSTEM
pto·maine /ˈtəʊmeɪn, təʊˈmeɪn/ *n* [A] concerning or caused by any of various poisonous substances formed by bacteria in decaying meat (usu. in the phr. **ptomaine poisoning**)
pub /pʌb/ also (*fml esp. BrE*) **public house**— *n* (esp. in Britain) a building (not a club or hotel) usu. containing 2 or more rooms where alcohol may be bought and drunk during fixed hours; inn —compare BAR[1] (10a)
pub-crawl[1] /ˈ· ˌ·/ *n sl, esp. BrE* a moving round from one PUB to another, usu. having a drink at each place: *Let's go on a pub-crawl tonight!*
pub-crawl[2] *v* [IØ] *sl, esp. BrE* to go on a PUB-CRAWL[1]: *They like (to go) pub-crawling* —**~er** *n*
pu·ber·ty /ˈpjuːbəti‖-ər-/ *n* [U] the time or stage of change in the human body from childhood to the state in which it is possible to produce children
pu·bic /ˈpjuːbɪk/ *adj* [Wa5;A] related to, or in a position near, the sexual organs: *pubic hair|the pubic bone*
pub·lic[1] /ˈpʌblɪk/ *adj* **1** [Wa5;A] of, to, by, for, or concerning people in general: *It is a matter of public importance that laws should be obeyed* **2** [Wa5;B] for the use of everyone; not private: *The town has its own public library and public gardens* **3** [B] in the sight or hearing of many people; not secret or private: *The minister will make a public statement soon about the new plans of the government.|This place is too public for talk about our personal affairs; anyone might hear what we're saying* **4** [B] known to all or to many: *The news of the ruler's death was not made public for several days* **5** [Wa5;A] connected or concerned with the affairs of the people, esp. with government: *How long has he held public office?* (= held (high) office in government) **6 go public** (of a company) to become a PUBLIC COMPANY **7 in the public eye** (of a person) much noticed by everyone as a result of one's activities —compare PRIVATE —**~ly** *adv*
public[2] *n* **1** [*the*+GU] people in general: *The town gardens are open to the public from sunrise to sunset daily.|The British public is interested in sport* **2** [S9;(S);(*the*) GU9;(GC)] a group in society considered for its interest in a particular person, activity, etc.: *The television public is increasing rapidly.|This famous young singer has an admiring public; he tries to please his public by singing its/their favourite songs. "My public want to hear me sing," he says.|Is there a public for that kind of activity?* **3 in public** in the presence of strangers; in the sight or hearing of many people —opposite **in private**
public-ad·dress sys·tem /ˌ·· ·ˈ· ˌ··/ *n* an electrically controlled apparatus used for making a speaker clearly heard by large groups of people, esp. out of doors
pub·li·can /ˈpʌblɪkən/ *n* **1** *esp. BrE* a person who (owns and) runs a PUB **2** *esp. bibl* (in the times of ancient Rome) a tax collector
public as·sis·tance /ˌ·· ·ˈ··/ *n* [U] money given by the state to people who cannot support themselves (now in Britain called **supplementary benefit**)
pub·li·ca·tion /ˌpʌblɪ̇ˈkeɪʃən/ *n* **1** [U (*of*)] the act or action of making something known (officially) to the public: *the publication of the results of the election* **2** [U] the offering for sale to the public of something printed: *A few mistakes in the printing of that book weren't noticed before publication* **3** [C] something PUBLISHed, such as a book or magazine
public bar /ˌ·· ˈ·/ *n BrE* a room in a PUB, inn, hotel etc., that is plainly furnished, and where the cheapest prices are charged for drinks —compare SALOON BAR
public com·pa·ny /ˌ·· ˈ···/ *n* a business company that offers shares in itself for sale to the public on the STOCK EXCHANGE
public con·ve·nience /ˌ·· ·ˈ··/ also **convenience**— *n* [*usu. pl. with sing. meaning*] *not AmE* public TOILETS provided by local government
public cor·po·ra·tion /ˌ·· ··ˈ··/ *n esp. BrE* a large company that provides services to the public and is owned by the government but supposed to be more independent than the ordinary NATIONALIZED industry: *The* BBC *is a public corporation* —compare PUBLIC UTILITY
public house /ˌ·· ˈ·/ *n BrE fml* PUB
pub·li·cist /ˈpʌblɪ̇sɪ̇st/ *n* a person whose business is to bring something to the attention of the public, esp. products for sale
pub·lic·i·ty /pʌˈblɪsɪ̇ti/ *n* [U] **1** public notice or attention: *The film actress's marriage got a lot of publicity, though she tried to keep it secret* **2** the business of bringing someone or something to (favourable) public notice, esp. for purposes of gain **3** ways used for doing this: *The concert was a good one, but because of bad publicity, very few people came*
publicity a·gent /·ˈ··· ˌ··/ *n* a person employed to get favourable PUBLICITY (1) for a person, a play, etc.
pub·li·cize, -cise /ˈpʌblɪ̇saɪz/ *v* [T1] to bring to public notice; get PUBLICITY (1) for
public nui·sance /ˌ·· ˈ··/ *n* **1** *law* an unlawful act or failure to act, which is harmful to everyone **2** *infml* a person who is generally troublesome to others
public o·pin·ion /ˌ·· ·ˈ··/ *n* [U] what most people think or believe: *A government may have to change its actions in order to fit in with changes in public opinion*
public own·er·ship /ˌ·· ˈ···/ *n* [U] ownership of businesses, property, etc., by the state: *The aircraft industry has been taken into public ownership*
public pros·e·cu·tor /ˌ·· ˈ····/ *n* (*often caps.*) a government lawyer who acts for the state in bringing charges against criminals in a court of law —compare ATTORNEY GENERAL
public purse /ˌ·· ˈ·/ *n* [*the*+R] money for national use collected by a government from taxes
public re·la·tions /ˌ·· ·ˈ··/ *n* **1** [P] the relations between an organization and the general public which must be kept friendly in various ways: *If we plant flowers in front of the factory it will be good (for) public relations* **2** [U] the work of keeping these relations friendly: *Public relations is big business today*
public relations of·fi·cer /ˌ·· ·ˈ·· ˌ···/ also (*infml*) **PRO**— *n* a person employed by a firm, government, etc., to keep its PUBLIC RELATIONS (1) friendly

public school /ˌ·· ˈ·/ *n* **1** (in Britain, esp. England) any of a limited number of private SECONDARY schools esp. for boys, who usu. live as well as study there **2** (esp. in Scotland and the US) a free local PRIMARY school supported by taxes, usu. for both boys and girls who study there but live at home

public ser·vant /ˌ·· ˈ··/ *n* a government official or a government worker —compare CIVIL SERVANT

public spir·it /ˌ·· ˈ··/ *n* [U] *apprec* willingness and desire to serve people and do what is necessary or helpful for all, without regard for personal advantage —**public-spirited** /ˌ·· ˈ···/ *adj*

public u·til·i·ty /ˌ·· ·ˈ···/ *n* a large company that provides services to the public and is controlled but not owned by the government —compare PUBLIC CORPORATION

public works /ˌ·· ˈ·/ *n* [P] buildings, roads, harbours, DRAINS[2] (1), and other such apparatus provided usu. by the government for public use, esp. as improvements or additions to what was there before

pub·lish /ˈpʌblɪʃ/ *v* **1** [T1;IØ] (of a kind of business firm) to choose, arrange, have printed, and offer for sale to the public (some kind of written work in the form of a book, magazine, newspaper, etc.): *This firm publishes educational books* **2** [T1] to sell the works of (a writer or musician) in this way **3** [T1;IØ] (of a writer or musician) to have (one's work) printed and put on sale: *She's only been writing for 18 months, but already she's published her 4th book* **4** [T1;IØ] (of a newspaper or magazine) to print (something written): *It's a good story, but we can't publish; it would offend too many people* **5** [T1 *often pass.*] to make known generally; give public notice of: *The death of the ruler was kept secret; the news wasn't published for several days*

pub·lish·er /ˈpʌblɪʃəʳ/ *n* a person or firm whose business is to PUBLISH (1) books, newspapers, etc., or (sometimes) to make and sell records or SHEET MUSIC

pub·lish·ing /ˈpʌblɪʃɪŋ/ *n* [U] the business or profession of PUBLISHing (1)

puce /pjuːs/ *n, adj* [Wa1;B;U] a dark brownish purple colour

puck /pʌk/ *n* a hard flat circular piece of rubber used instead of a ball in playing the game of ICE HOCKEY

Puck *n* [R] (in old stories) a small male fairy believed in former times to enjoy playing tricks on people

puck·er[1] /ˈpʌkəʳ/ *v* [T1;IØ: (UP)] to tighten into (unwanted) folds: *If you pucker up your lips like that you'll get lasting lines round your mouth*

pucker[2] *n* a small unwanted fold

puck·ish /ˈpʌkɪʃ/ *adj lit* playful; full of harmless tricks —**~ly** *adv*

pud /pʊd/ *n* [U;(C)] *BrE infml* PUDDING (1,2,3)

pud·ding /ˈpʊdɪŋ/ *n* **1** [U;(C)] *BrE* the sweet dish in a meal, served after meat or fish and before cheese; DESSERT: *She eats too much pudding, that's why she's fat.|What's for pudding, mother?* **2** [C;(U)] (*usu. in comb.*) a usu. solid sweet dish based on pastry, rice, bread, etc., with fat and (dried) fruit or other substances added, baked, boiled, or STEAMEd[2] (3), and served hot: *an apple pudding|a rice pudding|a bread and butter pudding* **3** [C;(U)] (*usu. in comb.*) an unsweetened dish of a mixture of flour, fat, etc., either covering or enclosing meat and boiled with it: *a* STEAK *and* KIDNEY *pudding* **4** [C9;U9] (*usu. in comb.*) a type of tubelike skin filled with meat cut small (SAUSAGE): BLACK PUDDING **5** [S;(U)] *infml* a soft wet mass or mixture: *We wanted to play football this afternoon, but it's rained so much that the ground is a real pudding, so we can't* **6** "**The proof of the pudding is in the eating**" "You won't really know whether something is good until you try it"

pudding head /ˈ·· ·/ *n* [C;N] *infml* a stupid person

pudding stone /ˈ·· ·/ *n* [U] a type of rock made of small rounded stones held together in a rocky mass; CONGLOMERATE

pud·dle[1] /ˈpʌdl/ *n* **1** [C] a small amount of rainwater lying in a hollow place in the ground **2** [U] a thick paste of sand, clay, and water spread over banks of earth, hollow places, etc., to prevent water from escaping through the earth

puddle[2] *v* [T1] **1** to mix (sand, clay, and water) into a mass to make PUDDLE[1] (2) **2** to move (melted iron) about with a long iron tool so that air gets in and the impure substances are separated

pu·den·dum /pjuːˈdendəm/ *n* **-da** /də/ [*usu. pl.*] the outer sexual organs, esp. of a woman

pudg·y /ˈpʌdʒi/ *adj* [Wa1] PODGY —**-iness** *n* [U]

pueb·lo /ˈpwebləʊ/ *n* **-los** the shared living place of some groups of American Indians in Mexico and the southwestern US, made up of a number of houses joined side by side and built one on top of the other

pu·er·ile /ˈpjʊəraɪl‖-rəl/ *adj fml* childish; fit only for children; silly

pu·er·il·i·ty /pjʊəˈrɪlɪ̆ti/ *n fml* **1** [U] childishness; silliness **2** [C *usu. pl.*] a childish or silly act, statement, thought, etc.

pu·er·per·al /pjuːˈɜːpərəl‖-ˈɜr-/ *adj* [Wa5;A] *med* of, after, or caused by CHILDBIRTH (esp. in the phr. **puerperal fever**)

puff[1] /pʌf/ *v* **1** [L9;(IØ)] to breathe rapidly and with effort, usu. during or after hurried movement **2** [L9, esp. AWAY, *at, on*;(T1)] to breathe in and out while smoking (a cigarette, pipe, etc.): *He puffed (away) at his pipe as he talked.|She puffed (at) a cigarette nervously* **3** [IØ;T1: (OUT)] **a** (of smoke or steam) to blow or come out repeatedly, esp. in small amounts **b** to cause (esp. smoke or steam) to come out repeatedly: *Don't puff cigarette smoke in my face.*|(fig.) *He puffed out a few words as he ran past me over the top of the hill* **4** [L9] to move (not very fast) sending out little clouds of smoke or breathing quick short breaths: *The railway train puffed into the station.|He puffed up the steep slope* **5** [X9] to make (one's way) by doing this: *The train puffed its way into the station* **6** [T1] *infml becoming rare* to praise (esp. something for sale) more than is deserved, in order to draw the attention of the public **7 puff and blow** also **puff and pant**— *infml* to breathe with difficulty in short deep breaths

puff[2] *n* **1** [C] an act of PUFFing[1] (1,2): *He blew out 3 candles with a single puff.|He took a puff at his cigarette* **2** [C] a sudden short rush or sending out of air, smoke, etc.: *I felt a sudden short puff of air from the open window* **3** [C] something light that is blown or pushed along: *There were little puffs of cloud in the blue sky* **4** [U] *infml humor* breath: *She had no puff left after climbing the hill* **5** [C] *infml becoming rare* written praise of a (new) book, play, etc., esp. as intended to increase sales **6** [C] an ornamental part of a garment made by drawing the cloth together so that it swells out in the middle **7** [C] (*usu. in comb.*) a hollow piece of light pastry that is filled with a soft (usu. sweet) mixture: *a cream puff|a* JAM *puff* —see also POWDER PUFF

puff ad·der /ˈ· ˌ··/ *n* a type of large poisonous African snake that swells out its body when annoyed

puff·ball /ˈpʌfbɔːl/ *n* a type of ball-shaped flowerless leafless plant (FUNGUS), which when ripe bursts in a dustlike cloud of fine powder —see picture at FUNGUS

puffed /pʌft/ adj [F] *infml* (esp. of a person) breathing with difficulty; out of breath

puff·er /ˈpʌfəʳ/ *n* **1** also **puffer fish** /ˈ·· ·/— a type of fish that swells up into a ball when annoyed **2** (*used esp. by or to children*) (a train pulled by) a steam engine

puf·fin /ˈpʌfən/ *n* a type of seabird of North Atlantic coasts that has a very large brightly coloured beak —see picture at WATER[1]

puff out *v adv* **1** [T1;I∅: (*with*)] to (cause to) enlarge, esp. with air: *The bird puffed out its feathers* **2** [T1] to arrange (a woman's hair) to give an effect of a thick mass **3** [T1] to put out the flame of (something) by blowing lightly

puff pas·try /ˌ· ˈ··/ *n* [U] a type of very light pastry made from a special mixture (**puff paste**) that rises and swells when cooked

puff up *v adv* **1** [T1 *usu. pass.*;I∅: (*with*)] to (cause to) swell **2 be puffed up** *usu. bibl* to be too proud

puff·y /ˈpʌfi/ *adj* [Wa1] **1** rather swollen **2** *infml* breathing with difficulty after effort —**puffily** *adv* —**puffiness** *n* [U]

pug[1] /pʌg/ also **pug dog** /ˈ· ·/— *n* a type of small short-haired fat dog with a wide flat face and a turned-up nose

pug[2] *n* [U] *tech* **1** wet clay mixed ready for brickmaking or other purposes **2** also **pug·ging** /ˈpʌgɪŋ/— material put under a floor or between walls to prevent sound from passing through

pug[3] *v* **-gg-** [T1] *tech* **1** to mix (clay) for use **2** to fill (a hollow floor or wall) with PUG[2] (2)

pug[4] *n Ind & PakE* a footmark (FOOTPRINT) of a wild animal (as noticed by a hunter)

pu·gi·lis·m /ˈpjuːdʒəlɪzəm/ *n* [U] **1** *fml* (in former times) the art or sport of fighting with bare tightly closed hands (FISTs) **2** *pomp* the art or sport of fighting with the hands, wearing special GLOVEs; BOXING —**-tic** /ˌpjuːdʒəˈlɪstɪk/ *adj*

pu·gi·list /ˈpjuːdʒələst/ *n fml or pomp* a person who practises PUGILISM; BOXER[4] (1)

pug mill /ˈ· ·/ *n tech* a machine with turning knives inside it, for mixing PUG[2]

pug·na·cious /pʌgˈneɪʃəs/ *adj fml* fond of, and ready to start, quarrelling and fighting, esp. in a way that shows great strength of will: *pugnacious people/behaviour* —**~ly** *adv*

pug·nac·i·ty /pʌgˈnæsəti/ also **pug·na·cious·ness** /pʌgˈneɪʃəsnəs/— *n* [U] *fml* the quality of being PUGNACIOUS

pug nose /ˌ· ˈ·/ *n* a short, rather flat nose —**pug-nosed** /ˌ· ˈ·◂/ *adj*

pu·is·sance[1] /ˈpjuːəsəns, ˈpwɪsəns/ *n* [U] *poet or old use* power or strength, esp. of a king

puis·sance[2] /ˈpwiːsəns/ *n* a type of competition in which riders have to jump their horses over very high fences

pu·is·sant /ˈpjuːəsənt, ˈpwɪsənt/ *adj* [B] *poet or old use* powerful

puke[1] /pjuːk/ *v* [T1;I∅] *sl* to be sick; bring back (food or drink) from the stomach through the mouth; VOMIT

puke[2] *n* [U] *sl* food or drink that has been brought back from the stomach through the mouth; VOMIT

puk·ka /ˈpʌkə/ *adj Ind & PakE, apprec* **1** good; dependable; of high quality **2** real; true; GENUINE

pul·chri·tude /ˈpʌlkrətjuːd‖-tuːd/ *n* [U] *fml* beauty (esp. of a woman)

pul·chri·tu·di·nous /ˌpʌlkrəˈtjuːdənəs‖-ˈtuː-/ *adj fml* (esp. of a woman) beautiful

pule /pjuːl/ *v* [I∅] *lit* (esp. of a baby) to cry weakly or make weak troubled noises

pull[1] /pʊl/ *v* **1** [T1;I∅] to draw (something) along behind or after one while moving: *The horse was pulling a cart; it was pulling steadily* **2** [T1;I∅;(X7)] to move (someone or something) to another place by holding and drawing along, sometimes with force: *He pulled his chair up to the table.|The cupboard door is stuck and I can't pull it open* **3** [T1; I∅ (*at*)] to seize and draw (someone or part of someone's body, garment, etc.) roughly towards one, sometimes with the desire to hurt: *The child pulled* (*at*) *its mother's coat.|The child pulled its mother by the coat* **4** [X9, esp. ON, OFF] to draw (esp. a (part of a) garment) to a different position with the hands: *He pulled his sock carefully over his swollen ankle.|He pulled on his boots/pulled his boots on* **5** [I∅] (of an apparatus) to move when drawn or pressed towards one: *The handle pulls so easily that a child could open the door* **6** [T1] to draw or press (something) towards one in order to cause an apparatus to work: *Aim the gun carefully before you pull the* TRIGGER **7** [T1] to stretch, and sometimes damage, by using force: *He's pulled a muscle as a result of trying to lift the end of the piano* **8** [T1 (OUT, UP)] to draw out of the earth: *She went into the garden to pull a few onions for dinner* **9** [T1 (OUT, OFF, AWAY)] to remove by drawing out: *That tooth is decayed and should be pulled out* **10** [T1] to hold back (a horse in a race, or a blow being aimed in BOXING) with the intention of avoiding victory **11** [T1;I∅] (esp. in GOLF) to strike (the ball) to the left of the intended direction (or to the right if one is left-handed) —compare SLICE **12** [T1;I∅] (in ball games such as cricket and BASEBALL) to hit (the ball) forward and across the body from right to left (or from left to right) **13** [T1;I∅] to row: *"Pull boys! Pull for the shore."|Will you pull me over to the island?* **14** [I∅] (of a horse) to struggle, esp. as a habit, and press its mouth hard against the metal bar (BIT) that is fixed in its mouth to control it **15** [D1 (*for*);T1] to draw (a measure of beer) out of a barrel or other large container, by moving a handle towards oneself **16** [T1 (*on*)] to draw out (a small weapon) into the open ready for use: *He pulled a gun on me* (=took out a gun and aimed it at me) **17** [T1] *sl, esp. AmE* to do or succeed in doing (a crime, something daring, something annoying or deceiving, etc.): *They pulled a bank job* (=robbed a bank).|*What are you trying to pull?* (=What deceiving trick are you trying to play on me?) **18** [T1 (IN)] to win, gain, or get (the attention, support, trade, votes, etc., of people): *The football match pulled in great crowds.|He's not popular enough to pull many votes at the council election* **19** [L9] (of a tobacco pipe) to allow smoke to pass through when the breath is drawn in **20** [T1] *tech* to print (a PROOF[1] (5) copy) **21 pull a fast one (on someone)** *infml* to get the advantage (over someone) by a trick **22 pull (something or someone) to pieces** to say or show that (something or someone) is bad, unpleasant, or not of high quality by pointing out the weak points or faults **23 pull one's weight** to do one's full share of work —see also PULL ABOUT, PULL AHEAD, PULL AT, PULL AWAY, PULL AWAY FROM, PULL BACK, PULL DOWN, **pull a** FACE (12), **pull something out of the** FIRE (19), PULL IN, **pull someone's** LEG[1] (17), PULL OFF, PULL ON, PULL OUT, PULL OVER, **pull one's** PUNCHES (4), **pull** STRINGS (9), PULL THROUGH, PULL TOGETHER, PULL UP, **pull the** WOOL (6) **over someone's eyes,** and compare PUSH[1]

pull[2] *n* **1** [C] an act of pulling with force in order to move something **2** [S9;(S)] a difficult steep climb: *It's a long pull up this hill* **3** [S9] force or effort used in moving or drawing something towards one: *You must keep up a steady pull on the rope* **4** [U9] a natural force that influences or causes movement: *Describe the effect of the moon's pull on the sea* **5** [U;S9] *infml* special influence; (unfair) personal advantage: *The importance of his family's name* *gives him a certain pull in this town/lots of pull in this town* **6** [S] *infml* a (short) journey made by rowing a boat, usu. for pleasure **7** [C *usu. sing.*] (esp. in GOLF) a misdirecting of the ball slightly to the left (or right if struck by a left-handed person) —compare SLICE **8** [C] (in cricket) a stroke that PULLs[1] (12) the ball **9** [C (*at*)] an act of drawing in tobacco smoke from a pipe, cigarette, etc., through the lips **10** [C (*at*)] an act of taking a long drink, esp. from a bottle **11** [C] (*usu. in comb.*) any article (such as a rope, a handle, etc.) used for pulling something or causing something to act by pulling: *a bellpull* **12** [C] *tech* a test copy of something printed but not yet examined for correctness —compare PUSH[2]

pull a·bout *v adv* [T1] to handle (someone or something) roughly

pull a·head *v adv* [I∅ (*of*)] to get in front by moving faster: *The powerful car soon pulled ahead of the local bus*

pull at *v prep* [T1] **1** to seize and pull sharply and repeatedly: *She pulled at the thread till it came out of the piece of cloth* **2** to draw tobacco smoke through the mouth while holding (a pipe) between the lips **3** to take a long continuous drink of beer or other liquid from (a container)

pull a·way *v adv* [I∅ (*from*)] **1** to free oneself; escape: *She tried to pull away from the man who was holding her* **2** (esp. of a road vehicle) to start to move off: *He jumped onto the bus just as it was pulling away*

pull away from *v adv prep* [T1] to go faster than and leave further behind

pull·back /ˈpʊlbæk/ *n* [*usu. sing.*] (of an army) an act of leaving a position and going back instead of advancing

pull back *v adv* [I∅] **1** to change one's mind and fail to keep a promise **2** (of an army) to leave a position and go back instead of advancing **3** to spend less money

pull down *v adv* [T1] **1** [Wv5] to weaken (someone) in health **2** to break in pieces and destroy (something built): *Half the houses in the street are being pulled down to make room for the new post office* **3** *infml, esp. AmE* PULL IN (5)

pul·let /ˈpʊlɨ̣t/ *n* a young hen during its first year of laying eggs

pul·ley /ˈpʊli/ *n* an apparatus consisting of a wheel over which a rope or chain can be moved, used for lifting heavy things —see picture at TOOL[1]

pulley block /ˈ·· ·/ *n* the wooden or metal frame that contains the wheel of a PULLEY —see picture at TOOL[1]

pull-in /ˈ· ·/ also **pull-up**— *n BrE infml* a place by the roadside where vehicles may stop and where drinks and light meals may be obtained —compare LAY-BY

pull in *v adv* **1** [I∅] (of a train) to arrive at a station **2** [I∅] also **pull over**— (of a vehicle or boat) to move to one side (and stop) **3** [T1] to seize (a possible criminal): *The police pulled him in for questioning* —compare NAB (1), PINCH (8) **4** [T1] to cause (esp. an animal) to go more slowly or to stop **5** [T1] *AmE* also **pull down**— *infml* to earn (money): *He's pulling in quite a bit in his new job* (=earning quite a lot of money) **6** [T1] to cause (oneself or one's stomach) to appear less fat by drawing in the stomach muscles —see also **tighten one's** BELT[1] (6), **pull in one's** HORNS[1] (8)

Pull·man /ˈpʊlmən/ *n* **-s** *tdmk* **1** [C] also **Pullman car** /ˈ·· ·/, *AmE* also **parlor car**— a specially comfortable railway carriage (esp. of former times) with separate chairs for each person, in which one could be served with food and drink **2** [C; *by*+U] a train (esp. of former times) which has one or more special carriages of this type **3** [C] *BrE now rare or AmE* a specially comfortable railway sleeping carriage

pull off *v adv* **1** [T1] *infml* to succeed in (a difficult attempt): *The trick looked impossible, but she pulled it off* **2** [I∅] to drive a vehicle onto the side of the road —compare PULL IN (2), PULL OVER

pull-on /ˈ· ·/ *adj* [Wa5;A] (of a garment) that is pulled on and fits tightly, without any fastenings

pull on *v prep* [T1] to draw (one end of something long) continuously and with force: *The coat was too tight, and the buttons pulled on the threads that held them*

pull·out /ˈpʊlaʊt/ *n* a part of a book, magazine, etc. that is complete in itself and may be unfolded for use or taken out separately

pull out *v adv* **1** [I∅] (of a train) to leave a station **2** [T1;I∅ (*of*)] to (cause to) leave a place or time of trouble: *Jim saw that the firm was going to be ruined, so he pulled out* —see also **pull one's** FINGER (11) **out, pull out (all) the** STOPS[2] (10)

pull·o·ver /ˈpʊlˌəʊvəʳ/ *n* a woollen garment for the top half of the body, that has no fastenings and is pulled on over the head and drawn down over the body —compare SWEATER, JUMPER

pull o·ver *v adv* [T1b;I∅] **a** to direct or move (one's vehicle) over to one side of the road **b** (of a vehicle) to move over to one side of the road

pull·through /ˈpʊlθruː/ *n esp. BrE* a thick strong string with a piece of cloth tied at one end, used for cleaning the inside of the barrel of a gun

pull through *v adv* [T1b;I∅] **1** also **pull round**— to (cause to) live in spite of illness or wounds; regain health: *He's very ill, but with careful nursing he'll pull through* —see also BRING THROUGH **2** to (help to) succeed in spite of difficulties: *Margaret had difficulty with her work for the examinations, but her teacher pulled her through*

pull to·geth·er *v adv* **1** [I∅] (of a group of people) to work so as to help a common effort **2** [T1b *no pass.*] to control the feelings of (oneself): *Stop acting like a baby! Pull yourself together!* **3** [T1] to cause to improve through proper organization: *The directors called in an experienced man to pull the department together*

pul·lu·late /ˈpʌljʊleɪt‖-jə-/ *v* [I∅] *fml* to breed or multiply esp. quickly and in great numbers —**-lation** /ˌpʌljʊˈleɪʃən‖-jə-/ *n* [U]

pull-up /ˈ· ·/ *n* **1** an arm-strengthening exercise in which a person pulls himself up until his chin is level with the bar he is holding onto **2** PULL-IN

pull up *v adv* **1** [T1;I∅] to (cause to) come to a stop: *The car pulled up outside the station* **2** [I∅ (*to, with*)] to come level (with another competitor in a race) **3** [T1] to stop (someone who is making mistakes, doing something badly, etc.); scold (someone) for a wrong act

pul·mo·na·ry /ˈpʌlmənəri‖ˈpʊlməneri, ˈpʌl-/ *adj* [Wa5;A;(B)] *med* of, concerning, or having an effect on the lungs —see picture at RESPIRATORY

pulp¹ /pʌlp/ *n* **1** [U] a soft almost liquid mass of plant or animal material, such as the soft inside part of many fruits or vegetables: *A banana is mainly pulp, except for its skin* **2** [U;S] the state or condition of being soft and liquid: *You've boiled these vegetables too long; you've boiled them to a pulp* **3** [U] wood or other vegetable materials (such as cotton cloth) softened and broken up by chemicals or other means, and used for making paper **4** [A] *derog* (of (a type of) book, magazine, etc.) cheaply produced on rough paper and containing matter of bad quality, esp. shocking stories about cruelty, sex, etc.: *pulp literature* **5 beat someone to a pulp** to beat and hit someone with hard blows **6 reduce someone to a pulp** to make someone completely helpless and unable to move, as a result of a shock to the feelings —**~y** *adj* [Wa1]

pulp[2] *v* [T1;IØ] to (cause to) become PULP[1] (2,3)

pul·pit /ˈpʊlpɪt/ *n* **1** [C] a small raised enclosure of wood or stone in a church, reached by a few steps, from which the priest addresses the worshippers at a service —see picture at CHURCH[1] **2** [*the*+R] *fml* **a** the teaching of religion, esp. by making speeches (SERMONs) in church about religious matters, as a work to which one gives oneself **b** Christian priests in general, as religious teachers in church

pul·sar /ˈpʌlsɑːʳ/ *n* a type of star that often cannot be seen, but is known to exist because of the regular radio signals that it gives out

pul·sate /pʌlˈseɪt‖ˈpʌlseɪt/ *v* [Wv4;IØ (*with*)] **1** to shake very regularly: *The air seemed to pulsate with the bright light.*|(fig.) *the pulsating beat of* LATIN AMERICAN *dance music* **2** to experience a strong excited sensation: *a pulsating finish to the cricket match* (=a very exciting finish) **3** PULSE[3] (1)

pul·sa·tion /pʌlˈseɪʃən/ *n* **1** [C] *esp. tech* a beat of the heart or any regular beat that can be measured **2** [U] the action of pulsating (PULSATE); pulsating movement

pulse[1] /pʌls/ *n* **1** [*usu. sing.*] the regular beating of blood in the main blood vessels carrying blood from the heart, esp. as felt by a doctor at the wrist: *His pulses raced* (=his heart beat very quickly).| *The doctor measured the woman's pulse rate* **2** a strong regular beat as in music, on a drum, etc. **3** a short sound as sent by radio or a small change in the quantity of electricity going through something **4 feel/take someone's pulse a** to measure or test someone's heartbeat by putting a finger on the blood vessel just above the wrist and counting the number of beats per minute **b** to try to find out the (political) opinions, intentions, etc., of someone or of a group at a certain moment **5 stir someone's pulses** to excite someone greatly; cause strong eager feelings

pulse[2] *n* **1** [U;(P)] the seeds of such plants as beans, PEAs, LENTILs, etc., used as food **2** [C *usu. pl.*] any of the plants from which these are obtained

pulse[3] *v* [IØ] **1** [(*through, with*)] to beat steadily as the heart does; move or flow with a steady and rather rapid beat and sound: *He could feel the blood pulsing through his body as he waited for the next explosion.*|*One could feel the excitement pulsing through the crowd.*|*pulsing with excitement* **2** (of a machine) to send out signals in regular PULSEs[1] (3)

pul·ver·ize, -ise /ˈpʌlvəraɪz/ *v* **1** [T1;IØ] to (cause to) become a fine powder or dust by crushing **2** [T1] *infml* **a** to defeat thoroughly in argument **b** to hit or beat severely —**-ization** /ˌpʌlvəraɪˈzeɪʃən‖-rə-/ *n* [U]

pu·ma /ˈpjuːmə/ *n* [Wn1] COUGAR

pum·ice /ˈpʌmɪ̣s/ also **pumice stone** /ˈ·· ·/— *n* [U] a type of very light, silver-grey rock, used in pieces or in powder form for cleaning and for rubbing surfaces smooth

pum·mel /ˈpʌməl/ also (*esp. AmE*) **pommel**— *v* **-ll-** (*AmE* **-l-**) [T1] to hit repeatedly, esp. with the closed hand

pump[1] /pʌmp/ *n* **1** [C] (*often in comb.*) a machine, usu. with a tube and a handle, for forcing liquids, air, or gas into or out of something: *At the farm there was an old-fashioned pump for drawing water from a well.*|*The heart is a kind of natural pump that moves the blood around the body.*|*a petrol pump*|*a stomach pump* —see picture at BICYCLE[1] **2** [S] an act of PUMPing[2] **3 All hands to the pump**(s)! everyone must help to get us out of this difficulty! **4 give someone's hand a pump** to shake someone's hand with force, moving it up and down —see also PRIME[3] (6) **the pump**

pump[2] *v* **1** [X9;(T1)] to move (liquids, air, or gas) by using a PUMP[1] (1): *If someone swallows poison, a doctor can sometimes pump it out of the stomach* **2** [X7,9] to empty or fill (something) with a liquid or gas by means of a PUMP[1] (1): *He pumped up his car tyres.*|*They had pumped the well dry, and could get no more water.*|(fig.) *He pumped his enemy full of lead* (=shot him many times) **3** [IØ (AWAY)] to work a PUMP[1] **4** [IØ (AWAY)] to work like a PUMP[1] (1): *His heart was pumping fast* **5** [L9] (of a liquid) to come out in short sudden flows as from a PUMP[1] (1) **6** [T1] to move (something) up and down like the handle of a PUMP[1] (1): *He took his friend's hand and pumped it up and down, saying how glad he was to see him* **7** [T1+*into* or *out of*] *infml* to force (something) steadily into or out of (someone): *Perhaps the new teacher can pump a few ideas into that lazy boy's head* **8** [T1] *infml* to ask (someone) questions in the hope of finding out something that one wants to know

pump[3] *n* [*usu. pl.*] **1** a type of light shoe used for dancing **2** *AmE* a type of woman's formal shoe with no fastener

pum·per·nick·el /ˈpʌmpənɪkəl‖ˈpʌmpər-/ *n* [U] a type of heavy dark brown bread, usu. cut into thin pieces before being sold

pump·kin /ˈpʌmpkɪ̣n/ *n* **1** [C;U] a type of very large dark yellow roundish fruit that grows on the ground **2** [C] the plant that produces this —see picture at VEGETABLE[1]

pump room /ˈ· ·/ *n* a room in a building connected with a natural spring of medicinal waters, where these waters are drunk by people as a cure for some illnesses: *The Pump Room in Bath is described in Jane Austen's stories*

pun[1] /pʌn/ also **play on words**— *n* an amusing use of a word or phrase that has 2 meanings, or of words having the same sound but different meanings: *He made the following pun: "7 days without water make one weak"* (=week)

pun[2] *v* **-nn-** [IØ (*on, upon*)] to make one or more PUNs[1]: *He punned on the likeness of "weak" and "week"*

punch[1] /pʌntʃ/ *v* **1** [T1;(IØ)] to strike (someone or something) hard with the closed hand (FIST): *He punched the man in the chest.*|*He punched him on the jaw.*|*The older boy was punching the smaller boy about* **2** [T1 (*in*)] to make (a hole) in (something) using a PUNCH[3] (1): *Did he punch your ticket?*|*Did he punch a hole in your ticket?* **3** [T1+IN or OUT] to drive (something) in or out using a PUNCH[3] (2): *All the nails have been punched in, so that the surface is quite smooth* **4** [IØ+IN or OUT] *esp. AmE* CLOCK IN or CLOCK OUT: *What time do you punch in in the morning?* —**~er** *n*

punch[2] *n* **1** [C (*in, on*)] a quick strong blow made with the closed hand (FIST): *I'd like to give that fellow a punch in the face.*|*Both fighters have strong punches: they both* **pack** (9) *quite* **a punch** (=they can both hit hard) **2** [U] *apprec* forcefulness; effective power: *That statement lacks punch; you should rewrite it to give it more punch* **3 beat someone to the punch a** (esp. in BOXING) to hit an opponent before he can hit you **b** to take action, speak, etc., before someone else can do so **4 pull one's punches** (*usu. neg.*) to blame, scold, or express an unfavourable opinion of someone or something less strongly than is deserved **5 roll with the punch** *not fml* to move back or sideways so as to soften the effect of a blow

punch[3] *n* **1** a steel tool for cutting holes in, or pressing a pattern onto, paper, leather, metal, etc.: *a ticket punch* **2** a tool for hammering the heads of nails below a surface **3** a tool for driving a BOLT[1] (1) out of a hole

punch[4] *n* [U] (*often in comb.*) a hot or cold drink made from fruit juice, sugar, water, and strong-tasting substances (SPICE*s*), usu. with wine or other drink containing alcohol added: *fruit punch*

Punch *n* [R] **1** the main male character (with a round unnaturally curved back and a long nose) in a PUNCH-AND-JUDY SHOW **2 as pleased/proud as Punch** very pleased/proud

Punch-and-Judy show /ˌpʌntʃ ən 'dʒuːdi ʃəʊ/ *n* a show for children in which the small character (PUPPET) PUNCH fights humorously with his wife Judy, usu. performed at the seaside

punch ball /'· ·/ also **punching ball**, *AmE* **punching bag** /'·· ·/— *n* a large leather ball, fixed on a spring or hung from a rope, which is PUNCHed[1] (1) for exercise or practice

punch bowl /'· ·/ *n* a large bowl in which PUNCH[4] is mixed and served

punch-drunk /'· ·/ *adj* **1** (of a person who fights as a sport (a BOXER)) showing unsteadiness, inability to think clearly, and other signs of brain damage from repeated blows on the head **2** *infml* confused, esp. because of continual misfortune or bad treatment

punched card /ˌ· '·/ also **punch card** /'· ·/— *n* a card with holes made in it in particular positions, each of which carries a particular piece of information to the electric calculator (COMPUTER) into which the card is put

punch line /'· ·/ *n* [*usu. sing.*] the last few words of a joke or story, that give meaning to the whole and cause amusement or surprise

punch-up /'· ·/ *n BrE infml* a fight

punch·y /'pʌntʃi/ *adj* [Wa1] *sl* PUNCH-DRUNK —**punchiness** *n* [U]

punc·til·i·o /pʌŋk'tɪliəʊ/ *n* **-lios** *fml* **1** [U] careful attention paid to every small exact detail of ceremonial behaviour, performance of duties, etc., however unimportant such attention may be **2** [C] an example of this

punc·til·i·ous /pʌŋk'tɪliəs/ *adj fml, usu. apprec* very exact and particular about details of behaviour or duty —**~ly** *adv* —**~ness** *n* [U]

punc·tu·al /'pʌŋktʃʊəl/ *adj* not late; arriving, happening, doing something, etc., at the exact or agreed time; PROMPT: *She's never punctual in answering letters; she's always late.|The cat makes a punctual appearance at mealtimes* —**~ity** /ˌpʌŋktʃʊ'ælɪ̌ti/ *n* [U] —**~ly** /'pʌŋktʃʊəli/ *adv*

punc·tu·ate /'pʌŋktʃʊeɪt/ *v* [T1] **1** to make or divide (written matter) into sentences, phrases, etc., by means of PUNCTUATION MARK*s* **2** [*usu. pass.*] to break repeatedly into (something that continues): *The football game was punctuated by the cheers of each team's supporters*

punctuate with *v prep* [D1] to interrupt (one's own speech) with (actions): *He punctuated his solemn remarks with a few well-chosen jokes*

punc·tu·a·tion /ˌpʌŋktʃʊ'eɪʃən/ *n* [U] **1** the art, practice, or system of punctuating (PUNCTUATE (1)) a piece of writing **2** the marks used in doing this: *If you produce a piece of writing without any punctuation, it's very difficult to understand*

punctuation mark /ˌ··'·· ·/ *n* any sign used in punctuating (PUNCTUATE (1)), such as a COMMA (,), a FULL STOP (.), a QUESTION MARK (?), a SEMICOLON (;), a HYPHEN (-), etc.

punc·ture[1] /'pʌŋktʃəʳ/ *n* a small hole made with a sharp point through a soft surface, esp. one made accidentally in a tyre

puncture[2] *v* **1** [Wv5;T1;I∅] to (cause to) burst or lose air as a result of a PUNCTURE[1]: *A nail on the road punctured the tyre.|The child's rubber ball punctured when it fell on a prickly bush* **2** [Wv5;T1] to make a small hole in (something) with a sharp point: *The person hurt in the car crash is suffering from a punctured lung* **3** [T1] to destroy suddenly: *His unexpected failure punctured his self-importance*

pun·dit /'pʌndɪ̌t/ *n often humor* **1** [C9] a person who knows a great deal about a particular subject and whose advice on it may be taken by others: *political pundits* **2** [C] a man of wisdom and knowledge

pun·gent /'pʌndʒənt/ *adj* **1** having a strong, sharp, stinging taste or smell, that may or may not seem unpleasant **2** (of speech or writing) producing a sharp direct effect that attracts interest or expresses an unfavourable opinion: *pungent remarks about my lateness* —**~ly** *adv* —**-gency** /pʌndʒənsi/ *n* [U]

Pu·nic /'pjuːnɪk/ *adj* [Wa5;A;(B)] of the ancient city of Carthage (in North Africa) or its people

pun·ish /'pʌnɪʃ/ *v* [T1] **1** [(*for*) *often pass.*] to cause (someone) to suffer for (a misdeed, fault, or crime): *Motorists should be punished severely for dangerous driving.|Dangerous driving should be severely punished* **2** to deal roughly with (an opponent), esp. by taking advantage of a weakness; damage with hard blows: *Our captain really punished the other side's* BOWLER*s* (=made a lot of runs very quickly)

pun·ish·a·ble /'pʌnɪʃəbəl/ *adj* [(*by, for*)] that may be punished by law: *Murder is punishable by death in some countries*

pun·ish·ing[1] /'pʌnɪʃɪŋ/ *adj infml* **1** that makes one thoroughly tired and weak: *It's a long and punishing climb up the mountain side* **2** (esp. in sports) hard-hitting: *a punishing* BATSMAN —**~ly** *adv*

punishing[2] *n* [S] *infml* a rough defeat; damage, esp. from blows: *Our team gave the opposing team a punishing.|"Your car seems to have taken a punishing." "Yes, I drove it into a wall by accident"*

pun·ish·ment /'pʌnɪʃmənt/ *n* **1** [U] the act of punishing or condition of being punished: *The boy bore his punishment without complaining* **2** [C] a way in which a person is punished: *A just judge will try to make the punishment fit the crime* **3** [U] *infml* rough treatment; damage: *The furniture in the house with 5 active children had taken a lot of punishment*

pu·ni·tive /'pjuːnɪ̌tɪv/ *adj* **1** intended as punishment **2** very severe; causing or intended to cause hardship: *punitive taxes* —compare PUTATIVE —**~ly** *adv*

punitive ex·pe·di·tion /'··· ··ˌ··/ *n* a sending of armed forces to punish groups who are acting against law and order in distant parts of a country

Pun·ja·bi /pʌn'dʒɑːbi/ *adj* [Wa5] of the Punjab, an area in northwestern India and Bangladesh

punk[1] /pʌŋk/ *n derog sl* **1** [C; *you*+N] *AmE* a rough and unpleasant young man or boy, esp. one in the habit of fighting and breaking the law (often in the phr. **young punk**) **2** [U] *rare* something worthless

punk[2] *adj* [Wa5,(1)] **1** [A] *AmE sl* worthless: *played a punk game* **2** [B] *AmE sl* being in poor health: *said that she was feeling punk* **3** [A] (in Britain in the 1970s) of a movement among certain young people who are opposed to the values of money-based society and who express this esp. in loud lively music (**punk rock**) that is often marked by violence, rude words, etc.

punk[3] *n* [U] *AmE* decayed wood (esp. in a soft mass) dry enough to be useful for starting fires

pun·kah /'pʌŋkə/ *n Ind & PakE* a type of FAN in the form of a long wooden bar with a cloth stretched across it, hung from the top of a room and moved by means of a rope pulled by a man (**punkah wallah**) employed to do so, used (esp. formerly) in hot countries to move and cool the air in a room

pun·net /ˈpʌnɨt/ *n esp. BrE* a small light square boxlike usu. wooden basket, used esp. for putting small soft fruits in when selling them

pun·ster /ˈpʌnstəʳ/ *n* a person who habitually makes PUNs

punt[1] /pʌnt/ *n* [C; *by*+U] a type of long narrow flat-bottomed river boat with square ends, moved by someone standing on it and pushing a long pole against the bottom of the river —see picture at BOAT[1]

punt[2] *v* **1** [I∅] to go for a (short) river journey by PUNT[1] **2** [T1] to move (a boat, esp. a PUNT[1]) by pushing a long pole against the bottom of the river **3** [X9] to carry (someone or something) in a PUNT[1] —**~er** *n*

punt[3] *v* [I∅] *BrE infml* to risk money (BET) on the result of a horse race —**~er** *n*

punt[4] *v* [T1;I∅] (esp. in RUGBY and AMERICAN FOOTBALL) to kick (a football) that has been dropped from the hands and has not yet hit the ground

punt[5] *n* (esp. in RUGBY and AMERICAN FOOTBALL) a kick made by PUNTing[4] —compare DROPKICK, PLACEKICK

pu·ny /ˈpjuːni/ *adj* [Wa1] *sometimes derog* small and weak; poorly developed: *puny little arms and legs|Puny man looks out at the universe* —**-nily** *adv* —**-niness** *n* [U]

pup[1] /pʌp/ *n* **1** a young SEAL[1] (1) or OTTER **2** PUPPY **3 in pup** (of a female dog) having young growing inside the body **4 sell someone a pup** *infml* to trick someone into buying something that is later found to be worthless

pup[2] *v* **-pp-** [I∅] (of a female dog) to give birth to young

pu·pa /ˈpjuːpə/ *n* **-pas** *or* **-pae** /piː/ (the state or form of) an insect in the middle stage of its development to a full-grown form, contained in and protected by a hard or soft covering —see picture at INSECT —**~l** *adj* [Wa5]: *in the pupal stage*

pu·pate /pjuːˈpeɪt‖ˈpjuːpeɪt/ *v* [I∅] *tech* (of a young insect) to become or be a PUPA —**-pation** /pjuːˈpeɪʃən/ *n* [U]

pu·pil[1] /ˈpjuːpəl/ *n* a person, esp. a child, who is being taught: *The school is large enough for about 500 pupils.|Miss Smith takes private pupils in singing and piano-playing* —see STUDENT (USAGE)

pupil[2] *n* the small black round opening in the middle of the coloured part of the eye, through which light passes and which can grow larger or smaller —see picture at EYE[1]

pup·pet /ˈpʌpɨt/ *n* **1** [C] a toylike jointed wooden or cloth figure of a person or animal, that is made to move by someone pulling wires or strings that are fixed to it —see also MARIONETTE and picture at THEATRE **2** [C] also **glove puppet**— a toylike cloth figure of a person or animal with a hollow inside into which the hand is put to move the figure **3** [C9] *often derog* a person or group that is controlled and directed by the will of someone else: *Are men the puppets of fate?* **4** [A] *derog* trying to give the appearance of acting independently, but really controlled and directed by the will of someone else: *a puppet government*

pup·pe·teer /ˌpʌpɨˈtɪəʳ/ *n* a person who performs with PUPPETs (1,(2))

pup·py /ˈpʌpi/ also **pup**— *n* **1** [C] a young dog: *Our dog Angus is over a year old: we can't really call him a puppy any more* **2** [C; *you*+N] *derog, becoming rare* a foolish self-important young man

puppy fat /ˈ·· ·/ *n* [U] *infml, often euph* fatness in boys and girls that usually disappears as they grow older

puppy love /ˈ·· ·/ also **calf love**— *n* [U] *sometimes derog* a young boy's or girl's feeling of love for a (usu. older) member of the opposite sex, which does not last for a very long time or lead to sexual relations

pur·blind /ˈpɜːblaɪnd‖ˈpɜr-/ *adj fml or lit* **1** dull; unable to understand things that are clear to most people **2** having very little power of sight; nearly blind

pur·chase[1] /ˈpɜːtʃɨs‖ˈpɜr-/ *v* **1** [T1;(D1 (*for*))] *fml or tech* to buy: *They've just purchased a new house in the country* **2** [T1 *often pass.*] *fml* to gain (something) at the cost of effort, suffering, or loss of something of value —**-chasable** *adj*

purchase[2] *n* **1** [U9] buying: *He gave his son some money for the purchase of his school books* **2** [C *often pl.*] **a** an act of buying: *She made several purchases in the dress shop* **b** an article that has just been bought: *The children helped to carry their mother's purchases from the shops* **3** [S;U] a firm hold for pulling, raising, or stopping something from slipping: *The climber tried to gain a purchase with his foot on a narrow edge of rock* **4** [U] *law* value of something (esp. land) calculated according to how much the yearly rent or income from it is **5 not worth a day's/an hour's purchase** (of a person's life) that has no hope of lasting

pur·chas·er /ˈpɜːtʃəsəʳ‖ˈpɜr-/ *n esp. tech* a person who buys goods from another

purchase tax /ˈ·· ·/ *n* [U] (in Britain until 1973) a tax on certain kinds of goods when sold in the shops (after 1973 changed to VALUE-ADDED TAX) —compare SALES TAX

pur·chas·ing pow·er /ˈ··· ˌ··/ *n* [U (*of*)] the value in goods that a particular standard amount of money can buy at a certain time

pur·dah /ˈpɜːdə, -dɑː‖ˈpɜr-/ *n* [U] *Ind & PakE* (esp. among Muslims) (the system of keeping women of rank in) a state of being kept out of public view

pure /pjʊəʳ/ *adj* **1** [Wa1;B] unmixed with any other substance: *pure silver|Is this garment made of pure wool, or of wool mixed with nylon?* **2** [Wa1;B] clean; free from dirt, dust, bacteria, or any harmful matter: *The air by the sea is pure and healthy.|pure drinking water* **3** [Wa1;B] of unmixed race: *a pure Arab horse|There's very little pure blood in any nation now* **4** [Wa1:B] free from evil; without sexual thoughts or experience: *She was still a pure young girl, pure in thought and deed* **5** [Wa1;B] (of colour or sound) clear; unmixed with other colours or sounds: *It was a sunny day with a cloudless sky of the purest blue* **6** [Wa1;B] (of a musical note) of exactly the correct highness or lowness: *The voices of the young boys singing in church were high and pure* **7** [Wa5;A] *infml* complete; thorough; only: *By pure chance he found the rare book he needed in a little shop* **8** [Wa5;A] (of an art or branch of study) considered only for its own nature as a skill or exercise of the mind, separate from any use that might be made of it: *pure science* —compare APPLIED **9** [Wa1;B] *fml* (of a thing) clean according to the rules of religious ceremony **10 pure and simple** *infml* thorough; and nothing else: *carelessness pure and simple*

pure·blood·ed /ˌpjʊəˈblʌdɨd◂‖ˌpjʊər-/ also **pure·blood** /ˈpjʊəblʌd‖ˈpjʊər-/— *adj* descending from one race with no mixture of other races —compare PUREBRED, THOROUGHBRED

pure·bred /ˈpjʊəbred‖ˈpjʊər-/ *n, adj becoming rare* (an animal) descended from one breed or kind with no mixture of other breeds —compare THOROUGHBRED

pu·ree[1] /ˈpjʊəreɪ‖pjʊˈreɪ/ *n* [U;C] (*often in comb.*) **1** soft food boiled to a soft half-liquid mass and rubbed through a fine wire frame: *an apple puree* **2** a thick vegetable soup made from this

puree² *v* [Wv5;T1] to make (food) into a PUREE¹

pure·ly /ˈpjʊəli‖ˈpjʊərli/ *adv* completely; wholly; only: *I don't want any reward for my help; I gave it purely (and simply) out of friendship*

pure·ness /ˈpjʊənəs‖ˈpjʊər-/ *n* [U] *rare* PURITY

pur·ga·tion /pɜːˈgeɪʃən‖pɜr-/ *n* [U] *fml* **1** the act or result of being made pure and free from evil **2** the act of purging (PURGE¹ (2)) the bowels

pur·ga·tive /ˈpɜːgətɪv‖ˈpɜr-/ *n, adj* (a medicine) that causes the bowels to empty: *The sick child needs a purgative.|This fruit often has a purgative effect*

pur·ga·to·ry /ˈpɜːgətəri‖ˈpɜrgətori/ *n* **1** [U] (*often cap.*) (esp. according to the ROMAN CATHOLIC church) a state or place in which the soul of a dead person must remain and be made pure by suffering for wrong-doing on earth, until it is fit to enter Heaven **2** [U;C] *often humor* a place, state, or time of suffering which is great but does not go on for ever: *Angela has a very thin sharp voice; it's purgatory to have to listen to her sing* —**-rial** /ˌpɜːgəˈtɔːriəl‖ˌpɜrgəˈto-/ *adj*

purge¹ /pɜːdʒ‖pɜrdʒ/ *v* **1** [D1+*from/of*;T1:(AWAY)] to make (someone, someone's soul, something, etc.) clean and free from (something evil or impure): *Try to purge your spirit (of hatred).|Try to purge (away) the hatred from your spirit, my son.|The people wished to purge their* SINs.|*The iron in the chemical compound must be purged* **2** [D1+*from/of*; T1] to clear (waste matter) from (the bowels) by means of medicine **3** [D1+*from/of*;T1] to get rid of (an unwanted person) in (a state, political party, group, etc.) by removal, often unjustly, from office, driving out of the country, killing, etc. **4** [T1] *law* to pay for (an act of wrong-doing) by suffering or punishment: *to purge one's crimes in prison*

purge² *n* **1** a medicine that quickly clears the bowels of waste matter **2** an act or set of actions intended to get rid of unwanted or undesirable members of a (political) group, suddenly, often unjustly, and often by force: *When the new president was appointed he at once carried out a purge of disloyal army officers*

pu·ri·fi·ca·tion /ˌpjʊərəfəˈkeɪʃən/ *n* [U (*of*)] the act of PURIFYing

pu·ri·fy /ˈpjʊərəfaɪ/ *v* [T1 (*of*)] to make PURE (esp. 2,4,9): *This salt has been specially purified for use in medicine.|This music seems to purify one's spirit of evil thoughts*

pur·ist /ˈpjʊərəst/ *n* a person who is always (too) careful to practise and preserve the correct, customary, or best way of doing something, esp. in matters of grammar, use of words, etc. —**-ism** *n* [U]

pu·ri·tan /ˈpjʊərətn/ *adj,n usu. derog* (of, like, or being) a person who has rather hard fixed standards of behaviour and self-control, and thinks any kind of pleasure is unnecessary or wrong: *Some people have a puritan belief that all sexual pleasure is wicked.|He's too much of a puritan to enjoy dancing or drinking alcohol* —**~ism** /ˈpjʊərətənɪzəm/ *n* [U]

Puritan *n, adj* [Wa5] (in England and New England in the 16th and 17th centuries) (a member) of a religious group that wished to make religion simpler and opposed the use of ceremony in church services —**~ism** *n* [U]

pu·ri·tan·i·cal /ˌpjʊərəˈtænɪkəl/ *adj derog* like a PURITAN: *a puritanical father who wouldn't allow his children to play games on a Sunday (God's day)* —**-cally** *adv* [Wa4]

pu·ri·ty /ˈpjʊərəti/ also **pureness**— *n* [U] the quality or state of being pure

purl¹ /pɜːl‖pɜrl/ *n, adj* [Wa5;B;U] *tech* the second of the 2 main stitches in KNITting in which the needle is put into the back of a stitch and the new stitch made there, leaving a raised pattern on the back: *a purl stitch|3* PLAIN³, *2 purl* —compare KNIT, PLAIN³

purl² *v tech* [T1;L9] (*often used in giving instructions*) to use PURL¹ as the stitch in KNITting (for a time): KNIT *one, purl one.|Purl (for) 3 rows* —see also KNIT, PLAIN³

purl³ *n* [(*the*) S] *lit* the sound of a stream PURLing⁴

purl⁴ *v* [Wv4;IØ] *lit* (of a small stream) to flow making a low gentle continuous noise

purl·er /ˈpɜːləʳ‖ˈpɜr-/ *n BrE infml* **1** [S] a heavy fall, usu. head first (esp. in the phr. **come a purler**) **2** [C] a heavy blow that knocks someone down

pur·lieus /ˈpɜːljuːz‖ˈpɜrluːz/ *n* [(*the*) P (*of*)] **1** *lit or pomp* the area in and around; neighbourhood (of a place) **2** *becoming rare* the parts (of a place) which lie near the edge or borders

pur·loin /pɜːˈlɔɪn, ˈpɜːlɔɪn‖-ɜr-/ *v* [T1] *fml* to steal (esp. something of small value): *"The Purloined Letter"* (story by E. A. Poe)

pur·ple¹ /ˈpɜːpəl‖ˈpɜr-/ *adj* [Wa1] of the colour purple —compare VIOLET

purple² *n* **1** [U] a dark colour made of a mixture of red and blue —compare VIOLET **2** [*the*+U] (in former times) dark red or purple garments as worn only by people of very high rank **3 born in the purple** *fml or lit* born of a kingly or princely family **4 raise someone to the purple** *fml* to make someone a CARDINAL in the ROMAN CATHOLIC church

purple heart /ˌ·· ˈ·/ *n BrE infml* a small heart-shaped ball (PILL) made of a type of mind-exciting drug

Purple Heart *n* a coinlike piece of metal (MEDAL) given as an honour to be worn by soldiers of the US wounded in battle

purple pas·sage /ˌ·· ˈ··/ also **purple patch** /ˌ·· ˈ·/— *n* (esp. in writing) a splendid, showy, or (too) high-sounding part in the middle of something plain or dull

pur·plish /ˈpɜːplɪʃ‖ˈpɜr-/ *adj* slightly purple

pur·port¹ /ˈpɜːpɔːt, -pət‖ˈpɜrport/ *n* [U9, esp. *of*] *fml* the general meaning or intention (of someone's words or actions): *I couldn't hear all that was said, but the purport of the message seemed to be this: . . .*

pur·port² /pɜːˈpɔːt‖pɜrˈport/ *v* [T3] to claim (doubtfully); have an (intended) appearance of being: *The orders, which purported to be signed by the general, were a trick of the enemy.|His plans are not what they purport to be*

pur·pose¹ /ˈpɜːpəs‖ˈpɜr-/ *n* **1** [C] an intention or plan; reason for an action: *Did you come to London for the purpose of seeing your family, or for business purposes?* **2** [C] use; effect; result: *Don't waste your money; put it to some good purpose* **3** [U] steady determined following of an aim; willpower **4 answer/fulfil/serve one's purpose(s)/the purpose** to be or do all that is needed: *I haven't got a pen here, but a pencil will answer the same purpose* **5 of set purpose** *fml, esp. BrE* with planned intention; for some special reason **6 on purpose a** intentionally; not by accident: *"I'm sorry I stepped on your toe; it was an accident." "It wasn't! You did it on purpose"* **b** with a particular stated intention: *I came here on purpose to see you* **7 to little/no/some/good purpose** with little/no/some/good result or effect **8 to the purpose** useful; connected with what is being considered or what is needed

purpose² *v* [T1,3,4,5] *fml* to have (something) as one's aim or intention: *He purposes to visit South America; later he purposes writing a book on his travels*

purpose-built /ˌ·· ˈ·◂/ *adj* [Wa5] *esp. BrE* specially made for a particular purpose: *We live in a* *purpose-built flat, not just a few rooms in a big old house*

pur·pose·ful /ˈpɜːpəsfəl‖ˈpɜr-/ *adj* **1** full of or expressing will **2** directed towards a (special) purpose —**~ly** *adv*

pur·pose·less /ˈpɜːpəsləs‖ˈpɜr-/ *adj* aimless; meaningless —**~ly** *adv* —**~ness** *n* [U]

pur·pose·ly /ˈpɜːpəsli‖ˈpɜr-/ *adv* **1** intentionally; not accidentally: *He said it was an accident, but we all know he did it purposely* **2** with a particular stated intention: *I purposely didn't come yesterday, as I knew you'd be out*

pur·po·sive /ˈpɜːpəsɪv‖ˈpɜr-/ *adj fml* PURPOSEFUL

purr[1] /pɜːʳ/ *n* **1** [C] a low continuous sound produced in the throat by a pleased cat **2** [S] a sound like this, made by a powerful machine that is working smoothly

purr[2] *v* **1** [I∅] to make the sound of a PURR[1]: *If you rub a cat under the chin, it will purr.|The big car purred along the road* **2** [I∅] (of a person) to show or express contentment in a pleasant low voice **3** [T1,5] (esp. of a woman) to express (a pleasant feeling or wish) in this way: *"Come again, won't you?" she purred*

purse[1] /pɜːs‖pɜrs/ *n* **1** [C] a small flattish leather or plastic bag used, esp. by women, for carrying money: *She carried her purse in her handbag* **2** [S] money supplies; money to spend: *That beautiful picture is beyond my purse; it's not within my purse* (=I can't afford it) **3** [C] an amount of money collected for some good purpose or offered as a gift or as a prize to a winner: *The* GOLF*er was unwilling to play for a purse of less than $10,000* **4** [C] *AmE* a woman's HANDBAG, esp. one without a shoulder STRAP; POCKETBOOK (3): *fits easily into pocket or purse* —see also PRIVY PURSE, PUBLIC PURSE

purse[2] *v* [T1] to draw (esp. the lips) together in little folds: *She pursed her lips to show her dislike*

purs·er /ˈpɜːsəʳ‖ˈpɜr-/ *n* [C;N] an officer on a passenger or trade ship who keeps the ship's accounts and is also in charge of the travellers' rooms, comfort, etc.

purse-snatch·er /ˈ· ˌ··/ *n AmE* a criminal who seizes a woman's HANDBAG while she is walking along, and tries to run off with it

purse strings /ˈ· ·/ *n* **1 hold the purse strings** to control the spending of the money of a family, a firm, etc. **2 loosen/tighten one's purse strings** be ready to spend more/less money; be more/less generous in spending

pur·su·ance /pəˈsjuːəns‖pərˈsuː-/ *n* **in (the) pursuance of** *fml* in the performing of, or continuing with: *He was wounded in the pursuance of his duty*

pur·su·ant to /pəˈsjuːənt tʊ, -tə‖pərˈsuː-/ *prep fml or pomp* in accordance with; following: *Pursuant to your instructions, I have placed an order for 10 cases of wine*

pur·sue /pəˈsjuː‖pərˈsuː/ *v* [T1] **1** to chase in order to catch, kill, or defeat: *The police are pursuing an escaped prisoner* **2** to follow closely; show continual attention to: *Wherever the travellers went in the Eastern city, they were pursued by beggars* **3** (of something harmful) to follow and cause suffering to: *Bad luck pursued us all through the year* **4** to make continual efforts to gain (something): *The poet has pursued fame all his life, but has never experienced it* **5** to continue (steadily) with; be busy with: *He is pursuing his studies at the university.|He could see he was losing the argument, so he said, "I'd rather not pursue the matter"* **6** *fml or lit* to follow or continue along (a way, path, etc.)

pur·su·er /pəˈsjuːəʳ‖pərˈsuːər/ *n* [C9;(C)] a person or animal that PURSUEs (1): *The deer ran faster than its pursuers*

pur·suit /pəˈsjuːt‖pərˈsuːt/ *n* **1** [U] the act of pursuing (PURSUE) someone or something (esp. in the phr. **in pursuit of**): *The police car raced through the streets in pursuit of another car* **2** [C] any activity to which one gives one's time, whether as work or for pleasure: *One of the boy's favourite pursuits is stamp collecting* **3** [A] used for chasing and attacking the enemy: *a pursuit plane* **4 in hot pursuit (of)** following after very quickly, closely, and eagerly

pu·ru·lent /ˈpjʊərələnt/ *adj med* forming, full of, or containing poisonous yellow matter (PUS) —compare PRURIENT —**-lence** *n* [U] —**-lently** *adv*

pur·vey /pɜːˈveɪ‖pɜr-/ *v* [T1 (*to*)] *fml or tech* to supply (food or other needed goods), esp. in large quantities

pur·vey·ance /pɜːˈveɪəns‖pɜr-/ *n* [U (*of*)] *fml or tech* the act or action of PURVEYing food

purvey for *v prep* [T1 *no pass.*] *old use* to supply food in large quantities to (a group) as a trade activity

pur·vey·or /pɜːˈveɪəʳ‖pɜr-/ *n* [C9, esp. *of* and/or *to*] *fml or tech* a seller or firm that supplies food to a large group: *purveyor to the Army*|(fig.) *He's well known as a purveyor of lies.|by appointment, purveyor of wine to Queen Elizabeth*

pur·view /ˈpɜːvjuː‖ˈpɜr-/ *n* [U9, esp. *of*] *fml or lit* the limits within which anything is effective or has power; limit of concern, activity, or interest (esp. in the phrs. **outside/within the purview of**)

pus /pʌs/ *n* [U] a thick yellowish-white liquid produced in an infected wound or poisoned part of the body

push[1] /pʊʃ/ *v* **1** [T1;I∅;X7] to use sudden or steady pressure in order to move (someone or something) forward, away from oneself, or to a different position: *He pushed me suddenly, and I fell into the water.|It's rather cold: please push the window up.|Don't push: wait your turn to get on the bus.|Please push the door shut* **2** [X9] **a** to make (one's way) by doing this: *He pushed his way to the front of the crowd* **b** to cause (oneself) to move by doing this: *He pushed himself to the front of the crowd* **3** [T1 (*into*);V3] to force (someone) to do something by continual urging: *I'm not pushing you; if you don't want this job, don't take it.|My friends are all pushing me to enter politics* **4** [T1;I∅] to force (someone or something) on the notice of others, as a means of success: *They aren't really pushing their business enough and are losing money on it; they ought to push their goods more* **5** [T1 (*for*)] to hurry or trouble (someone) by continual urging: *If you push a worker too hard, he may make mistakes.|He keeps pushing me for payment of the debt* —compare PUSH FOR **6** [I∅ (DOWN)] (of a woman giving birth) to use pressure of the muscles in order to help a baby to move downward and out of one's body **7** [T1; (I∅)] *infml* to sell (unlawful drugs) by acting as a connection between the suppliers and the people who need to or can be persuaded to buy **8 be pushing (a stated age, usu. over 30)** *infml* to be nearly (the stated number of years) old: *You wouldn't think so to look at him, but he's pushing 40* **9 push one's luck** to take an increasing risk: *I know you beat Bloggs easily, but if you agreed to fight Ali I think you'd be pushing your luck* —see also PUSH ALONG, PUSH AROUND, PUSH BACK, PUSH FOR, PUSH FORWARD, PUSH IN, PUSH OFF, PUSH ON[1,2], PUSH OUT, PUSH THROUGH, PUSH UP, and compare PULL[1]

push[2] *n* **1** [C] an act of pushing: *They gave the car a push to get it started.|The door opened at a slight push* **2** [(*the*) S] the action of pushing steadily or continuously: *the push of the water against the sea wall* **3** [C] a planned attack and advance of great strength by an army in the course of a war **4** [U] *infml* active will to succeed, esp. by forcing oneself and one's wishes on others **5** [U] help or influence in someone's favour **6 at a push** *infml, esp. BrE* if really necessary; if forced by special conditions: *I can finish the work by next month at a push, but that would mean I must lose my holiday* —compare **at a** PINCH² (4) **7 get the push** *sl* to be dismissed from one's job **8 give someone the push** *sl* to dismiss someone from his job **9 if/when it comes/came to the push** if/when there is a moment of special need: *I haven't a great deal of money in the bank, but if it came to the push I could lend you £100* **10 make a push** *becoming rare* to make a determined effort to do something —compare PULL²

push a·long *v adv* **1** [I∅ (*to*)] also **push a·head, push forward, push on**— to continue one's journey or march, steadily or with effort **2** [I∅] *infml* to leave: *It's getting late; we must be pushing along*

push a·round *v adv* [T1b] *infml* to treat (someone) roughly and unfairly as if of no importance, esp. in order to force obedience; ORDER ABOUT

push back *v adv* [T1] to cause (an enemy) to move back and lose ground

push·bike /ˈpʊʃbaɪk/ *n* [C; *by*+U] *BrE infml* a bicycle that is worked by pressing on the PEDALs, not by a motor

push-but·ton /ˈ· ˌ··/ *adj* [Wa5;A] **1** being or put into operation by a small round object (**push button**) that one presses with the finger: *This machine has a push-button starter* **2** *often derog* using or having a lot of machinery, so that people do not have to make an effort to do things by hand: *People say that we live now in a push-button age* **3** (of war) carried out by means of explosives that can be fired over very long distances, not by personal fighting

push·cart /ˈpʊʃkɑːt‖-kɑrt/ *n* a small cart pushed by hand, as used by a street tradesman selling fruit, for carrying shopping in a large store, etc.

push·chair /ˈpʊʃ-tʃeəʳ/ (*AmE* **stroller**)— *n BrE* a small folding chair on wheels for pushing a small child about

pushed /pʊʃt/ *adj infml* **1** [F+*for*] having difficulty in finding enough (money, time, etc.): *I'm always rather pushed for money at the end of the month* **2** [F] having no free time; busy: *I'd like to stop for a longer talk, but I'm rather pushed today* **3** [F3] having difficulty, esp. because of lack of time: *You'll be pushed to finish that long job by this evening*

push·er /ˈpʊʃəʳ/ *n* **1** *infml, often derog* a person who uses every means and effort to gain success for himself **2** *sl* a person who PUSHes¹ (7) unlawful drugs **3** a small tool for pushing food onto a spoon at meals, used by a child who is too young to handle a knife and fork

push for *v prep* [T1 *pass. rare*] to demand urgently and forcefully; try to get: *People living near the airport are pushing for new rules about night flights* —compare PUSH¹ (5)

push for·ward *v adv* **1** [T1b] *often derog* to try to attract attention to (someone, esp. oneself) **2** [I∅] (of a BATSMAN in cricket) to step forward and make a defending stroke at the ball **3** [I∅ (*to*)] PUSH ALONG (1)

push in *v adv* [I∅] *infml* to interrupt rudely

push off *v adv* [I∅] **1** *sl* (*used esp. in giving or reporting an order*) to go away: *What are you doing in this garden? Push off at once!* **2** also **push out**— to set sail in a small boat

push on¹ *v adv* **1** [I∅] to hurry: *We're late; we must push on* **2** [T1;V3] to encourage (someone) (to do something) **3** [I∅ (*to*)] PUSH ALONG (1)

push on² also **push on·to**— *v prep* [D1 (OFF)] to force (something) on (someone): *They've pushed all the work on me again: they've pushed it all off onto me*

push out *v adv* [T1 *often pass.*] to dismiss or get rid of (someone), often unfairly —see also **push the** BOAT (5) **out**

push·o·ver /ˈpʊʃˌəʊvəʳ/ *n* [S;(C)] *infml* **1** something that is very easy to do or win: *The examination was a pushover: I knew the answers to most of the questions* **2** someone who is easily influenced or deceived: *Charles is a pushover for girls with blue eyes*

push through *v adv; prep* **1** [T1b;D1] to force acceptance of (someone or something): *push the matter through|push the student through* **2** [I∅] (of a plant) to begin to come up through the ground

push up *v adv* [T1] to force (something) to rise: *What is pushing up the price of oil?* —see also **push up the daisies** (DAISY (3))

push-up /ˈ· ·/ *n esp. AmE* PRESS-UP

push·y /ˈpʊʃi/ also **push·ing** /ˈpʊʃɪŋ/, (*now rare*) **push·ful** /ˈpʊʃfəl/— *adj* [Wa1] *usu. derog* too eager to make oneself noticed; active and forceful in getting things done, esp. for one's own advantage —**-ily** *adv* —**-iness** *n* [U]

pu·sil·lan·i·mous /ˌpjuːsəˈlænəməs/ *adj fml derog* cowardly and weak; fearful of taking the slightest risk —**~ly** *adv* —**-mity** /ˌpjuːsələˈnɪməti/ *n* [U]

puss¹ /pʊs/ *n infml* **1** [N;R] PUSSY¹ (1,2): *Here puss, puss, puss!* **2** [C] a girl: *She's a clever little puss*

puss² *n* [*usu. sing.*] *sl, usu. humor* (someone's) face: *He hit him in the puss*

pus·sy¹ /ˈpʊsi/ *n infml* **1** [N] also **puss, pussycat**— (a word used for calling a cat): *"Here, pussy!" she called, but it did not come* **2** [R] also **puss**— (a name for a cat, esp. in children's stories) **3** [C] also **pussycat**— (*used esp. by or to children*) a cat

pussy² *n taboo sl* **1** [C] the outer female sex organs **2** [U] *esp. AmE* the act of having sex

pus·sy·cat /ˈpʊsikæt/ *n infml* **1** [N;C] PUSSY¹ (1,3) **2** [N] a person, esp. a female: *"What's New, Pussycat?"* (title of a cinema film)

pus·sy·foot /ˈpʊsifʊt/ *v* [I∅ (*round*)] *infml* to be too careful or afraid to act or to express one's opinions

pussy wil·low /ˈ·· ˌ··/ *n* **1** [C] a type of tree that has very small soft furry white or greyish flowers on stems **2** [U] stems of this, esp. as taken from the tree and used for ornament

pus·tule /ˈpʌstjuːl‖-tʃuːl/ *n med* a small raised or swollen spot on the skin containing poisonous matter

put¹ /pʊt/ *v* **put,** *pres. p.* **-tt- 1** [X9] to move, set, place, lay, or fix (someone or something) in, on, or to a stated place: *Put the chair nearer the fire.|He put some more wood on the fire.|You put too much salt in this food.|The police have put the thief in prison.|She undressed the children and put them to bed.|He put a match to his cigarette* (=lit it).*|Put that newspaper down while I'm talking to you!* **2** [X9] *tech* to turn, guide, or direct (a boat or horse) in a stated direction: *The captain put the ship back to port for repairs* **3** [X9] to push or send (with force): *She put her pen through the mis-spelt word* (=crossed it out).*|He fired, and put a bullet through the animal's head* **4** [X9] to make, place, set, or fix (something or someone) in connection with something else as an act of will or the mind: *It's time to put an end to the meeting* (=end it).*|You won't succeed with the work if you don't put your mind to it* (=study it).*|Never put your trust in a stranger* (=trust him).*|I didn't break the window, but everyone has put the blame on me* (=blamed me).*|I'll soon put a stop to that* (=stop it).*|Whatever put such a strange idea into your head?|His dirty clothes put his wife to shame.|The prisoner was put to death* (=was killed).*|He was put to the sword* (=killed with a sword).*|The murderer will be put on trial.|I* *may have been wrong, but put yourself in my place; what other action could I have taken?* **5** [X(7),9] to cause to be (in the stated condition): *He put his books in order.*|*"You've made a mistake." "I'll put it right at once."*|*He's put his knowledge of French to good use while he's been in France* **6** [X9;(T1)] to ask (officially) for (something) to be considered: *The lawyer put several questions to the witness.*|(*fml*) *I ask that the question be now put* —see also PUT TO² (1,2) **7** [X9] to express (something) in words, esp. in a particular and exact way: *She is—how shall I put it?—not exactly fat, but rather well-built for her age.*|*His ideas were cleverly put.*|*I want to know how to put this in French* (=say, translate).|*trying to put her feelings into words* **8** [X9;(T1)] to write down; make (a written mark of some kind): *Put a cross opposite each spelling mistake.*|*"What shall I put at the end of the sentence?" "Put a question mark."*|*I don't know what to put* **9** [X9] to cause (a person or animal) to be busy; set to some kind of regular arrangement or work: *If I really put myself to it, I can finish this work today.*|*Can we put the horse out for hire?*|*Put all the boys to work* **10** [T1] to throw (a heavy metal ball (SHOT)) as a form of sporting competition **11 put it there** *infml* (*used esp. in coming to an agreement*) please shake hands with me **12 put paid to** *BrE* to ruin; finish completely: *His accident has put paid to his chances of taking part in the race* —see also PUT ABOUT, PUT ACROSS¹·², PUT AHEAD, PUT ASIDE, PUT AT, PUT AWAY, PUT BACK, PUT BY, PUT DOWN, PUT DOWN AS, PUT DOWN FOR, PUT DOWN TO, PUT FORTH, PUT FORWARD, PUT IN, PUT IN FOR, PUT INTO, PUT OFF¹·², PUT ON¹·², PUT ONTO, PUT OUT, PUT OVER, PUT OVER ON, PUT THROUGH¹·², PUT TO¹·², PUT TOGETHER, PUT UP, PUT UPON, PUT UP TO, PUT UP WITH

put² *n* [*usu. sing.*] an act of PUTting¹ (10) a heavy metal ball

put³ *adj* **stay put** *infml* to remain where placed: *She placed the child in the chair and told him to stay put.*|*The row of books wouldn't stay put; it kept falling over*

put a·bout *v adv* **1** [I∅;T1] **a** (of a ship) to change direction **b** to cause (a ship) to change direction **2** [T1,5] *infml* to spread (bad or false news): *"It's being put about that she was secretly married." "Who put that lie about?"* **3** [T1 *usu. pass.*] *esp. ScotE* to cause to worry; make anxious **4 put it/oneself about** *BrE sl* (esp. of a woman) to be sexually active: *Who's this new secretary? She puts it about a bit, doesn't she!*

put a·cross¹ also **put over**— *v adv* [T1] **1** to cause to be understood; explain: *I'm not putting my meaning across very well.*|*That speaker doesn't know how to put himself across* **2** to perform so as to cause admiration: *Billie Holliday put that song across better than anyone else*

put across² also **put over on**— *v prep* [D1] *infml, esp. BrE* to deceive (someone) into believing or doing (something) (esp. in the phrs. **put it/one/that across someone**): *The woman in the market put it across me by selling me some bad eggs.*|*You can't put that old story across your employer* (=make him believe it)

put a·head *v adv* [T1] PUT FORWARD (5)

put a·side *v adv* [T1] **1** to save (money, time, etc.), usu. for a special purpose: *He has a little money put aside and intends to take a holiday.*|*Put the rest of the cake aside for tomorrow.*|*I've put aside 5 minutes to talk to you* —compare PUT AWAY (2), PUT BY **2** to pay no attention to (something)

put at *v prep* [X1] to guess (something) to be (something): *I'd put her age at 33*

pu·ta·tive /ˈpjuːtətɪv/ *adj* [Wa5;A] *fml* **1** generally accepted or supposed to be: *his putative parents* **2** supposed to exist or have existed: *The putative language from which modern Chinese arose*

put a·way *v adv* [T1] **1** to remove (something) to a place where it is usually stored: *Put the books away neatly in the cupboard* **2** also **put by**— to save (esp. money) for later use —compare PUT ASIDE (1) **3** *infml* to eat (usu. large quantities of food) **4** *fml* to cease to consider or use: *Put away these foolish ideas!* **5** *euph* to place (someone) in prison or in a hospital for mad people **6** also **put down**— *euph* to kill (an animal), esp. because of old age or illness **7** *bibl* to end one's marriage to (one's wife) by law

put back *v adv* **1** [T1] to cause to show an earlier time: *put the clocks back* —compare PUT FORWARD (4) **2** [T1] also **put be·hind**— to delay: *The fire in the factory has put back production* —compare PUT FORWARD (5) **3** [I∅;T1 (*to*)] **a** (of a ship) to return: *The ship put back to port* **b** to cause (a ship) to return **4** [T1 (*to, till, until*)] PUT OFF¹ (1): *The meeting has been put back until next week*

put by *v adv* [T1] PUT AWAY (2)

put-down /ˈ· ·/ *n infml, esp. AmE* an act of saying that someone or something is worthless and unimportant: *After that put-down, I don't see how he can ever face her again!*

put down *v adv* **1** [T1] to write (something) down: *Let me put down your telephone number before I forget it* **2** [T1] to control; defeat: *put down the opposition* **3** [T1] to store or start a supply of (esp. food or drink): *put down some wine* **4** [T1] to pay (an amount) as part of the cost of something, with a promise to pay the rest over a period of time —see also DOWN PAYMENT **5** [X9] to allow (someone) to leave a vehicle: *You needn't drive the car up to the house; just put me down at the garden gate* —compare DROP² (6) **6** [T1] *sl* to make (someone) feel humble **7** [T1;I∅] **a** to cause (an aircraft) to land **b** (of an aircraft) to land **8** [T1] PUT AWAY (6) —see also **put one's** FOOT (23) **down**

put down as *v adv prep* [X1,7;V4b] to consider (someone) as (something or doing something): *I'd put him down as an uneducated man* —compare PUT DOWN FOR (3)

put down for *v adv prep* **1** [D1] to write the name of (someone) in a list of people willing to give (an amount of money): *Put me down for £5* **2** [D1] to put (someone or someone's name) on a waiting list for (something, such as a race, a school, etc.): *He's put his son down for Eton* **3** [X1] to consider (someone) as (something): *I'd put him down for an uneducated man* —compare PUT DOWN AS

put down to *v adv prep* **1** [D1;V4b] to state that (something) is caused by (something): *I put his bad temper down to his recent illness/to having had an unhappy childhood* **2** [D1] to charge (something) to (someone's account) **3** [D1] *tech* to use (a place) for (a purpose): *The farmer put the field down to grass*

put forth *v adv* [T1] *fml or lit* **1** to use; bring into action or effect: *The government urged the nation to put forth every effort to help the war* **2** to produce and send out: *In spring the bush put forth new leaves*

put for·ward *v adv* [T1] **1** to offer (an idea, suggestion, etc.) for consideration **2** to offer (someone or oneself) for a position: *May I put your name forward as a possible chairman of the committee?* **3** to move (some event) to an earlier date or time **4** also **put on**— to cause to show a later time: *put the clocks forward* —compare PUT BACK (1) **5** also **put ahead**— to make (something) advance: *The warm weather has put the crops forward by a month* —compare PUT BACK (2) **6** to make (someone) noticed; bring (someone) to the attention of others: *You should put yourself forward more if you want to improve your chances in the firm*

put in *v adv* **1** [T1,5] to interrupt by saying: *"Don't forget us," she put in* **2** [I∅ (*at*)] **a** (of a ship) to enter a port: *The ship puts in at Bombay and remains there for a day* **b** *infml* to enter and make a short stop: *The motorist decided to put in at the next hotel for a meal* **3** [T1] *not fml* to make or send (a request or claim): *If the goods were damaged in the post, you can put in a claim to the post office* **4** [T1] to strike: *put in a blow* **5** [T1] to do, make, or spend, esp. for a purpose: *put in 3 years' work* **6** [T1] to spend (time or money): *put in an hour at one's studies* **7** [T1] to elect (a government or political party) **8 put in an appearance** to allow oneself to be seen at an occasion where one is expected —see also INPUT, **put the** BOOT[2] (10) **in, put one's** FOOT[1] (24) **in it, put in** MIND[1] (25) **of, put/stick one's** OAR (2) **in**

put in for *v adv prep* **1** [T1] to make a formal request for; APPLY (1) for: *They've put in for membership of the club* **2** [D1] *not fml* to cause (someone or something) to compete for or in: *I'm putting some of my best roses in for the flower show* **3 put in a good word for someone** to speak in someone's favour or support

put in·to *v prep* **1** [D1] also **put in**— to add (something) to (something): *Put more effort into your work!* **2** [D1] also **put in**— to give or lend (money) to (something, such as a group or idea): *He's put £1000 into his brother's business* **3** [D1] to translate into **4** [T1;D1] **a** (of a ship) to enter (a port): *The boat had to put into Sydney for supplies* **b** to cause (a ship) to enter (a port) **5 put oneself/one's back/one's heart into something** to work very hard and with great keenness at something **6 put something into execution** *fml* to carry out something, such as a plan **7 put words into someone's mouth** to make statements that one claims are the opinions of someone else with whom one is speaking

put-off /ˈ· ·/ *n infml* a pretended reason for not doing something; excuse

put off[1] *v adv* **1** [T1,4 (*till, until*)] to move to a later date; delay: *If it rains, the match must be put off.|I'll have to put off going till next month* **2** [T1] to delay a meeting with (someone) till a later time: *We've invited them to dinner, but we shall have to put them off because the baby's sick* **3** [I∅] *tech* to set sail **4** [T1] to stop and allow (someone) to leave a vehicle or boat **5** [T1] to make excuses to (someone) in order to avoid a duty: *"I promise to pay you next week." "I won't be put off with a promise that you don't intend to keep!"* **6** [T1] **a** to discourage (someone): *The speaker was trying to make a serious point, but people kept putting him off by shouting* **b** to cause dislike: *Those smelly animals put me off.|His bad manners put her (right) off* —see also OFF-PUTTING **7** [T1] TURN OFF (1,2) —opposite **put on 8** [T1] *lit or old use* PUT AWAY (4)

put off[2] *v prep* [D1;V4b] to discourage (someone) from (something or someone): *The smell puts me (right) off my food.|Don't talk, it puts him off his game.|The smell put me off eating for a week!*

put-on /ˈ· ·/ *n infml* **1** [S] a pretended act or show of feeling, intended to deceive **2** [C] *AmE* something not intended seriously; joke —**put-on** *adj* [A]

put on[1] *v adv* [T1] **1** to pretend to have (an opinion, quality, etc.): *She claims to be ill, but really there's nothing wrong with her: she puts it on in order to gain attention* **2** to increase: *put on speed|put on weight* **3** to perform (a play, show, etc.) on a stage **4** to ask (someone) to perform or play a game: *I'm putting you on next* **5** to cover (part of) the body with (something, esp. clothing); wear or place (something) on the body: *She put her hat and coat on.|He put on his glasses to read the letter.|Mary puts on too much face powder* —opposite **take off**; see DRESS (USAGE) **6** to add: *They put on 50 runs in the last hour of play.|So many people wanted to go to the match that another train had to be put on* **7** *AmE sl* to play a trick on (someone); deceive: *"My dog can speak 7 languages." "No, you're putting me on!"* —compare HAVE ON[1] (1) **8** PUT FORWARD (4) **9** TURN ON (1,2): *Put on the light/the radio* —opposite **put out 10 put it on** *infml* **a** to get fat: *You'll soon put it on if you eat so many cakes* **b** to charge too much: *Don't buy from that shop; they put it on* **11 put on years** *infml* to seem older —see also **put on an** ACT[2] (5)

put on[2] *v prep* **1** [D1] to add to: *The war put at least £50,000,000 on the taxes.|Your silly behaviour puts years on me!* (=makes me feel very old and tired) **2** [D1] to risk (something, esp. money) on (someone or something); BET **3** [D1] to state or guess at (the price, value, etc.) of (something): *What price would you put on this fine old silver cup?* **4** [T1] also **put upon**— *esp. BrE* to be a trouble to (someone): *You're sure I won't be putting on you if I stay to dinner?* **5 put money on something** to be certain about something —see also **put one's** FINGER (12) **on something, put one's** SHIRT (3) **on something**

put on·to *v prep* [D1] *infml* to give (someone) information about (someone or something good): *I can't advise you in this matter, but I can put you onto a good lawyer*

put out *v adv* **1** [T1] to make (something) stop burning: *She put the light out and went to sleep.|Put the fire out* **2** [T1 *usu. pass.*] to worry or annoy (someone): *She was so put out by the man's rudeness that she didn't know what to say* **3** [T1] to trouble (someone): *Will it put you out if I bring another guest?* **4** [T1] to put out of place; DISLOCATE: *I can't play tennis today, I've put my shoulder out* **5** [T1] to remove or destroy the sight of (an eye) **6** [T1] to produce: *The company puts out 13 new machines every month* **7** [T1] to broadcast or print: *The government will put out a new statement next week* **8** [T1] to send (work) to be done in another place **9** [I∅ (*to*)] to set sail: *put out to sea* **10** [T1 (*at*)] to lend (money) so as to gain interest **11** [T1] THROW OUT: *If you can't be quiet I'll have you put out!* **12** [L9, esp. *for*] *AmE sl* (of a woman) to (be willing to) have sex with someone: *She acts like she's a real lady, but she puts out for him all right!* **13 put oneself out** to take trouble: *No one likes her; she never puts herself out to help people*

put o·ver *v adv* **1** [I∅ (*to*)] (of a ship) to move to one side **2** [T1] PUT ACROSS[1]: *He wasn't elected because he didn't put his ideas over clearly enough*

put o·ver on *v adv prep* [D1] *infml* PUT ACROSS[2] (esp. in the phr. **put one over on someone**): *Wilson tried to put one over on me yesterday by selling me a worthless car*

pu·tre·fac·tion /ˌpjuːtrə̇ˈfækʃən/ *n* [U] *fml or tech* **1** the chemical breaking up and decaying of the substances in dead plants or animal bodies, causing the formation of bad-smelling chemical compounds **2** PUTRID (1) matter

pu·tre·fac·tive /ˌpjuːtrə̇ˈfæktɪv/ *adj fml or tech* causing PUTREFACTION (1) —**~ly** *adv*

pu·tre·fy /ˈpjuːtrə̇faɪ/ *v* [T1;I∅] to decay; (cause to) become PUTRID (1): *In tropical countries dead bodies must be buried at once as they quickly putrefy in the heat; the heat helps to putrefy them*

pu·tres·cent /pjuːˈtresənt/ *adj fml or tech* beginning to decay and smell bad: *a putrescent mass of fish* —**-cence** *n* [U]

pu·trid /ˈpjuːtrə̇d/ *adj* **1** (esp. of an animal or plant substance) very decayed and bad-smelling **2** *sl* worthless; very much disliked: *That play last night was really putrid!* —**~ity** /pjuːˈtrɪdʒ̍ti/ *n* [U]

putsch /pʊtʃ/ *n* a sudden and secretly planned attempt to remove a government from power, esp. by force

putt¹ /pʌt/ *n* (in the game of GOLF) **1** an act of PUTTing² (1) the ball: *It took 3 putts before he got the ball in the hole* **2** the result of this: *That putt didn't go into the hole.|His putt was too short*

putt² *v* [T1;IØ] (in the game of GOLF) **1** to strike (the ball) gently along the ground towards or into the hole **2** (*in comb.*) to take a stated number of PUTTs¹ (1) to hit the ball into (the hole): *Jacklin 3-putted the 17th hole*

put·tee /ˈpʌti, pʌˈtiː/ *n* [*usu. pl.*] a long narrow piece of cloth wound round the leg from ankle to knee for support and protection, esp. as part of an army uniform

put·ter¹ /ˈpʊtəʳ/ *n* [C9] a person who puts: *a putter of questions*

putt·er² /ˈpʌtəʳ/ *n* (in the game of GOLF) **1** a special short GOLF CLUB with a flat metal head used in PUTTing² (1) a ball **2** a person who PUTTs² (1): *She wins because she's such a good putter*

put·ter a·bout /ˈpʌtəʳ/ *v adv* [IØ] *AmE* POTTER ABOUT

putter a·way /ˈpʌtəʳ/ *v adv* [T1] *esp. AmE* POTTER AWAY

put through¹ *v adv* **1** [T1] to complete (a piece of business) successfully **2** [T1 (*to*)] **a** to connect (a telephone call(er)) by telephone: *Can you put me through to this number?* **b** to make (a telephone call): *I have several calls to put through*

put through² *v prep* [D1] **1** to make (something) pass through (something): *put the suggested law through Parliament|put the string through the hole in the handle of the brush* **2** to cause (someone) to experience (something): *put all the students through the examination* **3** to cause (someone) to suffer (something): *You've put him through a lot of pain* **4 put someone through it** *infml* to give someone a severe test of courage or ability —see also **put someone through his** PACES¹ (6)

putting green /ˈpʌtɪŋ griːn/ *n* (in the game of GOLF) a smooth grassy area containing the hole into which the ball must be played, usu. by PUTTing² (1)

put·to /ˈpʊtəʊ/ *n* **-ti** /ti/ [*usu. pl.*] *It* (in art) CHERUB

put to¹ *v adv* **1** [T1] *not fml* to close (a door, window, etc.) firmly **2** [IØ;T1] **a** (of a ship) to go towards the shore **b** to cause (a ship) to go towards the shore

put to² *v prep* [D1] **1** to ask (a question) of or make (an offer) to **2** to test (something or someone) by using the stated means: *Let's put the matter to a vote* **3** to cause (someone) to be in (a certain place or condition, esp. of sleep, rest, or death): *She put the child to bed.|The government put the criminal to death by hanging him* **4 put it to someone (that)** to suggest; invite someone to consider (that): *I put it to you that you haven't told the whole truth. What have you to say to that?* **5 be (hard) put to it to (do something)** to find it difficult to (do something): *You'd be hard put to it to find any snow in a desert* —see also **put to** SLEEP¹ (7)

put to·geth·er *v adv* [T1] **1** to form; make a group of: *put a team together* **2** to gather: *put my thoughts together* **3** [*usu. pass.*] to combine: *His share was more than all the others' put together* **4 put one's heads together** (of 2 or more people) to combine ideas —see also **put** TWO (4) **and two together**

put·ty¹ /ˈpʌti/ *n* [U] **1** a soft easily shaped pale-coloured oily paste, used esp. in fixing glass to window frames **2 be putty in someone's hands** to be easily influenced or controlled by someone **3 give someone/deserve a putty medal** *humor or derog, esp. BrE, becoming rare* to give someone/earn praise for some worthless action

putty² *v* **1** [X9, esp. *in*] to fix in a place with PUTTY¹ **2** [T1] to fill with PUTTY¹

put up *v adv* **1** [T1] to raise: *put up a tent* **2** [T1] to put in a public place: *put up a notice* **3** [T1] to increase (a price) **4** [T1] *becoming rare* to pack: *Put up some food for us.|Put up the apples in barrels* **5** [T1] to provide food and lodging for (someone): *I'm afraid I can't put you up; you'll have to go to a hotel* **6** [L9] *esp. BrE* to find food and lodging: *We'll put up here for the night.|We'll put up at an inn* —compare PUT UP WITH **7** [IØ (*for*)] *esp. BrE* to offer oneself for election: *My brother is putting up for Parliament at the next election* **8** [T1] to supply (money needed for something): *The plans for the new theatre are all prepared, but who will put up the money?* **9** [T1] to offer, show, make, or give, esp. in a struggle: *What a coward; he didn't put up much of a fight!* **10** [L9;(T1)] to offer for sale: *She's putting her house up (for sale)* **11** [T1 (*for*)] to suggest (someone) for a job, position, etc.: *Will you put Tom up for the cricket club* (=suggest him as a member)? **12** [T1] to place in safe-keeping or PUT AWAY (1): *Put up your sword* **13** [T1] *becoming rare* to preserve and store (fruit, food, etc.) **14** [T1] to call (a prisoner) to be examined in court **15** [T1] *tech* to make (a hunted animal or bird) leave a hiding place: *Hunters use dogs to put up birds* —see also **put someone's** BACK¹ (17) **up**

put-up job /ˌ· · ˈ·/ *n* [*usu. sing.*] *infml* something dishonestly arranged in advance in order to trick someone

put-up·on /ˈ· ·ˌ·/ *adj* [F] (of a person) used for someone else's advantage; taken advantage of: *The way his neighbour always expects him to lend things to her makes him feel put-upon*

put up·on *v prep* [T1] PUT ON² (4)

put up to *v adv prep* **1** [D1;V4b] to give (someone) the idea of (something or doing something, esp. something bad): *Who put you up to this trick?|Who put you up to cheating?* **2** [D1] to suggest (something) to (someone)

put up with *v adv prep* [T1 *pass. rare*] *not fml* to suffer (someone or something) without complaining: *I can't put up with your rudeness any more; leave the room.|That woman has a lot to put up with* (=has many troubles to bear).|*That's the kind of rude behaviour that I just will not put up with!* —compare PUT UP (6)

puz·zle¹ /ˈpʌzəl/ *v* [Wv3] **1** [Wv4;T1 *often pass.*] to cause difficulty of thought and a feeling of helplessness to (someone) in the effort to explain or understand: *The woman's illness puzzled the doctor; he couldn't find the cause* **2** [T1] to use (esp. one's mind) with great effort in order to understand or find the answer to something difficult: *I've puzzled my brain all day about this matter, but I still don't know how to act* **3** [L9, esp. *about, over, as to*] to make a great effort of the mind in order to understand or find the answer to a difficult question: *He was studying the map and puzzling about the easiest way to cross the mountains* —**puzzled** *adj* [B;F6b]: *a puzzled expression on his face|I'm puzzled (about) what to do next*

puzzle² *n* **1** [C *usu. sing.*] something that one cannot understand or explain: *No one has yet succeeded in explaining the puzzle of how life began* **2** [C] (*often in comb.*) a game, toy, or apparatus in which parts must be fitted together correctly, intended to amuse or exercise the mind and test how clever one is: *a* CROSSWORD *puzzle|a book of puzzles|a* JIGSAW PUZZLE **3** [S] the state of being

PUZZLED[1] (1): *I'm in a puzzle as to what to do next*
puz·zle·ment /ˈpʌzəlmənt/ *n* [U] the state of being PUZZLED[1] (1)
puzzle out *v adv* [T1,6a,b] to find the answer to (something) by thinking hard: *I've tried for weeks to puzzle out what could have made Eric so angry that he hasn't written to us*
puzzle o·ver *v prep* [T1] to think hard about (something confusing)
puz·zler /ˈpʌzləʳ/ *n infml* a person who or thing that PUZZLES[1] (1) one: *That woman is a puzzler; I don't understand her.|That last question was a real puzzler*
PVC /ˌpiː viː ˈsiː/ *n* [U] a type of plastic: *PVC film|This film is (made of) PVC*
P X /ˌpiː ˈeks/ *n* **P Xs** /ˌpiː ˈeksɨz/ post exchange; a shop at a US military establishment: *bought it at the PX* —compare NAAFI
pyg·my, pigmy /ˈpɪgmi/ *n* **1** [C] a member of a race of very small people **2** [C] any person or animal of much less than usual height **3** [C] a person of no importance, esp. with regard to skill or brain power: *He considers himself a great singer, but he's really a pygmy when compared with real musicians* **4** [A] *often tech or humor* very small: *a pygmy elephant|Don't expect my pygmy brain to understand these scientific matters*
Pygmy *n, adj* [Wa5;A] (a member of) a tribal race living in the forests of central Africa, whose average height is 1·4 metres or 4 feet 6 inches
py·ja·ma, *AmE* usu. **pajama** /pəˈdʒɑːmə‖-ˈdʒæ-, -ˈdʒɑ-/ *adj* [Wa5;A] of PYJAMAS: *pyjama bottoms* (=pyjama trousers)
py·ja·mas, *AmE* usu. **pajamas** /pəˈdʒɑːməz‖-ˈdʒæ-, -ˈdʒɑ-/ *n* [P] **1** a soft loose-fitting pair of trousers and short coat made to be worn in bed, esp. by men **2** loose cotton or silk trousers tied round the waist, worn by Muslim men and women —see PAIR (USAGE)
py·lon /ˈpaɪlən‖-lɑn, -lən/ *n* **1** a tall framework of steel bars used for supporting wires that carry electricity over stretches of land **2** a high tower or post used as a guiding mark for air pilots coming down to land **3 a** a gateway to an ancient temple of Egypt **b** any gate tower or large gateway in a building
py·or·rhoe·a, -rhe·a /ˌpaɪəˈrɪə/ *n* [U] a disease of the flesh surrounding the roots of the teeth, which may cause the teeth to become loose or fall out
pyr·a·mid /ˈpɪrəmɪd/ *n* **1** (in GEOMETRY) a solid figure with a flat usu. square base and straight flat 3-angled sides that slope upwards to meet at a point —see picture at GEOMETRY **2** a pile of objects in the shape of this **3** (*often cap.*) a type of very large ancient stone building in the shape of this, used formerly, esp. in Egypt, as the burial place of a king **4** any of several other types of ancient stone building like this in shape, found in various areas, esp. Latin America
pyramid sell·ing /ˈ··· ˌ··/ *n* [U] *tech* a method of selling goods in which a person buys a right to sell a company's goods and then sells part of that right to other people
pyre /paɪəʳ/ *n* a high mass of wood for the ceremonial burning of a dead body
Py·rex /ˈpaɪəreks/ *n* [U] *tdmk* a special kind of glass that does not crack in great heat, and so is used in making cooking containers: *a Pyrex bowl*
py·rex·i·a /paɪˈreksɪə/ *n* [U] *med* a feverish condition; rise in temperature
py·ri·tes /paɪˈraɪtiːz‖pə-/ *n* [U] (*often in comb.*) a natural compound of SULPHUR with any one of certain metals, esp. iron (**iron pyrites**) or copper (**copper pyrites**), found in the earth and having a shiny yellow look, like gold
py·ro·ma·ni·a /ˌpaɪərəʊˈmeɪnɪə‖-rə-/ *n* [U] a disease of the mind causing an uncontrollable desire to start fires
py·ro·ma·ni·ac /ˌpaɪərəʊˈmeɪniæk‖-rə-/ *n* a person suffering from PYROMANIA
py·ro·tech·nic /ˌpaɪərəʊˈteknɪk‖-rə-/ also **py·ro·tech·ni·cal** /-kəl/— *adj* [A;(B)] of or concerning PYROTECHNICS
py·ro·tech·nics /ˌpaɪərəʊˈteknɪks‖-rə-/ *n* **1** [U] the art or practice of making bright explosive lights, as used for amusement for large numbers of people (FIREWORK*s*) or as signals by and for ships, aircraft, soldiers, etc. **2** [P] *fml or tech* a public show of FIREWORK*s* for amusement **3** [P] a (too) splendid show of skill in words, music, etc.
Pyr·rhic vic·to·ry /ˌpɪrɪk ˈvɪktəri/ *n* a victory or success in which the winner is left in a worse state than before
py·thon /ˈpaɪθən‖-θɑn, -θən/ *n* [Wn1] any of several types of large non-poisonous tropical snakes that kill small animals for food by winding round them and crushing them
pyx /pɪks/ *n tech* a vessel in which the holy bread used for a particular Christian church service (COMMUNION) is kept

Q, q

Q, q /kjuː/ **Q's, q's** *or* **Qs, qs** **1** the 17th letter of the English alphabet **2 mind one's p's and q's** to be careful in what one says so as to avoid displeasing others
q *written abbrev. for:* question: *Answer q 1 first*
Q *written abbrev. for:* (in the games of CHESS and BRIDGE) queen
Q.C. /ˌkjuː ˈsiː/ also (*fml*) **Queen's Counsel**— *n* [C; E] (the title given, while a queen is ruling, to) a British lawyer (BARRISTER) of high rank: *Sir John Smithers, Q.C.| She's very young to be a Q.C.* —compare K.C.
QED *abbrev. for:* (*Lat*) **quod erat demonstrandum;** there is the answer to your/the question; your/the question has been answered
qq *written abbrev. for:* questions
qr *written abbrev. for:* quarter
qt *written abbrev. for:* **1** quantity **2** QUART
q.t. /ˌkjuː ˈtiː/ *n* **on the q.t.** on the QUIET[1] (2): *Don't say I told you: it's supposed to be on the q.t.*
qty *written abbrev. for:* quantity
qu *written abbrev. for:* question
qua /kweɪ, kwɑː‖kwɑː/ *prep* when thought of particularly as the thing, type, etc., already mentioned; by itself: *Money, qua money, cannot provide happiness*
quack[1] /kwæk/ *v* [IØ] to make the sound that ducks make
quack[2] *n* the sound made by a duck
quack[3] *n* a person dishonestly claiming to have special, esp. medical, knowledge and practising a skill he does not have: *a quack doctor*
quack·er·y /ˈkwækəri/ *n* [U] the behaviour of a QUACK[3]
quad[1] /kwɒd‖kwɑd/ *n infml, esp. BrE* a square

open place with buildings around it, esp. in a college of a university
quad² *n infml* QUADRUPLET
Quad·ra·ges·i·ma /ˌkwɒdrəˈdʒesɨ̇mə‖ˌkwɑ-/ also **Quadragesima Sun·day** /··ˌ··· ˈ··/— *n* [R] the first Sunday in LENT
quad·ran·gle /ˈkwɒdræŋgəl‖ˈkwɑ-/ *n* **1** a QUADRILATERAL, such as a square **2** *fml, esp. BrE* QUAD¹
quad·ran·gu·lar /kwɒˈdræŋgjələʳ‖kwɑ-/ *adj* [Wa5] having the shape of a QUADRANGLE (1)
quad·rant /ˈkwɒdrənt‖ˈkwɑ-/ *n* **1** a quarter of a circle —see WEIGHTS & MEASURES TABLE **2** an instrument for measuring angles
quad·rat·ic e·qua·tion /kwɒˌdrætɪk ɪˈkweɪʒən‖kwɑ-/ *n* an EQUATION of the form $ax^2+bx+c = y$, where x is to be found
quad·ri- /ˈkwɒdrɨ̇‖ˈkwɑ-/ also **quadru-** /ˈkwɒrʊ‖ˈkwɑdrə/, **quadr-** /ˈkwɒdr‖ˈkwɑ-/— *comb. form* 4: QUADRILATERAL|QUADRUPED
quad·ri·lat·er·al /ˌkwɒdrɨ̇ˈlætərəl‖ˌkwɑ-/ *adj, n* [Wa5] (a figure) with 4 sides —see picture at GEOMETRY
qua·drille /kwəˈdrɪl‖kwɑ-/ *n* a dance in which the dancers form a square
qua·dril·li·on /kwɒˈdrɪlɪən‖kwɑ-/ *n, determiner, pron* **quadrillion** *or* **quadrillions** [See NUMBER TABLE 2] **1** *BrE* the number one followed by 24 zeros; 10^{24}: *several/9 quadrillion/quadrillions* **2** *AmE* the number one followed by 15 zeros; 10^{15}
qua·droon /kwɒˈdruːn‖kwɑ-/ *n old use* a person one of whose 4 GRANDPARENT*s* was black (of African origin)
quad·ru·ped /ˈkwɒdrʊped‖ˈkwɑdrə-/ *n* an animal (MAMMAL) with 4 legs
quad·ru·ple¹ /ˈkwɒdrʊpəl, kwɒˈdruː-‖kwɑˈdruː-/ *v* [T1;IØ] to multiply (a number or amount) by 4
quadruple² *adj, predeterminer, n, adv* [Wa5;B;U] (an amount which is) 4 times as big as something mentioned or usual: *a quadruple amount of cake|quadruple the amount of cake* —**-ply** *adv* [Wa5]
quad·ru·plet /ˈkwɒdrʊplɨ̇t‖kwɑˈdrʌp-/ *n* [*usu. pl.*] one of 4 children born of the same mother at the same time
quadruple time /·ˌ·· ˈ·/ *n* [U] a musical time with 4 BEATS² (3)
qua·dru·pli·cate /kwɒˈdruːplɪkət‖kwɑ-/ *n* **in quadruplicate** in 4 copies
quaff /kwɒf, kwɑːf/ *v* [T1] *lit* to drink deeply
quag·ga /ˈkwægə/ *n* [Wn1] a type of animal which formerly lived in South Africa, related to the donkey (and the ZEBRA)
quag·mire /ˈkwægmaɪəʳ, ˈkwɒg-‖ˈkwæg-/ *n* a piece of soft wet ground; BOG
quail¹ /kweɪl/ *n* **quail** *or* **quails** [Wn2;C;U] (meat of) a kind of small bird
quail² *v* [IØ (*with, at*)] to be afraid; tremble: *to quail with fear at the thought*
quaint /kweɪnt/ *adj* [Wa1] unusual and attractive, esp. because old: *a quaint old lady|quaint village customs* —**~ly** *adv* —**~ness** *n* [U]
quake¹ /kweɪk/ *v* [IØ (*with, at*)] to shake; tremble: *to quake with fear at the thought*
quake² *n infml* EARTHQUAKE
Quak·er /ˈkweɪkəʳ/ *n, adj* [Wa5] (a member) of a Christian religious group which opposes violence and spends most of its religious services (**Quaker meetings**) in silence
qual·i·fi·ca·tion /ˌkwɒlɨ̇fɨ̇ˈkeɪʃən‖ˌkwɑ-/ *n* **1** [U] the act of QUALIFYing **2** [C] something which qualifies (QUALIFY (2)) or limits something said or suggested: *I agree, with qualifications* **3** [C] a proof that one has passed examinations and gained a certain degree of knowledge: *a medical qualification*
qual·i·fi·ca·tions /ˌkwɒlɨ̇fɨ̇ˈkeɪʃənz‖ˌkwɑ-/ *n* [P (*for*), P3] the necessary ability, experience, or knowledge: *He has the right qualifications for the job/to do the job*
qual·i·fied /ˈkwɒlɨ̇faɪd‖ˈkwɑ-/ *adj* **1** [B] limited: *He gave qualified agreement* **2** [B (*for*);F3] having suitable knowledge or QUALIFICATIONS esp. for a job: *He's well qualified to do/for the job.|a highly qualified man*
qual·i·fi·er /ˈkwɒlɨ̇faɪəʳ‖ˈkwɑ-/ *n* (in grammar) an adjective or adverb which limits the meaning of another word
qual·i·fy /ˈkwɒlɨ̇faɪ‖ˈkwɑ-/ *v* **1** [IØ (*as*), 3;V3] to (cause to) gain a certain level of knowledge, ability, or performance, or a QUALIFICATION (3): *Being the son of a member of parliament doesn't qualify him to talk about politics.|He qualified in medicine/as a doctor this year.| Will our team qualify for the second* ROUND⁴ (6) *of the competition?|a qualifying match* (=the team/person who wins it will be allowed to go on to the next or main stage of the competition) **2** [T1] to limit (esp. the meaning of something stated): *Adjectives qualify nouns.|Qualify that statement—it's too strong*
qual·i·ta·tive /ˈkwɒlɨ̇tətɪv‖ˈkwɑlɨ̇teɪ-/ *adj* [Wa5] of or about quality: *a qualitative judgment* —**~ly** *adv*
qual·i·ty /ˈkwɒlɨ̇ti‖ˈkwɑ-/ *n* **1** [U;C] a (high) degree of goodness: *Quality is more important than quantity.|material of low quality* **2** [C] something typical of a person or material: *Sympathy is his best quality.|moral qualities|qualities of leadership*
qualm /kwɑːm‖kwɑm, kwɑlm/ *n* [(*about*) *often pl.*] an unpleasant feeling, often of being nervous or unsure before doing something: *He had no qualms about working in a foreign country*
quan·da·ry /ˈkwɒndəri‖ˈkwɑn-/ *n* [(*about*)] a state of difficulty and inability to decide; feeling of not knowing what to do (esp. in the phr. **to be in a quandary**): *I was in a quandary about whether to go*
quan·ti·fy /ˈkwɒntɨ̇faɪ‖ˈkwɑn-/ *v* [T1] to measure (an amount or quantity): *Can pleasure be quantified?* —**-fiable** *adj* —**-fication** /ˌkwɒntɨ̇fɨ̇ˈkeɪʃən‖ˌkwɑn-/ *n* [U]
quan·ti·ta·tive /ˈkwɒntɨ̇tətɪv‖ˈkwɑntɨ̇teɪ-/ *adj* [Wa5] of or about quantity —**~ly** *adv*
quan·ti·ty /ˈkwɒntɨ̇ti‖ˈkwɑn-/ *n* **1** [U] a measurable property of something: *These goods are greater in quantity than in quality* **2** [C] **a** an amount or number: *a large quantity of beer* **b** *old use* a large amount or number: *Quantities of food were on the table* **3 an unknown quantity a** something or someone whose typical properties are yet to be found out **b** (in MATHEMATICS) a number represented by the letter X
quantity sur·vey·or /ˈ··· ·ˌ··/ *n* a person who gives the probable cost of materials for future building
quan·tum /ˈkwɒntəm‖ˈkwɑn-/ *n* **-ta** /tə/ *tech* (esp. in PHYSICS) a fixed amount
quantum the·o·ry /ˈ·· ˌ···/ *n* [*the*+R] the idea that ENERGY (3) travels in fixed amounts (QUANTA)
quar·an·tine¹ /ˈkwɒrəntiːn‖ˈkwɑ-/ *n* [U;S] a period of time when someone or something that may be carrying disease is kept separate from others so that the disease cannot spread: *Animals entering Britain from abroad are put in quarantine for 6 months to prevent the spread of diseases such as* RABIES
quarantine² *v* [T1 *often pass.*] to put in QUARANTINE¹
quark /kwɑːk, kwɔːk‖kwɑrk, kwɔrk/ *n tech* the smallest possible piece of material forming the substances of which atoms are made
quar·rel¹ /ˈkwɒrəl‖ˈkwɔ-, ˈkwɑ-/ *n* **1** [(*with*)] an argument: *to have a quarrel with an official* **2** [+

with; nonassertive] a cause for or point of disagreement: *I have no quarrel with his opinion* **3 pick a quarrel (with someone)** to make an argument happen

quarrel[2] *v* **-ll-** (*AmE* **-l-**) [I∅ (*about/over* and/or *with*)] to have an argument: *He quarrelled about politics with George.|They quarrelled (with each other)*

quar·rel·some /ˈkwɒrəlsəm‖ˈkwɔ-, ˈkwɑ-/ *adj* (of a person) likely to argue; often arguing

quarrel with *v prep* [T1] to disagree with; complain about: *I don't quarrel with your right to speak, but with your way of speaking*

quar·ry[1] /ˈkwɒri‖ˈkwɔ-, ˈkwɑ-/ *n* a (usu. living) thing which is being hunted

quarry[2] *n* a place from which stone, sand, etc., are dug out

quarry[3] *v* [T1;(I∅)] to dig out (stone, sand, etc.)

quart /kwɔːt‖kwɔrt/ *n* **1** a measure for liquids which is ¼ of a GALLON; 2 PINTS —see WEIGHTS & MEASURES TABLE **2 put a quart into a pint pot** *infml* to attempt the impossible: *You can't put a quart into a pint pot*

quar·ter[1] /ˈkwɔːtəʳ‖ˈkwɔr-/ *n* **1** [C] a 4th part of a whole; ¼: *a quarter of a mile|a mile and a quarter|not a quarter as good* **2** [C] 15 minutes before or after the hour: *The buses come on the quarter.|The clock strikes the quarters.|It's (a) quarter past 10* (=10.15)|*(a) quarter to 10*=(*AmE* also) *a quarter of 10* (=9.45)|*in 3 quarters of an hour* (45 minutes) **3** [C] 3 months of the year, esp. for making payments: *I pay my rent by the quarter* **4** [C] (in the US and Canada) a coin worth 25 cents (=¼ of a dollar) **5** [C] (*often in comb.*) ¼ of an animal including a leg: HINDQUARTERS **6** [C *often pl.*] a place or person(s), often from which something comes or may be expected: *Workers are arriving from all quarters of the earth* **7** [C] a part of a town, often typical of certain people: *the student quarter* **8** [C] the period twice a month when the moon shows ¼ of its surface (=½ the side facing the earth): *In the first week the moon is in its first quarter, in the third it is in its last quarter* **9** [U] mercy; the act of giving life to a defeated enemy: *to give/ask no quarter* **10** [C] a measure which is **a** *rare* ¼ of a HUNDREDWEIGHT; 2 STONES; 28 pounds —see WEIGHTS & MEASURES TABLE **b** ¼ of a pound; 4 OUNCES: *A quarter of sweets for the children, please* **11** [C] *tech* the side of a ship towards the back **12 at close quarters** near together —see also QUARTERS

quarter[2] *v* [T1] **1** to divide into 4 parts **2** to cut (an animal or human body) into 4 **3** to provide lodgings for (esp. soldiers)

quarter day /ˈ·· ·/ *n BrE* a day which officially begins a 3-month period of the year, and on which payments of esp. rent are made

quar·ter·deck /ˈkwɔːtədek‖ˈkwɔrtər-/ *n* [*the*+R] *tech* part of the highest level of a ship, used only by officers

quar·ter·fi·nal /ˌkwɔːtəˈfaɪnl‖-ər-/ *n* any of 4 matches in a competition of which the winners will play in the 2 SEMIFINAL matches: *the quarterfinals|a quarterfinal match*

quar·ter·ing /ˈkwɔːtərɪŋ‖ˈkwɔr-/ *n* [U] **1** the act of dividing into 4 —compare QUARTER² (1, 2) **2** the giving or finding of lodgings —compare QUARTER² (3)

quar·ter·ly[1] /ˈkwɔːtəli‖ˈkwɔrtər-/ *adj, adv* [Wa5] (happening, appearing, etc.) every 3 months (=4 times a year)

quarterly[2] *n* a magazine appearing every 3 months (= 4 times a year)

quar·ter·mas·ter /ˈkwɔːtəˌmɑːstəʳ‖ˈkwɔrtərˌmæ-/ *n* **1** a military officer in charge of provisions **2** a seaman in charge of STEERing

quartermaster-gen·e·ral /ˌ···· ˈ···/ *n* **quartermasters-general** an officer in charge of provisions for a whole army

quarter note /ˈ·· ·/ *n AmE* (in music) CROTCHET (1)

quar·ters /ˈkwɔːtəz‖ˈkwɔrtərz/ *n* [P] **1** lodgings (esp. in the phr. **married quarters** (=houses where soldiers live with their families)) **2** positions for fighting taken by sailors: *The seamen went each to his quarters*

quarter ses·sions /ˈ·· ˌ··/ *n* [P] a law court held every 3 months

quar·ter·staff /ˈkwɔːtəstɑːf‖ˈkwɔrtərstæf/ *n* **-staves** /steɪvz/ a long wooden pole used as a weapon, esp. in former times

quar·tet, -tette /kwɔːˈtet‖kwɔr-/ *n* (a piece of music written for) a group of 4 people playing instruments or singing together

quar·to /ˈkwɔːtəʊ‖ˈkwɔr-/ *n* **-tos** the size of paper produced by folding a sheet twice, so as to give 4 sheets: *Quarto books are kept separately in libraries because they are so big*

quartz /kwɔːts‖kwɔrts/ *n* [U] a hard mineral substance, now used in making very exact timekeeping instruments (**quartz watch**es, **quartz clocks**)

qua·sar /ˈkweɪzɑːʳ/ *n tech* any of many mysterious objects outside our star system (GALAXY), whose exact nature is unknown but which produce radio and electric waves rather like those of a star

quash /kwɒʃ‖kwɑʃ, kwɔʃ/ *v* [T1] **1** to make nothing of or officially refuse to accept (esp. something which has been decided): *The high court judge quashed the decision of the lower court* **2** SUPPRESS

qua·si- /ˈkweɪzaɪ, ˈkwɑːzi‖ˈkweɪzaɪ, ˈkwɑzi/ *comb. form often derog* seeming like: *quasi-scientific ideas that seem good but are not really based on facts*

quat·er·cen·te·na·ry /ˌkwætəsenˈtiːnəri‖ˌkwɑtərsenˈte-/ *n* the day or year exactly 400 years after a particular event: *1964 was the quatercentenary of Shakespeare's birth*

quat·rain /ˈkwɒtreɪn‖ˈkwɑ-/ *n* a group of 4 lines which is a whole poem, or part of a poem

qua·ver[1] /ˈkweɪvəʳ/ *v* **1** [I∅] (of a voice, or music) to sing, speak, or be played in a shaky way **2** [T1] to say in a shaky way —**~y** *adj*: *a quavery voice*

quaver[2] *n* **1** a shaking in the voice **2** *AmE* usu. **eighth note**— a musical note which is half a CROTCHET —see picture at NOTATION

quay /kiː/ *n* a fixed place where boats can land, often a stone-built area running out into a seaharbour

quean /kwiːn/ *n old use* a badly behaved woman, esp. one who is sexually immoral

quea·sy /ˈkwiːzi/ *adj* [Wa1] **1** feeling sickness or dislike **2** [(*about, at*)] finding it unpleasant to do something: *I was queasy about the whole idea of the party* —**-sily** *adv* —**-siness** *n* [U]

queen[1] /kwiːn/ *n* **1** [C;A] **a** (the title of) a female ruler of a country: *Queen Elizabeth the Second of England* **b** the wife of a king: *Queen Marie Antoinette of France was the wife of Louis the 16th* **2** [C] the leading female, often chosen in a competition (esp. in the phr. **beauty queen**): (fig.) *London is the queen of British cities* **3** [C] (*often in comb.*) the leading female insect of a group which is large and lays eggs: *the queen ant/bee/*WASP|(fig.) *She is the queen bee of her group, and everyone tries to meet her at parties* **4** [C] any of the 4 playing cards of a high rank with a picture supposed to be that of a female ruler and which ranks next in value after the king: *the queen of hearts* —see CARDS

(USAGE) **5** [C] the most powerful piece in the game of CHESS —see CHESS (USAGE) **6** [C] *humor derog sl* a male HOMOSEXUAL

queen² *v* [T1] **1** (in the game of CHESS) to change (a PAWN which has succeeded in crossing the board) to a QUEEN **2 queen it over someone** *derog infml* (of a woman) to act as if of higher rank or greater worth than someone

queen con·sort /ˌ· ˈ··/ *n* **queens consort** [C; *the*+R] *tech* (*often caps.*) a special title sometimes given to the wife of a ruling king —compare PRINCE CONSORT

queen·ly /ˈkwiːnli/ *adj* like, or suitable for, a queen

queen moth·er /ˌ· ˈ··/ *n* the mother of a ruler

Queen's Bench /ˌ· ˈ·/ also **Queen's Bench Di·vi·sion** /ˌ· ˈ· ·ˌ··/— *n* [*the*+R] (the name given, while a queen is ruling, to) a division of the High Court of Justice in England —compare KING'S BENCH

Queens·ber·ry rules /ˌkwiːnzbəri ˈruːlz‖-beri-/ *n* [P] **1** the rules of fair fighting in BOXING **2** rules of fair competition generally: *When will you learn that the game of politics is not played according to the Queensbury rules?*

Queen's Coun·sel /ˌ· ˈ··/ *n fml* Q.C.

queen's ev·i·dence /ˌ· ˈ···/ *n* [U] see KING'S EVIDENCE

queer¹ /kwɪəʳ/ *adj* [Wa1] **1** strange: *What a queer story!* **2** *infml* not well: *I'm feeling queer: I think I'll go home* **3** *infml* mad (esp. in the phr. **queer in the head**) **4** *infml usu. derog* (being, or typical of, a man who is) HOMOSEXUAL **5 in queer street** *BrE sl* **a** in debt; owing money **b** in trouble, esp. over money matters —**~ly** *adv* —**~ness** *n* [U]

queer² *v* [T1] to cause to go wrong or fail (esp. in the phr. **queer someone's/one's own pitch** (=spoil someone's/one's own plans or chances))

queer³ *n infml usu. derog* a male HOMOSEXUAL

quell /kwel/ *v* [T1] to cause to cease; put down; SUPPRESS: *"Minister Quells Opposition Attempt to Defeat Government* (title of newspaper story)

quench /kwentʃ/ *v* [T1 (*with, in*)] to take away the heat of (flames, steel, desire, etc.) with water or by other methods: *to quench one's thirst with a glass of water|in a pool of water*

quench·less /ˈkwentʃləs/ *adj lit* unQUENCHable; endless

quer·u·lous /ˈkwerʊləs/ *adj* complaining —**~ly** *adv* —**~ness** *n* [U]

que·ry¹ /ˈkwɪəri/ *n* a question or doubt

query² *v* **1** [T1] to question or raise a doubt about, sometimes by marking (?) on a piece of writing: *to query a point* **2** [T6a] to put as a question: *He queried whether she could sing.|"Can she sing?" he queried* **3** [T1] *esp. AmE* to ask questions of (esp. someone with power): *querying the President about his intentions*

quest¹ /kwest/ *n* [(*of, for*)] *lit* a search, attempt to find (esp. in the phr. **in quest of**): *The quest for gold was long and difficult*

quest² *v* [IØ (*for*)] *lit* to search

ques·tion¹ /ˈkwestʃən/ *n* **1** a sentence or phrase which asks for information: *I asked you a question and you didn't answer* **2** a difficulty or matter to be settled; PROBLEM (1): *It's a question of finding enough time.|If it's only a question of a few minutes, I can stay* **3** a doubt: *There's no question about it.|There was some question as to his honesty.|His honesty is beyond/past all question* **4 in question** under consideration; being talked about: *That is not the point in question* **5 call (something) in/into question** to raise doubts about (something): *His honesty was called in question* **6 come into question** to come under consideration; come to be talked about: *A new point came into question* **7 out of the question** impossible: *Their victory is out of the question: they've lost too many men* **8 there's no question about/that** there's no doubt about/that: *There's no question about Doctor Johnson('s) having been in Edinburgh in 1768* **9 there's no question of** there's no possibility of: *There's no question of Doctor Johnson('s) having been in Edinburgh in 1768*

question² *v* **1** [T1 (*about*)] to ask (someone) a question/questions **2** [T1,6a] to raise doubts about: *I question whether he could have arrived in time.|I would never question his honesty* —see ASK (USAGE)

ques·tion·a·ble /ˈkwestʃənəbəl/ *adj* **1** that may be QUESTIONed² (2); not certain: *a questionable idea* **2** of doubtful honesty: *questionable friends|questionable behaviour in money matters* —**-bly**

ques·tion·er /ˈkwestʃənəʳ/ *n* a person who QUESTIONs² (1)

ques·tion·ing /ˈkwestʃənɪŋ/ *adj* appearing to question: *She gave him a questioning look* —**~ly** *adv*

question mark /ˈ·· ·/ *n* the mark (?): (fig.) *There is a question mark hanging over the future of the prices and incomes plan* (= its future is uncertain)

question mas·ter /ˈ·· ˌ··/ *AmE* usu. **quizmaster**— *n* the chairman of a game where questions are put (by him)

ques·tion·naire /ˌkwestʃəˈneəʳ, ˌkes-/ *n* a piece of paper showing a set of questions to be answered, often by several people, so that information will be gained

question tag /ˈ·· ·/ *n* TAG¹ (6)

question time /ˈ·· ·/ *n* [R] (in Parliament) the period of time when ministers answer questions put by members of Parliament

quet·zal /ˈketsəl, ˈkwet-‖ketˈsɑːl (*Sp* ketˈsal)/ *n* **1** a type of Central American bird with bright feathers **2** a coin which is the standard measure of money in Guatemala —see MONEY TABLE

queue¹ /kjuː/ *n BrE* **1** a line of people, cars, etc., usu. waiting to move on, or into somewhere; set of people waiting for something: (fig.) *There's a queue of people for new houses* (= a long waiting-list) **2** a tail of hair hanging down from the back of the head, worn by a man in former times **3 jump the queue** to go ahead of people who have been in line longer than you have; do or get anything unfairly, without waiting for your turn

queue² *v* **queued, queuing** *or* **queueing** [IØ (UP, *for*)] *BrE* to form or join a line while waiting: *We queued (up) for the bus.|We queued for hours*

quib·ble¹ /ˈkwɪbəl/ *n* **1** an argument about a small point, often to avoid an honest answer **2** the small point argued about

quibble² *v* [Wv3;IØ (*about/over* and/or *with*)] to argue about small points: *Don't quibble about unimportant things with me* —**quibbler** *n* —**quibbling** *adj*

quick¹ /kwɪk/ *adj* **1** [Wa1;B (*about, at, with*);F3] swift; soon finished: *a quick worker|a quick drink|a quick answer|quick to learn|quick to show anger|quick at learning|quick with his hands* **2** [Wa1;B] easily showing anger (in the phrs. **a quick temper, quick tempered**) **3** [Wa5; *the*+P] *old use* living (people): *the quick and the dead* **4** [Wa5;F (*with*)] *old use* containing life: *quick with child* —**~ly** *adv* —**~ness** *n* [U]

quick² *n* [(*the*) U] **1** living matter, usu. the flesh to which the fingernails and toenails are joined **2 cut (a person) to the quick** to hurt a person's feelings deeply: *He cut me to the quick with that unkind remark*

quick³ *adv* [Wa1] **a** quickly (note the phr. **get rich quick**): *Come quick: something terrible has happened!* **b** (*in comb.*): *a quick-acting medicine*

quick-change /ˌ· ˈ·/ *adj* [A] (of an actor) frequently changing clothes during a performance: *a quick-change artist*
quick·en /ˈkwɪkən/ *v* [T1] **1** to (cause to) become quick: *Her singing quickened* **2** *old use or lit* to (cause to) show life
quick-freeze /ˈ· ·/ *v* **-froze** /frəʊz/, **-frozen** /ˌfrəʊzən/ [Wv5;T1] to freeze (food) swiftly so as not to spoil the natural values or taste: *I bought a quick-frozen chicken, and it was almost as good as the real thing!*
quick·ie /ˈkwɪki/ *n infml* an act taking a very short time, or the object which results, such as a story, film, etc.
quick·lime /ˈkwɪk-laɪm/ *n* [U] LIME[1] (1)
quick·sand /ˈkwɪksænd/ *n* [U;C *often pl. with sing. meaning*] wet sand which pulls in any beings which try to cross it (note the phr. **a bed of quicksand** (= an area of quicksand))
quick·set hedge /ˌkwɪkset ˈhedʒ/ *n esp. BrE* a line of growing bushes as a fence for a field or garden
quick·sil·ver /ˈkwɪkˌsɪlvəʳ/ *n* [U] MERCURY (2)
quick·step /ˈkwɪkstep/ *n* **1** [*usu. sing.*] a dance with swift steps **2** music for this dance
quick time /ˈ· ·/ *n* [U] marching time for soldiers, usu. 120 steps a minute or more
quick-wit·ted /ˌ· ˈ··◂/ *adj* clever; swift to understand and act
quid[1] /kwɪd/ *n* **quid** [Wn3] *BrE infml* a whole pound (in money); £1: *She earns at least 50 quid a week*
quid[2] *n* a lump of tobacco for CHEWing
quid pro quo /ˌkwɪd prəʊ ˈkwəʊ/ *n* **quid pro quos** *Lat* something given or received in exchange for something else
qui·es·cent /kwaɪˈesənt/ *adj* still; at rest —**quiescence** *n* [U] —**quiescently** *adv*
qui·et[1] /ˈkwaɪət/ *n* [U] **1** state of being quiet; quietness (often in the phr. **peace and quiet**) **2 on the quiet** *not fml* without telling anyone; secretly
quiet[2] *adj* [Wa1] **1** with little noise: *quiet music|a quiet voice* **2** without (unwanted) activity; at rest; calm: *a quiet life|The sea seems quieter now.|The trains are quiet in the afternoon* **3** not making oneself/itself noticed by activity: *quiet behaviour|a quiet thought* **4** (of colours) not bright —**~ly** *adv* —**~ness** *n* [U]
quiet[3] *v* [T1;IØ: (DOWN)] *esp. AmE* QUIETEN
qui·et·en /ˈkwaɪətn/ *v* [T1;IØ: (DOWN)] *esp. BrE* to (cause to) become QUIET[2] (1,2,3): *They were shouting at first but they quietened down after a while.|She quietened her behaviour.|I quietened her fears*
qui·et·is·m /ˈkwaɪətɪzəm/ *n* [U] **1** a (religious) practice which includes calm acceptance of things, without any effort to change them **2** *often derog* a state of calmness or inactivity: *political quietism* —**quietist** *n*
qui·e·tude /ˈkwaɪətjuːd‖-tuːd/ *n* [U] calmness; stillness
qui·e·tus /kwaɪˈiːtəs/ *n* [*usu. sing.*] *lit* **1** death, or the act which brings it **2** a state of inactivity
quiff /kwɪf/ *n BrE* the part of a man's hairstyle where the hair stands up at the front over the forehead
quill /kwɪl/ *n* **1** a bird's feather, esp. a long stiff one taken from the wing or tail **2** also **quill pen** /ˌ· ˈ·/— a pen made from this, used in former times **3** a sharp prickle on some animals, such as the PORCUPINE
quilt /kwɪlt/ *n* a cover for a bed made of 2 pieces of cloth with soft, warm material between —see picture at BEDROOM
quilt·ed /ˈkwɪltɨd/ *adj* [Wa5] made with cloth containing soft material and stitched across, often in diamond-shaped lines of stitching: *a quilted* HOUSECOAT
quin /kwɪn/ *n* (*AmE* **quint** /kwɪnt/) *BrE infml* QUINTUPLET
quince /kwɪns/ *n* a hard fruit related to the apple, which is used in jelly
quin·ine /ˈkwɪniːn‖ˈkwaɪnaɪn/ *n* [U] a drug used for treating fevers, esp. MALARIA
Quin·qua·ges·i·ma /ˌwɪŋkwəˈdʒesɨmə/ also **Quinquagesima Sun·day** /··ˌ··· ˈ··/— *n* [R] *tech* the Sunday before LENT
quin·sy /ˈkwɪnzi/ *n* [U] severe infection of the TONSILs
quin·tal /ˈkwɪntl/ *n* a weight of one HUNDREDWEIGHT or 100 kilos
quin·tes·sence /kwɪnˈtesəns/ *n* **the quintessence of** the perfect type or example of: *the quintessence of good manners* —**-sential** /ˌkwɪntɨˈsentʃəl/ *adj* [Wa5] —**-sentially** *adv*
quin·tet, -tette /kwɪnˈtet/ *n* (a piece of music written for) a group of 5 people playing instruments or singing together
quin·tu·plet /ˈkwɪntjʊplɨt, kwɪnˈtjuːp-‖kwɪnˈtʌp-/ *n* [*usu. pl.*] one of 5 children born of the same mother at the same time
quip[1] /kwɪp/ *n* a remark meant to sound clever
quip[2] *v* **-pp-** [IØ] to make clever-sounding remarks
quire /kwaɪəʳ/ *n* a group of 24 pieces of paper
quirk /kwɜːk‖kwɜrk/ *n* **1** a strange happening or accident: *By some quirk of fate the 2 of us were on the same train* **2** a strange type of behaviour or tendency to behave strangely: *He has some unusual quirks in his character*
quis·ling /ˈkwɪzlɪŋ/ *n* someone who helps another country against his own
quit[1] /kwɪt/ *adj* [Wa5;F+*of*] finished with; free of: *We're quit of all our difficulties*
quit[2] *v* **quitted** *or* **quit** (*AmE* **quit**), *pres. p.* **quitting** **1** [T1,4;IØ] *infml* to stop (doing something) and leave: *I've quit my job.|I've quit working.|I'd had enough, so I quit* **2** [T1] *old use* to leave **3 notice to quit** an instruction that one must leave a house, job, etc.
quite /kwaɪt/ *predeterminer, adv* [Wa5] **1** [H] completely; perfectly: *If you've quite finished . . . !* (= said to stop somebody doing something).*|I'm quite ready to go if you are.|not quite dead|You're quite right.|If you want to go alone, that's quite all right with me.|not quite all/enough/so much|not quite the man he thought he was|The answer has gone quite out of my mind.|I don't quite know what to say.|quite the dullest man I've ever met* **2** more than usually; rather: *It's really quite good: much better than we expected.|really quite a good story|quite small|There were quite a lot of* (=quite a few) *people at Louis's party.|Now she really quite enjoys her job.|It takes quite a/some time* **3** *esp. BrE* more or less; to some degree: *It was quite good, but there are better ones.|She quite enjoys her job, but she's looking for a new one* **4 quite a/an** *AmE infml* also **quite some**— *often apprec* (used just before a singular [C] noun without adjectives, to show that a person or thing is unusual or more than the average of the type): *That was quite a party* (= It was unusually noisy or nice or interesting or long or wild, etc.)*|That's quite a story.|She's quite a girl* **5 Quite (so)** *esp. BrE* (*as an answer to a suggestion*) agreed; certainly; that's right: *"I always think, when it's hot, you should rest instead of running about." "Quite"* **6 quite something** *infml* unusual; surprising; very good: *It's quite something to be made a government minister while still less than 30*
quits /kwɪts/ *adj* [Wa5;F (*with*)] **1** back on an even level with another or each other after a fight to settle an argument, after repaying money which

is owed, etc.: *Now we're quits.|I'm quits with him* **2 call it quits** *not fml* agree that an argument is settled: *Hit him back and call it quits* **3 double or quits** see DOUBLE² (11)

quit·tance /ˈkwɪtəns/ *n* **1** *law* a (written) statement freeing someone from repayment of money or other things **2 give someone his quittance** to tell someone to get out (often out of the speaker's house)

quit·ter /ˈkwɪtəʳ/ *n infml* a person who doesn't have the courage to finish things once started, esp. when difficulties arise

quiv·er¹ /ˈkwɪvəʳ/ *n* the container for arrows which is carried on the back: *a quiver(ful) of arrows*

quiver² *v* **1** [Wv4;I∅ (*with* and/or *at*)] to tremble a little: *I quivered (with pleasure/fear) at the sound* **2** [T1] (of an animal) to move a delicate part of the body: *The rabbit quivered its nose*

quiver³ *n* [*usu. sing.*] a trembling movement: *I felt a quiver of excitement*

qui vive /ˌkiː ˈviːv/ *n Fr* **on the qui vive** watchful

quix·ot·ic /kwɪkˈsɒtɪk‖-ˈsɑ-/ *adj* trying to do the impossible, often so as to be generous to others while oneself running into danger —**~ally** *adv* [Wa4]

quiz¹ /kwɪz/ *n* **-zz-** a competition or game where questions are put

quiz² *v* **-zz-** [T1 (*about*)] to ask questions of (someone): *He quizzed me about where I'd been last night*

quiz·mas·ter /ˈkwɪzmɑːstəʳ‖-mæ-/ *n esp. AmE* QUESTION MASTER

quiz·zi·cal /ˈkwɪzɪkəl/ *adj* (of a smile or look) suggesting or giving the idea **a** that one knows something and/or is laughing at the other person **b** that one is asking a question without saying anything: *a quizzical* GLANCE² (1) —**-cally** *adv* [Wa4]

quod /kwɒd‖kwɑd/ *n* **in quod** *BrE sl* in prison

quoit /kwɔɪt, kɔɪt/ *n* a ring to be thrown over a small upright post in a game often played on ships

quoits /kwɔɪts, kɔɪts/ *n* [U] a game using QUOITs

quon·dam /ˈkwɒndəm, -dæm‖ˈkwɑn-/ *adj pomp* (at) one time; former: *a quondam interest of mine—but that was many years ago!*

Quon·set hut /ˌkwɒnset ˈhʌt‖ˈkwɑn-/ *n AmE tdmk* a large shelter with a cement floor and a round roof made of iron sheets —compare NISSEN HUT

quo·rum /ˈkwɔːrəm‖ˈkworəm/ *n* a stated number of persons, without whom a meeting cannot be held

quo·ta /ˈkwəʊtə/ *n* a stated number or amount, or a limit on numbers: *The quota of foreigners allowed into the country has been reduced*

quo·ta·ble /ˈkwəʊtəbəl/ *adj* that can be, or is worthy of being, QUOTEd —**-bility** /ˌkwəʊtəˈbɪlɪ̈ti/ *n* [U]

quo·ta·tion /kwəʊˈteɪʃən/ *n* **1** [U] the act of quoting (QUOTE¹) **2** [C] a sentence drawn from literature or a piece taken from a work of art such as music **3** [C] the price of something **a** as at present known: *the latest quotations on the foreign exchange market* **b** probable in the future: *He gave me a quotation for a new house which was too high*

quotation mark /·ˈ·· ·/ *n* either of a pair of marks (" ") or (' ') showing the beginning and end of words said or written by someone else (esp. in the phr. **in quotation marks**)

quote¹ /kwəʊt/ *v* **1** [I∅ (*from*);T1] to repeat in speech or writing (the words of (another person, esp. a powerful or important person)): *He quotes (from) the Bible to support his beliefs* **2** [T1] to mention (the actions of (someone)) to add power to one's own point of view: *She quoted me several examples of his behaviour* **3** [D1 (*to*);T1] to give a price: *I can quote you a price lower than anyone else's!*

quote² *n infml* **1** QUOTATION (2) **2 in quotes** in QUOTATION MARKs

quote³ *adv* [Wa5] (a word used in speech for showing that one is starting a QUOTATION (2)): *The figures given are (quote) "not to be trusted"* (UNQUOTE), *according to this writer*

quoth /kwəʊθ/ *v* **quoth I/he/she/it** *old use* said I/he/she/it: *"Here shall I stay for ever," quoth the magic bird*

quo·tid·i·an /kwəʊˈtɪdɪən/ *adj* [Wa5;A] *fml* daily: *quotidian duties*

quo·tient /ˈkwəʊʃənt/ *n* a number which is the result when one number is divided by another

q.v. *abbrev. for:* (*Lat*) **quod vide**; which see; (used for telling readers to look in another place to find something out)

R, r

R, r /ɑːʳ/ **R's, r's** *or* **Rs, rs** **1** the 18th letter of the English alphabet **2 the 3 R's** reading, (w)riting and (A)RITHMETIC, said to form the beginning of a child's education

r *abbrev. for:* RECTO

R **1** *abbrev. for:* royal, as in R.A.F. **2** *written abbrev. for:* (on a map) river **3** *abbrev. for:* REX or REGINA: *Elizabeth R*

rab·bi /ˈræbaɪ/ *n* [C;N] in the Jewish religion, (the title of) a trained religious leader and teacher of the Jewish law

rab·bin·i·cal /rəˈbɪnɪkəl/ *adj* [Wa5] of or related to (the writings, teaching, etc., of the) RABBIs

rab·bit¹ /ˈræbɪ̈t/ *n* **1** [C] a common type of small long-eared animal of the HARE family that lives in a hole (BURROW) in the ground —see picture at MAMMAL **2** [U] **a** the fur of this animal: *My collar is only (made of) rabbit* **b** its meat used as food: *Have another piece of rabbit* —compare WELSH RAREBIT **3** [C] *infml* someone who plays a game badly: *I'm just a rabbit at tennis*

rabbit² *v* **-tt-** [I∅] **1** to hunt rabbits: *The dog went rabbitting in the wood* **2** [(ON, *about*)] *infml derog* to talk in a dull and esp. complaining way: *He keeps rabbitting (on) about his health*

rabbit hutch /ˈ·· ·/ *n* a wooden cage for pet rabbits

rabbit punch /ˈ·· ·/ *n* a quick blow with the closed hand (FIST) on the back of the neck: *He gave him a rabbit punch*

rabbit war·ren /ˈ·· ˌ··/ *n* an area where a group of wild rabbits live in their holes (BURROWs): (fig.) *The old part of the city is a real rabbit warren* (=consists of many narrow winding streets)

rab·ble /ˈræbəl/ *n* **1** [C] a disordered crowd of noisy people **2** [*the*+R] *derog* the lower classes; the common people

rabble-rous·er /ˈ·· ˌ··/ *n* a RABBLE-ROUSING speaker

rabble-rous·ing /ˈ·· ˌ··/ *adj* [A] (of a speaker or his words) exciting the mass of the people to hatred and violence: *a rabble-rousing speech*

Ra·be·lai·si·an /ˌræbəˈleɪzɪən, -ʒən/ *adj* (of stories, writings, etc.) full of jokes about sex and the body that are dirty but healthy and harmless, like the work of the French writer Rabelais (1490–1553): *Rabelaisian humour*

rab·id /'ræbɨd/ *adj* **1** [Wa5] suffering from RABIES: *a rabid dog* **2** [A] *derog* (of someone's feelings or opinions) unreasonably violent: *a rabid* TORY

ra·bies /'reɪbiːz/ also (*fml*) **hydrophobia**— *n* [U] a disease of the nervous system of warm-blooded animals, passed on by the bite of an infected animal and causing madness and death

RAC /ˌɑːr eɪ 'siː/ *abbrev. for:* ROYAL AUTOMOBILE CLUB

rac·coon, *BrE* also **racoon** /rə'kuːn, ræ-‖ræ-/ also (*AmE infml*) **coon**— *n* **1** [C] a type of small meat-eating North American animal with a long tail, and covered with thick fur **2** [U] the fur of this animal: *a raccoon coat*

race¹ /reɪs/ *n* **1** [(*against, between, with*)] a competition in speed: *have/run/lose/win a race|a 10-mile race|a boat-race* **2** a strong flow of water: *A mill-race is the fast stream of water driving the wheel of a water-mill* **3** *lit* an onward course as of time or life: *The old man's race of life was nearly run* **4 a race against time** an effort to do something before a certain time

race² *v* **1** [I∅;T1] to compete in, esp. run a race (against): *She's a very good swimmer and often races.|I'll race you to the end of the road* **2** [I∅] (of 2 or more people, vehicles, etc.) to run a race against each other: *Let's race!* **3** [I∅,3;L9;X9] to (cause to) go (somewhere) very fast: *He came racing across the road.|We raced the sick woman to hospital.|*(fig.) *The holidays raced by* **4** [T1] to cause (an animal or vehicle) to run a race: *My horse has hurt his foot so I can't race him* **5** [I∅] (of an engine) to work too fast because the machine that it drives is disconnected or not being used

race³ *n* **1** [C] one of a number of divisions of human beings, each with a different type of body: *the black/white/brown races* **2** [C9] a breed or type of animal or plant, esp. one useful to man for producing young of the same type: *breed an improved race of cattle* **3** [C] a group of people with the same history, language, customs, etc.: *the German race|The British are a sea-going race* **4** [A] of or between divisions of human beings with different types of body: *race relations* **5** [C9] a (stated) type of creature: *the human race* (=man in general)|*the feathered race* (*humor*=birds) —see FOLK (USAGE)

race card /'· ·/ *n* the printed list of events at a RACE MEETING, showing the events and the horses' names

race·course /'reɪs-kɔːs‖-kors/ *n* a prepared track on which horses race

race·horse /'reɪshɔːs‖-hɔrs/ *n* a horse specially bred or kept for racing

ra·ceme /'ræsiːm, ræ'siːm, rə-‖reɪ'siːm, rə-/ *n* a group of flowers growing on short stems coming from one main stem, with the lowest flowers opening first

race meet·ing /'· ˌ··/ *n* an occasion when several horse races are held at a particular place

rac·er /'reɪsəʳ/ *n* an animal bred and trained for racing, or a vehicle planned for use in races

rac·es /'reɪsɨz/ *n* [*the*+P] *not fml* RACE MEETING: *have a good day at the races*

race·track /'reɪs-træk/ *n esp. AmE* a course round which horses, cars, etc., race

ra·cial /'reɪʃəl/ *adj* [Wa5] connected with one's race, or with the different races of people: *racial pride/customs/origin/type*

ra·cial·is·m /'reɪʃəlɪzəm/ also (*esp. AmE*) **ra·cism** /'reɪsɪzəm/— *n* [U] *derog* political and social practices based on differences between the races of people, and on the belief that one's own race is the best —**racialist, racist** *adj, n* [B;C;*you*+N]: *You racialist!|That book is racialist*

ra·cial·ly /'reɪʃəli/ *adv* in connection with the different races of people: *Racially, there is no difference between those 2 nations*

rac·ing /'reɪsɪŋ/ *n* [A] **1** used for racing in competitions: *a racing car|a racing* YACHT|*a racing* PIGEON (1) **2** interested in or concerned with racing in competitions: *a racing club|A racing man is someone who likes going to the races*

racing sta·ble /'·· ˌ··/ *n* an establishment where horses are kept and trained for racing: *keep a racing stable*

rack¹ /ræk/ *n* [U] *lit* floating cloud

rack² *n* **1** [C] a framework with bars, hooks, etc., for holding things: *He washed the dishes and put them in the plate rack to dry* **2** [C] a shelf over the seats in a plane, railway carriage, or long-distance bus: *Put this box on the* (LUGGAGE) *rack for me, please* **3** [*the*+R] (in former times) (punishment by means of) an instrument of TORTURE (=great pain) consisting of a frame on which people were stretched by turning its wheels **4** [C] a bar with teeth on one edge, moved along by a wheel with teeth round its edge (a PINION) —see picture at MACHINERY **5 on the rack** suffering very severely from pain or anxiety

rack³ *v* [T1] **1** [Wv4 *often pass*+*by, with*] to cause great pain: *a racking headache|He was racked with pain/by doubts* **2** *derog* to charge too much rent: *He racked his* TENANT*s* **3 rack one's brains** to think very deeply or for a long time

rack⁴, wrack *n* [U] (usu. of buildings) the ruined state caused by lack of care (in the phr. **rack and ruin**): *The house went to/is in rack and ruin*

rack·et¹, racquet /'rækɨt/ *n* a light instrument consisting of a network usu. of nylon stretched in a frame with a handle, used for hitting the ball in various games such as tennis —see TENNIS, BADMINTON (USAGE) and picture at TENNIS

racket² *n* **1** [S] a loud noise: *Stop making such a racket! I can't sleep* **2** [U9] great social activity and hurry: *He hates the racket of modern life* **3** *infml derog* a dishonest way of getting money, as by threatening or cheating people or selling them useless goods **4** *humor derog* business or trade: *What racket are you in?|He got rich in the advertising racket* **5 on the racket** *infml* having a wild gay social life: *Mary's out on the racket as usual* **6 stand the racket** *infml* **a** to succeed in a test **b** to take the blame or pay the costs: *Why don't we go to a restaurant?—Bill will stand the racket*

rack·e·teer /ˌrækɨ'tɪəʳ/ *n derog* someone who works a RACKET² (3): *Al Capone was a famous racketeer in Chicago*

rack·e·teer·ing /ˌrækɨ'tɪərɪŋ/ *n* [U] *derog* the activity of working a RACKET² (3)

rack·ets, racquets /'rækɨts/ *n* [U] a ball game for 2 or 4 players in an enclosed court, smaller than for SQUASH² (3), played with a hard ball: *Rackets is a fast game*

rack rail·way /'· ˌ··/ *n* [C; *by*+U] a railway up a mountain side worked by a RACK² (4) and PINION: *go up the mountain by rack railway/on a rack railway*

rack rent /'· ·/ *n* [C;U] *derog* too much rent: *pay (a) rack rent|charge rack rents* —compare RACK³ (2)

rack up *v adv infml* to SCORE² (2)

rac·on·teur /ˌrækɒn'tɜːʳ‖ˌrækɑn- (*Fr.* ʀakɔ̃tœʀ)/ *n Fr* someone good at telling stories: *a great raconteur*

ra·coon /rə'kuːn, ræ-‖ræ-/ *n BrE* RACCOON

rac·y /'reɪsi/ *adj* (of speech or writing) amusing, full of life, and perhaps rather dirty: *Paul shocked* *the ladies with his racy stories* —**racily** *adv* —**raciness** *n* [U]

ra·dar /ˈreɪdɑːʳ/ also **radiolocation**— *n* [U] a method of finding the position of solid objects by receiving and measuring the speed of radio waves seen on a glass plate (SCREEN)

ra·di·al¹ /ˈreɪdɪəl/ *adj* [Wa5] arranged like a wheel; with bars, lines, etc., coming from one centre —**~ly** *adv*

radial² also **radial tyre** /ˌ··· ˈ·/— *n* a car tyre shaped with hollow lines in the rubber that are RADIAL to the wheel, so as to give better control of the car on slippery road surfaces

ra·di·ance /ˈreɪdɪəns/ *n* [U] the quality of being RADIANT (1,3)

ra·di·ant /ˈreɪdɪənt/ *adj* **1** [Wa5;A] sending out light or heat in all directions; shining: *the radiant sun* **2** [Wa5;A] *tech* sent out by RADIATION: *radiant heat* **3** [B (*with*)] (of a person or his appearance) showing love and happiness: *her radiant face|She was radiant with joy* —**~ly** *adv*

ra·di·ate /ˈreɪdieɪt/ *v* [T1] to send out (light or heat): (fig.) *She radiates joy*

radiate from *v prep* [T1] (*no pass.*) to come out or spread in all directions from (something): *Heat radiates from the fire*

ra·di·a·tion /ˌreɪdiˈeɪʃən/ *n* **1** [U] (the act of) radiating (RADIATE) heat, light, etc. **2** [C] something which is radiated: *This apparatus produces harmful radiations* **3** [U] RADIOACTIVITY: *the effects of (atomic) radiation*

radiation sick·ness /··ˈ·· ˌ··/ *n* [U] the illness caused by the effects of RADIOACTIVITY

ra·di·a·tor /ˈreɪdieɪtəʳ/ *n* **1** an apparatus consisting of pipes with steam or hot water passing through them, used for heating buildings —see picture at LIVING ROOM **2** an electric heater for the same purpose **3** an apparatus which keeps the engine of a motor vehicle cool —see picture at CAR

rad·i·cal¹ /ˈrædɪkəl/ *adj* **1** (of changes) thorough and complete: *make radical improvements* **2** (of a person or his opinions) in favour of thorough and complete political change: *a radical politician|His opinions are very radical* —**~ly** *adv* [Wa4]

radical² *n* **1** [*often cap.*] a person who wishes to make great and rapid changes in the government of the country **2** *tech* a group of atoms that is found unchanged in a number of compounds and acts like a single atom **3** (in MATHEMATICS) **a** the SQUARE ROOT of the quantity: *3 and −3 are radicals of 9* **b** the sign √ that means this

rad·i·cal·is·m /ˈrædɪkəlɪzəm/ *n* [U] **1** the quality of being politically RADICAL¹ (2) **2** (*often cap.*) the political ideas of RADICALs² (1)

rad·i·cal·ize, -ise /ˈrædɪkəlaɪz/ *v* [T1] to make (a person or group) RADICAL¹ (2)

rad·i·cle /ˈrædɪkəl/ *n* the root of a young plant, esp. before it comes out of the seed

rad·i·i /ˈreɪdiaɪ/ *pl. of* RADIUS

ra·di·o¹ /ˈreɪdiəʊ/ *n* **-os** **1** [U] (the method of) sending or receiving sounds through the air by means of electrical waves: *police talking to each other by radio* **2** [C] also **radio set** /ˈ··· ·/— an apparatus to receive sounds broadcast in this way: *buy a new radio* —see picture at SOUND³ **3** [U] the radio broadcasting industry: *get a job in radio|listen to Radio Peking* **4 on the radio a** (of a sound) broadcast: *I heard it on the radio* **b** (of a person) broadcasting: *John was on the radio again today* —compare **on the** TELEVISION

radio² *v* **1** [I∅;T1] to send (a message) through the air by means of electrical waves: *The ship radioed for help.|We must radio the message at once* **2** [T1] to send a message to (a place or person) in this way: *They radioed London for advice*

radio- *comb. form* **1** [*n*→*n, adj*→*adj*] connected with radio: RADIOGRAM (1) **2** [*n*→*n, adj*→*adj*] connected with RADIOACTIVITY: RADIOISOTOPE

ra·di·o·ac·tive /ˌreɪdiəʊˈæktɪv/ *adj* (of a substance) possessing RADIOACTIVITY: *This material is very radioactive.|radioactive dust* —**~ly** *adv*

ra·di·o·ac·tiv·i·ty /ˌreɪdiəʊækˈtɪvɪ̈ti/ *n* [U] the quality that some simple substances (ELEMENTs) have of giving out force (ENERGY (3)) by the breaking up of atoms, and which can harm living things

radio bea·con /ˈ··· ˌ··/ *n* a station that sends out radio signals to help planes to find their way

radio fre·quen·cy /ˈ··· ˌ···/ *n* the FREQUENCY of the radio waves commonly used in broadcasting

ra·di·o·gram /ˈreɪdiəʊgræm/ *n* **1** *BrE* (esp. in former times) a piece of furniture combining a radio and a GRAMOPHONE record player **2** *AmE* a message that has been radioed **3** RADIOGRAPH

ra·di·o·graph /ˈreɪdiəʊgrɑːf‖-græf/ *n* a photograph made with short waves (X-RAYs) that will pass through solid things

ra·di·og·ra·pher /ˌreɪdiˈɒgrəfəʳ‖-ˈɑg-/ *n* [C;U] *not AmE* (the job of) a person who takes RADIOGRAPHs, usu. for medical reasons

ra·di·og·ra·phy /ˌreɪdiˈɒgrəfi‖-ˈɑg-/ *n* [U] the taking of RADIOGRAPHS

ra·di·o·i·so·tope /ˌreɪdiəʊˈaɪsətəʊp/ *n tech* any of the RADIOACTIVE forms of a simple substance (ELEMENT) —see also ISOTOPE

ra·di·o·lo·ca·tion /ˌreɪdiəʊləʊˈkeɪʃən/ *n* RADAR

ra·di·ol·o·gy /ˌreɪdiˈɒlədʒi‖-ˈɑ-/ *n* [U] the use of RADIOACTIVITY in finding and treating a person's illness —**-gist** *n*

radio tel·e·scope /ˌ··· ˈ···/ *n* a radio receiver used for following the movements of the stars and of space vehicles

ra·di·o·ther·a·pist /ˌreɪdiəʊˈθerəpɪ̈st/ *n* a person who treats diseases by RADIOACTIVE substances or X-RAYs

ra·di·o·ther·a·py /ˌreɪdiəʊˈθerəpi/ *n* [U] **1** the job of a RADIOTHERAPIST **2** the treatment of diseases by this

rad·ish /ˈrædɪʃ/ *n* **1** a small vegetable whose red or white hot-tasting root is eaten raw: *a bunch of radishes* **2** the root of this vegetable

ra·di·um /ˈreɪdiəm/ *n* [U] a rare shining white metal that is a simple substance (ELEMENT), RADIOACTIVE, and used in the treatment of certain diseases, esp. CANCER: *to have radium treatment*

ra·di·us /ˈreɪdiəs/ *n* **-dii** /diaɪ/ **1** [C] (the line marking) the distance from the centre of a circle or SPHERE (1) to its edge or surface —see picture at GEOMETRY **2** [(*within*) C9] *not fml* a circular area measured from its centre point: *He lives somewhere within a 2-mile radius|within a radius of 2 miles from the town* **3** [C] *med* the long bone in the arm from the elbow to the thumb joint —see picture at SKELETON

R.A.F. /ˌɑːr eɪ ˈef, *infml* ræf/ *n* [*the*+R] (in Britain) *abbrev. for:* Royal Air Force: *join the R.A.F.*

raf·fi·a /ˈræfɪə/ *n* [U] the soft string-like substance from the leaf stems of a kind of PALM tree, used for tying up plants and making hats, baskets, etc.

raf·fish /ˈræfɪʃ/ *adj usu. derog* (of a person or his behaviour or appearance) happy, wild, and not very respectable: *a raffish young man|give lots of raffish parties* —**~ly** *adv* —**~ness** *n* [U]

raf·fle¹ /ˈræfəl/ *n* a sale of an article of some value by selling many low-priced numbered tickets of which one is chosen by chance to be the winner: *win a raffle|buy raffle tickets|win a pig in the raffle* —compare LOTTERY

raffle² *v* [T1 (OFF)] to sell in a RAFFLE: *raffle (off) a television set*

raft¹ /rɑːft‖ræft/ *n* **1** a flat boat made of large

rough pieces of wood: *escape from the wrecked ship on a raft* **2** also **life raft**— a flat rubber boat that can be filled with air, carried by planes and ships to save life **3** a flat floating framework used as a landing place for swimmers and for people with small boats **4** a number of tree trunks or logs fastened together to be sent floating down the river **5 a raft of** *AmE infml* a large number or amount of: *A whole raft of people came for drinks* —compare SLEW[3]

raft[2] *v* **1** [X9] to carry (something) on a RAFT (1) (somewhere): *raft the stores over to the island* **2** [X9] to send (wood) in the form of a RAFT (4) (somewhere): *raft the logs down the river* **3** [T1] to cross (water) on a RAFT (1): *They rafted the lake* **4** [L9] to travel (somewhere) on a RAFT (1): *They rafted down the river to New Orleans*

raf·ter /ˈrɑːftəʳ‖ˈræf-/ *n* one of the large sloping beams that hold up a roof —see picture at ROOF[1]

raf·tered /ˈrɑːftəd‖ˈræftərd/ *adj* [Wa5] (of a roof, room, etc.) having RAFTERs, esp. where these can be seen from below: *an ancient raftered hall*

rafts·man /ˈrɑːftsmən‖ˈræf-/ *n* **-men** /mən/ a man who RAFTs[2] (2) logs

rag[1] /ræg/ *n* **1** [C;U] (a small piece of) old cloth: *He cleaned the car with an oily rag|a piece of oily rag* **2** [C *usu. pl*] an old worn-out garment: *The beggar was dressed in rags* **3** [C] *infml derog* a stupid or badly-written newspaper: *Why are you reading that rag?* **4** [C] a small broken piece: (fig.) *There isn't a rag of proof that he did it* —compare SHRED **5 feel like a wet rag** *infml* feel very tired **6 glad rags** best clothes: *wear one's glad rags for the party* **7 like a red rag to a bull** *infml* causing uncontrollable fierce anger: *Any statement against the government is like a red rag to a bull to that minister*

rag[2] *v* **-gg-** *esp. BrE* **1** [I∅] to play about noisily and foolishly: *They don't do any work in that office, they're always ragging* **2** [T1 (*about, for*)] to play rough tricks on or make fun of; to TEASE: *They ragged him about his big ears|for having such big ears*

rag[3] *n esp. BrE* **1** a rough noisy but harmless trick: *They pushed him into the river for|as a rag* **2** an amusing procession of college students through the streets on some special day in the year, collecting money for some purpose: *On* **rag day** *we collected £300 for the hospital*

rag[4] *n* a piece of music written in RAGTIME

ra·ga /ˈrɑːgə/ *n* **1** any one of the many ancient patterns of notes in Indian music **2** a piece of music based on one of these patterns: *play an evening raga*

rag·a·muf·fin /ˈrægəˌmʌfɨn/ *n* a dirty young child, in torn clothes

rag·bag /ˈrægbæg/ *n* **1** a bag in which small bits of old cloth are kept for mending clothes **2** [(*of*)] *often derog* a confused mixture: *Her mind is a ragbag of disconnected facts*

rage[1] /reɪdʒ/ *n* **1** [C;U] (a sudden feeling of) wild uncontrollable anger: *The child wept with rage.|Father's in one of his rages.|*(fig.) *the rage of the storm* —see ANGRY (USAGE) **2** [S9 esp. *for*] a strong but not lasting interest (in) or urge for: *have a rage for collecting stamps* **3** [C] *infml* a fashion: *one of the latest rages* **4 (all) the rage** *infml* very fashionable: *Long hair is (all) the rage now* **5 be in/fly into a rage** to be/become very angry

rage[2] *v* **1** [I∅ (*against, at*)] to be in a state of RAGE[1] (1) **2** [Wv4;I∅] (of bad weather, pain, infectious diseases, etc.) to be very violent: *The battle raged.|a raging headache|The disease raged through the city for months* **3** [X9, esp. OUT] to stop being violent at last; to become quiet after a RAGE[1] (1): *He raged himself to a* STANDSTILL.|*The storm raged itself out*

rag·ged /ˈrægɨd/ *adj* **1** (of clothes) old and torn: *a ragged shirt* **2** (of a person) dressed in old torn clothes: *a ragged little boy* **3** with uneven edges or surfaces: *a ragged beard|ragged clouds in the sky after the storm* **4** (of work that needs effort of the mind) seeming unfinished and imperfect; with the parts not combining smoothly together: *The musicians gave a ragged performance* —**~ly** *adv*: *raggedly dressed* —**~ness** *n* [U]

rag·lan /ˈræglən/ *adj* [Wa5] (with or of an arm of a garment) that is joined with 2 sideways lines of sewing from the arm to the neck of the garment, instead of being sewn on at the shoulder: *a coat with raglan* SLEEVES|*a raglan coat*/JACKET

ra·gout /ræˈguː, ˈræguː‖ræˈguː/ *n* [C;U] *Fr* (a) mixture of vegetables and bits of meat boiled together; (a) STEW: *an excellent ragout*

rag·tag /ˈrægtæg/ *n* [*the*+P] *derog* the common people (in the phr. **ragtag and bobtail**)

rag·time /ˈrægtaɪm/ *n* [U] the form of music, song, and dance of black US origin, popular in the 1920's, in which the strong note of the tune comes just before the main beat of the music played with it (SYNCOPATION): *a ragtime band|a song written in ragtime*

rag trade /ˈ· ·/ *n* [*the*+R] *infml* the garment industry, esp. the making and selling of women's outer clothes —compare COUTURE

rag week /ˈ· ·/ *n* [C;R] the week in the year during which a student RAG is held —compare **rag day** (RAG[3] (2))

raid[1] /reɪd/ *n* [(*on*)] **1** a quick attack on an enemy position, not to seize the place but to do damage: *make a raid on the enemy coast* **2** also **air raid**— an attack by planes, in which bombs are dropped **3** a rapid visit to a place, to carry something away secretly or by force: *The hungry children made a raid on the kitchen and took all the cakes* **4** an unexpected visit by the police, in search of criminals or forbidden goods: *During their raid on the house, the police found a lot of dangerous drugs* **5** the using of money by someone in power, for a purpose for which it was not intended: *The Chief Minister made a raid on the road tax to help pay for the railways*

raid[2] *v* [I∅;T1] to visit or attack (a place) on a RAID: *raid a bank*

raid·er /ˈreɪdəʳ/ *n* a person, ship or plane that makes a RAID

rail[1] /reɪl/ *n* **1** [C] a fixed bar, to hang things on or for protection: *Keep your hand on the rail as you climb the steps* **2** [C] one of the pair of metal bars fixed to the ground, along which a train runs: *The accident was caused by some of the rails becoming bent in the heat* **3** [A] connected with the railway: *rail travel* **4 by rail** in a train; by train: *send it/travel by rail*

rail[2] *v* [T1 (IN, OFF)] to enclose or separate (a place) with RAILs[1] (1): *rail in/off the garden|The cliff edge is dangerous and should be railed*

rail[3] *v* [I∅ (*against, at*)] to curse or complain noisily: *He's always railing against the Government*

rail car /ˈ· ·/ *n* [C;U] a single railway carriage that can be used alone, worked by oil or electricity: *travel by rail car/in a rail car*

rail·head /ˈreɪlhed/ *n* the end of a railway track

rail·ing[1] /ˈreɪlɪŋ/ *n* [*often pl.*] one RAIL[1] (1) in a set making up a fence to protect people or keep them in or out: *The dog got its head stuck between the railings*

railing[2] *n* [C *usu. pl.*; U: (*against, at*)] a case or the action of RAILing[3]: *She wastes her time in useless railing(s) against her husband*

rail·le·ry /ˈreɪləri/ *n* [C *usu. pl.*; U] (a case of) friendly joking at someone's weakness; teasing (TEASE)

rail·road /ˈreɪlrəʊd/ *v* [T1] **1** *AmE* to send (goods) by railway **2** [(*into*)] to hurry (someone) unfairly: *The workers were railroaded into signing the agreement* **3** [(*through*)] to pass (a law) or carry out (a plan) quickly in spite of opposition: *The chairman railroaded the plan through the committee* **4** *AmE* to get (an enemy) sent to prison on untrue charges: *railroad a member of the political opposition*

rails /reɪlz/ *n* [P] **1** railway track **2 go off the rails a** (of a train) to leave the track **b** (of a person) to become disordered in mind, strange in behaviour, or completely mistaken **3 jump the rails** (of a train) to leave the track suddenly (and dangerously)

rail·way /ˈreɪlweɪ/ (*AmE* **railroad**)— *n BrE* **1** a track for trains **2** a system of these tracks, with its engines, stations, etc.: *get a job as a clerk on the railway*

rai·ment /ˈreɪmənt/ *n* [U] *lit* clothes

rain¹ /reɪn/ *n* **1** [U] water falling in separate drops from the clouds; the fall of these drops: *The crops need rain.|She went out in the rain without a coat* —compare DEW **2** [C9] a fall of rain of the stated type: *A heavy rain began to fall* **3** [S9+*of*] a thick fall of anything: *a rain of arrows/of questions* **4 as right as rain** *infml* in perfect health: *Jane's been ill, but she's as right as rain now* **5 look like rain** *not fml* to seem as if it will rain: *Don't go out—it looks like rain* —**~less** *adj*

rain² *v* **1** [*it*+IØ] (of rain) to fall: *It's raining.|It began to rain (hard)* **2** [*it*+T1] to drop (something) like rain: *They say it sometimes rains small fish* **3** [X9;L9 esp. DOWN: (*on, upon*)] to (cause to) fall like rain: *The bombs came raining down.|Tears rained down her cheeks.|Gifts rained (down) on the children.|Their rich uncle rained (down) gifts upon the children* **4 it never rains but it pours** events of the same (esp. bad) kind seem to come together **5 rain cats and dogs** to rain very heavily —see also RAIN DOWN, RAIN OFF, RAIN ON, RAIN OUT

rain·bow /ˈreɪnbəʊ/ *n* **1** an arch of different colours that sometimes appears in the sky opposite the sun esp. after rain **2 all the colours of a rainbow** *infml* many bright colours: *to paint the house (in) all the colours of the rainbow*

rainbow trout /ˈ·· ·/ *n* [Wn1] a food fish with black spots and pink or red lines on its body

rain check /ˈ· ·/ *n AmE* **1** a ticket for a later performance, when rain has stopped a public match or show **2** *infml* an agreement that one may claim later something that is being offered now: *I don't want a cigarette now, thank you, but I'll take a rain check on it*

rain·coat /ˈreɪnkəʊt/ *n* a light coat worn to keep the rain out

rain down also **hail down**— *v adv* [T1;IØ (*on*)] to (cause to) fall in great quantities: *She rained down curses on their heads.|troubles rained down* —see also RAIN ON

rain·drop /ˈreɪndrɒp‖-drɑp/ *n* a single drop of rain

rain·fall /ˈreɪnfɔːl/ *n* [C;U] the amount of rain, HAIL or snow that falls in an area in a certain time, as measured in inches or CENTIMETRE*s* of depth per year: *This area has (a) very heavy rainfall*

rain for·est /ˈ· ˌ··/ *n* a wet tropical forest with tall trees growing thickly together

rain gauge /ˈ· ·/ *n* an instrument for measuring the RAINFALL

rain off also (*esp. AmE*) **rain out**— *v adv BrE infml* [T1 *usu. pass.*] to cause to cease activity: *The game was rained off*

rain on also **rain down on**— *v prep* [D1] to cause to fall in great quantities: *to rain blows on the door* —see also RAIN DOWN

rain out *v adv* **1** [it+T1b *no pass.*] (of rain) to bring (itself) to a stop: *It will soon rain itself out and then we can have our walk* **2** *esp. AmE* RAIN OFF

rain·proof /ˈreɪnpruːf/ *adj* [Wa5] that keeps rain out: *The roof is no longer rainproof*

rains /reɪnz/ *n* [*the*+P] the season in tropical countries when rain falls continually; the MONSOON: *The rains have started early this year*

rain·storm /ˈreɪnstɔːm‖-ɔrm/ *n* a sudden heavy fall of rain

rain·wa·ter /ˈreɪnwɔːtəʳ‖-wɔ-, -wɑ-/ *n* [U] water fallen as rain: *wash one's hair in rainwater*

rain·y /ˈreɪni/ *adj* [Wa1] **1** having a lot of rain: *a very rainy day/place* **2 for a rainy day** for a time when money may be needed: *save up for a rainy day*

raise¹ /reɪz/ *v* [T1] **1** to lift, push, or move upward: *raise the window|raise the lid of a box|raise one's hat* **2** to move (a part of the body) upward, often as a sign: *She raised her finger to her lips as a sign for silence* **3** to set in an upright position: *He raised the fallen child to its feet* **4** to cause to rise: *The wind raised the fallen leaves from the ground* **5** [(*to*)] to make higher in amount, degree, size, etc.: *raise the rent/the temperature/someone's pay/the standard of English|raise Bob to the rank of captain* **6** to collect together: *raise an army|raise enough money for a holiday* **7** *esp. AmE* to produce, cause to grow or increase, and look after (living things); BRING UP (1) (children): *raise a family|raise horses|raise wheat* **8** to bring up and talk about (a subject): *There's an important point I want to raise* **9** *fml* to build (something high and noticeable): *raise a castle|raise a* MONUMENT **10** to make (a noise): *The men raised a cheer/a shout* **11** to cause people to make (a noise): *tell a funny story so as to raise a laugh* **12** to cause people to have (feelings): *His long absence raised doubts/fears about his safety* **13** to cause to end (an official rule forbidding something): *raise an* EMBARGO (=order forbidding movement of ships or trade or the broadcasting of a piece of news) **14** to bring back to life (a dead person): *Jesus was said to raise people from the dead* **15** to make a higher statement of what one expects to win (BID) than (a player in a game of cards): *I'll raise you!* **16 raise Cain/the devil/hell/the roof** *infml* to become very angry: *Mother will raise hell if you wake the baby* **17 raise (a number) to the power of (another number)** to multiply (it by itself) the stated number of times: *2 raised to the power of 3* (2^3) *is 8* —see RISE (USAGE)

raise² *n AmE* RISE

-rais·er /ˌreɪzəʳ/ *comb. form* **1** [*n*→*n*] a person who RAISE*s*¹ (6,7): *a cattle-raiser* **2** [*n*→*n*] a person who causes: *A fire-raiser is someone that sets fire to buildings on purpose* (ARSONIST) —see also CURTAIN RAISER

rai·sin /ˈreɪzən/ *n* a sweet dried fruit (GRAPE) used in cakes, bread, etc.

rai·son d'et·re /ˌreɪzɔ̃ ˈdetrə, -zɒn-‖-zəʊn- (*Fr* rɛzɔ̃dɛtr)/ *n Fr* a reason for existing: *He loves his work so much that it seems to be his only raison d'etre*

raj /rɑːdʒ/ *n* [(*the*) R] *Ind & PakE* (a period of) rule, esp. British rule in India: *The days of the (British) raj are ended*

ra·jah, raja /ˈrɑːdʒə/ *n* [C;R] (the title of) an Indian ruler: *All the rajahs attended the ceremony.|He became rajah after the death of his father* —see also RANEE

rake¹ /reɪk/ *n* **1** a gardening tool consisting of a row of teeth at the end of a long handle, used for making the soil level, gathering up dead leaves, etc. —see picture at GARDEN¹ **2** the same kind of tool on wheels, pulled by a horse or by a machine (TRACTOR) **3** the same kind of tool used to draw together the money on the table during a game of chance

rake² *v* **1** [IØ;T1;X7] to make (a place) level with a RAKE¹ (1,2): *rake the garden paths (smooth)|You rake and I'll dig* **2** [T1+TOGETHER, UP] to collect (as if) with a RAKE¹ (1): *rake up the dead leaves|rake the money together* **3** [IØ+ABOUT, AROUND, *among, over, through,* etc.] to search carefully (as if) by turning over and mixing up a mass: *I'll rake about/around among my papers and see if I can find it* **4** [T1 (*with*)] to examine or shoot in a continuous sweeping movement along the whole length of: *The police raked the hillside with powerful glasses but did not see the escaped prisoner*

rake³ *v* [Wv5;T1;IØ] **1 a** (of the stage of a theatre) to slope upwards towards the back **b** to cause (the stage of a theatre) to slope upward towards the back **2 a** (of a ship's centre poles (MASTs) or chimneys (FUNNELs)) to slope towards the back **b** to cause (a ship's MASTs or FUNNELs) to slope towards the back **3 a** (of the front (BOW) or back (STERN) of a ship) to slope outward from the water **b** to cause (a ship's BOW or STERN) to slope outward from the water

rake⁴ *n* [S] the angle of a slope: *the rake of the stage*

rake⁵ *n old use* a man (esp. rich and of good family) who has led a wild life with regard to drink and women

rake in *v adv* [T1] *infml* **1** to earn or gain (a lot of money): *He must be raking in £500 a week!* **2 rake it in** *infml* earn or gain a lot of money: *He must be raking it in!*

rake-off /ˈ· ·/ *n* a share of profits gained usu. dishonestly: *The taxi-driver gets a rake-off from the hotel if he brings travellers there*

rake out *v adv* [T1] *infml* to find by searching: *rake out some interesting facts|I'll try and rake out something for you to wear*

rake up *v adv* [T1] *infml* **1** to produce with difficulty by searching: *rake up some players for the team|rake up enough money for the rent* **2** *infml* to remember and talk about (something that should be forgotten): *Please don't rake up that old quarrel*

rak·ish /ˈreɪkɪʃ/ *adj* **1** like (that of) a RAKE⁵: *lead a rakish life|have a rakish look* **2** (of a person's appearance) bold, gay, and informal: *She wore her cap at a rakish angle* (=sideways on her head) **3** (of a ship or its shape) built for speed; looking neat and bold: *a rakish vessel* —**~ly** *adv* —**~ness** *n* [U]

ral·len·tan·do /ˌrælənˈtændəʊ‖ˌrɑlənˈtɑndəʊ/ *n, adv, adj* **-dos** [Wa5] *It* (a part of a piece of music) becoming slower

ral·ly¹ /ˈræli/ *v* **1** [IØ;T1] to come or bring together for a purpose: *The whole nation rallied to the government.|The government rallied the nation round it* **2** [IØ;T1] to come or bring back into order, ready to make another effort: *The tired soldiers rallied and drove the enemy back* **3** [IØ] to recover, as from illness or unhappiness: *He soon rallied from the shock of his father's death*

rally² *n* **1** [S] an act of RALLYing¹ **2** [C] a large (esp. political) public meeting **3** [C] a motor race over public roads **4** [C] (in tennis) a long struggle to gain a point, with each player hitting the ball again and again

rally³ *v* [T1 (*about, on*)] *pomp* to joke in a friendly way at (a person); TEASE: *They rallied him about/on his strange appearance*

rally round *v adv* [IØ] *infml* (esp. of a group) to come to someone's help: *Her friends all rallied round when she was ill*

ram¹ /ræm/ *n* **1** a fully-grown male sheep that can be the father of young —compare EWE and see picture at FARMYARD **2** BATTERING RAM **3** any machine that repeatedly drops or pushes a weight onto or into something **4** a machine that uses water pressure for lifting

ram² *v* **-mm- 1** [T1] to run into (something) very hard: *His car rammed mine* **2** [X9 esp. DOWN] to force into place with heavy pressure: *He rammed down the soil round the newly planted bush with his boots* **3 ram something down someone's throat** to force an unwanted idea or plan on someone: *Father keeps ramming it down my throat that I should become a doctor*

Ram [*the*+R] a group of stars forming the 1st of the 12 signs of the ZODIAC

Ram·a·dan /ˈræmədæn, -dɑːn, ˌræməˈdɑːn, -ˈdæn/ *n* [R] the 9th month of the Muslim year, during which no food or drink may be taken between sunrise and sunset

ram·ble¹ /ˈræmbəl/ *v* [IØ] **1** [(ABOUT, *through, among*)] to go on a RAMBLE²: *They rambled through the woods.|ramble about for hours in the old foreign city* **2** [(*about*)] to talk or write in a disordered and wandering way: *The old lady began to ramble (about the days of her youth)* **3** [Wv6] (of a plant) to grow loosely in all directions: *The wild roses rambled all over the fence|a rambling rose* —see also RAMBLER (2) —**-bling** *n* [U]: *to enjoy tennis and rambling*

ramble² *n* a (long) walk for enjoyment, often in the country: *go for/on a ramble through the woods*

ramble on *v adv* [IØ] **1** to continue to RAMBLE¹ (1): *The children rambled on across the fields* **2** [(*about*)] to continue to RAMBLE¹ (2): *He rambled on for hours (about his troubles)*

ram·bler /ˈræmbləʳ/ *n* **1** a person that RAMBLEs¹ (1) **2** also **rambler rose** /ˌ·· ˈ·/— a rose bush that RAMBLEs¹ (3)

ram·bling /ˈræmblɪŋ/ *adj* **1** (of speech or writing) disordered and wandering: *a long and very rambling letter* **2** (of houses, streets, etc.) of irregular shape; twisting and winding: *The old building was full of rambling passages*

ram·bunc·tious /ræmˈbʌŋkʃəs/ *adj humor* (of a person or his behaviour) noisy, uncontrollable and full of life —**~ly** *adv* —**~ness** *n* [U]

ram·e·kin /ˈræmɨkɨn, ˈræmkɨn/ *n* (a small dish for one person containing) a baked mixture of cheese, eggs, bread, etc.: *Have another of these excellent little ramekins*

ram·i·fi·ca·tion /ˌræmɨfɨˈkeɪʃən/ *n* [*usu. pl.*] a branch of a system (esp. of ideas, rules, etc.) that has many parts; part of a network: *the ramifications of a business/of a railway system*

ram·i·fy /ˈræmɨfaɪ/ *v* [IØ, T1] to (cause to) branch out in all directions; to form a network

ram·jet /ˈræm-dʒet/ also **ramjet en·gine** /ˈ·· ˌ··/— *n* a plane's JET engine, through which a flow of air is forced by the forward movement of the plane

ramp¹ /ræmp/ *n BrE infml* a dishonest trick to make people pay a high price: *They're charging too much rent—it's all a ramp* —compare RACKET² (3)

ramp² *n* a man-made slope used instead of steps to connect 2 levels: *Drive the car up the ramp*

ramp a·bout *v adv* [IØ] HORSE AROUND

ram·page¹ /ræmˈpeɪdʒ, ˈræmpeɪdʒ/ *v* [IØ] to rush about wildly or angrily: *The elephants rampaged through the forest*

rampage² /ˈræmpeɪdʒ, ræmˈpeɪdʒ/ *n* [(*the*) S] excited and violent behaviour (usu. in the phr. **be/go on the rampage**): *football crowds on the rampage* —**-pageous** /ræmˈpeɪdʒəs/ *adj*

ram·pant /ˈræmpənt/ *adj* **1** (of crime, disease, beliefs, etc.) widespread and impossible to control: *Sickness was rampant in the village* **2** [E] (of an animal drawn on a shield or flag in HERALDRY) standing on the back legs with the front legs raised as if to strike: *2 lions rampant* **3** (of plants) growing too freely —**~ly** *adv*

ram·part /ˈræmpɑːt‖-ɑrt/ *n* [usu. *pl.*] a wide bank of earth built to protect a fort or city

ram·rod /ˈræmrɒd‖-rɑd/ *n* **1** a stick for pushing the gunpowder into an old-fashioned gun **2** a stick for cleaning a small gun **3 stiff as a ramrod a** standing up very straight **b** very severe in behaviour

ram·shack·le /ˈræmʃækəl/ *adj* (of a building or vehicle) badly made or needing repair; falling to pieces: (fig.) *a ramshackle business*

ran /ræn/ *past t. of* RUN

ranch /rɑːntʃ‖ræntʃ/ *n* **1** [C] (in the western US and Canada) a very large farm where sheep, cattle or horses are produced **2** [C9] *AmE* any farm that produces one (stated) thing: *a fruit/chicken ranch*

ranch·er /ˈrɑːntʃəʳ‖ˈræn-/ *n* a man who owns or works on a RANCH: *a cattle rancher*

ranch house /ˈ· ·/ *n AmE* a house built on one level, usu. with a roof that does not slope much

ran·cid /ˈrænsɨd/ *adj* (of oily food or its taste or smell) not fresh; (tasting or smelling) unpleasant: *rancid butter|a rancid taste|smell/taste/go slightly rancid* —**~ity** /rænˈsɪdɨti/ *n* [U]

ran·cor·ous /ˈræŋkərəs/ *adj* bitter; feeling or showing RANCOUR —**~ly** *adv*

ran·cour, *AmE* **-cor** /ˈræŋkəʳ/ *n* [U] the feeling of bitter, unforgiving spite and hatred: *feel rancour against someone*

rand /rænd/ *n* [Wn3] the standard coin of South Africa, divided into 100 cents

ran·dom¹ /ˈrændəm/ *adj* [A] made or done aimlessly, without any plan: *fire a few random shots|make a random choice* —**~ly** *adv* —**~ness** *n* [U]

random² *n* **at random** aimlessly; without any plan: *make a choice/ask questions at random*

random samp·le /ˌ·· ˈ··/ *n* a set chosen from a group each member of which is equally likely to be chosen: *ask a random sample of people in the street what they think about the government*

rand·y /ˈrændi/ *adj infml* (of a person or his feelings) full of sexual desire: *to feel a bit randy* —**randiness** *n* [U]

ra·nee, rani /ˈrɑːniː, rɑːˈniː/ (the title of) **a** a female RAJAH **b** the wife of a RAJAH

rang /ræŋ/ *past t. of* RING

range¹ /reɪndʒ/ *n* **1** [C9] a connected line (of mountains, hills, etc.): *a high mountain range|2 ranges of hills* **2** [C] an area where shooting is practised, or where MISSILE*s* are tested **3** [C] (in North America) a wide stretch of grassy land where cattle feed **4** [S9;U,U9] the distance that a gun can fire, or between a gun and the object aimed at: *This sports gun has a range of 200 m.|shoot one's enemy at short/close/long range|He's still out of/beyond/in/within range (of my gun)* **5** [S9;U9] the distance at which one can see or hear: *Shout as soon as she comes within range* **6** [S9] the area within which a type of animal lives, or a type of plant grows: *The range of this flower is northern Europe* **7** [S9] the measurable limits between which something varies: *a country with a wide range of temperature|people in the £3000–£4000 income range* **8** [C9] a set of different objects of the same kind: *a complete range of gardening tools* **9** (esp. in former times) an iron fireplace with all the parts needed for various ways of cooking, built into a chimney in a kitchen

range² *v* **1** [Wv6;L9 (*across, from/to*)] (of mountains or hills) to lie in a RANGE¹ (1) **2** [T1] (in N. America) to keep (cattle, horses, etc.) on a RANGE¹ (3): *range 1000 cattle* **3** [Wv6;L1] (of a gun) to be able to fire (a distance): *This gun ranges 4 miles* **4** [Wv6;L9+*from & to, between & and*] to vary (between limits); to stretch or reach (from one limit to another): *The children's ages range from 5 to 15/between 5 and 15* **5** [L9 (through, over); T1 (*no pass.*)] to wander freely (through, over): *The children ranged the hills and valleys.|range through the forests/over the mountains* **6** [T1] to set in order or position; to place or arrange: *range the goods neatly in the shop window*

range find·er /ˈ· ˌ··/ *n* an instrument for finding the distance of an object **a** when shooting **b** when taking photographs

range o·ver *v prep* [T1] (of thoughts or speech) to be concerned with; to include, one after the other: *Our conversation ranged over many subjects*

rang·er /ˈreɪndʒəʳ/ *n* **1** (in Britain) the keeper of a royal forest **2** (in N. America) **a** a forest guard **b** a policeman who rides through country areas to see that the law is kept **3** (in the US) a COMMANDO **4** an older member of the GIRL GUIDE*s*

rank¹ /ræŋk/ *adj* [Wa1] **1** [B] (of a plant) too thick and widespread: *cut the rank grass* **2** [B *with*)] (of land) thickly covered (with useless plants): *rank soil|The field was rank with* WEED*s* **3** [B] (of smell or taste) very strong and unpleasant: *rank tobacco* **4** [A] having mistakenly the bad nature of what is named: *He's a rank beginner at the job, but he'll learn* —**~ly** *adv* —**~ness** *n* [U]

rank² *n* **1** [C;U] (a) degree of value, ability, importance, etc., in a group: *He will become a soldier of the top rank.|Each rank has a name.|hold the rank of general|He's above me in rank* **2** [C;U] (high) social position: *a person of rank|a person of low rank|people of all ranks* **3** a line (of policemen, soldiers, etc.) standing side by side **4** a line (of people or things): *Taxis stand in a (taxi) rank waiting to be hired* **5 keep/break rank(s)** (of soldiers) to stay in line/fail to stay in line: *The enemy broke rank(s) and ran* **6 of the first rank** among the best: *a writer of the first rank* **7 pull one's rank (on someone)** *infml* to use unfairly (on someone) the advantage of one's higher position

rank³ *v* **1** [L9;X9 (*as, among, above, etc.*)] to be or put (in a certain class): *Where do you rank Wordsworth/Where does Wordsworth rank as a poet? I rank him/He ranks below Goethe.|This town ranks (high) among the English beauty spots* **2** [T1; X9 *often pass.*] to arrange in regular order: *The cups were ranked neatly on the shelf* **3** [T1] *AmE* (of an officer) to be of higher rank than: *A general ranks a captain*

rank and file /ˌ· · ˈ·/ *n* [*the*+GU] **1** the common soldiers —compare ENLISTED MAN **2** the people in an organization who are not the leaders: *a member of the rank and file|the rank-and-file members of a trade union*

rank·er /ˈræŋkəʳ/ *n* an officer who has risen from being a common soldier

rank·ing /ˈræŋkɪŋ/ *adj* [A] *AmE* (of an officer) of highest rank present: *Who's the ranking officer here?*

ran·kle /ˈræŋkəl/ *v* [IØ] to continue to be remembered with bitterness and anger: *Their defeat still rankles*

ranks /ræŋks/ *n* **1** [P9, esp. *of*] *pomp* (the) class or group (of): *join the ranks of the unemployed* **2 reduce (someone) to the ranks** to reduce (a NON-COMMISSIONED OFFICER) to the rank of common soldier, as a punishment **3 rise from the ranks** to rise from the rank of a common soldier to that of an officer **4 the/other ranks** common soldiers below the rank of SERGEANT

ran·sack /ˈrænsæk/ *v* [T1] **1** to search (a place) thoroughly and roughly: *ransack one's pockets for the keys* **2** to search through and rob (a place): *Enemy soldiers ransacked the town*

ran·som¹ /ˈrænsəm/ *n* **1** [C] a sum of money paid to free a prisoner: *pay a large ransom* **2** [U] the freeing of a prisoner for money **3 hold someone to ransom** to keep someone prisoner so as to demand payment: *They took away* (KIDNAP*ped*) *the boy and held him to ransom* **4 a king's ransom** *pomp* a great deal of money: *cost/be worth a king's ransom*

ransom² *v* [T1] to set (someone) free by paying a RANSOM —**~er** *n*

rant¹ /rænt/ *v* **1** [I∅] to talk in a loud excited way, using grand but meaningless phrases: *The priest ranted about the devil and all his works* **2** [I∅;T1] (of an actor) to perform (his part in the play) in this way: *Try not to rant (the speech) so much* **3 rant and rave** *pomp* to talk loudly and angrily —**~er** *n*

rant² *n* [U] RANTing talk

rap¹ /ræp/ *n* **1** (the sound of) a quick light blow: *hear a rap on the door|The teacher gave me a rap over the head with her pencil* **2 beat the rap** *AmE sl* to escape punishment **3 get/give a rap on/over the knuckles** get/give a scolding **4 take a rap** *AmE infml* to suffer a blow: *He took a bad rap on the head when he fell* **5 take the rap (for)** *infml* to receive the punishment (for someone else's crime)

rap² *v* **-pp- 1** [L9 (*at, on*); X9 (*on, over*)] to strike quickly and lightly: *someone rapping loudly at the door/on the table|rap someone on/over the head* **2** [T1] *not fml* (esp. in newspaper style) to speak severely to: *The judge rapped the police for their treatment of the witness*

rap³ *n infml* the least bit (in such phrs. as **not care/give a rap, it doesn't matter a rap**): *I don't care/give a rap for him.|It doesn't matter a rap what he says*

rap⁴ *v* **-pp-** [I∅] *AmE* to talk freely and easily

ra·pa·cious /rəˈpeɪʃəs/ *adj fml* (typical of a person) who takes everything he can, esp. by force: *a rapacious band of robbers|rapacious behaviour* —**~ly** *adv* —**~ness** *n* [U]

ra·pa·ci·ty /rəˈpæsɨti/ *n* [U] the quality of being RAPACIOUS

rape¹ /reɪp/ *n* [U] a type of European plant grown as food for sheep and pigs and for the oil produced from its seeds: *grow a crop of rape*

rape² *v* [T1] to have sex with, against the woman's will

rape³ *n* [C;U] **1** (a case of) the act and crime of raping (RAPE²): *He was sent to prison for rape* **2** spoiling: *the rape of our beautiful forests*

rap·id¹ /ˈræpɨd/ *adj* **1** quick-moving; fast: *a rapid journey/worker|The improvement was rapid.|to ask questions in rapid* SUCCESSION **2** (of actions) done in a short time: *The school promised rapid results in the learning of languages* **3** (of a slope) descending steeply **4 rapid-fire a** (of a gun) able to fire shots quickly one after the other **b** (of questions, jokes, etc.,) spoken quickly one after the other —**~ity** /rəˈpɪdɨti/ *n* [U] —**~ly** /ˈræpɨdli/ *adv*

rapid² *n* [*usu. pl.*] **1** a part of a river where the water moves very fast over rocks **2 shoot the rapids** (of a boat) to pass quickly down this part of a river

ra·pi·er /ˈreɪpɪəʳ/ *n* **1** a long light thin 2-edged sword with a sharp point, used for driving (THRUSTing) into the body **2 rapier-thrust a** an attack with the point of this sword **b** a swift sharp amusing remark or answer

rap·ine /ˈræpaɪn‖ˈræpɨn/ *n* [U] *lit* the carrying away of property by force; PLUNDER

rap·ist /ˈreɪpɨst/ *n* a man guilty of RAPE³ (1)

rap out *v adv* [T1] **1** to say sharply and suddenly: *The officer rapped out an order* **2** to express (a message) by means of RAPs¹ (1)

rap·port /ræˈpɔː‖-or (*Fr.* rapɔr)/ *n* [U (*between, with*)] *Fr* close agreement and understanding: *be in/feel/develop rapport with someone*

rap·proche·ment /ræˈprɒʃmɑ̃, ræˈprəʊʃ-‖ˌræprəʊʃˈmɑ̃/ *n Fr* a coming together again in friendship of former enemies: *At last there are signs of a rapprochement between our 2 countries*

rap·scal·li·on /ræpˈskælɪən/ *n* [C; *you*+N] *humor & old use* a worthless fellow whom one is rather fond of; a RASCAL (2): *You've been drinking again, you rapscallion!*

rapt /ræpt/ *adj* [(*in*)] (typical of a person) giving his whole mind (to): *We listened with rapt attention* —**~ly** *adv* —**~ness** *n* [U]

rap·ture /ˈræptʃəʳ/ *n* **1** [U] great joy and delight: *He was filled with rapture.|the rapture of our first kiss* **2** [(*at, about, over*)] **be in/go into raptures** to be/become full of great joy and delight: *She went into raptures at the news*

rap·tur·ous /ˈræptʃərəs/ *adj* causing or showing RAPTURE: *hear the rapturous news|give him a rapturous welcome* —**~ly** *adv*: *rapturously happy*

rare¹ /reəʳ/ *adj* (of meat, esp. STEAK) lightly cooked: *I want my* STEAK *very rare, please*

rare² *adj* **1** unusual; uncommon: *a rare event|collect rare books|It's very rare for him to be late* **2** *infml* unusually good: *The party was rare fun* **3** (esp. of air) thin; light: *the rare air of the mountains* **4 rare old** *infml* unusually good/bad: *have a rare old time at the party* —**~ness** [U] *n*

USAGE Uncommon and perhaps valuable things are **rare**: *a* **rare** *bird/coin.* Common useful things that we have not got enough of are **scarce**: *Potatoes were* **scarce** *last winter.* We can use **rare**, but not **scarce**, about time: *one of my* **rare** (=not happening often) *visits to Paris.* Note that **rarely** means "not often" while **scarcely** means "hardly; only just".

rare·bit /ˈreəbɨt‖ˈreər-/ *n fml* WELSH RABBIT

rare earth /ˌ· ˈ·/ any member of a group of RARE² (1) metal substances (ELEMENT*s*)

rar·e·fied /ˈreərɨfaɪd/ *adj often humor* very high and pure; grand: *He moves in very rarefied circles; his friends are all lords*

rar·e·fy /ˈreərɨfaɪ/ *v* [Wv5;T1] to make (a substance, esp. air) thinner, more widely spread, etc.

rare·ly /ˈreəli‖ˈreərli/ *adv* **1** not often: *I have rarely seen (fml Rarely have I seen) such a beautiful sunset* **2** *fml* uncommonly; to a RARE² (1) degree: *a rarely beautiful girl*

USAGE Notice the word order of a sentence beginning with **rarely** or **seldom**, which is that of a question: **Rarely/Seldom** *have I heard such a strange story.*

rar·ing /ˈreərɪŋ/ *adj* [F3] *infml* **1** very eager: *The children were raring to get out into the snow* **2 raring to go** eager to start

rar·i·ty /ˈreərɨti/ *n* **1** [U] the quality of being RARE² (1) **2** [C;S] something uncommon: *Women who bake their own bread are becoming a rarity*

ras·cal /ˈrɑːskəl‖ˈræs-/ *n* [C; *you*+N] **1** a dishonest person **2** *humor* a person who plays tricks or misbehaves: *You little rascal! Where have you hidden my shoes?*

ras·cal·ly /ˈrɑːskəli‖ˈræs-/ *adj* like or of a RASCAL (1): *What a rascally trick!*

rash¹ /ræʃ/ *adj* **1** (of a person or his behaviour) foolishly bold; not thinking enough of the results: *make/take a rash decision|a rash young soldier* **2 in a rash moment** without thinking enough of the results: *I promised in a rash moment to buy the children a pet monkey* —**~ly** *adv* —**~ness** *n* [U]

rash² *n* **1** [S] a set of red spots on the face or body or both, caused by illness: *a heat rash* **2** [S9+*of*] a sudden unpleasant appearance of the stated thing in large numbers: *a rash of complaints* **3 come out**

in a rash to become covered with small red spots
rash·er /ˈræʃəʳ/ *n* a thin piece of salted or smoked meat (HAM or BACON) from the back, side, or leg of a pig: *cook a few rashers (of* BACON*) for breakfast*
rasp¹ /rɑːsp‖ræsp/ *v* **1** [T1] to rub (as if) with a RASP²: *The shoe mender rasped the heel of my shoe.|The cat's tongue rasped my hand* **2** [X9 (AWAY, OFF)] to remove with a RASP²: *rasp away the rough corners* **3** [T1;I∅ (*on, upon*)] to have an annoying effect like the sound of a RASP² (on): *Her loud voice rasped (on) the sick man's nerves.|a rasping sound* **4** [T1 (OUT)] to say in a rough voice: *The officer rasped (out) an order.|"Leave the room!" he rasped* —**~ingly** *adv*
rasp² *n* **1** [C] a tool used for smoothing wood, metal, etc., with a long narrow metal blade covered with sharp points **2** [S] a sound that might be made by this tool: *hear a rasp of metal on stone*
rasp·ber·ry /ˈrɑːzbəri‖ˈræzberi/ *n* **1** a type of bush bearing a soft sweet red or yellow berry **2** the fruit of this bush: *raspberries and cream* —see picture at BERRY **3** *sl* a rude sound made by putting one's tongue out and blowing: *blow a raspberry at the General|get/give a raspberry*
rat¹ /ræt/ *n* **1** [C] any of several types of long-tailed animal (RODENT) related to but larger than the mouse —see picture at MAMMAL **2** [C; *you*+N] a low worthless disloyal man: *But you promised to help us, you rat!* **3** **(look) like a drowned rat** (to look) wet and cold and uncomfortable **4** **smell a rat** *infml* to guess that something wrong is happening
rat² *v* **-tt-** [I∅] **1** [(*on*)] *infml* to act in a disloyal way; to break a promise: *They said they'd help but they've ratted (on us)* **2** to hunt RATs¹ (1): *The dogs went ratting*
rat-a-tat /ˌræt ə ˈtæt/ also **rat-a-tat-tat** /ˌræt ə tæt ˈtæt/— *n* RAT-TAT
ratch·et /ˈrætʃ$\frac{1}{3}$t/ *n* **1** a toothed wheel or bar provided with a piece of metal (PAWL) that can fit between the teeth so as to allow movement in one direction but not the other —see picture at MACHINERY **2** also **ratchet wheel** /ˈ·· ·/— a wheel fitted in this way
rate¹ /reɪt/ *v* [I∅;T1] *becoming rare* to scold (someone) violently; BERATE —**rating** *n* [C]: *give him a good rating for what he did*
rate² *n* **1** [C9 esp. *of*] a value, cost, speed, etc., measured by its relation to some other amount: *travel at the rate of 100 km an hour|The birth rate is the number of births compared to the number of the people* **2** [C9] a (stated) speed: *drive at a steady rate* **3** [C9] a charge or payment fixed according to a standard scale: *Night telephone rates are cheaper than day rates.|to increase the rate of pay for the workers* **4** [C *usu. pl.*] *BrE* a local tax paid by owners of buildings: *The rates have gone up.|The water rate is the tax we pay for water* **5** [A9] of the (numbered) quality: *a first-rate performer|That's a very second-rate team so we'll beat them easily* **6** **at any rate** in any case; whatever happens: *At any rate we can go out when it stops raining* **7** **at this/that rate** if events continue in the same way as now/then: *At this rate we won't be able to afford a holiday* **8** **rate of exchange** the relationship between the money of 2 countries: *What's the rate of exchange today between the £ and the $?*
rate³ *v* [X7,9] **1** to consider; set a value on: *I rate him high(ly) as a poet* **2** [*usu. pass.*] *BrE* to fix a RATE² (4) on (a building): *My house is rated rather high|at £500*
ra·tea·ble, ratable /ˈreɪtəbəl/ *adj* (of a building or its value) on which RATEs² (4) are charged: *What's the rateable value of this shop?*
rate·pay·er /ˈreɪtˌpeɪəʳ/ *n BrE* a person who pays RATEs² (4)
ra·ther¹ /ˈrɑːðəʳ‖ˈræðər/ *predeterminer, adv* [Wa5] **1** a little; QUITE (2); slightly: **a** (with an adj, adv, or prep) *a rather cold day|rather a cold day|rather cold weather|the rather cold weather we've been having|to drive rather fast|These shoes are rather too big.|I'm feeling rather better.|It's rather like a potato.|She's getting rather fat* **b** (with a sing. n or a v) *rather a pity|rather a lot of money|She's rather a fool.|I rather thought he'd say that.|It rather surprised me.|I rather like grammar, actually!* **2** (*often with* would *and sometimes with* had) more willingly: *I'd rather play tennis than swim.|"Have a drink?" "No thanks, I would rather not."|Rather than cause trouble, he left* —compare SOONer (3) **3** more; in a greater degree (in the phr. **rather than**): *John ought to go rather than Jean.|It was what he meant rather than what he said.|These shoes are comfortable rather than pretty.|He ran rather than walked* **4** more exactly; more truly; it would be better to say (in the phr. **or rather**): *He came home very late last night, or rather very early this morning*
USAGE 1 In some of the examples for 1**a**, one could say **fairly**: *a* **fairly** *cold day|***fairly** *cold weather|the* **fairly** *cold weather|to drive* **fairly** *fast.* This would mean that the coldness and speed of driving were not too great; a "**fairly** *cold*" day is "cold enough", but a "**rather** *cold*" day may be "too cold". Many British speakers, however, use **rather** about things they like very much: *I was* **rather** *pleased when I won the* NOBEL PRIZE. 2 *I would* **rather** is usual in *BrE*, though *I had* **rather** is not wrong even there, and the second may be equally common in *AmE*. The short form *I'd* **rather** stands for both.
ra·ther² /rɑːˈðɜːʳ‖ræ-/ *interj esp. BrE* Yes, certainly!: *"Isn't she beautiful?" "Rather!"|"Would you like a swim?" "Rather!"*
rat·i·fy /ˈræt$\frac{1}{3}$faɪ/ *v* [T1] *fml* to approve and make official by signing (a written agreement): *The heads of the 2 governments met to ratify the* TREATY —**-fication** /ˌræt$\frac{1}{3}$f$\frac{1}{3}$ˈkeɪʃən/ *n* [U]
rat·ing¹ /ˈreɪtɪŋ/ *n* **1** [C;U] the value of a building for tax (RATEs): *The rating officer came to look at the farm.|get a very low rating* **2** [C] the class in which a ship or machine is placed according to its size: *a ship with a rating of 500,000* TONs **3** [C] the position given to a radio or television PROGRAMME, or to a GRAMOPHONE record, showing how popular it is: *This song's been getting very good ratings* **4** [C] (in the British navy) a sailor who is not an officer: *a group of naval ratings drinking beer* **5** [C] *AmE* the business responsibility that a person or firm is thought to have: *a good* CREDIT¹ (6) *rating*
ra·ti·o /ˈreɪʃiəʊ‖ˈreɪʃəʊ/ *n* **-os** a figure showing the number of times one quantity contains another: *The ratio of 10 to 5 is 2 to 1* —compare PROPORTION
ra·ti·o·ci·na·tion /ˌrætiɒs$\frac{1}{3}$ˈneɪʃən‖ˌræʃiɑs$\frac{1}{3}$-, ˌræti-əʊs$\frac{1}{3}$-/ *n* [U] *fml* exact and METHODICAL thinking
ra·tion¹ /ˈræʃən‖ˈræ-, ˈreɪ-/ *n* a share (of food, petrol, etc.) allowed to one person for a period
ration² *v* [T1] **1** [(*to*)] to limit (someone) to a fixed RATION¹: *ration them to 2 eggs a week* **2** to limit and control (supplies): *They had to ration petrol* —compare RATION OUT
ra·tion·al /ˈræʃənəl/ *adj* **1** (of people) able to reason: *A rational woman wouldn't weep just because her husband had forgotten her birthday* **2** (of ideas and behaviour) sensible; according to reason: *offer a rational suggestion|explanation|not a very rational thing to do* —opposite **irrational** —**~ly** *adv* —**~ity** /ˌræʃəˈnæl$\frac{1}{3}$ti/ *n* [U]
ra·tio·nale /ˌræʃəˈnɑːl‖-ˈnæl/ *n* [C;U] the reason(s)

on which a system or practice is based

ra·tion·al·is·m /ˈræʃənəlɪzəm/ *n* [U] the quality or practice of being (a) RATIONALIST: *the period of 18th century rationalism in Europe*

ra·tion·al·ist /ˈræʃənəlɨst/ *adj, n* [B;C] (typical of) a person who bases his opinions and actions on reason, rather than on feelings or on religious belief —**~ic** /ˌræʃənəˈlɪstɪk/ *adj*

ra·tion·al·ize, -ise /ˈræʃənəlaɪz/ *v* **1** [IØ;T1] to find reasons (for one's own unreasonable behaviour or opinions): *to rationalize one's fears* **2** [T1] *esp. BrE* to make (a method or system) more modern and sensible and less wasteful: *to rationalize the organization of the firm* —**-ization** /ˌræʃənəlaɪˈzeɪʃən‖-lə-/ *n* [C;U]

ration book /ˈ·· ·/ *n* a book of tickets allowing one to buy RATIONS[1]

ration out *v adv* [T1] to give out (supplies) in RATIONS[1]: *He rationed out the water to the sailors* —compare RATION[2] (2)

ra·tions /ˈræʃənz‖ˈræ-, ˈreɪ-/ *n* [P] **1** the food supplied to members of the armed forces: *The men are complaining about their rations again, sir* **2 be on short rations** to be allowed less food than usual

rat·line, -lin /ˈrætlɨn/ *n* [*usu. pl.*] one of a set of short ropes forming a rope ladder for sailors to climb the SHROUDs of a ship

rat race /ˈ· ·/ *n* [*the*+R] *infml* the endless competition for success among fellow-workers in business: *Paul and Charles got so tired of the rat race that they left their jobs and went to work on a farm*

rats /ræts/ *interj sl* Nonsense! I don't believe it!

rat-tailed /ˈ· ·/ *n* (of a spoon) with a raised line along the back of the bowl

rat·tan /ræˈtæn, rə-/ *n* **1** [C] a type of tropical plant with a strong stem that is easily bent **2** [C] a walking-stick made from the stem of this plant **3** [U] these stems used for making baskets, furniture, etc.

rat-tat /ˌræt ˈtæt/ also **rat-a-tat, rat-a-tat-tat**— *n* [S] a sound of knocking, esp. on a door: *to hear a loud rat-tat*

rat·ter /ˈrætəʳ/ *n* a dog or cat that catches rats

rat·tle[1] /ˈrætl/ *v* **1** [IØ;T1] to (cause to) make a lot of quick little noises as of small hard objects hitting each other: *The beggar rattled the coins in his tin.|The windows rattled in the wind* **2** [L9] to move quickly while making these noises: *The cart rattled along the stony road* **3** [Wv5;T1] *infml* to make nervous or anxious: *Keep calm—don't get rattled*

rattle[2] *n* **1** [C] a baby's toy that RATTLEs[1] (1) **2** [C] an instrument that RATTLEs[1] (1), as used for making a happy noise by people watching a football match **3** [S] a rattling noise (RATTLE[1] (1)): *a rattle of milk bottles* **4** [C] the horny rings in a RATTLESNAKE's tail that make a noise

rat·tle·brained /ˈrætlbreɪnd/ *adj* (of a person) foolish and always talking

rattle off also **reel off**— *v adv* [T1] to repeat quickly and easily from memory: *He rattled off the poem*

rattle on also **rattle a·way**— *v adv* [IØ] to talk quickly and continuously: *He kept rattling away in French*

rattle·snake /ˈrætlsneɪk/ also (*esp. AmE*) **rat·tler** /ˈrætləʳ/— *n* a poisonous American snake that makes a noise with its tail when it is angry —see also RATTLE[2] (4)

rattle through *v prep* [T1] to perform quickly: *to rattle through his speech/her work*

rat·tle·trap /ˈrætltræp/ *n infml* a noisy old vehicle, esp. a car

rat·tling[1] /ˈrætlɪŋ/ *adj* [A] *infml apprec* (of movement or events) quick and busy: *The shop was doing a rattling trade*

rattling[2] *adv infml apprec* very: *a rattling good horse*

rat·ty /ˈræti/ *adj* [Wa1] **1** *BrE infml* annoyed: *Mother got a bit ratty when I broke those plates* **2** full of or reminding one of rats

rau·cous /ˈrɔːkəs/ *adj* (of voices) rough and unpleasant: *raucous shouts* —**~ly** *adv* —**~ness** *n* [U]

raunch·y /ˈrɔːntʃi/ *adj* [Wa1] *AmE sl* having or showing a strong desire for sex —**raunchiness** *n* [U]

rav·age /ˈrævɪdʒ/ *v* [T1 *often pass.*] **1** to ruin and destroy: *crops ravaged by storms* **2** (of an army or large crowd) to rob with violence (an area): *The conquering army ravaged the whole country*

rav·ag·es /ˈrævɪdʒɨz/ *n* [P9+*of*] the destroying effects of: *the ravages of fire/war*

rave[1] /reɪv/ *v* **1** [IØ (*about, against, at*)] to talk wildly as if mad: *He raved all night in his fever.|Father's raving at/against the Government again* **2** [X7,9] to put (oneself) into the stated condition by talking wildly: *He raved himself* HOARSE/*into a high fever*

rave[2] *n* **1** [A] *infml* very eager praise (esp. of a work of art): *His new play has been getting rave notices in the papers* **2** [C] *sl* a wild exciting party **3 in a rave about** *sl* full of admiration (for)

rave a·bout *v prep* [T1] *infml* to speak about with (too) great admiration: *All the girls raved about the new singer*

rav·el /ˈrævəl/ *v* **-ll-** (*AmE* **-l-**) [IØ;T1] **1** to UNRAVEL: *a rope that is ravelling at its end* **2** [(UP)] **a** to cause (threads, hair, etc.) to become twisted and knotted: *Don't let the cat ravel that ball of wool up* **b** (of threads, hair, etc.) to become twisted and knotted

ra·ven /ˈreɪvən/ *n* **1** [C] a type of large shiny black bird with a black beak and a deep unmusical voice (CROAK) **2** [A] *lit* the shiny black colour of this bird

raven-haired /ˌ·· ˈ·◂/ *adj lit* with shiny black hair

rav·e·ning /ˈrævənɪŋ/ *adj* [A] fierce and dangerous because of hunger: *ravening tigers*

rav·e·nous /ˈrævənəs/ *adj* very hungry —**~ly** *adv*

rav·er /ˈreɪvəʳ/ *n infml* an exciting person who leads an exciting life, esp. a modern person with social and sexual freedom

rave-up /ˈ· ·/ *n sl* a very wild party

ra·vine /rəˈviːn/ *n* a deep narrow valley with steep sides —see VALLEY (USAGE)

rav·ing /ˈreɪvɪŋ/ *adj, adv infml* (up to the point of) talking wildly: *a raving madman|He's raving (mad)* —see MAD (USAGE)

rav·ings /ˈreɪvɪŋz/ *n* [P] wild uncontrolled talk: *His ravings are impossible to understand.|the ravings of a madman/of the sick man*

rav·i·o·li /ˌræviˈəʊli/ *n* [U] a food in the form of small cases of flour paste (PASTA) filled with meat and boiled: *a big plateful of ravioli* —compare SPAGHETTI, MACARONI

rav·ish /ˈrævɪʃ/ *v* [T1] **1** *lit* to RAPE **2** *lit* to seize or rob with violence **3** [*usu. pass.*+*by, with*] to fill with delight: *ravished by her beauty*

rav·ish·ing /ˈrævɪʃɪŋ/ *adj* very beautiful; causing great delight: *a ravishing sight* —**~ly** *adv*

rav·ish·ment /ˈrævɪʃmənt/ *n* [U] the event of RAVISHing or being RAVISHed

raw[1] /rɔː/ *adj* [Wa5] **1** (of food) not cooked: *raw vegetables* **2** in the natural state; not yet treated for use: *raw silk/cotton* **3** (of a person) not yet trained; not experienced: *a raw* RECRUIT *who has just joined the army* **4** (of a part of the body) without skin; painful: *a raw wound|hands raw with cold* **5** (of weather) cold and wet: *a raw winter day* —**~ly** *adv* —**~ness** *n* [U]

raw² *n* [*the*+R] **1 in the raw a** without civilization: *see life in the raw among those wild tribes* **b** without clothes: *go swimming in the raw* **2 touch (someone) on the raw** to hurt (someone's) feelings by mentioning a subject on which he is sensitive

raw-boned /ˌ· ˈ·◂/ *adj* [Wa5] having large bones whose shape shows under the skin: *a big raw-boned woman*

raw deal /ˌ· ˈ·/ *n infml* a case of unfair or cruel treatment: *have/get (rather) a raw deal*

raw·hide /ˈrɔːhaɪd/ *n* **1** [U] natural untreated cow's leather: *a rawhide belt|boots made of rawhide* **2** [C] *esp. AmE* a whip made of this

raw ma·te·ri·al /ˌ· ·ˈ···/ *n* [*often pl.*] the natural substance(s) from which an article is made: *Coal and oil are important raw materials for the plastics industry*

ray¹ /reɪ/ *n* any of various types of large flat sea fish with a long pointed tail, related to the SHARK

ray² *n* [C9 esp. *of*] **1** a narrow beam (of light), esp. one of a group going out like a wheel from the same centre: *the sun's rays* **2** (in science) a line (of the stated force): *take an* X-RAY *photograph|to kill with a magic death ray* **3** a very small bit (of hope or comfort): *There isn't a ray of hope left for us*

ray·on /ˈreɪɒn‖-ɑn/ *n* [U] a smooth silk-like material made from wool or cotton (CELLULOSE)

raze /reɪz/ *v* [T1] *fml* to flatten (buildings, towns, etc.) (usu. in the phr. **raze to the ground**): *a bomb attack that razed the city to the ground*

ra·zor /ˈreɪzəʳ/ *n* a sharp sometimes electric instrument for removing hair from the skin: SHAVE (=cut) *off my beard with an electric razor* —see SAFETY RAZOR and picture at BATHROOM

ra·zor·back /ˈreɪzəbæk‖-ər-/ *n* **1** *BrE* a kind of large sea animal (WHALE) **2** *AmE* a type of partly wild pig of the south US

razor-backed /ˌ·· ˈ·◂/ *adj* with a narrow sharp-edged back: *razor-backed pigs*

razor edge /ˌ·· ˈ·◂/ also **razor's edge** /ˌ·· ˈ·◂/— *n* a difficult position between success and failure: *Edward nearly died in the accident—his life was on a razor edge for days.|a razor edge* SITUATION *between peace and war*

raz·zle /ˈræzəl/ *n* [*the*+R] a noisy pleasure party (in the phrs. **be/go on the razzle**): *After the football team won the match they all went on the razzle*

R.C. *n abbrev. for*: ROMAN CATHOLIC

Rd *written abbrev. for*: ROAD (2)

-rd *written suffix* (forms ORDINAL numbers with 3): *a 3rd* (=a third)|*the 23rd of June*

re¹ /reɪ/ *n* [C;U] the 2nd note in the (SOL-FA) musical SCALE: *sing (a) re*

re² /riː/ *prep* (esp. in business letters) on the subject of; with regard to: *re your enquiry of the 19th October*

re- /riː, rɪ/ *prefix* [*v→v, n→n*] **1** again: *to reboil the water|to hear a rebroadcast of a radio play* **2** again in a better way: *to rearrange the furniture|to rewrite the letter* **3** back to the former state: *to rebury the body*

USAGE When a word formed with **re-** has the same meaning as before with the addition of "again", "back", etc., then **re-** is pronounced /riː/. Other words already began with **re-** when they were borrowed from another language; it is then no longer possible to guess their meaning from their parts, and **re-** is pronounced /rɪ/. Compare **recover** (=to get better) /rɪˈkʌvəʳ/; **re-cover** (=to cover again)/ˌriːˈkʌvəʳ/.

're /əʳ/ *v contr. of* are: *We're ready but they're not.|"Are you Spanish?" "Yes, we are"* (not ***we're**)

USAGE Forms with **'re** are now used everywhere except in the most *fml* or *tech* writing. —see CONTR. (USAGE)

reach¹ /riːtʃ/ *v* **1** [L9] to stretch out a hand or arm for some purpose: *reach across the table and pick up the book|The shopkeeper reached for a packet of tea.|I reached up and put the parcel on top of the cupboard.|*(fig.) *to reach out towards a new idea* **2** [IØ;T1] to touch (something) by stretching out a hand or arm: *"Can you reach that apple on the tree?" "No, I'm not tall enough to reach (it)"* **3** [D1; T1: (DOWN)] to get or give by stretching out a hand or arm: *reach down the child's cap from the hook|Please reach me the coffee pot* **4** [L9;T1] (of things or places) to be big enough to touch; stretch out as far as: *The ladder won't quite reach (as far as) the window.|The forest reaches for many kilometres.|The garden reaches down to the lake* **5** [T1] to arrive at; get to: *They reached London on Thursday.|to reach the end of the book|The news only reached me yesterday.|reach the age of 50* **6** [T1] to get a message to; get in touch with (someone): *He can always be reached on the office telephone* **7 as far as the eye can reach** to the horizon: *see nothing but houses as far as the eye can reach*

reach² *n* **1** [U (*of*)] the distance that one can reach: *put the bottle within/beyond/out of (his) reach|to live within easy reach of the shops|*(fig.) *beyond the reach of my imagination* **2** [S] the length of one's arm: *He has a longer reach than I have so he can climb better* **3** [C] a straight stretch of water between 2 bends in a river

reach-me-down /ˈ· · ˌ·/ *n* [*usu. pl.*] *BrE infml* **1** a cheap ready-made garment usu. of poor quality **2** (*AmE* **hand-me-down**)— a garment used by one person after belonging to another: *wearing my big brother's reach-me-downs*

reach out *v adv* [T1 (*for*)] *no pass.* to stretch out (a hand or arm): *The monkey reached out a hand through the bars and took the banana*

re·act /riˈækt/ *v* [IØ] **1** [(*to*)] to act in reply; to behave differently as a result: *When the sun comes out the flowers react by opening wide.|How did he react to your suggestion?* **2** [(*with*)] *tech* (of a substance) to change when mixed with another: *An acid can react with a* BASE *to form a salt*

react a·gainst *v prep* [T1] to show feelings of opposition against; to take action against: *He reacted against his father's influence by becoming a priest*

re·ac·tion /riˈækʃən/ *n* **1** [C (*to*)] a case of REACTing (1): *What was your reaction to the news?* **2** [S;U] **a** (a) change back to a former condition **b** sudden weakness, tiredness, low spirits, etc., coming after unusual activity, esp. of the mind **3** [U] the quality of being REACTIONARY: *His efforts were defeated by the forces of reaction* **4** [C;U] (in science) **a** (a) force exercised by a body in reply to another force: *Action and reaction are equal and opposite* (Newton) **b** (a) change caused in a chemical substance by the action of another

re·ac·tion·a·ry /riˈækʃənəri‖-ʃəneri/ *adj, n* (a person) against or preventing (esp. political) changes in society

re·ac·tiv·ate /riˈæktɨveɪt/ *v* [IØ;T1] to make or become active again: *to reactivate the old arrangement|The chemicals reactivate when heated*

re·ac·tive /riˈæktɪv/ *adj* (of a chemical substance) that REACTs (2) —**~ly** *adv* —**~ness** *n*

react on also **react up·on**— *v prep* [T1] (of things or events) to have an effect on: *The rise in oil costs reacted on the price of food*

re·ac·tor /riˈæktəʳ/ *n* **1** NUCLEAR REACTOR **2** a container for a chemical REACTION

read¹ /riːd/ *v* **read** /red/ **1** [IØ;T1] (often+*can*) to understand (language in print or writing): *The child can read/is reading quite well now.|He reads well for a 6-year old.|to read a book* **2** [Wv6;T1] to understand (something printed or written): *to read music|to read a map|I can read French but I can't speak it.|(fig.) I can read your thoughts (from your face)* **3** [D1 (*to*); L9, esp. *to*; T1: (ALOUD)] to say (printed or written words) esp. to give pleasure to others: *She read the children a story.|The teacher read the poem aloud to the class* —compare READ OUT (1) **4** [I∅;T1,5,6b] to get (the stated information) from (print or writing): *read about the murder|read the account of the murder in the paper|read that the murderer has been caught|read how to make pastry* **5** [Wv6;L9] (of something written) to influence people (in the stated way): *Her letters always read well/always read as if she copied them from books* **6** [T1] to study (a subject) at university level: *John's reading History/Law at Oxford* —compare READ FOR **7** [L1,9] (of written words) to be or mean when said: *The name reads "Benson" not "Fenton".|The 2 copies read the same/differently* **8** [T1] (of measuring instruments) to show: *The* THERMOMETER *reads 33 degrees* **9** [T1 (*as*)] *fml* (to a person, +*please*) to understand the stated printed or written words to be a mistake for: *For £50 please read £15.|Please read £50 as £15.|£50 was read (as) £15* **10 read between the lines** to find a meaning that is not expressed: *If you read between the lines, this letter is really a request for money* **11 read oneself/someone to sleep** to make oneself/someone go to sleep by reading **12 take something as read** to declare something to be satisfactory or to be what it claims to be, without any need to consider it further: *We can take his ability as read, but is his character suitable for the job?*

read² *n esp. BrE infml* **1** [S] an act or period of reading: *Can I have a read of your paper?* **2** [S9] something (of the stated kind) to be read: *It's not great literature but it's a very good read*

-read /red/ *comb. form* **1** (of a person) informed to the stated degree by reading: *a well-read man|widely-read in Greek literature* **2** (of a piece of writing) read to the stated degree: *a widely-read newspaper*

rea·da·ble /ˈriːdəbəl/ *adj* **1** interesting or easy to read: *a readable article on metal, without too many scientific words* **2** LEGIBLE —**-bility** /ˌriːdəˈbɪlɪ̇ti/ *n* [U]

re·ad·dress /ˌriːəˈdres/ also **redirect**— *v* [T1 (*to*)] to write a different address on (a letter); to send, by writing a different address: *Readdress my letters (to the new house)*

read·er /ˈriːdəʳ/ *n* **1** [C9] a person who reads (a stated thing or in a stated way): *Are you a fast reader?|My brother's a great reader—he's always at the library.|We have received many letters on this subject from our readers* (in a newspaper) **2** [C;U] (the job of) a person who reads books to put mistakes right before printing or to decide whether to print (PUBLISH) them **3** [C;U (*in*)] (*often cap.*) *BrE* (the job of) a university teacher above the rank of LECTURER: *reader in French* **4** [C] a type of schoolbook for beginners: *Open your poetry readers at page 14*

read·er·ship /ˈriːdəʃɪp‖-ər-/ *n* **1** [S9] the (stated) number of READERs (1) of a newspaper: *The paper has a readership of 5000* **2** [C (*in*)] the position of a READER (3): *offer him a readership in modern languages*

read for *v prep* [T1] *esp. BrE* to study towards: *read for a university degree* —compare READ¹ (6)

read·i·ly /ˈredɪ̇li/ *adv* **1** willingly: *He readily promised to help* **2** with no difficulty: *They can readily be bought anywhere*

read·i·ness /ˈredinɪ̇s/ *n* **1** [S;U:3] (a) willingness: *show (a) great readiness to learn* **2** [S;U:9+*of*] (a) quickness: *her readiness of tongue* —see READY¹ (3) **3** [(*in*) U] the state of being ready: *to have everything in readiness for the party*

read·ing /ˈriːdɪŋ/ *n* **1** [U] the act or practice of reading: *Children learn reading and writing at school* **2** [U] knowledge obtained through books: *a man of little reading but much practical experience* **3** [C+*of*] an opinion about the meaning of (writing or events): *My reading of the law is that we needn't pay* **4** [C] a figure shown by a measuring instrument: *What are the temperature readings for the week?* **5** [U9] matter (of the stated type) to be read: *suitable reading for children* **6** [C] a gathering of people at which literature is read aloud: *to give public readings of Dickens's works|to have play-readings on Saturdays* **7** [C] (in Parliament) one of the 3 official occasions on which a suggested new law (BILL) is read aloud and considered: *the 3rd reading of the Industrial Relations* BILL **8** [A] for reading: *go and work in the reading room at the library|put the reading lamp on the table*

reading desk /ˈ·· ·/ LECTERN

read in·to *v prep* [D1] to believe (something) to be meant though not expressed (by something else): *Don't read more into her letter than she intended*

re·ad·just /ˌriːəˈdʒʌst/ *v* [I∅;T1: (*to*)] to get or put back into the proper position: *readjust the driving mirror|readjust (oneself) to school life after the holidays* —**~ment** *n* [C;U]: *a period of readjustment|make various readjustments*

read·out /ˈriːd-aʊt/ *n* [U] **1** the work of removing information from a machine that stores and produces it (COMPUTER) and of showing it in an understandable form **2** the information produced in this way

read out *v adv* [T1] **1** to read (a short piece of writing or a few facts) for others to hear: *read out the football results* —compare READ¹ (3) **2** *esp. AmE* to dismiss (as) from a political party: *They threatened to read him out (of the party)*

read through also **read o·ver**— *v adv* [T1] to practise (a play) using the words without movements —**read-through** /ˈ· ·/ *n* [S]: *Let's have a read-through*

read up *v adv* [T1;I∅+*on*] *infml* to study (a subject) thoroughly; to find out about by reading: *read up (on) the habits of elephants*

read·y¹ /ˈredi/ *adj* **1** [(*for*), F3] prepared and fit (for use): *Is breakfast ready?|The letters are ready for the post/ready to be signed.|I'm not ready yet. Where are my shoes?* **2** [F3] (of a person) willing (to do something): *She's always ready to help* **3** [A] (of thoughts or their expression) quick: *She has a ready tongue* (=can talk well).|*a man of ready* WIT **4** [F+*with*] (of a person) eager (to give): *She's too ready with advice* **5** [F] within reach: *He slept with his sword ready* **6 make ready** to prepare oneself: *They made ready for the attack*

ready² *interj BrE* **Ready, steady, go!** also **on your mark(s), get set, go!**— (used when telling people to begin a race): *Now, children, get in line. Ready, steady, go!*

ready³ *v* [T1] *esp. AmE* to prepare (oneself or something)

ready⁴ *n* [*the*+R] the state of being ready (in the phr. **at the ready**, of a gun)

ready⁵ *adv* (*used before a past p.*) in advance: *buy the meat ready cut|a ready-cooked dinner*

ready-made¹ /ˌ·· ˈ·◂/ *adj* [Wa5] **1** (of something bought, esp. of clothes) not made specially for the buyer; able to be used at once: *Most people wear ready-made shoes.|(fig.) His second wife had 3 children already, so when he married her he had a ready-made family* **2** *derog* not original: *ready-made opinions*

ready-made² /ˈ·· ·/ *n* a READY-MADE¹ (1) garment

ready mon·ey /ˌ·· ˈ··/ also **ready cash** /ˌ·· ˈ·/— *n* money that can be paid at once in actual coins and notes, and not owed: *sell it quickly for ready money*

ready reck·on·er /ˌ·· ˈ···/ *n* a book of tables to save the trouble of calculating

ready-to-wear /ˌ·· · ˈ·◂/ *adj* [Wa5;A] (of clothes) READY-MADE[1] (1): *a ready-to-wear suit*

re·af·for·est /ˌriːəˈfɒrəst‖-ˈfɔ-, -ˈfɑ-/ also (*esp. AmE*) **reforest**— *v* [T1] *esp. BrE* to plant (land) again with forest trees —**~ation** /ˌriːəfɒrəˈsteɪʃən‖-fɔ-, -fɑ-/ *n* [U]: *the reafforestation of Scotland*

re·a·gent /riːˈeɪdʒənt/ *n tech* a substance that by causing chemical REACTION (4) in a compound shows the presence of another substance

real[1] /rɪəl/ *adj* actually existing; true not false: *Is your ring brass or real gold?|What was the real reason for your absence?|The real amount was only £50.|a story of real life* —**~ness** *n* [U]

real[2] /rɪəl/ *n esp. AmE infml* **for real** **a** seriously: *They were fighting for real* **b** serious: *He couldn't believe their threats were for real*

real[3] /rɪəl/ *adv esp. AmE infml* very: *I'm real sorry!*

re·al[4] /reɪˈɑːl/ *n* (the value of) a coin formerly used in Spain and its Empire

real es·tate /ˈ· ·ˌ·/ *n* [U] **1** also **real property**— *fml & law* property in land and houses —compare PERSONAL PROPERTY **2** *esp. AmE* houses to be bought: *sell real estate*

real estate a·gent /ˈ· ·· ˌ··/ *n AmE* ESTATE AGENT

re·align /ˌriːəˈlaɪn/ *v* [T1] to form into new groups, regular arrangements, etc: *to realign one's forces on the battlefield* —**~ment** *n* [U]

re·a·lis·m /ˈrɪəlɪzəm/ *n* [U] **1** determination to face facts and deal with them practically, without being influenced by feelings or false ideas **2** (*often cap.*) (in art and literature) the showing of things as they really are: *Realism sometimes tends to show unpleasant details* —compare ROMANTICISM, CLASSICISM **3** (in PHILOSOPHY (1)) the belief that matter really exists outside our own minds —compare IDEALISM

re·a·list /ˈrɪələst/ *n* **1** a person whose social, political, and artistic ideas are based on REALISM (1) **2** an artist or writer whose work is based on REALISM (2)

re·a·lis·tic /rɪəˈlɪstɪk/ *adj* **1** showing REALISM (1): *Our income has got smaller, so we must be realistic and give up our car* **2** (of art or literature) life-like: *a realistic drawing of a horse* —**~ally** *adv* [Wa4]

re·al·i·ty /riˈæləti/ *n* **1** [U] the quality or state of being real; real existence: *She believes in the reality of fairies* **2** [C] something real: *Her dream of marrying Frederick became a reality* **3** [U] everything that is real: *try to escape from reality by going to the cinema* **4 in reality** in actual fact; in spite of what was thought: *Everyone liked the stranger, but in reality he was a criminal*

re·a·li·za·ble, -sable /ˈrɪəlaɪzəbəl/ *adj* that can be REALIZED: *His hopes are hardly realizable.|not realizable property*

re·a·li·za·tion, -sation /ˌrɪəlaɪˈzeɪʃən‖-lə-/ *n* **1** [S; U:9 (*esp. of*); *the*+U5] (an experience of) understanding and believing: (*a*) *full realization of his guilt|the full realization that he was guilty* **2** [*the*+U+*of*] (of a hope or purpose) becoming real: *the realization of my hopes* **3** [*the*+U+*of*] *fml* the act of selling (property) or of getting (money for selling property): *the realization of the house/of £1000*

re·a·lize, -ise /ˈrɪəlaɪz/ *v* **1** [T1,5a,6a] to understand and believe (a fact): *He didn't realize his mistake.|Do you realize it's Saturday?|I didn't realize how late it was* **2** [T1] to carry out; make real (a hope or purpose): *She realized her intention of becoming an actress* **3** [T1] *fml* **a** to sell: *He realized the house* **b** to get (money by selling): *He realized a profit* **4** [T1] *fml* (of something sold) to bring (money): *The house realized a profit*

realize on *v prep fml* **1** [T1] to sell (property), so as to get money: *He realized on the house* **2** [D1] to get (money) by selling (property): *He realized a profit on the house*

real·ly /ˈrɪəli/ *adv* [Wa5] **1** in actual fact; truly: *Did he really say that?|I really don't/I don't really want any more beer.|really rather a nice boy* **2** very (much); thoroughly: *It's really cold today.|I really hate him* **3** (*used for giving force to* ought *or* should) more correctly: *You ought really to have asked me first, you know* **4** (used for showing interest, doubt, surprise, or slight displeasure): *"I collect rare coins." "Really?"|Well, really! What a nasty thing to do*

realm /relm/ *n* **1** (*often cap.*) *lit & law* a kingdom: *the defence of the Realm* **2** [*often pl. with sing. meaning*] a world; area: *the realm of science|Fairies belong to the realms of the imagination*

re·al·pol·i·tik /reɪˈɑːlpɒlɪtiːk‖-pɑ- (*Ger* reˈaːlpoliːtiːk)/ *n* [U] politics based on practical and material facts rather than on ideas or moral aims, and directed towards the material success and greatness of one's own nation

real prop·er·ty /ˌ· ˈ···/ *n* [U] *fml, esp. law* REAL ESTATE (1)

real time /ˈ· ·/ *n tech* the actual time in which an event takes place (used of events controlled by COMPUTERs)

real·tor /ˈrɪəltəʳ, -tɔːʳ/ *n AmE tdmk* ESTATE AGENT

real·ty /ˈrɪəlti/ *n* [U] *law* REAL ESTATE

ream /riːm/ *n* **1** a measure for sheets of paper **a** (in Britain) 480 sheets **b** (in the US) 500 sheets **2** [*usu. pl. with sing. meaning*] *infml* a lot (of writing): *write reams of poetry*

re·an·i·mate /riːˈænəmeɪt/ *v* [T1] to fill with new strength or courage; bring back to life: *The new leader reanimated the political party*

reap /riːp/ *v* [I∅;T1] to cut and gather (a crop of grain): *to reap the corn|The men were all out reaping.|*(fig.) *to reap a reward/a profit*

reap·er /ˈriːpəʳ/ *n* **1** a machine that REAPs **2** *becoming rare* a person who REAPs

reaper and bind·er /ˌ·· · ˈ··/ *n* a machine that cuts the crop and binds it into sheaves (SHEAF)

reaping hook /ˈ·· ·/ *AmE* usu. **reap·hook** /ˈriːphʊk/— *n* SICKLE

re·ap·pear /ˌriːəˈpɪəʳ/ *v* [I∅] to appear again after absence —**~ance** /ˌriːəˈpɪərəns/ *n* [U]

re·ap·prais·al /ˌriːəˈpreɪzəl/ *n fml* **1** [U] the act of examining something again to see whether one should change one's opinion of it: *Our relations with Japan need reappraisal* **2** [C] a new judgment formed in this way

rear[1] /rɪəʳ/ *v* **1** [T1] to care for until fully grown: *He rears all types of birds.|to rear a large family* —compare RAISE[1] (esp. 7) **2** [T1] to lift up (one's head) esp. so as to be noticed: *A lion suddenly reared its head from among the long grass* **3** [I∅] (of a 4-legged animal) to rise upright on the back legs: *The horse reared and threw me off* **4** [T1] *fml* to build (something high): *to rear a tower*

rear[2] *n* **1** [U] the back: *a garden at the rear of the house|a rear window|the rear wheel of a bicycle* **2** [C] *euph* the part of the body where one sits; BUTTOCKS **3 bring up the rear** to come last (as in a procession)

USAGE British speakers say **at the rear** for something that is behind and beyond: *a garden* **at the rear** *of the house*, and **in the rear** for the back part of something: *walk* **in the rear** *of the procession.* American speakers generally say **in the rear** for both.

rear ad·mi·ral /ˌ· ˈ···◂/ *n* [C;A;N] (*often cap.*) an

officer of high rank in the navy: *Rear Admiral Jones|What do you think, Rear Admiral?|2 rear admirals on one ship*
rear·guard /ˈrɪəgɑːd‖ˈrɪərgɑrd/ *n* **1** a formation of soldiers protecting the REAR² (1) of an army —compare VANGUARD **2 rearguard action** a fight by the REAR of an army that is being driven back by a victorious enemy: (fig.) *to fight a rearguard action against political change*
re·arm /riːˈɑːm‖-ˈɑrm/ *v* [I∅;T1 (*with*)] to provide (oneself or others) with weapons again, or with new weapons: *If we want to fight we must rearm.|to rearm them with modern guns*
re·ar·ma·ment /riːˈɑːməmənt‖-ˈɑr-/ *n* [U] the action of REARMing a nation
rear·most /ˈrɪəməʊst‖ˈrɪər-/ *adj* [Wa5;A] last; furthest back: *sit in the rearmost carriage of the train*
re·ar·range /ˌriːəˈreɪndʒ/ *v* [T1] **1** to put into a different order: *Let's rearrange the room and have the desk by the window* **2** *rare* to put back in order —**~ment** *n* [C;U]: *to make various rearrangements|to need a lot of rearrangement*
rear·ward /ˈrɪəwəd‖ˈrɪərwərd/ *adj, n* [Wa5;A;U] **1** (in or towards) the REAR² (1) direction: *in a rearward direction|to point to (the) rearward* **2 to rearward of** some way behind
rear·wards /ˈrɪəwədz‖ˈrɪərwərdz/ also **rearward**— *adv* towards the REAR: *"Cavendish took a few more steps rearwards"* (SEU W.)
rea·son¹ /ˈriːzən/ *n* **1** [C (*for*), C3,5,6a+**why**; U3] the cause of an event; the explanation or excuse for an action: *The reason for the flood was all that heavy rain.|I have many reasons to fear him.|The reason that/The reason why he died was lack of medical care.|There is/We have reason to believe that he was murdered.|She's lied to me before. For this/that reason, I don't believe her now* **2** [C (*for*), C3,5] what makes one decide on an action; the cause of an intention: *What is your reason for wanting to enter the country?* **3** [U] the power to think, understand, and form opinions: *People are different from animals because they possess the quality of reason* **4** [*one's*+U] a healthy mind that is not mad (esp. in such phrs. as **lose one's reason**) **5** [U] good sense: *There's a great deal of reason in his advice* **6 beyond/past all reason** quite unreasonable; much more than is sensible: *Their demands are/go beyond all reason!* **7 bring someone to reason** to persuade someone to be sensible **8 by reason of** *fml* because of: *He escaped punishment, by reason of his youth* **9 do anything within reason** to do anything that is not too much to expect: *He'll do anything within reason for me but he won't break the law* **10 it/that stands to reason** it/that is clear to all sensible people: *It stands to reason that he won't go if we don't pay him* **11 listen to/hear reason** to allow oneself to be persuaded by (good) advice: *Why won't you listen to reason?* **12 with reason** (of something said or believed) rightly: *He thinks, with reason, that I don't like him*
USAGE Some people think a sentence such as *The* **reason** *for my absence was* **because** *I was ill* is bad English. It may be better to say: *The* **reason** *for my absence was* **that** *I was ill.* —compare CAUSE; see EXCUSE (USAGE)
reason² *v* **1** [I∅] to use one's REASON¹ (3): *She can reason very clearly* **2** [T5] to argue (that); give an opinion based on REASON¹ (3) (that): *I reasoned that since she had not answered my letter she must be angry with me* **3** [T1+*into* or *out of*] to persuade (someone) to do/not to do: *Try to reason him out of that idea/into going away quietly* —**~er** *n* [C9]: *a clever reasoner*
rea·so·na·ble /ˈriːzənəbəl/ *adj* **1** (of a person or his behaviour) sensible: *a reasonable man|a perfectly reasonable thing to do* —opposite **unreasonable**; see LOGICAL (USAGE) **2** (esp. of prices) fair; not too much: *to charge a very reasonable price* —**-bleness** *n* [U]
rea·son·a·bly /ˈriːzənəbli/ *adv* **1** sensibly **2** *apprec* fairly; rather: *The car is in reasonably good order*
rea·soned /ˈriːzənd/ *adj* [A] (of a statement, argument, etc.,) clearly thought out: *a (well-)reasoned statement*
rea·son·ing /ˈriːzənɪŋ/ *n* [U] the use of one's REASON¹ (3): *show great power of reasoning|Your reasoning was quite correct*
reason out *v adv* [T1b] to find an answer to (something) by thinking of all possible arguments: *Let's reason the matter out*
reason with *v prep* [T1] to try to persuade (someone) by fair argument: *You should reason with the child instead of just telling him to obey*
re·as·sure /ˌriːəˈʃʊəʳ/ *v* [T1 (*about*)] to comfort and make free from fear (someone anxious): *The doctor reassured the sick man (about his health)* —**-surance** /ˌriːəˈʃʊərəns/ *n* [C;U]: *She won't believe it in spite of all our reassurance(s)* —**-suringly** *adv*: *"You'll be all right," he said reassuringly*
re·bar·ba·tive /rɪˈbɑːbətɪv‖-ɑr-/ *adj fml* unattractive; fierce; offensive: *a rebarbative character*
re·bate /ˈriːbeɪt/ *n* an official return of part of a payment: *claim a rebate of 5% on your tax* —compare DISCOUNT
reb·el¹ /ˈrebəl/ *n* a person who REBELs: *The rebels have seized the Post Office.|a rebel army*
re·bel² /rɪˈbel/ *v* **-ll-** [I∅ (*against*)] to fight with violence (against anyone in power, esp. the government): *The slaves rebelled against their masters and killed them all*
re·bel·lion /rɪˈbeljən/ *n* [C;U] an act or the state of REBELling: *be in rebellion against|A little rebellion now and then is a good thing* (Thomas Jefferson) —compare REVOLUTION (1,2)
re·bel·lious /rɪˈbeljəs/ *adj* (seeming) disobedient and hard to control: *rebellious behaviour* —**~ly** *adv* —**~ness** *n* [U]
re·bind /ˌriːˈbaɪnd/ *v* **-bound** /ˈbaʊnd/ [T1] to put a new cover (BINDING) onto (a book)
re·birth /ˌriːˈbɜːθ‖-ɜrθ/ *n* [S] a renewal of life; change of spirit: *the rebirth of learning in the Western world*
re·born /ˌriːˈbɔːn‖-ɔrn/ *adj* [Wa5;F] as if born again: *Our hopes were reborn*
re·bound¹ /rɪˈbaʊnd/ *v* [I∅] to fly back after hitting something: *The ball rebounded from the wall and I caught it*
re·bound² /ˈriːbaʊnd/ *n* **on the rebound a** while REBOUNDing¹: *catch the ball on the rebound* **b** as a quick action in reply to failure or unpleasantness: *marry a different girl on the rebound*
rebound on /rɪˈbaʊnd/ also **rebound up·on**— *v prep* [T1] *no pass.* (of an action) to have an unexpected effect on: *His lies rebounded on himself because nobody trusted him any more*
re·buff¹ /rɪˈbʌf/ *v* [T1] to give a REBUFF to: *She rebuffed all my offers of friendship*
rebuff² *n* a rough or cruel answer when one is trying to be friendly or is asking for help: *meet with/suffer a rebuff*
re·build /ˌriːˈbɪld/ *v* **-built** /ˈbɪlt/ [T1] **1** to build again or build new parts to: *to rebuild a house after a fire|to rebuild a house, making it more modern* **2** to form newly: *to rebuild one's hopes on hearing of victory|News of the battle rebuilt her hopes that he might be alive.|a political party that wants to rebuild society*
re·buke¹ /rɪˈbjuːk/ *v* [T1 (*for*)] *fml* to give a REBUKE to: *to rebuke the child for his disobedience*

rebuke² *n fml* a few severe words; a short scolding esp. given officially: *to* ADMINISTER (=give) *a rebuke*

re·bus /'ri:bəs/ *n* any word game or PUZZLE in which words have to be guessed from pictures or letters that suggest the sounds that make them: *"R U 18" is a rebus for "Are you 18?"*

re·but /rɪ'bʌt/ *v* **-tt-** [T1] to prove the falsity of (a statement or charge); REFUTE

re·but·tal /rɪ'bʌtl/ *n* an act of REBUTting; proof that REBUTs

re·cal·ci·trance /rɪ'kælsɨtrəns/ also **re·cal·ci·tran·cy** /-si/— *n* [U] the quality of being RECALCITRANT

re·cal·ci·trant /rɪ'kælsɨtrənt/ *adj, n* (a person) that is disobedient, refusing to obey or be controlled: *recalcitrant behaviour*

re·call¹ /rɪ'kɔ:l/ *v* **1** [Wv6;T1,4,5,6a,b] to remember: *I can't recall his face/seeing him/that he came/where he lives/how to do it* **2** [T1 (*from, to*)] to call back (someone): *The government recalled the general after he lost the battle* **3** [T1] to send for or take back (something): *The makers have recalled a lot of cars that were unsafe* **4** [T1] to take back (an order or decision) —**~able** *adj*

re·call² /rɪ'kɔ:l‖rɪ'kɔl, 'ri:kɔl/ *n* **1** [S;U] (a) call to return: *the recall of the general from abroad* **2** [U] the power to remember something learned or experienced: *John has total recall and never forgets anything* **3** [*the*+R] a signal to soldiers to come back, made by blowing a metal horn (BUGLE): *sound the recall* **4 beyond/past recall** (so as to be) impossible to bring back or remember

re·cant /rɪ'kænt/ *v* [I∅;T1] to say publicly that one no longer holds (a former political or religious opinion): *He recanted (his faith) and became a Muslim/Christian* —**~ation** /ˌri:kæn'teɪʃən/ *n* [C;U]

re·cap¹ /'ri:kæp/ *v* **-pp-** [I∅;T1] *infml* RECAPITULATE

recap² *n infml* RECAPITULATION: *Can't you give us a recap of what he said?*

re·cap³ /ˌri:'kæp/ *v* [T1] *AmE infml* RETREAD —**recap** /'ri:kæp/ *n*

re·ca·pit·u·late /ˌri:kə'pɪtʃʊleɪt‖-tʃə-/ *v* [I∅;T1] to repeat (the chief points of something that has been said): *He recapitulated (the main arguments for joining the navy)*

re·ca·pit·u·la·tion /ˌri:kəpɪtʃʊ'leɪʃən‖-tʃə-/ *n* [C;U] (a case of) recapitulating (RECAPITULATE)

re·cap·ture /ri:'kæptʃəʳ/ *v* [T1] **1** to get into one's power again; CAPTURE² (1,2) again: *The soldiers recaptured the fort* **2 a** to bring back into the mind: *to recapture the happiness of one's youth* **b** to cause others to experience again: *He recaptured (for us) the way Mozart used to play this piece of music*

re·cast /ˌri:'kɑ:st‖ˌri:'kæst/ *v* **-cast** [T1] **1** to give a new shape to (as if) by CASTing¹ (7): *to recast a cracked church bell*|(fig.) *to recast a sentence* **2** to change the actors in (a play)

rec·ce /'reki/ *n BrE sl* a RECONNAISSANCE

recd *written abbrev. for:* received

re·cede /rɪ'si:d/ *v* [I∅ (*from*)] **1** (of things) to move back or away; go further off: *His hair is beginning to recede from his forehead* **2** [Wv4] to slope backwards: *a receding chin*

re·ceipt¹ /rɪ'si:t/ *n* **1** [C] a written statement that one has received money: *Ask the shop for a receipt when you pay the bill* **2** [U (*of*)] the event of receiving: *The receipt of the cheque was a pleasant surprise* **3** [C] *old use* RECIPE **4 be in receipt of** *pomp* to have received: *We are in receipt of your letter of the 17th* **5 make out a receipt** to write a RECEIPT¹ (1) **6 on receipt of** *fml* when one receives: *On receipt of your instructions he will send the goods*

receipt² *v* [T1] to mark as paid: *He receipted the bill*

re·ceipts /rɪ'si:ts/ *n* [P] the money received from a business: *The receipts have increased since last year*

re·cei·va·ble /rɪ'si:vəbəl/ *adj* **1** able or fit to be received **2** *tech* (of bills or accounts) on which money is to be received —compare PAYABLE

re·ceive /rɪ'si:v/ *v* **1** [T1] to get (something given or sent to one): *receive a letter|receive a lot of attention* —compare RECIPIENT **2** [T1] to suffer; be the subject of: *receive a heavy blow on the head from a falling stone|receive a scolding* **3** [T1] to provide room for; hold: *The lake receives the water from this river* **4** [T1;(I∅)] *fml* to accept as a visitor or member; act as host to; welcome: *Lady Jones receives on Monday afternoons.|He was received into the Church* **5** [T1] (of a radio or television set) to turn (radio waves) sent by (someone) into sound or pictures: *Are you receiving me?* **6 on the receiving end (of)** *infml* suffering (unpleasant actions done to one): *on the receiving end of several complaints*

re·ceived /rɪ'si:vd/ *adj* [Wa5;A] *fml or tech* being the generally accepted standard: *received pronunciation*

re·ceiv·er /rɪ'si:vəʳ/ *n* **1** [C] a person who deals in stolen property **2** [C] the part of a telephone that is held to one's ear —see picture at LIVING ROOM **3** [C] the part of a radio or television set that produces sound or pictures **4** [*the*+R] also **official receiver** (*often cap.*)— (in British law) the person officially appointed to take charge of affairs of a BANKRUPT¹ (1): *His business has failed and is in the hands of the receiver*

re·ceiv·er·ship /rɪ'si:vəʃɪp‖-ər-/ *n* [U] **1** the position of a RECEIVER (4) **2** the condition of being in the hands of the RECEIVER (4)

re·ceiv·ing /rɪ'si:vɪŋ/ *n* [U] the crime of being a RECEIVER (1): *The police charged him with receiving*

receiving set /·'·· ·/ *n* a radio or television RECEIVER (3)

re·cent /'ri:sənt/ *adj* having happened or come into existence only a short time ago: *recent history|a recent event|a recent copy of the newspaper* —**~ness** *n* [U]

re·cent·ly /'ri:səntli/ *adv* not long ago; lately: *I've only recently begun to learn French*

re·cep·ta·cle /rɪ'septəkəl/ *n tech or fml* a container for keeping things in

re·cep·tion /rɪ'sepʃən/ *n* **1** [C9 *usu. sing.*] an act of receiving; welcome: *get a very friendly reception* **2** [C] a large formal party: *give/hold a reception|a wedding reception* **3** [U] the office or department that receives visitors to a hotel or large organization: *Leave your key at reception* **4** [U] the receiving of radio or television signals: *Radio reception isn't very good here*

reception desk /·'·· ·/ *n* the desk just inside a hotel where guests are received

re·cep·tion·ist /rɪ'sepʃənɨst/ *n* a person who receives people arriving in a hotel, visiting a doctor, etc.

reception room /·'·· ·/ *n* (*used by people selling houses*) a living room; any room that is not a kitchen, bedroom, or bathroom

re·cep·tive /rɪ'septɪv/ *adj* [(*of, to*)] (of a person or his mind) willing to receive new ideas: *a receptive mind|He's not very receptive to my suggestions* —**~ly** *adv* —**~ness** *n* [U] —**-tivity** /ˌri:sep'tɪvɨti/ *n* [U]

re·cess¹ /rɪ'ses‖'ri:ses/ *n* **1** [C;U] a pause for rest during the working day or the working year: *Parliament is in recess now* **2** [U] (in the US) the school or university holidays **3** [C] a space in the wall of a room for shelves, cupboards, etc. **4** [C *often pl.*] *lit* a secret inner part of a place, that is hard to reach

re·cess² /rɪ'ses/ *v* **1** [Wv5;T1] to make or put into a RECESS¹ (3): *a recessed bookshelf* **2** [I∅] *esp. AmE* to take a RECESS¹ (1)

re·ces·sion /rɪ'seʃən/ *n* **1** [C] a period of reduced activity of trade; SLUMP² (1) **2** [U] the act of receding (RECEDE)

re·ces·sion·al /rɪ'seʃənəl/ *n* a holy song (HYMN) sung at the end of a Christian church service

re·ces·sive /rɪ'sesɪv/ *adj* [Wa5] (of groups of qualities passed on from parent to child) being the quality that is less likely to appear in the child when more than one are passed on: *Blue eyes are recessive and brown eyes are* DOMINANT¹ (3)

re·charge /ˌriː'tʃɑːdʒ‖-ɑr-/ *v* [T1] to put a new charge of electricity into (a BATTERY)

re·cher·ché /rə'ʃeəʃeɪ‖rə'ʃeər-, rəˌʃeər'ʃeɪ (*Fr* rəʃɛrʃe)/ *adj Fr* (esp. of words, ideas, etc., or of food) carefully chosen and perhaps too rare and strange: *a recherché meal of chocolate-covered ants*

re·cid·i·vist /rɪ'sɪdɪ̀vɪ̀st/ *n* a person who keeps going back to a life of crime; incurable criminal: *show recidivist tendencies* —**-vism** *n* [U]

re·ci·pe /'resɪ̀pi/ *n* [(*for*)] a set of instructions for cooking a dish: *follow a recipe|a collection of fish recipes|*(fig.) *a recipe for a happy marriage*

re·cip·i·ent /rɪ'sɪpɪənt/ *n* [(*of*)] a person who receives something

re·cip·ro·cal /rɪ'sɪprəkəl/ *adj* [Wa5] given and received in return; exchanged between 2 people or groups; MUTUAL: *a reciprocal trade agreement between 2 nations|feel a reciprocal liking for each other* —**~ly** *adv* [Wa4,5]

re·cip·ro·cate /rɪ'sɪprəkeɪt/ *v* **1** [T1;I∅] *fml* to give (something) in return: *He reciprocated my good wishes.|I reciprocated by wishing him a happy Christmas* **2** [I∅] (of a machine part) to move backwards and forwards in a straight line, like a PISTON in an engine —**-cation** /rɪˌsɪprə'keɪʃən/ *n* [U]

reciprocating en·gine /·'···· ˌ··/ *n* an engine in which a part moves backwards and forwards

re·ci·pro·ci·ty /ˌresɪ̀'prɒsɪ̀ti‖-'prɑ-/ *n* [U] the principle or practice of giving and taking advantages, or of buying and selling from and to each other (esp. among nations)

re·cit·al /rɪ'saɪtl/ *n* **1** a performance of poetry or esp. music, given by one performer or written by one writer: *give a piano recital* **2** *fml* a telling of a set of facts or events; account: *He gave us a terrible recital of his experiences*

re·ci·ta·tion /ˌresɪ̀'teɪʃən/ *n* **1** [U] the act of reciting (RECITE): *the art of recitation* **2** [C] a piece of literature (to be) RECITED: *give recitations from Shakespeare* **3** [C] (in the US) a school exercise in which pupils give spoken answers to questions on a lesson they have studied

re·ci·ta·tive /ˌresɪ̀tə'tiːv/ *n* [C;U] (a) speech set to music but not to a tune, that continues the story of a musical play (OPERA) between the songs

re·cite /rɪ'saɪt/ *v* **1** [I∅;T1] to say (something learned) aloud from memory: *recite a poem|I don't like reciting in public* **2** [T1] to give a list of: *recite his complaints* **3** [I∅] (in the US) to answer a teacher's questions; speak in class: *It's your turn to recite, Mr Kaplan* —**reciter** *n*

reck /rek/ *v* [I∅;T1: (*of*)] *lit* (*with* not *or* little, *or in questions*) to care; mind: *They recked nothing|little of the danger*

reck·less /'rekləs/ *adj* [(*of*)] (of a person or his behaviour) too hasty; not caring about danger: *reckless of danger|of what may happen|reckless driving* —**~ly** *adv* —**~ness** *n* [U]

reck·on /'rekən/ *v* **1** [X (*to be*) 1, (*to be*) 7,9 esp. *among, as*] to consider; regard: *He is reckoned (to be) a great actor.|She was reckoned (to be) very beautiful.|I reckon him as a friend|among my friends* **2** [T5a] *infml* to guess; suppose; calculate (a number) without counting exactly: *I reckon (that) he'll come soon.|How much do you reckon (that) she earns?* **3** [T1] to calculate; add up (an amount, cost, etc.): *My pay is reckoned from the 1st of the month*

reck·on·er /'rekənəʳ/ *n* [C9] a person who RECKONs (3): *He's a very quick reckoner* —compare READY RECKONER

reckon in¹ *v prep* [D1] to include in; take (an amount) into account in (a sum): *Have you reckoned the cost of postage in the total?*

reckon in² *v adv* [T1] to add (an amount) in: *Have you reckoned in the cost of postage?*

reck·on·ing /'rekənɪŋ/ *n* **1** [U] the act of calculating: *By my reckoning, it must be 60 kilometres from here to the coast* **2** [C] *old use* a bill: *pay one's reckoning|*(fig.) *You'll have a heavy reckoning to pay if you offend the President* **3** [U] the calculation of a ship's position —compare DEAD RECKONING **4** **day of reckoning** the time when one must suffer for a mistake **5** **out in one's reckoning** mistaken in one's calculations

reckon on *v prep* **1** [T1;V3] to trust (someone) (to do something); COUNT ON: *You can always reckon on me (to help you)* **2** [T1,4] to expect; depend on (something happening or getting something); BANK ON: *We're reckoning on a large profit|on being ½ an hour late.|You can't reckon on seeing him*

reckon up *v adv* [T1] *BrE infml* RECKON (3): *He reckoned up the cost*

reckon with *v prep* [T1] **1** to be faced with or opposed by; have to deal with: *If you hit the child again you'll have me to reckon with* **2** **to be reckoned with** to be taken into account seriously as a possible opponent, competitor, danger, etc.: *She's a woman to be reckoned with*

reckon with·out *v prep* [T1] **1** to fail to consider: *When he decided to go he reckoned without Mary, who refused to let him* **2** **reckon without one's host** to make a plan without asking the person most concerned

re·claim /rɪ'kleɪm/ *v* [T1 (*from*)] **1** to bring back from wrong behaviour: *reclaim former criminals* **2** to claim the return of: *reclaim some of the tax* **3** to make (land) fit for use: *reclaim land from the sea* **4** to obtain (materials) from a waste product: *reclaim rubber from old tyres*

rec·la·ma·tion /ˌreklə'meɪʃən/ *n* [U] the practice or act of RECLAIMing

re·cline /rɪ'klaɪn/ *v* **1** [L9 esp. *against, on*] to lie back or down; be or put oneself in a position of rest: *recline on the bed|in a reclining position* **2** [X9 esp. *against, on*] to lean (a part of oneself): *She reclined her head against his shoulder*

re·cluse /rɪ'kluːs‖'rekluːs/ *n* a person who lives alone away from the world on purpose —compare HERMIT

rec·og·ni·tion /ˌrekəg'nɪʃən/ *n* **1** [U] the power to recognize or state of being recognized: *The school hopes for recognition by the Department of Education* **2** [S;U] (a) reward given in order to recognize someone's behaviour: *Please accept this cheque in recognition of|as a recognition of your services* **3** **change beyond/out of all recognition** to change so as to be impossible to recognize: *Illness and age had changed her out of all recognition*

re·cog·ni·zance /rɪ'kɒgnɪzəns‖rɪ'kɑg-/ *n* [*usu. pl. with sing. meaning*] *law* a promise to attend the court, obey the law, etc., and, if the promise is broken, to pay an agreed sum of money: *enter into recognizances*

rec·og·nize, -nise /'rekəgnaɪz/ *v* **1** [T1] to know

again (someone or something one has met before): *I recognized Mary in the photograph.|Dogs recognize people by their smell* **2** [Wv5;T1 (*as*)] to admit (someone or something) as being real or having the right to be the stated thing: *They refused to recognize our government.|recognize him as king|a recognized method of teaching English* **3** [T5;V3] to see clearly; be prepared to agree: *I recognize him to be|I recognize that he is cleverer than I am* **4** [T1] to show official gratefulness for: *The government recognized his services by making him a lord* —**-nizable** *adj* —**-nizably** *adv*

re·coil[1] /rɪˈkɔɪl/ *v* [I∅] **1** [(*from*)] to draw back suddenly as in fear or dislike: *She recoiled at the sight of the snake|recoiled from the snake* **2** (of a gun) to spring back (when fired)

re·coil[2] /ˈriːkɔɪl, rɪˈkɔɪl/ *n* [S;U] (a) sudden backward movement, esp. of a gun after firing

recoil on *v prep* [T1 *no pass.*] (of a harmful action) to come back to and have a like effect on: *His lies recoiled on him because nobody would believe him any more*

rec·ol·lect /ˌrekəˈlekt/ *v* [Wv6;T1,4,5a,6a,b] to remember (something past): *Do you recollect her name?|meeting her?|where she lives?|how to get there?|As far as I (can) recollect, her name is Juliet*

rec·ol·lec·tion /ˌrekəˈlekʃən/ *n* **1** [U] the power or action of remembering the past: *enjoy the pleasures of recollection|His recollection goes back 80 years* **2** [C] something in one's memory of the past: *That evening together is one of my happiest recollections* **3** **to the best of my recollection** if I remember right: *To the best of my recollection the Norman Conquest happened in 1066*

rec·om·mend /ˌrekəˈmend/ *v* **1** [D1 (*to*); T1: (*as, for*)] to speak (to someone) in favour of; praise (as being good for a purpose): *Can you recommend me a good dictionary?|Can you recommend a good dictionary (to me)?|They recommended him for the job|as a good lawyer* **2** [T4,5c;V3] to advise or suggest: *I recommend buying this dictionary|you to buy this dictionary|that everyone (should) buy this dictionary* **3** [T1 (*to*)] (of a quality) to make attractive: *This hotel has nothing to recommend it (to travellers) except cheapness*

rec·om·men·da·tion /ˌrekəmenˈdeɪʃən/ *n* **1** [U] advice; the act of RECOMMENDing (1,2): *buy the car on Paul's recommendation* **2** [C] a letter or statement that RECOMMENDs (1) (esp. someone for a job): *write him a recommendation* **3** [C] a quality that RECOMMENDs (3): *Her 2 great recommendations are youth and beauty*

recommend to *v prep* [D1] *fml* to give in charge to; COMMEND to: *The dying man recommended his soul to God*

rec·om·pense[1] /ˈrekəmpens/ *v* [T1 (*for*)] *fml* to give a RECOMPENSE to: *recompense them (for their trouble)*

recompense[2] *n* [S;U: (*for*)] *fml* (a) reward or payment (for trouble or suffering): *receive £500 in recompense|as a recompense (for his help)*

rec·on·cile /ˈrekənsaɪl/ *v* [Wv5;T1 (*with*)] **1** to make peace between; make friendly again: *They quarrelled but now they're completely reconciled* **2** to find agreement between (2 actions or ideas): *I can't reconcile those 2 ideas.|How do you reconcile your principles with your behaviour?* —**-cilable** /ˌrekənˈsaɪləbəl/ *adj*

reconcile to *v prep* [D1] to cause to accept: *He became reconciled to the loss of his wife*

rec·on·cil·i·a·tion /ˌrekənsɪliˈeɪʃən/ also **rec·on·cile·ment** /ˈrekənsaɪlmənt/— *n* [S;U] (a) peacemaking: *try to cause* (BRING ABOUT) *a reconciliation between the 2 families*

rec·on·dite /ˈrekəndaɪt, rɪˈkɒn-‖ˈrekən-, rɪˈkɑn-/ *adj fml* (of ideas, knowledge, etc.) not commonly known; difficult to understand: *a recondite subject* —**~ness** *adj* [U]

re·con·di·tion /ˌriːkənˈdɪʃən/ *v* [Wv5;T1] to repair and bring back into working order: *A reconditioned engine is cheaper than a new one*

re·con·nais·sance /rɪˈkɒnɨ̇səns‖rɪˈkɑ-/ *n* [C;U] (an) act of reconnoitring (RECONNOITRE): *make a reconnaissance|After reconnaissance we decided not to attack*

re·con·noi·tre, *AmE* **-ter** /ˌrekəˈnɔɪtəʳ‖ˌriː-/ *v* [I∅; T1] (of a group of soldiers, ships, or aircraft) to go near (the place where an enemy is) in order to find out the enemy's numbers, position, etc.: *reconnoitre the area*

re·con·sid·er /ˌriːkənˈsɪdəʳ/ *v* [I∅;T1] to think again and change one's mind about (a subject): *Won't you reconsider your decision to leave the club?* —**~ation** /ˌriːkənsɪdəˈreɪʃən/ *n* [U]

re·con·sti·tute /riːˈkɒnstɨ̇tjuːt‖riːˈkɑnstɨ̇tuːt/ *v* [T1] **1** to bring back into existence: *reconstitute the committee under a new chairman* **2** [Wv5] to bring back (dried food) into its former condition by adding water: *reconstitute dried eggs|milk powder*

re·con·struct /ˌriːkənˈstrʌkt/ *v* [T1] **1** to rebuild after destruction or damage **2** to build up a complete description or picture of (something only partly known): *reconstruct a crime from known facts*

re·con·struc·tion /ˌriːkənˈstrʌkʃən/ *n* **1** [U] the act of RECONSTRUCTing **2** [C] something RECONSTRUCTed: *a reconstruction of what must have happened* **3** [R] (*usu. cap.*) the period of reorganization of the Southern United States after their defeat in the American CIVIL War

re·cord[1] /rɪˈkɔːd‖-ərd/ *v* **1** [T1,6a] to write down so that it will be known: *record the events of the past|What became of him|how he died is not recorded* **2** [I∅;T1] to preserve (sound or a television broadcast) so that it can be heard and/or seen again: *The machine is recording now.|a recorded* (compare LIVE[2] (5)) *broadcast|She has recorded several songs* **3** [T1] (of an instrument) to show by measuring: *The* THERMOMETER *recorded a temperature of 90 degrees*

rec·ord[2] /ˈrekɔːd‖-ərd/ *n* **1** [C] a written statement of facts, events, etc.: *Keep a record of how much you spend* **2** [C] the known facts about someone's past behaviour: *John and Peter both have fine military records* **3** [C] anything that provides information about the past: *dig up the records of ancient civilizations* **4** [U] the state of being recorded in writing and so established as fact: *It is a matter of record* (=known to be true) *that nobody has ever failed this examination* **5** [C] (often in sport) the best yet done; the highest/lowest figure ever reached: *break|make|establish a record for long distance swimming* **6** also **gramophone record, disc**— a circular piece of plastic on which sound is stored in the form of a narrow line (GROOVE) cut in it and can be turned back into sound by a RECORD PLAYER: *play|put on some records of dance music* —see picture at SOUND[3] **7** **for the record** to be reported as official: *Just for the record, I think the President is a fool* **8** **off the record** *infml* unofficial(ly); speaking/spoken privately: *My remarks were off the record and are not to be printed.|He told us off the record that the firm was doing badly this year* **9** **on record** **a** (of facts or events) (ever) recorded: *the coldest winter on record|Let's place that on record* (=record that) **b** (of a person) having publicly said, as if for written records: *He is|went|was put on record as having said that he opposed high taxation*

rec·ord[3] /ˈrekɔːd‖-ərd/ *adj* [Wa5;A] more, faster, better, etc., than ever before; that is a RECORD[2]

(5): *A record number of people attended the concert.*| *a record crop of corn*

record-break·ing /'·· ˌ··/ *adj* [Wa5] (usu. in sport) that goes beyond the former RECORD² (5): *a record-breaking speed*

recorded de·liv·er·y /·ˌ·· ·'···/ *n* [U] *BrE* the method of sending 1st class mail, by which proof that it has been delivered is obtained but not more than £2 is claimed in case of loss: *send it by recorded delivery* —compare CERTIFIED MAIL

re·cord·er /rɪ'kɔːdəʳ‖-ɔr-/ *n* **1** a type of wooden musical instrument like a whistle, with 8 holes for the fingers —see picture at WIND INSTRUMENT **2** (*often cap.*) the title of a judge in some city courts both in Britain and in the US **3** TAPE RECORDER

re·cord·ing /rɪ'kɔːdɪŋ‖-ɔr-/ *n* (esp. in broadcasting) a performance, speech, or piece of music that has been RECORDed¹ (2): *make a recording of her voice*| *listen to some recordings of early Italian music*

record li·bra·ry /'·· ˌ···/ *n* a collection of RECORD*s*² (6) for people to borrow: *Start a small record library at the school*

record play·er /'·· ˌ··/ also (*esp. BrE*) **gramophone**, (*esp. AmE*) **phonograph**— *n* an instrument which can turn the information stored in the long narrow line (GROOVE) of a RECORD back into the original sounds, music, etc., by letting a special needle travel along it

re·count¹ /rɪ'kaʊnt/ *v* [T1] to tell (a story); give an account of

re·count² /ˌriː'kaʊnt/ *v* [T1] to count again: *They had to recount the votes*

re·count³ /'riːkaʊnt/ *n* a 2nd or fresh count, esp. of votes: *I demand a recount*

re·coup /rɪ'kuːp/ *v* [T1] **1** to win back; regain (what one has lost, esp. money): *I shall recoup my travelling* EXPENSES *from my employers* **2** to provide (oneself) again with money: *Charles stole the diamonds to recoup himself for his losses at Monte Carlo*

re·course /rɪ'kɔːs‖'riːkors/ *n* [U] a means of help (esp. in the phr. **have recourse to** = make use of as a means of help): *The sick man had recourse to drugs to lessen his pain* —compare RESORT (3); see RESOURCE (USAGE)

re·cov·er /rɪ'kʌvəʳ/ *v* **1** [T1] to get back (something lost or taken away): *The police recovered the stolen jewellery.*|*When he recovered consciousness after the accident he asked "Where am I?"*|*She's beginning to recover her strength after her fever* **2** [I∅ (*from*)] to return to the usual state of health, strength, ability, etc.: *He is very ill and unlikely to recover.*|*He has recovered from his bad cold and can go out tomorrow.*|(fig.) *Has the country recovered yet from the effects of the war?* **3** [T1] to get (oneself) back into a proper state or position: *He almost fell, but succeeded in recovering himself.*|*She soon recovered herself and stopped crying* —**~able** *adj* [Wa5]

re-cov·er /ˌriː'kʌvəʳ/ *v* [T1] to put a new cover on: *re-cover all the chairs in purple silk*

re·cov·er·y /rɪ'kʌvəri/ *n* **1** [U (*of*)] RECOVERing or being RECOVERed (1): *the recovery of the stolen jewels* **2** [S (*from*)] RECOVERing (2): *make a quick recovery from her fever*

rec·re·ant /'rekrɪənt/ *n* [C;N] *lit* a cowardly and unfaithful person: *Yield, recreant (fool), and let the lady go!*

re-cre·ate /ˌriːkriː'eɪt/ *v* [T1] to make again: *recreate the scenes of the past in one's imagination*

rec·re·a·tion /ˌrekri'eɪʃən/ *n* [C;U] (a form of) amusement, or way of spending free time: *I am too busy for recreation.*|*His only recreations are drinking beer and working in the garden* —see HOBBY (USAGE)

rec·re·a·tion·al /ˌrekri'eɪʃənəl/ *adj* [Wa5] (of an activity) providing RECREATION

recreation ground /··'·· ·/ *n esp. BrE* a piece of public land set aside for games: *play football on the recreation ground*

recreation room /··'·· ·/ *n AmE* a room in a private house, used for playing games such as table tennis

re·crim·i·nate /rɪ'krɪmɪ̈neɪt/ *v* [I∅ (*against*)] to blame or make a charge against (a person who has blamed or made a charge against oneself): *recriminate against one's employers for one's dismissal for dishonesty* —**-natory** /nətəri‖-tori/ *adj*: *a few recriminatory remarks*

re·crim·i·na·tion /rɪˌkrɪmɪ̈'neɪʃən/ *n* [C *usu. pl.*;U] (an act of) quarrelling and blaming one another: *Let's make friends, instead of wasting our time on recrimination(s)*

re·cru·des·cence /ˌriːkruː'desəns/ *n* [C9, esp. *of*] *fml* a fresh OUTBREAK (of something unpleasant): *There has been a recrudescence of stealing in the big shops*

re·cruit¹ /rɪ'kruːt/ *n* **1** someone who has just joined one of the armed forces, esp. of his own free will, and is still being trained: *give the recruits their uniforms* **2** [(*to*)] a new member (of any organization): *New recruits to our music club are always welcome*

recruit² *v* **1** [I∅] to find RECRUIT*s*: *a recruiting drive* (=special effort) *for the army* **2** [T1] **a** to get (someone) as a RECRUIT: *recruit some new members* **b** to form (a group) with new members: *recruit an army*|*a new political party* **3** [I∅;T1] *fml & old use* to recover (one's health, strength, etc.) as by rest and good food —**~ment** *n* [U]

rec·tal /'rektl/ *adj* [Wa5] *med* of the RECTUM

rec·tan·gle /'rektæŋgəl/ *n tech* a figure with 4 straight sides forming 4 right angles —see picture at GEOMETRY

rec·tan·gu·lar /rek'tæŋgjʊləʳ‖-gjə-/ *adj* [Wa5] *tech* in the shape of a RECTANGLE

rec·ti·fi·ca·tion /ˌrektɪ̈fɪ̈'keɪʃən/ *n* [C;U] (a case of) RECTIFYing or being rectified (RECTIFY): *the rectification of mistakes*|*of alcohol*|*make several rectifications in the plan for the new town*

rec·ti·fi·er /'rektɪ̈faɪəʳ/ *n* **1** someone or something that rectifies (RECTIFY (1,2)) **2** *tech* an instrument that rectifies (RECTIFY (3))

rec·ti·fy /'rektɪ̈faɪ/ *v* [T1] **1** to put right: *rectify the mistakes in my bill* **2** [Wv5] *tech* to make pure: *rectified alcohol* **3** *tech* to change (the flow of electricity to and fro along a wire (ALTERNATING CURRENT)) so that it flows only one way (DIRECT CURRENT)

rec·ti·lin·e·ar /ˌrektɪ̈'lɪnɪəʳ/ *adj* [Wa5] *fml & tech* forming or moving in a straight line; having or made of straight lines

rec·ti·tude /'rektɪ̈tjuːd‖-tuːd/ *n* [U] *fml* honesty of character; moral correctness: *a man of rectitude*

rec·to /'rektəʊ/ *adj, n* **-tos** [Wa5;A;C] (being) a right-hand page of a book: *written on the recto (side)*—compare VERSO

rec·tor /'rektəʳ/ *n* [C;N] (*the title of*) **1** (in the CHURCH OF ENGLAND) the priest in charge of a PARISH from which he receives his income directly: *Have some more tea, Rector!* —compare VICAR **2** the head of certain colleges and schools

rec·to·ry /'rektəri/ *n* the house where a RECTOR (1) lives

rec·tum /'rektəm/ *n med* the lowest end of the large bowel, through which solid waste matter passes from the COLON to the ANUS —see picture at DIGESTIVE SYSTEM

re·cum·bent /rɪ'kʌmbənt/ *adj* [Wa5] *fml* (of a

person or his position) lying down on the back or side: *a recumbent figure on the bed*

re·cu·pe·rate /rɪˈkjuːpəreɪt, -ˈkuː-/ *v* [I∅;T1] to get well again after illness or difficulty; get back (one's health, strength, etc.): *He went to the mountains to recuperate (his strength)* —**-ration** /rɪˌkjuːpəˈreɪʃən‖-ˌkuː-/ *n* [U]

re·cu·pe·ra·tive /rɪˈkjuːpərətɪv‖rɪˈkuːpəreɪtɪv/ *adj* [Wa5] (of actions or events) helping one to RECUPERATE: *a recuperative holiday*

re·cur /rɪˈkɜːʳ/ *v* **-rr-** [I∅] **1** to happen again, or more than once: *If the pain should recur, take this medicine* **2** (of a DECIMAL) to be repeated for ever in the same order: *In 5·1515 . . . (also written 5·1̇5̇) the figures 15 recur, and the number can be read "5·15 recurring"*

re·cur·rence /rɪˈkʌrəns‖-ˈkɜr-/ *n* [U;C] the quality or an example of RECURring (1): *the frequent recurrence of the pain*

re·cur·rent /rɪˈkʌrənt‖-ˈkɜr-/ *adj* [Wa5] (of events) RECURring (1): *He suffers from recurrent pain(s) in his head* —**~ly** *adv*

recur to *v prep* [T1 *no pass.*] **1** to return in thought to (something): *Let us recur to what was said at this morning's meeting* **2** (of a memory, idea, etc.) to return to (someone's mind): *The thought of a trip round the world has often recurred to my mind*

re·curved /riːˈkɜːvd‖-ɜr-/ *adj tech* curved backwards or inwards: *recurved horns*

re·cu·sant /ˈrekjʊzənt‖-kjə-/ *adj, n* [Wa5] *fml & old use* (someone) refusing to obey official rules or esp. to accept official religious beliefs: *People who refused to belong to the* CHURCH OF ENGLAND *were once called "recusants"*

re·cy·cle /ˌriːˈsaɪkəl/ *v* [I∅;T1] **a** (of a substance that has already been used) to pass through a system of treatment so that it is fit to use again **b** to treat (such a substance) in this way: *recycle empty tins and bottles so as to use the metal and glass*

red[1] /red/ *adj* **-dd-** [Wa1] **1** of the colour of blood or of fire: *a red dress|Let's paint the door red* **2** (of hair) of a bright brownish orange or copper colour **3** (of the human skin, lips, or tongue) pink: *to turn red with shame or anger|eyes* (= the skin round the eyes) *red with weeping* **4** [Wa5] (of wine) of a dark purple colour —see also **red** HERRING —**~ness** *n* [U]

red[2] *n* **1** [C;U] (a) red colour: *the reds and yellows of the evening sky|mix red and yellow to make orange* **2** [U] red clothes: *I shall wear red for the ceremony* **3** [*the*+R] the state of being in debt, or of owing money to the bank: *be in/get into the red|We'll soon be/get out of the red* **4 paint the town red** *infml* to go out and get drunk and behave noisily **5 see red** to become angry suddenly and lose control of oneself

Red[1] *adj* **1** [Wa5] concerning the U.S.S.R., China, and other COMMUNIST countries: *The Red Army is the army of the U.S.S.R.* **2** *often derog* (of a person or his beliefs) COMMUNIST

Red[2] *n* **1** *derog* a COMMUNIST **2 Reds under the bed(s)** the (imaginary) danger that secret COMMUNISTs are hiding in one's country

red ad·mi·ral /ˌ· ˈ···/ *n* a kind of BUTTERFLY with bright red bands on its black wings, common in Europe and America

red blood cell /ˌ· ˈ· ·/ also **red cor·pus·cle** /ˌ· ˈ···/— *n* one of the cells in the blood which carry oxygen to every part of the body so that food can be used to give strength —see also WHITE BLOOD CELL, HEMOGLOBIN

red-blood·ed /ˌ· ˈ··◂/ *adj apprec* (of a person, his behaviour, etc.) bold, strong, and like (that of) a male: *a few red-blooded curses*

red·breast /ˈredbrest/ *n lit* ROBIN

red·brick /ˈredˌbrɪk/ *n* (*often cap.*) any English university started in the late 19th century in a city outside London: *go to a redbrick (university)* —compare OXBRIDGE

red·cap /ˈredkæp/ *n* **1** (in Britain) a military policeman **2** (in the US) a man who carries things for travellers at a railway station; PORTER

red car·pet /ˌ· ˈ··/ *n* [*the*+R] a special ceremonial welcome to a guest: *roll out the red carpet when the President comes|give him red-carpet treatment*

red cent /ˌ· ˈ·/ *n* [S *neg.*] *infml* something of the least possible value (in such phrs. as **not worth a red cent, I wouldn't give a red cent**)

red·coat /ˈredkəʊt/ *n* (in former times) a British soldier

Red Cres·cent /ˌ· ˈ··/ *n* [(*the*) GU] an international Muslim organization that does the same work as the RED CROSS

Red Cross /ˌ· ˈ·/ *n* [(*the*) GU] an international Christian organization that looks after sick, hurt, and wounded people

red·cur·rant /ˌredˈkʌrənt◂‖-ˈkɜr-/ *n* **1** a kind of small red berry that grows in bunches on a bush: *redcurrant wine* **2** the bush on which this fruit grows

red deer /ˌ· ˈ·/ *n* **-deer** [Wn3] a type of large deer common in northern Europe and Asia, with a reddish brown coat

red·den /ˈredn/ *v* [I∅;T1] to (cause to) turn red: *She reddened at the sound of their praises.|The sunset reddened the clouds*

red·dish /ˈredɪʃ/ *adj* slightly red

re·dec·o·rate /riːˈdekəreɪt/ *v* [I∅;T1] to put new paint, paper, etc., on (the inside of a building): *redecorate the bathroom|We always redecorate in the Spring*

re·deem /rɪˈdiːm/ *v* [T1] **1** to buy or gain the freedom of, esp. (in the Christian religion) the freedom from evil: *redeem a slave|redeem from* SIN **2** [(*from*)] to regain with money (what was given in exchange for money (PAWNed or MORTGAGEd)): *redeem my watch from the* PAWNSHOP **3** to carry out; fulfil: *redeem one's promise* —**~able** *adj*

Re·deem·er /rɪˈdiːməʳ/ *n* [*the, our*+R] Jesus Christ

redeeming fea·ture /ˌ··· ˈ··/ *n* something good in a person or thing that is bad in all other ways: *His only redeeming feature is his honesty*

re·demp·tion /rɪˈdempʃən/ *n* [U] **1** REDEEMing or being REDEEMed **2 beyond/past redemption** too evil to be REDEEMed (1): *a criminal past all redemption*

re·demp·tive /rɪˈdemptɪv/ *adj* [Wa5] *fml* that REDEEMs (1)

red en·sign /ˌ· ˈ··/ *n* [*the*+R] the flag used by British non-naval ships —compare WHITE ENSIGN

re·de·ploy /ˌriːdɪˈplɔɪ/ *v* [T1] to rearrange (soldiers, workers in industry, etc.) in a more effective way —**~ment** *n* [U]

red flag /ˌ· ˈ·/ *n* **1** [C] a flag of a red colour, used as a danger signal **2** [*the*+R] (*often cap.*) **a** the flag of the political LEFT[2] (3) **b** the party song of the political LEFT[2] (3)

red gi·ant /ˌ· ˈ··/ *n* a coolish star, near to the middle of its life, larger and less solid than the sun —compare WHITE DWARF

red-hand·ed /ˌ· ˈ··◂/ *adj* [Wa5;F] in the act of doing something wrong (in the phr. **catch someone red-handed**): *They caught the thief red-handed while he was just putting the diamonds in his pocket*

red·head /ˈredhed/ *n infml* a person with RED[1] (2) hair: *He married a beautiful redhead*

red-hot /ˌ· ˈ·◂/ *adj* [Wa5] (of metal) so hot that it shines red: (fig.) *red-hot keenness on dancing* —compare WHITE HEAT

re·dif·fu·sion /ˌriːdɪˈfjuːʒən/ *n* [U] *esp. BrE* the system of broadcasting both sound and television

from a central receiving apparatus to other receivers in public places
Red In·di·an /ˌ· ˈ···/ *n* INDIAN (2)
re·di·rect /ˌriːdaɪˈrekt, -də-/ *v* [T1] READDRESS
re·dis·trib·ute /ˌriːdɪˈstrɪbjuːt/ *v* [T1] to share out again in a different way —**-ution** /ˌriːdɪstrəˈbjuːʃən/ *n* [U]: *the redistribution of wealth in the country*
red lead /ˌred ˈled/ *n* [U] a poisonous red powder (LEAD OXIDE, Pb_3O_4) used in paint and to protect seeds against insects
red-let·ter day /ˌ· ˈ·· ·/ *n* a specially happy day that will be remembered: *It was a red-letter day for us when Paul came home*
red light /ˌ· ˈ·/ *n* **1** a light of a red colour used **a** at night as a danger signal **b** to stop vehicles **2 see the red light** to understand the danger of going on with what one is doing, and therefore stop
red-light dis·trict /ˌ· ˈ· ˌ··/ *n* the part of a town where one can hire women for sexual pleasure (PROSTITUTE*s*)
red meat /ˌ· ˈ·/ *n* [U] the meat of sheep (MUTTON) or of fully-grown cows (BEEF) —compare WHITE MEAT
re·do /riːˈduː/ *v* **-did** /ˈdɪd/, **-done** /ˈdʌn/, *3rd pers. sing.* **-does** /ˈdʌz/ [T1] to do again: *redo the bathroom in pink* (=paint it again)|*redo a piece of work/one's hair*
red·o·lence /ˈredələns/ *n* [U] *fml* the quality of being REDOLENT
red·o·lent /ˈredələnt/ *adj* [F+*of*] *fml* smelling of; making one think of: *The kitchen was redolent of onions.*|*an old house redolent of mystery*
re·doub·le /riːˈdʌbəl/ *v* [I∅;T1] to (cause to) increase greatly: *The noise redoubled.*|*The police redoubled their efforts to find the missing child*
re·doubt /rɪˈdaʊt/ *n* a small fort, forming part of a larger system of defences
re·doub·ta·ble /rɪˈdaʊtəbəl/ *adj lit & humor* greatly respected and feared: *a redoubtable opponent*
re·dound to /rɪˈdaʊnd/ *v prep* [T1] *fml* (of an event or action) to add to; increase (fame, honour, CREDIT[1] (3), etc.): *Any help you can give us will redound to your own good name* (=make people admire you)
red pep·per /ˌ· ˈ··/ *n* **1** [U] a hot-tasting powder made from the dried red seed cases (POD*s*) of a plant of the pepper family, used for giving taste to food: *put red pepper on your dinner* **2** [C] the plant that produces this powder **3** [C] the red fruit of the CAPSICUM plant, used as a vegetable
re·dress[1] /rɪˈdres/ *v* [T1] *fml* **1** to put right (a wrong, injustice, etc.) **2 redress the balance** to make things equal again
re·dress[2] /rɪˈdres‖ˈriːdres/ *n* [U] *fml* satisfaction or repayment for a wrong that has been done: *You must* SEEK *redress in the law courts for the damage to your car*
red set·ter /ˌ· ˈ··/ *n* a type of large dog with a red fur, often used for hunting
red·skin /ˈredˌskɪn/ *n old use* INDIAN (2)
red squir·rel /ˌ· ˈ··/ *n* **1** (in Europe) a type of small animal with a long bushy tail and red fur that lives in trees **2** (in America) a small animal of the same type, with the upper parts mostly red
red tape /ˌ· ˈ·/ *n* [U] silly rules, full of details, that delay (esp. government) business
re·duce /rɪˈdjuːs‖rɪˈduːs/ *v* **1** [T1 (*from* and/or *to*)] to make smaller, cheaper, etc. (from a larger to a smaller amount or number): *reduce the weight of a parcel by taking something out*|*I bought this shirt because it was reduced* (*from £3 to £2*).|*He won't reduce the rent of our house* **2** [I∅] *infml* (of a person) to lose weight on purpose: *No sugar, thank you—I'm trying to reduce* **3** [T1] (esp. in former times) to conquer (a place): *reduce a fort by bombing* —**reducible** *adj*
reduced cir·cum·stanc·es /ˌ·ˌ· ˈ····/ *n* [P] *old use* a poorer way of life than one formerly had
reduce to *v prep* **1** [D1] to bring (something) to (a smaller number or amount): *The great fire reduced the forest to a few trees* **2** [D1] to change (something) to (its parts): *reduce £'s to pence*|*We can reduce his statement to 3 simple facts.*|*reduce the rocks to dust* **3** [D1 *usu. pass.*] to bring (esp. someone) to (esp. a weaker or unfavourable state): *The class was reduced to silence/to order.*|*The captain was reduced to the ranks* (=made an ordinary soldier, not an officer) **4** [V4b *usu. pass.*] to force (someone) into (doing something humble, unpleasant, or dishonourable): *She was reduced to begging for her living* **5 reduce someone to tears** to make someone weep
re·duc·ti·o ad ab·sur·dum /rɪˌdʌktiəʊ æd əbˈsɜːdəm‖-ɜr-/ *n* [U] *Lat* the disproof of a piece of reasoning by showing that it leads to a silly result: *I can prove you're wrong by reductio ad absurdum—if everyone gave up their jobs and just sat in the sun like you, we'd all die of hunger*
re·duc·tion /rɪˈdʌkʃən/ *n* **1** [C;U] (a case of) making or becoming smaller; the amount taken off in making something smaller: *some/a slight reduction in the price of food*|*price reductions* **2** [C] a smaller copy (of a picture, map, or photograph) —opposite **enlargement**
re·dun·dan·cy /rɪˈdʌndənsi/ *n* **1** [C;U] (esp. of words) (a case of) being REDUNDANT (1): *the redundancy/the many redundancies of his style* **2** [C; U] *esp. BrE* (a case of) being REDUNDANT (2): *The increased use of oil will cause a lot of redundancy/many redundancies among coalminers* **3** [U] (of something made up of many parts) the quality of containing additional parts that will make the system work if other parts fail: *the redundancy of the English language*
redundancy pay /·ˈ···· ·/ *n* [U] *esp. BrE* additional payment made by an employer to a REDUNDANT (2) worker, according to age and length of employment
re·dun·dant /rɪˈdʌndənt/ *adj* **1** not needed; more than is necessary: *In the sentence "She lives alone by herself", the word "alone" is redundant* **2** [Wa5] *esp. BrE* (of a worker or group of workers) not needed because there is not enough work: *redundant labour* —**~ly** *adv*
re·du·pli·cate /rɪˈdjuːplɪkeɪt‖rɪˈduː-/ *v* [T1] to make again; repeat: *reduplicate his efforts* —**-cation** /rɪˌdjuːplɪˈkeɪʃən‖rɪˌduː-/ *n* [U]
red·wing /ˈredˌwɪŋ/ *n* a type of European THRUSH with red parts on its wings
red·wood /ˈredwʊd/ *n* **1** [C] any of several types of tall CONIFEROUS tree that grow in California **2** [U] the reddish wood of this tree
re·ech·o /riːˈekəʊ/ *v* [I∅;T1] to (cause to) be repeated again and again as an ECHO: *Their cries* ECHO*ed and reechoed among the lonely hills*
reed /riːd/ *n* **1** (the tall strong hollow stem of) any of various grasslike plants that grow in wet places **2** (in a musical instrument) a thin piece of wood or metal that produces sound by shaking (VIBRATION (1,2)) when air is blown over it —see picture at WIND INSTRUMENT **3 broken reed** *infml* a helper who cannot be trusted
reed in·stru·ment /ˈ· ˌ···/ *n* a musical instrument such as the OBOE, BASSOON, or CLARINET, in which sound is produced by the movement of a REED (2)
reeds /riːdz/ *n* [P] dried REED*s* (1) or, in some places, wheat stems used as a covering (THATCH) for roofs
re·ed·u·cate /riːˈedʒʊkeɪt‖-dʒə-/ *v* [T1;V3] to train

(someone) again; teach (someone) to do something that has now become necessary: *reeducate young criminals (to take their place in society)* —**-cation** /ˌriːedʒʊˈkeɪʃən‖-dʒə-/ *n* [U]

reed·y /ˈriːdi/ *adj* [Wa1] **1** (of a place) full of REEDs (1): *a reedy lake* **2** (of a sound) thin and high: *a reedy voice* —**reediness** *n* [U]

reef[1] /riːf/ *n* a reduction (in the area of a sail) made by REEFing[2]

reef[2] *v* [T1] to tie up (part of a sail) so as to reduce the size: *Reef your sails! The wind's getting stronger*

reef[3] *n* a line of sharp rocks or bank of sand, at or near the surface of the sea: *The ship was wrecked on a reef*

ree·fer[1] /ˈriːfəʳ/ *n* a short thick close-fitting coat, as worn by sailors

reefer[2] *n infml* a cigarette containing the drug MARIJUANA

reef knot /ˈ· ·/ *AmE* usu. **square knot**— *n esp. BrE* a kind of double knot that will not come undone easily: *tie the rope in a reef knot*

reek[1] /riːk/ *n* [S] **1** a strong unpleasant smell: *a reek of tobacco and beer* **2** *lit & ScotE* a thick smoke

reek[2] *v* [I∅] to give out smoke: *a reeking chimney*

reek of *v prep* [T1 *no pass.*] to smell strongly and unpleasantly of: *His breath reeks of onions.*|(fig.) *That business deal reeks of dishonesty*

reek with *v prep* [T1 *no pass.*] to be covered with (something wet and unpleasant): (fig.) *The government's action reeks with injustice*

reel[1] /riːl/ *n* **1** a round object on which a length of wire, cinema film, fishing line, recording TAPE[1] (3), etc., can be wound —see picture at SOUND[3] **2** (*AmE* **spool**)— *BrE* a usu. small wooden or plastic one of these on which sewing thread is sold **3** the amount that any of these will hold: *use up a whole reel of sewing cotton* **4** the length of time it takes to show this amount of cinema film: *The boy gets the girl at the end of the 8th reel*

reel[2] *v* [X9 esp. IN, UP, *off*, etc.] to put into the stated condition by winding: *reel in the line|reel up the fish|reel some more thread off the machine*

reel[3] *v* **1** [L9] to walk unsteadily as if drunk: *He came reeling up the street* **2** [I∅ (BACK)] to step away suddenly and unsteadily, as after a blow or shock: *When she hit him he reeled (back) and almost fell* **3** [I∅] to be confused in the mind: *Numbers always make my head reel* **4** [I∅] to seem to go round and round: *The room reeled before my eyes and I became unconscious*

reel[4] *n* (the music for) a high-spirited Scottish or Irish dance: *They were dancing reels in the kitchen*

reel off *v adv* [T1] RATTLE OFF: *He could reel off the dates of the kings of England*

re·en·try /riːˈentri/ *n* [C;U] **1** an act or the action of reentering **2** (of a space vehicle) an act or the action of returning into the earth's ATMOSPHERE (1): *make a successful reentry*

reeve /riːv/ *n* **1** (in former times) the chief law officer of an English town or larger area **2** (in Canada) the president of a town council

ref /ref/ *n* [C;N] *infml* REFEREE[1] (1)

ref. *abbrev. for:* REFERENCE

re·face /riːˈfeɪs/ *v* [T1] to put a new surface on: *reface worn stonework on a building*

re·fash·ion /riːˈfæʃən/ *v* [T1] *fml* to make again in a different way, esp. from old materials

re·fec·to·ry /rɪˈfektəri/ *n* (in schools, colleges, etc.) a large hall in which meals are served

ref·er·ee[1] /ˌrefəˈriː/ *n* **1** a judge in charge of a team game such as football —compare UMPIRE **2** a person who is asked to settle a disagreement **3** *BrE* REFERENCE (3b)

USAGE This word is used in connection with **basketball, billiards, boxing, football, hockey, rugby**, and **wrestling.**

referee[2] *v* [I∅;T1] to act as REFEREE[1] (1) for (a game): *John will referee (the football match)*

ref·er·ence /ˈrefərəns/ *n* **1** [C;U: (*to*)] (a case of) mentioning: *Did you hear all those nasty references to me that Janet kept making?* **2** [C;U: (*to*)] (a case of) looking at for information: *Keep this dictionary on your desk for easy reference* **3** [C] **a** a piece of written information about someone's character, ability, etc., esp. when he is looking for employment: *Your references show that you're just the man we want!|We will lend you the money if you bring a banker's reference* (=a note from the bank to say that there is money in your account) **b** a person who provides such information: *Ask Dr Ilson if he will act as one of your references* **4 in/with reference to** in connection with **5 without reference to** not connected with

USAGE A **testimonial** is kinder than a **reference**, because it is shown to the person it describes. A **reference** is more truthful, because it is not shown to him. But the 2 words are coming to be used with the same meaning.

reference book /ˈ··· ·/ *n* a book that is looked at for information: *This dictionary is a useful reference book*

reference li·bra·ry /ˈ··· ˌ···/ *n* **1** (the place containing) a collection of books that may not be taken away but must be studied in the place where they are kept: *Meet me in the reference library* **2** a collection of REFERENCE BOOKs: *Add this dictionary to your reference library*

reference mark /ˈ··· ·/ *n* a printed mark that directs the reader's attention to a note: *, †, ‡, § *are reference marks*

ref·e·ren·dum /ˌrefəˈrendəm/ *n* **-da** /də/ *or* **-dums** [C;*by*+U] a direct vote by all the people of a nation or area on some particular political question, such as a suggested law: *hold a referendum on this matter|decide the question by referendum* —compare PLEBISCITE

re·fer to /rɪˈfɜːʳ/ *v prep* **-rr-** **1** [T1] to mention; speak about: *Don't refer to your sister as a silly cow!* **2** [T1] to look at for information: *If you don't know what this means, refer to the dictionary* **3** [T1] to concern; be directed towards: *The new law does not refer to land used for farming* **4** [D1 (BACK)] to send (someone or something) to (usu. someone else) for decision or action: *The shop referred the complaint (back) to the makers of the article* **5** [D1] *rare* ATTRIBUTE TO —**~able to** *adj*

re·fill[1] /ˌriːˈfɪl/ *v* [T1] to fill again: *I'll refill my cigarette lighter with petrol*

re·fill[2] /ˈriːfɪl/ *n* a quantity of ink, petrol, etc., to REFILL something, often packed in a special container: *2 refills for my pen*

re·fine /rɪˈfaɪn/ *v* [T1] to make pure: *Oil must be refined before it can be used*

re·fined /rɪˈfaɪnd/ *adj* **1** [Wa5] made pure: *refined oil* **2** *sometimes derog* (of a person, his behaviour, etc.) having or showing education, delicacy of feeling, and gentleness of manners: *a refined way of speaking|She's so refined that she always eats cake with a fork*

re·fine·ment /rɪˈfaɪnmənt/ *n* **1** [U] the act of making pure: *the refinement of sugar* **2** [U] the quality of being REFINED (2): *a woman of some refinement* **3** [C (*on*)] a clever addition or improvement: *The new car has many added refinements such as a radio*

refine on also **refine up·on**— *v prep* [T1] to improve (a method, plan, etc.) esp. in details; make REFINEMENTs (3) to

re·fin·er /rɪˈfaɪnəʳ/ *n* [C9] **1** a person whose work is to REFINE something: *a rich oil refiner* **2** a machine that REFINEs something

re·fin·e·ry /rɪ'faɪnəri/ *n* a building and apparatus for refining (REFINE) metals, oil, or sugar: *a sugar refinery*

re·fit[1] /ˌriː'fɪt/ *v* **-tt-** [I∅;T1] **a** (esp. of a ship) to be made ready for further use: *sail into port to refit* **b** to make (esp. a ship) ready for further use

re·fit[2] /'riːfɪt/ *n* a case of REFITting: *sail into port for a refit*

refl. *written abbrev. for:* REFLEXIVE

re·flate /riː'fleɪt/ *v* [T1;I∅] to increase the supply of money in (a money system) to a former or desirable level

re·fla·tion /riː'fleɪʃən/ *n* [U] the official practice of increasing the amount of money to a desirable level in relation to the amount of goods, in order to improve industrial activity —compare DEFLATION, INFLATION

re·flect /rɪ'flekt/ *v* **1** [T1] to throw back (heat, light, sound, or an image): *The mirror reflects my face* **2** [T1,6] to express; give an idea of: *Does this letter reflect your real opinions/reflect how you really think?* **3** [I∅;T5] to consider carefully: *After reflecting for a time he decided not to go.|She reflected that life is short*

reflecting tel·e·scope /·'·· ˌ···/ *n* an instrument for seeing distant objects (TELESCOPE) in which the image is REFLECTed (1) in a mirror and made bigger —compare REFRACTING TELESCOPE

re·flec·tion /rɪ'flekʃən/ *n* **1** [U] the REFLECTing (1) of heat, light, sound, or an image: *The moon is bright only by reflection* **2** [C] an image REFLECTed (1) in a mirror or polished surface: *We looked at our reflections in the lake* **3** [C;U] (a) deep and careful thought: *He told us his reflections on Indian politics.|On reflection, he agreed to lend them the money.|I am sorry that I spoke too quickly and without reflection* **4 be/cast a reflection on** (of an event or action) to make people think badly of: *Your silly letter is/casts a reflection on your common sense* **5 cast reflections on** (of a person) to say bad things about: *You shouldn't have cast reflections on my wife*

re·flec·tive /rɪ'flektɪv/ *adj* (of a person or his mind) thoughtful

reflect on also **reflect up·on**— *v prep* **1** [T1,6a,b] to consider carefully: *I have been reflecting on the matter/on what you said/on why he did it/on how to get there* **2** [T1] (of an action or event) to bring blame on: *The lie that you told reflects on your honesty* **3** [D1] (of an action or event) to bring (CREDIT[1] (2) or DISCREDIT) on: *The welcome they gave us reflected great* CREDIT *on their good nature*

re·flec·tor /rɪ'flektəʳ/ *n* a surface that REFLECTs (1) light —see picture at BICYCLE[1]

re·flex /'riːfleks/ also **reflex ac·tion** /'·· ˌ··/— *n* a movement that is made in reply to some outside influence, without meaning to make it and without power to prevent it (=by INSTINCT): *I can't help shaking when I'm cold—it's a reflex (action)* —see also CONDITIONED REFLEX

reflex cam·e·ra /'·· ˌ···/ *n* a hand camera that shows the image on a small glass SCREEN by means of a mirror, so that the photographer can see it just as it will appear when the picture has been taken

re·flex·es /'riːfleks½z/ *n* [P] actions done in reply to an outside influence, esp. considered for their speed: *Tennis players need quick reflexes.|Don't drink alcohol before driving—it's bad for your reflexes.|The doctor hit his knee with a hammer to test his reflexes*

re·flex·ive /rɪ'fleksɪv/ *n, adj* [Wa5] (in grammar) (a word) showing that the action in the sentence has its effect on the person or thing that does the action: *In "I enjoyed myself"* **enjoy** *is a reflexive/is a* **reflexive verb**, *and the* PRONOUN **myself** *is also reflexive/is a* **reflexive pronoun**

re·float /ˌriː'fləʊt/ *v* [I∅;T1] **a** to cause (a boat or ship) to float again after sinking or getting stuck on the ground **b** (of a boat or ship) to float again in this way

re·foot /ˌriː'fʊt/ *v* [T1] to make (KNIT) a new foot on (an old sock or stocking)

re·for·est /riː'fɒr½st‖-'fɔ-, -'fɑ-/ *v* [T1] *AmE* REAFFOREST —**~ation** /riːˌfɒr½'steɪʃən‖-ˌfɔ-, -ˌfɑ-/ *n*

re·form[1] /rɪ'fɔːm‖-ɔrm/ *v* **1** [Wv5;I∅;T1] to (cause to) improve; make or become right: *We should try to reform criminals rather than punish them.|Harry has completely reformed/is a completely reformed character now—he's stopped taking drugs and got a regular job* **2** [T1] to cause REFORMs[2] in: *try to reform society* —see REFORM[2] (USAGE) —**~er** *n*: *Beatrice Webb was a famous social reformer*

reform[2] *n* [C;U] (a) social action which does or should improve conditions, remove unfairness, etc., in a society: *The new law brought many social reforms*

USAGE The noun **reform** is used particularly of social and religious improvement, while **reformation** is used also of improvement in a person's character and behaviour. The verb **reform** has both meanings.

re-form /ˌriː'fɔːm‖-ɔrm/ *v* [I∅;T1] to (cause to) form again, esp. into ranks: *The company reformed, ready to attack again*

ref·or·ma·tion /ˌrefə'meɪʃən‖-fər-/ *n* [C;U] (an) improvement; the act of REFORMing[1] (1) or state of being reformed: *Do you notice the complete reformation in Harry's character?* —see REFORM[2] (USAGE)

Reformation *n* [*the*+R] (the period of) the religious movement in Europe in the 16th century leading to the establishment of the REFORMed[1] (2) or PROTESTANT churches

re·for·ma·to·ry[1] /rɪ'fɔːmətəri‖rɪ'fɔrmətori/ also **re·for·ma·tive** /rɪ'fɔːmətɪv‖-'fɔr-/— *adj* [Wa5] (of an action) of or leading to REFORM[2]

reformatory[2] *n old use & AmE* APPROVED SCHOOL

re·fract /rɪ'frækt/ *v* [T1] (of water, glass, etc.) to cause (light) to change direction when passing through at an angle —**~ion** /rɪ'frækʃən/ *n* [U]: *Refraction makes a straight stick look bent if it is partly in water*

refracting tel·e·scope /·'·· ˌ···/ *n* an instrument for seeing distant objects (TELESCOPE) in which the image is bent (REFRACTed) by passing through a piece of glass (LENS) —compare REFLECTING TELESCOPE

re·frac·to·ry /rɪ'fræktəri/ *adj* **1** disobedient and troublesome: *a refractory horse* **2** (of diseases) difficult to cure **3** *tech* (of materials, esp. metals) difficult to melt; able to bear high temperatures

refractory brick /·ˌ··· '·/ *n* [C;U] (a) brick that will bear high temperatures and is used to form the inner part of FURNACEs

re·frain[1] /rɪ'freɪn/ *v* [I∅ (*from*)] to hold oneself back (from); avoid: *to refrain from smoking*

refrain[2] *n* a part of a song that is repeated, esp. at the end of each VERSE: *They all sang the refrain*

re·fresh /rɪ'freʃ/ *v* [T1] **1** to get rid of the tiredness of; make fresh again: *A glass of beer/A hot bath will refresh you.|He refreshed himself with a glass of beer* **2 refresh one's memory** to cause oneself to remember again: *I looked at the map to refresh my memory of the road*

re·fresh·er /rɪ'freʃəʳ/ *n tech* (in Britain) an additional payment made to a lawyer (BARRISTER) during a law case

refresher course /·'·· ·/ *n* a training course given

to a group of members of the same profession to bring their knowledge up to date: *to hold/attend a refresher course on modern teaching methods*

re·fresh·ing /rɪˈfreʃɪŋ/ *adj* **1** producing a feeling of comfort and new strength: *had a very refreshing sleep* **2** pleasantly new and interesting: *It's refreshing to meet a girl these days who doesn't wear eye* MAKEUP —**~ly** *adv*

re·fresh·ment /rɪˈfreʃmənt/ *n* [U] **1** (the experience of) being REFRESHed **2** food and drink: *to work all day without refreshment|got some coffee in the refreshment room at the railway station*

re·fresh·ments /rɪˈfreʃmənts/ *n* [P] (esp. light) food and drink: *Refreshments will be served after the meeting*

re·fri·ge·rant /rɪˈfrɪdʒərənt/ *n* a substance that is used to REFRIGERATE, such as solid CARBON DIOXIDE

re·fri·ge·rate /rɪˈfrɪdʒəreɪt/ *v* [Wv5;T1] to make cold; freeze (food, liquid, etc.) as a way of preserving: *refrigerated meat/beer*

re·fri·ge·ra·tion /rɪˌfrɪdʒəˈreɪʃən/ *n* [U] the keeping of food cool to preserve it: *Keep this meat under refrigeration.|the refrigeration industry*

re·fri·ge·ra·tor /rɪˈfrɪdʒəreɪtəʳ/ also (*infml, esp. BrE*) **fridge**, *AmE infml* also **icebox**— *n* a large box, cupboard, or room in which food or drink can be kept for a time at a low temperature: *There's some milk in the refrigerator* —compare FREEZER and see picture at KITCHEN

reft /reft/ *adj* [F (*of*)] *lit* BEREFT

re·fu·el /ˌriːˈfjuːəl/ *v* **-ll-** (*AmE* **-l-**) [I0;T1] to (cause to) fill up again with FUEL: *The aircraft made a stop to refuel*

ref·uge /ˈrefjuːdʒ/ *n* **1** [C;U] (a place that provides) protection or shelter from danger: *a mountain refuge for climbers|Where can we find refuge from the storm?* **2** [C] (*AmE* **safety island**)— *BrE tech* a place in the middle of a street where people can wait until it is safe to cross the rest of the way **3 take refuge (in)** to find shelter (in): *They took refuge under the bed.*|(fig.) *He took refuge in telling lies*

ref·u·gee /ˌrefjʊˈdʒiː/ *n* a person who has been driven from his country for political reasons or during a war

re·ful·gence /rɪˈfʌldʒəns‖rɪˈfʊl-/ *n* [U] *lit* the quality of being REFULGENT; bright light

re·ful·gent /rɪˈfʌldʒənt‖rɪˈfʊl-/ *adj lit* (of light) very bright: *the refulgent glory of the midday sun*

re·fund¹ /rɪˈfʌnd/ *v* [D1 (*to*); T1] to give (money) as a REFUND²: *They refunded (us) our money*

re·fund² /ˈriːfʌnd/ *n* [C;(U)] (a) repayment: *to demand a refund on unsatisfactory goods*

re·fur·bish /ˌriːˈfɜːbɪʃ‖-ɜr-/ *v* [T1] to polish up or make bright again (something old): (fig.) *He's going to Paris to refurbish his French*

re·fus·al /rɪˈfjuːzəl/ *n* [C;U:(3)] **1** (a case of) refusing: *My offer met with a cold refusal.|Refusal was impossible—I had to do what they asked* **2** (**the**) **first refusal** (the) right of deciding whether to buy something before it is offered to other people: *If you sell your house will you let me have (the) first refusal?*

re·fuse¹ /rɪˈfjuːz/ *v* [I0;T1,3;D1] not to accept or do or give: *He asked her to marry him but she refused (to marry him).|She refused his offer.|She refused him even a kiss*

USAGE One can **refuse** or **decline** to do something, but one must **decline** (opposite **agree**) in words: *The horse* **refused** (not ***declined** or ***agreed**) *to jump the wall.* One can **refuse** or **decline**, not **reject**, an invitation (opposite **accept**); **refuse** (not **decline** or **reject**) permission; **decline** or **reject** (not **refuse**) a suggestion; **refuse**, **reject**, or **decline** an offer (opposite **accept**); **reject** (not **refuse** or **decline**) a plan or PROPOSAL. One need not **reject** in words: *The horse* **refused/rejected** (not ***declined**) *the apple* (opposite **accepted**). One **denies** a statement or story, **admits** only a statement: *He* **denied** (not ***admitted**) *the story.|He* **denied/admitted** (*the fact*) *that he had murdered the king.|He* **denied/admitted** *having murdered the king.*

ref·use² /ˈrefjuːs/ *n* [U] *fml* waste material: *a heap of kitchen refuse|"Refuse collector" sounds better than* "DUSTMAN"

refuse dump /ˈ·· ·/ *n* a place where the REFUSE² collected from a town is put

re·fu·ta·ble /ˈrefjʊtəbəl, rɪˈfjuː-‖rɪˈfjuː-, ˈrefjə-/ *adj* (of a statement) that can be REFUTEd: *an argument that is easily refutable* —opposite **irrefutable**

ref·u·ta·tion /ˌrefjʊˈteɪʃən/ *n* [C;U] (a) proof that something is untrue

re·fute /rɪˈfjuːt/ *v* [T1] to prove **a** (someone) to be mistaken: *I refuted him easily* **b** (a statement) to be untrue: *I refuted his claim that the world was flat*

re·gain /rɪˈgeɪn/ *v* [T1] **1** to get or win back (something): *to regain one's health/one's consciousness* **2** to get back to; reach (a place) again: *to regain the shore* **3 regain one's footing/balance** to get back on one's feet after slipping or beginning to fall

re·gal /ˈriːgəl/ *adj* very splendid; of or suitable for a king or queen: *a regal old lady* —**~ly** *adv*

re·gale with /rɪˈgeɪl/ also **regale on**— *v prep* [D1] to give enjoyment to (oneself or another) with (something pleasant): *He regaled us with some stories about his youth.|She was regaling herself on cream cakes*

re·ga·li·a /rɪˈgeɪlɪə/ *n* **1** [U;(P)] the ornaments, crown, etc., worn or carried by a king or queen at royal ceremonies **2** [U;(P):(9)] the ceremonial clothes and ornaments that show one's (stated) official position: *a* MAYOR*'s regalia*

re·gard¹ /rɪˈgɑːd‖-ɑrd/ *n* [U] **1** respect: *I hold her in high/low/the greatest regard* **2** [+*for* or *to*] respectful attention: *You have no regard for my feelings!* **3** *lit* long look without moving one's eyes: *Her regard was fixed on the crowd* **4 in this regard** *fml* on this subject **5 in/with regard to** REGARDING —see AS FOR (USAGE)

regard² *v* **1** [X9] *fml* to look at (in the stated way): *She regarded him thoughtfully* **2** [X9 esp. *with*] to consider (in the stated way): *I have always regarded him highly/with the greatest admiration* **3** [T1 *usu. neg.*] *fml* to pay attention to (thoughts, ideas, etc.): *You never regard what I say!*

regard as *v prep* [V4b;X1,7,9] to consider (someone or something) as being (something): *I regard him as my brother/as stupid.|She regarded him as (being) without principles*

re·gard·ful /rɪˈgɑːdfəl‖-ɑr-/ *adj* [F+*of*] *fml* full of REGARD¹ (2): *You should be more regardful of your father's wishes*

re·gard·ing /rɪˈgɑːdɪŋ‖-ɑr-/ also **as regards**— *prep fml* (esp. in business letters) on the subject of; in connection with: *Regarding your recent enquiry . . .*

re·gard·less /rɪˈgɑːdləs‖-ɑr-/ *adv* [Wa5] *infml* whatever may happen: *Get the money, regardless!*

regardless of *prep* careless of; without worrying about: *Regardless of danger, he climbed the tower*

re·gards /rɪˈgɑːdz‖-ɑr-/ *n* [P] **1** good wishes: *Give him my (best) regards* **2 With kind regards** (a friendly but not very informal way of ending a letter)

re·gat·ta /rɪˈgætə/ *n* a meeting for races between rowing or sailing boats

re·gen·cy /ˈriːdʒənsi/ *n* [U] (the period of) government by a REGENT

Regency *n* **1** [*the*+R] (in Britain) the period

1811–1820 **2** [A] of the British style of the period 1810–1830: *a graceful Regency chair*

re·gen·e·rate¹ /rɪˈdʒenərɪ̈t/ *adj fml* having been REGENERATED² —opposite **unregenerate**

re·gen·e·rate² /rɪˈdʒenəreɪt/ *v* [IØ;T1] *fml* **1** to (cause to) improve morally **2** to give or obtain new life; grow again: *This creature's tail will regenerate if it's cut off* —**-ration** /rɪˌdʒenəˈreɪʃən/ *n* [U]: *the regeneration of our society*

re·gent¹ /ˈriːdʒənt/ *n* (*often cap.*) a person who governs in place of a king (or ruling queen) when he/she is not able to do so, as because of illness or absence or because he/she is still a child

regent² *adj* [Wa5;E] (*often cap.*) governing as a REGENT¹: *a queen regent|the Prince Regent*

reg·gae /ˈregeɪ/ *n* [U] (*often cap.*) popular dance and music from the West Indies

re·gi·cide /ˈredʒɪ̈saɪd/ *n* **1** [U] the crime of killing a king or queen **2** [C] a person who does this

re·gime /reɪˈʒiːm (*Fr* reʒim)/ *n* [C9] *Fr* **1** a particular (type of) government: *Things will change under the new regime* **2** REGIMEN

re·gi·men /redʒɪ̈mɪ̈n/ *n* [C9] a fixed plan of food, sleep, etc., in order to improve one's health: *to follow a* STRICT *regimen*

re·gi·ment¹ /ˈredʒɪ̈mənt/ *n* [GC] **1** a large military group, commanded by a COLONEL **2** a military organization, usu. drawn from one area of a country, that sends BATTALIONs of men to serve in an army **3** [(*of*)] a very large number (of living creatures): *a whole regiment of ants*

re·gi·ment² /ˈredʒɪ̈ment/ *v* [T1 *often pass.*] *derog* to control (people) firmly: *Modern children don't like being regimented* —**~ation** /ˌredʒɪ̈menˈteɪʃən‖-mən-/ *n* [U]

re·gi·ment·al /ˌredʒɪ̈ˈmentl/ *adj* [Wa5;A] of a REGIMENT¹ (1): *to listen to the regimental band*

re·gi·ment·als /ˌredʒɪ̈ˈmentlz/ *n* [P] the uniform worn by the men of a particular REGIMENT¹ (1): *He arrived at the party in full regimentals*

Re·gi·na /rɪˈdʒaɪnə/ *n Lat* (in Britain) **1** [E] (the title used after the name of a ruling queen): *Elizabeth Regina* **2** [R] *law* (used, when a queen is ruling, in titles of LAWSUITs) the State; the CROWN¹ (4): *in the action Regina v Ilson* (=the Crown against Ilson) —compare REX

re·gion /ˈriːdʒən/ *n* [C9] **1** a largish (stated) area, esp. of land, as a part of a country: *a tropical region|the region of the heart* **2 in the region of** about: *It will cost in the region of $500* **3 the lower regions** *euph* HELL¹ (1)

re·gion·al /ˈriːdʒənəl/ *adj* [Wa5] of a REGION or the REGIONS: *strange regional customs* —**~ly** *adv*

re·gions /ˈriːdʒənz/ *n* [(*the*) P] the parts of a country away from the capital: *reports coming in from the regions*

re·gis·ter¹ /ˈredʒɪ̈stəʳ/ *n* **1** [C] a record or list: *to keep a register of births and deaths* **2** [C] a book containing such a record: *The teacher can't find his school attendance register* —see also CASH REGISTER **3** [C] the range of a human voice or musical instrument: *That note is outside my register|is in the upper register of this instrument* **4** [C] a movable metal plate for controlling the flow of air in a pipe, as in a heating system **5** [C;U] *tech* the words, style, and grammar used by speakers and writers in particular conditions: *to write in (a) formal register|in the register of informal speech*

register² *v* **1** [T1] to put into an official list or record: *to register the birth of a baby|Is the car registered?* **2** [IØ] to enter one's name on a list: *to register at a hotel|as an elector* **3** [T1] (of machines or instruments) to show; record: *The* THERMOMETER *registered 35°C* **4** [T1] (of a person or his face) to express: *She|Her face registered anxiety* **5** [Wv5;T1] to send by REGISTERED POST: *You'd better register this parcel.|a registered letter* **6** [IØ *usu. neg.*] *infml* to have an effect (on a person); be noticed: *He told me he was married but I'm afraid it didn't register*

registered nurse /ˌ··· ˈ·/ *n* (in the US) a trained person who is officially allowed to practise as a nurse —compare STATE REGISTERED NURSE

registered post /ˌ··· ˈ·/ (*AmE* **registered mail**)— *n* [U] *BrE* a postal service for which an additional charge is made and which protects the sender of a valuable letter or parcel against loss

register of·fice /ˈ··· ˌ··/ also **registry of·fice** /ˈ··· ˌ··/— *n* an office where marriages can lawfully take place and where births, marriages, and deaths are recorded

re·gis·trar /ˌredʒɪ̈ˈstrɑːʳ‖ˈredʒɪ̈strɑr/ *n* a keeper of official records, as in a REGISTER OFFICE or a college

re·gis·tra·tion /ˌredʒɪ̈ˈstreɪʃən/ *n* **1** [U] the act of REGISTERing² (1,2,5): *The registration of students for the course will begin on Thursday morning* **2** [C] a fact that has been REGISTERed² (1,2)

registration book /··ˈ·· ·/ also **log book**— *n* (in Britain) a thin official book containing details about a car and recording all owners of that car

registration num·ber /··ˈ·· ˌ··/ *n* the official set of figures and letters that must be shown on the front and back of a car —see picture at CAR

re·gis·try /ˈredʒɪ̈stri/ *n* a place where records are kept

Re·gi·us pro·fes·sor /ˌriːdʒɪəs prəˈfesəʳ/ *n* [C;U] (*often cap.*) (the title of) a certain kind of university teacher of high rank (PROFESSOR) at Oxford and Cambridge: *David hopes to become Regius Professor of Latin.|3 Regius professors drinking wine*

reg·nant /ˈregnənt/ *adj* [Wa5;E] *fml* ruling, esp. (of a queen) in her own right and not as the king's wife

re·gress /rɪˈgres/ *v* [IØ] to return to a worse or less developed earlier state —**~ion** /rɪˈgreʃən/ *n* [U]

re·gres·sive /rɪˈgresɪv/ *adj* (of behaviour) that REGRESSes

re·gret¹ /rɪˈgret/ *v* **-tt-** **1** [T1,4,5a] to be sorry about (a sad fact or event): *to regret someone's death|We've always regretted selling the farm.|I regret having called* (=that I called) *him a thief, but I regret even more his stealing my watch!|She regrets that she can't come* **2** [T1] to be sorry that one has lost; miss very much: *I don't mind living in the city, but I do regret not being able to go for long walks* **3 I/We regret to say/to inform you/to tell you** *fml* (used when bad news is to follow): *We regret to inform you that you are to be dismissed next week*

regret² *n* [U (*at*)] **1** unhappiness (at the loss of something, or because something has or has not happened): *They said goodbye with great regret.|We heard with regret that you had failed the examination.|to feel regret at her absence* **2 (much/greatly) to one's regret** one is sorry to say: *Much to my regret, I must leave you now* —**~ful** *adj*: *He was sorry to leave, when he saw their regretful faces* —**~fully** *adv* —**~fulness** *n* [U]

re·grets /rɪˈgrets/ *n* [P] **1** (used in polite expressions of refusal) a note or message refusing an invitation: *to send one's regrets|I can't come—please give them my regrets* **2 have no regrets** not to feel sorry about what has happened

re·gret·ta·ble /rɪˈgretəbəl/ *adj* that one should feel sorry about; worthy of blame: *Your choice of friends is most regrettable*

re·gret·ta·bly /rɪˈgretəbli/ *adv* [Wa5] **1** in a REGRETTABLE manner; to a REGRETTABLE degree: *to get regrettably drunk* **2** it is REGRETTABLE that: *Regrettably, we had forgotten all about Randolph*

re·group /ˌriːˈgruːp/ *v* [I∅;T1] to (cause to) form into new groups or into groups again

reg·u·lar[1] /ˈregjʊləʳ‖-gjə-/ *adj* **1** [B] happening often with the same length of time between the occasions: *the regular noise* (TICK) *of the clock* **2** [B] happening, coming, doing something, again and again at the same times each day, week, etc.: *a regular customer|regular working hours* **3** [B] happening every time: *regular attendance at church* **4** [B] not varying: *to drive at a regular speed* **5** [B] proper; according to rule or custom: *He knows a lot about the law but he's not a regular lawyer* **6** [B] *apprec* evenly shaped: *Her nose is very regular.|regular* FEATURE*s* (=of the face) **7** [Wa5;A] *infml* complete; thorough: *His wife is a regular slave—she always has to bring him tea in bed* **8** [Wa5;A] professional; not just employed for a time: *the regular army* **9** [B] *esp. AmE* ordinary: *Do you want the regular size or this big one?* **10** [Wa5;B] living under a particular religious rule of life: *Ordinary* ROMAN CATHOLIC *priests are not members of the regular* CLERGY, *but* MONK*s are* —compare SECULAR **11** [Wa5;B] (in grammar) following a common pattern: *The verb "dance" is regular, but the verb "be" is not regular* (=is **irregular**) **12 keep regular hours** to follow the same quiet sensible way of life all the time

regular[2] *n* **1** a soldier who is a member of an army kept by a country all the time **2** *infml* a REGULAR[1] (2) visitor, customer, etc.: *Gordon is one of our regulars—he comes in for a drink about this time every night*

reg·u·lar·i·ty /ˌregjʊˈlærǝ̇ti‖-jə-/ *n* [U] the quality of being REGULAR[1]

reg·u·lar·ize, -ise /ˈregjʊləraɪz‖-gjə-/ *v* [T1] to make lawful and official (a state of affairs that has already gone on for some time): *We've been living together for years—let's regularize the* POSITION[1] (5) *and get married!* —**-ization** /ˌregjʊləraɪˈzeɪʃən‖-gjələrə-/ *n* [U]

reg·u·lar·ly /ˈregjʊləli‖-jələrli/ *adv* **1** at REGULAR[1] (2) times: *Take the medicine regularly 3 times a day.|She writes to me as regularly as clockwork every Thursday* **2** in a REGULAR[1] (6) way: *Her nose is regularly shaped*

reg·u·late /ˈregjʊleɪt‖-gjə-/ *v* [T1] **1** to fix or control; bring order or method to: *to regulate one's habits|to regulate the pressure of the tyres|a well-regulated family* **2** to make (a machine, esp. a clock or watch) work correctly: *Your watch is always slow; it needs to be regulated*

reg·u·la·tion /ˌregjʊˈleɪʃən‖-gjə-/ *n* **1** [U] control; the bringing of order: *the regulation of public spending* **2** [C] an esp. official rule or order: *regulations governing the sale of guns* **3** [A] official: *drive at the regulation speed*
USAGE Note the word order in this fixed phrase: **rules and regulations**.

reg·u·la·tor /ˈregjʊleɪtəʳ‖-gjə-/ *n* any type of instrument that controls, esp. the part of a clock that controls its speed

reg·u·lo /ˈregjʊləʊ‖-gjə-/ *n* [C9] *BrE* a degree of heat in a gas cooker, shown by the stated number: *Cook this meat on regulo 4*

re·gur·gi·tate /rɪˈgɜːdʒǝ̇teɪt‖-ɜr-/ *v* [T1] *fml* to pour out again from the mouth (food already swallowed): (fig.) *She just regurgitates everything the teacher says, instead of thinking for herself* —**-tation** /rɪˌgɜːdʒǝ̇ˈteɪʃən‖-ɜr-/ *n* [U]

re·ha·bil·i·tate /ˌriːhəˈbɪlǝ̇teɪt/ *v* [T1] **1** to put back into good condition: *to rehabilitate old houses* **2** to make able to live an ordinary life again, as by training: *to rehabilitate soldiers who have lost a limb in the war* **3** to put back to a former high rank, position, and fame: *He was suddenly let out of prison and rehabilitated as chief minister* —**-tation** /ˌriːhəbɪlǝ̇ˈteɪʃən/ *n* [U]

re·hash[1] /riːˈhæʃ/ *v* [T1] *infml* to use (ideas) again in a new form but without real change or improvement: *a politician who keeps rehashing the same old speech*

re·hash[2] /ˈriːhæʃ/ *n* [*usu. sing.*] *infml* a (product of) REHASHing[1]: *His second book is just a rehash of his first*

re·hear /ˌriːˈhɪəʳ/ *v* [T1] to try (a case in a law court) again

re·hears·al /rɪˈhɜːsəl‖-ɜr-/ *n* [C;U] **1** the act or an occasion of rehearsing (REHEARSE (1)): *This play will need a lot of rehearsal(s).|The play is in rehearsal now.|We'll meet after rehearsal* —see also DRESS REHEARSAL **2** *fml* the action of rehearsing or something REHEARSED (2): *The rehearsal of his adventures will take all night*

re·hearse /rɪˈhɜːs‖-ɜrs/ *v* **1** [I∅;T1] **a** to learn and practise (something) for later performance: *to rehearse a play|The actors were rehearsing in the tent* **b** to cause (someone) to do this: *She rehearsed the musicians* **2** [T1] *fml* to tell fully (events or a story): *He rehearsed (the story of) all his sufferings in prison*

re·house /ˌriːˈhaʊz/ *v* [T1] to put (someone) into a new or better house: *a plan to rehouse poor people in better homes*

Reich /raɪk (*Ger* raɪx)/ *n Ger* **1** [*the*+R] the German state or kingdom **2** [*the*+R9] the German State during one of 3 periods: *The 1st Reich lasted from the 10th century until 1806, the 2nd Reich from 1871–1918, and the 3rd Reich from 1933–45*

re·i·fi·ca·tion /ˌriːǝ̇fǝ̇ˈkeɪʃən, ˌreɪ-/ *n* [U] *tech, often derog* the action or result of REIFYing

re·i·fy /ˈriːǝ̇faɪ, ˈreɪ-/ *v* [T1] *tech, often derog* (in PHILOSOPHY (1)) to regard (something in the mind) as a material thing: *to reify* ECONOMIC *conditions that are caused by people and can be changed by people*

reign[1] /reɪn/ *n* **1** a period of REIGNing: *during the reign of King George* **2 reign of terror a** a period of political cruelty and official killing for no reason **b** a period of killings and other violent crimes done by a particular person or group, that cause great fear among the public

reign[2] *v* [I∅] **1** [(*over*)] to be the king or queen: *Our Queen reigns but does not rule.|to reign over a small kingdom* **2** to exist noticeably: *The thunder died away and quietness reigned once more*

re·im·burse /ˌriːǝ̇mˈbɜːs‖-ɜrs/ *v* [D1 (*to*); T1] to pay (money) back to (a spender): *We will reimburse you (for) the cost.|We will reimburse the cost (to you).|You/The cost will be reimbursed*

re·im·burse·ment /ˌriːǝ̇mˈbɜːsmənt‖-ɜr-/ *n* [C;U] (a) repayment (of a spender or of money): *We have to make some reimbursements.|the reimbursement of Harry|of the money*

rein /reɪn/ *n* [*often pl. with sing. meaning*] **1** a long narrow band usu. of leather, by which a horse (or sometimes a small child) is controlled and guided —see picture at HORSE **2 draw rein** to go more slowly: *He never drew rein for a moment till he reached the river* **3 give (free) rein to** to give freedom to (feelings or desires): *to give free rein to one's imagination* **4 keep a tight rein on** to control firmly **5 take the reins** to become (or make oneself) the leader and make the decisions **6 the reins of government** *pomp* political power: *to* ASSUME (2)*/drop/hold the reins of government*

rein back also **rein up**— *v adv* [T1] to cause (a horse) to stop by pulling the REIN*s*

re·in·car·nate[1] /ˌriːɪnˈkɑːneɪt‖-ɑr-/ *v* [T1 (*as*) *usu. pass.*] to cause to become again a living creature with a body, after death, esp. according to religious beliefs: *Perhaps you will be reincarnated as a snake*

re·in·car·nate² /ˌriːɪnˈkɑːnɪ̈t, riːˈɪnkɑː-‖-ɑr-/ *adj* [Wa5] *lit & old use* REINCARNATED

re·in·car·na·tion /ˌriːɪnkɑːˈneɪʃən‖-ɑr-/ *n* **1** [U] the act of being REINCARNATED¹: *Some Buddhists believe in the reincarnation of a man as an animal* **2** [C] the creature that results: *He believes he may not kill an animal, as it may be a reincarnation of a man* **3** [C] the life that the soul may have in this way: *What shall I be in my next reincarnation?*

rein·deer /ˈreɪndɪəʳ/ *n* **reindeer** [Wn3] a type of large deer with long branching horns that is used in the coldest parts of Europe for its milk, meat, and skin, and for pulling carriages (SLEDGE*s*) across the snow

re·in·force /ˌriːɪ̈nˈfɔːs‖-ˈfors-/ *v* [T1] to strengthen by adding **a** materials: *to reinforce a coat by sewing pieces of leather on the elbows*|(fig.) *to reinforce an argument with facts* **b** men, ships, etc.: *to reinforce an army*

reinforced con·crete /ˌ··· ˈ··/ also **ferroconcrete**— *n* [U] stonelike material (CONCRETE) strengthened by metal bars placed in it before it hardens, and used in building

re·in·force·ment /ˌriːɪ̈nˈfɔːsmənt‖-ˈfors-/ *n* [U] the act of reinforcing (REINFORCE): *This roof needs some reinforcement*

re·in·force·ments /ˌriːɪ̈nˈfɔːsmənts‖-ˈfors-/ *n* [P] more men sent to REINFORCE an army

rein in *v adv* [T1] to cause (a horse) to go more slowly by pulling the REIN*s*

reins /reɪnz/ *n* [P] LEADING REINS

re·in·state /ˌriːɪ̈nˈsteɪt/ *v* [T1 (*as, in*)] to put back (into a position formerly held): *He was dismissed, but was later reinstated (as a toolmaker/in his former job)* —**~ment** *n* [C;U]

re·in·sure /ˌriːɪ̈nˈʃʊəʳ/ *v* [T1] *tech* to INSURE again with another insurance company, so that the risk of loss will be shared —**-surance** /ˌriːɪ̈nˈʃʊərəns/ *n* [U]

re·is·sue¹ /ˌriːˈɪʃuː/ *v* [T1] *esp. BrE* to send out or print (ISSUE) again after a time: *to reissue a book in a new cover but without changing what is inside*

reissue² *n* something REISSUED: *a reissue of stamps*

re·it·e·rate /riːˈɪtəreɪt/ *v* [T1] to repeat several or many times: *"Go away! Go away!" he reiterated* —**-ration** /riːˌɪtəˈreɪʃən/ *n* [C;U]: *After much reiteration/many reiterations of the same thing, he succeeded in making them understand*

re·ject¹ /rɪˈdʒekt/ *v* [T1] **1** to refuse to accept: *She rejected my suggestion.|He was rejected for the army because of his bad eyes* **2** to throw away as useless or imperfect: *to choose the good apples and reject the bad ones* —see REFUSE (USAGE)

re·ject² /ˈriːdʒekt/ *n* something REJECTed¹ (2)

re·jec·tion /rɪˈdʒekʃən/ *n* [C;U] (a cause of) REJECTing: *I've had so many rejections I've stopped offering to help her.|a feeling of rejection*

rejection slip /·ˈ·· ·/ *n* a printed message REJECTing¹ (1) something that one has offered for printing and sale (PUBLICATION): *a young writer discouraged by so many rejection slips*

re·joice /rɪˈdʒɔɪs/ *v* [I∅ (*at, over*); T3,5] *fml & lit* **1** to feel or show great joy: *"Rejoice with me; for I have found my sheep which was lost."* (the Bible)|*to rejoice at/over good news|I rejoice (to hear) that you are coming home* **2 rejoice someone's heart/the heart of someone** to make someone feel glad: *The victory rejoiced the heart of the whole nation*

rejoice in *v prep* [T1 *no pass.*] *humor* (of a person) to possess (esp. in the phr. **rejoice in the name of ...**): *He rejoices in the name of Pigg* (used when the name sounds silly)

re·joic·ing /rɪˈdʒɔɪsɪŋ/ *n* [U] *fml* great joy, esp. shown by a number of people

re·joic·ings /rɪˈdʒɔɪsɪŋz/ *n* [P] *fml* feasting, dancing, etc., as signs of joy

re·join /rɪˈdʒɔɪn/ *v* **1** [T5a] (usu. used when the actual words are given) to answer: *"Not at all," he rejoined rudely* —see ANSWER (USAGE) **2** [I∅] *law* to answer a charge in a law court **3** [T1] *esp. BrE* to go back to (one's army camp, ship, etc.)

re-join /ˌriːˈdʒɔɪn/ *v* [T1] to join together again (things that are separated): *to re-join the 2 wires*

re·join·der /rɪˈdʒɔɪndəʳ/ *n* an answer, esp. a rude one

re·ju·ve·nate /rɪˈdʒuːvəneɪt/ *v* [T1 (*often pass.*); (I∅)] to make or become young again: *The mountain air will rejuvenate you* —**-nation** /rɪˌdʒuːvəˈneɪʃən/ *n* [S;U]

re·kin·dle /riːˈkɪndl/ *v* [T1;I∅] to (cause to) light again: *to rekindle the fire*|(fig.) *His interest in her rekindled*

re·laid /ˌriːˈleɪd/ *past t. & p. of* RELAY³

re·lapse¹ /rɪˈlæps/ *n* a return to a former and worse state esp. of health, after an improvement

relapse² *v* [I∅ (*into*)] to fall back (into evil or illness) after an improvement; return: *He relapsed into his old bad habits*

re·late /rɪˈleɪt/ *v* [T1] *fml* **1** [(*to*)] to tell (a story): *He related (to us) the story of his escape from the enemy* **2** to see or show a connection between: *I can't relate those 2 ideas* **3 Strange to relate** (used before telling a surprising story): *Strange to relate, Robert once shot a lion*

re·lat·ed /rɪˈleɪtɪ̈d/ *adj* [Wa5; (*by, to*)] connected; of the same family or kind: *Where to go, and what to do when we get there, are 2 related questions.|She is related to me by marriage* —opposite **unrelated** —**~ness** *n* [U]

relate to *v prep* **1** [T1 *often neg.*] to have a friendly relationship with; get on with: *She doesn't relate very well to her mother* **2** [D1,6a] also **relate with**— to connect (something) to (something else, as, a cause): *I can't relate what he does to what he says/to how he says he will act* **3** [T1] REFER TO (3)

re·la·tion /rɪˈleɪʃən/ *n* **1** [C] a member of one's family: *to invite all your relations to dinner* **2** [U (*between*)] connection: *the relation between wages and prices* —see USAGE **3** [C;U] *fml* (the act of telling) a story: *the/an exciting relation of his adventures in Africa* **4 bear no/little/some relation to** to match not at all/not much/partly, in number, amount, or size: *The actual cost bears no relation to what we thought it was going to be* **5 in/with relation to** *fml* (used in business letters) concerning; with regard to

USAGE Both **relation** and **relationship** (the more modern word) can mean "connection". To avoid confusion, it may be better to use **relative** rather than **relation** to mean "a member of one's family".

re·la·tion·al /rɪˈleɪʃənəl/ *adj* [Wa5] *tech* (of a word) used as part of a sentence but without a meaning of its own: *"Have" in "I have gone" is a relational word* —compare NOTIONAL

re·la·tions /rɪˈleɪʃənz/ *n* [P (*between, with*)] **1** way of treating and thinking of each other: *to have/establish friendly relations with someone|The relations between our 2 countries are not good just now* **2** connections; affairs together: *They have business relations with our firm* **3 have (sexual) relations with** *fml* to have sex with

re·la·tion·ship /rɪˈleɪʃənʃɪp/ *n* [C;U] **1** family connection: *I'm not going to give my son the job just because of our relationship* **2** RELATION (2)

rel·a·tive¹ /ˈrelətɪv/ *n fml* RELATION (1): *My uncle is my nearest relative* —see RELATION (USAGE)

relative² *adj* [Wa5] **1** [B] compared to each other

or to something else: *the relative costs of building in stone and in brick|After his troubles, he's now living in relative comfort* —opposite **absolute** **2** [F+*to*] *fml* connected (with); on the subject (of): *the facts that are relative to this question*

relative ad·verb /ˌ··· ˈ··/ *n tech* (an adverb like **where**, **when**, etc., in this sentence): *The house where he was born was very old*

relative clause /ˌ··· ˈ·/ *n tech* a part of a sentence that has a verb in it, and is joined to the rest of the sentence by a RELATIVE ADVERB or RELATIVE PRONOUN: *In "The man who lives next door is a doctor" the words "who lives next door" form a relative clause*

rel·a·tive·ly /ˈrelətɪvli/ *adv* [Wa5] quite; when compared to other people or things: *She walks relatively fast for a child of 3.|Relatively (speaking) it's a fine day.|a relatively fine day for the time of year*

relative pro·noun /ˌ··· ˈ··/ *n tech* (a word like **who**, **which**, **that**, etc., in this sentence): *The man who lives next door is a doctor*

rel·a·tiv·is·m /ˈrelətɪvɪzəm/ *n* [U] the belief that knowledge and moral truths depend on the limited nature of the human mind

rel·a·tiv·is·tic /ˌrelətɪˈvɪstɪk/ *adj* [Wa5] moving so fast that the size and other qualities change in accordance with Einstein's teachings on RELATIVITY

rel·a·tiv·i·ty /ˌreləˈtɪvɨti/ *n* [U] (*often cap.*) the relationship between time, size, and mass, which are said to change with increased speed: *Einstein's* THEORY *of Relativity*

re·lax /rɪˈlæks/ *v* **1** [Wv5;I∅;T1] **a** (of a person) to become less active and stop worrying: *Sit down and relax!|He was lying in the sun looking very relaxed and happy* **b** to make (someone) do this: *The music will help to relax you* —compare UNWIND **2** [I∅;T1] to make or become less stiff or tight: *His muscles relaxed.|He relaxed his hold on the wheel* **3** [T1] to make (effort or control) less severe: *You must not relax your efforts for a moment*

re·lax·a·tion /ˌriːlækˈseɪʃən/ *n* **1** [U9] the act of RELAXing (2,3) or condition of being RELAXed (2,3): *the relaxation of control over industry* **2** [C; U] (something done for) rest and amusement: *He plays the piano for a bit of relaxation. It's one of his favourite relaxations*

re·lax·ing /rɪˈlæksɪŋ/ *adj* (of weather or CLIMATE) making people feel lazy —opposite **bracing**

re·lay¹ /ˈriːleɪ/ *n* **1** [C; *in*, *by*+U] one part of a team or organization, that takes its turn in keeping an activity going continuously, a fresh group replacing a tired one: *groups of men working in/by relay(s) to clear the blocked railway line* **2** [C; *by*+U] an electrical arrangement or apparatus that receives messages by telephone, radio, etc., and passes them on over a further distance **3** [C] *infml* a RELAY RACE: *Who won the relay?* **4** [C] a broadcast sent out by RELAY¹ (2): *to listen to a relay of the concert*

re·lay² /ˈriːleɪ/ *v* [T1] to send out by RELAY¹ (2): *to relay a broadcast*

re·lay³ /ˌriːˈleɪ/ *v* **-laid** /ˈleɪd/ [T1] to lay again (esp. a CARPET¹ (1,2) or CABLE¹ (2))

relay race /ˈriːleɪ reɪs/ *n* a race in which each member of 2 or more teams runs part of the distance

relay sta·tion /ˈriːleɪ ˌsteɪʃən/ *n* a place that receives and rebroadcasts radio PROGRAMMEs

re·lease¹ /rɪˈliːs/ *v* **1** [T1 (*from*)] to set free; allow to come out: *to release a bear from a trap/a man from a promise|The aircraft released its bombs* **2** [T1] to allow **a** (a new film or record) to be shown or bought publicly **b** (a news story) to be known and printed **3** [T1] to press (a handle) so as to let something go: *to release the* HANDBRAKE *of the car* **4** [T1] *law* to give up (property, or a right)

release² *n* **1** [S;U: (*from*)] a setting free: *After his release from prison he came home.|After my examination I had a feeling of release* **2** [C] a letter or message that sets free: *The governor of the prison was signing releases* **3** [C] a new film or record that has been RELEASED¹ (2): *to see some of the latest releases* **4** [C] a handle, button, etc. that can be pressed to RELEASE¹ (3) part of a machine: *Press the release button* **5** [C] PRESS RELEASE **6 on general release** (of a film) able to be seen at all the cinemas in an area

rel·e·gate /ˈrelɨgeɪt/ *v* [T1 (*to*) *usu. pass.*] (in British football) to put (a team) into a lower division: *Everyone was surprised when Manchester United were relegated* —**-gation** /ˌrelɨˈgeɪʃən/ *n* [U (*to*)]

relegate to *v prep* [D1] to put (someone or something) into (a lower or worse position): *to relegate the old furniture to the children's room*

re·lent /rɪˈlent/ *v* [I∅] to have or show pity; become less cruel: (fig.) *In the morning the storm relented a little*

re·lent·less /rɪˈlentləs/ *adj* without pity: *a relentless enemy* —**~ly** *adv*: *He beat the child relentlessly* —**~ness** *n* [S;U]: *a surprising relentlessness*

rel·e·vance /ˈrelɨvəns/ also **rel·e·van·cy** /-si/— *n* [U (*to*)] the quality of being RELEVANT: *What you say has no relevance to what we're talking about*

rel·e·vant /ˈrelɨvənt/ *adj* **1** [B] connected with the subject: *I know he's black but it's not relevant. Is he a good lawyer?* —opposite **irrelevant** **2** [F+*to*] connected (with): *His colour isn't relevant to whether he's a good lawyer* —**~ly** *adv*

re·li·a·bil·i·ty /rɪˌlaɪəˈbɪlɨti/ *n* [U] the quality of being RELIABLE —opposite **unreliability**

re·li·a·ble /rɪˈlaɪəbəl/ *adj* fit to be trusted; dependable: *She may forget—she's not very reliable.|a reliable pair of boots* —**-bly** *adv*: *I am reliably informed that he takes drugs*

re·li·ance /rɪˈlaɪəns/ *n* [U (*on*)] trust: *I place complete reliance on his judgment*

re·li·ant /rɪˈlaɪənt/ *adj* [F+*on*] depending on; RELYing ON: *We should not be reliant on military power alone* —compare SELF-RELIANT

rel·ic /ˈrelɪk/ *n* **1** a part of the body or clothing of a holy person, or something that belonged to him, which is kept and respected after his death **2** something old that reminds us of the past: *This stone axe/This custom is a relic of ancient times*

rel·ics /ˈrelɪks/ *n* [P] *lit* the bones and other remains of a dead person

rel·ict¹ /ˈrelɪkt/ *n* [C9] *old use* (someone's) WIDOW (=woman whose husband is dead): *John Smith's relict|the relict of John Smith*

relict² *adj* [Wa5;A] *tech* remaining in existence after most others of the same type have ceased to exist: *a relict* SPECIES *of fish*

re·lief /rɪˈliːf/ *n* **1** [S;U] (a) feeling of comfort at the ending of anxiety, fear, or pain: *This medicine will give/bring some/a little relief.|a drug for the relief of pain|It was a great relief to me when/I gave* (HEAVEd¹ (4)) *a* SIGH *of relief when I heard he was safe.|You're safe! What a relief!* **2** [GC] a person or group taking over a duty for another: *The relief for the military guard is/are expected soon.|a relief driver|They had to provide a relief bus because there were so many passengers to carry* **3** [U] help for people in trouble: *send relief* (=money, food, clothes) *to the people who lost their homes in the flood|to start a relief* FUND (=collection of money) **4** [U+*of*] the act of relieving (RELIEVE (3)): *the relief of the city* **5** [C] (in art) a shape or ornament cut in wood or stone, or shaped in metal, so that it stands out above the rest of the surface it is on, as on a coin **6** [U] (*AmE* **benefit**)— *BrE* money that one is allowed not to pay in taxes, for some special reason: *He receives tax relief because he supports his old mother* **7 in bold/sharp relief** (in art) painted so that it seems to stand out clearly from the rest of the picture: *black trees standing out in bold relief against the snow* **8 in (high/low) relief** (in art) cut so that it stands out (a long way/a little) above the rest of the surface it is on —compare BAS-RELIEF **9 light relief** pleasant and amusing change: *Shakespeare put funny scenes into his serious plays to provide a little light relief* **10 (much) to one's relief/to one's (great) relief** making one feel (much) happier: *Much to my relief, he is safe now*

relief map /·ˈ· ·/ *n* a map with the mountains and high parts either cut in RELIEF (8) or painted to look like that

relief road /·ˈ· ·/ *n* a road made in order to take away some of the heavy traffic from another road

relief works /·ˈ· ·/ *n* [P] public buildings, bridges, roads, etc., made in order to provide jobs for people without work

re·lieve /rɪˈliːv/ *v* [T1] **1** to lessen (pain or trouble): *a drug that relieves headaches* **2** to take over a duty from (someone) as a RELIEF (2): *The guard will be relieved at midnight* **3** to drive away the enemy from (a town, fort, etc.) **4** to give variety to; make more interesting: *to relieve a dull evening with a little dancing* **5 relieve oneself** *fml & euph* to URINATE or empty the bowels **6 relieve one's feelings** to make one's feelings easier to bear by expressing them openly: *Shout if you want to—it'll relieve your feelings* **7 relieve someone's mind** to free someone from anxiety

re·lieved /rɪˈliːvd/ *adj* [F,F3,5a;(B)] (esp. of a person) given RELIEF (1): *Your mother will be very relieved.|I was relieved (to hear) that they were safe.|She had a relieved look on her face*

relieve of *v prep* [D1] **1** to take from (someone) (something heavy to carry or hard to do): *Let me relieve you of that heavy parcel.|You'd better relieve Mary of some of the housework* **2** *fml humor* to rob (someone) of (something): *A thief relieved me of £5* **3** [*often pass.*] *euph* to dismiss (someone) from (a position): *He was relieved of his employment*

re·li·gion /rɪˈlɪdʒən/ *n* **1** [U] belief in one or more gods, esp. the belief that he/they made the world and control it and give men life after death **2** [C] a particular system of belief and the worship, behaviour, etc., connected with it **3** [U] the life of a RELIGIOUS[2]: *Sister Ursula is in her 20th year of religion* **4** [S] something that one takes very seriously, often as a matter of conscience: *Cricket is a religion with John; he makes a religion of it*

re·li·gious[1] /rɪˈlɪdʒəs/ *adj* **1** [Wa5;A;(B)] of or concerning religion: *a religious service* **2** [B] (of a person or his behaviour) obeying the rules of a religion very carefully: *a very religious man* —opposite **irreligious** **3** [A;(B)] (typical of a person) performing the stated duties very carefully, as a matter of conscience: *She washes the floor with religious care every morning*

re·li·gious[2] *n* **-gious** [Wn3] *tech* a person who has given his life to the service of God, by making certain promises; a MONK or NUN: *Several religious live in this religious house established in the 15th century*

religious lib·er·ty /·,·· ˈ···/ *n* [U] the freedom to follow one's own religious beliefs

re·li·gious·ly /rɪˈlɪdʒəsli/ *adv* **1** faithfully and regularly: *She washes the floor religiously every morning* **2** [Wa5] firmly and seriously: *I religiously hope never to meet her again!*

re·line /ˌriːˈlaɪn/ *v* [T1] to put a new inside covering (LINING) into: *to reline an old coat*

re·lin·quish /rɪˈlɪŋkwɪʃ/ *v* [T1] *fml* to give up; yield: *to relinquish hopes/beliefs/habits|He relinquished his claim to the land/his hold on my hair.|He relinquished all control over the family business to his daughter*

rel·i·qua·ry /ˈrelɪ̈kwəri‖-kweri/ *n* a container for religious RELICs (1)

rel·ish[1] /ˈrelɪʃ/ *n* **1** [S;U] (a great deal of) enjoyment, esp. of food; pleasure: *He drank up the wine with (a) relish.|The danger added (a) relish to the adventure* **2** [U+*for, usu. neg.*] liking for: *I have no relish for seeing people being whipped* **3** [C;U] (a kind of) substance eaten with a meal, such as PICKLEs or SAUCE, to add taste and interest: *a spoonful of relish|3 different relishes*

relish[2] *v* [T1,4] to enjoy; be pleased with: *to relish a funny story|Hilary won't relish having to wash all those dishes*

re·live /ˌriːˈlɪv/ *v* [T1] to experience again, as in the imagination: *to relive one's school days in conversation with an old friend*

re·load /ˌriːˈləʊd/ *v* [IØ;T1] to load (a gun) again: *to reload the gun|How long does it take you to reload?*

re·lo·cate /ˌriːləʊˈkeɪt‖riːˈləʊkeɪt/ *v* [IØ;T1] to move to or set up in a new place: *to relocate the factory outside Bristol|We're relocating outside Bristol* —**-cation** /ˌriːləʊˈkeɪʃən/ *n* [U]: *the relocation of population away from a military area*

re·luc·tance /rɪˈlʌktəns/ *n* [S;U] (a degree of) unwillingness: *He agreed to help, but with great reluctance/with a certain reluctance*

re·luc·tant /rɪˈlʌktənt/ *adj* [B;F3] unwilling, and therefore perhaps slow to act: *reluctant helpers|to give a reluctant promise|He was very reluctant to help*

re·luc·tant·ly /rɪˈlʌktəntli/ *adv* **1** unwillingly: *She agreed, very reluctantly, to help* **2** (used before saying something one does not want to say) unfortunately; speaking unwillingly: *Reluctantly, I must refuse your invitation*

re·ly on /rɪˈlaɪ/ also **rely up·on**— *v prep* **1** [T1,4; V4a] to depend on (something, or something happening): *You can't rely on the weather.|I think I can come, but don't rely on it.|Don't rely on going to India* (=perhaps you won't go).*|Don't rely on me/my going to India* (=perhaps I won't go) **2** [T1;V3] to trust (someone, or someone to do something): *You may rely on me (to help you)*
USAGE Some people think **rely on/count on** *my going* is better English than **rely on** *me going*; but in **rely on/count on** *me to go* one can only use *me*.

re·main /rɪˈmeɪn/ *v* **1** [IØ] to stay or be left behind after others have gone or been removed: *Of the 7 brothers only 4 now remain; the rest are dead.|When the others had gone, Mary remained and put back the furniture.|It only remains for me to say that . . .* (=all that is left for me to say is . . .) **2** [L1,7,9] to continue to be (in an unchanged state): *Peter became a judge but John remained a fisherman.|If you won't eat you'll just have to remain hungry!|You can't let the room remain like this!* —see STAY (USAGE) **3 it remains to be seen** we shall know later on

re·main·der[1] /rɪˈmeɪndəʳ/ *n* [(*the*) GU] what is left over; the rest: *The remainder of the food will do for tomorrow.|10 people in our class are Arabs and the remainder are Germans*

remainder[2] *v* [T1 *usu. pass.*] to sell (esp. books) at a low price so as to get rid of them quickly

re·mains /rɪˈmeɪnz/ *n* [P] **1** [(*of*)] parts which are left: *the remains of dinner/of an old castle* **2** *fml* a dead body, usu. of a human being: *His remains lie in the churchyard*

re·make /ˌriːˈmeɪk/ *v* **-made** /ˈmeɪd/ [T1] to make (esp. a film) again: *I've heard they're remaking "Gone with the Wind"* —**remake** /ˈriːmeɪk/ *n*: *to see a remake of "Gone with the Wind"*
re·mand¹ /rɪˈmɑːnd‖rɪˈmænd/ *v* [T1 *usu. pass.*] to send back to prison from a court of law, to be tried later after further enquiries have been made (often in the phr. **remanded in custody**)
remand² *n* [C;U] **1** (a) decision to REMAND¹ someone, or the action of REMANDing: *Ask for* (*a*) *remand* **2 on remand** held in prison and waiting for trial
remand home /·ˈ· ·/ *n* (in Britain) a place where young people who have broken the law are sent for a while, till the court has decided what to do with them
re·mark¹ /rɪˈmɑːk‖-ɑrk/ *v* [T5] to say (not in answer to anything): *He remarked that it was getting late.*|*"It's getting late," he remarked*
remark² *n* **1** [C (*about, on*)] a spoken or written opinion: *to make/pass rude remarks about her appearance* **2** [U] *fml* notice: *Her absence of hair could hardly escape remark/was worthy of remark*
re·mar·ka·ble /rɪˈmɑːkəbəl‖-ɑr-/ *adj* [(*for*)] worth speaking of; unusual: *a most remarkable sunset*|*She is remarkable for her sweet temper*
re·mar·ka·bly /rɪˈmɑːkəbli‖-ɑr-/ *adv* (*used with adjectives and adverbs*) unusually; noticeably: *sings remarkably well*|*a remarkably fine day*
remark on also **remark up·on**— *v prep* [T1] to say or write something about: *Everyone remarked loudly on his absence*
re·mar·ry /ˌriːˈmæri/ *v* **1** [I∅] to marry again, as after the death of a former husband or wife: *He decided to remarry after her death for the good of the children* **2** [I∅;T1] **a** to marry (one's former husband or wife) again **b** (of 2 people) to marry each other again after DIVORCE
re·me·di·a·ble /rɪˈmiːdɪəbəl/ *adj* that can be put right or cured: *a remediable weakness in the eyes* —opposite **irremediable**
re·me·di·al /rɪˈmiːdɪəl/ *adj* [Wa5] curing or helping; providing a REMEDY: *to do remedial exercises for a weak back* —**~ly** *adv*
rem·e·dy¹ /ˈremɪ̈di/ *n* [C;U: (*for*)] **1** a way of curing (pain or disease): *Alcohol is the best remedy for colds* **2** a way of setting right (anything bad): *evils that are beyond/past remedy*|*The law provides no remedy for this injustice*
remedy² *v* [T1] to put or make right (anything bad): *to remedy an injustice/a fault/a loss*
re·mem·ber /rɪˈmembəʳ/ *v* **1** [T1 (*as*), 4,5a,6a,b; V4] to keep in the memory; call back into the mind: *I shall always remember that terrible day.*|*Certainly I posted your letter—I remember posting it.*|*I can't remember how to get there/where she lives/what happened then.*|*Do you remember me/my asking you that same question?*|*I remember him, as* (=when he was) *a child, playing the piano beautifully.*|*I remember* (*that*) *she wore a green hat* **2** [I∅; T3] to take care not to forget: *"Don't forget to post my letter. Please remember!" "Yes, I promise I'll remember to post your letter"* **3** [T1] *often euph* to give money or a present to: *Please remember the taxi driver!*|*She always remembers me at Christmas* **4 remember someone in one's prayers** to pray for someone **5 remember someone in one's will** to leave someone something (in one's WILL² (6)) after one's death
USAGE Note the difference between **remember** *posting a letter* (1) and **remember** *to post a letter* (2). In the first case the letter is already posted, while in the second case it has not been posted yet.
remember as *v prep* [X1,7;V4b] to think of (someone or something) as (being what they were in the past): *Is she really Chief Minister now? I remember her as a fat little girl!*|*How thin she is! I remember her as* (*being*) *fatter than that*
remember to *v prep* [D1] *infml* to send (someone's) greetings to: *Please remember me to your mother.*|*He asked to be remembered to you*
re·mem·brance /rɪˈmembrəns/ *n* **1** [C;U:+*of*] (a) memory; the state or act of remembering: *Christians eat bread and drink wine in remembrance of Jesus.*|*I have many happy remembrances of our days together* —see MEMORY **2** [C (*of*)] something kept or given to remind one: *He gave me his photograph as a remembrance* (*of him*)
Remembrance Day /·ˈ·· ·/ also **Remembrance Sunday** /·ˌ·· ˈ··/— *n* [R] (in Britain and Canada) the Sunday nearest to November 11th, when people remember those killed in the 2 world wars —compare MEMORIAL DAY
re·mil·i·tar·ize, -ise /ˌriːˈmɪlɪ̈təraɪz/ *v* [T1] to provide (esp. a nation) again with, or move again into (a place) with, armed forces and military apparatus —**-ization** /riːˌmɪlɪ̈tərai'zeɪʃən‖-tərə-/ *n* [U]
re·mind /rɪˈmaɪnd/ *v* [T1 (*of*); D5;V3] **1** (of a person) to tell or cause (someone) to remember (a fact, or to do something): *I must write to Mother—will you remind me?*|*Remind me to write to Mother.*|*She reminded me that I hadn't written to Mother.*|*"You haven't written to Mother," she reminded me.*|*I've forgotten what you said; will you remind me* (*of it*)? **2** (of a thing or event) to make (someone) remember (a fact, or to do something): *The sight of the clock reminded me that I was late/reminded me to leave at once.*|*What a big elephant! That reminds me—have you been to India lately?*
re·mind·er /rɪˈmaɪndəʳ/ *n* something, esp. a letter, to make one remember: *He hadn't paid the bill, so the shop sent him a reminder*
remind of *v prep* [D1] to make (someone) remember (someone or something) by seeming the same: *This hotel reminds me of the one we stayed in last year*
rem·i·nisce /ˌremɪ̈ˈnɪs/ *v* [I∅] to talk pleasantly about the past: *2 old friends reminiscing* (*about their youth*)
rem·i·nis·cence /ˌremɪ̈ˈnɪsəns/ *n* [U] memory of past events: *to enjoy the pleasures of reminiscence*
rem·i·nis·cenc·es /ˌremɪ̈ˈnɪsəns/ *n* [P] a spoken or written account of one's past life: *to write one's reminiscences* —compare MEMOIRS
rem·i·nis·cent /ˌremɪ̈ˈnɪsənt/ *adj* **1** [F+*of*] that reminds one of; like: *This hotel is reminiscent of the one we stayed in last year* **2** [A] (showing that one is) remembering something: *"Did you enjoy yourself in Paris?" "Yes," he said with a reminiscent smile*
re·miss /rɪˈmɪs/ *adj* [F] (typical of a person) that does not do his duty; careless: *He is very remiss in answering letters* —**~ness** *n* [U]
re·mis·sion /rɪˈmɪʃən/ *n* **1** [U] the act of REMITting (1) **2** [U9] (esp. in Christianity) forgiveness: *the remission of* SINs¹ (1,2) **3** [C] a period when a REMITTENT illness is less severe **4** [C;U] (a) lessening of the time a person has to stay in prison: *6 months' remission for good behaviour*
re·mit /rɪˈmɪt/ *v* **-tt-** **1** [T1] to free someone from (a debt or punishment) **2** [I∅;D1 (*to*);T1] to send (money) by post (to): *to remit a cheque*|*to remit by cheque*|*Remit me the money* **3** [T1] *fml* to stop for a while (an action): *They decided to remit their search for the missing man till daylight*
re·mit·tance /rɪˈmɪtəns/ *n* **1** [U] the REMITting (2) of money **2** [C] an amount of money REMITted (2): *Send her a small remittance each month*
remittance man /·ˈ·· ·/ *n derog* (esp. in former

times) a man living in a distant country on money regularly posted to him from home

re·mit·tent /rɪˈmɪtənt/ *adj* [Wa5] (of a fever or other disease) sometimes getting better and sometimes worse

remit to *v prep* [D1] *law* to send (a case) to (another court) for a decision

rem·nant /ˈremnənt/ *n* **1** [C9 esp. *of*] a part that remains: *to eat up the remnants of the feast* **2** [C] a small piece of cloth left over from a larger piece and sold cheap: *to go to a remnant sale*

re·mod·el /ˌriːˈmɒdl‖ˌriːˈmadl/ *v* **-ll-** (*AmE* **-l-**) [T1] to change the shape of: *to remodel an old house|an actress who had her nose remodelled*

re·mon·strance /rɪˈmɒnstrəns‖rɪˈman-/ *n* [C;U] (a) complaint: *many remonstrances|loud cries of remonstrance*

rem·on·strate /ˈremənstreɪt‖rɪˈman-/ *v* [IØ (*against, with*)] to complain: *to remonstrate against his behaviour|to remonstrate with Paul* (=complain to him) *about his behaviour*

re·morse /rɪˈmɔːs‖-ɔrs/ *n* [U (*for*)] **1** sorrow for having done wrong: *He felt|He was filled with remorse for his evil deed* **2 without remorse** without mercy —**~less** *adj* —**~lessly** *adv* —**~lessness** *n* [S;U]

re·morse·ful /rɪˈmɔːsfəl‖-ɔr-/ *adj* feeling or showing REMORSE: *a remorseful cry* —**~ly** *adv* —**~ness** *n* [U]

re·mote /rɪˈməʊt/ *adj* [Wa2; (*from*)] **1** distant in space or time: *remote stars|the remote future* **2** quiet and lonely; far from the city: *a remote village* **3** widely separated (from); not close: *The connection between these 2 ideas is very remote|something remote from his experience* **4** (of behaviour) not showing interest in others: *Her manner was polite but remote* **5** [*often superl.*] (esp. of a chance or possibility) slight: *I haven't the remotest idea what you mean.|I'm afraid your chances of success are rather remote* —**~ness** *n* [U]

remote con·trol /·ˌ· ·ˈ·/ *n* [U] a system for controlling machinery from a distance by radio signals

re·mote·ly /rɪˈməʊtli/ *adv* [*often neg.*] to a very small degree: *She isn't remotely interested in what you're saying*

re·mould, *AmE* **remold** /ˌriːˈməʊld/ *v* [T1] *BrE* RETREAD —**remould** /ˈriːməʊld/ *n*

re·mount¹ /ˌriːˈmaʊnt/ *v* **1** [IØ;T1] to get onto (a horse or bicycle) again; climb (a ladder, hill, etc.) again: *He remounted (his horse) and rode away* **2** [T1] to supply a fresh horse or horses for (a person or army) **3** [T1] to fix (a picture, photograph, etc.) on a new piece of cardboard (MOUNT² (6))

re·mount² /ˈriːmaʊnt/ *n* a fresh horse

re·mov·al /rɪˈmuːvəl/ *n* [C;U] (an) act of removing (REMOVE¹): *Removals are unpleasant, but it will be nice when we get into the new house*

removal van /·ˈ·· ·/ *BrE* also **pantechnicon,** *Br & AmE* **moving van**— *n BrE* a large covered vehicle (VAN) used for taking furniture usu. from one house to another

re·move¹ /rɪˈmuːv/ *v* **1** [T1 (*from*)] to take away (from a place); take off: *Remove your hat.|Remove your shoes in the mosque.|to remove a child from a class* **2** [T1 (*from*)] to get rid of; clean off: *to remove mud from your shoes* **3** [T1 (*from*)] *fml* to dismiss: *That officer must be removed (from his position)* **4** [IØ (*from, to*)] *fml* to go to live or work in another place: *Our office has removed (from London to Harlow)/removed (to Harlow from London)* **5 once/twice/etc., removed** (of COUSINs) different by 1, 2, etc., GENERATIONs (2): *My second* COUSIN *once removed is the child of my second* COUSIN —see TABLE OF FAMILY RELATIONSHIPS **6 removed from** distant from: *What you say is far removed from what you said before* —**removable** /rɪˈmuːvəbəl/ *adj*

remove² *n* **1** [C9] (*always with a statement of number*) a stage or degree (in such phrs. as **only one remove from, several removes from**): *Great cleverness is only one remove from madness* **2** [*the*+R] (*often cap.*) (in some schools in Britain) a class into which pupils are put after they have left a lower class but before they are ready to go into the next highest one

re·mov·er /rɪˈmuːvəʳ/ *n* someone whose work is moving furniture from one house to another when people REMOVE¹ (4)

-remover *comb. form* (a) substance for cleaning off (the stated substance): *a bottle of paint-remover*

re·mu·ne·rate /rɪˈmjuːnəreɪt/ *v* [T1 (*for*)] *fml* to reward; to pay (someone) for work or trouble —**-ration** /rɪˌmjuːnəˈreɪʃən/ *n* [S;U]: *to receive (a small) remuneration* —see PAY (USAGE)

re·mu·ne·ra·tive /rɪˈmjuːnərətɪv‖-reɪtɪv/ *adj* (of work) well-paid; profitable —**~ly** *adv*

re·nais·sance /rɪˈneɪsəns‖ˌrenəˈsɑns (*Fr* rənɛsɑ̃s)/ also **re·nas·cence** /rɪˈnæsəns/— *n Fr* a renewal of interest in some particular kind of art, literature, etc.

Renaissance *n* [*the*+R] the period in Europe between the 14th and 17th centuries, when the art, literature, and ideas of ancient Greece were discovered again and widely studied, causing a rebirth of activity in all these things —compare MIDDLE AGES

re·nal /ˈriːnl/ *adj* [Wa5] *med* of, near, or concerning the parts of the body (KIDNEYs) that separate waste matter from the blood and send it out of the body in a liquid form

re·name /riːˈneɪm/ *v* [T1] to give a new name to

re·nas·cent /rɪˈnæsənt/ *adj fml* (of an idea or feeling) springing up again; reborn after being forgotten: *He felt a renascent love for his children*

rend /rend/ *v* **rent** /rent/ *lit* **1** [T1 (APART)] to divide by force; split: *She wept and rent her garments.|A terrible cry rent the air* **2** [X9 esp. *from,* OFF] to pull violently: *The cruel soldiers were rending babies from their mothers' arms*

ren·der /ˈrendəʳ/ *v fml* **1** [X7] to cause to be: *His fatness renders him unable to touch his toes* **2** [T1] to give a RENDERING (1) of; perform: *to render the song beautifully* **3** [D1 (to); T1] to give (esp. help): *You have rendered me a service.|"Render to Caesar the things that are Caesar's"* (The Bible) **4** [T1] *tech* to put a thickness of PLASTER or cement directly onto: *The builders were rendering the walls* **5 render an account** to send an account of money that is owed **6 render thanks** to thank someone, esp. God

render down *v adv* [T1] to make (fat) pure by melting

ren·der·ing /ˈrendərɪŋ/ *n* [(*of*)] **1** a performance (of a play or piece of music): *gave a splendid rendering of the song* **2** a translation (of a piece of writing): *an English rendering of a Greek poem*

render in·to *v prep* [D1] *fml* to translate (a piece of writing) into (a language): *to render the Bible into Gujarati*

render up *v adv* [T1] **1** *fml* to say; offer (a prayer) **2** *old use* to yield; give up (something), esp. to an enemy: *to render up a city to a conqueror*

ren·dez·vous¹ /ˈrɒndɪ̈vuː, -deɪ-‖ˈrɑn- (*Fr* rɑ̃devu)/ *n* **-vous** /vuːz/ **1** an arrangement to meet at a certain time and place: *Let's make a rendezvous—where and when can we meet?* **2** the place (and time) chosen for meeting: *John arrived late for his rendezvous with Joan under the station clock*

3 a popular place for people to meet: *This club is a rendezvous for writers*
rendezvous² *v* [I∅] *tech* (usu. used of military affairs) to meet by arrangement: *The 2* SPACECRAFT *rendezvoused successfully*
ren·di·tion /ren'dɪʃən/ *n* [(*of*)] RENDERING (1)
ren·e·gade /'renɪ̈geɪd/ *n* [C; (*you*) N] *derog* a person who deserts one country or belief to join another; TRAITOR
re·nege, renegue /rɪ'niːg, rɪ'neɪg‖rɪ'nɪg, rɪ'niːg/ *v* [I∅] **1** [(*on*)] *fml* to break a promise: *You said you'd come—you can't renege now!* **2** (in card games) REVOKE
re·new /rɪ'njuː‖rɪ'nuː/ *v* [T1] **1** [Wv5] to give new life and freshness to; make as good as new again: *to come back from one's holiday with renewed strength* **2** to replace (something old, worn out, or used up) with something new of the same kind: *to renew one's library ticket* **3** to repeat (an action): *In the morning the enemy renewed their attack*
re·new·a·ble /rɪ'njuːəbəl‖rɪ'nuː-/ *adj* [Wa5] **1** that can be RENEWed (esp. 2) **2** [Wv5] that must be RENEWed (esp. 2): *This ticket is renewable after 12 months*
re·new·al /rɪ'njuːəl‖rɪ'nuːəl/ *n* **1** [U] the act of RENEWing **2** [C] something RENEWed
ren·net /'renɪ̈t/ *n* [U] a substance used for thickening milk to make cheese, JUNKET, etc.
re·nounce /rɪ'naʊns/ *v* [T1] **1** to give up (a claim); say formally that one does not own: *He renounced his claim to the property* **2** to say formally that one has no more connection with: *He renounced his religion and became a Muslim*
ren·o·vate /'renəveɪt/ *v* [T1] to repair; put back into good condition: *to renovate an old house* —**-vation** /ˌrenə'veɪʃən/ *n* [C;U]: *do some costly renovation(s) of old houses*
re·nown /rɪ'naʊn/ *n* [U] fame: *He won renown as a painter.|a painter of some/great/high renown*
re·nowned /rɪ'naʊnd/ *adj* [(*as, for*)] famous: *Edison was renowned as an inventor/renowned for his inventions*
rent¹ /rent/ *n* [C *usu. sing.*;U] **1** (a stated sum of) money paid regularly for the use of a room, building, television set, or piece of land: *Do you own your house or do you pay rent?|to let the house at a rent of £20.00 a week|to pay a high/low rent|to pay more/less rent|a rent collector* **2** *esp. AmE* money paid in this way for the use of a car, boat, suit of clothes, etc. **3 free of rent** (of a room, building, or piece of land) that is used without payment: *to live in a flat free of rent*
rent² *v* **1** [T1 (*from*)] to pay rent for the use of: *to rent a room from Mrs. Jones* **2** [D1 (*to*); T1] to allow to be used in return for rent; LET³ (5): *to rent a room to Mrs. Smith* **3** [L9, esp. *at*] (of a building, land, etc.) to bring in (the stated) rent: *This house rents at £100 a month* **4** [T1] *esp. AmE* to pay money for the use of (a car, boat, suit of clothes, etc.) for a short time; HIRE: *to rent some evening trousers* —see HIRE (USAGE) —**~able** *adj*
rent³ *n* a large tear, in or as if in cloth: *several great rents in the curtains*|(fig.) *a rent in a political party*
rent⁴ *past t. & p. of* REND
rent·al /'rentl/ *n fml* a sum of money fixed to be paid as rent: *to pay the television rental*
rent·er /'rentəʳ/ *n* a person in the cinema industry who rents films
rent-free /ˌ· '·◂/ *adv, adj* [Wa5] (used) without payment of rent: *to live rent-free|a rent-free flat*
ren·ti·er /'rɒntieɪ‖'rɑntjeɪ (*Fr* rɑ̃tie)/ *n Fr, often derog* a person who lives without working, on INVESTMENTs (=money lent to business or the government and bringing in an income)
rent out *v adv* [T1] *AmE* LET³ (5); HIRE OUT —see HIRE (USAGE)
rent roll /'· ·/ *n* (esp. in former times) **1** a list of people paying rent to one property owner, and of the amounts they all pay **2** the income from these people's rents
rent strike /'· ·/ *n* a refusal, by all the people living in a block of flats or group of houses, to pay their rent, because they hope the law will decide that it is too high
re·nun·ci·a·tion /rɪˌnʌnsi'eɪʃən/ *n* [C;U] a case or the act of renouncing (RENOUNCE (1)): *to make a renunciation|the moral beauty of renunciation*
re·o·pen /riː'əʊpən/ *v* [I∅;T1] to (cause to) open again after closing
re·or·gan·ize, -ise /riː'ɔːgənaɪz‖-'ɔr-/ *v* [I∅;T1] to ORGANIZE (something) again, perhaps in a new way —**-ization** /riːˌɔːgənaɪ'zeɪʃən‖riːˌɔrgənə-/ *n* [U]
rep¹, repp /rep/ *n* [U] a strong material used esp. for covering chairs
rep² *n sl* salesman: *Our rep will call on Monday*
rep³ *n infml* **1** [C] a REPERTORY (1) theatre or company: *the local rep* **2** [U] REPERTORY (1): *She acts in rep*
re·paid /rɪ'peɪd/ *past t. & p. of* REPAY
re·pair¹ /rɪ'peəʳ/ *v* **1** [I∅;T1] **a** to mend (something worn or broken): *to repair a broken watch/a road/old shoes* **b** (of something broken or worn) to be able to be mended: *This shirt is so old it won't repair* **2** [T1] *fml* to put right (a wrong, mistake, etc.): *How can I repair the wrong I have done her?* —**~able** *adj* —**~er** *n*
repair² *n* **1** [*often pl.*] an act or result of mending: *to carry out the repairs to my damaged car* **2 in (a) good/bad (state of) repair** in good/bad condition **3 under repair** being repaired: *"Road Under Repair"* (sign)
repair to *v prep* [T1] *fml* to go to (a place), often or in large numbers: *We all repaired to a restaurant and drank coffee together*
rep·a·ra·ble /'repərəbəl/ *adj* [*usu. sing.*] (of a wrong, mistake, etc.) that can be REPAIRed¹ (2) —opposite **irreparable**
rep·a·ra·tion /ˌrepə'reɪʃən/ *n* [U] *fml* repayment for loss or wrong: *to ask/make reparation for the sorrow one has caused*
rep·a·ra·tions /ˌrepə'reɪʃənz/ *n* [P] money paid by a defeated nation after a war
rep·ar·tee /ˌrepɑː'tiː‖repər'tiː/ *n* **1** [U] (the power to make) quick amusing answers in conversation: *listening to their* WITTY *repartee* **2** [C] an answer of this kind
re·past /rɪ'pɑːst‖rɪ'pæst/ *n fml* a meal
re·pat·ri·ate /riː'pætrieɪt‖riː'peɪ-/ *v* [T1] to bring or send (someone) back to his own country, or to the country of which he is a citizen —**-ation** /ˌriːpætri'eɪʃən‖ˌriːpeɪ-/ *n* [U]
re·pay /rɪ'peɪ/ *v* **-paid** /'peɪd/ **1** [D1 (*to*); T1] to pay (money) back: *When will you repay me the $5 I lent you?* **2** [T1] to pay (someone) back: *When will you repay me?* **3** [T1 (*by, for, with*)] to reward **a** (someone) (for an action): *How can I ever repay you (for your kindness)?* **b** (an action): *He repaid her kindness with blows/by hitting her*
re·pay·a·ble /rɪ'peɪəbəl/ *adj* [Wa5] (of money) that can or must be paid back: *The debt is repayable at the end of the month*
re·pay·ment /rɪ'peɪmənt/ *n* [C;U] the action of paying back; something paid back: *a/some small repayment for all you have done*
re·peal¹ /rɪ'piːl/ *v* [T1] to put an official end to (a law): *Sir Robert Peel repealed the Corn Laws*
repeal² *n* [U] the action of REPEALing: *the repeal of the Corn Laws*

re·peat[1] /rɪ'piːt/ *v* **1** [T1,5] to say or do again: *to repeat a word|a mistake|He repeated several times that he was busy* **2** [T1] to say (something heard or learnt): *Don't repeat what I told you* **3** [I∅] *infml* (of food that one has eaten) to be tasted afterwards in the mouth: *I find that onions repeat* **4** [I∅] (of numbers, esp. DECIMALs) RECUR **5 not bear repeating** (of words) to be too bad to say again **6 repeat a course/a year** (in education) to remain in the same class for a further year **7 repeat an order** (in business) to supply the same article(s) again **8 repeat oneself** to say or be the same thing again and again: *History seems to be repeating itself*

repeat[2] *n* **1** a REPEATed[1] (1) performance: *to give a repeat performance* **2** (in music) (a sign (:‖) showing) a passage to be played again

re·peat·ed /rɪ'piːtɨd/ *adj* [Wa5;A] done again and again: *His repeated failure is very sad*

re·peat·ed·ly /rɪ'piːtɨdli/ *adv* often; over and over again: *He repeatedly fails to pass the examination*

re·peat·er /rɪ'piːtəʳ/ *n* **1** a REPEATING (1) gun **2** REPEATING (2) watch or clock

re·peat·ing /rɪ'piːtɪŋ/ *adj* [Wa5;A] **1** (of a gun (REVOLVER or RIFLE)) that can be fired several times without reloading **2** (of a watch or clock, esp. in former times) that strikes the latest hour and quarter-hours when a spring is pressed **3** (of a number, esp. a DECIMAL) RECURring

re·pel /rɪ'pel/ *v* **-ll-** [T1] **1** to drive back by or as if by force: *to repel an attack* **2** to cause feelings of dislike in: *Let go at once! You repel me* —see REPULSE (USAGE)

re·pel·lent[1] /rɪ'pelənt/ *adj* [(*to*)] causing dislike (in); nasty: *a plate of repellent cold potatoes|His spotty face was repellent to her*

repellent[2] *n* [C;U] (a type of) substance that drives (something, esp. insects) away: *Do you know a good mosquito repellent?*

re·pent /rɪ'pent/ *v* [I∅ (*of*); T1,4] *fml* to be sorry for (wrongdoing): *He repented (of) his wickedness.|I have nothing to repent of.|He repented what he had done.|He repented having shot the bird*

re·pent·ance /rɪ'pentəns/ *n* [U] sorrow for wrongdoing

re·pen·tant /rɪ'pentənt/ *adj* [B; (*the*+P)] feeling or showing sorrow for wrongdoing: *her repentant face|The repentant put ashes on their foreheads and wore shirts made of hair*

re·per·cus·sion /ˌriːpə'kʌʃən‖ˌriːpər-/ *n* **1** [C] a far-reaching and unexpected effect (of some action or event) **2** [C;U] springing or being thrown back; something (esp. a sound) thrown back: *heard the repercussion(s) of the shot*

rep·er·toire /'repətwɑːʳ‖-ər-/ *n* the collection of plays, pieces of music, etc., that a performer or theatre company has learned and can perform: (fig.) *He has a large repertoire of funny stories*

rep·er·to·ry /'repətəri‖'repərtori/ *n* **1** [U] also (*infml*) **rep**— the practice of giving several plays, with the same company of actors and in the same theatres, one after the other on different days: *got a job in repertory|a repertory theatre/company* **2** [C] REPERTOIRE

rep·e·ti·tion /ˌrepɨ'tɪʃən/ *n* **1** [C;U] the act or an act of REPEATing[1] (1): *The performance improved with each repetition.|Let there be no repetition of this behaviour* **2** [U] the exercise of REPEATing[1] (2) words learned thoroughly

rep·e·ti·tious /ˌrepɨ'tɪʃəs/ also **re·pet·i·tive** /rɪ'petɨtɪv/— *adj derog* containing parts that are said or done too many times: *a repetitious speech* —**~ness** *n* [U]: *the repetitiousness of his job*

re·pine /rɪ'paɪn/ *v* [I∅ (*against, at*)] *fml or lit* to feel very discontented (at something); complain silently: *to repine against his cruel fate*

re·place /rɪ'pleɪs/ *v* [T1] **1** to put (something) back in the right place: *He replaced the book on the shelf* **2** to take the place of: *George has replaced Edward as captain of the team* —see DISPLACE (USAGE) —**~able** *adj* —opposite **irreplaceable**

re·place·ment /rɪ'pleɪsmənt/ *n* **1** [U] the act of putting someone or something in the place of someone or something else: *Your worn-out tyres need replacement* **2** [C] someone or something that REPLACEs (2): *We need a replacement for the officer who was shot*

replace with also **replace by**— *v prep* [D1] to change (something) for (something else instead): *We have replaced slave labour with/by machines*

re·play[1] /ˌriː'pleɪ/ *v* **1** [T1;I∅] to play (a match) again: *The teams finished level at the end, so they'll replay (the match) on Wednesday* **2** [T1] to play (a piece of music) again

re·play[2] /'riːpleɪ/ *n* **1** a match played again **2** PLAYBACK

re·plen·ish /rɪ'plenɪʃ/ *v* [T1] to fill up again; put new supplies into: *to replenish the food cupboard* —**~ment** *n* [U]

re·plete /rɪ'pliːt/ *adj* [F (*with*)] *fml* quite full, esp. of food: *felt replete with food and drink*

re·ple·tion /rɪ'pliːʃən/ *n* [U] *fml* the state of being REPLETE: *He ate to repletion*

rep·li·ca /'replɪkə/ *n* a close copy, esp. of a painting or other work of art, often made by the same artist

rep·li·cate /'replɨkeɪt/ *v* [T1] *tech* to repeat; DUPLICATE

re·ply[1] /rɪ'plaɪ/ *v* [I∅ (*to*); T5] to answer; say or do as an answer: *I asked him where to go, but he didn't reply.|"Of course not," she replied.|She replied that she was not amused.|Have you replied to his letter?* —see ANSWER (USAGE)

reply[2] *n* [C; *in*+U: (*to*)] an act of replying: *I asked him, but he made no reply.|What did you say in reply to his suggestion?*

reply for *v prep* [T1 *no pass.*] (of one of a group) to give an answer for (the others): *Shall I reply for you all?*

reply-paid /ˌ·ˌ· '·‿/ *adj* [Wa5] (esp. of a telegram) with the cost of the answer paid by the sender

re·point /riː'pɔɪnt/ *v* [T1] to put fresh MORTAR (=a mixture of sand, lime, and water) between the bricks or stones of (a wall)

re·port[1] /rɪ'pɔːt‖-ort/ *n* **1** [C] an account or description of events, experiences, etc.: *to read some newspaper reports of the accident|a business company's report for the year* **2** [C] the noise of an explosion or shot: *a loud report* **3** [C;U] (a piece of) talk that spreads without official support; RUMOUR **4** [C] (in education) SCHOOL REPORT **5 of good/evil report** *fml* said to be good/evil: *a man of evil report*

report[2] *v* **1** [T1,4,5;V3] (*not used with the actual words spoken*) to tell of; make known: *They reported the appearance of a star in the East/seeing a star in the East/that they had seen a star in the East/a star to have appeared in the East/what they had seen* —compare REPORT ON **2** [I∅ (*for, to*)] to go somewhere and say (to someone) that one is there (and ready for work or duty): *to report to the police|They report for work at 8.0 a.m.|What time do you have to report?* **3** [T1 (*for, to*)] to make a complaint about (someone or something) (to someone else): *He reported the boy (to the head teacher) (for making a noise)* **4** [T1] (of a REPORTER) to write an account of (a piece of news): *to report the Minister's speech for a newspaper* **5 report progress** to say what has been done up to now

re·port·age /rɪ'pɔːtɪdʒ, ˌrepɔː'tɑːdʒ‖-'por-, ˌrepər'tɑʒ/ *n* [U] **1** the art of REPORTing[2] (4) news **2** the style in which this is usually done **3** writing in this style, intended to give an exciting account of an event

report back *v adv* [I∅;T1,5] to bring back an account (of); come back and describe: *Go and find out the truth and report back quickly!|Columbus reported back that he had discovered America/what he had discovered*

report card /·ˈ· ·/ *n AmE* SCHOOL REPORT

re·port·ed·ly /rɪˈpɔːtɪ̣dli‖-ˈpor-/ *adv* [Wa5] according to what is said

reported speech /·ˌ·· ˈ·/ *n* [U] INDIRECT SPEECH

re·port·er /rɪˈpɔːtəʳ‖-ˈpor-/ *n* a person who collects and writes about news for a newspaper, or for radio or television —compare JOURNALIST

report on also **report up·on**— *v prep* [T1 (*to*)] to give information about (something) (to someone): *He reported on the whole event* (*to the minister*) —compare REPORT² (1)

re·pose¹ /rɪˈpəʊz/ *v fml* **1** [L9] to lie still and rest comfortably: *The cat is reposing on my knee* **2** [X9] to place (a part of oneself) for a rest: *She reposed her head on his shoulder* **3** [L9] *euph* to lie dead: *His body reposes in the local church*

repose² *n* [U] **1** *fml* comfortable rest; sleep: *a night's repose* **2** calm; quiet: *the repose of a hot summer afternoon|Try to develop more repose of manner—stop shouting like that!* **3 in repose** (of someone's face) when not showing feelings —**~ful** *adj*: *a reposeful Sunday in bed*

repose in *v prep* [D1] *fml* to place (trust, hopes, etc.) in: *to repose our trust in God*

repose on *v prep* [T1 *no pass.*] *fml* (of a proof or argument) REST ON

re·pos·i·to·ry /rɪˈpɒzɪ̣təri‖rɪˈpɑzɪ̣tori/ *n* **1** a place where things are stored: *a furniture repository* **2** [+ *of*] a person to whom knowledge of (something) is specially given: *Her brother was the repository of her hopes and fears*

re·pos·sess /ˌriːpəˈzes/ *v* [T1] to regain possession of (property), as when rent has not been paid: *The* LANDLORD *is threatening to repossess the farm* —**~ion** /ˌriːpəˈzeʃən/ *n* [U]

re·pot /ˌriːˈpɒt‖ˌriːˈpɑt/ *v* **-tt-** [T1] to put (a plant) into another (larger) pot

rep·re·hend /ˌreprɪˈhend/ *v* [T1] *fml* to blame; scold: *The boy deserves to be severely reprehended*

rep·re·hen·si·ble /ˌreprɪˈhensəbəl/ *adj* (of a person or his behaviour) deserving to be REPREHENDED: *a reprehensible deed* —**-bly** *adv*

rep·re·sent /ˌreprɪˈzent/ *v* **1** [T1;V4] (esp. of a painting) to show; be a picture of: *This painting represents a storm at sea/Icarus falling into the sea.|a tall stone figure representing Victory* **2** [T1] to be a sign of; stand for: *The red lines on the map represent railways* **3** [T1] **a** to act officially for (another person or people): *to represent one's fellow-workers at the Union meeting* **b** to be the Member of Parliament for (a place): *Does Mr. Walker still represent Worcester?* **4** [T1 *usu. pass.*] (of a member of a group) to be present as an example of (that group): *"a soup in which 20 kinds of vegetables were represented"* (Hawthorne) **5** [T1] *fml* to act the part of: *He represented Brutus in the school play* **6** [V3] *fml* to declare (someone or something), perhaps falsely, (to be): *He represented himself to be the Son of God* —see REPRESENT AS (USAGE)

re-pre·sent /ˌriːprɪˈzent/ *v* [T1] to send in again: *to re-present a bill for payment*

represent as *v prep* [X1,7;V4b] to describe (someone or something), perhaps falsely, as: *He represented himself as a friend of/as being friendly to the workers, but now we know the truth*

USAGE This is very close in meaning to REPRESENT (6). Perhaps if one **represents X as Y** one says what it is like, giving a description, while if one **represents X to be Y** one says what it is. Compare: *He represented me as cruel/as a cruel father.|He represented me to be his father.*

rep·re·sen·ta·tion /ˌreprɪzenˈteɪʃən/ *n* **1** [U] the act or condition of REPRESENTing (3) or being REPRESENTED (3): *"No taxation without representation" means that if people pay taxes they should be represented in Parliament* **2** [C (*of*)] something that REPRESENTS (1,5): *This painting is a representation of a storm at sea*

rep·re·sen·ta·tion·al /ˌreprɪzenˈteɪʃənəl/ *adj* (of a style of art, a painting, etc.) showing things just as they look in real life —compare ABSTRACT

rep·re·sen·ta·tions /ˌreprɪzenˈteɪʃənz/ *n* [P (*about, to*)] polite official complaints (esp. in the phr. **make representations**): *to make representations to the college cook about the bad food*

rep·re·sen·ta·tive¹ /ˌreprɪˈzentətɪv/ *adj* **1** [(*of*)] typical; being an example (of what others are like): *a representative collection of ancient Greek art|Are your opinions representative of those of the other students?* —opposite **unrepresentative** **2** [Wa5] (of a system of government) in which the people and their opinions are REPRESENTED (3)

representative² *n* [(*of*)] a person acting in place of one or more others: *sent a representative to the meeting* —see also SALESMAN

represent to *v prep* [D1,5] *fml* (*not used with the actual words spoken*) to express (something) to (someone); point out to, often angrily or complainingly: *to represent one's complaints to Head Office|I represented to him that it would be dangerous to do what he suggested*

re·press /rɪˈpres/ *v* [T1] **1 a** to rule (a person) by holding back from natural feelings, actions, etc.: *They are repressed by their parents, who prevent them from playing or shouting* **b** to control (a feeling or desire): *I could hardly repress my laughter* **2** to put down by force: *to repress a rising of the people with the help of the army*

re·pressed /rɪˈprest/ *adj tech* **1** (of a person) suffering from REPRESSION (2): *a very repressed little boy who never speaks* **2** [Wa5] (of a feeling or desire) in the state of REPRESSION (2): *to have a repressed desire to steal*

re·pres·sion /rɪˈpreʃən/ *n* **1** [U] the act of REPRESSing or state of being REPRESSED: *the repression of my feelings/of a rising of the people* **2** [C;U] *tech* (in PSYCHOLOGY) **a** the forcing of feelings or desires of which one is ashamed out of the conscious mind into the unconscious mind, with odd effects upon one's behaviour: *to suffer from sex-repression* **b** a feeling or desire that is in this state

re·pres·sive /rɪˈpresɪv/ *adj derog* (of a law or other kind of control) hard and cruel: *a repressive political system that allows no freedom* —**~ly** *adv* —**~ness** *n* [U]

re·prieve¹ /rɪˈpriːv/ *v* [T1] to give a REPRIEVE² to: *to reprieve the prisoner|*(fig.) *The doctor has reprieved me—I'm not going to die after all*

reprieve² *n* an official order delaying the punishment of a prisoner who was to die: *to* GRANT¹ (1) *him a reprieve|*(fig.) *He thought he was losing his sight, but received an unexpected reprieve*

rep·ri·mand¹ /ˈreprɪ̣mɑːnd‖-mænd/ *n* [C;U] (a) severe official scolding: *to receive a reprimand|We can't let his behaviour go without reprimand*

reprimand² *v* [T1] to scold officially and severely

re·print¹ /ˌriːˈprɪnt/ *v* [I∅;T1] **a** to print (a book) again when supplies have run out: *I hope this dictionary will often be reprinted!* **b** (of a book) to be printed again: *The book is reprinting—you'll be able to buy one soon*

re·print² /ˈriːˌprɪnt/ *n* a REPRINTed book —compare EDITION

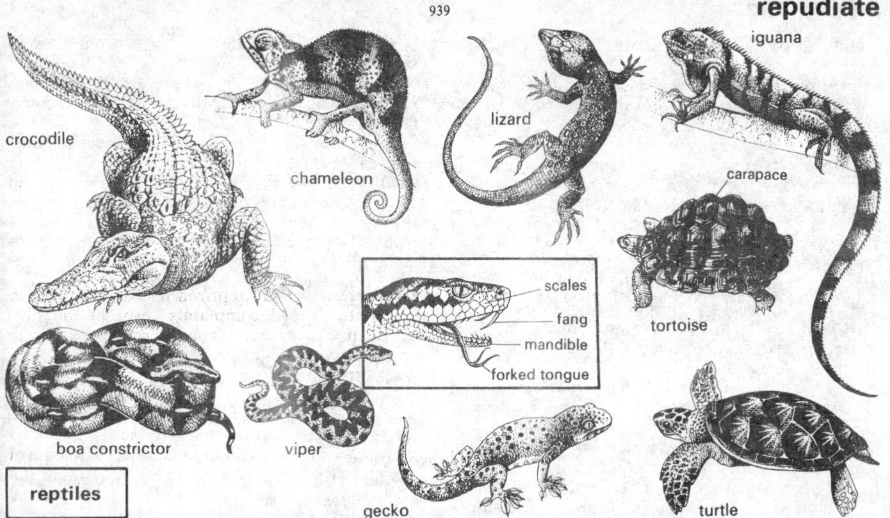

reptiles

re·pri·sal /rɪˈpraɪzəl/ *n* [C;U *often pl. with sing. meaning*] (an act of) punishing others for harm done to oneself, esp. of a political or military kind: *threatened with reprisals|to drop bombs on an enemy village in reprisal/as a reprisal*

re·prise /rɪˈpriːz/ *n* a repeating of all or part of a piece of music

re·proach¹ /rɪˈprəʊtʃ/ *n* **1** [U] blame: *She gave me a look of reproach.|to try to escape reproach* **2** [C] a word or words of blame: *When he came home drunk his wife greeted him with loud reproaches* **3** [S+*to*] something that brings shame (to): *These old ruined houses are a reproach to the city* **4 above/beyond reproach** perfect: *His manners are beyond reproach—I've never met anyone so polite* —**~ful** *adj* —**~fully** *adv*

reproach² *v* [T1 (*for, with*)] to blame (someone), not angrily but sadly: *It wasn't your fault—you have nothing to reproach yourself with.|He reproached her with laziness/for being lazy*

rep·ro·bate¹ /ˈreprəbeɪt/ *v* [T1] *rare & fml* to disapprove strongly and rightly of: *We reprobate his evil behaviour* —**-bation** /ˌreprəˈbeɪʃən/ *n* [U]

reprobate² *adj, n* [Wa5;A;C] *usu. humor* (typical of) a person of bad character: *a man of reprobate habits|Gordon is an old reprobate and spends all his money on beer*

re·pro·duce /ˌriːprəˈdjuːs‖-ˈduːs/ *v* [T1;IØ] **1** to produce the young of (oneself or one's (own) kind): *Some tropical fish reproduce (themselves/their kind) by laying eggs* **2** to (cause to) produce a copy (of); cause to be seen or heard again: *I wonder if this photograph will reproduce?|to reproduce a painting by photography* —**-ducible** *adj*

re·pro·duc·er /ˌriːprəˈdjuːsəʳ‖-ˈduː-/ *n* **1** a creature that REPRODUCE*s* (1) **2** a machine that REPRODUCE*s* (2)

re·pro·duc·tion /ˌriːprəˈdʌkʃən/ *n* **1** [U] the act or method of producing young: *a lesson at school on the reproduction of the rabbit* **2** [U] copying: *The quality of reproduction isn't very good on this recording* **3** [C] a copy, esp. of a work of art, less exact than a REPLICA: *a cheap reproduction of a great painting*

re·pro·duc·tive /ˌriːprəˈdʌktɪv/ *adj* [Wa5;A] **1** (of organs and natural actions) concerned with producing young: *the female reproductive system* **2** concerned with copying: *to print a book by modern reproductive methods*

re·proof¹ /rɪˈpruːf/ *n* [C;U] *fml* (an expression of) blame; scolding: *behaviour that deserves reproof*

re·proof² /ˌriːˈpruːf/ *v* [T1] to make (a coat, tent, etc.) able to keep out water again, usu. by treating with chemicals

re·prove /rɪˈpruːv/ *v* [T1 (*for*)] *fml* to scold (for bad behaviour): *to reprove a boy (for staying out late)*

re·prov·ing /rɪˈpruːvɪŋ/ *adj fml* expressing REPROOF¹: *to speak in a very reproving voice* —**~ly** *adv*

rep·tile /ˈreptaɪl‖ˈreptl/ *n* a type of creature whose blood changes temperature according to the temperature around it, which is covered in rough skin, and typically goes along on the ground or near it

rep·til·i·an¹ /repˈtɪlɪən/ *adj* **1** [Wa5] of or being a REPTILE: *A snake has reptilian skin* **2** *derog or humor* looking like (that of) a REPTILE: *a funny little reptilian old man*

reptilian² *n tech* REPTILE

re·pub·lic /rɪˈpʌblɪk/ *n* **1** a state completely governed by elected representatives **2** a nation whose chief of state is not a king but a president

Republic *n* [*the*+R9] the French State during one of 5 periods: *The 1st Republic lasted from 1789–1804, the 2nd Republic from 1848–1852, the 3rd Republic from 1871–1940, the 4th Republic from 1947–1958, and the 5th Republic from 1958 until the present day*

re·pub·li·can¹ /rɪˈpʌblɪkən/ *adj* **1** [Wa5] belonging to a REPUBLIC (2,3): *a republican system of government* **2** in favour of REPUBLIC*s* (2,3) as the best form of government: *republican ideas*

republican² *n* a person who disapproves of kings, and believes in government by elected representatives only

Republican¹ *adj* [Wa5] of, related to, or favouring the **Republican party**, one of the 2 largest political parties of the US: *He votes Republican at every election* —compare DEMOCRATIC

Republican² *n* a member or supporter of the REPUBLICAN¹ party —compare DEMOCRAT

re·pub·li·can·is·m /rɪˈpʌblɪkənɪzəm/ *n* [U] the beliefs or practices of REPUBLICAN*s*²

Republicanism *n* [U] the beliefs or practices of the REPUBLICAN¹ party of the US

re·pu·di·ate /rɪˈpjuːdieɪt/ *v* [T1] **1** to refuse to accept: *to repudiate offers of friendship* **2** to refuse to meet or recognize; state that one has no connection with (someone): *to repudiate one's wife* **3** to state that (something) is untrue or unjust: *to repudiate the charge of having shot his sister* **4** to refuse to pay (a debt) —**-ation** /rɪˌpjuːdiˈeɪʃən/ *n* [U]

re·pug·nance /rɪˈpʌgnəns/ *n* [S;U: (*to*)] the feeling of strong dislike: *She turned away from him in repugnance.|I feel a great repugnance to your suggestion*

re·pug·nant /rɪˈpʌgnənt/ *adj* [(*to*)] nasty; causing REPUGNANCE: *Of course I won't marry him—he's repugnant to me.|I find his opinions repugnant*

re·pulse[1] /rɪˈpʌls/ *v* [T1] **1** to drive back (an enemy attack) **2** to refuse coldly; push away (a friendly person, or an offer of friendship)
USAGE One can **repel** or **repulse** an enemy, but one can only **repulse** an offer of friendship.

repulse[2] *n* **1** the military defeat of an attack: *After several repulses we conquered the town* **2** a rude refusal of friendship

re·pul·sion /rɪˈpʌlʃən/ *n* **1** [S;U] strong dislike and fear (of something unpleasant): *to feel (a certain) repulsion at the sight of a diseased animal* **2** [U] *tech* (in science) the force by which bodies drive each other away —opposite **attraction**

re·pul·sive /rɪˈpʌlsɪv/ *adj* **1** very unpleasant; causing REPULSION (1): *a repulsive character|a repulsive skin disease* **2** [Wa5] *tech* (in science) exercising REPULSION (2): *repulsive forces* —**~ly** *adv* —**~ness** *n* [U]

rep·u·ta·ble /ˈrepjʊtəbəl‖-pjə-/ *adj* having a good name; well spoken of: *a reputable firm of builders* —**-bly** *adv*

rep·u·ta·tion /repjʊˈteɪʃən‖-pjə-/ *n* [S;U] **1** (an) opinion held by others (about someone or something); the degree to which one is well thought of: *to have a high reputation as a farmer|a man of evil reputation|He has the reputation of being a coward.|She has (quite) a reputation/some reputation for being amusing.|If people find out what you're doing it will be bad for your reputation* —compare CHARACTER, CHARACTERISTIC **2 live up to one's reputation** to behave in the way people have come to expect

re·pute /rɪˈpjuːt/ *n* [U] *fml* **1** REPUTATION (often in such phrs. as **of good/bad/evil repute**): *a man of evil repute|He is held in high repute.|I know her only by repute* (=I have not met her) **2** good REPUTATION: *a hotel of (some) repute*

re·put·ed /rɪˈpjuːtɨd/ *adj* [Wa5] **1** [A] generally supposed, but with some doubt: *the reputed father of her baby* **2** [F3,9 esp. *as*] reported to; considered (as): *He is reputed to keep a lot of money under his bed.|He is well/highly reputed in the town.|She is reputed to be/as the best singer in Europe*

re·put·ed·ly /rɪˈpjuːtɨdli/ *adv* [Wa5] according to what people say: *Reputedly, she is very stupid*

re·quest[1] /rɪˈkwest/ *n* **1** [C,C5c] a polite demand: *made a request for help|her repeated requests that I should play with her|to* GRANT[1] (1) *his requests* **2** [C] something that has been asked for: *Do they play requests on this radio show* (=records that have been asked for by listeners)? **3 at someone's request** because someone asked: *I bought it at your request/at the request of my father* **4 by request (of)** because asked for (by): *The band are playing this song by request of the Queen* **5 in (great) request** also **much in request**— popular; being asked for by many people: *These yellow socks have been much in request lately* **6 on request** when asked for: *The band will play on request*

request[2] *v* [T1,5c: (*of*); V3] (*not used with the actual words spoken*) to demand politely: *May I request your attention?|I requested (of him) that he (should) leave.|I requested them to stop making such a noise*

request stop /·ˈ· ·/ *n* (in Britain) a place where a bus will stop, but only if REQUESTED[2] (as b signalling with one's hand)

req·ui·em /ˈrekwɪəm, ˈrekwiem/ also **requiem mas** /ˌ··· ˈ·/— *n* **1** a Christian religious ceremon (MASS) for a dead person, at which people pra that his soul shall rest quietly **2** a piece of musi written for this ceremony

re·quire /rɪˈkwaɪəʳ/ *v* [Wv5] **1** [T1,4,5c] to need *This suggestion requires careful thought.|The floo requires washing.|His health requires that h (should) go to bed early.|I'm looking for the require ladder* **2** [T1 (*of*), 5c;V3] *fml* to demand; order expecting obedience: *All passengers are required t show their tickets.|Do you require anything of me?|t pass the required examinations to become a doctor He requires that they (should) work all night*

re·quire·ment /rɪˈkwaɪəmənt‖-ər-/ *n* **1** somethin needed: *This shop can supply all your requirement* **2** something demanded: *to obey all the requirement of the law* **3 meet someone's requirements** to do o be what someone REQUIRES

req·ui·site /ˈrekwɨzɨt/ *n, adj* [(*for*)] (something needed (for a purpose): *sports requisites|ever requisite for camping*

req·ui·si·tion[1] /ˌrekwɨˈzɪʃən/ *n* [C;U: (*for, on*) (a) formal demand, esp. by the army: *If you wan this new part for the plane, you'll have to fill in requisition paper.|made a requisition on the village fo horses|*(fig.) *The car is in/under continual requisitio when the boys are at home*

requisition[2] *v* [T1] to demand or take officially esp. for the army: *to requisition the stores of petrol*

re·quit·al /rɪˈkwaɪtl/ *n* [U] *fml* repayment: *I hav made full requital.|I gave him £10 in requital of hi help*

re·quite /rɪˈkwaɪt/ *v* [T1 (*with*)] *fml* to pay bac (something) (with something): *He requited m kindness only with cruel words* —see als UNREQUITED

rere·dos /ˈrɪədɒs‖ˈrɪərdɑs, ˈreərədɑs/ *n* an ornamental wall or large wall-like work of art behin an ALTAR in a church —see picture at CHURCH[1]

re·run[1] /riːˈrʌn/ *v* **-ran** /ˈræn/, **-run** /ˈrʌn/, *pres. p* **-running** [T1] **1** to show (a film or recordec television show) again **2** to run (a race) again *One of the competitors was found to have cheated, s the race had to be rerun*

re·run[2] /ˈriːrʌn/ *n* a film or recorded televisior show that is RERUN[1] (1)

re·scind /rɪˈsɪnd/ *v* [T1] *law* to put an end to REPEAL (a law, decision, or agreement)

re·script /ˈriːˌskrɪpt/ *n tech* **1** an official declaration or order, made by a government **2** a writter answer by the head of the ROMAN CATHOLIC church (POPE) to a question on law or morals

res·cue[1] /ˈreskjuː/ *v* [T1 (*from*)] to save (from harm or danger); set free: *to rescue a man from drowning|a cat from a high tree|one's stamp collection from a burning house* —**-cuer** *n* [C;(N)]

rescue[2] *n* **1** an act of rescuing (RESCUE[1]): *A rescue team are trying to reach the trapped miners* **2 come/go to someone's rescue** to come/go and help someone: *Jean couldn't do her Latin exercise, but her father came to her rescue*

re·search[1] /rɪˈsɜːtʃ‖-3r-/ *n* **1** [U] advanced study of a subject, so as to learn new facts or scientific laws: *a piece of research|research students/workers to do some research on diseases of the blood/in ancient history* **2** [C *usu. pl. with sing. meaning*] a piece of work of this kind: *to carry out a research* (=some researches) *into the causes of brain damage|My researches were directed towards finding a cure for headaches*

research[2] *v* **1** [I∅ (*into, on*)] to do RESEARCH[1]: *to research on/into the effects of cigarette smoking*

We've been researching for 3 years with no result **2** [T1] to do RESEARCH[1] on or for: *to research a subject|This book has been very well researched* —**~er** *n*

re·seat /ˌriːˈsiːt/ *v* [T1] **1** to put a new seat into: *to reseat a chair* **2** to give a new seat to; cause to sit again: *As soon as you're all reseated, we'll hear the rest of the music*

re·sem·blance /rɪˈzembləns/ *n* [C;U: (*between*)] (a) likeness: *"There's a strong resemblance between Viola and Sebastian." "I don't see the resemblance!"*

re·sem·ble /rɪˈzembəl/ *v* [T1 (*in*)] to look or be like: *She resembles her sister in appearance but not in character*

re·sent /rɪˈzent/ *v* [T1,4] to feel angry or bitter at: *He resents being called a fool.|I (strongly|bitterly) resent your remarks* —**~ful** *adj*: *to give him a resentful look|Don't be so resentful* —**~fully** *adv* —**~fulness** *n* [U]

re·sent·ment /rɪˈzentmənt/ *n* [U] the feeling of RESENTing bad treatment: *I don't bear you any resentment*

res·er·va·tion /ˌrezəˈveɪʃən‖-ər-/ *n* **1** [C;U:5] (a) limiting condition: *I accept your offer completely and without reservation(s)* **2** [C] a private doubt in one's mind: *I have some reservations about the truth of his story* **3** [U;C] (*often cap.*) the practice in ROMAN CATHOLIC churches of keeping some of the holy bread for later use: *Reservation of the* SACRAMENT **4** [C] (in the US) a piece of land set apart for N. American Indians to live in **5** [C] *esp. AmE* BOOKING: *made the reservations for our holiday*

re·serve[1] /rɪˈzɜːv‖-ɜrv/ *v* [T1] **1** to keep (for a special purpose): *These seats are reserved for old and sick people* **2** *esp. AmE* BOOK[2] (1): *to reserve a seat on the plane*

reserve[2] *n* **1** [C (*of*), *often pl. with sing. meaning*] a quantity (of something) kept for future use; store: *to keep a reserve* (=some reserves) *of food* **2** [*the*+R *often pl. with sing. meaning*] (*often cap.*) the military force that a country keeps for use if needed: *He's in/on the Reserve.|to call out the reserve(s)* —see also RESERVIST **3** [C (*of*)] a price limit below which something is not to be sold: *He put a reserve of £10,000 on the house* **4** [C9] a piece of land RESERVEd for a (stated) purpose: *to go and see the lions in the nature reserve* **5** [U] (of a person or his character) the quality of being RESERVED (1): *the well-known reserve of the Scots* **6** [C] a player whose job is to play in a team game instead of any member who is hurt or cannot play **7 in reserve** ready for use if needed **8 without reserve** *fml* **a** freely and openly: *She told me all about it without reserve* **b** without conditions: *I believe your story without reserve*

re·served /rɪˈzɜːvd‖-ɜr-/ *adj* **1** (typical of a person) that does not like to talk about himself or to make his feelings known: *Bob is very reserved—you never know what he's thinking* **2** [Wa5] having been RESERVED[1] (2): *reserved seats* —see also UNRESERVED

re·serv·ed·ly /rɪˈzɜːvɪ̈dli‖-ɜr-/ *adv* in a RESERVED (1) way —compare UNRESERVEDLY

re·serv·ist /rɪˈzɜːvɪ̈st‖-ɜr-/ *n* a soldier who can be or is called at any time of difficulty to serve in the country's army

res·er·voir /ˈrezəvwɑːʳ‖-ərvɑr, -vɔr/ *n* **1** a place where liquid is stored, esp. water for a city: *to go sailing on the local reservoir* **2** [+*of*] a large supply (of facts or knowledge): *This dictionary is a reservoir of information about the English language*

re·set /ˌriːˈset/ *v* **-set** /ˈset/, *pres. p.* **-setting** [T1] **1** to sharpen again (the blade of a tool, esp. a SAW) **2** to put (a jewel) into a new ornament: *to have my diamonds reset in a ring* **3** to put (a broken bone) back in place for a 2nd time: *His leg has not mended properly and will have to be reset* **4** to make up TYPE again for (something to be printed): *The book will have to be reset because there were so many mistakes in the first printing*

re·set·tle /riːˈsetl/ *v* [I∅;T1] to (help to) settle in a new country: *to resettle Ugandan Asians in Canada*

re·shuf·fle[1] /riːˈʃʌfəl/ *v* **1** [I∅;T1] to SHUFFLE (playing cards) again: *to reshuffle (the cards)* **2** [T1] *not fml* to change around; have a RESHUFFLE[2] of

reshuffle[2] *n not fml* a changing around of the positions of people employed in an organization: *a reshuffle in the Government*

re·side /rɪˈzaɪd/ *v* [L9] *fml* to have one's home (at, in a place): *to reside abroad|to reside at 8, The Mount Square* —see LIVE (USAGE)

reside in *v prep* [T1 *no pass.*] *fml* (of powers, rights, etc.) to belong to: *The power to change the law resides in Parliament*

res·i·dence /ˈrezɪ̈dəns/ *n* **1** [C] *fml* the place where one lives; a house, esp. a large grand one: (*humor*) *How nice of you to visit me at my humble residence!| "This desirable town residence for sale"* (advertisement) —see VILLA (USAGE) **2** [U] the state of residing (RESIDE): *took up residence in Jamaica* **3 in residence** actually living in a place, esp. **a** (of an official) in his official house **b** (of students) at the university: *The students are not in residence during the holidays*

res·i·den·cy /ˈrezɪ̈dənsi/ *n* (*often cap.*) (esp. in former times) the official house in a foreign country where a British political representative (RESIDENT) lives —compare EMBASSY

res·i·dent[1] /ˈrezɪ̈dənt/ *adj* [Wa5; (*in*)] living (in a place): *I've been resident in this hotel for 5 years.|a resident doctor* (=living in the hospital)

resident[2] *n* a person who lives (in a place) and is not just a visitor: *This hotel serves meals to residents only* (=only to people who sleep there)

Resident *n* [C9] (esp. in former times) a political representative (of a stated country) living abroad as an adviser

res·i·den·tial /ˌrezɪ̈ˈdenʃəl/ *adj often apprec* (of part of a town) consisting of private houses, without offices or factories

residential qual·i·fi·ca·tions /‥ˈ‥ ‥ˌ‥/ *n* [P] the condition of actually living in a place, that allows one to vote there

re·sid·u·al /rɪˈzɪdʒʊəl/ *adj* [Wa5] left over; remaining

re·sid·u·a·ry /rɪˈzɪdʒʊəri‖-dʒeri/ *adj* [Wa5;A] *law* having the right to what is left after a dead person's debts and earlier BEQUESTs have been settled (in the phr. **residuary legatee**): *I leave you £10,000, and George will be my residuary* LEGATEE *and get the rest of the money*

res·i·due /ˈrezɪ̈djuː‖-duː/ *n* [*usu. sing.*] *tech* what is left, esp. **a** *law* after a dead person's debts and earlier BEQUESTs have been settled **b** (in science) after chemical treatment

re·sign /rɪˈzaɪn/ *v* **1** [I∅ (*from*); T1] to give up (a job or position): *to resign from a committee|to resign one's post|If Paul resigns, who will get the job?* **2 resign (oneself or another) to** *fml* to hand (oneself or another) over to: *I resign my children to the care of the State* **3 resign oneself to** also **reconcile oneself to**— to become RESIGNED to: *You must resign yourselves to waiting a bit longer*

res·ig·na·tion /ˌrezɪgˈneɪʃən/ *n* **1** [U] the state of being RESIGNED: *to accept one's fate with resignation* **2** [C;U] (an act of) RESIGNing (1): *You have the choice between resignation and dismissal.|What have things been like since Bill's resignation?* **3** [C] a written statement that one RESIGNs (1): *to hand in/send in my resignation*

re·signed /rɪ'zaɪnd/ *adj* [(*to*)] (typical of a person) patiently prepared (for something unpleasant); calmly suffering without complaint: *He seems quite resigned (to his mother's death)* —**~ly** /rɪ'zaɪnᵻdli/ *adv*

re·sil·i·ence /rɪ'zɪlɪəns/ also **re·sil·i·en·cy** /-si/— *n* [S;U] (a) quality of being RESILIENT: *Rubber has more resilience than wood*

re·sil·i·ent /rɪ'zɪlɪənt/ *adj* **1** (of a substance) able to spring back to the former shape or position when pressure is removed: *Rubber is more resilient than wood* **2** (of living things) strong enough to recover from difficulty, disease, etc.: *He has a resilient character and will soon be cheerful again* —**~ly** *adv*

res·in /'rezᵻn/ *n* **1** [U] a thick sticky liquid that comes out of certain trees such as the FIR, and later becomes hard like yellow wax. It is used for making paint, in medicine, and as ROSIN **2** [C] any of various man-made plastic substances, produced chemically and used in industry —**~ous** /'rezᵻnəs/ *adj*

res·in·at·ed /'rezᵻneɪtᵻd/ *adj* [Wa5] mixed with or tasting of RESIN (1): *resinated wine*

re·sist /rɪ'zɪst/ *v* [T1,4] **1** to oppose; stand or fight against (force): *to resist an enemy attack|to resist being carried off* **2** to remain unchanged or unharmed by: *the power to resist disease|a roof that will resist the weather* **3** [*often neg.*] (of a living creature) to refuse to yield to: *She could hardly resist laughing* **4** [*usu. neg.*] to force or allow oneself not to accept: *I can't resist baked apples* —**~er** *n* —**~ible** *adj* —opposite **irresistible**

re·sist·ance /rɪ'zɪstəns/ *n* **1** [S;U] (an act of) RESISTing (1): *The defenders put up (a) strong resistance* **2** [U9] the (stated) force opposed to anything moving: *wind resistance to an aircraft* **3** [U] the determination to refuse; opposition: *There has been much resistance to this new law* —see also SALES RESISTANCE, PASSIVE RESISTANCE **4** [U] the ability (of a living body) to RESIST (2) disease: *Mary has great powers of resistance and will get well quickly* **5** [U] the power of a substance to RESIST (2) the passing through it of an electric current: *Copper has less resistance to electricity than lead has* —see also VOLTAGE **6** [(*the*) GU] (*often cap.*) an organization that fights secretly against enemy armies that have conquered and now control its country **7** [C] RESISTOR **8 the line of least resistance** the easiest way: *Let's take the line of least resistance and pay him the money instead of fighting*

re·sis·tant /rɪ'zɪstənt/ *adj* [(*to*)] having or showing RESISTANCE (to): *rats that are resistant to poison*

re·sis·tor /rɪ'zɪstəʳ/ *n* a piece of wire or other material used for increasing electrical RESISTANCE —see picture at ELECTRICITY

re·sole /ˌriː'səʊl/ *v* [T1] to put a new SOLE (=the under part) onto (a shoe)

res·o·lute /'rezəluːt/ *adj* [(*for*)] (of a person or his character) firm; determined in purpose: *resolute for victory* —compare IRRESOLUTE —**~ly** *adv* —**~ness** *n* [U]

res·o·lu·tion /ˌrezə'luːʃən/ *n* **1** [U] the quality of being RESOLUTE: *You should show more resolution.|She lacks resolution.|a man of great resolution* **2** [U+*of*] the action of resolving (RESOLVE[1] (3)): *The lawyer's advice led to the resolution of all our difficulties* **3** [C,C3,5c] a formal decision made by a group vote: *The Committee have passed/carried/* ADOPT*ed* (3)/REJECT*ed a resolution to build a new library.|a resolution for/against building a new library|a resolution that a new library (should) be built* **4** [C,C3] a decision; something one makes up one's mind to do or stop doing: *She's always making good resolutions but she never carries them out.|my New Year resolution* (=one made on January 1st for the year ahead) *to stop smoking* —compare RESOLVE[2] **5** [U+*of, into*] (in science) breaking up into parts: *the resolution of a chemical mixture into simple substances*

re·sol·va·ble /rɪ'zɒlvəbəl‖-'zɑl-, -'zɔl-/ *adj* **1** that can be RESOLVEd[1] (3): *This difficulty should be easily resolvable* **2** [Wa5;+*into*] that can be RESOLVEd INTO: *This mixture is resolvable into 2 simple substances*

re·solve[1] /rɪ'zɒlv‖rɪ'zɑlv, rɪ'zɔlv/ *v* **1** [L9 esp. *on*; T3,5,6b] to decide: *He resolved on/against going out.|to resolve to work harder/that one will work harder|Have you resolved where to go next?* **2** [L9 esp. *on*; T3,5] (of a committee or public body) to make a RESOLUTION (3) (that): *The committee resolved on/against appointing a new secretary.|Parliament has resolved that . . .* **3** [T1] to settle or clear up (a difficulty): *The matter was resolved by making George sleep on the floor*

resolve[2] *n fml* **1** [C,C3] RESOLUTION (4): *a firm resolve to avoid doing anything dishonest* **2** [U] RESOLUTION (1)

resolve in·to *v prep* [D1;T1] to separate or become separated into (parts): *We can resolve this difficulty into 2 areas of misunderstanding.|This mixture will resolve into 2 simple substances*

res·o·nance /'rezənəns/ *n* **1** [U] the quality of being RESONANT (1): *The bell-like resonance of his voice filled the great church* **2** [C;U] (a) sound produced or increased in one body by sound waves from another: *Playing the piano sets up resonance(s) in those glass ornaments*

res·o·nant /'rezənənt/ *adj* **1** [B] (of a sound) deep, full, clear, and continuing: *the resonant note of a bell* **2** [B] producing RESONANCE (2) **3** [F+*with*] (of a place) filled (with the stated sound): *The air was resonant with the shouts of children* —**~ly** *adv*

res·o·nate /'rezəneɪt/ *v* [IØ] **1** to produce sound by RESONANCE (2) **2** (of a sound) to be RESONANT (1)

res·o·na·tor /'rezəneɪtəʳ/ *n* an apparatus for increasing the RESONANCE (2) of sound, as in a musical instrument

re·sort /rɪ'zɔːt‖-ɔrt/ *n* **1** [C] a holiday place, or place considered good for the health: *a health/mountain resort* **2** [C9] a place that one visits regularly: *This restaurant is one of his favourite resorts* **3** [U+*to*] the action of RESORTing TO (1): *to pass the examination without resort to cheating* —compare RECOURSE; see RESOURCE (USAGE) **4** [C] someone or something RESORTed TO (1): *Her only resorts when she is alone are sewing and watching television* **5 as a/in the last resort** if everything else fails: *In the last resort we can always swim back* **6 have resort to** *fml* to RESORT TO (1)

resort to *v prep* **1** [T1,4] to make use of; turn to (often something bad) for help: *When his wife left him he resorted to drink.|She resorted to stealing when she had no more money* **2** [T1 *no pass.*] to go to (a pleasant place); visit (often): *We resorted to the hotel for some coffee*

re·sound /rɪ'zaʊnd/ *v* **1** [L9 esp. *through, throughout*] (of a musical instrument, a sound, etc.) to be loudly and clearly heard: *The (notes of the) hunting horn resounded through the forest.|(fig.) The name of the young singer resounded* THROUGHOUT/*all over the country* **2** [IØ (*with*)] (of a place) to give back sound; be filled (with sound): *The hall resounded with laughter and whistles*

re·sound·ing /rɪ'zaʊndɪŋ/ *adj* [A] **1** (of a sound) loud and clear; ECHOing[2] (1): *They all gave 3 resounding cheers* **2** very great: *a resounding success* —**~ly** *adv*

re·source /rɪ'zɔːs, -'sɔːs‖-ors/ *n* **1** [C] a part of

one's RESOURCES: *Oil is Kuwait's most important natural resource* **2** [C] a means of comfort or help: *Religion is her only resource now* **3** [C] something that one does to pass the time: *Music and sewing are her favourite resources* **4** [U] cleverness in finding a way round difficulties: *Robinson Crusoe was a man of great resource*
USAGE **Resort**, **recourse**, and **resource** can all mean something like "the means used to reach one's end, when others have failed"; but they are each used in different phrs.: *to have* **resort/recourse** *to violence|without* **resort/recourse** *to war|in the last* **resort**|*as a last* **resource.**

re·source·ful /rɪ'zɔːsfəl, -'sɔːs-‖-ors-/ *adj apprec* (typical of a person) that can find a way round difficulties: *a resourceful man|What a very resourceful thing to do!* —**~ly** *adv* —**~ness** *n* [U]

re·sourc·es /rɪ'zɔːsɪ̈z, -'sɔː-‖-or-/ *n* [P] **1** possessions (esp. of a country), in the form of wealth and goods, that help one to do what one wants: *spent all his resources on educating his children|to waste resources and* MANPOWER *on building old-fashioned ships|a country rich in natural resources* (=minerals, water, etc.) **2 leave someone to his own resources** to leave someone alone to pass the time as he wishes

re·spect¹ /rɪ'spekt/ *n* **1** [S;U: (*for*)] admiration; feeling of honour: *to show respect for one's parents|He is held in the greatest respect by the whole village* **2** [U (*for, to*)] attention (to); care (for): *to have no respect for the speed limit* —compare SELF-RESPECT **3** [C] a detail; point (in such phrs. as **in one/no respect, in several/many/all respects**): *This room is fine except in one respect—what can I sit on?* **4 in respect of** *fml* **a** concerning; with regard to: *His work is good in respect of quality but bad in respect of quantity* **b** (esp. in business letters) in payment for: *give him £100 in respect of the work he has done* **5 without respect to** without considering; without regard to: *Everybody can come to this school, without respect to class, race, or sex* **6 with respect to** *fml* (introducing a new subject, esp. in business letters) when we come to speak of: *With respect to the recent flood, please report the number of sheep that were drowned* —see AS FOR (USAGE)

respect² *v* [T1] **1** to feel RESPECT¹ (1) for (esp. a person or his qualities): *I deeply respect his courage* **2** to show RESPECT¹ (2) for: *I promise to respect your wishes* **3** to have SELF-RESPECT: *No girl who respected herself would go out dressed like that*

re·spec·ta·bil·i·ty /rɪˌspektə'bɪlɪ̈ti/ *n* [U] the quality of being RESPECTABLE (1): *to marry him for the respectability of his social connections*

re·spec·ta·ble /rɪ'spektəbəl/ *adj* **1** *not always apprec* showing or having character and standards acceptable to society: *How dare you talk to a respectable woman like that?|It's not respectable to be drunk in the street.|to put on a clean shirt and look respectable|I'd never marry her; she's too respectable!* **2** quite good; enough in amount or quality: *England made 346 for 7—quite a respectable total* (cricket report).|*a respectable income* —**-bly** *adv* —**~ness** *n* [U]

re·spect·er /rɪ'spektəʳ/ *n derog* someone who shows RESPECT¹ (1) for rich or important people: *"God is no respecter of persons"* (The Bible)

re·spect·ful /rɪ'spektfəl/ *adj* [(*to*)] feeling or showing RESPECT¹ (1) (to): *to wait in respectful silence for the great man to speak* —**~ly** *adv*: *Yours respectfully . . .* (at the end of a letter to a more important person, esp. in former times) —**~ness** *n* [S;U]: *to show respectfulness|a respectfulness that surprised me*

re·spect·ing /rɪ'spektɪŋ/ *prep* with RESPECT¹ (6) to

re·spec·tive /rɪ'spektɪv/ *adj* [Wa5;A] of or for each one; particular and separate: *My husband and I are each going to visit our respective mothers*
USAGE **Respective** is nearly always followed by a pl.: *They went home to their* **respective** *houses* not **She went home to her* **respective** *house.*

re·spec·tive·ly /rɪ'spektɪvli/ *adv* each separately in the order mentioned: *She gave a glass of beer to the man and a toy rabbit to the baby, respectively*

re·spects /rɪ'spekts/ *n* [P] **1** polite formal greetings: *Give my respects to your wife.|Please send them my respects when you write* **2 pay one's respects to** *fml* to pay a polite visit to (a person)

res·pi·ra·tion /ˌrespɪ̈'reɪʃən/ *n fml & tech* **1** [U] the action of breathing: *Respiration is difficult at great heights* —see also ARTIFICIAL RESPIRATION **2** [C] a single breath in and out

res·pi·ra·tor /'respɪ̈reɪtəʳ/ *n* an apparatus that is worn over the nose and mouth, to help people to breathe in spite of gas, smoke, etc.

re·spi·ra·to·ry /rɪ'spɪrətəri, 'respɪ̈reɪtəri, rɪ'spaɪərə-‖'respərərori, rɪ'spaɪərə-/ *adj* [Wa5;A] connected with breathing: *respiratory diseases|the respiratory organs*
See next page for picture

re·spire /rɪ'spaɪəʳ/ *v* [IØ] *tech* to breathe

res·pite /'respɪt, -paɪt‖-pɪt/ *n* [C *usu. sing.*; U] **1** [(*from*)] (a short period of) pause or rest, during a time of great effort, pain, or trouble: *a welcome respite from hard work|The noise went on all night without a moment's respite* **2** a welcome period of delay, before suffering a punishment or fulfilling a duty: *The office will be shut till Monday, so we have a few days' respite before we need to pay the rent*

re·splen·dence /rɪ'splendəns/ also **re·splen·den·cy** /si/— *n* [U] the quality of being RESPLENDENT

re·splen·dent /rɪ'splendənt/ *adj* gloriously bright and shining; splendid: (fig.) *George arrived, resplendent in a new white suit* —**~ly** *adv*: *resplendently dressed in purple silk*

re·spond /rɪ'spɒnd‖rɪ'spɑnd/ *v* **1** [IØ (*to*); T5] to answer: *I offered him a drink but he didn't respond* (*to my offer*).|*"I can't marry you," she responded sadly* —see ANSWER (USAGE) **2** [IØ (*by, to, with*)] to act in answer: *He responded* (*to my suggestion*) *with a laugh/by laughing* **3** [IØ;T5] (of people at a religious service) to make RESPONSES (3): *The priest says "The Lord be with you," and the people respond, "And also with you"*

re·spon·dent /rɪ'spɒndənt‖rɪ'spɑn-/ *n law* a person who has to answer a charge in a law court, esp. in a DIVORCE¹ (1) case; DEFENDANT —compare CORESPONDENT

respond to *v prep* [T1 *no pass.*] (esp. of a disease, or a part of the body that is hurt) to get better or do the right thing as a result of: *The disease failed to respond to drugs.|Is Mother's leg responding to treatment?|*(fig.) *The horse responded to his control*

re·sponse /rɪ'spɒns‖rɪ'spɑns/ *n* **1** [C (*to*)] an answer: *He made/gave no response* (*to my question*).|*There have been several responses* (*to our advertisement*) **2** [C;U: (*to*)] (an) action done in answer: *There has been very little response to our call for help* **3** [C *usu. pl.*] one of the parts of a religious service that are said or sung by the people, in answer to the parts sung by the priest **4 in response to** as an answer to: *to open the door in response to a knock|"In response to your enquiry . . ."* (in a business letter)

re·spon·si·bil·i·ty /rɪˌspɒnsə'bɪlɪ̈ti‖rɪˌspɑn-/ *n* **1** [U (*for, to*)] the condition of being RESPONSIBLE (1): *I take full responsibility for this action* **2** [U] the quality of being RESPONSIBLE (2): *Now that you're 13 you should have more sense of responsibility* —opposite **irresponsibility** **3** [U] the quality of being RESPONSIBLE (3): *He holds a position of great responsibility in the Government* **4** [C] something

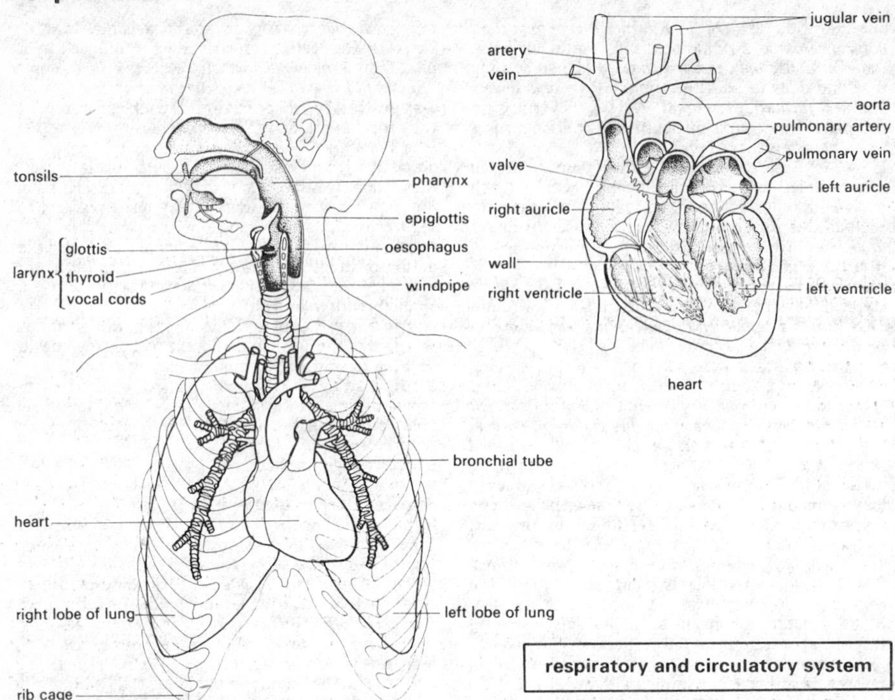

respiratory and circulatory system

for which one is RESPONSIBLE (1): *The father of a family has many responsibilities* **5 do something on one's own responsibility** to do something without being told to

re·spon·si·ble /rɪˈspɒnsəbəl‖rɪˈspɑn-/ *adj* **1** [F (*for, to*)] having the duty of looking after someone or something, so that one can be blamed (by the stated person) if things go wrong: *You are responsible to your mother for keeping the house tidy* **2** [B] (of a person or his character) trustworthy: *He is a responsible person and can be trusted to carry out orders* —opposite **irresponsible** **3** [B] (of a job) needing a trustworthy person to do it: *He holds a very responsible position in the firm* **4 be responsible for** to be the cause of: *Who is responsible for breaking the mirror?*

re·spon·si·bly /rɪˈspɒnsəbli‖rɪˈspɑn-/ *adv* in a RESPONSIBLE (2) way: *I'll trust you to behave responsibly while I'm out* —opposite **irresponsibly**

re·spon·sive /rɪˈspɒnsɪv‖rɪˈspɑn-/ *adj* **1** [(*to*)] (of a person or his character) sensitive (to); answering readily with words or feelings (to): *The child has a very responsive nature and will soon become fond of you.|She is very responsive to kindness* **2** [Wa5] RESPONDing (2): *She answered with a responsive smile* —**~ly** *adv* —**~ness** *n* [U]

rest¹ /rest/ *n* **1** [C;U: (*from*)] freedom from anything tiring; quiet; sleep: *to take/have a rest|to get a good night's rest|Sunday is my rest day.|some rest from one's labours* **2** [C9] (*often in comb.*) a support (for the stated thing): *an armrest|headrest|This wall will do as a rest for your camera* **3** [C] (in music) **a** a period of silence of a fixed length **b** one of a set of signs (such as 𝄾) that mark the length of these periods —see picture at NOTATION **4 at rest a** not moving: *The machine is at rest* **b** *euph* dead: *"At Rest"* (written on gravestones) **5 come to rest** (of something moving) to stop moving; come to a natural stop: *The car rolled down the hill by itself and came to rest at the bottom* **6 lay someone to rest** *euph* to bury someone's dead body **7 set someone's mind/fears at rest** to free someone from anxiety

rest² *v* **1** [IØ (*from*)] to take a REST¹ (1): *I always rest for an hour after dinner* **2** [T1] to allow to REST² (1): *Sit down and rest your feet.|May God rest his soul* (= a prayer that God will give peace to a dead person) **3** [X9 esp. *against, on*] to lean or support: *Rest your head against the wall/on your hands* **4** [L9] *euph* to lie buried: *Let his bones rest in peace* **5** [L9] to stop being active; come to REST¹ (5): *Let the argument rest there, because we shall never agree* **6** [IØ;T1] *law* **a** to stop explaining (one's case) to the court, because enough has been said: *I rest my case, my lord* **b** (of a case) to have been fully explained: *My case rests* **7** [IØ;T1] **a** to allow (farming land) to have nothing planted in it: *Rest the field for a year* **b** (of farming land) to have nothing planted in it: *Let the field rest for a year* **8 not to rest** to have no peace of mind: *I shall not rest until this matter is settled* **9 rest assured** *usu. imper* to be certain: *Rest assured/You can rest assured that we will do all we can* —see also REST ON, REST WITH

rest³ *n* [*the*+GU (*of*)] **1** what is left; the ones that still remain: *We'll eat some of the butter and keep the rest (of it) for breakfast.|He's only got one shirt, because all the rest (of them) are being washed.|John's English and the rest of us are Welsh* **2 for the rest** apart from what has already been mentioned; as for everything else

re·stage /ˌriːˈsteɪdʒ/ *v* [T1] to put (a play) on the stage again

re·state /ˌriːˈsteɪt/ *v* [T1] (*not used with the actual words spoken*) to say again, perhaps in different words: *to restate one's opinions* —**~ment** *n* [C;U]: (*a*) *restatement of one's opinions*

res·tau·rant /ˈrestərɔ̃, -rɒnt‖-rənt, -rɑnt (*Fr* rɛstɔrɑ̃)/ *n Fr* a place where food is sold and eaten

restaurant car /ˈ····ˌ·/ *n* DINING CAR

res·tau·ra·teur /ˌrestərəˈtɜːʳ/ *n* the owner of a restaurant, esp. one who runs it himself

rest cure /ˈ· ·/ *n* a course of treatment, often for people with illnesses of the mind, consisting of rest from one's usual activities

rest·ful /ˈrestfəl/ *adj* peaceful; giving one a feeling of REST[1] (1): *to spend a restful evening watching television* —**~ly** *adv* —**~ness** *n* [U]

rest home /ˈ· ·/ *n* an establishment where old or sick people are looked after

rest house /ˈ· ·/ *n* a house where travellers can stay, in a place where there are no hotels

resting-place /ˈ·· ·/ *n euph* a grave

res·ti·tu·tion /ˌrestəˈtjuːʃən‖-ˈtuːʃən/ *n* [U (*of*)] *fml* the act of returning something lost or stolen to its owner, or of paying for damage: *to make restitution* (*of something, to someone*)

res·tive /ˈrestɪv/ *adj* restless; unwilling to keep still or be controlled: *a restive horse* —**~ly** *adv* —**~ness** *n* [U]

rest·less /ˈrestləs/ *adj* **1** never quiet; always moving about: *the restless sea|a very restless night* **2** (seeming) unwilling or unable to stay still: *After listening to him for 3 hours they became restless* —**~ly** *adv* —**~ness** *n* [U]

re·stock /ˌriːˈstɒk‖ˌriːˈstɑk/ *v* [I∅;T1: (*with*)] **a** to get a new store (STOCK[1] (1)): *The food cupboard's nearly empty—we must restock* **b** to put new STOCK[1] (6) into: *to restock the park with deer*

rest on also **rest up·on**— *v prep* [T1] **1** to lean on; be supported by: *The bridge rests on stone arches.|Her hand rested lightly upon his shoulder* **2** (of sight or the eyes) to be directed on; fall on: *His eyes rested on the peaceful valley below* **3** also **repose on**— (of a proof, argument, etc.) to depend on; be based on: *His decision to sail west rested on his belief that the world was round* **4 rest on one's oars a** to stop rowing for a while **b** to stop working after effort or success; be satisfied with what is done, and do no more

res·to·ra·tion /ˌrestəˈreɪʃən/ *n* **1** [U] the act of giving something back: *the restoration of a borrowed book* **2** [U] the act of introducing again: *the restoration of public order after a time of violence* **3** [U+*to*] the act of putting or being put back to a former state or position: *He hopes for restoration to his old job.|I'm glad to hear of your restoration to health* **4** [C;U] **a** the act or work of putting old buildings, furniture, or works of art back into the original state: *the restoration of a painting|gave money to the church restoration* FUND[1] (2) **b** a piece of work of this kind: *The restorations to the castle took a year and cost a lot of money* **5** [C] a copy that shows what an earlier original must have been like: *a restoration of the ancient woolly elephant*

Restoration *n* [*the*+R] (the period in England following) the return of Charles II as king in 1660: *a Restoration play*

re·sto·ra·tive[1] /rɪˈstɔːrətɪv‖-ˈsto-/ *adj* [Wa5] that brings back health and strength: *a few restorative days by the sea*

restorative[2] *n* a RESTORATIVE[1] food, medicine, etc.

re·store /rɪˈstɔːʳ‖rɪˈstor/ *v* [T1] **1** [(*to*)] to give back: *to restore stolen property* **2** to bring back into use; introduce again: *to restore an old custom|to call in the army to restore law and order* **3** [(*to*) *usu. pass.*] to bring back to a proper state, esp. of health: *I feel quite restored* (*to health*) *after my holiday* **4** [(*to*)] to put back into a former position: *to restore him* (*to his old job*)*|restored the book to the shelf* **5** to put (old buildings, furniture, or works of art) back into the original state: *to restore an old oil painting|a ruined temple*

re·stor·er /rɪˈstɔːrəʳ‖rɪˈstorər/ *n* a person whose work is to RESTORE (5) things: *a picture restorer*

re·strain /rɪˈstreɪn/ *v* [T1 (*from*)] to control; hold back (from doing something): *If you can't restrain your dog* (*from biting the milkman*) *you must lock him up*

re·strained /rɪˈstreɪnd/ *adj* **1** (of a person or his behaviour) calm and controlled; not showing strong feelings —opposite **unrestrained** **2** not forceful or showy in style: *a room painted in restrained colours*

re·straint /rɪˈstreɪnt/ *n* **1** [U] *apprec* the quality of being RESTRAINED or RESTRAINing oneself: *I think you showed great restraint in not hitting him after what he said.|wage restraint* (=holding back from giving or asking for higher wages) **2** [C] *often derog* something that RESTRAINs: *He hates the restraints of life in a small town* **3** [U] the experience of being RESTRAINED: *You shouldn't keep birds in cages—they don't like restraint any more than we do* **4 be put/kept under restraint** *euph* (of a mad person) to be put/kept in a MENTAL hospital **5 without restraint** freely: *She told me without restraint all about her married life*

re·strict /rɪˈstrɪkt/ *v* [T1 (*to*)] to keep within limits; keep (to a certain limit): *to restrict oneself to* (*smoking*) *2 cigarettes a day|laws to restrict the sale of alcohol*

re·strict·ed /rɪˈstrɪktəd/ *adj* **1** [Wa5] controlled, esp. by law: *The sale of alcohol is restricted in Britain* **2** [Wa5; (*to*)] for a particular purpose, or for the use of a particular group only: *a restricted area, where only the army are allowed to go* **3** limited; not general: *The demand for fur boots is very restricted in the tropics* **4** *derog* narrow and shut in: *to live in a restricted space|*(fig.) *to lead a very restricted life*

re·stric·tion /rɪˈstrɪkʃən/ *n* **1** [U] the act of RESTRICTing or state of being RESTRICTED: *allowed to drink without restriction* **2** [C (*against*)] something that RESTRICTs, such as a law or rule: *a restriction against bringing dogs into the country|the many restrictions of army life*

re·stric·tive /rɪˈstrɪktɪv/ *adj* **1** *often derog* that RESTRICTs: *He finds life in a small town too restrictive* **2** [Wa5] (in grammar) that limits; DEFINING: *In "The man who came to dinner" the words "who came to dinner" are a restrictive* CLAUSE, *because they tell us which man is meant* —compare NONRESTRICTIVE —**~ly** *adv* —**~ness** *n* [U]

rest room /ˈ· ·/ *n AmE* a public LAVATORY (2), not in the street but in a hotel, restaurant, etc. —compare COMFORT STATION, PUBLIC CONVENIENCE

re·struc·ture /ˌriːˈstrʌktʃəʳ/ *v* [T1] to arrange (a system or organization) in a new way; give a new STRUCTURE to: *to restructure the ship-building industry*

rest with *v prep* [T1 *no pass.*] to be the responsibility of: *The decision rests with you.|The fate of these prisoners rests with the judge*

re·sult[1] /rɪˈzʌlt/ *v* [I∅] to happen as an effect or RESULT[2] (1): *If the police leave, disorder will result*

result[2] *n* **1** [C;U] what happens because of an action or event: *His illness is a/the result of bad food/of living in a cave* **2** [C;U] (a) noticeable good effect: *I've been trying to open the door, but without* (*much*) *result so far* **3** [C *usu. pl.*] (the news of) a person's or team's success or failure in an examination, sports match, etc.: *heard the football results on the radio|The result* (*of the match*) *was 1–0 to England.|How did you get on in the examination, and when will you know your results?* **4** [C] *BrE sl* (esp. in football) a win: *If we don't get a result tonight we'll be put down into a lower division* **5** [C] the answer to a sum: *Let's both add it up and see if we get the same result* **6 as a result (of)** *fml* because (of); therefore: *He was late as a result of the snow* **7 with the result that** *fml* so that: *I was in the bath,* *with the result that I didn't hear the telephone*

re·sul·tant /rɪ'zʌltənt/ *adj* [Wa5;A] happening as an effect, esp. as the total effect of many causes: *The O'Learys are fighting upstairs and the Cohens are performing a concert downstairs and the resultant noise is beyond anything*

result from *v prep* [T1,4: *no pass.*] to be the RESULT (1) of; happen because of: *His illness resulted from bad food|from living in a cave*

result in *v prep* [T1;V4a: *no pass.*] to have as a RESULT (1); cause: *The accident resulted in the death of 2 passengers|in 2 passengers dying*

re·sume /rɪ'zjuːm‖rɪ'zuːm/ *v fml* **1** [I∅;T1,4] to begin (something, or doing something) again after a pause: *We resumed our journey after a short rest.|We'll stop now and resume (working) at 2 o'clock* **2** [T1] to take again: *to resume one's seat*

ré·su·mé /'rezjʊmeɪ, 'reɪ-‖ˌrezʊ'meɪ (*Fr* rezyme)/ *n Fr* **1** a shortened form of a speech, book, etc.; SUMMARY **2** *esp. AmE* CURRICULUM VITAE

re·sump·tion /rɪ'zʌmpʃən/ *n* [U] the act of resuming (RESUME (1)): *the resumption of business after a holiday*

re·sur·face /ˌriː'sɜːfɨs‖-ɜr-/ *v* **1** [T1] to put a new surface on (a road) **2** [I∅] (of an undersea ship (SUBMARINE)) to come back to the surface

re·sur·gence /rɪ'sɜːdʒəns‖-ɜr-/ *n* [S;U] (esp. of ideas, beliefs, etc.) a return to power, life, and activity: (*a*) *resurgence of nationalist feeling*

re·sur·gent /rɪ'sɜːdʒənt‖-ɜr-/ *adj* [Wa5;A;(B)] in a state of RESURGENCE: *our resurgent hopes of victory*

res·ur·rect /ˌrezə'rekt/ *v* [T1] **1** to bring back into use, fashion, or attention: *to resurrect an old custom* **2** *humor* to dig up again: *a dog resurrecting a buried bone* **3** *rare* to bring back to life

res·ur·rec·tion /ˌrezə'rekʃən/ *n* **1** [U] renewal (of life, hope, etc.) **2** [*the*+R] (*often cap.*) (in Christian belief) the rising from the grave of all dead people at the end of the world: *"I believe in . . . the resurrection of the body, and the life everlasting"* (The CREED)

Resurrection *n* [*the*+R] the rising of Christ from his grave, which is remembered with ceremonies on EASTER Sunday

re·sus·ci·tate /rɪ'sʌsɨteɪt/ *v* [T1] to bring (a creature that is almost dead) back to life: *to try to resuscitate a drowned man*|(fig.) *to resuscitate old ideas* —**-tation** /rɪˌsʌsɨ'teɪʃən/ *n* [U]: *attempts at resuscitation*

re·tail¹ /'riːteɪl/ *v* [T1] *tech* to sell by RETAIL²: *to keep a little shop, and retail tobacco*

retail² *n* [U] the sale of goods in shops to CUSTOMERS, for their own use and not for resale: *the retail of goods|retail prices|a small retail business* —compare WHOLESALE

retail³ *adv* [Wa5] by RETAIL²; from a RETAILER: *to buy it retail*

re·tail⁴ /rɪ'teɪl/ *v* [T1] *fml* to pass on (amusing or damaging news) to other people

retail at /'riːteɪl/ *v prep* [T1 *no pass.*] to be sold at (a RETAIL² price): *These socks retail at $5 a pair*

re·tail·er /'riːteɪləʳ/ *n* someone who sells things by RETAIL²; shopkeeper

re·tain /rɪ'teɪn/ *v* [T1] **1** to keep possession of; avoid losing: *to retain one's balance|a memory that retains facts* —see also RETENTION **2** to hold in place: *built a wall to retain the water of the lake* **3** *law* to employ (a lawyer) to act for one, by paying in advance

re·tain·er /rɪ'teɪnəʳ/ *n* **1** (in former times) a servant, esp. one who has always worked for a particular person or family: *He called his old retainer and told him to bring in the wine* **2** *law* a sum of money paid to a lawyer (in Britain, to a BARRISTER) for his advice and help

re·take¹ /ˌriː'teɪk/ *v* **-took** /'tʊk/, **-taken** /'teɪkən/ [T1] **1** to regain possession of (a place lost in war): *to retake the city after severe fighting* **2** to photograph again

re·take² /'riːteɪk/ *n* a second photograph, esp. of a scene in cinema or television

re·tal·i·ate /rɪ'tælieɪt/ *v* [I∅ (*against, by*)] to pay back evil with evil: *Mary kicked Susan, and Susan retaliated (against her) (by biting)*

re·tal·i·a·tion /rɪˌtæli'eɪʃən/ *n* [U] the action of retaliating (RETALIATE)

re·tal·i·a·to·ry /rɪ'tæliətəri‖-tori/ also **re·tal·i·a·tive** /rɪ'tæliətɪv‖rɪ'tæli-eɪtɪv/— *adj* [Wa5] (of an action) that RETALIATEs

re·tard /rɪ'tɑːd‖-ɑrd/ *v* [T1] *esp. fml or tech* to make slow; cause to happen later: *Cold weather retards the growth of the crops* —**~ation** /ˌriːtɑː'deɪʃən‖-ɑr-/ *n* [U]

re·tard·ed /rɪ'tɑːdɨd‖-ɑr-/ *adj* (of a child) slower in development than others: *Lucy is very retarded and can't read yet*

retch /retʃ/ *v* [I∅] to try to be sick (VOMIT) but without success

retd *written abbrev. for:* RETIRED

re·tell /ˌriː'tel/ *v* **-told** /'təʊld/ [T1] to tell (a story) again in a new way or different language: *German fairy stories retold in English*

re·ten·tion /rɪ'tenʃən/ *n* [U] the state or action of RETAINing: **Retention of urine** *is the inability to pass liquid waste matter out of the body*

re·ten·tive /rɪ'tentɪv/ *adj* able to RETAIN things, esp. facts in the mind: *a very retentive memory* —**~ly** *adv* —**~ness** *n* [U]

re·think¹ /ˌriː'θɪŋk/ *v* **-thought** /'θɔːt/ [I∅;T1] to think again; reconsider (a subject): *We'd better rethink the whole plan.|If that's what he wants, he'll have to rethink*

re·think² /'riːˌθɪŋk/ *n* [S] *not fml* an act of RETHINKing: *have a rethink on this matter*

ret·i·cence /'retɨsəns/ *n* [C *usu. sing.*;U] a case or the quality of being RETICENT: *felt a certain/some reticence about telling the child the truth*

ret·i·cent /'retɨsənt/ *adj* (of a person or his behaviour) silent; not saying as much as is known or felt: *was reticent about the reasons for the quarrel* —**~ly** *adv*

re·tic·u·lated /rɪ'tɪkjʊleɪtɨd‖-kjə-/ *adj* [Wa5] *tech* forming or covered with a netlike pattern of squares and lines

re·tic·u·la·tion /rɪˌtɪkjʊ'leɪʃən‖-kjə-/ *n* [C *often pl.*; U] *tech* (a) netlike pattern: *a snake covered with beautiful orange and black reticulations*

ret·i·cule /'retɪkjuːl/ *n old use or humor* a small handbag

ret·i·na /'retɨnə/ *n* **-nas** *or* **-nae** /niː/ the light-sensitive area of nerve-endings at the back of the eye —see picture at EYE¹

ret·i·nue /'retɪnjuː‖-nuː/ *n* [GC] a group of servants and followers travelling with an important person: *The King's retinue consists of noble lords.|The President's retinue all carry guns*

re·tire /rɪ'taɪəʳ/ *v* **1** [I∅ (*from, to*)] to go away (to a quiet place): *to retire to one's own room* **2** [I∅] (esp. of an army) to go back, but without being forced to: *Our armies have retired to form themselves into new groups before attacking again.|He retired* (=from the cricket match) *after making 150 runs* —compare RETREAT **3** [I∅] *fml* to go to bed: *My dear, let us retire early tonight* **4** [I∅;T1] to (cause to) stop working at one's job, profession, etc., usu. because of age: *My father retired at the age of 60* **5** **retire into oneself** to become silent because one is thinking

re·tired /rɪ'taɪəd‖-ərd/ *adj* **1** [Wa5] (of a person) having stopped working, usu. because of age: *a* *retired general* **2** (of a place) far from crowds and large towns: *They live in a very retired spot; you'll never find it*

re·tire·ment /rɪ'taɪəmənt‖-ər-/ *n* **1** [C;U] a case or the act of retiring (RETIRE (4)): *His employers gave him a gold watch on his retirement.|We've had 2 retirements in our office this year* **2** [U] the period after one has RETIRED (4): *to write a book during one's retirement*

re·tir·ing /rɪ'taɪərɪŋ/ *adj* **1** [B] (typical of a person) that likes to avoid the company of others: *Jane is a retiring girl/has a retiring nature, and hates parties* **2** [Wa5;A] at which one RETIREs (4) (in the phr. **retiring age**): *What's the retiring age for miners?*

re·tort[1] /rɪ'tɔːt‖-ɔrt/ *v* [T5] (*used with the actual words spoken*) to make a RETORT[2]: *"Of course not," she retorted.|He retorted that it was all my fault* —see ANSWER (USAGE)

retort[2] *n* a quick, rather angry, and often amusing answer

retort[3] *n* a bottle with a long narrow bent neck, used for heating chemicals

re·touch /ˌriː'tʌtʃ/ *v* [T1] to improve (a picture or photograph) by adding small strokes with a brush or pencil

re·trace /rɪ'treɪs, riː-/ *v* [T1] **1** to go over again; go back over: *to retrace past events in one's mind* **2** **retrace one's steps** to go back in the direction from which one came

re·tract /rɪ'trækt/ *v* [IØ;T1] **1** to (cause to) draw back or in: *retract the wheels of an aircraft|A cat can retract its* CLAWs, *but a dog can't* **2** to take back (WITHDRAW) (a statement or offer that one has made): *Even when he was threatened with death, the political prisoner refused to retract* (*his speeches against the government*)

re·trac·ta·ble /rɪ'træktəbəl/ *adj* [Wa5] **1** (esp. of wheels) that can be RETRACTed (1): *an aircraft with retractable wheels* **2** (of a statement, offer, etc.) that can be RETRACTed (2)

re·trac·tile /rɪ'træktaɪl‖-tl/ *adj* [Wa5] that can be RETRACTed (1): *retractile* CLAWs

re·trac·tion /rɪ'trækʃən/ *n* **1** [U] the act of RETRACTing (1) **2** [C;U] a case or the act of RETRACTing (2): *The prisoner has written and signed a retraction of what he said*

re·tread[1] /ˌriː'tred/ *AmE infml* also **recap**; *BrE* also **remould**— *v* [T1] to renew the rubber covering (TREAD) on the bare surface of (a worn tyre)

re·tread[2] /'riːtred/ *AmE infml* also **recap**; *BrE* also **remould**— *n* a tyre that has been RETREADed[1]

re·treat[1] /rɪ'triːt/ *n* **1** [C;U: (*from, to*)] (an act of) RETREATing[2]: *Napoleon's retreat from Moscow* **2** [*the*+R] a military signal for RETREATing[2] (1) (often in the phr. **sound the retreat**=to give this signal, as by beating a drum) **3** [C] a place into which one can go for peace and safety **4** [C;U] (in the ROMAN CATHOLIC religion) (the practice of spending) a period of prayer, thought, and religious study, with a group of other Christians: *went into retreat|spent a few days in retreat* **5** **beat a retreat** to RETREAT[2], esp. quickly so as to avoid something unpleasant: *When they saw the teacher coming, they beat a hasty retreat* **6** **in full retreat** running away **7** **make good one's retreat** to RETREAT[2] successfully from danger

retreat[2] *v* **1** [IØ (*from, to*)] (esp. of an army) to move back; go back, esp. when forced to do so: *The defeated army had to retreat hastily* (*from the field of battle to the coast*) —compare RETIRE **2** [L9 esp. *from* and/or *to*] to go away; escape (from something unpleasant): *to retreat to a warmer country in winter*

re·trench /rɪ'trentʃ/ *v* [IØ;T1] *fml* to arrange to lessen (one's spending): *My dear, we must unfortunately retrench* (*our* EXPENSEs); *let us sell the horses* —**~ment** [C;U]: *to make a few retrenchments| Retrenchment will be necessary*

re·tri·al /ˌriː'traɪəl/ *n* an act of trying a law case again; new trial

ret·ri·bu·tion /ˌretrɨ'bjuːʃən/ *n* [S;U: (*for*)] *fml* (a) deserved punishment: *Do evil actions bring retribution after death?|If you don't give up drugs you will suffer a terrible retribution*

re·trib·u·tive /rɪ'trɪbjʊtɪv‖-bjə-/ *adj* [Wa5] *fml* done as a deserved punishment: *took retributive action against the men who threw the bomb*

re·triev·al /rɪ'triːvəl/ *n* [U] **1** the act of retrieving (RETRIEVE): *the retrieval of his hat/of his mistake* **2** **beyond/past retrieval** impossible to get back or put right

retrieval sys·tem /·'·· ˌ··/ *n tech* any of various methods of finding stored information when it is needed

re·trieve /rɪ'triːv/ *v* **1** [T1 (*from*)] to regain; find and bring back: *to retrieve the bag I left in the train|* (fig.) *to retrieve a poor girl from moral ruin* **2** [T1] to put right; make up for (a mistake, loss, defeat, etc.) **3** [IØ;T1] (of a RETRIEVER) to bring back (shot birds): *a dog that retrieves well* **4** **retrieve one's fortunes** to get money again after losing it by bad luck: *When he lost his job he tried to retrieve his fortunes by robbing a bank* —**retrievable** *adj*

re·triev·er /rɪ'triːvəʳ/ *n* any of several types of specially bred middle-sized hunting dog, trained to bring back shot birds

ret·ro- /'retrəʊ, 'retrə/ *prefix* [*n*→*n*;*v*→*v*;*adj*→*adj*] **1** back towards the past: RETROACTIVE|RETROSPECT **2** back towards an earlier and worse state: RETROGRESS|RETROGRADE **3** backwards: RETROFLEX **4** causing backward pressure: RETRO-ROCKET

ret·ro·ac·tive /ˌretrəʊ'æktɪv/ *adj* [Wa5] (esp. of a law) having effect on the past as well as on the future: *a retroactive pay increase* —**~ly** *adv*

ret·ro·flex /'retrəfleks/ also **ret·ro·flexed** /-flekst/— *adj* [Wa5] *tech* (of a speech sound) made with the point (TIP) of the tongue curled upwards and backwards

ret·ro·grade /'retrəgreɪd/ *adj* moving back towards an earlier and worse state

ret·ro·gress /ˌretrə'gres/ *v* [IØ (*to*)] *esp. fml or tech* to go back (to an earlier and worse state) —**~ion** /retrə'greʃən/ *n* [U]

ret·ro·gres·sive /ˌretrə'gresɪv/ *adj esp. fml or tech* showing a return to an earlier and worse state: *retrogressive childish behaviour in old people* —**~ly** *adv*

retro-rock·et /'retrəʊ ˌrɒkɨt‖-ˌrɑ-/ *n* a ROCKET that is used for slowing down an aircraft or SPACECRAFT

ret·ro·spect /'retrəspekt/ *n* [U] the act of looking back towards the past (in the phr. **in retrospect**): *One's school life seems happier in retrospect than in reality*

ret·ro·spec·tion /ˌretrə'spekʃən/ *n* [U] thought about the past: *to enjoy the pleasures of retrospection*

retro·spec·tive /ˌretrə'spektɪv/ *adj* [Wa5] **1** concerned with the past: *retrospective thoughts|a retrospective* EXHIBITION *of Lowry's paintings* (=a show of paintings from the earliest stages of his work up to the time of his death **2** (esp. of a law) RETROACTIVE —**~ly** *adv*

re·trous·sé /rə'truːseɪ‖rəˌtruː'seɪ (*Fr* rətruse)/ *adj Fr* (of a nose) turned back and up at the lower end

ret·ro·ver·sion /ˌretrəʊ'vɜːʃən‖-'vɜrʒən/ *n* [U] *tech* the state of being turned back; pointing backwards

ret·si·na /ret'siːnə/ *n* [U] a type of Greek wine that

tastes of the juice (RESIN) of certain trees

re·turn¹ /rɪˈtɜːn‖-ɜrn/ *v* **1** [I∅ (*from, to*)] to come or go back: *to return home|to return to London|What time does your husband return (from work)?* **2** [D1 (*to*);T1] to give or send back: *Don't forget to return (me) my keys!|We returned the empty bottles (to the shop)* **3** [I∅] to happen again: *Spring will soon return* **4** [T5] (*used with the actual words spoken*) to answer: *"Yes, if you like!" she returned, smiling* **5** [T1] (of a place) to elect (someone) as a Member of Parliament or to a political position: *A* COMMUNIST *has been returned as member for Cheltenham* **6** [T1;X7] (of the 12 people (JURY) who decide questions of fact in a lawcourt) **a** to give (a judgment=VERDICT): *They returned a* VERDICT *of "Not Guilty"* **b** to judge (someone) to be: *They returned the prisoner guilty (of murder)* **7** [T1] to bring in as a profit: *These shares return a good rate of interest* **8** [T1] to state officially (an amount of money) esp. in answer to a demand: *He returned his earnings as £3,000 on the tax declaration.|Don't forget to return the details of what you spend* **9 return a favour** to do a kind action in return for another **10 return thanks** *fml* to say that one is grateful, as in a speech or a prayer

return² *n* **1** [C (*from, to*)] an act of RETURNing¹ (1): *We look forward to your return (from China).|On his return he found her asleep.|Keep some food to eat on the return journey* **2** [U] the act of RETURNing¹ (2) something: *The library are demanding the return of the books* **3** [C+*of*] a case of happening again: *the return of spring|There has been a return of fever now that the weather is hot* **4** [C *often pl.*] a sum of money RETURNed² (7) as a profit: *These shares bring in a good return|good returns* **5** [C] an official statement or set of figures RETURNed¹ (8): *entered the money for writing this dictionary on her tax return* **6** [C] *not fml* a RETURN³ ticket **7 by return (of post)** by the next post: *Please answer his letter by return* **8 in return (for)** in exchange (for); in payment (for): *give her some roses in return for her kindness*

return³ (*AmE* **round-trip**)— *adj* [Wa5] *BrE* (of a ticket or its cost) for a trip from one place to another and back again: *The price is £1 single and £1.80 return*

re·tur·na·ble /rɪˈtɜːnəbəl‖-ɜr-/ *adj* [Wa5] **1** that must be given or sent back **2** that can be given or sent back, often for reuse: *returnable bottles*

returning of·fi·cer /·ˈ·· ˌ···/ *n* (in Britain) the official in each town or area who arranges an election to Parliament and gives out the result

return match /·ˌ· ˈ·/ *n* a second game played between 2 teams

re·turns /rɪˈtɜːnz‖-ɜr-/ *n* [P9] RETURNs² (3) of one's birthday; more birthdays (in the phr. **Many happy returns (of the day)!**, used as a birthday greeting)

return to *v prep* **1** [D1] to put (something) back (somewhere): *He returned the gun to his pocket* **2** [T1] to come or go back to (a former or usual state): *The temperature soon returned to the seasonal average* **3** [T1] to talk about again: *Let's return to the subject of camels*

re·u·ni·on /riːˈjuːnɪən/ *n* **1** [U] the state of being together again **2** [C] a meeting of friends or fellow-workers after a separation: *to hold a reunion of former students of the college*

re·u·nite /ˌriːjuːˈnaɪt/ *v* [Wv5;I∅;T1: (*with*)] to (cause to) come or join together again: *George and Mary are reunited at last.|Do you think the 2 parts of Ireland will reunite?*

re·use /ˌriːˈjuːz/ *v* [T1] to use again or RECYCLE —**reusable** *adj*

rev¹ /rev/ *n infml* REVOLUTION (4): *Play these song records at 33⅓ revs per minute* (r.p.m.)

rev² *v* **-vv-** [T1 (UP)] *infml* to increase the speed of (an engine): *Don't rev (up) your engine so loudly—you'll wake the baby* —see also REV UP

Rev¹ *n* [*the*+R;N;(A)] *BrE sl* REVEREND: *Ask the Rev about that.|Good morning, Rev!*

Rev² *written abbrev for:* REVEREND: *the Rev D. Macleod*

re·val·ue /riːˈvæljuː/ *v* [T1] **1** to find or say again the value of: *to revalue our possessions for insurance purposes* **2** to make the value of (money) more, esp. in relation to gold: *to revalue the dollar* —compare DEVALUE —**-uation** /riːˌvæljuːˈeɪʃən/ *n* [U;(C)]

re·vamp /riːˈvæmp/ *v* [T1] *infml* to mend and improve; give a new form to (something old): *to revamp an old play|We should revamp our whole method of production*

re·veal /rɪˈviːl/ *v* **1** [T1] to allow to be seen: *a dress that reveals part of her stomach|The curtains opened, to reveal a darkened stage* **2** [T1 (*as*), 5a;X (*to be*) 1, (*to be*) 7] (*not used with actual spoken words*) to make known (to be): *to reveal a secret|She suddenly revealed (the fact) that she was not married.|These letters reveal him as|reveal him to be an honest man*

revealed re·li·gion /·ˌ· ·ˈ··/ *n* [U] religious truth that is said to have been REVEALed (2) by God

re·veal·ing /rɪˈviːlɪŋ/ *adj* **1** allowing parts to be seen which are usually kept covered: *a very revealing dress* **2** full of meaning; giving some knowledge of facts which had been unknown: *revealing remarks which tell me a lot about the person who made them*

re·veil·le /rɪˈvæli‖ˈrevəli/ *n* [(*the*) R] the music played as a signal to waken soldiers in the morning: *Sound (the) reveille!*

rev·el¹ /ˈrevəl/ *v* **-ll-** (*AmE* **-l-**) [I∅] *old use or humor* to pass the time in dancing, feasting, etc.: *They were drinking and revelling all night* —**~ler** (*AmE* **~er**)— *n*: *a crowd of noisy revellers*

revel² *n* [C *often pl. with sing. meaning*;(U)] *old use or humor* a wild noisy party; REVELling¹

rev·e·la·tion /ˌrevəˈleɪʃən/ *n* **1** [U (*of*)] the making known (of something secret): *truths known by revelation* **2** [C; *the*+C5] a (surprising) fact that is made known: *We listened to her strange revelations about her past.|The revelation that the world is round surprised them*

Revelation also **Rev·e·la·tions** /ˌrevəˈleɪʃənz/— *n* [R] the last book of the Christian Bible, said to have been written by SAINT John

revel in *v prep* [T1,4] to enjoy greatly: *She revels in tennis|in meeting new friends*

rev·el·ry /ˈrevəlri/ *n* [U *often pl. with sing. meaning*] wild noisy dancing and feasting; REVELling¹

re·venge¹ /rɪˈvendʒ/ *v* [T1] **1** to do something in REVENGE² for (some harm done to oneself): *to revenge a defeat|an injustice* **2** to do something in REVENGE² for harm done to: *Hamlet revenged his dead father* (=killed the man who killed him)

USAGE **Avenge** has more of the idea of a deserved though unofficial punishment than **revenge**, which just means hurting someone who has harmed one. They have the same pattern: *He* **avenged/revenged** *himself on the murderer.|He* **avenged/revenged** *(the murder of) his sister.*

revenge² *n* [S;U: (*for, on*)] **1** (a) punishment given to someone in return for harm done to oneself: *angry thoughts of revenge|Hamlet wanted revenge for his father's murder.|I'll have my revenge on you for what you did.|They took a terrible revenge on the people of the village* **2 in/out of revenge (for)** as a punishment (for harm done to oneself): *We bombed their village in revenge for their attack on ours* **3 give someone his revenge** (in sport) to play another game against a defeated opponent —**~ful**

adj: *revengeful thoughts* —**~fully** *adv* —**~fulness** *n* [U]

revenge on *v prep* [D1 (*for*) *often pass.*] to give (oneself) REVENGE² on (someone who has harmed one): *Hamlet revenged himself on his father's murderer.|I'll be revenged on the whole lot of you for this!*

rev·e·nue /ˈrevɪ̈njuː‖-nuː/ *n* [U *sometimes pl. with sing. meaning*] income, esp. that which the government receives as tax

revenue of·fi·cer /ˈ··· ˌ···/ *n* CUSTOMS OFFICER

revenue tar·iff /ˈ··· ˌ··/ also **revenue tax** /ˈ··· ˌ·/— *n* a tax intended to increase a country's income, rather than to protect its trade —compare PROTECTIVE TARIFF

re·ver·be·rant /rɪˈvɜːbərənt‖-ɜr-/ *adj lit* reverberating (REVERBERATE)

re·ver·be·rate /rɪˈvɜːbəreɪt‖-ɜr-/ *v* [IØ] (of sound) to be thrown back again and again: ECHO² (1) repeatedly: *The thunder reverberated across the valley*

re·ver·be·ra·tion /rɪˌvɜːbəˈreɪʃən‖-ɜr-/ *n* [U;C *usu. pl.*] (a) sound heard again and again: *The reverberation(s) of the shot died away slowly*

re·vere /rɪˈvɪəʳ/ *v* [Wv5;T1] *fml* to give great respect and admiration to: *her revered father*

rev·e·rence¹ /ˈrevərəns/ *n* **1** [S;U: (*for*)] great respect and admiration mixed with love: *They hold him in great reverence/look on him with reverence.|They all have/show (a certain) reverence for her* **2** [C] *old use* a sign of respect, such as a CURTSY **3** [C;N:9] *old use, humor, or IrE* (the title used when speaking to or of a priest, in the phrs. **his reverence; your reverence(s); their reverences**): *Have some more wine, your reverence!*

reverence² *v* [T1] REVERE: *People still reverence the name of Mahatma Gandhi*

rev·e·rend /ˈrevərənd/ *adj* [A] *fml* **1** worthy of great respect; REVERED: *a reverend old gentleman with white hair* **2** [Wa5] being a priest: *A reverend gentleman is here to see you, sir!*

Reverend *n* [A;N; (*the*+R)] (a title of respect for) a religious person of importance: *(The) Reverend Donald Jones has moved to a new church.|When will the new church be finished, Reverend?|Will the* NUNS *accept the changes, Reverend Mother?|Ask the Reverend about that*

rev·e·rent /ˈrevərənt/ *adj* having or showing a feeling of REVERENCE¹ (1): *reverent behaviour* —**~ly** *adv*

rev·e·ren·tial /ˌrevəˈrenʃəl/ *adj* respectful; expressing REVERENCE¹ (1): *a reverential movement of the head* —**~ly** *adv*

rev·e·rie /ˈrevəri/ *n* **1** [U;C: (*about*)] (a state or occasion of) pleasant thoughts and dreams while awake: *She fell into a reverie about the past.|He was sunk in reverie and did not hear me* **2** [C] a piece of quiet thoughtful music

re·vers /rɪˈvɪəʳ/ *n* **-vers** /ˈvɪəz‖ˈvɪərz/ [*usu. pl.*] a part of a coat or dress turned back at the neck to show the inside, which may be a different colour from the rest —compare LAPEL

re·vers·al /rɪˈvɜːsəl‖-ɜr-/ *n* [C;U: (*of*)] (a case of) being REVERSED²: *He suffered a reversal of fortune and lost all his money*

re·verse¹ /rɪˈvɜːs‖-ɜrs/ *adj* [Wa5;A;(B (*to*))] **1** opposite in position; back; being the REVERSE³ (1,4): *the reverse side of the cloth* **2 in reverse order** from the end to the beginning: *We could begin at Z and write the dictionary in reverse order*

reverse² *v* **1** [IØ;T1] **a** to cause (a vehicle) to go backwards: *He reversed the car through the gate* **b** (of a vehicle) to go backwards: *The car reversed through the gate* **2** [IØ] (in dancing) to turn round in the opposite direction: *When I try to reverse, she steps on my toes* **3** [T1] to turn (something) over, so as to show the back: *She reversed the sheet of paper* **4** [T1] to change (a decision or judgment) to the opposite: *He reversed the judgment and set the prisoner free after all* **5** [T1] to change round (proper order or positions): *Shall we reverse the order and put Z at the beginning of this dictionary?* **6** [usu. imper.] **reverse arms** (of a soldier) to point one's gun downwards **7 reverse the charges** *AmE* also **call collect**— to make a telephone call to be paid for by the person receiving it —**reversible** *adj*: *This coat is reversible. You can wear it inside out* —**reversibility** /rɪˌvɜːsəˈbɪlɪ̈ti‖rɪˌvɜr-/ *n* [U]

reverse³ *n* **1** [*the*+U] the opposite in position; the back: *the reverse of the cloth* **2** [*the*+U (*of*)] the opposite; the other way round: *Yes, Edwin is afraid of Angela, but the reverse is also true: Angela is afraid of Edwin.|He did the reverse of what we expected: instead of being angry, he bought us a drink* **3** [C] a defeat or change for the worse: *The failure of his business was a serious reverse for him.|After several reverses the enemy was forced to fall back* **4** [*the*+U] the side (of a coin) that does not show the ruler's head: *The 10 pence piece has a lion on the reverse* —opposite **obverse** **5** [U] the position of the controls that causes backward movement, such as the REVERSE GEAR in a car: *Put the car into reverse*

reverse gear /·ˌ· ˈ·/ *n* [C;U] the GEAR (=arrangement that controls the speed and direction of the vehicle's movement without a change in the engine speed) for making a car go backwards: *My car has 4 forward* GEAR*s and a reverse gear.|How do you change into reverse gear in this car?*

re·ver·sion /rɪˈvɜːʃən‖rɪˈvɜrʒən/ *n* **1** [U+*to*] return to (a former condition or habit, or a former subject of conversation): *reversion to bad habits* **2** [U+*to*] *law* the REVERTing of property TO (an owner) **3** [C] *law* a right to own property in the future, on the death of the present owner

re·ver·sion·a·ry /rɪˈvɜːʃənəri‖rɪˈvɜrʒəneri/ *adj* [Wa5] *law* concerning a REVERSION (3): *His son has a reversionary right to the land*

re·vert to /rɪˈvɜːt‖-ɜrt/ *v prep* **1** [T1,4] to go back to (a former condition or habit): *He's stopped taking drugs now, but he may revert to taking them again* **2** [T1] to talk about again; go back to (a former subject of conversation): *Reverting to your earlier remark about camels, do you think . . ?* **3** [T1] *law* (of property) to go back to (an owner): *When he dies his land will revert to the state* **4 revert to type** to go back to the original state or pattern: *Mary tried to become an actress but she soon reverted to type and became a farmer like her father*

re·vet·ment /rɪˈvetmənt/ *n tech* a surface of stone or other building material added for strength to a wall that holds back loose earth, water, etc.

re·view¹ /rɪˈvjuː/ *n* **1** [C] an act of REVIEWing² (1): *After a careful review of political events he decided not to vote at all* **2** [C] a grand show of the armed forces, in the presence of a king or an important general: *held a naval review* **3** [C] **a** a regularly appearing magazine that contains articles giving judgments on new books, plays, and public events: *The New York Review of Books* **b** an article of the kind printed in this sort of magazine: *I hope your new book gets good reviews* **4** [U] the practice of REVIEWing² (3): *A* **review copy** *of a book is one that is sent to a magazine for review/for review purposes* **5 be/come under review** to be/start to be considered and judged: *The State medical service has been very much under review recently*

review² *v* **1** [T1] to consider and judge (an event or state of affairs); go over again in the mind: *He reviewed the whole of his past life* **2** [T1] to hold a REVIEW¹ (2) of (armed forces) **3** [T1;IØ] **a** to write a REVIEW[1] (3b) of (a play, book, etc.): *The play was well reviewed* (= praised) **b** to write REVIEWS[1] (3b): *Susan has been doing some reviewing for "The Times"* **4** [T1;I∅] *AmE* REVISE[1] (3)

re·view·er /rɪˈvjuːəʳ/ *n* a person who writes REVIEWS[1] (3b)

re·vile /rɪˈvaɪl/ *v* [T1] *fml* to curse; speak very strongly and angrily to or of: *a newspaper article reviling the Government* —**reviler** *n*

re·vise[1] /rɪˈvaɪz/ *v* **1** [T1] to read through (a piece of writing) carefully, making improvements and putting mistakes right **2** [T1] to change (opinions, intentions, etc.) because of new information or more thought: *I can see I'll have to revise my ideas about Tom—he's really quite clever after all* **3** [T1; I∅] *BrE* to study again (lessons already learnt): *I must revise for the examination.|to revise my history notes* —**reviser** *n*

revise[2] *n tech* (in printing) a printed page in which the mistakes have been put right

Revised Ver·sion /·,· ˈ··/ *n* [*the*+R] the form of the English Bible made in Britain in 1870–84 as a REVISION (2) of the AUTHORIZED VERSION

re·vi·sion /rɪˈvɪʒən/ *n* **1** [C;U] (an act of) revising (REVISE[1] (1)): *That book needs a lot of revision/has already had 3 revisions* **2** [C] a piece of writing that has been REVISED[1] (1) **3** [U] *BrE* the work of studying again lessons already learnt: *did some revision for the examination*

re·vi·sion·is·m /rɪˈvɪʒənɪzəm/ *n* [U] *often derog* any political movement of the LEFT[2] (3) that questions the main beliefs of an already existing MARXIST political system —**-t** *adj, n*: *revisionist opinions|He became a revisionist*

re·vi·tal·ize, -ise /riːˈvaɪtəl-aɪz/ *v* [T1] to put new strength or power into —**-ization** /riː,vaɪtəl-aɪˈzeɪʃən‖-tələ-/ *n* [U]

re·vi·val /rɪˈvaɪvəl/ *n* **1** [C;U: 9 esp. *of*] (a) rebirth or renewal; reviving or being REVIVED: *There has been a/some revival of interest in ancient music* **2** [C] a performance of an old play after many years **3** [C] a public religious meeting, with music, famous speakers, etc., intended to waken and increase people's interest in Christianity: *to play the drum at a revival (meeting)*

re·vi·val·ist /rɪˈvaɪvəlɪ̈st/ *n* a person who holds REVIVAL (3) meetings

Revival of Learn·ing /·,·· · ˈ··/ *n* [*the*+R] RENAISSANCE

re·vive /rɪˈvaɪv/ *v* **1** [I∅;T1] to make or become conscious or healthy again: *The fresh air soon revived him.|That rose will revive if you water it* **2** [I∅;T1] to bring or come back into use or existence: *to revive an old custom|Interest in ancient music has revived recently* **3** [T1] to perform (an old play) again after many years

re·viv·i·fy /riːˈvɪvɪ̈faɪ/ *v* [T1] *fml* to give new life and health to

rev·o·ca·ble /ˈrevəkəbəl/ *adj* [Wa5] *rare* that can be REVOKED (1) —opposite **irrevocable**

rev·o·ca·tion /,revəˈkeɪʃən/ *n* [C;U] (an act of) revoking (REVOKE (1)): *the revocation of an order*

re·voke /rɪˈvəʊk/ *v* **1** [T1] to put an end to (a law, decision, permission, etc.); CANCEL (2): *to revoke an order* **2** [I∅] (in card games such as BRIDGE) to break the rules by playing a card of the wrong kind (SUIT) when one has a card of the right kind

re·volt[1] /rɪˈvəʊlt/ *v* **1** [I∅ (*against*)] to act violently against those in power so as to take power from them: *The people revolted against the cruel king* **2** [T1 *often pass.*] to shock; cause (someone) to feel violent dislike and sickness: *Such cruelty revolted him* —see also REVULSION (2) **3** [L9 esp. *at, from, against*] to feel sick and shocked (at); turn (from, against) with violent dislike: *All civilized people will revolt at/from/against this terrible crime*

revolt[2] *n* [C;U: (*against*)] **1** (an example of) the act of REVOLTing[1] (1): *2 revolts in 3 years|The whole nation is in (a state of) revolt* **2 in revolt a** in the act of REVOLTing[1] (1) **b** feeling sick and shocked: *She turned away in revolt from the nasty old man*

re·volt·ing /rɪˈvəʊltɪŋ/ *adj* [(*to*)] very nasty: *a revolting smell of bad eggs|Their sexual practices seemed revolting to her* —**~ly** *adv*: *Your socks are revoltingly dirty*

rev·o·lu·tion /,revəˈluːʃən/ *n* **1** [C;U] (a time of) great social change, esp. the changing of a ruler and/or political system by force: *After a revolution, things can never be the same again.|Nothing less than revolution will satisfy us!* **2** [C (*in*)] a complete change (in ways of thinking or acting): *The invention of air travel caused a revolution in our way of living* **3** [C;U] (one complete) circular movement round a fixed point: *the revolution of the moon round the earth|The earth makes one revolution round the sun each year* —see also REVOLVE (1) **4** [C] also (*infml*) **rev**— (in a machine) one complete circular movement on a central point, as of a wheel: *a speed of 100 revolutions/revs per minute* —see also REVOLVE (1)

rev·o·lu·tion·a·ry[1] /,revəˈluːʃənəri‖-ʃəneri/ *adj* **1** [Wa5;A] connected with (a) REVOLUTION (1): *a revolutionary army|suffered for his revolutionary principles* **2** [B] completely new and different; being a REVOLUTION (2): *a revolutionary new way of growing rice*

revolutionary[2] *n* a person who favours and tries to bring about a REVOLUTION (1): *The revolutionaries are attacking the palace*

rev·o·lu·tion·ize, -ise /,revəˈluːʃənaɪz/ *v* [T1] **1** to cause a complete change in; cause a REVOLUTION (2) in: *The discovery of the new drug has revolutionized the treatment of many diseases* **2** to fill (people) with belief in REVOLUTION (1): *travel round the country revolutionizing the workers*

re·volve /rɪˈvɒlv‖rɪˈvɑlv/ *v* **1** [I∅;T1: (*on*)] to (cause to) spin round (on a central point); make REVOLUTIONs (4): *The wheels began to revolve slowly.|The earth revolves on its own* AXIS *once every 24 hours* **2** [T1] *fml* to consider carefully: *He revolved the main points in his mind* —compare TURN OVER (1) **3** [L9] (of several thoughts) to be considered in turn: *All sorts of mad ideas revolved in my mind*

revolve a·round *v prep* [Wv6;T1 *no pass.*] **1** to have as a centre or main subject: *A baby's life revolves mainly around its mother* **2** *AmE* REVOLVE ROUND

re·volv·er /rɪˈvɒlvəʳ‖rɪˈvɑl-/ *n* a type of small gun (PISTOL) containing several shots in a barrel that turns round after each one is fired, so that one need not reload every time

revolve round also **revolve a·bout**— *v prep* [T1 *no pass.*] to make REVOLUTIONs (3) round (a fixed point); move in circles round: *The moon revolves round the earth*

re·volv·ing /rɪˈvɒlvɪŋ‖rɪˈvɑl-/ *adj* [Wa5;A] that REVOLVEs (1): *a theatre with a revolving stage|went through the revolving doors*

re·vue /rɪˈvjuː/ *n* **1** [C] a light theatrical show with songs and dances but no story. It usually contains jokes about the events and fashions of the moment **2** [U] this kind of show: *She's been appearing/performing a lot in revue lately*

re·vul·sion /rɪˈvʌlʃən/ *n* [S;U] **1** [(*against*)] (a) feeling of being shocked and REVOLTed[1] (2): *She turned away from the dirty food in revulsion.|He was filled with a violent revulsion against such cruelty* **2** *fml* (a) sudden change (of feeling or opinion):

There has been a revulsion of public opinion in favour of punishment by hanging

rev up *v adv* -vv- [IØ] *infml* **1** (of an engine) to increase speed: *He heard the car revving up* **2** to increase the speed of an engine: *Don't rev up so noisily—you'll wake the baby*

re·ward[1] /rɪ'wɔːd‖-ɔrd/ *v* **1** [T1 (*for, with*)] to give a REWARD[2] to (someone): *He rewarded the boy (with £1) (for bringing back the lost dog)* **2** [T1 (*with*)] to give a REWARD[2] for (an action): *How can I reward your kindness?*

reward[2] *n* **1** [C;U: (*for*)] (something gained as) return for work or service: *received a title as a reward (for his services to the nation)|got nothing in reward (for her kindness)|He will expect some reward after working so hard* **2** [C (*for, of*)] an amount of money given to someone who helps the police or brings back lost property: *He gave the boy a reward (of £1) (for bringing back the lost dog)*

re·ward·ing /rɪ'wɔːdɪŋ‖-ɔr-/ *adj* (of an experience or action) worth doing or having; WORTHWHILE: *Nursing can be a very rewarding job*

re·wards /rɪ'wɔːdz‖-ɔr-/ *n* [P (*of*)] gains that come as a result (of something, or of doing something): *The rewards of art/of being an artist are not to be measured in money*

re·wire /ˌriː'waɪəʳ/ *v* [T1] to put new electric wires into (a building): *The whole house needs rewiring/needs to be rewired*

re·word /ˌriː'wɜːd‖-'wɜrd/ *v* [T1] to say or write again in different words: *to reword a letter so as to make the meaning clearer*

re·write /ˌriː'raɪt/ *v* [T1] to write (a piece of writing) again in a different and more suitable way —**rewrite** /'riːraɪt/ *n*: *a modern rewrite of an old story*

Rex /reks/ *n Lat* (in Britain) **1** [E] (the title used after the name of a ruling king): *George Rex* **2** [R] *law* (used, when a king is ruling, in titles of LAWSUITS) the State; the CROWN[1] (3): *in the action Rex v Jones* (=the Crown against Jones) —compare REGINA

rh *written abbrev. for*: right hand

rhap·so·dize, -dise /'ræpsədaɪz/ *v* [IØ (*about, over*)] *sometimes derog* to express (too) great praise and wild excitement: *Mother rhapsodized about/over your beautiful kitchen*

rhap·so·dy /'ræpsədi/ *n* **1** [(*about, over*) *often pl. with sing. meaning*] *sometimes derog* an expression of (too) great praise and wild excitement: *Mother went into* (=expressed) *a rhapsody over the beauty of the scene* **2** (*often cap.*) (a name sometimes given to) a piece of music of irregular form: *Gershwin's "Rhapsody in Blue" is a popular concert piece*

rhe·a /'rɪə/ *n* any of several kinds of large South American bird like the OSTRICH but smaller, with a long neck and long legs and 3 toes on each foot —see picture at EXOTIC

Rhen·ish /'renɪʃ/ *n* [U] *old use* HOCK[2]

rhe·o·stat /'rɪəstæt/ *n* an instrument that controls the loudness of radio sound or the brightness of electric light, by limiting the flow of electric current —see also RESISTANCE

rhe·sus /'riːsəs/ also **rhesus mon·key** /'·· ˌ··/— *n* a type of small short-tailed pale brown North Indian monkey, often used in scientific tests —see picture at PRIMATE[2]

Rhesus fac·tor /'·· ˌ··/ also **Rh factor** /ˌɑːr'eɪtʃ-/— *n* [*the*+R] *tech* a substance whose presence (**Rhesus positive**) or absence (**Rhesus negative**) in the red blood cells may have dangerous effects for some newborn babies or when one person receives blood from another

rhet·o·ric /'retərɪk/ *n* [U] **1** the art of speaking or writing so as to persuade people effectively **2** *derog* speech or writing that sounds fine and important, but is really insincere or without meaning

rhe·tor·i·cal /rɪ'tɒrɪkəl‖-'tɔ-, -'tɑ-/ *adj* **1** [Wa5;A] connected with RHETORIC (1): *The speaker showed great rhetorical skill* **2** [B] *derog* showing or using RHETORIC (2): *Don't be so rhetorical—just tell us what you mean in plain English!*

rhe·tor·i·cally /rɪ'tɒrɪkli‖-'tɔ-, -'tɑ-/ *adv* **1** [Wa5] in connection with RHETORIC (1): *Rhetorically, his speech was excellent* **2** *derog* in a way that shows RHETORIC (2): *He addressed the crowd very rhetorically, shouting and waving his arms* **3** [Wa5] not with serious intention, but only for the effect of the words: *I was only asking rhetorically; I didn't really expect an answer.|"I'd rather die than eat this terrible food!" he cried rhetorically*

rhetorical ques·tion /·ˌ··· '··/ *n* a question asked only for effect, and not expecting any answer

rhet·o·ri·cian /ˌretə'rɪʃən/ *n* a person trained and skilled in RHETORIC (1)

rheum /ruːm/ *n* [U] *old use* (the condition of having) water running from the nose and eyes, as when one has a cold

rheu·mat·ic[1] /ruː'mætɪk/ *adj* **1** [Wa5] connected with RHEUMATISM: *a rheumatic condition of the joints* **2** having RHEUMATISM, or open to attacks of RHEUMATISM: *a rheumatic old woman who can't walk very fast*

rheumatic[2] *n not fml* a person suffering from RHEUMATISM

rheumatic fe·ver /·ˌ·· '··/ *n* [U] a serious infectious disease, esp. in children, with fever, swelling of the joints, and possible damage to the heart

rheu·mat·ick·y /ruː'mætɪki/ *adj infml* RHEUMATIC[1] (2)

rheu·mat·ics /ruː'mætɪks/ *n* [P] *infml* RHEUMATISM: *My rheumatics are terrible this winter—I can hardly move*

rheu·ma·tis·m /'ruːmətɪzəm/ *n* [U] any of various diseases causing pain and stiffness in the joints or muscles of the body

rheu·ma·toid /'ruːmətɔɪd/ *adj* [Wa5] *tech* of or concerning RHEUMATISM or the long-continuing disease (**rheumatoid arthritis**) causing pain and stiffness in the joints of the legs and arms and often making them lose their proper shape

rhine·stone /'raɪnstəʊn/ *n* **1** [C] a piece of transparent rock (QUARTZ) **2** [C;U] a (type of) shining colourless jewel, made from this rock or from glass or paste

Rhine wine /ˌraɪn 'waɪn/ *n* [U] HOCK[2]

rhi·no·ce·ros /raɪ'nɒsərəs‖-'nɑ-/ also (*infml*) **rhi·no** /'raɪnəʊ/— *n* **-ros** *or* **-roses** [Wn2] one of several kinds of large, heavy, thick-skinned animal of Africa or Asia, with either 1 or 2 horns on its nose —see picture at RUMINANT

rhi·zome /'raɪzəʊm/ *n tech* the thick stem of some plants such as the IRIS, which lies flat along the ground with roots and leaves growing from it

rho·do·den·dron /ˌrəʊdə'dendrən/ *n* any one of a family of bushes that are grown for their large bright flowers, and keep their leaves in winter (are EVERGREEN)

rhom·boid[1] /'rɒmbɔɪd‖'rɑm-/ *n tech* (in GEOMETRY) a 4-sided figure whose opposite sides are equal; PARALLELOGRAM

rhomboid[2] also **rhom·boid·al** /-dl/— *adj* [Wa5] *tech* in the shape of a RHOMBUS

rhom·bus /'rɒmbəs‖'rɑm-/ *n tech* (in GEOMETRY) a figure with 4 equal straight sides and unequal angles —see picture at GEOMETRY

rhu·barb /'ruːbɑːb‖-ɑrb/ *n* [U] **1** a type of broad-leaved garden plant whose thick juicy stems are boiled with sugar and eaten as food **2** *infml* the sound of many people talking at the same time; noisy argument

rhyme¹ /raɪm/ *n* **1** [C (*for*)] a word that RHYMEs² (1) with another: *"Bold" and "cold" are rhymes.|I can't find a rhyme for "donkey"* **2** [U] (the use of) words that RHYME² (1) at the ends of the lines in poetry: *Rhyme was not used in ancient English poetry.|Shakespeare sometimes wrote in rhyme.|"Poets making beautiful old rhyme in praise of ladies dead."* (Shakespeare) **3** [C] a short and not serious piece of writing, using words that RHYME² (1): *make up silly little rhymes to amuse the children* **4** **rhyme or reason** [*nonassertive*] (any) sense or meaning: *There doesn't seem to be any rhyme or reason in his demands—is he mad?*

rhyme² *v* **1** [Wv6;I∅ (*with*)] (of words or lines of poetry) to end with the same sound (as another word, or as each other), including a vowel: *"House" rhymes with "mouse".|"School" and "fool" rhyme.|The last 2 lines of this poem don't rhyme properly* **2** [Wv6;T1 (*and, with*)] to put together (2 words that end with the same sound, including a vowel, or a word with another that does this): *You can rhyme "duty" with "beauty" but you can't rhyme "box" and "backs"* **3** [I∅] *lit & old use* to write poetry

rhymed /raɪmd/ *adj* [Wa5] written in lines that RHYME² (1)

rhyme·ster /ˈraɪmstəʳ/ *n old use* a writer of bad poems

rhyming coup·let /ˌ·· ˈ··/ *n* [*usu. pl.*] 2 lines of poetry next to each other that RHYME² (1): *"Nature and Nature's laws lay hid in night: God said 'Let Newton be!' and all was light" is a rhyming couplet by Pope*

rhyming slang /ˈ·· ·/ *n* [U] a secret language using words and phrases that RHYME² (1) with those really meant: *"Plates of meat" is rhyming slang for "feet"*

rhyth·m /ˈrɪðəm/ *n* **1** [U] (of sounds or movements in speech, dancing, music, etc.) the quality of happening at regular periods of time: (fig.) *the rhythm of the seasons* **2** [C] a particular pattern of this kind: *the exciting rhythms of African drum music*

rhyth·mic /ˈrɪðmɪk/ also **rhyth·mi·cal** /-kəl/— *adj* having RHYTHM (1): *the rhythmic beating of one's heart* —**~ally** *adv* [Wa4]

rib¹ /rɪb/ *n* **1** [C] one of the 12 pairs of bones running round the chest of a man or animal, from the BACKBONE to where they join at the front **2** [C] a piece of meat cut so as to include one of these bones: *a rib of* BEEF **3** [C] a curved rod used for strengthening a framework: *the ribs of a boat/of an* UMBRELLA **4** [C;U] (one long thin raised line in a) RIBBED pattern, as in KNITting: *the ribs of a leaf|socks made in rib* **5** **dig/poke someone in the ribs** to push someone with a finger or the elbow so as to attract attention esp. to a joke

rib² *v* **-bb-** [T1] *infml* to make fun of in a friendly way; laugh at (someone): *All the boys ribbed him for keeping a pet pig*

rib·ald /ˈrɪbəld/ *adj* **1** (of humorous speech or behaviour) rude in a low and disrespectful way: *ribald jokes|the ribald laughter of the drunk men* **2** (of a person) offending others by speaking or behaving in this way: *a crowd of ribald soldiers*

rib·ald·ry /ˈrɪbəldri/ *n* [U] RIBALD (1) language or jokes: *We've had enough of this ribaldry—try to control yourself in front of the priest!*

ribbed /rɪbd/ *adj* [Wa5] with RIBlike¹ (1) markings; in a pattern of long thin raised lines: *ribbed socks|"the ribbed sea sand"* (Coleridge)

rib·bing /ˈrɪbɪŋ/ *n* [U] a pattern of long thin raised lines in KNITting: *the ribbing round the tops of his socks*

rib·bon /ˈrɪbən/ also (*old use*) **rib·and** /ˈrɪbənd/— *n* **1** [C;U] (a piece of) silk or other cloth woven in a long narrow band and used for tying things, for ornament, etc.: *a black* TYPEWRITER *ribbon* **2** [C9] a piece of this in a special colour or pattern, worn in order to show that one has received a particular title or military honour: *wear the ribbon of the Victoria Cross on his chest* —see also MEDAL **3** [C] a long irregular narrow band: *old torn curtains hanging in ribbons|a ribbon of mist along the river bank*

ribbon de·vel·op·ment /ˌ·· ·ˈ···/ *n* [U] *usu. derog* (the practice of building) long lines of houses along the sides of main roads leading out of a city

rib cage /ˈ· ·/ *n* the wall of RIBs that encloses and protects the lungs

ri·bo·fla·vin /ˌraɪbəʊˈfleɪvɪ̵n‖ˌraɪbə-/ *n* [U] *tech* a substance (VITAMIN B_2) that exists naturally in meat, milk, and certain vegetables, and is important for human health

rice /raɪs/ *n* [U] **1** any of several kinds of food grain grown in wet tropical places, esp. in India and China —see picture at CEREAL **2** the seed of this, which is cooked and eaten as food everywhere in the world: *a plate of boiled rice|***Brown rice** *or* **unpolished rice** *has still got the outer covering of the seed,* **polished rice** *has had it removed, and* **ground rice** *has been turned to powder by crushing*

rice pa·per /ˈ· ˌ··/ *n* [U] **1** a kind of thin paper made esp. in China and used by artists there **2** a special form of this that can be eaten, and is used in cooking

rice pud·ding /ˌ· ˈ··/ *n* [C;U] a (type of) sweet dish made by baking rice in milk and sugar

rich /rɪtʃ/ *adj* [Wa1] **1** [B] (of a person) wealthy; possessing a lot of money or property **2** [F+*in*] possessing or containing a lot (of the stated thing): *This fish is rich in oil.|a city rich in ancient buildings* **3** [B] (of possessions) costly, valuable, and beautiful: *rich silk/furniture* **4** [B] (of food) containing a lot of cream, sugar, eggs, etc.: *a very rich Christmas cake* **5** [B] (of land) good for growing plants in: *rich soil|*(fig.) *This subject offers a rich field for advanced study* **6** [B] (of a sound or colour) deep, strong, and beautiful: *the rich notes of the church* ORGAN *(4)|a rich dark red* **7** [F;(B)] *infml becoming rare* amusing (esp. in the rather bad-tempered remark **That's rich!**): *"They've made John the captain." "That's rich! He doesn't know any more about football than a donkey"* **8** [*the*+P] wealthy people: *The rich are not always generous to the poor* **9** **rich and poor** rich people and/as well as poor people

rich·es /ˈrɪtʃɪ̵z/ *n* [P] *esp. lit* wealth; things that make one rich: *All his riches are no good to him if he is so ill.|*(fig.) *the riches of English poetry*

rich·ly /ˈrɪtʃli/ *adv* **1** splendidly; in a large quantity: *a queen's dress richly ornamented with jewels* **2** **richly deserve** to deserve fully (usu. something unpleasant): *You richly deserve to be punished*

rich·ness /ˈrɪtʃnɪ̵s/ *n* [U] the quality of being RICH (not usu. sense 1): *the richness of her dress/of the soil/of the food*

rick¹ /rɪk/ *n* a large pile of wheat stems (STRAW) or dried grass (HAY), often shaped like a little house, that stands out in the open air until it is needed

rick² *v* [T1] to build into a RICK¹: *rick the early corn*

rick³ *v* [T1] *esp. BrE* to twist (a joint or part of the body) slightly: *I've ricked my back/my ankle*

rick·ets /ˈrɪkɪ̵ts/ *n* [U;(P)] a children's disease caused by lack of the VITAMIN D provided by sunshine, butter, fresh milk, etc., which makes the bones become soft and bent: *Rickets is/are quite rare now*

rick·et·y /ˈrɪkɪ̇ti/ *adj* weak in the joints and likely to break: *a rickety old cart*

rick·shaw, *AmE* **-sha** /ˈrɪkʃɔː/ *n* a small 2-wheeled vehicle for 1 or 2 passengers, whose power comes from a man either pulling or cycling. They are used in East Asia
USAGE One **pulls** a **rickshaw**, or **pedals** it if it is the kind like a bicycle. The passengers *travel* or *ride* in it, and *get into/out of* it

ric·o·chet¹ /ˈrɪkəʃeɪ/ *n* **1** a sudden jumping change in the direction of a moving object such as a stone or bullet when it hits a surface at an angle **2** a blow from an object to which this has happened: *wounded by a ricochet, not by a direct hit*

ricochet² *v* **-cheted** /ʃeɪd/ *or* **-chetted** /ʃetɪ̇d/ [I∅ (*off*)] to change direction in a RICOCHET¹: *The bullet ricocheted off the bridge*

rid·dance /ˈrɪdəns/ *n* [S;U] *infml* (a) clearing away of something unwanted (usu. in the phr. **Good riddance!**): "*They've gone at last.*" "*Good riddance to the lot of them!*" (= I'm glad they've gone) —compare RID OF

rid·den /ˈrɪdn/ *comb. form* [*n→adj*] *derog* **1** too much in the power of or concerned with: *science-ridden* **2** too full of: *This house is insect-ridden*

rid·dle¹ /ˈrɪdl/ *n* **1** a difficult and amusing question to which one must guess the answer **2** a mystery; something one cannot understand: *Robert's character is a complete riddle to me* **3 read a riddle** to discover an answer or meaning

riddle² *n* a large SIEVE, as used for separating earth from stones in the garden

riddle³ *v* [T1] **1** to pass (earth, corn, ashes, etc.) through a RIDDLE² **2** to shake (the frame (GRATE) that holds a fire) so as to make the ashes go through

riddle with *v prep* [D1 *often pass.*] **1** to make many holes in (someone or something) by means of: *If you move I'll riddle you with bullets!* **2** to make full of (holes): *The tent's riddled with holes and the rain's coming in*

ride¹ /raɪd/ *v* **rode** /rəʊd/, **ridden** /ˈrɪdn/ **1** [T1] to travel along, controlling and sitting on (a horse, or other animal, a bicycle, or a motorcycle): *Can you ride a bicycle?|I'll ride your horse and you ride mine* —compare DRIVE **2** [I∅] to travel along controlling and sitting on a horse, for exercise and pleasure: *teach the children to ride|We're going (horse-)riding on Saturday* —see also SIDESADDLE, ASTRIDE **3** [L9] to go (somewhere) controlling and sitting on esp. a horse: *We rode across the fields.|He got on his bicycle and rode slowly down the road* **4** [T1] to go along, across, or all over (a place) on a horse: *He rides the borders/the* RANGES¹ (3) **5** [L9] (of a vehicle) to travel over a surface (in the stated manner): *This car rides smoothly* **6** [T1] *lit* (of a ship) to move or float on: *The boat rode the waves lightly* —see also ANCHOR¹ (5) **7** [L1] *tech* (of a professional rider in races (JOCKEY)) to weigh when ready for racing: *George rides 115 pounds* **8** [L7] (of a racetrack) to be (in a stated condition) for horse-racing: *The course will ride very hard, this weather* **9** [T1] *not fml, esp. AmE* to cause intentional and continual difficulty to; annoy: *Leave her alone and stop riding her—she's doing her best!* **10** [T1] *not fml* to move back so as to lessen the force of (a blow) **11 let something ride** *infml* to let something continue; take no action about something
USAGE One **rides** horses, bicycles, or anything else that one sits on top of with one's legs hanging down. A person who sits inside a wheeled vehicle and controls it is **driving** it: *to* **drive** *a car/a train/a cart.* The passengers inside are *travelling* or *riding* in it or being *driven,* though they may say *We went for a* **drive** *in the car.|We* **drove** *to Cambridge* (= by car, not in a public vehicle like a bus). —see LEAD (USAGE)

ride² *n* **1** [C (*on, in*)] a journey (on an animal, in a vehicle, etc.): *go for a ride|He lives only a short bus ride away.|Give me a ride on your back!|He takes her out for little rides in the car* —compare DRIVE **2** [C] a path through a wood, with a soft surface suitable for riding a horse on but not for vehicles **3** [C9] an animal that can be ridden on (of the stated quality, or with the stated result): *This horse is an easy ride* **4 take someone for a ride** *infml* **a** to deceive someone **b** *euph, esp. AmE* to remove someone by force and murder him

ride down *v adv* [T1] **1** to chase and reach (someone) on one's horse **2** to knock (someone) down with one's horse: *Get out of my way or I'll ride you down!*

ride in *v prep* [T1] to be carried along sitting in (a car, cart, boat, or aircraft not controlled by oneself): *She gets sick when she rides in a bus* —compare DRIVE

ride on *v prep* **1** [T1] to be carried as if riding (RIDE¹ (1)): *The little boy rode on his father's shoulders* **2** [D1] to carry (someone) as if riding (RIDE¹ (1)): *Shall I ride you on my back?* **3** [T1] to RIDE¹ (1) (esp. a donkey, camel, etc.): *the king riding on an elephant*

ride out *v adv* [T1] **1** (of a ship) to keep floating till the end of; last safely through (bad weather): *to ride out the storm* **2** to come safely through (trouble or difficult times) without taking any violent action

rid·er /ˈraɪdəʳ/ *n* **1** [C] a person who rides esp. a horse: *That's John's horse all right, but I can't see who the rider is* **2** [C9] a person who rides esp. a horse (with the stated skill): *a good/bold/poor rider|I'm afraid George is no rider* **3** [C,C4,5c] *law* a statement, opinion, or piece of advice added to an official declaration or judgment: *The* CORONER *decided that the child had been drowned, and added a rider (advising) that the lake should be filled in*

rid·er·less /ˈraɪdələs‖-dər-/ *adj* [Wa5] (of an animal) without a RIDER (1): *several riderless horses*

ride up *v adv* [I∅] (of clothing) to move upward out of place into an uncomfortable position: *a tight skirt that rides up when she sits down*

ridge¹ /rɪdʒ/ *n* a long narrow raised part of any surface, such as the top of a range of mountains or of a sloping roof where the 2 sloping surfaces meet: *He walked along the mountain ridge/sat on the ridge of the roof* —see picture at MOUNTAIN

ridge² *v* [T1] to make a RIDGE¹ or ridges in: *His forehead was ridged with anxiety*

ridge·pole /ˈrɪdʒpəʊl/ *n* the pole along the top of the sloped roof of a long tent

ridge tile /ˈ· ·/ *n* one of a set of specially shaped TILEs (=pieces of baked earth) which form the RIDGE¹ along the top of a sloped roof

rid·i·cule¹ /ˈrɪdɪ̇kjuːl/ *n* [U] **1** unkind laughter; being made fun of: *His behaviour deserves ridicule rather than blame* **2 hold someone up to ridicule** to invite people to laugh unkindly at someone: *It's not fair to hold me up to ridicule because I can't spell!* **3 lay oneself open to ridicule** to do things that will make people laugh at one

ridicule² *v* [T1] to laugh unkindly at; make unkind fun of: *They all ridiculed the idea*

ri·dic·u·lous /rɪˈdɪkjʊləs‖-kjə-/ *adj derog* silly; deserving RIDICULE¹ (1): *She looks ridiculous in those tight trousers* —**~ly** *adv*: *The examination was ridiculously easy* —**~ness** *n* [U]

ri·ding¹ /ˈraɪdɪŋ/ *n* [C; *the*+R9] (*usu. cap.*) (until 1974) any one of the 3 divisions of Yorkshire (=a large COUNTY in the North of England) for local government purposes: *the North/West/East Riding of Yorkshire*

rid·ing² *n* [U] the skill or exercise of travelling on a horse: *Let's do some riding*

riding breech·es /ˈ·· ˌ··/ *n* [P] trousers worn for RIDING²: *a new pair of riding breeches* —see PAIR (USAGE) and picture at HORSE

riding light /ˈ·· ·/ *n* a light on a ship that is floating but not moving because it is ANCHORed

rid of /rɪd/ *v prep* **rid of** *or* **ridded of, rid of,** *pres. p.* **ridding of** [D1] **1** to make (someone or something) free of: *He promised to rid the town of rats.|You must rid yourself of these old-fashioned ideas.|He's gone, and I'm glad to be rid of him* (=to be free of him again) **2 get rid of a** to free oneself from (something unwanted): *Try to get rid of your nasty cold* **b** to drive, send, throw, or give away or destroy; DISPOSE OF: *How can I get rid of those beggars/that lazy servant/my old coat/the flies in the kitchen?*

Ries·ling /ˈriːslɪŋ/ *n* [U;(C)] a type of white wine, usu. not sweet, made from the **Riesling grape**: *a cool glass of Riesling*

rife /raɪf/ *adj* [F] *esp. lit* **1** (of bad things) widespread; common: *Disease and violence were rife in the city* **2** [+*with*] full (of bad things): *The city was rife with disease and violence*

riff /rɪf/ *n* a repeated phrase in popular or JAZZ music

rif·fle through /ˈrɪfəl/ *v prep* [Wv3;T1] to turn over (papers, pages, etc.) quickly with one's finger

riff·raff /ˈrɪfræf/ *n* [*the*+P] badly-behaved people of the lowest class

ri·fle¹ /ˈraɪfəl/ *v* [Wv3;T1 (*of*)] to search through and steal everything valuable out of (a place): *The thieves rifled his pockets (of all their contents)*

rifle² *v* [Wv3,5;T1] to make curved cuts (GROOVE*s*) inside (the barrel of a gun) so as to make the bullets spin: *a rifled barrel*

rifle³ *n* a type of esp. military gun fired from the shoulder, with a long RIFLEd² barrel

ri·fle·man /ˈraɪfəlmən/ *n* **-men** /mən/ **1** [C] a soldier armed with a RIFLE³ **2** [C;A;N] (*often cap.*) (the title of) a soldier in a REGIMENT of RIFLES: *Come here, Rifleman Harding*

rifle range /ˈ·· ·/ *n* **1** [C] a place where people practise shooting with RIFLE*s*³ **2** [U] RIFLE SHOT (2)

ri·fles /ˈraɪfəlz/ *n* [P] (*often cap.*) (part of the title of) certain large bodies (REGIMENT*s*) of soldiers armed with RIFLE*s*³

rifle shot /ˈ·· ·/ *n* **1** [C] a shot fired from a RIFLE³: *We heard a single rifle shot* **2** [U] the distance that a RIFLE³ can shoot: *The hunter crept to within rifle shot of the tiger*

ri·fling /ˈraɪflɪŋ/ *n* [U] the cuts (GROOVE*s*) inside the barrel of a RIFLEd² gun

rift /rɪft/ *n* [(*between, in*)] *fml & lit* a crack; narrow opening made by breaking: *The sun appeared through a rift in the clouds.|(fig.) I'm afraid there's been a rift between us—my wife's run away*

rift val·ley /ˈ· ˌ··/ *n* a valley with very steep sides, formed by the cracking and slipping of the earth's surface

rig¹ /rɪg/ *v* **-gg-** [Wv5;T1;IØ] **a** to fit out (a ship) with the necessary ropes, sails, etc.: *a fully-rigged vessel* **b** (of a ship) to get ready in this way: *The "Victory" has nearly finished rigging and will sail tomorrow*

rig² *n* **1** [C] the way a ship's sails and the poles that carry them (MAST*s*) are arranged: *That boat looks like a fishing vessel from her rig* **2** [C9] (*usu. in comb.*) a piece of apparatus (for the stated purpose): *an* OILRIG **3** [C9] *infml* a set of clothes; the way a person is dressed: *That's a very attractive rig you've got on!*

rig³ *v* **-gg-** [T1] **1** to arrange (an event) dishonestly for one's own advantage: *They complained that the election had been rigged* **2 rig the market** to make industrial SHARES¹ (2) go up or down for one's own unlawful profit —see also RIG OUT, RIG UP

rig·ging /ˈrɪgɪŋ/ *n* [(*the*) U] all the ropes, sails, etc., with which a ship is RIGged¹: *The ship lost most of her rigging in the storm* —see picture at SAIL²

right¹ /raɪt/ *adj* **1** [Wa5;A] on or belonging to the side of the body that does not contain the heart: *his right foot, not his left* **2** [Wa5;A] on, by, or in the direction of this side: *a right turn, not a left turn|The right bank of the river Thames is on the south side because the river flows east* **3** [B] (*often cap.*) belonging to, connected with, or favouring the RIGHT² (3) in politics: *She's very right.|She votes Right, not Left* —opposite **left**

right² *n* **1** [(*the*) U] the RIGHT¹ (2) side or direction: *Keep to the right!|Take the second turning on the right* **2** [C] the right hand: *Hit him with your right* **3** [(*the*) GU] (*often cap.*) political parties or groups (such as the CONSERVATIVE or REPUBLICAN parties) that favour fewer political changes and less State control, and generally support the employers or those in official positions rather than the workers: *The right oppose(s) the new taxes.|a new party of the far Right* —opposite **left**

right³ *adj* **1** [F (*in*), F3] just; morally good: *I'll try to do whatever is right.|It's not right, but wrong, to tell lies.|I was right in selling/right to sell the farm.|It seemed only right to give her something* **2** [B (*in*), B3] correct; true: *Is that the right time?|He gave the right answer.|Would I be right to say/be right in saying that she's rather stupid?|"Is your name Alfred?" "Yes, that's right"* **3** [B] most suitable; best for a particular purpose: *Are we going in the right direction?* **4 put right** also **set right**— **a** to put into the correct position: *Put the picture right—it's not straight|Put the clock right* (=make the hands show the correct time) **b** to cure: *A week by the sea will soon put you right again* **c** also **put straight**— to give correct information to (someone who has a wrong opinion), often rather sharply: *He thought it was Thursday, but I soon put him right* **5 (quite) right in the/one's head** [*nonassertive*] *infml* sensible; not mad: *How can he say anything so silly? Is the man right in his head?* **6 (quite) right in the/one's mind/in one's right mind** altogether sensible; [*nonassertive*] not mad (used more seriously than (5)): *I'm afraid Mother isn't quite in her right mind these days* **7 right as rain** *infml* perfectly healthy; quite well **8 right enough a** satisfactory: *The bed was right enough but the food was nasty* **b** also **sure enough** — as was expected: *I told him to come, and right enough he arrived the next morning* **9 Right you are!** also **Right oh!**— *infml* Yes; I will; I agree: *"Shut the window, please." "Right you are!"* —**~ness** *n* [(*the*) U]: *I believe in the rightness of what she's doing*

right⁴ *n* **1** [U] what is RIGHT³ (1): *old enough to know the difference between right and wrong* **2** [S; U: (*of, to,* 3)] (a) morally just or lawful claim: *She has a right/has no right/has less right than I have to say that.|She has a right/the right to half your money.|The king gave them the right of cutting sticks in the forest* **3 as of right** because of a just claim **4 by right of** owing to; because of (something that gives a just claim): *She is British by right of marriage* **5 in one's own right** because of a personal claim that does not depend on anyone else: *Elizabeth II is queen of England in her own right* (=not because she is married to a king) **6 be in the right** to have justice on one's side; not deserve blame: *I must find out which of them was in the right* —opposite **in the wrong** —see also RIGHTS

right[5] *adv* [Wa5] **1** towards the RIGHT[2] (1): *He turned right* —opposite **left** **2** [H] *not fml* exactly: *right in the middle|Do it right now.|He's right here* **3** [H] *not fml* directly; straight: *Go right home at once!|There's the house, right in front of you.|right after breakfast* **4** properly; correctly: *to guess (quite) right|He doesn't treat her right.|Did I do it right?* —opposite **wrong** **5** [H] completely; all the way: *Go right to the end of the road.|Go right back to the beginning.|I haven't read the book right through* **6** *old use or NEngE* very: *The sailors were right glad to see land.|The Right Honourable John Jones* (=a title) **7 all right a** also **right, right you are**— Yes; I will; I agree; Good: *"Come tomorrow." "(All) right!"* **b** (*used with* but) certainly: *She's pretty, all right, but I don't like her* **c** well enough; satisfactorily: *Can he swim all right now?* **d** well in health: *Are you feeling all right?* **8 Eyes right** (military command) Turn your heads to the right **9 right and left** everywhere; on all sides: *We're losing money right and left* **10 right on** *sl* (used as an encouragement to a speaker): *When he promised them free beer all round, the crowd shouted "Right on!"* —compare **Hear! Hear!** (HEAR (6)) **11 too right** *esp. AustrE* You are correct; I agree

right[6] *v* [T1] to put (something) right or upright again: *The cat righted itself during the fall, and landed on its feet.|I hope your troubles will soon right themselves/soon be righted*

right-a·bout turn /ˌ· ·· ˈ·/ also **right-about face**— *n* [S] a complete turn that leaves one facing in the opposite direction: *to do a right-about turn*

right an·gle /ˈ· ˌ··/ *n* an angle of 90 degrees, as at any of the 4 corners of a square —see WEIGHTS & MEASURES TABLE and picture at GEOMETRY —**right-angled** /ˈ· ˌ··/ *adj* [Wa5]: *a right-angled* TRIANGLE (1)

right a·way /ˌ· ·ˈ·/ also (*esp. AmE*) **right off**— *adv* [Wa5] at once; without delay

right·eous /ˈraɪtʃəs/ *adj* [Wa5] *lit & bibl* **1** (of people and behaviour) (doing what is) lawful and morally good: *a righteous man|The righteous shall go to Heaven.|"I never drink or smoke," he said in a righteous voice* **2** (of feelings) morally blameless; having just cause: *righteous anger* —**~ly** *adv* —**~ness** *n* [U]: *"hunger and thirst after righteousness"* (The Bible)

right·ful /ˈraɪtfəl/ *adj* [Wa5;A] lawful; according to a just claim: *to take one's rightful share and not more|Who is the rightful owner of this car?* —**~ly** *adv* —**~ness** *n* [U]: *the rightfulness of his claim to the money*

right-hand /ˌ· ˈ·◂/ *adj* [Wa5;A] **1** on or to the right side: *Take a right-hand turn.|a car with a right-hand* DRIVE[2] (10) **2** of, for, with, or done by the right hand **3** turning the same way as the hands of a clock: *a right-hand screw* **4 one's right-hand man** one's most useful and valuable helper

right hand /ˌ· ˈ·/ *n* **1** the hand on the right-hand side of the body: *Most people write with the right hand* **2** RIGHT-HAND (4) man: *Mary is her mother's right hand*

right-hand·ed /ˌ· ˈ··◂/ *adj* [Wa5] **1** using the right hand (for most actions) rather than the left: *Most people are right-handed.|a right-handed blow* **2** made for use by a person who does this: *right-handed scissors* —**~ly** *adv* —**~ness** *n* [U]

right-hand·er /ˌ· ˈ··/ *n* **1** a person who usu. uses his right hand rather than his left **2** a blow or stroke given with the right hand

right·ist /ˈraɪtəst/ *adj, n* (*often cap.*) (a supporter) of the RIGHT[2] (3) in politics: *She is very rightist in her opinions*

right·ly /ˈraɪtli/ *adv* **1** [Wa5] correctly; truly: *If I am rightly informed . . .|He believed, rightly or wrongly, that she was guilty* **2** justly: *He was punished, and (very) rightly so* **3** [Wa5; *nonassertive*] *infml* for certain: *I can't rightly say whether it was Tuesday or Wednesday*

right-mind·ed /ˌ· ˈ··◂/ *adj* [Wa5;A] having the right opinions, principles, habits, etc.: *All right-minded children enjoy being dirty* —**~ness** *n* [U]

right of com·mon /ˌ· · ˈ··/ *n* [U] *law* the right of a person or people to use a particular area of land: *This village has right of common in the forest*

right off /ˌ· ˈ·/ *adv* [Wa5] *esp. AmE* RIGHT AWAY

right of pri·mo·gen·i·ture /ˌ· · ··ˈ···/ *n* [U] PRIMOGENITURE (1)

right of way /ˌ· · ˈ·/ *n* **rights of way** **1** [C] **a** a right to follow a path across someone else's private land: *We have a right of way across his field to our house* **b** a path over which someone holds this right: *2 public rights of way through the forest* **2** [(*the*)U] the right of traffic to drive, cross, pass, etc., before other vehicles

rights /raɪts/ *n* [P] **1** the political, social, etc., advantages to which someone has a just claim, morally or in law: *to fight for women's rights* **2 by rights** in justice; if things were done properly: *I shouldn't by rights be at this party at all—I'm on duty tonight* **3 set/put someone/something to rights** to make someone/something just, healthy, correct, etc.: *This medicine will soon put you to rights.|We need a new leader to set the country to rights again* **4 stand on one's rights** to say what one's just claims are and refuse to give them up **5 the rights and wrongs of** the true facts of: *I am determined to find out the rights and wrongs of this matter. Whose fault was it really?* **6 within one's rights** not going beyond one's just claims: *You'd be quite within your rights to refuse to work on Sunday*

right side /ˌ· ˈ·◂/ *n* **1** the outer side of a garment or material, usu. smoother and more attractive and meant to be looked at —compare WRONG SIDE **2 get on the right side of someone** to win someone's favour —compare **get on the** WRONG SIDE **of** **3 on the right side of (an age)** younger than: *She's still on the right side of 40* —compare **on the** WRONG SIDE **of** **4 keep on the right side of the law** not to break the law

right·ward /ˈraɪtwəd‖-ərd/ *adj* [Wa5;A;(B)] on or towards the right: *a rightward turn*

right·wards /ˈraɪtwədz‖-ər-/ *AmE* usu. **rightward**— *adv* [Wa5] on or towards the right

right wing /ˌ· ˈ·◂/ *adj, n* **1** [B;(*the*) GU] (the group of members) of a political party (esp. a CONSERVATIVE or REPUBLICAN party) or group, favouring fewer political changes: *a right wing politician|the right wing of the party* **2** [B;(*the*) GU] (of) the political party or group itself; RIGHT[1,2] (3): *very right wing ideas* **3** [Wa5;A;C] (in games like football) (of) **a** the position on the edge of the right of the field **b** a player in this position

right-wing·er /ˌ· ˈ··/ *n* **1** a member of a political RIGHT WING **2** a RIGHT WING (3b)

ri·gid /ˈrɪdʒəd/ *adj* **1** stiff; not easy to bend: *a tent supported on a rigid framework|She was rigid with fear* **2** (of a person or his character or opinion) firm; fixed; not easy to change: *He's very rigid in his ideas on marriage.|the rigid* DISCIPLINE[1] (2) *of army life* **3 shake someone rigid** *infml* to cause someone to have very great fear and/or surprise —**~ly** *adv*: *He was rigidly opposed to all new ideas*

ri·gid·i·ty /rəˈdʒɪdəti/ *n* [U] the quality of being

RIGID (1): *the rigidity of the framework/of her opinions*

rig·ma·role /ˈrɪgmərəʊl/ *n infml derog* **1** [S;U] a long confused story without much meaning: *She told me some rigmarole or other about having lost her keys* **2** [U] a long meaningless set of actions: *He had to go through all the rigmarole of swearing in front of the judge and kissing the Bible*

rig·or mor·tis /ˌrɪgə ˈmɔːtɪ̈s, ˌraɪgɔː-‖ˌrɪgər ˈmɔr-/ *n* [U] *Lat* the stiffening of the muscles after death: *Bury him before rigor mortis* SETs IN (=before he gets stiff)

rig·or·ous /ˈrɪgərəs/ *adj* **1** severe; painful: *the rigorous hardships of the journey* **2** careful and exact: *He made a rigorous study of the plants in the area* —**~ly** *adv*

rig·our, *AmE* **-or** /ˈrɪgəʳ/ *n* **1** [U] hardness; lack of mercy: *He deserves to be punished with the full rigour of the law* **2** [*the*+U9 *often pl. with sing. meaning*] severe conditions: *to suffer all the rigour(s) of winter/of army life* **3** [U] (in a subject of study) exactness that demands clear thinking: *the rigour of a scientific proof*

rig-out /ˈrɪg aʊt/ *n infml, often derog* a set of clothes: *You can't go to the party in that rig-out!*

rig out *v adv* **1** [T1 (*in, with*)] *not fml* to dress (someone); give clothes to: *If your clothes are all wet, I'm sure my mother can rig you out* **2** [X9 esp. *as, in*] to dress (someone) in (special or funny clothes); DRESS UP (1,2) (as): *She was rigged out/She rigged herself out in a silly orange uniform.|They rigged the little boy out as a sailor*

rig up *v adv* [T1] **1** *not fml* to put together the parts of (a boat or aircraft) **2** *infml* to put together (something) for a short time out of materials easily found: *Let's try to rig up some sort of shelter for the sheep*

rile /raɪl/ *v* [T1] *infml* to annoy; make angry: *It riles me when he won't stop whistling* —see ANGRY (USAGE)

rill /rɪl/ *n poet* a small stream

rim¹ /rɪm/ *n* the outside edge or border of esp. a round or circular object: *the rim of a cup|the rim of a wheel, round which the tyre fits* —**~less** *adj* [Wa5]: *She wore rimless glasses*

rim² *v* **-mm-** [T1] to be round the edge of (esp. something round or circular): *Trees rimmed the pool*

rime¹ /raɪm/ *n* [U] *lit* white FROST¹ (3)

rime² *n, v* [C;U;T1;I∅] *old use or poet* RHYME

-rimmed /rɪmd/ *comb. form* having a RIM¹ or rims of: *horn-rimmed glasses*

rind /raɪnd/ *n* **1** [U] the thick, sometimes hard, outer covering of certain fruits, esp. of the MELON and LEMON: *a piece of* LEMON *rind* **2** [C] a skin of one fruit of this type **3** [C;U] (a piece of) the thick outer skin, which cannot be eaten, of certain foods: *cheese rind*

USAGE Although the skin of the orange is of this type, it is more often called PEEL.

rin·der·pest /ˈrɪndəpest‖-ər-/ *n* [U] a disease of cattle that is passed on by touch (is CONTAGIOUS)

ring¹ /rɪŋ/ *n* **1** [C] a circular line, mark, or arrangement: *children dancing in a ring|count the rings of a tree when it is cut across* **2** [C] a circular band (esp. of the stated substance or for the stated purpose): *rings of oil round a wrecked ship|the rings of the* PLANET *Saturn|to smoke a cigarette and blow smoke rings|a rubber ring|A key ring is for carrying keys on* **3** [C] a circle worn on the finger. It is often **a** made of the stated metal: *5 gold rings* **b** ornamented with the stated precious stone: *a diamond ring* **c** worn to show the stated fact: *She wears a wedding ring to show that she's married* **4** [*the*+R] any closed-in central space where things are shown or performances take place, as in a CIRCUS (1,2,3) or dog show **5** [*the*+R] the small space closed in with ropes in which 2 men fight with their hands (BOX) —see BOXING, WRESTLING (USAGE) **6** [C] any group of people who work together, often dishonestly, to control (esp. the stated) business affairs for their own advantage: *join a drug ring* **7** [*the*+R] (*often cap.*) all the people (BOOKMAKERs) whose business is making money by taking BETs at horse-races **8 make/run rings round someone** to do things much better and faster than someone **9 throw one's hat into the ring** to (declare one's intention to) join in and compete

ring² *v* [T1 (*with*)] **1** to make or be a ring round: *Ring the spelling mistakes with red ink.|Police ringed the building.|an old house ringed (about) with trees* **2** to put a ring in the nose of (an animal): *to ring a pig* **3** to put a ring round the leg of (a bird) **4** (in games) to throw a ring over (a mark, wooden nail, etc.)

ring³ *v* **rang** /ræŋ/, **rung** /rʌŋ/ **1** [T1 (*for*)] to cause (a bell) to sound: *The cyclist rang his bell loudly.|Ring the bell for* (=to call) *your secretary* **2** [I∅] (of a bell, telephone, etc.) to sound: *The telephone's ringing.|The bell rang loudly* **3** [I∅ (*at, for*)] to ring a bell as a sign that one wants something: *She rang for the cook/for a drink* **4** [I∅ (*with*)] (of the ears) to be filled with a continuous sound: *The crash really made my ears ring.|My ears rang with their shouts* **5** [I∅;T1: (UP)] *AmE* usu. **call**— to telephone (someone): *Please ring (up) the doctor.|I'll ring you (back)* (=telephone you again) *when I know the answer.|I wonder when mother will ring?|He rang round all his friends* (=telephoned them all) *to see who could come to the party* **6** [T1] (of a clock) to mark (hours) by striking **7 ring a bell** *infml* to remind one of something: *Smith-Fortescue—the name rings a bell: I've heard it before* **8 ring hollow** to sound untrue: *His promises always ring hollow* **9 ring in one's ears** to make a loud hollow sound: *His unkind laughter rang in my ears* **10 ring the changes (on)** to introduce variety (in); give the same thing in a different form or different things in regular order: *I ring the changes (on my clothes) by wearing this coat with the other trousers* **11 ring up/down the curtain** to start/end a play by signalling for the theatre curtain to go up/down **12 ring true/false** to sound true/untrue: *His words rang true and I accepted his excuse* —see also RING IN, RING OFF, RING OUT, RING UP, RING WITH

ring⁴ *n* **1** [C] (an act of making) the sound of a bell: *He gave several loud rings at the door* **2** [S9, esp. *of*] a bell-like sound (of the stated kind): *the ring of horseshoes on the street* **3** [S9, esp. *of*] a loud clear sound (of the stated kind): *a ring of happy laughter* **4** [S9] a quality: *Her story had a ring of truth about it* **5** [C] a set (of church bells): *We have a full ring of 8 bells at our church* **6 give someone a ring** *not fml* to telephone someone: *I'll give you a ring tonight*

ring bind·er /ˈ· ˌ··/ *n* a notebook whose loose pages are held in position by metal rings fastened to a metal back

ring·er /ˈrɪŋəʳ/ *n* **1** a person who rings bells, as in a church: *The 8 ringers climbed the ladder to the tower* **2** *AmE* a person who enters a sports competition against the rules **3 a dead ringer for** *sl* a person who looks very like (someone else)

ring fin·ger /ˈ· ˌ··/ *n* the third finger of the left hand (or, in some parts of the world, the right hand)

ring in *v adv* **rang in, rung in** [T1] to mark the beginning of, with church bells (in the phr. **ring in the New Year**) —compare RING OUT (2)

ring·lead·er /ˈrɪŋˌliːdəʳ/ *n* a person who leads

others to do wrong or make trouble: *That big fellow with the beard is their ringleader—try to shoot him first!*

ring·let /'rɪŋlɪ̈t/ *n* a long hanging curl of hair: *a pretty child with golden ringlets*

ring·mas·ter /'rɪŋ,mɑːstəʳ‖-,mæ-/ *n* a person, esp. a man, whose job is directing performances in the CIRCUS (1,2,3) ring

ring off *v adv* **rang off, rung off** [IØ] *BrE* to end a telephone conversation: *I'd better ring off now—the baby's crying*

ring out *v adv* **rang out, rung out** **1** [IØ] (of a voice or bell) to sound loudly and clearly: *The word of command rang out* **2** [T1] to mark the end of, with church bells (in the phr. **ring out the Old Year**) —compare RING IN

ring road /'· ·/ (*AmE* **beltway**)— *n BrE* a road that goes round the edge of a large town so that traffic need not pass through the centre

ring·side /'rɪŋsaɪd/ *adj, adv, n* [Wa5;A;(B); *the*+R] (at) the edge of a RING¹ (4,5) where things are happening (esp. in the phr. **a ringside seat**): *We had ringside seats/seats by the ringside for the big fight, and saw it all*

ring up *v adv* **rang up, rung up** [T1] to record (money paid) on a machine which strikes a bell when the amount has been noted: *He sold me the shoes and rang up £10* —see also RING³ (5)

ring with *v prep* **rang with, rung with** [T1 *no pass.*] to be filled with the sound of: *The cinema rang with the children's laughter*

ring·worm /'rɪŋwɜːm‖-wɜrm/ *n* [U] a skin disease passed on by touch, and causing red rings often on the head

rink /rɪŋk/ *n* a specially prepared surface of **a** ice, for skating (SKATE) **b** any hard material, for roller-skating (ROLLER-SKATE): *I'll meet you on the rink*

rinse¹ /rɪns/ *v* **1** [T1 (OUT)] to wash (esp. clothes) in clean water so as to take away soap, dirt, etc.: *I'll just rinse (out) these shirts.|Rinse your mouth (out)* **2** [X9, esp. OUT or *out of*] to wash (soap, dirt, etc.) out (of something) with clean water: *Rinse the soap out of these shirts.|to rinse out the sea water from one's bathing-suit*

rinse² *n* **1** [C] an act of rinsing (RINSE¹): *Give the shirts at least 3 rinses* **2** [C;U: 9] (a) liquid for colouring the hair: *a (bottle of) blue rinse for grey hair*

rinse down *v adv* [T1 (*with*)] to swallow (food) down (with a drink): *Have a glass of beer to rinse your dinner down*

ri·ot¹ /'raɪət/ *n* **1** [C] a lot of violent actions, noisy behaviour, etc., by a number of people together, esp. in a public place: *call in the army to* PUT DOWN (2) *a riot* **2** [S] *infml* a very funny and successful occasion or person: *I hear the new show is a riot—do let's go and see it!* **3 a riot of colour** a plentiful usu. disordered show of colour: *The garden is a riot of colour with all those roses* **4 run riot a** to become violent and uncontrollable: *The football supporters ran riot through the town after the defeat of their team* **b** (of a plant) to grow too thick and tall

riot² *v* [IØ] to take part in a RIOT¹ (1): *The crowds are rioting for more pay/rioting against the Government* —**~er** *n*

riot act /'·· ·/ *n* **read the riot act** *humor* to warn (esp. children) to stop making a noise: *Goodness, did you hear that? I'd better go upstairs and read (them) the riot act*

riot in *v prep* [T1] *fml* (esp. bad things) to enjoy very much: *a wicked king who rioted in evil living* —compare REVEL IN

ri·ot·ous /'raɪətəs/ *adj* **1** (of people or behaviour) wild and disorderly: *a riotous crowd* **2** *apprec* (of an occasion) noisy and exciting: *They spent a riotous night drinking and singing* —**~ly** *adv* —**~ness** *n* [U]

rip¹ /rɪp/ *v* **-pp-** **1** [IØ] to be torn quickly and violently: *The sail ripped under the force of the wind* **2** [T1] to cause to tear quickly and violently: *He ripped the cloth with his knife.|I ripped my stocking on a nail* **3** [X9 *esp.* OFF] to put into the stated condition by quick and violent tearing: *He ripped the cover from the book.|*(fig.) *She ripped off her dress.|I ripped the letter open.|He ripped the curtains to/into pieces.|I ripped the paper in 2* **4 let her/it rip** *infml* to let (a car, boat, etc.) go at top speed **5 let things rip** *infml* to remove control and let things develop in their own way: *They'll be dancing all night—we'd better just go to bed and let things rip!* —see also RIP ALONG, RIP OFF, RIP UP

rip² *n* a long tear or cut: *a rip in the tyre caused by a sharp stone*

rip³ *n tech* a piece of rough water where 2 currents meet, in the sea or at the mouth of a river —see also RIPTIDE

rip⁴ *n* [C; *you*+N9] *sl becoming rare* a wild fellow: *3 wives at once! You old rip!*

RIP /,ɑːr aɪ 'piː/ *abbrev. for*: rest in peace (written on gravestones)

rip a·long *v adv* [IØ] *not fml* (of a car, boat, etc.) to go very fast or at top speed

ri·par·i·an /raɪ'peərɪən‖rɪ̈-/ *adj* [Wa5] *fml or tech* on or of the banks of a river, lake, etc.: *He owns a riparian property*

riparian rights /·,··· '·/ *n* [P] *law* the right to swim, catch fish, etc., in a piece of water because one owns the bank(s)

rip·cord /'rɪpkɔːd‖-kɔrd/ *n* **1** the cord that one pulls to open a PARACHUTE (=big circle of cloth used for jumping from an aircraft) when descending **2** the cord that one pulls to let gas out of a BALLOON (=big bag of gas used for air travel)

ripe /raɪp/ *adj* **1** [Wa1;B] (of fruit and crops) fully grown and ready to be eaten: *a field of ripe corn* (fig.) *her ripe red lips* —opposite **unripe** **2** [Wa1;B] (of cheese or wine) old enough to be eaten or drunk **3** [Wa1;B] (of a quality) fully developed: *I must ask someone of riper judgment/*SCHOLARSHIP (2) *than myself what to do* **4** [Wa5;F+*for*] ready for; fit for: *land ripe for industrial development|She is not yet ripe for marriage* **5** [Wa1;F+*in*] *fml* having grown to the possession (of): *a man ripe in experience* **6** [Wa1;B] *infml euph* concerned with or expressing such matters as sex, the passing of waste matter from the body, etc., in a shocking and/or amusing way: *That joke was rather ripe* **7 of ripe age** grown-up and experienced **8 of ripe(r) years** *euph or humor* no longer young **9 the time is ripe (for)** it is time (for); things are ready (for): *I won't tell her the news until the time is ripe (for it)* —**~ly** *adv* —**~ness** *n* [U]

rip·en /'raɪpən/ *v* [IØ;T1] to make or become ripe: *The sun ripens the corn.|The corn ripens in the sun*

rip-off /'· ·/ *n sl* **1** *esp. AmE* an act of stealing **2** an act of charging too much

rip off *v adv* [T1] *sl* **1** to rob (someone); charge (someone) too much: *They really ripped us off at that hotel!* **2** *esp. AmE* to steal: *Someone ripped off my bicycle*

ri·poste¹ /rɪ'pɒst, rɪ'pəʊst‖rɪ'pəʊst/ *n* **1** a quick return stroke with a sword in FENCING (1) **2** a quick, clever, and not very friendly reply

riposte² *v* **1** [IØ] to make a RIPOSTE¹ (1) **2** [IØ; T5a] (*sometimes used with the actual words spoken*) to reply as a RIPOSTE¹ (2): *"Nobody asked you, sir!" she riposted daringly*

rip·ple¹ /'rɪpəl/ *v* [Wv3] **1** [IØ;T1] to (cause to)

move in RIPPLEs² (1): *The lake rippled gently.|The wind rippled the surface of the cornfield* **2** [Wv5;T1] to form RIPPLEs² (2) on: *the rippled surface of the sand* **3** [IØ] to make a sound like gently running water: *a rippling stream|The water rippled over the stones*

ripple² *n* **1** [C] a very small wave; gentle waving movement: *ripples on a pool when the wind blows* **2** [C] a wavelike mark: *The sea leaves ripples on the sand* **3** [S9] a sound of or like gently running water: *I heard the ripple of the stream*

rip-roar·ing /ˌ· ˈ··/ *adj infml* noisy and exciting: *a rip-roaring party|They had a rip-roaring time spending all their wages in one night*

rip·saw /ˈrɪpsɔː/ *n* a coarse tool (SAW) that cuts wood along the direction of growth (GRAIN (5))

rip·tide /ˈrɪptaɪd/ *n* a TIDE (=regular rise and fall of the sea) that makes rough water and currents: *You'll never get the boat out; there's a riptide running tonight*

rip up *v adv* [T1] to tear violently into pieces: *Angrily she ripped the letter up.|*(fig.) *We must rip up our plan and start again*

rise¹ /raɪz/ *v* **rose** /rəʊz/, **risen** /ˈrɪzən/ **1** [IØ] (of the sun, moon, or stars) to come up; appear above the horizon: *The sun rises in the east* —opposite **set** **2** [IØ] to go up; get higher: *The river is rising after the rain.|Smoke rose from the factory chimneys.|Her voice rose higher and higher with excitement.|New factories have risen on the edge of the town* **3** [IØ] *fml* to get out of bed; get up: *She rises before it is light* **4** [IØ (UP)] also (*fml*) **arise**— to stand up from lying, kneeling, or sitting: *He rose from his knees.|She rose to greet her guests.|I cannot rise because of my broken leg* **5** [IØ] *fml* (of a group of people) to end a meeting: *We/The court will now rise for dinner* **6** [IØ] (of price, amount, temperature, etc.) to increase; get higher: *Tea/The price of tea has risen by 5 pence/has risen to 30 pence* —opposite **fall** **7** [Wv4;IØ] (of land) to slope upward: *The road rises steeply from the village* **8** [Wv6;L9] (of a river) to begin: *The River Rhine rises in Switzerland.|*(fig.) *The quarrel rose from/out of a misunderstanding* **9** [Wv6;L9] to show above the surroundings: *trees rising over the roof-tops* **10** [IØ] to come up to the surface of a liquid: *The fish are rising; perhaps we'll catch one* **11** [L9 esp. *from, to*] to move up in rank: *He rose from the rank of captain/to the rank of general* —see also RANKS **12** [IØ] (of uncooked bread) to swell as the YEAST works: *The bread won't rise properly* **13** [IØ] (of feelings) to become more cheerful: *My spirits rose when I saw the result* **14** [IØ] (of wind or storms) to get stronger **15** [IØ (*to*)] to show weakness or annoyance in reply to someone's intentionally nasty words or behaviour: *It's no good making jokes about John's mother—you won't get him to rise* —compare RISE² (6) **16** **rise again** also **rise from the dead**— to come back to life after being dead **17** **rise to the occasion** to show that one can deal with a difficult matter: *When the unexpected guests came, Mother rose to the occasion by making soup*

USAGE **raise** [T1] is used when someone/something places some other person or thing in a higher position. Compare this with **rise** [IØ], (*fml* **arise**) which is used when the person himself or thing itself moves to a higher position: *He* **raised** *the child from the ground.|The child* **rose** *from the ground.* But note: *He* **raised** *himself from the ground.*

rise² *n* **1** [U9] the act of growing greater or more powerful: *the rise and fall of the Roman Empire* **2** [C9 esp. *in*] an increase (in price, amount, temperature, etc.): *a rise in the cost of living* **3** [C] an upward slope; small hill: *a rise in the road|sit at the top of a small rise* **4** [C] (*AmE* **raise**)— *BrE not fml* an increase in wages: *We all got a £6-a-week rise last month.|I've had 2 rises this year* **5** [C] (esp. of fish) an act of rising to the surface of water: *There are lots of fish in the river but I haven't had a rise yet* **6** **get/take a rise out of someone** *not fml* intentionally to make someone show weakness or annoyance by one's words or behaviour: *You can always get a rise out of John by making jokes about his mother* **7** **give rise to** to be the cause of; lead to (esp. bad things): *These bad conditions have given rise to a lot of crime*

USAGE Note the word order in the fixed phr. **rise and fall**: *The water rose and fell.|The rise and fall of the temperature is caused by the wind.*

rise a·bove *v prep* [T1,4: *no pass*] to reach a higher standard than; conquer (faults, difficulties, etc.): *I thought you had risen above lying to your mother*

rise a·gainst *v prep* [T1] to REBEL against (rule or rulers); begin to oppose: *The people rose (up) against their leaders*

ris·er /ˈraɪzəʳ/ *n* **1** [C] the upright part of a step, between 2 flat parts (TREADs) **2** **early/late riser** a person who gets out of bed early/late in the morning

ris·i·bil·i·ty /ˌrɪzəˈbɪlǝ̍ti/ *n* [U *often pl. with sing. meaning*] *fml or pomp* the ability or desire to laugh

ris·i·ble /ˈrɪzəbəl/ *adj fml or pomp* **1** [B] funny; causing laughter **2** [Wa5;A] of or concerning laughter: *the risible muscles*

ris·ing¹ /ˈraɪzɪŋ/ *n* an occasion of rising against (RISE AGAINST) the rulers, esp. the government; (small) INSURRECTION

rising² *prep* nearly (the stated age): *My daughter is rising 7*

rising damp /ˌ·· ˈ·/ *n* [U] water that comes up from the ground into the walls of a building

rising gen·e·ra·tion /ˌ·· ··ˈ··/ *n* [*the*+GU] *pomp* young people who are growing up: *The rising generation have/has some funny ideas*

risk¹ /rɪsk/ *n* **1** [S;U: (*of,* 5)] a danger (of); something that may have a (stated) bad result: *There's some/a great/no/not much risk (of fire)* **2** [C] a danger: *Fishermen face a lot of risks in their daily lives* **3** [C9] (in insurance and insurance contracts) **a** (stated) danger: *fire risk|war risk|to* INSURE *it for all risks* **b** a person or thing that is a (stated) danger for the insurance company: *I'm afraid I'm a poor risk for life insurance—my health is so bad* **4** **at one's own risk** agreeing to bear any loss or danger: *"Anyone swimming in this lake does so at his own risk"* (notice) **5** **at owner's risk** (of goods sent by railway) with the owner agreeing to bear any loss or damage **6** **at risk** *fml* in danger: *The disease is spreading, and all children under 5 are at risk* **7** **at the risk of** **a** with danger of: *He saved my life at the risk of losing his own.|At the risk of seeming rude, I must say . . .* **b** also **at risk to**— with danger to: *He saved my life at the risk of his own/at (great) risk to his own* **8** **run/take risks/a risk** to do dangerous things; take chances/a chance: *You have to take a lot of risks in my job.|You're running a big risk in trusting him.|We'll just have to take the risk that George may come home* **9** **run/take the risk of doing something** to do (something dangerous): *I don't want to run the risk of meeting George*

risk² *v* **1** [T1] to place in danger: *to risk one's health|to risk one's money at cards* **2** [T1,4] to take the chance of: *to risk failure|He risked his parents' anger by marrying me*

risk·y /ˈrɪski/ *adj* [Wa2] *not fml* (esp. of an action) dangerous: *Robbing banks is risky as well as wrong* —**riskily** *adv* —**riskiness** *n* [U]

ri·sot·to /rɪˈzɒtəʊ‖-sɔ-/ *n* **-tos** [C;U] (a) food made of rice cooked with cheese, onions, chicken, etc.

ris·qué /ˈrɪskeɪ‖rɪˈskeɪ/ *adj Fr* (of a joke, story,

etc.) slightly rude and dirty; concerned with sex: *a rather risqué conversation*

ris·sole /ˈrɪsəʊl/ *n* a small round flat mass of cut-up meat (or fish), mixed with potato, egg, etc., and cooked in hot fat

rite /raɪt/ *n* [*often pl. with sing. meaning*] a form of behaviour with a fixed pattern, usu. for a religious purpose: *funeral rites*

rit·u·al[1] /ˈrɪtʃʊəl/ *adj* [Wa5;A] connected with RITUAL[2]; done as a RITE: *ritual dances|ritual murder* —**~ly** *adv*: *ritually killed*

ritual[2] *n* [C;U] one or more ceremonies or customary acts which are often repeated in the same form: *She went through the ritual of warming the teapot before she put the tea in.|Christian ritual* (=the form of church services)

rit·u·al·is·m /ˈrɪtʃʊəlɪzəm/ *n* [U] *often derog* great interest in or obedience to RITUAL[2]: *There's too much ritualism for me in that religion* —**-istic** /ˌrɪtʃʊəˈlɪstɪk/ *adj* —**-istically** *adv* [Wa4]

ritz·y /ˈrɪtsi/ *adj* [Wa1] *sl, becoming rare* beautiful and costly: *a very ritzy new car/flat*

ri·val[1] /ˈraɪvəl/ *n* [(*for, in*)] a person with whom one competes: *Bob and I were rivals for the job/in the painting competition/in love*

rival[2] *adj* [Wa5;A] competing: *If you aren't careful, I'll take my business to a rival firm of printers!*

rival[3] *v* **-ll-** (*AmE* **-l-**) [T1] to equal; be as good as: *Ships can't rival aircraft for speed*

ri·val·ry /ˈraɪvəlri/ *n* [C;U: (*in, with*)] competition; (a case of) being RIVALS[1]: *the many rivalries of office life|Should we encourage international rivalry in sport?|I don't want to enter into rivalry with you over Mildred—she's not worth it*

rive /raɪv/ *v* **rived, riv·en** /ˈrɪvən/ [T1 *usu. pass.*] *old use* to cause to split violently apart: *rocks riven by fire*|(fig.) *Her heart was riven by sorrow*

riv·er /ˈrɪvəʳ/ *n* **1** a wide natural stream of water flowing between banks into a lake, into another wider stream, or into the sea: *to go swimming in the river|sailing on the river|the river Amazon*|(fig.) *Rivers of blood flowed during the war* **2 sell someone down the river** to cause someone great disadvantage by being disloyal or unfaithful; BETRAY (1) someone

river ba·sin /ˈ·· ˌ··/ *n* an area from which all the water flows into the same river

riv·er·bed /ˈrɪvəbed‖-ər-/ *n* the ground over which a river flows between its banks

riv·er·side /ˈrɪvəsaɪd‖-ər-/ *n, adj* [Wa5;A; *the*+R] (the land) on or near the banks of a river: *to tie up the boat by the riverside|an old riverside inn*

riv·et[1] /ˈrɪvɪ̈t/ *n* a metal pin for fastening metal plates (as when building a ship), its ends being hammered flat after fixing, so that they spread and hold firmly —see picture at MACHINERY

rivet[2] *v* **1** [T1;X9] to cause to fasten with RIVETs[1]: *He riveted the metal sheets* (*on/together/to the ship's bottom*) **2** [T1] to attract and hold (someone's attention) strongly: *The strange sound riveted the attention of a passing policeman*

riv·et·er /ˈrɪvɪ̈təʳ/ *n* a person whose job is fastening RIVETs[1]

riv·et·ing /ˈrɪvɪ̈tɪŋ/ *adj not fml* very interesting and exciting: *He gave us a riveting account of his escape from the lion*

rivet on *v prep* [D1 *often pass.*] to fix (eyes or attention) firmly on: *He riveted his eyes on her.|All attention was riveted on the royal pair*

ri·vi·e·ra /ˌrɪviˈeərə/ *n* a warm stretch of coast that is popular with holidaymakers: *the Cornish Riviera*

riv·u·let /ˈrɪvjʊlɪ̈t‖-vjə-/ *n lit* a very small stream

RN [E] *abbrev. for*: Royal Navy (=the British navy): *Captain Anstruther, RN*

RNA *n* [U] *tech* ribonucleic acid; an important chemical found in all living cells; form of NUCLEIC ACID

roach[1] /rəʊtʃ/ *n* **roach** *or* **roaches** [Wn2] a kind of European fresh-water fish related to the CARP —see picture at FISH[1]

roach[2] *n* **1** *sl* the end of a MARIJUANA cigarette **2** *infml* COCKROACH

road /rəʊd/ *n* **1** [C; *by*+U] a smooth prepared track or way along which wheeled vehicles can travel, usu. between towns rather than within one: *It takes 3 hours by train and 4 by road* (=driving).|*It's not really a road, only a path.|a road map of Western Europe|There have been so many road accidents lately that you must teach the children about road safety* —see STREET (USAGE) **2** [S9] *becoming rare* (one's) way; space: *Get out of my road; I want to pass* **3** [C *usu. pl. with sing. meaning*] also **roadstead**— an open stretch of deep water, as at the mouth of a river, where ships can float at ANCHOR **4 on the road a** on a journey; travelling, esp. for one's work **b** (of esp. a theatrical company) TOURing; giving a number of planned performances at different places: *get the show on the road* **5 royal road (to)** an easy way (to): *There's no royal road to success in this trade, my boy!* **6 rule(s) of the road** the agreement(s) as to which side vehicles or ships should take when meeting, passing, etc.: *According to the rule of the road you must drive on the left in Britain* **7 take to the road** to become a TRAMP (=a homeless poor person without work who walks from place to place) —**~less** *adj* [Wa5]

Road *n* **1** [*the*+R9] (part of the name of) the road leading to a particular named place: *The Cambridge Road* **2** [R9] (part of the name of) a street in a town: *39 Forest Road*

road·bed /ˈrəʊdbed/ *n* [*usu. sing.*] the base of hard materials on which a road surface is laid

road·block /ˈrəʊdblɒk‖-blɑk/ *n* a bar or other object(s) used for closing a road to stop traffic, an enemy, etc.

road hog /ˈ· ·/ *n* [C;N] *not fml* a fast, selfish, and careless car driver

road·house /ˈrəʊdhaʊs/ *n* **-houses** /ˌhaʊzɪ̈z/ an inn on a main road outside a city, to which one goes to eat, drink, dance, etc.

road·man /ˈrəʊdmən/ also **road mend·er** /ˈ· ˌ··/— *n* **-men** /mən/ a man whose job is mending roads

road man·a·ger /ˈ· ···/ also (*infml*) **road·ie** /ˈrəʊdi/— *n* a person whose job is making arrangements for a GROUP[1] (3) when they are travelling

road met·al /ˈ· ··/ *n* [U] the stone used for making and mending roads

road sense /ˈ· ·/ *n* [U] the power to avoid accidents when walking or driving among traffic

road·side /ˈrəʊdsaɪd/ *n, adj* [Wa5;A; *the*+R] (at or near) the edge of the road: *We ate our meal by the roadside/at a roadside inn*

road·stead /ˈrəʊdsted/ *n* ROAD (3)

road·ster /ˈrəʊdstəʳ/ *n now rare* an open car with 2 seats

road·way /ˈrəʊdweɪ/ *n* [*the*+R] the middle part of a road where vehicles drive: *Don't stop on the roadway; go to the side* —compare FOOTPATH, PAVEMENT

road works /ˈrəʊdwɜːks‖-ɜr-/ *n* [P] (often seen on a warning sign for motorists) road repairs being carried out

road·wor·thy /ˈrəʊdˌwɜːði‖-ɜr-/ *adj* (of a vehicle) in a fit condition to be driven on the road —**-thiness** *n* [U]

roam /rəʊm/ *v* [IØ (*through, around*);T1] (of a person) to wander with no very clear aim (through, around, etc.): *The lovers roamed around/*

across/through/over the fields in complete forgetfulness of the time.|*to roam from place to place* —**~er** *n*: *Stanley is a roamer by nature and will never settle down*

roan[1] /rəʊn/ *adj, n* [Wa5;B;U] (of a horse or cow) (of) a mixed colour, esp. brown with white hairs in it: *a roan cow*

roan[2] *n* **1** [C] a ROAN[1] horse: *Who's that riding the roan?* **2** [U] a kind of soft leather made from SHEEPSKIN and used for binding books

roar[1] /rɔːʳ‖ror/ *v* **1** [Wv4;I∅] to give a ROAR[2] (1): *The lion/The football crowd/The engine roared.*|*a roaring wind in the trees* **2** [L9] to go along making a ROAR[2] (1): *The traffic roars past/along/down the hill* **3** [T1,5: (OUT)] (*often used with the actual words spoken*) (usu. of men or groups) to say or express with a ROAR[2] (1): *The crowd roared their approval.*|*He roared out the word of command* **4** [I∅] *infml* to laugh long and loudly: *Mother will roar when she hears what happened to your socks!* **5** [I∅] *not fml* (of a child) to weep noisily: *Billy began to roar when I took the chocolate away* **6** [X7] to cause oneself to become by shouting: *He roared himself* HOARSE (=made his throat sore and his voice rough) **7 do a roaring trade** *not fml* to do very good business; sell one's goods very fast

roar[2] *n* **1** a deep loud continuing sound: *the roar of an angry lion/of a football crowd/of an aircraft engine/of the wind and waves* **2** [+*of*] a deep loud sound of the stated kind: *roars of laughter* **3 set the room/the table in a roar** to make everyone in the room/at the table laugh loudly

roar down *v adv* [T1] to drown the voice of (a speaker) by shouting

roar for *v prep* [T1] to shout for; demand with a ROAR[2] (1): *He roared for mercy*

roar·ing[1] /ˈrɔːrɪŋ‖ˈrorɪŋ/ *n* [S] an uninterrupted ROAR[2] (1): *a roaring in one's ears*

roaring[2] *adv* [Wa5] *not fml* very (esp. in the phr. **roaring drunk**): *He came home roaring drunk and beat his wife*

roaring for·ties /ˌ·· ˈ··/ *n* [*the* + P] the part of the oceans between 40 and 50 degrees south of the EQUATOR where storms are very common

roaring suc·cess /ˌ·· ·ˈ·/ *n* [S] a very great success

roar with *v prep* [T1] to express with a ROAR[2] (in such phrs. as **roar with laughter/pain/anger**)

roast[1] /rəʊst/ *v* **1** [Wv5;T1;I∅] **a** to cook (esp. meat) by dry heat, either in front of an open fire or in a hot iron box (OVEN): *to roast a chicken*|*roasted coffee beans*|(fig.) *to roast oneself in the sun* **b** (esp. of meat) to be cooked in this way: *The meat is roasting nicely* —see COOK (USAGE) **2 fit to roast an ox** (of a fire) very big and hot **3 give someone a (good/real) roasting** to scold someone severely

roast[2] *n* **1** [C] a large piece of ROASTed[1] (1) meat: *Let's have a nice roast for Sunday dinner* **2** [A] ROASTed[1] (1): *a roast chicken*|*roast potatoes* **3** [C9] *esp. AmE* a meal eaten out of doors where the stated food is ROASTed[1] (1) over an open fire

roast·er /ˈrəʊstəʳ/ *n* **1** an apparatus for ROASTing[1] (1) food **2** a piece of meat suitable for ROASTing[1] (1)

roast·ing /ˈrəʊstɪŋ/ *adj, adv* [Wa5] very (hot): *a roasting (hot) summer day*

rob /rɒb‖rab/ *v* **-bb-** [T1 (*of*);(I∅)] to take the property of (a person or organization) unlawfully, with or without violence or threats: *to rob a bank*|*They knocked him down and robbed him of his watch* (compare *They stole his watch*).|(fig.) *You have robbed me of my happiness!* (compare *You have taken away my happiness* —see STEAL (USAGE)

rob·ber /ˈrɒbəʳ‖ˈra-/ *n* a person who robs or has robbed: *a band/a* GANG (2) *of robbers*

rob·ber·y /ˈrɒbəri‖ˈra-/ *n* **1** [U] the crime of taking someone else's property; robbing: *He was charged with robbery with violence* **2** [C] an example of this **3 daylight robbery** *infml* charging too much money: *£3 for a beer? It's daylight robbery!*

robe[1] /rəʊb/ *n* **1** a long flowing indoor garment for informal occasions: *a bath robe* **2** [*often pl. with sing. meaning*] such a garment when worn for official or ceremonial occasions: *a judge's black robes* **3** *esp. AmE* a warm covering for the lower body, often made of fur, used when sitting out of doors

robe[2] *v* [Wv5;I∅;T1: (*in*)] to dress (oneself or another) in ROBEs; put on a ROBE: *the king and queen robed in red*

rob·in /ˈrɒbɪ̣n‖ˈra-/ also (*used esp. to children*) **robin red·breast** /ˌ·· ˈ··/— *n* **1** a common type of fat little European bird, with a brown back and wings and a red breast —see picture at BIRD **2** any of various larger birds of the THRUSH family that look like this, in the US and other English-speaking countries

ro·bot /ˈrəʊbɒt‖-bat, -bət/ *n* **1** a machine that can move and do some of the work of a man, esp. an imaginary machine figure that moves and acts as if alive: *invent a robot to do the cleaning*|*A robot bomb is a small* UNMANNED *aircraft that can find its own way to the place where it is to fall as a bomb* **2** a person who acts without thought or feeling, as if he were a machine

ro·bust /rəˈbʌst, ˈrəʊbʌst/ *adj* **1** having or showing very good health: *a robust young man* **2** *not derog, often euph* (of jokes, conversation, etc.) rather rude; not suited to polite society —**~ly** *adv*: *He laughed robustly at her silly fears* —**~ness** *n* [U]

rock[1] /rɒk‖rak/ *v* **1** [I∅;T1] to (cause to) move regularly backwards and forwards or from side to side: *She rocked the child in her arms.*|*He rocked the* CRADLE[1] (1).|*The boat rocked (to and fro) on the water* **2** [T1] to cause great shock and surprise to: *The news of the President's murder rocked the nation* **3** [I∅] to dance to ROCK 'N' ROLL music **4 rock someone to sleep** to move someone, esp. a baby, to and fro so as to bring sleep **5 rock the boat** *derog* (of a member of a group) to do something that makes it hard for the group to work together: *Even if you don't agree with me, you mustn't rock the boat at this difficult time*

rock[2] *n* [U] ROCK 'N' ROLL

rock[3] *n* **1** [U] stone forming part of the earth's surface: *a passage cut through (the) solid rock*|*an interesting rock formation* **2** [C] (*often cap.*) a large mass of stone standing up above the level of its surroundings: *Edinburgh Castle stands on the Castle Rock* **3** [C] a large separate piece of stone: *danger from falling rocks* **4** [C] *AmE* a stone: *throw rocks at the teacher* **5** [U] (in Britain) a hard sticky kind of sweet made in long round bars and sold esp. at the seaside with the name of the place marked in it: *a stick of (Brighton) rock* **6 as firm/steady/solid as a rock a** perfectly firm and hard; unlikely to move **b** (of people) trustworthy

rock and roll /ˌ·· · ˈ·/ *n* [U] ROCK 'N' ROLL

rock bot·tom /ˌ· ˈ··/ *n* [R] (esp. of prices) the lowest point; the bottom: *Prices have reached rock bottom*

rock·bound /ˈrɒkbaʊnd‖ˈrak-/ *adj* [Wa5] (of a coast) bordered with rocks

rock cake /ˈ· ·/ also **rock bun**— *n* a type of small hard cake with a rough surface

rock-climb·ing /ˈ· ˌ··/ *n* [U] the sport of climbing rocks with ropes, special boots, etc.

rock crys·tal /ˈ· ˌ··/ *n* [U] a type of clear precious stone like glass; kind of QUARTZ

rock·er /ˈrɒkəʳ‖ˈra-/ *n* **1** one of the curved pieces of wood underneath a ROCKING CHAIR, ROCKING HORSE, or CRADLE[1] (1), which causes movement to and fro when pushed **2** *AmE* ROCKING CHAIR **3** **off one's rocker** *sl* out of one's mind; mad

rock·e·ry /ˈrɒkəri‖ˈrɑ-/ also **rock gar·den** /ˈ· ˌ··/— *n* a (part of a) garden laid out as a heap of rocks with suitable low-growing plants growing between them —see picture at GARDEN[1]

rock·et[1] /ˈrɒk$\frac{1}{2}$t‖ˈrɑ-/ *n* **1** a tube-shaped case packed with gunpowder, and with a stick fixed to it, that is shot high into the air and lets out stars of coloured flame; kind of FIREWORK: *We'll let off rockets on your birthday* **2** a machine of this kind driven by burning gases and carrying its own oxygen, used as a form of power for aircraft engines, and for space travel **3** a bomb or MISSILE (1) that is driven in this way **4** **give someone/get a rocket** *BrE infml* to scold someone/be scolded severely

rocket[2] *v* **1** [IØ (UP)] (esp. of levels, amounts, etc.) to rise quickly and suddenly: *The price of sugar has rocketed (up)* **2** [L9] to move very fast: *The train rocketed through the station at 90 miles an hour*

rocket base /ˈ·· ·/ *n* a military base for ROCKETs[1] (3)

rock·et·ry /ˈrɒk$\frac{1}{2}$tri‖ˈrɑ-/ *n* [U] the science of using ROCKETs[1] (2) for space travel

rocking chair /ˈrɒkɪŋ tʃeəʳ‖ˈrɑ-/ *AmE* also **rocker**— *n* a chair fitted with ROCKERs (1)

rocking horse /ˈ·· ·/ *n* a wooden horse fitted with ROCKERs (1), for a child to ride on

rock 'n' roll /ˌrɒk ən ˈrəʊl‖ˌrɑk-/ also **rock and roll**— *n* [U] a kind of popular modern dance music played loudly on electrical instruments. It has a strong beat, and goes on repeating the same few simple phrases

rock plant /ˈ· ·/ *n* any of those kinds of plant that grow naturally among rocks and can be planted in a ROCKERY

rocks /rɒks‖rɑks/ *n* [P] **1** a line of ROCK[3] under or beside the sea: *ships driven onto the rocks by a storm* **2** **on the rocks** **a** in difficulties over money **b** (of alcoholic drinks) with ice but no water: WHISKY *on the rocks* **c** (of a marriage) likely to break up soon

rock sal·mon /ˌ· ˈ··/ *n* [U] *BrE euph* (the trade name for) any of several types of fish such as DOGFISH, when sold as food

rock salt /ˈ· ·/ *n* [U] common salt as found in mines, not in the sea

rock·y[1] /ˈrɒki‖ˈrɑki/ *adj* [Wa1] **1** full of rocks; made of rock: *a rocky path up the mountain* **2** hard like rock —**rockiness** *n* [U]

rocky[2] *adj* [Wa1] *not fml* unsteady; not firm: *Be careful of that chair—it's a bit rocky.|I feel very rocky on my legs after that fall*

ro·co·co /rəˈkəʊkəʊ/ *adj* [Wa5] (of buildings, furniture, etc.) of a style fashionable in Europe from the late 17th to the 18th century, with a great deal of curling ornament

rod /rɒd‖rɑd/ *n* **1** [C] a long thin pole or bar of any stiff material such as wood, metal, or plastic: *to go fishing with rod and line|*PISTON-*rods in an engine* **2** [C] a stick used for beating people **3** [*the*+R] a beating given as a punishment: *The rod is not allowed in this school* **4** [C] also **perch, pole**— *esp. BrE, now rare* a measure of length equal to 5½ yards or 5·03 metres **5** [C] *AmE sl* PISTOL **6** **have a rod in pickle for someone** *becoming rare* to have a punishment ready for someone later on **7** **make a rod for one's own back** to prepare trouble for oneself in the future **8** **"Spare the rod and spoil the child"** (old saying) A child who is never punished will grow up with bad habits

rode /rəʊd/ *past t. of* RIDE

ro·dent /ˈrəʊdənt/ *n* a member of the family of small plant-eating animals with strong sharp teeth, that includes rats, mice, and rabbits —see picture at MAMMAL

ro·de·o /rəʊˈdeɪ-əʊ, ˈrəʊdi-əʊ/ *n* **-os** (in Canada and the western US) **1** a gathering together of cattle **2** a public performance at which COWBOYs ride wild horses, catch cattle with ropes, etc.

ro·do·mon·tade /ˌrɒdəmɒnˈteɪd, -ˈtɑːd‖ˌrɑdəmən-/ *n* [U] *fml & derog* the claim to be specially brave or clever; BOASTful talk: *a stupid piece of rodomontade*

roe[1] /rəʊ/ *n* [Wn1] ROE DEER

roe[2] *n* [C;U] (a) mass of eggs or male seed (SPERM) in a fish, often eaten as food

roe·buck /ˈrəʊbʌk/ *n* [Wn1] a male ROE DEER

roe deer /ˈ· ·/ *n* **-deer** [Wn3] a kind of small European and Asian forest deer

roent·gen[1], **röntgen** /ˈrɒntjən‖ˈrentgən/ *adj* [Wa5;A] *tech* (*often cap.*) of or concerning X-RAYs (1)

roentgen[2], **röntgen** *n tech* the international measure for X-RAYs (1)

ro·ga·tion /rəʊˈgeɪʃən/ *n* [*usu. pl. with sing. meaning*] the holy words regularly sung in Christian churches during the week (**Rogation week**) before the day in early summer (ASCENSION DAY) on which Jesus is said to have left the earth and gone to heaven

ro·ger /ˈrɒdʒəʳ‖ˈrɑ-/ *interj* (the male first name used in radio and signalling to show that a) message has been received and understood

rogue[1] /rəʊg/ *n* **1** [C; *you*+N] a very dishonest person, esp. a man: *Don't buy a used car from that rogue* **2** [C9; *you*+N9] *humor, becoming rare* a boy who likes playing tricks: *You little rogue—where are my shoes?*

rogue[2] *adj* [Wa5;A] (of a wild animal) living apart from the rest and having a very bad temper: *a rogue elephant*

rogu·e·ry /ˈrəʊgəri/ *n* [C;U] (a piece of) behaviour typical of a ROGUE[1]: *I've never heard of such roguery.|another of his rogueries*

rogu·ish /ˈrəʊgɪʃ/ *adj becoming rare* (typical of a person) who is playful and fond of playing tricks: *a merry roguish laugh|a roguish little dog pretending to bite my finger* —**~ly** *adv* —**~ness** *n* [U]

rois·ter·er /ˈrɔɪstərəʳ/ *n* a rough cheerful noisy person: *a crowd of drunk roisterers*

role /rəʊl/ *n* the part taken by someone in life or in any activity, esp. the part of some particular actor in a play: *Olivier played the role of Hamlet.|to fulfil her role as a mother* —see also TITLE ROLE

roll[1] /rəʊl/ *n* **1** [C+*of*] a flat piece (of the stated material) that has been ROLLed[2] (4) into a tube shape: *a roll of film|of paper|of cloth* **2** [C] a small loaf for one person, either long or in the shape of a ball: *breakfast rolls|a brown roll* **3** [C9] a small loaf for one person, cut through and filled with the stated food: *cheese rolls* —compare SAUSAGE ROLL **4** [C] (*often cap.*) an official list of names: *The College Roll shows the names of all the students* **5** **call the roll** to read aloud an official list of names to see who is there; hold ROLL CALL

roll[2] *v* **1** [L9;X9] to (cause to) move along by turning over and over: *We rolled the barrels of oil onto the ship.|The ball rolled into the hole.|Tears were rolling down her cheeks.|The big wave rolled me over and over* **2** [L9;(IØ)] to turn oneself over and over or from side to side: *The dog rolled on the floor|in the mud.|This horse likes to roll (on its back).|It's good for the baby to roll about* **3** [L9] to move steadily and smoothly along (as) on wheels: *The train rolled slowly into the station.|The clouds are rolling away.|The waves rolled over the sand* **4** [T1;X9: (UP)] to form into a tube or other (stated) shape by curling round and round: *He rolled (up) his* UMBRELLA.|*Roll up the map!*|*The cat rolled itself into a ball and went to sleep* —opposite **unroll** **5** [D1 (*for*);T1] to make (a tubelike object) by curling round and round between 2 moving surfaces such as one's hands: *to roll cigarettes*|*Please roll me a cigarette* **6** [IØ;L9] **a** (of a ship) to swing from side to side with the movement of the waves: *The ship rolled so heavily that we were all sick* —compare PITCH² (9) **b** to walk along swinging like this: *The* DRUNKEN *man rolled home to bed* **7** [IØ;T1;X7] **a** to make (a surface) (flat) by pressing with a ROLLER (1): *roll the grass in the garden*|*roll the road surface flat* **b** to be made flat in this way: *The pastry is so wet it won't roll* —compare ROLL OUT (1) **8** [IØ] to make a long deep sound by or like that of a lot of quick strokes: *The thunder/The drums rolled* **9** [T1] to cause (esp. film cameras) to begin working: *We're ready—roll the cameras* **10** [IØ (ABOUT)] *infml* to be helpless with laughter: *His jokes kept us simply rolling (about) all evening* —see also **roll in the** AISLEs **11** [T1] *AmE sl* to rob (a sleeping or unconscious person): *roll a drunk* **12** [T1] to throw (DICE) **13** [T1;IØ] **a** to cause (the eyes) to move round and round: *Stop rolling your eyes at me, girl!* **b** (of the eyes) to move round and round: *His eyes were rolling with fear* **14 keep the ball rolling** to keep things active and moving **15 roll one's r's** to pronounce the sound /r/ with the tongue beating rapidly against the roof of the mouth, as is common in Scotland **16 set the ball rolling** to be the first to do something, hoping that others will follow: *I'll sing a song first, just to set the ball rolling* —see also ROLL BACK, ROLL BY, ROLL IN, ROLL ON, ROLL OUT, ROLL UP

roll³ *n* **1** [(*the*) S+of] a long deep sound as of a lot of quick strokes: *a roll of thunder/of drums*|*hear the distant roll of the big guns* **2** [C] **a** a rolling movement, over and over or to and fro sideways: *a young horse having a roll on the grass*|*the slow roll of a ship on the rough sea* **b** an action which includes this movement: *another roll of the* DICE —compare PITCH² (9)

roll back *v adv* [T1] **1** to force (opposition) to move back; push back (an enemy's front) **2** *AmE* to reduce (prices)

roll bar /ˈ· ·/ *n* a metal bar on the top of a car, to protect the people inside if the car turns over

roll by *v adv* [IØ] **1** to move steadily and smoothly past, (as) on wheels: *watching the cars roll by* **2** (of time) to go past: *The years rolled by* —compare ROLL ON (1,2)

roll call /ˈ· ·/ *n* [C;R] the time or act of reading out a list of names to see who is there: *We'd better have a roll call now.*|*I'll see you after roll call*

rolled gold /ˌrəʊld ˈgəʊld/ *n* [U] a thin covering of gold on the surface of another metal: *My watch is only rolled gold* (=has a covering of gold), *not solid gold*

roll·er /ˈrəʊləʳ/ *n* **1** a tube-shaped piece of wood, metal, hard rubber, etc., that rolls over and over, as used **a** in a machine, for crushing, pressing, printing, etc. **b** for smoothing the surface of grass or roads **c** for moving heavy things that have no wheels: *push the boat down to the water on rollers* **d** for shaping: *She puts her hair into rollers to make it curl* **2** a rod round which something is rolled up: *a big map on a roller* **3** a long heavy wave on the coast: *to swim along/among the Atlantic rollers*

roller ban·dage /ˈ·· ˌ··/ *n* a long rolled band of woven material for use on wounds (BANDAGE) that is rolled up when not in use

roller blind /ˈ·· ·/ *n BrE* a kind of curtain (BLIND) that rolls up and down over a window —compare SHADE¹ (2)

roller coast·er /ˈ·· ˌ··/ also (*esp. AmE*) **coaster**— *n* a kind of small railway with sharp slopes and curves, popular in amusement parks

roller-skate /ˈ·· ·/ *v* [IØ;L9] to go on ROLLER SKATEs: *They roller-skated down the street* —**~r** *n*

roller skate *n* [*usu. pl.*] a frame with 4 wheels for fitting under a shoe, or a shoe with wheels fixed on, for using on any smooth surface in the way that ordinary SKATEs are used on ice

roller tow·el /ˈ·· ˌ··/ *n* a cloth (TOWEL) for drying the hands, that has joined ends and is hung on a ROLLER (2)

rol·lick·ing /ˈrɒlɪkɪŋ‖ˈrɑ-/ *adj* [A;(B)] noisy and merry: *a rollicking song about life at sea*

roll in¹ *v adv* [IØ] *not fml* to come or arrive in large quantities: *Invitations kept rolling in* —compare ROLL UP (2,3)

roll in² *v prep* **1** [D1 (UP)] to wrap up (something) in (something) by curling over and over: *roll the baby in a warm covering* **2** [D1] to cover (something) in (something) by rolling about: *roll the cake in sugar* **3** [T1 *no pass., usu. pres. p.*] *not fml* to have plenty of (money)

roll·ing /ˈrəʊlɪŋ/ *adj* **1** [A] (of land) rising and falling in long gentle slopes: *a rolling plain* **2** [F] *infml* (of a person) very rich; ROLLing IN² (3) money: *He can afford anything—he's simply rolling*

rolling mill /ˈ·· ·/ *n* a factory where metal is ROLLed OUT (1) into plates

rolling pin /ˈ·· ·/ *n* a tube-shaped piece of wood, glass, or other material, about ⅓ metre long, for spreading pastry out flat and thin before cooking

rolling stock /ˈ·· ·/ *n* [U] everything on wheels that belongs to a railway, such as engines and carriages

rolling stone /ˌ·· ˈ·/ *n not fml* a person who travels around a lot and has no fixed address or responsibilities —see also **a rolling stone gathers no** MOSS

roll of hon·our /ˌ· · ˈ··/ *n* a list of the names of people who have earned praise, as by passing an examination, showing bravery in battle, etc.

roll-on /ˈ· ·/ *n* a woman's short elastic undergarment that is ROLLed ON (3), for supporting the lower part of the body

roll on *v adv* **1** [IØ] to (seem to) flow on in a large continuous stream: *The great river rolled on* **2** [IØ *imper.*] *not fml* (addressed to a time or date) to come soon; hurry up: *Roll on, Spring!* **3** [T1] to put on (a garment) by rolling

roll out *v adv* [T1] **1** to spread (a piece of material) out flat and thin by pressing with a ROLLER (1) or a ROLLING PIN: *roll out the pastry* —compare ROLL² (7) **2** *sometimes derog* to say or sing with a full deep voice: *He rolled out the song/the noble words* **3** *infml* to produce in large quantities: *They keep rolling out these new types of camera*

rolls /rəʊlz/ *n* [*the*+P] (*often cap.*) the official list of lawyers who are allowed to practise their profession (often in the phr. **strike** (a lawyer) **off the rolls**=not to allow him to practise any more)

roll·top desk /ˌrəʊltɒp ˈdesk‖-tɑp-/ *n* a desk whose cover rolls back out of the way when it is opened

roll up *v adv* **1** [Wv5;T1] to roll (SLEEVEs (1)) up one's arms; roll (trousers) up one's legs: *He rolled up his* SLEEVEs *and washed the dishes* **2** [IØ] *infml* to arrive (esp. late, drunk, or in any unacceptable way): *I might have known you wouldn't roll up until the meeting had nearly finished* **3** [IØ *usu. imper.*] (used esp. when asking people to come inside and see a show at a CIRCUS (2,3), FAIR³ (1), etc.) to come in: *Roll up, ladies and gentlemen, to see the fat lady!*

ro·ly-po·ly¹ /ˌrəʊli ˈpəʊli◂/ also **roly-poly pud·ding** /ˌ·· ·· ˈ··/— *n* [C;U] (in Britain) (a) sweet food made of JAM (=fruit boiled with sugar) that is rolled up in pastry and then baked or boiled

roly-poly² *adj* [A;(B)] *apprec* (of a person) fat and round: *a roly-poly baby*

Ro·ma·ic /rəʊˈmeɪ-ɪk/ *adj, n* [Wa5;B;U] (of or in) the modern Greek language; DEMOTIC

ro·man /ˈrəʊmən/ *n* [U] (the ordinary style of) printing with small upright letters like the ones used for the words up to here: *printed in roman| roman letters* —compare ITALICS, CAPITALS

Roman¹ *adj* [Wa5] **1** connected with **a** the ancient empire of Rome: *Britain during the Roman period* **b** the city of Rome: *modern Roman life* **2** (of a nose) curving out near the top (= at the ARCH) **3** (of an arch) shaped like a half-circle at the top **4** ROMAN CATHOLIC

Roman² *n* **1** a citizen of **a** the ancient Roman Empire **b** the city of Rome **2** *not fml* a ROMAN CATHOLIC

Roman Cath·o·lic¹ /ˌ·· ˈ···/ *adj* [Wa5] connected with the branch of the Christian religion (the **Roman Catholic Church**) whose leader (POPE) rules from Rome: *Her family are Roman Catholic*

Roman Catholic² *n* a member of the ROMAN CATHOLIC¹ Church: *Her family are all Roman Catholics*

ro·mance¹ /rəʊˈmæns, rə-/ *n* **1** [C] a story of love, adventure, strange happenings, etc., often set in a distant time or place, whose events are happier or grander or more exciting than those of real life: *a romance about a king who married a beggar girl* **2** [U] the quality that such stories have; the quality in the human mind that hopes for such experiences in real life: *the romance of life in the Wild West* **3** [C] a love affair: *How is your little romance with Julia going?*

romance² *v* [I∅] **1** [(*about*)] to tell improbable stories or ROMANCEs¹ (1): *Is he telling the truth or romancing about his famous relations?* **2** [(*with*)] to carry on a love affair

Romance *adj* [Wa5] (of a language) having grown out of Latin, the language of ancient Rome: *French and Portuguese are Romance languages*

Ro·man·esque /ˌrəʊməˈnesk/ *n* [U] the style of building with round arches and thick pillars that was common in Western Europe in about the 11th century

Roman nu·me·ral /ˌ·· ˈ···/ *n* a sign used, in ancient Rome and sometimes now, for numbers, as in I, II, III, IV, V, VI, VII, VIII, IX, X —compare ARABIC NUMERAL

Ro·ma·no- /rəˈmɑːnəʊ/ *comb. form* Roman; of (ancient) Rome: *Romano-British art*

ro·man·tic¹ /rəʊˈmæntɪk, rə-/ *adj* **1** [B] belonging to or suggesting ROMANCE¹ (1): *a very romantic love story* **2** [B] *sometimes derog* fanciful; not practical; showing (too much) liking for dreams of love, adventure, etc.: *She has romantic ideas about becoming a famous actress* **3** [Wa5;A;(B)] (*often cap.*) marked by ROMANTICISM: *romantic poetry* —**~ally** *adv* [Wa4]

romantic² *n* **1** a ROMANTIC¹ (2) person: *He was a romantic who went off to the South Seas to paint pictures* **2** (*often cap.*) a writer, painter, etc., whose work shows ROMANTICISM

ro·man·ti·cis·m /rəʊˈmæntǰsɪzəm, rə-/ *n* [U] (*often cap.*) (in art and literature) the quality of admiring feeling rather than thought, and wild beauty rather than things made by man —compare REALISM, CLASSICISM —**-cist** *n*

ro·man·ti·cize, -cise /rəʊˈmæntǰsaɪz, rə-/ *v* [I∅;T1] *derog* to tell improbable and ROMANTIC¹ (2) stories (about); make (an event) sound more ROMANTIC by adding interesting or exciting details: *Just keep to the facts and stop romanticizing!*

Romantic Move·ment /·ˌ·· ˈ··/ *n* [*the*+R] the period at the beginning of the 19th century when Western European art and literature were marked by ROMANTICISM

Ro·ma·ny /ˈrəʊməni‖ˈrɑ-/ *n* **1** [U] the language of the wandering race of GIPSY people: *to speak Romany* **2** [A] of or related to this people or this language

Rom·ish /ˈrəʊmɪʃ/ *adj* [Wa5] *derog* typical of ROMAN CATHOLICs²: *these Romish practices like lighting candles*

romp¹ /rɒmp‖rɑmp/ *n* **1** an occasion of ROMPing² (1): *Let's have a romp with the children* **2** *becoming rare* a child who ROMPs² (1): *She's a little romp*

romp² *v* [I∅ (ABOUT, AROUND)] **1** to play noisily and roughly with a lot of running and jumping: *hear the children romping (about) upstairs* **2 romp home** to win a race easily

romp·er /ˈrɒmpəʳ‖ˈrɑm-/ *n* a pair of ROMPERS: *a blue romper*

romp·ers /ˈrɒmpəz‖ˈrɑmpərz/ *n* [P] a one-piece garment for babies combining a top and short trouser-like bottom: *a pair of rompers* —see PAIR (USAGE)

romp through *v prep* [T1] *not fml* to succeed in, quickly and without effort

ron·deau /ˈrɒndəʊ‖ˈrɑn-/ *n* **-deaux** /dəʊz/ *Fr* a short poem consisting of 10 or 13 lines. It contains only 2 RHYMEs (= sounds of the words at the line endings) and the opening words are repeated twice later in the poem

ron·do /ˈrɒndəʊ‖ˈrɑn-/ *n* **-dos** a piece of music that repeats the main tune several times, and may sometimes form part of a longer musical work such as a CONCERTO

ro·ne·o¹ /ˈrəʊniəʊ/ (*AmE* **mimeograph**)— *n* **-os** *BrE* a copy made on a **Roneo machine** (*tdmk*), which presses ink through the holes in a STENCIL

roneo² (*AmE* **mimeograph**)— *v* **-oed** *BrE* [T1] to copy (printed or written material) on a **Roneo machine** (*tdmk*): *roneo 50 copies of the report*

rönt·gen /ˈrɒntjən‖ˈrentgən/ *adj, n* ROENTGEN¹·²

rood /ruːd/ *n* **1** *old use or tech* a Christian cross or CRUCIFIX (=cross with the figure of Jesus nailed to it) usu. in a church **2** *now rare* a British measure of land equal to ¼ of an ACRE (about 1,011 square metres)

rood·screen /ˈruːdskriːn/ *n* a wooden or stone ornamental wall in a Christian church, which divides the part containing the singers (CHOIR) from the part where the other worshippers sit, and often has a ROOD (1) on the top of it

roof¹ /ruːf/ *n* **1** the outside covering on top of a building: *The rain's coming in—the roof must need mending* —compare CEILING **2** the top covering of a tent, a closed vehicle, etc. —see picture at CAR **3** house; home: *She and I can't live under the same roof* **4 a/no roof over one's head** somewhere/nowhere to live **5 raise the roof** to make a loud noise, esp. of angry or excited complaint: *Father will raise the roof when he hears what you've done!* **6 the roof of the/one's mouth** the bony upper part of the inside of the mouth; PALATE

See next page for picture

roof² *v* [Wv5;T1 (*with*)] to put a roof on; be a roof for: *a house roofed with wood*

roof gar·den /ˈ· ˌ··/ *n* a garden on the flat top of a building

roof in also **roof o·ver**— *v adv* [T1] to enclose by putting a roof on (an open place): *roof in the yard to make a garage*

roof·ing /ˈruːfɪŋ/ *n* [U] material for making or covering roofs

roof·less /ˈruːfləs/ *adj* [Wa5] **1** [B] (of a building) with no roof **2** [F] (of a person) with no home

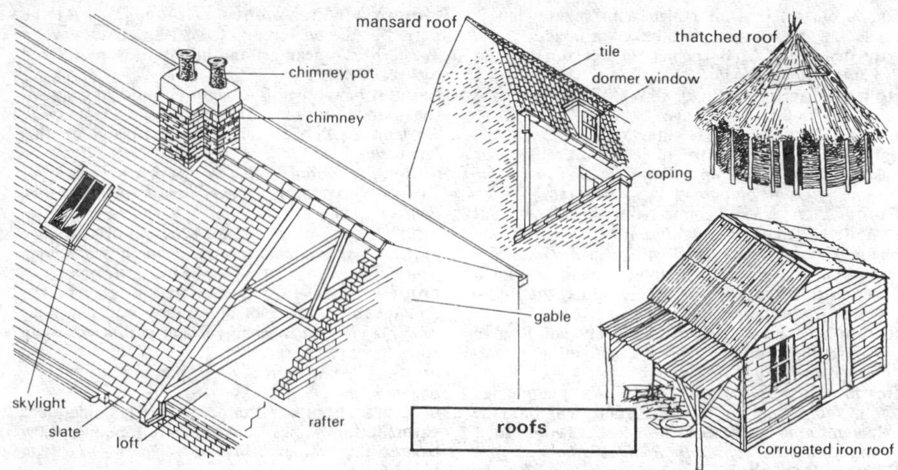

roof rack /ˈ· ·/ *n esp. BrE* a metal frame fixed on top of a car roof, for carrying things: *tie it to the roof rack* —see picture at CAR

roof·tree /ˈruːftriː/ *n lit* **1** the beam that runs along the highest point of a sloping roof; RIDGEPOLE **2** **under one's rooftree** in one's home

rook¹ /rʊk/ *n* a kind of large black European bird like a CROW, which flies about in groups that build their nests together in a ROOKERY

rook² *v* [T1 (*of*)] to cheat (someone), as by charging a very high price or by winning money at card games: *£5?! You've been rooked!|He rooked the young soldier of his pay*

rook³ also **castle**— *n* (in the game of CHESS) a piece that can move any distance but only in a straight line parallel to a side of the board —see CHESS (USAGE)

rook·e·ry /ˈrʊkəri/ *n* **1** a collection of ROOK*s*'¹ nests, high up in a group of trees **2** a place where a group of PENGUIN*s* or SEAL*s* live together

rook·ie /ˈrʊki/ *n AmE sl* a new soldier; RECRUIT

room¹ /ruːm, rʊm/ *n* **1** [C] (*often in comb.*) a division of a building, with its own walls, floor, and CEILING: *I want a double room* (=for 2 people) *with a view* **2** [P] (*often cap.*) the people in one such division of a hotel or large office building: *Ask Room 107 if they want coffee* **3** [U (*for*), U3] space that could be filled, or that is enough for any purpose: *There's room for 3 on the back seat.|There's no room to move.|Move along and make room for me!|A piano takes up a lot of room* **4** [U3] the chance (to do something): *He needs room to develop his skill as a painter* **5** [U+*for*] **a** need for: *There's plenty of room for improvement in his work* **b** reason for: *There's no room for doubt* —see PLACE (USAGE) —**~ful** *n* [(*of*)]: *a roomful of noisy children/of furniture*

room² *v* [L9 esp. *at, with*] *AmE* to lodge: have a room or rooms (at, with): *He's rooming at our house/with us*

-roomed /ruːmd, rʊmd/ *comb. form* with the stated number of rooms: *a 6-roomed house*

room·er /ˈruːməʳ/ *n AmE* a lodger; person who lives in a rented room

rooming house /ˈ·· ·/ *n AmE* a lodging house; building divided into separate rooms that can be rented

room·mate /ˈruːmˌmeɪt, ˈrʊm-/ *n* a person not a member of one's family with whom one shares a lodging: *Bill and I are roommates*

rooms /ruːmz, rʊmz/ *n* [P] *esp. BrE* a rented set of rooms in a larger building; lodgings: *He left his mother and moved into rooms*

room ser·vice /ˈ· ˌ··/ *n* **1** [U] a service provided by a hotel, by which food, drink, etc., are sent up to a person's room **2** [GU] the people (STAFF² (1)) who provide such a service

room·y /ˈruːmi/ *adj* [Wa1] with plenty of space: *a roomy house/cupboard/car* —**roominess** *n* [U]

roost¹ /ruːst/ *n* [C;U] **1** a bar, branch, etc., on which birds settle at night, esp. one for hens in a special little house (HEN HOUSE): *a hen roost|birds at roost in the trees* **2** **come home to roost** (of a bad action) to have a bad effect on the doer, esp. after a period of time **3** **rule the roost** *not fml* to be the leader: *It's Bill's wife who really rules the roost in that family*

roost² *v* [IØ] (of a bird) to sit and sleep for the night

roost·er /ˈruːstəʳ/ *n esp. AmE* COCK¹ (1)

root¹ /ruːt/ *n* **1** [*often pl.*] the part of a plant that grows down into the soil in search of food and water: *the roots of a flower|pull the plant up by the/by its roots* —see picture at FLOWER¹ **2** the part of a tooth, hair, or organ that holds it to the rest of the body: *the root of one's tongue* —see picture at TOOTH **3** origin; cause; central part or base: *"The love of money is the root of all evil" (the Bible).|Let's get to/get at the root of this matter* **4** *tech* (in MATHEMATICS) a number that when multiplied by itself a stated number of times gives another stated number: *2 is the 4th root of 16* **5** *tech* (in grammar) the base part of a word to which other parts can be added: *"Music" is the root of "musician" and of "unmusical"* **6** **root and branch** (of something bad that must be got rid of) thoroughly: *destroy this evil system root and branch* **7** **take/strike root** (of plants or ideas) to become established and begin to grow —see also ROOTS

root² *v* [IØ;T1] to (cause to) form roots: *Try to root this plant in the garden.|Do roses root easily?*

root³ also **root·le** /ˈruːtl/— *v* [L9 esp. ABOUT, AROUND, *for*] **1** (esp. of pigs) to search (for food) by digging with the nose: *pigs rooting in the earth (for potatoes)|Pigs need somewhere to root around* **2** to search (for something) by turning things over: *Who's been rooting about among my papers?*

root beer /ˈ· ·/ *n* [U] (esp. in the US) a sweet gassy non-alcoholic drink made from various roots

root crop /ˈ· ·/ *n* a crop that is grown for its roots, such as CARROTS

root·ed /ˈruːtɪ̇d/ *adj* **1** [Wa5;F (*to*)] fixed as if by roots: *He stood rooted (to the spot)* **2** [B] (of ideas, principles, etc.) firmly fixed and unchangeable: *He had a deeply rooted belief in free trade*

root for *v prep* [T1] *AmE* to cheer for (one's team)

root·less /ˈruːtləs/ *adj* [Wa5] homeless and without ROOTS —**~ness** *n* [U]

root out *v adv* **1** [T1] to get rid of completely; destroy (something bad): *This disease could easily be rooted out* **2** [D1 (*for*);T1] to find (something) by searching: *I'll try and root you out something dry to wear*

roots /ruːts/ *n* [P] **1** the feeling of belonging by origin to one particular place: *Her roots are in Scotland where she was born* **2 pull up one's roots** to move to a new place from one's settled home **3 put down (new) roots** to establish a (new) place by joining in local activities, making friends, etc.

root up *v adv* [T1] UPROOT

rope[1] /rəʊp/ *n* **1** [U] strong thick cord made by twisting: *Tie the horse to the gate with this piece of rope* **2** [C] a piece of this: *3 climbers on the same rope* (= fastened together)|*metal ropes* **3** [C+*of*] a fat twisted string (esp. of the stated jewels): *ropes of* PEARLS[1] (1)|*a rope/string of onions* **4** [*the*+R] hanging as a punishment **5 give someone enough rope to hang himself** to allow freedom to a fool or evil person in the hope that this will make him show how mistaken he is **6 give someone (plenty of) rope** to allow someone (plenty of) freedom to act **7 money for old rope** *infml* money that is easily earned: *You only have to walk on that stage and tell them about your experiences—it'll be money for old rope!* —see also ROPES

rope[2] *v* **1** [Wv5;T1 (UP)] to tie up with a rope: *roped chests of gold coins* **2** [I∅ (UP)] (of 2 or more mountain climbers) to be fastened together with the same rope: *We'd better rope (up) for this difficult bit* **3** [L9 esp. UP, DOWN, *up, down*] (of a mountain climber) to travel by means of a rope: *She roped down the rock face* **4** [T1] *esp. AmE* to catch (an animal) with a rope; LASSO[2]: *rope the cattle*

rope·danc·er /ˈrəʊpˌdɑːnsəʳ‖-ˌdæn-/ also **rope·walk·er** /ˈrəʊpˌwɔːkəʳ/— *n* a performer on a tightly stretched rope or wire —compare TIGHTROPE WALKER

rope in *v adv* [T1] *infml* to make (someone) help in one's plans or join an activity: *I've been roped in to help sell the tickets*

rope lad·der /ˈ· ˌ··/ *n* a ladder made of 2 long ropes connected by cross pieces of wood, rope, or metal

rope off *v adv* [T1] to separate (an area) from the rest with ropes: *They've roped off one end of the room*

ropes /rəʊps/ *n* [*the*+P] **1** the rope fence that surrounds a sports ring: *drive him up against the ropes* **2 know the ropes** to know from experience the rules and customs in some place or activity: *I've been to China before so I know the ropes; can I help you?*

rope to *v prep* [D1] to tie (something or someone) to (something) with a rope: *They roped him to a tree*

rope·walk /ˈrəʊpwɔːk/ also **rope·yard** /ˈrəʊpjɑːd‖-ɑrd/— *n* a long covered space where rope is made by twisting

rope·way /ˈrəʊpweɪ/ *n* a system of moving things around in buckets hanging from metal ropes, as in a factory or mine

rop·y, ropey /ˈrəʊpi/ *adj* [Wa1] *BrE infml* in bad condition; of bad quality: *a ropy old suit* —**ropiness** *n* [U]

Roque·fort /ˈrɒkfɔːʳ‖ˈrəʊkfərt/ *n* [U] a kind of strong French cheese with blue lines in it

Ror·schach test /ˈrɔːʃæk test‖ˈrɔr-/ *n* a method of testing a person's brains and character by making him say what various irregular spots of ink remind him of

ro·sa·ry /ˈrəʊzəri/ *n* **1** a string of BEADS (= small ornamental balls) used esp. by ROMAN CATHOLICS for counting prayers: *The priest blessed their new rosaries* **2** (*often cap.*) **a** a ROMAN CATHOLIC religious practice that consists of saying the set of prayers that are counted in this way, while thinking holy thoughts: *She says the Rosary every night for the health of her family* **b** a book containing this form of worship

rose[1] /rəʊz/ *n* **1** [C] any of various wild or cultivated bushes with strong prickly stems, divided leaves, and beautiful often sweet-smelling flowers —see pictures at FLOWER[1] and PLANT[2] **2** [C] the red, white, pink, or yellow flower of this bush, which also appears as the national sign of England on coins, stamps, etc.: *a bunch of red roses* **3** [C9] (*in comb.*) any of several plants that have flowers that look like this flower: *Christmas rose|rock rose* **4** [C] a circular piece of metal with holes in it that is fitted to the end of a pipe or WATERING CAN for watering gardens: *Put on the rose before you water the seeds* **5 a bed of roses** a very pleasant state to be in **6 be not all roses** (of a job, state of affairs, etc.) to include some unpleasant things **7 There's no rose without a thorn** Everything has its disadvantages **8 under the rose** *fml* secretly; SUB ROSA

rose[2] *adj* [Wa5] **1** (*usu. in comb.*) (of a colour) from pink to a deep purplish red: *rose-pink*|*"a rose-red city half as old as time"* (J. W. Burgon) **2 see (something, esp. the world) through rose-coloured spectacles/glasses** to think (something) is pleasanter than it really is

rose[3] *past t. of* RISE

ro·sé /ˈrəʊzeɪ‖rəʊˈzeɪ/ *n* [U] *Fr* any of several kinds of light pink wine: *another glass of rosé*

ro·se·ate /ˈrəʊziɪ̇t/ *adj lit* ROSY: *the roseate evening sky*

rose·bud /ˈrəʊzbʌd/ *n* a rose (the flower) that has not fully opened yet: *gather rosebuds*

rose hip /ˈ· ·/ *n* the red fruit of some kinds of rose bush

rose·leaf /ˈrəʊzliːf/ *n* a rose PETAL (= one of the coloured divisions of the flower)

rose·ma·ry /ˈrəʊzməri‖-meri/ *n* [U] a kind of low bush whose sweet-smelling leaves are used in cooking: *a bunch of rosemary*

ro·sette /rəʊˈzet/ *n* **1** a bunch of narrow silk bands (RIBBONS) made up in the form of a rose and worn for ornament or as a sign of something **2** a shape like this in stone or wood, cut on a building as an ornament

rose·wa·ter /ˈrəʊzˌwɔːtəʳ‖-ˌwɔ-, -ˌwɑ-/ *n* [U] a liquid made from roses and used for its pleasant smell

rose win·dow /ˈ· ˌ··/ *n* a circular ornamental window in a church, usu. containing a pattern of small divisions spreading out from a centre and filled in with coloured glass —see picture at WINDOW

rose·wood /ˈrəʊzwʊd/ *n* [U] any of several kinds of valuable hard dark red tropical wood, used for making fine furniture. It is not the wood of the rose bush: *an 18th century rosewood desk*

ros·in[1] /ˈrɒzɪ̇n‖ˈrɑ-/ *n* [U] RESIN (1) (when used in a solid form on the strings of musical instruments)

rosin[2] *v* [T1] to rub (the strings of a musical instrument) with ROSIN[1]

ros·ter /ˈrɒstəʳ‖ˈrɑ-/ *n* a list of people's names that shows what jobs they are to do in turn, and when

ros·trum /ˈrɒstrəm‖ˈrɑ-/ *n* **-trums** *or* **-tra** /trə/ a raised place (PLATFORM) for a public speaker, CONDUCTOR (1), etc.: *the teacher on his rostrum*

ros·y /ˈrəʊzi/ *adj* [Wa1] **1** (esp. of the human skin) pink: *rosy children|rosy lips and cheeks* **2** (esp. of the future) giving hope: *Things don't look very rosy down at the old firm; I'm looking for another job* —**rosiness** *n* [U]

rot¹ /rɒt‖rɑt/ *v* **-tt-** **1** [IØ] to decay naturally or as the result of some outside influence: (fig.) *They left him to rot in prison for 20 years* —see also ROTTEN **2** [T1] to cause to decay: *The rain has rotted the roof beams.|This cheap wine will rot your stomach* —compare ROTGUT; see also ROT AWAY, ROT OFF

rot² *n* **1** [U] (the action of) decay: *an old hollow tree full of rot*|(fig.) *How can we stop the rot in our society?* **2** [U9] decay or disease (of the stated kind) in plants or animals: *a sheep with foot rot|Dry rot has set in in the roof beams* **3** [U] *BrE sl* foolish remarks or ideas: *Don't talk rot!|That's complete rot* **4 the rot sets in** things begin to go wrong one after another: *I'll tell you what, old man, the rot really set in when we admitted women to the club!*

ro·ta /ˈrəʊtə/ *n esp. BrE* ROSTER

ro·ta·ry¹ /ˈrəʊtəri/ *adj* [Wa5] **1** (of movement) turning round a fixed point, like a wheel: *the rotary movement of the blades* **2** being or having a moving part that does this: *rotary blades|cut the grass with a rotary cutter*

rotary² *n AmE* a circular road at a point where roads meet: ROUNDABOUT

ro·tate /rəʊˈteɪt‖ˈrəʊteɪt/ *v* [IØ;T1] **1** to (cause to) turn round a fixed point: *The earth rotates once every 24 hours.|You can rotate the wheel with your hand* **2** to (cause to) take turns or come round in regular order: *rotate the crops*

ro·ta·tion /rəʊˈteɪʃən/ *n* **1** [U] the action of rotating (ROTATE): *the rotation of the earth* **2** [C] one complete turn round a fixed point: *make 10 rotations a second* **3 in rotation** (of events) coming round one after the other in regular order: *The seasons follow each other in rotation* **4 the rotation of crops** planting different crops in a field each year so as to keep the soil healthy

ro·ta·to·ry /rəʊˈteɪtəri, ˈrəʊtə-‖ˈrəʊtətori/ *adj* [Wa5] ROTARY¹ (1)

rot a·way *v adv* [IØ;T1] to (cause to) disappear by decay: *The old dog's teeth have all rotted away and he can't bite*

rote /rəʊt/ *n* [U] repeated study using memory rather than understanding (in such phrs. as **by rote, rote learning**): *I passed the examination by learning everything off by rote*

rot·gut /ˈrɒtgʌt‖ˈrɑt-/ *n* [U] *infml* strong cheap alcohol that is bad for the stomach (GUTS)

ro·tis·ser·ie /rəʊˈtɪsəri/ *n* **1** an apparatus for cooking meat by turning it over and over on a bar (SPIT¹ (1)), over direct heat **2** a restaurant whose speciality is meat cooked in this way

rot off *v adv* [IØ] to fall off through decay: *The branches have all rotted off*

ro·to·gra·vure /ˌrəʊtəʊgrəˈvjʊəʳ‖-tə-/ *n* **1** [U] the method of printing copies of a picture by pressure from a turning metal CYLINDER (= tube-shaped object) on which the lines of the picture have been cut with acid **2** [C] a picture printed in this way

ro·tor /ˈrəʊtəʳ/ *n* **1** a part (of a machine) that ROTATES (1) —see picture at AIRCRAFT **2** the system of blades that raise a HELICOPTER into the air by turning round and round

rot·ten /ˈrɒtn‖ˈrɑtn/ *adj* [Wa2] **1** decayed; gone bad: *rotten eggs|a rotten branch* **2** (of behaviour) bad; unkind: *What a rotten thing to do to her!* **3** *sl* bad; nasty: *What rotten weather!|How rotten for you!|Paul's a rotten driver* **4 feel rotten** to feel ill, tired, or unhappy **5 rotten to the core** completely bad morally —**~ness** *n* [U]

rotten bor·ough /ˌ·· ˈ··/ *n* (in Britain before 1832) any of a number of places (BOROUGHs) which elected a Member of Parliament although they had hardly any voters

rot·ten·ly /ˈrɒtnli‖ˈrɑ-/ *adv* unkindly; badly in a moral way: *He treats his wife rottenly*

rot·ter /ˈrɒtəʳ‖ˈrɑ-/ *n* [C; *you*+N] *BrE old public-school sl or humor* a bad worthless person

ro·tund /rəʊˈtʌnd/ *adj fml or humor* **1** (of a person) round (because fat) **2** (of the voice) sounding deep and full —**~ity** *n* [S;U] —**~ly** *adv*

ro·tun·da /rəʊˈtʌndə/ *n* a round building or hall, esp. one with a rounded bowl-shaped roof (DOME)

rou·ble, ruble /ˈruːbəl/ *n* (a coin or note worth) a measure of money in the USSR on which the money system there is based

rou·é /ˈruːeɪ‖ruːˈeɪ/ *n* [C; *you*+N9] *Fr, old use or humor* a man of wild social and sexual habits

rouge¹ /ruːʒ/ *n* [U] a red substance used by women and actors for colouring the cheeks

rouge² *v* [Wv5;T1;(IØ)] to put ROUGE¹ on (one's face): *her heavily rouged cheeks*

rough¹ /rʌf/ *adj* **1** [Wa1;B] having an uneven surface; not smooth: *the cat's rough tongue|rough grass|a dog with rough fur|The rough road made the cart shake* **2** [Wa1;B] (of weather, the sea, or a sea journey) stormy and violent; not calm: *rough winds|a very rough crossing to France* **3** [Wa1;B] *not always derog* (of people or behaviour) not gentle, tender, or polite; using force; (typical of someone) strong and simple: *a few rough words|rough kindness|a certain rough humour|Play nicely and don't be rough!* **4** [Wa1;B] (of food and living conditions) not delicate; simple; suitable only for strong people: *a rough but filling dinner|a rough country wine|Life was rough out in the Wild West when I was a boy* **5** [Wa5;A;(B)] (of plans, calculations, etc.) not (yet) in detail; unpolished; not in the finished form: *a rough drawing|a first rough attempt|a very rough translation|I've a rough idea where it is* **6** [Wa5;A] (of paper) for making the first attempts at drawing or writing something: *Try it on a bit of rough paper* **7** [Wa1;B] (of sounds) not gentle or tuneful: *a rough voice* **8** [Wa1;B] *infml* unfortunate and hard to bear: *to have a very rough time|What rough luck!|You lost all your money? That was a bit rough* **9 give someone the rough side of one's tongue** to speak severely to someone **10 rough and ready** simple and without comfort; ROUGH¹ (4): *The living conditions were a bit rough and ready, as there were no beds* —see also **rough** DIAMOND **11 rough on** *infml* unfortunate for (someone): *It's a bit rough on him, losing his toe!*

rough² *n* **1** [C] a violent noisy man: *a crowd of young roughs fighting at a football match* **2** [(*the*) U] the uneven ground with long grass on a GOLF course: *He lost his ball in the rough.|a lot of rough* **3** [C] ROUGH¹ (5) attempts at writing or drawing something: *It's under that pile of roughs* **4** [*the*+R] *becoming rare* the heavy work in a house: *a woman to help with the rough* **5 in rough** on ROUGH¹ (6) paper: *Write it out in rough and then copy it* **6 in the rough** (of a work of art) in an unfinished state **7 take the rough with the smooth** to accept bad things as well as good things without complaining

rough³ *v* **rough it** *not fml* to live in a simple and not very comfortable way: *The boys will have to rough it at camp* —*see also* ROUGH IN, ROUGH OUT, ROUGH UP

rough⁴ *adv* [Wa5] **1** in ROUGH¹ (4) conditions, esp. out of doors: *We can live rough for a bit* **2** in a ROUGH¹ (3) way; using (too much) force: *Those* *boys certainly play (it) rough!* **3 cut up rough** *infml* to become angry **4 sleep rough** (esp. of a homeless wanderer in a city) to sleep out of doors not from choice

rough·age /ˈrʌfɪdʒ/ *n* [U] coarse matter contained in food, that does not actually feed (NOURISH) the eater, but helps the bowels to work: *Potato skins provide valuable roughage*

rough-and-tum·ble /ˌ·· ˈ··/ *adj, n* [B;U;C] (an occasion of being) noisily violent; not (being) calm and gentle: *the rough-and-tumble of school life*

rough·cast[1] /ˈrʌfkɑːst‖-kæst/ *n* [U] a type of rough surface on the outside of a building, made of coarse PLASTER and little stones

roughcast[2] *v* **-cast** [Wv5;T1] to cover (a wall) with ROUGHCAST[1]: *a roughcast wall*

rough-dry /ˈ· ·/ *v* [Wv5;T1] to dry (washed clothes) without ironing

rough·en /ˈrʌfən/ *v* [IØ;T1] to make or become rough: *The cold wind roughened her skin*

rough-hewn /ˌ· ˈ·◂/ *adj* [Wa5] (of wood or stone) roughly cut; not made smooth: *a wall of rough-hewn blocks*|(fig.) *the noble rough-hewn face of Abraham Lincoln*

rough·house[1] /ˈrʌfhaʊs/ *n* [S] *not fml* a noisy disorderly fight, not usu. with weapons: *There's been a bit of a roughhouse and one of the boys got kicked in the head*

roughhouse[2] *v* [IØ] *not fml* to have a ROUGHHOUSE[1]

rough in *v adv* [T1] to put in (a few practice lines in a drawing): *I'll just rough in the shape of the head and you can paint the sky round it* —compare ROUGH OUT

rough·ly /ˈrʌfli/ *adv* **1** in a rough manner: *He pushed her roughly away* **2** [Wa5] about; more or less but not exactly: *There were roughly 200 people there.*|*How many people, roughly?*|*Roughly speaking I'd say 200*

rough·neck /ˈrʌfnek/ *n AmE infml* **1** a rough bad-tempered man **2** a member, not the leader, of a team who are making (DRILLing[1] (2)) an oil well

rough·ness /ˈrʌfnɪ̱s/ *n* **1** [U] the quality of being rough **2** [C] a ROUGH[1] (1) place: *a small roughness on the back of my hand*

rough out *v adv* [T1] to make (a first practice drawing): *I'll just rough out the whole picture and you can do the details* —compare ROUGH IN

rough·rid·er /ˈrʌfˌraɪdəʳ/ *n* a person who trains wild horses or rides them at sports meetings, esp. at RODEOs

rough·shod /ˈrʌfʃɒd‖-ʃɑd/ *adv* [Wa5] **ride roughshod over** to disregard (something or someone) in a way that hurts the feelings: *He rode roughshod over all our arguments*

rough stuff /ˈ· ·/ *n* [U] *BrE infml* violence; violent behaviour

rough up *v adv* [T1] **1** *infml* to attack (someone) roughly, usu. as a threat **2** to make untidy or uneven: *He roughed up the path by kicking at the stones*

rou·lette /ruːˈlet/ *n* [U] a game of chance in which a small ball is spun round a moving wheel and falls into a hole marked with a number —see also RUSSIAN ROULETTE

round[1] /raʊnd/ *adj* **1** [Wa1;B] circular: *a round plate* **2** [Wa1;B] shaped like a ball **3** [Wa1;B] (of parts of the body) fat and curved: *the child's round red cheeks* **4** [Wa5;A] (of numbers) full; complete: *a round* DOZEN **5 in round figures** (of numbers) not exactly, but to the nearest 10, 100, 1,000, etc., without troubling about small amounts: *The car cost £9,878—that's £10,000 in round figures* —**~ness** *n* [U]

round[2] *AmE* usu. **around**— *adv* [Wa5] **1** with a circular movement or movements; spinning in or as if in a circle: *The earth turns round once in 24 hours.*|*The wheels went round (and round).*|(fig.) *Your birthday will be/come round again soon* **2** in a circular position; surrounding a central point: *a field with a fence (all) round*|*The children gathered round to hear the story* **3** all over the place; in or into all parts; everywhere or to everyone in an area: *Hand round the glasses.*|*Send the invitations round.*|*A strange story has been going round.*|*Let's go into the palace and have a look round* **4** so as to face the other or stated way: *Turn the picture round (to face the wall)* **5** (*used after a word expressing distance*) in circular measurement: *a tree 5 feet round* **6** (of a journey) **a** not going the straightest way: *to walk/go/drive round by the cinema instead of coming straight home* **b** to someone's home: *Come round and see me sometime!*|*They invited us round for drinks* **7 all the year round** during the whole year: *John works all the year round, without a holiday* **8 round (about)** *not fml* in the neighbourhood: *He lives somewhere round (about)* **9 the other/wrong/right/opposite way round a** facing in the stated way: *He's got his hat on the wrong way round.*|*Turn the bed the other way round so he can see out of the window* **b** (of events) happening in the stated order or relationship: *George didn't shoot the General. It was the other way round: the General shot George!*

round[3] *AmE* usu. **around**— *prep* **1** with a circular movement about (a central point): *The earth goes round the sun.*|*Drake sailed (right/all) round the world and came back to England.*|*They danced round (and round) the holy tree* **2** in a circular position on all or some sides of (a central point): *to sit round the fire/round the table*|*Tie the belt round your waist.*|*"Is there a footpath round the coast?"* (SEU W.)|*Put something round your shoulders—it's cold* **3** into all parts of; all over (a place): *Have a look round the shop.*|*Let him show you (all) round the castle.*|*"just wandering round Lyme"* (SEU S.) **4** to or at the other side of, not going straight but changing direction: *He disappeared round the corner.*|*She'll be coming round the mountain* (= not over or through *the mountain*).|*The car's round the back of the house* **5** (with times, places, etc.) **a** also **round a·bout** /ˈ· ·ˌ·/— more or less; about: *They arrived round (about) 5 o'clock.*|*It'll cost somewhere round (about) £50* **b** in the neighbourhood of; near: *"I've just arrived round here"* (SEU S.) **6** *BrE nonstandard* to; round to: *I'm just going round the shops for some sugar* **7 round the clock** all the time: *We're working (right/all) round the clock to finish this dictionary!* —compare ROUND-THE-CLOCK

USAGE British speakers and writers often use **about** or **round** (both adv and prep) where Americans would use **around**. People who use both **round** and **around** often make a difference between **round** for "circular movement" or "measurement": *He turned* **round**.|*a tree 5 feet* **round**, and **around** meaning "in the area" or "near a centre": *He lives somewhere* **around**. Compare: *I travelled (all)* **around** *the world for a few years* (=all over the place); *The spaceship travelled (right)* **round** *the world in 40 minutes* (=in one complete circle).

round[4] *n* **1** something ROUND[1] (1,2) like a plate or ball **2** a complete piece cut off the end (of a loaf of bread): *eat 6 whole rounds of bread and butter* **3** a regular journey to a number of houses, offices, etc., in a town: *do a paper round* (=deliver newspapers to houses) —compare ROUNDS, ROUNDSMAN **4** [+ *of*] a number or set (of the stated activity or events): *a continual round of parties*|*a second round of wage claims* (= by trade unions for their members) **5** a share given out to everyone present (often in the phr. **round of drinks**): *I'll* STAND *you all* (= pay for you to have) *a round of beer!|What'll you have?—It's my round* (= I'm paying) **6** (in sport) one stage, period, or game, as **a** (in GOLF) a complete game including all the holes **b** (in BOXING) one of the periods of fighting in a match, separated by short rests: *a match of 15 rounds|knocked out in the 2nd round* —see BOXING (USAGE) **c** (in football) one of several sets of matches, of which all the winners will play against each other until one team is victorious: *the first round of the Football Cup* **7** one single shot: *He fired round after round.|I've only 2 rounds left* (=bullets for 2 shots).|(fig.) *another round of cheers* **8** [(*of*)] a piece of BEEF (= cow's meat) cut from the upper part of the back leg: *a nice round of* BEEF *for dinner* **9** a type of song for 3 or 4 voices, in which each sings the same tune, one starting a line after another has just finished it **10** RUNG **11 in the round a** with the stage in the middle and the people sitting on (almost) all sides (esp. in the phr. **theatre in the round**) **b** (in SCULPTURE, of a figure cut out of stone) not part of a wall but solid and separate so that it can be seen from all sides **12 the/one's daily round** the/one's duties that must be done every day: *her daily round of cooking and cleaning*

round[5] *v* **1** [Wv5;I∅;T1] to make or become round: *round one's lips to whistle|The child's eyes rounded with excitement.|rounded stones in the bed of the river|her rounded breasts* **2** [T1] *not fml* to travel round: *She rounded the corner at 95 miles per hour* —see also ROUND DOWN, ROUND OFF, ROUND ON, ROUND OUT, ROUND UP

round·a·bout[1] /ˈraʊndəbaʊt/ *n BrE* **1** (*AmE* **merry-go-round**) *BrE* also **merry-go-round**, *AmE* also **carousel**— a machine in an amusement park on which children can ride round and round sitting on wooden animals **2** (*AmE* **(traffic) circle, rotary**)— a central space at a road crossing, which makes cars go in a circle round it and not straight across —see picture at INTERCHANGE[2]

roundabout[2] *adj* (of the way to somewhere) indirect; not the shortest: *take a roundabout course to avoid the flood*|(fig.) *I heard the news in a roundabout way*

round-arm /ˈ· ·/ *adj, adv* (in cricket) (thrown or BOWLed) with the arm coming round at shoulder height

round brack·et /ˌ· ˈ··/ *n* [*usu. pl.*] *BrE* PARENTHESIS (2)

round down *v adv* [T1(*to*)] to reduce (an amount) to the nearest whole number: *If your income is £2,386·46, it will be rounded down to £2,386 for tax purposes*

roun·del /ˈraʊndl/ *n* **1** a small raised circle cut into wood or stone as an ornament **2** a coloured circle showing the nationality of a military aircraft

roun·de·lay /ˈraʊndǝleɪ/ *n becoming rare* a short simple song or poem with a REFRAIN (= certain lines repeated several times at the end of the parts)

roun·ders /ˈraʊndəz‖-ərz/ *n* [U] a British ball game like BASEBALL, usu. played by children, in which a player hits the ball and then runs round the edge of a square area

round-eyed /ˌ· ˈ·◂/ *adj* with the eyes wide open, as in surprise or wonder

Round·head /ˈraʊndhed/ *n* a supporter of the Parliament against the King in the English CIVIL War in the 17th Century —compare CAVALIER

round·house /ˈraʊndhaʊs/ *n* **-houses** /haʊzǝz/ **1** a round building where railway engines are kept and repaired **2** (esp. in former times) a small hut (CABIN) built on the open top DECK (= floor) of a sailing ship

round·ish /ˈraʊndɪʃ/ *adj* fairly or rather round in shape

round·ly /ˈraʊndli/ *adv* **1** strongly and forcefully: *She cursed him roundly* **2** completely (esp. in such phrs. as **roundly defeated**)

round off *v adv* [T1] **1** [(*by, with*)] to end (something) suitably and satisfactorily: *round off the evening with a hot drink|by singing a song* **2** to change (an exact figure) into the nearest whole number

round on also **round up·on**— *v prep* [T1] **1** to turn and attack: *The lion suddenly rounded on the hunters* **2** to scold or blame suddenly: *His wife rounded on him when he came home drunk*

round out *v adv* **1** [I∅;T1] to (cause to) swell or become round: *The sun is rounding out the corn.|The corn is rounding out nicely* **2** [T1] to complete: *He rounded out his education by spending a year in Paris*

round rob·in /ˌ· ˈ··/ *n* a letter expressing opinions or complaints, which is signed by many people and handed into an official body

rounds /raʊndz/ *n* **1 do/go/make one's rounds** to make a customary tour; make one's usual visits: *the policeman making his nightly rounds of the village* **2 go the rounds** (esp. of news) to be passed on

round-shoul·dered /ˌ· ˈ··◂/ *adj* with bent shoulders; with a back that is not upright: *a very round-shouldered girl*

rounds·man /ˈraʊndzmən/ *n* **-men** /mən/ a man employed by a shop to go round delivering goods to people's houses: *the baker's roundsman*

round ta·ble /ˌ· ˈ··◂/ *n* a table that makes everyone sitting round it seem of equal importance, because nobody can be at its head: *a round-table* DISCUSSION/CONFERENCE

round-the-clock /ˌ· · ˈ·◂/ *adj* [Wa5;A] done or happening all the time, both day and night: *keep a round-the-clock watch on the house* —compare ROUND[3] (7) **the clock**

round-trip /ˌ· ˈ·◂/ *adj* [Wa5] *AmE* RETURN[3]: *a round-trip ticket*

round trip *n* **1** a journey to a place and back again **2** a journey to a place and back by a different way

round·up /ˈraʊndʌp/ *n* a gathering together of scattered things or people, esp. of cattle by men on horses: *a roundup of all the sheep|of the criminals concerned in the robbery*

round up *v adv* [T1] **1** to gather together (scattered things, people, or animals, esp. cattle): *Round up a few friends to help you!* **2** to catch (a number of criminals) **3** [(*to*)] to change (an exact figure) to the next highest whole number: *round up* $47\frac{1}{2}$*p to 48p*

roup /ruːp/ *n* [U] a disease of hens

rouse /raʊz/ *v* **1** [T1 (*from, out of*)] to waken (someone): *The noise roused me* (*from/out of a deep sleep*).|*He's very hard to rouse in the mornings* **2** [T1 (*from, out of*)] to make (someone) more active, interested, or excited: *The speaker tried to rouse the masses* (*from their lack of interest*).|*I'm a dangerous woman when I'm roused* (= when something makes me angry) **3** [I∅] *rare* to wake up: *I roused early this morning* —see also AROUSE

rouse to *v prep* [D1] to make (someone) feel or do (something): *You must rouse yourself to action.|He's not easily roused to anger*

rous·ing /ˈraʊzɪŋ/ *adj* **1** [B] that makes people excited: *a very rousing speech about freedom* **2** [Wa5;A] (of a cheer) loud and eager: *When they heard the news they all gave 3 rousing cheers.|a rousing welcome*

rous·ta·bout /ˈraʊstəbaʊt/ *n AmE* a man who does heavy unskilled work, esp. at a seaport or in an oil field

rout¹ /raʊt/ *n* **1** a complete defeat and disorderly flight: *the total rout of the enemy forces* **2** [+*of*] *old use* a noisy disorderly crowd (of the stated people): *a rout of* DRUNKEN *sailors* **3** *old use* a large evening party: *Lady Fairlamb was holding a fashionable rout at her town house* **4 put someone to rout** to defeat completely and drive away someone

rout² *v* [T1] to defeat completely and drive away: *They routed the enemy*

route¹ /ruːt‖ruːt, raʊt/ *n* a way planned or followed from one place to another: *the shortest route from London to Edinburgh.*|*They were on route to* (= going to) *Paris when I met them*

route² *v* [X9 esp. *by, through*] to send (by a particular ROUTE¹): *They routed the goods through Italy/by way of Germany*

route march /ˈ· ·/ *n* a long march by soldiers in training

rou·tine¹ /ruːˈtiːn/ *n* **1** [U] the regular fixed ordinary way of working or doing things: *do it according to routine* **2** [C] a set of steps learnt and practised by a dancer for public performance: *do this little dance routine*

routine² *adj* [Wa5;A] **1** regular; according to rule: *a routine medical examination* **2** not unusual or exciting: *a dull routine job* —**~ly** *adv*

rout out *v adv* [T1 (*of*)] to get (someone) out (of bed or hiding): *Harry's been in the bath long enough—go and rout him out!*

roux /ruː/ *n* **roux** /ruːz/ [C;U] *Fr* (a) liquid mixture of fat and flour used for thickening soups and SAUCE*s*

rove /rəʊv/ *v* [Wv4;I∅;T1] *often lit* to wander; move continually (around): *to rove the seas in search of adventure*|*to come home after years of roving*|*His eyes roved about the room*

rov·er /ˈrəʊvəʳ/ *n lit* a wanderer

roving com·mis·sion /ˌ·· ·ˈ··/ *n* **1** *tech* permission, given to a person who is inquiring (officially) into a matter, to travel when necessary **2** *infml* a job that takes one all over the place

roving eye /ˌ·· ˈ·/ *n* [S] sexual interests that pass quickly from one person to another (in the phr. **have a roving eye**)

row¹ /rəʊ/ *v* **1** [I∅;T1] to move (a boat) through the water with OAR*s* (= long poles with flat ends): *You must learn to row (a boat)* **2** [L9;X9] to travel in this way; carry (someone or something) in this way: *He rowed (the boat) across the lake.*|*Shall I row you home?* **3** [I∅;T1: (*against*)] to have (a race of this kind): *row (a race) against Harvard*

row² /rəʊ/ *n* [*usu. sing.*] a trip or journey in a ROWING BOAT: *Come for a row!*

row³ /rəʊ/ *n* **1** [(*of*)] a neat line (of people or things) side by side: *a row of houses/of cups on a shelf*|*Children standing hand in hand in a row* (= side by side, not one behind the other) **2 a hard row to hoe** *becoming rare* a life full of difficulties: *Mary's got a hard row to hoe, with four small children*

row⁴ /raʊ/ *n infml* **1** [C] a noisy quarrel, sometimes with violent actions: *He's always having rows with his wife* **2** [S] a noise: *Stop making such a row; I can't sleep!* **3** [C] a case of being scolded: *You'll get in a row if the teacher hears about this* **4 kick up/make a row** *sl* to cause trouble, esp. by complaining loudly or angrily

row⁵ /raʊ/ *v* [I∅ (*with*)] *infml* to quarrel, often noisily or violently: *They're rowing again.*|*She always breaks dishes after rowing with her husband*

Row /rəʊ/ *n* [R9] (in an address) Street: *They live at 17 Fox Row*

row·an /ˈrəʊən, ˈraʊən/ *n* **1** also **mountain ash**— any of various small trees of the rose family with bunches of bright red berries in the autumn **2** the berry of this tree

row·an·ber·ry /ˈrəʊənberi, ˈraʊ-/ *n* ROWAN (2)

row·dy¹ /ˈraʊdi/ *adj* [Wa2] *not fml* (of a person or his behaviour) noisy and rough: *She was afraid of the big rowdy boys.*|*We live in a rowdy neighbourhood* —**rowdily** *adv* —**rowdiness** *n* [U]

rowdy² *n sl* a ROWDY¹ person

row·dy·is·m /ˈraʊdi-ɪzəm/ *n* [U] ROWDY¹ behaviour: *rowdyism at football matches*

row·el /ˈraʊəl/ *n* a small wheel with pointed teeth on it at the back of a SPUR (= instrument worn on a rider's heel, for urging a horse to go faster)

row·er /ˈrəʊəʳ/ *n* a person who rows: *8 strong rowers*

row·ing /ˈrəʊɪŋ/ *adj* [Wa5;A] for or connected with ROWing¹ (1): *join a rowing club*

rowing boat /ˈ·· ˌ·/ also (*esp. AmE*) **row·boat** /ˈrəʊbəʊt/— *n* a small boat that is moved through the water with OAR*s* (= long poles with flat ends): *"Rowing Boats for Hire"* (on a notice) —see picture at BOAT¹

row·lock /ˈrɒlək‖ˈrɑ-; *not tech* ˈrəʊlɒk‖-lɑk/ (*AmE* **oarlock**)— *n BrE* a pin or U-shaped rest on the side of a boat, for holding an OAR in place —see picture at BOAT¹

roy·al¹ /ˈrɔɪəl/ *adj* [Wa5;A] **1** (*often cap.*) for, belonging to, supported by, or connected with a king or queen: *the royal palaces*|*the Royal Navy* **2** (**right**) **royal(ly)** splendid(ly) (esp. in such phrs. as **a right royal feast, a royal welcome**): *They welcomed us right royally* —**~ly** *adv*

royal² *n infml* a member of the royal family: *The royals are now turning to face the television cameras*

Royal Au·to·mo·bile Club /ˌ·· ˈ···· ·, ˌ· ···ˈ· ·/ *n* [*the*+R] a British club for motorists, providing various advantages such as help with repairs on the road

royal flush /ˌ·· ˈ·/ *n* (in the card game of POKER) a set of cards dealt to a person which are the 5 highest cards in one of the 4 different types (SUIT*s*)

Royal High·ness /ˌ·· ˈ··/ *n* [C9; *Your*+N] (the words used when speaking to or of) a prince or princess (in the phrs. **Your Royal Highness; His/Her Royal Highness; Their Royal Highnesses**)

roy·al·ist /ˈrɔɪəlɪ̣st/ *adj, n* (typical of) someone who supports a king or queen, as in a CIVIL (1) war, or who believes that a country should be ruled by one

royal jel·ly /ˌ·· ˈ··/ *n* [U] the food on which bees feed a young queen bee

royal pre·rog·a·tive /ˌ·· ·ˈ···/ *n* [*the*+R] (*often caps.*) (one of) the special rights of a king or queen: *In Britain it is the royal prerogative to order Parliament to meet*

Royal So·ci·e·ty /ˌ·· ·ˈ···/ *n* [*the*+R] a British organization for the advancement of science. The important scientists who are its members have the title **Fellow of the Royal Society** (*abbrev.* FRS)

roy·al·ty /ˈrɔɪəlti/ *n* **1** [U] royal power and rank **2** [GU] people of the royal family: *The flag is only raised in the presence of royalty/when royalty are/is present* **3** [C] **a** a part of the price of a book, paid to the writer on each copy sold. It is also paid to the writer of a play or piece of music, when it is performed: *to receive royalties/a royalty of 5% on one's new book* **b** a share of the profits, as of an oil well or a mine or a new machine, paid in this way to an owner or inventor

RPM *abbrev. for:* REVOLUTION*s* (4) per minute, a measure of engine speed

RSM *abbrev. for:* REGIMENTAL SERGEANT MAJOR

RSVP *abbrev. for:* répondez s'il vous plaît (*Fr*); (written on invitations) please reply to this invitation

rub¹ /rʌb/ *v* **-bb-** **1** [T1 (*with*)] to slide one surface with pressure, to and fro or round and round against (another): *She rubbed the window (with a* *cloth*) **2** [T1 (TOGETHER)] to slide (2 surfaces against each other) in this way: *He rubbed his hands (together) to warm them/with pleasure* **3** [I∅ (*against, on*)] (of a surface) to slide in this way (against/on another) esp. so as to cause pain or wear out: *My shoe's rubbing* (=against my heel).| *This tyre seems badly worn; it must be rubbing (against/on something)* **4** [X9] to put (paste or liquid) on/over/into (a surface) in this way: *He rubbed polish on the table* —compare RUB IN (1) **5** [X9, esp. *in*] to cause (a hole) in this way: *You've rubbed a hole in the elbow of your coat/in your elbow* **6** [X7 (*with*)] to make (something) (clean, dry, etc.) in this way: *Rub your hair dry (with this cloth)* **7** [X9 esp. AWAY, OFF, *off*] to cause to disappear in this way: *Rub away that dirty mark.|Rub the mud off your boots* —see also RUB AGAINST, RUB ALONG, RUB DOWN, RUB IN, RUB OFF, RUB OUT, RUB UP, RUB UP AGAINST, **rub** SHOULDERS[1] (8) **with**

rub² *n* **1** [S] *not fml* an act of rubbing: *Give the table a good rub with this polish* **2** [*the*+R] the difficulty or cause of trouble (in the phr. **There's the rub**)

rub a·gainst *v prep* [D1;T1] to slide (something) with pressure against: *Don't rub (your shoulder) against the wet paint*

rub a·long *v adv* [Wv6;I∅] *BrE, not fml* **1** [(*by, on*)] to continue to do what is necessary, but with difficulty; SURVIVE: *He's not a good student; he can only just rub along in class.|She was able to rub along on the money her father gave her/by giving English lessons* **2** [(*with*)] to have a fairly good relationship (with someone); succeed in living together: *My wife and I seem to rub along (together) all right*

rub·ber¹ /ˈrʌbəʳ/ *n* **1** [U] a substance, made from the juice of a tropical tree, which keeps out water and springs back into position when stretched **2** [U] a substance with the same qualities as this, but made chemically **3** [C] *esp. BrE* a piece of this substance used for removing pencil marks; ERASER **4** [C *usu. pl.*] a shoe of this substance, either **a** *AmE* worn over another shoe to keep it dry or **b** (in British rockclimbing) PLIMSOLL or SNEAKER —see PAIR (USAGE) **5** [C] a piece of material used for rubbing surfaces to clean them: *a board rubber* (= for cleaning BLACKBOARD*s*) **6** [C] a person or machine that rubs **7** [C] *infml, esp. AmE* CONDOM

rubber² *n* **1** (when playing cards) **a** a set of 3 games of WHIST or BRIDGE. The winner of 2 games wins the set: *We've time for 1 more rubber* **b** 2 games won out of the 3 **c** the 3rd game which decides the winner **2** (in cricket) a set of international matches played one after the other: *a 5-match rubber between England and Australia*

rubber band /ˌ·· ˈ·/ *n* a thin circular piece of rubber used for fastening things together: *Put a rubber band round your hair/round this bunch of flowers*

rubber din·ghy /ˌ·· ˈ··/ *n* a small rubber boat blown up with air

rub·ber·ize, -ise /ˈrʌbəraɪz/ *v* [Wv5;T1] to cover (cloth) with a rubber surface

rub·ber·neck¹ /ˈrʌbənek‖-ər-/ *n AmE not fml* a person who RUBBERNECK*s*²

rubberneck² *v* [I∅] *AmE not fml* **1** to look about or watch something with too much interest: *They all gathered round the hole to rubberneck* **2** to go on a pleasure trip as one of a group with a guide

rubber plant /ˈ·· ·/ *n* a type of ornamental house plant of the RUBBER TREE family with large shiny dark green leaves

rubber sheath /ˌ·· ˈ·/ *n* CONDOM

rubber-stamp /ˌ·· ˈ·/ *v* [T1] *usu. derog* to approve or support officially (a decision) without really thinking about it

rubber stamp *n* **1** a piece of rubber on a handle, with raised letters or figures, used for printing the same thing (such as a name or date) again and again **2** *usu. derog* a person or body that acts only to make official the decisions already made by another

rubber tree /ˈ·· ·/ *n* a type of tropical tree from which rubber is obtained

rub·ber·y /ˈrʌbəri/ *adj often derog* strong and springy like rubber: *The meat's a bit rubbery—you cooked it too long!*

rub·bing /ˈrʌbɪŋ/ *n* a copy made from a raised shape or pattern in stone or (the stated) metal, esp. brass, by rubbing a piece of paper laid over the shape with wax, chalk, etc.: *a set of beautiful brass rubbings|Can you make a rubbing of this coin?*

rub·bish¹ /ˈrʌbɪʃ/ *n* [U] **1** waste material to be thrown away: *to burn the rubbish|Throw it on the garden rubbish heap* **2** silly remarks; nonsense: *He's talking rubbish*

rubbish² *v* [T1] *AustrE sl* to say that (someone or something) is bad or worthless; CRITICIZE

rubbish³ *interj* How silly!

rubbish bin /ˈ·· ·/ *n BrE* DUSTBIN

rub·bish·y /ˈrʌbɪʃi/ *adj infml* worthless and silly: *a rubbishy love story*

rub·ble /ˈrʌbəl/ *n* [U] (a mass of) broken stones or bricks: *After the bombing her house was just a heap of rubble*

rub·down /ˈrʌbdaʊn/ also **rub down** /ˌ· ˈ·/— *n* [S] an act of RUBbing DOWN: *a rub down with a wet cloth*

rub down *v adv* **1** [T1;(I∅)] to dry (oneself or an animal) by rubbing: *rubbing herself down after a swim* **2** [T1] to make (a surface) smooth by rubbing: *Rub the door down before you paint it*

ru·bel·la /ruːˈbelə/ *n* [U] *med* GERMAN MEASLES

Ru·bi·con /ˈruːbɪkən, -kɒn‖-kɑn/ *n* **cross/pass the Rubicon** to make a decision or take an action that cannot later be changed

ru·bi·cund /ˈruːbɪkənd/ *adj fml or humor* (of a person or esp. his face) fat, red, and healthy-looking: *a group of rubicund farmers*

rub in *v adv* **1** [T1] to make (liquid) go into a surface by rubbing: *Rub the polish well in* —compare RUB¹ (4) **2** [T1,5] (*not used with the actual words spoken*) to say repeatedly: *Mother kept rubbing (it) in that we mustn't talk to strangers* **3 rub it in** *infml* to keep talking about something that another person wants to forget: *"We'll be late." "I know; don't rub it in!"*

ru·ble /ˈruːbəl/ *n* ROUBLE

rub off *v adv* [I∅ (*on, onto*)] to come off a surface (onto another) by rubbing: *The mud will rub off quite easily.*|(fig.) *I hope that some of her good qualities will rub off onto you* —compare RUB¹ (7)

rub out *v adv* **1** [T1;I∅] *BrE* **a** to remove (esp. pencil writing) with a piece of rubber: *to rub out a word/a mistake/a dirty mark on the paper* **b** (esp. of pencil writing) to disappear in this way: *It won't rub out!* **2** [T1] *AmE sl* to murder (someone)

ru·bric /ˈruːbrɪk/ *n* a set of rules printed in some special way and telling one what to do, as in a prayerbook or examination paper

rub up *v adv* [T1] **1** to polish by rubbing: *The silver needs rubbing up* **2** BRUSH UP: *I must rub up my French* **3 rub someone up the wrong way** *not fml* to annoy someone —**rub-up** /ˈ· ·/ *n* [S]

rub up a·gainst *v adv prep* [T1 *no pass.*] *not fml* to meet (someone) by chance in company: *You rub up against a lot of famous people at Robert's parties*

ru·by /ˈruːbi/ *n* **1** [C] a deep red precious stone: *a ruby ring* **2** [A] the colour of this stone: *ruby wine*

ruck¹ /rʌk/ *n rare* an unwanted fold (in cloth): *rucks in the tablecloth*

ruck² *n* **1** [*the*+R] the ordinary level of life: *to get out of the (common) ruck and become famous as a singer* **2** [S+*of*] (esp. in football) a disordered group (of people): *Channon shot* (= kicked the ball) *from out of a ruck of players* **3** [C] (in RUGBY) a group of players from both teams who compete to get possession of the ball

ruck³ *v* [I∅] to take part in a RUCK² (3)

ruck·sack /ˈrʌksæk/ *n* a bag fastened to the shoulders and now usu. built on a light frame, in which climbers and walkers can carry their belongings —see picture at CAMP²

ruck up *v adv* [I∅] (of cloth) to form RUCKs¹: *Your coat's all rucked up at the back*

ruck·us /ˈrʌkəs/ *n* [*usu. sing.*] *AmE sl* a noisy complaint or FUSS¹ (1): *to raise a ruckus*

ruc·tion /ˈrʌkʃən/ *n* [S] *AmE infml* RUCTIONS: *There'll be a ruction if you don't give him some more chocolate*

ruc·tions /ˈrʌkʃənz/ *n* [P] *infml* noisy complaints and anger: *There'll be ructions if you don't give him some more chocolate*

rud·der /ˈrʌdəʳ/ *n* **1** a wooden or metal blade at the back of a ship that swings to and fro to control the direction —see picture at FREIGHTER **2** an apparatus for the same purpose on an aircraft —see picture at AIRCRAFT —**~less** *adj* [Wa5]

rud·dle¹ /ˈrʌdl/ *n* [U] the red paint used for marking sheep

ruddle² *v* [T1] to put RUDDLE¹ onto (a sheep)

rud·dy¹ /ˈrʌdi/ *adj* [Wa2] **1** (of the face) pink and healthy-looking: *the ruddy cheeks of the children* **2** *esp. lit* red or reddish: *the ruddy flames of the fire* —**ruddiness** *n* [U]

ruddy² *adj, adv* [Wa5;A] *BrE euph* (used, not in polite conversation, as an almost meaningless addition to speech): *Where's that ruddy elephant gone?*

rude /ruːd/ *adj* **1** [Wa1;B] (of a person or his behaviour) not at all polite: *It's rude to say you don't like hot food, when she spent so long preparing it.|Don't make rude remarks.|Don't be so rude to your father* **2** [Wa5;A] simple and roughly made: *a rude hut* **3** [Wa5;A] (of people) wild and untaught: *a rude mountain tribe* **4** [Wa5;A] raw; in the natural state: *rude cotton* **5** [Wa1;A] sudden and violent (in the phrs. **a rude shock, a rude awakening**) **6** [Wa1;B] (*used esp. by or to children*) causing sexual shame: *to tell a very rude story* **7 in rude health** very healthy —**~ness** *n* [U]

rude·ly /ˈruːdli/ *adv* **1** in a RUDE (1) way: *Don't speak so rudely to your father* **2** in a RUDE (2) way: *a figure rudely cut out of rough wood* **3** in a RUDE (5) way: *I was rudely* AWAKE*ned by the sound of a bell*

ru·di·ment /ˈruːdʒmənt/ *n tech* a RUDIMENTARY (2) bodily organ or part

ru·di·men·ta·ry /ˌruːdʒˈmentəri/ *adj* **1** (of facts, knowledge, etc.) simple; coming or learnt first: *I have only the most rudimentary knowledge of chemistry* **2** [Wa5] not (yet) developed: *an unborn mouse with a rudimentary tail*

ru·di·ments /ˈruːdʒmənts/ *n* [*the*+P+*of*] the RUDIMENTARY (1) parts (of a subject): *to learn the rudiments of grammar/of Italian*

rue¹ /ruː/ *v* [T1,4] *old use & humor* **1** to be sorry about (something one has done or not done): *I never went to school, and I've rued it bitterly all my life.|You'll rue having kicked that policeman* **2 rue the day (when one did something)** to be sorry (that one did something): *He'll rue the day he married her*

rue² *n* [U] a type of small strong-smelling European bush with bitter-tasting leaves, formerly used in medicine

rue·ful /ˈruːfəl/ *adj* feeling or showing that one RUEs something —**~ly** *adv*

ruff /rʌf/ *n* **1** a kind of stiff wheel-shaped white collar worn in Europe in the 16th century **2** a ring of hair or feathers round the neck of an animal or bird

ruf·fi·an /ˈrʌfɪən/ *n becoming rare* a bad, perhaps violent, man: *He was attacked in a dark street by a band of ruffians*

ruf·fi·an·ly /ˈrʌfɪənli/ *adj fml, becoming rare* (of a person or his behaviour) seeming like (that of) a RUFFIAN

ruf·fle¹ /ˈrʌfəl/ *v* [Wv5] **1** [T1 (UP)] to move the smooth surface of; make uneven: *He fondly ruffled the child's hair.|The bird ruffled (up) its feathers.|The wind-ruffled surface of the lake* **2** [I∅;T1] to cause slight anger in (someone or his feelings); (cause to) become rather angry: *Don't get so ruffled; you shouldn't ruffle so easily*

ruffle² *n* a band of fine cloth sewn in folds as an ornament round the edge of something, esp. at the neck or wrists of a garment; FRILL

rug /rʌg/ *n* **1** a thick usu. woollen floor mat, smaller than a CARPET¹ (2) —see picture at LIVING ROOM **2** a large warm woollen covering to wrap round oneself when travelling or camping: *Put this rug over your knees*

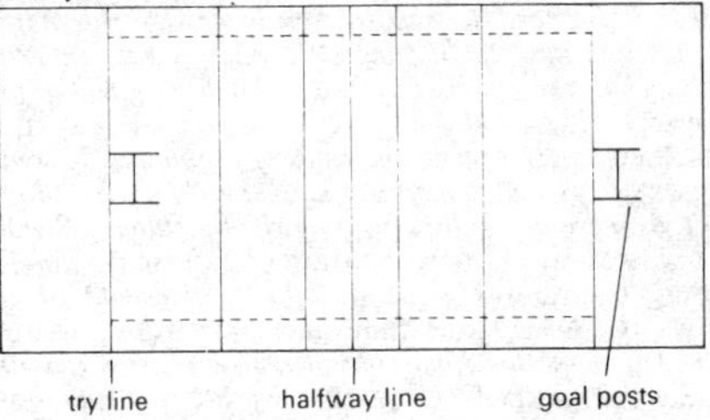

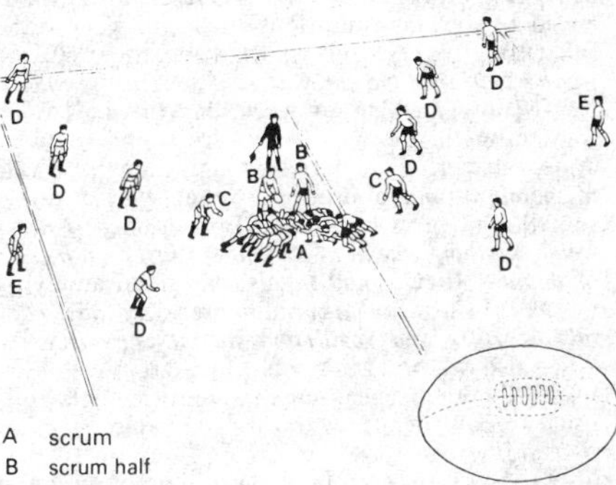

rugby

rug·by /ˈrʌgbi/ also (*fml*) **rugby foot·ball** /ˌ·· ˈ··/, (*infml*) **rug·ger** /ˈrʌgəʳ/— *n* [U] (*sometimes cap.*) a type of football played with an oval ball, by 2 teams of either 13 men (**rugby league**) or 15 men (**rugby union**)

USAGE One plays **rugby** on a *field*, with a **rugby** *football* or **rugger** *ball*, and one SCOREs² (1) *points*. In a *match* the person in charge is called the **referee**.

rug·ged /ˈrʌgɪ̈d/ *adj* **1** (of a thing) large, rough, unpolished, and strong-looking: (fig.) *a fierce rugged face* **2** (of a person or his character) rough but strong and good: *He's rugged but kind* —**~ly** *adv* —**~ness** *n* [U]

ru·in¹ /ˈruːɪ̇n/ *n* **1** [U] (the cause, state, or event of) destruction and decay: *an ancient temple which has fallen into ruin|Drink was your father's ruin and it will be the ruin of you too!* **2** [C] a RUINed² (1) building: *an interesting old ruin on top of the hill*

ruin² *v* [Wv5;T1] **1** to destroy and spoil (completely): *an ancient ruined city|She poured water all over my painting and ruined it* **2** to cause total loss of money to: *I was ruined by that law case; I'm a ruined man!*

ru·in·a·tion /ˌruːɪ̇nˈeɪʃən/ *n* [U] *not fml* (the cause of) being RUINed² (2): *You'll be the ruination of me, spending all that money!*

ru·in·ous /ˈruːɪ̇nəs/ *adj* **1** [Wa5] causing or so as to cause destruction or total loss of money: *The cost will be ruinous.|a ruinous war|ruinous debts|the ruinous stupidity of his action* **2** (of a building) partly or completely RUINed² (1) —**~ly** *adv*: *ruinously costly*

ru·ins /ˈruːɪ̇nz/ *n* [P] **1** remains (of a building or buildings): *the ruins of an ancient castle|a goat wandering among the ruins* **2 in ruins** (of a building) RUINed² (1): *The castle is now in ruins.|*(fig.) *Our plans are in ruins*

rule¹ /ruːl/ *n* **1** [C,C5,5c] a principle or order which guides behaviour, says how things are to be done, etc.: *It's against the rules to pick up the ball.|the rules of tennis|He makes it an invariable rule not to give anything to beggars.|We have a rule that the loser of the game buys/that the loser should buy everyone a drink* **2** [C,C5] the usual way that something happens: *the rules of grammar|He sometimes pays and sometimes not; there's no rule about it.|Is there a rule that pretty girls are stupid?* **3** [U9] (possession of) power to RULE² (1): *under foreign rule* (=by foreigners)|*to obtain the rule of the country* **4** [U9] the time or way of ruling (RULE² (1)): *under the kind rule of a new master|His rule lasted 20 years* **5** [C] RULER (2): *a 2 foot rule* —see also SLIDE RULE **6 as a rule** usually; generally **7 bend/stretch the rules** to allow oneself to be influenced by special conditions in deciding how the rule (RULE¹ (1)) is to be put into practice: *Usually we don't do this, but for you we'll stretch the rules a bit* **8 (do something) by/according to rule** (to do something) in the way things are supposed to be done, but perhaps without enough thought **9 rule of thumb** a quick and not very exact way of doing something, learnt by practical experience: *I never weigh anything when I'm cooking—I just do it by rule of thumb* **10 rules and regulations** small annoying RULEs¹ (1) usu. in large numbers: *You must obey all the rules and regulations about car insurance* —see also GOLDEN RULE, **rule of the** ROAD⁸

USAGE When speaking of scientific facts it is usual to call them laws rather than **rules**: *the law that oil floats on water.*

rule² *v* **1** [T1;I∅ (*over*)] to have and use the highest form of power over (a country, people, etc.), esp. as a king/queen or government: *In ancient times the kings of England ruled without a parliament, having complete power.|*(fig.) *to rule (over) one's children* **2** [T5;L9 esp. *on, against*] (esp. in law) to decide officially: *The judge ruled that he must stop beating his wife.|Perhaps you would care to rule on this matter, My Lord?* —compare RULING¹ **3** [Wv5;T1] **a** to draw (a line) with the help of a RULER (2) or like straight edge **b** to draw parallel lines on (paper) **4 be ruled by** to be guided or influenced by: *Don't let yourself be ruled by your feelings in this matter* **5 rule (esp. a group) with a rod of iron/with an iron hand** to govern (esp. a group) in a very severe way

rule·book /ˈruːlbʊk/ *n* **1** [C] a book of RULEs¹ (1) esp. one given to workers on a job **2** [*the*+R] the set of all the RULEs¹ (1) of a particular activity

rule off *v adv* [T1] to draw a line at the end of (something on a page): *He added up the list of figures and ruled it off neatly*

rule out *v adv* [T1] to declare the nonexistence of; EXCLUDE (2) (often in the phr. **rule out the possibility**): *We can't rule out the possibility that he'll come after all.|That idea can be completely ruled out*

rul·er /ˈruːləʳ/ *n* **1** a person who RULEs² (1) **2** a long narrow flat piece of hard material with straight edges. It is marked with inches or CENTIMETREs, and used for measuring things or for drawing straight lines: *a 12-inch ruler* —see picture at MATHEMATICAL

rul·ing¹ /ˈruːlɪŋ/ *n* [C (*on*), C5,5c] an official decision: *The judge has made/given several rulings on these matters.|a ruling that women are not allowed in the club/that he should stop beating his wife* —compare RULE² (2)

ruling² *adj* [Wa5;A] most powerful: *a member of the ruling class in this country|His garden is his ruling* PASSION (4) (=interest)

rum¹ /rʌm/ also **rummy**— *adj* [Wa1] *esp. BrE sl, becoming rare* unusual; strange

rum² *n* [U] **1** a strong alcoholic drink made from the juice of the sugar CANE (=plant) **2** *AmE* any kind of alcoholic drink

rum·ba /ˈrʌmbə/ *n* (the music for) a popular dance invented by the black people in Cuba

rum·ble¹ /ˈrʌmbəl/ *v* **1** [I∅] to make a deep continuous rolling sound: *The thunder/The big guns rumbled in the distance.|I'm hungry—my stomach's rumbling* **2** [L9] to go along making this sound: *The heavy cart rumbled down the rough street* **3** [T1,5a: (OUT)] (*used with the actual words spoken*) to say in a voice of this kind

rumble² *n* **1** [S] a rumbling (RUMBLE¹ (1)) sound: *a rumble of thunder* **2** [C] *esp. AmE* DICKY¹ (2) **3** [C] *AmE sl* a street fight

rumble³ *v* [T1] *BrE infml* to understand the hidden nature of; not be deceived by: *She's charming but insincere; I soon rumbled her*

rum·bling /ˈrʌmblɪŋ/ *n* **1** [S] a rumbling (RUMBLE¹ (1)) sound **2** [U9 esp. *about, often pl. with sing. meaning*] widespread unofficial talk or complaint: *There's been a lot of rumbling lately about bad working conditions.|rumblings of* DISCONTENT **3** [C5 *usu. pl.*] RUMOUR: *I've heard rumblings that Tim may leave the company*

rum·bus·tious /rʌmˈbʌstʃəs/ *adj infml, esp. BrE* (of a person or his behaviour) noisy and cheerful: *The children get very rumbustious after tea*

ru·mi·nant /ˈruːmɪ̇nənt/ *adj, n* [Wa5] (an animal) that RUMINATEs (1): *ruminant creatures|The cow is a ruminant*

See next page for picture

ru·mi·nate /ˈruːmɪ̇neɪt/ *v* [I∅] **1** (of cattle, deer, etc.) to bring back food (CUD) from the stomach and bite it over and over again **2** [(*about, over*)] (of a person) to think deeply: *Let me ruminate over this plan of yours* —**-nation** /ˌruːmɪ̇ˈneɪʃən/ *n* [U]

ru·mi·na·tive /ˈruːmɪ̇nətɪv‖-neɪ-/ *adj* (of a person or his behaviour) seeming thoughtful: *a man of ruminative habits* —**~ly** *adv*: *"I wonder . . ." he said ruminatively*

rum·mage¹ /ˈrʌmɪdʒ/ *n not fml* **1** [S (ABOUT, AROUND)] a case of rummaging (RUMMAGE²): *I'll have a good rummage (around) and see what I can find* **2** [U] *esp. AmE* old clothes and other things found by rummaging (RUMMAGE²) about

rummage² *v not fml* **1** [L9 esp. ABOUT, *through, among*] to turn things over and look into all the corners while trying to find something: *Who's been rummaging about among my papers?* **2** [T1] to

African elephant
Indian elephant
rhinoceros
Indian water buffalo
zebra
African buffalo
antelope
bison
giraffe
Bactrian camel
warthog
dromedary
cow
hippopotamus
deer

some hooved and ruminant mammals

search (a place, esp. a ship) thoroughly: *The officers rummaged the ship in search of drugs*

rummage sale /ˈ·· ·/ *n AmE* JUMBLE SALE

rum·my¹ /ˈrʌmi/ *adj* [Wa1] *esp. BrE sl, becoming rare* RUM¹

rummy² *n* [U] any of several simple card games for 2 or more players, played with 2 sets (PACKs) of cards

ru·mour, *AmE* **rumor** /ˈruːməʳ/ *n* **1** [U] unofficial news; common talk, perhaps untrue: *Rumour has it that Jean's getting married again* **2** [C (*about, of*), C5] a story that reaches one through this: *All kinds of strange rumours about Jean are going around*

ru·moured, *AmE* **rumored** /ˈruːməd‖-ərd/ *adj* [Wa5;B;F3,5,5b] reported unofficially: *a rumoured marriage between the prince and the dancer|It's rumoured that Jean's in love again*

ru·mour·mon·ger, *AmE* **rumor-** /ˈruːməˌmʌŋgəʳ‖-mərˌmɑŋ-, -ˌmʌŋ-/ *n* [C; *you*+N9] a person who spreads RUMOURs

rump /rʌmp/ *n* **1** the part of an animal at the back just above the legs. When we eat this part of a cow it is called a/some **rump steak** **2** *humor* (of a human being) the part of the body one sits on; BOTTOM (5b) **3** the remaining bad or worthless part of something, esp. of a public body or organization

rum·ple /ˈrʌmpəl/ *v* [Wv5;T1] to disarrange (hair, clothes, etc.); make untidy: *her rumpled curls|Don't rumple my dress, dear*

rum·pus /ˈrʌmpəs/ *n* [S] *infml* a noisy argument, quarrel, or disagreement: *to kick up|cause|make a rumpus|Who's making all that rumpus?*

rumpus room /ˈ·· ·/ *n AmE* a room usu. below ground level in a house, used for active games and parties

run¹ /rʌn/ *v* **ran** /ræn/, **run** /rʌn/, *pres. p.* **running** **1** [IØ] to move on one's legs at a speed faster than walking: *"Don't try to run before you can walk"* (saying).|*He ran to catch the bus.|The children came running when she called them.|The insect ran up my leg.|They ran to her help.|The child ran off to get his brother* **2** [L1] to travel (a distance) in this way: *He ran a mile in 4 minutes* **3** [T1] **a** to take part in (a race) in this way: *The children ran races in the park* **b** to cause (an animal) to take part in a race: *We won't run this horse in any races this season.|* (fig.) *The Party is running 3* CANDIDATEs (= people trying to get elected) *in the next election* **c** to cause (a race) to happen: *The bicycle race will be run in*

Holland next year **4** [L9;X9] **a** to cause (esp. a ship or wheeled vehicle) to advance quickly: *I'll run the car into the car park* **b** (esp. of a ship or wheeled vehicle) to advance quickly: *The car ran down the hill.|The train ran past the signal.|The boat ran into port* —compare **run before the** WIND[1] (12) **5** [L9;X9] to (cause to) move quickly: *A thought ran through my mind.|He ran his eyes over the list of figures* **6** [IØ;T1] **a** (of a machine) to work; be in movement: *Don't touch the engine while it's running* **b** to cause (a machine) to work or be in movement: *I'll just run the engine for a minute* **7** [L9;X9: esp. *by, on*] **a** (of a machine) to work (in a stated way, or by a stated form of power): *The motor isn't running smoothly.|This machine runs by electricity/runs off the electric light.|*(fig.) *Is everything running well in your office?* **b** to cause (a machine) to work (in a stated way, or by a stated form of power): *Do you run the trains on oil or by steam?* **8** [IØ;T1] **a** (of a public vehicle) to travel as arranged; go to and fro: *The trains don't run on Sundays/aren't running today.|This bus runs between Manchester and Liverpool/from here to the Town Hall* **b** to cause (a public vehicle) to travel in this way: *They're running a special train to the football match* **9** [Wv4; L9] (of liquids, sand, etc.) to flow: *to wash in running water|The tears ran down his face.|The water runs out of the pipe into the bucket.|*(fig.) *Your arguments run off her "like water off a duck's back"* (=without having any effect) (saying) **10** [L7] (of liquids, sand, etc.) to become by flowing: *The water ran cold/hot* **11** [IØ;L7] (of a container) **a** to pour out liquid: *Your nose is running.|Is the* TAP[1] (1) *still running?* **b** to reach (a state) by pouring out liquid: *The well has run dry* **12** [T1;D1] **a** to cause (liquids, sand, etc.) to flow, esp. from a TAP[1] (1): *Run the water till it gets hot* **b** to fill (a bath) for someone: *Please run me a nice hot bath* **13** [IØ] to melt and spread by the action of heat or water: *The butter will run if you put it near the fire.|I'm afraid the colours ran when I washed this shirt* **14** [Wv6;L9] to pass; stretch; continue: *a long passage running from end to end of the house| The road runs along the river bank/over the mountains/through a* TUNNEL **15** [T1] to own and drive (a car): *Mr Coakley runs a blue Volkswagen* **16** [L9;X9] *not fml* **a** to take (somebody or something, to somewhere) in a vehicle: *Can I run you home?* **b** to go quickly (to somewhere), esp. in a vehicle: *Why not run over and see us one evening?|I'll just run across to Mary's house and borrow some sugar* **17** [T1 (*across, into*)] to bring (something) into a country, unlawfully and secretly: *to run drugs/guns/arms (across the border/into Ireland)* **18** [T1] to control; be in charge of and cause to work (an organization or system): *Who's running this country?|to run a hotel/a youth club|We're running a new system of payment.|I don't want to run your life for you!* **19** [L9 esp. *for*] to have official force (during a period of time): *The insurance has only another month to run* **20** [IØ] (of a play, film, etc.) to be continuously performed: *His play is running in New York now and I hope it runs for years.|Is that film still running?* **21** [IØ (*against, for, in*)] *esp. AmE* to be or become a CANDIDATE (= a person trying to get elected) (in an election); compete (for an office, against someone else) in this way; STAND[1] (18): *to run for President|to run in the next election| to run against Ford|Johnson didn't run a second time* **22** [IØ] (of a hole in woven cloth, esp. in a stocking) to become a LADDER[1] (2) **23** [L9;T5a] (*used with the actual words given*) (of words in fixed order, as in a poem or law) to be; consist of: *How does the first line run?|The story runs like this . . .| The line runs "Time and the bell have buried the day"* **24 be run off one's feet** *infml* to be very busy; have to work too hard, esp. actively **25 run (a competitor) close/hard** to be nearly equal to (a competitor): *Paul won the prize, but Charles ran him very close* **26 run for it** *not fml* to escape by running **27 run for one's life/for dear life** *not fml* to run very fast to save oneself: *He's got a gun! Run for your lives!* **28 run foul/afoul of** **a** to become mixed in a disorderly way with: *The chain has run foul of plants in the water* **b** to meet difficulty in: *The chairman's plans have run afoul of opposition* **29 run (someone) (clean) off (someone's) feet/legs** *infml* to tire someone out with running **30 run (oneself or another) into the ground** to tire (oneself or someone else) out with hard work **31 run the chance/danger of** to take the risk of —see also RUN ACROSS, RUN AFTER, RUN ALONG, **run** AMOK, RUN AROUND, RUN AT, RUN AWAY, RUN AWAY WITH, RUN BACK, RUN BACK OVER, **make someone's** BLOOD[1] (11) **run cold,** RUN DOWN, **run it** FINE[4] (3), **run the** GAUNTLET[2], **run** HIGH[2] (3), RUN IN, RUN INTO, **run** LOW[3] (5), RUN OFF, RUN OFF WITH, RUN ON, RUN OUT, RUN OUT OF, RUN OUT ON, RUN OVER, **run** RINGS **round, run** RIOT, **run** RISKS, **run to** SEED, **run** SHORT[2] (6), **run a** TEMPERATURE, RUN THROUGH, RUN TO, RUN UP, RUN UP AGAINST, **run to** WASTE, **run before the** WIND

run² *n* **1** [C] the action of RUNning[1] (1): *to go for a run/to take the dog for a run before breakfast|A cross-country run is a run across the fields* **2** [C9] a (stated) period spent or distance travelled in this way: *a 10-minute run|a 3-mile run* **3** [S9] a short pleasure journey (of the stated kind): *Let's go for a run in the car* **4** [S9] a (stated) time taken or distance travelled by esp. a train or ship: *It's a 60-minute run/a 60-mile run to Brighton* **5** [*the*+C9] the journey to a (stated) place by train or ship: *a ship on the San Francisco run|They don't serve dinner on the Inverness or Edinburgh runs* **6** [C9] a (usu. enclosed) area where the (stated) animals are kept: *a hen run|a rabbit run|a sheep run* **7** [S+*on*] **a** an eager demand (for): *There's been a great run on beer this hot weather* **b** (in the money market) a general desire to sell: *a run on the £* **8** [C] a point won **a** (in cricket) by 2 players running from one WICKET to the other, passing each other on the way: *to* SCORE (= make) *10 runs* **b** (in BASEBALL) by a player reaching the home base safely **9** [C] (in card games) a set of cards dealt to a person, in which the numbers on all the cards follow on from each other: *A run in which all the cards are of the same type* (SUIT) *is called a* **running flush** —compare FLUSH[6] **10** [S9] a continuous set or SUCCESSION **a** of performances of a play, film, etc.: *The play had a run of 3 months* **b** of things produced in a factory **c** of like events: *a run of bad luck* **11** [C] *AmE* a stream **12** [C9] a sloping course for the (stated) downhill sport: *a* SKI-*run* **13** [C] (in music) a set of notes played or sung quickly up or down the SCALE[5] (5) without a break **14** [C9] *tech* a group of (the stated) fish travelling together: *a run of* SALMON *on their way up the river* **15** [C] *AmE* LADDER[1] (2): *a run in my new stockings* **16 a (good) run for one's money** *not fml* **a** to treat or serve (someone) in a satisfactory manner, esp. to be a worthy opponent of (someone) in a competition **b** to be treated or served in a satisfactory manner **17 a run on the bank** a sudden demand by many people to have their money back from the bank **18 at a run** RUNning[1] (1): *She left the house at a run* **19 be on the run** **a** to be trying to escape, or to hide, esp. from the police: *We've got the enemy on the run now!|The escaped murderer has been on the run for 3 weeks* **b** in a hurry: *She's on the run from morning till night* —compare **on the** GO[2] (10) **20 in the long run** after enough time; in the end: *It'll be cheaper in the long* *run to use real leather* **21 in the short run** for the near future: *Of course cardboard's cheaper than leather in the short run, but . . .* **22 the common/ordinary run (of)** the usual sort (of): *She's different from the common run of students.|This dictionary will be quite out of the ordinary run* **23 the run of (a place)** the freedom to visit or use (a place): *He's given our children the run of his garden.|I have the run of the university library* —see also RUNS

run-a·bout /ˈ· ·ˌ·/ *n not fml* a small light car

run a·cross *v prep* [T1] to find or meet by chance (esp. someone or something pleasant): *I ran across an old friend in the street* —compare COME ACROSS

run af·ter *v prep* [T1] **1** to chase: *a dog running after rabbits* (compare *a dog running behind my horse*) **2** *not fml* to try to gain the attention and company of: *He's always running after women* **3** *not fml* to perform the duties of a servant for: *I can't keep running after you all day!*

run a·long *v adv* [IØ *often imper.*] *infml* (*used esp. to children*) to leave; go away: *Run along now, all of you! I'm busy*

run-a·round /ˈ· ·ˌ·/ *n* [*the*+R] *infml* **1** the sort of treatment that consists in keeping a person waiting and refusing to see him or to answer his questions: *Don't give me the run-around, young man! Do you know who I am?* **2 give/get the run-around** to deceive/be deceived by one's husband or wife

run a·round *v adv* [L9] to go about in company (with, together): *I don't want you running around with my daughter, young man!*

run at *v prep* [T1 *no pass.*] to attack suddenly: *The dog ran at the visitor and bit him*

run·a·way /ˈrʌnəweɪ/ *adj* [Wa5;A] **1** out of control: *a runaway horse|a runaway increase in prices* **2** done by RUNning AWAY: *a runaway marriage* **3** having RUN AWAY: *a runaway child*

run-a·way *n* a person who has RUN AWAY: *The little run-away was brought back home in a police car*

run a·way *v adv* [IØ (*from*)] to escape by running: *She hit the child and he ran away* (compare *She kissed the child and he ran off*)

run a·way with also **run off with**— *v adv prep* [T1] **1** to get out of control and carry off (someone): (fig.) *Don't let your temper run away with you* **2** to take (someone of the opposite sex) away: *He ran away with his teacher's wife* **3** to steal and carry off (something): *He's run away with all my jewels* **4** to use; cost: *Your education runs away with most of my money* **5** to win (a game or competition) easily **6** [*usu. neg.*] to believe too easily: *Don't run away with the idea that you needn't work*

run back *v adv* **1** [T1b] to wind (film or TAPE¹ (3)) back **2** [IØ] (of share prices) to become lower

run back o·ver *v adv prep* [T1] to think and talk again about: *to let one's thoughts run back over one's childhood*

run-down¹ /ˈ· ·/ *n* **1** [(*the*) S (*of*)] the RUNning DOWN (5) of something: *the run-down of the plastics industry* **2** [C] *not fml* a detailed report of a set of events: *He gave me a run-down on everything that had happened while I was away*

run-down² /ˌ· ˈ·◂/ *adj* **1** [F;(B)] (of a person) tired and weak and in poor health: *You need a holiday; you look a bit run-down* **2** [B] (of a thing) old and broken or in bad condition: *They live in an old run-down hotel by the railway bridge*

run down *v adv* **1** [T1] to knock down and hurt (a person or animal) with one's vehicle —compare RUN INTO, RUN OVER **2** [T1] **a** to chase and catch (a person or animal): *to run down a criminal* **b** to find by searching: *to run down a book in the library* **3** [T1] to say rude or unfair things about; speak of as being less valuable, important, etc., than appears: *She's jealous of your success; that's why she's always running you down* **4** [IØ] (esp. of a clock, or of an electric BATTERY) to lose power and stop working, as because of the need for winding up **5** [IØ;T1] to (allow to) stop working gradually: *The coal industry is running down/is being run down*

rune /ruːn/ *n* **1** any of the letters of an alphabet cut on stone, wood, etc., once used by the peoples of Northern Europe **2** a magic charm written or spoken mysteriously —**runic** *adj* [Wa5]: *runic writing*

rung¹ /rʌŋ/ also **round**— *n* **1** one of the cross-bars that form the steps of a ladder **2** a bar like this between the legs of a chair **3 the highest/top/lowest/bottom rung of the ladder** the highest/lowest level in an organization or profession: *He made his son start at the bottom rung of the ladder*

rung² *past p. of* RING

run-in /ˈ· ·/ *n* **1** [C] *AmE infml* a quarrel or disagreement, esp. with the police or an official body **2** [*the*+R (*to*);(C)] *esp. BrE* RUN-UP (1)

run in *v adv* [T1] **1** to bring (an engine) slowly into full use: *I'm running my new car in* **2** *infml* (of the police) to catch (a criminal); ARREST¹ (1): *He was run in for being in possession of drugs*

run in·to *v prep* **1** [D1;T1] **a** to push (something sharp) into: *He ran the knife into his enemy* **b** (of something sharp) to go into: *The needle ran into her finger* —compare RUN THROUGH¹·² **2** [D1;T1] **a** to cause (a vehicle) to meet (something) with force: *to run one's car into a tree* **b** (of a vehicle) to meet (something) with force: *to run into a lamp-post|* (fig.) *You'll run into trouble if you don't take care* —compare RUN DOWN, RUN OVER **3** [T1] also **run to**— to add up to; reach (a length or amount): *a debt running into 1,000's of pounds* **4** [T1] *infml* to meet (someone) by chance

run·nel /ˈrʌnl/ *n* **1** *esp. lit* a small stream **2** an open DRAIN (= passage dug to carry away water) beside the road

run·ner /ˈrʌnəʳ/ *n* **1** a person who runs, esp. **a** in a race or as a sport: *only 6 runners in the race|a long-distance runner* **b** (esp. in former times) to carry messages: *They sent a runner from Marathon to Athens to carry the news* **2** one of the 2 thin blades on which a SLEDGE (= wheel-less carriage) slides over the snow or the single blade on which a SKATE slides over the ice **3** one of the stems with which a plant like the STRAWBERRY spreads itself along the ground **4** any of various long narrow pieces of plain or ornamental cloth, used for covering the tops of tables or for laying along the floor in passages or on stairs

-runner *comb. form* [*n*→*n*] a person who RUNs¹ (17) the stated goods into a country; SMUGGLEr: *a gun-runner|a* RUM-*runner* —compare BLOCKADE-RUNNER

runner bean /ˌ·· ˈ·/ also **scarlet runner** (*AmE* **string bean**)— *n BrE* a type of climbing bean with usu. bright red flowers and long green PODs (= seed containers) which are used as food —see picture at FLOWER¹

runner-up /ˌ·· ˈ·/ *n* **runners-up** *or* **runner-ups** the person or team that comes second in a race or competition

run·ning¹ /ˈrʌnɪŋ/ *n* **1** [U] the act or sport of running: *Paul used to practise running when he was at college* **2 in/out of the running** *not fml* with some/no hope of winning: *Charles is still in the running as a possible next head of the firm* **3 make the running** to set the speed at which a race is run, a relationship develops, etc.: *If you want to be friends with her you'll have to make (all) the running*

running² *adj* [Wa5;A] **1** (of water) **a** flowing: *We could hear the running water of the stream* **b** flowing from TAPs¹ (1): *This hotel has hot and cold running* *water in every room* **2** done while one is running along: *a running jump/fight/kick* **3** continuous: *He has a running battle with his wife over which of them is to use the car.|A* **running commentary** *is an account of a (sports) event given by a broadcaster while it is actually happening* **4** (of money) spent or needed to keep something working: *The running costs of that big car must be very high* **5** joined together continuously: *running stitch|to write in a running* HAND¹ (3) (=with joined letters) **6** for or concerned with running as a sport: *Where are my running shoes?* **7** giving out liquid: *a running nose/sore* **8 in running order** (of a machine) working properly **9 take a running jump a** to run to the point where one starts a jump **b** *sl, imper.* Go away! You annoy me

running³ *adv* [Wa5] (*after a pl. noun with a number*) one after the other without a break: *to win the prize 3 times running*

running board /ˈ·· ·/ *n* one of the steps running along each side of an old car: *to climb onto the running board*

running mate /ˈ·· ·/ *n* **1** (in US politics) a person with whom another is RUNning¹ (21) for a pair of political positions of greater and less importance, esp. those of President and VICE-President: *Nixon and Agnew were running mates in 1972* **2** the less important of these 2 people: *Agnew was Nixon's running mate in 1972*

run·ny /ˈrʌni/ *adj* [Wa1] *infml* **1** more liquid than is usual or expected: *runny butter* **2** (of the nose or eyes) producing liquid, as when one has a cold

run-off /ˈ· ·/ *n* a last race or competition to decide the winner, because 2 or more people have won an equal number of points, races, etc.

run off *v adv* **1** [T1] to allow (liquid) to flow out: *to run off a bucket of water from the barrel* **2** [D1 (*for*);T1] *not fml* to print (copies): *I'll run (you) off 100 of these notices* **3** [T1] to hold (a race, or esp. the early parts of a competition): *We'll run off the first* HEATS² (7) *in the morning* **4** [IØ] *esp. CanE* (of ice and snow) to melt

run off with *v adv prep* [T1] RUN AWAY WITH

run-of-the-mill /ˌ· · · ˈ·/ *adj often derog* ordinary; not special in any way: *The actor's performance was rather run-of-the-mill; there was nothing very exciting about it.|a run-of-the-mill job in an office*

run on¹ *v adv* **1** [IØ] **a** to continue: *This disease can run on for months* **b** (of time) to pass **2** [IØ] *not fml* to talk without stopping: *She'll run on for hours about her family if you let her* **3** [T1] to join (sentences or written letters) together: *It's bad style to keep running on your sentences with* COMMAS

run on² also **run up·on**— *v prep* [T1 *no pass.*] (of thoughts or conversation) to be concerned with: *His mind keeps running on the past*

run out *v adv* **1** [IØ] **a** to come to an end, so that there is no more: *Our food soon ran out* (compare *We ran out of food*).*|Have you nearly finished? Time is running out.|The contract runs out next week* **b** (of a person) to have no more: *Can you give me a cigarette? I've run out* **2** [IØ;T1] **a** (esp. of a rope) to unwind esp. as the result of pulling: *The line ran out into the water as a fish swallowed the hook* **b** to allow or cause (esp. a rope) to unwind in this way: *The firemen ran a* HOSE (= pipe) *out from the pump to the burning building* **3** [T1] (in cricket) to cause (a player who is in the middle of making a RUN² (8)) to leave the field by hitting the WICKET with the ball: *The Yorkshire captain was run out*

run out of *v adv prep* **1** [T1] (of a person) to use all one's supply of; have no more of: *We're running out of time.|to run out of petrol* **2** [D1] *infml* to force (someone) to leave (a place): *They ran him out of town*

run out on also **walk out on**— *v adv prep* [T1] *sl* to leave or desert (someone or something for whom/which one is responsible): *Patrick ran out on his poor wife*

run o·ver *v adv* **1** [IØ] (of liquids or their containers) to overflow: *The water/The cup ran over* **2** [T1] (of a vehicle or its driver) to knock down and pass over the top of (esp. a creature): *He was run over by a bus.|The bus ran him over/ran over him* —compare RUN INTO, RUN DOWN

runs /rʌnz/ *n* [*the*+P] *infml* DIARRHOEA: *I seem to have the runs*

runt /rʌnt/ *n* [C] a small badly-developed animal (esp. the smallest of its family)

run-through /ˈ· ·/ *n* an act of RUNning THROUGH¹ (2) something: *We need one more run-through before the performance*

run through¹ *v prep* **1** [T1] to spend (money) fast (and carelessly): *He soon ran through all his father's money* **2** [T1] also **run over**— to repeat for practice: *Let's run through the first scene again* **3** [T1] to read or examine quickly: *I'll just run through this list of figures* **4** [D1;T1] **a** to pass or draw (something) right through (something): *She ran her fingers through her hair/a pen through the word.|I ran the sword through his body* **b** to pass or go right through (something): *The needle ran through my finger* —compare RUN INTO (1) **5** [T1 *no pass.*] to be part of; spread right through: *A feeling of sadness runs through his poetry*

run through² *v adv* [T1b] to stick one's sword right through (someone): *I ran him through (and through)*

run to *v prep* [T1] **1** [Wv6] **a** (of money) to be enough to pay for: *My wages won't run to a car* **b** (of a person) to have enough money to pay for: *We can't run to a car* **2** to have a tendency towards: *The writer runs to descriptive details.|You are running to fat* —compare **run to** SEED¹ (8b) **3** RUN INTO (3)

run-up /ˈ· ·/ *n* **1** [*the*+R (*to*);(C)] also (*esp. BrE*) **run-in**— (the activities in) the period of time leading up to an event: *during the run-up to the election* **2** [C] (in sports) an act or distance of running in order to gain enough speed for a particular activity: *a jumper's run-up*

run up *v adv* [T1] **1** to raise (a flag): *They ran up the national flag in honour of the victory* **2** *not fml* to make quickly, esp. by sewing: *I ran this dress up in one evening* **3** to cause oneself to have (bills or debts): *She ran up a large bill for all her new clothes* **4** to cause to grow; force up (prices, BIDS³ (1), etc.) **5 run up a score** to cause oneself to have a bill to pay

run up a·gainst *v adv prep* [T1] **1** to strike with force: *The car ran up against a tree* **2** *infml* to meet (someone) by chance: *I ran up against old Bill in the market* **3** *infml* to meet (something difficult): *I thought we would be successful, but we ran up against a lack of money*

run·way /ˈrʌnweɪ/ *n* an area with a specially prepared hard surface, on which aircraft land and TAKE OFF (= leave the ground)

ru·pee /ruːˈpiː/ *n* (a note or coin worth) a measure of money in India, Pakistan, Sri Lanka, etc.: *It cost 500 rupees|(fml) rupees 500*

rup·ture¹ /ˈrʌptʃəʳ/ *n* **1** [C;U] (a) sudden breaking apart or bursting: *the rupture of a blood vessel|*(fig.) *The friendship between our 2 nations has ended in (a) rupture* **2** [C] a lump in the front wall of the stomach, formed by part of the bowel pushing itself out through a weak place in the muscles; HERNIA

rupture² *v* **1** [IØ;T1] **a** to cause (esp. a muscle) to break or burst: *He'll rupture a blood vessel if he goes* *on shouting like that!*|(fig.) *Our happy relationship has been ruptured* **b** (esp. of a muscle) to break or burst **2** [T1] to cause (oneself) to have a RUPTURE[1] (2): *She ruptured herself lifting a heavy weight*

ru·ral /ˈrʊərəl/ *adj often apprec* of or like the COUNTRYSIDE; concerning country or village life: *people living in rural areas* —compare URBAN, RUSTIC —**~ly** *adv*

rural dean /ˌ·· ˈ·/ *n* [C;U] (in the CHURCH OF ENGLAND) (the rank of) a priest who is under an ARCHDEACON and is responsible for several PARISHes (= pieces of country that each have their own church and usu. one ordinary priest)

Ru·ri·ta·ni·an /ˌrʊərəˈteɪnɪən/ *adj* of or typical of Ruritania, an imaginary small European kingdom of former times, full of exciting adventures, beautiful ladies, and fighting with swords: *Sasha's long black beard and flashing eyes give him a very Ruritanian appearance*

ruse /ruːz‖ruːs, ruːz/ *n* a trick to deceive an opponent: *The fox pretended to be dead as a clever ruse to catch the rabbit*

rush[1] /rʌʃ/ *n* any of several types of grasslike water plant whose long thin hollow stems are often dried and made into mats, baskets, and the seats of chairs —**rushy** *adj* [Wa2]

rush[2] *v* **1** [IØ] to hurry; act quickly: *There's plenty of time; we needn't rush* **2** [L9;X9] to (cause to) move suddenly and hastily in the stated direction: *They rushed up the stairs/out into the street/towards their mother/all over the place.*|*Doctors and medical supplies were rushed to the place of the accident* **3** [Wv5;T1] to do (a job) hastily and perhaps not carefully: *Let the butter melt slowly; you mustn't rush it* **4** [T1 (*into*)] to force (someone) to act or decide hastily: *Let me think about it and don't rush me.*|*I was rushed into buying these fur boots* **5** [T1] to attack suddenly and all together: *Perhaps if we all rush him at once he'll drop his gun* **6 rush someone off his feet** to make someone hurry too much or work too hard: *I've been rushed off my feet all day at the office and I'm tired*

rush[3] *n* **1** [C] a sudden rapid hasty movement: *The cat made little rushes to and fro after the ball* **2** [U] (too much) haste: *We needn't leave yet; what's all the rush?*|*We've got to paint the kitchen before tomorrow; it's a rush job* **3** [U] great activity and excitement: *I hate shopping during the Christmas rush when everyone's buying presents* **4** [S3,9] a sudden great demand: *There's been a rush to see the new play.*|*the rush for tickets for the football match* **5 give someone the bum's rush** *AmE sl* to throw someone out, esp. from a BAR (= drinking shop) —see also GOLD RUSH

rush·es /ˈrʌʃəz/ *n* [P] (in film-making) the first prints of a film before it has been cut: *I saw some of the rushes of "Dangerous Wedding" and they looked good*

rush hour /ˈ· ·/ *n* [(*the*)] one of the 2 periods in the day when people are travelling to and from work in a city and the streets are crowded: *to get to work before the rush hour/before the rush-hour traffic starts*

rush in·to *v prep* [T1] **1** to go into (a state or condition) hastily and without enough thought (in phrs. like **rush into marriage**) **2 rush into print** to have one's writing printed too hastily

rush·light /ˈrʌʃlaɪt/ also **rush can·dle** /ˌ· ˈ··/— *n* a kind of candle made (esp. in former times) by dipping the inside part of a RUSH[1] into melted fat

rush out *v adv* [T1] to produce hastily and in large numbers, as by printing or copying: *They rushed out 1,000 cheap copies of the Queen's wedding dress*

rush through *v adv* [T1] to complete (a job) hastily: *We'll try to rush the contract/your order through before Saturday*

rusk /rʌsk/ *n* a kind of hard dry BISCUIT, often made from a piece of bread baked hard, often given to babies

rus·set[1] /ˈrʌsət/ *n* any of various kinds of RUSSET-coloured winter apple with a rough skin: *a basket of russets*

russet[2] *n, adj* [S;U;B] *esp. lit* (of) a reddish brown or golden brown colour

Rus·sian /ˈrʌʃən/ *adj* [Wa5] of or related to **a** the language and people of Russia **b** the chief language, people, and country of the USSR: *the Russian language*|*the Russian Church*

Russian rou·lette /ˌ·· ··ˈ·/ *n* [U] a dangerous game in which one fires at one's own head a gun (REVOLVER) with a bullet in only one of the CHAMBERs (= set of spaces for bullets)

Rus·so- /ˈrʌsəʊ/ *comb. form* **1** Russian; of Russia: *a Russo*PHILE **2** Russian and: *Russo-American trade*

rust[1] /rʌst/ *n* [U] **1** the reddish brown surface that forms on iron and some other metals when attacked by water and air —compare RUSTY **2** (*usu. in comb.*) the colour of this: *a rust-coloured dress* **3** any of various diseases of plants, causing spots of this colour: *wheat rust*

rust[2] *v* [IØ;T1] to (cause to) become covered with RUST[1] (1): *The rain will rust the iron roof.*|*The lock has rusted and needs oil*

rust a·way *v adv* [IØ;T1] to (cause to) disappear through the action of RUST[1] (1): *The ancient lock had completely rusted away so the door opened easily*

rus·tic[1] /ˈrʌstɪk/ *adj* **1** [B] connected with or suitable for the country; RURAL: *The village has a certain rustic charm* **2** [B] *not apprec* simple and rough compared to (that of) the town: *their rustic voices*|*She looks very rustic in those big boots* —compare URBAN, RURAL **3** [Wa5;A] (of furniture and wooden objects) roughly made out of wood with its outer skin (BARK) left on: *a rustic bridge*|*a rustic garden seat* —**~ity** /rʌˈstɪsəti/ *n* [U]

rustic[2] *n often derog* a person from the country, esp. a farm worker: *a crowd of happy rustics drinking beer at the inn*|*You can't expect these rustics to understand Shakespeare*

rus·ti·cate /ˈrʌstɪkeɪt/ *v* **1** [IØ] *esp. humor or pomp* to (go to) live in the country far from town life **2** [T1] to send (a student) away from a university for a while as a punishment **3** [T1 *usu. pass.*] (in building) to form (the blocks of stone in the walls or at the corners of a building) with sloping rough-looking edges

rus·ti·ca·tion /ˌrʌstɪˈkeɪʃən/ *n* **1** [U] the action of **a** rusticating (RUSTICATE (1)) or of **b** rusticating (RUSTICATE (2)) a student: *He was threatened with rustication* **2** [C] (in building) a RUSTICATED (3) wall or corner of a building: *He climbed to her bedroom up the rustications*

rus·tle[1] /ˈrʌsəl/ *v* [Wv3] **1** [IØ;T1] **a** (of paper, dry leaves, silk, etc.) to make slight sounds when moved or rubbed together: *Her long silk skirt rustled as she walked* **b** to cause (paper, dry leaves, silk, etc.) to make these sounds: *The wind rustled the dead leaves.*|*Stop rustling that newspaper!* **2** [L9] to move along making these sounds: *The tiger rustled through the bushes* **3** [T1] *esp. AmE* to steal (cattle or horses that are left loose in open country)

rustle[2] *n* [(*the*) S] a sound of rustling (RUSTLE[1] (1)): *We heard a rustle of leaves*

rus·tler /ˈrʌsləʳ/ *n esp. AmE* a cattle thief; person who RUSTLEs[1] (3)

rust·less /ˈrʌstləs/ *adj* [Wa5] **1** (of metals) of a kind that does not form RUST[1] (1) **2** not having formed RUST[1] (1) —compare RUSTPROOF

rustle up *v adv* [D1 (*for*);T1a] *not fml* to find a supply of (something) (for someone): *I'll try and rustle (you) up something to eat*
rus·tling /ˈrʌslɪŋ/ *n* **1** [U] the sound of something that RUSTLE*s*[1] (1,2): *He heard the rustling of a mouse among his papers* **2** [C *often pl.*] a single sound of this kind: *I keep hearing strange rustlings in the bushes* **3** [U] *esp. AmE* the crime of stealing cattle or horses: *There's been a lot of rustling in these parts lately, Elmer, so take your gun*
rust·proof[1] /ˈrʌstpruːf/ *adj* (of metals) protected from RUST[1] (1) by special treatment —compare RUSTLESS
rustproof[2] *v* [T1] to make (metal) RUSTPROOF[1]
rust·y /ˈrʌsti/ *adj* [Wa1] **1** [B] covered with RUST[1] (1): *a rusty nail* **2** [F (*on*)] *not fml* **a** (of a person) having forgotten most of a subject: *I'm a bit rusty (on Greek history)* **b** (of one's knowledge of a subject) mostly forgotten: *My Greek history is a bit rusty* **3** [B] (of black cloth) having become brown with age —**rustiness** *n* [U]
rut[1] /rʌt/ *n* [U] *tech* the season of sexual excitement for animals, esp. male deer
rut[2] *n* **1** a deep narrow track left in soft ground by a wheel: *The farm carts have worn ruts in this field* **2 be in/get into a rut** to be in/get into a fixed and dull way of life, and be unable to do or think anything new: *You mustn't let yourself get into a rut, young man. Join the Navy and see the world!*
rut[3] *v* **-tt-** [Wv5;T1] to form RUT*s*[2] in: *the rutted surface of the road*
ruth·less /ˈruːθləs/ *adj* **1** (of a person or his behaviour) very cruel; without pity: *a ruthless enemy|his ruthless treatment of the conquered nation* **2** *not derog* firm in taking unpleasant decisions, esp. when something is to be reduced or taken out: *We must be ruthless this year and give Christmas presents only to the children* —**~ly** *adv* —**~ness** *n* [U]
rut·ting /ˈrʌtɪŋ/ *adj* [Wa5;A] of or during RUT[1]: *a battle between rutting* STAG*s* (1)
Rx *written abbrev. for: tech* RECIPE (used before a list of things to be mixed together to make a medicine)
-ry /ri/ *suffix* -ERY
rye /raɪ/ *n* **1** [U] a type of grass plant grown in cold countries **2** [U] the grain of this plant, used for making flour —see picture at CEREAL **3** [C;U] *esp. AmE* (a glass of) RYE WHISKY: *2 double ryes, please!* **4** [U] *esp. AmE* RYE BREAD: *hot salt* BEEF *on rye*
rye bread /ˈ· ·, ˌ· ˈ·/ *n* [U] dark bread made from RYE flour: *a* SLICE *of rye bread*
rye whis·ky /ˌ· ˈ··/ *n* [U] a strong drink (WHISKY) made from RYE grain

S, s

S, s /es/ **S's, s's** *or* **Ss, ss** the 19th letter of the English alphabet
S *written abbrev. for*: south(ern)
-s /z, s/ **1** (forms the *pl.* of a noun): *cats|dogs|2 girls* **2** (forms the third person sing. of the present tense of most verbs): *sits|takes|plays* **3** *esp. AmE* (*forms an adverb to describe a period of time*) during, during the: *Do you work Sundays?|Summers we go to the sea*
USAGE **-s, 's, s'** added to the end of a word (*dog***s**, *come***s**, *John***'s**) have the sound /z/ except 1 after words ending with the sounds /p, t, k, f, θ/. Here they are pronounced /s/ as in *cats* /kæts/. 2 after words ending with the sounds /s, z, ʃ, ʒ, tʃ, dʒ/. Here **-s** is added when the word ends in *-e* (*rose***s**) and **-es** when it does not (*push***es**). After these words, both **-s** and **-es** are pronounced /ɨz/: *rose***s** /ˈrəʊzɨz/; *push***es** /ˈpʊʃɨz/. The poss. ending **'s** has the same sound as **-s**, but is never spelt **-es**. Compare *match***es** (pl.), *match***'s** (poss.) —see also -ES
-'s[1] /z, s/ *contr. of* **1** is: *Father's here.|What's that?* **2** has: *Mother's gone out* **3** (*in questions after* who, what, when, *etc.*) does: *How's he plan to do it?* —see -S, CONTR. (USAGE)
USAGE The short forms **'re**, **'m**, **'ll**, **'d**, and **'s**, standing for **are**, **am**, **will**, **had**, **would**, **has**, and **is**, are not used at the end of a sentence: *I'm not coming but they* **are**.|*They're not coming but I* **am**.|*She's wondering where he* **is**.
-'s[2] *suffix contr. of* us (only in the phr. **let's**) —see LET[3], -S (USAGE)
-'s[3] **1** (forms the poss. case of sing. nouns, and of pl. nouns that do not end in *-s*): *the dog's bone|yesterday's lesson|the children's bedroom|the man in the corner's coat* (=the coat belonging to the man in the corner) —see OF (USAGE) **2** *BrE* (forms a word for a shop or somebody's home): *I bought it at the baker's.* (=at the baker's shop)|*I met him at Mary's* (=at Mary's house) —see -S (USAGE)
-s' *suffix* (forms the poss. pl. of most [C] nouns): *a boys' club* —see OF, -S (USAGE)
sab·ba·tar·i·an /ˌsæbəˈteərɪən/ *adj, n* (*often cap.*) (of or concerning) a person who believes in keeping the SABBATH (1,2) as a holy day
Sab·bath /ˈsæbəθ/ *n* [*the*+R;C] **1** the 7th day of the week; Saturday, kept as a day of rest and worship by Jews and some Christians **2** Sunday, kept as such a day by most Christian churches **3 keep/break the Sabbath** to keep/break the religious rules which limit work and play on this day
sab·bat·i·cal[1] /səˈbætɪkəl/ *adj* [A] *rare* of or concerning the SABBATH, esp. as a day when no work should be done
sabbatical[2] *n* [C; *on*+U] a period, often 1 year in each 7, allowed with pay esp. to a university teacher when he has no ordinary duties and may travel and study
sa·ble[1] /ˈseɪbəl/ *n* **1** [C] a type of small animal of northern Europe and Asia with beautiful dark fur **2** [U] the fur or hair of this animal: *an artist's sable(-hair) brush*
sable[2] *adj* **1** (in HERALDRY) black **2** *poet* black or very dark
sab·ot /ˈsæbəʊ/ *n* a shoe cut out from a block of wood, worn esp. by farmers, workers, etc., in some parts of Europe —compare CLOG
sab·o·tage[1] /ˈsæbətɑːʒ/ *n* [U] **1** intentional usu. secretly carried-out damage to machines, buildings, etc., esp. to weaken a business or a country in wartime **2** intentional indirect or secret action to prevent or ruin a plan; SUBVERSION
sabotage[2] *v* [T1] to practise SABOTAGE on
sab·o·teur /ˌsæbəˈtɜːʳ/ *n* a person who practises SABOTAGE
sa·bra /ˈsɑːbrə/ *n infml, esp. AmE* a native-born citizen of Israel
sa·bre[1], *AmE* usu. **-ber** /ˈseɪbəʳ/ *n* **1** [C] a heavy military sword with a curved blade used in former times **2** [C] a sword like this used in FENCING

—compare FOIL, ÉPÉE **3** [U] the art of using this sword —see FENCING (USAGE)

sabre[2], *AmE* usu. **-ber** *v* [T1] to strike or cut with a SABRE

sabre-rat·tling /ˈ·· ˌ··/ *adj, n* [U;A] (the action of) showing or talking about (military) power in a threatening way

sabre-toothed ti·ger /ˌ·· · ˈ··/ *n* a type of large tiger that lived very long ago, and had 2 long curved teeth in the upper jaw

sac /sæk/ *n tech* a part shaped like a bag inside a plant or animal, usu. containing a particular liquid

sac·cha·rin /ˈsækərɨn/ *n* [U] a very sweet-tasting chemical used in place of sugar esp. by people who want to reduce their weight or must not eat sugar

sac·cha·rine /ˈsækəriːn/ *adj* **1** very sweet or unpleasantly sweet **2** unpleasantly or too friendly, nice, kind, happy, etc.

sac·er·do·tal /ˌsækəˈdəʊtl‖-kər-/ *adj* [Wa5] *tech* **1** being, of, or concerning a priest or priests **2** of or concerning SACERDOTALISM

sac·er·do·tal·is·m /ˌsækəˈdəʊtl-ɪzəm‖-kər-/ *n usu. derog* belief in the great importance or holy powers of priests

sach·et /ˈsæʃeɪ‖sæˈʃeɪ/ *n* **1** a small usu. plastic bag holding just enough of a liquid (as SHAMPOO) to be used at one time **2** a small packet of sweet-smelling powder or pieces of dried flowers, leaves, etc., for putting among clothes in a cupboard to give them a pleasant smell

sack[1] /sæk/ *n* **1** [C] **a** a large bag, usu. of strong cloth or leather, used for storing or moving flour, coal, vegetables, grain, etc. **b** also **sackful**— the amount in one of these: *Coal used to cost 3 shillings a sack* **c** *esp. AmE* a bag of strong usu. brown paper with a flat bottom, such as large food shops give to people for carrying away the food they have bought: *a* GROCERY *sack|a paper sack* **2** [*the*+R] *infml BrE* the taking away of (some)one's job by an employer: *If you're late again tomorrow, he'll give you the sack/you'll get the sack* **3** [*the*+R] *infml esp. AmE* bed **4 hit the sack** *infml* to go to bed

sack[2] *v* [T1] *BrE, not fml* (of an employer) to take away the job of; dismiss

sack[3] *n* [U] any of various white wines brought to England esp. from Spain and the Canary Islands in the 16th and 17th centuries

sack[4] *n* [(*the*) S] the action of SACKing[5] a city: *put the city to the sack* (=SACK the city)

sack[5] *v* [T1] (esp. of an army in former times) to destroy buildings, take things of value, and usu. harm or kill people in (a conquered place, esp. a city); PLUNDER

sack·but /ˈsækbʌt/ *n* an early (MEDIEVAL) form of TROMBONE (a brass musical instrument)

sack·cloth /ˈsæk-klɒθ‖-klɔθ/ also **sack·ing** /ˈsækɪŋ/— *n* [U] **1** rough cloth for making SACK*s* and (in former times) clothing to show sorrow at someone's death **2 sackcloth and ashes** a spirit of sorrow or lack of pride

sack out *v adv* [IØ] *AmE sl* to go to sleep, esp. for the night

sack race /ˈ· ·/ *n* a race in which each person has to keep both legs inside a SACK and make short jumps forward

sa·cral /ˈseɪkrəl/ *adj tech* of, related to, or according to the rules of a religion

sac·ra·ment /ˈsækrəmənt/ *n* (used esp. in the CATHOLIC church) any of several Christian ceremonies (including BAPTISM, the EUCHARIST, and marriage) considered as started by Jesus Christ or as signs of blessing or truth

Sacrament also **Blessed Sacrament**— *n* [*the*+R] (used esp. in the CATHOLIC church) the holy bread eaten at MASS

sac·ra·men·tal /ˌsækrəˈmentl/ *adj* of, related to, or being a SACRAMENT

sa·cred /ˈseɪkrɨd/ *adj* **1** [Wa5;A;(B)] religious in nature or use: *sacred music|sacred history* (=the history of the church or religion) —opposite **secular** **2** [B] holy by connection with God: *sacred writings|sacred animals in some Eastern religions* **3** [B] serious, solemn, and important in the way religious things are: *a sacred promise|Is nothing sacred any more?* **4** [Wa5;F+*to*] for the honour of a stated person or god: *a temple sacred to the gods| "sacred to the memory of . . ."* (used on gravestones) —**~ly** *adv* —**~ness** *n* [U]

sacred cow /ˌ·· ˈ·/ *n derog* a thing or idea so much accepted that not even honest doubts about it are allowed

sac·ri·fice[1] /ˈsækrɨfaɪs/ *n* **1** [C;U] (an) offering to God or a god, esp. of an animal by killing it in a ceremony **2** [C] something offered in this way **3** [C;U] a/the loss or giving up of something of value, esp. for a particular purpose: *Success is not worth the sacrifice of your health* **4** [C] something given up or lost in this way: *His parents made many sacrifices to send him to a private school* **5 sell (something) at a sacrifice** to sell (something) at a price lower than its value or than one has paid

sacrifice[2] *v* **1** [T1;IØ] to make an offering of (something) as a SACRIFICE[1] (2) **2** [T1] to give up or lose, esp. for some good purpose or belief: *He sacrificed his life to save the child from the fire* **3** [T1;IØ] *infml* to sell (something) at less than its cost or value: *I need the money and I'm having to sacrifice (on the price of) my car*

sac·ri·fi·cial /ˌsækrɨˈfɪʃəl/ *adj* of, related to, or being (a) SACRIFICE[1]: *a sacrificial lamb* —**~ly** *adv*

sac·ri·lege /ˈsækrɨlɪdʒ/ *n* [U;C] (an example of) the act of treating a holy place or thing without respect; desecration (DESECRATE): (fig.) *Destroying this beautiful old building would be (a great) sacrilege*

sac·ri·le·gious /ˌsækrɨˈlɪdʒəs/ *adj* showing no respect for what is holy: *a sacrilegious act, wearing shoes inside a mosque* —**~ly** *adv*

sac·ris·tan /ˈsækrɨstən/ *n* a person in a church whose job is to take care of the articles used in worship, and sometimes of the whole church building

sac·ris·ty /ˈsækrɨsti/ *n* VESTRY (1)

sac·ro·il·i·ac /ˌsækrəʊˈɪliæk/ *n* the area of the body at the bottom of the BACKBONE where it meets the HIP*s*

sac·ro·sanct /ˈsækrəʊsæŋkt/ *adj often derog or humor* too holy or important to be allowed to suffer any harm or disrespect; not to be VIOLATED: *Don't call on him in the afternoon; he considers that time sacrosanct*

sad /sæd/ *adj* **-dd-** [Wa1] **1** [B] feeling, showing, or causing grief or sorrow; unhappy: *It makes me sad to hear you have to go away.|a sad day for our team when it lost the match* **2** [A] deserving blame; bad; DEPLORABLE: *a sad state of affairs when children aren't taught to read properly* **3 sadder but wiser** *infml* having learned from unpleasant experience **4 sad to say** (usu. at the beginning of a sentence) unfortunately: *Sad to say, the weather here has been nothing but rain all this week* —**~ness** *n* [U]

sad·den /ˈsædn/ *v* [T1;IØ] to make or become sad: *His later years were saddened by the death of his wife*

sad·dle[1] /ˈsædl/ *n* **1** [C] a usu. leather seat made to fit over the back of a horse, camel, etc., for a rider to sit on —see picture at HORSE **2** [C] the part of an animal's back where this is placed **3** [C;U] *esp. BrE* (a piece of) meat cut from the back of a deer or sheep just in front of the back legs (in the phrs. **(a) saddle of mutton/lamb/venison**) **4** [C] a seat on a bicycle, motorcycle, etc. —see picture at BICYCLE[1] **5** a narrow stretch of hill connecting 2 higher points —see picture at MOUNTAIN **6 in the saddle a** sitting on a SADDLE (1) on an animal's back **b** *infml* in a position to direct a job; in control

saddle² *v* **1** [T1 (UP)] to put a SADDLE upon (an animal): *saddled (up) his horse and rode away* —see also SADDLE UP **2** [D1+*with*/(*up*)*on*] to give (someone) (an unpleasant duty, responsibility, etc.): *He's saddled with a large house which he can't sell or keep repaired.|Don't saddle me with taking the children to school again*

sad·dle·bag /ˈsædlbæg/ *n* **1** either of a joined pair of bags placed over an animal's back so that one hangs on each side below a SADDLE **2** a bag fixed to a bicycle, motorcycle, etc., behind the seat or in a pair over the back wheel —see picture at BICYCLE[1]

sad·dler /ˈsædləʳ/ *n* a maker of SADDLEs and other leather articles for horses

sad·dler·y /ˈsædləri/ *n* **1** [U] the job or skill of a SADDLER **2** [U] goods made by a SADDLER **3** [C] a SADDLER'*s* shop

saddle-sore /ˈ·· ·/ *adj* (of a person) sore and painfully stiff from riding

saddle stitch /ˈ·· ·/ *n* **1** a fastening together as of a magazine by wire STAPLEs through the fold in its back **2** a type of ornamental stitch close to the edge of a piece of cloth or leather

saddle up *v adv* [IØ] to put a SADDLE upon a horse

Sad·du·cee /ˈsædjʊsiː‖-djə-/ *n* a member of a Jewish party of priests of the upper class at about the time of Christ —compare PHARISEE

sa·dhu /ˈsɑːduː/ *n* a poor wandering Hindu holy man

sa·dis·m /ˈseɪdɪzəm/ *n* [U] **1** unnatural fondness for cruelty to other people **2** *tech* the unnatural idea or action of getting sexual pleasure from hurting the person one loves —compare MASOCHISM —**sadist** *n* —**sadistic** /səˈdɪstɪk/ *adj* —**sadistically** *adv*

sad·ly /ˈsædli/ *adv* **1** in a sad manner: *He walked sadly away* **2** [Wa5] unfortunately: *Sadly, our plan failed* **3 sadly mistaken** having a very wrong idea: *If you think you can get money from him you're sadly mistaken; he never lends to anyone*

sa·do·mas·o·chis·m /ˌseɪdəʊˈmæsəkɪzəm/ *n* [U] the gaining of (sexual) pleasure from hurting oneself (or other people)

s.a.e. *written abbrev. for*: stamped addressed envelope

sa·fa·ri /səˈfɑːri/ *n* **1** [C; *on*+U] a trip through wild country, esp. in east or central Africa and usu. for hunting big animals **2** [C] the people, vehicles, animals, etc., making such a trip

safari park /·ˈ·· ·/ *n* a park in which large groups of wild animals are kept, so that one can drive round in a car and look at them

safe¹ /seɪf/ *adj* [Wa1] **1** [F (*from*)] out of danger; not threatened by harm; not able to be hurt; protected **2** [F] not hurt; unharmed: *came through the storm* **safe and sound** (= safe) **3** [B (*for*);B3] not allowing danger or harm: *a safe place to swim|Keep these papers in a safe place* **4** [B,B3] not likely to cause risk or disagreement: *It's safe to say/a* **safe bet** *that crime will continue at a high rate this year* **5** [B] (of a seat in Parliament) certain to be won in an election by a particular party **6** [B] (in BASEBALL) successful in reaching a BASE —opposite **out 7 as safe as houses** *infml* very safe from risk: *Your money will be as safe as houses in that company* **8 on the safe side** *not fml* taking no risks; being more careful than may be necessary: *Let's be on the safe side and take more money than we think we'll need* **9 play it safe** *infml* to take no risks —**~ly** *adv* —**~ness** *n* [U]

safe² *n* **1** a box or cupboard with thick metal sides and a lock, sometimes built as part of a wall, used for protecting valuable things from thieves and fire **2** a food cupboard with sides of fine net to keep out flies but allow air to enter

safe·break·er /ˈseɪfˌbreɪkəʳ/ also (*esp. AmE*) **safe·crack·er** /ˈseɪfˌkrækəʳ/— *n BrE* a person who breaks into SAFEs² (1) to steal

safe-con·duct /ˌ· ˈ··/ *n* **1** [U] official protection given to a person, such as an enemy in wartime, passing through a particular area **2** [C] a written order giving this

safe-de·pos·it /ˌ· ·ˈ·/ *n* [U] safe storing of small valuable objects, usu. in small boxes (**safe-deposit boxes**) in a special room in a bank

safe·guard¹ /ˈseɪfgɑːd‖-gɑrd/ *n* [(*against*)] a means of protection against something unwanted: *a new law containing safeguards against the misuse of government power*

safeguard² *v* [T1] to be a SAFEGUARD for; protect

safe·keep·ing /ˌseɪfˈkiːpɪŋ/ *n* [U] the action or state of protection from harm or loss for things of value: *Put your important papers in the bank for safekeeping*

safe·ty /ˈseɪfti/ *n* **1** [U] the condition of being safe; freedom from danger, harm, or risk: *The safety of the ship is the captain's responsibility.|Let's try to stay together as a group: there's* **safety in numbers**.| **road safety** *rules* (=rules for safe driving) **2** [C] also **safety catch** /ˈ·· ·/— a lock (usu. like a SWITCH[1] (1)) on a weapon to keep it from being fired accidentally **3** [C] (in American football) a play which ends with the ball behind the GOAL LINE of the team carrying it, and giving 2 points to the other team

safety belt /ˈ·· ·/ *n* **1** a belt for fastening to something solid, worn by someone working high up to keep him from falling **2** SEAT BELT

safety cur·tain /ˈ·· ˌ··/ *n* a theatre curtain made of material which will not burn, and which (in Britain) may be lowered between parts of a performance

safety-first /ˌ·· ˈ·/ *adj* [Wa5;A] *often derog* marked by a wish to take no risks; CAUTIOUS

safety glass /ˈ·· ·/ *n* [U] strong (usu. LAMINATED) glass that breaks only into small pieces which are not sharp

safety is·land /ˈ·· ˌ··/ *n AmE* REFUGE (2)

safety lamp /ˈ·· ·/ *n* a miner's lamp made so that its flame cannot explode the gases found underground

safety match /ˈ·· ·/ *n* a match which can be lighted only when rubbed along a special surface on its box or packet

safety pin /ˈ·· ·/ *n* a wire pin with a cover at one end and bent round so that its point can be held inside the cover

safety ra·zor /ˈ·· ˌ··/ *n* an instrument for removing hair from the skin (RAZOR) with a cover fitting over the thin blade to protect the skin from being cut —see picture at BATHROOM

safety valve /ˈ·· ·/ *n* **1** a part of a machine, esp. of a steam engine, which allows gas, steam, etc., to escape when the pressure becomes too great **2** something that allows feelings or forces to act, be expressed, etc., in a safe or nonviolent way: *Sport may be a safety valve for people's violent feelings*

saf·fron /ˈsæfrən/ *n* [U] **1** powder of a deep orange colour obtained from a flower (a kind of CROCUS) and used for colouring and for giving a special taste to food **2** orange-yellow colour

sag¹ /sæg/ *v* **-gg-** [IØ] **1** [(DOWN)] to sink, settle, or bend downward, esp. from the usual or correct

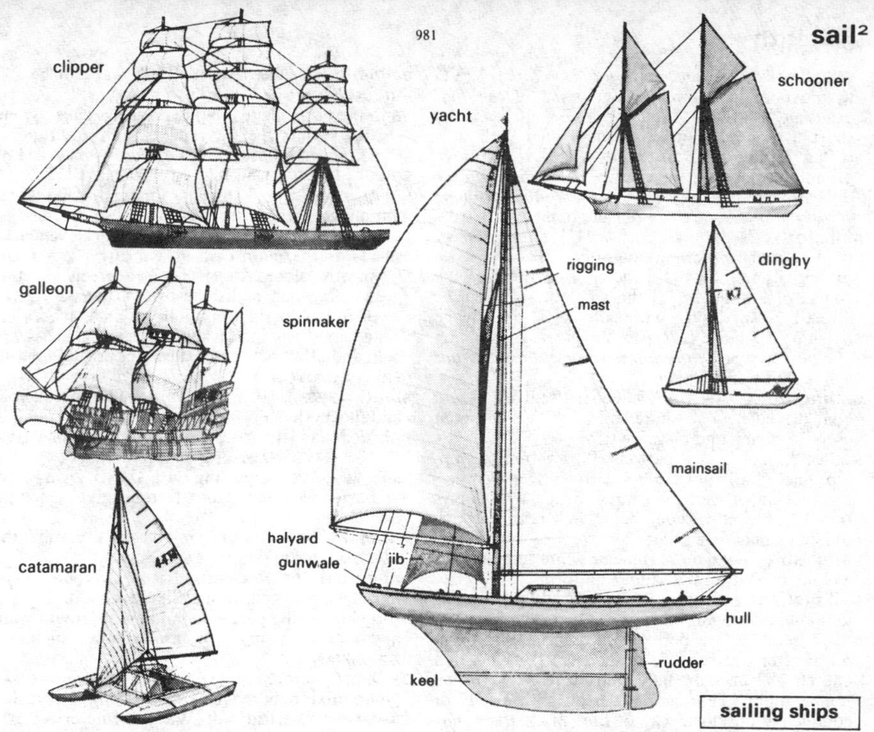

position: *The branch sagged (down) under the weight of the apples.|His trousers sag at the knees where he's been kneeling* **2** to lessen or become lower, less active or happy, etc.: *My spirits sagged when I saw the amount of work I had to do.|The sale of thick clothes always sags in the summer* **3** (of a book, performance, etc.) to become uninteresting during part of the length: *I finished the book even though it sagged in the middle and I almost stopped reading*

sag² *n* [S;(U): (*in*)] (a) downward bending or sinking: *a sag in the door|in the trousers|There's a lot of sag in that wall: it'll fall down soon*

sa·ga /ˈsɑːgə/ *n* **1** **a** any of the oldest stories of the deeds of the VIKINGs of Norway and Iceland **b** any long story of exciting and brave action **2** a long story about a particular place, time in history, group of people, etc.

sa·ga·cious /səˈgeɪʃəs/ *adj lit* having or showing deep understanding and good judgment; wise —**~ly** *adv*

sa·ga·ci·ty /səˈgæsɪ̈ti/ *n* [U] *lit* quality of being SAGACIOUS; good judgment and understanding: *a general|a battle plan of great sagacity*

sage¹ /seɪdʒ/ *adj* [A;(B)] *esp. lit* wise, esp. as a result of long thinking and experience —**~ly** *adv*

sage² *n* [*often pl.*] a person, esp. an old man or historical person, well known for his wisdom and long experience

sage³ *n* [U] a type of plant with grey-green leaves which are used in cooking to give a taste to food

sage·brush /ˈseɪdʒbrʌʃ/ *n* [U] a type of short bushy plant very common on the dry plains of the western US

Sa·git·tar·i·us /ˌsædʒɪ̈ˈteərɪəs/ *n* **1** [R] **a** the ancient sign, a half-horse half-human animal (CENTAUR) shooting an arrow, representing the 9th division of the ZODIAC belt of stars **b** the group of stars (CONSTELLATION) formerly in this division **2** [C] a person born under the influence of this sign —see picture at PLANET

sa·go /ˈseɪgəʊ/ *n* [U] a white food substance (STARCH) made from the stems of certain PALM trees (esp. the **sago palm**) and used in the form of grains or powder for making sweet dishes with milk and for stiffening cloth

sahib /sɑːb‖ˈsɑ-ɪb/ *n Ind & PakE* (*usu. cap.*) **1** [E] (used in India esp. in former times as a title of respect for males, following a name or title): *General Sahib|Jones Sahib* **2** [C;N] (in India in former times) a male European, esp. with some official position or rank

said¹ /sed/ *adj* [Wa5; (*the*) A] *fml* the particular (person, thing, etc.) spoken of before: *John James Smith is charged with stealing. The said John Smith was seen leaving the shop at the times stated* —compare AFORESAID

said² *past t. and past p. of* SAY

sail¹ /seɪl/ *n* **1** [C;U] a piece of strong cloth (like CANVAS or NYLON) fixed in position on a ship to move it through the water by the force of the wind: *a ship* **in full sail** (=with all its sails spread) **2** [Wn2;C] *tech* a boat driven by these: *The fishing boats were 15 sail in number* **3** [S] a short trip, usu. for pleasure, in a boat with these: *let's go for a sail this afternoon* **4** [U;S] distance at sea measured by the time a ship would take to travel it **5** [C] any of the broad wind-catching blades of a WINDMILL **6** **set sail** to begin a trip or a new course at sea **7** **take the wind from/out of someone's sails** *infml* to take away someone's pride or advantage by words or actions of one's own **8** **under sail** driven by sails and wind

sail² *v* **1** [L;X:9] **a** (of any ship) to travel on the water: *watch the ships sail by* **b** to command or direct (any ship) on the water): *The captain sailed his ship through the narrow passage* **2** [L9] (of people) to travel by ship: *We sailed across the Atlantic in 5 days* **3** [IØ] to begin a voyage: *We* *sail/Our ship sails tomorrow (for New York)* **4** [T1] to move or travel on (water): *one of the first men/ships to sail the Atlantic Ocean* **5** [I0] to make short trips as a sport in a small boat with sails (often in the phr. **go sailing**) **6** [L9] to move proudly, smoothly, or easily: *sailed through the difficult examination with no mistakes|birds sailing across the sky* —see also **sail close to the** WIND [1] (3)

sail·cloth /ˈseɪlklɒθ‖-klɔθ/ *n* [U] strong heavy CANVAS used esp. for making sails

sail·ing /ˈseɪlɪŋ/ *n* **1** [U] the skill of directing the course of a ship **2** [U] the sport of riding in or directing a small boat with sails **3** [C] **a** a voyage by ship: *a 5 days' sailing to New York* **b** a leaving of a port by a ship: *the dates and times of sailing this month from Southampton*

sailing boat /ˈ·· ·/ *AmE* **sail·boat** /ˈseɪlbəʊt/— *n* a boat driven by 1 or more sails, esp. a small boat used for racing and pleasure trips

sail·or /ˈseɪləʳ/ *n* **1** a person with a job on a ship, esp. one who is not a ship's officer **2** a member, esp. not an officer, of a navy **3** one who enjoys travel by water without being sick (esp. in such phrs. as **a good/bad sailor**)

sailor suit /ˈ·· ·/ *n* a usu. blue or white suit, esp. for a child, copied from a sailor's uniform

sail·plane /ˈseɪlpleɪn/ *n* a type of GLIDER plane for long flights using upward movements of air

saint /seɪnt/ *n* **1** a person who is officially recognized after death by (a branch of) the Christian church as specially holy and worthy of formal honour in the church **2** a person with a holy or completely unselfish way of life: *My mother, may she rest in peace, was a real saint* **3** [*usu. pl.*] a member of a particular usu. small religious group (used esp. by members of that group, such as early Christians, PURITAN*s*, and MORMON*s*) —**~hood** *n* [U]

Saint /sənt; *strong* seɪnt/ *n* [A] (a title before a SAINT*'s* (1) name): *Saint Joan of Arc* —see also the words following ST.

saint·ed /ˈseɪntɪ̣d/ *adj* [Wa5] **1** [A] (of one who has died) entered into heaven; to be regarded as a SAINT (3): *our sainted mother* **2** [B] made a SAINT (1); CANONIZED

saint·ly /ˈseɪntli/ *adj* [Wa2] of, like, or suitable to a SAINT (1,2): *a saintly man/life* —**-liness** *n* [U]

saint's day /ˈ· ·/ *n* the day each year on which the church honours a particular SAINT (1)

saith /seθ/ *old use or bibl* says

sake[1] /seɪk/ *n* **1 for the sake of a** for the good or advantage of: *If you won't do it for your own sake* (=to help yourself), *then do it for my sake* (=to please me).|*For both our sakes, please do as I ask.*|*My art does not try to serve society: it's just art for art's sake* **b** for the purpose of: *Please listen: I'm not talking just for talking's sake or for the sake of hearing myself!|Just for argument's sake, let's suppose* . . . **2 for God's/Christ's/goodness/pity('s) sake** *infml* (used for giving force to an urgent request, or sometimes an expression of annoyance): *For goodness sake, stop arguing!|What do you want from me, for God's sake?*

USAGE **for Christ's sake** is a rather strong expression, and should be used with care. The gentlest expression in this list is **for goodness sake**.

sa·ke[2], **saki** /ˈsɑːki/ *n* [U] a Japanese alcoholic drink made from rice and usu. served warm

sa·laam[1] /səˈlɑːm/ *n* **1** (a greeting, meaning "peace" in Arabic, used in the East) **2** a deep bending of the body while putting the inside of the right hand on the forehead, used as a respectful greeting

salaam[2] *v* [I0] to make a SALAAM (2)

sa·la·ble, saleable /ˈseɪləbəl/ *adj* that can be sold; fit for sale

sa·la·cious /səˈleɪʃəs/ *adj* expressing, causing, etc., strong sexual feelings usu. in an improper or shocking way; OBSCENE —**~ly** *adv* —**~ness** *n* [U]

sa·la·ci·ty /səˈlæsɪ̣ti/ *n lit* SALACIOUSness

sal·ad /ˈsæləd/ *n* **1** [U;C] a mixture of foods, usu. mainly vegetables, served cold and sometimes, esp. when other foods are added (as in **a chicken/cheese salad**) as the main dish at a meal: *a* **green salad** (=mostly of LETTUCE) **2** [C] a green vegetable grown for such a dish, esp. LETTUCE **3** [U;(C)] *AmE* a soft mixture, mainly of small pieces of a stated food (as in **chicken/tuna/egg salad**), served cold and often between 2 pieces of bread —see also FRUIT SALAD (1,2)

salad days /ˈ·· ·/ *n* [P] *infml* one's time of youth and inexperience

salad dress·ing /ˈ·· ˌ··/ *n* [U] **1** also **salad cream** /ˈ·· ·/— MAYONNAISE or a mixture like it of eggs, oil, and VINEGAR for putting on a SALAD **2** any liquid or pastelike, often strong-tasting mixture for putting on a SALAD

salad oil /ˈ·· ·/ *n* [U] a vegetable oil, usu. other than OLIVE oil, for making SALAD DRESSING

sal·a·man·der /ˈsæləmændəʳ/ *n* a type of small harmless 4-legged animal like a LIZARD but with soft skin, living partly on land and partly in water, and eating worms and insects —see picture at AMPHIBIAN

sa·la·mi /səˈlɑːmi/ *n* [U] a kind of large SAUSAGE (solid mixture of meats) with a strong salty taste

sal·a·ried /ˈsælərid/ *adj* [Wa5] having or receiving a SALARY, usu. as opposed to wages: *salaried workers/positions*

sal·a·ry /ˈsæləri/ *n* [C;U] fixed regular pay each month, 3 months, year, or sometimes each week, for a job, esp. as for workers of higher skill and rank: *a company paying good salaries|How much salary does the job pay?* —compare WAGE —see PAY (USAGE)

sale /seɪl/ *n* **1** an act of selling; contract or agreement exchanging something for money: *The sale of my house hasn't been easy but now Mr. Smith is interested and I hope I'll make the sale today* —see also BILL OF SALE **2** a special offering of goods in a shop at lower prices than usual: *I got this hat cheap at a sale.|regular price £3, sale price £1.49* —see also JUMBLE SALE **3** a selling of articles to whoever offers the highest price; AUCTION **4** [*often pl. with sing. meaning*] the total amount sold of something offered to be sold: *we're hoping for a large sale* (=large sales of our new product) **5 for sale** offered to be sold, esp. by a private owner: *The sign on that house says "For Sale"; shall we find out the price?* **6 on sale a** offered to be sold, esp. in a shop: *Will the new product be on sale as early as next month?* **b** *AmE* at or in a SALE (2): *I got this hat on sale; it was very cheap* **7 (on) sale or return** obtained from a seller in such a way that what is needed or used can be paid for, and the rest can be sent back without payment

sale·a·ble /ˈseɪləbəl/ *adj* SALABLE

sale of work /ˌ· · ˈ·/ *n* a sale in which small articles, food, etc., made at home are sold in order to make money for a particular purpose

sale·room /ˈseɪlrʊm, -ruːm/ also (*esp. AmE*) **sales·room** /ˈseɪlzrʊm, -ruːm/— *n* a place where AUCTION sales are held

sales /seɪlz/ *adj* [Wa5;A] of, for, or related to selling: *the sales department of a company|a sales representative*

sales·clerk /ˈseɪlzklɑːk‖-klɜrk/ *n AmE* SHOP ASSISTANT

sales·girl /ˈseɪlzgɜːl‖-ɜrl/ *n* a usu. young female SHOP ASSISTANT

sales·la·dy /ˈseɪlz,leɪdi/ *n polite* a female SHOP ASSISTANT

sales·man /ˈseɪlzmən/ *fem.* **sales·wom·an** /-,wʊmən/— *n* **-men** /mən/ **1** also (*fml*) **sales rep·re·sen·ta·tive** /ˈ· ··,···/— a man whose job is to sell a company's goods to businesses, homes, etc. **2** a usu. skilled SHOP ASSISTANT

sales·man·ship /ˈseɪlzmənʃɪp/ *n* [U] skill in selling or persuading: *It took some good salesmanship to get our plan accepted by the chairman*

sales re·sist·ance /ˈ· ·,··/ *n* [U] unwillingness to buy something; ability to keep oneself from being persuaded by a skilful salesman

sales slip /ˈ· ·/ *n AmE* a receipt given in a shop

sales talk /ˈ· ·/ *n* [U;C] talking intended to persuade or sell, esp. by praising what is for sale

sales tax /ˈ· ·/ *n* [U;C] (as in most places in the US) (an amount or rate of) money charged as tax in addition to the ordinary price of an article for sale —compare VAT

sa·li·ent[1] /ˈseɪlɪənt/ *adj* **1** standing out most noticeably or importantly: *the salient points of the speech* **2** *lit* pointing outward or upward, esp. beyond a general line, level, etc.: *a salient angle forming a sharp outside corner of the building*

salient[2] *n* an angle pointing outward, esp. in a line of battle or in the wall of a fort

sa·lif·e·rous /səˈlɪfərəs/ *adj tech* containing or producing salt

sal·i·fy /ˈsælǥfaɪ/ *v* [T1] *tech* to make chemically into a SALT[1] (1)

sa·line /ˈseɪlaɪn/ *adj* of, related to, or containing salt —**salinity** /səˈlɪnǥti/ *n* [U]

sal·i·nom·e·ter /,sælǥˈnɒmǥtəʳ‖-ˈnɑ-/ *n tech* an instrument, esp. a type of HYDROMETER, for measuring the amount of salt in a liquid

sa·li·va /səˈlaɪvə/ *n* [U] the natural watery liquid produced in the mouth

sa·li·va·ry /səˈlaɪvəri‖ˈsælǥveri/ *adj* of or concerning SALIVA or the organs (**salivary glands**) producing it —see picture at DIGESTIVE SYSTEM

sal·i·vate /ˈsælǥveɪt/ *v* [IØ] to produce (an increased amount of) SALIVA in the mouth —**-vation** /,sælǥˈveɪʃən/ *n* [U]

sal·low[1] /ˈsæləʊ/ *n* any of several types of WILLOW tree

sallow[2] *adj* (of the skin) yellow and unhealthy-looking —**~ness** *n* [U]

sallow[3] *v* [T1 *usu. pass.*] to make (the appearance of the skin) SALLOW: *a face sallowed by fever*

sal·ly /ˈsæli/ *n* **1** a quick attack and return to a position of defence; SORTIE **2** [(*of*)] a rush into action or expression; OUTBURST: *a sally of kisses* **3** *infml* a little trip; JAUNT **4** a clever remark of a usu. harmless kind; QUIP

sally forth also **sally out**— *v* [IØ] *old use or humor* to make a SALLY; rush out or set out: *I must sally forth into town and buy my week's food*

Sally Lunn /,sæli ˈlʌn/ *n* a slightly sweet breadlike cake (TEACAKE) served hot with butter

salm·on /ˈsæmən /*n* **salmon** **1** [Wn2] a type of large fish of the northern oceans with silvery skin and yellowish-pink flesh, which swims up rivers to lay its eggs —see picture at FISH[1] **2** [U] the pink flesh of this fish, valued as very good-tasting **3** [U] a yellowish-pink colour like that of this flesh

sal·mo·nel·la /,sælməˈnelə/ *n* [U] a type of bacteria mainly connected with food poisoning, stomach pains, etc.

salmon trout /ˈ·· ·/ *n* [Wn2;C;U] any of several kinds of large TROUT

sal·on /ˈsælɒn‖səˈlɑn (*Fr* salɔ̃)/ *n* **1** a stylish or fashionable business: *a shoe salon|a beauty salon* —see BEAUTY PARLOUR **2** (typically in France in the 18th century) a regularly-held fashionable gathering, esp. writers, artists, etc., at the home of a well-known lady **3** a large living room, esp. in a French house

sa·loon /səˈluːn/ *n* **1** a grandly furnished room for the social use of a ship's passengers **2** (*AmE* **sedan**) also **saloon car** /·ˈ· ·/— a car for 4 to 7 passengers, with a roof, closed sides, and windows —see picture at INTERCHANGE[2] **3** (typically in a town in the American wild west) a large public drinking place **4** a fancy shop or place of business; SALON (3) **5** *now rare & lit* a large and grand living room

saloon bar /·ˈ· ·/ also **saloon, lounge bar**— *n BrE* a better more pleasantly furnished room in an inn, public drinking place, etc., where drinks usu. cost more than in the PUBLIC BAR

sal·si·fy /ˈsælsǥfaɪ‖-fi/ *n* [U] a type of European purple-flowered plant whose long fleshy root is eaten as a vegetable

salt[1] /sɔːlt/ *n* **1** [U] a very common colourless or white solid substance (SODIUM CHLORIDE) found in the earth and in seawater and with many uses including preserving food and improving its taste: *The vegetables need more salt.|Please pass the salt.|* ROCK SALT|**table salt** (=in grains, usu. with small amounts of other chemicals added) **2** [C] *tech* a container for this at the table **3** [C] any of a class of chemical substances which may be formed by the combining of an acid and a BASE[1] (10) or metal **4** [U] (something giving) pleasant excitement or interest: *He says dangerous sports give salt to life* **5** [U] *infml* unwillingness to believe what is stated (esp. in such phrs. as **take with a grain/pinch of salt**): *You must take this "true story" with a large grain of salt; most of it is the writer's imagination* **6** [C] *infml* experienced sailor (esp. in the phr. **an old salt**) **7 rub salt in someone's wound**(**s**) to make someone's sorrow, pain, etc., even worse **8 the salt of the earth** *pomp* a person or people regarded as admirable or making the world a better place **9 worth one's salt** *infml* worthy of respect, or of one's pay

salt[2] *v* [T1] **1** to add salt to; put salt on: *Have you salted the vegetables?* **2** [Wv5; (DOWN)] to preserve with salt: *They salted down most of the meat for their use later* **3** [*usu. pass.* (*with*)] to add interest or excitement to: *a long report, but salted with interesting case studies* **4** to give a dishonest appearance of value to (something, esp. a mine by placing a small amount of a valuable mineral in it where it can be easily found)

salt[3] *adj* **1** [B] containing, full of, or tasting of salt; salty: *salt tears/butter/air/water* **2** [Wa5;A] formed by salty water: *a salt lake* —**~ness** [U]

salt a·way *v adv* [T1] *infml* to save (as money) for the future

salt·cel·lar /ˈsɔlt,seləʳ/ *n* a vessel for salt on a table, such as **a** *BrE* a container with 1 or more holes in the top for shaking salt out **b** a small open dish

sal·tire /ˈsɔːltaɪəʳ/ *n* (esp. in HERALDRY) an X-shaped cross

salt·lick /ˈsɔːlt,lɪk/ *n* **1** a large block of a salty substance for sheep and cows to touch with their tongues **2** a naturally salty piece of ground where animals get salt in this way

salt·pan /ˈsɔːltpæn/ *n* a natural or man-made hollow place from which salt water dries up leaving a surface of salt

salt·pe·tre, *AmE* **-ter** /,sɔːltˈpiːtəʳ/ *n* [U] a salty-tasting powdery substance (**potassium nitrate**) used in making GUNPOWDER, matches, and in preserving meat

salts /sɔːlts/ *n* [P] any of various chemical salts used as medicines, esp. EPSOM SALTs and SMELLING SALTS

salt·shak·er /ˈsɔːltˌʃeɪkəʳ/ *n AmE* SALTCELLAR (a)

salt·wa·ter /ˈsɔːltˌwɔːtəʳ/ *adj* [Wa5;A;(B)] being, of, belonging to, etc., salty water

salt·y /ˈsɔːlti/ *adj* [Wa1] **1** of, containing, or tasting of salt **2** *infml* of or concerning the sea or sailors: *a salty look provided by his sailor hat* **3** (of talk, stories, etc.) slightly improper in an amusing or exciting way; RACY: *salty humour* —**saltiness** *n* [U]

sa·lu·bri·ous /səˈluːbrɪəs/ *adj fml or lit* favourable to good health; WHOLESOME —**~ness**, —**-ty** *n* [U]

sal·u·ta·ry /ˈsæljʊtəri‖-jəteri/ *adj* favourable; causing improvement or a good effect, as to health: *It was a salutary experience for him to be forced to work hard*

sal·u·ta·tion /ˌsæljʊˈteɪʃən‖-ljə-/ *n* **1** [C;U] (an) expression of greeting by words or action **2** [C] the words, such as "Dear Sir", "Dear Miss Jones", etc., at the beginning of a letter

sa·lute[1] /səˈluːt/ *v* **1** [I∅;T1] to make a SALUTE[2] (1a) (to): *salute an officer|learn to salute properly* **2** [T1] *lit* to greet, esp. with polite words or with a sign: *saluted his friend with a wave of the hand* **3** [T1] *lit* to honour in a formal or ceremonial way: *a dinner to salute the president on his birthday*

salute[2] *n* **1** [C] any of several military signs of recognition, such as **a** a raising of the right hand to the forehead in a fixed way, directed to an officer of higher rank or returning such an action by another **b** a ceremonial firing of guns or lowering of flags in honour of a person of very high rank **c** an action of PRESENTing[2] (9) arms **2** [C;U] *lit* a greeting; SALUTATION **3** [C; *in*+U] a sign or ceremony expressing good feelings or respect: *held his hands together above his head in salute* **4** [C] *AmE* FIRECRACKER; BANGER (2) **5 take the salute** (of a person of high rank) to stand while being SALUTED[1] (1) by soldiers marching past

sal·vage[1] /ˈsælvɪdʒ/ *n* [U] **1** the act of saving a wrecked ship or its goods from the sea **2** the act of saving from destruction: *had no time for the salvage of his goods from the fire* **3** useful or valuable property saved from being destroyed: *a sale of salvage from the wreck*

salvage[2] *v* [T1] **1** to save from loss or damage by wrecking, fire, etc. **2** to save (a sick or wounded person, part of the body, etc.) medically: *"We'll try to salvage your leg", said the doctor to the trapped man*

sal·va·tion /sælˈveɪʃən/ *n* **1** [U] *tech* (esp. in the Christian religion) the saving or state of being saved from the power and effect of evil (SIN) **2** [U] saving or preservation from loss, ruin, or failure: *You're in trouble: your salvation depends on quick action* **3** [C *usu. sing.*] something that saves; a cause or means of saving: *That cup of tea was my salvation! Now I feel much better*

Salvation Ar·my /·ˌ·· ˈ··/ *n* [*the*+R] a Christian organization that has military uniforms and ranks, holds simple religious services with music, and is best known for its help to poor people

sal·va·tion·ist /sælˈveɪʃənɪ̵st/ *n* (*often cap.*) a member of the SALVATION ARMY

salve[1] /sɑːv‖sæv/ *n* [U;C] (an) oily paste for putting on a cut, wound, etc., to help the forming of new skin; OINTMENT

salve[2] *v* [T1] *usu. lit* to make (esp. feelings) less painful; SOOTHE: *He tried to* **salve his conscience** *with weak excuses to himself, but he knew he was doing wrong*

sal·ver /ˈsælvəʳ/ *n* a usu. fine metal plate for serving food, drink, etc., formally

sal·vi·a /ˈsælvɪə/ *n* [U] a type of ornamental garden plant with red or blue flowers

sal·vo /ˈsælvəʊ/ *n* **-vos** *or* **-voes** [(*of*)] **1** a firing of several guns at once, in a ceremony or battle **2** a sudden burst (as of cheers, shouts, etc.)

sal vo·lat·i·le /ˌsæl vəˈlætɪ̵li/ *n* [U] a liquid containing a form of AMMONIA and used (esp. formerly) as a cure for faintness —compare SMELLING SALTS

Sa·mar·i·tan /səˈmærɪ̵tn/ *n* **1** a member of the SAMARITANS **2 good Samaritan** (from a story told by Jesus) a person who gives kind and unselfish help to someone in need

Sa·mar·i·tans /səˈmærɪ̵tnz/ *n* [*the*+P] an organization helping people who are in great trouble of mind and have no one to share their feelings with

sam·ba /ˈsæmbə/ *n* **1** [*the*+R;C] a (type of) quick dance of Brazilian origin **2** [C] a piece of music for this dance

same[1] /seɪm/ *adj* **1** [*the*+B] being (always) only one single thing, person, etc.: *Father sits in the same chair every evening.|The broadcast was heard in the whole country at the same time.|The word is the same but it has 2 different spellings.|She wears the same red dress to every party.|"Are you still on the same telephone number?"* (SEU S.) **2** [*the, this, that, these, those*+B (*as, that*)] **a** being the particular one, or one already mentioned; not (an)other: *We have lived in this same town for 20 years.|Is this John Smith in the paper the same (one) that I went to school with?|You've made the same mistakes as last time/that you made last time.|That* VERY[2] (2) *same place where father shot the tiger* **b** like something else in every way; alike in (almost) every way; not different or changed: *We eat (much) the same thing for breakfast every day.|Men and women now get the same pay for doing the same jobs.|At the party she saw another woman wearing the same dress (as herself).|"Is your wife still ill?" "Yes, she's about the same—not any better"* **3 amount/come to the same thing** to have the same result or meaning **4 not the same without someone** *not fml* not so pleasant since someone left **5 one and the same** exactly the same; that one **6 same here** *infml* the same with me; me too: *"I think I ate too much." "Same here. I did too"* —see also ALL[3] (9) **the same to, (all) in the same** BOAT, **the same old** STORY, **at the same** TIME, **by the same** TOKEN

USAGE It is considered better English to use *as* after **same**, rather than *that*: *the* **same** *hat as/that you wore yesterday. As* must of course be used when no verb follows: *His car cost the* **same** *(amount) as mine.*

same[2] *pron* **1** (*with* the) the same thing, person, etc.: *Shall I play some different kind of music or would you like more of the same?|Thanks for helping me: I'll do the same for you sometime* **2** *now rare or humor* (*without* the) the things mentioned: *He was good at spending money but not so good at earning same* **3 (The) same again, please** *infml* (an order for another drink of the same kind) **4 same to you!** *infml* I wish you the same thing (a greeting or sometimes an angry wish): *"Happy Christmas!" "Same to you!"*

same[3] *adv* **1 the same (as)** in the same way (as): *2 different words but spelt the same|The 2 brothers look/speak the same as each other* **2 same as** *infml* the same as: *I have my pride, same as anyone else*

same·ness /ˈseɪmnɪ̵s/ *n* [U] **1** the state of being the same; very close likeness or IDENTITY: *I mistook one book for the other because of the sameness of their covers* **2** usu. unpleasant lack of variety; MONOTONY: *Don't you ever get tired of the sameness of the work in this office?*

sam·o·var /ˈsæməvɑːʳ/ *n* a large metal container

with a tube at the centre for hot coals or other heat, used esp. in Russia to boil water for making tea

sam·pan /ˈsæmpæn/ *n* a light flat-bottomed boat used along the coasts and rivers in China, Japan, etc. —see picture at BOAT[1]

sam·ple[1] /ˈsɑːmpəl‖ˈsæm-/ *n* **1** a small part representing the whole; typical small quantity, thing, event, etc.: *The nurse took a sample of my blood/a blood sample|I'd like to see some samples of your work* **2** a small trial amount of a product given away free: *free samples/sample bottles of a new kind of cooking oil*

sample[2] *v* [T1] **1** to take and examine a SAMPLE (1) of; test: *sampled the wine before giving it to others* **2** to get to know about by experience; TRY OUT: *sample the pleasures of country life* **3** to calculate by taking a SAMPLE (1) from: *sampled the population to find out the state of public opinion*

sam·pler /ˈsɑːmpləʳ‖ˈsæm-/ *n* an ornamental piece of cloth with the alphabet, family names and dates, a picture, etc., stitched on it with thread, as done by a girl to show her sewing skill

sam·u·rai /ˈsæmʊraɪ/ *n* **-rai** *or* **-rais** [Wn2] a member of a class of military noblemen in Japan in former times

san·a·to·ri·um, *AmE* also **san·i-** /ˌsænəˈtɔːrɪəm‖-ˈtor-/ *AmE* also **san·a·tar·i·um** /ˌsænəˈteərɪəm/— *n* **-iums** *or* **-ia** /rɪə/ an establishment for sick people who need long periods of treatment or rest, fresh air, exercise, etc.

sanc·ti·fy /ˈsæŋktɪ̈faɪ/ *v* [T1] **1** to make holy; HALLOW: *"God blessed the 7th day and sanctified it"* (The Bible) **2** [*usu. pass.*] to make completely acceptable; SANCTION: (fig.) *a stupid custom but sanctified by long use* **3** *tech* (in Christian thought) to make (a person) free from evil (SIN) —**-fication** /ˌsæŋktɪ̈fɪˈkeɪʃən/ *n* [U]

sanc·ti·mo·ni·ous /ˌsæŋktɪ̈ˈməʊnɪəs/ *adj* making a show of being religious; pretending to be holy —**~ly** *adv* —**~ness** *n* [U]

sanc·tion[1] /ˈsæŋkʃən/ *n* **1** [U] permission, approval, or acceptance: *The army acts only with the sanction of Parliament* **2** [C *usu. pl.*] an action, such as the stopping of trade, taken by 1 or more countries against a country which is breaking international law **3** [C] a formal action or punishment (to be) ordered when a law or rule is broken: *establish sanctions against union members who don't go to meetings* **4** [C] something that forces the keeping of a rule or standard: *societies where shame is the only sanction against wrongdoing*

sanction[2] *v* [T1] to accept, approve, or permit: *The church would not sanction the king's second marriage*

sanc·ti·ties /ˈsæŋktɪ̈tiz/ *n* [P] duties, rules, etc., considered to have great importance or SANCTITY (1): *a good father, respecting the sanctities of parenthood*

sanc·ti·ty /ˈsæŋktɪ̈ti/ *n* [U] **1** holiness; SACREDness: *an air of sanctity in the old church building|the sanctity of marriage* **2** holiness of life; PIETY

sanc·tu·a·ry /ˈsæŋktʃʊəri‖-tʃʊeri/ *n* **1** [C] the part of a religious building considered most holy, as in a Christian church **a** the area in front of the ALTAR **b** *esp. AmE* the room where the main meetings for worship are held **2** [C;U] (a place of) protection or safety from harm, esp. for a person escaping from officers of the law **3** [C] an area for birds or other kinds of animals where they may not be hunted and their animal enemies are controlled

sanc·tum /ˈsæŋktəm/ *n* **1** a holy place **2** *not fml* a private place or room where one can be quiet and alone

Sanc·tus /ˈsæŋktəs/ *n* [*the*+R] the 4th part of the religious service called the MASS, esp. when performed with music

sand[1] /sænd/ *n* [U] **1** loose material of very small fine grains, found in broad masses along seacoasts and in deserts, used for making cement and glass and for rubbing away roughness (in ABRASIVEs) —see also SANDS and picture at SITE[1] **2 build on sand** to plan or do something without any good reason to believe in its success

sand[2] *v* **1** [T1;X7: (DOWN)] to make smoother by rubbing with a rough surface, esp. SANDPAPER **2** [T1] to put sand on, esp. to prevent slipping: *The roads were sanded after the snowstorm*

san·dal /ˈsændl/ *n* a light shoe made of a flat bottom and bands to hold it on the foot

san·dal·wood /ˈsændlwʊd/ *n* [U] **1** a type of hard yellowish sweet-smelling south Asian wood used in making small boxes, figures, etc., and for its oil used in soap **2** a brown colour

sand·bag[1] /ˈsændbæg/ *n* a bag filled with sand or earth, esp. as used for piling up to form a wall or protection against explosions, rising water, etc.

sandbag[2] *v* **-gg-** [T1] **1** to put SANDBAGs on: *Workers were sandbagging the riverbanks to prevent flooding* **2** [(*into*)] *AmE infml* to force someone roughly to do something: *I didn't want to go but was sandbagged (into going) by my brother*

sand·bank /ˈsændbæŋk/ *n* a high underwater bank of sand in a river, harbour, etc.

sand·bar /ˈsændbɑːʳ/ *n* a stretch of sand formed by moving currents esp. across the mouth of a river

sand·blast /ˈsændblɑːst‖-blæst/ *v* [T1] to clean or cut metal, glass, etc., with a machine sending out a high-speed stream of sand

sand·box /ˈsændbɒks‖-bɑks/ *n AmE* a low box often with a cloth shade over it, holding sand for children to play in

sand·boy /ˈsændbɔɪ/ *n* (**as**) **happy as a sandboy** *infml* very happy

sand·cas·tle /ˈsændˌkɑːsəl‖-ˌkæ-/ *n* a small model, esp. of a castle, built in sand by children

sand dune /ˈ· ·/ *n* DUNE

sand·er /ˈsændəʳ/ also **sanding ma·chine** /ˈ·· ·ˌ·/— *n* a machine with a fastmoving rough surface (like SANDPAPER) for making surfaces smoother

sand fly /ˈ· ·/ *n* a small 2-winged biting fly common on seashores

sand·glass /ˈsændglɑːs‖-glæs/ *n* GLASS (4)

sand·man /ˈsændmæn/ *n* [*the*+R] (in children's stories) the man who causes children to go to sleep

sand·pa·per[1] /ˈsændˌpeɪpəʳ/ *n* [U] paper with a firmly stuck-on covering on one side of sand or fine grainy material like it, used for rubbing over surfaces to make them smoother

sandpaper[2] *v* [T1;X7: (DOWN)] to rub with SANDPAPER

sand·pip·er /ˈsændˌpaɪpəʳ/ *n* any of various types of small bird found esp. around muddy and sandy shores, having long legs and a long beak

sand·pit /ˈsændˌpɪt/ *n BrE* a box, hollow place in the ground, etc., with sand for children to play in

sands /sændz/ *n* [P] **1** a stretch of sand: *across the burning sands of the desert* **2** moments in time (as measured by sand in an HOURGLASS; esp. in such phrs. as **the sands of life are running out** =there is not long to live)

sand·shoe /ˈsændʃuː/ *n BrE* a light cloth shoe such as a PLIMSOLL

sand·stone /ˈsændstəʊn/ *n* [U] rock of a kind formed by sand fixed in a natural cement

sand·storm /ˈsændstɔːm‖-ɔrm/ *n* a windstorm in which sand is blown about in a desert

sand trap /ˈ· ·/ *n AmE* BUNKER (2)

sand·wich[1] /ˈsænwɪdʒ‖ˈsændwɪtʃ, ˈsænwɪtʃ/ *n* **1** 2 flat pieces of bread with some other usu. cold food between them, eaten with the hands **2** *BrE* a cake of 2 flat parts with JAM³ (1) or cream between them

sandwich² *v* [X9, esp. IN, *between*] *not fml* **1** to put tightly in between 2 things of a different kind: *a film of plastic sandwiched between 2 pieces of glass* **2** to find time for, among other events: *I'm very busy today but I'll try to sandwich that job in after tea*

sandwich board /'·· ·/ *n* a pair of large advertising signs for hanging at the front and back over the shoulders of a person (**sandwich man**) who walks about in public

sandwich course /'·· ·/ *n BrE* a course of business or industrial study including periods of usu. 3 or 6 months spent in working for a company

sand·y /'sændi/ *adj* [Wa1] **1** containing or full of sand **2** (esp. of hair) yellowish-brown in colour, like sand —**sandiness** *n* [U]

sane /seɪn/ *adj* [Wa1] **1** healthy in mind; not mad **2** produced by good reasonable thinking; sensible —**~ly** *adv*

sang /sæŋ/ *past t. of* SING

sang·froid /ˌsɒŋ'frwɑː‖ˌsɔŋ'frwɑː (*Fr.* sɑ̃frwa)/ *n* [U] *Fr* calm courage; great self-control during danger or difficulty

san·gri·a /sæŋ'griːə, sæn-, 'sæŋgrɪə/ *n* [U] *Sp* a cold drink made from red wine, fruit juice, and CARBONATED water

san·gui·na·ry /'sæŋgwənəri‖-neri/ *adj lit* **1** marked by, or fond of, much wounding and killing **2** *BrE* (of language) rude and marked by curses like "BLOODY"

san·guine /'sæŋgwən/ *adj* **1** eagerly hopeful; expecting the best; OPTIMISTIC: *a man of a sanguine temper* **2** (of the skin) of a healthy red colour **3** *lit* of or like blood —**-guinity** /sæŋ'gwɪnəti/ [U]

san·i·ta·ry /'sænətəri‖-teri/ *adj* **1** [Wa5] of or concerning health, esp. the treatment of human waste substances, dirt, or infection harmful to health: *sanitary* FITTINGs (=esp. the WC) *in a house* **2** clean; free from danger to health: *It's not sanitary to let flies come near food*

sanitary tow·el /'···· ˌ··/ *AmE* also **sanitary napkin**— *n* a small mass of soft paper worn between a woman's legs during her PERIOD¹ (5) to take up the flow from the WOMB

san·i·ta·tion /ˌsænə'teɪʃən/ *n* [U] the use of means for protecting public health, esp. by the removing and treatment of waste

san·i·to·ri·um /ˌsænə'tɔːrɪəm‖-'tor-/ also **san·i·tar·i·um** /-'teərɪəm/— *n* **-iums** *or* **-ia** /-rɪə/ *AmE* SANATORIUM

san·i·ty /'sænəti/ *n* [U] the quality of being SANE

sank /sæŋk/ *past t. of* SINK

sans /sænz/ *prep Fr, lit* without

San·skrit /'sænskrɪt/ *adj, n* [Wa5;B;R] (of or in) the ancient holy language of India

sans ser·if /ˌsæn 'serəf, ˌsænz-/ also (*infml*) **sans**— *n* [C;U] (in printing) a letter, or type of letter, without SERIFs and with all strokes of equal thickness, like the letters used for the main words in this dictionary

San·ta Claus /'sæntə klɔːz‖'sænti klɔz, 'sæntə-/ *n* FATHER CHRISTMAS

sap¹ /sæp/ *n* **1** [U] the watery juice carrying food, chemical products, etc., through a plant **2** [U] active strength, as of a young person: *the sap of youth* **3** [C;N] *infml* a stupid person likely to be tricked or treated unfairly: *Didn't you know I was joking, you sap?* **4** [C] *AmE* a heavy object made to hit with: *a sap made of small rocks in a cloth bag*

sap² *n* a long passage dug to get nearer to, or underneath, an enemy fort or position

sap³ *v* **-pp-** [T1] **1** to weaken by wearing or digging away at the base **2** to weaken or destroy, esp. during a long time **3** to act against by a SAP²

sa·pi·ence /'seɪpɪəns/ *n* [U] *lit* the quality of being SAPIENT; wisdom

sa·pi·ent /'seɪpɪənt/ *adj lit* wise and full of deep knowledge —**~ly** *adv*

sap·less /'sæpləs/ *adj* (appearing) dry and lifeless: *a sapless-looking old lady*

sap·ling /'sæplɪŋ/ *n* a young tree

sap·per /'sæpəʳ/ *n* **1** *BrE infml* a member, esp. of the lowest rank, of the branch of the Army (the ENGINEERs¹ (1)) doing digging and building **2** *AmE* a soldier skilled in getting secretly through the defences around an enemy camp

sap·phic /'sæfɪk/ *adj* [Wa5] **1** *tech* of or concerning a type of 4-line form of poetry used by the Greek poetess Sappho **2** *lit* LESBIAN

sap·phire /'sæfaɪəʳ/ *n* [C;U] a kind of precious stone of a transparent bright blue colour

sap·py /'sæpi/ *adj* [Wa1] **1** full of SAP¹ (1) **2** *BrE infml* strong and active **3** *AmE infml* silly or foolish

sap·wood /'sæpwʊd/ *n* [U] the younger outer wood in a tree, which is lighter and softer than the HEARTWOOD

sar·a·band, -bande /'særəbænd/ *n* **1** a Spanish court dance of the 17th–18th centuries **2** a piece of music for this, esp. as part of a typical SUITE

sar·cas·m /'sɑːkæzəm‖'sɑr-/ *n* [U] speaking or writing which tries to hurt someone's feelings, esp. by expressions which clearly mean the opposite to what is felt

sar·cas·tic /sɑː'kæstɪk‖sɑr-/ *adj* using or marked by SARCASM —**~ally** *adv* [Wa4]

sar·coph·a·gus /sɑː'kɒfəgəs‖sɑr'kɑ-/ *n* **-gi** /gaɪ/ *or* **-guses** a usu. ornamented stone box for a dead body, as used in ancient times

sar·dine /sɑː'diːn‖sɑr-/ *n* **1** any of various young small fish, esp. the PILCHARD, esp. as food preserved in oil in flat tins —see picture at FISH¹ **2** **like sardines** *infml* packed, crowded, etc., very tightly together

sar·don·ic /sɑː'dɒnɪk‖sɑr'dɑnɪk/ *adj* using or marked by a claim or feeling of being too good or important to consider a matter, person, etc., seriously; SCORNful; CYNICAL —**~ally** *adv* [Wa4]

sarge /sɑːdʒ‖sɑrdʒ/ *n* [C;N] *infml* SERGEANT

sa·ri /'sɑːri/ *n* a length of light cloth wrapped gracefully around the body, worn esp. by Hindu women

sar·ky /'sɑːki‖'sɑr-/ *adj* [Wa1] *BrE sl* SARCASTIC

sa·rong /sə'rɒŋ‖sə'rɔŋ, sə'rɑŋ/ *n* a length of cloth wrapped around the waist to form a loose skirt, as worn by Malayan women and men

sarsa·pa·ril·la /ˌsɑːspə'rɪlə, ˌsæs-‖ˌsæs-, ˌsɑrs-/ *n* [U;C] a sweet drink (like ROOT BEER) (tasting as if) made from the roots of a central or South American climbing plant

sar·to·ri·al /sɑː'tɔːrɪəl‖sɑr'tor-/ *adj lit* of or concerning the making or esp. wearing of men's formal clothes —**~ly** *adv*

sash¹ /sæʃ/ *n* a beltlike length of cloth worn around the waist as part of a garment, or (in ceremonial dress and usu. as a mark of some honour) over one shoulder

sash² *n* a frame into which sheets of glass are fixed to form part of a window, door, etc.

sa·shay /sæ'ʃeɪ/ *v* [L9 (ON)] *AmE infml* to move or go, esp. smoothly or easily

sash win·dow /'· ˌ··/ *n* a window of 2 SASHes² which opens by sliding one up or down behind or in front of the other. The SASHes are attached to weights inside the frame by a **sash cord** so that they do not fall down —compare CASEMENT WINDOW

sass¹ /sæs/ *n* [U] *AmE sl* SAUCE¹ (2)

sass² *v* [T1] *AmE sl* SAUCE²

sas·sa·fras /'sæsəfræs/ *n* [U] (the dried outer

covering of the root of) a type of small tree of Asia and North America, used for its taste to make a kind of tea

sass·y /ˈsæsi/ *adj* [Wa1] *AmE* SAUCY

sat /sæt/ *past t. and p. of* SIT

Sa·tan /ˈseɪtn/ *n* [R;N] *esp. fml or tech* the devil, esp. considered as the chief evil power or God's opponent

sa·tan·ic /səˈtænɪk/ *adj* very cruel, evil, or wicked; FIENDISH —**-ically** *adv* [Wa4]

Sat·an·is·m /ˈseɪtənɪzəm/ *n* [U] the worship of the devil —**-ist** *adj n*

satch·el /ˈsætʃəl/ *n* a small bag of strong cloth or leather, usu. with a band for carrying over the shoulder: *carried his books in his school satchel*

sate /seɪt/ *v* [T1 *usu. pass.* (*with*)] to satisfy with more than enough, or unpleasantly much, of something: *I've been to the theatre every night for 2 weeks and I'm now feeling rather sated with plays*

sa·teen /səˈtiːn‖sæ-/ *n* [U] shiny cotton cloth made to look like SATIN

sat·el·lite /ˈsætəlaɪt/ *n* **1** [C] a heavenly body moving around a larger one (a PLANET); MOON (1, esp. 3): *The moon is a satellite of the earth* **2** [C; *by*+U] a man-made object intended to move around the earth, moon, etc., for some purpose: *an unMANned satellite|a COMMUNICATIONS and weather satellite|The broadcast came from America by satellite and was heard at the same time in Europe* **3** [C] something, esp. a country, that is in, and depends on, the power or influence of another

sa·tia·ble /ˈseɪʃəbəl/ *adj fml* that can be satisfied —opposite **insatiable**

sa·ti·ate /ˈseɪʃieɪt/ *v* [T1 *usu. pass.*] to satisfy fully or sometimes too fully

sa·ti·e·ty /səˈtaɪəti/ *n* [U] the state of being (too much) filled or satisfied: *filled to (the point of) satiety by the big dinner*

sat·in /ˈsætən/ *n, adj* [Wa5;U;B] (made of) a kind of very fine smooth cloth mainly of silk, which is shiny on the front and dull on the back

sat·in·wood /ˈsætənwʊd/ *n* [U;C] (the very hard smooth wood of) a kind of East Indian tree, used esp. in fine furniture

sat·in·y /ˈsætəni/ also **satin**— *adj* very pleasantly smooth, shiny, and soft

sat·ire /ˈsætaɪəʳ/ *n* [C (*on*); U] (a work of) literature, theatre, speaking, etc., intended to show the foolishness or evil of some establishment or practice in an amusing way —compare SATYR

sa·tir·i·cal /səˈtɪrɪkəl/ also **sa·tir·ic** /səˈtɪrɪk/— *adj* fond of, being, using, etc., SATIRE —**~ly** *adv* [Wa4]

sat·ir·ize, -ise /ˈsætəraɪz/ *v* [T1] to write or speak using SATIRE against

sat·is·fac·tion /ˌsætəsˈfækʃən/ *n* **1** [U] contentment; pleasure: *He took great satisfaction from playing the piano well* **2** [C] something that pleases: *Playing the piano well was one of his greatest satisfactions* **3** [U] *fml* fulfilment of a need, desire, etc.: *satisfaction of public demand* **4** [U] *fml* condition of being fully persuaded; certainty: *It's been proved to my satisfaction* (=I am certain) *that you're telling the truth* **5** [U] *fml* payment of a claim, money owed, etc. **6** [U] *fml* the chance to defend one's honour (as by fighting a DUEL): *Sir, you are lying about me: I demand satisfaction!*

sat·is·fac·to·ry /ˌsætəsˈfæktəri/ *adj* good enough to be pleasing, or for a purpose, rule, standard, etc.: *a satisfactory excuse for his absence|of all the pens he tried, only one was satisfactory|Sales are up 20% from last year: that's very satisfactory* —**-rily** *adv*

sat·is·fy /ˈsætəsfaɪ/ *v* **1** [T1;I0] to make (someone) happy; please: *I didn't like the story: it didn't satisfy me. But perhaps I am hard to satisfy* **2** [T1] to be or give enough for; fulfil (a need, desire, etc.): *Just to satisfy my CURIOSITY, how much did you pay for your car?|He satisfied the examiner in his examination* **3** [T1] to be correct or good enough for (a demand, rule, standard, etc.); meet: *You can't vote until you have satisfied all the formal conditions.|x=2 satisfies the EQUATION $x^2=4$* **4** [D5;T1 (*of*) *usu. pass.*] to persuade fully: *Are you satisfied of my truthfulness/that I am telling the truth?* **5** [T1] to pay (money owed or charged): *a payment of £100 to satisfy his claim against the insurance company*

sat·is·fy·ing /ˈsætəsfaɪ-ɪŋ/ *adj* giving satisfaction: *a satisfying meal/experience* —**~ly** *adv*

sat·rap /ˈsætrəp‖ˈseɪtræp/ *n* a governor in the ancient Persian empire

sat·su·ma /sætˈsuːmə/ *n esp. BrE* a type of small seedless orange-like fruit (MANDARIN (4))

sat·u·rate /ˈsætʃəreɪt/ *v* [T1 *often pass.* (*with*)] **1** to put as much liquid as possible into; make completely wet; SOAK[1] (2): *The blood had saturated his shirt around the wound* **2** to fill completely so that no more can be held: *He says it's hard to sell a house now: the house* MARKET[1] (4) *is saturated* **3** [Wv5] *tech* to put into (a chemical SOLUTION) as much of the solid substance as possible

sat·u·ra·tion /ˌsætʃəˈreɪʃən/ *n* [U] **1** the act or result of saturating (SATURATE) **2** *tech* (of a colour) freedom from mixture with white; VIVIDNESS (1) **3** very heavy military force used against an enemy: *saturation of the area with heavy bombing*

saturation point /‥ˈ‥ ·/ *n* **reach a/the/one's saturation point** to be so full that further things cannot be accepted, contained, etc.

Sat·ur·day /ˈsætədi‖-ər-/ *n* **1** [R] the 7th and last day of the present week; day before next Sunday or last Sunday: *He'll arrive (on) Saturday.|He arrived on Saturday morning* (=during the morning of last Saturday) **2** [C] the 7th and last day of any week, or of the week that is being spoken of: *We do our shopping on Saturdays.|(BrE) He arrived on the Saturday and left on the Monday* (=arrived on the 7th day of the week being spoken of).*|He arrived on a Saturday.* (=not a Friday, Sunday, etc.)|*(esp. AmE) I work Saturdays*

Sat·urn /ˈsætən‖-ərn/ *n* [R] the PLANET which is 6th in order from the sun and is surrounded by large rings —see picture at PLANET

sat·ur·na·li·a /ˌsætəˈneɪlɪə‖-tər-/ *n* **-lias** *or* **-lia** /lɪə/ [Wn2] *lit* an occasion of wild merriment; ORGY

sat·ur·nine /ˈsætənaɪn‖-ər-/ *adj esp. lit* sad and solemn by nature; SULLEN; GLOOMY

sat·yr /ˈsætəʳ/ *n* **1** (in ancient literature) a god usu. represented as half human and half goat **2** *lit* a man with very strong sexual desires —compare SATIRE

sauce[1] /sɔːs/ *n* **1** [U;C] any of various kinds of usu. cooked, more or less thick, liquids put on or eaten with food: TOMATO *sauce|a white sauce for fish|*TARTAR SAUCE*|apple sauce|ice cream with chocolate sauce* **2** [U] *AmE sl* usu. **sass**— *not fml* rude (but often harmless) disrespectful talk, as to a parent, teacher, etc.; BACKCHAT: *None of your sauce, my girl!* **3 What's sauce for the goose (is sauce for the gander)** If one person is allowed to behave in a certain way, then so is the other person

sauce[2] *AmE sl* usu. **sass**— *v* [T1] *not fml* to speak rudely to (a parent, teacher, etc.): *Good boys don't sauce their mothers!*

sauce·pan /ˈsɔːspæn/ *n* a deep usu. round metal cooking pot with a handle and usu. a lid —see picture at KITCHEN

sau·cer /ˈsɔːsəʳ/ *n* a small plate with edges curving up, made for setting a cup on

sauc·y /ˈsɔːsi/ *AmE* also **sassy**— *adj* [Wa1] **1** fond of, or marked by, rude or disrespectful talk **2** *infml* producing sexual interest in an amusing way **3** *infml lit* stylish and good-looking: *a fast and saucy new car* —**saucily** *adv* —**sauciness** *n* [U]

sau·er·kraut /ˈsaʊəkraʊt‖-ər-/ *n* [U] *Ger* a dish made from small pieces of a leafy vegetable (CABBAGE) allowed to become sour by keeping them in salt

sau·na /ˈsaʊnə, ˈsɔːnə‖ˈsaʊnə/ also **sauna bath** /ˈ·· ·/— *n* **1** a Finnish type of bath in steam **2** a room or building for this

saun·ter[1] /ˈsɔːntəʳ/ *v* [L9] to walk in an unhurried way —**~er** *n*

saunter[2] *n* [S] an unhurried walk for pleasure; STROLL

sau·ri·an /ˈsɔːrɪən/ *n, adj* [Wa5] *tech* (of or like) a LIZARD or other animal of its family

saus·age /ˈsɒsɪdʒ‖ˈsɔ-/ *n* **1** [C] a thin eatable tube of animal skin filled with a mixture (**sausage meat**) of meat and bread-like materials, SPICEs, etc., and twisted at both ends: *a string of sausages* (=a chain of them made in the same tube) **2** [U] this meat mixture, usu. in such a form or as cut-off pieces: *We often eat sausage for breakfast*

sausage dog /ˈ·· ·/ *n BrE infml* DACHSHUND

sausage roll /ˌ·· ˈ·/ *n* a small piece of SAUSAGE meat in a covering of pastry (eaten esp. in Britain as an informal food)

sau·té[1] /ˈsəʊteɪ‖səʊˈteɪ/ *n* a SAUTÉed dish: *a sauté of potatoes and onions|sauté potatoes*

sauté[2] *v* **-téed** *or* **téd** [Wv5;T1] to cook quickly in a little hot oil or fat: *sauté the onions for 5 minutes*

Sau·ternes, -terne /səʊˈtɜːn‖-ɜrn/ *n* [U] a type of sweet gold-coloured French wine

sav·age[1] /ˈsævɪdʒ/ *adj* **1** [B] forcefully cruel or violent; uncontrollable; fierce; FEROCIOUS: *a savage attack in the newspapers|a savage dog|savage anger* **2** [A;(B)] (typical) of an uncivilized place or people: *savage people/customs/scenery* **3** [B] *BrE infml* very angry: *Her rudeness really makes me savage* —**~ly** *adv* —**~ness** *n* [U]

savage[2] *n* **1** a member of an uncivilized or undeveloped tribe or group **2** one thought to be like such a person, as by being cruel, violent, or wild

savage[3] *v* [T1] (esp. of an animal) to attack and bite fiercely: *savaged by a mad dog*

sav·ag·e·ry /ˈsævɪdʒəri/ *n* [U;C *usu. pl.*] an act, or the quality, of one who is SAVAGE: *beat his wife with great savagery|the savageries of ancient war*

sa·van·na, -nah /səˈvænə/ *n* [C;U] (an open flat stretch of) grassy land in a warm and sometimes wet part of the world

sav·ant /ˈsævənt‖səˈvɑnt, sæ- (*Fr* savɑ̃)/ *n Fr, lit* a person (supposedly) having great knowledge of some subject

save[1] /seɪv/ *v* **1** [T1 (*from*)] to make safe from danger: *Help! Save me!|"God save the King"|saved his friend from falling* **2** [IØ (UP, *for*)] to keep and add to an amount of money for later use: *Children should learn to save.|We're saving (up) for a new car* **3** [D1;T1: (*for*)] to keep and not spend or use, as for a special purpose or use later: *It'll save me 50p if I buy the large-size box.|saved his strength for an effort in the last minute of the race|It will save time if we drive the car instead of walking* **4** [D1;T1 (*from*); T4; (*esp. BrE*) X4] to make unnecessary (for (someone)): *Will you go to the shop for me? It'll save (me) a trip=It'll save (me) going into town.|A brush with a long handle will save you from having to bend down so far to clean the floor|a labour-saving instrument* **5** [IØ;T1 (*from*)] (in Christianity and some other religions) to free (a person) from the power or effect of evil (SIN); REDEEM (1): *"Jesus saves!"|"Christ came to save us from our SINs"* —see also **save** FACE[1] (3)

save[2] *n* (in football) a quick action by the GOALKEEPER which prevents the opponents' making a point

save[3] also **saving**— *prep lit & old use* **1** except (for): *answered all the questions save one|I agree with you, save that you have got 1 or 2 facts wrong* **2** **saving your presence** without meaning any offence to you —see BUT (USAGE)

sav·e·loy /ˈsævəlɔɪ/ *n BrE* a special kind of dry cooked SAUSAGE (1)

save on *v prep* [D1;T1] to save and not use so much, esp. by spending or costing less money: *Living near the shops saves us lots of money on petrol*

sav·er /ˈseɪvəʳ/ *n* **1** (*often in comb.*) something that prevents loss or waste: *Our new washing machine is a real time- and money-saver* **2** a person who saves money

sav·ing /ˈseɪvɪŋ/ *adj* [Wa5;A] that makes good or acceptable in spite of weakness, faults, etc.; REDEEMing: *an unpleasant subject, but treated with a saving sense of humour*

saving grace /ˌ·· ˈ·/ *n* a SAVING quality or fact: *a bad party, but with the saving grace of having served good food*

sav·ings /ˈseɪvɪŋz/ *n* [P] money saved, esp. as in a bank

savings ac·count /ˈ·· ·ˌ·/ *n* **1** *BrE* any of various kinds of bank accounts earning higher interest than a DEPOSIT ACCOUNT **2** *AmE* any interest-earning account

savings bank /ˈ·· ·/ *n* a bank which has only interest-earning kinds of accounts

sa·viour, *AmE* **-vior** /ˈseɪvɪəʳ/ *n* **1** [C] a person or thing that saves from danger or loss: *a country at war with itself, needing a political saviour* **2** [(*the*) R] (*usu. cap.*) (in the Christian religion) Jesus Christ

sav·oir-faire /ˌsævwɑː ˈfeəʳ‖-wɑr-/ *n* [U] *Fr* the ability to do and say the proper and polite thing on every social occasion

sa·vo·ry /ˈseɪvəri/ *n* [U] a type of MINT plant used in cooking to add taste to meat, beans, etc.

sa·vour[1], *AmE* **-vor** /ˈseɪvəʳ/ *n* [S;U] *BrE* **1** a taste or smell: *The meat had cooked too long and lost its savour* **2** (power to excite) interest: *He used to say that argument adds (a) savour to conversation, but now argument has lost its savour for him*

savour[2], *AmE* **-vor** *v* [T1] to enjoy, as by tasting, slowly and purposefully: *drank the wine slowly, savouring every drop|savoured the pleasures of country life in the summer*

savour of *v prep* [T1] to have a (slight) quality of, as in a taste, smell, etc.: *disliked any law that savoured of more government control*

sa·vour·y[1], *AmE* **-vory** /ˈseɪvəri/ *adj* **1** [Wa2] pleasant or attractive in taste **2** [Wa2] *not fml* morally attractive or good: WHOLESOME —opposite **unsavoury** **3** [Wa5] *BrE* (of a dish) having the taste of meat, cheese, vegetables, etc., without sugar —opposite **sweet**

savoury[2], *AmE* **-vory** *n BrE* a small salty dish, sometimes served at the end of a formal meal

sa·voy /səˈvɔɪ/ *n* [C;(U)] a type of vegetable (CABBAGE) with curled leaves

sav·vy[1] /ˈsævi/ *v* [IØ] *sl* to understand; get the meaning: *I never want to see you again! Savvy?*

savvy[2] *n* [U] *infml* practical knowledge and ability: KNOW-HOW

saw[1] /sɔː/ *n* a hand- or power-driven tool for cutting hard materials, having a thin flat blade with a row of V-shaped teeth on the edge

saw[2] *v* **sawed, sawn** /sɔːn/ (*esp. BrE*) *or* **sawed** (*esp. AmE*) **1** [T1 (UP, AWAY, OFF, THROUGH); IØ] to cut with a SAW: *He sawed the logs up into little pieces.|She was busy sawing logs* (=sawing a long piece of wood into logs).*|In 10 minutes of sawing, the tree*

say¹ USAGE Compare, **say, tell, speak, talk,** and (*fml*) **inform:**

[I0 (*to, with* and/or *about*)] *He* **spoke/ talked** (*to/ with me*) (*about dogs*)	[T1 (*to*)] *He* **said** "*Yes*". | *He* **said** *something* (*to me*)	[T1] *He* **said** *a prayer*. | *He* **told** *a lie*. | He **spoke/ talked** *French*	[T1 (*of*)] *He* **told/** (*fml*)**in-formed** *me* (*of the fact*)	[(D1 (to)] *He* **told** *me the news*. | *He* **told** *the news to me*	[D5] (*fml*) *He* **informed** *me that he was coming*	[T5a] *He* **said** (*that*) *he was coming*
[T5b] *He* **said** *so*	[D5a] *He* **told** *me* (*that*) *he was coming*	[D5b] *He* **told** *me so*	[D6a] *He* **told** *me where I was*	[D6b] *He* **told** *me where to go*	[V3] *He* **told** *me to go*	

Notice **a** **Say** is the only one that is used with the actual words spoken. It must have a direct object, and that object is words, not a person.

b **Tell** is the only one that is used for commands. It must have one or 2 objects: either words, or a person, or both.

c **Talk** gives the idea of a whole conversation or discussion, but it has the same grammar as **speak.** These 2 verbs need not have an object.

was nearly sawn through.|*tried to saw off a dead branch from the tree* **2** [I0 (*at*)] to move one's hand forwards and backwards (as if) cutting with a SAW: *sawed at the loaf of bread with his dull knife* **3** [L9] (of a material) to be able to cut by a SAW: *Soft wood saws easily*

saw³ *n* a short well-known saying (esp. in the phr. **old saw**): *the old saw that it's better to be safe than sorry*

saw⁴ *past t. of* SEE

saw·bones /ˈsɔːbəʊnz/ *n* **sawbones** [Wn3] *humor, esp. AmE* a doctor or SURGEON

saw·buck /ˈsɔːbʌk/ *n AmE sl* a $10 note

saw·dust /ˈsɔːdʌst/ *n* [U] dust or very small pieces (as of wood) made by a SAW in cutting

saw·horse /ˈsɔːhɔːs‖-hɔrs/ *n* a movable frame for supporting wood to be SAWn

saw·mill /ˈsɔːˌmɪl/ *n* a factory where logs are cut into boards by a power-driven SAW

sawn-off shot·gun /ˌ· · ˈ··/ *AmE* **sawed-off shot·gun** //— *n* a SHOTGUN with a barrel cut short, as carried as a weapon by criminals

saw·pit /ˈsɔːˌpɪt/ *n* (esp. in former times) a deep long hole in the ground in which one of a pair of men stands, who are cutting up, with a 2-handled SAW, a very large log placed over the hole

saw·yer /ˈsɔːjəʳ/ *n* a person whose job is SAWing logs

sax·i·frage /ˈsæksɪ̇frɪdʒ/ *n* [U] any of various types of small plant with bright flowers, growing esp. in rocky places

Sax·on /ˈsæksən/ *adj* [Wa5] of or concerning a people of north Germany who conquered and settled in England in the 5th century —see also ANGLO-SAXON

sax·o·phone /ˈsæksəfəʊn/ also (*infml*) **sax** /sæks/— *n* a metal musical instrument of various sizes and curved shapes, played with a REED and most usu. used in JAZZ, military, and dance music —see picture at WIND INSTRUMENT

sax·oph·o·nist /sækˈsɒfənɪ̇st‖ˈsæksəfəʊnɪ̇st/ *n fml* a SAXOPHONE-player

say¹ /seɪ/ *v* **said** /sed/, *3rd pers. pres. t.* **says** /sez/ **1** [T1 (*to*)] to pronounce (a sound, word, etc.): *What did you say? I said, "You're standing on my toe!"*|*You must learn to say "please", young man!*|*Have you said your prayers?* **2** [T1,5a,b,6a,b;I0 *nonassertive*] to express (a thought, intention, opinion, question, etc.) in words: *Don't believe anything he says.*|*He said* (*that*) *I was standing on his toe.*|*"Will it rain?" "I should say so/not."*|*"Will your party win the election?" "I'd rather not say."*|*"Who can say?"*|*"It's not for me to say."* **3** [T1,5a,b,6a,b; I0 *nonassertive*] *not fml* to show; INDICATE (1): *What time does your watch say?*|*She was smiling but her eyes said she was unhappy* **4** [T1,5a: *imper.*] *not fml* to suppose; ASSUME (1): (*Let's*) *say your plan fails: then what do we do?*|*Would you take an offer of, say, £100 for your car?*|*Can you come to dinner? Say, 7.30?* **5** [Wv6;T3] *not fml* to direct or instruct someone: *She says to meet her at the station.*|*It says on the bottle to take a spoonful every 4 hours* **6 I say** *infml BrE* **a** (a rather weak expression of surprise, interest, anger, sorrow, etc.): *"My husband is ill today." "I say! I'm sorry to hear that"* **b** (used for calling someone's attention): *I say, isn't it getting late?*|*I say, I've just had a wonderful idea!* **7 it goes without saying** *not fml* of course; clearly: *It goes without saying that our plans depend on the weather* **8 I wouldn't say no** *infml BrE* yes, please; I'd like it/some: *"Have another drink." "Well, I wouldn't say no"* **9 say for oneself/something** to offer as an excuse or as something in favour or defence: *You're late again! What have you got to say for yourself?*|*a bad idea with very little to be said for it* **10 say no more!** *infml* your/the meaning is very clear!: *I saw him leaving her flat at 6.30 in the morning." "Say no more!"* **11 say to oneself** *not fml* to think: *I woke up early and said to myself, "Shall I get up?"* **12 say what you like** *not fml* even though you may not agree **13 that is to say** also (*abbrev.*) **i.e.**— in other words; expressed another (more exact) way: *working as hard as before, that is to say not very hard* **14 they say** *not fml* people say; it's usually thought **15 what do you say?** *infml* you'll agree, won't you?: *Let's go into business together.*|*What do you say?*|*What do you say we go into business?*|*What do you say to going into business together?* **16 you don't say (so)!** *infml* (an expression of slight surprise) **17 you said it** *infml, esp. AmE* you're right; I agree: *"Let's go home." "You said it! I'm tired"* —see also NOT **to say, to say** NOTHING **of, say the** WORD, **not to have a good** WORD (21) **to say for**

say² *n* [S;U] **1** (a) power or right of (sharing in) acting or deciding: *She had no say in the choice of a husband; her parents had all the say* **2 have/say one's say** *not fml* to have/use the chance to say something, esp. to express one's opinion

say³ *interj AmE infml* (used for expressing surprise

or a sudden idea): *Say, haven't I seen you before somewhere?*

say·ing /ˈseɪ-ɪŋ/ *n* a well-known wise statement, ADAGE; PROVERB: *As the saying goes, "There's no smoke without fire"*

say on *v adv* [IØ *usu. imper.*] *infml* to keep talking; continue: *Say on! We're all listening*

say-so /ˈ· ·/ *n* [(*on*) S9, esp. *of*] *not fml* **1** a personal statement without proof: *Why should I believe what you say just on your say-so?* **2** permission: *allowed to come home from hospital on the doctor's say-so*

scab[1] /skæb/ *n* **1** [C;U] a hard mass mainly of dried blood which forms over a cut or wound on the skin while it is getting better **2** [U] **a** any of various diseases causing hard spots on plants **b** SCABIES in animals **3** [C;N] *derog sl* a worker who refuses to join a trade union, works in worse conditions than a union permits, or does the work of one who is on STRIKE[2] (2); BLACKLEG

scab[2] *v* **-bb-** [IØ] *AmE derog sl* to work as a SCAB (3)

scab·bard /ˈskæbəd‖-ərd/ *n* a usu. leather or metal tube, as hung from the belt, enclosing the blade of a sword, knife, etc.

scab·by /ˈskæbi/ *adj* [Wa1] covered with SCABs[1] (1) or having SCAB[1] (2) or SCABIES

sca·bies /ˈskeɪbiz/ *n* [U] a skin disease marked by SCABs[1] (1) and an unpleasant pricking sensation

sca·bi·ous /ˈskeɪbɪəs/ *n* [U] any of various types of tall European plant with usu. light purple flowers

sca·brous /ˈskeɪbrəs/ *adj lit* **1** rough-feeling because of small raised points, SCABs[1] (1,2), etc. on the surface: *a scabrous leaf* **2** unpleasant by association with improper or shocking subjects; RISQUÉ: *a scabrous description of his past life*

scads /skædz/ *n* [P] *AmE infml* large numbers or amounts

scaf·fold /ˈskæfəld, -fəʊld/ *n* **1** [C] a framework built up from wooden or metal poles and boards, as around a house being built, painted, or repaired, for workmen to stand on **2** [C] a board for a workman to stand on when working high up, usu. hung from ropes **3** [C] a raised stage for the killing of criminals (esp. in former times) by cutting off their heads or by hanging **4** [*the*+R] *lit* death in either of these ways: *a life of murder that led him at last to the scaffold*

scaf·fold·ing /ˈskæfəldɪŋ/ *n* [U] poles and boards (to be) built into a system of SCAFFOLDs (1) —see picture at SITE[1]

sca·lar /ˈskeɪləʳ/ *adj, n* [Wa5] *tech* (of or concerning) a number without an ASSOCIATED direction (as opposed to a VECTOR)

scal·a·wag /ˈskæləwæg/ *n* [C;N] *esp. AmE* SCALLYWAG

scald[1] /skɔːld/ *v* **1** [T1;IØ] to burn with hot liquid: *He scalded his tongue on/with the hot coffee.|Someone could be scalded to death by steam from that burst pipe.|Be careful that you don't touch that water: it's hot enough to scald!* **2** [T1] to clean or treat with boiling water or steam **3** [T1] to heat (esp. milk) almost to boiling

scald[2] *n* **1** [C] a skin burn from hot liquid or steam **2** [U] any of several plant diseases making marks that look like the effects of heat

scald·ing /ˈskɔːldɪŋ/ *adj* **1** (seeming to be) boiling or as hot as boiling: **scalding hot** *water/weather* **2** fierce in attacking in words: *a scalding report on the standard of work*

scale[1] /skeɪl/ *n* [*often pl. with sing. meaning*] **1** a pair of pans for weighing an object by comparing it with a known weight; BALANCE —see PAIR (USAGE) —see picture at KITCHEN **2** any weighing machine —see picture at BATHROOM **3 turn/tip the scales** *not fml* to be the fact, action, etc., that decides a result in favour of one thing or the other: *The American declaration of war in 1917 tipped the scales against Germany* **4 tip the scales at** *infml lit* to weigh

scale[2] *v* [L1] (esp. of a sports fighter) to weigh

scale[3] *n* **1** [C] one of the small nearly flat stiff pieces forming (part of) the outer body covering of some animals, esp. fish and snakes (REPTILEs) —see pictures at FISH[1] and REPTILE **2** [U] material forming a more or less removable covering of a surface, as **a** solid chemicals sticking to metal or stone in some conditions **b** greyish material forming around the inside of a pot in which water is boiled, hot water pipes, etc. —see also FUR[2] (5) **3** [U;C *usu. pl.*] (a small piece of) dry skin which comes away from the healthy skin below, as in some diseases **4** [U] damage or attack to plants by a type of small insects (**scale insects**) **5 the scales fell from my eyes** *infml lit* I was suddenly able to see what had always been clear

scale[4] *v* **1** [T1] to remove the SCALEs[3] (1) from: *scaled the fish before cooking them* **2** [X9;L9: esp. OFF] **a** to remove from a surface in thin small pieces: *He scaled (off) the paint from the wall* **b** to come off a surface in this way: *The paint scaled off easily with a knife* **3** [T1 *usu. pass.*] to cover with SCALE[3] (2): *heavily scaled water pipes* —see also DESCALE

scale[5] *n* **1** [C] a set of numbers or standards for measuring or comparing: *a pay scale for all the workers in the company|wind forces measured on a standard scale of 0–12* **2** [C] **a** a set of marks, esp. numbers, on an instrument at exactly fixed distances apart, as for measuring: *a ruler with a metric scale* **b** a piece of wood, plastic, etc., with such marks on the edge **3** [C] a rule or set of numbers comparing measurements on a map or model with actual measurements: *a scale of 1 inch to the mile|a scale of 1:25 000|a* **scale model/drawing** (=made according to a scale)|*a large-/small-scale map* **4** [C;U] size, esp. in relation to other things or to what is usual: *a large-scale business operation|business on a large/grand scale* **5** [C] a set of musical notes in upward and downward order and at fixed separations (different for MAJOR and MINOR scales): *the scale of A* (=with A for its base) **6 to scale** according to a fixed rule for reducing the size of something in a drawing, model, etc.: *carefully drawn to scale except one part which was* **out of scale**

scale[6] *v* **1** [T1] to climb up: *scale a wall/ladder* **2** [X9, esp. UP, DOWN] to increase or reduce, esp. by a fixed rate: *scale up/down taxes*

sca·lene /ˈskeɪliːn/ *adj* [Wa5] *tech* (of a TRIANGLE (1)) having no 2 equal sides

scal·li·on /ˈskælɪən/ *n AmE & old use* an onion whose round white part is small, esp. a SPRING ONION

scal·lop[1], **scol-** /ˈskɒləp‖ˈskɑ-/ *n* **1** a sea animal (a MOLLUSC) good for food and having a pair of rounded shells with raised lines meeting at one edge **2** (one of) a row of small curves forming an edge or pattern: *a dress with scallops around the neck*

scallop[2], **scol-** *v* [Wv5;T1] **1** to bake in a creamy mixture (SAUCE): *scalloped potatoes* **2** to cut or make SCALLOPs (2) in (an edge or line): *a dress with a scalloped neck*

scal·ly·wag /ˈskæliwæg/ *AmE* usu. **scalawag**— *n usu. humor* a trouble-making or dishonest person; RASCAL

scalp[1] /skælp/ *n* **1** the skin on the top of the human head, where hair grows **2** *infml* a mark of victory over someone: *He called for the minister's scalp* (=wanted him to admit defeat and leave his job)

scalp² *v* [T1] **1** (as of American Indians in former times) to cut off the SCALP¹ (1) of (a dead enemy) as a mark of victory **2** *AmE not fml* to buy and then resell (as theatre tickets) at very high prices for profit

scal·pel /ˈskælpəl/ *n* a small delicate knife used by doctors in operations —see picture at MEDICAL¹

scal·y /ˈskeɪli/ *adj* [Wa1] covered with SCALE*s*³ (1) or SCALE³ (2,3,4) —**scaliness** *n* [U]

scamp /skæmp/ *n* [C; (*you*) N] a trouble-making but usu. playful (young) person

scam·per /ˈskæmpəʳ/ *v* [L9] to run quickly and usu. playfully: *The mouse scampered into its hole*

scam·pi /ˈskæmpi/ *n* [U;(P)] *BrE* (a dish made from) large PRAWN*s* (small sea animals)

scan¹ /skæn/ *v* **-nn- 1** [T1] to examine closely, esp. in search: *scanned the doctor's face for a sign of hope*|RADAR *scanning the sky* **2** [T1] to look at quickly without careful reading **3** [T1;I∅] **a** to examine ((a line of) a poem) to show the pattern of music-like beats in each line **b** to have a regular pattern of this kind: *The poem scans very well.* **4** [T1] (of a beam of ELECTRON*s*) to be directed to (a surface) so as to cover with lines which are close together (as in the making of a television picture)

scan² *n* [S] an act of SCAN*ning*, esp. a searching look

scan·dal /ˈskændl/ *n* **1** [C;U] a state or action which offends people's ideas of what is right and proper **2** [C] a public feeling or action caused by such behaviour: *The news about the minister's private life caused a scandal* **3** [U] true or false talk which brings harm, shame, or disrespect to another: *I wish you'd stop repeating scandal about your neighbours!*

scan·dal·ize, -ise /ˈskændəl-aɪz/ *v* [T1 *usu. pass.*] to offend (someone's) feelings of what is right or proper

scan·dal·mon·ger /ˈskændəlˌmʌŋgəʳ/ *n derog* a person who spreads SCANDAL (3)

scan·dal·ous /ˈskændələs/ *adj* offensive to feelings of what is right or proper —**~ly** *adv*

Scan·di·na·vi·an /ˌskændəˈneɪvɪən/ *adj* [Wa5] of or concerning the countries Denmark, Norway, Sweden, and Iceland in N Europe, or their people or language

scan·ner /ˈskænəʳ/ *n* an instrument for SCAN*ning*¹ (1,4): *a* RADAR *scanner*

scan·sion /ˈskænʃən/ *n* [U] (the act of showing) the way a line of a poem SCAN*s*¹ (3b)

scant¹ /skænt/ *adj* [Wa2; (*of*)] (having) hardly enough: *paid scant attention to what was said*

scant² *v* [T1] to use, treat, or supply in a SCANTY way: *a subject scanted in most schoolbooks*

scant·y /ˈskænti/ *adj* [Wa1] hardly (big) enough; almost too small, few, etc.: *a scanty breakfast* —**scantily** *adv* —**scantiness** *n* [U]

-scape /skeɪp/ *comb. form* a SCENIC view, as in a picture: *a cityscape*

scape·goat /ˈskeɪpgəʊt/ *n* a person or thing taking the blame for the fault of others —see also WHIPPING BOY

scape·grace /ˈskeɪpgreɪs/ *n* [C;N] *becoming rare* a worthless or dishonest person

scap·u·la /ˈskæpjʊlə‖-pjələ/ *n med* SHOULDER BLADE —see picture at SKELETON

scar¹ /skɑːʳ/ *n* **1** a mark (formed from **scar tissue**) remaining on the skin or an organ from a wound, cut, etc. **2** a mark of damage like this: *scars on the polished tabletop*|(fig.) *a country showing the scars of recent war*

scar² *v* **-rr-** [T1;L9] to (cause to) be marked with a SCAR

scar·ab /ˈskærəb/ *n* **1** also **scarab bee·tle** /ˈ·· ˌ··/— a type of large black BEETLE (insect with hard shiny wing-covers) **2** a representation of this, often in a small stone, used in ancient Egypt as an ornament and sign of life after death

scarce¹ /skeəs‖skeərs/ *adj* [Wa1] **1** not much or many compared with what is wanted; hard to find; not PLENTIFUL: *Good fruit is scarce just now, and costs a lot* **2 make oneself scarce** *infml* to go away or keep away (from someone) —see RARE (USAGE)

scarce² *adv lit* hardly; SCARCELY: *I could scarce believe my eyes*

scarce·ly /ˈskeəsli‖-ər-/ *adv* [Wa5] **1** hardly; almost not; BARELY: *Scarcely had he arrived when he had to leave again.*|*She spoke scarcely a word of English* **2** *esp. pomp* (almost) certainly not: *You could scarcely have found a better person for the job than Miss Winkle* —see HARDLY (USAGE)

scar·ci·ty /ˈskeəsəti‖-ər-/ *n* [U;C] a state of being SCARCE; lack: *scarcities of all kinds of necessary goods*

scare¹ /skeəʳ/ *v not fml* **1** [T1;I∅] **a** to cause sudden fear to; FRIGHTEN: *Don't let the noise scare you: it's only the wind* **b** to become fearful: *a man who doesn't scare* (*easily*) **2** [X9 esp. OFF, AWAY] to drive, cause to go or become, etc., (as) by fear: *He got a gun and scared off the thief.*|*The high price is scaring away possible buyers*

scare² *n not fml* **1** [S] a sudden feeling of fear: *What a scare you gave me, appearing suddenly in the dark!* **2** [C] a usu. mistaken or unreasonable public fear: *At last war was avoided but only after several war scares*

scare³ *adj* [Wa5;A] *not fml* intended to cause fear: *scare stories about war, printed in the newspapers*

scare·crow /ˈskeəkrəʊ‖-ər-/ *n* an object (often old clothes hung on sticks) in the shape of a man, set up in a field to keep birds away from crops

scared /skeəd‖skeərd/ *adj* [B (*of*); F3,5,7] *not fml* put into, or being in, a state of fear or anxiety (often (*infml*) followed by **stiff/silly/out of one's wits/to death** for added force): *"Why won't you come on the trip? Are you scared?*|*What are you scared of?"*|*"I'm scared to fly in a plane—scared that it might crash"*

scare·mon·ger /ˈskeəˌmʌŋgəʳ‖-ər-/ *n derog* a person who spreads reports intended to cause a public SCARE²; ALARMIST

scare up *v adv* [T1 (*from*)] *not fml, esp. AmE* to make from things that are hard to find or not easy to use: *scare up a meal from the bits of food in the kitchen*

scarf /skɑːf‖skɑrf/ *n* **scarfs** *or* **scarves** /skɑːvz‖skɑrvz/ a piece of cloth, usu. (for men) long and narrow or (for women) square, for wearing around the neck, head, or shoulders for protection or ornament

scar·i·fy /ˈskeərəfaɪ, ˈskærəfaɪ/ *v* [T1] **1** *med* to make small cuts on (an area of skin) with a sharp knife **2** *lit* to attack fiercely in words **3** to break up and loosen the surface of (a road or field) with a pointed tool

scar·let /ˈskɑːlət‖-ɑr-/ *adj, n* [U] (of) a very bright red colour, often connected with marks of rank, office, etc.

scarlet fe·ver /ˌ·· ˈ··/ also **scar·la·ti·na** /ˌskɑːləˈtiːnə‖-ɑr-/— *n* [U] a serious and easily-spread disease, esp. of children, marked by a painful throat and red spots on the skin

scarlet pim·per·nel /ˌ·· ˈ···/ *n* a type of PIMPERNEL with bright red flowers

scarlet run·ner /ˌ·· ˈ··/ *n esp. BrE* RUNNER BEAN

scarlet wom·an /ˌ·· ˈ··/ *n euph & humor* a woman who is not modest or who does not have proper morals, esp. a PROSTITUTE

scarp /skɑːp‖skɑrp/ *n* a line of natural cliffs —compare ESCARPMENT

scar·per /ˈskɑːpəʳ‖-ɑr-/ *v* [IØ] *BrE sl* to run away: *"Go on, scarper! Get out!"*

scar·y /ˈskeəri/ *adj* [Wa1] *not fml* **1** causing or marked by fear: *a scary dark street|the scariest story I ever heard* **2** easily SCAREd; afraid: *Don't be so scary; we're quite safe*

scat /skæt/ *v* **-tt-** [IØ *usu. imper.*] *infml* to go away fast; *It's getting late; we'd better scat!*

scath·ing /ˈskeɪðɪŋ/ *adj* (of speech or writing) bitterly cruel in judgment —**~ly** *adv*

sca·tol·o·gy /skæˈtɒlədʒi‖-ˈtɑ-/ *n* [U] great interest in human bowels, body waste, etc. —**-gical** /ˌskætəˈlɒdʒɪkəl‖-ˈlɑ-/ *adj*

scat·ter¹ /ˈskætəʳ/ *v* **1** [T1;IØ] **a** to cause (a group) to separate widely: *The gunshot scattered the birds* **b** (of a group) to do this: *The birds scattered at the sound of the gun* **2** [D1+*with/on* or *over*; T1] to spread widely in all directions (on) (as if) by throwing: *scatter seed on the field/scatter the field with seed*|(fig.) *He scatters money about as if he were rich*

scatter² also **scat·ter·ing** /ˈskætərɪŋ/— *n* [S] a small number or amount separated widely (as if) by SCATTERing¹ (2): *a scatter(ing) of telephone calls during the day*

scat·ter·brain /ˈskætəbreɪn‖-ər-/ *n infml* a likeable but careless, forgetful, or unthinking person

scat·ter·brained /ˈskætəbreɪnd‖-ər-/ *adj infml* being or typical of a SCATTERBRAIN, esp. not (the result of) thinking carefully

scat·tered /ˈskætəd‖-ərd/ *adj* small and far apart; widely and irregularly separated: *scattered towns among the hills|The weather report says we'll have scattered* SHOWERs *today*

scat·ty /ˈskæti/ *adj* [Wa1] *infml BrE* slightly mad or SCATTERBRAINED —**-tiness** *n* [U]

scav·enge /ˈskævɪ̈ndʒ/ *v* [IØ;T1] **1** to search for or find (usable objects) at no cost, esp. among waste or unwanted things —compare SCROUNGE **2** (of animals) to feed as a SCAVENGER (1) (on): *homeless dogs scavenging on kitchen waste*

scav·eng·er /ˈskævɪ̈ndʒəʳ/ *n* **1** a creature (such as the VULTURE or JACKAL) which feeds on waste or decaying flesh **2** a person who SCAVENGEs (1)

sce·na·ri·o /sɪ̈ˈnɑːriəʊ‖-ˈnæ-, -ˈne-/ *n* **-rios** **1** a written description of the action to take place in a film, play, etc. **2** a description of a possible course of action or events

sce·nar·ist /sɪ̈ˈnɑːrɪ̈st, ˈsiːnə-‖sɪ̈ˈnærɪ̈st, -ˈne-/ *n tech* a writer of SCENARIOs (1)

scene /siːn/ *n* **1** [C] **a** (in a play) any of the divisions, often within an act, during which there is no change of place **b** (in a film, broadcast, etc.) a single piece of action in one place **2** [C] the background for (part of) the action of a play; SET³ (9a): *a play with few scene changes* **3** [C] a view of a place: *a beautiful scene from our hotel window|a painter of street scenes* **4** [C] a place where an event or action happens: *objects found at the scene of the crime* **5** [C] an event or course of action regarded as like something in a play or film: *angry scenes in Parliament* **6** [C] *not fml* a show of anger or feelings, esp. between 2 people in public: *I'm ashamed of you, making a scene in the restaurant like that* **7** [S9] *infml* an area of activity; place regarded as where a kind of thing happens or is interesting: *What's new on the film scene? Any new films?* **8 behind the scenes** *not fml* out of sight; secretly: *decisions made behind the scenes, without public knowledge* **9 make the scene** *sl* to be present, esp. to take part in something: *"Glad you could make the scene, man!"* **10 on the scene** *infml* present; appearing: *a broadcast from Africa by a news reporter on the scene|This great leader came on the scene just when his country needed him* **11 set the scene** *not fml* to prepare; make ready: *The unjust peace agreement set the scene for another war* **12 steal the scene** *infml* to take attention away from who or what ought to be most important —see SCENERY (USAGE)

sce·ne·ry /ˈsiːnəri/ *n* [U] **1** the set of painted backgrounds and other articles used on a theatre stage —see picture at THEATRE **2** natural surroundings, esp. in beautiful and open country

USAGE The general appearance of the country, considered from the point of view of beauty, is **scenery**: *the beautiful* **scenery** *of the English Lakes.* A **view** is the part of the **scenery** that can be seen from one place, esp. in the distance, as from a window: *a fine* **view** *of the river.* A **scene** is also what one sees from one place, but it is more likely to include people and movement: *a happy* **scene** *of children playing in the garden.* —see VIEW (USAGE)

scene·shift·er /ˈsiːnˌʃɪftəʳ/ *n* a worker who moves SCENERY (1) in a theatre

sce·nic /ˈsiːnɪk/ *adj* **1** of, concerning, or showing natural SCENERY: *a scenic road along the coast* **2** showing a scene: *scenic wallpaper* **3** of or concerning stage SCENERY —**~ally** *adv* [Wa4]

scent¹ /sent/ *v* **1** [T1] (esp. of animals) to smell, esp. to tell the presence of by smelling: *dogs scenting a fox* **2** [T1,5] to get a feeling or belief of the presence or fact (of): *She scented danger/scented that all was not well* **3** [Wv5;T1 (*with*) *usu. pass.*] to fill with a SCENT² (1b,5): *The air was scented with spring flowers*

scent² *n* **1** [C] a smell, esp. **a** as left by an animal and followed by hunting dogs **b** a particular usu. pleasant smell: *the scent of roses* **2** [(*the*) S] *not fml* a way to the discovering; TRACK² (1): *a scientist who thinks he's* **on the scent** *of a cure for heart disease, although others think he's following* **a false scent** **3** [S] (of animals) a power of smelling: *a dog with a good scent* **4** [S (*of*)] a feeling of the presence (of something): *a scent of danger* **5** [U; (C)] *esp. BrE* PERFUME —**~less** *adj* [Wa5]

scep·tic, *AmE* **skep-** /ˈskeptɪk/ *n* a SCEPTICAL person, esp. about the claims of a religion

scep·ti·cal, *AmE* **skep-** /ˈskeptɪkəl/ *adj* [(*of, about*)] unwilling (habitually) to believe a claim or promise; doubting; distrustful: *I'm sceptical of/about the team's chances of winning* —**~ly** *adv* [Wa4]

scep·ti·cis·m, *AmE* **skep-** /ˈskeptɪ̈sɪzəm/ *n* [U;S] a doubting state or habit of mind; dislike of believing without certainty; doubt

scep·tre, *AmE* **-ter** /ˈseptəʳ/ *n* a short rod carried by a ruler on ceremonial occasions as a sign of power

sched·ule¹ /ˈʃedjuːl‖ˈskedʒʊl, -dʒəl/ *n* **1** a timetable of things to be done, dealt with, etc.; PROGRAMME¹ (3): *a factory production schedule* **2** a formal list, as **a** a list of prices: *a schedule of postal charges* **b** *esp. AmE* a timetable of trains, buses, etc. **c** *fml* a list of details related to some other matter in writing **3 ahead of/on/behind schedule** before/at/after the planned or expected time

schedule² *v* **1** [T1 (*for*); V3: *usu. pass.*] to plan for a certain future time **2** [Wv5;T1] to put (a flight, train, etc.) into a timetable; make a regular service: *Are you going by a scheduled flight or by* CHARTER¹ (3)?

sche·ma /ˈskiːmə/ *n* **-mata** /mətə/ *fml* a representation of an arrangement or plan; DIAGRAM

sche·mat·ic /skiːˈmætɪk, skɪ-/ *adj* of or like a SCHEME¹ (3) or SCHEMA —**~ally** *adv* [Wa4]

sche·ma·tize /ˈskiːmətaɪz/ *v* [Wv5;T1] to express or show in a very simple, formal, (too) neat way

scheme¹ /skiːm/ *n* **1** a clever dishonest plan: *a*

scheme to escape taxes **2** *BrE* a formal, official, or business plan: *a health insurance scheme* **3** a plan in a simple form; a general arrangement; system: *It's hard to see any scheme in what this writer has written: it's very confused* —see also COLOUR SCHEME **4 the scheme of things** the way things are, regarded as an ordered system

scheme² *v* [Wv4;IØ (*for, against*), 3] to make clever dishonest plans; PLOT² (5) —**schemer** *n*

scher·zo /ˈskeətsəʊ‖-eər-/ *n* **-zos** /səʊz/ a quick playful piece of music for instruments, usu. part of a longer piece

schis·m /ˈsɪzəm, ˈskɪzəm/ *n* **1** [C;U] (a) separation between parts originally of the same group, esp. the Christian church **2** [U] the action of causing this

schis·mat·ic¹ /sɪzˈmætɪk, skɪz-/ *n* a person taking part in a religious SCHISM

schismatic² *adj* typical of, fond of, or taking part in SCHISM: *schismatic churches/teachings*

schist /ʃɪst/ *n* [U] *tech* any of several types of rock that naturally break apart into thin flat pieces

schiz·oid /ˈskɪtsɔɪd/ *adj tech* (typical) of or like SCHIZOPHRENIA or a SPLIT PERSONALITY

schiz·o·phre·ni·a /ˌskɪtsəʊˈfriːnɪə, -sə-/ *n* [U] *tech* a disorder of the mind marked by a separation of a person's mind and feelings, causing at last a drawing away from other people into a life in the imagination only —compare SPLIT PERSONALITY

schiz·o·phren·ic /ˌskɪtsəʊˈfrenɪk, -sə-/ *adj, n tech* (typical of) a person with SCHIZOPHRENIA —**~ally** *adv* [Wa4]

schmaltz, schmalz /ʃmɔːlts, ʃmælts‖ʃmɔlts, ʃmɑlts (*Ger* ʃmalts)/ *n* [U] *Ger, not fml* art or esp. music which brings out feelings in a too easy, not serious or delicate, way —**schmaltzy** *adj* [Wa1]

schnapps /ʃnæps/ *n* [U] a kind of strong alcoholic drink rather like GIN

schnit·zel /ˈʃnɪtsəl/ *n* [C; (*AmE*) U] a small piece of VEAL (= meat of a young cow) covered with bits of bread for quick cooking (FRYing) in oil

schnor·kel /ˈsnɔːkəl‖-ɔr-/ *n now rare* SNORKEL

schol·ar /ˈskɒləʳ‖ˈskɑ-/ *n* **1** a person with great knowledge of, and skill in studying, a subject, esp. other than a science: LEARNED person **2** the holder of a SCHOLARSHIP (1) **3** *lit & old use* a child in school **4** [*usu. neg.*] *infml* a clever and educated person: *I'm afraid I've never been much of a scholar* —see STUDENT (USAGE)

schol·ar·ly /ˈskɒləli‖ˈskɑlərli/ *adj* **1** concerned with serious detailed study —opposite **popular** **2** *usu. apprec* of or like a SCHOLAR (1)

schol·ar·ship /ˈskɒləʃɪp‖ˈskɑlər-/ *n* **1** [C] (*often cap. as part of a name*) a sum of money or other prize given to a student by an official body, esp. to pay (partly) for a course of study **2** [U] the knowledge, work, or method of SCHOLARS (1); exact and serious study; LEARNING: *a study which is a fine piece of scholarship*

scho·las·tic /skəˈlæstɪk/ *adj* **1** [Wa5;A] of or concerning schools and teaching **2** [Wa5;A] of or concerning SCHOLASTICISM **3** [B] too concerned with unimportant details; PEDANTIC: *a long and scholastic argument*

scho·las·ti·cis·m /skəˈlæstɪ̇sɪzəm/ *n* [U] the study of general questions (PHILOSOPHY (1)) starting from ancient writings and Christian teaching, as done in Europe from the 9th to 17th centuries

school¹ /skuːl/ *n* **1** [C] a place of education for children: *a* PRIMARY/SECONDARY SCHOOL|SUNDAY SCHOOL|*new schools built by the government*|*children of school age* = *old enough to attend school*|(fig.) *He had learned everything in the school of experience* **2** [U] **a** attendance or study at such a place; a course of learning at such a place: *He began school at the age of 5.*|*She always found school difficult* **b** one day's course at such a place: *School begins at 8:30.*|*walk home after school* **3** [GC] the body of students (and teachers) at such a place: *a teacher liked by the whole school* **4** [C;U] an establishment for teaching a particular subject, skill, etc.: *She goes to (an) art school at night.*|NIGHTSCHOOL|FINISHING SCHOOL **5** [C] (in certain universities) a department concerned with a particular subject: (*fml*) *the School of Law*|*He went to medical school for 3 years* **6** [C] a group of people with the same methods, opinions, (of artists) style, etc.: *Rembrandt and his school*|*a modern school of political thought*|SCHOOL OF THOUGHT **7** [C;U] *AmE* UNIVERSITY —see also OLD SCHOOL

school² *v* [T1 (*in*); V3] to teach, train, or bring under control: *a dog well schooled in obedience*|*He schooled himself to listen to others because he knew he talked too much*

school³ *n* [(*of*)] a large group of one kind of fish or certain other sea animals swimming together

school board /ˈ· ·/ *n* (in the US but not now in Britain) a local government body in charge of schools

school·boy /ˈskuːlbɔɪ/ (*fem.* **school·girl** /-gɜːl‖-gɜrl/)— *n* a boy attending school, esp. regarded as one who is not yet grown up

school·house /ˈskuːlhaʊs/ *n* **-houses** /ˌhaʊzɪ̇z/ a school building, esp. for a small village school

school·ing /ˈskuːlɪŋ/ *n* [U] education or attendance at school: *He had only 5 years of schooling*

school·man /ˈskuːlmæn/ *n* **-men** /men/ (*often cap.*) a teacher of SCHOLASTICISM

school·marm /ˈskuːlmɑːm‖-mɑrm/ *n infml & humor* **1** a woman teacher at a school **2** a woman thought to be like this, esp. in being commanding, old-fashioned, exact, and easily shocked

school·mas·ter /ˈskuːlˌmɑːstəʳ‖-ˌmæ-/ (*fem.* **school·mis·tress** /-ˌmɪstrɪ̇s/)— *n esp. BrE* a male teacher at a school

school·mas·ter·ing /ˈskuːlˌmɑːstərɪŋ‖-ˌmæ-/ *n* [U] *esp. BrE* the profession of being a SCHOOLMASTER

school·mate /ˈskuːlmeɪt/ also **school·fel·low** /ˈskuːlˌfeləʊ/— *n* a child at the same school: *We were schoolmates 20 years ago*

school of thought /ˌ· · ˈ·/ *n* **schools of thought** a group of people with the same way of thinking, opinion, etc.: *There are different schools of thought on the best method of educating children*

school re·port /ˌ· ·ˈ·/ also **report** (*AmE* **report card**)— *n BrE* (in education) a written statement by teachers about a child's work at school

school·work /ˈskuːlwɜːk‖-wɜrk/ *n* [U] study for or during school classes

schoo·ner /ˈskuːnəʳ/ *n* **1** a fast sailing ship with 2 or sometimes more MASTs (upright poles supporting the sails) and sails set along the length of rather than across the ship —see picture at SAIL² **2** a large tall drinking glass, esp. for SHERRY or sometimes beer

schwa /ʃwɑː/ *n* [C;U] (in English) a vowel sounded typically in word parts (SYLLABLEs) spoken without special force (STRESS) (as the *a* in *about*) and shown in this dictionary as /ə/ or /ə/

sci·at·ic /saɪˈætɪk/ *adj med* of or concerning the HIPs² (1) (the upper parts of the legs where they join the body at the side): *the* **sciatic nerve** (along the back of the upper legs)

sci·at·i·ca /saɪˈætɪkə/ *n* [U] *not fml* pain in the area of the lower back, HIPs² (1), and legs

sci·ence /ˈsaɪəns/ *n* **1** [U] (the study of) knowledge which can be made into a system and which usu. depends on seeing and testing facts and stating general natural laws **2** [C;U] a branch of

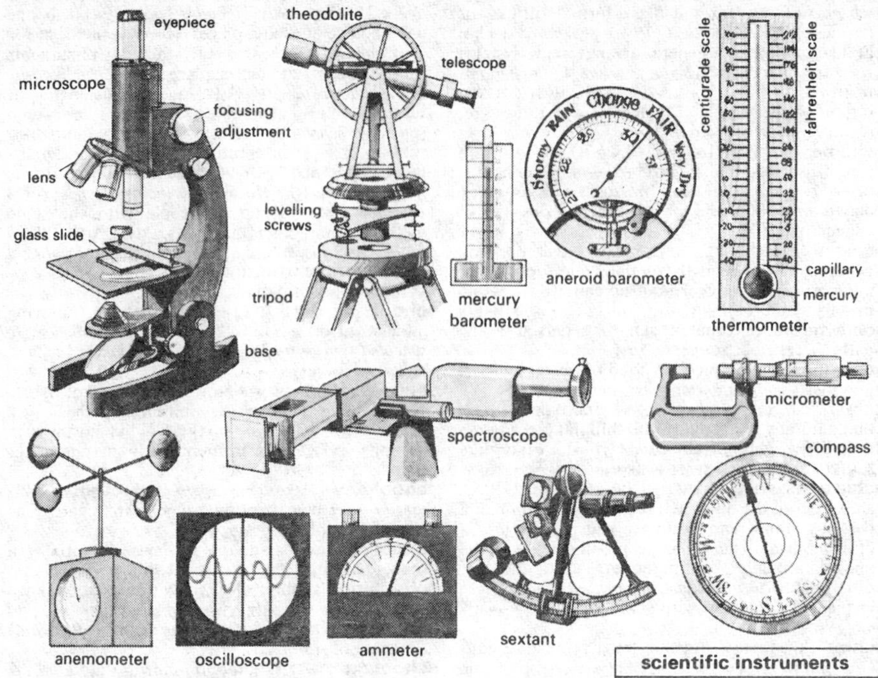

scientific instruments

such knowledge, esp. **a** anything which may be studied exactly: *the science of cooking|military science|Driving a car is an art, not a science* —see also SOCIAL SCIENCE **b** any of the branches usu. studied at universities, such as PHYSICS, BIOLOGY, chemistry, ENGINEERING, and sometimes MATHEMATICS (**the sciences**): *studying a science subject|government support for the sciences* —compare ARTS; see also NATURAL SCIENCE **3 have something down to a science** to have a complete exact knowledge of something, esp. a skill: *He seems to have writing popular books down to a science* (=He writes one good-selling book after another)

science fic·tion /ˌ·· ˈ··/ also (*infml*) **sci-fi** /ˌsaɪ ˈfaɪ/— *n* [U] literature, esp. NOVEL*s* and stories, which deals with imaginary future developments in science and their effect on life

sci·en·tif·ic /ˌsaɪənˈtɪfɪk/ *adj* **1** [Wa5;A;(B)] of, being, or concerning science or its principles or rules: *The microscope is a scientific instrument.|He had a scientific education and learned chemistry at the age of 13* **2** [B] needing or showing exact knowledge, skill, or use of a system: *scientific baby care|They were scientific in their search, looking in all the possible places in order* —**~ally** *adv* [Wa4]

sci·en·tist /ˈsaɪəntɪ̵st/ *n* a person who does work (esp. new work) in a science, esp. PHYSICS, chemistry, or BIOLOGY

sci·en·tol·o·gy /ˌsaɪənˈtɒlədʒi‖-ˈtɑ-/ *n* [U] a religious movement which claims to be able to free people from personal difficulties, increase human abilities, and quicken the curing of diseases of the body and mind —**-gist** *n*

scim·i·tar /ˈsɪmɪ̵təʳ/ *n* a sword with a curved blade that is sharp on the outer edge, formerly used in Turkey, Persia, etc.

scin·til·la /sɪnˈtɪlə/ *n* [S] a slightest bit; IOTA: *There's not a scintilla of truth in what he says; his statement lacks any scintilla of proof*

scin·til·late /ˈsɪntɪ̵leɪt/ *v* [Wv4;IØ (*with*); (T1)] **1** *usu. lit.* to send out (as) quick flashes of light or SPARK*s*[1] (1,2), SPARKLE (with): *The stars scintillated (their light) in the winter sky* **2** to make (as) quick and clever remarks or conversation: *I enjoy reading his books: he always scintillates (with) good ideas.|scintillating conversation* —**-lation** /ˌsɪntɪ̵ˈleɪʃən/ *n* [U]

sci·on /ˈsaɪən/ *n* **1** [C] a living part (usu. a young SHOOT) of a plant that is cut off, esp. for fixing (GRAFTing) onto another plant **2** [C9, esp. *of*] *lit* a young or most recent member (of a usu. noble or famous family)

scis·sor /ˈsɪzəʳ/ *v* [X9, esp. OUT, OFF] to cut (as) with scissors: *scissored the photograph out of the newspaper*

scis·sors /ˈsɪzəz‖-ərz/ *n* **1** [P] 2 sharp blades having handles at one end with holes for the fingers, fastened at the centre so that they open in the shape of the letter X and cut when they close: *I need scissors|some scissors|a pair of scissors* —compare SHEARS; see PAIR (USAGE) **2** [S] a movement of the body in certain sports, as **a** (in WRESTLING) a hold in which a person locks his legs around his opponent **b** (in HIGH JUMPing) a way of jumping in which the leg nearest the bar goes over first **3 scissors-and-paste** *infml & derog* of or being writing put together from pieces of other writings: *nothing new in the book, just a scissors-and-paste job*

scle·ro·sis /sklɪ̵ˈrəʊsɪ̵s/ *n* **-ses** /siːz/ [U;C] *med* (a) hardening of some usu. soft organ or part of the body —see also ARTERIOSCLEROSIS, MULTIPLE SCLEROSIS

scoff[1] /skɒf‖skɔf, skɑf/ *n* **1** [C *usu. pl.*] a SCOFFing[2] remark **2** [(*the*) S] and object of SCOFFing[2]: *ideas which were the scoff of the scientific world*

scoff[2] *v* [IØ(*at*)] to speak or act disrespectfully; laugh (at); RIDICULE[2]: *I came to the meeting to scoff but the speech persuaded me to listen* —**~er** *n* [*usu. pl.*]

scoff[3] *v* [T1 (UP)] *infml* to eat eagerly and fast: *The* *dog scoffed the plate of food with a few movements of its tongue*

scold¹ /skəʊld/ *n* [*usu. sing.*] a person, typically a woman, who scolds

scold² *v* [I∅ (*at*); T1] to speak in an angry and complaining way (to (someone)), esp. to blame: *Our neighbours are always making a noise, scolding their children.|I hate to scold (at you), son, but you mustn't stay out so late at night!* —~**ing** *n* [C;U]

scol·lop /ˈskɒləp‖ˈskɑ-/ *n, v* SCALLOP

sconce /skɒns‖skɑns/ *n* a usu. fancy holder which may be fixed to a wall, for 1 or more candles or electric lights

scone /skɒn, skəʊn‖skəʊn, skɑn/ (*AmE* **biscuit**)— *n* a soft usu. round breadlike cake of a size for one person, made of flour, salt, milk, fat, and sometimes sugar, dried fruit, etc., and baked

scoop¹ /skuːp/ *n* **1** [C] any of various containers or tools for holding and moving liquids or loose materials, as **a** a small deep SHOVEL-shaped tool held in the hand for digging out corn, flour, etc.: *a kitchen scoop|a measuring scoop* **b** a deep round spoon for dipping out soft food: *an ice-cream scoop* **c** a container for loose things weighed on scales **d** the bucket on an earth-moving machine **e** also **scoopful** /ˈskuːpfʊl/— the amount held by any of these: *2 scoops of ice cream* **2** [C] an action of taking (as) with one of these: *made a scoop with her hand and picked up what she had dropped* **3** [C] *not fml* a usu. exciting news report made by a newspaper before any other newspapers —compare EXCLUSIVE² (1) **4** [S] *infml* a successful piece of business, esp. one done by acting faster than others **5** [C] a FUNNEL-shaped opening at the front of some cars for air to enter the engine

scoop² *v* **1** [X9, esp. UP, OUT, *out of*] to take up or out, or make, (as) with a SCOOP¹ (1,5): *scoop up a handful of sand|scoop out some sugar from the bag|scoop some sugar out of the bag|He scooped his books up off the floor* **2** [T1] *not fml* (of a newspaper) to make a news report before (another newspaper): *The "News" scooped the other newspapers with an early report on the Australian election* **3** [T1] *infml* to win against, esp. by being faster; BEAT¹ (7): *scooped the other companies by making a good offer for the contract* **4** [I∅] *infml* (of a singer) to go from one note to another by singing all the notes in between, producing an unpleasant sliding sound

scoot /skuːt/ *v* [I∅ (UP, DOWN, AWAY, etc.); X9] *infml* to (cause to) move quickly and suddenly: *Here's the bus; you'll have to scoot if you want to catch it!*

scoot·er /ˈskuːtəʳ/ *n* **1** a child's vehicle with 2 small wheels, an upright handle fixed to the front wheel, and a narrow board for one foot, pushed by the other foot touching the ground **2** MOTOR SCOOTER —see BICYCLE (USAGE)

scope¹ /skəʊp/ *n* [U] **1** the area within the limits of a question, subject, action, etc.; RANGE¹ (7): *The politics of a country would be outside the scope of a book for tourists* **2** [(*for*)] space or chance for action or thought: *There's not much scope for selling coal in tropical countries*

scope² *n infml* any of various instruments for seeing, esp. a TELESCOPE, microscope, or PERISCOPE

scor·bu·tic /skɔːˈbjuːtɪk‖-ɔr-/ *adj* [Wa5] *tech* of, concerning, or having SCURVY

scorch¹ /skɔːtʃ‖-ɔr-/ *v* **1** [T1;I∅] **a** to burn (part of) a surface so as to change its colour, taste, or feeling but not completely destroy it: *scorch a shirt with an iron that's too hot|The meat was black and scorched on the outside but still raw inside* **b** (of such a surface) to burn in this way: *The meat is likely to scorch if you leave it cooking too long* **2** [T1] to dry up and take the life out of (plants) with a strong dry heat: *fields scorched by the hot summer sun* **3** [L9] *infml* to travel very fast: *The car scorched down the road at 90 miles an hour*

scorch² *n* **1** [C] a SCORCHed place; mark made by burning on a surface **2** [U] the appearance of SCORCHing produced by some plant diseases: *a plant suffering from scorch*

scorched earth /ˌ· ˈ·/ *n* [U] the destruction by an army of all useful things, esp. crops, in an area before leaving it to an advancing enemy (esp. in the phr. **scorched earth policy**)

scorch·er /ˈskɔːtʃəʳ‖-ɔr-/ *n* [S] **1** *infml* a very hot day **2** *sl* something which seems to SCORCH in being very exciting, angry, fast, powerful, etc.: *the best tennis match of the year, a real scorcher|a hard-hit ball, a scorcher his opponent couldn't handle*

scorch·ing /ˈskɔːtʃɪŋ‖-ɔr-/ *adj* **1** that SCORCHes: *scorching heat* **2** *not fml* very angry and powerful; SCATHING

score¹ /skɔːʳ‖skor/ *n* **1** the number of points, runs, GOALs (3), etc., made by opponents in a game, competition, sport, etc.: *The score stood at/was 2 to 1 with a minute left in the game* **2** [*usu. sing.*] one of these points, GOALs (3), etc.: *made a score in the last minute of the game* **3** a total of points won esp. in an examination: *a hard test in which the class all made low scores|a perfect score, 100 out of 100* **4** [(*off, against*)] *not fml* a successful and clever remark or action, esp. in an argument: *He couldn't make a score off his opponent, who seemed to know all his arguments already* **5** also **score mark** /ˈ· ·/— a line made or cut on a surface with a sharp instrument: *scores on the floor where a chair had been moved across it* **6** [*usu. sing.*] a reason; account (esp. in the phrs. **on this/that score, on the score of**): *On the score of money, don't worry; we have enough.|It's not the colour I wanted but it's no less pretty on that score* **7** *now rare* a bill or amount to be paid, as in a restaurant: *left early, leaving his friends to pay the score* **8** an old disagreement or hurt kept in mind; GRUDGE² (1): *I've got a score to settle with him* (=I want to make sure he is punished) **9 a** a written copy of a piece of music, esp. for a large group of performers: *a full score* (= showing all the parts in separate lines on the page)|*a* VOCAL *score* (=showing only the singers' parts) **b** a long piece or group of pieces of music for a film or play: *There were some good songs in that film: Who wrote the score?* **10 know the score** *infml* to understand the true and usu. unfavourable facts of a matter —see also RUN UP **a score**

score² *v* **1** [I∅;T1] to gain (one or more points, GOALs (2), etc.) in a sport, game, or competition: *scored 3 points/times in the last half of the game|score a* CENTURY *in cricket* **2** [D1 (*for, to*); (T1)] to give (a certain number of points) to (someone) in a sport, game, or competition: *The East German judge scored him 15/scored 15 to/for him.|What did the West German judge score?* **3** [I∅] to keep an official record of the SCORE¹ (1) of a sports match as it is played **4** [L9;T1] to win (a total of points) in an examination: *scored high/scored well on the test* **5** [I∅;T1] to gain or win (a success, victory, prize, etc.): *The bomb scored a hit on the railway bridge.|This writer has scored again with another popular book* **6** [L9;X9: (*off, against, over*)] to make (a clever and successful point), esp. in an argument against someone: *I hate conversations where people try to score (points) off each other* **7** [T1] to mark or cut 1 or more lines (as) with a sharp instrument: *score the paper to make it easy to fold|score the meat with a knife before cooking it* **8** [T1] *AmE, not fml* to scold; blame; BERATE: *He was scored by the newspapers for his unpopular opinions*

9 [I∅ (*with*)] *sl* (of a man) to have sex with a woman

score³ *determiner, n* **score** *or* **scores** [see NUMBER TABLE 4C] **1** (*often in comb.*) (a group of) 20: THREE*score or* THREE *score* (=60) **2 scores (and scores) (of)** large numbers (of); numbers (of) which are larger than DOZEN*s* but smaller than HUNDRED*s*: *scores of people, perhaps 80 or more* **3 three score years and ten** 70 years (a desirable length of life, according to the Bible)

score·board /ˈskɔːbɔːd‖ˈskorbord/ *n* a sign on which the SCORE¹ (1) of a game is recorded as it is played

score·book /ˈskɔːbʊk‖ˈskor-/ *n* a book in which the SCORE¹ (1) of a game, esp. cricket, is recorded as it is played

score·card /ˈskɔːkɑːd‖ˈskorkɑrd/ *n* a printed card used by someone watching a sports match, race, etc., to record what happens in it

score for *v prep* [D1 *usu. pass.*] to write (a piece of music) to be performed by (particular kinds of performers): *a piece scored for full* ORCHESTRA| *scored for 2 pianos*

score·keep·er /ˈskɔːˌkiːpəʳ‖ˈskor-/ *n* SCORER (1)

score·less /ˈskɔːləs‖ˈskor-/ *adj* [Wa5] (*used esp. in newspapers and broadcasting*) (of a sports match) without any points; with the SCORE¹ (1) of 0-0

score out also **score through**— *v adv* [T1] *fml* to draw a line through (one or more written words) to show that they should not be read; CROSS OUT

scor·er /ˈskɔːrəʳ‖ˈskorər/ *n* **1** a person who keeps the official record of a sports match and its SCORE¹ (1) as it is played **2** a player who scores points, GOAL*s*, etc.

scorn¹ /skɔːn‖skorn/ *n* **1** [U] strong, usu. angry feeling of disrespect; CONTEMPT **2** [*the*+S9, esp *of*] an object of such a feeling: *a small weak child, the scorn of its brothers* **3 laugh someone/something to scorn** also **pour scorn on**— *lit* to express scorn for; treat with scorn —**~ful** *adj* —**~fully** *adv*

scorn² *v usu. lit* **1** [T1,3,4] to refuse because of pride as something not worthy: *scorn offers of help* **2** [T1] to feel SCORN¹ (1) for: *He seemed to scorn women, and never married*

Scor·pi·o /ˈskɔːpiəʊ‖-ɔr-/ *n* **-os** **1** [R] **a** the ancient sign, a type of insect (SCORPION), representing the 8th division of the ZODIAC belt of stars **b** the group of stars (CONSTELLATION) formerly in this division **2** [C] a person born under the influence of this sign —see picture at PLANET

scor·pi·on /ˈskɔːpɪən‖-ɔr-/ *n* any of several types of tropical insect having a long body and curving tail which stings poisonously —see picture at ARACHNID

scotch /skɒtʃ‖skɑtʃ/ *v* [T1] **1** to take strong action to stop; put an end to: *scotch a false story by giving a true report of the facts* **2** to wound but not kill: *scotch a snake*

Scotch *n* **1** [U] also (*fml*) **Scotch whis·ky** /ˌ· ˈ··/— a type of strong alcoholic drink (WHISKY) made in Scotland **2** [C] a glass of this

Scotch broth /ˌ· ˈ·/ *n* [U] thick soup made from vegetables, BEEF¹ (1), or MUTTON, and BARLEY

Scotch egg /ˌ· ˈ·/ *n BrE* a dish made from a boiled egg cooked inside a covering of SAUSAGE meat

Scotch mist /ˌ· ˈ·/ *n* [C;U] a type of thick mist mixed with light rain

scotch tape /ˌ· ˈ·, ˈ· ·/ *n, v AmE tdmk* (*sometimes cap.* S) SELLOTAPE

Scotch wood·cock /ˌ· ˈ··/ *n* [U] a dish made of eggs beaten and cooked usu. with butter and milk (SCRAMBLED) served on a piece of TOASTED¹ (1) bread on which a fish (ANCHOVY) paste has been spread

scot-free /ˌ· ˈ·/ *adj* [Wa5;F] *infml* without harm or esp. punishment (esp. in such phrs. as **get off/escape/go scot-free**): *The man got off scot-free when the charges against him couldn't be proved in court*

Scot·land Yard /ˌskɒtlənd ˈjɑːd‖ˌskɑtlənd ˈjɑrd/ *n* [GU] (the main office of) the London police and esp. the division dealing with serious or difficult cases of crime

Scot·tish /ˈskɒtɪʃ‖ˈskɑtɪʃ/ also **Scots** /skɒts‖skɑts/, **Scotch**— *adj* **1** [Wa5] of, being, concerning, or typical of Scotland, its people, or English as spoken there **2** *taboo or humor* not liking to spend money; STINGY: *I asked for a pin, and she said she'd lend me one. How very Scottish of her!*

USAGE *Scotch* is sometimes, esp. in Scotland, regarded as *derog*, but it is often used without any such idea, esp. of the products of Scotland (as *Scotch wool*). *Scottish* and *Scots* are rather polite. *Scots* is usu. only of people (*a Scots lawyer|a Scottish plant*).

Scottish ter·ri·er /ˌ·· ˈ···/ *n* a type of small dog (TERRIER) with short legs and tail and wirelike hair

scoun·drel /ˈskaʊndrəl/ *n* [C;*you*+N] a wicked, esp. bold and selfish, man; VILLAIN (4): *What a scoundrel, to go away and leave his wife and 3 children!*

scoun·drel·ly /ˈskaʊndrəli/ *adj lit & pomp* (as) of or being a SCOUNDREL

scour¹ /skaʊəʳ/ *v* **1** [T1 (*for*)] to go through (an area) thoroughly in search of something **2** [L9 (ABOUT), esp. *after, for*] to hurry in search of something: *dogs scouring through the field after the rabbit*

scour² *v* **1** [T1 (DOWN, OUT)] to clean (a surface) by hard rubbing with a rough material: *scour down the walls with a stiff brush|scour out a dirty pan* **2** [X9, esp. *from, off,* OUT] to remove (dirt, oil, etc.) in this way: *scour off the dirt from the floor* **3** [T1 (OUT)] (of a stream of water) to form by wearing or washing away: *Water had scoured out a passage in the soft sand*

scour³ *n* [S] an act of SCOURing² (1)

scour·er /ˈskaʊərəʳ/ *n* a tool, esp. a small ball of plastic wire or net, for cleaning cooking pots and pans

scourge¹ /skɜːdʒ‖-ɜr-/ *n* **1** a whip used formerly for punishment **2** a cause of great punishment, harm, or suffering: *the scourge of war|Eye diseases have always been a scourge in tropical countries*

scourge² *v* [T1] **1** to beat with a whip **2** *lit* to punish **3** to cause great harm or suffering to: *a country scourged by disease and war*

scout¹ /skaʊt/ *v* **1** [L9, esp. AROUND, ABOUT, *for*] to go looking for something: *Scout around for a shop that's open late* **2** [T1 (OUT, *for*)] to go through or look carefully at (a place) to get information about it: *scout (out) the area to look for water*

scout² *n* **1** [C] a soldier sent out to search the land ahead of an army, esp. for information about the enemy **2** [C] a person who gets information for a sports team about young players who should be hired **3** [C] also **talent scout**— a person who visits small shows, plays, etc. to look for young actors, singers, etc. for more important places **4** [C] **a** BOY SCOUT **b** *AmE* GIRL SCOUT **5** [C] a servant at Oxford University who looks after students living in college rooms —compare GYP **6** [S (AROUND, *BrE* ROUND)] an act of SCOUTing: *took a scout round to see what he could see* **7 good scout** *infml* a helpful dependable person: *I'll ask Mary to help, she's a good scout*

scout·mas·ter /ˈskaʊtˌmɑːstəʳ‖-ˌmæ-/ *n* a grown-up leader of a group of BOY SCOUT*s*

scout out *v adv* [T1] to find by SCOUTing: *scouted out the enemy force only 3 miles away*

scow /skaʊ/ *n* a large boat with a flat bottom and square ends, used for carrying sand, rock, and waste materials

scowl¹ /skaʊl/ *v* **1** [IØ (*at*)] to make a SCOWL on one's face; FROWN¹ (1) angrily **2** [T1] to express in this way: *He scowled his displeasure*

scowl² *n* an angry threatening expression of the face; angry FROWN¹ (1)

scrab·ble¹ /ˈskræbəl/ *v* [IØ (ABOUT)] *infml* to move wildly and quickly (as if) looking for something; FUMBLE (1); SCRAMBLE¹ (1): *scrabbled about on the floor picking up the coins she'd dropped*

scrabble² *n* [S] *infml* SCRAMBLE² (1,2)

Scrabble *n* [R] *tdmk* a game in which players make points by putting rows of separate letters on the squares of a board to form words

scrag¹ /skræg/ also **scrag end** /ˌ· ˈ·/— *n* [U;C] the bony part of a sheep's neck, used usu. for boiling to make STEW or soup

scrag² *v* **-gg-** [T1] **1** to kill by twisting the neck (as of an animal) **2** *infml* to handle roughly by the neck

scrag·gly /ˈskrægəli/ *adj* [Wa1] *infml AmE* (esp. of things that grow) poor and uneven-looking; badly grown

scrag·gy /ˈskrægi/ *adj* [Wa1] thin and bony; SCRAWNY

scram /skræm/ *v* **-mm-** [IØ] *sl* to get away fast; run away: *You're not wanted here, so scram!|Let's scram!*

scram·ble¹ /ˈskræmbəl/ *v* **1** [L9] to move or climb quickly, esp. over a rough or steep surface: *I scrambled up the rock for a better look at the sea* **2** [I3;L9, esp. *for*] to struggle or compete with others eagerly or against difficulty: *people scrambling for shelter/scrambling to get out of the way* **3** [Wa5;T1] to mix together without order; JUMBLE: *He stood looking at the scrambled pages of his speech and didn't know where to begin* **4** [Wa5;T1] to mix the white and yellow parts of (1 or more eggs) together while cooking them **5** [Wa5;T1] to change the order of the signals in (a radio or telephone message) with a machine (a **scrambler**) so that it cannot be understood without being received on a special instrument

scramble² *n* **1** [S] an act of moving or climbing, esp. over a rough surface: *It's quite a scramble to get to the top of the hill* **2** [S] an eager and disorderly struggle: *a scramble for the best seats* **3** [C] a MOTORCYCLE race over very rough ground

scrap¹ /skræp/ *n* **1** [C] a small piece; bit: *a scrap of paper|scraps of news|*(fig.) *not a scrap of truth in what he says* **2** [U] material which cannot be used for its original purpose but which may have some value: *sold his car for scrap/for its scrap value* (=as metal to be used again) —see also SCRAPS, SCRAP PAPER

scrap² *v* **-pp-** [T1] **1** to get rid of as no longer useful or wanted; DISCARD¹ (1) **2** to make into SCRAP¹ (2)

scrap³ *n infml* a usu. sudden, short, not serious fight or quarrel

scrap⁴ *v* **-pp-** [IØ (*with*)] *infml* to quarrel or fight

scrap·book /ˈskræpbʊk/ *n* a book of empty pages in which a collection of photographs, newspaper articles, etc., is/may be fastened

scrape¹ /skreɪp/ *v* **1** [X9] to remove (material) from a surface by pulling or pushing an edge firmly across it repeatedly: *I scraped the mud from my boots.|I scraped the skin off the vegetables* **2** [T1 (DOWN); X7] to clean or make (a surface) smooth in this way: *She scraped the door (down) before painting it again.|He scraped his boots clean before coming in the house* **3** [L9, esp. *on, against*; T1 (*on, against*)] to (cause to) rub roughly: *a chair scraping on the floor|He scraped his chair against the wall* **4** [T1] to hurt or damage in this way: *He scraped his knee when he fell* **5** [T1 (OUT)] to make in this way: *She scraped (out) a hollow place in the ground* **6** [L9, esp. ALONG, BY, THROUGH, *through*] **a** live, keep a business, etc., with no more than the necessary money: *scraping by on very small wages* **b** to succeed in a class by doing work of the lowest acceptable quality: *She just scraped through the examination by one mark* **7 scrape a living** to get just enough food or money to stay alive **8 scrape the bottom of the barrel** *infml* to take, use, suggest, etc., something of the lowest quality: *Is he the best speaker they could get for the meeting? This time they've really scraped the bottom of the barrel!* —see also BOW¹ (5) **and scrape**

scrape² *n* **1** an act or sound of scraping (SCRAPE) **2** a hurt made by scraping (SCRAPE): *suffered a few cuts and scrapes* **3** *infml* an unpleasant position or affair, esp. caused by one's breaking a rule: *She got into a scrape with the police for parking her car in the middle of the road*

scrap·er /ˈskreɪpəʳ/ *n* a tool for scraping (SCRAPE¹ (1,2)), such as: **a** a fixed metal edge near the front door of a house for removing mud, snow, etc., from shoes —see picture at DOOR **b** a kitchen tool with a rubber blade for removing food from the sides of a bowl **c** a tool with a sharp metal blade for removing paint

scrape up also **scrape to·geth·er**— *v adv* [T1] *not fml* to gather (a total, esp. of money) with difficulty by putting small amounts together

scrap heap /ˈ· ·/ *n* **1** [C] a pile of waste material, esp. metal **2** [*the*+R] the place regarded as where unwanted things, people, or ideas go: *Put that plan on the scrap heap: it'll never work*

scrap·ings /ˈskreɪpɪŋz/ *n* [P] things (to be) SCRAPED¹ (1,2) from a surface: *scrapings taken from the paint for chemical tests*

scrap pa·per /ˈ· ˌ··/ *n* [U] **1** *AmE* usu. **scratch paper**— paper, esp. in small sheets already used on one side, which may be used for informal notes **2** waste paper which is sold and used in making new paper

scrap·py¹ /ˈskræpi/ *adj* [Wa1] *not fml* (appearing to be) made of small pieces; not well arranged or planned: *a scrappy, badly-written report*

scrappy² *adj* [Wa1] *AmE infml* liking to fight; SPIRITED

scraps /skræps/ *n* [P] pieces of food not eaten at a meal, and thrown away

scratch¹ /skrætʃ/ *v* **1** [T1;IØ] to rub and tear or mark (a surface) with something pointed or rough, as with CLAWs or FINGERNAILs: *Careful of the cat: he'll scratch (you)!|an accident in which the table top was scratched* **2** [IØ (ABOUT)] to make a sound or movement as if doing this: *a dog scratching at the door to be let in|chickens scratching (about) on the ground* **3** [X9, esp. *off*] to remove in this way: *scratched the paint off the wall|*(fig.) *scratched my name off/from the list* **4** [T1] to hurt in this way: *scratched her elbow on the point of a nail* **5** [T1] to write or make in this way: *scratched his name on the tree with a knife* **6** [T1;(IØ)] to rub lightly (a part of the body) as to stop ITCHing¹ (1): *The cat likes to be scratched behind its ears.|He scratched the place where he had been bitten by an insect* **7** [IØ;T1] to remove (oneself, a horse, etc.) from a race or competition before it starts: *The horse (was) scratched on the day before the race* **8** [IØ] (in BILLIARDS) to make a SCRATCH² (4) **9 scratch a living** to SCRAPE¹ (7) a living **10 scratch the surface** *not fml* to deal with only the beginning of a matter or only a few of many cases

scratch² *n* **1** [C] a mark or INJURY made by

SCRATCHing[1] (1): *a scratch on the table top made by her ring|got a few cuts and scratches from the accident* **2** [C] a sound (as if) made by SCRATCHing[1] (2): *a poor recording with the music spoiled by scratches* **3** [S] an act of SCRATCHing[1] (6): *a dog having a scratch* (=SCRATCHing itself with a back leg) **4** [C] (in BILLIARD*s*) a shot which results in a player having points given to his opponent **5** [C] a person, horse, etc., that SCRATCHes[1] (7) **6** [A] (in GOLF, of a very good player) having a HANDICAP[1] (2) of zero **7** [A] made or put together in a hurry using whatever could be found: *just time for a scratch meal before we have to catch the train|a scratch cricket team* **8** [U] *AmE sl* money **9 from scratch** *infml* starting from zero or with nothing **10 up to scratch** *infml* in(to) good condition or at/to an acceptable standard: *The piano player was not feeling well and his performance wasn't up to scratch* **11 without a scratch** *infml* without even the smallest amount of hurt or damage

scratch out *v adv* [T1] *not fml* to make marks over (something already written) to show that it should not be read —compare CROSS OUT

scratch·pad /ˈskrætʃpæd/ *n esp. AmE* a small pile of loosely joined sheets of paper (PAD) for writing informal notes

scratch pa·per /ˈ· ˌ··/ *n* [U] *AmE* SCRAP PAPER (1)

scratch up *v adv* [T1] *infml* SCRAPE UP

scratch·y /ˈskrætʃi/ *adj* [Wa1] **1** (of writing) (as if) made by SCRATCHing[1] (5); badly written: *What's her name? I can't read this scratchy signature* **2** (of a recording or its sound) marked by SCRATCHes[2] (1,2) **3** (of clothes) hot, rough, and pricking —**scratchiness** *n* [U]

scrawl[1] /skrɔːl/ *v* [T1] to write in a careless, irregular, awkward, or unskilful way

scrawl[2] *n* **1** [C *usu. sing.*] something written awkwardly, or fast and carelessly: *just a scrawl on a card to say she was having a good time* **2** [S] an awkward or irregular way of writing: *This letter must be from Frank: I recognize his scrawl*

scraw·ny /ˈskrɔːni/ *adj* [Wa1] *derog* (of people, animals, or parts of the body) without much flesh on the bones; thin; LEAN[3] (1)

scream[1] /skriːm/ *v* **1** [I∅] to cry out loudly on a high note, as in fear, pain, great excitement or anger, or sometimes laughter: *scream for help|screamed with laughter at the good joke*|(fig.) *The wind screamed down the chimney* **2** [T1,5: (OUT)] to say or express in this way: *He screamed (out) a warning not to touch the electric wire* **3** [T1,5: (OUT); (I∅)] to draw attention, as by such a cry (to): *The newspapers screamed (out) the news in large letters* **4** [I∅;3] to make a loud noise of anger, complaint, demand, etc.; CLAMOUR: *screaming about the loss of powers under the new law*

scream[2] *n* **1** [C] a sudden loud cry expressing anger, pain, fear, or sometimes laughter: *Her loud screams could be heard all over the house.*|(fig.) *the scream of the big electric* SAW *as it cut the log* **2** [S] *sl* a very funny person, thing, joke, etc.: *She thought it was a scream when I fell off my chair, but I failed to see the joke*

scream·ing·ly /ˈskriːmɪŋli/ *adv* **screamingly funny** *not fml* causing loud laughter; very funny

scree /skriː/ *n* [U] a mass of small loose broken rocks on the side of a mountain —see picture at MOUNTAIN

screech[1] /skriːtʃ/ *v* [I∅;T1] **1** [(OUT)] to cry out on a very high sharp note, as in terror or pain: *"Leave me alone!" she screeched.|birds screeching in the trees* **2 a** (of machines, esp. of tyres and BRAKE*s*) to make a noise like this **b** to cause (BRAKE*s*) to make a noise like this **3 screech to a halt/standstill/stop** also **come to a screeching halt**— *infml* to stop very suddenly (as if) making this noise: *The work on the new house came to a screeching stop when the builder had used all the money*

screech[2] *n* a very high unpleasant sound (as) of SCREECHing: *The forest seemed full of monkeys' screeches.|A screech of* BRAKE*s made us look to see what had happened in the street*

screech owl /ˈ· ·/ *n* any of various kinds of common birds active at night (OWL*s*) whose cry is a SCREECH

screed /skriːd/ *n* [*often pl. with sing. meaning*] *not fml* a long and usu. dull speech or piece of writing

screen[1] /skriːn/ *n* **1** [C] any of various kinds of upright frames, sometimes made of folding parts, which are used as small usu. movable walls for dividing a room, protecting people from view, from cold air, or from SPARK*s*[1] (1) from a fire **2** [C] something that protects, shelters, or hides: *a screen of trees to keep out the wind|put on a smile as a screen for his anger* **3** [C] a large flat usu. cloth or plastic surface on which a cinema film is shown: *first appeared on the screen* (=acted in his first film) *10 years ago* —see picture at PHOTOGRAPHIC **4** [(*the*) R] *esp. pomp* the cinema industry or the making of cinema films: *a star* (=well-known performer) *of stage, screen* (=in plays and films), *and radio|a play written for the screen* (=to be shown as a film)|*a* **screen test** (=test of one's ability to act in films) **5** [C] the front surface of an electrical instrument showing information, esp. the surface of a television on which the picture appears **6** [C] a frame holding a fine wire net, put into a window to keep out insects when the window is open **7** [C] also **sightscreen**— (in cricket) either of 2 large movable white walls placed at the ends of the field to make it easier for players to see the ball **8** [C] a frame holding a net or surface with holes, used for separating large things, which do not pass through the holes, from small things, which do —see also WINDSCREEN, SMOKESCREEN, CHOIR SCREEN

screen[2] *v* [T1] **1** [(*from*)] to shelter or protect, as from light, wind, etc.: *He screened his eyes with his hand* **2** [(OFF, *from*)] to hide from view, (as) with a SCREEN (1): *His movements were screened by a large rock between him and the others.|Part of the room was screened off as a place for the new baby* **3** [(*from*)] to (try to) protect (someone) from harm or punishment: *He admitted the crime in order to screen his wife, who was the real criminal* **4** [*often pass.*] to examine or prove the ability or SUITABILITY of (people for a job, requests to be allowed to do something, etc.): *100 carefully screened people were invited to have dinner with the President* **5** to provide (a window, room, etc.) with 1 or more SCREEN*s* (6): *windows screened to keep out insects* **6** [*usu. pass.*] to show (a film) for a group of people to see: *a new film, first screened only last year*

screen·ing /ˈskriːnɪŋ/ *n* [U;C] a/the showing of a film: *a new film, ready for screening next year*

screen out *v adv* [T1] **1** to stop coming through by a covering or SCREEN[1] (1,2): *The curtains screen out the sunlight* **2** to get rid of (an unsuitable person, request, etc.) by SCREENing[2] (4): *a test to screen out people who would not do the job well*

screen·play /ˈskriːnpleɪ/ *n* a story written in a form suitable for its production as a film

screw[1] /skruː/ *n* **1** [C] a usu. metal pin having a head usu. with a cut (SLOT) straight across it, often a point at the other end, and a raised edge (THREAD[1] (4)) going round and round it, so that when twisted and pressed (usu. with a SCREWDRIVER) into a material it holds firmly and can fasten the material to something else —see also THUMBSCREW, CORKSCREW and picture at MACHINERY **2**

[C] an act of turning one of these; turn: *gave it another screw to tighten it* **3** [C] a PROPELLER, esp. on a ship —see picture at FREIGHTER **4** [C] *sl* (used by prisoners) a prison guard **5** [C (*of*)] *BrE* **a** a small twisted piece (of paper) **b** the amount contained by one of these **6** [U] *BrE sl* pay; wages **7** [C] *BrE infml* a weak old horse **8** [C] *BrE infml* SCROOGE **9 a screw loose** *humor* something wrong or not working properly (esp. in one's mind): *He's got a screw loose* (=is slightly mad) **10 put the screws on/to someone** *sl* to force someone to do as one wishes, esp. by threatening

screw² *v* **1** [X9] to fasten with 1 or more screws: *The table legs are screwed to the top.|screw a lock on the door* **2** [X9;L9] **a** to turn or tighten (a screw or something that moves in the same way): *Screw the 2 pipes together end to end* **b** (of such a thing) to turn or tighten: *The 2 pieces screw together* **3** [X9, esp. UP] to twist **a** (a part of the face), as to express disapproval or uncertainty: *She screwed up her eyes to try to read the sign* **b** (paper or cloth) carelessly or to make a ball; WAD¹ (2) **4** [X9, esp. *out of*] to get by forcing or twisting or by great effort or threats: *He screwed the others out of their fair shares* **5** [T1 *often pass.*] *sl* to cheat; take something unfairly from; deal unfairly with (someone): *I'm afraid you got screwed, friend* **6** [I∅;T1] *taboo sl* **a** (of 2 people) to have sex **b** (esp. of a man) to have sex with (someone) **7 have one's head screwed on (right)** to be sensible; do nothing foolish

screw·ball /ˈskruːbɔːl/ *n* **1** (in BASEBALL) a throw (PITCH² (4)) which spins and curves in the opposite direction to a CURVE² (2) **2** *infml, esp. AmE* a person whose ideas or actions seem wild or mad, usu. in a harmless way

screw·driv·er /ˈskruːˌdraɪvəʳ/ *n* a tool with a narrow blade at one end which fits into the cut (SLOT) in the heads of SCREWs¹ (1) for turning them into and out of their places —see picture at TOOL¹

screw top /ˌ· ˈ·/ *n* **1** a cover which is made to be twisted tightly onto the top of a bottle or other container **2** an opening of a container made for such a cover to twist onto

screw up *v adv* **1** [T1 *usu. pass.*] *sl* to turn into disorder; MESS UP: *Things are screwed up, as usual* **2 screw up one's courage** to stop oneself from being afraid

screw·y /ˈskruːi/ *adj* [Wa1] *infml* (esp. of ideas and people) seeming unusual, strange, and often funny or annoying; CRAZY (1,2): *lots of mad ideas, each one screwier than the last|Something has gone screwy in my calculation: this can't be the right answer*

scrib·ble¹ /ˈskrɪbəl/ *v* **1** [I∅;T1] to write (meaningless marks): *The child can't write yet but she loves to scribble with a pencil* **2** [T1] to write carelessly or in a hurry (usu. something that is hard to read)

scribble² *n* **1** [C *often pl. with sing. meaning*] a meaningless written marking **2** [S;U] (a way of) writing which is careless and hard to read: *His writing is nothing but (a) scribble*

scrib·bler /ˈskrɪbləʳ/ *n derog & humor* a writer

scribe¹ /skraɪb/ *n* **1** a person employed to copy things in writing, esp. in times before the invention of printing **2** (*usu. cap.*) a Jewish non-priestly religious teacher and lawyer before and during the time of Jesus

scribe² *v* [T1] to mark (a line) on (wood or metal) by cutting into the surface, esp. with a pointed metal tool (**scriber**)

scrim·mage¹ /ˈskrɪmɪdʒ/ *n* **1** a disorderly fight between 2 or usu. more people **2** (in American football) a practice game among members of a team **3** *now rare* SCRUM (2)

scrimmage² *v* [I∅] to take part in a SCRIMMAGE¹ (1,2)

scrimp /skrɪmp/ *v* [I∅;T1] **1** to save (money) slowly and with difficulty, esp. by living poorly: *She had to* **scrimp and save** *to pay for her holiday* **2** SKIMP

scrim·shank /ˈskrɪmʃæŋk/ *v* [I∅] *BrE sl, becoming rare* to try to avoid doing the jobs one is supposed to be doing —**~er** *n*

scrim·shaw /ˈskrɪmʃɔː/ *n* [U] careful work with a knife in cutting shapes in and ornamenting pieces of bone, IVORY, etc., done by sailors on long sea voyages

scrip /skrɪp/ *n* [U] any of various kinds of paper which allow the holder to get something, esp. paper printed for use as money in certain shops, at certain times, etc.

script /skrɪpt/ *n* **1** [U] (way of) writing done by hand, esp. as in English with the letters of words joined **2** [C9;U9] the set of letters used in writing a language; ALPHABET: *words printed in Arabic script* **3** [C] a written form of a speech, play, or broadcast to be spoken **4** [C *usu. pl.*] *BrE* a piece of writing done by a student in an examination, to be read and given a mark by a teacher

script·ed /ˈskrɪptɨd/ *adj* [Wa5] (esp. of a speech or broadcast) having, or read from, a SCRIPT (3)

scrip·tur·al /ˈskrɪptʃərəl/ *adj* [Wa5] (*sometimes cap.*) of, found in, or according to a holy writing, esp. the Bible

scrip·ture /ˈskrɪptʃəʳ/ *n* **1** [U; *the*+P] (*usu. cap.*) (used by Christians) the Bible **2** [C] (*sometimes cap.*) a statement in the Bible **3** [U9 *usu. pl. with sing. meaning*] the holy books of a religion: *Buddhist scriptures*

script·writ·er /ˈskrɪptˌraɪtəʳ/ *n* a writer of plays or other material to be spoken on radio or television or in a film

scriv·en·er /ˈskrɪvənəʳ/ *n* **1** (in former times) a person who wrote letters for people who could not write **2** *obs* NOTARY

scrof·u·la /ˈskrɒfjʊlə‖ˈskrɔfjələ, ˈskrɑf-/ *n* [U] a disease in which organs in the neck become swollen

scrof·u·lous /ˈskrɒfjʊləs‖ˈskrɔfjələs, ˈskrɑf-/ *adj* [Wa5] of or suffering from SCROFULA

scroll /skrəʊl/ *n* **1** a long straight piece of animal skin, PAPYRUS (2), or (rarely) paper, often rolled around handles at 1 or both ends and used esp. in ancient times for writing books, records, and other formal writings **2** an ornament or shape with a curve like this (as often at the top of a pillar, at the end of the arm of a chair, or the end of a VIOLIN)

scroll·work /ˈskrəʊlwɜːk‖-wɜrk/ *n* [U] ornament marked by patterns with fancy curves

scrooge /skruːdʒ/ *n infml & derog* (*sometimes cap.*) MISER

scro·tum /ˈskrəʊtəm/ *n* **-ta** /tə/ *or* **-tums** *tech* the bag of flesh holding the TESTICLEs of male animals

scrounge /skraʊndʒ/ *v* **1** [T1] *often derog* to collect or get unofficially, without spending money, or by persuading others **2** [I∅ (AROUND)] to go looking for things: *scrounged around in people's desks looking for a pen* —**scrounger** *n*

scrub¹ /skrʌb/ *n* **1** [U] low-growing plants including bushes and short trees growing in poor soil and usu. forming a thick covering of the ground **2** [A] of small size and growing in such ways and places: *scrub* PINE|*scrub* OAK **3** [S9] *infml* a person of small size or importance; RUNT

scrub² *v* **-bb-** **1** [I∅;T1;X7] to clean by hard rubbing, as with a stiff brush: *scrubbed the floor clean|scrubbed the shirt to remove the spot* **2** [X9 esp. OUT] to remove in this way: *scrubbed the spot out|scrubbed the dirt off the floor* **3** [T1] to remove from consideration or from a list; CANCEL (1): *We've had to scrub our plans to go abroad this year; we've got no money* **4** [IØ;T1:(UP)] (of a doctor) to wash (the hands and arms) before doing an operation

scrub³ *n* [S] an act of SCRUBbing² (1,2): *Give that dirt/that floor a good hard scrub*

scrub·ber /ˈskrʌbəʳ/ *n BrE sl* **1** a woman who is too willing to have sex; woman whose sexual morals are considered socially unacceptable **2** PROSTITUTE

scrubbing brush /ˈ·· ·/ *AmE* usu. **scrub brush** /ˈ· ·/— *n* a stiff brush for heavy cleaning jobs (like SCRUBbing² (1,2) floors)

scrub·by /ˈskrʌbi/ *adj* [Wa1] **1** covered by, made of, or like SCRUB¹ (1,2) **2** (*infml & derog*) of small size or importance **3** SCRUFFY

scruff¹ /skrʌf/ *n* **the scruff of the neck** the flesh at the back of the neck

scruff² *n BrE infml* a dirty and untidy person

scruf·fy /ˈskrʌfi/ *adj* [Wa1] *not fml* dirty and untidy; SHABBY: *The hotel looked rather scruffy so we decided not to stay there*

scrum /skrʌm/ also (*fml*) **scrummage**— *n* **1** (in RUGBY) a group formed at certain times in the game by the front players (FORWARDs³) of both teams pushing against each other with heads down and shoulders together, to try to get the ball which is thrown onto the ground between them —see picture at RUGBY **2** *infml* a disorderly struggling crowd

scrum·cap /ˈskrʌmkæp/ *n* a tight-fitting head-covering worn by RUGBY players to protect the head and ears

scrum·half /ˌskrʌmˈhɑːf‖-ˈhæf/ *n* a player whose job is to put the ball into the SCRUM (1), and to pass it out quickly to other players

scrum·mage /ˈskrʌmɪdʒ/ *v* [IØ] (of a player or group of players) to take part in SCRUM (1)

scrump·tious /ˈskrʌmpʃəs/ *adj infml* (esp. of food) very fine; very DELICIOUS

scrum·py /ˈskrʌmpi/ *n* [U] a strong kind of alcoholic apple drink (CIDER) of South West England

scrunch¹ /skrʌntʃ/ *v not fml* **1** [T1] to crush; CRUNCH **2** [IØ] to make a sound/an action like this: *small loose rocks scrunching as we walked on them* **3** [T1 (UP)] to press into a ball in the hand; CRUMPLE

scrunch² *n* [S] *not fml* an act or sound of SCRUNCHing

scru·ple¹ /ˈskruːpəl/ *n fml* a measure of weight used for medicines, equal to 1·3 grams

scruple² *n* **1** [C *usu. pl. with sing. meaning*] a moral principle which keeps one from doing something; a doubt about the rightness of an action: *a man with no scruples, who will do anything to get what he wants* **2** [U] (*used esp. after words like* no *and* without) the desire to do what is right; conscience; SCRUPULOUSness: *acted wrongly and without scruple*

scruple³ *v* [I3;L9, esp. *about*: *usu. nonassertive*] to raise a moral argument against doing something; be unwilling because of SCRUPLEs² (1): *He wouldn't scruple to charge you much more than that table is worth, if he thought you'd pay*

scru·pu·lous /ˈskruːpjʊləs‖-pjə-/ *adj* **1** carefully doing only what is right; exactly honest; CONSCIENTIOUS: *A less scrupulous man wouldn't have given the money back to its owner* **2** correct even in the smallest detail; exact; PAINSTAKING (1): *The nurse treated the wound with the most scrupulous care* —**~ly** *adv* —**~ness** *n* [U]

scru·ti·neer /ˌskruːtəˈnɪəʳ/ *n BrE* an official examiner or counter of votes in an election

scru·ti·nize, -nise /ˈskruːtənaɪz/ *v* [T1] to give SCRUTINY to; examine closely

scru·ti·ny /ˈskruːtəni/ *n* **1** [U:(C)] (a) close study or look; (a) careful and thorough examination **2** [C] *BrE* an official re-counting of votes in an election

scu·ba /ˈskjuːbə‖ˈskuːbə/ *n* [A;(C)] an instrument used for breathing while swimming under water, made of 1 or more containers of air under pressure fastened to the back and connected by a rubber pipe to the mouth

scud¹ /skʌd/ *v* **-dd-** [IØ (*before*)] (esp. of clouds and ships) to move along quickly as if driven: *The boat scudded before the strong west wind*

scud² *n* **1** [C *often pl. with sing. meaning*] a fall of rain driven by the wind: *Scuds of rain beat down across the open street* **2** [U] light cloud driven by the wind **3** [S] an act of SCUDding; a rush

scuff¹ /skʌf/ *v* **1** [T1 (UP)] to make a rough mark or marks on the smooth surface of (shoes, furniture, a floor, etc.); SCRAPE¹ (3,4): *The floor was badly scuffed (up) where they had been dancing* **2** [IØ (UP)] (of shoes, floors, etc.) to be damaged in this way

scuff² also **scuff·mark** /ˈskʌfmɑːk‖-mark/— *n* a mark made by SCUFFing

scuf·fle¹ /ˈskʌfəl/ *v* [IØ] to be in a SCUFFLE²; fight: *a quarrel during the football match with players scuffling on the field*

scuffle² *n* a disorderly fight, usu. not serious or long

scull¹ /skʌl/ *n* **1** [C] either of a pair of short OARs (poles with blades) held and moved, one in each hand, by a person to row a boat **2** [C] a small light racing boat for 1 person rowing with a pair of these **3** [S] an act of rowing with these: *a scull on the lake*

scull² *v* [IØ;T1] to row (a boat) with SCULLs¹ (1) —**~er** *n*

scul·le·ry /ˈskʌləri/ *n* a room next to the kitchen, esp. in large or older house, for cleaning and keeping dishes and cooking pots, and for other rough cleaning jobs

scul·li·on /ˈskʌlɪən/ *n* (in former times) a boy doing cleaning work in a kitchen

sculp·tor /ˈskʌlptəʳ/ (*fem.* **sculp·tress** /-trəs/)— *n* an artist who makes works of SCULPTURE

sculp·tur·al /ˈskʌlptʃərəl/ *adj* of, concerning, or looking like SCULPTURE

sculp·ture¹ /ˈskʌlptʃəʳ/ *n* **1** [U] the art of shaping solid figures (as people or things) out of stone, wood, clay, metal, etc.: *to study sculpture as a class in art school* **2** [U;C] (a piece of) work produced by this art: *There's some interesting sculpture in this church*

sculpture² also **sculpt** /skʌlpt/— *v* **1** [Wv5;T1] to make by shaping: *sculptured pillars*|(fig.) *The water had sculptured the rocks into strange shapes* **2** [T1] to make a figure of (a person or thing) in SCULPTURE: *The king was sculpted by the artist over a period of several weeks* **3** [IØ] to make works of SCULPTURE: *tools for sculpturing in wood and clay*

scum /skʌm/ *n* **1** [U;S] a filmy covering that typically forms over a pool of still water **2** [U;S] impure or unwanted material in a liquid which rises and floats as a covering on the surface: *scum left on the shore by the waves* **3** [GU] *often taboo* worthless evil people: *He says people who are too lazy to work are* **the scum of the earth** (=the worst people in the world) **4** [*you*+N] a worthless evil person —**~my** *adj* [Wa2]

scup·per¹ /ˈskʌpəʳ/ *n usu. pl.* an opening in the side of a ship at the level of the DECK (upper floor) to allow water to run off it into the sea

scupper² *v* [T1] *BrE* **1** to sink (one's ship)

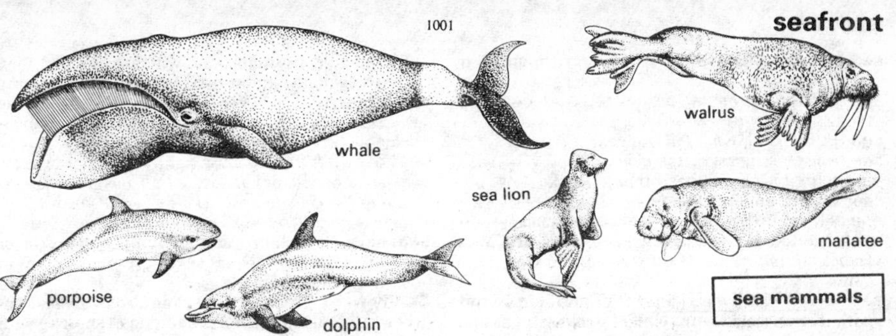

intentionally **2** [*usu. pass.*] *infml* to wreck or ruin (a plan)

scurf /skɜːf‖skɜrf/ *n* [U] dead skin in small dry bits (such as DANDRUFF in the hair) that loosen and come away from the skin underneath —**~y** *adj*

scur·ril·i·ty /skəˈrɪlə̇ti, skʌ-/ *n* [U] **1** SCURRILOUSness **2** SCURRILOUS language

scur·ri·lous /ˈskʌrə̇ləs/ *adj* making or containing very low, rude, improper, or evil statements; VULGAR (2): *a scurrilous attack in writing* —**~ly** *adv* —**~ness** [U]

scur·ry¹ /ˈskʌri/ *v* [L9] to move in haste, esp. with short quick steps; hurry: *The mouse scurried into its hole when the cat appeared*

scurry² *n* [(*the*) S,S3] a movement or esp. sound of SCURRYing: *heard the scurry of feet in the hall*

scur·vy¹ /ˈskɜːvi‖-ɜr-/ *adj* [Wa2;A] *not fml* dishonourable; deserving no respect; UNWORTHY; MEAN¹ (1,2): *What a scurvy trick to let your friend take the blame for your mistake!* —**scurvily** *adv*

scurvy² *n* [U] a disease (formerly common among sailors) which results in bleeding and caused by not eating fruit and vegetables (with VITAMIN C) —see also SCORBUTIC

scut /skʌt/ *n* the short upright tail of some animals, like the rabbit and deer

scutch·eon /ˈskʌtʃən/ *n* ESCUTCHEON

scut·tle¹ /ˈskʌtl/ *n* COALSCUTTLE

scuttle² *n* a small opening with a movable tight cover in the DECK (upper floor), outside, or bottom of a ship

scuttle³ *v* [T1] to sink (a ship, esp. one's own) by making holes in the bottom

scuttle⁴ *v* [L9] to rush in short quick movements, esp. to escape; SCURRY: *The children scuttled off/away when they saw the policeman*

scuttle⁵ *n* [S] an act of rushing away

Scyl·la /ˈsɪlə/ *n* **Scylla and Charybdis** *lit* a pair of dangers, of which a person may run into one by trying to avoid the other

scythe¹ /saɪð/ *n* a tool having a long curving blade fixed to a long wooden pole worked with a swinging movement to cut grain or long grass

scythe² *v* **1** [T1 (DOWN, OFF); IØ] to cut (grass or grain) with a SCYTHE **2** [Wv4;L9 (AWAY), esp. *at*] to make a wide sweeping forceful movement with the arm(s): *He aimed a scything blow at his opponent*

SE *written abbrev. for:* southeast(ern)

sea /siː/ *n* **1** [*the*+R;U *often pl. with sing. meaning*] the great body of salty water that covers much of the earth's surface; the water of the earth as opposed to the land; ocean: *boats sailing on the sea|Most of the earth is covered by sea.|sea water|sea travel|The sea seems quiet today.|sailed into quieter seas|the warm sea(s) around the south of France|(a) seacoast* —see also HIGH SEAS **2** [C] (*often cap., esp. as part of a name*) a large body of water smaller than an ocean, as **a** part of the ocean: *the North Sea* (northeast of Britain) **b** a body of water (mostly) enclosed by land: *the Dead Sea|the Mediterranean Sea* —see picture at GLOBE **3** [S9, esp. *of*] a large mass or quantity regarded as being like one of these: *The actor looked out from the stage onto a sea of faces* **4** [*the*+R; *to*+U] the job of a sailor or member of a navy: *went to sea at the age of 17* **5** [(*the*) R] the shore of the ocean: SEASIDE (often in names of towns in the phr. **-on-sea**): *a town with a beautiful position on the sea|Clacton-on-Sea* **6** [C9 *often pl. with sing. meaning*] movement of waves on the surface of a body of salt water: *The ship ran into strong winds and heavy seas* **7** [C] (*usu. cap. as part of a name*) any of a number of broad plains on the moon: *the Sea of Tranquillity* **8 at sea a** during a ship's voyage on the sea: *a ship lost at sea|spent 3 months at sea* **b** *infml* lost in mind; not understanding; BEWILDERed: *I don't understand politics: I'm (all) at sea when people talk about the government* **9 beyond the sea(s)** *lit & pomp* far away across the sea; in a distant country **10 by sea** on a ship or using ships: *He went by plane/by air, and sent his heavy boxes by ship/by sea* **11 put (out) to sea** to go out into the sea on a boat

sea a·nem·o·ne /ˈ· ·ˌ···/ *n* a type of simple sea animal with a jelly-like body (POLYP) and brightly-coloured flower-like parts that can often sting

sea·bed /ˈsiːbed/ *n* [*the*+R] the floor of the sea; the land at the bottom of the sea

sea·bird /ˈsiːbɜːd‖-bɜrd/ *n* any of the birds living near the sea or finding food in it

sea·board /ˈsiːbɔːd‖-bord/ *n* the part of a country along a seacoast

sea·borne /ˈsiːbɔːn‖-born/ *n* [Wa5] carried or brought in ships: *a seaborne attack|seaborne trade*

sea breeze /ˈ· ·/ *n* a cool light wind (BREEZE) blowing from the sea into the land, esp. in the daytime

sea cap·tain /ˈ· ˌ··/ *n not fml* a captain of a non-military (MERCHANT) ship

sea change /ˈ· ·/ *n esp. lit* a complete and usu. sudden change

sea cow /ˈ· ·/ *n not fml* any of various breast-feeding animals with warm blood (MAMMALs), such as the MANATEE, living in the sea

sea dog /ˈ· ·/ *n lit & humor* a sailor with long experience

sea·far·ing /ˈsiːˌfeərɪŋ/ *adj* [Wa5;A] *esp. lit* **1** of, about, or doing the job of a sailor: *a seafaring man|a story from my seafaring days* **2** having strong connections with the sea and sailing: *seafaring nations*

sea fog /ˈ· ·/ *n* [U;C] (a) thick mist (FOG) on land coming from the sea or caused by a warm wind from the sea

sea·food /ˈsiːfuːd/ *n* [U] fish and fishlike animals (esp. SHELLFISH) from the sea (suitable) as food

sea·front /ˈsiːfrʌnt/ *n* [C;U] the part of a coastal town that is on the edge of the sea, often with a broad path along it for holiday visitors

sea·girt /ˈsiːgɜːt‖-gɜrt/ *n* [Wa5] *poet* surrounded by the sea

sea·go·ing /ˈsiːˌgəʊɪŋ/ *adj* [Wa5;A] **1** OCEANGOING **2** SEAFARING

sea·gull /ˈsiːgʌl/ *n not fml* GULL

sea·horse /ˈsiːhɔːs‖-hɔrs/ *n* a type of very small fish with a neck and head that look like those of a horse —see picture at FISH[1]

sea is·land cot·ton /ˌ·· ˈ··/ also **sea island** /ˈ· ˌ··/— *n* [U] cotton of a kind grown in the US and West Indies having long soft threads and making a fine cloth

sea·kale /ˈsiːkeɪl/ *n* [U] a plant of northern Europe with thick nearly white stems, eaten esp. in Britain as a vegetable

seal[1] /siːl/ *n* **1** [Wn1;C] any of several types of large fish-eating animals living mostly on cool seacoasts and floating ice, with broad flat limbs (FLIPPER*s*) suitable for swimming **2** [U] SEALSKIN

seal[2] *n* **1** **a** an official often round pattern (EMBLEM) as of a government, university, company, or (esp. in former times) a powerful person **b** a piece of usu. red wax or soft metal into which such a pattern is pressed and which is fixed to some formal and official writings **c** such a pattern pressed into a piece of writing on paper to make it official **d** a circle of coloured paper with or without such a pattern, fixed to a piece of writing usu. for the same purpose **2** a metal tool with such a pattern for pressing it into paper or hot metal or wax —compare SIGNET **3** a small piece of paper or wax which is fixed across an opening, as of an envelope or packet, or a metal wire which is fastened around an opening, and which must be broken in order to open it **4** **a** a part of a machine for keeping a gas or liquid in or out **b** a tight connection allowing no liquid or gas to escape **5** a mark or sign, esp. expressing proof: *a kiss as the seal of his love* **6** **given under my hand and seal** *law* (of a statement or order in writing) signed by me and with a seal put on by me **7** **set the seal on** *lit* to bring to an end in a suitable way; formally end

seal[3] *v* **1** [T1] to make or fix a SEAL[2] (1) onto: *an official statement signed and sealed* **2** [Wv5;T1 (UP, DOWN); X7] to fasten or close (as) with a SEAL[2] (3,4) or a tight cover or band of something: *sealed the parcel (shut) with sticky* TAPE|*a sealed envelope|bottle|birds who seal (up) the holes and cracks in their nests with mud*|(fig.) *I promised not to tell you, and* **my lips are sealed***: I won't tell you.|sealed orders* (=secret orders not to be read until a particular time or place) **3** [T1] to settle; make (more) certain, formal, or solemn: *sealed their agreement by shaking hands* **4** **seal someone's doom/fate** *infml* to make someone's death or punishment certain

sea legs /ˈ· ·/ *n* [P] *infml* the ability to walk, feel comfortable, and not be sick (SEASICK) on a moving ship

seal·er /ˈsiːləʳ/ *n* [U;C] a thing or material which SEAL*s*[3] (2), esp. (a covering of) paint, paste, polish, etc., on a surface to keep other liquids from going into or through it

sea lev·el /ˈ· ˌ··/ *n* [R] the average height of the sea, used as a standard for measuring heights on land: *Mount Everest, 29,028 feet above sea level| Death Valley, California, 280 feet below sea level*

seal in *v adv* [T1] to keep inside or contained without a chance to escape, as with a SEAL[2] (3,4): *boats sealed in as early as November by ice on the river|Cook the meat quickly at first to seal in the juices.|"Our new plastic container will seal in freshness and* **seal out** *other smells"*

seal·ing /ˈsiːlɪŋ/ *n* [U] the hunting or catching of SEALS[1]

sealing wax /ˈ·· ·/ *n* [U] a solid substance, often red and sold in small bars, which melts and then hardens quickly, and is used for SEAL*s*[2] (1b,3)

sea li·on /ˈ· ˌ··/ *n* [Wn1] a type of SEAL[1] of the Pacific Ocean, with quite large ears and without valuable fur —see picture at SEA

seal off *v adv* [T1] to close tightly so as not to allow entrance or escape: *He sealed off the glass tube by melting the ends together.|Police sealed the area off where the murderer was known to be hiding*

seal·skin /ˈsiːlˌskɪn/ also **seal**— *n* [U] the skin or fur of certain kinds of SEAL*s*[1], esp. as used in clothing or made into leather

Sea·ly·ham /ˈsiːlɪəm‖ˈsiːlihæm/ also **Sealyham terri·er** /ˌ··· ˈ···/— a type of small dog (TERRIER) with a long head and body, short legs, and white fur

seam[1] /siːm/ *n* **1** a line of stitches joining 2 pieces of cloth, leather, etc., at or near their edges: *trousers coming apart at the seams* **2** the crack, line, or raised mark where 2 edges meet: *He made such a good job of sticking the sheets of paper together that the seams hardly showed* **3** a narrow band of one kind of mineral, esp. coal, between masses of other rocks **4** **burst at the seams** *infml* to be very, almost too full: *There were so many people that the hall was bursting at the seams* —**~less** *adj* [Wa5]

seam[2] *v* [T1] **1** [*usu. pass.* (*with*)] to mark with lines like SEAM*s*[1] (2,3): *a valley seamed by/with small streams of water* **2** [(TOGETHER)] to sew 1 or more SEAM*s*[1] (1) in: *seam 2 pieces of cloth together*

sea·man /ˈsiːmən/ *n* **-men** /mən/ **1** [C] a sailor on a ship, other than an officer **2** [C;A] a member of a navy with any of the lowest group of ranks (below PETTY OFFICER) **3** [C] a man skilled in handling ships at sea

sea·man·like /ˈsiːmənlaɪk/ *adj* typical of a good and skilful seaman

sea·man·ship /ˈsiːmənʃɪp/ *n* [U] the skill of handling a ship and directing its course

seam bowl·er /ˈ· ˌ··/ also **seam·er** /ˈsiːməʳ/— *n* (in cricket) a person who BOWL*s* the ball at quite a fast speed in such a way that when it hits the ground its hard SEAM[1] (1,2) makes it change direction

sea mile /ˈ· ·/ *n* NAUTICAL MILE

sea mist /ˈ· ·/ *n* [U;C] (a) mist on land coming in from the sea or caused by a warm wind from the sea

seam·stress /ˈsiːmstrɪ̣s/ also (*esp. BrE*) **sempstress**— *n* a woman whose job is sewing

seam·y /ˈsiːmi/ *adj* [Wa1] less pleasant; rougher; worse (esp. in the phr. **the seamy side**): *a description of the seamy side of city life* —**seaminess** *n* [U]

sé·ance /ˈseɪɑ̃s, ˈseɪɒns‖ˈseɪɑns (*Fr* seɑ̃s)/ *n Fr* a meeting with someone claiming to have special powers (MEDIUM), where people try to talk to or receive messages from the dead

sea·plane /ˈsiːpleɪn/ *n* an aircraft built to rise from and come down on water

sea·port /ˈsiːpɔːt‖-port/ *n* a large town on a coast or connected to a coast by water, with a harbour used by large ships

sea pow·er /ˈ· ˌ··/ *n* **1** [U] the strength of a country's navy **2** [C] a country with a powerful navy

sear[1] /sɪəʳ/ *adj* SERE

sear[2] *v* [T1] **1** to burn with a sudden powerful heat, as **a** to treat (a wound); CAUTERIZE **b** to hurt or damage in this way: *a bad burn where he had been seared on the hot iron* **c** to cook outside of (a piece of meat) quickly **2** to dry up (plants); cause to WITHER

search[1] /sɜːtʃ‖sɜrtʃ/ *v* **1** [IØ (*through, into*); T1: (*for, after*)] to look at, through, into, etc., or examine (a place) carefully and thoroughly to try to find something: *searched the woods for the lost child|searched (through) his pockets for a cigarette|*

searched her Bible for a word of comfort|The police searched the thief but found no weapon on him.| scientists searching for a cure to the common cold| (fig.) spent his life searching after fame|I've searched my conscience (=tried to find fault with myself) and I still think I did the right thing **2 search me!** *infml* I don't know!: *"What's the time?" "Search me: I haven't got a watch"* —**~er** *n*

search² *n* [C; *in*+U9, *esp. of*] an act of searching: *a long search for the lost child|went in search of a doctor for his sick wife|birds flying south in search of winter sun*

search·ing /ˈsɜːtʃɪŋ‖ˈsɜr-/ *adj* sharp and thorough; anxious to discover the truth: *She gave me a searching look, as if doubting what I told her* —**~ly** *adv*

search·light /ˈsɜːtʃlaɪt‖ˈsɜr-/ *n* a large light with a powerful beam which can be turned in any direction

search out *v adv* [T1] to find (out) or uncover by searching: *The lawyer searched out the weaknesses in the witness's statement*

search par·ty /ˈ· ˌ··/ *n* [GC] a group of people searching, esp. for a lost person

search war·rant /ˈ· ˌ··/ *n* a written order sometimes given by a court to police to allow them to search a place, as to look for stolen goods

sear·ing /ˈsɪərɪŋ/ *adj* **1** burning; unpleasantly hot **2** *infml* causing or describing very strong feelings, esp. of a sexual kind

sea·scape /ˈsiːskeɪp/ *n* a picture of a scene at sea —compare LANDSCAPE

sea·shell /ˈsiːʃel/ *n* a shell of a small sea animal (esp. a MOLLUSC), esp. as found on the shore

sea·shore /ˈsiːʃɔː‖-ʃor/ *n* [U] land along the edge of the sea

sea·sick /ˈsiːˌsɪk/ *adj* feeling sick, esp. in the stomach, because of the movement of a ship on water —**~ness** *n* [U]

sea·side /ˈsiːsaɪd/ *n* [A; *the*+R] *esp. BrE* the edge of the sea, esp. as a holiday place: *a seaside town|a holiday at/by the seaside* —see SHORE (USAGE)

sea·son¹ /ˈsiːzən/ *n* **1** [C;R] a period of time each year, as **a** spring, summer, autumn, or winter, marked by different weather and hours of daylight **b** marked by weather: *the cold season* **c** of greater or lesser activity: *the quiet business season after Christmas* **d** for some farming job: *the planting season* **e** of some animal activity: *the breeding season* **f** when a sport is played: *(The) football season begins next week* **g** for hunting, fishing, etc.: *During the deer season he goes shooting each week* **h** around a holiday, esp. Christmas: *Christmas time is called the* **season of good cheer**|*bank holiday season in August* **2** [C] *lit* a period of time: *The last 3 years have been a good season for the company* **3 for a season** *lit* for a while, for a short time **4 in season** **a** (of fresh foods) at the time of usual fitness for eating: *Fruit is cheapest in season* **b** (esp. of holiday business) at the busiest time of year: *Hotels cost more in season* **c** (of certain female animals) on HEAT¹ (5) **d** (of animals) permitted to be hunted at the time —opposite **out of season** **5 Season's Greetings!** (a greeting on a Christmas card)—compare CLOSE SEASON, OPEN SEASON, HIGH SEASON, LOW SEASON

season² *v* **1** [T1 (*with*)] to give special taste to (a food) by adding salt, pepper, a SPICE, etc. **2** [T1; I0] **a** to make (wood) hard and fit for use by gradual drying **b** (of wood) to become hard and fit for use **3** [Wv5;T1] to give long experience to: *a seasoned traveller/soldier*

sea·so·na·ble /ˈsiːzənəbəl/ *adj* **1** suitable or useful for the time of year **2** *fml* coming at a good or proper time; OPPORTUNE: *seasonable advice* —compare SEASONAL —**-bly** *adv*

sea·son·al /ˈsiːzənəl/ *adj* depending on the seasons, esp. happening or active at a particular season: *seasonal employment at a holiday camp* —compare SEASONABLE

sea·son·ing /ˈsiːzənɪŋ/ *n* **1** [U;C] something that SEASONs food **2** [U] the act or way of becoming SEASONed

season tick·et /ˈ·· ˌ··‖ˌ·· ˈ··/ also (*BrE infml*) **season**— *n* a ticket usable any number of times (as for railway or bus trips between 2 places, entrance to sports matches, etc.) during a fixed period of time

seat¹ /siːt/ *n* **1** a place for sitting: *Using all our chairs we'll have seats for 10 people.|the front/back seat of a car|2 tickets for good seats at the theatre* —see picture at CAR **2** the part on which one sits: *My seat is rather sore from riding a horse.|The seat of the trousers wears out quickly* **3** [(*of*)] a place of a particular power or activity; CENTRE¹ (2): *a famous university and* **seat of learning**|*London is the British seat of government* **4** a place as a member of an official body: *win/lose a seat in Parliament in an election|appointed to a seat on a government committee* **5** *tech* a way of sitting on a horse **6 take/have a seat** please sit down **7 in the driver's seat** *infml* in charge; in control **8 take a back seat (to someone)** *infml* to allow someone else to take control or have the more important job —see also COUNTRY SEAT, **by the seat of one's** PANTS

seat² *v* [T1] **1** [*often pass.*] to cause or help to sit: *He seated himself near the window.|(fml) Please be seated* (=sit down) **2** (of a room, table, etc.) to have room for seats for (a certain number of people): *a large room which will seat/seats 1,000* **3** to fit (esp. a machine part) into a hole or closefitting place: *Make sure the* WASHER (2) *is firmly seated before tightening the pipe* —see SIT (USAGE)

seat belt /ˈ· ·/ also **safety belt**— *n* a belt fixed to a seat (as in a car or plane) and fastened around a person for safety in case of sudden movement —see picture at CAR

-seat·er /ˈsiːtəʳ/ *comb. form* (something) having the stated number of seats of places to sit: *a 3-seater* SOFA

seat·ing /ˈsiːtɪŋ/ *n* [U] provision or arranging of seats: *Do we have enough seating/seating room for the guests?*

sea ur·chin /ˈ· ˌ··/ *n* any of several types of small ball-shaped sea animals having a hard shell with many sharp points

sea·wall /ˌsiːˈwɔːl‖ˈsiːwɔl/ *n* a wall built along the edge of the sea to keep it from flowing over an area of land

sea·ward /ˈsiːwəd‖-ərd/ *adj* [Wa5] going towards the sea

sea·wards /ˈsiːwədz‖-ərdz/ also **seaward**— *adv* [Wa5] towards the sea

sea·wa·ter /ˈsiːˌwɔːtəʳ‖-ˌwɔ-, -ˌwɑ-/ *n* [U] water in or from the sea, containing about 3% salt

sea·way /ˈsiːweɪ/ *n* **1** [C] a course followed by ship traffic on the sea **2** [C] a deep waterway, such as a river, allowing ocean ships to travel far inside land **3** [U] speed on the sea: *The ship was making good seaway in spite of strong winds*

sea·weed /ˈsiːwiːd/ *n* [U] any of various (masses of) plants, esp. dark green with long stems, growing in the sea —see picture at PLANT²

sea·wor·thy /ˈsiːwɜːði‖-ɜr-/ *adj* (of a ship) in good condition and fit for a sea voyage

sec /sek/ *n infml* SECOND² (3): *Just wait a sec, will you?*

sec *abbrev. for:* SECRETARY (3)

sec·a·teurs /ˈsekətɜːz‖ˌsekəˈtɜrz/ *n* [P] *BrE* strong scissors for cutting parts of garden plants —see PAIR (USAGE) and picture at GARDEN[1]

se·cede /sɪˈsiːd/ *v* [I∅ (*from*)] *fml* to leave a group or organization; officially separate, esp. because of disagreement

se·ces·sion /sɪˈseʃən/ *n* [U] formal separation from a group or organization: *The secession of some southern states from the U.S.A. in the 1860's led to a* CIVIL WAR —**~ist** *n*

se·clude /sɪˈkluːd/ *v* [T1] to keep from association with others: *He's secluded himself in his room to write his report*

se·clud·ed /sɪˈkluːdɪ̣d/ *adj* hidden or apart from view; very quiet and private: *a secluded country house|a secluded life*

se·clu·sion /sɪˈkluːʒən/ *n* [U] **1** the state of being SECLUDED **2** the act of keeping away from others: *a country where the seclusion of women is still the custom*

se·clu·sive /sɪˈkluːsɪv/ *adj fml* fond of SECLUSION (1); liking to be away from others —**~ly** *adv* —**~ness** *n* [U]

sec·ond[1] /ˈsekənd/ *determiner, adv, n, pron* **1** [see NUMBER TABLE 3] 2nd **2** [C] a person who helps another (a **principal**), esp. someone who is fighting in a match or DUEL[1] (1) **3** [C *usu. pl.*] an article of imperfect quality for sale at a lower price: *If you want to buy dishes cheaply, you ought to get factory seconds* **4** [S] a formal action of SECONDing[3] (1) a MOTION[1] (3) in a meeting **5** [C] a British university examination result of middle to good quality **6 second to none** *infml* the best: *As a football player John is second to none*

second[2] *n* **1** a length of time equal to 1/60 of a minute **2** a measure of an angle equal to 1/3600 of a degree (or 1/60 of a MINUTE[1] (1)) —see WEIGHTS & MEASURES TABLE **3** [usu. sing] a moment: *I'll be back in a second*

second[3] *v* [T1] **1** to make a second person's statement in favour of (a formal suggestion (MOTION[1] (3)) made in a meeting), so that, under the rules of order, argument or voting may follow: *"Will anyone second this* MOTION*?" "I second it, Mr Chairman."* **2** [*usu. sing pass.*] to support in an argument, decision, or effort: *He was seconded in his offer of help by several other friends* **3** to act as a SECOND[1] (2) to (a fighter) —**~er** *n*

se·cond[4] /sɪˈkɒnd‖sɪˈkɑnd/ *v* [T1 *usu. pass.*] *fml BrE* to move (someone) from usual duties to a special duty, usu. for a limited time: *If Mr. Adams is ill much longer, someone will have to be seconded from another department to do his work* —**~ment** *n* [C;U]

sec·ond·a·ry /ˈsekəndəri‖-deri/ *adj* [Wa5] **1** [(*to*)] of 2nd, or less than 1st, rank, value, importance, etc.: *In addition to the main question, there are various secondary matters to talk about* **2** later than, developing from, taken from, etc., something earlier or original: *a secondary infection brought on by a cold* **3** (of education or a school) for children over 11 years old: *secondary schools/teachers* —compare PRIMARY (3) **4** (of a flow of electricity) produced by another connection by INDUCTION —**-arily** /ˈsekəndərɪ̣li‖ˌsekənˈderɪ̣li/ *adv*

secondary mod·ern /ˌ····ˈ··/ also (*infml*) **secondary mod** /ˌ····ˈ·/— *n* (formerly in England) a SECONDARY school which does not prepare students for university or further study

secondary stress /ˌ····ˈ·/ also **secondary ac·cent** /ˌ····ˈ··/— *n tech* the next to the strongest force (STRESS) given in speech to part of a compound or long word, and shown in this dictionary by the mark ˌ

second best /ˌ··ˈ·◂/ *adj* [Wa5] **1** next to the best; 2nd in value, importance, etc.: *The shop didn't have quite what we wanted so we had to* **settle for second best** **2 come off second best** *not fml* to be defeated by someone else

second child·hood /ˌ··ˈ··/ *n* [S] *euph* the period when an old person's mind becomes weak and childish; DOTAGE

second-class /ˌ··ˈ·◂/ *adj not fml* regarded as below a standard; INFERIOR

second class *n* **1** [U] a class of mail **a** (in Britain) for letters delivered slower than FIRST CLASS **b** (in the US and Canada) for newspapers and magazines **2** [U] the ordinary type of seating, furnishing, etc. (cheaper than FIRST CLASS), esp. on a train: *a second-class carriage|We're travelling second class* **3** [C] *fml* SECOND[1] (5)

Second Com·ing /ˌ··ˈ··/ *n* a future glorious coming of Christ from heaven, expected by many Christians

second cous·in /ˌ··ˈ··/ *n* see TABLE OF FAMILY RELATIONSHIPS

second-de·gree /ˌ···ˈ·◂/ *adj* [Wa5] of the next to the most serious kind: *second-degree burns*

second-hand[1] /ˌ··ˈ·◂/ *adj, adv* [Wa5] **1** used or worn by an earlier owner; not new; USED: *a second-hand car|I got this book second-hand* **2** (got) from somewhere other than the original place or person: *It was a second-hand report, based on what others had told him of what happened* —see also HAND[1] (15)

second-hand[2] *adj* [A] dealing in SECOND-HAND[1] goods: *a second-hand shop*

second-in-com·mand /ˌ····ˈ·/ *n* a person, esp. a military officer, next in rank to the commander or director

second lieu·ten·ant /ˌ···ˈ··/ *n* [C;U] (an officer of) the lowest rank in the army, American AIR-FORCE, or MARINE CORPS

second na·ture /ˌ··ˈ··/ [U] *not fml* a very firmly fixed habit: *It's second nature for me to look twice to see if I've locked the doors at night*

second per·son /ˌ··ˈ··/ *n* [*the*+R;A] a form of verb or PRONOUN (word standing for a noun) showing the person or thing spoken to: *"You" is a second person* PRONOUN

second-rate /ˌ··ˈ·◂/ *adj not fml* of less than the best quality; INFERIOR[1] (2)

sec·onds /ˈsekəndz/ *n* [P] *infml* 2nd servings of food at a meal: *He quickly ate everything on his plate and asked for seconds*

second sight /ˌ··ˈ·/ *n* [U] the supposed ability to see future or far-away things; CLAIRVOYANCE

second-string /ˌ··ˈ·◂/ *adj esp. AmE* not (good enough to be) playing in all matches but used for taking the place of others

second thought /ˌ··ˈ·/ *n* [C;U] a thought that a past decision or opinion may not be right (esp. in the phrs. **to have second thoughts** and **on second thoughts** (*AmE* **thought**)): *I said I wouldn't do it, but on second thoughts I think I will*

se·cre·cy /ˈsiːkrɪ̣si/ *n* [U] **1** the practice of keeping secrets: *Secrecy is important to our plans* **2** the state of being secret: *The secrecy of the plan was closely guarded*

se·cret[1] /ˈsiːkrɪ̣t/ *adj* **1** [B (*from*)] kept from the view or knowledge of others, or of all except a few: *secret plans|These plans must be kept secret (from the enemy).*|TOP-SECRET|*a secret passage behind the wall* **2** [Wa5;A] (of a person) undeclared; unadmitted: *John is a secret admirer of Helen, though he has never spoken to her* **3** [F (*about*); (B)] *not fml* careful in keeping secrets; SECRETIVE: *He's rather secret about his private affairs* —**~ly** *adv*

secret[2] *n* **1** [C] something kept hidden or known only to a few: *Our plan must remain a secret.|Can* *you keep* (=not tell) *a secret?|The new chairman hasn't been formally appointed, but it's an open secret* (=everyone knows) *that it'll be Mr Smith* **2** [C] something (so far) unexplained; mystery: *the secret of how life on earth began* **3** [S] a single or most important means of gaining a good result; KEY[1] (3): *What is the secret of your success?* **4 in secret** in a private way or place; unknown to (most) others: *plans made in secret*

secret a·gent /ˌ·· ˈ··/ *n* a person gathering information secretly or doing secret jobs, esp. for a foreign government; SPY

sec·re·tar·i·al /ˌsekrəˈteərɪəl/ *adj* [Wa5] of or concerning (the work of) a secretary

sec·re·tar·i·at /ˌsekrəˈteərɪət/ *n* an official office or department with a SECRETARY (2) or esp. SECRETARY-GENERAL as its head: *The United Nations Secretariat in New York*

sec·re·ta·ry /ˈsekrətəri‖-teri/ *n* **1** a person with the job of preparing letters, keeping records, arranging meetings, etc., for another: *a job as* **private secretary** *to the company chairman* **2** any of various government officers, as **a** (in Britain) a minister (*fml* **Secretary of State**), or the highest nonelected officer (the **Permanent Secretary**) in a department: *the Home/Foreign Secretary|the Secretary of State for Home/Foreign Affairs* **b** (in the US) a nonelected director of a large department: *the Secretary of the* TREASURY|*the Secretary of State* (dealing with foreign affairs) **c** a government representative below the rank of AMBASSADOR: *the First* (*or 2nd, 3rd, etc.*) *Secretary at the British* EMBASSY **3** an officer of an organization who keeps records, writes official letters, etc.

secretary-gen·e·ral /ˌ···· ˈ···/ *n* **secretaries-general** the chief officer in charge of running a large organization (esp. an international organization)

se·crete[1] /sɪˈkriːt/ *v* [T1] (esp. of an animal or plant organ) to produce (a usu. liquid substance): *Tears are secreted by an organ under the upper eyelid*

secrete[2] *v* [T1] to put into a hidden place; hide; CONCEAL

se·cre·tion /sɪˈkriːʃən/ *n* **1** [U;C] **a** the production of some usu. liquid material by part of a plant or animal **b** such a product **2** [U] the act of hiding something

se·cre·tive /ˈsiːkrɪ̵tɪv, sɪˈkriːtɪv/ *adj* fond of keeping secrets; choosing to hide one's intentions or plans —**~ly** *adv* —**~ness** *n* [U]

secret ser·vice /ˌ·· ˈ··/ *n* [*the*+R;A] a government department dealing with special kinds of police work, esp. (in the US) protecting high government officers

sect /sekt/ *n often derog* a smaller group of people having a special set of teachings and practices, usu. within or separated from a larger (esp. religious) group

sec·tar·i·an[1] /sekˈteərɪən/ *adj* (typical) of, or connected with, 1 or more SECTs, esp. in relation to great strength and narrowness of beliefs

sectarian[2] also **sec·ta·ry** /ˈsektəri/— *n* a member of a SECT, esp. a person with fixed and narrow opinions —**~ism** *n* [U]

sec·tion[1] /ˈsekʃən/ *n* **1** [C] a part of a larger object, place, group, etc., that is (regarded as) more or less separate: *the business section of a city|a politician liked by all sections of the country|the population|the brass section* (=those who play brass instruments) *of a band|a bookcase which comes apart into sections|signals controlling each section of railway track|the section of an office dealing with record-keeping* **2** [C] any of the natural equal parts of some fruits, such as an orange **3** [C] a representation of something as if it were cut from top to bottom and looked at from the side **4** [C;U] (a) cutting by a doctor in an operation: CESARIAN SECTION|*the section of a blood vessel* **5** [C] (in MATHEMATICS) the figure formed by the points where a solid body is cut by a flat surface: CONIC *sections* **6** [C] a very thin flat piece cut from skin, plant growth, etc., to be looked at under a microscope **7** [C] *esp. AmE* a small class into which a large group of students is divided **8 in section** in the view shown by a SECTION[1] (3)

section[2] *v* [T1] **1** to cut or divide into SECTIONs **2** to cut or show a SECTION[1] (3,6) from

sec·tion·al /ˈsekʃənəl/ *adj* **1** [Wa5] made up of SECTIONs to put together or take apart: *sectional furniture* **2** of or connected with 1 or more SECTIONs, esp. areas of a country; local rather than national: *sectional quarrels/interests* **3** [Wa5] of or based on a SECTION (3): *a sectional view of the bands of rock in the earth*

sec·tion·al·is·m /ˈsekʃənəlɪzəm/ *n* [U] (too) great loyalty or shared interest within only 1 SECTION of a group, esp. an area of a country

section gang /ˈ·· ·/ *n AmE* a group of workmen keeping one section of a railway line repaired

sec·tor /ˈsektəʳ/ *n* **1** a part of a field of activity, esp. of business, trade, etc.: *employment in the public and private sectors* (=those controlled by the government, and by private business)|*the banking sector* **2** an area in a circle enclosed by 2 straight lines drawn from the centre to the edge —compare SEGMENT and see picture at GEOMETRY **3** an area of military operation: *the British sector in the city of Berlin*

sec·u·lar /ˈsekjʊləʳ‖-kjə-/ *adj* **1** not connected with or controlled by a church; not religious **2** favouring SECULARISM: *our modern secular society* **3** [Wa5] (of priests) living among ordinary people (rather than as MONKs)

sec·u·lar·is·m /ˈsekjʊlərɪzəm‖-kjə-/ *n* [U] a system of social teaching or organization which allows no part for religion or the church —**-ist** *n, adj*

sec·u·lar·ize, -ise /ˈsekjʊləraɪz‖-kjə-/ *v* [Wv5;T1] **1** to influence in favour of SECULARISM: *Western society has become secularized in modern times* **2** to remove from the control of the church: *secularized education* —**-ization** /ˌsekjʊləraɪˈzeɪʃən‖ˌsekjələrə-/ *n* [U] —**-izer** *n*

se·cure[1] /sɪˈkjʊəʳ/ *adj* [Wa2] **1** [(*from, against*)] safe; protected against danger or risk: *a castle secure from attack* **2** closed, firm, or tight enough for safety: *Make the windows secure before leaving the house* **3** having no doubt, fear, or anxiety: CONFIDENT: *a secure belief|The child felt secure near its parents* **4** sure to be won or not to be lost; certain; ASSURED[1]: *a secure job in the government|His place in history is now secure* —**~ly** *adv*

secure[2] *v* **1** [D1 (*for*); T1] *fml* to get, esp. as the result of effort: *He's lucky to have secured himself such a good job* **2** [T1 (*from, against*)] to make safe: *The officer in charge secured the camp against attack* **3** [T1] to hold or close tightly: *They secured the windows when the storm began to blow*

se·cu·ri·ty /sɪˈkjʊərɪ̵ti/ *n* **1** [U] the state of being SECURE: *the security that religion gave to his mind* **2** [U] something which protects or makes SECURE: *The money I've saved is my security against hardship* **3** [U] property of value promised to a lender in case repayment is not made or other conditions are not met **4** [U] protection against lawbreaking, violence, enemy acts, escape from prison, etc.: *For security reasons* (=reasons of security) *the passengers have to be searched.|Tight security was in force during the President's visit.|a* MAXIMUM/MINIMUM *security prison|The security forces* (= police and army) *were unable to keep order in the streets* **5** [C *usu. pl.*] a paper (esp. a BOND or piece of STOCK[1]

(10)) giving the owner the right to some property: *trade in government securities*

Security Coun·cil /·'··· ˌ··/ *n* [*the*+GU] a body within the United Nations having 15 member countries and concerned with peacekeeping

security risk /·'··· ˌ·/ *n* a person whose loyalty is doubtful and who cannot be given certain government jobs

se·dan /sɪ'dæn/ *n AmE* SALOON (2)

sedan chair /·ˌ· '·/ also **sedan**— *n* an enclosed seat carried on poles by 2 men, 1 in front and 1 behind, used in former times for carrying a person through the streets

se·date[1] /sɪ'deɪt/ *adj* [Wa2] not (easily) troubled; calm; quiet: *a sedate old lady|an old lady of sedate manner* —**~ly** *adv* —**~ness** *n* [U]

sedate[2] *v* [T1 *often pass.*] to cause to become sleepy or calm, esp. with a SEDATIVE

se·da·tion /sɪ'deɪʃən/ *n* [U] the causing of a sleepy or calm state, esp. with a SEDATIVE (esp. in the phr. **under sedation**): *He's under sedation and resting quietly in bed*

sed·a·tive /'sedətɪv/ *adj, n* [B;C;(U)] (a drug) acting against nervousness, excitement, or pain and usu. causing sleep: *The doctor gave the sick man a sedative to help him sleep.|medicine with sedative effects*

sed·en·ta·ry /'sedəntəri‖-teri/ *adj* **1** used to, or needing, long sitting and only slight activity **2** not moving from one place to another; settled

sedge /sedʒ/ *n* [U] any of various grasslike plants with 3-sided stems growing usu. in groups on lowlying wet ground —**sedgy** *adj* [Wa1]

sed·i·ment /'sedɪ̣mənt/ *n* **1** [U;S] solid material that settles to the bottom of a liquid: (*a*) *brown sediment in the bottom of the coffee cup* **2** [U] material carried along and then left in a place by moving water or ice

sed·i·men·ta·ry /ˌsedɪ̣'mentəri/ *adj* [Wa5] (made) of, or concerning, SEDIMENT (2): *sedimentary rock*

sed·i·men·ta·tion /ˌsedɪ̣mən'teɪʃən/ *n* [U] the forming or coming down of SEDIMENT

se·di·tion /sɪ'dɪʃən/ *n* [U] speaking, writing, or action intended to cause disobedience or violence against a government

se·di·tious /sɪ'dɪʃəs/ *adj* guilty of, causing, or likely to cause SEDITION: *a seditious speech/speaker* —**~ly** *adv* —**~ness** *n* [U]

se·duce /sɪ'djuːs/ *v* **1** [T1] to persuade (usu. someone young and without sexual experience) to have sex with one: *She was seduced by a man who never kept his promise to marry her* **2** [X9;V3] to cause or persuade (someone) to do something more or less wrong by making it seem attractive; ENTICE: *He was seduced into leaving the company by the offer of higher pay elsewhere.|The warm weather seduced me away from my studies to take a walk* —**seducer** *n*

se·duc·tion /sɪ'dʌkʃən/ *n* **1** [C;U] the action or an act of seducing (SEDUCE) **2** [C *usu. pl.*] a thing or quality that attracts by its charm: *the seductions of articles in shop windows*

se·duc·tive /sɪ'dʌktɪv/ *adj* having qualities likely to SEDUCE; very desirable or attractive: *a woman's seductive voice|a seductive offer of higher pay* —**~ly** *adv* —**~ness** *n* [U]

sed·u·lous /'sedjʊləs‖'sedʒə-/ *adj fml or lit* marked by steady attention, care, and determination; DILIGENT: *a sedulous workman* —**~ly** *adv*

see[1] /siː/ *v* **saw** /sɔː/, **seen** /siːn/ **1** [Wv6;IØ] to use the eyes; have or use the power of sight: *See! Here comes the train.|so dark he could hardly see (to do his work)|He doesn't see very well in his right eye.|She claims to see into the future* (=know what is to happen) **2** [Wv6;T1,5a,6a;V2,3 (*fml & only pass.*), 4,8] to look at; get sight of; notice, examine, or recognize by looking: *I looked for her but I couldn't see her in the crowd.|I saw the train come/coming into the station.|Can you see what's going on over there?|Let me see your ticket, please.|(fml) The prisoner was seen to take the money.|I could see (that) my friend needed my help.|I saw the whole accident with my own eyes: I saw the man knocked down and the driver driving away.|"For more information see page 153"* **3** [Wv6;IØ; T1,5a,b,6a] to understand or recognize: *"Do you see what I mean?" "Yes: now I see."|I see in the paper (that) the government lost a vote in Parliament.|Try to see the matter my way* **4** [IØ;T6a,b] to (try to) find out or determine: *Will you see if you can repair my car?|I'll see what I can do/see what the trouble is.|I'm not sure if I can lend you that much money: I'll have to see* **5** [Wv6;T5a] to make sure; take care: *See that you're ready at 8 o'clock.|I promise to see that the job is done on time* **6** [Wv6; T1,4;V4,8] *not fml* to form a picture in the mind of; imagine: *I can't see (myself) lending her money: can you see her ever paying it back?* (=It's unlikely)|*I can see a great future for you in music* **7** [Wv6; T1,4: *usu. neg.*] *not fml* to be in favour of: *I put my opinion to the chairman but he couldn't see it* **8** [Wv6;T1] *lit* to be an occasion of (an event or course in history): *The 5th century saw the end of the Roman Empire in the West* **9** [Wv6;T1] to have experience of; UNDERGO: *You and I have seen some good times together.|This old house has* **seen better days***: now it's in bad repair.|(infml) I don't know her age for sure, but she'll never see 40 again* (=she's older than 40) **10** [T1] to visit, call upon, or meet: *The doctor can't see you yet: he's seeing someone else at the moment.|Mrs. Johnson, may I see you a moment, please?* **11** [X9] to go with; ACCOMPANY (1): *Someone ought to see the old lady safely home.|Please see this troublesome fellow out of the office and tell him not to come back* **12** [T1] (in the game of POKER) to answer (an opponent) by risking an equal amount of money **13 (I'll) see you/be seeing you (later/soon/next week, etc.)** *infml* (used when leaving a friend): *"See you later, Mary." "Be seeing you, John"* **14 I'll see you dead/in hell before that happens!** I will never agree to that! **15 let me see** (used for expressing a pause for thought): *"Do you recognize this music?" "Let me see . . . Yes, now I do"* **16 see here** *usu. pomp* (used for expressing warning or disapproval): *See here, boys, you mustn't ever do that again* **17 Seeing is believing** *infml* **a** I'll believe it when I see it, and not before **b** Now I've seen it, so I believe it **18 see nothing/little/a lot/more/less of someone** *infml* to see, or be in company with, a person never/rarely/often/more often/less often: *Where's John? I've seen nothing of him all week.|They're good friends and see a lot of one another.|I'd like to see more of that girl* **19 see something in someone** *nonassertive infml* to like or be fond of someone: *I wonder why she fell in love with him: I'll never know what she sees in him* **20 see the back/last of** *infml* to be through with; have no more to do with: *I haven't liked dealing with this company and I'll be glad to see the back of them* **21 see things** *not fml* to think that one sees something that is not there: *I must be seeing things: I can't believe the neighbours have got a new car!* **22 so I see** What you say is already clear or easy to see: *"I'm afraid I'm a bit late." "So I see"* **23 you see** *not fml* (used with rather weak meaning in explanations) *"Why are you so late?" "Well, you see, the bus broke down."|I've got to stay with my mother, you see, so I can't come along*

USAGE 1 To **see** is to experience with the eyes, and it does not depend on the will. In this meaning, one can say *Can you* **see** *anything?* but not **Are you* **seeing** *anything?* When one uses the eyes on purpose and with attention, one is **looking at** something: *Stop* **looking** *at me like that!* To **watch** is to **look at** something that is moving: one **watches** television or a football match. 2 **See**, **feel**, **hear**, and **watch** can all be used in the patterns [V2] and [V4], but the meaning is different. Compare: *I* **saw** *him cross the road* (=I saw the whole journey from one side to the other).|*I* **saw** *him crossing the road* (=I saw him at a moment when he was in the middle) —see also SEE ABOUT, SEE OFF, SEE OUT, SEE OVER, SEE THROUGH, SEE TO, **see** FIT[2] (11), **see one's** WAY[1] (59), **see** RED[2] (13), **see** STARS

see[2] *n* the office of, area governed by, or centre of government of a BISHOP (Christian priest in charge of a large area) —compare DIOCESE; see also HOLY SEE

see a·bout *v prep* **1** [T1,4] to attend to; make arrangements for; deal with: *It's time for me to see about dinner|to see about cooking dinner* **2** to consider further: *"Father, will you take us to the football match tomorrow?" "Well, I'll see about that"* (=perhaps) **3 We'll see about that!** *infml* I will put a stop to that!

seed[1] /siːd/ *n* **1** [C;U] the part, usu. small and hard, of some plants that may grow into a new plant of the same kind, esp. as used for planting: *a large bag of grass seed* —see picture at FRUIT,[1] VEGETABLE[1] **2** [U] *old use & lit* SEMEN; SPERM **3** [P; (U)] *bibl* descendants, esp. those forming a race: *According to the Bible we are all the seed of Adam* **4** [C] something from which growth or development begins; beginning; GERM (2): *seeds of future trouble* **5** [C] a SEEDed[2] (5) player in a competition **6** [A] kept for planting or producing seeds: *seed potatoes/corn* **7** [A] small and incompletely developed: *seed eggs|seed* PEARL*s* **8 go/run to seed a** (of a plant) to produce seed, as usu. past the time when flowers are produced **b** (of a person) to lose one's power of freshness, esp. by becoming lazy, careless, or old **9 in seed** (of a plant) in the condition of bearing seeds —**~less** *adj* [Wa5]

USAGE Although **seed** has a plural, it is a [U] noun when one speaks of a large quantity, as used in farming. Compare: *a handful of* **seeds**|*a large bag of grass* **seed**.

seed[2] *v* **1** [I∅] (of a plant) to grow and produce seed **2** [T1 (*with*) *often pass.*] to plant seeds in (a piece of ground) **3** [T1] to remove seeds from (fruit) **4** [T1 (*with*)] to cause to be filled or scattered with something that grows or produces a result **5** [Wv5;T1;X1: *usu. pass.*] to place (a sports, esp. tennis, player at the start of a competition) in order of likelihood to win: *He was an unknown player who wasn't seeded* (=wasn't among the seeded players)

seed·bed /ˈsiːdbed/ *n* **1** an area of ground, esp. specially prepared, where seeds begin to grow **2** a place or favourable condition for development

seed·cake /ˈsiːdkeɪk/ *n* [C;U] (a) sweet cake containing strong-tasting (usu. CARAWAY) seeds

seed·ling /ˈsiːdlɪŋ/ *n* a young plant grown from a seed and not from a part cut off another plant

seeds·man /ˈsiːdzmən/ *n* **-men** /mən/ a dealer in seeds, esp. for flowers and vegetables

seed·y /ˈsiːdi/ *adj* [Wa1] **1** *not fml* having a poor, uncared for, worn-out appearance: *a rather seedy and unpleasant part of town* **2** full of seeds: *a seedy orange* **3** *infml* slightly unwell; under the WEATHER[1] (4) —**seedily** *adv* —**seediness** *n* [U]

see·ing /siːɪŋ/ also **seeing that** /ˈ·· ·/, (*infml*) **seeing as** /ˈ·· ·/, (*nonstandard*) **seeing as how** /ˈ·· · ˌ·/— *conj* considering the fact (that); INASMUCH as; because: *Seeing (that) she's lawfully old enough to get married, I don't see how you can stop her*

USAGE **Since**[3] (2) and **seeing** (*that*) are used only of facts that we know are true. They could not be used instead of **because**, in a question like this: *Did he come because he wanted money?* (=Was that the reason?)

seek /siːk/ *v* **sought** /sɔːt/ **1** [T1 (OUT); I∅ (*after, for*)] *usu. fml, old use, or lit* to make a search (for); look (for); try to find or get (something): *"Seek and you shall find."* (the Bible)|*sought shelter from the rain|sought out his friend in the crowd|seek (after) the truth in the matter|seek public office|seeking among his untidy papers for the right one* **2** [T1] *fml* to ask for; go to request: *You should seek advice from your lawyer on this matter* **3** [T3] *esp. lit* to try; make an attempt: *They sought to punish him for his crime but he escaped* **4** [T1] to move naturally towards: *Water seeks its own level.|The compass* POINTER *always seeks the north* **5 not far to seek** easily seen or understood; at HAND[1] (14): *The reason for his failure was not far to seek: he was ill during the examination* —see also **seek one's** FORTUNE, HIDE-AND-SEEK, SOUGHT AFTER —**~er** *n*

seem /siːm/ *v* [Wv6] **1** [I3;L (*to be*) 1,7,9] to give the idea or effect of being; be in appearance; appear: *She always seems (to be) sad.|I seem to have caught a cold.|There seems (to be) every hope that business will get better.|Things are not always what they seem.|You must do whatever seems right to you.|It seems like years since I last saw you* **2** [*it*+ I5a,b,6a (**as if**)] to appear to be true: *"It seems (as if) there will be an election soon." "So it seems."|"It would seem* (=it seems) *that there is no way out of our difficulty." "I agree: it seems not"*

seem·ing /ˈsiːmɪŋ/ *adj* [Wa5;A] that seems to be so, usu. as opposed to what is: *a seeming piece of good luck which later led to all kinds of trouble*

seem·ing·ly /ˈsiːmɪŋli/ *adv* [Wa5] **1** as far as one can tell; EVIDENTly: *Seemingly there is nothing we can do to stop the plan going ahead* **2** according to what appears, usu. opposed to what actually is so: *Some seemingly good luck brought us nothing but trouble*

seem·ly /ˈsiːmli/ *adj* [Wa2] (esp. of behaviour) pleasing by being suitable to an occasion or to social standards —**seemliness** *n* [U]

seen /siːn/ *past p. of* SEE[1]

see off *v adv* [T1] **1** [(*at*)] to go to the airport, station, etc., with (someone who is beginning a trip): *saw his friend off at the bus station* **2** to remain unharmed until (something or someone dangerous) has ceased to be active; WITHSTAND: *They saw off 3 enemy attacks within 3 days*

see out *v adv* [T1] **1** to last until the end of: *Will our supplies see the winter out?|It was such a bad play we couldn't see out the performance and we left early* **2** to go to the door with (someone who is leaving): (fig.) *We stayed up until midnight on December 31 to see the old year out and the new year in*

see o·ver *v adv* [T1a] **1** to examine: *I'd like to see over your report before it goes to the chief* **2** also **see round**— to visit and examine: *Would you like to see over the old castle?*

seep /siːp/ *v* [L9] (of a liquid) to flow slowly through small openings in a material; OOZE[2]: *Water had seeped into the house through the walls and roof*

seep·age /ˈsiːpɪdʒ/ *n* [U;S] (a) slow flow of a liquid by SEEPing: *water lost through seepage out of the container*

seer /ˈsɪəʳ/ *n lit & old use* one who knows about the future; PROPHET (5)

seer·suck·er /ˈsɪəˌsʌkəʳ‖ˈsɪər-/ *n* [U] a kind of light usu. cotton cloth with bands of a flat surface between bands of a surface with small folds

see·saw¹ /ˈsiːsɔː/ *n* **1** [C] a board balanced in the middle for children to sit on at opposite ends so that when one end goes up the other goes down **2** [U] children's play on such a board **3** [C] a movement backwards and forwards, as in a battle, game, etc., where now one side and now the other is winning

seesaw² *v* [IØ] **1** to move backwards and forwards, up and down, or between opponents or opposite sides: *seesawing prices* **2** to play SEESAW¹ (2)

seethe /siːð/ *v* **1** [Wv4;IØ] (of a liquid) to move about as if boiling; CHURN² (2): *looked down into the seething sea around the rocks* **2** [IØ;T1] *old use* to cook by boiling; STEW **3** [IØ (*with*)] to be very excited or angry: *a country seething with political unrest*

see-through /ˈ· ·/ *adj* [A] *not fml* that can be seen through; allowing what is inside to be (partly) seen

see through¹ *v prep* **1** [T1] to recognize the truth about (an excuse, (partly) false statement, etc.); not be FOOLed² (1) by **2** [D1] to provide for, support, or help until the end of (a time or difficulty): *enough money to see him through a year abroad*

see through² *v adv* [T1b] to SEE THROUGH¹ (2) a time or difficulty: *enough money to see him through*

see to *v prep* [T1,4] to attend to; take care of: *You ought to have your eyes seen to by a doctor.|If I see to getting the car out, will you see to closing the windows?*

seg·ment¹ /ˈsegmənt/ *n* **1** any of the parts into which something may be cut or divided; SECTION¹ (2): *a dish of orange segments|The runner went faster on the middle segment of the course* —see picture at FRUIT¹ **2** the area inside a circle between its edge and a straight line across it (CHORD) —see picture at GEOMETRY **3** the part of a line between 2 points on the line

seg·ment² /segˈment/ *v* [IØ;T1] to divide into pieces; separate into SEGMENT*s*¹ (1): *Oranges usually segment/may be segmented into 10 or 12 pieces*

seg·men·ta·tion /ˌsegmənˈteɪʃən/ *n* [U;S] division into SEGMENT*s*: *a segmentation of the job which allowed each part to be carried out separately*

seg·re·gate /ˈsegrɪgeɪt/ *v* [T1*usu. pass.*;(IØ)] to separate or (be) set apart, esp. from the rest of a social group: *an educational system where boys and girls were segregated*

seg·re·gat·ed /ˈsegrɪgeɪtɪ̵d/ *adj* **1** separated or kept apart **2 a** making separate arrangements for different, esp. racial, groups **b** for the use of only one such group: *In the U.S.A., blacks and whites used to go to segregated schools*

seg·re·ga·tion /ˌsegrɪˈgeɪʃən/ *n* **1** [U;S] an/the act or state of separation **2** [U] the separation of a social or esp. racial group from others, as by laws against using the same schools, (parts of) hotels, buses, etc. —opposite **integration**; compare APARTHEID

sei·gneur /seˈnjɜːʳ‖seɪ-/ *n* [C;N] (in a FEUDAL system) a nobleman or landowner; lord

seine /seɪn/ also **seine net** /ˈ· ·/— *n* a fishing net with weights along one edge causing it to hang straight down and enclose fish when the ends are drawn together

seis·mic /ˈsaɪzmɪk/ *adj* [Wa5] *tech* of, concerning, or caused by sudden shakings of the ground (EARTHQUAKE*s*)

seis·mo·graph /ˈsaɪzməgrɑːf‖-græf/ *n* an instrument for recording and measuring shaking of the ground (as in an EARTHQUAKE)

seis·mol·o·gy /saɪzˈmɒlədʒi‖-ˈmɑ-/ *n* [U] *tech* the scientific study of shaking movements in the surface of the earth —**-gist** *n*

seize /siːz/ *v* [T1] **1** to take possession of **a** by official order: *The weapons found in the house were seized by the police* **b** by force: *The enemy army seized the fort* **2** to take hold of eagerly, quickly, or forcefully; GRAB; GRASP¹ (1): *He seized my hand, shook it, and said how glad he was to see me.|She seized (hold of) the child and pulled it back from the edge of the cliff* **3** [*often pass.* (*with*)] to attack or take control of (someone's body or mind); OVERCOME: *He was seized with sudden chest pains.|The desire to be a singer had seized her* (=she was seized with the idea) **4** [*usu. pass.* (*of*)] also **seise**— *fml or law* to give ownership (of property) to: *You stand seized of the farm as of this date*

seize on also **seize up·on**— *v prep* [T1] to take and use eagerly: *She had always wanted to go to London, so she seized on the offer of a free trip*

seize up *v adv* [IØ] *esp. BrE* (as of (part of) a machine) to become stuck and fail to move or work; JAM¹ (4)

sei·zure /ˈsiːʒəʳ/ *n* **1** [U] the act or result of seizing (SEIZE): *The courts ordered the seizure of all her property* **2** [C] a sudden attack of an illness: *died of a heart seizure* (=of heart disease)

sel·dom /ˈseldəm/ *adv* not often; rarely: *Very seldom* (=hardly ever) *does he eat any breakfast.|The road is not seldom* (=is often) *flooded in winter.|She seldom, if ever, reads a book* —see RARELY (USAGE)

se·lect¹ /sɪ̵ˈlekt/ *adj* **1** [Wa5;A] chosen, or choosing, from a larger group: *a select collection of poems* **2** [B] limited to members of the best quality, often according to social class; EXCLUSIVE¹ (1)

select² *v* [T1;V3] to choose as best, most suitable, etc., from a group: *He selected a pair of socks to match his suit*

select com·mit·tee /·ˌ· ·ˈ··/ *n* [GC] a committee of Parliament appointed to consider a particular matter

se·lec·tion /sɪ̵ˈlekʃən/ *n* **1** [U] the act of SELECTing **2** [C] one that is SELECTed; choice: *The performance included some musical selections* **3** [C *usu. sing.*] a collection of things of a kind, as of goods for sale: *The shop has a fine selection of cheeses* —see also NATURAL SELECTION

se·lec·tive /sɪ̵ˈlektɪv/ *adj* **1** acting with, or concerning, only certain articles; not general: *selective controls on goods brought into the country for sale|a tax selective in its effects* **2** careful in choosing: *With 30 people wanting the job, the employer could afford to be selective in his choice* **3** *tech* (of a radio) able to receive a broadcast from one station without sounds from other stations (close to it in FREQUENCY) —**~ly** *adv* —**~ness** *n* [U] —**-tivity** /sɪ̵ˌləkˈtɪvɪ̵ti/ *n* [U]

Selective Ser·vice /·ˌ·· ˈ··/ [U] *AmE* NATIONAL SERVICE (1)

se·lec·tor /sɪ̵ˈlektəʳ/ *n* a person or instrument that SELECTs, esp. a member of a committee choosing a sports team

se·le·ni·um /sɪ̵ˈliːnɪəm/ *n* [U] a poisonous simple substance (ELEMENT) that is not a metal and is used esp. in light-sensitive electrical instruments and as a colouring material

self /self/ *n* **selves** /selvz/ **1** [U;C9] a person with his own nature, character, abilities, etc.: *He put his whole self into the job, working night and day.|Knowledge of self increases as one gets older* **2** [C9] a particular or typical part of one's nature: *I'm feeling better but I'm still not quite my old self* (=as I was before my illness) *yet.|their weaker/better/true selves* **3** [U] one's own advantage or profit:

She always thinks of others, never of self **4** [U] (written; esp. in business matters) the person concerned; the signer: *"Paid by: John Robinson. Deliver to: self"*

self- *comb. form* **1** oneself or itself: SELF-LOCKING|*self-loving* **2** by (means of) oneself or itself: *self-taught|self-*PROPEL*led* **3** of, to, with, for, or in oneself or itself: *self-*CONSISTENT|SELF-CONTAINED| SELF-ADDRESSED|*self-* RESTRAINT

self-ab·sorbed /ˌ· ·ˈ·◂/ *adj* paying all one's attention to oneself and one's own affairs

self-ab·sorp·tion /ˌ· ·ˈ··/ *n* [U] attention to oneself and to nothing else

self-a·buse /ˌ· ·ˈ·/ *n* [U] *euph* MASTURBATION

self-act·ing /ˌ· ˈ··◂/ *n* working by itself; AUTOMATIC[1] (1)

self-ad·dressed /ˌ· ·ˈ·◂/ *adj* [Wa5] addressed for return to the sender: *Please enclose a self-addressed envelope with your order*

self-ap·point·ed /ˌ· ·ˈ··◂/ *adj* [Wa5] *not fml* chosen for the job by oneself, unasked and usu. unwanted

self-as·ser·tion /ˌ· ·ˈ··/ *n* [U] the action of pushing forward one's own claims or abilities over those of others

self-as·ser·tive /ˌ· ·ˈ··◂/ *adj* forceful in making others take notice of oneself or in claiming things for oneself —**~ness** *n* [U]

self-as·sur·ance /ˌ· ·ˈ··/ *n* [U] sure belief in one's own abilities; undoubting SELF-CONFIDENCE

self-as·sured /ˌ· ·ˈ·◂/ *adj* sure of one's own abilities —**~ness** *n* [U]

self-cen·tred /ˌ· ˈ··◂/ *adj* interested only in oneself; SELFISH —**~ness** *n* [U]

self-col·oured /ˌ· ˈ··◂/ *adj* [Wa5] of a single colour: *a self-coloured flower|cloth*

self-com·mand /ˌ· ·ˈ·/ *n* [U] command over one's feelings; SELF-CONTROL

self-com·pla·cent /ˌ· ·ˈ··/ *adj* too pleased and satisfied by one's own position or success

self-con·fessed /ˌ· ·ˈ·◂/ *adj* [Wa5;A] admitted by oneself to be the stated kind of person; AVOWED: *a self-confessed drug taker*

self-con·fi·dence /ˌ· ˈ···/ *n* [U] a feeling of power to do things successfully

self-con·fi·dent /ˌ· ˈ···/ *adj* sure of one's own power to succeed

self-con·scious /ˌ· ˈ··◂/ *adj* **1** having knowledge or thought about oneself or itself; CONSCIOUS **2** nervous and uncomfortable about oneself as seen by others: *I could never be an actor: I'm too self-conscious* —**~ly** *adv* —**~ness** *n* [U]

self-con·tained /ˌ· ·ˈ·◂/ *adj* **1** complete in itself; having no part shared with anything else: *a self-contained flat with its own entrance, kitchen, bathroom, etc.* **2** (of a person) habitually not showing feelings or depending on others' friendship

self-con·tra·dic·to·ry /ˌ· ··ˈ···/ *adj* [Wa5] containing 2 opposite parts or statements which cannot both be true

self-con·trol /ˌ· ·ˈ·/ *n* [U] control over one's feelings; power to hold back the expression of strong feelings

self-con·trolled /ˌ· ·ˈ·◂/ *adj* showing SELF-CONTROL

self-de·feat·ing /ˌ· ·ˈ··◂/ *adj* having the effect of preventing its own success

self-de·fence /ˌ· ·ˈ·/ *n* [U] the act or skill of defending oneself, one's actions, rights, etc.: *the art of self-defence* (=BOXING, JUDO, etc.)|*He shot the man in self-defence* (=only to protect himself)

self-de·ni·al /ˌ· ·ˈ··/ *n* [U] the act or habit of not allowing oneself pleasures or not satisfying one's own desires

self-de·ny·ing /ˌ· ·ˈ··/ *adj* showing SELF-DENIAL

self-de·ter·min·a·tion /ˌ· ···ˈ··/ *n* [U] the right or action of the people of a place to make a free decision about the form of their government, esp. whether or not to be independent of another country

self-dis·ci·pline /ˌ· ˈ···/ *n* [U] the training of oneself to control one's habits and actions

self-drive /ˌ· ˈ·◂/ *adj* [Wa5] *BrE* (of a vehicle) hired or for hire to be driven by oneself (and not by a CHAUFFEUR)

self-ed·u·cat·ed /ˌ· ˈ····◂/ *adj* educated by one's own efforts and not formally in school

self-ef·fac·ing /ˌ· ·ˈ··◂/ *adj* avoiding the attention of others; keeping oneself from seeming important

self-em·ployed /ˌ· ·ˈ·◂/ *adj* [B; (*the*) P] earning money from one's own business and not as pay from an employer

self-es·teem /ˌ· ·ˈ·/ *n* [U] one's good or too good opinion of one's own worth

self-ev·i·dent /ˌ· ˈ···◂/ *adj* plainly true without need of proof; clear from the statement itself: *"We hold these truths to be self-evident, that all men are* CREATE*d equal . . ."* (US Declaration of Independence)

self-ex·am·in·a·tion /ˌ· ···ˈ··/ *n* [U] consideration of one's own actions, esp. to judge them according to some standards, religious beliefs, etc.

self-ex·plan·a·to·ry /ˌ· ·ˈ····/ *adj* (esp. of speaking or writing) explaining itself; needing no further explanation

self-gov·ern·ing /ˌ· ˈ···◂/ *adj* [Wa5] directing its own affairs; free from outside control; AUTONOMOUS

self-gov·ern·ment /ˌ· ˈ···/ also **self-rule**— *n* [U] government free from outside control or influence; independence; AUTONOMY

self-help /ˌ· ˈ·/ *n* [U] the action of providing for or helping oneself without depending on others

self-im·port·ance /ˌ· ·ˈ··/ *n* [U] too high an opinion of one's own importance

self-im·port·ant /ˌ· ·ˈ··◂/ *adj* showing SELF-IMPORTANCE; POMPOUS —**~ly** *adv*

self-im·posed /ˌ· ·ˈ·◂/ *adj* that one has forced oneself to accept: *a self-imposed limit of 3 cigarettes a day*

self-in·dul·gence /ˌ· ·ˈ··/ *n* [U] the too easy allowance of pleasure or comfort to oneself

self-in·dul·gent /ˌ· ·ˈ··◂/ *adj* showing SELF-INDULGENCE —**~ly** *adv*

self-in·terest /ˌ· ˈ··/ *n* [U] concern for what is best for, or to the advantage of, one's own self; selfishness: *Self-interest should prevent you from being rude to your employer*

self-in·terest·ed /ˌ· ˈ···◂/ *adj* showing SELF-INTEREST; selfish

self·ish /ˈselfɪʃ/ *adj* concerned with or directed towards one's own advantage without care for others —**~ly** *adv* —**~ness** *n* [U]

self·less /ˈselfləs/ *adj* caring only for others and not for oneself; completely unselfish —**~ly** *adv* —**~ness** *n* [U]

self-lock·ing /ˌ· ˈ··◂/ *adj* [Wa5] (as of a door) locking by its own action when closed

self-made /ˌ· ˈ·◂/ *adj* raised to success and wealth by one's own efforts starting without education, money, or social position (esp. in the phr. **a self-made man**)

self-o·pin·ion·at·ed /ˌ· ·ˈ····◂/ *adj* holding firmly on to one's own opinions even when possibly wrong

self-pit·y /ˌ· ˈ··/ *n* [U] too strongly felt or expressed pity for one's own sorrows or troubles

self-pos·sessed /ˌ· ·ˈ·◂/ *adj* showing SELF-POSSESSION; calm; COMPOSED (4)

self-pos·ses·sion /ˌ· ·ˈ··/ *n* [U] firm control over

one's own feelings and actions, esp. in difficult or unexpected conditions; COMPOSURE

self-pres·er·va·tion /ˌ· ··ˈ··/ *n* [U] the keeping of oneself from death or harm, esp. as an action done naturally (INSTINCT) by living things

self-rais·ing flour /ˌ· ˈ·· ˌ·/ *AmE* **self-rising flour**— *n* [U] flour that contains BAKING POWDER —compare PLAIN FLOUR

self-re·li·ance /ˌ· ·ˈ··/ *n* [U] the use of one's own powers of action and judgment without depending on others

self-re·li·ant /ˌ· ·ˈ··/ *adj* able to act without depending on the help of others

self-re·spect /ˌ· ·ˈ·/ *n* [U] proper respect for, or pride in, oneself; concern for one's worth as a person

self-re·spect·ing /ˌ· ·ˈ··◂/ *adj* [A] keeping up proper standards; not needing to feel shame

self-right·eous /ˌ· ˈ··/ *adj derog* proudly sure of one's own rightness or goodness, esp. in opposition to the beliefs and actions of others —**~ly** *adv* —**~ness** *n* [U]

self-rule /ˌ· ˈ·/ *n* [U] SELF-GOVERNMENT

self-sac·ri·fice /ˌ· ˈ···/ *n* [U] the giving up of one's pleasure or interests in favour of others or of a worthier purpose

self-sac·ri·fic·ing /ˌ· ˈ····/ *adj* showing SELF-SACRIFICE

self-same /ˈselfseɪm/ *adj* [Wa5; *the* + B] *lit* exactly same; VERY[2] (1) same: *2 great victories on the self-same day*

self-sat·is·fac·tion /ˌ· ··ˈ··/ *n* [U] a too satisfied opinion about one's own success or position

self-sat·is·fied /ˌ· ˈ···/ *adj* too pleased with one-self; SMUG; COMPLACENT

self-seek·er /ˌ· ˈ··/ *n* a person who acts only for his own interest or advantage

self-seek·ing /ˌ· ˈ··◂/ *n, adj* [U;B] (action) that works only for one's own advantage: *a dishonourable self-seeking politician*

self-serv·ice /ˌ· ˈ··◂/ *adj, n* [Wa5;B;U] (working by) the system in many restaurants, shops, petrol stations, etc., in which buyers collect what they want and then pay at 1 or more special desks

self-sown /ˌ· ˈ·◂/ *adj* [Wa5] (of a plant) growing from seeds dropped by the parent plant or carried by the wind or animals; not planted (SOWN) by people

self-start·er /ˌ· ˈ··/ *n* **1** a usu. electric apparatus for starting a car engine without turning it (with a CRANK[1] (1)) by hand **2** a vehicle with such an apparatus

self-styled /ˌ· ˈ·◂/ *adj* [Wa5;A] given the stated title by oneself, usu. without any right to it

self-suf·fi·cien·cy /ˌ· ·ˈ···/ *n* [U] the state or quality of being SELF-SUFFICIENT

self-suf·fi·cient /ˌ· ·ˈ··◂/ also **self-suf·fic·ing**— *adj* [(*in*)] able to provide for one's needs without outside help, esp. (of a country) without buying goods and services from abroad

self-sup·port·ing /ˌ· ·ˈ··◂/ *adj* earning enough money to pay its/one's costs without getting into debt or needing money from outside

self-will /ˌ· ˈ·/ *n* [U] strong unreasonable determination to follow one's own wishes, esp. in opposition to others —**~ed** *adj*

self-wind·ing /ˌ· ˈ··◂/ *adj* (of a wristwatch) winding itself as a result of being in movement on the arm

sell[1] /sel/ *v* **sold** /səʊld/ **1** [D1 (*to*); T1;X7;IØ] to give up (property or goods) to another for money or other value: *to sell one's house/car/business/books/ I sold my brother my car for £100.|I sold my car to my brother for £100.|dishonest voters who sell their votes to whoever pays most|I'd like to buy your house if you're willing to sell* **2** [T1] to help or cause (something) to be bought: *Bad news sells newspapers.|That name on the cover is enough to sell the book* **3** [T1;IØ] to offer (goods) for sale: *My job is selling insurance.|Do you sell cigarettes in this shop?* **4** [IØ (*at, for*)] to be bought; get a buyer or buyers; gain a sale: *a newspaper selling for/at 10p|The tickets cost too much and sold badly/wouldn't sell* **5** [T1 (*on*)] *infml* to persuade (someone) to like, believe, or agree to something: *Can you sell the chief on your plan?|I'm completely sold on the need to exercise every day* **6** [D1 (*to*); T1] *infml* to persuade of the truth or goodness of (a new, unlikely, or strange suggestion, idea, etc.): *Can you sell the chief your new idea?|What an excuse! You'll never sell that to anyone* **7** [T1 *usu. pass.*] *infml* trick; cheat; deceive: *The things we bought are no good: we've been sold!* **8 sell oneself a** to make oneself or one's ideas seem attractive to others **b** to give up one's principles for money or other gain **9 sell one's soul (to the devil)** to act dishonourably in exchange for money, power, fame, etc. **10 sell short** to sell something, esp. shares (STOCK[1] (10)) in a company, not yet owned but expected to be bought later at a lower price **11 sell something/someone short** to value something or someone too low: *"John is a fool." "I don't think so: you're selling him short"* —see also **sell like hot** CAKE*s*[1] (6), **sell someone down the** RIVER

sell[2] *n* [S] *infml* a deception: *The prize was supposed to be a free trip to Europe, but it turned out to be just a picture book of London. What a sell!* —see also HARD SELL, SOFT SELL

sell·er /ˈseləʳ/ *n* **1** [C] a person who sells **2** [C] a product with large sales: *The book surprised us by being such a seller* **3** [C9] (*sometimes in comb.*) a product with the stated type or amount of sales: BEST-SELLER|*He hopes his new book will be a bigger seller than the last*

seller's mar·ket /ˌ·· ˈ··/ *n* [S] a state of affairs in which goods are scarce, buyers have little choice, and prices are high —compare BUYER'S MARKET

selling point /ˈ·· ·/ *n* something which is pointed to in favour of a product to help it to be sold

sell off *v adv* [T1] to get rid of (goods) by selling, usu. cheaply

sel·lo·tape[1] /ˈseləteɪp, ˈseləʊ-/ (*AmE tdmk* **scotch tape**)— *n* [U] *tdmk* (*often cap.*) sticky thin clear material (CELLULOID) in long narrow lengths sold in rolls, for sticking paper, mending light objects, etc.

sellotape[2] (*AmE tdmk* **scotch tape**)— *v* [T1;X7] *tdmk* to put SELLOTAPE on; put together or mend with this

sell-out /ˈ· ·/ *n* [*usu. sing.*] *not fml* **1** a performance, sports match, etc., for which all tickets are sold **2** an act of disloyalty or unfaithfulness to one's purposes or friends; BETRAYAL

sell out *v adv* **1** [Wv5;T1;IØ: (*of*)] **a** to (cause to) sell all of (what was for sale): *The shop sold out all their shirts.=The shop sold out of shirts.|Sorry, we're all sold out of shirts in your size.|Sorry, the tickets are sold out: there are no more left.* **b** (of things for sale) to be all bought: *The shirts were cheap and sold out fast* **2** [IØ;T1] to sell (one's share in a business): *At 65 he sold out (his shop) and moved to Cornwall* **3** [T1;IØ] to be disloyal or unfaithful to (one's purposes or friends), esp. for money: *a good writer who sold out (his artistic standards) and now just writes for money*

sell up *v adv* **1** [T1;IØ] to sell (something, esp. a business) completely **2** [T1] to force (someone) to sell everything to pay a debt

sel·vage, -vedge /ˈselvɪdʒ/ *n* the edge on both sides of a length of cloth that is strengthened and finished to prevent threads from coming out

selves /selvz/ *pl. of* SELF

se·man·tic /sɪˈmæntɪk/ *adj* [Wa5] of or related to meaning in language

se·man·tics /sɪˈmæntɪks/ *n* [U] **1** the study of the meanings of words and other parts of language **2** the general study of signs and what they stand for

sem·a·phore[1] /ˈseməfɔːʳ‖-for/ *n* **1** [C] a tall post with coloured lights and an arm movable to different positions, used as a signal on railways **2** [U] a system of sending messages, using 2 flags held 1 in each hand in various positions to represent letters and numbers

semaphore[2] *v* [IØ;T1] to send (a message) by SEMAPHORE (2)

sem·blance /ˈsembləns/ *n* [S9, esp. *of*] an appearance; outward form or seeming likeness: *a pile of papers all over the desk with no semblance of order*

se·men /ˈsiːmən/ *n* [U] the liquid produced by the sex organs of the male, carrying SPERM and passed into the female during sexual union

se·mes·ter /sɨˈmestəʳ/ *n* either of the 2 periods into which a year at universities, esp. in the US, is divided —compare TERM

sem·i- /ˈsemɪ/ *prefix* **1** exactly half: SEMICIRCLE|SEMIQUAVER **2** part(ly) but not complete(ly): *semidarkness|semi*LITERATE|*semiliquid|semiprecious jewels* **3** happening, appearing, etc., twice in each period: *a semiweekly visit|semi*ANNUAL

sem·i·breve /ˈsemɪbriːv/ *AmE* **whole note**— *n BrE* a musical note with a time value equal to 2 MINIM*s* —see picture at NOTATION

sem·i·cir·cle /ˈsemɪˌsɜːkəl‖-ɜr-/ *n* **1** the part of a circle from one end of a line through the centre to the other; half a circle —see picture at GEOMETRY **2** a group arranged in the form of this: *The family sat around the fire in a semicircle* —**-cular** /ˌsemɪˈsɜːkjʊləʳ‖-ˈsɜrkjə-/ *adj*

sem·i·co·lon /ˌsemɪˈkəʊlən‖ˈsemɪˌkəʊlən/ *n* a mark (;) used in writing and printing to separate different members of lists and sometimes independent parts of a sentence

sem·i·con·duc·tor /ˌsemɪkənˈdʌktəʳ/ *n* a substance which allows the passing of an electric current more easily at high temperatures

sem·i·de·tached[1] /ˌsemɪdɪˈtætʃt/ *adj* [Wa5] (of a house) joined to another house by 1 shared wall; being one of a pair of joined houses —see picture at HOUSE[1]

semidetached[2] also (*infml*) **sem·i** /ˈsemɪ/— *n esp. BrE* a SEMIDETACHED house

sem·i·fi·nal /ˌsemɪˈfaɪnl◂‖ˈsemɪˌfaɪnl/ *n* (either of) a pair of matches whose winners then compete against one another to decide the winner of the whole competition

sem·i·fi·nal·ist /ˌsemɪˈfaɪnl-ɨst/ *n* a player who reaches the SEMIFINAL*s* in a competition

sem·i·nal /ˈsemɨnəl/ *adj* **1** containing the seeds of later development; influencing others in a new way; ORIGINAL[1] (2,3) **2** [Wa5] of or containing SEMEN

sem·i·nar /ˈsemɨnɑːʳ/ *n* a small class of usu. advanced students meeting to study some subject with a teacher

sem·i·nar·ist /ˈsemɨnərɨst/ also (*esp. AmE*) **sem·i·nar·i·an** /ˌsemɨˈneərɪən/— *n* a student at a SEMINARY, esp. of the ROMAN CATHOLIC Church

sem·i·na·ry /ˈsemɨnəri‖-neri/ *n* **1** [C] **a** a college for training ROMAN CATHOLIC priests **b** *AmE* a college for training other priests, usu. of a particular branch of the church (DENOMINATION) **2** *pomp & old use* a private school for girls: *a young ladies' seminary*

sem·i·ol·o·gy, semeiology /ˌsemiˈɒlədʒi‖ˌsiːmiˈɑ-/ also **sem·i·ot·ics** /ˌsemiˈɒtɪks‖-ˈɑtɪks/— *n* [U] *tech* the study of signs in general, esp. as they are related to language

sem·i·pre·cious /ˌsemɪˈpreʃəs◂/ *adj* [Wa5] (of a jewel, stone, etc.) of lower value than a PRECIOUS STONE

sem·i·qua·ver /ˈsemɪˌkweɪvəʳ/ *AmE* **sixteenth note**— *n BrE* a musical note ♬, with a time value half as long as a QUAVER

Se·mit·ic /sɨˈmɪtɪk/ *adj* **1** [Wa5] of or concerning a race of people including Jews and Arabs and (in ancient times) others including Babylonians and Assyrians, or any of their languages **2** Jewish —compare ANTI-SEMITISM

sem·i·tone /ˈsemɪtəʊn/ *AmE* **half step**— *n BrE* a difference in PITCH[3] (7) (highness of a musical note) equal to that between 2 notes which are next to each other on a piano

sem·i·trop·i·cal /ˌsemɪˈtrɒpɪkəl◂‖-ˈtrɑ-/ *adj* [Wa5] SUBTROPICAL

sem·i·vow·el /ˈsemɪˌvaʊəl/ *n tech* a sound like a vowel sound made with the tongue close to the top of the mouth, but moving quickly on to another position, as w or j in English

sem·i·week·ly /ˌsemɪˈwiːkli/ *adv, adj* [Wa5] appearing or happening twice a week —compare BIWEEKLY

sem·o·li·na /ˌseməˈliːnə/ *n* [U] hard grains of crushed wheat used in making certain food pastes (PASTA) and smooth cooked milky dishes: *semolina* PUDDING (2)

semp·stress /ˈsempstrɨs/ *n esp. BrE* SEAMSTRESS

SEN /ˌes iː ˈen/ *abbrev. for*: STATE ENROLLED NURSE

sen·ate /ˈsenɨt/ *n* (*usu. cap.*) **1** [(*the*) GC] the smaller (UPPER) of the 2 law-making groups (HOUSE*s*[1] (6a)) in some countries such as Australia, Canada, France, and the US: *a speech on the floor of the Senate* (=in the Senate) **2** [*the*+GU] the highest council of state in ancient Rome **3** [(*the*) GC] the governing council at some universities

sen·a·tor /ˈsenətəʳ/ *n* [C;A;N] (*often cap.*) a member of a SENATE (1,2)

sen·a·to·ri·al /ˌsenəˈtɔːrɪəl‖-ˈto-/ *adj* [Wa5] of or concerning a SENATE or SENATOR

send /send/ *v* **sent** /sent/ **1** [D1 (*to*); T1;V3,4] to cause to go or be taken to a place, in a direction, etc.: *If you need money I'll send it|I'll send you some.|You should send your shoes to be repaired.|The explosion sent glass flying everywhere* **2** [X9;V3,4] to cause, direct, order, etc., (a person) to go: *sent his army into battle|sent his children to good schools|The child was sent to buy some milk.|The accident sent me looking for a new car* **3** [X7,9, esp. *into*; V4] to cause to have a particular feeling or be in a particular state: *The news sent the family into great excitement.|The victory sent our spirits rising.|This noise will send me mad!* **4** [IØ (*for*), 3] to cause a message, request, or direction to go out; give a command, request, etc.: *The King sent and had the man brought to him.|He sent to tell us he couldn't come.|Send for a doctor!* **5** [X9, esp. OUT, FORTH] (of a natural object) to produce from itself: *the sun sending out light|branches sending* FORTH *their fruit* **6** [T1] *infml* (esp. of art or music) to be very pleasing and exciting to (someone): *Man, his playing really sends me!* **7** [D1 (*to*); T1,5a] *lit* (esp. of God) to give or provide; GRANT[1] (1): *Heaven send that we'll arrive safely!|Heaven send us a safe journey!* **8** [IØ;T1] (of a (person using a) radio apparatus) to TRANSMIT: *The ship's radio sent out signals for help* **9 send word** to send a message

send a·way also **send off**— *v adv* **1** [T1] to send to another place: *He sent his son away/off to school in Germany* **2** [IØ (*for*), 3] to order (goods) to be sent by post: *I couldn't get this kind of lamp in town, so I sent away for it*

send down *v adv* **1** [T1] to cause to go down: *Send these orders down to our branch office.|Bad news sent market prices down* **2** [I∅ (*to*)] to send a message, order, etc., to some lower place: *I'll send down to the kitchen to get some more coffee* **3** [T1 *usu. pass.*] *BrE* to dismiss (a student) from a university for bad behaviour **4** [T1 (*for*)] *infml BrE* to send (someone) to prison: *sent down for 10 years for robbing a bank* —see DOWN (USAGE)

send·er /ˈsendəʳ/ *n fml* a person who sends esp. a letter, parcel, message, etc.

send in *v adv* [T1] **1** to send (a letter, piece of work for a competition, etc.) to some central place **2** to give (one's name or card) to a servant when making a formal visit

send-off /ˈ· ·/ *n not fml* a usu. planned show of good wishes at the start of a trip, new business, etc.

send off *v adv* **1** [T1] to post (a letter, parcel, message, etc.) **2** [T1] *BrE* (esp. in football) to cause (a player) to leave the field because of a serious breaking of the rules **3** [T1;I∅ (*for*), 3] SEND AWAY **4** [T1] SEE OFF

send on *v adv* [T1] **1** to send (a letter) to the receiver's next address: *When he moved he left instructions for his letters to be sent on to his new address* **2** to send (belongings) in advance to a point on a trip

send out *v adv* **1** [T1] to send from a central point: *send out invitations/orders* **2** [I∅ (*for*)] to (try to) obtain something from somewhere else: *When we want coffee we send out (for it) to a local restaurant*

send-up /ˈ· ·/ *n infml BrE* something which SENDs UP (2) a subject, person, etc.; PARODY

send up *v adv* [T1] **1** to cause to go up: *a fire sending up smoke into the air|Good news sent prices up on the market* **2** *BrE* to copy the funny or silly qualities, actions, etc. of (a subject, person, etc.) to call attention to them in a joking way; make fun of **3** *infml AmE* to send (someone) to prison

se·nes·cence /sɪ̈ˈnesəns/ *n* [U] *fml & med* the condition of being SENESCENT; beginning of old age

se·nes·cent /sɪ̈ˈnesənt/ *adj fml & med* growing old; showing signs of old age

sen·e·schal /ˈsenɪ̈ʃəl/ *n* an important servant and sometimes representative in matters of law of a nobleman in the MIDDLE AGES

se·nile /ˈsiːnaɪl/ *adj* of or coming from old age; showing the weakness of body or esp. of mind connected with old age

se·nil·i·ty /sɪˈnɪlɪ̈ti/ *n* [U] the weakness of mind or body connected with old age

se·ni·or[1] /ˈsiːnɪəʳ/ *n* **1** a person who is older than another **2** *AmE* a student in the last year of a school or university course

senior[2] *adj* **1** [Wa5;F (*to*)] **a** older **b** of higher rank **c** having done longer service in an organization **2** [B] **a** old: *too senior to try for a young man's job* **b** of high rank: *a meeting of the most senior army officers*

Senior *n* [E] the older: *John Smith Senior is the father of John Smith*

senior cit·i·zen /ˌ··· ˈ···/ *n euph* an old person, esp. one over the age of 60 (for a woman) or 65 (for a man)

se·ni·or·i·ty /ˌsiːniˈɒrɪ̈ti‖-ˈɔ-, -ˈɑ-/ *n* [U] **1** the condition of being SENIOR[2] (1) in rank or age **2** official advantage coming from the length of one's service in an organization

sen·na /ˈsenə/ *n* [U] dried leaves from a type of tropical plant, used as a medicine to help the action of the bowels (a LAXATIVE)

Se·ñor /seˈnjɔːʳ‖seɪˈnjor (*Span* seˈɲor)/ *n* **-ñores** /ˈnjɔːreɪz‖ˈnjoreɪz/ (*Span* seˈɲores)/ *or* **-ñors** [A] the title of a Spanish(-speaking) man

Se·ño·ra /seˈnjɔːrə‖seɪˈnjorə (*Span* seˈɲora)/ *n* [A] the title of a (married) Spanish(-speaking) woman

Se·ño·ri·ta /ˌsenjɔːˈriːtə‖ˌsenjo- (*Span* seɲoˈrita)/ *n* [A] the title of an unmarried Spanish(-speaking) girl

sen·sa·tion /senˈseɪʃən/ *n* **1** [U;C] (a) direct feeling (as of heat or pain) coming from the senses: *could feel no sensation in his arm* **2** [C] a general feeling in the mind or body that one cannot describe exactly: *I knew the train had stopped, but I had the sensation that it was moving backwards* **3** [C] (a cause of) a state of excited interest: *The new discovery was/caused a great sensation*

sen·sa·tion·al /senˈseɪʃənəl/ *adj* **1** *often derog* causing excited interest or attention: *a sensational murder* **2** (esp. of writing or news reports) intended to cause quick excitement or shock **3** *sl* wonderful; very good or exciting: *Your team won? That's sensational!* **4** [Wa5] *tech* of or concerning the senses —**~ly** *adv*

sen·sa·tion·al·is·m /senˈseɪʃənəlɪzəm/ *n* [U] the intentional producing of excitement or shock, as by books, magazines, etc., of low quality —**-ist** *n*

sense[1] /sens/ *n* **1** [C] **a** an intended meaning: *The sense of the sentence was hard to understand* **b** any of several (different kinds of) meanings: *"man" in its broadest sense, including both men and women* **c** any of the parts of an explanation of a word separated as in this dictionary by the numbers **1**, **2**, etc. **2** [C9, esp. *of*] any of the 5 SENSES: *the senses of taste and smell* —see also SIXTH SENSE **3** [C9;U9, esp *of*] power to understand and make judgments about something: *a sense of values/direction|a successful man with good business sense* **4** [S+*of*; S5] a feeling, esp. one that is hard to describe exactly: *a sense that someone was standing behind him|a sense of* WARMTH *near the fire* **5** [U] good and esp. practical understanding and judgment: *Haven't you got enough sense to come in out of the rain?* —see also COMMON SENSE, HORSE SENSE **6** [U] the agreed opinion of a group (esp. in the phr. **the sense of the meeting**) **7 in a sense** in one way of speaking; partly: *You are right in a sense, but you don't know all the facts* **8 make sense a** to have a clear meaning: *No matter how you read it, this sentence doesn't make (any) sense* **b** *not fml* to be a wise course of action: *It makes sense to take care of your health* **9 make sense (out) of** to understand: *Can you make sense of what this writer is saying?* **10 (there's) no sense (in)** *infml* no good reason for: *no sense (in) looking for the coin under the table: you won't find it there* **11 talk sense** *infml* to speak reasonably *"Perhaps we shouldn't go out in this bad weather." "Now you're talking sense!"*

sense[2] *v* **1** [T1,5,6a,b] to have a feeling, without being told directly, (of): *The horse sensed danger and stopped.|She sensed what her husband was thinking* **2** [T1] (esp. of a machine) to discover and record; DETECT: *an apparatus to sense the presence of poisonous gases*

sense·less /ˈsensləs/ *adj* **1** [Wa5] in a sleeplike state, as after a blow on the head; unconscious **2** marked by a lack of meaning or thinking; foolish; purposeless —**~ly** *adv* —**~ness** *n* [U]

sense or·gan /ˈ· ˌ··/ *n* a part of the body (such as the eye, nose, tongue, or ear) from which the brain receives messages from the outside world

sens·es /ˈsensɪ̈z/ *n* **1** [(*the*) P] the 5 natural powers (sight, hearing, feeling, tasting, and smelling) which give a person or animal information about the outside world **2** [P9] one's powers of (reasonable) thinking: *Are you mad? Have you taken leave of/lost your senses?|She felt faint in the hot room but the fresh air made her come to her senses again*

sen·si·bil·i·ty /ˌsensəˈbɪlɨti/ *n* **1** [U;C *usu. pl.*] (a) tender or delicate feeling about what is correct, as in art or behaviour: *plays the piano with great sensibility|a man of sensibility/-ities* **2** [U (*to*)] sensitiveness: *sensibility to pain* **3** [U (*of, to*)] *fml* the condition of recognizing; AWAREness: *our sensibility to your trouble* —see SENSIBLE (USAGE)

sen·si·ble /ˈsensəbəl/ *adj* **1** [B] reasonable; having or showing good sense **2** [F+*of*] *fml* knowing; recognizing; AWARE: *sensible of the trouble he caused* **3** [B] noticeable; that can be SENSEd: *a sensible increase in temperature* **4** [B] SENSITIVE —**-bly** *adv*

USAGE **Sensibility** is not related to **sensible** in its meaning of "reasonable and practical" but is closer to **sensible** *of* ="conscious of". A **sensitive** person has great **sensibility**; he has delicate feelings and is quick to enjoy or suffer. **Sensuous** and **sensual** are also connected with the **senses**, but **sensual** means "of the body rather than of the mind or spirit" and is often bad, while **sensuous** may be used about the beauties of colour, sound, etc.

sen·si·tive /ˈsensɨtɪv/ *adj* **1** [(*to*)] quick to show or feel the effect of a force or of the presence of something: *sensitive to cold/pain|light-sensitive photographic paper* **2** (of an apparatus) measuring exactly: *a sensitive pair of scales* **3** showing delicate feelings or judgment: *a sensitive performance/actor* **4** *sometimes derog* (of a person) easily hurt in the feelings, esp. of self-respect; easily offended —compare HYPERSENSITIVE **5** dealing with secret government work: *sensitive official papers* —**~ly** *adv* —see SENSIBLE (USAGE)

sen·si·tiv·i·ty /ˌsensɨˈtɪvɨti/ also **sen·si·tive·ness** /ˈsensɨtɪvnɨs/— *n* [U] the quality, state, or degree of being sensitive

sen·si·tize, -tise /ˈsensɨtaɪz/ *v* [Wv5;T1] to make sensitive: *sensitized photographic film|I've now become sensitized to strange sounds in the night, and I often wake up*

sen·sor /ˈsensəʳ/ *n tech* any apparatus used for discovering the presence of a particular quality or effect (such as light, heat, sound, etc.)

sen·so·ry /ˈsensəri/ *adj* [Wa5] of, from, or concerning the bodily senses or their use: *sensory* PERCEPTION

sen·su·al /ˈsenʃʊəl/ *adj* **1** *lit & usu. derog* interested in, related to, etc., giving pleasure to one's own body, as by sex, food, and drink —compare SENSUOUS **2** [Wa5] of, or seen, felt, etc. by the senses: *sensual objects/experiences* —see SENSIBLE (USAGE)

sen·su·al·ist /ˈsenʃʊəlɨst/ *n derog* a person very interested in SENSUAL pleasure

sen·su·al·i·ty /ˌsenʃʊˈælɨti/ *n* [U] the state of being SENSUAL; fondness for SENSUAL pleasure

sen·su·ous /ˈsenʃʊəs/ *adj lit* being, of, concerning, causing, interested in, etc., feelings esp. of pleasure by the senses: *The cat stretched itself with sensuous pleasure in the warm sun* —see SENSIBLE (USAGE) —**~ly** *adv* —**~ness** *n* [U]

sent /sent/ *past t. and past p. of* SEND

sen·tence[1] /ˈsentəns/ *n* **1** (an order given by a judge which fixes) a punishment for a criminal found guilty in court: *He received a heavy/light* (=long/short) *sentence.|The sentence was 10 years* (*in prison*) *and a* FINE (=payment) *of £1000* **2** a group of words that forms a statement, command, EXCLAMATION, or question, usu. contains a subject and a verb, and (in writing) begins with a capital letter and ends with one of the marks ".!?" *The following are all sentences: "Sing the song again." "Birds sing." "How well he sings!" "Who sang at the concert last night?"* **3 a life sentence** an order to spend an unlimited period of time in prison **4 a/the death sentence** an order to be killed as a punishment **5 give/pass/pronounce sentence** (of a judge) to say the order for a punishment **6 under sentence of death** having received a death sentence

sentence[2] *v* [T1 *often pass.* (*to*); (I∅)] (of a judge or court) to give a punishment (to): *He was sentenced to 3 years in prison*

sen·ten·tious /senˈtenʃəs/ *adj* **1** showing too great care about what is right and wrong; full of supposedly wise moral remarks; moralizing (MORALIZE) **2** *now rare* marked by short neat expressions of general meaning; APHORISTIC —**~ly** *adv*

sen·tient /ˈsenʃənt/ *adj* **1** having feelings and some kind of consciousness **2** [(*of*)] *lit* recognizing; AWARE: *a young boy beginning to be sentient of the wide world around him*

sen·ti·ment /ˈsentɨmənt/ *n* **1** [U;C *often pl. with sing. meaning*] (a) thought or judgment arising from or marked by feeling: *noble sentiments|strong public sentiment on the question of higher taxes* **2** [U;C] (a) tender or fine feeling, as of pity, love, sadness, or imaginative remembrance of the past: *There's no place for sentiment in business affairs!|It's not a beautiful watch, but I wear it for sentiment because it was my father's* **3** [C *usu. pl. with sing. meaning*] an opinion about a matter: *"That's an ugly house." "I share your sentiments."|"(Those are) My sentiments exactly"* **4** [C *sometimes pl. with sing. meaning*] a phrase or expression of a wish or feeling: *A birthday card usually has a suitable sentiment like "Happy Birthday" on it*

sen·ti·ment·al /ˌsentɨˈmentl/ *adj* **1** marked by or arising from tender feelings, esp. rather than reasonable or practical ones **2** showing too much of such feelings, esp. of a weak or unreal kind: *sentimental love stories* —**~ly** *adv*

sen·ti·ment·al·is·m /ˌsentɨˈmentəl-ɪzəm/ *n* [U] the quality of being SENTIMENTAL; fondness for what is SENTIMENTAL: *19th century sentimentalism in literature* —**-ist** *n*

sen·ti·men·tal·i·ty /ˌsentɨmənˈtælɨti/ *n* [U] *often derog* SENTIMENTALISM

sen·ti·ment·al·ize, -ise /ˌsentɨˈmentəlaɪz/ *v derog* **1** [I∅ (*over, about*)] to think or behave SENTIMENTALly: *sentimentalizing about his childhood* **2** [Wv5; T1] to treat or consider in a SENTIMENTAL way: *a sentimentalized description of what was really a terrible time to live*

sen·ti·nel /ˈsentɪnəl/ *n lit & old use* a guard; SENTRY

sen·try /ˈsentri/ *n* **1** a soldier standing as a guard, as outside a building or entrance **2 on sentry-go** *BrE* on duty as a guard

sentry box /ˈ·· ·/ *n* a narrow shelter for a SENTRY to stand in while on duty

se·pal /ˈsepəl/ *n tech* any of the leaves forming a CALYX —see picture at FLOWER[1]

sep·a·ra·ble /ˈsepərəbəl/ *adj* that can be made or considered separate —**-bly** *adv* —**-bility** /ˌsepərəˈbɪlɨti/ [U]

sep·a·rate[1] /ˈsepəreɪt/ *v* **1** [T1;I∅: (*from*)] to set or move apart; (cause to) become disconnected: *separate the 2 pipes by unscrewing them|2 branches of the church which separated in the 15th century* **2** [T1 *often pass.*] to keep apart; mark a division between: *two towns separated by a river|a wall separating the rooms* **3** [T1;I∅: (UP, *into*)] to break or divide up into the parts forming the whole (of a mass or group): *a machine to separate the grains of* *wheat into heaps according to size|An orange separates (up) into 10 or 12 pieces.|The rope began to separate under the heavy load* **4** [IØ;T1: (OUT)] **a** to cause (a part of a mixture) to leave a mixture and form a mass by itself **b** (of a part of a mixture) to do this **5** [IØ] (of people) to go in different directions away from one another **6** [IØ;T1 *usu. pass.*] **a** (of a husband and wife) to live apart, esp. by a formal agreement **b** to cause (a husband and wife) to do this

sep·a·rate² /ˈsepərɨ̈t/ *adj* **1** [Wa5;B] not the same, different; DISTINCT (1): *This word has 3 separate meanings.|a list of 10 separate ways to kill rats* **2** [Wa5;A] not shared with another; INDIVIDUAL: *everyone thinking of his own separate interests|We went our separate ways home from the theatre* **3** [F (*from*)] apart; not joined: *Keep the onions separate from the bread or they'll make it smell* —**~ness** *n* [U] —**~ly** *adv* [Wa5]

sep·a·ra·tion /ˌsepəˈreɪʃən/ *n* **1** [U;C] (a) breaking or coming apart: *This fastening allows (an) easy separation of the 2 parts* **2** [C] a distance apart: *separations of ¼ inch between the lines on the paper* **3** [C;U: (*from*)] (a time of) (esp. a person's) being or living apart: *unhappy because of his separation from his mother* **4** [C] *law* a formal agreement by a husband and wife to live apart —compare DIVORCE **5 separation of church and state** formal independence of religious bodies and the government, as in the US, but not in countries like Britain with an ESTABLISHED (6) church

sep·a·rat·is·m /ˈsepərətɪzəm/ *n* [U] **1** the belief or aim of a group that wants to become separate from a political or religious body **2** belief in keeping (groups of people) apart: *racial and class separatism* —**-ist** *n*

sep·a·ra·tor /ˈsepəreɪtəʳ/ *n* any of various (parts of) machines for separating or keeping separate, esp. a machine to separate cream from milk

se·pi·a /ˈsiːpɪə/ *n* [U] **1** a brown paint or ink made from liquid produced by CUTTLEFISH: *a sepia drawing* (=one made with this) **2** the colour of this: *an old-fashioned sepia photograph*

se·poy /ˈsiːpɔɪ/ *n* an Indian soldier in a European army in India, esp. the British army there before 1947

sep·sis /ˈsepsɨ̈s/ *n* **-ses** /siːz/ [U;C] *med* a poisoning of part of the body by disease bacteria, often producing a yellowish substance (PUS) there

Sep·tem·ber /sepˈtembəʳ/ *n* [R;(C)] the 9th month of the year

sep·tet /sepˈtet/ *n* (a piece of music written for) a group of 7 people playing instruments or singing together

sep·tic /ˈseptɪk/ *adj* **1** *esp. BrE* infected; marked by SEPSIS **2** [Wa5] causing, related to, or being certain natural chemical changes (DECOMPOSITION) caused by bacteria

sep·ti·cae·mi·a, *AmE* **-cemia** /ˌseptɨ̈ˈsiːmɪə/ *n* [U] *tech* BLOOD POISONING

septic tank /ˈ·· ·/ *n* a large container built underground, esp. near buildings in country areas, where body waste matter carried by pipes is broken up and chemically changed by the action of bacteria

sep·tu·a·ge·nar·i·an /ˌseptʃʊədʒɨ̈ˈneərɪən/ *adj, n* [Wa5] (a person who is) between 70 and 79 years old

Sep·tu·a·ges·i·ma /ˌseptʃʊəˈdʒesɨ̈mə/ *n* [R] *tech* the 3rd Sunday before LENT

Sep·tu·a·gint /ˈseptʃʊədʒɪnt/ *n* [*the*+R] the OLD TESTAMENT in its most ancient translation into Greek

se·pul·chral /sɨ̈ˈpʌlkrəl/ *adj* **1** [Wa5] of, related to, or being a reminder of the dead **2** like, suitable for, etc., a grave

sep·ul·chre, *AmE* **-cher** /ˈsepəlkəʳ/ *n old use & bibl* a burial place; TOMB

se·quel /ˈsiːkwəl/ *n* **1** a story, film, etc., which continues the course of action, or has the same characters, as an earlier one **2** [(*to*)] something that follows something else, esp. as a result

se·quence /ˈsiːkwəns/ *n* **1** [C] a group of things arranged in an order, esp. following one another in time: *a sequence of historical plays by Shakespeare|bad luck with a whole sequence of misfortunes* **2** [U] the order in which things or esp. events follow one another; SUCCESSION: *Please keep the numbered cards in sequence: don't mix them up.|The sequence of events on the night of the murder still isn't known* **3** [C] a part of a story, esp. in a film, dealing with a single subject or action; scene; EPISODE **4** [C] (in MATHEMATICS) a set with quantities in the fixed order 1, 2, 3, etc. *the sequence* $1, x, x^2, x^3, \ldots$

se·quenc·ing /ˈsiːkwənsɪŋ/ *n* [U] arrangement in an order, esp. in time: *a busy railway station where the sequencing of trains was a difficult job*

se·quent /ˈsiːkwənt/ *adj* [Wa5] *lit* following in an order, esp. as a result

se·quen·tial /sɪˈkwenʃəl/ *adj* [Wa5] of, forming, or following in (a) SEQUENCE (1,2,4) —**~ly** *adv*

se·ques·ter /sɪˈkwestəʳ/ *v* [T1] **1** [Wv5] *lit* to hide from public view; keep apart from (other) people **2** SEQUESTRATE

se·ques·trate /sɪˈkwestreɪt, ˈsiːkwɨ̈-/ *v* [T1 *usu. pass.*] *law* to seize or take control, by the order of a court, of (property), as of a debtor, until the claims on it are settled

se·ques·tra·tion /ˌsiːkwɨ̈ˈstreɪʃən/ *n* [C;U] **1** the state, or a period of time, of being SEQUESTERed **2** *law* **a** an act of sequestrating (SEQUESTRATE) **b** the state of being SEQUESTRATEd

se·quin /ˈsiːkwɨ̈n/ *n* a very small flat round shiny ornament of metal or plastic used for sewing onto a piece of clothing (often over a large area) for ornament —**~ed** *adj*

se·quoi·a /sɪˈkwɔɪə/ *n* [C;U] any of several types of very large long-living tree of the western US, including the REDWOOD

se·ra·gli·o /sɨ̈ˈrɑːljəʊ/ *n* **-glios** HAREM

ser·aph /ˈserəf/ *n* **-aphs** *or* **-aphim** /-rəfɪm/ *bibl & lit* any of the 6-winged heavenly beings (ANGELs) of the highest rank guarding the seat of God

se·raph·ic /sɨ̈ˈræfɪk/ *adj* **1** *lit* like or suitable to a SERAPH (1), esp. in beauty or purity; SUBLIME (1): *a seraphic smile|child* **2** [Wa5] *bibl & lit* of or concerning SERAPHs

sere, sear /sɪəʳ/ *adj esp. lit* dried up; WITHEREd (1): *leaves become sere in the hot dry weather*

ser·e·nade¹ /ˌserɨ̈ˈneɪd/ *n* **1** a song or other music (to be) sung or played in the open air at night, esp. to a woman by a lover **2** a piece of music, usu. in several parts, (to be) played by a small group of instruments

serenade² *v* [T1] to sing or play a SERENADE (1) to

ser·en·dip·i·ty /ˌserənˈdɪpɨ̈ti/ *n* [U] the natural ability to find interesting or valuable things which one is not looking for

se·rene /sɨ̈ˈriːn/ *adj* **1** [B] completely calm and peaceful without trouble, sudden activity, or change: *a serene summer night|a serene trust in God* **2** [Wa5;A] (part of a royal title in some countries): *His Serene Highness* —**~ly** *adv* —**serenity** /sɨ̈ˈrenɨ̈ti/ *n* [U]

serf /sɜːf‖sɜrf/ *n* a person (not quite a slave) forced to stay and work on his master's land, esp. in a FEUDAL system or in the 17th and 18th centuries in eastern Europe

serf·dom /ˈsɜːfdəm‖ˈsɜr-/ *n* [U] the state or fact of being a SERF

serge /sɜːdʒ‖sɜrdʒ/ *n* [U] a type of strong cloth,

usu. woven from wool, and used esp. for suits, coats, and dresses

ser·geant /ˈsɑːdʒənt‖ˈsɑr-/ *n* [C;N;A] **1** a NONCOMMISSIONED OFFICER of upper rank in the army, airforce, or MARINES, usu. having 3 v-shaped marks on the upper arm of the uniform **2** a police officer with next to the lowest rank, typically also having such uniform marks

sergeant-at-arms /ˌ··· ˈ·/ *n* SERJEANT-AT-ARMS

sergeant ma·jor /ˌ·· ˈ··/ *n* [C;N;A] **1** a WARRANT OFFICER in the British army or ROYAL MARINES **2** a NONCOMMISSIONED OFFICER of the highest rank in the US army or MARINE CORPS

se·ri·al[1] /ˈsɪərɪəl/ *adj* [Wa5] **1** [B] of, happening or arranged in, or concerning a SERIES or row of things in order: *placed in serial order* **2** [A] of, being, or concerning a SERIAL[2] —**~ly** *adv*

serial[2] *n* **1** a written or broadcast story appearing in parts at fixed times: *"The Archers" is a British radio serial that has been heard every day for many years* **2** *tech* (used in libraries) (a book, magazine, etc. printed as one of) a continuing set with a single name and numbered 1, 2, 3, etc.

se·ri·al·ize, -ise /ˈsɪərɪəlaɪz/ *v* [T1 *often pass.*] to print or broadcast (a book already written) as a SERIAL[2] (1) —**-ization** /ˌsɪərɪəlaɪˈzeɪʃən‖-lə-/ *n* [U;C]

serial num·ber /ˈ··· ˌ··/ *n* a particular number given to one of a large group

serial rights /ˈ··· ·/ *n* [P] the lawful right to print (a long piece of writing) as a SERIAL[2] (1)

se·ri·a·tim /ˌsɪəriˈeɪtɪm/ *adv* [Wa5] *fml* one by one; one after another

ser·i·cul·ture /ˈserɪˌkʌltʃə^r/ *n* [U] *tech* the production of raw silk by breeding SILKWORM*s*

se·ries /ˈsɪəriːz/ *n* **series** [Wn3] **1** a group of things of the same kind or related in some way, coming one after another or in order: *a concert series* (=a series of concerts)|*a television series* (=a series of shows on television) **2** [C] a group of books printed by one company in the same style and often under a single name **3** [C] a set of coins or stamps, esp. of interest to a collector **4** [C] (in MATHEMATICS) the sum of the members of a SEQUENCE (4): *The series* $1+x+x^2+x^3+\ldots$ **5** [*in*+U;A] an electrical arrangement connected without branches, so that the same electricity passes through each part: *lamps in series*|*a series connection* —compare PARALLEL[2] (4) **6** [C] (in cricket and BASEBALL) a group of specially important games played one after another

ser·if /ˈserɪ̇f/ *n* **1** [C] a short line at the upper or lower end of the stroke of some types of printed letters **2** [C;U] (in printing) a letter, or type of letter, that has such lines and whose strokes are of different thicknesses, like the letters that this is printed in —compare SANS SERIF

se·ri·o·com·ic /ˌsɪəriəʊˈkɒmɪk‖-ˈkɑ-/ also **se·ri·o·com·ic·al** /ˌsɪəriəʊˈkɒmɪkəl‖-ˈkɑ-/— *adj* both serious and funny

se·ri·ous /ˈsɪərɪəs/ *adj* **1** (esp. of a person's manner or character) thoughtful; solemn; not gay or cheerful; GRAVE[2] (1) **2** not joking or funny; (intended) to be considered as sincere: *After a few jokes his speech became serious* **3** not (to be) easily or lightly dealt with; not slight: *serious damage done by the storm*|*serious crime* **4** of an important kind; needing or having great skill or thought: *This subject has never been paid any serious attention.*|*a serious artist/piece of art* —**~ness** [U]

se·ri·ous·ly /ˈsɪərɪəsli/ *adv* **1** in a serious way: *study music seriously*|*seriously wounded* **2** *infml* (used at the beginning of a sentence to turn attention from a joke or to a serious statement or subject): *Seriously now, you ought to take more care of your health* **3 take something seriously a** to treat (remarks, questions, etc.) as important and needing thought **b** to treat something as a great difficulty

ser·jeant-at-arms, sergeant- /ˌsɑːdʒənt ət ˈɑːmz‖ˌsɑrdʒənt ət ˈɑrmz/ *n* **serjeants-at-arms** an officer of a law court, parliament, etc., with the duty of keeping order during meetings

ser·mon /ˈsɜːmən‖ˈsɜr-/ *n* **1** a talk usu. based on a sentence from the Bible and given (PREACHed) as part of a church service **2** *infml* a (too) long and solemn warning or piece of advice

ser·mon·ize, -ise /ˈsɜːmənaɪz‖ˈsɜr-/ *v* [I∅] to try to teach moral lessons, esp. in a too long and solemn way; PREACH (3, esp. 4)

se·rous /ˈsɪərəs/ *adj* **1** (of a liquid) thin and watery **2** [Wa5] of or related to SERUM

ser·pent /ˈsɜːpənt‖ˈsɜr-/ *n* **1** a snake, esp. a large one **2** (from the beginning of the Bible, where the Devil appears as a creature like this) a wicked person who leads people to do wrong or harms those who are kind to him

ser·pen·tine /ˈsɜːpəntaɪn‖ˈsɜrpəntiːn/ *adj lit* twisting like a snake; turning one way and another; TORTUOUS: *the serpentine course of the river*

ser·rat·ed /sɪ̇ˈreɪtɪ̇d, se-/ *adj* having a row of connected V-shapes like teeth (as on a SAW[1]) (on the edge)

ser·ried /ˈserid/ *adj* [Wa5;A] *lit* **1** pressed closely together; CROWDED: *trees planted in serried rows* **2 serried ranks** rows (as of people) close together

se·rum /ˈsɪərəm/ *n* **-rums** *or* **-ra** /rə/ **1** [U] the watery part of an animal or plant liquid (as of blood) **2** [U;C] such (a) liquid from animal blood containing disease-fighting substances and prepared for putting into a person's or other animal's blood —compare VACCINE

ser·val /ˈsɜːvəl‖ˈsɜr-/ *n* a type of long-legged African animal of the cat family, smaller than a lion, having large ears and brown fur with black markings

ser·vant /ˈsɜːvənt‖ˈsɜr-/ *n* **1** a person who works for another, esp. in the other's house, receiving wages and (esp. in former times) food and lodgings: *They keep 2 servants: a cook and a gardener* **2** [(*of*)] *lit* a person or thing (willing to be) used for the service or purposes of another: *A politician should be a servant of the people* **3 Your (humble/obedient) servant** *now rare & pomp* **a** (an expression of good wishes or willingness to deal with someone) **b** (used before one's name at the end of a formal letter) —see also CIVIL SERVANT, PUBLIC SERVANT

serve[1] /sɜːv‖sɜrv/ *v* **1** [T1 (*as*)] to work (faithfully) for; do a useful job for: *Serve your country.*|*Our gardener has served the family for 20 years* **2** [I∅ (*on, in, as, under*)] to do a duty; have an office or job: *served in the army/on the committee*|*served under the old king* **3** [T1 (*with*)] to provide with something necessary or useful; to (try to) fill a need: *a single pipeline serving all the houses with water* **4** [X9, esp. *as, in*] to spend (a period of time) in a job or office: *served 2* TERMS[1] (3) *as President*|*served 10 years in Parliament* **5** [I∅;T1: (*for, as*); I3] to be good enough or satisfying for (a purpose or the needs) of (someone); SUFFICE (for): *One room had to serve as/for both bedroom and living room.*|*a bad roof which doesn't even serve to keep the rain out*|*I haven't got a hammer, but this stone should serve (my purpose)* **6** [I∅;T1 (*with*)] to give food to or be food for (people) as or at a meal: *In our family Mother always serves (at table).*|*This dish will serve 6 (people)* **7** [D1 (*to*); T1;X7: (UP, OUT)] to offer (food, a meal, etc.) for eating: *Be sure to serve the coffee hot.*|*What time is breakfast served in this* *hotel?* **8** [T1 *usu. pass.*] (of a person in a shop) to attend to (someone buying something); WAIT ON: *Are you being served?* (=Has someone else already taken your order?) **9** [T1 (*for*)] to spend (a period of time) in prison: *served 10 years|a long* SENTENCE¹ (1) *for his crime* **10** [I0;T1] (in tennis, VOLLEYBALL, etc.) to begin play by striking (the ball) to the opponent **11** [I0] to act as a SERVER (3) in church **12** [D1 (*with/on*)] *law* to deliver (an official order to appear in court) to (someone): *serve a* SUMMONS *on him|serve him (with) a* SUMMONS **13** [T1] *tech* (of a male animal, usu. hired for the purpose) to MATE³ with (a female) **14 as (the) occasion serves** at suitable times **15 if (my) memory serves (me)** *not fml* if I remember correctly **16 serve someone right** *infml* to be a good punishment for someone: *After all you've eaten it'll serve you right if you get a pain in your stomach* **17 serve time (for a crime)** *sl* to be in prison (as punishment for a crime)

serve² *n* an act or manner of serving (SERVE (10)), as in tennis; SERVICE¹ (14)

serve out *v adv* [T1] to work until the end of (a period of time fixed for a duty, esp. one already begun)

serv·er /ˈsɜːvəʳ‖ˈsɜr-/ *n* **1** a person who serves food **2** a player who SERVES¹ (10), as in tennis **3** a person who helps a priest during the EUCHARIST; ACOLYTE **4** something used in serving food, esp. **a** a specially-shaped tool for putting a particular kind of food onto a plate **b** a flat plate (TRAY) for carrying dishes, glasses, etc.

ser·ve·ry /ˈsɜːvəri‖ˈsɜr-/ *n* the part of an informal eating place where people get food to take back to their tables for eating

ser·vice¹ /ˈsɜːv$\frac{1}{2}$s‖ˈsɜr-/ *n* **1** [U] work or duty done for someone: *spent a life of service to others|died in the service of his country|This old coat has seen a lot of service* **2** [C *usu. pl.*] *fml* an act or job done in favour of someone: *may need the services of a lawyer in this affair|rewarded for his services to the government* **3** [U] *now rare* employment as a servant in someone's home **4** [C] any of the ARMED SERVICES: *The Royal Navy is sometimes called the* **Senior Service** **5** [U] duty in the army, navy, etc.: *He saw active service in several battles in the last war.*|NATIONAL SERVICE **6** [C9] *esp. BrE* any of several government departments: *the* DIPLOMATIC (1) *service|the* SOCIAL SERVICES **7** [U] attention to buyers in a shop or esp. to guests in a hotel, restaurant, etc.: *The service in this place is slow/bad: sometimes you have to wait 10 minutes for service* **8** [C9, esp. *for*] the dishes, tools, etc., needed to serve a stated food, meal, or number of people: *a silver tea service* **9** [C *AmE sometimes pl. with sing. meaning*] a fixed form of public worship; a religious ceremony: *a thanksgiving service to be held next Sunday|Our church has 3 services each Sunday* **10** [C;U] (the operation of) a business or organization doing useful work or supplying a need: *Is there any railway service here on Sundays?|a good postal service* **11** [C *usu. pl.*; A] a useful business or job that does not produce goods: *The value of a country's goods and services is its* GNP| *a service industry* **12** [A] something for the use of people working in a place, rather than the public: *a service entrance|service stairs* **13** [U;C] a/the repair of a machine: *Take your car for (a) service/for regular services.|the service department* (in a shop)| *The service on these machines is very poor in England* **14** [C] an act or manner of serving (SERVE¹ (10)), as in tennis: *He has a good fast service.|It's your service* (= your turn for service) **15** [C;U] *law* (a) delivering of an order to appear in court **16** [U] *tech* the act of serving (SERVE¹ (13)) a female animal **17 at your service** *polite or pomp* yours to command or use: *If you need any help, I and my car are at your service* **18 do someone a service** to do something which helps someone: *Thank you very much: you've done me a great service* **19 in the services** *BrE* in the army, navy, etc. **20 of service** of use; helpful: (*polite*) *Can I be of service to you?*

service² *v* [T1] to repair or put in good condition

ser·vi·cea·ble /ˈsɜːv$\frac{1}{2}$səbəl/ *adj* **1** that can be used; fit for (long or hard) use **2** useful; helpful: *a serviceable tool with many uses* —**-bility** /ˌsɜːv$\frac{1}{2}$səˈbɪl$\frac{1}{2}$ti‖ˌsɜr-/ *n* [U] —**~ness** /ˈsɜːv$\frac{1}{2}$səbəln$\frac{1}{2}$s‖ˈsɜr-/ *n* [U] —**-bly** /ˈsɜːv$\frac{1}{2}$səbli‖ˈsɜr-/ *adv*

service charge /ˈ·· ·/ *n* an amount of money charged for a particular service, sometimes in addition to a standard charge: *The bank makes a service charge on cheques which are returned.|a 10% service charge added to the hotel bill*

service flat /ˈ·· ·/ *n BrE* a flat of which the rent includes a charge for certain services, such as cleaning, providing food, etc.

ser·vice·man /ˈsɜːv$\frac{1}{2}$smən‖ˈsɜr-/ *n* **-men** /mən/ a male member of the army, navy, etc.

service road /ˈ·· ·/ *n* a small road along one side of a main road with few places to enter or leave it (such as a MOTORWAY), for the use of local traffic

service sta·tion /ˈ·· ˌ··/ *n* FILLING STATION

ser·vi·ette /ˌsɜːviˈet‖ˌsɜr-/ *n BrE, not fml* a table NAPKIN (1)

ser·vile /ˈsɜːvaɪl‖ˈsɜrvəl, -vaɪl/ *adj* **1** [(*to*)] behaving like a slave; allowing complete control by another: *servile expressions of praise for his employer* **2** of or concerning slaves or slavery: *The Hebrews were once brought to a servile condition in ancient Egypt* **3** (esp. in art, writing, etc.) following others without showing anything new; SLAVISH (2) —**-vility** /sɜːˈvɪl$\frac{1}{2}$ti‖sɜr-/ *n* [U] —**~ly** /ˈsɜːvaɪl-li‖ˈsɜrvəl-li, -vaɪl-li/ *adv*

serv·ing /ˈsɜːvɪŋ‖ˈsɜr-/ *n* **1** [U] the act of a person who serves: *the art of serving a meal* **2** [C] an amount of food for 1 person; HELPING

ser·vi·tor /ˈsɜːv$\frac{1}{2}$tər‖ˈsɜr-/ *n old use* a male servant

ser·vi·tude /ˈsɜːv$\frac{1}{2}$tjuːd‖ˈsɜrv$\frac{1}{2}$tuːd/ *n* [U (*to*)] *lit* the condition of a slave or one who is forced to obey another: *a life of servitude to the enemy conquerers*

ser·vo·mech·a·nis·m /ˈsɜːvəʊˌmekənɪzəm‖ˈsɜr-/ *n* an apparatus that supplies power to (part of) a machine and controls its operation

ser·vo·mo·tor /ˈsɜːvəʊˌməʊtəʳ‖ˈsɜr-/ also **ser·vo** /ˈsɜːvəʊ‖ˈsɜr-/— *n* a machine which allows a heavy operation to be done with only a slight effort by the user

ses·a·me /ˈsesəmi/ *n* [U] a type of tropical plant grown for its seeds and their oil, used esp. in cooking —see also OPEN SESAME

ses·qui- /ˈseskw$\frac{1}{2}$/ *prefix* 1½ times: *Our business began in 1825 and we had our 150th year, our sesqui*CENTENNIAL, *in 1975*

ses·sion /ˈseʃən/ *n* **1** [C, *in, out of*+U] **a** a formal meeting of an organization, esp. a law-making body or court: *Be seated! This court is now in session* **b** a time, esp. a part of a year, during which such meetings take place: *Parliament will not be in session again until after Christmas* **2** [C] *AmE & ScotE* one of the parts of the year when teaching is given at a university **3** [C] a meeting or period of time used esp. by a group for a particular purpose: *a dancing session*

ses·sions /ˈseʃənz/ *n* [P] *law* any of certain meetings of English courts of law

set¹ /set/ *v* **set,** *pres. p.* **setting** **1** [X9] to put (to stay) in a place: *set a lamp on the table|a dish to be set before a king|set guards around the gate|The boat set us on the shore.|set pen to paper* (=begin to write)|*set a match to the papers and watch them burn*|(fig.) *set him as leader over the group*|*His great height sets him apart* (=makes him clearly different) *from the others.*|*He set duty before pleasure in his mind* **2** [X7,9] to make to be in a stated condition: *opened the cage and set the bird free*|*set the mixed-up pages in order*|*set the mistake right*|*set the papers on fire* **3** [T1] to fix or determine (a rule, time, standard, number, etc.): *set a wedding day*|*set conditions for the agreement*|*set a high value on your life*|*set the price at £1000*|*set a new land speed record* **4** [D1;T1;V3] to give (a piece of work) for (someone) to do: *Who set (the questions for) the examination?*|*The teacher set the class various exercises. He then set them to write reports on what they'd done* **5** [T1] to put into a position, esp. into order for use: *set the clock (by the time given on the radio)*|*set the camera for a long-distance shot*|*set the table for dinner*|*The stage is set for the next part of the play* **6** [T1;I∅] **a** to put (a broken bone or limb) into a fixed position for proper joining **b** (of a broken bone or limb) to become joined in a fixed position **7** [T1] to fix firmly (a part of the body, esp. regarded as showing one's intention, feelings, etc.): *He set his jaw and refused to agree to anything I said.*|*She's* **set her face against** (=she opposes) *her daughter's marriage.*|*The child has* **set his heart** *on that toy: I wish I could buy it for him.*|*I've* **set my mind** *on this plan and I don't want to give it up* **8** [V4] to put into action: *Your remarks have set me thinking.*|*He set the machine going with a push* **9** [X7;T1;I∅] **a** to cause (a liquid, paste, soft material, etc.) to become solid: *Set the jelly by putting it in a cold place* **b** (of such materials) to harden or become solid **10** [T1;I∅] **a** to fix (a colour) against being changed as by water **b** (of a colour or colouring matter) to become fixed: *This chemical is used to set a* DYE[1] (1)/*make a* DYE *set* **11** [T1] *tech* to put (a bird) on eggs to HATCH[2] them **12** [I∅] (of a heavenly body) to pass downwards out of sight: *In the winter the sun sets early* —opposite **rise** **13** [T1 (UP)] to arrange ((in) metal letters (TYPE)) for printing: *Today most books are set (up) by machine* **14** [T1;I∅] **a** to arrange (hair) when wet to give the desired style when dry **b** (of hair) to dry after being arranged in this way: *straight hair that doesn't set easily* **15** [T1 (*to*)] to write or provide (music) for a poem or other words to be sung: *"Has the poem ever been set (to music)?" "Yes: it was set to an old working song tune"* **16** [D1+*in*/*with*] to fix (a precious stone) into (a piece of jewellery): *set a diamond in a ring*|*a ring set with 3 diamonds*|(fig.) *a dark sky set with bright stars* **17** [I∅] (of a plant) to form and develop seed or fruit: *Our apple trees set well last year even though there was a water* SHORTAGE **18** [X9 *often pass.*] to give a particular SETTING (3) to (a story, play, etc.): *The (action of) the book is set in 17th century Spain* **19** [I∅;T1] (of a dog) to point out the position of (a bird) with the nose while keeping still —see SIT (USAGE) —see also **set one's** CAP[1] (11) **at someone, set** FOOT[1] (25) **on, set at** NAUGHT, **set the** PACE[1] (7), **set something/someone to** RIGHTS, **set** SAIL[1] (6), SET ABOUT, SET AGAINST, SET ASIDE, SET BACK, SET BESIDE, SET DOWN, SET OFF, SET ON, SET OUT, SET TO, SET UP, SET UP AS, **set** STORE[2] (8) **by, set someone** STRAIGHT, **set someone's** TEETH[1] (8) **on edge, set to** WORK[1] (9)

set² *adj* **1** [Wa5;F9] placed; fixed; LOCATED (2): *a city set on a hill*|*eyes set deep in his head* **2** [F+*on, upon*] determined; of a fixed intention: *He's very set on going, and I can't make him see that it's a bad idea* **3** [Wa5;B] fixed; PRESCRIBED (2): *wages set by law*|*I must study at set hours each day* **4** [Wa5; B] given or fixed for study: *The examination will have questions on the set subjects/books* **5** [B] (of part of the body, manner, state of mind, etc.) fixed in position; unmoving: *She greeted her 50 guests with a set smile.*|*She's a woman of set opinions and won't change her mind now* —see also **set in one's** WAYS[1] (31) **6** [Wa5;(*all*):B (*for*);B3] ready; prepared: *Are you all set? Then let's go!*|*I was (all) set to leave the house when the telephone rang.*|*I've done my work and I'm set for the examination* **7** [Wa5;A] *BrE* (of a restaurant meal) complete and at a fixed price: *a set dinner*

set³ *n* **1** [C] a group of naturally connected things; group forming a whole: *a set of gardening tools*|*6 matching wine glasses in a set*|*a set of* FINGERPRINTS|*a 21-piece tea set* (=cups, plates, teapot, etc.) **2** *tech* (in MATHEMATICS) a formal object which is a collection of members: *the set of all numbers greater than 3*|*the set {x, y} with 2 members*|*the* NULL SET **3** [(*the*) GS9] *not fml* a group of people of a social type: *He goes around with a rather wild set.*|*the* JET SET **4** [U] a natural position of part of the body: *From the set of her shoulders it was clear that she was tired* **5** [U] the way in which (part of) a garment fits the body: *I don't like the set of this collar: it doesn't quite fit* **6** [(*the*) S] a direction, as of **a** movement, pointing, bending, etc.: *The wind had a western set* **b** thinking, opinion, etc.: *The set of public opinion is against building up the army* **7** [S] the hardening of a liquid, paste, soft solid, etc.: *You won't get a good set if you don't keep the jelly cold* **8** [C] an electrical apparatus, esp. a radio or television: *a colour television set*|*a* CRYSTAL SET| *Is your set* (=television) *working?* **9** [C] **a** something built and provided with furniture, scenery, etc., to represent the scene of (part of) the action of a play **b** a place (of this kind or in natural surroundings) where a film is acted: *Everyone must be on the set ready to begin filming at 10 o'clock* **10** [C] a part of a tennis match which may be won by a SCORE of 6 games to 0, 1, 2, 3, or 4, or 7–5, 8–6, 9–7, etc. **11** [C] a young plant to be SET OUT: *potato sets* **12** [U] the act of SETting[1] (19) by a hunting dog **13** [C] also **sett**— a type of square stone used for floors, roads, etc. **14** [S] an act or result of SETting[1] (14) hair: *I'd like a* SHAMPOO[2] (1) *and set, please* **15** [U] *poet* the going down in the sky of a heavenly body: *That will be before set of sun* —see also SUNSET **16** **make a dead set at** *BrE* **a** to combine to attack (someone): *The newspapers have made a dead set at this politician for using his official car for private purposes* **b** to try to gain the favour of (someone of the opposite sex): *Jean's making a dead set at Charles*

set about *v prep* [T1,4] to begin to do or deal with; start: *She set about her housework straight after breakfast*

set a·gainst *v prep* [D1] **1** [(OFF)] to balance (something) against (something opposite); subtract from: *Certain business losses can be set (off) against taxes* **2** to cause to oppose: *a religious war which set family against family*

set a·side *v adv* [T1] **1** also **set by**— to save for a special purpose: *set aside a little time/money each week* **2** to pay no attention to: *Setting aside my wishes in the matter, what would you really like to do?* **3** *law* to declare to be of no effect: *The judge set aside the decision of the lower court*

set·back /ˈsetbæk/ *n* **1** a going or return to a less good or advanced position than before: *She seemed better after her illness but then she had a sudden setback* **2** a defeat; REVERSE[3] (3): *The team has won 5 games, against 3 setbacks*

set back *v adv* **1** [T1] to put back (esp. by the stated distance or period); place at a distance behind something: *a house set 15 feet back from the* *road* **2** [T1] to delay the advance or development of (esp. by the stated period); make late by a certain amount: *The bad weather will set back our building plans (3 weeks)/(by 3 weeks)* **3** [D1;X9: *no pass.*] *infml* to cost (someone) (a large amount of money): *"That's a nice suit: it must have set you back quite a lot." "Yes, it set me back about £75"*

set be·side *v prep* [D1 *usu. pass.*] to compare with: *There is no one to set beside him as an actor. Set beside him, no one seems any good*

set down *v adv* [T1] **1** to put or lay down: *Set down your heavy bags and take a rest* **2** to write; make a record of: *I have set down everything that happened, as I remember it* **3** *BrE* (of a vehicle or its driver) to stop and let (a passenger) get out: *The bus sets the children down just outside the school gate*

set in *v adv* [I∅] (of a disease, unfavourable weather, or other natural condition) to begin and (probably) continue: *Winter sets in early in the north.|The sky looks as if a storm may be setting in.|Fortunately the wound was treated before infection could set in*

set off *v adv* **1** [I∅] also **set out**, (*esp. lit*) **set forth**— to begin a journey: *set off in search of the lost child|set off on a trip across Europe* **2** [T1] to cause to explode: *The bomb could be set off by the slightest touch* **3** [T1] to cause (sudden activity): *The discovery of gold in California set off a rush to get there* **4** [T1] to make (something) more noticeable or pleasing to the eye by putting it near something different: *The black cloth sets off the jewels.|a white belt to set off her blue dress* **5** [T1 *usu. pass.* (*in, by*)] to separate (a group of written words): *a sentence set off in/by* INVERTED COMMA*s*

set on *v prep* **1** [T1] (esp. of a group) to attack: *He was set on by robbers who took all his money* **2** [D1] to cause to attack or chase: *If you dare to come to my house again, I'll set the dog/the police on you!*

set out *v adv* **1** [T1] to put (young plants) into the ground separately for growing outside **2** [I3] to begin a course of action: *He set out to paint the whole house but finished only the front part* **3** [T1] also (*fml or pomp*) **set forth**— to explain (facts, reasons, etc.) in order, esp. in writing: *The reasons for my decision are set out in my report* **4** [T1] to arrange or spread out in order: *Set out the chairs for the meeting in rows of 10.|The meal was set out on a long table*

set piece /ˌ· ˈ·/ *n* **1** a work of art, literature, etc., with a well-known formal pattern or style: *Shakespeare's great set pieces|a set-piece description of a battle* **2** an arrangement of FIREWORK*s* to form a pattern when burning **3** *BrE* any of certain football plays which take place when the ordinary action of the game is stopped, such as a CORNER[1] (6) or FREE KICK

set·screw /ˈsetˌskruː/ *n* a screw for holding 2 machine parts fixed against one another or at a distance apart, or for controlling the tightness of a spring

set·square /ˈsetskweəʳ/ (*AmE* **triangle**)— *n* a flat 3-sided usu. plastic plate having one right angle and used for drawing straight lines and angles exactly —see picture at MATHEMATICAL

sett /set/ *n* SET[3] (12)

set·tee /seˈtiː/ *n* a long seat with a back and usu. arms for more than 1 person, esp. a small SOFA

set·ter /ˈsetəʳ/ *n* **1** any of 3 types of long-haired dogs often trained to point out the positions of animals for shooting —compare ENGLISH SETTER, IRISH SETTER **2** (*often in comb.*) a person or thing that sets: *a setter of traps/of fashions|a* TYPE*setter*[1] (3)

set the·o·ry /ˈ· ˌ···/ *n* [U] the branch of MATHEMATICS that deals with SET*s*[3] (2)

set·ting /ˈsetɪŋ/ *n* **1** [U] the action of a person or thing that sets: *the setting of the sun* **2** [C] the way or position in which something, esp. an instrument, is set: *This machine has 2 settings, fast and slow* **3** [C *usu. sing.*] **a** a set of surroundings: *high mountains forming a beautiful setting for a holiday trip* **b** the time and place where the action of a book, film, etc., is shown as happening: *Our story has its setting in ancient Rome* **4** [C] a set of articles (dishes, knives, forks, spoons, etc.) (to be) arranged on a table or at one place on a table for eating **5** a piece of metal holding a stone in a piece of jewellery: *a diamond in a gold setting*

set·tle[1] /ˈsetl/ *n* a long wooden seat with a high solid back, and a bottom part which is a chest having the seat for its lid

settle[2] *v* [Wv3] **1** [L9;(X9)] to (cause to) live in a place: *The conquerors settled their own people in the land.|got married and settled near Manchester* **2** [T1 *often pass.*] to provide people to live in (a place): *The American West was hardly settled until the 19th century* **3** [X9;L9] to (place so as to) stay or be comfortable: *settled himself in his chair|settled his hat on the back of his head* **4** [I∅((*up*) *on, over*)] to come to rest, esp. from above, from flight, etc.: *A bird settled on the branch.|Dust had settled on the tables and chairs.|Her cold had settled in her chest* (=hurt there but no longer in her nose or throat) **5** [I∅;T1: (DOWN)] to make or become quiet, calm, still, etc.: *This medicine should settle your nerves/your stomach.|We won't know what's really happened until the noise and excitement have settled down* **6** [T1;I∅] **a** to cause (the loose contents of something) to come closer together: *Shake the bag to settle the sugar in it: then you can pour more in* **b** (of such contents) to do this: *Shaking the bag makes the sugar settle slightly* **7 a** to separate (solid material or a liquid containing it) each from the other, usu. by causing the solid material to fall slowly to the bottom: *To settle the wine/*DREGS*, keep the bottle quite still on a shelf for 1 day* **b** (of the solid or liquid) to separate like this: *The wine/the* DREGS *will then settle* **8** [I∅] (of a building, the ground, etc.) to sink slowly to a lower level; SUBSIDE: *The crack in the wall is caused by the stone/the ground settling* **9** [T1,5,6a,b] to decide on; fix; make the last arrangements about: *We've settled that we'll go to Wales, but we haven't settled how to get there.|I'll be glad when it's* **all settled** **10** [T1;L9 (*with*)] to end (an argument, esp. in law); bring (a matter) to an agreement: *They settled their quarrel in a friendly way.|The 2 companies settled their disagreement* **out of court** (=without bringing it to court formally).|*On his unpaid taxes, he settled with the government for 50p in the £* **11** [T1] to pay (a bill or money claimed): *The insurance company settled the claim quickly, and for the full amount of the claim* **12 settle one's affairs** to put all one's business matters into order, esp. for the last time: *He settled his affairs before joining the army in 1940* **13 That settles it!** *infml* That has decided the matter!: *"The car won't start." "That settles it: we can't go out tonight"*

set·tled /ˈsetld/ *adj* **1** unlikely to change: *settled weather/habits* **2** not moving about: *a desert with no settled population* **3** [Wa5] (of a place) having people living in homes: *the settled coastal areas of Australia* **4** established; decided; fixed: *settled principles of law*

settle down *v adv* **1** [I∅;T1] to (cause to) sit comfortably: *She settled (herself) down in a chair with a book and a cup of tea* **2** [I∅] to establish a home and live a quiet life: *I hate all this travel: I* *want to get married and settle down* **3** [I∅] to become used to a way of life, job, etc.: *I'm sure the child will soon settle down in his new school* **4** [I∅ (*to*)] to give one's serious or whole attention (to a job, working, etc.): *I must settle down this morning and do the cleaning* —see also SETTLE² (5)

settle for *v prep* [T1 *no pass.*] to accept or agree to (something less than the best, or than hoped for): *I want £500 for my car and I won't settle for less.|I could never settle for such a quiet life: I want excitement*

settle in *v adv* [I∅;T1] to (help or cause to) move comfortably into or get used to a new home, job, etc.: *I haven't yet settled in/got settled in in my new job: I still find it all rather strange*

settle in·to *v prep* [T1] to get used to (new surroundings, a new job, etc.): *to settle into a new house/office*

set·tle·ment /ˈsetlmənt/ *n* **1** [U] the movement of a new population into a place to live there: *the settlement of the American West* **2** [C] a usu. recently-built small village in an area with few people: *a few settlements on the edge of the desert* **3** [U] the falling to the bottom of solid material in a liquid: *allow the wine time for settlement* **4** [U] the slow sinking of a building, the earth under it, etc. **5** [C] an agreement or decision ending an argument, question, etc.: *a settlement of a law case* **6** [C; *in*+U] a payment of money claimed: *a settlement of his tax bill* **7** [C] a formal gift or giving of money or property: *made a settlement on his daughter when she married* **8** [C] a usu. private organization in an inner city area to provide social services

settle on also **settle up·on**— *v prep* **1** [T1] to decide or agree on; choose: *She wanted blue and I wanted yellow, so we settled on green* **2** [D1] to give (money, property, etc.) to (someone) formally in law: *She settled a small yearly sum on each of her children* —compare MAKE OVER

set·tler /ˈsetləʳ/ *n* **1** a person who settles: *a settler of questions of law* **2** one of a (new) population, esp. in an area with few people: *19th century white settlers in Africa*

settle up *v adv* [I∅ (*with*)] **1** to pay what is owed on an account or bill: *settle up with the waiter after a meal* **2** (of a group) to pay and receive what is owed: *You bought the tickets and I paid for the meal. Shall we settle up now?*

set-to /ˈ· ·/ *n* [S] *not fml* a usu. short fight or quarrel

set to *v adv* [I∅] *not fml* **1** to begin eagerly or with determination: *If we all set to, we can finish cleaning the house in an hour* **2** to begin a quarrel or fight: *The angry women set to and began to pull each other's hair*

set-up /ˈ· ·/ *n* [*usu. sing.*] **1** an arrangement or organization: *He's new to the office and doesn't know the set-up yet* **2** (in tennis, VOLLEYBALL, etc.) a ball played so as to allow the next play to be easily or well made

set up *v adv* **1** [T1] to raise into position: *to set up a gravestone|*ROADBLOCK*s were set up by the police to catch the escaped prisoner* **2** [T1] to prepare (an instrument, machine, etc.) for use: *All this electrical wiring will take a day to set up* **3** [T1] to establish (an organization, business, etc.): *A new government was set up after the war.|to set up a school for young children* **4** [X9 *often pass.*, esp. *with, for*] to provide (someone) with what is necessary or useful: *enough apples from the tree to set us up for a long time|We're well set up for/with apples* **5** [T1] to produce; cause: *The high winds set up some dangerous driving conditions* **6** [T1] to SET¹ (13) (TYPE¹ (3) for printing)

set up as *v adv prep* **1** [D1;L1] to establish (oneself) in business as: *He set (himself) up as a house painter and soon made a success of it* **2** [Wv6; D1 *no pass.*] to show (oneself) (perhaps falsely) as; make a claim for (oneself) to be: *He sets himself up as a house painter but he never really does any work*

sev·en /ˈsevən/ *determiner, n, pron* [see NUMBER TABLE 1] (the number) 7 —**~th** *determiner, n, pron, adv* [see NUMBER TABLE 3]

sev·en·teen /ˌsevənˈtiːn◂/ *determiner, n, pron* [see NUMBER TABLE 1] (the number) 17 —**~th** *determiner, n, pron, adv* [see NUMBER TABLE 3]

seventh heav·en /ˌ·· ˈ··/ *n* [(*the*) R] *infml* the place of highest happiness; HEAVEN (4): *I'm in (the) seventh heaven when I listen to Mozart's music*

sev·en·ty /ˈsevənti/ *determiner, n, pron* [see NUMBER TABLE 1] (the number) 70 —**-tieth** *determiner, n, pron, adv* [see NUMBER TABLE 3]

seventy-eight /ˌ··· ˈ·/ *n infml* also **78**— a type of record, now old-fashioned, that is played by causing it to turn round 78 times every minute —compare FORTY-FIVE (2)

seven-year itch /ˌ·· · ˈ·/ *n* [(*the*) R] the dissatisfaction with one's marriage that is said to develop after about 7 years

sev·er /ˈsevəʳ/ *v* [T1;I∅] **1** to break or (be) cut up, esp. into 2 parts: *used scissors to sever the threads|The rope severed under the heavy weight* **2** [(*from*)] to (cause to) go apart, esp. with force; separate; disjoin: *The handle of the cup severed when it hit the floor.|an island severed from the* MAINLAND *by 50 miles of water*

sev·e·ral¹ /ˈsevərəl/ *adj* [Wa5;A;(B)] *fml* (*with pl. nouns*) **1** of the stated people or things; separate; RESPECTIVE: *stated their several opinions one at a time|shook hands and went their several ways|"busy with their several jobs"* (SEU W.) **2** *lit or fml* various; different: *walls built at several times by different people|sharing the work among the several members of the committee*

several² *determiner* more than 2 but fewer than many: *several visits each year to London|several* HUNDRED *times*

several³ *pron* a few but not many; some: *Several of the apples are bad, and several more have worm holes*

sev·e·ral·ly /ˈsevərəli/ *adv* [Wa5] *fml* separately; each by itself: *Shall we consider these questions severally, or all at once?*

sev·er·ance /ˈsevərəns/ *n* **1** [U;C] the/an act or result of SEVERing: *violence which led to (a) severance of relations between the 2 countries* **2** [U] *fml* the ending of a contract, esp. for employment

severance pay /ˈ··· ·/ *n* [U] money paid by a company to a worker losing his job through no fault of his own

se·vere /səˈvɪəʳ/ *adj* [Wa2] **1** not kind or gentle in treatment; not allowing failure or change in rules, standards, etc.; STERN; STRICT (1): *a severe look on her face|severe military rules* **2** very harmful or painful; serious or uncomfortable: *severe pain|the severest winter for 10 years* **3** needing effort; difficult: *a severe test of ability|severe competition* **4** plain; without ornament; AUSTERE: *the severe beauty of a simple church building* **5** expressing a strongly unfavourable judgment; very CRITICAL (1,4): *"The Times" certainly doesn't like the new film: their remarks are very severe* —compare STRICT (1) —**~ly** *adv*

se·ver·i·ty /səˈverəti/ *n* **1** [U] the state or quality of being SEVERE: *treated them with severity|The severity of his punishment was undeserved* **2** [C *usu. pl.*] a SEVERE (1,2,3) act or condition: *the severities of army life*

sew /səʊ/ *v* **sewed, sewn** /səʊn/ **1** [T1;I∅] to join or fasten (cloth, leather, paper, etc.) by stitches made with thread; make or mend (esp. pieces of clothing) with needle and thread: *a needle too large for sewing fine silk|Would you sew on this button/sew this button onto my shirt?* **2** [L9] to enclose in this way: *sewed a £5 note inside/into his coat pocket* —**~er** *n*

sew·age /ˈsjuːɪdʒ, ˈsuː-‖ˈsuː-/ *n* [U] the waste material and water carried in SEWERs. Before chemical treatment it is called **raw sewage**

sew·er /ˈsjuːəʳ, ˈsuːəʳ‖ˈsuːər/ *n* a man-made passage or large pipe under the ground for carrying water and waste material, esp. in a city, away to a body of natural water or for chemical treatment (**sewage disposal**), sometimes by turning the waste onto an area of ground (at a **sewage farm**)

sew·er·age /ˈsjuːərɪdʒ, ˈsuː-‖ˈsuː-/ *n* [U] the (system of) removing and dealing with waste matter and water through SEWERs: *a town with a modern sewerage system*

sew·ing /ˈsəʊɪŋ/ *n* [U] **1** the act or way of making, mending, etc., with thread, by hand or machine **2** work made in this way

sewing ma·chine /ˈ·· ·ˌ·/ *n* a machine for stitching material, worked with the hand or foot or (now usu.) by electricity

sew up *v adv* [T1] **1** to (en)close by sewing: *to sew up (the feathers inside) the bag* **2** *infml* to put into one's control; arrange to get certain hold of; determine or settle: *I want to sew up as many votes as possible: I want to have the election sewn up before I even put my name on the list*

sex[1] /seks/ *n* **1** [U] the condition of being either male or female: *a list of club members by name, age, and sex|In the space marked "sex", put an "M" for male or an "F" for female* **2** [C] the set of all male or female people: *a battle of the sexes* (= between men and women)|*a member of the opposite sex* **3** [A] connected with the bodily system of producing children: *sex organs* **4** [U] the act of SEXUAL INTERCOURSE between people: *Do you think sex outside marriage is always wrong?* **5** [U] all the activity between males and females which is connected with this act: *a lot of sex and violence in modern films* **6 have sex (with someone)** *not fml* to perform this act (with someone)

sex[2] *v* [T1] *esp. tech* to find out whether (esp. an animal) is male or female: *sexing day-old chickens*

sex·a·ge·nar·i·an /ˌseksədʒɪ̇ˈneərɪən/ *adj, n* [Wa5] (a person who is) between 60 and 69 years old

Sex·a·ges·i·ma /ˌseksəˈdʒesɪ̇mə/ *n* [R] *tech* the second Sunday before LENT

sex ap·peal /ˈ· ·ˌ·/ *n* [U] *not fml* power of being sexually exciting; attractiveness to one of the opposite sex: *She's a nice girl, but with no sex appeal, I'm sorry to say*

-sexed /sekst/ *comb. form* having the stated amount of sexual desire: *highly-sexed|over-sexed*

sex·is·m /ˈseksɪzəm/ *n* [U] the opinion that one sex is not as good as the other, esp. that women are less able in most ways than men

sex·ist /ˈseksɪ̇st/ *adj, n* (a person, esp. a man) showing SEXISM

sex·less /ˈseksləs/ *adj* **1** sexually uninteresting; not SEXY **2** [Wa5] not male or female; NEUTER[1] (2)

sex·tant /ˈsekstənt/ *n* an instrument for measuring angles, as between stars, used on a ship or aircraft to calculate its position —see picture at SCIENTIFIC

sex·tet /seksˈtet/ *n* (a piece of music written for) a group of 6 people playing instruments or singing together

sex·ton /ˈsekstən/ *n* a person with the job of taking care of a church building and sometimes of ringing the bell and digging graves

sex·tu·plet /sekˈstjuːplɪ̇t‖-ˈstʌ-/ *n* one of 6 people (or animals) born at one birth

sex·u·al /ˈsekʃʊəl, -sjʊəl‖ˈsekʃʊəl/ *adj* **1** [Wa5] of, related to, needing, or having sex as the quality of being male or female: *sexual* REPRODUCTION (1) **2** of or concerning sex as male and female activity: *sexual excitement* —see EROTIC (USAGE) —**~ly** *adv*

sexual in·ter·course /ˌ··· ˈ···/ also **intercourse**— *n* [U] the bodily act between 2 animals or people in which the male sex organ enters the female

sex·u·al·i·ty /ˌsekʃʊˈælɪ̇ti, -sjʊ-‖ˌsekʃʊ-/ *n* [U] fondness or readiness for, or interest in, sexual activity

sex·y /ˈseksi/ *adj* [Wa1] *not fml* exciting in a sexual way: *sexy girls/pictures/clothes* —see EROTIC (USAGE) —**sexily** *adv* —**sexiness** *n* [U]

SF *abbrev. for:* (*often not cap.*) SCIENCE FICTION

sfor·zan·do /sfɔːtˈsændəʊ‖sfɔrtˈsɑn-, -ˈsæn-/ *n, adj, adv* **-dos** *pr* **-di** /di/ ((a musical note) played) with additional force

Sgt *written abbrev. for:* SERGEANT

sh, shh, ssh /ʃ/ *interj* (used for demanding or asking for silence or less noise): *Sh! You'll wake the baby!* —compare SHUSH

shab·by /ˈʃæbi/ *adj* [Wa1] **1** appearing poor because of long wear or lack of care: *a shabby old hat* **2** (of a person) wearing such clothes **3** ungenerous or not worthy; dishonourable; unfair; MEAN[1] (1,2): *What a shabby trick, driving off and leaving me to walk home!* —**-bily** *adv* —**-biness** *n* [U]

shack /ʃæk/ *n* **1** [C] a small roughly built house; hut; SHANTY[1] **2** [C9] a small building for a person or purpose: *a gardener's shack*

shack·le[1] /ˈʃækəl/ *n* **1** a band for fastening around the wrist or ankle (as of an animal, prisoner, etc.) to something else (such as the other one in a pair) by a chain, to prevent movement **2** any of several kinds of U-shaped fasteners, such as the movable part of a PADLOCK **3** [*usu. pl.*] *lit* something that prevents freedom of action or expression

shackle[2] *v* [Wv3;T1 *usu. pass.*] to bind (as if) with SHACKLEs: *hands shackled together|shackled by old customs*

shack up *v adv* [IØ (*with,* TOGETHER)] *infml* (of a person, or man and woman) to live together while unmarried; COHABIT: *She's shacking up with her boyfriend; they're shacking up*

shad /ʃæd/ *n* **shad** [Wn3] a type of common food fish (related to the HERRING) of the north Atlantic

shade[1] /ʃeɪd/ *n* **1** [U] slight darkness or shelter from direct light, esp. from sunlight outdoors, made by something blocking it: *sitting in the shade of a tree/wall|no shade to be found in the desert* **2** [C] (*often in comb.*) something that keeps out light or its full brightness: *a* LAMPSHADE|*a window shade* (= BLIND[1] (3))|*a green eyeshade* **3** [U;C *usu. pl.*] representation of shadow or darkness in a picture, painting, etc.: *an artist using shade to good effect* **4** [C9] a slightly different colour: *The walls were light blue and the door a deeper shade* **5** [C9, esp. *of*] a slight (degree of) difference or varying; NUANCE: *a word with several shades of meaning* **6** [C] *esp. lit* the spirit of a dead person; GHOST **7** [C *usu. sing.*] *not fml* (*often before adjectives or adverbs*) a little bit: *He spoke with a shade of anxiety.|That music is just a shade too loud* **8 put someone/something in(to) the shade** *infml* to make someone/something seem much less important by comparison

USAGE **Shade** is any place sheltered from the sun. The clear shape made by the **shade** of something is a **shadow**. One cannot say **The dog saw his* **shade** *on the grass.*

shade[2] *v* **1** [T1] to shelter from direct light or heat: *She shaded her eyes from the sun with her hand* **2** [T1 (IN)] to represent the effect of shade or shadow on (an object in a picture): *a shaded-in background adding depth to the drawing* **3** [L9 (OFF), esp. *into*] to change slowly or by slight degrees (into something else): *a question where right and wrong shade into one another|blue shading off into grey*

shades /ʃeɪdz/ *n* **1** [P] *lit* darkness at the end of the day: *the shades of evening* **2** [*the*+P] *lit* the place of the dead; NETHERworld **3** [P] *infml* SUNGLASSES **4 shades of** *infml* this reminds me of (something in the past): *Shades of my old father! He would have agreed with all you've said*

shade tree /ˈ· ·/ *n* a tree (such as the ELM) grown mainly for shade from the sun

shad·ing /ˈʃeɪdɪŋ/ *n* [U] the filling in of an area in a picture to represent darkness

shad·ow¹ /ˈʃædəʊ/ *n* **1** [U *often pl. with sing. meaning*] greater darkness where direct light, esp. sunlight, is blocked by something: *The sun came through the small window but most of the room stayed in shadow.|He walked along in the shadows hoping no one would recognize him* **2** [C] a dark shape made on a surface by something between it and direct light: *As the sun set, the shadows became larger.|The tree* CAST (=produced) *its shadow on the wall* **3** [C] a dark place having the effect of this: *shadows under the eyes caused by lack of sleep* **4** [C] a form without substance or from which the real substance has gone: *After his illness he was only a shadow of his former self.|She wore herself down to a shadow with hard work* **5** [C] a person or thing who follows another closely: *The dog was his master's shadow* **6** [S *nonassertive*] a slightest bit; TRACE² (2): *true* **beyond the shadow of a doubt** **7** [C] the very strong power or influence of someone or something: *He lives in the shadow of his famous father* **8** [C] an unhappy or threatened feeling: *the shadow of coming war* **9 be afraid of one's own shadow** *not fml* to be habitually fearful or nervous see SHADOW (USAGE)

shadow² *v* [T1] **1** to make a shadow on; darken (as) with a shadow **2** to follow and watch closely, esp. secretly: *He felt he was being shadowed, but he couldn't see anyone behind him*

shadow³ *adj* [Wa5;A] **1** belonging to a group of politicians (the **shadow cabinet**) in the opposition party in Parliament who each study the work of a particular minister and are themselves ready to form a government **2** able to be active or become the stated thing when the proper or expected occasion comes: *a shadow army*

shad·ow·box /ˈʃædəʊbɒks‖-bɑks/ *v* [I∅] to fight with an imaginary opponent, esp. for training in BOXING —**~ing** *n* [U]

shad·ow·y /ˈʃædəʊi/ *adj* [Wa2] **1** hard to see or know about clearly; not DISTINCT (2): *a shadowy and little-known historical figure* **2** full of shade; in shadow: *the shadowy depths of the forest*

shad·y /ˈʃeɪdi/ *adj* [Wa1] **1** in or producing shade: *shady trees* **2** *not fml* of very doubtful honesty or character: *a shady politician*

shaft¹ /ʃɑːft‖ʃæft/ *n* **1** a long or thin pole forming the body of a spear, arrow, or weapon like these **2** the long handle of a hammer, axe, GOLF CLUB, or tool like these **3** one of the pair of poles that an animal is fastened between to pull a vehicle **4** a bar which turns, or around which a belt or wheel turns, to pass power through a machine: *a* PROPELLER *shaft|a* CRANKSHAFT **5** (the main body of) a pillar in a building **6** the stem of a feather **7** a beam of light coming through an opening: *a shaft of sunlight* **8** a flash (of lightning) **9** *lit* something shot like an arrow: *well-aimed shafts of* WIT² (3) *against those who argued with him* **10** a long passage, usu. in an up and down or sloping direction: *a mine shaft|a* VENTILATOR *shaft|a* LIFT² (4) *shaft* **11 give someone/get the shaft** *AmE sl* to treat someone/be treated unfairly and severely

shaft² *v* [T1 *often pass.*] *AmE sl* to treat unfairly and severely; punish undeservedly: *We got shafted on that sale: they tricked us into paying too much*

shag¹ /ʃæg/ *n* [U] rough strong tobacco cut into small thin pieces

shag² *v* **-gg-** [T1] *taboo sl* to have sex with

shagged /ʃægd/ also **shagged out** /ˌ· ˈ·ˈ/— *adj* [F] *BrE sl* very tired

shag·gy /ˈʃægi/ *adj* [Wa1] **1** being or covered with long, uneven, and untidy hair: *a shaggy beard/dog* **2** having a rough furlike surface: *a shaggy coat/mat* —**-gily** *adv* —**-giness** *n* [U]

shaggy-dog sto·ry /ˌ·· ˈ· ˌ··/ *n* a long joke **a** which is not so funny as the teller thinks **b** which has an ending that is purposely without point

sha·green /ʃəˈgriːn, ʃæ-/ *n* [U] a type of leather with a rough surface, often coloured green

shah /ʃɑː/ *n* (the title of) the ruler of Iran

shake¹ /ʃeɪk/ *v* **shook** /ʃʊk/, **shaken** /ˈʃeɪkən/ **1** [I∅; T1;X7] to (cause to) move quickly up and down and to and fro: *The explosion shook the house: the house shook.|She was shaking with laughter/anger/fear.|The wet dog shook himself.|The medicine is to be shaken before use.|The angry crowd shook their* FISTs (=closed hands) *at the police* **2** [X9] to put or remove by this kind of action: *He shook salt on his food.|She shook the sand out of her shoes* **3** [I∅;T1] to take and hold (someone's right hand) in one's own for a moment, sometimes moving it up and down, as a sign of greeting, goodbye, agreement, or pleasure (esp. in the phr. **shake hands** (**with someone**)): *The 2 men shook hands* (*with each other*)=*shook each other's hands*=*shook each other by the hand.*|(*infml*) *If you agree, let's shake* (*on it*) **4** [T1 (UP) *often pass.*] to trouble the mind or feelings of; upset: *She was badly shaken* (*up*) *by the accident/by the bad news* **5** [T1] to make less certain; weaken: *a faith in God which he says nothing can shake* **6** [T1] *infml* SHAKE OFF: *If you can shake* (*off*) *your friend I'd like to speak to you alone* **7 shake one's head** to move one's head from side to side to answer "no" or show disapproval —see also **shake a** LEG¹ (18)

shake² *n* **1** [C *usu. sing.*] an action of shaking: *answered "no" with a shake of the head* **2** [C] *infml* a moment: *I'll be ready in 2 shakes* **3** [C] *infml AmE* MILK SHAKE **4** [S9] *infml AmE* a type of treatment; DEAL³ (2): *a dealer who'll give you a fair shake*

shake·down /ˈʃeɪkdaʊn/ *n* **1** [C] *not fml* a place prepared as a bed **2** [C] *infml AmE* an act of getting money dishonestly, esp. by threats **3** [C] *infml AmE* a thorough search **4** [C;A] a last test operation of a new ship or aircraft: *a shakedown voyage/flight*

shake down *v adv* **1** [L9] *not fml* to use something prepared in a hurry as a bed: *shake down on the floor* **2** [I∅] *not fml* to become used to new surroundings; SETTLE DOWN (2,3): *He's new in the office but he'll soon shake down* **3** [T1] *infml AmE* to get money by a trick or threats from **4** [T1] *infml AmE* to search thoroughly **5** [T1] to take on a SHAKEDOWN (4) voyage

shake off *v adv* [T1] to get rid of; free oneself from; escape from

shake out *v adv* [T1] to open or spread with a shaking movement: *He took the dirty mat out of doors and shook it out*

shak·er /ˈʃeɪkəʳ/ *n* a container or instrument used in shaking: *mixed a drink in a* COCKTAIL *shaker|*(*AmE*) SALTSHAKER

shakes /ʃeɪks/ *n infml* **1** [*the*+P] nervous shaking of the body from disease, fear, strong drink, etc.: *I* *began to get the shakes just thinking about the test* **2 no great shakes** not very good, skilful, effective, etc.: *I'm no great shakes as a piano player, but I can sing well*

shake-up /ˈ· ·/ *n not fml* a rearrangement of an organization: *a government shake-up with 3 ministers losing their jobs*

shake up *v adv* [T1] **1** *not fml* to rearrange; make changes in (an organization): *The new chairman will shake up the company* **2** to mix by shaking **3 shake it up** *infml* hurry up

sha·ko /ˈʃeɪkəʊ/ *n* **-os** *or* **-oes** a high stiff military cap with a feather

shak·y /ˈʃeɪki/ *adj* [Wa1] **1** shaking or unsteady, as from nervousness or weakness **2** not solid or firm; weak and easily shaken; undependable: *an unsafe shaky ladder|shaky in her beliefs* —**shakily** *adv* —**shakiness** *n* [U]

shale /ʃeɪl/ *n* [U] soft rock made of hardened mud or clay which naturally divides into thin sheets

shale oil /ˈ· ·/ *n* [U] impure oil produced from SHALE by heating

shall /ʃəl; *strong* ʃæl/ *v neg. contr.* **shan't** [Wv2;I∅,2] **1** (used with *I* and *we* to express the simple future t.): *"When shall we 3 meet again?"* (Shakespeare)|*I shall have finished my work by next Friday* **2** *fml* (used with the 2nd and 3rd pers. to express) **a** (a promise or strong intention): *It shall be done as you wish* **b** (what will certainly be or happen): *That day shall come* **c** (a command or what must be done): *This law shall have effect in Scotland* **3** (used in questions or offers, esp. with *I* and *we*, asking the hearer to decide): *"Shall we go?" "Yes, let's."|"Shall I get you a chair?" "Yes, please."|"I'll be there at 3 o'clock, shall I?"* —see also SHALT, SHOULD

USAGE In *fml* speaking and writing, **shall** is used as stated above. In this case **will** is used for the simple future (1st meaning) of the 2nd and 3rd persons: *The meeting* **will** *be held tomorrow.|You* **will** *probably not like this book* and for the 2nd meaning with *I* and *we*: *I* **will** *be there, whatever happens.* (See the examples at **will**.) In ordinary modern use, **will** is more often used than **shall** in the 1st and 2nd meanings: *I* **will** *probably not be able to go.|We* **will** *plan to be there.* The 2nd meaning is usually expressed in speech by a degree of force on **shall** or **will**: *I want that prize and I* shall *win it!* or by adding words like **certainly**: *You* **will certainly** *be punished*; or by using instead words like **must** or **have to**. In the 3rd meaning, **shall** is always used.

shal·lop /ˈʃæləp/ *n esp. lit* a small light open boat for sailing or rowing

shal·lot /ʃəˈlɒt‖ʃəˈlɑt/ *n* a kind of small onion-like vegetable containing small round parts (BULBS) used for their taste in cooking

shal·low¹ /ˈʃæləʊ/ *adj* [Wa1] **1** not deep; not far from top to bottom: *a shallow river/dish|The shallow end of a swimming pool* **2** lacking deep or serious thinking; SUPERFICIAL: *shallow arguments|a shallow thinker whose opinions aren't worth much* **3** (of breathing) not taking much air into the lungs —**~ly** *adv* —**~ness** *n* [U]

shallow² *v* [I∅] to become SHALLOW¹ (1): *The river shallows at this point*

shal·lows /ˈʃæləʊz/ *n* [P] a SHALLOW¹ (1) area in a body of water: *a ship wrecked in the shallows that lie near the mouth of the river*

sha·lom /ʃæˈlɒm‖ʃæˈləʊm/ *interj* (a Jewish greeting or goodbye meaning "peace" in Hebrew)

shalt /ʃəlt; *strong* ʃælt/ [Wv2] **thou shalt** *old use or bibl* (when talking to one person) you shall

sham¹ /ʃæm/ *n* **1** [S] something false pretending to be the real thing; piece of deceit: *The agreement was a sham: neither side intended to keep to it* **2** [U] falseness; PRETENCE (1): *an honest man with a hatred of sham* **3** [A] not real; IMITATION (3); MOCK³: *sham jewellery|a sham battle*

sham² *v* **-mm-** [I∅;L7;T1] to put on the false appearance of (some disease, condition, etc.); FEIGN (1): *He isn't really ill: he's only shamming*

sha·man /ˈʃɑːmən/ *n* a priest, esp. in a form of religion practised in North East Asia, who uses magic to control or describe future events, cure sick people, etc.

sham·ble /ˈʃæmbəl/ *v* [L9] to walk awkwardly, dragging the feet: *shambling along the street*

sham·bles /ˈʃæmbəlz/ *n* [S] a place or scene of great disorder, (as if) the result of wrecking; wreck; MESS¹ (1): *After the noisy party the house was a shambles.|She did a very poor job: she made a shambles of it*

shame¹ /ʃeɪm/ *n* **1** [U] painful feeling of the guilt, wrongness, inability, or failure of oneself or a close friend, relative, etc.: *I feel no shame for my action: I did what was right* **2** [U *nonassertive*] the ability to feel this: *He had no shame and never felt guilty* **3** [U] the condition in which this should be felt; DISGRACE: *bad behaviour which brings shame on all of us* **4** [S] something that deserves blame; something that ought not to be: *What a shame that it rained on the day of your garden party!* **5 put someone/something to shame a** to cause shame to someone/something: *His son's crimes put the old man to shame* **b** to show someone/something to be lacking in ability, quality, etc., by comparison: *Your beautiful garden puts my few little flowers to shame* **6 Shame (shame)!** (called out against a speaker) You ought to be ashamed to say that!: *The minister's speech brought cries of "Shame"* **7 Shame on you!** also (*pomp or lit*) **For shame!**—You ought to be ashamed

shame² *v* [T1] **1** to bring dishonour to; DISGRACE: *He shamed his family by being sent to prison* **2** to appear very much better than: *a record of industrial peace which shames other companies* **3** to cause to feel shame: *It shames me to say it, but I told a lie* **4** [+*into* or *out of*] to force or urge by causing feelings of shame: *I tried to shame her into voting in the election, but she has no sense of public duty*

shame·faced /ˌʃeɪmˈfeɪst◂/ *adj* showing suitable shame or unsureness about oneself: *made his excuses in a shamefaced way* —**~ly** *adv*

shame·ful /ˈʃeɪmfəl/ *adj* deserving blame; causing the feeling or condition of shame —**~ly** *adv* —**~ness** *n* [U]

shame·less /ˈʃeɪmləs/ *adj* **1** (of a person) unable to feel shame; BRAZEN (2): *an immodest and shameless woman* **2** done without shame; inDECENT: *shameless disloyalty* —**~ly** *adv* —**~ness** *n* [U]

sham·my /ˈʃæmi/ *n* [C;U] CHAMOIS²

sham·poo¹ /ʃæmˈpuː/ *v* **-pooed,** *pres. p.* **-pooing,** *3rd pers. sing. pres. t.* **-poos** [T1] **1** to wash (the head and hair) **2** to clean (heavy woven material) with SHAMPOO² (2): *She shampooed the* CARPET

shampoo² *n* **-poos 1** [C] an act of SHAMPOOing¹: *gave herself* (=her own hair) *a shampoo* **2** [U;C] a usu. liquid soaplike product used for SHAMPOOing¹: *creamy shampoo for dry hair|*RUG *shampoo*

sham·rock /ˈʃæmrɒk‖-rɑk/ *n* [U;C] any of various plants (esp. a type of CLOVER) with 3 leaves on each stem and taken for the national sign of Ireland

shan·dy /ˈʃændi/ *n* [C;U] *esp. BrE* a drink made from a mixture of beer and GINGER ALE or LEMONADE (1)

shang·hai /ʃæŋˈhaɪ/ *v* [T1] **1** (esp. in former times) to make senseless by a blow or by drink and then put on a ship to serve as a sailor **2** [(*into*)] *infml* to trick or force into doing something unwillingly: *She shanghaied him into taking her mother to a film*

Shan·gri-La /ˌʃæŋgri ˈlɑː/ *n* [R] a distant beautiful imaginary place where everything is pleasant

shank /ʃæŋk/ *n* **1** [C] *esp. tech* a straight long or narrow usu. central or connecting part of something, such as **a** the straight part of a nail **b** the smooth part of a SCREW[1] (1) **c** the stem of a drinking glass **d** the smooth end of a DRILL[2] (1) where it is to be turned **e** the long straight central part of an ANCHOR[1] (1) —see picture at MACHINERY **2** [C;U] (a piece of) meat cut from the leg of an animal **3** [C] *old use* the part of the leg between the knee and ankle —see picture at HORSE

shanks's po·ny /ˌʃæŋksɨz ˈpəʊni/ *n* [U (*often cap.* S)] *BrE infml, usu. humor* one's own legs as a method of going from place to place: *The car's broken down so we'll have to use shanks's pony*

shan't /ʃɑːnt‖ʃænt/ [Wv2 *contr. of*] shall not: *I shall have to get ready on Thursday, . . . shan't I?* —see CONTR. (USAGE)

shan·tung /ʃænˈtʌŋ/ *n* [U] a type of silk cloth with a slightly rough surface

shan·ty[1] /ˈʃænti/ *n* a small roughly or badly built usu. wooden house; SHACK (1)

shanty[2], **chanty,** *AmE* also **-tey** *n* a song formerly sung by sailors in time to their work on a sailing ship

shan·ty·town /ˈʃæntitaʊn/ *n* (a part of) a town made up of badly built houses of thin metal, wood, etc., where poor people live

shape[1] /ʃeɪp/ *v* **1** [D1+*from/into*; V3] to make in a particular usu. finished shape or form: *The bird shaped its nest from mud and sticks/shaped mud and sticks into a nest/to make a nest* **2** [T1] to influence and determine the course or form of: *a powerful person who can shape events|time at school which shaped my future* **3** [T1 *usu. pass.*] to make (a piece of clothing) fit the body closely: *a dress shaped at the waist and not needing a belt* **4** [L9 (UP)] to develop well or in the stated way; take shape: *Our holiday plans are shaping (up) well.| "How is the new work system shaping?" "It's shaping into a good system"*

shape[2] *n* **1** [C;(U)] the appearance or form of something that is seen: *Houses come* (=are built) *in all shapes and sizes.|a cake in the shape of a heart| We saw a shape through the mist but we couldn't see who it was* **2** [U] the organization or form in which something is expressed, arranged, thought, etc.: *the shape of an argument|What shape will future society have?* **3** [(*in*) U9] *not fml* condition: *Our garden is in good shape after the rain* **4** [S] a way of appearing; form; GUISE (1): *ready to meet death in any shape|good luck in the shape of a job offer* **5** **get/put something into shape** to arrange or plan something properly **6** **in any shape or form** *not fml nonassertive* of any kind; at all: *I'm not looking for trouble in any shape or form* **7** **in(to)/out of shape** in(to)/out of good condition of the body and muscles: *going rock-climbing so as to get/stay in shape|I get tired easily: I must be out of shape* **8** **take shape** to begin to have a shape, esp. to begin to be like the finished form: *ideas taking shape in his mind* —**~less** *adj* —**~lessly** *adv* —**~lessness** *n* [U]

shaped /ʃeɪpt/ *adj* [Wa5] (*often in comb.*) having the stated shape: *a cloud shaped like a camel|a heart-shaped cake*

shape·ly /ˈʃeɪpli/ *adj* [Wa1] (esp. of a woman's body or legs) having a good-looking shape —**shapeliness** *n* [U]

shape up *v adv* [IØ] (esp. in anger, threats, etc.) to begin to do right: *You'd better shape up, young man, or expect to be punished!* —see also SHAPE[1] (4)

shard /ʃɑːd‖ʃɑrd/ also **sherd**— *n* a broken piece of a vessel of glass or POTTERY

share[1] /ʃeəʳ/ *n* **1** [S] the part belonging or owed to, or done by, a person: *If you want a share in/of the pay, you'll have to do your fair share of the work.|I had no share in this trick: I had nothing to do with it* **2** [C] any of the equal parts into which the ownership of a company may be divided: *owns 50 shares in the business|a* DIVIDEND (1) *of 50 pence per share* **3** [A] *BrE* of or concerning SHARES: *Share prices rose in heavy* TRADING **4** **go shares** *BrE* to divide the cost, ownership, profit, etc., among 2 or more people: *I went shares with 2 others in hiring a car for the day*

share[2] *v* **1** [IØ;T1: (*with/among/between*)] to use, pay, have, take part in, etc., (with others) or among a group: *We haven't enough books for everyone: some of you will have to share.|Everyone in the house shares the bathroom.|I have to share the bathroom with the rest of the family* **2** [T1 (OUT, *among/between*)] to divide and give out in shares: *At his death his property was shared (out) between his children* **3** [IØ;T1 (*with*)] to give a share (of) to 1 or more others: *Children should be taught to share.|Please share your newspaper with me* **4** [T1 (*with*)] to tell 1 or more others about: *I'd like to share with you something that happened last week* **5** [T1 (*with*)] to be among those who have (esp. an opinion or idea): *I'm sorry: I can't share your faith that everything will be all right* **6** **share and share alike** **a** *esp. law* to be held in equal shares **b** *infml* to have an equal share in everything —**sharer** *n*

share[3] *n* PLOUGHSHARE

share·crop·per /ˈʃeəˌkrɒpəʳ‖ˈʃeərˌkrɑ-/ *n* a farmer, esp. in the southern US, who lives on and farms the land of another, is given tools and supplies by him, and is paid a certain share of the crop

share·hold·er /ˈʃeəˌhəʊldəʳ‖ˈʃeər-/ *AmE* also **stockholder**— *n* an owner of 1 or more shares in a business

share in *v prep* [T1] to have a share in; take part in: *to share in a meal*

share-out /ˈ· ·/ *n* [S (*of*)] an act of giving out shares of something: *thieves quarrelling over the share-out of the stolen goods*

shares /ʃeəz‖ʃeərz/ *n* [P] *BrE* ownership rights in companies, bought and sold in the form of printed statements (**share certificates**)

shark[1] /ʃɑːk‖ʃɑrk/ *n* any of a number of kinds of large usu. grey fish that live esp. in warm seas, have several rows of sharp teeth, and are often dangerous to people —see picture at FISH[1]

shark[2] *n infml* a person clever at getting money from others in dishonest or merciless ways, as by lending money at high rates

shark·skin /ˈʃɑːkˌskɪn‖ˈʃɑrk-/ *n* [U] a type of smooth woollen, cotton, or RAYON cloth with small patterns, used for outer clothes

sharp[1] /ʃɑːp‖ʃɑrp/ *adj* [Wa1] **1** **a** having or being a thin cutting edge; KEEN: *a sharp knife/stone* **b** having or being a fine point: *a sharp pin|a sharp-pointed needle* **2** quick and sensitive in thinking, seeing, hearing, etc.: *a sharp mind|sharp eyes/sight* **3** causing a sensation like that of cutting, biting, pricking, or stinging: *a sharp wind/*FROST[1] (1)*|a sharp acid-like taste|a sharp crack when the branch of the tree broke* **4** *esp. AmE* (of cheese) having a strong taste **5** **a** not rounded; marked by angles: *an unattractive face with a sharp nose* **b** (of an angle) pointed; ACUTE (6) **c** having or showing a quick change in direction: *to make a sharp right turn* **6** steep and sudden: *a, sharp rise/fall in prices|There's a sharp drop over the cliff* **7** clear in shape or detail; DISTINCT (2); MARKED (2):

sharp dark shadows|a sharp photographic image|a sharp CONTRAST¹ (1) *between what is and what ought to be* **8** (of a pain) severe and sudden —opposite **dull** **9** quick and strong: *a sharp blow on the head|a sharp push on the door* **10** (as of words) intended to hurt; angry; severe; HARSH: *a sharp scolding|She was sharp with her son who was late for dinner.|a* **sharp-tongued** *woman* **11** clever, esp. to the point of dishonesty: *This sale sounds like* **sharp practice** *to me and I want nothing to do with it* **12** *infml* neat in action or appearance; fine; SMART² (3): *sharp-looking soldiers|a sharp piece of work* **13** [Wa5;E] (of a note in music) raised by ½ TONE (in the phrs. **F sharp, C sharp**, etc.): *to play an F-sharp* —compare FLAT¹ (6) —**~ly** *adv* —**~ness** *n* [U]

sharp² *adv* **1** [Wa5;E] exactly at the stated time: *The meeting starts at 3 o'clock sharp: don't be late!* **2** sharply (esp. in such phrs. as **turn sharp left/right**) **3** higher than the correct note: *She ruined her performance by singing sharp* **4 look sharp** *infml* **a** to watch out; be careful **b** to hurry up: *You'll have to look sharp if you want to be on time*

sharp³ *n* (in music) **1** a note higher by ½ TONE than a named note; the next black note to the right of a white note on the piano **2** a sign, (♯), used before a note to raise it by this amount —compare FLAT¹ (6) and see picture at NOTATION

sharp·en /ˈʃɑːpən‖ˈʃɑr-/ *v* [T1;I∅] to make or become SHARP or SHARPer: *to sharpen a pencil/knife|Cold weather sharpens the pain in my knee.|Her voice sharpened as she became impatient*

sharp·en·er /ˈʃɑːpənəʳ, ˈʃɑːpnəʳ‖ˈʃɑr-/ *n* a machine or tool for SHARPENing

sharp·er /ˈʃɑːpəʳ‖ˈʃɑr-/ also (*esp. AmE*) **sharp**— *n* a cheater, esp. a CARDSHARPER

sharp-eyed /ˌ· ˈ·◂/ *adj* [Wa2] quick and clear in seeing

sharp·shoot·er /ˈʃɑːpˌʃuːtəʳ‖ˈʃɑrp-/ *n* a person skilful in shooting; good MARKSMAN, esp. one with the job of firing exactly-aimed single shots at an enemy

shat·ter /ˈʃætəʳ/ *v* **1** [T1;I∅] to break suddenly into small pieces; SMASH: *A stone shattered the window: the glass shattered* **2** [T1;I∅] to damage badly; ruin; wreck: *a long illness which shattered his health* **3** [Wv4,5;T1] *infml* to shock; have a strong effect on the feelings of: *a shattered look on his face* **4** [Wv4,5;T1] *infml, esp. BrE* to cause to be very tired and weak: *I feel completely shattered after that run up the hill*

shave¹ /ʃeɪv/ *v* **1** [T1 (OFF); I∅] to cut off (hair or beard) close to the skin with a RAZOR: *I've decided to shave off my beard* **2** [T1] to cut off hair from the face of (oneself or another person) **3** [T1;L9] to cut all the hair from (a part of the body): *She shaves her legs and under her arms* **4** [T1 (OFF)] to cut off in very thin pieces from a surface: *shaved off some ice from a large block* **5** [T1] to cut such pieces from (a surface): *shaved the bottom of the door to make it close properly* **6** [T1] *infml* to come close to or touch in passing: *The car just shaved the corner of the wall while turning*

shave² *n* **1** [*usu. sing.*] an act or result of shaving (SHAVE) **2 a close/narrow shave** *infml* an almost unsuccessful escape or avoiding of something bad; narrow escape

-shav·en /ˈʃeɪvən/ *comb. form* SHAVEd: *a cleanshaven face* (=with no beard)

shav·er /ˈʃeɪvəʳ/ *n* **1** a tool for shaving (SHAVE), esp. an electric-powered instrument held in the hand for shaving hair **2** *becoming rare* a boy; YOUNGSTER

shav·ing /ˈʃeɪvɪŋ/ *n* **1** [U] the act of closely cutting off hair **2** [C *usu. pl.*] a very thin piece cut from a surface as with a sharp blade: *wood shavings made with a* PLANE³

shaving cream /ˈ·· ·/ *n* [U] paste made mostly of soap for putting on the face (sometimes with a **shaving brush**) to keep the hair soft and wet during SHAVING (1)

shawl /ʃɔːl/ *n* a piece of usu. soft heavy cloth, either square or long and narrow, for wearing over a woman's head or shoulders or wrapping round a baby

shay /ʃeɪ/ *n infml, esp. AmE* CHAISE

she¹ /ʃi; *strong* ʃiː/ *pron* [Wp1] (*used as the subject of a sentence*) **1** that female person or animal: *It's the farmer's best cow: she gives lots of milk.|She's certainly a pretty girl. Who is she?* **2** (used esp. of vehicles and countries) that thing regarded as female: *What's wrong with the car? She won't start.|Our country needs strong leaders: may she always have them!*

she² *n* **1** [S] *infml* a female: *Is the new baby a he or a she?* **2** [A] (*in comb., esp. with animal names*) female: *a she-goat|a she-devil* (=an evil woman)

sheaf /ʃiːf/ *n* **sheaves** /ʃiːvz/ **1** a bunch of grain plants tied together, esp. to stand up in a field to dry after gathering **2** [(*of*)] a handful or more of long or thin things laid or tied together; BUNDLE¹ (1): *The speaker had a sheaf of notes on the desk in front of him*

shear /ʃɪəʳ/ *v* **sheared, sheared** *or* **shorn** /ʃɔːn‖ʃorn/ **1** [T1] to cut off wool from (sheep) **2** [T1] *esp. lit* to cut off (hair) or hair from: *the day when her baby curls were shorn|He looked strange with his closely shorn head* **3** [I∅;T1: (OFF)] *tech* **a** (esp. of thin rods, pins, etc.) to break in 2 under a sideways or twisting force **b** to cause (esp. a thin rod, pin, etc.) to break in this way **4 be shorn of** to lose by the action of another; be STRIPPed¹ (1) of: *The king was shorn of his power by his nobles*

shears /ʃɪəz‖ʃɪərz/ *n* [P] **1** large scissors **2** any of various heavier cutting tools which work like scissors —see PAIR (USAGE) and picture at GARDEN¹

sheath /ʃiːθ/ *n* **sheaths** /ʃiːðz/ **1** a closefitting case for a knife or sword blade or the sharp part of a tool **2** a part of a plant, animal organ, or machine that acts as a covering like this **3** a simple closefitting woman's dress **4** a usu. rubber covering worn over a man's sex organ when having sex to keep the woman from having a child and to prevent infection; CONDOM

sheathe /ʃiːð/ *v* [T1] **1** to put into a SHEATH (1): *sheathed his sword* **2** [(*with, in*)] to enclose in a protective outer cover

sheath·ing /ˈʃiːðɪŋ/ *n* [U] **1** the action of a person who SHEATHEs **2** material (to be) made into a protective cover

sheath knife /ˈ· ·/ *n* a knife with a fixed (not folding) blade for carrying in a SHEATH (1)

she·bang /ʃɪ̵ˈbæŋ/ *n* **the whole shebang** *infml esp. AmE* all of it; the whole thing or affair

she·been /ʃɪ̵ˈbiːn/ *n esp. IrE* an unlawfully-kept drinking place

shed¹ /ʃed/ *v* **shed;** *pres. p.* **shedding** **1** [T1] *lit* to cause to flow out; pour out: *She shed tears of sorrow for what she did.|arguments which shed new light on the question* (=make it clearer) **2** [Wv6; T1] (of a surface) to keep (a liquid) from entering; REPEL: *A duck's back sheds water* **3** [T1;I∅] (as of a plant or animal) to throw off or get rid of naturally (outer skin, leaves, hair, etc.): *trees shedding their leaves in autumn|Some snakes shed their skin each year* **4** [T1] *BrE* (of a vehicle) to drop (a load of goods) by accident: *a road blocked where a large* LORRY *had shed its load* **5 shed blood** to cause wounding or esp. killing: *They wanted to bring* *down the government, but without shedding blood* —see also BLOODSHED

shed² *n* (*often in comb.*) a lightly built (partly) enclosed building, usu. for storing things: *a toolshed/cattle shed/woodshed/garden shed*

she'd /ʃid; *strong* ʃiːd/ [Wv2] *contr. of* (*in compound tenses*) **1** she would **2** she had —see CONTR. (USAGE)

sheen /ʃiːn/ *n* [U;S] (a) bright or shiny condition on a surface; LUSTRE (1): *hair with a beautiful sheen*

sheep /ʃiːp/ *n* **sheep** [Wn3] **1** a type of grass-eating animal that is farmed for its wool and its meat (MUTTON, lamb) and that moves about in a group (FLOCK) —compare RAM, EWE; see MEAT (USAGE) and picture at FARMYARD **2 a black sheep** *not fml* a person regarded with disfavour or shame compared to others in a group **3 make/cast sheep's eyes at someone** *infml* to behave fondly towards someone, esp. in an awkward or foolish way **4 may/might as well be hanged for a sheep as a lamb** *infml* may as well go ahead and do something very wrong if the punishment is the same as for something less **5 the sheep and the goats** those who are good, able, successful, etc., and those who are not: *a hard examination intended to separate the sheep from the goats*

sheep·dip /ˈʃiːpˌdɪp/ *n* [C;U] a chemical (used in a) bath for sheep to kill harmful insects in their wool

sheep·dog /ˈʃiːpdɒg‖-dɔg/ *n* a dog trained to drive sheep and keep them together

sheep·fold /ˈʃiːpfəʊld/ *n* a shelter or fenced area surrounded by a fence for sheep

sheep·ish /ˈʃiːpɪʃ/ *adj* uncomfortable, as from being slightly ashamed or fearful of others: *a sheepish smile* —**~ly** *adv* —**~ness** *n* [U]

sheep·skin /ˈʃiːpˌskɪn/ *n* **1** [U;(C)] the skin of a sheep, made into leather, esp. **a** with the wool left on **b** as a paper-thin writing material **2** [C] *AmE humor* DIPLOMA

sheer¹ /ʃɪəʳ/ *adj* [Wa1] **1** [B] very thin, fine, light in weight, and almost transparent: *ladies' sheer stockings* **2** [A] pure; unmixed with anything else; nothing but; UTTER¹: *He won by sheer luck/determination* **3** [B] very steep; (almost) straight up and down without a break: *a sheer cliff*

sheer² *adv* [Wa1] straight up or down: *The mountain rises sheer from the plain*

sheer³ *v* [L9, esp. OFF, AWAY] to turn (as if) to avoid hitting something; change direction quickly: *The boat came close to the rocks and then sheered away*

sheet¹ /ʃiːt/ *n* **1** [C] a large 4-sided piece of usu. cotton cloth used in a pair on a bed, 1 above and 1 below a person lying in it: *We change the sheets* (=put clean ones on the bed) *every week* —see picture at BEDROOM **2** [C;A] a piece of paper, esp. of some standard size: *wrapped in a sheet of newspaper* **3** [C;A] a broad stretch or piece of something thin: *a sheet of ice over the lake*|**sheet metal** (=metal in sheets) **4** [C *often pl.*] a moving or powerful wide mass: *rain coming down in sheets*|*A sheet of flame blocked his way out of the burning house* **5** [C] a piece of paper printed as 50, 100, etc., postage stamps before they are torn off one by one **6** [C] *sl* a newspaper **7 (as) white as a sheet** *infml* very pale in the face, as because of fear or a shock

sheet² *n tech* a rope or chain controlling the angle between a sail and the wind

sheet an·chor /ˈ· ˌ··/ *n* **1** a ship's largest ANCHOR used only in time of danger **2** something that is a main or only support in trouble

sheet·ing /ˈʃiːtɪŋ/ *n* [U] (cloth or other material for making) SHEETs¹ (1,3): *metal sheeting*

sheet light·ning /ˌ· ˈ··, ˈ· ˌ··/ *n* [U] lightning in the form of a sudden flash of brightness that covers the whole sky —compare FORKED LIGHTNING

sheet mu·sic /ˈ· ˌ··, ˌ· ˈ··/ *n* [U] music printed on single sheets and not bound in book form

sheikh, sheik /ʃeɪk‖ʃiːk/ *n* [C;A;(N)] **1** an Arab chief or prince **2** a Muslim religious leader or teacher

sheikh·dom, sheikdom /ˈʃeɪkdəm‖ˈʃiːk-/ *n* a place under the government of a SHEIKH (1)

shei·la /ˈʃiːlə/ *n sl, esp. AustrE* a girl

shek·els /ˈʃekəlz/ *n* [P] *humor* money

shel·duck /ˈʃeldʌk/ (*masc.* **shel·drake** /ˈʃeldreɪk/)— *n* [Wn1] a type of large often brightly-coloured European duck

shelf /ʃelf/ *n* **shelves** /ʃelvz/ **1** a flat usu. long and narrow board fixed against a wall or in a frame, for placing things on **2** a group of things filling one of these: *a 5-foot shelf of books* **3** something in nature with a shape like one of these, esp. a narrow surface (LEDGE) of rock or underwater bank —compare CONTINENTAL SHELF **4 on the shelf** *infml* (esp. of a person) not active, esp. put aside by others as of no use: *She never married; she's been left on the shelf*

shell¹ /ʃel/ *n* **1** [C;U] (*often in comb.*) a hard covering of an animal, or of an egg, fruit, nut, or seed: *a* SNAIL/OYSTER *shell*|*a* NUTSHELL|*some pieces of eggshell* —see also SEASHELL and picture at FRUIT¹, NUT¹ **2** [C] something regarded as the outer surface as opposed to the contents or substance: *only the shell of a man, with no tender feelings* **3** [C] the outside frame of a building: *The builders want to finish the shell before winter* **4** [C] **a** an explosive for firing from a large gun: *shells bursting all around* **b** *esp. AmE* a bullet, esp. the case holding the part to be fired from the weapon **5** [C] a light racing boat for rowing by 1 or more people **6** [C] an outer case made of pastry or cake for certain prepared dishes **7** [C] **come out of one's shell** *infml* to begin to be friendly or interested in others

shell² *v* **1** [T1] to remove from a natural covering like a shell or POD: *to shell* PEAS/OYSTERs **2** [T1;I∅] to fire SHELLs¹ (4a) (at): *The enemy lines were weakened by shelling before the attack*

she'll /ʃil; *strong* ʃiːl/ [Wv2] *contr. of* **1** she will: *She'll come if she can* **2** she shall —see CONTR. (USAGE)

shel·lac¹ /ʃəˈlæk/ *n* [U] a kind of thick orange or clear alcohol-based liquid used like paint as a shiny protective covering

shellac² *v* **-ck-** [T1] **1** to cover with SHELLAC **2** *AmE infml* to defeat severely

shel·lack·ing /ʃəˈlækɪŋ/ *n* [C *usu. sing.*] *AmE infml* a severe defeat

shell·fish /ˈʃelˌfɪʃ/ *n* **shellfish** **1** [Wn3;C] any animal without a BACKBONE that lives in water and has a shell (a MOLLUSC or CRUSTACEAN): *The* LOBSTER *is a shellfish* **2** [U] such animals as food: *I'd like (some) shellfish for dinner*

shell out *v adv* [T1;I∅] *infml* to pay (money needed or asked for): *We agreed to share the cost but later he wouldn't shell out*|*shell out £2 for his share*

shell·shock /ˈʃelʃɒk‖-ʃɑk/ *n* [U] *not fml* illness of the mind or nerves, esp. in soldiers, caused by the experience of war

shel·ter¹ /ˈʃeltəʳ/ *n* **1** [C] a building or enclosure offering protection: *a wooden shelter in a public garden*|*a bus shelter* (=roofed enclosure at a bus stop) **2** [U] protection or the state of being protected: *In the storm I looked for the shelter of a tree*|*took shelter under a tree* **3** [U] the providing of a place to live or stay; ACCOMMODATION (1): HOUSING (1): *our need for food, clothing, and shelter*

shelter² *v* **1** [T1 (*from*)] to protect from harm; give shelter to: *to shelter a plant from direct sunlight|sheltering the homeless* **2** [L9, esp. *from*] to take shelter; find protection: *In the rain people were sheltering in the doorways of shops*

shel·tered /ˈʃeltəd‖-ərd/ *adj* kept away from harm, risk, or unpleasantness: *a sheltered life with no worries about money*

shelve /ʃelv/ *v* **1** [T1] to put on a shelf; arrange on shelves **2** [T1] to put aside, esp. as not to be used or considered: *We've shelved our holiday plans because the baby is ill* **3** [Wv4;I∅ (DOWN, UP)] (of land) to slope gradually

shelves /ʃelvz/ *pl. of* SHELF

shelv·ing /ˈʃelvɪŋ/ *n* [U] (material for) shelves

she·nan·i·gan /ʃə̇ˈnænɪgən/ *n* [*usu. pl*] *infml* **1** a funny and attention-getting act; MONKEY BUSINESS: *an hour of amusing shenanigans from 2 fine performers* **2** a practice or trick of doubtful honesty

shep·herd¹ /ˈʃepəd‖-ərd/ *n* a man or boy who takes care of sheep in the field

shepherd² *v* [X9] to lead, guide, or take care of like sheep: *The teacher was shepherding the group of children into the bus*

shep·herd·ess /ˈʃepədes‖-ərdə̇s/ *n* (esp. in poetry and art) a woman or girl who takes care of sheep in the field

shepherd's pie /ˌ·· ˈ·/ also **cottage pie**— *n* [U] *BrE* a dish made of finely cut-up cooked meat covered with a thick paste of cooked potato and baked

shepherd's plaid /ˌ·· ˈ·/ also **shepherd's check**— *n* [C;U] a pattern of small black and white squares woven in woollen cloth

Sher·a·ton /ˈʃerətn/ *adj* [Wa5] of the graceful style of furniture made in Britain around 1800 by Thomas Sheraton: *a Sheraton card table*

sher·bet /ˈʃɜːbət‖ˈʃɜr-/ *n* [U] **1** *esp. BrE* sweet powder for adding to water to make a cool drink, esp. for children **2** esp. AmE SORBET

sherd /ʃɜːd‖ʃɜrd/ *n tech* (esp. in ARCHAEOLOGY) SHARD —see also POTSHERD

sher·iff /ˈʃerə̇f/ *n* **1** [C (*of*)] (in Britain) HIGH SHERIFF **2** [C;A;N] (in the US) an elected officer in a local area (COUNTY) with duties including carrying out the orders of courts and preserving public order

Sher·pa /ˈʃɜːpə‖ˈʃɜr-/ *n* [C;A] a member of a Himalayan tribe who are very good at climbing mountains, and are often employed to guide other mountain climbers

sher·ry /ˈʃeri/ *n* [U;C] a pale or dark brown strong wine of a kind originally from Spain, often drunk in Britain before a meal

she's /ʃiz; *strong* ʃiːz/ *contr. of:* **1** [Wv1] she is: *She's working in an office* **2** [Wv2] (*in compound tenses*) she has: *She's got a new job* —see CONTR. (USAGE)

Shet·land po·ny /ˌʃetlənd ˈpəʊni/ *n* a type of rough-haired strong very small horse

Shetland wool /ˌ·· ˈ·/ *n* [U] soft wool from sheep bred in the Shetland Islands north of Scotland

shew /ʃəʊ/ *v* **shewed** /ʃəʊd/, **shewn** /ʃəʊn/ *now rare* SHOW

shib·bo·leth /ˈʃɪbəleθ‖ˈʃɪbələ̇θ/ *n* a once-important old phrase or custom which no longer has much meaning

shield¹ /ʃiːld/ *n* **1** a broad piece of metal, wood, or leather carried by soldiers in former times as a protection from arrows, blows, etc. **2** a representation of this used for a COAT OF ARMS, BADGE, (in the US) road sign, etc. **3** a protective cover, esp. a plate on a machine to protect the person working it from moving parts

shield² *v* [T1 (*from*)] to protect or hide from harm or danger: *She lied to the police to shield her guilty friend.|He raised his arm to shield himself from the blow*

shift¹ /ʃɪft/ *v* **1** [I∅;T1] to change in position or direction; move from one place to another: *He shifted impatiently in his seat during the long speech.|Fasten the load down to keep it from shifting at high speed.|The wind shifted and blew the mist away.|Don't try to shift the blame onto me!* **2** [I∅] to take care of oneself; live as one can; GET ALONG (3); MANAGE (3) (esp. in the phr. **shift for oneself**): *He's had to shift for himself since his mother died* **3** [I∅ (UP/DOWN; *into, to*)] *esp. AmE* CHANGE¹ (9) **4 shift gear(s)** *esp. AmE* CHANGE¹ (10) **gear(s)**

shift² *n* **1** a change in position or direction; an act or result of SHIFTing¹ (1): *a shift in the wind/in political opinion* **2 a** a group of workers which takes turns with 1 or more other groups: *I work on the day/night shift at the factory* **b** the period of time worked by such a group **3 a** *old use* a woman's dresslike undergarment **b** a loosefitting straight simple woman's dress **4** a means or trick used in a time of difficulty; EXPEDIENT **5 make shift (with)** to use what can be found, for lack of anything better; MAKE DO (with): *We had no chairs so we had to make shift: we made shift with old boxes* —compare MAKESHIFT

shift key /ˈ· ·/ *n* the part (KEY¹ (2)) of a TYPEWRITER which is pressed in order to print a capital letter

shift·less /ˈʃɪftləs/ *adj* lacking in purpose, ability, or effort to get things done —**~ly** *adv* —**~ness** *n* [U]

shift·y /ˈʃɪfti/ *adj* [Wa1] showing a habit of tricks and deceit: *a shifty-eyed* (=shifty) *man who shouldn't be trusted* —**shiftily** *adv* —**shiftiness** *n* [U]

shil·ling /ˈʃɪlɪŋ/ *n* **1** an amount of money in use in Britain until 1971, equal to 12 (old) pence and 1/20 of £1: *£1 6s 3d = 1 pound 6 shillings and 3 pence* **2** a coin worth this amount, now 5 decimal pence; 5p coin **3** an amount of money in Kenya, Uganda, Tanzania, and Somalia, equal to 100 cents —see MONEY TABLE

USAGE Since the change to decimal money in Britain the shilling has had its place taken by the 5 pence piece, a coin of the same size and value (at the time of introduction) but with a different pattern stamped on it; but this new coin is still sometimes called a shilling. In the same way, a 10p piece has taken the place of the 2 shilling coin.

shil·ly-shal·ly /ˈʃɪli ˌʃæli/ *v* [I∅] *infml* to waste time without reaching a decision or taking action

shim·mer¹ /ˈʃɪməʳ/ *v* [Wv4;I∅] to shine with a soft trembling light: *shimmering water in the moonlight*

shimmer² *n* [U] a soft trembling shining effect: *the shimmer of glasses in the candlelight*

shin¹ /ʃɪn/ *n* the bony front part of the leg between the knee and ankle —see picture at HUMAN²

shin² *AmE* also **shinny**— *v* **-nn-** [L9, esp. UP, DOWN, *up, down*] to climb (a tree, pole, etc.), esp. quickly and easily, using the hands and legs: *shinned up a tree to get a better view*

shin·bone /ˈʃɪnbəʊn/ also (*med*) **tibia**— *n* the front bone in the leg below the knee —see picture at SKELETON

shin·dig /ˈʃɪndɪg/ *n infml & becoming rare* **1** a party, dance, or other gay social occasion **2** SHINDY

shin·dy /ˈʃɪndi/ *n BrE infml* a noisy quarrel or disagreement

shine¹ /ʃaɪn/ *v* **shone** /ʃɒn‖ʃəʊn/ **1** [I∅] to give off light; look bright: *a fine morning with the sun shining (down)|The polished surface shone in the sun* **2** [X9] to direct (a lamp, beam of light, etc.) **3** [Wv6;I∅] to appear clearly as excellent: *He's a pretty good student, but sports are where he really shines*

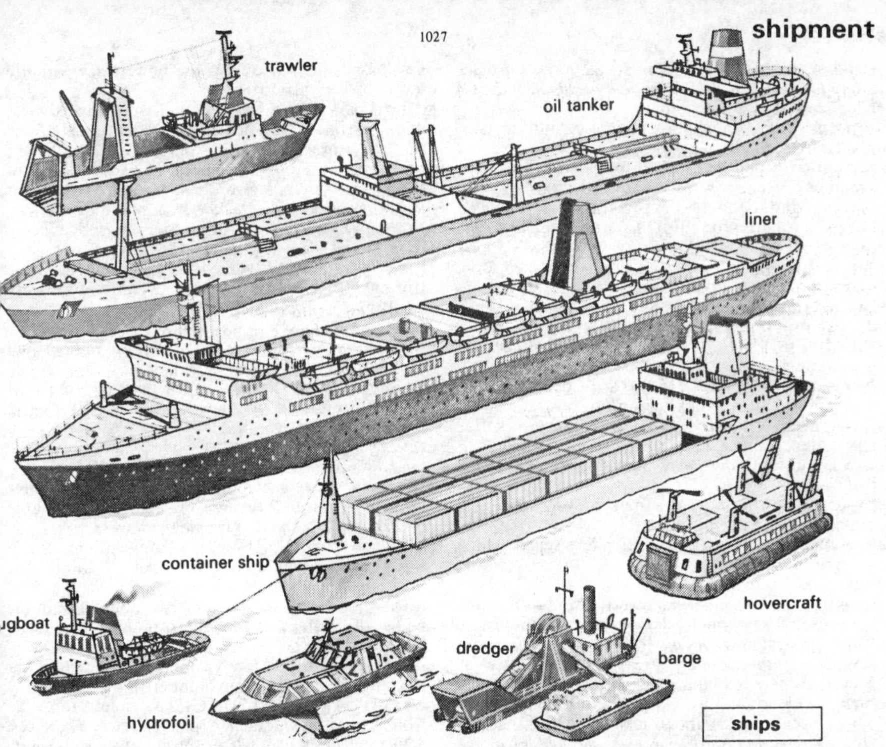

ships

shine[2] *v* **shined** [T1] to polish; make bright by rubbing: *Shine your shoes before going out*

shine[3] *n* **1** [S;(U)] brightness; shining quality: *The wooden surface had a beautiful shine* **2** [S] an act of polishing, esp. of shoes: *These shoes need a shine* **3 (come) rain or shine** *not fml* in good or bad weather; whatever happens: *I promise we'll be there at 8, rain or shine* **4 take a shine to someone** *infml, esp. AmE* to like someone, esp. at once or without any clear reason

shin·er /ˈʃaɪnəʳ/ *n infml* BLACK EYE (1)

shin·gle[1] /ˈʃɪŋgəl/ *n* **1** a small thin piece of building material (such as wood or ASBESTOS) laid in rows to cover a roof or wall **2 hang up/out one's shingle** *infml AmE* to establish an office as a doctor or lawyer

shingle[2] *v* [T1] to cover (esp. a roof) with SHINGLES[1]

shingle[3] *n* [U] small rough rounded pieces of stone (larger than GRAVEL) lying in masses along a seashore —**-gly** *adj* [Wa1]

shin·gles /ˈʃɪŋgəlz/ *n* [U] a disease caused by an infection of certain nerves and producing painful red spots often in a band around the waist

shin·ing /ˈʃaɪnɪŋ/ *adj* **1** [B] giving off light; bright **2** [A] excellent; noticeably fine: *a shining example of courage*

shin·ny /ˈʃɪni/ *v AmE* SHIN[2]

Shin·to /ˈʃɪntəʊ/ also **Shin·to·is·m** /ˈʃɪntəʊɪzəm/— [R] the ancient religion of Japan, including the worship of spirits of nature and of the past members of one's family

shin·y /ˈʃaɪni/ *adj* [Wa1] (esp. of a smooth surface) looking as if polished; bright: *a shiny new 10p coin* —**shininess** *n* [U]

ship[1] /ʃɪp/ *n* **1** [C; *by, on board*+U] a large boat for carrying people or goods on the sea **2** [C] *infml* a large aircraft or space vehicle **3 when one's ship comes in/home** *infml* when one becomes rich —see TRAIN, VESSEL (USAGE)

ship[2] *v* **-pp- 1** [T1] to cause to be carried by ship: *I'm flying to America but my car is being shipped* **2** [T1] to send (esp. a large article) over some distance by post or other means: *We ship our products anywhere within Great Britain* **3** [X9 (OFF)] *not fml* to order (someone) to go; send (someone): *He joined the army and was shipped off to training camp* **4** [T1] (of a boat) to take (water) over the side: *The boat began to ship water and threatened to sink* **5** [L9] to take a job on a ship's voyage: *escaped his family and shipped on a voyage to Australia* **6** [T1] to hold (one's OARs) to the side of the boat without rowing

-ship *suffix* [*n*, (*adj*)→*n*[C;U]] **1** the state or quality of: FRIENDSHIP|*to live under a* DICTATORSHIP|*to suffer* HARDSHIPs **2** the position or profession of: *Full* MEMBERSHIP *of the club costs £5 a year.*|*2 new* PROFESSORSHIPs *at the university* **3** the time in the office, rank, position, or profession of: *during his* DICTATORSHIP/PROFESSORSHIP **4** the whole group of: *a large* MEMBERSHIP|*a* READERSHIP *of 5,000*|*The full* MEMBERSHIP *of the club came to the meeting* **5** the art or skill of: SEAMANSHIP|*a man of great* SCHOLARSHIP|HORSEMANSHIP —compare -MANSHIP **6** (forming part of certain titles): *your* LADYSHIP

ship bis·cuit /ˈ· ˌ··/ also (*esp. BrE*) **ship's biscuit, hard tack**— *n* [U] a kind of hard-baked bread eaten esp. formerly by sailors at sea

ship·board /ˈʃɪpbɔːd‖-bord/ *n* **on shipboard** on board ship; on a ship: *goods stored on shipboard*

ship·brok·er /ˈʃɪpˌbrəʊkəʳ/ *n* the representative of a ship owner who takes goods for SHIPMENT, arranges for insurance, etc.

ship·build·ing /ˈʃɪpˌbɪldɪŋ/ *n* [U] the business or job of building (=making) ships

ship ca·nal /ˈ· ·ˌ·/ *n* a man-made waterway large enough for ships that travel on the sea

ship·mate /ˈʃɪpmeɪt/ *n* a fellow sailor on the same ship

ship·ment /ˈʃɪpmənt/ *n* **1** [U;(C)] the action of

sending, carrying, and delivering goods: *articles ready for shipment|delayed or lost in shipment* **2** [C] a load of goods sent together

ship·per /ˈʃɪpəʳ/ *n* a dealer who makes SHIPMENT*s* of goods: *wine shippers*

ship·ping /ˈʃɪpɪŋ/ *n* [U] **1** ship traffic; ships as a group **2** the business of making SHIPMENT*s* **3** the sending and delivery of something: *a shipping charge* (=charge for shipping) *of £1 added to the price*

shipping a·gent /ˈ·· ˌ··/ *n* a business representative of a shipowner at a port

ship's chand·ler /ˌ· ˈ··/ also **ship chandler**— *n* a dealer in supplies for ships

ship·shape /ˈʃɪpʃeɪp/ *adj not fml* clean and neat; in good order

ship·wreck[1] /ˈʃɪp-rek/ *n* [C;U] a/the destruction of a ship, as by hitting rocks or sinking

shipwreck[2] *v* [T1 *usu. pass.*] **1** to cause to suffer SHIPWRECK: *sailors shipwrecked on an island* **2** to wreck; ruin: *All our hopes were shipwrecked by the bad news*

ship·wright /ˈʃɪp-raɪt/ *n* a person who works on building and repairing ships

ship·yard /ˈʃɪp-jɑːd‖-jɑrd/ *n* a place where ships are built or repaired

shire /ʃaɪəʳ/ *n old use* COUNTY (1)

shire horse /ˈ· ·/ *n* a large powerful kind of English horse used for pulling loads

shires /ʃaɪəz‖ʃaɪərz/ *n* [*the*+P] *BrE becoming rare* (*usu. cap.*) the country areas in the centre of England where fox hunting is popular

shirk /ʃɜːk‖ʃɜrk/ *v* [T1,4;IØ] to avoid (unpleasant work) because of laziness, lack of determination, etc.: *We mustn't shirk our cleaning job|doing our cleaning* —**~er**

shir·ring /ˈʃɜːrɪŋ/ *n* [U] the gathering of cloth into small folds made by drawing it along 2 or more rows of threads pulled tight or by stitching in rows of tight rubber thread

shirt /ʃɜːt‖ʃɜrt/ *n* **1** a piece of clothing for the upper part of the body, usu. of light cloth with a collar and SLEEVE*s* (covering the arms), usu. worn by a man, inside a coat —compare SWEATSHIRT, NIGHTSHIRT, UNDERSHIRT **2 lose one's shirt** *infml* to lose all one has; lose a lot of money **3 put one's shirt on something** *infml* to risk all one's money, esp. on a horse in a race **4 stuffed shirt** *infml* a person who acts grand and important; POMPOUS person —see also KEEP[1] (19) **your shirt on**

shirt·front /ˈʃɜːtfrʌnt‖ˈʃɜrt-/ also **front**— *n* the part of a shirt covering the chest, esp. the stiff front part of a formal white shirt

shirt·ing /ˈʃɜːtɪŋ‖ˈʃɜr-/ *n* [U;C] *tech* cloth, such as light cotton, for making shirts

shirt·sleeve /ˈʃɜːtˌsliːv‖ˈʃɜrt-/ *n infml* **1** the sleeve of a shirt **2** [A] being without, or showing no need for, coats, as because of hot weather or informality: *a shirtsleeve crowd to watch the cricket match* **3 in one's shirtsleeves** wearing nothing over one's shirt: *On such a hot day the men in the office were working in their shirtsleeves*

shirt·tail /ˈʃɜːt-teɪl‖ˈʃɜrt-/ *n* the front or back part of a shirt below the wearer's waist

shirt·waist /ˈʃɜːtˌweɪst‖ˈʃɜrt-/ *n AmE* **1** a plain shirt made for a woman **2** SHIRTWAISTER

shirt·waist·er /ʃɜːtˌweɪstəʳ‖ˈʃɜrt-/ *n* a woman's dress in the style of a man's shirt

shirt·y /ˈʃɜːti‖ˈʃɜr/ *adj* [Wa1] *infml* bad-tempered; angry and rude

shish ke·bab /ˈʃɪʃ kə̇ˌbæb‖-bɑb/ *n* KEBAB

shit[1] /ʃɪt/ *v* **shit,** *pres. p.* **shitting** *taboo* **1** [IØ;(T1)] to pass (solid waste) from the bowels; DEFECATE **2** [T1] to make dirty, by passing solid waste from the bowels into: *He's shit his trousers* **3 shit oneself** **a** to pass solid waste from the bowels accidentally **b** *sl* to be very afraid

shit[2] *n taboo* **1** [U] solid waste from the bowels; EXCREMENT **2** [S] an act of passing this waste from the body: *to go and have a shit* **3** [U] stupid talk; NONSENSE (1,2) **4** [S] something of no value (in such phrs. as **don't give a shit** (=don't care) and **not worth a shit**) **5** [C; *you*+N] a worthless person

shit[3] *interj taboo* (expressing anger or annoyance)

shits /ʃɪts/ *n* [*the*+GU] *taboo* DIARRHOEA

shit·ty /ˈʃɪti/ *adj* [Wa1] *taboo* unpleasant; nasty

shiv·er[1] /ˈʃɪvəʳ/ *n* [*usu. pl.*] *now rare* any of the very small pieces into which something is broken by a blow or fall

shiver[2] *v* [IØ;T1] *now rare* to break into many small pieces; SHATTER (1)

shiver[3] *v* [IØ] to shake, esp. (of people) from cold or fear; tremble: *Our enemies must be* **shivering in their shoes** (=very afraid)

shiver[4] *n* a feeling of SHIVERing[3]: *That strange noise sends* **shivers (up and) down my spine** (=back)

shiv·ers /ˈʃɪvəz‖-ərz/ *n* [*the*+P] *infml* **1** tremblings typical of a fever **2** feelings of strong unreasonable dislike or fear: *Snakes give me the shivers*

shiv·er·y /ˈʃɪvəri/ *adj* [Wa2] **1** (of weather) cold: *a shivery winter day* **2** (of a person) trembling as if feverish

shoal[1] /ʃəʊl/ *n* an underwater bank of sand not far below the surface of the water, making it dangerous to boats

shoal[2] *n* [(*of*)] **1** a large group (of fish) swimming together **2** *not fml* a large number

shock[1] /ʃɒk‖ʃɑk/ *n* **1** [U;(C)] (a) violent force, as from a hard blow, crash, explosion, etc.: *The shock of the explosion was felt far away: the shock waves spread for miles* **2** [U] the state or strong feeling caused by something unexpected and usu. very unpleasant: *The bad news left us all speechless from shock* **3** [C] something causing this; an unpleasant piece of news: *His death was a shock to us all* **4** [C; U] the sudden violent effect of electricity passing through the body **5** [U] *med* the weakened state of the body with less activity of the heart, lungs, etc., usu. following damage to the body **6** *infml* SHOCK ABSORBER

shock[2] *v* **1** [T1;IØ] to cause usu. unpleasant or angry surprise to (someone): *I was shocked by his sudden illness|his rudeness|his wild ideas.|It shocked me to see how my neighbours treated their children* **2** [T1 *usu. pass.*] to give an electric shock to: *got shocked when he touched the wire*

shock[3] *n* [(*of*)] a thick bushy mass (of hair)

shock ab·sorb·er /ˈ· ·ˌ··/ *n* an apparatus made usu. of a rod moving in and out of a tube of liquid, fixed near each wheel of a vehicle to lessen the effect of rough roads or on an aircraft to make a smoother landing —see picture at CAR

shock·er /ˈʃɒkəʳ‖ˈʃɑ-/ *n becoming rare or humor* a person or thing that shocks as being improper, wild, or immoral

shock·head·ed /ˌʃɒkˈhedə̇d◂‖ˌʃɑk-/ *n* having a SHOCK[3] of hair on the head

shock·ing /ˈʃɒkɪŋ‖ˈʃɑ-/ *adj* **1** causing SHOCK[1] (2); very improper, wrong, or sad: *a shocking accident* **2** *not fml* very bad (though not evil): *What a shocking waste of time!* —**~ly** *adv*: *shockingly rude behaviour|(not fml) shockingly bad grammar*

shock·proof /ˈʃɒkpruːf‖ˈʃɑk-/ *adj* (esp. of a watch) not easily damaged by being dropped, hit, shaken, etc.

shock treat·ment /ˈ· ˌ··/ also **shock ther·a·py** /ˈ· ˌ···/— *n* [U] *med* treatment of some disorders of the mind by using powerful drugs or electric shocks

shock troops /ˈ· ·/ *n* [P] soldiers chosen and trained for use in sudden forceful attacking

shod /ʃɒd‖ʃɑd/ *adj* [Wa5;B9] *usu. lit* wearing or provided with shoes: *poor badly-shod children*

shod·dy[1] /'ʃɒdi‖'ʃɑdi/ *n* [U] **1** cloth made using wool from old used cloth: *an armchair filled with shoddy* **2** cheap material of poor quality

shoddy[2] *adj* [Wa1] **1** made or done cheaply and badly, usu. to look like something better: *shoddy workmanship that won't bear close examination* **2** ungenerous or not worthy; dishonourable; SHABBY (3): *He played a shoddy trick on his employers.* —**-dily** *adv* —**-diness** *n* [U]

shoe[1] /ʃu:/ *n* **1** an outer covering for the human foot, usu. of leather and having a hard base (SOLE) and a support (HEEL) under the heel of the foot: *to put on/take off one's shoes* —compare BOOT[2] (1), SANDAL, SLIPPER **2** either of the pair of curved plates (in the BRAKE) around a vehicle wheel which may press against it to stop it or slow it down: *an accident caused by worn* BRAKE *shoes* —see picture at BICYCLE[1] **3** *tech* the part of an electric train that slides along the track or wire to pick up electricity **4** HORSESHOE: *The horse has cast* (=lost) *a shoe* **5 to fill someone's shoes** *not fml* to take the place and do the job of someone: *Will anyone be able to fill the director's shoes now that he's left the company?* **6 If the shoe fits (wear it)** *AmE infml* If the **cap** FITs[3] (7) (wear it) **7 in someone's shoes** *not fml* in someone's position; experiencing what another has to experience: *I'm glad I'm not in his shoes just now!* **8 where the shoe pinches** *not fml* where the particular difficulty is

shoe[2] *v* **shod** /ʃɒd‖ʃɑd/ *or* **shoed,** *pres. p.* **shoeing** [T1] to fix a SHOE[1] (4) on (an animal): *A man who shoes horses is called a* FARRIER

shoe·black /'ʃu:blæk/ *n* BOOTBLACK

shoe·horn /'ʃu:hɔ:n‖-hɔrn/ *n* a curved piece of metal or plastic for putting inside the back of a shoe when slipping it on, to help the heel go in easily

shoe·lace /'ʃu:leɪs/ *n* a thin cord or piece of leather (to be) passed through holes on both sides of the front opening of a shoe and tied to fasten the shoe on

shoe·mak·er /'ʃu:ˌmeɪkəʳ/ *n* a person who makes shoes and boots

shoe·shine /'ʃu:ʃaɪn/ *n* an act of polishing the shoes

shoe·string /'ʃu:ˌstrɪŋ/ *n* **1** [C] *esp. AmE* SHOELACE **2** [*on*+S;A] *not fml* a very small amount of money: *He started his business on a shoestring and built it up* **3** [A] *AmE* long and thin: *shoestring potatoes* (=thin CHIPs[1] (4))|*a shoestring* TIE[1] (1)

shone /ʃɒn‖ʃəʊn/ *past t. and past p. of* SHINE[1]

shoo[1] /ʃu:/ *interj* (said, usu. not angrily, to animals or small children) go away!

shoo[2] *v* [X9] *not fml* to drive away (as if) by saying "SHOO": *shooed the birds off the bushes|shooed the children out of the kitchen*

shook /ʃʊk/ *past t. of* SHAKE

shoot[1] /ʃu:t/ *v* **shot** /ʃɒt‖ʃɑt/ **1** [T1 (OFF); L9] to let fly with force (a bullet, arrow, etc.): *This gun shoots (off) bullets.|I shot an arrow at the spot on the wall* **2** [T1;I∅: (*at*)] to fire (a weapon): *I'm coming out with my hands up: don't shoot!|Can you shoot a* BOW[3] (1)*?|He shot at a bird, but missed it* (compare *He shot a bird and killed it*).|*If the police see the dangerous murderer, they'll shoot to kill* **3** [T1] to hit, wound, or kill with something as from a gun: *He shot a bird.|He was shot 3 times in the arm* **4** [T1] *esp. BrE* **a** to kill (a kind of animal) in this way for sport: *He goes to Scotland every year to shoot wild duck* **b** to do this on (an area of land): *They're shooting the woods behind the farm* —see HUNT (USAGE) **5** [X9] to make (one's way) by firing a gun at anyone in the way: *He shot his way out of prison* **6** [X7,9] to cause to go or become by hitting with something from a gun: *Part of his foot was shot away* (=off) *in battle.|She shot him dead* **7** [D1;X9] to send out as from a gun: *She shot him a distrustful look.|a meeting where everyone shot questions at the chairman* **8** [L9] to go fast or suddenly: *Blood shot out of the wound.|He shot past me in his fast car* **9** [T1;I∅] to kick, throw, etc., a ball aimed to make (a point) in a game: *in a good position to shoot* **10** [Wv4;L9] (of pain) to move fast along a nerve: *Pain shot through his arm* **11** [T1;I∅] to make a photograph or film (of): *This film was shot in California* **12** [T1] *infml* (in GOLF) to make (the stated number of strokes) in playing a complete game: *Miller shot a 69 today* **13** [T1] *AmE* to play (a game of, esp. BILLIARDS, CRAPS, POOL[2] (3), MARBLES): *Let's shoot some/a game of* POOL **14** [T1] to pass quickly by or along: *a car shooting traffic lights* (=when they are signalling cars to stop)|*a boat shooting the* RAPIDs[2] (2) **15** [I∅] (esp. in cricket) (of a ball) scarcely to rise from the ground after hitting it; keep very low after bouncing (BOUNCE) **16** [T1;I∅] **a** to move (a sliding locking bar (BOLT[1] (2))) across **b** (of such a bar) to move across **17** [I∅ *usu. imper.*] *infml* to speak out; say what is to be said: *"May I ask a question?" "Certainly. Shoot!"* **18** [I∅] (of a plant) to put out SHOOTs[2] (1) **19** [T1] *tech* to aim at (a star) with an instrument to find one's position **20** [T1] *drug-users' sl* to take (a drug) directly into the BLOODSTREAM by using a needle: *to shoot* HEROIN **21 shoot one's bolt/(*AmE*) wad** *infml* to use up all one's strength, arguments, etc., and have nothing left **22 shoot the bull** *AmE infml* to have an informal not very serious conversation: *They sat around shooting the bull until late at night* **23 shoot the works** *infml, esp. AmE* **a** to risk all one's money in a game **b** to use all one's effort —see also **shoot a** LINE[2] (38), SHOOT DOWN, SHOOT FOR, SHOOT OFF, SHOOT OUT, SHOOT UP, SHOT

shoot[2] *n* **1** a new growth from (a part of) a plant, esp. a young stem and leaves —see picture at FLOWER[1] **2** an occasion for shooting (of animals, in competition, military training, etc.): *a weekend shoot* **3** *esp. AmE* a sending up of a space vehicle or ROCKET[1] (2) SHOT[1] (4): *a moon shoot* (=for a voyage to the moon) **4** an area of land where animals are shot for sport

shoot down *v adv* [T1] **1** to bring down and destroy (an aircraft) by shooting **2** *infml* to say "no" firmly to (a person or idea): *another idea shot down by the chairman*

-shooter /'ʃu:təʳ/ *comb. form* a person or weapon that shoots: *a* RIFLE*shooter*|PEASHOOTER|SIX-SHOOTER|SHARPSHOOTER

shoot for also **shoot at**— *v prep* [T1] *not fml, esp. AmE* to try to reach; have a GOAL (1); aim at: *We're shooting this year for a 50% increase in sales*

shooting box /'·· ·/ also **shooting lodge** /'·· ·/— *n BrE* a small house in the country for use by sportsmen during the shooting season

shooting brake /'·· ·/ *n BrE, becoming rare* ESTATE CAR

shooting gal·le·ry /'·· ˌ···/ *n* an enclosed place (esp. at a FAIR[3]) where people shoot guns at fixed or moving objects to win prizes, for practice, etc.

shooting match /'·· ·/ *n* **the whole shooting match** *infml* the whole thing or affair

shooting star /ˌ·· '·/ also **falling star**— *n not fml* a small piece of material (a METEOR) from space which burns brightly as it passes through the earth's air

shooting stick /'·· ·/ *n* a pointed walking-stick with a top which opens out to form a seat, for sitting outdoors

shooting war /ˈ·· ·/ *n not fml* a war in which there is actual fighting

shoot off *v adv* [T1] **1** to fire (a weapon) or explode (esp. FIREWORK*s*), into the air without aiming: *shot off their weapons as a sign of victory* —see also SHOOT[1] (2,4) **2 shoot one's mouth off** *infml* to talk foolishly about what one does not know about or should not talk about

shoot-out /ˈ· ·/ *n not fml* a battle or formal exchange of shots between gunfighters

shoot out *v adv* **1** [T1;I∅] to (cause to) come out suddenly: *The snake shot out its tongue. Its tongue shot out* **2** [T1 (*with*)] *not fml* to decide (a quarrel) by shooting: *The boys are going to shoot it out (with each other)*

shoot up *v adv* **1** [I∅] to go upwards, increase, or grow quickly: *Flames shot up into the air.|Prices have shot up lately* **2** [T1] *not fml* to shoot wildly and freely in (a place): *gunfighters shooting up the town*

shop[1] /ʃɒp‖ʃɑp/ *n* **1** [C] (*AmE* **store**)— a room or building where goods are regularly kept and sold: *the local village shop|The shops in town close at 5.30.|(in comb.) a bookshop|a sweetshop* **2** [C] also (*pomp, esp. in names*) **shoppe**— *AmE* such a place, esp. small or selling special kinds of goods: *a beauty shop* (=SALON)|*a gift shoppe* **3** [C] a place where things are made or repaired; WORKSHOP: *the body shop in a car factory|a repair shop* **4** [C] *infml* a place of business, such as an office: *The director's office is a smooth-running shop* —compare CLOSED SHOP **5** [U] business; activity (esp. in the phrs. **set up shop, close/shut up shop**): *He's set up shop as a lawyer in town.|The whole country shuts up shop on Christmas Day* **6** (**talk**) **shop** (to talk about) one's work **7 all over the shop** *BrE infml* **a** scattered in disorder: *Don't leave your things all over the shop; put them away in the cupboard* **b** everywhere; in all directions: *I've been all over the shop trying to find that pen* **8 the right/wrong shop** *infml* the right/wrong person to give help, advice, etc.: *If you want help with French, you've come to the wrong shop: I don't know a word of it*

shop[2] *v* **-pp- 1** [I∅ (*for*)] to visit 1 or more shops in order to buy; buy goods (often in the phr. **go shopping**): *I went shopping today in town.|I was shopping for some new clothes, but I couldn't find anything* —compare WINDOW-SHOP **2** [T1] *AmE* to visit (1 or more shops) in order to buy: *We shopped all the main shops* **3** [T1] *BrE sl* to tell the police about (a criminal); INFORM AGAINST: *The murderer was shopped by his girlfriend* —**~per** *n*

shop a·round *v adv* [I∅] to compare prices or values in different shops before buying: (fig.) *We shopped around before deciding which church to join*

shop as·sis·tant /ˈ· ·ˌ··/ (*AmE* **salesclerk**)— *n BrE* a person who serves buyers in a shop —see OFFICER (USAGE)

shop floor /ˌ· ˈ·ˈ/ *n* [*the*+R] *not fml* the place regarded as where ordinary workers (not those who direct them, the MANAGEMENT) do their work: *What's the feeling on the shop floor about the rise in pay?*

shop·keep·er /ˈʃɒpˌkiːpəʳ‖ˈʃɑp-/ *AmE* usu. **storekeeper**— *n* a person, usu. the owner (the PROPRIETOR), in charge of a small shop

shop·lift /ˈʃɒpˌlɪft‖ˈʃɑp-/ *v* [I∅;T1] to take (goods) from a shop without paying; steal from a shop —**~er** *n*

shoppe /ʃɒp‖ʃɑp/ *n AmE pomp* (*esp. in names*) SHOP[1] (2)

shopping cen·tre /ˈ·· ˌ··/ *n* a group of shops of different kinds, usu. outside the centre of a town and planned and built as a whole

shop·soiled /ˈʃɒpsɔɪld‖ˈʃɑp-/ *adj BrE* slightly damaged or dirty from being handled or kept on view in a shop for a long time

shop stew·ard /ˌ· ˈ··/ *n* a trade union officer who is elected by the members of his union in a particular place of work to represent them

shop·worn /ˈʃɒpwɔːn‖ˈʃɑpworn/ *adj* **1** (as of ideas) no longer fresh, interesting, or valuable: *shopworn phrases that don't persuade anyone any longer* **2** *AmE* SHOPSOILED

shore[1] /ʃɔːʳ‖ʃor/ *n* **1** [C;U] the land along the edge of a large stretch of water: *to walk along the shore|to see a boat about a mile from/off the shore* **2 on shore** on land; away from one's ship: *The sailors were warned not to get into trouble while they were on shore* —see also ASHORE, OFFSHORE, ONSHORE

USAGE The edge of the land where it meets the water is the **shore** or **coast**. One can speak of the **shore** or the **coast** of the sea, but the edge of a lake must be the **shore**. **Coast** is the word used in connection with maps, weather, or naval defence: *to walk on the* **shore** *collecting shells|a holiday on the north* **coast** *of Spain.* The **seaside** is the area by the sea considered as a place of enjoyment: *digging in the sand at the* **seaside**. A **beach** is part of the **coast** that is smooth, without cliffs or rocks. It may consist either of sand or of small stones.

shore[2] *v* [T1 (UP)] **1** to support with a SHORE[3]: *shored up the damaged fence* **2** to strengthen or give support to (something weak or in danger of failing); keep from failing or falling: *government action to shore up farm prices*

shore[3] *n* a length of usu. wood placed under or against something to prevent its falling down; support; PROP[1] (1)

shore leave /ˈ· ·/ *n* [U] time allowed to a sailor or ship's officer to spend on shore

shorn /ʃɔːn‖ʃorn/ *past p. of* SHEAR

short[1] /ʃɔːt‖ʃort/ *adj* [Wa1] **1** [B] not far from one end to the other: little in distance or length (opposite **long**) or height (opposite **tall**): *writes in short sentences|only a short way/distance from here|had her hair cut short|A straight line is the shortest distance between 2 points.|He's a short man, shorter than his wife* **2** [B] lasting only a little time; BRIEF: *a short visit of only half an hour|only a short time ago|I have such a short memory: I can't remember what you told me yesterday* —opposite **long 3** [B;E: (*of*)] lacking enough; not reaching far enough or to a standard; INSUFFICIENT or DEFICIENT: *"I'm short of money this week: can you lend me some?" "Sorry: I'm rather short myself."|a shopkeeper found guilty of using short weights/measures|These goods are in short supply: the price will be high.|I need £1 but I'm 5p short: I've only got 95p.|Our car broke down only 2 miles short of where we wanted to go* —see LACK (USAGE) **4** [B] rudely impatient; CURT; BRUSQUE: *I'm sorry I was short with you: I ought to have answered your question more politely.|a* **short-tempered** *fellow who's likely to get angry* **5** [B] pronounced quickly or without force, as opposed to the other (**long**) one in a pair of vowel sounds **6** [B] (of pastry) falling easily into pieces; CRUMBLY **7** [A] (of a drink) of a kind (such as SPIRITS[1] (12)) usu. served in a small glass —compare LONG DRINK **8** [B] (in cricket) **a** (of a fielder) in a position close to the hitter —opposites **long, deep b** (of a BOWLed ball) hitting the ground quite far from the hitter **9 for short** as a shorter way of saying the same: *My name is Alexander, "Al" for short* **10 in short** to put it into a few words; all I mean is: *You can't make me! I won't do it! In short—no!* **11 little/nothing short of** *pomp* little/nothing less than; almost/completely **12 make short work of** *not fml* to deal with or defeat quickly **13 short and sweet** *not fml* not wasting words or time; short and direct in expression **14 short on** *not fml* without very much or enough (of): *He's a nice fellow but short on brains* (=not clever) **15 short for** a shorter form of, or way of saying: *The usual word* "PUB" *is short for "public house"* —**~ness** *n* [U]

short² *adv* **1** [Wa5] suddenly; ABRUPTly (1): *The driver stopped short when the child ran into the street.|The rider pulled his horse up short* **2 be taken/caught short** *BrE infml* to have a sudden and strong need to empty the bowels or esp. pass water from the body **3 cut short** to stop suddenly before the end: *The accident forced them to cut their holiday short* **4 fall short (of)** to be less than (good) enough (for): *Our income may well fall short of our needs* **5 go short (of)** to be without enough (of): *I'm giving my dinner to the children; they mustn't go short (of food)* **6 run short (of) a** to use almost all one has (of) and not have enough left: *We've run short of oil* **b** to become less than enough: *The supply of oil is running short (of what we need)*—see also SELL¹ (10) **short**

short³ *n not fml* **1** a short film shown before the main film at a cinema **2** a drink of strong alcohol, such as WHISKY or RUM —compare LONG DRINK **3** SHORT CIRCUIT —see also **the** LONG³ (4) **and (the) short of it**

short·age /'ʃɔːtɪdʒ‖'ʃɔr-/ *n* [C;U: (*of*)] a condition of having less than needed; an amount lacking: *food shortages during the war|Shortage of skilled workers is our main difficulty*

short·bread /'ʃɔːtbred‖'ʃɔrt-/ *n* [U] a thin hard kind of sweet cake (a kind of BISCUIT) made with a lot of butter

short·cake /'ʃɔːtkeɪk‖'ʃɔrt-/ *n* [U] **1** *BrE* usu. thick SHORTBREAD **2** *AmE* cake (usu. of a kind like SCONE*s*) over which sweetened fruit is poured: STRAWBERRY *shortcake*

short-change /ˌ· '·/ *v* [T1] *not fml* to give back less than enough money (CHANGE² (4)) to (a buyer who pays for something with a large note or coin)

short-cir·cuit /ˌ· '··/ *v* **1** [T1;I0] to (cause to) have a SHORT CIRCUIT **2** [T1] to do something without going through; BYPASS: *to short-circuit all the formality by a simple telephone call*

short circuit *n* a faulty electrical connection that makes too short a path for the current between 2 points and so usu. puts the power supply out of operation

short·com·ing /'ʃɔːtˌkʌmɪŋ‖'ʃɔrt-/ *n* [*usu. pl.*] a failing to reach what is expected or right; DEFECT: *In spite of all my friend's shortcomings I still like him*

short cut /ˌ· '·, '· ·‖'· ·/ *n not fml* a quicker more direct way

short·en /'ʃɔːtn‖'ʃɔrtn/ *v* [T1;I0] to make or become short or shorter: *She shortened the skirt by an inch.|Shorten this report to 2000 words*

short·ening /'ʃɔːtnɪŋ‖'ʃɔrt-/ *n* [U] *esp. AmE* fat for combining with flour in pastry mixtures

short·fall /'ʃɔːtfɔːl‖'ʃɔrt-/ *n* an amount lacking to reach the amount needed, expected, or hoped for: *We hoped to make £1000 but after our bad luck there'll be a shortfall of at least £200*

short·hand /'ʃɔːthænd‖'ʃɔrt/ *n* [U] rapid writing in a system using signs or shorter forms for letters, words, phrases, etc.; STENOGRAPHY: *The secretary took down in shorthand what was said: she made shorthand notes* —compare LONGHAND

short·hand·ed /ˌʃɔːt'hændɪ̵d◂‖ˌʃɔrt-/ *adj* lacking the needed number of helpers or workers

shorthand typ·ist /ˌ·· '··/ also (*esp. AmE*) **stenographer**— *n* a person who records speech in SHORTHAND and then makes a copy on a TYPEWRITER

short·horn /'ʃɔːthɔːn‖'ʃɔrthɔrn/ *n* any of several kinds of milk- and BEEF-producing cattle with short horns

short·ie /'ʃɔːti‖'ʃɔrti/ *n* SHORTY

short-list /'· ·/ *v* [T1 *usu. pass.*] *BrE* to put on a SHORT LIST

short list *n BrE* a list of the most suitable people for an appointment, chosen from all those who were considered at first and from among whom 1 or more successful ones are chosen

short-lived /ˌ· '·◂/ *adj* [Wa2] lasting only a short time

short·ly /'ʃɔːtli‖'ʃɔrt-/ *adv* **1** [Wa5] soon; (in) a little time: *Mr. Jones will be back shortly* **2** [Wa5] at a short distance: *Make a right turn shortly beyond the village* **3** in a few words; BRIEFly¹ (1): *He explained his meaning shortly but clearly* **4** impatiently; not politely: *He answered shortly that he didn't care what I thought*

short of /'· ·/ *prep* **1** not quite reaching to; up to but not including: *threats of every action short of war* **2** except for; without: *Short of calling a meeting I don't know how we can get our plan approved*

short or·der /ˌ· '··◂/ *n AmE* **1** an order for quickly-cooked food, as in an informal eating place **2 in short order** quickly and with no trouble: *He finished his work in short order*

short-range /ˌ· '·◂/ *adj* [Wa2] of, concerning, or covering a short distance of time

shorts /ʃɔːts‖ʃɔrts/ *n* [P] **1** trousers ending at or above the knees (worn in playing games, in hot weather, by children, etc.) **2** *esp. AmE* men's UNDERPANTS of this kind

short shrift /ˌ· '·/ *n* [U] unfairly quick treatment; little attention (esp. in the phrs. **get/give short shrift**): *Some thought that the armed forces were getting all the government money and education was getting short shrift*

short·sight·ed /ˌʃɔːt'saɪtɪ̵d◂‖ˌʃɔrt-/ *adj* **1** also (*esp. AmE*) **nearsighted**— *esp. BrE* unable to see objects clearly or read things in writing if they are not close to the eyes —opposite **longsighted 2** not considering the likely future effects of present action: *It's very shortsighted not to spend money on repairing your house* —opposite **farsighted** —**~ly** *adv* —**~ness** *n* [U]

short sto·ry /ˌ· '··/ *n* a short invented story usu. containing only a few characters and dealing with feelings rather than events

short-term /ˌ· '·◂/ *adj* [Wa2] (esp. in money matters) happening in, dealing with, or concerning a short period of time; in or for the near future: *short-term planning|borrowing*

short time /ˌ· '·◂/ *n* [U] work at a factory, office, etc., for a shorter than usual period each day or week: *Workers were put on short time at the factory while raw materials were scarce*

short wave /ˌ· '·◂/ *n* [U] radio broadcasting or receiving on waves of less than 60 metres in length: *a short-wave radio|to listen to broadcasts on short wave*

short-wind·ed /ˌ· '··◂/ *adj* quickly becoming tired and out of breath after a little running

short·y, shortie /'ʃɔːti‖'ʃɔrti/ *n infml* **1** [N] *derog* a short person **2** [A] (of a garment) short: *shortie* NIGHTDRESS

shot¹ /ʃɒt‖ʃɑt/ *n* **1** [C] an action of shooting a weapon: *fired 3 shots|wounded by a shot in the leg* **2** [C9] a person who shoots with the stated degree of skill: *She's a good*/CRACK³/*poor shot* —see also DEAD SHOT **3** [C] a kick, throw, etc., of a ball intended to make a point in the game: *His shot went to the right of the* GOAL.|*a* PENALTY *shot* **4** [C] a sending up of a space vehicle or ROCKET: *a moon shot* (=for a voyage to the moon) **5** [C] a chance or effort to do something; TRY² (1); GO² (3) (often in such phr. as **have a shot at**): *It's a hard job but I'd like a shot at it* **6** [U] nonexplosive metal in the form of balls for shooting from some kinds of guns, esp. CANNONs in former times and SHOTGUNs —see also BUCKSHOT, GRAPESHOT **7** [C] the heavy metal ball used in the SHOT PUT **8** [C] a photograph: *fashion shots* **9** [C] a single part of a cinema film made by one camera without interruption: *an action shot* **10** [C] *not fml* a taking of a drug into the bloodstream through a needle; INJECTION: *a shot of* PENICILLIN **11** [C] *infml* a bill for drinks (esp. in the phr. **pay one's shot**) **12** [C9] a chance at the stated degree of risk: *The horse is an 8 to 5 shot to win the race* —see also LONG SHOT **13** [C] *not fml* a small drink (esp. of WHISKY) for swallowing at once **14 a shot in the arm** *not fml* something which acts to bring back a happy active condition: *a big sale which was a shot in the arm to the failing company* **15 a shot in the dark** *not fml* a guess unsupported by arguments; wild guess **16 big shot** *derog* an important person **17 call one's shot** *AmE infml* to state exactly what one intends to do **18 like a shot** *not fml* quickly or without any delay: *The dog was off like a shot after the rabbit*

shot² *adj* **1** [Wa5;B (*with*)] woven in 2 different colours (one along and one across the material), giving a changing effect of colour: *a dress of shot silk: it was blue shot with green* **2** [F (THROUGH)+*with*] *esp. lit* having a lot of in a mixture; full of: *His stories are shot through with fine descriptions* **3** [F] *AmE infml* ruined or completely worn by hard use: *My nerves are shot: I need a holiday* **4** [F+*of*] *infml* rid of; finished with: *glad to be shot of the job*

shot³ *past t. and past p. of* SHOOT

shot·gun /ˈʃɒtgʌn‖ˈʃɑt-/ *n* a gun fired from the shoulder, which is smooth inside its 1 or usu. 2 barrels, fires a quantity of small metal balls (SHOT¹ (6)) together for a quite short distance, and is used esp. for shooting birds

shot put /ˈ· ·/ *n* [*the*+R] a competition to throw (PUT¹ (10)) a heavy metal ball (SHOT¹ (7)) the furthest distance

shot tow·er /ˈ· ˌ··/ *n* a tower in which SHOT¹ (6) is made by pouring melted lead through a framework of small holes into water far below

should /ʃəd; *strong* ʃʊd/ *v neg. contr.* **shouldn't** [Wv2;I∅,2] **1** (in reported speech) SHALL: *I knew if I kept at it I should succeed.*|(*fml*) *He said he should return, and he did return* **2** (used usu. with *that*, after adjectives and verbs marked [5c] like *intend, desire, demand, be anxious*): *It's odd that you should mention that.*|*I was anxious that our plan should not fail.*|*I suggest that John should go*|(*AmE* also) *that John go* **3** (used with *I* and *we* in CONDITIONAL sentences with a past t., or about the past): *We should never have won without your help.*|*I shouldn't see him if we didn't go to the same school.*|*I should stay out of trouble if I were you* **4** (expressing duty or what is necessary) ought to: *That was stupid: you shouldn't have done it.*|*Why shouldn't I say what I think?*|*If you see anything strange you should call the police* **5** (expressing what is likely) will probably: *The effect of the tax should be felt in higher prices.*|*We needn't get ready yet; the guests shouldn't come for another hour* **6** (used for expressing what is possible but not likely, in CONDITIONAL sentences about the future): *"If I should die before I wake. . ."* (child's prayer)|*I don't think it will happen, but if it should, what shall we do?*|(*fml*) *Should you be interested, I have a book on the subject you might like to see* **7** (used in phrs. like the following, to express humour or surprise): *As I left the house, who should come to meet me but my old friend Sam!*|*At that point, what should happen but* (*that*) *the car wouldn't start* **8** *humor* (expressing the opposite meaning) ought not to; needn't (esp. in the phr. **should worry**): *With all his money, he should worry about a little thing like £5!* **9 I should** (used when giving advice) you ought to: *I should keep the money* (*if I were you*) **10 I should have thought** *esp. BrE* (in remarks expressing surprise): *20 degrees? I should have thought it was colder than that* (*if you hadn't told me*) **11 I should like** I want: *I should like to ask the minister a question.*|*I should like a bath* —see LIKE (USAGE) **12 I should think** (expressing doubt) I believe: *I should think she must be at least 40.*|*"Can you come?" "Yes, I should think so"* **13 I should (just) think so!/not!** Of course!/Of course not!: *"Mother never climbs trees." "I should think not, at her age!"*

USAGE 1 in meanings 2–9, 12, and 13, only **should** is used. In meanings 1, 3, 10, and 11, the same rules are followed as for **shall** and **will** in *fml* speech and writing, although in ordinary use **would** is more common, esp. in meanings 1 and 3. 2 In meanings 4 and 5, **should** is weaker than **ought to** and much weaker than **must** or **have to**. 3 Avoid meaning 3 (CONDITIONAL) where it might be confused with meaning 4 (ought to). A sentence like *I* **should** *help you if I had time* could mean either. 4 *I'd, he'd*, etc., are short for *I/he* **had** or *I/he* **would**, but not for *I/he* **should**. —see OUGHT, LIKE, SHALL (USAGE)

shoul·der¹ /ˈʃəʊldəʳ/ *n* **1** [C] **a** the part of the body at each side of the neck where the arms are connected **b** the part of a garment that covers this part of the body: *a coat split across the shoulders* **2** [C *usu. pl. with sing. meaning*] the upper part of the back including these, esp. considered as where loads are carried: *He was bent over with the weight of the load on his shoulders* —see picture at HUMAN² **3** [C] something like these in shape, such as **a** a slope on a mountain near the top —see picture at MOUNTAIN **b** the outward curve on a bottle below the neck **4** [C *usu. sing.*] either edge of a road outside the travelled part: *He drove the car onto the hard shoulder of the* MOTORWAY *and waited for help* **5** [C;U] the upper part of the front leg of an animal as meat: *a shoulder of lamb* **6 head and shoulders above** *not fml* very much better than: *This book stands/is head and shoulders above all others on the subject* **7 open one's shoulders** (of a person hitting a ball) to hit with the full force of one's shoulders and upper body, not just one's arm **8 rub shoulders with** *not fml* to meet socially; be in the same company with **9 shoulder to shoulder** *not fml* **a** side by side; close together **b** together; with the same intentions **10 (straight) from the shoulder** *not fml* expressed plainly and directly without trying to avoid unpleasantness —see also COLD SHOULDER, **put one's shoulder to the** WHEEL² (8)

shoulder² *v* **1** [T1] to place (as a load) on the shoulder(s): (fig.) *to shoulder the responsibility of high political office* **2** [X9] to push with the shoulders: *He shouldered his way to the front, shouldering others aside* **3 shoulder arms** [*usu. imper.*] (of a soldier) **a** *BrE* to hold a weapon upright at one's side with the right hand at about the middle of the weapon **b** *AmE* to hold a weapon by the end with the barrel resting on the front of one shoulder

shoulder blade /ˈ·· ·/ also (*med*) **scapula**— *n* either of the 2 flat 3-sided bones on each side of the upper back —see picture at SKELETON

shoulder strap /ˈ·· ·/ *n* a narrow band for passing over the shoulder, esp. in a pair on a woman's dress, undergarment, etc., for holding it up

should·n't /ˈʃʊdnt/ [Wv2] *contr. of* should not —see CONTR. (USAGE)

shouldst /ʃədst; *strong* ʃʊdst/ [Wv2] **thou shouldst** *old use or bibl* (when talking to one person) you should

shout¹ /ʃaʊt/ *v* **1** [IØ;T1,5:(OUT)] to give a loud cry (of); speak or say very loudly: *I can hear you all right: there's no need to shout.|"Help!" he shouted = He shouted for help = He shouted to us to help him* **2** [T1;IØ] *AustrE infml* to order and pay for (a drink) for someone else **3 shout oneself hoarse** to shout until one's voice loses its strength

shout² *n* **1** [C] a loud cry or call: *a warning shout|shouts of delight from the football crowd* **2** [S9] *BrE & AustrE infml* a particular person's turn to buy alcoholic drinks for others: *"Whose shout is it?" "It's my shout; would you like another beer?"*

shout down *v adv* [T1] to shout so as to make (someone) stop speaking: *The crowd shouted down the unpopular speaker*

shout·ing /ˈʃaʊtɪŋ/ *n* **1** [U] shouts **2 all over bar the shouting** the important or interesting part (of a struggle, competition, event, etc.) has now been (successfully) completed, and the result is no longer in doubt **3 within shouting distance** near enough for a shout to be heard

shove¹ /ʃʌv/ *v* **1** [IØ;X9] to push, esp. in a rough or careless way: *There was a lot of* **pushing and shoving** *to get on the bus.|Help me shove this furniture aside* **2** [L9, esp. OVER] *infml* to move oneself: *Shove over, friend, and let me sit on the seat beside you*

shove² *n* [*usu. sing.*] a strong push: *We gave the car a good shove and moved it out of the mud*

shove a·round *v adv* [T1b] *infml* PUSH AROUND; ORDER ABOUT

shove-ha'penny /ˌʃʌv ˈheɪpni/ *n* [U] the original form of SHUFFLEBOARD, played with coins on a table esp. in inns

shov·el¹ /ˈʃʌvəl/ *n* **1** a long-handled tool with a broad usu. square or rounded blade for lifting and moving loose material —compare SPADE **2 a** a part like this on a digging or earth-moving machine **b** such a machine itself **3** also **shovelful** /ˈʃʌvəlfʊl/— the amount of material carried in any of these

shovel² -ll- (*AmE* -l-) **1** [T1;IØ] to take up, move, make, or work with a SHOVEL: *He shovelled a path through the snow* **2** [X9] to move roughly as if with a SHOVEL: *He shovelled the papers into his desk*

shov·el·board /ˈʃʌvəlbɔːd‖-bord/ *n* [U] SHUFFLEBOARD

shove off *v adv* [IØ] **1** (of (a person in) a boat) to leave the shore **2** [*usu. imper.*] *infml* to go away; leave: *Shove off! I'm busy*

show¹ /ʃəʊ/ *v* **showed, shown** /ʃəʊn/ **1** [D1 (*to*); T1,6a;V3,4] to offer for seeing; allow or cause to be seen: *He showed his ticket at the door.|She never shows her feelings.|The photograph showed the baby laughing.|Can you show me the book you mean?|Show me where your leg hurts.|The weather is showing signs of spring.|His record shows him to have worked hard at school* **2** [IØ;L7] to appear; be in or come into view; be VISIBLE: *The lights showed faintly through the mist.|a well-mended break that hardly shows|His happiness showed in his smile.|She did very little work on this report, and it shows!|The sky began to show red in the early morning* **3** [T1] to point to as a mark or number; INDICATE: *The clock showed 20 minutes past 2* **4** [X9] to go with and guide or direct: *May I show you to your seat?|Show the gentleman in/out, please* —see also SHOW AROUND, SHOW OVER **5** [D1,5;T1,5,6a] to state or prove: *His speech showed (us) that he didn't understand the subject.|The result that mass and* ENERGY (3) *are related was shown by Einstein.|a fine piece of work that shows what is possible in the subject* **6** [D; T:(1,6a,b)] to explain; make clear to (someone) by words or esp. actions; DEMONSTRATE: *Will you show me how to use this machine/how I should use it? Don't just tell me how: show me.|The purpose of a dictionary is to show (the reader) the meaning of words* **7** [T1;IØ] **a** to offer as a performance **b** (esp. of a cinema film) to be offered at present: *"What's showing at the cinema?" "They're showing a Marx Brothers film"* **8** [Wv6;T1] (esp. of a material) to allow to be easily seen: *This light-coloured dress will show dirt, I'm sorry to say* **9** [X (*to be*) 1,7] to prove (oneself) to be: *He showed himself brave/a brave soldier in battle* **10** [D1 (*to*); T1] *lit* to make to be felt in one's actions: *"Lord, show your mercy upon us"* (prayer)|*They showed their enemies pity and kindness* **11** [IØ] *sl* to arrive; SHOW UP (3): *I came to meet my friend, but he never showed* **12** [IØ] *AmE* to finish in 3rd place in a horse or dog race —compare PLACE² (9) **13 it goes to show** *not fml* it proves the point: *It all goes to show that crime doesn't pay* **14 to show for** [*usu. nonassertive*] as a profit or reward from: *nothing to show for his life's work except a lot of memories* **15 show one's face** to be present in a company: *Since he lost all his money he's been ashamed to show his face in society* **16 show the way** *lit* to set an example for others' future work —see also SHOW AROUND, SHOW OFF, SHOW OVER, SHOW ROUND, SHOW UP

show² *n* **1** [S9] a showing of some quality; DISPLAY: *The army put on a show of strength.|He answered with a show of amusement at the question* **2** [S] an outward appearance, esp. as opposed to what is really true, happening, etc.: *I made a show of interest, but I really couldn't have cared less.|He put on a good show, but he didn't deceive anyone* **3** [(*for*) U] grandness; splendid appearance or ceremony; POMP (2): *All this ceremony is just empty show: it's all done for show; it doesn't mean a thing* **4** [C] a public showing; collection of things for looking at; EXHIBITION (1): *a cat/flower/car show|a one-woman show of her paintings at the* GALLERY (1,2)|*not up to show standards* (= not good enough to be in a *show*) **5** [C] *not fml* a performance, esp. in a theatre or NIGHTCLUB or on radio or television: *What television shows do you usually watch?|Let's go out and see a show, or perhaps a film* **6** [S] *infml* an organization or activity: *He's the chief, in charge of the whole show* **7** [S9] *infml* an effort; act of trying (often in such phrs. as **put up a good/poor show**): *Last year's sales totals were a rather poor show, I'm afraid* **8 get this show on the road** *infml* to start to work; get going **9 Good show!** *BrE infml* Very good! Well done! **10 on show** in place for seeing by the public **11 steal the show** *not fml* to get all the attention and praise expected by someone else, at a show or other event **12 the greatest show on earth** *pomp* the CIRCUS (1,2,3)

show a·round also (*esp. BrE*) **show round**— *v prep; adv* [D1;T1] to be a guide to (someone) on a first visit to (a place): *Before you start work, I'll show you around (the office) so that you can meet everyone*

show·boat /ˈʃəʊbəʊt/ *n* (esp. in the US) a riverboat containing a theatre where performances are given at towns along the river

show busi·ness /ˈ· ˌ··/ also (*infml*) **show biz** /ˈʃəʊ bɪz/— *n* [U] the business of performing; the job of people who work in television, films, the theatre,etc.

show·case /ˈʃəʊkeɪs/ *n* a set of one or more shelves enclosed with glass in which objects are placed for looking at in a shop or MUSEUM

show·down /ˈʃəʊdaʊn/ *n* [*usu. sing.*] *not fml* a settlement of a quarrel or matter of disagreement in an open direct way

show·er¹ /ˈʃaʊəʳ/ *n* **1** [C *often pl.*] a short-lasting fall of rain or snow: *Scattered showers are expected this afternoon* **2** [C (*of*)] a fall of many small things or drops of liquid: *The bucket fell over, sending a shower of paint on the men below the ladder* **3** [C (*of*)] a quantity or rush of things coming at the same time: *a shower of letters on her birthday* **4** [C] **a** a washing of the body by standing under an opening from which water comes out in many small streams: *to take/have a shower* **b** an apparatus for this, with controls for water and usu. built as an enclosure in a bathroom —see picture at BATHROOM **5** [C] *AmE* a party given on some occasion by a woman's friends at which they give her suitable gifts: *a baby/*ENGAGEMENT (1) *shower* **6** [GS] *BrE infml derog* a group of unpleasant, untidy, lazy, etc., people: *You're a real shower; get your hair cut, all of you!*

shower² *v* **1** [IØ] to rain or pour down in SHOWERs: *It's started to shower: I'm sure to get wet.|Nuts showered down when the tree was shaken* **2** [D1+*with/on*] **a** to pour (on), scatter heavily (on): *They showered the married pair with rice* **b** to give in large quantity: *They showered gifts on her/showered her with gifts* **3** [IØ] to take a SHOWER (4a)

show·er·y /ˈʃaʊəri/ *adj* [Wa2] (as of weather) bringing rain from time to time but not for long

show·girl /ˈʃəʊgɜːl‖-gɜrl/ *n* a girl in a group of singers or dancers, usu. in very fancy dress, in a musical show

show·ing /ˈʃəʊɪŋ/ *n* **1** [C] an act of putting on view: *a showing of new fashions* **2** [S] a record of success or quality; performance: *a good/poor showing by the local team* **3** [*on*+S] a statement or understanding of a state of affairs: *On any showing it'll be an interesting election.|On the government's own showing they won't win by very many votes*

show jump·ing /ˈ· ˌ··/ *n* [U] a form of horseriding competition judged on ability and often speed in jumping a course of fences —**-er** *n*

show·man /ˈʃəʊmən/ *n* **-men** /mən/ *not fml* **1** a person whose business is producing plays, musical shows, etc. **2** a person who behaves always as if performing for others

show·man·ship /ˈʃəʊmənʃɪp/ *n* [U] skill in drawing public attention

shown /ʃəʊn/ *past p. of* SHOW¹

show-off /ˈ· ·/ *n infml* a person who SHOWs OFF

show off *v adv* **1** [IØ] to behave so as to try to get admiration for oneself, one's abilities, etc. **2** [T1] to show, esp. as something fine, beautiful, etc.: *The white dress showed off her dark skin*

show of hands /ˌ· · ˈ·/ *n* a vote taken by counting the raised hands of voters

show o·ver *v prep* [D1] *esp. BrE* to guide through (esp. an interesting building or a house for sale); take on a visit to

show·piece /ˈʃəʊpiːs/ *n* a fine example fit to be admired by everyone

show·place /ˈʃəʊpleɪs/ *n* a place to be admired for its beauty or for some quality

show·room /ˈʃəʊrʊm, -ruːm/ *n* a room where examples of goods for sale may be looked at

show round *v prep; adv* [D1;T1] *esp. BrE* SHOW AROUND

show up *v adv* **1** [T1;IØ] to (cause to) be easily seen: *The cracks in the wall show up in the sunlight: the sunlight shows them up* **2** [T1] to uncover; make clear the (esp. unpleasant) truth about: *I intend to show up this liar/this deception* **3** [IØ] *infml* to arrive; be present: *Did everyone you invited show up?* **4** [T1] *esp. BrE* to make (someone) feel shame: *When we go to dinner parties my husband always shows me up with the rude jokes he tells*

show·y /ˈʃəʊi/ *adj* [Wa1] too colourful, bright, attention-getting, etc., usu. without much real beauty —**showily** *adv* —**showiness** *n* [U]

shrank /ʃræŋk/ *past t. of* SHRINK

shrap·nel /ˈʃræpnəl/ *n* [U] metal scattered in small pieces from an exploding bomb or esp. SHELL¹ (4) fired from a large gun

shred¹ /ʃred/ *n* **1** [C *often pl.*] a small narrow piece torn or roughly cut off: *a shred of tobacco/cloth* **2** [S *nonassertive*] a smallest piece; bit: *not a shred of truth in his statement*

shred² *v* **-dd-** [Wv5;T1] to cut or tear into SHREDs: *a dish with shredded* CABBAGE

shred·der /ˈʃredəʳ/ *n* **1** a coarse kitchen GRATER **2** a machine which tears paper (such as secret papers to be thrown away) into very small pieces which cannot be read

shrew /ʃruː/ *n* **1** any of several types of very small mouselike animal with a long pointed nose —see picture at MAMMAL **2** a bad-tempered scolding woman

shrewd /ʃruːd/ *adj* [Wa1] **1** clever in judgment, esp. of what is to one's own advantage: *a shrewd lawyer who knows all the tricks* **2** well-reasoned and likely to be right: *a shrewd guess* —**~ly** *adv* —**~ness** *n* [U]

shrew·ish /ˈʃruːɪʃ/ *adj* typical of a bad-tempered woman (SHREW (2)) —**~ly** *adv* —**~ness** *n* [U]

shriek¹ /ʃriːk/ *v* [IØ;T1] to cry out with a high sound; SCREECH: *"Help!" she shrieked.|They were all shrieking with laughter*

shriek² *n* a wild high cry (as of pain or terror)

shrift /ʃrɪft/ *n* see SHORT SHRIFT

shrike /ʃraɪk/ *n* any of several kinds of mostly greyish birds with hooked strong beaks, which feed on insects and other small creatures

shrill /ʃrɪl/ *adj* [Wa1] **1** (of a sound) high and sounding sharp or even painful to the ear; PIERCING: *a shrill whistle* **2** (of words) marked by continuous complaining: *The newspapers became ever shriller in their attacks* —**shrilly** /ˈʃrɪl-li, ˈʃrɪli/ *adv* —**~ness** *n* [U]

shrimp /ʃrɪmp/ *n* **shrimps** *or* **shrimp** **1** [Wn2;C] any of many types of small sea creature with long legs and a fanlike tail —compare PRAWN, SCAMPI —see picture at CRUSTACEAN **2** [C;(N)] *usu. derog* a small person

shrine¹ /ʃraɪn/ *n* **1** a chest containing the remains of a holy person's body **2** a place for worship; place held in respect for its religious or other connections: *Stratford, the shrine of Shakespeare*

shrine² *v* [T1] *esp. lit* ENSHRINE

shrink¹ /ʃrɪŋk/ *v* **shrank** /ʃræŋk/, **shrunk** /ʃrʌŋk/ *or* **shrunken** /ʃrʌŋkən/ **1** [IØ;T1] to (cause to) become smaller, as from the effect of heat or water: *Washing wool in hot water will shrink it = make it shrink.|Meat shrinks by losing some of its fat in cooking* **2** [L9] to move back and away: RETIRE (1): *Fearing a beating, the dog shrank into a corner*

shrink² *n AmE humor sl* HEADSHRINKER (1); PSYCHIATRIST

shrink·age /ˈʃrɪŋkɪdʒ/ *n* [U;S] the/an act or amount of SHRINKing¹ (1); loss in size

shrink from *v prep* [T1,4] to be afraid of; avoid because of fear; RECOIL from: *He shrank from (the thought of) having to kill anyone*

shrive /ʃraɪv/ *v* **shrove** /ʃrəʊv/, **shriven** /ˈʃrɪvən/ [T1] *old use* (of a priest) to listen to a CONFESSION (an admitting of wrongdoing) from, and give God's forgiveness to (someone)

shriv·el /ˈʃrɪvəl/ *v* **-ll-** (*AmE* **-l-**) [Wv5;IØ;T1: (UP)] to (cause to) dry out and become smaller by twisting into small folds: *plants shrivelling (up) in the dry heat*

shroud¹ /ʃraʊd/ *n* **1** also **winding sheet**— the cloth for covering a dead body at burial **2** something that covers and hides: *A shroud of secrecy hangs over/surrounds the plan* **3** any of the supporting ropes in pairs connecting a ship's central poles (MASTs) to its sides

shroud² *v* [T1 *usu. pass.*] to cover and hide: *hills shrouded in mist|a history shrouded in uncertainty*

Shrove Tues·day /ˌʃrəʊv ˈtjuːzdi‖-ˈtuː-/ *n* [R] (in the Christian year) the day before ASH WEDNESDAY; the last day before the solemn period of LENT

shrub /ʃrʌb/ *n* a low bush with several woody stems —see picture at GARDEN¹

shrub·be·ry /ˈʃrʌbəri/ *n* [U;(C)] (part of a garden planted with) SHRUBs forming a mass or group

shrug¹ /ʃrʌg/ *v* **-gg-** [I∅;T1] to raise (one's shoulders), esp. as an expression of doubt or lack of interest: *He shrugged (his shoulders), saying he didn't know and didn't care*

shrug² *n* an act of SHRUGging: *to answer with a shrug (of the shoulders)*

shrug off *v adv* [T1] to treat as easy or not important: *She can shrug off her troubles and keep smiling*

shuck¹ /ʃʌk/ *n esp. AmE* an outer covering on a plant or animal; shell, POD, or HUSK

shuck² *v* [T1] *esp. AmE* to remove from an outer covering: *to shuck corn/PEAs*

shucks /ʃʌks/ *interj AmE infml* (an inoffensive expression of annoyance or disappointment)

shud·der¹ /ˈʃʌdəʳ/ *v* [I∅ (*at*), 3] to shake uncontrollably for a moment, as from fear, cold, or strong dislike; tremble: *She shuddered at the sight of the dead body*

shudder² *n* an act of SHUDDERing

shuf·fle¹ /ˈʃʌfəl/ *v* **1** [I∅;T1] to mix up the order of (playing cards) so as to produce a chance order ready for a game to begin **2** [X9] to move or push to and fro or to different positions: *looked busy shuffling papers from one pile to another on his desk* **3** [T1;L9] to walk by dragging (one's feet) slowly along: *walked along shuffling his feet* —**-fler** *n*

shuffle² *n* **1** [S] **a** a slow dragging walk **b** a dance with this kind of step **2** [C] an act of shuffling (SHUFFLE¹ (1)) cards **3** [C] RESHUFFLE; SHAKE-UP: *a shuffle of government ministers*

shuf·fle·board /ˈʃʌfəlbɔːd‖-bord/ also **shovelboard**— *n* [U] a game, played esp. on ships, in which round flat wooden pieces are driven by means of a long-handled pusher, along a smooth surface to try to make them come to rest on numbered areas

shuf·ty /ˈʃʊfti/ *n* [S] *BrE sl* a quick view or look (esp. in the phrs. **have/take a shufty (at)**)

shun /ʃʌn/ *v* **-nn-** [T1,4] to avoid with determination; keep away from: *shunned all society|shunned seeing other people*

shunt /ʃʌnt/ *v* **1** [T1 *usu. pass.*; I∅] **a** to turn (a railway train or carriage) from one track to another, esp. to a SIDING **b** (of a train) to be turned in this way **2** [X9;L9] to (cause to) go to one side, off course, or out of action: *Smith has been shunted to a smaller branch office of the company*

shunt·er /ˈʃʌntəʳ/ *n BrE* a railway SHUNTing engine or its driver

shush /ʃʊʃ/ *v not fml* **1** [I∅ *usu. imper.*] to become quiet; HUSH: *Shush, now. Don't cry* **2** [T1] to tell to be quiet, as by saying "SH"

shut /ʃʌt/ *v* **shut,** *pres. p.* **shutting** **1** [T1;I∅] to move into a covered, blocked, or folded-together position; close: *Shut the gate so that the dog can't get out.|He shut his eyes and tried to sleep.|The wood has swollen and the door won't shut.|He shut the book and put it away* **2** [X9] to keep or hold by closing: *He shut himself in his room to think.|Shut out all wicked thoughts from your mind.|She shut her skirt in the door and tore the edge* **3** [T1;I∅] to stop in operation; SHUT DOWN or SHUT UP (4): *in the evening when the shops have shut|a factory that was shut in 1931* —see also SHUT AWAY, SHUT DOWN, SHUT OFF, SHUT UP —see OPEN (USAGE)

shut a·way *v adv* [T1] to keep guarded away from others; ISOLATE (2): *He shut himself away in his country house with no telephone*

shut·down /ˈʃʌtdaʊn/ *n* a stopping of work, as in a factory because of a labour quarrel, holiday, repairs, lack of demand, etc.

shut down *v adv* **1** [I∅] (as of a business or factory) to stop operation, esp. for a long time or forever: *The whole company shuts down for 3 weeks' summer holiday* **2** [T1] to cause to do this: *A STRIKE² (1) has shut down several car factories* —compare SHUT UP (4)

shut-eye /ˈ· ·/ *n* [U] *infml* sleep

shut off *v adv* **1** [T1;I∅] to stop in flow or operation, as by turning a handle or pressing a button: *They shut off the gas and electricity in their house before leaving on holiday* **2** [T1 (*from*)] to keep separate or away: *a valley shut off by mountains from the rest of the world|It's nice to be shut off from daily pressures while on holiday*

shut·ter¹ /ˈʃʌtəʳ/ *n* **1** a wood or metal cover that can be placed, usu. by unfolding in pairs, in front of a window to block the view or keep out the light **2** a part of a camera which opens for an exact usu. very short time in taking a picture to let light fall on the film **3 put up the shutters** *infml* to close a business at the end of the day or forever

shutter² *v* [T1 *usu. pass.*] to close (as) with SHUTTERs (1): *a sad sight, with all the shops shuttered and the people gone*

shut·tle¹ /ˈʃʌtl/ *n* **1** a pointed instrument used in weaving to pass the thread across and between the threads that form the length of the cloth **2** a sliding thread carrier on a sewing machine for the lower of the 2 threads which lock to make a stitch **3** a regular going to and fro by air, railway, bus, etc., along a way between 2 points: *There is a shuttle (bus service) between the town centre and the station* **4** SHUTTLECOCK

shuttle² *v* [L9;X9] **1** to move to and fro often or regularly: *When she's at home she shuttles between the kitchen and the garden* **2** to move by a SHUTTLE¹ (3): *shuttling passengers across the country*

shut·tle·cock /ˈʃʌtlkɒk‖-kɑk/ *n* a small light feathered object with a round base, for hitting across a net in a game of BADMINTON —see BADMINTON (USAGE)

shut up *v adv* **1** [I∅ *often imper.*] *sl* to stop talking; be quiet: *Shut up! I'm trying to think* **2** [T1] *infml* to make (someone) stop talking: *Can't you shut your friend up?* **3** [T1] to keep enclosed: *He shut himself up in his room* **4** [I∅;T1] to make (a place) safe before leaving, as a shop at the end of a business day: *Business was slow so he shut up (the shop) early for the day* —see also **shut up** SHOP¹ (5)

shy¹ /ʃaɪ/ *adj* **shyer, shyest** **1** [Wa1;B] not bold; nervous in the company of others; not putting oneself forward; BASHFUL; DIFFIDENT **2** [Wa1;B] expressing this quality: *a shy smile* **3** [Wa1;F+*of*] having doubts or distrust; WARY: *I'm shy of saying too much on this delicate subject* **4** [Wa1;B] (of animals) unwilling to come near people **5** [Wa5; F+*of*; E] *esp. AmE* lacking; short: *We're still 3 votes shy (of the number we need to win)* **6 fight shy of** to try to avoid **7 Once bitten, twice shy** *infml* A person who has been tricked will be more careful in the future —**~ly** *adv* —**~ness** *n* [U]

shy² *v* **1** [I∅ (*at*)] (esp. of a horse) to make a sudden movement, as from fear: *The horse shied at the loud noise and threw its rider* **2** [L9, esp. OFF, AWAY, *at*] to avoid something unpleasant, as by moving aside: *They shied away from buying the house when they learnt the full price*

shy³ *v* [X9;(T1)] *infml* to throw with a quick movement: *boys shying stones over the surface of the water*

shy⁴ *n infml* **1** a throw **2** an attempt: *to have a shy at a new job* —see also COCONUT SHY

-shy *comb. form* fearing or disliking: *camera-shy|girl-shy|gun-shy*

shys·ter /ˈʃaɪstəʳ/ *n AmE infml* a dishonest person, esp. a lawyer

si /siː/ *n* [C;U] TI (1)

Si·a·mese /ˌsaɪəˈmiːz◂/ *n* **Siamese** [Wn3] SIAMESE CAT

Siamese cat /ˌ··· ˈ·/ *n* a type of blue-eyed, short-haired cat, pale grey or light brown —see picture at CAT

Siamese twin /ˌ··· ˈ·/ *n* either of a pair of people (TWIN*s*) joined together from birth at some part of their bodies

sib·i·lant¹ /ˈsɪbʒlənt/ *adj* making or being a sound like that of *s* or *sh*: *a sibilant whistling sound*

sibilant² *n tech* a SIBILANT sound, such as /s, z, ʃ, ʒ, tʃ, dʒ/ in English

sib·ling /ˈsɪblɪŋ/ *n fml* a brother or sister

sib·yl /ˈsɪbɪl, -bəl/ *n* any of several women in the ancient world who were thought to know the future

sib·yl·line /ˈsɪbʒlaɪn/ *adj* of, written by, or typical of SIBYL*s*: *sibylline* RIDDLES¹ (1)/ORACLE*s* (1)

sic /sɪk/ *adv* [Wa5] *Lat* (usu. in BRACKET*s* after a word in writing) written in this wrong or strange way intentionally; not my mistake: *The writer tells us that the war lasted from 939* (sic) *to 1945!*

sick /sɪk/ *adj* [Wa1] **1** [(*BrE*) A; (*AmE*) B; *the*+P] not well; ill; having a disease: *to visit a sick uncle in hospital|a sick tree* **2** [F] upset in the stomach so as to want to throw up what is in it; NAUSEATED (*AmE* usu. in the phr. **sick to one's stomach**): *He began to feel sick as soon as the ship started to move* —see also **be** SICK (8) **3** [A] causing or typical of this feeling: *a sick smell/feeling* **4** [F (*at*)] feeling something so unpleasant as (almost) to cause this feeling: *I'm sick at having to refuse you, but I must* **5** [F+*of*] having a dislike from too much of something (note the phr. **sick and tired of**): *I'm sick of winter: why doesn't spring come?* **6** [B] unhealthy; unnaturally cruel in likings, humour, etc.; MORBID: *a sick joke/mind* **7** [Wa5;A] for or related to illness: SICK PAY|SICK LEAVE **8 be sick** *esp. BrE* to throw up what is in the stomach; VOMIT: *He suddenly felt sick, and was sick twice before he could even get into bed* **9 go/report sick** to excuse oneself from work because of illness **10 look sick** *infml* look worthless by comparison: *He's such a good swimmer he makes me look sick* **11 make someone sick** *infml* to be strongly displeasing to someone: *Your complaining makes me sick! Why don't you be quiet?* **12 on the sick list** *not fml* (absent because) ill **13 take sick** (*usu. past t.*) *becoming rare* to become ill: *He took sick and died a week later* **14 worried sick** very worried —see also SICK UP

USAGE 1 In *BrE to be/feel* **sick** is to VOMIT or feel that one is going to VOMIT. It is therefore confusing to say *I was* **sick** *yesterday* meaning "I was **ill**", but all right to use **sick** in this meaning before a noun: *a* **sick** *child.* 2 A **sick** person has a disease, not for example a wound or a broken leg, although one may be on **sick leave**, or receive **sick pay**, for these reasons too. 3 One can speak of the **sick** (=**sick** people) but not of **the* **ill.**

-sick *comb. form* feeling sick in the stomach from the stated kind of travel: AIRSICK|CARSICK|SEASICK —**~ness** [U]

sick·bay /ˈsɪkbeɪ/ *n* a room, as on a ship, with beds usu. in rows for people who are ill

sick·bed /ˈsɪkbed/ *n* the bed where a person lies ill

sick call /ˈ· ·/ *n* [U] *AmE* SICK PARADE

sick·en /ˈsɪkən/ *v* **1** [T1] to cause strong (almost) sick feelings of dislike in; NAUSEATE **2** [I∅ (*BrE* (*for*))] to become ill; show signs of a disease: *The animal began to sicken and soon died*

sick·en·ing /ˈsɪkənɪŋ ˈsɪknɪŋ/ *adj* which SICKEN*s* (1) a person; very displeasing or unpleasant: *It's sickening to see such cruelty.|the sickening sound of the fine old teapot breaking to pieces on the floor* —**~ly** *adv*

sicken of *v prep* [T1,4 *no pass.*] to become tired of: *At last he sickened of waiting for her, and went away*

sick head·ache /ˌ· ˈ··/ *n not fml, esp. AmE* a headache (such as MIGRAINE) with a feeling of sickness in the stomach

sick·le /ˈsɪkəl/ *n* a tool with a hook-shaped blade, held in the hand, used for cutting grain or long grass —compare SCYTHE

sick leave /ˈ· ·/ *n* [(*on*) U] (permitted amount of) time spent away from a job during illness

sickle-cell a·nae·mi·a /ˌ·· · ·ˈ···/ *n* [U] a condition, found esp. in black races, in which the red blood cells have a curved shape, causing general weakness and illness

sick·ly /ˈsɪkli/ *adj* [Wa1] **1** habitually ill; weak and unhealthy: *a sickly child|a sickly-looking plant* **2** unpleasantly weak, pale, or silly: *His face was a sickly yellow* **3** causing a sick feeling: *a sickly smell*

sick·ness /ˈsɪknʒs/ *n* **1** [C;U] a/the condition of being ill; illness or disease: *a strange sickness for which no cure is known|absence owing to sickness* **2** [U] the condition of feeling sick; NAUSEA: (*lit*) *He felt a wave of sickness come over him*

sickness ben·e·fit /ˈ·· ˌ···/ *n* [U] *BrE* money paid, esp. by the government, to someone who is too ill to work

sick pa·rade /ˈ· ·ˌ·/ (*AmE* **sick call** /ˈ· ·/)— *n* [U] *BrE* the daily time or place for soldiers to report themselves as ill (esp. in the phr. **go on sick parade**)

sick pay /ˈ· ·/ *n* [U] pay for time spent away from a job during illness

sick·room /ˈsɪk-rʊm, -ruːm/ *n* a room where someone lies ill in bed

sick up *v adv* [T1] *BrE sl* to VOMIT (something)

side¹ /saɪd/ *n* **1** [C] (*sometimes in comb.*) a more or less upright surface of something, not the top, bottom, front, or back: *The front door is locked: we'll have to go around to the side.|They threw the box over the side of the ship into the sea.|The sides of the bowl were beautifully painted.|The house was halfway up the side of the hill/up the hillside* **2** [C] any of the flat surfaces of something: *Which side of the box is up?* (=which is the top) **3** [C] a part, place, or division according to a real or imaginary central line: *the other side of town|the left/right side of his face|Cars drive on the left side of the road in England.|I saw her on the far side of the room* **4** [C] the right or left part of the body, esp. from the shoulder to the top of the leg: *a pain in his left side* **5** [C *usu. sing.*] the place next to someone, often regarded as the place of a helper, friend, tool, etc.: *walking along with his wife at his side|During her illness he never left her side* **6** [C] (*often in comb.*) an edge or border: *A square has 4 equal sides.|I sat on the side of the road/on the roadside* —see picture at GEOMETRY **7** [C] either of the 2 surfaces of a thin flat object: *the rough/smooth side of a piece of leather|Write on only one side of the paper.|Which side of the coin is up?* **8** [C] the inside or outside of a piece of clothing: *One sock was on wrong side out* (=so that the inside and not the outside was showing) **9** [C] a page of writing; one side of a sheet of paper **10** [C] a part to be considered, usu. in opposition to another; ASPECT (2): *Try to look at all sides of the question before deciding.|His kindness was a side of his character that few knew about* **11** [C] (a group which holds) a position in a quarrel, disagreement, war, etc.: *The US entered the war on England's side in 1941: it was the winning side.|Your opinions don't make much sense: whose side are you on in this question?* **12** [GC] **a** either of 2 opposing sports teams **b** *BrE* a sports team: *Our school has a good cricket side* **13** [C9] the part of a line of a family that is related to a particular person: *He's Scottish on his mother's side* **14** [C] either half of an animal body cut along the BACKBONE: *a side of* BEEF/BACON **15** [U] *BrE becoming rare* unpleasantly proud grand behaviour towards others (esp. in the phrs. **put on side, have no/be without side**) **16 every side/all sides** every place, person, direction, etc.: *bullets being fired from all sides* **17 hold/split one's sides** to be weak with uncontrollable laughter **18 on the side a** *esp. AmE* beside or in addition to the main thing, job, etc.: *an evening job to bring in a little money on the side* **b** *BrE* as a usu. cheating or dishonest additional activity: *He makes a little money on the side by not reporting all his income to the taxman* **19 on the . . . side** rather; too: *I like the house but I think the price is on the high side* **20 put on/to one side** to take out of consideration, for the present; keep for possible use later **21 side by side** next to (one) another: *The 2 bottles stood side by side on the table* **22 take sides (with)** to be on one side or the other in a quarrel: *Mother took sides with David against Father in the argument* **23 this side of** *infml* without going as far as: *the best Chinese food this side of Peking* —see also ALONGSIDE, ASIDE, BACKSIDE, BESIDE, COUNTRYSIDE, INSIDE, OUTSIDE

side[2] *adj* [Wa5;A] **1** at, from, towards, etc., the side: *a side door|a side view of an object* **2** beside or in addition to the main or regular thing: *a* SIDE ISSUE|*a side remark|a* SIDE EFFECT|*The main dish was meat, with various vegetables as side dishes*

side[3] *v* [IØ+*with* or *against*] to be in a party in a quarrel, disagreement, etc.; take a side: *Mother sided with David (against Father) in the argument*

side·arm /ˈsaɪd-ɑːm‖-ɑrm/ *n* [*usu. pl.*] a weapon carried or worn at one's side, such as a sword or PISTOL

side·board /ˈsaɪdbɔːd‖-bord/ *n* a piece of DINING ROOM furniture like a long table with a cupboard below to hold dishes, glasses, etc. —see picture at LIVING ROOM

side·boards /ˈsaɪdbɔːdz‖-bordz/ (*AmE* **side·burns** /ˈsaɪdbɜːnz‖-bɜrnz/)— *n* [P] *BrE* growths of hair on the sides of a man's face in front of the ears esp. worn long

side·car /ˈsaɪdkɑːʳ/ *n* a usu. one-wheeled enclosed seat fastened to the side of a motorcycle to hold a passenger

-sid·ed /ˈsaɪdɪ̣d/ *comb. form* having the stated kind or usu. number of sides: *a steep-sided mountain|a 4-sided enclosure*

side ef·fect /ˈ· ·ˌ·/ *n* an effect in addition to the intended one: *Sleeping drugs often have harmful habit-forming side effects*

side horse /ˈ· ·/ *n AmE* POMMEL HORSE

side is·sue /ˈ· ˌ··/ *n* a question or subject apart from the main one; something of not much importance

side·kick /ˈsaɪdˌkɪk/ *n AmE* a usu. less important helper or companion

side·light /ˈsaɪdlaɪt/ *n* **1** [U] light coming from the side **2** [C *often pl.*; U] (a piece of) interesting though not very important information: *The study of uniforms can give some interesting sidelights on military history* **3** [C] a narrow window beside a door or other window **4** [C] either of a pair of lamps at the sides of a vehicle —compare HEADLIGHT and see picture at CAR

side·line /ˈsaɪdlaɪn/ *n* **1** a line marking the limit of play at the side of a football field, tennis court, etc. **2** [*usu. pl. with sing. meaning*] the area just outside this and out of play: *The* COACH[1] (4) *stood on the sideline(s) shouting to his players* **3** an activity in addition to one's regular job

side·long /ˈsaɪdlɒŋ‖-lɔŋ/ *adv, adj* [Wa5] directed sideways: *a sidelong blow/smile|He looked at her sidelong*

side or·der /ˈ· ˌ··/ *n AmE* a restaurant order for a separate dish in addition to the main dish

si·der·e·al /saɪˈdɪərɪəl/ *adj* [Wa5;A] *tech* related to or calculated by the stars. Sidereal measurements of time are based on the **sidereal day**, equal to 23 hours 56 minutes 4·09 seconds

side·sad·dle[1] /ˈsaɪdˌsædl/ *n* a woman's SADDLE (=seat for putting on a horse) on which both legs are placed on the same side of the horse's back

sidesaddle[2] *adv* [Wa5] (as if) on a SIDESADDLE: *She rode sidesaddle*

side·show /ˈsaɪdʃəʊ/ *n* **1** a separate small show at a fair or CIRCUS (3), usu. with strange people (a sword swallower, bearded lady, etc.) on view **2** a usu. amusing activity beside a more serious main one

side·slip[1] /ˈsaɪdˌslɪp/ *v* **-pp-** [IØ] to slip, slide, or SKID[2] (1) sideways, as in a car or on SKIs

sideslip[2] *n* a SIDESLIPping movement

sides·man /ˈsaɪdzmən/ *n* **-men** /mən/ (in the CHURCH OF ENGLAND) a man who collects offerings of money in church

side·split·ting /ˈsaɪdˌsplɪtɪŋ/ *adj* causing uncontrollable laughter; very funny: *a sidesplitting joke*

side·step /ˈsaɪdstep/ *v* **-pp-** [T1;IØ] **1** to take a step to the side, (as) to avoid (a blow) **2** *not fml* to avoid (an unwelcome question, duty, etc.) as if by moving aside; EVADE (2,3)

side street /ˈ· ·/ *n* a narrow less-travelled street, esp. one that meets a main street —compare BACK STREET

side·stroke /ˈsaɪdstrəʊk/ *n* [*usu. sing.*] a way of swimming by lying on one side moving the arms one by one forward and backward under the water, and kicking the legs like scissors

side·swipe[1] /ˈsaɪdswaɪp/ *v* [T1] *AmE not fml* to strike with a blow directed along the side: *sideswipe a parked car*

sideswipe[2] *n* **1** *esp. AmE not fml* a blow directed along the side **2** *infml* an attacking remark made in the course of making other statements about something completely different

side·track[1] /ˈsaɪdtræk/ *n* **1** an unimportant line of thinking followed instead of keeping on a more important one **2** SIDING (1)

sidetrack[2] *v* [T1 *usu. pass.*] **1** to cause to leave a more important or purposeful line of thought and follow some unimportant one **2** to move to a SIDING (1)

side·walk /ˈsaɪdwɔːk/ *n AmE* PAVEMENT (1)

side·ward /ˈsaɪdwəd‖-ərd/ *adj* [Wa5] directed or moving to one side: *a sideward look to see who was sitting on his right*

side·wards /ˈsaɪdwədz‖-ərdz/ also (*esp. AmE*) **sideward**— *adv* [Wa5] to one side: *moved the piano sidewards*

side·ways /ˈsaɪdweɪz/ *adv, adj* [Wa5] **1** [(ON)] with one side (and not the front or back) forward or up: *She was so fat that she could only get through the door sideways (on)* **2** to or towards one side: *stepped sideways|sideways jump*

sid·ing /ˈsaɪdɪŋ/ *n* **1** [C] a short railway track connected to a main track, used for loading and unloading, for carriages not in use, etc. **2** [U] *AmE* wood or metal in lengths for nailing up to form the sides of a building

si·dle /ˈsaɪdl/ *v* [L9 (UP)] to walk as if ready to turn and go the other way, esp. secretively or nervously: *He sidled up to the stranger in the street and tried to sell him the stolen ring*

siege /siːdʒ/ *n* **1** an operation by an army surrounding a defended place to force it to yield, by repeated attacks, blocking of its supplies, etc. **2 lay siege to** to be a SIEGE of; BESIEGE (1) **3 raise a siege a** to cease to surround a fort or city **b** to drive away the enemy surrounding a fort or city

si·en·na /siˈenə/ *n* [U] earthy material which is brownish yellow (in the form of **raw sienna**), and reddish brown when burned (**burnt sienna**), used as colouring matter for paint

si·er·ra /siˈerə/ *n* [*often pl.*] *Sp* a row, range, or area of sharply-pointed mountains

si·es·ta /siˈestə/ *n Sp* a short sleep after the midday meal, as is the custom in hot countries

sieve[1] /sɪv/ *n* **1** a tool of wire or plastic net on a frame, or of a solid sheet with holes, used for separating large and small solid bits, or solid things from liquid **2 a head/memory like a sieve** *infml* a mind that forgets quickly

sieve[2] *v* **1** [T1] to put through a SIEVE **2** [X9, esp. OUT] to separate using a SIEVE: *Sieve the earth in order to sieve out the stones from the soil*

sift /sɪft/ *v* **1** [T1;I∅] to put (something) through a SIEVE, SIFTER, or net **2** [I∅ (*through*); T1] to make a close examination of (things in a mass or group): *He sifted through his papers to find the lost letter* **3** [X9, esp. OUT] to separate or get rid of in either of these ways: *to sift (out) the stones from the earth/the truth from the lies* **4** [L9] (of a fine-grained material) to pass (as) through a SIEVE: *Snow sifted through the crack in the roof into the room*

sift·er /ˈsɪftəʳ/ *n* (*often in comb.*) a container with many small holes in the top, for scattering powdery foods

sigh[1] /saɪ/ *v* [I∅] **1** to let out a deep breath slowly and with a sound, usu. expressing tiredness, sadness, or satisfaction **2** (as of the wind) to make a sound like this **3** [(*for*)] *lit* to feel fondly sorry, esp. about something past, far away, etc.; grieve: *sighing for his youth*

sigh[2] *n* an act or sound of SIGHing (1): *We all* HEAVEd[1] (4) *a sigh of* RELIEF (1) *when the work was done*

sight[1] /saɪt/ *n* **1** [C] something that is seen: *What a beautiful sight those roses make!|the familiar sight of the postman going along the street* **2** [U;S] the seeing of something: *The crowd waited for a sight of the Queen passing by.|The house is hidden from sight behind trees* **3** [U] the sense of seeing; the power of the eye; EYESIGHT; VISION (1): *to have one's sight tested by a doctor|good sight for a man of age 80* —see also SECOND SIGHT **4** [U] presence in one's view; the range of what can be seen: *She's too careful with her children, never letting them out of her sight.|The boat was within sight of land.|The train came round the bend into sight* **5** [C *usu. pl.*] something worth seeing, esp. a place visited by tourists: *to see the sights of London* —see SIGHTSEE (USAGE) **6** [S] something which looks very bad or laughable: *What a sight you are, with paint all over your clothes!|This room looks a sight: it's the untidiest place I've ever seen* **7** [C *often pl.*] a part of an instrument or weapon which guides the eye in aiming: *To aim, line up the front and* REAR[2] (1) *sights on the gun.|I had the deer* **in my sights**, *but it moved before I could fire* **8** [S] a lot; a great deal (esp. in such phrs. as **a sight better/more . . . than**): *This car is costing me a* DARN[3] *sight more to run than I expected* **9** [A] to be done, dealt with, etc., as soon as seen or received: *a sight* DRAFT[1] (2) **10 a sight for sore eyes** *infml* a person or thing that one is glad to see at last; a welcome sight **11 at first sight** at the first time of seeing or considering: *They fell in love as soon as they met: it was love at first sight.|At first sight the difficulty looks greater than it really is* **12 at/on sight** as soon as seen or shown, without delay: *The guard had orders to shoot on sight* (=without finding out who was there) **13 catch sight of** to see for a moment; get a GLIMPSE of: *I caught sight of her hurrying away but I didn't try to speak to her* **14 in sight a** in view; VISIBLE (1) **b** within a little of being reached; near: *peace in sight at last after 2 years of war* **15 in the sight of** *lit* in the judgment or opinion of: *punishable in the sight of law* **16 know someone by sight** to recognize someone without knowing him personally or without knowing his name **17 lose sight of a** to cease to see **b** to cease to have news about; lose touch with: *lost sight of her school friends over the years* **c** to forget; fail to consider: *In the heat of the argument we mustn't lose sight of our main purpose* **18 out of sight a** out of the range of being seen: *Stay out of sight: she mustn't see us* **b** *infml* very high, great, etc.: *The chairman said that labour costs had gone out of sight in the past year* **c** *sl, esp. AmE* very good; wonderful: *A party? That would be out of sight! I'd love it* **19 set one's sights (on)** aim (at); direct one's efforts (towards) **20 sight unseen** without a chance of seeing or examining

sight[2] *v* **1** [T1] to get a view of, esp. after a time of looking; see for the first time: *The sailors gave a shout when they sighted land.|Several rare birds have been sighted in this area* **2** [L9, esp. *along*] to aim or look in a certain direction: *Sight along the gun barrel/along the edge to see if it's straight* —**~ing** *n*

sight·ed /ˈsaɪtɨd/ *adj* [Wa5] (of a person) able to see; not blind

-sighted *comb. form* showing or having the stated kind of ability to see: *weak-sighted|a clear-sighted judgment*|SHORTSIGHTED

sight·less /ˈsaɪtləs/ *adj lit* unable to see; blind

sight·ly /ˈsaɪtli/ *adj* [Wa1] pleasant-looking; good in appearance —opposite **unsightly** —**-liness** *n* [U]

sight-read /ˈsaɪt riːd/ *v* **sight-read** /ˈsaɪt red/ [I∅; T1] to play or sing (written music) at first sight without practice —**~er** /ˈsaɪt ˌriːdəʳ/ *n* —**~ing** *n* [U]

sight·screen /ˈsaɪtskriːn/ *n* SCREEN[1] (7)

sight·see /ˈsaɪtsiː/ *v* [I∅] to go about, as on holiday, visiting places of interest (esp. in the phr. **go sightseeing**) —**~ing** *n* [U]

USAGE The forms ***sightsees**, ***sightsaw**, ***sightseen** do not exist. One should say instead *He* **goes/went/has been sightseeing**, or *She sees/saw/has seen the* **sights.**

sight·se·er /ˈsaɪtˌsiːəʳ/ *n* a person who goes SIGHTSEEing

sign[1] /saɪn/ *n* **1** a standard mark; something which is seen and represents a known meaning; SYMBOL: *Crowns, stars,* STRIPEs, *etc., are signs of military rank.|The number −5 begins with the sign −, the* MINUS[2] (1) *sign.|Written music uses lots of signs, like* ♭, 𝄞, *and* ♯ **2** [C3] a movement of the body intended to express a meaning; signal: *Don't ring the bell yet: wait until I give the sign.|She put her finger to her lips as a sign to be quiet* **3** a board or other notice giving information, warning, directions, etc.: *Pay attention to the traffic/road signs.|Can't you read that sign? It says "No Smoking"* **4** something that shows a quality, or the presence or coming of something else: *All the signs are that* *business will get better.|Swollen ankles can be a sign of heart disease* **5** also **sign of the zodiac**— any of the 12 divisions of the year represented by groups of stars **6** *esp. bibl* a wonderful act of God; MIRACLE **7 a sign of the times** something that is typical of the way things are just now

sign[2] *v* **1** [IØ;T1] to write (one's name) on (a written paper), esp. for official purposes, to show one's agreement, show that one is the writer, etc.: *The papers are ready to be signed.|Sign here, please.|He signed his name on the cheque/signed the cheque* **2** [V3 (*to, for*)] to make a movement as a sign to (someone); signal: *The policeman signed (to/for) me to stop* **3** [IØ,3;T1;V3] to SIGN UP or SIGN ON (1): *Arsenal (=a famous football team) has signed 2 new players: the players signed with Arsenal yesterday* —see also SIGN AWAY, SIGN FOR, SIGN IN, SIGN OFF, SIGN OUT, SIGN OVER

sig·nal[1] /ˈsɪgnəl/ *n* **1** [C] a sound or action intended to warn, command, or give a message: *A red lamp is often used as a danger signal.|American Indians sometimes used to send smoke signals.|She made a signal with her arm for a left turn* **2** [C (*for*), C3] an action which causes something else to happen: *His scolding was a signal for the girl to start crying.|When I look at my watch, it's a signal (for us) to leave* **3** [C] a railway apparatus (usu. with coloured lights) near the track to direct train drivers **4** TRAFFIC LIGHT **5** [C] a sound, image, or message sent by waves, as in radio or television: *We live too far from the city to get a strong television signal*

signal[2] *v* **-ll-** (*AmE* **-l-**) **1** [IØ (*to, for*)] to give a signal: *The general signalled to his officers for the attack to begin.|She was signalling wildly, waving her arms* **2** [V3 (*to*); D5 (*to*); T1,3,5] to express, warn, or tell by a signal or signals: *The policeman signalled (to) the traffic to move forward slowly.|The thief signalled (his friend) that the police were coming* **3** [T1] to be a sign of; MARK: *The defeat of 1066 signalled the end of Saxon rule in England*

signal[3] *adj* [A] **1** *lit* noticeable, important, and usu. excellent; OUTSTANDING (1,2): *a signal example of courage* **2** [Wa5] used for signalling: *signal fires*

signal box /ˈ·· ·/ (*AmE* **signal tow·er** /ˈ·· ˌ··/)— *n BrE* a small raised building near a railway from which traffic on the line is controlled

sig·nal·ize, -ise /ˈsɪgnəlaɪz/ *v* [T1 *usu. pass.*] to make known; draw attention to; show as important: *The crowning of the new king was signalized by a public holiday*

sig·nal·ler, *AmE* **signaler** /ˈsɪgnələʳ/ *n* a member of the army or navy trained in signalling

sig·nal·ly /ˈsɪgnəli/ *adv lit* very noticeably; unmistakably

sig·nal·man /ˈsɪgnəlmən/ *n* **-men** /mən/ **1** *BrE* a man who controls railway traffic and signals **2** SIGNALLER

sig·na·to·ry /ˈsɪgnətəri‖-tori/ *n* any of the signers of an agreement, esp. among nations

sig·na·ture /ˈsɪgnətʃəʳ/ *n* **1** a person's name written by his own hand, as at the end of a written statement, letter, cheque, etc. **2** the act of signing one's name: *to witness someone's signature* **3** *tech* a sheet which is folded after printing to form usu. 8, 16, or 32 pages of a book —see also KEY SIGNATURE, TIME SIGNATURE

signature tune /ˈ··· ·/ *n* a short piece of music used regularly in broadcasting to begin and end a particular show or as the special mark of a radio station

sign a·way *v adv* [T1] to give up formally (ownership, a claim, right, etc.), esp. by signing a paper: *She signed away her share in the property*

sign·er /ˈsaɪnəʳ/ *n* a person whose signature appears on something

sig·net /ˈsɪgn½t/ *n* an object used for printing a small pattern in wax as an official or private SEAL[2] (1a), and often fixed to or part of a finger ring (a **signet ring**)

sign for *v prep* [T1] to sign one's name to show the receipt of; formally accept: *Certain classes of mail have to be signed for when they are delivered*

sig·nif·i·cance /sɪgˈnɪfɪkəns/ *n* [U;S] importance; meaning; value: *an industry of great significance to the country|Don't read significance into* (=try to find it in) *every careless remark*

sig·nif·i·cant /sɪgˈnɪfɪkənt/ *adj* **1** of noticeable importance or effect: *a significant increase in crime|one of the most significant studies of the subject* **2** having a special meaning: *a significant smile* —**~ly** *adv*

sig·nif·i·ca·tion /ˌsɪgnɪf½ˈkeɪʃən/ *n lit* the intended meaning of a word; SENSE[1] (1a)

sig·ni·fy /ˈsɪgn½faɪ/ *v* **1** [T1,5] *fml* to be a sign of; represent; mean; DENOTE: *What does this strange mark signify?|A fever usually signifies a disorder of the body/that there is something wrong with the body* **2** [T1;IØ] *fml* to make known (esp. an opinion) by an action: *Will those in favour of the suggestion please signify (their agreement) by raising their hands?* **3** [IØ;T1: *usu. nonassertive*] *infml* to matter; have importance (for): *What does it signify if you're rich or poor, as long as you're happy?|Never mind that mistake; it doesn't signify*

sign in *v adv* [IØ] to record one's name when arriving —opposite **sign out**

sign lan·guage /ˈ· ˌ··/ *n* [U] any of various systems of hand movements for expressing meanings, as used by the DEAF (1) and DUMB (1), by some American Indians, etc.

sign off *v adv* [IØ] **1** (of a radio or television station) to cease broadcasting, esp. for the day **2** to end a letter, as with a signature: *"I'd better sign off now. Love, John"*

sign of the zo·di·ac /ˌ· · · ˈ···/ *n* SIGN[1] (5)

sign on *v adv* **1** [IØ;T1] to (cause to) join (a working force), by signing a paper; ENLIST (1): *He signed on as a sailor* **2** [IØ] (of a radio or television station) to begin broadcasting for the day

Si·gnor /siːˈnjɔːʳ, ˈsiːnjɔːʳ (*Ital* siˈɲor)/ *n* [A;N] the title of an Italian (-speaking) man

Si·gno·ra /siːˈnjɔːrə (*Ital* siˈɲora)/ *n* [A;N] the title of a (married) Italian(-speaking) woman

Si·gno·ri·na /ˌsiːnjɔːˈriːnə‖-njə- (*Ital* siɲoˈrina)/ *n* [A;N] the title of an unmarried Italian(-speaking) girl

sign out *v adv* [IØ] to record one's name when leaving —opposite **sign in** —**sign-out** /ˈ· ·/ *adj* [Wa5;A]

sign o·ver *v adv* [T1 (*to*)] to give formally (one's rights, ownership, etc.) to another, esp. by signing a paper

sign·post /ˈsaɪnpəʊst/ *n* a sign showing directions and distances, as at a meeting of roads

sign·post·ed /ˈsaɪnˌpəʊst½d/ *adj* [F] *esp. BrE* provided with SIGNPOSTs to guide the driver

sign up *v adv* [IØ,3;T1;V3] to (cause to) sign an agreement to take part in something, or to take a job; ENLIST (1): *There was an attempt to sign up more men for the police force, but few signed up.|I've signed up to take a course at the local college* —**sign-up** /ˈ· ·/ *adj* [Wa5;A]

si·lage /ˈsaɪlɪdʒ/ *n* [U] grass or other plants (FODDER) cut and stored in a SILO away from air for preservation as winter food for cattle

si·lence[1] /ˈsaɪləns/ *n* **1** [U] absence of sound; stillness: *nothing but silence in the empty house|The silence was broken by a loud cry* **2** [U] the state of not speaking or making a noise: *She received the bad news in silence.|His forceful arguments reduced his opponent to silence* **3** [U] failure to write a letter or letters: *What can his silence mean? I hope he's not ill* **4** [U] failure to mention or say a particular thing: *I can't understand the government's silence on such an important matter* **5** [C] a moment or period of any of these conditions: *a one-minute's silence|long silences between letters* —see also CONSPIRACY OF SILENCE

silence² *v* [T1] **1** to cause or force to stop making a noise: *Can you silence the children so that I can work?|The enemy's guns were silenced by repeated bombings* **2** to force to stop expressing opinions, making opposing statements, etc.: *The king silenced his opponents by having them put in prison*

si·lenc·er /ˈsaɪlənsəʳ/ *n* an apparatus for reducing noise, such as **a** a part for fitting around the end of the barrel of a small gun **b** *AmE* **muffler**— a part of a petrol engine which fits onto the pipe where burnt gases come out —see picture at CAR

si·lent¹ /ˈsaɪlənt/ *adj* **1** not speaking; not using spoken expression: *What's wrong? Why are you so silent?|a silent prayer|silent reading* **2** free from noise; quiet: *silent laughter|the silent hours of the night* **3** making no statement; expressing no opinion, decision, etc.: *The law is silent on this difficult point* **4** [Wa5] (of a letter in a word) not having a sound; not pronounced: *silent "w" in "wreck"* **5** [Wa5] being or concerning films with no sound: *the days of the silent* SCREEN/*films* —**~ly** *adv*

silent² *n* [*usu. pl.*] *infml* a SILENT¹ (5) film

silent part·ner /ˌ·· ˈ··/ *n AmE* SLEEPING PARTNER

sil·hou·ette¹ /ˌsɪluːˈet/ *n* **1** a shadow-like representation of the shape of something, filled in with a solid colour, usu. black: *silhouettes cut from paper|His silhouette appeared on the curtain* **2** a shape or figure; PROFILE¹ (1): *a car with a low silhouette|a dress with a fashionable silhouette* **3 in silhouette** as a dark shape against a light background

silhouette² *v* [T1 *usu. pass.*] to cause to appear as a SILHOUETTE: *birds silhouetted against the bright sky*

sil·i·ca /ˈsɪlɪkə/ also (*tech*) **silicon di·ox·ide** /ˌ··· ·ˈ··/— *n* [U] the substance found naturally as sand, QUARTZ, and FLINT

sil·i·cate /ˈsɪlɪkeɪt, -kɨt/ *n* [C;U] *tech* any of a large group of solid substances making up most of the earth and most building materials

sil·i·con /ˈsɪlɪkən/ *n* [U] a simple substance (ELEMENT) that is nonmetallic and found in combined forms in nature in great quantities

sil·i·cone /ˈsɪlɨkəʊn/ *n* [U;C] any of a group of chemicals unchanged by heat and cold, and used in making types of rubber, oil, and RESIN (2)

sil·i·co·sis /ˌsɪlɨˈkəʊsɨs/ *n* [U] a lung disease (esp. among miners, stonecutters, etc.) caused by long breathing of SILICA dust

silk /sɪlk/ *n* **1** [U] **a** fine thread which is produced by a kind of insect (SILKWORM) and made into thread for sewing and into cloth **b** smooth soft cloth made from this: *10 yards of the finest silk* **2** [U] the fine light hair on MAIZE (a type of corn) **3** [C] a KING'S/QUEEN'S COUNSEL: *His father was a well-known silk* **4 take silk** to become a KING'S/QUEEN'S COUNSEL **5 silk and satins** *lit* fine rich clothes

silk·en /ˈsɪlkən/ *adj* [Wa5] *lit* **1** soft, smooth, or shiny like silk; SILKY: *silken hair* **2** made of silk: *silken garments*

silk screen /ˌ· ˈ·◂/ *n* [U] a way of printing on a surface by forcing paint or ink through a specially prepared stretched piece of cloth onto it

silk·worm /ˈsɪlkwɜːm‖-wɜrm/ *n* a type of insect (CATERPILLAR) bred originally in China which produces a COCOON (covering for its body) of silk

silk·y /ˈsɪlki/ *adj* [Wa1] like silk; soft, smooth, or shiny: *a dress of some silky material|the cat's fine silky fur* —**silkiness** *n* [U]

sill /sɪl/ *n* the flat piece at the base of an opening or frame, esp. a WINDOWSILL —see picture at WINDOW

sil·la·bub, syl- /ˈsɪləbʌb/ *n* [C;U] a dish made of sweetened cream or milk mixed with wine and usu. egg whites

sil·ly¹ /ˈsɪli/ *adj* **1** [Wa1;B] having or showing little judgment; foolish; stupid; not serious; not sensible; RIDICULOUS: *It's silly to go out in the rain if you don't have to.|The book's title sounded silly but it was really a serious study* **2** [Wa1;B] *becoming rare* weak-minded: *The poor old man is getting rather silly* **3** [Wa5;F] *infml* senseless; STUNned (2,3) (in such phrases as **knock/bore someone silly**) **4** [Wa5; A] (of a player or his position in cricket) very close to the BATSMAN (in the phrs. **silly point, silly mid-off, silly mid-on**)

silly² *n* [C;N] (an inoffensive word for) a silly person: *No, silly, I didn't mean that!*

si·lo /ˈsaɪləʊ/ *n* **-los** **1** a usu. round tower-like enclosure on a farm for storing SILAGE (=green winter food for cattle) —see picture at FARMYARD **2** an underground base from which a GUIDED MISSILE may be fired

silt /sɪlt/ *n* [U] loose sand, mud, soil, etc., carried in running water and then dropped (as at the entrance to a harbour, bend in a river, etc.)

silt up *v adv* [IØ;T1] to fill or become filled with SILT: *The old harbour silted up years ago: it's now all silted up*

sil·van /ˈsɪlvən/ *adj* [Wa5] *esp. lit* SYLVAN

sil·ver¹ /ˈsɪlvəʳ/ *n* [U] **1** a soft whitish precious metal that is a simple substance (ELEMENT), carries electricity very well, can be brightly polished, and is used esp. in ornaments and coins **2** silver money; coins made of this, or of some white metal like it, and not of copper: *For this £5 note could you give me 4 £1 notes and £1 in silver, please?* **3** spoons, forks, dishes, etc., for the table, made of this or a metal like it **4 a silver spoon (in one's mouth)** wealth; a comfortable life: *She was born with a silver spoon in her mouth*

silver² also (*lit*) **sil·vern** /ˈsɪlvən‖-ərn/— *adj* [Wa5] **1** made of silver: *polished silver forks|Is your ring silver?* **2** like silver in colour: *a silver-haired old man|the silver fox* **3** *lit* pleasantly musical; SILVERY (1)

silver³ *v* **1** [T1] to cover with a thin shiny silver-coloured surface: *to silver the back of a mirror* **2** [T1;IØ] *lit* to (cause to) become silver-coloured: *hair silvered by old age*

silver birch /ˌ·· ˈ·/ *n* the common white BIRCH tree, which has a silvery-white trunk and branches

sil·ver·fish /ˈsɪlvəˌfɪʃ -ər-/ *n* [Wn2] a type of small silver-coloured wingless insect found about houses and sometimes harmful to paper and cloth

silver ju·bi·lee /ˌ·· ˈ···/ *n* the return after 25 years of the date of some important personal event, esp. of becoming a king or queen —compare GOLDEN JUBILEE, DIAMOND JUBILEE

silver pa·per /ˌ·· ˈ··◂/ also **silver foil** /ˌ·· ˈ·◂/— *n* [U] paper with one bright metallic surface, as used in packets for cigarettes, food, etc.

silver plate /ˌ·· ˈ·◂/ *n* [U] metal with a thin outer surface of silver

sil·ver·side /ˈsɪlvəsaɪd‖-ər-/ *n* [U] *BrE* the top side of meat (BEEF) cut from the leg of cattle

sil·ver·smith /ˈsɪlvəˌsmɪθ‖-ər-/ *n* a maker of vessels, jewellery, etc., in silver

silver-tongued /ˌ·· ˈ·◂/ *adj esp. lit* able to give fine persuading speeches: ELOQUENT

sil·ver·ware /ˈsɪlvəweəʳ‖-ər-/ *n* [U] *AmE* CUTLERY

silver wed·ding /ˌ·· ˈ··/ also **silver wedding an·ni·ver·sa·ry** /ˌ·· ˈ·· ··ˌ···/— *n* the return after 25 years of the date of a wedding —compare GOLDEN WEDDING, DIAMOND WEDDING

sil·ver·y /ˈsɪlvəri/ *adj* **1** having a pleasant musical sound **2** like silver in shine and colour

sim·i·an /ˈsɪmɪən/ *adj, n tech* (of, concerning, or like) a monkey or APE

sim·i·lar /ˈsɪmələʳ, ˈsɪmɪləʳ/ *adj* **1** [(*to*)] like or alike; of the same kind; partly or almost the same: *bread, cake, and other similar foods|We have similar opinions; my opinions are similar to his.|Boys wear fashionable clothes to attract girls. In a similar way, some birds have bright feathers* **2** [Wa5] *tech* exactly the same in shape but not size: *Similar* TRIANGLES (1) *have equal angles*

sim·i·lar·i·ty /ˌsɪmɨˈlærɨti/ *n* **1** [U] the quality of being alike or like something else; RESEMBLANCE: *How much similarity is there between the 2 religions?* **2** [C] a point of likeness: *Their differences are more noticeable than their similarities*

sim·i·lar·ly /ˈsɪmɨləli‖-ərli/ *adv* **1** in a similar way **2** as is similar: *Boys wear fashionable clothes. Similarly, some birds have bright feathers*

sim·i·le /ˈsɪmɨli/ *n* an expression making a comparison in the imagination between 2 things, using the words *like* or *as*: *"As white as snow" is a simile* —compare METAPHOR

si·mil·i·tude /sɨˈmɪlɨtjuːd‖-tuːd/ *n lit* **1** [U] likeness; appearance like something else: *the Devil in the similitude of a snake* **2** [C] a comparison made by an expression or story, as in a SIMILE or PARABLE: *Jesus often spoke in similitudes*

sim·mer¹ /ˈsɪməʳ/ *v* **1** [IØ;T1] to (cause to) cook gently in liquid at or just below boiling heat: *The soup was left to simmer* —see COOK (USAGE) **2** [IØ (*with*)] to be filled (with hardly controlled excitement, anger, etc.): *He was simmering with anger and could hardly speak politely*

simmer² *n* [S] a heat just below boiling; condition of SIMMERing: *Bring the vegetables to a simmer*

simmer down *v adv* [IØ *often imper.*] to become calmer; control one's excitement: *Simmer down, Mary: it won't help to lose your temper*

si·mo·ny /ˈsɪməni, ˈsaɪ-/ *n* [U] (in former times) the buying and selling of church appointments

sim·per¹ /ˈsɪmpəʳ/ *v* [IØ] to smile in a silly unnatural way —**~ingly** *adv*

simper² *n* a silly foolish-looking smile

sim·ple¹ /ˈsɪmpəl/ *adj* [Wa3] **1** [Wa1] not ornamented; plain: *simple but well-prepared food|buildings in a simple style* **2** [Wa1] easy to understand or do; not difficult: *a simple explanation|The plan sounds simple enough but it won't be so simple to put it into action* **3** [Wa1] of the ordinary kind, without special qualities, rules, difficulties, etc.; not COMPLICATED; BASIC: *Bacteria are simple forms of life.|a simple case of stealing|A knife is one of the simplest of tools* **4** [Wa5] not (able to be) divided; of only one thing or part: *A simple sentence has only 1 verb* —compare COMPOUND³ (1), COMPLEX² (1) **5** [Wa5] not mixed with anything else; with nothing added; pure: *a simple statement of the facts|The simple truth is, I don't know* **6** [Wa1] sincere; natural and honest: *a child's simple trust|a woman of simple goodness* **7** [Wa1] easily tricked; foolish; GULLIBLE: *You may be joking but she's simple enough to believe you* **8** [Wa1] *lit* of low rank or unimportant position: *a simple farm worker* **9** [Wa1] *euph old use* weak-minded **10 the simple life** *infml* life considered as better without the difficulties of having many possessions, using machines, etc. —see also PURE **and simple**

simple² *n old use* a wild plant used as medicine

simple-heart·ed /ˌ·· ˈ··◂/ *adj lit* not wise, but honest and naturally trusting

simple in·terest /ˌ·· ˈ··/ *n* [U] interest calculated on an original sum of money without first adding in the interest already earned —compare COMPOUND INTEREST

simple ma·chine /ˌ·· ·ˈ·/ *n tech* any of the several machine parts (such as the wheel, LEVER¹ (1), screw, etc.) of which all machinery is made

simple-mind·ed /ˌ·· ˈ··◂/ *adj* [B; *the*+P] **1** foolish; unthinking; FEEBLEMINDED: *a simple-minded mistake* **2** not wise; simple and trusting in mind: *a clever dealer who tricked many simple-minded buyers*

sim·ple·ton /ˈsɪmpəltən/ *n now rare* a weak-minded trusting person; NITWIT

sim·pli·ci·ty /sɪmˈplɪsɨti/ *n* [U] **1** the state of being simple: *a beautiful simplicity of style|He believes everything with childlike simplicity* **2 simplicity itself** *infml* very easy: *The plan was simplicity itself: how could it fail?*

sim·pli·fy /ˈsɪmplɨfaɪ/ *v* [Wv5;T1] to make plainer, easier, or less full of detail: *Try to simplify your explanation for the children* —see also OVERSIMPLIFY —**-fication** /ˌsɪmplɨfɨˈkeɪʃən/ *n* [C;U]

sim·ply /ˈsɪmpli/ *adv* **1** in a simple way; easily, plainly, clearly, or naturally: *On her small income they live very simply.|This cake is made quite simply* **2** [Wa5] just; only: *I don't like driving: I do it simply to get to work each day* **3** [Wa5] really; very (much): *My dear, it's simply wonderful to see you!*

sim·u·la·crum /ˌsɪmjʊˈleɪkrəm‖-mjə-/ *n* **-crums** *or* **-cra** /krə/ *lit* a likeness or representation of something

sim·u·late /ˈsɪmjʊleɪt‖-mjə-/ *v* [T1] to give the effect or appearance of; IMITATE: *A sheet of metal was shaken to simulate the noise of thunder*

sim·u·lat·ed /ˈsɪmjʊleɪtɨd‖-mjə-/ *adj* [Wa5] that is something made to look, feel, etc., like the real thing: *simulated diamonds made of glass*

sim·u·la·tion /ˌsɪmjʊˈleɪʃən‖-mjə-/ *n* [U;C] **1** (a) representation; pretending; IMITATION (3) **2** (a) study of, or way of studying, long courses of events in business, science, etc., by high-speed calculation (on a COMPUTER) of the effects of possible future changes or decisions

sim·u·la·tor /ˈsɪmjʊleɪtəʳ‖-mjə-/ *n* an apparatus which allows a person in training to feel what real conditions are like (in traffic, in an aircraft, space vehicle, etc.)

sim·ul·ta·ne·ous /ˌsɪməlˈteɪnɪəs‖ˌsaɪ-/ *adj* [Wa5] happening or done at the same moment: *the simultaneous appearance of 2 books on the same subject* —**~ly** *adv* —**-ity** /ˌsɪməltəˈniɨti‖ˌsaɪ-/, **~ness** *n* [U]

sin¹ /sɪn/ *n* **1** [U] disobedience to God; the breaking of law regarded as holy: *"keep us this day without sin"* (Book of Common Prayer) **2** [C] an example of this; an offence against a religious law: *guilty of the sin of pride|to* COMMIT (1) *a sin* —compare CRIME **3** [C] *esp. humor* something that should not be done; a serious offence: *She thinks it's a sin to end a sentence with a* PREPOSITION **4 live in sin** *usu. euph or humor* (of 2 unmarried people) to live together as if married

sin² *v* **-nn-** [IØ (*against*)] to break God's laws; do wrong according to some standard: *"We have sinned against you and against our fellow men"* (prayer)

since¹ /sɪns/ *adv* [Wa5] (*with* PERFECT¹ (7) *tenses*) **a** at a time between then and now; SUBSEQUENTLY: *Her husband died 10 years ago but she's since remarried.|I saw him on Wednesday, but we haven't met since* **b** from then until now (often in the phr. **ever since**): *He came to England 3 years ago and has lived here ever since* **c** ago (esp. in the phr. **long**

since): *I've long since forgotten what our quarrel was about*

since² *prep* (*with the present or* PERFECT¹ (7) *tenses*) from (a point in past time) until now; during the period after: *I haven't seen her since last week|since her illness.|Until last week I hadn't seen her since 1973. Since then I had wondered where she was living.|It's a long time since breakfast* —compare FOR¹ (25)

since³ *conj* **1** (*with the present or* PERFECT¹ (7) *tenses*) **a** after the past time when: *It's been years since I enjoyed myself so much as last night.|Since leaving Paris, we've visited Brussels and Amsterdam* **b** continuously from the time when (often in the phr. **ever since**): *We've been friends ever since we met at school* **2** as; as it is a fact that: *Since you can't answer the question, perhaps we'd better ask someone else* —see SEEING (USAGE)

sin·cere /sɪnˈsɪəʳ/ *adj* [Wa2] (of a person, feelings, or behaviour) free from deceit or falseness; real, true, or honest; GENUINE: *a sincere admiration of his opponent's qualities|She was not completely sincere in what she said*

sin·cere·ly /sɪnˈsɪəli‖-ər-/ *adv* **1** in a sincere way; truly: *I sincerely hope your father will be well again soon* **2 Yours sincerely** (written at the end of a letter, just before the signature, addressed to someone by name)

sin·cer·i·ty /sɪnˈserɪ̈ti/ *n* [U] the quality of being sincere; honesty: *I may say* **in all sincerity** *that you've been my most loyal friend*

sine /saɪn/ *n* [(*of*)] *tech* the FRACTION (2) calculated for an angle by dividing the length of the side opposite it in a right-angled TRIANGLE (1) by the length of the side opposite the right angle —see picture at TRIGONOMETRY

si·ne·cure /ˈsaɪnɪkjʊəʳ, ˈsɪn-/ *n* a position usu. giving an income but with few or no duties; easy, well-paid job

si·ne di·e /ˌsaɪni ˈdaɪ-iː, ˌsɪni ˈdiːeɪ/ *adv* [Wa5] *Lat* without fixing a date for a next meeting; INDEFINITELY: *The meeting was* ADJOURN*ed* (=ended) *sine die*

sin·e qua non /ˌsɪni kwɑː ˈnəʊn‖-ˈnɑn/ *n Lat* a necessary condition; what must be had; what cannot be done without: *A good knowledge of Italian is a sine qua non for the job in our Rome office*

sin·ew /ˈsɪnjuː/ *n* **1** [C;U] a strong cord in the body connecting a muscle to a bone; TENDON **2** [C *usu. pl. with sing. meaning*;U] *lit* means of strength; part of a powerful framework: *the strong sinew(s) of our national defence*

sin·ew·y /ˈsɪnjuːi/ *adj* **1** (of meat) containing SINEW (1); not easy to cut or eat **2** strong, (as if) having strong muscles

sin·ful /ˈsɪnfəl/ *adj* **1** guilty of, or being, SIN¹ (2) **2** *infml* shameful; seriously wrong or bad: *a sinful waste of time and money* —**~ly** *adv* —**~ness** *n* [U]

sing /sɪŋ/ *v* **sang** /sæŋ/, **sung** /sʌŋ/ **1** [D1 (*to, for*); T1;I0] to produce (music, musical sounds, songs, etc.) with the voice: *Birds sing loudest in the early morning.|I like to sing, although I don't sing well.|My sister can't sing a note* (=can't *sing* at all) **2** [X9] to cause to go by this means: *She sang her baby to sleep.|Sing your troubles away* **3** [I0] to make or be filled with a ringing sound: *An enemy bullet sang past my ear.|My ears are still singing from the loud noise* **4** [Wv4;I0] (of speech or writing) to sound fine and pleasant: *a fine writer with a singing style* **5** [I0 (*of*); T1] *lit* to speak, tell about, or praise in poetry: *Poets sang the king's praises; they sang of his brave deeds* **6** [I0] *AmE sl* (of a criminal) to give information to the police —see also SING OUT, SING UP —**~able** *adj* —**~er** *n*

sing. *written abbrev. for:* singular

singe¹ /sɪndʒ/ *v* **singed,** *pres. p.* **singeing** [T1] **1** to burn off the ends from (hair, threads, etc.) by passing near a flame: *He got too near the fire and singed his beard* **2** to burn lightly on the surface; SCORCH¹ (1): *singed the shirt with a hot iron*

singe² *n* a slight burn; an act or mark of SINGEing

Sing·ha·lese /ˌsɪŋəˈliːz/ *adj* [Wa5] SINHALESE

sing·ing /ˈsɪŋɪŋ/ *n* **1** [U] the art of the singer: *to study singing|a poor singing voice* **2** [U;C] the act or sound of voices in song: *The ceremony ended with the singing of "God Save the Queen"* **3** [U] ringing noise: *the singing of the wind in the chimney*

sin·gle¹ /ˈsɪŋgəl/ *adj* [Wa5] **1** [A] being (the) only one: *The letter was written on a single sheet of paper.|A single tree gave shade from the sun.|His single aim was to make money.|Not a single one of her neighbours gave her any help* **2** [B] having only one part, quality, etc.; not double or MULTIPLE¹: *For a strong sewing job use double, not single, thread.|A single flower has only 1 set of* PETALS **3** [A] separate; considered by itself: *Food is our most important single need.|There's no need to write down every single word I say* **4** [B] unmarried **5** [A] for the use of only one person: *a single bed* **6** [A] *AmE* **one-way**— (of a ticket or its cost) for a trip from one place to another but not back again —opposite **return**

single² *n* **1** *BrE* a SINGLE¹ (6) ticket: *A single to London, please* **2** (in cricket) a single run: *They ran a few quick singles* **3** a BASEBALL hit that allows the hitter to reach first BASE **4** [*usu. pl.*] *infml* a $1 or £1 note: *One £5 note and the other £5 in singles, please* **5** a record with only one short song on each side —opposite **LP** **6** *infml* a SINGLE¹ (5) room

single-breast·ed /ˌ·· ˈ··◂/ *adj* [Wa5] (of a coat) closing in the centre at the front with only one row of buttons —compare DOUBLE-BREASTED

single-deck·er /ˌ·· ˈ·◂·/ *n* [C; *by*+U] a bus with only one floor —compare DOUBLE-DECKER

single file /ˌ·· ˈ·/ also **Indian file**— *n, adv* [Wa5;C; *in*+U] (moving or standing in) a line of people, vehicles, etc., one behind another: *to form a single file|to go (in) single file along the narrow passage*

single-hand·ed /ˌ·· ˈ··◂/ *adj, adv* done by one person; working alone; without help from others: *a single-handed sailing voyage*

single-mind·ed /ˌ·· ˈ··◂/ *adj* having or showing one clear purpose and effort to serve it —**~ly** *adv* —**~ness** *n* [U]

sin·gle·ness /ˈsɪŋgəlnɪ̈s/ *n* [U] **1** the directing of thoughts, efforts, etc., together; CONCENTRATION (1): *to study with singleness of mind|He worked with singleness of purpose for his friend's election* **2** the condition of being alone or single

single out *v adv* [T1 (*for*)] to separate or choose from a group, esp. for special treatment or notice: *They all did wrong: why single him out for punishment?*

sin·gles /ˈsɪŋgəlz/ *n* **singles** [Wn3;C] a match or competition made up of matches, esp. of tennis, with one player against one —compare DOUBLES

sin·gle·stick /ˈsɪŋgəlˌstɪk/ *n* [U] fighting with a wooden stick used like a sword, popular in former times

sin·glet /ˈsɪŋglɪ̈t/ *n BrE* a man's garment without sleeves worn as a VEST or as an outer shirt when playing some sports

sin·gle·ton /ˈsɪŋgəltən/ *n tech* (in card games) a card that is the only one of its SUIT held by a player

sin·gly /ˈsɪŋgli/ *adv* [Wa5] separately; by itself or themselves; one by one: *Some guests came singly, others in groups*

sing out *v adv* [I0;T1] to sing or call loudly: *The waiter sang out our order to the kitchen*

sing·song /ˈsɪŋsɒŋ‖-sɔŋ/ *n* **1** [S;A] a dull repeated rising and falling of the voice in speaking **2** [C] *BrE* an informal gathering or party for singing songs

sin·gu·lar[1] /ˈsɪŋgjʊləʳ‖-gjə-/ *adj* **1** [Wa5] of or being a word or form representing exactly one: *The noun "mouse" is singular: it is the singular form of "mice"* —opposite **plural** **2** of unusual quality; EXTRAORDINARY (2): *a woman of singular beauty* **3** *becoming rare* very unusual or strange; peculiar: *the singular events leading up to the murder* —**~ity** /ˌsɪŋgjʊˈlærɪ̣ti‖-jə-/ *n* [U;C]

singular[2] *n* (a word in) a form representing exactly one: *"Trousers" has no singular: it can't be expressed in the singular*

sin·gu·lar·ly /ˈsɪŋgjʊləli‖-gjələrli/ *adv* **1** particularly; very (much): *a singularly beautiful woman|singularly wet weather for the time of year* **2** strangely; in an unusual way: *Is he mad? He's certainly behaving singularly*

sing up *v adv* [I∅] *esp. BrE* to sing (more) loudly; SING OUT

Sin·ha·lese /ˌsɪnhəˈliːz/ also **Singhalese**— *adj* [Wa5] of or concerning the language, people, etc., of Sri Lanka —see NATIONALITY TABLE

sin·is·ter /ˈsɪnɪ̣stəʳ/ *adj* [B] threatening, intending, or leading to evil: *a sinister look on his face|a sinister-looking crack in the roof*

sink[1] /sɪŋk/ *v* **sank** /sæŋk/, **sunk** /sʌŋk/ **1** [I∅;T1] to (cause to) go down below a surface, out of sight, or to the bottom (of water): *This rubber ball won't sink: it floats.|The enemy sank the ship: it sank with the loss of 100 lives.|The moon sank below the hills* **2** [I∅ (DOWN)] to fall to a lower level or position: *The flames at last sank down and the fire went out* **3** [I∅ (*to*)] to get smaller; go down in number, value, strength, etc.: *The population of the island has sunk from 100 to 20.|His voice sank to a whisper* **4** [L9] to fall (as) from lack of strength: *She fainted and sank to the ground.|He sank onto the chair and fell asleep at once* **5** [I∅] to become weaker; fail: *He's sinking fast and won't live much longer* **6** [T1] to dig out or force into the earth: *to sink fence posts|a well|a mine* SHAFT[1] (10) **7** [T1 *often pass.*] *not fml* to cause to fail; ruin; spoil: *The lack of money will certainly sink our plans* **8** [T1] to stop considering; forget: *Can't we sink our disagreements and work together?* **9** [T1 (*in, into*)] to put (money, labour, etc.) into; INVEST: *I've sunk all my money into buying a new house: I hope I won't be sorry* **10** [T1] (in games like GOLF and BILLIARDS) to cause (a ball) to go into a hole **11** **sink or swim** to fail or succeed without help from others: *He was left by his family to sink or swim by himself* —see also SUNKEN —**~able** *adj*

sink[2] *n* **1** **a** a large basin in a kitchen, for washing pots, vegetables, etc., fixed to a wall and usu. with pipes to supply and carry away water **b** *AmE* WASHBASIN —see picture at KITCHEN **2** *esp. lit* an evil place; DEN (2): *a sink of wickedness* —see also **everything but the** KITCHEN **sink**

sink·er /ˈsɪŋkəʳ/ *n* a weight fixed to a fishing line or net to keep the end down under water

sink in *v adv* [I∅] **1** to enter a solid through the surface: *If the ink sinks in it'll be hard to remove the spot from the cloth* **2** *not fml* to become understood, get a firm place in the mind: *I think the lesson has sunk in: he won't make the same mistake again*

sinking fund /ˈ·· ·/ *n* a sum of money saved by a government, company, etc., and added to regularly, for paying a debt at a future time

sink in·to *v prep* **1** [D1;T1] to put, force, or go below (a surface) or into (a solid): *He sank the knife into her back.|I'm hungry. I'd like to sink my teeth into a hot meal right now!* **2** [T1] to reach (a lower or less active state): *to sink into sleep|to sink into disuse*

sin·less /ˈsɪnləs/ *adj* free from SIN[1] (1); pure and holy —**~ness** *n* [U]

sin·ner /ˈsɪnəʳ/ *n* a person who SINs; one who has disobeyed God; wrongdoer

Sinn Fein /ˌʃɪn ˈfeɪn/ *n* [R] an Irish nationalist organization

Si·no- /ˈsaɪnəʊ/ *comb. form* **1** Chinese; of China: SINOLOGY **2** Chinese and: *Sino-Japanese trade*

Si·nol·o·gy /saɪˈnɒlədʒi‖-ˈnɑ-/ *n* [U] the study of Chinese language, history, literature, etc. —**-gist** *n*

sin·u·ous /ˈsɪnjʊəs/ *adj* twisting like a snake; full of curves; winding: *a sinuous road among the mountains|a dancer's sinuous grace* —**sinuosity** /ˌsɪnjʊˈɒsɪ̣ti‖-ˈɑ-/ *n* [C;U]

si·nus /ˈsaɪnəs/ *n* a hollow place inside a bone, esp. any of the air-filled spaces in the bones of the face that have an opening into the nose

sip[1] /sɪp/ *v* **-pp-** [I∅ (*at*); T1] to drink, taking only a little at a time into the front of the mouth: *sipping at her drink just to be polite*

sip[2] *n* a very small amount of a drink; slight taste: *May I taste your drink? I'll only take a sip (of it)*

si·phon[1], **syphon** /ˈsaɪfən/ *n* **1** a tube bent so that a liquid is drawn upward and then downward through it to a lower level **2** a kind of bottle for holding SODA-WATER and forcing it out by gas pressure **3** any of various tubelike organs, esp. in water animals, for taking in and carrying away liquids

siphon[2], **syphon** *v* [T1 (OFF, OUT)] to draw off or take away by a SIPHON[1] (1): *to siphon (out) petrol from a* TANK (1)|*(fig.) a new road to siphon off some of the traffic through the town centre*

sir /səʳ; *strong* sɜːʳ/ *n* [N] **1** (a respectful address to an older man or one of higher rank; to an officer by a soldier; to a male teacher by a British school child; to a male buyer in a shop; etc.): *Yes, sir.|Thank you, sir.|Will that be all, sir?* **2** *pomp* (an angry scolding form of address): *Come here at once, sir!* **3** **no sir!** *AmE infml* certainly not!: *I won't have any of that cheap plastic, no sir!*

Sir *n* **1** [A] (a title used before the name of a KNIGHT[1] (1,2) or BARONET): *Sir Harold Wilson|(not fml) Sir Harold* **2** [N] (used at the beginning of a formal letter, in such phrs. as **Dear Sir(s)** or **My dear Sir**)

sire[1] /ˈsaɪəʳ/ *n* **1** [C] the father of an animal, esp. of a horse —compare DAM[1] **2** [N] *old use* (a form of address to a king)

sire[2] *v* [T1] (esp. of a horse) to be the father of: *This horse has sired several race winners*

si·ren /ˈsaɪərən/ *n* **1** an apparatus for making a loud long warning sound, as used on ships, police cars, fire engines, and for air-attack warnings **2** (in ancient Greek literature) any of a group of woman-like creatures whose sweet singing charmed sailors and caused the wreck of their ships **3** a dangerous beautiful woman; FEMME FATALE

sir·loin /ˈsɜːlɔɪn‖ˈsɜr-/ also **sirloin steak** /ˌ·· ˈ·/— *n* [C;U] (a piece of) meat from cattle (BEEF) cut from the best part of the lower back

si·roc·co /sɪ̣ˈrɒkəʊ‖-ˈrɑ-/ *n* **-cos** a hot wind blowing from the desert of North Africa across to S Europe

sir·rah /ˈsɪrə/ *n* [N] *obs* (an angry disrespectful address to a man)

sis /sɪs/ *n* [N] *infml* sister

si·sal /ˈsaɪsəl, -zəl/ *n* [U] (a plant of the West Indies whose leaves produce) a strong white thread-like substance used in making cord, rope, and mats

sis·sy[1], **cissy** /ˈsɪsi/ *n* [C;N] *infml* a boy who looks

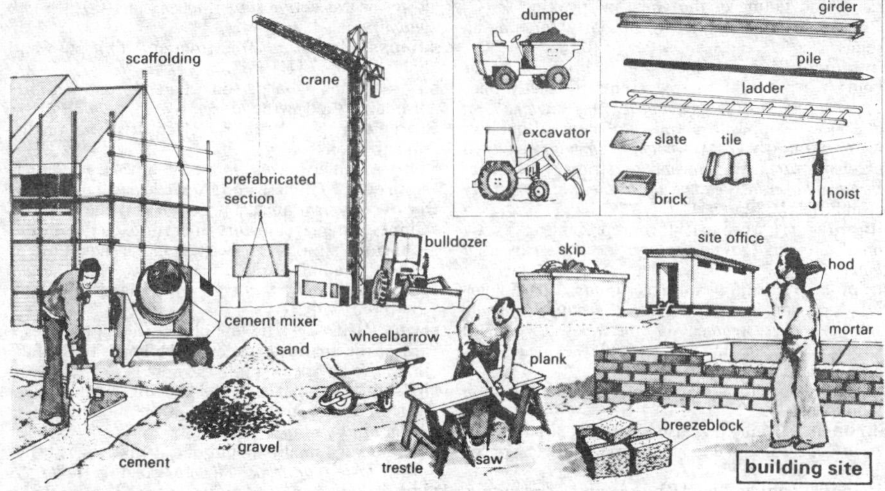

or acts like a girl in some way; one who seems silly and unmanly

sissy² also **sis·si·fied** /ˈsɪsɪfaɪd/— *adj* [Wa1] *infml* typical of a SISSY; girlish; EFFEMINATE

sis·ter /ˈsɪstəʳ/ *n* **1** [C] a female relative with the same parents: *Joan and Mary are sisters.|Joan is Mary's sister.|Mary has a sister* —see TABLE OF FAMILY RELATIONSHIPS **2** [C;N] a woman in close association with the speaker (used esp. by followers of WOMEN'S LIB): *Keep fighting for your rights, sisters!* **3** [A] (of women or things considered female) with the same purpose; in the same group; fellow: *a sister ship|sister societies in various cities* **4** [C;N;A] *BrE* (a title for) a nurse in charge of a department (WARD) of a hospital: *Sister Brown|the night sister* **5** [C;N;A] (a title for) a woman member of a religious group, esp. a NUN: *Sister Mary Grace|a Christian sister* **6** [N] *AmE sl* a woman; girl: *All right, sister, drop that gun!*
USAGE When **sister** means a nurse of a particular rank in a hospital (*def.* 4), it may be a man.

sis·ter·hood /ˈsɪstəhʊd‖-ər-/ *n* **1** [GC] a society of women leading a religious life **2** [C] a group of things regarded as female: *the sisterhood of developing countries* **3** [U] a sisterly relationship, esp. as claimed among women working for WOMEN'S LIB

sister-in-law /ˈ·· · ˌ·/ *n* **sisters-in-law** **1** the sister of one's husband or wife **2** the wife of one's brother **3** the wife of the brother of one's husband or wife —see TABLE OF FAMILY RELATIONSHIPS

sis·ter·ly /ˈsɪstəli‖-ər-/ *adj* of or like a sister; typical of a loving sister

sit /sɪt/ *v* **sat** /sæt/, *pres. p.* **sitting** **1** [L9] to rest in a position with the upper body upright and supported at the bottom of the back, as on a chair or other seat: *They all sat keeping warm by the fire.|We sat on the floor.|He sat at his desk working* **2** [L9;X9: esp. DOWN] to (cause to) go into this position; (cause to) take a seat: *Sit down, please: sit in that chair there.|She sat the baby (down) on the grass* **3** [I∅] (of an animal or bird) to be in or go into a position with the tail end of the body resting on a surface **4** [L9] to have a position in an official body: *He sits on several committees* —see also SIT FOR (1) **5** [I∅] (of an official body) to have 1 or more meetings: *The court sat until all the arguments for both sides had been heard* **6** [I∅] to lie; rest; have a place (and not move): *left the papers sitting on the desk|books sitting unread on the shelf|a village sitting on the side of a hill|The coat doesn't sit well* (= fits badly) *on you* **7** [I∅(*for*)] to have one's picture painted or photographed; POSE¹ (1): *to sit for a photographer|to sit for one's* PORTRAIT **8** [T1] *BrE* to take (a written examination): *to sit one's* A-LEVELS —see also SIT FOR (2) **9** [T1] to keep one's seat on (a horse): *to sit on her horse gracefully* **10** [I∅] (of a hen) to cover eggs to bring young birds to life: *Don't go near the hens while they're sitting* **11** **sit on one's hands** *infml* to take no action; SIT BY **12** **sit pretty** *not fml* to be in a very good position: *With profits up 125% their company is sitting pretty* **13** **sit tight** *not fml* to keep in the same position; not move: *If your car breaks down, just sit tight and wait for the police to come along* —see also SIT ABOUT, SIT BACK, SIT BY, SIT DOWN UNDER, SIT FOR, SIT IN, SIT IN ON, SIT ON, SIT OUT, SIT UP, SIT WITH
USAGE 1 One **sits** *at* a table or desk; *on* a chair, a BENCH, a SOFA, a branch, the BEACH, or the ground; *in* a tree or an armchair. *He was* **seated** means "He was in a **sitting** position". *He* **seated** *himself* means "He **sat** down". 2 To **seat** usually means "to provide **seats** for": *This hall will* **seat** *100 people.* When one means "to place in a sitting position" a better word is **set**: *He* **set** *the child on his knee.*

sit a·bout also **sit a·round**— *v adv* [I∅] *infml* to do nothing, esp. while waiting or while others act

si·tar /ˈsɪtɑːʳ, sɪˈtɑːʳ/ *n* a N Indian stringed instrument with a long neck and a number of metal strings —see picture at STRINGED INSTRUMENT

sit back *v adv* [I∅] **1** to rest one's back in a comfortable chair **2** to take no more active part; rest: *to sit back and enjoy the results of hard work*

sit by *v adv* [I∅] to fail to take proper or needed action; be IDLE¹ (1)

sit-down /ˈ· ·/ *n* **1** [C] also **sit-down strike** /ˌ· · ˈ·/— a stopping of work by workers in an office, factory, etc., who refuse to leave until their demands are met **2** [A] (of a meal) at which people are served while seated at a table —compare BUFFET³

sit down un·der *v adv prep* [T1] to suffer without complaining; PUT UP WITH

site¹ /saɪt/ *n* **1** a place where something was or happened: *the site of the Battle of Waterloo|digging on an* ARCHAEOLOGICAL *site* **2** a piece of ground for building on: *the site of a new planned town*

site² *v* [T1 *usu. pass.*] to provide with a SITE¹ (2);

LOCATE (2): *a house beautifully sited to catch the sunshine*

sit for *v prep* [T1] *BrE* **1** to be a member of Parliament for (a place): *He sits for a town in Cambridgeshire* **2** to (prepare to) take an examination for: *sat for a* SCHOLARSHIP (1) *but failed to win it* —see also SIT (8)

sit-in /ˈ· ·/ *n* an act of social dissatisfaction and anger by a group of people who enter a public place, stop its usual business, and refuse to leave

sit in *v adv* [IØ] **1** [(*for, as*)] to take another's regular place, as in a meeting or office job: *The president is ill tonight so the secretary will be sitting in for her (as chairman at the meeting)* **2** to take part in a SIT-IN

sit in on *v adv prep* [T1] to attend (as a meeting) without taking an active part: *Members of the public are allowed to sit in on some Town Council meetings*

sit on *v prep* [T1] **1** *not fml* to delay taking action on: *He's been sitting on my letter for months: Why doesn't he answer it?* —see also SIT (4,12) **2** also **sit up·on**— *fml* (of an official body) to consider or examine (a case): *The court are sitting on the question of permission to build the new road* **3** *infml* to force rudely into silence or inactivity: *always sat on by her elder brothers*

sit out *v adv* [T1] **1** to remain seated during (a dance); not take part in **2** also **sit through**— to stay until the end of (a performance), esp. without enjoyment

sit·ter /ˈsɪtəʳ/ *n* **1** a person whose picture is taken or painted; one who sits for an artist or photographer **2** *infml* (in cricket) an easy catch **3** BABY-SITTER

sit·ting[1] /ˈsɪtɪŋ/ *n* **1** a period of time spent seated in a chair: *I read the book in/at a single sitting* **2** an act or period of time of having one's picture made **3** a serving of a meal for a number of people at one time: *2 sittings of dinner, one at 7 and one at 8* **4** a meeting of an official body; SESSION

sitting[2] *adj* [Wa5;A] **1** that now has a seat on an official body (such as Parliament): *The sitting member will be hard to defeat in the election* **2** *BrE* that now lives in a place: *Sitting* TENANTs *are protected by law in various ways*

sitting duck /ˌ·· ˈ·/ *n* someone or something easy to attack or cheat

sitting room /ˈ·· ·/ *n esp. BrE* LIVING ROOM

sit·u·at·ed /ˈsɪtʃʊeɪtɨd/ *adj* [F9] **1** in a particular place; LOCATED (2) **2** *usu. infml* placed among possibilities; in a condition

sit·u·a·tion /ˌsɪtʃʊˈeɪʃən/ *n* **1** a position or condition at the moment; state of affairs: *I'm in a difficult situation and I don't know what to do* —see CONDITIONS (USAGE) **2** *now rare or fml* a job; position in work: *to look at the "Situations Wanted" and "Situation* VACANT*" advertisements in the newspaper* **3** a position with regard to surroundings: *The defence of Britain is helped by its island situation*

situation com·e·dy /··ˌ·· ˈ···/ *n* [C;U] a (form of) humorous television or radio show typically having a number of standard characters who appear in different stories each week

sit-up /ˈ· ·/ *n* a muscle-training movement in which a person sits up from a lying position keeping his legs straight and on the floor

sit up *v adv* **1** [IØ;T1b] to (cause or help to) rise to a sitting position: *The loud noise woke her up and made her sit up in bed.|She sat the old man up in bed* **2** [IØ (STRAIGHT)] to sit properly upright in a chair: *Sit up straight, son!* **3** [IØ (*for*)] to stay up late; not go to bed: *Don't sit up (for me) if I'm late* **4** [IØ (*at, to*)] to take one's seat at a table: *Dinner's ready! Come and sit up (at/to the table)* **5 sit up and take notice** to become surprised, excited, or afraid

sit-up·on /ˈ· ·ˌ·/ *n BrE humor euph* BOTTOM (5b)

sit with *v prep* [T1] to help to nurse (a sick person)

six /sɪks/ *determiner, n, pron* [see NUMBER TABLE 1] **1** (the number) 6 **2** a cricket hit that is worth 6 runs, esp. one that crosses the edge of the playing area before touching the ground **3 at sixes and sevens** *infml* in disorder, esp. of mind; confused or undecided: *I'm all at sixes and sevens about what to do* —**~th** *determiner, n, pron, adv* [see NUMBER TABLE 3]

six-foot·er /ˌ· ˈ··/ *n infml* a tall person, more than 6 feet tall

six-pack /ˈ· ·/ *n esp. AmE* a set of 6 bottles or cases of a drink sold in a paper or plastic case for carrying

six·pence /ˈsɪkspəns/ *n* **1** [U] (in Britain until 1971) the sum of 6 pennies; 6d **2** [C] a small silver-coloured coin with this value, now 2½p

six-shoot·er /ˈ· ˌ··/ also **six·gun** /ˈsɪksgʌn/— *n* a type of small gun (REVOLVER) holding 6 bullets

six·teen /ˌsɪkˈstiːn◂/ *determiner, n, pron* [see NUMBER TABLE 1] (the number) 16 —**~th** *determiner, n, pron, adv* [see NUMBER TABLE 3]

sixteenth note /·ˈ· ·/ *n AmE* SEMIQUAVER

sixth form /ˈ· ·/ *n* [GC] the highest level (FORM[1] (11)) in a British school; the group of students usu. aged 16 or older who have taken O LEVEL*s*

sixth sense /ˌ· ˈ·/ *n* [S] *not fml* an ability to see or know that does not come from the 5 senses; INTUITION

six·ty /ˈsɪksti/ *determiner, n, pron* [see NUMBER TABLE 1] **1** (the number) 60 **2 like sixty** *AmE infml* with great speed or force —**-tieth** *determiner, n, pron, adv* [see NUMBER TABLE 3]

sixty-four /ˌ·· ˈ·◂/ *determiner, n, pron* [see NUMBER TABLE 1] **1** (the number) 64 **2 the sixty-four-thousand-dollar question** *AmE* also (*now rare*) **the sixty-four-dollar question**— *infml* the most important question; question on whose answer a very great deal depends —**sixty-fourth** *determiner, n, pron, adv* [see NUMBER TABLE 3]

siz·a·ble, sizeable /ˈsaɪzəbəl/ *adj* rather large; CONSIDERABLE

size[1] /saɪz/ *n* **1** [U;C] (a degree of) bigness or smallness: *What's the size of his book collection?| rocks of all sizes* **2** [U] bigness: *None of the jewels were of any size.|a town of some size* **3** [C] any of a set of measures in which objects are made (such as clothes, for fitting people): *dresses in women's and children's sizes|I take a size 8 shoe.|What size bottle would you like? The small size is 25p and the large size is 45p* **4 cut someone down to size** to show someone to be really less good, important, etc. **5 That's about the size of it** *infml* That's a fair statement of the matter

size[2] also **siz·ing** /ˈsaɪzɪŋ/— *n* [U] pastelike material used for giving stiffness and a hard shiny surface to paper, cloth, etc.

size[3] *v* [T1] to cover or treat with SIZE[2]

-sized /saɪzd/ *comb. form* of the stated size or number: *a good-sized* (=large) *crowd|a large-sized envelope*

size up *v adv* [T1] *not fml* to form an opinion or judgment about; get an idea of: *to size up the possibilities for action|the goods for sale*

siz·zle /ˈsɪzəl/ *v* [Wv4;IØ] to make a HISSing[1] (1) sound, as of water falling on hot metal or food cooking in hot fat: *meat sizzling on the fire*

siz·zler /ˈsɪzləʳ/ *n infml* a very hot day; SCORCHER: *Yesterday was a real sizzler!*

SJ *abbrev. for:* (after the name of a JESUIT (1)) Society of Jesus: *Francis Xavier, SJ*

skate[1] /skeɪt/ *n* **skate** *or* **skates** [Wn2;C;U] any of a large family of large flat sea fish useful as food —see picture at FISH¹

skate² *n* **1** also **ice skate**— either of a pair of metal blades fitted to the bottom of shoes for allowing the wearer to go swiftly on ice **2** ROLLER SKATE **3** **get/put one's skates on** *infml* to hurry

skate³ *v* [I∅] to move on SKATE*s*²: *to skate across the lake|to go skating* —~r *n*

skate·board /ˈskeɪtbɔːd‖-bord/ *n* a short board with 2 small wheels at each end for standing on and riding

skate o·ver also **skate round**— *v prep* [T1] to avoid treating seriously; make to seem unimportant; GLOSS OVER

ske·dad·dle /skɪˈdædl/ *v* [I∅] *infml* to run away; hurry off

skeet /skiːt/ also **skeet shoot·ing** /ˈ· ˌ··/— *n* [U] the sport of shooting at clay objects thrown into the air to give the effect of flying birds; a kind of CLAY-PIGEON shooting

skein /skeɪn/ *n* [(*of*)] **1** a loosely wound length (of thread or YARN) **2** a large group (of wild GEESE) flying in the sky

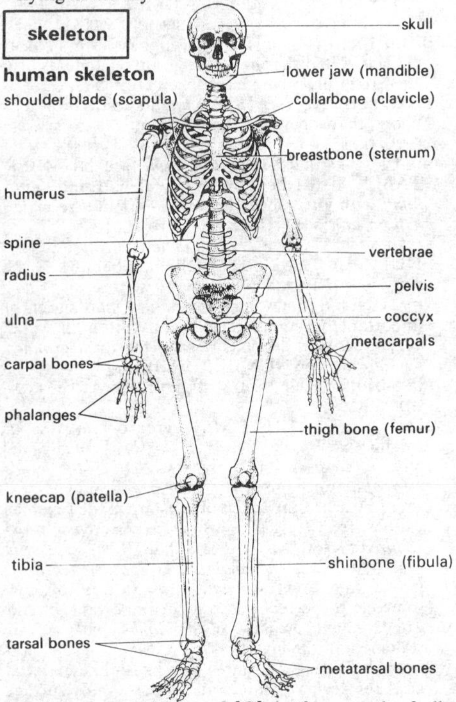

skeleton

human skeleton

skull
lower jaw (mandible)
shoulder blade (scapula)
collarbone (clavicle)
breastbone (sternum)
humerus
spine
vertebrae
radius
pelvis
ulna
coccyx
metacarpals
carpal bones
phalanges
thigh bone (femur)
kneecap (patella)
tibia
shinbone (fibula)
tarsal bones
metatarsal bones

skel·e·ton /ˈskelɪ̇tn/ *n* **1** [C] the framework of all the bones in a human or animal body **2** [C] a set of these bones (or models of them) held in their positions, as for use by medical students **3** [C] *not fml* an unnaturally very thin person: *The poor old man was just a skeleton* **4** [C] something forming a framework: *the steel skeleton of a tall building|I've written the skeleton of my report, but I have to fill in the details* **5** [A] enough to keep an operation or organization going, and no more: *During the labour quarrel British Rail is offering only a skeleton service with 5 trains a day* **6** [C] *infml* a secret of which a person or family is ashamed (esp. in the phr. **skeleton in the cupboard/**(*AmE*) **closet**): *It's time to bring the family skeleton out of the cupboard* (=to make known the shameful family secret)

skeleton key /ˈ··· ·/ *n* a key made to open a number of different locks

skep·tic /ˈskeptɪk/ *n AmE* SCEPTIC

skep·ti·cal /ˈskeptɪkəl/ *adj AmE* SCEPTICAL —**~ly** *adv* [Wa4]

skep·ti·cis·m /ˈskeptɪ̇sɪzəm/ *n AmE* SCEPTICISM

sketch¹ /sketʃ/ *n* **1** a rough not detailed drawing: *Rembrandt's sketches for his paintings* **2** a short description in words: *The speaker amused us with a sketch of city life in the 1890s* **3** a short informal piece of literature or stage acting: *travel sketches in a magazine|The performance included some funny sketches*

sketch² *v* **1** [I∅] to draw SKETCHes¹ (1) **2** [T1] to make a SKETCH¹ (1) of **3** [T1 (IN, OUT)] to describe roughly with few details: *to sketch in/out the main points of our plan* —**~er** *n*

sketch·pad /ˈsketʃpæd/ also **sketch·book** /ˈsketʃbʊk/— *n* a number of fastened-together sheets of paper for making SKETCHes¹ (1) on

sketch·y /ˈsketʃi/ *adj* [Wa1] not thorough or complete; lacking details; rough —**sketchily** *adv* —**sketchiness** *n* [U]

skew /skjuː/ *adj* **1** not straight; sloping or twisted; OBLIQUE¹ (2): *a skew arch* **2** **on the skew** in such a position; ASKEW —**~ness** *n* [U]

skew·bald /ˈskjuːbɔːld/ *adj, n* [Wa5] (a horse) coloured with large white and esp. brown shapes (PATCHes) —compare PIEBALD

skew·er¹ /ˈskjuːəʳ/ *n* a long wooden or metal pin for holding meat together while cooking or for putting through small pieces of meat and vegetables (as SHISH KEBAB) for cooking

skewer² *v* [T1] to fasten or make a hole through (as) with a SKEWER¹: *Skewer the meat before cooking*

skew-whiff /ˌ· ˈ·ˈ/ *adj BrE infml, usu. humor* SKEW: *She came in out of the wind with her hat rather skew-whiff*

ski¹ /skiː/ *n* **skis** either of a pair of long thin narrow pieces of wood, plastic, or metal curving up in front, for fastening to a boot for travelling (often in sports) on snow

ski² *v* **skied** /skiːd/, *pres. p.* **skiing** [I∅] to go on SKI*s* for travel or sport: *to go skiing|to ski down a hill|learning to ski* —see also WATER SKIING —**~er** *n*

ski·bob /ˈskiːbɒb‖-bab/ *n* a bicycle-like vehicle with SKI*s* instead of wheels and ridden by a person wearing short SKI*s* for balance

skid¹ /skɪd/ *n* **1** [*usu. pl.*] a piece of usu. wood placed under a heavy object for raising it off the floor or for moving it on **2** a block placed against a vehicle wheel (as on a hill) to keep it from turning **3** [*usu. sing.*] an act or path of SKIDding: *The car went into a skid.|skid marks on the road* **4** **put the skids on/under** *infml* **a** to stop or defeat; FRUSTRATE (1) **b** to force to hurry

skid² *v* **-dd-** [I∅] (of a vehicle or a wheel) to fail to stay in control on a road; slip sideways out of control

skid·lid /ˈskɪdˌlɪd/ *n BrE infml* a motorcyclist's protective hat; CRASH HELMET

skid·pan /ˈskɪdpæn/ *n BrE* a prepared slippery surface where drivers practise controlling SKIDding² (1) vehicles

skid row /ˌskɪd ˈrəʊ/ *n* [R] *AmE not fml* a poor dirty part of town where unemployed and alcoholic people gather

skiff /skɪf/ *n* a small light boat for rowing or sailing by one person

skif·fle /ˈskɪfəl/ *n* [U] *esp. BrE* music popular in the late 1950's, based on American FOLK² music and played partly on instruments made by the performers

ski jump /ˈ· ·/ *n* **1** [U] competition in jumping on

SKIs at high speed from a steep downward slope ending in a cliff **2** [C] the slope and cliff set up for this event

skil·ful, *AmE* **skillful** /ˈskɪlfəl/ *adj* having or showing skill —**~ly** *adv*

ski lift /ˈ· ·/ *n* a power-driven endless wire rope with seats for carrying SKIers to the top of a slope

skill /skɪl/ *n* [U;C] (a use of) practical knowledge and power; ability to do something (well): *a writer of great skill|a test of your skill with numbers|to learn the skill of flying a plane|Reading and writing are 2 different skills* —see GENIUS (USAGE)

skilled /skɪld/ *adj* [(*in*)] having or needing skill: *skilled workmen/jobs*

skil·let /ˈskɪlǝ̣t/ *n AmE* FRYING PAN

skim /skɪm/ *v* **-mm-** **1** [T1 (OFF)] to remove (floating fat or solids) from the surface of a liquid: *to skim (off) the cream from the milk|*(fig.) *Does private education skim off all the best students from the state system?* **2** [T1] to remove unwanted floating material from (liquid): *Skim the boiling rice from time to time* **3** [T1;IØ (*through, over*)] to read quickly to get the main ideas; SCAN[1] (2) **4** [L9;T1] to (cause to) move swiftly in a path near or touching (a surface): *to skim little stones over a lake|birds skimming the waves looking for food|planes skimming the treetops*

skimmed milk /ˌ· ˈ·/ also **skim milk**— *n* [U] milk from which the cream has been removed

skim·mer /ˈskɪməʳ/ *n* **1** a flat spoon with holes in it, for SKIMming liquids **2** a kind of sea bird that flies along water with its lower beak under the surface to catch insects

skimp /skɪmp/ *v* [IØ (*on*); T1] to spend, provide, or use less (of) than is really needed: *to skimp the material when making a cheap suit|to skimp on food to save money*

skimp·y /ˈskɪmpi/ *adj* [Wa1] having been SKIMPed (on); not being enough; SCANTY; MEAGRE: *it was a skimpy meal with hardly enough for everyone* —**skimpily** *adv* —**skimpiness** *n* [U]

skin[1] /skɪn/ *n* **1** [U;(C)] the natural outer covering of an animal or human body, from which hair may grow: *a skin disease|Women like to have soft skin* **2** [C;U] (*sometimes in comb.*) this part of an animal body for use as leather, fur, a WINESKIN, etc.: *many skins needed to make a fur coat|a coat made of sheepskin* **3** [C] a natural outer covering of some fruits and vegetables; PEEL: *banana skins|onions skins* —see picture at FRUIT[1] **4** [C] an outer surface built over a framework or solid inside: *aircraft wings with metal or cloth skins|the mostly glass skin of an office building* —see picture at PERCUSSION **5** [U;C] the more solid surface that forms over a liquid, as when it gets cool: *Do you like skin on your rice* PUDDING (1,2)? **6** a case for a SAUSAGE **7 by the skin of one's teeth** *infml* narrowly; only just: *We had to run for the train, and caught it by the skin of our teeth* **8 get under someone's skin** *infml* to annoy or excite someone deeply **9 save one's skin** *infml* to save oneself, esp. in a cowardly way, from death, ruin, punishment, etc. **10 skin and bone(s)** *infml* thinness of body: *You're all skin and bones, son: don't they feed you well at school?* **11 under the skin** beneath the outside appearance; at heart —**~less** *adj* [Wa5]

skin[2] *v* **-nn-** [T1] **1** to remove the skin from: *to skin a deer/an onion* **2** to hurt by rubbing off some skin: *He skinned his knee when he fell* **3** *infml* to cheat of money; FLEECE: *got skinned at cards last night* —see also EYES (9)

skin-deep /ˌ· ˈ·◂/ *adj* [Wa5] *not fml* not going deep; on the surface only; SUPERFICIAL: *Their differences of opinion are only skin-deep: they really believe the same things*

skin-dive /ˈ· ·/ *v* [IØ] to go deep under water without heavy breathing apparatus and not wearing a protective suit: *to go skin-diving* —compare FROGMAN —**skin-diver** *n* —**skin-diving** *n* [U]

skin flick /ˈ· ·/ *n AmE sl* a film showing a lot of sex

skin·flint /ˈskɪnˌflɪnt/ *n derog* a person who is not generous; one who will not spend money; MISER

skin·ful /ˈskɪnfʊl/ *n* [S] *infml* an amount of alcohol to make one drunk: *Father's singing his old army songs again; he must have had a skinful*

skin game /ˈ· ·/ *n infml* a cheating game in which a player is sure to lose his money

skin graft /ˈ· ·/ *n* an operation to repair a burn, wound, etc., by taking a piece of healthy skin to put in place of the damaged skin

skin·head /ˈskɪnhed/ *n* (in Britain in the early 1970's) a youth (usu. a boy) with his hair cut very short who behaved violently

-skinned /skɪnd/ *comb. form* having the stated kind of skin: *dark-skinned* —see also THICK-/THIN-SKINNED

skin·ny /ˈskɪni/ *adj* [Wa1] *derog* (esp. of people) thin; without much flesh

skint /skɪnt/ *adj* [Wa5;F] *BrE sl* completely without money; BROKE

skin-tight /ˌ· ˈ·◂/ *adj* (of clothes) fitting tightly against the body

skip[1] /skɪp/ *v* **-pp-** **1** [IØ] to move in a light dancing way, as with quick steps and jumps: *The little girl skipped along at her mother's side* **2** [L9, esp. AROUND] to move in no fixed order: *The speech skipped around: it skipped from one subject to another* **3** [IØ (*over*); T1] to pass over or leave out (something in order); not do or deal with (the next thing): *to skip (over) an uninteresting description in a book|Every time the record comes to that part of the music, the needle skips* **4** [T1] to fail to attend or to take part in (an activity); miss: *to skip a meeting/a meal* **5** [(*BrE*) IØ; (*AmE*)T1] to jump over (a rope) passed repeatedly beneath one's feet **6** [IØ (OFF, OUT); T1] *infml* to leave hastily and secretly, esp. to avoid being punished or paying money: *She skipped off/out without paying her bill*

skip[2] *n* a light quick stepping and jumping movement

skip[3] *n esp. BrE* a builder's large metal container for carrying heavy materials, esp. old bricks, wood, etc., to be taken away —see picture at SITE[1]

skip[4] *n* the captain of a BOWLS team

ski plane /ˈ· ·/ *n* an aircraft with SKIs instead of wheels, for landing on snow

skip·per[1] /ˈskɪpəʳ/ *n* [C;N] *infml* **1** a ship's captain **2 a** *BrE* a captain of a sports team **b** *AmE* a MANAGER (1) or captain of a sports team

skipper[2] *v* [T1] *infml* to be the SKIPPER of; lead: *He skippered his team to victory*

skirl /skɜːl‖skɜrl/ *n* [(*the*) S (*of*)] a loud high sound as made by BAGPIPES

skir·mish[1] /ˈskɜːmɪʃ‖-ɜr-/ *n* **1** a fight between small groups of soldiers, ships, etc., at a distance from the main forces and not part of a large battle **2** a slight or unplanned exchange of arguments between opponents

skirmish[2] *v* [IØ (*with*)] to fight in a SKIRMISH: *skirmished with his opponent* —**~er** *n*

skirt[1] /skɜːt‖skɜrt/ *n* **1** [C] a woman's outer garment that fits around the waist and hangs down with one lower edge all round **2** [C] a part of a coat or dress that hangs below the waist **3** [C] any of various guarding or covering parts of a vehicle or machine **4** [C *usu. pl.*] an area on the outer edge of something; OUTSKIRTS **5** [U] *sl* girls or women considered as sexual objects (esp. in the phrs. **a piece/bit of skirt** (=a girl)): *a nice bit of skirt|skirt-chasing*

skirt² *v* [T1] **1** to be or go around the outside of; go around: *a road/mountains skirting the town* **2** to avoid (a question, subject, difficulty, etc.): *The speech was disappointing: it skirted all the main questions*

skirting board /ˈ·· ·/ (*AmE* **baseboard**)— *n* [C;U] *BrE* (a) board fixed along the base of a wall where it meets the floor of a room —see picture at LIVING ROOM

skirt round also **skirt a·round**— *v prep* [T1] SKIRT²

ski stick /ˈ· ·/ (*AmE* **ski pole** /ˈ· ·/)— *n BrE* either of a pair of pointed short poles held by a SKIer for balance and for pushing against the snow

skit /skɪt/ *n* [(*on*)] a short usu. humorous acted-out scene, often copying and making fun of something

skit·ter /ˈskɪtəʳ/ *v* [L9;X9] **a** (of a small creature) to run quickly and lightly **b** to draw (the hook of a fishing line, across water) in this way

skit·tish /ˈskɪtɪʃ/ *adj* **1** not serious or responsible; silly and changeable in mind: *a charming but skittish young woman* **2** (esp. of a horse) easily excited and made afraid —**~ly** *adv* —**~ness** *n* [U]

skit·tle /ˈskɪtl/ also **skittle pin** /ˈ·· ·/— *n* a bottle-shaped object used in SKITTLES

skittle out *v adv* [T1] (in cricket) to dismiss (a whole team) quickly for very few runs

skit·tles /ˈskɪtlz/ *n* [U] **1** an English usu. informal game in which a player tries to knock down 9 SKITTLE*s* by throwing a ball or other object at them **2 not all beer and skittles** *BrE* not just a matter of enjoying oneself: *An actor's life is not all beer and skittles*

skive /skaɪv/ *v* [I∅ (OFF)] *BrE infml* to avoid work, often by staying out of the way of others who are working —**skiver** *n*

skiv·vy¹ /ˈskɪvi/ *n BrE derog* a servant, esp. a girl, who does only the dirty unpleasant jobs in a house

skivvy² *v* [I∅] *BrE infml* (esp. of a woman) to do the dirty unpleasant jobs in a house: *I don't see why I should spend my time skivvying for you*

sku·a /ˈskjuːə/ *n* a kind of large N Atlantic seabird

skul·dug·ge·ry, skullduggery /ˌskʌlˈdʌgəri/ *n* [U] *esp. humor* secretly dishonest or unfair action: *Some skulduggery no doubt went on during the election*

skulk /skʌlk/ *v* [L9;(I∅)] to move about secretly or hide, through fear or for some evil purpose: *robbers skulking around the corners, ready to jump out* —**~er** *n*

skull /skʌl/ *n* **1** the bone of the head which encloses the brain —see picture at SKELETON **2** *infml* this regarded as the mind or its covering: *Can't you get it into your thick skull that we can't afford it?*

skull and cross·bones /ˌ· · ˈ··/ *n* a sign for death or danger, used esp. **a** on bottles containing poison **b** on PIRATE*s*'¹ (1) flags in former times

skull·cap /ˈskʌlkæp/ *n* a simple closefitting cap for the top of the head, as worn sometimes by old men, some priests, Jewish men, etc.

skunk¹ /skʌŋk/ *n* **1** [C] a type of small black and white N American animal which gives out a powerful bad-smelling liquid as a defence when attacked —see picture at CARNIVOROUS **2** [C; *you*+N] *usu. humor* a person who is bad, unfair, unkind, etc.

skunk² *v* [T1] *AmE infml* to keep (an opponent) from making any points; defeat completely

sky¹ /skaɪ/ *n* **1** [(*the*) U;C *often pl. with sing. meaning*] the upper air; the space above the earth where clouds and the sun, moon, and stars appear: *The sky turned dark as the storm came near.|There's a bit of blue sky between the clouds.|We expect sunny skies for the next 2 days=skies should remain sunny* —compare HEAVEN **2 praise someone to the skies** to express the strongest praise for someone **3 The sky's the limit** *infml* There is no upper limit (esp. to the amount of money that may be spent)

sky² *v* [T1] to knock (a ball) high into the air in a game, esp. by mistake

sky blue /ˌ· ˈ·◂/ *n* [U] the pleasant bright blue colour of a clear sunny sky —**sky-blue** *adj*

sky·div·ing /ˈskaɪˌdaɪvɪŋ/ *n* [U] the sport of jumping from an aircraft and making movements while falling before opening a PARACHUTE —**skydiver** *n*

sky-high /ˌ· ˈ·◂/ *adv infml* very high; to a very high level: *Prices have gone sky-high*

sky·hook /ˈskaɪhʊk/ *n AmE humor* a hook or support imagined as coming from the sky: *How will we ever keep this wall up? Skyhooks?*

sky·jack /ˈskaɪdʒæk/ *v* [T1] *not fml* to HIJACK (an aircraft) —**~er** *n* [C] —**~ing** *n* [U;C]

sky·lark¹ /ˈskaɪlɑːk‖-lɑrk/ *n* a kind of well-known small bird (LARK) that sings while flying upward

skylark² *v* [I∅ (ABOUT)] *infml* to play rather wildly; have fun; LARK ABOUT

sky·light /ˈskaɪlaɪt/ *n* a glass-covered opening in a roof to let in light —see picture at ROOF¹

sky·line /ˈskaɪlaɪn/ *n* a shape or picture made by scenery (esp. tall city buildings) against the background of the sky

sky·rock·et /ˈskaɪˌrɒkɪ̣t‖-ˌrɑ-/ *v* [I∅] *infml* to go up suddenly and steeply

sky·scrap·er /ˈskaɪˌskreɪpəʳ/ *n* a very tall city building

sky·writ·ing /ˈskaɪˌraɪtɪŋ/ *n* [U] the making of words, pictures, etc., in the sky with lines of smoke from an aircraft, usu. for advertising

slab /slæb/ *n* **1** [C (*of*)] a thick flat usu. 4-sided piece of metal, stone, wood, food, etc.: *a house built on a cement slab|a slab of cake/cheese|The top of the table was formed by a stone slab* **2** [*the*+R] *infml* the often stone table top on which a dead body is laid in a hospital or MORTUARY

slack¹ /slæk/ *adj* [Wa1] **1** (of a rope, wire, etc.) not pulled tight **2** not firm; weak; loose: *slack laws/control* **3** not busy or active: *Winter is the slack season at most hotels.|Business is slack just now* **4** not properly careful or quick: *be slack in doing one's duty* —**~ly** *adv* —**~ness** *n* [U]

slack² *v* **1** [I∅] to be lazy; not work well or quickly enough: *scolded for slacking* **2** [L9;X9: esp. OFF, UP] to reduce (in) speed, effort, or tightness; SLACKEN: *to slack off towards the end of a hard day's work|The train slacked off (its speed) as it came into the station*

slack³ *n* [U] the part of a rope, wire, etc., that hangs loose: *There's too much slack in the thread: pull it tight to take up/in the slack*

slack⁴ *n* [U] coal dust

slack·en /ˈslækən/ *v* [I∅;T1: (OFF, UP)] to make or become SLACK; reduce in activity, force, etc., or in tightness: *The train slackened speed.|Slacken (up) the tent ropes before it rains*

slack·er /ˈslækəʳ/ *n* a person who is lazy or avoids work

slacks /slæks/ *n* [P] trousers, esp. of a loosefitting informal kind —see PAIR (USAGE)

slack wa·ter /ˌ· ˈ··/ *n* [R] the time of still water when the TIDE is turning: *at/after slack water*

slag /slæg/ *n* **1** [U] lighter glasslike waste material left when metal is separated from its natural rock **2** [C] *BrE derog sl* an unpleasant ugly woman, esp. one with socially unacceptable sexual morals

slag·heap /ˈslæghiːp/ *n esp. BrE* a pile of SLAG, as at a mine, factory, etc.

slain /sleɪn/ *past p. of* SLAY

slake /sleɪk/ *v* **1** [T1] to satisfy (thirst) with a drink; QUENCH **2** [Wv5;T1;I∅] **a** to change (lime) chemically by adding water; HYDRATE **b** (of lime) to be changed in this way

sla·lom /ˈslɑːləm/ *n* [(*the*) U] a kind of SKIing race down a winding course marked out by flags

slam¹ /slæm/ *n* [S] the act or loud noise of a door closing violently

slam² *v* **-mm- 1** [IØ;T1;L7] to shut loudly and with force: *Please don't slam the door.|The door slammed (shut)* **2** [X9] to push, move, etc., hurriedly and with great force: *She slammed on the* BRAKE*s and the car came to a stop.|He slammed the papers down on the desk and angrily walked out* **3** [T1] (used in newspapers) to attack with words: *The paper says, "Minister slams Local Government Spending."* **4 slam the door (in someone's face)** to refuse rudely to meet someone, accept an offer, etc.

slam³ *n* (in the card game of BRIDGE) a taking of 12 (**small slam** or **little slam**) or 13 (**grand slam**) TRICK*s*

slan·der¹ /ˈslɑːndəʳ‖ˈslæn-/ *n* **1** [C] an intentional false spoken report, story, etc., which unfairly damages the good opinion held about a person by others **2** [U] the making of such a statement, esp. as an offence in law —compare LIBEL

slander² *v* [T1] to speak SLANDER against; harm by making a false statement —**~er** *n*

slan·der·ous /ˈslɑːndərəs‖ˈslæn-/ *adj* being or containing SLANDER —**~ly** *adv*

slang¹ /slæŋ/ *n* [U] language that is not usu. acceptable in serious speech or writing, including words, expressions, etc., regarded as very informal or not polite, and those used among particular groups of people. These are marked *sl* in this dictionary: *There are lots of slang words for money, like "*BREAD*" and "*DOUGH*".|army/schoolboy slang|Slang often goes in and out of fashion quickly*

slang² *v* [T1] *BrE infml* to attack (someone) with rude angry words: *The 2 opponents got angry and started a* **slanging match**, *each saying rude things about the other*

slang·y /ˈslæŋi/ *adj* [Wa1] **1** being or like SLANG: *a rather slangy word* **2** using esp. rude and impolite SLANG: *a rude and slangy attack* —**slanginess** *n* [U]

slant¹ /slɑːnt‖slænt/ *v* **1** [Wa4,5;IØ;T1] to (cause to) be at an angle from straight up and down across; (cause to) SLOPE: *The roof line slants upwards from left to right* **2** [T1 *usu. pass.*] to express (facts, a report, etc.) in a way favourable to a particular opinion: *The news of the meeting was slanted to make it seem that an agreement was reached* —**~ingly** *adv*

slant² *n* **1** [S] a SLANTing direction or position: *a steep upward slant|a line drawn at/on a slant* **2** [C] a particular (fair or unfair) way of looking at or expressing (facts or a state of affairs): *an interesting new slant on the news*

slant·wise /ˈslɑːnt-waɪz‖ˈslænt-/ *adv, adj* at a SLANT; in a SLANTing direction

slap¹ /slæp/ *n* **1** a quick blow with the flat part of the hand: *He gave her a slap on the cheek and she began to cry* **2 slap in the face** *not fml* an action (seeming to be) aimed directly against someone else; REBUFF: *The minister's decision was a slap in the face to those who had tried to change his mind* **3 slap on the wrist** *not fml* a gentle punishment or warning: *This law ought to be tighter: it mustn't give criminals just a slap on the wrist!*

slap² *v* **-pp- 1** [T1] to strike quickly with the flat part of the hand: *to slap someone in the face/on the cheek/on the back* **2** [X9, esp. *on*] to place quickly, roughly, or carelessly: *to slap paint thickly on a wall*

slap³ *adv* [H] *infml* directly; right; SMACK⁴ (1): *to run slap up to the edge of the cliff and then stop*

slap and tick·le /ˌ·· · ˈ··/ *n* [U] *BrE infml, usu. humor* playful lovemaking: *a bit of slap and tickle in the back row of the cinema*

slap-bang /ˌ· ˈ·/ *adv* [Wa5;H] *infml* suddenly and violently: *ran slap-bang into the wall*

slap·dash /ˈslæpdæʃ/ *adj* done, made, etc., in a hasty careless way

slap down *v adv* [T1] *not fml* to stop or keep from acting, esp. rudely or forcefully: *to try to slap down political opposition*

slap·hap·py /ˈslæpˌhæpi/ *adj infml* **1** wildly and carelessly happy **2** *BrE* SLAPDASH

slap·stick /ˈslæpˌstɪk/ *n* [U] humorous acting (COMEDY (1,2)) that depends on rather violent fast action and simple jokes

slap-up /ˈ· ·/ *adj* [A] *BrE infml* excellent; fine and esp. fancy: *a slap-up meal at a good restaurant*

slash¹ /slæʃ/ *v* **1** [T1;IØ (*at*)] to cut with long sweeping forceful strokes, as with a knife or sword: *to slash at the bushes with a stick|The paintings had been slashed and ruined.|His opponent's sword slashed his arm* **2** [T1] to move or force with this kind of cutting movement: *He slashed his way through the high grass.|He was slashing his sword about wildly* **3** [Wv4;T1] to attack fiercely in words: *a slashing attack on the government* **4** [T1 *usu. pass.*] to reduce (an amount, price, etc.) steeply: *"This week only: prices slashed!"* (shop advertisement) **5** [T1 (*with*) *usu. pass.*] to cut (a garment), so as to sew in or show a different colour in the opening: *a blue skirt slashed with red* **6** [Wv4;L9] (esp. of rain) to come hard down and across; DRIVE¹ (10): *The rain slashed against the window*

slash² *n* **1** [C] a long sweeping cut or blow **2** [C] a straight cut making an opening in a garment **3** [S] *BrE taboo* an act of passing water from the body **4** [C;U] also **slash mark** /ˈ· ·/— OBLIQUE²

slat /slæt/ *n* a thin narrow flat piece of usu. wood, esp. in furniture or VENETIAN BLIND*s* —**~ted** *adj*

slate¹ /sleɪt/ *n* **1** [U] heavy rock formed from mud by pressure and easily split into flat thin pieces **2** [C] a small piece of this or other material used for laying in rows to cover a roof —see picture at ROOF¹ **3** [C] a small board made of this or of wood, used for writing on with chalk **4** [C] *AmE* a list of people, esp. those of the same party, entered in an election **5** [C] an imaginary record of the past, esp. of mistakes, faults, disagreements, etc. (usu. in the phrs. **a clean slate, wipe the slate clean**): *Let's wipe the slate clean and forget our past quarrels*

slate² *v* **1** [T1] to cover (a roof) with SLATE*s* (2) **2** [T1 (*for*); V3: *usu. pass.*] *AmE not fml* **a** to choose for a purpose or office: *She's slated to be the next chairman* **b** to expect or plan to happen: *a meeting slated to take place/slated for next week*

slate³ *v* [T1 (*for*)] *BrE not fml* to blame severely or attack in words; BERATE: *slated the government for their failure to act*

slat·tern /ˈslætən‖-ərn/ *n lit* a dirty untidy woman —**~ly** *adj*

slat·y /ˈsleɪti/ *adj* [Wa1] containing or like SLATE (1)

slaugh·ter¹ /ˈslɔːtəʳ/ *n* **1** [U;C] (a) killing of many people or animals, esp. cruelly, wrongly, or as in a battle; MASSACRE **2** [C *usu. sing.*] *infml* a severe defeat **3** [U] the killing of animals for meat

slaughter² *v* [T1] **1** to kill (animals) for food; BUTCHER **2** to kill (esp. many people) cruelly or wrongly; MASSACRE: *many people needlessly slaughtered each year in road accidents* **3** *infml* to defeat severely in a game

slaugh·ter·house /ˈslɔːtəhaʊs‖-ər-/ also **abattoir**— *n* **-houses** /haʊzɪ̇z/ a building where animals are killed for meat

slave¹ /sleɪv/ *n* **1** a person owned in law by another; servant without personal freedom **2** [(*of, to*)] a person completely in the control of another person or thing; one who must obey: *We're all the slaves of habit.|a slave to duty/fashion* **3** *usu. humor* a person who works hard at uninteresting work for another: *a dull job as an office slave*

slave² *v* [IØ (AWAY)] *not fml* to work like a slave; work hard with little rest: *slaved away all weekend digging in the garden*

slave driv·er /'· ,··/ *n* **1** *infml* a person who demands hard work from those in his employment or under him **2** a person in charge of slaves at work

slave la·bour /,· '··/ *n* [U] **1** work by slaves **2** *humor* hard work done for little or no pay, or forced to be done

slav·er¹ /'slævəʳ/ *v* [IØ] **1** to let liquid (SALIVA) come out of the mouth; DROOL **2** [(*over*)] *usu. derog* to be eager or excited

slaver² *n* [U] liquid (SALIVA) running down from the mouth

slav·er³ /'sleɪvəʳ/ *n* a person or esp. a ship in the business of carrying or selling slaves

sla·ve·ry /'sleɪvəri/ *n* [U] **1** the system of having slaves **2** the condition of being a slave: *"No one shall be held in slavery . . ."* (United Nations declaration)

slave trade /'· ·/ also **slave traf·fic** /'· ,··/— *n* [U] the buying and selling of slaves, esp. the forced carrying away of Africans as slaves in the 17th–19th centuries

Sla·vic /'slɑːvɪk, 'slæ-/ also **Sla·von·ic** /slə'vɒnɪk‖-'vɑ-/— *adj* of or concerning the E European people (**Slavs**) including Russians, Czechs, Poles, Yugoslavs, etc., or their languages

slav·ish /'sleɪvɪʃ/ *adj* **1** slavelike; needing or showing hard work, complete dependence on others, etc. **2** copying or copied very closely or exactly from something else; not fresh or changed: *a slavish translation: very faithful to the original but hardly understandable in English* —**~ly** *adv*

slay /sleɪ/ *v* **slew** /sluː/, **slain** /sleɪn/ *lit* to kill, esp. violently; put to death —**~er** *n*

slea·zy /'sliːzi/ *adj* [Wa1] cheap and poor-looking; DISREPUTABLE; SHABBY (1): *a sleazy hotel in a dirty dark street* —**-ziness** *n* [U]

sled¹ /sled/ *n BrE & AmE* SLEDGE¹ (1)

sled² *v* **-dd-** [IØ] *BrE & AmE* SLEDGE² (1)

sledge¹ /sledʒ/ *n* **1** *BrE* a vehicle made for sliding along snow or ice on 2 metal blades. Small light kinds are used in play and sport for going fast down slopes **2** *AmE* one of these made for carrying heavy loads across snow

sledge² *v* **1** [IØ] *BrE* to go or race down slopes on a SLEDGE¹ (1) (esp. in the phr. **go sledging**) **2** [IØ; T1] *AmE* to travel or carry on a SLEDGE¹ (2)

sledge·ham·mer /'sledʒ,hæməʳ/ *n* a large heavy hammer for swinging with both hands to drive in posts, break stones, etc.

sleek¹ /sliːk/ *v* [X9] to cause (hair or fur) to be smooth and shining: *He sleeked down/back his hair with water before going in to meet her*

sleek² *adj* [Wa1] **1** (esp. of hair or fur) smooth and shining, as from good health and care **2** (too) neat, fashionable, or stylish in appearance —**~ly** *adv* —**~ness** *n* [U]

sleep¹ /sliːp/ *n* **1** [U] the natural resting state of unconsciousness of the body: *to get 8 hours' sleep a night|I haven't had enough sleep lately* **2** [S] a period of time of this: *a good night's sleep* **3** [U] *not fml* the substance that sometimes gathers in the corners of the eyes when one is tired or asleep: *a little bit of sleep in one's eye* **4 get to sleep** [*usu. nonassertive*] to succeed in sleeping: *I couldn't get to sleep last night: I was too excited* **5 go to sleep a** to begin to sleep; fall asleep **b** *not fml* (of an arm, leg, etc.) to become unable to feel, or to feel PINS AND NEEDLES **6 lose sleep over something** [*nonassertive*] *infml* to be very worried, sorry, anxious, etc., about something **7 put to sleep a** *euph* to kill (a suffering animal) mercifully **b** (*said to or by children*) to make (a person) unconscious, as for an operation **8 the big/long sleep** *pomp* death —see also ASLEEP (3b)

sleep² *v* **slept** /slept/ **1** [IØ] to rest in sleep; be naturally unconscious, as at night: *He likes to sleep (for) an hour in the afternoon.|I didn't sleep well last night* **2** [T1] to provide beds or places for sleep for (a number of people): *The back seat of the car folds down to sleep 2* —see also SLEEP AROUND, SLEEP IN, SLEEP OFF, SLEEP ON, SLEEP OUT, SLEEP THROUGH, SLEEP TOGETHER, SLEEP WITH

sleep a·round *v adv* [IØ] *infml* to have sex with a lot of different people; be PROMISCUOUS

sleep·er /'sliːpəʳ/ *n* **1** a person sleeping **2** [C9] a person who sleeps in the stated way: *I'm a heavy/*SOUND¹ (5) *sleeper: you'll have trouble waking me up* **3** *AmE* also **tie**— any of the row of heavy pieces of wood, metal, etc., supporting a railway track **4** a heavy piece of wood used as a support in building **5** a train with beds for sleeping through the night **6** *AmE not fml* something (as a book, play, etc.) that has a delayed or unexpected success **7** a small ring worn in the ear, so as to keep open a hole made there for an EARRING

sleep in *v adv* [IØ] **1** to sleep at one's place of work: *a big house with 2 servants who slept in* —opposite **sleep out** **2** to sleep late in the morning; LIE IN (1)

sleeping bag /'·· ·/ *n* a large thick envelope or bag of warm material for sleeping in when camping —see picture at CAMP²

sleeping car /'·· ·/ *n* a railway carriage with beds for passengers

sleeping part·ner /,·· '··/ (*AmE* **silent partner**)— *n BrE* a partner in a business who takes no active part in its operation

sleeping pill /'·· ·/ also **sleeping tab·let** /'·· ,··/— *n* a PILL which helps a person to sleep

sleeping po·lice·man /,·· ·'··/ *n esp. CarE* a narrow raised part placed across a road to force traffic to move slowly

sleeping sick·ness /'·· ,··/ *n* [U] *not fml* any of various serious diseases, esp. one in Africa carried by the TSETSE FLY, causing loss of weight, fever, and esp. great tiredness

sleep·less /'sliːpləs/ *adj* [Wa5] **1** not providing sleep (esp. in the phr. **a sleepless night**): *I've spent many sleepless nights worrying about what I should do* **2** *lit* not sleeping or able to sleep: *lay sleepless on his bed* —**~ly** *adv* —**~ness** *n* [U]

sleep off *v adv* [T1] **1** to get rid of (a feeling or effect of something) by sleeping: *to sleep off last night's big dinner* **2 sleep it off** *infml* to sleep until one is no longer drunk

sleep on *v prep* [T1] *not fml* to delay deciding on (a question) until the next day; spend a night considering

sleep out *v adv* [IØ] **1** to sleep away from one's place of work —opposite **sleep in** **2** to sleep away from home or outdoors

sleep through *v prep* [T1] to fail to wake up during; be asleep and miss hearing, seeing, etc.

sleep to·geth·er *v adv* [IØ] *euph* (of 2 people) to have sex

sleep·walk·er /'sliːp,wɔːkəʳ/ *n* a person who gets up and walks about while asleep —**-ing** *n* [U]

sleep with *v prep* [T1] *euph* to have sex with (another person)

sleep·y /'sliːpi/ *adj* [Wa1] **1** tired and ready for sleep **2** quiet; inactive or slow-moving: *a sleepy country town* **3** (of fruit) past ripeness; beginning to spoil —**sleepily** *adv* —**sleepiness** *n* [U]

sleep·y·head /ˈsliːpihed/ *n* [C;N] a sleepy person, esp. a child

sleet[1] /sliːt/ *n* [U] partly frozen rain; ice falling in fine bits mixed with water —**sleety** *adj* [Wa1]

sleet[2] *v* [*it*+IØ] (of SLEET) to fall

sleeve /sliːv/ *n* **1** a part of a garment for covering (part of) an arm: *a dress with short/long sleeves* **2** *AmE* usu. **jacket**— a stiff envelope for keeping a GRAMOPHONE record in and usu. with printed information (**sleeve notes**) about the contents **3** a closefitting stiff case for a book **4** a tube with 2 open ends for enclosing something, esp. a machine part **5 have/keep something up one's sleeve** *not fml* to keep secret for use at the right time in the future **6 laugh up one's sleeve** *not fml* to laugh to oneself; be secretly amused **7 roll up one's sleeves** *not fml* to get to work; prepare to do the really hard job **8 wear one's heart on one's sleeve** to be in the habit of showing one's feelings to others —**~less** *adj* [Wa5]

-sleeved /sliːvd/ *comb. form* having SLEEVEs of the stated kind: *a long-/short-sleeved shirt*

sleigh[1] /sleɪ/ *n* a vehicle which slides along snow on 2 metal blades, esp. for carrying people and for pulling by a horse —compare SLEDGE

sleigh[2] *v* [IØ] to go in a SLEIGH

sleight of hand /ˌslaɪt əv ˈhænd/ *n* **1** [U] skill and quickness of the hands in doing tricks, as with cards: *to make a coin disappear by sleight of hand* **2** [C;U] clever deception: *to deceive the voters with a (piece of) political sleight of hand*

slen·der /ˈslendəʳ/ *adj* [Wa2] **1** delicately or gracefully thin in the body; not fat; SLIM: *a slender woman/figure* —see THIN (USAGE) **2** pleasingly thin compared to length or height; not wide or thick: *a slender book of only 50 pages* **3** slight; small and hardly enough: *a person of slender means* (=without much money)|*only the slenderest chance of success* —**~ly** *adv* —**~ness** *n* [U]

slen·der·ize, -ise /ˈslendəraɪz/ *v* [IØ;T1] *AmE infml* to make (oneself) thinner by eating less, playing sports, etc.

slept /slept/ *past t. and p. of* SLEEP

sleuth /sluːθ/ *n humor* DETECTIVE

slew[1], *AmE* **slue** /sluː/ *v* [IØ;T1: (ROUND, AROUND)] to (cause to) turn or swing violently: *lost control of the car and it slewed round*

slew[2] *past t. of* SLAY

slew[3] *n* [(*of*) *usu. sing.*] *infml, esp. AmE* a large number; lot: *a whole slew of difficulties*

slewed /sluːd/ *adj* [F] *sl* drunk

slice[1] /slaɪs/ *n* **1** [(*of*)] a thin flat piece cut from something: *a slice of bread* **2** a kitchen tool with a broad blade for lifting and serving pieces of food **3** (in sports like GOLF and tennis) a flight of a ball away from a course straight ahead and towards the side of the player's stronger hand —compare HOOK **4 a slice of life** a representation or experience of life as it really is: *a show to amuse you, not to give you a slice of life*

slice[2] *v* **1** [Wv5;T1;X7: (UP)] to cut into SLICEs[1] (1): *to slice up a cake|It's thin-sliced bread: it's been sliced thin.|A loaf of sliced bread, please* **2** [X9, esp. OFF] to cut off as a SLICE[1] (1): *to slice off a thick piece from the loaf* **3** [T1;L9, esp. *into*] to cut with a knife: *He sliced (into) his fingers by accident when cutting vegetables* **4** [T1;IØ] to hit (a ball) in a SLICE[1] (3) **5 any way you slice it** *AmE infml* however you consider it

slick[1] /slɪk/ *adj* [Wa1] **1** smooth and slippery: *slick icy places on the roads* **2** good-looking on the surface but without much depth; GLIB **3** clever or effective (but often not honest): *a slick job of selling* **4** *tech* (of a tyre used in car racing) completely smooth —**~ly** *adv* —**~ness** *n* [U]

slick[2] *n* **1** [C] OIL SLICK **2** [C *usu. pl.*; A] *AmE infml* a magazine printed on shiny paper, esp. with popular articles, colour pictures, love stories, etc. —compare PULP[1] (4)

slick down *v adv* [T1] to make (esp. hair) shiny with water, oil, etc.

slick·er /ˈslɪkəʳ/ *n infml* **1** a well-dressed fast-talking person who should not be trusted **2** *AmE* a shiny plastic or rubber coat for keeping out rain

slide[1] /slaɪd/ *v* **slid** /slɪd/ **1** [IØ;T1] to (cause to) go smoothly over a surface: *He slid along the ice.|He slid his glass across the table top* **2** [L9] to pass smoothly or continuously; go slowly and unnoticed; slip: *She slid out of the room when no one was looking.|He slid over/around the question without answering it* **3 let something slide** *infml* to let a course or condition go its own way, esp. get worse; pay no attention; do nothing

slide[2] *n* **1** a downward turn; fall: *to stop the slide in living standards* **2** a slipping movement over a surface: *The car went into a slide on the ice* **3** a sliding machine part, such as the U-shaped tube on a TROMBONE —see picture at WIND INSTRUMENT **4** a track or apparatus for sliding down: *a* SKI *slide|a log slide|a children's* PLAYGROUND *slide* **5** a usu. square piece of film in a frame for passing strong light through to show a picture on a surface: *a camera that takes colour slides|a slide show|They showed slides of their holiday* **6** a small piece of thin glass to put an object on for seeing under a microscope —see picture at SCIENTIFIC **7** (*usu. in comb.*) a sudden fall of a mass, as down a hill: *a landslide/snowslide/rockslide* **8** HAIR SLIDE

slide rule /ˈ· ·/ *n* an instrument for calculating numbers, usu. made of a ruler (marked with LOGARITHMs) with a middle part that slides along its length —see picture at MATHEMATICAL

sliding door /ˌ·· ˈ·/ *n* a door that slides across an opening rather than swinging from one side of it

sliding scale /ˌ·· ˈ·/ *n* a system of pay, taxes, etc., calculated by rates which may vary or depend on outside facts

slight[1] /slaɪt/ *adj* [Wa1] **1** not strong-looking; thin; FRAIL (1,3): *The wind seemed about to lift her slight body* **2** not great; not considerable; small or weak: *a slight book that's hardly worth reading|a slight pain|a slight smell of petrol* **3 in the slightest** [*nonassertive*] at all: *"Do you mind if I open the window?" "Not in the slightest: please do"* —**~ness** *n* [U]

slight[2] *v* [T1] to treat rudely, without respect, or as if unimportant —**~ingly** *adv*

slight[3] *n* a SLIGHTing act, a treatment as unimportant; INSULT: *I'm afraid he took your remark as a slight to/on his work*

slight·ly /ˈslaɪtli/ *adv* **1** [Wa5] to a slight degree; a bit; rather: *to feel slightly ill|just slightly too much salt in the soup* **2** in a slight way: *a slightly-built framework*

slim[1] /slɪm/ *adj* **-mm-** [Wa1] **1** (esp. of people) attractively thin; not fat —see THIN (USAGE) **2** (of hope, probability, etc.) poor; slight; not considerable: *Our chances of winning are slim: we have only the slimmest chance* —**~ly** *adv* —**~ness** *n* [U]

slim[2] *v* **-mm-** [IØ] to (try to) make oneself SLIM (1); lose weight: *I don't want any cake: I'm slimming/trying to slim* —**~mer** *n* —**~ming** *n* [U]

slime /slaɪm/ *n* [U] **1** partly liquid mud, esp. regarded as ugly, bad-smelling, etc. **2** thick sticky liquid produced by the skin of various fish and SNAILs

slim·y /ˈslaɪmi/ *adj* [Wa1] **1** like, being, or covered with SLIME; unpleasantly slippery **2** very unpleasant and offensive; DISGUSTING —**sliminess** *n* [U]

sling[1] /slɪŋ/ *v* **slung** /slʌŋ/ **1** [D1 (*to*); X9] to throw, esp. roughly or with effort: *He slung his coat over his shoulder* **2** [X9] to throw (a stone) in a SLING² (4) **3 sling mud at** *infml* to say unfair and damaging things about (esp. a political opponent) **4 sling one's hook** *BrE sl* to go away —**~er** *n*

sling² *n* **1** a piece of material for hanging from the neck to support a damaged arm or hand —see picture at MEDICAL¹ **2** an apparatus of ropes, bands, etc., for holding heavy objects to be lifted or carried **3** a cloth band on a weapon for carrying it upright behind the shoulder or across the back **4** a length of cord with a piece of leather in the middle, held at the ends and swung, for throwing stones with force

sling³ *v* **slung** [T1 (UP) *often pass.*] to move or hold in a SLING² (2,3): *The line of flags was slung (up) between 2 trees.|with his gun slung over his shoulder*

sling·shot /ˈslɪŋʃɒt‖-ʃɑt/ *n AmE* CATAPULT¹ (1)

slink /slɪŋk/ *v* **slunk** /slʌŋk/ [L9] to move quietly and secretly, as if fearful or ashamed; STEAL¹ (3): *to slink away into the night*

slip¹ /slɪp/ *v* **-pp- 1** [I∅] to slide out of place or fall by sliding: *My foot slipped and I nearly fell.|It was icy, and people were* **slipping and sliding** *all along the street* **2** [L9;X9] to move slidingly, smoothly, secretly, or unnoticed: *She slipped into/out of the room when no one was looking.|As the years slipped by/past, I thought less about her* **3** [I∅+*into* or *out of*; T1+ON or OFF] *not fml* to put on or take off (a garment): *He slipped off his good clothes, slipped into a dirty old pair of trousers, and went to dig in the garden* **4** [I∅] to fall from a standard; get worse or lower: *He has slipped in my opinion since I found out more about him* **5** [I∅ (UP)] to make a slight mistake: *The office slipped up and the letter was never sent* **6** [D1 (*to*)] to give secretly: *He slipped the waiter £1 to get a good table* **7** [T1] to get free from (a fastening): *The dog slipped his collar and ran away* **8** [T1] to escape from (one's attention, memory, etc.); be forgotten or unnoticed by: *I'm sorry I forgot his birthday: the date completely slipped my mind* **9 let slip a** to fail to follow (a chance, offer, etc.) **b** to say without intending **10 slip a disc** to get a SLIPPED DISC **11 slip something over on someone** *AmE infml* to trick someone

slip² *n* **1** [C] an act of slipping or sliding **2** [C] a usu. slight mistake: *"Too" was a slip of the pen: I meant to write "to"* **3** [C] a woman's undergarment like a short dress not covering the arms or neck **4** [C *usu. pl. with sing. meaning*] a long surface built to slope down into water, for moving ships into or out of water, or for ships to land at **5** [U;C] (the position of) a cricket fielder who stands close behind and to the right of a (right-handed) hitter, for catching balls that come off the edge of the BAT —see picture at CRICKET² **6 give someone the slip** *infml* to escape from someone —see also PILLOWCASE, GYMSLIP

slip³ *n* **1** a usu. small or narrow piece of paper: *a slip marking his place in the book* **2** a small branch cut for planting; CUTTING¹ (1) **3** [+*of, usu. sing.*] *becoming rare* a small thin one: *a little slip of a boy*

slip⁴ *n* [U] a mixture of clay and water used in POTTERY-making for ornamenting a surface and as cement

slip·cov·er /ˈslɪpˌkʌvəʳ/ *n* a removable closefitting cloth cover for a piece of furniture

slip·knot /ˈslɪpnɒt‖-nɑt/ *n* a knot that can be tightened round something by pulling one of its ends

slip-on /ˈ· ·/ *adj* [Wa5;A] (of a garment) made so that it can be put on easily

slip·o·ver /ˈslɪpˌəʊvəʳ/ *n* a garment which one puts on by putting one's head through it; PULLOVER

slipped disc /ˌ· ˈ·/ *n* [S] a painful displacement of one of the connecting parts (DISCs (4) between VERTEBRAE) in the back

slip·per /ˈslɪpəʳ/ also (*fml*) **carpet slipper**— *n* a light shoe with the top made from soft material, usu. worn indoors

slip·per·y /ˈslɪpəri/ *adj* [Wa2] **1** difficult to hold or to stand, drive, etc., on without slipping: *Drive very carefully: the roads are wet and slippery* **2** *not fml* difficult to understand exactly; ELUSIVE **3** *infml* not to be trusted; SHIFTY **4 a/the slippery slope** *esp. BrE humor* a course that may seem good at first but then cannot be stopped and leads to ruin —**-iness** *n* [U]

slip·py /ˈslɪpi/ *adj* **Look slippy!** *BrE infml* Be quick about it!; Hurry up!

slip road /ˈ· ·/ *n BrE* a road for driving onto or off a MOTORWAY —see picture at INTERCHANGE²

slips /slɪps/ *n* [*the*+P] **1** the part of a cricket field where the SLIPs² (5) stand **2** *BrE* the sides of the uppermost level of seating in some theatres

slip·shod /ˈslɪpʃɒd‖-ʃɑd/ *adj* careless; not exact or thorough

slip·stream /ˈslɪpstriːm/ *n* **1** the area just behind a fast-moving racing car where a following driver may keep up his speed easily **2** a stream of air driven backwards by an aircraft engine

slip-up /ˈ· ·/ *n* a usu. slight mistake

slip·way /ˈslɪpweɪ/ *n* a track sloping down into the water for moving ships into or out of water

slit¹ /slɪt/ *v* **slit**, *pres. p.* **-tt-** [T1;X7] to make a SLIT in; make a cut along: *to slit an envelope (open) with a knife|Her long dress was slit up to the knee in Chinese style*

slit² *n* a narrow cut or opening

slith·er /ˈslɪðəʳ/ *v* [L9] **1** to move in a slipping or twisting way like a snake **2** to slide unsteadily: *slithered across the ice*

slith·er·y /ˈslɪðəri/ *adj* slippery in appearance or feeling

sliv·er¹ /ˈslɪvəʳ/ *n* [(*of*)] a small thin sharp piece cut or torn off

sliver² *v* [I∅;T1] to break or (be) cut into SLIVERs: *The stone slivered the glass*

sliv·o·vitz /ˈslɪvəvɪts, ˈsliː-/ *n* [U] a strong alcoholic drink made in SE Europe; kind of PLUM BRANDY

slob /slɒb‖slɑb/ *n* [C; *you*+N] *infml* a man who is rude, lazy, dirty, or carelessly-dressed

slob·ber¹ /ˈslɒbəʳ‖ˈslɑ-/ *v* **1** [I∅;T1] to let (liquid) fall from the lips **2** [T1] to make wet in this way: *The baby has slobbered her dress* **3** [I∅ (OVER)] to express fond feelings too openly and indelicately: *bad poetry, slobbering over the beauties of nature*

slobber² *n* [U] liquid that runs down from the mouth; SLAVER

sloe /sləʊ/ *n* a small bitter kind of PLUM with dark purple skin that is the fruit of the BLACKTHORN

sloe gin /ˌ· ˈ·/ *n* [U] a sweet reddish alcoholic drink made from GIN and SLOEs

slog¹ /slɒg‖slɑg/ *v* **-gg-** *esp. BrE* **1** [L9] to do hard dull work without stopping; make one's way by continuous effort: *to slog away at a job* **2** [T1;I∅] (esp. in cricket) to hit (the ball) hard and wildly —**~ger** *n*

slog² *n BrE not fml* **1** [S;U] (a time or course of) hard dull work without stopping: *I always found school difficult: it was a hard slog* **2** [C] (esp. in cricket) a wild hard hit

slo·gan /ˈsləʊgən/ *n* a short phrase expressing a usu. political or advertising message

sloop /sluːp/ *n* **1** a small kind of sailing ship with one central pole (MAST) and sails along its length **2** a small armed ship such as a CUTTER (2)

slop¹ /slɒp‖slɑp/ *n* [U] **1** [*usu. pl. with sing. meaning*] **a** food waste, esp. for feeding to animals **b** liquid food for sick people **2** *derog* tasteless liquid food **3** [*usu. pl. with sing. meaning*] human solid and liquid waste

slop² *v* **-pp-** **1** [T1] to cause some of (a liquid) to go over the side of a container; SPILL¹ (1); SPLASH¹ (1): *I moved the soup bowl and slopped some of the soup* **2** [L9] (of a liquid) to do this **3** [T1] to make wet in this way **4** [L9] *not fml* to go in mud or wetness; SLOSH **5** [T1] to feed with food waste

slop ba·sin /'· ,··/ also **slop bowl** /'· ·/— *n BrE* a bowl used at table for holding the waste tea or coffee poured back from the bottoms of cups

slope¹ /sləʊp/ *v* [Wv4;I∅] **1** to lie or move in a sloping direction; be or go at an angle: *a sloping roof|The railway slopes up/down slightly at this point* **2 slope arms** [*usu. imper.*] *BrE* (of a soldier) to hold a weapon by the end with the barrel resting at a slope on the left shoulder

slope² *n* **1** a surface that slopes; a piece of ground going up or down: *to climb a steep slope|a* SKI *slope* **2** a degree of sloping; a measure of an angle from a level direction: *a slope of 30 degrees = a slope of 1 in 2* **3 at the slope** *BrE* (of a soldier or a weapon) (with the weapon) held sloping on one shoulder

slope off *v adv* [I∅] *BrE infml* to go away secretly, as to escape or avoid work

slop out *v adv* [T1;I∅] *BrE* (of a prisoner) to remove SLOPS¹ (3) from (a room)

slop·py /'slɒpi‖'slɑpi/ *adj* [Wa1] **1** (as of clothes) loose, informal, and careless- or dirty-looking **2** not careful or thorough enough **3** wet and dirty **4** silly in showing feelings —**-pily** *adv* —**-piness** *n* [U]

slosh /slɒʃ‖slɑʃ/ *v* **1** [L9] to go through water or mud: *sloshing along in our rubber boots* **2** [I∅;T1] **a** (of liquid) to move about as against the sides of a container **b** to cause (a liquid) to do this **3** [T1] *BrE sl* to hit; PUNCH¹ (1); BASH

sloshed /slɒʃt‖slɑʃt/ *adj* [F] *infml* drunk

slot¹ /slɒt‖slɑt/ *n* **1** a long straight narrow opening or hollow place, esp. in a machine or tool: *to put a coin in the slot|a slot in the top of a screw* **2** *infml* a place or position in a list, system, organization, etc.: *The 7 o'clock time slot on the radio is usually filled with a news broadcast*

slot² *v* **-tt-** **1** [Wv5;T1] to cut a SLOT (1) in: *a slotted screw* **2** [X9] to put into a SLOT (1): *slot a lid into the top of the box* **3** [X9] *esp. BrE* to put into a SLOT (2); find a place for: *I'm going to try to slot in some reading on my holiday*

sloth /sləʊθ/ *n* **1** [U] *esp. lit* unwillingness to work; dislike of doing things actively; laziness **2** [C] any of several types of slow-moving animal of central and S America that live in trees and hang by all 4 legs from branches

sloth·ful /'sləʊθfəl/ *adj esp. lit* unwilling to work or be active; lazy —**~ly** *adv* —**~ness** *n* [U]

slot ma·chine /'· ·,·/ *n* **1** *BrE* a machine, esp. for selling drinks, cigarettes, etc., which is made to work by putting a coin into it; VENDING MACHINE —see picture at STREET **2** *AmE* FRUIT MACHINE

slouch¹ /slaʊtʃ/ *n* **1** [S] a tired-looking round-shouldered way of standing or walking **2** [C *usu. neg.*] *not fml* a lazy, untidy, or useless person

slouch² *v* [Wv4;I∅] to carry the body at a SLOUCH¹ (1): *a slouching figure asleep in the chair* —**~ingly** *adv*

slouch hat /,· '·/ *n* a man's soft hat with a wide part (BRIM) around the bottom that can be pulled down

slough¹ /slaʊ‖sluː, slaʊ/ *n* **1** a place of deep mud or very wet ground **2** a bad condition from which one cannot easily get free: *She had got herself into a slough of self-pity* **3 the slough of despond** *lit* a state of great sorrow, anxiety, etc.

slough² /slʌf/ *n* the thrown-off skin of a snake or other animal that regularly loses its outer skin

slough off /slʌf/ *v adv* [T1] **1** to throw off (dead outer skin) **2** *esp. lit* to get rid of as something worn out or unwanted

slov·en /'slʌvən/ *n lit* a person of untidy habits; one who is careless in dress or appearance

slov·en·ly /'slʌvənli/ *adj* [Wa2] like a SLOVEN; not neat or orderly; untidy —**-liness** *n* [U]

slow¹ /sləʊ/ *adj* [Wa1] **1** [B] not moving or going on quickly; having less than a usual or standard speed: *slow music/growth/poison|a slow train/walk/death* **2** [B+*in*; B3] taking a long time or too long: *The government was slow in acting/slow to act* **3** [B] not good or quick in understanding; dull in mind **4** [B] not very active; dull; not BRISK: *Business is slow just now* **5** [F;E] (of a clock) showing a time that is earlier than the true time (often by a stated amount): *The station clocks are 2 minutes slow* **6** [B] (of a surface) not allowing quick movement: *a slow* WICKET (1b) **7 slow off the mark** (*AmE* usu. **slow on the uptake**)—slow to understand (esp. the point of a joke) —**~ly** *adv* —**~ness** *n* [U]

slow² *adv* [Wa1] slowly —see also GO SLOW, GO-SLOW, SLOW-DOWN

USAGE **Slow** (adv) is used only **a** after (not before) verbs: *to drive* **slow b** with **how**: *How* **slow** *he drives!* **c** in comb.: **slow**-*moving*. Otherwise, use **slowly**.

slow³ *v* [I∅;T1: (UP, DOWN)] to make or become slower: *The train slowed (its speed) as it went around the curve.|Business slows up/down at this time of year*

slow·coach /'sləʊkəʊtʃ/ (*AmE* **slow·poke** /'sləʊpəʊk/)— *n* [C;N] *BrE infml* a person who seems to be moving too slowly

slow-down /'· ·/ *n* **1** a lessening of speed or activity; slowing down: *a business slow-down* **2** *AmE* GO-SLOW

slow mo·tion /,· '··/ *n* [U] action which takes place at a much slower speed than in real life, esp. as shown for special effect in films

slow·worm /'sləʊwɜːm‖-ɜrm/ *n* a type of small harmless European LIZARD with very small eyes and no legs, that moves like a snake

sludge /slʌdʒ/ *n* [U] **1** thick mud **2** the product of waste (SEWAGE) treatment **3** dirty waste oil in an engine

slue /sluː/ *v* [I∅;T1: (ROUND, AROUND)] *AmE* SLEW¹

slug¹ /slʌg/ *n* any of several types of small limbless plant-eating creature, related to the SNAIL but with no shell, that often do damage to gardens —see picture of MOLLUSC

slug² *n* a lump or piece of metal, esp. **a** *AmE* a coin-shaped object unlawfully put into a machine in place of a coin **b** *tech* a machine-made piece of metal with a row of letters along the edge for printing **c** *sl, esp. AmE* a bullet

slug³ *v* **-gg-** [T1] *AmE infml* **1** to strike with a heavy blow, esp. with the closed hand and so as to make unconscious **2 slug it out** to fight fiercely to the end

slug·gard /'slʌgəd‖-ərd/ *n lit* a habitually lazy person

slug·gish /'slʌgɪʃ/ *adj* slow-moving; not very active or quick: *a sluggish stream/car engine|feeling rather sluggish in the heat of the day* —**~ly** *adv* —**~ness** *n* [U]

sluice¹ /sluːs/ *n* a passage for water with an opening (a **sluice gate** or **sluice valve**) through which the flow can be controlled or stopped

sluice² *v* **1** [T1 (OUT, DOWN)] to wash with floods or streams of water, as from a SLUICE **2** [L9] (of water) to come (as if) from a SLUICE; come in streams

sluice·way /'sluːs-weɪ/ *n* a man-made stream filled

with water from a SLUICE, as in mining for washing earth containing gold

slum¹ /slʌm/ *n* **1** [*often pl. with sing. meaning*] a city area of poor living conditions and dirty unrepaired buildings **2** *infml* a very untidy place

slum² *v* **-mm-** *infml* **1** [I∅ *usu. pres. p.*] to amuse oneself by visiting a place on a much lower social level **2 slum it** to live very cheaply, not having things that others find necessary

slum·ber¹ /ˈslʌmbəʳ/ *v* [I∅] *lit* to lie asleep; sleep peacefully —**~er** *n*

slumber² *n* [U;C *often pl. with sing. meaning*] *lit* a state of sleep: *waking from her slumber(s)|a deep slumber*

slum·ber·ous /ˈslʌmbərəs/ also **slum·brous** /ˈslʌmbrəs/— *adj lit* sleepy; wanting or suggesting sleep

slum·my /ˈslʌmi/ *adj* [Wa1] *infml* **1** of or like SLUMS¹ (1) **2** dirty and untidy

slump¹ /slʌmp/ *v* **1** [L9 (DOWN)] to sink down; fall heavily or in a heap; COLLAPSE¹ (1): *He slumped in his chair asleep* **2** [I∅] to go down in number or strength; fall off; DECLINE¹ (2): *Sales have slumped in the last month*

slump² *n* **1** a time of seriously bad business conditions and unemployment; DEPRESSION (5) **2** *esp. AmE* a lowering of activity, number, force, etc.

slung /slʌŋ/ *past t. and p. of* SLING

slunk /slʌŋk/ *past t. and p. of* SLINK

slur¹ /slɜːʳ/ *v* **-rr-** [T1] **1** [Wa5] to write a SLUR² (1) over (musical notes) **2** to sing or play (notes) connectedly **3** to pronounce (a sound in a word) unclearly or not at all

slur² *n* **1** [C] a curved line, ⌒ or ⌣, written over or under musical notes directing them to be played smoothly without separation —compare TIE¹ (7) **2** [S] a SLURring¹ (3) way of speaking

slur³ *v* **-rr-** [T1] to say unfair bad things about

slur⁴ *n* an unfair damaging remark

slurp /slɜːp‖slɜrp/ *v* [I∅;T1] *not fml* to eat (soft food) or drink noisily: *slurping sounds|children slurping their milk*

slur·ry /ˈslʌri‖ˈslɜri/ *n* [U] a watery mixture, esp. of clay, mud, lime, or PLASTER

slush /slʌʃ/ *n* [U] **1** partly melted snow; watery snow **2** literature, films, etc., concerned with silly love stories; MUSH¹ (3) —**slushy** *adj* [Wa1]

slush fund /ˈ· ·/ *n* [esp. AmE] *AmE* a sum of money (**slush money**) secretly kept for dishonest use, such as by a politician in an election

slut /slʌt/ *n* **1** a woman who acts immodestly or immorally **2** an untidy lazy woman; SLATTERN —**~tish** *adj*

sly /slaɪ/ *adj* [Wa1] **1** clever in deceiving; dishonestly tricky; CRAFTY: *a sly old fox* **2** playfully unkind: *a sly joke* **3 on the sly** secretly (as of something done dishonestly or unlawfully) —**~ly** *adv* —**~ness** *n* [U]

smack¹ /smæk/ *n* [(*of*)] a particular taste; FLAVOUR

smack² *v* **1** [T1] to open and close (one's lips) noisily **2** [T1] to strike loudly, as with the flat part of the hand **3** [X9] to put so as to make a short loud sound: *He smacked the book angrily on the table*

smack³ *n* **1** a quick loud noise, sound of SMACKing² (3): *The book hit the floor with a smack* **2** a loud kiss: *a smack on the cheek* **3** a quick loud forceful blow **4** *infml* an attempt (in the phr. **have a smack at**)

smack⁴ *adv* [H] *infml* **1** with force: *run smack into a wall* **2** (*esp. AmE*) **smack-dab** /ˌ· ˈ·/— squarely; directly; right: *There it was, smack-dab* in the middle of the room

smack⁵ *n* a small sailing boat used for fishing

smack·er /ˈsmækəʳ/ *n sl* **1** [*usu. pl.*] a pound or a dollar: *a debt of 1000 smackers* **2** a loud kiss

smack of *v prep* [T1] to have a taste or suggestion of: *wine that seems to smack of sunny hillsides|a plan that smacks of disloyalty*

small¹ /smɔːl/ *adj* [Wa1] **1** [B] little in size, weight, force, importance, etc.; not large: *a small man, only 5 feet tall|a book written for small children|The girl is small for her age.|a small number of people|the smallest shoe size in the shop|The space is big enough only for the smallest of cars* **2** [A] doing only a limited amount of a business or activity: *to be a small businessman=own a small business|a small farmer* **3** [A] (*esp. with nouns marked* [U]) very little; slight: *had small hope of success* **4** [Wa5;B] (of letters) LOWER CASE: *"Church" is sometimes written with a capital* C *and sometimes with a small* c **5 feel small** to feel ashamed or humble **6 in a small way** modestly; not grandly **7 small wonder** no wonder; of course: *You've been eating far too much: small wonder you're putting on weight* —see also **small** BEER (4), SMALLS —**~ness** *n* [U]

small² *adv* [Wa1] in a small manner: *He writes so small I can't read it*

small³ *n* [*the*+R9, esp. *of*] the small narrow part of something, esp. the lower part of the back where it curves in: *a pain in the small of the back*

small ad /ˈ· ·/ *n BrE* CLASSIFIED AD

small arms /ˈ· ·‖ˌ· ˈ·/ *n* [P] guns made to be held in one or both hands for firing

small change /ˌ· ˈ·/ *n* [U] money in coins of small value

small fry /ˈ· ·/ *n* [Wn3;C *usu. pl.*] *infml* a young or unimportant person

small·hold·er /ˈsmɔːlˌhəʊldəʳ/ *n BrE* a person who owns or rents a SMALLHOLDING

small·hold·ing /ˈsmɔːlˌhəʊldɪŋ/ *n BrE* a piece of farmland smaller than an ordinary farm (usu. less than 50 ACREs)

small hours /ˈ· ·/ *n* [*the*+P] the early morning hours just after midnight

small in·tes·tine /ˌ· ·ˈ··/ *n* the long narrow twisting tube in the body, into which food first passes from the stomach and where most of its chemical change takes place —compare LARGE INTESTINE and see picture at DIGESTIVE SYSTEM

small-mind·ed /ˌ· ˈ··◂/ *adj* having narrow selfish interests; unwilling to change one's mind or listen to others —compare OPEN-MINDED, BROADMINDED —**~ness** *n* [U]

small·pox /ˈsmɔːlpɒks‖-pɑks/ *n* [U] a serious infectious disease (esp. in former times), causing spots which leave marks on the skin

smalls /smɔːlz/ *n* [P] *BrE infml* small pieces of underclothing, handkerchiefs, etc., esp. for washing: *to wash one's smalls*

small talk /ˈ· ·/ *n* [U] *not fml* light conversation on unimportant or nonserious subjects

small-time /ˌ· ˈ·◂/ *adj* limited in activity, profits, wealth, ability, etc.; unimportant —**-timer** *n*

smarm·y /ˈsmɑːmi‖-ɑr-/ *adj* [Wa1] *BrE sl* unpleasantly and falsely polite; UNCTUOUS

smart¹ /smɑːt‖smɑrt/ *v* [I∅] **1** to cause or feel a painful stinging sensation, usu. in one part of the body and not lasting long: *The place where he had cut his knee was smarting* **2** [(*under, over*)] to be hurt in one's feelings; suffer in mind: *She was still smarting under/over his unkind words*

smart² *adj* [Wa1] **1** quick or forceful; LIVELY (1); VIGOROUS (1): *a smart blow on the head|a smart rise/fall in prices* **2** good or quick in thinking; clever; BRIGHT (5); INTELLIGENT **3** neat and stylish in appearance; SPRUCE²: *You look very smart in that new shirt* **4** used by, concerning, etc., very fashionable people **5 play it smart** *not fml,* *esp. AmE* to act wisely; to do the right thing: *You ought to play it smart and stop smoking* —**~ly** *adv* —**~ness** *n* [U]

smart[3] *n* **1** a SMARTing[1] (1) pain **2** something that hurts the feelings or pride: *the smart of being defeated*

smart al·eck /ˈsmɑːt ˌælɪ̈k‖-ɑr-/ *n infml* a person who annoys others by claiming to know everything and trying to sound clever —**smart-alecky** *adj*

smart·en up /ˈsmɑːtn‖-ɑr-/ *v adv* [T1;I∅] to (cause to) become good looking, neat, or stylish; SPRUCE UP: *Some new paint should smarten up the house*

smash[1] /smæʃ/ *v* **1** [I∅;T1: (UP)] to (cause to) break into pieces violently; SHATTER (1): *The dish smashed (up) on the floor* **2** [X9;L9] to go, drive, throw, or hit forcefully, as against something solid; crash: *He smashed his foot through the thin door.*|*They smashed their way out of the building* **3** [T1; I∅: (UP)] to (cause to) be destroyed or ruined; wreck: *to smash (up) one's car|to smash the enemy's defences* **4** [T1;(I∅)] (in games like tennis) to hit (the ball) with a SMASH[2] (4) **5** [T1] to split (atoms)

smash[2] *n* **1** a powerful blow: *a smash that sent his opponent to the floor* **2** a breaking into pieces; crash: *the smash of glasses breaking on the floor* **3** also **smash hit** /ˌ· ˈ·/— *not fml* a great success, as of a new play, book, film, etc.; HIT[2] (3): *a new musical smash* **4** a hard downward attacking shot, as in tennis **5** a failure of a business: *had to sell their house after the smash* **6** SMASH-UP

smash-and-grab /ˌ· · ˈ·/ *adj* [Wa5;A] *esp. BrE* (of a robbery) done by quickly breaking a shop window, taking the valuable things inside it, and running away

smashed /ˈsmæʃt/ *adj infml* drunk

smash·er /ˈsmæʃəʳ/ *n infml* a person or thing that is very fine

smash·ing /ˈsmæʃɪŋ/ *adj infml, esp. BrE* very fine; wonderful; excellent

smash-up /ˈ· ·/ *n* **1** a ruining or wrecking; COLLAPSE[1] (1,4): *the smash-up of the German empire* **2** a road or railway accident: *a 5-car smash-up*

smat·ter·ing /ˈsmætərɪŋ/ *n* [(*of*)] a small amount (esp. of knowledge)

smear[1] /smɪəʳ/ *n* **1** a spot made by an oily or sticky material; mark made by SMEARing **2** *esp. med* a small bit of some material prepared for examining under a microscope **3** an unproved charge made intentionally to try to turn public feelings against someone

smear[2] *v* **1** [D1 + *with/on* or *over*; T1;I∅] **a** to cause (a sticky or oily material) to spread on or go across (a surface): *She smeared butter on/over the bottom of the dish.*|*Be careful: if you touch the wall you'll smear the fresh paint* **b** (of such material) to do this: *Be careful: the paint may smear* **2** [T1;I∅] to (cause to) lose clearness in this way or by rubbing: *Several words had/were smeared and I couldn't read them* **3** [T1] to make a SMEAR[1] (3) against; charge unfairly

smear test /ˈ· ·/ *n* a medical test made by examining a SMEAR[1] (2), esp. of material from a woman's VAGINA for discovering CANCER (2)

smell[1] /smel/ *v* **smelled** *or* **smelt** /smelt/ [Wv6] **1** [I∅] to use the nose; have or use the sense of the nose: *Here, smell: what do you think this liquid is?*|*an old dog who can hardly smell any longer* **2** [T1,4,5,6a;V4] to notice, examine, discover, or recognize by this sense: *to smell cooking|I could smell that the milk wasn't fresh.*|*He can always smell when rain is coming* **3** [T1,4,5;V4] to notice, come to know of, recognize, etc., by some natural unexplained ability: *a writer who can always smell a good idea|I could smell trouble coming* —see also RAT[1] (4) **4** [L7,9 esp. *of, like*] to have an effect on the nose; have a particular smell: *a sweet-smelling flower|This book smells old* **5** [I∅ (*of*)] to have an offensive effect on the nose; have an unpleasant smell; STINK[1] (1): *The meat had been left out for days and had started to smell*

USAGE **Smelt** is more common in *BrE* than **smelled**, except in literature, but **smelled** is more common in *AmE*.

smell[2] *n* **1** [U] the power of using the nose; the sense that can discover the presence of gases in the air: *dogs that track by smell alone* **2** [C] a quality that has an effect on the nose; something that excites this sense: *Some flowers have stronger smells than others* **3** [C *usu. sing.*] an act of SMELLing (2) something: *Have a smell of this wine: does it seem all right?*

smelling salts /ˈ·· ·/ *n* [P] a strong-smelling chemical (esp. AMMONIA), formerly often carried in a small bottle, for curing faintness

smell out *v adv* [T1] **1** to discover or find (as if) by smelling: *to smell out a fox* **2** to cause (a place) to be unpleasant because of a bad smell: *Those old socks are really smelling the room out*

smell·y /ˈsmeli/ *adj* [Wa1] unpleasant-smelling —**smelliness** *n* [U]

smelt[1] /smelt/ *v* [T1] to melt (metal-containing earth (ORE)) for separating and removing the metal, as is done in large factories (**smelters**)

smelt[2] *n* **smelt** *or* **smelts** [Wn2] any of various small important food fishes of lakes and coasts

smile[1] /smaɪl/ *v* **1** [I∅;(T1)] to have or make (a smile): *She smiled at me: how wonderful!*|*It's rare to see him smile* —compare GRIN **2** [I∅ (*at*), 3] to have a feeling which a smile expresses; consider something slightly funny or silly: *He smiled to think what a fool he'd been* **3** [I∅ (*on*)] to act or look favourably: *The weather smiled on us: it was a fine day* **4** [T1] to express with a smile: *She smiled a greeting* —**smilingly** *adv*

smile[2] *n* **1** an expression of the face with the mouth turned up at the ends and the eyes bright, that usu. expresses amusement, happiness, approval, or sometimes bitter feelings **2 all smiles** very happy-looking: *The winner was all smiles as he heard the results of the voting*

smirch[1] /smɜːtʃ‖-ɜr-/ *v* [T1] to bring dishonour on; DISGRACE[2] (1); DISCREDIT[1] (1)

smirch[2] *n* harm done to someone's character; BLOT[2] (1)

smirk[1] /smɜːk‖smɜrk/ *v* [I∅] to smile in a false or too satisfied way

smirk[2] *n* a SMIRKing expression; silly proud smile

smite /smaɪt/ *v* **smote** /sməʊt/, **smitten** /ˈsmɪtn/ [T1] **1** *old use & lit* to strike hard: *smote his enemy with the sword* **2** *esp. bibl & lit* to destroy, attack, or punish as if by a blow **3** [*usu. pass.* (*by, with*)] to have a powerful sudden effect on: *He was so smitten by/with the view that he stopped and took out his camera* —see also SMITTEN

smith /smɪθ/ *n* (*usu. in comb.*) **1** a worker in metal: BLACKSMITH|GOLDSMITH **2** a maker: GUNSMITH

smith·e·reens /ˌsmɪðəˈriːnz/ *n* (**in**)**to smithereens** *infml* into small bits; to complete destruction: *to bomb a building into smithereens*

smith·y /ˈsmɪði‖-θi, -ði/ *n* a BLACKSMITH'S place of work

smit·ten /ˈsmɪtn/ *adj esp. humor* in love, esp. suddenly fond of a person —see also SMITE[1] (3)

smock /smɒk‖smɑk/ *n* **1** a light loose coatlike garment for putting on over one's other clothing while working **2** a woman's loose shirtlike garment, often worn by future mothers to hide their shape

smock·ing /ˈsmɒkɪŋ‖ˈsmɑ-/ *n* [U] ornamentation, esp. on dresses, made by gathering cloth into small regular folds held tightly with fancy stitching

smog /smɒg‖smɑg, smɔg/ *n* [U] the unhealthy dark mixture of gases (esp. FOG[1] (1), smoke, and vehicle waste gases) in the air in some large cities

smoke[1] /sməʊk/ *n* **1** [U] gas mixed with very small bits of solid material (esp. CARBON[1] (1)) that can be seen in the air and is usu. given off by burning: *smoke from a chimney|the smell of tobacco smoke* **2** [C] **a** *infml* something (esp. a cigarette) for smoking **b** an act of smoking: *a short smoke on his pipe* **3 go up in smoke** to end or fail without results, esp. suddenly **4 There's no smoke without fire** also **Where there's smoke there's fire**— If unfavourable things are being said about someone or something, they are probably at least partly true —**~less** *adj* [Wa5]

smoke[2] *v* **1** [T1;IØ] to suck or breathe in smoke from (esp. tobacco, as in cigarettes, a pipe, etc.): *I don't smoke now, though I used to smoke 20 cigarettes a day* —see also SMOKING **2** [L9] (as of a pipe) to allow this in a stated way: *This pipe smokes poorly/easily* **3** [Wv4;IØ] to give off smoke: *the sight of smoking chimneys* **4** [Wv4;IØ] to give off too much smoke, as because of poor burning: *a smoking fireplace* **5** [Wv5;T1] to darken with smoke, esp. by allowing smoke to settle on and cover a surface: *to look at a bright light only through smoked glass* **6** [Wv5;T1] to preserve and give a special taste to (meat) by hanging in smoke

smoke out *v adv* [T1] **1** to fill a place with smoke to force (a person, animal, etc.) to come out **2** to bring into public view: *The old war criminal was at last smoked out from his hiding place abroad and brought to trial*

smok·er /ˈsməʊkəʳ/ *n* **1** a person who smokes **2** *not fml* a railway carriage where smoking is allowed **3** *now rare* an informal party for men only

smoke·screen /ˈsməʊkskriːn/ *n* **1** a cloud of smoke produced for hiding a place or activity from enemy sight **2** something for others to see, hear, etc., which hides one's real intentions

smoke·stack /ˈsməʊkstæk/ *n* **1** a tall chimney for taking off smoke, esp. from a factory or ship **2** *AmE* the FUNNEL[1] (1) of a railway steam engine

smok·ing /ˈsməʊkɪŋ/ *n* **1** [U] the practice or habit of sucking in tobacco smoke from cigarettes, a pipe, etc. **2** [A] (of a place) allowing this; where one may smoke: *a railway* **smoking compartment**|*a smoking room*

smoking jack·et /ˈ·· ˌ··/ *n* a man's short usu. fancy coat for wearing at home indoors

smok·y /ˈsməʊki/ *adj* [Wa1] **1** filled with or producing (too much) smoke **2** with the taste or appearance of smoke: *a smoky mist|smoky-tasting fish* —**smokiness** *n* [U]

smol·der /sməʊldəʳ/ *n, v AmE* SMOULDER

smooch[1] /smuːtʃ/ *v* [IØ] *infml* to kiss and hold someone lovingly: *a couple smooching* (*with each other*) *in the back row of the cinema* —**~er** *n*

smooch[2] *n* [S] *infml* an act of SMOOCHing[1] —**~y** [Wa1]

smooth[1] /smuːð/ *adj* [Wa1] **1** having an even surface without sharply raised or lowered places, points, lumps, etc.; not rough: *The sea looks calm and smooth.|a smooth road*|(fig.) *make the way smooth to reaching an agreement* **2** even in movement without sudden changes or breaks: *bring a car to a smooth stop|a smooth dancer* **3** (of a liquid mixture) without lumps; evenly thick: *Beat until smooth* **4** (of a taste) not bitter or sour; pleasant in the mouth: *a smooth pipe tobacco* **5** very or too pleasant, polite, or untroubled in manner; avoiding or not showing difficulties: *Distrust a very smooth salesman* —see also **take the** ROUGH[2] (1) **with the smooth** —**~ly** *adv* —**~ness** *n* [U]

smooth[2] *v* [T1] **1** [(OUT, DOWN)] to make smooth(er): *smooth out a tablecloth|smooth down boards before painting* **2** [(AWAY)] to remove (roughness) from a surface: *a face cream that claims to smooth away* WRINKLEs

smooth·ie, smoothy /ˈsmuːði/ *n infml* a person with smooth manners; one who behaves with (too) easy grace

smooth o·ver *v adv* [T1] to make (difficulties) seem small or unimportant: *smooth over the bad feelings between opponents*

smor·gas·bord /ˈsmɔːgəsbɔːd‖ˈsmɔrgəsbord/ *n* [(C);U] (a restaurant meal in which people serve themselves from) a large number of different Scandinavian dishes

smote /sməʊt/ *past t. of* SMITE

smoth·er[1] /ˈsmʌðəʳ/ *n* [S] a SMOTHERing[2] (1) mass: *nearly covered in a smother of flowers thrown at her*

smother[2] *v* **1** [T1] to cover thickly or heavily: *cake smothered with/in cream* **2** [T1;IØ] to die or kill from lack of air; SUFFOCATE: *a baby smothered in bed accidentally* **3** [T1] to keep from developing, growing, or getting out; SUPPRESS: *succeed in smothering all opposition* **4** [T1] to put out or keep down (a fire) by keeping out air

smoul·der[1], *AmE* **smol-** /ˈsməʊldəʳ/ *n* [*usu. sing.*] a SMOULDERing[2] (1) fire

smoulder[2], *AmE* **smol-** *v* [Wv4;IØ] **1** to burn slowly without a flame **2** to have, be, or show violent feelings that are kept from being expressed: *smouldering anger|smouldering eyes*

smudge[1] /smʌdʒ/ *v* [T1;IØ] **1** to make or become dirty with a mark of rubbing: *He smudged the paper with his dirty hands.*|(fig.) *an accident smudging our clean safety record* **2** to (cause to) make such a mark

smudge[2] *n* **1** a dirty mark **2** *esp. AmE* a slow-burning outdoor fire for keeping away insects or (built in a **smudgepot**) for keeping fruit trees from freezing —**smudgy** *adj* [Wa1]

smug /smʌg/ *adj* **-gg-** [Wa1] too pleased with oneself; showing too much satisfaction with one's own qualities, position, etc. —**~ly** *adv* —**~ness** *n* [U]

smug·gle /ˈsmʌgəl/ *v* [X9] to take from one country to another unlawfully (esp. goods without paying the necessary tax (DUTY)): *It's a serious crime to smuggle an animal into Britain* —**-gler** *n* —**-gling** *n* [U]

smut[1] /smʌt/ *v* **-tt-** [T1] to get SMUT on; mark with SMUT

smut[2] *n* **1** [C;U] (a small piece of) material like dirt or SOOT that blackens or makes dark marks **2** [U] any of various FUNGUS diseases of grasses and grains that turn plant parts into black dust **3** [U] material for reading, hearing, or seeing that is morally improper and offensive

smut·ty /ˈsmʌti/ *adj* [Wa1] morally improper; OBSCENE: *a smutty joke/book* —**-tily** *adv* —**-tiness** *n* [U]

snack[1] /snæk/ *v* [IØ] *AmE* to eat small amounts between or instead of meals

snack[2] *n* an amount of food smaller than a meal; something eaten informally between meals

snack bar /ˈ· ·/ *n* an informal public eating place that serves SNACKs; place for buying and eating SANDWICHes, drinks, etc.

snaf·fle[1] /ˈsnæfəl/ also **snaffle bit** /ˈ·· ·/— *n* a kind of BIT[1] (1) made of 2 short joined bars, for putting in a horse's mouth

snaffle[2] *v* [T1] *BrE sl* **1** to take (a catch); catch (a ball), esp. easily **2** to steal; PINCH[1] (7)

snag[1] /snæg/ *n* **1** a dangerous rough sharp part of something that may catch and hold or cut things passing against it **2** a pulled thread in a cloth, esp.

a stocking **3** *esp. BrE* a hidden or unexpected difficulty

snag² *v* **-gg-** **1** [T1] to catch on a SNAG¹ (1): *The fishing line got snagged under water and had to be cut* **2** [D1 (*for*); T1] *AmE infml* to catch or get, esp. by quick action: *She snagged a nice profit on the sale*

snail /sneɪl/ *n* **1** any of several kinds of small animal (MOLLUSC) with a soft body, no limbs, and usu. a hard SPIRAL¹ (1)-shaped shell on its back —see picture at MOLLUSC **2 a snail's pace** *not fml* a very slow speed

snake¹ /sneɪk/ *n* **1** any of many kinds of cold-blooded animals (REPTILE*s*) with a long limbless body, large mouth, and fork-shaped tongue, usu. feeding on other animals and often with a poisonous bite **2** a tool with a very long ropelike metal end for twisting inside and unblocking pipes **3** a system in which the values of certain countries' money are allowed to vary against each other within narrow limits **4 a snake in the grass** *usu. humor* a false friend —see picture at REPTILE

snake² *v* [L9;X9] to move in a twisting way; wind (one's way or body) in moving: *a train snaking (its way) through the mountains*

snake·bite /ˈsneɪkbaɪt/ *n* [A;U] the result or condition of being bitten by a poisonous snake

snake charm·er /ˈ· ˌ··/ *n* a person who controls snakes, usu. by playing music

snakes and lad·ders /ˌ· · ˈ··/ *n* [U] a board game in which players may move pieces upwards and forwards along pictures of ladders and be forced downwards and backwards along pictures of snakes

snaky /ˈsneɪki/ *adj* [Wa1] like a snake, esp. in winding or twisting: *a snaky road|movement*

snap¹ /snæp/ *v* **-pp-** **1** [IØ (*at*);X9] to close the jaws quickly (on): *The dog snapped at my ankles|snapped the ball away and ran* **2** [IØ;T1] to (cause to) break suddenly off or in 2: *The branch snapped under all that snow: its weight was enough to snap it.*|(fig.) *My nerves at last snapped under the pressure of work* **3** [IØ;T1] to (cause to) make a sound as of either of these actions: *snap a whip* **4** [L9;X9] to move so as to cause such a short sound: *The lid snapped shut* **5** [T1] to say quickly, usu. in an annoyed or angry way **6** [T1] *infml* to photograph; take a SNAPSHOT of **7 snap one's fingers** to make a noise by moving the second finger quickly along the thumb **8 snap one's fingers at** to show no respect for: *If you continue to snap your fingers at your teachers you'll be severely punished!* **9 snap out of it** *infml* to make oneself quickly get free from a bad state of mind **10 snap someone's head off** *infml* to answer someone in a short rude way: *I just asked a simple question: there's no need to snap my head off!* **11 snap to it** (*AmE* also **snap it up**)— to hurry up: *Come on, men, snap to it!* —see also SNAP AT, SNAP BACK, SNAP UP

snap² *n* **1** [C] an act or sound of SNAPping¹ **2** [C] also **snap fas·tener** /ˌ· ˈ··/— a fastening made of 2 usu. small round metal parts that close and hold when pressed together **3** [C9] (*in comb.*) any of several kinds of thin dry sweet BISCUIT*s* (1) **4** [U] (in Britain) a type of card game in which players lay down cards one after the other and try to be the first to notice and call out SNAP⁴ (1) when 2 like cards are laid down together **5** [U] *infml* eager effort; ZIP² (3): *Come on, men: put some snap in it!* **6** [S] *AmE infml* a very easy task **7** [C;U] *NEngE* a worker's small meal for eating while working **8** [C] *infml* SNAPSHOT —see also COLD SNAP

snap³ *adj* [A] done, made, arrived at, etc., in haste or without (long) warning: *call a snap election to take place in 3 weeks*

snap⁴ *interj BrE* **1** (said in the game of SNAP² (4) when one notices that 2 like cards have been laid down) **2** *infml* (said when one notices 2 like things together): *Snap! You're wearing the same hat as me!*

snap at *v prep* [T1] **1** to accept or take eagerly: *snap at an invitation to the palace* **2** to answer (someone) rudely: *Don't try to be friendly to him: you'll only be snapped at*

snap·drag·on /ˈsnæpˌdrægən/ *n* also **antirrhinum**— a kind of garden plant with white, red, or yellow flowers suggesting the face of a DRAGON (1)

snap·per /ˈsnæpəʳ/ *n* [Wn2] any of a family of sport and food fish found in warm seas

snap·pish /ˈsnæpɪʃ/ *adj* speaking habitually in a rude annoyed way; bad-tempered; TESTY —**~ly** *adv* —**~ness** *n* [U]

snap·py /ˈsnæpi/ *adj* [Wa1] **1** full of SNAP² (5); LIVELY (1): *snappy conversation* **2** stylish; fashionable: *a snappy dresser* **3 Make it snappy!** (*BrE* also **Look snappy!**)— *infml* Hurry up! —**-pily** *adv* —**-piness** *n* [U]

snap·shot /ˈsnæpʃɒt‖-ʃɑt/ *n* an informal picture taken with a hand-held camera

snap up *v adv* [T1] to take or buy quickly and eagerly: *snap up a* BARGAIN¹ (2)

snare¹ /ˈsneəʳ/ *n* **1** a trap for catching an animal, esp. an apparatus with a rope which catches the animal's foot **2** [*often pl. with sing. meaning*] something in which one may be caught; a course which leads to being trapped **3** any of the metal strings on the bottom of a SNARE DRUM

snare² *v* [T1] **1** to catch (as if) in a SNARE¹ (1): *to snare a rabbit* **2** to get by skilful action: *snare a good job*

snare drum /ˈ· ·/ *n* a small flat military kind of drum used also in bands, having metal springs stretched across the bottom to allow a continuous sound —see picture at PERCUSSION

snarl¹ /snɑːl‖snɑrl/ *n* [*usu. sing.*] a knotty twisted confused mass or state; TANGLE

snarl² *v* [T1 (UP) *usu. pass.*] to put into a SNARL¹; make confused or difficult; TANGLE: *Traffic was badly snarled (up) near the accident*

snarl³ *v* **1** [IØ] (of an animal) to make a low angry sound while showing the teeth **2** [IØ;T1] (of a person) to speak or say in an angry bad-tempered way

snarl⁴ *n* an act or sound of SNARLing³; angry GROWL

snarl-up /ˈ· ·/ *n* a confused state, esp. of traffic

snatch¹ /snætʃ/ *v* **1** [T1;IØ] to get hold of (something) hastily; take in a hurry, esp. forcefully: *The thief snatched her handbag and ran.|The boy was snatched from his home by 2 armed men* **2** [T1] to take quickly as chance allows, often wrongfully or without permission: *snatch a kiss|Death snatched him at a young age* —**~er** *n*

snatch² *n* **1** [(*at*)] an act of SNATCHing (at) something: *He made a brave snatch at victory but failed at last* **2** [*usu. pl.*] a short period of time or activity: *to sleep in snatches, waking up often* **3** a short and incomplete part of something that is seen or heard

snatch at *v prep* [T1] to try to SNATCH; make every effort to get: *snatch at a chance*

snaz·zy /ˈsnæzi/ *adj* [Wa1] *infml* good-looking in a neat, stylish, or showy way

sneak¹ /sniːk/ *v* **1** [L9;X9] to (cause to) go quietly and secretly; go or take so as not to be seen: *sneak past a guard|sneak around to the back door* **2** [T1] *sl* to steal secretly: *a boy caught sneaking an apple from a shop* **3** [IØ (*on*)] *BrE school sl* to give information, esp. to a teacher, about the wrongdoings (of another pupil)

sneak² *n* **1** [C] *not fml* a SNEAKY person; one who acts secretly and should not be trusted **2** [A] *not*

fml unexpected; secret until the last moment; surprise **3** [C] *BrE school sl* a person who SNEAKs[1] (3)
sneak·er /ˈsniːkəʳ/ *n esp. AmE* a cloth shoe with a bendable rubber bottom, worn esp. for sports
sneak·ing /ˈsniːkɪŋ/ *adj* [A] **1** secret; not expressed, as if shameful: *a sneaking desire to go into politics* **2** (of a feeling or SUSPICION (1,2)) not proved but probably right: *a sneaking feeling that the plan won't work*
sneak thief /ˈ· ·/ *n* a thief who takes things within reach without using force
sneak up *v adv* [I∅ (*on*)] to come near (to someone), keeping out of sight until the last moment: *Don't sneak up on/behind me like that! You gave me quite a shock!*
sneak·y /ˈsniːki/ *adj* [Wa1] *not fml* acting or done secretly and deceitfully —**sneakiness** *n* [U]
sneer[1] /snɪəʳ/ *v* [I∅] **1** to express proud dislike by a kind of usu. one-sided smile **2** [(*at*)] to act proudly; treat something as if not worthy of serious notice: *a piece of work not to be sneered at* —**~er** *n* —**~ingly** *adv*
sneer[2] *n* a SNEERing expression of the face, way of speaking, or remark
sneeze[1] /sniːz/ *v* [I∅] **1** to have a sudden uncontrolled burst of air out of the nose and mouth, usu. caused by discomfort in the nose: *The dust made him sneeze* **2 not to be sneezed at** *infml, often humor* worthy of consideration; not to be considered unfavourably
sneeze[2] *n* an act, sound, etc., of sneezing (SNEEZE)
snick[1] /snɪk/ *v* [T1] **1** to make a small cut or mark on **2** (in cricket) to hit (the ball) off the edge of the BAT
snick[2] *n* **1** a small cut or mark: NICK[2] (1) **2** (in cricket) a hit made off the edge of the BAT
snick·er /ˈsnɪkəʳ/ *v, n* [I∅;C] **1** *esp. BrE* ((of a horse) to make) a long low sound; WHINNY **2** [(*at*)] *esp. AmE* SNIGGER
snide /snaɪd/ *adj* [Wa1] intending or intended to hurt the feelings in a pretendedly funny way; MEAN[1] (2); INSINUATING —**~ly** *adv* —**~ness** *n* [U]
sniff[1] /snɪf/ *v* **1** [I∅ (*at*)] to draw air into the nose with a sound, esp. in short repeated actions **2** [T1] to do this to discover a smell in or on: *dogs sniffing the ground* **3** [T1] to say in a proud complaining way: *"I expected something rather nicer," she sniffed* **4** [T1] *sl* to take (a harmful drug) through the nose; INHALE —**~er** *n*
sniff[2] *n* an act or sound of SNIFFing
sniff at *v prep* [T1] to dislike or refuse proudly (esp. in the phr. **not to be sniffed at**): *You shouldn't sniff at such a good offer*
snif·fle[1] /ˈsnɪfəl/ also **snuffle**— *v* [I∅] to SNIFF repeatedly in order to keep liquid from running out the nose, as when one is crying or has a cold —**-fler** *n*
sniffle[2] also **snuffle**— *n* an act or sound of sniffling (SNIFFLE)
snif·fles /ˈsnɪfəlz/ also **snuffles**— *n* [(*the*) P] *not fml* the signs of a cold in the nose; liquid blocking or running from the nose
sniff·y /ˈsnɪfi/ *adj* [Wa1] *infml* **1** unpleasantly proud by habit **2** *BrE* having a bad smell, esp. as a result of long disuse or spoiling
snif·ter /ˈsnɪftəʳ/ *n* **1** *esp. BrE* a small amount of an alcoholic drink **2** *AmE* a short-stemmed bowl-like glass that grows narrower at the top, for drinking BRANDY
snig·ger[1] /ˈsnɪgəʳ/ also (*esp. AmE*) **snicker**— *v* [I∅ (*at*)] to laugh in a disrespectful more or less secret way
snigger[2] also (*esp. AmE*) **snicker**— *n* an act or sound of SNIGGERing
snip[1] /snɪp/ *n* **1** a short quick cut with scissors: *make a snip in the cloth* **2** a small piece (cut off); bit **3** [*usu. sing.*] *BrE infml* an attractive and surprisingly cheap article for sale; BARGAIN[1] (2)
snip[2] *v* **-pp-** [X9, esp. OFF] to cut (as if) with scissors, esp. in short quick strokes: *snip off the corner of a packet|snip a hole in the paper*
snipe[1] /snaɪp/ *n* [Wn2] any of several birds with very long thin beaks, living in wet places and often shot for sport
snipe[2] *v* [I∅ (*at*)] **1** to shoot from a hidden position at unprotected people (such as an enemy not in battle) **2** to attack a person or thing in an indirect way; make repeated small attacks —**sniper** *n*
snip·pet /ˈsnɪpɪ̈t/ *n* [(*of*)] a small bit of something, esp. a short piece from something spoken or written
snips /snɪps/ *n* [P] heavy scissors for cutting metal sheets —see PAIR (USAGE)
snitch[1] /snɪtʃ/ *v infml* **1** [I∅ (*on*)] to tell about the wrongdoings of a friend **2** [T1] to steal (esp. something of no great value)
snitch[2] *n BrE infml, usu. humor* nose
sniv·el /ˈsnɪvəl/ *v* **-ll-** (*AmE* **-l-**) [I∅] **1** to have liquid blocking or coming from the nose; SNIFFLE **2** to act or speak in a weak complaining crying way: *If you fail, don't come snivelling back to me* —**~ler** (*AmE* **~er**) *n*
snob /snɒb‖snɑb/ *n* **1** a person who dislikes or keeps away from those he feels to be of lower social class **2** *now rare* a person who admires people of a higher social class **3** [C9] a person who is too proud of having special knowledge or judgment in a subject: *a kind of musical snob who thinks that no one after Mozart was any good*
snob·be·ry /ˈsnɒbəri‖ˈsnɑb-/ *n* [U] the practice or talk of SNOBs; SNOBBISH action or language
snob·bish /ˈsnɒbɪʃ‖ˈsnɑ-/ also **snob·by** /ˈsnɒbi‖ˈsnɑbi/— *adj* [Wa1] typical of a SNOB, esp. proud about one's social position or knowledge —**~ly** *adv* —**~ness** *n* [U]
snog[1] /snɒg‖snɑg/ *v* **-gg-** [I∅] *BrE infml* to kiss
snog[2] *n* [S] *BrE infml* an act of SNOGging[1]
snood /snuːd/ *n* an ornamental thick net for holding in a woman's hair at the back; type of HAIRNET
snook /snuːk‖snʊk, snuːk/ *n* **cock a snook at** *esp. BrE* to express disrespect for, as by spreading one hand out with the thumb touching the nose
snoo·ker[1] /ˈsnuːkəʳ‖ˈsnʊ-/ *n* [U] a BILLIARDS game played on a table with 6 pockets, with 15 red balls and 6 balls of other colours
snooker[2] *v* [T1 *often pass.*] *infml* to put into a difficult position; trap, trick, or defeat (someone, a plan, etc.)
snoop[1] /snuːp/ *v* [I∅] *not fml* to search, look into, or concern oneself with others' property without permission, or something not one's concern
snoop[2] *n infml* a person who SNOOPs, esp. one employed as a DETECTIVE, SPY, etc.
snoop·er /ˈsnuːpəʳ/ *n infml* a person who SNOOPs
snoot /snuːt/ *n sl, esp. AmE* the nose
snoot·y /ˈsnuːti/ *adj* [Wa1] *infml* proudly rude; SUPERCILIOUS: *He's too snooty to be interested in his old friends now he's rich* —**snootily** *adv* —**snootiness** *n* [U]
snooze[1] /snuːz/ *v* [I∅] *infml* to have a short sleep; DOZE
snooze[2] *n* [*usu. sing.*] *infml* a short sleep; NAP
snore[1] /snɔːʳ‖snor/ *v* [I∅] to breathe heavily and noisily through the nose and mouth while asleep —**snorer** *n*
snore[2] *n* a noisy way of breathing when asleep; a noise of snoring (SNORE)
snor·kel /ˈsnɔːkəl‖-ɔr-/ *n* an air tube that can rise

above the surface of water, as for allowing a swimmer under water to breathe or for carrying air to a SUBMARINE

snort[1] /snɔːt‖snɔrt/ *v* **1** [IØ] to make a rough noise by blowing air down the nose **2** [IØ;T1] to express (esp. impatience or anger, or sometimes amusement) (as) by this sound: *"Certainly not," he snorted*

snort[2] *n* **1** an act or sound of SNORTing **2** *infml* a drink of strong alcohol taken with one act of swallowing

snort·er /ˈsnɔːtəʳ‖-ɔr-/ *n* [*usu. sing.*] *infml* something that is unusually fine or esp. violent, powerful, difficult, etc.

snot /snɒt‖snɑt/ *n* [U] *taboo* the thick liquid (MUCUS) produced in the nose

snot·ty /ˈsnɒti‖ˈsnɑti/ *adj* [Wa1] *sl* **1** also **snotty-nosed** /ˈ·· ·/— trying to act as if one is important; rude **2** wet with SNOT: *a snotty nose*

snout[1] /snaʊt/ *n* the long nose of any of various animals (such as pigs) —see picture at FARMYARD

snout[2] *n BrE sl* **1** [U] tobacco **2** [C] a cigarette

snow[1] /snəʊ/ *n* **1** [U] water frozen into small flat 6-sided white bits (FLAKEs) that fall like rain in cold weather and may cover the ground thickly **2** [C] a fall of this: *one of the heaviest snows this winter* **3** [U] *sl* COCAINE in powder form

snow[2] *v* **1** [*it*+IØ] (of snow) to fall: *Look! It's snowing* **2** [T1] *AmE sl* to persuade or win the respect of (someone), as by making oneself sound important: *I was really snowed by his smooth manners and wild stories* —see also SNOW IN, SNOW UNDER

snow·ball[1] /ˈsnəʊbɔːl/ *n* **1** a ball pressed or rolled together from snow, as thrown at each other by children **2 a snowball's chance in hell** *infml* no chance at all (of succeeding, lasting, etc.)

snowball[2] *v* [IØ] *not fml* to increase in size faster and faster or uncontrolledly: *The effect of rising prices has snowballed*

snow·ber·ry /ˈsnəʊbəri, -beri‖-ˌberi/ *n* a type of garden bush with pink flowers and white berries

snow-blind /ˈ· ·/ *adj* suffering from SNOW BLINDNESS

snow blind·ness /ˈ· ˌ··/ *n* [U] pain and (near) blindness for a time, caused by long looking at snow in bright sunlight

snow·bound /ˈsnəʊbaʊnd/ *adj* blocked or kept indoors by heavy snow

snow-capped /ˈ· ·/ *adj* [Wa5] *lit* (of a mountain) covered in snow at the top

snow-clad /ˈ· ·/ *adj lit* covered in snow

snow·drift /ˈsnəʊˌdrɪft/ *n* a deep bank or mass of snow formed by the wind

snow·drop /ˈsnəʊdrɒp‖-drɑp/ *n* a type of European small white flower which appears in the early spring, often when snow is still on the ground

snow·fall /ˈsnəʊfɔːl/ *n* **1** [C] a fall of snow **2** [U; S] the amount of snow that falls: *an average snowfall of 5 inches per year*

snow·field /ˈsnəʊfiːld/ *n* a wide stretch of ground always covered in snow

snow·flake /ˈsnəʊfleɪk/ *n* one of, or a small mass of, the small flat 6-sided bits of frozen water which fall as snow

snow in also **snow up**— *v adv* [T1 *usu. pass.*] (as of snow) to pile up on the ground, roads, etc., so as to keep (people) from travelling or prevent going to or from (a place): *The valley is snowed in most of the winter*

snow leop·ard /ˈ· ˌ··/ also **ounce**— *n* a type of large wild cat that lives in the high areas of central Asia, and has pale greyish-white fur with dark spots

snow·line /ˈsnəʊlaɪn/ *n* [*the*+R] the imaginary line (as on a mountainside) above which snow never melts

snow·man /ˈsnəʊmæn/ *n* **-men** /men/ a figure of a man made out of snow, esp. by children

snow·plough, *AmE* **-plow** /ˈsnəʊplaʊ/ *n* an apparatus or vehicle for pushing snow off roads or railways

snow·shoe /ˈsnəʊʃuː/ *n* a light flat frame around a strong net, for fastening in pairs under the shoes, to allow a person to walk on snow without sinking in

snow·storm /ˈsnəʊstɔːm‖-ɔrm/ *n* a very heavy fall of snow, esp. blown by strong winds

snow un·der *v adv* [T1 (*with*) *usu. pass.*] *not fml* to load too heavily (as with work or things to do); OVERWHELM (3): *snowed under with invitations to parties*

snow-white /ˌ· ˈ·◂/ *adj* as white as snow; pure white

snow·y /ˈsnəʊi/ *adj* [Wa1] **1** full of snow or snowing **2** pure (white): *snowy (white) hair* —**snowiness** *n* [U]

Snr *BrE written abbrev. for:* SENIOR

snub[1] /snʌb/ *v* **-bb-** [T1 *often pass.*] to treat rudely as by paying no attention to

snub[2] *n* an act of SNUBbing

snub[3] *adj* [Wa5;A;(B)] (of a nose) flat and short; STUBBY

snub-nosed /ˌ· ˈ·◂/ *adj* **1** having a SNUB[3] nose **2** [Wa5] (of a handgun) having a very short barrel

snuff[1] /snʌf/ *v* [T1] **1** to cut the black burnt end of the central string (WICK) from (a candle), usu. with a scissor-like tool (a pair of **snuffers**) **2 snuff it** *BrE sl* to die

snuff[2] *v* [T1;IØ] (esp. of animals) to draw (air or a smell) into the nose with a sound; SNIFF

snuff[3] *n* [*usu. sing.*] an act of SNUFFing; a breath taken in

snuff[4] *n* [U] tobacco made into powder for breathing into the nose, esp. used in former times

snuff·er /ˈsnʌfəʳ/ *n* a tool with a small bell-shaped end on a handle, for putting out candles

snuf·fle /ˈsnʌfəl/ *v, n* [IØ;C] SNIFFLE

snuff out *v adv* [T1] **1** to put out (a candle flame), esp. by pressing a cover over it for a moment or by pressing it with the fingers **2** to put an end to; EXTINGUISH: *the time when the learning of the ancient world had been snuffed out*

snug[1] /snʌg/ *adj* [Wa1] **1** giving or enjoying WARMTH, comfort, peace, protection, etc.; COSY: *a snug little room with a fire going|sitting snug by the fire* **2** (as of clothes) fitting closely, or sometimes too tightly —**~ly** *adv* —**~ness** *n* [U]

snug[2] *n BrE* a small room or enclosed place for sitting privately, esp. in an inn

snug·gle /ˈsnʌgəl/ *v* [L9, esp. UP; X9] to move or lie close for WARMTH and comfort; NESTLE: *children snuggling up/down in bed|She snuggled (her cheek) against his shoulder*

so[1] /səʊ/ *adv* [Wa5] **1** in the way I show: *Watch me do it: you should push the needle through (just) so.|(infml) Cut the apples up like so* **2** in that way; in the way stated: *She was washing her hair. While she was so employed, she heard a noise* **3** (often in the phrs. **so . . . that, so . . . as to**) **a** to such a degree: *The statement was so clear (that) it couldn't be misunderstood.|The windows are so small as not to admit much light at all.|He couldn't get through the door, he was so fat.|He held his hands a foot apart, and said "The fish was so long."|Don't be so silly!|(fml) I've never seen so beautiful a child.|You mustn't worry so.|So much more difficult* —see SUCH (USAGE) **b** in such a way: *The book is so written as to give a quite wrong idea of the facts.|It (so) happens that we have the same birthday.|As it (so)* *happens, we have the same birthday* **4** (used in place of an idea, expression, etc., stated already, esp. after a verb marked [5b]): *He hopes he'll win and I hope so too.|If you're going to go out you'd better do so quickly.|Are you married? If so* (= If that is true), *give your wife's name.|If you say so I'll have to believe it.|"God said, 'Let the dry land appear.' And it was so"* (The Bible).|*Martha's got a job, or so she tells me* —compare NOT **5** (*followed by* be, have, do, *or a* MODAL *verb and then its subject*) in the same way; also: *You have pride and so have I.|I enjoyed the book and so did my wife.|If my brother is allowed to go out, so should I be.|"The Irish were tribes." "Well, so were the Scots"* (SEU S.) **6** (*followed by a subject and then* have, do, *or a* MODAL *verb*) indeed; certainly: *"Father, you promised!" "Well, so I did."|I hoped to win and so I shall* **7** *infml* very: *We're so glad you could come!|Thank you; you've been so (very) kind* **8** up to a limit; to a certain degree: *Stop telling me to hurry up; my legs will go just so fast and no faster!* **9** *not SEngE* (*used esp. by children, for answering a charge or statement with* not): *"I didn't do it." "You did so! You did so do it!"* **10 and so on/forth** and other things of this kind; and continuing: *things like pots, pans, dishes, and so forth|He counted 1, 2, 3, and so on up to 100* **11 as . . . so** in the way/time that . . ., in that same way/time: *As the wind blew harder, so the sea grew rougher* **12 even so** even in this case: *Even if you're right—even so, it doesn't prove anything* **13 just as . . . so** as it is true that . . . it is equally true that: *Just as French people enjoy their wine, so the British enjoy their beer* **14 Just so** also **Quite so**—*BrE* Yes; I agree **15 or so** more or less; about: *It'll only cost 15p or so* **16 so . . . as** [*usu. nonassertive*] (in comparisons) as . . . as: *not so foolish as I thought|He's never again written so good a book as his first one* —see also **so** LONG² (3) **as, in so** FAR¹ (10) **as**; see AS (USAGE) **17 so as to a** in order to: *The test questions are kept secret, so as to prevent cheating* **b** in such a way as to: *The day was dark, so as to make a good photograph hard to get* —see ORDER (USAGE) **18 So long!** *infml* Goodbye! —see also LONG **19 so many/much a** a certain number/amount: *a charge of so much per day* **b** an amount equal to; all: *All these silly books are just so much waste paper!* —see also FAR, **so** MUCH¹ (9) **for, so** MUCH² (10) **as, so** MUCH² (9) **the**

so² *conj* **1** with the result that: *I had broken my glasses, so (I) couldn't see what was happening.|I'm busy today, so can you come tomorrow?|He wrote a famous book, and so got a place in history* **2** with the purpose (that): *I packed him a little food so (that) he wouldn't get hungry* **3** therefore: *I had a headache, so I went to bed* **4** (*used at the beginning of a sentence*) **a** (with weak meaning): *So here we are again* **b** (to express discovery): *So now I see what's been happening!* **c** what if?; what does it matter that?: *So, I made a mistake. What are you going to do about it?* **5 just so** *not fml* as long as; if only: *Just so he gets his 3 meals a day he doesn't care what happens* **6 so what?** *infml* Why is that important? Why should I care?

so³ *adj* [F] **1** [Wa5] in agreement with the facts; true: *some statements that just aren't so|If what you say is really so, I'll have to change my plans* **2** (used in place of an adjective already stated): *Of all the careless people no one is more so than Bill.|He's clever—probably too much so for his own good* **3 just so** arranged exactly and tidily: *If everything is not just so, he'll be angry*·

soak¹ /səʊk/ *v* **1** [I∅;T1: (*in*)] to (cause to) remain in a liquid, esp. to become soft or completely wet: *Leave the dirty clothes to soak.|He likes to soak himself in a warm bath* **2** [L9, esp. IN, *into, through*; T1 *usu. pass*] (of a liquid) to enter (a solid) through the material of a surface: *The ink had soaked through the thin paper.|a rain-soaked field* **3** [X9, esp. OUT] to remove by keeping or washing well in water: *The packet says this soap is the best for soaking out dirt* **4** [T1] *infml* to charge a very high amount of money to: *an unpleasant town where they enjoy soaking the tourists* —see also SOAKED

soak² *n* **1** an act or state of SOAKing (1) **2** *sl* a person who is often or usually drunk

soaked /səʊkt/ *adj* [F] **1** thoroughly wet, as from rain: *My dear, you're soaked! Take off those wet clothes!* **2** [+*with* or *in*] full; RIFE; STEEPed: *a place soaked in memories* **3** *sl* drunk

soak·ing /ˈsəʊkɪŋ/ *adv, adj* very wet

soak up *v adv* [T1] **1** to draw in (as a liquid) through a surface: *He got out his handkerchief to soak up the blood.|The ground soaked up the rain* **2** to receive (blows, an attack, etc.) without suffering too much harm: *The fighter had to soak up a lot of punishment* (= hard blows) *towards the end of the fight*

so-and-so /ˈ· · ˌ·/ *n* **so-and-sos** **1** [U] someone or something; a certain one (not to be named): *a list of givers, with so-and-so saying he'll give £5, so-and-so £2, etc.* —compare SUCH AND SUCH **2** [C] *euph* (used instead of a stronger word like BASTARD¹) a rude, wicked, etc., person: *John's usually all right but he can be a so-and-so at times*

soap¹ /səʊp/ *n* [U] **1** a product made from fat and ALKALI, for use with water to clean the body or other things: *a* BAR/TABLET/*cake of soap|soap powder|a box of soap* FLAKE*s for washing clothes* —compare DETERGENT and see picture at BATHROOM **2 no soap** *AmE infml* no results or success: *I tried to persuade him, but no soap* —see also SOFT SOAP

soap² *v* [T1 (UP)] to rub soap on or over: *soap (up) one's hands and make a* LATHER

soap·box /ˈsəʊpbɒks‖-bɑks/ *n not fml* **1** [C] a real or imaginary box for someone to stand on to give a speech to a crowd outdoors: *He got on his soapbox and told the people in Hyde Park what he thought* **2** [A] of or concerning informal outdoor speech-making

soap bub·ble /ˈ· ˌ··/ *n* a ball of air enclosed by a film of soap

soap op·e·ra /ˈ· ˌ···/ *n not fml* a daily or weekly continuing television or radio story (SERIAL) which is usu. about the characters' private troubles

soap·stone /ˈsəʊpstəʊn/ *n* [U] a kind of soft stone which feels like soap

soap·suds /ˈsəʊpsʌdz/ *n* [P] SUDS

soap·y /ˈsəʊpi/ *adj* [Wa1] **1** containing or full of soap **2** like soap **3** *infml* falsely or too pleasant: *a soapy voice* **4** *infml* like SOAP OPERA; MELODRAMATIC —**soapiness** *n* [U]

soar /sɔːʳ‖sor/ *v* [I∅] *esp. lit* **1** to fly; go fast or high (as) on wings; sail in the air: *birds soaring over the hills* **2** [Wv4] to go upward, esp. far or fast: *The temperature soared to 80° on May 1* **3** [Wv4] to go beyond what is ordinary or limiting: *a soaring imagination* **4** [Wv4,6] to be very high; TOWER: *soaring mountains/buildings|The cliffs soar 500 feet into the air* **5** (of a motorless aircraft (GLIDER) or people in it) to go through the air

sob¹ /sɒb‖sɑb/ *v* **-bb-** **1** [I∅] to breathe while weeping, in sudden short bursts making a sound in the throat: *a little girl sitting and sobbing in the corner* **2** [T1 (OUT)] to say or tell by weeping: *He sobbed out the whole sad story* **3** [X9] to bring by weeping: *She sobbed herself to sleep* —**sobbingly** *adv*

sob² *n* an uncontrolled short breath while weeping; a sound of SOBbing

so·ber¹ /ˈsəʊbəʳ/ *adj* [Wa2] **1** in control of oneself;

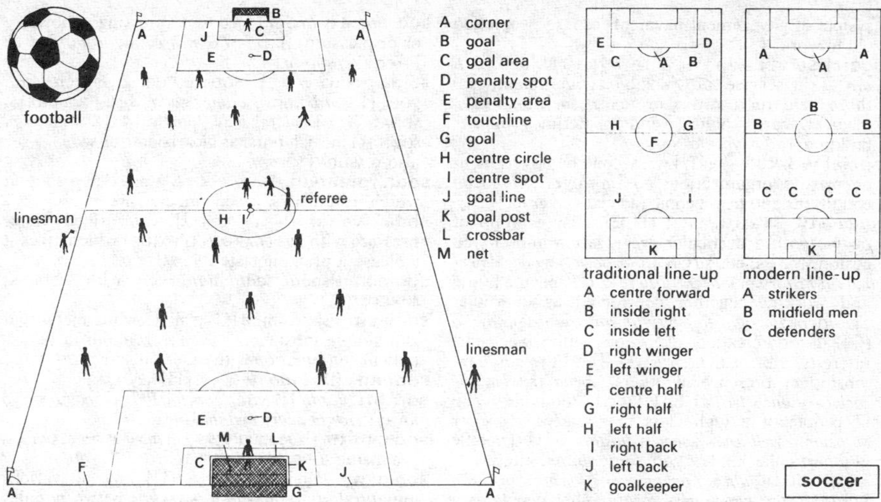

not drunk **2** thoughtful, serious, or solemn; not silly; GRAVE² (1) **3** not ornamental or brightly-coloured; RESTRAINED —**~ly** *adv*

sober² *v* [Wv4;T1;IØ: (DOWN)] to make or become serious or thoughtful: *Her illness had a sobering effect on her spirits*

sober up *v adv* [T1;IØ] *not fml* to make or become SOBER¹ (1); get or be rid of the effect of alcohol: *I hope this coffee may sober him up*

so·bri·e·ty /səˈbraɪəti/ *n* [U] *usu. lit* the quality or state of being SOBER¹ (1)

so·bri·quet /ˈsəʊbrɪkeɪ/ also **soubriquet**— *n lit* an unofficial name or title; NICKNAME

sob sto·ry /ˈ· ˌ··/ *n not fml* a story intended to make the hearer or reader cry, feel pity, or feel sorry

so-called /ˌ· ˈ·◂/ *adj* [Wa5;A] **1** called or named the stated thing: *the so-called "Social Contract" between the government and unions* **2** improperly or falsely named so: *so-called Christians who show no love to anyone*

soc·cer /ˈsɒkəʳ‖ˈsɑ-/ *BrE* also **football, Association Football**— *n* [U] a football game between 2 teams of 11 players who kick or touch a round ball without using the arms or hands

so·cia·ble /ˈsəʊʃəbəl/ *adj* fond of being with others; enjoying social life; friendly —**-bility** /ˌsəʊʃəˈbɪlɪ̈ti/ *n* [U] —**-bly** /ˈsəʊʃəbli/ *adv*
USAGE It is better to use **sociable**, rather than **social**, to mean "cheerful and friendly": *to spend a* **sociable** *evening drinking.* **Social** is never used of people: *We're very* **sociable** (not ***social**) *in our office!* Use **social** to mean **a** "connected with society": **social** *history* **b** "connected with living in a group and meeting people": *her busy* **social** *life.*

so·cial¹ /ˈsəʊʃəl/ *adj* **1** [Wa5;B] of or concerning human society, its organization, or quality of life: *opinions on various social questions* **2** [Wa5;B] based on rank in society (sometimes different from wealth or political power): *Marriage isn't always easy between 2 people of different social class(es)* **3** [B] of, concerning, or spent in time or activities with friends: *social drinking|proper social behaviour* **4** [Wa5;A] for or concerned with friendly or nonbusiness gatherings: *a social club* **5** [B] forming groups or living together by nature: *social insects like ants* **6** [B] fond of being with others; SOCIABLE: *I'm not feeling very social this evening* —**~ly** *adv*

social² *AmE* also **sociable**— *n* a planned informal friendly gathering of members of a group or esp. church

social an·thro·pol·o·gy /ˌ·· ··ˈ···/ *n* [U] the study of the customs, beliefs, behaviour, and organization of human societies —compare PHYSICAL ANTHROPOLOGY

social climb·er /ˌ·· ˈ··/ *n derog* a person who spends money or tries to make friends in order to be accepted in society of a higher class

social de·moc·ra·cy /ˌ·· ·ˈ···/ *n* [U] the aim of politicians (**social democrats**), esp. in W Europe, who support many of the aims of SOCIALISM

so·cial·is·m /ˈsəʊʃəlɪzəm/ *n* [U] (*sometimes cap.*) any of various beliefs or systems (sometimes considered to include COMMUNISM) aiming at public ownership of the means of production and the establishment of a society in which every person is equal

so·cial·ist¹ /ˈsəʊʃəlɪ̈st/ *n* **1** a believer in SOCIALISM **2** (*usu. cap.*) a member of a SOCIALIST political party —see also SOCIALIST² (USAGE)

socialist² *adj* **1** of, concerning, or following SOCIALISM **2** [Wa5] (*usu. cap.*) of, concerning, or favouring any of various esp. W European parties who support more equality of wealth and government ownership of business
USAGE The British LABOUR PARTY is sometimes informally called **the Socialist Party** or **the Socialists**, esp. by its opponents.

so·cia·lite /ˈsəʊʃəl-aɪt/ *n* a person well known for going to many fashionable parties

so·cial·ize, -ise /ˈsəʊʃəl-aɪz/ *v* **1** [T1 *usu. pass.*] to bring into public ownership: *Some services must be socialized for the public good* **2** [IØ (*with*)] to spend time with others in a friendly way: *There will be no socializing during business hours!* **3** [T1] *tech* to cause to fit into a society: *Schools do part of the job of socializing children* —**-ization** /ˌsəʊʃəlaɪˈzeɪʃən‖-ʃələ-/ *n* [U]

socialized medi·cine /ˌ··· ˈ··/ *n* [U] *AmE* medical care provided by a government and paid for by taxes —compare NATIONAL HEALTH SERVICE

social sci·ence /ˌ·· ˈ··‖ˈ·· ˌ··/ *n* **1** [U] also **social stud·ies** /ˈ·· ˌ··/— the study of people in society, usu. including history, politics, ECONOMICS, SOCIOLOGY, and ANTHROPOLOGY **2** [C] any of these: *the social sciences*

social se·cu·ri·ty /ˌ·· ·ˈ···/ *n* [U] **1** (*AmE* **welfare**)— *BrE* government money paid to people without jobs, old, ill, etc. **2** *AmE* (*often cap.*) the system of government payments esp. to people too old to work

social serv·ice /ˌ·· ˈ··‖ˈ·· ˌ··/ *n* [*usu. pl.*] *esp. BrE* any of the services provided by a government, esp. those paid for (partly) by taxes, such as roads, medical care, police, and sometimes house-building, railways, etc.

social work /ˈ·· ·/ *n* [U] work done by government or private organizations to improve bad social conditions and help people in need —**~er** *n*

so·ci·e·ty /səˈsaɪəti/ *n* **1** [U;C] a large group of people with a particular organization and shared customs, laws, etc.: *Is Western society going downhill?|a history of ancient society* **2** [U] people living and working together considered as a whole: *Society has a right to expect obedience of the law* **3** [C] an organization of people with like aims, interests, etc.: *a film society* **4** [U9] the companionship or presence of others: *spend time in the society of one's friends* **5** [U] the fashionable group of people of a high class in a place: *a society occasion|a well-known society hostess* **6** [U9] people of a particular kind or with some shared interest: *a remark that would not pass in polite society*

USAGE *The* **community** means other people as a whole, compared to one single person: *Keep the streets clean for the good of the* **community**. It is a less general word than **society**, though both may often be used: *the treatment of young criminals in the modern* **community**/*in modern* **society**. **Mankind** means everyone who is human, without political considerations; it is the most general word of all: *a great medical discovery for the good of* **mankind**.

so·cio- /ˈsəʊʃəʊ/ *comb. form usu. tech* **1** [→*adj*] social and: *sociopolitical causes of unrest|a family anxious not to lose its socio*ECONOMIC *position* **2** [→*n, adj*] social; of society: SOCIOLOGY

so·ci·ol·o·gy /ˌsəʊsiˈɒlədʒi, ˌsəʊʃi-‖-ˈɑlə-/ *n* [U] the scientific study of societies and human behaviour in groups —**-gical** /ˌsəʊsɪəˈlɒdʒɪkəl, ˌsəʊʃɪə-‖-ˈlɑ-/ *adj* [Wa5] —**-gically** *adv* [Wa4] —**-gist** /ˌsəʊsiˈɒlədʒəst, ˌsəʊʃi-‖-ˈɑl-/ *n*

sock¹ /sɒk‖sɑk/ *n* **1** a covering of soft material for the foot and usu. part of the lower leg, usu. worn inside a shoe: *knee socks* (coming up to the knee) **2 pull one's socks up** *BrE infml* to make an effort to put oneself right **3 put a sock in it** *humor, esp. BrE* to keep quiet; stop talking

sock² *v* [T1] *infml* **1** to strike hard: *He socked his opponent on the jaw* **2 sock it to someone** *esp. AmE* to express oneself or behave forcefully: *It was a great performance: you really socked it to them!*

sock³ *n* [*usu. sing.*] *infml* a forceful blow, esp. with the closed hand

sock⁴ *adv* [Wa5;H] *sl, esp. BrE* (of the giving of a blow) firmly and exactly: *He hit him sock on the jaw*

sock·et /ˈsɒkət‖ˈsɑ-/ *n* an opening, hollow place, or machine part that forms a holder or into which something fits: *His eyes nearly jumped from their sockets in surprise.|bone/tooth sockets|fit a candle/an electric light* BULB *into a socket* —see picture at ELECTRICITY, TOOL¹

So·crat·ic meth·od /səˌkrætɪk ˈmeθəd/ *n* [*the*+R] the method (used by the Greek PHILOSOPHER (2) Socrates) of discovering unexpected truths or proving a point by asking clever questions

sod¹ /sɒd‖sɑd/ *n* **1** [U] earth with grass and roots growing in it **2** [C] a piece of this

sod² *n BrE sl* **1** a man thought to be foolish and/or annoying: *You (selfish) sod!|a lot of silly sods* **2** (used in expressions of good or kind feeling) fellow: *a nice old sod* **3** something that causes a lot of trouble or difficulty: *That job's a real sod!* **4 not give/care a sod** not to care at all

sod³ *v* **sod it** *BrE sl* (used for expressing annoyance or displeasure) HELL²: *I've missed my train. Sod it!* —see also SOD OFF

so·da /səʊdə/ *n* **1** [U] SODA WATER **2** [U] *esp. AmE* POP² (2): *a bottle of orange soda* **3** [C] ICE-CREAM SODA: *A chocolate soda, please* **4** [U] *not fml* SODIUM (in such phrs. as **bicarbonate of soda**) —see also WASHING SODA

soda foun·tain /ˈ·· ˌ··/ *n AmE* a place in a shop at which fruit drinks, ice cream, etc., are served

soda wa·ter /ˈ·· ˌ··/ *n* [U] water filled under pressure with gas (CARBON DIOXIDE) which gives it a pleasant pricking taste

sod·den /ˈsɒdn‖ˈsɑdn/ *adj* heavy with wetness; SOAKed¹ (2)

so·di·um /ˈsəʊdɪəm/ *n* [U] a silver-white metal that is a simple substance (ELEMENT), found in nature only in combination with other substances

sodium chlo·ride /ˌ··· ˈ··/ *n* [U] *tech* SALT

sod off *v adv* [IØ *usu. imper.*] *BrE taboo sl* to go away: *He got angry and told me to sod off*

sod·o·mite /ˈsɒdəmaɪt‖ˈsɑ-/ *n now rare* a person practising SODOMY

sod·o·my /ˈsɒdəmi‖ˈsɑ-/ *n* [U] any of various unnatural sexual acts, esp. ANAL sex between males

so·ev·er /səʊˈevəʳ/ *adv* [Wa5] *usu. lit* **1** (*usu. in comb.*) ever: *Wheresoever he may go* **2** (after *any*) of any kind; WHATEVER³: *any place soever*

so·fa /ˈsəʊfə/ *n* a comfortable seat with raised arms and a back and wide enough for usu. 2 or 3 people —see picture at LIVING ROOM

soft /sɒft‖sɔft/ *adj* [Wa1] **1** not firm against pressure; giving in to the touch; changeable in shape; not hard or stiff: *a soft chair/bed|His foot sank slightly into the soft ground.|a book with a soft cover* **2** less hard than average: *Lead is one of the softer metals* **3** smooth and delicate to the touch: *soft skin* **4** restful and pleasant to the senses, esp. the eyes: *soft lights|a soft summer evening* **5** quiet; not making much noise; not loud: *a whisper so soft I could hardly hear* **6** not violent; gentle: *soft winds from the south* **7** not angry or excited; making calm: *a soft answer to an angry question* **8** *not fml* not showing or needing hard work; easy **9** weak in condition of the body; in poor SHAPE² (7) **10** *not fml* easily persuaded; easy to make agree or do what one wishes; weak **11** *infml* dealing with opinions, ideas, etc., rather than numbers and facts: *one of the soft sciences like* PSYCHOLOGY **12** [F+*on*] *infml* not firmly set in one's mind on or against something: *His American political enemies said he was soft on* COMMUNISM **13** [Wa5] (of a drink) containing no alcohol and usu. sweet **14** [Wa5] *not tech* **a** (of *c*) having the sound /s/ and not /k/: *soft* c *in* acid **b** (of *g*) having the sound /dʒ/ and not /g/: *soft* g *in* age **15** (of water) free from certain minerals; allowing soap to act easily: *We're lucky that the local water is quite soft* —opposite **hard** **16** *not fml* not of the worst, most harmful, etc., kind: *soft* PORNOGRAPHY|*soft drugs like* CANNABIS **17** *infml* foolish or mad: *Have you gone soft in the head?* —**~ly** *adv* —**~ness** *n* [U]

soft·ball /ˈsɒftbɔːl‖ˈsɔft-/ *n* [U] a game like BASEBALL but played on a smaller field with a slightly larger and softer ball

soft-boiled /ˌ· ˈ·◂/ *adj* [Wa5] (of an egg) boiled not long enough for the inside to become solid

soft coal /ˌ· ˈ·/ *n infml* BITUMINOUS COAL

soft·en /ˈsɒfən‖ˈsɔ-/ *v* [T1;IØ (UP)] to (cause to) become soft(er), gentle, less stiff, or less severe: *a cream for softening dry skin|He softened the blow by telling her the bad news gently.|In the heat the frozen ground began to soften (up).|The water can be softened by adding a chemical (a* **softener***)*

soften up *v adv* [T1] **1** to weaken (an enemy's

defences), as by bombing, before an attack **2** *not fml* to prepare (someone) for persuasion; break down the opposition of (someone): *Mother has promised to soften Father up a bit, and then we'll ask him for the money*

soft fur·nish·ings /ˌ· ˈ···/ *n* [P] the curtains, mats, seat covers, etc., used in ornamenting a room

soft·heart·ed /ˌsɒftˈhɑːtɨ̣d◂‖ˌsɔftˈhɑr-/ *adj* [Wa2] having tender feelings; easily moved to pity; merciful —**~ness** *n* [U]

soft·ie /ˈsɒfti‖ˈsɔf-/ *n* SOFTY

soft land·ing /ˌ· ˈ··/ *n* a slow coming down of a space vehicle to earth, the moon, etc., without damage

soft pal·ate /ˌ· ˈ··/ *n* the back part of the PALATE (1) (=top of the mouth) —see also HARD PALATE

soft-ped·al /ˌ· ˈ··‖ˈ· ˌ··/ *v* **-ll-** (*AmE* **-l-**) [T1 *usu. pass.*] *infml* to make (a subject, fact, suggestion, etc.) seem unimportant; PLAY DOWN

soft sell /ˌ· ˈ·◂/ *n* [(*the*) U] selling by suggestion or gentle persuading of buyers —opposite **hard sell**

soft-soap /ˈ· ·/ *v* [T1] *infml* to persuade by saying nice things

soft soap /ˌ· ˈ·/ *n* [U] *infml* persuading by gentle means such as FLATTERY

soft-spok·en /ˌ· ˈ··◂/ *adj* [Wa2] having a gentle voice; speaking usu. kindly or without showing anger

soft spot /ˈ· ·/ *n* [(*for*)] *infml* a feeling of special kindness or liking; fondness: *I have a soft spot for people from my native village*

soft·ware /ˈsɒftweəʳ‖ˈsɔft-/ *n* [U] *tech* the set of systems (in the form of PROGRAM*s* rather than machine parts) which control the operation of a COMPUTER —opposite **hardware**

soft·wood /ˈsɒftwʊd‖ˈsɔft-/ *n* [U] wood from EVERGREEN trees (such as PINE and FIR) that is cheap and easy to cut —opposite **hardwood**

soft·y, softie /ˈsɒfti‖ˈsɔfti/ *n* [C;N] *infml* a weak or very easily persuaded person

sog·gy /ˈsɒgi‖ˈsɑgi/ *adj* [Wa1] completely wet; heavy and usu. unpleasant with wetness: *soggy ground after the heavy rain* —**-gily** *adv* —**-giness** *n* [U]

soi·gné, -gnée /ˈswɑːnjeɪ‖swɑnˈjeɪ (*Fr* swaɲe)/ *adj Fr* dressed or arranged fashionably and with care in detail

soil¹ /sɔɪl/ *v* [Wv5;T1;IØ] to make or become dirty, esp. slightly or on the surface: *a sale of soiled goods*|*The shirt collar was badly soiled and would never be white again*

soil² *n* [U] **1** the state of being SOIL*ed* **2** material that SOIL*s*; dirt **3** human waste; SEWAGE: *Soil is carried away from a house by a* **soilpipe**

soil³ *n* **1** [U] the top covering of the earth in which plants grow; ground: *an area of rich/sandy soil* **2** [*the*+R] *usu. pomp* where a farmer works; the life or land of a farm: *She makes her living from the soil* **3** [U;C] *usu. pomp* a place or country: *my native soil* —see LAND (USAGE)

soi·ree, -rée /ˈswɑːreɪ‖swɑˈreɪ (*Fr* sware)/ *n Fr* an evening party, usu. of a quiet polite kind

soj·ourn¹ /ˈsɒdʒɜːn‖ˈsəʊdʒɜrn/ *n* [C9] *esp. lit* a stay in a place other than one's home for a time

sojourn² *v* [L9] *lit* to live for a time in a place: *She sojourned with some relatives in London for 2 months* —**~er** *n*

sol /sɒl‖sɑl/ *n* [C;U] the 5th note in the (SOL-FA) musical SCALE: *sing (a) sol*

Sol *n* [R] *lit* the sun

sol·ace¹ /ˈsɒlɨ̣s‖ˈsɑ-/ *n* **1** [U] comfort in grief or anxiety; lessening of trouble in the mind **2** [C] something that provides this

solace² *v* [T1] to give comfort in mind to or for

so·lar /ˈsəʊləʳ/ *adj* [Wa5] **1** of, from, or concerning the sun: *solar time* **2** using the power of the sun's light and heat: *a solar power system*|*a solar* FURNACE

solar cell /ˌ·· ˈ·/ *n* an apparatus for producing electric power from sunlight

so·lar·i·um /səʊˈleərɪəm/ *n* **-ia** /rɪə/ *or* **-iums** a usu. glass-enclosed room in a house or esp. a hospital, where one can sit in bright sunlight

solar plex·us /ˌ·· ˈ··/ *n* [*the*+R] **1** the system of nerves between the stomach and the BACKBONE **2** *infml* the stomach

solar sys·tem /ˈ·· ˌ··/ *n* **1** [(*the*) S] the sun together with the bodies (PLANET*s*) going around it **2** [C] such a system around another star —see picture at PLANET

solar year /ˌ·· ˈ·/ *n tech* the length of time in which the earth goes once around the sun, equal to 365 days 5 hours 49 minutes

sold /səʊld/ *past t. and p. of* SELL

sol·der¹ /ˈsɒldəʳ, ˈsəʊl-‖ˈsɑdər/ *n* [U] soft metal, usu. a mixture of lead and tin, used when melted for joining other metal surfaces

solder² *v* [T1 (UP)] to join or repair with SOLDER: *solder an electrical connection*|*solder 2 wires together*

soldering i·ron /ˈ··· ˌ··/ *n* a hand tool with a copper end which is heated in a flame or by electricity for melting and putting on SOLDER

sol·dier¹ /ˈsəʊldʒəʳ/ *n* **1** a member of an army, esp. a man and esp. one of low rank (not an officer) **2** a hard worker for some purpose: *a soldier in the* CAUSE¹ (3) *of women's rights*

soldier² *v* [IØ] to serve as a soldier

sol·dier·ly /ˈsəʊldʒəli‖-ərli/ also **sol·dier·like** /ˈsəʊldʒəlaɪk‖-ər-/— *adj lit* typical or worthy of a good soldier

soldier of for·tune /ˌ·· · ˈ··/ *n not fml* a person who travels in search of military action, for adventure or pay

soldier on *v adv* [IØ] *not fml, esp. BrE* to continue working; work steadily, esp. in spite of difficulties: *He doesn't like the job but he'll soldier on until the work is done*

sol·dier·y /ˈsəʊldʒəri/ *n* [(*the*) GU] *lit* soldiers, esp. of the stated (usu. bad) type: *rude soldiery*

sole¹ /səʊl/ *n* **1** the bottom surface of the foot, esp. the part on which one walks or stands —see picture at HUMAN² **2** the part of a piece of footwear covering this, esp. the flat bottom part of a shoe not including the heel

sole² *v* [T1 *usu. pass.*] to put a SOLE¹ on (a shoe): *have one's shoes soled*

sole³ *n* [Wn2;C;U] any of various kinds of flat fishes with small mouths, eyes, and FIN*s*, of which large types make fine food —see picture at FISH¹

sole⁴ *adj* [Wa5;A] **1** having no sharer; being the only one **2** belonging or allowed to one and no other; unshared: *The sole responsibility for this job is yours*

so·le·cis·m /ˈsɒlɨ̣sɪzəm‖ˈsɑ-/ *n* a breaking of rules about what is proper, as in grammar or social politeness

-soled /səʊld/ *comb. form* having such SOLE*s*¹: *rubber-/thick-soled shoes*

sole·ly /ˈsəʊl-li/ *adv* [Wa5] not including others; only; EXCLUSIVELY

sol·emn /ˈsɒləm‖ˈsɑ-/ *adj* **1** done, made, etc., seriously, having a sense of religious-like importance **2** too serious for humour; GRAVE² (1): *a solemn moment in history* **3** of the grandest most formal kind: *a solemn church* FESTIVAL/*royal dinner* —**~ly** *adv* —**~ness** *n* [U]

so·lem·ni·ty /səˈlemnɨ̣ti/ *n* **1** [U] the quality of being solemn; formality or seriousness **2** [C *usu. pl.*] a formal act or quality proper for a grand or solemn event: *all the solemnities of the occasion*

sol·em·nize, -nise /ˈsɒləmnaɪz‖ˈsɑ-/ *v* [T1] *lit or fml* to perform a formal religious ceremony of (esp. marriage) —**-nization** /ˌsɒləmnaɪˈzeɪʃən‖ˌsɑləmnə-/ *n* [U]

sol-fa /ˌsɒl ˈfɑː‖ˌsəʊl-/ *n* [R] the system which represents each note of the musical SCALE by one of 7 short words, esp. for singing

so·li·cit /səˈlɪsɨt/ *v* **1** [I∅;T1: (*for*)] to ask for (money, help, a favour, etc.) from (a person): *May I solicit your advice on a matter of importance.*| *Beggars are not allowed to solicit in public places* **2** [I∅] (esp. of a woman) to offer oneself for sex for pay; advertise oneself as a PROSTITUTE —**~ation** /səˌlɪsɨˈteɪʃən/ *n* [U;C]

so·lic·i·tor /səˈlɪsɨtəʳ/ *n* **1** (esp. in England) a kind of lawyer who gives advice, appears in lower courts, and prepares cases for a BARRISTER to argue in a high court **2** *AmE* a person who comes to people's doors to sell or SOLICIT (1)

so·lic·i·tor gen·e·ral /·ˌ··· ˈ···/ *n* **solicitors general** the chief law officer next below the ATTORNEY GENERAL of a country

so·lic·i·tous /səˈlɪsɨtəs/ *adj* [(*about, of, for*)] **1** taking eager, kind, or helpful care **2** anxious; carefully interested —**~ly** *adv* —**~ness** *n* [U]

so·lic·i·tude /səˈlɪsɨtjuːd‖-tuːd/ *n* [U] anxious, kind, or eager care

sol·id[1] /ˈsɒlɨd‖ˈsɑ-/ *adj* **1** not needing a container to hold its shape; not liquid or gas: *The milk in the bottles had frozen solid* **2** [Wa5] having an inside filled up; not hollow: *Children's bicycles sometimes have solid rubber tyres* **3** made of material tight together; DENSE (1); COMPACT[1] (1): *They dug down until they hit solid rock* **4** [Wa5] without spaces or breaks; CONTINUOUS: *I waited for 3 solid hours and then went home* **5** of good quality; (as if) firm and well-done or -made: *solid furniture*|*a solid wall*|*a solid piece of writing* **6** that may be depended on; REPUTABLE: *solid citizens of the town* **7** needing or showing serious attention; not silly or light: *a solid report, which will make solid reading* **8** [Wa5;A] **a** completely of the stated material without mixture of others: *a solid gold watch* **b** *AmE* completely of the stated colour without mixture of others: *a solid blue dress* **9** [(*for, against*)] in or showing complete agreement: *The members were solid against the idea.*|*solid agreement* **10** [Wa5] being or concerning space with length, width, and height; 3-DIMENSIONAL: *A* SPHERE *is a solid figure.*|**Solid geometry** *is the study of lines, figures, angles, measurements, etc., in space* **11** [Wa5;F] written or printed as 1 word without a HYPHEN: *"Doghouse" used to be written "dog-house", but now it is usually written solid* —**~ly** *adv* —**~ness** *n* [U]

solid[2] *n* **1** a SOLID (1) object; something that does not flow: *At what temperature does alcohol become a solid?* **2** [*usu. pl.*] any of the solid material in a liquid: *milk solids*|*the solids in blood* **3** (esp. in GEOMETRY) an object that takes up space; object with length, width, and height **4** [*usu. pl.*] an article of non-liquid food: *He's still too ill to take solids*

sol·i·dar·i·ty /ˌsɒlɨˈdærɨti‖ˌsɑ-/ *n* [U] agreement of interests, aims, or standards

so·lid·i·fy /səˈlɪdɨfaɪ/ *v* [T1;I∅] to (cause to) become solid, hard, or firm: *Cold should solidify the jelly.*|*Opinion on the question had begun to solidify* —**-fication** /səˌlɪdɨfɨˈkeɪʃən/ *n* [U]

so·lid·i·ty /səˈlɪdɨti/ *n* [U] the quality or state of being firm, not hollow, well made, dependable, or in agreement

solid-state /ˌ·· ˈ·ˈ/ *adj* [Wa5] of, being, or having electrical parts (esp. TRANSISTOR*s*) that run without heating or moving parts

sol·i·dus /ˈsɒlɨdəs‖ˈsɑ-/ *n* **-di** /daɪ/ OBLIQUE[2]

so·lil·o·quize, -quise /səˈlɪləkwaɪz/ *v* [I∅;T1] to speak or say in SOLILOQUY

so·lil·o·quy /səˈlɪləkwi/ *n* [C;U] an act or the action of talking to oneself alone, esp. a speech in a play in which a character's thoughts are spoken to those watching the play

sol·ip·sis·m /ˈsɒlɨpsɪzəm‖ˈsəʊ-, ˈsɑ-/ *n* [U] **1** *tech* any of various systems of thought that admit only the self as something existing or knowable **2** *not fml* too great attention to oneself rather than relations with others —**-sist** *n* —**-sistic** /ˌsɒlɨpˈsɪstɪk‖ˌsəʊ-, ˌsɑ-/ *adj*

sol·i·taire /ˌsɒlɨˈteəʳ‖ˌsɑ-/ *n* **1** [C] (of a piece of jewellery having) a single jewel, esp. a diamond **2** [U] *AmE* PATIENCE (4)

sol·i·ta·ry[1] /ˈsɒlɨtəri‖ˈsɑlɨteri/ *adj* **1** [Wa5;A;(B)] alone without companions **2** [B] fond of, or habitually, being alone **3** [B] in a lonely place **4** [Wa5;A *nonassertive*] single; SOLE[4]: *Can you give me one solitary piece of proof for what you say?* —see ALONE (USAGE) —**-tarily** /ˈsɒlɨtərli‖ˌsɑlɨˈterɨli/ *adv*

solitary[2] *n* **1** [C] a person who lives completely alone; ANCHORITE; HERMIT **2** [U] *sl* SOLITARY CONFINEMENT

solitary con·fine·ment /ˌ···· ·ˈ··/ *n* [U] the keeping of a person in a closed place without any chance of seeing or talking to others

sol·i·tude /ˈsɒlɨtjuːd‖ˈsɑlɨtuːd/ *n* [U] the quality or state of being alone away from companionship

so·lo[1] /ˈsəʊləʊ/ *n* **-los** **1** a (part of) a piece of music (to be) played or sung by one person **2** a job or performance, esp. an aircraft flight, done by one person alone

solo[2] *adj, adv* [Wa5] **1** without a companion **2** of, for, or played or heard as, a musical SOLO: *She has a fine solo voice.*|*This phrase is to be played solo by the piano*

solo[3] *v* [I∅] *infml* to perform alone, esp. in flying an aircraft by oneself

solo[4] *n* [U] a card game like WHIST but in which each player plays on his own and states how many TRICK*s* he hopes to make

so·lo·ist /ˈsəʊləʊɨst/ *n* a performer of a musical SOLO

sol·stice /ˈsɒlstɨs‖ˈsɑl-/ *n* the times each year when days are longest or shortest. The **summer solstice** is on June 22 and the **winter solstice** on December 22

sol·u·ble /ˈsɒljʊbəl‖ˈsɑljə-/ *adj* **1** [(*in*)] that can be DISSOLVED (2) **2** solvable (SOLVE) —**-bility** /ˌsɒljʊˈbɪlɨti‖ˌsɑljə-/ *n* [U]

so·lu·tion /səˈluːʃən/ *n* **1** [C;(U)] an act or way of finding an answer to a difficulty or PROBLEM (1,2): *a sheet of practice questions provided with solutions*| *It's a difficulty that hardly admits solution* **2** [C;U] (a) liquid containing a solid or gas mixed (DISSOLVED (2a)) into it, usu. without chemical change: *a weak sugar solution* (=with little sugar in the water) **3** [U] the state or action of being mixed into liquid like this: *sugar in solution in water*

solve /sɒlv‖sɑlv, sɔlv/ *v* [T1] to find a SOLUTION (1) to; come to an answer, explanation, or way of dealing with (something): *solve a* PROBLEM/PUZZLE/*mystery* —**solvable** *adj* —**solver** *n*

sol·ven·cy /ˈsɒlvənsi‖ˈsɑl-, ˈsɔl-/ *n* [U] the quality or state of being SOLVENT

sol·vent[1] /ˈsɒlvənt‖ˈsɑl-, ˈsɔl-/ *adj* having enough to pay all money owed; not in debt

solvent[2] *n* [C;(U)] (a) liquid able to break down and bring a solid substance into SOLUTION (3): *Alcohol and petrol are useful solvents for spots that will not come off in water*

som·bre, *AmE* **-ber** /ˈsɒmbəʳ‖ˈsɑm-/ *adj* **1** sadly serious; GRAVE[2] (1); GLOOMY **2** (of colours or sights) like or full of shadows; dark —**~ly** *adv* —**~ness** *n* [U]

som·bre·ro /sɒm'breərəʊ‖sɑm-/ *n* **-ros** a man's high usu. cloth hat with a very wide flat shade (BRIM) around it, rolled up at the edges, worn esp. in Mexico

some[1] /sʌm/ *determiner* **1** certain but not all: *Some French wine is quite sweet.*|*Some days you win, and some days you lose* **2** an unknown or unstated one; a(n): *Can you give me some idea of the cost?*|*Go away! Come back some other time.*|*There must be some reason for what he's done* **3** (*before nouns expressing measurement*) quite a large number or amount of: *This fine gift should go some way* (=quite a long way) *towards paying our costs.*|*The fire went on for some time* (=several hours) *before it was brought under control* **4** *infml* (*used before a noun at the beginning of a sentence*) no kind of; no . . . at all: *Some help that is! We're no further than we were before!*|*Some friend you are! You won't even lend me £1!* **5** *infml* a fine or important; quite a: *That was some speech you made!*|*It was* (*quite*) *some party!* **6 some . . . or (an)other** (*sometimes in comb.*) one or several which the speaker cannot or does not care to state exactly: *I'm not making this story up; I must have heard it somewhere or other*|*He's staying with some friends or other in the country* USAGE In neg. sentences, **any** or **no** are used instead of **some**: *I haven't* **any**/*I have* **no** *socks.* If **some**, **somebody**, etc., are used in questions, it means that we think the answer will be "yes". Compare: *Is there* **something** *to eat?* (I can smell food!)|*Is there* **anything** *to eat?* (I'm hungry!)

some[2] /səm; *strong* sʌm/ *determiner* a little, few, or certain or small number or amount of: *They own some land in London.*|*I saw some people* (compare *a person*) *I knew.*|*May I offer you some tea?*

some[3] /sʌm/ *pron* **1** a little, few, or certain or small amount: *He asked for money and I gave him some* (compare *but I didn't give him any*).|*I looked everywhere for fresh fruit before I found some* **2** [(*of*)] certain ones or a certain part but not all: *You can trick some of the people some of the time . . .*|*I took some of the cake but left most of it.*|*Some say "Only fools fall in love", but I don't believe it.*|*In this collection of stories some were very good and some of the others fairly good.*|*"There will be some who will break loose"* (SEU S.)

some[4] /səm; *strong* sʌm/ *adv* [Wa5] **1** (used usu. before a number) about: *There were some 40 or 50 people there* **2** *AmE* rather; SOMEWHAT: *I'm feeling some better today, thanks* **3 some little/few** quite a lot of: *I hope this is the last we see of him for some little time!*

-some[1] /səm/ *suffix* [*n→adj*] showing a stated quality, action, or thing: AWESOME|BURDENSOME|TROUBLESOME

-some[2] *suffix* [*determiner→n*] a group of (so many) members, esp. players: *a* GOLF FOUR*some*

some·bod·y /'sʌmbɒdi‖-bɑdi/ also **some·one** /'sʌmwʌn/— *pron* **1** a person; some but no particular or known person: *If you don't know the answer, ask somebody.*|*Somebody lost his/their coat.*|*There's somebody on the telephone for you* **2 or somebody** or a person of that sort: *This job needs a repairman or a builder or somebody* —compare SOME[1] (6); see EVERYBODY, SOME (USAGE)

some·day /'sʌmdeɪ/ *adv* [Wa5] at some future time: *Perhaps someday I'll be rich*

some·how /'sʌmhaʊ/ *adv* [Wa5] *not fml* **1** by some means; in some way not yet known or stated: *I can't see how, but we'll have to reach an agreement somehow* (*or other*).|*"The library copy has somehow disappeared"* (SEU S.) —compare SOME[1] (6); see SOME (USAGE) **2** for some reason that is not clear: *Somehow I seem to have 2 knives and no fork.*|*I think she's right but somehow I'm not completely sure*

som·er·sault[1] /'sʌməsɔːlt‖-ər-/ *n* a jump or rolling backward or forward movement in which the feet go over the head before the body returns upright

somersault[2] *v* [L9;(I∅)] to move in or do a SOMERSAULT[1]: *somersault through a window*

some·thing[1] /'sʌmθɪŋ/ *pron* **1** some unstated or unknown thing: *I think I dropped something.*|*Something must be done!*|*I was looking for something cheaper* —compare SOME[1] (2); see SOME (USAGE) **2** (used instead of (part of) a word, name, or number that one has forgotten): *What's his name? Jim something—yes, Jim Taylor* **3** a valuable thing; thing better than nothing: *At least we didn't lose any money. That's something!* **4** some food or drink: *You must be thirsty: are you sure I can't offer you something?* **5 make something of it** *sl* to start a fight about something: *Yes, I stole your girl, want to make something of it?* **6 make something of oneself/one's life** to be successful **7 or something** *infml* **a** (showing that the speaker is not sure): *"might go to Buttermere or something"* (SEU S.) **b** (showing that the speaker does not believe the meaning of a word): *Girls like her are supposed to be* LIBERATEd (1) *or something* **8 see something of someone** to see someone from time to time: *If you're going to be in London next year perhaps we may see something of each other* **9 something for nothing** a profit without risk or effort: *Some people will never learn that you can't get something for nothing* **10 something of a(n)** *infml* rather a(n); a fairly good: *He's something of a book collector* **11 something tells me** *infml* I think that: *Something tells me my watch isn't quite right* **12 something to/in** some truth or value in (as a statement): *There's something to/in what you say: I'll take your advice* **13 something to do with a** *BrE* a person or thing connected with: *I think Guy Fawkes was something to do with a plan to blow up Parliament* **b** a connection with: *Guy Fawkes Day has something to do with a plan to blow up Parliament*

something[2] *adv* [Wa5] **1** [H] rather; a bit; SOMEWHAT: *cost something over £3* **2 something like a** rather like: *The building looked something like a church* **b** *infml, esp. BrE* about; APPROXIMATEly: *something like 1000 people present*

some·time[1] /'sʌmtaɪm/ *adv* [Wa5] at some uncertain or unstated time **a** in the future: *We'll take our holiday sometime in August, I think* **b** in the past: *Our house was built sometime around 1905*

sometime[2] *adj* [Wa5;A] *fml* having been once but now no longer; former: *Sir Richard Marsh, sometime chairman of British Rail*

some·times /'sʌmtaɪmz/ *adv* [Wa5] at times; now and then; OCCASIONALly: *Sometimes I wonder why I ever listen to him.*|*Sometimes he comes by train and sometimes by car*

some·way /'sʌmweɪ/ *adv* [Wa5] *AmE infml* SOMEHOW (1)

some·what /'sʌmwɒt‖-wɑt/ *adv* [Wa5] **1** by some degree or amount; a little; rather: *a price somewhat higher than expected*|*suffering somewhat from the heat* **2 more than somewhat** *pomp* to quite a large degree: *His behaviour displeased me more than somewhat* **3 somewhat of** *not fml,* a kind of; rather: *The cake we made was somewhat of a failure*

some·where /'sʌmweəʳ/ *AmE* also **some·place** /'sʌmpleɪs/— *adv* [Wa5] **1** (in/at/to) some place: *Where is my pen? It must be somewhere here.*|*Not finding what he wanted here he went somewhere else.*|*"Ian needed somewhere to stay"* (SEU S.) **2** some number or amount: *somewhere between 1½ and 2 litres of milk* **3 get somewhere** *infml* to begin to get good results; succeed: *Now at last we know the murder weapon; now we're getting somewhere!* **4 or somewhere** or in/at/to some other place: *"They're going away to Greece or somewhere* (SEU S.) —see SOME (USAGE)

som·nam·bu·lis·m /sɒm'næmbjʊlɪzəm‖sɑm'næmbjə-/ *n* [U] the action or habit of walking about while asleep —**-list** *n*

som·no·lent /'sɒmnələnt‖'sɑm-/ *adj lit* **1** nearly falling asleep; DROWSY **2** causing or suggesting sleep: *a somnolent country scene* —**~ly** *adv*

son /sʌn/ *n* **1** [C;N] a male child —see TABLE OF FAMILY RELATIONSHIPS **2** [C *usu. pl.*] a male descendant: *The sons of the first discoverers are still on the islands after centuries* **3** [*the*+R] (*usu. cap.*) (in the Christian religion) the 2nd person of the TRINITY; Christ **4** [C (*of*)] *lit* a usu. male person coming from or in association with a thing, place, or quality: *Britain weeping for her sons fallen in battle|a son of the soil* (=one brought up on a farm) **5** [N] (used by an older man in speaking to a much younger man or boy): *What's your name, son?*

so·nar /'səʊnɑːʳ, -nəʳ/ *n* [U] an apparatus using sound waves for finding the position of underwater objects (like MINE*s*[3] (3) or SUBMARINE*s*)

so·na·ta /sə'nɑːtə/ *n* a piece of music for 1 or 2 instruments, one of which is a piano, made up of usu. 3 or 4 short parts of varying speeds played in order

son et lu·mi·ere /ˌsɒn eɪ 'luːmjɛəʳ‖ˌsɑn- (*Fr* sɔ̃ e lymjɛr)/ *n Fr, esp. BrE* a performance which uses lights and recorded sounds to tell the stories of historical events

song /sɒŋ‖sɔŋ/ *n* **1** [C] (*often in comb.*) a usu. short piece of music with words for singing: *a lovesong/* FOLK*song|the best song in the show|a book of 16th century English songs* **2** [C] a poem suitable or prepared for singing to music **3** [U] the act or art of singing: *burst into song* **4** [U;C] the music-like sound of a bird or birds: *a study of birdsong* **5 for a song** *infml* for a very small price; very cheaply: *He found the car going for a song and bought it* **6 song and dance** *infml* an unnecessary, useless, or unwelcome expression of excitement, anger, impatience, etc.

song·bird /'sɒŋbɜːd‖'sɔŋbərd/ *n* any of the many kinds of birds that can produce musical sounds

song·book /'sɒŋbʊk‖sɔŋ-/ *n* a book of songs with music for singing

song·ster /'sɒŋstəʳ‖'sɔŋ-/ (*fem.* **song·stress** /-strɨs/)— *n lit* **1** a singer or writer of songs **2** SONGBIRD

son·ic /'sɒnɪk‖'sɑ-/ *adj* [Wa5] **1** (*usu. in comb*) of or concerning the speed of sound in air, about 741 miles per hour: SUBSONIC/SUPERSONIC *flight* **2** of or concerning sound waves

sonic boom /ˌ·· '·/ *BrE* also **sonic bang** /ˌ·· '·/— *n* an explosive sound produced by the shock wave from an aircraft beginning to go faster than the speed of sound

son-in-law /'· · ˌ·/ *n* **sons-in-law** the husband of one's daughter —see TABLE OF FAMILY RELATIONSHIPS

son·net /'sɒnɨt‖'sɑ-/ *n* a 14-line poem with any of several fixed formal patterns of line endings (RHYME*s*)

son·ny /'sʌni/ *n* [N] *becoming rare* (used in speaking to a young boy): *Better go home to your mother, sonny*

son of a bitch /ˌ· · · '·/ *n* **sons of bitches** /'· · '··/ [C; *you*+N] *taboo* a wicked person; BASTARD[1] (2): *That son of a bitch stole my car!|You son of a bitch!*

son of a gun /ˌ· · · '·/ *n* **son of a guns, sons of guns** /ˌ· · '·/ [C; *you*+N] *infml* (*used esp. by a man to a close male friend*) a fellow who wins the social approval of his group, as being manly, daring, humorous, etc.

so·nor·i·ty /sə'nɒrɨti‖sə'nɔ-/ *n* [U] the quality of being SONOROUS

so·nor·ous /'sɒnərəs, sə'nɔːrəs‖sə'nɔrəs, 'sɑnərəs/ *adj* having a pleasantly full loud sound: *a sonorous bell/voice* —**~ly** *adv*

son·sy /'sɒnsi‖'sɑn-/ *adj* [Wa1] *ScotE* (of a woman) cheerful and pretty; nicely fat; BUXOM

soon /suːn/ *adv* **1** [Wa5;H] before long; within a short time: *I'll be going soon so I won't have another drink.|soon after the party|It soon became clear that . . .|"They should be home very soon"* (SEU W.) **2** [Wa1] quickly; early: *Please get this done* **as soon as** *possible:* **the sooner the better.**|*not until after tomorrow at the soonest|He got married as soon as he left university* **3** [Wa1] (*in phrases expressing comparisons*) readily; willingly: *I'd sooner die than marry you!|"Will you dance?" "I'd just as soon not, if you don't mind"* **4 no sooner . . . than** when . . . at once: *No sooner had we sat down than we found it was time to go.|No sooner said than done!* (=It'll be done/It has been done very fast) —see HARDLY (USAGE) **5 sooner or later** at some time certainly; if not soon then later **6 speak too soon** to accept a fact, result, etc., as true before it is certain: *I hope I'll get the job, but I mustn't speak too soon*

soot[1] /sʊt/ *n* [U] black powder produced by burning, and carried into the air and left on surfaces by smoke —**~y** *adj* [Wa1]

soot[2] *v* [T1 (UP) *usu. pass*] to cover or make dirty with SOOT

soothe /suːð/ *v* [Wv4;T1] **1** to make less angry, excited, or anxious; comfort or calm: *soothe one's feelings|soothing words* **2** to make less painful: *soothe a sore throat|soothing medicine* —**soothingly** *adv*

sooth·say·er /'suːθˌseɪəʳ/ *n old use* a person believed to be able to tell the future

sop[1] /sɒp‖sɑp/ *n* **1** [(*to*)] something offered to a displeased person to win his favour **2** a piece of food dipped into a liquid

sop[2] *v* **-pp-** [T1] to dip and fill with a liquid: *sop bread in* GRAVY (1) —see also SOP UP

soph·is·m /'sɒfɪzəm‖'sɑ-/ *n* **1** [C] an argument which looks correct but is false, esp. one intended to deceive **2** [U] SOPHISTRY (1) —**-ist** *n*

so·phis·ti·cate /sə'fɪstɨkeɪt/ *n* a SOPHISTICATED (1) person

so·phis·ti·cat·ed /sə'fɪstɨkeɪtɨd/ *adj* **1** having or showing a knowledge of social life and behaviour; WORLDLY-WISE; URBANE: *a child quite sophisticated for his age|sophisticated clothes* **2** having many parts; COMPLICATED; COMPLEX[1] (1,2): *sophisticated machinery|arguments*

so·phis·ti·ca·tion /səˌfɪstɨ'keɪʃən/ *n* [U] the quality of being SOPHISTICATED

soph·ist·ry /'sɒfɨstri‖'sɑ-/ *n* **1** [U] the use of false deceptive arguments **2** [C *usu. pl.*] SOPHISM (1)

soph·o·more /'sɒfəmɔːʳ‖'sɑfəmor/ *n* a student in the second year of a course in a US college or high school

sop·o·rif·ic /ˌsɒpə'rɪfɪk‖ˌsɑ-/ *adj* causing or tending to sleep: *a soporific drug/speech* —**~ally** *adv* [Wa4]

sop·ping /'sɒpɪŋ‖'sɑ-/ *adv, adj infml* very wet: *We were caught in the storm and got our clothes sopping (wet)*

sop·py /'sɒpi‖'sɑpi/ *adj* [Wa1] *BrE infml* **1** foolish **2** (as of a story) too full of expressions of tender feelings like sorrow, love, etc.

so·pra·no[1] /sə'prɑːnəʊ‖-'præ-/ *n* **-nos** **1** (a woman or child with, or a musical part for) a singing voice in the highest usual range, above ALTO **2** (of a family of instruments) the instrument which plays notes in the highest range

soprano² *adj* [Wa5] of, for, concerning, or having the range or part of a SOPRANO

sop up *v adv* [T1] to take (a liquid) into a solid so as to leave a dry surface: *sop up the water with a cloth or* MOP¹ (1)

sor·bet /ˈsɔːbɨt, ˈsɔːbeɪ‖ˈsɔrbɨt (*Fr* sɔrbe)/ *AmE* **sherbet**— *n* [U;C] *Fr* a dish usu. with the taste of a fruit, made like ice cream using mostly water instead of cream

sor·cer·er /ˈsɔːsərəʳ‖ˈsɔr-/ *fem.* **sor·cer·ess** /-rɨs/— *n* a person believed to do magic by using the power of evil spirits

sor·cer·y /ˈsɔːsəri‖ˈsɔr-/ *n* [U] the practice of a SORCERER; magic done by evil spirits

sor·did /ˈsɔːdɨd‖ˈsɔr-/ *adj* **1** marked by unpleasantness and esp. shameful qualities; BASE²; VILE (1): *a sordid murder* **2** very dirty or poor: *sordid living conditions* —**~ly** *adv* —**~ness** *n* [U]

sore¹ /sɔːʳ‖sor/ *adj* [Wa1] **1** [B] painful or aching from a wound, infection, or (of muscles) hard use: *a sore throat from a cold|I'm sore from all that running yesterday* **2** [A;(B)] *old use* causing great difficulty or anxiety; GRIEVOUS (1): *sore trouble* **3** [A] likely to cause pain of mind or offence: *Don't joke about his weight: it's a rather sore subject with him* **4** [F] *infml, esp. AmE* angry, esp. from feeling unjustly treated: *Don't get sore: I meant no harm* —**~ness** *n* [U]

sore² *n* a painful usu. infected place on the body

sore·head /ˈsɔːhed‖ˈsor-/ *n AmE infml* a bad-tempered person

sore·ly /ˈsɔːli‖ˈsorli/ also (*old use*) **sore**— *adv* severely or painfully; very

sor·ghum /ˈsɔːgəm‖ˈsɔr-/ *n* [U] (thick sweet liquid made from) a type of corn grown in warm areas —see picture at CEREAL

so·ror·i·ty /səˈrɒrɨti‖səˈrɔ-/ *n* [GC] (at some American universities) a club of women students usu. living in the same house —compare FRATERNITY (4)

sor·rel¹ /ˈsɒrəl‖ˈsɔ-, ˈsɑ-/ *adj, n* [Wa5] (a horse whose colour is) bright reddish-brown, often with a white tail

sorrel² *n* [U] any of various plants with sour-tasting leaves used in cooking

sor·row¹ /ˈsɒrəʊ‖ˈsɑ-, ˈsɔ-/ *n* [U;C *often pl.*: (*over, at, for*)] (a cause of) unhappiness over loss or wrongdoing; sadness; grief: *sorrow at the death of a friend|the joys and sorrows of life|His son has been a sorrow to him.|He expressed his sorrow over what he had done* —**~ful** *adj* —**~fully** *adv* —**~fulness** *n* [U]

sorrow² *v* [Wv4;I∅ (*over, at, for*)] *esp. lit* to feel or express sorrow; grieve: *a sorrowing heart|the sorrowing relatives at the funeral*

sor·ry¹ /ˈsɒri‖ˈsɑri, ˈsɔri/ *adj* **1** [F (*about*), F3,5a] grieved; sad: *"How's your cat?" "It died." "I am sorry."|I'm sorry to say that our efforts have failed.|I was sorry to hear your bad news* **2** [F (*for, about*), F5a] having a sincere feeling of shame or unhappiness at one's past actions, and expressing a wish that one had not done them: *If you say you're really sorry, I'll forgive you.|I'm sorry I broke your pen.|I'm sorry I ever came here; I wish I'd stayed at home* **3** [Wa5;F] (used for expressing polite refusal, disagreement, excusing of oneself, etc.) (esp. in the phr. **I'm sorry**): *I'm sorry but I don't agree* **4** [Wa1; A;(B)] causing pity mixed with disapproval: *a car in the sorriest of conditions|He was a sorry sight in his dirty and torn old clothes* **5 be/feel sorry for** to feel pity towards: *I feel sorry for whoever marries her!*

USAGE One says *I'm* **sorry** when one steps on someone's toe, or (in a suitable voice) *I'm very* **sorry** (*to hear that*) when told of a death. To feel pity for someone is to feel **sorry** *for* him. **Sorrowful**, a much stronger word, is not used in any of these meanings, and indeed would not be used of oneself: *her* **sorrowful** *face|"He's gone!" she replied* **sorrowfully**.

sorry² *interj* **1** (used for expressing polite refusal, disagreement, excusing of oneself, etc.): *Sorry; you can't come in.|Sorry; did I step on your toe?* **2** *esp. BrE* (used for asking someone to repeat something one has not heard properly): *"I'm cold." "Sorry?" "I said, I'm cold"*

sort¹ /sɔːt‖sɔrt/ *n* **1** [C (*of*)] a group of people, things, etc., all having certain qualities; type; kind: *a cheap sort of paper|That's just the sort of thing I want.|people of all sorts/all sorts of people|* (nonstandard) *those sort of books|"to decide what sort of fruit was poisonous"* (SEU S.) —see KIND (USAGE) **2** [C9, *usu. sing.*] *infml* person; one: *That was nice of her: she's not such a bad sort after all* **3** [C] *tech* a single piece of printer's TYPE **4 a sort of** a weak, unexplained, or unusual kind of: *I had a sort of feeling you'd say that.|*(nonstandard) *a sort of a feeling|a big ugly sort of castle* —see also SORT OF **5 it takes all sorts (to make a world)** any society consists of people who vary greatly in their habits, characters, opinions, etc.: *"He has a long beard and wears flowers in his hair!" "Well, it takes all sorts"* **6 of sorts/a sort** of a poor or doubtful kind: *It's a painting of sorts, but hard to describe* **7 out of sorts** in a bad temper; feeling unwell or annoyed

sort² *v* **1** [T1 (OUT); I∅ (*through, over*)] to put (things) in order; place according to kind, rank, etc.; arrange: *sort (through) old papers to see what can be thrown away|a job sorting letters in the Post Office* —see also SORT OUT **2** [T1] *ScotE* to mend; repair: *have one's washing machine sorted* —**~er** *n*

sor·tie /ˈsɔːti‖ˈsɔrti/ *n* **1** a short trip into an unfamiliar or unfriendly place: *returning from a sortie abroad|*(fig.) *the government's first sortie into industrial lawmaking* **2** a flight to bomb an enemy centre **3** a short attack made by an army from a position of defence

sort of /ˈ· ·/ *adv* [Wa5] *infml* in some way or degree; rather; KIND OF: *feeling sort of ill|I sort of thought you might say that.|"sort of the colour of that wall"* (SEU S.)|*"sort of 7 to half past"* (SEU S.)

sort-out /ˈ· ·/ *n* [*usu. sing.*] *BrE* an act of putting things in order: *This room's very untidy; it needs a good sort-out*

sort out *v adv* **1** [T1 (*from*)] to separate from a mass or group: *sort out the papers to be thrown away, and put the rest back* —see also SORT² (1) **2** [T1,6a] *BrE* to put in order; put right; deal with: *a silly quarrel that's now been sorted out* **3** [T1] *BrE sl* to attack and defeat: *Let me get my hands on them! I'll sort them out!*

SOS /ˌes əʊ ˈes/ *n* **1** the letters *SOS* as an international signal calling for help, used esp. by ships in trouble **2** an urgent message from someone in trouble: *The radio often broadcasts SOS messages to find the relatives of someone very ill*

so-so /ˈ· ·/ *adj, adv infml* not very bad(ly) but also not very good/well: *a so-so tennis player|Business is only just so-so*

sot /sɒt‖sɑt/ *n* a person who is habitually drunk and unable to think clearly

sot·tish /ˈsɒtɪʃ‖ˈsɑ-/ *adj* stupid like a SOT —**~ly** *adv* —**~ness** *n* [U]

sot·to vo·ce /ˌsɒtəʊ ˈvəʊtʃi‖ˌsɑ-/ *adv It* in a soft voice not to be heard by everyone; ASIDE² (2)

sou /suː/ *n* [S *nonassertive*] *infml* the smallest amount of money

sou·brette /suːˈbret/ *n Fr* a female part, usu. that

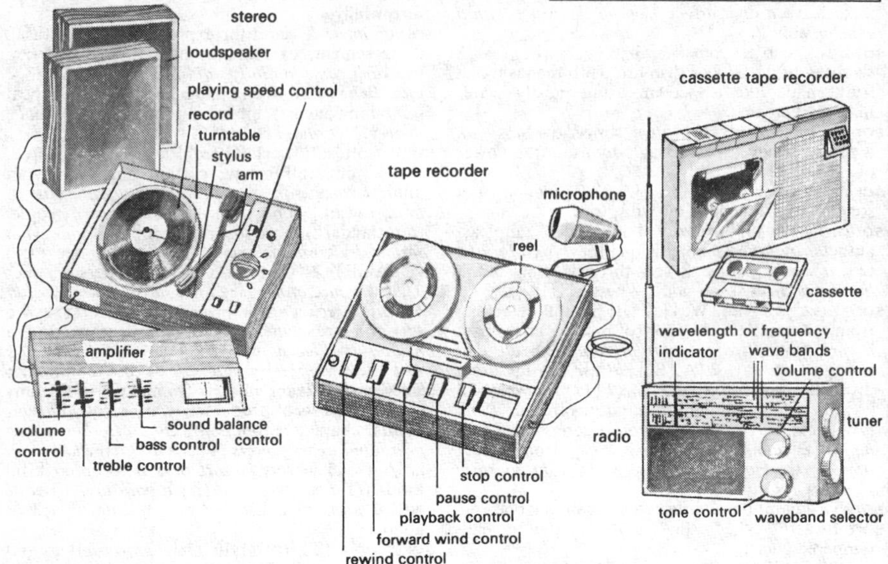

of a gay pretty servant girl, in a humorous play

sou·bri·quet /ˈsuːbrɪkeɪ/ *n* SOBRIQUET

souf·flé /ˈsuːfleɪ‖suːˈfleɪ/ *n* [C;U] a light airy dish made from eggs, flour, milk, and usu. cheese or some other food to give taste, baked and eaten at once while hot

sough /sʌf, saʊ/ *v, n* [I∅;C] *lit* (to make) the sound of the wind in trees

sought /sɔːt/ *past t. and p. of* SEEK

sought af·ter /ˈ· ˌ··/ *adj* [F] *esp. BrE* highly regarded, wanted, or popular because of rarity or high quality: *one of the articles most sought after by collectors* —**sought-after** *adj* [A]

soul¹ /səʊl/ *n* **1** [C] the part of a person that is not the body and is thought not to die: *"What good does it do a man if he gains the whole world but loses his soul?"* (The Bible)|*souls resting in heaven* **2** [C (*of*)] a central, most important or most active part: *He's such a good joke teller, he's* **the life and soul of** *any party* **3** [U] *not fml* the attractive quality produced by honesty or true deep feeling: *a stylish performance but lacking in soul* **4** [C9] a person: *She's a dear old soul* **5** [C *usu. pl. with numbers or nonassertive*] a person: *a population of 300 souls|You mustn't tell this to a soul* **6** [*the*+S+*of*] a fine example; EMBODIMENT: *Mary will help you: she's the soul of kindness* **7** [U] SOUL MUSIC: *the sound of soul|a soul group* **8 heart and soul** (with) all one's power and feeling: *to put heart and soul into a performance* **9 keep body and soul together** to have enough money, food, etc., to live **10 sell one's soul** to act against one's conscience for money, power, etc. **11 upon my soul!** *now rare* (used for expressing great surprise or shock)

soul² *adj* [Wa5;A] *AmE infml* of or concerning black people: *soul food*

soul broth·er /ˈ· ˌ··/ *fem.* **soul sis·ter** /ˈ· ˌ··/— *n AmE sl* (*used esp. among young black people*) a black person

soul-des·troy·ing /ˈ· ·ˌ··/ *adj not fml* giving no chance for the mind to work; very uninteresting

soul·ful /ˈsəʊlfəl/ *adj* full of feeling; expressing deep feeling: *a soulful look|song* —**~ly** *adv* —**~ness** *n* [U]

soul·less /ˈsəʊl-ləs/ *adj* having or showing no attractive or tender human qualities: *a big soulless business* —**~ly** *adv* —**~ness** *n* [U]

soul mu·sic /ˈ· ˌ··/ *n* [U] a type of popular music usu. performed by black singers and supposed to show feelings strongly and directly

soul-search·ing /ˈ· ˌ··/ *adj, n* [B;U] (making a) deep examination of one's mind and conscience: *hours of soul-searching*

sound¹ /saʊnd/ *adj* [Wa1] **1** in good condition; without disease or damage: *in sound health|being of sound mind* (=not mad) **2** solid; firm; strong: *a sound beginning for further study* **3** based on truth or good judgment; not wrong: *sound opinions|advice|reasoning|judgment* **4** [(*on*)] (of a person) having the right opinions: *a sound person to have on the committee* **5** (of sleep) deep and untroubled **6** severe; hard: *a sound* SLAP —**~ly** *adv* —**~ness** *n* [U]

sound² *adv* [Wa1] SOUNDly¹ (5) (esp. in the phr. **sound asleep**)

sound³ *n* **1** [U;C] what is or may be heard; (something that causes) a sensation in the ear: *hear the sound of voices|strange sounds from the next room|Sound travels* (in **sound waves**) *at 1,100 feet per second in air.|a language with many consonant sounds* —see NOISE (USAGE) **2** [S9] a quality of something read or heard: *His remarks had a worried sound.|music with a* SOUL *sound|Just from the sound of it, I'd say the matter was serious* **3** [A] (of recording, films, etc.) for listening to and not (only) seeing —**~less** *adj* [Wa5] —**~lessly** *adv* [Wa5]

sound⁴ *v* **1** [Wv6;L1,7,9] to have the effect of being; seem when heard: *a voice that sounds too loud in a small room|Your idea sounds (like) a good* *one.|Does this sentence sound right?|It sounds as if the government don't know what to do* **2** [I∅] to make a sound; produce an effect that can be heard: *His advice seemed to keep sounding in my ears.|The bell sounded at 8 o'clock for dinner* **3** [T1] to cause (esp. a musical instrument) to make a sound: *A bell is sounded at 8 o'clock.|Sound your horn to warn the other driver* **4** [T1] to signal by making sounds: *sound the "all clear" after an air attack* **5** [T1 *usu. pass.*] to express as a sound; pronounce: *The "s" in "island" is not sounded: it's* SILENT[1] (4) **6** [T1] *poet* make known; tell: *to sound God's praise*

sound[5] *n* **1** a fairly broad stretch of sea water mostly surrounded by coast **2** a water passage connecting 2 larger bodies of water and wider than a STRAIT

sound[6] *v* [T1] to measure the depth of (esp. the bottom of a body of water), as by using a weighted line (**sounding line**)

sound bar·ri·er /'· ,···/ *n* [*the*+R] the sudden increase in the force opposing an object in flight as it gets near the speed of sound: *to break the sound barrier* (=go faster than sound)

sound ef·fects /'· ·,·/ *n* [P] sounds produced by people or machines to give the effect of natural sounds needed in a radio or television broadcast or a film

sounding board /'·· ·/ *n* **1** a means used for spreading news or opinions: *to use the letters page of the newspaper as a sounding board* **2** a board fixed over and behind a stage, PULPIT (1), etc., to allow a speaker or performer to be heard more loudly and clearly

sound·ings /'saʊndɪŋz/ *n* [P] **1** measurements made by SOUNDing[6] **2** a part of a body of water where the bottom may be reached with a SOUNDing[6] line

sound off *v adv* [I∅ (*on, about*)] *not fml* to express an opinion freely and forcefully

sound out *v adv* [T1 (*on, about*)] to try to find out the opinion or intention of (someone)

sound·proof[1] /'saʊndpruːf/ *adj* keeping sound from getting in or out

soundproof[2] *v* [Wv5;T1] to make SOUNDPROOF

sound·track /'saʊndtræk/ *n* **1** the band near the edge of a film where sound is recorded **2** the recorded music from a film

sound wave /'· ·/ *n* [*usu. pl.*] a pressure wave of esp. sound, made in the air or in any other material that will carry it

soup /suːp/ *n* [U] **1** liquid cooked food containing small pieces of meat, fish, or vegetables **2 from soup to nuts** *AmE infml* from beginning to end, completely and in detail **3 in the soup** *infml* in trouble

soup·çon /'suːpsɒn‖-sɑn (*Fr* supsɔ̃)/ *n* [S (*of*)] *Fr* a little bit; TRACE[2] (2): *to add just a soupçon of salt*

soup kitch·en /'· ,··/ *n* a place where people with no money may get free food

soup up *v adv* [Wv5;T1] **1** to increase the power of (an engine) or the engine of (a car), as with a SUPERCHARGER **2** *infml* to make bigger, more exciting, more attractive, etc.: *His second book is just his first one again, in souped-up form*

sour[1] /saʊəʳ/ *adj* [Wa1] **1** having the taste that is not bitter, salty, or sweet, and is produced esp. by acids: *sour green apples* —see also **sour** GRAPES **2** having the taste of chemical action by bacteria (FERMENTATION): *This milk has gone sour: it has a sour taste* **3** *not fml* turning out to be bad or wrong; disappointing (esp. in the phrs. **go/turn sour**) **4** having or expressing a bad temper; unsmiling —**~ly** *adv* —**~ness** *n* [U]

sour[2] *v* [T1;I∅] to (cause to) become sour: *The milk has soured overnight*

source /sɔːs‖sors/ *n* **1** [(*of*)] a place from which something comes; producing place or force: *We'll have to find a new source of income.|to find the source of the engine trouble* **2** the place where a stream of water starts: *Follow up the river to discover its source* —compare SPRING[2] (1) **3** [*usu. pl.*] a person or thing that supplies information

sour cream /,· '·/ *BrE* also **soured cream**— *n* [U] cream made sour by adding a kind of bacteria, and used in various foods

sour·dough /'saʊədəʊ‖-ər-/ *n* **1** [U] *NW AmE & CanE* a kind of slightly alcoholic flour mixture for making bread **2** [C] a person with long experience of living or esp. looking for gold, in Alaska or N Canada

sour on *v prep* [D1] *AmE* to turn the opinion of (someone) against (something): *That experience soured me on camping for the rest of my life!*

sour·puss /'saʊəpʊs‖-ər-/ *n humor* a person with no sense of humour, who always complains and is never satisfied

sou·sa·phone /'suːzəfəʊn/ *n* a type of very large brass musical instrument, played by blowing, used esp. in bands, and usu. fitted round the player's left shoulder

souse /saʊs/ *v* [T1] **1** to dip in water or pour water over; make completely wet **2** [Wa5] to preserve (esp. fish) by placing in salted water, VINEGAR, etc.

soused /saʊst/ *adj sl* drunk

south[1] /saʊθ/ *adv* [Wa5] **1** (*often cap.*) towards the south: *to travel south|Brighton is south of London* **2 down south** *infml* to or in the south: *to spend the winter down south* —see NORTH (USAGE)

south[2] *n* (*often cap.*) **1** [(*the*) R] (the direction of) one of the 4 main points of the compass, on the right of a person facing the rising sun **2** [*the*+R; A] (of a wind) (coming from) this direction: *a warm south wind|The wind's in the south* —compare SOUTHERLY

South *n* [*the*+R] **1** the part of a country which is further south than the rest **2** the southeastern states of the US where there used to be black slaves —see NORTH (USAGE)

south·bound /'saʊθbaʊnd/ *adj* [Wa5] travelling towards the south

south·east[1] /,saʊθ'iːst◂/ *adv* [Wa5] (*often cap.*) towards the southeast: *windows facing southeast*

southeast[2] *n* (*often cap.*) **1** [(*the*) R] (the direction of) the point of the compass that is halfway between south and east **2** [*the*+R;A] (of a wind) (coming from) this direction —compare SOUTHEASTERLY

south·east·er /,saʊθ'iːstəʳ/ *n* a strong wind or storm coming from the southeast

south·east·er·ly /,saʊθ'iːstəli‖-ər-/ *adj* **1** towards or in the southeast **2** [Wa5] (of a wind) coming from the southeast

south·east·ern /,saʊθ'iːstən‖-ərn/ *adj* (*often cap.*) of or belonging to the southeast part, esp. of a country

south·east·ward /,saʊθ'iːstwəd‖-ərd/ *adj* going towards the southeast —compare SOUTHEASTERLY

south·east·wards /,saʊθ'iːstwədz‖-ərdz/ *AmE* also **southeastward**— *adv* (towards the) southeast

south·er·ly /'sʌðəli‖-ər-/ *adj* **1** towards or in the south: *the southerly shore of the lake* **2** [Wa5] (of a wind) coming from the south

south·ern /'sʌðən‖-ərn/ *adj* (*often cap.*) of or belonging to the south part, esp. of the world or a country: *the southern US|the warm southern sun* —see NORTH (USAGE)

South·ern·er /'sʌðənəʳ‖-ər-/ *n* a person who lives

in or comes from the southern part of a country

southern lights /ˌ·· ˈ·/ *n* [*the*+P] (*usu. caps.*) see AURORA

south·ern·most /ˈsʌðənməʊst‖-ər-/ *adj* [Wa5] *fml* furthest south

south·paw /ˈsaʊθpɔː/ *n* **1** *BrE* a LEFT-HANDED (1) fighter, esp. a boxer (BOX[4] (1)) **2** *AmE infml* a LEFT-HANDED (1) person

south pole /ˌ· ˈ·/ *n* **1** [*the*+R;C] (*usu. caps.*) (the lands around) the most southern point on the surface of the earth, or of another chief heavenly body (PLANET) **2** [*the*+R] the point in the sky to the south around which stars seem to turn

south·ward /ˈsaʊθwəd‖-ərd/ *adj* [Wa5] going towards the south —compare SOUTHERLY (1)

south·wards /ˈsaʊθwədz‖-ərdz/ *AmE* also **southward**— *adv* [Wa5] towards the south

south·west[1] /ˌsaʊθˈwest◂/ *adv* [Wa5] (*often cap.*) towards the southwest: *to sail southwest*

southwest[2] *n* **1** [(*the*) R] (*often cap.*) (the direction of) the point of the compass which is halfway between south and west **2** [*the*+R;A] (of a wind) (coming from) this direction —compare SOUTHWESTERLY

south·west·er /ˌsaʊθˈwestəʳ/ *n* a strong wind or storm from the southwest

south·west·er·ly /ˌsaʊθˈwestəli‖-ərli/ *adj* **1** towards or in the southwest **2** [Wa5] (of a wind) coming from the southwest

south·west·ern /ˌsaʊθˈwestən‖-ərn/ *adj* (*often cap.*) of or belonging to the southwest part, esp. of a country

south·west·ward /ˌsaʊθˈwestwəd‖-ərd/ *adj* going towards the southwest —compare SOUTHWESTERLY

south·west·wards /ˌsaʊθˈwestwədz‖-ərdz/ *AmE* also **southwestward**— *adv* (towards the) southwest: *sail southwestwards*

sou·ve·nir /ˌsuːvəˈnɪəʳ, ˈsuːvənɪəʳ/ *n* an object (to be) kept as a reminder of an event, trip, place, etc.

sou'west·er /saʊˈwestəʳ/ *n* **1** a hat of shiny material (OILSKIN) with a wide band coming far down over the neck and worn esp. by sailors in storms **2** SOUTHWESTER

sove·reign[1] /ˈsɒvrɪ̵n‖ˈsɑv-/ *n* **1** the person with the highest political power in a country; a ruler such as a king or queen; MONARCH **2** a former British gold coin worth £1

sovereign[2] *adj* **1** [Wa5] in control of a country; ruling: *Sovereign power must lie with the people* **2** [Wa5] (of a country) independent and self-governing **3** *lit or pomp* having wonderful powers, esp. of curing: *a sovereign* REMEDY

sove·reign·ty /ˈsɒvrənti‖ˈsɑv-/ *n* [U] **1** complete freedom and power to act or govern: *the sovereignty of God|of Parliament* **2** the quality of being an independent self-governing country

so·vi·et /ˈsəʊvɪ̵t, ˈsɒ-‖ˈsəʊ-, ˈsɑ-/ *n* an elected council at any of various levels in COMMUNIST countries

Soviet *adj* [Wa5] of or concerning the USSR (the **Soviet Union** /ˌ··· ˈ··/) or its people

sow[1] /saʊ/ *n* a fully grown female pig —compare BOAR, HOG

sow[2] /səʊ/ *v* **sowed, sown** /səʊn/ *or* **sowed** [T1;I∅] **1** to plant or scatter (seeds) on (a piece of ground) **2** *lit* to set in movement; cause to begin: *"Whatever a man sows, that he will also* REAP*"* (The Bible) —**~er** *n*

sox /sɒks‖sɑks/ *n* [P] *nonstandard or in tdmks, esp. AmE* socks

soy /sɔɪ/ also **soy·a** /sɔɪə/— *n* [U] SOYBEAN*s*: *soya flour*

soy·bean /ˈsɔɪbiːn/ also **soya bean** /ˈ·· ·/— *n* (the bean of) a plant native to Asia grown for food from its seeds which produce oil and are rich in PROTEIN —see picture at VEGETABLE[1]

soy sauce /ˈ· ·/ *n* [U] dark brown liquid made from SOYBEAN*s* allowed to become sour-tasting in salt water, and eaten esp. with E Asian food

soz·zled /ˈsɒzəld‖ˈsɑ-/ *adj BrE sl* drunk

spa /spɑː/ also **watering place**— *n* a usu. fashionable place with a spring of mineral water where people come for cures of various diseases

space[1] /speɪs/ *n* **1** [U;C] something limited and measurable in length, width, or depth and regarded as not filled up; distance, area, or VOLUME (3); room: *In the space of 10 miles the road goes up 1,000 feet.|enough space at the table for 10 people|Keep some space between you and the car ahead* **2** [U; C:(9)] a quantity or bit of this for a particular purpose: *to find a parking space|to fly in a country's air space* **3** [U] that which surrounds all objects and continues outward in all directions: *fall out of the window into space|I don't think he saw me: he was just looking out into space* **4** [U] (*often in comb.*) what is outside the earth's air; where other heavenly bodies move: *to travel through space to the moon|a space station|*SPACECRAFT*|in outer space* **5** [U;C *often pl.*] (an area of) land not built on (esp. in the phr. **open space**): *a town planned to have some open space near the centre|a holiday in the wide open spaces* **6** [U;C] a period of time: *the spaces between meals|a large increase during the space of 2 years* **7** [C] **a** an area or distance left between written or printed words, lines, etc. **b** the width of a letter on a TYPEWRITER: *The word "the" takes 3 spaces*

space[2] *v* [X9 esp. OUT, *usu. pass.*] to place apart; arrange with spaces between: *10 lines of writing spaced out to fill the page*

space·craft /ˈspeɪs-krɑːft‖-kræft/ *n* **spacecraft** [Wn3] a vehicle able to travel in SPACE[1] (4)

spaced out /ˌ· ˈ·/ *adj sl, esp. AmE* in a state of mind such as that caused by taking mind-influencing drugs; HIGH[1] (8b)

space heat·er /ˈ· ˌ··/ *n* an electric or FUEL-burning machine for heating an enclosed area or room

space probe /ˈ· ·/ *n* PROBE[1] (3)

space·ship /ˈspeɪsˌʃɪp/ *n* (esp. in stories) a SPACE[1] (4) vehicle for carrying people

space·suit /ˈspeɪs-suːt, -sjuːt‖-suːt/ *n* a suit for wearing in SPACE[1] (4), covering the whole body and provided with an air supply

spac·ing /ˈspeɪsɪŋ/ *n* [U] placement or arrangement apart, esp. of written or TYPED[2] (1) lines (in the phrs. **single/double/triple spacing**=lines with 0/1/2 empty lines between)

spa·cious /ˈspeɪʃəs/ *adj* having a lot of room; not narrow; ROOMY —**~ly** *adv* —**~ness** *n* [U]

spade[1] /speɪd/ *n* **1** a tool like a SHOVEL (1) for digging earth, with a broad metal blade for pushing with the foot into the ground —see picture at GARDEN[1] **2** also **spadeful** /ˈspeɪdfʊl/— the amount (as of earth) carried by this **3 call a spade a spade** *infml* to speak the plain truth without being delicate or sensitive

spade[2] *v* [I∅;T1] to dig, move, or work with a SPADE[1] (1)

spade[3] *n* **1** a playing card with 1 or more figures shaped like a pointed leaf printed on it in black: *the 6 of spades|only one spade left in the player's hand* —see CARDS (USAGE) **2** *taboo derog sl* a black-skinned person

spade·work /ˈspeɪd-wɜːk‖-ɜrk/ *n* [U] hard work done in preparation for an event or course of action

spa·ghet·ti /spəˈgeti/ *n* [U] an Italian food made of flour paste (PASTA) in long strings, usu. sold in dry form for making soft again in boiling water —compare MACARONI, VERMICELLI

spake /speɪk/ *old use or poet past t. of* SPEAK

spam /spæm/ *n* [U] *tdmk* a kind of tinned meat usu. eaten cold

span¹ /spæn/ *n* **1** [C] a stretch between 2 limits, esp. in time: *over a span of 3 years* —compare WINGSPAN **2** [C9] a length of time over which something continues or works well: *a short attention/interest/memory span* **3** [C] (the length of) a bridge, arch, etc., between supports **4** [C] the distance from the end of the thumb to the end of the little finger in a spread hand; about 9 inches or 0·23 metres

span² *v* **-nn-** [T1] **1** to form an arch or bridge over: *A bridge spanned the stream* **2** to enclose in space or time; reach over: *His interests spanned many subjects, and his active life spanned most of the Victorian period*

span³ *adj* see SPICK-AND-SPAN

span·gle¹ /ˈspæŋɡəl/ *n* a small piece of shiny metal or plastic sewn in large numbers esp. on dresses to give a shining effect; SEQUIN

spangle² *v* [Wv5;T1 (*with*)] to give a shining effect to, (as if) with SPANGLE*s*; ornament with shining objects

span·iel /ˈspænɪəl/ *n* any of various breeds of small short-legged dogs with long ears and long wavy hair

Span·ish /ˈspænɪʃ/ *adj* of or belonging to Spain or its language —see NATIONALITY TABLE

spank¹ /spæŋk/ *v* [T1] to strike with quick force (as if) with the open hand, esp. on the BUTTOCK*s* —**spank** *n* —**~ing** *n* [U;C]

spank² *v* [L9, esp. ALONG] to go or esp. sail quickly

spank·ing¹ /ˈspæŋkɪŋ/ *adj* [A] quickly moving; BRISK (1); SMART² (1); LIVELY (1): *a spanking wind*

spanking² *adv* [Wa5] (*used before adjectives like* new, clean, fine, *etc.*) very; completely: *a spanking new car*

span·ner /ˈspænəʳ/ (*AmE* **wrench**)— *n BrE* **1** a metal hand tool with jaws (**open-ended spanner**) or a hollow end (**ring spanner**), for fitting over and twisting screwed machine parts (NUT*s*¹ (2)) —see picture at TOOL¹ **2 a spanner in the works** *BrE infml* a cause of confusion or ruin to a plan or operation

span roof /ˈ· ·/ *n* a roof with 2 opposite slopes

spar¹ /spɑːʳ/ *n* a thick pole, esp. one used on a ship to support sails or ropes —compare MAST

spar² *v* **-rr-** [I∅ (*with*)] **1** to BOX (=fight with thick GLOVE*s*) without hitting hard, as in practice (between **sparring partners**) or in testing an opponent's defence **2** to fight with words; WRANGLE: *a minister sparring with newspaper reporters*

spar³ *n* [U] any of various nonmetallic rather shiny minerals, esp. found naturally along with metal

spare¹ /speəʳ/ *v* **1** [T1] to keep from punishing, harming, or attacking: *Take my money but spare my life!* **2** [D1] to save (someone) (need or trouble): *Use the telephone and spare yourself a visit* **3** [D1] to keep from giving (someone) (something unwelcome): *Please spare me your opinions: just tell me the facts* **4** [D1;T1] to give up as not completely needed; afford to give: *Can you spare me 5 minutes? I want your advice.|We're so busy that no one in the office can be spared for any other work* **5** [T1 *nonassertive*] to keep from using, spending, etc.: *Nothing/No trouble was spared to make sure the guests enjoyed themselves* **6 enough and to spare** more than enough **7 to spare** left over; EXTRA¹: *We have just enough money to buy it, with 11 pence to spare*

spare² *adj* **1** [Wa5] not in use but kept for use: *a spare tyre/bedroom* **2** [Wa5] not needed for use; free: *something to do in her spare time* **3** [Wa1] rather thin; LEAN³ (1): *a kind of beauty in her spare figure* **4** [Wa1] not in plenty; MEAGRE (2); SPARING: *a spare meal of bread and cheese* **5 go spare** *BrE sl* to become very anxious and/or angry

spare³ *n* **1** a second object of the same kind that is kept for possible use **2** SPARE TYRE (1) **3** [*often pl.*] *BrE* SPARE PART a part which can be used in place of an old or broken part of a car, machine, etc.

spare-part sur·ge·ry /ˌ· · ˈ···/ *n* [U] *infml* the fixing of organs (such as a heart) from dead people into the body to take the place of organs that are diseased or damaged

spare·ribs /ˈspeəˌrɪbz/ *n* [P] (some of) a pig's RIB*s* with the meat which sticks to them

spare tyre /ˌ· ˈ·/ *n* **1** a 5th tyre carried in a vehicle for use if a tyre is damaged on the road **2** *humor* a noticeably fat waist —compare MIDDLE AGE SPREAD

spar·ing /ˈspeərɪŋ/ *adj* [(*in, of*)] using or giving little; FRUGAL (1): *sparing of praise* —**~ly** *adv*

spark¹ /spɑːk‖spɑrk/ *n* **1** a small bit of burning material thrown out by a fire or by the striking together of 2 hard objects **2** a light-producing passage of electricity across a space **3** a direct cause of an event regarded as a fire or explosion: *The spark that* SET OFF (3) *the war was the murder of the prince* **4** [(*of*)] a very small but important bit, esp. of a quality: *a spark of cleverness/politeness* **5 bright spark** /ˈ· ·/ *BrE infml* a clever or cheerful person

spark² *v* **1** [Wv4;I∅] to throw out SPARK*s* (1) **2** [I∅] to produce a SPARK (2) **3** [X9, esp. *to, into*] to lead into action; INCITE: *a player sparking his team to victory* **4** [T1] *esp. AmE* SPARK OFF

sparking plug /ˈ·· ·/ *AmE* **spark plug** /ˈ· ·/— *n BrE* a part which screws into a petrol engine and makes an electric SPARK to explode the petrol mixture —see picture at PETROL

spar·kle¹ /ˈspɑːkəl‖ˈspɑr-/ *v* [I∅] **1** to shine in small flashes: *a diamond that sparkled in the sunlight* **2** [Wv4] (of a drink) to give off gas in small BUBBLE*s*¹ (1): *sparkling wine* —compare STILL¹ (4) **3** [(*with*)] to show spirit and excitement; be bright: *a conversation sparkling with humour|eyes sparkling with pleasure*

sparkle² *n* [C;U] an act, or the quality, of sparkling (SPARKLE (3)): *the sparkle of a diamond|frequent sparkles of humour*

spar·kler /ˈspɑːkləʳ‖ˈspɑr-/ *n* **1** a kind of stick made to give off harmless bright SPARK*s*¹ (1) as it burns down **2** *sl* a diamond

spark off *v adv* [T1] *esp. BrE, not fml* to lead to; be the direct cause of: *What sparked off the quarrel?*

sparks /spɑːks‖spɑrks/ *n* [C;N] an electrician or radio OPERATOR

spar·row /ˈspærəʊ/ *n* any of various kinds of small brownish birds very common in many parts of the world —see picture at BIRD¹

sparse /spɑːs‖spɑrs/ *adj* [Wa1] scattered; with few members; thin; SCANTY: *lots of bare floor and only sparse furniture|an unattractive sparse beard* —**~ly** *adv* —**~ness, sparsity** *n* [U]

spar·tan /ˈspɑːtn‖-ɑr-/ *adj* (*often cap.*) simple and without attention to comfort; severe

spas·m /ˈspæzəm/ *n* **1** [C;(*tech*) U] a sudden uncontrolled tightening of muscles **2** [C (*of*)] a sudden violent effort, feeling, or act; FIT¹ (1): *spasms of grief/laughter/coughing*

spas·mod·ic /spæzˈmɒdɪk‖-ˈmɑ-/ *adj* **1** of or like a SPASM: *spasmodic pain* **2** not continuous; irregular; INTERMITTENT; FITFUL: *spasmodic growth in population* —**~ally** *adv* [Wa4]

spas·tic /ˈspæstɪk/ *n, adj* **1** [Wa5] (a person) suffering from a disease (**spastic paralysis**) in which some parts of the body will not move because the muscles stay tightened **2** *sl* (*used esp. by children*) (a person who is) foolish, lacking in skill, etc.

spat[1] *n* a cloth covering for the ankle, worn esp. formerly by men above a shoe, fastened by side buttons and a band under the shoe
spat[2] *n AmE* a short unimportant quarrel
spat[3] *past t. and p. of* SPIT
spatch·cock /ˈspætʃkɒk‖-kɑk/ *v* [X9, esp. *into*] *infml* to fit (words) into an existing framework; INTERPOLATE: *spatchcocked some new facts into his prepared speech*
spate /speɪt/ *n* [S9, esp. *of*] **1** *esp. BrE* a large number or amount, esp. coming together in time: *a spate of accidents on a dangerous stretch of road* **2 in spate** flooding; full of rushing water: *a river in full spate*
spa·tial /ˈspeɪʃəl/ *adj* [Wa5] *fml* of, concerning, or being in space —**~ly** *adv*
spat·ter[1] /ˈspætəʳ/ *v* **1** [D1 + *with/on*; T1] to scatter (drops of a liquid) on (a surface): *The car spattered my clothes with mud.|Some paint was spattered on the floor: the floor was all spattered with paint* **2** [IØ] (of a liquid) to fall or be thrown off in drops onto a surface: *A little of the hot cooking oil spattered on the wall*
spatter[2] *n* **1** a SPATTERed drop or spot **2** [*usu. sing.*] a small amount; SPRINKLE: *a spatter of rain*
spat·u·la /ˈspætjʊlə‖-tʃələ/ *n* any of various tools with a dull-edged wide flat blade, for spreading, mixing, or lifting soft substances —see picture at MEDICAL[1]
spav·in /ˈspævɪn, -vən/ *n* a bony swelling on a horse's HOCK[1] (2) —**~ed** *adj*
spawn[1] /spɔːn/ *v* **1** [T1;IØ] (of water animals like fishes and FROGs) to lay (eggs) in large quantities together **2** [T1] to produce, esp. in large numbers; GENERATE: *a mystery that spawned lots of guesses about what really happened*
spawn[2] *n* [U] **1** the eggs of water animals like fishes and FROGs, laid together in a soft mass —see picture at AMPHIBIAN **2** rootlike parts of MUSHROOMs, esp. prepared for growing
spay /speɪ/ *v* [T1] to remove (part of) the sex organs of (a female animal): *to have a cat spayed*
speak /spiːk/ *v* **spoke** /spəʊk/, **spoken** /ˈspəʊkən/ **1** [IØ (*to/with* and/or *about*)] to say things; express thoughts aloud; use the voice; talk: *Don't speak with your mouth full of food.|to speak to a friend in the street|a chance to speak to/with the chairman about my idea* —see SAY (USAGE) **2** [IØ] to express thoughts, ideas, etc., in some other way than this: *The book speaks of the writer's childhood.|Actions speak louder than words.|Everything at the party spoke of careful planning* **3** [IØ] to make a speech: *I've invited her to speak to our club on any subject she likes: I hope she'll speak about 20 minutes and then answer questions* **4** [T1] to be able to talk in (a language): *to speak English|a place where no English is spoken|We need a French-speaking secretary* **5** [T1] to express or say: *to speak the truth|hardly able to speak a word* **6** [IØ (*to*)] to be **on speaking terms**: *After their fight, they're not speaking (to each other)* **7** [IØ] (esp. of a gun or musical instrument) to make a sound **8** [T1] to say from memory; RECITE (1) (esp. in the phr. **speak a piece**) **9** [L9] to mean in the stated way what is said (in such phrs. as **generally/properly speaking**): *Generally speaking, I think you're right.|I think, personally speaking, it's a good idea* **10 on speaking terms a** [*nonassertive*] willing to talk and be polite to another, esp. after a quarrel: *She and her mother are not on speaking terms after last night* **b** good enough friends to exchange greetings **11 so to speak** as one might say; rather: *up to his neck, so to speak, in debt* **12 speak one's mind** to express one's thoughts directly: *I'm angry and I want a chance to speak my mind to the director* **13 to speak of** [*nonassertive*] worth mentioning; of much value: *no rain to speak of, only a few drops*
speak·eas·y /ˈspiːkˌiːzi/ *n* (esp. in the US in the 1920's and 1930's) an unlawful place for going to buy and drink alcohol
speak·er /ˈspiːkəʳ/ *n* **1** a person making a speech, or who makes speeches in a stated way: *an interesting speaker* **2** a person who speaks a language: *a speaker of English* **3** (*often cap.*) the person who controls the course of business in a lawmaking body (note the phr. **Mr Speaker**) **4** LOUDSPEAKER
speak·er·ship /ˈspiːkəʃɪp‖-ər-/ *n* the office of speaker in a lawmaking body
speak for *v prep* [T1] **1** to express the thoughts, opinions, etc., of: *a powerless group with no one to speak for them* **2** to be a witness of; say things about; give an idea of: *a fine job which speaks well for the workers and for the company's future* **3** [*usu. pass.*] to get the right to (something) in advance; RESERVE[1]: *The first 300 cars of this new model have already been spoken for* **4 speak for itself/themselves** to need no further explanation: *Look at the facts and decide: they speak for themselves*
speaking tube /ˈ·· ·/ *n* a pipe through which people in different rooms (as on a ship) may speak to one another
speak out *v adv* [IØ] to speak boldly, freely, and plainly: *speak out against our real enemies*
speak to *v prep* [T1] **1** *fml* to direct one's remarks to; talk about: *We haven't much time: please speak to the subject* **2** *euph* to speak severely to; ADMONISH: *He was late again today: it's time you spoke to that boy* **3** *not fml* to be interesting or attractive to; APPEAL[2] (2) to: *I'm afraid this kind of art doesn't really speak to me*
speak up *v adv* [IØ] **1** to speak more loudly: *Speak up, please: I can't hear you* **2** to speak boldly; SPEAK OUT: *spoke up in defence of her political beliefs*
spear[1] /spɪəʳ/ *n* a pole with a sharp point at one end used esp. formerly for throwing as a weapon
spear[2] *v* **1** [T1] to make a hole in or catch (as) with the point of a spear; IMPALE: *He reached out and speared a piece of meat with his fork* **2** [L9] *not fml* to move swiftly as if towards something aimed at: *a boat spearing through the water*
spear[3] *n* a young thin pointed leaf (of grass or other plants) growing directly from the ground
spear·head[1] /ˈspɪəhed‖ˈspɪər-/ *n* [*usu. sing.*] something that begins an attack or course of action forcefully; a leading force
spearhead[2] *v* [T1] to act as a SPEARHEAD for; lead forcefully
spear·mint /ˈspɪəˌmɪnt‖ˈspɪər-/ *n* [U] a common MINT plant widely grown and used for its fresh taste, as in some CHEWING GUM
spec /spek/ *n* **on spec** /ˌ· ˈ·/ *infml BrE* as a risk or SPECULATION (2): *to buy oil-company shares on spec*
spe·cial[1] /ˈspeʃəl/ *adj* **1** [Wa5] of a particular kind; not ordinary or usual: *a special reason for the request|a special case deserving special treatment|a special printing of a newspaper* **2** also (*fml*) **especial**— particularly great or fine; EXCEPTIONAL: *Tonight is a special occasion, and we have something very special for dinner.|a special friend of mine*
special[2] *n* **1** something that is not of the regular or ordinary kind: *a 2-hour television special* **2** *AmE infml* an advertised reduced price in a shop (often in the phr. **on special**): *Ice cream is on special this week only!|They're having a special on ice-cream this week*
special de·liv·er·y /ˌ·· ·ˈ···/ *n* [U] the delivering of a piece of mail by a special carrier before it would ordinarily come in the next post
spe·cial·ist /ˈspeʃəlɪ̈st/ *n* **1** a person who has

special interests or skills in a limited field of work or study; EXPERT **2** a doctor who gives treatment in a particular way or to certain kinds of people or diseases: *a heart specialist*

spe·cial·i·ty /ˌspeʃiˈælǝ̇ti/ *AmE* usu. **spe·cial·ty** /ˈspeʃǝlti/— *n* **1** a special field of work or study: *Her speciality is ancient Greek poetry* **2** [(*of*)] a particularly fine or best product: *Fish baked in pastry is the speciality of this restaurant*

spe·cial·ize, -ise /ˈspeʃǝlaɪz/ *v* [IØ (*in*)] to limit all or most of one's study, business, etc., to particular things or subjects —**-ization** /ˌspeʃǝlaɪˈzeɪʃǝn‖-lǝ-/ *n* [U;(C)]

spe·cial·ized, -ised /ˈspeʃǝlaɪzd/ *adj* fit or developed for one particular use: *specialized tools/knowledge*

special li·cence /ˌ·· ˈ··/ *n* [C; *by*+U] *law* an official permission given by the Church of England for a marriage at a time or place not usu. allowed

spe·cial·ly /ˈspeʃǝli/ *adv* **1** [Wa5] for one particular purpose: *I made a chocolate cake specially for you* **2** (*often in comb.*) in a special way: *I made this cake specially, with brown sugar instead of white* **3** ESPECIALLY: *not specially hot today*

special plead·ing /ˌ·· ˈ··/ *n* [U] unfair use of the words of an argument to make one side stronger

special stu·dent /ˌ·· ˈ··/ *n* a student in an American university who is not in a course leading to a degree

spe·cie /ˈspiːʃi/ *n* [U] *fml* money in coins: *payment in specie*

spe·cies /ˈspiːʃiːz/ *n* **-cies** [Wn3; (*of*)] **1** a group of plants or animals that are of the same kind, which are alike in all important ways, and which can breed together to produce young of the same kind —compare GENUS **2** *not fml* a type; sort: *a strange species of car*

spe·cif·ic¹ /spǝ̇ˈsɪfɪk/ *adj* **1** [B] detailed and exact; clear in meaning; careful in explanation; not VAGUE (1,2) **2** [Wa5;A] particular; certain; fixed, determined, or named: *a specific tool for each job* —**~ity** /ˌspesǝ̇ˈfɪsǝ̇ti/ *n* [U]

specific² *n* [(*for*)] *fml or tech* a drug that has an effect on a particular disease —see also SPECIFICS

spe·cif·ic·ally /spǝ̇ˈsɪfɪkli/ *adv* **1** exactly and clearly **2** (*before adjectives*) of the stated kind and no other; particularly: *not a specifically Christian idea but found in many religions* **3** speaking more exactly; NAMELY: *several countries, specifically the US, Britain and France*

spe·ci·fi·ca·tion /ˌspesǝ̇fǝ̇ˈkeɪʃǝn/ *n* **1** [U (*of*)] the action of SPECIFYing **2** [C *usu. pl.*] any of the parts of a detailed plan or set of descriptions or directions: *specifications for a building/car*

specific grav·i·ty /·ˌ·· ˈ···/ *n tech* the weight of a material divided by the weight of the amount of water which would fill the same space; DENSITY (2) compared with water

spe·cif·ics /spǝ̇ˈsɪfɪks/ *n* [P] matters to be decided exactly; details: *Now that we've generally agreed, let's get down to specifics and make a plan*

spe·ci·fy /ˈspesǝ̇faɪ/ *v* [T1,6a,b] to mention exactly; describe fully so as to choose or name: *to specify* HARDWOOD *floors for a house to be built|Please specify when you will be away/the dates of your absence*

spe·ci·men /ˈspesǝ̇mǝn/ *n* **1** [C] a single typical thing or example: *He's still a fine specimen of health* **2** [C] one or a piece or amount of something for being shown, tested, etc. **3** [C9] *infml* a person unusual in some way: *She's a strange specimen, isn't she?*

spe·cious /ˈspiːʃǝs/ *adj fml* seeming right or correct but not so in fact; PLAUSIBLE —**~ly** *adv* —**~ness** *n* [U]

speck /spek/ *n* [(*of*)] **1** a small spot, coloured mark, or dot: *a speck of dirt on my shirt/in my eye* **2** [*usu. nonassertive*] a very small bit: *not a speck of truth in the claim*

speck·le /ˈspekǝl/ *n* a small irregular mark; coloured SPECK, esp. in a large number covering a surface —**-led** *adj*

spec·ta·cle /ˈspektǝkǝl/ *n* **1** [C] a grand public show or scene **2** [C] a silly sight; object of laughing or disrespect: *to make a spectacle of oneself* **3** [A] of or for SPECTACLEs: *a spectacle case*

spec·ta·cled /ˈspektǝkǝld/ *adj* [Wa5] wearing SPECTACLES

spec·ta·cles /ˈspektǝkǝlz/ also **glasses**, (*infml*) **specs** /speks/— *n* [P] glasses, esp. of the usual kind with side parts fitting on top of the ears: *to get a new pair of spectacles=some new spectacles* —see PAIR (USAGE)

spec·tac·u·lar¹ /spekˈtækjʊlǝʳ‖-jǝ-/ *adj* grandly out of the ordinary; attracting excited notice —**~ly** *adv*

spectacular² *n* a SPECTACULAR entertainment: *a television spectacular with lots of famous stars*

spec·ta·tor /spekˈteɪtǝʳ‖ˈspekteɪtǝr/ *n* a person who watches (esp. an event or sport) without taking part

spec·tral /ˈspektrǝl/ *adj* **1** of or like a SPECTRE **2** [Wa5] *tech* of or made by a SPECTRUM (1,2)

spec·tre, *AmE* **-ter** /ˈspektǝʳ/ *n* **1** a spirit without a body; GHOST¹ (1) **2** something that is seen in the mind and causes fear

spec·tro·scope /ˈspektrǝskǝʊp/ *n* an apparatus for forming and looking at spectra (SPECTRUM (1)) —see picture at SCIENTIFIC —**-scopic** /ˌspektrǝˈskɒpɪk‖-ˈskɑ-/ *adj* [Wa5]

spec·trum /ˈspektrǝm/ *n* **-tra** /trǝ/ **1** a set of bands of coloured light in the order of their WAVELENGTHs, into which a beam of light may be separated (as by a PRISM (2)) —see picture at OPTICS **2** a range of any of various kinds of waves: *a radio/sound spectrum* **3** an arrangement of unseparated members along a line; continuous range: *a wide spectrum of opinion(s) on this question*

spec·u·late /ˈspekjʊleɪt‖-jǝ-/ *v* **1** [IØ;T5] to think (about a matter) in a light way or without facts that would lead to a firm result: *I was just speculating that this might be my last chance* **2** [IØ (*in*)] to buy or deal in goods, SHAREs¹ (2), etc., whose future price is still very uncertain, in the hope of a large profit: *speculating in gold mines* —**-lator** *n*

spec·u·la·tion /ˌspekjʊˈleɪʃǝn‖-jǝ-/ *n* **1** [U;C:(5)] (an example of) reasoning lightly or without all the facts **2** [U;C] (a case of) business trading in the hope of profit from price rises rather than from actual business earnings

spec·u·la·tive /ˈspekjʊlǝtɪv‖-jǝ-/ *adj* **1** [B] of or being SPECULATION (2): *a speculative guess/sale* **2** [Wa5;A] based on reason alone and not facts about the world: *speculative* PHILOSOPHY (1) —**~ly** *adv*

speech /spiːtʃ/ *n* **1** [U] the act or power of speaking; spoken language: *Speech was impossible with so much noise around* **2** [U] the way of speaking of a person or group: *By your speech I can tell you're from Liverpool* **3** [C] **a** an act of speaking formally to a group of listeners: *to give/make a speech* **b** the words so spoken: *The minister's speech was sent to the newspapers in advance* **4** [C] a usu. long set of lines for an actor to say in a play

spee·chi·fy /ˈspiːtʃǝ̇faɪ/ *v* [IØ] *infml & humor* to

make a speech or speeches, esp. in a (too) proud fine-sounding way

speech·less /ˈspiːtʃləs/ *adj* **1** [F (*with*); (B)] unable for the moment to speak because of strong feeling, shock, etc. **2** [A] too great to allow speech or expression: *speechless wonder* —**~ly** *adv* —**~ness** *n* [U]

speech ther·a·py /ˌ· ˈ···, ˈ· ˌ···/ *n* [U] treatment for helping people with various kinds of difficulties in speaking plainly —**-pist** *n*

speed¹ /spiːd/ *n* **1** [C] rate of movement; distance divided by time of travel: *to keep to a speed of 55 miles per hour|to move along at a slow but steady speed* **2** [U] the action, ability, or state of moving swiftly: *a football player with good speed|He made his escape by speed rather than cleverness* **3** [C] GEAR¹ (3) (esp. in such phr. as **3/4/5-speed**): *a 10-speed bicycle* **4** [U] *drug-users' sl* AMPHETAMINE **5 at speed** /ˌ· ˈ·/ fast; swiftly

speed² *v* **speeded** *or* **sped** /sped/ **1** [L9;X9] to (cause to) go or pass quickly: *saw a car speeding away|The time sped quickly by* **2** [I∅ *usu. used in pres. p.*] to go or drive too fast; break the speed limit: *Was I really speeding officer?* —see also SPEED UP

speed- *comb. form* **1** of a kind allowing a fast speed: *speed-reading* **2** of a kind judged by speed: *speed-skating* (SKATE)

speed·boat /ˈspiːdbəʊt/ *n* a small power-driven boat built for high speed

speed·ing /ˈspiːdɪŋ/ *n* [U] the offence of driving faster than the lawful limit: *found guilty of speeding* —**speeder** *n*

speed lim·it /ˈ· ˌ··/ *n* the fastest speed allowed by law on a particular stretch of road: *to keep within*/EXCEED (2) *the speed limit*

speed·om·e·ter /spɪˈdɒmɪ̇təʳ, ˈspiːdɒ-‖-ˈdɑ-/ *BrE infml* also **spee·do** /ˈspiːdəʊ/— *n* an instrument in a vehicle for telling its speed —see picture at CAR

speed trap /ˈ· ·/ *n* a stretch of road watched by hidden policemen to catch drivers going too fast

speed-up /ˈ· ·/ *n* an act of going faster; ACCELERATION: *a speed-up in house-building to meet the demand*

speed up *v adv* [I∅;T1] to (cause to) move or go faster

speed·way /ˈspiːdweɪ/ *n* **1** [C] a track for racing motor vehicles, esp. motorcycles **2** [U] the sport of racing motorcycles on such a track

speed·well /ˈspiːdwel/ *n* [U] a kind of small European wild plant with light bluish flowers

speed·y /ˈspiːdi/ *adj* [Wa1] going, working, or passing fast; quick; swift: *a speedy journey* —**speedily** *adv* —**speediness** *n* [U]

spe·le·ol·o·gy, spelae- /ˌspiːliˈɒlədʒi‖-ˈɑlə-/ *n* [U] **1** the scientific study of caves **2** the sport of walking and climbing in caves —**-logical** /ˌspiːlɪəˈlɒdʒɪkəl‖-ˈlɑ-/ *adj* [Wa5] —**-ogist** /ˌspiːliˈɒlədʒɪ̇st‖-ˈɑlə-/ *n*

spell¹ /spel/ *n* **1 a** a condition caused by magical power; ENCHANTMENT **b** the magic words producing this condition **2** [*usu. sing.*] a strong attractive power: *to fall under the spell of such wonderful storytelling*

spell² *v* **spelt** /spelt/ *or* **spelled** (*AmE* **spelled**) **1** [D1;T1 (*with*)] to name in order (the letters) of (esp. a word): *My name is spelt S-M-Y-T-H* **2** [T1 (OUT) *no pass.*] (of letters in order) to form (a word): *B-O-O-K spells "book"* **3** [I∅] to form words (correctly) from letters: *to learn to spell|children who can't spell well* **4** [T1] *not fml* to add up to (a result); mean: *His disapproval spells defeat for our plan* —**~er** *n*

USAGE **Spelt** is more common in *BrE* than **spelled**, but **spelled** is the regular form in *AmE*.

spell³ *v* **spelled** [T1] to take the turn of; allow (another) to rest by taking over work; RELIEVE (2): *Let me spell you on duty so that you can have your tea*

spell⁴ *n* **1** [C] an unbroken period of time of usu. unstated length: *a spell of work abroad* **2** [C9] a usu. quickly-passing period of illness, fainting, etc.; ATTACK² (4): *a coughing spell*

spell·bind /ˈspelbaɪnd/ *v* [Wv4,5;T1] to hold the complete attention of; FASCINATE —**~er** *n*

spell·ing /ˈspelɪŋ/ *n* **1** [U] the action or proper way of forming words from letters: *Her spelling has improved* **2** [C] an ordered set of letters forming a word: *a word for which British and American spellings are different*

spell out *v adv* [T1] **1** to explain in the plainest or most detailed way: *to spell out the government's plans in a speech* **2** to write or say (a word) letter by letter

spend /spend/ *v* **spent** /spent/ **1** [T1 (*on, for*); I∅] to give out (esp. money) in payment: *to spend £2,000 for/on a new car|to spend 10p on chocolate|cuts in government spending* **2** [T1 (*in*)] to pass or use (time): *to spend a pleasant hour (in) talking with friends|to spend 3 years in prison|He's spent his life writing this book* **3** [T1] *esp. fml or lit* to wear out or use completely: *The storm soon spent itself/its force*

spend·er /ˈspendəʳ/ *n* [C9] a person who spends money in the stated amounts or ways: *a shop for big spenders*

spending mon·ey /ˈ·· ˌ··/ *n* [U] POCKET MONEY (1)

spend·thrift /ˈspendˌθrɪft/ *n* a person who spends money wastefully

spent /spent/ *adj* **1** worn out; EXHAUSTed: *to come home tired and spent* **2** [Wa5] already used; no longer for use: *spent bullets*

sperm /spɜːm‖spɜrm/ *n* **sperm** *or* **sperms** **1** [Wn2; C] a cell produced by the sex organs of a male animal, which usu. swims in a liquid and is able to unite with the female egg to produce new life **2** [U] the liquid from the male sex organs in which these swim; SEMEN

sper·ma·cet·i /ˌspɜːməˈseti‖-ɜr-/ *n* [U] a waxy material found in the head of the SPERM WHALE and used in making skin creams, candles, etc.

sper·ma·to·zo·a /ˌspɜːmətəˈzəʊə‖-ɜr-/ *n sing.* **-zoon** /ˈzəʊən/ [P] *tech* SPERM (1)

sperm whale /ˈ· ·/ *n* a kind of large WHALE up to 60 feet long which is hunted for the oil in its head, for fat, and for SPERMACETI and AMBERGRIS

spew /spjuː/ *v* **1** [L9;X9] to (cause to) come out in a rush or flood; (cause to) GUSH¹ (1): *The burst pipe was spewing out dirty water* **2** [I∅;T1: (UP)] *sl* to VOMIT

sphag·num /ˈsfægnəm/ *n* [U] any of a large group of MOSSes growing in wet areas which can go to make up PEAT and which are used by gardeners for packing plants

sphere /sfɪəʳ/ *n* **1** a round figure in space; ball-shaped mass; solid figure all points of which are equally distant from a centre —see picture at GEOMETRY **2** an area or range of existence, force, meaning, action, etc.: COMPASS² (4), PROVINCE (5): *famous in many spheres* **3** (in ancient science) any of the transparent shells which were thought to turn around the earth with the heavenly bodies fixed in them

-sphere *comb. form* [→*n*] **1** of a SPHERE: HEMISPHERE **2** SPHERICAL: BATHYSPHERE

spher·i·cal /ˈsferɪkəl/ *adj* having the form of a SPHERE (1)

sphe·roid /ˈsfɪərɔɪd/ *n* a figure which is not quite a SPHERE (1), esp. one that is longer in one direction and has 2 endpoints

sphinc·ter /ˈsfɪŋktəʳ/ *n* a muscle which surrounds

and can tighten to close a passage in the body —see picture at DIGESTIVE SYSTEM

sphinx /sfɪŋks/ *n* **1** an ancient Egyptian image of a lion, lying down, with a human head **2** a person who behaves or speaks in a mysterious way

spice¹ /spaɪs/ *n* **1** [C;U] any of various vegetable products used esp. in powder form for giving a taste to other foods **2** [U;S] interest or excitement, esp. as added to something else: *a few good stories to add spice to the speech*

spice² *v* [T1 (UP, *with*)] to add SPICE to

spick-and-span /ˌspɪk ən ˈspæn/ *adj not fml* clean and bright; like new

spic·y /ˈspaɪsi/ *adj* [Wa1] **1** containing or tasting like SPICE (1) **2** exciting, esp. from being slightly improper or rude; RACY —**spicily** *adv* —**spiciness** *n* [U]

spi·der /ˈspaɪdəʳ/ *n* **1** any of many kinds of small 8-legged creatures which make silk threads, sometimes into nets for catching insects to eat —see picture at ARACHNID **2** *AmE* an iron FRYING PAN

spi·der·y /ˈspaɪdəri/ *adj* [Wa2] long and thin like a SPIDER'*s* (1) legs or suggesting a pattern like its WEB: *the old lady's spidery writing*

spiel /ʃpiːl, spiːl/ *n* [C;U] *sl* a fast-flowing line of talk, esp. intended to persuade

spig·ot /ˈspɪgət/ *n* an apparatus for turning on and off a flow of liquid, esp. from a container such as a barrel; TAP¹ (1)

spike¹ /spaɪk/ *n* **1** a long pointed piece of metal with an outward or upward point: *spikes along the top of a fence* **2** any of several pieces of metal fixed in the bottom of shoes for holding the ground, esp. in sports **3** a very large nail or pin for fastening **4** a sharp esp. upward point on a line (GRAPH) describing a change

spike² *v* [T1] **1** [Wv5] to fix with SPIKEs¹ (1,2); drive SPIKEs into **2** to damage by using the SPIKEs on one's shoes **3** *esp. AmE* to add a strong alcoholic drink to (a weak or nonalcoholic one) **4** **spike someone's guns** to prevent someone from attacking; take away an opponent's power

spike³ *n* an ear of grain

spike·nard /ˈspaɪknɑːd‖-ɑrd/ *n* [U] **1** a kind of valuable sweet-smelling oil used in ancient times **2** an E Indian plant from whose roots and stems this was probably made

spik·y /ˈspaɪki/ *adj* [Wa1] **1** having sharp points **2** *infml* having fixed opinions and hard to please; easily offended

spill¹ /spɪl/ *v* **spilled** *or* **spilt** /spɪlt/ **1** [T1;IØ] to (cause to) pour out accidentally, as over the edge of a container, and be lost: *My hand slipped and spilt my drink* (=made my drink spill) **2** [L9, esp. OVER] to spread or rush beyond limits: *The crowd spilt over from the church into the streets* **3** [T1 *often pass.*] *esp. lit* to cause (blood) to flow by wounding: *A lot of blood was spilled in that battle* **4** [T1;IØ] *infml* to let out or tell (secret information): *He threatened to spill* (*what he knew*) *to the police* **5** [T1] (esp. of a horse) to cause (a rider) to fall **6** **spill the beans** *infml* to tell a secret too soon or to the wrong person

USAGE **Spilt** is more common in *BrE* than **spilled**, except in literature, but **spilled** is more common in *AmE*.

spill² *n* **1** an act or amount of SPILLing¹ (1): *to clean up coffee spills* **2** a fall from a horse, bicycle, etc.: *to take/have a spill*

spill³ *n* a thin piece of wood or twisted paper for lighting lamps, pipes, etc.

spill·o·ver /ˈspɪlˌəʊvəʳ/ *n* [U;C] an amount that SPILLs¹ (1,2) over or goes beyond limits into something else

spill·way /ˈspɪlweɪ/ *n* a passage for water over or around a DAM (=wall for holding back water)

spin¹ /spɪn/ *v* **spun** /spʌn/, *pres. p.* **spinning** **1** [IØ; T1] to make (thread) by twisting (cotton, wool, etc.): *to spin thread|to spin wool into thread|a spinning mill* **2** [T1] (of a SPIDER or SILKWORM) to produce (thread, esp. in a mass or net) **3** [IØ;T1] to (cause to) turn round and round fast; WHIRL¹ (1): *to spin a* TOP⁴ (1)|*a wheel spinning on its* AXLE|*I spun round to see who had spoken* **4** [L9] to move fast on wheels: *to spin along at 50 miles per hour* **5** [T1] to produce in the mind and express; FABRICATE (1): *to spin a* YARN (=story)|*to spin a fine* THEORY (1) *which may be false* **6** [Wv5;T1] to produce in a threadlike form: *to spin* FIBREGLASS|*spun gold/nylon*

spin² *n* **1** [C] an act of spinning: *Try your luck on a spin of the wheel* (=at a game of ROULETTE)! **2** [U; S] fast turning movement: *to throw a cricket ball with lots of spin|a spin of 10 turns per second* **3** [S] a short trip for pleasure: *Take a spin in my new car* **4** [C] a fall by an aircraft in a steep circular path: *to go into/come out of a spin* **5** [S] a steep drop; PLUNGE² (1): *bad news which sent prices into a spin* **6** [A] (in cricket) depending on a spinning movement of the ball: *a spin* BOWLER **7** [S] *infml* a confused racing state of mind; PANIC¹ (1) (esp. in the phr. **in a (flat) spin**)

spi·na bif·i·da /ˌspaɪnə ˈbɪfɪ̈də/ *n* [U] *med* a serious condition in which the BACKBONE is split down the middle from birth, leaving the SPINAL CORD unprotected

spin·ach /ˈspɪnɪdʒ, -ɪtʃ‖-ɪtʃ/ *n* [U] a type of widely-grown vegetable whose broad green leaves are eaten —see picture at VEGETABLE¹

spin·al /ˈspaɪnl/ *adj* [Wa5] of, for, or concerning the SPINE (1): *spinal disease*

spinal cord /ˌ·· ˈ·/ *n* the thick cord enclosed in the SPINE by which nervous messages are carried

spin·dle /ˈspɪndl/ *n* **1** a round pointed rod used for twisting the thread in SPINning (1) **2** a machine part around which something turns **3** any of various machine parts that are thin rods

spindle tree /ˈ·· ·/ *n* a type of small tree of Europe and Asia with a bright reddish berry (**spindleberry**) and strong white wood

spin·dly /ˈspɪndli/ *adj* [Wa1] long, thin, and weak-looking: *a young horse standing unsteadily on its spindly legs*

spin-dry /ˌ· ˈ·/ *v* [T1] to remove water from (clothes) after washing, esp. in a washing machine with a special part (**spin dryer** /ˌ· ˈ··/), that spins round and round fast

spine /spaɪn/ *n* **1** also **spinal col·umn** /ˌ·· ˈ··/— the row of bones in the centre of the back of higher animals that supports the body and protects the SPINAL CORD —see picture at SKELETON **2** the end of a book where the pages are fastened and the title is usu. printed **3** any of various stiff sharp-pointed plant or animal parts; prickle

spine·less /ˈspaɪnləs/ *adj* **1** without moral strength or courage **2** [Wa5] (of an animal) having no BACKBONE —**~ly** *adv* —**~ness** *n* [U]

spi·net /spɪˈnet‖ˈspɪnɪ̈t/ *n* **1** a small HARPSICHORD **2** *AmE* a low upright piano

spin·na·ker /ˈspɪnəkəʳ/ *n* a large 3-sided sail that has a rounded shape when blown out by the wind, carried on some racing boats for going with the force of the wind —see picture at SAIL²

spin·ner /ˈspɪnəʳ/ *n* **1** a person that SPINs¹ (1) material for cloth **2** **a** a cricket ball thrown with a spinning action **b** a BOWLER of such balls **3** (in some games) a movable arrow which is spun and stops showing the number, kind, etc., of moves to be made —see also MONEY-SPINNER

spin·ney /ˈspɪni/ *n BrE* a small area full of trees and low plants

spinning jen·ny /ˈ·· ˌ··/ *n* an early machine allowing one person to SPIN a number of threads at once

spinning wheel /ˈ·· ·/ *n* a small machine used esp. formerly at home for SPINning thread, in which a foot-driven wheel moves a SPINDLE

spin-off /ˈ· ·/ *n* a usu. useful product or result other than the main one; BY-PRODUCT (1)

spin out *v adv* [T1] to make longer; draw out; stretch; EXTEND (2): *to spin out a story to make a book*

spin·ster /ˈspɪnstəʳ/ *n* **1** *law* an unmarried woman **2** *sometimes derog* an unmarried woman who is no longer young; OLD MAID (1) —**~hood** *n* [U]

spin·y /ˈspaɪni/ *adj* [Wa1] like or full of SPINEs (3)

spi·ral[1] /ˈspaɪərəl/ *n* **1** a curve formed by a point winding round a centre and getting always closer to or further from it: *a spiral watch-spring* **2** a curve in space winding round a central line: *a spiral* NEBULA (=stars and gases in a spiral)|*a spiral* STAIRCASE **3** a continuous upward or downward change: *the spiral of increasing raw-material prices*

spiral[2] *v* **-ll-** (*AmE* **-l-**) **1** [L9] to move in a SPIRAL[1] (1,2); rise or fall in a winding way: *The stairs spiralled round the central pillar.*|*The damaged plane spiralled to earth* **2** [Wv4;IØ] to fall or esp. rise continuously: *spiralling prices*

spire /spaɪəʳ/ *n* a roof rising steeply to a point on top of a tower, as on a church; (the top of a) STEEPLE —see picture at CHURCH

spir·it[1] /ˈspɪrɨt/ *n* **1** [C; *in*+U] *lit* a person apart from the body; one's mind or soul: *I wish I could stop smoking: the spirit is willing but the flesh is weak.*|*a person troubled in spirit* **2** [C] a being without a body, such as a GHOST[1] (1) **3** [C] a dead person regarded as still alive apart from the body **4** [C] a power regarded as able to take control of a person: *one possessed by a spirit* **5** [U] (*sometimes cap.*) life or thought regarded as independently existing: *the belief that spirit is everywhere and in everything* **6** [C9] a person of the stated kind or temper: *She's such a kind spirit* **7** [S9] an intention or feeling in the mind; ATTITUDE (2): *to take a remark in the right spirit, without offence* **8** [U] excitement, force, or effort shown; ENERGY (1,2); liveliness (LIVELY (1)) **9** [U9] excited loyalty: *team/school spirit* **10** [C] the central quality or force of something: *the 17th-century spirit of enquiry* **11** [(*the*) S (*of*)] the real intended meaning of a law, rule, etc., rather than what it actually says: *Obey the spirit of the law* —opposite **letter** **12** [C *usu. pl., sometimes with sing. meaning*] an alcoholic drink (such as WHISKY or BRANDY) produced by boiling (DISTILLATION) from a weaker alcohol-containing drink or mixture **13** [U] any of various liquids such as alcohol used esp. for breaking down solids or as FUELs —see also METHYLATED SPIRITS, WHITE SPIRIT **14 in spirit** in one's thoughts or imagination: *I can't come to your wedding, but I'll be there in spirit: I'll think about you*

spirit[2] *v* [X9, esp. AWAY, OFF] to carry away; take, esp. in a secret or mysterious way; MAKE OFF WITH: *They spirited him away/out of town before the crowd arrived*

Spirit *n* [*the*+R] HOLY SPIRIT

spir·it·ed /ˈspɪrɨtɨd/ *adj* full of SPIRIT[1] (8); forceful; ANIMATED (1): *a spirited quarrel/defence*

-spirited *comb. form* [*adj*→*adj*] having the stated kind of feelings or temper: HIGH-SPIRITED|PUBLIC SPIRITed

spir·it·less /ˈspɪrɨtləs/ *adj* **1** weak or lazy; without SPIRIT (8) **2** sad; not cheerful; in low SPIRITS —**~ly** *adv* —**~ness** *n* [U]

spirit lev·el /ˈ·· ˌ··/ also (*esp. AmE*) **level**— *n* a tool for testing whether a surface is level, made of a bar containing a short glass tube of liquid with a BUBBLE[2] (1) which will be in the centre if the surface is level —see picture at TOOL[1]

spir·its /ˈspɪrɨts/ *n* **1** [P] the cheerful or sad state of one's mind: *in high* (=cheerful) *spirits*|*a friendly letter which raised my spirits* **2** [U9, esp. *of*] SPIRIT[1] (13): *spirits of* TURPENTINE

spir·i·tu·al[1] /ˈspɪrɨtʃʊəl/ *adj* **1** [B] nonmaterial; of the nature of spirit: *one's spiritual nature* —compare INTELLECTUAL **2** [Wa5;B] religious; SACRED: *spiritual songs*|*an adviser in spiritual matters* **3** [Wa5;A] related or close in spirit; connected by qualities or interests of a deep kind: *The theatre is her spiritual home* **4** [Wa5;B;E] *fml* of the church (often in the phr. **lords spiritual** (=BISHOPs)) —opposite **temporal, lay** —**~ly** *adv*

spiritual[2] *n* a religious song of the type sung originally by the black peoples of the US

spir·i·tual·is·m /ˈspɪrɨtʃʊlɪzəm/ *n* [U] the belief that the dead may send messages to living people usu. through a person (MEDIUM) with special powers and often using a system (**spirit rapping**) of knocking noises on a table —**-ist** *n* —**-istic** /ˌspɪrɨtʃʊˈlɪstɪk/ *adj*

spir·i·tu·al·i·ty /ˌspɪrɨtʃʊˈælɨti/ *n* [U] fondness for religious things, worship, prayer, etc.; DEVOTION

spir·i·tual·ize, -ise /ˈspɪrɨtʃʊlaɪz‖-tʃə-/ *v* [T1 *usu. pass*] to give a purer, more religious, less material meaning to: *Ancient ideas of gods became more and more spiritualized* —**-ization** /ˌspɪrɪtʃʊlaɪˈzeɪʃən/ *n* [U]

spir·i·tu·ous /ˈspɪrɨtʃʊəs/ *adj fml or tech* being or containing alcoholic SPIRITs[1] (12)

spirt /spɜːt‖spɜrt/ *n, v rare* SPURT

spit[1] /spɪt/ *n* **1** a thin pointed rod for sticking meat onto and turning, for cooking over a fire **2** a small usu. sandy point of land running out into a stretch of water **3** a depth of earth equal to that of a spade's blade: *to dig a hole 2 spits deep*

spit[2] *v* **-tt-** [T1] to fix or stick with a SPIT[1] (1)

spit[3] *v* **spat** /spæt/ *or* **spit** **1** [T1 (OUT); IØ] to force (liquid) from the mouth: *to spit on the ground*|*to spit (out) tobacco juice*|*He's very ill and spitting blood* **2** [T1 (OUT)] to say or express with effort, force, or anger, as if doing this: *She could hardly spit out the hateful word* —see also SPIT UP **3 spit it out** *infml* Go ahead and say what is on your mind

spit[4] *n* **1** [U] the liquid in the mouth; SALIVA **2** [U] *infml* a whitish liquid produced on the stems and leaves of plants by some insects —compare CUCKOO-SPIT **3** [C] *infml* the exact likeness (esp. in the phrs. **the spit and image of**, (*BrE*) **the dead spit of**): *That boy is the spit and image of his father* —see also SPITTING IMAGE

spit and pol·ish /ˌ· · ˈ··/ *n* [U] *not fml* **1** hard cleaning and polishing **2** (too) great attention to a clean and shiny appearance, as esp. in the army, navy, etc.

spite[1] /spaɪt/ *n* [U] **1** unreasonable dislike for and desire to annoy another person, esp. in some small way: *I'm sure he took my parking space just out of/from spite* **2 in spite of** in opposition to the presence or efforts of; DESPITE: *I went out in spite of the rain* —**~ful** *adj* —**~fully** *adv* —**~fulness** *n* [U]

spite[2] *v* [T1] to treat with SPITE; annoy intentionally

spit·fire /ˈspɪtfaɪəʳ/ *n* a person with a fierce temper

spitting im·age /ˌ·· ˈ··/ *n* [(*the*) S (*of*)] an exact likeness; SPIT[4] (3) and image

spit·tle /ˈspɪtl/ *n* [U] SPIT[4] (1); SALIVA

spit·toon /spɪˈtuːn/ *AmE* also **cuspidor**— *n* a vessel usu. set on the floor in a public room for SPITting³ (1) tobacco juice into

spit up *v adv* **1** [T1] to SPIT³ (1) from the lungs, stomach, etc.: *to spit up blood* **2** [T1;IØ] *euph* VOMIT

spiv /spɪv/ *n BrE sl, becoming rare* a man who lives by cheating society, making money in small rather dishonest ways —**~vy** *adj* [Wa1]

splash¹ /splæʃ/ *v* **1** [IØ] to move or hit usu. noisily in a liquid: *children splashing in the bath* **2** [IØ;T1] **a** (of a liquid) to fall, strike, or move noisily, in drops, waves, etc.: *The rain splashed on the window* **b** to cause (a liquid) to do this: *one of the modern painters who just seems to splash paint about* **3** [T1 (*with*)] to throw a liquid against (something): *He splashed his face with cold water to try to wake himself up* **4** [T1] *infml* to give a lot of space to (esp. a news story); report as if very important: *The paper splashed the story on page one* **5** [IØ;T1 (ABOUT): (OUT, *on*)] *esp. BrE* to spend (money) on unnecessary but fine things: *She doesn't mind splashing her money about.|They were cheap enough, so I splashed out (£5) and got 2*

splash² *n* **1** a SPLASHing¹ act, movement, or noise: *go into the water with a splash* **2** a mark made by SPLASHing¹: *a splash of paint on the floor* **3** *not fml* a forceful favourable effect; occasion of becoming quickly well-known: *to make a splash in society* **4** *infml* a treatment in a newspaper as very important: *a page-one splash|splash* HEADLINE*s* **5** *esp. BrE* a small added amount, as of water to a drink

splash³ *adv* [H] with a SPLASH: *fell splash into the lake*

splash down *v adv* [IØ] (esp. of a space vehicle) to land in the sea —**splashdown** /ˈsplæʃdaʊn/ *n*

splash·y /ˈsplæʃi/ *adj* [Wa1] *esp. AmE* big, bright, and eye-catching

splat /splæt/ *n; adv* [S;H] (with) a noise as of something wet hitting a surface and being flattened

splat·ter /ˈsplætəʳ/ *v* [T1;IØ] SPATTER¹; SPLASH¹ (2)

splay¹ /spleɪ/ *v* [T1;IØ: (OUT)] to (cause to) spread out or become larger at one end: *The house has a narrow front but it splays out at the back*

splay² *n* an outward spreading at one end or side of esp. a window or door

splay·foot /ˈspleɪfʊt/ *n* **-feet** /fiːt/ a foot with a very flat spread-out shape —**~ed** /ˌspleɪˈfʊtɪ̣d◂/ *adj*

spleen /spliːn/ *n* **1** [C] a small organ near the upper end of the stomach that controls the quality of the blood supply and produces certain blood cells —see picture at DIGESTIVE SYSTEM **2** [U] violent anger, esp. expressed suddenly (esp. in the phr. **vent one's spleen** = to express one's annoyance)

splen·did /ˈsplendɪ̣d/ *adj* **1** grand in appearance; glorious; SUMPTUOUS **2** *not fml* very fine; excellent: *a splendid example of stupidity* —**~ly** *adv*

splen·dif·e·rous /splenˈdɪfərəs/ *adj not fml* grand; SPLENDID (1)

splen·dour, *AmE* **-dor** /ˈsplendəʳ/ *n* [U *often pl. with sing. meaning*] excellent or grand beauty; MAGNIFICENCE: *the splendour(s) of the high distant mountains*

sple·net·ic /splɪ̣ˈnetɪk/ *adj lit* bad-tempered; habitually angry or unpleasant

splice¹ /splaɪs/ *v* [T1] **1** [(*to, onto,* TOGETHER)] to fasten end to end to make one continuous length, as by weaving (ropes), sticking (pieces of film), nailing (beams), etc. **2** [*usu. pass.*] *infml* to join in marriage **3 splice the main brace** *humor sl* to drink or give out strong alcoholic drink, esp. at the end of a hard day's effort as formerly on board ships

splice² *n* an act or place of joining end to end

splic·er /ˈsplaɪsəʳ/ *n* an apparatus for fastening pieces of film or recording TAPE together neatly

splint /splɪnt/ *n* a flat piece of wood, metal, etc., used for protecting and keeping a damaged part of the body, esp. a broken bone, in position —see picture at MEDICAL¹

splin·ter¹ /ˈsplɪntəʳ/ *n* **1** [C] a small needle-like piece broken off something; SLIVER: *get a splinter in one's finger* **2** [A] (of a group) that has separated from a larger body

splinter² *v* **1** [IØ;T1] to (cause to) break into small needle-like pieces **2** [IØ (OFF)] to separate from a larger organization

split¹ /splɪt/ *v* **split;** *pres. p.* **splitting** **1** [T1;IØ] to (cause to) divide along a length, esp. with force or by a blow or tear: *This soft wood splits easily.|His coat had split down the back* **2** [IØ;T1: (UP, *into*)] to divide into separate parts: *to split (up) a book into* CHAPTER*s|The stream splits into 3 smaller streams at this point* **3** [T1;IØ] to separate into opposing groups or parties: *a quarrel which split the Labour Party|The judges split on the decision, 2 for and 2 against* **4** [T1] to divide among people; share: *We'll split the cost and profits among all of us* **5** [T1] to break up (an atom) by FISSION **6** [IØ] *AmE* (of shares in the ownership of a company) to be multiplied so that each holder gets a certain, often stated, number for each one held: *The* STOCK *has lately split 2 for 1* **7** [IØ (UP, WITH)] to end a friendship, marriage, etc.: *I'm afraid he's split with his former friends and won't even see them* **8** [IØ (*on*)] *BrE sl* to tell secret information (about someone): *If I tell you where I'm going this morning, promise you won't split on me to my teacher* **9** [Wv6; IØ] *sl* to leave quickly: *I'm getting tired of this place: let's split* **10 split an infinitive** to put a word such as an adverb between "to" and its following verb: *I said "to quietly go", but the teacher said I should avoid splitting* INFINITIVE*s like that* —see also **split the** DIFFERENCE, **split** HAIR*s*, **split one's** SIDE*s*¹ (17)

split² *n* **1** a cut or break made by splitting: *to mend a split in the tabletop* **2** a division or separation, esp. **a** within a usu. undivided group **b** between 2 different things: *the split between what is and what ought to be* **3** *AmE* the SPLITting (6) of shares in a company **4** a dish made from fruit (esp. a banana) cut into 2 pieces with ice cream on top

split-lev·el /ˌ· ˈ··◂/ *adj* [Wa5] (of a building) having floors at different heights in different parts

split pea /ˌ· ˈ·◂/ *n* a dried PEA separated into its 2 natural halves

split per·son·al·i·ty /ˌ· ··ˈ···/ *n not fml* a set of 2 very different ways of behaving present in one person at different times —compare SCHIZOPHRENIA

split ring /ˌ· ˈ·/ *n* a metal ring of 2 turns pressed flat together, used for holding and slipping keys on and off

splits /splɪts/ *n* [(*the*) P] a movement in which a person's legs are spread wide and touch the floor along their whole length: *Can you do the splits?*

split sec·ond /ˌ· ˈ··◂/ *n not fml* a small part of a second; FLASH; INSTANT¹ (1) —**split-second** *adj*

split·ting /ˈsplɪtɪŋ/ *adj* (esp. of a headache) giving the feeling of a sharp blow; very painful

splotch /splɒtʃ‖splɑtʃ/ *BrE* also **splodge** /splɒdʒ‖splɑdʒ/— *n* an irregular coloured or dirty mark or spot; BLOTCH —**~y** *adj* [Wa1]

splurge¹ /splɜːdʒ‖-ɜr-/ *n not fml* **1** an act of splurging (SPLURGE); EXTRAVAGANCE: *a splurge in a good restaurant* **2** a grand show or effort: *one of the film splurges of the 1950's*

splurge² *v* [IØ;T1: (*on*)] *not fml* to spend more (money) than one can usually afford

splut·ter¹ /ˈsplʌtəʳ/ *n* a SPITting³ noise; SPUTTER: *The fire went out with a few splutters as the rain began to fall*

splutter[2] *v* **1** [T1;I∅] to say or talk quickly and as if confused: *"But—but . . ." he spluttered* **2** [I∅] to make a light explosive noise; SPUTTER

spoil[1] /spɔɪl/ *n* [U *usu. pl. with same meaning*] things taken without payment, as **a** by an army from a defeated enemy or place: *the spoils of victory* **b** by thieves: *to divide up the spoil*

spoil[2] *v* **spoilt** /spɔɪlt/ *or* **spoiled** **1** [T1] to cause to become of no use or value; ruin: *The visit was spoilt by an argument* **2** [I∅;T1] to (cause to) decay or lose goodness: *The fruit has spoilt in the hot sun: the heat was enough to spoil it* **3** [Wv5;T1] to make (esp. a child) selfish from having too much attention or praise **4** [T1] to treat very or too well; CODDLE (2): *This hotel advertises that it spoils its guests* —**~er** *n*
USAGE A thing that is **spoiled** may be only slightly damaged, but if we say that something is **spoilt** it sounds as if it were completely ruined.

spoil[3] *v* **spoilt** *or* **spoiled** [T1 (*of*)] *old use & lit* to rob: *to spoil a rich man of his goods*

spoil·age /ˈspɔɪlɪdʒ/ *n* [U] the action, or waste resulting from, SPOILing[2] (1)

spoil for *v prep* **1** [T1] to be very eager for (esp. in the phr. **be spoiling for a fight**) **2** [D1] to cause to be unsatisfied with: *This fine French wine spoils you for the cheaper kinds*

spoils /spɔɪlz/ *n* [P] the rewards of getting political power, esp. public offices for giving to friends, party workers, etc.

spoil·sport /ˈspɔɪlspɔːt‖-ort/ *n* [C;N] a person who puts an end to another's jokes or fun

spoke[1] /spəʊk/ *n* **1** any of the bars which connect the outer ring of a wheel to the centre, as on a bicycle —see picture at BICYCLE[1] **2 put a spoke in someone's wheel** to keep someone from going ahead with plans

spoke[2] *past t. of* SPEAK

spok·en /ˈspəʊkən/ *past p. of* SPEAK

-spoken *comb. form* [*adv→adj*] speaking with the stated degree of EXCELLENCE: *a well-spoken girl*

spoke·shave /ˈspəʊkʃeɪv/ *n* a tool with a blade between 2 handles, used for making curved surfaces smooth

spokes·man /ˈspəʊksmən/ *fem.* **spokes·wom·an** /-ˌwʊmən/— *n* **-men** /mən/ a person chosen to speak and represent the opinions of others officially

spo·li·a·tion /ˌspəʊliˈeɪʃən/ *n* [U] *fml* the action of violent SPOILing[2] (1) or destruction

spon·dee /ˈspɒndiː‖ˈspɑndiː/ *n* a measure of poetry consisting of 2 strong (or long) beats —**-daic** /spɒnˈdeɪ-ɪk‖spɑn-/ *adj* [Wa5]

sponge[1] /spʌndʒ/ *n* **1** [C] any of a large group of simple sea creatures which stay in one place and grow a spreading rubber-like frame (SKELETON (1)) full of small holes **2** [C;U] a piece of this animal's frame or of rubber or plastic like it, which can hold a lot of water and is usu. used in washing surfaces **3** [C] *infml* a person who SPONGEs[2] (3) **4** [C;U] *BrE* SPONGE CAKE **5 throw in** (*BrE* also **up**) **the sponge** *not fml* to accept defeat

sponge[2] *v* **1** [T1 (OFF, OUT, DOWN)] to clean or pass over (as if) with a wet cloth or SPONGE[1] (2): *to sponge down the car before turning the water on it* **2** [T1 (UP)] to remove (liquid) with a cloth, SPONGE[1] (2), etc.: *to sponge (up) blood from a wound* **3** [I∅;T1:(*on, from*)] *not fml* to live or get (money, meals, etc.) free by taking advantage of another's good nature or weakness —**sponger** *n*: *a sponger on his friends*

sponge bag /ˈ· ·/ *n BrE* a small usu. plastic bag for carrying one's soap, toothbrush, etc.

sponge cake /ˈ· ·/ *n* [U;C] (a) light cake made from eggs, sugar, and flour but often no fat

spong·y /ˈspʌndʒi/ *adj* [Wa1] like a SPONGE[1] (1); soft, full of holes, and often rather wet; not firm —**sponginess** *n* [U]

spon·sor[1] /ˈspɒnsəʳ‖ˈspɑn-/ *n* **1** a person who takes responsibility for a person or thing: *the sponsor of a* BILL *in Parliament* **2** a business which pays for a show, broadcast, sports event, etc., usu. in return for advertising —**~ship** *n* [U]

sponsor[2] *v* [T1] to act as SPONSOR for

spon·ta·ne·i·ty /ˌspɒntəˈniːɘ̆ti‖ˌspɑn-/ *n* [U] the quality of being SPONTANEOUS

spon·ta·ne·ous /spɒnˈteɪnɪəs‖spɑn-/ *adj* produced from natural feelings or causes without outside force, esp. quickly and (as if) unplanned: *a spontaneous cheer from the crowd* —**~ly** *adv* —**~ness** *n* [U]

spoof[1] /spuːf/ *v* [I∅;T1] *not fml* to make fun of (a person or thing); talk in a humorously false way (about)

spoof[2] *n not fml* a humorous misrepresentation; SEND-UP; PARODY[1] (1): *a magazine spoof of university life*

spook[1] /spuːk/ *n usu. infml* a spirit; GHOST[1] (1)

spook[2] *v* [T1] *not fml, esp. AmE* to cause (an animal) to be suddenly afraid and run away

spook·y /ˈspuːki/ *adj* [Wa1] *infml* causing fear in a strange way; suggesting GHOSTs; EERIE

spool /spuːl/ *n* **1** a round object usu. with a hole through the centre and raised circular edges on each end, for winding a length of electric wire, recording TAPE, camera film, etc., round **2** *AmE* REEL[1] (2) **3** an amount held by any of these: *2 spools of thread*

spoon[1] /spuːn/ *n* **1** (*often in comb.*) a tool for mixing, serving, and eating food, consisting of a small bowl with a handle: *a silver/plastic/wooden spoon*|TEASPOON|TABLESPOON **2** SPOONFUL: *2 spoons of sugar* —see also WOODEN SPOON

spoon[2] *v* **1** [X9, esp. UP, OUT] to take up or move with a spoon: *Spoon (out) the mixture into glasses.*|*Mother was spooning up the soup* **2** [I∅ (*with*)] *now rare* to touch and talk fondly; NECK[2]

spoo·ner·is·m /ˈspuːnərɪzəm/ *n* an expression in which the first sounds of 2 words have changed places usu. with a funny result (as in *sew you to a sheet* for *show you to a seat*)

spoon-feed /ˈ· ·/ *v* **-fed** [T1] **1** to feed (esp. a baby) with a spoon **2** [Wv5] to offer (a subject) to (students) in very easy lessons that need no thinking

spoon·ful /ˈspuːnfʊl/ *n* **-s** *or* **spoonsful** /ˈspuːnzfʊl/ (*often in comb.*) the amount that a spoon will hold: *2* TEASPOONFULs *of sugar*

spoor /spɔːʳ, spʊəʳ/ *n* a mark or waste droppings (as left by a wild animal) which can be followed; track

spo·rad·ic /spəˈrædɪk/ *adj* happening irregularly; scattered in time: *only sporadic fighting/cases of fever* —**~ally** *adv* [Wa4]

spore /spɔːʳ‖spor/ *n* a very small seedlike usu. single cell produced by some plants and simple animals and able to develop into a new plant or animal, often after living through bad conditions for a time

spor·ran /ˈspɒrən‖ˈspɔ-, ˈspɑ-/ *n* a fur-covered bag worn as a PURSE[1] (1) in front of a KILT

sport[1] /spɔːt‖sport/ *v* **1** [T1] to wear or show publicly; show off: *She came in today sporting a fur coat* **2** [I∅] *usu. lit* to have fun; play; FROLIC: *lambs sporting in the field*

sport[2] *n* **1** [C;U] an outdoor or indoor game, competition, or activity carried on by rules and needing bodily effort and skill: *Do you really think cricket is an exciting sport?*|*famous men in the world of sport* —see HOBBY (USAGE) **2** [U] active amusement; play: *It's great sport, swimming in the sea* **3** [U] joking fun: *The older girls were making sport of her* **4** [C] a generous-minded person of a kind who accepts defeat or a joke good-temperedly, or in the stated way: *You've been a real sport to laugh at the trick we played on you* **5** [(*BrE becoming rare*) N9; (*AustrE*) N] *infml* fellow; friend: *How are you, old sport!* **6** [C] *tech* a plant or animal that is different in some important way from its usual type: *This insect's a sport; it has 7 legs* **7 the sport of kings** *pomp* horse racing

sport·ing /ˈspɔːtɪŋ‖ˈspor-/ *adj* **1** [B] offering the kind of fair risk that is usual in a game: *a sporting chance of winning* **2** [Wa5;A] of, concerning, or fond of field sports like hunting or horse racing: *a painter of sporting scenes* —**~ly** *adv*

spor·tive /ˈspɔːtɪv‖ˈspor-/ *adj esp. lit* being or fond of SPORT² (2); playful: *a sportive little dog* —**~ly** *adv* —**~ness** *n* [U]

sports /spɔːts‖sports/ *n* **1** [P] *BrE* a meeting at which people compete in running, jumping, throwing, etc. (ATHLETICS): *The school sports are next week* **2** [A] (*sometimes in comb.*) of, for, or connected with 1 or more sports: *the sports page of the paper* **3** [A] *AmE* also **sport**— (*sometimes in comb.*; esp. of clothes) informal in style: *Must I wear a suit to the dinner, or will a sport(s)* JACKET *be good enough?*

sports car /ˈ· ·/ *n* a low usu. open car for travelling with high power and speed —see picture at INTERCHANGE²

sports·man /ˈspɔːtsmən‖ˈspor-/ *fem.* **sports·wom·an** /-ˌwʊmən/— *n* **-men** /mən/ **1** a good SPORT² (4); one who plays sports in a fair and graceful spirit **2** a person who plays or enjoys sports, esp. outdoor sports like shooting, hunting, horseracing, etc.

sports·man·like /ˈspɔːtsmənlaɪk‖ˈspor-/ *adj* showing good SPORTSMANSHIP; like a good SPORTSMAN (1)

sports·man·ship /ˈspɔːtsmənʃɪp‖ˈspor-/ *n* [U] a spirit of honest fair play and graceful winning and losing

sport·y /ˈspɔːt‖ˈsporti/ *adj* [Wa1] *not fml* good-looking in a bright informal way: *sporty new trousers* —**sportiness** *n* [U]

spot¹ /spɒt‖spɑt/ *n* **1** [C] a part or area different from the main surface, as in colour, usu. of a round shape: *a white dress with blue spots|a sticky spot on the floor* **2** [C] a particular place: *Spain is our favourite holiday spot.|X marks the spot.|trouble spots in the world|the exact spot where it happened* **3** [C] a small or limited part of something: *one of the brighter spots in the news* **4** [C] a dirty or bad-looking mark: *clean off ink spots with soap and water* **5** [C] *euph* PIMPLE: *annoyed to find a spot on her nose* **6** [S9] an area of mind or feelings: *I have a soft spot (in my heart) for my old school* **7** [C] a position, as in an organization or order: *a good spot as the director's secretary* **8** [C] a usu. difficult position or state of affairs; FIX² (1): *Now we're really in a spot!* **9** [S] *BrE infml* a little bit; small amount: *have a spot of tea|a spot of* BOTHER² (1) **10** [C] a place in a broadcast: *a guest spot on a well-known show* **11** [C] *infml* SPOTLIGHT¹ (1) **12** [A] being or done in the place where the action is: *spot reporting on the election|spot control of traffic* **13** [A] for buying and paying at once: *spot* CASH| *spot wheat|spot prices* **14** [A] limited to a few times or places as representing all: *We needn't test everyone; we'll just make spot* CHECKs¹ (3) **15 change one's spots** [*nonassertive*] change one's qualities or way of life **16 knock spots off** *BrE infml* to defeat easily; be very much better than **17 on the spot** *not fml* **a** at once: *Anyone breaking the rules will be asked to leave on the spot* **b** at the place of the action: *Wherever she's needed she's quickly on the spot* **c** in a position of having to make the right action or answer: *The question put me on the spot: I couldn't make an excuse or lie*

spot² *v* **-tt-** **1** [T1] to pick out, esp. with the eye; see; recognize: *a tall man easy to spot in a crowd|a good eye for spotting mistakes* **2** [T1;I∅] to mark or be marked with coloured or dirty spots: *white cloth spotted with green|a floor covering that spots rather too easily* **3** [X9 *usu. pass.*] to place in position: *Guards were spotted around the building* **4** [*it*+I∅ (*with*)] *BrE* (of rain) to fall lightly and irregularly (esp. in the phr. **it's spotting with rain**) **5** [T1 (UP, OUT)] *AmE tech* to remove (a spot) from (paper, cloth, etc.): *a chemical for spotting clothes/ink* **6** [D1] *AmE* to allow as an advantage in a game: *He spotted his opponent 3 points and still won*

spot³ *adv* [Wa5;H] *BrE infml* exactly (in the phr. **spot on**): *She arrived spot on time*

spot-check /ˌ· ˈ·‖ˈ· ˌ·/ *v* [T1] to give a SPOT¹ (14) CHECK to; test as a typical case: *spot-checking income tax calculations*

spot·less /ˈspɒtləs‖ˈspɑt-/ *adj* completely clean —**~ly** *adv* —**~ness** *n* [U]

spot·light¹ /ˈspɒtlaɪt‖ˈspɑt-/ *n* **1** [C] (a bright round area of light made by) a lamp with a directable narrow beam —see picture at THEATRE, LIVING ROOM **2** [*the*+R] public attention: *in the political spotlight this week*

spotlight² *v* [T1] to direct attention to, (as if) with a SPOTLIGHT: *an article spotlighting the difficulties of school-leavers*

spot-on /ˌ· ˈ·◂/ *adj, adv* [Wa5] *BrE infml* exactly (right): *Your judgment turned out to be spot-on*

spot·ted /ˈspɒtɨd‖ˈspɑ-/ *adj* marked with coloured or dirty spots

spotted dick /ˌspɒtɨd ˈdɪk‖ˌspɑ-/ also **spotted dog** /ˌ·· ˈ·/— *n* [C;U] *BrE* a kind of boiled heavy sweet dish with CURRANTs

spot·ter /ˈspɒtəʳ‖ˈspɑ-/ *n* **1** [C9] a person who keeps watch for the stated thing: *a bird spotter* **2** [A] used for keeping watch on an enemy's actions: *a spotter plane*

spot·ty /ˈspɒti‖ˈspɑti/ *adj* [Wa1] **1** *AmE* with some spots different from others; irregular; PATCHY: *The book was spotty—some good parts and some bad* **2** *BrE infml* having, or being still of the age to have, ACNE (=spots on the face)

spouse /spaʊs, spaʊz/ *n usu. fml or law* a husband or wife

spout¹ /spaʊt/ *v* **1** [I∅;T1: (OUT)] to throw or come out in a forceful stream: *a well spouting oil| water spouting out from the pipe* **2** [T1] to pour out in a stream of words: *He's always spouting Shakespeare* —**~er** *n*

spout² *n* **1** an opening from which liquid comes out, such as a tube, pipe, or small U- or V-shaped lip for pouring liquid from a container: *the spout of a teapot* **2** a forceful esp. rising stream of liquid —see also WATERSPOUT **3 up the spout** *infml* ruined; in a hopeless condition

sprain¹ /spreɪn/ *n* an act or result of SPRAINing a joint —compare STRAIN² (4)

sprain² *v* [Wv5;T1] to damage (a joint in the body) by sudden twisting: *have a sprained ankle| sprain one's ankle*

sprang /spræŋ/ *past t. of* SPRING¹

sprat /spræt/ *n* a small kind of European HERRING (a food fish)

sprawl¹ /sprɔːl/ *v* **1** [X9 *usu. pass.*; L9: (OUT)] to stretch out (oneself or one's limbs) awkwardly in lying or sitting: *He found her sprawled out in a comfortable chair asleep* **2** [Wv4;L9 (OUT)] to spread ungracefully: *The city sprawls for miles in each direction*

sprawl² *n* [*usu. sing.*] **1** a SPRAWLing² (1) position **2** an irregular spreading mass or group: *a sprawl of buildings*

spray¹ /spreɪ/ *n* (an arrangement of flowers, jewels, etc., in the shape of) a small branch with its leaves and flowers

spray² *n* **1** [U] water in very small drops blown from the sea, a waterfall, etc. **2** [U;C] (a can or other container holding) liquid to be SPRAYed³ out under pressure: *a quick-drying spray paint|Did you bring along some insect spray?*

spray³ *v* **1** [X9;L9: esp. *on*] **a** to scatter (liquid) in small drops under pressure: *spray paint on a wall* **b** (of liquid) to be scattered in this way: *The water sprayed out over the garden* **2** [D1 (+*with/on*); IØ] to throw or force out liquid in small drops upon (a surface, person, field of crops, etc.): *spray a wall with paint|Our wheat needs spraying soon*

spray·er /ˈspreɪəʳ/ *n* a person or apparatus that SPRAYs³ out a liquid: *use a paint sprayer*

spray gun /ˈ· ·/ *n* an apparatus like a gun for pumping to SPRAY³ out liquid

spread¹ /spred/ *v* **spread** **1** [IØ;T1: (OUT)] to (cause to) open, reach, or stretch out; (cause to) be longer, broader, wider, etc.: *a ship with sails spread|In 20 years the city has spread quickly to the north* **2** [L9, esp. *over, for*] to cover a large area or period of time: *The city spreads (for) 10 miles to the north.|His interests now spread over several subjects* **3** [D1+*with/on*] to put (a covering) on (a surface): *spread butter on bread/spread a piece of bread with butter* **4** [T1 (*over, among*)] to scatter, share, or divide over an area, period of time, etc.; DISTRIBUTE: *spread the cost over 3 years* **5** [T1;IØ] to make or become (more) widely known: *The news of the gold discovery quickly spread.|If I tell you this secret, don't spread it around* **6** [T1;IØ] to (cause to) have a wider effect: *an infectious easily-spread disease|The fire soon spread through the whole part of town* **7** [T1] to prepare (a table or meal) for eating: *The table was spread for tea* **8** **spread oneself** to spend money, effort, etc., freely to produce a good effect —**~able** *adj*

spread² *n* **1** [(*the*) S] the act or action of spreading: *the spread of a disease/one's interests/the city* **2** [C *usu. sing.*] a distance, area, or time of spreading: *a tree with a spread of 100 feet|a 1,000-*ACRE *spread in Texas|The various dealers' prices show a wide spread* —see also MIDDLE AGE SPREAD **3** [C] a newspaper or magazine article or advertisement usu. running across one or more pages and with pictures: *a 2-page spread* **4** [C] a large or grand meal; table spread with food: *Our host had a fine spread waiting for us* **5** [C] a cloth for covering something in a house, esp. a BEDSPREAD **6** [U;C] a soft food for spreading on bread: *a tube of cheese spread*

spread-ea·gle /ˌ· ˈ··‖ˈ· ˌ··/ *v* [T1 *usu. pass.*; IØ] to put (someone, esp. oneself) or go into a position with arms and legs spread out: *lie spread-eagled on the bed*

spread eagle /ˌ· ˈ··/ *n* a picture (used officially esp. in the US) of an EAGLE with wings and legs spread out —**spread-eagle** *adj* [Wa5;A]

spree /spriː/ *n* a time of free and wild fun, spending, drinking, etc.

sprig /sprɪg/ *n* **1** a small end of a stem or branch with leaves: *soup with a sprig of* PARSLEY **2** one of a set of small metal points fixed to the bottom of a shoe used in certain sports

sprigged /sprɪgd/ *adj* (esp. of fine cloth) having an ornamented pattern of plant SPRIGs (1)

spright·ly /ˈspraɪtli/ *adj* [Wa1] gay and light; LIVELY (1): *a sprightly dance/story/young girl* —**-liness** *n* [U]

spring¹ /sprɪŋ/ *v* **sprang** /spræŋ/, **sprung** /sprʌŋ/ **1** [L9] to move quickly as if by jumping; BOUND⁵ (1): *He sprang to his feet/sprang to the door/sprang over the wall* **2** [L9, esp. UP] to come into being or action quickly or from nothing; arise: *A wind suddenly sprang up.|Towns had sprung up in what was a dry desert.|I turned the key and the engine sprang into life* **3** [L9, esp. *from*] to be a product or result: *What unhappiness can spring from the love of money!* **4** [L9, esp. *from*] to come out (as if) in a spring of water; ISSUE² (1): *Tears sprang from her eyes* **5** [T1;IØ] to crack or split: *The heavy weight sprang one of the beams* **6** [T1;L7;X7] to open or close (as if) by the force of a spring: *The box sprang open when I touched the button* **7** [T1] *sl* to cause to leave prison, lawfully or by escaping **8** [T1 (*on*)] to produce as a surprise; make known unexpectedly (to): *spring a surprise party on someone|He sprang his marriage on his parents* **9** **spring a leak** (of a ship, container, etc.) to begin to let liquid through a crack, hole, etc.

spring² *n* **1** [C *often pl.*] a place where water comes up naturally from the ground **2** [R;C;(U)] the season between winter and summer in which leaves and flowers appear **3** [C] an object, usu. a length of metal wound around, which tends to push, pull, or twist against a force and return to its original shape: *the springs of a car/watch* **4** [U] the quality of this object; ELASTICITY: *not much spring in this old bed* **5** [S;U] an active healthy quality (esp. in the phr. **a spring in one's step**) **6** [C] an act of springing: *The cat made a spring at the mouse* —**~less** *adj* [Wa5]

spring·board /ˈsprɪŋbɔːd‖-bord/ *n* **1** a strong bendable board for jumping off to give height to a DIVE¹ (1) or jump **2** [(*to*)] a starting point where power is built up

spring·bok /ˈsprɪŋbɒk‖-bɑk/ *n* [Wn1] a swift graceful kind of S African GAZELLE

spring-clean¹ /ˌ· ˈ·/ *v* [T1;(IØ)] to clean (a place) thoroughly, as people often clean houses in the spring

spring-clean² /ˈ· ·/ *AmE* **spring-clean·ing** /ˌ· ˈ··/— *n* [S] a thorough cleaning

springer span·iel /ˌ·· ˈ··/ *n* either of 2 breeds of sporting dogs, of middle size, usu. partly white and with flat or wavy hair

spring on·ion /ˌ· ˈ··/ *n BrE* a kind of onion with a small white round part (BULB) and green stem, usu. eaten raw

spring roll /ˈ· ·/ *BrE* also **pancake roll** (*AmE* **egg roll**)— *n BrE* a Chinese dish made of a thin case of egg pastry filled with bits of vegetable and often meat and usu. cooked in oil

spring tide /ˌ· ˈ·/ *n* a large rise and fall (TIDE) of the sea at or soon following the times of the new and full moon —compare NEAP TIDE

spring·time /ˈsprɪŋtaɪm/ *n* [(*the*) U] *not fml* the season of spring; time of spring weather: *I like (the) springtime best of all*

spring·y /ˈsprɪŋi/ *adj* [Wa1] having SPRING² (4); coming back to an original shape: *a springy floor, good for dancing*

sprin·kle¹ /ˈsprɪŋkəl/ *v* **1** [X9] to scatter in drops or small grains: *sprinkle water on the grass|sprinkle sand along the icy path* **2** [T1 (*with*)] to scatter liquid, small bits, etc., on or among: *sprinkle the path with sand|a beautiful area sprinkled with lakes|* (fig.) *a book sprinkled with humour* **3** [*it*+IØ] to rain lightly

sprinkle² *n* **1** a light rain **2** SPRINKLING

sprin·kler /ˈsprɪŋkləʳ/ *n* **1** any of various apparatuses for scattering drops of water: *a garden* *sprinkler* **2** a system of fire protection inside a building with water openings which are turned on by high heat

sprin·kling /ˈsprɪŋklɪŋ/ *n* [(*of*), *usu. sing.*] a small scattered group or amount: *a sprinkling of snow|of new faces in the crowd*

sprint[1] /sprɪnt/ *v* [IØ] to run at one's fastest speed, esp. for a short distance —**~er** *n*

sprint[2] *n* **1** an act of SPRINTing: *He made a sprint to catch the bus* **2** a short race; DASH[2] (1)

sprite /spraɪt/ *n* a fairy, esp. a playful graceful one

sprock·et /ˈsprɒkɪ̇t‖ˈsprɑ-/ *n* **1** also **sprocket wheel** /ˈ·· ·/— a wheel with 1 or more rows of teeth for fitting into and turning a chain, photographic film with holes, etc. —see picture at BICYCLE[1] **2** a single one of these teeth

sprout[1] /spraʊt/ *v* **1** [IØ;T1: (*from,* UP)] to (cause to) grow or come out: *leaves beginning to sprout from trees|You've sprouted a beard since I last saw you* **2** [IØ;T1] to (cause to) send up new growth, as from a seed; BUD: *These old potatoes have begun to sprout*

sprout[2] *n* **1** a new growth on a plant; SHOOT[2] (1) **2** *infml* a young person **3** BRUSSELS SPROUT

spruce[1] /spruːs/ *n* **1** [C] any of about 40 kinds of ornamental and wood-producing trees found in colder northern parts of the world and having short needle-shaped leaves that remain in winter and grow singly around the branches **2** [U] the light soft wood of this tree

spruce[2] *adj* [Wa2] tidy and clean, esp. in appearance; SMART[2] (3); TRIM[2]: *a banker in his spruce coat and hat* —**~ly** *adv* —**~ness** *n* [U]

spruce[3] *v* [T1 (UP)] *not fml* to make (something or oneself) SPRUCE[2]; clean and neaten (something or oneself) up: *get spruced up|spruce oneself (up) for a party*

spruce up *v adv* [IØ] *not fml* to make oneself SPRUCE[2]

sprung[1] /sprʌŋ/ *past p. of* SPRING

sprung[2] *adj* [Wa5] supported or kept in shape by springs: *a sprung* MATTRESS

spry /spraɪ/ *adj* [Wa1] active; quick in movement: *He's 75 years old and still spry as a cat* —**~ly** *adv* —**~ness** *n* [U]

spud /spʌd/ *n* **1** a long-handled tool like a SPADE with a narrow blade for digging up roots and unwanted plants **2** *infml* a potato

spume /spjuːm/ *n* [U] *esp. lit* white air-filled matter on the top of a liquid, esp. on the sea; FOAM; FROTH

spun /spʌn/ *past t. and past p. of* SPIN

spunk /spʌŋk/ *n* [U] **1** *infml* courage; PLUCK[2] (1) **2** *BrE taboo* SEMEN —**spunky** *adj* [Wa1]

spur[1] /spɜːʳ/ *n* **1** a U-shaped object with a point or toothed wheel for fastening around the heel of a rider's boot to urge on or direct a horse **2** a stiff sharp growth on the back of some birds' legs **3** a force leading to action; INCENTIVE: *good news which will be a spur to continued effort* **4** a railway track that goes away from a main line **5** a length of high ground coming out from a range of higher mountains **6 on the spur of the moment** without preparation; as the moment calls for **7 win one's spurs** to earn the right to a position, reward, or title; gain honour

spur[2] *v* **-rr- 1** [T1] to prick (a horse) with SPUR*s*[1] (1) to go faster **2** [T1;V3: (ON)] to urge to (faster) action or (greater) effort: *He spurred his players to fight harder* **3** [L9] *esp. lit* to ride fast on a horse: *They spurred through the forest*

spu·ri·ous /ˈspjʊərɪəs/ *adj* **1** not really the product of the time, writer, etc., shown or claimed: *spurious lines in an ancient poem, added later* **2** like something else but falsely so; false **3** bad in reasoning; wrong —**~ly** *adv* —**~ness** *n* [U]

spurn /spɜːn‖spɜrn/ *v* [T1] to treat or refuse with angry pride; SCORN[2] (1): *spurned all offers of help|a spurned lover*

spur-of-the-mo·ment /ˌ· · · ˈ··/ *adj* [A;(B)] *infml* done, made, or happening without preparation

spurt[1] /spɜːt‖spɜrt/ *n* a short sudden increase of activity, effort, or speed; BURST[2]: *He does his work in spurts between days of inactivity*

spurt[2] *v* [IØ] to make a SPURT[1]: *a runner spurting past his opponent*

spurt[3], **spirt** *v* [L9;(X9): esp. OUT, *from*] to (cause to) flow out suddenly or violently; GUSH; SPOUT: *water spurting from the broken pipe*

spurt[4], **spirt** *n* a sudden usu. short coming out, as of liquid; SURGE[1] (1): *a spurt of steam from the teapot*

sput·ter[1] /ˈspʌtəʳ/ *v* **1** [T1;IØ] to say or speak in confusion; SPLUTTER[2] (1) **2** [IØ] to make repeated soft explosive sounds: *The car's engine started, sputtered for a moment, and died again*

sputter[2] *n* a SPUTTERing noise or way of speaking: *the sputter of hot fat in the pan*

spu·tum /ˈspjuːtəm/ *n* [U] liquid from the mouth, esp. coughed up from the lungs in some diseases

spy[1] /spaɪ/ *v* **1** [IØ (*into, on, upon*)] to watch secretly: *spy on one's neighbours|spy into others' affairs* **2** [IØ (*on, upon*)] to try to get information secretly from an unfriendly place **3** [T1;V4] to catch sight of; discover after some looking: *She was quick to spy her friend in the crowd*

spy[2] *n* **1** a person employed to find out secret information, as from an enemy or company in competition **2** a person who keeps watch secretly

spy·glass /ˈspaɪglɑːs‖-glæs/ *n* a tube-shaped instrument for seeing things in the distance with one eye; small TELESCOPE

spy out *v adv* [T1] to travel in (a place) quietly or secretly getting information (esp. in the phr. **spy out the land**)

sq *written abbrev. for:* square: *6 sq metres*

squab /skwɒb‖skwɑb/ *n* a young PIGEON (=kind of bird), esp. as food

squab·ble[1] /ˈskwɒbəl‖ˈskwɑ-/ *n not fml* a continuing quarrel, esp. over something unimportant

squabble[2] *v* [IØ] to quarrel, esp. noisily and unreasonably

squad /skwɒd‖skwɑd/ *n* [GC;N] **1** a group of soldiers smaller than a PLATOON and often doing a particular duty **2** a group of people working as a team: *a police bomb squad|a fire-fighting squad|* FLYING SQUAD

squad car /ˈ· ·/ *n esp. AmE* a car used by police on duty; PATROL CAR

squad·ron /ˈskwɒdrən‖ˈskwɑ-/ *n* [GC] **1** a body of soldiers with TANK*s* (2) or (formerly) horses of the same size as a BATTALION **2** a large group of warships; any of the largest parts of a FLEET **3** the main size of a fighting organization in an airforce; any of the parts of a WING[1] (4)

squadron lead·er /ˈ·· ˌ··/ *n* [C;A;N] an officer of lower middle rank in the Royal Air Force

squal·id /ˈskwɒlɪ̇d‖ˈskwɑ-/ *adj* **1** very dirty and uncared-for; FILTHY: *squalid living conditions* **2** having, expressing, or about low moral standards; SORDID: *a squalid story of sex and violence* —**~ly** *adv*

squall[1] /skwɔːl/ *v* [IØ] to cry (out) noisily —**~er** *n*

squall[2] *n* a loud unpleasant cry: *the squall of the seabirds*

squall[3] *n* a sudden strong wind often bringing rain or snow —**squally** *adj* [Wa1]

squal·or /ˈskwɒləʳ‖ˈskwɑ-/ *n* [U] the condition of being SQUALID (1): *a part of the city now sunk into squalor*

squan·der /ˈskwɒndəʳ‖ˈskwɑn-/ *v* [T1] to spend foolishly; use up wastefully —**~er** *n*

square¹ /skweəʳ/ *n* **1** a figure with 4 straight equal sides forming 4 right angles **2** a piece of material in this shape: *a square of cloth|a head square* (=SCARF) **3** a group of soldiers formed tightly into this shape and facing outwards **4** a straight-edged often L-shaped tool for drawing and measuring right angles —see also SETSQUARE, T-SQUARE **5** a broad open place at the meeting of streets: *a band playing in the town square* **6** the buildings surrounding this: *a fine house in Berkeley Square* **7** a number equal to another number multiplied by itself: *16 is the square of 4* —see also SQUARE ROOT **8** a space on a game board: *move 2 squares forward* **9** *sl becoming rare* a person who does not know or follow the latest ideas, styles, etc. **10 on the square** *infml* honest(ly); fair(ly) **11 square one** *BrE* the very beginning; starting point: *All my papers were lost in the fire so now I'm back to square one with the work*

square² *adj* **1** [Wa5;B] having 4 equal sides and 4 right angles; being a square: *A handkerchief is usually square.|a square tower* **2** [Wa1;B] forming a (nearly) right angle: *a square corner|a square jaw* **3** [Wa5;A] being a measurement of area equal to that of a square with sides of the stated length: *144 square inches equals 1 square foot* —see WEIGHTS & MEASURES TABLE **4** [Wa5;E] being the stated length from a corner in both directions: *The room is 10 feet square* **5** [Wa1;B] fair; honest: *a square* DEAL³ (1)|*Are you being square with me?* —see also FAIR² (4) **and square** **6** [Wa5;F] paid and settled: *Our account is all square* **7** [Wa5;F] equal in points; TIED² (6): *The teams are all square at 1 match each* **8** [Wa1;B] *infml* of or like a SQUARE¹ (9); old-fashioned: *She's rather square in what she likes* **9** [Wa1;B] (in cricket) in a position at (about) right angles to the hitter —see picture at CRICKET² **10 a square meal** a good satisfying meal: *get 3 square meals a day* —**~ly** *adv* —**~ness** *n* [U]

square³ *v* **1** [T1 (UP)] to put into a shape with straight lines and right angles: *square up a wall|"I won't be threatened," she said, squaring her shoulders/jaw* **2** [Wv5;T1 (OFF)] to mark squares on; divide into squares: *a game played on squared paper* **3** [T1 *usu. pass.*] to multiply (a number) by itself once: *2 squared equals 4* (written $2^2=4$) **4** [T1;I∅: (*with*)] to (cause to) fit to a particular explanation or standard; RECONCILE or be RECONCILEd: *His arguments don't square with the facts* **5** [T1] to pay or pay for; settle: *square an account* **6** [T1] to pay or settle dishonestly, as by a BRIBE: *government officers who will have to be squared* **7** [T1] to cause (totals of points or games won) to be equal: *Britain won the second match to square the* SERIES (6) *at one each* —see also SQUARE AWAY, SQUARE UP, SQUARE UP TO

square⁴ also **squarely**— *adv infml* **1** fairly; honestly: *You've treated me very square* —see also FAIR² (4) **and square** **2** [H] directly; with nothing in the way: *He looked her square in the eye*

square a·way *v adv* [T1 *often pass.*] *AmE infml* to put in order; settle correctly: *help a new man to get himself/his things squared away*

square-bash·ing /ˈ· ˌ··/ *n* [U] *BrE infml* practice, esp. in marching, by soldiers; DRILL² (2)

square brack·et /ˌ· ˈ··/ *n* [*usu. pl.*] BRACKET¹ (2a)

square dance /ˈ· ·/ *n* a dance in which 4 pairs of dancers face each other to form a square

square knot /ˈ· ·/ *n AmE* REEF KNOT

square-rigged /ˌ· ˈ·◂/ *adj* [Wa5] (of a ship) having sails set across rather than along the length of the ship

square root /ˌ· ˈ·/ *n* the number not less than 0 which when multiplied by itself equals a particular number or the stated number: *3 is the square root of 9|how to calculate square roots*

square up *v adv* [I∅] **1** *infml* to pay what is owed; settle a bill or a disagreement: *Let's square up: how much is the bill?* **2** [(*to*)] also **square off**— to stand as if ready to begin fighting

square up to *v adv prep* [T1] to face with determination: *square up to the possibility of failure*

squash¹ /skwɒʃ‖skwɑʃ, skwɔʃ/ *v* **1** [T1;I∅] to force or be forced into a flat shape; crush: *I sat on my hat and squashed it* **2** [X9;L9] to push or fit into a small space; SQUEEZE¹ (2): *May I squash in next to you?* **3** [T1] to force into silence or inactivity; PUT DOWN (2): *squashed by an unkind remark*

squash² *n* **1** [C] an act or sound of SQUASHing: *I heard a squash when I dropped the bag* **2** [S] a crowd of people in a small space: *a squash of 100 reporters all asking questions at once* **3** [U] also (*fml*) **squash rack·ets** /ˈ· ˌ··/— a game played in a 4-walled court by 2 or 4 people with RACKETs¹ (smaller than for tennis) and a small dark rather soft rubber ball **4** [U] *BrE* a sweet fruit drink without alcohol: *a glass of (orange) squash*

squash³ *n* [Wn2;C;U] any of a group of large fairly solid vegetables including MARROWs and PUMPKINs

squash·y /ˈskwɒʃi‖ˈskwɑʃi, ˈskwɔʃi/ *adj* [Wa1] **1** soft and easy to press or crush **2** (of ground) wet and soft —**squashiness** *n* [U]

squat¹ /skwɒt‖skwɑt/ *v* **-tt-** [I∅] **1** to sit on a surface with legs drawn fully up or under the body, esp. balancing on the front of the feet **2** to live in a place without owning it, paying rent, or getting permission; be a SQUATTER **3** *BrE infml* to sit

squat² *n* **1** [S] a SQUATting position **2** [C] *BrE sl* an empty building for SQUATting¹ (2)

squat³ *adj* **1** [Wa1;B] ungracefully short or low and thick: *an ugly squat building* **2** [Wa5;F;(B)] in a SQUATting¹ (1) position: *sitting squat around the fire*

squat·ter /ˈskwɒtəʳ‖ˈskwɑ-/ *n* **1** a person who lives in an empty building without permission or payment of rent **2** a settler on unowned land who does not pay rent but has rights over it in law (**squatter's rights**) and may sometimes become its owner **3** an Australian sheep farmer

squaw /skwɔː/ *n* **1** an American Indian woman **2** *AmE humor* a wife or older woman

squawk¹ /skwɔːk/ *v* [I∅] **1** (esp. of some birds) to make a loud rough-sounding cry: *hens squawking at the sight of the cat* **2** *infml* to complain loudly —**~er** *n*

squawk² *n* an act or noise of SQUAWKing: *the squawks of ducks/of taxpayers*

squeak¹ /skwiːk/ *v* **1** [I∅] to make a short very high but not loud sound: *a squeaking door|These old bedsprings squeak whenever I move* **2** [I∅] *sl* to tell a secret to avoid punishment; SQUEAL¹ (2) **3** [L9, esp. BY, THROUGH] *not fml* to succeed, pass, or win narrowly —**~er** *n*

squeak² *n* **1** a short very high soft noise: *the squeak of a mouse* **2 a narrow squeak** a narrow escape; NEAR THING —see also BUBBLE AND SQUEAK

squeak·y /ˈskwiːki/ *adj* [Wa1] **1** tending to SQUEAK¹ (1): *a squeaky door/voice* **2 squeaky clean** *infml, esp. AmE* very clean

squeal¹ /skwiːl/ *v* [I∅] **1** to make a long very high sound or cry: *squealing tyres/pigs|The children squealed with delight* **2** [(*on*)] *sl* to tell criminal secrets; SQUEAK¹ (2); INFORM: *He squealed on his former friends to the police* —**~er** *n*

squeal² *n* a long very high cry or noise: *squeals of delight from the children|a squeal of tyres turning the corner at high speed*

squeam·ish /ˈskwiːmɪʃ/ *adj* easily shocked or made

to feel sick; unable to stand unpleasantness —**~ly** *adv* —**~ness** *n* [U]

squee·gee[1] /ˈskwiːdʒiː/ *n* a tool with a straight-edged rubber blade and short handle, for removing or spreading liquid on a surface (as in window washing)

squeegee[2] *v* [T1] to move (liquid) or clean (a surface) with a SQUEEGEE

squeeze[1] /skwiːz/ *v* **1** [T1] to press together, esp. from opposite sides; COMPRESS[1] (1): *squeeze an orange|squeeze out a wet cloth* **2** [L9;X9] to fit by forcing, CROWDing, or pressing: *She tries to squeeze her feet into shoes that are too small.|Is the car full or can I squeeze in?* **3** [X9, esp. *from, out of*] to get or force out (as if) by pressure: *squeeze the juice from an orange|squeeze* TOOTHPASTE *out of a tube|squeeze 10 pages out of a small subject* **4** [X9, esp. IN] to put in a small place; find space or time for: *You'll find the shop squeezed between 2 big office buildings.|How can you squeeze (in) so many things into a day?* **5** [T1] to cause money difficulties to: *a business squeezed by high costs and reduced sales*

squeeze[2] *n* **1** [C] an act of pressing in from opposite sides or around: *He gave her hand a gentle squeeze* **2** [C] a small amount SQUEEZED[1] (3) out: *a squeeze of* LEMON *in the tea* **3** [S] *not fml* a condition of CROWDing or pressing; SQUASH[2] (2): *There's room for one more, but it'll be a squeeze* **4** [C *usu. sing.*] a difficult state of affairs caused by short supplies, tight controls, or high costs: *a* HOUSING/CREDIT *squeeze* **5 a tight squeeze** *not fml* a difficulty which one is narrowly able to get through

squeez·er /ˈskwiːzəʳ/ *n* an instrument which SQUEEZE*s*[1] (3) the juice from fruit, esp. oranges and LEMON*s*

squelch[1] /skweltʃ/ *n* **1** an act of SQUELCHing[2] (1) **2** a sound of SQUELCHing[2] (2)

squelch[2] *v* **1** [T1] to force into silence or inactivity; crush: *a desire for freedom which nothing could squelch* **2** [IØ] to make, or move making, a sound of partly liquid material being pressed down and drawn up (as when stepping through mud)

squib /skwɪb/ *n* **1** a small BANGER (=toy explosive) **2** a short not usu. serious piece of writing, esp. attacking a politician or political party **3 a damp squib** *BrE infml* something that fails to have its intended effect

squid /skwɪd/ *n* [Wn2] a sea creature of sizes from very large to very small with 10 arms at one end of a long body strengthened by a featherlike shell inside —see picture at MOLLUSC

squidg·y /ˈskwɪdʒi/ *adj* [Wa1] *BrE infml* pastelike; soft and wet

squif·fy /ˈskwɪfi/ *adj* [Wa1] *BrE infml* slightly drunk

squig·gle /ˈskwɪgəl/ *n infml* a short wavy or twisting line, esp. written or printed: *What do these squiggles on the map mean?* —**-gly** *adj* [Wa1]

squint[1] /skwɪnt/ *v* [IØ] **1** to look with almost closed eyes, as at a bright light or in aiming a gun **2** [Wv6] to have a SQUINT[2] (1)

squint[2] *n* **1** [C;(U)] a disorder of the eye muscles causing the eyes to look in 2 different directions **2** [C (*at*)] **a** an act of looking hard through nearly closed eyes **b** *BrE infml* an act of looking (esp. in the phrs. **have/take a squint at**) —**~y** *adj* [Wa1]

squire[1] /skwaɪəʳ/ *n* **1** [C] (esp. formerly) the main landowner in an English village or country place **2** [C] (in former times) a KNIGHT'*s* armour-bearer **3** [N] *BrE infml* (used esp. by market shopkeepers, salesmen, etc., in addressing a man, sometimes not very respectfully): *You sure you can afford all this, squire?*

squire[2] *v* [T1] *infml lit* to go with (a woman) in public to a party, etc.; ESCORT

squire·ar·chy, squirarchy /ˈskwaɪərɑːki‖-ɑr-/ *n* [GC] the class of country landowners holding political power, esp. in England until 1832

squirm[1] /skwɜːm‖-ɜrm/ *v* [IØ] to twist the body about, as from discomfort, shame, or nervousness; WRITHE: *hard and direct questions that made him squirm*|(fig.) *The police have got him this time: he'll never squirm out of this charge*

squirm[2] *n* a twisting movement of the body

squir·rel /ˈskwɪrəl‖ˈskwɜrəl/ *n* any of a family of small 4-legged animals with long furry tails that climb trees and eat nuts which they also store for the winter —see picture at MAMMAL

squirt[1] /skwɜːt‖-ɜrt/ *v* **1** [T1;IØ] to force or be forced out in a thin stream: *squirt oil into a lock* **2** [T1 (*with*)] to hit or cover with such a stream of liquid: *I was squirted with water from the false flower in his buttonhole*

squirt[2] *n* **1** a quick thin stream; JET[3] (1) **2** *infml* a young person, esp. one who makes big claims or puts himself forward

squirt·er /ˈskwɜːtəʳ‖-ɜr-/ *n* a machine or container for SQUIRTing out liquid

Sr *written abbrev. for:* **1** [E] SENIOR **2** [A] SISTER (4, 5) **3** [A] *Ind & PakE* SRI

Sri /ʃriː/ *n* [A] *Ind & PakE* Mr

SRN *abbrev. for:* STATE REGISTERED NURSE

SS [A] *abbrev. for:* STEAMSHIP

Ssh /ʃ/ *interj* SH

-st /ˌst/ *suffix* **1** (the form used for -EST (1) after *-e*) **2** *old use or bibl* -EST (2) **3** (forms ORDINAL numbers with 1): *the 1st* (=first) *prize|my 21st birthday*

St *written abbrev. for:* **1** [E] Street **2** [A] SAINT

stab[1] /stæb/ *n* **1** a wound made by a pointed weapon: *a stab in the chest* **2** an act of STABbing: *made several stabs at his enemy* **3** a sudden painful feeling; PANG: *a stab of guilt* **4** *not fml* an act or chance of trying; GO[2] (3): *have/make a stab at the job* **5 a stab in the back** an attack from someone supposed to be a friend; BETRAYAL

stab[2] *v* **-bb-** [T1;IØ (*at*)] to (move as if to) strike forcefully into with something pointed, esp. with a weapon to wound: *Caesar was stabbed to death.|He stabbed a piece of meat from the plate with his fork* —**~ber** *n*

stab·bing /ˈstæbɪŋ/ *adj* (esp. of pain) as if made by a knife; sharp and sudden

sta·bil·i·ty /stəˈbɪlɪti/ *n* [U;S] the quality or state of being STABLE[3]: *a marriage that gave stability to his life*

sta·bil·ize, -ise /ˈsteɪbɪlaɪz/ *v* [T1;IØ] to (cause to) become firm, steady, or unchanging; (cause to) keep in balance: *a ship stabilized with a* GYROSCOPE —**-ization** /ˌsteɪbɪlaɪˈzeɪʃən‖-lə-/ *n* [U]

sta·bil·iz·er, -iser /ˈsteɪbɪlaɪzəʳ/ *n* an apparatus or chemical that STABILIZE*s* something

sta·ble[1] /ˈsteɪbəl/ *n* **1** [*often pl. with sing. meaning*] a (part of a) building for keeping and feeding animals, esp. horses, in —see picture at FARMYARD **2** [*often pl. with sing. meaning*] a group of racing horses with one owner or trainer **3** [(*of*) *usu. sing.*] *not fml* a group of things with one owner or people in one organization: *a big businessman who owns a stable of newspapers*

stable[2] *v* [T1] to put or keep (animals) in a STABLE[1] (1)

stable[3] *adj* [Wa2] **1** not easily moved, upset, or changed; firm; steady: *a stable ladder|government|rate of exchange for money* **2** clear and purposeful in mind; dependable: *I'm glad she's become such a stable character* **3** (of a substance) tending to keep the same chemical or atomic state; not breaking down naturally —opposite **unstable** —**-bly** *adv*

stable boy /ˈ·· ·/ also **stable lad**— *n* a man who

works in a STABLE[1] (1), looks after horses, etc.
sta·bling /ˈsteɪbəlɪŋ/ *n* [U] space in STABLEs[1] (1): *stabling for 5 horses*
stac·cat·o /stəˈkɑːtəʊ/ *adj, adv* (of music) (having notes) cut short in playing; disconnected(ly): —compare LEGATO
stack[1] /stæk/ *n* **1** [(*of*)] a usu. orderly pile or heap of things one above another: *a stack of papers/dishes* **2** a large pile of grain, grass, etc., for storing outdoors **3** [(*of*) *often pl.*] *infml* a large amount or number **4** a pipe, or group of pipes in a chimney, for carrying away smoke: *tall factory stacks* **5** [*usu. pl.*] a part of a library where books are stored close together
stack[2] *v* **1** [T1;IØ: (UP)] to make into or form a neat pile; arrange in a STACK: *stack (up) books against the wall* **2** [T1 (*with*)] to put piles of things on or in (a place): *The floor was stacked with boxes* **3** [T1(*against*)] *infml, esp. AmE* to arrange unfairly and dishonestly: *He said his opponent had cheated, had stacked the cards* **4** [IØ;T1:(UP)] **a** (of an aircraft) to fly in a pattern with others waiting for a turn to land at an airport **b** to make (an aircraft) wait like this
stack up *v adv* **1** [IØ (*against*)] *infml AmE* to compare; measure; match: *How does their product stack up against the competition of other firms?* **2** [IØ;T1] to (cause to) form a usu. waiting crowd or line: *Traffic was stacked up for miles because of the accident* **3** [IØ] *infml AmE* to be as a result or condition: *That's how things stack up today*
sta·di·um /ˈsteɪdɪəm/ *n* **-diums** *or* **-dia** /dɪə/ a large usu. unroofed building with rows of seats surrounding a sports field
staff[1] /stɑːf‖stæf/ *n* **staves** /steɪvz/ *or* **staffs** **1** a thick stick of the kind carried in the hand when walking, or used as a mark of office **2** a pole for flying a flag on **3** also **stave**— a set of one or more groups of the 5 lines on which music is written —see picture at NOTATION **4 the staff of life** *pomp* bread
staff[2] *n* **1** [GC] the group of workers who carry on a job or do the work of an organization: *The school's teaching staff is/are excellent.|a staff of 15* **2** [P] *BrE* members of such a group: *in charge of about 20 staff|complaints by staff about working conditions* **3** [GC] a group of officers having duties with a higher commander rather than commands of their own: *a staff officer*
staff[3] *v* [T1 (*with*) *usu. pass.*] to supply with STAFF[2]; provide the workers for: *a well-staffed office|a hospital staffed with 20 doctors*
staff ser·geant /ˈ· ˌ··/ *n* [C;A;N] **1** a sergeant of the highest rank in the British army **2** a sergeant of middle rank in the US army, airforce, or MARINE CORPS
stag /stæg/ *n* **1** [Wn1;C] a fully grown male deer —see MEAT (USAGE) **2** [A] for men only: *a stag dinner/party* **3** [A] full of sex and suitable for men only: *stag films/books* **4** [C] *BrE* a person who buys shares in a new company hoping to sell them quickly at a profit
stage[1] /steɪdʒ/ *n* **1** [C] a period or part in a course of action or events; state reached at a particular time: *The plan is still in its early stages/at an early stage.|the most serious stage of the disease* **2** [C; *on/off*+U] the raised floor on which plays are performed in a theatre: *a stage set for an indoor scene|The actor was on stage for most of the play* —see picture at THEATRE **3** [*the*+R] *usu. lit* the art or life of an actor; work in the theatre: *"Don't put you daughter on the stage, Mrs. Worthington."* (Noel Coward) **4** [C] *usu. lit* a centre of action or attention: *a case on the centre of the medical stage* **5** [C] a part of a trip: *We travelled by (easy) stages, stopping often along the way* **6** [C] a self-contained driving part of a ROCKET[1] (2): *a 3-stage* ROCKET **7** [C; *by*+U] STAGECOACH **8 set the stage for** to prepare for; make possible: *an unjust peace which set the stage for another war* **9 stage left/right** the left/right of an actor on stage facing the theatre seats
stage[2] *v* [T1] **1** to perform or arrange for public show; put on: *stage a play/an art show/a football match* **2** to cause to happen, esp. for show or public effect: *stage a 1-day* STRIKE[2] (1)/*a return to public life*
stage·coach /ˈsteɪdʒkəʊtʃ/ *n* [C; *by*+U] (in former times) a horse-drawn closed vehicle carrying passengers on regular services between fixed places
stage di·rec·tion /ˈ· ·ˌ··/ *n* a description or direction for performance put into the written form of a play
stage door /ˌ· ˈ·/ *n* the side or back door in a theatre, used by actors and stage workers
stage fright /ˈ· ·/ *n* [U] nervousness felt by someone (going to be) performing in public
stage-man·age /ˈ· ˌ··/ *v* [T1] *not fml* to direct, arrange, or show for public effect, esp. secretly or without taking part: *a cleverly stage-managed robbery*
stage man·ag·er /ˈ· ˌ···/ *n* the person in charge of a theatre stage during a performance
stag·er /ˈsteɪdʒəʳ/ *n infml, esp. BrE* a person with experience (esp. in the phr. **an old stager**)
stage·struck /ˈsteɪdʒstrʌk/ *adj* in love with the theatre and esp. with the idea of being an actor
stage whis·per /ˌ· ˈ··/ *n* **1** an actor's loud whisper supposedly not heard by others on stage **2** a loud whisper intended to be heard by everyone
stag·ger[1] /ˈstægəʳ/ *v* **1** [IØ] to have trouble standing or walking; move unsteadily on one's feet: *I was so tired I could hardly stagger to my feet* **2** [T1] to cause to doubt or wonder; seem almost unbelievable to; shock: *a story that staggers the imagination* **3** [Wv5;T1] to arrange not to come at the same place or time: *Working hours are staggered so that not everyone is in the office at once*
stagger[2] *n* an unsteady movement of a person having trouble walking or standing: *She gave a stagger as she began to feel faint*
stag·ger·ing /ˈstægərɪŋ/ *adj* almost unbelievable; very surprising and shocking; ASTONISHING —**~ly** *adv*
stag·gers /ˈstægəz‖-ərz/ *n* [*the*+P] a disorder of an animal's nervous system causing unsteady walking
stag·ing /ˈsteɪdʒɪŋ/ *n* **1** [C;U] the action or art of performing a play: *a new staging of Shakespeare's "Hamlet"* **2** [U] movable boards and frames for standing on; SCAFFOLDING **3** [C;U] the orderly gathering of an army in one place (**staging area**) for a forward movement
staging post /ˈ·· ·/ *n* **1** a place at which regular stops are made on long journeys, esp. by aircraft: *Bahrain is a staging post on the flight from Britain to Australia* **2** any state, event, etc., which is a point in the development of something
stag·nant /ˈstægnənt/ *adj* **1** (as of water) not flowing or moving, and often bad-smelling **2** not developing or growing; inactive: *how to put some life back into our stagnant industry* —**~ly** *adv*
stag·nate /stægˈneɪt‖ˈstægneɪt/ *v* [IØ] to become STAGNANT; stop moving or developing —**-nation** /stægˈneɪʃən/ *n* [U]
stag·y /ˈsteɪdʒi/ *adj* [Wa1] as if acting or acted on stage; not natural; THEATRICAL —**stagily** *adv* —**staginess** *n* [U]
staid /steɪd/ *adj* settled and unexciting; serious and dull by habit —**~ly** *adv* —**~ness** *n* [U]

stain[1] /steɪn/ *v* [T1;IØ] **1** to discolour in a way that is lasting or not easy to repair: *stain one's fingers and clothes with berry juice|teeth stained by years of smoking* **2** to change, esp. by darkening chemically: *stain the chairs to match the dark table*

stain[2] *n* **1** [C;U] a STAINed place or spot: *blood stains at the scene of the murder* **2** [U;C] a chemical for darkening (esp. wood, or material for looking at under a microscope) **3** [C] *lit* a mark of guilt or shame; TAINT: *the stain upon his honour*

stained glass /ˌ· ˈ·◂/ *n* [U] glass coloured in its production and used esp. artistically in church windows —see picture at CHURCH

stain·less /ˈsteɪnləs/ *adj* **1** of a kind not easily broken down chemically (esp. RUSTed) by air and water: *a set of stainless (steel) knives and forks* **2** *lit* without a STAIN[1] (2); spotless

stair /steəʳ/ *n* **1** [A;C] STAIRS: *climb down the steep winding stair|a stair* CARPET **2** [C] any of the steps in a set of stairs

stair·case /ˈsteəkeɪs‖-ər-/ also **stair·way** /-weɪ/— *n* a length of stairs with its supports and side parts for holding on to —see also MOVING STAIRCASE

stairs /steəz‖-ərz/ *n* [P;(S)] **1** a fixed length of steps built for going from one level to another, esp. inside a building (often in the phr. **a flight of stairs**): *go up and down the stairs|There's a light at the head* (=top) *of the stairs* —see also DOWNSTAIRS, UPSTAIRS **2 above/below stairs** /·ˈ· ·/ (esp. formerly) in the masters'/servants' part of the house

stair·well /ˈsteəwel‖-ər-/ *n* the space going up through the floors of a building where the stairs are

stake[1] /steɪk/ *n* **1** [C] a pointed piece of wood, metal, etc., for driving into the ground (as a mark, for holding a rope, etc.) **2** [C] (in former times) a post to which a person was bound for being killed, esp. by burning **3** [*the*+R] punishment by death in this way **4** [C] something that may be gained or lost; INTEREST[1] (5): *Profit-sharing allows workers a stake in their company's business.|He lost his stake* (=money he had STAKED[2] (1)) *when the horse finished last* **5 at stake** at risk; dependent on what happens; able to be changed or lost **6 pull up stakes** *infml* to leave one's home and job and move away

stake[2] *v* **1** [T1 (*on*); D5a] to risk (money, one's life, etc.) on a result; BET: *You mustn't fail: I've staked all my hopes on you* **2** [T1] to fasten or strengthen with STAKEs[1] (1): *stake (up) a young tree* **3** [T1 (OUT, OFF)] to mark (an area of ground) with STAKEs[1] (1): *stake off part of a field for building on* **4 stake (out) one's/a claim** to make a claim; state that something is one's by right: *He staked a claim to the land where he'd found the gold*

stake·hold·er /ˈsteɪkˌhəʊldəʳ/ *n* **1** a person chosen to hold the money given by opponents in a race, BET, etc., and give it all to the winner **2** *law* a person, usu. a lawyer, who takes charge for a time of property in a quarrel or sale

stake out *v adv* [T1] *sl* to cause (a place) to be watched secretly all the time by police —**stakeout** /ˈsteɪk-aʊt/ *n*

stakes /steɪks/ *n* **1** [P] the amounts risked in a game **2** [S] (esp. in names) a horse race in which the prize money is made up equally by the owners of the horses **3** [P] the prize in this or any race, competition, etc.

stake to *v prep* [D1] *AmE* to pay for (something) for (someone else); TREAT[1] (5) to: *Father promised to stake me to a new car when I'm 18*

stal·ac·tite /ˈstæləktaɪt‖stəˈlæktaɪt/ *n* a sharp downward-pointing part of a cave roof (like an ICICLE), formed over a long time by mineral-containing water dropping from the roof

stal·ag·mite /ˈstæləgmaɪt‖stəˈlægmaɪt/ *n* an upward-pointing part of a cave floor formed by drops from a STALACTITE and often joining it to form a solid pillar

stale /steɪl/ *adj* [Wa1] **1** no longer fresh; not good to eat, smell, etc., any longer: *bits of stale bread for the birds* **2** no longer interesting; not new or exciting: *the same stale jokes I've heard 50 times before|stale news* **3** (of a person) worn out and less active than before; without new ideas: *I'm getting stale: I need a change* —**~ness** *n* [U]

stale·mate[1] /ˈsteɪlmeɪt/ *n* [C;U] **1** (in the game of CHESS) a position from which a player can only move into CHECK and back again, and which means that neither player wins **2** a condition in which neither side in a quarrel, argument, etc., can get an advantage; DEADLOCK

stalemate[2] *v* [T1 *usu. pass.*] to bring to a STALEMATE

stalk[1] /stɔːk/ *v* **1** [T1] to hunt (an animal) by following quietly and staying hidden: (fig.) *stalk a criminal* **2** [L9] to walk stiffly, proudly, or with long steps **3** [T1;IØ] *lit* (of GHOSTs and evils regarded as living things) to move silently (through): *The disease stalked (through) the city* —**~er** *n*

stalk[2] *n* **1** (*often in comb.*) the main upright part of a plant (not a tree): *a beanstalk* **2** a long narrow part of a plant supporting one or more leaves, fruits, or flowers; stem —see pictures at FLOWER[1] and FRUIT[1]

stall[1] /stɔːl/ *n* **1** [C] an indoor enclosure (as in a BARN or STABLE) for one animal: *cattle in their stalls* **2** [C] a small enclosure inside a room: *a* SHOWER[1] (4b) *stall in a changing room at the sports centre* **3** [C] *esp. BrE* (*often in comb.*) a table or small open-fronted shop in a public place: *a market stall|a station bookstall* **4** [C] any in a row of fixed usu. roofed enclosed seats along the sides in the central part of some large churches, esp. the seats for the use of CANONs **5** [A] *BrE* in or of the STALLS in a theatre: *a front stall seat* **6** [C] FINGERSTALL

stall[2] *v* [IØ;T1] **1 a** (of an engine) to stop for lack of power or speed to keep going **b** to cause or force (an engine) to do this **2** to force or be forced to stop moving or going along: *a car stalled in deep snow* **3** to (cause to) go into a STALL[3]

stall[3] *n* a loss of control in an aircraft caused by trying to climb too steeply too slowly

stall[4] *v infml* **1** [IØ] to delay; intentionally take little or no action: *Stop stalling and answer my question!* **2** [T1] to put off; deal with by delaying: *Perhaps we can stall the seller/the sale until we can be sure we have the money*

stall·hold·er /ˈstɔːlˌhəʊldəʳ/ *n BrE* a person who rents and keeps a market STALL[1] (3)

stal·li·on /ˈstælɪən/ *n* a fully-grown male horse kept for breeding

stalls /stɔːlz/ *n* [P] *BrE* the seats in the front part of the main level of a theatre: *We bought seats in the stalls to see the play*

stal·wart[1] /ˈstɔːlwət‖-ərt/ *adj* strong and unmoving in body, mind, purpose, etc.: *a stalwart supporter/fighter* —**~ly** *adv* —**~ness** *n* [U]

stalwart[2] *n* a firm dependable follower, esp. of a political party

sta·men /ˈsteɪmən/ *n tech* the male POLLEN-producing part of a flower —see picture at FLOWER[1]

stam·i·na /ˈstæmɨnə/ *n* [U] the strength of body or mind to fight tiredness, discouragement, or illness; staying power: *You need great stamina to run the 10,000 metres*

stam·mer[1] /ˈstæməʳ/ *v* **1** [IØ] to speak with pauses and repeated sounds, either habitually or because of excitement, fear, etc.: *She stammers when she feels nervous* —compare STUTTER **2** [T1 (OUT)] to say while doing this: *He stammered his thanks.|"Th-th-thank you", he stammered* —**~er** *n* —**~ingly** *adv*

stammer² *n* [*usu. sing.*] the fault of STAMMERing in speech

stamp¹ /stæmp/ *v* **1** [L9, esp. *on*] to put the feet down hard; step with force: *He was stamping about in the cold trying to keep his feet warm* **2** [T1] to strike (esp. a surface) downwards with (the foot): *She stamped her feet in anger.|He stamped the mud off his shoes* **3** [D1+*with/on*; T1] to mark (a pattern, sign, letters, etc.) on (an object or surface) by pressing: *The office stamps the date on all incoming letters* (=stamps all the letters with the date).|*The title was stamped in gold on the book* **4** [Wv5;T1] to stick a stamp onto: *different bags for stamped and unstamped mail* **5** [T1;X (*as*) 1] to put into a class; CATEGORIZE; DISTINGUISH (3): *His manners stamped him (as) a military man* **6** [T1 (OUT)] to produce by a forceful blow (as by factory machinery): *stamp out a car body*

stamp² *n* **1** also (*fml*) **postage stamp**— a small usu. 4-sided piece of paper sold by post offices in various values for sticking on a piece of mail to be sent **2** a piece of paper like this for sticking to certain official papers to show that tax (**stamp duty**) has been paid **3** also (*fml*) **trading stamp**— a piece of paper like this given (as a means of encouraging trade) by a shop to a buyer at a fixed rate (such as 1 for each 2½ pence spent), for sticking in a book and later exchanging for goods or money **4** an instrument or tool for pressing or printing onto a surface —see also RUBBER STAMP **5** a mark or pattern made by this: *The stamp in the library book shows it must be returned tomorrow* **6** an act of stamping, as with the foot **7** [*usu. sing.*] a sign typical of something; MARK¹ (2): *remarks which bear the stamp of truth* **8** [*usu. sing.*] a lasting result; effect: *The events left their stamp on his mind* **9** a kind; sort: *I don't much like books of that stamp*

stam·pede¹ /stæm'piːd/ *n* **1** a sudden rush of fearful animals **2** a sudden mad rush or mass movement: *There's been a stampede to buy gold before the price goes up*

stampede² *v* [I∅;T1: (*into*)] to (cause to) go in a STAMPEDE or unreasonable rush: *We mustn't be stampeded into doing anything foolish*

stamping ground /'·· ·/ *n* [*often pl.*] *infml* a favourite very familiar place

stamp out *v adv* [T1] to put an end to completely: DO AWAY WITH; ERADICATE

stance /stɑːns‖stæns/ *n* [*usu. sing.*] **1** a way of standing, esp. in various sports: *a tennis stance for receiving the ball* **2** a way of thinking: STANDPOINT; ATTITUDE (3)

stanch¹ /stɑːntʃ‖stɔntʃ, stɑntʃ/ *v esp. AmE* STAUNCH¹

stanch² *adj* STAUNCH² —**~ly** *adv* —**~ness** *n* [U]

stan·chion /'stɑːntʃən‖'stæn-/ *n* **1** any strong bar standing straight up as a support **2** a metal frame that fits around a cow's neck to keep the cow from moving too far forwards or backwards in an enclosure

stand¹ /stænd/ *v* **stood** /stʊd/ **1** [I∅] to support oneself on the feet upright: *Please remain standing.|Don't just stand there; help me!|I couldn't get a seat on the bus, so I had to stand* **2** [I∅;(T1): (UP)] to (cause to) rise to a position of doing this: *He stood (up) politely when the lady entered the room.|He stood the child on the wall so that she could see* **3** [L9] to be in or take a stated position (of doing this): *Stand back and let the man through.|The soldiers stood at/to attention.|Stand* CLEAR¹ (11) *of the doors, please.|Stand firm: don't let them push you around* **4** [L1,9] to be in height: *He stands 5 feet 10 inches.|The building stands over 200 feet high* **5** [L7,9] to be in a particular state of affairs or condition: *How do things stand at the moment?|My bank account stands at 36 pence* **6** [Wv6;L9, esp. *for, against*] to feel in a particular way; hold an opinion, belief, etc.: *Sometimes I wonder what Christianity really stands for* **7** [L7,9] to have a rank or position in a range of values: *This book stands high in my opinion.|How does Britain stand among football-playing countries?* **8** [I3] to be in a position to gain or lose: *If this new law is passed, we stand to lose our tax advantage* **9** [I∅;T1;L7] to (cause to) rest in a position, esp. upright or on a base: *Few houses were left standing after the bomb hit.|The table stood in the corner* **10** [I∅;L7] to remain unmoving: *The car stood in the garage for weeks with no one to drive it.|Some of the machinery is standing* IDLE¹ (1) (=unused) **11** [Wv4;I∅] (of a liquid) to be still; not flow or be moved: *water in standing pools|leave the mixture to stand overnight* **12** [Wv6;T1,3,4: *usu. nonassertive*] to accept successfully; bear; TOLERATE; WITHSTAND: *This work will hardly stand close examination.|Could you stand to go there again tomorrow?|He wants to marry me but I can't stand the sight of him* —see BEAR (USAGE) **13** [T1] to do or take part in (a duty) by standing or walking: *stand guard/watch|The soldiers had to stand a weekly* INSPECTION **14** [L9] to hold a course at sea; sail: *stand out from the shore* **15** [Wv6;I∅] to be found in a particular form in writing: *Copy the words just as they stand on the original list.|We needn't change those words: let them stand* **16** [Wv6;I∅] to remain true or in force: *Don't forget: my offer of help still stands.|The House of Lords ruled that the law should be allowed to stand* **17** [D1 (*for*); T1] to pay the cost of (something) for (someone else); give as a TREAT² (1): *Let me stand you a dinner* **18** [I∅ (*for*)] also (*esp. AmE*) **run**— *BrE* to make oneself a choice in an election; be a CANDIDATE: *stand for Parliament/for club president|He stood unsuccessfully in 2 elections* **19** [I∅] *AmE* (of a vehicle) to park for a short time, as for waiting or loading (used esp. on signs in the phr. **no standing**) **20 know how/where one stands (with someone)** to know how someone feels about one: *He always says what he thinks, and you always know where you stand with him* **21 stand a chance** to have a chance: *You don't stand a chance of getting the job!|She stands a good chance of winning* **22 stand on one's hands/head** to support oneself on the hands/head and hands, with the feet in the air **23 stand on one's own (two) feet/legs** to be able to do without help from others **24 stand something on its head** to change or upset violently: *It was a discovery which stood the whole of chemistry on its head* —see also STAND BY, STAND DOWN, STAND FOR, STAND IN, STAND OUT, STAND UP, STAND UP FOR, **stands to** REASON¹ (10), **stand** TRIAL (7), **stand** EASY² (8), *stand one's* GROUND¹ (19), **stand** PAT³ (3), **stand and** DELIVER —**~er** *n*

stand² *n* **1** a strong effort or position of defence: *In February 1916 the French Army made a stand at Verdun.|a stand of 135 runs by the England cricketers Greig and Knott* **2** a fixed public decision or opinion (often in the phr. **take a stand**): *If he wants my vote he'll have to take a stand on the question of East-West relations* **3** a place or act of standing: *When I came in the president had taken his stand at the end of the table* **4** a raised stage, esp. at a public place or ceremony: *a judges' stand* **5** a small often outdoor shop or place for showing things; STALL¹ (3): *a fruit stand by the road* **6** (*often in comb.*) a frame, desk, base, or other piece of furniture for putting something on: *a hatstand|a music stand* (for holding sheets of music) **7** a place where taxis wait to be hired **8** [*often pl. with sing. meaning*] an open-fronted building at a sports ground with rows of seats or standing space rising behind each other: *hit a ball into the stands* **9** *AmE* WITNESS BOX: *Will the next witness please take the stand?* —see also ONE-NIGHT STAND

stan·dard[1] /ˈstændəd‖-ərd/ *n* **1** [often pl.] a level or degree of quality that is considered proper or acceptable: *We work to a high standard of exactness.|a teacher who sets high standards for his pupils* **2** something fixed as a rule for measuring weight, value, purity, etc.: *The government has an official standard for the purity of silver* **3** any of various ceremonial flags: *the royal standard* **4** a pole with an image or shape at the top formerly carried by armies **5** the system of using one particular material (esp. gold) for fixing the value of a country's money: *Britain went off the gold standard in 1931* **6** a base for holding something; STAND[2] (6): *candles lit in their standards* **7** a bush grown with an upright main stem to look like a tree

standard[2] *adj* **1** [B] ordinary; of the usual kind; not rare or special: *These nails come in 3 standard sizes* **2** [A] generally recognized as excellent, correct, or acceptable: *It's one of the standard books on the subject.|standard spelling/pronunciation|standard English* —compare NONSTANDARD **3** [Wa5;B] *BrE* (up to the end of 1977) (of eggs) of an ordinary average size, as measured by law

standard-bear·er /ˈ·· ˌ··/ *n infml lit* the leader of an organization, esp. a political party

stan·dard·ize, -ise /ˈstændədaɪz‖-ər-/ *v* [Wv5;T1] to cause to fit a single standard; make to be alike in every case: *a system of standardized road signs| Efforts to standardize English spellings did not at first succeed* —**-ization** /ˌstændədaɪˈzeɪʃən‖-dərdə-/ *n* [U]

standard lamp /ˈ·· ·/ *n BrE* a lamp on a tall base which stands on the floor of a room—see picture at LIVING ROOM

standard of liv·ing /ˌ·· · ˈ··/ also **living standard**— *n* the degree of wealth and comfort in everyday life enjoyed by a person, group, country, etc.: *have a high/low standard of living*

standard time /ˌ·· ˈ·/ *n* [U] the time calculated as the average according to the sun in a particular area of the world, and to which all clocks in the area are set —compare SUMMER TIME

stand·by /ˈstændbaɪ/ *n* **-bys** **1** a person or thing that is kept ready and can always be called on and used: *If the electricity fails, the hospital has a standby power apparatus* **2 on standby** ready to be called on at any time: *A special team of police were kept on standby during the time of violence*

stand by[1] *v adv* [IØ] **1** to be present or near: *There were several people standing by when the accident happened* **2** to remain inactive when action is needed: *How can you stand by and watch the country go to ruin?* **3** (esp. in radio and military use) to wait; stay ready: *stand by to receive a message/to fire*

stand by[2] *v prep* [T1] **1** to try to help and support: *Please stand by me in my hour of need* **2** to be faithful or loyal to: *I'll stand by my promise*

stand down *v adv* **1** [IØ] to yield one's position or chance of election **2** [IØ] to leave the witness box in court **3** [T1;IØ] *esp. BrE* **a** to send (soldiers) off after a period of being on duty **b** (of soldiers) to go off duty

stand for *v prep* **1** [T1] to be a sign or short form of; represent; mean: *What does* "PTO" *stand for?* **2** [T1,4: *nonassertive*] to allow to go on; accept; PUT UP WITH: *I won't stand for any more of your rudeness/for being treated like a child* **3** [T1] to have as a principle; support: *Before we elect him to parliament, we want to know what he stands for*

stand-in /ˈ· ·/ *n* **1** a person who takes the part of an actor at certain unimportant or dangerous moments in a film **2** a person who takes the place or job of another for a time

stand in *v adv* [IØ (*for*)] to act as a STAND-IN: *I'm standing in for the regular man while he's on holiday this week*

stand·ing[1] /ˈstændɪŋ/ *adj* [Wa5;A] **1** remaining; kept in use or force: *We have a standing invitation: we can visit them whenever we like.|Before the days of standing armies there were only small local forces in peacetime* **2** done from a standing position: *a race from a standing* (=not running) *start|a standing* OVATION

standing[2] *n* [U] **1** rank, esp. based on experience or others' respect; position in a system, organization, or list: *a student of first-year standing in the university|a lawyer of high standing* **2** continuance; time during which something has kept on; DURATION (esp. in such phrs. as **of long standing**): *friends of 20 years' standing* **3 in good standing** having kept all the rules, paid the necessary money, etc.: *a club member in good standing* **4 of standing** respected; of high rank; EMINENT

standing or·der /ˌ·· ˈ··/ *n* **1** [C *usu. pl.*] a rule or order that stays in force and is not repeated for each case: *a standing order for milk to be delivered daily* **2** [C; *by*+U] *BrE* an order to pay a fixed amount from a bank account each month, year, etc.: *pay one's insurance by standing order*

standing room /ˈ·· ·/ *n* [U] space for standing in a theatre, sports ground, etc., usu. sold after all seats have been filled

stand off *v adv* [T1] *BrE* to stop employing (a worker), esp. for a period in which there is little work; LAY OFF (1)

stand·off half /ˌstændɒf ˈhɑːf‖ˌstændɔf ˈhæf/ *n* FLY HALF

stand·off·ish /stændˈɒfɪʃ‖-ˈɔfɪʃ/ *adj not fml* rather unfriendly; coldly formal; ALOOF —**~ly** *adv* —**~ness** *n* [U]

stand out *v adv* [IØ] **1** to have an easily-seen shape, colour, etc.: *The road sign is easy to read: the words stand out well* **2** [(*from, among*)] to be much better or the best: *Among mystery writers, Agatha Christie stood out as a real master* **3** [(*for, against*)] to be firm in opposition; not yield: *I'm standing out against his idea: I'm standing out for my own, which is better*

stand·pipe /ˈstændpaɪp/ *n* a pipe connected directly to a water supply and providing water to a central or public place

stand·point /ˈstændpɔɪnt/ *n* a position from which things are seen and opinions formed; POINT OF VIEW: *Let's look at this from a historical standpoint/ from the standpoint of the ordinary man*

stand·still /ˈstændˌstɪl/ *n* [S] a condition of no movement; stop: *bring the car to a standstill*

stand to *v adv tech, esp. BrE* **1** [IØ] (of soldiers) to take up a position ready for action **2** [T1] to cause (soldiers) to do this

stand-up /ˈ· ·/ *adj* [A] **1** (of a collar) made to stand stiffly up without folding **2** [Wa5] (of COMEDY (1) or its performer) depending on telling jokes rather than on acting **3** [Wa5] for use by people standing up

stand up *v adv* **1** [L9 esp. *to, under*] to stay in good condition after testing or hard use; wear or last well: *a good floor wax that will stand up to continual passing to and fro* **2** [IØ] to be accepted as true or proven: *The charges you've made would never stand* *up in court* **3** [T1] *infml* to fail to meet (someone, esp. of the opposite sex) as arranged: *Where is he? If that man has stood me up I'll never speak to him again*

stand up for *v adv prep* [T1] to defend against attack; SUPPORT (3); STICK UP FOR: *You must stand up for your rights!*

stank /stæŋk/ *past t. of* STINK

stan·za /ˈstænzə/ *n* a group of lines in a repeating pattern forming a division of a poem

sta·ple[1] /ˈsteɪpəl/ *n* **1** a small bit of thin wire with 2 square corners which is driven into sheets of light material (esp. paper) and usu. bent over on the other side to hold them together **2** a small U-shaped piece of strong wire with pointed ends for driving with a hammer, as for holding other wire in place

staple[2] *v* [T1] to fasten with one or more STAPLE*s*

staple[3] *n* **1** [C *usu. pl.*; A] a main product that is produced or sold: *the staples among British farm products* **2** [C *usu. pl.*; A] a food that is used and needed in the kitchen all the time: *Don't forget staples/staple foods like sugar and salt when you go to the shops* **3** [C *usu. pl.*; A] something that forms the main or most important part: *a staple* DIET *of rice and vegetables* **4** [C *usu. sing.*] the length of one FIBRE of a kind of thread: *shirts of long-staple cotton*

sta·pler /ˈsteɪplər/ *n* a usu. small hand instrument for driving STAPLE*s*[1] (1) into paper

star[1] /stɑːr/ *n* **1** [C] a brightly-burning heavenly body of great size, such as the sun but esp. one very far away (a FIXED STAR) **2** [C] *infml* any heavenly body (such as a PLANET) that appears as a bright point in the sky —see also SHOOTING STAR **3** [C] a 5- or more pointed figure **4** [C] a piece of metal in this shape for wearing as a mark of office, rank, honour, etc. **5** [C *usu. pl.*] a heavenly body regarded as determining one's fate: *She was born under an unlucky star* **6** [S] one's success or fame or chance of getting it: *His star has now set and people have begun to forget him* **7** [C] a sign used with numbers from usu. 1 to 5 in various systems, and in the imagination, to judge quality: *The guidebook gives this hotel 3 stars* **8** [C] a famous or very skilful performer: *a film/football star|an* ALL-STAR *performance* **9** [C] ASTERISK —see also STARS —**~less** *adj*

star[2] *v* **-rr-** **1** [Wv5;T1] to mark with one or more stars; ASTERISK: *In the list the starred questions* (*like* *5) *are the most difficult* **2** [T1] to have as a main performer; FEATURE[2] (1): *one of my favourite old films starring Charlie Chaplin* **3** [IØ (*in*)] to appear as a main performer: *Humphrey Bogart starred in a number of fine films*

star·board /ˈstɑːbəd‖ˈstɑrbərd/ *n* [R] the right side of a ship or aircraft as one faces forward —compare PORT[5]

starch[1] /stɑːtʃ‖-ɑr-/ *v* [Wv5;T1] to stiffen with STARCH[2] (3)

starch[2] *n* **1** [U] a white tasteless substance forming an important part of foods such as grain, rice, beans, and potatoes **2** [U;C] (a) food containing this: *You're getting too fat: avoid sweets and starches* **3** [U] a product made from this, usu. in powder form, for stiffening cloth: *I like a lot of starch in my shirts|a can of* SPRAY *starch*

star cham·ber /ˌ· ˈ··/ *n* (*often caps.*) a court or like body that acts in secret and without public responsibility, and gives severe judgments

starch·y /ˈstɑːtʃi‖ˈstɑr-/ *adj* [Wa1] **1** full of, or like, STARCH **2** *infml* stiffly correct and formal; STUFFY (2)

star-crossed /ˈ· ·/ *adj lit* unlucky; ILL-FATED

star·dom /ˈstɑːdəm‖ˈstɑr-/ *n* [U] the position of a famous performer

star·dust /ˈstɑːdʌst‖ˈstɑr-/ *n* [U] something that is light, fine, and airy; a dreamlike magic quality or feeling

stare[1] /steər/ *v* **1** [IØ (*at*)] to look fixedly with wide-open eyes, as in wonder, fear, or deep thought: *It's rude to stare* (*at other people*).|*He sat staring into space, thinking* **2** [X9] to look at (someone) in this way: *The teacher stared the class into silence* **3 stare one in the face** to be so near as to be very easily seen or unavoidable: *a lost key that was staring me in the face all the time*

stare[2] *n* an act or way of staring (STARE); long fixed look: *a beautiful girl who always gets admiring stares from men*

stare out *AmE* **stare down**— *v adv* [T1] to make (someone) look away under the power of a long steady look

star·fish /ˈʃtɑːˌfɪʃ‖ˈstɑr-/ *n* [Wn2] any of several types of flat sea animal with 5 arms forming a star shape and a mouth and rows of tube feet on the lower surface

star·gaz·er /ˈstɑːˌgeɪzər‖ˈstɑr-/ *n humor* **1** ASTRONOMER **2** ASTROLOGER

star·gaz·ing /ˈstɑːgeɪzɪŋ‖ˈstɑr-/ *n* [U] (the habit or practice of) thinking about impractical ideas instead of giving one's full attention to one's present duties

star·ing /ˈsteərɪŋ/ *adj esp. BrE* unpleasantly bright and noticeable to the eye: *a staring white building*

stark[1] /stɑːk‖stɑrk/ *adj* [Wa1] **1** [B] hard, bare, or severe in appearance; not made soft or pleasant, as by ornament: *the stark shape of rocks against the sky* **2** [A] pure; complete; UTTER: *stark terror/madness/nonsense* —**~ly** *adv*

stark[2] *adv* **1 stark naked** *infml* without any clothes; completely NAKED **2 stark staring mad** *humor* completely mad

stark·ers /ˈstɑːkəz‖ˈstɑrkərz/ *adj* [F] *BrE humor sl* NAKED (1)

star·let /ˈstɑːlɪ̥ət‖ˈstɑr-/ *n* a young actress who plays small usu. sexy parts in films, hoping to become famous

star·light /ˈstɑ-laɪt‖ˈstɑr-/ *n* [U] the light given by the stars

star·ling /ˈstɑːlɪŋ‖ˈstɑr-/ *n* a very common kind of usu. greenish-black bird originally of Europe that eats harmful insects but also damages fruit and grain crops —see picture at BIRD[1]

star·lit /ˈstɑːˌlɪt‖ˈstɑr-/ *adj lit* lighted by the stars; bright with many stars: *one starlit night*

star·ry /ˈstɑːri/ *adj* [Wa1] filled with stars: *a starry winter sky*

starry-eyed /ˌ·· ˈ·◂/ *adj* [Wa2] full of unreasonable or silly hopes

stars /stɑːz‖stɑrz/ *n* [*the*+P] **1** *lit* a far-away unreachable aim: *reach for the stars* **2 thank one's lucky stars** to be grateful, esp. for some lucky escape: *You can thank your lucky stars* (*that*) *I'm feeling generous today* **3 stars in one's eyes** an unthinking feeling that some wonderful thing is really possible **4 see stars** to see flashes of light, esp. as the result of being hit on the head

Stars and Stripes /ˌ· · ˈ·/ *n* [*the*+R;*the*+P] *AmE pomp* the flag of the US

Star-Span·gled Ban·ner /ˌ· ·· ˈ··/ *n* [*the*+R] **1** the NATIONAL ANTHEM (=Song) of the US **2** *AmE pomp* the flag of the US

star-stud·ded /ˈ· ˌ··/ *adj infml* filled with famous performers: *a star-studded* CAST[2] (2)

start[1] /stɑːt‖stɑrt/ *v* **1** [IØ;T1,3: (OFF, OUT, *for*); L7] to begin (a course, journey, etc.); set out (on): *It's a long trip: we'll have to start out/off early and start back for home in the afternoon.|He started poor but quickly became rich.|She started for the door before I could stop her* **2** [IØ;T1: (UP)] to (cause to) come into being; begin: *How did the trouble start?|It takes dry materials to start a fire.|I'm no good at starting up conversations* **3** [IØ;T1,3,4;V4: (*with*)] to (cause to) go into (movement or activity); begin: *We start (work) at 8.30 every morning.|It's started to rain/started raining.|You should start saving money now.|Give it a push to start it going.|How shall we start the meeting? Let's start with business from last time.|The clock keeps starting and stopping: what's wrong with it?* **4** [IØ (IN, *on*)] to begin doing a job or a piece of work: *You're hired: when can you start?|Will I have time to start (in) on digging the garden tonight?* **5** [L9, esp. *at, from*] to go from a particular point; have a beginning or lower limit: *Prices start at £5.|The railway line starts from the coastal city* **6** [T1] to begin using: *We've finished this bottle of wine: shall we start a new one?|Start each page on the 2nd line* **7** [IØ;T1] to (cause to) play on a team at the beginning of a match: *the starting 11 for England|hurt and unable to start* **8** [IØ (*at*)] to make a quick uncontrolled movement, as from sudden surprise; be STARTLEd: *She started at the noise.|The touch on his shoulder made him start* **9** [L9] *esp. lit* to move suddenly and violently from rest: *He started angrily to his feet on hearing the speaker's words.|Blood started from the wound* **10** [T1] *tech* to drive (an animal) from hiding into the open **11 to start with** also **for a start**— (used before the first in a list of facts, reasons, etc.). *It won't work: to start with, it's a bad idea, and secondly it'll cost too much* **12 start (all) over again** *AmE* also **start (all) over**— to begin again as before or as at the first **13 start something** *infml* to make trouble; start a fight: *Are you trying to start something, friend?*

USAGE 1 Both **start** and **begin** are used in the patterns [T3] and [T4] with the same meaning; but [T3] is better when **a** the subject is a thing, not a person: *The ice* **began/started** *to melt* or **b** the 1st verb is in the -ing form: *I'm* **beginning/starting** *to cook the dinner* or **c** the 2nd verb deals with feelings or the mind: *I* **began** *to understand . . .|She* **started** *to wonder . . .* 2 **Begin** cannot be used instead of **start** in the meanings **a** to begin a journey or race: *They* **started** *(out) for London.* **b** to bring into existence: *to* **start** *a swimming club.* **c** to (cause to) begin working: *The car won't* **start**. **Commence** is used like **begin**, not like **start**. It is very *fml*.

start² *n* **1** [C] a beginning of activity or development; condition, act, or place of starting: *The runners lined up at the start.|The start of the film was quite exciting.|It was love from the very start* —see also FALSE START **2** [C *usu. sing.*] a sudden uncontrolled movement, as of surprise: *I woke up from the bad dream with a start* **3** [C] a sudden quick movement from stillness **4** [C;U: (*on, over*)] HEAD START: *The thieves have had (a) 3 days' start and their track will be hard for the police to follow*

start·er /ˈstɑːtəʳ‖ˈstɑr-/ *n* **1** a person, horse, car, etc., in a race or match at the start: *Of 8 starters, only 3 finished the race* **2** a person who gives the signal for a race to begin **3** [C9] a person who begins doing something: *He's a slow starter but what he learns he learns well* **4** an instrument for starting a machine, esp. an electric motor for starting a petrol engine —see picture at CAR **5** *infml* something that is just a beginning or a first step: *That bad joke was just a starter: we had to listen to much worse ones later* **6** [*nonassertive*] *BrE* a possibility with any chance of success: *I'm afraid your idea isn't a starter* —opposite **nonstarter**; compare BEGINNER

start·ers /ˈstɑːtəz‖ˈstɑrtərz/ *n* [P] *BrE infml* **1** the first part of a 3- or more part meal, usu. soup, fruit juice, or fish **2 for starters** first of all; to begin with

starting block /ˈ·· ·/ *n* one of a pair of blocks fixed to the ground against which a runner's feet push off at the start of a race

starting gate /ˈ·· ·/ *n* a set of gates which open at the same moment to start a horse or dog race

starting price /ˈ·· ·/ *n* a PRICE¹ (3) that is in effect just as a (horse) race begins

start·le /ˈstɑːtl‖ˈstɑrtl/ *v* [T1] to cause to jump or be quickly surprised; give an unexpected slight shock to: *You startled me! I didn't hear you come in* —**-lingly** *adv*

starv·a·tion /stɑːˈveɪʃən‖stɑr-/ *n* **1** [U] suffering or death from lack of food **2** [A] (of wages) not enough to pay for the things necessary for life

starve /stɑːv‖stɑrv/ *v* [IØ;T1] **1** to (cause to) die from lack of food: *They got lost in the desert and starved to death* **2** to (cause to) suffer from great hunger: *I'd rather starve than work for that company!|She's starving herself trying to lose weight* **3** [(*for, of*)] to (cause to) suffer from not having some stated thing: *She's lonely, and starving for companionship.|The engine was starved of petrol and wouldn't start*

starve·ling /ˈstɑːvlɪŋ‖ˈstɑr-/ *n lit* a person or animal that is thin and unhealthy from lack of food

stash /stæʃ/ *v* [T1 (AWAY)] *not fml* to store secretly; hide: *He keeps his money stashed (away) under the bed*

state¹ /steɪt/ *n* **1** [C] a condition in which a person or thing is; way of being: *the state of the nation|the state of one's health|a happy state of mind|How is the cricket match coming along? What's the state of play?* **2** [C *usu. sing.*] *infml* a very nervous, anxious, or excited condition (esp. in the phrs. **in/into a state**): *She let herself get into a state before the examinations began* **3** [(*the*): C;U] (*often cap.*) the government of a country: *Locke and Hobbes had different ideas of the state.|Should industry be controlled by the state?|state-owned railways|matters of state|state secrets|What is the proper relationship between Church and State?|life in the* WELFARE STATE| *a* POLICE STATE **4** [C] a country considered as a political organization: *the development of Britain into a modern state* **5** [U] the grandness and ceremony connected with high-level government: *The Queen drove to the palace in state.|*ROBEs *of state|the President's state visit to Britain* **6** [C] (*often cap.*) any of the smaller partly self-governing parts making up certain nations: *the 50 states of the US|Queensland is one of the states of Australia* —see FOLK (USAGE)

state² *v* **1** [T1,5,6a,b] to say, express, or put into words, esp. formally: *State your name and address.|This book states the case for women's rights very clearly* **2** [Wv5;T1] to set in advance; fix; SPECIFY: *Theatre tickets must be used on the stated date*

State *n* [U] the branch of the US government dealing with foreign affairs (in the phrs. **Secretary of State, Department of State**) —see also SECRETARY OF STATE

state·craft /ˈsteɪtkrɑːft‖-kræft/ *n* [U] the art of government; STATESMANship

State En·rolled Nurse /ˌ· ·· ˈ·/ *n* (in Britain) (the title of) a trained person who is officially allowed to practise as a nurse, lower in rank than a STATE REGISTERED NURSE

state·hood /ˈsteɪthʊd/ *n* [U] the condition of being **a** an independent nation **b** one of the states making up a nation (such as the US)

state·less /ˈsteɪtləs/ *adj* [Wa5] having no citizenship; not belonging to any country: *a stateless person with few rights* —**~ness** *n* [U]

state·ly /ˈsteɪtli/ *adj* [Wa1] **1** formal; ceremonious: DIGNIFIED: *a stately old lady|walk at a stately speed* **2** grand in style or size; NOBLE[1] (2): *a row of stately tall trees* —**-liness** *n* [U]

stately home /ˌ·· ˈ·/ *n* a large country house, usu. of historical interest and containing fine works of art, which people pay to visit

state·ment /ˈsteɪtmənt/ *n* **1** [C] something that is stated; a written or spoken declaration, esp. of a formal kind: *Do you believe the witness's statement?|The punishment for making false statements to the tax officer can be severe* **2** [C] a list showing amounts of money paid, received, owing, etc., and their total: *I get a statement from my bank every month* **3** [U] expression in words: *The details of the agreement need more exact statement* **4** [C] the introduction of the main phrase or tune in a piece of music

State Reg·is·tered Nurse /ˌ· ··· ˈ·/ *n* (in Britain) (the title of) a fully-trained person who is officially allowed to practise as a nurse

state·room /ˈsteɪtrʊm, -ruːm/ *n* a passenger's private room on a ship; CABIN

States /steɪts/ *n* [*the*+R] *infml* the US: *He spent a year in the States studying in Boston*

state's ev·i·dence /ˌ· ˈ···/ *n* **turn state's evidence** *AmE* to make statements in court against one's former criminal friends, esp. in order to get safety from punishment oneself —compare KING'S EVIDENCE

state·side /ˈsteɪtsaɪd/ *adj, adv* [Wa5] *sl* of, in, or towards the United States of America

states·man /ˈsteɪtsmən/ *n* **-men** /mən/ a political or government leader, esp. one who is wise and fair-minded —**~ship** *n* [U]

stat·ic[1] /ˈstætɪk/ *adj* **1** not moving or changing; STATIONARY **2** lacking the effect of action or movement, and usu. uninteresting: *a rather dull and static style of writing* —opposite **dynamic** **3** [Wa5] of or being electricity not flowing in a current: *static electricity in some people's hair* **4** [Wa5] *tech* of or concerning objects at rest: *static forces*/FRICTION

static[2] *n* [U] radio noise caused by electricity in the air and making regular signals harder to hear

stat·ics /ˈstætɪks/ *n* [U] the branch of science (MECHANICS) dealing with the forces that produce balance in objects at rest

sta·tion[1] /ˈsteɪʃən/ *n* **1** [C] *AmE* also **depot**— a building on a railway (or bus) line where passengers or goods are taken on: *Can you tell me the way to the (railway) station?|a station hotel*/PLATFORM **2** [C9;(C)] a building that is a centre for the stated kind of service: *a police/fire/*LIFEBOAT*/petrol station* **3** [C] a company or apparatus that broadcasts on television or radio: *I can't get* (=hear) *many foreign stations on this little radio* **4** [C] a place or building for some special scientific work: *a* RESEARCH *station* **5** [C] a settlement or place of business in wild country: *a fur-trading station in Oregon in the 1840's* **6** [C] a place of duty: *The army is* **at action stations** (=ready for action) *because it has been told to expect an enemy attack* **7** [C] a usu. small military establishment: *a naval station* **8** [C; *of*+U] *lit* one's position in life; social rank: *She married beneath her station* (=someone of lower rank) **9** [C] a large sheep or cattle farm in Australia **10** [C] a branch post office in the US **11** [U] *tech* (esp. of a warship) position in relation to others in a group: *keep (on) station*

station[2] *v* [T1 *often pass.*] to put into a certain place; POST[6]: *Guards were stationed around the prison*

sta·tion·a·ry /ˈsteɪʃənəri‖-neri/ *adj* [Wa5] **1** standing still; not moving: *A stationary object is easiest to aim at* **2** for staying in one place; not PORTABLE: *a stationary gun*

station break /ˈ·· ·/ *n AmE* a pause during a radio or television broadcast for local stations to give their names

sta·tion·er /ˈsteɪʃənəʳ/ *n* a person or shop that sells STATIONERY

sta·tion·er·y /ˈsteɪʃənəri‖-neri/ *n* [U] **1** materials for writing; paper, ink, pencils, etc. **2** paper for writing letters, usu. with matching envelopes: *a letter on hotel stationery*

sta·tion·mas·ter /ˈsteɪʃənˌmɑːstəʳ‖-ˌmæs-/ *n* the person in charge of a railway (or bus) station

stations of the Cross /ˌ·· · · ˈ·/ *n* [(*the*) P] (*often cap.* S) 14 or more pictures of happenings during Jesus's last sufferings and death, usu. put up in order around the walls inside a church

station wag·on /ˈ·· ˌ··/ *n AmE* ESTATE CAR

sta·tis·tic /stəˈtɪstɪk/ *n* a single number in a collection of STATISTICS (1)

stat·is·ti·cian /ˌstætɪ̵sˈtɪʃən/ *n* a person who works with STATISTICS

sta·tis·tics /stəˈtɪstɪks/ *n* **1** [P] collected numbers which represent facts or measurements: *These statistics show deaths per 1,000 of population* —see also VITAL STATISTICS **2** [U] the science of dealing with masses of such numbers: *Statistics is a rather modern branch of* MATHEMATICS —**-tical** *adj* —**-tically** *adv* [Wa4,5]

stat·u·a·ry[1] /ˈstætʃʊəri‖-tʃʊeri/ *n* [U] **1** STATUE*s* as a group **2** the art of making STATUE*s*

statuary[2] *adj* [Wa5] *tech* of, for, or concerning STATUE*s*

stat·ue /ˈstætʃuː/ *n* a usu. large likeness esp. of a person or animal, made in some solid material (such as stone, metal, or plastic)

stat·u·esque /ˌstætʃʊˈesk/ *adj* like a STATUE in grace, formal beauty, grandness, etc.

stat·u·ette /ˌstætʃʊˈet/ *n* a very small STATUE for putting on a table or shelf

stat·ure /ˈstætʃəʳ/ *n* [U;(C)] **1** a person's natural height: *grow to (one's) full stature* **2** quality or position gained by development or proved worth: *a man of (high) stature, respected by others*

sta·tus /ˈsteɪtəs/ *n* **1** [C;U] a condition that determines one's formal position; position in relation to others: *What's your status in this country? Are you a citizen?* **2** [U] high social position; recognition and respect by others; PRESTIGE: *Her family name gave her status in the group* **3** [C] a state of affairs: *What's the status of the talks between the government and the unions?*

status quo /ˌsteɪtəs ˈkwəʊ/ *n* [*the*+R] *Lat* the state of things as they are; existing state of affairs

stat·ute /ˈstætʃuːt/ *n* [C; *by*+U] *fml* a law passed by a lawmaking body and formally written down

statute book /ˈ·· ·/ *n* [(*the*)] *not fml* a real or imaginary written collection of the STATUTE*s* in force

statute law /ˈ·· ·/ *n* [U] *law* the body of written laws established by Parliament —compare COMMON LAW

stat·u·to·ry /ˈstætʃʊtəri‖-tʃətori/ *adj* [Wa5] fixed or controlled by STATUTE: *statutory control of wages|a statutory age limit*

staunch[1] /stɔːntʃ‖stɔntʃ, stɑntʃ/ also (*esp. AmE*) **stanch**— *v* [T1] to stop the flow of (esp. blood)

staunch[2] also **stanch**— *adj* [Wa1] dependably loyal; firm: *a staunch friend/Christian/supporter of his political party* —**~ly** *adv* —**~ness** *n* [U]

stave /steɪv/ *n* **1** any of the thin curved pieces of wood fitted edge to edge to form the sides of a barrel **2** STAFF[1] (3)

stave in *v adv* **staved** *or* **stove** /stəʊv/ [T1;I∅] to break or be broken inwards: *The ship's side was stove in by the crash*

stave off *v adv* **staved** [T1] to keep away; hold at a distance; keep back for a time; FEND OFF: *enough food to stave off hunger pains*

staves /steɪvz/ *pl. of* STAFF¹

stay¹ /steɪ/ *n* a strong rope used for supporting an upright pole (MAST) on a ship

stay² *v* **1** [IØ] to stop and remain rather than go on or leave: *I stayed late at the party last night.|Can you stay for/to dinner, or must you go?* **2** [L1,7,9] to continue to be; remain; keep or be kept: *Don't turn here: stay on the same road.|Please stay seated.|The temperature has stayed hot this week.|Get out and stay out!|The men stayed out on* STRIKE² (1) *for a week.|You'll have to keep working hard to stay ahead of the others* **3** [IØ] to live in a place for a while; be a visitor or guest: *My wife's mother is staying (with us) this week.|stay at a hotel* **4** [L9] to do this for (the stated time): *stay the night at a friend's house* **5** [T1] to last out; continue for the whole length of: *stay the course in a mile race* **6** [T1] to stop from going on, moving, or having effect; hold back: *The lawyer asked for the punishment to be stayed* (=officially delayed).|(*lit*) *Stay your hand! Don't hurt her* **7** [T1] *esp. lit* to satisfy (hunger, thirst, etc.) for a time: *stay one's stomach with a piece of bread* **8** [IØ *usu. imper.*] *old use* to stop; wait a moment: *But stay! What's this?* **9 be here/come to stay** *not fml* to become generally accepted: *Are short dresses here to stay, or will fashion change again?* **10 stay put** to remain in one place; not move: *I like to stay put by the fire on a cold day*
USAGE 1 One **stays** *at a hotel*, but *with friends* (=in their house): *"Where are you* **staying**?" *"At the Grand Hotel"|"With George"|"At George's"* (=his house). You can also use **stop** with this meaning, but it is often felt to be less good English. 2 **Remain** is more *fml* than **stay**, and cannot always be used in those expressions where **stay** means "continue to be (in a place or condition)": *The door* **stayed/remained** *closed.|to* **stay** (not ***remain**) *put|to* **stay** (not ***remain**) *home. BrE* also uses **stop** with this meaning.

stay³ *n* **1** [C *usu. sing.*] a usu. limited time of living in a place: *a short stay in hospital* **2** [C;U] a stopping or delay by order of a judge: *The prisoner was given (a) stay of* EXECUTION *because new facts in his case had come to light*

stay⁴ *n lit* a person or thing that acts as a support: *She was her husband's stay in all his troubles*

stay⁵ *v* [T1] *lit* to provide support for: *stay one's trust on God*

stay-at-home /ˈ·· ˌ·/ *n infml* a person in the habit of staying at home and not liking to travel

stay·er /ˈsteɪəʳ/ *n not fml* a horse or person who can keep going to the end of a long race, course, etc.

staying pow·er /ˈ·· ˌ··/ *n* [U] the power to keep going to the end; ENDURANCE; STAMINA

stay on *v adv* [IØ] to remain after the usual or expected time for leaving: *Sir John is 65 next month but is staying on as chairman*

stays /steɪz/ *n* [P] a lady's old-fashioned undergarment stiffened by pieces of bone and worn tight around the waist

St Ber·nard /ˌsənt ˈbɜːnəd‖ˌseɪnt bərˈnɑrd/ *n* a Swiss breed of large strong dog used esp. formerly for helping lost mountain travellers

std *written abbrev. for:* STANDARD

STD *n* [R] subscriber trunk dialling; the telephone system in Britain allowing people to connect their own long-distance calls

stead /ˈsted/ *n* **1 in someone's stead** in someone's place; instead of someone: *While the chief is away, another director will act in his stead* **2 stand one in good stead** to be of good use when needed: *I took careful notes which later stood me in good stead* —see also INSTEAD

stead·fast /ˈstedfɑːst‖-fæst/ *adj* **1** faithful; steadily loyal **2** fixed; not moving or movable —**~ly** *adv* —**~ness** *n* [U]

stead·y¹ /ˈstedi/ *adj* [Wa1] **1** firm; sure in position or movement; not shaking: *Hold that candle steady.|a delicate job needing a steady hand/steady nerves|take steady aim* **2** moving or developing evenly; not wildly varying; regular: *keep up a steady speed|steady growth in industry|a steady east wind* **3** not changing; STABLE: *a steady income/job* **4** dependable; of good habits; not silly; serious: *She needs to marry someone steady* —**steadily** *adv* —**steadiness** *n*

steady² *v* [T1;IØ] to make or become steady, settled, regular, or less changing: *He started to fall, then steadied himself.|He needs a wife to steady him.|A cup of tea will steady your nerves*

steady³ *adv* [Wa5] **go steady** *becoming rare* (of a boy and girl) to go with one another socially all the time: *She's been going steady with him for a long time: do you think they'll get married soon?*

steady⁴ *n becoming rare* a person of the other sex with whom one spends time regularly; person with whom one goes STEADY³

steady⁵ also **steady on** /ˌ·· ˈ·/— *interj BrE infml* be careful; watch what you're doing: *Steady (on)! You nearly knocked the glass out of my hand*

steady state the·o·ry /ˌ·· ˈ· ˌ···/ *n* [*the*+R] the idea that things in space have always existed and always been going further apart as new atoms come into being —compare BIG BANG THEORY

steak /steɪk/ *n* **1** [C;U] a flat piece of meat from cattle or a stated animal or fish, cut from the fleshy part and in a direction across the animal: *Steak costs too much to have very often.|2* GAMMON *steaks, please* **2** [U] *BrE* such cattle meat of a less good quality, usu. used in small pieces in dishes with vegetable or pastry

steal¹ /stiːl/ *v* **stole** /stəʊl/, **stolen** /ˈstəʊlən/ **1** [T1; IØ] to take (what belongs to another) without any right: *My bicycle was stolen while I was in the shop.|She used to steal money from her father's desk drawer* **2** [T1] to take quickly, without permission, or not quite properly: *steal a kiss|steal a look at the pretty girl across the table* **3** [L9] to move secretly or quietly: *He stole out of the house without anyone seeing him.|The evening shadows begin to steal across the ground* —see also **steal a** MARCH³ (8), **steal the** SCENE (12), **steal the** SHOW² (11), **steal someone's** THUNDER¹ (7)
USAGE One **steals** things. One **robs** people (of things): *I've been* **robbed**! *He* **robbed** *me of my watch! He* **stole** *my watch!*

steal² *n* [S] *infml, esp. AmE* something for sale very cheaply: *At £5 this camera was a steal!*

stealth /ˈstelθ/ *n* [U] the action of going or acting secretly or unseen (esp. in the phr. **by stealth**): *gain one's purposes by stealth*

stealth·y /ˈstelθi/ *adj* [Wa1] quiet and secret; (trying to be) unseen —**stealthily** *adv*

steam¹ /stiːm/ *n* **1** [U] water in the state of a gas produced by boiling **2** [A] using this under pressure to produce power or heat: *a steam engine* **3** [U] the mist formed by water becoming cool: *Steam formed on the inside of the kitchen windows* **4** [U] railway operation by STEAM¹ (2) engines **5** [U] *infml* feelings and power considered as trapped by self-control (esp. in the phrs. **let off/work off steam**): *I was so angry I worked off steam by taking a long walk* **6 full steam ahead** forward at the fastest speed **7 get up steam** to begin to move with power and speed: *our plans are beginning to get up* *steam* **8 under one's/its own steam** by one's/its own power or effort

steam² *v* **1** [Wv4;IØ] to give off steam, esp. when very hot: *The pan of boiling water was steaming away on the fire.|steaming hot coffee* **2** [L9] to travel by steam power: *The ship steamed into the harbour* **3** [Wv5;T1] to cook by allowing steam to heat: *a steamed* PUDDING*|steamed rice* **4** [X7,9] to use steam on, esp. for unsticking or softening: *steam open a letter|steam a stamp off an envelope* —see also STEAM UP

steam·boat /ˈstiːmbəʊt/ *n* a steam-powered boat made for going on rivers and along coasts

steam·er /ˈstiːməʳ/ *n* **1** a vessel for holding food for cooking with steam **2** STEAMSHIP

steam i·ron /ˈ· ˌ··/ *n* an electric iron that holds water and makes steam which goes into the clothes for easier pressing

steam·roll·er¹ /ˈstiːmˌrəʊləʳ/ *n* **1** a heavy usu. steam-powered machine with very wide wheels for driving over and flattening road surfaces **2** *infml* a force that crushes all opposition

steamroller² *v* [T1] *infml* to crush or force using very great power or pressure

steam·ship /ˈstiːmˌʃɪp/ *n* a large non-naval ship driven by steam power

steam shov·el /ˈ· ˌ··/ *n AmE* EXCAVATOR (2)

steam up *v adv* **1** [T1;IØ] to cover or be covered with steam: *His glasses (became) steamed up when he came into the warm room* **2** [T1 *usu. pass.*] *not fml* to make angry or excited: *Don't get all steamed up about it: it's not important*

steed /stiːd/ *n usu. poet* a horse, esp. for riding

steel¹ /stiːl/ *n* [U] **1** iron in a hard strong form containing some CARBON and sometimes other metals, and used in building materials, cutting tools, machines, etc. **2** *lit* fighting weapons: *give the enemy a taste of our steel* **3** great strength: *a man of steel*

steel² *v* [T1;V3] to make hard, unfeeling, or determined: *He steeled himself to go in and say he was sorry*

steel band /ˈ· ·/ *n* [GC] a band playing drums cut from metal oil barrels to sound particular notes, and heard esp. in Trinidad and other Caribbean islands

steel wool /ˌ· ˈ·/ *n* [U] material that is a mass of fine sharp-edged steel threads for using to rub a surface smooth, remove paint, etc.

steel·work·er /ˈstiːlˌwɜːkəʳ‖-ɜr-/ *n* a person who works in the steel-producing industry

steel·works /ˈstiːlwɜːks‖-ɜrks/ *n* **steelworks** [Wn3; C *often pl. with sing. meaning*] a factory where steel is made

steel·y /ˈstiːli/ *adj* [Wa1] like steel, esp. in colour or hardness: *steely blue eyes|steely determination*

steel·yard /ˈstiːljɑːd‖-ɑrd/ *n* a scale for hanging from a hook or from the user's hand and having 2 arms unequally long

steen·bok /ˈstiːnbɒk‖-bɑk/ also **steinbok**— *n* [Wn1] a kind of small S and E African ANTELOPE

steep¹ /stiːp/ *adj* [Wa1] **1** rising or falling quickly or at a large angle; PRECIPITOUS: *a steep rise in prices|a steep drop in living standards|too steep a hill to get up on a bicycle* **2** *infml* (of a demand or esp. a price) unreasonable; too much: *He's asking £500 for his old car, which I think is a bit steep* —**~ly** *adv* —**~ness** *n* [U]

steep² *v* **1** [T1;IØ: (*in*)] to (let) stay in a liquid, for softening, cleaning, bringing out a taste, etc.; SOAK: *Steep the coffee: leave the coffee to steep for 5 minutes* **2 steeped in** thoroughly filled or familiar with: *a place steeped in mystery|a mind steeped in law*

steep·en /ˈstiːpən/ *v* [T1;IØ] to make or become steeper: *The climb steepened as we went higher*

stee·ple /ˈstiːpəl/ *n* a church tower with a top part rising to a usu. high sharp point —see picture at CHURCH¹

stee·ple·chase /ˈstiːpəltʃeɪs/ *n* **1** a 3000-metre footrace with 35 high and long jumps to be made during the run **2** a horserace over a course of more than 2 miles with about 15 various jumps to be made

stee·ple·jack /ˈstiːpəldʒæk/ *n* a person whose work is building, painting, or repairing towers, tall chimneys, STEEPLEs, etc.

steer¹ /stɪəʳ/ *n* a male animal of the cattle family with its sexual organs removed, esp. a young one raised for its meat —compare OX, BULLOCK

steer² *v* **1** [X9;L9] to direct the course of (as a ship or vehicle): *steer a boat into the wind/by the stars|steer a car round a corner|steer a conversation into a favourite subject* **2** [X9;L9] to go in or hold to (a course); follow (a way): *a boat steering (a course) for the harbour|We turned the car round and steered for home* **3** [L9] (of a ship or vehicle) to allow being directed: *How does your car steer? Does it take the corners well?* **4 steer clear (of)** *not fml* to keep away from; avoid: *Steer clear of all doubtful questions*

steer³ *n* **a bum steer** *infml, esp. AmE* a piece of bad advice or misleading information: *give someone a bum steer*

steer·age /ˈstɪərɪdʒ/ *n* [U] (esp. in former times) the part of a passenger ship for those with the cheapest tickets

steer·age·way /ˈstɪərɪdʒweɪ/ *n* [U] *naut* the amount of movement forward which a ship needs to be STEERed properly

steering com·mit·tee /ˈ·· ·ˌ··/ *n* a committee which arranges in what order the business at a formal meeting shall be dealt with

steering gear /ˈ·· ·/ *n* [U] the RUDDER and other parts of a ship used for STEERing it

steering wheel /ˈ·· ·/ *n* the wheel which controls a car or ship's movement, when turned one way or the other —see picture at CAR

steers·man /ˈstɪəzmən‖ˈstɪərz-/ *n* **-men** /mən/ a person who STEERs, esp. a HELMSMAN

stein /staɪn/ *n* a tall thick cup for beer, often ornamented

stein·bok /ˈstaɪnbɒk‖-bɑk/ *n* [Wn1] STEENBOK

ste·le /ˈstiːli‖stiːl, ˈstiːli/ *n* **-lae** /liː/ a stone standing up straight, with writing or pictures cut into it, esp. an ancient Greek gravestone

stel·lar /ˈsteləʳ/ *adj* [Wa5] *tech* of or concerning the stars

stem¹ /stem/ *n* **1** the central part of a plant above the ground, from which the leaves grow, or the smaller part which supports leaf or flower —see picture at FLOWER¹ **2** any narrow upright part which supports another: *the stem of a wine glass* **3** the narrow part of a tobacco pipe **4** the part of a word which remains the same, while combining with different endings **5** a large block of wood set upright in the BOW (front) of a ship **6** *esp. bibl* a family or line of those descended from a family **7 from stem to stern** all the way from the front to the back (esp. of a ship)

stem² *v* **-mm-** [T1] **1** to stop (the flow of): *to stem the blood|to stem the flow of blood from the wound* **2** to prevent; stand against (esp. in the phr. **to stem the tide of**): *to stem the* TIDE *of public opinion against them*

stem from *v prep* [T1,4] to have as origin: *Her interest in flowers stems from her childhood in the country*

-stemmed /stemd/ *comb. form* having the stated type or number of stems: *hairy-stemmed*

stench /stentʃ/ *n* [*usu. sing.*] *fml* a (strong) bad smell

sten·cil[1] /ˈstensəl/ *n* **1** a piece of material, esp. WAXed paper or metal, in which patterns or letters have been cut **2** the pattern or letters made by putting paint or ink through the spaces in this

stencil[2] *v* **-ll-** (*AmE* **-l-**) [T1] to make (a copy of) by using a STENCIL[1] (1)

Sten gun /ˈsten ˌgʌn/ *n* a type of small MACHINE-GUN

ste·nog·ra·pher /stəˈnɒgrəfəʳ‖-ˈnɑ-/ *n esp. old use & AmE* SHORTHAND TYPIST

ste·nog·ra·phy /stəˈnɒgrəfi‖-ˈnɑ-/ *n* [U] SHORTHAND writing

sten·to·ri·an /stenˈtɔːrɪən‖-ˈto-/ *adj* [Wa5] *fml or lit* (of the voice) very loud; powerful

step[1] /step/ *n* **1** the act of putting one foot in front of the other in order to move along: *Take 2 steps forward and 2 steps back* **2** the sound this makes: *I heard a step* —compare FOOTSTEP **3 a** the distance between the feet when stepping: *The door is 3 steps away* **b** short distance: *It's just a step from my house to his* —compare PACE **4** a flat edge, esp. in a set of surfaces each higher than the other, on which the foot is placed for climbing up and down; stair, RUNG of a ladder, etc.: *Mind the step outside the door* **5** an act, esp. in a set of actions, which should produce a certain result: *Our first step must be a change in working hours; then we must decide how to improve conditions* **6** a degree on a scale: *A step in temperature on the Fahrenheit scale is smaller than a step on the Centigrade scale* **7** a type of movement of the feet in dancing: *a fast step|Do you know this step?* **8** *tech & AmE infml* (in music) a TONE **9 break step** to stop marching together in step **10 in step/out of step a** (esp. of soldiers) stepping with the left and right leg at the same time/a different time as one or more others **b** (of a person or behaviour) in/not in accordance or agreement with others: *He is out of step with modern life* **11 keep step** to march together in step **12 step by step** gradually **13 take steps (to do something)** to take action: *We must take steps to help the families of those who were hurt* **14 watch one's step** to behave or act carefully

step[2] *v* **-pp- 1** [L9] to put one foot down usu. in front of the other, in order to move along: *step forward/aside* **2** [L9] to walk: *Step into the house while you're waiting* **3** [L9 esp. *on*] to bring the foot down (on) TREAD: *She stepped on a loose stone and twisted her ankle* **4** [T1;I∅] *rare* to dance (esp. in the phrs. **step a measure, step it out** (=to dance gaily and actively)) **5 step on it** *infml* to go faster **6 step out of line** to act differently from others or from what is expected —see also STEP DOWN, STEP IN, STEP OUT, STEP UP

step- *comb. form* related not by blood but by parent who has remarried: *a stepbrother|a stepmother* —see TABLE OF FAMILY RELATIONSHIPS

step·broth·er /ˈstepˌbrʌðəʳ/ *n* a male whose father or mother has married one's mother or father —see TABLE OF FAMILY RELATIONSHIPS

step·child /ˈsteptʃaɪld/ *n* **-children** /tʃɪldrən/ the child of one's husband/wife by an earlier marriage; a **stepson** or **stepdaughter**

step down also **step a·side**— *v adv* [I∅ (*in favour of*)] to give one's place to another person, esp. in elections

step in *v adv* [I∅] **1** to enter (usu.) a house **2** to enter an argument, plan, etc., between other people by saying or doing something: *Father stepped in and forbade me to go camping*

step·lad·der /ˈstepˌlædəʳ/ *n* a sloping framework of 2 parts, one of which is like a ladder, which can be folded together for storing and used in the house for reaching high places —see picture at HOUSEHOLD

step out *v adv* [I∅] **1** to start walking fast **2** *infml* (*esp. in the* -ing *form*) to enjoy oneself in an active social life

step·par·ent /ˈstepˌpeərənt/ *n* the person to whom one's father or mother has been remarried; one's **stepmother** or **stepfather**

steppe /step/ *n* [*usu. pl. with sing. meaning*] a large area of land without trees, esp. that belonging to Russia and covering parts of Europe and Asia

stepping-stone /ˈ·· ·/ *n* **1** one of a row of large stones with a level top, which one walks on to cross a river or stream **2** a way of improvement or getting ahead

steps /steps/ *n* [P] **1** a number of STEP*s* (4), usu. outside and made of stone (often in the phr. **a flight of steps**): *He took a photograph of her on the church steps* —compare STAIR, STAIRCASE **2** *BrE* STEPLADDER —see PAIR (USAGE)

step·sis·ter /ˈstepˌsɪstəʳ/ *n* a female whose father or mother has married one's mother or father —see TABLE OF FAMILY RELATIONSHIPS

step up *v adv* [T1] *infml* to increase (an amount of something) in size or speed: *to step up the work*

-ster /stəʳ/ *suffix* **1** a person of a certain type: *a* YOUNGSTER **2** a person of a certain trade or interests: *a* TRICKSTER

ster·e·o[1] /ˈsteriəʊ, ˈstɪər-/ also **stereo set** /ˈ··· ·/— *n* **-os** a record player which gives out sound from 2 places by means of 2 LOUDSPEAKER*s* —see picture at SOUND[3]

stereo[2] also (*fml*) **ster·e·o·phon·ic** /ˌsterɪəˈfɒnɪk‖-ˈfɑ-/— *adj* [Wa5] which gives out, or is given out as, sound coming from 2 different places: *a stereo recording|a stereo record player*

ster·e·o- /ˈsterɪə/ *prefix tech* having 3 DIMENSION*s* (1); having a solid form

ster·e·o·scope /ˈsterɪəskəʊp/ *n* an apparatus which shows a scene as if real, with distance, depth, etc., by showing a separate picture to each eye, as if seen from slightly different viewpoints at the same time

ster·e·o·scop·ic /ˌsterɪəˈskɒpɪk‖-ˈskɑ-/ *adj* [Wa5] in 3 DIMENSION*s* (1); seen or seeing with depth and distance

ster·e·o·type[1] /ˈsterɪətaɪp/ *n* **1** a fixed pattern which is believed to represent a type of person or event: *She believes that she is not a good mother because she does not fit the stereotype of a woman who spends all her time with her children* **2** *tech* a metal plate for printing from, made by taking the shape from a set of movable letters (TYPE)

stereotype[2] *v* [Wv5;T1] **1** to fix in one form or type: *It's wrong to stereotype people, as if they were all alike.|She has a stereotyped view of teachers, believing that they are all as unfair as hers were when she was a girl* **2** *tech* to print from a STEREOTYPE[1] (2)

ster·ile /ˈsteraɪl‖-rəl/ *adj* **1** [Wa5] (of living things) which cannot produce young: *A* MULE *is the sterile young of a horse and donkey* **2** made free from all very small (sometimes harmful) living things (GERM*s* and bacteria): *sterile soil for planting seeds* **3** (of land) not producing crops **4** (of ideas or speech) lacking new thought, imagination, etc.

ste·ril·i·ty /stəˈrɪlɪ̈ti/ *n* [U] the state of being STERILE

ster·il·ize, -ise /ˈsterɪ̈laɪz/ *v* [T1] to make STERILE (1,2): *He didn't want to have any more children, so he had an operation to sterilize him.|Have these instruments been sterilized, nurse?* —**-ization** /ˌsterɪ̈laɪˈzeɪʃən‖-lə-/ *n* [U]

ster·ling[1] /ˈstɜːlɪŋ‖-ɜr-/ *n* [U;E] *tech* the type of money used in Britain, based on the pound (£):

The value of sterling has risen.|the pound sterling

sterling² *adj* [Wa5;A] **1** *tech* (of gold and esp. silver) of standard value **2** of good true qualities: *a sterling helper*

sterling ar·e·a /'·· ,···/ *n* [*the*+R] (esp. in former times) a group of countries, some in the British COMMONWEALTH and some out of it, who used British money as a standard for the value of their own money

stern¹ /stɜːn||stɜrn/ *adj* [Wa1] **1** very firm or hard towards others' behaviour: *a stern teacher* **2** difficult or hard to bear: *a stern punishment* **3** showing firmness, esp. with disapproval: *a stern look* —**~ly** *adv* —**~ness** *n* [U]

stern² *n* **1** the back end of a ship —compare BOW and see picture at FREIGHTER **2** *infml, often humor* the part of the body on which one sits; bottom

ster·num /'stɜːnəm||-ɜr-/ *n* **-nums** *or* **-na** /nə/ *med* BREASTBONE —see picture at SKELETON

ste·roid /'stɪərɔɪd/ *n, adj* [Wa5] (of) a type of substance in the body related to fats, each of which has a certain effect

ster·to·rous /'stɜːtərəs||-ɜr-/ *adj lit or humor* making a noisy sound while breathing: *a stertorous sleeper* —compare SNORE —**~ly** *adv*

stet¹ /stet/ *interj* (used as a note for asking a printer not to remove or change writing which has been crossed out) let it stay or remain

stet² *v* **-tt-** [T1] *tech* to ask a printer to print (a word, letter, etc., that has been crossed out) by writing "STET"

steth·o·scope /'steθəskəʊp/ *n* a medical instrument with 2 pipelike parts to be fitted into the doctor's ears and another to be placed on someone's chest, so that the doctor may hear the sound of the heartbeat —see picture at MEDICAL¹

stet·son /'stetsən/ *n* a type of hat for a man, with a wide edge (BRIM) standing out round the head, seen esp. in films of the American west, worn by COWBOYS

ste·ve·dore /'stiːvɪ̈dɔːʳ||-dor/ *n* a person whose job is loading and unloading ships

stew¹ /stjuː||stuː/ *n* **1** [C;U] a meal with meat, vegetables, etc., cooked together in liquid **2** [S] *infml* a confused anxious state of mind (in the phr. **in a stew**)

stew² *v* [T1;I∅] **1** to cook (something) slowly and gently in liquid in a closed vessel **2 stew in one's own juice** *infml* to (be left to) suffer as a result of one's own actions

stew·ard¹ /'stjuːəd||'stuːərd/ *n* **1** a man who controls supplies of food in a place such as a club or college **2** one of a number of men who serve passengers on a ship or plane **3** one of a number of men who arrange a public amusement, such as a horse race, a meeting, etc. **4** a man who is employed to look after a house and lands, such as a farm

steward² *v* [I∅] to act as a STEWARD¹

stew·ard·ess /,stjuːə'des||'stuːərdɪ̈s/ *n* a woman who serves passengers on a plane

stew·ard·ship /'stjuːədʃɪp||'stuərd-/ *n* [U] **1** the office of STEWARD¹ (4), esp. of a house and lands **2** the duties of a STEWARD¹ (4)

stewed /stjuːd||stuːd/ *adj* **1** [B] *BrE* (of tea) kept too long before pouring, thus being strong-tasting **2** [F] *infml* drunk

stick¹ /stɪk/ *n* **1** a small thin piece of wood **2** a thin rod of wood used for supporting the body when walking; WALKING STICK **3** such a rod used as a tool or for any other purpose: *He beat him with a stick* **4** [(*of*)] a thin rod of any material: *a stick of* ROCK (=a hard kind of sweet)|*a stick of chalk*|*a stick of* CELERY **5** an uninteresting person (in the phrs. **dull/dry old stick**) **6 get the wrong end of the stick** to misunderstand **7** (**wield**) **a/the big stick** (to use) (the threat of) force

stick² *v* **stuck** /stʌk/ **1** [X9] to push (in) (esp. a pointed object): *to stick pins into the material* **2** [Wv5;T1] *esp. infml* to STAB in order to kill **3** [X9; I∅] to (cause to) be fixed with a sticky substance: *Stick a piece of paper over the old address and write the new one on it* **4** [L9] to remain fixed: *The paper's sticking to my hand/has stuck on my hand* **5** [L9;(I∅)] to become fixed in position: *His head stuck in the window* **6** [I∅] to stop moving or working: *The door has stuck, and I can't get out* **7** [X9] *infml* to put: *Stick it on the table.|Stick it down.|He stuck a flower in his buttonhole* **8** [T1,4: *nonassertive*] *infml* to bear (a person or activity): *I can't stick his voice.|I can't stick waiting around* —compare STAND **9 stick in one's throat a** to be hard to accept: *Having to pay out £50 for such a small thing really sticks in my throat* **b** to be hard to say —see also STICK AROUND, STICK AT, STICK BY, STICK OUT, STICK OUT FOR, STICK TO, STICK TOGETHER, STICK UP, STICK UP FOR, STICK WITH, STUCK

stick³ *n* [U] *infml* hard punishment or experience (in the phrs. **give someone stick, get/take stick**): *She'll give him some stick when she finds out about his behaviour*

stick a·round *v adv* [I∅] *infml* to stay or wait in a place

stick at *v prep* [T1] **1** to continue to work hard at: *to stick at the job* **2** to stop at or be discouraged by esp. something wrong (usu. in the phr. **stick at nothing**): *a criminal who would stick at nothing, even murder*

stick by *v prep* [T1] *infml* to continue to support: *to stick by one's beliefs|to stick by a friend*

stick·er /'stɪkəʳ/ *n* **1** a person or thing which sticks **2** a small piece of paper or other material (LABEL) with sticky material on the back and a picture or message on the front: *His car is covered with stickers with the names of the places he's visited*

stick·ing plas·ter /'·· ,··/ also **plaster**, (*now rare*) **patch**— *n* [C;U] *BrE* (a thin band of) material that can be stuck to the skin to protect small wounds —see picture at MEDICAL¹

stick-in-the-mud /'· · · ,·/ *n infml* a person who will not change or accept new things

stick·le·back /'stɪkəlbæk/ *n* any of several types of small fierce fish with a number of prickles on their backs

stick·ler /'stɪkləʳ/ *n* [(*for*)] a person who has a strong determination to get a particular quality from others: *He's a stickler for the truth*

stick-on /'· ·/ *adj* [Wa5;A;(B)] with a sticky substance on the back by which to be fixed: *a stick-on price* LABEL

stick out *v adv* **1** [T1;I∅] to (cause to) be positioned beyond the rest; (cause to) reach further than usual: *Her ears stick out* **2** [I∅] *infml* to be clearly seen: *It sticks out a mile that we aren't really welcome here* **3** [T1] to continue to the end (of something difficult): *Try to stick out the evening*

stick out for *v adv prep* [T1] to continue action to get (what one asked for): *They say she's too young but she's sticking out for the job*

stick·pin /'stɪk,pɪn/ *n AmE* TIEPIN

sticks /stɪks/ *n* **1** [*the*+P] a country area far from the modern life **2** [P] also **sticks of fur·ni·ture** /,·· '···/— *infml* furniture, esp. of little value or importance: *We were left with nothing after the fire, just a few sticks (of furniture)*

stick shift /'· ·/ *n AmE* a way of working GEARS¹ (3) in a car by means of a GEAR LEVER

stick to *v prep* [T1] to refuse to leave or change: *stick to one's plans|to stick to one's promise*

stick to·geth·er *v adv infml* (of 2 or more people) to stay loyal to each other
stick up *v adv* [T1] **1** to rob or threaten with a gun: *to stick up a bank* **2** to raise (the hands) when threatened with a gun (esp. in the phr. **stick 'em up**) —**stick-up** /ˈ· ·/ *n*
stick up for *v adv prep* [T1] to defend by words or actions: *When they hit you, stick up for yourself instead of crying*
stick with *v prep* [T1] to stay loyal to
stick·y /ˈstɪki/ *adj* [Wa1] **1** [B] made of or containing material which can stick to or around anything else: *She fell in the sticky mud.|His fingers are sticky with sweets*|JAM ³ **2** [B] *infml* difficult; awkward: *It was a bit sticky when that car came out right in front of us; I thought we weren't going to make it!* (=might crash) **3** [F] *infml* not willing to help, be generous, etc.: *I asked him to lend me some money, but he was a bit sticky about it* **4** (**come to/meet**) **a sticky end** *infml* (at last to suffer) ruin, dishonour, death, etc. —**stickily** *adv* —**stickiness** *n* [U]
sticky wick·et /ˌ·· ˈ··/ *n* **1** (in cricket) a WICKET that has been made wet, and is then being quickly dried by hot sun, and is therefore very difficult to play on **2 be/bat on a sticky wicket** *BrE infml* to be in a state of affairs that is or may become difficult
stiff¹ /stɪf/ *adj* [Wa1] **1** [B] not easily bent: *stiff paper|shoes are often stiff when they're new* **2** [B] painful when moving or moved: *stiff aching muscles* **3** [B] not easily moved; firm: *Beat the eggs until stiff* **4** [B] formal; not friendly: *a stiff smile* **5** [A;(B)] *infml* (of a drink of strong alcohol) large and without water or other liquid added: *a stiff* WHISKY **6** [B] difficult to do: *a stiff job|stiff reading* **7** [F] *infml* too much to accept; unusual in degree: *It's a bit stiff to expect us to go out again at this time of night* —see also THICK, STEEP —**~ly** *adv* —**~ness** *n* [U]
stiff² *adv* **1 bore someone stiff** to make someone very tired with dull talk **2 scare someone stiff** to make someone very afraid
stiff³ *n sl* a dead body
stiff·en /ˈstɪfən/ *v* **1** [T1;I0] to (cause to) become hard or firm: *The dress is made of a very light material, but it's stiffened with a thicker material underneath* **2** [T1;I0: (*up*)] to (cause to) become stiff and painful: *The long march stiffened me (up)* **3** [I0] to become anxious or less friendly, as when afraid or offended: *He stiffened at her rude remarks*
stiff·en·er /ˈstɪfənəʳ/ *n* a thing which stiffens: *a pair of collar stiffeners*
stiff·en·ing /ˈstɪfənɪŋ/ *n* [U] material which stiffens esp. clothing
stiff-necked /ˌ· ˈ·◂/ *adj* proudly OBSTINATE
sti·fle /ˈstaɪfəl/ *v* **1** [Wv4;T1;I0] to (cause to) stop breathing properly: *The gas stifled them.|a stifling (hot) day* **2** [T1] to prevent from happening or continuing: *Their ideas were stifled*
stig·ma /ˈstɪgmə/ *n* **1** a sign of shame; feeling of being ashamed: *There is a sort of stigma about having to ask for money* **2** the top of the centre part of a flower which receives POLLEN which allows it to form new seeds
stig·ma·ta /ˈstɪgmətə, stɪgˈmɑːtə/ *n* [P] the marks on Christ's body caused by nails, said to have been produced in the same form on the bodies of certain very holy men (SAINT*s*)
stig·ma·tize, -tise /ˈstɪgmətaɪz/ *v* [T1] to mark (a person) out by a sign of shame; tell or show that (someone) is shameful: *They stigmatized their opponent as a liar so as to make him unpopular*
stile /staɪl/ *n* an arrangement of (usu. 2) high steps which must be climbed to cross a fence or wall outdoors, esp. between fields
sti·let·to /stə̇ˈletəʊ/ *n* **-tos** **1** a knife used as a weapon, with a long thin sharp point; small DAGGER **2** *infml* a shoe with a STILETTO HEEL
stiletto heel /·ˌ·· ˈ·/ *n* a high thin metal piece forming the heel of a shoe for women
still¹ /stɪl/ *adj* **1 a** not moving: *Keep still while I fasten your shoe* **b** without wind: *a hot still airless day* **2** calm: *a still mind* **3** quiet or silent: *The room was still at the end of the speech* **4** (of drinks) not containing gas: *still orange (juice)* —**~ness** *n* [U]
still² *v* [T1] **1** to make quiet or calm: *The food stilled the baby's cries* **2** to prevent from moving: *The wind was stilled*
still³ *adv* [Wa5] **1** (even) up to now/then and at this/that moment: *Are you still here? You should have gone home hours ago* **2** even so: *We knew he was unlikely to win, but it's still unfair that he didn't get a higher mark* **3** even (more/less): *Just as we thought the sun would sink it grew still redder* **4** however; NEVERTHELESS: *It's a very unpleasant affair. Still, we can't change it* **5** besides; yet: *He gave still another reason*
USAGE At any moment in time, one can use **still** to express surprise that something has continued later than expected, or **already** to express surprise that it has begun earlier than expected: *The coffee's* **still** *hot.|The coffee's* **already** *cold.* **Yet** is like **already**, but is *nonassertive* in this meaning: *The coffee's not cold* **yet**.|*Is the coffee cold* **yet**? **Yet** can be used, in its 4th meaning, like **still**: *I have* **yet/still** *to find out the truth.*
still⁴ *n* **1** [*the*+R+*of*] quietness or calm: *the still of the evening* **2** [C] a photograph advertising a moving picture film
still⁵ *n* an apparatus for making alcohol
still·birth /ˈstɪlbɜːθ, ˌstɪlˈbɜːθ‖-ərθ/ *n* a child born dead
still·born /ˈstɪlbɔːn, ˌstɪlˈbɔːn‖-ərn/ *adj* [Wa5] born dead
still life /ˌ· ˈ·◂/ *n* **still lifes** [U;C] a (type of) painting, esp. of flowers and fruit in special arrangements: *a still life painting*
still·room /ˈstɪlrʊm, -ruːm/ *n* **1** a room where a STILL⁵ is used **2** a storeroom near the kitchen in a large house, as for home-preserved foods
stil·ly /ˈstɪli/ *adj poet* still, quiet, or calm
stilt /stɪlt/ *n* [*usu. pl.*] one of a pair of poles, with supporting pieces for the foot, which can allow the user to walk raised above the ground
stilt·ed /ˈstɪltə̇d/ *adj* (of a style of writing or speaking) very formal and unnatural —**~ly** *adv*
Stil·ton /ˈstɪltən/ *n* [U] a type of cheese which is thick and white with greenish marks in it
stim·u·lant /ˈstɪmjʊlənt‖-jə-/ *n* **1** anything taken into the body, usu. (containing) a drug, which gives it more power to be active for a time **2** anything which encourages further or greater activity
stim·u·late /ˈstɪmjʊleɪt‖-jə-/ *v* [Wv4;T1] **1** to increase in activity: *Exercise is stimulating.|The cold air stimulates the blood* **2** to excite (the body or mind): *Some plants are stimulated by light* **3** to encourage: *He was stimulated into new efforts* —**-lation** /ˌstɪmjʊˈleɪʃən‖-jə-/ *n* [U]
stim·u·lus /ˈstɪmjʊləs‖-jə-/ *n* **-li** /laɪ/ something which is the cause of activity: *Light is a stimulus to growth in plants*
sting¹ /stɪŋ/ *v* **stung** /stʌŋ/ **1** [T1] to cause sharp pain to: *The whip stung him.|The smoke is stinging my eyes* **2** [T1] to prick with a STING² (1): *An insect stung me* **3** [I0] to have a STING² (1,2): *Some insects sting.|a stinging* NETTLE **4** [I0] to feel a sharp pain: *My eyes are stinging from the smoke* **5** [T1] *sl* to take too much money from: *They stung him for 1000 dollars*
sting² *n* **1** a sharp organ used as a weapon by some

animals, often poisonous: *Does a bee die when it loses its sting?* **2** a pain-producing substance contained in hairs on a plant's surface: NETTLE*s have a sting* **3** a sharp pain, wound, or mark caused by a plant or animal **4** a strong burning pain, usu. on the outer skin: *the sting of salt rubbed into a wound* **5** an ability to cause pain or hurt feelings: *the sting of her tongue* (=way of speaking) **6 a sting in its tail** (esp. of a story or suggestion) a part which is unexpectedly harmful or unpleasant, esp. to the hearer: *The plan has a sting in its tail: it means we lose one day's holiday*

sting·er /ˈstɪŋəʳ/ *n infml* a blow which makes the skin feel sharp pain

stin·go /ˈstɪŋgəʊ/ *n* [U] *esp. BrE* (a type of) strong beer

sting·ray /ˈstɪŋreɪ/ *n* a type of large seafish with a tail which can be used as a weapon against enemies, causing pain

stin·gy /ˈstɪndʒi/ *adj* [Wa1] *infml* having or showing unwillingness to give, esp. money: *a stingy person|a stingy meal* (=a small one of rather bad quality) —**-gily** *adv* —**-giness** *n* [U]

stink[1] /stɪŋk/ *v* **stank** /stæŋk/, **stunk** /stʌŋk/ [IØ] **1** [(*of*)] to give a strong bad smell: *The place stank of decayed fish* **2** *sl* to be very unpleasant or bad: *Your plan stinks* **3** *sl* to be disliked very much: *He stinks|His name stinks*

stink[2] *n* **1** a strong unpleasant smell **2 raise a stink** *infml* to make trouble by complaining

stink·ing[1] /ˈstɪŋkɪŋ/ *adj* [Wa5;A;(B)] **1** having a very bad smell **2** *sl* very unpleasant or bad: *a stinking idea*

stinking[2] *adv* [Wa5] very (in the phr. **stinking rich**)

stink out *v adv* [T1] *infml* **1** to fill with a bad smell: *The burning pan has stunk the house out* **2** (of something which smells bad) to drive away: *The smell of his cooking is enough to stink us all out!*

stint[1] /stɪnt/ *v* [T1 (*of*)] to give too small an amount (of): *to stint the food|Don't stint yourself; take all you want*

stint[2] *n* **1** [U] a limit (in the phr. **without stint**) **2** [C] a limited or fixed amount, esp. of work which is shared: *doing a stint in the army*

sti·pend /ˈstaɪpend/ *n* money paid for professional work, esp. to a priest

sti·pen·di·a·ry[1] /staɪˈpendɪəri‖-diːeri/ *adj* [Wa5] receiving a STIPEND

stipendiary[2] also **stipendiary ma·gi·strate** /·ˌ····ˈ···/— *n* a MAGISTRATE paid by the state

stip·ple /ˈstɪpəl/ *v* [Wv5;T1;IØ] to draw or paint (a picture, pattern, etc.) on (something) by using dots to make areas of colour, darkness, etc., instead of lines

stip·u·late /ˈstɪpjʊleɪt‖-jə-/ *v* [T1,5] to demand as a condition: *He stipulates 3 things before he can agree to go*

stip·u·la·tion /ˌstɪpjʊˈleɪʃən‖-jə-/ *n* **1** [U] the act of stipulating (STIPULATE): *By stipulation of time and place we may be sure of meeting* **2** [C,C5] a condition of agreement: *agreed, but with several stipulations*

stir[1] /stɜːʳ/ *v* **-rr-** **1** [T1] to move around and mix (esp. something mainly liquid) by means of an object such as a spoon: *to stir the* PUDDING (*mixture*) **2** [X9] to put in by such a movement: *to stir the milk into the tea|to stir nuts into a cake* **3** [IØ] to move from a position: *She stirred in her sleep.*|(fig.) *Interest began to stir among the listeners* **4** [T1;IØ] *infml* to cause (oneself) to move or wake: *It's too cold to stir from the fire|the house* **5** [T1] *infml* to cause to wake or move: *She's still asleep and no one can stir her* **6** [T1] to set moving: *The wind stirred her hair* **7** [T1 (*to*)] to excite (the feelings) (of): *He was stirred by stories of battle.|The story stirred her sympathy* **8** [IØ] *sl* to cause trouble between others, esp. by telling stories: *He enjoys stirring* —see also STIRRER **9 stir one's stumps** *infml* to step or walk fast **10 stir the blood** to excite the feelings

stir[2] *n* **1** [C] an act of STIRring[1]: *Give the mixture a few stirs* **2** [C *usu. sing.*] a movement: *a stir of excitement/interest* **3** [S] (public) excitement (esp. in the phr. **cause a stir**)

stir[3] *n* **in stir** *sl* in prison

stir·rer /ˈstɜːrəʳ/ *n sl* a person who causes trouble between others

stir·ring /ˈstɜːrɪŋ/ *adj* which excites the feelings: *stirring music* —**~ly** *adv*

stir·rup /ˈstɪrəp‖ˈstɜ-/ *n* **1** a metal piece for the rider's foot to go in, hanging from the sides of a horse's SADDLE —see picture at HORSE **2** a bone inside the ear which carries sound further inside

stirrup cup /ˈ·· ·/ *n* a cupful of strong drink, usu. wine, given to someone setting out on a journey, esp. (originally) a rider

stir up *v adv* [T1] to cause (trouble): *Don't stir up trouble unnecessarily* —see also STIR[1] (8)

stitch[1] /stɪtʃ/ *n* **1** [C] a movement of a needle and thread into cloth at one point and out at another in sewing: *to put a stitch in something* **2** [C] a turn of the wool round the needle in KNITting: *to drop* (=lose) *a stitch* **3** [C] the piece of thread or wool seen in place after the completion of such a movement: *a short stitch|a loose stitch* **4** [C;U] a particular style of sewing or KNITting and the effect which it gives: *feather stitch in sewing* **5** [C *usu. pl.*] *tech.* a piece of thread which sews the edges of a wound together **6** [S] a sharp pain in the side, esp. caused by running **7** [C *usu. sing.*] *infml* clothes (esp. in the phrs. **haven't got a stitch, not a stitch on**) **8 in stitches** laughing helplessly

stitch[2] *v* [T1;IØ] to sew; put stitches on to fasten together or for ornamental effect: *stitch a garment|stitch a button on a shirt*

stoat /stəʊt/ *n* a type of small brown furry animal that eats other animals —compare ERMINE and see picture at CARNIVOROUS

stock[1] /stɒk‖stɑk/ *n* **1** [C (*of*) *often pl.*] a supply (of something) for use: *a good stock of food* **2** [U] goods for sale: *Some of the stock is being taken without being paid for* **3** [C] the thick part of a tree trunk **4** [C] **a** a piece of wood used as a support or handle, as for a gun or tool **b** the piece which goes across the top of an ANCHOR[1] (1) from side to side **5** [C] **a** a plant from which CUTTING*s* are grown **b** a stem onto which another plant is GRAFTed **6** [U] a group of animals used for breeding **7** [U] farm animals, usu. cattle; LIVESTOCK **8** [U9] a family line, esp. of the stated character **9** [C;U] money lent to a government at a fixed rate of interest **10** [C;U] the money (CAPITAL) owned by a company, divided into SHARE*s* **11** [C] a type of garden flower with a sweet smell **12** [C;U] a liquid made from the juices of meat, bones, etc., used in cooking **13** [C] (in former times) a stiff cloth worn by men round the neck of a shirt —compare TIE **14 in/out of stock** kept/not kept in the shop at the present moment and therefore able/not able to be bought: *"Have you any blue shirts in stock?" "No, I'm afraid they're out of stock, but we shall be having some more in next month"* **15 out of stock** having none for sale: *"Have you any blue shirts in stock?" "No, I'm afraid we're out of stock* (*of them*) *at the moment"* **16 take stock** (**of**) to consider the state of things so as to take a decision (often in the phr. **take stock of the situation**) —compare STOCKTAKING; see also LAUGHINGSTOCK, LOCK[2] (8), **stock, and barrel**

stock[2] *v* [T1] **1** to keep supplies of: *They stock all* *types of shoes* **2** [(UP)] to supply: *a shop well stocked with goods* **3** [(UP)] to store: *They've stocked their crops in the* BARN —see also STOCK UP

stock[3] *adj* [Wa5;A] **1** commonly used, esp. without much meaning: *a stock greeting such as "Good morning"* **2** kept in STOCK[1] (14), esp. because of a standard or average type: *stock sizes*

stock·ade[1] /stɒˈkeɪd‖stɑ-/ *n* a wall or fence of upright pieces of wood (STAKE*s*) built for defence

stockade[2] *v* [T1] to put a STOCKADE[1] round for defence

stock·breed·er /ˈstɒkˌbriːdəʳ‖ˈstɑk-/ *n* a farmer who breeds cattle

stock·brok·er /ˈstɒkˌbrəʊkəʳ‖ˈstɑk-/ *n* a man whose job is buying and selling STOCK*s*[1] (10) and SHARE*s*[1] (2)

stock·car /ˈstɒk-kɑːʳ‖ˈstɑk-/ *n* **1** a car of an ordinary type that has had changes made to it in order to take part in a special type of rough car race (**stockcar racing**) **2** *AmE* a railway carriage (TRUCK) for carrying cattle

stock com·pa·ny /ˈ· ˌ···/ *n AmE* **1** [GC] a group of actors who perform a certain set of plays **2** [C] JOINT-STOCK COMPANY

stock cube /ˈ· ·/ *n* a solid lump of dried material which when mixed with water forms a STOCK[1] (12)

stock ex·change /ˈ· ·ˌ·/ also **stock mar·ket**— *n* [*the*+R] (*usu. caps.*) **1** the place where STOCK*s*[1] (10) and SHARE*s*[1] (2) are bought and sold **2** the business of doing this (esp. in the phr. **on the stock exchange**): *made some money on the Stock Exchange*

stock·fish /ˈstɒkˌfɪʃ‖ˈstɑk-/ *n* [U;(Wn2;C)] (a) fish dried naturally in the sun for use as food

stock·hold·er /ˈstɒkˌhəʊldəʳ‖ˈstɑk-/ *n AmE* SHAREHOLDER

stock·i·ly /ˈstɒkɪ̈li‖ˈstɑ-/ *adv* in a STOCKY way (esp. in the phr. **stockily built**=having a STOCKY body)

stock·i·net, -nette /ˌstɒkɪ̈ˈnet‖ˌstɑ-/ *n* [U] a type of material which stretches, because the stitches are KNITted together

stock·ing /ˈstɒkɪŋ‖ˈstɑ-/ *n* **1** a garment for a woman's foot and leg which is shaped to fit closely —compare SOCK **2 in one's stocking/stockinged feet** wearing no shoes

stock-in-trade /ˌ· · ˈ·/ *n* [U] **1** things used in carrying on a business **2** ways or actions habitually used: *Silly jokes are his stock-in-trade*

stock·ist /ˈstɒkɪ̈st‖ˈstɑ-/ *n* a person or firm that keeps certain goods for sale: *stockist of large sizes in shoes*

stock·job·ber /ˈstɒkˌdʒɒbəʳ‖ˈstɑkˌdʒɑ-/ *n* a person who buys and sells for a STOCKBROKER

stock·man /ˈstɒkmən‖ˈstɑk-/ *n* **-men** /mən/ a man employed to look after farm animals

stock·pile[1] /ˈstɒkpaɪl‖ˈstɑk-/ *n* a large store of materials for future use, esp. ones which may become difficult to obtain

stockpile[2] *v* [T1] to keep adding to a store of (materials), esp. in case of future need

stock·pot /ˈstɒkpɒt‖ˈstɑkpɑt/ *n* a container used in cooking for keeping STOCK[1] (12)

stock·room /ˈstɒkrʊm, -ruːm‖ˈstɑk-/ *n* a store room, esp. for goods in a shop: *Some library books are not kept on the shelves, but in the stockroom*

stocks /stɒks‖stɑks/ *n* [*the*+P] **1** a wooden frame in which criminals were in former times imprisoned by the feet **2** a framework in which a ship is held while being built (esp. in the phr. **on the stocks**)

stock-still /ˌ· ˈ·/ *adv* [Wa5] without the slightest movement: *He stood stock-still and listened*

stock·tak·ing /ˈstɒkˌteɪkɪŋ‖ˈstɑk-/ *n* [U] **1** the making of a list of goods held in a business **2** the act of considering the state of one's affairs

stock up *v* [I∅ (*with*)] to make a full store of goods: *We must stock up with food for the holiday*

stock·y /ˈstɒki‖ˈstɑ-/ *adj* [Wa1] thick, short, and strong (in body) —**stockily** *adv* —**stockiness** *n* [U]

stock·yard /ˈstɒkjɑːd‖ˈstɑkjɑrd/ *n* place where cattle or sheep are kept before being taken away

stodge /stɒdʒ‖stɑdʒ/ *n* [U] *infml* **1** food that is unpleasantly heavy and uninteresting **2** something difficult to learn, read, etc.

stodg·y /ˈstɒdʒi‖ˈstɑ-/ *adj* [Wa1] *infml* **1** (of food) thick, heavy, and sticky **2** uninteresting and difficult **3** (of a person) dull; lacking excitement —**stodginess** *n* [U]

sto·ic /ˈstəʊɪk/ *n* a person who shows no feelings of dislike, worry, etc., when faced with something unpleasant, but always remains calm

sto·ic·al /ˈstəʊɪkəl/ also **stoic**— *adj* of or like a STOIC; patient when suffering —**~ally** *adv* [Wa4]

sto·i·cis·m /ˈstəʊɪ̈sɪzəm/ *n* [U] the behaviour of a STOIC; patience and courage when suffering: *bear all one's misfortunes with stoicism*

stoke /stəʊk/ *v* [T1 (UP)] to fill (an enclosed fire) with material (FUEL) which is burned to give heat, power, etc.: *to stoke up the fire* (*with coal*)

stoke·hold /ˈstəʊkhəʊld/ also **stoke·hole** /ˈstəʊkhəʊl/— *n* a room in a ship where heat and power are produced from FURNACE*s*

stok·er /ˈstəʊkəʳ/ a person or machine that puts FUEL into a FURNACE —see also STOKE

stoke up *v adv* [I∅] to STOKE a fire, steam engine, etc.: *Don't forget to stoke up before going to bed*

stole[1] /stəʊl/ *n* **1** a long straight piece of material worn on the shoulders by women, esp. worn with fine clothes for a social occasion **2** a straight band of silk worn round the neck by some Christian priests during church services

stole[2] *past t. of* STEAL

sto·len /ˈstəʊlən/ *past p. of* STEAL

stol·id /ˈstɒlɪ̈d‖ˈstɑ-/ *adj* showing no excitement when strong feelings might be expected —**~ly** *adv* —**~ness** *or* **~ity** /stəˈlɪdɪ̈ti/ *n* [U]

stom·ach[1] /ˈstʌmək/ *n* **1** [C] a baglike organ in the body where food is DIGESTed (=broken down for use by the body) after being eaten —see picture at DIGESTIVE SYSTEM **2** [C] *infml* the front part of the body below the chest; ABDOMEN —see picture at HUMAN[2] **3** [U;S:+*for, nonassertive*] **a** desire to eat: *I've no stomach for this heavy food* **b** liking; acceptance: *He's got no stomach for a fight*

stomach[2] *v* [T1 *usu. nonassertive*] **1** to eat without dislike or illness: *I can't stomach heavy food* **2** to accept without displeasure: *I can't stomach his jokes*

stom·ach·ache /ˈstʌmək-eɪk/ *n* [C;U] (a) continuing pain in the ABDOMEN, esp. because of food passing through the body —see ACHE (USAGE)

stom·ach·ful /ˈstʌməkfʊl/ *n* [S+*of*] *infml* as much as can be borne: *I've had a/my stomachful of your bad behaviour*

stomach pump /ˈ·· ·/ *n* an apparatus with a tube for drawing out the contents of the stomach, as after taking poison

stomp[1] /stɒmp‖stɑmp, stɔmp/ *v* [L9 esp. ABOUT] *infml* to walk or dance with a heavy step: *stomping up the stairs*

stomp[2] *n* a dance with heavy stepping movements

stone[1] /stəʊn/ *n* **1** [C] a piece of rock, esp. not very large, either of natural shape or cut out specially for building: *Stones fell down from the edge of the cliff.|He threw a stone at the dog* **2** [U] (*often in comb.*) solid mineral material; (a type of) rock; SANDSTONE|LIMESTONE|*a stone surface* **3** [C] a single hard seed inside some fruits, such as the CHERRY, PLUM, and PEACH —see picture at FRUIT[1]

4 a piece of hard material formed in an organ of the body, esp. the BLADDER or KIDNEY —see also GALLSTONE **5** [C] PRECIOUS STONE **6** [C] GRAVESTONE: *to put a stone above the grave* —see also HAILSTONE, MILLSTONE, STEPPING-STONE **7 leave no stone unturned (to do)** to try every way possible (of doing) **8 rolling stone** a person who has no settled home and way of life

stone² *v* [T1] **1** to throw stones at (someone), esp. as a punishment: *The criminal was stoned to death* **2** [Wv5] to take the seeds or STONEs¹ (3) out of (usu. dried fruit): *stoned fruit*

stone³ *n* **stone** *or* **stones** [Wn2] (in Britain) (a measure of weight equal to) 14 pounds (lbs): *He weighs 13 stone(s).|a 20-stone man* —see WEIGHTS & MEASURES TABLE

stone- *comb. form* completely: **stone-cold** /ˌ· ˈ·◂/| **stone-**DEAF /ˌ· ˈ·◂/

Stone Age /ˈ· ·/ *n* [*the*+R] the earliest known time in the history of man, when only stone was used for making tools, weapons, etc. —compare IRON AGE

stone·break·er /ˈstəʊnˌbreɪkəʳ/ *n* a person or machine that breaks or crushes stones into small pieces for making the surface of a road

stone·cut·ter /ˈstəʊnˌkʌtəʳ/ *n* a person or machine that shapes stone into blocks for use in building

stoned /stəʊnd/ *adj* [F] *sl* **1** very drunk **2** excited by the use of drugs

stone fruit /ˈ· ·/ *n* [U] the type of fruit which has a STONE¹ (3)

stone·less /ˈstəʊnləs/ *adj* [Wa5] (of fruit) without STONEs¹ (3); STONED² (2)

stone·ma·son /ˈstəʊnˌmeɪsən/ also **mason**— *n* a person whose job is cutting stone into shape for building

stone's throw /ˈ· ·/ *n* [S] a short distance

stone·wall /ˌstəʊnˈwɔːl/ *v* [I∅] *esp. BrE* **1** (in cricket) to be slow and careful when BATting **2** to make a long speech or question so as to slow down the business of a meeting, parliament, etc. —**~er** *n*

stone·ware /ˈstəʊnweəʳ/ *n* [U] pots and other vessels made from a special hard clay that contains a type of hard stone (FLINT)

stone·work /ˈstəʊnwɜːk‖-ɜrk/ *n* [U] the parts of a building, esp. those ornamented with special shapes, made of stone

ston·y /ˈstəʊni/ *adj* [Wa1] **1** containing or covered with stones: *stony ground* **2** (*sometimes in comb.*) cruel; showing no pity or feeling: *a stony* STARE|*a stony heart* —**stonily** *adv*

stony broke /ˌ·· ˈ·/ *adj* [Wa5;F] *sl* having no money at all

stood /ˈstʊd/ *past p. and t. of* STAND

stooge¹ /stuːdʒ/ *n* **1** a person who acts as partner in a COMEDY act, who is made to seem silly by the jokes of the other partner, and who is generally laughed at **2** a person who does what another person wants **3** a person who is made to seem foolish, esp. by agreeing habitually to another person's unreasonable wishes

stooge² *v* **1** [I∅ (*for*)] to be a STOOGE¹ on stage **2** [L9 esp. AROUND, ABOUT] *BrE sl* **a** (of a pilot) to fly to and fro over quite a small area: *stooging around at 25,000 feet, waiting for the enemy planes* **b** to walk or go to and fro without any fixed purpose

stool /stuːl/ *n* **1** a seat without a supporting part for the back or arms: *a piano stool* —see picture at BEDROOM **2** *fml & tech* a piece of solid waste matter passed from the body **3** *old use* a place for emptying the bowels, esp. a COMMODE (2) **4** FOOTSTOOL **5 fall between two stools** to fail to take either of the 2 chances which one has had

stool·pi·geon /ˈstuːlˌpɪdʒ̍ən/ also (*AmE sl*) **stool·ie** /ˈstuːli/— *n sl* a person, such as a criminal, who helps the police to trap another

stoop¹ /stuːp/ *v* **1** [T1;I∅] to bend (the head and shoulders) forwards and down **2** [I∅] to stand habitually with the head and shoulders bent over: *He used to stoop, but he did exercises to make his shoulders straight* **3** [T3 *nonassertive*] to allow oneself (to do something), so falling to a low standard of behaviour: *I wouldn't stoop to talk to such a woman* **4** [I∅] *tech* (of a bird) to fly steeply downwards, esp. in order to attack

stoop² *n* [S] a habitual position with the shoulders bent or rounded

stoop to *v prep* [T1,4] to fall to a low standard of behaviour by (doing): *I wouldn't stoop to borrowing money*

stop¹ /stɒp‖stɑp/ *v* **-pp- 1** [T1,4;I∅] to (cause to) cease moving or continuing an activity: *He put his hand out as a signal to the bus to stop.|He put his hand out to stop the bus.|We stopped working at teatime.|Stop, thief!* **2** [T1;V (*from*) 4] to prevent: *I'm going; you can't stop me.|You must stop her telling them* **3** [T1;I∅] to (cause to) end: *The rain stopped.|We stopped the fight* **4** [I∅] to pause: *I stopped at the first word I didn't recognize* **5** [L9] to remain: *I'm feeling a little tired; I think I'll stop here a few minutes more.|I've such a lot of work to do—I'll have to stop in tonight* **6** [I∅] *infml or nonstandard* to stay, esp. for a short visit: *Are you stopping to tea?|I'm not stopping* **7** [T1 (UP)] to block: *There's something inside stopping (up) the pipe* **8** [T1] to hold back (the flow of blood) or the blood inside (a wound): *Can't you stop the blood?* **9** [T1] *becoming rare* to fill (a decayed tooth) with a special compound: *to have a tooth stopped* **10** [T1] to prevent from being given or paid: *to stop someone's electricity supply|to stop a cheque* **11** [T1] (in music) to use the fingers on (holes or strings) in order to change the note played by an instrument **12 stop at nothing (to do something)** to be ready to take any risk (in order to do something) **13 stop short of (doing)/short at (something)** to decide against (a strong action): *She wouldn't stop short of stealing if she thought it would help her children* —**~pable** *adj* [Wa5]

USAGE Note the difference of meaning between these patterns with **stop**: **a** (*followed by* to+*infin*) *He* **stopped** *to listen.|He* **stopped** *there to listen* (=he paused, in order to listen). **b** [T4] *He* **stopped** *listening* (=he didn't listen any more).|*He* **stopped** *there listening* (=he paused, and was listening. The adverb changes the meaning.) **c** [V4] *He* **stopped** *me (from) listening* (=he didn't allow me to listen) —see STAY² (USAGE)

stop² *n* **1** the act of stopping or state of being stopped: *to make a stop on the way* **2** a place on a road where buses or other public vehicles stop for passengers **3** a dot as a mark of PUNCTUATION, esp. a FULL STOP **4** a movable part of a musical instrument used for changing the level of the notes (PITCH) **5** a set of pipes on an ORGAN (4) with a movable part to provide a certain type of notes —see picture at KEYBOARD¹ **6** the part of a camera which moves to control the amount of light entering —compare APERTURE **7** (*often in comb.*) an object which prevents movement: *a doorstop* **8** a point or sign at which to stop: *There's a stop up ahead* **9** a consonant sound made by holding back air and letting it go suddenly from the mouth: */p/, /t/, and /k/ are stops/stop consonants* **10 pull all the stops out** to do everything possible to complete an effect or action: *He pulled all the stops out to complete the work in time*

stop by¹ also **stop round**— *v adv* [I∅] *esp. AmE* to make a short visit, esp. to someone's home

stop by[2] *v prep* [T1] *esp. AmE* to make a short visit to (someone's house)

stop·cock /ˈstɒpkɒk‖ˈstɑpkɑk/ *BrE* also **turncock**— *n* a VALVE or TAP which controls the flow of water in a pipe

stop·gap /ˈstɒpgæp‖ˈstɑp-/ *n* something or someone that fills a need for a time: *Let's make a stopgap arrangement for you to stay here tonight and go on tomorrow morning.|act as a stopgap while the secretary's away*

stop-go /ˌ· ˈ·◂/ *adj, n* [Wa5;A;C] *BrE not fml* (of or being) a time in which periods of a large supply of money and rising prices (INFLATION) and of a smaller supply of money and steady prices (DEFLATION) quickly follow each other: *the government's stop-go* POLICY

stop off *v adv* [I∅ (*at*)] *infml* to make a short visit to a place while making a journey somewhere else: *We need some matches; we'll stop off when we see a shop*

stop·o·ver /ˈstɒpˌəʊvəʳ‖ˈstɑp-/ *n* a short stay between parts of a journey, as on a long plane journey

stop o·ver *v adv* [I∅] *esp. AmE* to make a short stay before continuing a journey

stop·page /ˈstɒpɪdʒ‖ˈstɑ-/ *n* **1** [C] a blocked state which stops movement, as in a waste pipe or a pipe in the body **2** [C] the state of being held back: *A stoppage of air is necessary to make certain consonant sounds* **3** [U] the act of preventing something being given, esp. money: *Stoppage of pay is no longer a lawful punishment in a firm* **4** [C] the act of stopping work, or the condition which results from having stopped work, as in a STRIKE

stop·per /ˈstɒpəʳ‖ˈstɑ-/ *n* **1** an object which fits in and closes the opening to esp. a bottle or JAR **2 put the stopper(s) on** *infml* to stop something happening, being known, etc., on purpose

stop·ping /ˈstɒpɪŋ‖ˈstɑ-/ *n becoming rare* a FILLING in a tooth

stop press /ˌ· ˈ·◂/ *n* [*the*+R] the last news added to a newspaper after the main part has been printed

stop·watch /ˈstɒpwɒtʃ‖ˈstɑpwɑtʃ, -wɔtʃ/ *n* a watch which can be stopped and started at any time, so that the time taken by an event or action can be measured exactly —see picture at CLOCK[1]

stor·age /ˈstɔːrɪdʒ‖ˈstor-/ *n* [U] **1** the act of storing: *storage space* **2** a place for storing goods (esp. in the phr. **in storage**): *His furniture is in storage while he finds a new house* **3** the price paid for having things, such as furniture, stored —see also COLD STORAGE

store[1] /stɔːʳ‖stor/ *v* [T1] **1** [(UP)] to make up and keep a supply of: *to store drinks in the cupboard* **2** to keep in a special place (WAREHOUSE): *to store one's furniture* **3** to fill with supplies: *to store one's cupboard with food* **4** to put away for future use: *to store one's winter clothes*

store[2] *n* **1** [(*of*)] a supply for future use: *This animal makes a store of nuts for the winter* **2** a place for keeping things: *My food store is in the kitchen* **3** a large building in which articles are stored; WAREHOUSE: *a furniture store* **4** a large shop: *a furniture store* —see also CHAIN STORE, STORES **5** *esp. AmE* a shop: *the local village store* **6** [(*of*)] a large number or amount: *That's just one from his store of silly jokes.|to have a store of adventures to write about* **7 in store a** kept ready (for future use): *to keep a few pounds in store for a rainy day* (=for a time of need) **b** about to happen: *There's a shock in store for him* **8 set . . . store by** to feel to be of (the stated amount of) importance: *He sets great store by his sister's ability*

store·house /ˈstɔːhaʊs‖ˈstor-/ *n* **-houses** /ˌhaʊzɪ̀z/ **1** [(*of*)] a place or person full of information: *The library is a storehouse of knowledge.|He is a storehouse of useful ideas* **2** STORE[2] (3)

store·keep·er /ˈstɔːˌkiːpəʳ‖ˈstor-/ *n esp. AmE* a shopkeeper

store·room /ˈstɔːrʊm, -ruːm‖ˈsto-/ *n* a room where goods are kept till needed

stores /stɔːz‖storz/ *n* **1** [P] military or naval apparatus, goods, and food: *ship's stores* **2** [*the*+GU] the building, room, etc., (in an army camp, ship, etc.) where these are kept **3** [S] a shop in which many different types of goods are sold: *There's a small general stores in the village where you can get anything from stamps to potatoes*

sto·rey, *AmE* **story** /ˈstɔːri‖ˈsto-/ *n* **1** a floor or level in a building: *There are 3 storeys including the ground floor* **2 the upper storey** *infml, often humor* the mind or brain: *He's a bit weak in the upper storey* (= is not very clever)

-sto·reyed, *AmE* **-storied** /ˈstɔːrid‖ˈstorid/ *comb. form* having the stated number of STOREYs: *4-storeyed houses*

stor·ied /ˈstɔːrid‖ˈstorid/ *adj* [Wa5;A] *lit* being the subject of many stories: *The storied greatness of King Arthur*

stork /stɔːk‖stɔrk/ *n* any of several types of large white bird, with a long beak, neck, and legs, which walk in water and some of which make nests in the summer among the high chimneys in northern Europe —see picture at WATER[1]

storm[1] /stɔːm‖stɔrm/ *n* **1 a** a rough weather condition with wind, rain, and often lightning **b** (*in comb.*) a rough weather condition with wind and the stated thing: *a* THUNDERSTORM|*a snowstorm|a* SANDSTORM **2** [(*of*)] a sudden violent show of feeling: *a storm of weeping/tears* **3** [(*of*)] a loud noise: *a storm of cries* **4 take by storm a** to conquer by a sudden violent attack: *The soldiers took the city by storm* **b** to win success from (those who watch a performance): *Her singing took New York/the theatre by storm* —see also **storm in a** TEACUP

storm[2] *v* **1** [T1] to attack with sudden violence: *to storm the city* **2** [L9] to blow violently: *The wind stormed around the house* **3** [I∅ (*at*)] to show or express violent anger: *"Get out and never come back!" he stormed.|He stormed about the house, breaking things*

storm·bound /ˈstɔːmbaʊnd‖-ɔr-/ *adj* prevented from travelling by stormy weather

storm cen·tre /ˈ· ˌ··/ *n* **1** the heart of a storm **2** the point or person where trouble begins or is worst

storm cloud /ˈ· ·/ *n* **1** a dark cloud which may bring rain **2** [*usu. pl.*] a sign of something dangerous: *the storm clouds of war*

storm lan·tern /ˈ· ˌ··/ *n* a lamp for carrying in the hand, in which the light is covered with glass so that wind cannot blow it out

storm troop·er /ˈ· ˌ··/ *n* (in Germany before and during World War 2) a soldier in a private political army, known for cruelty and violence

storm·y /ˈstɔːmi‖-ɔr-/ *adj* [Wa1] **1** having one or more storms: *stormy weather|a stormy day* **2** showing noisy expressions of feeling: *a stormy quarrel|stormy tears* —**stormily** *adv*

stormy pet·rel /ˌ·· ˈ··/ *n* **1** also **Mother Cary's chicken, storm petrel** /ˈ· ˌ··/— a type of small black and white seabird of the north Atlantic Ocean and the Mediterranean Sea **2** a person whose presence excites discontentment, quarrelling, etc., in a social group

sto·ry[1] /ˈstɔːri‖ˈstori/ *n* **1** an account of events, real or imagined **2** *infml* (*used by and to children*) a lie (esp. in the phr. **to tell stories**)—see also TALL

STORY **3** the PLOT¹ (3) of a book, film, play, etc.: *The film is a love story* —see also STORY LINE **4** (material for) an article in a newspaper, magazine, etc.: *This event will be a good story for the paper* **5** **the same old story** the usual excuse or difficulty —see HISTORY (USAGE)

story² *n AmE* STOREY

sto·ry·book /ˈstɔːrɪbʊk‖ˈsto-/ *adj* [Wa5;A] as perfectly happy as in a fairy story for children, which usually ends with the words "They married and lived happily ever after": *a storybook* ROMANCE

story line /ˈ·· ·/ *n* the type of PLOT¹ (3) in a film, book, or play: *The story line is a love affair between 2 foreigners*

sto·ry·tell·er /ˈstɔːriˌteləʳ‖ˈsto-/ *n* **1** a person who is or was telling a story, esp. to children **2** a person, esp. a child, who tells lies

stoup /stuːp/ *n* **1** a drinking vessel used in former times, or the amount it contained **2** a container for holy water (=blessed by a priest) inside the entrance to a church

stout¹ /staʊt/ *adj* [Wa1] **1** [B] rather fat and heavy: *She became stout as she grew older* **2** [B] strong; thick; too solid to break: *He cut a stout stick to help him walk* **3** [A:(B)] brave; determined: *a stout supporter of the team* —**~ly** *adv* —**~ness** *n* [U]

stout² *n* [U] a kind of strong dark beer

stout·heart·ed /ˌstaʊtˈhɑːtɪ̈d◂‖-ɑr-/ *adj esp. lit* brave; of a firm character

stove¹ /stəʊv/ *n* an enclosed apparatus for cooking or heating which works by burning coal, oil, gas, etc., or by electricity —see also COOKER, HEATER —see picture at CAMP²

stove² *past t. and past p. of* STAVE

stove·pipe /ˈstəʊvpaɪp/ *n* **1** a pipe which carries away smoke from a STOVE **2** *infml* a TOP HAT

stow /stəʊ/ *v* [X9 (AWAY)] **1** to put away or pack, esp. for some time: *to stow goods (away) in boxes* **2** **stow it!** *sl* Be quiet!

stow·age /ˈstəʊɪdʒ/ *n* [U] **1** the act of STOWING goods **2** the space allowed for keeping goods, as on a ship: *not enough stowage* **3** the price paid for having goods kept in a special place, as on a ship

stow·a·way /ˈstəʊəweɪ/ *n* a person who hides on a ship or plane to get a free journey

stow a·way *v adv* [I∅] to hide on a ship or plane in order to make a free journey, unknown to anyone

strad·dle /ˈstrædl/ *v* **1** [T1;I∅] to sit, stand, or move with the legs out at the sides (of): *to straddle a horse|to sit straddling the fence* **2** [T1] to be, land, etc., on either side of (something), rather than the middle: *The shots straddled the* TARGET

Strad·i·va·ri·us /ˌstrædɪ̈ˈveərɪəs, -ˈvɑːr-/ also (*infml*) **Strad** /stræd/— *n* **-ri·i** /riːi/ a VIOLIN (or other like instrument) of high quality, made by the Italian maker Antonio Stradivari (1644–1737)

strafe /strɑːf‖streɪf/ *v* [T1] to attack with heavy gunfire from a low-flying aircraft

strag·gle /ˈstrægəl/ *v* [Wv3] **1** [Wv4;L9] to move or spread untidily, without ordered shape: *straggling branches/houses* **2** [I∅] to fall (back) away from the main group while walking or marching: *to straggle over the fields instead of staying on the road* —**-gler** *n*

strag·gly /ˈstrægəli/ *adj* [Wa1] growing or lying out in an untidy shape: *straggly hair|straggly branches*

straight¹ /streɪt/ *adj* **1** [Wa1;B] not bent or curved: *A straight line is the shortest distance between 2 points.|She has straight, not curly hair* **2** [Wa1;F;(B)] level or upright: *Put the mirror straight.|Put the pole up straight* **3** [Wa1;F] tidy; neat: *Put your hair straight* **4** [Wa1;B] honest; truthful: *Are you being straight with me?|a straight answer* —compare LEVEL **5** [Wa1;F] correct (esp. in the phrs. **set/put someone/the record straight**): *Just to put the record straight, this is what really happened.|Let me set you straight about that* **6** [Wa5;B] (of alcohol) without added water: *a straight* WHISKY*|to drink* WHISKY *straight* —compare NEAT (6) **7** [Wa5;A] (in the theatre) serious, of the established kind: *the straight theatre|a straight play* **8** [Wa1;B] (of the face) not laughing; with a serious expression: *We couldn't keep our faces straight when he fell over the dog* —**~ness** *n* [U]

straight² *adv* [Wa5;H] **1** in a straight line: *straight down the road|Sit up straight.|*(fig.) *I'm too tired to think straight* **2** directly: *Go straight to school without stopping.|He went straight to the point* (=said what he thought) **3** **go straight** to leave a life of crime **4** **tell someone straight** *infml* to speak to someone clearly and boldly, even about what may offend

straight³ *n* [*usu. sing.*] a straight part or place, esp. on a race track

straight and nar·row /ˌ· · ˈ··/ *n* **on the straight and narrow** behaving or living honestly, not as a criminal

straight·a·way /ˌstreɪtəˈweɪ/ also (*infml*) **straight off** /ˌ· ˈ·/— *adv* [Wa5] at once

straight·edge /ˈstreɪt-edʒ/ *n* a measure or ruler which is also used for testing whether things are level

straight·en /ˈstreɪtn/ *v* [T1 (UP); I∅: (OUT)] to (cause to) become straight, level, or tidy: *Straighten your hat.|Straighten your room up* —see also STRAIGHTEN UP

straighten out *v adv* [T1] **1** to remove (the confusions or difficulties in): *to straighten out one's business affairs* **2** to remove difficulties, esp. bad behaviour or worries, in the life of: *He's refusing to go after all his promises? Let me see him; I'll soon straighten him out*

straighten up *v adv* **1** [I∅] to get up from a bent over position **2** [T1] to improve or make more powerful: *Straighten up your ideas!*

straight fight /ˌ· ˈ·/ *n* a competition, as in an election, between only 2 people or parties

straight·for·ward /ˌstreɪtˈfɔːwəd‖-ˈfɔrwərd/ *adj* **1** honest, without hidden meanings **2** expressed or understood in a direct way, without difficulties —**~ly** *adv*

straight out /ˌ· ˈ·◂/ *adj, adv* open(ly); direct(ly) in speech: *a straight-out answer|to say straight out what you think*

straight up /ˌ· ˈ·/ *adv* [Wa5] *BrE sl* (used esp. in asking or replying to a question) honestly; truly: *"I only paid £400 for that car." "Straight up?"* (=is that really true?) *"Yes, straight up"*

straight·way /ˈstreɪt-weɪ/ *adv* [Wa5] *old use & bibl* at once

strain¹ /streɪn/ *n* **1** [S9 *often pl. with sing. meaning*] *esp. lit* a tune; notes of music: *the strains of a well-known song|a pleasant strain* **2** [S9] a manner or style of using words: *Her letters were written in a happy strain* **3** [C] a breed or type of plant or animal: *This strain (of wheat) can grow even during a cold spring* **4** [S9 (*of*)] a quality which tends to develop, esp. one passed down a family: *a strain of madness in her family*

strain² *v* **1** [X9] to stretch or pull tightly: *They strained the cover over the top* **2** [T1] to use the whole of: *to strain one's ears for a sound* **3** [L9] to make great efforts: *to strain to hear|straining to understand* **4** [T1] to damage or weaken (a part of the body): *to strain a muscle|All exercise strains the heart* **5** [L9 esp. *against*] to press oneself closely: *to strain against the prison bars|against the ropes which tied him* **6** [X9] to hold tightly: *She strained the* *child to her* **7** [T1] to force beyond acceptable or truthful limits: *to strain the truth for one's own purposes* **8** [T1] to separate (a liquid and solid) by pouring through a narrow space, esp. the fine holes in a STRAINER: *to strain the potatoes/vegetables*

strain³ *n* **1** [C;U] **a** the condition of being STRAINed² (1): *The rope broke under the strain* **b** the force causing this: *to measure the strain on the materials of which a house is built* **2** [C (*on*)] a fact or state which tests the powers, esp. of mind and body: *The additional work put a great strain on him* **3** [U] a state of TENSION (3): *She's under a lot of strain at the moment; her child's very ill* **4** [C;U] damage to a part of the body caused by too great effort and often stretching of muscles: *heart strain|a strain of the lower leg* —compare SPRAIN

strain at *v prep* [T1] **1** to stretch or pull tightly: *He strained at the rope* **2 straining at the leash** eager to be free, esp. to do what one wants

strained /streɪnd/ *adj* **1** not natural in behaviour; unfriendly: *His manner was strained* **2** forced beyond acceptable limits: *The meaning you give to the story is rather strained* **3** nervous or tired: *a strained face at the end of the day*

strain·er /ˈstreɪnəʳ/ *n* an instrument for separating solids from liquids, with small spaces in the material it is made of, such as a SIEVE made of fine wire, a COLANDER, or a FILTER¹ (1)

strait¹ /streɪt/ *adj* [Wa1] *esp. bibl* narrow or difficult

strait² *n* [*usu. pl. with sing. meaning*] (*often cap. as part of a name*) a narrow passage of water between land and (esp.) connecting 2 seas: *the Straits of Dover* —see also STRAITS

strait·ened /ˈstreɪtnd/ *adj* lacking money (usu. in the phr. **in straitened circumstances**)

strait·jack·et /ˈstreɪtˌdʒækɨ̇t/ *n* **1** a garment which holds the arms down, preventing the wearer, esp. a madman, from violent movement **2** something which prevents free development: *the straitjacket of* POVERTY (1)

strait·laced /ˌstreɪtˈleɪst◂/ *adj derog* having very firm ideas about morals, esp. the belief that many things must not be done

straits /streɪts/ *n* [P] a difficult position in life such as illness or lack of money (esp. in the phr. **in . . . straits**): *Now that father's lost his job, we're in serious straits*

strand¹ /strænd/ *n esp. poet* a shore or BEACH beside the sea, a lake, or river

strand² *v* [T1] *tech* to cause (a ship) to run onto the shore

strand³ *n* [(*of*)] a single piece or thread (of a material made up of many threads, wires, etc.): *Many strands are twisted together to form a rope*

strand·ed /ˈstrændɨ̇d/ *adj* [Wa5] in a helpless position, unable to get away: *a* WHALE *stranded on the shore|stranded in the middle of the traffic*

strange /streɪndʒ/ *adj* **1** [Wa1;B] hard to accept or understand; surprising: *It's strange you've never met him.|What a strange idea!* **2** [Wa5;B] not known or experienced before; unfamiliar: *The street he stood in was strange to him. He stood in a strange street* **3** [Wa5;F+*to*] not experienced (in) or accustomed (to): *strange to one's duties* **4** [Wa5;B] *old use* foreign: *a traveller in a strange country* —**~ly** *adv*: *Strangely, I've never seen that popular television show* —**~ness** *n* [U]

strang·er /ˈstreɪndʒəʳ/ *n* [C;(N)] **1** a person who is unfamiliar: *They never talk to strangers. "Have you met each other before?" "No, we're strangers"* **2** a person in a new or unfamiliar place: *I'm a stranger in this town. Can you tell me the way to the station?*

stran·gle /ˈstræŋgəl/ *v* [T1] to kill by pressing on the throat

stran·gle·hold /ˈstræŋgəlhəʊld/ *n* **1** a strong hold round the neck **2** a strong control which prevents action: *the stranglehold of large firms on industry*

stran·gu·late /ˈstræŋgjʊleɪt‖-gjə-/ *v* [Wv5;I∅; (T1)] *med* to (cause to) become tightly pressed so as to stop the flow of blood: *a strangulated* HERNIA

stran·gu·la·tion /ˌstræŋgjʊˈleɪʃən‖-gjə-/ *n* [U] the act of strangling (STRANGLE) or fact of being strangled: *Death was caused by strangulation*

strap¹ /stræp/ *n* **1** [C] a strong narrow band of material, such as leather, used as a fastening: *a watch strap|Fasten the straps round the case.|One of the silk straps on her dress has slipped off her shoulder* —see picture at CLOCK¹ **2** [*the*+R] the giving of punishment by beating with a thick narrow piece of leather

strap² *v* **-pp-** **1** [X9] to fasten in place with one or more STRAPs¹: *to strap a bag onto one's back|Make sure you're firmly strapped in before the plane takes off* **2** [T1] to beat with a STRAP¹ **3** [T1 (UP), *often pass.*] (*AmE* **tape**)—*BrE* to bind (a part of the body that has been hurt, esp. a limb) with BANDAGEs

strap·hang·ing /ˈstræpˌhæŋɪŋ/ *n* [U] the position in travelling on public vehicles in which one stands and holds a STRAP¹ (1) which hangs from the roof —**straphanger** *n*

strap·less /ˈstræpləs/ *adj* [Wa5] (of a dress or garment which covers the top part of a woman's body) without pieces of material over the shoulders joining the front and back; not covering the shoulders

strap·ping /ˈstræpɪŋ/ *adj* [A;(B)] big and strong: *a fine, strapping man*

stra·ta /ˈstrɑːtə‖ˈstreɪtə/ *n pl. of* STRATUM

strat·a·gem /ˈstrætədʒəm/ *n* a trick or plan to deceive an enemy or to gain an advantage

stra·te·gic /strəˈtiːdʒɪk/ also **stra·te·gi·cal** /-kəl/— *adj* [Wa5] (done) for reasons of STRATEGY; not general, but part of a plan (of war): *a strategic decision* —**~ally** *adv* [Wa4]

strat·e·gist /ˈstrætɨ̇dʒɨ̇st/ *n* a person skilled in planning, esp. military movements

strat·e·gy /ˈstrætɨ̇dʒi/ *n* **1** [U] the art of planning movements of armies or forces in war: *a general who was a master of strategy* —compare TACTICS **2** [C] a particular plan for winning success in a particular activity, as in war, a game, a competition, or for personal advantage: *Why should he give me a present? It must be a strategy to make me let him go on holiday alone* **3** [U] skilful planning generally: *She uses strategy to get what she wants*

strat·i·fi·ca·tion /ˌstrætɨ̇fɨ̇ˈkeɪʃən/ *n* [U] **1** the act of STRATIFYing or state of being stratified **2** **a** arrangement in strata (STRATUM) **b** the positioning of different strata in relation to one another

strat·i·fy /ˈstrætɨ̇faɪ/ *v* [Wv5;T1;I∅] to arrange or become arranged in separate levels or strata (STRATUM): *a stratified society|stratified rock*

strat·os·phere /ˈstrætəsfɪəʳ/ *n* [*the*+R] the outer part of the air which surrounds the earth, starting at about 6 miles (10 kilometres) above the earth —compare ATMOSPHERE

stra·tum /ˈstrɑːtəm‖ˈstreɪ-/ *n* **-ta** /tə/ **1** a band of rock of a certain kind, esp. with other types above and below it in the ground **2** a level of earth, such as one where remains of an ancient civilization are found by digging **3** a level of people in society; social class

straw /strɔː/ *n* **1** [U] dried stems of grain plants, such as wheat, used for animals to sleep on, for making baskets, mats, etc.: *a straw hat* **2** [C] **a** one stem of wheat, rice, etc. **b** a thin tube of paper or plastic for sucking up liquid **3** [S *nonassertive*] the smallest value: *I don't care a straw* *for your opinion* **4 clutch at straws** to attempt to save oneself from trouble by means which cannot succeed **5 make bricks without straw** to (try to) do work without the necessary instruments or money **6 man of straw** a man who appears important in position but is in fact without power **7 a straw in the wind** a suggestion or sign of what may happen **8 the last straw (that breaks the camel's back)** an addition to a set of troubles which makes them at last too much to bear

straw·ber·ry /ˈstrɔːbəri‖-beri, -bəri/ *n* **1** [C] a type of plant which grows near the ground, bearing a red juicy fruit **2** [C] the fruit of this, red with small yellow seeds in the surface, eaten fresh and in JAM —see picture at BERRY **3** [U] a dark pink colour

strawberry mark /ˈ··· ·/ *n* a reddish area of skin, present from birth (BIRTHMARK)

straw·board /ˈstrɔːbɔːd‖-bord/ *n* [U] a type of thick paper or card made from STRAW (1), used esp. for packing

straw-col·oured /ˈ· ˌ··/ *adj* light yellow

straw poll /ˌ· ˈ·/ also **straw vote**— *n* an unofficial examination of opinions before an election, to see what the result is likely to be

stray[1] /streɪ/ *v* **1** [L9 esp. *from*] to wander away: *Our dog is lost; he strayed away from home when we left the door open* **2** [I∅] (of thoughts or conversation) to move away from the subject: *Her mind strayed on the scene outside*

stray[2] *n* **1** an animal lost from its home **2** a child without a home (in the phr. **waifs and strays**) **3** any person or thing which has got separated from others of the kind: *This book on English history must be a stray; it's on the dictionary shelf in the library*

stray[3] *adj* [Wa5;A] **1** lost; separated from home or others of the kind: *stray cats* **2** met by chance; scattered: *hit by a stray shot|a few stray birds on the trees*

streak[1] /striːk/ *n* [(*of*)] **1** a thin line or band, different from what surrounds it: *streaks of grey appearing in her black hair* **2** a quality which sometimes appears among different qualities of character: *a streak of cruelty* **3 like a streak of lightning** very quickly: *He disappeared round the corner like a streak of lightning* **4 a winning/losing streak** repeated success/failure during a time of good/bad luck

streak[2] *v* **1** [L9] to move very fast: *The cat streaked across the road with the dog behind it* **2** [Wv5;T1] to cover with STREAK*s*[1] (1): *a face streaked with dirt* **3** [I∅] (in the 1970's) to run swiftly across a public place with no clothes on, except possibly on the feet or head

streak·er /ˈstriːkəʳ/ *n* a person who is STREAKing[2] (3)

streak·y /ˈstriːki/ *adj* [Wa1] **1** marked with STREAK*s*[1] (1): *streaky* BACON (=with lines of fat among the meat) **2** (of a shot made in cricket) hit off the edge of the BAT

stream[1] /striːm/ *n* **1** a natural flow of water, usu. smaller than a river: *to cross a stream* **2** [(*of*)] anything flowing or moving on continuously: *a stream of people into and out of the house* **3** [*usu. sing.*] (the direction of) a current of water: *floating along with the stream* —see also DOWNSTREAM, UPSTREAM **4** [*usu. sing.*] a general way of thinking, behaving, etc., in society (esp. in the phrs. **go with/against the stream**): *He hasn't the courage to go against the stream* **5** *esp. BrE* (in schools) a level of ability within a group of pupils of the same age, esp. of a class: *She is in the top stream, but her French is so bad she has to change classes and take that subject with the bottom stream* **6 on stream** *tech* in(to) production: *The supply of oil from the North Sea has now come on stream*

stream[2] *v* **1** [L9] to flow fast and strong; pour out: *The pipe broke and water streamed onto the floor* **2** [L9] to move in a continuous flowing mass: *They streamed out of the cinema* **3** [L9] to float in the air: *The wind caught her* SCARF*/hair, and it streamed out* **4** [T1] *esp. BrE* to group in STREAMs[1] (5): *The pupils are streamed into 5 ability groups*

stream·er /ˈstriːməʳ/ *n* **1** a long narrow piece of coloured paper or material; narrow flag or BANNER, used for ornament on buildings at a time of public enjoyment **2** *tech* a beam of coloured light in the night sky in the far north or south —see also AURORA **borealis**

stream·line /ˈstriːmlaɪn/ *v* [T1] **1** to form into a smooth shape which moves easily through water or air: *They streamlined the racing car so that it moved even faster* **2** to make (a business, organization, etc.) more simple but more effective in working: *Can't we streamline this arrangement so that it doesn't take so long to get the work back from the printers?*

stream·lined /ˈstriːmlaɪnd/ *adj* smooth and regular (in shape) with nothing which prevents easy movement in water and air: *A fish or a bird is more streamlined than a ship or a plane can ever be*

stream of con·scious·ness /ˌ· · ˈ···/ *n* [*the*+R] (esp. in literature) (the expression of) thoughts, feelings, etc., in a person's mind in a continuous flow during his waking time

street /striːt/ *n* **1** a road with houses or other town buildings on one or both sides: *a street map of Brighton* (=showing the names and positions of all the roads)|*101 Oxford Street, London* **2 be on/walk the streets a** to be homeless **b** to be a STREETWALKER **3 not in the same street (as)** not of the same good standard (as) **4 streets ahead of** much better than **5 up one's street** in one's area of interest or activity: *Ask his advice on gardening; that's right up his street* —compare **in one's** LINE[2] (26)

USAGE A **street** is in the middle of a town, and a **road** is usually in the country, between one town and another: (*BrE*) *in the* **road**|*in Oxford* **Street**| (*AmE*) *on the* **road**|*on Main* **Street**. The **way** to a place is either **a** the direction, and the instructions needed for getting there: *Can you tell me the* **way** *to Buckingham Palace?* or **b** one's journey from one place to another: *A funny thing happened to me on my* **way** *to the theatre!*

See next page for picture

street·car /ˈstriːtkɑːʳ/ *n AmE* TRAM

street·walk·er /ˈstriːtˌwɔːkəʳ/ *n* a PROSTITUTE who waits for business in the streets

strength /streŋθ, strenθ/ *n* [C;U] **1** the quality or degree of being strong: *He can lift heavy weights because of his strength.|strength of character* **2** something providing strength or power: *His personal knowledge is the strength of his argument* **3** force, esp. measured in numbers: *They came in strength to see the fight.|The police force is 400 men below strength* **4 on the strength** being a member of an organization, firm, armed force, etc.: *"Are you on the strength here?" "No, I'm just helping out for a week"* **5 on the strength of a** because of: *I bought it on the strength of his advice* **b** in the likelihood of: *I baked a cake on the strength of their coming*

strength·en /ˈstreŋθən, ˈstrenθən/ *v* **1** [T1] to make strong or stronger: *to strengthen a fence* **2** [I∅] to gain strength: *The wind strengthened during the night*

stren·u·ous /ˈstrenjʊəs/ *adj* **1** taking great effort: *a strenuous day* **2** showing great activity: *a strenuous supporter of women's rights* —**~ly** *adv* —**~ness** *n* [U]

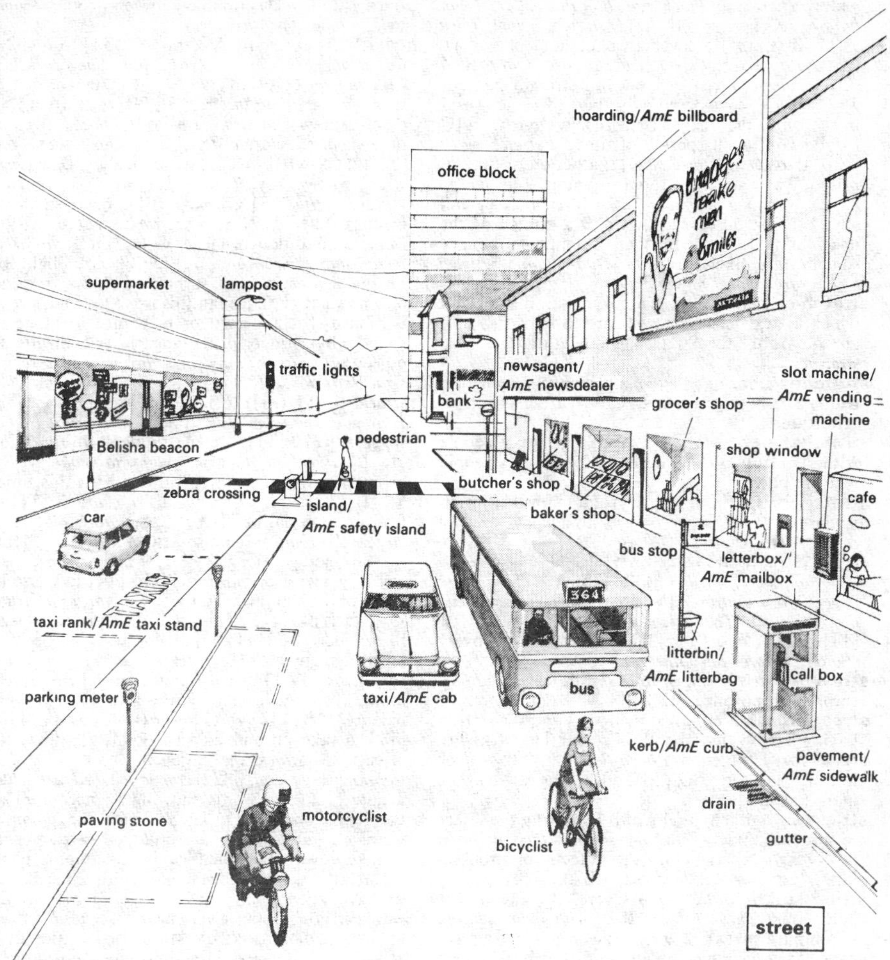

strep·to·coc·cus /ˌstreptəˈkɒkəs‖-ˈkɑ-/ *n* **-ci** /-ˈkɒksaɪ, -ˈkɒsaɪ‖-ˈkɑ-/ a type of bacterium growing in chains that causes various infections, esp. in the throat —**-cal** /-ˈkɒkəl‖-ˈkɑ-/ *adj* [Wa5]

strep·to·my·cin /ˌstreptəʊˈmaɪsə̇n, -tə-/ *n* [U] a strong drug used in medicine for killing harmful bacteria

stress¹ /stres/ *n* **1** [C;U] force or pressure caused by difficulties in life: *He's under stress because his wife is very ill* **2** [C;U] force of weight caused by something heavy: *The vehicles passing over put stress on the material of the bridge* **3** [U] a sense of special importance (esp. in the phr. **lay stress on**): *not enough stress on the need for exactness* **4** [C;U] the degree of force put on a part of a word, making it seem stronger than other parts: *In "under", the main stress is on "un"*

stress² *v* [T1] **1** to give a sense of importance to (a certain matter): *He stressed the need for careful spending if they were not to find themselves without money* **2** to give force to (a (part of a) word): *He stressed the first vowel of "object", which was the wrong pronunciation for the verb* **3** *rare* to put STRESS¹ (2) on: *The weight stressed the bridge to the point of damaging it*

stress mark /ˈ· ·/ *n* a mark (ˋ *or* ˈ *or* ˌ) to show that STRESS¹ (4) falls on a certain part of a word

stretch¹ /stretʃ/ *v* **1** [T1;I∅] to (cause to) become wider or longer: *My wool coat stretched when I washed it* **2** [X9 (OUT)] to cause to reach full length or width: *to stretch a rope between 2 poles*|(fig.) *You are stretching my patience to the limit* **3** [L9] to spread out: *The waters of the sea stretched round them as far as the eye could see* **4** [I∅] to be elastic: *Rubber bands stretch* **5** [T1;I∅: (OUT)] to straighten (the limbs or body) to full length: *She got out of bed and stretched.*|*The cat stretched out in front of the fire* **6** [T1] to cause to go beyond a limit (of rule, or time): *to stretch the rules and leave work early* **7** [L9] to last: *His visits stretched over 3 months* **8 stretch one's legs** *not fml* to have a walk, esp. after sitting for a time **9 stretch a point** also (*infml*) **stretch it a bit**— to make a rule, remark, etc., mean what one wants it to: *We'll stretch a point and let the baby travel free, though you should have bought him a ticket.*|*Is that true? Aren't you stretching it a bit?* —**~able** *adj*

stretch² *n* **1** [C *usu. sing.*] an act of stretching, esp. the body: *to get out of bed and have a good stretch* **2** [U] the (degree of) ability to increase in length or width: *There's not much stretch in this collar; I can hardly get it over my head.|stretch nylon|stretch socks* **3** [C (*of*) a level area (of land or water): *a pleasant stretch of country|a wide stretch of road* **4** [C *usu. sing.*] (a part, esp. one of 2 straight sides, of a race track, considered as) a part of a race (esp. in the phrs. **the final/finishing/home stretch**) **5** [C (*of*)] a continuous period of time: *a stretch of 10 years abroad* **6** [C *usu. sing.*] *sl* a period of time in prison **7 at a stretch** without stopping: *They had to remain standing for hours at a stretch* **8 at full stretch** using all one's powers **9 a stretch of the imagination** [*nonassertive*] an attempt to believe something unlikely to be so: *That couldn't be true, by any stretch of the imagination*

stretch·er /ˈstretʃəʳ/ *n* **1** a covered framework on which a sick person can be carried lying down **2** an apparatus for stretching something: *a shoe stretcher*

stretcher-bear·er /ˈ·· ˌ··/ *n* a person (usu. one of a team of 2) whose job is to carry (a person on) a STRETCHER

stretcher par·ty /ˈ·· ˌ··/ *n* [GC] a group of people with STRETCHERs (1) who go to the help of people who are hurt

stretch·y /ˈstretʃi/ *adj* [Wa1] (of a material) which is elastic: *It was made of very fashionable stretchy cotton* —**stretchiness** *n* [U]

strew /struː/ *v* **strewed, strewn** /struːn/ *or* **strewed** **1** [D1+*on, over, (in)/with*] to scatter: *There were papers strewn all over the floor.|They strewed seeds over the earth.|They strewed the earth with seeds* **2** [T1] *esp. lit or poet* to lie scattered on or over: *Flowers strewed the path*

strewth /struːθ/ *interj BrE sl* (an expression of surprise, annoyance, etc.)

stri·at·ed /straɪˈeɪtɨd‖ˈstraɪeɪtɨd/ *adj* [Wa5] *tech* having narrow lines, bands of colour, etc.; STRIPED

stri·a·tion /straɪˈeɪʃən/ *n tech* **1** [C] a STRIPE (1) or line **2** [U] the condition of having STRIPEs or markings in lines

strick·en /ˈstrɪkən/ *adj* [Wa5] **1** showing the effect of trouble, anxiety, etc.: *her stricken face* **2** (*often in comb.*) experiencing the effects of trouble, illness, etc.: *stricken by debts|grief-stricken*

strict /strɪkt/ *adj* [Wa1] **1** severe, esp. in rules of behaviour: *They are very strict with their children* —compare SEVERE **2 a** exact: *a strict* INTERPRETATION *of the facts* **b** complete; not to be broken: *He told me about it in strict secrecy* —**~ly** *adv*: *Strictly speaking, it's not allowed, but we won't prevent it* —**~ness** *n* [U]

stric·ture /ˈstrɪktʃəʳ/ *n* **1** [*often pl.*] (an expression of) blame or judgment: *the strictures of the public on the private lives of the famous* **2** *tech* a place where a tube in the body becomes narrower

stride[1] /straɪd/ *v* **strode** /strəʊd/, **stridden** /ˈstrɪdn/ **1** [L9] to walk with long steps or cross with one long step: *He strode out.|He strode over the stream* **2** [T1] *rare* BESTRIDE

stride[2] *n* **1** a long step in walking **2 make great strides** to improve or do well **3 take (something/it all) in one's stride** to accept and deal with easily: *Some people would have been shocked and unable to work, but he takes everything in his stride*

stri·den·cy /ˈstraɪdənsi/ also **stri·dence** /ˈstraɪdəns/— *n* [C;U] the quality of being STRIDENT

stri·dent /ˈstraɪdənt/ *adj* with a hard sharp sound or voice, esp. containing a high unpleasant note: *a strident woman/speaker* —**~ly** *adv*

strid·u·late /ˈstrɪdjʊleɪt‖-dʒə-/ *v* [I∅] *tech* (of certain insects) to make a rough high sound by rubbing parts of the body together —**-lation** /ˌstrɪdjʊˈleɪʃən‖-dʒə-/ *n* [U]

strife /straɪf/ *n* [U] trouble between people: *family strife|a time of political strife*

strike[1] /straɪk/ *v* **struck** /strʌk/ **1** [T1] to hit: *He was so angry he wanted to strike him.|She struck him with an axe* **2** [X9] to give a blow by means of: *He struck his axe into the tree* **3** [T1;D1;I∅ (OUT)] to give (a blow): *to strike a blow|He moved away as the animal struck.|He struck out at his attackers* **4** [T1;I∅;(DOWN)] to harm suddenly: *They were struck (down) by illness.|They were happy until* POVERTY *struck* **5** [X7 *usu. pass.*] to make suddenly or unexpectedly: *They were struck silent* **6** [X9] to cause a condition of (fear, worry, etc.): *to strike terror into their hearts* **7** [T1;I∅] **a** to light by hitting against a hard surface: *to strike a match* **b** to produce (a flame) in this way: *to strike a light* **8** [T1;I∅] (of a person or machine) to make (a sound), by a finger or moving part which hits an object: *He struck a note on the piano.|The clock struck|struck 12|12 (=12 notes=12 o'clock) has struck* **9** [T1 (*as*)] to have a (strong) effect on: *How does the room strike you?|I was struck by her suggestion* **10** [T1] to come suddenly to the mind of: *It struck me that we ought to make a new arrangement.|A thought strikes me* (=at this time) **11** [L7] to seem: *The room struck cold* **12** [T1] to find (a material or place): *They struck oil.|We've struck the road* —see also STRIKE ON **13** [T1;L9] to start going (along): *They struck off on a new course* —see also STRIKE OUT **14** [T1] to cause (a piece of a plant) to take root: *The gardener struck some* CUTTINGs **15** [T1] *tech* to produce (a coin or like object) **16** [I∅ (*for*)] to stop working because of disagreement: *They struck for better working conditions* **17** [T1] to produce or reach (agreement) (esp. in the phrs. **strike a bargain, strike a balance**) **18** [T1] *tech* to lower (sails or a flag) **19** [T1] to take up and hold (a bodily position) for effect: *He struck the customary* POSE[2] (1) *of a well-known general, and everyone laughed* **20 strike a note of** to say words showing (a need for) (a quality): *a book that strikes a warning note|a note of warning against modern immorality* **21 strike camp** to take down tents when leaving a camping place **22 strike it rich** to find sudden wealth **23 strike oil** to have good luck, esp. in making money **24 within striking distance** very near —see also STRICKEN, STRIKE OFF, STRIKE ON, STRIKE OUT, STRIKE UP

strike[2] *n* **1** [C; *on*+U] a time when no work is done because of disagreement, as over pay or working conditions (esp. in the phr. **(go) on strike**) **2** [C] an attack, esp. by aircraft whose bombs hit the place attacked **3** [C] success in finding esp. a mineral in the earth: *an oil strike*

strike·bound /ˈstraɪkbaʊnd/ *adj* [Wa5] unable to move, act, or travel because of a STRIKE[2] (1): *strikebound when the trains stopped running*

strike·break·er /ˈstraɪkˌbreɪkəʳ/ *n* a person who works when most others are on STRIKE[2] (1) —see also BLACKLEG

strike·break·ing /ˈstraɪkˌbreɪkɪŋ/ *n* [U] the act of working or bringing others to work during a STRIKE[2] (1)

strike off *v adv* [T1] **1** [*often pass.*] to remove (as a name) from an official list: *The doctor was struck off for making love to a married woman he was treating* (=he had his name taken off the list of doctors and was no longer allowed to practise) **2** to print (copies of something)

strike on also **strike up·on**— *v prep* [T1] to discover; HIT ON: *I've struck on a plan*

strike out *v adv* **1** [L9] to swim hard in a certain direction: *He struck out towards the ship* **2** [T1] also **strike through**— *fml* to CROSS OUT (a mistake in writing, an unwanted piece of writing, etc.):

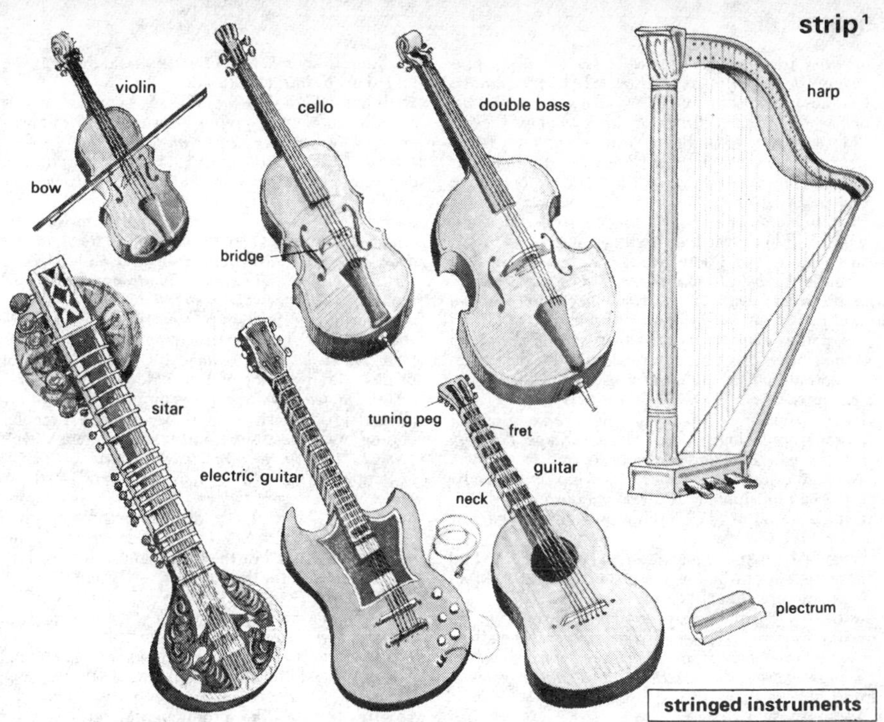

stringed instruments

Strike out the old address and write in the new one —see also SCORE OUT **3** [IØ] to take up an independent life, or a new activity (esp. in the phr. **strike out on one's own**)

strike pay /ˈ· ·/ *n* [U] money paid to workmen on STRIKE² (1) from their trade union's **strike fund(s)**

strik·er /ˈstraɪkəʳ/ *n* **1** a person on STRIKE² (1) **2** a FORWARD in football —see picture at SOCCER

strike up *v adv* **1** [T1;IØ] to begin playing or singing: *to strike up a song* **2** [T1 (*with*)] to start to make (a friendship): *They struck up an* ACQUAINTANCE (*with each other*) *on the plane*

strik·ing /ˈstraɪkɪŋ/ *adj* which draws the attention, esp. because of being attractive or unusual: *a very striking woman|a striking idea* —**~ly** *adv*

string¹ /strɪŋ/ *n* **1** [C;U] (a) thin cord: PUPPETs *are worked by strings.|pictures hung on string* **2** [C; U] anything like this, esp. used for tying things up: *nylon string* **3** [C] a thin piece of material, often one of several, stretched across a musical instrument, to give sound —see also STRINGS **4** [C (*of*)] a set (of things) connected together on a thread: *a string of onions*/BEADS **5** [C (*of*)] a set (of words, actions, etc.) following each other closely: *a string of curses/prayers/complaints* **6 have (someone) on a string** to make (someone) act as one wishes: *The little boy has his mother on a string* **7 no strings attached** (esp. of an agreement) with no limiting conditions **8 play second string** to take or have a position of less importance than the main one: *All his life he had played second string to his brother in the family business until he left and started his own firm* **9 pull strings/wires** to use influence, esp. secretly, with people concerned with something one needs: *He had to pull a few strings to get that job* **10 two strings/a second string to one's bow** an additional interest, ability, or idea which can be used, as well as the main one: *He had 2 strings to his bow, so when he lost his job as a toolmaker he became a gardener* —see also SECOND-STRING

string² *v* **strung** /strʌŋ/ [T1] **1** to put one or more STRINGS¹ (3) on (a musical instrument) **2** to thread (BEADs) on a string: (fig.) *to string phrases/words together* **3 highly strung** (of a person) very sensitive and easily excited, hurt in feelings, etc. **4 strung up** very excited, nervous, or worried —see also STRING ALONG, STRING OUT, STRING UP

string a·long *v adv infml* **1** [T1] to encourage (someone's) hopes deceitfully: *He will never be paid the money they promised him; they're just stringing him along* **2** [IØ (*with*)] to go (with someone else) for a time, esp. for convenience: *I'll string along with someone who's driving into the next town*

string band /ˌ· ˈ·/ *n* [GC] a group of players of different STRINGED INSTRUMENTs

string bean /ˌ· ˈ·/ *n AmE* RUNNER BEAN

stringed in·stru·ment /ˌ· ˈ···/ *n* a musical instrument with one or more STRINGs¹ (3): *A* VIOLIN *is a stringed instrument* —see also STRINGS

strin·gen·cy /ˈstrɪndʒənsi/ *n* [U] the quality of being STRINGENT: *the stringency of wartime rules*

strin·gent /ˈstrɪndʒənt/ *adj* **1** (of rules) severe; which must be obeyed **2** (of the supply of money for business) lacking in amount of money —**~ly** *adv*

string or·ches·tra /ˌ· ˈ···/ *n* a large group of players of different STRINGED INSTRUMENTs

string out *v adv* [T1;IØ] to spread (something) out in a line: *She strung out 12 pairs of socks along the washing line*

strings /strɪŋz/ *n* [P] the set of (players with) STRINGED INSTRUMENTs in an ORCHESTRA

string up *v adv* [T1] **1** to hang (something) high: *They strung up coloured lights round the room* **2** *infml* to put to death by hanging, as a punishment

string·y /ˈstrɪŋi/ *adj* [Wa1] having threadlike flesh or muscle: *His stringy arms are weak* —**stringiness** *n* [U]

strip¹ /strɪp/ *v* **-pp- 1** [T1 (*of*, OFF)] to remove (the covering or parts of): *Elephants strip the leaves* *off|from trees.|Elephants strip trees (of leaves).|to strip the leaves off|a stripped tree* **2** [X9] to remove (clothes) from someone: *They stripped his shirt off and beat him.|They stripped his shirt from his back* **3** [T1;I0 (OFF)] to undress, usu. completely: *She stripped to her bathing suit.|When the sun came out the little boy stripped off* **4** [T1 (DOWN)] to remove the parts of (esp. an engine); DISMANTLE: *He bought an old car and spent his free time stripping it down* **5** [T1] to tear the twisting THREAD¹ (4) from (a GEAR¹ (3) or SCREW¹ (1)): *She was careless in repairing her bicycle and stripped the* GEARS

strip² *n* **1** [(*of*)] a narrow piece: *a strip of land|paper* **2** an occasion or performance of taking the clothes off, esp. as in STRIPTEASE: *to do a strip* **3** the clothes of a particular colour worn by a team in football: *a blue and white strip*

strip car·toon /ˌ· ·ˈ·/ *n BrE* COMIC STRIP

stripe /straɪp/ *n* **1** a band of colour, among one or more other colours: *Tigers have orange fur with black stripes* **2** a band of colour worn on a uniform as a sign of rank **3** a stroke of a whip on the body, esp. as a punishment: *10 stripes on the back*

striped /straɪpt/ *adj* having STRIPE*s* of colour: *striped silk*

strip light·ing /ˈ· ˌ··, ˌ· ˈ··/ *n* [U] a method of lighting a room by long, esp. FLUORESCENT, tubes —see picture at ELECTRICITY

strip·ling /ˈstrɪplɪŋ/ *n* a young man or youth

strip of *v prep* [D1] to take away (something) from (someone): *The robbers stripped him of all he possessed|stripped the house of all valuable articles*

strip·per /ˈstrɪpəʳ/ also **strip art·ist** /ˈ· ˌ··/— *n infml* a STRIPTEASE performer

strip·tease /ˈstrɪptiːz, ˌstrɪpˈtiːz/ also **strip show** [C] /ˈ· ·/— *n* [C;U] (a) removal of clothes by a person, esp. a woman, performed as a show

strip·y /ˈstraɪpi/ *adj* [Wa1] covered in STRIPE*s* of colour: *a stripy pattern*

strive /straɪv/ *v* **strove** /strəʊv/, **striven** /strɪvən/ **1** [L9 esp. *after, for/against*;I3] to struggle hard (to get or conquer): *He strove for recognition as an artist/to be recognized as an artist.|a swimmer striving against the current* **2** [I0 (*with*)] *old use* to fight —**striver** *n*

strobe light /ˈstrəʊb ˌlaɪt/ *n* a light which goes on and off very quickly

strode /strəʊd/ *past t. of* STRIDE

stroke¹ /strəʊk/ *v* [T1] to pass the hand over gently, esp. for pleasure: *The cat likes being stroked*

stroke² *n* **1** [C] a blow, esp. with (the edge of) a weapon: *a stroke of the whip|an axe stroke* **2** [C] a sudden illness in part of the brain which damages it and can cause loss of the ability to move some part of the body **3** [S+*of*] an unexpected piece (of luck) **4** [S] one act, esp. of work: *He changed things at a stroke* (=with one direct action) **5** [C] a single movement which is repeated, esp. in a sport or game: *She can't swim yet but has made a few strokes with her arms.|With a stroke of its wings the bird flew away* **6** [C] a line made by a single movement of a pen or brush in writing or painting: *She drew his face with a few strokes* **7** [C] a mark or line made in writing or printing **8** [C] OBLIQUE² **9** [C] a rower who sets the speed for others rowing with him: *He was (the) stroke in the winning boat* **10** [C] the sound made by a clock on the hour: *to arrive on the stroke of 12* (=exactly at 12) —compare STRIKE

stroke³ *v* **1** [T1] to act as STROKE² (9) to ((the rowers in) a boat) **2** [X9] to hit (a ball): *He stroked the ball easily past the fielder*

stroll /strəʊl/ *v* [I0] to walk, esp. slowly, for pleasure —**stroll** *n* [*usu. sing.*]

stroll·er /ˈstrəʊləʳ/ *n* **1** a person who STROLL*s* or is strolling **2 a** *BrE* a light PUSHCHAIR that can be folded up **b** *AmE* PUSHCHAIR

stroll·ing /ˈstrəʊlɪŋ/ *adj* [Wa5;A] who travels around the country giving informal performances on the way: *strolling players|musicians*

strong /strɒŋ‖strɔŋ/ *adj* **1** [Wa1;B] having (a degree of) power, esp. of the body: *She is not very strong after her illness* **2** [Wa1;B] powerful against harm; not easily broken, spoilt, moved or changed: *strong shoes|strong beliefs|He held the door back with his strong arm* **3** [Wa1;E] of a certain number: *Our club is 50 strong* **4** [Wa1;B] violent: *a strong wind|a strong blow* **5** [Wa1;B] **a** powerful or effective: *a strong argument|a strong smell* **b** unacceptable: *It's a bit strong to punish them for such a small thing* **6** [Wa1;B] (esp. of drinks) having a lot of the material which gives taste: *The tea is too strong* —compare WEAK (4) **7** [Wa5;B] (of a verb) which does not add a regular ending in the past tense, but may change a vowel: *"Speak" is a strong verb; its past tense is "spoke"* —compare WEAK (6) **8** [Wa1;B] *tech* of worth: *Is the pound stronger today?* **9 (still) going strong** active and powerful, esp. after some time or when old: *Grandfather's clock is still going strong* **10 the strong arm of the law** the police and forces of law, esp. considered for their power —**~ly** *adv*

strong·arm /ˈstrɒŋɑːm‖ˈstrɔŋarm/ *adj* [Wa5;A] using (unnecessary) force: *the use of strongarm methods to make him admit his guilt*

strong·box /ˈstrɒŋbɒks‖ˈstrɔŋbaks/ *n* a usu. metal box or SAFE² (1) for keeping valuable things, such as jewels

strong form /ˈ· ·/ *n* a pronunciation with a longer SYLLABLE and/or clearer vowel sound than the WEAK FORM

strong·hold /ˈstrɒŋhəʊld‖ˈstrɔŋ-/ *n* **1** a fort **2** [+*of*] a place where an activity is common or general: *The village is a stronghold of old beliefs and customs*

strong lan·guage /ˌ· ˈ··/ *n* [U] *often euph* swearing; curses

strong-mind·ed /ˌ· ˈ··◂/ *adj* firm in beliefs, wishes, etc.: *He is very strong-minded and will never agree to changes in his way of work* —**~ly** *adv* —**~ness** *n* [U]

strong point /ˈ· ·/ *n* a skill, quality, etc., which one possesses to a high degree: *Languages are not her strong point*

strong room /ˈ· ·/ *n* a room, as in a bank, with a special thick door and walls, where valuable objects can be kept

stron·ti·um /ˈstrɒntɪəm‖ˈstrantʃɪəm, -tɪəm/ *n* [U] a type of soft metal that is a simple substance (ELEMENT)

strontium 90 /ˌ··· ˈ··/ *n* [U] the form of STRONTIUM which is given off by atomic explosions and is thought to have harmful effects on people and animals

strop¹ /strɒp‖strap/ *n* a narrow piece of leather for sharpening RAZOR*s* on

strop² *v* **-pp-** [T1] to sharpen on a STROP¹

stro·phe /ˈstrəʊfi/ *n* **1** (esp. in ancient Greek plays) a song by a group of actors, answered by another group in the same way **2** a group of lines in a poem

strop·py /ˈstrɒpi‖ˈstrapi/ *adj* [Wa1] *BrE infml* rather forceful in behaviour, esp. going against others: *He's being a bit stroppy today and refusing to look after his sister*

strove /strəʊv/ *past t. of* STRIVE

struck /strʌk/ *past t. and p. of* STRIKE

struc·tur·al /ˈstrʌktʃərəl/ *adj* [Wa5] of or concerning STRUCTURE, esp. of the main part of a building: *a structural fault* —**~ly** *adv*

struc·ture¹ /ˈstrʌktʃəʳ/ *n* **1** [U (*of*)] the way in which parts are formed into a whole: *the structure of the brain|cell structure|the structure of a sentence* **2** [C] anything formed of many parts, esp. a building: *a tall structure*

structure² *v* [Wv5;T1] to form (esp. ideas) into a whole form, in which each part is related to others: *to structure one's arguments*

stru·del /ˈstruːdl/ *n* [C;U] a sweet food, with fruit inside a light kind of pastry, particularly **apple strudel** as made in Austria

strug·gle¹ /ˈstrʌgəl/ *v* [IØ] to make violent movements, esp. when fighting against a person or thing: *He struggled to the surface as the water dragged him down.|She struggled out of the net which had trapped her.|*(fig.) *They struggled against* POVERTY (=lack of money).*|I'll carry you if you don't struggle*

struggle² *n* **1** a hard fight or bodily effort: *the struggle between the 2 teams* **2** [*usu. sing.*] an effort: *With a struggle, he controlled his feelings*

strum /strʌm/ *v* **-mm-** [IØ (*on*); T1] to play (a STRINGED INSTRUMENT) carelessly or informally, esp. without skill: *strumming* (*on*) *a* GUITAR

strum·pet /ˈstrʌmpɪ̣t/ *n old use* a PROSTITUTE

strung /strʌŋ/ *past t. and p. of* STRING

strut¹ /strʌt/ *v* **-tt-** [IØ] to walk in a proud strong way, esp. with the chest out and trying to look important: *The male bird strutted in front of the female*

strut² *n* **1** a piece of wood or metal holding the weight of another in a part of a building, an aircraft, etc. —see picture at AIRCRAFT **2** [*usu. sing.*] a strutting (STRUT¹) way of walking

strych·nine /ˈstrɪkniːn‖-naɪn, -niːn/ *n* [U] a type of poisonous drug used as a medicine in very small amounts

stub¹ /stʌb/ *n* **1** a short end left when something has been used, esp. of a cigarette or pencil **2** the piece of a cheque or ticket left in a book of these as a record after use

stub² *v* **-bb-** [T1] to hurt (one's toe) by hitting against something

stub·ble /ˈstʌbəl/ *n* [U] short stiff pieces of something which grows, esp. a short beard or the remains of wheat after being cut —**~bly** *adv* [Wa2]

stub·born /ˈstʌbən‖-ərn/ *adj* **1** determined; with a strong will: *a stubborn child who won't obey his mother* **2** difficult to use, move, change, etc.: *This lock's rather stubborn; it needs oiling* —**~ly** *adv* —**~ness** *n* [U]

stub·by /ˈstʌbi/ *adj* [Wa1] short and thick: *his stubby finger*

stub out *v adv* [T1] to stop (a cigarette) burning by pressing down the end

stuc·co /ˈstʌkəʊ/ *n* [U] material (PLASTER) used on buildings to cover walls and form ornamental shapes

stuck¹ /stʌk/ *adj* [Wa5] **1** [F] fixed in place, not moving: *The door's stuck.|His head is/has got stuck in the window* **2** [F9] fixed by sticky material: *The paper is stuck to my finger.|There is a sweet stuck on that chair* **3** [F] unable to go or do anything further, esp. because of difficulties: *I'm stuck; can you give me some help with this sum, Father?* **4** [F+*with*] *infml* having to do or have, esp. unwillingly: *We were stuck with relatives who came to stay unexpectedly* **5** [F+*on*] *BrE infml* having a great liking (for); fond (of) (esp. someone of the opposite sex): *Jane's really stuck on her new teacher* **6 get stuck in(to)** *infml* to start work or action (on) forcefully: *Here's your dinner, get stuck in!*

stuck² *past t. and p. of* STICK

stuck-up /ˌ· ˈ·◂/ *adj infml* proud in manner, as though thinking others of less worth: *too stuck-up to speak to her old friends*

stud¹ /stʌd/ *n* **1** a number of horses or other animals kept for breeding **2** *esp. AmE* a male horse kept for breeding **3** *taboo* a man considered for his part in the sexual act: *He's not much of a stud* —compare FUCK² (2)

stud² *n* **1** a type of fastener used instead of a button and button hole, esp. one of 2 flat pieces joined by a narrow part (**collarstud**) or one of 2 separate parts which are pressed together (**press stud**) **2** a nail or flat-topped object, esp. those used for marking off parts of a road, or anything like this used as an ornament

stud³ *v* **-dd-** [Wv5;T1] to cover with (something like) STUDs²: *a star-studded sky|a sky studded with stars|*(fig.) *a star-studded film*

stud·book /ˈstʌdbʊk/ *n* a list of names of animals, esp. race horses, from which other animals have been bred —see also PEDIGREE

stu·dent /ˈstjuːdənt‖ˈstuː-/ *n* **1** a person who is studying at a place of education or training **2** *BrE* a person studying at a university or college **3** *AmE* a person studying at a school or college **4** [+*of*] a person with a stated interest: *a student of human nature*

USAGE Anyone studying at a college or university is a **student**. In the US, this word is also used for children who are too young for college, but in Britain these are **pupils**. Grown-up people studying under a famous musician may also be called his **pupils**. A **scholar** is either **a** (*BrE old use*) a **pupil** or **b** someone whose education is being paid for in some special way because he has done so well, or **c** someone who makes a profession of study, and knows a great deal about his subject. This person may be quite old.

students' u·ni·on /ˌ·· ˈ···/ *n BrE* **1** the association of students, esp. in a college or university or combining those in many places of education **2** a (part of a) building where students have a social life together

stud farm /ˈ· ·/ *n* a place where horses are bred

stud·ied /ˈstʌdid/ *adj* [Wa5] carefully thought or considered, esp. before being expressed: *a studied remark|She spoke with studied politeness*

stu·di·o /ˈstjuːdiəʊ‖ˈstuː-/ *n* **-os** **1** a workroom for a painter, photographer, etc. **2** a room from which broadcasts are made: *a television studio* **3** [*often pl.*] a room or place where cinema films are made: *Pinewood studios*

studio a·part·ment /ˈ··· ·ˌ··/ *n AmE* a 1-room flat; BED-SITTER

studio au·di·ence /ˈ··· ˌ···/ *n* [GC] people at a radio or television performance (PROGRAMME) when it is made, whose laughter and so on is broadcast with it or recorded

studio couch /ˈ··· ·/ *n* a piece of furniture for sitting on, which can be made into a bed: *We have a studio couch in our living room*

stu·di·ous /ˈstjuːdɪəs‖ˈstuː-/ *adj* **1** eager to study and habitually doing so **2** *fml* careful: *to pay studious attention to detail* —**~ly** *adv* —**~ness** *n* [U]

stud·y¹ /ˈstʌdi/ *n* **1** [U] the act of studying one or more subjects: *He spent the afternoon in study* **2** [U;C *often pl.*] a subject studied: *to give time to one's studies* **3** [C] a thorough enquiry into, esp. including a piece of writing on, a particular subject: *to make a study of Shakespeare's plays* **4** [C] a room used for studying and work **5** [C] a drawing or painting of a detail, esp. for combining later into a larger picture: *a study of a flower* **6** [C] a piece of music for practice in method and TECHNIQUE

study² *v* **1** [T1;IØ] to spend time in learning (one

or more subjects): *He studies French* **2** [T1] to examine carefully: *He studied the shape of the wound* **3** [T1] to act with concern for: *to study someone's needs*

stuff¹ /stʌf/ *n* [U] **1** *infml* things in a mass; matter: *I can't carry all my stuff alone.|The meat is good stuff* **2** material of any sort, of which something is made: (fig.) *Such experiences are the stuff of life* **3** *esp. old use* cloth **4 do one's stuff** to show one's ability as expected **5 That's the stuff!** /ˈ· · ˌ·/ *infml* That's the right thing to do/say! **6 know one's stuff** *infml* to be good at what one is concerned in **7 Stuff and nonsense!** /ˌ· · ˈ··/ That's a stupid idea!

stuff² *v* **1** [T1 (*with*)] to fill with a substance: *to stuff a* PILLOW|*to stuff a shoe with newspaper* **2** [X9 esp. *into*] to push, esp. as filling material: *Don't stuff anything else in, or the bag will burst* **3** [Wv5; T1] to fill the skin of (a dead animal), to make it look real: *a stuffed elephant* **4** [T1] to put STUFFING (2) inside: *to stuff a chicken* **5** [T1] *taboo sl* to have sex with (a woman) **6** [T1;IØ] *infml* to cause (oneself) to eat as much as possible **7 Get stuffed!** *sl* (an expression of dislike, esp. for what someone has said)

stuffed shirt /ˌ· ˈ·, ˈ· ·/ *n* a dull person, esp. a man, who thinks himself important

stuff·ing /ˈstʌfɪŋ/ *n* [U] **1** material used as a filling for something: *use feathers as stuffing* **2** finely cut-up food with a special taste placed inside a bird or piece of meat before cooking **3 knock the stuffing out of someone** to make someone weak or powerless, in a fight or by illness or effort

stuff up *v adv* [T1 *often pass.*] to block completely: *to stuff up a hole|to be stuffed up|have a stuffed up nose* (=have the nose blocked because of a cold)

stuff·y /ˈstʌfi/ *adj* [Wa1] **1** (having air) which is not fresh: *a stuffy room*/ATMOSPHERE (2) **2** (having a way of thought) which is dull, old-fashioned, etc. —**stuffily** *adv* —**stuffiness** *n* [U]

stul·ti·fy /ˈstʌltǰfaɪ/ *v* [T1] **1** to make stupid or dull in mind: *the stultifying effect of uninteresting work* **2** *fml* to cause to seem foolish or useless: *The changes stultify all the work we did* —**-fication** /ˌstʌltǰfǰˈkeɪʃən/ *n* [U]

stum·ble¹ /ˈstʌmbəl/ *v* [IØ] **1** to catch the foot on the ground while moving along and start to fall: *He stumbled and fell.|He stumbled on a stone* **2** [(*at*)] to stop and/or make mistakes in speaking or reading aloud: *She stumbled and stopped reading.|She stumbled at/over the long word* **3** *lit* do something wrong, as a mistake or moral fault: *Any man may stumble into crime when among criminals* —**-bler** *n*

stumble² *n* an act of stumbling (STUMBLE¹)

stumble a·cross also **stumble up·on, stumble on**— *v prep* [T1] to meet or discover by chance: *Guess who I stumbled across?*

stumbling block /ˈ·· ·/ *n* **1** something which prevents action: *The stumbling block is my inability to drive a car: how can I get there?* **2** something which causes worry, dislike, etc.: *Her strange way of walking is her stumbling block*

stump¹ /stʌmp/ *n* **1** the base of a tree left after the rest has been cut down **2** the remaining part of a limb which has been cut off **3** the STUB of a pencil or the useless end of something long which has been worn down, such as a tooth **4** (in cricket) one of the 3 upright pieces of wood at which the ball is thrown —see picture at CRICKET² **5 stir one's stumps** to walk (fast); move the legs

stump² *v* **1** [L9] to move, esp. heavily: *He stumped angrily up the stairs* **2** [T1] to make political speeches on a special tour of (an area): *stumping the country before the election* **3** [T1] (in cricket) to end the turn to hit of (a BATSMAN) who has moved outside the hitting area, by touching the STUMPS¹ (4) with the ball **4** [T1] *infml* to put an unanswerable question or point to: *His foolishness stumps me/It stumps me how he can be so foolish and not get hurt*

stump·er /ˈstʌmpəʳ/ *n* **1** a question which is too difficult or strange to answer **2** *infml, becoming rare* a WICKET KEEPER

stump up *v adv* [T1;IØ] *infml, esp. BrE* to pay (money). esp. unwillingly: *He stumped up £5 after being persuaded the money would be used well*

stump·y /ˈstʌmpi/ *adj* [Wa1] short and thick in body

stun /stʌn/ *v* **-nn-** [T1] **1** to make unconscious by hitting the head: *They stunned the animal before shooting it, so that it would not suffer* **2** to cause to lose the senses or sense of balance: *He sat stunned for a moment holding his head* **3** to shock into helplessness: *He was stunned by the unfairness of their judgment* **4** [*often pass.*] to delight: *stunned by her beauty*

stung /stʌŋ/ *past t. and p. of* STING

stunk /stʌŋk/ *past p. of* STINK

stun·ner /ˈstʌnəʳ/ *n infml* a very attractive person, esp. a woman, or thing

stun·ning /ˈstʌnɪŋ/ *adj* very attractive; delightful; beautiful —**~ly** *adv*

stunt¹ /stʌnt/ *v* [Wv5;T1] to prevent (full growth) (of): *Lack of food may stunt the growth/stunt the body*

stunt² *n* **1** act of bodily skill, often dangerous: *In the film he had to drive a car into the sea, and other dangerous stunts* **2** an action which gains attention, as in advertising: *These newspaper articles are part of a stunt to raise interest in new products* **3** any trick movement, as of a plane: *The plane flew upside down, turned over twice, and did a few more stunts before landing* **4 pull a stunt** to do a trick, sometimes silly

stunt man /ˈ· ·/ (*fem.* **stunt wom·an** /ˈ· ˌ··/)— *n* a person who does dangerous acts in a film so that the actor does not have to take risks

stu·pe·fac·tion /ˌstjuːpǰˈfækʃən‖ˌstuː/ *n* [U] the act of STUPEFYing or state of being stupefied

stu·pe·fy /ˈstjuːpǰfaɪ‖ˈstuː-/ *v* [T1 *often pass.*] **1** to make unable to think: *stupefied with tiredness* **2** to surprise very much: *I was stupefied at the sight of so much gold*

stu·pen·dous /stjuːˈpendəs‖stuː-/ *adj* surprisingly great: *a stupendous mistake* —**~ly** *adv*

stu·pid /ˈstjuːpǰd‖ˈstuː-/ *adj* [Wa2] **1** [B;N] silly or foolish, either generally or in a certain action: *a stupid person|That was stupid of you* **2** [F] *becoming rare* lacking in power of mind, either by nature or through the influence of something which prevents the mind being clear: *born stupid|still stupid with sleep* —see also STUPOR —**~ly** *adv*

stu·pid·i·ty /stjuːˈpɪdǰti‖stuː-/ *n* **1** [U] the state or quality of being stupid **2** [C *usu. pl.*; U] (an example or act of) stupid behaviour

stu·por /ˈstjuːpəʳ‖ˈstuː-/ *n* [C;(U)] a state in which one cannot think or use the senses: *in a* DRUNKEN *stupor|He lay in a sort of stupor caused by the heat*

stur·dy /ˈstɜːdi‖-ɜr-/ *adj* [Wa1] **1** strong and firm, esp. in body: *running on his sturdy legs* **2** determined in action: *They kept up a sturdy opposition to the plan* —**sturdily** *adv* —**sturdiness** *n* [U]

stur·geon /ˈstɜːdʒən‖-ɜr-/ *n* [C;U] a type of large fish which can be eaten, from which CAVIAR and ISINGLASS are obtained

stut·ter¹ /ˈstʌtəʳ/ *v* [IØ] to speak with difficulty in producing sounds, esp. habitually holding back the first consonant —compare STAMMER —**~er** *n* —**~ingly** *adv*

stutter² *n* the fault of STUTTERing¹ in speech: *a nervous stutter|exercises to cure a child's stutter*

sty¹ /staɪ/ *n* PIGSTY (1)

sty², stye *n* an infected place on the edge of the eyelid, usu. red and swollen

Sty·gi·an /ˈstɪdʒɪən/ *adj* [Wa5] *lit* unpleasantly dark

style¹ /staɪl/ *n* **1** [C;U] a type of choice of words, esp. which marks out the speaker, or writer as different from others: *The letter is expressed in a formal style* **2** [C;U] a general manner or way of doing anything which is typical or representative of a person or group, time in history, etc.: *the modern style of building* **3** [U] high quality of social behaviour, appearance, or manners: *He has great style: he wears hand-made clothes, drives a beautiful car, and goes to the best parties* **4** [C] fashion, esp. in clothes: *the style of the 30's* **5** [C] a type or sort, esp. of goods: *They sell every style of mirror.|a hair style* **6** [C] *fml* a correct title: *He takes the style of "Lord"* **7** [C] the rodlike part inside a flower which supports the STIGMA at the top —see picture at FLOWER¹ **8** [C] STYLUS (1) **9 in style** in a grand way: *She gives dinner parties in style, with the best food and wine* —**~less** *adj* [Wa5]

style² *v* **1** [X9] to form in a certain (good) pattern, shape, etc.: *They styled their house in the Portuguese manner.|The dress is carefully styled* **2** [X1] to give (a title) to: *He styles himself "Lord"*

-style *comb. form* in a certain form or manner like that of the stated person, place, etc.: *She sat down on the floor Indian-style*

styl·ish /ˈstaɪlɪʃ/ *adj* fashionable —**~ly** *adv* —**~ness** *n* [U]

styl·ist /ˈstaɪlɪ̵st/ *n* **1** a person who carefully develops a good style of writing **2** (*in comb.*) a person who is concerned with styles of appearance: *a hair stylist*

styl·is·tic /staɪˈlɪstɪk/ *adj* [Wa5] of or concerning style, esp. in writing or art: *A stylistic change will not improve the subject matter* —**~ally** *adv* [Wa4]

styl·is·tics /staɪˈlɪstɪks/ *n* [U] the study of style, esp. in writing

styl·ize, -ise /ˈstaɪlaɪz/ *v* [Wv5;T1] (in art or description) to treat or present in a fixed style, not in a natural representation: *a stylized representation of a heart on playing cards*

sty·lus /ˈstaɪləs/ *n* **1** a pointed instrument used in ancient times for writing on wax **2** the needle-like instrument, with a hard jewel, such as a diamond, on the end, that is the part of a RECORD PLAYER that picks up the sound signals from a record —see picture at SOUND³

sty·mie¹ /ˈstaɪmi/ *n* (in GOLF) an occasion when an opponent's ball is in the way, preventing the player's ball reaching the hole

stymie² *v* [T1] **1** (in GOLF) cause (someone or oneself) to be stopped by positioning the balls in a STYMIE¹ **2** to prevent from taking or being put into action; stop: *His plan for improving the business was stymied by his employer's lack of interest*

styp·tic /ˈstɪptɪk/ *adj, n* [Wa5] (a substance) which stops bleeding

sua·sion /ˈsweɪʒən/ *n* [U] *rare* the act of persuading; PERSUASION: *moral suasion*

suave /swɑːv/ *adj* having or showing very good smooth manners which please people, sometimes in spite of bad character —**suavity** *n* [U] —**~ly** *adv*

sub¹ /sʌb/ *n infml* **1** an amount of money paid to a worker from his wages before the usual day of payment —compare SUBSIDY **2** SUBSCRIPTION (2) **3** SUBEDITOR **4** SUBMARINE² **5** (esp. in sport) SUBSTITUTE¹

sub² *v* **-bb-** *infml* **1** [I∅] to act as a SUBSTITUTE¹ **2** [T1;I∅] to give or receive (a SUB¹ (1)) **3** [T1] SUBEDIT

sub- *prefix* **1** under; below: *subzero* (*temperatures*)| SUBSOIL **2** almost: *sub*ARCTIC (*conditions*) **3** less (important or powerful) than: SUBCOMMITTEE|SUBEDITOR

sub·al·tern /ˈsʌbəltən‖səˈbɔltərn/ *n* [C;N] an officer in the army lower in rank than a captain

sub·a·tom·ic /ˌsʌbəˈtɒmɪk‖-ˈtɑ-/ *adj* [Wa5] *tech* (of very small parts of matter) smaller than an atom

sub·com·mit·tee /ˈsʌbkəˌmɪti/ *n* [GC] a smaller group formed from a larger committee to deal with a certain matter in more detail

sub·con·scious¹ /sʌbˈkɒnʃəs‖-ˈkɑn-/ *adj* [Wa5] (of thoughts, feelings, etc.) not fully known or understood by the mind in its conscious workings; present at a hidden level of the mind —see CONSCIOUS (USAGE) —**~ly** *adv*

subconscious² also **unconscious**— *n* [*the*+R] the hidden level of the mind and the thoughts that go on there, beyond conscious knowledge

sub·con·ti·nent /ˌsʌbˈkɒntɪ̵nənt‖-ˈkɑn-/ *n* a large mass of land not quite large enough to be called a CONTINENT

sub·con·tract¹ /ˌsʌbkənˈtrækt‖-ˈkɑntrækt/ *v* [T1; I∅] to hire another CONTRACTOR to fulfil (a contract or part of it)

sub·con·tract² /sʌbˈkɒntrækt‖-ˈkɑn-/ *n* a contract which another CONTRACTOR, not the original, is employed to fulfil

sub·con·trac·tor /ˌsʌbkənˈtræktəʳ‖-ˈkɑntræk-/ *n* a person who takes on a SUBCONTRACT²

sub·cu·ta·ne·ous /ˌsʌbkjuːˈteɪnɪəs/ *adj* [Wa5] *tech* beneath the skin: *subcutaneous fat* —**~ly** *adv*

sub·di·vide /ˌsʌbdɪ̵ˈvaɪd/ *v* [T1;I∅] to divide (something that is already divided) into smaller parts: *subdivide a house into flats* —**-vision** /ˈvɪʒən/ *n* [U]

sub·due /səbˈdjuː‖-ˈduː/ *v* [T1] **1** to conquer or control the actions of: *Fear subdued them.|Napoleon subdued much of Europe* **2** to make gentler or less rough in effect

sub·dued /səbˈdjuːd‖-ˈduːd/ *adj* **1** gentle; reduced in strength of light, sound, movement, etc.: *subdued lighting|a subdued voice* **2** quiet in behaviour, not forceful, esp. unnaturally or not habitually so: *You seem very subdued tonight: is anything worrying you?*

sub·ed·it /ˌsʌbˈedɪ̵t/ also (*infml*) **sub**— *v* [T1] to look at and put right (others' writing) as a SUBEDITOR

sub·ed·i·tor /ˌsʌbˈedɪ̵təʳ/ also (*infml*) **sub**— *n* a person who looks at and puts right others' work, such as newspaper articles, esp. one who helps a main EDITOR

sub·head·ing /ˈsʌbˌhedɪŋ/ *n* a usu. smaller written title phrase lower down in the body of a piece of writing that has a main title phrase at the beginning

sub·hu·man /sʌbˈhjuːmən/ *adj* [Wa5] **1** of less than human qualities: *subhuman behaviour* **2** at a point of development between man and animal: *The old bones they found are like those of a man, but are thought to be subhuman*

sub·ject¹ /ˈsʌbdʒɪkt/ *n* **1** a person owing loyalty to a certain state or royal ruler: *a subject of the United Kingdom* —compare CITIZEN **2** something being considered, as in conversation: *Don't change the subject; answer the question* **3** a branch of knowledge studied, as in a system of education: *She's taking 3 subjects in her examinations* **4** a cause: *His strange clothes were the subject of great amusement|a subject for amusement* **5** the main area of interest treated in a work, esp. written: *a book on the subject of love* **6** a certain occasion, object, etc., represented in art: *The subject of the painting is the Battle of Waterloo* **7** a person or animal chosen to experience something or to be studied in an EXPERIMENT: *The subject of their cruelty was a small bird* **8** *rare* a person having or likely to have a certain disease or disorder: *a nervous/sensitive/*BILIOUS *subject* **9** (in music) a group of notes forming the tune on which a longer piece is based **10** (in grammar) the noun, PRONOUN, etc., which is most closely related to the verb in forming a sentence

subject² *adj* [Wa5] **1** [A] governed by someone else; not independent: *a subject race* **2** [F+*to*] ruled (by): *subject to the laws on political meetings* **3** [F+*to*] tending or likely (to have): *He's subject to ill health.|The arrangements are subject to change*

sub·ject³ /səb'dʒekt/ *v* [T1] to cause to be controlled or ruled: *These people have been subjected by another tribe*

sub·jec·tion /səb'dʒekʃən/ *n* [U] **1** the act of SUBJECTing³ or state of being subjected **2** [(*to*)] a state of dependence, esp. when ruled by another's will: *The children lived in complete subjection while their father was alive*

sub·jec·tive /səb'dʒektɪv/ *adj* **1** existing only in the mind; imaginary: *a subjective image of water in the desert* **2** influenced by personal feelings: *This is a very subjective judgment of her abilities* —compare OBJECTIVE **3** [Wa5] *rare* (in grammar) of the subject —**~ly** *adv* —**-tivity** /ˌsʌbdʒek'tɪvɪ̆ti/ *n* [U]

subject mat·ter /'·· ˌ··/ *n* [U] anything being considered in speech or writing or represented in art: *His speech was clever, although the subject matter wasn't interesting in itself*

subject to¹ /'sʌbdʒɪkt tə, tʊ, tuː (*as for* **to**)/ *prep* depending on; on condition that (there is): *Our plans may change subject to the weather*

subject to² /səb'dʒekt/ *v prep* [D1 *often pass.*] to cause to experience: *They were subjected to great suffering*

sub·join /ˌsʌb'dʒɔɪn/ *v* [T1 (*to*)] *fml* to add (a sentence or phrase) at the end: *He subjoined a message at the bottom of the page*

sub ju·di·ce /ˌsʌb 'dʒuːdɪsi‖ˌsʊb 'juːdɪkeɪ/ *adj* [Wa5;F] *law, Lat* (of a case in court) now being considered in law, and therefore not allowed to be mentioned (as in a newspaper)

sub·ju·gate /'sʌbdʒʊgeɪt‖-dʒə-/ *v* [T1] to conquer or take power over: *a subjugated people|to subjugate the opposition* —**-gation** /ˌsʌbdʒʊ'geɪʃən‖-dʒə-/ *n* [U]

sub·junc·tive¹ /səb'dʒʌŋktɪv/ *adj* [Wa5] being or concerning a special form (MOOD) of the verb used in certain languages, often to express doubt, wishes, a dependent verb, etc.

subjunctive² *n* **1** [*the*+R] the special form of the verb used in certain languages to express a SUBJUNCTIVE MOOD² **2** [C] a verb which is in the SUBJUNCTIVE MOOD²: *In the sentence "I wish I were a bird", "were" is a subjunctive*

sub·lease¹ /'sʌb-liːs‖sʌb'liːs/ *n* an agreement by which someone who rents property from its owner, himself rents (part of) that property to someone else —see also LEASE

sublease² /sʌb'liːs/ *v* [T1;I∅] to SUBLET (a place)

sub·let /sʌb'let/ *v* **-tt-** [T1;I∅] (of a person who rents property from its owner) to rent ((part of) a property) to someone else: *He rents the house and sublets a room to a friend* —see also LET⁴

sub·lieu·ten·ant /ˌsʌb-lə'tenənt, -lef-‖-luː-/ *n* [C;A] an officer of the lowest rank in the British navy

sub·li·mate¹ /'sʌblɪ̆meɪt/ *v* [T1] **1** (in chemistry) to change (a solid substance) to a gas by heating and back to a solid, in order to make pure **2** to make pure **3** to replace (natural urges, esp. sexual) with socially acceptable activities —**-mation** /ˌsʌblɪ̆'meɪʃən/ *n* [U]

sub·li·mate² /'sʌblɪ̆mɪ̆t/ *n* a solid after being SUBLIMATED¹ (1)

sub·lime /sə'blaɪm/ *adj* **1** [B] very noble or wonderful; of the highest quality; which causes pride, joy, etc.: *sublime music* **2** [Wa5;A] *infml & often derog* which causes great surprise: *What a sublime lack of understanding!* **3 from the sublime to the ridiculous** (when comparing 2 things, occasions, etc.) starting with something wonderful, but followed by something silly —**~ly** *adv* —**~ness** *n* [U] —**-limity** /sə'blɪmɪ̆ti/ *n* [U]

sub·lim·i·nal /sʌb'lɪmɪ̆nəl/ *adj* [Wa5] (shown) at a level of the mind which the senses are not conscious of: *subliminal advertising* (=too quick to have a conscious effect)

sub·ma·chine gun /ˌsʌbmə'ʃiːn gʌn/ *n* a type of light MACHINEGUN

sub·ma·rine¹ /'sʌbməriːn, ˌsʌbmə'riːn/ *adj* [Wa5] *tech* growing or used under or in the sea: *submarine plant life|a submarine* CABLE¹ (2)

submarine² also (*infml*) **sub**— *n* a ship, esp. a warship, which can stay under water

submarine pen /'··· ·, ··'· ·/ also **pen**— *n* a protective shelter where SUBMARINE*s*² are kept safe from enemy attack

sub·mar·i·ner /sʌb'mærɪnəʳ‖'sʌbməriːnər/ *n* a sailor working and living in a SUBMARINE²

sub·merge /səb'mɜːdʒ‖-ɜr-/ *v* **1** [Wv5;T1;I∅] to (cause to) go under the surface of water: *He submerged the cups in the bowl.|The ship submerged, then rose to the surface.|dangerous submerged rocks* **2** [T1] to cover or completely hide: *Her happiness at seeing him submerged her former worries*

sub·merg·ence /səb'mɜːdʒəns‖-ɜr-/ also **sub·mer·sion** /səb'mɜːʃən‖-'mɜrʒən/— *n* [U] the act of submerging or state of being SUBMERGEd

sub·mer·si·ble /səb'mɜːsəbəl‖-ɜr-/ *n, adj* [Wa5] (a boat) which can go under water

sub·mis·sion /səb'mɪʃən/ *n* **1** [U;(C)] the/an act of SUBMITting or the state of being submitted **2** [U (*to*)] obedience **3** [C,C5] *fml* a suggestion

sub·mis·sive /səb'mɪsɪv/ *adj* gentle, willing to take orders from others, etc. —**~ly** *adv* —**~ness** *n* [U]

sub·mit /səb'mɪt/ *v* **-tt-** **1** [I∅;T1: (*to*)] to cause (oneself) to yield or agree to obey: *to submit (oneself) to another's wishes|He was losing the fight but he would not submit* **2** [T1 (*to*)] to offer for consideration: *to submit new plans* **3** [T5] *law* to suggest or say: *We wish to submit that the case cannot be proved*

sub·nor·mal /ˌsʌb'nɔːməl‖-ɔr-/ *adj* [Wa5] less than is usual, average, etc., esp. in power of the mind: *He was born subnormal and will never learn to speak*

sub·or·bital /sʌb'ɔːbɪ̆tl‖-'ɔr-/ *adj* [Wa5] *tech* being or concerning less than one complete journey (ORBIT) round the earth or a like heavenly body: *a suborbital space flight*

sub·or·di·nate¹ /sə'bɔːdɪ̆nət‖-ɔr-/ *adj* [Wa5; (*to*)] of a lower rank or position —**~ly** *adv*

subordinate² *n* a person who is of lower rank in a job, and takes orders from his SUPERIOR (=the person higher in rank) —see also INFERIOR

sub·or·din·ate³ /sə'bɔːdɪ̆neɪt‖-ɔr-/ *v* [T1] **1** [(*to*)] to put in a position of less importance: *He subordinated his wishes to the general good of the group* **2** to consider of less importance —**-ation** /səˌbɔːdɪ̆'neɪʃən‖-ɔr-/ *n* [U] —**-ative** /sə'bɔːdɪ̆nətɪv‖-ɔrdɪ̆neɪtɪv/ *adj* [Wa5]

subordinate clause /·,··· '·/ *n* DEPENDENT CLAUSE

sub·orn /sə'bɔːn‖-ɔrn/ *v* [T1] *fml* to persuade (another person) to do wrong, esp. to tell lies in a court of law, usu. for payment —**~ation** /ˌsʌbɔː'neɪʃən‖-ɔr-/ *n* [U]

sub·plot /'sʌbplɒt‖-plɑt/ *n* a set of events (PLOT)

that is of less importance than and separate from the main PLOT of a play, story, etc.

sub·poe·na[1] /sə'piːnə, səb-/ *n* (in law) a written order to attend a court of law

subpoena[2] *v* **-naed** [T1] to order to court by a SUBPOENA[1]

sub ro·sa /ˌsʌb 'rəʊzə/ *adv* [Wa5] *fml, Lat* (when something is said or written) to be treated as a secret

sub·scribe /səb'skraɪb/ *v* **1** [I∅ (*to*)] to pay money regularly (in support of some good aim): *He subscribes to an animal protection society* **2** [T1 (*to*)] to give (money): *He subscribed a large amount* (*to the collection for the hospital*) **3** [I∅ (*to*)] to pay regularly in order to receive a magazine, newspaper, etc.: *I subscribe to "Language and Speech".|Do they all subscribe?* **4** [T1;X1] *fml* to sign (the name of) oneself: *to subscribe one's name* (*as X*)|*to subscribe oneself X*

subscribe for *v prep* [T1] *fml* to SUBSCRIBE (2): *"How much did you subscribe for?" "I subscribed for £2"*

sub·scrib·er /səb'skraɪbəʳ/ *n* **1** a person who SUBSCRIBEs or has subscribed **2** a person who receives the use of a service over a period of time, for which he pays: *a telephone subscriber*

subscribe to *v prep* [T1, 4 *often nonassertive*] to agree with; approve of: *I can't subscribe to unnecessary killing*

sub·scrip·tion /səb'skrɪpʃən/ *n* **1** [U] the act of subscribing (SUBSCRIBE) **2** [C] also (*infml*) **sub**— an amount of money given, esp. regularly to a society **3** [C] an agreement to pay regularly for something: *a subscription dance* (=only for people who pay to go regularly) **4** *fml* a signature

sub·se·quent /'sʌbsɪ̵kwənt/ *adj* [Wa5;A;F+*to*] coming after something else, sometimes as a result of it: *We made plans for a visit, but subsequent difficulties with the car prevented it* —**~ly** *adv*

sub·ser·vi·ence /səb'sɜːvɪəns‖-ɜr-/ *n* [U] the state or quality of being SUBSERVIENT

sub·ser·vi·ent /səb'sɜːvɪənt‖-ɜr-/ *adj* [(*to*)] **1** habitually willing to do what others want; tending to obey others' wishes **2** useful in gaining a purpose —**~ly** *adv*

sub·side /səb'saɪd/ *v* **1** [I∅] (of a building) to sink bit by bit further into the ground **2** [I∅] (of land) to fall away suddenly, because of lack of support: *The road tends to subside in the mountains* **3** [I∅] (of bad weather or other violent conditions) to go back to the usual level: *The floods subsided* (=went down).|*The wind subsided* (=died down).|*His anger quickly subsided* **4** [L9] *infml* to sink down; settle: *She was thoroughly tired, and subsided into a chair*

sub·si·dence /səb'saɪdəns, 'sʌbsɪ̵dəns/ *n* **1** [U] the act of subsiding (SUBSIDE (1,2)) or the state which results; COLLAPSE[1] (1) of land or buildings **2** [C] an example of this: *subsidences over an old coal mine*

sub·sid·i·a·ry[1] /səb'sɪdɪəri‖-dieri/ *adj* [Wa5: (*to*)] connected but of second importance to the main company, plan, work, etc.

subsidiary[2] *n* anything which is SUBSIDIARY[1], esp. a company: *British Tyres is a subsidiary of the British Rubber Company*

sub·si·dize, -dise /'sʌbsɪ̵daɪz/ *v* [Wv5;T1] (of someone other than the buyer) to pay part of the costs of (something) for (someone): *In our school you can buy subsidized meals* —**-dization** /ˌsʌbsɪ̵daɪ'zeɪʃən‖-də-/ *n* [U] —**-dizer** /'sʌbsɪ̵daɪzəʳ/ *n*

sub·si·dy /'sʌbsɪ̵di/ *n* money paid, esp. by the government or an organization, to make prices lower, make it cheaper to produce goods, etc.

sub·sist /səb'sɪst/ *v* [I∅ (*on*)] to keep alive, esp. when having small amounts of money or food: *They subsisted on bread and water/on £20 a week*

sub·sis·tence /səb'sɪstəns/ *n* [U] **1** the ability to live, esp. with little money or food: *Subsistence is not possible in such conditions* **2** the state of living with little money or food: *living at subsistence level*

subsistence crop /·'·· ·/ *n* a crop grown for use by the grower rather than for sale

sub·soil /'sʌbsɔɪl/ *n* [U] the lower level of soil, coarser than that on the surface, but above the hard rock

sub·son·ic /ˌsʌb'sɒnɪk‖-'sɑ-/ *adj* [Wa5] (flying at a speed) below the speed of sound: *subsonic flight/aircraft*

sub·stance /'sʌbstəns/ *n* **1** [C] a material; type of matter: *Salt is a useful substance* **2** [U] the important part or quality; strength: *no substance in the speech* **3** [*the*+R (*of*)] the real meaning, without the unimportant details: *The substance of what he said was that too many people have too little money* **4** [U] solidity: *a soft cloth with little substance in it* **5** [U] *esp. old use* wealth: *a man of substance*

sub·stan·dard /ˌsʌb'stændəd‖-ərd/ *adj* [Wa5] **1** not as good as the average **2** not of an acceptable sort

sub·stan·tial /səb'stænʃəl/ *adj* **1** [B] solid; strongly made: *a substantial desk* **2** [B] big enough to be satisfactory: *a substantial supply of food* **3** [B] noticeable; important; of some size or value: *to make substantial changes* **4** [Wa5;A] concerning the important part or meaning: *Though they disagreed on details, they were in substantial agreement over the plan* **5** [B] wealthy: *a very substantial family in the wool trade* **6** [Wa5;A] *fml* of material existence: *The plans were fulfilled and the dream house became a substantial building*

sub·stan·tial·ly /səb'stænʃəli/ *adv* [Wa5] **1** mainly; in the important part: *not substantially different* **2** quite a lot: *to help substantially*

sub·stan·ti·ate /səb'stænʃieɪt/ *v* [T1] to prove the truth of (something said, claimed, etc.): *Can you substantiate your claim in a court of law?* —**-ation** /səbˌstænʃi'eɪʃən/ *n* [U]

sub·stan·tiv·al /ˌsʌbstən'taɪvəl/ *adj* [Wa5] of or acting as a SUBSTANTIVE[1]

sub·stan·tive[1] /səb'stæntɪv‖'sʌbstəntɪv/ *n* a noun

sub·stan·tive[2] /'sʌbstəntɪv/ *adj* [Wa5] *fml or tech* **1** having existence as a separate being **2** (in grammar) expressing existence: *The substantive verb is "to be"* —**~ly** *adv*

substantive rank /·ˌ·· '·‖ˌ··· '·/ *n BrE* an actual paid position in the army (as compared with a rank in which one might be acting for a time, or receive as an honour)

sub·sta·tion /'sʌbˌsteɪʃən/ *n* a place where electricity is passed on from a generating (GENERATE) station into the general system

sub·sti·tute[1] /'sʌbstɪ̵tjuːt‖-tuːt/ *n* [(*for*)] a person or thing acting in place of another: *He is the doctor's substitute during holiday times.|There is no substitute for good food and exercise*

substitute[2] *v* **1** [T1 (*for*)] to put (something or someone) in place of another: *We substituted red balls for blue, to see if the baby would notice.|They don't like potatoes, so we substituted rice* **2** [I∅ (*for*)] to act as a SUBSTITUTE[1]; be used instead of: *He substituted for the worker who was ill* —see DISPLACE (USAGE) —**-tution** *n* [C;U]

sub·stra·tum /ˌsʌb'strɑːtəm‖-'streɪ-/ *n* **-ta** /tə/ **1** an idea, quality, etc., which forms the hidden base of something else: *It's not a good argument, but it has a substratum of truth* **2** a level (STRATUM) lying beneath another, esp. in the earth

sub·struc·ture /'sʌbˌstrʌktʃəʳ/ *n* a solid base

underground which supports something above ground

sub·sume /səb'sjuːm‖-'suːm/ *v* [T1(*under*)] *fml* to include as a member of a group or type

sub·ten·ant /ˌsʌb'tenənt/ *n* a person to whom a place is SUBLET by the TENANT; person who pays rent to the original renter

sub·tend /səb'tend/ *v* [T1] *tech* (in GEOMETRY) to have (the stated angle or ARC[1] (1)) opposite to it: *This side of the figure subtends an angle of 30 degrees*

sub·ter·fuge /'sʌbtəfjuːdʒ‖-ər-/ *n* **1** [C] a trick or dishonest way of succeeding in something **2** [U] the attempt to gain one's aims secretly

sub·ter·ra·ne·an /ˌsʌbtə'reɪnɪən/ *adj* [Wa5] underground: *subterranean rivers*

sub·ti·tle /'sʌbˌtaɪtl/ *n rare* a title printed beneath the main title of a book

sub·ti·tles /'sʌbˌtaɪtlz/ *n* [P] words printed over a film in a foreign language to translate what is being said: *a French film with English subtitles*

sub·tle /'sʌtl/ *adj* [Wa1] **1** delicate, hardly noticeable, and esp. pleasant: *a subtle taste|subtle differences in meaning* **2** very clever in noticing and understanding: *a subtle mind* **3** clever in arrangement: *a subtle plan* **4** *old use & bibl* wicked in a clever hidden way: *the subtle* SERPENT (= snake) *in the Bible* —**-tly** *adv*: *subtly different*

sub·tle·ty /'sʌtəlti/ *n* **1** [U] the quality of being SUBTLE: *the subtlety of his argument* **2** [C *often pl.*] a SUBTLE idea, thought, or detail

sub·to·pi·a /sʌb'təʊpɪə/ *n* [C;U] a modern area of houses, esp. which has been planned for many people to live in but which is not very interesting to see —compare SUBURB, UTOPIA

sub·tract /səb'trækt/ *v* [T1 (*from*)] to take (a part or amount) from something larger: *Subtract 10 and add 1, what is the result?|to subtract 10 from 30|to subtract a quarter of the money for one's own use* —compare DEDUCT

sub·trac·tion /səb'trækʃən/ *n* **1** [U] the act of subtracting or state of being subtracted **2** [C] an act of taking one number away from a larger one

sub·trop·i·cal /ˌsʌb'trɒpɪkəl‖-'trɑ-/ also **semitropical**— *adj* [Wa5] of or suited to an area near the tropics

sub·urb /'sʌbɜːb‖-ɜrb/ *n* an outer area of a town or city, where people live: *Blackheath is a suburb of London*

sub·ur·ban /sə'bɜːbən‖-ɜr-/ *adj* [Wa5;A] of or in the SUBURBS, esp. when considered uninteresting and full of dull ideas, lack of change, etc.: *a suburban traveller|suburban streets with houses all the same|suburban life*

sub·ur·ban·ite /sə'bɜːbənaɪt‖-ɜr-/ *n infml* a person who lives in the SUBURBS

sub·ur·bi·a /sə'bɜːbɪə‖-ɜr-/ *n* [U] *often derog* **1** the SUBURBS **2** the life and ways of people who live there

sub·urbs /'sʌbɜːbz‖-ɜr-/ *n* [*the*+P] the area generally where most people live, on the edge of any city, as opposed to the shopping and business centre

sub·ven·tion /səb'venʃən/ *n fml* a SUBSIDY or gift of money for a special use

sub·ver·sive /səb'vɜːsɪv‖-ɜr-/ *adj* which may cause, or attempts to cause, the destruction of those in power or of established ideas: *The government dislikes this magazine because it prints subversive ideas* —**~ly** *adv* —**~ness** *n* [U]

sub·vert /səb'vɜːt‖-ɜrt/ *v* [T1] *fml* **1** to try to destroy the power and influence of (esp. a governing body) **2** *rare* to make less loyal, esp. to a person in power: *The king's men had been subverted and they killed him in the night* —**-version** /səb'vɜːʃən‖-'vɜrʒən/ *n* [U]

sub·way /'sʌbweɪ/ *n* **1** [C] a path under a road or railway by which it can be safely crossed **2** [*the*+R; C; *by*+U] *AmE* an underground railway —compare UNDERGROUND, TUBE

suc·ceed /sək'siːd/ *v* **1** [I∅ (*in*)] to gain a purpose or reach an aim: *She succeeded the second time she took the examination* **2** [I∅] to do well, esp. in gaining position or popularity in life: *He is the type of person who succeeds anywhere* **3** [T1] to follow after: *A silence succeeded his words* **4** [T1;I∅ (*to*)] to be the next HEIR after, or the next to take a position or rank: *Mr. Smith succeeded Mr. Jones as our teacher.|to succeed to the property* —see COULD (USAGE)

suc·cess /sək'ses/ *n* **1** [U] the act of succeeding in something **2** [U] a good result **3** [C] a person or thing that succeeds or has succeeded: *His book has come out/his play has been performed and it's a success* **4** [U9] *esp. old use* a result: *What success?|His play had poor success*

suc·cess·ful /sək'sesfəl/ *adj* **1** having succeeded; having gained an aim **2** having gained a position or popularity in life: *Her ability makes her successful in everything she does* —**~ly** *adv*

suc·ces·sion /sək'seʃən/ *n* **1** [U] the act of following one after the other: *His words came out in quick succession* **2** [C (*of*), *usu. sing.*] a number (of persons or things) following on one after the other **3** [U] the act of SUCCEEDing (4) to an office or position

suc·ces·sive /sək'sesɪv/ *adj* [Wa5] following one after the other: *2 visits on successive days* —compare CONSECUTIVE —**~ly** *adv*

suc·ces·sor /sək'sesə[r]/ *n* **1** a person or thing that comes after another: *Last week's storm was bad, but its successor yesterday was even worse* **2** a person who takes an office or position formerly held by another

suc·cinct /sək'sɪŋkt/ *adj* clearly expressed in few words —**~ly** *adv* —**~ness** *n* [U]

suc·cour[1], *AmE* **-cor** /'sʌkə[r]/ *n* [U] *fml & lit* help given in difficulty

succour[2], *AmE* **-cor** *v* [T1] *fml & lit* to give help to (someone in difficulty)

suc·cu·bus /'sʌkjʊbəs‖-kjə-/ *n* **-bi** /baɪ/ a female devil supposed to have sex with a sleeping man —compare INCUBUS

suc·cu·lence /'sʌkjʊləns‖-kjə-/ *n* [U] the state of being SUCCULENT

suc·cu·lent[1] /'sʌkjʊlənt‖-kjə-/ *adj* **1** *apprec* juicy: *a succulent fruit/piece of meat* **2** [Wa5] *tech* (of a plant) thick and fleshy

succulent[2] *n tech* a SUCCULENT[1] (2) plant, such as a CACTUS

suc·cumb /sə'kʌm/ *v* [I∅ (*to*)] **1** to yield: *He succumbed to persuasion* **2** to die (because of): *He succumbed to the illness*

such[1] /sʌtʃ/ *determiner, pron* **1** (*sometimes with* as *or* that) so good, bad, or unusual: *His kindness was such that we will never forget him/was such as to make us all love him.|He wrote to her every day, such was his love for her* **2** (*sometimes with* as) of the same kind; like: *chairs, tables, and all such necessary furniture|They will plant flowers such as roses,* SUNFLOWERS*, etc.|people such as my sister|such people as my sister* **3 and such** and SUCHLIKE[2] **4 any/no/some such** any/no/some (person or thing) like that: *He said "Get out!" or some such rude remark.|No such person exists.|They want beer, but don't give them any such thing—tea's good enough* **5 as such** in that form or kind: *He's a good man and is known as such to everyone.|It's not an agreement as such, but it will serve as one* **6 such . . . as** *fml* any that: *such food/such of the food as they can eat|Such girls as he knew were teachers* **7 such as it is/they**

are although it/they may not be of much worth: *He won't refuse to give you his help, such as it is* —compare **for what it's** WORTH

such² *predeterminer* **1** (*sometimes with* as *or* that) to so great a degree: *Don't be such a fool!|I don't want such a lot of money as that.|We haven't had such a good time for years.|He told us such a funny story/such funny stories that we all laughed.|"His wife is such a dull stupid lump"* (SEU W.)|*It wasn't such a hard test after all* —compare SO¹ (3) **2** (*sometimes with* as) of the same kind; of that kind: *such a paper as "The Times"|She's dirty and untidy; I can't understand such a person/such people!*

USAGE Compare **such** and **so** in these examples: **a** *It was* **such** *an interesting meeting. The meeting was* **so** *interesting.* **b** *There were* **such** *a lot of people. There were* **so** *many people.* **c** *It was* **such** *a shock. It was* **so** *shocking.* **d** *His courage was* **such** *that . . . His courage was* **so** *great that . . .* **e** **such** *a nice man . . .* (*fml*) **so** *nice a man . . .*

such and such /ˈ· · ˌ·/ *predeterminer infml* a certain (time, amount, etc.) not named: *If they tell you to come on such and such a day, don't agree if it's not convenient*

such·like¹ /ˈsʌtʃlaɪk/ *adj* [Wa5;A] *infml* of that kind: *tennis and cricket and suchlike summer sports*

suchlike² *pron infml* things of that kind: *Do you enjoy plays, films, and suchlike?*

suck¹ /sʌk/ *v* **1** [T1;I∅] to draw (liquid) into the mouth by using the tongue, lips, and muscles at the side of the mouth, with the lips tightened into a small hole: *to suck milk through a* STRAW¹ (2b) **2** [T1;I∅ (AWAY, *at*)] to eat (something) by holding in the mouth and melting by movements of the tongue: *sucking (away at) a sweet*|(fig.) *The baby was sucking its thumb* **3** [X9] to draw into a position: *The tree sucked up the rain.|The current sucked them under (the water)*

suck² *n* **1** an act of sucking **2 give suck (to)** *old use* to SUCKLE

suck·er /ˈsʌkəʳ/ *n* **1** [C] a person or thing that sucks **2** [C] an organ by which some animals can hold on to a surface: *This fly has suckers on its feet* **3** [C] a flat piece which sticks to a surface by SUCTION: *You stick this hook to the wall with a sucker, then hang something from it* **4** [C] a SHOOT growing out through the ground from the root or lower stem of a plant **5** [C;N] *infml* a foolish person who is or has been easily cheated

sucking pig /ˈ·· ·/ *n* [C;U] (a) young pig still taking milk from its mother, esp. used as special food, as at Christmas according to custom

suck·le /ˈsʌkəl/ *v* [T1;I∅] to give milk to (the young) from the mother's breast or milk-producing organ —see also NURSE² (1)

suck·ling /ˈsʌklɪŋ/ *n* a young human or animal still taking milk from the mother

suck up *v adv* [I∅ (*to*)] *infml* to try to make oneself liked, esp. by unnaturally nice behaviour to someone: *She's always sucking up to her teacher*

su·crose /ˈsuːkrəʊz, ˈsjuː-‖ˈsuː-/ *n* [U] the common form of sugar

suc·tion /ˈsʌkʃən/ *n* [U] the act of drawing air or liquid away so that another gas or liquid enters or a solid sticks to another surface, because of the pressure of the air outside

suction pump /ˈ·· ·/ *n* a pump which works when air is drawn out to make a VACUUM

sud·den /ˈsʌdn/ *adj* **1** happening, done, etc., unexpectedly: *a sudden illness* **2 all of a sudden** suddenly —**~ly** *adv* —**~ness** *n* [U]

suds /sʌdz/ also **soapsuds**— *n* [P] the form taken by soap when mixed with water, esp. the part on top containing air (soap BUBBLEs) —**sudsy** *adj* [Wa1]

sue /suː, sjuː‖suː/ *v* **1** [T1 (*for*)] to bring a claim in law against, esp. for an amount of money: *If you spoil his property you may be sued* **2** [I∅ (*for*)] to beg or ask (for something), esp. officially in court: *to sue for* PARDON¹ (2)

suede, suède /sweɪd/ *n* [U] soft leather with a rough surface: *suede shoes*

su·et /ˈsuːɪ̤t, ˈsjuːɪ̤t‖ˈsuː-/ *n* [U] a kind of hard fat used in cooking, from the KIDNEYs of an animal —**suety** *adj*

suf·fer /ˈsʌfəʳ/ *v* **1** [I∅ (*for*)] to experience pain or difficulty: *She was very generous to him but she suffered for it when he ran away with all her money* **2** [T1] to experience (something painful): *She suffered the loss of her pupils' respect* —see also SUFFER FROM **3** [I∅] to grow worse; lessen in quality: *He spent his time enjoying himself and his work suffered* **4** [V3] *bibl* to allow **5** [T1] to accept without dislike (esp. in the phr. **to suffer fools (gladly)**)

suf·fe·ra·ble /ˈsʌfərəbəl/ *adj* which can be SUFFERed (5) or borne —see also INSUFFERABLE

suf·fer·ance /ˈsʌfərəns/ *n* **on sufferance** with permission, though not welcomed

suf·fer·er /ˈsʌfərəʳ/ *n* a person who is suffering, or often suffers, as from an illness

suffer from *v prep* [T1] to experience (something unpleasant, such as an illness), esp. over a period of time: *She suffers from headaches*

suf·fer·ing /ˈsʌfərɪŋ/ *n* **1** [U] pain and difficulty generally **2** [C *usu. pl.*] an experience of pain: *severe sufferings*

suf·fice /səˈfaɪs/ *v fml* **1** [I∅ (*for*)] to be enough **2** [T1] (esp. of food) to satisfy: *They were not sufficed* **3 suffice it to say that . . .** I will say only that . . .

suf·fi·cien·cy /səˈfɪʃənsi/ *n* **1** [U] the state of being or having enough **2** [S (*of*)] a supply which satisfies

USAGE There may be a **sufficiency** of something, or an **insufficiency** of it, but one cannot say **my* **insufficiency** *of soap* in the way that one can say *my* **lack** *of soap.*

suf·fi·cient /səˈfɪʃənt/ *adj* [Wa5;B (*for*),B3] enough: *sufficient for everybody* —see ENOUGH (USAGE)

suf·fix /ˈsʌfɪks/ *n* an AFFIX that is placed at the end of a word —compare PREFIX

suf·fo·cate /ˈsʌfəkeɪt/ *v* [T1;I∅] to (cause to) lose one's life because of lack of air —**-cation** /ˌsʌfəˈkeɪʃən/ *n* [U]

suf·fra·gan /ˈsʌfrəgən/ *adj* [Wa5;A;E] (of a BISHOP) helping a higher BISHOP in his work

suf·frage /ˈsʌfrɪdʒ/ *n* **1** [U] the right to vote in national elections **2** [C] *fml* a vote of approval

suf·fra·gette /ˌsʌfrəˈdʒet/ *n* (in Britain in the early 20th century) a woman who was a member of a group which tried to gain the right to vote, esp. by acts bringing them to public notice

suf·fuse /səˈfjuːz/ *v* [T1] to cover or spread over, esp. with a colour or liquid: *The light of the setting sun suffused the clouds* —**-fusion** /səˈfjuːʒən/ *n* [U]

sug·ar¹ /ˈʃʊgəʳ/ *n* **1** [U] a sweet usu. white substance used in food; SUCROSE, as obtained from SUGARCANE and SUGAR BEET **2** [C] *tech* any of several types of sweet substance formed in plants —compare GLUCOSE **3** [N] *infml* (a word used for addressing a person one likes) —compare HONEY —**~less** *adj* [Wa5]

sugar² *v* [T1] **1** to put sugar in: *to sugar one's tea* **2** to make less unpleasant (esp. in the phr. **to sugar the pill**)

sugar beet /ˈ·· ·/ *n* [U] a type of plant which grows under the ground and from which **beet sugar** is obtained

sug·ar·cane /ˈʃʊgəkeɪn‖-ər-/ *n* [U] a type of tall upright tropical plant from whose stems **cane sugar** is obtained

sug·ar·coat·ed /ˌʃʊgəˈkəʊtɪ̣d◂‖-ər-/ *adj* [Wa5] **1** (of food or drugs) covered with a hard coat of sugar **2** having its unpleasantness hidden

sugar dad·dy /ˈ·· ˌ··/ *n infml* an older man who has a relationship, esp. sexual, with a younger woman, providing her with money and presents

sug·ar·loaf /ˈʃʊgələʊf‖-ər-/ *n* a mass of LOAFSUGAR; LOAF[1] (2)

sug·ar·y /ˈʃʊgəri/ *adj* **1** (as if) containing sugar **2** too sweet, nice, kind, etc., in manner to be acceptable

sug·gest /səˈdʒest‖səgˈdʒest/ *v* **1** [T1] to cause to come to the mind: *The sight of the birds suggested a new idea for flying machines* **2** [T1,4,5a,c,6a,b] to say or write (an idea to be considered): *I suggest bringing/(that) we bring the meeting to an end* **3** [T1] to bring (itself) to the mind: *An idea suggested itself* **4** [T1,5a] to give signs (of): *Her expression suggested anger/(that) she was angry*

sug·ges·ti·ble /səˈdʒestəbəl‖səg-/ *adj* who can be influenced easily

sug·ges·tion /səˈdʒestʃən‖səg-/ *n* **1** [U] the act of suggesting **2** [C,C5] something suggested **3** [C (*of*)] a slight sign: *Her face held a suggestion of anger* **4** [U] (in PSYCHOLOGY) a way of causing an idea to be accepted by the mind by indirect connection with other ideas

sug·ges·tive /səˈdʒestɪv‖səg-/ *adj* **1** which brings new ideas to the mind, in addition to what is expressed **2** which suggests immorality or (unacceptable) thoughts of sex —**~ly** *adv*

su·i·cid·al /ˌsuːɪ̣ˈsaɪdl, ˌsjuː-‖ˌsuː-/ *adj* **1** [Wa5] of or with a tendency to SUICIDE **2** wishing to kill oneself **3** which leads or will lead to death or destruction —**~ly** *adv*

su·i·cide /ˈsuːɪ̣saɪd, ˈsjuː-‖ˈsuː-/ *n* **1** [U] the act of killing oneself: *to* COMMIT (1) *suicide* **2** [C] an example of this **3** [C] *law* a person who does this **4** [U] an act which destroys the position of the person concerned: *It would be suicide to admit guilt*

suit[1] /suːt, sjuːt‖suːt/ *n* **1 a** a set of outer clothes which match, usu. including a short coat (JACKET) with trousers or skirt **b** (*usu. in comb.*) a garment or set of garments for a special purpose: *a bathing suit|a space suit* (=for travelling through space) **2** a set (of armour) (in the phrs. **suit of armour/mail**) **3** one of the 4 sets of cards used in games —see CARDS (USAGE) **4** *fml* a request **5** *old use* the act of asking a woman to marry (esp. in the phr. **plead/press one's suit**) **6** LAWSUIT **7 follow suit** to do the same as someone else has

suit[2] *v* **1** [T1;I∅] to satisfy or please; be convenient for: *It's a small house but it suits our needs* **2** [T1] to match or look right with: *That colour doesn't suit her* **3** [T1] to be good for (the health of): *Rich food doesn't suit my stomach* **4** [T1 (*to*)] to make suitable: *to suit the garment to the cloth* **5** [Wv5;T1 (*to, for*)] to make fit: *He isn't suited to such a hard life* **6 suit oneself** *infml* to do what one likes, esp. when different from other people

sui·ta·bil·i·ty /ˌsuːtəˈbɪlɪ̣ti, ˌsjuː‖ˌsuː-/ *n* [U] the fact or degree of being suitable

sui·ta·ble /ˈsuːtəbəl, ˈsjuː-‖ˈsuː-/ *adj* [(*for*)] fit (for a purpose); right; convenient: *Is she suitable for the job?* —**~ness** *n* [U] —**-bly** *adv*

suit·case /ˈsuːtkeɪs, ˈsjuːt-‖ˈsuːt-/ *n* a flat bag for carrying clothes and possessions when travelling —see also CASE

suite /swiːt/ *n* **1** [(*of*)] a set (of furniture) for a room, esp. a SETTEE and 2 chairs (**3-piece suite**) **2** [(*of*)] a set (of rooms), esp. in a hotel **3** (in music) a piece of music with several loosely connected parts **4** *rare* the people with an important person; band of followers: *the President and his suite* —see also RETINUE

suit·ing /ˈsuːtɪŋ, ˈsjuː-‖ˈsuː-/ *n* [U;C] material, esp. woven wool, for (men's) clothing

sui·tor /ˈsuːtəʳ, ˈsjuː-‖ˈsuː-/ *n* **1** *esp. old use* a man wishing to marry a woman **2** *fml* a person bringing a LAWSUIT in a court of law

sulk /sʌlk/ *v* [I∅] to show lasting annoyance against others, esp. silently and for slight cause

sulks /sʌlks/ *n* [*the*+P] a state of bad temper, esp. refusing to speak to others (esp. in the phrs. **have/be in a fit of the sulks**)

sulk·y[1] /ˈsʌlki/ *adj* [Wa1] **1** showing that one is SULKing **2** tending to SULK —**sulkily** *adv* —**sulkiness** *n* [U]

sulky[2] *n* (in former times) a light horse-drawn carriage with 2 wheels, for 1 rider

sul·len /ˈsʌlən/ *adj* **1** silently showing dislike, lack of cheerfulness and interest, etc., esp. over a period of time **2** dark and unpleasant: *a sullen sky* —**~ly** *adv* —**~ness** *n* [U]

sul·ly /ˈsʌli/ *v* [T1] *esp. lit* to spoil or reduce the (high) value of: *The accident sullied her record as a driver*

sul·pha drug, *AmE* **sulfa drug** /ˈsʌlfə drʌg/ also **sul·phon·a·mide,** (*AmE* **-fon-**) /sʌlˈfɒnəmaɪd‖-ˈfɑ-/— *n* any of a group of drugs which are used against diseases caused by bacteria

sul·phate, *AmE* **-fate** /ˈsʌlfeɪt/ *n* [C;U] a SALT[1] (3) formed from SULPHURIC ACID

sul·phide, *AmE* **-fide** /ˈsʌlfaɪd/ *n* [C;U] a mixture of SULPHUR with another substance

sul·phur, *AmE* **-fur** /ˈsʌlfəʳ/ *n* [U] a simple substance (ELEMENT) that is found in different forms (esp. a light yellow powder) and is used in the chemical and paper industries and in medicines

sul·phu·ret, *AmE* **-fu-** /ˈsʌlfjʌret‖-ˈfjə-/ *v* **-tt-** (*AmE* **-t-**) [Wv5;T1] *tech* to combine with SULPHUR

sul·phu·ric ac·id, *AmE* **-fu-** /sʌlˌfjʊərɪk ˈæsɪ̣d/ *n* [U] a type of powerful acid —see also VITRIOL

sul·phu·rous, *AmE* **-fu-** /ˈsʌlfərəs/ also **sul·phu·re·ous,** *AmE* **-fu-** /sʌlˈfjʊərɪəs/— *adj* [Wa5] of, like, or with SULPHUR

sul·tan /ˈsʌltən/ *n* a Muslim ruler, as formerly in Turkey

sul·ta·na /sʌlˈtɑːnə‖-ˈtænə/ *n* **1** the wife, mother, or daughter of a SULTAN **2** a small seedless kind of RAISIN (dried fruit) used in baking

sul·tan·ate /ˈsʌltəneɪt, -nɪ̣t/ *n* **1** [C *usu. sing.*; *the*+R] the position of or rule by a SULTAN: *during his sultanate|to reach the sultanate* **2** [C] a country ruled by a SULTAN

sul·try /ˈsʌltri/ *adj* [Wa1] **1** (of weather) hot, with a lack of air or air which is hard to breathe **2** causing strong sexual attraction or desire —**-trily** *adv* —**-triness** *n* [U]

sum /sʌm/ *n* **1** [*the*+R (*of*)] the total produced when numbers, amounts, etc., are added together: *The sum of 6 and 4 is 10* **2** [C (*of*) *sometimes pl. with sing. meaning*] an amount: *I had to spend a large sum/large sums of money to get it back* **3** [C] a usu. simple calculation, adding, multiplying, dividing, etc.: *learning to do sums at school* **4** [*the*+R (*of*)] the whole; a complete SUMMARY (esp. in the phr. **sum total**): *The sum (total) of his experience is one year working abroad* **5 in sum** (to say) in a short phrase —see also SUM UP

su·mac, sumach /ˈsuːmæk, ˈʃuː-/ *n* a kind of small tree or bush

sum·mar·ize, -ise /ˈsʌməraɪz/ *v* [T1] to be or make a short general account out of (something longer or more detailed) —see also SUM UP

sum·ma·ry[1] /ˈsʌməri/ *adj* [Wa5] *fml* **1** short; expressed as a SUMMARY: *a summary description* **2** done at once without attention to formalities or details, esp. (of punishments) without considering

mercy: *summary dismissal* —**-rily** /ˈsʌmərɪ̈li‖sʌˈme-/ *adv*
summary² *n* [(*of*)] a short account giving the main points
sum·mat /ˈsʌmət/ *pron BrE dial or infml* something
sum·ma·tion /səˈmeɪʃən/ *n fml* **1** [U] the action of adding **2** [C] the result of this **3** [C] a SUMMARY of a speech, usu. by the speaker; SUMMING-UP
sum·mer¹ /ˈsʌməʳ/ *n* **1** [U;C] the season between spring and autumn when the sun is hot and there are many flowers: *in high summer* (=the warmest time) **2** [C *usu. pl.*] *esp. old use & lit* a year of one's age: *He looked younger than his 70 summers* **3** [*the*+R (*of*)] *esp. lit* the best time (of a person's life, for a certain activity, etc.): *That was the high summer of English literature*
summer² *v rare* **1** [L9] to spend the summer: *We summered by Lake Geneva* **2** [X9] to cause (animals) to live and feed during the summer
sum·mer·house /ˈsʌməhaʊs‖-ər-/ *n* **-houses** /ˌhaʊzɪ̈z/ a small building in a garden, with seats in the shade —see picture at GARDEN¹
summer school /ˈ·· ·/ *n* a course of lessons, LECTURES, etc., arranged in addition to the year's work in a university or college after the start of the summer holiday (VACATION)
sum·mer·time /ˈsʌmətaɪm‖-ər-/ *n* [(*the*) U] *not fml* the season of summer; the time of hot weather
summer time /ˈ·· ·/ (*AmE* **daylight saving time**)—*n* [U] **1** the system of having the time on the clocks usu. one hour later than natural time according to the sun, so as to make use of daylight hours in the summer **2** the time during which this continues: *When does summer time start?*
sum·mer·y /ˈsʌməri/ *adj* like or suitable for summer
summing-up /ˌ·· ˈ·/ *n* **summings-up** a SUMMARY spoken at the end of a speech or (esp.) by the judge at the end of a court case
sum·mit /ˈsʌmɪ̈t/ *n* **1** [C (*of*)] the top, esp. the highest part on the top of a mountain —see picture at MOUNTAIN **2** [*the*+R (*of*)] the highest point, degree, etc. **3** [*the*+R] the official position of heads of state: *the summit powers* (=the leaders) **4** [C] a meeting between heads of state **5** [A] between heads of state: *a summit meeting*
sum·mon /ˈsʌmən/ *v* [T1 (*to*); V3 *often pass.*] *fml* **1** to give an official order (to come, do, etc.): *to be summoned (in)to the presence of the Queen|to summon a servant* **2** SUMMONS²
sum·mons¹ /ˈsʌmənz/ *n* **-mons·es** an order to appear, esp. in court, often written: *They served a summons on him*
summons² *v* [T1;(V3): *often pass.*] to give a SUMMONS¹ to; order to appear in court
summon up *v adv* [T1] to draw (a quality) out of oneself, esp. with an effort: *He had to summon up all his strength to jump the stream*
sump /sʌmp/ *n* **1** a place at the bottom, as of a mine, where water collects **2** a part of an engine, at the bottom, which holds the supply of oil —see picture at PETROL
sump·tu·a·ry /ˈsʌmptʃʊəri‖-tʃʊeri/ *adj* [Wa5] *fml & law* limiting the amount of money which can be spent
sump·tu·ous /ˈsʌmptʃʊəs/ *adj* costly and great in amount; showing great value, generosity, etc.; grand —**~ly** *adv* —**~ness** *n* [U]
sum up *v adv* **-mm-** **1** [T1;IØ] to give the main points of (something); SUMMARIZE, esp. as a judge at the end of a court case —see also SUMMING-UP **2** [T1] to consider and judge quickly: *to sum up the* SITUATION (1)|*I'd sum him up as a fool*
sun¹ /sʌn/ *n* **1** [(*the*) R] a burning star in the sky, which the earth goes round and from which it receives light and heat —see picture at PLANET **2** [(*the*) R;U] **a** a light and heat from the sun: *to feel the sun on one's head* **b** a place with sunlight: *Let's walk over to the sun on the other side of the street* **3** [C] a star round which PLANETs may turn **4 a place in the sun** a fortunate position which gives favourable chances in life **5 under the sun** anywhere; at all **6 with the sun** at sunrise and/or sunset: *He gets up/goes to bed with the sun*
sun² *v* **-nn-** [T1] to place (oneself) or stay in sunlight; allow sunlight to fall on (oneself): *She sat sunning herself in the garden*
sun·baked /ˈsʌnbeɪkt/ *adj* **1** [Wa5] hardened by strong sunlight **2** also **sundrenched** /ˈsʌndrentʃt/—*infml* having much hot sunshine: *the sunbaked shores of the Caribbean*
sun·bathe /ˈsʌnbeɪð/ *v* [IØ] to spend time in strong sunlight, usu. sitting or lying, in order to make the body brown —**-bather** *n*
sun·beam /ˈsʌnbiːm/ *n* a beam of sunlight
sun·blind /ˈsʌnblaɪnd/ *n* a piece of material (SHADE¹ (2)) which can be pulled over a window or door to keep out sunlight, such as a movable one which can be made to stand out from the wall outside a shop
sun·bon·net /ˈsʌnˌbɒnɪ̈t‖-ˌbɑ-/ *n* a cloth garment covering the whole head with a piece at the edge standing out to keep the sun off the face and neck, esp. worn by babies
sun·burn /ˈsʌnbɜːn‖-ɜrn/ *n* [U] **1** the condition of having sore skin after experiencing the effects of strong sunlight **2** an area of skin made sore in this way
sun·burnt /ˈsʌnbɜːnt‖-ɜrnt/ also **sun·burned** /-bɜːnd‖-ɜrnd/— *adj* **1** *BrE* having a brown skin; SUNTANNed **2** *AmE* suffering from SUNBURN
sun·dae /ˈsʌndeɪ‖-di/ *n* a dish made from ice cream with fruit, sweet-tasting juice, nuts, etc.
Sun·day /ˈsʌndi/ *n* **1** [R] the first day of the present week; day before next Monday or last Monday: *He'll arrive (on) Sunday.|He'll arrive late Sunday night* (=during the latter part of next Sunday evening) **2** [C] the first day of any week or of the week that is being spoken of, on which Christians worship: *She arrived on the Sunday and left on the Tuesday* (=arrived on the first day of the week being spoken of).|*She arrived on a Sunday* (=not a Saturday, Monday, etc.)|(*esp. AmE*) *She sleeps late Sunday* —see also MONTH (3) **of Sundays**
Sunday best /ˌ·· ˈ·/ also **Sunday clothes** /ˈ·· ·/— *n* **in one's Sunday best** wearing very good clothes, which are only worn on special occasions, esp. (originally) for church
Sunday school /ˈ·· ·/ *n* [C;U] (a) place or occasion for giving children religious teaching on a Sunday
sun·deck /ˈsʌndek/ *n* **1** the upper level of a passenger ship where the sun is strongest **2** a flat roof where one may lie in the sun
sun·der /ˈsʌndəʳ/ *v* [T1] *fml & lit* to separate or break into 2 parts —see also ASUNDER
sun·dew /ˈsʌndjuː‖-duː/ *n* a type of plant that catches insects in its sticky leaves and eats them
sun·dial /ˈsʌndaɪəl/ *n* an apparatus used esp. in former times which shows the time according to where the shadow of a pointer falls when the sun shines on it —see picture at GARDEN¹
sun·down /ˈsʌndaʊn/ *n* [R] sunset
sun·down·er /ˈsʌnˌdaʊnəʳ/ *n* **1** *infml, esp. BrE* an alcoholic drink taken in the evening **2** *AustrE* a wanderer (TRAMP² (4)) who often asks for a place to sleep
sun·drenched /ˈsʌndrentʃt/ *adj infml* SUNBAKED (2)

sun·dries /ˈsʌndriz/ *n* **1** small articles of any type, esp. for sale or as bought but not named separately in an account **2** various small matters that do not need special mention
sun·dry[1] /ˈsʌndri/ *adj* [Wa5;A] **1** various: *books, pens, and sundry other articles* **2 all and sundry** all types of people; everybody
sundry[2] *n AustrE* EXTRA[2] (4)
sun·fish /ˈsʌnˌfɪʃ/ *n* [Wn2] a type of very large fish with an almost circular body
sun·flow·er /ˈsʌnˌflaʊəʳ/ *n* a type of garden plant which grows very tall, with a large yellow flower which turns towards the sun —see picture at FLOWER[1]
sung /sʌŋ/ *past p. of* SING
sun·glass·es /ˈsʌnˌglɑːsɨ̵z‖-ˌglæ-/ *n* [P] glasses with dark glass in them to protect the eyes from sunlight —see PAIR (USAGE)
sun god /ˈ· ·/ *n* a god in some ancient religions who was considered to represent and/or have power over the sun
sun hel·met /ˈ· ˌ··/ also **topee, topi**— *n* a hard hat for protecting the head in tropical sunshine
sunk /sʌŋk/ *past p. of* SINK
sunk·en /ˈsʌŋkən/ *adj* **1** [Wa5;A] which has (been) sunk: *a sunken ship* **2** [B] hollow; having fallen inwards or lower than the surface: *sunken eyes* **3** [Wa5;A] built below the surrounding level: *a sunken garden*
sun·lamp /ˈsʌnlæmp/ also **sunray lamp** /ˈ·· ·/— *n* a lamp which gives out ULTRAVIOLET light which browns and gives health to the skin like that of the sun itself
sun·less /ˈsʌnləs/ *adj* [Wa5] **1** lacking natural light **2** lacking cheerfulness
sun·light /ˈsʌnlaɪt/ *n* [U] natural light from the sun
sun·lit /ˈsʌnˌlɪt/ *adj* brightly lit by the sun
sun lounge /ˈ· ·/ (*AmE* **sun porch**, **sun par·lor** /ˈ· ˌ··/)— *n BrE* a room with large windows which let in a lot of bright sunlight
sun·ny /ˈsʌni/ *adj* [Wa1] **1** having bright sunlight: *a sunny room|a sunny day* **2** cloudless: *a sunny sky* **3** cheerful: *a sunny smile* **4 the sunny side of life** the cheerful pleasant things one experiences —compare BRIGHT (7) —**-nily** *adv* —**-niness** *n* [U]
sunny-side up /ˌ·· · ˈ·/ *adj* [Wa5;F;(B)] *AmE* (of an egg) fried (FRY = cooked in hot fat) on one side only, not turned over in the pan
sun·ray /ˈsʌnreɪ/ *n* [A] ULTRAVIOLET light: *sunray treatment* —see also SUNLAMP
sun·rise /ˈsʌnraɪz/ also (*infml*) **sun-up** /ˈ· ·/— *n* [R;C] the time when the sun is seen to appear after the night
sun·roof /ˈsʌnruːf/ *n* **1** a flat roof of a building where one may enjoy the sun **2** also **sunshine roof** /ˈ·· ·/— a part in the top of a car which can be moved back to let in air and light
sun·set /ˈsʌnset/ *n* [R;C] the time when the sun is seen to disappear as night begins: *They stopped work at sunset.|a beautiful sunset*
sun·shade /ˈsʌnʃeɪd/ *n* **1** a light folding circular frame covered with usu. ornamental cloth and held over the head to protect a person from the sun —compare PARASOL, UMBRELLA **2** a SUNBLIND over a shop
sun·shine /ˈsʌnʃaɪn/ *n* [U] **1** strong sunlight, as when there are no clouds **2** a place where there is bright light and heat from the sun **3 a ray of sunshine a** pleasure, beauty, or joy, esp. among unhappiness or dullness: *Her smile brought a ray of sunshine into the room* **b** *infml* a cheerful person
sun·spot /ˈsʌnspɒt‖-spɑt/ *n* **1** one of the small dark areas on the sun's surface **2** *BrE infml* a place with much sunshine and heat, where people like to go on holiday
sun·stroke /ˈsʌnstrəʊk/ also **heatstroke**— *n* [U] an illness with fever, weakness, headache, etc., caused by the effects of too much strong sunlight, esp. on the head
sun·tan /ˈsʌntæn/ *n* the brownness of the skin after the effects of sunshine —**suntanned** *adj*
sun·trap /ˈsʌntræp/ *n* a place which is unusually sunny
sun wor·ship /ˈ· ˌ··/ *n* [U] **1** the worship of the sun as a god **2** *infml* love of sunbathing (SUNBATHE) —**~per** *n*
sup[1] /sʌp/ *v* **-pp-** [T1;IØ: (UP)] *Scot & N EngE* to drink: *supping his beer*
sup[2] *n* [(*of*)] *Scot & N EngE* a mouthful (of liquid): *to have a sup of soup*
sup[3] *v* **-pp-** [IØ (*on* or *off*)] *old use* to eat (as) supper: *supping on/off bread and cheese*
su·per[1] /ˈsuːpəʳ, ˈsjuː-‖ˈsuː-/ *n infml* **1** [C;N] a police or other SUPERINTENDENT **2** [C] an additional actor taking small parts; SUPERNUMERARY (2)
super[2] *adj infml* (used in speech) wonderful
super- *prefix* greater or more than usual: *the superpowers* (= powerful nations)|*superheated*
su·per·a·bun·dance /ˌsuːpərəˈbʌndəns, ˌsjuː-‖ˌsuː-/ *n* [S (*of*); *in* + U] *fml* a very large amount, even more than necessary: *a superabundance of food|food in superabundance*
su·per·a·bun·dant /ˌsuːpərəˈbʌndənt, ˌsjuː-‖ˌsuː-/ *adj* [Wa5] *fml* more than enough in amount or number
su·per·an·nu·ate /ˌsuːpərˈænjʊeɪt, ˌsjuː-‖ˌsuː-/ *v* [T1] to cause (someone) to leave work, esp. to RETIRE (4) in old age
su·per·an·nu·at·ed /ˌsuːpərˈænjʊeɪtɨ̵d, ˌsjuː-‖ˌsuː-/ *adj* [Wa5] **1** too old for work **2** old-fashioned: *superannuated ideas*
su·per·an·nu·a·tion /ˌsuːpərænjʊˈeɪʃən, ˌsjuː-‖ˌsuː-/ *n* [U] **1** the giving up of, or dismissing from, work in old age **2** money paid as a PENSION, esp. from one's place of work, when one leaves work in old age
su·perb /suːˈpɜːb, sjuː-‖suˈpɜrb/ *adj* perfect in form, quality, etc.; wonderful: *The food was superb* —**~ly** *adv*
su·per·charged /ˈsuːpətʃɑːdʒd, ˈsjuː-‖ˈsuːpərtʃɑrdʒd/ *adj* [Wa5] unusually full of power, as of an engine with additional FUEL, or a person who is very full of life, acts quickly, etc.
su·per·charg·er /ˈsuːpəˌtʃɑːdʒəʳ, ˈsjuː-‖ˈsuːpərˌtʃɑr-/ *n* an apparatus for producing more power from an engine by forcing air into the place where the FUEL, such as petrol, burns
su·per·cil·i·ous /ˌsuːpəˈsɪlɪəs, ˌsjuː-‖ˌsuːpər-/ *adj* (as if) thinking others of little importance; SCORNful[1]; HAUGHTY —**~ly** *adv* —**~ness** *n* [U]
su·per·con·duc·tiv·i·ty /ˌsuːpəkɒndʌkˈtɪvɨ̵ti, ˌsjuː-‖ˌsuːpərkɑn-/ *n* [U] the ability of certain metals to allow electricity to pass freely (without RESISTANCE) when at the lowest temperatures possible (near ABSOLUTE ZERO)
su·per·du·per /ˌsuːpəˈduːpəʳ, ˌsjuː-◂‖ˌsuːpər-/ *adj* [Wa5] *sl* wonderful; SUPER
su·per·e·go /ˌsuːpərˈiːgəʊ, -ˈegəʊ, ˌsjuː-‖ˌsuː-/ *n* **-os** (in FREUDIAN PSYCHOLOGY) the moral self or conscience; the one of the 3 parts of the mind that is partly conscious and that rewards and punishes us by our feelings of guilt or rightness, according to our respect for the rules of society —compare ID, EGO
su·per·fi·cial /ˌsuːpəˈfɪʃəl, ˌsjuː-‖ˌsuːpər-/ *adj* **1** [Wa5] on the surface; not deep **2** not serious, complete, or searching in thought, ideas, etc. —**~ity** /ˌsuːpəfɪʃiˈælɨ̵ti, ˌsjuː-‖ˌsuːpər-/ *n* [U] —**~ly** /ˌsuːpəˈfɪʃəli, ˌsjuː-‖ˌsuːpər-/ *adv*

su·per·fi·cies /ˌsuːpəˈfɪʃiːz, -ʃi-iːz, ˌsjuː-‖ˌsuːpər-/ *n* **-cies** [Wn3] *fml* a surface or outer part

su·per·fine /ˈsuːpəfaɪn, ˈsjuː-‖ˈsuːpər-/ *adj* **1** very fine, esp. of smooth quality: *superfine flour* **2** too detailed or small for fair judgment —compare FINE

su·per·flu·i·ty /ˌsuːpəˈfluːɪ̵ti, ˈsjuː-‖ˌsuːpər-/ *n* [C; U: (*of*)] a greater amount than is needed

su·per·flu·ous /suːˈpɜːflʊəs, sjuː-‖suːˈpɜr-/ *adj* [Wa5] more than is necessary; not needed or wanted —**~ly** *adv* —**~ness** *n* [U]

su·per·hu·man /ˌsuːpəˈhjuːmən, ˌsjuː-‖ˌsuːpər-ˈhjuː-, -ˈjuː-/ *adj* [Wa5] (as if) beyond or better than human powers: *a superhuman attempt to move the stone*

su·per·im·pose /ˌsuːpərɪmˈpəʊz, ˌsjuː-‖ˌsuː-/ *v* [T1 (*on*)] to put over something else or over each other, esp. so as to show the form of both: *to superimpose one film image on another*

su·per·in·tend /ˌsuːpərɪnˈtend, ˌsjuː-‖ˌsuː-/ *v* [T1] to be in charge of and direct (work or people working): *The gardener superintends the children who come to help him*

su·per·in·tend·ent /ˌsuːpərɪnˈtendənt, ˌsjuː-‖ˌsuː-/ *n* **1** [C] a person in charge of some work, building, hospital, home for criminal children, etc. **2** [C;N] a British police officer of middle rank

su·pe·ri·or[1] /suːˈpɪəriəʳ, sjuː-‖sʊ-/ *adj* **1** [Wa5;A] *fml & tech* higher in position; upper: *The superior limbs of man are the arms* **2** [Wa5;B (*to*)] (of people and things) good or better in quality or value: *He thinks he's superior to us because his father's an important man* **3** [Wa5;A] of higher rank or class: *the superior classes* **4** [Wa5;B] of high quality: *superior wool* **5** [B] (as if) thinking oneself better than others: *a superior smile* **6** [Wa5;F+*to*] strong enough in character to be against something one might be persuaded into: *They talk of their neighbours in a cruel way, but she is superior to all that* —opposite **inferior** —**~ity** /suːˌpɪəriˈɒrɪ̵ti, sjuː-‖sʊˌpɪəriˈɔ-, -ˈɑ-/ *n* [U]

superior[2] *n* **1** [C9] a person of higher rank, esp. in a job **2** [C;E] (*usu. cap.*) (a title for) the head of a religious group: *Mother Superior|Father Superior*

su·pe·ri·o·ri·ty com·plex /·ˌ··ˈ··· ˌ··/ *n infml* a condition of the mind which someone is believed to have because he seems to want power over others, as he gives them orders roughly, likes his own way of doing things, etc. —compare INFERIORITY COMPLEX

su·perl. *written abbrev for*: SUPERLATIVE[2] (1)

su·per·la·tive[1] /suːˈpɜːlətɪv, sjuː-‖sʊˈpɜr-/ *adj* **1** best; most good: *of superlative quality* **2** [Wa5] of the SUPERLATIVE[2] (1)

superlative[2] *n* **1** [*the*+R] also (*rare*) **superlative de·gree** /·ˌ··· ·ˈ·/— the highest degree of comparison of an adjective or adverb: *"Good" becomes "best" in the superlative* **2** [C] an example of this; word in this form: *She thought the country wonderful and described it in her letters home with a list of superlatives*

su·per·la·tive·ly /suːˈpɜːlətɪvli, sjuː-‖sʊˈpɜr-/ *adv* [Wa5] (esp. of something good) to a very high degree: *superlatively good*

su·per·man /ˈsuːpəmæn, ˈsjuː-‖ˈsuːpər-/ *n* **-men** /men/ **1** (in stories) a man with powers of mind and body much greater than others' **2** *infml* a man of great ability

su·per·mar·ket /ˈsuːpəˌmɑːkɪ̵t, ˈsjuː-‖ˈsuːpər-ˌmɑr-/ *n* a large shop where one serves oneself with food and goods —see picture at STREET

su·per·nal /suːˈpɜːnl, sjuː-‖sʊˈpɜrnəl/ *adj lit or poet* (as if) coming from heaven

su·per·nat·u·ral /ˌsuːpəˈnætʃərəl, ˌsjuː-‖ˌsuːpər-/ *adj* [Wa5] **1** [B] not explained by natural laws but (esp.) by the powers of spirits, gods, and magic **2** [*the*+U] matters and experiences connected with unknown forces and spirits: *an interest in the supernatural* —**~ly** *adv*

su·per·no·va /ˌsuːpəˈnəʊvə, ˌsjuː-‖ˌsuːpər-/ *n* a very large exploding star seen in the sky as a bright mass for a while —compare NOVA

su·per·nu·me·ra·ry /ˌsuːpəˈnjuːmərəri, ˌsjuː-‖ˌsuːpərˈnjuːməreri/ *adj, n* [Wa5] **1** (a person or thing) additional to the usual number **2** (an actor) having a small part with nothing to say

su·per·scrip·tion /ˌsuːpəˈskrɪpʃən, ˌsjuː-‖ˌsuːpər-/ *n* words written on (top of or on the outside of) something

su·per·sede /ˌsuːpəˈsiːd, ˌsjuː-‖ˌsuːpər-/ *v* [T1 *often pass.*] to replace, esp. as an improvement on: *The old methods have been superseded*

su·per·ses·sion /ˌsuːpəˈseʃən, ˌsjuː-‖ˌsuːpər-/ *n* [U (*of*)] *fml* the act of superseding or state of being SUPERSEDED

su·per·son·ic /ˌsuːpəˈsɒnɪk, ˌsjuː-‖ˌsuːpərˈsɑ-/ *adj* [Wa5] faster than the speed of sound: *supersonic flight|a supersonic aircraft*

su·per·star /ˈsuːpəstɑːʳ, ˈsjuː-‖ˈsuːpər-/ *n* an unusually famous and popular performer

su·per·sti·tion /ˌsuːpəˈstɪʃən, ˌsjuː-‖ˌsuːpər-/ *n* [U;C] (a) belief which is not based on reason or fact but on association of ideas, as in magic

su·per·sti·tious /ˌsuːpəˈstɪʃəs, ˌsjuː-‖ˌsuːpər-/ *adj* (tending to be) full of SUPERSTITIONS —**~ly** *adv*

su·per·struc·ture /ˈsuːpəˌstrʌktʃəʳ, ˈsjuː-‖ˈsuːpər-/ *n* **1** an arrangement of parts built up on top of another, such as the upper parts of a ship **2** the part of a building above the ground **3** an important arrangement, system, etc., which has grown from a certain base: *a superstructure of religion based on nature worship*

su·per·tax /ˈsuːpətæks, ˈsjuː-‖ˈsuːpər-/ *n* [U] (in Britain in former times) additional income tax only on very high incomes —compare SURTAX

su·per·vene /ˌsuːpəˈviːn, ˌsjuː-‖ˌsuːpər-/ *v* [IØ] *fml* (of an event) to come into a state of affairs causing a change to it: *The meeting went on until lack of time supervened*

su·per·vise /ˈsuːpəvaɪz, ˈsjuː-‖ˈsuːpər-/ *v* [T1;IØ] to keep watch over (work and workers) as the person in charge —**-vision** /ˌsuːpəˈvɪʒən, ˌsjuː-‖ˌsuːpər-/ *n* [U] —**-visor** /ˈsuːpəvaɪzəʳ, ˈsjuː-‖ˈsuːpər-/ *n*

su·per·vi·so·ry /ˌsuːpəˈvaɪzəri, ˌsjuː-‖ˌsuːpər-/ *adj* [Wa5] of or as a person who SUPERVISES

su·pine /ˈsuːpaɪn, ˈsjuː-‖suːˈpaɪn/ *adj* **1** [Wa5] lying on the back looking upwards —compare PRONE (1) **2** lacking in action, strength, etc.; lazy —**~ly** *adv*

sup·per /ˈsʌpəʳ/ *n* [C;U] the last meal of the day, taken in the evening —**~less** *adj* [Wa5]

sup·plant /səˈplɑːnt‖səˈplænt/ *v* [T1] to take the place of, often by tricks or deceit —**~er** *n*

sup·ple /ˈsʌpəl/ *adj* [Wa1] **1** bending or moving easily, esp. in the joints of the body **2** quick in thinking, changing one's ideas, values, etc. —**~ness** *n* [U]

sup·ple·ment[1] /ˈsʌplɪ̵mənt/ *n* **1** an additional amount of something **2** an additional written part, at the end of a book, or as a separate part of a newspaper, magazine, etc.

sup·ple·ment[2] /ˈsʌplɪ̵ment/ *v* [T1 (*by, with*)] to make additions to: *She supplements her* DIET (=food) *with eggs and fruit from the farm*

sup·ple·men·ta·ry /ˌsʌplɪ̵ˈmentəri/ *adj* [Wa5 (*to*)] **1** additional: *a supplementary water supply for use if the main supply fails* **2** (of angles or an angle) making up 180° together, or with the other angle: *This angle is supplementary to that.|They are supplementary angles*

supplementary ben·e·fit /··ˌ··· ˈ··/ *n* [U] (in

Britain) additional money given by the state to someone who already receives money from it, but not enough to live on

sup·pli·ant /ˈsʌpliənt/ *adj, n esp. lit* (a person) begging, praying, or requesting

sup·pli·cant /ˈsʌplɪkənt/ *n* a person begging for something, esp. from a person in power or God

sup·pli·cate /ˈsʌplɪkeɪt/ *v fml or lit* **1** [T1;I∅: (*for*); V3] to beg (someone), esp. for help **2** [T1] to beg someone for —**-cation** /ˌsʌplɪˈkeɪʃən/ *n* [C;U]

sup·pli·er /səˈplaɪəʳ/ *n* [*often pl. with sing. meaning*] a person or firm that supplies something, esp. goods: *The suppliers were Bradford and Dyson*

sup·plies /səˈplaɪz/ *n* [P] food and/or necessary materials for daily life, esp. for a group of people over a period of time

sup·ply[1] /səˈplaɪ/ *v* [T1] **1** [(*to*)] to provide (something): *In Britain milk is supplied to each house in bottles* **2** [(*with*)] to give things to (a person) for use: *The firm who used to supply us have closed their business* **3** to satisfy (a need) **4 supply the place of** *fml* to (be) put instead of

supply[2] *n* **1** [C (*of*)] a store which can be used: *a water supply* (=a system of pipes bringing water to houses and buildings)|*a food supply* **2** [C (*of*), *usu. sing.*] an amount: *Bring a large supply of food with you* **3** [U] the rate at which an amount is provided: *We often have little food, but we eat according to supply* —see also SUPPLIES **4 in short supply** scarce

supply and de·mand /·ˌ· · ·ˈ·/ *n* [U] the balance between the amount of goods and how much is needed, esp. as shown in price changes

supply teach·er /·ˈ· ˌ··/ *n* a teacher who takes the place of regular teachers for short periods while they are away

sup·port[1] /səˈpɔːt‖-ort/ *v* [T1] **1** to bear the weight of, esp. preventing from falling: *You support the bottom of the box while I lift the top* **2 a** to provide money for (a person) to live on: *to support a family* **b** to help, with sympathy, or practical advice, money, food, etc: *to support him in his trouble* **3** to approve of and encourage: *to support the new political party|to support birth control* **4** to be in favour of: *The results support my original idea* **5** to be loyal to, esp. by attending matches or performances: *They support the local theatre* **6** (with *can/cannot*) to bear: *I can't support this heat*

support[2] *n* **1** [U] the act of SUPPORTing[1] (1) **2** [C] a piece of material which bears the weight of something: *the supports of the bridge* **3** [C] an apparatus which holds a weak or displaced part of the body **4** [U] money to live: *a means of support* (such as a job) **5** [C] a person who provides money to live, esp. for his family **6** [U] encouragement and help: *to give his suggestion more support* **7** [U] the amount of attendance or number of people who are loyal attenders: *The theatre gets a lot of support* —compare SUPPORTER

sup·por·ta·ble /səˈpɔːtəbəl‖-or-/ *adj* [*usu. neg.*] *fml* bearable —compare INSUPPORTABLE

sup·port·er /səˈpɔːtəʳ‖-or-/ *n* **1** [C9] a person who gives loyalty and attendance to (an activity), defends (a principle), etc. **2** [C] (in HERALDRY) one of 2 figures of men or animals on either side of a shield

supporting part /·ˌ·· ˈ·/ also **supporting role** /·ˌ·· ˈ·/— *n* a small part in a play, for a less important actor

supporting pro·gramme /·ˌ·· ˈ··/ *n* a short film or less important part of a performance, as opposed to the main film or part

sup·por·tive /səˈpɔːtɪv‖-or-/ *adj* [Wa5;A;(B)] *fml* which gives (additional) encouragement, help, etc.: *They won a prize to travel abroad but would never have been able to go without the supportive efforts of their firm*

sup·pose[1] /səˈpəʊz/ *v* **1** [T5a,b;V3] to take as likely; consider as true: *We suppose he's gone home.*|*"He must be dead, then." "Yes, I suppose so"* **2** [T5a,b;V3 *often pass.*; X1,7,9] to believe: *I suppose that's true.*|*I supposed him to be a workman, but he was in fact a thief.*|*He was commonly supposed* (*to be*) *foolish* **3** [V3 *pass.*] **a** to expect, because of duty, responsibility, law, or other conditions: *Everyone is supposed to wear a seat belt in the car* **b** [*neg.*] to allow: *You're not supposed to smoke in here* **4** [T1] *fml* to have as a condition; PRESUPPOSE: *Every effect supposes a cause*

suppose[2] *conj* **1** why not?; I suggest: *Suppose we wait a while* **2** if: *Suppose it rains, what shall we do?* **3** what would/will happen if?: *Suppose a lion should come out of the forest?* (*What then?*)

sup·posed /səˈpəʊzd/ *adj* [Wa5;A] believed to be (so), though without much proof: *Her supposed wealth is a very small sum*

sup·pos·ed·ly /səˈpəʊzɪdli/ *adv* [Wa5] as believed; as it appears: *Supposedly, she's a rich woman*

sup·pos·ing /səˈpəʊzɪŋ/ *conj* SUPPOSE[2] (2,3)

sup·po·si·tion /ˌsʌpəˈzɪʃən/ *n* **1** [U,U5] the act of supposing (SUPPOSE[1] (1)) or guessing **2** [C] an idea which is a result of this: *My supposition is that he took the money, meaning to pay it back later*

sup·pos·i·to·ry /səˈpɒzɪtəri‖səˈpɑzɪtori/ *n* a form of medicine shaped into a small piece to be placed inside a lower opening of the body, usu. the RECTUM

sup·press /səˈpres/ *v* [T1] **1** to crush (esp. an action or state) by force: *to suppress one's feelings of guilt* **2** to prevent from appearing: *to suppress the truth/a smile* **3** to prevent from being printed and made public

sup·pres·sion /səˈpreʃən/ *n* [U] the act of SUPPRESSing or state of being suppressed

sup·pres·sive /səˈpresɪv/ *adj fml or tech* which tends to SUPPRESS: *a suppressive cough medicine* —**~ness** *n* [U]

sup·pres·sor /səˈpresəʳ/ *n* **1** a person or thing that SUPPRESSes **2** a small apparatus which prevents an electrical machine from causing bad quality (INTERFERENCE) on a television or radio set, one type of which is fitted to this machine, another to the television or radio

sup·pu·rate /ˈsʌpjʊreɪt‖-pjə-/ *v* [I∅] (of a wound) to give out infected material (PUS) —**-ration** /ˌsʌpjʊˈreɪʃən‖-pjə-/ *n* [U]

su·pra·na·tion·al /ˌsuːprəˈnæʃənəl, ˌsjuː-‖ˌsuː-/ *adj* [Wa5] higher than or going beyond national power, interest, borders, etc.

su·prem·a·cist /səˈpreməsɪst/ *n* [C9] a person who believes in the SUPREMACY of a certain group: *a white supremacist*

su·prem·a·cy /səˈpreməsi/ *n* [U] **1** the state of being SUPREME: *the supremacy of the state* **2** [(*over*)] the highest level of power; highest position: *to gain supremacy over others*

su·preme /suːˈpriːm, sjuː-, sə-‖sʊ-, suː-/ *adj* [Wa5] **1** (*often cap.*) highest in position, esp. of power: *the supreme command* (=power of commanding, as in an army) **2** highest in degree: *supreme happiness/courage* **3** greatest possible (esp. in the phr. **the supreme sacrifice**=giving one's life) —**~ly** *adv*

Supreme Be·ing /·ˌ· ˈ··/ *n* [*the*+R] *lit* God

Supreme Court /·ˌ· ˈ·/ *n* [*the*+R] the highest court of law in a state of the US or in the US as a whole

sur- /sɜː‖sɜr/ *prefix* [*n*→*n*] *rare* over; above: SURCHARGE|SURTAX —compare SUPER-

sur·charge[1] /ˈsɜːtʃɑːdʒ‖ˈsɜrtʃɑrdʒ/ *v* [T1 (*on*)] to make an additional charge to or for: *He was surcharged on the parcel*

surcharge² *n* **1** an amount charged in addition to the usual amount or the amount already paid, as for a letter with too few stamps on it for the weight **2** a mark on a letter showing this

sur·coat /ˈsɜːkəʊt‖ˈsɜr-/ *n* an armless garment worn over armour

surd /sɜːd‖sɜrd/ *n tech* a quantity which cannot be shown in whole numbers

sure¹ /ʃʊəʳ/ *adj* **1** [Wa5;F,F5a,6a,b] having no doubt: *I think so, but I'm not sure.|I'm sure he'll come.|Are you quite sure who she is?|I'm not sure whether to go* **2** [Wa5;F3] certain (to happen): *He is sure to come.|It's sure to rain* **3** [Wa1;F+*of*] certain (of having): *I've never felt surer of success* **4** [Wa1;B] certain in effect; to be trusted: *One thing is sure; he can't have gone far.|He made a sure step out of the mud* **5 make sure of something/that a** to find out for certain: *Make sure of the time* **b** to arrange so: *Make sure (that) you get here* **c** *esp. old use* to believe as certain: *He made sure it was true* **6 sure of oneself** certain that one's actions are right, acceptable, etc.; (too) CONFIDENT —see also SELF-ASSURED **7 to be sure a** it must be accepted (that): *To be sure, some people may disagree, but that doesn't mean I'm wrong* **b** *now rare* (an expression of surprise) —**~ness** *n* [U]
USAGE 1 In *BrE*, **certainly** and *I'm* **certain** are used when one really knows the truth; **surely** and *I'm* **sure** when one has only a strong hope or belief: *I'm* **certain** *he didn't steal it/He* **certainly** *didn't steal it: I stole it myself!|I'm* **sure** *he didn't steal it/***Surely** *he didn't steal it: he's not that kind of person.* 2 **Sure** and **certain** have the same meaning in the following NEGATIVE² (1) patterns: [F5] *I'm not* **sure/certain** *where he is.*|[F6] *I'm not* **sure/certain** *how to do it.* **Sure** cannot be used of events: *It is* **certain** (not ***sure**) *that ....* 3 In *BrE*, **certainly** is used when giving a firm "yes" or "no", and the use of **sure** or **surely** in this meaning is thought to be rather American: *"May I borrow your knife?"* **"Certainly!"**/(*esp. AmE*) **"Sure!"**|*"Can you dance?" "I* **certainly** *can!"*/(*esp. AmE infml*) *"I* **sure** *can!"*

sure² *adv* [Wa5] **1** *infml esp. AmE* certainly: *Sure I will.|Are you all right? Sure.|He sure is tall* **2 as sure as** (used for giving force to an expression): *That's the truth, as sure as I'm standing here* **3 for sure** certainly so: *He won't live long, and that's for sure* **4 sure enough** RIGHT³ (8b) **enough**

sure·fire /ˈʃʊəfaɪəʳ‖ˈʃʊər-/ *adj* [A] *infml* certain to happen or succeed: *a surefire winner/cure*

sure·foot·ed /ˌʃʊəˈfʊtɨd◂‖ˌʃʊər-/ *adj* FOOTSURE —**~ly** *adv* —**~ness** *n* [U]

sure·ly /ˈʃʊəli‖ˈʃʊərli/ *adv* **1** safely: *slowly but surely* **2** [Wa5] certainly **3** [Wa5] *esp. AmE* of course **4** [Wa5] I believe or hope (something must be or become so): *Surely you remember him?|You know him, surely?* —see SURE¹ (USAGE)

sure thing /ˌ· ˈ·/ *n* [S] *infml* a certainty: *That race is a sure thing for me; I'm certain to win it*

sur·e·ty /ˈʃʊərɨti/ *n* **1** [C;U] a person who takes responsibility for another's behaviour **2** [C;U] money given to make sure that a person will appear in court —see also BAIL **3** [S] *old use* certainty (in the phr. **of a surety**=certainly)

surf¹ /sɜːf‖sɜrf/ *n* [U] the white airfilled water (FOAM) formed by waves when they break on rocks, a shore, etc.

surf² also **surf ride** /ˈsɜːf-raɪd‖ˈsɜrf-/— *v* [IØ] to ride as a sport over breaking waves near the shore, on a SURFBOARD (esp. in the phr. **go surfing**) —see also SURFER

sur·face¹ /ˈsɜːfɨs‖ˈsɜr-/ *n* **1** [C] the outer part: *a rough surface|the earth's surface|marks on the surface of the table|It's only a surface wound.|the surface workers at a coal mine* (=those who work above ground) **2** [C] the top of a body of liquid: *A wave broke across the surface of the pool.|surface* TENSION (=the holding power of the surface) **3** [*the*+R] what is easily seen, not the main (hidden) part (esp. in the phr. **on the surface**): *He seems quiet on the surface, but he's quite different when you get to know him.|surface difficulties|surface friendliness* —see also SUPERFICIAL

surface² *v* **1** [IØ] to come to the surface of water: *fish surfacing to catch insects* **2** [T1] to cover (esp. a road) with hard material **3** [IØ] *infml, often humor* to make an appearance, esp. for the first time on a particular day by getting out of bed: *old arguments that have surfaced once again|He doesn't usually surface until 10 o'clock*

surface³ *adj* [Wa5] (of post) travelling by land and sea: *surface mail|to send a letter surface|It went surface, which takes much longer than* AIRMAIL

surface-to-air /ˌ·· · ˈ·/ *adj* [Wa5;A] (of a weapon) fired from the earth towards aircraft: *surface to air* MISSILE*s*

surf·board /ˈsɜːfbɔːd‖ˈsɜrfbord/ *n* a narrow piece of wood, plastic, etc., for riding over the waves as they break on the shore

surf·boat /ˈsɜːfbəʊt‖ˈsɜrf-/ *n* a light boat which will float on SURF

sur·feit¹ /ˈsɜːfɨt‖ˈsɜr-/ *n* [C (*of*) *usu. sing.*] too large an amount, esp. of food

surfeit² *v* [T1 (*with*)] to fill with too much of something

surf·er /ˈsɜːfəʳ‖ˈsɜr-/ *n* a person who is SURFing² or habitually goes surfing

surge¹ /sɜːdʒ‖sɜrdʒ/ *n* [(*of*) *usu. sing.*] **1** a forward rolling movement, of or like a wave: *a surge of people|a surge of electric current* —compare TIDE **2** a sudden example of strong increasing feeling: *a surge of love*

surge² *v* [L9] **1** to move, esp. forward, in or like powerful waves: *The crowd surged past him* **2** [(*up*)] (of a feeling) to arise powerfully: *Anger surged (up) within him*

sur·geon /ˈsɜːdʒən‖ˈsɜr-/ *n* **1** a doctor whose job is to practise SURGERY (3) **2** a medical officer in the army or navy —see also **dental surgeon** (DENTIST), HOUSE SURGEON

sur·ge·ry /ˈsɜːdʒəri‖ˈsɜr-/ *n* **1** [C] *BrE* a place where one or a group of doctors or DENTIST*s* receives people to give them advice on their health and medicines to treat illnesses **2** [C;U] *BrE* the time during which this takes place **3** [U] the skill and practice of performing medical operations: *Many lives have been saved by surgery* **4** [U] the performing of such an operation, usu. including the cutting open of the skin: *The condition is serious; it will need surgery*

sur·gi·cal /ˈsɜːdʒɪkəl‖ˈsɜr-/ *adj* [Wa5] **1** [B] of, by, or for SURGERY **2** [A] (of a garment) made and worn as a treatment for a particular bodily condition: *a surgical boot* (=for fitting and/or improving a badly shaped foot)|*surgical stockings* —**~ly** *adv* [Wa4]

surgical spir·it /ˌ··· ˈ··/ *n* [U] alcohol used for cleaning wounds or skin in hospital

sur·ly /ˈsɜːli‖ˈsɜrli/ *adj* [Wa1] seeming angry, bad-mannered, etc., esp. habitually: *a surly fellow|a surly look*

sur·mise¹ /səˈmaɪz‖sər-/ *v* [T1,5b;IØ] *fml* to suppose as a reasonable guess: *It may not be true; he was only surmising*

surmise² /səˈmaɪz, ˈsɜːmaɪz‖sər-, ˈsɜr-/ *n fml* a guess

sur·mount /səˈmaʊnt‖sər-/ *v* [T1] **1** to conquer

(esp. difficulties): *With patience and determination we can surmount every difficulty* **2** to get over or above: *The rider's horse easily surmounted the fence* **3** [*usu. pass.*] to be over or on top of: *a house surmounted by a tall chimney* —**~able** *adj*

sur·name /ˈsɜːneɪm‖ˈsɜr-/ *n* the name one shares with the other members of one's family, often the last name: *Alan Smith's surname is Smith* —compare FORENAME

sur·pass /səˈpɑːs‖sərˈpæs/ *v* [T1] to go beyond, in amount or degree: *to surpass all expectation*

sur·pass·ing /səˈpɑːsɪŋ‖sərˈpæ-/ *adj* [Wa5;A] *lit* to a degree above anything else —**~ly** *adv*

sur·plice /ˈsɜːplɪ̵s‖ˈsɜr-/ *n* a garment made of white material worn over a darker garment during religious services by some priests and CHOIRBOYs —see also VESTMENT —**-pliced** *adj* [Wa5]

sur·plus /ˈsɜːpləs‖ˈsɜr-/ *n, adj* [Wa5; (*to*)] (an amount) additional to what is needed or used, as of money

sur·prise¹ /səˈpraɪz‖sər-/ *n* **1** [U] the feeling caused by an unexpected event **2** [C] an unexpected event **3** [U;A] the act of coming on (someone, often an enemy) unprepared (esp. in the phr. **take by surprise**): *They took the animals by surprise and hunting them was easy.|They took the animals by surprise attack* —see also SURPRISE² (3)

surprise² *v* [T1] **1** [Wv5] to cause surprise to: *The taste surprised him; it was not as he'd imagined it* **2** [Wv5] to shock or cause to disbelieve: *Your behaviour surprises me* **3** to come on or attack when unprepared: *They surprised the animals at their food.|They surprised us with a visit*

sur·pris·ing /səˈpraɪzɪŋ‖sər-/ *adj* unusual; causing surprise —**~ly** *adv*

sur·real /səˈrɪəl/ *adj* SURREALISTIC (1)

sur·real·is·m /səˈrɪəlɪzəm/ *n* [U] a modern type of art and literature in which the artist represents, in a dreamlike way, unrelated images and objects in the mind

sur·real·ist /səˈrɪəlɪ̵st/ *adj, n* (an artist or writer) concerned with SURREALISM

sur·real·is·tic /səˌrɪəˈlɪstɪk/ *adj* **1** of a dreamlike quality, esp. strange and causing fear **2** as if concerning SURREALISM

sur·ren·der¹ /səˈrendəʳ/ *v* **1** [T1;IØ: (*to*)] to yield to the power of esp. an enemy, as a sign of defeat: *to surrender (oneself/one's army) to the enemy* **2** [T1] *fml* to give up possession of (esp. a paper, in return for money or services): *to surrender one's claim to the money|Surrender your ticket before going in.|to surrender a* POLICY/INSURANCE POLICY **3** [T1;IØ: (*to*)] to yield (oneself) to the power of a feeling, state, etc.: *He should have fought for his rights, but he surrendered to political pressure* —see also GIVE UP

surrender² *n* [U] the act of SURRENDERing

sur·rep·ti·tious /ˌsʌrəpˈtɪʃəs/ *adj* done, gained, etc., secretly, esp. for dishonest reasons: *a surreptitious look to see if he was watching as she took 2 more of his sweets* —**~ly** *adv* —**~ness** *n* [U]

sur·rey /ˈsʌri/ *n AmE* (in former times) a light horse-drawn carriage with 4 wheels and 2 seats

sur·ro·gate /ˈsʌrəgeɪt‖ˈsɜr-/ *n, adj* [Wa5;C;A] **1** (a person) acting for another, such as a priest or judge **2** (a person or thing) acting or used in place of another; SUBSTITUTE: *a surrogate material|a food surrogate*

sur·round¹ /səˈraʊnd/ *v* [T1 *often pass.*] **1** to be all around on every side: *The trees surround the house* **2** to go around on every side: *The soldiers surrounded the enemy* **3** to be easily found nearby: *We are surrounded by comforts*

surround² *n* an edge, esp. ornamental as part of the furnishing in a house, or an open space around a CARPET: *to make a surround for a fireplace*

sur·round·ing /səˈraʊndɪŋ/ *adj* [Wa5;A] around and nearby: *in the surrounding area*

sur·round·ings /səˈraʊndɪŋz/ *n* [P] the place and conditions of life: *The surroundings a child grows up in may have an effect on his development* —see ENVIRONMENT (USAGE)

sur·tax /ˈsɜːtæks‖ˈsɜr-/ *n* [U] an additional tax on high incomes —compare SUPERTAX

sur·veil·lance /sɜːˈveɪləns‖sɜr-/ *n* [U] a close watch kept on someone, esp. a prisoner (esp. in the phr. **under surveillance**)

sur·vey¹ /səˈveɪ‖sər-/ *v* [T1] **1** to look at (a person, group, place, or condition) as a whole: *to survey the view* **2** to examine the condition of and give a value for (a building): *The house has been surveyed* **3** to measure, judge, and record on a map the details of (an area of land): *to survey the east coast*

sur·vey² /ˈsɜːveɪ‖ˈsɜr-/ *n* **1** [C] a general view or considering (of a place or condition) **2** [C;U] (an) examination of a house, esp. for someone who may buy it: *The house is still under survey* **3** [C;U] (an) act of SURVEYing¹ (3) land **4** [C] a map showing the details and nature of such land —see also ORDNANCE SURVEY

sur·vey·or /səˈveɪəʳ‖sər-/ *n* **1** a person whose job is to examine buildings, esp. houses for sale **2** a person whose job is to measure land, record details in maps, etc. **3** [(*of*)] (*often cap.*) an official or skilled person who examines (the stated thing); INSPECTOR

sur·viv·al /səˈvaɪvəl‖sər-/ *n* **1** [U] the fact or likelihood of surviving (SURVIVE): *hopes of survival* **2** [C] something which has continued to exist from an earlier time, (esp.) which is not useful now: *The old man is a survival of a past age/an age long gone.|That fashion is a survival from 1910*

survival kit /·ˈ·· ·/ *n* a packet of limited articles needed to keep one alive, as when lost or hurt during adventurous travelling

survival of the fit·test /·ˌ·· · · ˈ··/ *n* [U] NATURAL SELECTION

sur·vive /səˈvaɪv‖sər-/ *v* **1** [IØ] to continue to live, esp. after coming close to death: *We survived, although others died in the accident* **2** [T1] to continue to live after: *We survived the accident.|She survived her sons*

sur·vi·vor /səˈvaɪvəʳ‖sər-/ *n* a person who has continued to live, esp. in spite of coming close to death

sus·cep·ti·bil·i·ties /səˌseptəˈbɪlɪ̵tiz/ *n* [P] sensitive or tender parts of a person's nature: *wounded in his deepest susceptibilities when she refused his love/when he failed the examination*

sus·cep·ti·bil·i·ty /səˌseptəˈbɪlɪ̵ti/ *n* [U (*to*)] the quality or state of being SUSCEPTIBLE

sus·cep·ti·ble /səˈseptəbəl/ *adj* **1** [B (*to*)] easily influenced: *susceptible to suggestion* **2** [B] likely to experience strong feelings, esp. to fall in love easily: *a susceptible girl* **3** [F+*to*] sensitive; likely to feel a strong effect (from): *susceptible to ill health|susceptible to the cold* **4** [F+*of*] *fml* which can have: *A signed agreement is not susceptible of change*

sus·pect¹ /ˈsʌspekt/ *adj* of uncertain truth, rightness, quality, etc.: *That is a rather suspect result; I don't believe he could have found the answer so easily.|His fitness is suspect, so we can't take the risk of including him in the team*

suspect² *n* a person who is SUSPECTed³ (2) of guilt, esp. in a crime

sus·pect³ /səˈspekt/ *v* **1** [T1,5a] to believe to exist or be true; think likely: *We suspected trouble.|We suspected that he was lost, even before we were told* **2** [T1 (*of*); X (*to be*) 1] to believe to be guilty: *They* *suspect him of murder.*|*They suspect him to be the murderer* **3** [T1] to be doubtful about the truth or value of: *I suspect his* MOTIVE*s* (=real reasons for what he does) **4** [T5a,b] *infml* to suppose or guess: *I suspect you may be right.*|*I suspect that's true*

sus·pend /sə'spend/ *v* **1** [X9 esp. *from, often pass.*] to hang from above: *to suspend a rope from a tree* **2** [T1 *usu. pass.*] to hold still in liquid or air: *The sun broke over the trees and dust could be seen suspended in the beam of light* **3** [Wv5;T1] to put off or stop (esp. the fulfilment of a decision) for a period of time: *to suspend the law*|*to suspend punishment* **4** [T1 *usu. pass.*] to prevent from taking part in a team, belonging to a group, etc., for a time, usu. because of misbehaviour or breaking rules: *He has been suspended from school*

sus·pend·er /sə'spendə^r/ *n* [*usu. pl.*] **1** a band (GARTER) with a fastener hanging down, formerly used by men to hold a sock up **2** a fastener hanging down from an undergarment to hold a woman's stockings up

suspender belt /·'·· ·/ *n* a light undergarment for women with SUSPENDER*s* (2) fixed to it

sus·pend·ers /sə'spendəz‖-ərz/ *n* [P] *AmE* BRACES —see PAIR (USAGE)

sus·pense /sə'spens/ *n* [U] a state of uncertain expectation: *We waited for the decision and the suspense was terrible.*|*He wouldn't tell them, but kept them in suspense all day*

sus·pen·sion /sə'spenʃən/ *n* **1** [U] the act of SUSPENDing or state of being suspended **2** [C] a liquid mixture with very small pieces of solid material contained but not combined in the liquid —see SUSPEND (2) **3** [U;C] the pieces of apparatus fixed to the wheels of a car, motorcycle, etc., to lessen the effects of rough road surfaces —see picture at CAR

sus·pen·sion bridge /·'·· ·/ *n* a bridge hung from strong steel ropes (CABLE*s*) fixed to towers

sus·pi·cion /sə'spɪʃən/ *n* **1** [U] **a** the act of SUSPECTing[3] or state of being suspected: *He is under suspicion of stealing* **b** lack of trust or willingness to accept: *She always treated us with suspicion* **2** [C,C5] **a** a feeling of SUSPECTing[3]: *I have a suspicion that he's right* **b** a belief about someone's guilt: *The police have not found the thief but they have their suspicions* **3** [S (*of*)] a slight amount (of something seen, heard, tasted, etc.): *a suspicion of tears in her eyes*

sus·pi·cious /sə'spɪʃəs/ *adj* **1** [(*of*)] not trusting: *She was always suspicious of us*/*our intentions* **2** likely to SUSPECT[3] (guilt): *We can't help being suspicious about someone who buys so many new clothes just after money was stolen from the office* **3** causing to SUSPECT[3] guilt, wrongness, etc.; SUSPECT[1]: *He is a suspicious character* (=person) —**~ly** *adv*

sus·tain /sə'steɪn/ *v* [T1] **1** **a** to bear (difficulty) **b** to do this without loss of strength: *to sustain severe damage in an accident* **2** to keep in continuance: *to sustain a note in music*|*a well-sustained attempt* **3** [Wv4] to keep strong; strengthen: *A light meal will not sustain us through the day* **4** *fml* to hold up (the weight of): *An old wall cannot sustain a new building* **5** *law* to establish as right: *to sustain a case*

sus·te·nance /'sʌstənəns/ *n* [U] **1** the ability (of food) to keep strong or strengthen **2** food which does this

sut·tee /'sʌtiː/ *n* **1** [U] the ancient custom in the Hindu religion of a wife being burnt with her dead husband **2** [C] a woman who did this

su·ture /'suːtʃə^r/ *n* **1** a (type of) thread used for stitching a wound together —see also GUT, CATGUT **2** the stitch(es) made with this

su·ze·rain /'suːzəreɪn‖-rən, -reɪn/ *n* **1** a state which controls the foreign affairs of another state **2** (in former times) a ruling lord

su·ze·rain·ty /'suːzərənti/ *n* [U] the fact or state of being a SUZERAIN

svelte /svelt/ *adj* (esp. of a woman) thin, graceful, and well-shaped

SW *written abbrev. for:* southwest(ern)

swab[1] /swɒb‖swɑb/ *n* **1** *med* a piece of material which will hold liquid to be tested for infection **2** *med* the liquid taken on this material **3** a cleaning cloth which will hold water, as for use on the floors of a ship

swab[2] *v* **-bb-** **1** [T1] to take liquid on a SWAB[1] (1) from (a part of the body) **2** [T1 (DOWN)] to clean (esp. the floors (DECK*s*) of a ship) **3** [X9 (UP)] to remove by cleaning in this way: *to swab the water from the floor*|*to swab it up*

swad·dle /'swɒdl‖'swɑdl/ *v* [T1] to wrap (a person) in many coverings, esp. (in former times) to wind (a baby) in narrow pieces of cloth

swaddling clothes /'·· ·/ also **swaddling bands**— *n* [P] *esp. bibl* the cloth(s) wound round SWADDLEd babies

swag /swæg/ *n* [U] **1** *sl* the goods obtained in a robbery **2** *AustrE* a set of clothes and belongings in a BUNDLE, as carried by travellers and wanderers

swag·ger[1] /'swægə^r/ *v* [I∅] **1** to walk with a swinging movement, as if proud: *He swaggered down the street after winning the fight* **2** to talk in a BOASTing[2] (1,2) way —**~er** *n* —**~ingly** *adv*

swagger[2] *n* [S] a proud manner of walking

swain /sweɪn/ *n esp. lit or poet* a young man in a country village, esp. a lover or admirer of a girl

swal·low[1] /'swɒləʊ‖'swɑ-/ *n* a type of small bird with pointed wings and a tail that comes to 2 points, which comes to the northern countries in summer —see picture at BIRD[1]

swallow[2] *v* **1** [T1] to move (food or drink) down the throat from the mouth: *to swallow a mouthful of bread*/*soup*|(fig.) *to swallow one's pride* (=to forget it, before doing something humble) **2** [I∅] to make the same movement of the throat, esp. as a sign of nervousness: *He swallowed, and stepped into the examination room* **3** [T1] **a** to accept patiently: *to swallow rude remarks* **b** *infml* to believe, in spite of doubt: *to swallow a story* (*whole*) —**~er** *n*

swallow[3] *n* **1** an act of swallowing **2** an amount swallowed

swallow dive /'·· ·/ (*AmE* **swan dive** /'· ·/)— *n BrE* a DIVE[2] (1), esp. a jump into water, starting with the arms stretched out from the sides of the body

swal·low·tailed /'swɒləʊteɪld‖'swɑ-/ *adj* [Wa5] **1** (of birds and some flying insects) having a tail with 2 points (FORKED) **2** (of a man's coat) having a long part at the back (TAIL), divided into 2 parts

swallow up *v adv* [T1 *often pass.*] to take in, causing to disappear: *Travel costs swallowed up their money*

swam /swæm/ *past t. of* SWIM

swa·mi /'swɑːmi/ *n* [C;A] (a title for) a Hindu religious teacher

swamp[1] /swɒmp‖swɑmp, swɔmp/ *n* [C;U] (an area of) soft wet land; (a) BOG: *The land is no use for growing crops; it's mainly swamp*

swamp[2] *v* [T1] **1** to fill with water, esp. causing to sink **2** [*usu. pass.*] to crush with a large amount, as of work or difficulties: *We were swamped with telephone calls after our advertisement was put in the paper*

swamp·y /'swɒmpi‖'swɑmpi, 'swɔmpi/ *adj* [Wa1] (of land) wet like a SWAMP

swan[1] /swɒn‖swɑn/ *n* a type of large white bird

with a long neck, which lives on rivers and lakes —see picture at WATER¹

swan² *v* **-nn-** [L9 (OFF)] *infml* to go or travel, esp. where and when one likes: *He just went swanning off to the races when he should have been working*

swan dive /ˈ· ·/ *n* SWALLOW DIVE

swank¹ /swæŋk/ *v* [I∅] *infml* to act or speak in an unpleasantly proud way: *swanking (about) in her new fur coat*

swank² *n infml* **1** [U] (the attempt to make people think well of one by) proud and showy behaviour, speech, etc. **2** [C] a person who BOASTs² (1,2)

swank·y /ˈswæŋki/ *adj* [Wa1] *infml* **1** liking or tending to act or speak in an unpleasantly proud way **2** also **swank**— costly or worth BOASTing² (3) of, esp. as being fashionable: *a really swanky party* —**swankiness** *n* [U]

swans·down /ˈswɒnzdaʊn‖ˈswɑnz-/ *n* [U] **1** soft small feathers which grow underneath the larger feathers of a SWAN, near its skin —compare DOWN⁶ **2** a very soft thick type of cloth

swan·song /ˈswɒnsɒŋ‖ˈswɑnsɔŋ/ *n* **1** the last piece of work or performance, of an artist, poet, etc. **2** a song supposed to be sung by a SWAN just before its death

swap¹, swop /swɒp‖swɑp/ *v* **-pp-** [T1 (*for*); I∅ (*nonstandard*) D1] *infml* to exchange (goods or positions): *I'll swap 6 old foreign stamps for 3 of the new ones.|I liked her coat and she liked mine, so we swapped.|I want to sit where you're sitting; shall we swap round?|I'll swap you 3 of mine for one of yours*

swap², swop *n infml* **1** [*usu. sing.*] an exchange: *to do a swap* **2** a thing that has been or may be exchanged

sward /swɔːd‖swɔrd/ *n old use & lit* a piece of grassy land

swarf /swɔːf‖swɔrf/ *n* [U] small bits of metal, plastic, etc., produced by a cutting tool in operation

swarm¹ /swɔːm‖swɔrm/ *n* [GC (*of*)] **1** a large group (of insects) moving in a mass, esp. bees with a QUEEN **2** a crowd (of people) or moving mass (of animals)

swarm² *v* **1** [I∅] (of bees) to leave the living place (HIVE) in a mass to find another **2** [L9] to move in a crowd or mass

swarm³ *v* [L9 esp. UP, *up*; (T1)] *becoming rare* to climb using the hands and feet: *He swarmed up the tree*

swarm with *v prep* [T1 *no pass.*] to be full of: *The place swarmed with tourists*

swar·thy /ˈswɔːði‖-ɔr-/ *adj* [Wa1] **1** (of the skin or face) dark-coloured **2** (of a person) having such a skin

swash·buck·ler /ˈswɒʃˌbʌkləʳ‖ˈswɑʃ-, ˈswɔʃ-/ *n* (esp. in films and stories) a daring fellow who is fond of showy adventures, sword fighting, etc.

swash·buck·ling /ˈswɒʃˌbʌklɪŋ‖ˈswɑʃ-, ˈswɔʃ-/ *adj* [Wa5] like or about a SWASHBUCKLER, esp. a PIRATE¹ (1)

swas·ti·ka /ˈswɒstɪkə‖ˈswɑ-/ *n* a pattern in the form of a cross with each arm bent back at a right angle, used as a sign for the sun in ancient times and for the NAZI Party in modern times

swat¹ /swɒt‖swɑt/ *v* **-tt-** [T1] to hit (an insect) with a flat object or hand, esp. so as to cause death

swat² *n* **1** an act of SWATting **2** a flat object with a wire handle, for killing flies

swatch /swɒtʃ‖swɑtʃ/ *n* [(*of*)] a piece (of cloth) as an example of a type or quality of material; SAMPLE

swath /swɒθ‖swɑθ/ also **swathe**— *n* **1** an amount of grass or crops cut with one movement of the hand, by SCYTHE **2** a line of grass or crops that has been cut by a machine **3 cut a swath through** to cause the main part of (something) to be destroyed: *The storm cut a (wide) swath through the town*

swathe /sweɪð‖swɑð, swɔð, sweɪð/ *v* [X9 esp. *in, usu. pass.*] *esp. lit or fml* to wrap round in cloth, esp. a BANDAGE: (fig.) *hills swathed in mist* —compare SWADDLE

swat·ter /ˈswɒtəʳ‖ˈswɑ-/ *n* SWAT² (2)

sway¹ /sweɪ/ *v* **1** [T1;I∅] to (cause to) swing from side to side: *The dancers swayed to the music* **2** [X9;L9] to (cause to) swing to one side: *The weight of the load swayed the cart to the right* **3** [T1] to influence: *When choosing a job don't be swayed by false promises of future high earnings* **4** [T1] *esp. old use* to rule: *His power sways the world*

sway² *n* [U] **1** SWAYing movement: *The sway of the ship made him fall over* **2** influence: *He changed his opinion under the sway of his friend's argument* **3** *old use & lit* power to rule: *under Caesar's sway*

sway·back /ˈsweɪbæk/ *n* a curving of the BACKBONE, esp. found in horses —**~ed** *adj* [Wa5]

swear /sweəʳ/ *v* **swore** /swɔːʳ‖swor/, **sworn** /swɔːn‖sworn/ **1** [T3,5a] to promise formally or by an OATH (1): *He swore to obey.|He swore by his honour/on his father's grave that he would always be loyal* **2** [T5a] *infml* to state firmly: *He said he was there all the time, but I'll swear I never saw him* **3** [T1 (*to*); I∅] to (cause to) take an OATH (1), as in court: *They swore him to silence* **4** [T1 (*on*)] **a** to take (an OATH (1)): *One swears the oath in court (with the right hand) on the Bible before giving* EVIDENCE **b** to declare the truth of by OATH (1): *a sworn statement* **5** [I∅ (*at*)] to curse: *Stop swearing in front of the children* —see also SWEAR BY, SWEAR IN, SWEAR OFF, SWEAR TO —**~er** *n*

swear by *v prep* [T1,4: *no pass.*] *infml* to trust in and encourage the use of: *She swears by hand washing, and won't have a machine*

swear in *v adv* [T1 *often pass.*] **1** to cause (a witness) to take the OATH (1) in court —see also SWEAR (3) **2** to cause to make a promise of responsible action, judgment, etc. (an OATH (1) of loyalty): *The elected President was sworn in*

swear off *v adv* [T1,4: *no pass.*] to state one's intention to stop (using): *He's sworn off (smoking) cigarettes for a month*

swear to *v prep* [T1,4: *no pass., usu. neg.*] to declare firmly the truth of (it): *I couldn't swear to its having been done*

swear·word /ˈsweəwɜːd‖ˈsweərwɜrd/ *n* a word used as a curse

sweat¹ /swet/ *v* **1** [I∅] to have SWEAT² (1) coming out through small holes in the skin: *sweating in the heat/with fear* **2** [T1] to cause to do this: *to sweat a horse* **3** [I∅] to show liquid on the surface, coming from inside: *The cheese is sweating* **4** [T1;I∅] to (force to) work very hard for little money —see also SWEATED, SWEATSHOP **5 sweat blood** *infml* to work unusually hard —see also SWEAT OUT

sweat² *n* **1** [U] also **perspiration**— liquid which comes out from the body through the skin to cool it **2** [U] liquid on a surface, esp. drawn out in drops by heat **3** [S] the action of SWEATing or (anxious) state which causes this: *in a cold sweat* **4** [C] fever and a feeling of heat along with loss of liquid through the skin: *Every 2 hours she had sudden sweats* **5** [S] *infml* hard work **6** [C] *infml* a man who has experience, esp. a soldier (in the phr. **old sweat**)

sweat·band /ˈswetbænd/ *n* a narrow piece of **a** leather around the inside of a hat, to prevent damage by SWEAT² (1) **b** cloth worn around the wrist or forehead to prevent SWEAT² (1) running down

sweat·ed /ˈswetɪ̵d/ *adj* [Wa5;A] (made by

workers) forced to work long hours for little money: *sweated labour*

sweat·er /ˈswetəʳ/ *n* **1** a heavy woollen garment for the top of the body, not usu. with a fastening; heavy JUMPER **2** a KNITted top garment of any material; JUMPER

sweat gland /ˈ· ·/ *n* any of the many small organs under the skin from which liquid is lost to cool the skin

sweat out *v adv* [T1] **1** to get rid of (an illness) by causing oneself to SWEAT¹ (1) **2 sweat it out** *infml* **a** to take hard exercise: *sweating it out in the* GYMNASIUM **b** to suffer unpleasantness until it ends: *He hated watching his first operation, but he had to sweat it out*

sweat·shirt /ˈswet-ʃɜːt‖-ɜrt/ *n* a loose cotton garment for the upper part of the body; sort of T-SHIRT

sweat·shop /ˈswet-ʃɒp‖-ʃɑp/ *n* a factory or workroom where workers produce goods by SWEATED labour, often in bad conditions

sweat·y /ˈsweti/ *adj* [Wa1] **1** (of a person) SWEATing¹ (1) **2** covered in or containing SWEAT² **3** smelly with SWEAT² **4** unpleasantly hot; causing one to SWEAT¹

swede /swiːd/ *n* [C;U] a type of round yellow vegetable like a TURNIP

sweep¹ /swiːp/ *v* **swept** /swept/ **1** [T1;X7] to clean by brushing: *to sweep a room|to sweep the house clean/clear of dirt* **2** [X9] **a** to remove by brushing: *to sweep the dirt away* **b** to remove with a brushing movement: *The wind swept the leaves away.|She swept up her child and ran off* **3** [X9] to cause to move with a swing: *to sweep a brush across a surface|to sweep one's arms above one's head* **4** [T1 (*of*)] *rare* to clear (of what is unwanted): (fig.) *to sweep the country of crime* **5** [L9] to move (over or past something) quickly; rush: *A storm swept over the country.*|(fig.) *Fear swept over him* **6** [T1] to cross completely: *The storm swept the country* **7** [T1] to win completely and easily, as in elections: *The new political party swept the country* **8** [T1] to move over and touch: *The branches swept the surface of the water* **9** [L9] to be in a curve across land: *The hills sweep round the hidden valley* **10** [L9] (of a person) to move (away) in a proud firm manner: *She swept from the room in her long dress* **11** [T1] to move across in watching or giving a view of: *The old man's eyes swept the distance* **12** [D1] to make (a BOW² (1) or CURTSEY) with a graceful movement: *to sweep someone a bow* **13 sweep the board** to win easily and completely, as in gambling (GAMBLE) **14 sweep someone off his feet a** to knock someone over **b** to cause someone to fall suddenly in love with one: *The young army captain has rather swept Anthea off her feet* **c** to persuade someone completely and suddenly: *The crowd were swept off their feet by the force of the speaker's arguments* —see also SWEEP UP

sweep² *n* **1** an act of sweeping: *This room needs a good sweep* **2 a** a swinging movement, as of the arm: *with a sweep of his sword* **b** the distance covered by this: (fig.) *the broad sweep of his argument* **3** [*usu. sing.*] a long curved line or area (of country) across land: *the long sweep of the distant hills* **4** a strong forward movement **5** an act of moving out over a broad area to search, attack, etc. **6** *tech* a long OAR for moving a boat **7** *tech* a pole forming a handle for raising the bucket of a well **8** *tech* one of the large broad arms of a WINDMILL **9** SWEEPSTAKE **10** *infml* CHIMNEYSWEEP **11 clean sweep** /ˌ· ˈ·/ **a** a complete removal: *We must make a clean sweep of all these old books; they're no use any more* **b** a complete victory in every place, event, etc.: *It's a clean sweep for Germany; they finish first, second, and third in the race*

sweep·er /ˈswiːpəʳ/ *n* **1** a person or thing that sweeps —compare CARPET SWEEPER **2** (in football) a player who defends from behind other defending players

sweep·ing /ˈswiːpɪŋ/ *adj* **1** including many things: *sweeping plans* **2** not careful or correct in detail; too general: *a sweeping statement* **3** without limit: *sweeping changes* —**~ly**

sweep·ings /ˈswiːpɪŋz/ *n* [P] dirt, dust, etc., which are swept up

sweep·stake /ˈswiːpsteɪk/ *n* a form of risking money, usu. on a horserace, in which those who hold tickets for the winners gain all the money paid by those who bought tickets

sweep·stakes /ˈswiːpsteɪks/ *n* **-stakes** [Wn3] SWEEPSTAKE

sweep up *v adv* [I∅] to clean a place, esp. sweeping the floor

sweet¹ /swiːt/ *adj* [Wa1] **1 a** having a taste like that of sugar: *sweet fruit* **b** containing sugar: *sweet tea* **2** having a pleasant taste and smell; fresh: *sweet water* **3** pleasing to see or hear: *sweet sounds|sweet music* **4** gentle or attractive in manner; lovable: *a very sweet person|to have a sweet temper* **5 a** having a light pleasant smell, like many garden flowers **b** (of wine) having a taste caused by the presence of sugar; not DRY¹ (9) **6** pleasant: *the sweet smell of success* **7 sweet on** /ˈ· ·/ *infml* in love with —see also SHORT¹ (13) **and sweet** —**~ly** *adv* —**~ness** *n* [U]

sweet² *n BrE* **1** [C] a small piece of sweet substance, mainly sugar or chocolate, eaten for pleasure —see also CANDY **2** [C;U] (a dish of) sweet food served at the end of a meal —see also PUDDING, DESSERT **3** [*my*+N] (a word used for addressing a loved one)

sweet-and-sour /ˌ· · ˈ·/ *adj* [Wa5] (of a SAUCE or food with this) having both gentle and strong tastes together

sweet·bread /ˈswiːtbred/ *n* an organ (the PANCREAS) from a sheep or young cow, used as food

sweet·bri·er, briar /ˈswiːtbraɪəʳ/ also **eglantine**— *n* a type of wild rose with sweet-smelling pink flowers

sweet corn /ˈ· ·/ *AmE* usu. **corn**— *n* [U] *esp. BrE* a type of MAIZE used as a vegetable

sweet·en /ˈswiːtn/ *n* **1** [T1] to make sweet, esp. by adding sugar **2** [I∅] to become (more) sweet: *Apples sweeten as they become ripe* **3** [T1] to make kinder, gentler, etc.: *A good meal sweetened his temper* **4** [T1] to make pleasanter: *Holidays sweeten life* **5** [T1] *infml* to give money or presents to, in order to persuade: *We sweetened him with the promise of a toy and he stopped crying*

sweet·en·er /ˈswiːtənəʳ/ *n* **1** a substance which is used instead of sugar to make food and drink taste sweet **2** *infml* money, a present, etc., given in order to persuade someone

sweet·en·ing /ˈswiːtənɪŋ/ *n* [U] any substance which makes food sweeter

sweet·heart /ˈswiːthɑːt‖-hart/ *n* **1** [C] *becoming rare* a person whom another loves: *They were sweethearts for 10 years before they married* **2** [N] DARLING

sweet·ie /ˈswiːti/ *n* **1** [C] *infml* (*used esp. by women*) a nice lovable person or thing **2** [C] *BrE infml* (*used esp. by and to children*) & *ScotE* a SWEET² (1) **3** [N] *infml* (*used esp. when addressing a woman*) DARLING

sweet·ish /ˈswiːtɪʃ/ *adj* rather sweet in taste, smell, etc., sometimes unpleasantly so

sweet·meat /ˈswiːtmiːt/ *n old use* a sweet or any food made of or preserved in sugar

sweet pea /ˌ· ˈ·‖ˈ· ·/ *n* a type of climbing plant with very sweet smelling flowers
sweet pep·per /ˌ· ˈ··/ *n* a GREEN PEPPER, or the less strong forms of RED PEPPER —see also PEPPER[1] (2)
sweet po·ta·to /ˌ· ·ˈ··, ˈ· ·ˌ··/ also **yam**— *n* **1** a type of climbing plant that grows in tropical countries **2** the root of that plant eaten as a vegetable
sweets /swiːts/ *n* [*the*+P (*of*)] *lit* pleasures; enjoyable things: *the sweets of victory/success*
sweet tooth /ˌ· ˈ·, ˈ· ·/ *n* [S] a liking for things that are sweet and sugary
sweet wil·li·am /ˌswiːt ˈwɪlɪəm/ *n* a type of garden plant with many small sets of flowers on one stem
swell[1] /swel/ *v* **swelled, swollen** /ˈswəʊlən/ *or* **swelled 1** [I∅ (UP)] to increase in fullness and roundness: *Her ankle swelled (up) after the fall* —see also SWOLLEN[1] **2** [T1] to increase the size or amount of: *He took a job to swell his pocket*/FUNDS (=money) **3** [T1 (OUT)] to fill, giving a round shape: *The wind swelled (out) the sails* **4** [T1;I∅] to fill (the heart) with strong feeling: *Her heart swelled with pride.|Pride swelled her heart*
swell[2] *n* **1** [(*the*) S] the movement of large stretches of the sea up and down, without separate waves **2** [(*the*) S (*of*)] an increase of sound: *the great swell of the* ORGAN (4) **3** [(*the*) S (*of*)] roundness and fullness: *the firm swell of her breasts* **4** [C] *sl old use* a fashionable or important person
swell[3] *adj* [Wa5] **1** *AmE infml* very good; of good quality: *a swell teacher* **2** *sl old use* fashionable
swelled head /ˌ· ˈ·/ *n* [*usu. sing.*] *esp. AmE* SWOLLEN HEAD —**~ed** /ˌ· ˈ··◂/ *adj* [Wa5]
swell·ing /ˈswelɪŋ/ *n* **1** [U] the act of swelling or state of being swollen **2** [C] a place on the body which has increased in size and usu. stands out from the rest
swel·ter /ˈsweltəʳ/ *v* [I∅] (of a person) to experience the effects of great heat: *Open the window, we're sweltering*
swel·ter·ing /ˈsweltərɪŋ/ *adj* [Wa5] very hot, causing unpleasantness
swept /swept/ *past t. and p. of* SWEEP
swept-back /ˌ· ˈ·◂/ *adj* **1** (of an aircraft's wing) having the front edge pointing backwards at an angle from the main body of the aircraft **2** (of hair) combed or brushed back so as not to be covering any part of the face
swerve[1] /swɜːv‖swɜrv/ *v* **1** [I∅] to turn suddenly to one side, when moving ahead: *A dog ran in front of the car and we swerved* **2** [T1;I∅: (*from*)] to (cause to) change from a course or purpose: *Nothing will swerve him from his aims*
swerve[2] *n* a swerving movement (SWERVE[1] (1)): *The bicycle gave a sudden swerve to the left*
swift[1] /swɪft/ *adj* [Wa1] **1** [B] rapid; fast: *swift running|a swift runner* **2** [B;F3] ready or quick in action: *a swift reply|He was swift to take offence* **3** [B] short or sudden: *a swift visit to the shops* —**~ly** *adv* —**~ness** *n* [U]
swift[2] *n* a type of small bird with long wings, which eats insects —see picture at BIRD[1]
swig[1] /swɪg/ *n* [(*of*)] *sl* a drink, esp. a large swallow: *a swig of beer*
swig[2] *v* **-gg-** [T1 (OFF, DOWN); I∅] *sl* to drink, esp. in large mouthfuls or all at once without taking a breath
swill[1] /swɪl/ *v* **1** [T1 (OUT, DOWN)] to wash by pouring large amounts of water on: *to swill the yard* **2** [T1 (DOWN); I∅] *sl* to drink, esp. in large amounts
swill[2] *n* **1** [S] also **swill down** /ˌ· ˈ·/, **swill out** /ˌ· ˈ·/— an act of SWILLing[1] (1) **2** [C (*of*)] *sl* an act of SWILLing[1] (2) **3** [U] pig food, mostly uneaten human food in partly liquid form
swim[1] /swɪm/ *v* **swam** /swæm/, **swum** /swʌm/; *pres. p.* **swimming 1** [I∅] to move through water by moving limbs and/or tail: *Some snakes can swim* **2** [T1] to cross or complete (a distance) by doing this: *to swim a river* **3** [X9] to cause or help to do this: *She swam him across, holding his head up* **4** [I∅ (*with, in*)] to be full of or covered with liquid: *meat swimming in fat* **5** [I∅] to cause one to feel DIZZY; (seem to) spin round: *He was hot and tired and his head was swimming* **6 swim with the tide** to follow the behaviour of other people around one —**~mer** *n*
swim[2] *n* **1** [*usu. sing.*] an act or occasion of swimming: *to go for a swim* **2 in the swim** knowing about and concerned in what is going on in modern life
swim·ming /ˈswɪmɪŋ/ *n* [U] the act or sport of those who swim
swimming bath /ˈ·· ·/ also **swimming baths**— *n* [Wn3] *BrE* a public SWIMMING POOL, usu. indoors —see also BATHS; see BATH (USAGE)
swimming cos·tume /ˈ·· ˌ··/ also **swim·suit** /ˈswɪmsuːt, -sjuːt‖-suːt/— *n* BATHING SUIT
swim·ming·ly /ˈswɪmɪŋli/ *adv* easily and well
swimming pool /ˈ·· ·/ *n* a special pool for swimming in, sometimes outdoors
swimming trunks /ˈ·· ·/ *n* [P] a man's garment, like very short trousers, for swimming —see PAIR (USAGE)
swin·dle[1] /ˈswɪndl/ *v* [T1 (*out of*)] to cheat (someone), esp. getting money unlawfully —**-dler** *n*
swindle[2] *n* **1** an example of swindling (SWINDLE): *a big bank swindle* **2** *infml* an article, service, or performance which is not of the value paid for: *These shoes are a swindle; they have a hole after being worn just a week* —compare FRAUD
swine /swaɪn/ *n* **swine** [Wn3] **1** [C] *old use or tech* a pig: *swine fever* **2** [C; *you*+N] *sl* a disliked unpleasant person
swine·herd /ˈswaɪnhɜːd‖-ɜrd/ *n* (in stories of former times) a man or boy who looks after pigs, esp. one who later becomes an important person
swing[1] /swɪŋ/ *v* **swung** /swʌŋ/ **1** [T1;I∅] to (cause to) move backwards and forwards or round and round, from a fixed point once or regularly: *The mirror swung round.|They were swinging their arms* **2** [X7,9;L7,9] to (cause to) move in a curve: *The door swung shut* **3** [X9;L9] **a** to move (oneself) while hanging from a fixed point: *They were swinging on the gate* **b** to move (oneself) forward from one fixed point to another by a movement through the air: *They swung themselves down from the top of the wall* **4** [I∅] to ride on a SWING[2] (5a) **5** [T1] to wave (something) around in the air, esp. as a weapon; BRANDISH or WIELD: *He swung his stick, hitting his enemy a crushing blow* **6** [I∅ (*for*)] *infml* to be hanged to death, as a punishment: *He'll swing (for that/it/his crime)* **7** [L9] to turn quickly: *He swung round and said "Why are you following me?"* **8** [L9] to walk rapidly and actively with light steps: *swinging gaily down the street* **9** [X9;L9] to (cause to) change to a large degree, once or regularly: *She swung from happiness to tears.|The value of the pound swung downwards* **10** [I∅] *infml* to have or play with a pleasing exciting beat: *That music/that band really swings* **11** [L9] to start smoothly and rapidly: *We're ready to swing into action at any time* **12 no/not enough room to swing a cat** *infml* very little space
swing[2] *n* **1** [U;C] the/an act or method of swinging once or regularly: *the swing of his arms|with a swing of his arms* **2** [C] the distance covered by a swinging movement: *a wide swing* **3** [U;S] a strong regular beat (esp. in the phr. **go with a swing**): *music that goes with a swing|He walked*

down the street with a swing **4** [U] a type of JAZZ music of the 1930's and 40's with a strong regular beat, usu. played by a big band **5** [C] **a** a seat, esp. for children, on which one can ride backwards and forwards, fixed (usu.) by ropes or chains from above: *to go on a swing* **b** a ride on this: *to have a swing* **6** [C] a large change: *a swing in prices/public opinion* **7 go with a swing** to happen successfully **8 in full swing** fully active: *The party was still in full swing at four o'clock in the morning*

swinge /swɪndʒ/ *v* [T1] *old use* to beat or whip

swinge·ing /ˈswɪndʒɪŋ/ *adj* (esp. of arrangements concerning money) very great in force, degree, etc.: *swingeing* CUTS (= reductions) *in public spending*

swing·er /ˈswɪŋəʳ/ *n* a person who lives a free modern life, including freedom in sex

swing·ing /ˈswɪŋɪŋ/ *adj* [Wa5] **1** gay and full of life: *a swinging party* **2** fashionably free and modern, esp. in sex life —**~ly** *adv*

swing-wing /ˌ· ˈ·◂/ *n, adj* [Wa5] (an aircraft) having wings that can be moved to different positions in flight for low speeds and speeds faster than sound

swin·ish /ˈswaɪnɪʃ/ *adj* [Wa5] badly behaved, unpleasant, etc.; like a SWINE (2) —**~ly** *adv* —**~ness** *n* [U]

swipe¹ /swaɪp/ *n* **1** a sweeping stroke or blow: *Give him a swipe round the ear!* **2** an attack in words

swipe² *v* **1** [T1;IØ (*at*)] to hit violently, esp. with a swing of the arm: *She swiped at his head, but he got out of the way* **2** [T1] *infml* to steal by seizing: *She swiped a cake while no one was looking*

swirl¹ /swɜːl‖swɜrl/ *n* **1** a SWIRLing² movement: *She danced with a swirl of her skirt* **2** [(*of*)] a twisting mass (of water, dust, etc.); EDDY: *swirls of smoke*

swirl² *v* **1** [L9] to move with twisting turns: *The water swirled about his feet* **2** [X9] to carry along while doing this: *He was swirled away on the current*

swish¹ /swɪʃ/ *v* **1** [T1;L9] to (cause to) cut through the air making a sharp whistling noise: *to swish past|the cow's swishing tail* **2** [IØ] (esp. of clothes) to make a soft sound in movement —**swish** *n*

swish² *adj infml* fashionable or costly-seeming

Swiss /swɪs/ *adj* [Wa5] of or from Switzerland —see NATIONALITY TABLE

Swiss chard /ˌ· ˈ·/ *n* CHARD

Swiss cheese /ˌ· ˈ·/ *n* [U] EMMENTALER

swiss roll /ˌ· ˈ·/ *n* a type of cake made without fat, baked in a thin piece and then rolled up with a sweet substance (JAM or cream) inside

switch¹ /swɪtʃ/ *n* **1** an apparatus for stopping an electric current from flowing, esp. one which is moved up or down with the hand —see picture at ELECTRICITY **2** an apparatus for causing a train to turn onto another railway line **3** a complete change, esp. unexpected: *a switch in the train times* **4** a small thin stick, esp. taken from a tree **5** a piece of false hair, usu. long

switch² *v* **1** [T1;L9] to change or exchange: *He switched positions/ideas.|He switched one argument for another* **2** [X9 *esp. to*] to move or change by a SWITCH¹ (1,2): *They switched the train to the other track.|He switched the lights from green to red* **3** [T1] **a** to hit with a SWITCH¹ (4): *He switched his horse to make it go faster* **b** to move quickly; TWITCH: *He switched his hand away* —see also SWITCH ON, SWITCH OFF, SWITCH OVER —**~able** *adj*

switch·back /ˈswɪtʃbæk/ *n* **1** a railway going up and down steep slopes, esp. for amusement at FAIRS³ (1) **2** anything changing direction steeply

switch·blade /ˈswɪtʃbleɪd/ *n AmE* FLICK KNIFE

switch·board /ˈswɪtʃbɔːd‖-bord/ *n* the arrangement of telephone lines, or the people who work it, on a central board for connections

switched-on /ˌ· ˈ·◂/ *adj* **1** *infml* alive to experience; AWARE and ALERT —compare SWITCH OFF (2) **2** *infml* modern and fashionable in point of view **3** *sl* under the influence of drugs

switch·gear /ˈswɪtʃgɪəʳ/ *n* [U] machinery for making electrical connections in a system

switch·man /ˈswɪtʃmən/ *n* **-men** /mən/ *AmE* POINTSMAN

switch off *v adv* **1** [T1;IØ] to turn off (esp. an electric light or apparatus) by means of a SWITCH¹ (1) —see OPEN (USAGE) **2** [IØ] *infml* to stop listening or feeling: *He just switches off when you try to talk to him*

switch on *v adv* [T1;IØ] to turn on (esp. an electric light or apparatus) by means of a SWITCH¹ (1) —see also SWITCHED-ON; see OPEN (USAGE)

switch o·ver *v adv* **1** [L9 esp. *to, from*] to change completely: *switch over to the opposite party in politics* **2** [IØ] to change from one radio or television CHANNEL to another —**switchover** /ˈswɪtʃ-əʊvəʳ/ *n*

swiv·el¹ /ˈswɪvəl/ *n* an apparatus joining 2 parts in such a way that they can turn independently

swivel² *v* **-ll-** (*AmE* **-l-**) [X9;L9: (ROUND)] to move round; PIVOT² (1): *The chair swivelled to the right when he tried it*

swiz /swɪz/ *n* [S] *BrE infml* something which cheats one's expectations; a disappointing state of affairs

swiz·zle /ˈswɪzəl/ *n* a mixed alcoholic drink

swizzle stick /ˈ·· ·/ *n* a stick or glass rod for mixing drinks

swol·len¹ /ˈswəʊlən/ *adj* **1** [B] of an increased size, often because of the presence of water or air within, which is not usually present: *Her foot was very swollen after her accident* **2** [A] too great or proud: *a swollen opinion of oneself* —**~ness** *n* [U]

swollen² *past p. of* SWELL

swollen head /ˌ·· ˈ·/ (*AmE* **swelled head**)— *n* [*usu. sing.*] *BrE* pride; a too great sense of one's own importance: *If you believe all the good things your teacher says about you, you'll get a swollen head* —**~ed** /ˌ·· ˈ··◂/ *adj* [Wa5]

swoon¹ /swuːn/ *v* [IØ] **1** *lit or humor* to experience deep effects of joy, desire, etc.: *The young girls swooned when they saw their favourite actor* **2** *now rare* to lose consciousness; FAINT² (1)

swoon² *n now rare* a FAINT³

swoop¹ /swuːp/ *v* [IØ] **1** to descend sharply, esp. in attack **2** [(*on*)] to rush on someone to attack —**~er** *n*

swoop² *n* **1** a SWOOPing action: *The police made their swoop at night and the robbers were caught* **2 at one fell swoop** all at once

swop /swɒp‖swɑp/ *v, n* SWAP

sword /sɔːd‖sord/ *n* **1** a weapon used esp. in former times with a long blade and a handle **2 at sword point** under threat of death **3 cross swords (with)** to be opposed (to), esp. in argument **4 draw one's sword** to remove the sword from its SHEATH in order to start a fight **5 put to the sword** *fml & lit* to kill

sword dance /ˈ· ·/ *n* **1** an esp. Scottish type of dance including jumping over swords laid on the ground **2** a dance in which swords are waved, hit together etc. —**sword dancer** *n*

sword·fish /ˈsɔːdˌfɪʃ‖-or-/ *n* [Wn2] a sort of large fish with a long sharp upper jaw like a sword

sword·play /ˈsɔːdpleɪ‖-or-/ *n* [U] the movement and skill used in fighting with swords

swords·man /ˈsɔːdzmən‖-or-/ *n* **-men** /mən/ a fighter with a sword, esp. a skilled one

swords·man·ship /ˈsɔːdzmənʃɪp‖-or-/ *n* [U] skill in fighting with a sword

sword·stick /ˈsɔːdˌstɪk‖-or-/ *n* a sword with a narrow blade enclosed in a walking stick

swore /swɔːʳ‖swor/ *past t. of* SWEAR

sworn[1] /swɔːn‖sworn/ *adj* [Wa5;A] complete; totally so: *sworn enemies*

sworn[2] *past p. of* SWEAR

swot[1] /swɒt‖swɑt/ (*AmE* **grind**)— *n BrE infml* a person who works (too) hard at his studies, as when trying to get good examination results and having no other interests

swot[2] (*AmE* **grind**)— *v* **-tt-** [IØ] *BrE infml* to study hard —**~ter** *n*

swot up *v adv* [T1] *BrE infml* to work hard in order to learn (a subject of one's studies), usu. before an examination

swum /swʌm/ *past p. of* SWIM

swung /swʌŋ/ *past p. & t. of* SWING

syb·a·rite /ˈsɪbəraɪt/ *n fml or lit* a person who lives in great comfort and costly surroundings

syb·a·rit·ic /ˌsɪbəˈrɪtɪk/ *adj fml or lit* of or like a SYBARITE

syc·a·more /ˈsɪkəmɔːʳ‖-mor/ *n* **1** [C] (in Europe) a type of MAPLE tree —see picture at TREE[1] **2** [C] (in America) a type of PLANE tree **3** [C] (in the lands east of the Mediterranean) a type of FIG tree **4** [U] the hard wood of any of these trees

syc·o·phant /ˈsɪkəfənt/ *n* a person who tries to please (FLATTERs) those more rich and powerful, so as to gain advantage for himself

syc·o·phan·tic /ˌsɪkəˈfæntɪk/ *adj* of or like (the behaviour of) a SYCOPHANT

syl·la·ba·ry /ˈsɪləbəri‖-beri/ *n tech* a list of signs, each representing a SYLLABLE; SYLLABIC alphabet —compare ALPHABET

syl·lab·ic /sɨ̇ˈlæbɪk/ *adj* [Wa5] having or forming one or more SYLLABLEs: *"N" is a syllabic consonant in "button"*

syl·lab·i·fy /sɨ̇ˈlæbɨ̇faɪ/ also **syl·lab·i·cate** /sɨ̇ˈlæbɨ̇keɪt/— *v* [T1] to divide (a word) into separate SYLLABLEs, esp. by special signs: *In this dictionary we use dots to syllabify words* —**-ification** /sɨ̇ˌlæbɨ̇fɨ̇ˈkeɪʃən/ *n* —**-ication** /sɨ̇ˌlæbɨ̇ˈkeɪʃən/

syl·la·ble /ˈsɪləbəl/ *n* a word or part of a word which contains a vowel sound or consonant acting as a vowel: *There are 2 syllables in "button"*

-syl·la·bled /ˈsɪləbəld/ *comb. form* having the stated type or number of SYLLABLEs

syl·la·bub /ˈsɪləbʌb/ *n* [C;U] SILLABUB

syl·la·bus /ˈsɪləbəs/ *n* **-buses** *or* **-bi** /baɪ/ **1** an arrangement of subjects for study, esp. over a period of time **2** a written account of subjects to be studied —see also TIMETABLE

syl·lo·gis·m /ˈsɪlədʒɪzəm/ *n* a reasoned argument in which there are 2 statements leading to a 3rd statement (CONCLUSION)

syl·lo·gis·tic /ˌsɪləˈdʒɪstɪk/ *adj* [Wa5] by means of or in the form of a SYLLOGISM

sylph /sɪlf/ *n* **1** (in ancient beliefs) a female spirit of the air; fairy **2** an attractively thin and graceful woman

sylph·like /ˈsɪlf-laɪk/ *adj* (of (the body of) a woman) attractively thin and graceful

syl·van, sil- /ˈsɪlvən/ *adj* [Wa5] *esp. lit* of or in woods and the country

sym- /sɪm/ also **syn-**— *prefix* together with; sharing: SYMPATHY|SYMBIOSIS

sym·bi·o·sis /ˌsɪmbiˈəʊsɨ̇s‖-baɪ-, -bi-/ *n* **-ses** /siːz/ [U;(C)] (a) state of life of 2 different living things which depend on each other for certain advantages, often with one living on the other's body

sym·bol /ˈsɪmbəl/ *n* **1** [(*of*)] a sign, shape, or object which represents a person, idea, value, etc.: *In the picture the tree is the symbol of life and the snake the symbol of evil* **2** a letter or figure which expresses a sound, number, or chemical substance: *"H_2O" is the symbol for water*

sym·bol·ic /sɪmˈbɒlɪk‖-ˈbɑ-/ also **sym·bol·i·cal** /-ɪkəl/— *adj* [(*of*)] of, as, or using a SYMBOL —**~ally** *adv* [Wa4]

sym·bol·is·m /ˈsɪmbəlɪzəm/ *n* **1** [U] the use of SYMBOLs **2** [R] (*often cap.*) a system of literature and art, esp. in 19th-century France, in which SYMBOLs (1) were used to represent real things, feelings, etc.

sym·bol·ist /ˈsɪmbəlɨ̇st/ *n* a writer or artist practising SYMBOLISM (2)

sym·bol·ize, -ise /ˈsɪmbəlaɪz/ *v* [T1] **1** to represent by one or more SYMBOLs **2** to be a SYMBOL of —**-ization** /ˌsɪmbəlaɪˈzeɪʃən‖-bələ-/ *n* [U]

sym·met·ri·cal /sɪˈmetrɪkəl/ also **sym·met·ric** /sɪˈmetrɪk/— *adj* **1** [Wa5] having both sides exactly alike —opposite **asymmetric** **2** beautifully balanced —**~ly** *adv* [Wa4]

sym·me·try /ˈsɪmɨ̇tri/ *n* [U] **1** exact likeness in size, shape, form, etc., between the opposite sides of something **2** the beauty in such a balance; pleasing balance

sym·pa·thet·ic /ˌsɪmpəˈθetɪk/ *adj* **1** [B (*to*)] of, feeling, or showing sympathy: *She was sympathetic to my aims* **2** [Wa5;A] connecting ideas or events as cause and result, because one follows the other: *sympathetic magic* **3** [B] *rare* sharing the same sort of feelings or qualities —**~ally** *adv* [Wa4]

sym·pa·thies /ˈsɪmpəθiz/ *n* [P] **1** feelings of support (esp. in the phr. **one's sympathies lie with**): *His sympathies lie with our political opponents* **2** a message of comfort in grief: *to send one's sympathies on the death of a friend's husband*

sym·pa·thize, -ise /ˈsɪmpəθaɪz/ *v* [IØ (*with*)] to feel or show sympathy or approval: *I know you feel angry, and I sympathize* —**-thizer** *n* —**-thizingly** *adv*

sym·pa·thy /ˈsɪmpəθi/ *n* [U] **1** the ability to share the feelings of another **2 a** pity: *He felt sympathy for her sufferings* **b** the expression of this: *He pressed her hand in sympathy* **3** agreement in feelings: *I have a lot of sympathy for his opinions, but I don't think his ideas will work* **4 come out in sympathy** to support workers who have stopped working (gone on STRIKE) by stopping work oneself

sym·phon·ic /sɪmˈfɒnɪk‖-ˈfɑ-/ *adj* [Wa5] of or like a SYMPHONY

sym·pho·ny /ˈsɪmfəni/ *n* a musical work for a large group of instruments (ORCHESTRA), usu. having 4 parts (MOVEMENTs)

sym·po·si·um /sɪmˈpəʊzɪəm/ *n* **-siums** *or* **-sia** /zɪə/ a meeting between scientists or those experienced in a particular subject, in order to talk about a certain area of interest

symp·tom /ˈsɪmptəm/ *n* [(*of*)] **1** an outward sign of inner change, new feelings, etc. **2** a change in body or mind which shows disease or disorder

symp·to·mat·ic /ˌsɪmptəˈmætɪk/ *adj* [Wa5; (*of*)] acting as a SYMPTOM: *The liking for small families is symptomatic of a change in our society* —**~ally** *adv* [Wa4]

syn- *prefix* SYM-: SYNCHRONIZE

syn·a·gogue /ˈsɪnəgɒg‖-gɑg/ *n* **1** [C] a place where Jews worship according to their religion; Jewish temple **2** [*the*+R] a meeting for such worship

sync, synch /sɪŋk/ *n* [U] *infml* synchronization (SYNCHRONIZE) (esp. in the phr. **out of sync**)

syn·chro·mesh /ˈsɪŋkrəʊmeʃ/ *n* [U] (the use of) a part of the GEARs in a car, which allows them to change smoothly

syn·chro·nize, -nise /ˈsɪŋkrənaɪz/ *v* **1** [T1;IØ] to

(cause to) happen at the same speed: *They synchronized their steps.|Their steps synchronized* **2** [T1] to set (clocks and watches) at the same time **3** [T1] **a** to fit (recorded sound) to the right parts of a piece of film: *to synchronize a* SOUNDTRACK **b** to do this to (a film): *a badly synchronized film* —**-nization** /ˌsɪŋkrənaɪˈzeɪʃən‖-krənə/ *n* [U]

syn·chro·tron /ˈsɪŋkrəʊtrɒn, -krə-‖-trɑn/ *n* an apparatus which makes ELECTRON*s* move very fast

syn·co·pate /ˈsɪŋkəpeɪt/ *v* [Wv5;T1] to change (the beat (RHYTHM)) of (music), by giving force to the usu. less forceful beats —**-pation** /ˌsɪŋkəˈpeɪʃən/ *n* [U]

syn·co·pe /ˈsɪŋkəpi/ *n* [U] *tech* **1** the removal of one or more sounds or letters from the middle of a word (as when "cannot" is changed to "can't") **2** the loss of consciousness in FAINTing

syn·dic /ˈsɪndɪk/ *n tech* **1** a person chosen to represent a firm or group's business interests **2** a certain sort of MAGISTRATE **3** a member of a committee in Cambridge University

syn·di·cal·is·m /ˈsɪndɪkəlɪzəm/ *n* [U] a type of TRADE UNIONism the aim of which is control of industry by the workers —**-ist** *adj, n* [Wa5]

syn·di·cate[1] /ˈsɪndɪkɨ̇t/ *n* [GC] **1** a group of businesses or people combined together for a particular purpose, esp. making money **2** an organization that sells articles to several newspapers at the same time

syn·di·cate[2] /ˈsɪndɨ̇keɪt/ *v* **1** [T1;IØ] to form into a SYNDICATE[1] (1) **2** [T1] to produce (articles) through a SYNDICATE[1] (2): *a syndicated report* —**-cation** /ˌsɪndɨ̇ˈkeɪʃən/ *n* [U]

syn·drome /ˈsɪndrəʊm/ *n* **1** a collection of medical SYMPTOM*s* (2) which represent a bodily disorder or disorder of the mind **2** any pattern of qualities, happenings, etc., typical of a general condition

syn·od /ˈsɪnəd/ *n* a meeting about church affairs to decide important matters for a whole group of churches

syn·o·nym /ˈsɪnənɪm/ *n* a word with the same or nearly the same meaning as another word in the same language: *"Sad" and "unhappy" are synonyms* —compare ANTONYM

sy·non·y·mous /sɨ̇ˈnɒnɨ̇məs‖-ˈnɑ-/ *adj* [Wa5; (*with*)] having the same or nearly the same meaning (as): *Being a soldier is synonymous with being a brave man, in his opinion* —**~ly** *adv*

sy·nop·sis /sɨ̇ˈnɒpsɨ̇s‖-ˈnɑp-/ *n* **-ses** /siːz/ a short account of something longer, esp. the story of a film, play, or book

sy·nop·tic /sɨ̇ˈnɒptɪk‖-ˈnɑp-/ *adj* [Wa5] *tech* of or as a SYNOPSIS —**~ally** *adv* [Wa4]

synoptic gos·pels /·ˌ·· ˈ··/ *n* [*the*+P] (*usu. cap.*) the accounts of Christ's life written by Matthew, Mark, and Luke (as opposed to John), which all tell very much the same story in the same way

syn·tac·tic /sɪnˈtæktɪk/ *adj* [Wa5] of or by the rules of SYNTAX —**~ally** *adv* [Wa4]

syn·tax /ˈsɪntæks/ *n* [U] the rules of grammar which are used for ordering and connecting words in a sentence

syn·the·sis /ˈsɪnθɨ̇sɨ̇s/ *n* **-ses** /siːz/ **1** [U] the combining of separate things, ideas, etc., into a complete whole —compare ANALYSIS **2** [C] something, such as a chemical material or an idea, made by combining or bringing together various parts

syn·the·size, -sise /ˈsɪnθɨ̇saɪz/ *v* [T1] **1** to make up or produce by combining parts: *No one has ever synthesized gold* —compare ANALYSE **2** to combine (parts) into something whole: *to synthesize the substances by heating them together* **3** to make (esp. something looking or acting like a natural product) by combining chemicals: *to synthesize a drug*

syn·the·siz·er, -siser /ˈsɪnθɨ̇saɪzəʳ/ *n* a person or machine that SYNTHESIZE*s* parts into a whole: *A sound synthesizer can produce the sound of a voice if the right measurements of power are given to it*

syn·thet·ic /sɪnˈθetɪk/ *adj* [Wa5] **1** of or concerning SYNTHESIS **2** produced by synthesizing (SYNTHESIZE (3)); not naturally produced; ARTIFICIAL (1) **3** (of a (type of) language) using endings on words rather than separate words, to express relationships: *Latin was a synthetic language, unlike modern English* —**~ally** *adv* [Wa4]

syph·i·lis /ˈsɪfəlɨ̇s/ *n* [U] a serious VENEREAL DISEASE (=disease of the sex organs), which can be passed on during sexual activity and also from parent to child by INHERITANCE (2)

syph·i·lit·ic /ˌsɪfəˈlɪtɪk/ *adj, n* [Wa5] (a person) suffering the effects of SYPHILIS

sy·phon /ˈsaɪfən/ *n, v* SIPHON

sy·ringe[1] /sɨ̇ˈrɪndʒ/ *n* a sort of pipe used in science and medicine, into which liquid can be drawn and from which it can be pushed out in a particular direction —see also HYPODERMIC and picture at MEDICAL

syringe[2] *v* [T1] to treat (a diseased part, wound, etc.) with liquid from a SYRINGE

syr·up /ˈsɪrəp‖ˈsɜ-, ˈsɪ-/ *n* [U] **1** sweet liquid, esp. sugar and water: *Tinned fruit usually has a lot of syrup with it* **2** TREACLE or SUGARCANE juice, used in foods **3** medicine in the form of thick sweet liquid

syr·up·y /ˈsɪrəpi‖ˈsɜ-, ˈsɪ-/ *adj* **1** like or containing SYRUP **2** too sweet in effect —compare SUGARY

sys·tem /ˈsɪstɨ̇m/ *n* **1** [C] a group of related parts working together: *the postal system* **2** [C (*of*)] an ordered set of ideas, methods, or ways of working: *a new system of elections* **3** [C] a plan: *He claims to have a special system for winning money on horse races* **4** [C] the body with its usual ways of working: *Her system was harmed by living abroad* **5** [U] orderly methods: *You need some system in your life if you want to succeed*

sys·te·mat·ic /ˌsɪstɨ̇ˈmætɪk/ *adj apprec* based on a regular plan or fixed method; thorough: *She goes from one thing to another, which is not very systematic, but natural for a small child.|The police made a systematic search of the room* —**~ally** *adv* [Wa4]

sys·te·ma·tize, -tise /ˈsɪstɨ̇mətaɪz/ *v* [T1] to arrange in a system or by a set method —**-tization** /ˌsɪstɨ̇mətaɪˈzeɪʃən‖-mətə-/ *n* [U]

sys·te·mic /sɪsˈtemɪk, -ˈtiːmɪk‖sɪsˈtemɪk/ *adj* [Wa5] *tech* closely concerned as part of a system, as of the body or a language

systems an·a·lyst /ˈ·· ˌ···/ *n* a COMPUTER worker who plans subjects for study by using sets of figures

T, t

T, t /tiː/ **T's, t's** *or* **Ts, ts** **1** the 20th letter of the English alphabet **2 to a T** *not fml* exactly; perfectly: *That dress fits Jean to a T* —see also CROSS[2] (12) **one's 't's and dot one's 'i's,** T-BONE, T-SHIRT

t. *written abbrev. for:* tense

't /t/ *pron* [Wp1] *old use & poet* it (in the phrs. **'tis, 'twas, 'twere, 'twill, 'twould**): *'Twere better you came at once, my Lord* (=It would be better that you came at once)

ta /tɑː/ *interj BrE sl* **1** thank you **2 Ta ever so** Thank you ever so much; Thank you very much

tab /tæb/ *n* **1** a small piece or narrow length of cloth, paper, etc., fixed at one or both ends to something to help in opening or handling, or as a sign of what it is, who owns it, etc.: *Hang your coat over the hook by the tab on the inside of the collar.*| *Before my first day at school my mother sewed tabs on all my clothes with my name on* **2** *infml* a bill; statement of money owed **3** *sl* TABULATOR **4 keep tabs/a tab on** *infml* to watch closely: *Remember to keep a tab on your spending*

tab·ard /ˈtæbəd, -ɑːd‖-ərd, -ɑrd/ *n* **1** a short armless outer garment with the wearer's COAT OF ARMS sewn on, worn in former times by noble soldiers (KNIGHT*s*) over their armour **2** a garment like this with a lord's COAT OF ARMS sewn on, worn by his HERALD

ta·bas·co /təˈbæskəʊ/ also **tabasco sauce** /·ˌ·· ˈ·/— *n* [U] *tdmk* a very hot-tasting liquid made from peppers, used for giving a special taste to food

tab·by /ˈtæbi/ *n* **1** a cat with greyish- or brownish-black bands and marks on its grey or brown fur **2** a female cat

tab·er·nac·le /ˈtæbənækəl‖-ər-/ *n* **1** (*often cap.*) a movable framework of wood hung with curtains, used in worship by the Jews before they settled in Palestine **2** (*often cap.*) the name used by several Christian churches for a building of worship: *the* BAPTIST *Tabernacle* **3** a small ornamental box in which the holy bread and wine that represents the body and blood of Christ are kept in certain Christian churches

ta·ble[1] /ˈteɪbəl/ *n* **1** [C] a piece of furniture with a flat top supported by one or more upright legs: *When we arrived at the restaurant we asked for a table for 2 in a corner.*|*a glass table*|*a table top* —see picture at LIVING ROOM **2** [A] made to be placed and used on such a piece of furniture: *a table lamp*| *a table (-model) radio*|*table wine* (=for drinking with a meal) **3** [C] such a piece of furniture specially made for the playing of various games: *a card table* **4** [S] the food served at a meal: *an excellent table*|*to choose something from the cold table* (*in a restaurant*) **5** [GC] the people sitting at a table: *John's clever stories kept the whole table amused* **6** [C] a printed or written collection of figures, facts, or information arranged in orderly rows across and down the page: *a bus* TIMETABLE| *There is a table of contents at the front of this dictionary* **7** [C] also **multiplication table**— a list which young children repeat to learn what number results when a number from 1 to 12 is multiplied by any of the numbers from 1 to 12: *The 3 times table starts: one* THREE *is* THREE, TWO THREE*s are* SIX, THREE THREE*s are* NINE ($1\times3=3$, $2\times3=6$, $3\times3=9$) **8** [C] TABLELAND **9 at table a** during a meal: *It is bad manners to blow your nose at table* **b** having a meal: *The President's at table now but will see you as soon as he's finished eating* **10 on the table** (of a matter before Parliament, a committee, etc.) **a** *BrE* being talked about, esp. in committee **b** *AmE* left for consideration until a later date or time **11 turn the tables (on someone)** to seize a position of strength formerly held (by someone else) when one was weak or in danger of defeat **12 under the table** *infml* **a** too drunk to act or behave properly **b** (of money) given in order to influence somebody dishonestly: *The businessmen offered me £500 under the table if I would vote against the government's plans* **13 drink someone under the table** to drink much more alcohol than someone without becoming drunk

table[2] *v* [T1] **1** *BrE* to suggest; bring forward (a matter, report, etc.) for consideration by a committee, Parliament, etc. **2** *esp. AmE* to leave (a matter, report, etc.) until a later date for consideration **3** to put (facts, figures, information, etc.) into the form of a TABLE[1] (6)

tab·leau /ˈtæbləʊ‖ˈtæbləʊ, tæˈbləʊ/ *n* **-leaux** /ləʊz/ *or* **-leaus** **1** a lifelike representation, on a stage, of a scene or event by a group of people who do not move or speak **2** an interesting or funny group of people, like a picture, suddenly formed: *George on his knees in front of Mary—what a tableau!*

ta·ble·cloth /ˈteɪbəlklɒθ‖-klɔθ/ *n* a cloth for covering a table, esp. during a meal

ta·ble d'hôte /ˌtɑːbəl ˈdəʊt (*Fr* tabl dot)/ *n* [A] *Fr* (of a complete meal of several dishes) served at a fixed price, as in a hotel or restaurant: *a very good table d'hôte meal* —compare À LA CARTE

ta·ble·land /ˈteɪbəl-lænd/ *n* [*often pl. with sing. meaning*] a large area of high flat land; PLATEAU

table lin·en /ˈ·· ˌ··/ *n* [U] tablecloths and NAPKIN*s*

table man·ners /ˈ·· ˌ··/ *n* [P] correct social behaviour at meals

ta·ble·mat /ˈteɪbəlmæt/ *n* a small mat made of material that will not let heat pass, placed under hot dishes to protect a table's surface

ta·ble·spoon /ˈteɪbəlspuːn/ *n* **1** a large spoon used for serving food from a bowl or dish onto plates **2** the amount held by this

ta·ble·spoon·ful /ˈteɪbəlˌspuːnfʊl/ *n* **-s** *or* **tablespoonsful** TABLESPOON (2)

tab·let /ˈtæblɪ̵t/ **1** a hard flat block of some substance, esp. a small round one of medicine: *The doctor told me to take 2 tablets before every meal.*|*a large tablet* (=bar) *of soap*|*chocolate*|*sucking a throat tablet for my cough* **2** a shaped flat piece of stone or metal with words cut into it, fastened to a wall to bring a particular event, person, etc., to memory **3** a thin sheet of clay or wax used as a writing surface in ancient times **4** *becoming rare* a number of sheets of writing paper fastened together along one edge: *a writing tablet* (=PAD)

table talk /ˈ·· ·/ *n* [U] informal conversation at meals

table ten·nis /ˈ·· ˌ··/ *n* [U] an indoor game played on a table by 2 or 4 players who use small BAT*s* to knock a very small hollow plastic ball to each other across a net

ta·ble·ware /ˈteɪbəlweəʳ/ *n* [U] the plates, glasses, knives, forks, spoons, etc., used in setting a table for a meal

tab·loid /ˈtæblɔɪd/ *n* a newspaper with about half the page size of an ordinary newspaper and usu.

containing many pictures and a limited amount of serious news

ta·boo[1] /tə'buː, tæ'buː/ *adj* **1** strongly forbidden by social custom, esp. for use in general conversation: *taboo words|a taboo act* **2** [Wa5] too holy or evil to be touched, named, or used: *This land is the burial place of tribal chiefs and is therefore taboo*

taboo[2] *n* **-boos** **1** [C;U] (a) strong social custom forbidding an act or the naming of certain things: *a taboo against sex before marriage* **2** [C;U] *tech* (one of the) religious, social, or magical rules forbidding the naming, use, or touching of a person or object considered too holy or evil: *That tree is under (a) taboo so people don't go near it* **3** [C] something which religion or social custom regards as forbidden: *Is sex before marriage a taboo in your country?*

ta·bor /'teɪbəʳ/ *n* a small drum beaten with the hand, usu. played along with a FIFE

tab·u·lar /'tæbjʊləʳ‖-bjə-/ *adj* [Wa5] arranged in the form of a table: *This information will be less confusing if it's produced in tabular form*

tab·u·late /'tæbjʊleɪt‖-bjə-/ *v* [T1] to arrange (facts, figures, information, etc.) in the form of a table —**-lation** /ˌtæbjʊ'leɪʃən‖-jə-/ *n* [U]

tab·u·la·tor /'tæbjʊleɪtəʳ‖-bjə-/ also (*sl*) **tab**— *n* an apparatus on a TYPEWRITER that moves the paper along a set number of spaces at a time, used for setting out matter in the form of a table

ta·cit /'tæsɨt/ *adj* [Wa5;A;(B)] expressed or understood without being put into words; not spoken or written: *a tacit agreement* —**~ly** *adv*

ta·ci·turn /'tæsɨtɜːn‖-ɜrn/ *adj fml* speaking little; usually silent; not liking to say a lot —**~ity** /ˌtæsɨ'tɜːnɨti‖-'ɜr-/ *n* [U] —**~ly** /'tæsɨtɜːnli‖-ɜr-/ *adv*

tack[1] /tæk/ *n* **1** [C] a small nail with a sharp point and flat head used for fastening light objects and materials to a solid surface: *hammered a tack into the wall and hung a small picture from it* **2** [C;U] the direction of a sailing ship as shown by the position of its sails: *The captain ordered a change of tack* **3** [C] a change in a sailing ship's direction made by changing the position of its sails **4** [C;U] a course of action: *Since they had failed to persuade the unions, the government tried the new tack of forcing them to agree* **5** [C] a long loose stitch used for fastening pieces of cloth together until they can be sewn together properly: *to put a few tacks in* —see also TACK[2] (3) **6 on the right/wrong tack** following the right/wrong course of action —see also HARD TACK, **get down to** BRASS TACKS

tack[2] *v* **1** [T1 (DOWN)] to fasten (something) to a solid surface with a TACK[1] (1): *tacked a notice to the board|tacked down the lid of the box* **2** [T1;IØ] to change the course of (a sailing ship) **3** [T1] to sew (cloth) with long loose straight stitches: *use a tacking stitch*

tack·i·ness /'tækinɨs/ *n* [U] **1** the quality of being TACKY[1] **2** the quality of being TACKY[2]

tack·le[1] /'tækəl/ *n* **1** [U] the apparatus used in a sport, such as the rod, line, hooks, etc., used in fishing: *Don't forget to bring your sports tackle tomorrow!* **2** [C;U] (a system of) ropes and wheels (PULLEYS) for working a ship's sails, raising heavy weights, etc. **3** [C] (in football) an act of taking the ball from an opponent **4** [C] (in RUGBY) an act of stopping the opponent carrying the ball by seizing him and bringing him down

tackle[2] *v* **1** [T1;IØ] (in football) to take the ball away from (an opponent) **2** [T1;IØ] (in RUGBY) to take the ball by seizing and bringing down (an opponent) **3** [T1] *not fml* **a** to deal with (a matter): *The question set by the teacher was so difficult that the pupils didn't know how to tackle it* **b** to deal with (a person) by speaking openly and forcefully: *If Bill's late again I'll have to tackle him about it* **4** [T1] *sl* to seize and attack: *The robber tried to run away but a man ran and tackled him*

tack on *v adv* [T1 (*to*)] *infml* to add (something) to the end of a speech, book, etc.

tack·y[1] /'tæki/ *adj* [Wa1] sticky: *The paint on the door is still tacky so don't touch it*

tacky[2] *adj* [Wa1] *AmE sl* SHABBY

tact /tækt/ *n* [U] the ability to do or say the right thing at the right time; skill in handling people without causing offence: *A minister of foreign affairs who lacks tact is a dangerous man* —**~ful** *adj* —**~fully** *adv* —**~less** *adj* —**~lessly** *adv* —**~lessness** *n* [U]

tac·tic /'tæktɪk/ *n* [*usu. pl.*] a means of getting a desired result: *Violent tactics are unlikely to help*

tac·tic·al /'tæktɪkəl/ *adj* [Wa5] **1** of or related to TACTICS (1): *Fred made a tactical decision to threaten to leave the company, in the hope that they would then offer him a better job* **2** of or related to TACTICS: *a tactical movement of forces|a general of great tactical skill* —**~ly** *adv* [Wa4]

tac·ti·cian /tæk'tɪʃən/ *n* a person skilled in TACTICS

tac·tics /'tæktɪks/ *n* [GU] **1** the art of arranging military forces for battle and moving them during battle: *the tactics of drawing an enemy into a trap* **2** the art of using existing means to get a desired result: *If you want to be a successful politician you must make yourself able in tactics* —compare STRATEGY

tac·tile /'tæktaɪl‖'tæktl/ *adj tech* **1** that can be felt by touch; experienced by touch: *a tactile sensation* **2** [Wa5] of or related to the sense of touch: *tactile organs*

tac·tu·al /'tæktʃʊəl/ *adj* [Wa5] *tech* TACTILE (2)

tad·pole /'tædpəʊl/ *n* a small black water creature with a long tail and round head that slowly develops limbs and loses its tail to become a fully-grown FROG or TOAD —see picture at AMPHIBIAN

taf·fe·ta /'tæfɨtə/ *n* thin shiny smooth stiff cloth made from silk, nylon, etc.: *a taffeta dress*

taff·rail /'tæfreɪl/ *n tech* the rail around the STERN (=back end) of a ship or boat

taf·fy /'tæfi/ *n* [U] *AmE* TOFFEE

Taffy *n* [C;N] *BrE sl* a Welshman

tag[1] /tæg/ *n* **1** a small narrow length of paper, material, etc., fixed to something to show what it is, who owns it, details about it, etc.: *a name tag|a price tag* **2** a metal or plastic point at the end of a cord, SHOELACE, etc. **3** a phrase or sentence spoken (too) often, esp. one in Latin; CLICHÉ **4** a loosely hanging piece of torn cloth or any other untidy end **5** a small mass of hair stuck together **6** also **question tag**— a phrase such as "isn't it", "won't it", etc., added to the end of a sentence to make it a question or ask for agreement

tag[2] *v* **-gg-** **1** [T1] to fasten a TAG[1] (1) to (something): *Tag the bottles now or we'll forget which is which* **2** [X9] to put (someone) into a kind or class: *Ever since she failed her examination she's been tagged as stupid* **3** [X9 esp. ON, *onto, to*] to fix (something) onto something else: *The speaker tagged a request for more money to the end of his talk* **4** [L9 (ALONG) esp. *behind*] to follow closely: *a baby elephant tagging along behind its mother* **5** [L9 esp. ALONG, ON, *to*] *infml* to go with someone without being invited: *What are you tagging along for? You weren't invited!*

tag[3] also **tick, tig, he**— *n* [U] a children's game in which one player chases the others until he touches one of them, who in turn becomes the person who chases

tail[1] /teɪl/ *n* **1** [C] the movable long growth at the back of a creature's body: *a dog's tail|Cut the tails off before you cook the fish* —see pictures at CAT and DOG **2** [C] anything like this in appearance, shape, or position: *the tails of a coat|a* COMET*'s tail* **3** [C] *sl* BACKSIDE: *sat down hard on his tail* **4** [C *usu. sing.*] the back, last, or lowest part of various things: *the tail of a plane/of the procession* **5** [C] the side of a coin which does not bear the head of a ruler (esp. in the phr. **heads or tails**) —compare HEAD¹ (6) **6** [C] *sl* a person employed to watch and follow someone, esp. a criminal: *The police have got a tail on me so they know my every move* **7** [U] *sl* **a** women considered as sexual objects (esp. in the phrs. **a bit/piece of tail** (=a woman)) **b** *taboo* the act of having sex **8 turn tail** to run away **9 with one's tail between one's legs** in a state of complete defeat —see also **not be able to make** HEAD¹ (32) **or tail of** —**~less** *adj* [Wa5]

tail² *v* [T1] *infml* **1** to follow closely behind (someone): *The police have been tailing me. They know I'm here* **2** to cut the stems off the bottom of (berries) (esp. in the phr. **top and tail**)

tail·back /ˈteɪlbæk/ *n* a line of traffic covering a certain distance on the road, esp. when the vehicle in front has been stopped by an accident or because the road is blocked

tail·board /ˈteɪlbɔːd‖-bord/ *AmE* **tail·gate** /ˈteɪl-geɪt/— *n* the board at the back of a cart or large vehicle that can be let down or removed to make loading and unloading easier

tail·coat /teɪlˈkəʊt, ˈteɪlkəʊt/ *n* a man's formal evening coat with a long shaped back divided into 2 below the waist

-tailed /teɪld/ *comb. form* having a tail of the stated sort: *a curly-tailed pig*

tail end /ˌ· ˈ·/ *n* [(*of*) *usu. sing.*] the last part: *the tail end of the procession|the tail end of summer*

tail·light /ˈteɪl-laɪt/ *n* a red light at the back of a vehicle so that it can be seen in the dark

tail off also **tail a·way**— *v adv* [I∅] to lessen in quantity, strength, or quality: *His voice tailed off as his courage failed*

tai·lor¹ /ˈteɪləʳ/ *n* a person who makes outer garments to order, esp. for men

tailor² *v* **1** [I∅;T1] to make (an outer garment) by cutting and sewing cloth, esp. fitting closely to the person's measurements **2** [X9] to prepare for a special purpose: *We can tailor our insurance to meet your special needs*

tailor-made /ˌ·· ˈ·ˈ/ *adj* [Wa5] **1** (of clothes) made specially for the buyer with special attention paid to getting an exact fit: *a tailor-made suit* —compare READY-MADE **2** [(*for*)] exactly suited to a special need: *John's tailor-made for this job*

tail·piece /ˈteɪlpiːs/ *n* **1** an ornamental picture or pattern printed in the empty space left at the end of a CHAPTER¹ (1) or the bottom of a page **2** any part added at the end: *He added a tailpiece describing what happened after the end of the war*

tails /teɪlz/ *n* [P] a TAILCOAT: *For a formal occasion at the palace you must wear tails*

tail·spin /ˈteɪlˌspɪn/ *n* an uncontrolled spinning fall by a plane, in which the tail spins in a wider circle than the front

tail·wind /ˈteɪlˌwɪnd/ *n* a wind coming from behind

taint¹ /teɪnt/ *v* [Wv5;T1] **1** to touch or infect as with something undesirable; make morally impure: *a character tainted with dishonesty|tainted money* **2** to spoil; make unfit for use: *The warm weather's tainted this meat*

taint² *n* [S;U: (*of*] (a) slight touch of decay, infection, or bad or immoral influence: *the taint of disloyalty|a taint of madness in the family|Is this meat free from taint?* —**~less** *adj* [Wa5]

take¹ /teɪk/ *v* **took** /tʊk/, **taken** /ˈteɪkən/ **1** [T1] to get possession of; gain; seize; win: *Now that the enemy forces have taken the airport the end of the war is nearer.|500 prisoners were taken in the battle.|John took second place in the race.|The general swore to take back the fort whatever the cost* **2** [T1] to hold with the hands; GRASP: *He took her arm and led her across the road.|The murderer took the woman by the throat and killed her.|He took a spade and planted the potatoes* **3** [T1] to borrow or use without asking permission or by mistake: *Someone took my hat by mistake so I had to wear theirs to go home in.|If you take things without asking the owner's permission then you're a thief* **4** [T1] to have room for; hold: *This bottle takes a litre.|How much petrol will the car take?* **5** [T1 (*to*)] to carry from one place to another: *Don't forget to take your bag with you.|We usually take the children to school in the car* —see BRING (USAGE) **6** [D1 (*to*)] to carry (to a person): *Take him another cup of tea* **7** [T1] to use as a way of getting from one place to another: *My husband goes to work on the bus but takes the train coming home* **8** [T1] to obtain; receive: *The princess takes the title of queen when she marries the king* **9** [T1] to buy or pay to have: *We decided to take a flat in London because of my husband's job.|We take 2 newspapers every morning* **10** [T1] to introduce into the body by swallowing, eating, drinking, breathing, etc.: *The doctor gave me some medicine to take for my cold.|It should be against the law to take dangerous drugs.|Every morning I open the window and take a breath of fresh air* **11** [T1] to have: *Mr Jones is taking a walk at present but should be back soon.|(esp. AmE) I usually take a bath in the mornings.|How soon does the medicine take effect?* —see HAVE (USAGE) **12** [T1] to find out by testing, measuring, etc.: *Nurse, take this man's temperature please* **13** [X9 esp. AWAY, *from*] to remove; subtract: *What do you get if you take 5 from 12?|Take 10 away and what do you have left?* **14** [T1] to choose: *Take any card from my hand!* **15** [T1] to have or pretend to have for oneself; accept; ASSUME (2,3): *Why should you take all the praise for our success?* **16** [T1] to perform; do: *The government took these measures to reduce unemployment.|a difficult course to take* **17** [T1] to swear (an OATH) **18** [X9;V3] to understand: *The girl took his smile to mean yes/took it for yes/took it as meaning yes* **19** [X9] to surprise; come upon suddenly: *My father's death took us all by surprise* **20** [T1 *often pass.* +*by, with*] to attract; delight: *The child was really taken by the little dog.|I was quite taken with that young man.|The little house took my fancy* **21** [T1] to study as a course: *Did you take history at school?* **22** [D1 (*for*);L1] to last; need (a period of time): *The journey from York to London takes 2 hours.|It took me 4 hours to drive from here to Edinburgh.|How long does the flight take?* —compare TAKE UP (5) **23** [T1] to need: *It takes a thief to know a thief.|That takes some believing* (=is hard to believe) **24** [D1 (*for*);T1] to cost: *It takes a lot of money to buy a house as big as that.|It took £12 for me to buy that coat/took me £12 to buy that coat* **25** [T1 (UP)] to use; OCCUPY (3,4): *Take a seat and make yourself comfortable.|We can't have a table in here because it takes up too much space* **26** [T1] to need for the best result; accept: *What sort of film does this camera take?|This machine only takes 5-pence coins* **27** [T1] (in grammar) to govern: *The verb "kill" takes a direct object* **28** [T1] to make by photography: *I had my picture taken this morning* **29** [T1] to accept and use: *You must take every chance that life offers.|Take my advice and tell the police exactly what happened* **30** [T1] to experience; have (a certain feeling): *Why do you always* *take offence when I make suggestions?* **31** [X9] to act towards in a certain way: *I always take your suggestions seriously* **32** [IØ] to have an intended effect; work: *The colour took and her white dress is now red.|Did the* VACCINATION *take?* **33** [L7] *esp. dial* to become: *John took sick and had to lie down* **34** [X7 *pass.*] to cause to become: *John was taken ill this morning so he stayed off work* **35** [T1 (DOWN)] to write down: *The policeman took my name and address down.|Take a letter, Miss Jones* **36** [X9 esp. *from*] to copy: *You took your article directly out of my book* **37** [T1 *usu. pass.*] *euph* to remove by death: *I knew my husband was ill but I didn't think he'd be taken so soon* **38** [X9] to effect a change in the person or condition of (someone): *His natural ability took him to the top* **39** [T1] to attempt to jump or get over or round (a wall, fence, stream, etc.): *The horse would have won the race if it had taken that last fence well* **40** [T1] (esp. of a man) to have sex with: *"Take me!" she breathed softly* **41** [IØ;T1] (of fish) to bite (the hook of a fisherman): *The fish don't seem to be taking today* **42** [T1] to accept responsibility for: *to take lodgers/private pupils/paying guests|Miss Jones is away today, so will you take her class for her?* **43** [T1] to accept as payment; receive: *I won't take less than £500 for my car* **44 be able to take (something)** to be able to face (something painful, sad, etc.) without weakening: *I don't think I can take any more bad news* **45 take a/one's chance (on something)** to attempt something though conscious of the possibility of failure: *I don't think I'll get the job but I'm willing to take a/my chance and ask for it* **46 take it from me** also **take my word** —believe me when I say: *You can take it from me that there won't be an election this year.|She'll never marry anyone else; take it from me* **47 take one's time (over) a** to use as much time as is necessary; not hurry **b** to take more time than is reasonable: *The workmen seem to be taking their time over building this road!* **48 take (something) as read** to agree without the need of hearing, reading, talking about, etc.: *We can take it as read that if you're well enough to go to the theatre you're well enough to go to work.|We didn't want to hear the secretary's report so we took it as read* **49 take to one's heels/legs** to run away at once —see also TAKE ABACK, TAKE AFTER, TAKE APART, TAKE AWAY FROM, TAKE BACK, TAKE DOWN, TAKE FOR, TAKE IN, TAKE OFF, TAKE ON, TAKE OUT, TAKE OUT ON, TAKE OVER, TAKE TO, TAKE UP, TAKE UP WITH —**taker** *n*

take[2] *n* **1** a scene that has been or is to be photographed for a moving picture: *6 takes before the director was satisfied* **2** [*usu. sing.*] the amount of money taken by a business, thief, etc. **3** [*usu. sing.*] a share of this: *My friend wants a bigger take of the money we stole*

take a·back *v adv* [T1 *often pass.*] to surprise and confuse (someone): *The price of the tickets rather took me aback*

take af·ter *v prep* [Wv6;T1] **1** to look or behave like (an older relative): *Mary really takes after her mother; she has the same eyes, nose, and hair* **2** *AmE* to chase

take a·part *v adv* [T1] **1** to separate (a small machine, clock, etc.) into pieces: *Take the watch apart and see if you can see what's wrong with it* —compare TAKE DOWN **2** *infml* to scold severely

take·a·way /ˈteɪkəweɪ/ (*AmE* **carryout**)— *adj, n* [Wa5;A;C] *BrE* (from) a shop where cooked meals are bought and taken away to be eaten: *I don't want to cook tonight so I think I'll go and get a meal from the takeaway.|a takeaway meal*

take a·way from *v adv prep* [T1] to lessen the effect of (something good or desirable): *His refusal to accept the prize does not take away from his success in winning it* —compare DETRACT FROM

take back *v adv* [T1] **1** to admit that one was wrong in (what one said); make as if (something) were never said: *After all your recent kindness I'd like to take back all the nasty things I said about you* —compare WITHDRAW (5) **2** to agree to receive back (goods which do not fit or are broken, someone who has run away, etc.): *This shop promises to take back any goods that don't satisfy the person who buys them.|I'd not take my husband back if he ever left me*

take down *v adv* [T1] to separate (a large machine or article) into pieces: *to take down a dangerous bridge* —compare TAKE APART; see also TAKE[1] (35), **take somebody down a** PEG **(or two)**

take for *v prep* [X1] **1** to regard (someone) as being (something); consider: *Why do you take me for a fool?|I'm not going to help you steal a car; what do you take me for?* (=I am not dishonest, even if you think I am) **2** to mistake (someone) for (someone else): *I took you for Mrs Brown when I saw you this morning. You look just like her* —see also **take someone for a** RIDE[2] (4), **take something/someone for** GRANT**ed**

take-home pay /·ˈ··/ *n* [U] pay left after all taxes, union payments, etc., have been paid

take in *v adv* **1** [T1] to receive and provide lodgings for (a person): *The kind old lady offered to take in the poor homeless stranger* **2** [T1] to accept (work) to be done in the home: *My wife makes £10 a week by taking in sewing* **3** [T1] to include: *The British Empire once took in a quarter of the world* **4** [T1] to reduce the size of (a garment, the sail of a ship, etc.): *Can you take in this dress for me? It's too loose round the waist* —compare LET OUT (1) **5** [T1,6a,b] to understand: *It took me a long time to take in what you were saying/how to do it* **6** [T1] *not fml* to deceive; cheat: *My mother was taken in by the businessman's offers of marriage and stupidly gave him most of her money* **7** [T1] to notice or see (something) fully: *It was amusing to see his surprise as he took in the scene* **8** [T1] to believe (something false): *Her husband takes in all her lies* —see also **take in** HAND[1] (43), **take something in one's** STRIDE, **take into** CARE[1] (10), **take the** LAW (16) **into one's own hands**

take·off /ˈteɪk-ɒf‖-ɔf/ *n* **1** [C;U] the beginning of a flight, when a plane, SPACECRAFT, etc., rises from the surface of the earth: *a smooth takeoff|We expect takeoff to be at 12 o'clock* **2** [C] *infml* a copy of someone's typical behaviour, usu. done to amuse others: *a funny takeoff of leading politicians*

take off *v adv* **1** [T1] to remove (a garment): *Take your coat off* —opposite **put on** **2** [T1] *infml* to copy (someone, esp. his speech or manners): *The actor made everyone laugh by taking off the members of the royal family* —compare IMPERSONATE, MIMIC[3] (1) **3** [IØ] (of a plane, SPACECRAFT, etc.) to rise into the air at the beginning of a flight **4** [T1] to remove (a train, bus, etc.) from public use **5** [IØ] to leave the ground in jumping —see also **take one's** HAT **off to someone, take one's** MIND[1] (29) **off, take the** EDGE **off, take one's** EYES **off, take the** GILT **off the gingerbread**

take on *v adv* **1** [T1] to start to employ: *We've decided to take on a new clerk in the accounts department* **2** [T1a] to begin to have (a quality or appearance): *These insects can take on the colour of their surroundings* **3** [T1] to start a quarrel or fight with: *Why don't you take on someone your own size?|Now that the government's defeated the employers it can take on the unions* **4** [T1] to accept (work, responsibility, etc.): *My doctor says I'm too tired and has advised me not to take any more work* on **5** [L9] *becoming rare* to be excited and worried: *Don't take on so; there's nothing to worry about* **6** [I∅] to become fashionable, popular, etc.: *The fashion for long skirts didn't take on for some time*

take out *v adv* [T1] **1** to remove from inside: *to have a tooth taken out* **2** to go somewhere with (a person): *My wife's taking me out to the theatre tonight.|She's too young to be taken out by boys* **3** to obtain officially or formally; get: *Have you taken out insurance on your possessions?* **4** *tech* to destroy or cause to be ineffective: *We took the factory out by bombing it.|The Italian striker was successfully taken out by the England defence, who kept getting the ball away from him* **5 take someone out of himself** to amuse or interest someone so that cares and worries are forgotten **6 take it out of someone** *infml* to use all the strength of someone: *The long journey seems to have taken it out of mother* —see also **take a** LEAF **out of someone's book, take the wind out of someone's** SAILS[1] (7)

take out on *v adv prep* [D1] to express (one's feelings) by making (someone else) suffer: *Why do you always take your annoyance out on me? It's not my fault you're angry.|I don't think it's fair that you should come home after a bad day at work and take it out on me and the children*

take·o·ver /ˈteɪkˌəʊvəʳ/ *n* an act of gaining control, esp. over a business company by buying most of the shares

take o·ver *v adv* [I∅;T1] to gain control over and responsibility for (someone or something): *Who do you think will take over now that the governor has been dismissed?|Our firm took over 2 fruit packing companies last year* —compare OVERTAKE

take to *v prep* **1** [T1] to be kind or favourable to; like: *Jean took to Paul as soon as they met* **2** [T1,4] to begin as a practice, habit, etc.: *John's taken to drinking too much lately* **3** [T1] to go for rest, hiding, escape, etc.: *Father's got a cold so has taken to his bed.|The criminal took to the woods to escape from the police* —see also **take to the** ROAD, **take someone to** TASK

take up *v adv* **1** [T1,4] to begin to spend time doing (something); interest oneself in: *John took up art while at school.|Alfred's just taken up sailing* **2** [T1] to continue: *I'll take up the story where I finished yesterday* **3** [T1 (*with*)] to raise consideration of (a matter): *I'd like to take Paul's case up with a lawyer* **4** [T1 (*on*)] to be willing to accept the offer of (a person) if made again in the future: *I can't come out with you tonight but I'd like to take you up on your offer another time* **5** [L1] (of activities or events) to fill (time), esp. unpleasantly: *Visiting grandfather will take up the whole of Sunday* **6** [T1] (of things) to collect and become filled with: *plants taking up water* **7 taken up (with)** very interested (in): *The government can't do anything about unemployment because it's too taken up with trying to keep prices down* —see also **take up** RESIDENCE, **take up the** CUDGELS **for**

take up with *v adv prep* [T1] to become friendly with

tak·ing /ˈteɪkɪŋ/ *adj esp. infml* attractive

tak·ings /ˈteɪkɪŋz/ *n* [P] receipts of money, esp. by a shop

talc /tælk/ *n* [U] **1** a soft smooth greenish grey mineral that feels like soap, used in making paints, plastics, and various body powders **2** TALCUM POWDER

tal·cum pow·der /ˈtælkəm ˌpaʊdəʳ/ also **talc powder** /ˈ· ˌ··/— *n* [U] a very fine powder of crushed TALC (1) made to have a pleasant smell, spread over the body to make it smell nice and feel smooth and dry

tale /teɪl/ *n* **1** a story of imaginary events: *a tale about good fairies|tales of adventure* **2** a lie; false story: *The wicked little girl was always telling her mother tales* **3** a report of events: *On returning from the war he told us tales of fear and sadness* **4** a piece of news, esp. when false or intended to hurt: *It was nasty of you to go round telling tales you knew weren't true*

tale·bear·er /ˈteɪlˌbeərəʳ/ also **tale·tell·er** /ˈteɪlˌteləʳ/— *n* a person who nastily spreads false or unkind pieces of news around

tal·ent /ˈtælənt/ *n* **1** [C;U: (*for*)] (a) special natural or learnt ability or skill, esp. of a high quality: *a talent for drawing|musical/artistic talent* —see GENIUS (USAGE) **2** [U] people of such ability: *There was a lack of local talent, so the acting club hired an actor from London to take the main part* **3** [GU] *sl* sexually attractive women: *We stood on the corner waiting for any talent that might pass by* **4** [C] an ancient coin or weight of various values, used among the Greeks, Romans, etc.: *50 talents of silver*

tal·ent·ed /ˈtæləntɪ̣d/ *adj* having or showing TALENT (1): *a very talented actor*

talent scout /ˈ·· ·/ *n* SCOUT[2] (3)

tal·is·man /ˈtælɪ̣zmən/ *n* **-s** an object often marked with special magical signs or words and believed to give unusual power or protection

talk[1] /tɔːk/ *v* **1** [I∅] to use human words; have the power of speech; produce words; speak: *Human beings can talk; animals can't* **2** [I∅ (*to/with* and/or *about*)] to make words, thoughts, ideas, etc., known by means of speech: *I'm talking seriously now!|When I'm talking to your father I expect you to be quiet.|There's an important matter I want to talk about with you* **3** [I∅] to copy human speech: *Have you taught your pet bird to talk?* **4** [I∅] to express thoughts as if by speech: *People who cannot speak or hear can talk by using signs* **5** [T1] to speak about: *We talked music all night* **6** [T1] to express in words: *Talk sense!* **7** [T1] to be able to speak (a language): *Do you talk French?* **8** [I∅] to give information, usu. unwillingly: *Have you persuaded the prisoners to talk yet?* **9** [I∅] to speak about other people's actions and private lives: *Don't do anything foolish. You know how people talk* **10 talk big** *infml* to speak with too much pride in oneself or one's actions; make oneself or one's actions seem more important than they are —see also TALK DOWN, TALK DOWN TO, TALK INTO, TALK OUT, TALK OUT OF, TALK OVER, TALK ROUND, **talk 19 to the** DOZEN, **talk** SHOP[1] (6), **talking through one's** HAT, **talk** TURKEY —see SAY (USAGE)

talk[2] *n* **1** [U] a particular way of speech or conversation: *baby talk* **2** [C] a conversation: *I met Mrs Jones at the shops and had a long talk with her* **3** [C (*on, about*)] an informal speech: *The teacher gave us a talk on sexual responsibility in the modern world* **4** [*the*+R9 esp. *of*] a subject of conversation: *Her sudden marriage is the talk of the street* **5** [U] empty or meaningless speech: *His threats were just talk. Don't worry!* **6** [U] sounds that are like human speech: *the talk of monkeys* —see also TALKS

talk·a·tive /ˈtɔːkətɪv/ *adj* liking to talk a lot —**~ness** *n* [U]

talk down *v adv* [T1] **1** to guide (a plane) safely to the ground when the pilot is unable to see well, by giving instructions by radio **2** *AmE* to make (someone speaking) silent by argument or loud speech

talk down to *v adv prep* [T1] to speak to (someone) in a way that makes one seem of higher rank or greater importance

talk·er /ˈtɔːkəʳ/ *n* **1** [C9] a person who talks: *a good/bad/poor talker|What a talker that man is!* **2**

[C] a bird that talks: *Which pet bird makes the best talker?*

talk·ie /ˈtɔːki/ *n old use infml* a moving picture with sounds and words

talking point /ˈ·· ·/ *n* a subject of argument or conversation

talking-to /ˈ·· ·/ *n* **-tos** *infml* a scolding

talk in·to *v prep* [V4b;D1] to persuade (someone) to do (something): *My wife talked me into buying her a new car* —compare TALK OUT OF

talk out *v adv* [T1] **1** to consider (a matter) thoroughly so that nothing new or useful can be said **2** to settle by talking: *Unions and employers usually try to talk out their differences before taking action against each other* **3** *BrE* to prevent (a law) from being accepted by talking in Parliament until there is no time left for voting

talk out of *v adv prep* [V4b;D1] **1** to persuade (someone) not to do (something): *The policeman talked the man out of jumping from the top of the building* —compare TALK INTO **2 talk one's way out of** to avoid or escape from (trouble) by talking: *The police asked me about the crime, but I talked my way out of it*

talk o·ver *v adv* [T1 (*with*)] **1** to consider (something) thoroughly; speak about: *Can I see you a moment? I've an important matter to talk over*

talk round[1] *v adv* [T1b (*to*)] to persuade (someone)

talk round[2] *v prep* [T1] to avoid speaking directly about (a matter)

talks /tɔːks/ *n* [P] a formal exchange of opinions and views: *The 2 presidents met in Paris for talks.|peace talks*

tall /tɔːl/ *adj* [Wa1] **1** [B] having a greater than average height: *Paul's the tallest man I've ever seen.|a tall building|a tall tree* **2** [E] having the stated height: *4 feet tall* —see HIGH (USAGE) —**~ish** *adj* [Wa5] —**~ness** *n* [U]

tall·boy /ˈtɔːlbɔɪ/ (*AmE* **highboy**)— *n BrE* a tall piece of wooden furniture containing several drawers

tall or·der /ˌ· ˈ··/ *n* a request that is unreasonably difficult to perform

tal·low /ˈtæləʊ/ *n* [U] hard animal fat used for making candles

tall sto·ry /ˌ· ˈ··/ also **tall tale** /ˌ· ˈ·/— *n* a story that is difficult to believe

tal·ly[1] /ˈtæli/ *n* **1** (in former times) a stick with cuts (NOTCHES) made in it to show an amount of money owed, a quantity of goods delivered, etc. **2** anything on which an account, record of points, or SCORE is kept **3** *not fml* an account; record of points; SCORE: *England's tally at the moment is 15 points, against Scotland's 11* **4** a ticket fastened to something to show what it is, who owns it, etc.; LABEL; TAG

tally[2] *v* [T1;IØ (*with*)] **1** to (cause to) agree or equal exactly: *We must tally our stories if we want the police to believe us.|Your figures don't tally with mine* **2** to calculate (points won, a total, an account, etc.); count

tal·ly·ho /ˌtæliˈhəʊ/ *interj* (an expression shouted by a fox hunter when he sees the fox)

tal·ly·man /ˈtælimən/ *n* **-men** /mən/ *BrE* **1** a person who sells cheap goods and collects weekly or monthly payments for them **2** a person who calculates totals or points won (TALLY[1] (3))

Tal·mud /ˈtælmʊd/ *n* [*the*+R] the body of Jewish law concerned with religious and nonreligious life

tal·on /ˈtælən/ *n* a sharp powerful curved nail on the feet of some hunting birds, used for seizing animals for food —see picture at PREY[1]

ta·ma·le /təˈmɑːli/ *n* [U] a strong-tasting Mexican dish made of corn and small pieces of meat mixed with crushed peppers, wrapped in corn leaves and cooked in steam

tam·a·rind /ˈtæmərɨnd/ *n* **1** [C] a type of tropical tree grown for its fruit, pleasant-smelling flowers, and wood **2** [U] the fruit of this tree eaten as food or crushed to make a cool drink

tam·a·risk /ˈtæmərɪsk/ *n* a type of bush or small tree with featherlike branches and masses of pink flowers, that grows esp. on sandy soils near the sea in warm areas

tam·bour /ˈtæmbʊəʳ/ *n* **1** a small circular frame made from 2 circles of wood, one of which fits inside the other to hold cloth firmly in place while patterns are being sewn on it **2** a drum **3** a rolling top or front for a piece of furniture (such as a desk), made from long narrow pieces of wood stuck onto strong cloth

tam·bou·rine /ˌtæmbəˈriːn/ *n* a circular wooden or metal frame with a skin stretched over and small metal plates fastened round the edge, held in one hand and beaten against the other hand or the body to produce a musical sound —see picture at PERCUSSION

tame[1] /teɪm/ *adj* [Wa1] **1** gentle and unafraid; not fierce; trained to live with man: *a tame lion/duck/fox* **2** not wild or uncontrollable; not dangerous **3** *infml* unexciting; uninteresting: *a tame book/play/article|The game was so tame that we left early* **4** spiritless: *a tame little man* —**~ly** *adv* —**~ness** *n* [U]

tame[2] *v* [T1] **1** to train (a wild, uncontrollable, or fierce animal) to be gentle and unafraid in man's presence **2** to make (something troublesome, dangerous, or uncontrollable) useful and safe: *One day man will tame nature* —**tamable** *or* **tameable** *adj* —**tamer** *n*

Tam·ma·ny /ˈtæməni/ *adj* [Wa5;A] *esp. AmE* of or related to an organization trying to win or keep political power in a city by dishonest and unfair methods

tam-o'-shan·ter /ˌtæm ə ˈʃæntəʳ/ also **tam·my** /ˈtæmi/— *n* a tight-fitting flat-topped hat of Scottish origin, usu. made from soft cloth

tamp /tæmp/ *v* **1** [X9, esp. DOWN] to pack tightly or force down by repeated light blows **2** [T1] to cover (an explosive in a hole) with sand, clay, etc., to make the explosion stronger

tam·per with /ˈtæmpəʳ/ *v prep* [T1] to make changes in (something) without official permission: *After the accident it was found that the car had been tampered with*

tam·pon /ˈtæmpɒn‖-pɑn/ *n* a mass of cotton or like material fitted into a woman's sex organ to take in (ABSORB) the monthly bleeding

tan[1] /tæn/ *v* **-nn-** **1** [T1] to change (animal skin) into leather by treating with TANNIN **2** [IØ;T1] to (cause to) become brown, esp. by sunlight: *Janet quickly tanned to a golden brown under the hot Spanish sun.|This special chemical liquid will tan you as you sleep* **3** [T1] *infml* to beat (someone) severely **4 tan someone's hide** also **tan the hide off someone**—*infml* to beat someone severely

tan[2] *n* **1** [U] a variable colour averaging a yellowish brown **2** [C] the brown colour given to the skin by sunlight: *All the people who went abroad for their holidays came back with nice tans*

tan[3] *adj* [Wa1] having a yellowish brown colour: *tan shoes*

tan[4] *abbrev. for:* TANGENT (2)

tan·dem[1] /ˈtændəm/ *n* a bicycle built for 2 riders sitting one behind the other

tandem[2] *adv* [Wa5] (of 2 people riding a bicycle, horses pulling a carriage, etc.) arranged one behind the other

tang /tæŋ/ *n* [*usu. sing.*] a strong taste or smell

special to something: *the tang of the sea air* —**~y** *adj* [Wa1]

tan·gent /ˈtændʒənt/ *n* **1** a straight line touching the edge of a curve but not cutting across it —see picture at GEOMETRY **2** [(*of*)] *tech* the FRACTION (2) calculated for an angle by dividing the lengths of the sides opposite and next to it in a right-angled TRIANGLE —see picture at TRIGONOMETRY **3 go/fly off at a tangent** *infml* to change suddenly from one course of action, thought, etc., to another

tan·gen·tial /tænˈdʒenʃəl/ *adj* [Wa5] **1** *tech* related to or having the nature of a TANGENT (1): *After you've drawn the circle, draw a line tangential to it* **2** *fml* moving or going out in different directions; showing DIVERGENCE: *Tangential forces are threatening the unity of our party* —**~ly** *adv*

tan·ge·rine /ˌtændʒəˈriːn‖ˈtændʒəriːn/ *n* **1** [C] a small sweet orange with a loose skin that comes off easily **2** [U] this fruit eaten as food **3** [U] a dark or reddish orange colour

tan·gi·ble /ˈtændʒəbəl/ *adj* **1** that can be felt by touch **2** clear and certain; real; not imaginary: *The police need tangible proof of his guilt before they can act against him* —**-bility** /ˌtændʒəˈbɪlǰti/ *n* [U] —**-bly** /ˈtændʒəbli/ *adv*

tangible as·sets /ˌ··· ˈ··/ *n* [P] the real property and possessions of a firm or company —compare GOODWILL (2)

tan·gle¹ /ˈtæŋgəl/ *v* [Wv5;T1;I∅] to (cause to) become a confused mass of disordered and twisted threads: *I don't like to sew with thread that tangles easily.*|*Your hair's so tangled that it doesn't look as if it's been combed for a week.*|(fig.) *After listening to his speech I thought his ideas and opinions were so tangled that I could not vote for him*

tangle² *n* **1** a confused mass of hair, thread, string, etc. **2** a confused disordered state: *The wool was in such a tangle as to be useless.*|*The centre party has a tangle of opinions on every question of political importance* **3** *infml* a quarrel; fight; disagreement: *My wife was very upset by a tangle with one of the neighbours*

tangle with *v prep* [T1] *infml* to quarrel, argue, or fight with (someone)

tan·go¹ /ˈtæŋgəʊ/ *n* **-gos 1** [C] a spirited dance of Spanish American origin **2** [C;U] (a piece of) music for this dance

tango² *v* [I∅] to dance the TANGO¹

tank /tæŋk/ *n* **1** a large container for storing liquid or gas: *The tank in my car holds 40 litres of petrol.*| *You should buy a tank for your tropical fish rather than keep them in a bowl* —see picture at CAR **2** an enclosed heavily armed armoured vehicle that moves on 2 endless metal belts —see CATERPILLAR TRACTOR **3** *esp. Ind & PakE* a large man-made pool for storing water

tan·kard /ˈtæŋkəd‖-ərd/ *n* **1** a large drinking cup, usu. with a handle and lid, esp. for drinking beer **2** the amount of liquid that this holds

tanked up /ˌ· ˈ·/ *adj* [F] *sl* drunk, esp. from drinking beer

tank·er /ˈtæŋkəʳ/ *n* [C; *by*+U] a ship, plane, or railway or road vehicle specially built to carry large quantities of gas or liquid, esp. oil —see pictures at SHIP¹ and INTERCHANGE²

tan·ner¹ /ˈtænəʳ/ *n* a person whose job is making animal skin into leather by TANning¹ (1)

tanner² *n old sl* SIXPENCE

tan·ne·ry /ˈtænəri/ *n* a place where animal skin is made into leather by TANning¹ (1)

tan·nin /ˈtænǰn/ also **tan·nic ac·id** /ˌtænɪk ˈæsǰd/— *n* [U] a reddish acid made from the outer covering (BARK) of certain trees, esp. the OAK, used in preparing leather, making ink, etc. It is also found naturally in tea leaves, GRAPE skins, etc.

tan·ning /ˈtænɪŋ/ *n sl* a beating

tan·noy /ˈtænɔɪ/ *n tdmk esp. BrE* a system of giving out information to the public by means of LOUDSPEAKERS

tan·sy /ˈtænzi/ *n* **1** [C] any of various types of wild plants with yellow flowers and finely divided leaves **2** [U] the bitter tasting leaves of this plant used in medicine and cooking

tan·ta·lize, -lise /ˈtæntl-aɪz/ *v* [Wv4,5;T1] to worry or annoy (a person or animal) by keeping something strongly desired just out of reach; cause anger by raising hopes that cannot be satisfied: *a tantalizing smell of food*|*If you continue to tantalize the dog with a bone you must expect to be bitten*

tan·ta·lus /ˈtæntəl-əs/ *n* a framework in which bottles of alcoholic drink may be kept locked up

tan·ta·mount /ˈtæntəmaʊnt/ *adj* [Wa5;F+*to*] equal in value, force, or effect: *Your answer is tantamount to a refusal*

tan·trum /ˈtæntrəm/ *n* a sudden uncontrolled attack of bad temper or anger

Tao·is·m /ˈtaʊɪzəm, ˈtɑːəʊ-/ *n* [U] a religion developed from a mixture of popular Chinese beliefs and Buddhism, concerned with obtaining a long life and good fortune, often by magical means —**-ist** *adj, n* [Wa5]

tap¹ /tæp/ *n* **1** *AmE* **faucet** —any apparatus for controlling the flow of liquid or gas from a pipe, barrel, etc. —see picture at BATHROOM **2** an object shaped like a PLUG¹ (1) made to fit and close the opening in a barrel **3 on tap a** (of beer) from a barrel **b** ready for use when needed: *By the way you buy new clothes you'd think we had money on tap*

tap² *v* **-pp-** [T1] **1** to open a barrel so as to draw off (liquid) **2** to open (a barrel) so as to draw off liquid **3** to use or draw from: *to tap the nation's natural mineral wealth* **4** to listen to conversations on a telephone by making connection to (the telephone, a telephone wire, etc.) **5** to listen to (a person, telephone conversation, etc.) by making a connection to a telephone wire —compare WIRETAP

tap³ *v* **-pp-** [T1;I∅: (*on*)] **1** to strike (the hand, foot, etc.) lightly against something: *The teacher tapped her fingers on the desk impatiently* **2** to strike (something) lightly with a quick short blow, esp. to attract attention: *I tapped on the window to let them know I'd arrived*

tap⁴ *n* [(*on*)] a short light blow: *a tap on the window*

tap danc·ing /ˈ· ˌ··/ *n* [U] stage dancing in which musical time is beaten on the floor by the feet of the dancer, who wears special shoes with pieces of metal on the bottom —**-er** *n*

tape¹ /teɪp/ *n* **1** [U] narrow material in the form of a band, used for tying up parcels, packets, etc. **2** [C] a string stretched across the winning line in a race and broken by the winner **3** [C;U] (a length of) narrow plastic material covered with a special MAGNETIC substance on which sound can be recorded **4** [C] also **tape re·cord·ing** /ˈ· ·ˌ··/— a length of this on which a performance, piece of music, speech, etc., has been taped: *heard some tapes of her songs* **5** [C] a TAPE MEASURE —see also RED TAPE

tape² *v* **1** [T1;I∅] also **tape-re·cord** /ˈ· ·ˌ·/— to record (sound) on TAPE¹ (3) by using a TAPE RECORDER **2** [T1 (UP)] to fasten or tie (a parcel, packet, etc.) with TAPE¹ (1): *Have you finished taping all the presents up yet?* **3** [T1 (UP), *often pass.*] *AmE* STRAP² (3) **4 have someone taped** *sl* to understand a person, their weakness and guilt, etc., thoroughly

tape deck /ˈ· ·/ *n* the apparatus in a TAPE RECORDER that records and plays back sound, and often has to be connected to a separate listening system

tape mea·sure /ˈ· ˌ··/ *n* a band of narrow cloth or bendable steel, marked with divisions of length, used for measuring —see picture at TOOL[1]

ta·per[1] /ˈteɪpəʳ/ *n* **1** a gradual decrease in the width of a long object **2** a length of string covered in wax, used for lighting candles, pipes, etc. **3** a very thin candle

taper[2] *v* [T1;IØ: (OFF)] to (cause to) become gradually narrower towards one end: *The animal's tail tapered off to a point*

tape re·cord·er /ˈ· ·ˌ··/ *n* an instrument which can record sound on and play sound back from TAPE[1] (3) —see picture at SOUND[3]

tap·es·try /ˈtæpɪ̈stri/ *n* [C;U] (a piece of) heavy cloth on which coloured threads are woven by hand to produce a picture, pattern, etc., hung on walls or used for covering furniture: *Gobelin tapestry|tapestry chair covers|The Bayeux tapestry tells the story of the Battle of Hastings in pictures* —**-tried** *adj* [Wa5]: *an ancient tapestried hall*

tape·worm /ˈteɪpwɜːm‖-wɜrm/ *n* any of various types of long flat worm that when fully-grown live in the bowels of man and other animals

tap·i·o·ca /ˌtæpiˈəʊkə/ *n* [U] small hard white grains of food made from the crushed dried roots of CASSAVA, esp. used for making sweet dishes

ta·pir /ˈteɪpəʳ/ *n* **tapir** *or* **tapirs** [Wn2] a type of piglike animal of tropical America, with thick legs, a short tail, and a long nose

tap·pet /ˈtæpɪ̈t/ *n* a part of a machine, such as an arm or other piece that stands out from the rest, used for passing on noncontinuous movement —see picture at PETROL

tap·room /ˈtæp-ruːm, -rʊm/ *n* a room in a hotel or inn where barrels are stored and cheaper drinks served

tap·root /ˈtæp-ruːt/ *n* the main root of a plant, growing straight down and giving off smaller side roots

taps /tæps/ *n* [GU] (in the US armed forces) the last signal of the day, blown on a BUGLE to signal that lights should be put out

tar[1] /tɑːʳ/ *n* **1** [U] a black substance, thick and sticky when hot and hard when cold, used for making roads, preserving wood, etc. **2** [C] JACK TAR

tar[2] *v* **-rr-** [T1;IØ] **1** to cover (something) with TAR[1] (1): *to tar a road* **2 tar and feather** to put TAR[1] (1) on (someone) and then cover with feathers as a punishment **3 tarred with the same brush** having the same faults

tar·an·tel·la /ˌtærənˈtelə/ also **tar·an·telle** /ˌtærənˈtel/— *n* **1** [C] a rapid Italian dance for 2 people **2** [C;U] (a piece of) music for this dance

ta·ran·tu·la /təˈræntjʊlə‖-tʃələ/ *n* a type of large hairy poisonous SPIDER from Southern Europe

tar·boosh /tɑːˈbuːʃ‖tɑr-/ *n* a hat without a part sticking out all round (BRIM), worn esp. by some Muslim men; type of FEZ

tar·dy /ˈtɑːdi‖ˈtɑrdi/ *adj* [Wa1] **1** *fml* slow in acting or happening **2** *AmE* late —**tardily** *adv* —**tardiness** *n* [U]

tare[1] /teəʳ/ *n* [*usu. pl.*] *bibl* an unwanted plant growing among corn; WEED[1] (1)

tare[2] *n* [*usu. sing.*] *tech* **1** the weight of wrapping material in which goods are packed **2** the weight of an unloaded goods vehicle **3** an amount subtracted for this when weighing a loaded goods vehicle

tar·get /ˈtɑːgɪ̈t‖ˈtɑr-/ *n* **1** anything fired at, esp. a round card or board with circles on it, used in shooting practice **2** [(*of*)] a person or thing that is made the object of unfavourable remarks, jokes, etc.: *This plan will be the target of many opposition attacks* **3** a total or object which one desires to reach: *I've set myself a target of saving £5 a week*

tar·iff /ˈtærɪ̈f/ *n* **1** a tax collected by a government on goods coming into or sometimes going out of a country **2** a list of fixed prices such as the cost of meals, rooms, etc., charged by a hotel, restaurant, etc.

tar·mac[1] /ˈtɑːmæk‖ˈtɑr-/ also (*fml*) **tar·ma·cad·am** /ˌtɑːməˈkædəm‖ˌtɑr-/— *adj, n* [Wa5;B;U] (made of) a mixture of TAR[1] (1) and crushed or very small stones used for making the surface of roads

tarmac[2] *n* [*usu. sing.*] an area covered with TARMAC[1], esp. one used for landing aircraft on (RUNWAY)

tarmac[3] also (*fml*) **tarmacadam**— *v* **-macked, -macking** [T1] to cover (a road's surface) with TARMAC[1]

tarn /tɑːn‖tɑrn/ *n* (*often cap. as part of a name*) a small mountain lake or pool esp. in the North of England: *Seathwaite Tarn*

tar·nish[1] /ˈtɑːnɪʃ‖ˈtɑr-/ *v* [Wv5;T1;IØ] to (cause to) become dull, discoloured, or less bright: *tarnished brass*|(fig.) *tarnished honour*

tarnish[2] *n* [S;U] dullness; loss of polish

ta·ro /ˈtɑːrəʊ/ *n* **taros** a type of tropical plant grown for its thick root which is boiled and eaten as food

tar·ot /ˈtærəʊ/ *n* any of a set of 22 cards used for telling the future

tar·pau·lin /tɑːˈpɔːlɪ̈n‖tɑr-/ *n* [C;U] (a sheet or cover of) heavy cloth covered with wax, paint, or TAR[1] (1) so that water will not pass through

tar·ra·gon /ˈtærəgən/ *n* [U] **1** a type of small European plant grown for its strong-smelling leaves **2** the leaves of this plant used for giving a special taste to food

tar·ry[1] /ˈtæri/ *v* [IØ] *old use & lit* **1** to stay in a place: *We wished we could have tarried longer on this beautiful island* **2** to delay or be slow in starting, going, coming, etc.

tar·ry[2] /ˈtɑːri/ *adj* [Wa1] covered with TAR[1]

tar·sal[1] /ˈtɑːsəl‖ˈtɑr-/ *n med* a bone in the ankle

tarsal[2] *adj* [Wa5] *med* of or related to the TARSUS

tar·sus /ˈtɑːsəs‖ˈtɑr-/ *n* **-si** /saɪ/ *med* a collection of 7 small bones in the ankle —see picture at SKELETON

tart[1] /tɑːt‖tɑrt/ *adj* **1** sharp to the taste; acid-tasting; not sweet **2** using bitter remarks to wound a person's feelings; SARCASTIC —**~ly** *adv* —**~ness** *n* [U]

tart[2] *n* **1** [C;U] *BrE* (a) fruit PIE: *Have some more apple tart* —see PIE (USAGE) **2** [C] a circle of pastry cooked with fruit, cheese, or JAM (=fruit preserved by cooking in sugar) on it **3** [C] *sl* a girl or woman who is regarded as having a sexually immoral character

tar·tan /ˈtɑːtn‖ˈtɑrtn/ *n* **1** [U] woollen cloth woven with bands of different colours and widths crossing each other at right angles, worn chiefly by Scottish Highlanders: *a tartan dress* **2** [C] a special pattern on this cloth worn by a particular Scottish CLAN, and known by the CLAN's name

tar·tar[1] /ˈtɑːtəʳ‖ˈtɑr-/ *n* [U] **1** a hard chalklike substance that forms on the teeth **2** the reddish-brown substance that forms on the insides of wine barrels **3** also **cream of tartar** /ˌ· · ˈ··/— a white powder made by treating this or from chemicals, used in making BAKING POWDER and in medicine

tartar[2] *n* (*often cap.*) a fierce person with a violent temper

tar·tar·ic ac·id /tɑːˌtærɪk ˈæsɪ̈d‖tɑr-/ *n* [U] a strong acid of plant origin used in preparing certain foods and medicines

tartar sauce, tartare sauce /tɑːˌtɑː ˈsɔːs‖ˈtɑrtəʳ sɔs/ *n* [U] very small pieces of vegetables mixed with MAYONNAISE, esp. eaten with fish

tart up /tɑːt‖tɑrt/ *v adv* [Wv5;T1] *sl* to make

(someone or something) too showy, by brightly painting, putting on cheap ornaments, colourful clothes, etc., often in an improper way

task /tɑːsk‖tæsk/ *n* **1** a piece of work (that must be) done, esp. if hard or unpleasant; duty: *Mother set me the task of sweeping the floors.|She finds looking after her old mother a difficult task* **2 take someone to task** to speak severely to someone for a fault or failure; scold someone

task force /ˈ· ·/ *n* [GC] **1** a military force under one commander sent to a place for a special purpose: *A combined naval and army task force was sent to attack the post* **2** (in Britain) a group of police that deals with serious crimes in a particular area

task·mas·ter /ˈtɑːskˌmɑːstəʳ‖ˈtæskˌmæstər/ *fem.* **task·mis·tress** /ˈtɑːskˌmɪstrɨs‖ˈtæsk-/— *n* a person who gives jobs, esp. hard and unpleasant ones, to other people: *Our teacher's a very hard taskmaster but he certainly gets good results from his pupils*

tas·sel /ˈtæsəl/ *n* a bunch of threads tied together into a round ball at one end and hung as an ornament on clothes, flags, curtains, etc. —**~led** (*AmE* **~ed**) *adj* [Wa5]

taste¹ /teɪst/ *v* **1** [T1] to test the TASTE² (2) of (food or drink) by taking a little into the mouth: *I always taste the wine before allowing the waiter to fill my glass.|I've never tasted goat but I know I wouldn't like it* **2** [Wv6;T1] to experience the TASTE² (2) of (something): *I've got a cold so I can't taste what I'm eating* **3** [Wv6;T1] to eat or drink (food or drink): *The prisoner had not tasted food in the 3 days since he'd escaped* **4** [L7,9 esp. *of*] to have a particular TASTE² (2): *These oranges taste nice.|This meat's been cooked too long and doesn't taste of anything.|This soup tastes of chicken but I thought you said it was vegetable* **5** [T1] to experience: *Once people have tasted freedom they're unwilling to become slaves again*

taste² *n* **1** [C;U] the special sense by which a person or animal knows one food from another by its sweetness, bitterness, saltiness, etc.: *I've got a cold, so my taste's quite gone* **2** [C;U] the sensation that is produced when food or drink is put in the mouth and that makes it different from other foods or drinks by its saltiness, sweetness, bitterness, etc: *Sugar has a sweet taste.|This cake has no/very little taste* **3** [C (*of*) *usu. sing.*] a small quantity of food or drink: *I had a taste of soup to see if it was nice* **4** [U] the ability to enjoy and judge beauty, style, art, music, etc.; ability to choose and use the best manners, behaviour, fashions, etc.: *His speech offended many people present and was in very bad taste.|You need good taste before you can enjoy this music* **5** [C;U:(*for, in*)] a personal liking for something: *a taste for music|She has costly tastes in clothes* **6** [C (*of*) *usu. sing.*] an experience: *Once you've had a taste of life in our country you won't want to return home*

taste bud /ˈ· ·/ *n* a group of cells on the tongue which can tell the difference between foods according to their taste

taste·ful /ˈteɪstfəl/ *adj* having or showing good TASTE² (4) —**~ly** *adv* —**~ness** *n* [U]

taste·less /ˈteɪstləs/ *adj* [Wa5] **1** having no taste **2** having or showing poor TASTE² (4) —**~ly** *adv* —**~ness** *n* [U]

USAGE When **tasteless** is used of food, it means "having no **taste**". When it is used of people, furniture, ornaments, etc., it means "having or showing bad **taste**": *The potatoes were* **tasteless** *without salt.|a* **tasteless** *over-furnished room*|**Distasteful** is not used in either of these meanings, but only of unpleasant things that must be done: *It is my* **distasteful** *duty to warn you . . .*

taste of *v prep* [T1] *fml* TASTE¹ (5)

tast·er /ˈteɪstəʳ/ *n* a person whose job is testing the quality of foods, teas, wines, etc., by tasting them

tast·y /ˈteɪsti/ *adj* [Wa1] **1** (esp. of salty rather than sugary food) having a pleasant noticeable taste; pleasing to the taste: *a tasty meal* **2** *infml* (esp. of news) interesting: *a tasty piece of news about our neighbour* —**tastily** *adv*

tat¹ /tæt/ *v* **-tt-** [T1;IØ] to make (something) by TATTING (2)

tat² *n* [U] *BrE sl* material or matter of poor quality

tat³ *n* see TIT FOR TAT

ta-ta /tæˈtɑː/ *interj infml* goodbye

tat·as /ˈtætɑːz/ *n* **go tatas** (*said by or to children*) to go for a walk

tat·ter /ˈtætəʳ/ *n* a piece of cloth, paper, etc., torn off or hanging loosely

tat·tered /ˈtætəd‖-ərd/ *adj* **1** (of clothes) old and torn **2** (of a person) dressed in old torn clothes

tat·ters /ˈtætəz‖-ərz/ *n* [P] **1** old worn-out clothing or bits of cloth **2 in tatters** (of clothes) old and torn

tat·ting /ˈtætɪŋ/ *n* [U] **1** a kind of knotted ornamental netlike cloth (LACE) made by hand **2** the art of making this

tat·tle /ˈtætl/ *v* **1** [IØ] to talk about small unimportant things, or other people's private affairs; GOSSIP **2** [T1] to let out (small secrets) in this way —**-ler** *n*

tat·too¹ /təˈtuː, tæˈtuː/ *n* **-toos** **1** a rapid beating of drums played late at night to signal that soldiers should go to their rooms **2** a rapid continuous beating of drums: *to play a tattoo* **3** an outdoor military show with music, usu. at night: *the Edinburgh tattoo*

tattoo² *n* **-toos** a pattern, picture, or message put on the skin by TATTOOing³: *The sailor had a tattoo saying "I love Anne" on his chest*

tattoo³ *v* **1** [T1] to make (a pattern, picture, message, etc.) on the skin by pricking with a pin and then pouring coloured DYEs in: *He had the words "I love Anne" tattooed on his chest* **2** [Wv5;T1] to mark (a person or his skin) by doing this: *I didn't see the criminal's face but I noted he had a tattooed hand*

tat·too·ist /təˈtuːɨst, tæ-/ *n* a person whose job is TATTOOing³

tat·ty /ˈtæti/ *adj* [Wa1] *infml* untidy; not well kept: *tatty clothes* —**-tily** *adv* —**-tiness** *n* [U]

taught /tɔːt/ *past t. & p. of* TEACH

taunt¹ /tɔːnt/ *v* [Wv4;T1 (*with*)] to try to make (someone) angry or upset by making unkind remarks, laughing at faults or failures, etc.: *They taunted her with her inability to swim* —**~ingly** *adv*

taunt² *n* [*often pl.*] a remark or joke intended to hurt someone's feelings or make him angry: *cruel taunts about her wooden leg*

Tau·rus /ˈtɔːrəs/ *n* **1** [R] **a** the ancient sign, a BULL¹, representing the 2nd division of the ZODIAC belt of stars **b** the group of stars (CONSTELLATION) formerly in this division **2** [C] a person born under the supposed influence of this sign —see picture at PLANET

taut /tɔːt/ *adj* **1** tightly drawn; stretched tight: *Pull the string taut!|taut muscles* **2** showing signs of worry or anxiety: *a taut expression on her face* —**~ly** *adv* —**~ness** *n* [U]

tau·to·lo·gi·cal /ˌtɔːtəˈlɒdʒɪkəl‖-ˈlɑ-/ *adj* of or using TAUTOLOGY

tau·tol·o·gy /tɔːˈtɒlədʒi‖tɔːˈtɑ-/ *n* [C;U] (an example of) repeating something in different words but without making the meaning clearer; (an) unnecessary repeating of the same idea in different words (as in *He sat alone by himself*)

tav·ern /ˈtævən‖-ərn/ *n old use* an inn

taw·dry /ˈtɔːdri/ *adj* [Wa1] cheaply showy; lacking good TASTE[2] (4): *tawdry jewellery* —**-drily** *adv* —**-driness** *n* [U]
taw·ny /ˈtɔːni/ *adj* [Wa1] having a brownish yellow colour
tawse /tɔːz/ *n ScotE* **1** [C] a leather belt with which children are beaten to be punished **2** [*the*+R] a beating with this given as a punishment
tax[1] /tæks/ *v* **1** [T1] to charge a tax on: *After it's been taxed my income is very small.|Tobacco and alcoholic drinks are taxed heavily in Britain.|Tax the rich!* **2** [Wv4;T1;I∅] to make heavy demands (on); tire: *Such a long journey would be too taxing for my old uncle.|You're taxing my patience by asking such stupid questions* —see also TAX WITH —**~ability** /ˌtæksəˈbɪlɨti/ *n* [U] —**~able** /ˈtæksəbəl/ *adj* [Wa5]
tax[2] *n* **1** [C;U] (a sum of) money paid in accordance with the law to the government according to income, property, goods bought, etc.: *The government plans to increase taxes by 5 per cent over the next year.|How much income tax do you pay?|Half of my wages go in tax* **2** [S+*on*] a heavy demand; demanding duty: *To travel a long way would be too much of a tax on my father's strength*
tax·a·tion /tækˈseɪʃən/ *n* [U] **1** the act of taxing **2** money raised from taxes: *We must increase taxation if we are to spend more on the health service*
tax col·lec·tor /ˈ· ·ˌ··/ *n* an official who collects taxes
tax-free /ˌ· ˈ·◂/ *adj, adv* [Wa5] free from taxation: *You can live on this little island tax-free*
tax ha·ven /ˈ· ˌ··/ *n* a place where many people choose to live because no taxes (or very low taxes) are paid there
tax·i /ˈtæksi/ also (*fml*) **tax·i·cab** /ˈtæksikæb/, (*esp. AmE*) **cab**— *n* [C; *by*+U] a car which may be hired by the public along with its driver, the price of a journey usu. being calculated by a special machine (TAXIMETER) —see CAR (USAGE) and picture at STREET
taxi[2] *v* **taxied**, *pres. p.* **taxiing** [I∅;T1] **a** (of a plane) to move along the ground before taking off or after landing **b** to pilot (a plane) along the ground before taking off or after landing
tax·i·der·mist /ˈtæksɨdɜːmɨst‖-ɜr-/ *n* a person who practises TAXIDERMY as a job
tax·i·der·my /ˈtæksɨdɜːmi‖-ɜr-/ *n* [U] the art of specially cleaning, preparing, and preserving the skins of fish, birds, and animals, and filling them with special material so that they look like the living creature
tax·i·meter /ˈtæksiˌmiːtəʳ/ *n* a small machine fitted to taxis to calculate the charge for each journey
taxi rank /ˈ·· ·/ also (*esp. AmE*) **taxi stand, cab-stand**— *n* a place where taxis wait to be hired —see picture at STREET
tax·on·o·my /tækˈsɒnəmi‖-ˈsɑ-/ *n* [U] the branch of science dealing with putting plants and animals into various classes according to their natural relationships
tax with *v prep* [D1;V4b] *fml* to charge (someone) with (something bad or doing wrong): *My teacher taxed me with being lazy*
TB *abbrev. for:* TUBERCULOSIS
T-bone /ˈtiː bəʊn/ also **T-bone steak** /ˌ· · ˈ·/— *n* a thinly cut piece of meat (BEEF) with a T-shaped bone in
tea /tiː/ *n* **1** [U] a type of white-flowered bush mainly grown in South and East Asia for its leaves **2** [U] the specially treated, dried, and finely cut leaves of this bush used for making TEA (3) **3** [U] a hot brown drink made by pouring boiling water onto this: *In Britain tea is usually drunk with milk and/or sugar in it.|a cup of tea* **4** [C *usu. pl.*] a cup of this: *3 teas and a coffee please, waiter!* **5** [C;U] a small meal, usu. served in the afternoon with a cup of TEA (3): *What are we having for tea today?|a funeral tea* **6** [U9] a medicinal drink made by putting plant parts, esp. roots and leaves, in hot water: HERB *tea* **7 one's cup of tea** the sort of thing one likes: *Playing cards isn't my cup of tea; let's watch television instead*
tea·bag /ˈtiːbæg/ *n* a small bag of cloth or paper with tea leaves inside, put into boiling water to make enough tea for one person
tea break /ˈ· ·/ also **coffee break**— *n* a short pause from work in the middle of the morning or afternoon for a drink, a rest, something light to eat, etc.
tea cad·dy /ˈ· ˌ··/ *n* a small box, tin, etc., in which tea is kept
tea·cake /ˈtiːkeɪk/ *n* a small round cake made of a sweetened breadlike mixture with pieces of dried fruit (CURRANT*s*, RAISIN*s*, etc.) in it, cut in 2, and eaten hot or cold with butter
teach /tiːtʃ/ *v* **taught** /tɔːt/ [D1 (*to*),5,6a,b;T1,4,5; V3,4;I∅] to give knowledge or skill of, or training or lessons in (a particular subject, how to do something, etc.) to (someone): *I teach boys history and my wife teaches girls French.|You can't teach an old dog new tricks.|John teaches politics to university students.|I would rather teach older than younger children.|His religion teaches (him) that war is wrong.|He taught the boys not to fight.|I taught them where they could find the best berries.|All children should be taught how to read and write.|He wants to be taught (to play) cricket.|She taught (me) singing.|My husband teaches at a local school*
teach·er /ˈtiːtʃəʳ/ *n* [C;N] a person who teaches, esp. as a profession: *My husband's a history teacher in a local school.|the University Teachers' Association*
tea chest /ˈ· ·/ *n* a large wooden chest in which tea is packed
teach-in /ˈ· ·/ *n infml* an exchange of opinions about a subject of interest, as held in a college by students, teachers, guest speakers, etc.
teach·ing /ˈtiːtʃɪŋ/ *n* **1** [U] the work of a teacher **2** [C *often pl. with sing. meaning*;U] that which is taught, esp. the moral, political, or religious beliefs taught by a person of historical importance: *to follow Christ's teaching/teachings|the teachings of Freud*
teaching hos·pi·tal /ˈ·· ˌ···/ *n BrE* a hospital where medical students can practise medicine under the guidance of experienced doctors
teaching ma·chine /ˈ·· ·ˌ·/ *n* a machine that presents the student with a piece of information followed by some questions and allows him to move to the next piece of information only when he has answered these questions correctly
tea cloth /ˈ· ·/ *n* **1** a small cloth for spreading over a small table from which tea is to be served **2** TEA TOWEL
tea co·sy /ˈ· ˌ··/ *n* a thick covering put over a teapot to keep the contents hot
tea·cup /ˈtiːkʌp/ *n* **1** a cup in which tea is served **2** TEACUPFUL **3 storm in a teacup** a lot of worry and nervous annoyance over something unimportant
tea·cup·ful /ˈtiːkʌpfʊl/ *n* **-s** *or* **teacupsful** /ˈtiːkʌpsfʊl/ the amount held by a teacup
tea·gar·den /ˈtiːˌgɑːdn‖-ɑr-/ *n* **1** an outdoor restaurant where drinks and light meals are served **2** a large area of land on which tea is grown; tea PLANTATION
tea·house /ˈtiːhaʊs/ *n* **-houses** /ˌhaʊzɨz/ a restaurant in China or Japan where tea is served
teak /tiːk/ *n* **1** [C] a type of large tree from India, Burma, and Malaysia, with very hard yellow wood that does not decay **2** [U] the wood of this tree

used for making furniture, ships, etc.
tea·ket·tle /ˈtiː,ketl/ *n* a KETTLE, esp. used for heating water for making tea
teal /tiːl/ *n* **teal** [Wn3] a type of small wild duck, very swift in flight
tea·leaf /ˈtiːliːf/ *n* **-leaves** /liːvz/ **1** one of the very finely cut pieces of leaf used for making tea, esp. when left in a teapot or teacup after tea has been drunk **2** *BrE sl* a thief
team /tiːm/ *n* [GC] **1** 2 or more animals pulling the same vehicle: *The carriage was drawn by a team of 4 white horses.|a team of oxen* **2** a group of people who work, play, or act together: *John's in the school cricket team.|The government is led by an able team of skilled politicians.|Cricket is a team game*
team spir·it /ˈ· ,··/ *n* [U] the spirit which leads each member of a team to think of the team's success before his own personal advantage
team·ster /ˈtiːmstəʳ/ *n* **1** a person who drives a team of animals **2** *AmE* a person who drives a LORRY (=a large road vehicle), esp. as a job
team up *v adv* [IØ (*with*)] *not fml* to work together; combine: *Your new hat and shoes team up nicely with your blue coat*
team·work /ˈtiːmwɜːk‖-wɜrk/ *n* [U] the ability of a group of people to work together effectively; combined effort
tea par·ty /ˈ· ,··/ *n* a social gathering in the afternoon, at which tea is drunk
tea·pot /ˈtiːpɒt‖ˈtiːpɑt/ *n* a vessel, usu. round, with a handle at one side and a SPOUT (=bent pouring pipe) at the other, in which tea is made and served
tear¹ /tɪəʳ/ *n* **1** a drop of salty liquid that flows from the eye during pain or sadness: *My wife burst into tears when she heard the bad news* **2 in tears** crying; weeping: *The little girl was in tears because she'd lost her mother*
tear² /teəʳ/ *v* **tore** /tɔːʳ‖tor/, **torn** /tɔːn‖torn/ **1** [Wv5;T1] to pull apart or into pieces by force, esp. so as to leave irregular edges: *Why did you tear the cloth when I'd advised you to cut it with scissors?|The boy tore the flesh on his legs climbing up a tree.|I've only got an old torn dress to wear so I can't go to the dance* **2** [X9] to make by doing this: *The girl tore a hole in her dress climbing over the wall* **3** [X9 esp. AWAY, *off*, OFF, OUT, UP] to remove by force: *The spiteful child tore some of the papers out of his brother's book.|Our roof was torn off in the storm.|* (fig.) *unhappy children torn from their parents* **4** [IØ] to become torn (TEAR² (1)): *This material tears easily, so be careful when you wear it* **5** [T1 (APART) *usu. pass.*] to divide by the pull of opposing forces; destroy the peace of: *a country torn apart by war|The prince was torn between loyalty to his family and his love for the girl* **6** [L9] to move excitedly with great speed: *The excited children tore noisily down the street.|I'm in a tearing hurry* (=a great hurry) **7 tear one's hair** to pull one's hair violently in grief or anger **8 tear one's hair out** to be very excited or anxious **9 tear oneself away** to leave unwillingly **10 tear someone's heart out** to fill someone with sadness —see also TEAR APART, TEAR AT, TEAR DOWN, TEAR INTO, TEAR OFF, TEAR UP
tear³ /teəʳ/ *n* a torn place in cloth, paper, etc.
tear a·part /teəʳ/ *v adv* [T1b] *infml* **1** to express a very poor opinion of (someone or his work) **2** to scold
tear at /teəʳ/ *v prep* [T1] to try to pull apart or in pieces by force: *The fighting girls tore at each other with their nails*
tear·a·way /ˈteərəweɪ/ *n sl* a noisy and violent youth
tear down /teəʳ/ *v adv* [T1] to pull down; destroy
tear·drop /ˈtɪədrɒp‖ˈtɪərdrɑp/ *n* a single tear
tear·ful /ˈtɪəfəl‖ˈtɪər-/ *adj* **1** crying; weeping; wet with tears: *a tearful young girl* **2** likely to weep: *Janet looked so tearful that I thought she was going to cry* —**~ly** *adv* —**~ness** *n* [U]
tear·gas /ˈtɪəgæs‖ˈtɪər-/ *n* [U] a stinging chemical gas that causes blindness for a short time by making the eyes produce tears, used by police to control violent crowds
tear in·to /teəʳ/ *v prep* [T1 *no pass.*] to attack (someone) violently with blows or words
tear·jerk·er /ˈtɪə,dʒɜːkəʳ‖ˈtɪər,dʒɜr-/ *n infml* a very sad book, play, broadcast, etc.
tear·less /ˈtɪələs‖ˈtɪər-/ *adj* [Wa5] *esp. lit* lacking tears; without tears —**~ly** *adv*
tear off /teəʳ/ *v adv* [T1] *infml* **1** to do (a job) rapidly: *The secretary tore off 2 letters before dinner* **2 tear someone off a strip** to scold someone severely
tea·room /ˈtiːruːm, -rʊm/ *n* a restaurant where tea and light meals are served
tear up /teəʳ/ *v adv* [T1] to destroy completely by tearing: *The magician tore up a pound note and then made it whole again.|*(fig.) *I believe the unions intend to tear up the agreement with the government*
tease /tiːz/ *v* **1** [T1;IØ] to make fun of (a person or animal) playfully or unkindly: *At school, the other children always teased me because I was fat* **2** [T1; (IØ)] to comb; separate and straighten the threads in (wool, cotton, etc.) **3** [T1;(IØ)] to make (cloth) soft by raising the threads on the surface by brushing **4** [T1] *AmE* BACKCOMB
tea·sel, -zel, -zle /ˈtiːzəl/ *n* **1** a type of plant with prickly leaves and flowers **2** a dried flower from this plant, used in former times for teasing (TEASE (2,3)) wool, cotton, cloth, etc.
teas·er /ˈtiːzəʳ/ *n* **1** *sl* a difficult question **2** also **tease**— a person who TEASEs (1) a lot or who likes teasing
tea ser·vice /ˈ· ,··/ also **tea set** /ˈ· ·/— *n* a matching set of cups, plates, teapot, etc., used in serving tea
tea·spoon /ˈtiːspuːn/ *n* **1** a small spoon used for mixing sugar into tea, coffee, etc. **2** TEASPOONFUL
tea·spoon·ful /ˈtiːspuːnfʊl/ *n* **-s** *or* **teaspoonsful** /ˈtiːspuːnzfʊl/ the amount held by one TEASPOON
tea strain·er /ˈ· ,··/ *n* a small metal or plastic bowl-shaped object with many very small holes in it, through which tea is poured to stop leaves from going into the cup
teat /tiːt/ *n* **1** a specially shaped rubber object with one or more holes in it, fixed to the end of a bottle so that a baby can drink liquids by sucking **2** a NIPPLE (1), or the part which serves the same purpose on an animal —see picture at FARMYARD
tea ta·ble /ˈ· ,··/ *n* a table at which tea is served
tea·time /ˈtiːtaɪm/ *n* [U] the time of day when tea is served: *I'll see you at teatime*
tea tow·el /ˈ· ,··/ also (*esp. AmE*) **dish towel**— *n* a cloth for drying cups, plates, etc., drying after they have been washed
tea tray /ˈ· ·/ *n* a TRAY on which articles for serving tea are carried
tea trol·ley /ˈ· ,··/ also (*esp. AmE*) **tea wag·on**— *n esp. BrE* a small table on wheels, from which food is served
tech /tek/ *n infml* (esp. in Britain) a college (**technical college**) providing courses in sciences, subjects needing skills of the hand rather than of the mind, art, social studies, etc., for students who have left school —compare POLYTECHNIC
techn- /tek-n/ also **tech·no-** /ˈteknə, tekˈnɒ‖-nə, -ˈnɑ-/— *comb. form* **1** of skill: TECHNICAL **2** of practical science: TECHNOLOGY
tech·ni·cal /ˈteknɪkəl/ *adj* **1** [Wa5] having special knowledge, esp. of an industrial or scientific subject: *technical* EXPERTs*|the Association of Scientific and Technical Workers* **2** of or related to a particular and esp. a practical or scientific subject;

concerning those subjects taught to provide skills for the hand rather than for the mind: *a technical college|technical training* —compare ACADEMIC¹ (2) **3** [Wa5] according to an unreasonably fixed acceptance of the rules: *The result was a technical defeat for the government, but otherwise of limited importance* **4** belonging to a particular art, science, profession, etc.: *This book is too technical for me* —**~ly** *adv* [Wa4]

tech·ni·cal·i·ty /ˌteknɨ̀ˈkælɨ̀ti/ *n* a TECHNICAL (2) point, detail, or expression: *The general explained the military technicalities of the matter to the newspaper reporters.|The fighter lost on a technicality* (=he perhaps deserved to win, but he broke a particular rule, and so lost)

technical knock·out /ˌ··· ˈ··/ *n* the ending of a BOXING⁴ match because one of the fighters cannot continue (as, for example, because he is too badly hurt) —see BOXING (USAGE)

tech·ni·cian /tekˈnɪʃən/ *n* a highly skilled scientific or industrial worker; specialist in the practical details of a subject

tech·nique /tekˈniːk/ *n* **1** [C] **a** the manner in which a subject is treated by a writer, artist, etc.; method of artistic expression used in writing, music, art, etc. **b** a method or manner of play in sport: *Boycott's perfect technique kept him out of trouble* **2** [U] skill in art or some specialist activity

tech·noc·ra·cy /tekˈnɒkrəsi‖-ˈnɑ-/ *n tech* **1** [U;C] (organization and control of industry by) a group of skilled specialists **2** [C] a country where industry is controlled by such a group

tech·no·crat /ˈteknəkræt/ *n tech* a member or supporter of (a) TECHNOCRACY (1)

tech·no·lo·gi·cal /ˌteknəˈlɒdʒɪkəl‖-ˈlɑ-/ *adj* of or related to TECHNOLOGY: *The development of the steam engine was the greatest technological advance of the 19th century* —**~ly** *adv* [Wa4]

tech·nol·o·gist /tekˈnɒlədʒɨ̀st‖-ˈnɑ-/ *n* a specialist in TECHNOLOGY

tech·nol·o·gy /tekˈnɒlədʒi‖-ˈnɑ-/ *n* [U;(C)] the branch of knowledge dealing with scientific and industrial methods and their practical use in industry; practical science

tech·y /ˈtetʃi/ *adj* [Wa1] TETCHY

ted·dy bear /ˈtedi beəʳ/ also **teddy**— *n* a toy bear filled with soft material

teddy boy /ˈ·· ·/ also (*sl*) **ted** /ted/— *n* (in Britain, in the 1950's) a young man who dressed in the style of the early 20th century

Te De·um /ˌtiː ˈdiːəm, ˌteɪ ˈdeɪəm/ *n* **-ums** *Lat* **1** an ancient Christian song of praise thanking God for his mercy and kindness **2** a piece of music written specially for this **3** a special service at which God is praised and thanked for his help

te·di·ous /ˈtiːdɪəs/ *adj* long and tiring; uninteresting: *a tedious book|politician|speaker* —**~ly** *adv* —**~ness** *n* [U]

te·di·um /ˈtiːdɪəm/ *n* [U] TEDIOUSness

tee /tiː/ *n* (in GOLF) (the area surrounding) a small heap of sand or a specially-shaped plastic or wooden object from which the ball is first driven at the beginning of each attempt to hit it into the hole

teem¹ /tiːm/ *v* [L9 esp. *in*] *esp. lit* to be present in large numbers; ABOUND: *Fish teem in this river*

teem² *v* [(*it*) IØ *usu. pres. p.*] *infml* to rain very heavily: *You can't go out without a coat on; it's teeming.|The rain teemed down for hours.|It's teeming with rain* (=it's raining very heavily)

teem·ing /ˈtiːmɪŋ/ *adj* [Wa5;F+*with*;(B)] *esp. lit* (of a river, wood, etc.) full of a type of creature; having a type of creature present in great numbers: *a forest teeming with deer|the teeming forest*

teem with *v prep* [T1 *no pass.*] *esp. lit* (of a river, wood, etc.) to have (a type of creature) present in great numbers: *This river teems with all kinds of fish in summer*

teen·age /ˈtiːneɪdʒ/ also **teen·aged** /ˈtiːneɪdʒd/— *adj* [Wa5;A] of, for, or being a TEENAGER: *teenage fashions|a teenage boy*

teen·ag·er /ˈtiːneɪdʒəʳ/ *n* a young person of between 13 and 19 years old

teens /tiːnz/ *n* [P] the period of one's life between and including the ages of 13 and 19: *She's in her teens*

tee·ny·bop·per /ˈtiːniˌbɒpəʳ‖-ˌbɑ-/ also **bopper**— *n sl* a young girl (between the ages of about 9 and 14) who is very interested in popular music and the groups who play it, the latest fashions, etc.

tee·ny wee·ny /ˌtiːni ˈwiːni◂/ also **teen·sy ween·sy** /ˌtiːnzi ˈwiːnzi◂/, **teeny, teensy**— *adj* [Wa1] (*used esp. to children*) very small

tee off *v adv* [IØ] (in GOLF) to drive the ball from a TEE

tee shirt /ˈtiː ʃɜːt‖-ʃɜrt/ *n* T-SHIRT

tee·ter /ˈtiːtəʳ/ *v* [IØ (*on*)] to stand or move in an unsteady way: *teetered along in her high shoes*|(fig.) *The government is teetering on the edge of defeat over its latest plans*

teeth¹ /tiːθ/ *n* [P] **1** *infml* effective force or power: *When will the police be given the necessary teeth to deal with young criminals?* **2 armed to the teeth** very heavily armed **3 cast/throw something in someone's teeth** to blame someone for something **4 escape by the skin of one's teeth** to have a narrow escape **5 get one's teeth into** to do (a job) very actively and purposefully **6 in the teeth of** against the strength of; in opposition to **7 lie in one's teeth/throat** to lie shamelessly **8 set someone's teeth on edge** to give someone the unpleasant sensation caused by certain acid tastes or high sounds: *Don't press so hard with the chalk when you write! The noise sets my teeth on edge* **9 show one's teeth** to act threateningly

teeth² *pl. of* TOOTH

teethe /tiːð/ *v* [IØ] (esp. of babies) to grow teeth

teething troub·les /ˈ·· ˌ··/ *n* [P] troubles and difficulties happening during the early stages of an activity or operation, as when a baby is growing teeth —see also TEETHE

tee·to·tal /ˌtiːˈtəʊtl◂/ *adj* [Wa5] never drinking, or opposed to the drinking of, alcohol

tee·to·tal·ler, *AmE* **-taler** /tiːˈtəʊtələʳ/ *n* a person who never drinks alcohol

tee up *v adv* **1** [T1;IØ] (in GOLF) to prepare to hit by placing (the ball) on a TEE **2** [T1] to prepare; arrange

Tef·lon /ˈteflɒn‖-lɑn/ *n* [U] *tdmk* a man-made substance which is used for MOULDing³ (1) things and to which food will not stick. The insides of pans are often given a covering of this to make cleaning them easy

teg·u·ment /ˈtegjʊmənt‖-gjə-/ *n tech* INTEGUMENT

tel·e /ˈteli/ *n* [C;U] *AmE* TELLY

tel·e- *comb. form* **1** over a distance: *telegram*| TELEPATHY|*television* **2** by television: TELECAST

tel·e·cast¹ /ˈtelikɑːst‖-kæst/ *v* [T1] *rare* to broadcast on television

telecast² *n* a broadcast on television

tel·e·com·mu·ni·ca·tions /ˌtelikəmjuːnɨ̀ˈkeɪʃənz/ *n* [P] the various methods of receiving or sending messages by telephone or telegraph, either by radio signals or by wires: *The Post Office makes a profit on telecommunications and a loss on delivering letters*

tel·e·gram /ˈtelɨ̀græm/ *n* **1** [C; *by*+U] a message sent by telegraph **2** [C] a piece of paper on which this message is delivered

tel·e·graph¹ /ˈtelɨ̀grɑːf‖-græf/ *n* **1** [U] a method

of sending messages along wire by electric signals: *by telegraph* **2** [C] the apparatus that receives or sends messages in this way **3** [C] *now rare* SCOREBOARD —see also BUSH TELEGRAPH

telegraph² *v* [D1 (*to*),5a;T1,5a;V3;IØ] to send (someone) (something) by TELEGRAPH¹ (1): *We telegraphed her the bad news.|Did you telegraph that father had died?|They telegraphed us to go as soon as possible*

te·leg·ra·pher /tǝ̇ˈlegrəfəʳ/ also **te·leg·ra·phist** /tǝ̇ˈlegrəfǝ̇st/— *n* a person employed to send and receive messages by telegraph

tel·e·graph·ese /ˌtelǝ̇grəˈfiːz‖-græfˈiːz/ *n* [U] a manner of writing used in telegrams, in which unnecessary words are not included (as in *Arriving Wednesday* for *I am arriving on Wednesday*)

tel·e·graph·ic /ˌtelǝ̇ˈgræfɪk/ *adj* [Wa5] of, for, like, or sent by a telegram: *telegraphic apparatus|a telegraphic message|Has your firm got a shortened telegraphic address?* —**~ally** *adv* [Wa4]

telegraph pole /ˈ··· ·/ also **telegraph post**— *n* a pole for supporting telephone and telegraph wires

te·lem·e·ter /tǝ̇ˈlemǝ̇təʳ‖ˈtelǝ̇ˌmiːtər/ *n tech* an instrument that measures quantities, esp. distances, and sends the results by radio to a home station

te·lem·e·try /tǝ̇ˈlemǝ̇tri/ *n* [U] *tech* the collection of information by TELEMETER

tel·e·ol·o·gy /ˌteliˈɒlədʒi‖-ˈɑ-/ *n* [U] *tech* the belief that all things and events were specially planned to fulfil a purpose —**-gical** /ˌteliəˈlɒdʒɪkəl‖-ˈlɑ-/ *adj* [Wa5] —**-gically** *adv* [Wa4] —**-gist** /ˌteliˈɒlədʒǝ̇st‖-ˈɑ-/ *n*

tel·e·path·ic /ˌtelǝ̇ˈpæθɪk/ *adj* **1** able to practise TELEPATHY **2** [Wa5] of, sent by, or like TELEPATHY —**~ally** *adv* [Wa4]

te·lep·a·thist /tǝ̇ˈlepəθǝ̇st/ *n* a person who practises TELEPATHY

te·lep·a·thy /tǝ̇ˈlepəθi/ *n* [U] the sending of thoughts, messages, etc., from one person's mind to another's without the ordinary use of the senses

tel·e·phone¹ /ˈtelǝ̇fəʊn/ also (*infml*) **phone**— *n* **1** [U] a method of sending sounds, and talking to others, over long distances by electrical means: *The captain could speak to policemen on the shore by radio telephone* **2** [C] the apparatus that receives or sends sound, esp. speech, in this way: *If the telephone rings, can you answer it?|Your mother was on the telephone earlier* (=she rang up earlier) —see picture at LIVING ROOM

telephone² also (*infml*) **phone**— *v* **1** [D1 (*to*);T1; V3;IØ] to speak (a message) to (someone) by telephone: *I telephoned your aunt the sad news of father's death.|Did you telephone Bob?|I telephoned mother to come as soon as she could.|John's just telephoned through to say he'll be late home tonight.|If you don't want to go to the shops today you can telephone your order and they'll deliver it* **2** [D1 (*to*); T1] to send (something) to (someone) by telephone: *We telephoned Jean a greetings telegram on her wedding day* **3** [L9;T1] to (try to) reach (a place or person) by telephone: *I've been telephoning all morning but I've not been able to speak to the minister.|You can't telephone Glasgow directly from here. You have to go through the* OPERATOR

telephone booth /ˈ··· ·/ *n* CALL BOX

telephone di·rec·to·ry /ˈ··· ·ˌ··/ also **telephone book** /ˈ··· ·/— *n* a book containing an alphabetical list of the names of all the people in an area who own a telephone, with their telephone numbers and addresses

telephone ex·change /ˈ··· ·ˌ·/ *n* a place where telephone connections are made

te·leph·o·nist /tǝ̇ˈlefənǝ̇st/ *n* a person who works at a TELEPHONE EXCHANGE

te·leph·o·ny /tǝ̇ˈlefəni/ *n* [U] the practice of using telephones

tel·e·pho·to·graph /ˌtelǝ̇ˈfəʊtəgrɑːf‖-græf/ also **tel·e·pho·to** /ˌtelǝ̇ˈfəʊtəʊ◂/— *n* **1** an enlarged picture of a distant object taken with a camera specially made for the purpose **2** a picture sent from one place to another by radio, telegraph wires, etc.

tel·e·pho·tog·ra·phy /ˌtelǝ̇fəˈtɒgrəfi‖-ˈtɑ-/ *n* [U] **1** the photography of objects too distant for ordinary cameras by means of cameras made specially for the purpose **2** the practice of sending photographs from one place to another by radio, telegraph wires, etc. —**-phic** /ˌtelǝ̇fəʊtəˈgræfɪk/ *adj* [Wa5]

telephoto lens /ˌ···· ˈ·/ *n* a special LENS that allows a camera to take clear enlarged pictures of objects too distant for ordinary cameras

tel·e·print·er /ˈtelǝ̇ˌprɪntəʳ/ *AmE* **tel·e·type·writ·er** /ˌtelǝ̇ˈtaɪpraɪtəʳ/— *n* [C; *by*+U] an apparatus with a number of buttons with letters on them (TYPEWRITER KEYBOARD) used for sending and receiving printed messages by telegraphic methods

Tel·e·prompt·er /ˈtelǝ̇prɒmptəʳ‖-prɑmp-/ *n tdmk* a machine that unrolls lines of enlarged writing, placed in front of a person appearing on television so that he can read it yet appear to be speaking naturally

tel·e·scope¹ /ˈtelǝ̇skəʊp/ *n* a tubelike scientific instrument used for seeing distant objects by making them appear nearer and larger —see picture at OPTICS

telescope² *v* **1** [IØ;T1] to (cause to) become shorter by crushing, as in a violent accident: *The 2 buses telescoped together, killing all the passengers* **2** [IØ] to become shorter by one part sliding over another: *This instrument will telescope small enough to fit into this box*

tel·e·scop·ic /ˌtelǝ̇ˈskɒpɪk‖-ˈskɑ-/ *adj* [Wa5] **1** of, like, or related to a TELESCOPE: *a telescopic* LENS **2** seen or obtained by means of a TELESCOPE: *a telescopic picture of the moon|a telescopic star* **3** made of parts that slide one over another so that the whole can be made shorter

tel·e·vise /ˈtelǝ̇vaɪz/ *v* **1** [T1] to broadcast by television: *The tennis match will be televised* **2** [L9] to be broadcast by television: *This play was written specially for television and should televise well*

tel·e·vi·sion /ˈtelǝ̇ˌvɪʒən, ˌtelǝ̇ˈvɪʒən/ also (*infml*) **telly**— *n* **1** [U] the method of broadcasting still and moving pictures and sound over a distance by means of electrical waves moving through the air **2** [U] the news, plays, advertisements, pictures, etc., broadcast in this way: *Watching television is how most people spend their free time.|the television news* **3** [C] also **television set** /ˈ··ˈ·· ·, ˈ···· ·/— a boxlike apparatus for receiving pictures and sound **4** [U] the industry of making and broadcasting plays, films, etc., on TELEVISION (1): *Jean works in television as a reporter* **5 on (the) television a** broadcast by TELEVISION (1): *What's on television tonight?* **b** broadcasting by TELEVISION (1): *The President spoke to the nation on television*

tel·e·vi·su·al /ˌtelǝ̇ˈvɪʒʊəl/ *adj* [Wa5] *esp. BrE* of, related to, or suitable for broadcasting by television

tel·ex¹ /ˈteleks/ *n* **1** [U] a telegraphic method of passing printed messages from one place to another by TELEPRINTER. Telex is an international service provided by the post offices of various countries **2** [C] a message received or sent in this way: *A telex has just arrived from Hong Kong*

telex² *v* [D1 (*to*),5a;T1,5a;V3;IØ] to send (a message, information, news, etc.) to (a person, place, firm, etc.) by TELEX[1] (1): *Telex Australia that prices are to be increased 10%*

tell /tel/ *v* **told** /təʊld/ **1** [D1 (*to*),5a,b;T1 (*of*)] to make (something) known in words to (someone); express in words; speak: *Did you tell Aunt Joan the news about Paul?|John told us he'd seen you in town.|I can't tell you how pleased I am to be here tonight* (=I'm very pleased).|*Can you tell me what time the party starts?|George Washington always told the truth.|I always tell my daughter a story before she goes to sleep.|Don't tell me you've missed the train!* (=I am worried by the fact that you seem to have missed the train)|*I'm right, I tell you!* (=you can be certain that I am right) **2** [T1;V3;D5a,b] to warn; advise: *I told you David would want a drink.|I told you that man was a fool but you wouldn't listen to me.|I told you not to print that story, and now look what's happened!|I told you so!* **3** [D6a,b;X9] to show; make known: *This light tells you if the machine is on or off.|Will you tell me how to do it?* **4** [Wv6;T1,6a,b] to find out; know: *It's impossible to tell who'll win the next election.|How do you tell which handle to turn when the light goes out?* **5** [V3; D6a,b;X9] to order; direct: *Do you think children should do as they're told?|I told you to get here early, so why are you late?|Don't try and tell me whether I can or not!* **6** [Wv6;T5a,6a (**whether**, **if**), b (**whether**);X9 esp. *from*; APART;IØ] to recognize; know: *It was so dark I couldn't tell it was you.|It's difficult to tell Jean from Joan, they look so alike.|I can't tell if it's him or not.|"Which team will win?" "Who can tell?"* **7** [IØ] to be noticeable; have an effect: *Her nervousness began to tell as soon as she entered the room* —see also TELL ON (1) **8** [IØ] to speak someone's secret to someone else: *If I whisper you my secret will you promise not to tell?* —see also TELL ON (2) **9** [T1] *old use* to count **10 all told** altogether; when all have been counted **11 tell me another** *infml* I don't believe you; I think you're joking **12 tell the time** to read the time from a clock or watch **13 there is/was/will be no telling** it is/was/will be impossible to know: *There's no telling what will happen if she meets him while she's in this temper* **14 you can never tell** also **you never can tell**— one can never be sure about something because one can easily be deceived without knowing it **15 you're telling me** *infml* (a strong way of saying) I know this already —see SAY (USAGE)

tell a·gainst *v prep* [T1 *no pass.*] to count in judgment against (someone): *Your bad skin will tell against you if you want to be an actress*

tell·er /ˈteləʳ/ *n* **1** *esp. AmE* a person employed to receive and pay out money in a bank **2** a person who counts votes, as at an election

tell·ing /ˈtelɪŋ/ *adj* **1** very effective: *a telling blow to the head|a telling argument* **2** that shows, perhaps unintentionally, one's feelings and opinions —**~ly** *adv*

tell off *v adv* **1** [T1b] *infml* to scold **2** [V3;X9] to separate (a group) from the whole body (for special work or to do something): *10 soldiers were told off to dig ditches* **3** [T1] also **tell o·ver**— *old use* to count one by one; measure

tell on *v prep* [T1] **1** also (*fml*) **tell up·on**— to have a bad effect on (someone or something): *All those late nights are telling on your work, Jean* **2** *infml* (*used esp. by children*) to inform against (someone): *If I'd known you were going to tell on me I'd never have told you my secret*

tell·tale[1] /ˈtelteɪl/ *n infml* a person who informs about other people's secrets, wrong actions, etc.

telltale[2] *adj* [Wa5;A] that makes a fact known: *It was clear from the telltale look in her eyes that she loved him*

tel·ly, *AmE* usu. **tele** /ˈteli/ *n* [C;U] *infml esp. BrE* television

tel·pher, telfer /ˈtelfəʳ/ *n* **1** a system of buckets hanging from moving wires in which stones, rocks, etc., are moved from one place to another **2** one of the buckets used in such a system

Tel·star /ˈtelstɑːʳ/ *n* [C; *by*+U] *tdmk* one of a number of man-made objects moving high above the earth, by which telephone messages and television can be passed over very long distances

te·me·ri·ty /təˈmerəti/ *n* [U] *fml* foolish boldness; RASHness: *had the temerity to ask for higher wages after only 3 days' work*

temp /temp/ *n not fml* a person, esp. a secretary, employed to work in an office for a short time while someone is absent, while there is a great deal of work, etc.

tem·per[1] /ˈtempəʳ/ *n* **1** [C] a particular state or condition of the mind with regard to anger: *Jean's in a bad temper because she missed the bus and had to walk to work.|He has a naturally sweet temper* (=is calm by nature) **2** [C;U] an angry, impatient, or bad state of mind: *John's in a temper today, so keep away from him* **3** [U] the degree to which a substance, esp. a metal, has been hardened or strengthened by TEMPERing[2] (1) **4 fly/get into a temper** to become angry quickly and suddenly **5 keep one's temper** to stay calm **6 lose one's temper** to become angry **7 out of temper** *fml* angry

temper[2] *v* [T1] **1** [Wv5] to bring (metal, clay, etc.) to the desired degree of hardness or firmness by special treatment: *Steel is tempered by heating and being put suddenly in cold water* **2** to soften; make less severe: *justice tempered with mercy*

tem·pe·ra /ˈtempərə/ *n* [U] *tech* **1** a type of heavy thick paint that can be made thinner with egg, water, etc. **2** painting done with this, esp. in FRESCOes

tem·pe·ra·ment /ˈtempərəmənt/ *n* [C;U] a person's nature, esp. as it influences how he thinks, behaves, or acts in general: *Many actors have excitable temperaments.|Whether a person likes Venice or not depends largely on temperament*

tem·pe·ra·men·tal /ˌtempərəˈmentl/ *adj* **1** [Wa5] caused by one's nature: *I have a temperamental dislike of sports* **2** having or showing frequent changes of temper: *The actress was so temperamental that many people refused to work with her* —**~ly** *adv*

tem·pe·rance /ˈtempərəns/ *n* [U] **1** self-control in speech, behaviour, or esp. the drinking of alcohol **2** total avoidance of alcoholic drinks: *a temperance hotel* (=where no alcohol is served)

tem·pe·rate /ˈtempərət/ *adj* **1** practising or showing self-control: *It is rare for so temperate a man to get angry* **2** (of parts of the world, CLIMATE, etc.) free from very high or very low temperatures: *The temperate areas of the world are found to the north and south of the tropics*

tem·pe·ra·ture /ˈtempərətʃəʳ/ *n* [C; *in, of*+U] **1** the degree of heat or coldness of a place, object, etc.: *What's the average temperature in London on a summer's day?|A sudden change in temperature could bring rain* **2 have/run a temperature** to have a bodily temperature higher than the correct one; have a fever **3 take someone's temperature** to measure the temperature of someone's body with a THERMOMETER

-tem·pered /ˈtempəd‖-ərd/ *comb. form* [*adj*→*adj*] having a temper of the stated kind: *a bad-tempered old man* —**~ly** *comb. form* [*adj*→*adv*]: *good-temperedly*

tem·pest /ˈtempəst/ *n lit* a violent storm

tem·pes·tu·ous /temˈpestʃʊəs/ *adj lit* very rough; stormy; violent: *the tempestuous sea/wind*|(fig.) *a* *tempestuous meeting of the council* —**~ly** *adv* —**~ness** *n* [U]

tem·plate, templet /ˈtemplᵻt/ *n* a thin board or plate of metal cut into a special shape or pattern, used as a guide for cutting metal, wood, clay, etc. —see picture at MATHEMATICAL

tem·ple[1] /ˈtempəl/ *n* a place for the worship of a god or gods, esp. in the Hindu, Buddhist, Mormon, or modern Jewish religions: *the Temple of Heavenly Peace in Peking*

temple[2] *n* one of the flattish places on each side of the forehead —see picture at HUMAN[2]

tem·po /ˈtempəʊ/ *n* **-pos** *or* **-pi** /piː/ **1** the rate or pattern of movement, work, or activity: *the busy tempo of city life* **2** the speed at which music is (to be) played

tem·po·ral /ˈtempərəl/ *adj* [Wa5] **1** [B] of or limited by time: *"When" and "while" are temporal* CONJUNCTIONs (1) **2** [B] of or related to practical material affairs as opposed to religious affairs: *the temporal power of the church* **3** [E] *fml* not of the church: *the Lords temporal* (=those members of the House of Lords who are not BISHOPs (1)) —compare SPIRITUAL[1] (4), TEMPORARY

tem·po·ra·ry /ˈtempərəri, -pəri‖-pəreri/ *adj* [Wa5] lasting only for a limited time: *Many students find temporary jobs during their summer holidays* —compare PERMANENT, TEMPORAL —**-rarily** /ˈtempərərᵻli‖ˌtempəˈreərᵻli/ *adv*: *I was temporarily delayed* —**-rariness** /ˈtempərərinᵻs‖-pəreri-/ *n* [U]

tem·po·rize, -rise /ˈtempəraɪz/ *v* [Wv4;IØ] *fml* to delay or avoid making a decision so as to gain time

tempt /tempt/ *v* **1** [T1;V3] to (try to) persuade (someone) to do something unwise or immoral: *The football club tried to tempt the player with offers of money.|Only proof of victory will tempt the government to call an election this year* **2** [Wv4;T1; V3] to attract: *a tempting meal|The warm sun tempted us to go swimming* **3 tempt Providence** to take an unnecessary risk —**~er** (*fem.* **~ress**) *n* —**~ingly** *adv*

temp·ta·tion /tempˈteɪʃən/ *n* **1** [U,U3] the act of TEMPTing or the state of being TEMPTed: *the temptation to smoke a cigarette* **2** [C,C3] something very attractive; something that TEMPTs: *the temptations of a big city|It's a great temptation for a young man to be surrounded by pretty women*

ten /ten/ *determiner, n, pron* [see NUMBER TABLE 1] **1** (the number) 10 **2 ten a penny** (*AmE* **a dime a dozen**)— *infml* very common; not at all unusual or valuable **3 ten to one** very likely: *Ten to one the train will be late* —**tenth** *determiner, n, pron, adv* [see NUMBER TABLE 3]

ten·a·ble /ˈtenəbəl/ *adj* **1** [B] that can be successfully defended against attack: *not a tenable argument* **2** [F9 esp. *for*] (of an office, position, etc.) that can be held by somebody (for a stated period of time): *How long is the post tenable (for)?*

te·na·cious /tᵻˈneɪʃəs/ *adj* **1** [B] unyielding; firm, esp. in a courageous way **2** [B] (of memory) able to keep or store much information **3** [F+*of*] *fml* holding firmly: *a man tenacious of the opinion that all change must be opposed* —**~ly** *adv* —**~ness** *n* [U]

te·na·ci·ty /tᵻˈnæsᵻti/ *n* [U] the quality of being TENACIOUS; TENACIOUSness

ten·an·cy /ˈtenənsi/ *n* **1** [C] the length of time during which a person uses a room, land, building, etc., for which he has paid rent **2** [U] the possession and use of a room, land, building, etc., for which rent is paid

ten·ant[1] /ˈtenənt/ *n* a person who pays rent for the use of a room, building, land, etc.: *Do you own your house or are you a tenant?*

tenant[2] *v* [Wv5;T1 *usu. pass.*] to pay rent for the use of (a room, building, land, etc.): *These houses are all tenanted by mine workers*

tenant farm·er /ˌ·· ˈ··/ *n* a person who farms land owned by someone else and pays rent in money or with a share of what he produces

ten·ant·ry /ˈtenəntri/ *n* [GC] all the TENANT FARMERs renting land from one person in one place

tench /tentʃ/ *n* **tench** *or* **tenches** [Wn2] **1** [C] a type of European fish that lives in lakes and rivers **2** [U] this fish cooked and eaten as food

tend[1] /tend/ *v* [T1] **1** to take care of; look after: *She tended her husband lovingly during his long illness.|The nurse skilfully tended the soldiers' wounds.|Who's tending the shop while you're away?|a farmer tending his sheep* —see also TEND TO **2** *AmE* to serve customers in (a shop, store, etc.)

tend[2] *v* **1** [L9] to move or develop one's course in a certain direction: *Interest rates are tending upwards* **2** [T3;L9 esp. *to, towards*] to have a tendency: *Janet tends to get very angry if you annoy her.|Arthur's books tend to dullness*

ten·den·cy /ˈtendənsi/ *n* **1** [C,C3] a natural likelihood of developing, acting, or moving, in a particular way: *She's always had a tendency to be fat* **2** [C (*towards*)] a special natural skill or cleverness: *an artistic tendency*

ten·den·tious /tenˈdenʃəs/ *adj derog* (of a speech, book, etc.) written to express a particular opinion; intended to influence the reader or hearer in a desired direction; specially prepared to help a political/moral/religious cause —**~ly** *adv* —**~ness** *n* [U]

ten·der[1] /ˈtendəʳ/ *adj* [Wa1] **1** [B] not hard or difficult to bite through: *Cook the meat a long time so that it's really tender* **2** [B] delicate; too easily crushed; needing careful handling: *tender flowers* **3** [B] painful; sore: *After riding such a long way on a bicycle his bottom was very tender* **4** [A] young; inexperienced: *a child of tender years* **5** [B] gentle and loving; sympathetic; kind: *a tender heart* **6** [B] that might offend or hurt people: *One should always avoid tender subjects of conversation at parties* —**~ly** *adv* —**~ness** *n* [U]

tender[2] *n* **1** a person who takes care of something **2** a vehicle carrying coal and/or water, pulled behind a railway engine **3** a small boat for carrying passengers, supplies, etc., between the shore and a larger boat

tender[3] *n* **1** a statement of the price one would charge for providing goods or services or for doing a job **2** LEGAL TENDER

tender[4] *v* [T1] *fml* **1** to offer in payment: *"Passengers should tender the exact amount of money. Change will not be given on this bus"* (notice) **2** to present for acceptance: *The minister tendered his* RESIGNATION (*2*) *to the king but the king asked him to reconsider his decision*

ten·der·foot /ˈtendəfʊt‖-ər-/ *n* **-foots** *or* **-feet** /fiːt/ **1** *AmE* a person who has recently arrived in a rough place, such as the western US, where life is hard **2** an inexperienced beginner: *a tenderfoot in the office*

tender for *v prep* [T1] to make a formal offer to do (something), fulfil (a contract), etc., at a certain price for acceptance

ten·der·heart·ed /ˌtendəˈhɑːtᵻd◂‖-dərˈhɑr-/ *adj* easily moved to love, pity, or sorrow —**~ly** *adv* —**~ness** *n* [U]

ten·der·ize, -ise /ˈtendəraɪz/ *v* [Wv5;T1] to make (meat) tender by special preparation

ten·der·loin /ˈtendəlɔɪn‖-ər-/ *n* [U] tender meat taken from each side of the backbone of cows or pigs

ten·don /ˈtendən/ *n* a thick strong cord that connects a muscle to a bone

ten·dril /ˈtendrɨl/ *n* a thin leafless curling stem by which a climbing plant fastens itself to a support

tend to *v prep* [T1] TEND¹ (1); attend to

ten·e·ment /ˈtenɨmənt/ *n* **1** also **tenement house** /ˈ··· ·/— a large building divided into flats, esp. in the poorer areas of a city **2** *tech* the property rented by a TENANT¹

ten·et /ˈtenɨt/ *n fml* a principle or belief held by a person or organization

ten·ner /ˈtenəʳ/ *n BrE infml* £10 or a 10 pound note

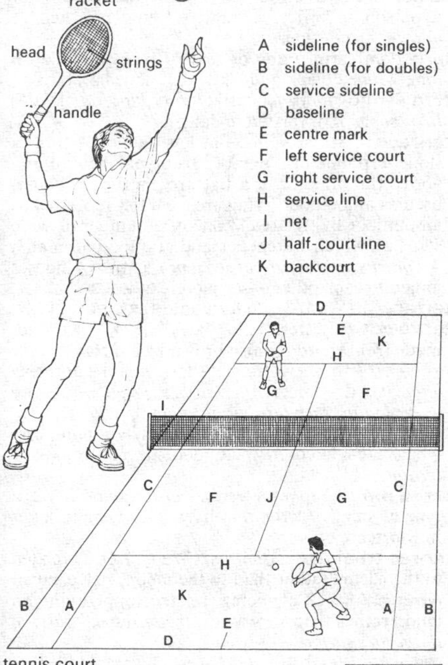

ten·nis /ˈtenɨs/ *n* [U] a game for 2 people (**singles**) or 2 pairs of people (**doubles**) who use RACKETs to hit a small soft ball backwards and forwards across a low net dividing a specially marked level court: *a tennis ball|a tennis court*
USAGE In an important **tennis** *match* the person in charge is called the **umpire**; the winner of such a *match* is the one who wins the larger number of *sets* (= groups of *games*).

tennis el·bow /ˌ·· ˈ··/ *n* [U;(C)] an uncomfortable medical condition of the elbow caused by too much effort when playing tennis or other like games

ten·on /ˈtenən/ *n* a specially cut end of a piece of wood made to fit exactly into a shaped opening (MORTISE) in another piece of wood and so form a joint

ten·or /ˈtenəʳ/ *n* **1** [C;U] (a man with) the highest male singing voice in general use **2** [C] an instrument with the same range of notes as this —see picture at NOTATION **3** [C *usu. sing.*] *fml* (esp. of a person's life) the general direction, course, or style **4** [C *usu. sing.*] *fml* (of something written or spoken) the general meaning: *I understood the tenor of his speech but not the details*

ten·pin /ˈtenˌpɪn/ *n* one of the 10 bottle-shaped wooden objects that one tries to knock down in BOWLING (2)

tenpin bowl·ing /ˌ·· ˈ··/ (*AmE* **ten·pins** /ˈtenˌpɪnz/)— *n* [U] *BrE* BOWLING (2)

tense¹ /tens/ *n* [C;U] any of the forms of a verb that show the time and continuance or completion of the action or state expressed by the verb: *"I am" is present tense, "I was" is past tense, "I will be" is future tense*

tense² *adj* [Wa1] **1** stretched tight; stiff: *tense muscles/nerves* **2** having, showing, or causing nervous anxiety: *I was so tense the night before my examinations that I couldn't sleep* —**~ly** *adv* —**~ness** *n* [U]

tense³ *v* [T1;I∅: (UP)] to (cause to) become TENSE²

tensed up /ˌ· ˈ·/ *adj* [F] nervously anxious: *John seems very tensed up; do you know what's worrying him?*

ten·sile /ˈtensaɪl‖ˈtensəl/ *adj tech* **1** [Wa5;A] of or related to TENSION (1,2): *The tensile strength of a rope tells you how much weight it can hold without breaking* **2** [B] that can be stretched: *tensile rubber*

ten·sion /ˈtenʃən/ *n* **1** [U] the degree of tightness or stiffness of a wire, rope, etc.: *If the tension of this string is increased it will break* **2** [U] the amount of a force stretching something: *This wire will take 50 pounds tension before breaking* **3** [U] (a feeling of) nervous anxiety, worry, or pressure: *The doctor said I was suffering from nervous tension* **4** [C *usu. pl.*;U] an anxious, untrusting, or possibly dangerous relationship between people, countries, etc.: *the racial tensions of a big American city|International tension should be reduced when this agreement is signed* **5** [U] electric power: *Danger. High tension wires. Keep clear!*

tent /tent/ *n* **1** a moveable shelter made of cloth supported by a framework of poles and ropes, used esp. by campers —see picture at CAMP² **2** any of various like-shaped frameworks used for giving support or protection, esp. in the treatment of illness: *Put a tent over his legs to stop them being rubbed by the sheets* —see also OXYGEN TENT

ten·ta·cle /ˈtentɨkəl/ *n* a long snakelike boneless jointless limb on certain creatures, used for moving, feeling, seizing, touching, etc.: *the tentacles of an* OCTOPUS —see picture at MOLLUSC

ten·ta·tive /ˈtentətɪv/ *adj* **1** made or done only as a suggestion to see the effect; not certain: *We've made tentative plans for a holiday but haven't decided anything certain yet* **2** HESITANT; not DECISIVE —**~ly** *adv* —**~ness** *n* [U]

ten·ter·hooks /ˈtentəhʊks‖-ər-/ *n* **on tenterhooks** in a worried, anxious, or nervous state of mind; in a state of anxious expectation

tent peg /ˈ· ·/ *n* PEG¹ (1c)

te·nu·i·ty /teˈnjuːɨti, tɨ-‖-ˈnuː-/ *n* [U] *fml* TENUOUSness

ten·u·ous /ˈtenjʊəs/ *adj* **1** very thin: *The* SPIDER *hung from a tenuous silky thread* **2** (of ideas, opinions, etc.) having little meaning; slight: *the tenuous nature of his political ideas* —**~ly** *adv* —**~ness** *n* [U]

ten·ure /ˈtenjəʳ, -jʊəʳ/ *n* [U] **1** the act or right of holding land or office: *the tenure of an office|conditions of tenure* **2** conditions on which this is held **3** the length of time one holds office **4** *AmE* the right to stay in an office without needing to have a new contract of employment, usu. given after a particular number of years

te·pee /ˈtiːpiː/ *n* a round tent of the type used by North American Indians

tep·id /ˈtepɨd/ *adj* (esp. of liquid) only slightly warm: (fig.) *Because of political differences David's relationship with his father was only tepid* —**~ity** /teˈpɪdɨti/ *n* [U] —**~ly** /ˈtepɨdli/ *adv* —**~ness** *n* [U]

te·qui·la /tɨˈkiːlə/ *n* [U] a strong alcoholic drink made in Mexico

ter·cen·te·na·ry /ˌtɜːsenˈtiːnəri‖ˌtɜrsenˈtenəri, tɜrˈsentneri/ also **tercentennial**— *n* (the day an event happened in) the 300th year after an event

ter·cen·ten·ni·al /ˌtɜːsenˈteniəl‖ˌtɜr-/ *adj* [Wa5] 300th (esp. in the phr. **tercentennial anniversary**)

term[1] /tɜːm‖tɜrm/ *n* **1** [C; *in, of, during*+U] one of the periods of time into which the school, university, or business year is divided: *the summer term|Are there any examinations at the end of term?* **2** [C] a period of time during which a court, parliament, etc., meets **3** [C] a fixed or limited period of time: *The President is elected for a 4 year term* **4** [C9] an agreed or set period of time at the end of a period, after which something is to happen, etc.: *Since our contract is getting near its term we must think of asking for a better one.|The doctor said my wife was too near her term* (= the day on which she is to give birth to a child) *to travel by air* **5** [C] a word or expression with a special meaning or used in a particular activity, job, profession, etc.: *a medical term* **6** [C] each of the various parts in an expression in the science of numbers **7 in the long/short term** over a long/short period of time: *In the short term we expect to lose money on this book but in the long term we hope to make large profits*

term[2] *v* [X1,7,9] to name; call; give (something) (a TERM[1] (5)): *The chairman of this parliament is termed the "Speaker".|"You wouldn't term this house beautiful, would you?" "No, but how/what would you term it?"*

ter·ma·gant /ˈtɜːməgənt‖ˈtɜr-/ *n* [C; (*you*) N] *esp. lit* a noisy quarrelsome woman

ter·mi·na·ble /ˈtɜːmɨnəbəl‖ˈtɜr-/ *adj* [Wa5] *fml or tech* that can be ended

ter·mi·nal[1] /ˈtɜːmɨnəl‖ˈtɜr-/ *adj* [Wa5] **1** *tech* for the TERM[1] (1); of or happening at the end of a TERM[1] (1): *Have you finished the terminal accounts yet?* **2** of, being, related to, or for an illness that will cause death: *the terminal* WARDs *of a hospital* **3** of or at the end or limit of something —**~ly** *adv*

terminal[2] *n* **1** a bus station in the centre of a town for passengers going to or arriving from an airport **2** a point at which connections can be made to an electric system (CIRCUIT) **3** an apparatus by which a user can give instructions to and get information from an electric thinking machine (COMPUTER)

ter·mi·nate /ˈtɜːmɨneɪt‖ˈtɜr-/ *v* [T1;L9] to (cause to) come to an end: *to terminate a contract|The council meeting terminated at 2 o'clock*

ter·mi·na·tion /ˌtɜːmɨˈneɪʃən‖ˌtɜr-/ *n* **1** [C;U] (an example of) the act of terminating (TERMINATE): *termination of a* PREGNANCY **2** [C] *tech* the last part or letter of a word

ter·mi·nol·o·gy /ˌtɜːmɨˈnɒlədʒi‖ˌtɜrmɨˈnɑ-/ *n* **1** [C;U] (a system of) specialized words and expressions used in a particular science, profession, activity, etc.: *I don't understand scientific terminology* **2** [U] the science that studies this —**-ogical** /ˌtɜːmɨnəˈlɒdʒɪkəl‖ˌtɜrmɨnəˈlɑ-/ *adj* [Wa5] —**-ogically** *adv* [Wa4;Wa5]

ter·mi·nus /ˈtɜːmɨnəs‖ˈtɜr-/ *n* **-ni** /naɪ/ *or* **-nuses** **1** the station at the end of a railway line **2** the last stop on a railway or bus line

ter·mite /ˈtɜːmaɪt‖ˈtɜr-/ *n* a type of antlike insect that lives in very large groups in tropical areas, that eats and destroys wood, and that builds large hills of hard earth —see picture at INSECT

terms /tɜːmz‖tɜrmz/ *n* [P] **1** the conditions of an agreement, contract, etc.: *According to the terms of the agreement British ships will be allowed to take a limited amount of fish each year* **2** conditions with regard to payment, prices, etc.: *We sell furniture at very reasonable terms* **3 bring to terms** to force (someone) to agree to stated conditions **4 come to terms/make terms** to reach an agreement **5 come to terms with** to accept (something one does not want to accept) **6 in no uncertain terms** clearly and usu. angrily: *He told me in no uncertain terms to stay away from his daughter* **7 in terms of/in . . . terms** with regard to: *In terms of money/in money terms we're quite rich, but not in terms of happiness* **8 on equal terms** as equals **9 on good/bad/speaking/friendly terms** having a relationship: *After their argument they weren't on speaking terms* **10 think in terms of** to consider or take as a course of action: *We're thinking in terms of moving to the south, as there are so few jobs in the north*

terms of ref·e·rence /ˌ· · ˈ···/ *n* [P] the subject that a person in office, committee, etc., is asked or allowed to consider

tern /tɜːn‖tɜrn/ *n* any of several types of smallish long-winged black and white fork-tailed seabird

terp·si·cho·re·an /ˌtɜːpsɪkəˈrɪən‖ˌtɜr-/ *adj* [Wa5] *lit or pomp* of or related to dancing

ter·race[1] /ˈterɨs/ *n* **1** a flat level area cut from a slope, esp. one of a number rising one behind and above the other **2 a** a flat area next to a house, used as an outdoor living area **b** a flat roof used as an outdoor living area **3** one of a number of wide steps on which watchers stand at a football match **4** (*often cap. as part of a name*) a row of houses joined to each other —see picture at HOUSE[1]

terrace[2] *v* [Wv5;T1] to form into TERRACEs[1] (1)

ter·ra·cot·ta /ˌterəˈkɒtə‖-ˈkɑ-/ *n* [U] (articles made from) hard reddish brown baked clay

ter·ra fir·ma /ˌterə ˈfɜːmə‖-ˈfɜr-/ *n* [U] *Lat, pomp or humor* dry land: *After such a rough voyage we were glad to reach terra firma again*

ter·rain /teˈreɪn, tɨ-/ *n* [C;U] a stretch of land, esp. when considered in relation to its nature: *rocky terrain*

ter·ra·pin /ˈterəpɨn/ *n* **terrapin** *or* **terrapins** [Wn2] a type of small TURTLE that lives in rivers and lakes in warm areas

ter·res·tri·al /tɨˈrestrɪəl/ *adj* [Wa5] **1** of or related to the earth (rather than to the moon, space, etc.): *terrestrial life* **2** of, being, related to, or living on land (rather than in water): *the terrestrial parts of the earth's surface* —**~ly** *adv*

ter·ri·ble /ˈterəbəl/ *adj* **1** very severe indeed: *a terrible war/accident|a terrible winter/cold* **2** unpleasant; nasty: *We had a terrible time on holiday* **3** *infml* very bad indeed: *a terrible play*

ter·ri·bly /ˈterəbli/ *adv* **1** very badly, severely, etc.: *He played that piece of music terribly* **2** [Wa5] *infml* very: *I've been terribly worried about you all day.|We were terribly lucky to find you here*

ter·ri·er /ˈterɪəʳ/ *n* any of several types of small active dogs originally used for hunting

ter·rif·ic /təˈrɪfɪk/ *adj infml* **1** very good; enjoyable; excellent: *a terrific play/book/party* **2** very great in size or degree: *He drove at a terrific speed*

ter·rif·i·cally /təˈrɪfɪkli/ *adv infml* very: *It's terrifically cold again today. It's like being in Siberia!*

ter·ri·fy /ˈterɨfaɪ/ *v* [Wa5;T1] to fill with terror or fear: *Heights terrify me*

ter·ri·to·ri·al[1] /ˌterɨˈtɔːrɪəl◂‖-ˈto-/ *adj* [Wa5] **1** [B] of or related to the land: *a country's territorial possessions* **2** [A] (*often cap.*) of, belonging to, or related to one of the US territories (TERRITORY (4)) **3** [A] (*often cap.*) of, belonging to, or related to the TERRITORIAL ARMY

territorial[2] *n* (*often cap.*) a member of the TERRITORIAL ARMY

Territorial Ar·my /ˌ····· ˈ··/ *n* [(*the*) GU] a military force of people who are trained in their free time to be able to defend Britain

territorial wa·ters /ˌ····· ˈ··/ *n* [P] the sea near a country's coast, in which foreigners are not allowed to fish

ter·ri·to·ry /ˈterɨtəri‖-tori/ *n* **1** [C;U] (an area of) land, esp. ruled by one government: *British territory|travelled through unknown territory* **2** [C;U] (an) area regarded by a person, animal, group, etc., as belonging to it alone and defended against others entering it: *The birds sang to warn other birds off their territory* **3** [C;U] (an) area for which one person or branch of an organization is responsible: *How much territory are the Newcastle police responsible for?* **4** [C] (*often cap.*) (esp. in former times) an area which is not yet admitted as a state of the US but which has its own elected law-making body with a governor and workers appointed by the US government

ter·ror /ˈterəʳ/ *n* **1** [U] very great fear: *The people ran from the enemy in terror* **2** [C] someone or something that causes such fear: *The criminal was the terror of the neighbourhood* **3** [C;N] *infml* an annoying person: *Your son's a real terror! Can't you control him any better?*

ter·ror·is·m /ˈterərɪzəm/ *n* [U] the practice of using (threats of) violence to obtain political demands —**-ist** *adj, n* [Wa5]: *Terrorists are thought to have been responsible for the bomb which exploded in the law court earlier today*

ter·ror·ize, -ise /ˈterəraɪz/ *v* [Wv5;T1] to fill (someone) with terror by threats or acts of violence

terror-strick·en /ˈ·· ˌ··/ also **terror-struck** /ˈ·· ·/— *adj* filled with uncontrollable terror

ter·ry·cloth /ˈteriklɒθ‖klɔθ/ also **ter·ry** /ˈteri/— *n* [U] a thick usu. cotton material with uncut threads on both sides, esp. used for making TOWELs, bath mats, etc.

terse /tɜːs‖tɜrs/ *adj* [Wa1] (of a speaker, his speech, or style) short; using few words —**~ly** *adv* —**~ness** *n* [U]

ter·tian /ˈtɜːʃən‖ˈtɜr-/ *adj* [Wa5] *tech* (of a fever) coming repeatedly in severe attacks every 2 days

ter·tia·ry /ˈtɜːʃəri‖ˈtɜrʃieri, -ʃəri/ *adj* [Wa5] **1** *fml* 3rd in place, degree, order, or rank **2** *med* severe: *tertiary burns*

Tertiary *adj* [Wa5] of or belonging to the 3rd historical period (**Tertiary period**) of the formation of rocks, between about 1,000,000 and 70,000,000 years ago

Te·ry·lene /ˈterɪ̈liːn/ *adj, n* [Wa5;U] *tdmk, BrE* (made of) a type of man-made cloth

tes·sel·la·ted /ˈtesɪ̈leɪtɪ̈d/ *adj* [Wa5] made of small flat pieces of variously coloured stones that form a pattern

test¹ /test/ *n* **1** a number of questions, jobs, etc., set to measure someone's skill, cleverness, or knowledge of a particular subject; short examination: *a history test|You can't drive by yourself until you've passed your driving test* **2** a short medical examination: *an eye test* **3** a practical examination or trial: *Before buying the car I went for a test drive.|atom bomb tests* **4** something used as a standard when judging or examining something else: *Employers will use this agreement as a test in dealing with future wage claims* **5** TEST MATCH **6 put something to the test** to find out the qualities of something by using it in certain conditions

test² *v* **1** [Wv5;T1] to study or examine by means of a test: *I must go to the hospital to have my eyes tested* **2** [Wv4;T1] to be a severe or difficult test of or for: *These wet roads really test a car's tyres.|These are testing times for our country* **3** [T1;IØ: (*for*)] to search by means of tests: *testing (the ground) for oil*

tes·ta·ment /ˈtestəmənt/ *n fml* WILL² (6) (esp. in the phr. **last will and testament**) —see also OLD TESTAMENT, NEW TESTAMENT

tes·ta·men·ta·ry /ˌtestəˈmentəri/ *adj* [Wa5] *tech* of, related to, or done according to a WILL² (6)

tes·tate /ˈtesteɪt, -tɪ̈t/ *adj* [Wa5] *tech* (of a person) having made a lawful WILL² (6) before dying —opposite **intestate**

tes·ta·tor /tesˈteɪtəʳ‖ˈtesteɪ-, tesˈteɪ-/ (*fem.* **tes·ta·trix** /tesˈteɪtrɪks/)— *n tech* the maker of a WILL² (6)

test ban /ˈ· ·/ *n* an agreement between states to stop testing atomic bombs: *a test-ban* TREATY

test case /ˈ· ·/ *n* a case in a court of law which establishes a particular principle and is then used as a standard against which other cases can be judged

test·er /ˈtestəʳ/ *n* a person or instrument that tests

tes·ti·cle /ˈtestɪkəl/ *n* one of the 2 round SPERM-producing organs in the male, enclosed in a bag of skin behind and below the PENIS

tes·ti·fy /ˈtestɪ̈faɪ/ *v* [IØ (*against, for, to*);T5] **1** to bear witness; make a solemn statement of what is true: *The teacher testified to the pupil's ability and willingness to work hard.|One witness testified that he'd seen the prisoner run out of the bank after it had been robbed* **2** to serve as proof: *Her red face testified to her guilt|that she was guilty*

tes·ti·mo·ni·al /ˌtestɪ̈ˈməʊnɪəl/ *n* **1** a formal written statement of a person's character, ability, willingness to work, etc. —see REFERENCE (USAGE) **2** something given or done as an expression of respect, praise, thanks, etc.

tes·ti·mo·ny /ˈtestɪ̈məni‖-məʊni/ *n* **1** [C;U] a formal statement that something is true, as made by a witness in a court of law **2** [U,U5] any information in support of a fact or statement; proof: *The cat's happy expression bore testimony that it had eaten the cream*

tes·tis /ˈtestɪ̈s/ *n* **-tes** /tiːz/ *tech* TESTICLE

test match /ˈ· ·/ also **test**— *n* a cricket (or RUGBY) match played between teams representing different countries

test pi·lot /ˈ· ˌ··/ *n* a pilot who flies new aircraft in order to test them

test tube /ˈ· ·/ *n* a small tube of thin glass, closed at one end, used in scientific tests —see picture at LABORATORY

test-tube ba·by /ˈ· · ˌ··/ *n* **1** a baby born as the result of ARTIFICIAL INSEMINATION **2** a baby started outside the body and then planted inside a female to develop naturally

tes·ty /ˈtesti/ *adj* [Wa1] **1** (of a person) impatient; quickly or easily annoyed **2** (of a remark, behaviour, etc.) showing impatience and annoyance —**-tily** *adv* —**-tiness** *n* [U]

tet·a·nus /ˈtetənəs/ also (*infml*) **lockjaw**— *n* [U] a serious disease caused by bacteria that enter the body through cuts and wounds. It stiffens, hardens, and tightens the muscles, esp. of the jaw, causing great pain and discomfort

tetch·y, techy /ˈtetʃi/ *adj* [Wa1] **1** (of a person) sensitive in a bad-tempered way **2** (of a remark, behaviour, etc.) showing bad-tempered sensitiveness —**-ily** *adv* —**-iness** *n* [U]

tête-à-tête¹ /ˌteɪt ɑː ˈteɪt, ˌteɪt ə ˈteɪt/ *adv* [Wa5] (of 2 people) together in private: *to sit tête-à-tête|The 2 Presidents had dinner tête-à-tête*

tête-à-tête² *n* a private conversation between 2 people

teth·er¹ /ˈteðəʳ/ *n* **1** a rope or chain to which an animal is tied so that it is free to move within a limited area **2 at the end of one's tether** unable to suffer any more

tether² *v* [Wv5;T1] to fasten (an animal) with a TETHER¹

Teu·ton·ic /tjuːˈtɒnɪk‖tuːˈtɑ-/ *adj* [Wa5] of or related to the peoples who lived in northwestern Europe in former times: *the ancient Teutonic languages*

text /tekst/ *n* **1** [C;U] the main body of writing in a book; words in a book written by the writer as opposed to notes, pictures, etc.: *Children won't like this book because there is too much text and too few pictures* **2** [C;U] the original words of a speech, article, etc.: *What the politician really meant will not be clear until we examine the text of his speech* **3** [C9] any of the various forms in which a book, article, etc., exists; copy: *the original text of "War and Peace"* **4** a sentence from the Bible to be read and talked about by a priest in church **5** TEXTBOOK

text·book /ˈtekstbʊk/ *n* a standard book for the study of a particular subject, esp. used in schools

tex·tile /ˈtekstaɪl/ *n* any material made by weaving: *a textile factory|We need to produce more textiles, especially silk and cotton*

tex·tu·al /ˈtekstʃʊəl/ *adj* [Wa5] of or related to the TEXT: *textual differences between the 2 copies of this book|textual* CRITICISM

tex·ture /ˈtekstʃəʳ/ *n* [U;C] **1** the degree of roughness or smoothness, coarseness or fineness, of a surface, esp. as felt by touch: *the delicate texture of her skin|the smooth texture of silk* **2** the way in which the threads of a cloth have been woven, esp. as regards roughness or smoothness: *cotton of (a) loose/firm/uneven texture*

-tex·tured /ˈtekstʃəd‖-ərd/ *comb. form* having a TEXTURE of the stated kind: *coarse-textured cloth*

-th /θ/ *suffix* (forms ORDINAL numbers, except with 1, 2, or 3): *the 17th of June|a 5th of the total* —compare -ND, -RD, -ST (3)

tha·lid·o·mide /θəˈlɪdəmaɪd/ *n* [U] a drug formerly used for making people calm or sleepy, until it was discovered that it caused unborn babies to develop wrongly, esp. without limbs

thalidomide ba·by /·ˈ··· ˌ··/ *n* a baby born wrongly formed, esp. without limbs, because its mother had taken THALIDOMIDE

than¹ /ðən; *strong* ðæn/ *conj* **1** (used for introducing the second part of a comparison of inequality): *I know him better than you.|Jean runs faster than John.|I've never met anyone cleverer than you (are).|Paul is taller than I (am).|Nothing is more unpleasant than finding/than to find insects in your bath.|They work better together than if they're alone* **2** (used for introducing the unwanted choice in statements of what one wants to do): *I'd rather play football than go swimming*
USAGE *She sees me more often* **than** *her father* may mean **a** *more often* **than** *she sees her father* or **b** *more often* **than** *her father sees me.* It is the same with **as**: *He likes her as much* **as** *Mary* may mean **a** *as much* **as** *he likes Mary* or **b** *as much* **as** *Mary likes her* —see ME, HARDLY (USAGE), DIFFERENT (USAGE 1)

than² *prep* **1** in comparison with: *Paul is taller than me.|They arrived earlier than usual* **2** (with measures and standards): *to drive at more than 100 miles per hour* **3 more often than not** usually **4 more X than Y** X but not really very Y (in phrs. like **more surprised than angry**): *I was more annoyed than worried when they didn't come home* (=annoyed but not really very worried) **5 no/none other than (the person named)** the person himself/herself: *It's no/none other than dear old Irving!* **6 nothing more or less than** only and completely: *He can work if he likes—it's nothing more or less than laziness* **7 than what** *BrE nonstandard* THAN¹: *I speak better English than what those foreigners do*

thane, thegn /θeɪn/ *n* **1** (in early English history) a member of a class of a rank between nobles and ordinary men, who held land from the King in return for military service **2** (in early Scottish history) a low-rank member of the noble class

thank /θæŋk/ *v* **1** [T1 (*for*)] to express one's gratefulness to (someone); give thanks to (someone): *The old lady thanked me for helping her across the road* —see also THANK YOU **2** [X9 esp. *for*;V3] (used when requesting something forcefully or rudely) you'd better do/give me what I want: *I'll thank you for that book.|I'll thank you to be quiet while I'm speaking* **3 have (oneself) to thank** to be responsible for something (oneself): *You've only got yourself to thank for the accident* **4 have (someone) to thank** to place blame or responsibility rightly on (someone): *You've got John to thank for your cold. He caught it first and passed it on to everyone* **5 thank God/goodness/heaven** (an expression of great thankfulness): *"Your son's alive." "Thank God"*

thank·ful /ˈθæŋkfəl/ *adj* **1** [B,B3,5] (of a person) showing, feeling, or expressing thanks; grateful: *You should be thankful to be/that you're alive* **2** [B] (of a person's manner, character, appearance, etc.) showing or expressing thanks; grateful: *a thankful look on her face* —**~ly** *adv* —**~ness** *n* [U]

thank·less /ˈθæŋkləs/ *adj* **1** not feeling or showing thanks; ungrateful **2** not likely to be rewarded with thanks: *a thankless job* —**~ly** *adv* —**~ness** *n* [U]

thanks /θæŋks/ *n* [P] **1** words expressing gratefulness: *Kneel down and give thanks to God.|to return a borrowed book with thanks* **2 thanks to** on account of; owing to; because of: *It was thanks to your stupidity that we lost the game*

thanks·giv·ing /ˌθæŋksˈgɪvɪŋ◂/ *n* [C;U] (an) expression of gratefulness, esp. to God

Thanksgiving also **Thanksgiving Day** /ˈ··· ˌ·/— *n* [R] the 4th Thursday in November, kept in the US as a holiday on which God is thanked for the crops which have been safely gathered in

thank·you /ˈθæŋkjuː/ *adj, n* [Wa5;A] (an act of) expressing thanks: *We owe Mrs Jones a special thankyou for all her help.|a thankyou card*

thank you /ˈ· ·/ also (*infml*) **thanks**— *interj* **1** (used politely to mean) I am grateful to you: *Thank you for the nice present you sent me.|Thank you for helping me across the road* **2 No, thank you** (used when refusing an offer politely): *"Would you like a cup of tea?" "No, thank you. I've just had one"*
USAGE If one is offered something that one does not want, one replies *"No,* **thank you**." A reply of **"Thank you"** means that one wants it: *"Have a drink!"* "**Thank you.** *Beer, please."*

that¹ /ðæt/ *determiner* **those** /ðəʊz/ **1** being the one or amount stated, shown, or understood: *Those sweets you gave me tasted very nice.|Have you eaten all that chocolate we bought?* **2** being the one of 2 or more people or things that is further away in time, place, thought, etc.: *This room (we're in) is a lot warmer than that one (across the passage).|Do you want to sit in this chair (here) or that one (over there)?* **3 at that point** then

that² /ðæt/ *pron* **those** **1** a thing, idea, etc., which is understood, stated, etc.: *So that's why you don't like him.|Who told you that?|Come at 6. That seems early enough* **2** (*used with* be, *when pointing to a thing or person*) one of 2 or more people, things, kinds, or ideas that is further away in place, time, thought, etc.: *That's your coat on the hook. This one's mine.|"Who's that?" "It's me"* **3** (*not used of people*) **a** the one or kind: *The best coal is that from Newcastle.|More apples? Have you eaten all those (which) we bought?* **b** the one over there: *Look at that!* (=at that picture! —compare *Look at that man!*) **4 after that** after what had happened; then **5 and all that** also (*BrE nonstandard*) **and that**— and so on; and all like things: *I used to take drugs and all that when I was young* **6 at that** **a** additionally; besides; as well: *It's an idea, and a good one at* *that* **b** with THAT² (10) **7 like that** in such a way; in the way just shown; thus: *Do they always dance like that in France?* **8 that is (to say)** in other words; more correctly **9 that's that** that is the end of the matter; that settles the matter **10 with that** also **at that**— when he had done that; then: *He kissed me and with that he left*

that³ /ðæt/ *adv* [Wa5] *infml* so; to such a degree: *I like him but not (all) that much!*|(*BrE dial*) *I was that hungry I could have eaten a horse!* —see THIS³ (USAGE)

that⁴ /ðət; *strong* ðæt/ *conj* **1** (*used for introducing various kinds of* CLAUSE): *It's true (that) he's French.*|*I will make certain (that) we're ready on time.*|*I believe (that) you want to leave.*|*He was so rude that she refused to speak to him.*|*Bring it closer so (that) I can see it better.*|(*fml*) *Bring it closer that I may see it better.*|*I'll give it you on condition (that) you don't break it.*|*The reason was that he was afraid* **2** *not fml* (*used as the subject of a* DEFINING RELATIVE CLAUSE, *to mean*) who or which: *It's Jean that makes the decisions here.*|*Did you see the letter that/which came today?*|*He's the greatest man that's/who has ever lived.*|*The man that told you that is lying!*|*There's a man (that) comes here every morning* **3** (*used as the object of a* DEFINING RELATIVE CLAUSE *containing* be, *to mean*) whom or which: *He's not the man that* (not **whom*) *he was* **4** *not fml* (*used as the object of a* DEFINING RELATIVE CLAUSE, *to mean*) whom or which: *Did you get the books (that) I sent you?*|*There are lots of things (that) I need to do before I leave tonight.*|*"It's the sort of book that people hide"* (SEU S.) **5** *not fml* (*used as the object of a* PREPOSITION *in a* RELATIVE CLAUSE, *to mean*) whom or which: *That's the man (that) I was telling you about* **6** *not fml* (*used for introducing a* DEFINING RELATIVE CLAUSE, *to mean*) in, on, for, or at which: *the day that he arrived*|*The speed (that) he drives I'm surprised he's not killed himself* **7** (*used for introducing some further information, esp. after nouns in patterns* [C5] *and* [U5]): (*The fact*) *that you don't like her has nothing to do with the matter.*|*There's no proof that she killed him* **8** *lit* (*used for introducing an expression of desire*): OH *that I could fly!*|"WOULD (*that*) *we were there*" (religious song)

USAGE Except in *fml* writing 1 **That** can be used as the subject of a DEFINING RELATIVE CLAUSE instead of **who** or **which**. It is particularly useful when it means both people and things: *the children and parcels* **that** *filled the car*. . . . It is never used as the subject of a NONDEFINING RELATIVE CLAUSE: *This is my father,* **who** (not ***that**) *lives in Glasgow.*| *He broke his leg,* **which** (not ***that**) *was very sad.* 2 **That** can also be used as the object of a DEFINING RELATIVE CLAUSE instead of **whom** or **which**. It can mean "when" in expressions of time: *the time* (**that**) *he stayed* or "in which" in expressions of manner: *the way* (**that**) *he talks.* It is not usually used without a PREPOSITION to mean "where": *the house* (**that**) *he lived in* . . . 3 It can be left out altogether **a** when it is the object, as in 2 above **b** in sentences with "There is/are": *There's a shop up the road* (**that**) *sells them.*

thatch¹ /θætʃ/ *v* [Wv5;T1] to cover (a roof) or the roof of (a building) with THATCH²: *Our house has a thatched roof*—see picture at ROOF¹

thatch² *n* **1** [U] roof covering of STRAW, REEDs, etc. **2** [C] *humor* a mass of thick or untidy hair (on the head)

thaw¹ /θɔː/ *v* **1** [T1;I0: (OUT)] **a** (of a frozen substance) to increase in temperature to above freezing point and so become liquid, soft, or bendable: *The snow is thawing* **b** to cause the temperature of (a frozen substance) to increase to above freezing point **2** [(*it*) I0] (of the weather) to become warm enough for snow and ice to melt: *It often doesn't thaw until June in Siberia* **3** [I0] (of a person) to become friendlier, less formal, etc.

thaw² *n* a period of warm weather during which snow and ice melt

the¹ /ðə, ði; *strong* ðiː/ *definite article, determiner* **1** (*used when it is clearly understood who or what is meant*): *We have a cat and a dog. The cat* (=our cat) *is black and the dog* (=our dog) *white.*|*the history of China* (=Chinese history)|*The Danes that I know work very hard.*|*Take these letters to the post office* (it is understood that you know which post office and where it is) **2** (*used with a person, thing, or group that is the only one of its kind*): *the moon*|*the sun*|*In the year 2000 I will be 49.*|*The Danes work very hard.*| *sitting on the ground* **3** (*used with or as a part of a title*): *The Queen of Denmark*|*His Royal Highness the Prince of Wales*|*George the First* (usu. written George I)|*Peter the Great* **4** (*used before a proper name as of a ship, building, river, etc.*): *the Rhine*|*the Atlantic*|*the Alps*|*the Tower of London*|*the leaning tower of Pisa*|*We sailed to America on the QEII* **5** (*used, often with strong pronunciation, for showing that the following noun is best, best-known, most approved, most important, most wanted, etc.*): *This is the life for me.*|*Her wedding was hardly the event of the century.*|*the business centre of Europe*|*a man called Julius Caesar —not to be confused with* the *Julius Caesar* **6** (*used esp. in neg. sentences with a noun to show what is needed or necessary*): *I haven't got the money for a car* **7** (*used instead of poss.* PRONOUNs *before the names of parts of the body or personal possessions*): *How's the arm today?* (=your arm)|*The car* (=my car) *broke down on the way to work again today.*|*to write with the* (=one's) *left hand*|*She hit him on the ear* **8** (*used with uncountable* [U] *nouns or words with general meanings in sentences like*): *"I was on the telephone to my mother last night." "I didn't know you had a telephone."*|*Turn the water/light/fire/gas on* **9** (*used with an adjective or participle to make it into a noun meaning all members of a group or class, usu. used with a plural verb*): *the dead*|*the poor*|*the hungry*|*The English drink a lot of beer* **10** (*used with a singular noun to make it general, followed by a singular verb*): *The lion is a wild animal from Africa* (compare *Man is a land animal*) —see USAGE 2 **11** (*used before an adjective to make it an* ABSTRACT (=expressing a quality) *noun*): *the beautiful*|*"The difficult we do at once. The impossible takes a little longer"* **12** *becoming rare* (*used with the names of diseases, nervous conditions, and illnesses, esp. those plural in form*): *He's got the* MUMPS/*the* JITTERS **13** (*used before nouns such as* "sea", "air", "wind", "sky", *etc., esp. when there is no adjective and the noun does not follow the words* "there is/are"): *The sea was rough* (=There was a rough sea).|*The sky was blue* (=There was a blue sky). **14** (*used in a* PREPOSITIONAL *phr. with a* UNIT (=fixed measure) *used in calculation*): *Eggs are sold by the* DOZEN.|*Our car does 30 miles to the* GALLON.|*cotton cloth sold by the yard or the metre* **15** (*used with the plural of the numbers* 20, 30, 40, *etc., to show a particular* DECADE (=a period of 10 years) *in a century or person's life*): *In the 30's there was great unemployment* **16** (*often used before the words* "North", "South", "West", "East" *and combinations of them to make them into nouns*): *In winter birds fly South/to the South.*|*What's it like working in the South (of England)?* **17** (*used with musical instruments after the verbs* "play", "like", *etc.*): *I play the piano* (compare *I play tennis*) **18** *esp. ScotE* (*used instead of* to-): *the day* (=today)| *the morrow* (=tomorrow)

USAGE 1 With certain words, **the** is not used except when there is something else before or after the noun that tells us which one or what kind is meant. This is true of the following: **a** ABSTRACT nouns, such as *music, history, time, beauty, work*. Compare: *Life is difficult*. **The** *life of a writer is difficult* **b** names of materials, such as *wine, silk, coal, gold, sugar*. Compare: *She gave us beer and cheese; I drank* **the** *beer but I didn't eat* **the** *cheese* **c** names of times, after *at, by, on*: *at sunset|by night|on Monday* (Compare *during* **the** *night|on* **the** *Monday after Christmas*.) **d** names of meals, after *at, before, during, for*, and the verb *have*: *after|at|before|during breakfast|coffee for breakfast|When do you have breakfast?* (Compare **The** *breakfast she gave us was good*). 2 **The** is not used **a** with most names of diseases: *He's got* SMALLPOX. **b** in many expressions about organizations and means of travelling: *by car|at school|in bed|in prison* **c** in expressions like *arm in arm, face to face, husband and wife, from beginning to end* **d** after [X1] verbs describing a change of state: *They made him President.|They crowned him king.|They appointed him captain* **e** when someone is directly addressed: *Come here, doctor!* **f** with **Man** or **Woman** in meaning 10 above. 3 Names and titles ([R] in this dictionary) either include **the** as part of the name, or they do not. These must be learnt. But note **a** Some ordinary words can be used like names. Compare: **the** *father of a family|I'll ask father!* **b** Names can be used like ordinary words. Compare: *London is a big city.*|**the** *London of my youth* (=London when I was young).

the² *adv* [Wa5] **1** (*used before each of a pair of* COMPARATIVE *adjectives or adverbs, to show that 2 things increase or decrease together*): *The more he has the more he wants* **2** (*used before a* COMPARATIVE *adjective or adverb, to mean*) in or by that; on that account; in or by so much; in some degree: *He's had a holiday and looks the better for it* **3** (*used before a* SUPERLATIVE *adjective or adverb, to mean*) **a** above all others: *He likes you the best* **b** very much: *"He has the greatest difficulty* (=very great difficulty) *with drugs"* (SEU S.)

the- /θi-/ *comb. form* THEO-

the·at·re, *AmE* **-ter** /ˈθɪətəʳ/ *n* **1** [C] a special building or place for the performance of plays: *London's theatres|an evening at the theatre* **2** [(*the*) U] the work or activity of people who write or act in plays: *the modern Russian theatre* **3** [C9] a scene of important military events: *the Pacific theatre of World War II* **4** [C; *in*+U] OPERATING THEATRE **5** [C] LECTURE THEATRE

the·at·re·go·er, *AmE* **-ter-** /ˈθɪətəˌgəʊəʳ‖-tər-/ *n* a person who regularly goes to the theatre

the·at·ri·cal /θiˈætrɪkəl/ *adj* **1** [Wa5] of, related to, or for the theatre: *a theatrical company* **2** (of behaviour, manner, a person, etc.) showy; not natural —**~ly** *adv* [Wa4]

the·at·ri·cals /θiˈætrɪkəlz/ *n* [P] stage performances, esp. as done by AMATEURs

thee /ðiː/ *pron* [Wp1] *old use* (*object form of* THOU) you: *"Shall I compare thee to a summer's day?"*

theft /θeft/ *n* [C;U] (an example of) the crime of taking someone else's property from a place

thegn /θeɪn/ *n* THANE

their /ðəʳ; *strong* ðeəʳ/ *determiner* [Wp1] (*poss. form of* THEY) belonging to them: *They ought to wash their faces.|cars with their engines at the back|Everyone must do their best*

theirs /ðeəz‖ðeərz/ *pron* [Wp1] (*poss. form of* THEY) that/those belonging to them: *The ship is theirs.|Those are theirs over there.|I do my duty and I expect everyone else to do theirs.|That is ours, not theirs* —see also OF (6)

the·is·m /ˈθiːɪzəm/ *n* [U] the belief that a personal God exists and that he has made his existence known through the Bible, church, dreams, etc. —**-ist** *n* —**-istic** /θiːˈɪstɪk/ *adj* [Wa5] —**-istically** *adv* [Wa4]

them[1] /ðəm; *strong* ðem/ *pron* [Wp1] (*object form of* THEY): *He bought them drinks.|He bought drinks for them.|Where are my shoes? I can't find them* —see ME, HIM (USAGE)

them[2] /ðem/ *determiner nonstandard* those: *Pass me them sweets, please*

theme /θiːm/ *n* **1** the subject of a talk or piece of writing **2** a short simple tune on which a piece of music is based

theme song /'· ·/ also **theme tune** /'· ·/— *n* a song or tune often repeated during a musical play, cinema picture, etc. —compare SIGNATURE TUNE

them·selves /ðəm'selvz/ *pron* [Wp1] **1** (*refl. form of* THEY): *The children seem to be enjoying themselves* **2** (*strong form of* THEY): *They built the house themselves.|Themselves a religious family, they were shocked at our behaviour* **3** *infml* (in) their usual state of mind or body (often in the phrs. **be themselves, come to themselves**): *When they came to themselves* (=regained consciousness) *they found their money had been stolen.|They don't feel themselves this morning after a night without sleep* **4** (**all**) **by themselves** alone, without help **5 in themselves** without considering the rest: *These little things aren't important in themselves, but they worry him because he's ill* —see YOURSELF (USAGE)

then[1] /ðen/ *adv* [Wa5] **1** at that time: *We lived in the country then.|I was still unmarried then.|Will you still be alive then?|I don't think I'll be married by/before then, do you?|When you see her, then you'll understand* **2** next in time, space, or order; afterwards: *Let's go for a drink and then go home.|The elephants were followed by the camels and then came the horses* **3** in that case: *If you want to go home, then go.|What shall we do, then? Swim?* **4** as a result; therefore: *If x=5 and y=3, then xy=15.|Go into the cave, (because) then they won't see you* **5** besides; and also: *You must ask John to the party, then Paul and Mark as well* **6 but then** (**again**) however: *I like watching television but then (again) I wouldn't miss it if I didn't have one* —see also NOW **and then**, NOW **then**, THERE **and then**

then[2] *adj* [Wa5;A] being so at the time: *the then capital of the country*

USAGE Some people think **then** should not be used as an adjective

thence /ðens/ *adv* [Wa5] *fml* **1** from that place on: *We can drive to London and thence to Paris by air* **2** therefore; for that reason: *He was recently in Africa; thence we may argue that it was there he caught this tropical disease*

thence·forth /ðens'fɔːθ‖'ðensforθ/ also **thence·forward** /ðens'fɔːwəd‖-'fɔrwərd/— *adv* [Wa5] from that time on

the·o- /θɪə, θi'ɒ‖θɪə, θi'ɑ/ also **the-**/θi/— *comb. form* of God or gods: THEOLOGY|THEISM

the·oc·ra·cy /θi'ɒkrəsi‖θi'ɑ-/ *n* **1** [U] government by priests or people that claim support from God **2** [C] a state governed in this way

the·o·crat·ic /θɪə'krætɪk/ *adj* of or related to THEOCRACY (1)

the·od·o·lite /θi'ɒdəlaɪt‖θi'ɑ-/ *n* an instrument used by SURVEYORs for measuring angles —see picture at SCIENTIFIC

the·o·lo·gian /θɪə'ləʊdʒən/ *n* a person who has studied THEOLOGY

the·ol·o·gy /θi'ɒlədʒi‖θi'ɑ-/ *n* **1** [U] the study of religion and religious ideas and beliefs; study of God and of God's relationship with man, esp. by studying the origin and development of a particular religion **2** [C;U(9)] a particular body of opinion about religion: *According to Muslim theology there is only one God* —**-ogical** /θɪə'lɒdʒɪkəl‖-'lɑ-/ *adj* [Wa5]—**-ogically** *adv* [Wa4]

the·o·rem /'θɪərəm/ *n tech* (in the science of numbers) a statement that can be shown to be true by reasoning

the·o·ret·i·cal /θɪə'retɪkəl/ also **the·o·ret·ic** /θɪə'retɪk/— *adj* **1** [Wa5] based on THEORY, not on practical experience: *theoretical science* **2** existing only in THEORY, not in practice; HYPOTHETICAL

the·o·ret·i·cal·ly /θɪə'retɪkəli/ *adv* **1** in a THEORETICAL way; not practically **2** according to THEORY but not really: *Theoretically he's in charge, but in fact his secretary takes all the decisions*

the·o·rist /'θɪərɪ̈st/ *n* a person who forms or deals with the THEORY of a subject: *a leading political theorist*

the·o·rize, -rise /'θɪəraɪz/ *v* [I∅ (*about, on*);T5] to form a THEORY or theories (THEORY (1))

the·o·ry /'θɪəri/ *n* **1** [C;S5] a statement or group of statements established by reasoned argument based on known facts, intended to explain a particular fact or event; explanation for which certain proof is still needed but which appears to be reasonable: *According to Darwin's theories man and monkeys are descended from the same ancient animal* **2** [U] the part of a science or art that deals with general principles and methods as opposed to practice; set of rules or principles for the study of a subject: *The government's plans seem good in theory but I doubt if they'll work in practice.|musical theory* **3** [C;S5] an opinion based on limited information or knowledge; something supposed: *He has a theory that the girl's the murderer but I think he's wrong* **4** [U] (in the science of numbers) a body of principles, THEOREMs, etc., belonging to one part of the subject

the·os·o·phy /θi'ɒsəfi‖θi'ɑ-/ *n* [U] any of various forms of religious thought claiming that a special relationship can be established between a person's soul and God, esp. by quiet thought and prayer —**-phical** /θiə'sɒfɪkəl‖-'sɑ-/ *adj* [Wa5] —**-phist** /θi'ɒsəfɪ̈st‖θi'ɑ-/ *n*

ther·a·peu·tic /ˌθerə'pjuːtɪk/ *adj* of or related to the treating or curing of disease: *a therapeutic bath* —**~ally** *adv* [Wa4]

ther·a·peu·tics /ˌθerə'pjuːtɪks/ *n* [U] the branch of medicine concerned with the treatment and cure of disease

ther·a·pist /'θerəpɪ̈st/ *n* a specialist in a particular branch of THERAPY: *a speech therapist*

ther·a·py /'θerəpi/ *n* [U;(C)] the treatment of illnesses of the mind or body, esp. without drugs or operations —see also OCCUPATIONAL THERAPY, RADIOTHERAPY

there[1] /ðeəʳ/ *adv* [Wa5] **1** to, at, or in that place: *Paul's hiding there, under the trees.|I like living there.|Go and stand over there* (compare *Come and stand over here*).|*"It's certainly very cold out there"* (SEU S.) **2** at that point of time: *I read to the bottom of the page and decided to stop there* **3** (used for drawing attention to someone or something, usu. followed by the verb if the subject is not a pron.): *There goes John.|There he goes.*|HELLO *there!* **4** *infml* (*usu. used after a noun*) being present in that place: *I live in that house there.*|(*nonstandard*) *When are you going to get that there hair cut?* **5 all there** [*usu. nonassertive*] *infml* healthy in the mind; able to make fair judgments: *I don't think she's all there* (=I think she's mad) **6 get there** to succeed in reaching an aim: *You'll get there in the end if you work hard!* **7 there and back** to a place and back again **8 there and then** also **then and there**— at that time and place: *There and then he kissed her and asked her to marry him* **9 There you are a** here is what you wanted: *There you are! A nice cup of tea* **b** I told you so: *There you are. I knew I was right* **10 there you go** *infml* you are doing again what you usually do: *There you go, talking* *about people behind their backs again*

there² /ðeəʳ, ðəʳ/ *pron* (*used as the first word in a sentence or* CLAUSE *or as the second word in a question, as the subject of the verb, esp. of* "be", "seem", *and* "appear", *when the real subject follows later*): *"There are fairies at the bottom of our garden"* (poem).|*There's a man at the door.*|*Is there something/anything wrong?*|*There's a hole in your trousers.*|*"There could be a bit of money in this."* (SEU W.)|*There's been a car stolen.*|*There's plenty to eat, isn't there?*|*I don't want there to be any doubt about this.*|*There's something (that) keeps making a funny noise.*|*There came a knock at the door*
USAGE 1 All these sentences tell us that someone or something that has not been mentioned before exists, happens, etc. In English this idea is usually expressed with **there**; it is more natural to say **There's** *a man at the door* than *A man is at the door.* 2 **It** is only used when the person or thing has already been mentioned or thought of. Compare: *"Is* **there** *anyone in the office?"* (=or is it empty?) *"Yes,* **there's** *Harry."*|*"***There's** *a man in the office!" "Yes,* **it's** *Harry."* 3 Do not confuse **there** in these sentences with **there** the adverb of place, which is spelt in the same way but pronounced differently. **There's** *Peter* can mean **a** "he exists" or **b** "I can see him."

there³ /ðeəʳ/ *interj* (used for comforting someone or for expressing victory, satisfaction, encouragement, sympathy, sadness, etc., the meaning changing according to the setting (CONTEXT) and the way it is expressed): *There! Do you feel better now?*|*There, there. Stop crying.*|*There. I told you I was right!*|*There. You've made me cry.*|*But there! What can you expect for £5?* —compare NOW¹ (3)

there·a·bouts /ˌðeərəˈbaʊts/ *AmE* also **there·a·bout** /ˌðeərəˈbaʊt/— *adv* [Wa5] *not fml* near that place, time, number, degree, etc.: *I'll see you at 9 o'clock or thereabouts.*|*The people who lived thereabouts were very worried about the whole affair*

there·af·ter /ðeəˈrɑːftəʳ‖-ˈræf-/ *adv* [Wa5] *fml* after that in time or order; afterwards: *"Thereafter we heard no more of this suggestion"* (SEU W.) —compare HEREAFTER¹

there·by /ðeəˈbaɪ, ˈðeəbaɪ‖-ər-/ *adv* [Wa5] **1** *fml or law* by that means; by doing or saying that: *He became a citizen, thereby gaining the right to vote* —compare HEREBY **2 (and) thereby hangs a tale** There is an interesting story connected with what I have just said

there·fore /ˈðeəfɔːʳ‖ˈðeər-/ *adv* [Wa5] **1** as a result; for that reason; so: *I've never been to China and therefore I don't know much about it.*|(*fml*) *As I don't know much about China, I therefore can't advise you.*|(*fml*) *Because he's younger, he therefore needs more sleep* **2** (used in reasoning) as this proves; it follows that: *I think. Therefore, I exist*

there·in /ðeəˈrɪn/ *adv* [Wa5] **1** *old use or law* in that (place or piece of writing): . . . *and everything therein contained* —compare HEREIN **2** *fml* in that particular matter: *She would never agree to marry him and therein lay the cause of his unhappiness*

there·in·af·ter /ˌðeərɪnˈɑːftəʳ‖-ˈæf-/ *adv* [Wa5] *law* later in the same official paper, statement, etc.

there·of /ðeəˈrɒv‖-ˈrɑv/ *adv* [Wa5] *fml* of that or it: *All citizens of the United Kingdom are ruled by the laws thereof* —compare HEREOF

there·on /ðeəˈrɒn‖-ˈrɑn/ *adv* [Wa5] *fml* **1** on that: *I read the report and wrote some remarks thereon* **2** THEREUPON (1)

there·to /ðeəˈtuː‖ðeərˈtuː/ *adv* [Wa5] *fml* **1** in addition to that; also **2** to that: *". . . any conditions* ATTACH*ing thereto . . ."* (SEU W.)

there·un·der /ðeəˈrʌndəʳ/ *adv* [Wa5] *fml or law* **1** under that, it, or them: *the land, with any coal found thereunder . . .* **2** below, following, or in accordance with (something written)

there·up·on /ˌðeərəˈpɒn, ˈðeərəpɒn‖-pɔn, -pɑn/ *adv* [Wa5] *fml* **1** as a result of that; about that matter: . . . *if all are agreed thereupon* . . . **2** without delay after that; then: *Thereupon she asked me to marry her* —compare HEREUPON

therm /θɜːm‖θɜrm/ *n* (a measurement of heat equal to) 100,000 BRITISH THERMAL UNIT*s*, used in Britain in measuring the amount of gas used by each user

therm- also **ther·mo-** /ˈθɜːməʊ, -mə, θɜˈmɒ‖ˈθɜrməʊ, -mə, θərˈmɑ/— *comb. form* of or related to heat: THERMODYNAMICS|THERMOMETER

ther·mal¹ /ˈθɜːməl‖ˈθɜr-/ *adj* [Wa5] **1** of, using, producing, or caused by heat; of or related to heat or temperature: *thermal power stations* **2** naturally warm or hot: *thermal springs*

thermal² *n* a rising current of warm air, esp. as used by GLIDER pilots to gain height

ther·mi·on·ic /ˌθɜːmiˈɒnɪk◂‖ˌθɜrmiˈɑ-/ *adj* [Wa5] *tech* of or related to THERMIONICS

ther·mi·on·ics /ˌθɜːmiˈɒnɪks‖ˌθɜrmiˈɑ-/ *n* [U] *tech* the branch of science that deals with the outward flow of ELECTRON*s* from heated metal

thermionic valve /ˌ···· ˈ·/ (*AmE* **thermionic tube** /ˌ···· ˈ·/)— *n BrE tech* a system of ELECTRODE*s* arranged in an airless glass or metal container, esp. used in radios and televisions

ther·mo·dy·nam·ics /ˌθɜːməʊdaɪˈnæmɪks‖ˌθɜr-/ *n* [U] the branch of science that deals with the relationship between heat and the power that works and drives machines, and the making of one into the other

ther·mom·e·ter /θəˈmɒmɨtəʳ‖θərˈmɑ-/ *n* an instrument for measuring and showing temperature, esp. a thin glass tube containing a special liquid (usu. MERCURY) that rises and falls as the temperature rises and falls —see also CLINICAL THERMOMETER —see picture at MEDICAL²

ther·mo·nu·cle·ar /ˌθɜːməʊˈnjuːkliəʳ‖ˌθɜrməʊˈnuː-/ *adj* [Wa5] of, using, or caused by the very high temperatures that result from **atomic** FUSION: *a thermonuclear bomb*

ther·mo·plas·tic /ˌθɜːməʊˈplæstɪk‖ˌθɜrmə-/ *adj, n* [Wa5;B;C;U] (a plastic that is) soft and bendable when heated

ther·mos /ˈθɜːməs‖ˈθɜr-/ *n tdmk* FLASK (4)

thermos bot·tle /ˈ·· ˌ··/ *n esp. AmE* FLASK (4)

ther·mo·set·ting /ˈθɜːməʊˌsetɪŋ‖ˈθɜr-/ *adj* [Wa5] (of plastic) that becomes hard and unbendable after having been heated and shaped

thermos flask /ˈ·· ·/ *n* FLASK (4)

ther·mo·stat /ˈθɜːməstæt‖ˈθɜr-/ *n* an apparatus that can be set to keep an even temperature at a particular level by disconnecting and reconnecting a supply of heat when necessary

the·sau·rus /θɪˈsɔːrəs/ *n* a collection of words put in groups together according to likenesses in their meaning rather than in an alphabetical list

these /ðiːz/ *pl. of* THIS: *"doing a hard day's work these days"* (=at the present time) (SEU S.)

the·sis /ˈθiːsɨs/ *n* **-ses** /siːz/ **1** an opinion or statement put forward and supported by reasoned argument **2** a long article written on a particular subject for a higher (POSTGRADUATE) university degree

thes·pi·an /ˈθespɪən/ *adj* [Wa5] *fml* (*often cap.*) of or related to acting or the theatre: *the thespian art*

thews /θjuːz‖θuːz/ *n* [P] *lit* **1** muscles **2** bodily strength

they /ðeɪ/ *pron* [Wp1] (*used as the subject of a sentence*) **1** those people, animals, or things: *My brother and sister are coming for their holidays. They arrive on Monday* **2** people in general: *They say* *prices are going to increase again.|John's as clever as they come* (=very clever)

they'd /ðeɪd/ [Wv2] *contr. of* (*in compound tenses*) **1** they had: *If only they'd been there* **2** they would: *They'd never believe you* —see CONTR. (USAGE)

they'll /ðeɪl/ [Wv2] *contr. of* **1** they will: *They'll arrive tomorrow* **2** they shall —see CONTR. (USAGE)

they're /ðəʳ; *strong* ðeəʳ, ðeɪəʳ/ [Wv1] *contr. of* they are: *They're the best you can buy* —see CONTR. (USAGE)

they've /ðeɪv/ [Wv2] *contr. of* (*esp. in compound tenses*) they have: *They've lost again.|They've a wonderful new house* —see CONTR. (USAGE)

thick[1] /θɪk/ *adj* [Wa1] **1** [B] **a** having a large distance between opposite surfaces; not thin: *a thick board* **b** (of a round object) wide in relation to length: *thick wire* **2** [E] measuring in depth, width, or from side to side: *ice 5* CENTIMETRE*s thick* **3** [B] (of liquid) not watery; not flowing easily; heavy: *thick soup* **4** [B] difficult to see through; DENSE: *thick mist* **5** [B] aching and/or unable to think clearly: *My head's rather thick this morning after all that beer I drank last night* **6** [B] (esp. of an ACCENT[1] (3)) very noticeable **7** [F+*with*] full of; covered with: *The air was thick with smoke.|furniture thick with dust* **8** [B] (of a voice) not clear in sound: *His voice sounded thick because of his cold* **9** [B] closely packed; made of many objects set close together: *a thick forest* **10** [B] *infml* (of a person) stupid **11** [F] *sl* beyond what is reasonable or satisfactory: *It's a bit thick to expect me to work till midnight!* **12** [B (*with*)] *infml* very friendly: *Jean and John seem very thick with each other* **13 as thick as two short planks** *sl* very stupid indeed **14 as thick as thieves** *infml* very friendly **15 lay it on thick** *infml* to praise, thank, etc., someone too much —**~ly** *adv*

thick[2] *adv* [Wa1] so as to be thick; thickly: *The flowers grew thickest near the wall*

thick[3] *n* **1** [(*the*) S] the part most packed with people, traffic, etc.; place or time of greatest activity: *in the thick of the fight* **2** [(*the*) S9] the thick part of anything: *the thick of his thumb* **3 through thick and thin** through both good and bad times; faithfully

thick ear /ˌ·ˈ·/ *n* [*usu. sing.*] *infml* a blow to the ear that causes it to swell

thick·en /ˈθɪkən/ *v* [T1;IØ] **1** to (cause to) become thick: *I always thicken my soups by adding flour.|The mist is thickening* **2** to (cause to) become more confused and difficult to understand: *The* PLOT[1] (3) *thickened*

thick·en·er /ˈθɪkənəʳ/ also **thick·en·ing** /ˈθɪkənɪŋ/— *n* [C;U] a substance used for thickening a liquid

thick·et /ˈθɪkɨt/ *n* a thick growth of bushes and small trees: *The fox hid in the thicket where the dogs could not reach it*

thick·head·ed /ˌθɪkˈhedɨd◂/ also **thick·wit·ted** /ˌθɪkˈwɪtɨd◂/— *adj* stupid

thick·ness /ˈθɪknɨs/ *n* **1** [C;U] the state, degree, or quality of being thick: *The beam has a thickness of 4 inches|is 4 inches in thickness* **2** [C] LAYER[1] (1): *wrapped it in 3 thicknesses of newspaper*

thick·set /ˌθɪkˈset◂/ *adj* **1** having a short broad body **2** set thickly or in close arrangement: *thickset rose bushes*

thick-skinned /ˌ·ˈ·◂/ *adj* [Wa2] *sometimes derog* insensitive, esp. to blame, disapproval, etc.; not easily offended

thief /θiːf/ *n* **thieves** /θiːvz/ a person who steals or has stolen, esp. without using violence

thieve /θiːv/ *v* **1** [IØ] to steal things; rob people; act as a thief **2** [T1] *nonstandard* to steal (something)

thiev·ing[1] /ˈθiːvɪŋ/ also (*esp. fml or lit*) **thiev·e·ry** /ˈθiːvəri/— *n* [U] the act or practice of stealing; THEFT

thieving[2] *adj* [Wa5;A] who habitually steals or has just stolen: *Come back here with my bicycle, you thieving boys!*

thiev·ish /ˈθiːvɪʃ/ *adj esp. lit* thieflike: *thievish habits* —**~ly** *adv* —**~ness** *n* [U]

thigh /θaɪ/ *n* **1** the top part of the human leg between the knee and the HIP[2] —see picture at HUMAN[2] **2** a part like this on the back legs of certain animals

thim·ble /ˈθɪmbəl/ *n* a very small protective metal or plastic cap put over the finger that pushes the needle during sewing

thim·ble·ful /ˈθɪmbəlfʊl/ *n* [(*of*)] *infml* a very small quantity (of liquid)

thin[1] /θɪn/ *adj* **-nn-** [Wa1] **1 a** having a small distance between opposite surfaces; not thick: *a thin board|thin ice* **b** (of a round object) narrow in relation to length; fine: *thin string/wire* **2** having little fat on the body; not fat: *She looked thin after her illness* —see USAGE **3** (of a liquid) watery; flowing easily; weak: *This beer's too thin to enjoy* **4** not closely packed; made of few objects widely separated: *Your hair's getting very thin.|a thin* AUDIENCE (1) **5** easy to see through; not DENSE (1,2): *thin mist|The air on top of the mountain was very thin* **6** (esp. of a sound or note) lacking in strength: *thin high notes* **7** lacking force or strength; poor: *The teacher said my excuse was too thin to believe* **8 have a thin time** *infml* to have an unpleasant, uncomfortable, or esp. unsuccessful time **9 thin on the ground** *infml* scarce: *Taxis seem very thin on the ground tonight—we'll have to walk* **10 thin on top** *infml* becoming BALD (=hairless) —**~ly** *adv*: *Spread the butter thinly* —**~ness** *n* [U]

USAGE **Thin** is a general word, the opposite of **fat** or **thick**. When one wishes to say that someone is **thin** in a beautiful way, the best words are **slim** or **slender**: *a* **slim** *young girl* (compare *a* **thin** *old horse*)|*her* **slender** *arms*. **Delicate** has also this meaning, but it suggests softness and perhaps weakness: *her* **delicate** *fingers*. **Delicate** and **fine** are used of things that are sharp and narrow and that give the idea of careful sensitive work: **fine** *silk thread*|*a* **delicate** *line drawing|to write the names on the map with a* **fine** *pen*.

thin[2] *adv* [Wa1] so as to be thin; thinly: *Don't cut the bread so thin*

thin[3] *v* **-nn-** **1** [T1;IØ] to (cause to) become thin: *We should wait until the mist thins before driving on.|to thin wine by adding water* **2** [T1 (OUT)] to pull up the weaker of (a mass of young plants) so that the stronger ones have room to grow freely

thine[1] /ðaɪn/ *pron* [Wp1] *old use, bibl, or poet* (*poss. form of* THOU) that/those belonging to THEE; yours: *"For thine is the kingdom, the power, and the glory"* (prayer)

thine[2] *determiner* [Wp1] *old use, bibl, or poet* (*before a vowel or* h) THY: *"Drink to me only with thine eyes"* (Ben Jonson)

thing /θɪŋ/ *n* **1** [C] any material object; an object that need not or cannot be named: *What's that thing you've got on your head?|What do you use this thing for?|"You can't leave that thing there," shouted the policeman* **2** [C] a garment; piece of clothing: *I've not got a thing to wear* **3** [C] that which is not material: *What a nasty thing to say to your sister!|I'm more interested in things of the mind than things of the body* **4** [C] a creature: *Your daughter's such a sweet little thing.|He's been very ill and weak, poor thing.|There wasn't a living thing in the woods* **5** [C] a subject; matter: *There's one more thing I wanted to say* **6** [C] an act; deed: *What's the next thing we* have to do?|I expect great things from you, son! **7** [the+R] that which is necessary: *I think I've got just the thing you need* **8** [C] an event: *The murder was a terrible thing wasn't it?* **9** [C] a product of work or activity: *My son likes making things* **10** [C] an aim or effort: *The next thing is for you to get well again* **11** [C] an idea: *He says the first thing that comes into his head* **12** [the+R (in)] *not fml* the fashion or custom: *She was wearing the latest thing in shoes.|It's not the thing to put your knife in your mouth when you eat* **13** [S9] *sl* an activity very satisfying to one personally: *What's your thing?|Everyone should be free to do their thing* **14 first thing** early; before anything else: *First thing in the morning I open the window and breathe deeply* **15 for one thing** (used for introducing a reason): *For one thing I think you're stupid, for another I don't like you* **16 have a thing about** to have a strong like or dislike for **17 it's a good thing** it's lucky: *It's a good thing George can't hear us!* **18 it's a good/bad thing to** it's sensible/not sensible to: *It's a good thing to clean your teeth after meals* **19 make a good thing (out) of** to get advantage or profit from **20 make a thing of** to give too much importance to: *I disagree with you, but don't let's make a thing of it!* **21 taking one thing with another** considering everything that needs to be considered

thing·a·ma·jig, thingumajig /ˈθɪŋəmɪ̈dʒɪg/ also **thing·a·ma·bob** /ˈθɪŋəmɪ̈bɒb‖-ˌbɑb/, **thing·um·my** /ˈθɪŋəmi/— *n infml* a person or thing, esp. one whose name one has forgotten or does not know: *this new thingamajig for opening beer bottles*

things /θɪŋz/ *n* **1** [P] personal possessions; belongings: *Pack your things. We're going to leave* **2** [P] the general state of affairs: *Things are getting worse and worse* **3** [P9] the dishes, cups, knives, etc., used for the stated meal: *Mother's washing up the tea things* **4 be seeing things** to see things which do not exist; have HALLUCINATIONs

think[1] /θɪŋk/ *v* **thought** /θɔːt/ **1** [IØ (*about*);T1] to use the power of reason; make judgments; use the mind to form opinions; have (a thought): *Do you still think in English when you're speaking French?|If animals can think, what do they think about?|thinking great thoughts* **2** [Wv6;T5a,b;X1,7] to believe; consider: *I think she's wrong, don't you?|He thinks himself a great poet.|"Do you think it will rain?" "Yes, I think so."|I thought her rather clever* **3** [T6a,b] (*used after* cannot *and* could not) to imagine; understand: *I can't think why you did it.|They couldn't think where to go* **4** [T6a] (*used in questions*) to believe: *Who do you think murdered the old lady?* **5** [T6a] to reason about; bring to mind: *Think how big and varied the world is* **6** [IØ; T6a,b] to consider carefully: *Think before you accept his offer!|The criminal was thinking what to do next when the police arrived* **7** [T5a,b, (*fml*) 3] to have as a half-formed intention or plan: *We thought to return early.|We thought we'd go swimming tomorrow.|"You'll go swimming tomorrow, will you?" "Yes, I thought so"* (=that is my intention) **8** [T6a,b] (*used after* cannot *and* could not *and in infin. after* try, want, *etc.*) to remember: *I can't think what his name is.|I'm trying to think what his address is/how to get there* **9** [T5a;L9] to expect: *Little did he think the police would be waiting for him.|We didn't think we'd be this late.|I thought as much* (used when one has heard some news, to mean "that's just what I expected") **10** [T1] to have as the centre of one's thoughts: *He thinks business all day* **11** [L9] *not fml* to direct the mind in a particular way: *to think big* —see also **see/think** FIT **to do** **12 I don't think** *sl* (used esp. when bitterly or nastily attacking someone, to mean) I certainly do not think so: *You're clever, I don't think* **13 to think aloud** to speak one's thoughts as they come **14 think twice** to think very carefully about something —**~er** *n*: *Bertrand Russell, one of the great thinkers of our age*

USAGE To make this word stronger, one says *He* **thought** *deeply.|He* **thought** *hard/very hard/very hard indeed.*

think[2] *n* [S (*about*)] *infml* an act of thinking, esp. about a difficulty or question; occasion or need for thinking: *I'll have to have a think about this before I give you an answer.|If you think I'm going to lend you a pound you've got another think coming* (=you'll have to think of someone else to ask, because I certainly won't lend you a pound)

think·a·ble /ˈθɪŋkəbəl/ *adj* that can be thought of or imagined; CONCEIVABLE

think·ing[1] /ˈθɪŋkɪŋ/ *n* [U] **1** the act of using one's mind to produce thoughts and ideas **2** opinion; judgment; thought: *What's the government's thinking on this matter?* **3 put on one's thinking cap** *not fml* to think seriously about something

thinking[2] *adj* [Wa5;A] thoughtful; reasoning; that can think clearly and seriously

think of *v prep* **1** [T1,4] also **think a·bout**— to consider seriously before making a decision: *We're thinking of going to France for our holidays but we've not decided for certain yet* **2** [X9] also **think a·bout**— to have as an opinion about: *What do you think of the government's latest offer to the unions?* **3** [T1] to take into account; have in one's mind: *Do be careful—think of your poor mother!* **4** [T1] (*used after* cannot *and* could not *and in infin. after* try, want, *etc.*) to remember: *I can't think of his name* **5** [T1,4] to suggest: *I was the first to think of going away for our holidays* **6 not think much of** to have a low opinion of **7 not think of** *infml* not consider; not be able to: *I wouldn't think of hurting a child!* **8 think better of someone** to have a higher opinion of someone: *People will think better of you if you say you're sorry* **9 think better of something** to change one's opinion about something; decide wisely against something: *I was going to ask a question but thought better of (doing) it* **10 think highly/well/little/poorly/etc. of someone or something** to have a good/bad/etc. opinion of someone or something **11 think nothing of** to regard as usual or easy: *He thinks nothing of walking 4 miles to work and back every day* **12 think nothing of it** do not trouble yourself to thank me for it **13 will/would/can/could not think of** to refuse to consider

think out also (*esp. AmE*) **think through**— *v adv* [T1] to consider (something) in detail, with care; reach a decision about (something) after much careful thought

think o·ver *v adv* [T1] to consider (something) seriously: *Your offer is very attractive but I need to think it over before I can let you know my decision*

think tank /ˈ· ·/ *n* a committee of people experienced in a particular subject, established to develop ideas and advise on matters related to that subject

think up *v adv* [T1] to invent (esp. an idea): *The prisoners tried to think up a plan for escape*

thin·ner /ˈθɪnəʳ/ *n* [U] a liquid, such as TURPENTINE, added to paint to make it spread more easily

thin-skinned /ˌ· ˈ·◂/ *adj* [Wa2] *sometimes derog* sensitive; easily offended

third /θɜːd‖θɜrd/ *determiner, adv, n, pron* **1** [see NUMBER TABLE 3] 3rd **2** [C] the lowest passing degree examination result at a British university

third de·gree /ˌ· ·ˈ·◂/ *n* [the+R] *not fml* rough treatment of a prisoner by the police in order to obtain information or a statement of guilt

third-degree burn /ˌ·· ˈ·/ *n* a very serious burn

third par·ty /ˌ· ˈ··◂/ *n tech* **1** a person in a law case other than the 2 main people concerned **2** a person not named in an insurance agreement but who will be protected by the insurance in the event of an accident

third per·son /ˌ· ˈ··/ *n* [*the*+R] *tech* a form of verb, or word representing a noun (PRONOUN), used for showing the person or thing spoken of (not the one who is spoken to or speaking): *"He is" is the third person present singular of "to be"*

third rail /ˌ· ˈ·/ *n* (in some railway systems) an additional RAIL laid beside or between the RAILs of the track, for carrying electric current

third-rate /ˌ· ˈ·◂/ *adj* [Wa5] of very poor quality

Third World /ˌ· ˈ·◂/ *n* [*the*+R] the industrially less developed countries of the world, esp. in Asia and Africa, that do not actively support either the COMMUNIST or CAPITALIST² (2) groups of countries —compare NONALIGNED

thirst¹ /θɜːst‖θɜrst/ *n* **1** [S;U;(C)] a sensation of dryness in the mouth caused by the need to drink; desire for drink: *After running 5 miles we really had a thirst* **2** [U] suffering caused by this being unsatisfied: *The soldiers died of thirst in the desert* **3** [(*the*) S+*for*] a strong desire: *the thirst for excitement*

thirst² *v* [Wv6;IØ] *old use* to feel a need to drink; be thirsty

thirst for also (*lit*) **thirst af·ter**— *v prep* [T1] to have a strong desire for: *Our people thirst for independence*

thirst·y /ˈθɜːsti‖ˈθɜr-/ *adj* [Wa1] **1** [B] feeling thirst: *Salty food makes one thirsty.*|(fig.) *The fields are thirsty for rain* **2** [A;(B)] causing thirst: *Cricket is a thirsty game to play on a hot day* **3** [F+*for*] having a strong desire for: *She was thirsty for news of her children* —**thirstily** *adv*

thir·teen /ˌθɜːˈtiːn◂‖ˌθɜr-/ *determiner, n, pron* [see NUMBER TABLE 1] (the number) 13. This is sometimes thought to be an unlucky number —**~th** *determiner, n, pron, adv* [see NUMBER TABLE 3]

thir·ty /ˈθɜːti‖ˈθɜrti/ *determiner, n, pron* [see NUMBER TABLE 1] (the number) 30 —**-tieth** *determiner, n, pron, adv* [see NUMBER TABLE 3]

this¹ /ðɪs/ *determiner* **these** /ðiːz/ **1** being the one or amount stated, going to be stated, shown, or understood: *I saw Mrs Jones this morning* (=before midday today).|*Wait until you've heard this story!*|*Who's this Mrs Bloggs we keep hearing about?* **2** being the one of 2 or more people or things that is nearer in time, place, thought, etc.: *You look in this box* (*here*) *and I'll look in that one* (*over there*).|*I'm surprised you like that picture. I like this one myself* **3** *infml* a certain: *Then this man came up to me in the street and started making rude suggestions . . .*|*There were these 2 Irishmen called Pat and Mike . . .* **4 at this point** now

this² *pron* **these** **1** a thing, idea, etc., understood, stated, going to be stated, etc.: *Who told you this?*|*Wait until you've heard this!*|*What's this?*|*This is what you must do . . .* **2** (*used with* be, *when showing or introducing a thing or person*) one of 2 or more people, things, kinds, or ideas that is nearer in place, time, thought, etc.: *This is your book—let me give it to you.*|*"This is my sister." "How do you do?"*|*This is more comfortable than that one over there.*|HULLO! *This is Naomi Robinson speaking . . .* **3** (*not used of people*) the one or kind here: *Please carry this/this box.* (Compare *Please carry this child.*)|*Do you know this?* (*=this book?* (Compare *Do you know this man?*)) **4 like this** in such a way; in the way shown; thus **5 this, that, and the other** also **this and that**— *infml* various things; all sorts of things: *We were sitting there talking about this, that, and the other . . .* **6 What's all this?** What is the trouble, matter, etc., here?

this³ *adv* [Wa5] *infml* so; this degree: *I've never been out this late before.*|*Cut off about this much thread . . .*

USAGE Some people think it is not very good English to use **this** and **that** as adverbs; instead of **this** *late* they say *as late as* **this**

this·tle /ˈθɪsəl/ *n* any of several types of wild plant with prickly leaves and yellow, white, or esp. purple flowers. The thistle is the national sign of Scotland

this·tle·down /ˈθɪsəldaʊn/ *n* [U] the soft feathery substance fastened to the seeds of the THISTLE, by means of which they float through the air

thith·er /ˈðɪðəʳ‖ˈθɪðər/ *adv* [Wa5] *old use* to that place; in that direction

thole /θəʊl/ also **thole·pin** /ˈθəʊlˌpɪn/— *n* **1** either of 2 pins on the side (GUNWALE) of a boat, between which an OAR is held in place **2** a single pin that fits through a hole in the OAR to keep it in place

thong /θɒŋ‖θɔŋ/ *n* a narrow length of leather used as a fastening, whip, etc.

tho·rax /ˈθɔːræks‖ˈθo-/ *n* **-races** /rəsiːz/ *or* **-raxes** *tech* **1** the part of the human body between the neck and ABDOMEN; chest **2** a part like this in other animals **3** the part of an insect's body that carries the legs and wings —see picture at INSECT

thorn /θɔːn‖θɔrn/ *n* **1** [C] a prickle growing on a plant; sharp pointed growth on the stem of a plant: *the thorns on a rose bush* —see picture at FLOWER¹ **2** [C;U] (*usu. in comb.*) any of various types of bush, plant, or tree having such prickles: HAWTHORN **3 a thorn in one's flesh/side** a continual cause of annoyance

thorn·y /ˈθɔːni‖ˈθɔrni/ *adj* [Wa1] **1** prickly; having THORNs (1) **2** difficult to handle; causing worry or trouble: *a thorny matter* —**thorniness** *n* [U]

thor·ough /ˈθʌrə‖ˈθʌrəʊ, ˈθʌrə/ *adj* **1** [B] complete in every way: *a thorough search* **2** [Wa5;A] being fully or completely (the stated thing): *a thorough fool* **3** [B] careful with regard to detail: *a thorough worker* —**~ly** *adv*: *After a hard day's work I feel thoroughly tired* —**~ness** *n* [U]

thor·ough·bred /ˈθʌrəbred‖ˈθʌrəʊ-, ˈθʌrə-/ *adj, n* [Wa5] (an animal, esp. a horse) descended from parents of one particular type with the best qualities; (animal) of pure breed

thor·ough·fare /ˈθʌrəfeəʳ‖ˈθʌrəʊ-, ˈθʌrə-/ *n* **1** a road for public traffic, esp. a busy main road: *Nevskii Prospekt is Leningrad's busiest thoroughfare* **2 No thoroughfare** (as written on signs) not open to the public; no way through; no entrance

thor·ough·go·ing /ˌθʌrəˈgəʊɪŋ◂/ *adj* **1** [B] very thorough; complete in every way: *a thoroughgoing search* **2** [Wa5;A] complete; UTTER: *a thoroughgoing fool*

those /ðəʊz/ *pl. of* THAT: *"We don't want all those Yorkshire miners out of work."* (SEU S.)|*Back in those days nobody was out of work for very long*

thou /ðaʊ/ *pron* [Wp1] *old use or bibl* (*used as the subject of a sentence with special old forms of verbs such as* ART¹, CANST, DIDST, *etc.*) the person to whom one is speaking, now usu. God; you: *"Thou* SHALT (=shall) *not kill"* (The Bible).|*Be thou ever near me, God!*

though¹ /ðəʊ/ *adv* [Wa5] *not fml* (*not used at the beginning of a* CLAUSE) in spite of the fact; NEVERTHELESS: *It's hard work. I enjoy it though.*|*He's a bad President. There's no reason, though, to shoot him*

though² *conj* **1** in spite of the fact that; even if: *Though/Even though it's hard work, I enjoy it.*|*He* *spoke firmly though pleasantly.|Poor though I am, I can afford beer* **2 as though** as if: *He behaves as though he were better than us*

thought¹ /ˈθɔːt/ *n* **1** [U] the act of thinking: *The priest sat, deep in thought* **2** [U] serious consideration: *Give his offer plenty of thought before you accept it* **3** [U (*of*)] intention: *I had no thought of annoying you* **4** [C;U] something that is thought; (a) product of thinking; idea, opinion, etc.: *Let me have your thoughts on the subject.|You must give up all thought of John* **5** [U9] the particular way of thinking of a social class, person, period, country, etc.: *ancient Greek thought* **6** [C;U: (*for*)] (an example of) attention; regard: *With no thought for her own safety she jumped into the river to save the drowning child* **7** [S9] *not fml* a little: *This soup needs a thought more salt* —see also SECOND THOUGHT

thought² *past t. and p. of* THINK

thought·ful /ˈθɔːtfəl/ *adj* **1** [B] given to or expressing thought: *The girl looked thoughtful for a moment and then answered* **2** [F+*of*] careful: *You should be more thoughtful of your safety* **3** [B] paying attention to the wishes, feelings, etc., of other people; taking other people into account: *It was very thoughtful of you to stop for me* —**~ly** *adv* —**~ness** *n* [U]

thought·less /ˈθɔːtləs/ *adj* **1** [(*of*)] not thinking; careless; showing lack of thought: *It was thoughtless of you to forget your sister's birthday.|A man with a wife and children can't afford to be thoughtless of the future* **2** selfish; failing to take other people into account; not paying enough attention to the wishes, feelings, etc., of others: *It was very thoughtless to eat all the cake and leave none for me* —**~ly** *adv* —**~ness** *n* [U]

thought-out /ˌ· ˈ·◂/ *adj* [Wa5;B9] produced or arrived at after the stated consideration: *a well thought-out plan*

thought-read·er /ˈ· ˌ··/ *n* a person who is thought to or claims to be able to know what another person is thinking without being told

thou·sand /ˈθaʊzənd/ *determiner, n, pron* **-sand** *or* **-sands** [see NUMBER TABLE 2] **1** (the number) 1,000 **2 one in a thousand** very good indeed —see HUNDRED (USAGE) —**~th** *determiner, n, pron, adv* [see NUMBER TABLE 3]

thral·dom, *AmE* **thralldom** /ˈθrɔːldəm/ *n* [U] slavery

thrall /θrɔːl/ *n* **1** [C (*to*)] a slave; SERF: (fig.) *He is a thrall to material wealth* **2** [U] slavery (esp. in the phr. **in thrall (to)**)

thrash /θræʃ/ *v* **1** [T1] to beat with or as if with a whip or stick, as a punishment **2** [T1] to defeat thoroughly **3** [L9 (ABOUT)] to move wildly or violently about: *The fishes thrashed about in the net*

thrash·ing /ˈθræʃɪŋ/ *n* **1** a severe beating **2** a severe defeat

thrash out *v adv* [T1] **1** to talk about (something) thoroughly to find an answer **2** to produce by much talk and consideration: *After a whole night of argument we thrashed out the following plan*

thread¹ /θred/ *n* **1** [C;U] (a length of) very fine cord made by spinning cotton, wool, silk, etc., used in sewing or weaving: *cotton/nylon thread* **2** [C9] anything with the fineness or thinness of this: *a thread of light passed through the crack* **3** [C] a line of reasoning connecting the parts of an argument or story: *to lose the thread of one's argument* **4** [C] a raised line that winds around the outside of a screw or the inside of a NUT¹ (2), BOLT¹ (1), etc. —see picture at MACHINERY **5 hang by a thread** to be in a very dangerous or unsafe position: *The old man's life hangs by a thread*

thread² *v* [T1] **1** to pass one end of a thread through the hole (EYE) of (a needle) **2** to put (a film) in place on a PROJECTOR **3** [(TOGETHER)] to connect by running a thread through: *The little girl threaded the shells together and wore them round her neck* **4** to cut a THREAD¹ (4) on (a screw, NUT¹ (2), BOLT¹ (1), etc.) **5 thread one's way through** to make one's way carefully through (streets, crowds, forests, etc.)

thread·bare /ˈθredbeəʳ/ *adj* **1** (of cloth, clothes, etc.) worn thin; very worn **2** having been so much used as to be no longer interesting; HACKNEYED: *threadbare jokes that are no longer funny*

thread·like /ˈθredlaɪk/ *adj* long and thin: *little threadlike worms*

threat /θret/ *n* **1** [C; *under*+U (*of*)] an expression of an intention to hurt, punish, cause pain, etc., esp. if one's instructions are not obeyed: *I obeyed his order but only under threat of punishment.|The Chinese do not take Soviet threats seriously* **2** [C (*to*) *usu. sing.*] a person, thing, or idea regarded as a possible danger: *While the killer goes free he is a threat to everyone in the town* **3** [C9 esp. *of, usu. sing.*] a sign or warning of coming danger: *The clouds brought a threat of rain*

threat·en /ˈθretn/ *v* **1** [Wv4,5;T1 (*with*)] to express a threat against (someone): *I was threatened with a beating if I didn't obey.|a threatening letter* **2** [Wv4,5;T1,3] to express (a threat) against someone: *The killer threatened to murder me if I didn't obey* **3** [Wv4;T1] to give warning of (something bad): *The black clouds threatened rain* **4** [Wv4;IØ] to seem likely to happen: *While danger threatens we must all take care* **5** [Wv4;T1] to be a threat against: *Noisy traffic threatens our way of life in this village* —**~ingly** *adv*

three /θriː/ *determiner, n, pron* [see NUMBER TABLE 1] (the number) 3

three-cor·nered /ˌ· ˈ··◂/ *adj* [Wa5] **1** having 3 corners: *a three-cornered hat* **2** having 3 competitors, parties, etc.: *a three-cornered political system*

three-D /ˌθriː ˈdiː◂/ also **3-D**— *n* [U] a THREE-DIMENSIONAL form or appearance

three-deck·er /ˌ· ˈ··◂/ *n* **1** *tech* (in former times) a type of sailing ship with 3 DECK*s* **2** a SANDWICH made of 3 pieces of bread with 2 thicknesses of filling between

three-di·men·sion·al /ˌ· ·ˈ···◂/ *adj* [Wa5] having or seeming to have length, depth, and height —see picture at GEOMETRY

three-half·pence /ˌ· ˈ··/ also **penny-halfpenny**— *n* [U;(C)] 1½d; (the value of) one and a half old pennies

three-leg·ged race /ˌ· ˈ·· ·/ *n* a race run by competitors in pairs, each pair having their inside legs tied together

three-line whip /ˌ· · ˈ·/ *n* an order given by party leaders to MEMBERS OF PARLIAMENT belonging to their party, telling them that they must vote in a particular way or be considered disloyal to their party

three·pence /ˈθrepəns, ˈθrʌ-, ˈθrʊ-, ˈθrɪ-/ *n* **1** [C] THREEPENNY BIT **2** [U] 3d; (the value of) 3 old pennies: *It cost threepence*

three·pen·ny bit /ˌθrepəni ˈbɪt, ˌθrʌ-, ˌθrʊ-, ˌθrɪ-/ *n* a small round silver coin or a small 12-sided coin formerly used in Britain with a value of 3 old pence (3d)

three-quar·ter¹ /ˌ· ˈ··◂/ *adj* [Wa5] consisting of 3 FOURTH*s* (¾) of the whole: *a three-quarter length coat*

three-quarter² /ˌ· ˈ··/ *n* (in RUGBY) one of a group of fast-running players whose main job is to get the ball over their opponents' line for a TRY² (2) —see picture at RUGBY

three R's /ˌθriː ˈɑːz‖-ˈɑrz/ *n* [*the*+P] reading,

writing, and ARITHMETIC (=working with numbers) considered as the base for children's education

thren·o·dy /ˈθrenədi/ *n lit* a funeral song for the dead

thresh /θreʃ/ *v* [IØ;T1] to separate the grain from (corn, wheat, or other grain-bearing plants) by beating

thresh·er /ˈθreʃəʳ/ *n* **1** a machine or person that THRESHes **2** a type of large SHARK[1] with a long tail

threshing ma·chine /ˈ·· ·ˌ·/ *n* a machine for separating the grain from wheat, corn, etc.

thresh·old /ˈθreʃhəʊld, -ʃəʊld/ *n* **1** a piece of wood or stone fixed beneath the door into a house or building **2** [*usu. sing.*] the place or point of beginning: *Scientists are now on the threshold of a better understanding of how the human brain works* **3** *tech* (in PSYCHOLOGY) limit; the lowest level at which an influence can be felt or produce an effect: *The sound was so loud it was on the threshold of pain*

threw /θruː/ *past t. of* THROW

thrice /θraɪs/ *predeterminer, adv* [Wa5] *becoming rare* 3 times: *"Weave a circle round him thrice."* (Coleridge)|*He earns thrice the amount I earn*

thrift /θrɪft/ *n* [U] **1** wise use of money and goods; avoidance of waste in the use of money **2** a type of plant with round groups of small pink or white flowers

thrift·y /ˈθrɪfti/ *adj* [Wa1] avoiding waste in the use of money; using money and goods wisely: *a thrifty housewife* —**thriftily** *adv* —**thriftiness** *n* [U]

thrill[1] /θrɪl/ *v* [Wv4;L9 esp. *at, to*;T1] to (cause to) feel a THRILL[2] or thrills: *a thrilling story of violence and murder* —**~ingly** *adv*

thrill[2] *n* a sudden very strong feeling of joy, fear, excitement, pleasure, etc., that seems to flow round the body like a wave

thrill·er /ˈθrɪləʳ/ *n* a book, play, or film that tells a very exciting story, esp. of crime and violence

thrive /θraɪv/ *v* **throve** /θrəʊv/ *or* **thrived, thrived** *or* **thriven** /θrɪvən/ [Wv4;IØ] to develop well and be healthy; be successful: *a thriving business*

throat /θrəʊt/ *n* **1** the passage from the back of the mouth down inside the neck, that divides into 2 passages, one taking air to the lungs, the other food to the stomach: *a sore throat* **2** the front of the neck: *The murderer cut the old man's throat* —see picture at HUMAN[2] **3 force/thrust/ram something down somebody's throat** to force someone to accept something, esp. one's ideas, opinions, etc., unwillingly **4 jump down someone's throat** to attack somebody in words, strongly and unexpectedly **5 lie in one's throat** to lie in one's TEETH **6 stick in one's throat** to be unacceptable

-throat·ed /ˈθrəʊtɪ̈d/ *comb. form* having a throat of the stated kind: *a red-throated bird*

throat·y /ˈθrəʊti/ *adj* [Wa1] *not fml* (of a person) having a low rough voice: *a throaty singer*|*You sound throaty today. Have you got a cold?* —**throatily** *adv* —**throatiness** *n* [U]

throb[1] /θrɒb‖θrɑb/ *v* **-bb-** [Wv4;IØ] (of the heart, a machine, etc.) to beat strongly and rapidly: *My heart was throbbing with excitement*

throb[2] *n* a strong low continuous beat: *the throb of machinery* —see also HEARTTHROB

throes /θrəʊz/ *n* [P] **1** *esp. lit* severe pains, esp. caused by dying (esp. in the phr. **death throes**) **2 in the throes of** struggling with (some difficulty): *a country in the throes of war*

throm·bo·sis /θrɒmˈbəʊsɪ̈s‖θrɑm-/ *n* **-ses** /siːz/ [U;C] the medical condition of having a blood CLOT (=a thickened or solid mass of blood) in a blood vessel or the heart

throne /θrəʊn/ *n* **1** [C] the ceremonial chair of a king, queen, BISHOP, etc. **2** [*the*+R] the rank or office of a king or queen: *He was only 15 when he came to the throne*

throng[1] /θrɒŋ‖θrɔŋ/ *n* [GC (*of*)] a large crowd (of people or things): *throngs of passengers at the railway station*

throng[2] *v* **1** [T1] to move (as if) in a crowd in: *Passengers thronged the station waiting for their trains* **2** [L9] to move (as if) in a crowd: *People thronged to see the new play*

thros·tle /ˈθrɒsəl‖ˈθrɑ-/ *n poet* THRUSH[1]

throt·tle[1] /ˈθrɒtl‖ˈθrɑtl/ *v* **1** [T1] to seize (someone) tightly by the throat to stop breathing; STRANGLE **2** [T1 (BACK);L9 esp. DOWN, BACK] to reduce the flow of petrol, oil, etc., to (an engine) so lessening speed

throttle[2] *n* a doorlike part of a pipe (VALVE) that opens and closes to control the flow of liquid, gas, oil, etc., into an engine

through[1] /θruː/ *prep* **1** in at one side, end, or surface of (something) and out at the other: *to go through a door*|*Water flows through this pipe.*|*He pushed his way through the crowd to the door.*|*We couldn't see through the mist.*|*Is it quicker to drive round the town, or straight through the middle?* **2** by way of: *The murderer must have climbed in through the open window* **3** by means of: *I got this book through the library.*|*It was through John that they found out* **4** as a result of; because of: *The war was lost through bad organization* **5** from the beginning to the end of: *I don't think the old man will live through the night.*|*I read right through/half way through the article but found it uninteresting* **6** over the surface of or within the limits of: *We travelled through France and Belgium on our holidays* **7** among or between the parts or single members of: *The monkeys swung through the trees.*|(fig.) *to search through my papers* **8** having finished, or so as to finish, successfully: *Did you get through your examinations?* **9** having reached, or so as to reach, the end of: *Are you through (with) your work yet?* **10** without stopping for: *to drive through a red light* **11** *AmE* (*esp. in expressions of time*) up to and including: *Wednesday through Saturday* —see INCLUSIVE (USAGE) **12** against and in spite of (a noise): *I could hear his voice through the crashing of the bombs* —see also THRU

through[2] *adv* [Wa5] **1** in at one side, end, or surface, and out at the other: *The soldier wouldn't let us through* **2** [(*to*)] all the way; along the whole distance: *Does this train go right through to London?* **3** from the beginning to the end; to completion: *Have you read the letter through?* **4** to a favourable or successful state: *"How did you do in your examinations?" "I got through with good marks"* **5** [(*to*)] *esp. BrE* (when telephoning) in a state of being connected to a person or place: *"Can you put me through to Mr Jones?" "You're through now"* **6** in every part; thoroughly (esp. in the phr. **wet through**): *I got wet through in the rain* **7 go through with** to do or continue (something) in spite of difficulties **8 see something through** to continue with something until the end **9 through and through** completely; in every way

USAGE When one is telephoning in Britain, *Are you* **through**? means "Are you connected to the other speaker?" In the US, it means "Have you finished?".

through[3] *adj* [Wa5] **1** [A] passing from one end or side to another: *a through beam* **2** [A] allowing a free or continuous journey: *a through road*|*Is this a through train or do I have to change?* **3** [F (*with*)] finished; done: *I'm not through just yet. I should be finished in an hour* **4** [F (*with*)] finished; no longer effective: *As far as racing is concerned your illness* *means you're through!* **5** [F (*with*)] *infml* having no further relationship: *Jane and I are through.|I'm through with men/alcohol/you*

through·out¹ /θruːˈaʊt/ *adv* [Wa5] (*usu. in end position*) right through; in every part; in, to, through or during every part: *The house is painted throughout.|The prince remained loyal throughout*

throughout² *prep* in, to, through, or during every part of: *It rained throughout the night.|The disease spread throughout the country*

through·put /ˈθruːpʊt/ *n* **1** the amount of materials passed through a factory in a given time **2** *tech* the work dealt with by a COMPUTER (=an electric calculating machine with a memory) in a given time

through·way /ˈθruːweɪ/ *n* THRUWAY

throw¹ /θrəʊ/ *v* **threw** /θruː/, **thrown** /θrəʊn/ **1** [D1 (*to*);T1;IØ] to send (something) through the air by a sudden movement or straightening of the arm: *It's my turn to throw.|He threw the ball 100 metres.|Throw me the ball* **2** [X9] to move (oneself or part of one's body) suddenly and with force: *The fighters threw themselves at each other* **3** [T1] to make (a voice) appear to be coming from somewhere other than its place of origin **4** [X9] to cause to go or come into some place, condition, position, etc., as if by THROWing¹ (1): *If you want to be an actor you must be able to throw your voice to the back of the largest theatre.|This new system has thrown us all into confusion* **5** [D1 (*at*)] to direct (words, looks, etc.) to (a particular person): *She threw me an angry look* **6** [X9 esp. ON, OFF, *over*] to put on or take off (a garment) hastily: *She threw off her clothes and jumped into the water* **7** [IØ;T1] *tech* (of an animal) to give birth to (a young one) **8** [T1] to move (a SWITCH, handle, etc.) in order to connect or disconnect parts of a machine, apparatus, etc. **9** [T1] to shape (an object) on a POTTER'S WHEEL **10** [D1 (*at*);T1] to strike (somebody) with (a blow, stroke, etc.): *He threw his opponent such a blow that he fell to the ground unconscious* **11** [T1] to cause to fall to the ground **12** [T1] to roll (a DICE) **13** [T1] to get (a particular number) by rolling a DICE **14** [T1] *infml* to arrange or give (a party, dinner, etc.) **15** [T1] *sl* to confuse; shock: *Your behaviour really threw me for a while* **16** [T1] *AmE* to lose (a fight) on purpose **17 throw a fit** to have a sudden attack of uncontrolled temper **18 throw oneself at someone a** to rush violently towards someone **b** to attempt forcefully to win the love of someone **19 throw oneself into** to work very busily at —see also THROW AWAY, THROW BACK ON, THROW IN, THROW OFF, THROW OPEN, THROW OUT, THROW OVER, THROW TOGETHER, THROW UP —**~er** *n*

throw² *n* **1** an act of throwing **2** [(*of*)] the distance to which something is thrown: *a throw of 100 metres|a record throw* **3** the result of throwing

throw·a·way¹ /ˈθrəʊəweɪ/ *n infml* an advertisement printed on a piece of paper and given out in the street, put through people's doors, etc.

throwaway² *adj* [Wa5;A;(B)] **1** (of a remark) said with false carelessness, seeming to have no regard for the effect **2** to be thrown away after use: *a throwaway paper cup*

throw a·way *v adv* [T1] **1** to put something in a DUSTBIN, LITTERBIN, etc., because you do not want it **2** to waste; lose by foolishness; fail to use; miss: *You threw away the chance of a good job by your stupidity*

throw·back /ˈθrəʊbæk/ *n* [(*to*)] *not fml* (an example of) a return to one or more of the typical qualities of a person in the past from whom one was descended

throw back on also **throw back up·on**— *v adv prep* [D1 *usu. pass.*] to cause (someone) to have to go back to (something) after something else has failed

throw-in /ˈ· ·/ *n* (in football) an act of throwing the ball back on from the side of the field after it has been kicked out of play

throw in *v adv* [T1] *infml* to supply (something) in addition to something else without increasing the price: *The charge for the room is £5 a night, with meals thrown in*

throw off *v adv* [T1] **1** to free oneself from (something bad); recover from: *It took me a week to throw off my cold* **2** to escape from (someone or something chasing one) **3** to say, write, or produce (something) easily: *to throw off a few lines of poetry*

throw o·pen *v adv* [T1] **1** to allow the general public to enter (a place): *The queen has thrown open her castle for the summer* **2** [(*to*)] to make open: *The competition was thrown open to sportsmen from all countries*

throw out *v adv* [T1] **1** to refuse to accept: *The committee threw out my suggestions* **2** to say (something) carelessly or without considering the result

throw o·ver also **throw o·ver·board**— *v adv* [T1] to end a relationship with (somebody)

throw to·geth·er *v adv* [T1 *often pass.*] **1** to build or make hastily: *I just threw the meal together so I hope it's all right* **2** to bring together: *Chance threw us together at a party*

throw up *v adv* **1** [T1] to produce (a famous person): *Our country has thrown up a number of great writers* **2** [T1] to give up: *I hear you've thrown up your job and are now looking for a new one* **3** [IØ] *sl* VOMIT

thru /θruː/ *adv, adj, prep* [Wa5] *AmE infml* through

thrum /θrʌm/ *v* **-mm- 1** [IØ] (esp. of a large machine) to make a low heavy continuous sound **2** [T1;IØ (*on*)] STRUM

thrush¹ /θrʌʃ/ *n* any of several types of singing birds with a brownish back and spotted breast —see picture at BIRD

thrush² *n* [U] **1** an infectious disease of the mouth and throat, esp. in children **2** *infml* a painful disease of the VAGINA

thrust¹ /θrʌst/ *v* **thrust 1** [X9] to push forcefully and suddenly: *We thrust our way through the crowd.|The murderer killed her by thrusting a knife in her back.|The actress said she was perfectly happy until fame was thrust upon her* **2** [IØ (*at*)] to make a sudden forward stroke with a sword, knife, etc. **3 thrust oneself forward** to draw attention to oneself

thrust² *n* **1** [C] an act of THRUSTing¹; forceful forward push **2** [U] **a** the force directing an object, esp. a plane, forward; forward-moving power of an engine **b** forceful pressure from one object onto another, as between the stones in an arch **3** [C] a swift forward stroke with a knife, sword, etc.

thrust·er /ˈθrʌstəʳ/ *n* **1** *sl* someone who rides too close to the dogs in fox hunting **2** a small ROCKET¹ (2) for controlling the height of a spaceship **3** *infml* a person who draws attention to himself to win advantage

thru·way, throughway /ˈθruːweɪ/ *n AmE* a very wide road for high speed traffic

thud¹ /θʌd/ *v* **-dd-** [Wv4;L9] to make a THUD² by beating, striking, landing, falling, etc.

thud² *n* a dull sound as caused by a heavy object striking something soft: *The dead man fell to the floor with a thud*

thug /θʌg/ *n* [C; (*you*) N] a violent criminal

thug·ge·ry /ˈθʌgəri/ *n* [U] (the use of) violence for criminal purposes

thumb¹ /θʌm/ *n* **1** a short thick movable part that is set apart from the fingers and can be moved to be opposite any of the fingers —see picture at

HUMAN[2] **2** the part of a GLOVE that fits over this **3 all thumbs** *not fml* awkward with the hands **4 stick out like a sore thumb** *infml* to seem very unsuitable, awkward, out of place, etc. **5 thumbs up** an expression of satisfaction, victory, or approval **6 under somebody's thumb** *infml* under the control, power, or influence of someone **7 twiddle one's thumbs** *infml* to do nothing useful or helpful; waste time

thumb² *v* **1** [IØ] *infml* to ask passing motorists for a ride by holding out one's hand with the thumb raised; HITCHHIKE **2** [T1] *infml* to get (a ride) by doing this **3** [IØ (*through*);T1] to look through (a book) quickly

thumb·nail /ˈθʌmneɪl/ *n* **1** [C] the nail on the upper outer end of the thumb **2** [A] quite small; short: *a thumbnail* SKETCH[1] (1,2)

thumb·screw /ˈθʌmskruː/ *n* an instrument used in former times to cause great pain by crushing the thumbs

thumb·tack /ˈθʌmtæk/ *n AmE* DRAWING PIN

thump¹ /θʌmp/ *v* **1** [T1;L9] to strike with a heavy blow: *I'll thump you if you annoy me any more.|The brick thumped against the tree* **2** [Wv4;IØ] to produce a repeated dull sound by beating, striking, falling, walking heavily, etc.: *The old man thumped noisily along the passage.*|(fig.) *I've got a thumping headache*

thump² *n* **1** a heavy blow **2** the dull sound produced by this

thump³ *adv* [Wa5;H] with a THUMP[2]: *The brick landed thump on his head*

thump·ing /ˈθʌmpɪŋ/ *adv* [Wa5] *infml* very: *a thumping great house*

thun·der¹ /ˈθʌndəʳ/ *n* **1** [U] the loud explosive noise that follows a flash of lightning: *After the lightning came the thunder.|There's thunder in the air* (=thunder seems likely) **2** [C *usu. pl.*;U] any loud noise like this: *the thunder of distant guns|thunders of* APPLAUSE **3** [U] *usu. fml* a person's anger: *If you disobey mother you risk her thunder* **4 by thunder** *infml* (express surprise or great satisfaction): *You're right, by thunder!* **5 in thunder** (used for giving force to a question): *What in thunder do you think you're doing?* **6 like/as black as thunder** *infml* very angry or annoyed **7 steal somebody's thunder** to spoil a person's attempt to produce an effect by doing what he had intended to do

USAGE Note the word order in this fixed phr.: **thunder and lightning**.

thunder² *v* **1** [*it*+IØ] to produce thunder: *My wife always hides under the bed when it thunders* **2** [Wa4;IØ (OUT)] to produce loud sounds like this: *The guns thundered in the distance* **3** [T1 (OUT)] to shout loudly **4** [IØ] to attack violently with words: *The politician thundered at the government's plans* —**~er** *n*

thun·der·bolt /ˈθʌndəbəʊlt‖-dər-/ *n* **1** a flash of lightning from which thunder is heard **2** a sudden event which causes great shock, anxiety, etc.

thun·der·clap /ˈθʌndəklæp‖-ər-/ *n* a single loud crash of thunder

thun·der·cloud /ˈθʌndəklaʊd‖-ər-/ *n* a large dark cloud producing thunder and lightning: (fig.) *The thunderclouds of war were coming nearer*

thun·der·ing /ˈθʌndərɪŋ/ *adj, adv* [Wa5;A] *infml* very (great, bad, severe, etc.): *The minister lives in a thundering big house in the country*

thun·der·ous /ˈθʌndərəs/ *adj* producing thunder or a loud noise like thunder: *thunderous* APPLAUSE —**~ly** *adv*

thun·der·storm /ˈθʌndəstɔːm‖-dərstɔrm/ *n* a storm of very heavy rain and thunder and lightning

thun·der·struck /ˈθʌndəstrʌk‖-ər-/ *adj* [F;(B)] very surprised indeed; shocked

thun·der·y /ˈθʌndəri/ *adj* (of the weather) giving signs that thunder is likely

thu·ri·ble /ˈθjʊərɨbəl‖ˈθuː-/ *n* a vessel in which INCENSE is burnt, esp. in a church

Thurs·day /ˈθɜːzdi‖ˈθɜr-/ *n* **1** [R] the 5th day of the present week; day before next Friday or last Friday: *He'll arrive* (*on*) *Thursday.|He'll arrive on Thursday afternoon* (=during the afternoon of next Thursday) **2** [C] the 5th day of any week, or of the week that is being spoken of: *I'm always in on Thursdays/on Thursday evenings.|He arrived on the Thursday and left on the Saturday* (=arrived on the 5th day of the week being spoken of).|*He arrived on a Thursday* (=not a Wednesday, Friday, etc.)| (*esp. AmE*) *She works Thursdays*

thus /ðʌs/ *adv* [Wa5] *fml* **1** in this manner; in the way or by the means stated: *We hope the new machine will work faster, thus reducing our costs.*| (*old use*) *Thus said the Lord . . .* **2** with this result; HENCE: *There has been no rain. Thus, the crops are likely to suffer* **3 thus far** until now; to this point

thwack /θwæk/ *n, v* WHACK

thwart¹ /θwɔːt‖θwɔrt/ *v* [T1] to oppose successfully: *I was thwarted in my plans by the weather*

thwart² *n tech* a seat across a rowing boat, for the rower

thy /ðaɪ/ *determiner* [Wp1] *old use* (*poss. form of* THOU) belonging to THEE; your: *Death, where is thy* STING[2] (5)*?*

thyme /taɪm/ *n* [U] **1** a type of small plant grown for its leaves **2** the dried crushed leaves of this plant used for giving a special taste to food

thy·roid /ˈθaɪrɔɪd/ also **thyroid gland** /ˈ·· ˌ·/— *n* an organ in the neck that controls the development of the mind and body —see picture at RESPIRATORY

thy·self /ðaɪˈself/ *pron* [Wp1] *old use* **1** (*refl. form of* THOU) **2** (*strong form of* THOU) —see YOURSELF (USAGE)

ti /tiː/ also **si**— *n* [C;U] the 7th note in the (SOL-FA) musical scale: *sing* (*a*) *ti*

Ti /ˌtiː ˈaɪ/ the chemical sign for TITANIUM

ti·a·ra /tiˈɑːrə/ *n* **1** a piece of jewellery that looks like a small crown, worn on the head by women at formal dances, dinners, etc. **2** the crown worn by the POPE

tib·i·a /ˈtɪbɪə/ *n* **-iae** /i-iː/ *or* **-ias** *med* SHINBONE

tic /tɪk/ *n* a sudden painless purposeless movement in the face or limbs caused by a tightening of the muscles, usu. because of a nervous illness

tick¹ /tɪk/ *n* **1** any of various types of very small insect-like animals that bury themselves in the skin of animals and suck their blood **2** *BrE infml* an annoying or worthless fellow

tick² *n* **1** a short sudden regularly repeated sound made by a clock or watch **2** a mark (usu. ✓) put against something, such as an answer, name on a list, etc., to show that it is correct **3** *infml, esp. BrE* a moment: *I'll be down in a tick.|I'm going to the shops but will only be a* COUPLE *of ticks*

tick³ *v* **1** [IØ] (of a clock, watch, etc.) to make a regularly repeated short sudden sound **2** [T1 (*off*)] to show that (an answer, name on a list, etc.) is correct by marking with a TICK[2] (2) **3 make someone or something tick** *infml* to provide a person or thing with reasons for acting, behaving, working, etc., in a particular way: *We're trying to find out what makes him tick* —see also TICK AWAY, TICK OFF, TICK OVER

tick⁴ *n* a strong thick coarse cloth cover of a MATTRESS, PILLOW, etc. —see also TICKING

tick⁵ *n* [U] *infml* CREDIT[1] (4): *Will you let me have these things on tick until I get paid tomorrow?*

tick⁶ *n* [U] TAG[3]

tick a·way *v adv* [T1] (of a clock, watch, etc.) to

show the passing of (minutes, seconds, etc.) by TICKing[3]

tick·er /ˈtɪkəʳ/ *n* **1** a telegraphic machine that prints information and news on long narrow lengths of paper **2** any of various modern machines that record information and news by electrical means **3** *sl* a watch **4** *sl* the heart: *She's got a weak ticker*

tick·er·tape /ˈtɪkəteɪp‖-ər-/ *n* [U] very long narrow lengths of paper used in a TICKER (1) and often thrown during public rejoicings

tick·et¹ /ˈtɪkɪ̠t/ *n* **1** [C; *by*+U] a printed piece of paper or card given to a person to show that he has paid for a service such as a journey on a bus, entrance into a cinema, etc.: *a bus/train/cinema ticket|Entrance to the theatre is by ticket only* **2** [C] a piece of card or paper fastened to and giving information such as price, size, quality, etc., about an object for sale in a shop **3** [C] *esp. AmE* a list of people supported by one political party in an election **4** [C] *not fml* a printed notice of an offence against the driving laws: *a parking ticket* **5** [*the*+R] *sl* the thing needed: *This piece of string is just the ticket. It's exactly what I need* **6** *sl* a PAWNBROKER'*s* receipt **7 get one's ticket** *infml* to be dismissed from the armed forces **8 work one's ticket** *sl old use* to avoid work, unpleasant duty, etc., by pretending to be ill, by giving other false reasons, etc.

ticket² *v* **1** [T1] to put a ticket, TAG, or LABEL on (something) **2** [X9] to intend (something) for a certain use: *These cars have been ticketed for sale abroad*

ticket col·lec·tor /ˈ·· ·ˌ··/ *n* a person employed to examine and collect tickets, esp. in a railway station

tick·ing /ˈtɪkɪŋ/ also **tick**— *n* [U] the thick strong coarse cloth used for making MATTRESS and PILLOW covers (TICK*s*⁴)

ticking off /ˌ·· ˈ·/ *n* **tickings off** a scolding

tick·le¹ /ˈtɪkəl/ *v* **1** [T1] to touch (someone, part of their body, etc.) lightly with the fingers, a feather, etc., to produce laughter, a feeling of nervous excitement, etc. **2** [T1;I∅] to (cause (someone) to) feel a sensation of nervous excitement in part of the body: *I don't like these rough sheets; they tickle* **3** [Wv5;T1] to delight or amuse; please; excite **4 tickled pink** *sl* delighted, very pleased, or amused

tickle² *n* [C;U] (an example of) the act or sensation of tickling (TICKLE¹ (1, 2))

tick·ler /ˈtɪkləʳ/ *n infml* a difficult question or state of affairs needing special care or attention

tick·lish /ˈtɪklɪʃ/ *adj not fml* **1** (of a (part of a) person) sensitive to tickling; easily TICKLEd¹ (1) **2** (of a question, state of affairs, etc.) difficult; needing special care and attention —**~ly** *adv* —**~ness** *n* [U]

tick off *v adv* [T1b] *infml* to scold

tick o·ver *v adv* [I∅] **1** (of a motor engine) to continue working at the slowest possible speed but without moving the vehicle **2** (of work, activity, etc.) to continue at a usual or slow rate; be rather quiet or inactive

tick-tack-toe, tic-tac-toe /ˌ· · ˈ·/ *n* [U] *AmE* NOUGHTS AND CROSSES

tid·al /ˈtaɪdl/ *adj* [Wa5] of, having, or related to the TIDE: *The river is tidal up to the 4th bridge.|tidal currents*

tidal wave /ˈ·· ·/ *n* a very large dangerous ocean wave caused by an underwater explosion, EARTHQUAKE, etc.: (fig.) *a tidal wave of public disapproval against the government's plans*

tid·bit /ˈtɪdˌbɪt/ *n AmE* TITBIT

tid·dler /ˈtɪdləʳ/ *n BrE* **1** [C] *infml* a very small fish **2** [C;N] *infml* a small child **3** [C] *sl* a ½ penny coin

tid·dly, -dley /ˈtɪdli/ *adj* [Wa1] *BrE infml* **1** slightly drunk **2** very small

tid·dly·winks, -dley- /ˈtɪdliwɪŋks/ *AmE* also **tiddledywinks** /ˈtɪdldiwɪŋks/— *n* [U] a game in which the players try to make small round pieces of plastic jump into a cup by pressing their edges down hard with a larger piece of plastic

tide /taɪd/ *n* **1** [C] the regular rise and fall of large areas of water, esp. the seas, caused by the pull of the moon and sun: *The sea comes right up to the cliffs when the tide is in* —see also HIGH TIDE, LOW TIDE **2** [C] a current of water caused by this: *Strong tides make swimming dangerous* **3** [C] a movement, as of public opinion: *We must wait for a change in the tide before introducing this unpopular law* **4** [U] *old use* (*esp. in comb.*) time; season: *at Christmastide* **5 swim/go with/against the tide** *infml* to act in accordance with/opposition to a general current of thought, custom, or what most other people are doing

tide·mark /ˈtaɪdmɑːk‖-mark/ *n* **1** the highest point reached by a TIDE (1) on the shore **2** *humor* a dirty mark left by incomplete washing: *a tidemark round the little boy's neck*

tide o·ver¹ *v adv* [T1b] to help (someone) through a difficult period

tide over² *v prep* [D1] to help (someone) through (a difficult period): *Can you lend me £10 to tide me over the next few days?*

tide·wa·ter /ˈtaɪdˌwɔːtəʳ‖-ˌwɔ-, -ˌwɑ-/ *n* [U] **1** water that flows onto the land when the TIDE is very high **2** the water in the TIDAL parts of rivers and streams **3** *AmE* low coastal land

tide·way /ˈtaɪdweɪ/ *n* **1** a narrow stretch of water in which a TIDAL current flows **2** a strong current running through such a stretch of water

tid·ings /ˈtaɪdɪŋz/ *n* [P] *old use* news: *glad tidings of joy*

ti·dy¹ /ˈtaɪdi/ *adj* **1** [Wa1] neatly arranged: *a tidy room|tidy thoughts* **2** [Wa1] (of a person, animal, their habits, etc.) liking things to be neatly arranged: *My son's very tidy and never goes out without combing his hair* **3** [Wa5] *infml* fairly large: *a tidy income* —**-dily** *adv* —**-diness** *n* [U]

tidy² *v* [I∅;T1: (UP)] to make (something or someone) neat

tidy³ *n* a small box in which small articles can be kept

tie¹ /taɪ/ *n* **1** also (*esp. AmE*) **necktie**— a band of cloth worn round the neck, usu. inside a shirt collar and tied in a knot at the front —compare BOW TIE, FOUR-IN-HAND **2** a cord, string, etc., used for fastening something **3** something that unites; BOND: *family ties|ties of friendship* **4** [*usu. sing.*] something that takes one's attention and limits one's freedom: *Young children can be a tie* **5** an equality of results, votes, etc.: *The result of the election was a tie* **6** a length of wood, metal, etc., that joins parts of a framework and gives support **7** a curved line (⁀) connecting the heads of 2 printed musical notes of the same level showing that they are to be played or sung as one unbroken note —compare SLUR² (1) **8** *AmE* SLEEPER (3)

tie² *v* **tied**; *pres. p.* **tying** **1** [X9 esp. UP] to fasten with a cord, rope, etc.: *Make sure the parcel's correctly tied up before you post it.|to tie a dog to the fence* **2** [T1] to fasten by drawing together and knotting string, LACE*s*, etc.: *Can you tie your own shoes yet?* **3** [I∅] to be fastened by string, LACE*s*, etc., that are drawn together and knotted: *My dress ties at the back* **4** [T1] to make (a knot or BOW³ (3)): *to tie a knot* **5** [T1] to form a knot or BOW³ (3) in (a string, TIE¹ (1), etc.): *to tie a* SCARF **6** [I∅ (*with, for*)] to be equal to an opponent or his result in a competition: *I tied for 2nd place in the* *examinations* **7** [T1 *usu. pass.*] to finish (a match, competition) with equal points **8** [T1] to connect (musical notes of the same level) so that there is no interruption in playing or singing —see also TIE DOWN, TIE IN, TIE TOGETHER, TIE UP

tie·break·er /ˈtaɪˌbreɪkəʳ/ also **tie·break** /ˈtaɪbreɪk/— *n* (in tennis) a number of quickly-played points (not part of a standard game), played to decide the winner of a SET³ (10) in which each side has won 6 games

tied cot·tage /ˌ· ˈ··/ *n* a house owned by a farmer and rented to one of his workers on the condition that he continues to be employed by the farmer

tied house /ˌ· ˈ·/ *n BrE* an inn that is controlled by a particular beer-making firm, and must sell the beer that it makes —compare FREE HOUSE

tie down *v adv* [T1b] **1** to limit the freedom of (someone) **2** [(*on, to*)] to force (someone) to take a particular position, accept the conditions of a contract, make a decision, etc.

tie-dye /ˈ· ·/ *v* [Wv5;T1] to tie (a garment) in knots and DYE so that some parts take more DYE than others

tie in *v adv* [I∅ (*with*)] to have a close connection (to): *This witness's information doesn't tie in with the facts*

tie-on /ˈ· ·/ *adj* [Wa5;A;(B)] (of a LABEL, TAG, etc.) fastened to an object by tying

tie·pin /ˈtaɪˌpɪn/ *AmE* also **stickpin**— *n* an ornamental pin for holding the 2 halves of a TIE¹ (1) together

tier /tɪəʳ/ *n* any of a number of rows, esp. of seats, shelves, etc., rising one behind or above another: *Her wedding cake had 3 tiers*

tie to·geth·er *v adv* [T1;I∅] to (cause to) match or be closely connected

tie-up /ˈ· ·/ *n* **1** a connection; LINK **2** a partnership; MERGER **3** *AmE* a short interruption in work because of an accident, industrial trouble, etc.

tie up *v adv* [T1 *often pass.*] **1** [(*in*)] to place (money) in an account, business, etc., where free use is limited **2** to limit the free use of (money, property, etc.) by lawful conditions **3** [(*with*)] to connect: *The police are trying to tie up his escape from prison with the murder* **4** to stop: *The traffic was tied up by the accident* **5 tied up** very busy

tiff /tɪf/ *n* a slight quarrel: *a lovers' tiff*

tif·fin /ˈtɪfɨn/ *n* [U] *Ind & PakE* a midday meal

tig /tɪg/ *n* [U] TAG³

ti·ger /ˈtaɪgəʳ/ (*fem.* **tigress**)— *n* **1** [Wn1] a type of very large fierce wild cat that has yellowish fur with black bands across and lives in Asia —see picture at CAT **2** a person like such an animal in fierceness, courage, etc. **3 paper tiger** *derog* (esp. in China and south-east Asia) an enemy which wishes to seem powerful, but is really not so **4 ride the tiger** *infml* to live in a very uncertain or dangerous way

ti·ger·ish /ˈtaɪgərɪʃ/ *adj* cruel; fierce; of or like a tiger

tiger lil·y /ˈ·· ˌ··/ *n* a type of tall LILY with black spotted orange flowers

tight¹ /taɪt/ *adj* [Wa1] **1** closely fastened, held, knotted, etc.; firmly fixed in place: *This drawer is so tight I can't open it* **2** drawn out as far as possible; fully stretched: *Pull the thread tight* **3** fitting part of the body (too) closely: *tight shoes* **4** leaving no free room or time; fully packed: *I've got a very tight* SCHEDULE *today so I can't see you until tomorrow.*|*Pack the cases as tight as possible* **5** (*esp. in comb.*) closely or firmly put together so that air, water, etc., cannot pass through: *Are you sure this joint*/*roof is completely tight?*|WATERTIGHT **6** having or producing an uncomfortable feeling of closeness in part of the body: *a tight feeling in the chest* **7** *tech* (of money) difficult to obtain, except at high rate of interest **8** *tech* (of goods) difficult to obtain **9** difficult to deal with or escape from: *The government found itself in a tight corner*/SPOT (=difficult position) *over its incomes plan* **10** marked by close competition: *a tight game*/*race* **11** *sl* drunk —**~ly** *adv* —**~ness** *n* [U]

tight² *adv* [Wa1] **1** closely; firmly; tightly: *She held him tight in her arms* **2** thoroughly; well: *Good night; sleep tight* **3 sit tight a** to stay where one is: *I'll sit tight while you go for the drinks* **b** to keep to one's own opinions, ideas, etc.: *Sit tight and don't be persuaded by him*

USAGE Some people think **tight** should not be used as an adverb. They say *fasten it* **tightly**/*more* **tightly**|*the most* **tightly** *shut*, and not *fasten it* **tight/tighter**|*the* **tightest** *shut*.

tight·en /ˈtaɪtn/ *v* [T1 (UP);I∅] to (cause to) become tight or tighter

tighten up *v adv* [T1;I∅ (*on*)] to (cause to) become firmer or more severe: *The government are tightening up (on) the driving laws*

tight·fist·ed /ˌtaɪtˈfɪstɨdˌ/ also **tight**— *adj infml* very ungenerous, esp. with money —**~ness** *n* [U]

tight-lipped /ˌ· ˈ·ˌ/ *adj* **1** having the lips pressed together **2** not wanting to talk; silent; not saying much

tight·rope /ˈtaɪt-rəʊp/ *n* a tightly stretched rope or wire, high above the ground, on which TIGHTROPE WALKER*s* perform

tightrope walk·er /ˈ·· ˌ··/ *n* a person skilled in walking or doing tricks on a TIGHTROPE

tights /taɪts/ *n* [P] **1** a very close fitting garment covering the legs and lower part of the body, as worn by girls and women **2** a very close fitting garment covering the legs and body, worn by ACROBAT*s*, BALLET dancers, etc. —see PAIR (USAGE)

tight·wad /ˈtaɪt-wɒd‖-wɑd/ *n sl* a very ungenerous person, esp. with regard to money

ti·gress /ˈtaɪgrɨs/ *n* a female tiger

tike /taɪk/ *n* TYKE

til·de /ˈtɪldə/ *n* a mark (˜) placed over a Spanish *n* as a sign that it is to be pronounced /nj/

tile¹ /taɪl/ *n* **1** a thin shaped piece of baked clay used for covering roofs, walls, floors, etc. —see pictures at SITE¹, ROOF¹ and BATHROOM **2** an object like this made from plastic, metal, etc. **3** a marked playing piece used in certain games **4 have a tile loose** *infml* to be slightly mad **5 (out) on the tiles** *infml* enjoying oneself in a wild manner

tile² *v* [Wv5;T1] to cover (a roof, floor, wall, etc.) with TILE*s*¹ (1,2) —**tiler** *n*

till¹ /tɪl/ *v* [T1] to cultivate (the ground) —**~er** *n*

till² /tɪl/ *n* **1** a drawer in a shop where money is kept **2 have one's fingers in the till** *infml* to steal money from the shop where one works **3 with one's fingers in the till** *infml* stealing money from the shop where one works: *I was caught with my fingers in the till and dismissed*

till³ /tɪl, tl/ *prep, conj not fml* UNTIL —see TO, INCLUSIVE (USAGE)

till·age /ˈtɪlɪdʒ/ *n* [U] **1** the act or practice of cultivating land **2** cultivated land

til·ler /ˈtɪləʳ/ *n* a long handle fastened to the top end of a small boat's RUDDER so that it can be turned easily

tilt¹ /tɪlt/ *v* [Wv4;T1;I∅] to (cause to) slope as by raising one end

tilt² *n* **1** [C;U] a slope: *She wore her hat at a tilt over her left eye* **2** [C] an act of TILTing¹; TILTing¹ movement **3** [C (*at*)] a charge with a LANCE **4** [C (*at*)] an attack in speech or writing: *The minister made a tilt at the opposition leader in Parliament* **5 (at) full tilt** *infml* at full speed; with full force

tilt at *v prep* [T1] **1** to attack (someone) in speech or writing **2** (in former times) to charge at (someone) with a LANCE **3 tilt at windmills** to fight imaginary enemies

tim·ber¹ /ˈtɪmbəʳ/ *n* **1** [U] wood for building **2** [U] growing trees, esp. considered as a supply of wood for building **3** [C] a wooden beam, esp. a curved piece forming part of a ship's framework **4** [U9] *fml or pomp* a person's character or qualities

timber² /ˌtɪmˈbɜːʳ/ *interj* (a warning shouted when a cut tree is about to fall down)

tim·bered /ˈtɪmbəd‖-ərd/ *adj* [Wa5] **1** (of a building) made partly of wood: *half-timbered old houses* **2** covered with growing trees

tim·ber·line /ˈtɪmbəlaɪn‖-ər-/ *n* [*the*+R] **1** the height above sea level beyond which trees will not grow **2** the northern or southern limit beyond which trees will not grow

tim·bre /ˈtæmbəʳ, ˈtɪm- (*Fr* tɛ̃br)/ *n* [U;C] *tech, Fr* the quality which allows one to tell the difference between sounds of the same level and loudness when made by different musical instruments or voices

tim·brel /ˈtɪmbrəl/ *n esp. old use* TAMBOURINE

time¹ /taɪm/ *n* **1** [U] a continuous measurable quantity from the past, through the present, and into the future: *The universe exists in space and time* **2** [U] the passing of the days, months, and years, taken as a whole **3** [U9] a system of measuring this: *British Summer Time* **4** [S9;U] a limited period as between 2 events, for the completion of an action, etc.: *It will take you a long time to learn French properly.|Take more time and care over your work* **5** [C *usu. pl.*] a period in history: *in ancient times|in Queen Victoria's time* **6** [C9 *often pl.*] a period or occasion and the particular experience connected with it: *We had a good time at the party.|The hard times of the 1930's* **7** [U9] the point at which something is expected to happen: *to die before one's time* **8** [U9] the regular period of work of a worker: *I work full time but my wife only works part time* **9** [U] the rate of pay received for an hour's work: *I get time and a half for working on Saturdays and double time for Sundays* **10** [U] *sl* a period of imprisonment: *to do/serve time* **11** [U] free or unfilled TIME¹ (4): *I doubt if he ever has time to watch television* **12** [(*the*) R] a particular point in the day stated in hours, minutes, seconds, etc.: *What's the time?| "What time's John coming to tea?" "About 4 o'clock"* **13** [U] (*often in comb.*) a particular point in the year, day, etc.; moment for a particular activity or event: *When it's time to go to bed we say it's bedtime.|summertime* **14** [C] the right occasion: *He's in a good temper, so now's the time to tell him you've made a serious mistake* **15** [R9] the particular moment at which something happens: *What time's opening time/closing time?* **16** [C] the period in which an action is completed, esp. a performance in a race: *His time was just under 4 minutes* **17** [U] an unlimited period in the future: *In time you'll forget him.|Only time will tell if you're right* **18** [U] *tech* the rate of speed of a piece of music: *You beat time and I'll play* —see picture at NOTATION **19** [U] *tech* the rate of speed of military marching **20 against time** in an effort to finish something within a certain period: *We're working against time to get this dictionary finished* **21 ahead of one's time** having ideas too modern or original for the period in which one is living **22 ahead of time** early **23 all the time** continuously **24 at one time** formerly **25 at the same time a** together **b** in spite of this; yet: *He can be very rude but at the same time, I can't help liking him* **26 at the time** at the moment when something happened: *I told you at the time that I thought you were stupid* **27 bide one's time** to wait for a suitable chance **28 for a time** for a short period **29 for the time being** for a limited period: *Can you share a room for the time being? We'll let you have one on your own next week* **30 from time to time** sometimes **31 have an easy time (of it)** *infml* to have money, possessions, a good job, etc., without having fought hard for them **32 have no time for** *infml* to not waste one's time in concerning oneself with (someone or something); dislike **33 in good time a** at the right time **b** early or soon enough: *Get to the concert in good time to make sure of a seat* **34 in one's own good time** *infml* when one is ready **35 in no time (at all)** very quickly **36 in time a** early or soon enough: *Will you be home in time to see the children before they go to bed?* **b** following the correct TIME¹ (18, 19): *to sing/march/play in time* **37 It's only a question/matter of time** It must happen; the only question is when **38 keep time a** (of a clock, watch, etc.) to work correctly **b** to follow the correct TIME¹ (18, 19) in music, marching, etc. **39 kill time** to make time pass quickly by doing something **40 make good time** to go at a speed that is satisfactory or better than expected **41 many a time** often; frequently **42 on time** at the right time: *Do the trains ever run on time here?* **43 once upon a time** (often used at the beginning of children's stories, to mean) at a time in the past **44 one/two/three/etc. at a time** singly/in groups of 2/3/etc. **45 pass the time of day** to have a short conversation **46 play for time** to act in a manner that delays a decision, event, etc., until a time more suitable to oneself **47 take one's time** to be slow; go at one's own speed **48 time after time** often; repeatedly **49 time and (time) again** often; repeatedly **50 the time of one's life** a very enjoyable experience

USAGE 1 When a busy person feels he is using time sensibly, or on things that are neither good or bad, he uses the verb **spend**: *You should* **spend** *an hour every day practising the piano.|I* **spend** *a lot of (my) time wondering about Colin.* The verbs **waste** and **lose** are also for busy people, and mean that time has been badly used: *I* **wasted** *a whole hour trying to find a garage.|Hurry up! We mustn't* **lose** *any more time!* The verb **pass** gives the idea of too much time that must be filled: *He* **passes** *his time (in) making plastic models.|Listening to the radio helps her to* **pass** *the time.* 2 At 11.45, it is *a quarter of/to 12* in *AmE, a quarter to 12* in *BrE*. At 12.15 it is *a quarter after/past 12* in *AmE, a quarter past 12* in *BrE*. —see also TIMES

time² *v* **1** [T1;V3 *usu. pass.*] to arrange or set the time at which (something) happens or is to happen: *The train is timed to arrive at 6 o'clock* **2** [T1] to record the speed of (something) **3** [T1] to record the time taken by/for (something or someone): *to time a journey|to time a runner in a race* **4** [T1] to hit (a ball) or make (a shot) at just the right moment, so as to make the most effective use of the force of one's blow

time bomb /ˈ· ·/ *n* **1** a bomb that can be set to explode at a particular time **2** a state of affairs, esp. political, that is likely to be very dangerous or difficult to handle

time card /ˈ· ·/ also **time sheet**— *n* a card or sheet on which the hours worked by a worker are recorded

time ex·po·sure /ˈ· ·ˌ··/ *n* **1** [C;U] (an) EXPOSURE of photographic film to the light for more than ½ a second when taking a photograph **2** [C] a picture made by doing this

time fuse /ˈ· ·/ *n* an apparatus screwed into a bomb, so fixed that it will cause an explosion at a certain time

time-hon·oured /ˈ· ˌ··/ *adj* [Wa5] respected because of age or long use: *a time-honoured custom*
time im·me·mo·ri·al /ˌ· ··ˈ···/ *n* [U9] the time beyond memory; long ago in the past: *From time immemorial the tribe have buried their dead on this island*
time·keep·er /ˈtaɪmˌkiːpəʳ/ *n* **1** a person who records the time of competitors in a race **2** a person employed to record the time worked by others **3** a clock or watch, esp. considered for its ability to tell the right time
time lag /ˈ· ·/ also **lag**— *n* the period of time between 2 closely connected events
time·less /ˈtaɪmləs/ *adj* [Wa5] **1** lasting for ever; independent of time; unending: *the timeless universe* **2** not changed by time: *the timeless beauty of Venice* —~**ly** *adv* —~**ness** *n* [U]
time lim·it /ˈ· ˌ··/ *n* a period of time within which something must be done
time·ly /ˈtaɪmli/ *adj* [Wa1] happening at just the right time: *Your timely warning saved our lives* —**-liness** *n* [U]
time·piece /ˈtaɪmpiːs/ *n tech or old use* a clock or watch
tim·er /ˈtaɪməʳ/ *n* a person or machine that measures or records time —see also EGG TIMER
times¹ /taɪmz/ *prep* multiplied by: *3 times* (usu. written ×) *3=9*
times² *n* [P] **1** the present: *a sign of the times* **2** occasions on which something was done: *I played cricket 5 times last week* **3 at times** sometimes **4 behind the times** old-fashioned **5 for old times' sake** because of or as a reminder of happy times in the past **6 march with the times** to develop at the same rate as changing fashions and social customs
USAGE This word is often used with a *cap.* in the name of a newspaper: *The New York* **Times**.
time·sav·ing /ˈtaɪmˌseɪvɪŋ/ *n* [Wa5] more effective and quicker; serving to reduce time
time·serv·er /ˈtaɪmˌsɜːvəʳ‖-ɜr-/ *n* a person who selfishly shapes his opinions and behaviour to please those in power at the time
time·serv·ing /ˈtaɪmˌsɜːvɪŋ‖-ɜr-/ *adj, n* [U] (the behaviour of a person) who is a TIMESERVER
time-shar·ing /ˈ· ˌ··/ *n* [U] the handling by a COMPUTER (=an electrical calculating machine with a memory) of more than one PROGRAM at the same time
time sheet /ˈ· ·/ *n* TIME CARD
time sig·nal /ˈ· ˌ··/ *n* a signal, esp. one sent by radio, showing an exact moment in time, so that clocks, watches, etc., may be set right
time sig·na·ture /ˈ· ˌ···/ *n tech* a mark, usu. in the form of a FRACTION, used when writing music, to show the number and value of BEATS² (3) in a BAR¹ (6) —see picture at NOTATION
time switch /ˈ· ·/ *n* a SWITCH that can be set to start a machine, activity, etc., at a particular time
time·ta·ble¹ /ˈtaɪmˌteɪbəl/ *n* **1** a table of the times at which buses, trains, planes, etc., arrive and leave **2** a table of the times of classes in a school, college, etc. **3** any plan having a list of the times at which stated events are to happen: *the government's timetable for Parliament*
timetable² *v* [T1;V3: *usu. pass.*] **1** [(*for*)] to plan for a certain future time **2** to arrange according to a TIMETABLE
time·work /ˈtaɪmwɜːk‖-wɜrk/ *n* [U] work paid for according to the time spent doing it
time·worn /ˈtaɪmwɔːn‖-worn/ *adj* showing signs of damage and decay through age
time zone /ˈ· ·/ *n* any of the 24 parts, each about 15° wide, into which the earth is divided for the purpose of keeping time
tim·id /ˈtɪm̥ɨd/ *adj* fearful; lacking courage —~**ity** /tɨˈmɪdɨti/ *n* [U] —~**ly** /ˈtɪmɨdli/ *adv* —~**ness** *n* [U]
tim·ing /ˈtaɪmɪŋ/ *n* [U] **1** the arrangement and control of events, actions, etc., to get the desired results; control over the rate of an activity **2** judgment in this: *Improve your timing and you could be a good dancer*
tim·o·rous /ˈtɪmərəs/ *adj* (of a person) fearful; nervous; lacking courage —~**ly** *adv* —~**ness** *n* [U]
tim·o·thy /ˈtɪməθi/ also **timothy grass** /ˈ··· ·/— *n* [U] a type of coarse grass used as cattle food
tim·pa·ni /ˈtɪmpəni/ *n* [GU] a set of 2, 3, or 4 KETTLEDRUMS played by one musician in a band
tim·pa·nist /ˈtɪmpənɨst/ *n* a person who plays a KETTLEDRUM
tin¹ /tɪn/ *n* **1** [U] a soft whitish metal that is a simple substance (ELEMENT), easily shaped and used to cover (PLATE) metal objects with a protective shiny surface **2** [C] *AmE* usu. **can**— a small metal box or container: *a tin of beans/of tobacco* **3** [U] *sl, esp. BrE* money
tin² *AmE* usu. **can**— *v* **-nn-** [Wv5;T1] to preserve (esp. food) by packing in tins: *tinned fruit/meat*
tin³ *adj* [Wa5] made of tin
tinc·ture¹ /ˈtɪŋktʃəʳ/ *n* **1** [C;U] a medical substance mixed with alcohol **2** [S (*of*)] *lit* a slight suggestion (of a colour, taste, etc.) **3** [C;U] *tech* any of the colours or metals used in a COAT OF ARMS
tincture² *v* [Wv5;T1] *lit* to give a slight colour or taste to (something)
tin·der /ˈtɪndəʳ/ *n* [U] any material that catches fire easily, esp. when prepared specially for use in a TINDERBOX: *The plants are as dry as tinder/are tinder dry after this long hot summer*
tin·der·box /ˈtɪndəbɒks‖-dərbɑks/ *n* **1** a box containing TINDER, a FLINT, and steel, used in former times instead of matches for providing a flame **2** a very dangerous uncontrollable place or state of affairs
tine /taɪn/ *n* a point or narrow pointed part, as of a fork or a deer's ANTLERS
tin·foil /ˈtɪnfɔɪl/ *n* a very thin bendable sheet of shiny metal, used as a protective wrapping, esp. for covering food before cooking it
ting /tɪŋ/ *v* [T1;IØ] to (cause to) make a high clear ringing sound —**ting** *n*
ting-a-ling /ˌtɪŋəˈlɪŋ/ *n* a high clear ringing sound, esp. as made by a small bell
tinge¹ /tɪndʒ/ *v* [Wv5;T1] **1** to give a slight degree of a colour to (an object or colour): *black hair tinged with grey* **2** to show signs of: *Her admiration for him was tinged with jealousy*
tinge² *n* [S (*of*)] a slight degree (of colour or some quality): *a tinge of sadness in her voice*
tin·gle¹ /ˈtɪŋgəl/ *v* [Wv3,4;IØ] to feel a slight prickly sensation: *The cold made my skin tingle*
tingle² *n* [S] a slightly prickly sensation
tin god /ˌ· ˈ·/ *n infml* **1** a person of limited importance who acts as though he were more important than he is **2** a person who is mistakenly made the object of praise, admiration, etc.
tin hat /ˌ· ˈ·/ *n not fml* a metal hat worn by soldiers for protection
tin·ker¹ /ˈtɪŋkəʳ/ *n* **1** [C] a person who travels from place to place mending metal pots, pans, etc. **2** [S; U] an act of TINKERing² **3** [C;(N)] *infml* a disobedient or annoying young child
tinker² *v* **1** [IØ] to do the work of a TINKER¹ **2** [IØ (*with*)] to try to repair without useful results: *Don't tinker with/at my television* **3** [L9] to pass the time aimlessly in an unproductive way: *to tinker about in the garden*
tin·kle¹ /ˈtɪŋkəl/ *v* [Wv3,4;IØ;T1] to (cause to) make light metallic sounds: *He tinkled the coins together*

tinkle² *n* [*usu. sing.*] **1** a tinkling (TINKLE¹) sound **2** *BrE infml euph* an act of passing liquid from the body
tin·ny /ˈtɪni/ *adj* [Wa1] **1** of, like, or containing tin **2** having a thin metallic sound: *a tinny bell* **3** *sl* worthless; of very poor quality —**-niness** *n* [U]
tin o·pen·er /ˈ· ˌ···/ (*AmE* **can opener**)— *n BrE* an apparatus for opening tins
tin pan al·ley /ˌ· · ˈ··/ *n* [R] (*often caps.*) writers, players, and producers of popular music
tin·plate /ˈtɪnpleɪt/ *n* [U] very thin sheets of iron or steel covered with tin
tin·sel /ˈtɪnsəl/ *n* [U] **1** very thin sheets, lengths, or threads of shiny material used for ornaments, esp. on special occasions **2** anything showy that is really worthless —**~ly** *adj*
tint¹ /tɪnt/ *n* **1** *esp. lit* a pale or delicate shade of a colour; slight degree of a colour **2** any of various weak DYE*s* for the hair **3** [*usu. sing.*] an act of giving the hair a special colour by TINTing²
tint² *v* [Wv5;T1] to give a slight or delicate colour to (the hair) —**~er** *n*
tin·tack /ˈtɪntæk/ *n* a short nail made of iron covered with tin
tin·tin·nab·u·la·tion /ˌtɪntɨnæbjʊˈleɪʃən‖-bjə-/ *n* [C;U] *tech or pomp* the sound or ringing of bells
ti·ny /ˈtaɪni/ *adj* [Wa1] very small indeed
tip¹ /tɪp/ *n* **1** the usu. pointed end of something: *to burn the tips of one's fingers* **2** a small piece or part serving as an end, cap, or point: *I only smoke cigarettes with tips* **3 have (something) on the tip of one's tongue** to be about to remember (a name, word, etc.)
tip² *v* **-pp-** [Wv5;T1] to supply a TIP¹ (1, 2) to (something): *tipped cigarettes*
tip³ *v* **-pp-** **1** [T1;I∅] to (cause to) lean at an angle: *The children tipped the table and the glasses fell off* **2** [T1;I∅: (OVER, UP)] to (cause to) upset; (cause to) fall over: *Who knocked the bottle over? It couldn't have tipped over by itself* **3** [T1] to throw or leave (unwanted articles) somewhere **4** [X9] to pour (a substance) from one container into another, onto a surface, etc.: *She weighed the flour and tipped it into the basin*
tip⁴ *n* a place where unwanted waste is left
tip⁵ *v* **-pp-** [T1] to strike lightly: *to tip the ball*
tip⁶ *v* **-pp-** [D1;T1;I∅] to give (a TIP⁷) to (a waiter, waitress, etc.): *I tipped the taxi driver (£1) for being so polite and helpful* —**~per** *n*
tip⁷ *n* a small amount of money given as a gift for a small service performed
tip⁸ *n* [C (*on*), C5] a helpful piece of advice: *Thanks for your tip on how to get ink out of shirts*
tip⁹ *v* **-pp-** [T1;V3] to give a helpful piece of advice by stating (what or who) one expects to do something: *Which horse are you tipping to win the race?|I'm tipping Mr Smith as the next President*
tip-off /ˈ· ·/ *n* a piece of helpful information; warning: *a tip-off about the enemy's attack*
tip off *v adv* **1** [T1;D5] to give (someone, as the police) a warning: *The police were tipped off that the criminals were planning to rob the bank* **2** [X9 esp. *about*;D5] to give (someone) private or secret information about something
tip·pet /ˈtɪpɨt/ *n* **1** *rare* a long piece of material or fur worn round the neck and shoulders with the end hanging down to the waist in front **2** *tech* an article of dress like this worn by judges, priests, etc.
tip·ple¹ /ˈtɪpəl/ *v* [Wv3;I∅] *infml* to drink (too much) alcohol habitually —**-pler** *n*
tipple² *n* [*usu. sing.*] *infml* an alcoholic drink: *What's your favourite tipple?*
tip·staff /ˈtɪpstɑːf‖-stæf/ *n* **-staves** /steɪvz/ *or* **-staffs** [C;N] an attendant with special duties in a court of law
tip·ster /ˈtɪpstəʳ/ *n* a person who gives information and advice about the likely winner of horse and dog races, esp. in return for money
tip·sy /ˈtɪpsi/ *adj* [Wa1] slightly drunk —**-sily** *adv* —**-siness** *n* [U]
tip·toe¹ /ˈtɪptəʊ/ *n* **on tiptoe** **a** on one's toes with the rest of the feet raised above the ground **b** eager; excited: *She was on tiptoe on the morning of her wedding*
tiptoe² *v* [I∅] to walk on one's toes with the rest of one's feet raised above the ground
tip-top /ˌ· ˈ·◂/ *adj* [Wa5] *infml* of the highest quality; excellent —**tip-top** *adv*
ti·rade /taɪˈreɪd, tɨ-‖ˈtaɪreɪd, tɨˈreɪd/ *n* a long very angry scolding speech
tire¹ /taɪəʳ/ *v* [Wv4;T1;I∅ (*of*)] to (cause to) become tired: *I've had a very tiring day at work.|After walking for 2 hours I began to tire.|Jean never tires of talking about her work*
tire² *n AmE* TYRE
tired /taɪəd‖taɪərd/ *adj* **1** [B] having or showing a lack of power in the mind or body, esp. after activity; having or showing a need for rest or sleep: *I'm so tired I could sleep for a week* **2** [F (*of*)] no longer interested; annoyed: *I'm tired of your stupid conversation* **3** [B] showing lack of imagination or new thought: *The same tired old subjects come up year after year* —**~ly** *adv* —**~ness** *n* [U]
tire·less /ˈtaɪələs‖ˈtaɪər-/ *adj* [Wa5] never or rarely getting tired: *a tireless worker* —**~ly** *adv*
tire out *v adv* [Wv5;T1] to cause to become completely tired: *Jean's tired out and should go to bed early*
tire·some /ˈtaɪəsəm‖ˈtaɪər-/ *adj* **1** annoying: *a tiresome child who won't do what she's told* **2** tiring or uninteresting, esp. because of length or dullness —**~ly** *adv*
ti·ro /ˈtaɪərəʊ/ *n* TYRO
tis·sue /ˈtɪʃuː, -sjuː‖-ʃuː/ *n* **1** [U] animal or plant cells, esp. those that are like in form and purpose and make up a particular organ: *lung tissue|leaf tissue* **2** [U] also **tissue pa·per** /ˈ·· ˌ··/— light thin paper used for wrapping, packing, etc. **3** [C] a piece of soft paper, esp. used for blowing the nose on **4** [C;U] (a) light thin cloth **5** [C (*of*)] *fml* something formed as if by weaving threads together; network: *a tissue of lies*
tit¹ /tɪt/ *n sl* **1** [C] also **titty**— **a** BREAST¹ (1) **b** NIPPLE **2** [C; (*you*) N] *BrE* a weak stupid person **3 get on one's tits** to annoy one greatly
tit² also (*fml*) **titmouse**— *n* any of several types of small European birds: *a blue tit|a great tit*
ti·tan /ˈtaɪtn/ *n* a person of great strength, importance, size, cleverness, etc.
ti·tan·ic /taɪˈtænɪk/ *adj* [Wa5] of great size, strength, power, importance, etc.
ti·ta·ni·um /taɪˈteɪnɪəm/ *n* [U] a type of silvery grey light strong metal that is a simple substance (ELEMENT (6)), used esp. for making compounds with other metals
tit·bit /ˈtɪtˌbɪt/ *AmE* **tidbit**— *n esp. BrE* **1** a small piece of particularly nice food **2** *infml* an interesting piece of news
tit·fer /ˈtɪtfəʳ/ *n BrE sl* a hat
tit for tat /ˌ· · ˈ·/ *n infml* **1** [C;U] something unpleasant, such as a blow, in return for something unpleasant one has suffered: *I didn't invite her to my party because she didn't invite me to hers. It was just tit for tat* **2** [C] an argument
tithe /taɪð/ *n* **1** a tax of 1/10 of one's yearly profit or income paid in former times for the support of the priest of the local church **2** [(*of*)] a 1/10 part (of anything)

tit·il·late /ˈtɪtǝ̣leɪt/ *v* [Wv4;T1] to excite pleasantly —**-lation** /ˌtɪtǝ̣ˈleɪʃən/ *n* [U]
tit·i·vate, tit·ti- /ˈtɪtǝ̣veɪt/ *v* [T1;I∅] *infml* to make (esp. oneself) pretty or tidy
ti·tle /ˈtaɪtl/ *n* **1** [C] a name given to a book, painting, play, etc.: *The title of this play is "Othello"* **2** [C] a word or name, such as "Mr", "Lord", "Doctor", "General", "Lady", etc., given to a person to be used before his name as a sign of rank, profession, etc. **3** [S;U: (*to*)] *tech* the lawful right to ownership or possession: *Has Britain any title to this island?* **4** [C] the position of unbeaten winner in certain sports competitions; CHAMPIONSHIP (3): *They're fighting for the world title tonight.*|*a title fight*
ti·tled /ˈtaɪtld/ *adj* [Wa5] having a noble title, such as "Lord": *titled ladies*
title deed /ˈ·· ·/ *n* a piece of paper giving proof of a person's right of ownership of property
ti·tle·hold·er /ˈtaɪtlˌhəʊldəʳ/ *n* a person or team who is at present the unbeaten winner of a sports competition
title page /ˈ·· ·/ *n* the page at the front of a book giving the title, writer's name, etc.
title role /ˈ·· ·/ *n* the chief part (ROLE) in a play, after which the play is named
tit·mouse /ˈtɪtmaʊs/ *n* **-mice** /maɪs/ *fml* TIT²
tit·ter /ˈtɪtəʳ/ *v* [I∅] to laugh very quietly from nervousness or badly controlled amusement —**titter** *n*: *That's enough of your titters, girls!*
tit·tle /ˈtɪtl/ *n* [S] a very small amount; bit (esp. in the phr. **not one/a jot or tittle**)
tittle-tat·tle¹ /ˈtɪtl ˌtætl/ *n* [U] *infml* GOSSIP¹ (1)
tittle-tattle² /ˌ·· ˈ··, ˈ·· ˌ··/ *v* [I∅] *infml* GOSSIP²
tit·ty /ˈtɪti/ *n sl* TIT¹
tit·u·lar /ˈtɪtʃʊləʳ‖-tʃə-/ *adj* [Wa5] **1** existing in name only; holding a title but not having the duties, responsibilities, or power of office **2** of, belonging to, or related to a title
tiz·zy /ˈtɪzi/ *n* [*usu. sing.*] *sl* a state of excited confusion
T-junc·tion /ˈtiː ˌdʒʌŋkʃən/ *n* a place where 2 roads, pipes, etc., join and form the shape of a letter T
TNT /ˌtiː en ˈtiː/ *n* [U] TRINITROTOLUENE, a type of powerful explosive
to¹ /tə, tʊ; *strong* tuː/ *prep* **1** in a direction towards: *the road to London*|*She stood up and walked to the window.*|*He pointed to the moon.*|*She threw the ball to me* (=for me to catch. Compare *She threw the stone at me*=to hurt me) **2** in the direction of; so as to have reached: *We're hoping to go to London for our holidays this year.*|*The robber was sent to prison for 5 years* **3** as far as: *The water came to our necks* **4** towards; reaching the state of: *He usually works hard but tends to laziness.*|*She sang the baby to sleep* **5** as far as the state of: *The child was kicked to death by the wild horse.*|*Wait until the lights change to green* **6** in a touching position with: *The 2 lovers danced cheek to cheek.*|*The paper stuck firmly to the wall* **7** facing or in front of: *They stood face to face/back to back.*|*Sitting with my back to the engine* **8** as far as; until and including: *Count (from 10) to 20.*|*I read the book from beginning to end.*|*They stayed from Friday night to/till Sunday morning.*|*It's 10 miles (from here) to London.*|*I'm wet to the skin.*|*They were killed to a man/to the last man* (=they were all killed) —see INCLUSIVE (USAGE) **9** for the attention or possession of: *Have you told all your news to John?*|*I want a present to give to my wife.*|*This is a letter to Mildred from George* **10** for; of: *Have you got the key to this lock?*|*a job as secretary to a doctor* **11** in relation with; in comparison with: *I know he's successful but he's nothing to what he could have been.*|*The result of the match was 5 points to 3.*|*This wine is second to none* (=is the best) **12** together with: *We sang the song to a new tune today.*|(*becoming rare*) *Do you want an egg to your tea?* **13** forming; making up; being in degree or amount: *There are 100 pence to every pound* **14** in accordance with: *Your dress isn't really to my liking.*|*You will hear of something to your advantage* **15** (*with words about addition*) as well as; and: *Add 2 to 4* (compare SUBTRACT *2 from 4*).|*In addition to John, there are the girls* **16** in honour of: *Let's drink to the health of our respected foreign guests.*|*They built a temple to Mars* **17** with the aim or purpose of: *a passing motorist came to our help* **18** for the possession of: *The prince has no right to the title* **19** (of time) before: *"It's 5 (minutes) to 4." "No, it's only 10 to (4)."*|*How long is it to/till dinner?* **20** in the position of: *Scotland is to the north of England* **21** per: *This car does 30 miles to the* GALLON **22** (*used like* by *after some* PASSIVE*s*): *He is well known to the police* **23** so as to cause (esp. a feeling): *He broke it, (greatly) to my annoyance.*|*To my great surprise, we won!* **24** as far as concerns: *To me this seemed silly.*|*It looked to him like a rabbit* **25** in connection with: *What's your answer to that?*|*She's always kind to animals.*|*This'll do a lot of good to your chest.*|*"things Arthur did to me"* (SEU S.) **26 (a number) to (a number) a** between (a number) and (a number): *in 10 to 12 feet of water*|*She's 40 to 45* **b** compared with: *It's 100 to 1 he'll lose* (=100 times as likely)
USAGE 1 Compare **to** and **till/until** with expressions of time; **to** is always used when speaking of the clock: *It's 5 minutes* **to** (not ***till**) *4* —opposite **past**. Otherwise, **to** is used of time only **a** with **from**: *We stayed* **from** *June* **to** *September* —see INCLUSIVE (USAGE) **b** when it means "so as to be on": *We've put the party off* **to/till** *Tuesday.*|*They've brought the date of the meeting forward* **to** (not ***till**) *the 17th.* **c** when considering the length of time before an event: *It's an hour* **to/till** *dinner.* **d** in certain expressions like **to the last**, **to this day**, **to date**. Use **till/until** in other expressions of time: *We stayed* **until** (not ***to**) *7.*|*I didn't see him* **till** (not ***to**) *last week.*|**Until** (not ***To**) *when does the concert go on?* 2 In the 9th meaning, the person actually receives the information, present, etc. When it is only intended that he shall receive it, use **for**: *I really bought these shoes* **for** *Mary, but I think I'll give them* **to** *Jane.* —see also ACCORDING TO, AS TO, CLOSE **to,** NEAR (*to*), DUE TO, OWING TO, PRIOR TO, SUBJECT TO, TO AND FRO; compare FROM
to² *adv* [Wa5] **1** into consciousness: *John didn't come to for half an hour after he'd fallen and hit his head* **2** into a shut position: *The wind blew the door to*
to³ (*used before a verb to show it is the* INFINITIVE, *but not before* can, could, may, might, will, would, shall, should, must, ought to; *sometimes left out when the verb is understood. Note the following patterns*): **a** (*after verbs*): [I3] *He lived to be 90.*|[T3] *It wants to be fed.*|[V3] (*usu. with reported commands*) *He told them to shoot* (=He said "Shoot!").|*He told them (not) to*|*"You're not allowed to put your head back"* (SEU S.)|[L (*to be*) 1] *He seems (to be) a fool.*|[L (*to be*) 7] *It proved (to be) possible.*|*"It just doesn't appear to be on anywhere"* (SEU S.)|[X (*to be*) 1] *They supposed her (to be) their daughter.*|[X (*to be*) 7] *They wished him (to be) dead* **b** (*after* how, where, who, whom, whose, which, when, what, *or* whether): [D6b] *Tell me where to go.*|[T6b] *He knows what to do.*|*I don't know how to.*|*She wondered whether or not to/whether to or not* **c** (*after nouns*): [C3] *an attempt to land*|[P3] *the* QUALIFICATION*s to drive*|[U3] *some reason to leave* **d** (*after adjectives*): [B3] *an easy thing to*

do||[F3] *I'm glad/sorry/happy to say* . . . **e** (*when speaking about the verb, as in grammar*): *"To find" takes a direct object.|To wear boots would be safest.|It would be safest (for you) to wear boots.|"What they really ought to have done was to refuse"* (SEU S.) **f** (*when speaking of purpose*) in order to: *They left early to catch the train.|I want some scissors to cut my nails (with)* **g** (*in the patterns* **used, ought, going+to**): *"I was going to make a very stupid remark"* (SEU S.) **h** (*in the patterns* **too . . . to . . ., . . . enough to . . .**): *He's too fat to dance.|It's cold enough to snow* **i** (in the pattern **to . . .**=if I can . . .): *To be honest, I don't know anything about it.|To put it another way, do you like him?|To begin with, let's* . . . **j** (in phrs. like **in order to, so as to**) **k** (in the pattern **There is**+noun+**to**): *There were plenty of things to eat.|There's Bob to consider* (=he must be considered)

USAGE Some people think it is bad English to put any other word, such as an adverb, between **to** and the verb that follows it, making a SPLIT **infinitive**: *He was wrong* **to** *suddenly say that.* But sometimes there is nowhere else to put the adverb: *Your job is* **to** *really understand these children.|He likes* **to** *half close his eyes.*

toad /təʊd/ *n* any of several types of animal like a large FROG (1), that usu. live on land, but go into water for breeding —see picture at AMPHIBIAN

toad-in-the-hole /ˌ· · · ˈ·/ *n* [C;U] (a British dish of) SAUSAGE*s* baked in BATTER (=a mixture of eggs, milk, and flour)

toad·stool /ˈtəʊdstuːl/ *n* any of several types of fleshy plant (FUNGUS) like the MUSHROOM, but often poisonous —see picture at FUNGUS

toad·y¹ /ˈtəʊdi/ *n* [C;N] *derog* a person too nice to people of higher rank, esp. for personal advantage

toady² *v* [IØ (*to*)] *derog* to be too nice to someone of higher rank, esp. for personal advantage

to-and-fro¹ /ˌ· · ˈ·/ *adj* [Wa5] forwards and backwards or from side to side: *a to-and-fro movement*

to-and-fro² *n* [*the*+U (*of*)] *infml* activity in which people or things move from place to place, pass in opposite directions, etc.: *the busy to-and-fro of passengers in the airport* —see also TO-ING AND FRO-ING

to and fro *adv* (of repeated movements or journeys) backwards and forwards; from side to side: *The teacher walked to and fro in front of the class as he talked*

toast¹ /təʊst/ *v* **1** [Wv5;T1] to make (bread, cheese, etc.) brown by holding close to heat **2** [T1] *not fml* to warm thoroughly: *to toast one's feet by the fire* —see COOK (USAGE)

toast² *n* **1** [U] bread made brown by being held in front of heat, usu. eaten hot with butter: *I like toast for breakfast* **2** [C] a call on other people to drink to a person or thing; words of loyalty, admiration, etc., spoken before drinking **3** [*the*+R] the person whose health is drunk

toast³ *v* [T1] to drink or suggest a drink to the success, happiness, health, or honour of (someone)

toast·er /ˈtəʊstəʳ/ *n* an apparatus for TOASTing¹ (1) bread electrically —see picture at KITCHEN

toasting fork /ˈ·· ·/ *n* a long-handled fork for TOASTing¹ (1) bread in front of the fire

toast·mas·ter /ˈtəʊstˌmɑːstəʳ||-ˌmæ-/ *n* a person who speaks the TOAST*s*² (2) and introduces speakers at a formal dinner

to·bac·co /təˈbækəʊ/ *n* **-os 1** [U] a type of plant grown for its large leaves, used chiefly in smoking **2** [U] the leaves of this plant, specially prepared for use in cigarettes, pipes, CHEWing, etc. **3** [C] a particular type of this

to·bac·co·nist /təˈbækənəst/ *n* a person who sells tobacco, cigarettes, etc.

to·bog·gan¹ /təˈbɒgən||-ˈbɑ-/ *n esp. AmE* a long light board curved up at the front, for carrying people over snow, esp. down slopes for sport

toboggan² *v* [IØ] **1** *esp. BrE* to go or race down slopes on a SLEDGE (1), as done by children or in the sport of **tobogganing 2** *AmE* to go on a TOBOGGAN

to·by jug /ˈtəʊbi dʒʌg/ *n* a small drinking vessel, in the form of a fat old man wearing a 3-cornered hat

toc·ca·ta /təˈkɑːtə (*It* tɔˈkata)/ *n* a special piece of music, esp. for the ORGAN, piano, or like instrument, in a free style with difficult passages that show the player's skill

toc·sin /ˈtɒksən||ˈtɑk-/ *n esp. lit* (a bell rung as) a warning signal

tod /tɒd||tɑd/ *n* **on one's tod** *BrE sl* alone; by oneself

to·day¹ /təˈdeɪ/ *adv* [Wa5] **1** during or on the present day: *Are we going shopping today?* **2** during or at the present time: *We sell more cars abroad today than we've ever done before*

today² *n* [R] **1** this present day: *Today's my birthday!* **2** this present time, period, etc.: *Young people of today are much more concerned about helping the old than their parents were*

tod·dle /ˈtɒdl||ˈtɑdl/ *v* **1** [IØ] to walk with short unsteady steps, as a small child does **2** [L9] *sl* to walk; go: *I'm just toddling over to Mary's. Why don't you come?*

tod·dler /ˈtɒdləʳ||ˈtɑd-/ *n* a child who has just learnt to walk

tod·dy /ˈtɒdi||ˈtɑdi/ *n* [U] **1** a sweetened mixture of WHISKY and hot water **2** a fresh or alcoholic drink made from the juice (SAP) of certain tropical Asian PALM trees

to-do /tə ˈduː/ *n* [*usu. sing.*] *sl* a state of excited confusion or annoyance

toe¹ /təʊ/ *n* **1** one of the 5 small movable parts at the end of each foot —see picture at HUMAN² **2** the part of a sock, shoe, etc., that fits over these **3 on one's toes** fully conscious and ready for action —see also TREAD **on someone's toes**

toe² *v* **toe the line** to obey orders; act in accordance with general custom

toe cap /ˈ· ·/ *n* a leather covering stitched over the toe of a shoe to strengthen it

toe·hold /ˈtəʊhəʊld/ *n* a very small place (as on a rock) just big enough to take part of the foot and thus give support to a climber —compare FOOTHOLD

toe·nail /ˈtəʊneɪl/ *n* the nail on any of the toes —see picture at HUMAN²

toff /tɒf||tɑf/ *n sl, esp. BrE* a well-dressed person of high social rank

tof·fee, toffy /ˈtɒfi||ˈtɑfi/ *n* **1** [C;U] *AmE* also **taffy**— (a piece of) a hard sticky sweet brown substance made by boiling sugar and butter with water **2** [C] *NWEngE* a sweet of any kind

toffee ap·ple /ˈ·· ˌ··/ *n* an apple covered with TOFFEE, held on a small stick

toffee-nosed /ˈ·· ·/ *adj sl* SNOBBISH

to·ga /ˈtəʊgə/ *n* a long loose flowing outer garment worn by the citizens of ancient Rome

to·geth·er /təˈgeðəʳ/ *adv* [Wa5] **1** in or into one group, body, or place: *The people gathered together.|John and Jean are living together but they have no plans to get married* **2** in or into union: *Tie the ends together.|Add these numbers together.|Multiply 5 and 17 together.|It's torn, but I'll stick it together again* **3** in or into relationship with one another: *We hope to bring the 2 enemies close enough together to make peace* **4** at the same time: *Why do all my troubles always come together?* **5** without interruption: *They worked for 8 hours together* **6** in agreement; combined: *We should all stand together to defend what we believe to be right* **7** considered as a whole; COLLECTIVELY: *The Soviet people did more to win the war than the rest of us (put) together* **8** into or in a condition of unity: *The argument does not hold together well* **9 close/near together** near each other —see also GET TOGETHER, PULL TOGETHER

to·geth·er·ness /tə'geðənɨs‖-ðər-/ *n* [U] a feeling of being united with other people; friendliness

together with /·'·· ·/ *prep* as well as; along with; in addition to: *He sent her some roses, together with a nice letter*

tog·gle /'tɒgəl‖'tɑ-/ *n* a short shaped bar of wood used in place of a button on a DUFFEL COAT

togs /tɒgz‖tɑgz, tɔgz/ *n* [P] *sl* clothes

tog up /tɒg‖tɑg, tɔg/ also **tog out**— *v adv* **-gg-** [T1b (*in*)] *infml* to dress (oneself) in specially nice or formal clothes

toil¹ /tɔɪl/ *n* [U] *esp. fml or lit* hard or continuous work —see WORK (USAGE)

toil² *v esp. fml or lit* **1** [Wv4;L9] to work hard and untiringly **2** [L9] to move with tiredness, difficulty, or pain: *The slaves toiled up the hill pulling the heavy blocks*

toi·let /'tɔɪlɨt/ *n* **1** [C] a large seatlike bowl fixed to the floor and connected to a pipe (DRAIN), used for getting rid of the body's waste matter —see picture at BATHROOM **2** [C] a room containing this **3** [U9] *fml* the act of washing and dressing oneself **4** [U9] *fml* a person's appearance with regard to style of dress, hair, etc.

toilet pa·per /'·· ˌ··/ *n* [U] thin paper, in a continuous length or single pieces, for cleaning the body when waste matter has been passed from it —see picture at BATHROOM

toi·let·ries /'tɔɪlɨtriz/ *n* [P] articles or substances used in dressing, washing, etc.

toilet roll /'·· ·/ *n* a rolled-up continuous length of TOILET PAPER

toi·let·ry /'tɔɪlɨtri/ *n* [A] of or for TOILETRIES: *the toiletry* COUNTER

toilet train /'·· ·/ *v* [Wv5;T1] to teach (a child) to pass waste matter from the body only when sitting on the TOILET

toilet wa·ter /'·· ˌ··/ *n* [U] a pleasant-smelling liquid used as a light PERFUME

toils /tɔɪlz/ *n* [P] *esp. lit* net: (fig.) *caught in the toils of the law*

to·ing and fro·ing /ˌtuːɪŋ ən 'frəʊɪŋ/ *n* **to·ings and fro·ings** [U;C *usu. pl.*] *infml* busy unproductive activity: *After a lot of to-ing and fro-ing they reached a decision*

To·kay /təʊ'keɪ/ *n* [U] a type of sweet Hungarian wine

to·ken /'təʊkən/ *n* **1** [A;C] an outward sign; something that represents some fact, event, feeling, etc.; small part representing something greater: *All the family wore black as a token of their grief.*|*a token payment*|*a token* STRIKE² **2** [C] something that serves as a reminder; KEEPSAKE; SOUVENIR: *My husband gave me a ring as a token of our first meeting* **3** [C] a piece of metal used instead of coins for a particular purpose **4** [C9] a receipt, usu. fixed to a greetings card, which one can exchange for the stated thing in a shop: *a £2* BOOK TOKEN|*a gift token* (=that one can exchange for anything in a particular shop) **5 by the same token** in the same way **6 in token of** as proof of

token mon·ey /'·· ˌ··/ *n* [U] metal coins formerly produced and used by people in trade and exchangeable for official money

told /təʊld/ *past t. & p. of* TELL

tol·e·ra·ble /'tɒlərəbəl‖'tɑ-/ *adj* [Wa5] fairly good; not too bad; that can be TOLERATED

tol·e·ra·bly /'tɒlərəbli‖'tɑ-/ *adv* [Wa5] to a limited degree; fairly: *I feel tolerably well today*

tol·e·rance /'tɒlərəns‖'tɑ-/ *n* **1** [C;U: (*of, to*)] the quality of being able to suffer pain, hardship, etc., without being damaged: *Many old people have a very limited tolerance to cold* **2** [U] the quality of allowing people to behave in a way that may not please one, without becoming annoyed **3** [C;U] *tech* (in building) the amount by which the measure of a value can vary from the amount intended, without causing difficulties: *This wooden beam was made to have a tolerance of 0·001 inches* **4** [C;U: (*to, of*)] *tech* the degree to which a cell, animal, plant, etc., can successfully oppose the effect of a poison, drug, etc. **5** [U] TOLERATION

tol·e·rant /'tɒlərənt‖'tɑ-/ *adj* showing or practising TOLERATION: *a tolerant father* —**~ly** *adv*

tol·e·rate /'tɒləreɪt‖'tɑ-/ *v* [T1] **1** to allow (something one does not agree with) to be practised or done freely without opposition; permit **2** to suffer (someone or something) without complaining: *I can't tolerate your bad manners any longer* —see BEAR (USAGE)

tol·e·ra·tion /ˌtɒlə'reɪʃən‖ˌtɑ-/ *n* [U] **1** the quality or practice of allowing opinions, beliefs, customs, behaviour, etc., different from one's own, to be held and practised freely: *religious toleration* **2** TOLERANCE (2)

toll¹ /təʊl/ *n* **1** [C] a tax paid for the right to use a road, harbour, etc. **2** [C9 *usu. sing.*] the cost in health, life, etc., from illness, an accident, etc.: *the holiday death toll on the roads*

toll² *v* **1** [Wv4;T1;IØ] **a** to ring (a bell) slowly and repeatedly **b** (of a bell) to ring slowly and repeatedly **2** [T1] to tell or make known by doing this: *The church bell tolled the hour*

toll³ *n* [(*the*) S] the sound of a TOLLing² (1) bell

toll·gate /'təʊlgeɪt/ *n* a gate across a road at which a TOLL¹ (1) must be paid

toll·house /'təʊlhaʊs/ *n* **-houses** /ˌhaʊzɨz/— a house at a TOLLGATE in which the person who collects TOLLS¹ (1) lives

tom·a·hawk /'tɒməhɔːk‖'tɑ-/ *n* a light axe used by North American Indians in war and hunting

to·ma·to /tə'mɑːtəʊ‖-'meɪ-/ *n* **-toes** **1** [C;U] (a type of) soft fleshy juicy red fruit eaten raw or cooked as a vegetable **2** [C] the type of hairy yellow-flowered plant on which this fruit grows —see picture at VEGETABLE¹

tomb /tuːm/ *n* a grave, esp. a large ornamental one built to have a large space inside where the dead person is placed

tom·bo·la /tɒm'bəʊlə‖tɑm-/ *n* [U] *esp. BrE* any of various games in which tickets are drawn by chance to win prizes or money

tom·boy /'tɒmbɔɪ‖'tɑm-/ *n* a spirited girl who likes rough and noisy games —**~ish** *adj*

tomb·stone /'tuːmstəʊn/ *n* GRAVESTONE

tom·cat /'tɒmkæt‖'tɑm-/ also (*infml*) **tom** /tɒm‖tɑm/— *n* a male cat

tome /təʊm/ *n esp. lit or humor* a large book

tom·fool·e·ry /tɒm'fuːləri‖tɑm-/ *n* **1** [U] foolish behaviour **2** [C *usu. pl.*] a foolish act

tom·my gun /'tɒmi gʌn‖'tɑ-/ *n sl* a light MACHINE-GUN

tom·my·rot /'tɒmirɒt‖'tɑmirɑt/ *n* [U] *infml* complete nonsense

to·mor·row¹ /tə'mɒrəʊ‖-'mɔ-, -'mɑ-/ *adv* [Wa5] during or on the day following today: *It rained yesterday and today so perhaps it will be sunny tomorrow.*|*"dreaming, perhaps, of the party tomorrow"* (SEU W.)

tomorrow² *n* **1** [R] the day following today: *Tomorrow will be my birthday!*|*"We washed the glasses ready for tomorrow"* (SEU W.) **2** [S;R] the future: *a brighter tomorrow*|*Tomorrow's world*|*the* *world of tomorrow will be very different from the present time*

tom·tit /ˈtɒm,tɪt‖ˈtɑm-/ *n infml* any of various types of small bird, esp. the blue TIT[2]

tom-tom /ˈtɒm tɒm‖ˈtɑm tɑm/ *n* **1** a long narrow American INDIAN or Asian drum played by being beaten with the hands **2** a large modern standing drum played with a stick —see picture at PERCUSSION

ton /tʌn/ *n* [see NUMBER TABLE 4B] **1** [Wn1;C] a measurement of weight equal in Britain to 2,240 pounds (**long ton**) and in the United States to 2,000 pounds (**short ton**) —see WEIGHTS & MEASURES TABLE **2** [Wn1;C] also **tonne, metric ton**— a measurement of weight equal to 1,000 kilos —see WEIGHTS & MEASURES TABLE **3** [Wn1;C] a measurement of **a** the size of a ship equal to 100 CUBIC feet **b** the amount of goods a ship can carry equal to 40 CUBIC feet **4** [C (*of*) *usu. pl. with sing. meaning*] *sl* a very large quantity (of anything): *I bought tons of fruit while it was cheap* **5** [S] *sl* a heavy weight: *This book weighs a ton* **6** [(*the*) S] *sl* 100 miles per hour: *The police caught me doing a ton so I have to go to court for breaking the speed limit* —see also TON-UP **7** [C] *sl* 100 runs made by one player in one INNINGS; CENTURY (3) **8 (come down) like a ton of bricks** *sl* (to act) with sudden crushing weight or force or in sudden anger

ton·al /ˈtəʊnl/ *adj* [Wa5] of or related to TONALITY or TONE

ton·al·i·ty /təʊˈnæl̩ti/ *n tech* **1** [U;C] the character of a tune depending on the musical KEY in which it is played **2** [C] a musical KEY

tone /təʊn/ *n* **1** [C] any sound considered with regard to its quality, highness or lowness, strength, etc. —see picture at SOUND[3] **2** [C] the quality or character of a particular instrument or singing voice as regards the sound it produces **3** [C] also (*esp. AmE*) **step**— *tech* a difference in the highness of a musical note equal to that between 2 notes which are 2 notes apart on a piano: *a tone between B and C sharp* **4** [C *often pl. with sing. meaning*] a particular quality of the voice as expressive of some feeling, meaning, etc.; manner of expression: *in ringing tones|I don't like your tone; don't take that tone (of voice) with me* (=what you are saying, and the way you are saying it, annoy me) **5** [C] a particular (change of) highness or lowness of a speech sound **6** [C] a variety of a colour, different from the ordinary colour because of more light or darkness, the addition of a slight quantity of another colour, etc.: *a picture painted in various tones of blue and no other colour* **7** [U] *tech* the effect in painting of light and shade together with colour **8** [U] the ordinary and proper state of firmness of the organs, muscles, etc., of the body **9** [U] the general quality or nature: *These new people, with their dirty habits and wild children, bring down the tone of the neighbourhood*

-toned /təʊnd/ *comb. form* having the stated type of TONE[1] (2)

tone-deaf /ˌ· ˈ·◂/ *adj* unable to tell the difference between different musical notes

tone down *v adv* [T1] to reduce the violence, excitement, or force of (something): *After I swore at the policeman he warned me to tone down my language*

tone in *v adv* [T1;IØ (*with*)] to (cause to) match: *I think black shoes would tone in better with your coat than red ones*

tone lan·guage /ˈ· ˌ··/ *n* any of those languages, such as Chinese or Yoruba, in which differences of musical tune (=TONE (5)) are used for expressing the difference between words that have the same spelling

tone·less /ˈtəʊnləs/ *adj* [Wa5] lacking colour, spirit, etc.; lifeless; dull: *a toneless voice/answer/reply* —**~ly** *adv*

tone po·em /ˈ· ˌ··/ *n* a piece of music written to represent musically a poetic idea, scene, etc.

tone up *v adv* [T1;IØ] to (cause to) become stronger, brighter, more effective, etc.: *Swimming is the best way to tone up your body*

tong /tɒŋ‖tɑŋ, tɔŋ/ *n* [GC] a Chinese secret society

tongs /tɒŋz‖tɑŋz, tɔŋz/ *n* [P] an instrument consisting of 2 movable arms joined at one end, used for holding or lifting various objects: *sugar tongs for picking up lumps of sugar* —see PAIR (USAGE) and picture at LABORATORY

tongue /tʌŋ/ *n* **1** [C] the movable fleshy organ in the mouth, used for tasting, moving food around, and, in human beings, for producing speech —see picture at HUMAN[2] **2** [C;U] this organ taken from an animal such as the ox, cooked as food **3** [C] any of various objects like a TONGUE (1) in shape or purpose, such as the piece of hanging metal in the middle of a bell or the piece of material under the LACE*s* in a shoe: *Tongues of flame shot out from the burning hut* **4** [C] a spoken language: *This dictionary is specially intended for people whose native tongue is not English* **5 bite one's tongue off** *infml* to be sorry for what one has just said **6 find one's tongue** to start to speak, esp. after a period when one has been too unsure of oneself or afraid to speak **7 get one's tongue around** *not fml* to pronounce (a difficult word, name, etc.) correctly **8 give tongue** *fml* to speak out loudly **9 hold one's tongue** *usu. imper.* to remain silent **10 keep a civil tongue (in one's head)** to be polite **11 set tongues wagging** to cause much interest and talk **12 (with) (one's) tongue in (one's) cheek** *infml* saying or doing something one does not seriously mean —see also **the** ROUGH[1] (9) **side of one's tongue, the** TIP[1] (3) **of one's tongue**

-tongued /tʌŋd/ *comb. form* **1** having a tongue of the stated kind: *a fork-tongued snake* **2** (habitually) speaking in the stated manner: *sharp-tongued women*

tongue-tied /ˈ· ·/ *adj* unable to speak freely, as through awkwardness in the presence of others

tongue twist·er /ˈ· ˌ··/ *n* a word or phrase difficult to speak quickly or correctly

ton·ic[1] /ˈtɒnɪk‖ˈtɑ-/ *adj* [Wa5] **1** *fml* strengthening: *the tonic quality of sea air* **2** (in music) of or based on the TONIC[2] (3)

tonic[2] *n* **1** anything which increases health or strength: *Country air is the best tonic for someone who lives in the city* **2** a medicine intended to give the body more strength, esp. when tired **3** the first note of a musical scale of 8 notes —compare DOMINANT[2]

tonic sol-fa /ˌ·· · ˈ·/ *n* [U] a method of showing musical notes by the first letters of the words in the SOL-FA system

tonic wa·ter /ˈ·· ˌ··/ also **tonic**— *n* [U] gassy water made bitter by the addition of QUININE, often added to strong alcoholic drinks: *a* GIN[2] *and tonic*

to·night[1] /təˈnaɪt/ *adv* [Wa5] on or during the night of today: *I've been really tired today so I think I'll go to bed early tonight.|at 9 o'clock tonight*

tonight[2] *n* [R] the night of today: *Tonight is a very special occasion.|on tonight's radio news*

ton·nage /ˈtʌnɪdʒ/ *n* [U;(C)] **1** the amount of goods a ship can carry, expressed in TON*s* (3b) **2** the size of a ship expressed in TON*s* (3a) **3** the total shipping of a navy, port, or country, expressed in TON*s* (3a) **4** a charge made for each TON (3b) of goods carried

tonne /tʌn/ *n* [Wn1] TON (2)

ton·sil /ˈtɒnsəl‖ˈtɑn-/ *n* either of 2 small roundish

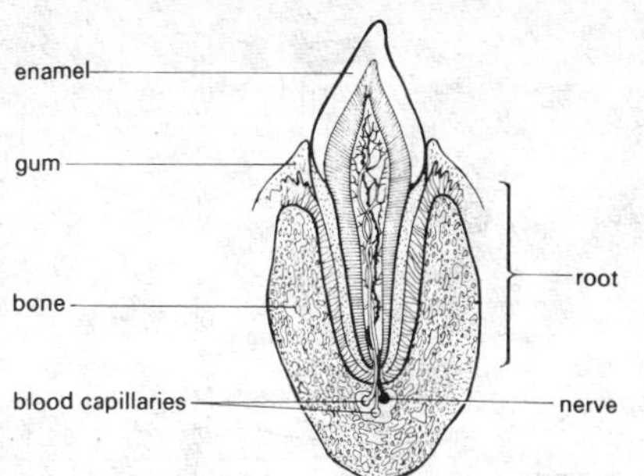

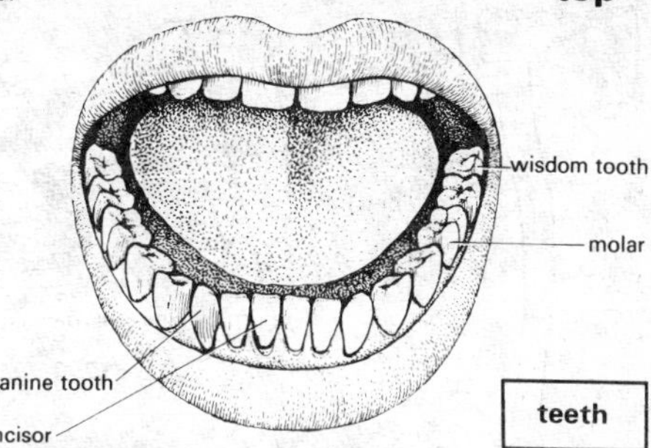

organs of flesh at the sides of the throat near the back of the tongue —see picture at RESPIRATORY

ton·sil·li·tis, tonsilitis /ˌtɒnsəˈlaɪtəs‖ˌtɑn-/ *n* [U] a painful soreness of the TONSILs

ton·so·ri·al /tɒnˈsɔːrɪəl‖tɑnˈso-/ *adj* [Wa5] *often humor* of or related to a men's HAIRDRESSER or his work

ton·sure¹ /ˈtɒnʃəʳ‖ˈtɑn-/ *n* **1** [U] the religious act of removing all the hair from the top part of the head as a sign one is a MONK **2** [C] the part of the head that has had the hair removed in this way

tonsure² *v* [Wv5;T1] to remove all the hair from the top part of the head of (someone) as a sign of being a MONK

ton·tine /ˈtɒntiːn, tɒnˈtiːn‖-ɑn-/ *n* a form of interest paid to those who have combined to lend a sum of money, arranged so that it increases as each lender dies, till the last one alive gets all that remains

ton-up /ˌtʌn ˈʌp◂/ *adj* [Wa5;A] (of a driver) liking to travel at high speeds, esp. over 100 miles per hour

too /tuː/ *adv* [Wa5] **1** [(*for*, 3)] (*before adjectives and adverbs*) more than enough; to a higher degree than is necessary or good; EXCESSIVEly: *You're going* (*much*) *too fast, slow down!*|*This dress is* (*a bit*) *too small* (=not big enough) *for me.*|*If the coffee's too hot, leave it to get cool.*|*There's been* (*far*) *too little rain lately and the crops are dying through lack of water.*|*It's too soon* (*for us*) *to tell whether you'll be found guilty or not.*|*It's too hot a day to work* (not **It's too hot weather.*)|*He's too much of a coward* (=too cowardly) *to fight.*|*"That didn't go too badly"* (=it went quite well) (SEU S.) **2** (*not at the beginning of a* CLAUSE) also; in addition; as well: *I can dance and sing too.*|*I can dance. I can sing too* (compare *I can't dance. I can't sing either.*)|*When I told her I'd been to Paris too* (=as well as London, Rome, etc.) *she was very jealous.*|*Have you been to Paris too* (=as well as me), *Jean?*|*It snowed yesterday; in October too!* **3** *infml, esp. AmE* indeed; so: *"I won't do it" "You will too!"* (=you must) **4 only too** very: *I'm only too pleased to be able to help you*

USAGE 1 One can say *The day is* **too** *hot* or *It's* **too** *hot a day* (notice the word order). **Too** cannot be used before ordinary adjectives in the pattern **too**+adjective+noun; one can say *The coffee is* **too** *sweet* but not **the* **too** *sweet coffee.* 2 *He's* **too** *much of a coward to shoot* means either **a** "for him to shoot others" or **b** "for others to shoot him".

took /tʊk/ *past t. of* TAKE

tool¹ /tuːl/ *n* **1** any instrument or apparatus such as an axe, hammer, spade, etc., held in the hands for doing special jobs —see MACHINE (USAGE) **2** anything necessary for doing one's job: *Words are his tools* **3** a person unfairly or dishonestly used by another for his own purposes: *The king was the tool of the military government* **4** *taboo sl* PENIS **5 down tools** to stop working, esp. suddenly and because one is discontented
See next page for picture

tool² *v* **1** [T1] to shape or make (something) with a tool: *The artist tooled a pattern onto the cover of the book with a hot needle* **2** [L9 esp. *along*, ALONG] *sl* to ride in or drive a large vehicle: *We were tooling along* (*the road*) *at 50 miles per hour*

tool up *v adv* [T1;I∅] to prepare (a factory) for production by providing the necessary tools and machinery

toot /tuːt/ *v* **1** [I∅] to make a short warning sound on a horn, whistle, etc. **2** [T1;I∅] **a** to cause (a horn, whistle, etc.) to produce a short warning sound: *The car drivers tooted their horns to show their anger at the delay* **b** (of a horn, whistle, etc.) to produce a short warning sound —**toot** *n*

tooth /tuːθ/ *n* **teeth** /tiːθ/ **1** one of the small hard bony objects growing in the upper and lower mouth of most animals, used for biting and tearing food **2** any of the narrow pointed parts that stand out from a comb, SAW, COG, etc. —see picture at MACHINERY **3 long in the tooth** *infml* old **4 tooth and nail** very violently: *The girls fought tooth and nail like wild cats* —see also TEETH —**~less** *adj* [Wa5]

tooth·ache /ˈtuːθ-eɪk/ *n* [U;C] (a) pain in a tooth —see ACHE (USAGE)

tooth·brush /ˈtuːθbrʌʃ/ *n* a small brush used for cleaning the teeth —see picture at BATHROOM

tooth·comb /ˈtuːθkəʊm/ *n* FINE-TOOTH COMB

-toothed /tuːθt, tuːðd/ *comb. form* having teeth of the stated sort or number

tooth·paste /ˈtuːθpeɪst/ *n* [U] a specially prepared substance used for cleaning the teeth —see picture at BATHROOM

tooth·pick /ˈtuːθˌpɪk/ *n* a short thin pointed piece of wood used for removing food stuck between the teeth

tooth pow·der /ˈ· ˌ··/ *n* [U] a specially prepared powder used for cleaning the teeth

tooth·some /ˈtuːθsəm/ *adj rare* (of food) having a pleasant taste

tooth·y /ˈtuːθi/ *adj* [Wa1] *infml* having or showing big teeth that stick out: *a toothy smile*

toot·le /ˈtuːtl/ *v infml* **1** [T1;I∅] to TOOT continuously and quietly: *tootling* (*on*) *his horn* **2** [L9] to go, drive, etc., in an unhurried manner: *I must just tootle down to the shops for some flour* —**tootle** *n*

toots /tuːts‖tʊts/ also **toot·sy** /ˈtuːtsi‖ˈtʊtsi/— *n* [N] *esp. AmE* DARLING

tootsie /ˈtʊtsi/ *n* (*used by or to a child*) a foot

top¹ /tɒp‖tɑp/ *n* **1** [(*the*) C] the highest part: *at the top of the mountain*|*Start reading at the top of the page.*|*The mountain tops were hidden in mist* **2** [A] the highest of several: *They live on the top floor* **3** [(*the*) C] the upper surface: *the top of my desk*|*the table top* **4** [(*the*) R (*of*)] the most important or worthiest part of anything: *He started life at the bottom and worked his way to the top* **5** [C *usu. pl.*] (of a plant) the highest part(s), usu. leaves: *birds*

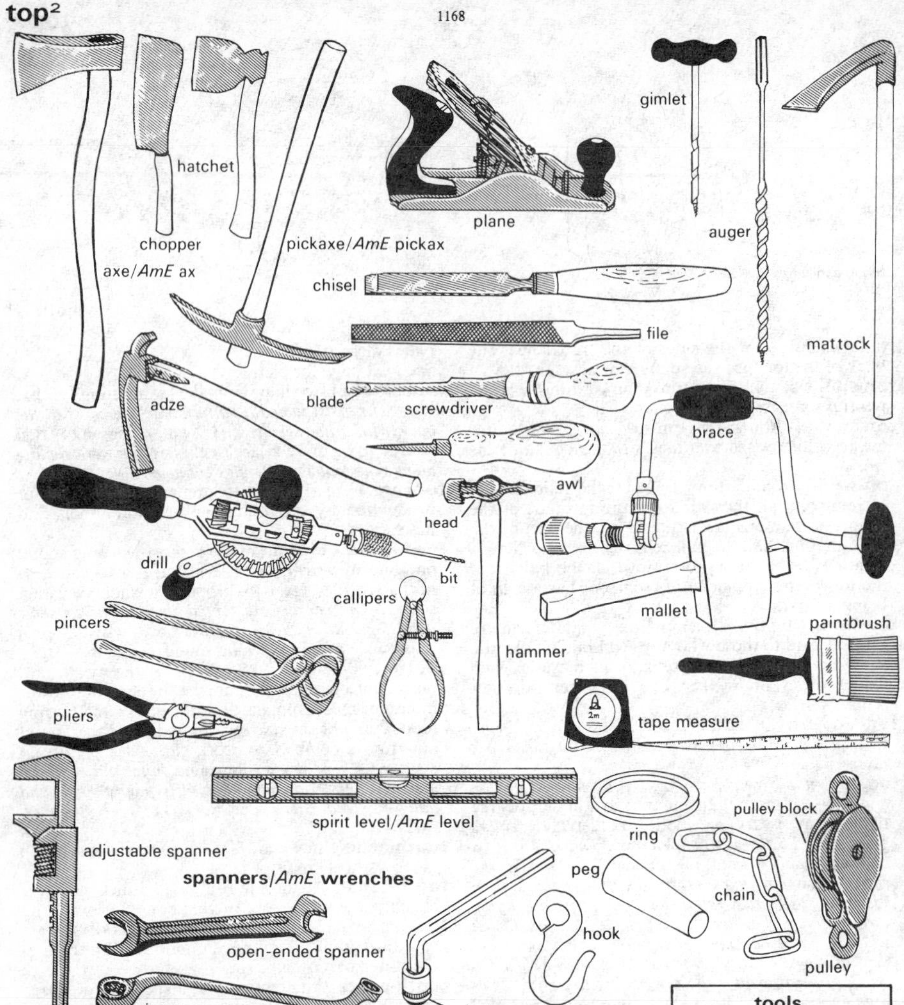

flying through treetops|vegetable tops **6** [(*the*) C] the cover: *I can't unscrew the top of this bottle* **7** [C] a garment worn on the upper part of the body **8 at the top of (one's) voice** as loudly as possible **9 at top speed** very fast **10 blow one's top** *infml* to explode with anger **11 from top to bottom** (of a place or organization) all through; completely **12 from top to toe** (of a person) completely: *She was dressed in green from top to toe* **13 get on top of** to conquer or be too much for: *Things have been rather getting on top of me lately* **14 in(to) top (gear)** (of a car) in(to) the highest GEAR¹ (3): (fig.) *He's been ill and hasn't got back into top gear yet* (=is not yet at his best) **15 on (the) top (of) a** over; above; resting on: *a glass of milk with cream on top* **b** in addition (to): *He lost his job and on top of that his wife left him* **16 on top of the world** very happy **17 the top of the tree** *infml* the highest position in a profession

top² *v* **-pp-** [T1] **1** to reach the top of: *When we topped the hill we had a beautiful view of the valley* **2** to provide a top for; form a top for: *The cake was topped with cream* **3** to be higher, better, or more than: *Our profits have topped £1,000 this year.|I can top your story with an even funnier one.|And to top it all, he said he loved her* **4** to remove the leafy top from (a vegetable, fruit, etc.) **5** (esp. in GOLF) to hit (a ball) above the centre: *He topped the ball and it went all along the ground* **6 top the bill** to be the chief actor or actress in a play —see also TOP OFF, TOP OUT, TOP UP

top³ *adj* [Wa5] of, related to, or being at the top: *Fred is our top man.|(BrE) George was bottom of the class and I was top.|Bob came out top in the examination*

top⁴ *n* **1** a type of child's toy that is made to spin and balance on its point by twisting it sharply with the fingers or with a string or by clockwork **2 sleep like a top** to sleep deeply

to·paz /ˈtəʊpæz/ *n* **1** [U] a transparent yellowish mineral **2** [C] a piece of this, specially cut and polished, considered to be a precious stone

top boot /ˈ· ·/ *n* a knee-length riding-boot with a broad pale band round the top

top brass /ˌ· ˈ·/ *n* [(*the*) GU] *sl* officers of high rank in the armed forces

top·coat /ˈtɒpkəʊt‖ˈtɑp-/ *n* **1** [C;U] the last covering of paint to be put on something —compare UNDERCOAT **2** [C] OVERCOAT

top dog /ˌ· ˈ·/ *n sl* the person in the highest or most

important position esp. after a struggle or effort
top drawer /ˌ· ˈ·◂/ *adj, n* [B; *the*+R] *infml* (of, being, or related to) the highest social rank
top-dress /ˌ· ˈ·‖ˈ· ·/ *v* [D1+*on/with*;T1 (*with*)] to spread (lime, sand, MANURE, etc.) over the surface of (a field)
top·dress·ing /ˌtɒpˈdresɪŋ‖ˈtɑpˌdresɪŋ/ *n* [U] a covering of lime, sand, MANURE, etc., spread over a field
tope /təʊp/ *n* [Wn2] a type of small SHARK[1]
to·pee, topi /ˈtəʊpiː‖təʊˈpiː/ *n* PITH HELMET
top-flight /ˌ· ˈ·◂/ *adj infml* first rate; of highest rank or quality: *top-flight scientists*
top·gal·lant /tɒpˈgælənt, təˈgælənt‖tɑp-, tə-/ *adj, n* [Wa5] *tech* (of, related to, or being) the 3rd sail or set of ropes (RIGGING) above the DECK on a sailing ship
top hat /ˌ· ˈ·/ *n* a man's tall silk hat, esp. worn on formal occasions
top-heav·y /ˌ· ˈ··◂/ *adj* [F;(B)] not properly balanced because of too much weight at the top; too heavy at the top in relation to the bottom
to·pi·a·ry /ˈtəʊpɪəri‖-pieri/ *adj, n* [Wa5;B;U] (of, related to, shaped by, or being) the art of cutting trees and bushes into ornamental shapes
top·ic /ˈtɒpɪk‖ˈtɑ-/ *n* a subject for conversation, talk, writing, etc.: *Politics or religion are always interesting topics of conversation*
top·ic·al /ˈtɒpɪkəl‖ˈtɑ-/ *adj* of, related to, dealing with, or being a subject of present interest: *The recent events in China have made this film very topical* —**~ly** *adv* [Wa4]
USAGE **Topical** has the same connection with time as **local** has with place: *of great* **topical** *interest* (=interesting now but not always)|*of great* **local** *interest* (=interesting here but not everywhere).
top·ic·al·i·ty /ˌtɒpəˈkælətiˌtɑ-/ *n* **1** [U] the quality or state of being TOPICAL **2** [C *usu. pl.*] a subject of present interest
top·knot /ˈtɒpnɒt‖ˈtɑpnɑt/ *n* a knot or bunch of hair, feathers, RIBBONs, etc., worn on the top of the head
top·less /ˈtɒpləs‖ˈtɑp-/ *adj* [Wa5] **1** (of a woman) having the upper part of the body, including the breasts, bare **2** (of a garment) leaving the upper part of a woman's body, including the breasts, uncovered
top·mast /ˈtɒpmɑːst‖ˈtɑpmæst/ *n tech* the second part of the MAST (=the pole that holds up the sails) above the DECK on a sailing ship
top·most /ˈtɒpməʊst‖ˈtɑp-/ *adj* [Wa5] highest; being right at the top
top-notch /ˌ· ˈ·◂/ *adj infml* first rate; of highest rank; being one of the best possible
top off *v adv* [T1] *AmE* **1** to complete successfully: *Let's top off the evening with a drink* **2** TOP OUT
to·pog·raph·er /təˈpɒgrəfəʳ‖-ˈpɑ-/ *n* a person skilled in TOPOGRAPHY
top·o·graph·i·cal /ˌtɒpəˈgræfɪkəl‖ˌtɑ-/ *adj* [Wa5] of or related to TOPOGRAPHY —**~ly** *adv* [Wa4]
to·pog·ra·phy /təˈpɒgrəfi‖-ˈpɑ-/ *n* [U] **1** the science of describing or representing the character of a particular place in detail, esp. as regards the shape and height of the land, as on a map **2** the character of a particular place in detail, esp. as regards the shape and height of the land
top out *v adv* [T1] to mark the completion of (a large building) with a special ceremony
top·per /ˈtɒpəʳ‖ˈtɑ-/ *n infml* TOP HAT
top·ping[1] /ˈtɒpɪŋ‖ˈtɑ-/ *n* [C;(U)] something put on top of food to make it look nicer, taste better, etc.
topping[2] *adj* [Wa5] *sl, esp. BrE, becoming rare* excellent
top·ple /ˈtɒpəl‖ˈtɑ-/ *v* [Wv3;IØ;T1: (OVER)] to (cause to) become unsteady and fall down
tops /tɒps‖tɑps/ *n* [*the*+R] *sl* the very best: *Anita acts as though she's the tops*
top·sail /ˈtɒpseɪl, -səl‖ˈtɑp-/ *n tech* the square sail second above the DECK on a sailing ship
top-se·cret /ˌ· ˈ··◂/ *adj* to be kept very secret indeed, usu. because of military value: *top-secret papers/information*
top·side /ˈtɒpsaɪd‖ˈtɑp-/ *n* [U] high quality meat (esp. BEEF) cut from the upper leg of an animal
top·soil /ˈtɒpsɔɪl‖ˈtɑp-/ *n* [U] (soil from) the upper level of soil, in which most plants have their roots
top·spin /ˈtɒpˌspɪn‖ˈtɑp-/ *n* [U] turning movement given to a ball in such a way that it spins forward in the air
top·sy-tur·vy /ˌtɒpsi ˈtɜːvi◂‖ˌtɑpsi ˈtɜrvi◂/ *adv, adj* (being) in a state of complete disorder and confusion: *The whole world's going topsy-turvy.*|*a topsy-turvy state of affairs*
top up *v adv* [T1] **1** [(*with*)] to fill (a partly empty container) with liquid **2** *infml* to put more drink into (a person's) glass: *Your glass is nearly empty; let me top you up!*
toque /təʊk/ *n* a woman's small round close-fitting BRIMless hat
tor /tɔːʳ/ *n* a small rocky hill
torch /tɔːtʃ‖tɔrtʃ/ *n* **1** *AmE* usu. **flashlight**— a small electric light in a tube carried in the hand to give light **2** a mass of burning material tied to a stick and carried by hand to give light: *The dry forest went up like a torch* (=burned very fiercely).|(fig.) *the torch of knowledge/learning* **3** *AmE* BLOWLAMP **4 carry a torch for** to be in love with (someone, esp. a person who does not return the love)
torch·light /ˈtɔːtʃlaɪt‖ˈtɔr-/ *n* [U] light produced by TORCHes (1, 2): *a torchlight procession to mark the great day*
tore /tɔːʳ‖tor/ *past t. of* TEAR
to·re·a·dor /ˈtɒrɪədɔːʳ‖ˈto-, ˈtɑ-/ *n* one of the men who takes part in a Spanish BULLFIGHT riding on a horse
tor·ment[1] /ˈtɔːment‖ˈtɔr-/ *n* **1** [C *usu. pl.*;U] (a) very great pain or suffering in mind or body **2** [C] something or someone that causes this: *That child is a torment to its parents*
tor·ment[2] /tɔːˈment‖tɔr-/ *v* [T1] **1** to cause to suffer great pain in mind or body **2** to annoy: *Stop tormenting your poor father with such stupid questions*
tor·men·tor /tɔːˈmentəʳ‖tɔr-/ *n* someone who TORMENTs[2] (1)
torn /tɔːn‖torn/ *past p. of* TEAR
tor·na·do /tɔːˈneɪdəʊ‖tɔr-/ *n* **-does** *or* **-dos** a very violent wind in the form of a very tall wide pipe of air that spins at speeds of 300 miles per hour and faster
tor·pe·do[1] /tɔːˈpiːdəʊ‖tɔr-/ *n* **-does** a long narrow explosive shell, driven along under the surface of the sea by its own motors, aimed at ships in order to destroy them
torpedo[2] *v* [T1] to attack or destroy (a ship) with a TORPEDO[1]: (fig.) *The opposition parties are expected to torpedo the government's plan in Parliament* (=attack it and make it ineffective)
torpedo boat /·ˈ·· ·/ *n* a small fast warship used mainly for TORPEDO[1] attacks
tor·pid /ˈtɔːpəd‖ˈtɔr-/ *adj* **1** inactive; slow; lazy; lacking in strength: *a torpid mind* **2** (esp. of animals that sleep through the winter) having lost the power of feeling or moving —**~ity** /tɔːˈpɪdəti‖tɔr-/ *or* —**~ness** /ˈtɔːpɪdnəs‖ˈtɔr-/ *n* [U] —**~ly** /ˈtɔːpədli‖ˈtɔr-/ *adv*
tor·por /ˈtɔːpəʳ‖ˈtɔr-/ *n* [U] the state of being TORPID; condition of lazy inactivity
torque /tɔːk‖tɔrk/ *n* **1** [C] an ornamental band of

twisted metal worn round the neck or arms by ancient Britons or Gauls **2** [U] the movement that causes a SHAFT (=a rod of metal) to spin in an engine; twisting force

tor·rent /ˈtɒrənt‖ˈtɔ-, ˈtɑ-/ *n* a violently rushing stream, esp. of water: *The rain fell in torrents.|A torrent of water swept down the valley.|*(fig.) *a torrent of tears/bad language*

tor·ren·tial /tɒˈrenʃəl‖tɔ-/ *adj* caused by or like a TORRENT: *torrential rain*

tor·rid /ˈtɒrɪ̈d‖ˈtɔ-, ˈtɑ-/ *adj* **1** very hot: *torrid weather* **2** strongly felt; uncontrollable: *a torrid relationship/love affair* **3** concerning or describing strong feelings and uncontrolled activity, esp. sexual: *a torrid story of sex and violence* —**~ly** *adv*

tor·sion /ˈtɔːʃən‖ˈtɔr-/ *n* [U] *tech* **1** the act of twisting or turning **2** the state of being twisted or turned **3** the spinning effect of a driving force in a motor on a rod of metal (SHAFT) **4** the force that moves a rod, wire, etc., back into the correct shape after it has been twisted out of shape

tor·so /ˈtɔːsəʊ‖ˈtɔr-/ *n* **-sos** **1** the human body without the head and limbs; TRUNK **2** a representation of this in stone, metal, etc. **3** *fml* any object, piece of work, etc., that has been partly destroyed or left unfinished

tort /tɔːt‖tɔrt/ *n law* any wrongful act that can be dealt with by a CIVIL action in a court of law

tor·til·la /tɔːˈtiːjə‖tɔr-/ *n* [C;U] (a) thin round flat cake made by baking a mixture of crushed corn and eggs, eaten esp. in Mexico

tor·toise /ˈtɔːtəs‖ˈtɔr-/ *n* a type of slow-moving land animal that has the body covered by a hard shell into which the legs, tail, and head can be pulled for protection —see picture at REPTILE

tor·toise·shell /ˈtɔːtəsʃel, ˈtɔːtəʃel‖ˈtɔr-/ *n* **1** [U] the hard shell of the TORTOISE or TURTLE, which is brown with yellowish marks, and is sometimes polished and used for making combs, small ornamental boxes, etc. **2** [C] a cat with brown, black, and yellowish fur **3** [C] a type of BUTTERFLY with brownish markings

tor·tu·ous /ˈtɔːtʃʊəs‖ˈtɔr-/ *adj* **1** twisted; winding; full of bends **2** not direct in speech, thought, or action; deceiving —**~ly** *adv* —**~ness** *n* [U]

tor·ture¹ /ˈtɔːtʃəʳ‖ˈtɔr-/ *n* **1** [U] the act of causing someone to feel severe pain, done out of cruelty, as a punishment, etc. **2** [C;U] (a) severe pain or suffering caused in the mind or body: *the tortures of jealousy* **3** [C] a method of causing such pain or suffering: *the Japanese water torture*

torture² *v* [Wv5;T1] to cause great pain or suffering to (a person or animal) out of cruelty, as a punishment, etc.: *The police tortured him to make him admit to the crime* —**~r** *n*

To·ry /ˈtɔːri‖ˈtori/ *n, adj* [Wa5] (a member) of the British CONSERVATIVE PARTY: *Tory principles* —**~ism** *n* [U]

toss¹ /tɒs‖tɔs/ *v* **1** [D1 (*to*);T1] to throw: *The children tossed the ball to each other.|I tossed him the ball/a catch* **2** [Wv4;T1;I∅] to (cause to) move about rapidly and pointlessly: *The boat was tossed about in the stormy sea.|My husband was tossing about all night. He couldn't get to sleep* **3** [X9] to move or lift (part of the body) rapidly: *The horse tossed its head back and smelt the wind* **4** [Wv5;T1] to mix lightly: *Toss the cooked vegetables with/in butter* **5** [T1;I∅ (UP, *for*)] to throw (a coin) to decide something according to which side lands face upwards: *There's only one cake and 2 of us, so let's toss (up) for it* —see also TOSS FOR

toss² *n* **1** [C] an act of TOSSING¹ (1, 2, 3): *a quick toss of the head* **2** [(*the*) S] a TOSSING¹ (2) movement: *the toss of the waves* **3** [*the*+R] an act of TOSSING¹ (5): *Our team won the toss so we play first* **4** [C] *rare* a fall, esp. as a result of being thrown from a horse (esp. in the phr. **take a toss**) **5 argue the toss** *infml* to argue about a decision that has already been made and cannot be changed

toss for *v prep* [D1] to compete with (someone) for possession or first choice of (something) by TOSSING¹ (5): *There's only one cake and 2 of us; I'll toss you for it*

toss off *v adv* [T1] **1** to produce (something) quickly with little effort **2** to drink quickly **3** *taboo sl* to MASTURBATE (someone or oneself)

toss-up /ˈ· ·/ *n* **1** [S] *sl* an even chance: *It's a toss-up between the 2 of them as to who will get the job* **2** [C *usu. sing.*] an act of TOSSING¹ (5)

tot /tɒt‖tɑt/ *n* **1** a very small child (esp. in the phr. **tiny tot**) **2** a small amount of a strong alcoholic drink: *a tot of* RUM/WHISKY —see also TOT UP, TOT UP TO

to·tal¹ /ˈtəʊtl/ *adj* [Wa5] complete; whole: *What is the total population of Britain?|When I tell you to be silent I expect that silence to be total* —**~ly** *adv*: *I totally agree with you*

total² *n* **1** a number or quantity obtained as the result of addition; complete amount: *Add these numbers together and tell me the total.|A total of 20,000 people visited the castle on the first day it was open to the public* **2 in total** when all have been added up: *In total, there must have been 20,000 people there*

total³ *v* **-ll-** (*AmE* **-l-**) **1** [L1] to equal a total of; add up to; be in numbers: *Your debts total £100,000* **2** [T1 (UP)] to find the total of; add up

to·tal·i·tar·i·an /təʊˌtælɪ̈ˈteərɪən/ *adj* [Wa5] of, being, or related to a political system in which a single person or political party controls all thought and action and does not allow opposition parties to exist: *a totalitarian government*

to·tal·i·tar·i·an·is·m /təʊˌtælɪ̈ˈteərɪənɪzəm/ *n* [U] the practices and principles of a TOTALITARIAN state

to·tal·i·ty /təʊˈtælɪ̈ti/ *n* **1** [U] the state of being whole; completeness **2** [C] *fml* a total amount; sum **3** [C] *tech* the period when the sun or moon is completely hidden in an ECLIPSE

to·tal·i·za·tor, -isator /ˌtəʊtəlaɪˈzeɪtəʳ‖-lə-/ *n fml* TOTE²

tote¹ /təʊt/ *v* [T1] *infml* to carry: *to tote a gun*

tote² *n* a machine that shows the number of BETs placed on each horse or dog in a race and the amount to be paid (less tax) to the people who risked money on the winners

to·tem /ˈtəʊtəm/ *n* **1** an animal, plant, or object thought by certain tribes, esp. North American Indians, to have a close relationship with the family group **2** a representation of this, esp. on wood

totem pole /ˈ·· ·/ *n* a tall pole of wood with the shapes of one or more TOTEMs (1) cut or painted on it, put up by the Indians of northwest North America

tot·ter /ˈtɒtəʳ‖ˈtɑ-/ *v* **1** [I∅] to move in an unsteady way from side to side as if about to fall: *The pile of books tottered then fell.|*(fig.) *The country is tottering on the edge of ruin* **2** [L9;(I∅)] to walk with weak unsteady steps: *The old lady tottered down the stairs*

tot·ter·y /ˈtɒtəri‖ˈtɑ-/ *adj* unsteady; shaky

tot up /tɒt‖tɑt/ *v adv* **-tt-** [T1] to add up (figures, money, etc.)

tot up to *v adv prep* [L1] to equal; add up to: *Your total debts tot up to £1,000*

tou·can /ˈtuːkən, -kæn/ *n* a type of tropical American bird with bright feathers and a very large beak —see picture at EXOTIC

touch¹ /tʌtʃ/ *v* **1** [I∅;T1] to be separated from

(something) by no space at all: *Stand so that your shoulders are touching.|The branches hung down and touched the water* **2** [IØ;T1] to feel with a part of the body, esp. the hands or fingers: *Don't touch!|Visitors are requested not to touch the paintings* **3** [T1] to strike lightly or quietly with the hand, finger, etc.; press with slight force: *You only need to touch the bell for it to ring* **4** [T1] to handle: *He swore he'd never touch a drink again.|I didn't touch her so I don't know why she's crying* **5** [T1 *usu. neg.*] to eat or drink a little of: *You haven't touched your food; I hope you're not ill* **6** [T1 *usu. neg.*] to compare with; be equal to: *Your work will never touch the standard set by Robert* **7** [T1] (esp. of a ship) to reach (esp. land): *We touched land after 3 months at sea* **8** [T1] *fml* to concern: *a serious matter that touches your future* **9** [Wv4;T1] to cause (someone or his heart) to feel pity, sympathy, etc.: *His sad story so touched my heart that I nearly wept* **10** [T1] to mark with light strokes; put in with a pencil or brush: *He drew her head, and quickly touched in the eyes, nose, and mouth* **11** [T1] *fml* to deal with or treat in speech or writing: *My history course didn't touch the 20th century* **12 touch bottom a** to reach the bottom: *The water was not very deep and the boat almost touched bottom* **b** to reach the lowest level: *After so many misfortunes his spirits touched bottom* **13 touch the spot** *sl* to be exactly what is needed: *A swim in the lake really touches the spot on a hot day like today* **14 touch wood** to touch something made of wood in order to turn away bad luck —see also TOUCH DOWN, TOUCH FOR, TOUCH OFF, TOUCH ON, TOUCH UP —**~able** *adj* —**~er** *n*

touch² *n* **1** [U] that sense by which a material object is felt and by which it is known to be hard, smooth, rough, etc. **2** [C *usu. sing.*] the effect caused by touching something; way something feels: *the silky touch of soft smooth cloth* **3** [C] an act of touching: *a touch of the hand* **4** [C] a way of touching: *a light touch* **5** [S (*of*)] a slight attack (as of an illness): *a touch of cold/fever* **6** [C] a slight stroke or blow: *He gave the horse a touch of the whip to make it go faster* **7** [C] an addition or detail that improves or completes something; slight added effort in finishing any piece of work: *a nice touch|I'm just putting the finishing touches to the cake* **8** [S9] a special ability to do something needing skill, esp. artistic work: *Your recent work's been bad. I hope you're not losing your touch.|The piano player had a firm/delicate touch* **9** [C] a person's particular way of doing things **10** [C (*of*)] a slight amount (of some quality or substance): *This soup could do with a touch more salt* **11** [U] (in SOCCER or RUGBY) the area of land outside the field of play **12 in/out of touch (with) a** regularly/not regularly exchanging news and information: *Please write, it would be nice to keep in touch* **b** having/not having information about something: *I would like to go back to teaching but I'm out of touch with my subject now* **13 lose touch** to stop exchanging news and information **14 to the touch** when felt: *A cat's fur is soft to the touch*

touch-and-go /ˌ· · ˈ·◂/ *adj* risky; of uncertain result: *a touch-and-go state of affairs|It was touch-and-go whether the doctor would get there in time*

touch·down /ˈtʌtʃdaʊn/ *n* [C;R] **1** (in RUGBY) an act of TOUCHing DOWN (1) **2** the landing of a plane

touch down *v adv* [IØ] **1** (in RUGBY) to press the ball to the ground behind one's opponent's GOAL in order to win a TRY **2** (of a plane) to land

tou·ché /ˈtuːʃeɪ‖tuːˈʃeɪ/ *interj* (an expression used when recognizing the force, strength, or rightness of a person's argument, reply, etc., to mean) that is a good point against me

touched /tʌtʃt/ *adj* [F] *sl* **1** slightly mad **2** feeling grateful: *I was very touched by their present*

touch for *v prep* [D1] *infml* to persuade (someone) to give one (a sum of money)

touch·ing /ˈtʌtʃɪŋ/ *prep fml or lit* concerning; regarding

touch·line /ˈtʌtʃlaɪn/ *n* a line along each of the 2 longer sides of a sports field, esp. in football —see picture at SOCCER

touch off *v adv* [T1a] **1** to cause to explode **2** to start; cause: *His stupid remarks touched off a fight*

touch on also (*fml*) **touch up·on**— *v prep* [T1,6] to talk about (something) shortly

touch·stone /ˈtʌtʃstəʊn/ *n* anything used as a test or standard; CRITERION

touch-type /ˈ· ·/ *v* [IØ] to TYPE without having to look at the letters on the TYPEWRITER; read and TYPE what one is reading at the same time

touch up *v adv* [T1] **1** to improve by making small changes or additions **2** *sl* to touch (a person of the opposite sex) as if making sexual advances

touch·y /ˈtʌtʃi/ *adj* [Wa1] **1** easily offended or annoyed; too sensitive **2** needing skilful or delicate handling: *a touchy state of affairs in Northern Ireland* —**touchily** *adv* —**touchiness** *n* [U]

tough¹ /tʌf/ *adj* [Wa1] **1** strong; not easily weakened; able to suffer uncomfortable conditions: *Only tough breeds of sheep can live in the mountains* **2** not easily cut, worn, or broken: *as tough as leather* **3** difficult to cut or eat: *tough meat* **4** difficult to do; not easy; demanding effort: *a tough lesson/job* **5** unyielding; hard; STUBBORN: *The government has threatened to get tough with people who try to avoid paying taxes* **6** rough; violent; disorderly: *a tough criminal* **7** *infml* too bad; unfortunate: *Tough luck!|It really is tough that it had to happen to you of all people* **8 as tough as old boots a** very tough **b** very strong **c** unable to feel pity, sympathy, etc. **9 tough as nails** hard as NAILs —**~ly** *adv* —**~ness** *n* [U]

tough² also **tough·ie** /ˈtʌfi/— *n infml* a rough violent disorderly person, esp. a criminal

tough·en /ˈtʌfən/ *v* [IØ;T1: (UP)] to (cause to) become TOUGH¹

tou·pee /ˈtuːpeɪ‖tuːˈpeɪ/ *n* a small WIG or HAIRPIECE specially shaped to fit exactly over a place on a man's head where the hair no longer grows

tour¹ /tʊəʳ/ *n* **1** [C (*round*)] a journey during which several places of interest are visited: *a tour round Europe* **2** [C (*round*)] a short trip to or through a place in order to see it: *We went on a guided tour round the castle* **3** [C9 esp. *in*] a period of duty at a single place or job, esp. abroad: *a 2-year tour in Germany* **4** [C; *on*+U] a journey from place to place as made by a company of actors in order to perform, by an important person to make official visits, by a sports team, etc.: *The National Youth Theatre is on tour in the North at present.|the England cricketers' tour of India*

tour² *v* [L9 esp. *round*;T1] to visit as a tourist: *We're touring (round) Italy for our holidays this year.|a touring holiday*

tour de force /ˌtʊə də ˈfɔːs‖ˌtʊər də ˈfors/ *n* [S] *Fr* a show of strength or great skill

tour·is·m /ˈtʊərɪzəm/ *n* [U] **1** the practice of travelling for pleasure, esp. on one's holidays **2** the business of providing holidays, tours, hotels, etc., for tourists

tour·ist /ˈtʊərɪst/ *n* **1** a person travelling for pleasure: *a cheap tourist hotel near the harbour* **2** a sportsman on TOUR¹ (4)

tourist class /ˈ·· ·/ *n* [U] the travelling conditions which are fairly cheap and suitable for ordinary travellers

tour·na·ment /ˈtʊənəmənt, ˈtɔː-‖ˈtɜr-, ˈtʊər-/ *n* **1**

a number of competitions of skill between players, the winner of one competition playing the winner of another, until the most skilful is found: *a tennis tournament* **2** (in former times) a competition of courage and skill between noble soldiers (KNIGHT*s*) fighting with weapons which usu. have the sharp edges covered

tour·ney /ˈtʊəni, ˈtɔː-‖ˈtɜr-, ˈtʊər-/ *n* **1** TOURNAMENT (2) **2** *fml or pomp* TOURNAMENT (1)

tour·ni·quet /ˈtʊənɪkeɪ, ˈtɔː-‖ˈtɜrnɪkɜ̍t, ˈtʊər-/ *n* anything, esp. a band of cloth with a small tightly packed mass (PAD) of cloth underneath, twisted tightly round a limb to stop bleeding

tou·sle /ˈtaʊzəl/ *v* [Wv3,5;T1] to disarrange (esp. the hair); make untidy

tout[1] /taʊt/ *v* **1** [I∅ (*for*)] to try repeatedly to persuade people to buy one's goods, use one's services, etc.: *touting for business* **2** [I∅;T1] to sell (information about horses) for use in BETting **3** [I∅;T1] to sell (tickets in short supply) at a price higher than usual, so making big profits

tout[2] *n* a person who TOUT*s*[1]: *A ticket tout offered me a £2 ticket for £10*

tout en·sem·ble /ˌtuːt ɒnˈsɒmbəl‖-ɑnˈsɑm- (*Fr* tut ɑ̃sɑ̃bl)/ *n* [*usu. sing.*] *Fr* ENSEMBLE (1)

tow[1] /təʊ/ *v* [T1] to pull (a vehicle) along by a rope or chain: *We towed the car to the nearest garage*

tow[2] *n* **1** [C] an act of TOWing; pull **2** [U] the state of being TOWed: *to take a boat in tow* **3 in tow** *infml* following closely behind: *She arrived with all her children in tow*

tow[3] *n* [U] short or broken pieces of FLAX, HEMP, etc., used esp. for making rope

to·wards /təˈwɔːdz‖tordz/ also **to·ward** /təˈwɔːd‖tord/— *prep* **1** in the direction of, without necessarily reaching: *She was walking towards town when I met her.|I hope we're not moving towards war again.|"the tendency towards disorder"* (SEU W.) **2** in a position facing: *He stood with his back towards me* **3** near; just before in time: *Towards the end of the 19th century people began to demand one man one vote* **4** in relation to; as regards: *What are his feelings towards us?* **5** for the purpose of; for part payment or fulfilment of: *We save £5 towards paying for our holidays each week*

tow·el[1] /ˈtaʊəl/ *n* **1** a piece of cloth or paper used for rubbing or drying wet skin, dishes, etc. —see picture at BATHROOM **2 throw in the towel/sponge** *infml* to admit defeat

towel[2] *v* **-ll-** (*AmE* **-l-**) [T1 (DOWN)] to rub or dry with a TOWEL[1]

tow·el·ling, *AmE* **toweling** /ˈtaʊəlɪŋ/ *n* [U] thickish cloth, used esp. for making TOWEL*s*

tow·er[1] /ˈtaʊəʳ/ *n* **1** a tall building standing alone or forming part of a castle, church, etc.: *the Tower of London* —see picture at CHURCH[1] **2** a tall metal framework, esp. used for signalling, broadcasting, etc.: *the Eiffel Tower|a radio/television tower* **3 tower of strength** a person who can always be depended on to give help, sympathy, and support in times of trouble

tower[2] *v* [L9 esp. *above, over,* ABOVE] to be very tall, esp. in relation to the height of the surroundings: *The high mountains towered over the little town.*|(fig.) *In ability he towers over the rest of them* (=he has much greater ability)

tower block /ˈ·· ·/ *n* a tall block of flats or offices

tow·er·ing /ˈtaʊərɪŋ/ *adj* [Wa5;A] **1** very tall: *towering trees* **2** very great: *in a towering temper* (=very angry indeed)

tow·line /ˈtəʊlaɪn/ also **tow·rope** /ˈtəʊrəʊp/— *n* a rope, chain, etc., by which anything is or may be TOWed[1]

town /taʊn/ *n* **1** [C] a large group of houses and other buildings where people live and work: *Preston is the largest town in Lancashire* **2** [R] the business or shopping centre of such a place: *We went to the town to do some shopping today.|Town was very busy today* **3** [R] the chief centre of an area (in England, esp. London): *I was in town on business last week* **4** [GC] the people who live in a TOWN (1): *The whole town is angry about the council's handling of education* **5** [*the*+R] life in TOWNS (1) and cities, as opposed to life in the country: *I like the town better than the country* **6** [*the*+R] TOWN*s* (1) and cities in general: *Many country people are leaving the country for the town* **7 go to town** *infml* to act or behave freely or wildly, esp. by spending a great deal of money **8 (out) on the town** *infml* enjoying oneself wildly, esp. at night **9 paint the town red** *infml* to have a very enjoyable time, esp. in a high-spirited and noisy manner

town clerk /ˌ· ˈ·/ *n* an official who keeps the records, advises on matters regarding the law, and acts as secretary of a town

town coun·cil /ˌ· ˈ··/ *n* [GC] *BrE* an elected governing body of a town

town cri·er /ˌ· ˈ··/ *n* (in former times) a person employed to walk about the streets shouting out news, warnings, etc.

town gas /ˌ· ˈ·/ *n* [U] gas produced by heating coal, for use in industry and the home

town hall /ˌ· ˈ·/ *n* a public building used for a town's local government offices and public meetings

town house /ˈ· ·/ *n* **1** a modern house with 2 or 3 floors, esp. suited to be built on a small piece of land in a town **2** a house in a town belonging to someone who also owns a house in the country

town·scape /ˈtaʊnˌskeɪp/ *n* a painting of a view of a town

town·ship /ˈtaʊnʃɪp/ *n* **1** (in Canada and the US) a town, or town and the area around it, that has certain powers of local government **2** (in South Africa) a place where nonwhite citizens live

towns·man /ˈtaʊnzmən/ (*fem.* **towns·wom·an** /-ˌwʊmən/)— *n* **-men** /mən/ a person who lives in a town

towns·peo·ple /ˈtaʊnzˌpiːpəl/ also **towns·folk** /-fəʊk/— *n* **1** [*the*+P] the people who live in a particular town considered as a group **2** [P] people who live in towns as opposed to the country

tow·path /ˈtəʊpɑːθ‖-pæθ/ *n* a path along the bank of a CANAL or river, used by horses pulling boats

tox·ae·mi·a, toxemia /tɒkˈsiːmɪə‖tɑk-/ *n* [U] a medical condition in which the blood contains poisons

tox·ic /ˈtɒksɪk‖ˈtɑk-/ *adj* **1** [Wa5] of, related to, or caused by poisonous substances **2** poisonous: *a toxic drug* —**~ity** /tɒkˈsɪsɜ̍ti‖tɑk-/ *n* [U]

tox·i·col·o·gist /ˌtɒksɪˈkɒlədʒɜ̍st‖ˌtɑksɪˈkɑ-/ *n* a student of or scientist whose special subject is TOXICOLOGY

tox·i·col·o·gy /ˌtɒksɪˈkɒlədʒi‖ˌtɑksɪˈkɑ-/ *n* [U] the scientific and medical study of poisons, their nature and effects, and the treatment of poisoning

tox·in /ˈtɒksɜ̍n‖ˈtɑk-/ *n* a poisonous substance, esp. one produced by bacteria in a living or dead plant or animal body and usu. causing a particular disease

toy /tɔɪ/ *n* **1** [C] an object for children to play with: *a toy soldier* **2** [A;(C)] (being) a small breed of dog kept as a pet: *a toy* POODLE

toy·shop /ˈtɔɪʃɒp‖-ʃɑp/ *n* a shop in which toys are sold

toy with *v prep* [T1] **1** to consider (an idea) not very seriously **2** to play with (something) purposelessly; handle (something) carelessly: *While he was talking to his secretary, he toyed with a pencil*

trace[1] /treɪs/ *v* [T1] **1** to follow the course or line of (something or someone): *The criminal was traced to London* **2** [(BACK)] to find the origins of by finding proof or by going back in time: *His family can trace its history back to the 10th century.*|*The whole false story was traced (back) to an opposition politician* **3** to follow the course, development, or history of: *to trace the beginnings of the Labour movement* **4** to find or discover: *I can't trace the letter you sent me* **5** to copy by drawing on transparent paper the lines on (a drawing, map, etc.) placed underneath **6** [(OUT)] to draw the course or shape of **7** to write slowly and with effort: *He traced his name slowly at the bottom of the page* —**~able** *adj* [Wa5]

trace² *n* **1** [C;U] a mark or sign showing the former presence or passing of some person, vehicle, or event: *Did the police find any trace of the murderer?*|*We've lost all trace of our daughter* (= we no longer know where she is).|*lost without trace in the forest* **2** [C] a very small amount of something: *There are traces of poison in the dead man's blood*

trace³ *n* **1** either of the ropes, chains, or lengths of leather by which a cart, carriage, etc., is fastened to an animal that is pulling it **2 kick over the traces** to free oneself from control

trace el·e·ment /ˈ· ˌ···/ *n* a simple chemical substance that is necessary for healthy growth and development, found in plants and animals in very small quantities

trac·er /ˈtreɪsəʳ/ *n* a bullet or SHELL¹ (4) that leaves a line of smoke or flame behind it so that its course can be seen

trac·e·ry /ˈtreɪsəri/ *n* [U;(C)] (a piece of) ornamental work done with branching and crossing lines, as in the upper parts of many church windows —see picture at WINDOW¹

tra·che·a /trəˈkɪə‖ˈtreɪkɪə/ *n med* WINDPIPE

tra·cho·ma /trəˈkəʊmə/ *n* [U] a painful disease that attacks the transparent covering over the EYEBALL and the inner surface of the eyelids

trac·ing /ˈtreɪsɪŋ/ *n* a copy of a map, drawing, etc., made by tracing (TRACE¹ (5))

tracing pa·per /ˈ·· ˌ··/ *n* [U] strong transparent paper used for tracing (TRACE¹ (5))

track¹ /træk/ *n* **1** [*often pl. with sing. meaning*] a line or number of marks left by a person, animal, vehicle, etc., that has passed before: *The dog followed the fox's tracks into the woods* **2** a rough path or road: *a bicycle track* **3** a course of action: *He's gone along in the same track year after year* **4** the metal lines on which a train runs **5** the course or line taken by something: *the track of the storm* **6** an endless belt used over the wheels of some very heavy farm, building, or military vehicles to make movement over rough ground easier **7** a course specially prepared for racing: *track events*|*a running track* **8** one of the pieces of music on a long-playing record or TAPE¹ (3): *I like the last track on this side* **9** one of the bands on which material can be recorded on a TAPE¹ (3) **10 cover (up) one's tracks** to keep one's movements or activities secret **11 in one's tracks** *infml* where one is; suddenly: *The criminal stopped in his tracks when the door opened behind him* **12 keep/lose track (of)** to keep/fail to keep oneself informed about a person, state of affairs, etc. **13 make tracks** *sl* to leave, esp. in a hurry **14 off the beaten track** not well-known or often visited **15 the wrong side of the tracks** *AmE* the less outwardly pleasant part of a town where the poorer people live **16 on somebody's track** following somebody: *The police are on the criminal's track and hope to catch him soon* **17 on the right/wrong track** thinking or working correctly/incorrectly **18 have a one-track/single-track mind** *infml* to give all one's attention to one subject

track² *v* **1** [T1] to follow the track of (an animal, plane, ship, person, etc.) **2** [IØ] (of a needle (STYLUS) on a record player) to follow the continuous cut (GROOVE) on a record **3** [L9] (of (a person working) a television or film camera) to move round while taking a distant picture —**~er** *n*

track down *v adv* [T1] to find (someone or something) by hunting or searching

tracking sta·tion /ˈ·· ˌ··/ *n* a special building with scientific instruments used for following the course of space vehicles

track·less /ˈtrækləs/ *adj* [Wa5] **1** without paths, roads, etc.: *a trackless forest* **2** not running on a railway: *a trackless engine*

track·suit /ˈtræksuːt/ *n* a loose-fitting suit of warm material worn by sportsmen when training but not when playing, racing, etc. —**~ed** *adj* [Wa5]: *tracksuited runners*

tract¹ /trækt/ *n* a short article, esp. one dealing with a religious or moral subject

tract² *n* **1** a wide stretch of land: *tracts of desert in Australia* **2** a system of related organs in an animal, with one particular purpose: *the* DIGESTIVE *tract*

trac·ta·ble /ˈtræktəbəl/ *adj* **1** *fml* that can be easily controlled or governed **2** *tech* that can be easily worked; MALLEABLE —**-tability** /ˌtræktəˈbɪlɪ̣ti/ *n* [U]

trac·tion /ˈtrækʃən/ *n* [U] **1** the act of drawing or pulling a heavy load over a surface **2** the form or type of power used for this: *steam traction* **3** the force that prevents a wheel from slipping over the surface on which it runs

traction en·gine /ˈ·· ˌ··/ *n* a large vehicle, usu. worked by steam power, used for pulling heavy loads along roads

trac·tor /ˈtræktəʳ/ *n* a powerful motor vehicle with large wheels and thick tyres used for pulling farm machinery (PLOUGH*s*, DRILL*s*⁴, etc.) or other heavy objects —see picture at FARMYARD

trad /træd/ *n* [U] a style of JAZZ originally played in New Orleans about 1920, marked by free expression within a set instrumental framework

trade¹ /treɪd/ *n* **1** [U] the business of buying, selling, or exchanging goods, within a country or between countries: *a trade agreement between England and France* **2** [*the* + R9] a particular business or industry: *He works in the cotton trade*/*tourist trade* **3** [(*the*) GU] the people who work in a particular business or industry: *This talk is only likely to be of interest to the trade* **4** [C; *by* + U] a job, esp. one needing special skill with the hands: *the trade of a printer*|*He's a printer by trade* **5** [S9] amount of business: *On the corner a girl was doing a good trade in flowers*

trade² *v* **1** [IØ] to carry on trade: *ships trading between England and Spain* **2** [T1 (*for*)] to buy, sell, or exchange (a product, goods, etc.): *The early settlers traded copper for corn* **3** [IØ (*at, with*)] *AmE* to shop regularly

trade gap /ˈ· ·/ *n* the difference between the value of that which a country buys and sells abroad when the former is the larger figure

trade in *v adv* [T1 (*for*)] to give (something) in part payment when buying something new: *He traded his old car in for a new one* —**trade-in** *n*

trade·mark /ˈtreɪdmɑːk‖-mark/ *n* **1** a special name, sign , word, etc., which is marked on a product to show that it is made by a particular producer, and may not be used by other producers **2** a particular sign, way of acting, etc., by which a person or his activities may habitually be recognized

trade name /ˈ· ·/ also **brand name**— *n* a name given by a producer to a particular product, by which it may be recognized from among like products made by other producers
trade on also (*fml*) **trade up·on**— *v prep* [T1] to take unfair advantage of (someone's good nature, sympathy, etc.)
trade price /ˈ· ·/ *n* the price at which goods are sold by producers to shops
trad·er /ˈtreɪdəʳ/ *n* a person who buys and sells goods, esp. in foreign countries
trades /treɪdz/ *n* [*the*+P] *infml* TRADE WIND*s*
trades·man /ˈtrəɪdzmən/ *n* **-men** /mən/ **1** a person who buys and sells goods, esp. a shopkeeper **2** a person who calls on private houses to deliver goods
trades·peo·ple /ˈtreɪdzˌpiːpəl/ *n* [P] people who buy and sell goods, esp. shopkeepers
Trades Un·i·on Con·gress /ˌ· ··· ˈ··/ *n* [*the*+R] the association of British trade unions
trade un·i·on /ˌ· ˈ···/ also **trades union,** *AmE* **labour union**— *n* an organization of workers to represent their interests and deal as a group with employers —**~ism** *n* [U] —**~ist** *n*
trade wind /ˈ· ·/ *n* a tropical wind that blows almost continually towards the EQUATOR (=the imaginary line running round the middle of the earth) from the northeast and southeast
trading es·tate /ˈ·· ·ˌ·/ *n* an industrial area containing factories that are built or paid for by the government or local council and usu. rented to firms
trading post /ˈ·· ·/ *n* POST[5] (2)
trading stamp /ˈ·· ·/ *n fml* STAMP[2] (3)
tra·di·tion /trəˈdɪʃən/ *n* **1** [U] the passing down of opinions, beliefs, practices, customs, etc., from the past to the present, esp. by word of mouth or practice **2** [C] an opinion, belief, custom, etc., passed down in this way: *It is a tradition that women get married in long white dresses* **3** [U] the body of principles, beliefs, practices, experience, etc., passed down from the past to the present
tra·di·tion·al /trəˈdɪʃənəl/ *adj* of or in accordance with TRADITION: *the traditional English breakfast* —**~ly** *adv*: *Traditionally, women are married in long white dresses*
tra·di·tion·al·is·m /trəˈdɪʃənəlɪzəm/ *n* [U] a very great respect for TRADITION (3), esp. in religious matters —**-ist** *n*
tra·duce /trəˈdjuːs‖-ˈduːs/ *v* [T1] *fml* to speak falsely of (someone, his character, etc.), esp in order to influence somebody's good opinion unfavourably; SLANDER —**-ducer** *n*
traf·fic /ˈtræfɪk/ *n* [U] **1** the movement of people or vehicles along roads or streets, of ships in the seas, planes in the sky, etc. —compare CIRCULATION (2) **2** the people, vehicles, etc., in this movement **3** trade; buying and selling: *the unlawful traffic in drugs* **4** business done by a railway, ship or air travel company, etc., in carrying goods or passengers: *passenger traffic*
traf·fi·ca·tor /ˈtræfɪkeɪtəʳ/ also **traffic in·di·ca·tor** /ˈ·· ˌ····/— *n* a flashing light on a car that shows a driver's intention of turning left or right
traffic cir·cle /ˈ·· ˌ··/ *n AmE* ROUNDABOUT[1] (2)
traffic in *v prep* **-ck-** [T1 (*with*)] to carry on trade, esp. of an unlawful or improper kind, in (a particular type of goods): *trafficking in stolen goods*
traf·fick·er /ˈtræfɪkəʳ/ *n* [(*in*)] a person who carries on trade, esp. in a particular type of goods which it is improper or unlawful to sell
traffic light /ˈ·· ·/ also **traffic sig·nal** /ˈ·· ˌ··/— *n* [*usu. pl.*] one of a set of coloured lights used for controlling and directing traffic, esp. where one road crosses another —see picture at STREET
traffic war·den /ˈ·· ˌ··/ *n* an official responsible for controlling the parking of vehicles on city streets
tra·ge·di·an /trəˈdʒiːdɪən/ *n* an actor or writer of TRAGEDY (2)
tra·ge·di·enne /trəˌdʒiːdiˈen/ *n* an actress of TRAGEDY (2)
tra·ge·dy /ˈtrædʒɨ̈di/ *n* **1** [C] a serious play that ends sadly, esp. with the main character's death: *"Hamlet" is one of Shakespeare's best known tragedies* **2** [U] such plays considered as a group **3** [U] the branch of the theatre dealing with such plays **4** [C;U] a terrible, unhappy, or unfortunate event: *Their holiday ended in tragedy when their hotel caught fire*
tra·gic /trædʒɪk/ *adj* **1** [Wa5;A] of or related to TRAGEDY (2): *a tragic actress* **2** [B] very sad, unfortunate, etc.: *a tragic accident* —**~ally** *adv* [Wa4]
tra·gi·com·e·dy /ˌtrædʒɪˈkɒmɨ̈di‖-ˈkɑ-/ *n* **1** [C] a play or story with both sad and funny parts **2** [U] such plays and stories considered as a group
trail[1] /treɪl/ *v* **1** [T1] to drag or allow to drag behind: *The child was trailing a toy car on a string* **2** [Wv4;I∅ (ALONG, BEHIND, *behind*)] to be dragged along behind: *Her long skirt was trailing along behind her* **3** [T1] to follow the tracks of: *The police trailed the criminal to the place where he was hiding* **4** [L9 esp. ALONG, BEHIND, *behind*] to walk tiredly: *The defeated army trailed back to camp* **5** [Wv4;I∅] (of a plant) to grow over or along the ground
trail[2] *n* **1** the track or smell of a person or animal, esp. as followed by a hunter **2** a path across rough country made by the passing of people or animals **3** a stream of dust, smoke, people, vehicles, etc., behind something moving: *The carriage left a trail of dust* **4 blaze a/the trail** to be the very first in doing something; lead the way in some activity or field of knowledge **5 hard/hot on someone's trail** following closely behind a person or thing
trail·er /ˈtreɪləʳ/ *n* **1** a TRAILing[1] (5) plant **2** an advertisement for a new film, usu. consisting of small pieces taken from it, and shown at a cinema **3** a vehicle pulled by another vehicle —see picture at FARMYARD **4** *AmE* CARAVAN (3)
trail off *v adv* [I∅] (esp. of a voice) to become gradually weaker and fade away: *Her interest in the work soon trailed off*
train[1] /treɪn/ *n* **1** [C; *by*+U] a line of connected railway carriages drawn by an engine —see USAGE **2** [C] a long line of moving people, vehicles, or animals **3** [C] a part of a long dress that spreads over the ground behind the wearer **4** [GC] a group of servants or officers attending a person of high rank **5** [C] a chain of related events, thoughts, actions, etc.: *The telephone rang and interrupted my train of thought* **6** [C] *tech* a line of gunpowder to lead fire to an explosive **7 in train** in preparation (for action): *Arrangements for the minister's visit are now in train*
USAGE One travels *in* (or, *esp. AmE, on*) a **train**, **bus**, **plane**, **boat**, or **ship**; note also the pattern *by* **train**, **boat**, etc. One *gets into/out of* it, or *on/onto/off* it. If it goes at fixed times one may *catch* it or *miss* it. The person in control *drives* a **train** or **bus**, PILOT*s* or *flies* (FLY) a **plane**, PILOT*s* or *sails* a **ship**.
train[2] *v* **1** [T1] to direct the growth of (a plant) by bending, cutting, tying, etc. **2** [T1;V3;D6b esp. **how**] to give teaching or practice, esp. in an act, profession, or skill; instruct: *At school they should train young children (how) to be good citizens.|to train a horse to jump fences* **3** [I∅,3] to be taught or given practice, esp. in an art, profession, or skill: *I trained to be a doctor but decided to become an actor instead* **4** [I∅;T1:(*for*)] to make ready for a test of skill: *Every morning John spends 2 hours training for*

the race **5** [T1 (*on, upon*)] to aim (a gun) at something or someone —**~able** *adj* —**~er** *n*

train·bear·er /ˈtreɪnˌbeərəʳ/ *n* an attendant who holds up or helps to hold up the TRAIN¹ (3) of a dress, esp. at a wedding

train·ee /treɪˈniː/ *n* a person who is being trained: *a trainee reporter*

train fer·ry /ˈ· ˌ··/ *n* [C; *by*+U] a ship for carrying trains over a stretch of water from one railway to another

train·ing /ˈtreɪnɪŋ/ *n* **1** [U;S] the act of TRAINing² (2,4) or being trained; instruction **2** [U] a course of special exercises, practice, food, etc., to keep sportsmen or animals healthy and fit **3 in/out of training** in/not in a good healthy condition for a sport, test of skill, etc. **4 go into training** to train oneself for a test of skill: *He went into training for the swimming competition*

training col·lege /ˈ·· ˌ··/ *n* [C;U] a college for training teachers

train·man /ˈtreɪnmən/ *n* **-men** /mən/ *AmE* a man who works on a railway train

traipse, trapse /treɪps/ *v* [L9] *infml* to walk tiredly

trait /treɪt/ *n* a particular quality of someone or something; CHARACTERISTIC: *Anne's generosity is one of her most pleasing traits*

trai·tor /ˈtreɪtəʳ/ *n* [C;N] a person who is disloyal, esp. to his country

trai·tor·ous /ˈtreɪtərəs/ *adj* [Wa5] *esp. lit* of or like a TRAITOR; TREACHEROUS —**~ly** *adv*

tra·jec·to·ry /trəˈdʒektəri/ *n* the curved path of an object fired or thrown through the air: *the trajectory of a bullet*

tram /træm/ also **tram·car** /ˈtræmkɑːʳ/ *AmE* usu. **streetcar**— *n* a public vehicle for many passengers, usu. driven by electricity, that runs along metal lines set in the road

tram·line /ˈtræmlaɪn/ *n* [*usu. pl.*] **1** *BrE* one of the lines, set in the road, along which a TRAM runs **2** *infml* one of the 2 pairs of lines on the edges of a tennis court, marking additional space used only when 4 people are playing

tram·mel /ˈtræməl/ *v* **-ll-** (*AmE* **-l-**) [T1] *fml* to prevent the free movement, action, or development of (someone or something)

tram·mels /ˈtræməlz/ *n* [P] *fml* something that TRAMMELs: *the trammels of material wealth*

tramp¹ /træmp/ *v* **1** [L9] to walk with firm heavy steps **2** [L9;T1] to walk steadily through or over: *The children tramped the woods looking for berries* **3** [L;X:9] to press repeatedly with the feet: *Someone tramped on my toes on the bus*

tramp² *n* **1** [(*the*) S] the sound of heavy walking **2** [C] a long walk **3** [C] also **tramp steam·er** /ˈ· ˌ··/— a ship that does not make regular trips but takes goods to any port **4** [C] *often derog* a person with no home or job, who wanders from place to place begging for food or money **5** [C] an immoral woman

tram·ple /træmpəl/ *v* [Wv3;T1 (DOWN);L9 esp. *on, upon, over*] to step heavily with the feet (on); crush under the feet: *The hunter was trampled to death by a wild elephant.*|(fig.) *to trample on someone's feelings*

tram·po·line /ˈtræmpəliːn‖ˌtræmpəˈliːn/ *n* an apparatus consisting of a sheet of material tightly stretched and held to a metal frame by strong springs, on which ACROBATs and GYMNASTs jump up and down to perform exercises

trance /trɑːns‖træns/ *n* a sleeplike condition of the mind in which one does not notice the things around one (esp. in the phr. **in a trance**)

tran·ny /ˈtræni/ *n BrE infml* TRANSISTOR (2)

tran·quil /ˈtræŋkwɨl/ *adj* calm; quiet; peaceful; free from anxiety, worry, etc.: *a tranquil life in the country*|*a tranquil lake*|*a tranquil smile* —**~lity** (*AmE* **~ity**) /træŋˈkwɪlɨti/ *n* [U] —**~ly** *adv*

tran·quil·lize, -lise, *AmE* **-quilize** /ˈtræŋkwɨlaɪz/ *v* [T1] to cause to become calm or peaceful

tran·quil·lizer, -liser, *AmE* **-quilizer** /ˈtræŋkwɨlaɪzəʳ/ *n* a drug used for reducing nervous anxiety, worry, etc., and for making a person calm and peaceful

trans- /træns, trænz, trɑːns, trɑːnz‖træns, trænz/ *prefix* across; beyond; over; on the far side of: *the trans-Siberian railway*|TRANSATLANTIC *flights*

trans·act /trænˈzækt/ *v* [T1] to carry (a piece of business, matter, etc.) through to an agreement

trans·ac·tion /trænˈzækʃən/ *n* **1** [U] the act of TRANSACTing **2** [C] something TRANSACTed; a piece of business; affair

trans·ac·tions /trænˈzækʃənz/ *n* [P] records of the meetings of a society: *the transactions of the Royal Historical Society*

trans·al·pine /trænzˈælpaɪn/ *adj* [Wa5] of, from, or related to the north of the Alps

trans·at·lan·tic /ˌtrænzətˈlæntɪk/ *adj* [Wa5] **1** on the other side of the Atlantic ocean: *a transatlantic military base*/*country* **2** crossing the Atlantic ocean: *transatlantic flights* **3** concerning countries on both sides of the Atlantic ocean: *a transatlantic agreement*

tran·scend /trænˈsend/ *v* [T1] **1** to go or be above or beyond (a limit, something within limits, etc.): *the joys of heaven that transcend all earthly happiness* **2** to go beyond in size, strength, goodness, quality, etc.: *work by a writer that transcends in wisdom anything else that he has produced*

tran·scen·dence /trænˈsendəns/ also **tran·scen·den·cy** /trænˈsendənsi/— *n* [U] the state or quality of being TRANSCENDENT

tran·scen·dent /trænˈsendənt/ *adj* [Wa5] going far beyond ordinary limits: *the transcendent* GENIUS *of Mozart* —**~ly** *adv*

tran·scen·den·tal /ˌtrænsenˈdentl/ *adj* [Wa5] going beyond human knowledge, thought, belief, and experience; such as cannot be discovered or understood by practical experience or reason: *transcendental* MEDITATION —**~ly** *adv*

tran·scen·den·tal·is·m /ˌtrænsenˈdentəl-ɪzəm/ *n* [U] the belief that knowledge and the principles of reality can be obtained by studying thought and not necessarily by practical experience —**-ist** *n*

trans·con·ti·nen·tal /ˌtrænzkɒntɨˈnentl, ˌtræns-‖-kɑn-/ *adj* [Wa5] crossing a CONTINENT: *a transcontinental railway*

tran·scribe /trænˈskraɪb/ *v* [T1] **1** to write a copy of **2** to make a full copy of (notes or recorded matter) **3** to represent (speech sounds) by means of special (PHONETIC) letters **4** [(*into*)] to write in the alphabet of another language **5** [(*for*)] to arrange (a piece of music) for some instrument or voice other than the original **6** to record (a radio or television play, talk, etc.) for future broadcast

tran·script /ˈtrænskrɪpt/ *n* a written or printed copy; something TRANSCRIBEd

tran·scrip·tion /trænˈskrɪpʃən/ *n* **1** [U] the act of transcribing (TRANSCRIBE) **2** [C] something TRANSCRIBEd

tran·sept /ˈtrænsept/ *n* the part of a cross-shaped church that crosses the main body of the church at right angles —see picture at CHURCH¹

trans·fer¹ /trænsˈfɜːʳ/ *v* **-rr-** **1** [T1;I∅] to move officially from one place, job, thing, etc., to another: *The office was transferred from Belfast to Dublin.*|*That football player is hoping to transfer*/*be transferred to another team soon* **2** [T1;I∅] to (cause to) move or change from one vehicle to another: *At London we transferred from the train to a bus* **3** [T1] to move (a pattern, set of marks, etc.) from one surface to another **4** [T1] to give the ownership of (property) to another person —**~ability** /træns,fɜːrəˈbɪlǝ̇ti/ *n* [U] —**~able** /trænsˈfɜːrəbəl/ *adj*

USAGE *I* **transferred** *to another school* probably means that it was my own choice; *I was* **transferred** *to another school* means that it was someone else's decision.

trans·fer² /ˈtrænsfɜːʳ/ *n* **1** [C;U] (an example of) the act of TRANSFERring: *This footballer wants a transfer to another team* **2** [C] someone or something that has TRANSFERred[1] (1) **3** [C] a ticket allowing a passenger to change from one bus, train, etc., to another without paying more money **4** [C] a drawing, pattern, etc., for sticking or printing onto a surface: *He had a transfer of Mickey Mouse on the back of his shirt*

trans·fer·ence /ˈtrænsfərəns‖trænsˈfɜr-/ *n* [U] the act of TRANSFERring or being TRANSFERred, esp. from one job to another

Trans·fig·u·ra·tion /,trænsfɪgjʊˈreɪʃən‖-gjə-/ *n* [*the*+R] **1** the glorious change in the appearance of Christ in the presence of 3 chosen followers, as described in the Bible **2** the day, usu. August 6th, on which the church solemnly remembers this event

trans·fig·ure /trænsˈfɪgəʳ‖-gjər/ *v* [T1] to change (someone or something) in outward form or appearance, esp. in order to make glorious or perfect: *a face transfigured with joy* —**-uration** *n* [C;U]

trans·fix /trænsˈfɪks/ *v* [T1] **1** to force a hole through as with a sharp pointed weapon **2** [(*usu. pass.*)] to cause to be unable to move or think because of terror, shock, etc.: *He was transfixed to the spot when I told him the terrible news*

trans·form /trænsˈfɔːm‖-fɔrm/ *v* [T1] to change completely in form, appearance, or nature: *The magician transformed the man into a rabbit.|A steam engine transforms heat into power* —**~able** *adj*

trans·for·ma·tion /,trænsfəˈmeɪʃən‖-ər-/ *n* [C;U] (an example of) the act of TRANSFORMING; complete change

trans·form·er /trænsˈfɔːməʳ‖-ɔr-/ *n* an apparatus for changing electrical force (VOLTAGE)

trans·fuse /trænsˈfjuːz/ *v* [T1] to put (the blood of one person) into the body of another —**-fusion** /ˈfjuːʒən/ *n* [C;U]: *The driver lost a lot of blood as a result of the accident so he was rushed to hospital for a (blood) transfusion*

trans·gress /trænzˈgres‖træns-/ *v fml* **1** [T1] to go beyond (a proper limit) **2** [T1] to break (a law, agreement, etc.) **3** [IØ] to do wrong; offend against a moral principle —**~ion** /trænzˈgreʃən‖træns-/ *n* [C;U] —**~or** /trænzˈgresəʳ‖træns-/ *n*

tran·ship, transship /trænˈʃɪp, trænsˈʃɪp/ *v* **-pp-** [T1] to move (goods) from one ship or vehicle to another —**~ment** *n* [U]

tran·si·ence /ˈtrænzɪəns‖ˈtrænʃəns/ also **tran·si·en·cy** /-si/— *n* [U] the state of being TRANSIENT

tran·si·ent¹ /ˈtrænzɪənt‖ˈtrænʃənt/ also **tran·si·to·ry** /ˈtrænzǝ̇təri‖-tori/— *adj* [Wa5] **1** lasting for only a short time: *transient happiness* **2** (of a person) passing through a place or staying for only a short time

transient² *n esp. AmE* a guest who stays in a hotel for only a short time

tran·sis·tor /trænˈzɪstəʳ, -ˈsɪstəʳ/ *n* **1** a small solid electrical apparatus, esp. used in radios, televisions, etc., for controlling the flow of an electrical current —compare VALVE **2** also **transistor ra·di·o** /·,·· ˈ···/— a radio that has these instead of VALVEs

tran·sis·tor·ize, -ise /trænˈzɪstəraɪz, -ˈsɪs-/ *v* [Wv5; T1] to provide with TRANSISTORs

tran·sit /ˈtrænsǝ̇t, -zǝ̇t/ *n* **1** [U] the act of passing over, across, or through: *There is a transit camp in Vienna for Jews who leave the Soviet Union and hope to settle in Israel* **2** [U] the moving of people or goods from one place to another, esp. on public vehicles: *His letter must have got lost in transit* **3** [C;U] *tech* (a) movement of a small heavenly body (PLANET) or moon across the face of a larger heavenly body

tran·si·tion /trænˈzɪʃən, -sɪ-/ *n* [C;U] (an example of) the act of changing or passing from one form, state, subject, or place to another: *Our party supports a peaceful transition to rule by elected representatives of the people* —**~al** *adj* [Wa5] —**~ally** *adv*

tran·si·tive /ˈtrænsǝ̇tɪv, -zǝ̇-/ *adj, n* [Wa5] (a verb) that takes a DIRECT OBJECT —compare INTRANSITIVE

trans·late /trænzˈleɪt, træns-/ *v* **1** [T1;IØ] to change (speech or writing) from one language into another: *This book was first translated from French into English in the 15th century* **2** [IØ] to be changed from one language into another **3** [T1] to explain; make clear **4** [T1] *fml* to bear or change from one place, state, or form to another —**-latable** *adj* —**-lation** /ˈleɪʃən/ *n* [C;U]: *I've only read Tolstoy in translation* (=in English, not in Russian)

trans·la·tor /trænzˈleɪtəʳ, træns-/ *n* a person who translates from one language to another, esp. as a profession

trans·lit·e·rate /trænzˈlɪtəreɪt‖træns-/ *v* [T1] to write (a word, name, sentence, etc.) in the alphabet of a different language or system: *Do we transliterate the Russian "X" into English as "kh"?* —**-ation** /,trænzlɪtəˈreɪʃən‖,træns-/ *n* [C;U]

trans·lu·cence /trænzˈlusəns‖træns-/ also **trans·lu·cen·cy** /-si/— *n* [U] the state of being TRANSLUCENT

trans·lu·cent /trænzˈlusənt‖træns-/ *adj* not transparent but clear enough to allow light to pass through: *translucent glass in their bathroom window*

trans·mi·gra·tion /,trænzmaɪˈgreɪʃən‖,træns-/ *n* [U] the passing of the soul at death into another body

trans·mis·sion /trænzˈmɪʃən‖træns-/ *n* **1** [U] the act of TRANSMITting or of being TRANSMITted **2** [C] something broadcast as by television or radio **3** [C] the parts by which power is carried from an engine to the wheels that produce movement in a vehicle or motor —see picture at CAR

trans·mit /trænzˈmɪt‖træns-/ *v* **-tt-** **1** [T1] to send or pass from one person, place, or thing to another: *to transmit a disease/infection/message* **2** [T1;IØ] to send out (electric signals, messages, news, etc.) by telegraphic wire or radio; broadcast **3** [T1] to allow to travel through or along itself: *Glass transmits light but not sound* **4** [T1] to carry (force, power, etc.) from one part of a machine to another

trans·mit·ter /trænzˈmɪtəʳ‖træns-/ *n* **1** someone or something that TRANSMITs **2** an instrument in a telegraphic system that sends out messages **3** an apparatus that sends out radio or television signals

trans·mog·ri·fy /trænzˈmɒgrǝ̇faɪ‖trænsˈmɑ-/ *v* [T1] *humor* to cause to change completely in form, appearance, or character by or as if by magic —**-fication** /trænz,mɒgrǝ̇fɪˈkeɪʃən‖træns,mɑ-/ *n* [C;U]

trans·mute /trænzˈmjuːt‖træns-/ *v* [T1] to change from one form, nature, substance, etc., into a usu. higher kind —**-mutable** *adj* —**-mutation** /,trænzmjuːˈteɪʃən‖,træns-/ *n* [C;U]

trans·o·ce·an·ic /,trænzəʊʃiˈænɪk‖,træns-/ *adj* [Wa5] **1** crossing an ocean **2** on another side of an ocean

tran·som /ˈtrænsəm/ *n* **1** a bar of wood separating a door from a window above; LINTEL **2** a bar of wood or stone fitted across a window to divide it in 2 —see picture at WINDOW **3** a window divided in this way **4** also **transom win·dow** /ˈ·· ˌ··/— *AmE* FANLIGHT

trans·par·en·cy /trænˈspærənsi, -ˈspeər-/ *n* **1** [U] the state of being transparent **2** [C] a piece of photographic film, usu. in a square holder, on which a picture, pattern, etc., can be seen when light is passed through from behind

trans·par·ent /trænˈspærənt, -ˈspeər-/ *adj* **1** allowing light to pass through so that objects behind can be clearly seen: *Glass is transparent* **2** thin or fine enough to be seen through: *Her silk dress was almost transparent* **3** clear; easily understood **4** about which there is no doubt; certain: *a transparent lie* —**~ly** *adv*

tran·spi·ra·tion /ˌtrænspəˈreɪʃən/ *n* [U] *tech* the act of transpiring (TRANSPIRE (1))

tran·spire /trænˈspaɪəʳ/ *v* **1** [I∅;T1] *tech* (of the body, plants, etc.) to give off (esp. watery waste matter) through the surface of the body, leaves, etc. **2** [*it*+I5] (of an event, secret, etc.) to become gradually known: *It later transpired that the minister had been ill with an incurable disease* **3** [I∅] *infml* to happen

USAGE Everyone agrees that it is bad English to use **transpire** when one means "happen", but the word is often used in this way.

trans·plant¹ /trænsˈplɑːnt‖-ˈplænt/ *v* [T1] **1** to move (a plant) from one place and plant in another **2** to move (an organ, piece of skin, hair, etc.) from one part of the body to another or from one person or animal to another: *to transplant a heart* **3** to move from one place and settle or introduce elsewhere: *Under the Tudors many English people were transplanted to Ireland* —**~ation** *n* [U]

trans·plant² /ˈtrænsplɑːnt‖-plænt/ *n* **1** something TRANSPLANTed¹ (1, 2), esp. an organ, piece of skin, hair, etc. **2** an act or operation of TRANSPLANTing¹ (2) an organ, piece of skin, hair, etc.: *a heart transplant*

trans·po·lar /trænzˈpəʊləʳ‖træns-/ *adj* [Wa5] across the (north or south) POLE or POLAR area

trans·port¹ /trænˈspɔːt‖-ort/ *v* [T1] **1** to carry (goods, people, etc.) from one place to another **2** (in former times) to send (a criminal) to a distant land as a punishment **3** [*usu. pass.*] *lit* to fill with delight, joy, or any strong feeling —**~able** *adj*

trans·port² /ˈtrænspɔːt‖-ort/ *n* **1** [U] also (*esp. AmE*) **transportation**—the act of TRANSPORTing¹ (1) or of being TRANSPORTed¹ (1): *The transport of goods by air is very costly* **2** [U] **a** also (*esp. AmE*) **transportation**— a means or system of carrying passengers or goods from one place to another: *Moscow's public transport system is among the finest in the world* **b** *infml* a method of being TRANSPORTed: *I'd like to go to the concert, but I've no transport* **3** [C] a ship or aircraft for carrying soldiers or supplies **4 in a transport/transports of** *lit* filled with (a very strong feeling as of joy, delight, etc.)

trans·por·ta·tion /ˌtrænspɔːˈteɪʃən‖-spər-/ *n* [U] (in former times) **1** the act of TRANSPORTing¹ (2) someone as a punishment **2** the period for which a person is TRANSPORTed¹ (2) as a punishment

transport caf·e /ˈ·· ˌ··/ *n* a cheap eating place on a main road, used mainly by long distance heavy vehicle drivers

trans·port·er /trænˈspɔːtəʳ‖-or-/ *n* a long vehicle on which a number of cars can be carried

transporter bridge /·ˈ·· ·/ also **transporter**— *n* a bridge consisting of a high tower on each bank connected by lengths of steel RAIL from which a flat carriage, level with the ground, hangs on chairs or ropes. Vehicles drive onto the carriage which then moves to the opposite side of the river

transporter crane /·ˈ·· ·/ also **transporter**— *n* a CRANE that can move on rails along the side of a train, ship, etc., to make loading and unloading easier

trans·pose /trænˈspəʊz/ *v* [T1] **1** to change the order or position of (2 or more things): *to transpose the letters of a word* **2** to write or perform (a piece of music) in a musical KEY other than the original —**-position** /ˌtrænspəˈzɪʃən/ *n* [C;U]

trans·ship /trænˈʃɪp, trænsˈʃɪp/ *v* **-pp-** [T1] TRANSHIP —**~ment** *n* [U]

tran·sub·stan·ti·a·tion /ˌtrænsəbstænʃiˈeɪʃən/ *n* [U] *tech* the belief that the bread and wine offered by the priest at the MASS (=a Christian religious service) becomes the body and blood of Christ —compare CONSUBSTANTIATION

trans·verse /trænzˈvɜːs‖trænsˈvɜrs/ *adj* [Wa5] lying or placed across: *a transverse beam* —**~ly** *adv*

trans·vest·is·m /trænzˈvestɪzəm‖træns-/ *n* [U] the unnatural desire to wear the clothing of the opposite sex

trans·ves·tite /trænzˈvestaɪt‖træns-/ *adj, n* [Wa5] (of or related to) a person who practises TRANSVESTISM

trap¹ /træp/ *n* **1** an apparatus for catching and holding animals: *a mouse caught in a trap* **2** a position in which one is caught by deception and cannot escape; plan for deceiving and tricking a person: *The police set a trap to catch the thief* **3** a U or S shaped part of a pipe, that holds water and prevents smelly gas from waste pipes escaping **4** a light 2-wheeled vehicle pulled by a horse **5** *sl* a mouth: *He'll keep his trap shut* (=won't tell the secret) **6** an apparatus from which a dog is set free at the beginning of a race **7** an apparatus containing a very powerful spring, that fires clay plates and balls into the air to be shot at, as in TRAPSHOOTING **8** an apparatus that separates solids from liquids in waste pipes, thus preventing the pipes from becoming blocked

trap² *v* **-pp-** **1** [T1] to catch by a trick or deception: *The police trapped the criminal down a narrow street from which he could not escape* **2** [T1] to hold back; block: *Sand and leaves trapped the water in the stream* **3** [T1;I∅] to catch (an animal) in a trap, esp. for food or fur or as a business

trap·door /ˈtræpdɔːʳ‖-dor/ *n* a small door covering an opening in the roof or floor

tra·peze /trəˈpiːz/ *n* a short bar hung from 2 ropes, used by ACROBATs and GYMNASTs for special exercises

tra·pe·zi·um /trəˈpiːzɪəm/ (*AmE* **trapezoid**)— **-iums** *or* **-ia** /ɪə/ *BrE tech* (in the science of numbers) a 4-sided figure in which only one pair of sides is parallel —see picture at GEOMETRY

trap·e·zoid /ˈtræpəzɔɪd/ (*AmE* **trapezium**)— *n BrE tech* (in the science of numbers) a 4-sided figure in which no sides are parallel

trap·per /ˈtræpəʳ/ *n* a person who traps wild animals, esp. for their fur, as a business

trap·pings /ˈtræpɪŋz/ *n* [P] articles of dress or ornamentation, esp. as a sign of public office: *He wore all the trappings of high office*

Trap·pist /ˈtræpəst/ *n* a member of a ROMAN CATHOLIC religious society (ORDER¹ (17)) whose members never speak, and live according to very severe rules

trapse /treɪps/ *v* [L9] TRAIPSE

trap·shoot·ing /ˈtræpˌʃuːtɪŋ/ *n* [U] the sport of shooting at clay plates or balls fired into the air by a powerful spring (TRAP¹ (7))

trash /træʃ/ *n* **1** [U] worthless material or writing; meaningless expressions or ideas; anything of low quality **2** [U] *AmE* waste material to be thrown

away; RUBBISH **3** [P] *AmE* worthless people
trash·can /ˈtræʃkæn/ *n AmE* DUSTBIN
trash·y /ˈtræʃi/ *adj* [Wa1] worthless: *trashy ideas* —**-iness** *n* [U]
trau·ma /ˈtrɔːmə, ˈtraʊmə/ *n* **-mas** *or* **-mata** /mətə/ *tech* **1** a damage to the mind caused by the body having been wounded, or by a sudden shock or terrible experience **2** a wound
trau·mat·ic /trɔːˈmætɪk/ *adj* (of an experience) deeply and unforgettably shocking; of or of the nature of a TRAUMA (1) —**~ally** *adv* [Wa4]
trav·ail /ˈtræveɪl/ *n* [U] *old use* the pains of giving birth to a child: *a woman in travail*
trav·el¹ /ˈtrævəl/ *v* **-ll-** (*AmE* **-l-**) [Wv3] **1** [I∅] to go from place to place, esp. to a distant place; make a journey: *to travel (round the world) for a year*|(fig.) *The old man's mind travelled over the recent events that had destroyed his home* **2** [L9] to pass, go, move, etc., as light, sound, etc.: *At what speed does light travel?*|*The news travelled fast* **3** [T1] to go through or over: *The theatre group travelled Europe from London to Athens* **4** [L9] to move (a stated distance): *We travelled 1,000 miles on our first day* **5** [Wv6;L9] to go from place to place in order to sell and take orders for one's firm's goods: *My husband travels for a London firm* —see also TRAVEL IN **6** [I∅] *sl* to go very quickly: *We were really travelling when the police caught us* **7 travel light** to travel without much LUGGAGE
travel² *n* [U] the act of travelling
USAGE The activity of moving about the world is **travel**. When one person does this for a while, we speak of his **travels**: *He came home after years of foreign* **travel**.|*Did you go to Persepolis during your* **travels**? A **journey** is the time spent and the distance covered in going from one particular place to another, and a **voyage** has the same meaning but is only by sea: *some books to read on the* **journey/voyage**|*Persepolis is 10 days'* **journey** *across the desert*.
travel a·gen·cy /ˈ·· ˌ···/ also **travel bu·reau** /ˈ·· ˌ··/— *n* [GC] a business that makes arrangements for other people's holidays and journeys, such as by buying tickets, finding hotel rooms, etc.
travel a·gent /ˈ·· ˌ··/ *n* a person who owns or works in a TRAVEL AGENCY
travel in *v prep* [Wv3,6;T1] to go from place to place selling and taking orders for (goods of the stated kind)
trav·elled, *AmE* **traveled** /ˈtrævəld/ *adj* [B9] **1** (of a person) experienced in travel: *a (widely) travelled writer* **2** (of a road, area, etc.) used or visited by travellers (to the stated degree): *a well-travelled road*
trav·el·ler, *AmE* **traveler** /ˈtrævələʳ/ *n* **1** a person on a journey **2** [(*in*)] also **travelling sales·man** /ˌ··· ˈ··/— a person who goes from place to place selling and taking orders for his firm's goods —compare TRAVEL¹ (5), TRAVEL IN
traveller's cheque /ˌ··· ˈ·/ *n* a cheque sold by a bank to a person intending to travel abroad, exchangeable at most banks and many hotels, restaurants, etc., for the money of the particular country
travelling fel·low·ship /ˌ··· ˈ···/ *n* a gift of money to be spent on educational travel, given by an educational organization to a worthy student
trav·el·ogue, *AmE* **-og** /ˈtrævəlɒg‖-lɔg, -lɑg/ *n* a talk or film describing travel in a particular country, a person's travels, etc.
trav·els /ˈtrævəlz/ *n* [P] travelling; journeys, esp. abroad: *things I saw on/during my travels* —see TRAVEL² (USAGE)
trav·el·sick /ˈtrævəlˌsɪk/ *adj* sick from the movement of a vehicle
tra·verse¹ /ˈtrævɜːs‖trəˈvɜrs/ *v* **1** [T1] to pass across, over, or through: *The lights traversed the sky searching for enemy planes* **2** [I∅] *tech* to make a TRAVERSE² (1)
tra·verse² /ˈtrævɜːs‖-ɜrs/ *n* **1** *tech* a movement to the side across the face of a very steep slope of rock or ice, to a place where climbing is easier **2** *tech* a change of direction in a TRENCH (=a deep ditch dug for soldiers to move about in) so that the enemy cannot fire directly along it **3** something such as a bar, beam, etc., placed or lying across something else: *a traverse beam*
trav·es·ty¹ /ˈtrævǝsti/ *n* a copy, account, or example of something that completely misrepresents the nature of the real thing in order to give false unfavourable ideas about it: *The politician's trial was a travesty of justice*
travesty² *v* [T1] to make a TRAVESTY¹ of (something)
trawl¹ /trɔːl/ *v* [I∅;T1] to fish with a TRAWL² (1): *boats out trawling (for fish)*|*to trawl the lake*
trawl² *n* **1** a large open-mouthed fishing net with a wide mouth that is drawn along the sea bottom **2** *AmE* also **trawl line** /ˈ· ·/— a long fishing line to which are fastened many smaller fishing lines
trawl·er /ˈtrɔːləʳ/ *n* a fishing vessel that uses a TRAWL² (1) —see picture at SHIP¹
tray /treɪ/ *n* **1** a flat piece of wood or metal with raised edges used for carrying small articles, esp. cups, plates, food, etc. **2** also **trayful**— the amount or number that this will hold: *a tray of glasses* **3** an open container of wood, metal, or plastic with a flat bottom and raised edges, placed on a desk to hold papers, letters, etc.
treach·e·rous /ˈtretʃərəs/ *adj* **1** disloyal; deceitful **2** dangerous: *treacherous currents* —**~ly** *adv*
treach·e·ry /ˈtretʃəri/ *n* **1** [U] disloyalty; deceit; unfaithfulness; falseness —compare TREASON **2** [C *usu. pl.*] a TREACHEROUS (1) action
trea·cle /ˈtriːkəl/ (*AmE* **molasses**)— *n* [U] *esp. BrE* a very thick sticky dark liquid produced when sugar is being REFINED (=made pure)
trea·cly /ˈtriːkli/ *adj* [Wa1] **1** thick and sticky; like TREACLE: *treacly black mud* **2** (of a drink or liquid food) too thick and sweet: (fig.) *a treacly voice*
tread¹ /tred/ *v* **trod** /trɒd‖trɑd/, **trodden** /ˈtrɒdn‖ˈtrɑdn/ **1** [T1] to walk on, over, or along: *Every day he trod the same path through the woods to school* **2** [L9] to walk or step: *Don't tread on the flowers!* **3** [T1] to press firmly with the feet; crush with the feet: *They crush the juice out of the fruit by treading it* **4** [X9] to press or crush (into a certain state or position) with the feet: *We must tread the fire out before we leave.*|*Don't tread mud into the* CARPET¹ **5** [T1] to make (a path) by walking **6 tread on air** *sl* to be very happy **7 tread on somebody's heels** to follow very closely behind somebody **8 tread on somebody's toes** to offend somebody; hurt the feelings of somebody **9 tread water** to stay upright in deep water with the head above the surface by moving the feet up and down as if one were riding a bicycle
tread² *n* **1** [S9] the act, manner, or sound of walking: *a noisy tread* **2** [C] the part of a step or stair on which the foot is placed **3** [C;U] the pattern of raised lines on a tyre that makes it hold the road better
trea·dle¹ /ˈtredl/ *n* an apparatus worked by the feet to drive a machine: *the treadle of a sewing machine*
treadle² *v* [I∅] to work a TREADLE¹ with the feet
tread·mill /ˈtredˌmɪl/ *n* **1** [C] a mill worked by people walking on steps fixed to the edge of a large wheel or by animals walking on a sloping endless belt **2** [*the*+R] (in former times) the use of such

an apparatus as an official punishment **3** [U] uninteresting work

trea·son /ˈtriːzən/ *n* [U] (the crime of) disloyalty to one's country, esp. by helping its enemies or by violent opposition to those in power —compare TREACHERY

trea·so·na·ble /ˈtriːzənəbəl/ also **trea·son·ous** /ˈtriːzənəs/— *adj* of, being, or related to TREASON: *a treasonable crime against the state* —**-bly** *adv*

trea·sure[1] /ˈtreʒəʳ/ *n* **1** [U] wealth in the form of gold, silver, jewels, etc.: *buried treasure* **2** [C] a very valuable object: *The library has many art treasures* **3** [C;N] *infml* a person considered very precious: *She's a real treasure.|Come here, treasure, and give me a kiss*

treasure[2] *v* [Wv5;T1] to keep as precious; regard (a possession) as valuable

treasure house /ˈ·· ·/ *n* a building where TREASURE[1] (1) was formerly stored: (fig.) *This library is a treasure house of knowledge*

trea·sur·er /ˈtreʒərəʳ/ *n* a person in charge of the money belonging to a club, organization, political party, etc.

treasure trove /ˈ·· ·/ *n* [U] money, gold, jewels, or other valuable objects found hidden in the ground and claimed by no one

treasure up *v adv* [T1] to store for future use, esp. as in one's mind

trea·su·ry /ˈtreʒəri/ *n* **1** [C] (esp. in former times) the place where the money of a government is kept and controlled **2** [C9, esp. *of*] a collection of valuable things: *This book is a treasury of useful information* **3** [*the*+GU] (*usu. cap.*) the government department that controls and spends public money —compare EXCHEQUER

treasury bill /ˈ··· ·/ *n* (*often cap.* T) (in Britain) a written order to pay money at regular dates (BILL OF EXCHANGE) sold by the TREASURY (3) to raise money for short periods

treat[1] /triːt/ *v* **1** [X9] to act or behave towards: *This firm has always treated its workers well.|She treats us as/like children* —compare BEHAVE **2** [X9] to deal with; handle: *We treat all requests in the order in which they are received.|This delicate glass must be treated with care* **3** [X9] to regard; consider: *My employer treated our request as a joke* **4** [T1] to try to cure by medical means: *Are they able to treat this disease?* **5** [T1;(I∅)] to buy or give (someone) something special, as a friendly act; pay for the food, drink, amusement, etc., of (someone) —see also TREAT TO **6** [Wv5;T1] to put (a substance) through a chemical or industrial action in order to change in some way: *treated pig skin* **7** [I∅ (*with*)] *fml* to talk in order to arrange an agreement or settlement —**~able** *adj* —**~er** *n*

treat[2] *n* **1** something that gives pleasure, joy, or delight, esp. when unexpected: *It's a great treat for her to go to London* **2 one's treat** one's act of TREATing[1] (5): *Now remember this is to be my treat, so I'll pay for everything*

trea·tise /ˈtriːtɨs, -tɨz/ *n* [(*on*)] a book or article that examines the facts and principles of a particular subject and gives the writer's opinions on it

treat·ment /ˈtriːtmənt/ *n* **1** [U] the act or manner of treating someone or something: *He's gone to hospital in London for (special) treatment* **2** [C] a substance or method used in treating someone medically

treat of *v prep* [T1] *fml* to be about; deal with: *a poem treating of love*

treat to *v prep* [D1] to buy for or give (someone) (something special) as a friendly act: *I'm going to treat myself to a holiday in Spain next year*

treat·y /ˈtriːti/ *n* **1** [C] an agreement made between countries and formally signed by their representatives **2** [U] *fml* agreement between people: *We sold the house by private treaty* **3 in treaty (with)** in the middle of TREATing[1] (7) (with)

treaty port /ˈ·· ·/ *n* a port that must be kept open to foreign trade according to international agreement

treb·le[1] /ˈtrebəl/ *n* **1** [C] (a person with or a musical part for) a high singing voice **2** [C] (of a family of instruments) the instrument with this range of notes **3** [U] the upper half of the whole range of musical notes —compare BASS[2]

treble[2] *adv, adj* [Wa5] (of a voice or musical instrument) high in sound

treble[3] *predeterminer* 3 times as big, as much, or as many as; multiplied by 3: *He earns treble my wages*

treble[4] *v* [Wv5;T1;I∅] to (cause to) become 3 times as great in number, size, or amount

treble chance /ˌ·· ˈ·/ *n* [*the*+R] (in Britain) a method of competing in the football POOLS by guessing which will be the DRAWN[1] (20) matches, with a higher value in points, and then which matches will be won away and at home, with a lower value in points

treble clef /ˌ·· ˈ·/ *n tech* a sign 𝄞 showing that the following musical notes are higher in PITCH than MIDDLE C —compare BASS CLEF and see picture at NOTATION

tree[1] /triː/ *n* **1** a type of tall plant with a wooden trunk and branches, that lives for many years: *an apple tree|the trees in the wood* **2** a bush or other plant with a treelike form: *a coconut tree|rose trees* **3** a wooden object with a special purpose, such as a SHOE TREE, CLOTHES TREE, etc. **4** a drawing with a branching form, esp. as used for showing family relationships —see also FAMILY TREE **5 up a (gum) tree** in a difficult position from which escape is difficult —**~less** *adj* [Wa5]

See next page for picture

tree[2] *v* [Wv5;T1] to chase or force up a tree

tree fern /ˈ· ·/ *n* a type of large tropical FERN that grows to the size of a tree

tre·foil /ˈtriːfɔɪl, ˈtrefɔɪl/ *n* **1** any of various types of plant, such as CLOVER, that have leaves divided into 3 little leaves **2** an ornamental shape like the leaf of such a plant, esp. used in patterns on stone

trek[1] /trek/ *n* a journey, esp. a long hard one

trek[2] *v* **-kk-** [L9] to make a long hard journey

trel·lis[1] /ˈtrelɨs/ *n* [C;U] (a) light upright framework of long narrow pieces of wood, esp. used as a support for climbing plants —see picture at GARDEN[1]

trellis[2] *v* [Wv5;T1] to support on a TRELLIS[1]: *trellised roses*

trem·ble[1] /ˈtrembəl/ *v* **1** [Wv3,4;I∅] to shake uncontrollably as from fear, cold, excitement, etc.: *The children trembled with fear when they saw the policeman* **2** [Wv3,4;I∅] to move backwards and forwards or from side to side; shake: *The whole house trembled as the train went by* **3** [Wv3,4; L9(*for*);I3] to feel fear or anxiety; be worried: *The fishermen's wives trembled for their husbands' safety.|I tremble to think what's going to happen* —**-blingly** *adv*

tremble[2] *n* [S] **1** an act of trembling (TREMBLE[1] (1,2)); SHUDDER **2 all of a tremble** *infml* trembling with excitement or nervousness

tre·men·dous /trɪˈmendəs/ *adj* **1** very great in size, amount, or degree: *to travel at a tremendous speed|a tremendous explosion|(infml) She's a tremendous talker* (=talks a great deal) **2** wonderful: *We went to a tremendous party last night* —**~ly** *adv*

trem·o·lo /ˈtreməlәʊ/ *n* **-los** *tech* a special slightly shaking effect produced by rapidly varying the loudness, level, or TONE of a musical note, esp.

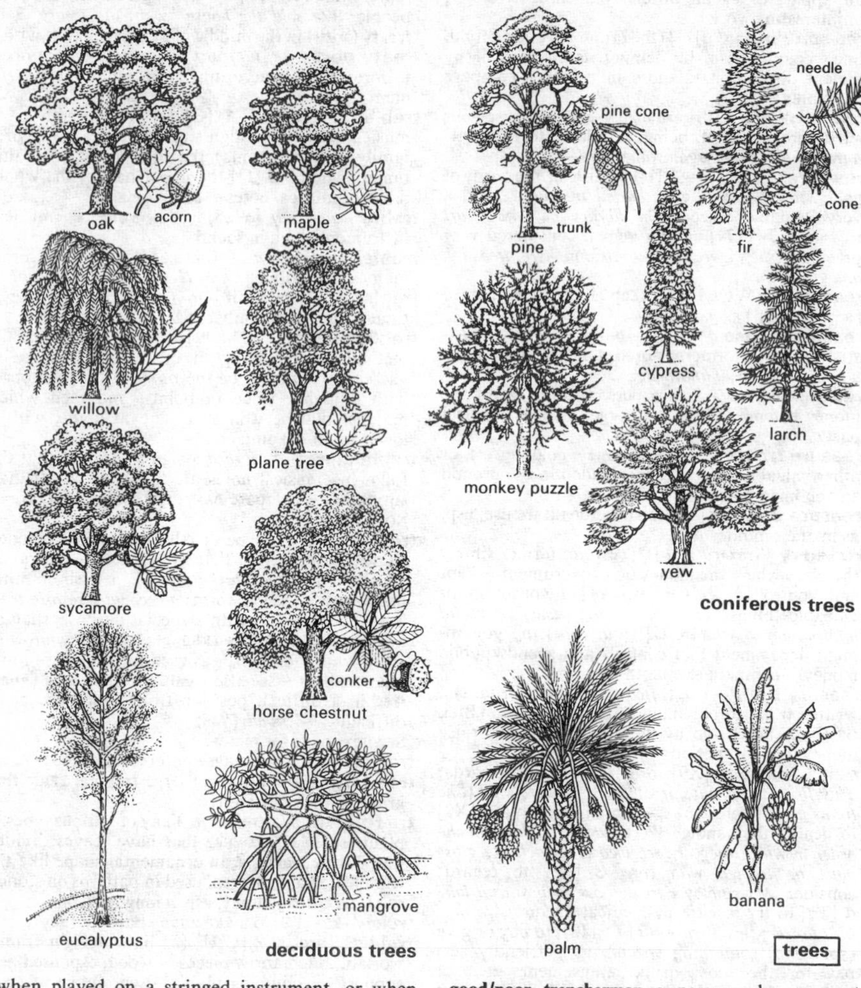

when played on a stringed instrument, or when sung

trem·or /ˈtreməʳ/ *n* **1** a shaking movement of the earth: *an earth tremor* **2** a shaking movement caused by fear, nervousness, illness, weakness, etc.: *The story was so terrible that it sent tremors down my* SPINE

trem·u·lous /ˈtremjʊləs‖-mjə-/ *adj* **1** slightly shaking **2** uncertain; nervous —**~ly** *adv* —**~ness** *n* [U]

trench¹ /trentʃ/ *n* **1** a long narrow hole cut in the ground; ditch **2** a deep ditch dug in the ground as a protection for soldiers: *In the First World War the soldiers fought in trenches*

trench² *v* [Wv5;T1] **1** to dig TRENCHES¹ (1) in **2** [Wv5] to protect with TRENCHES¹ (2): *a trenched camp*

tren·chant /ˈtrenʃənt/ *adj* (of language) forceful; effective; sharp; to the point: *a trenchant argument/speech* —**~ly** *adv* —**-chancy** /ˈtrenʃənsi/ *n* [U]

trench coat /ˈ· ·/ *n* a loose-fitting coat with a belt and pockets, esp. made in a military style, in a material through which water cannot pass

trench·er /ˈtrenʃəʳ/ *n* a large wooden plate used, esp. in former times, for serving food

trench·er·man /ˈtrenʃəmən‖-ʃər-/ *n* **-men** /mən/ **good/poor trencherman** a person who usu. eats much/little

trend¹ /trend/ *v* [L9] to have a certain tendency, course, or direction of development; tend

trend² *n* **1** a general direction or course of development; tendency: *The trend of wages is still upwards* **2 set the trend** to start or popularize a fashion

trend·set·ter /ˈtrendˌsetəʳ/ *n infml* a person who starts or popularizes the latest fashion

trend·y¹ /ˈtrendi/ *adj* [Wa1] *esp. BrE infml* very fashionable; very influenced by the latest fashions: *a trendy dress/girl* —**trendiness** *n* [U]

trendy² *n esp. BrE infml* a TRENDY¹ person: *a restaurant full of young trendies*

tre·pan /trɪˈpæn/ *v* **-nn-** [T1] TREPHINE²

tre·phine¹ /trɪˈfiːn‖-ˈfaɪn/ *n tech* a special medical instrument with a sharp fine-toothed circular cutting edge used in trephining (TREPHINE²)

trephine² *v* [T1] to cut a round piece of bone out of (the SKULL) (=the bone in the head) as part of a medical operation

trep·i·da·tion /ˌtrepɪ̈ˈdeɪʃən/ *n* [U] a state of anxiety or fear

tres·pass¹ /ˈtrespəs, -pæs/ *n* **1** [C;U] (an example

of) the act of TRESPASSing² (1) **2** [C] *old use & bibl* a SIN; wicked or wrong action: *Forgive us our trespasses*

trespass² *v* [IØ] **1** [(*upon*)] to go onto privately-owned land without permission **2** *old use & bibl* to do wrong; SIN —**~er** *n*: *a fierce dog to bite trespassers*

trespass up·on also **trespass on**— *v prep* [T1] to take more of (something) than what is right, proper, or usual; make too much use of: *It would be trespassing upon their generosity to accept any more from them*

tress·es /ˈtresǰz/ *n* [P] *lit* a woman's long hair

tres·tle /ˈtresəl/ *n* a wooden beam fixed at each end to a pair of spreading legs, used, usu. in pairs, as a removable support for a table or other flat surface —see picture at SITE¹

trestle bridge /ˌ·· ˈ·/ also **trestle**— *n* a framework of steel or wood for carrying a road or railway over a valley

trestle ta·ble /ˌ·· ˈ··/ *n* a table made of wooden boards laid on TRESTLE*s*

trews /truːz/ *n* [P] close fitting TARTAN trousers —see PAIR (USAGE)

tri- /traɪ/ *prefix* [*n→n, adj→adj, v→v*] 3: TRIAD| TRIANGLE|TRISECT

tri·ad /ˈtraɪæd/ *n* [GC] *rare* a group of 3 closely related people or things

tri·al /ˈtraɪəl/ *n* **1** [C;U] (an example of) the act of hearing and judging a person, case, or point of law in a court: *The murder trial lasted 6 weeks.|trial by a military court* **2** [C;U] (an example of) the act of testing to find quality, value, usefulness, etc.: *She did so well in the horse trials she might be chosen to represent England abroad.|I've appointed a secretary for a trial period to see how she does the job* **3** [C] an attempt; effort; try: *He succeeded on his 3rd trial* **4** [C] an annoying thing or person; cause of worry or trouble: *That child is a trial to his parents* **5 on trial a** for the purpose of testing: *He took the car on trial but didn't like it so brought it back* **b** being tried in a court of law **6 put (somebody) on trial** to try (somebody) in a court of law **7 stand trial** to be tried: *to stand trial for murder* **8 trial and error** a method of getting the most satisfactory results by trying several methods and, having learnt from one's mistakes, choosing the best: *to cook by trial and error*

trial mar·riage /ˌ·· ˈ··/ *n* **1** [U] the custom of a man and woman living together as husband and wife for a short period to find out if they are suitable marriage partners **2** [C;U] a case or period of this

trial run /ˌ·· ˈ·/ *n* an act of driving a vehicle to test it

tri·an·gle /ˈtraɪæŋgəl/ *n* **1** a flat figure with 3 straight sides and 3 angles —see picture at GEOMETRY **2** any 3-cornered or 3-sided figure, object, or piece: *a triangle of land* **3** a 3-sided musical instrument made of a bent steel rod played by being struck with another steel rod —see picture at PERCUSSION **4** a group of 3; TRIAD —see also ETERNAL TRIANGLE **5** *AmE* SETSQUARE

tri·an·gu·lar /traɪˈæŋgjʊləʳ‖-gjə-/ *adj* [Wa5] **1** of or shaped like a TRIANGLE (1) **2** having 3 people or groups: *a triangular trade agreement between 3 countries*

trib·al¹ /ˈtraɪbəl/ *adj* [Wa5] of or related to a tribe or tribes: *a tribal dance|a tribal chief*

tribal² *n esp. Ind & PakE* someone in a TRIBAL¹ stage of social development

trib·al·is·m /ˈtraɪbəl-ɪzəm/ *n* [U] the organization of a social group into a tribe

tribe /traɪb/ *n* [GC] **1** a social group made up of people of the same race, beliefs, customs, language, etc., usu. of a fairly low level of civilization, under the leadership of a chief or chiefs: *American Indian tribes|The whole tribe is/are angry about it* —see FOLK (USAGE) **2** a group of related plants or animals: *the cat tribe* **3** *often derog* a group of people with the same common character, profession, etc.: *the tribe of teachers*

tribes·man /ˈtraɪbzmən/ *n* **-men** /mən/ a (male) member of a tribe

trib·u·la·tion /ˌtrɪbjʊˈleɪʃən‖-bjə-/ *n* [C;U] (a cause of) trouble, grief, worry, suffering, etc.

tri·bu·nal /traɪˈbjuːnəl/ *n* [GC] a court of people appointed officially, judges, etc., with powers to deal with special matters: *The rent tribunal ordered that my rent be reduced.*|(fig.) *Increasing unemployment is opposed by the tribunal of public opinion*

trib·une¹ /ˈtrɪbjuːn/ *n* **1** an official of Ancient Rome elected by the ordinary people to protect their interests **2** a popular leader; person who defends popular rights and interests

tribune² *n* a raised stage for people speaking to a meeting

trib·u·ta·ry¹ /ˈtrɪbjʊtəri‖-bjəteri/ *adj* [Wa5;A;(F+*to*)] **1** (of a stream or river) flowing into another **2** (of a person, country, etc.) paying TRIBUTE (1) to another

tributary² *n* **1** a stream or river that flows into a larger stream or river: *the tributaries of the Rhine* **2** [(*to*)] a person, state, etc., that pays TRIBUTE (1) to another

trib·ute /ˈtrɪbjuːt/ *n* **1** [C;U] (a) payment made by one ruler, government, or country to another as the price of peace, protection, etc. **2** [C] something done, said, or given to show respect or admiration for someone —see also FLORAL TRIBUTE **3 pay (a) tribute** to show one's respect or admiration for or gratefulness to someone or something

trice /traɪs/ *n* **in a trice** *not fml* in a moment; in the shortest possible time

tri·ceps /ˈtraɪseps/ *n* **-es** *or* **triceps** [Wn1] the large muscle that runs along the back of the upper arm

trich·i·no·sis /ˌtrɪkǰˈnəʊsǰs/ *n* [U] a disease that results from eating incompletely cooked PORK (=the flesh of the pig) and causes pain, fever, swelling muscles, and sleeplessness

trick¹ /trɪk/ *n* **1** an act needing special skill, esp. done to confuse or amuse: *magic tricks|No one understood how I did the card tricks* **2** a special skill: *John taught me the trick of pouring wine without dropping any* **3** something done to deceive or cheat someone: *He got the money by a trick.*|(fig.) *a trick of the heat in the desert* **4** something done to someone to make him look stupid and thus give amusement to others: *The children loved playing tricks on their teacher* **5** [(*of*)] a strange or typical habit: *He has a trick of looking at people straight in the eye to make them feel guilty* **6** a stupid or childish act: *What a nasty trick to play on someone who's supposed to be your friend!* —see also DIRTY TRICK **7** the cards (one from each player) played or won in one ROUND⁴ (6) of cards —see CARDS (USAGE) **8** *tech* (among sailors) a period of duty at the wheel of the ship **9 a trick worth two of that** a cleverer way of doing it than that **10 do the trick** *infml* to fulfil one's purpose or intention: *This medicine ought to do the trick* (=cure the disease) **11 not/never miss a trick** *infml* to know everything that is going on

trick² *adj* [Wa5;A] *not fml* **1** made for playing tricks: *a trick spoon that melts in hot liquid* **2** (esp. of a bone or joint) weak and likely to fail suddenly **3** full of hidden and unexpected difficulties: *a trick question in an examination paper* **4** of, concerned with, or related to a TRICK¹ (2) or TRICK*s*¹ (2): *He*

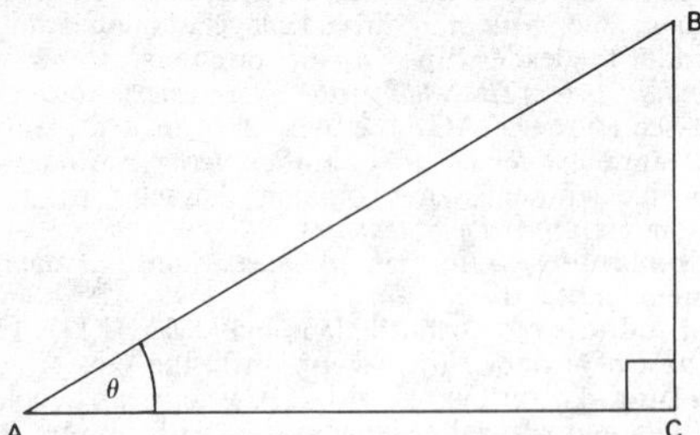

for θ

AB = hypotenuse (hyp)

AC = adjacent side (adj)

BC = opposite side (opp)

AĈB = 90°

(sin) sine θ = BC/AB (opp/hyp)

(cos) cosine θ = AC/AB (adj/hyp)

(tan) tangent θ = BC/AC (opp/adj)

trigonometry

won the competition because of his trick riding

trick³ *v* [T1 (*into*)] to cheat (someone): *Mother tricked me into taking my medicine*

trick·e·ry /ˈtrɪkəri/ *n* [U] the use of tricks to deceive or cheat

trick·le¹ /ˈtrɪkəl/ *v* [Wv3] **1** [L9] to flow in drops or in a thin stream: *Blood trickled down his face.*|(fig.) *The children trickled into the classroom* **2** [X9] to cause (esp. liquid) to flow in this way

trickle² *n* [S] a small thin flow; small, slow, or irregular quantity of anything coming, going, or moving

trick out also **trick up**— *v adv* [X9, esp *in*] to dress (someone or something) showily; ornament

trick·ster /ˈtrɪkstəʳ/ *n* a person who deceives or cheats people

trick·y /ˈtrɪki/ *adj* [Wa1] **1** (of a difficulty, work, state of affairs, etc.) difficult to handle or deal with; delicate; full of hidden or unexpected difficulties **2** (of a person or his actions) deceitful; clever in cheating; SLY: *a tricky politician* —**trickiness** *n* [U]

tri·col·our, *AmE* **-or** /ˈtrɪkələʳ‖ˈtraɪˌkʌlər/ *n* **1** [C] a flag with 3 equal bands of different colours **2** [*the*+R] (*usu. cap.*) the national flag of France

tri·cy·cle /ˈtraɪsɪkəl/ *n* [C; *by*+U] a bicycle with 3 wheels, 2 at the back and one at the front

tri·dent /ˈtraɪdənt/ *n* a forklike instrument or weapon with 3 points

tried¹ /traɪd/ *adj* [Wa5] found to be good or trustworthy by experience or testing: *a tried method*

tried² *past t. & p. of* TRY

tri·en·ni·al /traɪˈeniəl/ *adj* [Wa5] **1** done or happening every 3 years **2** lasting for 3 years

tri·er /ˈtraɪəʳ/ *n* a person who tries hard; someone who always does his best

tri·fle /ˈtraɪfəl/ *n* **1** [C] an article or thing of little value or slight importance, matter of slight importance: *wasting one's money on trifles* **2** [C] a very small amount of money **3** [C;U] (esp. in Britain) a dish of plain cakes set in fruit and jelly (usu. containing SHERRY), covered with cream or CUSTARD and sometimes crushed nuts or chocolate **4 a trifle** to some degree; rather: *He's a trifle angry*

trifle a·way *v adv* [Wv3;T1] to waste; FRITTER AWAY

tri·fler /ˈtraɪfləʳ/ *n* a person who TRIFLE*s* WITH someone or something

trifle with *v prep* [Wv3;T1] **1** to deal lightly with (someone) without the necessary seriousness or respect: *The general is not a man to be trifled with* **2** to handle (something) carelessly or needlessly

tri·fling /ˈtraɪflɪŋ/ *adj* of slight importance; of little value

trig·ger¹ /ˈtrɪgəʳ/ *n* **1** the small tongue of metal pressed by the finger to fire a gun **2 quick on the trigger** able to shoot quickly

trigger² *v* [T1 (OFF)] to start (something, esp. a chain of events); set off: *Large price increases will trigger off demands for even larger wage increases*

trigger-hap·py /ˈ·· ˌ··/ *adj* **1** too ready to shoot; ready to shoot for the slightest reason **2** not responsible enough, esp. in matters which could lead to war; too dependent on violent methods: *Their government's trigger-happy methods may lead to war*

trig·o·nom·e·try /ˌtrɪgəˈnɒmətri‖-ˈnɑ-/ *n* [U] the branch of MATHEMATICS (=the science of numbers) that deals with the relationship between the sides and angles of TRIANGLE*s* (=3-sided figures)

trike /traɪk/ *n BrE infml* TRICYCLE

tri·lat·e·ral /ˌtraɪˈlætərəl/ *adj* [Wa5] having 3 sides: *a trilateral agreement* —**-rally** *adv* [Wa5]

tril·by /ˈtrɪlbi/ also **trilby hat** /ˌ·· ˈ·/— *n esp. BrE* a man's soft hat, esp. made of FELT, with a fold in the top

tri·lin·gu·al /ˌtraɪˈlɪŋgwəl/ *adj* of, using, or able to speak, 3 languages: *a trilingual secretary/newspaper* —**~ly** *adv* [Wa5]

trill¹ /trɪl/ *n* **1** (in singing or instrumental music) the rapid repeating of 2 musical notes, for special effect **2** a sound or number of repeated sounds like this, esp. as made by a bird **3** a speech sound like this, such as that produced by the point of the tongue against the part of the mouth just behind the upper front teeth

trill² *v* [Wv5;IØ;T1] to sing, play, or pronounce with a TRILL

tril·lion /ˈtrɪljən/ *determiner, n, pron* **trillion** *or* **trillions** [see NUMBER TABLE 2] **1** *BrE* 1,000,000,000,000,000,000; 10^{18} **2** *esp. AmE* 1,000,000,000,000; 10^{12}

tri·lo·bite /ˈtraɪləbaɪt/ *n* a type of small sea creature of very long ago, whose remains are found in large numbers in some areas

tril·o·gy /ˈtrɪlədʒi/ *n* a group of 3 related books, plays, etc., connected by common subject matter but each complete in itself

trim¹ /trɪm/ *v* **-mm- 1** [T1] to make neat, even, or tidy by cutting: *have one's hair trimmed* **2** [T1 (OFF)] to remove by cutting: *to trim off loose threads* **3** [Wv5;T1:(*with*)] to ornament: *a coat trimmed with fur* **4** [T1;(IØ)] **a** to move (a sail) into the desired position **b** (of a sail) to move into the desired position **5** [T1;(IØ)] **a** to arrange the load of (a ship or aircraft) so as to give the desired balance in the water or air **b** (of a ship or aircraft) to balance in this way **6** [T1] *not fml* to defeat completely, esp. in sport **7** [T1;IØ] to change (one's opinions and principles) for one's own advantage and popular approval **8** [T1] to reduce: *You must trim your costs if you want to make bigger profits*

trim² *adj* **-mm-** [Wa1] tidy; in good order; pleasingly neat in appearance: *a trim sailing ship/figure/garden* —**~ly** *adv*

trim³ *n* **1** [S] an act of cutting **2** [U] proper shape, order, or condition; readiness; fitness: *The team was in (good) trim for the match*

tri·ma·ran /'traɪmərӕn/ *n* a type of fast pleasure boat with a flat usu. wooden surface (DECK) supported by 3 narrow parallel HULL*s* (=floating surfaces) with a space between them, and moved by sails

tri·mes·ter /traɪ'mestəʳ/ *n AmE* a TERM of 3 months at a school or college

trim·mer /'trɪməʳ/ *n* **1** a person or machine that TRIM*s*[1] (1,2), esp. a machine that TRIM*s*[1] (1,2) wood **2** a person who changes his opinions and principles for his own advantage or to win approval

trim·ming /'trɪmɪŋ/ *n* [*usu. pl.*] **1** something used for TRIMming[1] (3); an ornament or pleasant addition: *duck served with all the trimmings* (=vegetables, potatoes, etc.) **2** a piece cut off from a larger piece

tri·ni·tro·tol·u·ene /ˌtraɪnaɪtrəʊ'tɒljʊ-iːn‖-'tɑ-/ *n* [U] *rare* TNT

trin·i·ty /'trɪnɪ̇ti/ *n* [GC] *fml & lit* a group of 3

Trinity *n* **1** [*the*+R] *tech* (in the Christian religion) the union of the 3 forms of God (the Father, Son and HOLY SPIRIT) as one God **2** [R] also **Trinity Sun·day** /ˌ··· '··/— the Sunday after WHITSUN (1)

trin·ket /'trɪŋkɪ̇t/ *n* a small ornament or piece of jewellery of low value

tri·o /'triːəʊ/ *n* **-os** **1** [GC] any group of 3 people or things: *a trio of friends* **2** [GC] a group of 3 singers or musicians **3** [C] a piece of music written for a group of 3 singers or musicians

trip[1] /trɪp/ *v* **-pp-** **1** [IØ (*over*);T1 (UP)] **a** to catch one's foot and lose one's balance: *The fisherman tripped over a root and fell into the river* **b** to cause (someone) to do this: *The boy put his leg out to trip the teacher* **2** [IØ;T1 (UP)] to (cause to) make a mistake as in a statement or behaviour: *This lawyer always tries to trip witnesses up by asking confusing questions* **3** [T1 (UP)] to catch or trap in a mistake **4** [L9] to move or dance with quick light steps: *The little girl tripped down the path* **5** [T1] to start or set free (a SWITCH[1] (1), spring, etc.): *A thief climbing in through the window tripped the wire and set the bells ringing*

trip[2] *n* **1** a journey from one place to another: *to go on a trip to Europe|a 500-mile trip* **2** a journey with a particular purpose or happening regularly: *to make a trip to the doctor's|a business trip* **3** a journey for pleasure: *a day trip to the country* **4** a mistake: *a trip of the tongue* **5** a fall; act of tripping **6** a SWITCH, wire, etc., for starting some apparatus or movement **7** *drug users' sl* a period under the influence of a mind-changing drug

tri·par·tite /traɪ'pɑːtaɪt‖-'ɑr-/ *adj* [Wa5] **1** having 3 parts: *a tripartite leaf* **2** (of an agreement) agreed on by 3 parties

tripe /traɪp/ *n* [U] **1** the rubbery wall of the stomach of the cow or ox, eaten as food: *boiled tripe and onions* **2** *infml* worthless or stupid talk, ideas, writing, etc.: *Why do you read such tripe?*

trip·le[1] /'trɪpəl/ *v* [IØ;T1] to (cause to) grow to 3 times the amount or number: *The firm tripled its profits last year*

triple[2] *adj* [Wa5] **1** having 3 parts or members **2** 3 times repeated: *a triple* DOSE (=amount) *of medicine*

triple jump /'·· ·/ *n* [*the*+R;S] an ATHLETICS event in which the competitors take off and land on one foot, follow it by jumping on one foot and landing on the other, and finish with a jump from both feet

trip·let /'trɪplɪ̇t/ *n* **1** [*usu. pl.*] any one of 3 children born of the same mother at the same time **2** *tech* a group of 3 musical notes to be played in the time of 2 ordinary notes **3** a group or set of 3 (as of lines in a poem)

triple time /'·· ·/ *n* [U] a musical time with 3 BEAT*s*

trip·lex[1] /'trɪpleks‖'trɪ-, 'traɪ-/ *n* [U] (*often cap.*) *BrE tdmk* a special safety glass made of a sheet of transparent plastic between 2 sheets of glass, esp. used in car windows

triplex[2] *n AmE* a group of rooms on 3 floors, used as a house —compare DUPLEX

trip·li·cate[1] /'trɪplɪ̇kɪ̇t/ *adj* [Wa5] consisting of or existing in 3 parts that are exactly alike: *triplicate copies of the contract*

trip·li·cate[2] /'trɪplɪ̇keɪt/ *v* [T1] **1** to make 2 exact copies of (something written) so that altogether there are 3 copies **2** to multiply by 3

trip·li·cate[3] /'trɪplɪ̇kɪ̇t/ *n* **1** one of 3 like things, esp. the 3rd of 3 exact copies of an article, paper, etc. **2 in triplicate** in 3 copies, one of which is the original

tri·pod /'traɪpɒd‖-pɑd/ *n* a 3-legged support, such as for a camera —see picture at LABORATORY

tri·pos /'traɪpɒs‖-pɑs/ *n* (a course of study for) the set of examinations for the BA degree at Cambridge University

trip out *v adv* [IØ] *drug users' sl* to experience the effect of a mind-changing drug

trip·per /'trɪpəʳ/ *n esp. BrE, often derog* a person on a pleasure trip, esp. one lasting only one day

trip·ping /'trɪpɪŋ/ *adj* [Wa5] **1** walking, running, or dancing with light easy movements **2** (of a step, movement, etc.) light and easy —**~ly** *adv*

trip·tych /'trɪptɪk/ *n* a picture or CARVING, usu. with a religious subject, done on 3 boards fixed side by side, so that the side ones can be folded inwards to cover the middle one

trip·wire /'trɪpˌwaɪəʳ/ *n* a wire stretched across the ground, that causes a trap, explosive, etc., to work if a person or animal touches it

tri·reme /'traɪriːm/ *n* [C; *by*+U] *tech* an ancient warship with 3 rows of OAR*s* on each side; kind of GALLEY

tri·sect /traɪ'sekt/ *v* [T1] to divide into 3 (esp. equal) parts

trite /traɪt/ *adj* [Wa1] (of remarks, ideas, etc.) too often repeated to be effective; too much used —**~ly** *adv* —**~ness** *n* [U]

tri·umph[1] /'traɪəmf/ *n* **1** [C] a complete victory or success: *a triumph over the enemy|his examination triumph* **2** [U] the joy or satisfaction caused by this: *shouts of triumph* **3** [C] (in ancient Rome) a procession in honour of a victorious general

triumph[2] *v* [IØ] **1** [(*over*)] to be victorious (over) **2** to show great joy and satisfaction because of success or victory; rejoice in victory

tri·um·phal /traɪ'ʌmfəl/ *adj* [Wa5] of, related to, or marking a TRIUMPH[1] (1,3): *a triumphal arch*

tri·um·phant /traɪ'ʌmfənt/ *adj* [Wa5] **1** victorious; successful: *The triumphant army marched into the enemy capital* **2** rejoicing in one's success or victory: *The victorious general made a triumphant return* —**~ly** *adv*

tri·um·vir /traɪ'ʌmvəʳ/ *n tech* (in ancient Rome) one of 3 men sharing the power of government

tri·um·vir·ate /traɪ'ʌmvɪ̇rɪ̇t/ *n* **1** [C] *tech* (in ancient Rome) the (period of) office of a TRIUMVIR **2** [GC] a group of 3 men together governing a country

triv·et /'trɪvɪ̇t/ *n* **1** a 3-legged stand for holding a pot or other vessel over a fire **2** a metal stand, usu. with short legs, placed under a hot pot or dish to protect a surface **3 as right as a trivet** *becoming rare* in perfectly good condition or health

triv·i·a /'trɪvɪə/ *n* [P] unimportant or useless things; TRIFLE*s* (1)

triv·i·al /'trɪvɪəl/ *adj* **1** of little worth or importance: *Why do you get angry over such trivial*

matters? **2** ordinary: *trivial everyday duties* —**~ly** *adv*
triv·i·al·i·ty /ˌtrɪviˈælǝ̇ti/ *n* **1** [C] something of little importance or worth; something TRIVIAL **2** [U] the state of being TRIVIAL (1)
triv·i·al·ize, -ise /ˈtrɪviǝlaɪz/ *v* [T1] to make TRIVIAL (1); reduce to unimportance
tro·cha·ic /trǝʊˈkeɪ-ɪk/ *adj, n* [Wa5;C] (a line of poetry) consisting of TROCHEE*s*
tro·chee /ˈtrǝʊkiː/ *n tech* a measure of poetry consisting of one strong (or long) beat followed by one weak (or short) beat, as in "father"
trod /trɒd‖trɑd/ *past t. & p. of* TREAD
trod·den /ˈtrɒdn‖ˈtrɑdn/ *past p. of* TREAD
trog·lo·dyte /ˈtrɒglǝdaɪt‖ˈtrɑg-/ *n* a person who lived in a cave in very ancient (PREHISTORIC) times
troi·ka /ˈtrɔɪkǝ/ *n* **1** [C] a Russian carriage drawn by a team of 3 horses side by side **2** [GC] a group of 3 people acting together for a common purpose; TRIUMVIRATE
Tro·jan /ˈtrǝʊdʒǝn/ *n* **work like a Trojan** to work very hard
troll[1] /trǝʊl/ *v* **1** [T1;I∅] to sing the lines of (a song), each singer starting slightly after the one before; sing (a song) as a ROUND **2** [I∅ (*for*)] to fish (for) by pulling a line through the water behind a slow-moving boat
troll[2] *n* (in ancient Scandinavian writings and stories) one of a race of beings with special powers, variously described as friendly or evil, as very small or very large, and as living in caves or hills
trol·ley /ˈtrɒli‖ˈtrɑli/ *n* **1** [C] any of various low 2- or 4-wheeled carts or vehicles, esp. one pushed by hand **2** [C] *esp. BrE* a small table on very small wheels (CASTER*s*) from which food and drinks are served **3** [C] a small low vehicle running on railway lines, esp. one worked by hand **4** [C] an apparatus, such as a wheel on the end of a pole, to carry current from a wire to an electrically driven vehicle **5** [C; *by*+U] *AmE* an electric TRAM
trol·ley·bus /ˈtrɒlibʌs‖ˈtrɑ-/ *n* [C; *by*+U] an electric bus that draws power from a pair of wires running above it
trol·lop /ˈtrɒlǝp‖ˈtrɑ-/ *n* [C; *you*+N] **1** a very untidy woman or girl **2** a sexually immoral woman or girl
trom·bone /trɒmˈbǝʊn‖trɑm-/ *n* a large brass musical instrument with a long sliding tube that is made longer or shorter to vary the note —see picture at WIND INSTRUMENT
trom·bon·ist /trɒmˈbǝʊnǝ̇st‖trɑm-/ *n* a person who plays a TROMBONE
troop[1] /truːp/ *n* **1** a band of people or wild animals, esp. when moving: *a troop of monkeys/children* **2** a body of soldiers, esp. a group of CAVALRY (=soldiers who fight on horses) or of soldiers in armoured vehicles, 2 or more making up a SQUADRON **3** a group of about 32 BOY SCOUT*s* under the guidance of a grown-up leader
troop[2] *v* **1** [L9] to move together in a band: *Everyone trooped into the meeting* **2** [T1] *BrE* to carry (the REGIMENTAL flag (**colour**)) in a ceremonial way before the REGIMENT
troop car·ri·er /ˈ· ˌ···/ *n* [C; *by*+U] a ship or aircraft used for carrying large numbers of soldiers
troop·er /ˈtruːpǝʳ/ *n* **1** [C;A] (the title of) a soldier of the lowest rank in the CAVALRY or the armoured REGIMENT*s* **2** [C] *AmE* a member of a STATE police force **3 swear like a trooper** to swear a great deal
troops /truːps/ *n* [P] soldiers
troop·ship /ˈtruːpˌʃɪp/ *n* [C; *by*+U] a ship for carrying a large number of soldiers
trope /trǝʊp/ *n tech* (a word or phrase used as) a FIGURE OF SPEECH
tro·phy /ˈtrǝʊfi/ *n* **1** a prize given for winning a race, competition, or test of skill **2** something taken after much effort, esp. in war or hunting: *hanging the lion's head on the wall as a trophy*
trop·ic /ˈtrɒpɪk‖ˈtrɑ-/ *n* one of the 2 imaginary lines (lines of LATITUDE) drawn around the world at about 23½° north (**the tropic of Cancer**) and south (**the tropic of Capricorn**) of the imaginary line round the middle of the world (EQUATOR) —see picture at GLOBE
trop·i·cal /ˈtrɒpɪkǝl‖ˈtrɑ-/ *adj* [Wa5] **1** of, related to, concerning, or living in the tropics: *tropical flowers|the tropical sun* **2** very hot: *tropical weather* —**~ly** *adv* [Wa4,5]
trop·ics /ˈtrɒpɪks‖ˈtrɑ-/ *n* [*the*+P] the area between the tropics; hottest part of the earth: *living in the tropics*
trot[1] /trɒt‖trɑt/ *n* **1** [S] (of a horse) a way of moving fairly quickly in which a front foot and the opposite back foot move as a pair; movement between a walk and a GALLOP **2** [C] a ride on a horse moving at this speed **3** [S] a fairly fast human speed between a walk and a run; slow run; quick walk **4** [C] a journey at this speed, esp. for exercise **5 have the trots** also **be on the trot**— *sl* to have DIARRHOEA **6 on the trot** *not fml* **a** in a state of continuous activity: *I've been on the trot all day at work* **b** one after another: *to win 3 races on the trot*
trot[2] *v* **-tt- 1** [I∅;T1] **a** (of a horse or its rider) to move at a TROT[1] (1) **b** to cause (a horse) to move at a TROT[1] (1) **2** [T1] to travel (a distance) at a TROT[1] (1,3) **3** [L9] *often humor & infml* (of a person) to move fairly quickly at a TROT[1] (3); hurry: *I must be trotting along now or I'll miss the bus*
troth /trǝʊθ‖trɔθ, trɑθ, trǝʊθ/ *n* [U] *old use* **1** faithfulness; loyalty: *by my troth* **2** truth: *in troth* —see also PLIGHT **one's troth**
trot out *v adv* [T1a] *infml* to say or write (something well-known already) in an uninteresting unchanged way
Trot·sky·ist /ˈtrɒtskiǝ̇st‖ˈtrɑt-, ˈtrɔt-/ also (*derog*) **Trot·sky·ite** /ˈtrɒtskiaɪt‖ˈtrɑt-, ˈtrɔt-/ (*derog sl*) **Trot**— *adj, n* [Wa5] (of or related to) a person who favours the political principles of Leon Trotsky, esp. his belief in the need for a working class seizure of state power right around the world if SOCIALISM is to be firmly established
trot·ter /ˈtrɒtǝʳ‖ˈtrɑ-/ *n* **1** [C] a horse specially bred and trained for TROTting[1] (1) **2** [C;U] (a) pig's foot used as food
trou·ba·dour /ˈtruːbǝdɔːr, -dʊǝʳ‖-dor, -dʊǝr/ *n* a singer and poet who travelled round the noble courts of Italy and Southern France in the 12th and 13th centuries
trou·ble[1] /ˈtrʌbǝl/ *v* **1** [Wv3,5;T1] to cause (someone) to be anxious, nervous, worried, etc.: *You look troubled; what's worrying you?* **2** [Wv3;T1 (*for*);V3] (esp. in polite expressions) to cause inconvenience to (someone): *I'm sorry to trouble you, but can you tell me the time?|Can I trouble you to shut the door?* (=Please shut it!)|*May I trouble you for the salt?* (=Please pass it to me) **3** [Wv3; I∅,3] to cause inconvenience to oneself: *Don't trouble to write when I'm gone* **4** [Wv3,5;T1] to cause (someone) pain as a disease does: *He's been troubled with a bad back since he was a child* **5** [Wv3,5;T1] to force into irregular or violent movement: *The wind troubled the surface of the lake* **6 fish in troubled waters** to try to win some advantage from a confused and difficult state of affairs **7 I'll trouble you to** (used in rude requests): *I'll trouble you to remember your manners!*
trouble[2] *n* **1** [C;U] (a) difficulty, worry, anxiety,

annoyance, etc.: *to have trouble getting the car started|Paying the rent is the least of my troubles at present* **2** [U] danger; risk; a difficulty or dangerous state of affairs: *The little boy looked in trouble so I swam out to save him* **3** [U (*with*)] the position where one is blamed for doing wrong or thought to have done wrong: *My son's always getting into trouble with the police.|He told a lie rather than get his friend into trouble* **4** [S;U] (an) inconvenience; (something that causes) more than usual work or effort: *I hope we've not put you to any trouble.|Some cakes are very nice to eat but a great trouble to bake* **5** [C;U] (an example of) political or social disorder: *There's been a lot of trouble in that country in the past year* **6** [U] failure to work properly: *The car's got some sort of engine trouble again* **7** [C (*with*)] a fault: *The trouble with you is that you're stupid. That's your trouble!* **8** [C;U] (a) medical condition; illness: *I've got heart trouble but it's nothing serious* **9 ask/look for trouble** to behave so as to cause difficulty or danger for oneself **10 get (a girl) into trouble** *infml* to make (a girl) PREGNANT **11 take trouble** to give oneself work and effort: *We must thank her for taking all that trouble.|You might have taken the trouble to tell us that the bridge was down!*

troub·le·mak·er /ˈtrʌbəlˌmeɪkəʳ/ *n* a person who habitually causes trouble, esp. by making others feel discontented

troub·le·shoot·er /ˈtrʌbəlˌʃuːtəʳ/ *n* a person employed to discover and remove causes of trouble in machines, organizations, etc.

troub·le·some /ˈtrʌbəlsəm/ *adj* **1** causing trouble or anxiety; annoying: *a troublesome child* **2** difficult to handle: *a troublesome state of affairs*

trough /trɒf‖trɔf/ *n* **1** a long narrow boxlike object, esp. for holding water or food for animals —see picture at FARMYARD **2** a long narrow hollow area, as between 2 waves; DEPRESSION **3** *tech* (in METEOROLOGY) a long area (of fairly low pressure) between 2 areas of high pressure **4** a long open pipe in which water that runs off a roof is caught and taken away

trounce /traʊns/ *v* [T1] **1** to beat or punish severely **2** to defeat completely

troupe /truːp/ *n* a company (of singers, actors, dancers, etc.)

troup·er /ˈtruːpəʳ/ *n* **1** a member of a TROUPE **2 a good trouper** a loyal fellow-worker

trou·ser /ˈtraʊzəʳ/ *n* [A] trousers: *a trouser leg|a trouser factory*

trouser press /ˈ·· ·/ *n* an apparatus for keeping a pair of trousers in when they are not being worn, in such a way that the cloth will be kept smooth

trou·sers /ˈtraʊzəz‖-ərz/ *n* [P] **1** an outer garment divided into 2 parts each fitting a leg, worn from the waist down, esp. by men and boys: *These trousers are dirty. I need some clean ones* —see PAIR (USAGE) **2 wear the trousers** *infml* to be in charge: *Who wears the trousers in your house. You or your wife?*

trous·seau /ˈtruːsəʊ, truːˈsəʊ/ *n* **-seaux** *or* **-seaus** the personal possessions, including clothes and articles for the home, that a woman brings with her when she marries

trout /traʊt/ *n* **1** [Wn3;C] any of various types of river (or sometimes sea) fish with darkish spots on their brown skins, highly regarded for sport and food —see picture at FISH[1] **2** [U] the flesh of this fish cooked as food **3** [C] a stupid ugly old woman (esp. in the phr. **old trout**)

trove /trəʊv/ *n* —see TREASURE TROVE

trow·el /ˈtraʊəl/ *n* **1** a tool with a flat blade for spreading cement, PLASTER, etc. **2** a garden tool like a small spade with a curved blade, for digging small holes, lifting up plants, etc. —see picture at GARDEN[1]

troy weight /ˈtrɔɪ weɪt/ *n* [U;E] a British system of measuring the weight of gold, silver, and jewels: *3 pounds troy weight* —compare AVOIRDUPOIS; see WEIGHTS & MEASURES TABLE

tru·an·cy /ˈtruːənsi/ *n* [U] the act of purposely staying away from school without permission

tru·ant /ˈtruːənt/ *n* **1** a pupil who purposely stays away from school without permission **2** *derog* a person who selfishly fails to do his work or duty **3 play truant** also (*AmE infml*) **play hookey**— to stay away from school on purpose, without permission

truce /truːs/ *n* [C;U] (an agreement between 2 enemies for) the stopping of fighting for a period

truck[1] /trʌk/ *n* [U] **1** goods used for BARTER (=exchange in a system in which money is not used) **2** *AmE* vegetables or fruit specially grown for the market; goods produced for sale in a MARKET GARDEN **3** payment made in goods rather than money **4 have no truck with** to have nothing to do with; avoid any business or social connections with

truck[2] *n* [C; (*by*+U)] **1** *BrE* an open railway vehicle for carrying goods: *coal trucks* **2** a simple vehicle for carrying goods, pulled or pushed by hand **3** a fairly large motor vehicle with an open back, used for carrying goods **4** *esp. AmE* LORRY

truck farm /ˈ· ·/ *n AmE* MARKET GARDEN

truck·ing /ˈtrʌkɪŋ/ *n* [U] *AmE* the business of carrying goods on motor vehicles

truck·le bed /ˈtrʌkəl bed/ (*AmE* **trundle bed**)— *n BrE* a low bed on wheels, pushed under another bed when not in use

truckle to *v prep* [Wv3;T1 *no pass.*] to yield weakly to; behave like a slave towards

truc·u·lence /ˈtrʌkjʊləns‖-kjə-/ also **truc·u·len·cy** /ˈtrʌkjʊlənsi‖-kjə-/— *n* [U] the state or quality of being TRUCULENT

truc·u·lent /ˈtrʌkjʊlənt‖-kjə-/ *adj* **1** cruel; fierce; violent **2** bitterly cruel in judgment: *a truculent newspaper article intended to hurt* **3** always willing to quarrel or attack; threatening; not afraid of opposition —**~ly** *adv*

trudge[1] /trʌdʒ/ *v* [L9] to walk with heavy steps, slowly and with effort: *The old man trudged through the deep snow back towards home.|to trudge (for) 20 miles*

trudge[2] *n* a long tiring walk

true[1] /truː/ *adj* [Wa1] **1** in accordance with fact or reality; actual: *a true story|Is the news true?|Is it true you're going abroad for your holidays?|"That singer's beautiful." "True, but she can't sing"* **2** real; not false: *true gold|True love should last for ever* **3** [(*to*)] faithful; loyal: *a true friend|John always stays true to his principles* **4** free from deceit; sincere: *I have a true interest in your future* **5** exact; exactly like an original or standard: *a true copy* **6** proper; correct: *He's religious in the truest sense* **7** unfailing; sure: *a true sign* **8** correctly fitted, placed, or formed: *If the door's not exactly true it won't close properly* **9 come true** to happen just as was wished, expected, dreamt, etc. **10 true to** in accordance with: *Your book is very true to life* **11 true to type** behaving or acting just as one would expect from a person or thing of that type

true[2] *n* [*the*+R] **1** that which is true: *the good, the beautiful, the true* **2 out of true** not having the exact position or correct shape or balance

true[3] *adv* **1** in a true manner; truthfully: *She speaks true* **2** carefully and exactly: *Try to sail straight and true!* **3** without varying from type: *to breed true*

true blue /ˌ· ˈ·/ *n BrE* a completely loyal CONSERVATIVE

true-blue /ˌ· ˈ·◂/ *adj* [Wa5] **1** completely honest or faithful **2** of, being, or related to a TRUE BLUE: *true-blue principles*

true·born /ˌtruːˈbɔːn‖-bɔrn◂/ *adj* [Wa5] actually so by birth; LEGITIMATE: *a trueborn Scot*

true·heart·ed /ˌtruːˈhɑːtɨ̥d◂‖-ˈhɑr-/ *adj* [Wa2] faithful; loyal

true-life /ˌ· ˈ· ◂/ *adj* [Wa5;A] based on fact: *a true-life adventure story*

true·love /ˈtruːlʌv/ *n* the person one loves; SWEETHEART

true up *v adv* [T1] to change (something) slightly in order to give a perfect shape or fit; make TRUE¹ (8)

truf·fle /ˈtrʌfəl/ *n* **1** a type of fleshy blackish or light brown FUNGUS that grows underground and is highly regarded as a food **2** a type of soft sweet, usu. made with RUM

trug /trʌg/ *n* a broad flattish basket used in gardens to carry flowers, tools, etc.

tru·is·m /ˈtruːɪzəm/ *n* a statement of something that is so clearly true that there is no need to mention it

tru·ly /ˈtruːli/ *adv* **1** exactly; in accordance with the truth: *A worm cannot truly be described as an insect* **2** sincerely: *I am truly grateful for all your help* **3** certainly; really: *There was a truly beautiful view from the window* **4 yours truly** (used at the end of a formal letter before the signature)

trump¹ /trʌmp/ *n lit* (a sound made by) a TRUMPET (esp. in the phr. **the last trump**=(the sound of TRUMPETs blown at) the end of the world)

trump² *n* **1** (in card games) any card of a SUIT chosen to be of higher rank than the other 3 SUITs **2** *sl, becoming rare* an excellent dependable person **3 no trump** (in the game of BRIDGE) an offer or attempt to play without any particular SUIT as TRUMPs

trump³ *v* [T1] to beat (a card) or win (a TRICK) by playing a TRUMP²

trump card /ˈ· ·/ *n* **1** an important advantage **2 play one's trump card** to use that which is most advantageous to one's cause in order to improve one's position

trump·e·ry /ˈtrʌmpəri/ *n, adj* [U;A;(B)] *lit* **1** (objects that are) showy but of very little value **2** (ideas, opinions, actions, etc., that are) worthless

trum·pet¹ /ˈtrʌmpɨ̥t/ *n* **1** a brass wind instrument consisting of a long metal tube curved round once or twice and ending in a bell, played by pressing 3 buttons on top of the tube in various combinations —see picture at WIND INSTRUMENT **2** something shaped like the bell-shaped end of this: *The old man puts a trumpet to his ear so that he can hear better* **3** the loud cry of an elephant **4 blow one's own trumpet** to praise oneself

trumpet² *v* **1** [IØ] to play a TRUMPET¹ (1) **2** [IØ] (of an elephant) to make a loud sound **3** [T1] to declare or shout loudly: *She's always trumpeting the cleverness of her son* —**~er** *n*

trumps /trʌmps/ *n* [P] **1** (in card games) a SUIT chosen to be of higher value than the other 3 SUITs **2 turn/come up trumps** to behave in a generous or helpful way, esp. unexpectedly

trump up *v adv* [Wv5;T1] to invent (a reason, charge, etc.) falsely or dishonestly

trun·cate /trʌŋˈkeɪt‖ˈtrʌŋkeɪt/ *v* [Wv5;T1] to shorten by cutting the top or end off (something): (fig.) *a badly truncated report*

trun·cheon /ˈtrʌnʃən/ *n* a short thick stick carried as a weapon by policemen

trun·dle /ˈtrʌndl/ *v* [L9;X9] **a** (of something heavy or awkward on wheels) to move or roll **b** to cause (something heavy or awkward on wheels) to move or roll: *The fruit seller trundled his cart along the street*

trundle bed /ˈ·· ·/ *n AmE* TRUCKLE BED

trunk /trʌŋk/ *n* **1** the thick wooden main stem of a tree —see picture at TREE¹ **2** the human body apart from the head and limbs —see picture at HUMAN² **3** a large case or box in which clothes or belongings are stored or packed for travel **4** the very long round MUSCULAR nose of an elephant, used for reaching leaves, grass, water, etc., and lifting them to the mouth **5** *AmE* BOOT² (2)

trunk call /ˈ· ·/ (*AmE* **long distance call**)— *n BrE* a telephone call made over a long distance

trunk line /ˈ· ·/ *n* **1** a telephone line between distant places **2** the main line of a railway

trunk road /ˈ· ·/ *n* a main road for long-distance travel

trunks /trʌŋks/ *n* [P] a very short trouser-like garment, either tight-fitting or loose, worn by men, esp. for swimming —see PAIR (USAGE)

truss¹ /trʌs/ *v* [T1] **1** [(UP)] to tie up firmly with cord, rope, etc. **2** [(UP)] to prepare (a chicken, duck, etc.) for cooking by tying the legs and wings in place **3** to support (a roof, bridge, etc.) with a TRUSS² (1)

truss² *n* **1** a framework of beams or bars built to support a roof, bridge, etc. **2** a special belt worn to support muscles in a case of HERNIA and prevent it growing or spreading **3** *BrE* a tied parcel of HAY or STRAW

trust¹ /trʌst/ *n* **1** [U (*in*)] firm belief in the honesty, goodness, worth, justice, power, etc., of someone or something; faith: *I don't place any trust in the government's promises* **2** [U] solemn responsibility: *a position of trust* **3** [U] a solemn responsibility given to someone: *to fulfil one's trust* **4** [U] the condition of being given to someone for care, protection, etc.: *I left my pets in trust with a neighbour while I went on holiday* **5** [U] care; keeping: *After my parents' death I was put in my grandmother's trust* **6** [U] the act of holding and controlling property or money for the advantage of someone else: *The money will be held in trust for you until you're 21* **7** [C] a group of people holding and controlling money or property for the advantage of others **8** [C] a property or sum of money held and controlled by someone or a group of people for the advantage of someone else **9** [U] belief in the ability or intention of a person to pay in the future for goods received now; CREDIT: *The goods were supplied on trust* **10** [C] a group of firms that have combined to reduce competition and control prices to their own advantage **11 take on trust** to accept without proof or close examination

trust² *v* **1** [Wv4;T1;V3] to believe in the honesty and worth of (someone or something); have faith in: *You shouldn't trust him, he's dishonest.|Trust my judgment!|You can't trust him to do anything right* **2** [T1;V3] to depend on: *You can't trust the trains (to run on time)* **3** [T1] to allow (someone) to have money or goods and to return or pay for them at a later date: *Can you trust me for a packet of cigarettes until Friday?* **4** [IØ;T5a] to hope: *Everything went all right, I trust.|I trust you enjoyed yourself*

trust·ee /trʌsˈtiː/ *n* **1** a person or firm that holds and controls property or money for the advantage of someone else; person to whom property or money is given in TRUST¹ (6) **2** a member of a group appointed to control the affairs of a company, firm, college, etc.

trust·ee·ship /trʌsˈtiːʃɪp/ *n* **1** [C;U] the position of TRUSTEE **2** [U] government of an area by a country or countries appointed by the United Nations **3** [C] also **trust ter·ri·to·ry** /ˈ· ˌ····/— an area under such government

trust·ful /ˈtrʌstfəl/ also **trust·ing** /ˈtrʌstɪŋ/— *adj* ready to trust others: *the trustful nature of a small child* —**~ly** *adv* —**~ness** *n* [U]

trust fund /ˈ· ·/ *n* money belonging to one person but held and controlled for his advantage by someone else (a TRUSTEE (1))

trust in *v prep* [T1] to have faith in; believe in

trust to *v prep* **1** [D1] to place (someone or something) in the care or keeping of (someone); ENTRUST to **2** [T1] to depend on: *You trust too much to luck/your memory*

trust·wor·thy /ˈtrʌstˌwɜːði‖-ɜr-/ worthy of trust; dependable —**-thiness** *n* [U]

trust·y¹ /ˈtrʌsti/ *adj* [Wa1] *esp. old use* that may be trusted; dependable; faithful

trusty² a prisoner given special rights because of good behaviour in prison

truth /truːθ/ *n* **truths** /truːðz, truːθs/ **1** [U] that which is true; the true facts: *You must always tell the truth* **2** [U] the state or quality of being true: *I don't doubt the truth of his information but I don't approve of the way he uses it* **3** [C] a fact or principle accepted as true or for which proof exists: *the truths of science* **4** [U] sincerity; honesty: *There was no truth in his expressions of friendship* **5 in truth** in fact; really **6 tell the truth and shame the devil** *infml* to speak the truth and pay no attention to one's fear of doing so **7 to tell the truth** *infml* (used for introducing a personal opinion or when admitting something, to mean) to be quite FRANK; I must admit that . . . : *To tell the truth, I don't really like her*

truth·ful /ˈtruːθfəl/ *adj* **1** (of a person) who habitually tells the truth: *a truthful boy* **2** (of a statement, account, etc.) true: *a truthful account of what happened* —**~ly** *adv* —**~ness** *n* [U]

try¹ /traɪ/ *v* **1** [T1,4] to test by use and experience, in order to find the quality, worth, effect, etc.: *Have you tried this new soap?|Have you tried this hotel?|We tried growing our own vegetables but soon found it was harder than we'd imagined* **2** [IØ;T3;(T1)] to attempt: *I don't think I can do it but I'll try.|I've tried time and time again but I still can't do it.|He tried to stand on his head but couldn't.|Try Mrs Jones. She might lend you £1* **3** [T4] to attempt and do; experience: *I tried standing on my head but it gave me a headache* **4** [T1] to attempt to open (a door, window, etc.): *I think the door's locked but I'll try it just in case* **5** [T1] to examine (a person thought guilty or a case) in a court of law: *They're going to try him for murder* **6** [Wv4;T1] to put (someone, his nerves, patience, etc.) to a severe test; stretch (someone's patience, nerves, etc.) almost to the limit; cause to suffer; annoy: *Sometimes you really try me.|I've had a very trying time at work today.|This small print tries my eyes* **7 try and (do)** *not fml* (*not used in verb forms with* tried *or* trying) to try to (do): *You must try and come to the party.|I always try and help her* (compare *I'm always trying to help her*).|*I'll try and telephone you* —see also **try one's** HAND (**at**)

USAGE 1 Note the ways of making this verb stronger: *He* **tried** *hard/very hard/very hard indeed.* 2 Unlike **go and** (GO (31)) the form **try and** cannot be used in all tenses. One can say **Try** *and stop me.*| **Try** *and make me do it.*|**Try** *and get some rest* but not **He* **tried** *and stopped me.* 3 Note the difference between *He* **tried** *to climb the mountain* (but he couldn't).|*He* **tried** *climbing the mountain* (he climbed it, to see what it was like at the top).

try² *n* **1** an attempt: *Let me have a try.|It was a good try but it didn't succeed* **2** (in RUGBY) 4 points won by pressing the ball to the ground behind the opposing team's GOALs, giving one the right to try to kick a GOAL —see picture at RUGBY

try for *v prep* [T1] *BrE* to make an attempt to get or win; compete for

try on *v adv* [T1] **1** to put on (a garment, hat, shoes, etc.) to test the fit, examine the appearance, etc. **2 try it on** *sl* to behave in a bold or disobedient manner, esp. to discover how far such behaviour will be allowed

try-out /ˈ· ·/ *n* [S] *infml* a trial or test of fitness for some purpose

try out *v adv* [T1] to test (something or someone) by use and experience: *The idea seems fine but we need to try it out in practice*

try out for *v adv prep* [T1] *AmE* TRY FOR

tryst /trɪst, traɪst/ *n old use or humor* **1** an appointment between lovers to meet at a secret place or time **2** the meeting or meeting place so arranged

tsar, czar, tzar /zɑːʳ, tsɑːʳ/ *n* [C;A;(N)] (until 1917) the male ruler of Russia

tsa·ri·na, czarina, tzarina /zɑːˈriːnə, tsɑː-/ *n* [C;(A; N)] (until 1917) **1** the female ruler of Russia **2** the wife of the TSAR

tset·se fly, tzetze fly /ˈtetsi flaɪ, ˈtsetsi-, ˈsetsi-/ also **tsetse**— *n* a type of blood-sucking African fly that causes SLEEPING SICKNESS and other serious diseases

T-shirt, tee shirt /ˈtiː ʃɜːt‖-ʃɜrt/ *n* a close-fitting collarless garment for the upper body, with short arms, worn esp. by men

tsp *written abbrev. for:* TEASPOON: *one tsp of salt*

T-square /ˈtiː skweəʳ/ *n* a large ruler shaped like a letter T, used esp. in drawing parallel lines

TT *abbrev. for:* TEETOTAL

tub /tʌb/ *n* **1** a large round usu. wooden vessel, for packing, storing, washing, etc. **2** *infml* the container in which one takes a bath **3** *infml* an awkward slow boat **4** *sl* a fat person **5** TUBFUL

tu·ba /ˈtjuːbə‖ˈtuːbə/ *n* a large brass wind instrument that produces low notes —see picture at WIND INSTRUMENT

tub·by /ˈtʌbi/ *adj* [Wa1] *infml* shortish and fattish

tube /tjuːb‖tuːb/ *n* **1** [C] a hollow round pipe of metal, glass, rubber, etc., used esp. for carrying or holding liquids **2** [C] a small soft metal container, closed at one end and fitted with a cap at the other for holding TOOTHPASTE, paint, etc., which are pushed out of the tube by tightly pressing the end opposite to the cap **3** [C] any hollow pipe or organ in the body: *the* BRONCHIAL *tubes* **4** [*the*+R;C; *by*+U] *BrE* (*sometimes cap.*) UNDERGROUND³: *a tube train|to travel by tube* **5** [C] VALVE (2) **6** [C] CATHODE RAY TUBE

tube·less /ˈtjuːbləs‖ˈtuːb-/ *adj* [Wa5] having no INNER TUBE*s*: *tubeless tyres*

tu·ber /ˈtjuːbəʳ‖ˈtuː-/ *n* a fleshy swollen underground stem, such as the potato, with small BUD*s* on from which new plants grow

tu·ber·cu·lar /tjuːˈbɜːkjʊləʳ‖tuːˈbɜrkjə-/ also **tu·ber·cu·lous** /tjuːˈbɜːkjʊləs‖tuːˈbɜrkjə-/— *adj* [Wa5] of, suffering from, or causing TUBERCULOSIS

tu·ber·cu·lo·sis /tjuːˌbɜːkjʊˈləʊsɪ̈s‖tuːˌbɜrkjə-/ *n* [U] a serious infectious disease that attacks many parts of the body, esp. the lungs

tub·ful /ˈtʌbfʊl/ also **tub**— *n* the amount that a TUB¹ (1) holds

tub·ing /ˈtjuːbɪŋ‖ˈtuː-/ *n* [U] metal, plastic, etc., in the form of a tube

tub-thump·er /ˈ· ˌ··/ *n infml* a violent public speaker who tries to excite his listeners by working on their feelings

tu·bu·lar /ˈtjuːbjʊləʳ‖ˈtuːbjə-/ *adj* [Wa5] of, being, or made of a tube or tubes: *tubular metal furniture|tubular bells*

T.U.C. /ˌtiː juː ˈsiː/ *abbrev. for:* TRADES UNION CONGRESS

tuck¹ /tʌk/ *v* **1** [X9] to put into a convenient

narrow space for protection, safety, etc.: *The bird tucked its head under its wings* **2** [X9] to take the edge or end of (a garment, piece of material, etc.) and put or push into a desired or convenient position, usu. a narrow space: *Tuck your shirt into your trousers* **3** [T1] to sew TUCKs² (1) into (a garment, piece of material, etc.) **4** [Wv5;X9 (AWAY)] to build (a building) in a private almost hidden place: *Our house is tucked away among the trees*

tuck² *n* **1** [C] a flat fold of material sewn into a garment for ornament or to give a special shape **2** [U] *BrE* food, esp. cakes, sweets, etc., as eaten by schoolboys

tuck a·way *v adv* [T1] **1** to store in a safe place: *She's got a lot of money tucked away* **2** *infml* to eat (a lot of food)

tuck·er /ˈtʌkəʳ/ *n* **one's best bib and tucker** *infml* one's best clothes

tuck·er·bag /ˈtʌkəbæg‖-ər-/ *n AustrE* any bag used for carrying food

tuck-in /ˈ· ·/ *n* [*usu. sing.*] *infml* a big meal

tuck in *v adv* **1** [IØ] *not fml* to eat eagerly **2** [T1] TUCK UP: *She tucked the little boy in*

tuck in·to *v prep* [T1] *not fml* to eat (something) eagerly

tuck shop /ˈ· ·/ *n BrE* a shop, esp. at a school, where sweets and cakes are sold

tuck up *v adv* [T1 (*in*)] to make (someone, esp. a child) comfortable in bed by pulling the bed clothes tight: *The children got into bed and then their father came into the bedroom and tucked them up*

-tude /tjuːd‖tuːd/ *suffix* [→*n*] the condition or degree of being: SERVITUDE|MAGNITUDE —compare -NESS

Tues·day /ˈtjuːzdiː‖ˈtuːz-/ *n* **1** [R] the third day of the present week; day before next Wednesday or last Wednesday: *He'll arrive* (*on*) *Tuesday.*|*He'll arrive on Tuesday morning* (=during the morning of next Tuesday) **2** [C] the third day of any week, or of the week that is being spoken of: *I usually go to the cinema on Tuesdays.*|*He arrived on the Tuesday and left on the Thursday* (=arrived on the 3rd day of the week being spoken of).|*He arrived on a Tuesday* (=not a Monday, Wednesday, etc.).| (*esp. AmE*) *She works Tuesdays*

tuft /tʌft/ *n* [(*of*)] a bunch (of hair, feathers, grass, etc.) growing or held closely together at a base —**~ed** *adj* [Wa5]: *a tufted duck*

tug¹ /tʌg/ *v* **-gg-** **1** [T1;IØ (*at*)] to pull hard with force or much effort: *She tugged* (*at*) *the chair until it moved* **2** [X9] to move by pulling with great effort: *The small child tugged the table across the room*

tug² *n* a sudden strong pull

tug·boat /ˈtʌgbəʊt/ also **tug**— *n* a small powerful boat used for guiding large vessels into a port, up rivers, etc. —see picture at SHIP¹

tug-of-war /ˌ· · ˈ·/ *n* [C;U] a test of strength in which 2 teams pull against each other on a rope, each trying to draw the other over the winning line

tu·i·tion /tjuːˈɪʃən‖tuː-/ *n* [U] **1** instruction; teaching **2** the charge made for this, esp. at a college or private school

tu·lip /ˈtjuːlɪ̣p‖ˈtuː-/ *n* **1** a type of garden plant that grows from a BULB and has large showy colourful cup-shaped flowers on top of tall stems **2** the flower of this plant

tulle /tjuːl‖tuːl/ *n* [U] a thin soft silk or nylon netlike material used for making dresses, VEILs, etc.

tum·ble¹ /ˈtʌmbəl/ *v* [Wv3] **1** [L9] to fall suddenly or helplessly; roll over or down quickly or violently: *The old lady tumbled down the stairs* **2** [L9] to move or go into confusion or disorder: *little cats tumbling over each other in their basket*|*The children tumbled off the bus at the park* **3** [Wv4;IØ] to fall rapidly in price: *Tumbling prices have meant reduced profits* **4** [X7,9] to throw about in a confused mass: *to tumble clothes dry in a machine* **5** [Wv4;IØ (DOWN)] to fall to pieces; fall down; COLLAPSE: *The hut tumbled down in the storm* **6** [IØ] to perform GYMNASTIC exercises, esp. rolling and turning **7** [IØ (*to*)] *sl* to understand suddenly: *It was a long time before she tumbled* (*to what I meant*)

tumble² *n* **1** [C] a fall **2** [S] a state of disorder and confusion

tum·ble·down /ˈtʌmbəldaʊn/ *adj* [Wa5] in a condition of near ruin: *a tumbledown old house*

tum·bler /ˈtʌmbləʳ/ *n* **1** a flat-bottomed drinking glass with no handle or stem **2** the part in a lock that must be turned by a key before the lock will open **3** an ACROBAT; GYMNAST

tum·ble·weed /ˈtʌmbəlwiːd/ *n* [U] a type of plant growing in the desert areas of North America whose upper branches fall off in autumn and are blown about by the wind

tum·brel, -bril /ˈtʌmbrɪ̣l/ *n* a type of simple cart used for taking prisoners to the GUILLOTINE in the French REVOLUTION

tu·mes·cent /tjuːˈmesənt‖tuː-/ *adj tech* swollen —**-cence** /tjuːˈmesəns‖tuː-/ *n* [U]

tu·mid /ˈtjuːmɪ̣d‖ˈtuː-/ *adj tech* (of a part of the body) swollen —**~ity** /tjuːˈmɪdɪ̣ti‖tuː-/ *n* [U]

tum·my /ˈtʌmi/ *n infml* stomach: *a tummy ache*

tu·mour, *AmE* **-mor** /ˈtjuːməʳ‖ˈtuː-/ *n* a mass of diseased cells in the body which have divided and increased too quickly, causing swelling and illness

tu·mult /ˈtjuːmʌlt‖ˈtuː-/ *n* [C;U] the confused noise and excitement of a big crowd, fighting, etc.; state of confusion and excitement

tu·mul·tu·ous /tjuːˈmʌltʃuəs‖tuː-/ *adj* disorderly; noisy: *a tumultuous welcome* —**~ly** *adv*

tu·mu·lus /ˈtjuːmjʊləs‖ˈtuːmjə-/ also **barrow**— *n* **-luses** *or* **-li** /laɪ/ a large pile of earth heaped over a grave by people in very ancient (PREHISTORIC) times

tun /tʌn/ *n* **1** a large barrel for holding liquids, esp. wine, beer, etc. **2** a measure equal to 252 GALLONs, used for measuring wine, beer, etc.

tu·na /ˈtjuːnə‖ˈtuːnə/ *n* **1** [Wn2;C] also **tunny**— a type of large sea fish caught in large numbers for food **2** [U] also **tunny, tuna fish** /ˈ·· ·/— the flesh of this fish, usu. sold ready-cooked in tins

tun·dra /ˈtʌndrə/ *n* [U; *the*+R] a cold treeless plain in the far north of Europe, Asia, and North America, frozen hard in winter and often flooded in summer

tune¹ /tjuːn‖tuːn/ *n* **1** a number of musical notes, one after the other, that produce a pleasing pattern of sound; arrangement of musical sounds: *Do you know the tune to this song?* **2** **call the tune** to be in a position to give orders, command, etc. **3** **change one's tune** also **sing another/a different tune**— to change one's opinion, decision, behaviour, etc. **4** **in/out of tune** **a** at/not at the correct musical level (PITCH): *The piano is out of tune* **b** in/not in agreement or sympathy: *His ideas were in tune with the period in which he lived* **5** **to the tune of** to the amount of: *We were robbed to the tune of £5,000*

tune² *v* [Wv5;T1 (UP)] **1** to set (a musical instrument) at the proper musical level (PITCH) **2** to put (an engine) in good working order for top speed and best performance **3** **tune oneself to** to change one's behaviour to match (that of one's surroundings)

tune·ful /ˈtjuːnfəl‖ˈtuːn-/ *adj* having a pleasing tune; pleasant to listen to —**~ly** *adv* —**~ness** *n* [U]

tune in *v adv* [Wv5;T1;IØ:(*to*)] **1** to set (a radio) to receive broadcasts from a particular radio station: *We always tune in at 10 o'clock to hear the news* **2 tuned in (to)** in touch with what people are thinking, saying, feeling, etc.: *A politician must keep tuned in to popular feeling if he is to be successful*

tune·less /ˈtjuːnləs‖ˈtuːn-/ *adj* **1** unmusical; unpleasant to listen to **2** not producing music: *a tuneless old piano* —**~ly** *adv*

tun·er /ˈtjuːnəʳ‖ˈtuː-/ *n* **1** [C] the part of a radio or television that receives the signals and changes them into sound and/or pictures **2** [C9] a person who TUNEs[2] (1) musical instruments of the stated kind: *a piano tuner*

tune-up /ˈ· ·/ *n* an act of tuning (TUNE[2] (2)) an engine

tune up *v adv* [IØ] to set an instrument at the proper musical level (PITCH)

tung·sten /ˈtʌŋstən/ also **wolfram**— *n* [U] a hard metal that is a simple substance (ELEMENT (6)), used esp. in the production of steel

tu·nic /ˈtjuːnɪk‖ˈtuː-/ *n* **1** a loose-fitting short-armed or armless outer garment reaching to the knees, worn by both sexes among the ancient Romans or Greeks **2** a specially-shaped short coat worn by policemen, soldiers, etc., as part of a uniform **3** a loose armless dress, esp. as worn by girls as part of a school uniform **4** a garment like this worn by women for sport, exercise, dancing, etc.

tuning fork /ˈ·· ·/ *n* a small steel instrument, consisting of a stem that divides into 2 and producing a pure musical note of fixed musical level (PITCH) when struck, used in tuning (TUNE[2] (1)) musical instruments

tun·nel[1] /ˈtʌnl/ *n* an underground or underwater passage; passage for a road, railway, etc., through or under a hill, river, town, mountain, etc.

tunnel[2] *v* **-ll-** (*AmE* **-l-**) **1** [T1;IØ] to make a TUNNEL[1] under or through (a hill, river, etc.): *to tunnel under the sea* **2** [T1] to make or form as or like a TUNNEL[1]: *to tunnel a passage* —**~ler** (*AmE* **~er**) *n*

tun·ny /ˈtʌni/ *n* [Wn2] TUNA

tup /tʌp/ *n tech* a male sheep

tup·pence /ˈtʌpəns/ *n BrE sl* TWOPENCE

tup·penny /ˈtʌpni/ *adj* [Wa5;A] *BrE sl* **1** TWOPENNY **2 not give/care a tuppenny damn** not to care at all

tur·ban /ˈtɜːbən‖ˈtɜr-/ *n* **1** a head-covering of Muslim origin, worn by men in parts of North Africa and southern Asia, consisting of a long length of cloth wound tightly round the head **2** a type of small tight-fitting hat worn by women —**~ed** *adj* [Wa5]

tur·bid /ˈtɜːbɨ̣d‖ˈtɜr-/ *adj* **1** (of a liquid) not clear or transparent; muddy; thick **2** confused: *turbid thoughts/feelings* **3** (of smoke, clouds, etc.) heavy; dark; thick —**~ness, ~ity** /tɜːˈbɪdɨ̣ti‖tɜr-/ *n* [U]

tur·bine /ˈtɜːbaɪn‖ˈtɜrbɨ̣n, -baɪn/ *n* an engine or motor in which the pressure of a liquid or gas, usu. at very high temperatures, drives a special wheel and thus changes into circular movement

tur·bo·jet /ˈtɜːbəʊdʒet‖ˈtɜr-/ *n* **1** a powerful engine that produces forward movement by forcing out a stream of hot air and gases behind itself, esp. used in aircraft **2** an aircraft getting power from such an engine

tur·bo·prop /ˈtɜːbəʊprɒp‖ˈtɜrbəʊprɑp/ *n* **1** a TURBINE engine that drives a PROPELLER **2** an aircraft getting power from such an engine

tur·bot /ˈtɜːbɒt, -bət‖ˈtɜrbət/ *n* **1** [Wn2;C] a type of large European fish with a flat diamond-shaped body, highly regarded as food **2** [U] the flesh of this fish eaten as food

tur·bu·lence /ˈtɜːbjʊləns‖ˈtɜrbjə-/ also **tur·bu·len·cy** /-si/— *n* [U] **1** the state of being TURBULENT **2** irregular and violent movement of the air: *The flight was very uncomfortable because of turbulence*

tur·bu·lent /ˈtɜːbjʊlənt‖ˈtɜrbjə-/ *adj* violent; disorderly; uncontrolled; stormy: *turbulent currents/weather/winds|a turbulent period of history|a turbulent crowd*

turd /tɜːd‖tɜrd/ *n* **1** [C] *taboo* a piece of solid waste material passed from the body **2** [C; (*you*) N] *taboo sl* an offensive person

tu·reen /tjʊˈriːn‖təˈriːn/ *n* a large deep dish with a lid, from which soup is served at table

turf[1] /tɜːf‖tɜrf/ *n* **-s** *or* **turves** /tɜːvz‖tɜrvz/ **1** [U] the surface of the soil with the grass and roots growing in it **2** [C] a piece of this **3** [C] a block or piece of PEAT dug to be burnt **4** [*the*+R] **a** horseracing **b** the grassy course over which horses race

turf[2] *v* [T1] to cover (a piece of land) with TURF[1] (1)

turf ac·coun·tant /ˈ· ·,··/ *n* BOOKMAKER

turf out *v adv* [T1] *infml* to throw out; get rid of: *He's been turfed out of the club for not paying for his drinks*

tur·gid /ˈtɜːdʒɨ̣d‖ˈtɜr-/ *adj* **1** swollen, as by a liquid or inner pressure **2** (of language or style) too solemn and self-important —**~ity** /tɜːˈdʒɪdɨ̣ti‖tɜr-/ *n* [U] —**~ly** *adv*

tur·key /ˈtɜːki‖ˈtɜrki/ *n* **1** [C] a type of large bird bred and kept on farms for its meat which is highly regarded as food, esp. for Christmas —see picture at DOMESTIC ANIMAL **2** [U] the flesh of this bird eaten cooked as food **3 cold turkey** *sl* **a** a method of curing drug dependence by stopping the drug completely and at once (esp. in the phr. **go cold turkey**) **b** the unpleasant sick feeling caused by doing this **4 talk turkey** *infml, esp. AmE* to speak seriously and plainly, esp. about business matters

Turk·ish /ˈtɜːkɪʃ‖ˈtɜr-/ *adj* [Wa5] of Turkey, its people, or their language

Turkish bath /,·· ˈ·/ *n* a type of bath in which one sits in a very hot steamy room, then washes the body thoroughly, and has a MASSAGE

Turkish de·light /,·· ·ˈ·/ *n* [U] a very sweet pink or white jelly-like substance covered in chocolate or powder sugar, eaten in lumps as a sweet

tur·me·ric /ˈtɜːmərɪk‖ˈtɜr-/ *n* [U] **1** a type of Asian plant **2** the yellowish root of this plant crushed to a fine powder and used for giving a special taste and colour to food, esp. curries (CURRY[2])

tur·moil /ˈtɜːmɔɪl‖ˈtɜr-/ *n* [S;U] a state of confusion, excitement, and trouble

turn[1] /tɜːn‖tɜrn/ *v* **1** [IØ;T1] to (cause to) move round a fixed point: *The wheel turned slowly.|Turn the hands of the clock until they point to 9 o'clock* **2** [IØ;T1] to (cause to) move round or partly round: *to turn a key in the lock* **3** [T1] to do or perform by moving round a fixed point: *She turned a neat circle on the ice* **4** [IØ (OVER)] to roll from side to side or backwards and forwards: *My husband* TOSS*ed and turned all night. He couldn't sleep because of the heat* **5** [IØ;T1] to (cause to) change direction: *to turn the car into a narrow street|The car turned into the hotel entrance.|The ball turned sharply when it hit the ground.|*(fig.) *Her condition turned for the worse* **6** [T1] to go round: *The car turned the corner* **7** [L9] to direct oneself in a particular direction: *Turn right here and left at the end of the street.|She turned away and wept.|*(fig.) *He turned to crime* (=became a criminal) **8** [IØ (ROUND)] to bend round; look round: *He turned and waved* **9** [X9] to aim; point; set or direct in a particular direction: *The police turned their guns on the bank robbers as they ran away* **10** [X;L:9] **a** to cause (one's attention, interest, mind, etc.) to be directed towards or away from something: *He turned his thoughts to home* **b** (of one's attention, interest, mind, etc.) to be directed towards or away from something: *His attention turned to the pretty young girl* **11** [X7;L1,7] to (cause to) become: *In autumn the leaves turn brown.|This heat will turn the grass brown.|a Christian turned Buddhist|to turn thief|He turns nasty if you laugh at him* **12** [T1;IØ] to (cause to) become sour: *The heat's turned the milk* **13** [T1] to shape (wood or metal); form: *to turn wood on a* LATHE **14** [T1] to hurt (one's ankle) by twisting **15** [T1;IØ] to (cause to) feel uncomfortable, sick, etc.: *Fatty food turns my stomach* **16** [T1 (*from, into*);L9 esp. *from, into*] to change the form or nature (of): *Success had turned him from a kind gentle person into a nasty unfair employer.|She turned her old dress into a skirt.|Don't let all this praise turn your head* (=make you become proud) **17** [Wv5,6;T1] to become; reach; pass (a certain age, time, amount, etc.): *a man turned 40|It's just turned 3 o'clock* (=is just after 3 o'clock) **18** [T1] to get by buying or selling; gain: *to turn a small profit* **19** [T1] to PLOUGH (the soil, field, etc.) **20** [Wv5;T1] to form or express gracefully: *a nicely-turned phrase|her well-turned ankles* **21** [X9 esp. AWAY, OUT] to cause to go; send; drive: *My father would turn me out if he knew I took drugs* **22** [X9] to throw into disorder or confusion: *The robbers had turned the room upside down* **23** [T1;IØ] to (cause to) change position so that the bottom becomes the top, the hidden side uncovered, the inner side the outer, etc.: *to turn the page|The page won't turn; it seems to be stuck.|to turn a worn collar* **24** [X9 esp. IN, DOWN, BACK] to fold: *He turned the corner of the page down so that he could find his place* —see also TURN AGAINST, TURN AWAY, TURN BACK, TURN DOWN, TURN IN, TURN OFF, TURN ON, TURN OUT, TURN OVER, TURN OVER TO, TURN TO[1,2], TURN UP

turn[2] *n* **1** [C] an act of turning; single movement completely round a fixed point **2** [C] a change of direction: *a turn in the road/river* **3** [*the*+R (*of*)] a point of change in time: *at the turn of the century* **4** [S] a movement or development in direction: *a turn for the worse|an unusual turn of events* **5** [U] an amount of turning: *There's a lot of turn in this* WICKET (=the ball will change direction sharply after hitting it) **6** [C,C3] a rightful chance or duty to do something; place or appointed time in a particular order: *It's my turn to drive next.|You've missed your turn so you'll have to wait* **7** [S] a particular style, habit, or tendency: *He's got an artistic turn so he's going to art college* **8** [S] a period of action or activity: *a turn at the wheel* **9** [C9] a deed or action with the stated effect: *a good turn* **10** [S] *infml* a shock: *You gave me quite a turn when you shouted out like that* **11** [C] *infml* an attack of illness: *She's had one of her turns again* **12 at every turn** in every place; at every moment **13 by turns** also **turn and turn about**— one after another; in order **14 on the turn a** about to turn or change **b** *not fml* (of milk) on the point of becoming sour **15 out of turn a** out of the correct order **b** at an unsuitable time or in an unsuitable way: *I hope I haven't spoken out of turn; I didn't know it was supposed to be secret* **16 take turns** to do something in regular order: *We took turns at driving the car* **17 to a turn** (esp. of food) perfectly cooked

turn·a·bout /ˈtɜːnəbaʊt‖ˈtɜrn-/ *n* an act of turning in a different or opposite direction: (fig.) *the government's sudden turnabout on unemployment*

turn a·gainst *v prep* **1** [T1] to become opposed to or an enemy of (someone or something) **2** [D1] to cause (someone) to become opposed to or an enemy of (someone or something)

turn a·way *v adv* **1** [T1] to refuse one's sympathy, help, or support to (someone) **2** [T1] to refuse to admit **3** [IØ] to refuse to look at something or someone

turn back *v adv* **1** [T1;IØ] to (cause to) return **2** [T1] to fold (esp. the corner of a page): *Turn the page back and it will mark your place*

turn·coat /ˈtɜːnkəʊt‖ˈtɜrn-/ *n* [C;N] *derog* a person who changes his party, principles, or loyalty

turn·cock /ˈtɜːnkɒk‖ˈtɜrnkɑk/ *n BrE* STOPCOCK

turn down *v adv* [T1] **1** to lessen the force, strength, loudness, etc., of (something) by using controls: *Turn that radio down at once!* **2** to refuse (a request, person, etc.): *I'll have to turn down your offer.|She turned him down!*

turn·er /ˈtɜːnə^r‖ˈtɜr-/ *n* a person who shapes wood or metal on a LATHE

turn in *v adv* **1** [IØ] *infml* to go to bed **2** [T1] to deliver (a person or thing) to the police **3** [T1] to give back; return: *You must turn in your uniform when you leave the army* **4** [T1] *esp. AmE* to hand in; give in: *This is a poor piece of work you've turned in*

turn·ing /ˈtɜːnɪŋ‖ˈtɜr-/ *n* a place where one road branches off from another

turning point /ˈ·· ·/ *n* a point in time at which a very important change takes place: *a turning point in our country's industrial development*

tur·nip /ˈtɜːnəp‖ˈtɜr-/ *n* **1** [C] a type of plant grown for its large round fleshy yellowish or white root **2** [C] the root of this plant used as a vegetable or for cattle food **3** [U] this root eaten, usu. cooked, as food

turn·key /ˈtɜːnkiː‖ˈtɜrn-/ *n now rare* a person who has charge of a prison's keys; JAILER

turn-off /ˈ· ·/ *n AmE* a smaller road branching off from a main road

turn off *v adv* **1** [Wv5;T1;(IØ)] to stop the flow of (water, gas, etc. in a pipe) by screwing a TAP tighter **2** [Wv5;T1;(IØ)] to stop (a radio, television, light, etc.), esp. by using a button or SWITCH —see OPEN (USAGE) **3** [T1;IØ] *infml* to (cause to) lose interest: *Popular music really turns me off* **4** [IØ;T1] to leave (one road) for another: *We turned off at Birmingham*

turn on[1] *v adv* **1** [Wv5;T1;(IØ)] to cause (water, gas, etc., in a pipe) to flow by unscrewing a TAP **2** [Wv5;T1;(IØ)] to start (a radio, light, etc.), esp. by using a button or SWITCH: (fig.) *She turns on her charm whenever she wants anything* —see OPEN (USAGE) **3** [T1] also **turn up·on**— to attack (someone) suddenly and without warning **4** [Wv5;T1] *sl* to excite or interest (a person) strongly, and often sexually **5** [Wv5;T1;IØ] *sl* to (cause to) have a very strong and unusual experience, esp, by taking a drug for the first time

turn on[2] *v prep* [T1] to depend on: *The success of a party turns on the guests invited*

turn·out /ˈtɜːnaʊt‖ˈtɜrn-/ *n* **1** [C9, esp. *of, usu. sing.*] the number of people who attend a meeting; people in attendance: *a poor turnout|They usually get a turnout of 500 and more at their union meetings* **2** [C] the manner or style in which a person is dressed: *a colourful turnout* **3** [C] an occasion on which one empties all the unwanted things from a room, drawer, etc. **4** [C] *AmE* a wide place in a narrow road where cars can pass or park **5** [S9] the amount of goods produced by a worker or factory; OUTPUT: *a large turnout*

turn out *v adv* **1** [T1] to stop (a gas, oil, or electric light, heating apparatus, etc.) **2** [T1] to drive out; send away **3** [IØ] to come out or gather as for a meeting, public event, etc.: *Crowds turned out for the procession* **4** [T1] to produce: *This factory can turn out 100 cars a day* **5** [T1] **a** to clear or empty (the contents) from a cupboard, drawer, etc. **b** to clear or empty the contents from (a cupboard, drawer, etc.) **6** [L1,3,7] to happen to be in the end: *His statement turned out to be false.|The party turned out a success.|He turned out to live in Hastings.|It's turned out nice and sunny again*

turn·o·ver /'tɜːnˌəʊvəʳ||'tɜrn-/ *n* **1** [C] an act of turning over **2** [S9, esp. *of*] the number of times a particular article is sold during a particular period **3** [S9, esp. *of*] the amount of business done in a particular period: *a turnover of £5,000 a week* **4** [S9] the number of workers that are hired by a firm to fill the places of workers who have left in a particular period: *a large turnover because of dissatisfied workers* **5** [C;U:9] a small PIE made by spreading some fruit on half of a round or square piece of pastry and then turning the other half over to cover it: *an apple turnover*

turn o·ver *v adv* **1** [T1] to think about; consider **2** [T1;IØ] **a** to cause (an engine) to run at lowest speed **b** (of an engine) to run at lowest speed **3** [T1 (*to*)] to deliver (someone or something) to the police **4** [T1] to do business or sell goods worth (the stated amount): *We turn over £1,000 every week*

turn over to *v adv prep* [D1] to give the control of (something) to (someone)

turn·pike /'tɜːnpaɪk||'tɜrn-/ also **pike, turnpike road** /ˌ·· '·/— *n AmE* a special road for the use of fast-travelling vehicles, esp. such a road which one has to pay to use

turn·stile /'tɜːnstaɪl||'tɜrn-/ *n* a small gate with 4 arms at right angles to each other, spinning round on a central post, set in an entrance to admit people one at a time, usu. after payment

turn·ta·ble /'tɜːnˌteɪbəl||'tɜrn-/ *n* **1** a large flat round table, sunk into the ground to be level with the surface, onto which railway engines run to be turned round or matched to different tracks on which they are supposed to run **2 a** the round spinning surface on which a record is placed to be played **b** a machine, including such a round surface, for spinning a record —see picture at SOUND[3]

turn to[1] *v prep* [T1] **1** to go to for help, advice, sympathy, comfort, etc.: *Who can I turn to in my hour of need?* **2** to look at (the stated page) in a book

turn to[2] *v adv* [IØ] to begin work; work: *The committee turned to and soon produced a plan*

turn-up /'· ·/ *n* **1** *AmE* **cuff**—a narrow band of cloth turned upwards at the bottom of a trouser leg **2** also **turn-up for the book** /ˌ· · · · '·/— *infml* an unexpected and surprising event

turn up *v adv* **1** [T1] to find: *The police have turned up a lot of new information about the wanted man* **2** [IØ] to be found: *The missing bag turned up, completely empty, in the lake* **3** [T1] to uncover by digging **4** [T1] to shorten (a garment) by folding up the bottom **5** [IØ] to arrive; make one's appearance: *She turns up late for everything* **6** [T1] to increase the force, strength, loudness, etc., of (something) by using controls **7** [IØ] to happen, esp. unexpectedly: *Don't worry, something's sure to turn up* **8** [T1] *BrE sl* to cause to be sick **9 turn up one's nose at (someone or something)** *infml* to suggest by one's behaviour and actions that (someone or something) is not good enough for one

tur·pen·tine /'tɜːpəntaɪn||'tɜr-/ also (*infml*) **turps** /tɜːps||tɜrps/— *n* [U] a thin oil made from the wood of certain trees, used for removing unwanted paint from clothes, brushes, etc., for mixing with paint to make it thinner, and in medicine

tur·pi·tude /'tɜːpɨ̣tjuːd||'tɜrpɨ̣tuːd/ *n* [U] shameful wickedness: *moral turpitude*

tur·quoise[1] /'tɜːkwɔɪz, -kwɑːz||'tɜrkwɔɪz/ *n* [C;U] (a shaped piece of) a mineral that is bluish-green or greenish-blue in colour and is regarded as precious

turquoise[2] *adj, n* [B;U] (of) the colour of TURQUOISE[1]

tur·ret /'tʌrɨ̣t/ *n* **1** a small tower, usu. at an angle of a larger building and often ornamental or for defence —see picture at CASTLE[1] **2** (on a TANK (2), plane, warship, etc.) a low heavily-armoured steel DOME, that spins round to allow its guns to be aimed in any direction

tur·tle /'tɜːtl||'tɜrtl/ *n* [Wn1] **1** any of various types of COLD-BLOODED animal of various sizes, living on land or esp. in water and having a soft body covered by a hard horny shell into which the head, legs, and tail can be pulled for protection —see picture at REPTILE **2 turn turtle** (of a ship) to turn over; CAPSIZE

tur·tle·dove /'tɜːtldʌv||'tɜr-/ *n* a type of wild bird (a DOVE) with a pleasing soft cry and a white-edged tail

tur·tle·neck /'tɜːtlnek||'tɜr-/ *n esp. AmE* **1** POLO NECK **2** a garment (esp. a SWEATER) with one of these

tush /tʌʃ/ *interj now rare* (an expression of dissatisfaction usu. mixed with blame)

tusk /tʌsk/ *n* a very long pointed tooth, usu. one of a pair, that comes out beyond the mouth in certain animals such as the elephant

tusk·er /'tʌskəʳ/ *n infml* an elephant

tus·sle[1] /'tʌsəl/ *v* [Wv3;IØ (*with*)] *infml* to fight roughly without weapons; struggle roughly

tussle[2] *n infml* a rough struggle or fight

tus·sock /'tʌsək/ *n* a small thick mass of grass

tut *interj* the sound of t made by sucking rather than explosion, and often read as /tʌt/, used for expressing slight disapproval or annoyance: *Tut (tut)! I've got some chalk on my coat*

tu·te·lage /'tjuːtɨ̣lɪdʒ||'tuː-,/ *n* **1** [U] responsibility for someone, his education, property, actions, etc., protection; GUARDIANship **2** [U;S] the state or period of being under someone's care and protection; state or period of being under a GUARDIAN

tu·te·la·ry /'tjuːtɨ̣ləri||'tuːtɨ̣leri/ also **tu·te·lar** /'tjuːtɨ̣ləʳ||'tuː-/— *adj* acting as someone or something that protects or looks after

tu·tor[1] /'tjuːtəʳ||'tuː-/ *n* **1** a teacher who gives private instruction to a single pupil or a very small class and who sometimes lives with the family of his pupil **2** (in British universities and colleges) a teacher who directs the studies of a number of students whom he also meets separately

tutor[2] *v* **1** [T1;(IØ):(*in*)] to act as a TUTOR[1] (1) to **2** [T1] to train in obedience: *to tutor a horse*

tu·to·ri·al[1] /tjuː'tɔːrɪəl||tuː'torɪəl/ *adj* [Wa5] of or related to a TUTOR[1] or his duties

tutorial[2] *n* (esp. in British universities and colleges) a period of instruction given by a TUTOR[1] (2)

tut·ti frut·ti /ˌtuːti 'fruːti/ *n* [U] ice cream with very small pieces of mixed fruit and sometimes crushed nuts mixed in

tut-tut[1] /ˌtʌt 'tʌt/ *interj* TUT

tut-tut[2] *v* **-tt-** [IØ;T1] to express impatience, annoyance, disapproval, etc., at (someone or something) by saying TUT-TUT

tu·tu /'tuːtuː/ *n* a short skirt made of many folds of stiffened material worn by women BALLET dancers

tu-whit tu-whoo /tə ˌwɪt tə 'wuː/ *interj* the sound made by an OWL

tux·e·do /tʌk'siːdəʊ/ also (*infml*) **tux** /tʌks/— *n* **-dos** *AmE* DINNER JACKET

TV *abbrev. for:* television

twad·dle /'twɒdl||'twɑdl/ *n* [U] foolish talk or writing; nonsense

twain /tweɪn/ *n old use & poet* a pair; set of 2: *"East is East, and West is West, and never the twain shall meet"* (R. Kipling)
twang¹ /twæŋ/ *n* **1** a quick ringing sound such as that made by pulling then suddenly freeing a very tight string or wire **2** a quality of sound of human speech produced by pronouncing the words at the very back of the mouth or through the nose
twang² *v* [IØ;T1] to (cause to) make a TWANG¹ (1): *"The next person to twang his ruler will be punished," shouted the teacher*
'twas /twɒz‖twɑz/ *contr. of* (*old use or poet*) it was —see CONTR. (USAGE)
twat /twɒt, twæt‖twɑt/ *n* [C; *you*+N] *taboo sl* a nasty unpleasant person —compare TWIT²
tweak¹ /twiːk/ *v* [T1] to seize, pull, and twist (the ear or nose) with a sudden movement
tweak² *n* a sudden pull and twist of the nose or ear; act of TWEAKing¹
twee /twiː/ *adj BrE infml* too delicate; unpleasantly DAINTY
tweed /twiːd/ *n* [U] a type of coarse woollen cloth woven from threads of several different colours: *a tweed suit*
tweeds /twiːdz/ *n* [P] (a suit of) TWEED clothes
tweed·y /'twiːdi/ *adj* [Wa1] **1** of or like TWEED **2** dressed frequently in TWEEDS: *She's a tweedy country type* **3** informal, or seeming to show a liking for the outdoors in habits or life style: *tweedy ladies with thick leather walking shoes*
'tween /twiːn/ *prep poet* between
tweet /twiːt/ *v, n* [IØ;C] (to make) the short weak high noise of a small bird; CHIRP
tweet·er /'twiːtəʳ/ *n* a LOUDSPEAKER that reproduces high radio or recorded sounds
twee·zers /'twiːzəz‖-ərz/ *n* [P] a small tool made from 2 narrow pieces of metal joined at one end, used for picking up, pulling out, and handling very small objects —see PAIR (USAGE) and picture at MEDICAL¹ —**tweezer** *n* [A]: *the tweezer handle*
twelfth /twelfθ/ *determiner, adv, n, pron* [see NUMBER TABLE 3] 12th
twelve /twelv/ *determiner, n, pron* [see NUMBER TABLE 1] (the number) 12
twelve·month /'twelvmʌnθ/ *n* [S] *not fml esp. BrE* a year
twen·ty /'twenti/ *determiner, n, pron* [see NUMBER TABLE 1] (the number) 20 —**-tieth** *determiner, n, pron, adv* [see NUMBER TABLE 3]
twenty-one /ˌ·· '·◂/ *determiner, n, pron* **1** [see NUMBER TABLE 1] (the number) 21 **2** [U] *AmE* PONTOON² (1)
twerp, twirp /twɜːp‖twɜrp/ *n* [C; *you*+N] *sl* an annoying unpleasant person; silly fool
twice /twaɪs/ *predeterminer, adv* [Wa5] 2 times: *I've read the book twice.|I work twice as hard as you.|Since his holiday he's been twice the man he was* (=he's been a lot stronger, better, more able, etc., since his holiday).|*He eats twice what you eat/twice the amount that you eat.|twice a day|twice daily|"I've only met her once or twice"* (SEU S.) —see also THINK **twice**
twice-told /ˌ· '·◂/ *adj* [Wa5;A] already told before; well-known (esp. in the phr. **a twice-told tale**)
twid·dle¹ /'twɪdl/ *v* [Wv3] **1** [T1] to move (the fingers) about aimlessly **2** [T1;IØ (*with*)] to play with (something) purposelessly with the hands: *Stop twiddling your pencil!|to twiddle with one's hair* —see also **twiddle one's** THUMBs
twiddle² *n* [S] an act of twiddling (TWIDDLE¹); purposeless movement of the fingers
twig¹ /twɪg/ *n* a small thin woody stem branching off from a branch on a tree or bush —**twiggy** *adj* [Wa1]
twig² *v* **-gg-** [IØ;T6a] *BrE sl* to understand
twi·light /'twaɪlaɪt/ *n* [U] **1** the time when night is about to become day or (more usually) day night **2** the faint darkish light in the sky during this time **3** a period or condition of decay, failure, etc., before or following one of growth, glory, success, etc.: *the twilight years of the Roman empire*
twill /twɪl/ *n* [U] strong cloth woven to have parallel sloping lines across its surface
twin¹ /twɪn/ *n* **1** either of 2 children born of the same mother at the same time: *The brothers looked so like each other that many people thought they were twins.|Jean and John are twins.|my twin sister* **2** either of 2 people or things closely related or connected, or very like each other: *twin towns*
twin² *v* **-nn-** [Wv5;T1 (*with*)] to join (a town) closely with another town in another country to encourage friendly relations: *Harlow in England is twinned with Stavanger in Norway*
twin bed /ˌ· '·/ *n* [*usu. pl.*] either of a pair of single beds in a room for 2 people —**twin-bedded** /ˌ· '··◂/ *adj* [Wa5]: *a twin-bedded room*
twine¹ /twaɪn/ *n* [U] strong cord or string made by twisting together 2 or more threads or strings
twine² *v* **1** [Wv4;L9] to twist; wind: *The stems twined round the tree trunk* **2** [T1] to twist; wind: *to make a rope by twining strings* **3** [T1] to make by twisting or winding
twinge /twɪndʒ/ *n* a sudden sharp pain (in the body or mind): *a twinge of conscience/toothache*
twin·kle¹ /'twɪŋkəl/ *v* [Wv3,4;IØ] **1** to shine with an unsteady light that rapidly changes from bright to faint: *the twinkling light of the stars* **2** [(*with*)] (of the eyes) to be bright with cheerfulness, amusement, pleasure, etc. **3** (of the eyelids, feet in dancing, etc.) to move rapidly up and down
twinkle² *n* [(*the*) S] **1** a repeated momentary bright shining of light **2** a brightness in the eyes as from cheerfulness, pleasure, amusement, etc.: *a twinkle of delight* **3** TWINKLING (1)
twin·kling /'twɪŋklɪŋ/ *n* **1** [S] a moment; very short period of time **2 in the twinkling of an eye** in a moment
twin set /'· ˌ·/ *n BrE* a woman's JUMPER² and CARDIGAN of the same colour and style, made to be worn together
twirl¹ /twɜːl‖twɜrl/ *v* [IØ;T1] **1** to (cause to) turn round and round quickly; (cause to) spin **2** to (cause to) curl: *She twirled his hair round her fingers* —**~er** *n*
twirl² *n* a sudden quick spin or circular movement —**~y** *adj* [Wa1]
twirp /twɜːp‖twɜrp/ *n* [C; *you*+N] *sl* TWERP
twist¹ /twɪst/ *v* **1** [T1 (TOGETHER)] to wind (a number of threads, stems, etc.) together: *to make a rope by twisting threads* **2** [T1] to make (something) by doing this: *to twist a rope* **3** [X9,esp. *round*] to wind (rope, cord, etc.) around something: *She twisted her hair round her fingers to make it curl* **4** [IØ] to move in a winding course: *a stream twisting across the fields* **5** [T1] to turn: *Twist the handle to the right and the box will open* **6** [L9] to move with a bending turning movement: *The dancer twisted sexily to the music* **7** [Wv5;T1] to hurt (a joint or limb) by pulling and turning sharply as in an accident **8** [IØ;T1] to (cause to) change shape by bending, curling, turning, etc.: *His mouth twisted down at the corners as though he was going to cry.|The child twisted the wire into the shape of a star* **9** [X9, esp. OFF] to pull or break off by turning and bending forcefully: *to twist an apple off a tree* **10** [T1] to change the true or intended meaning of (a statement, words, etc.): *The police twisted my words to make me look guilty* **11** [IØ] to dance the TWIST² (7) **12 twist somebody's arm a** to

bend somebody's arm up and behind the back to cause pain **b** to persuade someone to do what one wants with friendly pressure **13 twist (somebody) round one's little finger** to be able to get (someone) to do what one wants

twist² *n* **1** [C] an act of twisting: *gave an unintended twist to my words* **2** [C;(U)] something, such as thread, rope, etc., made by twisting 2 or more lengths together: *a twist of tobacco* (=a roll of tobacco leaves twisted together) **3** [C;(U)] a twisted baked piece of pastry or loaf of bread **4** [C9] a particular tendency of mind or character: *a criminal twist* **5** [C] a bend: *a road with a lot of twists in it* **6** [C] an unexpected change or development: *a strange twist of fate/events* **7** [C;U] (a) special spinning movement given to a ball when throwing to make it take a curved path **8** [*the*+R] a dance, popular in the 1960s, in which the dancers twist arms, legs, and bottom in time with fast noisy music, but remain in the same place —**twisty** *adj* [Wa1]: *a twisty road*

twist·er /ˈtwɪstəʳ/ *n* **1** a dishonest person who cheats other people **2** a difficult job; difficulty: *Our teacher set us some real twisters in the examinations* —see also TONGUE TWISTER **3** *AmE infml* a TORNADO or WHIRLWIND **4** a person who twists, esp. one who dances the TWIST² (7) **5** a thing that twists, esp. a ball with a forward and spinning movement

twit¹ /twɪt/ *v* **-tt-** [T1 (*about, on, with*)] *not fml* to make fun of (someone) because of behaviour, a mistake, a fault, etc.

twit² *n* [C; *you*+N] *sl* a stupid fool

twitch¹ /twɪtʃ/ *v* **1** [T1;I∅] to (cause to) move suddenly and quickly, usu. without conscious control: *The horse twitched its ears.|His face twitched with pain* **2** [T1] also **twitch at**— to give a sudden quick pull to (something): *The wind twitched the paper out of my hand.|I felt someone twitch at my coat* —**~er** *n*

twitch² *n* **1** a repeated short sudden movement of a muscle, done without conscious control —compare TIC **2** a sudden quick pull

twit·ter¹ /ˈtwɪtəʳ/ *v* [I∅] **1** (of a bird) to make a number of short rapid sounds **2** [(ON and/or *about*)] (of a person) to talk rapidly, as from nervous excitement: *always twittering on about some unimportant difficulty* —**~er** *n*

twitter² *n* **1** [U;(*the*) S] short high rapid sounds made by birds; sound of TWITTERing¹ (1) **2** [S] a state of nervous excitement **3 all of a twitter** in a very excited state —**~y** *adj*

twixt /twɪkst/ *prep old use & poet* between

two /tuː/ *determiner, n, pron* **twos** [see NUMBER TABLE 1] **1** (the number) 2 **2 in two** into 2 parts: *cut it in two* **3 one or two** a few: *I've invited one or two friends round this evening* **4 put two and two together** to calculate the meaning of what one sees or hears: *"How did you know I was going abroad for my holidays?" "I saw you had a travel book about Spain, and put two and two together"* **5 two can play at that game** (used as a threat to someone who has been unfair, unkind, etc., to one)

two-bit /ˈ· ·/ *adj* [Wa5;A] *AmE sl* of small importance; INSIGNIFICANT

two-edged /ˌ· ˈ··◂/ *adj* [Wa5] **1** having 2 cutting edges **2** having 2 possible meanings or results, one favourable and one unfavourable

two·faced /ˌtuːˈfeɪst◂/ *adj* [Wa5] deceitful; insincere; HYPOCRITICAL

two-hand·ed /ˌ· ˈ··◂/ *adj* [Wa5] **1** used with both hands: *a heavy two-handed sword* **2** (esp. of a tool) needing or worked by 2 people: *a two-handed* SAW **3** having, or able to work effectively with, 2 hands

two·pence, *BrE* also **tuppence** /ˈtʌpəns‖ˈtʌpəns, ˈtuːpens/ *n* **1** [U] 2 pence (old or new) **2** [C] also **twopenny piece** /ˌ·· ˈ·/— a British coin worth 2 new pence **3 not care twopence** *infml* not to care at all

two·penny, *BrE* also **tuppenny** /ˈtʌpəni‖ˈtʌpəni, ˈtuːpeni—/ *adj* [Wa5;A] **1** costing 2 pence: *a twopenny ticket* **2** also **twopenny-half·penny** /ˌ·· ˈ··/— almost worthless; of very little value

two-piece¹ /ˌ· ˈ·◂/ *adj* [Wa5;A] consisting of 2 matching parts, as a suit: *a two-piece suit*

two-piece² /ˈ· ·/ *n* a matching pair of outer garments to be worn together

two-ply /ˈ· ˌ·/ *adj, n* [Wa5] consisting of 2 sets of thread or 2 thicknesses

two·some /ˈtuːsəm/ *n* [*usu. sing.*] *infml* a group of 2 people or things: *John and Helen make a nice twosome, don't you think?*

two-step /ˈ· ·/ *n* (a piece of music for) a dance with long sliding steps

two-time /ˈ· ·/ *v* [Wv4;I∅;T1] *infml* to be deceitfully unfaithful to (a girlfriend or boyfriend) by having a relationship with somebody else —**two-timer** *n* [C; *you*+N]

two-tone /ˈ· ·/ *adj* [Wa5;A] coloured in 2 colours or in 2 varieties of one colour: *two-tone shoes*

two-way /ˌ· ˈ·◂/ *adj* [Wa5] **1** moving or allowing movement in both directions: *a two-way street|two-way traffic* **2** (of radio apparatus) for sending and receiving signals

ty·coon /taɪˈkuːn/ *n* a businessman or industrialist with great wealth and power

ty·ing /taɪ-ɪŋ/ *pres. p. of* TIE

tyke, tike /taɪk/ *n* **1** [C; *you*+N] *esp. NEngE* a badly-behaved or worthless person **2** [C] a worthless dog of mixed breed **3** [C] *esp. AmE* a small child **4** [C] *BrE* (*often cap.*) a person from Yorkshire, in northern England

tym·pa·num /ˈtɪmpənəm/ *n* **-na** /nə/ *or* **-nums** *med* **1** EARDRUM **2** MIDDLE EAR

type¹ /taɪp/ *n* **1** [C] a particular kind, class, or group; group or class of people or things very like each other and different from those outside the group or class: *a new type of dictionary* (=a dictionary of a new type)*|What type of plant is this?|any of several types of large flesh-eating animal|I like Italian (type) ice cream* **2** [C] a person or thing considered an example of such a group or class: *Abraham Lincoln is the type of politician who rises to power from humble origins* **3** [C] a small block of metal or wood with the shape of a letter on the upper end, dipped in ink and pressed on paper to print the letter **4** [U] many such blocks used in printing **5** [U] printed words **6 true to type** showing the nature, behaviour, or appearance expected of the group to which a person or thing belongs

type² *v* **1** [Wv5;T1;I∅] to write (something) with a TYPEWRITER **2** [T1] to find out the type of (something): *The doctor was unable to type the rare disease* **3** [T1 (*as*)] to consider (someone or something) as belonging to the stated type: *I was always typed as a thief in every play I acted in*

type·cast /ˈtaɪpkɑːst‖-kæst/ *v* **-cast** [Wv5;T1] to repeatedly give (an actor) the same kind of part: *They always typecast me as a murderer because my face looks evil*

type·face /ˈtaɪpfeɪs/ *n* the size and style of the letters used in printing

type·script /ˈtaɪpˌskrɪpt/ *n* **1** [C] a TYPEWRITTEN copy of something, esp. as prepared for the printer **2** [U] TYPEWRITTEN material, esp. as prepared for the printer

type·set·ter /ˈtaɪpˌsetəʳ/ *n* a person who arranges or sets TYPE¹ (4) for printing; COMPOSITOR

type·writ·er /ˈtaɪpˌraɪtəʳ/ *n* **1** a machine that prints letters by means of keys which when struck by the fingers press onto paper through an ink-filled RIBBON (=a long narrow piece of material) **2** *now rare* TYPIST

type·writ·ten /ˈtaɪpˌrɪtn/ *adj* [Wa5] written on a TYPEWRITER

ty·phoid /ˈtaɪfɔɪd/ also **typhoid fe·ver** /ˌ·· ˈ··/— *n* [U] an infectious disease that attacks the bowel causing fever, severe discomfort, and often death, produced by bacteria introduced into the body by food or drink

ty·phoon /taɪˈfuːn/ *n* a very violent tropical storm in the western Pacific

USAGE There are many words for a violent tropical circular wind. A **whirlwind** is small, a **cyclone** may be very large, bringing rain and great destruction. When it happens in the western Atlantic Ocean it is called a **hurricane**, and the same thing happening in the western Pacific or China Sea is a **typhoon**. When shaped like a pipe and passing in a narrow path, it is a **tornado** if it goes over land, and a **waterspout** if it goes over water.

ty·phus /ˈtaɪfəs/ *n* [U] an infectious disease, carried by lice (LOUSE) and FLEA*s*, that causes severe fever, very bad headaches, red spots over the body, and nervous sickness

typ·i·cal /ˈtɪpɪkəl/ *adj* [(*of*)] **1** combining and showing the main signs of a particular kind, group, or class: *a typical British summer|a typical 18th-century church* **2** showing the usual behaviour or manner; CHARACTERISTIC: *It was typical of him to be so rude* —compare FORMAL (5), CONVENTIONAL

typ·i·cally /ˈtɪpɪkli/ *adv* **1** in a typical manner: *typically American* **2** on a typical occasion; in typical conditions: *Typically, he would come in late and then say he was sorry* **3** in a typical case or example; if true to TYPE: *a large vessel usu. made of clay and typically having a long curved neck*

typ·i·fy /ˈtɪpɨ̄faɪ/ *v* [T1] **1** to represent in a typical manner (as by an image, form, model, or likeness): *In this book we have tried to typify the main classes of verbs* **2** [Wv6] to be a typical mark or sign of: *The high quality that typifies all his work* **3** [Wv6] to serve as a typical example of: *Abraham Lincoln typifies the politician who rises from humble origins to a position of power and influence*

typing pool /ˈ·· ·/ *n* a group of TYPIST*s* in a large office who TYPE² (1) letters for any members of the office

typ·ist /ˈtaɪpɨ̄st/ *n* **1** a secretary employed mainly for typing (TYPE² (1)) letters **2** a person skilled at using a TYPEWRITER

ty·pog·ra·pher /taɪˈpɒgrəfəʳ‖-ˈpɑ-/ *n* **1** a printer **2** TYPESETTER; COMPOSITOR

ty·po·graph·ic /ˌtaɪpəˈgræfɪk◂/ also **ty·po·graph·ic·al** /-kəl/— *adj* [Wa5] of, related to, or caused by TYPOGRAPHY (note the phr. **a typographic error**) —**~ally** *adv* [Wa4,5]

ty·pog·ra·phy /taɪˈpɒgrəfi‖-ˈpɑ-/ *n* [U] **1** the work of preparing and setting matter for printing **2** the arrangement, style, and appearance of printed matter

ty·ran·ni·cal /tɨ̄ˈrænɪkəl/ also **tyr·an·nous** /ˈtɪrənəs/— *adj* severely and unjustly cruel in governing; of or related to TYRANNY —**-cally** *adv* [Wa4]

tyr·an·nize, -nise /ˈtɪrənaɪz/ *v* [IØ (*over*);T1] to use power over (a person, country, people, etc.) with unjust cruelty

ty·ran·no·sau·rus /tɨ̄ˌrænəˈsɔːrəs/ also **tyrannosaurus rex** /···ˌ·· ˈ·/— *n* a type of large fierce flesh-eating DINOSAUR with small front legs, a large head, and sharp teeth, that walked on its powerful back legs

tyr·an·ny /ˈtɪrəni/ *n* **1** [U] the use of cruel or unjust power to rule a person or country **2** [C *often pl.*] a cruel or unjust act, esp. from a person in power **3** [U] government by a ruler with complete power, usu. gained by unjust means: (fig.) *the tyranny of the clock, which makes us get up when we don't want to* **4** [C] an ancient Greek state governed in his way

ty·rant /ˈtaɪərənt/ *n* a person with complete power, usu. gained unjustly by force, who rules cruelly and unjustly

tyre, *AmE* **tire** /taɪəʳ/ *n* **1** a thick rubber band, solid or filled with air, that fits round the outside edge of a wheel, esp. on a motor vehicle or bicycle, as a running surface and to soften shocks —see picture at CAR **2** a protective metal band fitted round a wooden wheel

ty·ro, tiro /ˈtaɪərəʊ/ *n* a beginner; person with little experience

tzar /zɑːr, tsɑːʳ/ *n* [C;A] TSAR

tza·ri·na /zɑːˈriːnə, tsɑː-/ *n* [C;A] TSARINA

tze·tze fly /ˈtetsi flaɪ, ˈtsetsi-, ˈsetsi/ *n* TSETSE FLY

U, u

U, u /juː/ **U's, u's** *or* **Us, us** the 21st letter of the English alphabet

U *n, adj* [Wa5;C;A] (in Britain) (a film) that children of any age may be admitted to see in a cinema: *"Goldilocks and the 3 Bears" is a U* —compare A, AA, X

u·biq·ui·tous /juːˈbɪkwɨ̄təs/ *adj* [Wa5] *usu. fml* appearing, happening, done, etc., everywhere

U-boat /ˈjuː bəʊt/ *n* a German SUBMARINE, as in the 2nd World War

UCCA /ˈʌkə/ *n* [GU] the Universities Central Council on Admissions; an official body which receives and deals with people's requests to do degrees and other courses at British universities

ud·der /ˈʌdəʳ/ *n* a baglike organ of a cow, female goat, etc., from which milk is produced —see picture at FARMYARD

UFO /ˈjuːfəʊ, ˌjuː ef ˈəʊ/ *n* **UFO's** unidentified (IDENTIFY) flying object; the name for something strange seen landing or in the sky, esp. when thought to come from another world in space

ugh /ʊx, ʌg/ *interj* (a shout of dislike): *Ugh! This medicine tastes nasty*

ug·ly /ˈʌgli/ *adj* [Wa1] **1** unpleasant to see: *an ugly face* **2** very unpleasant: *an ugly scene* (=argument) *developed* **3** threatening; bad-tempered: *an ugly customer* (= person)|*an ugly temper|an ugly sky, threatening rain* —**-liness** *n* [U]

ugly duck·ling /ˌ·· ˈ··/ *n* a person less attractive, skilful, etc., than others in early life but developing beyond them later

UHF /ˌjuː eɪtʃ ˈef/ also (*fml*) **ultrahigh frequency**— *n* [U] (the sending out of radio waves at) the rate of 300,000,000 to 3,000,000,000 HERTZ, producing excellent sound quality: *a UHF television set* —compare VHF

UK *abbrev. for*: United Kingdom (of Great Britain and Northern Ireland)

u·ku·le·le /ˌjuːkəˈleɪli/ *n* a type of musical instrument with 4 strings, like a small GUITAR, used in playing non-serious music
-u·lar /jʊləʳ/ *suffix* [→*adj*] see -AR
ul·cer /ˈʌlsəʳ/ *n* a rough place on the skin inside or outside the body which may bleed or produce poisonous matter: *a stomach ulcer|mouth ulcers*
ul·cer·ate /ˈʌlsəreɪt/ *v* **1** [IØ] to form one or more ULCERs: *The sore place ulcerated* **2** [Wv5;T1,IØ] to (cause to) become covered by one or more ULCERs: *The leg ulcerated.|The damage to the skin ulcerated the leg* —**-ation** /ˌʌlsəˈreɪʃən/ *n* [U]
ul·cer·ous /ˈʌlsərəs/ *adj* [Wa5] having or producing ULCERs: *ulcerous skin|an ulcerous condition*
ul·lage /ˈʌlɪdʒ/ *n* [U] *tech* the amount by which the liquid (esp. wine) in an unopened bottle does not come up to the top; amount of air in a bottle
ul·na /ˈʌlnə/ *n med* the inner bone of the arm (on the side opposite to the thumb), in man, or front leg, in animals —see picture at SKELETON
ult /ʌlt/ *abbrev. for*: ULTIMO: *your letter of the 23rd ult*
ul·te·ri·or /ʌlˈtɪərɪəʳ/ *adj* [Wa5;A;(B)] **1** *tech* later in time or more distant in space; beyond **2** *infml* hidden or kept secret, esp. because bad: *He has an ulterior* MOTIVE (= reason or intention) *for wanting to see her: he's going to ask to borrow some money*
ul·ti·mate /ˈʌltɪmɪt/ *adj* [Wa5;A;(B)] **1** (the) last or farthest distant; being at the end or happening in the end: *The ultimate point of land before the sea begins.|After many defeats, the war ended for us in ultimate victory* **2** considered as an origin or base; FUNDAMENTAL: *The sun is the ultimate store of power.|The ultimate responsibility lies with the President* **3** *not fml* greatest; after which no other can be considered: *He's done stupid things before, but to look for the escaping gas with a match really was the ultimate silliness*
ul·ti·mate·ly /ˈʌltɪmɪtli/ *adv* [Wa5] in the end; after all else or all others: *We considered all their plans, but ultimately we chose to follow our own.|Many gave their opinions, but ultimately the decision lay with the President*
ul·ti·ma·tum /ˌʌltɪˈmeɪtəm/ *n* **-tums** *or* **-ta** /tə/ a statement of conditions to be met, esp. under threat of force, as when one nation threatens war if another does not agree
ul·ti·mo /ˈʌltɪməʊ/ *adj* [Wa5;E] *pomp or fml* (in business letters) of last month
ul·tra- /ˈʌltrə/ *prefix* beyond; very: *ultrasound|ultrahigh|ultramodern*
ul·tra·high fre·quen·cy /ˌʌltrəhaɪ ˈfriːkwənsi/ *n* [U;(C)] *fml* (*often caps.*) UHF
ul·tra·ma·rine /ˌʌltrəməˈriːn/ *adj, n* [U] (of) a very bright blue colour
ul·tra·son·ic /ˌʌltrəˈsɒnɪk‖-ˈsɑ-/ *adj* [Wa5] (of sound waves) beyond the range of human hearing
ul·tra·vi·o·let /ˌʌltrəˈvaɪəlɪt/ *adj* [Wa5] **1** [B] (of light that is) beyond the purple end of the range of colours (SPECTRUM) that make up light that can be seen by human beings: *ultraviolet* RAYs —compare INFRARED **2** [A] using such light to cure certain skin diseases, examine faded writing, etc.: *an ultraviolet lamp*
um·ber /ˈʌmbəʳ/ *n, adj* [U] (of) a brown earthlike colour, esp. as used in painting
um·bil·i·cal cord /ʌmˌbɪlɪkəl ˈkɔːd‖-ˈkɔrd/ *n* the tube of flesh which joins the young to the organ which feeds it inside the mother, before birth
um·brage /ˈʌmbrɪdʒ/ *n* [U] offence (in the phr. **take umbrage (at)**)
um·brel·la /ʌmˈbrelə/ *n* **1** an arrangement of cloth over a folding frame with a handle, used for keeping rain off the head **2** a protecting power or influence; protection: *a new country formed under the political umbrella of the United Nations* **3** anything which covers or includes a wide range of different parts: *a business umbrella formed of many different firms*
um·laut /ˈʊmlaʊt/ *n* [U;C] **1** (a) change of quality in a vowel sound, caused by the influence of a following vowel, esp. in GERMANIC languages **2** the sign showing such a change; DIAERESIS
um·pire¹ /ˈʌmpaɪəʳ/ *n* a judge in charge of a game such as cricket or tennis or of a swimming competition —see picture at CRICKET²
USAGE This word is used in connection with **badminton, baseball, cricket, table tennis, tennis,** and **volleyball**. —compare REFEREE
umpire² *v* [T1;IØ] to act as UMPIRE¹ for (a game or competition)
ump·teen¹ /ˌʌmpˈtiːn◂/ *determiner infml* a large number of: *She's got umpteen storybooks about the sea* —**~th** *n, determiner*: *That's the umpteenth time I've told you not to do that!*
umpteen² *pron infml* a very large number: *She doesn't need to borrow a book when she's got umpteen waiting to be read at home*
'un /ən/ *pron infml & nonstandard* ONE: *He's a bad 'un* (= a wicked immoral person).|*I'll take those apples; they look like good 'uns*
un- /ʌn/ *prefix* **1** [*adj→adj;adv→adv*] not: *unfair|unhappy|unfortunately* **2** [*v→v*] (showing the opposite action): *unwind|to unblock a pipe*
USAGE 1 Compare: *He wants a nonscientific* (=not connected with science) *job as a swimming teacher.|It was very unscientific* (=on a low level as regards science) *not to measure your results!* A bomb can be *nonatomic* but not **unatomic*; either it is *atomic* or it is not. 2 An *unwrapped* parcel has either not been *wrapped* or it has been *unwrapped*. An *unwashed* shirt has not been *washed*, because there is no verb **to unwash*.
UN /ˌjuː ˈen/ *abbrev. for*: United Nations
un·a·bashed /ˌʌnəˈbæʃt◂/ *adj* fearless, not discouraged or ashamed, etc., esp. when something unusual happens: *He lost his trousers but was quite unabashed* —see also ABASH
un·a·bat·ed /ˌʌnəˈbeɪtɪd/ *adj* [Wa5] (of a wind, a person's strength, etc.) without losing force: *The storm was|continued unabated* —see also ABATE
un·a·ble /ʌnˈeɪbəl/ *adj* [Wa5;F3] not able: *He seems unable to understand you.|I'd like to go, but I'm unable to* —compare INABILITY
un·a·bridged /ˌʌnəˈbrɪdʒd◂/ *adj* [Wa5] (esp. of something written, a speech, etc.) given in full form, not shortened —see also ABRIDGE
un·ac·com·pa·nied /ˌʌnəˈkʌmpənid◂/ *adj* [Wa5] **1** without a COMPANION: *Unaccompanied ladies|ladies unaccompanied by a man will not be admitted* **2** without music as ACCOMPANIMENT: *an unaccompanied song* —see also ACCOMPANY (1,3)
un·ac·coun·ta·ble /ˌʌnəˈkaʊntəbəl/ *adj* surprising; not easily explained: *He has an unaccountable interest in old customs* —compare ACCOUNT FOR (2) —**-bly** *adv*: *Unaccountably, he never mentioned the accident.|He was unaccountably worried*
un·ac·cus·tomed /ˌʌnəˈkʌstəmd◂/ *adj* **1** [Wa5;A] unusual: *his unaccustomed expression of anger* —compare ACCUSTOMED **2** [F +*to*] not accustomed
un·a·dopt·ed /ˌʌnəˈdɒptɪd◂‖-ˈdɑp-/ *adj* [Wa5] (of a street surface) not to be repaired by the town council workmen, but the responsibility of those who live there
un·a·dul·te·rat·ed /ˌʌnəˈdʌltəreɪtɪd/ *adj* **1** [Wa5;B] (esp. of food) not mixed with impure or less pure substances **2** [A] complete; UTTER: *What you say is unadulterated nonsense*
un·ad·vised /ˌʌnədˈvaɪzd/ *adj* not sensible; done

without taking thought or advice: *an unadvised haste in marrying* —compare ADVISEDLY —**~ly** /ˌʌnədˈvaɪzɨ̣dli/ *adv*

un·af·fect·ed /ˌʌnəˈfektɨ̣d/ *adj* **1** natural in behaviour or character: *the unaffected delight of a child* —compare AFFECTED (1) **2** not AFFECTed (2) —**~ly** *adv*

un·al·loyed /ˌʌnəˈlɔɪd◂/ *adj* [Wa5] *esp. lit* not mixed, esp. with unpleasant feelings —compare ALLOY[2] (2)

un-A·mer·i·can /ˌ• •ˈ•••◂/ *adj* [Wa5] (esp. of political activity and loyalty) unfavourable to the US; against American customs and ways: *Some men used to be imprisoned for un-American activities*

u·na·nim·i·ty /ˌjuːnəˈnɪmɨ̣ti/ *n* [U] the state or fact of being UNANIMOUS

u·nan·i·mous /juːˈnænɨ̣məs/ *adj* [Wa5] **1** (of people) all agreeing: *They were (completely) unanimous in asking for more holidays* **2** (of agreements, statements, etc.) supported by everyone in the same way: *The vote was unanimous* —**~ly** *adv*

un·an·nounced /ˌʌnəˈnaʊnst◂/ *adj* [Wa5] having given no sign of arriving or being present; appearing unexpectedly: *He walked up to her quite unannounced and started an argument*

un·an·swe·ra·ble /ʌnˈɑːnsərəbəl‖ʌnˈæn-/ *adj* [Wa5] **1** which cannot be answered or argued against, esp. (of a charge) because true or right: *an unanswerable case in law* **2** (of a question) having no answer

un·ap·proa·cha·ble /ˌʌnəˈprəʊtʃəbəl◂/ *adj* (of a person) hard to talk to; not seeming to encourage friendliness

un·armed /ˌʌnˈɑːmd◂‖-ˈɑr-/ *adj* [Wa5] **1** not carrying a weapon **2** using no weapons: *unarmed* COMBAT (= fighting)

un·asked /ʌnˈɑːskt, -ˈɑːst‖-ˈæskt, -ˈæst/ *adj* [Wa5] **1** [F] without being asked to do something: *She came to help quite unasked* **2** [B (FOR)] not asked for: *an unasked present|Your advice was quite unasked for*

un·as·sum·ing /ˌʌnəˈsjuːmɪŋ◂, -ˈsuː-‖-ˈsuː-/ *adj* not showing a wish to be noticed; quiet in manner: *She drew no attention to herself with her unassuming ways* —**~ly** *adv*

un·at·tached /ˌʌnəˈtætʃt◂/ *adj* [Wa5] **1** not connected **2** not married or ENGAGED (4)

un·at·tend·ed /ˌʌnəˈtendɨ̣d◂/ *adj* [Wa5] alone, without people present or in charge (esp. in the phr. **leave someone/something unattended**): *Your car will be damaged if you leave it unattended here*

un·a·vail·ing /ˌʌnəˈveɪlɪŋ◂/ *adj* [Wa5] not having any effect: *an unavailing attempt to save her|with unavailing courage* —see also AVAIL[2]

un·a·wares /ˌʌnəˈweəz‖-ˈweərz/ *adv* [Wa5] **1** unintentionally or without noticing: *He dropped it unawares* **2 take someone unawares** to surprise someone by one's presence

un·bal·ance /ˌʌnˈbæləns/ *v* [Wv5;T1] to cause to have a lack of NORMAL values (in the mind), esp. shown by sudden changes in behaviour: *His terrible experience unbalanced him/his mind.|an unbalanced person/character/mind* —compare BALANCED

un·bar /ˌʌnˈbɑːʳ/ *v* **-rr-** [T1] **1** to remove a (locking) bar from (a door or gate) **2** to make open for something to come in: *to unbar the way to peace*

un·bear·a·ble /ʌnˈbeərəbəl/ *adj* which is too bad, esp. in behaviour, to be borne: *He is unbearable when he's in a bad temper.|unbearable heat|unbearable pain*

un·bear·a·bly /ʌnˈbeərəbli/ *adv* to a degree which is too bad to bear: *unbearably rude*

un·be·known /ˌʌnbɪˈnəʊn/ also **un·be·knownst** /ˌʌnbɪˈnəʊnst/— *adj, adv* [Wa5;F (*to*)] without the knowledge of the person stated: *Unbeknown to his father, he had run away from school*

un·be·lief /ˌʌnbɨ̣ˈliːf/ *n* [U] lack of belief in matters of religious faith

USAGE **Unbelief** is the opposite of **belief** only when one speaks of religious matters. Otherwise the opposite is **disbelief** (*in* the existence of something, *of* the truth of something). One can **believe in a** the existence of something: *Do you* **believe in** *fairies?* **b** the usefulness or rightness of something: *I don't* **believe in** *giving wine to children.*

un·be·lie·va·ble /ˌʌnbɨ̣ˈliːvəbəl/ *adj* very surprising: *It's unbelievable how many cats she has!|Her singing voice is unbelievable* —**-bly** *adv*: *Her singing voice is unbelievably good*

un·be·liev·er /ˌʌnbɨ̣ˈliːvəʳ/ *n* a person who has no faith (in something, esp. religion) —compare BELIEVER

un·be·liev·ing /ˌʌnbɨ̣ˈliːvɪŋ/ *adj* [Wa5] having no faith, esp. in religion —**~ly** *adv*

un·bend /ʌnˈbend/ *v* **-bent** /ˈbent/ [IØ] to behave in an informal manner, esp. when usu. formal; RELAX: *She finds it hard to unbend, even at parties, so people don't like her*

un·bend·ing /ʌnˈbendɪŋ/ *adj* unable to change opinions, decisions, etc., esp. refusing to do so

un·bid·den /ˌʌnˈbɪdn/ *adj* [Wa5] *esp. lit* **1** not asked for or expected: *He spoke out unbidden in the middle of the meeting* **2** uninvited: *They arrived unbidden at midnight* —compare BID[1]

un·bind /ˌʌnˈbaɪnd/ *v* **-bound** /ˈbaʊnd/ [T1] to loosen the fastenings of; free from something that binds: *He unbound the prisoner/the wound* —compare BIND

un·blush·ing /ˌʌnˈblʌʃɪŋ/ *adj* [Wa5] without showing any sense of shame; bold: *unblushing lies|She was quite unblushing about her behaviour* —**~ly** *adv*

un·born /ˌʌnˈbɔːn◂‖-ɔrn/ *adj* [Wa5] **1** not yet born **2** in or of the future: *nations yet unborn*

un·bos·om /ˌʌnˈbʊzəm/ *v* [T1 (*to*)] to tell the secret feelings, esp. troubles and worries, of (oneself)

un·bound·ed /ʌnˈbaʊndɨ̣d/ *adj* [Wa5] limitless; far-reaching: *Her unbounded love of music takes in every type, ancient and modern* —compare BOUND[2]

un·bowed /ˌʌnˈbaʊd◂/ *adj* [Wa5] *esp. lit* not conquered or defeated: *His body is hurt but his spirit is unbowed* —see also BOW[1] (6)

un·bri·dled /ʌnˈbraɪdld/ *adj* [Wa5] not controlled, and (esp.) too active or violent: *an unbridled tongue* (=speech)|*unbridled anger* —compare BRIDLE[2] (2)

un·buck·le /ˌʌnˈbʌkəl/ *v* [T1] to undo by loosening one or more BUCKLEs

un·bur·den /ˌʌnˈbɜːdn‖-ɜr-/ also **disburden**— *v* [T1 (*of*)] **1** to take away a load or worry from: *We unburdened him of his bags so that he could sit down* **2** to free (oneself, one's mind, etc.) by talking about a secret trouble: *She unburdened herself of her terrible secret.|He unburdened his heart to his friends*

un·but·toned /ˌʌnˈbʌtnd/ *adj* **1** [Wa5] with buttons unfastened **2** *rare* RELAXed; not formal

un·called-for /ʌnˈkɔːld fɔːʳ/ *adj* not deserved or right: *Such rudeness is quite uncalled-for*

un·can·ny /ʌnˈkæni/ *adj* [Wa1] mysterious; not natural or usual: *It seemed uncanny to hear her voice from the other side of the world* —**-nily** *adv*

un·cared-for /ʌnˈkeəd fɔːʳ‖-ˈkeərd-/ *adj* (as if) not well looked after: *His face is dirty and his hair uncared-for.|The garden has an uncared-for appearance*

un·ce·re·mo·ni·ous /ˌʌnserɨ̣ˈməʊnɪəs/ *adj* **1** informal: *an unceremonious but sincere welcome* **2** not done politely; rudely quick: *She finished the meal with unceremonious haste* —**~ly** *adv*: *He was kicked* *out unceremoniously into the street* —**~ness** *n* [U]

un·cer·tain /ʌn'sɜːtn‖-ɜr-/ *adj* **1** [Wa5;F+*of*, F6a,b] not certain; doubtful: *I'm uncertain what time he's coming.|I'm uncertain of his intentions/wishes.|I'm uncertain how to get there* **2** [B] changeable: *uncertain weather* **3** [B] undecided or unable to decide (a particular thing or things generally): *She feels uncertain when she's left alone in a strange place.|Our plans for our holidays are uncertain* **4 of uncertain age** *euph* (of a woman) not young, but not yet old, esp. if not admitting her age —**~ly** *adv* —**~ness** *n* [U]

un·cer·tain·ty /ʌn'sɜːtənti‖-ɜr-/ *n* **1** [U,U6a,b] the state or quality of being uncertain: *some uncertainty whether she knows|the uncertainty of the weather* **2** [C *often pl.*] a fact or condition which is doubtful, undecided, etc.: *Whether she comes is still an uncertainty.|the uncertainties of life*

un·char·i·ta·ble /ʌn'tʃærɪ̈təbəl/ *adj* not kind, helpful, fair in judging others, etc.; not CHARITABLE: *He said she had a large nose, which was a rather uncharitable remark* —**-bly** *adv*

un·chart·ed /ʌn'tʃɑːtɪ̈d‖-ɑr-/ *adj* [Wa5] *esp. lit* (of a place) not known well enough for records, esp. maps, to be made: *the uncharted forest lands of Brazil* —see also CHART[2]

un·checked /ˌʌn'tʃekt◂/ *adj* [Wa5] **1** not prevented from moving, developing, etc.: *an unchecked flow of blood|The disease spread unchecked* —see also CHECK[1] (1) **2** not tested for quality, correctness, etc.: *The goods should not have left the factory unchecked* —see also CHECK[1] (3)

un·chris·tian /ʌn'krɪstɪən/ *adj* **1** not kind, helpful, generous, etc.: *unchristian behaviour* **2** showing lack of kind helpful feelings: *an unchristian interruption* —compare CHRISTIAN[2] (3)

un·clad /ˌʌn'klæd◂/ *adj* [Wa5] *fml or pomp* not wearing any clothes —compare CLAD, UNSHOD

un·cle /'ʌŋkəl/ *n* **1** [C;A;N] (*often cap.*) the brother of one's father or mother, the husband of one's aunt, or a man whose brother or sister has a child: *He's my uncle.|I'm now an uncle.|Take me swimming, Uncle (Jack)!* —see TABLE OF FAMILY RELATIONSHIPS **2** [A;(C;N)] (*often cap.*) a man who is a friend or neighbour of a small child or its parents: *He's uncle to all the little boys who like to play football with him* **3** [C;A;N] *often derog* a man who takes the place of a father, esp. in relation to the children of a woman who is or was married to someone else: *The child has had too many uncles; he needs a real father* **4 say uncle** *AmE infml* to admit defeat; give up

un·clean /ˌʌn'kliːn◂/ *adj* **1** *bibl* (esp. in the Jewish religion) (of animals) that cannot be eaten; forbidden **2** (of people) not considered pure, esp. in a religious way, often because of a condition of the body which may infect others: *In ancient times* LEPERS *were thought unclean* —compare CLEAN[1] (7) —**~ness** [U]

Uncle Sam /ˌ·· '·/ *n* [R] *infml lit* the US

Uncle Tom /ˌ·· '·/ *n often derog* (a name for) a black person (NEGRO) who is very friendly to white people

un·cloud·ed /ʌn'klaʊdɪ̈d/ *adj* [Wa5] **1** clear: *His sight was unclouded at 90 years of age* —compare CLOUD[2] (2) **2** untroubled: *unclouded happiness*

un·col·oured, *AmE* **uncolored** /ʌn'kʌləd‖-ərd/ *adj* [Wa5] *usu. fml* plain, esp. not with a special effect added: *His account was uncoloured by his personal feelings* —compare COLOUR[2] (3)

un·com·for·ta·ble /ʌn'kʌmftəbəl/ *adj* **1** not comfortable: *an uncomfortable chair|I'm uncomfortable in this chair* **2** troubled by one's position in relation to others; SHY or EMBARRASSed: *I felt uncomfortable when I had to admit my guilt* —**-bly** *adv*

un·com·mit·ted /ˌʌnkə'mɪtɪ̈d◂/ *adj* [(*to*)] **1** not having given loyalty to any one thing, group, political belief, etc.: *She has no family and is quite uncommitted.|She will join the club when she has free time, but at the moment wants to remain uncommitted* —compare COMMITTED **2** [Wa5] not having given a promise: *We are examining the goods, but until we sign an agreement are uncommitted to buying*

un·com·mon·ly /ʌn'kɒmənli‖-'kɑ-/ *adv fml* very; unusually: *That's uncommonly kind of you*

un·com·pro·mis·ing /ʌn'kɒmprəmaɪzɪŋ‖-'kɑm-/ *adj* refusing to change ideas or decisions; firm in beliefs, ways, etc.: *He is too uncompromising to excuse the children's mistakes.|He has uncompromising opinions about what is right* —**~ly** *adv*

un·con·cerned /ˌʌnkən'sɜːnd‖-ɜr-/ *adj* **1** [B (*about*)] not worried or anxious: *She must have hurt herself, but seemed quite unconcerned* **2** [Wa5;F (*with*)] not interested or taking part: *She is unconcerned with school affairs* **3** [Wa5;F+*with*] not about: *The report is unconcerned with details* —compare CONCERNED —**~ly** /ˌʌnkən'sɜːnɪ̈dli‖-ɜr-/ *adv*

un·con·di·tion·al /ˌʌnkən'dɪʃənəl/ *adj* [Wa5] not limited by any conditions: *unconditional freedom* —**~ly** *adv*

un·con·scio·na·ble /ʌn'kɒnʃənəbəl‖-'kɑn-/ *adj* [Wa5] *usu. fml* unreasonable in degree or amount: *an unconscionable time to spend shopping* —**-bly** *adv*

un·con·scious[1] /ʌn'kɒnʃəs‖-'kɑn/ *adj* [Wa5] **1** having lost consciousness: *She hit her head and was unconscious for several minutes* **2** not intentional: *an unconscious action* —see CONSCIOUS (USAGE) —**~ly** *adv* —**~ness** *n* [U]

unconscious[2] *n* [*the* +R] SUBCONSCIOUS

un·con·sid·ered /ˌʌnkən'sɪdəd‖-ərd/ *adj* [Wa5] **1** not carefully thought out: *an unconsidered action* **2** disregarded; unnoticed: *a few unconsidered objects left lying about* —compare CONSIDERED

un·cork /ʌn'kɔːk‖-ɔrk/ *v* [T1] to open (esp. a bottle or barrel) by removing the CORK[1] (2) —compare CORK[2]

un·coup·le /ʌn'kʌpəl/ *v* [T1] to separate (esp. joined railway carriages); free from a fastening: *to uncouple the engine (from the carriages)|to uncouple the chain from the wall* —compare COUPLE[1] (1)

un·couth /ʌn'kuːθ/ *adj* not having good manners; rough in speech and ways —**~ly** *adv* —**~ness** *n* [U]

un·cov·er /ʌn'kʌvə^r/ *v* [T1] **1** to remove a covering from **2** to find out (something unknown or kept secret); discover: *The police have uncovered a plan to steal £1,000,000*

un·crit·i·cal /ʌn'krɪtɪkəl/ *adj* [(*of*)] not making or showing any judgments; (unwisely) accepting, without deciding if good or bad: *She is quite uncritical of his behaviour.|an uncritical eye for paintings*

un·crowned /ˌʌn'kraʊnd◂/ *adj* [Wa5] **1** not crowned as king, but with the power of a ruler or leader **2 the uncrowned king/queen (of)** the person generally considered to be the best, most famous, etc., in a particular activity: *Christine Evert, the uncrowned queen of women's tennis in the late 1970's*

un·crush·a·ble /ʌn'krʌʃəbəl/ *adj* [Wa5] **1** (of materials and cloth) which stays smooth; which does not form unwanted folds **2** *esp. lit* (of a person, a person's will, etc.) that will not yield: *uncrushable desire for success*

unc·tion /'ʌŋkʃən/ *n* [U] the act of putting oil on a person (ANOINTing him) as a religious ceremony, esp. (in the CATHOLIC church) at the end of life (**extreme unction**)

unc·tu·ous /'ʌŋktʃʊəs/ *adj* **1** smooth in speech, esp. not sincere but showing kindness, interest, etc., for effect: *unctuous praise* **2** *tech* oily —**~ly** *adv* —**~ness** *n* [U]

un·cut /ˌʌnˈkʌt◂/ *adj* [Wa5] **1** (of a book) with the edges of the pages still joined together **2** (of a film or story) not made shorter, as when **a** newly made and not arranged in its best form for showing **b** shown including some scenes which at other times have been removed **3** (of a diamond or precious stone) not shaped and formed for wearing, use in jewellery, etc.

un·daunt·ed /ʌnˈdɔːntɨd/ *adj* [Wa5] not at all discouraged by danger or difficulty; bold —see also DAUNT

un·de·ceive /ˌʌndɪˈsiːv/ *v* [T1] *fml* to inform of the truth, esp. when mistaken: *She thought he was a famous man, but I had to undeceive her*

un·de·cid·ed /ˌʌndɪˈsaɪdɨd/ *adj* [Wa5] **1** [F (*about*), F6a,b;(B)] in doubt: *I'm undecided whether to go to France or Italy for my holidays* **2** [B] without a result; with neither side winning: *The match was left undecided* —**~ly** *adv* —**~ness** *n* [U]

un·de·clared /ˌʌndɪˈkleəd‖-ərd/ *adj* [Wa5] (of goods) which have not been officially shown or made known when entering a country so that tax (CUSTOMS DUTY) can be paid on them

un·de·ni·a·ble /ˌʌndɪˈnaɪəbəl/ *adj* [Wa5] certainly so, in existence, etc.: *His skill is undeniable, but he works too slowly* —**-bly** *adv*

un·der[1] /ˈʌndəʳ/ *adv* [Wa5] in or to a lower place; directly below —see also DOWN[1] (24) **under**, GO UNDER, KEEP UNDER

under[2] *prep* **1** in or to a lower place than; directly below: *The box is under the table.*|*to come out from under the trees*|*to breathe under water* **2** less than: *under £5*|*a temperature* (*of*) *under 30°*|*boys of 10 and under* —opposite **over**; compare BELOW **3** lower in rank than; serving or obeying: *They work under a kind leader/under his kind leadership.*|*We're under orders to leave.*|*Under the rules, he can't be dismissed.*|*"Is everything under control?"* (SEU W.) **4** beneath the surface or covering of: *What are you wearing under your coat?*|(fig.) *She wrote the book under the name of "George Eliot"* **5** during the rule of: *Spain under Franco* **6** during; in the state or act of: *under* DISCUSSION|*under contract* **7** *tech* (of land) bearing (a crop): *Many parts of Asia are kept under rice* **8** in the class of (often in the phr. **under the heading of**): *Rabbits come under* (*the heading of*) *animals* **9** in; during; because of: *Under present conditions no change is possible.*|*under/in the* CIRCUMSTANCES|*under the influence of alcohol* **10** having (often a mistaken idea): *You were under a* MISAPPREHENSION/*mistaken* IMPRESSION.|*I was under the* IMPRESSION *that . . .*|*He goes under the name of Smith* (= calls himself Smith, though this may not be his real name).|*He lives under* (*the*) *threat of disease.*|*to work under great difficulties* **11 under age** too young in law, esp. for drinking alcohol, entering certain public places alone, driving a car, etc. **12 under cover (of)** hidden or sheltered (by): *They escaped under cover of darkness* —compare BELOW, BENEATH

under- *prefix* **1** [*n*→*n*] (of a person) less important or lower in rank: *a head* GARDENER *and 3 under*-GARDENERS **2** [*n*→*n*] (of a thing or place) going or being below: UNDERPASS **3** [*v*→*v*;*adj* (*n*+-ed)→*adj*] too little: *to undercook*|*underworked*|UNDERPRIVILEGED

un·der·act /ˌʌndərˈækt/ *v* [T1;IØ] to act on stage with a small amount of force, sometimes considered a fault, sometimes an advantage: *In a play about strong feelings, it's a mistake to underact.*|*He cleverly underacted the part, so that there was a strong effect of hidden feelings*

un·der·arm[1] /ˈʌndərɑːm‖-ɑrm/ also **underhand**— *adj, adv* (esp. in sports) (done, thrown, or hit) with the hand not moving above the shoulder

underarm[2] *n* [A] *euph* (of the) ARMPIT

un·der·bel·ly /ˈʌndəˌbeli‖-ər-/ *n* **1** the softest part of the BELLY, underneath an animal **2** [(*of*)] the weak or undefended part of a place, a plan, etc.: *The soft underbelly of Europe risks attack*

un·der·brush /ˈʌndəbrʌʃ‖-ər-/ *n* [U] thick UNDERGROWTH in a forest

un·der·car·riage /ˈʌndəˌkærɪdʒ‖-ər-/ also (*infml*) **un·der·cart** /ˈʌndəkɑːt‖ˈʌndərkɑrt/— *n* the wheels and lower part of an aircraft, which support it when it lands —see picture at AIRCRAFT

und·er·charge /ˌʌndəˈtʃɑːdʒ‖ˌʌndərˈtʃɑrdʒ/ *v* [T1; (D1);IØ] to take or ask too small an amount of money from (someone); charge too little: *He undercharged me on the bus.*|*I was undercharged* (*by*) *10 pence.*|*I think he undercharged by mistake.*|*They forgot the prices had risen, and undercharged*

un·der·clothes /ˈʌndəkləʊðz, -kləʊz‖-dər-/ also **un·der·cloth·ing** [U] /ˈʌndəˌkləʊðɪŋ‖-dər-/— *n* [P] UNDERWEAR

un·der·coat /ˈʌndəkəʊt‖-dər-/ *n* [C;U] a covering of paint put onto a surface as a base for a top covering of paint

un·der·cov·er /ˌʌndəˈkʌvəʳ◂‖-dər-/ *adj* [Wa5] acting or done secretly, not publicly, esp. as a SPY or for gain: *undercover meetings*|*an undercover* AGENT|*undercover payments*

un·der·cur·rent /ˈʌndəˌkʌrənt‖-dər-/ *n* **1** a hidden current of water beneath the surface **2** a hidden tendency in general feelings, opinions, etc.: *an undercurrent of discontent*

un·der·cut[1] /ˌʌndəˈkʌt‖-ər-/ *v* **-cut**; *pres. p.* **-cutting** [T1] to sell goods more cheaply or to work for smaller wages than (someone doing the same)

un·der·cut[2] /ˈʌndəkʌt‖-ər-/ *n* an underneath piece of SIRLOIN (meat)

un·der·de·vel·oped coun·try /ˌʌndədɪˌveləpt ˈkʌntri‖-dər-/ also **underdeveloped na·tion** /ˌ····ˈ··/— *n* DEVELOPING COUNTRY

un·der·dog /ˈʌndədɒg‖ˈʌndərdɔg/ *n* a person, country, etc., which is treated badly by or gets the worst deal in any activity

un·der·done /ˌʌndəˈdʌn◂‖-ər-/ *adj* [Wa5] not cooked until completely brown, sometimes (of meat) thought to have a better taste, sometimes (esp. of baking) spoilt

un·der·es·ti·mate[1] /ˌʌndərˈestɨmeɪt/ *v* **1** [T1] to have too low an opinion of the degree or number of: *I underestimated his strength/her abilities* **2** [T1; IØ] to give too low a value for (an amount): *I underestimated* (*the cost of the journey*), *and am left with no money* —see also ESTIMATE

un·der·es·ti·mate[2] /ˌʌndərˈestɨmɨt/ *n* an ESTIMATE which is too small

un·der·felt /ˈʌndəfelt‖-ər-/ *n* [U] soft rough material placed between a CARPET and the floor

un·der·floor /ˌʌndəˈflɔːʳ◂‖-ər-/ *adj* [Wa5] (esp. of heating systems) laid beneath the surface of the floor: *underfloor heating* —see also CENTRAL HEATING

un·der·foot /ˌʌndəˈfʊt‖-ər-/ *adv* [Wa5] **1** under the foot, esp. against the ground: *He crushed the fallen nuts from the tree underfoot* **2** below one's feet; for walking on: *The ground was stony underfoot* **3** in the way, so as to be annoying: *The children are always getting underfoot*

un·der·gar·ment /ˈʌndəˌgɑːmənt‖ˈʌndərgɑr-/ *n* *sometimes euph* an article of UNDERWEAR

un·der·go /ˌʌndəˈgəʊ‖-dər-/ *v* **-went** /ˈwent/, **-gone** /ˈgɒn‖ˈgɔn/ [T1] to experience (esp. suffering or difficulty): *She underwent a thorough examination at the hospital.*|*The building must undergo modern changes*

un·der·grad·u·ate /ˌʌndəˈgrædʒʊɨt‖-ər-/ also

(*infml*) **un·der·grad** /ˌʌndəˈgræd‖-ər-/— *n* a university student who has not yet taken his first degree: *undergraduate humour*

un·der·ground[1] /ˌʌndəˈgraʊnd‖-ər-/ *adv* **1** under the earth's surface: *Mines can be a long way underground* **2** secretly: *The news has been passed on underground, but not in the official newspapers* **3 go underground** to hide from public view or leave ordinary life for a time, esp. during an official search

un·der·ground[2] /ˈʌndəgraʊnd‖-ər-/ *adj* [Wa5] **1** below the surface of the earth: *an underground passage* **2** representing a political view which is not publicly accepted, as of a RESISTANCE group in wartime or modern groups which concern themselves with human rights: *the underground* PRESS (= newspapers)

underground[3] /ˈʌndəgraʊnd‖-ər-/ also **tube**, (*AmE* **subway**)— *n* [*the* +R;C; *by* +U] *BrE* (*often cap.*) a railway system in which the trains run in tubes under the earth, esp. (in Britain) the one in London: *We went on the Underground.*|*We went by underground* —compare METRO

un·der·growth /ˈʌndəgrəʊθ‖-dər-/ *n* [U] bushes, tall plants, etc., smaller than the trees around them

un·der·hand /ˌʌndəˈhænd◂‖-ər-/ *adj, adv* [Wa5] UNDERARM[1]

un·der·hand·ed /ˌʌndəˈhændɨ̇d◂‖-ər-/ also **underhand**— *adj* dishonest, esp. secretly: *I don't believe in getting what you want by underhanded methods; it's better not to have it at all* —**~ly** *adv* —**~ness** *n* [U]

un·der·hung /ˌʌndəˈhʌŋ‖-ər-/ *adj* [Wa5] (of the lower jaw) standing out beyond the upper jaw

un·der·lay /ˈʌndəleɪ‖-ər-/ *n* [U;C] (a piece of) material to be kept under a CARPET, esp. to preserve the quality of the CARPET and to keep heat in

un·der·lie /ˌʌndəˈlaɪ‖-ər-/ *v* **-lay** /ˈleɪ/, **-lain** /ˈleɪn/ [Wv4;T1] (of feelings and qualities) to be present as an explanation or real meaning of: *An underlying uncertainty made him act in a nervous manner.*| *Does some personal difficulty underlie his lack of interest in work?*

un·der·line /ˌʌndəˈlaɪn‖-ər-/ also **underscore**— *v* [T1] **1** to mark (one or more words) by drawing a line underneath, esp. to show importance or to give force **2** to give force to (an idea, feeling, etc., which has been expressed or shown): *His refusal to go underlined his dislike of the place*

un·der·ling /ˈʌndəlɪŋ‖-ər-/ *n derog* a person of low rank or position in relation to another, such as a servant

un·der·manned /ˌʌndəˈmænd‖-ər-/ *adj* [Wa5] **1** (of a ship) having less than the usual number of sailors **2** (of a factory or place of work) not having enough workers; UNDERSTAFFED —see also MAN[2]

un·der·men·tioned /ˌʌndəˈmenʃənd◂‖-ər-/ *adj* [Wa5;A] which is mentioned later in the same piece of writing: *Please supply me with the undermentioned goods: . . .*

un·der·mine /ˌʌndəˈmaɪn‖-ər-/ *v* [T1] **1** to wear away the earth beneath, removing support: *The house is unsafe since the* FOUNDATIONS *were undermined by floods* **2** to weaken or destroy by stages: *Illness undermined his strength*

un·der·neath[1] /ˌʌndəˈniːθ‖-ər-/ *prep, adv* (so as to go) under (something): *"The letter was pushed underneath the church door."* (SEU S.)|*She wore a fur coat with nothing underneath.*|*The insect crept further underneath*

underneath[2] *n* [(*the*) S] *not fml* the lower part of something; bottom surface: *There's a crack on the underneath of the bowl/on its underneath*

un·der·nour·ish /ˌʌndəˈnʌrɪʃ‖-ər-/ *v* [Wv5;T1] to give too little and/or bad quality food, causing lack of growth and development —**~ment** *n* [U]

un·der·pants /ˈʌndəpænts‖-ər-/ *n* [P] short underclothes for men, covering the lower part of the body and sometimes the tops of the legs —see PAIR (USAGE)

un·der·pass /ˈʌndəpɑːs‖ˈʌndərpæs/ *n* a way under a road, either another road or (esp.) a path for walkers (SUBWAY)

un·der·pin /ˌʌndəˈpɪn‖-ər-/ *v* **-nn-** [T1] **1** to use a solid piece of material to support (esp. a wall) **2** to give strength or support to (an argument): *His presence at the crime underpins the case against him*

un·der·play /ˌʌndəˈpleɪ‖-ər-/ *v* [T1] **1** to give less force in expressing than one could: *to underplay the importance of money in life* **2** to UNDERACT (a part) **3 underplay one's hand** to act carefully, showing less of one's plans, intentions, powers, etc., than one could

un·der·priv·i·leged /ˌʌndəˈprɪvɨ̇lɪdʒd‖-dər-/ *adj* (of people) not having the advantages of the ordinary person's life; lacking in good chances for education, social life, etc.

un·der·proof /ˌʌndəˈpruːf‖-ər-/ *adj* [Wa5;B;E] (of alcoholic drinks) less strong than PROOF SPIRIT: *10 degrees underproof*

un·der·quote /ˌʌndəˈkwəʊt‖-dər-/ also **underbid** /ˌʌndəˈbɪd‖-ər-/— *v* [T1] (in business) to make an offer to sell at a lower price than (someone else) selling the same

un·der·rate /ˌʌndəˈreɪt/ *v* [T1] to give too low a value to, esp. in one's opinion of a degree or amount of, (ability, strength, etc.): *We underrated his powers as a speaker*

un·der·score /ˌʌndəˈskɔːʳ‖ˌʌndərˈskor/ *v* [T1] UNDERLINE

un·der·sec·re·ta·ry /ˌʌndəˈsekrətəri‖ˌʌndərˈsekrəteri/ *n* (*often cap.*) a person who is in charge of the daily work of a government department (either a member of parliament of the government party (**parliamentary undersecretary**) or a CIVIL SERVANT (**permanent undersecretary**)) and helps and advises a minister

un·der·sell /ˌʌndəˈsel‖-ər-/ *v* **-sold** /ˈsəʊld/ [T1] to sell goods at a lower price than (a business competitor)

un·der·sexed /ˌʌndəˈsekst◂‖-ər-/ *adj* [Wa5] having less sexual desire than usual —compare OVERSEXED

un·der·shirt /ˈʌndəʃɜːt‖ˈʌndərʃɜrt/ *n AmE* VEST

un·der·side /ˈʌndəsaɪd‖-ər-/ *n* [(*the*)] the part underneath; lower side or surface

un·der·signed /ˈʌndəsaɪnd‖-ər-/ *adj* [Wa5;A; *the* +GU] whose signature is/are lower on the paper, beneath the writing: *The undersigned (persons) wish to be considered for election: John Smith, Joe Brown, Mary Bloggs*

un·der·sized /ˌʌndəˈsaɪzd◂‖-ər-/ also **un·der·size** /-ˈsaɪz◂/— *adj* [Wa5] too small or smaller than usual, esp. because of lack of growth

un·der·slung /ˌʌndəˈslʌŋ◂‖-ər-/ *adj* [Wa5] (of the frame of a motor vehicle) connected to the AXLE*s* from below

un·der·staffed /ˌʌndəˈstɑːft‖ˌʌndərˈstæft/ *adj* having too few workers, or fewer than usual: *The office is understaffed since the last secretary left* —compare UNDERMANNED

un·der·stand /ˌʌndəˈstænd‖-ər-/ *v* **-stood** /ˈstʊd/ [Wv6] **1** [T1;I0̸] to know or get the meaning of (something): *Do you understand (this word)?*|*I can't understand modern literature* **2** [T1,6a] to know or feel closely the nature of (a person, feelings, etc.): *I can't understand him when he behaves so badly.*|*I understand how you feel* **3** [T5a,b;V3] *often fml or polite* to have been informed; have found out (a fact): *I understand you're coming to work for us.*|*"I'm coming to work* *for you." "So I understand."|I understood he was married, but I find I was misinformed* **4** [T1 (*by*), 5a;V3 *often pass.*] to take or judge (as the meaning): *What do you understand by the order to move on—where do they want us to go?|By "children" it's understood (that) they mean people under 14.|"Children" is understood to mean those under 14.|We understood them to mean that they would wait for us* **5** [T1 *often pass.*] to add (esp. a word) in the mind for completion: *When I say "Come and help", the object "me" is understood* **6 give someone to understand** *fml* to cause someone to judge or believe: *He gave me to understand that he would be here by 3—can I have misunderstood?* **7 make oneself understood** to make one's meaning clear to others, esp. in speech **8 understand one another/each other** to know what is wished, esp. to agree: *Now we understand one another, we can make the right changes* —**~able** *adj* —**~ably** *adv* [Wa3]

un·der·stand·ing /ˌʌndəˈstændɪŋ‖-ər-/ *n* **1** [U] the act of understanding; power to judge: *According to my understanding of the letter, it means something quite different* **2** [C] power of the brain; INTELLIGENCE: *beyond a child's understanding* **3** [S;U] sympathy: *There is (a) deep understanding between them* **4** [C *usu. sing.*] a private, not formal, agreement: *We have come to an understanding* (=reached an agreement).|*I lent him money on the understanding that* (=on condition that) *he paid it back the next month*

un·der·state /ˌʌndəˈsteɪt‖-ər-/ *v* [T1] **1** to cause to seem of less importance or strength than is so: *They understated the seriousness of the crime* **2** to express while holding back the feelings: *In an understated speech he made clear his feelings*

un·der·state·ment /ˌʌndəˈsteɪtmənt‖-dər-/ *n* [C; (U)] **1** (a) statement which is not strong enough to express facts or feelings with full force (such as *not bad* meaning *rather good*) **2 the understatement of the year** a point which is true, but which could be much more forceful: *You call him rich? That's the understatement of the year; he owns more than any man in Britain*

un·der·stud·y[1] /ˈʌndəˌstʌdi‖-ər-/ *v* [T1] to act as UNDERSTUDY to (an actor or actress) in (a part): *She understudied (Maggie Smith as) Desdemona*

understudy[2] *n* an actor or actress learning an important part in a play so as to be able if necessary to take the place of the actor who plays that part: *The* LEADING **man** *has been taken ill; call the understudy|his understudy to go on stage*

un·der·take /ˌʌndəˈteɪk‖-ər-/ *v* **-took** /ˈtʊk/, **-taken** /ˈteɪkən/ **1** [T1] to take up (a position); start on (work): *He undertook the responsibility for changes* **2** [T3,5] to promise or agree: *He undertook to improve the working arrangements*

un·der·tak·er /ˈʌndəteɪkəʳ‖-dər-/ *n* a person whose job it is to arrange funerals

un·der·tak·ing[1] /ˌʌndəˈteɪkɪŋ‖ˈʌndərteɪ-/ *n* **1** [C *usu. sing.*] a TASK, piece of work, or something needing effort: *To start a new farm with no help is rather a large undertaking, isn't it?* **2** [C,C3,5] a promise: *Will you give me an undertaking not to see that young man again/that you won't see him again?*

un·der·tak·ing[2] /ˈʌndəˌteɪkɪŋ‖-ər-/ *n* [U] the business of an UNDERTAKER

under-the-coun·ter /ˌ·· · ˈ··◂/ *adj* [Wa5] *infml* (bought or sold) secretly, esp. against the law: *under-the-counter sales* —see also COUNTER[1] (3)

un·der·tone /ˈʌndətəʊn‖-dər-/ *n* **1** a low voice: *He spoke in an undertone.|They spoke in undertones/an undertone* **2** [(*of*)] a hidden feeling or meaning: *There was an undertone of sadness in her letter* —compare OVERTONES **3** a colour which shows through another: *green with a slight undertone of yellow* —compare OVERTONE

un·der·tow /ˈʌndətəʊ‖-dər-/ *n* [S] the current beneath the surface which pulls back towards the sea as a wave breaks on the shore

un·der·wa·ter /ˌʌndəˈwɔːtəʳ◂‖-dər-/ *adj, adv* (used, done, etc.) below the surface of a stretch of water: *underwater swimming|underwater films|underwater cameras/fishing|The ship was underwater when they reached her.|The ship lay underwater.|They swam underwater*

un·der·wear /ˈʌndəweəʳ‖-dər-/ also **underclothes** [P], **underclothing**— *n* [U] the clothes worn next to the body under other clothes, such as VESTs, UNDERPANTS, BRAs, etc. —see also UNDIES

un·der·weight /ˌʌndəˈweɪt◂‖-ər-/ *adj* [B;E] weighing too little or less than is usual: *He is several pounds underweight.|The potatoes are underweight* —compare OVERWEIGHT

un·der·went /ˌʌndəˈwent‖-ər-/ *past t. of* UNDERGO

un·der·world /ˈʌndəwɜːld‖ˈʌndərwɜrld/ *n* [*the* + R] **1** (*usu. cap.*) (in ancient Greek stories) the place where the spirits of the dead live **2** the criminal world, esp. those whose profession is crime when considered as a social group separate from the rest of society

un·der·write /ˌʌndəˈraɪt/ *v* **-wrote** /ˈrəʊt/, **-writ·ten** /ˈrɪtən/ [T1] **1** to agree to buy from a company (all new shares not bought by the public) **2** to take responsibility for fulfilling (an insurance agreement, esp. against loss of SHIPPING)

un·der·writ·er /ˈʌndəˌraɪtəʳ‖-dər-/ *n* **1** a person who buys new shares from a company when not sold to the public **2** an insurance AGENT, esp. one who makes agreements to repay losses of SHIPPING firms

un·de·si·ra·ble[1] /ˌʌndɪˈzaɪərəbəl/ *adj usu. fml* unpleasant; not wanted: *Long delays are undesirable, but sometimes necessary.|It is undesirable to wear heavy clothes in a hot country* —compare DESIRABLE (1) —**-bility** /ˌʌndɪzaɪərəˈbɪlɪ̈ti/ *n* [U] —**-bly** /ˌʌndɪˈzaɪərəbli/ *adv* [Wa3]

undesirable[2] *n* a person not thought good or useful; person not wanted or liked by society generally

un·de·vel·oped /ˌʌndɪˈveləpt/ *adj* [Wa5] (usu. of a place) in its natural state, esp. not having industry, mining, building, modern farming, etc. —compare UNDERDEVELOPED COUNTRY, DEVELOP (4), DEVELOPER

un·dies /ˈʌndiːz/ *n* [P] *infml* articles of (esp. women's) UNDERWEAR generally

un·dis·charged /ˌʌndɪsˈtʃɑːdʒd◂‖-ɑr-/ *adj* [Wa5] **1** (esp. of goods on a ship) not unloaded —compare DISCHARGE[1] (8) **2** (of a gun) not fired —compare DISCHARGE[1] (6) **3** (of an account or debt) not paid —compare DISCHARGE[1] (4) **4** (of a person who owes money) not yet allowed by the court to stop repayments; still in debt by law: *an undischarged* BANKRUPT

un·dis·tin·guished /ˌʌndɪˈstɪŋgwɪʃt◂/ *adj* not marked by good qualities; with no signs of excellent ability, character, etc.: *an undistinguished performance|an undistinguished writer* —compare DISTINGUISH (5), DISTINGUISHED

un·di·vid·ed /ˌʌndɪˈvaɪdɪ̈d◂/ *adj* [Wa5] complete: *Give me your undivided attention*

un·do /ʌnˈduː/ *v* **-did** /dɪd/, **-done** /ˈdʌn/ [T1] **1** to unfasten (what is tied or wrapped): *to undo the string round a parcel|He undid the parcel* —see also UNDONE, DO UP (1,3) **2** to remove the effects of: *In 10 minutes he undid my whole day's work* **3** [*usu. pass.*] *esp. old use* to ruin the position and esp. the good name of (a person): *I am undone! My secret has been discovered!*

un·do·ing /ʌn'duːɪŋ/ *n* [S9 *usu. with poss.*] the cause of ruin, shame, failure, etc.: *Our attempt to climb higher was our undoing, as we weren't experienced enough and fell to the bottom of the hill*

un·do·mes·ti·cat·ed /ˌʌndə'mestɪkeɪtɨd/ *adj* [Wa5] **1** (of an animal) not serving man; not TAME **2** (of a person) not interested in cooking, housework, etc. —compare DOMESTICATE (2)

un·done /ˌʌn'dʌn◂/ *adj* [Wa5] **1** [F] unfastened or loose: *One button is undone.|There's a button undone.|Your button has come undone.|You've got 2 buttons undone* **2** [B] not done: *a pile of undone work*

un·doubt·ed /ʌn'daʊtɨd/ *adj* [Wa5] known for certain to be (so): *his undoubted wealth* —**~ly** *adv*: *That is undoubtedly true*

un·dreamed-of /ʌn'driːmd əv, -ɒv‖-əv, -ɑv/ also **un·dreamt-of** /ʌn'dremt əv, -ɒv‖-əv, -ɑv/— *adj* [Wa5;A;(B)] which is beyond, and esp. better or more than, what might be imagined: *undreamed-of happiness*

un·dress[1] /ʌn'dres/ *v* **1** [IØ] to take one's clothes off **2** [T1] to take the clothes off (someone): *She undressed the baby and put him in his bath*

undress[2] *n* [U] **1** *fml* lack of clothes: *The little boy ran out of the door, still in a state of undress* **2** *tech* military uniform not for ceremonial occasions

un·dressed /ˌʌn'drest◂/ *adj* [Wa5] **1** not wearing any clothes, esp. ordinary day clothes: *When he saw she was undressed he shut the door again quickly* **2** (of some meat, esp. from birds, and foods, esp. SALADS) not prepared for cooking or eating —see also DRESS[1] (9,11) **3** (of animal skins) not yet fully treated or preserved as leather **4** (of wounds) not treated with drugs and covered —see also DRESS[1] (12) **5 get undressed** to take one's clothes off

un·due /ˌʌn'djuː◂‖-duː◂/ *adj* [Wa5;A] too much; not suitable: *with undue haste*

un·du·late /'ʌndjʊleɪt‖-dʒə-/ *v* [Wv4;IØ] to move or lie like waves rising and falling: *undulating hills*

un·du·la·tion /ˌʌndjʊ'leɪʃən‖-dʒə-/ *n* **1** [U] a rising and falling movement or shape, like waves **2** [C *often pl.*] (something with) a smooth curve among a number of others

un·du·ly /ʌn'djuːli‖-'duː-/ *adv* [Wa5] too much (so); very: *not unduly worried|not worried unduly*

un·dy·ing /ʌn'daɪ-ɪŋ/ *adj* [Wa5;A;(B)] which will never end: *our undying love|undying fame*

un·earth /ʌn'ɜːθ‖-'ɜrθ/ *v* [T1] **1** to dig up: *to unearth a box buried under a tree* **2** to discover: *to unearth a secret*

un·earth·ly /ʌn'ɜːθli‖-'ɜr-/ *adj* **1** not natural; as if of a spirit world; GHOSTLY: *the unearthly brightness of the night|to feel an unearthly presence in the room* **2** *infml* (of time) very inconvenient, esp. because too early or late: *What an unearthly time of night to call!* —**-liness** *n* [U]

un·ease /ʌn'iːz/ *n* [U] *lit* uneasiness (UNEASY)

un·eas·y /ʌn'iːzi/ *adj* [Wa1] **1** not comfortable or at rest: *The sleeper gave an uneasy movement* **2** worried; anxious: *uneasy about the future* —**-ily** *adv* —**-iness** *n* [U]

un·e·co·nom·ic /ˌʌniːkə'nɒmɪk, ˌʌnekə-‖-'nɑ-/ also **un·e·co·nom·i·cal** /-kəl/— *adj* **1** resulting in loss of money or not producing (enough) profit —compare ECONOMIC (2) **2** wasteful: *an uneconomic use of time* —compare ECONOMICAL —**~ally** *adv* [Wa4]

un·ed·u·cat·ed /ʌn'edʒʊkeɪtɨd‖-dʒə-/ *adj* showing a lack of (good) education; not socially well trained: *uneducated speech*

un·em·ployed /ˌʌnɪm'plɔɪd/ *adj* [Wa5] **1** [B; *the* +P] not having a job: *trying to find work for the unemployed* **2** [B] not being used profitably

un·em·ploy·ment /ˌʌnɪm'plɔɪmənt/ *n* [U] **1** the condition of lacking a job: *He was thrown into unemployment when the factory closed* **2** a lack of jobs for numbers of people in society: *Unemployment became worse as industries failed*

un·en·light·ened /ˌʌnɪn'laɪtənd/ *adj* [Wa5] **1** not having been informed of a certain piece of knowledge: *In his unenlightened state he went on believing she disliked him, though she was hiding the fact that she loved him* —compare ENLIGHTEN **2** not having knowledge generally, because uneducated; IGNORANT **3** having wrong beliefs and unable to change, because of lack of knowledge; SUPERSTITIOUS or PREJUDICED —compare ENLIGHTENED

un·en·vi·a·ble /ʌn'enviəbəl/ *adj* unpleasant; not to be wished for, esp. because of difficulty: *Telling a woman that her husband's been killed is an unenviable job*

un·e·qual /ʌn'iːkwəl/ *adj* **1** [Wa5;B (*in, to*)] not of equal size, value, etc.: *unequal amounts|amounts unequal in size|amounts unequal to each other* **2** [F +*to*] (of a person) not having enough strength, ability, etc.: *He was unequal to the job* **3** [B] UNEVEN —compare EQUAL[1] —**~ly** *adv* —**~ness** *n* [U]

un·e·qualled, *AmE* **unequaled** /ʌn'iːkwəld/ *adj* [Wa5] too good, clever, etc., for anything to be found of equal quality: *unequalled courage* —see also EQUAL[3] (2)

un·e·quiv·o·cal /ˌʌnɪ'kwɪvəkəl/ *adj* [Wa5] which is plain in meaning —compare EQUIVOCAL —**~ly** *adv* [Wa4]

un·er·ring /ʌn'ɜːrɪŋ/ *adj* [Wa5] without making a mistake; unable to fail, esp. to hit something or reach the right point: *With unerring judgment/aim he threw the ball through the hole* —**~ly** *adv*

UNESCO /juː'neskəʊ/ *n* [R] United Nations Educational, Scientific, and CULTURAL Organization

un·e·ven /ʌn'iːvən/ *adj* **1** not smooth or even: *Her hair has been badly cut and the ends are uneven* **2** irregular: *His heart beat at an uneven rate* —compare EVEN[2] (2) **3** *sometimes euph* tending to change in quality or in type: *His work has been rather uneven this year* (= has often been bad) **4** (of numbers) ODD —**~ly** *adv* —**~ness** *n* [U]

un·e·vent·ful /ˌʌnɪ'ventfəl/ *adj* not having any important events; dull or calm: *an uneventful life* —compare EVENTFUL —**~ly** *adv* —**~ness** *n* [U]

un·ex·am·pled /ˌʌnɪg'zɑːmpəld‖-'zæm-/ *adj* [Wa5] *fml* better than anything else that has happened; EXCEPTIONAL: *unexampled bravery*

un·ex·cep·tio·na·ble /ˌʌnɪk'sepʃənəbəl/ *adj* [Wa5] too good to be found lacking in any way; quite satisfactory: *unexceptionable behaviour* —compare *un*EXCEPTIONAL —**-bly** *adv* [Wa3,5]

un·fail·ing /ʌn'feɪlɪŋ/ *adj* [Wa5] (esp. of something good) never ceasing to be (so): *with unfailing interest/courage|an unfailing admirer of modern art* —compare FAIL[1] (5) —**~ly** *adv*

un·faith·ful /ʌn'feɪθfəl/ *adj* [(*to*)] **1** [Wa5] disloyal to one's marriage partner by having a sexual experience or relationship with another person: *In court they asked how many times he had been unfaithful with this other woman.|She was unfaithful for years before he found out* **2** *rare* not faithful or loyal —compare FAITHFUL (1,2) —**~ly** *adv* —**~ness** *n* [U]

un·fal·ter·ing /ʌn'fɔːltərɪŋ/ *adj* [Wa5] not stopping or holding back; unhesitating (HESITATE): *unfaltering steps|an unfaltering speech* —see also FALTER —**~ly** *adv*

un·fath·o·ma·ble /ʌn'fæðəməbəl/ *adj* [Wa5] which cannot be understood; the meaning of which cannot be reached: *an unfathomable mystery* —compare FATHOM[2] —**-bly** *adv* [Wa3,5]

un·fath·omed /ʌn'fæðəmd/ *adj* [Wa5] the nature of which or reason for which has not been understood: *the unfathomed depths of the mind* —compare FATHOM[2]

un·fa·vou·ra·ble, *AmE* **-vorable** /ʌnˈfeɪvərəbəl/ *adj* [(*to, for*)] not favourable: *The weather is unfavourable to our plans/for a holiday.|an unfavourable report on the new plan* —opposite **favourable** —**-bly** *adv* [Wa3]

un·feel·ing /ʌnˈfiːlɪŋ/ *adj* cruel; hard; not sympathetic towards others: *The unfeeling teacher made them all stay in after school on a sunny day* —compare FEEL FOR —**~ly** *adv*

un·fet·tered /ʌnˈfetəd‖-ərd/ *adj* [Wa5] free from care or responsibility: *She lived a gay unfettered life travelling round the world* —compare FETTER[2]

unfit for /ʌnˈfɪt/ *v prep* **-tt-** [D1;V4b] to make unfit for: *Years of work in Africa unfitted him for life in a cold country*

un·flag·ging /ʌnˈflægɪŋ/ *adj* [Wa5] without tiring or stopping: *She gave her unflagging attention to the job all afternoon* —**~ly** *adv*

un·flap·pa·ble /ʌnˈflæpəbəl/ *adj not fml esp. BrE* never losing a calm manner; never showing signs of worry in affairs which might cause anxiety: *My secretary is quite unflappable and would keep working if the office was burning down* —**-bly** *adv* [Wa3]

un·flinch·ing /ʌnˈflɪntʃɪŋ/ *adj* [Wa5] fearless; firm, without fear: *Her expression was unflinching.|unflinching eyes|unflinching courage* —**~ly** *adv*

un·fold /ʌnˈfəʊld/ *v* **1** [T1] to open from a folded position: *to open an envelope and unfold the letter inside* **2** [T1;I∅] to (cause to) become clear, more fully known, etc.: *The story unfolds as the film goes on.|to unfold all one's secrets* **3** [I∅] (of a BUD) to open into a flower: *Modern films can show a rose unfolding*

un·fore·seen /ˌʌnfɔːˈsiːn◂‖-ˈfor-/ *adj* [Wa5] unexpected: *unforeseen delays|unforeseen joys*

un·for·get·ta·ble /ˌʌnfəˈgetəbəl‖-fər-/ *adj* (of an experience) too strong in effect, good or bad, to be forgotten: *The colours of Africa/England in the spring are unforgettable.|We went to a beautiful town and spent an unforgettable day* —**-bly** *adv* [Wa3]

un·for·tu·nate[1] /ʌnˈfɔːtʃʊnɨ̍t‖-ˈfɔrtʃə-/ *adj* **1** unlucky: *You were unfortunate in missing the concert.|an unfortunate accident* **2** deserving of pity: *The unfortunate man has a twisted leg* **3** unsuitable: *to make an unfortunate remark* **4** unsuccessful: *an unfortunate business* VENTURE *which ended with everyone losing their money*

unfortunate[2] *n* an unlucky person, esp. who has no social advantages, has no home, etc.

un·for·tu·nate·ly /ʌnˈfɔːtʃʊnɨ̍tli‖-ˈfɔrtʃə-/ *adv* **1** by bad luck: *I was unfortunately delayed* **2** [Wa5] it is/was a bad thing that . . .; I am afraid that . . .: *Unfortunately, we never found out the truth* —compare FORTUNATELY

un·found·ed /ʌnˈfaʊndɨ̍d/ *adj* [Wa5] not supported by facts; baseless: *an unfounded report of carelessness among the workmen|The suggestion that I wanted her to leave is quite unfounded*

un·fre·quent·ed /ˌʌnfriˈkwentɨ̍d/ *adj* [Wa5] not often visited by many people: *They chose an unfrequented spot to put up the tent* —see also FREQUENT[2]

un·frock /ʌnˈfrɒk‖ʌnˈfrɑk/ also **defrock, disfrock**— *v* [T1] to remove from the position of priest in the church, as a punishment for unsuitable behaviour or beliefs —see also FROCK (2)

un·furl /ʌnˈfɜːl‖-ɜrl/ *v* [T1] to unroll and open (a flag, sail, etc.) —see also FURL

un·gain·ly /ʌnˈgeɪnli/ *adj* [Wa2] not graceful; awkward in movement; CLUMSY —**-liness** *n* [U]

un·gen·e·rous /ʌnˈdʒenərəs/ *adj* **1** not generous; selfish **2** unfair: *an ungenerous remark|It's ungenerous to say he doesn't work hard: he's just slower and produces less* —**~ly** *adv*

un·god·ly /ʌnˈgɒdli‖-ˈgɑd-/ *adj* [Wa2] **1** [B] showing lack of respect for God and religion; wicked —compare GODLY **2** [A;(B)] *infml* surprisingly unpleasant: *What an ungodly noise!* **3** [A;(B)] *infml* unreasonable: *I had to get up at an ungodly hour this morning* (= very early)

un·gov·er·na·ble /ʌnˈgʌvənəbəl‖-vər-/ *adj* uncontrollable: *an ungovernable temper* —see also GOVERN (2)

un·gra·cious /ʌnˈgreɪʃəs/ *adj* not polite: *an ungracious refusal|ungracious in her acceptance of the explanation* —**~ly** *adv*

un·grate·ful /ʌnˈgreɪtfəl/ *adj* **1** not grateful **2** *esp. fml or lit* (of work or action) unpleasant; giving no reward or result —compare THANKLESS —**~ly** *adv* —**~ness** *n* [U]

un·grudg·ing /ʌnˈgrʌdʒɪŋ/ *adj* [Wa5] generous; willing: *ungrudging efforts|She was ungrudging in giving her time*

un·guard·ed /ʌnˈgɑːdɨ̍d‖-ɑr-/ *adj* [Wa5] careless over what is made known, esp. when usually careful (often in the phr. **in an unguarded moment**): *An unguarded remark let everyone know his secret*

un·guent /ˈʌŋgwənt/ *n* [C;(U)] *often lit* a thick oily substance used on the skin; OINTMENT —see also UNCTUOUS

un·hal·lowed /ʌnˈhæləʊd/ *adj* [Wa5] **1** [B] *tech* not made holy by a special church ceremony: *unhallowed ground* (= where those refused membership of a church can be buried in a GRAVEYARD) **2** [A] *lit* wicked

un·hand /ʌnˈhænd/ *v* [T1 *usu. imper.*] *old use or humor* to take the hands off (someone); stop holding: *Unhand my daughter!*

un·hap·pi·ly /ʌnˈhæpɨ̍li/ *adv* **1** in an unhappy way **2** [Wa5] UNFORTUNATELY (2): *Unhappily, we never saw her again*

un·hap·py /ʌnˈhæpi/ *adj* [Wa1] **1** not happy **2** unlucky: *an unhappy meeting at the wrong time* **3** unsuitable: *an unhappy statement, which was certain to hurt someone's feelings* —**-piness** *n* [U]

un·health·y /ʌnˈhelθi/ *adj* [Wa1] **1** not strong, often ill; not generally in good health: *They're unhealthy children, always ill, because they don't get good food and fresh air* —compare HEALTHY **2 a** not likely to give good health: *a hot wet unhealthy place* —compare HEALTHFUL **b** not good for the mind or body: *an unhealthy habit of eating raw meat* **c** unnatural: *an unhealthy interest in cruel punishments* **3** showing illness or poor health: *an unhealthy yellow skin|He's (His face is) an unhealthy colour* —**unhealthily** *adv* —**unhealthiness** *n* [U]

un·heard /ˈʌnˈhɜːd◂‖-ɜrd/ *adj* [Wa5] **1** not heard, esp. in court —see also HEAR (3) **2** not listened to: *Her complaints went unheard*

unheard-of /·ˈ· ·/ *adj* [Wa5] very strange and unusual; never having happened in the past: *It's unheard-of to pass the examination so young*

un·hinge /ʌnˈhɪndʒ/ *v* [T1] **1** to remove (a door) from HINGEs **2** [Wv5] *not fml* to drive (a person) mad or to UNBALANCE (the mind): *The experience unhinged his mind.|He is quite unhinged*

un·ho·ly /ʌnˈhəʊli/ *adj* **1** [Wa5;B] *esp. lit* wicked **2** [Wa2;A;(B)] *infml* UNGODLY (2): *an unholy noise* —compare HOLY (3) —**-liness** *n* [U]

un·hook /ʌnˈhʊk/ *v* [T1] **1** to remove from a hook: *to unhook the meat* **2** to unfasten the hooks of: *to unhook a dress* —compare HOOK

un·hoped-for /·ˈ· ·/ *adj* [Wa5] too good to be expected: *unhoped-for success*

un·horse /ʌnˈhɔːs‖-ɔrs/ *v* [T1] to cause to fall from

a horse: *He was unhorsed while jumping (over) a fence*

u·ni- /ˈjuːnɨ̥/ *prefix* one; single

UNICEF /ˈjuːnɨ̥sef/ *n* [R] United Nations International Children's EMERGENCY FUND

u·ni·corn /ˈjuːnɨ̥kɔːn‖-ɔrn/ *n* an imaginary horse-like animal, told of in stories, with one horn growing from its forehead

un·i·den·ti·fied /ˌʌnaɪˈdentɨ̥faɪd/ *adj* [Wa5] of which the name, nature, or origin has not been found or given: *An unidentified man was seen near the scene of the murder.|There's an unidentified box under the table; is it yours?* —see also UFO

u·ni·fi·ca·tion /ˌjuːnɨ̥fɨ̥ˈkeɪʃən/ *n* [U] the act or result of UNIFYing or uniting: *The unification of Italy resulted in one country instead of several kingdoms*

u·ni·form¹ /ˈjuːnɨ̥fɔːm‖-ɔrm/ *adj* [Wa5] **1** with every part the same; even; regular: *a uniform colour* **2** the same in every way: *They were of uniform value.|rows of uniform houses* —**~ity** /ˌjuːnɨ̥ˈfɔːmɨ̥ti‖-ɔr-/ *n* [U]: *to bring the 2 systems into uniformity (with each other)* —**~ly** /ˈjuːnɨ̥fɔːmli‖-ɔr-/ *adv*

uniform² *n* [C; (*in*) U] a certain type of clothing which all members of a group wear, esp. in the army, a school, or the police: *They all wear uniforms at my school.|Policemen and postmen wear dark blue uniforms.|He was in uniform 3 years* (= in the armed forces)

u·ni·formed /ˈjuːnɨ̥fɔːmd◂‖-ɔr-/ *adj* [Wa5] habitually wearing/having to wear the uniform of a group: *a line of uniformed soldiers*

u·ni·fy /ˈjuːnɨ̥faɪ/ *v* [T1] **1** to make all the same: *to unify the systems* **2** to make (parts) into one (whole): *to unify the country*

u·ni·lat·e·ral /ˌjuːnɨ̥ˈlætərəl/ *adj* [Wa5] done by or having an effect on only one of the groups in an agreement: *a unilateral declaration of independence* (**UDI**) *by a member country* —**~ly** *adv*

unilateral dis·ar·ma·ment /··ˌ····ˈ···/ *n* [U] the act by one nation alone of giving up defence by weapons (esp. NUCLEAR)

un·im·pea·cha·ble /ˌʌnɪmˈpiːtʃəbəl/ *adj* [Wa5] *fml* (of a person or personal qualities) blameless; that cannot be doubted: *an unimpeachable character/witness* —compare IMPEACH —**-bly** *adv* [Wa3,5]

un·in·formed /ˌʌnɪnˈfɔːmd◂‖-ɔr-/ *adj* [Wa5] **1** (done) without related or enough knowledge: *an uninformed guess* —compare INFORMED **2** lacking knowledge; IGNORANT

un·in·hab·i·ta·ble /ˌʌnɪnˈhæbɨ̥təbəl/ *adj* [Wa5] unfit to be lived in —compare INHABIT, HABITABLE

un·in·hib·it·ed /ˌʌnɪnˈhɪbɨ̥tɨ̥d/ *adj* free in action and behaviour, esp. doing and saying what one likes without worrying about what other people think —compare INHIBITED —**~ly** *adv*

un·in·te·rest·ed /ʌnˈɪntrɨ̥stɨ̥d/ *adj* [(*in*)] not interested —see DISINTERESTED

un·in·ter·rupt·ed /ˌʌnɪntəˈrʌptɨ̥d/ *adj* [Wa5] continuous —**~ly** *adv*

u·ni·on /ˈjuːnɪən/ *n* **1** [U] the act of joining or state of being joined into one: *"In union there is strength"* (old saying) **2** [C] (*often cap.*) a group of countries or states joined together: *The President gave his speech on the state of the Union* (=the US) **3** [U] a state of agreement and unity: *They lived in unspoilt union* **4** [C;U] (unity in) marriage: *joined in perfect union|a union blessed by children* **5** [GC] (*often cap.*) (esp. in names and titles) a club or society: *to join the Students' Union* **6** [C] *tech* a connecting part for pipes **7** [GC] TRADE UNION: *to join a union|the Post Office workers' union*

U·ni·on·is·m /ˈjuːnɪənɪzəm/ *n* [U] **1** a former political movement giving support for the union of Great Britain and Ireland **2** support for the FEDERAL union (=the North) of the United States during the CIVIL WAR **3** (*usu. not cap.*) TRADE UNIONism —**-ist** *n, adj* [Wa5]: *Unionist members of parliament*

u·ni·on·ist /ˈjuːnɪənɨ̥st/ *n* TRADE UNIONist

u·ni·on·ize, -ise /ˈjuːnɪənaɪz/ *v* [Wv5;T1;IØ] to (cause to) form a TRADE UNION —**-ization** /ˌjuːnɪənaɪˈzeɪʃən‖ˌjuːnɪənə-/ *n* [U]

Union Jack /ˌ··· ˈ·/ also (*tech*) **Union Flag** /ˈ··· ·/— *n* the national flag of Great Britain

u·nique /juːˈniːk/ *adj* **1** [Wa5] being the only one of its type: *This stamp is unique; all others like it have been lost or destroyed* **2** *infml often considered nonstandard* unusual: *I am in a rather unique position, as my job is different from anyone else's* **3** *sometimes considered nonstandard* UNEQUALLED: *a unique knowledge of ancient European coins* —**~ly** *adv* —**~ness** *n* [U]

u·ni·sex /ˈjuːnɨ̥seks/ *adj* [Wa5] **1** (esp. of clothes) of one type which can be used by both male and female **2** selling, using, etc., such a type: *a unisex shop|the unisex* GENERATION (3b)

u·ni·son /ˈjuːnɨ̥sən, -zən/ *n* [U] **1** the singing of the same note by everybody at the same time (esp. in the phr. **in unison**) —compare HARMONY **2** perfect agreement (esp. in the phr. **in unison**)

u·nit /ˈjuːnɨ̥t/ *n* **1** [C] one complete thing: *3 more units of it ought to be enough* **2** [GC] a group of things or people forming a complete whole but usu. part of a larger group: *an army unit sent ahead into enemy country|The family is the smallest social unit.|an* X-RAY *unit* **3** [C] **a** the smallest whole number; the number 1 **b** any whole number less than 10 **4** [C] an amount or quantity taken as a standard of measurement: *The pound is the standard unit of money in Britain* **5** [C] (*usu. in comb.*) a rather large article, esp. of furniture, which can be fitted with others of the same type: *a kitchen unit|unit furniture*

U·ni·tar·i·an /ˌjuːnɨ̥ˈteərɪən/ *adj, n* [Wa5] (a member) of a branch of the Christian church which does not believe in the TRINITY

u·nite /juːˈnaɪt/ *v* **1** [T1;IØ] to join together into one: *They united the 2 pipes.|The 2 colours mixed and united.|A piece of wood unites the parts* **2** [IØ (*in*), I3] to act together for a purpose: *They united (in their attempts) to form a club* **3** [T1] to join in marriage: *They were united by the local priest* **4** [IØ] to join in an agreement: *The countries united for business purposes*

u·nit·ed /juːˈnaɪtɨ̥d/ *adj* **1** [B] in agreement: *They are a united family* **2** [Wa5;A;(B)] with everyone concerned having the same aim: *to make a united effort|Manchester United* (football club) **3** [Wa5;A] (*cap. in names*) joined in a political organization **a** of states or countries into a nation: *the United States (of America)|the United Kingdom (of Great Britain and Northern Ireland)* **b** of countries for a certain purpose: *the United Nations* —**~ly** *adv*

unit trust /ˌ·· ˈ·/ (*AmE* **mutual fund**)— *n BrE* a company formed to control INVESTMENTs of many different types

u·ni·ty /ˈjuːnɨ̥ti/ *n* **1** [U;C] the state of being one complete whole or condition of being united: *church unity|a new unity between different branches of the church|unity of colour in a picture* **2** [U] agreement of aims and interests: *The argument spoilt their former unity* **3** [U] *tech* the number one: *greater than unity*

u·ni·ver·sal /ˌjuːnɨ̥ˈvɜːsəl◂‖-ɜr-/ *adj* [Wa5] **1** concerning all members of a group: *universal agreement as to who should become chairman* **2** for all people or every purpose; widespread: *It's a subject of universal interest.|This machine has a universal use*

in the home **3** (done, found, etc.) in all parts of the world: *universal travel* —**~ity** /ˌjuːnɪ̈vɜː'sælɪ̈ti‖-ɜr-/ *n* [U]
universal joint /ˌ···· '·/ *n* a JOINT, as in a machine, which can turn in all directions
u·ni·ver·sal·ly /ˌjuːnɪ̈'vɜːsəli‖-ɜr-/ *adv* [Wa5] **1** everywhere: *universally present* **2** by everyone: *universally accepted*
u·ni·verse /'juːnɪ̈vɜːs‖-ɜrs/ *n* **1** [*the* +R] (*often cap.*) all space and the matter which exists in it: *God made the universe* **2** [C] a star system; GALAXY: *a story of travellers in time who reached a new universe*
u·ni·ver·si·ty /ˌjuːnɪ̈'vɜːsɪ̈ti◂‖-ɜr-/ *n* **1** [C] a place of education at the highest level, where degrees are given: *Several new universities have been built* **2** [U] such a place when attended for a course of study: (*BrE*) *to go to university* (=(*BrE & AmE*) *to go to a university*) **3** [*the*+GU] the members of this place, students and teachers: *The whole university is against the changes*
un·kempt /ˌʌn'kempt◂/ *adj* **1** having untidy clothes and hair **2** (of the hair) untidy
un·kind /ˌʌn'kaɪnd◂/ *adj* [Wa1] not kind; cruel or thoughtless
un·kind·ly /ʌn'kaɪndli/ *adv* **1** in an unkind way: *She spoke unkindly* **2** [Wa5] as if to appear unkind: *She didn't mean it unkindly*
un·know·ing /ˌʌn'nəʊɪŋ◂/ *adj* [Wa5] not knowing something: *Unknowing, she walked into danger* —**~ly** *adv*: *unknowingly deceived*
un·known[1] /ˌʌn'nəʊn◂/ *adj* [Wa5] whose name, value, or origin is not known: *An unknown man has stolen all our money.|an unknown quantity*
unknown[2] *n* an unknown person or thing
un·law·ful /ʌn'lɔːfəl/ *adj* [Wa5] against the law —**~ly** *adv*
un·learn /ˌʌn'lɜːn‖-ɜrn/ *v* [T1] to forget on purpose (something learnt, such as a fact or habit) —compare LEARN (2)
un·leash /ʌn'liːʃ/ *v* [T1] **1** to remove (a dog) from a LEAD[2] (10) **2** [(*on, upon*)] to set free from control (feelings, forces, etc.); RELEASE: *All his anger was unleashed upon us.|The armies unleashed violence on the city*
un·leav·ened /ʌn'levənd/ *adj* **1** (of bread) made without YEAST, and therefore flat and unrisen **2** not mixed, esp. not improved, by new influences: *a dull life unleavened by a little amusement* —see also LEAVEN[2]
un·less /ʌn'les, ən-/ *conj* if . . . not; except in the case that: *I will leave at 9, unless you want to go earlier.|I won't write unless he writes first.|Do not leave the building unless instructed to do so*
USAGE **Unless** is not used of imaginary events. We can say *If she weren't so silly she would understand.|If I hadn't stopped her she would have jumped;* but not ***Unless** she were so silly . . .| ***Unless** *I had stopped her . . .*
un·let·tered /ʌn'letəd‖-ərd/ *adj* [Wa5] **1** not well educated —compare LETTERED **2** not able to read; ILLITERATE
un·like /ˌʌn'laɪk◂/ *adj, prep* not like; different (from): *"as unlike as chalk and cheese"|She's very unlike her mother; they're completely unlike (each other).|It's unlike him to be late: he's usually on time*
un·like·ly /ʌn'laɪkli/ *adj* [Wa2] **1** [F,F3] not expected; improbable: *He may come, but it's very unlikely.|They're unlikely to marry.|It seems unlikely that they're in* —opposite **likely** **2** [B] not likely to happen or be true: *an unlikely possibility|an unlikely story* —**-liness** *n* also **-lihood** [U]
un·load /ʌn'ləʊd/ *v* **1** [T1] to remove (a load) from (something): *to unload the books|to unload the car* **2** [T1;I∅] to have (a load) removed: *The car is unloading (its passengers) in front of the house* **3** [T1 (*on*)] **a** to get rid of (something unwanted): *He unloaded his possessions on me to be stored* **b** to express (inner feelings): *He unloaded his anger on me* **4** [T1; I∅] to remove the CHARGE from (a gun) or film from (a camera) —compare LOAD[2] —**~er** *n*
un·lock /ʌn'lɒk‖-lɑk/ *v* [T1] to unfasten the lock of; open or make ready for opening by unfastening the lock: *She unlocked 'the door and turned the handle to open it* —compare LOCK[3] (1)
un·looked-for /ʌn'lʊkt fɔːʳ/ *adj* [Wa5] *esp. lit* unexpected
un·loose /ʌn'luːs/ *v* [T1] *esp. lit* to set free
un·loos·en /ʌn'luːsən/ *v* [T1] to loosen: *He sat down and unloosened his belt*
un·luck·y /ˌʌn'lʌki/ *adj* [Wa1] not lucky
un·made /ˌʌn'meɪd◂/ *adj* (of a bed) not put in order ready for sleeping
un·man·ner·ly /ʌn'mænəli‖-ər-/ *adj fml* of bad social manners; impolite: *unmannerly behaviour* —compare MANNERLY
un·mar·ried /ˌʌn'mærid◂/ *adj* [Wa5] not married; SINGLE: *unmarried mothers* —compare MARRIED
un·mask /ʌn'mɑːsk‖-mæsk/ *v* [T1] **1** to remove a MASK[1] from **2** to show the hidden truth about: *to unmask the thief* —compare MASK[2] (2)
un·matched /ˌʌn'mætʃt◂/ *adj* [Wa5] with no equal: *unmatched courage* —compare MATCH[2] (1), MATCHLESS
un·mea·sured /ʌn'meʒəd‖-ərd/ *adj* [Wa5] (of a quality) without limit; beyond measure: *unmeasured greatness* —compare MEASURELESS
un·men·tio·na·ble /ʌn'menʃənəbəl/ *adj* [Wa5] too unpleasant, bad, terrible, shocking, etc., to be spoken of
un·men·tio·na·bles /ʌn'menʃənəbəlz/ *n* [P] **1** *old euph or humor* UNDERCLOTHES **2** *old euph* trousers
un·mind·ful /ʌn'maɪndfəl/ *adj* [Wa5;F+*of*] *fml* forgetting or not taking into account: *unmindful of her wishes|unmindful of difficulties* —compare HEEDless
un·mis·ta·ka·ble /ˌʌnmɪ̈'steɪkəbəl/ *adj* [Wa5] clearly recognizable; that cannot be thought to be otherwise: *He shouted in unmistakable anger.|There was an unmistakable fault in the material* —**-bly** *adv* [Wa3,5]
un·mit·i·gat·ed /ʌn'mɪtɪ̈geɪtɪ̈d/ *adj* [Wa5;A] in every way (bad); not lessened or excused in any way: *an unmitigated criminal|grief unmitigated by the passing of time* —compare MITIGATE —**~ly** *adv*
un·moved /ʌn'muːvd/ *adj* **1** not having feelings of pity —compare MOVE[1] (9) **2** not worried; calm
un·nat·u·ral /ˌʌn'nætʃərəl/ *adj* **1** not natural; unusual: *a head of unnatural size* **2** against ordinary good ways of behaving: *an unnatural mother|unnatural sexual practices* —**~ly** *adv*: *an unnaturally large head|He'd expected, not unnaturally, that she'd be there to meet him*
un·ne·ces·sa·ry /ʌn'nesəsəri‖-seri/ *adj* [Wa5] not necessary or wanted; additional to what is needed or expected: *That was an unnecessary remark; it would have been better to keep silent* —**-rily** /ʌn'nesəsərəli‖ˌʌn-nesə'serəli/ *adv*: *unnecessarily rude*
un·nerve /ˌʌn'nɜːv‖-ɜrv/ *v* [Wv4;T1] to take away the courage of or power to act
un·num·bered /ˌʌn'nʌmbəd‖-ərd/ *adj* [Wa5] **1** too many to be counted; NUMBERLESS; INNUMERABLE **2** not having a number marked
UNO /'juːnəʊ/ *now rare* UN
un·ob·tru·sive /ˌʌnəb'truːsɪv/ *adj* **1** not too easily seen or noticed **2** politely avoiding making others worried by one's presence; DISCREET: *to make oneself unobtrusive|With an unobtrusive remark about the weather, she kept the conversation going* —**~ly** *adv* —**~ness** *n* [U]

un·of·fi·cial /ˌʌnəˈfɪʃəl◂/ *adj* [Wa5] **1** not official; informal: *an unofficial meeting* **2** not yet said to be true by those in charge; unCONFIRMed: *It's unofficial, but I know he's got the job* —**~ly** *adv*

un·or·tho·dox /ʌnˈɔːθədɒks‖ʌnˈɔrθədɑks/ *adj* not according to usual beliefs, methods, etc.: *He's a very unorthodox runner, but he usually wins the race* —compare ORTHODOX

un·pack /ʌnˈpæk/ *v* [T1;IØ] to remove (possessions) from (a container): *to unpack after a holiday|to unpack one's clothes|to unpack one's case*

un·par·al·leled /ʌnˈpærəleld/ *adj* [Wa5] too great to be equalled: *unparalleled changes|unparalleled rudeness*

un·par·lia·men·ta·ry /ˌʌnpɑːləˈmentəri‖-pɑr-/ *adj* [Wa5] (of something said or done in Parliament) not suitable; showing bad behaviour

un·per·son /ˌʌnˈpɜːsən‖-3r-/ *n* **-s** *not fml* a real person whose existence is not officially admitted: *After her attacks on the government, the newspapers began to treat her as an unperson, and her name was no longer mentioned in public*
USAGE The pl. of this word is **unpersons**, not ***unpeople.**

un·pick /ʌnˈpɪk/ *v* [T1] to take out (the stitches) from (something): *She unpicked the side* SEAM.|*She unpicked 3 stitches*

un·placed /ʌnˈpleɪst/ *adj* [Wa5] not one of the first 3 in a race or competition; not PLACED

un·play·a·ble /ʌnˈpleɪəbəl/ *adj* **1** (in sports) (of a ball) too well thrown, hit, etc., to be hit back; too difficult to hit **2** (of ground) unfit to be played on **3** (of a record) that cannot be played satisfactorily because damaged or of poor sound quality **4** (of music) that cannot be played because too difficult

un·pleas·ant /ʌnˈplezənt/ *adj* **1** causing dislike; not enjoyable; displeasing: *unpleasant smells/weather* **2** wishing to quarrel; unkind: *She was rather unpleasant with me.|a few unpleasant words* —**~ly** *adv* —**~ness** *n* [C;U]: *Don't let the recent unpleasantness end our friendship!*

un·plumbed /ˌʌnˈplʌmd◂/ *adj* [Wa5] UNFATHOMED

un·prac·tised, *AmE* usu. **-ticed** /ʌnˈpræktɪ̵st/ *adj* [Wa5] not skilful because of lack of experience: *She pulled out the stitches with an unpractised hand* (= she did it unskilfully) —opposite **practised**

un·pre·ce·dent·ed /ʌnˈpresɪ̵dentɪ̵d/ *adj* [Wa5] never having happened before: *unprecedented rainfall/changes* —see also PRECEDENT —**~ly** *adv*

un·prej·udiced /ʌnˈpredʒədɪ̵st/ *adj* [Wa5] not showing unfair judgment; not PREJUDICED: *my unprejudiced opinion*

un·pre·ten·tious /ˌʌnprɪˈtenʃəs/ *adj* not showing signs of wealth, size, importance, etc., or not wishing to do so: *an unpretentious house with a small number of rooms and simple furniture|They are rich but have an unpretentious style of living* —**~ly** *adv* —**~ness** *n* [U]

un·prin·ci·pled /ʌnˈprɪnsɪ̵pəld/ *adj* (done) without regard to moral values, standards of honourable behaviour, etc. —see also PRINCIPLE (4)

un·prin·ta·ble /ʌnˈprɪntəbəl/ *adj* [Wa5] (of words) unacceptable for being seen in print, usu. because morally offensive

un·pro·fes·sion·al /ˌʌnprəˈfeʃənəl/ *adj* not typical of the behaviour which is suitable in a certain profession or activity —**~ly** *adv*

un·prompt·ed /ʌnˈprɒmptɪ̵d‖ʌnˈprɑmp-/ *adj* [Wa5] (esp. of words or actions) produced without being asked for, suggested, etc.

un·pro·voked /ˌʌnprəˈvəʊkt◂/ *adj* [Wa5] (esp. of a bad action) (done) without being caused or forced by another action —compare PROVOKE

un·qual·i·fied /ʌnˈkwɒlɪ̵faɪd‖-ˈkwɑ-/ *adj* [Wa5] **1** [B] not limited: *We are in unqualified agreement* **2** [B (*for*); F3] not having suitable knowledge or QUALIFICATIONS: *an unqualified nurse|I am quite unqualified to talk on this subject* —opposite **qualified**

un·ques·tio·na·ble /ʌnˈkwestʃənəbəl/ *adj* [Wa5] which cannot be QUESTIONed[2] (2); certain: *The fact is unquestionable* —compare QUESTIONABLE —**-bly** *adv*: *He is unquestionably the best cricketer in England*

un·ques·tion·ing /ʌnˈkwestʃənɪŋ/ *adj* [Wa5] (done) without doubt or worry: *unquestioning trust in God* —compare QUESTION[2] (2)

un·qui·et /ʌnˈkwaɪɪ̵t/ *adj* [Wa5] *esp. lit* not calm or at rest

un·quote /ˌʌnˈkwəʊt/ *adv* [Wa5] (a word used in speech for showing that one has come to the end of a QUOTATION (2)): *The figures given are* (QUOTE[3]) *"not to be trusted"* (*unquote*), *according to this writer*

un·rav·el /ʌnˈrævəl/ *v* **-ll-** (*AmE* **-l-**) **1** [T1;IØ] also **ravel**— **a** to cause (threads, cloth, etc.) to become separated or unwoven **b** (of threads, cloth, etc.) to become separated or unwoven **2** [T1] to make clear (a mystery)

un·rea·da·ble /ʌnˈriːdəbəl/ *adj* **1** too dull to be read **2** ILLEGIBLE —**-bly** *adv*

un·real /ˌʌnˈrɪəl◂/ *adj* (of an experience) (as if) imaginary or unlike reality, as when the mind is confused by tiredness and unusual changes

un·rea·so·na·ble /ʌnˈriːzənəbəl/ *adj* **1** unfair in demands; not sensible —compare REASON[1] (5) **2** (of prices, costs, etc.) too great —opposite **reasonable** —**-bly** *adv* —**~ness** *n* [U]

un·rea·son·ing /ʌnˈriːzənɪŋ/ *adj* [Wa5] thoughtless; not using the power of reason: *unreasoning anger*

un·re·lent·ing /ˌʌnrɪˈlentɪŋ/ *adj* [Wa5] continuous, without decreasing in power: *a week of unrelenting activity* —compare RELENT, RELENTLESS —**~ly** *adv*

un·re·lieved /ˌʌnrɪˈliːvd◂/ *adj* [Wa5] not varied in any way; continuous or complete: *unrelieved anxiety|unrelieved darkness* —see also RELIEVE (4) —**~ly** /ˌʌnrɪˈliːvɪ̵dli/ *adv*: *unrelievedly dull*

un·re·mit·ting /ˌʌnrɪˈmɪtɪŋ◂/ *adj* [Wa5] never stopping: *unremitting activity* —see also REMIT (3) —**~ly** *adv*

un·re·quit·ed /ˌʌnrɪˈkwaɪtɪ̵d◂/ *adj* [Wa5] not given in return (esp. in the phr. **unrequited love**) —see also REQUITE

un·re·served /ˌʌnrɪˈzɜːvd◂‖-3r-/ *adj* [Wa5] **1** without limits or RESERVATIONs: *to give one's unreserved attention* **2** open (in speech); FRANK —**~ly** /ˌʌnrɪˈzɜːvɪ̵dli‖-3r-/ *adv*

un·rest /ʌnˈrest/ *n* [U] **1** lack of calmness **2** dissatisfaction, esp. socially: *In the 30's there were hunger marches and signs of unrest among the poor and unemployed*

un·re·strained /ˌʌnrɪˈstreɪnd◂/ *adj* [Wa5] not held back or reduced: *unrestrained anger/violence*

un·rip /ʌnˈrɪp/ *v* **-pp-** [T1] **1** to tear open **2** to pull stitches out of, so as to open: *to unrip a* SEAM

un·ri·valled, *AmE* **-valed** /ʌnˈraɪvəld/ *adj* [Wa5] unequalled; very good: *an unrivalled knowledge of Chinese art* —see also RIVAL[3]

un·roll /ʌnˈrəʊl/ *v* [T1;IØ] to open from a rolled position: *The picture is rolled up inside the cloth; unroll it and hang it up.|The paper unrolled and something fell out from inside*

un·ruf·fled /ʌnˈrʌfəld/ *adj* calm; not worried —see also RUFFLE[1] (2)

un·ru·ly /ʌnˈruːli/ *adj* [Wa2] **1** wild in behaviour: *these unruly children* **2** not easily kept in place: *unruly hair* —**-liness** *n* [U]

un·sad·dle /ʌnˈsædl/ *v* **1** [T1;IØ] to remove the SADDLE from (a horse) **2** [T1] UNSEAT (1a)

un·said /ʌn'sed/ *adj* [Wa5] (thought of but) not spoken about

un·sa·vour·y, *AmE* **-vory** /ʌn'seɪvəri/ *adj* unpleasant or unacceptable in moral values: *an unsavoury character* (= person)|*unsavoury activities*

un·say /ʌn'seɪ/ *v* **-said** /'sed/ [T1] *esp. lit* to make (a statement) as if never expressed: *If only I could unsay my words of anger*

un·scathed /ʌn'skeɪðd/ *adj* [Wa5] not harmed

un·schooled /ˌʌn'sku:ld◂/ *adj* [Wa5; (*in*)] untrained; not experienced —compare SCHOOL[2]

un·scram·ble /ʌn'skræmbəl/ *v* [T1] to put (esp. a message in CODE) back into order so as to be understood —see also SCRAMBLE[1] (5)

un·screw /ʌn'skru:/ *v* [T1] **1** to remove the screw(s) from (something) **2** to undo by twisting: *I can't unscrew* (*the top of*) *this bottle*

un·script·ed /ˌʌn'skrɪptɨd◂/ *adj* [Wa5] (of a broadcast talk or conversation) not written or planned before; spoken naturally —opposite **scripted**

un·scru·pu·lous /ʌn'skru:pjʊləs‖-pjə-/ *adj* not careful in details, esp. not caring about honesty and fairness in getting something: *unscrupulous methods* —opposite **scrupulous** —**~ly** *adv* —**~ness** *n* [U]

un·seat /ʌn'si:t/ *v* [T1] **1 a** also **unsaddle**— (of a horse) to throw off (a rider) **b** to cause a horse to throw off (a rider): *The fence unseated the rider* **2** to remove from a position of power, as from a seat in Parliament

un·see·ing /ˌʌn'si:ɪŋ◂/ *adj* [Wa5] not noticing; (as if) blind: *She was looking ahead with unseeing eyes when she fell over.*|*She looked, unseeing, at the window* —**~ly** *adv*

un·seem·ly /ʌn'si:mli/ *adj* [Wa2] not suitable (in behaviour): *It used to be thought unseemly for women to go to church without a hat* —opposite **seemly** —**-liness** *n* [U]

un·seen /ˌʌn'si:n/ *n* **1** [C] *not fml* a piece of writing to be translated into one's own language without having been seen before and prepared (as in an examination): *a Latin unseen* **2** [*the* + U] the world of spirits

un·ser·vi·cea·ble /ʌn'sɜ:vɨsəbəl‖-ɜr-/ *adj* [Wa5] not able to be used, because broken, worn out, etc.

un·set·tle /ʌn'setl/ *v* [T1] **1** [Wv4] to make less calm, more dissatisfied, etc.: *The sudden changes unsettled her/her mind.*|*many unsettling changes* **2** to cause illness to (esp. the stomach): *Foreign food always unsettles my stomach/me* —compare SETTLE[2] (5)

un·set·tled /ˌʌn'setld◂/ *adj* (of weather) changeable —opposite **settled**

un·sex /ʌn'seks/ *v* [T1] *lit* to take away the power to have sex or the typical qualities of one's sex

un·sexed /ˌʌn'sekst◂/ *adj* [Wa5] (of very young chickens) not separated by sex

un·sha·kea·ble, -kable /ʌn'ʃeɪkəbəl/ *adj* firm (in belief)

un·shod /ˌʌn'ʃɒd◂‖-'ʃɑd◂/ *adj* [Wa5] **1** *lit* (of a person) wearing no shoes; barefoot —opposite **shod** **2** (of a horse) not having had horseshoes fitted —see also SHOE[2]

un·sight·ly /ʌn'saɪtli/ *adj* [Wa2] not pleasant to look at; ugly —opposite **sightly** —**-liness** *n* [U]

un·skilled /ˌʌn'skɪld◂/ *adj* [Wa5] **1** not having training for a particular type of job **2** not needing special skill: *an unskilled job* —compare SKILLED

un·so·cia·ble /ʌn'səʊʃəbəl/ *adj* not friendly; not fond of being with people —opposite **sociable**

un·so·cial /ˌʌn'səʊʃəl◂/ *adj* [Wa5] not suitable for combining with family and social life (esp. in the phr. **unsocial hours**): *He receives more money for working unsocial hours, but it doesn't make up for his never seeing his family*

un·so·phis·ti·cat·ed /ˌʌnsə'fɪstɨkeɪtɨd◂/ *adj* [Wa5] simple in ways, likes, dislikes, etc.; inexperienced in the world and social life —opposite **sophisticated**

un·sound /ˌʌn'saʊnd◂/ *adj* [Wa5] **1** (of the body) not healthy **2** (of buildings, solid objects, etc.) not strong, esp. likely to fall **3** (of ideas) not having a firm base in fact **4** *rare* (of sleep) not deep or continuous **5 of unsound mind** *law* mad, and therefore not responsible for one's actions

un·spar·ing /ʌn'speərɪŋ/ *adj* [Wa5] **1** giving no mercy —see also SPARE[1] **2** holding nothing back, esp. money or help: *She gave out the food with an unsparing hand* (= generously).|*unsparing of one's time* —**~ly** *adv*

un·spea·ka·ble /ʌn'spi:kəbəl/ *adj* [Wa5] terrible: *unspeakable pain* —**-bly** *adv*: *unspeakably cruel*

un·spot·ted /ˌʌn'spɒtɨd/ *adj* [Wa5] *esp. old use* morally pure; blameless

un·stop /ˌʌn'stɒp‖ˌʌn'stɑp/ *v* **-pp-** [T1] **1** to open (something closed by a STOPPER): *to unstop a bottle* **2** to remove something that stops a flow in —compare STOP[1] (7)

un·strung /ˌʌn'strʌŋ◂/ *adj* [Wa5] **1** (of a musical instrument) without strings, or with the strings loosened **2** having lost control over the nerves and feelings

un·stuck /ˌʌn'stʌk◂/ *adj* [Wa5] **1** not fastened or stuck on —see also STICK[2] (3,4) **2 come unstuck** to go wrong; be unsuccessful: *He/His plans came unstuck*

un·stud·ied /ˌʌn'stʌdɨd/ *adj* [Wa5] natural: *unstudied grace* —compare STUDIED

un·sul·lied /ˌʌn'sʌlɨd/ *adj* [Wa5] *esp. lit* unspoilt; pure; without blame

un·sung /ˌʌn'sʌŋ◂/ *adj* [Wa5] not praised formally, esp. in poetry; undeservedly not famous (esp. in the phr. **unsung hero**)

un·swerv·ing /ʌn'swɜ:vɪŋ‖-ɜr-/ *adj* [Wa5] firm in purpose, esp. loyal —see also SWERVE[1] (2)

un·tan·gle /ˌʌn'tæŋgəl/ *v* [T1] to remove TANGLEs from; make smooth and free from twisted parts

un·tapped /ˌʌn'tæpt◂/ *adj* [Wa5] not used or drawn from: *He has untapped depths of experience which our firm could use* —see also TAP[2] (3)

un·ten·a·ble /ʌn'tenəbəl/ *adj* [Wa5] (of a position, esp. in an argument) which cannot be defended; which will fall to attack

un·thin·ka·ble /ʌn'θɪŋkəbəl/ *adj* not acceptable; which one cannot believe has happened, or cannot wish to happen: *Of course you can't go on holiday next week; it's quite unthinkable.*|*Defeat is unthinkable*

un·think·ing /ʌn'θɪŋkɪŋ/ *adj* careless; (done) without considering the effect; THOUGHTLESS —**~ly** *adv*

un·thought-of /ʌn'θɔ:t ɒv, -əv‖-ɑv, -əv/ *adj* [Wa5] quite unexpected; not imagined

un·ti·dy /ˌʌn'taɪdi/ *adj* [Wa1] not tidy

un·tie /ʌn'taɪ/ *v* [T1] to undo (a knot or something tied): *Untie the string.*|*Untie me from the chair*

un·til /ʌn'tɪl, ən-/ also (*not fml*) **till**— *prep, conj* **1** up to (the time that): *Wait until 10/tea/tomorrow.*|*Wait until I call.*|*We won't start until Bob comes.*|*He stayed from Monday till Friday.*|*She didn't arrive until 6 o'clock.*|*Until when?*|(*fml*) *Do not leave the building until instructed to do so.*|(*infml*) *He was here up until last week* **2** as far as; up to (a place to which one is going, or a place thought of as an event in time): *Stay on the train until* (*we get to*) *Birmingham* —see TO (USAGE)

un·time·ly /ʌn'taɪmli/ *adj* **1** not suitable for the time or occasion: *an untimely show of temper* **2** happening too soon: *The accident put an untimely* *end to the party* —compare TIMELY —**-liness** *n* [U]

un·tinged /ʌn'tɪndʒd/ *adj* [Wa5; (*by*)] **1** not showing any signs at all: *a meeting untinged by sadness* **2 not untinged with** showing signs of: *a meeting not untinged with grief*

un·tir·ing /ʌn'taɪərɪŋ/ *adj* [Wa5] not showing or experiencing tiredness, esp. in spite of hard work —**~ly** *adv*

un·to /'ʌntuː/ *prep obs & bibl* to: *She spoke unto him*

un·told /ˌʌn'təʊld◂/ *adj* [Wa5] **1** not told or expressed: *an untold story* **2** too great to be counted; limitless: *untold wealth*

un·tou·cha·ble /ʌn'tʌtʃəbəl/ *adj, n* [Wa5] (a person) of the lowest social group, esp. in the Hindu CASTE system

un·to·ward /ˌʌntə'wɔːd‖ˌʌn'tord/ *adj* [Wa5] unfortunate; not wanted: *an untoward event* —**~ly** *adv* —**~ness** *n* [U]

un·truth /ʌn'truːθ, 'ʌntruːθ/ *n fml euph* a lie

un·truth·ful /ʌn'truːθfəl/ *adj* **1** lying, esp. habitually: *an untruthful boy* **2** [Wa5] not true: *an untruthful story* —opposite **truthful** —**~ly** *adv*

un·tu·tored /ˌʌn'tjuːtəd◂‖ˌʌn'tuːtərd◂/ *adj* [Wa5] *esp. lit* (as if) not trained or educated: *Mistakes fell from his untutored tongue*

un·used¹ /ˌʌn'juːzd◂/ *adj* [Wa5] not having been used: *Put away the unused plates and cups* —compare USED¹

un·used² /ˌʌn'juːst/ *adj* [F+*to*] not accustomed: *She's unused to flying and gets a little anxious in planes* —compare USED²

un·u·su·al /ʌn'juːʒʊəl, -ʒəl/ *adj* **1** [Wa5] rare; not common **2** interesting because different from others; DISTINCTIVE: *I like that painting; it's most unusual*

un·u·su·al·ly /ʌn'juːʒʊəli, -ʒəli/ *adv* [Wa5] **1** in an unusual way **2** very; more than is common: *My dog's unusually fond of chocolate*

un·ut·te·ra·ble /ʌn'ʌtərəbəl/ *adj* [Wa5;A] **1** terrible: *in unutterable pain* **2** *infml* complete: *an unutterable fool* —**-bly** *adv*

un·var·nished /ˌʌn'vɑːnɪʃt◂‖-ɑr-/ *adj* [Wa5] plain; without additional description: *to give the unvarnished truth* —compare VARNISH² (2)

un·veil /ˌʌn'veɪl/ *v* **1** [I∅] to take off one's VEIL **2** [T1] to remove a VEIL or covering from (a person or something new): *They unveiled the picture.*|(fig.) *She was unveiled as the one responsible*

un·versed /ˌʌn'vɜːst‖-ɜr-/ *adj* [F +*in*] *fml & lit* not experienced or informed: *unversed in the ways of city life/the world of business*

un·voiced /ˌʌn'vɔɪst◂/ *adj* [Wa5] not spoken —compare VOICE²

un·war·rant·ed /ʌn'wɒrəntɨd/ *adj* [Wa5] (done) without good reason; not with just cause: *an unwarranted interruption*

un·wed /ˌʌn'wed◂/ *adj* [Wa5] *esp. old use* (esp. of a woman) not (yet) married

un·well /ʌn'wel/ *adj* [Wa5;F] **1** ill, esp. for a short time **2** *euph* menstruating (MENSTRUATE)

un·wiel·dy /ʌn'wiːldi/ *adj* **1** awkward to move, esp. because large, heavy, a strange shape, etc.: *an unwieldy box* **2** difficult to use; awkward in practice: *an unwieldy argument/method* —**-diness** *n* [U]

un·wind /ʌn'waɪnd/ *v* **-wound** /ʌn'waʊnd/ **1** [T1; I∅] **a** to undo (something that has been wound round): *She unwound the wool from the ball* **b** (of something wound round) to come undone **2** [I∅] to become clear, esp. if twisting or detailed: *The path unwound before them.*|*The story/film unwound before their eyes* **3** [I∅] *infml* to stop being nervous; RELAX

un·wit·ting /ˌʌn'wɪtɪŋ◂/ *adj* [Wa5;A;(B)] not knowing or intended: *unwitting rudeness* —**~ly** *adv*

un·wont·ed /ʌn'wəʊntɨd/ *adj* [Wa5;A;(B)] *esp. fml* unaccustomed; unusual

un·writ·ten law /ˌʌnrɪtn 'lɔː/ *n* a custom followed as a rule, though not formally so: *the unwritten law that women and children are saved first from a sinking ship*

un·zip /ˌʌn'zɪp/ *v* **-pp-** [T1] to open by undoing a ZIP (fastener)

up¹ /ʌp/ *adv* [Wa5] **1** towards or into a higher position; from below to a higher place: *Can you lift that box up onto the shelf for me?*|*The boy climbed up to a higher branch on the tree.*|*It gets hot quickly when the sun comes up.*|*Up you come!* **2** above; at or in a higher position: *flying 30,000 feet up*|*What's going on up there?* **3** to, into, or in a sitting or standing position: *He got up from his chair.*|*Please sit up straight.*|*Stand up when the teacher comes in!*|*I don't want to stand up for a whole hour* **4** from or off a surface: *Please pick that plate up (off the table)* **5** to the surface from below it: *He swam a long way under water and then came up for air.*|*The miners climbed up out of the mine* **6** from or away from the floor, the ground, the ground floor, or the bottom: *The sleeping dog jumped up when it saw its master.*|*Up,*/*Up with you, you lazy girl!* **7** so as to be completely finished: *The money's all used up.*|*The party ended up with a song.*|*He won't eat up his vegetables.*|*"Drink up, Jane!"* (SEU W.) **8** so as to be all in small pieces: *to tear up the newspaper*|*"The examinations are divided up into 3 parts"* (SEU S.) **9** out of the stomach through the mouth, when VOMITing (= being sick): *I'm afraid he's brought his dinner up again* **10** in or towards (the north): *He's flying up to Glasgow from London.*|*I'll be up in Scotland all the week.*|*up North* —compare DOWN¹ (7) **11** *BrE* (esp. of London, Oxford, or Cambridge) to or in a city or place of importance, from or compared with one supposed to be of less importance: *We usually go (from the country) up to London for a week every Christmas.*|*When is John going up to Oxford?*|*"Whatever you may see up in London"* (SEU S.) **12** to or towards a point away from the speaker, esp. a point at a higher level: *Will you walk up to the shop with me?* **13** towards and as far as the speaker: *He came right up (to me) and asked my name* **14** (*with verbs of fixing or fastening*) firmly; tightly; so as to be closed, covered, or joined: *to tie up a parcel*|*He nailed up the door so they couldn't open it* **15** (showing or making an increase or higher level of price, quantity, or quality): *I'm afraid the price of food is going up (and up)* **16** to a state of greater activity, force, strength, power, etc.: *The fire was burning up brightly.*|*Please turn the radio up* (=louder) *a bit* **17** so as to be together: *Please add up/count up these figures.*|*to collect up the fallen apples* **18** to or in a higher or better condition: *That family has certainly come up in the world* (= socially) **19** so as to be in a raised position: *He turned up his collar to keep his neck dry* **20** more loudly (in phrs. like **Speak up!**) **21** (so as to be) on top (in phrs. like **right side up, wrong end up**) **22 up and down a** higher and lower: *to jump up and down* **b** backwards and forwards: *to walk up and down (in a room)* —see also UPS AND DOWNS **23 Up (with)** We want or approve of: *Up the workers!* —see also UP TO

up² *adj* [Wa5] **1** [F] in a raised position; so as to be in place or be seen: *high up in the mountains*|*right up in the sky*|*to hang/put a picture up (on the wall)*|*The flag's up* (= on its pole).|*Hands up (if you know the answer)!*|*There's a notice up (on the board) about it.*|*The new house hasn't been up* (= built) *long* **2** [F] above the horizon (esp. in the phr. **The sun is up**) **3** [F] out of bed: *It's very early in the* *morning and no one is up yet* **4** [A;E] directed or going up: *the road up|the up stairs|(BrE) the up train (to London)* **5** [F] at a higher level: *Sales are up.|The temperature is up 10 degrees today* **6** [F] finished; ended: *Time's up!|It's all up with him now—nothing can save him from prison* **7** [F] *lit* prepared to fight: *The whole country was up, ready to drive out the enemy* **8** [F] (of a road) being repaired; with a broken surface: *"Road Up"* (sign) **9** [F] (in horse racing) riding: *Here comes the Queen's horse, with Lester Piggott up!* **10** [F] *not fml* charged with an offence; in court: *up before the judge|to be had up for stealing* **11 be up** *infml* to be happening; be the matter: *What's up? Why is Maisie crying?|I knew something was up when I saw the smoke* **12 be well up in/on** to know a lot about **13 not up** (in tennis and like games) (of a ball) having hit the ground (BOUNCEd) more than once before being hit **14 up and about** out of bed (again) and able to walk —compare OUT **and about** **15 up for** intended or being considered for: *The house is up for sale.|This subject will be up for* DISCUSSION *at the next meeting*

up[3] *v* **-pp-** *infml* **1** [T1] to raise; increase: *to up the price of petrol* **2** [Wv6;I∅+*and*] (used for adding force to the account of a surprising action) to get or jump up (and): *He upped and left.|I upped and told him what I thought of him!*

up[4] *prep* **1** to or in a higher or rising position; along; to the far end of: *He climbed up the hill/the stairs/the ladder.|His office is up the stairs.|They live just up the road* **2** against the direction of the current: *to go/be up (the) river|sailing up the Seine* **3** *BrE nonstandard* to; up to: *I'm going up the West End tonight* **4 up and down** away and back along: *His eyes moved up and down the rows of people, looking for his son's face* **5 up yours** *BrE taboo sl* (used for expressing great dislike for or annoyance at a person)

up[5] *n* [*the* +R] the part of a ball's course in which it is still rising after having hit the ground (BOUNCED): *He hit the ball on the up* —see also UP-AND-UP

up- *prefix* **1** [*v*→*v, adj, n*] so as to be above or in a higher position: UPGRADE|UPBRINGING|*to* UPHOLD —see USAGE **2** [*n*→*adj, adv*] being or going (farther) up: UPHILL|UPSTREAM|UPSTAIRS **3** [*n, v*→*v*] so as to be out of place or upside down: UPTURNED|UPROOT|UPEND **4** [*n*→*n, adj, adv*] (in) the higher or better part (of the): UPLAND|UPTOWN
USAGE These words are often formed from a *v adv* or from a verb that can be followed by **up**: *bring up*→*upbringing*.

up-and-com·ing /ˌ· · ˈ··◂/ *adj* [Wa5;A;(B)] showing signs of being about to succeed, when at the beginning of a profession, activity, etc. —compare UPCOMING

up-and-up /ˌ· · ˈ·/ *n* **on the up-and-up** *infml* **a** *BrE* improving; succeeding **b** *AmE* honest

up·beat /ˈʌpbiːt/ *n* [*the*+R;(C)] the beat in music which does not have the force, when the CONDUCTOR'*s* hand is raised —compare DOWNBEAT

up·braid /ˌʌpˈbreɪd/ *v* [T1 (*with*)] *fml* to scold

up·bring·ing /ˈʌpbrɪŋɪŋ/ *n* [S] (a way of) training and caring (for a child): *He blames his failure on his upbringing.|a good upbringing*

up·com·ing /ˈʌpˌkʌmɪŋ/ *adj* [Wa5;A] *AmE* about to happen —compare UP-AND-COMING

up-coun·try /ˌ· ˈ··◂/ *adj, adv* [Wa5] **1** in or from the inner parts of the country, away from the coast **2** not civilized; from an area with few people, towns, etc.

up·date /ˌʌpˈdeɪt/ *v* [T1] to make more modern or UP TO DATE

up·end /ʌpˈend/ *v* [T1] **1** to cause to stand on end or on any part that does not usually stand on the floor **2** to knock down: *He upended his opponent with one blow*

up·grade /ˌʌpˈgreɪd/ *v* [T1] to give a higher position to (esp. an employed person)

up·heav·al /ʌpˈhiːvəl/ *n* [C;U] (a) great change and movement: *all the upheaval of moving house|What an upheaval when they moved house!|a lot of upheaval to change offices*

up·hill[1] /ˌʌpˈhɪl/ *adv* [Wa5] **1** on an upward slope: *walking uphill* **2** forward with difficulty: *It's uphill all the way in this job*

up·hill[2] /ˌʌpˈhɪl◂/ *adj* [Wa5] **1** [B] on an upward slope: *an uphill path* **2** [A;(B)] difficult (esp. in the phr. **an uphill task**)

up·hold /ˌʌpˈhəʊld/ *v* **-held** /ʌpˈheld/ **1** [T1] to support; prevent from being weakened or taken away: *to uphold a right* **2** [T1] to declare to be right; CONFIRM: *The judge upheld the lower court's decision* **3** [T5a] *NEng & ScotE* to declare; MAINTAIN —**~er** *n*

up·hol·ster /ʌpˈhəʊlstəʳ/ *v* [T1] **1** to furnish (a room) with CARPET*s*, curtains, etc. **2** [Wa5] to fit (a chair) with soft coverings over filling material (PADDING) **3 well upholstered** (of a person) fat; fleshy

up·hol·ster·er /ʌpˈhəʊlstərəʳ/ *n* a person whose job is STUFFing and covering chairs and furniture

up·hol·ster·y /ʌpˈhəʊlstəri/ *n* [U] **1** CARPET*s*, curtains, soft chairs, etc. **2** the trade of an UPHOLSTERER

up·keep /ˈʌpkiːp/ *n* [U (*of*)] **1** the act of keeping something repaired and in order **2** the cost of this

up·land /ˈʌplənd/ *n* [U *often pl. with sing. meaning*] the higher land in an area: *broad sunlit uplands|the upland areas of the country*

up·lift[1] /ˌʌpˈlɪft/ *v* [T1] **1** *fml & lit* to raise high **2** [Wv4] to encourage cheerful or holy feelings in: *uplifting words*

up·lift[2] /ˈʌpˌlɪft/ *n* [U] **1** upward support: *an uplift* BRA|*a* BRA *giving enough uplift* **2** (something which gives) a sense of joy or moral improvement

up·on /əˈpɒn‖əˈpɑn/ *prep fml* ON[1] (1a,2,3,4,5b,6,7, 8b,10,12b,13,15,16) —see also **upon my** WORD[1] (19)

up·per[1] /ˈʌpəʳ/ *adj* [Wa5;A] **1** in a higher position (than something lower): *the upper arm* —see also **the upper** STOREY (2) **2** farther from the sea: *the upper* REACH*es* (=areas) *of the Nile* **3** of greater importance or higher rank —opposite **lower**

upper[2] *n* **1** the top part of a shoe or boot above the HEEL and SOLE **2 (down) on one's uppers** *infml* very poor

upper[3] *n infml* a drug which produces feelings of happiness or lack of anxiety —compare DOWNER

upper case /ˌ·· ˈ·◂/ *n* [U] (writing in) capital letters —compare LOWER CASE

upper class /ˌ·· ˈ·◂/ *adj, n* [B;(*the*) GU *often pl. with sing. meaning*] (of) a small social class whose members belong to a few old (and usu. noble) families, may own a great deal of land, and are usu. thought of as being very rich

upper crust /ˌ·· ˈ·◂/ *adj, n* [B;(*the*) GU] *infml & often humor* (of or belonging to) the higher classes of society; (of or belonging to) the ARISTOCRACY

up·per·cut /ˈʌpəkʌt‖-ər-/ *n* (in BOXING) a blow with the hand moving upward to the chin

upper hand /ˌ·· ˈ·/ *n* [*the* +R] control (esp. in the phrs. **have/get the upper hand**)

Upper House /ˌ·· ˈ·/ also **Upper Cham·ber** /ˌ·· ˈ··/— *n* [*the* +R] one of the 2 branches of a parliament, esp. the one that is smaller, less representative, and weaker: *The* HOUSE OF LORDS *is the British Upper House*

up·per·most /ˈʌpəməʊst‖-pər-/ also **up·most**

/ˈʌpməʊst/— *adv, adj* [Wa5] **1** in the highest or strongest position **2 come uppermost** to appear first and most clearly in the mind: *to say what comes uppermost*

up·pish /ˈʌpɪʃ/ *adj* **1** *infml* too proud, behaving badly with others, etc. **2** (in cricket) (of a stroke) hit in the air, esp. unintentionally, and in danger of being caught —**~ly** *adv* —**~ness** *n* [U]

up·pi·ty /ˈʌpəti/ *adj infml* UPPISH (1)

up·right[1] /ˈʌp-raɪt/ *adj* [Wa5] **1** (standing) straight up, esp. habitually: *a tall upright old man|an upright walk* **2** honest, fair, responsible, etc.: *an upright citizen* —**~ly** *adv* —**~ness** *n* [U]

upright[2] *adv* [Wa5] straight up; not bent

upright[3] *n* a supporting beam which stands straight up

upright pi·an·o /ˌ·· ·ˈ··/ *n* a piano with strings that are set in an up and down direction —compare GRAND PIANO

up·ris·ing /ˈʌpˌraɪzɪŋ/ *n* a RISING

up·roar /ˈʌp-rɔːʳ‖ˈʌp-ror/ *n* [S;U] confused noisy activity, esp. shouts

up·roar·i·ous /ʌpˈrɔːrɪəs‖ˌʌpˈro-/ *adj* **1** noisy, esp. with laughter **2** very amusing; causing loud laughter —**~ly** *adv*

up·root /ˌʌpˈruːt/ *v* [T1] **1** also **root up**— to tear up by the roots **2** to remove from one's home, settled habits, etc.: *to uproot oneself and settle abroad*

ups and downs /ˌ· · ˈ·/ *n* [P] good and bad periods: *Life is full of ups and downs*

up·set[1] /ʌpˈset/ *v* **-set**; *pres. p.* **-setting** **1** [T1] **a** to turn over, causing confusion: *to upset a dish/cup|* (fig.) *Her plans were upset by the change in the weather* **b** to cause to overflow or scatter by a knock: *He upset the milk/the sugar* **2** [IØ] **a** to be turned over: *The dish upset when you kicked it* **b** to overflow or scatter by a knock: *The milk upset when you kicked the dish* **3** [T1] to cause to worry, not be calm, etc.: *Do what he wants, or you'll upset him* **4** [T1] to make ill, usu. in the stomach: *The foreign food upset him/his stomach* —compare UNSETTLE

up·set[2] /ˌʌpˈset◂/ *adj* **1** [F] worried; anxious; feeling unhappy about something **2** [B] slightly ill: *an upset stomach*

upset[3] /ˈʌpset/ *n* **1** [C;U] the act of upsetting or putting into confusion or state of being so: *a complete upset of our plans* **2** [C] *infml* a quarrel **3** [C] a slight illness, usu. of the stomach: *a stomach upset*

up·shot /ˈʌpʃɒt‖ˈʌpʃɑt/ *n* [(*the*) S (*of*)] *not fml* the result in the end; OUTCOME: *What was the upshot of all that talk? Was anything decided?*

up·side down /ˌʌpsaɪd ˈdaʊn/ *adv* **1** [Wa5] in a position with the top turned to the bottom **2** in disorder: *Everything's upside down in this house* **3 turn somewhere upside down** to throw somewhere into disorder, esp. when searching: *She turned the house upside down, but couldn't find the hat*

up·stage[1] /ˌʌpˈsteɪdʒ/ *adv* towards the back of the stage in the theatre

upstage[2] /ˌʌpˈsteɪdʒ◂/ *adj infml* **1** too proud; HAUGHTY **2 upstage and county** *BrE* making a show of being (or pretending to be) of high social rank; SNOBbish

upstage[3] /ʌpˈsteɪdʒ/ *v* [T1] to take attention away from (someone else) for oneself

up·stairs[1] /ˌʌpˈsteəz◂‖-ərz/ *adv* [Wa5;F] at or to the upper floor(s) of a building: *He ran upstairs.|My room is upstairs*

upstairs[2] *adj* [Wa5;A] on a higher floor: *a house with 3 upstairs bedrooms* —**upstairs** *n* [Wn3;C]: *The upstairs of this house is all new*

up·stand·ing /ˌʌpˈstændɪŋ◂/ *adj* [Wa5] **1** tall and strong **2** honest and responsible —compare UPRIGHT[1] (2)

up·start /ˈʌpstɑːt‖-ɑrt/ *n derog* a person who has risen suddenly or unexpectedly to a high position and who is felt to be taking advantage of the power he has gained

up·stream /ˌʌpˈstriːm◂/ *adv, adj* [Wa5] (moving) against the current, towards the beginning of a river, stream, etc.

up·surge /ˈʌpsɜːdʒ‖-ɜr-/ *n* [(*of*)] an act of rising suddenly or violently to the surface, esp. of the mind, usu. with expression of a feeling

up·swing /ˈʌpˌswɪŋ/ *n* [(*in*)] a change to a higher stronger degree or greater number of something: *an upswing in votes for the new party*

up·take /ˈʌpteɪk/ *n* [*the* +R] ability to understand esp. something new (in the phrs. **quick/slow on the uptake**)

up·tight /ˈʌptaɪt, ʌpˈtaɪt/ *adj infml* very worried, nervous, anxious, etc., esp. about a particular thing

up to /ˈ· ·/ *prep* **1** as far as; to and including **a** a number: *Up to 10 men can sleep in this tent* **b** a higher degree or position in a set: *Everyone works, from the boy who sweeps the floor up to the President* **2** also **up till** /ˈ· ·/— until **3** [*usu. nonassertive*] equal to; good, well, clever enough (for): *Michael's not really up to that job.|My German isn't up to translating that letter.|Do you feel up to going out, or does your head hurt?* **4** the duty or responsibility of (in the phr. **be up to someone**): *It's up to you whether you decide to take the job* **5 be/get up to** to do (something bad): *What in the world are you up to? Stop it at once!|The children are always getting up to* MISCHIEF

USAGE **Up to** or **up till/until** are used with expressions of time when we mean that something was happening/not happening before a certain moment: **Up to** *now I've never met him.|I thought* **up until** *last week that there were no lions in India.*

up to date /ˌ· · ˈ·◂/ *adj* **1** modern **2 bring someone/something up to date** to tell someone/include in something the latest information

up to the min·ute /ˌ· · · ˈ··◂/ *adj* **1** very modern **2** including all the latest information

up·town /ˌʌpˈtaʊn◂/ *adj, adv AmE* at or in the living areas of a city or town, not the business centre —compare DOWNTOWN

up·turn /ˈʌptɜːn‖-ɜrn/ *n* [(*in*)] a favourable change: *an upturn in the exchange value of the pound*

up·turned /ˌʌpˈtɜːnd◂‖-ɜr-/ *adj* **1** [B] turning upwards at the end: *an upturned nose* **2** [Wa5;A] having been turned over

up·ward /ˈʌpwəd‖-ərd/ also **upwards**— *adj* [Wa5] increasing, getting higher, etc.; going up: *an upward movement of the hand*

up·wards /ˈʌpwədz‖-ər-/ *AmE* usu. **-ward** *adv* [Wa5] towards a higher level, position, or price: *A tree grows upwards while its roots grow down.|Costs are moving upwards*

upwards of /ˈ·· ·/ also **upward of**— *prep* more than, esp. in number or price: *upwards of £50|upwards of 50 years old*

u·ra·ni·um /jʊˈreɪnɪəm/ *n* [U] a heavy white metal that is a simple substance (ELEMENT (6)), is RADIOACTIVE, and is used in the production of atomic power

U·ra·nus /jʊˈreɪnəs/ *n* [R] the PLANET 7th in order from the sun —see picture at PLANET[1]

ur·ban /ˈɜːbən‖ˈɜr-/ *adj* [Wa5;A;(B)] of a town or city: *urban life*

ur·bane /ɜːˈbeɪn‖ɜr-/ *adj* having very good social manners; of smooth polite behaviour —**~ly** *adv* —**-banity** /ɜːˈbænəti‖ɜr-/ *n* [U]

ur·ban·ize, -ise /ˈɜːbənaɪz‖ˈɜr-/ *v* [Wv5;T1] to

cause to have or belong to towns or cities and their ways of living and behaviour, esp. when originally of or from the country —**-ization** /ˌɜːbənaɪˈzeɪʃən‖ˌɜrbənə-/ *n* [U]

ur·chin /ˈɜːtʃ$\frac{1}{2}$n‖ˈɜr-/ *n* a small boy, esp. one who gets into trouble and/or is dirty and untidy —see also SEA URCHIN

-ure /jəʳ/ *suffix* [*v*→*n*] **1** the act or condition of: *to fear* EXPOSURE|*the* CLOSURE *of the factory* **2** the body responsible for: *the* LEGISLATURE

urge[1] /ɜːdʒ‖ɜrdʒ/ *v* **1** [X9 (ON)] to drive or force (forward): *to urge the horses on with whips* **2** [V3] to beg or persuade with force: *They urged us to go with them* **3** [T1 (*on*)] to tell of with force; STRESS: *She urged the importance of speed.|She urged on us the need for speed*

urge[2] *n* [C;(*the*) S3] a strong wish or need (for something): *powerful sexual urges|She'd often felt the/an urge to hit him*

ur·gent /ˈɜːdʒənt‖ˈɜr-/ *adj* **1** very important, esp. which must be dealt with quickly or first: *It's not urgent; it can wait till tomorrow* **2** showing that something must be done or dealt with quickly: *He was urgent in his demands* —**~ly** *adv* —**-gency** /ˈɜːdʒənsi‖ˈɜr-/ *n* [U]

u·ric /ˈjʊərɪk/ *adj* [Wa5;A] *tech* of or found in URINE: *uric acid*

u·ri·nal /ˈjʊər$\frac{1}{2}$nəl, jʊˈraɪ-‖ˈjʊər$\frac{1}{2}$-/ *n* **1** a building for use by men as a LAVATORY for passing URINE **2** a vessel into which men may pass URINE

u·ri·na·ry /ˈjʊər$\frac{1}{2}$nəri‖-neri/ *adj* [Wa5] concerning the organs and passages of the body used for collecting and passing out URINE

u·ri·nate /ˈjʊər$\frac{1}{2}$neɪt/ *v* [IØ] to pass URINE from the body —**-nation** /ˌjʊər$\frac{1}{2}$ˈneɪʃən/ *n* [U]

u·rine /ˈjʊər$\frac{1}{2}$n/ *n* [U] liquid containing waste material, passed from the body

urn /ɜːn‖ɜrn/ *n* **1** any large metal container in which large quantities of tea or coffee may be heated and kept **2** a large container (VASE) with handles in which the ashes of a burnt dead body are kept, in ancient times often ornamental, in modern use plainer

u·ro- /ˈjʊərəʊ, jʊˈrɒ/ also **ur-** /jʊˈr-/— *comb. form* of or concerning URINE or the parts of the body where this is produced and passed out

Ur·sa Ma·jor /ˌɜːsə ˈmeɪdʒəʳ‖ˌɜr-/ also **Great Bear**— *n* [R] PLOUGH

us /əs, s; *strong* ʌs/ *pron* [Wp1] **1** (*object form of* WE): *He bought us a drink.|He bought a drink for us.|Us do a thing like that? Never!* **2** *BrE nonstandard* (*used esp. as an* INDIRECT *object*) me: *"Lend us a pound", he said* —see ME, HIM (USAGE)

US[1] /ˌjuː ˈes◂/ *abbrev. for:* UNSERVICEABLE

US[2] *abbrev. for:* **1** also **USA** /ˌjuː es ˈeɪ/— the United States (of America) **2** of the United States: *the US navy*

us·age /ˈjuːzɪdʒ, ˈjuːsɪdʒ/ *n* **1** [U] the way of using something; the type or degree of use **2** [C;U] one or more standards practised by users, esp. in using a language: *modern English usage* **3** [C;U] customs of behaviour: *Meals based on rice are not in common usage in England*

use[1] /juːs/ *n* **1** [U] the act of using or state of being used: *the use of water* **2** [U] the ability or right to use something: *to be given the use of the library* **3** [C;U] the purpose or reason for using something: *What use does this tool have/*SERVE*?|This book has a use as an ornament* **4** [U] the usefulness or advantage given by something: *Is this book any use?|What's the use of worrying?|It's no use (your) complaining; they won't do anything about it* **5** [U] custom; habit; practice **6 have no use for (esp. a person)** to think of no value; dislike **7 in use** being used **8 make use of** to use well; take advantage of **9 of use** useful: *I think you'll find this tool of use (to you)* **10 out of use** no longer used: *That expression has gone out of use*

use[2] /juːz/ *v* **1** [T1] to employ; put to use: *a pot used for cooking eggs/used to cook eggs|Stop touching; you use your eyes to look, not your hands.|I use the buses a lot.|The camera uses a new type of film* **2** [X9] *fml* to treat in the stated manner: *to use someone ill* (=badly) **3** [T1] to finish: *All the paper has been used* —see also USE UP **4** [T1] to treat (someone) with consideration only for one's own advantage —**usable** *adj*

use[3] /juːs/ *v* **used** /juːst/, *BrE neg. contr.* **usedn't, usen't** /ˈjuːsənt/ [I3 *past t.*] (*used for expressing a former fact or state*) to do regularly or habitually: *I (never/always) used to be interested in ships.|I used to go on Saturdays (but now I no longer do so).|He used not to like fish (but now he does).|It used to be thought that the earth was flat.|He doesn't work here now, but he used to.|Didn't she use to live in Coventry?|I'm surprised to see you smoking; you didn't use to/used not to.|Used there to be a hotel on that corner?|I use(d)n't to like wine, but I'm quite fond of it now*

USAGE 1 **Used** *to* and **would** are both used of habits or states that existed in the past and have now ceased, but **would** is not used at the beginning of a story: *We* **used** *to swim every day when we were children. We* **would** *run down to the lake and jump in* . . . 2 Of the various neg. forms, some people think *He* **used** *not to* is better than *He didn't* **used/use** *to*, but all are possible. *He never* **used** *to* expresses the same idea. The best question form is probably *Did/Didn't he* **use/used** *to*? but **Used/Usen't** *he to*? **Used** *he not to?* also exist.

used[1] /juːzd/ *adj* (usu. of goods) which has already had an owner; SECOND-HAND: *used cars*

used[2] /juːst/ *adj* [F +*to*] accustomed: *to get used to English food|"I'm not used to drinking."* (SEU S.)|*a man used to country life* —compare UNUSED[2]

use·ful /ˈjuːsfəl/ *adj* **1** effective in use: *a useful idea|Money is always useful* **2** helpful: *He's a useful person to have around* —**~ly** *adv*

use·ful·ness /ˈjuːsfəln$\frac{1}{2}$s/ *n* [U] **1** the state or quality of being useful **2 outlive/outlast its (one's) usefulness** to continue to be present when old and no longer effective

use·less /ˈjuːsləs/ *adj* **1** [Wa5] not of any use **2** [Wa5] not giving hope of success: *This method of working is useless* **3** *infml* not able to do anything properly: *You're useless! You've done it wrong again!* —**~ly** *adv* —**~ness** *n* [U]

us·er /ˈjuːzəʳ/ *n* a person or thing that uses: *the biggest user of oil* (=the country, industry, etc. that uses the most)

use up *v adv* [T1] to finish completely

ush·er[1] /ˈʌʃəʳ/ *n* **1** a man who shows people to their seats on an important occasion, as in church at weddings **2** a person who keeps order in a law court **3** *old use* a man who walks ahead of an important person

usher[2] *v* [X9 esp. IN, OUT] *fml* to bring; come, bringing or causing to enter: *Rain ushered in the summer.|When was the atomic age ushered in?*

ush·er·ette /ˌʌʃəˈret/ *n* a woman or girl whose job is in a cinema, taking tickets, selling ice cream, and showing people to their seats in the dark

USSR *abbrev. for:* Union of Soviet Socialist Republics (Soviet Union) —see NATIONALITIES TABLE

usu. *written abbrev. for:* usually

u·su·al /ˈjuːʒʊəl, ˈjuːʒəl/ *adj* **1** customary: *We will meet at the usual time.|"Is it usual to have milk with meals?" "Wine would be more usual"* **2 as usual** as is common or has happened before: *As usual, he arrived last*

u·su·al·ly /ˈjuːʒʊəli, ˈjuːʒəli/ *adv* often; generally: *I'm not usually so late.|I'm not late, usually*

u·sur·er /ˈjuːʒərəʳ/ *n derog* a person who lends money, esp. which must be paid back at an unfairly high rate of interest

u·su·ri·ous /juːˈzjʊəriəs‖juːˈʒʊər-/ *adj fml derog* **1** of or concerning USURY **2** typical of a USURER **3** (of a price) too high —**~ly** *adv* —**~ness** *n* [U]

u·surp /juːˈzɜːp‖-ɜrp/ *v* [T1] *fml* to seize for oneself (power or position), esp. unlawfully —**~ation** /ˌjuːzɜːˈpeɪʃən‖-ɜr-/ *n* [U] —**~er** /juːˈzɜːpəʳ‖-ɜr-/ *n*

u·su·ry /ˈjuːʒəri/ *n* [U] *derog* the practice of lending money to be paid back at a high rate of interest

u·ten·sil /juːˈtensəl/ *n fml or tech* **1** an object for use in a particular way, esp. a tool: *to buy all the utensils for gardening* **2** any tool, container, etc., used in the house, esp. for cooking: *to wash the kitchen utensils*

u·te·rine /ˈjuːtərɪn, -raɪn/ *adj* [Wa5] **1** of the WOMB or UTERUS **2** *tech* (of relatives or relationships) related through the same mother, not the same father: *uterine sisters*

u·te·rus /ˈjuːtərəs/ *n* **-ri** /raɪ/ *or* **-ruses** *tech* WOMB

u·til·i·tar·i·an /juːˌtɪlɨˈteəriən/ *adj* **1** concerned with practical use, not made for or interested in perfect forms, thoughts, etc. **2** believing in UTILITARIANISM —compare MATERIALISTIC

u·til·i·tar·i·an·is·m /juːˌtɪlɨˈteəriənɪzəm/ *n* [U] a belief that an act is better according to the number of people it helps

u·til·i·ty /juːˈtɪlɨti/ *n* **1** [U] the degree of usefulness **2** [C *often pl.*] any useful service for the public, such as supplies of water to the home, the bus service, etc.

u·til·ize, -ise /ˈjuːtɨlaɪz/ *v* [T1] *fml* to make (good) use of; use: *to utilize one's abilities in a suitable job* —**-izable** *adj* [Wa5] —**-ization** /ˌjuːtɨlaɪˈzeɪʃən‖-lə-/ *n* [U]

ut·most¹ /ˈʌtməʊst/ also (*esp. lit*) **ut·ter·most** /ˈʌtəməʊst‖-tər-/— *adj* [Wa5;A] of the greatest degree: *with her utmost strength|to the utmost limits*

utmost² also (*esp. lit*) **uttermost**— *n* [(*the*) R] the most that can be done (esp. in the phr. **to do one's utmost**)

u·to·pi·a /juːˈtəʊpiə/ *n* [R;(C)] (*often cap.*) (an idea of) a perfect society

u·to·pi·an /juːˈtəʊpiən/ *adj* [Wa5] concerning ideas of perfection, esp. socially, which are not practical —compare IDEALISTIC

ut·ter¹ /ˈʌtəʳ/ *adj* [Wa5;A] complete: *It's an utter mystery.|You're an utter fool*

utter² *v* [T1] **1** to speak (sound) **2** *tech* to produce and spread (false money)

ut·ter·ance /ˈʌtərəns/ *n esp. fml or tech* **1** [U] the act of speaking (esp. in the phr. **give utterance to**=express) **2** [C] something spoken: *the utterances of the mad* **3** [S] a way of speaking

ut·ter·ly /ˈʌtəli‖-ər-/ *adv* [Wa5] completely: *You're utterly mad!*

U-turn /ˈjuː tɜːn‖-ɜr-/ *n* **1** a turning movement in a car on a road taking one back in the direction one came from **2** *infml, usu. derog* a complete change, resulting in the opposite of what has gone before

u·vu·la /ˈjuːvjʊlə‖-vjə-/ *n* **-las** *or* **-lae** /liː/ a small soft piece of flesh which hangs down from the top of the mouth at the back —see picture at HUMAN²

u·vu·lar /ˈjuːvjʊləʳ‖-vjə-/ *adj, n tech* (a consonant) produced with the back of the tongue touching or nearly touching the UVULA

ux·o·ri·ous /ʌkˈsɔːriəs‖-ˈso-/ *adj lit or fml* unusually fond of one's wife —**~ly** *adv* —**~ness** *n* [U]

V, v

V, v /viː/ **V's, v's** *or* **Vs, vs** **1** the 22nd letter of the English alphabet **2** the ROMAN NUMERAL (number) for 5

v *written abbrev. for:* **1** VELOCITY **2** verb **3** *infml* very **4** VERSO **5** VOLUME **6** VIDE

V¹ *n* a thing or part shaped like the letter V: *She cut the material out in a V* —see also V-NECK, V-SIGN

V² *written abbrev for:* VOLT

v. (*AmE* **vs.**)— *abbrev for:* (esp. in sport) VERSUS (against): *The big cricket match is starting today; it's England v. Australia*

V-1 /ˌviː ˈwʌn/ also (*infml BrE, esp. humor*) **doodle-bug**— *n* a type of flying bomb used by the Germans in World War II

V-2 /ˌviː ˈtuː/ *n* a type of flying weapon (ROCKET) used by the Germans in World War II

vac /væk/ *n infml BrE* a university VACATION¹ (1a)

va·can·cy /ˈveɪkənsi/ *n* **1** [U] the state of being VACANT **2** [C] an empty space, where something is lacking **3** [C] an unfilled place, such as a hotel room that is not being used **4** [C] an unfilled position in a factory, office, etc.: *We've only got vacancies for metal workers; all the other positions are filled* **5** [U] emptiness of mind; lack of thought or interest

va·cant /ˈveɪkənt/ *adj* **1** empty; not filled with anything **2** [Wa5] (of a house, room, or seat) not being used or lived in **3** [Wa5] (of a position in employment) not at present filled **4** **a** (of the mind) not thinking; empty **b** showing lack of active or serious thought: *a vacant look* **c** foolish; senseless: *The madman gave a vacant laugh* —**~ly** *adv*

vacant pos·ses·sion /ˌ·· ·ˈ··/ *n* [U] *BrE law* the right of a buyer of a house or other building to move into it

va·cate /vəˈkeɪt, veɪ-‖ˈveɪkeɪt/ *v* [T1] **1** to cease to use or live in: *You must vacate the room by Friday as my son wants it.|As soon as she vacated her seat on the bus, it was taken by someone else* **2** to give up (something, such as a job or position)

va·ca·tion¹ /vəˈkeɪʃən‖veɪˈkeɪʃən/ *n* **1** [C; *on*+U] **a** *esp. BrE* one of the periods of holiday when universities (or law courts) are closed —see also LONG VACATION **b** *esp. AmE* any period of holiday **2** [C;U] *fml* an act or the action of vacating (VACATE) —see HOLIDAY (USAGE)

vacation² *v* [IØ (*at, in*)] *esp. AmE* to have a VACATION¹ (1b) —**~er** *n*

vac·cin·ate /ˈvæksɨneɪt/ *v* [T1 (*against*)] to introduce VACCINE into the body of (someone), as a protection against a disease

vac·cin·a·tion /ˌvæksɨˈneɪʃən/ *n* [C;U: (*against*)] (an example of) the act of vaccinating (VACCINATE)

vac·cine /ˈvæksiːn‖vækˈsiːn/ *n* [U;C] any of several types of poisonous substance (containing a VIRUS) used for protecting people against diseases (esp. SMALLPOX)

vac·il·late /ˈvæsɨleɪt/ *v* [IØ (*between*)] to be continually changing from one opinion or feeling to another; be uncertain of what action to take —**-lation** /ˌvæsɜ̇ˈleɪʃən/ *n* [U;C]

va·cu·i·ty /vəˈkjuːɜ̇ti, væ-‖væ-/ *n* **1** [U] *fml* lack of imagination or ideas **2** [C *usu. pl.*] *fml* a foolish remark, action, or idea **3** [U;C *usu. pl.*] *fml or lit* emptiness, as of the universe: *It is difficult to think of the great vacuities that exist in outer space*

vac·u·ous /ˈvækjʊəs/ *adj fml* **1** foolish, esp. in showing no sign of ideas, thought, or feeling: *a vacuous expression* **2** without purpose; meaningless: *the vacuous life of many rich people* —**~ly** *adv* —**~ness** *n* [U]

vac·u·um¹ /ˈvækjʊəm/ *n* **-u·ums** *or* (*tech*) **-u·a** /jʊə/ **1** [C] a space that is completely (or almost completely) empty of all gas, esp. from which all air has been taken away **2** [S] emptiness; lack: *Her death left a vacuum in his life*

vacuum² *v* [T1 (OUT); I∅] *infml* to clean (a house, room, floor, etc.) using a VACUUM CLEANER: *She vacuumed the room (out) yesterday.|I've been vacuuming all morning*

vacuum clean·er /ˈ··· ˌ··/ also (*infml, tdmk*) **hoover**— *n* an apparatus which cleans floors and floor coverings by drawing up the dirt from them in air —see picture at HOUSEHOLD

vacuum flask /ˈ··· ·/ *n* FLASK (4)

vacuum-packed /ˈ··· ·‖ˌ··· ˈ·/ *adj* [Wa5] (esp. of food offered for sale in shops) packed in a wrapping from which most of the air has been removed

vacuum pump /ˈ··· ·/ *n* a pump for removing air or gas from an enclosed space

vacuum tube /ˈ··· ·/ *n* VALVE (2)

va·de me·cum /ˌvɑːdi ˈmeɪkəm, ˌveɪdi ˈmiːkəm/ *n* (esp. in former times) a small book intended to be carried about and used for giving one quickly the facts needed on some subject

vag·a·bond /ˈvægəbɒnd‖-bɑnd/ *n* a person who lives an irregular or wandering life, esp. one who is thought to be lazy or worthless —compare VAGRANT

va·ga·ry /ˈveɪgəri/ *n* [*often pl.*] an unusual, purposeless, or unexpected idea, act, or thought: *The building of this house in the shape of a temple was a rich man's vagary.|the vagaries of love*

va·gi·na /vəˈdʒaɪnə/ *n* the passage which leads from the outer sex organs of women or female animals, to the organ (WOMB) in which young are formed

va·gi·nal /veˈdʒaɪnl‖ˈvædʒɜ̇nl/ *adj* [Wa5] of, related to, or having an effect on the VAGINA

va·gran·cy /ˈveɪgrənsi/ *n* [U] the state or offence of being a VAGRANT²

va·grant¹ /ˈveɪgrənt/ *adj* [A] **1** going from place to place with no fixed purpose: *a vagrant life* **2** *esp. lit* wandering or aimless: *vagrant fancies*

vagrant² *n* **1** a person who lives a wandering life with no steady home or work, esp. one who is poor and begs —compare VAGABOND **2** *law* anyone (such as a drunk person) who is found by the police wandering about without any lawful means of support, and who may be charged with the offence of VAGRANCY

vague /veɪg/ *adj* **1** [B] not clear in shape or form: *On the hillside, he could see the vague shapes of sheep coming through the mist* **2** [B] not clearly described, expressed, felt, or understood: *I couldn't recognize the woman from the vague description of her that you gave me* **3** [B] unable to express oneself clearly: *She's so vague that I can never understand what she's trying to say* **4** [A *usu. superl.*] *infml* slight; small: *I haven't the vaguest idea where I've left my pen* —**~ly** *adv* —**~ness** *n* [U]

vain /veɪn/ *adj* **1** full of self-admiration; thinking too highly of one's appearance, abilities, etc. **2** without result; useless: *After a number of vain attempts to climb the mountain we were forced to return to camp* **3** *fml derog* unimportant; slight; empty: *He wasted his time in the vain pleasures of smoking and drinking* **4 in vain** uselessly; without a successful result **5 take God's name in vain a** to speak of God without proper respect **b** to use God's name in cursing **6 take someone's name in vain** to talk disrespectfully about someone, without his knowledge, to another person —**~ly** *adv*

USAGE Note the word order of a sentence beginning with **vainly**, which may be that of a question: **Vainly** *he tried/did he try to open the door.*

vain·glo·ri·ous /veɪnˈglɔːrɪəs‖-ˈglo-/ *adj esp. lit or old use* showing too much pride in one's abilities —**~ly** *adv*

vain·glo·ry /veɪnˈglɔːri‖ˈveɪnglori/ *n* [U] *esp. lit or old use* too great a show of pride or VANITY

val·ance /ˈvæləns/ *n* **1** a narrow length of cloth hanging as a border from the edge of a shelf, or from the frame of a bed to the floor **2** *AmE* PELMET

vale /veɪl/ *n* **1** (as part of place name or in poetry) a broad low valley: *the Vale of Evesham* **2 this vale of tears** *lit or humor* the world; the daily life of men and women

val·e·dic·tion /ˌvælɜ̇ˈdɪkʃən/ *n fml* **1** [C] a speech or remark used in this act **2** [U] the act of saying goodbye, esp. on very important or formal occasions

val·e·dic·to·ry /ˌvælɜ̇ˈdɪktəri/ *adj fml or lit* in the manner or form of, or suited to, a VALEDICTION: *valedictory remarks*

va·len·cy /ˈveɪlənsi/ also (*esp. AmE*) **va·lence** /-ləns/— *n esp. BrE* the measure of the power of atoms to combine together to form compounds

val·en·tine /ˈvæləntaɪn/ *n* **1** (*often cap.*) a lover chosen on **Saint Valentine's Day** (February 14th): *Will you be my Valentine?* **2** an ornamental greeting card sent (usu. unsigned) to arrive on February 14th, declaring one's love for someone of the opposite sex

va·le·ri·an /vəˈlɪərɪən/ *n* **1** [C;U] any of several types of plant with strong-smelling red or white flowers **2** [U] a medicinal substance made from the roots of this

val·et¹ /ˈvælɜ̇t, ˈvæleɪ/ *n* **1** also **gentleman's gentleman**— a gentleman's personal male servant, who looks after his clothes, cooks his food, etc. **2** a male hotel worker who cleans and presses the clothes of people staying there

valet² *v* **1** [T1] to act as a VALET¹ to (someone) **2** [T1;I∅] to clean, repair, and brush (a person's clothes)

val·e·tu·di·nar·i·an¹ /ˌvælɜ̇tjuːdɜ̇ˈneərɪən‖-tuːdn-ˈeə-/ *n fml* **1** a person who has poor health **2** a person who is always thinking about the state of his health, even when this is not really necessary

valetudinarian² also **val·e·tu·di·nar·y** /ˌvælɜ̇ˈtjuːdɜ̇nəri‖-ˈtuːdneri/— *adj fml* having an unusual concern for one's health

val·i·ant /ˈvælɪənt/ also **val·or·ous** /ˈvælərəs/— *adj esp. fml or lit* (of a person or act) very brave, esp. in war; showing active and lasting courage

val·i·ant·ly /ˈvælɪəntli/ *adv* **1** *esp. fml or lit* very bravely **2 try valiantly** to try very hard; try with great effort (often with no success)

val·id /ˈvælɜ̇d/ *adj* **1** (of a reason, argument, etc.) having a strong firm base; that can be defended: *If you can't give me a valid reason for breaking your promise, I shan't trust you again* **2** *law* written or done in a proper manner so that a court of law would agree with it **3** having value; that can be used lawfully for a stated period or in certain conditions: *a train ticket valid for 3 months* —**~ity**

/və'lɪdǝ̈ti/ *n* [U (*of*)]: *You don't know enough about the subject to question the validity of my statements* —**~ly** /'vælǝ̈dli/ *adv*

val·i·date /'vælǝ̈deɪt/ *v* [T1] to make VALID: *In order to validate the agreement between yourself and your employer, you must both sign it* —**-dation** /ˌvælǝ̈'deɪʃən/ *n* [C;U]

va·lise /və'liːz‖və'liːs/ *n becoming rare* a small bag used while travelling, esp. for carrying clothes

val·ley /'væli/ *n* **1** [C] the land lying between 2 lines of hills or mountains, often with a river running through it —see picture at MOUNTAIN **2** [C9 *usu. sing.*] the land through which a stated river or great river system flows: *the Thames valley* USAGE A deep narrow mountain **valley**, with steep sides, is a **ravine** or **gorge**. If it is very small and steep it is a **gully**; if it is very large it is a **canyon**. **Cwm** is a Welsh word for **valley**, and **ghyll** is a *NWEngE* word for **ravine**.

val·our, *AmE* **-or** /'vælə^r/ *n* [U] *esp. fml or lit* great bravery, esp. in war

valse /væls/ *n Fr* a type of dance tune (WALTZ), esp. one written to be performed at a concert

val·u·a·ble[1] /'væljuəbəl, -jubəl‖'væljəbəl/ *adj* **1** worth a lot of money **2** [(*for, to*)] having great usefulness or value: *years of valuable service|You'll find this little tool very valuable for cutting out small shapes* —see WORTHLESS (USAGE)

valuable[2] *n* [*usu. pl.*] something (esp. something small, such as a piece of jewellery) that is worth a lot of money: *If you want to make sure that your valuables are safe, put them in the bank*

val·u·a·tion /ˌvælju'eɪʃən/ *n* **1** [U (*of*)] the action of calculating how much money something is worth **2** [C (*of*)] a value or price decided upon: *I was offered a piece of land at the reasonable valuation of £1500* **3** [C (*of*)] the opinion or idea one has of someone's worth in regard to ability or character

val·ue[1] /'væljuː/ *n* **1** [(*of*) U] the (degree of) usefulness of something, esp. in comparison with other things: *You'll find this instrument of great value in making certain kinds of measurement.|Smoking has little value except in helping to calm the nerves* **2** [U] that quality in something which makes it helpful, useful, or desirable: *In choosing employment he always set a high value on the interest of the work and a much lower value on the pay offered* **3** [C; (*of*) U] the worth of something in money or as compared with other goods for which it might be changed: *The value of the British pound is less than it was 100 years ago.|Will the value of houses and land continue to increase?|land values|I paid him £50 for the painting, but its real value must be about £500.|Jewels are articles of value; they are articles of great value.|These old ornaments are of little value* **4** [U9] worth compared with the amount paid (often in the phr. **value for money**): *If your coat wore out in less than a year it certainly wasn't good value; it was poor value for money.|You always get value for money at that shop* (=the goods are always worth the price charged) **5** [C *usu. pl.*] a standard or idea which most people have about the worth of good qualities: *One way of judging a society is to consider its values* (=the worth which its people think that justice, kindness, freedom, etc., have) **6** [C] the exact meaning or effect of a word **7** [C] the length of a musical note **8** [C] (in the science of numbers) the quantity expressed by a letter of the alphabet or other sign: *Let "x" have the value 25* **9** [C] *tech* the way in which light and shade (and sometimes different degrees of colour) are used in a picture or drawing —see COST (USAGE), WORTHLESS (USAGE) —**~less** *adj*

value[2] *v* **1** [T1 (*at*)] to calculate the value, price, or worth of (something): *If you want to sell your collection of stamps you should begin by having it valued.|He valued the house and its contents at £12,000* **2** [Wv5;T1] to consider (someone or something) to be of great worth: *I've always valued your friendship very highly.|a valued friend*

value-ad·ded tax /ˌ·· '·· ·‖ˌ·· ·· '·/ also **VAT**— *n* [R;U] (in Britain and some other European countries) a tax (such as 10 per cent added to the price) paid by the buyer to the seller of an article, and to the government by those who make and sell the article

val·u·er /'væljuə^r/ *n* a person whose work is to decide how much money things are worth

valve /vælv/ *n* **1** a doorlike part of a pipe (or of a pipelike part inside the body), which opens and shuts so as to control the flow of liquid, air, gas, etc., through the pipe: *You put air into a bicycle tyre through the valve in the tyre.|The valves of the heart and blood vessels allow the blood to pass in one direction only* —see pictures at PETROL, WIND INSTRUMENT and RESPIRATORY **2** also **vacuum tube**, (*esp. AmE*) **tube**— a closed glass tube with no air in it, used for controlling a flow of electricity, as in radio or television **3** a hard shell protecting the soft body of certain sea creatures, esp. one of 2 enclosing the animal —see also BIVALVE

val·vu·lar /'vælvjulə^r‖-vjə-/ *adj* [Wa5] connected with a VALVE or valves, esp. of the heart

va·moose /væ'muːs, və-/ *v* [IØ *often imper.*] *AmE sl* to go away hastily

vamp[1] /væmp/ *n* **1** *tech* **a** the front upper part of a boot or shoe **b** a piece of leather used for repairing this part **2** *infml* **a** a not very skilful way of playing a musical instrument, esp. a piano, in simple sets of notes invented by the player **b** a short informal piece of music that introduces a song

vamp[2] *v* **1** [T1] *tech* to repair (a boot or shoe) by using a VAMP[1] (1*b*) **2** [T1 (OUT, UP); IØ] *infml* to play (a tune) in the manner of a VAMP[1] (2)

vamp[3] *n* (esp. in the 1920s and 1930s) a woman who intentionally uses her charm to make men do things for her or give her money

vam·pire /'væmpaɪə^r/ *n* **1** an evil spirit which is believed to live in the bodies of dead people and suck the blood of people while they are asleep at night **2** an evil person who lives by forcing others to give him money, or takes from them time or strength which they cannot afford

vampire bat /'·· ·/ also **vampire**— *n* any of various South American animals like a flying mouse (BAT) which suck the blood of other animals

vamp up *v adv* [T1] *infml* to invent (something) from little material: *She can always vamp up some new excuse for coming late*

van[1] /væn/ *n* [*the*+U] *fml or lit* VANGUARD (2,3) (esp. in the phr. **in the van (of)**)

van[2] *n* (*often in comb.*) **1** a covered road vehicle for carrying goods and sometimes people: *a baker's van|a police van|Chris brought 6 people to the party in his van* —compare LORRY and see picture at INTERCHANGE **2** *esp. BrE* a covered railway carriage for goods and sometimes people: *a* LUGGAGE *van|the guard's van*

va·na·di·um /və'neɪdɪəm/ *n* [U] a type of hard silvery metal used in making certain kinds of steel and DYEs

van·dal /'vændl/ *n* a person who intentionally damages or destroys beautiful or useful things belonging to others, makes beautiful places ugly, etc.

van·dal·is·m /'vændəl-ɪzəm/ *n* [U] intentional

needless and usu. widespread damage and destruction, esp. of public buildings and other public property

van·dal·ize, -ise /ˈvændəl-aɪz/ *v* [T1 *often pass.*] to damage or destroy (esp. a piece of public property) intentionally: *We can't use any of the public telephones round here; they've all been vandalized*

vane /veɪn/ *n* **1** a bladelike part of certain machines, which has a flat surface that makes it possible to use the force of wind or water as the driving power: *the vanes of a* PROPELLER **2** WEATHER VANE

van·guard /ˈvængɑːd‖-ɑrd/ *n* **1** [G;C] the soldiers marching at the front of an army, or sent on ahead to protect it against surprise attack —compare REARGUARD **2** [*the*+U] the leading part of an army or of any marching body of people, or of ships in battle (often in the phr. **in the vanguard**) **3** [*the*+U] the leading part of any kind of advancement in human affairs (esp. in the phr. **in the vanguard (of)**): *In the modern world the scientists are in the vanguard of all industrial development*

va·nil·la /vəˈnɪlə/ *n* **1** [C] any of several types of climbing plant with sweet-smelling flowers, that grow esp. in tropical America **2** [U] a substance or liquid made from the beans of this plant, used for improving the taste of certain sweet foods **3** [A] (of a food) made to taste of this: *vanilla ice cream|vanilla cakes*

van·ish /ˈvænɪʃ/ *v* [IØ] **1** to disappear; go out of sight: *With a wave of his hand, the magician made the rabbit vanish* **2** to cease to exist; come to an end: *Many types of animal have now vanished from the earth*

vanishing cream /ˈ··· ·/ *n* [U] a thick creamy substance used by women to make their skin soft, which is quickly taken in by the surface of the skin without making it shine

vanishing point /ˈ··· ·/ *n* [*usu. sing.*] **1** the place or point at which something goes out of sight or comes to an end: *After that steep climb my strength reached vanishing point* **2** (in the drawing of solid objects) the point in the distance at which parallel lines appear to the human eye to meet, and are therefore represented as doing so

van·i·ty /ˈvænɨ̣ti/ *n* **1** [U] the quality or state of being too proud of oneself or one's appearance, abilities, etc.: *"She's always looking at herself in the mirror." "What vanity!"* **2** [U] the quality or state of being without true lasting value: *the vanity of human wishes|Fame, power, wealth; all is vanity* **3** [C] a thing or act that is without true lasting value

vanity case /ˈ··· ·/ also **vanity bag**— *n* a small bag or case used by women for carrying articles and substances (MAKE-UP) used in making the face more beautiful

van·quish /ˈvæŋkwɪʃ/ *v* [T1] *esp. lit* to conquer; defeat completely

van·tage·point /ˈvɑːntɪdʒpɔɪnt‖ˈvæn-/ *n* **1** also **point of vantage**, (*fml*) **coign of vantage**— a good position from which to attack, defend, or see something: *If we climb to the top of the rising ground it will give us a vantagepoint from which to see the race* **2** point of view: *I quite agree that from your vantagepoint his action must have seemed rather unwise*

vap·id /ˈvæpɨ̣d/ *adj* (of speech or writing, or of a person) lacking force, interest, or ideas; dull —**~ly** *adv* —**~ness** *n* [U]

va·pid·i·ty /vəˈpɪdɨ̣ti/ *n* **1** [U] the state or quality of being VAPID **2** [C *usu. pl.*] a VAPID remark

va·por·ize, -ise /ˈveɪpəraɪz/ *v* [T1;IØ] to (cause to) change into VAPOUR (1,2): *Water vaporizes when boiled* —**-ization** /ˌveɪpəraɪˈzeɪʃən‖-rə-/ *n* [U]

va·por·ous /ˈveɪpərəs/ *adj* **1** having the nature of VAPOUR (1,2): *Vaporous clouds rose from the lake* **2** *now rare* full of strange or useless fancies

va·pour, *AmE* **-por** /ˈveɪpəʳ/ *n* **1** [U;C] a gaslike form of a liquid (such as mist or steam), often caused by a sudden change of temperature: *A cloud is a mass of vapour in the sky.|Strange vapours rose from the dark lake* **2** [U9] *tech* the gas to which the stated liquid or solid can be changed by the action of heat: *water vapour* **3** [C] *now rare* a passing fancy; unreal or empty product of the imagination

va·pours, *AmE* **-pors** /ˈveɪpəz‖-ərz/ *n* [*the*+P] *old use or humor* (*used esp. of women*) a state of feeling suddenly faint

vapour trail /ˈ·· ·/ *n* a line of water VAPOUR formed in the air by a high-flying aircraft

var. *written abbrev for:* VARIANT

var·i·a·bil·i·ty /ˌveərɪəˈbɪlɨ̣ti/ *n* [U] the quality or condition of being VARIABLE[1]; probability that something will vary

var·i·a·ble[1] /ˈveərɪəbəl/ *adj* **1** changeable; not staying the same; not steady: *The winds today will be light and variable* **2** that can be intentionally varied: *The amount of heat produced by this electrical apparatus is variable at will by turning a small handle* **3** *euph* usually good, but often bad: *That actor's performances are rather variable* —**-bly** *adv* —**~ness** *n* [U]

variable[2] *n usu. tech* **1** something which represents something (such as temperature) which can vary in quantity or size **2** a letter representing this

var·i·ance /ˈveərɪəns/ *n* **at variance (with)** in opposition (to); not in agreement (with): *Though they were friends for many years, they're now completely at variance.|What he did was at variance with what he'd promised to do*

var·i·ant[1] /ˈveərɪənt/ *adj* [Wa5;A] different; varying: *variant spellings*

variant[2] *n* a (slightly) different form, as of a word, phrase, or part of a story or piece of writing: *"Favor" is the American variant of the British "favour"*

var·i·a·tion /ˌveəriˈeɪʃən/ *n* **1** [U] the action of varying **2** [C] an example or degree of this: *If you go to a number of different shops you'll often find great variations of price for the same articles* **3** [C] one of a set of repeated parts of part of a simple piece of music, sometimes written by someone else, each with certain different ornamental changes or developments made to it: *Elgar wrote a piece of music called the "Enigma Variations"* **4** [C; U] (an example of) change from what is usual in the form of a group or kind of living things, such as animals

var·i·col·oured, *AmE* **-ored** /ˈveəriˌkʌləd‖-ərd/ *adj* of many different colours

var·i·cose /ˈværɨ̣kəʊs/ *adj* (of a blood vessel, esp. in the leg) that has become greatly and incurably swollen (esp. in the phr. **varicose veins**)

var·ied /ˈveərid/ *adj* **1** of different kinds: *varied ideas about what is important in life* **2** not staying the same; changing: *a varied life*

var·ie·gat·ed /ˈveərɪəgeɪtɨ̣d/ *adj* (esp. of a flower or leaf) marked irregularly in spots, lines, masses, etc., of different colours

var·ie·ga·tion /ˌveərɪəˈgeɪʃən/ *n* [U] irregular colour marking, esp. in plants

va·ri·e·ty /vəˈraɪəti/ *n* **1** [U] the state of varying; difference of condition or quality: *She didn't like the work, because it lacked variety; she was doing the same things all the time* **2** [S (*of*)] a group or collection containing different sorts of the same thing or people: *Everyone arrived late at the party, for a variety of reasons* **3** [C] a type which is different from others in a group to which it belongs: *An eager farmer is always looking for new varieties of wheat* **4** [U] (*AmE* also **vaudeville**)— a kind of theatre or television show in which a number of amusing short performances are given (such as singing, music, dancing, acts of skill, telling jokes, etc.)

variety meat /·ˈ··· ·/ *n* [C;U] *AmE euph* (a type of) OFFAL

variety show /·ˈ··· ·/ *n* a show in which VARIETY (4) is performed

var·i·form /ˈveərᵻfɔːm‖-ɔrm/ *adj tech or fml* having various forms: *variform plants*

var·i·o·rum /ˌveəriˈɔːrəm‖-ˈorəm/ also **variorum e·di·tion** /··ˌ·· ·ˈ··/— *n* a book, often the collected works of a great writer, with explanations and remarks by various people who have made a special study of literature: *a Shakespeare variorum*

var·i·ous /ˈveərɪəs/ *adj* **1** [A;(F)] different from each other; of (many) different kinds: *Of all the various ways of cooking an egg, I like boiling best.|Your reasons for not wanting to meet Smith may be many and various, but you must still meet him* **2** [Wa5;A] several; a number of: *Various people among those present thought they'd heard the aircraft* —see DIFFERENT (USAGE)

var·i·ous·ly /ˈveərɪəsli/ *adv* **1** in various ways or at various times; differently: *The depth of this cave has been variously calculated at from 200 metres to 500 metres* **2** by various names: *Queen Elizabeth I of England, known variously as "the* VIRGIN *Queen" and "Good Queen Bess"*

var·let /ˈvɑːlᵻt‖ˈvɑr-/ *n* [C;N] *old use* a wicked or worthless man; KNAVE

var·mint /ˈvɑːmᵻnt‖ˈvɑr-/ *n* [C; *you*+N] *infml or dial* a troublesome worthless person or animal (esp. a young male)

var·nish¹ /ˈvɑːnɪʃ‖ˈvɑr-/ *n* **1** [U;C] (any of several types of) liquid made by mixing various substances with oil, which, when brushed onto articles made esp. of wood and allowed to dry, gives a clear hard bright surface —see also NAIL VARNISH **2** [(*the*) S] the shiny appearance produced by using this substance: *Hot plates may spoil the varnish on a table* **3** [S;(U)] a smooth or shiny appearance, esp. when it is thought to be only on the surface, covering something rough or of poor quality

varnish² *v* **1** [T1] to cover with VARNISH¹ or with NAIL VARNISH **2** [T1 (OVER)] to cover (something unpleasant) over with a smooth appearance: *Though the members of the committee disagreed on several points, the chairman did his best to varnish this over in the report* —see also UNVARNISHED

var·si·ty /ˈvɑːsᵻti‖ˈvɑr-/ *n* **1** [*the*+R;C;A] *infml or pomp BrE* (*often cap.*) a university (esp. Oxford or Cambridge): *the Varsity match* (=a match between Oxford and Cambridge) **2** [A;(C)] *AmE* the chief group or team representing a university, college, school, or club, esp. in a sport: *the varsity football team*

var·y /ˈveəri/ *v* **1** [I∅ (*in*)] to be different; have qualities that are not the same as each other: *Opinions on this matter vary.|Houses vary in size.|This student never varies; his work is always very good* **2** [Wv4;T1;I∅ (*from*)] to (cause to) become different; change (continually): *Her health varies from good to rather weak.|Old people don't like to vary their habits*

vas·cu·lar /ˈvæskjʊləʳ‖-kjə-/ *adj* [Wa5] *tech* concerning or containing vessels through which liquids move in the bodies of animals or plants: *a vascular system*

vase /vɑːz‖veɪs, veɪz/ *n* a container, usu. shaped like a deep pot with a rather narrow opening at the top and usu. made of glass or baked clay, used either to put flowers in or as an ornament

va·sec·to·my /vəˈsektəmi/ *n* [C;U] (an operation for) removing a male's ability to become a father by cutting the small tube that carries the male seeds (SPERM)

Vas·e·line /ˈvæsᵻliːn/ *n* [U] *tdmk* a type of soft yellow or white jelly used for various medical and other purposes

vas·sal /ˈvæsəl/ *n* **1** [C;A] (during the MIDDLE AGES) (a person) who promised to be loyal to a lord and to serve him or fight for him and who in return was given land by the lord: *a vassal kingdom* **2** [C] a person who serves another in a slavelike way

vas·sal·age /ˈvæsəlɪdʒ/ *n* [U] **1** the state of being a VASSAL **2** the loyalty or services that had to be given by a VASSAL (1)

vast /vɑːst‖væst/ *adj* [Wa1] very large and wide; great in size or amount; spreading a great distance: *The vast plains stretch for 600 miles.|The actors were brought from New York to London at vast cost*

vast·ly /ˈvɑːstli‖ˈvæstli/ *adv* very greatly: *His piano playing has improved vastly since last year*

vast·ness /ˈvɑːstnᵻs‖ˈvæst-/ *n* **1** [U] the quality or state of being VAST **2** [C *usu. pl.*] a great empty area: *the vastnesses of space*

vat /væt/ *n* a very large barrel or container for holding liquids (such as beer, WHISKY, DYE, etc.), esp. when they are being made

VAT /ˌviː eɪ ˈtiː, væt/ *n* [R;U] VALUE-ADDED TAX

Vat·i·can /ˈvætɪkən/ *n* **1** [*the*+R] the large palace in which the POPE lives, in Rome, Italy **2** [(*the*+) GU] the POPE's government or office

vau·de·ville /ˈvɔːdəvɪl, ˈvəʊ-/ *n* [U] *AmE* VARIETY (4): *a vaudeville singer*

vault¹ /vɔːlt/ *n* **1** [C] **a** a number of arches built so that they form a roof **b** a roof or CEILING made in this manner, as in most churches **2** [C] an underground room **a** beneath the floor of a church or in a CHURCHYARD, in which the bodies of the dead are placed **b** in which things are stored to keep them at the same cool temperature: *a wine vault* **3** [C] a room with thick walls and a heavy door to protect it against fire and thieves, in which money, jewels, important papers, etc., are kept at a bank **4** [(*the*) S] *poet* a covering like a large curved roof: *In former times, poets often called the sky "the vault of heaven"*

vault² *v* [T1;L9] to jump over (something) in one movement using the hands or a pole to gain more height: *He put his hand on the gate and vaulted it easily.|When he was young he could vault onto the back of a horse* —**~er** *n*

vault³ *n* a jump made by VAULTing² —see also POLE VAULT

vault·ed /ˈvɔːltᵻd/ *adj* [Wa5] **1** in the form of a VAULT¹ (1): *a vaulted roof* **2** covered with a curved roof: *a vaulted passage*

vault·ing¹ /ˈvɔːltɪŋ/ *n* [U] **1** the VAULTs¹ (1a) in a roof **2** framework in the form of a VAULT¹ (1)

vaulting² *adj* [A;(F)] *esp. lit* (of a non-material thing) reaching or stretching out for the highest point (esp. in the phr. **vaulting ambition**)

vaulting horse /ˈ·· ·/ also **horse**— *n* a wooden apparatus which people can VAULT² over for exercise —compare POMMEL HORSE, SIDE HORSE

vaunt¹ /vɔːnt/ also (*v prep*) **vaunt of, vaunt about**— *v* [Wv5;T1] *esp. lit* to praise (something) too much; BOAST about: *I was surprised to find that his much-vaunted car was old and of a rather common kind* —**~er** *n* —**~ingly** *adv*

vaunt² *n lit* an example of VAUNTing¹; BOAST

VC /ˌviː ˈsiː/ *n* VICTORIA CROSS

VD /ˌviː ˈdiː/ *n* [U] VENEREAL DISEASE

-'ve /v, əv/ [Wv2] *contr. of* (*in compound tenses*) have —see CONTR. (USAGE)

veal /viːl/ *n* [U] meat from the young of a cow (CALF) —see MEAT (USAGE)

vec·tor /ˈvektəʳ/ *n* **1** (in science) a quantity which has direction as well as size and which can be represented by an arrow the length of which has a direct relationship with the size **2** an insect (such as a fly or mosquito) which can carry a disease from one living thing to another **3** *tech* the course of an aircraft

veer /vɪəʳ/ *v* **1** [L9] (of a traveller, vehicle, or road) to turn or change direction: *The car was out of control and suddenly veered across the road* **2** [L9] (of a person, or of opinion, talk, etc.) to change from one intention, course, plan, or opinion to another: *We were talking about food, and then suddenly the conversation veered round to stomach diseases* **3** [T1;L9] to (cause (a ship) to) change course, esp. away from the wind **4** [IØ] *tech* (of the wind) to change direction, moving round the compass in the order North–East–South–West —compare BACK⁴ (6)

veg /vedʒ/ *n* **veg** [Wn3;C *usu. pl.*; U] *infml BrE* (a type of) vegetable, usu. when cooked: *meat and 2 veg*

ve·gan /ˈviːgən‖ˈviːdʒən/ *n* a person who believes in and practises VEGETARIANISM but who also does not eat eggs or cheese or drink milk —compare VEGETARIAN

vege·ta·ble¹ /ˈvedʒtəbəl/ *n* **1** [C *usu. pl.*] a (part of a) plant that is grown for food to be eaten with the main part of a meal, usu. of a type which grows in or near the ground: *meat and vegetables|2 vegetables on a plate; both are onions* **2** [C] a type of this: *We grow many different vegetables; potatoes, onions, beans, etc.* **3** [U] plant life (esp. in the phr. **animal, vegetable, or mineral**) **4** [C] a human being who exists but has little or no power of thought (or sometimes also movement)
See next page for picture

vegetable² *adj* [Wa5;A] of, related to, growing like, or made or obtained from plants: *vegetable life|vegetable oils*

vegetable king·dom /ˈ··· ˌ··/ *n* [*the*+R] one of the 3 divisions into which the world can be divided; all plant life considered as a group —compare ANIMAL KINGDOM, MINERAL KINGDOM

vegetable mar·row /ˌ··· ˈ··/ *n fml or tech* MARROW (3)

veg·e·tar·i·an¹ /ˌvedʒəˈteərɪən/ *n* a person who believes in and practises VEGETARIANISM —compare VEGAN

vegetarian² *adj* [Wa5] **1** of, for, or related to VEGETARIANs¹: *vegetarian beliefs|a vegetarian restaurant* **2** made up only of vegetables: *a vegetarian meal*

veg·e·tar·i·an·is·m /ˌvedʒəˈteərɪənɪzəm/ *n* [U] the belief in and practice of eating only fruit, vegetables, nuts, etc., or of avoiding eating meat and fish, usu. for reasons of health or religion

veg·e·tate /ˈvedʒəteɪt/ *v* [IØ] to live in the manner of a plant, without activity of mind or body; have a dull life without interests or social activity

veg·e·ta·tion /ˌvedʒəˈteɪʃən/ *n* [U] **1** plant life in general **2** all the plants in a particular place: *The strange and colourful vegetation of the tropical forest*

ve·he·ment /ˈvɪəmənt/ *adj* **1** fiercely strong or eager in support of or esp. in opposition to someone or something: *I have a vehement hatred of people who are cruel to animals* **2** *esp. lit* coming with great, sudden, and unpleasant force; violent: *a vehement wind* —**~ly** *adv* —**-mence** /ˈvɪəməns/ *n* [U]

ve·hi·cle /ˈviːɪkəl/ *n* **1** [C] something in or on which people or goods can be carried from one place to another, esp. **a** along roads, usu. having wheels (such as a carriage, bicycle, car, cart, taxi, or bus) but sometimes made to slide over snow or ice **b** through space (esp. in the phr. **space vehicle**) **2** [C (*for*)] something by means of which something else can be passed on or spread: *Television has become an important vehicle for spreading political ideas* **3** [C (*for*)] a means for showing off a person's abilities: *The writer wrote this big part in his play simply as a vehicle for the famous actress*

ve·hic·u·lar /viːˈhɪkjʊləʳ‖-kjə-/ *adj* [Wa5] *fml* concerning or connected with vehicles on roads: *vehicular traffic*

veil¹ /veɪl/ *n* **1** [C] a covering of fine cloth or net for all or part of the head or face, worn esp. by women, often for reasons of fashion or religion **2** [S (*of*)] something which covers or hides something else: *As the mountains were covered with a veil of cloud we couldn't see their tops.|After the police started to question people, a veil of secrecy came down over the whole village; no one was willing to talk* **3** [C] a covering or curtain that hides holy things **4 draw a veil over something** to avoid speaking about or describing something unpleasant **5 take the veil** (of a woman) to become a NUN **6 under the veil of** under the (deceiving) appearance of

veil² *v* [T1] to cover (as if) with a VEIL¹ (1,2)

veiled /veɪld/ *adj* **1** [Wa5] wearing a VEIL¹ (1) **2** (partly) hidden; expressed indirectly: *veiled threats*

vein /veɪn/ *n* **1** [C] a tube that carries blood from any part of the body to the heart —compare ARTERY and see picture at RESPIRATORY **2** [C] one of a system of thin lines which run in a forked pattern through leaves and the wings of certain insects **3** [C] a thin coloured line found in some kinds of stone and certain other substances **4** [C] a crack in rock, filled with useful metal or rock: *a vein of silver* **5** [S+*of*] a small but noticeable amount (of some quality): *There's a vein of cruelty in his nature* **6** [*in*+ :S9; *the*+R] a state of mind; MOOD: *speaking in a sad vein|We asked him to tell us a few jokes, but he wasn't in the (right) vein*

veined /veɪnd/ *adj* having or marked with VEINs (esp. 2,3) or VEINs of the stated kind or number: *a veined leaf|the many-veined wings of the bee*

vein·ing /ˈveɪnɪŋ/ *n* [U] a pattern of VEINs (esp. 2,3)

ve·lar /ˈviːləʳ/ *adj, n* **1** [Wa5;B] *tech* concerning the soft part of the roof of the mouth (PALATE) **2** [B; C] (a speech sound) made with the back of the tongue touching or nearly touching this part: */k/ and /g/ are velars*

ve·lar·ize /ˈviːləraɪz/ *v* [Wv5;T1;(IØ)] to produce (a sound) with the tongue raised at the back —compare NASALIZE, PALATALIZE

veld, veldt /velt/ *n* [*the*+R;C] (a stretch of) the wild, high, flat, mostly treeless grassland of South Africa

vel·lum /ˈveləm/ *n* [U] **1** a material of fine quality made from the skins of the young of cows (or of goats or sheep), used for book covers, lampshades, etc., and (esp. in former times) for writing on **2** thick smooth paper of fine quality, esp. for writing letters on

ve·loc·i·pede /vəˈlɒsəpiːd‖vəˈlɑ-/ *n* **1 a** a very early kind of bicycle, often pushed forward by the rider's feet pressing against the ground **b** *obs or humor* a bicycle **2** *AmE* a child's 3-wheeled bicycle

ve·loc·i·ty /vəˈlɒsəti‖vəˈlɑ-/ *n* **1** [C] *tech* speed in a certain direction; rate of movement **2** [S;U] **a** high speed (as of a moving vehicle): *The car came round the corner at such a velocity that the driver was unable to keep it on the road* **b** *esp. lit or*

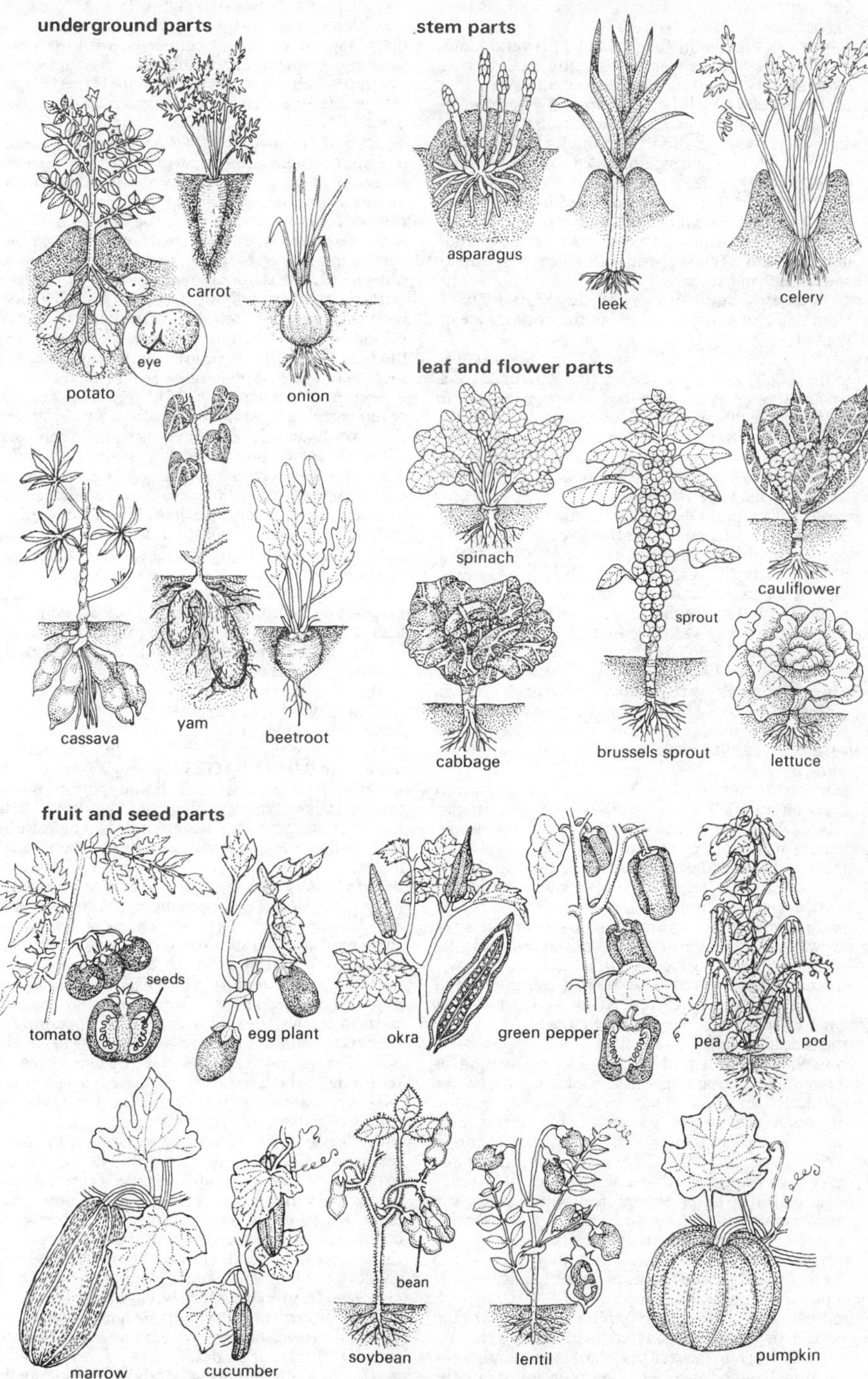

vegetables (according to the parts that are eaten)

fml swiftness (as of events) —see also ESCAPE VELOCITY, MUZZLE VELOCITY

ve·lour, velours /vəˈlʊəʳ/ *n* [U] any of several kinds of heavy cloth made from silk, cotton, etc., having a soft slightly raised surface usu. on both sides

vel·vet /ˈvelvɨt/ *n* [U] **1** a type of fine closely-woven cloth made esp. of silk but also of nylon, cotton, etc., having a short soft thick raised surface of cut threads on one side only **2 be on velvet** *infml* to be in a very safe favourable position, esp. with regard to money **3 the/an iron hand in the/a velvet glove** firmness, strength, and even cruelty, hidden under an appearance of good manners or gentleness **4 (walk)/(move) with (a) velvet tread** *lit* to walk softly and silently

vel·ve·teen /ˌvelvɨˈtiːn/ *n* [U] a cheap kind of cloth made of cotton but having the appearance of VELVET

vel·vet·y /ˈvelvɨti/ *adj* **1** (of a thing which is soft to the touch) looking or feeling like VELVET **2** (of a colour) having a soft deep look: *The dog had gentle eyes of velvety brown* **3** (of musical sound or playing) very full and soft; lacking sharpness: *The singer poured out a stream of rich velvety notes* **4** (of a wine or other strong alcoholic drink) very smooth to the taste; not acid

ve·nal /ˈviːnl/ *adj fml* **1** (of an action, practice, or behaviour) done, not for the proper or honest reasons, but in order to gain money **2** (of a person) acting or ready to act unfairly or wrongly, esp. by using power or position in favour of other people, in return for money or other reward: *venal judges* —compare VENIAL —**~ity** /viːˈnælɨti/ *n* [U] —**~ly** /ˈviːnəli/ *adv*

vend /vend/ *v* [T1] **1** *esp. fml* to offer (small articles) for sale, usu. in public places: *After he lost his money, he lived by vending matches in the street* **2** *law* to sell (land or other property)

vend·ee /venˈdiː/ *n law* a person to whom something is sold

ven·det·ta /venˈdetə/ *n* **1** a long-lasting quarrel between families (esp. in Italy and the Italian islands) in which the members of one family believe it to be their duty to kill those of the other family **2** a long-lasting state of affairs in which one person always does his best to harm another

vending ma·chine /ˈ·· ·ˌ·/ *n* a machine in a public place from which articles such as packets of cigarettes, containers of milk, stamps, etc., can be obtained by putting a coin into it

vend·or, -er /ˈvendəʳ/ *n* **1** [C9] a seller of small articles that can be carried about or pushed on a cart: *a fruit vendor* —see also NEWSVENDOR **2** *law* the seller of a house, land, etc.

ve·neer[1] /vɨˈnɪəʳ/ *n* **1** [C;U] a thin covering of good quality wood, used for forming the outer surface of an article made either of cheaper wood of poorer quality and less pleasing appearance or of some other material such as plastic or a wood-based board **2** [C (*of*) *usu. sing.*] a surface covering meant to hide some roughness or weakness beneath; outer appearance which hides the unpleasant reality: *Under a veneer of good manners and speech Mr Wilson was a coarse fellow*

veneer[2] *v* **1** [Wv5;T1] to cover with a VENEER[1] (1) **2** [T1 (*with*)] to hide (an unpleasant quality) under a pleasing appearance

ven·e·ra·ble /ˈvenərəbəl/ *adj* **1** [B] (of an old person or thing) considered to deserve great respect or honour, because of character, religious or historical importance, etc. **2** [Wa5;A] **a** (in the CHURCH OF ENGLAND) (the title given to a priest) having the rank of ARCHDEACON **b** (in the ROMAN CATHOLIC Church) (the title given to a dead person) who is going to be declared a SAINT (=holy person)—see OLD (USAGE)

ven·e·rate /ˈvenəreɪt/ *v* [T1] to treat (a person or thing, esp. that is old or connected with the past) with great respect and honour, and sometimes worship —**-ration** /ˌvenəˈreɪʃən/ *n* [U]: *The Chinese people hold their* FOREFATHERs *in great veneration*

ve·ne·re·al /vɨˈnɪəriəl/ *adj* [Wa5;A] *med* **1** resulting from or passed on by sexual activity: *venereal infections* **2** of or related to VENEREAL DISEASE: *There's a very high venereal rate in this city*

venereal dis·ease /·ˌ··· ·ˈ·/ also **VD**— *n* [C;U] (any of several types of) disease passed from one person to another during sexual activity: GONORRHEA *and* SYPHILIS *are venereal diseases*

ve·ne·tian blind /vɨˌniːʃən ˈblaɪnd/ *n* a window covering made of long thin flat bars of metal, plastic, or wood fixed to strings in such a way that the bars can be raised or lowered, or turned either to let in or shut out light and air

ven·geance /ˈvendʒəns/ *n* **1** [U] very severe harm or damage done to another person as a punishment for harm he has done to oneself, one's family, etc. **2** [S] an act of punishment: *He swore a terrible vengeance on the enemy who had ruined his farm* **3 take vengeance on/upon someone** to punish someone severely for harm he has done to oneself **4 with a vengeance** *infml* to a high degree; with greater force than is usual: *The wind's blowing with a vengeance; it's almost impossible to walk against it* —see REVENGE

venge·ful /ˈvendʒfəl/ *adj esp. lit* (of an action or feeling) based on a fierce desire to punish a person for the harm he has done to oneself; REVENGEful —**~ly** *adv* —**~ness** *n* [U]

ve·ni·al /ˈviːniəl/ *adj* (of a fault, mistake, wrongdoing, etc.) of only slight importance and therefore forgivable —compare VENAL

ven·i·son /ˈvenɨsən/ *n* [U] the flesh of a deer as food —see MEAT (USAGE)

ven·om /ˈvenəm/ *n* [U] **1** liquid poison which certain snakes, insects, and other creatures use in biting or stinging **2** a strong and bitter desire to hurt or harm someone by speech or action; great hatred

ven·om·ous /ˈvenəməs/ *adj* **1** (of a creature) having an organ that produces poison; able to attack with poison **2** (of speech, behaviour, etc.) showing a strong and bitter desire to hurt or harm someone: *a venomous look* **3** *sometimes humor* nasty; unpleasant: *What a venomous meal! I haven't tasted anything so bad for a long time* —**~ly** *adv*

ve·nous /ˈviːnəs/ *adj* **1** [Wa5] *med* **a** concerning or connected with the bloodvessels (VEINs (1)) of the body —see also INTRAVENOUS **b** (of blood) that is returning to the heart: *Venous blood is usually dark red* —compare ARTERIAL (1b) **2** (of a leaf) having (many or noticeable) VEINs (2)

vent[1] /vent/ *v* [T1] **1** to give expression to (one's feelings) **2** *tech* to make a VENT[2] (1) in

vent[2] *n* **1** a hole, opening, or pipe which forms a means by which gases, smoke, air, or liquid can enter or escape from an enclosed space or a container —see picture at CAMP **2** *tech* the opening through which small animals, birds, fishes, and snakes get rid of waste matter from their bodies **3 give vent to** to express freely (a strong feeling or natural desire for activity): *He gave vent to his anger by tearing up the unwelcome letter that demanded payment of his debt*

vent[3] *n tech* a long narrow straight opening at the bottom of a coat, at the sides or back

ven·ti·late /ˈventɨleɪt‖-tl-eɪt/ *v* [T1] **1** to allow or cause fresh air to enter and move around inside (a room, building, etc.), thus driving out bad air, smoke, gas, etc. **2** to permit or cause full public examination of (a subject or question); allow the free expression of all sides of (an argument)

ven·ti·la·tion /ˌventǝ̇ˈleɪʃǝn‖-tlˈeɪ-/ *n* [U] **1** (the system or apparatus that is used for) the passing into and around a room, building, etc., of fresh air **2** full public expression of opinions on a subject: *The workers requested that they should be allowed full ventilation of all their difficulties*

ven·ti·la·tor /ˈventǝ̇leɪtǝʳ‖-tl-eɪ-/ *n* any arrangement or apparatus for the ventilating (VENTILATE (1)) of a room, building, etc.

vent on *v prep* [D1] to express (a feeling) at the cost of (someone or something): *It's wrong to vent your anger on the children*

ven·tri·cle /ˈventrɪkǝl/ *n* **1** either of the 2 spaces in the bottom of the heart that receive blood from the AURICLES and then push it out into the main bloodvessels of the body —see picture at RESPIRATORY **2** any of various small hollow places in an animal body or organ, esp. in the brain

ven·tril·o·quis·m /venˈtrɪlǝkwɪzǝm/ *n* [U] the art of speaking or singing with little or no movement of the lips or jaws, in such a way that the sound seems to come from someone else or from some distance away

ven·tril·o·quist /venˈtrɪlǝkwǝ̇st/ *n* a person who practises VENTRILOQUISM, usu. in the theatre to amuse the public

ven·ture¹ /ˈventʃǝʳ/ *v* **1** [L9] to risk going somewhere or doing something (dangerous): *Don't venture too near the edge of the well; you might fall in.*|*Today's the first time I've ventured out of doors since my illness* **2** [T1,3] to take the risk of saying (something that may be opposed or considered foolish): *If I may venture an opinion, I must say that the future of man depends on his finding a new religious belief.*|*I venture to say that by the year 2500 there'll be more men living on the moon than on the earth* **3** [T1] *fml* to take the risk of harming or losing (something): *The main cause of his ruin was his habit of venturing large sums of money on horse racing* **4** [T3] *fml* to be bold enough (to do something): *He ventured to touch the fierce dog and was bitten on the hand* **5 nothing ventured, nothing gained** if one never takes any risks, one will never have any success

venture² *n* **1** an attempt; course of action (esp. in business) of which the result is uncertain and there is risk of loss or failure as well as chance of gain or success **2 draw a bow at a venture** to make a guess
USAGE **Venture**, both verb and noun, carries the idea of risk to one's life or money: *a business* **venture**|*Nobody* **ventured** (=dared) *to speak to the angry king*. An **adventure** (the more general word) suggests excitement, with or without some danger. In the pl. it means the life and activities of a character in a story: *"The* **Adventures** *of Sinbad the Sailor"*.

venture on also **venture up·on**— *v prep* [T1] to attempt (something dangerous or risky)

ven·tur·er /ˈventʃǝrǝʳ/ *n* a person who takes great risks, esp. (in former times) one who risked his life, money, ships, etc., in distant places

ven·ture·some /ˈventʃǝsǝm‖-tʃǝr-/ also **ven·tur·ous** /ˈventʃǝrǝs/— *adj esp. lit* **1** (of an action) risky **2** (of a person) daring; ready to take risks —**~ness** *n* [U]

ven·ue /ˈvenjuː/ *n* **1** a meeting place arranged for some purpose or activity: *The venue of the big match is the football ground at Wembley* **2** *law* the area where a law case is tried

Ve·nus /ˈviːnǝs/ *n* [R] the PLANET 2nd in order from the sun, and next to the earth —see picture at PLANET

ve·ra·cious /vǝˈreɪʃǝs/ *adj fml* **1** (of a person) truthful: *a veracious witness* **2** (of a statement) true and exact —**~ly** *adv*

ve·rac·i·ty /vǝˈræsǝ̇ti/ *n* [(*the*) U (*of*)] *fml* truthfulness

ve·ran·da, -dah /vǝˈrændǝ/ *n* an addition to a house, built out from any of the walls, having a floor and a roof (usu. supported by pillars) but no outside wall

verb /vɜːb‖vɜrb/ *n* a word or phrase that tells what someone or something is, does, or experiences: *In "She is tired" and "He wrote a letter", "is" and "wrote" are verbs*

verb·al¹ /ˈvɜːbǝl‖ˈvɜr-/ *adj* [Wa5] **1** spoken, not written: *a verbal description* **2** connected with words and their use: *verbal skill* **3** that produces the exact words of something: *a verbal translation* **4** concerned with the actual words in which something is expressed, and not with the real meaning: *There is a big verbal difference between "late in the afternoon" and "early in the evening", but the meanings are nearly the same* **5** of, coming from, or connected with a verb —compare VERBOSE

verbal² *n* **1** *infml* a spoken statement that one is guilty of a crime **2** *humor* an exchange of angry words; quarrel

verb·al·ize, -ise /ˈvɜːbǝl-aɪz‖ˈvɜr-/ *v* [T1;IØ] to express (something) in words

verb·al·ly /ˈvɜbǝl-i‖ˈvɜr-/ *adv* **1** in spoken words and not in writing **2** as a verb

verbal noun /ˌ·· ˈ·/ also **gerund**— *n* a noun which describes an action or experience and has the form of a present participle: *"Building" is a verbal noun in "The building of the bridge was slow work", but not in "The bank was a tall building"*

ver·ba·tim /vɜːˈbeɪtǝ̇m‖vɜr-/ *adj, adv* [Wa5] repeating the actual words (spoken or written) exactly: *His memory was so good that he could repeat many plays of Shakespeare verbatim*

ver·be·na /vɜːˈbiːnǝ‖vɜr-/ *n* any of several types of garden plant, some of which have flowers of many different colours

ver·bi·age /ˈvɜːbi-ɪdʒ‖ˈvɜr-/ *n* [U] too many unnecessary words in speech or writing

ver·bose /vɜːˈbǝʊs‖vɜr-/ *adj* using or containing too many words —compare VERBAL —**~ly** *adv*

ver·bos·i·ty /vɜːˈbɒsǝ̇ti‖vɜrˈbɑ-/ also **ver·bose·ness** /vɜːˈbǝʊsnǝ̇s‖vɜr-/— *n* [U] the quality of being VERBOSE

ver·dant /ˈvɜːdǝnt‖ˈvɜr-/ *adj lit or poet* **1** (of land) covered with freshly growing green plants or grass: *the verdant fields* **2** (of colour) of a fresh leafy or grassy green —**-dancy** /ˈvɜːdǝnsi‖ˈvɜr-/ *n* [U]

ver·dict /ˈvɜːdɪkt‖ˈvɜr-/ *n* **1** the official decision made by a JURY in a court of law, declared to the judge at the end of a trial: *Gentlemen of the* JURY, *what is your verdict? Guilty, or not guilty?* —see also OPEN VERDICT **2** *infml* a statement of (carefully considered) opinion; judgment or decision given on any matter: *The general verdict on the party was that it had been very enjoyable*

ver·di·gris /ˈvɜːdǝ̇gris‖ˈvɜr-/ *n* [U] a greenish-blue substance which forms a thin covering on articles of copper or brass as a result of age, or of being unprotected from wet conditions

ver·dure /ˈvɜːdʒǝʳ‖ˈvɜr-/ *n* [U] *lit or poet* (the fresh green colour of) growing grass, plants, trees, etc.

verge /vɜːdʒ‖vɜrdʒ/ *n* **1** the edge or border (esp. of a road, path, etc.) **2 on the verge of** very near to (the stated (change of) condition or action): *She tried to hide her grief, but she was on the verge of tears*

verge on also **verge up·on**— *v prep* [T1] to be near to (the stated quality or condition): *Her strange* *behaviour sometimes verges on madness.|dark grey, verging on black*

ver·ger /ˈvɜːdʒəʳ‖ˈvɜr-/ *n* **1** a person paid to look after the inside of a church, and to perform small duties such as showing worshippers where they may sit **2** *esp. BrE* an official person who walks in front of the head of a university, CATHEDRAL, etc., in ceremonial processions

ver·i·fy /ˈverɨfaɪ/ *v* **1** [T1,5,6a] to make sure that (a fact, statement, etc.) is correct or true: *The police are verifying the prisoner's statements by questioning several witnesses.|Before the bank was willing to lend him money, it verified that he was the true owner of the house* **2** [T1 *often pass.*] (of an event) to prove the truth of (something that was stated or believed to be a probability) **3** [T1] *law* to prove that (an object, piece of writing, weapon, etc., which is being produced by a lawyer during a court case) is really what is claimed —**-fiable** *adj* —**-fication** /ˌverɨfɨˈkeɪʃən/ *n* [U]

ver·i·ly /ˈverɨli/ *adv bibl or old use* really; truly

ver·i·si·mil·i·tude /ˌverɨsɨˈmɪlɨtjuːd‖-tuːd/ *n fml* **1** [U] the quality of seeming to be true; likeness to reality or real things **2** [C] a statement that only appears to be true

ver·i·ta·ble /ˈverɨtəbəl/ *adj* [Wa5;A] (used to give force to an expression) that may be described as; that may really be compared to; real: *Thank you for such a fine meal; it was a veritable feast* —**-bly** *adv*: *After being without food for so long, they were veritably dying of hunger*

ver·i·ty /ˈverɨti/ *n* **1** [C *usu. pl.*] *lit* an accepted truth; general law or truth on which religious teachings, standards of right behaviour, etc., are based **2** [U (*of*)] *lit or fml, now rare* truth

ver·mi·cel·li /ˌvɜːmɨˈseli, -ˈtʃeli‖ˌvɜr-/ *n* [U] a food made from flour paste (PASTA) in the form of very thin strings which have been dried and are made soft again by boiling —compare MACARONI, SPAGHETTI

ver·mic·u·lite /vɜːˈmɪkjʊlaɪt‖vɜrˈmɪkjə-/ *n* [U] a type of MICA that is a very light material made up of threadlike parts, that can be used for keeping heat inside buildings, growing seeds in, etc.

ver·mi·form /ˈvɜːmɨfɔːm‖ˈvɜrmɨfɔrm/ *adj* shaped rather like a worm

vermiform ap·pen·dix /ˌ···ˈ··/ *n* APPENDIX[1]

ver·mi·fuge /ˈvɜːmɨfjuːdʒ‖ˈvɜr-/ *n* [C;U] a drug for driving worms out of the body of man or animals

ver·mil·i·on /vəˈmɪlɪən‖vər-/ *adj, n* [B;U] bright reddish-orange (colour)

ver·min /ˈvɜːmɨn‖ˈvɜr-/ *n* [GU] **1** any kind of unpleasant biting insect (such as a FLEA, LOUSE, etc.) that lives on the body of man or animals, usu. by drawing out blood **2** any usu. small kind of animal or bird that destroys crops, spoils food, or does other damage, and is difficult to control: *To a farmer a fox is vermin because it steals and kills chickens* **3** *derog* useless unpleasant people who are a trouble to society: *His opinion is that all beggars are vermin*

ver·min·ous /ˈvɜːmɨnəs‖ˈvɜr-/ *adj* **1** full of VERMIN (esp. 1): *The prison was a verminous old wooden building, and from living in such a place the prisoners themselves became verminous* **2** [Wa5] (of a disease) caused by VERMIN (1) **3** *derog* (of a person) very unpleasant; unlikeable; nasty

ver·mouth /ˈvɜːməθ‖vərˈmuːθ/ *n* [U] a type of pale yellow or dark red drink, usu. drunk before a meal, made from wine with the addition of bitter or strong-tasting substances from roots and HERBs

ver·nac·u·lar[1] /vəˈnækjʊləʳ‖vərˈnækjələr/ *adj* [Wa5] using the common speech of a country or area: *The* ROMAN CATHOLIC *Church now uses vernacular services, but until recently all their services were in Latin*

vernacular[2] *n* [*the*+R;C] the native spoken language of the (stated or understood) country or area, esp. as compared with a foreign language: *Having lived in England for a long time he had got used to speaking English, but when he returned home to Italy he soon* LAPSE*d into the vernacular* (= began to speak Italian again).|*The vernaculars of these African tribes have never been written down*

ver·nal /ˈvɜːnl‖ˈvɜrnl/ *adj* [Wa5] *lit or tech* of, like, or appearing in the spring season: *the vernal wood*

ver·o·nal /ˈverənl‖-nɔl/ *n* [U] *tdmk* (*often cap.*) a type of drug used, esp. formerly, for helping people to sleep

ve·ron·i·ca /vəˈrɒnɪkə‖vəˈrɑ-/ *n* [U;C] any of a number of related plants and bushes, most of which have blue, purple, or pink flowers

ver·ru·ca /vəˈruːkə/ *n* **-cas** *or* **-cae** /kiː/ a small hard often infectious growth on the skin, usu. on the bottom of the feet

ver·sa·tile /ˈvɜːsətaɪl‖ˈvɜrsətl/ *adj* **1** having many different kinds of skill or ability; easily able to change from one kind of activity to another: *He's a very versatile performer; he can act, sing, dance, and play the piano* **2** having many different uses: *Nylon is a versatile material* —**-tility** /ˌvɜːsəˈtɪlɨti‖ˌvɜr-/ *n* [U]

verse /vɜːs‖vɜrs/ *n* **1** [U] writing arranged in regular lines, with a pattern of repeated beats (as in music) and words of matching sound at the end of some lines; language in the form of poetry: *Not all verse is great poetry* —see also BLANK VERSE, FREE VERSE **2** [C] **a** a set of lines of poetry which forms one part of a poem, and usu. has a pattern that is repeated in the other parts: *Today I learned 3 verses of a poem at school* **b** a set of such lines forming the words to which the tune of a song is sung **3** [C] *tech* a line of poetry: *In this poem, each verse has 5 beats* **4** [C] one of the numbered single sentences or groups of sentences that together form one numbered division (CHAPTER) of a holy book, esp. one of the books of the Bible **5 give/quote chapter and verse (for something)** to tell exactly where to find support for or proof of something stated or reported

versed /vɜːst‖vɜrst/ *adj* [F+*in*] possessing a thorough knowledge (of) or skill (in a subject, an art, etc.); experienced (esp. in the phr. **well versed in**)

ver·si·fi·ca·tion /ˌvɜːsɨfɨˈkeɪʃən‖ˌvɜr-/ *n* **1** [U] the art or practice of VERSIFYing **2** [U9] the particular pattern or way in which a poem is written: *a study of the versification of Coleridge's poem, "The Ancient Mariner"*

ver·si·fy /ˈvɜːsɨfaɪ‖ˈvɜr-/ *v* **1** [T1] to turn into the form of poetry: *My mother often versified fairy stories for us when we were children* **2** [I∅] *often derog* to write in the form of poetry, though not always with skill —**-fier** *n*

ver·sion /ˈvɜːʃən‖ˈvɜrʒən/ *n* [C (*of*)] **1** one person's account of an event, as compared with that of another person: *The 2 newspapers gave different versions of what happened* **2 a** a translation: *The play was in German, but I'd read an English version, so I was able to understand most of the action* **b** (*usu. cap.*) an official translation of (part of) the Bible: *The King James Version of the Bible first appeared in 1611* **3** a form of a written or musical work that exists in more than one form: *Did you read the whole book or only the short version?* **4** a slightly different form, copy, or style of an article: *This dress is a cheaper version of the one we saw in the shop* **5** a performer's particular way of understanding and expressing some famous piece of music, character in a play, etc.

ver·so /ˈvɜːsəʊ‖ˈvɜr-/ *adj, n* **-sos** [Wa5;A;C] (being) a left-hand page of a book: *written on the verso (side)* —compare RECTO
ver·sus /ˈvɜːsəs‖ˈvɜr-/ *prep fml* v.
ver·te·bra /ˈvɜːtəbrə‖ˈvɜr-/ *n* **-brae** /briː, breɪ/ one of the small hollow bones down the centre of the back which form the BACKBONE (3) or SPINE —see picture at SKELETON —**-bral** *adj* [Wa5]
ver·te·brate /ˈvɜːtəbrət, -breɪt‖ˈvɜr-/ *adj, n* [Wa5] *tech* (an animal, bird, fish, etc.) which has a BACKBONE (3) —compare INVERTEBRATE
ver·tex /ˈvɜːteks‖ˈvɜr-/ *n* **-texes** *or* **-tices** /təsiːz/ [(*of*)] **1** *tech* **a** the angle opposite the base (of any figure, such as a PYRAMID, CONE, TRIANGLE, etc.) **b** the meeting point of the 2 lines (of an angle) **2** *med* the top (of the head) **3** *tech or fml* the highest point: *the vertex of an arch|the vertex of a hill*
ver·ti·cal[1] /ˈvɜːtɪkəl‖ˈvɜr-/ *adj* [Wa5] **1** (of an object) standing upright: *Telegraph poles must be set in the ground so that they are vertical* **2** (of a line or surface) forming an angle of 90 degrees with the level ground, or with a straight line in a figure: *For a car that went over the edge of the road, there was a vertical fall to the sea below* —compare HORIZONTAL **3** pointing or moving directly upwards or downwards: *A vertical takeoff aircraft is one that can rise straight from the ground, without first running along for some distance* —**~ly** *adv* [Wa4]
vertical[2] *n* **1** *esp. tech* a VERTICAL[1] (2) line, surface, or position **2 out of the vertical** not exactly upright
ver·tig·i·nous /vɜːˈtɪdʒənəs‖vɜr-/ *adj fml* causing VERTIGO, esp. by being unpleasantly far above the ground: *looking from those vertiginous heights at the people below*
ver·ti·go /ˈvɜːtɪgəʊ‖ˈvɜr-/ *n* [U] a feeling of great unsteadiness, as though one's head were spinning round, often giving one at the same time a sensation of sickness and faintness, and caused usu. by looking down from a great height
verve /vɜːv‖vɜrv/ *n* [U] a strong feeling of life, force, and eager enjoyment, expressed through some activity or shown in some form of art
ve·ry[1] /ˈveri/ *adj* **1** [Wa5;A] (used for giving force to an expression): *This is the very pen he used when he was writing the book. He used this very pen.|I'll go this very minute* (=at once).|*They say he died in that very bed.|I found it at the very bottom of the box.|She died at the very height of her fame.|The very walls of the old city are full of history.|She was afraid of the very idea of going home alone.|It's her very cleverness that makes it difficult for her to work with other people* **2** [Wa1;A] *poet* correctly named; rightly so-called; being truly that which is stated: *The veriest child should be able to understand such a simple thing* **3 the very idea** *infml* (used for expressing surprise or shock at something said or suggested by someone else): *Of course you can't stay out of doors till 2 in the morning. The very idea!*
very[2] *adv* **1** (used to give force to an adj, a pres. p. or past p. used as an adj. or another adv, but not to a COMPARATIVE adj or to a past p. that is not fully adj in use, for which *much* or very *much* is used instead) especially; in a high degree: *It's very foolish to smoke, as it's known to be dangerous to health.|This is a very good cake; may I have another piece, please?|I feel very tired after all that effort.|a very exciting book|She's a clever girl, and has learnt the new work very quickly.|I feel very much better today.|"It is I think very very different."* (SEU S.)| *"Thanks very much"* (SEU S.) **2** (used to give force to a superl. adj, or to *same*) in the greatest possible degree: *The cake ought to be good, because I used the very best butter.|This is the very last time I offer to help you.|There have been 3 accidents in this very same place* **3 not very a** in no way; exactly the opposite of: *The teacher wasn't very pleased when he found a dead mouse on his desk* **b** only slightly; to a small degree: *"Was the play interesting?" "Not very"* **4 one's very own** (used by or to a child) shared with no one else: *You're a lucky boy to have your very own boat.|Can I have this dog for my very own?* **5 very good** (used as a respectful form of agreement) of course; certainly: *"Please send this letter off at once." "Very good, Sir"* **6 very well** (used as a form of agreement, but often with some degree of unwillingness) all right (but I don't particularly want to): *"You ought to take a coat with you." "*OH, *very well, if I must"*
very high fre·quen·cy /ˌ·· · ˈ···/ *n* [U;(C)] (*often cap.*) *fml* VHF
Ver·y light /ˈvɪəri laɪt‖ˌveri ˈlaɪt, ˌvɪəri-/ *n* (a bright, sometimes coloured, light produced by) a special sort of burning bullet that is fired high into the air from a small gun (**Very pistol**), used for lighting up a wide space for a short time at night, as for an aircraft to land, or as a signal that someone is in danger and needs help
ves·i·cle /ˈvesɪkəl/ *n med* a small hollow part in an organ or other bodily part, or a small swelling on the skin, usu. filled with liquid
ve·sic·u·lar /vəˈsɪkjʊləʳ‖-kjə-/ *adj* [Wa5] *med* of, related to, or marked by the formation of VESICLES: *pigs suffering from vesicular disease*
ves·per /ˈvespəʳ/ *adj* [Wa5;A] of or related to VESPERS
ves·pers /ˈvespəz‖-ərz/ *n* [U;(P)] (in some divisions of the Christian church) the evening service
ves·sel /ˈvesəl/ *n fml* **1** a usu. round container, such as a glass, pot, cup, bottle, bucket, or barrel, used esp. for holding liquids: *a drinking vessel* **2** a ship or large boat: *The Port of London is filled with vessels of all kinds.|a fishing vessel|a motor vessel* **3** a tube (such as a VEIN) that carries blood or other liquid through the body, or plant juice (SAP) through a plant —see also BLOOD VESSEL
USAGE This is a very *fml* word, which should be avoided by students. Instead, use **ship** or **boat**. A **ship** is usually larger than a **boat**, though one may say *We went to the US by* **boat**.|*We were 6 days on the* **boat**—meaning a large passenger **ship** or LINER.
vest[1] /vest/ *v* [T1;IØ] *tech, old use, or poet* to dress (oneself), usu. in long garments, for a ceremony (as in church) —see also VEST IN, VEST WITH
vest[2] *n* **1** (*AmE* **undershirt**)— *BrE* a short under-garment, usu. without coverings for the arms, worn on the upper part of the body next to the skin **2** *AmE* WAISTCOAT
ves·tal vir·gin /ˌvestl ˈvɜːdʒən‖-ɜr-/ also **vestal**— *n* one of the young women who promised to remain unmarried, and whose duty was to keep the holy fire always burning in the temple of Vesta, the Roman goddess of the house
vested in·terest /ˌ·· ˈ··/ *n often derog* a share or right already held in something, that is of advantage to the holder: *It was difficult to end the system of slavery because the people who owned the slaves had a vested interest in keeping it*
vested in·terests /ˌ·· ˈ··/ *n* [P] *usu. derog* all the people having a VESTED INTEREST in a particular business or state of affairs, which they are unwilling to lose even for the good of the public: *It would be impossible to make a law forbidding smoking, because of the powerful vested interests who own the tobacco companies*
ves·ti·bule /ˈvestəbjuːl/ *n* **1** a wide passage or small room just inside the outer door of a (public) building through which all other rooms are

reached; entrance hall: *I can't deal with Mr McGregor just now; ask him to wait in the vestibule* **2** (in the body) a hollow that leads to another hollow, esp. the central hollow of the inner ear **3** *AmE* an enclosed passage at each end of a railway carriage which connects it with the next carriage

ves·tige /ˈvestɪdʒ/ *n* [(*of*)] **1** a sign, mark, track, or other proof that someone or something formerly existed or was present: *Some upright stones in wild places are the vestiges of ancient religions* **2** the very small slight remains (of something): *The police sent the vestiges of the meal on the dead man's plate to be tested for poison* **3** [*usu. neg.*] the smallest possible amount: *There's not a vestige of truth in the witness's statement* **4** the remains or imperfectly developed form of some limb or organ that was formerly important but is not now used

ves·ti·gi·al /veˈstɪdʒɪəl, -dʒəl/ *adj* [Wa5] *esp. med* that remains as a VESTIGE (esp. 4): *Some snakes have vestigial legs* —**~ly** *adv*

vest in *v prep fml* **1** [D1 *usu. pass.*] to give the official and lawful right to possess or use (power, property, etc.) to (someone): *In Britain, the right to make new laws is vested in the representatives of the people* **2** [T1 *no pass.*] (of power, property, etc.) to belong by right to (someone): *This power vested in the Church* —compare VEST WITH

vest·ment /ˈvestmənt/ *n* [*often pl.*] *fml* a ceremonial garment, esp. as worn by priests for church services

ves·try /ˈvestri/ *n* **1** [C] also **sacristy**— a small room in a church where holy vessels, official records, etc., are stored, and where the priest and church singers put on their ceremonial garments —see picture at CHURCH[1] **2** [C] any room connected with a church building, which is used for prayer meetings, church business, etc. **3** [GC] (the group of) church members or representatives who meet to consider the business of their particular church area (PARISH)

ves·try·man /ˈvestrimən/ *n* **-men** /mən/ a member of the VESTRY (3)

ves·ture /ˈvestʃəʳ/ *n* [U] *lit or poet* clothing; general covering

vest with *v prep* [D1 *usu. pass.*] *fml* to give (someone) the official and lawful right to possess or use (power, property, etc.) —compare VEST IN

vet[1] /vet/ also (*fml BrE*) **veterinary sur·geon** /ˌ···· ˈ··/, (*fml AmE*) **vet·e·ri·nar·i·an** /ˌvetərɪ̇ˈneərɪən/— *n* a trained animal doctor who can also perform operations

vet[2] *v* **-tt-** [T1] *esp. BrE* **1** to treat (an animal) medically **2** *infml* (of a doctor) to give (someone) a medical examination, esp. for some purpose **3** *infml* to examine (something or someone) carefully for correctness, past record, etc.: *The foreigners were thoroughly vetted before they were allowed into the country*

vetch /vetʃ/ *n* any of several types of beanlike climbing plant, some of which are used for cattle food

vet·e·ran /ˈvetərən/ *n, adj* [Wa5] **1** [C (*of*); A] (an old man) who in the past has had experience in the stated form of activity, esp. in war; old soldier: *Grandfather is a veteran of the First and Second World Wars.*|*veteran officers* **2** [C;A] (a person) who had had long experience in some form of activity: *At the age of 12 the boy was already a veteran traveller, having flown all over the world with his father* **3** [C] *AmE* also (*infml*) **vet**— any person, young or old, who has served any length of time in the armed forces, esp. during a war **4** [C;A] (a thing) that has grown old with long use: *Every year a race is held in England for veteran cars* (=those made in or before 1904).|*This sewing machine is a real veteran* —compare VINTAGE[2] (4)

Veterans Day /ˈ··· ·/ *n* [R] (in the US and Canada) a day (11th November) set aside for remembering the end of fighting in the First World War

vet·e·ri·na·ry /ˈvetərɪ̇nəri‖-neri/ *adj* [Wa5;A] connected with the medical care and treatment of sick animals (esp. farm animals and pets): *veterinary science* —see also VET[1]

ve·to[1] /ˈviːtəʊ/ *n* **-toes** **1** [C (*on*)] a refusal to give permission for something, or to allow something to be done; act of forbidding something completely: *I've put a veto on football in the garden in case the children break any more windows* **2** [U] (esp. in international politics) the official right or power to refuse permission for an action, or to forbid something to be done

veto[2] *v* [T1] to prevent or forbid (some action); refuse to allow (something) —**vetoer** *n*

vex /veks/ *v* [T1] **1** to displease (someone); cause (someone) to feel angry or bad-tempered **2** [*often pass.*] to trouble (someone) continually; keep in discomfort or without rest: *Travellers in the desert are often vexed by flies* **3** to cause (someone) to have to think hard; PUZZLE —see ANGRY (USAGE)

vex·a·tion /vekˈseɪʃən/ *n* **1** [U] the feeling, fact, or state of being VEXed; displeasure **2** [C *often pl.*] something that causes the feeling of being VEXed

vex·a·tious /vekˈseɪʃəs/ *adj* displeasing; troublesome; causing VEXATION: *After many vexatious delays, the building of the house was begun* —**~ly** *adv*

vexed ques·tion /ˌ· ˈ··/ *n* something that has caused much fierce argument and is difficult to decide; troublesome matter or question

VHF /ˌviː eɪtʃ ˈef/ also (*fml*) **very high frequency**— *n* [U] (the sending out of radio waves at) the rate of 30,000,000 to 300,000,000 HERTZ: *This radio station broadcasts only on VHF.*|*a VHF radio* —compare UHF

vi·a /ˈvaɪə‖ˈvɪə/ *prep* **1** travelling or sent through (a place) on the way: *We flew to Athens via Paris and Rome* **2** by means of; using: *I've read this French play via an English translation.*|*I sent a message to Mary via her sister*

vi·a·ble /ˈvaɪəbəl/ *adj* **1** able to succeed in operation: *This plan looks all right in principle, but in practice it wouldn't be viable* **2** *tech* able to continue to exist as or develop into a living thing: *a viable newborn child* —**-bility** /ˌvaɪəˈbɪlɪ̇ti/ *n* [U] —**-bly** /ˈvaɪəbli/ *adv*

vi·a·duct /ˈvaɪədʌkt/ *n* a long high bridge which carries a road or railway line across a valley

vi·al /ˈvaɪəl/ *n AmE becoming rare* PHIAL

vi·ands /ˈvaɪəndz/ *n* [P] *old use or pomp* articles of food, esp. of a rare or fine kind: *The shops were full of Christmas viands*

vibes /vaɪbz/ *n* **vibes** *infml* **1** [Wn3;GC *usu. sing.*] a VIBRAPHONE: *Charlie plays vibes in our band* **2** [P] VIBRATIONs (3)

vi·bran·cy /ˈvaɪbrənsi/ *n* [U] the quality of being VIBRANT (esp. 2,3): *the vibrancy of her character*

vi·brant /ˈvaɪbrənt/ *adj* **1** *lit* strongly vibrating (VIBRATE (1)), esp. so as to produce sound: *the vibrant strings of this instrument* **2** (of colour or light) bright and strong, esp. pleasantly so **3** alive; forceful; powerful and exciting: *a city vibrant with life*|*a youthful vibrant voice* —**~ly** *adv*

vi·bra·phone /ˈvaɪbrəfəʊn/ also (*infml*) **vibes**— *n* a type of musical instrument consisting of a set of metal bars set in a frame, which are struck to produce notes that are made to VIBRATE (1) by a special apparatus

vi·brate /vaɪˈbreɪt‖ˈvaɪbreɪt/ *v* **1** [T1;IØ] to (cause to) shake continuously and very rapidly with a fine slight movement that may often be felt or heard rather than seen: *Tom's heavy footsteps upstairs make the old house vibrate.|The air in the desert seemed to vibrate in the midday heat* **2** [IØ (*to*)] *infml* to feel the effect or influence of something excitedly

vi·bra·tion /vaɪˈbreɪʃən/ *n* **1** [C;U] (a) slight continuous shaky movement **2** [C;U] (a single) regular to and fro movement of a stretched or touched wire **3** [C *usu. pl.*] *infml* an influence, favourable or unfavourable, felt by a sensitive person as coming from someone or something else: *I feel really drawn to that girl; I get good vibrations from her*

vi·bra·to /vɪˈbrɑːtəʊ/ *n* **-tos** *tech* (in music) a slightly shaking effect given to the sound of the voice, or of stringed or wind instruments, for added expressiveness, produced by varying the loudness or the force used in producing the same note

vi·brat·or /vaɪˈbreɪtəʳ‖ˈvaɪbreɪtər/ *n* an instrument used for producing VIBRATION*s* (1), esp. an electrical apparatus used on the skin to produce pleasing sensations

vi·bro- /ˈvaɪbrəʊ/ *comb. form esp. med* working by means of VIBRATION (1): *vibro*MASSAGE

vic·ar /ˈvɪkəʳ/ *n* **1** [C;N] (in the CHURCH OF ENGLAND) a priest in charge of a church and the area (PARISH) belonging to it, who receives a yearly payment (STIPEND) for his duties **2** [C] (in the ROMAN CATHOLIC Church) a representative: *The* POPE *is known as the vicar of Christ*

vic·ar·age /ˈvɪkərɪdʒ/ *n* a VICAR'*s* (1) house

vi·car·i·ous /vɪˈkeərɪəs‖vaɪ-/ *adj* **1** experienced by the imagination through watching or reading about other people; indirect: *He gets vicarious pleasure by going to watch films about sex* **2** *fml & becoming rare* experienced for other people: *Christ's vicarious sufferings on the cross* **3** *fml & becoming rare* **a** (of a person) taking the place of another; acting as the representative of someone else **b** done, used, or held by someone as someone else's representative —**~ly** *adv* —**~ness** *n* [U]

vice¹ /vaɪs/ *n* **1** [C;U] (any particular kind of) evil living, esp. in sexual practices, taking of harmful drugs, uncontrolled drinking habits, etc.: *In spite of the police, there's usually a certain amount of vice in all big cities.|Continual smoking can become a vice* **2** [U] wickedness of character —opposite **virtue** **3** [C] **a** a serious fault of character: *His laziness is so great as to be almost a vice* —opposite **virtue** **b** *infml, often humor* a bad habit: *I love drinking coffee; it's one of my vices* **4** [C] *infml* a weakness in a system, way of working, etc. **5** [C;U] *tech* (any particular kind of) fixed bad habits that make a horse, dog, or farm animal untrustworthy

vice², *AmE* **vise** *n esp. BrE* a type of tool with metal jaws that can be tightened by a screw, used for holding a piece of wood or metal firmly so that it can be worked on with both hands

vice- *prefix* **1** the person next in official rank below the stated person, who has the power to represent him or act in place of him: *the vice-president|Vice-President Mondale|the vice-captain of the cricket team* **2** the office next in rank below the stated office: *vice-governorship*

vice-chan·cel·lor /ˌ· ˈ···/ *n* [C;N] (*often cap.* V & C) (in Britain) the officer who actually controls the affairs of a university; real head of a university (since the CHANCELLOR (3) is appointed only as an honour)

vice·like /ˈvaɪs-laɪk/ *adj* very firm; giving no chance of movement or escape (esp. in the phr. **a vicelike grip**)

vice·re·gal /vaɪsˈriːgəl/ *adj* connected with or belonging to a VICEROY: *the viceregal palace*

vice·reine /vaɪsˈreɪn‖ˈvaɪsreɪn/ *n* the wife of a VICEROY

vice·roy /ˈvaɪsrɔɪ/ *n* a king's representative ruling for him in another country: *When Britain ruled India, the British king was represented there by a viceroy*

vice squad /ˈ· ·/ *n* [GC] a band of police whose duty is to see that the laws against VICE¹ (1) are obeyed

vice ver·sa /ˌvaɪs ˈvɜːsə, ˌvaɪsi-‖-ɜr-/ *adv Lat* in the opposite way from that just stated: *When she wants to go out, he wants to stay in, and vice versa* (=when he wants to go out, she wants to stay in)

vi·cin·i·ty /vəˈsɪnəti/ *n* **1** [*in*+(*the*) U (*of*) *often pl. with sing. meaning*] the surroundings; area very near to or around the stated place; neighbourhood: *"Are there any shops in this vicinity?" "Not really; the nearest is 3 miles away"* **2** [U (*of, to*)] *fml* nearness **3 in the vicinity of** *pomp* about: *His income is in the vicinity of £5000 a year*

vi·cious /ˈvɪʃəs/ *adj* **1** cruel; having or showing hate and the desire to hurt: *He gave the dog a vicious blow with his stick* **2** dangerous; able or likely to cause severe hurt: *a vicious-looking knife* **3** **a** (of a horse) having a fault that makes control difficult **b** (of other animals) dangerous; bad-tempered; which may attack people **4** *fml & becoming rare* full of evil habits or behaviour: *vicious practices* —**~ly** *adv* —**~ness** *n* [U]

vicious cir·cle /ˌ·· ˈ··/ *n* a set of events in which cause and effect follow each other until this results in a return to the first (undesirable or unpleasant) position and the whole matter begins again: *"Crime leads to prison, which leads to unemployment, which leads to crime. It's a vicious circle"*

vi·cis·si·tudes /vəˈsɪsətjuːdz‖-tuːdz/ *n* [P *sometimes sing.*] changes from good to bad and bad to good in one's condition of life

vic·tim /ˈvɪktəm/ *n* **1** [C (*of*)] a person, animal, or thing that suffers pain, death, harm, destruction, etc., as a result of other people's actions, or of illness, bad luck, etc.: *We took the victims of the storm into our house for the night.|Many 1000s of animals have been victims of this strange new disease.|That fine old building was knocked down last year, a victim of the council's desire for modern planning* **2** [C] a person or animal killed and offered as a gift to a god **3 fall victim to** to suffer because of (an action): *She fell victim to her desire for new clothes (and found herself without money)*

vic·tim·ize, -ise /ˈvɪktəmaɪz/ *v* [T1] **1** to cause (someone) to suffer unfairly **2** to cause (someone) unfairly to receive punishment or blame which should really be shared by many others —**-ization** /ˌvɪktəmaɪˈzeɪʃən‖-mə-/ *n* [U]

vic·tor /ˈvɪktəʳ/ *n esp. fml, lit, or pomp* **1** a conqueror in battle **2** a winner in a race, game, competition, or other kind of struggle

Vic·to·ri·a Cross /vɪkˌtɔːrɪə ˈkrɒs‖-ˌtorɪə ˈkrɔs/ also **VC**— *n* a special MEDAL given to members of the British armed forces who have done acts of great bravery in the presence of the enemy

Vic·to·ri·an /vɪkˈtɔːrɪən‖-ˈto-/ *adj, n* **1** [Wa5;B;C] (any English person) of or living in the time when Queen Victoria ruled (1837–1901): *Victorian furniture|Florence Nightingale and William Gladstone were famous Victorians* **2** [B] like the middle-class society in the time of Queen Victoria; very respectable and religious in a formal way that sometimes only pretends to be good and pure (esp. in matters of sex): *His opinions are very Victorian*

victoria plum /·ˌ··· ˈ·/ also (*infml*) **victoria**— *n* a large, sweet, dark red type of PLUM

vic·to·ri·ous /vɪkˈtɔːrɪəs‖-ˈto-/ *adj* **1** [Wa5;B (*in, over*)] having won or conquered: *the victorious team* —opposite **vanquish**ed **2** [A] of, related to, or showing victory: *a victorious shout* —**~ly** *adv*

vic·to·ry /ˈvɪktəri/ *n* **1** [U (*in, over*)] the act of winning or state of having won (in war or in any kind of struggle): *The officers led their men to victory in battle* **2** [C (*in, over*)] a success in a struggle: *He had a narrow victory in the election; he won by only a few votes.*|*The industrial agreement was a victory for good sense; it prevented more loss of money by both employers and workers* —opposite **defeat**

vict·ual /ˈvɪtl/ *v* **-ll-** (*AmE* **-l-**) *tech* **1** [T1] to supply (usu. a large number of people) with food **2** [I∅] to take in and store supplies of food and drink

vict·ual·ler, *AmE* **-ualer** /ˈvɪtələʳ/ *n tech* a person who deals in or supplies VICTUALS —see also LICENSED VICTUALLER

vict·uals /ˈvɪtlz/ *n* [P] *old use or dial* (supplies of) food and drink

vi·cu·ña, -na /vɪˈkjuːnə‖vɪˈkuː-/ *n* **1** [C] a type of large South American animal (related to the LLAMA) from which soft, very good quality wool is obtained **2** [U] the cloth made from this wool: *a vicuña coat*

vi·de /ˈvaɪdi, ˈviːdi/ *v* [T1 *only imper.*] *Lat* (used for telling a reader where to find more about the subject) see; look at: *Vide page 32*

vide in·fra /ˌ·· ˈ··/ *interj Lat* (used for telling the reader where to find more about the subject) look at a later place in the book

vi·de·li·cet /vɨ̇ˈdiːlɨ̇set, -ket‖-ˈde-/ *adv Lat fml* VIZ.

vid·e·o /ˈvɪdiəʊ/ *adj* [Wa5;A] **1** *tech* connected with or used in the showing of pictures by television: *a video* DISPLAY *system* —compare AUDIO **2** using VIDEOTAPE^1: *a video recording*

vid·e·o·tape^1 /ˈvɪdiəʊteɪp/ *n* [U] a long narrow band of MAGNETIC material on which television pictures (and sound) are recorded for broadcasting at a later date

videotape^2 *v* [T1] to make a recording of (a television show) on VIDEOTAPE^1

vide su·pra /ˌ·· ˈ··/ *interj Lat* (used for telling a reader where to find more about the subject) look at an earlier place in the book

vie /vaɪ/ *v* **vied**; *pres. p.* **vying** [L9 esp. *with, for*] to compete (against someone) (for something): *They are vying (with each other) for the lead*

view^1 /vjuː/ *n* **1** [U] ability (esp. of the person or thing stated) to see or be seen from a particular place; sight: *My view of the stage was blocked by the big hat of the woman sitting in front of me.*|*The car turned the corner and was lost to our view/passed out of view* (=could not be seen any more).|*The valley was hidden from view in the mist.*|*When we reached the top of the mountain, we came in view of* (=were able to see) *a wide plain below/a wide plain came into view* (=was able to be seen).|*He fell off his horse in full view of his friends* (=seen by all, and himself able to see all of them).|*There was no shelter within view* (=that could be seen) *anywhere* **2** [C (*of*)] **a** something seen from a particular place, esp. a stretch of pleasant country: *There's no view from my bedroom window except of some factory chimneys* **b** a picture or photograph of a piece of scenery, a building, etc. **3** [S (*of*)] a special chance to see or examine someone or something: *If we stand at this window, we'll get a better view (of the procession)* **4** [C (*of*) *usu. sing.*] a general consideration of a matter in all its details: *The lawyer hasn't yet formed a clear view of the case* **5** [C (*about, on*)] a personal opinion, belief, idea, etc., about something: *In my view, he's a fool.*|*What are your views on free university education?* **6 fall in with (or meet) someone's views** *fml* to agree to do as someone wishes **7 in view** already planned or suggested: *He wants to find work, but he has nothing particular in view* **8 in view of** considering; taking into consideration: *In view of his youth, the police have decided not to continue with the case against him* **9 keep something in view** to remember something as a possibility or for future consideration if a favourable chance comes **10 on view** being shown to the public; offered to be seen and examined **11 take a dim/poor view of** *infml* to think unfavourably about **12 take the long view (of something)** not to think only of the results which will follow at once from some action, but also of its effects in the more distant future **13 with a view to doing something** with the intention of doing something; in order to do something: *With a view to improving his ability to speak French, he spends most of his holidays in France*

USAGE The **aspect** or **outlook** of a house is the way it faces: *a room with a southern* **aspect**. What one sees from the windows is a **view**. All these words also have fig. meanings: *What are your* **views** (=your opinions) *on education?*|*We must consider this suggestion from every* **aspect** (=way of looking at it). What is expected to happen in the future is the **outlook** or the **prospect**: *Trade's bad, and the* **outlook** *for next year is even worse.*|*I don't look forward to the* **prospect** *of 3 weeks alone in a boat with Mildred!* —see SCENERY (USAGE)

view^2 *v* **1** [T1] *esp. tech* to examine; look at thoroughly: *Several possible buyers have come to view the house* —see also ORDER TO VIEW **2** [X9, esp. *as, with*] to consider; regard; think about: *He viewed his son's lawless behaviour as an attack on himself.*|*As the man and his wife grew older they viewed the future with some anxiety, because they'd saved very little money.*|*How do you view this matter?* (=what is your opinion about it?) **3** [T1; I∅] to watch (esp. television)

view·er /ˈvjuːəʳ/ *n* **1** a person watching television **2** an apparatus for looking at transparent colour photographs

view·find·er /ˈvjuːˌfaɪndəʳ/ *n* a piece of apparatus on a camera, which shows a small picture of what is to be photographed —see picture at PHOTOGRAPHIC

view·less /ˈvjuːləs/ *adj AmE* expressing no opinions

view·point /ˈvjuːpɔɪnt/ *n* POINT OF VIEW

vig·il /ˈvɪdʒɨ̇l/ *n* **1** [C;U] (an act of) remaining watchful for some purpose (as on guard, in prayer, looking after sick people, etc.), esp. while staying awake during the night (esp. in the phrs. **keep vigil, all-night vigil**) **2** [*the*+R+*of*] *old use* the day or night before (a Christian holy day), as spent in prayer and without food: *on the vigil of Christmas*

vig·i·lance /ˈvɪdʒɨ̇ləns/ *n* [U] watchful care; continual attentiveness

vig·i·lant /ˈvɪdʒɨ̇lənt/ *adj* continually watchful or on guard; always prepared for possible danger: *A vigilant police force helps to control crime* —**~ly** *adv*

vig·i·lan·te /ˌvɪdʒɨ̇ˈlænti/ *n esp. derog* a member of a group of people who form themselves into an unofficial organization to keep order and punish crime in an area where an official body either does not exist or does not work properly

vi·gnette /vɪˈnjet (*Fr* viɲɛt)/ *n* **1** an ornamental pattern or drawing without a border, set into a book, esp. at the beginning or end of a CHAPTER **2** a drawing or photograph of a scene or of someone's head and shoulders, the edges of which fade gradually into the unprinted paper **3** a short effective written description of a character or scene

vig·or·ous /ˈvɪgərəs/ *adj* **1** forceful; strong; healthy and active: *As a cricketer he's vigorous rather than skilful* **2** using or needing forcefulness and strength: *The politician made a vigorous speech in defence of the government* **3** (of a plant) healthy; growing strongly —**~ly** *adv*

vig·our, *AmE* **-or** /ˈvɪgəʳ/ *n* [U] forcefulness; strength shown in power of action in body or mind

Vi·king /ˈvaɪkɪŋ/ *n* a man belonging to a race of Scandinavian people who attacked and sometimes settled along the coasts of northern and western Europe from the 8th to the 10th centuries: *Viking ships*

vile /vaɪl/ *adj* [Wa1] **1** hateful; shameful; evil; low and worthless: *Would you be so vile as to steal a coat from a sick man?* **2** *infml* very bad, nasty, or unpleasant: *She has a vile temper; it's impossible to live with her.|This food is vile; I can't bear to eat it!* —**~ly** /ˈvaɪl-li/ *adv* —**~ness** *n* [U]

vil·i·fi·ca·tion /ˌvɪlə̇fə̇ˈkeɪʃən/ *n fml* **1** [U] the act of VILIFYing **2** [C] an example of this

vil·i·fy /ˈvɪlə̇faɪ/ *v* [T1] *fml* to speak evil of (someone or something) without good cause, esp. in order to influence others unfavourably

vil·la /ˈvɪlə/ *n* **1** a pleasant country house in its own garden, often used for only part of the year for holidays, esp. in southern Europe: *We're renting a villa in the south of France for the summer holidays* **2** (*often cap. as part of the name of a house*) (in Britain) a house on the edge of a town, either standing by itself or joined to another, and having a garden, usu. built before 1914: *South Villa|fine old 19th century villas* **3** a large ancient Roman country house with the buildings and (farm)land belonging to it

USAGE People selling a house like to call it a **villa**, which sounds as if it were separate from other houses and probably on the edge of a town or in the country; or a **residence**, which is a *fml* word for a large house. A **mansion** also is large, grand, and often ancient. A **bungalow** is a house all on one floor, with no stairs.

vil·lage /ˈvɪlɪdʒ/ *n* **1** [C] a collection of houses and other buildings (such as a church, inn, school, and one or more shops) in a country area, smaller than a town: *the village schoolmaster|village life* **2** [GC] the people in this place as forming a little society of their own: *The whole village is going to the baker's funeral today*

vil·lag·er /ˈvɪlɪdʒəʳ/ *n* a person who lives in a village

vil·lain /ˈvɪlən/ *n* **1** [*the*+R;C] (in old plays, films, and stories) a man who is the (or a) main bad character: *The villain carried off the pure young girl and tied her to the railway line* —opposite **hero** **2** [C] *infml BrE* a criminal: *The police have caught the villains* **3** [C;*you*+N] *infml* (used for expressing amused or loving blame) a troublesome young person or animal: *Stop eating all those sweets, you young villain!* **4** [C;*you*+N] *fml* a thoroughly wicked man who harms others **5 the villain of the piece** *infml, often humor* the person or thing to be blamed; the one that has caused all the trouble on some occasion

vil·lain·ies /ˈvɪləniz/ *n* [P] *esp. lit* evil or wicked acts

vil·lain·ous /ˈvɪlənəs/ *adj derog* **1** *esp. lit* evil; like or fitting the character of a VILLAIN (4) **2** *infml* of very bad quality: *This is a villainous pair of shoes; they've ruined my feet*

vil·lain·y /ˈvɪləni/ *n* [U] *esp. lit* evil or wicked behaviour

-ville /vɪl/ *suffix* [*adj*+s,*n*+s→*n*[U]] *sl, esp. AmE* a place or thing of the stated quality: *This party is really dullsville*

vil·lein /ˈvɪlə̇n, ˈvɪleɪn/ *n* a land worker in Europe in the MIDDLE AGES who was given a small amount of land of his own in return for work on the land of a large landowner, and who was not allowed to leave the place

vil·lein·age, *AmE* **-lenage** /ˈvɪlə̇nɪdʒ/ *n* [U] the state of being a VILLEIN

vim /vɪm/ *n* [U] *infml* active bodily force; healthy good spirits and readiness for activity (often in the phr. **vim and vigour**)

vin·ai·grette /ˌvɪnə̇ˈgret, ˌvɪneɪ-/ *n* [U] a sharp-tasting mixture of oil, VINEGAR, salt, pepper, etc., sometimes with added HERBs, served with some cold dishes of meat, fish, and vegetables

vin·di·cate /ˈvɪndə̇keɪt/ *v* [T1] **1** to show that charges made against (someone or something) are untrue; free from blame: *The report of the committee of enquiry completely vindicates him and declares his action to have been right and proper* **2** *fml* to prove (something that was in doubt) to be true or right: *The success of the operation completely vindicates my faith in the doctor*

vin·di·ca·tion /ˌvɪndə̇ˈkeɪʃən/ *n* **1** [U (*of*)] the act of vindicating or being VINDICATEd **2** [S (*of*)] a fact that VINDICATEs

vin·dic·tive /vɪnˈdɪktɪv/ *adj* too unwilling to forgive; having or showing the desire to harm someone from whom harm has been received —**~ly** *adv* —**~ness** *n* [U]

vine /vaɪn/ *n* **1** also **grapevine**— a type of climbing plant with a woody stem that produces bunches of juicy green or purple fruit (GRAPEs) **2 a** any creeping or climbing plant with thin twisting stems (such as the IVY, the CUCUMBER, the MELON, etc.) **b** (*often in comb.*) the main stem itself: *a* HOP³ *vine*

vin·e·gar /ˈvɪnɪgəʳ/ *n* [U] an acid-tasting liquid made usu. from MALT or sour wine, used in preparing and preserving vegetables, for putting on food, etc.

vin·e·gar·y /ˈvɪnɪgəri/ *adj* **1** of or like VINEGAR; very sour: *This wine bottle has been opened too long; the wine has a vinegary taste* **2** unkind; bitter; sharp-tempered: *vinegary remarks*

vin·e·ry /ˈvaɪnəri/ *n* a usu. heated room or small building, made mostly of glass, where VINEs (1) are grown in cold countries

vine·yard /ˈvɪnjəd‖-jərd/ *n* a piece of land planted with VINEs (1) for wine production

vi·no /ˈviːnəʊ/ *n* **-noes** [U;(C)] *infml* (any type of) cheap ordinary wine —see also PLONK⁴

vi·nous /ˈvaɪnəs/ *adj fml, tech, or humor* like, caused by, connected with, or coloured like wine: *sounds of vinous laughter*

vin·tage¹ /ˈvɪntɪdʒ/ *n* **1** (a fine wine made in) a particular year, and named by the date of the year: *This red wine is of 1929 vintage; it's a very good vintage.|He has some rare old vintages in his collection of wines* **2** [*usu. sing.*] *tech* **a** the yearly gathering of GRAPEs in an area and the making of new wine from them: *All the people from the surrounding villages come to help with the vintage* **b** the season when this is done: *The unusually hot weather caused an early vintage* **c** the crop of GRAPEs in a particular year: *The vintage last year was harmed by disease* **3** *infml* the past time or age to which someone or something belongs: *"When did you go to university?" "I'm of the 1950 vintage"*

vintage² *adj* [Wa5;A] **1 a** (of PORT⁶ or CHAMPAGNE) of high enough quality in a particular year to be sold without being mixed with wines from other years **b** *infml* (of other wines) of a type that is of a high enough quality to be given a named

VINTAGE[1] (1) **2** produced in or being a time famous for high quality and lasting value: *a vintage silent film|This has been a vintage year for the theatre in London; so many good plays have been produced* **3** showing all the best qualities of the work of (the stated person): *This piece of music is vintage Brahms* **4** (of a car) made between 1919 and 1930 —compare VETERAN (4)

vint·ner /ˈvɪntnəʳ/ *n* a person whose business is buying and selling wines

vi·nyl /ˈvaɪnǀl/ *n* [C;U] (any of several types of) firm bendable plastic used instead of leather, rubber, wood, etc.: *vinyl floor covering*

vi·ol /ˈvaɪəl/ *n* a type of stringed musical instrument of the 16th and 17th centuries, from which the modern VIOLIN was developed

vi·o·la¹ /viˈəʊlə/ *n* a type of stringed musical instrument, like the VIOLIN but a little larger and producing a slightly deeper sound

vi·o·la² /ˈvaɪələ, vaɪˈəʊlə/ *n* any of several types of low-growing garden plants with single small white, yellow, or purple flowers, rather like small pansies (PANSY)

vi·o·late /ˈvaɪəleɪt/ *v* [T1] **1** to disregard or act against (something solemnly promised, accepted as right, etc.): *A country isn't respected if it violates an international agreement* **2** *fml* to break open, into, or through (something that ought to be respected or left untouched): *The thieves violated many graves in their search for the gold* **3** *esp. lit* to break, spoil, or destroy (a calm or sheltered condition) **4** *lit or euph* to have sex with (a woman) by force; RAPE —**-lation** /ˌvaɪəˈleɪʃən/ *n* [U;C: (*of*)]

vi·o·lence /ˈvaɪələns/ *n* [U] **1** very great force in action or feeling: *The wind blew with great violence* **2** rough treatment; use of bodily force on others, esp. (unlawfully) to hurt or harm: *The police were said to have used unnecessary violence on the crowd.|Many people say too much violence is shown on television.|crimes of violence|robbery with violence* **3** **do violence to** **a** to spoil; have a harmful effect on: *These modern boxlike buildings do violence to the beauty of the old city* **b** to damage; twist (meaning or facts): *This careless newspaper report does violence to the truth*

vi·o·lent /ˈvaɪələnt/ *adj* **1** (of a person) uncontrollably fierce (and dangerous) in action: *The madman was violent and had to be locked up* **2** acting with or using great damaging force: *a violent storm|a violent kick* **3** forceful beyond what is usual or necessary: *a violent quarrel|violent language* **4** produced by or being the effect of damaging force: *He died a violent death, murdered by an enemy* **5** (of feelings) unusually strong or difficult to control: *a violent pain|She was in a violent temper and began throwing things about* —**~ly** *adv*

vi·o·let /ˈvaɪəlǀt/ *n, adj* **1** [C] a type of small plant with sweet-smelling dark purplish-blue flowers **2** [U;B] (having) a purplish-blue colour **3** [C9] *humor* a person who does not draw attention to his or her abilities (esp. in the phrs. **shrinking/modest violet**)

vi·o·lin /ˌvaɪəˈlɪn/ *n* **1** a type of 4-stringed wooden musical instrument, supported between the left shoulder and the chin and played by drawing a BOW³ (2) across the strings —see picture at STRINGED INSTRUMENT **2** [*usu. pl.*] *infml* a person who plays this instrument in a band —**~ist** *n*: *He is one of the best violinists in the world*

vi·o·lon·cel·lo /ˌvaɪələnˈtʃeləʊ/ *n* **-los** *fml* CELLO —**violoncellist** *n*

VIP /ˌviː aɪ ˈpiː/ *n infml* a very important person; person of great influence or fame

vi·per /ˈvaɪpəʳ/ *n* **1** any of several types of small poisonous snake —see picture at REPTILE **2** a wicked or ungrateful person who does harm to others

vi·ra·go /vǀˈrɑːgəʊ/ *n* **-goes** *or* **-gos** a fierce-tempered scolding woman with a loud voice

vir·gin¹ /ˈvɜːdʒǀn‖ˈvɜr-/ *n* a person (esp. a woman or girl) who has not had sexual relations with a member of the opposite sex

virgin² *adj* [Wa5] **1** [A] without sexual experience: *a book called "The Virgin Soldiers"* **2** [B] fresh; unspoiled; unchanged by human activity: *no footmarks on the virgin snow*|(fig.) *The mind of a child is virgin soil; it's not full of firmly held ideas and opinions that prevent it receiving new ones*

vir·gin·al¹ /ˈvɜːdʒǀnl‖ˈvɜr-/ *adj apprec* of, concerning, or suitable to a VIRGIN: *virginal pureness*

virginal² *n* a type of small square legless piano-like musical instrument popular in the 16th and 17th centuries

vir·gin·als /ˈvɜːdʒǀnlz‖ˈvɜr-/ *n* **virginals** [Wn3;C] VIRGINAL²

virgin birth /ˌ·· ˈ·/ *n* [*the*+R] (*often caps*) the religious belief that Christ was caused to be born of the VIRGIN MARY by God, and not by means of ordinary sexual union

Vir·gin·i·a /vəˈdʒɪnɪə‖vər-/ also (*fml*) **Virginia to·bac·co** /·ˌ·· ·ˈ··/— *n* [U;C] any of several types of tobacco grown esp. in the state of Virginia, US: *a Virginia cigarette*

virginia creep·er /·ˌ·· ˈ··/ (*AmE* **woodbine**)— *n* [U] a type of climbing garden plant often grown on walls, with large leaves that turn deep red in autumn

vir·gin·i·ty /vɜːˈdʒɪnǀti‖vɜr-/ *n* [U] the state of being a VIRGIN: *She was 19 when she lost her virginity* (=had sex with a man for the first time)

Virgin Mar·y /ˌ·· ˈ··/ also **Blessed Virgin Mary**— *n* [*the*+R] (in the Christian religion) Mary, the mother of Christ

Vir·go /ˈvɜːgəʊ‖ˈvɜr-/ *n* **-gos** **1** [R] **a** the ancient sign, a young girl (VIRGIN), representing the 6th division in the ZODIAC belt of stars **b** the group of stars (CONSTELLATION) formerly in this division **2** [C] a person born under the influence of this sign —see picture at PLANET

vir·gule /ˈvɜːgjuːl‖ˈvɜr-/ *n* a sign (/) used for separating 2 or more words between which a choice has to be made

vir·ile /ˈvɪraɪl‖ˈvɪrəl/ *adj usu. apprec* **1** (of a man) having the full amount of strong and forceful qualities expected of a man, esp. in matters of sex: *She admired the virile young swimmer* **2** *sometimes euph* forceful; manly; full of active strength: *His style of singing is very virile, but he doesn't have much feeling for the expressiveness of the words.|The way in which the footballer robbed his opponent of the ball was rather "virile"* (=too rough)

vi·ril·i·ty /vǀˈrɪlǀti/ *n* [U] *usu. apprec* male sexual power; manly qualities

vi·rol·o·gist /vaɪəˈrɒlədʒɪst‖-ˈrɑ-/ *n* a person who is skilled in VIROLOGY

vi·rol·o·gy /vaɪəˈrɒlədʒi‖-ˈrɑ-/ *n* [U] the scientific study of VIRUSes, and of diseases caused by them

vir·tu /vɜːˈtuː‖vɜr-/ *n* see OBJECT OF VIRTU

vir·tu·al /ˈvɜːtʃʊəl‖ˈvɜr-/ *adj* [Wa5;A] almost what is stated; in fact though not in name: *The king was so much under the influence of his wife that she was the virtual ruler of the country*

vir·tu·al·ly /ˈvɜːtʃʊəli‖ˈvɜr-/ *adv* almost; very nearly; in every way that is really important: *My book's virtually finished; I've only a few changes to make in the writing*

vir·tue /ˈvɜːtʃuː‖ˈvɜr-/ *n* **1** [U] goodness, nobleness, and worth of character as shown in right behaviour: *You can trust him; he's a man of the* *highest virtue* —opposite **vice** **2** [C] any good quality of character or behaviour: *Among her many virtues are loyalty, courage, and truthfulness* **3** [U; C] (an) advantage: *One of the virtues of this curtain material is that it's easily washable* **4** [U;C] (an) effectiveness in producing a particular good result; power: *Many people doubt the virtue of ancient country medicines in curing the sick* **5 by virtue of** also (*fml*) **in virtue of**— as a result of; by means of: *Though she isn't British by birth, she's a British citizen by virtue of her marriage to an Englishman* **6 woman of easy virtue** *euph, becoming rare* a woman who has sexual experience with many men —see also **make a virtue of** NECESSITY

vir·tu·os·i·ty /ˌvɜːtʃʊˈɒsɨti‖ˌvɜrtʃʊˈɑ-/ *n* [U] a very high degree of skill in performance in one of the arts

vir·tu·o·so /ˌvɜːtʃʊˈəʊzəʊ‖ˌvɜrtʃʊˈəʊsəʊ/ *n* **-sos** *or* **-si** /zi‖si/ a person who has a very high degree of skill as a performer in one of the arts, esp. music

vir·tu·ous /ˈvɜːtʃʊəs‖ˈvɜr-/ *adj* **1** possessing, showing, or practising VIRTUE(*s*) (1,2) **2** *derog* (too) satisfied with one's own good behaviour, and expressing this in one's manner towards those who have done wrong —**~ly** *adv*

vir·u·lence /ˈvɪrʊləns‖ˈvɪrə-/ also **vir·u·len·cy** /-si/— *n* [U] the quality or state of being VIRULENT

vir·u·lent /ˈvɪrʊlənt‖ˈvɪrə-/ *adj* **1** (of a poison, a disease caused by bacteria, etc.) very powerful, quick-acting, and dangerous to life or health **2** (of a feeling or its expression) very bitter; full of hatred —**~ly** *adv*

vi·rus /ˈvaɪərəs/ *n* a tiny disease-causing object smaller than bacteria which infects living cells in the body, in plants, etc.: *the common cold virus|virus infections* —compare GERM

vi·sa¹ /ˈviːzə/ *n* an official mark put onto a PASSPORT by a representative of a country, giving a foreigner permission to enter, pass through, or leave that country

visa² *v* **-saed** /zəd/ [T1] to provide a VISA¹ for (a PASSPORT)

vis·age /ˈvɪzɪdʒ/ *n lit* the human face, esp. with regard to its expression or appearance: *a smiling visage|his hairy visage*

-vis·aged /ˈvɪzɪdʒd/ *comb. form lit or fml* having the kind of face described: *a dark-visaged Indian*

vis-à-vis /ˌviːz ɑː ˈviː, ˌviːz ə ˈviː/ *prep fml or pomp* with regard to; when compared to: *This year's income shows an improvement vis-à-vis last year's*

vis·ce·ra /ˈvɪsərə/ *n* [(*the*) P] **1** the large inside organs of the body, such as the heart, lungs, stomach, etc. **2** *infml* the bowels

vis·ce·ral /ˈvɪsərəl/ *adj* [Wa5] *med* belonging to or connected with the VISCERA

vis·cos·i·ty /vɪsˈkɒsɨti‖-ˈkɑ-/ *n* **1** [C;U] (a measure of) the unwillingness of a thick liquid or a gas to obey forces that try to make it flow **2** [U] the quality of being sticky

vis·count /ˈvaɪkaʊnt/ *n* [C;A] (*often cap.*) (the title of) a British nobleman next in rank below an EARL: *Viscount Montgomery of Alamein*

vis·count·cy /ˈvaɪkaʊntsi/ *n* the rank or title of VISCOUNT

vis·count·ess /ˈvaɪkaʊntɨs/ *n* [C;A] (*often cap.*) (the title of) **a** the wife of a VISCOUNT **b** a woman of the rank of VISCOUNT in her own right

vis·cous /ˈvɪskəs/ also (*tech*) **vis·cid** /ˈvɪsɨd/— *adj* (of a liquid) thick and sticky; that does not flow easily

vise /vaɪs/ *n AmE* VICE²

vis·i·bil·i·ty /ˌvɪzəˈbɪlɨti/ *n* **1** [U] ability to give a clear view **2** [U;C] (esp. in official weather reports) the degree of clearness (often measured in distance) with which objects can be seen according to the condition of the air and the weather: *We had a splendid view of the mountains because of the very good visibility* **3** [U] *rare* the quality, state, or fact of being VISIBLE (1)

vis·i·ble /ˈvɪzəbəl/ *adj* [(*to*)] **1** that can be seen; noticeable to the eye —opposite **invisible** **2** noticeable to the mind: *What is this object? It seems to serve no visible purpose*

vis·i·bly /ˈvɪzəbli/ *adv* noticeably: *He was visibly anxious about the examination*

vi·sion /ˈvɪʒən/ *n* **1** [U] (the) ability to see: *I've had my eyes tested and the report says that my vision is perfect* **2** [U] power of imagination and expression; wisdom in understanding the true meaning of facts, esp. with regard to the future: *We need a man of vision as president* **3** [C] something that is without bodily reality, seen (as) in a dream, when in a sleeplike state, or as a religious experience: *She saw/had a vision in which God seemed to appear before her* **4** [C+*of*] a picture seen in the mind; idea, esp. as a fulfilment of a desire: *He has a clear vision of the future he wants for his children.|The student had visions of getting a degree with first class honours* **5** [C (*of*) *usu. sing.*] *lit* something seen, esp. an unexpectedly strange, rare, or beautiful sight: *For a moment we had a vision of the mountaintop before the mist hid it again.|What a vision of hopelessness the old man looked.|She really is a vision* (=is very beautiful) —see also FIELD OF VISION

vi·sion·a·ry¹ /ˈvɪʒənəri‖-neri/ *adj* **1** *apprec* having or showing VISION (2) **2** fanciful; existing in the mind only and improbable of fulfilment

visionary² *n* **1** a person whose aims for the future are noble or excellent but lack reality or are not easy to put into practice **2** a (holy) person who sees VISIONs (3)

vis·it¹ /ˈvɪzɨt/ *v* **1** [T1;I∅] to (go and) spend some time in (a place or, as a guest, someone's house): *While we're in Europe we ought to visit Holland.|Aunt Jane usually visits us for 2 or 3 weeks in the spring.|"Do you live in this town?" "No, we're only visiting"* **2** [T1;I∅] to go to see (someone) or look at (a building or other place) for a short time: *When we were in London we visited the Tower twice* **3** [L9] *AmE* to stay: *Anyone who's visiting in Edinburgh ought to go and see the castle.|We always visit at the Savoy Hotel when we're in London* —see also VISIT WITH **4** [T1] to go to (a place) in order to make an official examination: *Schools have to be visited from time to time by education officers* **5** [T1 *usu. pass.*] *lit* **a** to attack (a place): *20 years ago this area was visited by a terrible disease* **b** to come into the mind of (someone): *Last night I was visited by a strange dream*

visit² *n* **1** [C (*to, from*)] an act or time of visiting: *He makes several business visits to America every year.|We've just had a visit from the police* (=the police have visited us) **2 go on a visit (to someone or something)** to visit (someone or something), esp. for a long stay **3 pay a visit (to someone or something)/pay (someone or something) a visit** to visit (someone or something) usu. for a short time and for a purpose

vis·i·tant /ˈvɪzɨtənt/ *n* **1** *lit* a person who, or thing that, visits, esp. one thought to be a spirit from the world of the dead **2** *tech* VISITOR (2)

vis·i·ta·tion /ˌvɪzɨˈteɪʃən/ *n* **1** [C (*by, of*)] a formal visit by someone in charge (esp. by a high official person to discover whether things are in good order) or by a priest **2** [C (*of*)] an event (usu. natural) believed to be an act of punishment (or sometimes of favour) from heaven: *The villagers thought that the storm was a visitation of God* **3** [C (*from*)] *infml, often humor* an unusually long social visit that is troublesome to the person visited

vis·it·ing /ˈvɪzɪ̆tɪŋ/ *n* [U] (*often in comb.*) the act of making visits: *In her free time Mrs Evans does prison visiting* (=visits prisoners and tries to make them happier, look after their interests, etc.).| *Visiting hours in this hospital* (=the times when sick people may be visited by their friends) *are from 4.30 to 6.00*

visiting card /ˈ··· ·/ also (*infml*) **card**— *n* a small card with one's name (and address) on it, which one gives to people one does not know when one goes to visit them or leaves if they aren't at home

visit on also **visit up·on**— *v prep* [D1] *esp. bibl* to direct (one's anger, a punishment, etc.) against (someone or something): *God has visited his anger on us*

vis·it·or /ˈvɪzɪ̆təʳ/ *n* [(*to, from*)] **1** a person who visits or is visiting (the stated or understood place or person): *Visitors to the castle are asked not to take photographs.*|*The castle gets lots of visitors from America* **2** a bird which spends only part of the year in a country

visitors' book /ˈ··· ·/ *n* a book in which visitors (esp. to a place of interest, or staying in a hotel) write their names and addresses

visit with *v prep* [T1 *no pass.*] *AmE* to talk socially with (someone)

vi·sor /ˈvaɪzəʳ/ *n* **1** (in a suit of armour) the part of the metal headcover (HELMET) which can be raised or lowered to show or to protect the face **2** also **sun visor** /ˈ· ˌ··/— a movable framework of dark glass or thick cloth, fitted to the top of a car's front window to protect the driver's eyes from very bright sunshine **3** the front part of a cap which protects the eyes from sunshine; PEAK

vis·ta /ˈvɪstə/ *n* [(*of*)] **1** a distant view, to which the eye is directed between narrow limits, as by rows of trees **2** a set of events stretching far into the future or back into the past, as seen in the imagination: *After her husband's death she saw her life as an endless vista of sadness and grief*

vi·su·al /ˈvɪʒʊəl/ *adj* [Wa5] **1** [B] gained by seeing: *Visual knowledge of a place of battle helps a general to plan his attack* **2** [B] connected with or having an effect on the sense of sight: *The visual arts are painting, dancing, etc., as opposed to music and literature* **3** [A] *tech* concerned with the power of sight: *the visual nerve*|*the visual organ* **4** [B] (esp. of the directing of aircraft) performed without the help of radio, calculating instruments, etc.: *a visual landing*|*visual bombing*

visual aid /ˌ·· ˈ·/ *n* (an apparatus for showing) any object that can be looked at, such as a picture, map, photograph, or film, used for helping people to learn, remember, etc.

vi·su·al·ize, -ise /ˈvɪʒʊəlaɪz/ *v* [T1 (*as*), 4,6;V4] to form a picture of (something or someone) in the mind; imagine: *Though he described the place carefully, I couldn't visualize it because it was so different from anything I'd known.*|*Try to visualize sailing through the sky on a cloud* —**-ization** /ˌvɪʒʊəlaɪˈzeɪʃən‖-lə-/ *n* [U]

vi·su·al·ly /ˈvɪʒʊəli/ *adv* **1** in appearance: *Visually the chair is very pleasing, but it's uncomfortable* **2** using VISUAL AIDs: *He explained the journey visually by the use of pictures and maps*

vi·tal /ˈvaɪtl/ *adj* **1** [B (*to, for*)] very necessary (for some purpose expressed or suggested); of the greatest importance: *If you're to avoid being discovered, it's vital that you should hide at once.*|*This point is vital to my argument.*|*Your support is vital for the success of my plan* **2** [B] full of life and force: *Their leader's vital and cheerful manner filled his men with courage* **3** [Wa5;A] necessary for life (in order to stay alive): *He was lucky that the bullet hadn't entered a vital organ* (=any organ without which life cannot continue, such as the heart, brain, etc.)

vital force /ˌ·· ˈ·/ also **vital prin·ci·ple** /ˌ·· ˈ···/— *n* [*the*+R] *esp. lit* that force in an animal or plant which is considered to be the cause of its life (as opposed to the chemical actions that work within it)

vi·tal·i·ty /vaɪˈtælɪ̆ti/ *n* [U] **1** gay forcefulness of character or manner: *That singer has no vitality; you could almost go to sleep while she's performing* **2** ability to stay alive or working in an effective way: *Continual tropical fevers weaken the vitality*

vi·tal·ize, -ise /ˈvaɪtl-aɪz/ *v* [T1] to give force to; bring (something or someone) to life: *How can we vitalize British industry?* —see also REVITALIZE

vi·tal·ly /ˈvaɪtl-i/ *adv* in the highest possible degree: *It was vitally important for him to pass his examination, as it would have a deciding effect on his future*

vi·tals /ˈvaɪtlz/ *n* [(*the*) P] *esp. old use or humor* the main bodily organs (the lungs, heart, brain, and esp. the stomach and bowels) without which a person cannot continue to live

vital spark /ˌ·· ˈ·/ *n* [*the*+R] *infml* the power of making music or characters in books or plays seem alive and exciting

vital sta·tis·tics /ˌ·· ·ˈ··/ *n* [P *sometimes sing.*] **1** *infml* the measurements of a woman's body round the chest, waist, and HIPs: *Jean's vital statistics are 38-24-38* (inches) **2** certain facts, officially collected and arranged, about people's lives, esp. their births, marriages, deaths, and length of life

vit·a·min /ˈvɪtəmɪ̆n, ˈvaɪ-‖ˈvaɪ-/ *n* **1** [C *usu. pl.*] any one of several chemical substances which are found in very small quantities in certain foods, and lack of which causes certain weaknesses and diseases in people and animals: *This type of bread has added vitamins.*|*vitamin* PILLs **2** [U9] any particular type of this, named by a letter of the alphabet (A, B, C, D, E, G, H, K, or P): *Oranges contain vitamin C*

vi·ti·ate /ˈvɪʃieɪt/ *v* [T1 *often pass.*] *fml* to weaken; spoil; harm the quality of: *All his attempts to improve were vitiated by his lack of willpower* —**-ation** /ˌvɪʃɪˈeɪʃən/ *n* [U]

vit·i·cul·ture /ˈvɪtɪ̆kʌltʃəʳ/ *n* [U] (the study and science of) the growing of GRAPEs, esp. for making wine

vit·re·ous /ˈvɪtrɪəs/ *adj tech* of, made of, or like glass: *Vitreous rocks are especially hard and shiny.*| *vitreous* CHINA

vit·ri·fy /ˈvɪtrɪ̆faɪ/ *v* [T1;I∅] to (cause to) change into glass or a glasslike substance, by means of heat

vit·ri·ol /ˈvɪtrɪəl/ *n* [U] **1** bitter cruel wounding quality of speech or writing **2 a** also **oil of vitriol** /ˌ· · ˈ···/— pure SULPHURIC ACID, which burns flesh deeply **b** (*usu. in comb.*) any of the SULPHATEs of metals used in medicine or for colouring: **Blue vitriol** *is copper* SULPHATE

vit·ri·ol·ic /ˌvɪtriˈɒlɪk‖-ˈɑlɪk/ *adj* (of a feeling or its expression) bitter and harmful; causing sharp pain to the mind

vi·tu·pe·rate /vɪˈtjuːpəreɪt‖vaɪˈtuː-/ *v* [Wv4;T1;I∅] *fml* to scold or blame (someone or something) fiercely; attack with curses

vi·tu·pe·ra·tion /vɪˌtjuːpəˈreɪʃən‖vaɪˌtuː-/ *n* [U] (the act of using) angry speech and cursing

vi·tu·pe·ra·tive /vɪˈtjuːpərətɪv‖vaɪˈtuː-/ *adj* **1** (of speech) containing VITUPERATION **2** (of a person) always ready to curse or use angry speech —**~ly** *adv*

vi·va·ce /viˈvɑːtʃi, -tʃeɪ/ *adv, adj* (in music) (that is to be played) quickly and with spirit

vi·va·cious /vɪ̆ˈveɪʃəs/ *adj* (esp. of a woman) gay;

full of life and high spirits —**~ly** *adv* —**vivacity** /vɨ̵ˈvæsɨ̵ti/ *n* [U] —**~ness** /vɨ̵ˈveɪʃəsnɨ̵s/ *n* [U]

vi·var·i·um /vaɪˈveərɪəm/ *n* **-iums** *or* **-ia** *tech* an enclosed place where animals are kept indoors in conditions similar to their natural surroundings

vi·va vo·ce¹ /ˌvaɪvə ˈvəʊtʃi, -ˈvəʊsi, ˌviːvə-/ *adv, adj* [Wa5] *Lat* (carried out) by means of speaking: *Writing to him isn't enough; I must argue the case with him viva voce.|There'll be both written and viva voce examinations in French*

viva voce² also (*infml*) **viva** /ˈvaɪvə/— *n Lat* a spoken examination

viv·id /ˈvɪvɨ̵d/ *adj* **1** (of light or colour) bright and strong; producing a sharp sensation on the eye: *a vivid flash of lightning|vivid red hair* **2** that produces or is able to produce sharp clear pictures in the mind; lifelike: *To the little boy's vivid imagination, the stick he held was a sword with which he was fighting enemies.|a vivid description* **3** (of a person's power of expression as having an effect on others) full of life and force: *The actor gave a vivid performance as the mad king* —**~ly** *adv* —**~ness** *n* [U]

vi·vip·a·rous /vɪˈvɪpərəs/ *adj* [Wa5] *tech* (of an animal) giving birth to living young ones (not by means of eggs): *a viviparous fish*

viv·i·sect /ˈvɪvɨ̵sekt/ *v* [T1;IØ] to perform an operation on (a living animal) not in order to cure a sickness, but as a scientific test, esp. in order to increase medical knowledge of human diseases

viv·i·sec·tion /ˌvɪvɨ̵ˈsekʃən/ *n* **1** [U] the art and practice of VIVISECTing **2** [C] an example of this

viv·i·sec·tion·ist /ˌvɪvɨ̵ˈsekʃənɨ̵st/ *n* a person who practises or supports VIVISECTION (1)

vix·en /ˈvɪksən/ *n* **1** a female fox **2** *derog* a nasty bad-tempered woman

vix·en·ish /ˈvɪksənɪʃ/ *adj* (of a woman) fierce and bad-tempered; fond of scolding

viz. /vɪz/ also (*fml*) **videlicet**— *adv* and it is/they are; that is to say: *On most English farms you'll find only 4 kinds of animal, viz. horses, sheep, cattle, and pigs*
USAGE Usually read aloud as "NAMELY".

vi·zi·er /vɨ̵ˈzɪəʳ/ *n* (in former times) (the title of) a minister in some Muslim countries

V-neck /ˈviː nek/ *n* a neck opening of a dress, shirt, etc., with the front cut in the shape of a V —**V-necked** *adj*: *a V-necked* SWEATER

vo·cab /ˈvəʊkæb/ *n infml* VOCABULARY (3)

vo·cab·u·la·ry /vəˈkæbjʊləri, vəʊ-‖-bjəleri/ *n* **1** all the words known to a particular person: *Our baby's just starting to talk; he's got a vocabulary of about 10 words* **2** the special set of words used in a particular kind of work, business, etc.: *I find it difficult to understand the vocabulary of the law-courts* **3** a list of words, usu. in alphabetical order and with explanations of their meanings, less complete than a dictionary

vo·cal¹ /ˈvəʊkəl/ *adj* **1** [Wa5;A] connected with the voice; used in speaking: *The tongue is one of the vocal organs* **2** [Wa5;B] produced by or for the voice; spoken, sung, or expressed aloud: *I like instrumental better than vocal music* **3** [B] *infml* expressing oneself freely and noisily in words; talking a great deal, usu. loudly —**~ly** *adv*

vocal² *n often pl.* a performance of a popular song by a singer, esp. as part of a performance by a band: *a performance by Pete Robertson's band, with vocals by Liz Forsyth*

vocal cords, vocal chords /ˈ·· ·, ˌ·· ˈ·/ *n* [P] thin bands of muscle in the boxlike part (LARYNX) at the upper end of a person's air passage (WINDPIPE) that can be made to move rapidly by the passing of air and thus produce sound —see picture at RESPIRATORY

vo·cal·ist /ˈvəʊkəlɨ̵st/ *n* a singer of popular songs, esp. one who sings with a band

vo·cal·ize, -ise /ˈvəʊkəl-aɪz/ *v fml* **1** [T1] to say or sing (words, sounds, etc.) **2** [IØ] to practise singing exercises **3** [T1] *tech* **a** to change (a consonant) into a vowel **b** to speak (a sound) with VOICE¹ (7)

vo·ca·tion /vəʊˈkeɪʃən/ *n* **1** [C] a job which one does because one thinks one has a special fitness or ability to give service to other people: *Teaching children ought to be a vocation as well as a way of earning money* **2** [S] a special call from, or choosing by, God for the religious life: *My friend ceased to be a priest because he ceased to believe in his vocation* **3** [S;U (*for*)] particular fitness or ability (for a certain kind of work, esp. of a worthy kind): *She's a good nurse because she has a real vocation for looking after the sick* **4** [C] a person's work or employment: *I know he writes for magazines, but what's his main vocation?*

vo·ca·tion·al /vəʊˈkeɪʃənəl/ *adj* [Wa5] preparing for or connected with a VOCATION (4): *vocational training*

voc·a·tive /ˈvɒkətɪv‖ˈvɑ-/ *adj, n* [Wa5] (a noun, or the special form of a noun) used in some languages (such as Latin) when addressing someone or something

vo·cif·er·ate /vəˈsɪfəreɪt, vəʊ-‖vəʊ-/ *v* [T1;IØ] *fml* to shout or speak (words) in a loud and very forceful way, esp. when complaining

vo·cif·er·a·tion /vəˌsɪfəˈreɪʃən, vəʊ-‖vəʊ-/ *n* [C;U] an act or the action of speaking loudly and forcefully, and usu. angrily and complainingly

vo·cif·er·ous /vəˈsɪfərəs, vəʊ-‖vəʊ-/ *adj* **1** noisy in the expression of one's feelings **2** expressed noisily in speech or by shouting: *vociferous demands for easier examinations* —**~ly** *adv* —**~ness** *n* [U]

vod·ka /ˈvɒdkə‖ˈvɑdkə/ *n* [U] a type of strong, colourless, and almost tasteless alcoholic drink, first made in (and very popular in) Russia and Poland

vogue /vəʊg/ *n* **1** [*the*+R;C] the generally accepted fashion or custom at a certain (usu. not lasting) time: *High boots were the vogue for women last year.|There seems to be a vogue for sailing small boats at present* **2** [S] the state of being in popular favour: *He used to have a great vogue as a film actor, but no one goes to the cinema to see him now* **3** [A] newly popular and much used, but likely soon to go out of favour: *vogue words* **4 all the vogue** *infml* very fashionable; very new and popular **5 come into/go out of vogue** to become/cease to be popular or fashionable **6 in vogue** fashionable; much used, worn, etc., at the present time: *Short skirts are no longer in vogue in Britain*

voice¹ /vɔɪs/ *n* **1** [U] the sound(s) produced by man in speaking and singing: *The human voice can express every possible kind of feeling* **2** [U] the ability of a person to produce such sound(s): *I have no voice today; I've lost my voice, as the result of a bad cold* **3** [U;C] (the quality or force of) such sound as particular to a certain person or creature: *She lowered her voice as she told me the secret; she spoke in a low voice.|She has an unpleasant voice.|We could hear the children's voices in the garden.|The boy's voice is breaking* (=becoming lower like a man's) **4** [U] (the expressing of) an opinion; the right to express an opinion, to vote, or to influence other opinions, decisions, etc.: *The crowd was large, but they were all of one voice.|I can't help you to get this job, as I have little voice in the decision of the directors* **5** [C] **a** ability as a singer: *He's got a good voice; he sings well* **b** a singer performing with others in a particular piece of music: *This song is arranged for singing by 3 voices* **6** [C (*of*)] an expression of something which is like the human voice either in sound or because it expresses human feelings, ideas, qualities, etc.: *He was very angry at first but in the end the voice of reason won, and he recognized that the suggestion was fair and just* **7** [U] the sound produced when a speaker makes his breath act on his VOCAL CORDS as it passes through them —see also VOICE² (2) **8** [C *usu. sing.*] the form of the verb which shows whether the subject of a sentence acts (**active voice**) or is acted on (**passive voice**) **9 at the top of one's voice** very loudly **10 give voice to** to express (feelings, thoughts, etc.) aloud **11 in good voice** speaking or singing at one's best **12 lift up one's voice** *old use* to sing or speak **13 raise one's voice a** to speak louder **b** to speak loudly and angrily (to someone): *Don't raise your voice to me* **c** to express one's displeasure, disagreement, etc.: *As no one raised his voice against the plan, it was agreed on* **14 with one voice** *lit* all together; with everyone expressing the same opinion

voice² *v* [T1] **1** to express in words, esp. forcefully: *The chairman voiced the feeling of the meeting when he demanded more pay* **2** [Wv5] to produce (a sound, esp. a consonant) with a movement of the VOCAL CORDS as well as with the breath: /d/ *and* /g/ *are voiced consonants, but* /t/ *and* /k/ *aren't*

voice box /ˈ· ·/ *n infml* LARYNX

-voiced /vɔɪst/ *comb. form* having a voice of the stated quality: *loud-voiced|soft-voiced|sweet-voiced*

voice·less /ˈvɔɪsləs/ *adj* **1** [Wa5] making no sound: *He sat there silent, making small voiceless movements with his lips* **2** having no chance, or no desire, to express opinions **3** [Wa5] (of a speech sound, esp. a consonant) produced without VOICE¹ (7): /f, k, t/ *are voiceless consonants*

voice-o·ver /ˌ· ˈ··/ *n* the voice of an unseen person on a film or television show, who makes remarks or gives information about what is being shown

void¹ /vɔɪd/ *adj* **1** [Wa1;F+*of*] empty (of); without; lacking: *That part of the town is completely void of interest for visitors* **2** [Wa5;B] *esp. law* (of any kind of official agreement) having no value or effect from the beginning: *An agreement signed by a child, to repay borrowed money, is void* —see also NULL AND VOID **3** [Wa5;B] *lit* completely empty: *The desert stretching away before the traveller seemed totally void* **4** [Wa5;F+*in*] (in the card game of BRIDGE) having no cards of the stated SUIT at the beginning of a game: *void in hearts*

void² *n* **1** [*the*+R] the space around our world and stretching out beyond the stars: *A ball of fire seemed to fall out of the void, disappearing before it reached the earth* **2** [C *usu. sing.*] an empty space: *The ground began to shake and a sudden void opened under his feet* **3** [C *usu. sing.*] a feeling of emptiness or loss: *The child's death left a painful void in his parents' lives*

void³ *v* [T1] **1** *fml or tech* to get rid of (the usu. unpleasant or unwanted contents of something) by emptying or pouring out through a hole, tube etc. **2** *law* to cause to be without effect; make VOID¹ (2)

voile /vɔɪl (*Fr* vwal)/ *n* [U] a very fine, thin, almost transparent material of cotton, silk, or wool, used esp. in making summer dresses

vol /vɒl‖vɑl/ *abbrev* (*often cap.*) VOLUME (1): *Dickens' work in 24 vols*

vol·a·tile /ˈvɒlətaɪl‖ˈvɑlətl/ *adj* **1** (of a person or his character) of a quickly-changing, undependable nature; variable in purpose or interest **2** (of a liquid or oil) easily changing into a gas: *Petrol is volatile* —**-tility** /ˌvɒləˈtɪlə̣ti‖ˌvɑ-/ *n* [U]

vol-au-vent /ˌvɒl əʊ ˈvɑ̃‖ˌvɑl- (*Fr* vɔlovɑ̃)/ *n* a very light small pastry case filled with meat, chicken, etc.

vol·can·ic /vɒlˈkænɪk‖vɑl-/ *adj* **1** of, from, produced, or caused by a VOLCANO: *volcanic rocks|volcanic activity* **2** violently forceful

vol·ca·no /vɒlˈkeɪnəʊ‖vɑl-/ *n* **-noes** *or* **-nos** a mountain with a large opening (CRATER) at the top (and often others on the sides) through which melting rock (LAVA), steam, gases, etc., escape from time to time with explosive force from inside the earth: *An* **active volcano** *may explode at any time.|A* **dormant volcano** *is quiet at present.|An* **extinct volcano** *has ceased to be able to explode*

vole /vəʊl/ *n* (*often in comb.*) any of several types of small thick-bodied short-tailed animal of the rat and mouse family, which live in fields, woods, banks of rivers, etc.: *a water vole|a bank vole* —see picture at MAMMAL

vo·li·tion /vəˈlɪʃən‖vəʊ-, və-/ *n* [U] *fml* the act of using one's will; one's power to control, decide, or choose (a course of action)

vo·li·tion·al /vəˈlɪʃənəl‖vəʊ-, və-/ *adj fml* resulting from choice or the use of will: *volitional movements*

vol·ley¹ /ˈvɒli‖ˈvɑli/ *n* **1** [C] a number of shots fired at the same time by soldiers, police, etc. **2** [C+*of*] **a** a like attack, but with named weapons, such as stones, spears, arrows, etc.: *The monkeys in the trees aimed volleys of fruit at the men passing below* **b** a number of blows given, words spoken, etc., quickly and with force, usu. with unpleasant intention: *When a car knocked over the fruitseller's cart, he directed a volley of curses at the driver.|a volley of blows* **3** [*the*+R] (of a ball) the condition of not having hit the ground after being thrown, kicked, or hit: *The footballer kicked the ball on the volley, and it flew into the back of the net* **4** [C] a kicking or hitting of a ball that is in this condition, esp., in tennis, a stroke by which the player returns the ball to his opponent without allowing it to touch the ground first —see also HALF VOLLEY

volley² *v* **1** [IØ] (of guns) to be fired all together **2** [L9] (of shots fired or objects thrown) to come flying together through the air **3** [X9] to hit or kick (a ball) on the VOLLEY¹ (3): *The footballer volleyed the ball into the back of the net* **4** [IØ;T1] (in tennis) to make a VOLLEY¹ (4) against (one's opponent): *Borg volleyed Connors as he came up to the net*

vol·ley·ball /ˈvɒlibɔːl‖ˈvɑ-/ *n* [U] a game in which a large ball is struck by hand backwards and forwards across a net without being allowed to touch the ground

USAGE One plays **volleyball** in a *court*, *scoring* (SCORE) *points* by hitting the *ball* over the *net* with one's hands in such a way that one's opponents cannot hit it back. In an important *match* the person in charge is called the **umpire**.

volt /vəʊlt/ *n* (a standard measure of electrical force used in causing a flow along wires, equal to) the amount needed to produce one AMPERE of electrical current where the RESISTANCE of the CONDUCTOR is one OHM

volt·age /ˈvəʊltɪdʒ/ *n* [C;U] electrical force measured in VOLTS

volte-face /ˌvɒlt ˈfɑːs‖ˌvəlt-/ *n* [*usu. sing.*] *Fr, esp. lit or fml* a change to a completely opposite opinion or course of action

vol·u·ble /ˈvɒljʊbəl‖ˈvɑljə-/ *adj often derog* having, always ready to produce, or expressed in a great flow of words: *Ted's a voluble speaker at meetings; he doesn't give much chance to others to say anything.|Her explanations for her failure to do the work were voluble but not easily believed* —**-bility** /ˌvɒljʊˈbɪlə̣ti‖ˌvɑljə-/ *n* [U] —**-bly** /ˈvɒljʊbli‖ˈvɑljə-/ *adv*

vol·ume /ˈvɒljuːm‖ˈvɑljəm/ *n* **1** [C] **a** one of a set of books of the same kind or together forming a whole: *We have a set of Dickens' works in 24* *volumes* **b** one of a set of collected reports, magazines, papers, etc., of the same kind put together in book form, often yearly: *the 1970 volume of the Notes of the Scientific Association* **2** [C] *often fml* a book, esp. a large one: *His library was full of rare old volumes* **3** [U (*of*)] size or quantity thought of as measurement of the space inside or filled by something: *The volume of this container is 100,000* CUBIC *metres* **4** [U;C] *esp. tech* amount produced by some kind of (industrial) activity: *The volume of passenger travel on the railways is decreasing* **5** [U] (degree of) fullness or loudness of sound: *The television is too loud; turn the volume down.|a voice that lacks volume* —see picture at SOUND³

vol·umes /ˈvɒljuːmz‖ˈvaljəmz/ *n* **1** [P (*of*)] a large quantity or mass (esp. of something that pours or flows) **2 speak volumes (for something)** to show or express (something) very clearly or fully: *Her refusal to become angry with that very unpleasant young man speaks volumes for her patience*

vo·lu·mi·nous /vəˈluːmɨ̣nəs, vəˈljuː-‖vəˈluː-/ *adj* **1** (of a (part of a) garment) very loose and full; using much cloth: *a voluminous skirt* **2** (of a container) very large; able to hold a lot: *a voluminous shopping bag* **3** *often derog* producing or containing much writing: *a voluminous writer|a voluminous report* —**~ly** *adv* —**~ness** *n* [U]

vol·un·ta·ry¹ /ˈvɒləntəri‖ˈvalənteri/ *adj* [Wa5] **1** [B] (of a person or an action) acting or done willingly, without payment and without (the doer) being forced: *He made a voluntary statement to the police* **2** [A] controlled or supported by people who give their money, services, etc., of their own free will: *Many social services are still provided by voluntary societies* **3** [B] *tech* under the control of the will: *the voluntary muscles|voluntary movements* —opposite **involuntary movements** —opposite **involuntary** —**-tarily** *adv*: *He made the promise quite voluntarily; I didn't force him to*

voluntary² *n* a piece of music played in church before or after the service, usu. on an ORGAN

vol·un·teer¹ /ˌvɒlənˈtɪəʳ‖ˌva-/ *n* **1** [C (*for*)] *sometimes humor* a person who VOLUNTEERS² (1): *This work costs us nothing; it's all done by volunteers.|Are there any volunteers for a swim before breakfast?* **2** [C] a person who VOLUNTEERS² (2) for service in the army, navy, etc.

volunteer² *v* **1** [I∅,3] to offer one's services or help without payment or reward; make a willing offer (to do something), esp. when others are unwilling **2** [I∅ (*for*), 3] to offer to join the army, navy, or airforce of one's own free will, without being forced to **3** [T1] to tell (something) without being asked: *My friend volunteered an interesting piece of news.|"It's not my car, it's my father's", she volunteered*

vo·lup·tu·a·ry /vəˈlʌptʃʊəri‖-tʃeri/ *n lit, usu. derog* a person who gets great enjoyment from comfort and costly living and delights in the pleasures of the senses

vo·lup·tu·ous /vəˈlʌptʃʊəs/ *adj* **1** of a kind (esp. connected with women) that suggests or expresses sexual pleasure or enjoyment: *The dancer's movements were slow and voluptuous.|She had a full voluptuous mouth.|her voluptuous curves* **2** (of a woman) having a beautiful soft rounded body that excites sexual feeling **3** too much concerned with the enjoyment of bodily (esp. sexual) pleasures: *the voluptuous life of the Romans in ancient times* **4 a** giving a fine delight to the senses: *the voluptuous feeling of pure soft silk* **b** giving a satisfying feeling of rest and enjoyment: *voluptuous comfort* —**~ly** *adv* —**~ness** *n* [U]

vo·lute /vəˈluːt/ *n tech* a kind of ornamentation used on the top of pillars (esp. in buildings in the ancient Greek form), shaped like the end view of a loose roll of paper —**voluted** *adj*: *voluted pillars*

vom·it¹ /ˈvɒmɨ̣t‖ˈva-/ *n* **1** [U] food or other matter that has been VOMITed² (1) **2** [C] an act of VOMITing

vomit² *v* **1** [T1;I∅] to throw up (the contents of the stomach) through the mouth; be sick: *The poor creature began to vomit blood.|The unpleasant smell made her feel so sick that she began to vomit* **2** [T1 (OUT)] to pour out suddenly with force and in great quantity (usu. something unpleasant or unwanted): *The ship's side vomited out a great mass of black oil into the sea*

voo·doo /ˈvuːduː/ *n* [U] (*often cap.*) a set of magical beliefs and practices, used as a form of religion, found particularly among some of the peoples of parts of the West Indies —**~ism** *n* [U]

vo·ra·cious /vəˈreɪʃəs, vɒ-‖vɔ-, və-/ *adj* **1** eating or desiring large quantities of food, from either hunger or lack of self-control: *Pigs are voracious feeders* **2** having or showing a limitless eagerness, like a hunger, for something: *She's a voracious reader of all kinds of love stories* —**~ly** *adv*

vo·rac·i·ty /vəˈræsɨ̣ti, vɒ-‖vɔ-, və-/ *n* [U] *fml* the state or quality of being VORACIOUS

vor·tex /ˈvɔːteks‖ˈvɔr-/ *n* **-texes** *or* **-tices** /tɨ̣siːz/ **1** [C] a mass of anything, esp. water or wind, making such forceful circular movement as to cause objects which it meets to be drawn into its hollow centre, as in a WHIRLPOOL or WHIRLWIND **2** [*the*+R (*of*)] *lit or pomp* a set of conditions, activities, interests, or feelings so forceful that one is helpless against them: *Against his will he was drawn into the vortex of war and spent 4 years as a soldier*

vo·ta·ry /ˈvəʊtəri/ *n* [(*of*)] **1** *fml or tech* a regular worshipper (of a particular god, holy person, or religion): *Roman soldiers were often votaries of Mars, the god of war* **2** *fml, pomp, or humor* an eager admirer or supporter (of some idea, belief, activity, etc.): *The course of the international football match was watched on television by all the votaries of the sport*

vote¹ /vəʊt/ *n* **1** [C (*on, about*)] an act of making a choice or decision on a matter by means of voting: *If we can't agree by the end of the meeting, a vote will have to be taken on the matter* —see also CARD VOTE **2** [C (*for, against*)] a (particular person's) choice or decision, as expressed by voting: *At the election I shall give my vote to Tom Smith* (=I shall vote for him) —see also CASTING VOTE **3** [C] the piece of paper on which a choice is expressed: *Members were asked to place their votes in the box* **4** [*the*+R9] **a** the whole number of such choices made either for or against someone or something: *The opposition vote seems to be growing* **b** the opinion represented by such choices, esp. those made by a particular set of people: *The women's vote will certainly be in favour of spending more on schools* **5** [*the*+R] a decision made by voting: *The vote yesterday went in his favour* **6** [*the*+R (*sometimes pl. with same meaning*)] the right to vote in political elections: *In Britain, young people are given the vote at the age of 18.|Some countries don't support the idea of votes for women* **7** [C9 *usu. sing.*] *tech* an amount of money VOTEd² (5) by Parliament for a particular purpose: *The vote for Education gets higher every year* **8 cast/record one's vote** *fml* to vote (as an act on a particular occasion) **9 put something to the vote** to decide to try to obtain a decision about something by asking everyone concerned to vote for or against it

vote² *v* **1** [I∅ (*for, against, on*), 3,5] to express one's choice officially from among the possibilities offered or suggested (usu. done by marking a piece of paper secretly, or by calling out or raising one's hand at a meeting): *You're only 16; you're too young to vote.|I shall vote for Heath because I think he's the better man.|As we can't all agree on this matter, let's vote on it.|We voted to give a concert to get some money for the hospital.|They voted that the school should continue* **2** [L9] *infml* to express one's choice in favour of (a person or political party) at an election: *Vote Macdonald, the man you can trust!* **3** [X9, esp. IN, *into*, ON, *onto*] to elect: *The people have just voted in a new government* **4** [X9, esp. OFF, *off*, OUT (*of*)] to dismiss by means of a vote or election: *The government are afraid they will be voted out of office at the next election* **5** [D1;T1] to agree, as the result of a vote, to provide (something): *Parliament has voted the town a large sum of money for a new road* **6** [D1 *often pass.*] *infml* to agree or state as the general opinion: *The party was voted a great success* **7** [I5a] *infml* (*usu. used after the pron* I) to suggest (a course of action): *I vote we go home* (=let's go home)

vote down *v adv* [T1] to defeat (someone or something) by voting

vote of cen·sure /ˌ· · ˈ··/ *n* **votes of censure** a declaration of blame against someone, expressed by voting

vote of con·fi·dence /ˌ· · ˈ···/ *n* **votes of confidence** a declaration of support for the actions of someone, usu. expressed by voting

vote of thanks /ˌ· · ˈ·/ *n* **votes of thanks** [*usu. sing.*] a public expression of thanks (esp. in the phr. **propose a vote of thanks**)

vot·er /ˈvəʊtəʳ/ *n* **1** a person who is voting **2** a person who has the right to vote, esp. in a political election

vote through *v adv* [T1] to accept (something) by voting

vo·tive /ˈvəʊtɪv/ *adj* [Wa5] given or done to fulfil a solemn promise made to God or a holy person (SAINT), usu. as thanks for a favour prayed for and received: *The church was full of votive candles.|a votive offering*

vouch·er /ˈvaʊtʃəʳ/ *n* **1** *BrE* a kind of ticket that may be used instead of money for a particular purpose: *a travel voucher|Some firms give their workers luncheon* (LUNCH) *vouchers, with which they can buy a meal in certain restaurants* **2** *BrE* a kind of ticket that gives a buyer the right to receive certain goods free or at a lower price during a limited time **3** *law* a receipt or official declaration, written or printed, given to prove that accounts are correct or that money has already been paid

vouch for /vaʊtʃ/ *v prep* [T1] **1** to declare one's belief in (someone or something), from one's own personal experience or knowledge: *I've read this report carefully and I can vouch for its correctness* **2** to take the responsibility for (someone's future behaviour)

vouch·safe /vaʊtʃˈseɪf/ *v* [D1 (*to*); T1,3] *lit or fml* to offer, give, say, or do (something) as an act of favour or kindness (esp. to someone lower in rank or position than oneself): *For all the mercies vouchsafed us, we are truly grateful to God*

vow[1] /vaʊ/ *n* **1** a solemn promise or declaration of intention: *All the men took/made a vow of loyalty to their leader* **2 take vows** to begin to live, with a group of others, apart from the world, in a religious house (as a MONK or NUN) **3 under a vow** in the state of having made a promise, esp. to God: *The members of this religious group are under a vow of silence*

vow[2] *v* **1** [T3,5a] to declare or swear solemnly (that one will do something): *He vowed to kill his wife's lover.|When young Ernie was caught stealing he vowed he'd never do it again* **2** [T1 (*to*)] *fml* to promise (something) by swearing solemnly, esp. to God: *Priests vow their lives to the service of the church*

vow·el /ˈvaʊəl/ *n* **1** any one of the human speech sounds in which the breath is let out without any stop or any closing of the air passage in the mouth or throat that can be heard: *The simple vowel sounds of British English are represented in this dictionary by* /iː, ɪ, e, æ, ɑː, ɒ, ɔː, ʊ, uː, ʌ, ɜː, ə/ **2** *infml* a letter used for representing any of these: *The vowels in the English alphabet are* a, e, i, o, u, *and, sometimes,* y —compare CONSONANT, DIPHTHONG

vox pop /ˌvɒks ˈpɒp‖ˌvɑks ˈpɑp/ *n infml* an enquiry carried out in the street by a television, radio, or newspaper reporter who tries to find out what people's opinions are on a matter of public interest

vox pop·u·li /ˌvɒks ˈpɒpjʊlaɪ, -liː‖ˌvɑks ˈpɑpjə-/ *n* [*the*+R] *Lat* public opinion

voy·age[1] /ˈvɔɪ-ɪdʒ/ *n* a journey, usu. long, made by boat or ship: *The voyage from England to India used to take 6 months.|When I give up work I am going on/shall make/shall take a long sea voyage*

voyage[2] *v* [Iø] *lit or fml* to make a long journey by (sea); travel over (the sea) —see TRAVEL (USAGE)

voy·ag·er /ˈvɔɪ-ɪdʒəʳ/ *n* a person who travels by sea (esp. where risks or difficulties may be met)

voy·ag·es /ˈvɔɪ-ɪdʒɨz/ *n* [(*the*) P (*of*)] an account of long journeys by land or sea to distant places: *The voyages of the early travellers make interesting reading*

voy·eur /vwɑːˈjɜːʳ (*Fr* vwajœr)/ *n* a person who obtains sexual excitement from watching the sexual activities of others, esp. in secret —**~istic** /ˌvwɑːjəˈrɪstɪk/ *adj* —**~istically** *adv* [Wa4]

vs. /ˈvɜːsəs‖ˈvɜr-/ *AmE* V.

V-sign /ˈviː saɪn/ *n* **1** a sign made by holding the hand up with the first 2 fingers spread in the shape of a V and the front (PALM) of the hand facing forwards, used for expressing victory or the hope of it **2** a like sign made with the back of the hand facing forwards, used for expressing great dislike or anger, and usu. thought to be very rude

VTOL /ˌviː tiː əʊ ˈel, ˈviːtɒl‖-tɑl/ *n, adj* [Wa5;U;A] vertical takeoff and landing; (working by means of) a system which makes it possible for an aircraft to take off and land without having to run for a certain distance along the ground (on a RUNWAY): *a VTOL aircraft*

vul·can·ite /ˈvʌlkənaɪt/ *n* [U] a type of rubber which has been specially treated to make a smooth hard compound for use in industry

vul·can·ize, -ise /ˈvʌlkənaɪz/ *v* [T1] to treat (rubber) at high temperature, with SULPHUR, so as to give strength for industrial use —**-ization** /ˌvʌlkənaɪˈzeɪʃən‖-nə-/ *n* [U]

vul·gar /ˈvʌlgəʳ/ *adj* **1** [B] (of a person) very rude, low, or having bad manners either by nature or from lack of training: *Mrs Atkins is a very vulgar woman, to shout like that at the top of her voice* **2** [B] (of speech or behaviour) displeasing; going against the accepted standards of polite society, esp. with regard to bodily habits, acts, etc.: *Putting food into one's mouth with a knife is considered vulgar in England* **3** [B] showing, esp. by drawing people's attention too noticeably, a lack of fine feeling or good judgment in the choice of what is suitable or beautiful, esp. in matters of art: *The house was full of costly, but very vulgar furniture* **4** [Wa5;A] *esp. lit* belonging to, generally accepted among, or used by, the common people: *vulgar opinion* —**~ly** *adv*

vulgar frac·tion /ˌ·· ˈ··/ *n* a FRACTION expressed by a number above and a number below a line (rather than as a DECIMAL): *¾ is a vulgar fraction*

vul·gar·i·an /vʌlˈgeərɪən/ *n fml* a person whose behaviour, in spite of his supposed wealth or social position, is considered unsuitable and VULGAR

vul·gar·is·m /ˈvʌlgərɪzəm/ *n fml* **1** [C] a word or expression not usu. used by educated people **2** [U] VULGARITY (1a)

vul·gar·i·ty /vʌlˈgærɪ̈ti/ *n derog* **1** [U] **a** the state or quality of being VULGAR (1,2,3) **b** VULGAR (1,2,3) speech or action **2** [C *often pl.*] a particular example of VULGAR (1,2,3) speech or action

vul·gar·ize, -ise /ˈvʌlgəraɪz/ *v* [T1] *derog* to spoil the quality of; lower the standard of (something that is good): *This beautiful piece of music has been vulgarized by being made into a popular dance tune* —**-ization** /ˌvʌlgəraɪˈzeɪʃən‖-gərə-/ *n* [U;C]

Vulgar Lat·in /ˌ·· ˈ··/ *n* [R] the form of Latin spoken in ancient Rome, esp. by the common people, as opposed to the written (CLASSICAL) language, and from which many modern languages, such as Italian, French, and Spanish, have developed

Vul·gate /ˈvʌlgeɪt, -gɪ̈t/ *n* [*the*+R] a special Latin translation of the Bible made in the 4th century, and commonly used in the ROMAN CATHOLIC Church

vul·ne·ra·ble /ˈvʌlnərəbəl/ *adj* [B (*to*)] **1** (of a place or thing) weak; not well protected; easily attacked: *We're in a vulnerable position here, with the enemy on the hill above us* **2** (of a person or his feelings) easily harmed, hurt, or wounded; sensitive: *She looked so young and vulnerable that he felt a great desire to protect her* —**-bility** /ˌvʌlnərəˈbɪlɪ̈ti/ *n* [U (*to*)] —**-bly** /ˈvʌlnərəbli/ *adv*

vul·pine /ˈvʌlpaɪn/ *adj* **1** *tech* of, related to, or like a fox **2** *esp. lit* like a fox in appearance or character; clever in a sharp tricky way

vul·ture /ˈvʌltʃəʳ/ *n* **1** any of several types of large ugly tropical birds with almost featherless heads and necks, which feed on dead animals —see picture at PREY¹ **2** a person who has no mercy and who uses people, esp. weak and helpless people, for his own advantage and gain: *Moneylenders are the vultures of society*

vul·va /ˈvʌlvə/ *n* **-vae** /viː/ *or* **-vas** the place where the passage leading to the female sex organs has its opening on the body

vy·ing /ˈvaɪ-ɪŋ/ *pres. p. of* VIE

W, w

W, w /ˈdʌbəljuː/ **W's, w's** *or* **Ws, ws** the 23rd letter of the English alphabet

W *written abbrev. for:* **a** west(ern) **b** WATT

WAC /wæk/ *n* a member of the (American) Women's Army CORPS (**the WACs**): *She's joined the WACs to help her country*

wack /wæk/ *n* [N] *NW EngE sl* (*used esp. in the city of Liverpool*) fellow; friend

wack·y /ˈwæki/ *adj* [Wa1] *infml, esp. AmE* (of people, ideas, behaviour, etc.) silly or strange —**wackiness** *n* [U]

wad¹ /wɒd‖wɑd/ *n* [(*of*)] **1** a thick soft mass of material pressed into a hole or crack, used for filling an empty space, etc.: *wads of cotton in one's ears to keep out noise* **2** a thick piece of cloth, or pieces of paper folded, pressed, or fastened together: *A wad of letters arrived today* **3** a rather large amount esp. of paper money rolled up: *He has wads of money!* —see also WADGE

wad² *v* **-dd-** [T1] **1** to make a WAD of: *Wad the newspaper and hit the flies with it* **2** [(*with*)] to fill with a WAD: *Wad the space with paper*

wad·ding /ˈwɒdɪŋ‖ˈwɑ-/ *n* [U] (any material used for) WADs, esp. if used for packing or in medicine: *Put some wadding into the empty space.|cotton wadding*

wad·dle¹ /ˈwɒdl‖ˈwɑdl/ *v* [IØ (ALONG)] to walk with short steps, bending from one side to the other, as if having short legs and a heavy body: *Ducks waddle*

waddle² *n* [*usu. sing.*] a heavy awkward way of walking, like that of a duck

wade /weɪd/ *v* [IØ] to walk through water: *Let's wade into/across/through this water*

wade in *v adv* [IØ] *infml* to begin something difficult or heavy in a determined manner: *The work won't wait: we'd better wade in now*

wade in·to *v prep* [T1] *infml* **1** to begin (something difficult or heavy) in a determined manner: *The work won't wait: let's wade into it now* **2** to start attacking (someone) with words or blows: *When I said that she just waded into me*

wad·er /ˈweɪdəʳ/ *n* **1** a person who WADEs **2** either of a pair of high rubber boots intended to protect the legs while wading (WADE) or fishing **3** WADING BIRD

wade through *v prep* [T1] *infml* to finish by making an effort (something long, unpleasant, or uninteresting): *I waded through that long report at last*

wadge /wɒdʒ‖wɑdʒ/ *n* [(*of*)] *infml BrE* a mass or amount of things pressed or rolled tightly together: *a wadge of papers*

wad·i, wady /ˈwɒdi‖ˈwɑdi/ *n* a usu. dry river bed of the sort common in desert countries

wad·ing bird /ˈ·· ·/ *n* any of various large birds with long legs and neck that WADE into water to find their food (such as the HERON and the CRANE)

wa·fer /ˈweɪfəʳ/ *n* **1** flour, sugar, etc., cooked in the form of a very thin cake: *ice cream with a wafer in it* **2** a thin round piece of special bread used with wine in the Christian religious ceremony of Holy COMMUNION **3** a small round piece of (often red) paper or other material stuck on the back of a letter to close it, or on a paper to show that it is official

waf·fle¹ /ˈwɒfəl‖ˈwɑ-/ *n* a large light sweet cake, usu. marked with raised squares, common in America and often covered with a sweet liquid

waffle² *v* [Wv3;IØ (ON)] *BrE sl* to talk nonsense expressed in words that sound good: *I asked him a question but he just went waffling on*

waffle³ *n* [U] *BrE sl* nonsense expressed in words that sound good: *Don't talk such waffle, man!*

waffle i·ron /ˈ·· ˌ··/ *n* a cooking apparatus with 2 joined metal parts that shut upon each other and mark a pattern of raised squares on WAFFLEs¹ that are being cooked

waft¹ /wɑːft, wɒft‖wɑft, wæft/ *v* [T1;IØ :(ALONG)] *fml or lit* to (cause to) move or go lightly on or as if on wind or waves: *Cooking smells wafted along the hall*

waft² *n* **1** *fml* a sudden not lasting smell, carried by moving air: *wafts of cigarette smoke* **2** *fml* a short light current of air **3** *lit* a single slow waving movement of the hand

wag¹ /wæg/ *v* **-gg-** [T1;I∅] **1** (of people and other living creatures) to (cause to) shake (esp. a movable body part) quickly and repeatedly from side to side: *The dog wagged its tail with pleasure.|The dog's tail wagged* **2 a case of the tail wagging the dog** *infml* a state of affairs in which the followers control the leader **3 Their tongues wagged** *infml* They talked a lot, esp. about something surprising or shocking

wag² *n* [*usu. sing.*] an act of WAGging¹; shake: *The dog greeted its master with a wag of its tail*

wag³ *n infml* a clever and amusing talker (usu. male): *Bob is a bit of a wag and we always laugh at his jokes*

wage¹ /weɪdʒ/ *v* [T1] to begin and continue (a struggle of some kind) (esp. in the phr. **wage war (on/against)**): *to wage war|to wage a war against crime and disease*

wage² *n* **1** [A] of or about wages: *a high wage level in this industry* **2** [S] wages: *What is your weekly wage?|a weekly wage of £50* **3 a living wage** an amount of pay large enough to buy the food, clothing, etc., needed for living: *We have a right to a living wage*

wage earn·er /ˈ· ˌ··/ *n* a person who works for wages or a SALARY: *In our family both my husband and I are wage earners*

wage freeze /ˈ· ·/ also (*BrE*) **wages freeze** /ˈ·· ·/— *n* an attempt, esp. by government, to keep pay from rising

wa·ger¹ /ˈweɪdʒəʳ/ *n* [C,C5] *fml* an amount of money risked on an uncertain result; BET

wager² *v* [D1,5a;T1 (*on*), 5a] *fml* to BET: *I'll wager (£5) he's there by now.|He's there by now, I'll wager.|I'll wager (you) (£5) that he's there*

wag·es /ˈweɪdʒɪ̈z/ *n* [P] a payment usu. of money for labour or services (usu. according to contract) calculated by the hour, day, week, or amount produced, and usu. received daily or weekly —see PAY (USAGE)

wage scale /ˈ· ·/ *n* **1** a list of rates or wages paid for related jobs **2** the level of wages paid by an employer

wage slave /ˈ· ·/ *n humor or derog* WAGE EARNER: *We wage slaves don't know what real freedom is*

wag·ge·ry /ˈwægəri/ *n* **1** [U] jokes and fun typical of a WAG³ **2** [C] a joke or funny trick typical of a WAG³

wag·gish /ˈwægɪʃ/ *adj* of, like, or typical of a WAG³: *waggish remarks* —**~ly** *adv* —**~ness** *n* [U]

wag·gle¹ /ˈwægəl/ *v* [T1;I∅] to (cause to) move frequently from side to side: *The dog waggled its tail.|The dog's tail waggled* —compare WAG

waggle² *n* [S] an act of waggling (WAGGLE)

wag·gon, *AmE* **wagon** /ˈwægən/ *n* [C; *by*+U] **1** a strong 4-wheeled road vehicle, mainly for heavy loads, drawn by horses or oxen **2** a small copy of this as a child's toy **3** *BrE* GOODS WAGGON **4** TROLLEY (2) **5 on/off the (water-) waggon** *sl* unwilling/no longer unwilling to drink alcohol: *He's been/gone on and off the waggon so many times you never know what to serve him at a party*

wag·gon·er, *AmE* **wagoner** /ˈwægənəʳ/ *n* the driver of a WAGGON

wag·gon·ette, *AmE* **wagonette** /ˌwægəˈnet/ *n* (in former times) a light 4-wheeled pleasure carriage drawn by horses, with side-seats facing inwards behind the driver, and a door at the back

wag·on-lit /ˌvægɒn ˈliː‖-gən- (*Fr* vagɔ̃ li)/ *n* **wagons-lits** (*same pronunciation*) *BrE* SLEEPING CAR

wag·tail /ˈwægteɪl/ *n* any of several types of small black and white European bird that move their tails quickly up and down as they walk

waif /weɪf/ *n esp. lit* **1** an uncared-for child or one without a home: *a pitiful little waif* **2 waifs and strays** children (or animals) without homes

wail¹ /weɪl/ *v* **1** [I∅ (*for, with*)] to make a usu. long cry or sound suggesting grief or pain: *to wail with sorrow|The wind wailed in the chimney all night* **2** [T1,5: (OUT)] to say, sing, or cry out in a way that suggests grief or pain: *"You've taken my apple," he wailed.|She kept wailing that she was lonely* **3** [I∅ (*over, about*), 5] *derog* to complain: *Don't wail over/about your misfortunes*

wail² *n* an act or sound of WAILing

wain /weɪn/ *n old use* a farm WAGGON

wain·scot /ˈweɪnskət, -skɒt‖-skət, -skɑt/ *n* **1** PANELLING, esp. on the lower half of the walls of a room in an old house **2** SKIRTING BOARD —**~ed** *adj*

waist /weɪst/ *n* **1** the narrow part of the human body just above the legs and HIPs —see picture at HUMAN² **2** (the size of) the part of a garment that goes round this part of the body: *to take in the waist of a dress* **3** the narrow middle part of any apparatus, such as a stringed musical instrument **4** *tech* the middle part of a ship

waist·band /ˈweɪstbænd/ *n* the thickened or strengthened part of a garment (trousers, a skirt, etc.) that fastens round the waist

waist·coat /ˈweɪskəʊt, ˈweskət‖ˈweskət/ *AmE* usu. **vest**— *n* a men's close-fitting garment without arms that reaches to the waist and is worn under the JACKET (short coat) of a 3-piece suit

waist·line /ˈweɪstlaɪn/ *n* **1** a line thought of as surrounding the waist at its narrowest part **2 a** the length of this line: *Your waistline is getting bigger* **b** its position: *a dress with a high waistline*

wait¹ /weɪt/ *v* **1** [I∅ (*for*, ABOUT, AROUND), 3] to stay somewhere without doing anything until somebody or something comes or something happens: *We waited and waited.|We waited (for) 20 minutes.|We waited for something (to happen).|We're waiting to go.|Don't keep her waiting* **2** [I∅ (*for*)] (usu. in *-ing*-form) to be ready: *Your tea is waiting (for you): don't let it get cold* **3** [I∅] to remain unspoken, unheard, or not dealt with: *This news can't wait until tomorrow.|The business can wait until after dinner* **4** [T1] to not act until (the stated occasion); AWAIT (esp. in the phr. **wait one's turn**): *just waiting his chance to strike* **5** [T1 (*for*)] *infml* to delay the beginning of (a meal): *Don't wait dinner for me: I shall be late* **6 wait and see** to delay an action or decision until the future becomes clearer: *He has a wait-and-see way of dealing with difficulties* **7 wait at table** to serve meals, esp. as a regular job USAGE One **awaits** (*fml*) or **waits for** someone who will come or something that will happen perhaps doing nothing else but **wait**: *"Why are you standing there?" "I'm* **waiting** *for John (to come)"* (=he'll be here soon and I want to see him).|*"I'm* **waiting** *to use that machine"* (=it's not my turn yet). To **expect** someone or something is to think that he will come or it will happen, whether or not one wants the person or the event: *I'm* **expecting** *guests.|We're* **expecting** *a cold winter.|I* **expect** *to* (=think I will) *be here for another hour.|Mother* **expects** *me to* (=has told me to and thinks I will) *feed the baby.* **Waiting** is a sort of activity, **expecting** is a state of mind

wait² *n* **1** an act or period of waiting: *a long wait for something to happen* **2 lie in wait (for someone)** to hide, waiting to attack (someone): *The robbers were lying in wait for the rich traveller*

wait·er /ˈweɪtəʳ/ (*fem.* **wait·ress** -trɪ̈s)— *n* [C;N] a person who serves food at the tables in a restaurant

waiting list /ˈ·· ·/ *n* a list of those who want something (such as theatre tickets or a job), often giving first the names of those who asked first

waiting room /ˈ·· ·/ *n* a room for those who are waiting (such as one in a doctor's office for people waiting to see the doctor)

wait on also **wait up·on**— *v prep* [T1] **1** to attend as a servant: *They all wait on the king* **2** to supply the needs of; serve: *They wait on you very well in this restaurant/shop* **3** *now rare* to make a formal visit to: *If convenient, I shall wait on you on Tuesday morning at 10 o'clock* **4** *lit* to follow as a result of: *Success waits on effort* **5 wait on someone hand and foot** to serve someone very humbly

waits /weɪts/ *n* [(*the*) P] *esp. BrE, now rare* CAROL singers who go round to people's houses

wait up *v adv* [IØ (*for*)] *infml* to delay going to bed: *Don't wait up (for me): I shall be coming home very late*

waive /weɪv/ *v* [T1] *esp. fml or tech* to give up willingly (a right, a rule, etc.): *We cannot waive this rule except in case of illness*

waiv·er /ˈweɪvəʳ/ *n law* **1** the act of waiving (WAIVE) a right, claim, etc. **2** an official written statement containing a declaration of such an act: *Please sign this waiver*

wake¹ /weɪk/ *v* **woke** /wəʊk/ *or* **waked, woken** /ˈwəʊkən/ *or* **waked 1** [T1;IØ :(UP)] to (cause to) cease to sleep: *She usually wakes early.|The children's shouts woke us out of/from our afternoon sleep.|*(fig.) *The noise was loud enough to wake the dead* —see USAGE **2** [IØ] *lit* to be or remain awake, esp. at night: *It makes no difference whether he sleeps or wakes* **3** [T1;IØ :(UP, *to*)] to (cause to) become conscious (of something): *The bad news woke the country to the danger of war.|At last we woke to the possibilities of the new invention* **4** [T1; IØ] to (cause to) become active: *The lonely child woke our pity.|At the sight of the enemy, the citizens' anger woke* **5** [T1;IØ] *lit* to (cause to) begin moving: *The wind woke the waves.|A light wind woke among the trees* **6** [T1] *lit* to spoil with noise the peace or quietness of: *The sound of gunfire woke the hills* **7 Wake up!** *infml* Listen!; Pay attention!

USAGE **Wake** (*up*), **waken** (*up*), **awake**, and **awaken** can all be used in the patterns [IØ] and [T1], though it may be better to use **awake** as an [IØ] verb and **waken** and **awaken** as [T1] verbs. The most common and least formal is **wake** (*up*), in both patterns. It should be used except in *fml* writing, in fig. meanings, or in the PASSIVE: *The baby* **woke** (*up*).|*The national spirit* **awoke**.|*I was* **wakened** *by their shouts.*

wake² *n* a gathering to watch and grieve over a dead person on the night before the burial, sometimes with feasting and drinking, esp. in Ireland and northern parts of Britain

wake³ *n* **1** a track or path, esp. the track left by a moving body (such as a ship) in a liquid (such as water): *the broad white wake of the great ship* **2 in the wake of a** close behind and in the same path of travel as: *The car left clouds of dust in its wake* **b** as a result of: *hunger and disease in the wake of the war*

wake·ful /ˈweɪkfəl/ *adj* not sleeping or able to sleep; sleepless: *a wakeful night/baby* —**~ly** *adv* —**~ness** *n* [U]

wak·en /ˈweɪkən/ *v* [T1;IØ: (UP)] *fml* to (cause to) wake —see WAKE (USAGE)

wak·ey wak·ey /ˌweɪki ˈweɪki/ *interj BrE humor sl* Wake up!

wak·ing /ˈweɪkɪŋ/ *adj* [Wa5;A] of the time when one is awake: *He spends all his waking hours working*

walk¹ /wɔːk/ *v* **1** [T1;IØ] to (cause to) move at a walk: *to walk to town|to walk a horse|to walk (for) 10 miles|He likes walking* **2** [T1] to pass over, through, or along on foot: *to walk the roads|to walk a* TIGHTROPE **3** [T1] to follow on foot for the purpose of measuring, examining, etc.: *to walk the border* **4** [L9] *lit* to follow a course of action or way of life: *to walk humbly in the sight of God* **5** [IØ] (of a spirit) to move about in a form that can be seen: *Do the spirits of the dead walk at night?* **6** [T1] to cause to move by holding while going on foot: *to walk a bicycle* **7** [T1] to take (an animal) for a walk; exercise: *He's walking the dog* **8** [T1] to cause to move in a manner suggesting a walk: *Let's walk this heavy ladder to the other end of the room* **9** [X9;(T1)] to go on foot with (someone), usu. to a stated place: *I walked her home* **10** [IØ] (in cricket) (of the player who hits the ball (BATSMAN)) to leave the field willingly after being caught out, without waiting for the UMPIRE'*s* decision **11 walk (someone) off (their) feet/legs** *infml* to tire (someone) by making (them) move about on foot too much —see also WALK AWAY FROM, WALK INTO, WALK OFF WITH, WALK OUT, WALK OUT ON, WALK OVER, WALK UP

walk² *n* **1** (of people and creatures with 2 legs) a natural and unhurried way of moving on foot in which the feet are lifted one at a time with one foot not off the ground before the other touches: *at a walk* **2** (of creatures with 4 legs) a way of moving forward in which there are always at least 2 feet on the ground **3** a (usu. short) journey on foot esp. for exercise or pleasure: *Let's go for/have/take a short walk* **4** a place, path, or course for walking: *There is a beautiful walk along the river* **5** a distance to be walked: *a 10-minute walk from here* **6** the manner or style of walking: *His walk is just like his father's* **7** a low rate of speed: *Production has decreased to a walk*

walk·a·bout /ˈwɔːkəbaʊt/ *n Austr & BrE infml* **1** a period spent, esp. by an Australian ABORIGINAL, away from regular work travelling about on foot through the country (often in the phr. **go walkabout**) **2** a walk through crowds by an important person, mixing and talking informally with the people

walk·a·way /ˈwɔːkəweɪ/ *n sl, esp. AmE* an easily won competition: *That race was just a walkaway for my horse*

walk a·way from *v adv prep* [T1] *sl, esp. AmE* **1** to run faster than or win over without difficulty: *My horse just walked away from all the others in that race* **2** to come out of (an accident) unhurt or almost unhurt: *to walk away from a car crash*

walk·er /ˈwɔːkəʳ/ *n* a person who walks, esp. for pleasure or exercise

walk·ie-talk·ie /ˌwɔːki ˈtɔːki/ *n infml* a 2-way radio that can be carried, allowing one to talk as well as listen

walk-in /ˈ· ·/ *adj* [Wa5;A] *sl, esp. AmE* **1** large enough to be walked into: *a walk-in cupboard* **2** easy (esp. in the phr. **walk-in victory**)

walk·ing /ˈwɔːkɪŋ/ *adj* [Wa5;A] **1** *infml* human: *She knows so many words that she's a walking dictionary!* **2** used for or in going on foot: *walking shoes* **3** consisting of or done by travelling on foot: *a walking holiday/tour*

walking pa·pers /ˈ·· ˌ··/ *n* [P9] *AmE infml* MARCHING ORDERS (2)

walking stick /ˈ·· ·/ *n* a stick used for supporting someone while walking

walk in·to *v prep* [T1] **1** to obtain (a particular job) very easily **2** to meet (something) through carelessness: *He walked right into the trap*

walk off with also **walk a·way with**— *v adv prep* [T1] *sl* **1** to steal and take away **2** to win easily: *He walked off with first prize*

walk of life /ˌ· · ˈ·/ *n fml* rank or employment (esp. in the phrs. **every walk of life, all walks of life**): *Our membership includes people from all walks of life*

walk-on /ˈ· ·/ *n* **1** a small, usu. non-speaking, part in a play: *a walk-on part* **2** a person who has such a part

walk·out /ˈwɔːk-aʊt/ *n* **1** a STRIKE[2] (1): *The walkout was caused by a disagreement over pay and working conditions* **2** the action of leaving a meeting or organization as an expression of disapproval

walk out *v adv* [I∅ (*of*)] **1** to go on STRIKE **2** to leave suddenly, esp. as an expression of disapproval

walk out on *v adv prep* [T1] *sl* to leave suddenly, esp. in a time of trouble; desert: *He just walked out on his wife and family without saying a word!*

walk·o·ver /ˈwɔːkˌəʊvəʳ/ *n sl* an easy victory

walk o·ver *v prep* [T1] *sl* **1** to win without difficulty against: *Our party just walked over the opposition in the elections* **2** to treat badly: *Don't let your husband walk (all) over you like that*

walk-up /ˈ· ·/ *n, adj* [Wa5;A;C] *AmE infml* **1** (a flat) in a tall block with no LIFT[2] (4): *It's not easy living in a 6th-floor walk-up* **2** (a block of flats) that is tall but has no LIFT[2] (4)

walk up *v adv* [I∅ *usu. imper.*] *infml* (used when inviting people to come in and see a performance, esp. outdoors, such as a CIRCUS) to enter: *Walk up, ladies and gentlemen!*

wall[1] /wɔːl/ *n* **1** an upright dividing surface (esp. of stone or brick) intended for defence or safety, or for enclosing something: *In some parts of England, fields are surrounded by stone walls.|the city wall of London* **2** the side of a building or a room: *Hang that picture on the wall* —see picture at LIVING ROOM **3** an upright mass of something: *the wall of the cliff|a wall of water|fire|the cliff wall* **4** something that separates or opposes; BARRIER: *a wall of silence|of ˈmisunderstanding|a* TARIFF *wall* **5** the covering or inner surface of something hollow: *the walls of a blood vessel* —see picture at RESPIRATORY **6 bang/run one's head against a (brick) wall** *infml* to try to do the impossible **7 (Even) (the) walls have ears** *infml* others may hear us **8 to the wall** into a hopeless position: *to go|to be driven|to be pushed to the wall* **9 up the wall** in or into a state of great anger or near madness **10 with one's back to the wall** fighting with no way of escape

wall[2] *v* **1** [Wv5;T1 (IN)] to provide, cover with, or surround with or as if with a wall: *an old walled town in Portugal* **2** [T1 (UP)] to close (an opening) with or as if with a wall: *to wall (up) a door* **3** [X9, esp. UP, IN, *in*] to enclose with or as if with a wall: *Let's wall the prisoner (up) in the castle*

wal·la·by /ˈwɒləbi‖ˈwɑ-/ *n* [Wn1] any of various types of KANGAROOs of small to middle size

wal·lah, -la /ˈwɒlə‖ˈwɑlə/ *n* [C9] *Ind and Pak E* a person (usu. male) who has a particular type of work or who does a particular duty or service: *The* **book wallah** *went from place to place selling books*

wal·let /ˈwɒlɪ̈t‖ˈwɑ-/ *n* **1** a small flat leather case which can usu. be folded, for holding papers and paper money, usu. carried by a man in his JACKET or back trouser pocket **2** a long leather case for official papers **3** *old use* a bag for food/clothes etc. formerly carried by travellers and beggars

wall-eyed /ˌ· ˈ·◂/ *adj derog sl* **1** having eyes that show an unusually large amount of white **2** having eyes that turn outward away from each other —opposite **cross-eyed**

wall·flow·er /ˈwɔːlˌflaʊəʳ/ *n* **1** a type of sweet-smelling European yellow or red flower that grows best near garden or house walls **2** a person who sits by the wall at a dance because no one has asked them to dance

wall off *v adv* [T1] **1** [(*from*)] to separate with or as if with one or more walls: *This room is walled off from the rest of the house* **2** [(*into*)] to divide into parts with or as if with one or more walls: *They walled off the large prison into lots of very small cells* **3** to make or give shape to with or as if with one or more walls: *In the large prison they walled off a little cell for each prisoner*

wal·lop[1] /ˈwɒləp‖ˈwɑ-/ *n sl* **1** [C] a powerful blow **2** [U] *BrE sl* beer

wallop[2] *v* [T1] *sl* **1** to hit with force once or more than once: *to wallop someone|to give someone a walloping* **2** [(*at*)] to defeat thoroughly, esp. in a game or match: *He walloped me at tennis*

wal·lop·ing /ˈwɒləpɪŋ‖ˈwɑ-/ *adj* [Wa5;A] *infml* very big: *a walloping great house in the country*

wal·low[1] /ˈwɒləʊ‖ˈwɑ-/ *v* [I∅ (*in*)] **1** (of a ship) to roll and struggle in a rough sea: *The ship wallowed helplessly among the great waves* **2** to move or roll about (with pleasure) in deep mud, dirt, water, etc., as some animals do: *The pigs are wallowing in the mud* **3 wallow in the mud** to lead a bad life

wallow[2] *n* **1** [(*in*)] an act or example of WALLOWing: *"I like a good wallow in mud now and then," said the pig* **2** a place where animals come to WALLOW

wallow in *v prep* [T1] *humor derog* **1** *infml* to enjoy too greatly: *He's really wallowing in the praise of his new book* **2 be wallowing in money/it** *sl* to be very rich

wall paint·ing /ˈ· ˌ··/ *n* **1** [C] a picture actually painted on a wall, not just hung on one, esp. a FRESCO **2** [U] the art of painting such pictures; FRESCO

wall·pa·per[1] /ˈwɔːlˌpeɪpəʳ/ *n* [U] ornamental paper to cover the walls of a room —see picture at LIVING ROOM

wallpaper[2] *v* [T1;(I∅)] to provide the walls of (a room) with wallpaper

Wall Street /ˈ· ·/ *n* [R] the influential American centre for money matters and the buying and selling of business shares, in New York City —compare the CITY (of London)

wall-to-wall /ˌ· · ˈ·◂/ *adj, adv* (of a floor covering) over the whole floor: *wall-to-wall* CARPET*s*

wal·nut /ˈwɔːlnʌt/ *n* **1** [C] an eatable nut, shaped like a human brain, with a rough shell which is easily divided into 2 parts —see picture at NUT[1] **2** [C] also **walnut tree** /ˈ·· ·/— the tree that produces these nuts **3** [U] the wood of this tree, of great value for furniture **4** [U] a reddish brown colour

wal·rus /ˈwɔːlrəs‖ˈwɒl-, ˈwɑl-/ *n* [Wn1] **1** [C] either of 2 types of large sea-animals (like a very large SEAL) with 2 long teeth standing out from the face and pointing downward —see picture at SEA **2** [A] hanging down at both ends (in the phr. **a walrus moustache**)

waltz[1] /wɔːls‖wɔlts/ *n* [C; *the*+R] **1** a social dance for a man and a woman, from Vienna, made up of 6 steps in 3/4 time: *I like dancing the waltz* **2** music for this dance: *They're playing a waltz by Strauss*

waltz[2] *v* **1** [I∅] to dance a WALTZ **2** [X9] to cause to dance in this way, or to move quickly, in or into the stated condition: *He waltzed her over to the band* **3** [L9] *infml* to move or advance easily, successfully, or showily: *We can't just waltz up to a complete stranger and introduce ourselves*

waltz off with *v adv prep* [T1] *infml* WALK OFF WITH

wam·pum /ˈwɒmpəm‖ˈwɑm-/ *n* [U] shells put into strings, belts, etc., and used as money or ornaments by North American Indians

wan /wɒn‖wɑn/ *adj esp. lit* (appearing) ill, weak, and tired: *a wan smile* —**-ly** *adv* —**-ness** *n* [U]

wand /wɒnd‖wɑnd/ *n* a thin stick carried in the hand, esp. by a person who does magic tricks

wan·der /ˈwɒndəʳ‖ˈwɑn-/ *v* **1** [I∅ (ABOUT);T1] to

move about (an area) without a fixed course, aim, or purpose: *We love wandering (about) (the hills)* **2** [I∅] (esp. of streams, roads, etc.) to follow a winding course: *The river wanders through some very beautiful country* **3** [I∅ (OFF)] to move away (from the main idea): *Don't wander off the point* **4** [I∅ (*from*)] to move away (from proper behaviour) **5** [I∅] (of people or thoughts) to be or become confused and unable to follow an ordinary conversation: *I'm afraid the sick man's mind is wandering*

wan·der·er /ˈwɒndərəʳ‖ˈwɑn-/ *n* a person who wanders, esp. for pleasure or because he is lost

wan·der·ing /ˈwɒndərɪŋ‖ˈwɑn-/ *adj* [A] **1** having or showing aimless, slow movement or movement that is not straight or regular: *the wandering course of a stream* **2** [Wa5] moving from place to place without staying in any one place very long: *wandering tribes|the wandering* MINSTRELs *of former times*

wan·der·ings /ˈwɒndərɪŋz‖ˈwɑn-/ *n* [P] movement from place to place or away from the proper or usual course or place: *You must have seen a lot of strange things in your wanderings*

wan·der·lust /ˈwɒndəlʌst‖ˈwɑndər-/ *n* [U;S] a strong desire to wander

wane¹ /weɪn/ *v* [Wv4] **1** [I∅ (AWAY)] to grow gradually smaller or less after being full or complete: *The moon* WAXes *and wanes.|the waning power of the Roman Empire in the 5th Century* **2** [L9, esp. *in*] to lose power, wealth, or influence: *The Roman Empire rapidly waned in power in the 5th Century*

wane² *n* **on the wane** becoming smaller, weaker, or less: *The sick man's strength is on the wane.|The power of the Roman Empire was on the wane in the 5th Century*

wan·gle¹ /ˈwæŋgəl/ *v sl* **1** [D1+(*into/out of*); T1(*out of*)] **a** to get (something) from someone, esp. by cleverness or a trick: *I wangled an invitation (out of George)* **b** to get (someone) to do, provide, or have something, esp. by cleverness or a trick: *I wangled George into giving me an invitation.|I wangled George into a good job* **2** [L9;X9 :(esp. *out of*)] to work (one's way) or get (oneself) out of a difficulty, esp. by cleverness or a trick: *All right, Buster Keaton, let's see you wangle (yourself/your way) out of this one!*

wangle² *n sl* an act, case, or example of wangling (WANGLE): *I got George a good job with a bit of a wangle*

wank¹ /wæŋk/ *v* [I∅] *BrE taboo sl* to MASTURBATE

wank² *n* [S;(C)] *BrE taboo sl* an act of WANKing

wank·er /ˈwæŋkəʳ/ *n BrE sl* **1** *taboo* a person who MASTURBATEs **2** a person who does not take a serious interest in things; DILETTANTE

want¹ /wɒnt‖wɔnt, wɑnt/ *v* [Wv6] **1** [T1,3;V3,8;X (*to be*) 7] to have a strong desire to or for; feel a strong desire to have: *He wanted (a chance) to rest.|I want him to rest.|I want this letter (to be) opened now!|I want the letter (to be) ready by tomorrow!|Say what you want, I still like him* **2** [V4 *neg.*] to be against: *I don't want people playing the piano at all hours of the day and night!* **3** [T1,4] to need: *The house wants painting/more paint.|Those criminals want a good beating.|This job wants doing* **4** [T3] ought: *You want to see a doctor about your cough.|You don't want to work so hard.|The work wants to be done with great care* **5** [T1] to suffer from the lack of: *Many people still want food and shelter* **6** [T1] *often fml* to be without; not have enough (of); lack: *His answer wants politeness* **7** [T1 (*often pass.*)] to wish or demand the presence of: *The servants will not be wanted this afternoon.|Don't go where you're not wanted.|Your country wants you* **8** [Wv5;T1 (*for*) *often pass.*] (esp. of the police) to hunt or look for in order to catch: *The police want him for murder.|He is wanted for murder.|He is a wanted man* **9** [*it*+T1] *AmE* to lack (for completion): *It wants 3 minutes to 12 o'clock* **10** [I∅] to lack enough food, clothing, shelter, etc.: *You shall never want while I am alive* **11** [I∅+IN or OUT] *AmE sl, ScotE* to desire to come or go: *The cat wants in.|The dog wants out* **12 want some doing** *infml* to need a great deal of effort: *This difficult job wants some doing*

want² *n* **1** [U; (*the*) S: (*of*)] lack, absence, or need (often in the phr. **for/from want of**): *The plants died for/from want of water.|I'll take this one for want of a better* **2** [U] severe lack of the things necessary to life; DESTITUTION (often in the phr. **in want**): *Want makes people unhappy.|How terrible to live in want!* —see LACK (USAGE) **3 in want of** in need of: *Are you in want of money?|The house is in want of repair* **4 a long-felt want** *often humor* something whose lack has been felt for a long time

want ad /ˈ· ·/ *n esp. AmE* a small newspaper advertisement stating that something or someone is wanted (such as a job, a person for a job, or a particular thing) —compare CLASSIFIED AD

want for *v prep* [Wv6;T1] *fml* **1** (*usu. in future tenses and with* no, not, *etc.*) (of a person) to lack (esp. food, clothing, shelter, money, love, attention, etc.): *You shall never want for food while I have any money left!* **2 want for nothing** (of a person) to lack nothing; have everything necessary: *He wanted for nothing while his mother was alive*

want·ing¹ /ˈwɒntɪŋ‖ˈwɔn-, ˈwɑn-/ *adj* [Wa5;F] **1** LACKING **2 be found (to be) wanting (in)** to be considered not good enough, strong enough, or full enough of

wanting² *prep* without: *a letter wanting a stamp*

wan·ton¹ /ˈwɒntən‖ˈwɔn-, ˈwɑn-/ *adj* **1** *lit* wild and full of fun: *a wanton mind* **2** uncontrolled: *wanton growth of plant life in the tropical rain forest* **3** (of a woman more than of a man) sexually improper: *She gave him a wanton look* **4** having no just cause or no good reason: *wanton cruelty|wanton waste of money* —**~ly** *adv* —**~ness** *n* [U]

wanton² *n lit* a woman of improper sexual behaviour

wants /wɒnts‖wɔnts, wɑnts/ *n* [P] needs: *My wants are few and are soon satisfied*

wap·i·ti /ˈwɒpɪ̣ti‖ˈwɑ-/ *n* [Wn1] *AmE* ELK (2)

war¹ /wɔːʳ/ *n* **1** [U] armed fighting between nations: *Is war necessary?|to put an end to war|a prisoner of war|an act of war|the art of war* **2** [C] an example or period of this: *He fought in both World Wars* **3** [U;C] a struggle between opposing forces or for a particular purpose: (a) *class war|a war against disease* **4 at war (with)** in a state of armed struggle (with each other or another country): *Those 2 countries have been at war (with each other/with Ruritania) for a long time* **5 carry the war into the enemy's camp** to attack someone who has been expecting to attack you **6 go to war (against)** to begin an armed struggle (against): *The king decided to go to war (against his enemies)* **7 make/wage war (on/upon/against) a** to direct an armed struggle (against) **b** to struggle (against): *to make war on disease* **8 (having) been in the wars** *infml* (having) been hurt or damaged

war² *v* **-rr-** [I∅ (*with, against, for*)] **1** *lit* to take part in or direct a war **2** [Wv4] to be in a strong or active struggle: *warring beliefs|to war against illness*

war ba·by /ˈ· ˌ··/ *n* a child born during or soon after a war

war·ble¹ /ˈwɔːbəl‖ˈwɔr-/ *n* [(*the*) S (*of*)] **1** the act or sound of warbling (WARBLE) **2** a bird's or birdlike song

warble² *v* [I∅ (AWAY);T1 (OUT)] **1** (esp. of birds)

to sing with a clear, continuous, yet varied note **2** (of people, esp. women) to sing while pouring out notes from the throat, sometimes in an untrained, uncontrolled way: *to warble (out) (a song)* —compare TRILL

war·bler /ˈwɔːbləʳ‖ˈwɔr-/ *n* **1** any of various types of songbirds **2** a person (esp. a woman) who WARBLEs

war bride /ˈ· ·/ *n* **1** a woman who marries a member of the armed forces who is ordered into active service in time of war **2** a woman who marries a member of the armed forces, esp. of a foreign nation, whom she has met in time of war

war cloud /ˈ· ·/ *n* [*usu. pl.*] a sign that war is getting nearer: *War clouds were gathering over Europe in the summer of 1939*

war crime /ˈ· ·/ *n* an inhuman act during a war, such as the mistreatment of prisoners or the murder of many harmless people

war cry /ˈ· ·/ also **battle cry**— *n* **1** a cry used by people fighting a war to show their courage and make the enemy afraid **2** a short statement, easy to remember, used for getting people to do something or oppose something, esp. in politics; SLOGAN: *"Equal Rights for Women!" was their war cry*

ward /wɔːd‖wɔrd/ *n* **1** a division of a hospital, esp. a large room usu. for people all needing treatment of the same kind: *the heart ward of a large teaching hospital* **2** a division of a city, esp. for political purposes: *ward politics* **3** a person, esp. a child, who is under the protection of another person or of a law court: *Everyone was shocked when he married his young ward.|They are wards of court/of the state* **4** a division of a prison (such as a block of CELLs): *waiting in the death ward* **5** *lit* the act or action of guarding (often in the phr. **keep watch and ward over someone**)

-ward /wəd‖wərd/ *suffix* [*n → adj, (esp. AmE) adv*] -WARDS: *a northward/downward movement|an earthward movement|(AmE) They moved downward*

war dance /ˈ· ·/ *n* a dance performed esp. by tribes in preparation for battle or after a victory

war·den /ˈwɔːdn‖ˈwɔrdn/ *n* **1** a person who looks after a place (and people): *the warden of an old people's home* **2** an official who helps to see that certain laws are obeyed: *A* **traffic warden** *sees that all cars are properly parked* **3** *BrE* the head of some older schools and colleges **4** *AmE* the head of a prison; GOVERNOR

ward·er /ˈwɔːdəʳ‖ˈwɔr-/ (*fem.* **ward·ress** /-drɨ̥s/)— *n BrE* a prison guard

ward off *v adv* [T1a] to prevent (something bad, as danger, a blow, a cold, etc.)

war·drobe /ˈwɔːdrəʊb‖ˈwɔr-/ *n* **1** a room, cupboard, or large upright box, with a door, in which one hangs up clothes —see picture at BEDROOM **2** a collection of clothes (esp. of one person or for one activity): *a new summer wardrobe* **3** a collection of special historical clothes (COSTUMEs) and ornaments to be worn in a theatre

ward·room /ˈwɔːdrʊm, -ruːm‖ˈwɔr-/ *n* the space in a warship where all the most important officers of the ship live and eat, except for the captain

-wards /wədz‖wərdz/ *suffix* [*n → adv*] towards the stated direction or place: *They moved* NORTHWARDS/DOWNWARDS/EARTHWARDS.|*skywards*

-ware /weəʳ/ *comb. form* [*n→n* [U]] **1** things of the same hard material, esp. for use in a house, hotel, restaurant, etc.: *tinware|ironware* **2** things used in the stated place for the preparation of food: *kitchenware|*OVEN*ware*

ware·house /ˈweəhaʊs‖ˈweər-/ *n* **-houses** /ˌhaʊzɨ̥z/ a place, esp. a building, for storing things, esp. to be sold or before being moved

wares /weəz‖weərz/ *n* [P] *rather lit* articles for sale, usu. not in a shop: *The baker travelled round the town selling his wares*

war·fare /ˈwɔːfeəʳ‖ˈwɔr-/ *n* [U] **1** war **2** struggle

war·head /ˈwɔːhed‖ˈwɔr-/ *n* the explosive front end of a bomb or esp. MISSILE

war·horse /ˈwɔːhɔːs‖ˈwɔrhɔrs/ *n* **1** (esp. in former times) a horse for use in war; CHARGER **2** a soldier or usu. male person in public life (such as a politician) who has seen a lot of action and is still eager for more

war·i·ly /ˈweərɨ̥li/ *adv* see WARY —**~iness** *n* [U]

war·like /ˈwɔːlaɪk‖ˈwɔr-/ *adj* **1** ready for war or threatening war: *a warlike appearance* **2** liking or skilled in war: *a warlike nation*

war·lock /ˈwɔːlɒk‖ˈwɔrlɑk/ *n* (esp. in stories) a male WITCH (1)

war·lord /ˈwɔːlɔːd‖ˈwɔrlɔrd/ *n usu. derog* **1** a high military leader **2** (esp. in China in the 1920s and '30s) a general or other military commander who gets and keeps political power in an area by force

warm[1] /wɔːm‖wɔrm/ *adj* [Wa1] **1** [B] having or producing enough heat or pleasant heat: *warm milk|a warm fire* **2** [B] able to keep in heat or keep out cold: *warm clothes* **3** [B] having or giving a feeling of heat: *We were warm from exercise.|It was a warm climb* **4** [B] showing or marked by strong feeling, esp. good feeling: *warm support for the local team|a warm supporter of the local team|warm friendship|warm friends|a warm welcome* **5** [B] marked by excitement or anger: *a warm argument* **6** [B] recently made; fresh (esp. in the phrs. **warm scent/smell/trail**) **7** [F] (esp. in children's games) near a hidden object, the right answer to a question, etc.: *You're getting warm, warmer—no, now you're getting cooler again* —opposite **cool** or **cold** **8** [B] giving a pleasant feeling of cheerfulness or friendliness: *warm colours|a warm voice|a warm invitation* —**~ish** *adj* —**~ly** *adv*: *They dressed warmly.|They greeted each other warmly* —**~ness** *n* [U]

warm[2] *v* **1** [Wv4;T1;(I∅)] to cause (someone or something) to become warm: *They warmed their hands/themselves by the open fire.|A hot drink warms on a cold day.|a warming fire/drink* **2** [I∅] (of things rather than people) to become warm: *The soup is warming in the pot over the fire*

warm[3] *n* **1** [*the*+R] a warm place, state, or condition: *Come into the warm, out of the cold* **2** [S] the act or action of making oneself warm: *Come and have a warm by the fire*

warm-blood·ed /ˌ· ˈ··◂/ *adj* [Wa5] *tech* (of birds, MAMMALs, etc.) able to keep the temperature of the body rather high whether the outside temperature is high or low —**~ly** *adv* —**~ness** *n* [U]

warm-heart·ed /ˌ· ˈ··◂/ *adj* having or showing warm, esp. friendly, feelings —**~ly** *adv* —**~ness** *n* [U]

warming pan /ˈ·· ·/ *n* a round covered copper vessel, containing hot coals, with a long wooden handle, formerly used to warm a bed

war·mon·ger /ˈwɔːˌmʌŋgəʳ‖ˈwɔrˌmʌŋ-, -ˌmɑŋ-/ *n derog, esp. AmE* a person who urges war or who tries to get a war started

warm o·ver *v adv* [Wv5;T1] *usu. derog, esp. AmE infml* **1** WARM UP (2) **2** to use (the same arguments) again: *He never has any new ideas but just keeps giving us the same ones warmed over*

warmth /wɔːmθ‖wɔrmθ/ *n* [U] the state or quality of being warm: *the warmth of the fire/of his feelings/of the arguments on both sides*

warm to *v prep* [T1 *pass. rare*] *infml* **1** also **warm towards**— to begin to like (a person): *I warmed to the new guest at once* **2** to become interested in: *The more he spoke, the more he warmed to his subject*

warm up *v adv* **1** [T1;I∅] **a** to cause (a thing) to become warm: *The sun warmed up the seat nicely* **b** (esp. of a thing) to become warm: *The seat warmed up nicely* **2** [T1;I∅] also (*AmE*) **warm over**— to (cause to) become reheated for eating: *Let's warm up the meat before we serve it again* **3** [T1;I∅] to (cause to) become ready for action or performance by exercise or operation before the real test comes: *The singers are warming up before the concert.|Let's warm up the car engine a bit before we start* **4** [T1;I∅ :(*to*)] to (cause to) become more excited or exciting: *He warmed up* (*to his subject*) *as he spoke on.|Let's warm up this party* **5** [T1] to make (a crowd) ready to accept a performance —**warm-up** /'· ·/ *n*: *After a warm-up* (*period*) *of 15 minutes, the game began*

warn /wɔːn‖wɔrn/ *v* **1** [Wv4;I∅;T1 :(*of, against*), 5a;D5a;V3] to tell (of something bad that may happen, or of how to prevent something bad): *to warn* (*someone*) (*of danger/against danger*)*|to warn someone against doing something|to warn someone not to do something|He warned* (*her*) (*that*) *he couldn't afford to marry her.|A red warning light flashed on and off.|He warned the firm that more oil would be needed that year* **2** [T1] to give knowledge to (often officially) of some future need or action: *If you warn the police when you go away on holiday, they will watch your house*

warn·ing /'wɔːnɪŋ‖'wɔr-/ *n* **1** [U;C,C3 :(*of*)] the act of warning or the state of being warned: *They attacked without warning/without giving a warning.|a warning not to go there* **2** [C (*of*), C3] something that warns: *Let that be a warning to you.|Take that for a warning of what may happen.|His life should be a warning to us all* **3** [C (*of*), C3] a person who is an example of what *not* to do: *He is a warning to us all of what happens to people who drink too much* **4** *old use* notice to leave, or to end an agreement: *gave his servant a month's warning*

warn off¹ also **warn a·way**— *v adv* [T1] to try to cause to stay away by warning or threats: *The road was closed to traffic after the accident, and the police were warning everyone off*

warn off² *v prep* [T1] to try to cause to stay away from, by warning or threats: *The farmer warned us off his fields*

war of nerves /ˌ· · '·/ *n* an attempt to worry the enemy and destroy his courage by threats, PROPAGANDA, etc.

warp¹ /wɔːp‖wɔrp/ *n* **1** [the+R] *tech* threads running along the length of cloth —compare WEFT **2** [S] a twist out of a true level or straight line: *a warp in a board* **3** [C] a rope or strong wire used for pulling a net along behind a fishing boat

warp² *v* [Wv5;T1;I∅] to (cause to) turn or twist out of shape: *This wood warps under pressure.|*(fig.) *a warped mind that cannot tell right from wrong*

war paint /'· ·/ *n* [U] **1** paint that members of some tribes put on their bodies before going to war, esp. in former times **2** *humor* MAKE-UP (3)

war·path /'wɔːpɑːθ‖'wɔrpæθ/ *n* [*pl. rare*] **1** the course taken by a group of American Indians going off to fight (esp. in the phr. **on the warpath**) **2** the course of action of a person who is ready to fight or struggle (esp. in the phr. **on the warpath**): *Those politicians are on the warpath for higher taxes again*

war·rant¹ /'wɒrənt‖'wɔ-, 'wɑ-/ *n* **1** [U] proper reason for action: *Do you consider that the wild behaviour of the crowd was warrant enough for the police to use force?* **2** [C] a written order signed by an official of the law, esp. allowing the police to take certain action: *You can't search my house without a warrant*

warrant² *v* **1** [T1,4] to cause (an action) to appear right or reasonable: *Her small income does not warrant her taking a long holiday* **2** [X (*to be*) 7; (T1),5a] to GUARANTEE: *The grower warrants these plants* (*to be*) *free from disease.|He warrants* (*that*) *they are free from disease* **3** [T5a;D5a] *infml* to declare as if certain: *I'll warrant* (*you*) (*that*) *he's back there drinking again.|He's back there drinking again, I'll warrant* (*you*)

war·rant·ee /ˌwɒrən'tiː‖ˌwɔ-, ˌwɑ-/ *n tech* a person who receives a WARRANTY

warrant of·fic·er /'·· ˌ···/ *n* **1** a member of the British army, airforce, or ROYAL MARINES with a rank between NONCOMMISSIONED OFFICER and COMMISSIONED OFFICER **2** a member of the US army, airforce, MARINE CORPS, or navy with such a rank

war·ran·tor /'wɒrəntɔːʳ, ˌwɒrən'tɔːʳ‖ˌwɔrən'tɔr, ˌwɑ-/ *n tech* a person who gives a WARRANTY

war·ran·ty /'wɒrənti‖'wɔ-, 'wɑ-/ *n* [C; *under*+U] *tech* a written GUARANTEE: *They'll repair this new car without charging because it's still under warranty*

war·ren /'wɒrən‖'wɔ-, 'wɑ-/ *n* **1** an area in which small animals are kept or live, esp. rabbits **2** *usu. derog* a place in which too many people live, or in which one gets lost easily: *a warren of narrow twisting old streets*

war·ri·or /'wɒrɪəʳ‖'wɔ-, 'wɑ-/ *n* **1** *lit* a soldier or experienced fighting man **2** a man who fights for his tribe: *The warriors charged bravely, but what could their spears do against our guns?*

war·ship /'wɔːˌʃɪp‖'wɔr-/ *n* a naval ship used for war, esp. one armed with guns

wart /wɔːt‖wɔrt/ *n* **1** [C] a small hard ugly swelling on the skin, esp. of the face or hands **2** [C] a swelling of the same kind or appearance, esp. on a tree **3** [C;N] *sl, now rare* an ugly man or boy, or one greatly disliked —**~y** *adj* [Wa2]

wart·hog /'wɔːthɒg‖'wɔrthɔg, -hɑg/ *n* [Wn1] a type of African wild pig with long front teeth that stick out of its mouth and some lumps on its face that look like WARTs —see picture at RUMINANT

war·time /'wɔːtaɪm‖'wɔr-/ *n* [U] a period during which a war is going on: *Life can be very hard in wartime*

war·y /'weəri/ *adj* [Wa2 (*of*)] careful; looking out for danger: *wild animals wary of traps|a wary old politician who never says too much* —**warily** *adv* —**wariness** *n* [U]

was /wəz; *strong* wɒz‖wəz; *strong* wɑz/ [Wv1] *past t. of* BE, 1st and 3rd pers. sing.: *I/He was* —compare WERE

wash¹ /wɒʃ‖wɔʃ, wɑʃ/ *v* **1** [T1 (DOWN, OFF, OUT, *with*)] to clean with or as if with liquid: *to wash clothes/one's car/a dog/one's hands/oneself* (*with soap and water*) **2** [I∅ (*with*)] to clean oneself or a part of one's body with liquid: *to wash* (*with soap and water*) *before dinner* **3** [L9;(I∅)] to bear cleaning with liquid without damage: *These clothes don't wash easily* **4** [I∅ (*with*) *nonassertive*] *infml* to be easy to believe: *His story just won't wash* (*with me*) **5** [I∅ (*against, over*);T1] to flow over or against (something) continually: *The waves washed* (*against/over*) *the shore* **6** [X9, esp. AWAY, OFF, *off*] to cause to be carried as stated, with or as if with liquid: *I washed the dirt off* (*my hands*)*.|The waves washed the swimmer away* (*over the rocks*) **7** [T1 (OUT)] to make by the continuous flow of liquid: *The waves had washed* (*out*) *a large hole in the rock* **8** [T1;I∅ :(*for*)] to pour water over (esp. small stones) in search of precious metal: *We kept washing* (*the* GRAVEL) (*for gold*)*, but found nothing* **9 wash one's hands of** *infml* to refuse to have anything more to do with or to accept responsibility for: *I wash my hands of you and all your wild ideas!* **10 wash clean** to wash until clean: *He washed* (*his face*) *clean before coming downstairs*

wash² *n* **1** [S] the act or action or an example of

washing or being washed: *Go upstairs and have a wash.|Give the car a good wash* **2** [(*the*) S] things to be washed, or being washed; LAUNDRY: *Have you done the wash yet? Then hang it out to dry* **3** [(*the*) S] the flow, sound, or action of a mass of water (such as a wave): *I heard the wash of the waves round our boat all night* **4** [S;U] water or waves thrown back (as when rowing a boat) **5** [S;U] a movement of air caused by an aircraft passing through it **6** [U] worthless, esp. liquid waste (sometimes used as food for animals) **7** [S;(U)] soup or other liquid food that is thin and tasteless: *Take this wash of yours back at once, waiter!* **8** [C] (*often in comb.*) the liquid with which something is washed or coloured: *They all kiss me now that I use that new mouthwash!|a copper-coloured hairwash* **9 come out in the wash** *infml* **a** (of something shameful) to become known **b** to turn out all right in the end **10 in the wash** being washed: *Your favourite shirt is in the wash, my dear*

wash³ *adj* [Wa5;A] *AmE infml* washable: *wash cotton*

wash·a·ble /ˈwɒʃəbəl‖ˈwɔ-, ˈwɑ-/ *adj* that can be washed without damage: *washable cotton|Is this shirt washable?*

wash a·way *v adv* [T1] to remove the effect of (something): *Prayer can wash away your* SINs

wash·ba·sin /ˈwɒʃˌbeɪsən‖ˈwɔʃ-, ˈwɑʃ-/ also (*AmE*) **sink**— *n* a large fixed basin for water for washing hands and face —see picture at BATHROOM

wash·board /ˈwɒʃbɔːd‖ˈwɔʃbord, ˈwɑʃ-/ *n* a movable board with a wavy surface against which clothes may be rubbed when washing

wash·bowl /ˈwɒʃbəʊl‖ˈwɔʃ-, ˈwɑʃ-/ *n AmE* WASHBASIN

wash·cloth /ˈwɒʃklɒθ‖ˈwɔʃklɔθ, ˈwɑʃ-/ *n AmE* FACECLOTH

wash·day /ˈwɒʃdeɪ‖ˈwɔʃ-, ˈwɑʃ-/ also **washing day** /ˈ·· ·/— *n* [R;(C)] the day when clothes are washed: *Monday is washday in our family*

wash down *v adv* [T1] **1** to clean (something large and hard) with a lot of water: *to wash down the car/the walls* **2** [(*with*)] to swallow (food or medicine) with the help of liquid: *Wash the dry cake down with tea*

wash draw·ing /ˈ· ˌ··/ *n* **1** [C] a drawing made in water paint of one colour **2** [U] the art of making such drawings

washed-out /ˌ· ˈ·◂/ *adj* **1** faded in colour, as from too much washing: *washed-out old curtains* **2** very tired: *She felt washed-out after working all night*

washed-up /ˌ· ˈ·◂/ *adj sl* (esp. of people) finished; with no further possibilities of success: *Let me tell you, friend, you're (all) washed-up in this town!*

wash·er /ˈwɒʃəʳ‖ˈwɔ-, ˈwɑ-/ *n* **1** a person who washes **2** a ring of metal, leather, rubber, etc., put over a BOLT or a screw to give a softer or larger pressing surface, or put between 2 pipes to make a better joint —see picture at MACHINERY **3** WASHING MACHINE

wash·er·wom·an /ˈwɒʃəˌwʊmən‖ˈwɔʃər-, ˈwɑ-/ also **washwoman**— *n* **-women** /ˌwɪmɨn/ (in former times) a woman whose job it was to wash clothes, often in her own home

wash·house /ˈwɒʃhaʊs‖ˈwɔʃ-, ˈwɑʃ-/ *n* **-houses** /ˌhaʊzɨz/ a room or building used for washing, esp. for washing clothes

wash·ing /ˈwɒʃɪŋ‖ˈwɔ-, ˈwɑ-/ *n* [U] things (esp. clothes) washed or to be washed: *Hang the washing out to dry*

washing ma·chine /ˈ·· ·ˌ·/ *n* a machine for washing clothes

washing so·da /ˈ·· ˌ··/ *n* [U] *not fml* a rough chemical powder (**sodium carbonate**) used esp. in washing very dirty things

washing-up /ˌ·· ˈ·/ *n* [U] *BrE infml* the act of washing dishes, plates, etc. after a meal, or the dishes, plates, etc. that are to be washed: *Who'll do the washing-up tonight?|There's a lot of washing-up to be done*

wash-leath·er /ˈ· ˌ··/ *n* [U;C] yellow, soft, oiled, esp. sheepskin leather used for polishing metal

wash·out /ˈwɒʃ-aʊt‖ˈwɔʃ-, ˈwɑʃ-/ *n sl* **1** a failure: *That whole plan of yours was a washout after all, and cost us a lot of money* **2** a person who fails, esp. in a course of training or study

wash out *v adv* **1** [T1] to cause to wash free of an unwanted substance, such as dirt: *Was she able to wash out her dirty coat?* **2** [T1 (*of*)] to remove by washing: *Was she able to wash the dirty mark out of her coat?* **3** [IØ (*of*)] to be removed by washing: *At last the dirty mark washed out of her coat* **4** [T1;IØ :(*of*)] to (cause to) fade by washing: *After the shirt had been cleaned, its bright blue was washed out* **5** [T1] to destroy, make useless, stop, or prevent by the force or action of water: *The bridge/The game was washed out by the storm.*|(fig.) *Let's wash out that idea and think again*

wash·room /ˈwɒʃrʊm, -ruːm‖ˈwɔʃ-, ˈwɑʃ-/ *n AmE euph* LAVATORY

wash·stand /ˈwɒʃstænd‖ˈwɔʃ-, ˈwɑʃ-/ *n* a table in a bedroom, holding things needed for washing face and hands, esp. in former times

wash up *v adv infml* **1** [Wv4;IØ] *BrE* to wash the dishes, plates, knives, forks, etc. after a meal: *Are you going to wash up tonight, then?* **2** [IØ] *AmE* to wash one's face and hands: *After crying so much, she had to wash up before coming downstairs* **3** [T1] (of waves) to bring in to the shore: *The sea washed up the body of the drowned sailor*

wash·wom·an /ˈwɒʃˌwʊmən‖ˈwɔʃ-, ˈwɑʃ-/ *n* **-women** /ˌwɪmɨn/ WASHERWOMAN

wash·y /ˈwɒʃi‖ˈwɔʃi, ˈwɑʃi/ *adj* [Wa2] *rare* **1** weak or watery: *washy soup* **2** pale: *a washy appearance* **3** lacking in life force, strength of character, or clearness of form: *washy ideas/people* —compare WISHY-WASHY

was·n't /ˈwɒzənt‖ˈwɑ-/ [Wv1] *contr. of* was not —see BE —see CONTR. (USAGE)

wasp /wɒsp‖wɑsp, wɔsp/ *n* any of many types of insect related to the bee, which fly and sting but do not produce sweet HONEY, and are usu. coloured yellow and black —see picture at INSECT

wasp·ish /ˈwɒspɪʃ‖ˈwɑ-, ˈwɔ-/ *adj usu. derog* **1** like a WASP in behaviour, esp. in tending to quarrel a lot: *a nasty waspish remark* **2** like a WASP in form, esp. in being thin —**~ly** *adv* —**~ness** *n* [U]

wasp-waist·ed /ˌ· ˈ··◂/ *adj now rare* (esp. of a woman) having a very thin waist, perhaps too thin

was·sail /ˈwɒseɪl‖ˈwɑsəl/ *n* **1** noisy merry feasting and drinking at Christmas time in England in former times **2** a shout, meaning "Good Health!" given by Englishmen when drinking together in former times **3 go wassailing** to go from house to house at Christmas, esp. in former times, singing CAROLS

wast /wəst; *strong* wɒst‖wəst; *strong* wɑst/ *v* [Wv1] *old use or poet past t. of* BE used with THOU

wast·age /ˈweɪstɪdʒ/ *n* [U;S] wasting or that which is wasted: *Think of the wastage represented by all those people who don't finish their university course!|a wastage of 25% of all the goods produced*

waste¹ /weɪst/ *n* **1** [C *often pl.*] *often lit* an unused or useless stretch of land; wide empty lonely stretch of water or land: *No crops will grow on these stony wastes* **2** [U;S] loss, wrong use, or lack of full use: *Waste of food is wicked while people are* *hungry.|It's a waste of John to employ him on this easy work when he is so clever.|Don't let all this good food go to waste!* **3** [U;C *often pl.*] used, damaged, or unwanted matter: *A lot of poisonous waste from the chemical works goes into the river.|Waste from the body passes out from the bowels* **4 go/run to waste** to be wasted —compare LAY WASTE, REFUSE[2]

waste[2] *v* **1** [T1 (*on*);IØ] to use wrongly, not use, or use too much of: *He wasted his money, time, and ability on (trying to help) worthless people.|Don't waste: save!* **2** [Wv4,5;T1] (esp. of a disease) to cause to lose flesh, muscle, strength, etc., slowly: *The strange disease wasted his whole body.|It was a wasting disease.|a wasted body* **3** [T1 *often pass.*] to make (farming land) useless by damage: *Long dry periods wasted the land* **4** [IØ] *rare* (of a supply of something) to be used without thought or lost: *If you don't turn the electricity off, it will waste while you are out* **5** [T1] *AmE sl* to kill **6 Waste not, want not** *infml* If you use too much now, you will have too little later **7 waste one's breath** *infml* to speak without persuading anyone or changing anything: *Don't waste your breath speaking to them: they never listen*

waste[3] *adj* [Wa5;A] **1** (esp. of areas of land) empty; not productive; ruined or destroyed: *waste land* **2** got rid of as worthless, damaged, or of no use: *waste material* **3** used for holding or carrying away what is worthless or no longer wanted: *waste pipes*

waste a·way *v adv* [IØ] (esp. of a person or a part of the body) to weaken or lose flesh, muscle, etc.: *Since my aunt became ill, she has been wasting away*

waste·ful /ˈweɪstfəl/ *adj* tending to waste or marked by waste: *wasteful habits* **—~ly** *adv* **—~ness** *n* [U]

waste pa·per /ˌ· ˈ··/ *n* [U] paper got rid of because used, not necessary, or not fit for use

wastepaper bas·ket /ˌweɪstˈpeɪpə ˌbɑːskɪ̈t, ˈweɪstˌpeɪpə-‖ˈweɪstˌpeɪpər ˌbæ-/ also (*esp. AmE*) **waste·bas·ket** /ˈweɪstˌbɑːskɪ̈t‖-ˌbæ-/— *n* a container for used or unnecessary material in a house or office, esp. WASTE PAPER

waste pipe /ˈ· ·/ *n* a pipe for carrying off liquid that one wants to get rid of

waste prod·uct /ˈ· ˌ··/ *n* something useless produced by the same action that produces something useful

wast·er /ˈweɪstəʳ/ *n* **1** a person or thing that uses wastefully, or causes or permits waste: *a way of doing things that is a waster of time|a time-waster* **2** *lit* a destroyer **3** *rare* WASTREL

was·trel /ˈweɪstrəl/ *n lit derog* a person who uses foolishly or too quickly the things that belong to him

watch[1] /wɒtʃ‖wɑtʃ, wɔtʃ/ *v* **1** [T1;V2,4;IØ] to look at (some activity, amusement, or event), usu. while sitting or standing: *Do you often watch television?|They watched the sun set/setting behind the trees.|Some were playing cards, and others were watching* —see SEE (USAGE) **2** [T1] to keep one's eyes fixed on (someone or something): *She watched the train till it disappeared from sight* **3** [T1,3] to look for; expect and wait (for): *She watched her chance/her moment to cross the road.|She watched to see what I would do* **4** [T1,5] to take care of, be careful with, or pay attention to: *I'll watch the baby while you are away.|You'd better watch Smith: I think he's a thief.|Watch that the milk doesn't boil over.|Watch your health as you grow older.|You have to watch your words when you talk to the general* **5** [T1,6a,b;V2,4] to attend carefully to (someone or someone's action): *Watch Jim.|Watch Jim do/doing it.|Watch how to do this.|Watch what I do, and then do the same* **6** [IØ (*at, by*)] *rather lit* to stay awake at night (for some purpose): *She watched beside her sick mother's bed for several nights* **7 watch it!** *infml* (usu. in giving or reporting orders) Be careful!: *Watch it with those boxes!* **8 watch one's step** *infml* to act with great care **9 watch the clock** *infml* to be waiting for one's working day to end instead of thinking about one's work —**~er** *n* —see SEE (USAGE)

watch[2] *n* **1** [C] (*often in comb.*) a small clock to be worn or carried: *a wristwatch|My watch has stopped: please set it (to the right time) and wind it so it will work again* —see CLOCK (USAGE) **2** [(*the*) S] one or more people ordered to watch a place or a person (esp. in the phr. **set a watch on**): *In spite of the watch set on the house, the thief escaped* **3** [(*the*) GU] also **night watch**— a form of police force doing duty in towns at night in former times, made up of citizens serving in turn, or else of paid men with no special training: *Call out the watch! There's been a crime* **4** [C *usu. pl.*] also **night watch**— *often poet* any of the periods into which the night was divided for this duty: *the slow watches of the night* **5** [C; *on*+U] (sailors who have to be on duty during) a period of 2 or 4 hours at sea: *You'll be on the first watch tonight.|Who's on watch now?* **6 keep (a) close/careful watch on** to fix one's attention on, carefully: *The government is keeping (a) close watch on the activities of that political party* **7 keep watch for** to look and wait for: *Keep watch for the milkman: I want to pay him today* **8 on the watch for** waiting for: *Be on the watch for thieves in this crowd*

watch·band /ˈwɒtʃbænd‖ˈwɑtʃ-, ˈwɔtʃ-/ also **watch·strap** /-stræp/— *n* a band of leather, cloth, metal etc., by which a wristwatch is kept fastened to the wrist

watch·dog /ˈwɒtʃdɒg‖ˈwɑtʃdɔg, ˈwɔtʃ-/ *n* **1** a fierce dog kept to guard property **2** a person or group that tries to guard against loss, waste, stealing, or undesirable practices: *a watchdog of public morals*

watch·es /ˈwɒtʃɪ̈z‖ˈwɑ-, ˈwɔ-/ *n* **in the watches of the night** *lit* during the sleepless periods of the night

watch for *v prep* [T1;V3] to look for; expect and wait for: *She watched for her chance/her moment to cross the road.|They watched for the bus to come along*

watch·ful /ˈwɒtʃfəl‖ˈwɑtʃ-, ˈwɔtʃ-/ *adj* [(*for*)] careful to notice things; on the watch: *Let's remain watchful for any sign of enemy activity* **—~ly** *adv* **—~ness** *n* [U]

watch·mak·er /ˈwɒtʃˌmeɪkəʳ‖ˈwɑtʃ-, ˈwɔtʃ-/ *n* a person who makes or repairs watches or clocks

watch·man /ˈwɒtʃmən‖ˈwɑtʃ-, ˈwɔtʃ-/ *n* **-men** /mən/ a guard, esp. of a building or an area with buildings on it: *Call the* **night watchman** *if there is any trouble tonight*

watch out *v adv* [IØ] *infml* (esp. in giving or reporting orders) to take care: *Watch out!—There's a car coming*

watch out for *v adv prep* [T1] to keep on looking for: *Watch out for a tall man in a black hat*

watch o·ver *v adv* [T1] to guard and protect; take care of (something or someone)

watch·tow·er /ˈwɒtʃˌtaʊəʳ‖ˈwɑtʃ-, ˈwɔtʃ-/ *n* a high tower from the top of which people can see what is coming a long way off, used esp. in former times

watch·word /ˈwɒtʃwɜːd‖ˈwɑtʃwɜrd, ˈwɔtʃ-/ *n* **1** a word or phrase used as a sign of recognition among members of the same society, class, or group; PASSWORD **2** a word or phrase that expresses a principle or guide to action of a person or group; SLOGAN: *"Equal Rights for Women" was their watchword*

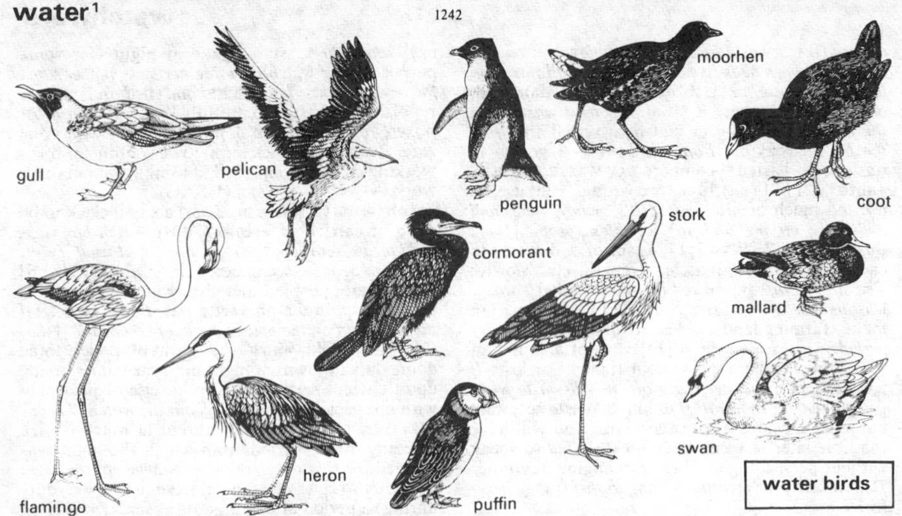

wa·ter¹ /ˈwɔːtəʳ‖ˈwɔ-, ˈwɑ-/ *n* [U] **1** the most common liquid, without colour, taste, or smell, which falls from the sky as rain, forms rivers, lakes, and seas, and is drunk by people and animals: *The prisoner was given only bread and water* **2** a supply of this liquid, esp. from pipes: *to threaten to turn off the water* **3** a mass of this liquid (esp. in the phrs. **by/on the water**): *Help! He's fallen in the water* **4** a liquid like or containing this liquid: *Waiter, take back this water that you call soup* **5** a liquid like or containing this liquid, produced by some part of the body **6** the movement of people or goods by river or sea rather than by land (often in the phr. **by water**): *Let's go by water this time* **7** the level of the sea (or some rivers) at a particular time; TIDE: *high/low water* **8** the stated degree of completeness or great ability (esp. in the phr. **of the first water**): *She is a scientist/thief of the first water* **9 above water** *infml* out of difficulty (esp. in the phr. **keep one's head above water** (=keep out of difficulty)): *In this business we don't make much money, but we are able to keep our heads above water* **10 in/into deep water(s)** *infml* in/into trouble because of the difficulty of completing or understanding something: *It was easy at first, but we're in deep water now* **11 in/into hot water** *sl* in/into trouble related to anger or punishment: *We'll get into hot water if she hears about this* **12 in low water** *BrE sl* lacking money **13 in smooth water** *sl, esp. BrE* free from trouble (after difficulties) **14 like water** *infml* in great quantity and/or without considering the cost: *The wine flowed like water at their party* **15 make/pass water** *old euph* to URINATE **16** [*nonassertive*] **hold water** *not fml* to be true or reasonable: *I'm sorry, but your story just doesn't hold water* **17 open water** water suitable for sailing, not full of islands, rocks, etc. **18 The water(s) closed over my head** I sank **19 throw cold water on** *infml* to speak against; point out difficulties in (a plan, idea, etc.) **20 water on the brain/knee/etc.** liquid on the brain, knee, etc. as the result of disease —see also WATERS, TREAD **water**

water² *v* **1** [T1;(IØ)] to pour water on (something, esp. an area of land): *It's very dry: we must water the garden/the roses* **2** [T1] to supply (esp. animals) with water: *to water the horses* **3** [IØ] (esp. of a ship) to get or take water: *Our ship watered at every port we visited* **4** [IØ] (esp. of the eyes or mouth) to form or let out water or something like water: *My eyes watered when I handled the onions* **5** [T1 *often pass.*] (esp. of rivers) to flow through and provide with water: *Colombia is watered by the Magdalena, Atrato, San Juan, and other rivers* **6** [Wv5;T1] *rare* to WATER DOWN (1) (esp. food): *Waiter, this soup has been watered!* **7** [Wv5;T1] to increase the value of (shares in one's business) to an improper degree: *watered shares* —see also WATER DOWN

-water *comb. form* **1** liquid made from the stated substance: *rosewater* **2** water for the stated thing or purpose: *bathwater|dishwater*

water bird /ˈ·· ·/ *n* any bird that swims or walks in the water —compare WATERFOWL

water bis·cuit /ˈ·· ˌ··/ *n* a BISCUIT made from flour and water and sometimes fat

water blis·ter /ˈ·· ˌ··/ *n* a BLISTER with watery contents that do not contain poisonous material (PUS) or blood

wa·ter·borne /ˈwɔːtəbɔːn‖ˈwɔtərborn, ˈwɑ-/ *adj* supported or carried by water: *waterborne trade/diseases*

water bot·tle /ˈ·· ˌ··/ *n* **1** a glass container for drinking water —see picture at CAMP² **2** a metal or plastic container for carrying drinking water on a journey, when camping, etc.

water buf·fa·lo /ˈ·· ˌ···/ *n* [Wn1] a type of Asian animal like an ox that is often kept and used by man —see picture at RUMINANT

water butt /ˈ·· ·/ *n* a barrel for collecting rainwater from the roof

water can·non /ˈ·· ˌ··/ *n* an apparatus for forcing a stream of water under very high pressure against objects and esp. people

water cart /ˈ·· ·/ also (*esp. AmE*) **water waggon**— *n* a vehicle carrying water, for sale or for washing roads

water clos·et /ˈ·· ˌ··/ *n fml* WC

wa·ter·col·our, *AmE* **-color** /ˈwɔːtəˌkʌləʳ‖ˈwɔtər-, ˈwɑ-/ *n* **1** [U;C *usu. pl.*] colours to be mixed with water, not oil, and used for painting pictures: *Look at these bright new watercolours* **2** [U] the art of painting such pictures **3** [C] a picture painted in this way: *Have you sold any more watercolours?*

wa·ter·course /ˈwɔːtəkɔːs‖ˈwɔtərkors, ˈwɑ-/ *n* **1** a natural or manmade passage through which water flows **2** a stream of water (such as a river or underground stream)

wa·ter·cress /ˈwɔːtəkres‖ˈwɔtər-, ˈwɑ-/ *n* [U] any of several kinds of hot-tasting plant grown in water and used as food without needing to be cooked, esp. in SALADs: *some nice fresh watercress*

water down *v adv* [T1 *often pass.*] **1** to weaken (a liquid) by adding water: *Waiter, this soup/beer/drink has been watered down!* **2** to weaken the effect of (something): *His political statement has been watered down so as not to offend anyone*

watered silk /ˌ·· ˈ·/ *n* [U] MOIRÉ

wa·ter·fall /ˈwɔːtəfɔːl‖ˈwɔtər-, ˈwɑ-/ *n* **1** water falling straight down over rocks, sometimes from a great height **2** a large quantity of something all arriving at once: *a waterfall of suggestions*

wa·ter·fowl /ˈwɔːtəfaʊl‖ˈwɔtər-, ˈwɑ-/ *n* **-fowl** *or* **-fowls** [Wn2;C *usu. pl.*] any swimming bird, esp. one shot by hunters

wa·ter·front /ˈwɔːtəfrʌnt‖ˈwɔtər-, ˈwɑ-/ *n* [*usu. sing.*] land, land with buildings, or a part of a town near a stretch of water, esp. when used as a port: *to buy fresh fish on the waterfront*

water hen /ˈ·· ·/ *n* MOORHEN

wa·ter·hole /ˈwɔːtəhəʊl‖ˈwɔtər-, ˈwɑ-/ *n* a small area of water in dry country, where wild animals go to drink

water ice /ˈ·· ·/ *n* [C;U] a frozen sweet made of fruit juice or water with colour and taste added

watering can /ˈ··· ·/ *n* a container from which water can be poured through a long SPOUT onto garden plants —see picture at GARDEN

watering place /ˈ··· ·/ *n* **1** a SPA **2** a WATERHOLE

water jack·et /ˈ·· ˌ··/ *n* a container filled with water which fits over part of a machine to cool it

water jump /ˈ·· ·/ *n* a test for men or horses, which shows how far they can jump as well as how high, since they must cross a stretch of water as they come down from a fence, usu. as part of a race or competition (esp. in a STEEPLECHASE or SHOW JUMPING)

water lev·el /ˈ·· ˌ··/ *n* the height to which a mass of water has risen or sunk

water lil·y /ˈ·· ˌ··/ *n* any of several types of plant which grow in water, with large flowers, often white but sometimes of other colours, and flat leaves, often seen floating on the surface of a pool in ornamental gardens

wa·ter·line /ˈwɔːtəlaɪn‖ˈwɔtər-, ˈwɑ-/ *n tech* the position which the water reaches along a ship's side

wa·ter·logged /ˈwɔːtəlɒgd‖ˈwɔtərlɔgd, ˈwɑ-, -lɑgd/ *adj* [Wa5] full of water, as of a floating object which can no longer float, or of wet earth

wa·ter·loo /ˌwɔːtəˈluː‖ˌwɔtər-, ˌwɑ-/ *n* **-loos** [C9 *usu. sing.*] (*usu. cap.*) an experience which (justly) crushes one after a time of unusual success

water main /ˈ·· ·/ *n* a large underground pipe carrying a supply of water

wa·ter·man /ˈwɔːtəmən‖ˈwɔtər-, ˈwɑ-/ *n* **-men** /mən/ a man who lives and works by a river, lake, etc., esp. one who rows people in a boat for money

wa·ter·mark /ˈwɔːtəmɑːk‖ˈwɔtərmɑrk, ˈwɑ-/ *n* **1** a mark made on paper by the maker, seen only when it is held up to the light **2 high/low watermark** a mark showing the highest/lowest level reached by a river or the sea

water mead·ow /ˈ·· ˌ··/ *n* a field which is often flooded

wa·ter·mel·on /ˈwɔːtəˌmelən‖ˈwɔtər-, ˈwɑ-/ *n* [C; U] a type of large round fruit with juicy red flesh and black seeds

wa·ter·mill /ˈwɔːtəˌmɪl‖ˈwɔtər-, ˈwɑ-/ *n* a mill whose power is gained from moving water

water po·lo /ˈ·· ˌ··/ *n* [U] a game played by 2 teams of swimmers with a ball

wa·ter·pow·er /ˈwɔːtəˌpaʊə^r‖ˈwɔtər-, ˈwɑ-/ *n* [U] the power from moving water which can be used for electricity and/or to work machines: *They built a* DAM *to produce waterpower to be used in making electricity*

wa·ter·proof¹ /ˈwɔːtəpruːf‖ˈwɔtər-, ˈwɑ-/ *adj, n* [Wa5] (an outer garment) which does not allow water, esp. rain, to go through: *Put on your waterproof (coat) before you go out in the rain*

waterproof² *v* [T1] to cause to be WATERPROOF¹, as by putting rubber onto a material

water rate /ˈ·· ·/ *n* (in Britain) the charge made to each house-owner by the water board, who supply the public with water

wa·ters /ˈwɔːtəz‖ˈwɔtərz, ˈwɑ-/ *n* **1** [P9] sea near (or belonging to) the stated country: *fishing in Icelandic waters* **2** [P9] the water of the stated river, lake, etc.: *This is where the waters of the Amazon flow out into the sea* **3** [*the*+P] water containing minerals supposed to be good for the health, which comes up out of the ground from a spring and is drunk at a particular place: *He's taking the waters at Bath* **4** [P] *lit or poet* seas: *sailing on great waters* **5 still waters run deep** people who do not talk much may, beneath their quietness, have strong feelings, be very clever, etc.

wa·ter·shed /ˈwɔːtəʃed‖ˈwɔtər-, ˈwɑ-/ *n* **1** the high land separating 2 river systems, from which each has its origin in many little streams **2** the point where there is, or must be, a change from one state of affairs to another

wa·ter·side /ˈwɔːtəsaɪd‖ˈwɔtər-, ˈwɑ-/ *n* [*the*+R] the edge of a natural body of water

water ski·ing /ˈ·· ˌ··/ *n* [U] the sport in which one travels over water on SKIs, pulled by a boat: *to go water skiing*

water sof·ten·er /ˈ·· ˌ···/ *n* a machine or chemical used for taking certain unwanted minerals (esp. chalk) out of water

water span·iel /ˈ·· ˌ··/ *n* a type of dog (SPANIEL) which is used for swimming back with birds shot by hunters over water

wa·ter·spout /ˈwɔːtəspaʊt‖ˈwɔtər-, ˈwɑ-/ *n* a wind condition (TORNADO) over the sea which carries water in a tall pipe-shaped turning mass —see TYPHOON (USAGE)

water sup·ply /ˈ·· ·ˌ·/ *n* the flow of water provided for a building or area, and the system of lakes, pipes, etc., that provides it: *to turn off the water supply*

water ta·ble /ˈ·· ˌ··/ *n* the level at and below which water can be found in the ground

wa·ter·tight /ˈwɔːtətaɪt‖ˈwɔtər-, ˈwɑ-/ *adj* [Wa5] **1** through which no water can go: *a watertight box* **2** allowing of no mistakes or reason for change: *a watertight argument/plan/excuse*

water tow·er /ˈ·· ˌ··/ *n* a tall tower on a high place which gives height to a supply of water so that it can flow in pipes to all places lower than that, for public use

water va·pour /ˈ·· ˌ··/ *n* [U] water in the form of gas in the air

water vole /ˈ·· ·/ also (*infml*) **water rat**— *n* a type of small animal which lives in holes near a river and can swim

water wag·gon /ˈ·· ˌ··/ *n* (*esp. AmE*) WATER CART

wa·ter·way /ˈwɔːtəweɪ‖ˈwɔtər-, ˈwɑ-/ *n* a stretch of water up which a ship can go, such as part of a river

wa·ter·wheel /ˈwɔːtəwiːl‖ˈwɔtər-, ˈwɑ-/ *n* a wheel which is turned by moving water, esp. to give power to machines

wa·ter·wings /ˈwɔːtəˌwɪŋz‖ˈwɔtər-, ˈwɑ-/ *n* [P] a joined pair of winglike plastic or rubber bags filled with air, worn under the arms to support a swimmer

wa·ter·works /ˈwɔːtəwɜːks‖ˈwɔtərwɜrks, ˈwɑ-/ *n* [P] **1** buildings, pipes, and supplies of water forming a public water system: *a job at the waterworks* **2** *euph* (esp. used of medical conditions) the body's system and organs for removing water from the body: *waterworks trouble* (= illness or disorder) **3 turn on the waterworks** *infml* to start to cry, esp. (in the opinion of the speaker) so as to get attention, or what one wants

wa·ter·y /ˈwɔːtəri‖ˈwɔ-, ˈwɑ-/ *adj* **1** [B] containing (too much) water: *watery soup/coffee/potatoes* **2** [B] full of water **3** [B] very pale in colour: *a watery sun* **4** [Wa5;A] *esp. lit* under the water (esp. in the phr. **a watery grave** (= the state of being drowned))

watt /wɒt‖wɑt/ *n* a measure of electrical power: *A* KILOWATT *is 1000 watts*

watt·age /ˈwɒtɪdʒ‖ˈwɑ-/ *n* [U;S] power in WATTS (of an electrical apparatus): *a wattage of 3* KILOWATTS

wat·tle /ˈwɒtl‖ˈwɑtl/ *n* **1** [U] a mixture of thin sticks woven over thicker poles to form a fence or wall **2** [U] a type of Australian plant (ACACIA) with yellow flowers, chosen as a sign to represent that country **3** [C] the red flesh growing from the head or throat of some birds, esp. males: *the* COCK*'s* COMB *and the* TURKEY*'s wattle*

wattle and daub /ˌ·· · ˈ·/ *n* [U] a mixture of WATTLE (1) with mud or clay, for the walls of houses, used esp. in former times

wave¹ /weɪv/ *v* **1** [I∅] to move in the air, backwards and forwards, up and down without moving from one place: *The grass waved in the wind* **2** [T1; I∅: (*at*)] to move ((something in) one's hand) as a signal, esp. in greeting: *She waved her hand towards the door.|He waved his stick in the air.|They're waving (at us).|Wave, then.|Wave to your father* **3** [T1;(D1 (*to*))] to express by waving the hand: *They waved goodbye.|She waved us goodbye* **4** [T1] to cause (hair) to lie in regular curves: *She waved her hair* **5** [I∅] to lie, grow, or be in regular curves: *Her hair waves naturally* **6** [X9] to signal to (a person) to move with a wave of the hand: *The policeman waved the traffic on.|She impatiently waved him away and went on with her work*

wave² *n* **1** a raised curving line of water on the surface, esp. of the sea, which is one of a number at even distances from each other: *The waves rose and fell on the shore* **2** the movement of the hand in waving: *a wave of the hand* **3** an evenly curved part of the hair: *natural/*PERMANENT *wave* **4** a suddenly rising and increasing feeling, way of behaviour, etc., passed on from person to person: *a wave of fear|a wave of violence* —see also HEAT WAVE **5** a form in which some forms of ENERGY, such as light and sound, move: *radio waves*

wave a·side *v adv* to push aside without giving attention to (esp. ideas, suggestions, etc.): *She waved his worries aside*

wave band /ˈ· ·/ *n* a set of waves of like lengths, esp. of sound: *Radio 2 can be heard on the long wave band* —see picture at SOUND³

wave·length /ˈweɪvleŋθ/ *n* **1** the distance between one WAVE² (5) and another **2** a radio signal sent out on radio WAVEs² (5) that are a particular distance apart: (fig.) *You and I are on different wavelengths* (=are completely different, do not agree about anything, cannot understand each other, etc.)

wa·ver /ˈweɪvəʳ/ *v* [Wv4] **1** [I∅] to be unsteady, burn unsteadily, etc.: *The flame wavered and went out* **2** [I∅ (*between*)] to be uncertain, esp. in deciding: *He wavered between accepting and refusing* —**waverer** *n* —**waveringly** *adv*

wav·y /ˈweɪvi/ *adj* [Wa1] in the shape of waves; having regular curves —**waviness** *n* [U]

wax¹ /wæks/ *n* [U] a solid material made of fats or oils and changing to a thick liquid when melted by heat: *a wax candle|wax in the ears* (=a natural substance) —see also BEESWAX

wax² *v* [T1] to put wax on, esp. as a polish: *to wax the floor*

wax³ *v* **1** [I∅] (esp. of the moon) to grow: *the waxing moon* —see also WANE **2** [L7] *esp. old use* (of a person) to become (usu. in the phrs. **wax merry, happy,** etc.)

USAGE Note the word order in this fixed phr. **wax and wane**: *The moon waxes and* WANE*s every month.*

wax⁴ *n BrE sl, esp. old use* a sudden burst of anger, bad temper, etc.

wax·en /ˈwæksən/ *adj* **1** [Wa5] made of wax **2** very pale, as if ill: *a waxen face*

wax pa·per /ˌ· ˈ··/ also **waxed paper**— *n* [U] paper containing wax, which prevents water from passing through, and is used in food wrapping

wax·works /ˈwækswɜːks‖-wɜrks/ *n* **waxworks** [Wn3;C *often pl. with sing. meaning*] (a place where one can see) models of human beings made in wax

wax·y¹ /ˈwæksi/ *adj* [Wa1] (pale) like wax —see also WAXEN —**waxiness** *n* [U]

waxy² *adj* [Wa1] *BrE sl, esp. old use* angry

way¹ /weɪ/ *n* **1** [C9] *rare* (except in names and comb.) a road or path: *a cycle way|Abercrombie Way* —see STREET (USAGE) —see also HIGHWAY, RAILWAY **2** [C9, esp. *to*] the (right) road(s), path(s), etc., to follow in order to reach a place: *Is this the way out?|the way to the shops* **3** [C9] (in) direction: *Which way is the house from here?|Come this way* **4** [S9] the distance to be travelled in order to reach a place or point: *a long way from home|Christmas is still a long way off* **5** [C9] method: *What's the right way (in which) to address the Queen?|What's the right way of addressing the Queen?|Do it this way.|Wash them in soapy water. In this/that way you can get rid of the dirty marks.|Foreign countries have a different way of life from ours.|(not fml) He doesn't speak the way I do* **6** [C9] the manner or degree of behaviour: *a pleasant way of speaking|I don't like the way that* (=in which) *you laugh at her.|He spoke in such a way as to offend them/in such a way that they were offended.|They both answered in the same way* **7** [S9] a condition, esp. of health (chiefly in the phr. **in a bad way**) **8** [U] forward movement; PROGRESS; HEADWAY (esp. in the phrs. **make one's way, make way, gather way**) **9** [C] (to) a degree or point: *In some ways I don't like him very much.|There's no way we can help him.|In a way I can see what you mean, even though I don't share your point of view* **10** [S9] (*used esp. when one wants to change verbs that usu. do not express movement, into verbs that do express movement*) path; course: *to make one's way|to go one's way|He laughs his way through life.|The acid bit its way through the metal* **11 by the way a** while travelling **b** (used to introduce a new subject in speech) in addition **12 by way of a** by going through: *by way of London* **b** as a sort of, or instead of: *by way of help* **c** with the intention of: *by way of helping* **13 get one's own way** to do or get what one wants, in spite of others **14 give way** to yield **15 go out of the/one's way (to do)** to take the trouble (to do), on purpose **16 have a way with one** to have an attractive quality which persuades others **17 have it both ways** to gain advantage from opposing opinions or actions (esp. in the phr. **you can't have it both ways**): *You'll have to decide whether you want to stay with your sister more than you want to go on holiday; you can't have it both ways* **18 in the family way** *euph* going to have a baby **19 out of/in the way (of)** (not) blocking space for the forward movement of: *Move out of my way so that I can get in the* *kitchen.|Her social life got in the way of her studies* **20 mend one's ways** to improve one's manners, behaviour, work, etc. **21 no way** *sl* no: *"Will you help me do this?" "No way, man!"* **22 on one's/the way (to)** moving (towards): *She put her coat on and set out on her way/went on her way* **23 out of the way** unusual or not commonly known: *do nothing out of the way* —see also OUT-OF-THE-WAY **24 pave the way (for)** to be a preparation (for): *Such opinions pave the way for social change* **25 pay one's way** never to owe money to others **26 the parting of the ways** the point at which things must change or at which 2 people must separate **27 put someone in the way of (doing) something** to give someone the chance of doing/getting something: *He put me in the way of a job* **28 put someone out of the way** to kill or get rid of someone **29 right of way** the right to pass along or over a place: *Motorists must stop, because those on foot have the right of way at a crossing* **30 see one's way (clear) to (doing)** to feel able to do; to believe or decide that one will **31 set in one's ways** (esp. of an old person) having very fixed habits **32 to my way of thinking** in my opinion **33 under way** moving forward

USAGE Speakers of *BrE* and *AmE* say *We travelled from London to Dover* or *We travelled all the way from London to Dover*. Speakers of *BrE* and *AmE* also say *Prices in this shop vary from $50 to $500*, but only speakers of *AmE* say *Prices in this shop vary all the way from $50 to $500*.

way² *adv* **1** [H] *esp. AmE* far: *way out|way back|way behind* **2** [E] near: *down Canterbury way*

way·bill /ˈweɪˌbɪl/ *n* a list of goods and passengers carried by the person delivering/taking them

way·far·er /ˈweɪˌfeərəʳ/ *n esp. old use & lit* a traveller on foot —compare PEDESTRIAN

way·far·ing /ˈweɪˌfeərɪŋ/ *adj* [Wa5] *esp. old use* travelling, esp. by habit and on foot: *a wayfaring stranger*

way·lay /weɪˈleɪ/ *v* **-laid** /ˈleɪd/ [T1] to stop (a person in a certain place, esp. one moving somewhere) for a special purpose: *She waylaid me after the lesson and asked where I had been the week before*

way-out /ˌ· ˈ·◂/ *adj sl* unusually good, strange, modern, etc.; good, strange, modern, etc., to a high degree

ways /weɪz/ *n* **1** [P] customs; habits: *Birds and their Ways* (title of a book) **2** [S] *AmE* WAY¹ (4): *We've a long ways to go yet* —see also WAY (20)

-ways *suffix* [*n, adj→adv*] in the stated way: *sideways*

ways and means /ˌ· · ˈ·/ *n* [P] methods of doing or obtaining something, esp. **a** tricks: *He hasn't got a job, but he seems to have ways and means of getting money* **b** *AmE* means of obtaining money, esp. for a club or government: *the Ways and Means Committee of the House of Representatives*

way·side /ˈweɪsaɪd/ *n* [*the*+R] **1** the side of the road: *"Tales of a Wayside Inn"* (Longfellow) **2 fall by the wayside** to fail and give up

way·ward /ˈweɪwəd‖-ərd/ *adj* changeable and not easy to guide (in character): *wayward behaviour|a wayward son*

WC /ˌdʌbəljuː ˈsiː/ also (*fml*) **water closet**— *n* a LAVATORY which is emptied by a flow of water from the pipes

we /wi; *strong* wiː/ *pron* [Wp1] (*used as the subject of a sentence*) **1** (*pl. of* I) the people speaking; oneself and one or more others: *Shall we* (= you and I) *sit together, Mary?|May we* (= I and the others) *go now, sir?* **2** *fml* (*used by a king or queen in official language*) I **3** (*used in writing*) **a** *fml and becoming rare* (*used by a writer who does not give his name*) I **b** you (the reader) and I: *"We saw on page 126 how the king persuaded his nobles to stop quarrelling . . ."* **4** (*used esp. to children and sick people, esp. when comforting them*) you: *Now, we must be a brave girl, and stop crying.|And how are we feeling today, Mr. Jones?*

weak /wiːk/ *adj* **1** [Wa1] not strong enough to work or last properly **a** (of parts of objects): *a weak wall* **b** (of organs of the body): *a weak heart|weak eyes* **2** [Wa1] not strong in character: *too weak to defend his rights* **3** [Wa1] not as well as usual in body, esp. after illness: *His legs felt weak* **4** [Wa1] containing mainly water: *weak soup* **5** [Wa1] not reaching a good standard: *weak in/at French* **6** [Wa5] (of a verb) forming the past t. and past p. in a regular way, with the usual endings: *Stepped is a weak form; swam and swum are* STRONG —**~ly** *adv*

weak·en /ˈwiːkən/ *v* **1** [T1;I∅] to (cause to) be weak in form, material, or health: *The illness weakened her heart.|She weakened as the illness grew worse* **2** [I∅] to become less determined: *She asked so many times that in the end we weakened and let her go*

weaker sex /ˈ·· ˌ·/ *n* [*the*+R] *euph & pomp* women in general; woman

weak form /ˈ· ·/ *n* a pronunciation with a shorter SYLLABLE and/or a less clear vowel sound than the STRONG FORM: *The weak form of "would" is written "'d"*

weak-kneed /ˌ· ˈ·◂/ *adj* habitually afraid and nervous; not strong in character; cowardly

weak·ling /ˈwiːk-lɪŋ/ *n* a person lacking strength in body or character

weak·ness /ˈwiːknɨ̥s/ *n* **1** [U] the state of being weak, esp. in mind, body, or character **2** [C] a weak part: *That's the only weakness in the system.|His heart is his weakness* **3** [C] a fault in character: *Drinking is his weakness* **4** [C (*for*)] a strong liking, esp. which is bad for one: *a weakness for chocolate*

weal¹ /wiːl/ *n* [U] *lit & old use* well-being

weal² *n* a mark on the skin; WELT

Weald /wiːld/ *n* [*the*+R] (in Britain) an area of open grassland, once wooded, covering parts of Sussex, Kent, and Surrey

wealth /welθ/ *n* **1** [U] (a large amount of) money and possessions: *his great wealth|a man of wealth* **2** [S (*of*)] a large number: *a wealth of examples*

wealth·y /ˈwelθi/ *adj* [Wa1] (of a person) rich —**wealthily** *adv*

wean /wiːn/ *v* [T1] to accustom (a young child, baby, or animal) to food instead of mother's milk

wean from *v prep* [D1 (AWAY);V4b] to cause (someone) to leave (an interest, habit, companion, etc., that one disapproves of): *She tried to wean him (away) from (playing) football*

weap·on /ˈwepən/ *n* a tool for harming or killing in attack or defence: *Guns are of little value against modern weapons in war* —**~less** *adj*

weap·on·ry /ˈwepənri/ *n* [U] weapons

wear¹ /weəʳ/ *v* **wore** /wɔːʳ‖wor/, **worn** /wɔːn‖worn/ **1** [T1] to have (esp. clothes) on the body: *He's wearing a new coat.|She wears her hair up.|She's wearing her diamonds* —see DRESS¹ USAGE —see also HAVE ON **2** [T1] **a** to have on the face: *She wore an angry expression* **b** to have (a type of look): (fig.) *The town wears an empty look* **3** [T1] to reduce the material of by continued use: *The water has worn the rocks.|*(fig.) *The noise wore her nerves (to nothing)* —see also WEAR AWAY, WEAR DOWN, WEAR OUT **4** [I∅] to be reduced by use: *I liked this shirt, but the neck has worn* —see also WEAR AWAY, WEAR DOWN, WEAR OUT **5** [X9] to produce by wear, use, rubbing, etc.: *You've worn a hole in your sock.|The villagers had worn a path through the fields*

6 [L9] to last in the stated condition: (fig.) *Considering her age, she has worn well* (=still looks young) **7** [T1 *nonassertive*] *infml* to accept; find acceptable; allow: *I was going to suggest Fiji for our holiday, but I don't think father will wear it* —**~able** *adj*

wear² *n* [U] **1** the act of wearing (clothes): *a year's wear before it wore out* **2** use which reduces the material: *This mat has had a lot of wear* **3** damage from use: *Look at the wear on these shoes* **4** the quality of lasting in use: *There's a lot of wear in these shoes* **5 the worse for wear** in bad condition after a period of time in use: *I spent the whole night at the party, but the next morning I was none the worse for wear* (=still fresh and active)

wear³ *n* [U9] **a** (used esp. in business) clothes of the stated type, or for the stated purpose: *men's wear|evening wear|holiday wear* **b** (*in comb.*): FOOTWEAR

wear and tear /ˌ· · ˈ·/ *n* [U] the damaging effects of ordinary use.|(fig.) *the wear and tear of modern city life*

wear a·way *v adv* [T1;I∅] to (cause to) disappear: *In the course of centuries, the wind has worn the rocks away*

wear down *v adv* **1** [T1;I∅] to (cause to) be reduced bit by bit: *He finished the wood by rubbing until he wore the surface down/until the surface wore down.*|(fig.) *The illness wore her down* **2** [T1] to reduce the force of: *We wore down their opposition after several hours' argument*

wear·ing /ˈweərɪŋ/ *adj* (very) tiring: *She's very wearing when she talks on and on.|It's a very wearing job* —see also HARDWEARING

wearing ap·par·el /ˈ·· ·ˌ··/ *n* [U] *fml or pomp* (also used in business) clothes

wear·i·some /ˈwɪərisəm/ *adj* which makes one feel tired and BOREd: *a wearisome day|a wearisome child who can't do anything right*

wear off *v adv* [I∅] to be reduced until it disappears: *The pain is wearing off*

wear on *v adv* [I∅] to pass slowly (in time): *The meeting wore on all afternoon*

wear out *v adv* [Wv5] **1** [T1;I∅] also **wear through**— to (cause to) be reduced to nothing or a useless state by use: *Her shoes wear out quickly when she goes walking.|worn-out old shoes* **2** [T1] to tire (someone) greatly: *All this talking wears me out* —see also OUTWORN, WORN-OUT

wear·y¹ /ˈwɪəri/ *adj* [Wa1;(*of*)] **1** very tired: *feeling weary|a weary smile* **2** which makes one tired: *weary weather|a weary day* —**wearily** *adv* —**weariness** *n* [U]

weary² *v* [T1 (*with*);I∅ (*of*)] to (cause to) become WEARY: *to weary someone with questions|to weary of work*

wea·sel /ˈwiːzəl/ *n* a type of small thin furry animal with a pointed face which can kill other small animals —see picture at CARNIVOROUS

weasel out *v adv* **-ll-** (*AmE* **-l**) [I∅ (*of*)] *AmE infml* to escape (from a duty): *He wants to weasel out of his responsibilities*

weath·er¹ /ˈweðəʳ/ *n* [U; *the*+R] **1** the condition of wind, rain, sunshine, snow, etc., at a certain time or over a period of time: *good weather|nice weather|a period of hot weather|What will the weather be like tomorrow?* —see also WEATHERS **2 keep one's/a weather eye open (for)** to be ready (for what may happen, such as trouble) **3 make heavy weather of** to make (something) seem difficult for oneself **4 under the weather** not very well and/or happy —see also FAIR-WEATHER, WEATHERS

weather² *v* **1** [T1] to pass safely through (a storm or difficulty): *Once the bad times were weathered, their life changed for the better* **2** [Wv5;T1] to leave open to the air: *weathered wood* **3** [I∅] to be changed by the air and weather: *Rocks weather until they are worn away* **4** [T1] (in sailing) to pass on the WINDWARD side of

weather-beat·en /ˈ·· ˌ··/ *adj* **1** marked or damaged by the force of wind, sun, etc.: *weather-beaten rocks* **2** (of a face or skin) made brown and lined by the wind and sun

weath·er·board /ˈweðəbɔːd‖-ərbord/ *n* **1** [U] also **weather boarding** /ˈ·· ˌ··/, *AmE* **clapboard**— a type of covering for the outer walls of a house, to protect the walls from rain **2** [C] a board or set of boards fixed across the bottom of a door, to prevent floods from getting inside

weather-bound /ˈ·· ·/ *adj* **1** having to stay at home because of bad weather **2** delayed (on a journey) by bad weather

weather bu·reau /ˈ·· ˌ··/ *n* an office where information about the weather is gathered for use in WEATHER FORECASTs

weath·er·cock /ˈweðəkɒk‖-ərkɑk/ *n* a movable arrangement of metal parts which is blown round to show the direction of the wind: (fig.) *As regards politics, he's a weathercock who keeps changing his opinions as a result of different influences* —see also WEATHER VANE

weather fore·cast /ˈ·· ˌ··/ *n* a description of weather conditions as they are expected to be by those who study them (METEOROLOGISTs) —**~er** *n*

weath·er·glass /ˈweðəglɑːs‖-ərglæs/ *n now rare* BAROMETER

weath·er·man /ˈweðəmæn‖-ər-/ *n* **-men** /men/ a WEATHER FORECASTer, as on television and the radio, or METEOROLOGIST

weath·er·proof¹ /ˈweðəpruːf‖-ər-/ *adj* (esp. of garments) which can keep out wind and rain —compare WATERPROOF

weatherproof² *v* [T1] to make (a material) WEATHERPROOF¹

weath·ers /ˈweðəz‖-ərz/ *n* [P] kinds of weather (esp. in the phr. **in all weathers**): *They have to be out in all weathers*

weather ship /ˈ·· ·/ *n* a ship at sea which reports on weather conditions

weather sta·tion /ˈ·· ˌ··/ *n* a place or building used for noting weather conditions

weather vane /ˈ·· ·/ *n* a WEATHERCOCK, esp. one not having a part shaped like an animal —see picture at CHURCH¹

weave¹ /wiːv/ *v* **wove** /wəʊv/, **woven** /ˈwəʊvən/ **1** [I∅] to form threads into material by drawing one thread at a time under and over a set of longer threads held out on a LOOM, from one side to the other **2** [T1] to make by doing this: *to weave a mat* **3** [X9] to twist or wind: *He wove branches together to form a roof* **4** [T1] to form by twisting: *to weave a nest out of sticks and feathers* **5** [X9 (*into*)] to introduce: *He weaves his own ideas into the official speeches* **6** [T1] to produce (a story), esp. from a suggestion **7** [T1] to make (a plan), esp. cleverly **8 get weaving** *BrE infml* to start working hard at something

weave² *n* the way in which a material is woven and the pattern formed by this: *a loose/fine/*HERRINGBONE *weave*

weave³ *v* **weaved** **1** [L9] to move along, turning and changing direction frequently: *weaving in and out between the cars* **2** [X9] to make (one's way) by doing this: *He weaved his way through the crowd*

weav·er /ˈwiːvəʳ/ *n* a person whose job is to weave cloth

web /web/ *n* **1** a net of thin threads spun (SPIN) by some insects and esp. SPIDERs —see picture at ARACHNID **2** a length of material still on a weaving frame —see also WEBBING **3** the skin filling the space between the toes of ducks and some other animals which use their feet for swimming **4** a detailed arrangement or network: *a web of deceit* (=a set of lies) **5** *tech* a large roll of paper for printing

webbed /webd/ *adj* [Wa5] having a WEB (3) (between the toes): *webbed feet|webbed toes*

web·bing /ˈwebɪŋ/ *n* [U] strong narrow woven material in bands, used for supporting springs in seats, for belts, etc.

web-foot·ed /ˌ· ˈ··ˈ/ also **web-toed** /ˌ· ˈ·ˈ/— *adj* [Wa5] (of animals) having WEBBED feet: *Ducks are web-footed* —see pictures at DOMESTIC ANIMAL and AMPHIBIAN

web off·set /ˌ· ˈ··/ *n* [U] a method of printing using one continuous roll of paper

wed /wed/ *v* **wedded** *or* (*esp. dial*) **wed** [T1;I0] *old use & lit* (also used in newspaper style) to marry: *He wedded a girl from Scotland.|They're expected to wed next week.|They were wed in the spring*

we'd /wid; *strong* wiːd/ [Wv2] *contr. of* (*in compound tenses*) **1** we had **2** we would —see CONTR. (USAGE)

Wed *written abbrev. for:* Wednesday

wed·ded /ˈwedɨd/ *adj* **1** [Wa5;A] having been lawfully married (esp. in the phrs. **(lawful) wedded husband/wife**) **2** [Wa5;F+*to*] united; closely connected: *This poem is a wonderful example of beauty wedded to truth* **3** [F+*to*] keen on; unable to give up (esp. an idea): *He's very wedded to the idea of free trade*

wed·ding /ˈwedɪŋ/ *n* a marriage ceremony, esp. with a party or meal after a church service

wedding break·fast /ˈ·· ˌ··/ *n* a meal after a marriage ceremony, for the families and guests

wedding ring /ˈ·· ·/ also **wedding band**— *n* a plain usu. gold ring placed on the third finger of a person's left hand by the person who is marrying one, during the marriage ceremony

wedge¹ /wedʒ/ *n* **1** a piece of (esp.) wood with a V-shaped edge, one end being thin and the other quite wide, used for making a space (to break something) or filling a space (to hold 2 things together): *Put a wedge in the door so that it will stay open* **2** something shaped like this: *shoes with wedge heels* **3** a GOLF CLUB with a heavy metal head for driving the ball high out of sand or rough ground **4 the thin end of the wedge** the part which seems least important but will open the way for more important or serious things of like kind

wedge² *v* **1** [T1;X7] to fix firmly with a WEDGE¹: *Wedge the door* (*open/shut*) **2** [X9, esp. IN, *into*] to cause to be unable to move from a place: *The people sitting close to me wedged me in/into the corner*

wedged /wedʒd/ *adj* [F] unable to move away because held in one place: *She sat in a low chair with high sides and when she tried to get out found she was wedged*

Wedg·wood /ˈwedʒwʊd/ *n* [U] *tdmk* a type of usu. ornamental plate or CHINA

wed·lock /ˈwedlɒk||-lɑk/ *n* [U] **1** the state of being (lawfully) married **2 born out of wedlock** *fml* born of unmarried parents; ILLEGITIMATE

Wednes·day /ˈwenzdi/ *n* **1** [R] the 4th day of the present week; day before next Thursday or last Thursday: *He'll arrive* (*on*) *Wednesday.|He'll arrive on Wednesday afternoon* (= during the afternoon of next Wednesday).|*She left* (*last*) *Wednesday* **2** [C] the 4th day of any week, or of the week that is being spoken of: *Many shops close on Wednesday afternoons.|He arrived on the Wednesday and left on the Friday* (= arrived on the 4th day of the week being spoken of).|*He arrived on a Wednesday* (= not a Tuesday, Thursday, etc.).|(*esp. AmE*) *She works Wednesdays*

wee¹ /wiː/ *adj* [Wa1;A] **1** *ScotE* very small: *a wee child* **2 a wee bit** *infml* rather: *I'm afraid he's a wee bit drunk*

wee² *n* **bide a wee** *ScotE* to stay a little longer

wee³ also **wee-wee** /ˈ· ·/— *v* [I0] *infml* (*used esp. by or to children*) to pass water from the body; URINATE —**wee** also **wee-wee** *n* [S]: *Have/Do a wee-wee*

weed¹ /wiːd/ *n* **1** [C] an unwanted wild plant, esp. one which prevents crops or garden flowers from growing properly **2** [the+R] cigarettes or (something made of) tobacco **3** [the+R] (cigarettes containing) MARIJUANA **4** [C] *usu. derog* a weak-bodied person, esp. a very thin and tall one

weed² *v* **1** [T1;I0] to remove WEEDs¹ (1) from (a place where crops or flowers grow): *to weed the garden|a morning spent weeding* **2** [X9] to remove (weeds): *to weed the grass out of/from the rose garden*

weed out *v adv* [T1] to get rid of (things or people of worse quality or less use): *He weeded out one by one the books he didn't want*

weeds /wiːdz/ *n* [P] black garments worn at a funeral and sometimes for a period of time after that

weed·y /ˈwiːdi/ *adj* [Wa1] *infml* **1** weak in body, or thought to be so **2** full of WEEDs¹ (1): *a weedy garden* —**weediness** *n* [U]

week /wiːk/ *n* **1** a period of 7 days (and nights), esp. from Sunday to Saturday: *twice a week* **2** also **working week**— the period of time during which one works, as in a factory or office: *He works a 60-hour week.|The 5-day week is usual in most firms* **3** (**the stated day**) **week** also **a week on** (**the stated day**)— *esp. BrE* a week after (the stated day); on the next (stated day): *She'll be here tomorrow week.|She's coming on Sunday week/a week on Sunday* **4** (**a**) **week last/next/this/on** (**the stated day**) a week before or after (the stated day): *It happened a week last Monday.|"How long ago did it happen?" "It will be a week on Thursday."|He's arriving 2 weeks next Saturday* **5 week in, week out** without change or rest

week·day /ˈwiːkdeɪ/ *n* **1** a day of the week, including Friday, not at the weekend: *There is one train timetable for weekdays, another for Saturdays, and another for Sundays* **2** a day of the week not Sunday: *In Leeds there is one train timetable for weekdays and another for Sundays*

USAGE Note the phr. **She works on weekdays** (*AmE* also **She works weekdays**).

week·end¹ /ˌwiːkˈend, ˈwiːkend||ˈwiːkend/ *n* **1** Saturday and Sunday, esp. when considered a holiday **2** this period of time with the addition of Friday evening from the time of stopping work

USAGE Note the phrs. (*BrE*) **She works at weekends**=(*AmE*) **She works (on) weekends**

weekend² *v* [L9] to pass a weekend: *weekending away from home*

week·end·er /ˌwiːkˈendəʳ||ˈwiːken-/ *n* a person spending one or more weekends in a particular place: *They don't live here: they're only weekenders*

week·ly¹ /ˈwiːkli/ *adj, adv* (happening or appearing) once a week or every week: *a weekly visit|They shop weekly in the town*

weekly² *n* a magazine or newspaper which appears once a week

week·night /ˈwiːknaɪt/ *n* a night not at the weekend

USAGE Note the phrs. **She works on weeknights** (*AmE* also **She works weeknights**).

wee·ny /ˈwiːni/ *adj* [Wa1] *infml* very small —see also TEENY WEENY

weep /wiːp/ *v* **wept** /wept/ **1** [T1;IØ (*over*)] *esp. fml* to let fall (tears) from the eyes: *He lost control of his feelings and began to weep.*|*They wept over/for their failure.*|(fig.) *to weep bitter tears* —compare CRY **2** [T1] *rare or lit* to cry for or because of: *He wept his fate* **3** [X7,9] to put into a certain state by crying: *She wept herself to sleep* **4** [Wv4;IØ] to lose liquid **a** *lit or poet* such as rain: *weeping skies* **b** from a part of the body, esp. because of illness: *The wound is weeping*

weep·ing /ˈwiːpɪŋ/ *adj* [Wa5] (of trees) with the branches hanging down: *a weeping* WILLOW

weep·y /ˈwiːpi/ *adj* [Wa1] *infml* **1** tending to cry, or crying often: *not very well, and feeling weepy* **2** (of a story, film, etc.) as if intended to make one sad

wee·vil /ˈwiːvəl/ *n* a type of small BEETLE which spoils grain, seeds, etc., by feeding on them

weft /weft/ *n* the threads of a material woven across the downward set of threads —see also WARP

weigh /weɪ/ *v* **1** [T1] to find the weight of, esp. by a machine: *to weigh oneself* **2** [L1] to have a certain weight: *It weighs 6 pounds.*|*I weigh less than I used to* **3** [X9, esp. *against*] to consider or compare carefully: *He weighed the ideas in his mind* **4** [L9, esp. *with*] to be important (to): *Your suggestion does not weigh with those in power* **5** [T1] to raise (an ANCHOR): *to weigh* ANCHOR —see also WEIGH UP **6 weigh one's words** to consider carefully before speaking

weigh·bridge /ˈweɪˌbrɪdʒ/ *n* a machine for weighing vehicles and their loads, including a flat area onto which the vehicles are driven

weigh down *v adv* [T1 (*with*) *often pass.*] to make or cause to feel heavy (with a load): *I was weighed down with the shopping.*|(fig.) *weighed down with grief*|*trees weighed down by snow*|(fig.) *lives weighed down by lack of money*

weigh in *v adv* **1** [IØ (*at*)] to test one's weight before a fight in BOXING, or a horse-race **2** [IØ (*with*)] to join in a fight or argument: *He weighed in (with information) to prove the point*

weigh on *v prep* [T1] to cause worry to: *The lack of money weighed on his mind.*|*His worries weighed on him*

weigh out *v adv* [T1] to measure in amounts by weight: *Our flour is sold in bags of a certain weight, but in the past they used to weigh it out in the shop*

weight[1] /weɪt/ *n* **1** [U] the heaviness of anything, esp. as measured by a certain system: *She never eats and is losing weight* **2** [U] *tech* the force with which a body is drawn towards the centre of the earth: *The weight of an object is related to the force of* GRAVITY, *which is fixed, and to its mass* **3** [C] a piece of metal of a standard heaviness, which can be balanced against a substance to measure equal heaviness of that substance: *a one-pound weight* **4** [C] (*sometimes in comb.*) a heavy object used for holding something down: *a paperweight* **5** [U] a system of standard measures of weight: TROY *weight*|*metric weight* **6** [U] value or importance: *an idea of weight*|*which bears weight with us*|*a man of political weight* **7** [C] (something with) a large amount of weight: *It's not sensible to lift weights after an operation* **8** [C] (something giving) a sense of worry or anxiety: *The loss of the money is a weight on my mind* **9 pull one's weight** to join in work or activity equally with others **10 put on/lose weight** (of a person) to become heavier/lighter **11 throw one's weight about/around** to give orders to others, because one thinks oneself important **12 under/over weight** too light/too heavy

weight[2] *v* [T1] **1** [Wv5;(*with*)] to put a weight on or add a heavy material to: *Fishing nets are weighted* **2** to make heavy

weight down *v adv* [T1 (*with*) *usu. pass.*] to load heavily; WEIGH DOWN: *weighted down with shopping*

weight·ed /ˈweɪtɪ̈d/ *adj* [Wa5;F (*towards, against*)] giving advantage: *These tests are weighted in favour of those people who have read the right books.*|*The competition was weighted against the younger children*

weight·ing /ˈweɪtɪŋ/ *n* [U;S] *esp. BrE* something additional, esp. additional pay given because of the high cost of living in a certain area: *They got a London weighting of £200 a year*

weight·less /ˈweɪtləs/ *adj* [Wa5] having no weight, as when in space, when free from the drawing power of the earth or any other large body: *a weightless flight in space* —**~ly** *adv* —**~ness** *n* [U]

weight lift·ing /ˈ· ˌ··/ *n* [U] the activity of lifting specially shaped weights in a certain manner and holding them above the head, esp. in sports competitions —**weight lifter** *n*

weight·y /ˈweɪti/ *adj* [Wa1] having or seeming to have importance: *weighty* PROBLEM*s* —**weightily** *adv* —**weightiness** *n* [U]

weigh up *v adv* [T1] to (try to) understand; form an opinion about: *I can't weigh him up*

weir /wɪəʳ/ *n* **1** a wall across a river, stopping or controlling the flow of the water above it **2** a wooden fence across a stream for catching fish

weird /wɪəd‖wɪərd/ *adj* [Wa1] **1** strange; unnatural **2** *infml* unusual and not sensible or acceptable: *She has some weird ideas* —**~ly** *adv* —**~ness** *n* [U]

weird·ie /ˈwɪədi‖ˈwɪərdi/ *n infml* a strange person, with unusual clothes, habits, etc.

weird·o /ˈwɪədəʊ‖ˈwɪər-/ *n* **-s** *sl* WEIRDIE

welch /welʃ/ *v* [IØ (*on*)] WELSH

wel·come[1] /ˈwelkəm/ *interj* [(*to*)] (an expression of pleasure when someone arrives in a place new to him, said by any person who belongs there): *Welcome to our home.*|*Welcome home/back* (when returning from another place).|*Welcome to England*

welcome[2] *v* **1** [T1] to greet (a person) when arriving in a new place: *The Queen welcomed the President as soon as he got off the plane* **2** [Wv4;T1] to meet or be found by (a visitor), esp. with pleasure: *They welcomed him with flowers.*|*a welcoming smile* **3** [T1] to receive (an idea): *Little interest welcomed his suggestion.*|*They welcomed the idea rudely/with little interest* **4** [X9] to receive (someone) into the stated place with greetings: *They opened the door and welcomed him in*

welcome[3] *adj* [Wa5] **1** [B] acceptable and wanted: *a welcome suggestion*|*All suggestions will be welcome.*|*You are always welcome at my house* **2** [B] pleasant and likeable: *a welcome change* **3** [F+*to*, F3] allowed freely (to have), sometimes because not wanted: *She's coming to visit you? You're welcome to her!*|*You're welcome to try, but you won't succeed* **4 You're welcome** (a polite expression when thanked for something): *"Thank you!" "You're welcome"* **5 make (someone) welcome** to receive (a guest) with friendliness

welcome[4] *n* **1** [C] a greeting on arrival: *The Queen gave a welcome to the foreign minister* **2** [C] a show of kind acceptance: *They gave him the same welcome as they would to their own son* **3** [C;(U)] a way of receiving or accepting: *They gave us a warm (=kind) welcome*

weld[1] /weld/ *v* [T1;IØ :(*to,* TOGETHER)] **a** to join (usu. metals) by pressure or melting together when hot **b** (of metals) to become joined in this way

weld[2] *n* the part joined in WELDING[1]

weld·er /ˈweldəʳ/ *n* a person whose job is to make WELDed[1] joints

wel·fare /ˈwelfeəʳ/ *n* [U] **1** well-being; comfort and happiness: *We only want his welfare* **2** help with living conditions, social difficulties, etc.: *Tell your troubles to the welfare officer in the factory.*| *welfare work* (=to improve life for the unfortunate) **3** (in the US) (the system of) additional government help for those in special need: *on welfare* —compare SUPPLEMENTARY BENEFIT

welfare state /ˌ·· ˈ·‖ˈ·· ·/ *n* [C; *the*+R] (a country with) a system of social help which is free, esp. one which gives money to the unfortunate

wel·kin /ˈwelkɪn/ *n* [*the*+R] *poet* the sky

well[1] /wel/ *n* **1** a place where water comes from underground: *to find a well in the desert*|*well water* **2 a** such a place with round walls leading down to the water **b** a hole like this through which oil is drawn from underground **3** an enclosed space in a building running straight up and down, as for a LIFT[2] (4) to travel in, or across which stairs turn: *the stairwell* **4** *BrE* the space in front of the judge in a law court

well[2] *v* **1** [L9, esp. OUT] (of liquid) to flow (from): *Blood welled (out) from the cut* **2** [Wv4;I∅ (UP)] to rise: *She was so angry that the tears welled (up)*

well[3] *adv* **better** /ˈbetəʳ/, **best** /best/ **1** in the right manner; satisfactorily: *well clothed*|*They spent their money well and were pleased with what they bought* **2** to a high standard: *She paints very well* **3** [Wa5] thoroughly: *Wash it well before you dry it.*|*"I don't know that part of the island very well"* (SEU W.)|*I know him well* **4** [Wa5;H] much; quite: *I can't reach it; it's well above my head.*|*He was well within the time* **5** with kindness or favour: *They speak well of him at school* **6** [Wa5] (*after* can't *or* couldn't) justly or suitably: *I couldn't very well say no when there was no one else whom she could ask* **7 as well** in addition; also; too: *I'm going to London and my sister's coming as well* **8 as well as** in addition to (being): *He came as well as his brother.*|*He was kind as well as sensible* **9 come off well** to be lucky in the end: *You came off well, with £1000.*|*The business arrangement came off well for everyone* **10 do well a** to succeed or improve **b** (*only in* -ing *form*) getting better in health **11 do oneself well/do well by someone**: to give oneself/someone good things, comfortable surroundings, etc.: *He does well by his guests* **12 do well out of** to gain profit from: *He did well out of the sale of his house* **13 do well to** to act wisely to: *You would do well to tell him.*|*You did well to tell him* **14 just as well** (as a reply) (There's) no harm done; (There's) no loss: *"We're too late to see the film." "Just as well: I hear it isn't very good"* —see also WELL[5] (3) **15 may well** could suitably: *You may well need a coat if it rains.*|*You may well ask!* (= we are all wondering).|*It may well rain before tonight* (= it is likely) **16 may (just) as well** could with the same result: *You might just as well ask for the moon as for a bicycle, because you're not going to get either.*|*You may as well tell me the worst* (= I'm already worried, or have guessed it) **17 pretty well** almost: *The work is pretty well finished* **18 well and truly** *not fml* completely: *George is well and truly drunk* **19 Well done!** (said when someone has been successful): *You've passed your examination, Robert. Well done!* **20 well away a** getting ahead: *We're well away on the rebuilding of the house* **b** *sl* starting to be drunk **21 well out of** lucky enough to be free from (an affair): *We'll never stop them arguing. I wish I were well out of it.*|*It's lucky you left before the trouble happened; you were well out of it* **22 well up in** well informed about: *well up in the latest fashions*

well[4] *interj* **1** an expression of surprise: *She's got a new job. Well, well!* **2** (used for introducing an expression of surprise, doubt, acceptance, etc.): *Well, what a surprise!*|*Well, I'm not sure.*|*Well, all right, I agree* **3** (used when continuing a story): *Well, then she said . . .* **4 Oh well!** (used for showing cheerfulness when something bad has happened): *"Oh well, I can't complain; I was lucky yesterday"* (SEU W.)

well[5] *adj* **better; best 1** [F;(B)] in good health: *She was ill for a month but she's looking well now/she looks better now.*|*I'm feeling very unwell.*|(*esp. AmE*) *I'm not a well man* **2** [Wa5;F] right; in an acceptable state (esp. in certain phrs., usu. with *all*): *All is not well with her since she lost her money* **3** [Wa5;F] most suitable (esp. in the phr. **(just) as well**): *It would be (just) as well to telephone them before we arrive* **4** [Wa5;F] *rare* favourable: *It was well for us that we took our holiday early* **5 It's all very well** (an expression of dissatisfaction when comparing what is practical to what is suggested): *It's all very well for you/It's all very well to say that, but what can I do?*

we'll /wil; *strong* wiːl/ [Wv2] *contr. of* **1** We will **2** We shall —see CONTR. (USAGE)

well-ad·vised /ˌ· ·ˈ·◂/ *adj* [Wa2] sensible: *You would be well-advised to tell him of your plans before you go*

well-ap·point·ed /ˌ· ·ˈ··◂/ *adj* [Wa2] having all the necessary objects, apparatus, or furniture: *a well-appointed hotel*

well-bal·anced /ˌ· ˈ··◂/ *adj* [Wa2] **1** (of people and their characters) strong in the mind; sensible in daily life and not controlled by unreasonable feelings **2** (of meals or ways of eating) containing the right amounts of what is good for the body: *a well-balanced* DIET

well-be·ing /ˌwelˈbiːɪŋ◂‖ˈwelˌbiːɪŋ/ *n* [U] personal and bodily comfort, esp. good health: *His walk in the sunshine gave him a sense of wellbeing*

well·born /ˌwelˈbɔːn◂‖ˈwelbɔrn/ *adj* [Wa5] coming from a family of social importance, esp. of the higher classes

well-bred /ˌ· ˈ·◂/ *adj* [Wa2] well-behaved or polite, probably the result of one's being well brought up: *He's very well-bred.*|*a well-bred voice*

well-cho·sen /ˌ· ˈ··◂/ *adj* [Wa2] **(a few) well-chosen words** a short but suitable speech: *She gave a few well-chosen words after dinner to the group*

well-con·nect·ed /ˌ· ·ˈ··◂/ *adj* [Wa2] knowing people of power and importance socially, esp. being related to them

well deck /ˈ· ·/ *n tech* a level (DECK) on a ship between other levels, forming a space between them

well-de·fined /ˌ· ·ˈ·◂/ *adj* [Wa2] clear in form; easily recognizable: *The trees are well-defined in the picture.*|*well-defined limits*

well-dis·posed /ˌ· ·ˈ·◂/ *adj* [Wa2;A;F (*towards*)] favouring; showing kindness: *a well-disposed nature*|*well-disposed towards strangers*

well-done /ˌ· ˈ·◂/ *adj* (of food, esp. meat) cooked for a longer rather than shorter period of time —compare RARE[1]

well-earned /ˌ· ˈ·◂/ *adj* [Wa2] much deserved: *a well-earned rest after so much hard work*

well-es·tab·lished /ˌ· ·ˈ··◂/ *adj* [Wa2] **1** having strong or satisfying proof: *well-established principles* **2** having been in existence for some time and doing well; long established: *a well-established business firm*

well-fa·voured /ˌ· ˈ··◂/ *adj old use* (of a person) good-looking

well-found /ˌ· ˈ·◂/ *adj* (esp. of a ship) having all the necessary apparatus; WELL-APPOINTED

well-found·ed /ˌ· ˈ··◂/ *adj* [Wa2] based on facts:

His suggestions are well-founded, but it's too late to change now

well-groomed /ˌ· ˈ·◂/ *adj* [Wa2] having a very neat clean appearance, as if special care has been taken

well-ground·ed /ˌ· ˈ··◂/ *adj* [Wa2] **1** [F (*in*)] instructed fully: *well-grounded in the skills needed to live in the desert* **2** [B] WELL-FOUNDED

well-heeled /ˌ· ˈ·◂/ *adj sl* rich

well-hung /ˌ· ˈ·◂/ *adj* [Wa2] *taboo apprec sl* **1** (of a woman) having large breasts **2** (of a man) having a large sex organ

well-in·formed /ˌ· ·ˈ·◂/ *adj* [Wa2] knowing a lot about several subjects or parts of a particular subject: *He's very well-informed; that's why he won the general knowledge competition*

wel·ling·ton /ˈwelɪŋtən/ also **wellington boot** /ˌ··· ˈ·/— *n* [*usu. pl.*] a boot usu. made of rubber which keeps water from the feet and lower part of the legs —see picture at GARDEN[1]

well-in·ten·tioned /ˌ· ·ˈ··◂/ *adj* [Wa2] acting in the hope of good results, though often failing: *It was a well-intentioned effort to help*

well-knit /ˌ· ˈ·◂/ also **well-set**— *adj* strong and with good muscles: *well-knit bodies/limbs*

well-known /ˌ· ˈ·◂/ *adj* [Wa2] known by many people: *a well-known fact* —see FAMOUS (USAGE)

well-lined /ˌ· ˈ·◂/ *adj infml* **1** full of money: *well-lined pockets* **2** (of the stomach) full of food

well-mean·ing /ˌ· ˈ··◂/ *adj* [Wa2] WELL-INTENTIONED: *a well-meaning person/effort* —see also MEAN **well**

well-meant /ˌ· ˈ·◂/ *adj* [Wa5] said or done for a good purpose, though not with a good result: *Her help was well-meant, but it just made the job take longer* —see also MEAN **well**

well-nigh /ˈ· ·/ *adv* [Wa5] *fml* almost: *well-nigh impossible*

well-off /ˌ· ˈ·◂/ *adj* [Wa2] **1** [F (*for*); (B)] rich: *well-off for money* **2** [F] lucky (esp. in the phr. **you don't know when you're well off** (= you're more fortunate than you know)) —opposite **badly-off** —compare OFF[3] (8)

well-oiled /ˌ· ˈ·◂/ *adj sl* drunk

well o·ver *v adv* [I∅] (of liquid) to overflow

well-pre·served /ˌ· ·ˈ·◂/ *adj* [Wa2] *apprec or euph* (of an old person) showing few of the usual weaknesses of old age

well-read /ˌ· ˈ·◂/ *adj* [Wa2] having read a lot of different types of books and gained much useful information, esp. in general knowledge

well-round·ed /ˌ· ˈ··◂/ *adj* **1** (esp. of a person) having a full, pleasantly curved shape **2** (esp. of social experience) full of different types of useful activity: *a well-rounded education*

well-spok·en /ˌ· ˈ··◂/ *adj* **1** having a way of speaking typical of a carefully educated person **2** *BrE* using a socially acceptable variety of English pronunciation

well·spring /ˈwelˌsprɪŋ/ *n* [(*of*)] *esp. lit* a never-ending supply

well-thought-of /ˌ· ˈ· ·◂/ *adj* [Wa2] (of a person) liked and admired generally

well-timed /ˌ· ˈ·◂/ *adj* [Wa2] said or done at the most suitable time: *well-timed advice*

well-to-do /ˌ·· ˈ·◂/ *adj infml* rich

well-tried /ˌ· ˈ·◂/ *adj* often used before and known to work well: *well-tried methods*

well-turned /ˌ· ˈ·◂/ *adj* [Wa2] (of a phrase) carefully formed and pleasantly expressed: *a well-turned phrase*

well-wish·er /ˈ· ˌ··/ *n* a person giving good wishes to another, esp. on a special occasion: *Crowds of well-wishers gathered as the Queen's ship entered the harbour*

well-worn /ˌ· ˈ·◂/ *adj* (of phrases) with little meaning, because over-used

welsh, welch /welʃ/ *v* [I∅ (*on*)] **1** to avoid payment: *He welshed on his debts* **2** to break one's word or promise: *She welshed on her promises* —**~er** *n* USAGE This verb is considered offensive by Welsh people.

Welsh *adj* [Wa5] of Wales, its people, or their CELTIC language

Welsh rab·bit /ˌ· ˈ··/ also **Welsh rare·bit** /ˌwelʃ ˈreəbɪ̈t‖-ˈreər-/— *n* a small meal of cheese melted on bread often with beer or other things added for special taste; cheese on TOAST

welt /welt/ *n* **1** a raised mark on the skin usu. from or as if from a stroke of a whip; WEAL **2** a piece of leather round the edge of a shoe to which the top and bottom are stitched

Welt·an·schau·ung /ˈveltˌænʃaʊ-ʊŋ/ *n Ger* the total idea of society, of the world and its purpose, etc., that a person or group has: *The Weltanschauung of the middle classes found expression in the public buildings of the Victorian period*

wel·ter[1] /ˈweltəʳ/ *v* [I∅ (*in*)] *rare* to WALLOW in something

welter[2] *n* [GS+*of*] a disordered mixture: *A welter of religions is/are represented in this crowd of people of different races*

wel·ter·weight /ˈweltəweɪt‖-ər-/ *n, adj* [Wa5] (in BOXING) a man weighing between 135 and 147 pounds

wen /wen/ *n* a small lump on the skin, esp. of the head, made of cells which have grown in too large numbers

wench[1] /wentʃ/ *n* [C;N] *old use & dial* a girl, esp. in the country

wench[2] *v* [I∅] *old use* to have sex with many women, such as PROSTITUTEs

wend /wend/ *v* **wend one's way** **a** *esp. lit* to move or travel over a distance, esp. slowly **b** to leave: *I must be wending my way*

Wens·ley·dale /ˈwenzlideɪl/ *n* **1** [U] a type of not very strong white cheese made from cow's milk and originally from Yorkshire **2** [C] a type of long-haired sheep

went /went/ *past t. of* GO

wept /wept/ *past t. and past p. of* WEEP

were /wəʳ; *strong* wɜːʳ/ *neg. contr.* **weren't** /wɜːnt‖ˈwɜrənt, wɜrnt/ [Wv1] *past t. of* BE —see CONTR. (USAGE)

we're /wɪəʳ; *strong* wiːəʳ/ [Wv1] *contr. of* we are —see CONTR. (USAGE)

were·wolf /ˈweəwʊlf, ˈwɪə-‖ˈweər-, ˈwɪər-/ *n* **-wolves** /wʊlvz/ (in stories) a man who sometimes turns into an animal (i.e. a WOLF)

wert /wɜːt‖wɜrt/ [Wv2] **thou wert** *old use or bibl* (when talking to one person) you were

Wes·ley·an /ˈwezlɪən/ *n, adj* [Wa5] (a member) of the branch of the PROTESTANT church established by John Wesley; METHODIST

west[1] /west/ *adv* [Wa5] (*often cap.*) **1** towards the west: *to travel west|He sat facing West, watching the sun go down.|Reading is (not far) west of London* **2** **go west** *humor* **a** to die **b** to be damaged or broken

west[2] *n* (*often cap.*) **1** [(*the*) R] one of the 4 main points of the compass, which is on the left of a person facing north: *the west door of the church|The sun sets in the west* **2** [*the*+R;(A)] (of a wind) (coming from) this direction

West *n* [*the*+R] **1** the western part of the world, esp. western Europe and the United States —compare OCCIDENT **2** the part of a country which is further west than the rest **3** (in the US) the part of the country west of the Mississippi; the areas of more recent settling than the eastern US, and with the population more thinly spread: *"How the West*

was Won" (film title) —see NORTH (USAGE)
west·bound /ˈwestbaʊnd/ *adj* [Wa5] travelling towards the west: *a westbound ship*
West Coun·try /ˈ· ˌ··/ *n* [*the*+R] the West of England
West End /ˌ· ˈ·/ *n* [*the*+R] the western part of central London, where the shops, theatres, offices, etc., are: *West-End shops*
west·er·ly /ˈwestəli‖-ərli/ *adj* [Wa5] **1** [A;(B)] towards or in the west: *the westerly shore of the lake|in a westerly direction* **2** [B] (of a wind) coming from the west: *a soft westerly wind*
west·ern¹ /ˈwestən‖-ərn/ *adj* (*often cap.*) of or belonging to the west part of the world or of a country: *the Western nations* —see NORTH (USAGE)
western² *n* (*often cap.*) a story, usu. on a film, about life in the WEST (3) in the past, esp. about cattle farms, horses, and gunfights
West·ern·er /ˈwestənəʳ‖-tər-/ *n AmE* someone who lives in or comes from the WEST (3)
west·ern·ize, -ise /ˈwestənaɪz‖-ər-/ *v* [Wv5;T1] to cause (esp. African or Asian people and countries) to have or copy the customs and ways typical of the western world (that is, America and Europe) —**-ization** /ˌwestənaɪˈzeɪʃən‖-ərnə-/ *n* [U]
west·ern·most /ˈwestənməʊst‖-ər-/ *adj* [Wa5] *fml* farthest west: *the westernmost parts of China*
West In·di·an /ˌ· ˈ···/ *adj* [Wa5] of or from the West Indies: *West Indian cooking*
west·ward /ˈwestwəd‖-ərd/ *adj* [Wa5] going towards the west: *in a westward direction* —compare WESTERLY
west·wards /ˈwestwədz‖-ər-/ *AmE* also **westward**— *adv* towards the west: *They travelled westwards*
wet¹ /wet/ *adj* **-tt-** **1** [Wa1] covered in or with liquid or not dry: *I can't go out till my hair's dry; it's still wet from being washed.|wet ground|wet paint|to get wet* **2** [Wa1] rainy: *wet weather|a wet day|We can't go out, it's too wet* **3** [Wa1] *infml derog* (of a person) lacking in strength (of mind); too weak or unwilling to get things done: *Don't be so wet! Of course you can do it, if you only stop saying you can't!* **4 wet through** completely covered in or with liquid: *Don't go out, you'll get wet through.|My coat is wet through* —**~ly** *adv* —**~ness** *n* [U]
wet² *n* **1** [*the*+R] rainy weather: *I can't go out, because the coat I brought is too thin to protect me from the wet* **2** [*the*+R] wet ground (esp. after rain): *Come and walk on the dry road, instead of going through the wet* **3** [S] *BrE sl* a drink (in the phr. **have a wet**)
wet³ *v* **wet** *or* **wetted** [T1] **1** to cause to be wet: *Wet your finger and hold it up; the side that dries is the side the wind's blowing from* **2 wet the bed** (esp. of children) to pass water from the body in bed, because of a loss of control while asleep
USAGE In *BrE* the past tense and past participle are usually **wetted** except in the phr. **wet the bed**: *Billy's* **wet the bed** *again!*
wet blan·ket /ˌ· ˈ··‖ˈ· ˌ··/ *n derog* a person who discourages others or prevents them enjoying what they do
wet dock /ˌ· ˈ·‖ˈ· ·/ *n* a DOCK (= place for keeping ships) which is kept full of water —compare DRY DOCK
wet dream /ˌ· ˈ·/ *n* a sexually exciting dream
weth·er /ˈweðəʳ/ *n* a male sheep (RAM) which has had its sexual organs removed (= has been CASTRATED)
wet nurse /ˈ· ·/ *n* a woman employed to give breast milk to another woman's baby
wet suit /ˈ· ·/ *n* a garment worn by underwater swimmers which allows some water to go through, but keeps the person warm by fitting close to the body
wet·ting /ˈwetɪŋ/ *n* the act of (a person's) being wetted unpleasantly by rain, sea, etc.
wetting a·gent /ˈ·· ˌ··/ *n* a chemical substance which, when spread on a solid surface, makes it hold liquid
we've /wiv; *strong* wiːv/ [Wv2] *contr. of* (in compound tenses) we have —see CONTR. (USAGE)
whack¹ /wæk/ also **thwack**— *v* [T1] to hit with a blow making a loud noise
whack² *n* **1** [C] also **thwack**— (the noise made by) a hard blow **2** [C9 *usu. sing.*] *infml* a (fair or equal) share: *Have you all had your whack?* **3** [C *usu. sing.*] *infml* a try; attempt: *If you can't open it, let me have a whack at it*
whacked /wækt/ also **whacked out** /ˌ· ˈ·/— *adj* [F] *infml* very tired: *I'm completely whacked*
whack·er /ˈwækəʳ/ *n infml* **1** something very big **2** a big lie
whack·ing¹ /ˈwækɪŋ/ *adj* [Wa5] *infml* very big: *a whacking (great) orange*
whacking² *n* a beating
whale /weɪl/ *n* **1** any of several types of very large animals which live in the sea, with a body like a fish's body but blood which does not change its temperature, because they are MAMMAL*s* —see picture at SEA **2 a whale of a time** (*infml*) a very enjoyable experience, such as a social occasion, party, etc.
whale·bone /ˈweɪlbəʊn/ *n* [U] a material taken from the upper jaw of WHALE*s*, used for keeping things stiff and in a certain shape
whal·er /ˈweɪləʳ/ *n* **1** a man who hunts WHALE*s* at sea **2** a ship or boat from which WHALE*s* are hunted
whal·ing /ˈweɪlɪŋ/ *n* [U] the hunting of WHALE*s* and the treatment of them at sea to produce oil and other materials
wham /wæm/ *n infml* (the sound made by) a hard blow
wharf /wɔːf‖wɔrf/ *n* **wharfs** *or* **wharves** /wɔːvz‖wɔrvz/ a place, usu. like a wide stone wall built along the edge of or out into the sea or river, where ships can be tied up to unload goods
what¹ /wɒt‖wɑt, wʌt/ *determiner, pron* [Wp2] **1** (*used in questions*) **a** (*when a choice is to be made from an unknown number or amount*) which (thing or person)?: *What fool told you that?|What time will you come?|What are you doing?|He asked me what I was* (not *what was I*) *doing.|What shoes are you going to wear?|What's the time?|What does this mean?|What (kind of) books do you like reading?|What am I sitting on?|What colour/shape is it?|What (ever) size shoes do you take?|"What are we going to do about this wreck?"* (SEU W.)|*"Look on it and tell me what the number is."* (SEU S.)|(*infml*) *Guess what—John refuses to pay!|I'll tell you what: let's hide the money!* **b** (*used for having words repeated when not heard, or when the hearer is surprised*): *What did you say?|"I got up at half past 4." "What?"* (Some people think *"What"* is not very polite here; compare PARDON) **c** (*used in surprise or anger*): *What? I don't believe it! They can't do that* **d** (*in questions about a person's job*): *"What are you?" "I'm a teacher"* (compare *"Who are you?" "I'm George Smith"*) **2** (*used for showing relationships between things*) that which; a/the thing that: *I believed what he told me.|He told me what to do.|He pointed to what looked like a tree.|Show me what* (= the things that) *you bought.|". . . if you see what I mean"* (SEU S.)|*"This one seems really fairly reasonable for what it is."* (SEU S.) *I gave him what I had/what books I had/what money I had* (not **what*

book I had) **3 and what not** *not fml* and other things; ETC.: *I bought sugar, tea, eggs, and what not* **4 give someone what for** *infml* to punish and/or scold someone: *Your father will give you what for if he finds out you've not been to school for 3 days* **5 so what?** also (*fml*) **what of it**— *infml* that is of no importance, is it?; how can that make any difference: *"He's won £1,000." "So what? He isn't any happier"* **6 what few/what little** those few which, or that little which: *I told him what little I knew on the subject.|He visits what few friends he has* **7 what (. . .) for?** *infml* **a** why?: *"I'm going to Paris." "What for?"|"Nobody knows for certain just what the British army is there for"* (SEU S.) **b** for which purpose? (in the phr. **what is something for?**): *What's this thing for?* (= Tell me its purpose) **8 what have you** *infml* anything (else) like that: *In his pocket I found a handkerchief, string, old sweets, and what have you* **9 what if?** what will happen if?: *What if we move the picture over here? Do you think it'll look better?* **10 what is/was something like?** (used when asking for a description): *"What's the new teacher like?" "He's got a red beard and he makes stupid jokes."|"What's it like flying alone?"* **11 what's his/her/their/its name** also **what d'you call him/her/them/it**— *infml* (used when speaking of a person or thing whose name one cannot remember): *I'll never forget what's his name.|Mary's gone out with what's his name—you know, the boy with the curly beard* —see also WHAT D'YOU CALL IT, WHAT'S IT **12 what's more** and this (in the phr. **what is more** = more important): *We invited a new speaker and, what's more, he was happy to come* **13 what's what** the important things (in the phr. **know what's what**) **14 what it takes** *infml* the qualities necessary for success (in the phr. **have (got) what it takes**) —compare **what** ABOUT **15 what the . . .?** (used with various words, such as HELL, *devil*, BLAZES, etc. when asking angry or surprised questions) what: *What the* HELL *do you want?|"Would the last gentleman kindly explain what the* HELL *he was talking about?"* (SEU S.) **16 what though** *lit* even if (used in comparing something bad with something better, which is stated next): *What though the battle* BE (= is) *lost? We can fight again!* —see WHICH (USAGE) **what/how** ABOUT

what[2] *predeterminer* **1** how surprisingly good/bad: *What weather!|What a face he made when he took the medicine!|What a pity!* **2** (*with an adjective*) how surprisingly: *What funny stories she tells!|What beautiful weather!|What a good idea!|I told him what a clever girl you are* —see HOW (USAGE)

what[3] *adv* [Wp2] **1** in what way?; to what degree?: *What do you care about it?* **2 what with** (used for introducing the causes of something, esp. something bad): *What with all this work and so little sleep at nights, I don't think I can go on much longer*

USAGE Both defs. are esp. used with derog. meaning—(1) tends to mean "in no way", "to no degree" (2) usu. introduces the causes of a *bad* state of affairs

what d'you call it /ˈwɒdʒə ˌkɔːl ɨt‖ˈwɑ-, ˈwʌ-/ also **what you may call it** /ˈwɒdʒə mə ˌkɔːl ɨt‖ˈwɑ-, ˈwʌ-/— *n infml* WHAT'S IT

what·ev·er[1] /wɒˈtevəʳ‖wɑ-, wʌ-/ also (*lit*) **what·so·ev·er** /ˌwɒtsəʊˈevəʳ‖ˌwɑt-, ˌwʌt-/— *determiner, pron* **1** any(thing) at all that: *They eat whatever (food) they can find.|"I believe she's cured of whatever was wrong with her"* (SEU W.) **2** no matter what: *Whatever I said, he'd disagree.|He refuses, for whatever reason*

whatever[2] *pron not fml* **1** anything (else) like that: *Anyone seen carrying bags, boxes, or whatever, was stopped by the police* —see also WHATNOT, WHAT[1] (8) **have you 2** (showing surprise) WHAT[1] (1a)?: *Look at that strange animal! Whatever is it?|John's getting married? Whatever next!* —see EVER (USAGE)

whatever[3] also **whatsoever**— *adj* [Wa5;E *nonassertive*] at all: *Have you any interest whatever?*

what·not /ˈwɒtnɒt‖ˈwɑtnɑt, ˈwʌt-/ *n* **1** [U] *infml* anything (else): *carrying his bags and whatnot* **2** [C] a piece of furniture with open shelves, used, esp. in Victorian times, for showing ornaments

what's it /ˈwɒts ɨt‖ˈwɑts-, ˈwʌts-/ also **what's its name** /ˈwɒts ɨts ˌneɪm‖ˈwɑts-, ˈwʌts-/— *n infml* (a word used for any small object, such as a small piece of machinery, esp. when one cannot remember its proper name): *I can't screw up the what's it: will you try?*

wheat /wiːt/ *n* [U] **1** a plant from whose grain flour is made: *a field of wheat* **2** the grain from this plant: *wheat of good quality* —see picture at CEREAL

wheat·en /ˈwiːtn/ *adj* [Wa5] *tech or lit* made from wheat (flour): *wheaten bread/products*

wheat germ /ˈ· ·/ *n* [U] the centre of the wheat grain, containing much of the goodness and food value (VITAMIN*s*)

whee·dle /ˈwiːdl/ *v* [IØ;X9] to (try to) make (someone) do what one wants by pleasant but insincere behaviour and words: *She wheedled him into going*

wheedle out *v adv* [T1 (*of*)] to obtain (something) from someone by insincerely pleasant persuading: *I wheedled a promise out of her*

wheel[1] /wiːl/ *v* **1** [T1] to move (a wheeled object) with the hands: *The nurse wheeled the table up to the bed* **2** [X9] to move (something) on a wheeled object: *The nurse wheeled his dinner up* **3** [IØ] to move in a WHEEL[2] (3): *The soldiers wheeled around the square* **4** [IØ (ROUND, AROUND, ABOUT)] to turn suddenly or change direction: *I called him as he was running away and he wheeled (to face me)* **5** [IØ] (of birds) to fly round and round in circles: *the* GULL*s wheeling over the sea*

wheel[2] *n* **1** [C] a circular object with an outer frame which turns around an inner part (HUB) to which it is joined, used for turning machinery, making vehicles move, etc. **2** [*the*+R] the STEERING WHEEL of a car or guiding wheel of a ship: *I'm rather tired; will you take the wheel* (= drive instead of me)? **3** [C] a type of movement, esp. of a body of soldiers on ceremonial occasions, where one end of a line moves as if round a circle, the other end remaining at the centre of the circle **4 at the wheel** driving or guiding (esp. a car) —see also STEERING WHEEL **5 oil the wheels** to make matters go more smoothly and without trouble **6 on wheels** in a car/by car: *meals on wheels* (= delivered to the homes of old people in Britain) **7 on oiled wheels** smoothly; without trouble **8 put one's shoulder to the wheel** to start work, esp. to help someone else **9 wheels within wheels** hidden influences having effects on surface behaviour or states of affairs: *They appear to be doing this simply to help their friends, but who knows the real reason—there are wheels within wheels*

wheel·bar·row /ˈwiːlˌbærəʊ/ also **barrow**— *n* a movable container with one wheel at the front, 2 handles at the back, 2 legs, and a 3-cornered part in which things can be carried, such as earth in a garden —see picture at SITE[1] and GARDEN[1]

wheel·base /ˈwiːlbeɪs/ *n* the distance between the front and back AXLE on a vehicle

wheel·chair /ˈwiːltʃeəʳ/ *n* a chair with large wheels which can be turned by the user; chair in which a person who cannot walk can be pushed from place to place

-wheel·er /ˈwiːləʳ/ *comb. form* a moving object with a certain number or type of wheels: *a 3-wheeler* (=a car with 3 wheels)

wheel·house /ˈwiːlhaʊs/ *n* **-houses** /ˌhaʊzɪ̆z/ the place on a small or not modern ship where the captain stands at the WHEEL² (2)

wheel·ing /ˈwiːlɪŋ/ *n* **wheeling and dealing** *infml* the act of getting what one wants by any methods, including unfair ones

wheels /wiːlz/ *n* [P] *sl* a car or like vehicle: *Are these your new wheels, man?*

wheel·wright /ˈwiːlraɪt/ *n* (esp. in former times) a person who makes and repairs wheels, esp. the wooden wheels for horse-drawn carts

wheeze¹ /wiːz/ *v* **1** [IØ] **a** (of people) to make a noisy sound when breathing, esp. a whistle in the chest **b** (of objects) to make any sound like this **2** [T1 (OUT)] to say while doing this: *succeeded in wheezing out a greeting*

wheeze² *n* **1** the act or sound of wheezing (WHEEZE¹) **2** *sl* a joke or trick

wheez·y /ˈwiːzi/ *adj* [Wa1] that WHEEZEs¹, esp, habitually: *a wheezy old bicycle pump* —**wheezily** *adv* —**wheeziness** *n* [U]

whelk /welk/ *n* a type of sea animal which lives in a shell, and is sometimes used as food —see picture at MOLLUSC

whelp¹ /welp/ *n* a young animal, esp. a dog or wild animal of a doglike or catlike type

whelp² *v* [IØ] (of animals) to give birth to WHELPs

when¹ /wen/ *adv* [Wa5] **1** (*in questions*) at what time; how soon: *When will they come?|Do you know when they're coming?* (not *. . . *when are they coming?*)|*Ask him when to open it* **2** (of time) at or on which: *at the time when we met|It's the sort of day when you'd like to stay in bed* —see THAT (USAGE)

when² *conj* **1** at the time at which: *Come in when you've taken your coat off.|She was beautiful when she was a girl.|I jumped up when she called.|When sleeping, I never hear a thing.|This dictionary will look nice when printed.|When in trouble, ask her for help.|When I came home she was cooking dinner* (compare *He came home while I was cooking dinner*).|*I'll tell him when he comes* (not *. . . *when he will come*) —see also WHENEVER **2** if (with present tense): *No one can make a dress when they haven't learnt how* **3** considering that; as; SINCE: *I can't tell you anything when you won't listen* **4** although: *She stopped trying, when she might have succeeded next time* **5** (after a COMMA) and then: *They arrive at 6, when we all have dinner* **6** **hardly/scarcely when** (of time) only just . . . when: *I had hardly opened the door|Hardly had I opened the door when he hit me* —see HARDLY (USAGE)

when³ *pron* **1** (*in questions*) what time?: *Since when has that been so?* **2** (*showing relationship*) which time: *I went to bed at 10, before when I was reading for an hour.|next summer, by when the new house should be ready*

when⁴ *n* **the when and where/and how** the time and place/method

whence /wens/ *adv* [Wa5] **1** *old use* from where?: *Whence come you?* **2** *rare* (from) which place; (from) where: *They returned to the land* (*from*) *whence they came* **3** from which: *the bridge over the river Cam, whence* (*came*) *the name of the town of Cambridge* **4** *rare* to the place from which: *They returned whence they came* —compare WHITHER
USAGE Some people think that **from whence** is bad English, and that **whence** is better alone

when·ev·er¹ /weˈnevəʳ/ *conj* **1** at any time at all that: *Come whenever you like.|I'd like to see you whenever* (*it's*) *convenient* —compare WHEN² (1) **2** every time: *Whenever we see him we speak to him*

whenever² *adv* [Wa5] *not fml* **1** at any such time: *Whether they arrive tonight, tomorrow, or whenever, they'll be welcome.|in 1922 or whenever* (*it was*) **2** (showing surprise) WHEN¹ (1): *Whenever did you find time to do it?* —see EVER (USAGE)

where¹ /weəʳ/ *adv* [Wa5] **1** (*in questions*) at/to what place, position, etc.: *Where can he be?|Where will all this trouble lead* (= what result will it have)*?|I wonder where he is* (*not* *. . . *where is he*).|*"I'm going now." "Where to?"|Where are they from?|Ask him where to go* **2** (of place) at or to which: *the office where I work|has reached the point where a change is needed|*(*infml*) *"some places where there aren't any buses to at all"* (SEU S.) —see THAT (USAGE)

where² *conj* **1** at, to the place (at) which: *Keep him where you can see him.|Where I live there are plenty of sheep* **2** or/to any place at all that: *Go where you like* —see also WHEREVER **3** WHEREAS (1): *They want a house, where we would rather live in a flat* **4** **where it's at** *sl* very good, esp. as being fashionable: *This party's really where it's at, man!*

where³ *n* **the where and when/how** the place and time/method

where·a·bouts¹ /ˌweərəˈbaʊts◂‖ˈweərəbaʊts/ *adv* [Wa5] (used when an exact answer is not expected) where?; in or to what place?: *Whereabouts did I leave my bag?|"I've got some rather rich relations." "Whereabouts?"* (SEU S.)|*"Whereabouts are you going?"* (SEU S.)|*I wonder whereabouts he is*

where·a·bouts² /ˈweərəbaʊts/ *n* [GU9] the place a person or thing is in: *The escaped prisoner's whereabouts is/are still unknown*

where·as /weəˈræz/ *conj* **1** (*used for introducing an opposite*) but: *They want a house, whereas we would rather live in a flat.|Whereas we want a flat, they would rather live in a house* **2** *law* (*at the beginning of a sentence*) since; because of the fact that

where·at /weəˈræt/ *adv, conj* [Wa5] *obs* **1** at which: *the place whereat he sits* **2** WHEREUPON

where·by /weəˈbaɪ‖weər-/ *adv* [Wa5] *fml* **1** by means of which: *a system whereby a new discovery may arise* **2** according to which: *a law whereby all children are to receive cheap milk*

where·fore /ˈweəfɔːʳ‖ˈweərfor/ *adv, conj* [Wa5] *old use* **1** why?: *Wherefore come you?* **2** for which reason

where·fores /ˈweəfɔːz‖ˈweərforz/ *n* **the whys and wherefores** the reasons, causes, etc.

where·in /weəˈrɪn/ *adv, conj esp. fml* **1** in what sense?; in what way?; how?: *Wherein lies the difficulty?* **2** in which: *the part wherein lies the fault*

where·of /weəˈrɒv‖weəˈrʌv, -ˈrɑv/ *adv, conj fml* of which/what

where·on /weəˈrɒn‖weəˈrɔn, weəˈrɑn/ *adv, conj* [Wa5] *old use or humor* **1** on which: *the table whereon lay the food* **2** WHEREUPON

where·so·ever /ˌweəsəʊˈevəʳ‖ˈweərsəʊˌevər/ *conj, adv esp. lit* WHEREVER²

where·to /weəˈtuː‖-ər-/ also (*old use*) **where·un·to** /weəˈrʌntʊ, ˌweərʌnˈtuː‖weəˈrʌntuː/— *adv, conj fml* **1** to what purpose? **2** in what direction? **3** to which

where·u·pon /ˌweərəˈpɒn‖ˈweərəpɑn, -pɔn/ *conj* (at once) after that: *He saw me coming, whereupon he offered me his seat*

wher·ev·er¹ /weəˈrevəʳ/ *adv* [Wa5] *not fml* **1** (showing surprise) where?: *Wherever did you get that idea?* **2** anywhere at all; any such place: *at home, at school, or wherever* —see EVER (USAGE)

wherever² *conj* **1** at/to all places/any place: *Wherever you go, I go too* **2** at/to any place at all that; WHERE² (2): *wherever possible|wherever you like*

where·with·al /ˈweəwɪðɔːl‖-ər-/ *n* [*the*+R; *the*+

R3] the necessary means (to do something), esp. money: *I'd like a new car but I lack the wherewithal (to pay for it)*

wher·ry /ˈweri/ *n* a type of BARGE[1] (1)

whet /wet/ *v* **-tt-** [T1] **1** to sharpen: *He whetted his knife on the stone* **2 whet someone's appetite** (of a taste or short experience) to make someone wish for more: *You'd think she'd never climb again after falling down the mountain, but it's just whetted her appetite*

wheth·er /ˈweðəʳ/ *conj* **1** if . . . or not: *He asked me whether she was coming.|He wondered whether to come.|It was uncertain whether he would come.|The decision whether to see her was mine alone.|I worry about whether I hurt her feelings.|"not knowing whether you'll get the tickets or not"* (SEU S.) **2 a** no matter if . . . (or) . . .: *I shall go, whether you come with me or stay at home* **b** (no one knows) if it can be . . . (or) (esp. in the phr. **whether by accident or design** = through luck or on purpose): *Whether by accident or design, they met.|Whether through choice or obedience I don't know, but he certainly did all the work very well* **3 whether or not/no** if so or not

USAGE **if** can be used instead in meaning 1, except **a** before INFINITIVE*s*: not (**the question* **if** *to go*) **b** after PREPOSITION*s*: not (**It depends on* **if** *he's ready*) **c** after nouns: not (**the question* **if** *he's ready*) **d** with **not**: not (***if** *or not he's ready*)

whet·stone /ˈwetstəʊn/ *n* a stone used for sharpening cutting tools

whew /hjuː/ *interj* PHEW

whey /weɪ/ *n* [U] the watery part of sour milk after the solid part has been removed —see also CURD

which /wɪtʃ/ *determiner, pron* [Wp2] **1** (*used in questions, when a choice is to be made from a known set of possibilities*) what (thing or person)?: *Which do you want?|Which girl/book do you like best?|Which shoes shall I wear, the red ones or the brown ones?|Which of these is yours?|Ask him which he wants* (not **which does he want*).*|I don't know which of them to buy* —compare WHAT **2** (*used for showing relationship between things*) being the one(s) that: *the house which/that is opposite|the house* (*which*) *I built|the house* (*which/that*) *I went into/into which I went|the rooms which/that are empty* **3** (*used esp. in written language, with* COMMA*s*) and/because it/they, them: *His age, which I think is 90* (=and I think it is 90)*, is the least noticeable thing about him.|Books, which you can change* (=because you can change them) *at the shop, make good presents.|This amount, above which I cannot go, is my last offer.|"There are 2 left, one of which is almost finished and the other of which is not quite"* (SEU S.) **4** (and) this: *He changed his mind, which made me very angry.|He changed his mind for the second time, after which I refused ever to go out with him again.|*(*fml*) *He believes in public ownership, which idea I am quite opposed to.|He may come, in which case I'll ask him* **5 which is which? a** what is the difference between the 2? **b** which is the one I am looking for?

USAGE Compare **which** and **what**: 1 **Which** is used when a choice is to be made from a known set of things or people: **Which** *colour do you want, red or blue?|***Which** *of these colours/***Which** *of his daughters do you like best?* **What** is used when the choice is from an unknown set: **What** *colour was it?|***What** *are you eating?* 2 **Which** can be followed by *of*, but **what** cannot: **Which** *of the girls/books do you like?* not (***What** *of the girls/books . . .?*) —see THAT (USAGE)

which·ev·er /wɪˈtʃevəʳ/ *determiner, pron* **1** any (one) (of a set of known possibilities) that: *Take whichever seat you like.|Have whichever you want.|Have 2, whichever you want.|Choose whichever of them you like best.|I'll give it to whichever of you wants it* **2** no matter which: *It has the same result, whichever way you do it.|Whichever you want is yours* **3** *not fml* (showing surprise) WHICH (1)?: *Whichever did you choose?* —see EVER (USAGE)

whiff[1] /wɪf/ *n* **1** [S (*of*)] a short-lasting smell or movement of air: *Something good must be cooking; I got a whiff of it through the window* **2** [C] *infml* a small CIGAR **3** [C *usu. pl.*] a breath in: *A few whiffs of this gas and she'll fall asleep until we've pulled the tooth out*

whiff[2] *v* **1** [T1] to breathe (esp. tobacco smoke) gently in or out **2** [I∅] *infml* to smell bad: *That fish whiffs a bit*

whif·fy /ˈwɪfi/ *adj* [Wa1] *infml BrE* having a bad smell; smelly: *That dog's a bit whiffy*

Whig /wɪg/ *n, adj* [Wa5] (a member) of the LIBERAL PARTY, a name used esp. in the last century and before the rise of the LABOUR PARTY but not in modern use

while[1] /waɪl/ *n* **1** [S] a time, esp. a short one: *Just wait for a while and then I'll help you* **2 all this while/this long while** *old use* all this time; (for) a long time **3 once in a while** sometimes, but not often **4 worth one's/someone's while** WORTHWHILE to one/someone (esp. in the phr. **make it worth your while** = pay you)

while[2] also (*esp. BrE*) **whilst** /waɪlst/— *conj* **1** the time that or during the whole of the time that: *While I was out he started to misbehave.|While I read, she sang.|I was reading the book while in hospital/while working on a ship* **2 a** (to introduce the first CLAUSE) although: *While I understand what you say, I can't agree with you* **b** (to introduce something different) but; WHEREAS (1): *You like sports, while I'd rather read.|While their country has plenty of oil, ours has none* **c** (to introduce something different in the second CLAUSE) and what is more: *They're having trouble at home, while abroad things are even worse*

while[3] *prep nonstandard NE EngE* until: *I can't see you while Friday*

while a·way, wile away *v adv* [T1] to pass (time) lazily: *to while away the hours*

whim /wɪm/ *n* a sudden idea or wish, often not reasonable: *to* INDULGE *his every whim|a sudden whim to buy a new hat*

whim·per[1] /ˈwɪmpəʳ/ *v* **1** [I∅] (esp. of a creature that is afraid) to make one or more small weak cries: *The little dog whimpered when I tried to bath it* **2** [I∅;T1] (of a person) to speak or say in a small trembling voice as if about to cry: *"Don't hurt me!" he whimpered*

whimper[2] *n* **1** a small weak cry, of pain or fear **2** an act of gentle weeping or weak-complaint

whim·si·cal /ˈwɪmzɪkəl/ *adj* fanciful; with strange ideas —**~ly** *adv* [Wa4]

whim·si·cal·i·ty /ˌwɪmzɪˈkæləti/ *n* **1** [U] the quality of being WHIMSICAL **2** [C *usu. pl.*] an act of WHIMSY

whim·sy, whimsey /ˈwɪmzi/ *n* **1** [U] strangeness in thought and behaviour, esp. making odd things seem humorous **2** [C] a strange act or idea

whin /wɪn/ *n* [U *often pl. with sing. meaning*] GORSE

whine[1] /waɪn/ *v* [I∅] **1** to make a high sad sound: *The dog whined at the door, asking to be let out* **2** to complain (too much) in an unnecessarily sad voice: *Stop whining, child!*

whine[2] *n* the sound of whining (WHINE[1])

whin·er /ˈwaɪnəʳ/ *n derog* a person who complains (WHINE[1] (2))

whin·ny /ˈwɪni/ *v* [I∅] to make a gentle sound which horses make —**whinny** *n*

whip[1] /wɪp/ *n* **1** a long piece of material, esp. rope or leather fastened to a long stiff handle, used for hitting animals or people **2** a person whose job is to control the HOUNDs (=hunting dogs) in a fox hunt **3** a member of Parliament who is responsible for making other members of his party attend at voting time **4** an order given to members of Parliament to attend and vote —see also THREE-LINE WHIP **5** a sweet food made of beaten eggs and other foods whipped together

whip² *v* **-pp-** **1** [T1] to beat with a WHIP¹ (1) **2** [T1] *esp. old use* to beat hard: *His father whipped him for misbehaviour* **3** [T1] *infml* to conquer; beat: *Ali really whipped Frazier* **4** [L9;X9] to move (something) quickly: *He whipped out into the street.|He whipped it into his pocket.|He whipped out his gun.|He whipped off his shoes* **5** [Wv5;T1] to beat until stiff (esp. cream or the white part of eggs): *whipped cream* —see also WHISK² (3), BEAT¹ (5) **6** [T1] **a** to sew over (the edge of material) with a close stitch **b** to cover (the end of a stick or rope) closely with thread, string, etc. **7** [L9] (of wind or rain) to move violently, beating down: *The wind whipped across the plain* **8** [T1] to cause (a TOP⁴) to spin by means of a piece of string fixed to a stick **9** [T1] *tech* to fish (a stream) with a rod and line

whip·cord /ˈwɪpkɔːd‖-kɔrd/ *n* [U] **1** a strong type of cord **2** a type of strong woollen material

whip hand /ˈ· ·/ *n* [*the*+R] control; power (in the phrs. **have/got the whip hand over someone**)

whip in *v adv* [T1] *tech* to keep control of (the HOUNDs) during a fox hunt

whip·lash /ˈwɪp-læʃ/ *n* **1** the blow (LASH) from a whip **2** a sudden shocking feeling: *the whiplash of fear* **3** also **whiplash in·ju·ry** /ˌ·· ˈ···/— any type of harm done to the body by the sudden violent movement of the head and neck, as in an accident

whip·per-in /ˌ·· ˈ·/ *n* **whippers-in** WHIP¹ (2)

whip·per·snap·per /ˈwɪpəˌsnæpəʳ‖ˈwɪpər-/ *n* [C; *you*+N9] a person, esp. young, not thought important, but who says and does too much so as to draw attention: *a whippersnapper clerk who thinks he rules the office*

whip·pet /ˈwɪpɪ̈t/ *n* a type of small thin racing dog like a GREYHOUND

whip·ping /ˈwɪpɪŋ/ *n* a beating, esp. as a punishment

whipping boy /ˈ·· ·/ *n* **1** a child who, in former times, was educated with and punished instead of a noble's son **2** anyone who gets most of the blame and/or punishment —see also SCAPEGOAT

whip·poor·will /ˈwɪpʊəˌwɪl‖ˈwɪpər-/ *n* a type of small bird of North America with a cry like its name, which comes out at night

whip·py /ˈwɪpi/ *adj* [Wa1] (of a rod, stem, etc.) which bends or springs back easily

whip-round /ˈ· ·/ *n esp. BrE* a collection of money among a group of people, as in a place of work, to give to one member, esp. when something has just happened to him of a sad or happy nature: *We're having a whip-round for old Fred, who's leaving the firm*

whip up *v adv* [T1] **1** to cause (feelings) to rise, become stronger, etc.: *to whip up interest* **2** to make quickly: *to whip up a meal/a plan*

whirl¹ /wɜːl‖wɜrl/ *v* **1** [X9;I∅] to (cause to) move round and round very fast: *the whirling dancers|The letter was picked up by the wind and whirled into the air* **2** [X9;L9] to (cause to) move away in a hurry: *The car whirled them off to the wedding* **3** [I∅] to give the feeling of turning fast until GIDDY: *His senses were whirling*

whirl² *n* **1** [S] the act or sensation of WHIRLing¹ (esp. in the phr. **in a whirl** = confused): *My head's in a whirl; I must sit down and think* **2** [C *usu. sing.*] very fast movement or activity, esp. of a rather confused sort: *a whirl of activity|the gay social whirl* **3** **give something a whirl** *infml* to try something; give something a chance

whir·li·gig /ˈwɜːlɪˌgɪg‖ˈwɜr-/ *n* **1** a toy which spins; spinning TOP **2** a ROUNDABOUT¹ (1)

whirl·pool /ˈwɜːlpuːl‖ˈwɜrl-/ *n* a place with circular currents of water in a sea or river, which can draw objects into it

whirl·wind /ˈwɜːlˌwɪnd‖ˈwɜrl-/ *n* a tall pipe-shaped body of air moving rapidly in a circle —see TYPHOON (USAGE)

whirl·y·bird /ˈwɜːliˌbɜːd‖ˈwɜrliˌbɜrd/ *n* [C; *by*+U] *AmE sl* a HELICOPTER

whirr¹, *AmE* **whir** /wɜːʳ/ *v* **whirred** [I∅] to make a regular sound like/by something beating against the air: *the whirring of the machinery*

whirr², *AmE* **whir** *n* the sound of WHIRRing¹: *the whirr of the sewing machine*

whisk¹ /wɪsk/ *n* **1** [*usu. sing.*] a quick movement, esp. to brush something off: *with a whisk of his hand* **2** a small brush consisting of a bunch of feathers, hair, etc., tied to a handle: *driving away flies with a fly whisk* **3** a small hand-held apparatus for beating eggs, whipping cream, etc.: *an egg whisk*

whisk² *v* **1** [T1] to move (something) quickly, esp. so as to brush something off: *The horse was whisking its tail* **2** [X9 esp. OFF, AWAY] to remove **a** by brushing lightly: *She whisked the dirt off* **b** by taking suddenly: *She whisked the cups away/whisked him (off) home* **3** [T1] to beat (esp. eggs), esp. with a WHISK¹ (3)

whis·ker /ˈwɪskəʳ/ *n* one of the long stiff hairs that grow near the mouth of a cat, rat, etc. —see picture at CAT

whis·kered /ˈwɪskəd‖-ərd/ *adj* having whiskers

whis·kers /ˈwɪskəz‖-ərz/ *n* [P] hair allowed to grow on the sides of a man's face, not meeting at the chin

whis·key /ˈwɪski/ *n* [U;C] WHISKY made in Ireland or the US

whis·ky /ˈwɪski/ *n* **1** [U] a type of strong alcoholic drink (SPIRIT) made from MALTed grain, such as BARLEY, produced esp. in Scotland **2** [C] an amount of this drunk in one glass

whis·per¹ /ˈwɪspəʳ/ *v* **1** [T1;I∅] to speak (words) with noisy breath, but not with the usual movements in the throat which produce the voice, so that only a person close by can hear: *Stop whispering in the corner; say whatever it is out loud.|She whispered a few words weakly before she fell unconscious.|"Listen!" she whispered* **2** [I∅] (usu. of the wind) to make a soft sound: *the wind whispering in the roof* **3** [X9 esp. ABOUT, *often pass.*] to tell (a secret) widely: *His adventures have been whispered through the village/whispered about/whispered everywhere* —**~er** *n*

whisper² *n* **1** [C] whispered words: *She said it in a whisper, so I couldn't hear* **2** [C *usu. sing.*] a soft windy sound: *the whisper of the wind in the roof* **3** [C] a piece of information passed secretly from one person to another; RUMOUR: *I've heard a whisper that old Bill's going to lose his job next month* **4** [U] *tech* the type of sound made by the throat when whispering

whispering cam·paign /ˈ··· ·ˌ·/ *n* an attack made against a person's position or good name by passing on accounts of bad behaviour, true or false, from one person to another

whist /wɪst/ *n* [U] a type of card game for 2 pairs of players

whist drive /ˈ· ·/ *n* a meeting to play WHIST between several pairs of partners who change opponents

whis·tle[1] /ˈwɪsəl/ *n* **1** a simple (musical) instrument for making a high sound by passing air or steam through **2** the high sound made by passing air or steam through a small tube-shaped area, either an instrument, a mouth, or a beak: *gave a loud whistle of surprise* **3 wet one's whistle** *humor* to drink (esp. alcohol)

whistle[2] *v* **1** [IØ] to make the sound of a WHISTLE[1] (2), esp. with the mouth, to make music or as a signal to draw attention **2** [T1] to produce (music) by doing this: *He whistled "God save the Queen"* **3** [X9] to cause to come by doing this: *He whistled his dog back* **4** [L9] to move with a noise like a WHISTLE[1] (2): *The wind whistled round them*

whistle for *v prep* **He/She/They can/will have to whistle for it** *infml* He, she, etc., won't get it, esp. payment: *"He wants his £5 back." "He'll have to whistle for it; I've no money left"*

whistle-stop /ˈ·· ·/ *n* **1** [C] *AmE* a small railway station where trains stop usu. only if given a signal **2** [C;A] a touring visit, esp. by a politician, with many short stops, esp. in small places: *a whistle-stop tour*

whistle up *v adv* [T1] to make (something) from poor or scarce material(s): *whistle up some new ideas for lessons* —compare WHIP UP

whit /wɪt/ *n* [S *nonassertive*] *esp. fml* (by) a small amount: *not a whit of common sense*

Whit *n* [R] WHITSUN: *the Whit weekend*

white[1] /waɪt/ *adj* **1** [Wa1] **a** of a colour which is like that of a clean cloud in a sunny sky; of the colour of milk; of the colour which contains all the colours: *white hair* (=when one is very old)|*white light* (= natural light) **b** pale in colour: *a white skin|white wine* **2** [Wa5] (of a person) of a pale-skinned race —see also FAIR[1] (7,8) **3** [Wa1] pale with fear: *She/Her face went white.|white-faced|white-lipped* **4** [Wa5] (of coffee) with milk or cream —opposite **black** **5** [Wa5] *esp. old use* pure; showing moral goodness: *a white wedding* (=when the BRIDE is dressed in white) —**~ness** *n* [U]

white[2] *n* **1** [U] the colour which is white **2** [C] a person of a pale-skinned race: *This seat is for whites only* **3** [C] the white part of the eye, which can be seen in animals when the eyes are turned up in fear, illness, etc., but in man can be seen all the time —see picture at EYE[1] **4** [C;U] (*usu. in comb.*) the part of an egg which is colourless, but white after cooking: *Beat 3 egg whites until stiff*

white al·loy /ˌ· ˈ··/ *n* [U;C] WHITE METAL

white ant /ˌ· ˈ·/ *n* TERMITE

white·bait /ˈwaɪtbeɪt/ *n* [U] very small young fish of several types, eaten as food

white blood cell /ˌ· ˈ· ·/ also **white cor·pus·cle** /ˌ· ˈ···, ˌ· ·ˈ··/— *n* one of the cells in the blood which fight against infection (not the ones which carry oxygen) —compare RED BLOOD CELL

white-col·lar /ˌ· ˈ··◂/ *adj* [Wa5;A;(F)] not of the people who work with their hands in jobs needing bodily strength and/or little thinking; of office workers, indoor workers, etc.: *a white-collar job* —compare BLUE-COLLAR

whited sep·ul·chre /ˌ·· ˈ···/ *n bibl* a person who has the appearance of a good man, though evil at heart

white dwarf /ˌ· ˈ·/ *n tech* a hot star, near the end of its life, more solid but less bright than the sun —compare RED GIANT

white el·e·phant /ˌ· ˈ···/ *n* a usu. big object not useful to its owner, though perhaps having cost money, or been given as a present, which the owner wants to get rid of

white en·sign /ˌ· ˈ··/ *n* the flag used by the British navy —compare RED ENSIGN

white feath·er /ˌ· ˈ··/ *n* [C; *the*+R] (a sign of) unwillingness to fight; lack of courage: *Don't show the white feather; fight for your beliefs*

white flag /ˌ· ˈ·/ *n* a sign that one accepts defeat (SURRENDERs): *They walked towards the enemy waving the white flag*

White·hall /ˈwaɪthɔːl, ˌwaɪtˈhɔːl/ *n* **1** [R] the street (near) where British government offices stand in London **2** [GU] the British government itself (esp. the government departments rather than the members of Parliament): *What action has/have Whitehall taken on this matter?*

white heat /ˌ· ˈ·/ *n* [U] the temperature at which a metal turns white, usu. after being red (when it becomes **white-hot** instead of **red-hot**)

white hope /ˌ· ˈ·/ *n* [C9 *usu. sing.*] the person who one expects will bring great success: *our great white hope for the future*

white horse /ˌ· ˈ·/ also **white-cap** /ˈwaɪtkæp/— *n* [*usu. pl.*] *esp. lit* a type of wave on the sea with a white top

White House /ˈ· ·/ *n* [*the*+R] the official home (in Washington) of the President of the United States

white hunt·er /ˌ· ˈ··/ *n* a white man who is paid to lead and advise a group of people hunting for animals in Africa

white lead /ˌwaɪt ˈled/ *n* [U] a compound of lead with CARBON and oxygen, formerly part of the old type of house paint, but no longer used because poisonous, esp. to young children

white lie /ˌ· ˈ·/ *n* a lie told so as not to hurt someone else, and therefore not thought of as a bad action

white-liv·ered /ˌ· ˈ··◂‖ˈ· ˌ··/ *adj* cowardly; LILY-LIVERED

white ma·gic /ˌ· ˈ··/ *n* [U] magic used for good purposes, to make good things happen, to cure diseases, etc.

white man /ˈ· ·/ *n* [C; (*the* + R)] a member of the race which has a pale skin, with little colouring matter in it, esp. one of the Europeans who took control of non-European countries

white meat /ˈ· ·/ *n* [U] **1** the very pale-coloured meat from those parts of a cooked bird which are nicest to eat, such as the breast of a chicken **2** certain types of pale-coloured meat (VEAL and PORK) —compare RED MEAT

white met·al /ˌ· ˈ··/ also **white alloy** /ˌ· ˈ··/— *n* [U; C] any silvery-coloured mixture of metals, containing tin

whit·en /ˈwaɪtn/ *v* [T1;IØ] to (cause to) become (more) white: *I must whiten my tennis shoes*

whit·en·ing /ˈwaɪtənɪŋ/ also **whiting**— *n* [U] white material, powder or liquid, which is used for giving a clean white colour: *to put whitening on tennis shoes*

White Pa·per /ˌ· ˈ··/ *n* an official report from the British government on a certain subject: *a government White Paper on education*

white pep·per /ˌ· ˈ··/ *n* [U] a type of PEPPER[1] (1a) made from crushed seeds from which the dark outer covering has been removed

whites /waɪts/ *n* [P] white clothing, esp. as worn for sports, such as long white trousers used in cricket

white sauce /ˌ· ˈ·‖ˈ· ·/ *n* [U] a thick white liquid cooked with flour, poured over certain types of food

white slav·e·ry /ˌ· ˈ···/ *n* [U] the action or business of taking girls to a foreign country and forcing them to be PROSTITUTEs (**white slaves**) there

white spir·it /ˌ· ˈ··/ *n* [U] *esp. BrE* a strong liquid made from petrol, used for making paint thinner and for removing marks on clothes

white·thorn /ˈwaɪtθɔːn‖-θɔrn/ *n* [C;U] HAWTHORN

white·throat /ˈwaɪtθrəʊt/ *n* any of several types of

small European bird with a pleasant song

white tie /ˌ· ˈ·◂/ *n* **1** [C] a small white tie (BOW TIE) worn by men at the neck, esp. for formal social occasions **2** [A;U] formal men's clothing for a social occasion: *a white-tie affair|to wear white tie and* TAILS —compare BLACK TIE

white·wash[1] /ˈwaɪtwɒʃ‖-wɔʃ, -wɑʃ/ *n* **1** [U] a white liquid mixture made from lime, used for covering walls and other parts of a house **2** [C;U] an attempt to hide something wrong: *That whole affair was a whitewash.|What he said was a load of whitewash*

whitewash[2] *v* [T1] **1** to cover with WHITEWASH[1] (1): *whitewashing the farm buildings* **2** to try to hide something wrong about (something or someone); make (what is bad) seem good: *The speech white-washed him so well I didn't believe a word of it*

whith·er /ˈwɪðəʳ/ *adv* [Wa5] *old use, poet, or humor* **1** to what place?: *Whither are you going?* **2** to which (place): *the place whither he went|"I joined the train at Crew, whither I went with Father and Julia by car"* (SEU W.) —compare WHENCE **3** (esp. in newspapers, political language, etc.; in titles, not in sentences) What is the likely future of?; where is (the stated person or thing) going?: *Whither France?|"Whither the movement?—into Space"* (SEU W.)

whi·ting[1] /ˈwaɪtɪŋ/ *n* **whiting** *or* **whitings** [Wn2;C] a type of sea fish used for food

whit·ing[2] *n* [U] WHITENING

whit·low /ˈwɪtləʊ/ *n* an infected piece of skin near a nail —see also HANGNAIL

Whit·sun /ˈwɪtsən/ also **Whit** /wɪt/— *n* [R] **1** also **Whit Sun·day** /ˌ· ˈ··/— the 7th Sunday after Easter **2** the public holiday or the whole week including and after this Sunday

Whit·sun·tide /ˈwɪtsəntaɪd/ *n* [R] WHITSUN (2)

whit·tle /ˈwɪtl/ *v* [T1 (DOWN, AWAY)] to cut (wood) to a smaller size by taking off small thin pieces: *whittling wood|whittling down a piece of wood|*(fig.) *Lack of sleep whittled his strength away* —**whittler** *n*

whiz, whizz /wɪz/ *v* **-zz-** [L9] *infml* to move very fast, often with a noisy sound: *She was whizzing down the road to the shop when she slipped and fell.|Cars were whizzing past*

whiz kid /ˈ· ·/ *n infml* a person who moves ahead in life and (esp.) in business very fast, because of clever ideas which succeed

who /huː/ *pron* [Wp2] **1** (*used in questions*) what person or people?: *Who's at the door?|Who will you take with you?|Who did you give it to?|"She's dancing." "Who with?"|Who are they?* **2** (*showing relationship*) that one (person)/those ones: *a man who wants to see you|a man* (*who*) *I know|"people who are living separate lives"* (SEU S.)*|the man* (*who*) *I sent it to* (compare *to whom I sent it*) **3** (*used esp. in written language, with* COMMAS) and/but he, she, etc.: *That man, who I may say I never met before, came to my party uninvited.|That's George's dog, who/which bit me* —see also WHOM

USAGE 1 **Who** is used as an object PRONOUN in *infml* English, except directly after a PREPOSITION: **Who** *did you see?|I wonder* **who** *he met?|I wonder* **who** *he's talking to*; but not **I wonder to* **who** *he's talking*. 2 When a word for a collection of people ([GU] or [GC]) is used with a pl. verb, use **who**: *a family* **who** *quarrel among themselves.* When it is used with a sing. verb, use **which**: *a family* **which** *has always lived here* —see THAT (USAGE)

WHO /ˌdʌbəljuː eɪtʃ ˈəʊ/ *abbrev. for*: the World Health Organization

whoa /wəʊ, həʊ/ *interj* (a call to a horse to) stop

who'd /huːd/ *contr. of* who had/would

who·dun·it /ˌhuːˈdʌnɪ̇t/ *n infml* a story, film, etc., about the mysteries of crimes, esp. concerned with finding out who was the criminal; a DETECTIVE story

who·ev·er /huːˈevəʳ/ *pron* **1** anybody that: *I'll take whoever wants to go.|"Could you get whoever it is to send them off?"* (SEU S.) **2** no matter who: *Whoever it is, I don't want to see them/him.|The business would be a success, whoever owned it* **3** *not fml* (*showing surprise*) WHO (1)?: *Whoever can that be knocking at the door?* —see EVER (USAGE)

whole[1] /həʊl/ *adj* [Wa5] **1** [B] not spoilt or divided: *a whole cake, not half of one|to swallow it whole* (= without breaking it up in the mouth/without CHEWing) **2** [A] not less than (a); all (the): *the whole day|the whole truth* **3** [B] *old use & bibl* healthy; HALE **4 swallow something whole** to accept something without thinking, esp. something that should be questioned

whole[2] *n* [*usu. sing.*] **1** [(of)] the complete amount, thing, etc.: *the whole of that area|We can't treat the group as a whole, but must pay attention to each member* **2** the sum of the parts: *2 halves make a whole* **3 as a whole** in general: *the country as a whole* **4 on the whole** generally; mostly: *On the whole, I like it*

whole-heart·ed /ˌ· ˈ··◂/ also **full-hearted**— *adj* with all one's ability, interest, sincerity, etc.: *whole-hearted attention/sympathy* —**~ly** *adv*

whole·meal /ˈhəʊlmiːl/ also *AmE* **whole wheat** /ˌ· ˈ·◂/— *adj* [Wa5;A] containing all the grain, from which flour is made; made without removing the covering of the grain: *wholemeal flour|wholemeal bread* (= a type of brown bread)

whole note /ˈ· ·/ *n AmE* SEMIBREVE

whole num·ber /ˌ· ˈ··/ *n* INTEGER

whole·sale[1] /ˈhəʊlseɪl/ *n* [U] the business of selling goods in large quantities, esp. to shopkeepers —compare RETAIL

wholesale[2] *adj, adv* [Wa5] **1** of or concerned in selling in large quantities or at the lower prices fixed for such sales: *They sell machines to the public wholesale* **2** in too large, unlimited numbers: *a wholesale rush from the burning cinema*

whole·sal·er /ˈhəʊlˌseɪləʳ/ *n* a businessman who sells WHOLESALE[2] goods

whole·some /ˈhəʊlsəm/ *adj* **1** good for the body: *Swimming is a wholesome pleasure.|wholesome food* **2** good in effect, esp. morally: *Such films are not wholesome for young children* —**~ness** *n* [U]

who'll /huːl/ *contr. of* who will

whol·ly /ˈhəʊl-li/ *adv* completely: *not wholly to blame for the accident*

whom /huːm/ *pron* [Wp2] (the object form of WHO, used esp. in writing and careful speech): *With whom?|the man with whom he talked|You saw whom?|Whom did they see?|the man* (*whom*) *they saw arriving|a man* (*whom*) *you may know of* —see THAT (USAGE)

whoop[1] /wuːp, huːp/ *v* [IØ] **1** to make a loud cry, as of joy **2 whoop it up** *infml* to enjoy oneself a lot

whoop[2] *n* **1** a loud shout (of joy) **2** a noisy breathless cough typical of WHOOPING COUGH

whoo·pee[1] /wʊˈpiː/ *interj* a cry of joy

whoop·ee[2] /ˈwʊpiː/ *n* **make whoopee** *infml* to go out enjoying oneself greatly

whoop·ing cough /ˈhuːpɪŋ kɒf‖-kɔf/ *n* [U] a disease, esp. caught by children, in which each attack of coughing is followed by a long noisy drawing in of the breath

whoosh /wʊʃ‖wuːʃ/ *n* [*usu. sing.*] a soft sound, as of air rushing out of something

whop[1] /wɒp‖wɑp/ *v* **-pp-** [T1] *sl* to beat or defeat

whop[2] *n AmE sl* a blow

whop·per /ˈwɒpəʳ‖ˈwɑ-/ *n infml* **1** a big thing: *Did you catch that fish? What a whopper!* **2** a big lie:

told a real whopper to excuse his lateness

whop·ping /ˈwɒpɪŋ‖ˈwɑ-/ *adj, adv* [Wa5;A] *infml* very (big): *a whopping (great) lie*

whore /hɔːʳ‖hor/ *n old use & bibl* a PROSTITUTE

who're /ˈhuːəʳ/ *contr. of* who are

whore·house /ˈhɔːhaʊs‖ˈhor-/ *n* **-houses** /ˌhaʊzɪ̈z/ *old use & bibl* a house of PROSTITUTE*s*; place or building where women provide sex for money

whore·mon·ger /ˈhɔːˌmʌŋgəʳ‖ˈhorˌmʌŋ-, -ˌmɑŋ-/ also **whore·mas·ter** /-ˌmɑːstəʳ‖-ˌmæ-/— *n old use & pomp* **1** a man who buys sex for money, esp. habitually **2** *derog* a man thought immoral in his sex life

whorl /wɜːl‖wɜrl/ *n* **1** a ring, esp. of leaves on a stem **2** the shape which a line makes when going round in a circle and continuing outward from the centre, not joining up, esp. on some fingers (a type of FINGERPRINT) or in the growth of some seashells

whor·tle·ber·ry /ˈwɜːtlˌberi‖ˈwɜr-/ *n* BILBERRY

who's /huːz/ *contr. of* **1** who is: *Who's he talking about?* **2** who has: *Who's he brought to dinner?* **3** who does?: *Who's he mean?*

whose /huːz/ *determiner, pron* [Wp2] **1** (*used in questions*) of or belonging to whom?: *Whose is this?|Whose house is this?|Whose shoes was he wearing?|I wonder whose we can* (not **whose can we*) *use.|I don't know whose to borrow* **2** (*used for showing relationship*) **a** of whom: *That's the man whose house was burned down.|"someone whose name he had forgotten"* (SEU S.) **b** of which: *That's the new machine whose parts are too small to be seen.|This factory, whose workers are all women, is closed for part of the school holidays*

USAGE Some people think it is bad English to use **whose** as in sense 2b

who·so·ev·er /ˌhuːsəʊˈevəʳ/ also **who·so** /ˈhuːsəʊ/— *pron old use* WHOEVER (1,2)

who've /huːv/ *contr. of* who have: *people who've been there|Who've you met?*

why¹ /waɪ/ *adv* [Wa5] for what reason?: *Why did you do it?|They asked him why he did it* (not **. . . why did he do it*)*.|Why didn't you stop him?|"Why risk breaking the law?"* (SEU W.)*|I can't think why she said that*

why² *conj* also **the reason why**— the reason(s) for which: *Is that why you did it?|Why he shot her isn't important.|I don't see why it shouldn't work*

why³ *interj* (expressing surprise): *I'm looking for my glasses; why, I was wearing them all the time!*

why not /ˌ· ˈ·/ *adv* [Wa5] (to suggest someone's doing something): *Why not make your dress, instead of buying it?*

whys /waɪz/ *n* **the whys and wherefores (of)** the reasons and explanation (for)

wick /wɪk/ *n* **1** a piece of twisted thread in a candle, which burns as the wax melts **2** a tubelike piece of material in an oil lamp which draws up oil while burning **3 get on someone's wick** *infml BrE* to annoy someone, esp. continually

wick·ed /ˈwɪkɪ̈d/ *adj* [Wa2] **1** very bad; evil: *wicked cruelty|a wicked man|*(fig.) *It's a wicked waste of money* **2** *infml, esp. old use* like a child behaving badly: *You wicked girl!* —**~ly** *adv* —**~ness** *n* [U]

USAGE This is a very strong word, for real moral evil. Noisy disobedient children are usually called not **wicked**, but **naughty**.

wick·er /ˈwɪkəʳ/ *n* [A] WICKERWORK: *a wicker basket*

wick·er·work /ˈwɪkəwɜːk‖ˈwɪkərwɜrk/ *n* [U;A] any example(s) of objects produced by weaving TWIG*s*, REED*s*, etc.: *a house full of wickerwork furniture|It's wickerwork, isn't it?*

wick·et /ˈwɪkɪ̈t/ *n* **1** (in cricket) **a** either of 2 sets of 3 sticks (STUMP*s*), with 2 small pieces of wood (BAIL*s*) on top, at which the ball is thrown (BOWL*ed*) **b** also **pitch**— the stretch of grass between these 2 sets —see CRICKET (USAGE) and picture **2** (in cricket) one turn of a player to hit the ball: *England have lost 3 wickets* (= 3 of their players are out)*.|Sussex won by 7 wickets* (= with 7 players left who have not completed, or yet started, their turn) **3** also **wicket gate** /ˈ·· ·/— a small gate or door which is part of a larger one **4 keep wicket** (in cricket) to act as a WICKET KEEPER

wicket keep·er /ˈ·· ˌ··/ *n* (in cricket) a player who stands behind the WICKET (1a) to catch the ball —see picture at CRICKET

wide¹ /waɪd/ *adj* [Wa1] **1** [B;E] large from side to side or edge to edge: *The skirt's too wide.|4 inches wide* **2** [B] covering a large space or range of things: *over the wide seas|wide interests* **3** [B] also **wide o·pen** /ˌ· ˈ··/— fully open: *wide eyes* **4** [B] (in sport) far from the right point: *a wide ball* **5** [B] *sl* clever in cheating: *a wide boy* **6 wide of the mark** not suitable, correct, etc., at all: *What he told me had happened was quite wide of the mark*

wide² *adv* **1** [(*of*)] (in sport) far away from the right point: *The ball went wide* (*of the field*) **2** completely (open), esp. the mouth: *open wide|wide open|*WIDE-EYED

wide³ *n* (in cricket) a ball that is thrown (BOWL*ed*) wide of the WICKET (1a)

wide-an·gle /ˌ· ˈ··◂/ *adj* [Wa1;A;(F)] (of the glass (LENS) in a camera) able to give a view of a wider angle than the ordinary

wide-a·wake /ˌ· ·ˈ·◂/ *adj* [Wa2] **1** fully awake **2** having or showing fully active senses; ALERT: *wide-awake ideas*

wide-eyed /ˌ· ˈ·◂/ *adj* [Wa2] with eyes fully open because of great surprise

wide·ly /ˈwaɪdli/ *adv* **1** over a wide space or range of things: *widely known|He is widely read|has read widely* (=many types of book) **2** to a large degree: *widely different*

wid·en /ˈwaɪdn/ *v* [T1] to make (wide or) wider: *to widen a road*

wide·spread /ˈwaɪdspred/ *adj* found, placed, etc., in many places: *a widespread disease*

wid·geon /ˈwɪdʒən/ *n* **widgeon** *or* **widgeons** [Wn2] a kind of duck which lives on freshwater lakes and pools

wid·ow /ˈwɪdəʊ/ *n* [C;(*old use*) A] a woman whose husband has died, and who has not married again

USAGE One can speak of a man's widow: *Margaret is John's* **widow**. If the woman dies first, one cannot say **John is Margaret's* **widower**, but only *John is a* **widower.**

wid·owed /ˈwɪdəʊd/ *adj* [Wa5] left alone after the death of one's husband/wife

wid·ow·er /ˈwɪdəʊəʳ/ *n* a man whose wife has died, and who has not married again —see WIDOW (USAGE)

wid·ow·hood /ˈwɪdəʊhʊd/ *n* [U] the state of being a WIDOW

width /wɪdθ/ *n* **1** [U;C] size from side to side: *What is its width?|We can't get the piano through the door because of its* (*great*) *width* **2** [C] a piece of material of the full width, as it was woven: *Half a width would do, but they won't cut it along the length of the cloth*

wield /wiːld/ *v* [T1] to control the action of: *to wield power|*(*old use & lit*) *to wield a weapon* —**~er** *n*

wife /waɪf/ *n* **wives** /waɪvz/ the woman to whom a man is married: *my/his/your wife* —see WOMAN (USAGE)—see TABLE OF FAMILY RELATIONSHIPS

wife·ly /ˈwaɪfli/ also **wife·like** /-laɪk/— *adj* having or showing the good qualities of a wife

wig /wɪg/ *n* an arrangement of false hair to make a covering for the head, to hide one's real hair or lack of hair: *The actress wore a black wig over her* BLOND *hair.*|*Judges wear wigs in court* —see also BIGWIG

wigged /wɪgd/ *adj* [Wa5] wearing a WIG

wig·ging /ˈwɪgɪŋ/ *n* [*usu. sing.*] *infml BrE* a severe scolding

wig·gle¹ /ˈwɪgəl/ *v* [T1;IØ] *not fml* to (cause to) move in small side to side, up and down, or turning movements: *to wiggle one's toes* —**-gler** *n*

wiggle² *n* a wiggling (WIGGLE¹) movement: *Her toes gave a wiggle*

wight /waɪt/ *n old use* a person

wig·wam /ˈwɪgwæm‖-wɑm/ *n* a tent of the type used by some North American Indians

wil·co /ˈwɪlkəʊ/ *interj* (used esp. on a 2-way radio, for saying that a message received has been understood and will be acted upon)

wild¹ /waɪld/ *adj* **1** [Wa5;B] usu. living in natural conditions and having natural qualities not produced by man, esp. (in animals) violence; not TAME or CULTIVATED: *a wild elephant*|*Some wild flowers are growing in a corner of the garden.*|*You may try to make a pet of a fox, but it's still a wild animal by nature* **2** [Wa1;B] (esp. of people and animals) **a** violent in behaviour; uncontrollable: *a wild dog* **b** not CIVILIZEd; SAVAGE: *wild tribes* **c** disordered in appearance or behaviour; *a wild party* **3** [Wa1;B] (of places) natural; without the presence of man, esp. because too cold, rocky, etc., to live in: *the wild hills* **4** [Wa1;B] (of natural forces) violent; strong: *a wild wind* **5** [Wa1;F;(A)] having or showing strong feelings, esp. of anger: *I felt so wild when she hit the baby* **6** [Wa1;B] having or showing lack of thought or control: *a wild idea*|*I'll make a wild guess* (= because I don't know any facts).|*a wild throw* **7** [Wa1;B] *infml* good; pleasing: *That was a really wild party last night!*|*That idea's really wild!* **8** [Wa1;F+*about*] having a great liking (for someone or something), often to an unreasonable degree: *wild about racing cars* —**~ness** *n* [U]

wild² *n* [*the*+R, *often pl.* (*of*) *with sing. meaning*] natural areas full of animals and plants, with few people: *The tiger escaped, driven by the call of the wild.*|*lost in the wilds* (*of an unknown country*)

wild³ *adv* **1** wildly **2 run wild** to behave as one likes, without control **3 go wild** to be filled with feeling, esp. anger or joy: *They went wild over his good looks*

wild boar /ˌ· ˈ·/ *n* a type of large fierce hairy European wild pig that is often hunted

wild·cat¹ /ˈwaɪldkæt/ *n* **1** a naturally wild type of cat looking like a pet cat, that is very fierce **2** a person who shows sudden violent bad temper

wildcat² *adj* [Wa5;A] **1** (in business) unlikely to succeed because of lack of thought; risky: *wildcat* SCHEMEs **2** (in industry) happening unofficially and unexpectedly: *wildcat* STRIKEs

wil·de·beest /ˈwɪldɨbiːst/ *n* **wildebeest** *or* **wildebeests** [Wn2] GNU

wil·der·ness /ˈwɪldənɨs‖-dər-/ *n* **1** [*the*+R] *old use & bibl* an area of land with little life, esp. a desert: *Jesus went out into the wilderness to think alone* **2** [C (*of*)] an unchanging stretch of land, water, etc., with no sign of human presence: *in a wilderness of houses*/(fig.) *pain*|*That garden's a wilderness* (= not controlled in growth) **3 in (to) the wilderness** (sent) out of political life, esp. for doing wrong

wild·fire /ˈwaɪldfaɪəʳ/ *n* **like wildfire** very fast: *The story spread*/*went round like wildfire*

wild·fowl /ˈwaɪldfaʊl/ *n* [P] birds that are shot for sport, esp. ones that live near water such as ducks

wild-goose chase /ˌ· ˈ· ·/ *n* (**lead someone**) **a wild-goose chase** (to cause someone) a useless search; MISLEAD someone

wild·life /ˈwaɪldlaɪf/ *n* [U] animals (and plants) which live and grow wild

wild·ly /ˈwaɪldli/ *adv* in a wild way: *He ran wildly down the street.*|*His answer was wildly wrong* (= very greatly)

wild oats /ˌ· ˈ·/ *n* **sow one's wild oats** to behave wildly (while young), esp. when expecting in the future to live a quiet ordinary life

wile a·way /waɪl/ *v adv* [T1] WHILE AWAY

wiles /waɪlz/ *n* [P] tricks; deceitful PERSUASION: *tricked by the salesman's wiles into buying worthless goods*

wil·ful, *AmE* **willful** /ˈwɪlfəl/ *adj* **1** [B] having or showing the intention of doing what one likes, in spite of other people: *a wilful child*|*wilful behaviour* **2** [A] done on purpose: *wilful misbehaviour* —**~ly** *adv* —**~ness** *n* [U]

wi·li·ness /ˈwaɪlinɨs/ *n* [U] the quality of being WILY

will¹ /wɪl/ *v* **would** /wʊd/, *3rd pers. sing.* **will**, *pres. t. neg. contr.* **won't** [Wv6;IØ,2] **1** (used for expressing the simple future tense): *They say that it will be good weather tomorrow.*|*If you study tomorrow, you will pass the examination next week.*|*They said it would be fine, but it rained.*|*If it came sooner, it would be better* **2 a** to be willing to: *I will come, when I can.* **b** (used for expressing a polite request or question): *Will you have some tea?*|*Will you telephone me this afternoon?* **c** (*with* STRESS¹ (4) *on* will *or* not) (used for expressing refusal to do or not to do): *No, I will* not*!* **3 a** is/are/proved or expected (to): *These things will happen.*|*Oil will float on water.*|*If people study, they will learn* (= If people study, they learn) **b** is/are suited to; has/have the power to: *This car will hold 6 people comfortably* **4** to be accustomed to: *Children will often be* (= usually are) *full of life when their parents are tired* **5** may likely (be): *The person you mentioned will be the father of the person with the same name, is that right?*|*This will be just what she wants.*|*That would be in 1967, I think* **6** *to have to* (*with* STRESS, *esp. as a command in the form of a question*): *Will you do as*/*what I say?*|*If you* will *go out without a coat, you'll naturally catch cold.*|*Shut the door, will you?* **7** (in special additions to statements): **a** (with *will* and *won't*): *You won't go there, will you?* (=I hope not)|*You'll go there, won't you?* (=I hope so) **b** (with statements related to orders): *Shut the door, will you!*|*Shut the door, won't you!*|*Have some tea, won't you?* —see also WOULD —see SHALL (USAGE)

will² *n* **1** [U;C] the power in the mind to choose one's actions: *Free will makes us able to choose our way of life* **2** [U;S] power to control one's mind and body: *His strong will makes him able to refuse all pleasures.*|*He did it by force of will* **3** [C;U,U3] intention or power to make things happen: *the will to live*|*She has such a strong will; she won't do what we say.*|*He didn't have the will to change* **4** [U9] what is wished or intended (by the stated person): *Her death is God's will.*|*to do God's will* **5** [S] force and interest (in the phr. **with a will**): *They set to work with a will* **6** [C] the wishes of a person in regard to sharing his property among other people after his death, esp. in an official written form: *Have you made your will yet* (= caused these wishes to be written down)? **7 at will** as one wishes **8 of one's own free will** according to one's own wishes, not those of someone else **9 where there's a will, there's a way** if you want to get or do something strongly enough you can find a way to get or do it

will³ *v* **1** [T1;I0] *old use* to wish (for/to be): *One of Shakespeare's plays is called "Twelfth Night or What you Will".|whether you will or no/not* **2** [T1,5,(5c); V3] to make or intend (to happen) esp. by power of the mind: *We willed him to stop, but he went past.|God has willed that the earth (should) turn once a day* **3** [D1 (*to*)] to leave (possessions or money) in a WILL² (6) to be given after one's death: *Grandfather willed me his watch* .

-willed /wɪld/ *comb. form* having a certain type or degree of will: *strong-willed*

wil·lies /ˈwɪliz/ *n* **give someone the willies** *infml* to cause fear in someone by being strange, dark, or lonely: *This place/that person/the way he speaks gives me the willies*

will·ing /ˈwɪlɪŋ/ *adj* **1** [B] eager: *a willing helper* **2** [F,F3,5c] ready; tending to favour: *Are you willing to help?|Are you willing that he (should) be allowed to join?* **3** [A] which is done or given gladly: *to give willing service* —**~ly** *adv* —**~ness** *n* [U,U3]

will-o'-the-wisp /ˌ· · · ˈ·/ *n* **1** a bluish moving light seen at night over wet ground because of the burning of waste gases from decayed plants **2** an undependable person or idea; aim that cannot be reached: *chasing the will-o'-the-wisp of perfection*

wil·low /ˈwɪləʊ/ *n* **1** [C] also **willow tree** /ˈ·· ·/— a type of tree which grows near water, with long thin branches —see picture at TREE¹ **2** [U] the wood from this tree

willow pat·tern /ˈ·· ˌ··/ *n* [U] a set of pictures with people, trees, water, etc., which represent a Chinese story and are put in blue on plates, cups, etc., in England

wil·low·y /ˈwɪləʊi/ *adj* pleasantly thin and graceful: *a willowy figure*

will·pow·er /ˈwɪlˌpaʊəʳ/ *n* [U] strength of WILL² (2): *She has a lot of willpower; she won't eat any cake, because she wants to be thin*

wil·ly-nil·ly /ˌwɪli ˈnɪli/ *adv* regardless of whether (generally) wanted, liked, etc., or not: *They introduced the new laws willy-nilly*

wilt¹ /wɪlt/ *v* **1** [T1;I0] **a** to cause (a plant) to become less fresh and start to die: *The heat wilted the flowers* **b** (of a plant) to become less fresh and start to die: *The flowers are wilting for lack of water* **2** [I0] (of a person) to become tired and weaker: *I'm wilting in this heat*

wilt² *v* [Wv2] **thou wilt** *old use or bibl* (when talking to one person) you will

wil·y /ˈwaɪli/ *adj* [Wa1] clever in tricks, esp. for getting what one wants: *a wily fox* —see also WILES —**wiliness** *n* [U]

wim·ple /ˈwɪmpəl/ *n* a covering of cloth over the head and arranged around the neck and face, formerly worn by women in the MIDDLE AGES, and now by some NUNs (=women living a life of religious work)

Wim·py /ˈwɪmpi/ *n BrE tdmk* a HAMBURGER

win¹ /wɪn/ *v* **won** /wʌn/, *pres. p.* **winning** **1** [Wv4; T1;I0] to be the best or first in (a struggle, competition, or race): *He won the race.|Who won?|Who won the war?|the winning team* **2** [T1] to gain (the stated place) in a competition or race: *I won first place.|They won a famous victory* **3** [T1] to be given (something) as the result of success in a competition, race, or game of chance: *He won a prize/cup/shield/£100* **4** [I0] to be right in a guess or argument: *The baby's a boy after all, so you win!* **5** [I0;T1] to guess successfully (the result of a race or game of chance), often so as to gain money (esp. in the phr. **win a bet**): *to win at cards* **6** [D1 (*for*);T1] to gain (for oneself) by effort or ability: *I can't win his friendship, though I've tried.|By her hard work she won a place for herself/won herself a place in the school team* **7** [T1] *fml or lit* to reach with effort: *They won the top of the mountain* **8 win hands down** to win easily **9 win the day** to succeed; have the victory —see also WIN THROUGH
USAGE One **wins** [T1] a **game**, a **war**, or a **prize**; after the event one can say [I0] *I've* **won**! One **beats** [T1] or **defeats** [T1] **people**; **defeat** is particularly used of enemies in war, and **beat** is the usual word for games: *The Americans* **defeated** *the British in 1781.|We* **beat** *their team by 10 points.* If one works for money or any other reward one **earns** [T1] it, and this word also carries the idea that one deserves what one has worked for: *He's* **earning** *£60 a week.|He's worked so hard that he's* **earned** (=he deserves) *a rest.* **Earn** is also used in the I0 pattern: *Her sons are both* **earning** (=being paid wages) *now.* To **gain** [T1] is to obtain (an advantage). This word is different from **earn**: **a** it is not used of money **b** one can **gain** things one does not deserve **c** one can **earn** (=deserve) things one does not actually receive: *to* **gain** *attention/knowledge/time/favour/*ADMISSION *to the university.* When there is an idea of successful competition, **win** or **earn** can be used instead of **gain**: *He* **won/gained/earned** *the admiration of the whole world by . . .*

win² *n* (esp. in sport) a victory or success: *3 wins and 2 defeats*

win back *v adv* [T1] to regain: *How can I win back the love she has given to this other man?*

wince¹ /wɪns/ *v* [I0 (*at*)] to move suddenly, (as if) drawing the body away from something unpleasant: *She winced as she touched the cold body.*|(fig.) *She winced* (MENTALly) *at his angry words* —compare JUMP, START¹ (8)

wince² *n* [S] a wincing (WINCE¹) movement

win·cey·ette /ˌwɪnsiˈet/ *n* [U] a fairly light material with a soft surface, used esp. for night clothes —compare FLANNELETTE

winch¹ /wɪntʃ/ *n* a machine for pulling up objects by means of a turning part —see picture at FREIGHTER

winch² *v* [X9 (UP, AWAY)] to pull by a WINCH¹: *winched the car out of the ditch*

wind¹ /wɪnd/ *n* **1** [U;C] strongly moving air: *high/strong/heavy winds* —compare BREEZE, AIR **2** [U] breath or breathing: *He couldn't get his wind* (= could not breathe properly, regularly) *after his run* —compare WINDPIPE **3** [U] (the condition of having) air or gas in the stomach, as when swallowed with food: *You get wind when you eat too quickly* **4** [U] *infml* words without meaning, or producers of them: *That speaker's a load of wind* **5** [*the*+GU] the group of WIND INSTRUMENT players in a band: *The wind is/are playing too loud* **6 break wind** *euph* to pass air or gas from the bowel **7 get wind of** *infml* to hear about, esp. accidentally or unofficially **8 (something) in the wind** (something secret) about to happen/being done **9 it's an ill wind (that blows no good/nobody any good)** even bad things may have some good results **10 put/get the wind up** *infml* to make/become afraid or anxious **11 raise the wind** to get needed money at once: *You could raise the wind by selling your stamp collection* **12 (sail/run) before the wind** *tech* (to sail) with the wind behind the ship **13 (sail) close to the wind** (to be) near to dishonesty or improper behaviour **14 second wind** **a** steady breathing regained during exercise which has at first made one breathless **b** ability to try hard again (esp. in the phr. **get one's second wind**) **15 see how the wind blows** to find out what is the general opinion **16 sound in wind and limb** healthy; not harmed in body **17 throw/fling something to the winds** to stop using some quality (esp. in the phr. **throw caution to the winds** (=to act without thought of the result, on

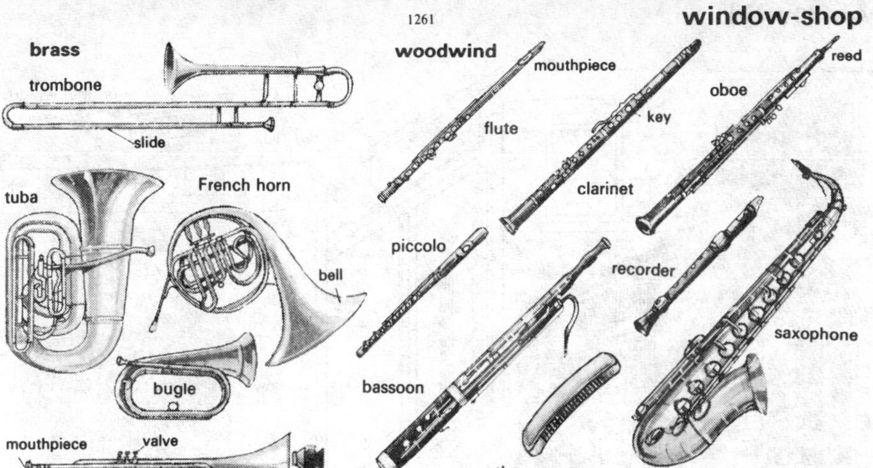

wind instruments

purpose) —see also **take the wind from/out of someone's** SAILS[1] (7)

wind² /wɪnd/ *v* [T1] **1** to cause to be breathless: *He hit him in the stomach and winded him* **2** to give (esp. a horse) time to breathe: *winded their animals at the top of the hill* **3** (esp. of HOUNDS) to smell the presence of: *to wind a fox*

wind³ /waɪnd/ *v* **winded** *or* **wound** /waʊnd/ *lit* to blow (a horn/a sound on a horn)

wind⁴ /waɪnd/ *v* **wound** /waʊnd/ **1** [T1] to turn round and round: *to wind the handle* **2** [T1] to make into a ball or twisted round shape: *to wind wool* **3** [L9] to follow a direction in a twisting shape: *The path winds through the woods* **4** [T1 (UP)] to tighten the working parts of by turning: *to wind a clock* **5** [X9] to move by turning a handle: *to wind a bucket from a well|wound down the car window* **6** [X9 esp. *round*] to place around several times: *to wind a cloth round the wounded arm|She wound the wool round the back of the chair* **7 wind one's way into someone's affections** to cause someone to like one, by cleverness **8 wind someone round one's little finger** to make someone do what one wants **9 wound up** very excited in mind, esp. worried, often expressing this by talking too much: *He thought he wasn't good enough to pass the examination, and got rather wound up about it* —see also WIND DOWN, WIND UP

wind⁵ /waɪnd/ *n* a bend or turn: *Give the handle a few more winds*

wind·bag /ˈwɪndbæg/ *n* [C; *you* + N] *infml* a person who talks too much, esp. about dull things —see also WIND[1] (4)

wind·break /ˈwɪndbreɪk/ *n* a fence, wall, line of trees, etc., intended to prevent the wind coming through with its full force

wind·cheat·er /ˈwɪndˌtʃiːtəʳ/ (*AmE* **wind·break·er** /-ˌbreɪkəʳ/)— *n BrE becoming rare* a short coat usu. fastened closely at wrists and neck, which is intended to keep out the wind —see also ANORAK, PARKA

wind down /waɪnd/ *v adv* **1** [I∅] (of a clock or watch) to work more slowly before at last stopping **2** [I∅] (of a person) to rest until calmer, after work or excitement **3** [T1] to cause to be no longer in operation, esp. gradually: *The company is winding down its business in Hong Kong* —compare WIND UP (1)

wind·fall /ˈwɪndfɔːl/ *n* **1** a piece of fruit blown down off a tree: *These apples are windfalls, but they're good* **2** an unexpected lucky gift, esp. money, from someone: *a windfall of £100 from a distant relative*

wind gauge /ˈwɪnd geɪdʒ/ *n* an instrument which measures the strength of the wind

wind·i·ly /ˈwɪndɨli/ *adv* see WINDY —**-ness** *n* [U]

wind·ing /ˈwaɪndɪŋ/ *adj* [Wa5] of a twisting turning shape: *a winding path|winding stairs* —see also WIND[4] (3)

winding sheet /ˈwaɪndɪŋ ʃiːt/ *n* SHROUD[1] (1)

wind in·stru·ment /ˈwɪnd ˌɪnstrʊmənt/ *n* any musical instrument played when air is being blown through it

wind·jam·mer /ˈwɪndˌdʒæməʳ/ *n* **1** a large sailing ship **2** WINDCHEATER

wind·lass /ˈwɪndləs/ *n* a machine for pulling or moving objects by means of a turning part, often with a handle —compare WINCH

wind·less /ˈwɪndləs/ *adj* [Wa5] without wind: *a windless sky, with no clouds moving|a windless day*

wind·mill /ˈwɪndˌmɪl/ *n* **1** a building containing a machine that crushes corn into flour and is driven by large sails which are turned round by the wind **2** *AmE* also **pinwheel**— a type of toy consisting of a stick with usu. 4 small curved pieces at the end which turn round when blown **3 tilt at windmills** to fight or argue unnecessarily against ideas or people imagined to be in opposition

win·dow /ˈwɪndəʊ/ *n* a space in a wall, esp. in a house, to let in light and air, esp. of glass which can be opened: *the front window|a car window*
See next page for picture

window box /ˈ·· ·/ *n* a box full of earth in which plants can be grown outside a window

window dress·ing /ˈ·· ˌ··/ *n* [U] **1** the art or practice of arranging goods in a shop window to give a good effect and attract people **2** material intended to attract people to an idea or activity: *This little book is the window dressing for his French course*

window en·ve·lope /ˈ·· ˌ···/ *n* an envelope with a transparent area on the front through which the address can be seen on the letter inside

win·dow·pane /ˈwɪndəʊpeɪn/ *n* one whole piece of glass in a window

window shade /ˈ·· ˌ·/ *n AmE* BLIND[3] (1)

window-shop /ˈ·· ·/ *v* **-pp-** [I∅] to look at the goods shown in (several) shop windows without necessarily intending to buy —**window shopper** *n* —**window shopping** *n* [U]: *to go window shopping*

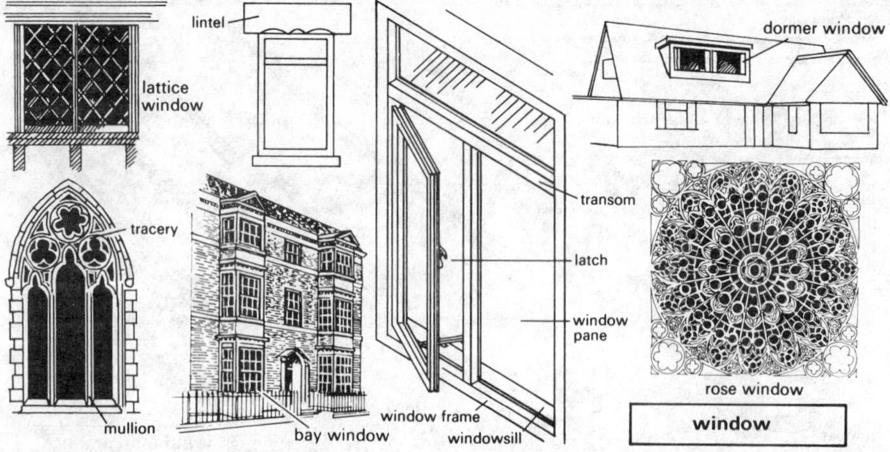

win·dow·sill /ˈwɪndəʊˌsɪl/ *n* the flat shelf formed by the wood or stone below a window, on the inside or outside

wind·pipe /ˈwɪndpaɪp/ *n* the tube which forms an air passage from the throat to the top of the lungs —see picture at RESPIRATORY

wind·screen /ˈwɪndskriːn/ *n BrE* the piece of glass or transparent material across the front of a car —see picture at CAR

windscreen wip·er /ˈ·· ˌ··/ also **wiper**— *n* one of the 2 movable arms which can be worked by machinery to clear rain from the WINDSCREEN of a car —see picture at CAR

wind·shield /ˈwɪndʃiːld/ *n* **1** the piece of transparent material fixed at the front of a motorcycle **2** *AmE* WINDSCREEN

wind·sock /ˈwɪndsɒk‖-sɑk/ also **wind·sleeve** /-sliːv/— *n* a piece of material, like a tube coming to a point at one end (a CONE), fastened to a pole at airports to show the direction of the wind by the way it blows

wind·storm /ˈwɪndstɔːm‖-ɔrm/ *n* a weather condition of high wind, with little rain

wind·swept /ˈwɪndswept/ *adj* **1** [Wa5] (of country) open to the wind, esp. where the soil can be blown off because there are no trees **2** (as if) blown into an untidy state: *a windswept appearance|She looked very windswept when she came in out of the storm*

wind tun·nel /ˈwɪnd ˌtʌnl/ *n* a manmade enclosed passage (TUNNEL) through which air is forced at fixed speeds to test aircraft and their parts

wind up /waɪnd/ *v adv* **1** [T1 (*with*)] to cause to be finished, on purpose: *to wind up the evening with a drink|to wind up a company* **2** [L4,7,9] *infml* to put oneself (in a certain state or place), accidentally: *He wound up feeling ashamed of himself.|He wound up drunk.|You'll wind up in hospital, if you drive so fast* —see also WIND⁴ (9), END UP

wind·ward¹ /ˈwɪndwəd‖-ərd/ *adv, adj* [Wa5] into or against the direction of the wind: *The strong wind held us against the windward side of the wall* —compare LEEWARD

windward² *n* [U] the direction from which the wind is blowing: *The wind was so strong we could not sail to windward*

wind·y /ˈwɪndi/ *adj* [Wa1] **1** with a lot of wind: *windy weather|a windy hillside* **2** *sl, esp. BrE* afraid —**windily** *adv* —**windiness** *n* [U]

wine¹ /waɪn/ *n* **1** [U;C] (any of many kinds of) alcoholic drink made from GRAPES: *a glass of wine|fine wine(s)|the wines of Alsace|my favourite wine* **2** [U9,(U);C9,(C)] (any of certain types of) alcoholic drink made from fruit, plants, etc.: *apple wine* **3** **wine, women, and song** gay enjoyment with drinking of alcohol, dancing, etc.

wine² *v* **wine and dine** to (cause to) have a meal and wine: *We wined and dined (them) until late into the night*

wine·bib·bing /ˈwaɪnˌbɪbɪŋ/ *n* [U] drinking (too much) wine —**winebibber** *n*

wine·glass /ˈwaɪnglɑːs‖-glæs/ *n* **1** a glass, usu. of a rounded shape with a stem and base, intended to hold wine **2** the amount that this holds

wine·press /ˈwaɪnpres/ *n* a container (VAT) in which the juice is pressed out of GRAPES, for making wine

wine·skin /ˈwaɪnˌskɪn/ *n* a bag made from an animal's skin, used for holding wine

wing¹ /wɪŋ/ *n* **1** one of the 2 feathered limbs by which a bird flies, or a transparent limb of flight on an insect —see pictures at BIRD and INSECT **2** one of the parts standing out from the side of a plane which support it in flight —see picture at AIRCRAFT **3** any part of an object or group which stands out from the side: *the west wing of the house* **4** a group of 3 SQUADRONS in an airforce **5** (in sport) the position or player on the far right or left of the field —see picture at SOCCER **6** a group in a political party who have more/less advanced opinions than the rest: *the right wing of the* LABOUR *party* (= those more like the CONSERVATIVES) **7** **on the wing** (of a bird) flying: *a bird on the wing* **8** **take wing**/(fig.) **take wings** to fly (away): *The bird took wing.|Time takes wings when you're enjoying yourself* **9** **under someone's wing** being protected, helped, etc., by someone: *to take the new member under one's wing* —**~less** *adj*

wing² *v* **1** [L9] to fly (as if) on wings **2** [Wv5;T1] to give wings to: *winged creatures* **3** [T1] to wound in the arm or wing

wing com·mand·er /ˈ· ·ˌ··/ *n* [C;A;N] an officer of middle rank in the Royal Air Force

wing·er /ˈwɪŋəʳ/ *n esp. BrE* (in games like football) a player in the area on the far left or right of the field —see also WING¹ (5)

-winger *comb. form* a person who belongs to the stated group (RIGHT WING or LEFT WING) in a political party

wing nut /ˈ· ·/ also **butterfly nut**— *n* a NUT¹ (2)

with sides which one can hold while turning it

wings /wɪŋz/ *n* [P] **1** the sign (BADGE) which a pilot can wear, to show he can fly an aircraft: *to get one's wings* **2** (either of) the sides of a stage, where an actor is hidden from view: *the right side of the wings* —see picture at THEATRE **3** speed (in the phrs. **give/lend wings to**): *Fear lent me wings* **4 in the wings** hidden and waiting for action

wing·span /ˈwɪŋspæn/ also **wing·spread** /-spred/— *n* the distance from the end of one wing to the end of the other, when both are stretched out

wink¹ /wɪŋk/ *v* **1** [IØ;(T1): (*at*)] to close and open (one eye) rapidly, usu. as a signal between people, esp. of amusement: *He winked at her, and she knew he was only pretending to be angry* **2** [X9] to remove by such a movement (a BLINK): *He winked something out of his eye* **3** [T1;IØ] *AmE* **blink**— *BrE* **a** to cause (a light) to flash on and off: *The driver's winking his lights; he's turning this way* **b** (of a light) to flash on and off: *A car's small lights on the right hand side wink when it turns right* **4** [IØ] *old use* to close one's eyes (in sleep)

wink² *n* **1** [C] a WINKing¹ movement: *with a wink of the eye|gave me a wink* **2** [S *nonassertive*] (used of sleep) a short time: *I didn't get a wink of sleep|sleep a wink* —see also FORTY WINKS **3 a nod's as good as a wink (to a blind man)** I understand the suggestion without words or signs being necessary **4 tip someone the wink** *infml* to give someone information or a sign about something: *tipped the wink to the police about a stolen car*

wink at *v prep* [T1] *fml becoming rare* to pretend not to notice (bad behaviour, qualities, etc.), suggesting approval: *To wink at rudeness in children is not sensible*

wink·ers /ˈwɪŋkəz‖-ərz/ (*AmE* **blinkers**)— *n* [P] *infml BrE* the small lights on a car which flash either on the right or left to show that it will move towards that direction

win·kle /ˈwɪŋkəl/ also **periwinkle**— *n* a type of small sea animal that lives in a shell and is eaten as food

winkle out *v adv* [T1 (*of*)] *infml* to get (information/a person) by force or hard work: *At last I winkled the truth out of him.|We'll winkle him out of there*

win·ner /ˈwɪnəʳ/ *n* **1** a person or animal that has won or is thought likely to win **2** something that is or is expected to be successful: *That idea's a real winner*

win·ning /ˈwɪnɪŋ/ *adj* [Wa5] which attract(s); which seem(s) to offer friendship: *winning ways|a winning smile*

win·nings /ˈwɪnɪŋz/ *n* [P] money which has been won in a game, by BETting on a (horse) race, etc.

win·now /ˈwɪnəʊ/ *v* [T1 (*from*)] **1** to blow the outer part (HUSKs) from (grain) **2** *bibl* to separate (the good from the bad)

win o·ver also **win round**— *v adv* [T1b (*to*)] to gain the support of (someone), often by persuading: *The thought of being alone in the winter won him over/round to the idea of staying with his daughter.|He disagrees, but we can win him round/over to our point of view*

win·some /ˈwɪnsəm/ *adj* nice-looking; attractive; bright: *a winsome appearance|a winsome girl* —**~ly** *adv* —**~ness** *n* [U]

win·ter¹ /ˈwɪntəʳ/ *n* [U;C] the season between autumn and spring when it is cold and most trees have lost their leaves: *I go on holiday in winter.|She'll be home by winter.|One winter we went to Switzerland.|a very cold winter|last winter|the last few winters|winter clothes*

winter² *v* [L9 esp. *in*] to spend the winter: *to winter in a warm country*

winter gar·den /ˈ·· ˌ··/ *n* an enclosed glass place where ornamental (esp. tropical) flowering plants are grown in winter, and where people may sit, esp. a large hotel room or separate public hall used for concerts and other amusements

win·ter·green /ˈwɪntəgriːn‖-ər-/ *n* [U] (a type of plant from North America producing) a strong-smelling oil which can be rubbed over sore muscles

winter sports /ˌ·· ˈ·/ *n* [P] sports which take place on snow or ice

win·ter·time /ˈwɪntətaɪm‖-ər-/ *n* [(*the*) U] *not fml* the winter season; the time of winter weather: *Heating bills are highest in (the) wintertime*

win through also **win out**— *v adv* [IØ] to succeed, esp. after some time or difficulties

win·try /ˈwɪntri/ also **win·ter·y** /ˈwɪntəri/— *adj* [Wa1] like winter, esp. cold or snowy: *wintry clouds|a wintry scene*

wipe¹ /waɪp/ *v* **1** [T1] to pass a cloth/other material against (something) to remove dirt, liquid, etc.: *Wipe your feet/shoes (on the mat).|Wipe your nose (on/with your handkerchief)* **2** [X9 esp. AWAY, OFF] to remove by doing this: *to wipe the tears away|Wipe the dirt off the table onto the floor* **3** [X7] to cause to be by doing this: *Wipe your face clean.|Wipe the floor dry* **4** [T1] *sl* to strike: *to wipe someone's face with a stick* **5 wipe the floor with someone** *infml* to make someone feel deeply ashamed, by severe scolding or by defeat in an argument

wipe² *n* a wiping (WIPE¹) movement: *Give your nose a good wipe*

wipe down *v adv* [T1] to clean (parts of a house) with a slightly wet cloth: *to wipe down the walls*

wipe off *v adv* [T1] to get rid of on purpose: *to wipe off a debt*

wipe out *v adv* [T1] **1** [*often pass.*] to destroy all of: *The enemy wiped out the whole nation* **2** to clean inside: *to wipe the bath out* **3** WIPE OFF

wip·er /ˈwaɪpəʳ/ *n* WINDSCREEN WIPER

wipe up *v adv* **1** [T1] to remove (liquid/dirt SPILLED or dropped) with a cloth **2** [T1;IØ] to dry (dishes, plates, etc., that have been washed) with a cloth

wire¹ /waɪəʳ/ *n* **1** [C;U] (a piece of) thin metal like a thread **2** [C] *infml, esp. AmE* a telegram **3 live wire** an active forceful person who is full of new ideas —see also LIVE² (4) **4 pull wires** —see **pull** STRINGS

wire² *v* **1** [T1] to connect up wires in (something), esp. in an electrical system: *to wire a house|to re-wire it* **2** [T1 (*to*/TOGETHER)] to fasten with wire(s) **3** [D1 (*to*), 5;T1] to send a telegram to: *He wired me (about) the results of the examination.|He wired me that I had passed.|Wire her to come home*

wire·cut·ters /ˈwaɪəˌkʌtəz‖ˈwaɪərˌkʌtərz/ *n* [P] a pair of moving parts forming a tool for cutting through wire —see PAIR (USAGE)

wire-haired /ˌ· ˈ·◂‖ˈ· ·/ *adj* [Wa5] (of certain types of dog) having stiff smooth hair, not soft or wool-like: *a wire-haired* TERRIER

wire in *v adv* [IØ (*to*)] *BrE infml, now rare* to start working hard: *They wired into the work.|Wire in, everybody, don't stand watching!*

wire·less¹ /ˈwaɪələs‖ˈwaɪər-/ *adj* [Wa5;A] *tech* without (using) wires; connected with radio

wireless² *n esp. BrE, becoming rare* **1** [U] the means of sending messages in sound, esp. across long distances, by radio waves around the earth **2** [C] also **wireless set** /ˈ·· ·/— a small machine for receiving sound broadcasting **3** [*the*+R] the means of information, amusement, etc., which radio broadcasts represent (esp. in the phr. **on the wireless**) —see also RADIO

wire net·ting /ˌ· ˈ··/ *n* [U] a material made of wires woven together into a network, with quite large spaces between them

wire·tap /ˈwaɪətæp‖-ər-/ *v* **-pp-** [I∅] *esp. AmE* to TAP telephone lines

wire-tap·ping /ˈ· ˌ··/ *n* [U] the skill or practice of listening to telephone messages by an unofficial connection —see also TAP[2] (4,5)

wire wool /ˌ· ˈ·/ *n* [U] a very fine sort of wire woven together and arranged in a sort of flat round solid piece (SCOURER) which is used for cleaning pans —compare STEEL WOOL

wire·worm /ˈwaɪəwɜːm‖ˈwaɪərwɜrm/ *n* any of several types of wormlike creatures, which are the young of insects, and destroy plants by eating them

wir·ing /ˈwaɪərɪŋ/ *n* [(*the*) U] the arrangement or quality of the wired electrical system in a building: *good wiring|old wiring*

wir·y /ˈwaɪəri/ *adj* [Wa1] rather thin, with strong muscles: *a wiry body* —**wiriness** *n* [U]

wis·dom /ˈwɪzdəm/ *n* [U] the quality of being wise

wisdom tooth /ˈ·· ·/ *n* one of the 4 large back teeth in man, which do not usu. appear until the rest of the body has stopped growing —see picture at TOOTH

wise[1] /waɪz/ *n* [S] *old use* way; manner (usu. in the phrs. **in this/no wise**)

wise[2] *adj* [Wa1] *usu. fml & polite* **1** having or showing good sense, cleverness, the ability to understand what happens and decide on the right action: *a wise man/decision|It was wise of you to leave when you did* **2 get wise to** *infml* to learn to understand the tricks of: *I've got wise to him and his game* (=cheating) **3 none the wiser** knowing no more, after being told **4 put someone wise** to inform someone properly, esp. when formerly wrongly informed **5 wise after the event** seeing what should have been done to prevent what has now happened: *If we hadn't bought the car we would have had enough money to repair the house. Well, it's easy to be wise after the event* —**~ly** *adv*

USAGE **Sensible** is the usual word in speech

-wise *comb. form* [*n*→*adv, adj*] **1** in the manner of: CRAB*wise* **2** in the position or direction of: *lengthwise* (LENGTHWAYS)|CLOCKWISE **3** in connection with; with regard to: *taxwise*

USAGE Many new adverbs are formed by adding **-wise** to nouns, with the meaning "in connection with", although some people think this is bad English: *taxwise|saleswise|moneywise|cricketwise.*

wise·crack /ˈwaɪzkræk/ *v, n* [T1;C] *infml* (to make) a joking remark or reply

wise guy /ˈ· ·/ also [C] **wise·a·cre** /ˈwaɪzˌeɪkəʳ/— *n* [N;C] *infml* a person who thinks he can supply information which shows he knows more than others, but which is in fact no use

wise up *v adv* [T1;I∅] *infml, esp. AmE* to (cause to) learn the right information (esp. in the phr. **get wised up**)

wish[1] /wɪʃ/ *v* **1** [Wv6;T5a,c] to want (what is at present impossible): *I wish we had a cat.|I wish I were a bird* **2** [I∅ (*for*)] to want and try to cause a particular thing, esp. when it can come only by magic, expressed in a special way or silently: *Go to the well and wish, and perhaps your desire will come true.|You have all you could wish for* **3** [Wv6;X7,9] to want (something or someone) to be: *We wished the work complete, but it wasn't.|We wished her anywhere except in our house!* **4** [D1 (*to*)] to hope that (someone) has (something), esp. expressed as a greeting: *We wish you a merry Christmas/good luck* **5** [Wv6;T3;V3;I∅; (*fml*) T1] *polite* to want: *Do you wish to eat alone?|Do you wish me to come back later? I will if you wish/(fml) if you wish it* **6 wish someone joy of it/him/etc.** (used when someone has chosen the wrong thing or person) to hope that someone will enjoy it/him/etc., more than one expects —see also **wish someone** FURTHER[1] (6)

USAGE In *BrE* it is rather *fml* to use *were* after **wish** in sentences like *I* **wish** *I were a cat*; but Americans would think it very bad English to use *was* in this sentence. —see HOPE (USAGE)

wish[2] *n* **1** [C,C3] a feeling of wanting, esp. what at present is impossible: *a wish to see the world|a wish to be alone|a wish for peace* **2** [C] a want for and attempt to make a particular thing happen, esp. when it can only come by magic, expressed in a special way or silently (esp. in the phr. **make a wish**) **3** [C9] what is wished for: *his last wish* (=before death)

wish·bone /ˈwɪʃbəʊn/ *n* a V-shaped bone in a cooked chicken or other farm bird, the ends of which are pulled apart by 2 people while they make a wish

wishful think·ing /ˌ·· ˈ··/ *n* [U] acting as though something is true or will happen because one would like it to be

wish on also (*fml*) **wish up·on**— *v prep* [D1] **1** [*usu. nonassertive*] to hope that (someone else) should have (something or someone): *She's a difficult person; I wouldn't wish her on my worst enemy* **2** to give, pass on, or leave (someone or something unwanted) to (someone else) because it suits one's own convenience: *She's wished her 2 children on me for the day, while she goes for a trip to London*

wish·y-wash·y /ˈwɪʃi ˌwɒʃi‖-ˌwɔʃi, -ˌwɑʃi/ *adj* [Wa1] without strength; weak: *wishy-washy tea*

wisp /wɪsp/ *n* [(*of*)] **1** a small twisted bunch (of HAY) **2** a small separate untidy piece: *a wisp of hair|wisps of grass* **3** a small thin twisting bit (of smoke or steam)

wisp·y /ˈwɪspi/ *adj* [Wa1] in a WISP or wisps; thin: *a wispy piece of grass*

wis·te·ri·a /wɪˈstɪəriə/ *n* [U;C] any of several kinds of climbing plant with purple or white flowers

wist·ful /ˈwɪstfəl/ *adj* having or showing a wish which may not be satisfied, or thoughts of past happiness which may not return —**~ly** *adv* —**~ness** *n* [U]

wit[1] /wɪt/ *v* **to wit** *usu. fml or tech, esp. law* that is (to say)

wit[2] *n* **1** [U *usu. pl. with sing. meaning*] power of thought; INTELLIGENCE: *He hadn't the wit to say no* **2** [U] the ability to make clever connections in the mind and express them well: *He had the wit to see the weak point in his opponent's argument at once* **3** [U] the ability to say things which are both clever and amusing at the same time: *conversation full of wit* **4** [C] a person who can do this: *As a wit, he is a popular after-dinner speaker* **5 at one's wits' end** made too worried by difficulties to know what to do next **6 have/keep one's wits about one** to be ready to act sensibly according to what may happen **7 live by one's wits** to gain what one needs by clever tricks rather than by work —see also WITTY

witch /wɪtʃ/ *n* **1** a woman who has, or is believed to have, magic powers, esp. who can CAST SPELLS on people (= make something bad happen to them, like an illness or accident) —compare WARLOCK, WIZARD **2** a woman who seems to have unusual power in attracting men —see also BEWITCH

witch·craft /ˈwɪtʃkrɑːft‖-kræft/ *n* [U] the practice of magic to make things (esp. bad things) happen

witch·doc·tor /ˈwɪtʃˌdɒktəʳ‖-ˌdɑk-/ *n* a man in an undeveloped society who is believed to have magical powers; MEDICINE MAN

witch·e·ry /ˈwɪtʃəri/ *n* [U] **1** charm; (exercise of) the power to attract **2** WITCHCRAFT

witch-ha·zel, wych-hazel /'· ,··/ *n* **1** [C] a type of tree which produces a liquid used for treating skin damaged by a blow **2** [U] the liquid produced

witch-hunt /'· ·/ *n* **1** (in former times) an act of searching out WITCHes[1] to kill them **2** a search for people with disliked political views, so that they may be removed from power —**witch-hunting** *n* [U]

witch·ing /'wɪtʃɪŋ/ *adj* **1** [Wa5;A] suited to WITCHes[1] (esp. in the phr. **the witching hour**) **2** [B] charming; BEWITCHing: *her witching ways*

with /wɪð, wɪθ/ *prep* **1** in the presence of; beside, near, among, or including: *staying with a friend|living with one's children|A man walked down the road with his dog.|He acted with a Shakespeare company.|It cost 3 pounds with wine.|Mix the flour with some milk.|He fought with the American navy during the war* **2** having, possessing, or showing: *a book with a green cover|a child with a dirty face|The man with the big dog came in.|She came in with a smile.|They fought with courage.|a factory with its chimney smoking* —opposite **without** **3** by means of: *to fight with a sword|to eat with a spoon|to hear with one's ears|I succeeded, with his advice.|Cut it with the scissors.|He was killed with an arrow* (= someone killed him; compare *He was killed by an enemy*).*|What will you buy with the money?* —opposite **without** **4** having as material or contents: *I filled it with sugar.|It was covered with dirt.|a cake made with eggs* **5** in support of; in favour of: *to vote with the government|The whole country is with the queen.|I agree with every word.|You're either with me or against me* **6** against: *Stop fighting with your brother.|Have a race with me.|to compete with foreign businesses* **7** in the same direction as: *to sail with the wind|carried along with the crowd* **8** at the same time (and rate) as: *With the dark nights comes the bad weather.|Her hair became grey with the passing of the years.|His earnings increased with his power* **9** equally by comparison to: *to compare chalk with cheese|to match a coat with a skirt|level with the street* —see also GO WITH **10** (separate) from: *to part with money|to break with the past/one's family* **11** in spite of: *With all your advantages, you are not a success.|With the best will* (= intention) *in the world, I can't make her like me* **12 a** because of: *singing with joy|grass wet with rain|eyes bright with excitement* **b** because of having: *With 3 children we can't afford new furniture.|With winter coming on, it's time to buy warm clothes.|I can't go out with all these dishes to wash!|With John away, we've got more room* **13** in the care of: *Your secret is safe with me.|Leave your little dog with me while you go on holiday.|to trust someone with a secret* **14** concerning; in the case of: *Be careful with that glass.|Be gentle with the baby.|There's a difficulty with this new timetable.|at peace with|in love with|patient with|What's wrong/the matter with you?* —see also BEAR WITH **15** (joined) to: *combine with|mix with|connect with* **16** (as a command) (esp. in the phr. **Down with** = Let's remove, destroy, etc.): *Down with school!|Off to bed with you!|Away with old ideas!|On with the dance!* **17** to be chosen by: *The decision is/rests with you* **18 in with** a friend of (a person or group), often one with bad habits: *She's in with/fallen in with some wild young people* **19 with it** *sl* dressing, thinking, behaving, or being in the most modern way **20 with me/you** *usu. nonassertive* following my/your argument: *Are you still with me?|I'm not with you; you go too fast* —see also WHAT[3] (2) **with**

USAGE *William was shot* **by** *the arrow* means the same as *The arrow shot William. William was shot* **with** *the arrow* **by** *Frederick* means the same as *Frederick shot William* **with** (=by means of) *the arrow*

with·al[1] /wɪ'ðɔːl/ *adv old use* besides; together with this

withal[2] *prep* [*usu. nonassertive*] *old use* (always used at the end of a CLAUSE) with: *He had nothing to feed himself withal*

with·draw /wɪð'drɔː, wɪθ-/ *v* **-drew** /'druː/, **-drawn** /'drɔːn/ **1** [IØ] to move or turn oneself slightly out of a certain direction: *She withdrew against the wall as the car passed close by* **2** [T1 (*from*)] to take away or back: *to withdraw £5 from a bank account* **3** [T1;IØ: (*from*)] to (cause to) move away or back: *to withdraw the army|The army withdrew.|The 2 men withdrew from the room while the meeting voted for which should be chairman* **4** [T1;IØ (*from*)] to (cause to) not join in: *He withdrew his horse from the race.|He withdrew from the race* **5** [T1;IØ] to make (a remark) as if unsaid; TAKE BACK: *to withdraw a remark|I withdraw that point.|"Will you withdraw, sir?" "No"*

with·draw·al /wɪð'drɔːəl, wɪθ-/ *n* **1** [U] the act of WITHDRAWing or state of being withdrawn **2** [C] an example of this

withdrawal symp·tom /·'·· ,··/ *n* [*usu. pl.*] a painful feeling of lacking something (esp. drugs) which one has become used to having

with·drawn /wɪð'drɔːn, wɪθ-/ *adj* habitually quiet and for a time seeming concerned not with other people, but with one's own thoughts

withe /wɪθ/ *n* WITHY

with·er /'wɪðə^r/ *v* **1** [T1;IØ (AWAY): (UP)] **a** to cause (esp. a plant) to become reduced in size, colour, etc.: *The cold withered the leaves.|*(fig.) *withered hopes* **b** (esp. of a plant) to become reduced in size, colour, etc.: *The flowers withered in the cold* —compare WILT **2** [T1] to cause to be silent and/or uncertain (by an expression on the face or remark): *One look withered her opponent*

with·er·ing /'wɪðərɪŋ/ *adj* which WITHER(*s*) (2): *withering remarks* —**~ly** *adv*

with·ers /'wɪðəz‖-ərz/ *n* [P] the high part above a horse's shoulders —see picture at HORSE

with·hold /wɪð'həʊld, wɪθ-/ *v* **-held** /'held/ [T1 (*from*)] **1** to keep (back) on purpose: *to withhold the money* (*from the owners*)*|to withhold the information/someone's rights* **2** to say that one refuses: *I withhold my agreement*

with·in[1] /wɪ'ðɪn‖wɪ'ðɪn, wɪ'θɪn/ *adv* [Wa5] *old use* inside a place: *within and without|the sadness within* (= inside a person)*|"This Building To Be Sold. Enquire Within"* (on a notice)

within[2] *prep* **1** inside the limits of (esp. time or distance); not beyond or more than: *He'll arrive within an/the hour.|within shouting distance|*(fig.) *to keep within* (= not break) *the law|somebody within the organization* **2** *esp. old use & lit* inside (a place): *Within the walls of this house lies a secret* —opposite **outside** or (old use) **without** —see INSIDE (USAGE)

with·out[1] /wɪ'ðaʊt‖wɪ'ðaut, wɪ'θaʊt/ *adv, prep* **1 a** not having; lacking: *to go out without a coat|a night without sleep|We couldn't have done it without John* **b** (*with the* -ing *form*) not: *He left without telling me.|Can you wash it without breaking it?|"You can't move in Millom without everybody knowing"* (SEU S.) **2** *old use* outside: *without a city wall|The king waits without!* —opposite **within** **3 do/go (etc.) without (something)** to continue as usual in spite of the lack (of): *I can't go without sleep for 2 nights.|If there's no coffee we'll have to do without (it).|"He had got along without women for quite a long time"* (SEU W.) **4 without number** too many to be counted: *stars without number*

without[2] *conj AmE, esp. dial* UNLESS

with·stand /wɪð'stænd, wɪθ-/ *v* **-stood** /'stʊd/ [T1]

1 to oppose without yielding: *to withstand an attack* **2** to continue in good condition in spite of: *Children's furniture must withstand kicks and blows* —see also RESIST

with·y /ˈwɪði/ also **withe**— *n* a stick from a WILLOW tree, which bends easily and may be used for weaving into baskets

wit·less /ˈwɪtləs/ *adj* [Wa5] (as if) lacking in ability to think: *a witless idea* —**~ly** *adv* —**~ness** *n* [U]

wit·ness¹ /ˈwɪtnɪ̈s/ *n* **1** [C (*of*)] also **eyewitness**— a person who is present when something happens: *a witness of the accident* **2** [C] a person who tells in a court of law what he saw happen or knows about someone **3** [C (*to*)] a person who is present at the making of and signs an official paper to show that he has seen the maker sign it: *a witness to the* WILL² (6) **4** [U] *fml* what is said about an event, person, etc., esp. in court (esp. in the phrs. **give witness, bear witness**): *He bore witness in the murder case* **5** [C (*to*)] a sign or proof (of) **6 bear witness to** to show or prove (a quality): *The success of the show bears witness to our good planning*

witness² *v* [T1] **1** to be present at the time of and notice: *We witnessed a strange change in her* **2** to be present as a WITNESS¹ (3) at the making of: *to witness the* WILL/*the signature* **3** to be a sign of: *His tears witnessed the shame he felt*

witness box /ˈ·· ·/ *AmE* usu. **witness stand** /ˈ·· ·/— *n* the raised area, enclosed at the sides, where witnesses stand in court when being questioned

witness to *v prep* **1** [T1,4] to tell and prove (what happened), esp. in a court of law: *to witness to the events of that evening|He witnessed to having seen the man enter the building* **2** [T1] WITNESS² (3)

-wit·ted /ˈwɪtɪ̈d/ *comb. form* having a certain type of mind or brain: *quick-witted*

wit·ti·cis·m /ˈwɪtɪ̈sɪzəm/ *n* a WITTY remark

wit·ting /ˈwɪtɪŋ/ *adj* [Wa5] *rare* done on purpose and with understanding —opposite **unwitting** —**~ly** *adv*

wit·ty /ˈwɪti/ *adj* [Wa1] having or showing a clever mind and amusing way of expressing thoughts: *a witty speaker|a witty remark* —**wittily** *adv* —**wittiness** *n* [U]

wives /waɪvz/ *pl. of* WIFE

wiz·ard /ˈwɪzəd‖-ərd/ *n* **1** (esp. in stories) a man who has magic powers, esp. to CAST SPELLs —see also WITCH **2** a person with unusual, almost magical, abilities of a certain kind: *He's a wizard at playing the piano*

wiz·ard·ry /ˈwɪzədri‖-ər-/ *n* [U] **1** the practice of magic **2** wonderful ability: *his football wizardry*

wiz·ened /ˈwɪzənd/ *adj* (as if) dried up, with lines in the skin: *wizened apples*

wk *written abbrev. for:* week

woad /wəʊd/ *n* [U] a blue colouring matter (DYE), esp. used in former times for colouring the body

wob·ble¹ /ˈwɒbəl‖ˈwɑ-/ *v* **1** [I∅] to move unsteadily from one direction to another: *The table's wobbling.|You're making the table wobble with your foot.|Her hand wobbled.|His voice wobbled when he sang* **2** [T1] to move (an object) in this way, esp. on purpose: *Don't wobble the table*

wobble² *n* a wobbling (WOBBLE¹) movement: *a wobble in her voice*

wob·bly /ˈwɒbli‖ˈwɑ-/ *adj* [Wa1] tending to WOBBLE¹: *wobbly handwriting*

woe /wəʊ/ *n* **1** [U] great sorrow: *a heart full of woe* **2** [C *usu. pl.*] a trouble: *she told him all her woes* **3 tale of woe** an experience of continued misfortune, told of by the one who suffered

woe·be·gone /ˈwəʊbɪgɒn‖-gɔn, -gɑn/ *adj* [Wa5] very sad in appearance

woe·ful /ˈwəʊfəl/ *adj* **1** very sad: *woeful eyes* **2** [Wa5] which makes one sorry, because it should not be: *a woeful lack of understanding* —**~ly** *adv*

wog /wɒg‖wɑg/ *n BrE taboo sl* a foreigner, esp. of a dark-skinned race

woke /wəʊk/ *past t. of* WAKE

wok·en /ˈwəʊkən/ *past p. of* WAKE

wold /wəʊld/ *n* [*often pl. with sing. meaning*] (*usu. cap. as part of a name*) an area of hilly open country: *the Yorkshire Wolds*

wolf¹ /wʊlf/ *n* **wolves** /wʊlvz/ **1** a type of wild animal of the dog family which hunts other animals in a group (PACK) —see picture at CARNIVOROUS **2** a man who charms women so as to use them for his own pleasure **3 cry wolf** to call for help unnecessarily, risking the possibility that a future real need will not be believed in **4 keep the wolf from the door** to earn enough to eat and live **5 a wolf in sheep's clothing** a person who seems harmless but is hiding the wish to hurt, take advantage, etc. —**~ish** *adj*

wolf² *v* [T1 (DOWN)] to eat quickly, in large amounts: *wolfed his meal*

wolf·hound /ˈwʊlfhaʊnd/ *n* a type of dog which is very large, originally used for hunting wolves (WOLF¹ (1))

wol·fram /ˈwʊlfrəm/ *n* [U] TUNGSTEN

wolfs·bane /ˈwʊlfsbeɪn/ *n* [U] a type of flowering plant related to the ACONITE

wolf whis·tle /ˈ· ˌ··/ *n* a way of whistling a high note followed by a falling note, which men sometimes use in the street to express admiration of the appearance of a woman who is passing

wom·an /ˈwʊmən/ *n* **women** /ˈwɪmɪ̈n/ **1** [C;(N)] a fully grown human female **2** [R] women in general: *Woman lives longer than man in most countries* **3** [C] a woman in employment in a house or who serves a queen: *The queen's women surrounded her* **4** [C; *the*+R] (a female person with) female nature or qualities, such as caring for weak creatures, personal attractiveness, and interest in people: *a man with something of a/the woman in him* **5** [A] female: *women workers* **6** [C9] a wife, lover, or woman with whom a man lives: *the woman in his life|the* SHEIKH *and all his women* **7 woman of the world** an experienced woman who knows how people behave

USAGE 1 Note the word order in this fixed phr.: **women and children**: *The women and children hid in the caves for safety* 2 A **woman** who is being married is called a **bride** during the actual marriage ceremony, and perhaps for a few weeks afterwards: *Here's George Philpotts and Mildred, his* **bride**. *Let's all kiss the* **bride**! After that, Mrs Philpotts is George Philpotts' **wife**. It is correct to call her a **woman**, but not **his* **woman** or **George Philpotts'* **woman**. —see LADY, PEOPLE (USAGE) —see also OLD WOMAN

wom·an·hood /ˈwʊmənhʊd/ *n* **1** [U] the condition or period of being a woman **2** [GU] *rare* all the women of a nation or the world, considered together as one body —see also MANHOOD

wom·an·ish /ˈwʊmənɪʃ/ *adj usu. derog* (of a man) like a woman in character, behaviour, appearance, etc.: *a womanish walk* —compare MANNISH, EFFEMINATE

wom·an·ize, -ise /ˈwʊmənaɪz/ *v* [I∅] (of men) to habitually spend time with many women, esp. in order to have a sexual relationship —**-izer** *n*

wom·an·kind /ˈwʊmənkaɪnd/ *n* [R] women considered together as one body —compare MANKIND

wom·an·ly /ˈwʊmənli/ *adj* having or showing the qualities suitable to a woman: *She showed a womanly concern for their health* —compare MANLY —**-liness** *n* [U]

womb /wuːm/ *n* the female sex organ of a MAMMAL

where her young can develop: (fig.) *the womb of time* (= the beginnings of history)

wom·bat /ˈwɒmbæt‖ˈwɑm-/ *n* a type of smallish animal of Australia with soft hair over a body shaped like a bear's, whose young live in a pocket of skin (POUCH) on its body

wom·en·folk /ˈwɪmɨnfəʊk/ *n* [P] **1** *infml* women **2** female relatives (of a man)

won /wʌn/ *past t. and past p. of* WIN

won·der[1] /ˈwʌndəʳ/ *n* **1** [U] a feeling of strangeness, surprise, etc., usu. combined with admiration and the wish to find out about the thing which excites this sensation: *filled with wonder at the sight of the great new aircraft* **2** [C] a wonderfully made object, perfect of its kind: *The temple of Diana and the hanging gardens of Babylon were 2 of 7 Wonders of the World in ancient times* **3** [C] a wonderful act or producer of such acts: (*infml*) *He's a wonder, the way he arranges everything all alone* **4 for a wonder** *becoming rare* surprisingly; unexpectedly **5 It's a wonder (that)** It's surprising: *It's a wonder you recognized me after all these years* **6 (It's) no wonder** naturally; of course: *It's no wonder you can't sleep when you eat so much* **7 work/do wonders** to bring unexpectedly good results: *He looked so tired before, but his holiday has worked wonders (in him)/done wonders (for him)*

wonder[2] *adj* [Wa5;A] *rare* which is unusually good of its kind: *the wonder horse|a wonder boy|wonder drugs*

wonder[3] *v* **1** [Wv4;IØ (*at*);T5a, (*nonassertive*) 6a (*if*)] to be surprised and want to know (why): *The men stood wondering before the ancient temple they'd discovered.|I wonder at his rudeness.|That the criminal was caught is not to be wondered at.|I wonder (that) he can come here after what happened.|"She left home." "I don't wonder, after the treatment she had* (= I find it natural)*."|I shouldn't wonder if he stayed in India* (= I rather expect him to) **2** [IØ (*about*);T6a,b] to express a wish to know, in words or silently: *"Does she know we're here?" "I'm just wondering."|I wonder what really happened.|I wonder who he is.|I was just wondering how to do it* **3** [IØ (*about*)] to suggest that it is not so; doubt: *Does she mean it? I wonder (about that)* —**~ingly** *adv*

USAGE To **wonder** is to ask oneself a question: *I* **wonder** *where . . . He* **wondered** *whether . . .* One can **wonder** *at* (=be very much surprised by) both good and bad things: *The country boy* **wondered** *at all the noisy traffic in the city.* One **admires** good things (=looks at them with pleasure and respect) without necessarily being surprised at them: *He* **admired** *the fine buildings, and the pretty girls in the streets.*

won·der·ful /ˈwʌndəfəl‖-dər-/ *adj* unusually good: *wonderful news* —**~ly** *adv*

won·der·land /ˈwʌndəlænd‖-ər-/ *n* **1** [R] fairyland **2** [C *usu. sing.*] a place which is unusually beautiful, rich, etc.

won·der·ment /ˈwʌndəmənt‖-dər-/ *n* [U] a feeling of surprise

won·ders /ˈwʌndəz‖-ərz/ *n* **wonders will never cease** (used for expressing surprise when the opposite of what one expects happens)

won·drous[1] /ˈwʌndrəs/ *adj poet* wonderful: *wondrous beauty*

wondrous[2] *adv poet* unusually; particularly: *wondrous rare*

won·ky /ˈwɒŋki‖ˈwɑŋki/ *adj* [Wa2] *BrE infml* not steady and likely to give way or fall: *a wonky table leg|wonky legs after being ill in bed*

wont[1] /wəʊnt‖wont/ *adj* [Wa5;F3] *becoming rare* likely or accustomed (to happen): *He is wont to arrive unexpectedly* —compare WONTED

wont[2] /wəʊnt‖wont/ *n* [S9] *fml* (the stated person's) habit or custom: *He spoke for too long, as is his wont*

won't /wəʊnt/ [Wv2] *contr. of* will not —see CONTR. (USAGE)

wont·ed /ˈwəʊntɨd‖ˈwon-/ *adj* [Wa5;A] *rare* customary: *He took his wonted walk round the park* —compare WONT[1]

woo /wuː/ *v* [T1] **1** *esp. old use* (of a man) to try to persuade (a woman) into love and marriage **2** to make efforts to gain (the support of): *to woo the voters before an election* —**~er** *n*

wood[1] /wʊd/ *n* **1** [U] the material of which trunks and branches of trees are made, which is cut and dried in various forms for making material for burning, for making paper or furniture, etc.: *Put some more wood on the fire* **2** [C *often pl. with sing. meaning*] a place where trees grow, smaller than a forest: *We went for a ride in the wood(s)* **3** [*the*+R] one or more barrels (in the phrs. **in/from the wood**): SHERRY *from the wood* (=not from bottles) **4** [C] one of the set of 4 GOLF CLUBs with wooden heads used for driving a ball long distances —compare IRON[1] (5) **5** [*the*+R] the wooden part of a tool, weapon, etc. **6 can't see the wood for the trees** missing what's clear by looking too closely **7 out of the wood** free from danger, difficulty, etc.

wood[2] *adj* [Wa5] WOODEN: *a wood chair*

wood al·co·hol /ˌ· ˈ···/ *n* METHYL ALCOHOL

wood·bine /ˈwʊdbaɪn/ *n* [U] **1** a type of HONEYSUCKLE, esp. the common European one **2** *AmE* VIRGINIA CREEPER

wood·block /ˈwʊdblɒk‖-blɑk/ *n* **1** a piece of wood with a shape cut on it for printing **2** a block of wood used in making the floor of a room (sometimes in a pattern)

wood·cock /ˈwʊdkɒk‖-kɑk/ *n* [Wn2] a type of brown woodland bird with a long thin beak, sometimes shot for food

wood·craft /ˈwʊdkrɑːft‖-kræft/ *n* [U] the skill of finding one's way in wooded country

wood·cut /ˈwʊdkʌt/ *n* **1** a picture or print which has been made by pressing down the shaped surface of a piece of wood on colouring matter (DYE) and then onto material or paper **2** WOODBLOCK (1)

wood·cut·ter /ˈwʊdˌkʌtəʳ/ *n* (esp. in fairy stories) a man whose job is to cut down trees in a forest

wood·ed /ˈwʊdɨd/ *adj* [Wa5] having woods; covered with growing trees: *wooded hills*

wood·en /ˈwʊdn/ *adj* **1** [Wa5] made of wood: *a wooden bed* **2** stiff; unbending: *wooden movements* —**~ly** *adv* —**~ness** *n* [U]

wood·en·head·ed /ˌwʊdnˈhedɨd◂/ *adj* stupid; unable to understand and therefore to act right

wooden spoon /ˌ·· ˈ·/ *n* [*the*+R;(C)] *BrE infml* an imaginary prize supposed to be given to the person or team that finishes last in a sports competition

wood·land /ˈwʊdlənd, -lænd/ *n* [U *often pl. with sing. meaning*] wooded country; area of land covered with growing trees: *large areas of woodland|birds of the woodland(s)|woodland birds*

wood·louse /ˈwʊdlaʊs/ *n* **-lice** /laɪs/ a type of very small insect-like animal with 14 legs which lives under wood, stones, etc. —see picture at CRUSTACEAN

wood·peck·er /ˈwʊdˌpekəʳ/ *n* any of several types of bird with a long beak, which can make holes in the wood of trees and pull out insects —see picture at BIRD

wood·pile /ˈwʊdpaɪl/ *n* **nigger in the woodpile** the part or person that causes difficulty

wood pulp /ˈ· ·/ *n* [U] broken bits of the soft parts of wood, used for making paper

wood·shed /ˈwʊdʃed/ *n* a place for storing firewood, esp. near a house

woods·man /ˈwʊdzmən/ also (*becoming rare*) **wood·man** /ˈwʊdmən/— *n* **-men** /mən/ a man whose job is in a wood or forest, protecting and/or cutting down trees

wood·wind /ˈwʊdˌwɪnd/ *n* [(*the*) GU] (the players of) the set of instruments in an ORCHESTRA which are usu. made of wood and are played by blowing: *The woodwind is/are too loud*

wood·work /ˈwʊdwɜːk‖-wɜrk/ *n* [U] **1** the skill of making wooden objects, esp. furniture; CARPENTRY **2** the objects produced **3** *not fml* the parts of a house that are made of wood: *a mouse behind/in the woodwork*

wood·worm /ˈwʊdwɜːm‖-wɜrm/ *n* **1** [Wn2;C *usu. pl.*] the small soft wormlike young (LARVA) of certain BEETLE*s*, which makes holes in wood **2** [U] the condition in which damage is done by these creatures

wood·y /ˈwʊdi/ *adj* [Wa1] **1** of or with woods: *a woody valley* **2** of or like wood: *plants with woody stems*

woo·er /ˈwuːəʳ/ *n old use* a man who WOO*s* (a woman): *her wooer*

woof¹ /wuːf‖wʊf, wuːf/ *n* [*the*+R] *tech* the threads which are woven across to make cloth using the WARP as a base

woof² /wʊf/ *n, interj infml* (a word used for describing the sound (BARK) made by a dog)

woof·er /ˈwuːfəʳ‖ˈwʊ-/ *n* an apparatus (LOUDSPEAKER) for giving out deep sounds

wool /wʊl/ *n* [U] **1** the soft thick type of hair which sheep and some goats have **2 a** material made up from this, or something like it, in the form of a long string: KNIT*ting wool*|*nylon* KNIT*ing wool*|ANGORA *wool* (from a special breed of goat) **b** material from sheep's wool woven into cloth: *a wool suit*|*This coat is wool* —see also WORSTED **3** soft material from plants, such as cotton before it is spun: *cotton wool* **4** *humor* a person's hair, esp. which is soft and stands out like wool **5 keep your wool on!** don't get angry! **6 pull the wool over someone's eyes** to trick someone or hide the facts from him —see also DYED-IN-THE-WOOL

wool·gath·er /ˈwʊlˌgæðəʳ/ *v* **be woolgathering** to be thinking of other things instead of what is being done, esp. when this leads to not hearing other people or doing things wrong

wool·gath·er·ing /ˈwʊlˌgæðərɪŋ/ *n* [U] the action of WOOLGATHERing

wool·len, *AmE* also **woolen** /ˈwʊlən/ *adj* [Wa5] **1** [B] made of wool: *a woollen coat* **2** [A] of materials made of wool: *woollen* MANUFACTURER*s*

wool·lens, *AmE* also **woolens** /ˈwʊlənz/ *n* [P] **1** garments made of wool, esp. KNITted —see also WOOLLY² **2** woollen cloth, esp. in large amounts

wool·ly¹ /ˈwʊli/ *adj* [Wa1] **1** of or like wool, esp. with a soft surface: *woolly socks* **2** (of thoughts) not clear in the mind: *His ideas are a bit woolly* —**-liness** *n* [U]

woolly² *n* [*usu. pl.*] *esp. infml* a garment made of wool, esp. KNITted: *winter woollies*

woolly-head·ed /ˌ·· ˈ··◂/ *adj* tending not to think clearly or have sensible ideas

wool·sack /ˈwʊlsæk/ *n* [*the*+R] the seat in the British Parliament on which the Lord CHANCELLOR sits in in the HOUSE OF LORDS

woo·zy /ˈwuːzi/ *adj* [Wa1] *infml* having an unsteady feeling in the head; DIZZY

wop /wɒp‖wɑp/ *n taboo derog* a foreigner, esp. an Italian or person with Italian-type looks

Worces·ter sauce /ˌwʊstə ˈsɔːs‖-tər-/ *n* [U] a dark strong-tasting liquid made from VINEGAR, SPICE*s*, and SOY, put on food to give an additional taste

word¹ /wɜːd‖wɜrd/ *n* **1** [C] one or more sounds which can be spoken (together) to represent an idea, object, action, etc.: *Tell me what happened in your own words.*|*Words fail me* (= I can't describe or answer that, esp. because of surprise or shock).|*Tired/angry/pleased isn't the word for the way I feel* (= the word doesn't describe the strength of feeling).|*I know the tune of the song, but I don't know the words* **2** [C] the written representation of this: *Can you read this word?*|*What does this word mean?* **3** [C] the shortest (type of) statement: *In a word, no.*|*I don't believe a word of it.*|*Don't say a word to anybody* **4** [C *often pl. with sing. meaning*] a short speech or conversation: *Can I have a few words with you?*|*a word with you?*|*a word in your ear* (= Let me give you some advice or information)|*We exchanged a few words.*|*a word of praise* **5** [U] a message or news (esp. in the phr. **send word** = in a letter): *Word came of his success abroad* **6** [*the*+R] the right word; PASSWORD: *He gave the word and they let him in* **7** [C *usu. sing.*] an order: *On the word of command/On his word they all moved forward* **8** [S9] a promise (esp. in the phrs. **give one's word, keep/break one's word to someone**): *I give you my word* (*of honour*) *I'll go.*|*I kept my word to her* **9** [C] a suggestion or RECOMMENDATION (esp. in the phrs. **put in/say a good word for someone**) **10 as good as one's word** true to one's promise **11 big words** BOASTing **12 eat one's words** to admit to having said something wrong **13 in other words** expressing the same thing in different words; which is the same as saying **14 (not) in so many words** (not) expressed with that meaning but only suggested: *"Did she say she liked him?" "Not in so many words,* (*but . . .*)*"* **15 (have) a word in someone's ear** *not fml* (to speak to someone) secretly, esp. giving advice or asking a question —see also MAN¹ (18) **of his word,** PLAY ON WORDS, **put words in(to) someone's** MOUTH¹ (7), **take the words out of someone's** MOUTH¹ (10), WORDS **16 (have) the last word (on)** (to make) the remark which finishes an argument or set of writings, speeches, etc.: *If I can have the last word on this subject, I'd just like to say . . .* **17 the last word in** the most recent development in **18 man of few words** a person who says very little **19 (upon) my word!** (an expression of surprise) **20 my word upon it** *old use* I promise that **21 not have a good word (to say) for** to be always expressing one's disapproval of **22 say the word** *infml* to give one's approval or a signal for something to be done or started **23 suit the action to the word** to do what one talked of doing: *As soon as she'd said it, she suited the action to the word and hit him as she'd threatened* **24 take someone at his word** to act on the belief that someone means what he said: *He says call in on him any time, but he doesn't expect you to take him at his word* **25 take someone's word for it** to accept what someone says as correct: *If you say there's no point going in because it's full, I'll take your word for it* **26 (get) a word in edgeways** *nonassertive* (to make) a remark made in spite of others who are speaking all the time: *He talks so much that no one else can get a word in edgeways*

word² *v* [X9;(T1)] to express in words: *He worded the explanation well*

word blind·ness /ˈ· ˌ··/ *n* [U] *not fml* DYSLEXIA

word for word /ˌ· · ˈ·◂/ *adv* **1** in the same words: *Tell me what she said, word for word* **2** also **word by word** /ˌ· · ˈ·◂/— giving a word in a foreign language for each word, rather than giving the meaning of whole phrases and sentences —**word-for-word** *adj* [Wa5]: *a word-for-word translation*

word·ing /ˈwɜːdɪŋ‖ˈwɜr-/ *n* [(*the*) S] the words chosen to express something and the phrases they form: *The wording of a business agreement should be exact*

word·less /ˈwɜːdləs‖ˈwɜrd-/ *adj* [Wa5] **1** [B] without using words: *Her look was a wordless question* **2** [A] unable to speak; speechless: *She looked at him in wordless disbelief* —**~ly** *adv* —**~ness** *n* [U]

word of mouth /ˌ·· ˈ·/ *n* [U] speech (as a means of making something known): *learnt the news by word of mouth*

word-per·fect /ˌ· ˈ··/ (*AmE* **letter-perfect**)— *adj* [Wa5] *BrE* having or showing correctness in repeating every word: *Her speech was word-perfect.*|*She was word-perfect in her speech*

word·play /ˈwɜːdpleɪ‖ˈwɜrd-/ *n* [U] joking about word meanings; PUNning

words /wɜːdz‖wɜrdz/ *n* **have words (with)** *euph* to argue angrily (with)

word·y /ˈwɜːdi‖ˈwɜrdi/ *adj* [Wa1] using or containing too many words: *a wordy explanation* —**wordily** *adv* —**wordiness** *n* [U]

wore /wɔːʳ‖wor/ *past t. of* WEAR

work¹ /wɜːk‖wɜrk/ *n* **1** [U] activity which uses effort, esp. with a special purpose, not for amusement: *It takes a lot of work to build a house* **2** [U not+*the*] (the nature or place of) a job or business: *My work is in medicine/as a doctor.*|*I go to work at 9.*|*What time do you get home from work?*|*I eat at work* **3** [U] what one is working on: *I hear you've changed jobs; is the work difficult at the new place?*|*I'm taking some work home to do this evening.*|*Don't stay inside to do your sewing; bring your work out with you* **4** [U] what is produced by work, esp. of the hands: *This mat is my own work* (= I made it).|*to sell one's work*|(fig.) *The broken window must be the work of that bad boy* **5** [U] *tech* force multiplied by distance **6** [C *usu. pl.*] a work of art; object produced by writing, painting, etc.: *Shakespeare's works include plays and poems* —see also WORKS **7 all in the day's work** as expected; which can be done; not unusual **8 at work (on)** doing something, esp. work: *Danger; men at work (on this road)* **9 go/set to work (on)** to start doing **10 have one's work cut out** to have something difficult to do, esp. in the time allowed **11 in work/out of work** having a job/unemployed **12 make hard work of** to find difficulties in (something not so difficult) **13 make short work of** to finish quickly and easily
USAGE This is a general word that can be used of activities of the mind and of the body. Both **labour** and **toil** can be used instead, but both express the idea of tiring and unpleasant effort. —see JOB (USAGE)

work² *v* **1** [IØ (*at/on*)] to do an activity which uses effort, esp. as employment: *working in a factory*|*working on a book*|*working at his French* (= school subject) **2** [IØ] (of a plan, machine, or moving part) to be active in the proper way, without failing: *Does this light work?*|*The clock hasn't been working since the electricity was off.*|*Your idea won't work in practice.*|*It works by electricity* —compare GO **3** [X9] to make (a person) work: *They work us too hard in this office* **4** [T1] to make (a machine) work: *Stand there, and work the machine.*|*Press there, that works the machine.*|*It's worked by electricity* **5** [X9] to get (through) by working or effort: *He worked his way to the front of the crowd.*|*He worked his way through college* (= paid by working) **6** [T1] to work in (a large place), usu. moving about: *They worked the whole country singing well-known songs* **7** [T1] to produce (an effect): *to work a change*|*This medicine works wonders*/MIRACLEs **8** [T1] *infml* to arrange, esp. unofficially: *How did you work it? 2 days additional holiday!*|*We'll work it so that we can all go together* **9** [T1] to keep (a place of work) in operation: *to work an oil well* **10** [X9;L9] to (cause to) reach a state or position by small movements: *Work the brush into the corner.*|*My hair works loose when I run.*|(fig.) *He worked himself into a temper* **11** [IØ] to tremble; express feeling by violent movement: *The child was very disappointed; her mouth worked and she started to cry* **12** [T1] to shape with the hands: *to work clay*|*to work* DOUGH **13** [T1 *often pass.*] to control with the hands: PUPPETs *are toy creatures worked by strings* **14** [T1 *often pass.*] to stitch: *a baby's dress worked by hand* **15** [IØ] *tech* to FERMENT¹ (1) **16** [L9] to move or act for a certain result: *Your lack of interest will work against you when your employer gets to know.*|*to work round to a new point of view* **17 work to rule** to obey the rules of one's work exactly in such a way that one causes inconvenience to others (usu. these rules are informally changed for convenience), in order to give force to a claim for more money, shorter working hours, etc.
USAGE To make this word stronger, one says *He* **worked** *hard/very hard/very hard indeed.* These expressions are used only of people, and of animals such as horses, not of machines. They give the idea of conscious effort

-work *comb. form* [*n*→*n*[U]] **1** work done using the stated materials or tools: WOODWORK (1)|NEEDLEWORK (1) **2** objects produced by doing such work: WOODWORK (2,3)|NEEDLEWORK (2)|PAINTWORK

wor·ka·ble /ˈwɜːkəbəl‖ˈwɜr-/ *adj* **1** which can work or be worked: *a workable machine* **2** which will work out; usable: *This plan isn't workable* **3** (of substances) which can be shaped with the hands: *workable clay for making pots* —**~ness** *n* [U]

work·a·day /ˈwɜːkədeɪ‖ˈwɜr-/ *adj* [Wa5;A] ordinary and/or dull: *this workaday world*

work·bag /ˈwɜːkbæg‖ˈwɜrk-/ *n* a bag for tools and objects used in activities with the hands, such as sewing

work·bas·ket /ˈwɜːkˌbɑːskɪ̄t‖ˈwɜrkˌbæs-/ also **work·box** /ˈwɜːkbɒks‖ˈwɜrkbɑks/— *n* a small stiff container, usu. in BASKETWORK, for small sewing objects such as needles and thread

work·bench /ˈwɜːkbentʃ‖ˈwɜrk-/ *n* (a table with) a hard surface for working on with tools: *a* CARPENTER *at his workbench*

work·book /ˈwɜːkbʊk‖ˈwɜrk-/ *n* **1** a book which tells how something works —compare HANDBOOK **2** a book which gives information about a subject and/or guidance to the student on work to do alone **3** a book kept, esp. by a student, as a record of work and studies

work·day /ˈwɜːkdeɪ‖ˈwɜrk-/ also **working day**— *n* **1** the amount of time during which one works each day **2** a day which is not a holiday

worked up /ˌ· ˈ·◂/ *adj* [F] very excited; showing strong feelings, esp. when worried (esp. in the phr. **get worked up**): *That child gets worked up about going to school and leaves the house crying every day*

work·er /ˈwɜːkəʳ‖ˈwɜr-/ *n* **1** a person or animal which works **2** a hard worker: *She's a real worker; she gets twice as much done as anybody else* **3** also **working man** /ˌ·· ˈ·/— a person who works with his hands rather than his mind; WORKING CLASS man: *a factory worker*

work force /ˈ· ·/ *n* [*the*+R] the people who work in factories and industry generally, considered as a body: *the work force of this country*

work·horse /ˈwɜːkhɔːs‖ˈwɜrkhɔrs/ *n* **1** a person who does most of the work in the group to which he belongs (often in the phr. **a willing workhorse**) **2** a vehicle, machine, etc., that is very useful, esp.

in performing ordinary continuous jobs
work·house /ˈwɜːkhaʊs‖ˈwɜrk-/ *n* **-houses** /ˌhaʊzɪ̇z/ [*the*+R;(C)] *BrE* (in former times) a place for the poor to live when they had no employment, esp. when old
work-in /ˈ· ·/ *n* the taking-over of a factory or other place of work by angry or dissatisfied workers who work in it according to their own methods and refuse to leave
work in *v adv* [T1] to include, by a clever arrangement of words: *to work in a mention of the help she gave* —see also WORK INTO, WORK IN WITH
work·ing /ˈwɜːkɪŋ‖ˈwɜr-/ *adj* [Wa5;A] **1** concerning or including work: *The visiting minister had a working breakfast with the head of government* **2** who works with the hands: *a working man* —see also WORKMAN **3** (of time) spent in work: *the working day* **4** used in work, business, etc.: *a working tool* **5** (of ideas) useful as a base for planning how to do something: *a working* THEORY
working class /ˌ·· ˈ·◂/ also **lower class**, (*fml & rare*) **labouring classes**— *n, adj* [*the*+GU *often pl. with sing. meaning*;B] (of) the social class to which people belong who work with their hands: *Not many students come from the working class.|a working-class home|Many people who are working class have cars.|"The working class is/the working classes are getting richer" he said*
working day /ˌ·· ˈ·◂‖ˈ·· ·/ *n* WORKDAY
working knowl·edge /ˌ·· ˈ··/ *n* [S] enough practical knowledge to do something: *He has a working knowledge of car engines and can do most repairs*
working or·der /ˌ·· ˈ··/ *n* [U] the state of working well, with no trouble (in the phr. **in working order**)
working-out /ˌ·· ˈ·/ *n* [U] the way of calculating or planning something: *the working-out of the total|the working-out of the plan*
working par·ty /ˈ·· ˌ··/ *n* a committee, as in a firm or in parliament, which examines a particular point and reports what it finds
work·ings /ˈwɜːkɪŋz‖ˈwɜr-/ *n* [P] **1** the way in which something works or acts: *I shall never understand the workings of an engine* **2** the parts of a mine which have been dug out
working week /ˌ·· ˈ·/ *n* WEEK (2)
work in·to *v prep* [D1] to include (something) in (something else), by a clever arrangement of words: *He worked a mention of her into his speech* —see also WORK IN
work in with *v adv prep* [T1] to be able to join in work or social activity with (other people)
work·man /ˈwɜːkmən‖ˈwɜrk-/ *n* **-men** /mən/ **1** [C] a man who works with his hands, esp. in a particular skill or trade: *The workmen fixed the water system* **2** [C9] a man who is skilled to a stated degree, esp. in work with the hands: *a clever workman|A bad workman always blames his tools*
work·man·like /ˈwɜːkmənlaɪk‖ˈwɜrk-/ *adj* having or showing the qualities of a good workman: *workmanlike methods*
work·man·ship /ˈwɜːkmənʃɪp‖ˈwɜrk-/ *n* [U] **1** (signs of) skill in making things: *good workmanship* **2** one or more objects produced by work
work off *v adv* [T1] to remove, by work or activity: *to work off one's anger|to work off a debt*
work·out /ˈwɜːkaʊt‖ˈwɜr-/ *n infml* a period of bodily exercise and training for a sport
work out *v adv* **1** [T1] to calculate the answer to: *to work out a sum* **2** [IØ] to have an answer which can be calculated: *The sum won't work out/doesn't work out* **3** [T1;IØ] to (cause to) have a good result: *Things will work themselves out.|I hope the new job works out for you* **4** [IØ] to have a result; develop; TURN OUT: *I wonder how their ideas worked out in practice?* **5** [T1;6a,b] to plan or decide: *to work out the details|I can't work out what he wants/how to do it* **6** [IØ] *infml* to exercise: *to work out in the* GYMNASIUM **7** [Wv5;T1] to complete the use of (esp. a mine): *The mine was worked out years ago*
work out at also **work out to**— *v adv prep* [L1] to come to (an amount or total): *The cost works out at £6 a night*
work o·ver *v adv* [T1] *infml, esp. AmE* to attack violently: *They worked him over*
work·peo·ple /ˈwɜːkˌpiːpəl‖ˈwɜrk-/ *n* [P] workers who are employed, esp. in a factory
work·room /ˈwɜːkrʊm, -ruːm‖ˈwɜrk-/ *n* a room which is specially kept for working in, esp. on a certain sort of work: *a photographic workroom*
works[1] /wɜːks‖wɜrks/ *n* **1** [*the*+P] the moving parts (of a machine) —see picture at CLOCK[1] **2** **give someone the works** *sl* **a** to tell someone all the information **b** to be violent to someone by shooting, beating, etc.
works[2] *n* **works** [Wn3;C *often pl. with sing. meaning*] (*often in comb.*) an industrial place of work; factory: *a gas works|the works* CANTEEN
work·shop /ˈwɜːkʃɒp‖ˈwɜrkʃɑp/ *n* a room or place, as in a factory or business, where heavy repairs and jobs on machines are done: *I'll have to send the broken sewing machine away to the workshop*
work-shy /ˈ· ·/ *adj* not liking work and trying to avoid it: *He's not at home because he's work-shy, but because he's ill*
work-stud·y /ˈ· ˌ··/ *n* [U] the skill or practice of making work more productive in less time by noting the way things are done by workers and suggesting improvements
work·top /ˈwɜːktɒp‖ˈwɜrktɑp/ *n* a flat surface on top of a piece of kitchen furniture, used for doing work on, such as preparing a meal —see picture at KITCHEN
work-to-rule /ˌ· · ˈ·/ *n* a form of working which causes activity to become slower, because attention is paid to every point in the rules, even when unnecessary —see also GO-SLOW
work up *v adv* **1** [T1] to excite the feelings, esp. anger, tears, etc., of (esp. oneself): *The politician worked the crowd up until they shouted together* —see also WORKED UP, WORK[2] (10) **2** [IØ (*to*)] to move or develop (towards): *She's working up to what she wants to say* —see also BUILD UP **3** [T1] to develop steadily: *He worked up the firm from nothing* —see also BUILD UP **4** [T1] to complete (a study) by degrees: *to work up the notes into a book* **5** **work up an appetite** to make oneself hungry by work or exercise
world /wɜːld‖wɜrld/ *n* **1** [(*the*) R] **a** the earth: *everyone in the world|English is a world language|the Second World War* **b** a particular part of it: *the Third World* (= the poor countries)|*the Old World* (= not America) **2** [(*the*) R] the universe: *The sun is the centre of our world* **3** [C] a PLANET or star system, esp. one which may contain life: *Is there life on other worlds?* **4** [*the*+R] people generally, esp. those known to the public: *The whole world knows about it* **5** [(*the*) R] human life and its affairs: *You must learn to live in the world as it is* **6** [C9 *usu. sing.*] a particular group with a common interest: *the cricket world* **7** [*the*+R9] a particular area of interest: *the world of cooking|cookery world* (esp. as the title of a regular article in a magazine) **8** [C] a state or place of existence: *The sea is the fishes' world* **9** [*the*+R] *fml* material standards (not SPIRITUAL): *to give up the world and serve God* **10** [(*the*) S9+*of*] a large number or amount: *The fire makes a world of difference.|The medicine did me a/the world of good* **11** [*the*+R9] a group of

living things: *the animal world* **12 (have) the best of both worlds** (to have) the advantages which each choice offers, without having to choose between them **13 in the world** (in a question expressing surprise): *Where in the world* (=wherever) *could he be?|What in the world* (=whatever) *are you doing?* **14 dead to the world** *infml* not noticing anything, because drunk or fast asleep **15 bring/come into the/this world** to give birth to (a child)/be born **16 for all the world as if/like** exactly as if/like **17 make one's way in the world** to succeed in life **18 not for the world** certainly not: *I wouldn't hurt her for the world* **19 on top of the world** very happy **20 all the world to** (means) everything of importance to: *My home is all the world to me* **21 out of this world** *infml* unusually good; wonderful **22 think the world of** to care about very much: *He may get angry sometimes, but he really thinks the world of you* **23 worlds apart** completely different: *Their ways of life are worlds apart* **24 world without end** (in prayers) for ever —see also MAN[1] (19) **of the world**

World Bank /ˌ· ˈ·/ *n* [*the*+R] an international bank formed in 1944 to give help to poorer nations

world-beat·er /ˈ· ˌ··/ *n* a person (esp. competitor) or thing thought so good as to be better than any other: *This runner is a world-beater*

world-class /ˌ· ˈ·◂/ *adj* [Wa5] among the best in the world: *That cricketer is world-class*

world·ly /ˈwɜːldli‖ˈwɜr-/ *adj* **1** [Wa5;A] of the material world: *all my worldly goods* **2** [Wa1;B] concerned with the ways of society, esp. social advantage; not SPIRITUAL —opposite **unworldly** —**-liness** *n* [U]

worldly-wise /ˌ·· ˈ·◂‖ˈ·· ·/ *adj* experienced in the ways of society: *too worldly-wise to expect too much of human nature*

world pow·er /ˌ· ˈ··/ *n* a nation which is important and whose trade, politics, etc., have an effect on many other parts of the world

world·shak·ing /ˈwɜːldˌʃeɪkɪŋ‖ˈwɜrld-/ *adj* EARTH-SHAKING

world war /ˌ· ˈ·/ *n* a war in which many nations of the world join

world-wear·y /ˌ· ˈ··◂/ *adj* [Wa5] tired of life —**-iness** *n* [U]

world·wide /ˌwɜːldˈwaɪd◂‖ˌwɜr-/ *adj, adv* [Wa5] in or over all the world: *French cheeses are famous worldwide*

worm[1] /wɜːm‖wɜrm/ *n* **1** a small thin creature with no backbone or limbs, like a round tube of flesh, esp. the one which lives in and moves through earth: *The (earth) worm turns the soil.|The dog has worms* (= which live inside the body) **2** a person who is thought worthless, cowardly, etc. **3** (*in comb.*) any of various sorts of small creature with no limbs or backbones: *silkworms|*TAPE-WORM*s* —see also HOOKWORM, GLOW-WORM **4** the curving line round a SCREW[1] (1)

worm[2] *v* **1** [T1] to remove living worms from the body of, esp. by chemical means: *You must worm the dog with a gentle drug* **2** [X9 esp. IN, *into*] **a** to move by twisting or effort: *He wormed his way into the space.|He wormed himself out of the way* **b** to make (oneself) accepted by degrees, through one's efforts: *He wormed himself into her heart.|He's not the right sort of person to have in this club. How did he worm his way in?*

worm cast /ˈ· ·/ *n* a heap of earth like a tube which has been passed through the body of an (earth) worm

worm-eat·en /ˈ· ˌ··/ *adj* **1** full of holes, esp. (of furniture) from WOODWORM **2** *sl* old

worm gear /ˈ· ·/ also **worm wheel**— *n* a sort of GEAR[1] (3) with an arrangement inside curving round and round

worm·hole /ˈwɜːmhəʊl‖ˈwɜrm-/ *n* **1** a hole in the ground left by a worm **2** a hole in wood made by WOODWORM

worm out *v adv* [T1 (*of*)] to obtain (all the information) by questioning, esp. over a period of time: *He wormed the secret out (of her)*

worm·wood /ˈwɜːmwʊd‖ˈwɜrm-/ *n* [U] **1** a kind of plant with a bitter taste, used in ABSINTH and some medicines **2** *lit* bitterness; something that causes deeply wounded feelings: *the wormwood of defeat*

worm·y /ˈwɜːmi‖ˈwɜrmi/ *adj* [Wa1] **1** of or like a worm **2** containing worms: *a wormy apple* **3** with holes made by worms; WORM-EATEN

worn /wɔːn‖worn/ *past p. of* WEAR

worn-out /ˌ· ˈ·◂/ *adj* [Wa5] **1** [B] completely finished by continued use: *worn-out shoes* **2** [F] very tired: *She was worn-out after 3 sleepless nights* —compare OUTWORN

wor·ried /ˈwʌrid‖ˈwɜrid/ *adj* [(*about*)] anxious: *a worried look|She seems very worried about something* —**~ly** *adv*

wor·ri·some /ˈwʌrisəm‖ˈwɜri-/ *adj* which troubles or makes anxious

wor·ry[1] /ˈwʌri‖ˈwɜri/ *v* **1** [Wv4;T1] to make anxious or uncomfortable: *Her late hours* (= coming home late) *worry me.|The (bad) smell doesn't worry him.|a very worrying state of affairs* **2** [IØ (*about, over*)] to be anxious, esp. over a period of time: *Worrying about your health can make you ill.|Don't worry!* **3** [T1] (esp. of a dog) to chase and bite (an animal): *The dog was found worrying sheep, and had to be shot.|many cases of sheep-worrying* **4** [T1 (*for*)] to keep trying to persuade: *She worried him for a present* —**~ingly** *adv*

worry[2] *n* **1** [U] a feeling of anxiety: *lines of worry on her face* **2** [C] a person or thing which makes one worried: *It's a worry to me having to leave the children alone in the house.|Money is just one of our worries* (= there are others)

worry at *v prep* [T1;V3] to keep attempting to conquer or persuade: *to worry at a* PROBLEM *until one finds an answer|She worried at her husband to buy her a new dress*

worse[1] /wɜːs‖wɜrs/ *adj* [Wa5] **1** [B] (*compar. of* BAD) more bad or less good: *Your face looks terrible but mine feels (even) worse.|It's not a bad mark, but it's worse than your usual one.|He may be late. Worse still, he may not come at all.|I'm worse at sums than Jean, but better at history* **2** [F] (*compar. of* ILL) more ill (than before): *He's getting steadily worse.|At least, he's no worse* **3 go from bad to worse** to get much worse even than before: *He used to steal when he was a child and now he's in prison. He's going from bad to worse* **4 none the worse (for)** not harmed (by): *He's none the worse (for the experience)/(for his fall from the window)* **5 the worse for wear** spoilt/not improved by time and use or work: *My coat is the worse for wear after sleeping in it.|He looks the worse for wear after years of hard work* —see also **worse** LUCK, **make** MATTER*s*[1] **worse**

worse[2] *n* [U] **1** something worse: *He thought everything bad had happened at once, but worse was to follow* **2 a change for the worse** a bad change

worse[3] *adv* (*compar. of* BADLY) [Wa5] **1** in a worse way: *You're working worse than I expected.|"People who behave worse than animals"* (SEU W.) **2** to a worse degree: *It's hurting worse than before*

USAGE Some people think that this word should not be used as an adverb, in expressions like *to behave* **worse**, and that it is better to say *to behave in a* **worse** *way*

wors·en /ˈwɜːsən‖ˈwɜr-/ *v* [T1;IØ] to (cause to)

become worse: *The difficulty has worsened.|The rain has worsened our difficulties*

wor·ship[1] /ˈwɜːʃɪp‖ˈwɜr-/ *n* [U] **1** great respect, admiration, etc., esp. to God or a god: *Sun worship can mean the worship of the sun as a god, but its modern meaning is a liking for sitting in the sun getting one's skin brown* **2** the act of showing this: *They joined in worship together* **3** a religious service: *They attended worship*

worship[2] *v* **-pp-** (*AmE* **-p-**) **1** [T1;L9 esp. *at*] to show great respect, admiration, etc.: (fig.) *She worships the ground he walks on.|His admirers worshipped at his feet* **2** [L9] to attend a church service: *to worship regularly* —**-per** *n*

Worship *n* **your/his Worship** *esp. BrE* (a title of respect used to/of certain official people such as a MAGISTRATE or a MAYOR)

wor·ship·ful /ˈwɜːʃɪpfəl‖ˈwɜr-/ *adj* [Wa5;A] *esp. BrE* (used as a respectful form of address): *the Worshipful the* MAYOR *of Brighton|the worshipful company of* GOLDSMITH*s*

worst[1] /wɜːst‖wɜrst/ *adj* (*superl. of* BAD) [Wa5;A] **1** (the) most bad: *This is the worst accident for years* **2 come off worst** to be defeated

worst[2] *n* [*the*+R (*of*)] **1** the most bad thing or part: *I've seen bad work, but this is the worst.|The worst of it is that I could have prevented the accident if I'd been earlier.|He was the worst of all in that game* **2 at (the) worst** if one thinks of it in the worst way: *He's a fool at (the) best, and at (the) worst he's a criminal* **3 do one's worst** to do as much harm as one can (esp. suggesting that very little harm can be done): *The enemy is coming, but let him do his worst; we are ready for him* **4 get the worst of (it)** to be defeated **5 if the worst comes to the worst** if the worst difficulties happen; if there is no better way: *If the worst comes to the worst, we can always go by bus tomorrow*

worst[3] *adv* (*superl. of* BADLY) [Wa5] most badly: *The others weren't good but she played (the) worst of anybody* (= worse than all the rest).|*Who suffered worst?|the worst-dressed woman*

worst[4] *v* [T1 *usu. pass.*] *esp. old use* to defeat: *worsted in battle*

wor·sted /ˈwʊstɪ̈d/ *n* [U] wool cloth: *a worsted suit*

wort /wɜːt‖wɜrt/ *n* [U] a sweet mixture of MALT and water which, when it has been chemically changed by FERMENTing, will become beer

worth[1] /wɜːθ‖wɜrθ/ *prep* **1** (*esp. after* be) of the value of: *It's worth much more than I paid for it.|"a piece of land worth £4,500"* (SEU W.) **2** having possessions amounting to: *He's worth £1,000,000* **3** (esp. with *-ing* form) deserving: *You're not worth helping.|It isn't worth waiting for him.|The food's not worth eating.|Don't lock the door; it isn't worth the trouble.|It's worth making an effort* **4 for all one is worth** with all possible effort **5 for what it's worth** though I'm not sure it's of value **6 worth it** useful; worth the trouble: *Don't lock the door; it isn't worth it* —see also **worth one's/someone's** WHILE[1] (4)

worth[2] *n* [U] value: *After his unkindness, I know the true worth of his friendship* (= It is worthless)

-worth /wəθ‖wərθ/ *comb. form* a certain amount of the stated value: *Will you change this pound note for a poundsworth of pennies?*

worth·less /ˈwɜːθləs‖ˈwɜrθ-/ *adj* **1** [Wa5] of no value: *a worthless action* **2** (of a person) of bad character: *a worthless member of society* —**~ly** *adv* —**~ness** *n* [U]

USAGE Things of great value are **priceless, valuable**, or **invaluable** (=very useful). Things of little or no value are **valueless** or **worthless.**

worth·while /ˌwɜːθˈwaɪl◂‖ˌwɜr-/ *adj* worth doing; worth the trouble taken: *a worthwhile job* —see also **worth one's/someone's** WHILE [1] (4)

wor·thy[1] /ˈwɜːði‖ˈwɜrði/ *adj* [Wa1] **1** [F+*of*, F3; A] deserving: *worthy of help/dislike|a worthy winner|not worthy to be chosen* **2** [B] *esp. old use* to be admired, respected, etc.: *a worthy man* —**-thily** *adv* —**-thiness** *n* [U]

worthy[2] *n sometimes humor* a person of importance

-worthy *comb. form* deserving: *praiseworthy*

wot /wɒt‖wɑt/ *v* **-tt-** [IØ (*of*)] *old use or pomp, esp. BrE* to know: *Other times which we wot not of*

wot·cher /ˈwɒtʃəʳ‖ˈwɑ-/ *interj BrE sl, becoming rare* HELLO

would /wʊd/ *v neg. contr.* **wouldn't** [Wv2;IØ,2] **1 a** *past t. of* WILL: *They said it would be fine* (actual words "*It will be fine*") **b** (used instead of WILL with a past tense verb): *They couldn't find anyone who would* (= who was willing to) *take the job.|She would be surprised if he came* **2** (shows what always happened) used to: *We used to work in the same office. We would often have coffee together* —see USE[3] (USAGE) **3** (used to show that one is annoyed at something that always happens or is typical): *That's exactly like Jocelyn— she* would *lose the key!* **4 would better** *AmE* had better (HAVE[1] (2)) **5 would rather** (expressing a choice): *Which would you rather do, go to the cinema or stay at home?|I'd rather not say what I think.|I'd rather you didn't tell him* **6 would that** *rare* We, they, etc., wish; if only . . . : *Would that we had seen her before she died* **7 would you** (expressing a polite request): *Would you please lend me your pencil?* —see LIKE[1]

would-be /ˈ· ·/ *adj* [Wa5;A] which one wishes to be, but is not: *a would-be musician*

would·n't /ˈwʊdnt/ [Wv2] *contr. of* would not —see CONTR. (USAGE)

wouldst /wʊdst/ [Wv2] **thou wouldst** *old use or bibl* (when talking to one person) you would

wound[1] /wuːnd/ *n* a damaged place in the body, usu. a hole or tear through the skin; esp. done on purpose by a weapon, such as a gun: *only a flesh wound* (= not deep)|(fig.) *a wound to her pride* —see also **rub** SALT [1] (7) **in someone's wounds**

USAGE One gets **wounded** or receives a **wound** in war or fighting. The word suggests being hurt, on purpose, by a bullet or with a sharp instrument such as a sword. One gets **injured** or receives an **injury** in an accident, and this suggests broken bones: *badly/seriously/severely/*FATAL*ly* **wounded/ injured.** Both words are more serious than **hurt**

wound[2] /wuːnd/ *v* [T1] to cause a wound to: *The shot wounded his arm.|He wounded him in the arm*

wound[3] /waʊnd/ *past t. and past p. of* WIND

wove /wəʊv/ *past t. of* WEAVE

wov·en /ˈwəʊvən/ *past p. of* WEAVE

wow[1] /waʊ/ *interj infml* an expression of surprise and admiration

wow[2] *n* [S] *infml* a great success

wow[3] *n* [U] faulty rising and falling sounds in a machine for playing recorded sound —compare FLUTTER[2] (4a)

WRAC /ræk/ *n* a member of the (British) Women's Royal Army Corps **(the WRACs)**

wrack[1] /ræk/ *n* [U] RACK[4]

wrack[2] *n* [U] any of several types of SEAWEED

wraith /reɪθ/ *n* **1** a shape like a person's body, esp. seen just before his death **2** a very thin person

wran·gle[1] /ˈræŋgəl/ *v* [IØ (*with*)] to argue, esp. angrily

wrangle[2] *n* an angry or noisy argument

wran·gler /ˈræŋgləʳ/ *n* **1** a person who WRANGLE*s* or is wrangling **2** *AmE* a COWBOY, esp. one who looks after horses **3** a Cambridge University student placed in the highest class of the MATHEMATICS examination (TRIPOS)

wrap[1] /ræp/ *v* **-pp-** **1** [T1 (UP, *in*)] to cover (in a material folded around): *I put the book in a box and* *wrapped it up in brown paper before I posted it.|They offered to wrap the shoes in the shop, but I wanted to wear them at once* **2** [X9 esp. *(a)round*] to fold (a material) over: *I wrapped the* RUG *around the sick man's legs to keep him warm*

wrap[2] *n* **1** *becoming rare* a garment or piece of material which is used as a covering, esp. a SCARF, SHAWL, or RUG **2 under wraps** *infml* hidden from the public

wrap·per /ˈræpəʳ/ *n* **1** a piece of paper which forms a loose cover on a book **2** a piece of paper, such as one with a sticky edge for folding over a rolled up newspaper, to be used as a covering when a book, newspaper, etc., is posted

wrap·ping /ˈræpɪŋ/ *n* [U;(C) *often pl. with sing. meaning*] material used for folding round and covering something

wrap up *v adv* **1** [I∅] to wear warm clothes: *In cold weather you should wrap up well* **2** [T1] to hide (an idea) in words: *He wrapped up his meaning in a fancy speech which I couldn't understand* **3** [T1] *esp. infml* to complete or finish (a business arrangement, a meeting, etc.): *Now the agreement is wrapped up all we have to do is wait for the first orders* **4** [I∅ *usu. imper.*] *sl* to be quiet; SHUT UP **5 wrapped up in** giving complete love or attention to: *She's so wrapped up in him she can't see his faults*

wrath /rɒθ‖ræθ/ *n lit* great anger: *the wrath of God* —**~ful** *adj* —**~fully** *adv*

wreak /riːk/ *v* [T1 (*on*)] to do (violence) or express (strong feelings) in violence: *to wreak* VENGEANCE *(on someone)*

wreath /riːθ/ *n* **1** an arrangement of flowers or leaves, esp. in a circle, such as one given at the funeral of a dead person **2** a circle of leaves or flowers placed on the head or round the neck of someone to honour him **3** a curl of smoke, mist, gas, etc.

wreathe /riːð/ *v esp. lit* **1** [Wv5+*in*;T1] to circle round and cover completely: *Mist wreathed the hilltops.*|(fig.) *She/her face was wreathed in smiles* **2** [X9 esp. *(a)round*] (of a snake) to move (itself) when twisted round and round **3** [L9] (of smoke, mist, gas, etc.) to move gently in circles: *The smoke wreathed round the street light*

wreck[1] /rek/ *n* **1** [C] a ship lost at sea or (partly) destroyed on rocks: *the wreck of the Mary Dere* —see also SHIPWRECK **2** [U] the state of being ruined or destroyed: *the wreck of all her hopes* **3** [C] *esp. infml* the parts of a thing, esp. a building, left after it has been partly destroyed: *My plan's a wreck; we can't go on with it* **4** [C] a person whose health is destroyed: *He is a complete wreck since his illness*

wreck[2] *v* **1** [Wv6;T1 *often pass.*] **a** to cause (a ship) to be destroyed: *The ship was wrecked on the rocks* **b** to cause (the people on a ship) to be in a SHIPWRECK: *We were wrecked off the coast of Africa* **2** [T1] to destroy: *The weather has completely wrecked our plans*

wreck·age /ˈrekɪdʒ/ *n* [U (*of*)] the broken parts of a destroyed thing: *the wreckage of the cars which were in the accident*|(fig.) *trying to put together the wreckage of my life*

wreck·er /ˈrekəʳ/ *n* **1** a person who destroys, esp. (in former times) one who tried to cause a ship to be caught on rocks in order to be able to steal from it **2** a person whose job it is to bring out goods from ships which have been WRECKed[2] (1), so that they will not be lost **3** *esp. AmE* a person employed to knock down buildings **4** *AmE* a vehicle used for moving other vehicles when these have broken down, or after accidents

wren /ren/ *n* any of several types of very small bird which sing

wrench[1] /rentʃ/ *v* **1** [X9] to pull hard with a twisting or turning movement: *He wrenched it from her hands.*|*to wrench it open/off* **2** [T1] to twist and damage (a joint of the body): *to wrench one's ankle*

wrench[2] *n* **1** an act of twisting and pulling **2** damage to a joint of the body by twisting: *I've given my knee a bad wrench* **3** painful grief at a separation: *the wrench of leaving one's family* **4 a** *AmE* SPANNER **b** *BrE* a SPANNER with jaws whose distance apart may be changed

wrest /rest/ *v* [X9 esp. *from, out of*] **1** to pull (away) violently: *He wrested it from her hands* **2** to obtain with difficulty: *to wrest the truth out of someone|to wrest crops from the soil* **3** to change the appearance of (facts): *This report wrests the facts out of their true meaning*

wres·tle /ˈresəl/ *v* **1** [I∅ (*with,* TOGETHER)] to fight by holding and throwing the body: *She wrestled with her attacker until she kicked his feet from under him and he fell to the ground.*|(fig.) *He wrestled with the fact of his failure.*|(fig.) *wrestling with a difficult examination paper* **2** [T1;I∅] to fight (someone) like this as a sport (**wrestling**) **3** [X9] to put into the stated condition by fighting like this: *She wrestled her attacker to the ground* —**wrestler** *n*
USAGE One **wrestles** in a **ring**. One loses the CONTEST by *falls*, SUBMISSION*s*, or a **knockout**. In an important *match*, the person in charge is called the **referee**.

wretch /retʃ/ *n* **1** a poor or unhappy person: *unlucky wretches with no homes* **2** *often humor* a person or animal disliked and thought bad and useless: *You wretch! You're late again*

wretch·ed /ˈretʃɪ̵d/ *adj* **1** [B] **a** very unhappy: *feeling wretched after an illness* **b** of a bad type which makes one unhappy: *a wretched life/headache* **2** [Wa5;A] of a type which is disliked: *Wretched child, why can't she behave?|What a wretched colour.|wretched weather* —**~ly** *adv* —**~ness** *n* [U]

wrig·gle[1] /ˈrɪgəl/ *v* **1** [I∅] to twist from side to side, either in one place or when moving along: *He wriggled uncomfortably on the hard chair* **2** [T1] to move (a part of the body) in this way; WIGGLE

wriggle[2] *n* a wriggling (WRIGGLE[1]) movement

wriggle out of *v adv prep* [T1,4] *infml* to escape (a difficulty) by clever tricks, by pretending, etc.: *You know you're to blame, so don't try to wriggle out of it*

wright /raɪt/ *n* (*usu. in comb.*) a maker: *a wheelwright|a playwright*

wring[1] /rɪŋ/ *v* **wrung** /rʌŋ/ **1** [T1] **a** to twist (esp. the neck, causing death): *I'll wring your neck if you don't behave* **b** to press hard on; SQUEEZE (esp. the hand): *He wrung my hand* (=when shaking hands in greeting).|*wringing one's hands in sorrow*|(fig.) *The baby's sufferings wrung its mother's heart* **2** [T1 (OUT, *from*)] **a** to twist and/or press (wet clothes) to remove water: *Wring those wet things out* **b** to press (water) from wet clothes: *Wring the water out (of the cloth).*|(fig.) *You can't wring blood from a stone* (= you can't get money from a hard person) **3** [X9 esp. *from, out of*] to force (a statement from a person): *They wrung the truth out of her in the end* **4 wringing wet** very wet, so that water can be pressed out

wring[2] *n* **1** an act of WRINGing **2** a machine (PRESS) which presses cheese into shape or presses the juice out of apples

wring·er /ˈrɪŋəʳ/ *n* a machine, often part of a washing machine, with rollers between which water is pressed from clothes, sheets, etc., being passed through —compare MANGLE[2]

wrin·kle[1] /ˈrɪŋkəl/ *n* **1** a line in something which is folded or crushed, esp. on the skin when a person is old **2** *infml* a useful small suggestion or HINT: *to know all the wrinkles* (= to know the best ways of doing something) —**-kly** *adj* [Wa1]

wrinkle² *v* **1** [T1 (UP)] to cause to form into lines, folds, etc., esp. for a short time: *She wrinkled her nose at the bad smell* **2** [I∅] (esp. of the skin) to form into lines, folds, etc.: *Too much sun dries the skin and it begins to wrinkle*

wrist /rɪst/ *n* **1** the joint between the hand and the lower part of the arm —see picture at HUMAN² **2** the lower edge of the part of a garment which covers the whole arm

wrist·band /ˈrɪstbænd/ *n* **1** a loose CUFF **2** a band used for fastening something, such as a watch, to the wrist

wrist·let /ˈrɪstlɪ̈t/ *n* a band made of metal parts joined together, used for fastening a watch (**wristlet watch**) to the wrist

wrist·watch /ˈrɪstwɒtʃ‖-wɑtʃ, -wɔtʃ/ *n* a watch made to be fastened on the wrist with a band (STRAP) of metal or leather or other material —see picture at CLOCK¹

wrist·y /ˈrɪsti/ *adj* [Wa1] (esp. in sport) having or showing strong movement of the wrist: *a wristy player*

writ /rɪt/ *n* an official paper given in law to tell someone to do or not to do a particular thing —see also HOLY WRIT

write /raɪt/ *v* **wrote** /rəʊt/, **written** /ˈrɪtn/ **1** [T1;I∅] to make (marks that represent letters or words) by using a tool held in the hand, esp. (in modern times) with a pen or pencil on paper **2** [T1] to express and record in this way, or sometimes by means of a TYPEWRITER: *to write a report|a cheque* **3** [T1;I∅] to be a writer of (books, plays, etc.): *He writes for the stage.|Charlotte Bronte wrote "Jane Eyre"* **4** [D1 (*to*);T1,3,5;I∅ (*to*), 4] to produce and send (a letter): *He writes me a letter every day.|He writes to me every day.|I wish he would write more often.|He wrote to ask me to come.|He wrote that he'd be coming on Tuesday.|He wrote asking me to come* **5** [T1;D5] *esp. AmE* to produce and send a letter to (someone): *He writes me every day.|George wrote me that he couldn't come* **6 be written on/all over** to be clearly showing because of the expression on: *Guilt was written all over his face* **7 writ large** *esp. lit or pomp* made more clearly noticeable; on a larger or grander scale —see also WRITE AWAY, WRITE BACK, WRITE DOWN, WRITE DOWN AS, WRITE IN, WRITE OFF, WRITE OUT, WRITE UP

write a·way *v adv* [I∅ (*for*)] to write to a far-off place, esp. to buy something one cannot get near home: *She wrote away for the book, because the shop didn't have it*

write back *v adv* [I∅,3,4,5] to reply in a letter: *I received his letter 2 weeks ago, but I forgot to write back*

write down *v adv* [T1] **1** to record in writing (esp. what has been said): *Write your idea down while it's clear in your mind* **2** *rare* MARK DOWN (*2*)

write down as *v adv prep* [X1,7] to describe as: *They wrote him down as a lazy worker|as lazy*

write-in /ˈ· ·/ *n AmE* a vote given by writing the name of the person voted for

write in *v adv* **1** [I∅ (*for*)] to send a letter to a firm, asking for something or giving an opinion: *We wrote in for a free book, but the firm never replied* **2** [T1] *AmE* **a** to vote for (someone) by writing the name on the voting paper **b** to add (a name) to a list in an election

write-off /ˈ· ·/ *n* anything which is completely ruined and cannot be repaired: *The car was a write-off after the accident*

write off *v adv* **1** [T1 (*as*)] to accept the loss or failure of: *We'll just have to write off the arrangement if we can't find the money for it* **2** [T1] to remove willingly (esp. the need for repayment): *to write off a debt* —compare WIPE OFF **3** [I∅ (*for*)] WRITE AWAY

write out *v adv* [T1] **1** to write in full: *to write out a report* **2** to write (something formal): *to write out a cheque|receipt*

writ·er /ˈraɪtəʳ/ *n* a person who writes as a job or who has written a particular thing: *He is a writer but he can't make enough money to live from his books*

writer's cramp /ˌ·· ˈ·/ *n* [U] stiffness of the hand after writing for a long time

write-up /ˈ· ·/ *n infml* a written report, esp. one giving a good judgment, as of goods or a play: *The concert got a good write-up in the local newspaper*

write up *v adv* **1** [T1] to write (again) in a complete and useful form: *to write up one's notes* **2** [T1] to write a report on (goods, a play, etc.), esp. giving a good judgment: *to write the play up in the local newspaper* **3** [I∅ (*to*)] WRITE IN (*1*): *We wrote up to the B.B.C.*

writhe /raɪð/ *v* [I∅] to twist the body, as when in great pain: *writhing with pain*

writ·ing /ˈraɪtɪŋ/ *n* [U] **1** the activity of writing, esp. books: *Writing is his life* **2** handwriting: *I can't read the doctor's writing* **3** written work or form: *a piece of writing|Put that down in writing* —see also WRITINGS

writing desk /ˈ·· ·/ *n* a desk, esp. with a place for writing materials

writing ma·te·ri·als /ˈ·· ·ˌ···/ *n* [P] pen, paper, and ink

writing pa·per /ˈ·· ˌ··/ also **notepaper**— *n* [U] paper for writing letters on, usu. smooth and of quite good quality and cut into various standard sizes

writ·ings /ˈraɪtɪŋz/ *n* [P9] works of literature or other written material, produced by the stated person: *Darwin's scientific writings*

writ·ten /ˈrɪtn/ *past p. of* WRITE

wrong¹ /rɒŋ‖rɔŋ/ *n* **1** [U] standards according to which some things are bad: *to know right from wrong* **2** [C] any bad action, esp. one which causes pain: *the wrongs done to men by fate* **3 in the wrong** mistaken or deserving blame —opposite **in the right** **4 two wrongs don't make a right** you ought not to harm someone as punishment for harming you

USAGE The words **fault** and **wrong** can both be used of bad actions, but **a wrong** expresses the idea of an unjust act, and is more seriously evil than a **fault**: *to* COMMIT *a great* **wrong**. **b fault,** but not **wrong**, is used of someone's small bad qualities: *With all her* **faults** *I love her still.* **c fault**, but not **wrong**, is used of someone's responsibility for bad results: *It's your* **fault** *we lost the way!* To **blame** someone is to say that it was his **fault**: *He refused to accept the* **blame** (=to admit that it was his **fault**).

wrong² *adj* [Wa2] **1** [B] not correct: *This sum is wrong.|the wrong answer|No, you're wrong; she didn't say that.|The clock's wrong; it's later than the time it shows* **2** [F] evil; against moral standards: *Telling lies is wrong|It's wrong to tell lies* **3** [B] not suitable: *This is the wrong time to make a visit* **4 be caught on the wrong foot** to have to act when unprepared **5 get (hold) of the wrong end of the stick** to misunderstand **6 get out of bed on the wrong side** to be in a bad temper all day —**~ly** *adv*

wrong³ *adv* **1** wrongly: *You've spelt the word wrong* **2 get it wrong** to misunderstand **3 go wrong a** to make a mistake, as in following a path, or a method: *The sum is wrong, but I can't see where I*

went wrong **b** to end badly: *The day down by the sea went wrong* **c** to stop working properly: *Our clock went wrong* **d** to act badly, immorally, etc.: *He met some bad friends and they helped him to go wrong*
wrong[4] *v* [T1] **1** to be unfair to or cause difficulty, pain, etc., to: *I wronged him by saying he could never improve his work* **2** to judge (someone) unfairly: *You wrong him by having such a low opinion of his work*
wrong·do·ing /ˈrɒŋˌduːɪŋ‖ˌrɔŋˈduːɪŋ/ *n* [C;U] (an example of) bad, evil, or unlawful behaviour —**-er** *n*
wrong·ful /ˈrɒŋfəl‖ˈrɔŋ-/ *adj* **1** unjust: *wrongful dismissal from a job* **2** unlawful: *wrongful imprisonment* —**~ly** *adv*
wrong·head·ed /ˌrɒŋˈhedɪ̣d◂‖ˌrɔŋ-/ *adj* **1** sticking in a determined way to a wrong idea or course of action: *wrongheaded students who think they can cure the world's evils by destroying society* **2** mistaken: *a wrongheaded idea* —**~ly** *adv* —**~ness** *n* [U]
wrong side /ˌ· ˈ·/ *n* [*the*+R] **1** the inner side of a garment or material, usu. rougher and not so attractive and not meant to be looked at —compare RIGHT SIDE (1) **2 get on the wrong side of someone** to lose someone's favour —compare **get on the** RIGHT SIDE (2) **of 3 on the wrong side of (the stated age)** older than: *She must be on the wrong side of 40 by now* —compare **on the** RIGHT SIDE (3) **of**
wrote /rəʊt/ *past t. of* WRITE
wroth /rɒθ‖rɔθ/ *adj* [F] *old use, bibl, or poet* very angry
wrought /rɔːt/ *adj* [Wa5;B (*of*)] *old use & lit* made or done: *carefully wrought works of literature*|*wrought by hand*|*wrought of stone*
wrought i·ron /ˌ· ˈ··◂/ *n* [U] iron shaped into a useful form or pleasing pattern: *a wrought-iron gate*
wrought-up /ˌ· ˈ·◂/ *adj* very nervous and excited —compare OVERWROUGHT, WORKED UP
wrung /rʌŋ/ *past t. and past p. of* WRING
wry /raɪ/ *adj* [Wa1;A;(F)] **1** showing dislike, lack of pleasure, etc.: *a wry face* (= expression)/*smile* **2** *rare* twisted —**~ly** *adv*
wt *written abbrev. for:* weight
wurst /wɜːst‖wɜrst (*Ger* vʊrst)/ *n* (a German name for) a type of SAUSAGE or mixture of cooked meat less commonly eaten in England than in the rest of Europe
wych-ha·zel /ˈwɪtʃ ˌheɪzəl/ *n* WITCH-HAZEL
wy·vern /ˈwaɪvən‖-ərn/ *n* a type of unreal animal written about in stories, looking like a 2-legged winged DRAGON (1)

X, x

X, x /eks/ **X's, x's** *or* **Xs, xs 1** the 24th letter of the English alphabet **2** the ROMAN NUMERAL (number) for 10 **3** (a mark written esp. on a letter or card, meaning) a kiss
x *n* [R] (in MATHEMATICS) a quantity that is unknown until a calculation has been made: *If* $3x=6, x=2$
X[1] *n* [R] a person whose name is not made known to the public: *At the trial, Mrs X, one of the witnesses, was allowed to keep her face covered*
X[2] *n, adj* [Wa5;C;A] (a film) that children under 18 may not be admitted to see in a cinema: *"Terrors of the Grave" is an X (film)* —compare A, AA, U
X chro·mo·some /ˈeks ˌkrəʊməsəʊm/ *n* a type of CHROMOSOME which exists in pairs in female cells and singly in male cells, and, after union of male and female, will produce a female when combined with another of its own type, and a male when combined with a Y CHROMOSOME
xen·on /ˈzenɒn‖ˈziːnɑn, ˈze-/ *n* [U] a type of rare gas sometimes used in photography to produce short flashes of light
xen·o·pho·bi·a /ˌzenəˈfəʊbɪə/ *n* [U] unreasonable fear and dislike of foreigners or strangers —**-c** *adj*
xe·rox[1] /ˈzɪərɒks, ˈze-‖ˈzɪərɑks, ˈziː-/ *v* [T1] *tdmk* (*often cap.*) to make a photographic copy of (printed or written matter) on a special electric copying machine
xerox[2] *n* (*often cap.*) a photographic copy made by XEROXing[1]
X·mas /ˈkrɪsməs, ˈeksməs/ *n* [R;(C)] *infml* Christmas
x-ray /ˈeks reɪ/ *v* [T1] (*often cap.*) to photograph, examine, or treat by means of X-RAYS: *They x-rayed her leg to find out if the bone was broken*
X-ray *n* **1** [*usu. pl.*] a powerful unseen beam of light which can pass through substances that are not transparent, and which is used for photographing conditions inside the body, for treating certain diseases, and for various purposes in industry: *an X-ray camera* **2** a photograph taken using this: *The doctor examined the X-rays, to see if they showed anything wrong with her lungs* **3** a medical examination made using this: *He had to go into hospital for an X-ray*
xy·lo·phone /ˈzaɪləfəʊn/ *n* a type of musical instrument made up of a set of flat wooden bars of different lengths tuned to produce a set of musical notes, played by striking the bars with small wooden hammers —see picture at PERCUSSION

Y, y

Y, y /waɪ/ **Y's, y's** *or* **Ys, ys** the 25th letter of the English alphabet
-y[1] /i/ also (*esp. after* -y) **-ey**— *suffix* [*n*→*adj* [Wa1]] **1** full of, covered with, or tending to: *dirty*|*hairy*|*sleepy* **2** like, like that of, or fond of: *a cold* WINTRY *day*|*a* HORSY *person*/*appearance* —**-ily** *suffix* [→*adv*] —**-iness** *suffix* [→*n* [U]]
-y[2] *suffix* **1** [*n*→*n*] also **-ie**— *infml* (*forming a pet name, used esp. by or to children*) dear little: *Johnny*|DADDY|*doggie*|PANTIES **2** [*v*→*n*] the action of (a verb): INQUIRY
yacht /jɒt‖jɑt/ *n* [C; *by*+U] **1** a light sailing boat, esp. one used for racing —see picture at SAIL[2] **2** a large, often motor-driven boat used for pleasure, such as one kept by a rich person
yacht·ing /ˈjɒtɪŋ‖ˈjɑtɪŋ/ *n* [U] (the act of) sailing, travelling, or racing in a YACHT: *She loves yachting.*|*She went yachting*
yachts·man /ˈjɒtsmən‖ˈjɑts-/ *fem.* **yachts·wom·an**

/-ˌwʊmən/— *n* **-men** /mən/ a person who owns or sails a YACHT

ya·hoo /jəˈhuː, ˈjɑːhuː‖ˈjɑhuː/ *n* **yahoos** *rare* a rude unpleasant person

yak¹ /jæk/ *n* a type of long-haired ox of central Asia

yak² *v* **-kk-** [IØ] *infml* to talk continuously about unimportant things; CHATTER

yam /jæm/ *n* **1** a type of climbing plant grown in the tropical parts of the world **2** the root of this plant eaten as a vegetable —see picture at VEGETABLE¹ **3** *AmE* SWEET POTATO

yam·mer /ˈjæməʳ/ *v* [IØ] *AmE* **1** to complain in a sad voice **2** to talk noisily and continuously

yang /jæŋ/ *n* [R] (in Chinese thought) the strong active male principle or force in the world —compare YIN

yank¹ /jæŋk/ *v infml* [X9;(T1;IØ)] to pull suddenly and sharply: *He yanked the nail out*

yank² *n infml* **1** a sudden sharp pull **2** (*usu. cap.*) YANKEE (1)

Yan·kee /ˈjæŋki/ *n infml* **1** a citizen of the United States of America **2** *AmE* a person born or living in the northern or northeastern states of the United States of America

yap¹ /jæp/ *v* **-pp-** [IØ] **1** (esp. of dogs) to make short sharp excited noises (sharp BARK*s*) **2** [ON or AWAY] *sl* to talk noisily about unimportant things

yap² *n* **1** [C] (of a dog) a short sharp noise (sharp BARK) **2** [U] *sl* noisy empty talk

yard¹ /jɑːd‖jɑrd/ *n* **1** a measure of length that is a little less than a METRE; 3 feet; 36 inches —see WEIGHTS & MEASURES TABLE **2** (esp. in the building trade) a measure that is a yard high, a yard wide, and a yard deep; a CUBIC yard: *We need 3 yards of sand* —see WEIGHTS & MEASURES TABLE **3** a long pole that supports a square sail

yard² *n* **1** an enclosed or partly enclosed area next to a building or group of buildings **2** *AmE* BACKYARD (2) **3** an area enclosed for a special purpose, activity, or business: *shipyard|coalyard*

yard·age /ˈjɑːdɪdʒ‖ˈjɑr-/ *n* the size of something measured in yards: *a large yardage*

yard·arm /ˈjɑːd-ɑːm‖ˈjɑrd-ɑrm/ *n* either end of the pole (YARD¹ (3)) that supports a square sail

yard goods /ˈ· ·/ *n* [P] *AmE* materials, such as cloth, sold in measures of a yard

yard·stick /ˈjɑːdˌstɪk‖ˈjɑrd-/ *n* **1** a stick that is one yard long and marked with smaller measures of length **2** any standard of measurement or comparison: *Is profit the only yardstick of success?*

yarn¹ /jɑːn‖jɑrn/ *n* **1** [U] a long continuous thread, as of wool or cotton, used in making cloth, mats, etc. **2** [C] *infml* a story, esp. one told by someone returning from an adventure or long travels (often in the phr. **spin a yarn**)

yarn² *v* [IØ] *infml* to tell YARNS¹ (2)

yar·row /ˈjærəʊ/ *n* [U] a type of plant with flat-topped groups of flowers, used in medicine

yash·mak /ˈjæʃmæk/ *n* a piece of cloth worn across the face by some Muslim women

yaw¹ /jɔː/ *v* [IØ] *tech* (of a ship, aircraft, etc.) to make a YAW² (1) —compare PITCH² (9), ROLL² (6a)

yaw² *n tech* **1** (of a ship, aircraft, etc.) a turn to the side, esp. out of the proper course **2** the amount of such a turn: *a yaw of 105°*

yawl /jɔːl/ *n* **1** a type of sailing boat with at least 2 sails, one of which is set well back **2** a small boat carried on a ship

yawn¹ /jɔːn/ *v* [IØ] **1** to open the mouth wide and breathe in deeply, as when tired or uninterested **2** [Wv4] to be or become wide open: *The hole yawned before him.|a yawning crack*

yawn² *n* an act of YAWNing

yaws /jɔːz/ *n* [U] a skin disease of the tropics

Y chro·mo·some /ˈwaɪ ˌkrəʊməsəʊm/ *n* a type of CHROMOSOME which exists singly in male cells, and, after union of male and female, will produce a male when combined with an X CHROMOSOME

yd *written abbrev. for*: YARD(*s*)¹ (1)

ye¹ /jiː/ *pron* [Wp1] *old use* (used esp. when addressing more than one person, usu. only as the subject of a sentence) you

ye² *determiner* (a word used esp. in the names of inns and shops, in order to make them seem old and historical, meaning) the: *Ye Old Dog and Duck* (inn sign)| *Ye Old Tea Shop*

yea¹ /jeɪ/ *adv old use* yes

yea² *n tech* a vote, voter, or reply in favour of an idea, plan, law, etc. —opposite **nay**; compare AYE³

yeah /jeə/ *adv infml* yes

year /jɪəʳ, jɜːʳ‖jɪər/ *n* **1** a measure of time equal to about 365¼ days, which is the amount of time it takes for the earth to travel completely round the sun **2** also **calendar year**— a period of 365 or 366 days divided into 12 months beginning on January 1st and ending on December 31st **3** a period of 365 days measured from any point: *I arrived here 2 years ago today* **4** a period of a year or about a year in the life of an organization: *The school year is broken up with many holidays* **5 all the year round** during the whole year **6 year in, year out** happening regularly each year —see also LEAP YEAR

USAGE When speaking of dates, one says *the* **year** *1977*, not **1977* **year**.

year·book /ˈjɪəbʊk, ˈjɜː-‖ˈjɪər-/ *n* a book printed once a year giving facts and information about the year just past: *Look! There's my photograph in the school yearbook*

year·ling /ˈjɪəlɪŋ, ˈjɜː-‖ˈjɪər-/ *n* an animal, esp. a young horse, between 1 and 2 years old

year·long /ˌjɪəˈlɒŋ◂, ˈjɜː-‖ˌjɪərˈlɔŋ◂/ *adj* [Wa5;A;(B)] lasting for a year or all through the year: *She came back after a yearlong absence*

year·ly /ˈjɪəli, ˈjɜː-‖ˈjɪərli/ *adj, adv* [Wa5;A;(B)] (happening, appearing, etc.) every year or once a year

yearn /jɜːn‖jɜrn/ *v* [IØ,3] to have a strong, loving, or sad desire: *They yearned to return home*

yearn for *v prep* [T1;V3] to have a strong, loving, or sad desire for: *She yearned for his presence|him|him to come home*

yearn·ing /ˈjɜːnɪŋ‖ˈjɜr-/ *n* [U;C] (a) strong usu. sad desire

years /jɪəz, jɜːz‖jɪərz/ *n* [P] age, esp. old age: *a young boy of 6 years|a woman of some years|He is very healthy for a man of his years*

yeast /jiːst/ *n* [U] a form of very small plant life that is used for producing alcohol in beer and wine and for making bread light and soft —see picture at FUNGUS

yeast·y /ˈjiːsti/ *adj* [Wa2] **1** of, like, or containing YEAST **2** having a surface of many small balls of air (BUBBLE*s*)

yell¹ /jel/ *v* **1** [IØ (*at*)] to make a loud cry or shout, as of fear or excitement: *Don't yell at me like that!* **2** [T1 (OUT, *at*)] to say or shout loudly: *He yelled (out) orders at everyone*

yell² *n* **1** a loud cry, as of fear or excitement **2** *AmE* a cheer or cry of fixed words or sounds, esp. one shouted to encourage a school team

yel·low¹ /ˈjeləʊ/ *n* [U;(C)] a colour like that of butter, gold, or the middle part (YOLK) of an egg

yellow² *adj* [Wa2] **1** having or being of the colour yellow **2** having a light brown or yellowish skin **3** *sl* also **yellow-bel·lied** /ˈ·· ˌ··/— not brave; cowardly

yellow³ *v* [T1;IØ] to (cause to) become yellow: *That paper has yellowed with age*

yellow fe·ver /ˌ·· ˈ··/ *n* [U] a dangerous disease of

tropical parts of the world, in which the skin turns yellow

yellow per·il /ˌ·· ˈ··/ *n* [*the*+R] the supposed danger that the very large number of people in eastern Asia will destroy or take over the civilizations of the western countries

yellow press /ˌ·· ˈ·/ *n* [*the*+GU] *becoming rare* newspapers that try to make all matters exciting rather than reporting them exactly

yelp[1] /jelp/ *v* [IØ] to make a short sharp high cry, as of pain or excitement: *The dog yelped and ran off*

yelp[2] *n* a short sharp cry, as of pain or excitement

yen[1] /jen/ *n* **yen** [Wn3;C] the standard amount (UNIT) of money in Japan

yen[2] *n* [S (*for*, 3)] a strong desire: *He has a yen to be alone in a boat*

yeo·man /ˈjəʊmən/ *n* **-men** /mən/ *BrE* **1** *rare* a farmer who owns and works his own land **2** *old use* a servant of high rank in the house of a royal or noble person

yeo·man·ry /ˈjəʊmənri/ *n* [*the*+GU] *BrE* the body of country landowners

yes[1] /jes/ *adv* **1** (used for showing agreement, willingness, etc., in answer to questions, or to remarks without *no* or *not*): *"Is this book a dictionary?" "Yes, it is."*|*"Hasn't she got beautiful eyes?" "Yes, hasn't she!"* (compare *"She's not pretty, is she?" "No, she isn't"*)|*"Wouldn't you like to go to the cinema?" "Yes, I would"* —opposite **no** **2** (used when partly agreeing, but going on to state a different opinion): . . . *"Yes, (yes,) what you say is right, but . . ."* **3** (used for showing that one has heard a command or call, and will obey or is paying attention): *"Go and close the door." "Yes, sir."*|*"Michael!" "Yes, mother?"* (=what do you want?)

yes[2] *n* a vote, voter, or reply in favour of an idea, plan, law, etc.

yes-man /ˈjes mæn/ *n* **-men** *derog* a person who always agrees with his employer, leader, etc.

yes please /ˌ· ˈ·/ *adv* PLEASE[2] (3)

yes·ter- /ˈjestəʳ/ *comb. form* the day, week, year, etc., before this one: *yesteryear*

yes·ter·day[1] /ˈjestədi‖-ər-/ *adv* [F] **1** on the day before this one: *It was only yesterday that I saw him.*|*Yesterday she came to tea* **2** only a short time ago: *I wasn't born yesterday* (=I'm not a fool)

yesterday[2] *n* **1** [Wa5;R] the day before this one: *I saw him at yesterday's meeting.*|*Today is Sunday so the day before yesterday was Friday* **2** [C] *old use* time that is not long past: *"All our yesterdays have lighted fools the way to dusty death"* (Shakespeare) **3** [A] (of) the day before this one: *Yesterday morning/afternoon/evening*

yet[1] /jet/ *adv* [Wa5] **1** *nonassertive* at this moment; now: *It is not time to go yet* (compare *It is time to go now*).|*"Have another?" "Not yet, thank you"* **2** *nonassertive* at or up to that moment; then: *It was not yet time to go.*|*When you left, had they arrived yet?* **3** *nonassertive* (not usu. with the past tense) up to this moment; so far: *He hasn't done much yet.*|(compare *He's done a lot now/already*).|*Is John here yet?*|*Has he arrived yet?*|(*AmE*) *Did you eat yet?* **4** *fml* at this time as at earlier times; still: *He is yet a child.*|*I have yet to hear the story* (=I have still not heard) **5** at a future time: *The plan may (even) yet succeed* **6** even; still: *Play it yet more softly* **7** in addition; again: *Sing it yet once more* (=for at least the 3rd time) **8 as yet** *nonassertive fml* up to this moment: *We have not succeeded as yet.*|*As yet, we have received no answer* —see STILL, JUST (USAGE)

yet[2] *conj* but even so; but: *strange yet true*|*She's a funny girl, (and/but) yet you can't help liking her*

yet·i /ˈjeti/ also **abominable snowman**— *n* a large hairy manlike animal supposed to live in the Himalaya mountains

yew /juː/ *n* **1** [C] also **yew tree** /ˈ· ·/— a type of tree with small leaves that are always dark green and small red berries —see picture at TREE[1] **2** [U] the wood of this tree

yid /jɪd/ *n taboo derog* a Jew

Yid·dish /ˈjɪdɪʃ/ *n* [R] a language spoken by Jews, esp. in eastern Europe

yield[1] /jiːld/ *v* **1** [T1;IØ] to give, produce, bear, etc.: *That tree yields plenty of fruit.*|*His business yields big profits* **2** [T1 (UP); IØ: (*to*)] to give up control (of); SURRENDER: *We yielded (up) our position to the enemy.*|*We were forced to yield* **3** [D1] *fml* to provide; furnish; give: *The empty house yielded us shelter* **4** [IØ] to bend, break, etc., because of a strong force: *The shelf is beginning to yield under that heavy weight* **5 yield up the ghost** *euph* to die

yield[2] *n* that which is produced or the amount that is produced, as of fruit or profit: *The trees gave a high yield this year*

yield·ing /ˈjiːldɪŋ/ *adj* **1** able to bend; not stiff or fixed **2** likely to agree with or give in to others: *He has a yielding character and will soon change his mind*

yin /jɪn/ *n* [R] (in Chinese thought) the soft inactive female principle or force in the world —compare YANG

yip·pee /jɪˈpiː‖ˈjɪpi/ *interj infml* a cry of delight, happiness, success, etc.

yob·bo /ˈjɒbəʊ‖ˈjɑ-/ also **yob** /jɒb‖jɑb/— *n* **-bos** *derog BrE* a young man who appears to have nothing to do and is rude or troublesome

yo·del[1] /ˈjəʊdl/ *v* **-ll-** (*AmE* **-l-**) [T1;IØ] to sing (a song or piece of music) with many rapid changes between the natural voice and a very high voice

yodel[2] *n* a song, piece of music, or cry sung or made by YODELling[1]

yo·ga /ˈjəʊgə/ *n* [U] a Hindu system of exercises to free the self from the body, will, and mind

yog·hurt, yogurt, yoghourt /ˈjɒgət‖ˈjəʊgərt/ *n* [U] milk that has turned thick and slightly acid through the action of certain bacteria, often eaten with fruit

yo·gi /ˈjəʊgi/ *n* a person who practises YOGA, esp. one who teaches it to others

yoke[1] /jəʊk/ *n* **1** [C] a wooden bar used for joining 2 animals, esp. oxen, together in order to pull heavy loads, farm vehicles, etc. **2** [Wn2;C] 2 animals joined together by such a bar: *6 yoke(s) of oxen* —see NUMBER TABLE 4B **3** [C] a frame fitted across a person's shoulders for carrying 2 equal loads **4** [C] that piece of a garment from which the rest hangs, as the part of a shirt around the shoulders **5** [*the*+R (*of*)] power, control, etc.: *They were brought under the yoke of the king* **6** [C (*of*) *usu. sing.*] something that binds people or things together: *The yoke of marriage* **7** [C] something that represents the position of slavery or of being under the power of someone

yoke[2] *v* [T1 (TOGETHER)] to join with or as if with a YOKE[1]: *Yoke the oxen together.*|*Yoke the oxen to the load*

yo·kel /ˈjəʊkəl/ *n humor or derog* a simple or foolish country man

yolk /jəʊk‖jəʊk, jelk/ *n* [C;U] the yellow central part of an egg

yon·der /ˈjɒndəʳ‖ˈjɑn-/ also **yon** /jɒn‖jɑn/— *adj, adv* [Wa5;A;E] *becoming rare* at a place or in a direction shown, suggested, or in view; over there: *He has walked to yonder hill*

yonks /jɒŋks‖jɑŋks/ *n* [U] *infml BrE* a very long time: *I haven't seen him for yonks; he's gone to live in Australia*

yore /jɔːʳ‖jor/ *n* [U] *lit* time long past (esp. in the phr. **of yore**): *in days of yore*

york·er /ˈjɔːkəʳ‖ˈjɔr-/ *n* (in cricket) a ball that is BOWLed in such a way that it passes underneath the BAT

York·shire pud·ding /ˌjɔːkʃə ˈpʊdɪŋ‖ˌjɔrkʃər-/ *n* [C;U] a baked mixture of flour and egg, usu. eaten with cow's meat (BEEF)

Yorkshire ter·rier /ˌ·· ˈ···/ *n* a type of short dog with fairly long hair

you /jə, jʊ; *strong* juː/ *pron* [Wp1] (*used as subject or object*) **1** the person or people being spoken to: *You are kind.|Would you like some tea?|Will you please stop that noise.|Only you can decide this.|I told you (the truth)* **2** *not fml* one; anyone: *You have to be careful with people you don't know* (compare *One has to be . . .*) **3** (used with nouns or phrases when addressing someone, esp. in an angry way): *You girls are always getting into trouble.|You fool!|You in the corner; come here!* —see HIM (USAGE)

you-all /ˈ· ·/ *pron S AmE* **1** (*to more than one person*) you: *You-all will about fill the aircraft* **2** *nonstandard* (*to one person*) you: *You-all are the most beautiful girl in the world!*

you'd /jəd, jʊd; *strong* juːd/ *contr. of* **1** you had **2** you would —see CONTR. (USAGE)

you'll /jəl, jʊl; *strong* juːl/ *contr. of* **1** you will **2** you shall —see CONTR. (USAGE)

young[1] /jʌŋ/ *adj* **younger** /ˈjʌŋgəʳ/, **youngest** /ˈjʌŋgɪ̵st/ **1** in an early stage of life, growth, development, etc.; recently born or begun: *a young girl/plant/country* —opposite **old** **2** of, for, concerning, or having the qualities of a young person: *a young manner* **3** fresh and good: *young vegetables* **4** having only a little experience: *young in crime* —**~ish** /ˈjʌŋɪʃ/ *adj*

young[2] *n* **1** [*the*+P] young people considered as a group **2** [P9] young animals: *The lion fought to protect her young.|the young of the elephant* **3** **with young** (esp. of animals) expecting to give birth; PREGNANT

young·er /ˈjʌŋgəʳ/ *adj* [Wa5; *the*+A; *the*+E] (*sometimes cap.*) used before or after a person's name to separate that person from a father or mother: *the younger Jones|Jones the younger* —compare ELDER[2] (2)

young·ster /ˈjʌŋstəʳ/ *n* a young person, esp. a boy

your /jəʳ; *strong* jɔːʳ‖jər; *strong* jʊər, jor/ *determiner* [Wa5;A] **1** (*poss. form of* YOU (1)) belonging to you: *Your hands are dirty.|You must all come and bring your wives|your book, not mine* **2** (*poss. form of* YOU (2)) belonging to one; one's **3** *infml* (used for giving force to an expression) a, an: *Your typical postage stamp is square|your actual English gentleman* **4** (used for showing disapproval, or for suggesting that something is not so good as is claimed): *If this is your famous French cooking, I don't think much of it*

you're /jəʳ; *strong* jɔːʳ‖jər; *strong* jʊər, jor/ *contr. of* you are —see CONTR. (USAGE)

yours /jɔːz‖jʊərz, jorz/ *pron* [Wp1] **1** (*poss. form of* YOU) *that which is of you: Is this yours?|Her daughter is rather stupid, but both of yours are very clever.|Is Paul a friend of yours?* **2** (*usu. cap.*) (written at the end of a letter with or without various other words): *Write "yours faithfully" or "yours truly" to strangers, "yours* SINCERE*ly" to people you have met, and "yours" or "yours ever" to friends* **3** **yours truly** /ˌ· ˈ··/ **a** (polite phr. written at the end of a letter) **b** *infml* I; me; myself: *I can take care of yours truly*

your·self /jəˈself‖jər-/ *pron* **-selves** /ˈselvz/ [Wp1] **1** (*refl. form of* YOU): *You'll hurt yourself if you play with the scissors.|"You consider yourself of no importance at all."* (SEU S.) *I hope you'll enjoy yourself* **2** (*strong form of* YOU): *You yourself know it couldn't be true.|You boys must learn to think for yourselves instead of just obeying orders.|"Shut the door will you?" "Shut it yourself!"* **3** *infml* (in) your usual state of mind or body (in such phrs. as **be oneself**, **come to oneself**, etc.): *Are you very tired? You don't seem yourself today.|I'll forgive you; I know you weren't yourself when you said that* **4** **(all) by yourself** alone; without help: *Do it by yourself.|Did you walk across the country all by yourself?*

USAGE Always use the REFLEXIVE **pronouns** like **yourself** with verbs that need a REFLEXIVE object: *to enjoy* **oneself**. With some verbs they can be put in or left out with no change of meaning: *He washed* (**himself**). They are also used after v preps: Compare: *Mary looked at* **herself** (=at Mary) *in the mirror*; *Mary looked at her* (=at another woman) *in the mirror*. These PRONOUN*s* are not otherwise used after PREPOSITION*s* that mean position or direction in space: *Shut the door behind you* (not **behind* **yourself**).

youth /juːθ/ *n* **youths** /juːðz‖juːðz, juːθs/ **1** [U] the period of being young, esp. the period between being a child and being fully grown; early life **2** [U] the appearance, health, etc., of someone who is young **3** [C] *often derog* a young person, esp. a young male: *a group of youths* **4** [(*the*) GU (*of*)] young men and women considered as a group: *The youth of the country is/are ready to fight*

youth·ful /ˈjuːθfəl/ *adj* **1** of or having the qualities of youth: *a youthful skin* **2** young —**~ly** *adv* —**~ness** *n* [U]

Youth Hos·tel /ˈ· ˌ··/ *n* a HOSTEL for usu. young people walking around country areas on holiday, for which they pay small amounts of money to the Youth Hostels Association (YHA) or to the International YHA

you've /jev; *strong* juːv/ *contr. of* you have —see CONTR. (USAGE)

yowl[1] /jaʊl/ *v* [IØ] (esp. of an animal) to make a long loud cry, as of pain or sadness

yowl[2] *n* a long loud cry

yo·yo /ˈjəʊjəʊ/ *n* **-yos** a toy made of a thick circular piece of wood, plastic, etc., that can be made to run up and down a string tied to it

yuc·ca /ˈjʌkə/ *n* a type of plant with long pointed leaves and large white flowers

yule /juːl/ *n* [R] *rare* (*sometimes cap.*) Christmas

yule log /ˈ· ·/ *n* **1** a log of wood burnt on the evening before Christmas **2** a cake made to look like this

yule·tide /ˈjuːltaɪd/ *n* [R] *esp. poet or pomp* (*sometimes cap.*) Christmas; CHRISTMASTIME: *Yuletide greetings*

Z, z

Z, z /zed‖ziː/ **Z's, z's** *or* **Zs, zs** the 26th and last letter of the English alphabet

za·ny[1] /ˈzeɪni/ *n* **1** (in former times) a character in amusing plays, esp. a CLOWN or ACROBAT **2** *rare* a person who tries to make others laugh by doing foolish things

zany[2] *adj* [Wa1] foolish in an amusing way: *Michael made us all laugh with his zany tricks*

zeal /ziːl/ *n* [U] eagerness; keenness: *He shows great zeal for knowledge*

zeal·ot /ˈzelət/ *n usu. derog* a person who is too eager in his beliefs

zeal·ot·ry /ˈzelətri/ *n* [U] *derog, now rare* the quality of being a ZEALOT: *show great zealotry*

zeal·ous /ˈzeləs/ *adj* [B (*for, in*), F3] eager; keen: *zealous for fame/in doing his duty/to succeed* —**~ly** *adv* —**~ness** *n* [U]

ze·bra /ˈziːbrə, ˈze-‖ˈziːbrə/ *n* [Wn1] any of several types of wild animal from Africa that look like a horse with broad dark brown and white lines all over the body: *shoot several zebra* —see picture at RUMINANT

zebra cross·ing /ˌ·· ˈ··/ *n* (in Britain) a place on a busy street, painted with black and white lines to show that people have the right to walk across there —see picture at STREET

ze·bu /ˈziːbjuː, ˈziːbuː/ *n* any of several types of Asian or East African cow, with a loose folded skin and a fleshy HUMP (=rounded, raised-up part) on the shoulders

zed /zed/ (*AmE* **zee** /ziː/)— *n BrE* the name of the letter Z

zeit·geist /ˈzaɪtgaist (*Ger* ˈtsaɪtgaɪst)/ *n* [*the*+R] *Ger* (*often cap.*) the general spirit of a period in history, as shown in people's ideas and beliefs

Zen /zen/ *n* [R] a Japanese form of the Buddhist religion, stating that one must look inside oneself for understanding, rather than depend on holy writings

ze·na·na /zeˈnɑːnə, zə-/ *n* (in former times) the women's part of an Indian or Persian house —compare HAREM

zen·ith /ˈzenəθ‖ˈziː-/ *n* **1** [*the*+R] the point in the heavens directly above a person on earth —opposite **nadir** **2** [C *usu. sing.*] the highest point, as of hope or fortune: *Our spirits rose to their zenith after the victory*

zeph·yr /ˈzefər/ *n poet* a soft gentle west wind

zep·pe·lin /ˈzepəlɪn/ *n* a type of large stiff AIRSHIP used by the Germans in World War I

ze·ro /ˈzɪərəʊ‖ˈziːrəʊ/ *n* **-ros** *or* **-roes** **1** the name of the sign 0 and of the number it stands for **2** the point between + and − on a scale; on the CENTIGRADE scale, the temperature at which water freezes: *It was 5 below zero last night* —compare ABSOLUTE ZERO **3** (often written 0) nothing; no size or quantity: *Our population has reached zero growth* (=it is not growing any more)

USAGE In saying a number, **zero** is generally used for 0 in scientific matters. In daily life, American speakers may use it in speech where a British speaker would favour NOUGHT, OH, or NIL. Compare: *Wolverhampton nil* (*BrE* football SCORE); *Detroit zero* (*AmE* BASEBALL SCORE).

zero hour /ˈ·· ·/ *n* [R] the hour at which an action or (military) operation is planned to begin: *Zero hour is fixed for midnight*

zero in on *v adv prep* [T1] **1** to aim gunfire directly at (something) **2** to aim one's attention directly towards (something)

zest /zest/ *n* **1** [S;U] (a quality of) being pleasant and exciting: *The danger of being caught gave/added (a) zest to the affair* **2** [S9;U] (a feeling of) being eager and excited: *He entered into the work with zest/with a zest which surprised us all* **3** the outer skin of an orange or LEMON used for giving a special taste to food

zig·gu·rat /ˈzɪgʊræt‖ˈzɪgə-/ *n* a PYRAMIDlike (3) tower in ancient Mesopotamia (=Iraq and parts of Syria) with a temple on top

zig·zag[1] /ˈzɪgzæg/ *n* a line shaped like a row of z's: *go in a zigzag|a zigzag path*

zigzag[2] *adv* in a ZIGZAG[1]

zigzag[3] *v* **-gg-** [IØ;L9] to go in a ZIGZAG[1]: *The path zigzags up the hill*

zinc /zɪŋk/ *n* [U] a bluish-white metal that is a simple substance (ELEMENT) used in the production of other metals, and to cover (PLATE) metal objects with a protective surface

zin·ni·a /ˈzɪnɪə/ *n* **1** any of several types of American garden plant related to the DAISY **2** the brightly-coloured long-lasting flower of this plant: *a bunch of zinnias*

Zi·on·is·m /ˈzaɪənɪzəm/ *n* [R] the political movement to establish and develop an independent state of Israel in Palestine for the Jews —**-ist** *adj, n*: *a group of young Zionists|This organization is not Zionist*

zip[1] /zɪp/ *v* **-pp-** **1** [X7] to put into the stated condition with a ZIP[2] (1): *He zipped the bag open/shut* **2** [L9] to make the sound of something moving quickly and suddenly through the air, or of cloth tearing: *The bullet zipped through the air*

zip[2] *n* **1** [C] also **zip fas·ten·er** /ˌ· ˈ···/— a fastener made of 2 sets of metal or plastic teeth and a sliding piece that joins the edges of an opening in material by drawing the teeth together **2** [C] a ZIPping[1] (2) sound: *We heard the zip of a bullet* **3** [U] *infml* quickness and activity: *David always seems active and healthy and full of zip*

zip code /ˈ· ·/ *n AmE* POSTCODE

zip·per /ˈzɪpər/ *n AmE* ZIP[2] (1)

zip·py /ˈzɪpi/ *adj* [Wa1] *infml* quick and active; full of ZIP[2] (3)

zip up *v adv* [T1] to fasten (a person into something) with a ZIP[2] (1): *Will you zip me up/zip up my dress?* —opposite **unzip**

zith·er /ˈzɪðər/ *n* a type of flat musical instrument with 30–40 strings, played with the fingers or with a PLECTRUM (=small piece of metal, bone, etc., worn on a finger)

zizz /zɪz/ *n* [S] *infml BrE* a short sleep (esp. in the phrs. **have/take a zizz**)

zo·di·ac /ˈzəʊdiæk/ *n* **1** [*the*+R] an imaginary belt through space along which the sun, the moon, and the nearest heavenly bodies (PLANET*s*) appear to travel and which is divided into 12 equal parts (SIGN*s*) each named after a group (CONSTELLATION) of stars which were once in them **2** [C] a circular representation of this with pictures and names for each part (SIGN), esp. as used by people (ASTROLOGER*s*) who believe in the influence of the stars on one's character and fate —see picture at PLANET —**~al** /zəʊˈdaɪəkəl/ *adj* [Wa5]

zom·bie, -bi /ˈzɒmbi‖ˈzɑm-/ *n* **1** [C] (according to certain African and Caribbean religions) a dead person who is made to move by magic **2** [C; *you*+N] *derog* someone who moves very slowly and behaves as if he were not really alive

zon·al /ˈzəʊnl/ *adj* with regard to or arranged in ZONE*s* (1); shaped like a ZONE

zone¹ /zəʊn/ *n* **1** [C] a division or area marked off from others by particular qualities **2** [C9] an area with the stated qualities: *a war/danger zone* **3** [C] one of the 5 divisions of the earth's surface according to temperature, marked by imaginary lines running round it from east to west: *the* TORRID *zone, the 2* TEMPERATE *zones and the 2* FRIGID *zones* **4** [C] (in the US) a division of the country for postal and telephone purposes

zone² *v* [T1] **1** to divide into ZONE*s*¹ (1) **2** [(*as, for*)] to give a special purpose to (an area, as in a town): *This part of the town has been zoned as a shopping area/for industrial development*

zon·ing /ˈzəʊnɪŋ/ *n* [U] the choosing of areas to be developed for different purposes, when planning a town

zonked /zɒŋkt‖zaŋkt/ *adj sl, esp. AmE* under the influence of alcohol or a drug, as LSD; HIGH

zoo /zuː/ also (*fml*) **zoological gar·dens** [P] /ˌ····· ˈ··, ··ˌ··· ˈ··/— *n* **zoos** [C] a park where many kinds of living animals are kept for show: *go to the zoo and watch the monkeys*

zo·ol·o·gist /zəʊˈɒlədʒɨst, zʊˈɒ-‖-ˈɑl-/ *n* a person who studies ZOOLOGY

zo·ol·o·gy /zəʊˈɒlədʒi, zʊˈɒ-‖-ˈɑl-/ *n* [U] the scientific study of the different kinds of animals, and of where and how they live —**-gical** /ˌzəʊəˈlɒdʒɪkəl, ˌzʊə-‖-ˈlɑ-/ *adj* [Wa5]

zoom¹ /zuːm/ *v* **1** [IØ] (of an aircraft) to go quickly upward: (fig.) *The cost of living zoomed* **2** [L9] *infml* (of a driver or vehicle) to go quickly: *Jack went zooming past in his new car* **3** [L9 esp. IN (*on*) or OUT] (of a cinema camera) to move quickly between a distant and a close-up view: *The camera zoomed in on the child's face*

zoom² *n* [S] (the deep low sound of) the upward flight of an aircraft

zoom lens /ˌ· ˈ·/ *n* a photographic LENS (=curved glass) that can move in from a distant to a close-up view while keeping what is being photographed in FOCUS (=clear)

zo·o·phyte /ˈzəʊəfaɪt/ *n tech* any of many types of plantlike sea creatures, such as the CORAL*s* and SPONGE*s*

Zou·ave /zuːˈɑːv, zwɑːv‖zuːˈɑv, zwɑv (*Fr* zwav)/ *n* a soldier in the part of the French army that used to be formed of Algerians

zuc·chi·ni /zuːˈkiːni‖zʊ- (*It* tsukˈkini)/ *n* [Wn2] *AmE* COURGETTE

Zu·lu /ˈzuːluː/ *adj* of or related to the language or people of Zululand in South Africa

List of words used in the dictionary

This is a list of the words that have been used for all the explanations and examples in this dictionary, except those words in SMALL CAPITAL letters.

A

a
ability
able
-able
about
above
abroad
absence
absent *adj*
accept
accident
accordance
according (to)
account *v,n*
accustom *v*
ache *v,n*
acid
across
act *v*
action
active
activity
actor, actress
actual
add
addition
address *v,n*
adjective
admiration
admire
admit
advance *v,n*
advantage
adventure *n*
adverb
advertise
advice
advise
affair(s)
afford
afraid
after *adv,prep,conj*
afternoon
afterwards
again
against
age *n*
ago
agree
ahead
aim *n,v*
air *n*
-al
alcohol(ic)
alike *adj,adv*
alive
all *adj,adv*
all right
allow
almost
alone
along
aloud
alphabet
already
also
although
altogether
always
among
amongst
amount *n*
amuse
amusing *adj*
an
-an
-ance
ancient
and
anger *n,v*
angle
angry
animal *n,adj*
ankle
annoy
another
answer *n,v*
ant
anxiety
anxious
any
anybody
anyhow
anyone
anything
anywhere
apart
apparatus
appear
appearance
apple
appoint
approve
April
-ar
arch, archway
area
argue
arise
arm *n,v*
armour *n,v*
arms
army
around *prep,adv*
arrange, arrange-ment(s)
arrive
arrow
art
article
artist
as
ashamed
ash(es)
aside *adv*
ask
asleep
association
at
-ate
-ation
atom(ic)
attack *n,v*
attempt *n,v*
attend
attention
attentive
attract(ive)
August
aunt
autumn
average *n,adj,v*
avoid
awake *adj*
away
awkward
axe *n*

B

baby
back *n,adv*
background
backward(s)
bacteria (-ium)
bad
bag *n*
bake
balance *n,v*
ball
banana
band *n*
bank
bar
bare
barrel
base *n,v*
basin
basket
bath *n*
bathe *v*
battle
be
beak
beam
bean
bear *n*
bear *v*
beard *n*
beat *v*
beautiful
beauty
because
become
bed
bee
beer
before
beg
begin
behave
behaviour
behind
belief
believe
bell *n*
belong
below
belt *n*
bend *n,v*
beneath
berry
beside
besides
best *adj,adv*
better *adj,adv*
between
beyond
Bible
bicycle
big
bill
bind
bird
birth
bit
bite *n,v*
bitter *adj*
black *adj*
blade
blame *n,v*
bleed *v*
bless
blind *adj,v*
block *n,v*
blood *n*
blow *n,v*
blue *n,adj*
board *n*
boat
body
boil *v*
bold
bomb *n,v*
bone *n*
book *n*
boot *n*
border *n,v*
born
borrow
both
bottle *n*
bottom *n*
bowel
bowl *n*
box *n*
boy
brain
branch *n,v*
brass
brave *adj*
bread
breadth
break *v*
breakfast *n*
breast *n*
breath
breathe
breed *n,v*
brick *n*
bridge *n,v*
bright *adj*
bring
British
broad
broadcast *n,v*
brother
brown *n,adj*
brush *n,v*
bucket
Buddhist, -ism
build
bullet
bunch *n*
burn *v,n*
burst *n,v*
bury
bus
bush *n*
busy
but
butter *n*
button *n,v*
buy *v*
by

C

cage *n*
cake *n*
calculate
call *n,v*
calm *adj*
camel
camera
camp *n,v*
can *v*
candle
cap *n*
capital *n*
captain *n*
car
card *n*
cardboard
care *n,v*
carriage
carry
cart *n*
case *n*
castle *n*
cat *n*
catch *v*
cattle
cause *n,v*
cave *n*
cease
cell
cement *n*
cent
centre *n*
century
ceremony *n*
certain *adj, determiner*
certainty
chain *n,v*
chair *n*
chairman
chalk *n*
chance *n*
change *n,v*
character
charge *n,v*
charm *n,v*
chase *v*

cheap
cheat *n,v*
cheek *n*
cheer *n,v*
cheerful
cheese
chemical *n,adj*
chemistry
cheque
chest
chicken
chief *n,adv*
child, children
chimney
chin
chocolate *n,adj*
choice *n*
choose
Christian,
  Christianity
Christmas
church
cigarette
cinema *n,adj*
circle *n*
circular *adj*
citizen
city
civilize
claim *n,v*
class *n*
clay
clean *v,adj*
clear *v,adj*
clerk
clever
cliff
climb
clock *n*
close *v,adj,adv*
cloth
clothes, clothing
cloud *n*
club *n*
coal
coarse *adj*
coast *n*
coat *n*
coconut
coffee
coin *n*
cold *n, adj*
collar *n*
collect *v*
college
colour *n,v*
comb *n,v*
combine *v*
come
comfort *n,v*
command *n,v*
committee
common *adj*
companion
company
compare
comparison
compass
compete
complain
complete *v,adj*
compound *n,adj*
concern *v*
concerning
concert *n*
condition
confuse
connect
conquer
conscience
conscious
consider
consist
consonant (sound)
contain
content *adj*
contents *n*
continue
contract *n*
control *n,v*
convenient
conversation
cook *n,v*
cool *adj*
copper *n,adj*
copy *n,v*
cord
corn
corner *n*
correct *adj*
cost *n,v*
cotton *n*
cough *n,v*
could
council
count *v*
country *n*
courage *n*
course
court *n*
cover *n,v*
cow *n*
coward
crack *n,v*
crash *n,v*
cream *n*
creature
creep *v*
cricket
crime
criminal *n,adj*
crop *n*
cross *n,v*
crowd *n*
crown *n,v*
cruel
crush *v*
cry *n,v*
cultivate
cup *n*
cupboard
cure *n,v*
curl *n,v*
current *n*
curse *n,v*
curtain *n*
curve *n,v*
custom *n*
cut *n,v*
cycle *v*

D

daily *adj*
damage *n,v*
dance *n,v*
danger
dare *v*
daring *n,adj*
dark *adj*
date *n*
daughter
day
dead *adj*
deal *n,v*
dear *adj*
death
debt
decay *n,v*
deceive
December
decide
decimal *n,adj*
declare
decrease *n,v*
deed
deep *adj*
deer
defeat *n,v*
defence
defend
degree
delay *n,v*
delicate
delight *n,v*
deliver
demand *n,v*
department
depend
dependent
depth
descend
describe
description
descriptive
desert *n*
desert *v*
deserve
desire *n,v*
desk
destroy
detail *n*
determine
develop
devil *n*
diamond
dictionary
die *v*
difference
different
difficult
difficulty
dig
dinner
dip *v*
direct *v,adj*
direction
dirt
dirty *adj*
dis-
disappoint
discourage
discover
disease *n*
dish *n*
dismiss
distance
distant
ditch *n*
divide *v*
division
do
doctor *n*
dog *n*
dollar
-dom
donkey
door
doorway
dot *n*
double *adj,adv,v*
doubt *n,v*
down *adv,prep*
drag *v*
draw
drawer
dream *n,v*
dress *n,v*
drink *n,v*
drive *v*
drop *n,v*
drown
drug *n*
drum *n,v*
drunk
dry *v,adj*
duck *n*
dull *adj*
during
dust *n*
duty

E

each *determiner,*
  pron
eager
ear
early *adj,adv*
earn
earth *n*
east *n,adj,adv*
eastern
easy
eat
-ed
edge *n*
educate
effect *n*
effective
effort
egg *n*
either
elastic *adj*
elbow *n*
elder *adj*
eldest
elect *v*
electric
electrical
electrician
electricity
elephant
else
empire
employ *v*
empty *v,adj*
en-
-en
-ence
enclose
encourage
end *n,v*
enemy
engine
English *n,adj*
enjoy
enough *n,adj,adv*
enquire
enter *v*
entrance
envelope
equal *n,v,adj*
-er
escape *n,v*
-ese
especially
-ess
establish
even *adj,adv*
evening
event
ever
every
evil *n,adj*
exact *adj*
examine
examination
example
excellent
except *prep,conj*
exchange *n,v*
excite
excuse *n,v*
exercise *n,v*
exist
expect
experience *n,v*
explain
explanation
explode
explosion
explosive *n,adj*
express *v*
expression
eye
eyelid

F

face *n,v*
fact
factory *n*
fade *v*
fail
failure
faint *adj*
fair *adj*
fairy
faith
faithful *adj*
fall *n,v*
false
fame
familiar *adj*
family
famous
fancy *n,v,adj*
far *adj,adv*
farm *n,v*
farmer
fashion(able)
fast *adj,adv*
fasten
fat *n,adj*
fate
father *n*
fault *n*
favour *n,v*
favourable
favourite *adj*
fear *n,v*
feast *n,v*
feather *n*
February
feed *v*
feel *v*
feelings
fellow *n*
female *n,adj*
fence *n*
fever *n*
few
field *n,adj*
fierce
fight *n,v*
figure *n*
fill
film *n,v*
find *v*
fine *adj*
finger *n*
finish *n,v*
fire *n,v*
firm *n,adj*
first *adj,adv*
fish *n,v*

fisherman
fit *v,adj*
fix *v*
flag *n*
flame *n,v*
flash *n,v*
flat *n,adj*
flesh *n*
flight
float *v*
flood *n,v*
floor *n*
flour
flow *n,v*
flower *n*
fly *n v*
fold *n,v*
follow *v*
fond
food *n*
fool *n*
foolish
foot
football
for *prep*
forbid
force *n,v*
fore-
forehead
foreign
foreigner
forest
forget
forgive
fork
form *n,v*
formal
former
formerly
fort
fortune
fortunate
forward(s) *adv*
fox *n*
frame *n*
framework
free *v,adj*
freeze
frequent *adj*
fresh
Friday
friend
fro
from
front *n,adj*
fruit *n*
-ful
fulfil
full
fun *n*
funny
funeral *n*
fur *n*
furnish
furniture
further *adj,adv*
future *n,adj*

G

gaiety
gain *n,v*
game *n*
garage *n,v*
garden *n*
garment
gas *n*
gate
gather
gay
general *n,adj*
generosity
generous
gentle *adj*
gentleman
get
gift
girl
give
glad
glass *n*
glorious
glory
go
goat
god & God
goddess
gold
golden
good
good-bye
goods
govern
government
grace
gradual(ly)
grain
gram
grammar
grand
grandfather
grandmother
grass
grateful
grave *n*
great
green *n,adj*
greet
grey *n,adj*
grief
grieve
ground
group *n*
grow
growth
guard *n,v*
guess *n,v*
guest
guide *n,v*
guilt
gun *n*
gunpowder

H

habit
habitual
hair
half *n,adj,adv*
hall
hammer *n,v*
hand *n,v*
handkerchief
handle *n,v*
hang
happen
happening
happiness
happy
harbour *n*
hard *adj,adv*
hardly
harm *n,v*
haste *n*
hasten
hastily
hasty
hat
hate *n,v*
hatred
have
he
head *n,adj*
health *n*
healthy
heap *n,v*
hear
heart
heat *n,v*
heaven
heavy
heel
height
help *n,v*
hen
her(s) *pron,adj*
here
hide *v*
high *adj,adv*
hill
him
Hindu(ism)
hire *v*
his
historical
history
hit *n,v*
hold *n,v*
hold *n*
holiday
hollow *adj*
holy
home *n.adj,adv*
honest
honesty
honour *n*
honourable
-hood
hook *n,v*
hope *n,v*
horizon
horn *n*
horse *n*
hospital
host
hot
hotel
hour
house *n*
how
human *adj*
humble *adj*
humour, humorous
hunger
hungry
hunt *v*
hurry *v*
hurt *v*
husband *n*
hut

I

I
-ible
-ic
-ical
ice *n*
icy
idea
if
ill *adj*
im-
image
imaginary
imagination
imagine
importance
important
improve
in
in-
inch *n*
include
including
income
increase *n,v*
indeed
indoor(s) *adj,adv*
industrial
industry
infect(ious)
influence *n,v*
influential
inform
information
-ing
ink *n*
inn
inner
inquire
inquiry
insect
inside *n,prep,adv*
instead
instruct
instrument
insurance
intend
intention
interest *n,v*
interesting
international
interrupt
into
introduce
introduction
invent
invitation
invite
inwards
-ion
ir-
iron *n,adj*
-ish
island
-ist
it
its
-ity
-ive
-ization
-ize

J

January
jaw(s) *n*
jealous(y)
jelly
Jew(ish)
jewel
jewellery
job *n*
join *n,v*
joint *n*
joke *n,v*
journey *n*
joy
judge *n,v*
judgment
juice
July
jump *n,v*
June
just *adj,adv*
justice

K

keen
keep *v*
key *n*
kick *n,v*
kill *v*
kilo
kilogram
kilometre
kind *n,adj*
king
kingdom
kiss *n,v*
kitchen
knee
kneel
knife *n*
knock *n,v*
knot *n,v*
know *v*
knowledge

L

labour *n*
lack *n,v*
ladder
lady
lake
lamb
lamp
land *n,v*
language
large
last *v,adj,adv*
late
lately
latter
laugh *n,v*
laughter
law
lawful
lawyer
lay *v*
lazy
lead *n*
lead *v*
leaf
lean *v*
learn
least
leather
leave *v*
left
leg
lend
length
less
-less
lesson
let *v*
letter
level *n,adj,adv*
library
lid
lie *v*
life
lift *v*
light *n,v,adj*
lightning
like *v,adj,adv, prep*
-like
likely
limb
lime *n*
limit *n,v*
line *n*

lion
lip
liquid *n,adj*
list *n*
listen *v*
literature
litre
little *n,adj,adv*
live *v*
load *n,v*
loaf *n*
local *adj*
lock *n,v*
lodge *v*
lodgings
log *n*
lonely
long *adj,adv*
look *n,v*
loose *adj*
lord *n*
lose
loss *n*
lot
loud *adj,adv*
love *n,v*
low *adj*
lower *v*
loyal
loyalty
luck
lump *n*
lung(s)
-ly

M

machine *n*
machinery
mad
magazine
magic *n,adj*
magician
mail *n,v*
main *adj*
make *v*
male *n,adj*
man *n*
manner
manners
many
map *n,v*
March
march *v*
mark *n,v*
market *n*
marriage
marry
mass
master *n*
mat
match *n,v*
material *n,adj*
matter *n,v*
may *v*
May
me
meal
mean *v*
meaning *n*
means *n*
measure *n,v*
meat
medicine *n*
meet *v*
meeting *n*
melt
member
memory
mend *v*
-ment
mention *n,v*
mercy
merry
message
messenger
metal *n*
method
metre
metric
microscope
mid-
middle *n,adj*
might *v*
mile
military *adj*
milk *n,v*
mill *n*
mind *n,v*
mine *pron,n*
mineral
minister
minute *n*
mirror *n*
mis-
Miss
miss *v*
mist
mistake *n,v*
mix *v*
mixture
model *n*
modern
moment(ary)
modest
Monday
money
monkey *n*
month
moon *n*
moral(s)
more
morning
mosque
mosquito
most
mother
motor *n*
mountain
mouse
mouth *n*
move
Mr
Mrs
much
mud
multiply
murder *n,v*
muscle *n*
music *n*
musician
Muslim *n,adj*
must *v*
my
mystery

N

nail *n,v*
name *n,v*
narrow *adj*
nasty
nation
native *n,adj*
nature
naval
navy
near *adj,adv,prep*
neat *adj*
necessary *adj*
neck
need *n,v*
needle *n*
neighbour *n*
neither
nerve *n*
nervous
-ness
nest *n*
net *n*
network
never
new
news
newspaper
next *adj,adv*
nice
night
no
noble *n,adj*
nobleman
nobody
noise *n*
non-
none
no one
nor
north *n,adj,adv*
northern
nose *n*
not
note *n,v*
nothing
notice *n,v*
noun
November
now
nowhere
number *n*
nurse *n,v*
nut
nylon

O

obey
object *n*
obtain
occasion *n*
ocean
o'clock
October
odd
of
off *adv,prep*
offence
offend
offensive *adj*
offer *n,v*
office
officer
official *adj*
often
oil *n,v*
old *adj*
on
once
one
onion
only *adj,adv*
open *v,adj*
operation
opinion
opponent
oppose
opposite *adj,prep*
opposition
or
-or
orange *n,adj*
order *n,v*
ordinary *adj*
organ
organization
origin
ornament *n,v*
other
otherwise *adv,conj*
ought
our(s)
-ous
out
outer *adj*
outside *n,adj,adv, prep*
outdoor(s) *adj,adv*
over *adv,prep*
overflow *n,v*
owe
owing to
own *v,adj*
ox(en)
oxygen

P

pack *v*
packet
page
pain *n*
paint *n,v*
pair *n*
palace
pale *adj*
pan *n*
paper *n*
parallel
parcel *n*
parent *n*
park *n,v*
parliament
part *n*
participle
particular *adj*
partner *n*
party
pass *v*
passage
passenger
past *n,adj,prep*
paste *n,v*
pastry
path
patient *adj*
pattern *n*
pause *n,v*
pay *n,v*
peace *n*
peculiar
pen *n*
pence
pencil *n*
penny
people *n*
pepper *n*
per
perfect *adj*
perform
perhaps
period
permission
permit *v*
person
personal
persuade
pet *n*
petrol
photograph *n,v*
photography
phrase *n*
piano *n*
pick *v*
picture *n*
piece *n*
pig
pile *n,v*
pillar
pilot *n,v*
pin *n,v*
pink
pipe *n*
pity *n,v*
place *n,v*
plain *n,adj*
plan *n,v*
plane *n*
plant *n,v*
plastic(s)
plate *n*
play *n,v*
pleasant
please *v,adv*
pleasure
plenty
plural
pocket *n*
poem
poet
poetry
point *n,v*
pointed
poison *n,v*
pole *n*
police *n*
policeman
polish *n,v*
polite *adj*
political
politician
politics
pool
poor *adj*
popular
popular
popularity
population
port *n*
position
possess
possessions
possible *adj*
possibility
post *n,v*
postage stamp
pot *n*
potato
pound *n*
pour
powder *n*
power
practical
practice
practise *v*
praise *n,v*
pray
prayer
precious *adj*
preparation
prepare *v*
presence
present *n,adj*
preserve *v*
president
press *v*
pretend
pretty *adj*

prevent
price *n*
pride *n*
prick *v*
prickle *n*
prickly
priest
prince
principle
print *v*
prison
private *adj*
prize *n*
probable
probability
procession
produce *v*
product
production
profession
profit *n*
promise *n,v*
pronounce
pronunciation
proof *n*
proper
property
protect
protection
protective *adj*
proud
prove
provide
provision(s)
public *n,adj*
pull *n,v*
pump *n,v*
punish
pupil
pure
purple
purpose *n*
push *n,v*
put

Q

quality
quantity
quarrel *n,v*
quarter *n*
queen *n*
question *n,v*
quick *adj*
quiet
quite

R

rabbit *n*
race *n,v*
radio *n,v*
railway
rain *n,v*
raise *v*
range *n*
rank *n*
rapid *adj*
rare
rat *n*
rate
rather
raw
re-
reach *n,v*
read
ready
real
reason *n,v*
receipt
receive
recent(ly)
recognition
recognize
record *n,v*
red
reduce
reduction
refusal
refuse *v*
regard *n,v*
regular
rejoice
related
relative(s)
relation
religion
religious
remain
remains
remark *n*
remember
remind
remove
rent *n,v*
repair *n,v*
repeat
reply *n,v*
report *n,v*
represent
representative *n, adj*
republic
request *n,v*
respect *n,v*
respectful
responsible
rest *n,v*
restaurant
result *n,v*
return *n,v*
reward *n,v*
rice
rich *adj*
rid
ride *n,v*
right *n,adj,adv*
ring *n,v*
ripe
rise *v*
risk *n,v*
river
road
rob
rock *n*
rod
roll *v*
roof
room
root *n*
rope
rose *n*
rough
round *adj,adv,prep*
row *n*
row *v*
royal
rub *v*
rubber
rude
ruin(s) *n,v*
rule *n,v*
ruler
run *n,v*
rush *n,v*
-ry

S

sad *adj*
safe *adj*
sail *n,v*
sale
salt *n,adj*
same *adj*
sand *n*
satisfaction
satisfactory
satisfy
Saturday
save *v*
say *v*
scale(s) *n*
scarce(ly)
scatter *v*
scene
scenery
school
science
scientific
scientist
scissors
scold *v*
screw *n,v*
sea
search *n,v*
season *n*
seat *n,v*
second *n,adj*
secrecy
secret *n,adj*
secretary
see *v*
seed *n*
seem
seize
self
sell
send *v*
sensation *n*
sense *n*
senseless
sensible
sensitive
sentence
separate *v,adj*
September
serious
servant
serve
service
set *n,v*
settle *v*
several
severe
sew
sex(ual)
shade *n,v*
shadow *n*
shake *n,v*
shall
shame *n*
shape
share *n,v*
sharp *adj*
she
sheep
sheet *n*
shelf
shell
shelter *n,v*
shield *n,v*
shilling
shine *v*
ship *n*
-ship
shirt
shock *n,v*
shoe *n*
shoot *v*
shop *n,v*
shore *n*
short *adj*
shot
should
shoulder
shout *n,v*
show *n,v*
shut *v,adj*
sick *adj*
side
sideways
sight *n*
sign *n,v*
signal *n,v*
signature
silence *n*
silent
silk
silly
silver
simple *adj*
since
sincere
sing
single *adj*
singular
sink *v*
sir
sister
sit
size *n*
skilful
skill
skin
skirt *n*
sky *n*
slave
sleep *n,v*
slide *v*
slight *adj*
slip *v*
slippery
slope *n,v*
slow *v,adj*
small
smell *n,v*
smile *n,v*
smoke *n,v*
smooth *adj*
snake
snow *n,v*
so
soap *n*
so-called
social
society
sock(s)
soft
soil *n*
soldier *n*
solemn
solid *n,adj*
some
somebody
somehow
someone
something
sometimes
somewhere
son
song
soon
sore *n,adj*
sorrow *n*
sorry
sort *n*
soul
sound *n,v*
soup
sour
south *n,adj,adv*
southern
space *n*
spade
speak
spear *n*
special *adj*
speech
speed *n*
spell *n*
spend *v*
spin *v*
spirit
spite
splendid
split *v*
spoil *v*
spoon
sport(s) *n*
spot *n*
spread *v*
spring *n,v*
square *n,adj*
stage *n*
stair(s)
stamp *n,v*
stand *v*
standard *n*
star
start *n,v*
state *n,v*
station *n*
stay *n,v*
steady *adj*
steal *v*
steam *n,v*
steel
steep *adj*
stem *n*
step *n,v*
stick *n,v*
sticky
stiff
still *adj,adv*
sting *v*
stitch *n,v*
stocking(s)
stomach *n*
stone *n*
stop *n,v*
store *n,v*
storm *n*
story
straight *adj,adv*
strange
stranger *n*
stream *n*
street
strength
stretch *n,v*
strike *v*
string *n*
stroke *n*
strong
struggle *n,v*
student
study *n,v*
stupid
stupidity
style *n*
subject *n*
substance
subtract
succeed
such
suck *v*

sudden
suffer
sugar *n*
suggest
suit *n,v*
sum
summer *n*
sun *n*
Sunday
supper
supply *n,v*
support *n,v*
suppose
sure
surface
surprise *n,v*
surround *v*
swallow *v*
swear
sweep *v*
sweet *n,adj*
swell *v*
swift *adj*
swim *v*
swing *v*
sword
sympathy, -etic
system

T

table *n*
tail *n*
take *v*
talk *n,v*
tall
taste *n,v*
tax *n,v*
taxi
tea
teach
team
tear *v*
tears *n*
telephone *n,v*
telegram
telegraph *v,n,attrib*
television
tell
temper *n*
temperature
temple
tend
tender *adj*
tennis
tense *n*
tent *n*
terrible
terror
test *n,v*
-th
than
thank
that *determiner pron,conj*
the
theatre
their(s)
them
then
there *adv*
therefore
these
they
thick
thief
thin *adj*
thing
think
third
thirst *n*
this
thorough
those
though
thought *n*
thread *n*
threat
throat
through
throw *n,v*
thumb *n*
thunder *n,v*
Thursday
thus
ticket *n*
tidy *v,adj*
tie *v*
tiger
tight *adj*
till *prep*
time
timetable
tin
tire *v*
title *n*
to
tobacco
today *n,adv*
toe *n*
together
tomorrow *n,adv*
tongue *n*
tonight *n,adv*
too
tool
tooth
top *n*
total *n,adj*
touch *n,v*
tour *n,v*
tourist
towards
tower *n,v*
town
toy *n*
track *n,v*
trade *n*
traffic *n*
train *n,v*
translate
transparent
trap *n,v*
travel *n,v*
treat *v*
treatment
tree *n*
tremble *v*
tribe *n*
trick *n,v*
trip *n*
tropic(s)
trouble *n,v*
troublesome
trousers
true
trunk
truth
trust *n,v*
trustworthy
try *v*
tube *n*
Tuesday
tune *n*
turn *n,v*
twice
twist *n,v*
type, typical
tyre

U

ugly
un-
uncle
under
underneath *prep, adv*
understand
undo
uniform *n,adj*
union
unite
unity
universe
university
until *prep,conj*
up
upon
upper
upright
upset *v*
upside-down
upstairs
-ure
urge
urgent
us
use *n,v*
usual

V

valley
value *n*
variety
various
vary
vegetable *n,adj*
vehicle
verb
very
vessel
vice-
victory
view *n*
village
violent, -ence
visit *n,v*
voice *n*
vote *n,v*
vowel (sound)
voyage *n*

W

wages
waist
wait *v*
wake *v*
walk *n,v*
wall *n*
wander *v*
want *v*
war
-ward(s)
warm *v,adj*
warn
wash *n,v*
waste *n,v,adj*
watch *n,v*
watchman
water *n*
wave *n,v*
wax *n*
way
we
weak *adj*
wealth
weapon
wear *v*
weather *n*
weave *v*
wedding
Wednesday
week
weep
weigh
weight
welcome *n,v,adj*
well *n,adj,adv*
well-
west *n,adj,adv*
western
wet *adj*
what *adj,pron, interj*
whatever
wheat
wheel *n*
when *adv,conj*
whenever
where *adv,conj*
wherever
whether
which *adj,pron*
whichever
while *conj*
whip *n,v*
whisper *n,v*
whistle *n,v*
white *n,adj*
who *pron*
whole *n,adj*
why *adv,interj,conj*
wicked *adj*
wide *adj,adv*
width
wife
wild
will *n,v*
willing
win *v*
wind *n*
wind *v*
window
wine *n*
wing *n*
winter *n*
wire *n*
wise
wish *n,v*
with
within
witness *n,v*
without
woman
wonder *n,v*
wood
wool
word *n*
work *n,v*
-work
world
worm *n*
worry *n,v*
worse
worst
worship *n,v*
worth
worthy (of)
would
wound *n,v*
wrap (up)
wreck *n,v*
wrist
write
wrong *n,adj,adv*

Y

-y
yard
year
yellow *n,adj*
yes
yesterday *n,adv*
yet
yield *v*
you
young *adj*
your(s)
youth

Z

zero

Irregular verb forms

(The pronunciation of each verb is shown at its own place in the dictionary)

Verb	Past tense	Past participle	Notes
abide	abode, abided	abode, abided	
arise	arose	arisen	
awake	awoke, awaked	awoken, awaked	
be	—	—	see table Wv1, p. xxxviii
bear	bore	borne	see USAGE
beat	beat	beaten	
become	became	become	
befall	befell	befallen	
beget	begot	begotten	
begin	began	began	
behold	beheld	beheld	
bend	bent	bent	
bereave	bereft, bereaved	bereft, bereaved	see USAGE
beseech	besought	besought	
beset	beset	beset	
bestride	bestrode	bestridden, bestrid, bestrode	
bet	bet (*BrE also* betted)	bet (*BrE also* betted)	
betake	betook	betaken	
bethink	bethought	bethought	
bid	bade, bid	bade, bid, bidden	
bide	bided, bode	bided	
bind	bound	bound	
bite	bit	bitten	
bleed	bled	bled	
bless	blessed, blest	blessed, blest	blessed /-ɪd/, *adj*
blow	blew	blown	
break	broke	broken	
breed	bred	bred	
bring	brought	brought	
broadcast	broadcast	broadcast	
build	built	built	
burn	(*esp. BrE*) burnt, (*esp. AmE*) burned	(*esp. BrE*) burnt, (*esp. AmE*) burned	
burst	burst	burst	
buy	bought	bought	
can	—	—	see table Wv2, p. xxxviii
cast	cast	cast	
catch	caught	caught	
chide	chid	chidden, chid	
choose	chose	chosen	
cleave	cleft, clove	cleft, cloven	
cling	clung	clung	
come	came	come	
cost	cost	cost	
creep	crept	crept	
cut	cut	cut	
dare	dared	dared	see table Wv2, p. xxxviii
deal	dealt /delt/	dealt	
dig	dug	dug	
dive	dived, (*AmE*) dove	dived	
do	did	done	see table Wv2, p. xxxviii
draw	drew	drawn	
dream	(*esp. BrE*) dreamt, (*esp. AmE*) dreamed	(*esp. BrE*) dreamt, (*esp. AmE*) dreamed	
drink	drank	drunk	drunken, *adj*
drive	drove	driven	
dwell	(*esp. BrE*) dwelt, (*esp. AmE*) dwelled	(*esp. BrE*) dwelt, (*esp. AmE*) dwelled	
eat	ate /et ‖ eɪt/	eaten	
fall	fell	fallen	
feed	fed	fed	
feel	felt	felt	
fight	fought	fought	
find	found	found	
flee	fled	fled	
fling	flung	flung	
fly	flew	flown	
forbear	forbore	foreborne	
forbid	forbade, forbad	forbidden	
forecast	forecast	forecast	
foreknow	foreknew	foreknown	
foresee	foresaw	foreseen	

Verb	Past tense	Past participle	Notes
foretell	foretold	foretold	
forget	forgot	forgotten	
forgive	forgave	forgiven	
forsake	forsook	forsaken	
forswear	forswore	forsworn	
freeze	froze	frozen	
gainsay	gainsaid	gainsaid	
get	got	got (*AmE also* gotten)	
gild	gilded	gilded	
gird	girded, girt	girded, girt	
give	gave	given	
go	went	gone	
grave	graved	graven, graved	
grind	ground	ground	
grow	grew	grown	
hamstring	hamstringed, -strung	hamstringed, -strung	
hang	hung, hanged	hung, hanged	hanged = killed by hanging
have	had	had	see table Wv2, p. xxxviii
hear	heard	heard	/hɜːd ‖ hɜrd/
heave	heaved, hove	heaved, hove	
hew	hewed	hewn, hewed	
hide	hid	hidden, hid	
hit	hit	hit	
hold	held	held	
hurt	hurt	hurt	
inlay	inlaid	inlaid	
keep	kept	kept	
kneel	knelt, (*esp. AmE*) kneeled	knelt, (*esp.AmE*) kneeled	
knit	knitted, knit	knitted, knit	
know	knew	known	
lay	laid	laid	
lead	led	led	
lean	(*esp. BrE*) leant /lent/, (*esp. AmE*) leaned /liːnd/	(*esp. BrE*) leant, (*esp. AmE*) leaned	
leap	leapt /lept/, (*esp. AmE*) leaped /liːpt/	leapt, (*esp. AmE*) leapt	
learn	learnt, (*esp. AmE*) learned	learnt, (*esp. AmE*) learned	learned /-ɪd/, *adj*
leave	left	left	
lend	lent	lent	
let	let	let	
lie	lay	lain	= be flat— see USAGE
light	lit, lighted	lit, lighted	
lose	lost	lost	
make	made	made	
may	—	—	see table Wv2, p. xxxviii
mean	meant	meant	/ment/
meet	met	met	
melt	melted	melted	molten, *adj*
miscast	miscast	miscast	
misdeal	misdealt	misdealt	
misgive	misgave	misgiven	
mislay	mislaid	mislaid	
mislead	misled	misled	
misspell	(*esp. BrE*) misspelt, (*esp. AmE*) misspelled	(*esp. BrE*) misspelt (*esp. AmE*) misspelled	
misspend	misspent	misspent	
mistake	mistook	mistaken	
misunderstand	misunderstood	misunderstood	
mow	mowed	mown, mowed	
outbid	outbade, outbid	outbidden, outbid	
outdo	outdid	outdone	(*3rd pers. sing. pres. t.*) outdoes
outgrow	outgrew	outgrown	
outrun	outran	outrun	
outshine	outshone	outshone	
overbear	overborne	overborne	
overcast	overcast	overcast	
overcome	overcome	overcome	
overdo	overdid	overdone	(*3rd pers. sing. pres. t.*) overdoes
overfeed	overfed	overfed	

Verb	Past tense	Past participle	Notes
overhang	overhung	overhung	
overrun	overran	overrun	
oversee	oversaw	overseen	
oversleep	overslept	overslept	
overtake	overtook	overtaken	
overthrow	overthrew	overthrown	
partake	partook	partaken	
pay	paid	paid	
prove	proved	proved	proven, *adj*
put	put	put	
read	read /red/	read /red/	
rebind	rebound	rebound	
rebuild	rebuilt	rebuilt	
recast	recast	recast	
redo	redid	redone	(*3rd pers. sing. pres. t.*) redoes
relay	relaid	relaid	
remake	remade	remade	
rend	rent	rent	
repay	repaid	repaid	
rerun	reran	rerun	
reset	reset	reset	
retell	retold	retold	
rewind	rewound	rewound	
rewrite	rewrote	rewritten	
rid	rid, ridded	rid, ridded	
ride	rode	ridden	
ring	rang	rung	
rise	rose	risen	
run	ran	run	
saw	sawed	sawn, sawed	
say	said	said	says = /sez/
see	saw	seen	
seek	sought	sought	
sell	sold	sold	
send	sent	sent	
set	set	set	
sew	sewed	sewn, sewed	
shake	shook	shaken	
shall	—	—	see table Wv2, p. xxxviii
shave	shaved	shaved	shaven, *adj*
shear	sheared	shorn, sheared	
shed	shed	shed	
shine	shone, shined	shone, shined	-ed = polished
shit	shit	shit	
shoe	shod	shod	
shoot	shot	shot	
show	showed	shown, showed	
shrink	shrank, shrunk	shrunk	shrunken, *adj*
shrive	shrove, shrived	shriven, shrived	
shut	shut	shut	
sing	sang	sung	
sink	sank	sunk	sunken *adj*
sit	sat	sat	
slay	slew	slain	
sleep	slept	slept	
slide	slid	slid	
sling	slung	slung	
slink	slunk	slunk	
slit	slit	slit	
smell	(*esp. BrE*) smelt, (*esp. AmE*) smelled	(*esp. BrE*) smelt, (*esp. AmE*) smelled	
smite	smote	smitten	
sow	sowed	sown, sowed	
speak	spoke	spoken	
speed	sped, speeded	sped, speeded	
spell	(*esp. BrE*) spelt, (*esp. AmE*) spelled	(*esp. BrE*) spelt, (*esp. AmE*) spelled	
spend	spent	spent	
spill	(*esp. BrE*) spilt, (*esp. AmE*) spilled	(*esp. BrE*) spilt, (*esp. AmE*) spilled	
spin	spun, span	spun	
spit	spat (*AmE also* spit)	spat (*AmE also* spit)	
split	split	split	
spoil	(*esp. BrE*) spoilt, (*esp. AmE*) spoiled	(*esp. BrE*) spoilt, (*esp. AmE*) spoiled	

Verb	Past tense	Past participle	Notes
spread	spread	spread	
spring	sprang (*AmE also* sprung)	sprung	
stand	stood	stood	
steal	stole	stolen	
stick	stuck	stuck	
sting	stung	stung	
stink	stank, stunk	stunk	
strew	strewed	strewn, strewed	
stride	strode	stridden, strid	
strike	struck	struck	stricken, *adj*
string	strung	strung	
strive	strove, strived	striven, strived	
sunburn	sunburned	sunburned	sunburnt, *adj*
swear	swore	sworn	
sweep	swept	swept	
swell	swelled	swollen, swelled	
swim	swam	swum	
swing	swung	swung	
take	took	taken	
teach	taught	taught	
tear	tore	torn	
tell	told	told	
think	thought	thought	
thrive	throve thrived	thrived, (*espBrE*) thriven	
throw	threw	thrown	
thrust	thrust	thrust	
tread	trod	trodden, trod	
unbend	unbent	unbent	
unbind	unbound	unbound	
underbid	underbid	underbid, -bidden	
undergo	underwent	undergone	
understand	understood	understood	
undertake	undertook	undertaken	
undo	undid	undone	(*3rd pers. sing. pres. t.*) undoes
unwind	unwound	unwound	
uphold	upheld	upheld	
upset	upset	upset	
wake	woke, waked	woken, waked	
waylay	waylaid	waylaid	
wear	wore	worn	
weave	wove	woven	
wed	wedded, wed	wedded, wed	
weep	wept	wept	
wet	wetted, wet	wetted, wet	
will	—	—	see table Wv2, p. xxxviii
win	won	won	
wind/waɪnd/	wound	wound	
withdraw	withdrew	withdrawn	
withhold	withheld	withheld	
withstand	withstood	withstood	
wring	wrung	wrung	
write	wrote	written	

Spelling table

To find in the dictionary a word that you have heard but not seen:

SOUND	AS IN	OTHER POSSIBLE SPELLINGS
iː	sh*ee*p	f*ie*ld, pol*i*ce, t*ea*m, k*ey*, p*eo*ple, sc*e*ne, qu*ay*, am*oe*ba, C*ae*sar, (*AmE*) bus*y*
ɪ	sh*i*p	sav*a*ge, w*o*men, carr*ia*ge, vall*ey*, mount*ai*n, vill*a*ge, for*ei*gn, alw*ay*s, coff*ee*, l*y*nch, g*ui*lt, s*ie*ve, b*u*sy (*BrE*) bus*y*, (*AmE*) app*ea*rance
e	b*e*d	*a*ny, s*ai*d, br*ea*d, s*ay*s, g*ue*st, b*u*ry, l*eo*pard, l*ei*sure, fr*ie*nds, (*AmE*) *ae*sthetic
æ	b*a*d	pl*ai*d, (*AmE*) l*au*gh, (*AmE*) c*a*lf
ɑː (*AmE* written /ɑ/, pronounced /ɑr/ when followed by "r")	c*al*m	f*a*ther, h*ea*rt, baz*aa*r, s*e*rgeant, Sh*ah*, (*BrE*) l*au*gh, (*AmE*) b*o*ther, (*AmE*) h*o*nest
ɒ (*BrE* only)	p*o*t	*e*ntree, bure*au*cracy, J*oh*n, w*a*tch, c*ou*gh, l*au*rel, y*ach*t h*o*nest (N.B. This sound does not exist in the variety of *AmE* described in this dictionary.)
ɔː (*AmE* written /ɔ/, pronounced /ɔr/ when followed by 'r")	c*augh*t	b*a*ll, b*oa*rd, dr*aw*, h*au*nt, f*ou*r, fl*oo*r, p*o*rt, extr*ao*rdinary, G*eo*rge, (*AmE*) d*o*g, *ough*t
ʊ	p*u*t	w*oo*d, w*o*lf, c*ou*ld
uː	b*oo*t	m*o*ve, sh*oe*, gr*ou*p, fl*ew*, bl*ue*, t*oo*, fr*ui*t, r*u*de, thr*ough*, rh*eu*matism, man*oeu*vre, n*ew* (=/njuː/), cw*m*, (*tech*) le*e*ward, (*AmE*) li*eu*tenant
ʌ	c*u*t	s*o*me, d*oe*s, bl*oo*d, y*ou*ng
ɜː (*AmE* pronounced /ɜr/)	b*ir*d	b*ur*n, f*er*n, w*or*m, j*our*nal, *ear*n, m*yr*tle, *err*, G*uer*nsey, conn*oi*ss*eur*, m*yrrh*, (*AmE*) chauff*eur*

SOUND	AS IN	OTHER POSSIBLE SPELLINGS
ə (*AmE* pronounced /ər/ when followed by "r")	*a*bout	fount*ai*n, clar*i*ty, (*AmE*) phys*i*cian, bur*eau*crat, parl*ia*ment, purp*o*se, lunch*eo*n, danger*ou*s, tort*oi*se, (*AmE*) mull*ei*n, nat*io*n, rest*au*rant, aut*u*mn, th*e*, serge*a*nt, cupb*oar*d, act*or*, theat*re*, bigg*er*, s*ur*prise, furnit*ure*, begg*ar*, sold*ie*r, col*our*, chauff*eu*r, guerr*i*lla, (*AmE*) colleg*ia*te
eɪ	m*a*ke	p*ay*, st*ea*k, v*ei*n, w*eigh*, str*aigh*t, pr*ey*, g*au*ge, g*ao*l, caf*é*, matin*ée*, tr*ai*n, G*ae*lic, *eh*, (*AmE*) mel*ee*
əʊ	n*o*te	s*ew*, s*oa*p, s*ou*l, gr*ow*, t*oe*, *oh*, br*oo*ch, b*eau*, y*eo*man, m*au*ve, *owe*, th*ough*, f*ol*k
aɪ	b*i*te	*eye*, p*ie*, b*uy*, *aye*, tr*y*, d*ye*, g*ui*de, s*igh*, h*eigh*t, *ai*sle, (*AmE*) c*oy*ote, (*AmE*) g*ey*ser
aʊ	n*ow*	*ou*nce, pl*ough*, sauerkr*au*t
ɔɪ	b*oy*	p*oi*son, l*aw*yer, b*uoy*
ɪə (*AmE* pronounced /ɪər,ɪr/ when followed by "r")	h*ere*	app*ear*, id*ea*, f*ie*rce, b*ee*r, souven*ir*, w*eir*, atmosph*ere*, th*eo*ry
eə (*AmE* pronounced /eər, er/)	th*ere*	h*air*, b*are*, wh*ere*, b*ear*, th*eir*, pr*ayer*, sc*ar*ce, *ae*roplane, m*ayor*, h*eir*
ʊə (*AmE* pronounced /ʊər, ʊr/ when followed by "r")	p*oor*	ins*ure*, t*our*, cr*ue*l, amat*eur* (= -tʃʊə, -tjʊə/)
eɪə (*AmE* pronounced /eɪər/ when followed by "r")	pl*ayer*	w*eigher*
əʊə (*AmE* pronounced /əʊər/ when followed by "r")	l*ower*	s*ewer*, b*oa*

SOUND	AS IN	OTHER POSSIBLE SPELLINGS
aɪə (*AmE* pronounced /aɪər/ when followed by "r")	*tire*	b*uy*er, d*y*er, h*igh*er, qu*i*et, l*i*on, g*i*ant, f*ie*ry, t*y*rant, (*BrE*) Is*aiah*
aʊə	t*ower*	*our*, h*our*, H*owar*d, s*auer*kraut
(*AmE* pronounced /aʊər/ when followed by "r")		
ɔɪə (*AmE* pronounced /ɔɪər/ when followed by "r")	empl*oyer*	l*awyer*, r*oyal*
p	*p*en	ha*pp*en, she*ph*erd
b	*b*ack	ru*bb*er, *bh*ang
t	*t*ea	bu*tt*er, *Th*omas, walk*ed*, yach*t*, *pt*armigan, dou*bt*, frig*ht*, (*AmE*) *phth*isic
d	*d*ay	la*dd*er, call*ed*, cou*ld*
k	*k*ey	*c*ool, s*ch*ool, bis*cu*it, lo*ck*, sa*cch*arine, toba*cc*o, che*que*, lou*gh*, wal*k*, la*cq*uer, *kh*aki, *q*ueen (=/kw/), *q*ueue (=/kj/)
g	*g*ay	bi*gg*er, *gh*ost, va*gue*, *gu*ard
tʃ	*ch*eer	na*t*ure, ma*tch*, ques*t*ion, *c*ello, *Cz*ech, righ*te*ous
dʒ	*j*ump	e*dge*, sol*di*er, a*ge*, exa*gg*erate, gra*du*al, a*dj*ust, sandwi*ch*
f	*f*ew	co*ff*ee, cou*gh*, *ph*ysics, hal*f*, o*ft*en
v	*v*iew	o*f*, Ste*ph*en, na*vv*y
θ	*th*ing	
ð	*th*en	ba*the*
s	*s*oon	*c*ity, ni*c*e, *ps*ychology, *sc*ene, me*ss*, *sch*ism, fa*st*en, *sw*ord
z	*z*ero	wa*s*, sci*ss*ors, *x*ylophone, da*zz*le, e*x*ample (=/gz/), (*AmE*) di*s*cern
ʃ	fi*sh*ing	o*c*ean, *s*ure, *ch*ivalry, sta*t*ion, ti*ss*ue, fa*sc*ism, fu*chs*ia, cons*ci*ous, pa*ss*ion, ten*s*ion, politi*c*ian, (*BrE*) *sch*edule, (*AmE*) nau*se*ous, lu*x*ury (=/kʃ/)

SOUND	AS IN	OTHER POSSIBLE SPELLINGS
ʒ	plea*s*ure	rou*g*e, vi*s*ion, sei*z*ure, u*s*ual, lu*x*urious (=/gzh/), (*AmE*) gla*zi*er
h	*h*ot	*wh*om
m	su*m*	bo*mb*, ha*mm*er, autu*mn*, ca*lm*, dra*chm*, phle*gm*, gover*nm*ent
n	su*n*	*kn*ow, *gn*aw, fu*nn*y, *pn*eumonia, *mn*emonic, kitt*en*, cert*ain*, cott*on*, ca*ñ*on (=/nj/)
ŋ	su*ng*	si*n*k, to*ngue*, ha*nd*kerchief
l	*l*ed	ba*ll*, battl*e*, ped*al*, tunn*el*
r	*r*ed	ma*rr*y, *wr*iggle, *rh*ubarb, dia*rrh*oea
j	*y*et	on*i*on, *E*urope, b*e*auty, *u*se, n*e*w, hallelu*j*a, stren*u*ous, torti*ll*a, q*u*eue (= /kj/)
w	*w*et	*o*ne, ch*o*ir, (= /kw/), q*u*een (= /kw/), *wh*en, Don *Ju*an, pat*o*is
ks	bo*x*	a*cc*ident, e*xc*ept, sti*cks*, for*ks*

Silent consonants

The following consonant letters have no sound at all in certain words:

b	as in bom*b*, dou*b*t
c	as in ya*c*ht, mus*c*le, s*c*ene, vi*c*tuals
g	as in si*g*n, *g*naw
gh	as in ou*gh*t, li*gh*t, throu*gh*, hi*gh*, Edinbur*gh*
h	as in *h*onest, *h*our, *h*eir; ex*h*austed, r*h*ubarb, yac*h*t, ve*h*icle, w*h*ich, Jo*h*n
k	as in *k*now
l	as in ha*l*f, wa*l*k, ca*l*m, cou*l*d
m	as in *m*nemonic
n	as in autum*n*, gover*n*ment
nc	as in bla*nc*mange
p	as in *p*sychology, *p*tarmigan, *p*neumonia, cor*p*s
r	in *BrE*, is pronounced only before a vowel, or at the end of a word when the next word in the phrase begins with a vowel: ca*r*, ca*r*d
s	as in ai*s*le, i*s*land, cor*p*s, patoi*s*
t	as in fas*t*en, of*t*en, balle*t*
th	as in as*th*ma
w	as in *w*rong, s*w*ord, ans*w*er, daw*n*
x	as in fau*x* pas

The commonest ways of pronouncing the 26 letters

		Letter Name
A, a	æ, ɑː, eɪ, eə	eɪ
B, b	b	biː
C, c	k, s	siː
D, d	d	diː
E, e	e, iː	iː
F, f	f, v	ef
G, g	g, dʒ	dʒiː
H, h	h	eɪtʃ
I, i	ɪ, iː, aɪ	aɪ

		Letter Name
J, j	dʒ	dʒeɪ
K, k	k	keɪ
L, l	l	el
M, m	m	em
N, n	n	en
O, o	o,ɔː, əʊ, (*AmE*) ɑ	əʊ
P, p	p	piː
Q, q	kw, k, kj	kjuː
R, r	r	ɑː, (*AmE*) ɑr

		Letter Name
S, s	s, z	es
T, t	t	tiː
U, u	ʌ, ʊ, uː	juː
V, v	v	viː
W, w	w	'dʌbljuː
X, x	ks, z	eks
Y, y	j, ɪ, aɪ	waɪ
Z, z	z	(*BrE*) zed, (*AmE*) ziː

Number table

1 CARDINALS: 1–99

Any of these can be used instead of nine in the following patterns. See *Note* below for the use of **one.**

1A Determiner & pronoun

There are nine (*of them*)[1]. | *The nine of them ordered dinner*[1]. | *All nine* (*of them*) *ordered dinner*[1]. | *the nine largest cities in the US* | *The boy is nine* (= 9 years old). | *They invited nine people to the party*[1]. | *on page nine* | *Nine of the boys came.* | *It costs nine 50* (= nine pounds and 50 pence *or* nine dollars and 50 cents). | *He paid nine and 4* (= 9 shillings and 4 pence, old British money). | *He paid 4 and nine*[1] (= 4 shillings and 9 pence). | *a nine-fold increase in production*[1] | *Production has increased ninefold*[1]

1B Noun

Nine is my favourite number. | *Nines are my favourite numbers.* | *2 nines is/are/make 18* (or 2 × 9 = 18). | *She wore a nine on her uniform* (= a written number 9). | *She wears/takes a* (*size/number*) *nine in shoes.* | *She played a nine*[1] (= a playing card with the number 9). | *4 nines beat 3 10's*[1] (= 4 of these playing cards). | *They marched in nines*[1] (= in groups of nine). | *He is in his nineties*[1] (= 90 to 99 years old). | *It happened in the 'nineties*[1] (of the last century) (= between 1890 and 1899). | *The temperature is in the* (*high/low/mid*) *nineties*[1]

Note: **one** is used with singular verbs and things: *There is* (*only*) *one of them* but *There are twenty-one of them.* | *They invited one person.* It cannot be used in the patterns marked[1].

2 CARDINALS: HUNDRED, THOUSAND, MILLION, BILLION, TRILLION

These can all be used in the following patterns.

2A Determiner and pronoun

There are a/one hundred (*of them*). | *There are 3 hundred and 50 of them.* | *The* (*one*) *hundred people came.* | *2 hundred of them came.* | *to buy by the hundred.* | *It's worth a few hundred/several hundred/at least 5 hundred* (= 500 pounds, dollars, etc.). | *"How many hundred do you want?" "Another 2 hundred."* | *I've told you a hundred times.* | *the hundred largest cities in the US* | *a hundredfold increase in production* | *Production has increased a hundredfold*

Note also: ten thousand (*people*) (= 10,000).

2B Noun

I can't read the hundred (= the number 100) *you've written.* | *I've told you hundreds* (*and hundreds*) *of times.* | *The hundreds* (*of people*) *came.* | *It's worth hundreds* (= of pounds, dollars, etc.). | *How many hundreds do you want?* (= groups of 100)

Note also: tens of thousands (*of people*) (= 10,000; 20,000; 30,000, etc.).

3 ORDINALS

1st–99th can all be used instead of ninth in the following patterns, and **thousandth, millionth, billionth, trillionth** instead of **hundredth.** See note below for the use of **first, second.**

3A Determiner, pronoun, and adverb

The ninth person got a prize. | *the* (*one*) *hundredth person* | *the 2 hundredth* (= *200th*) *person* | *King Louis the Ninth* | *She was* (*the*) *ninth in the exam.* | *He came/finished ninth in the race.* | *Ninth*(*ly*) *and last*(*ly*) *let me say …* | *the ninth largest city in the US*[1] | *He arrived on the ninth* (= the 9th day of month). | *the ninth of May* = (*esp. BrE*) *May the ninth* = (*esp. AmE*) *May ninth* | *every ninth year* (= in 1970, 1979, 1988, etc.)

3B Noun

He wants a ninth of the money[1] (= 1/9). | *2 ninths of the money*[1] (= 2/9) | *a/one hundredth of the money* (= 1/100) | *a/one 2 hundredth of the money* (= 1/200) | *2 hundredths of the money* (= 2/100) | *He was the ninth to climb the mountain.* | *2 musical notes a ninth* (= 9 notes) *apart*

Note: **first** cannot be used in the patterns marked[1]; but **second** can be used in all patterns except those for FRACTIONS: $\frac{1}{2}$ is *a/one* **half.**

Note also: He put the car into second (GEAR) *and then changed into third.*

4

4A dozen

Determiner

There is/are a/one dozen (eggs). | *a dozen of them* | *half a dozen* | *a dozen and a half* | *one/2 dozen and a half* | *one/2 and a half dozen* | *The (one) dozen people came.* | *another 2 dozen eggs* | *several dozen* | *How many dozen do you want?* | *to buy by the dozen*

Noun

I've told you dozens (and dozens) of times. | *The dozens who came enjoyed themselves.* | *How many dozens (of eggs) do you want?* (= how many groups of 12) | *Eggs are sold in dozens.* | *His friends arrived in (their) dozens*

4B gross, head, brace, ton, hundredweight, stone, yoke

Determiner

a/one gross (of envelopes) | *There is a gross (of them).* | *Another 2/3/5 gross (of envelopes)* | *How many gross do you want?* | *bought/sold by the gross*

Noun

sold in grosses | *How many grosses (of envelopes) do you want?* (= how many groups of 144)

4C Score:

Determiner

a score (of years) | *There are/is a score (of them)* | *another 2/3/5 score* | *letters by the score* | *3 score years and 10* (= 70 years) | *4 score and 7 years ago* (= 87 years ago)

Noun

scores (and scores) of friends | *They arrived in (their) scores*

Note the following ways of mentioning uncertain numbers. If the number is large, it should not be too exact: *90-odd people* but not **97-odd people*:

Age: He's nineish, nine or so/or thereabouts (= about 8–10 years old)
He's ninetyish, ninety or so/or thereabouts (= about 88–95)

Dates: on the ninth of May or thereabouts/(*esp. Br E*) or so (= between about the 8th and the 11th)
in 1890 or thereabouts/(*esp Br E*) or so (= between about 1888 and 1895)

Time: at nineish, nine or thereabouts/(*esp. Br E*) or so (= at 9 o'clock or slightly later)

Money: £9 or so/or thereabouts, some £9, a good £9, £9 odd (= nine pounds odd = between £9 and £10)
£90 odd (=90-odd pounds=between about £90 and £98)

General: 9/90 people or so/or thereabouts, 9/90 or so people, some 9/90 people, a good 9/90 people, 90-odd people.

Weights and measures tables

Words in **heavy letters** in the centre are the most common ones in general speech.

BRITISH

LINEAR MEASURE

		1 **inch**	=	2.54 cm
12 inches	=	1 **foot**	=	0.3048 m
3 feet	=	1 **yard**	=	0.9144 m
5½ yards	=	1 rod, pole, or perch	=	5.029 m
22 yards	=	1 chain	=	20.12 m
10 chains	=	1 **furlong**	=	0.2012 km
8 furlongs	=	1 **mile**	=	1.609 km
6076.12 feet	=	1 nautical mile	=	1852 m

SQUARE MEASURE

		1 square inch	=	645.16 mm^2
144 in^2	=	1 square foot	=	0.0929 m^2
9 ft^2	=	1 square yard	=	0.8361 m^2
4840 yd^2	=	1 acre	=	4047 m^2
640 acres	=	1 square mile	=	259 ha

CUBIC MEASURE

		1 cubic inch	=	16.39 cm^3		
1728 in^3	=	1 cubic foot	=	0.02832 m^3	=	28.32 dm^3
27 ft^3	=	1 cubic yard	=	0.7646 m^3	=	764.6 dm^3

CAPACITY MEASURE

		1 fluid ounce	=	28.41 cm^3
5 fluid oz.	=	1 gill	=	0.1421 dm^3
4 gills	=	1 **pint**	=	0.5683 dm^3
2 pints	=	1 **quart**	=	1.137 dm^3
4 quarts	=	1 (UK) **gallon**	=	4.546 dm^3
231 in^3	=	1 (US) **gallon**	=	3.785 dm^3
8 gallons	=	1 bushel	=	36.369 dm^3

AVOIRDUPOIS WEIGHT (MASS)

		1 grain	=	64.8 mg
		1 dram	=	1.772 g
16 drams	=	1 **ounce**	=	28.35 g
16* ounces	=	1 **pound**	=	0.4536 kg
14 pounds	=	1 **stone**	=	6.350 kg
2 stones	=	1 quarter	=	12.70 kg
4 quarters	=	1 (long) **hundredweight**	=	50.80 kg
20 hundredweight	=	1 (long) **ton**	=	1.016 tonnes
100 pounds	=	1 (short) **hundredweight**	=	45.36 kg
2000 pounds	=	1 (short) **ton**	=	0.9072 tonnes

(*7000 grains = 16 ounces)

The short hundredweight and ton are more common in the US.

TEMPERATURE

$$°\textit{Fahrenheit} = \left(\frac{9}{5}°C\right) + 32$$

$$°\textit{Centigrade} = \left(\frac{5}{9}\right)(°F - 32)$$

$$\text{Kelvin} = °C + 273.15$$

US DRY MEASURE

1 pint	=	0.9689 UK pint	=	0.5506 dm^3
1 bushel	=	0.9689 UK bushel	=	35.238 dm^3

US LIQUID MEASURE

	1 fluid ounce	= 1.0408 UK fluid oz.	= 0.0296 dm^3
16 fluid oz.	= 1 pint	= 0.8327 UK pint	= 0.4732 dm^3
8 pints	= 1 gallon	= 0.8327 UK gallon	= 3.7853 dm^3

CIRCULAR MEASURE

		1 second	= 4.860 μrad.
60 seconds	=	1 minute	= 0.2909 μrad.
60 minutes	=	1 degree	= 17.45 μrad. = $\pi/180$ rad.
45 degrees	=	1 oxtant	= $\pi/4$ rad.
60 degrees	=	1 sextant	= $\pi/3$ rad.
90 degrees	=	1 quadrant or 1 right angle	= $\pi/2$ rad.
360 degrees	=	1 circle or 1 circumference	= 2 π rad.
1 grade or gon	=	1/100th of a right angle	= $\pi/200$ rad.

METRIC

LINEAR MEASURE

		1 **millimetre**	=	0.03937 in
10 mm	=	1 **centimetre**	=	0.3937 in
10 cm	=	1 decimetre	=	3.937 in
10 dm	=	1 **metre**	=	39.37 in
10 m	=	1 decametre	=	10.94 yd
10 dam	=	1 hectometre	=	109.4 yd
10 hm	=	1 **kilometre**	=	0.6214 mile

SQUARE MEASURE

		1 square millimetre	= 0.00155 in^2
100 mm^2		= 1 square centimetre	= 0.1550 in^2
100 cm^2		= 1 square metre	= 1.196 yd^2
100 m^2		= 1 are	= 119.6 yd^2
10,000 m^2	= 100 ares	= 1 hectare	= 2.471 acres
100 ha		= 1 square kilometre	= 247.1 acres

CUBIC MEASURE

		1 cubic centimetre	=	0.06102 in^3
1000 cm^3	=	1 cubic decimetre	=	0.03532 ft^3
1000 dm^3	=	1 cubic metre	=	1.308 yd^3

Note: In 1964 the litre was recognized as being 1 dm^3. Britain still has the 1901 value of the litre: 1 litre = 1.00028 dm^3.

CAPACITY MEASURE

	1 millilitre	= 0.00176 pint	
10 ml	= 1 centilitre	= 0.0176 pint	
10 cl	= 1 decilitre	= 0.176 pint	
10 dl	= 1 **litre**	= 1.76 pint	= 0.22 UK gallon
10 l	= 1 decalitre	= 2.20 gallon	
10 dal	= 1 hectolitre	= 22.0 gallon	
10 hl	= 1 kilolitre	= 220.0 gallon	

MASS

	1 **milligram**	= 0.015 grain	
10 mg	= 1 centigram	= 0.154 grain	
10 cg	= 1 decigram	= 1.543 grain	
10 dg	= 1 **gram**	= 15.43 grain	= 0.035 oz
10g	= 1 decagram	= 0.353 oz	
10 dag	= 1 hectogram	= 3.527 oz	
10 hg	= 1 **kilogram**	= 2.205 pound	
1000 kg	= 1 **tonne** (metric ton)	= 0.984 (long) ton = 2204.62 lb	

CIRCULAR MEASURE

	1 micro-radian	= 0.206 seconds
1000 μ rad	= 1 milli-radian	= 3.437 minutes
1000 m rad	= 1 radian	= 57.296 degrees = $180/\pi$ degrees

METRIC PREFIXES

	Abbreviation	*Factor*
tera-	T	10^{12}
giga-	G	10^9
mega-	M	10^6
kilo-	k	10^3
hecto-	h	10^2
deca-	da	10^1
deci-	d	10^{-1}
centi-	c	10^{-2}
milli-	m	10^{-3}
micro-	μ	10^{-6}
nano-	n	10^{-9}
pico-	p	10^{-12}
femto-	f	10^{-15}
atto-	a	10^{-18}

Note: The British system, unlike the metric one, is not built up in 10's: 1 lb = 16 oz = 7000 grains. The metric system is built up by adding PREFIXes which are the same for every kind of measure. These PREFIXes should be used in steps (MULTIPLE*s*) of ± 3: milli-, micro-, mega-; rather than in the smaller steps hecto-, deca-, deci-, or centi-.

Animal table

ANIMAL	MALE	FEMALE	YOUNG	GROUP NOUN	NOISE—all are verb and noun: some are also interjections
cat	**tom(cat)**	**queen**	**kitten**		**purr** **miaow** *interj*
cattle (*pl.*)	**bull**	**cow**	**calf**	**herd**	**bellow** (of bull) **moo** (of cow) *interj*
chicken	**cock**	**hen**	**chick**	**brood** (of young)	**crow** (of cock) **cockadoodledoo** (of cock) *interj* **cluck** (of hen) *interj* **cackle** (of hen) **cheep** (of chicks) *interj*
dog	**dog**	**bitch**	**pup(py)**		**bark** **whine** **growl** **bowwow** *interj*
dolphin, porpoise, whale	**bull**	**cow**	**calf**	**school**	
donkey					**heehaw** *interj* **bray**
duck	**drake**	**duck**	**duckling**		**quack** *interj*
deer (*pl.* **deer**)	**buck** **stag**	**doe** **hind** (esp. of red deer)		**herd**	
fish				**shoal**	
fox	**dog**	**vixen**	**cub**		**bark**
goat	**billy (goat)**	**nanny (goat)**	**kid**	**herd**	**bleat**
goose (pl. geese)	**gander**	**goose**	**gosling**	**flock** **gaggle**	**hiss** **honk**
horse	**stallion**	**mare**	**foal**	**herd** (esp. in the wild)	**neigh** **whinny**
lion	**lion**	**lioness**	**cub**	**pride**	**roar**
pig	**boar**	**sow**	**piglet**	**herd**	**grunt** **oink** *interj*
rabbit	**buck**	**doe**			
seal	**bull**	**cow**	**pup**	**colony**	**bark**
sheep	**ram**	**ewe**	**lamb**	**flock**	**bleat** **baa** *interj*

Table of family relationships

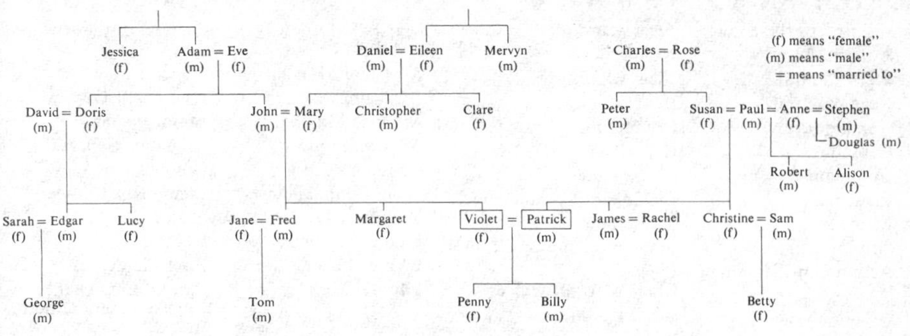

THE FAMILY

Mother: Mary is VIOLET's mother. VIOLET is Billy's mother.
Father: Paul is PATRICK's father. PATRICK is Penny's father.
Sister: Margaret is VIOLET's sister. Christine is PATRICK's sister.
Brother: Fred is VIOLET's brother. James is PATRICK's brother.
Aunt: Clare is VIOLET's aunt. VIOLET is Tom's aunt
Uncle: Peter is PATRICK's uncle. PATRICK is Betty's uncle.
Niece: Betty is PATRICK's niece. VIOLET is Clare's niece.
Nephew: Tom is VIOLET's nephew. PATRICK is Peter's nephew.

PATRICK is married to VIOLET. He is her **husband** and she is his **wife.** They have two children, Penny and Billy. Patrick and Violet are the **parents** of these children: PATRICK is their **father** and VIOLET is their **mother.** The children call PATRICK **Dad, Daddy, father,** etc., and they call VIOLET **Mum, Mummy, Mother,** (*AmE*) **Mom,** etc.

Billy is PATRICK's and VIOLET's **son**, and Penny is their **daughter.**

PATRICK has a **brother,** James, and a **sister,** Christine. VIOLET has a **sister** Margaret, and a **brother,** Fred. (Note: There is no special word to show whether one brother or sister is older than another.)

PATRICK has one **uncle:** Peter (his mother's brother). He calls him **Uncle** Peter, or just **Uncle.** He is Peter's **nephew.**

VIOLET has one **uncle** and 2 **aunts**: Christopher (her mother's brother), Clare (her mother's sister) and Doris (her father's sister). She is their niece. She calls the aunts **Aunt Clare** and **Aunt Doris,** or just **Auntie.**

VIOLET has 2 **grandfathers** = Adam (her father's father) and Daniel (her mother's father). She calls them **Grandpa, Grandad, Grandfather,** etc.

VIOLET has also 2 **grandmothers:** Eve (her father's mother) and Eileen (her mother's mother). She calls them **Grandma, Granny, Grandmother,** etc. She is Adam's, Eve's, Daniel's and Eileen's **granddaughter,** and they are her **grandparents.**

PATRICK is the **grandson** of Charles and Rose (his mother's parents). (His other 2 grandparents are not shown here.)

PATRICK and VIOLET's children, Penny and Billy, are the **great-grandchildren** or **great-grandson** and **great-granddaughter,** of Adam, Eileen, Rose, etc. Adam is one of these children's **great-grandfathers,** and Rose is one of their **great-grandmothers.**

PATRICK has a **father-in-law:** John (his wife's father). He has also a **mother-in-law:** Mary (his wife's mother). He is John and Mary's **son-in-law.**

VIOLET is the **daughter-in-law** of Paul and Susan (her husband's parents).

PATRICK has 2 **sisters-in-law:** Margaret (his wife's sister) and Rachel (his brother's wife). He has also 2 **brothers-in-law:** Fred (his wife's brother) and Sam (his sister's husband). (Note: there is not a special word for the relationship between John and Paul, or between Susan and Mary, even though their children are married to each other.)

VIOLET is the **great-niece** of Mervyn (the brother of a grandparent) and of Jessica (the sister of another grandparent). Mervyn is VIOLET's **great-uncle,** and Jessica is VIOLET's **great-aunt.**

VIOLET has **2 cousins,** or **first cousins:** Lucy and Edgar (the children of an aunt or uncle; in this case, of her aunt Doris). Violet's children Pènny and Billy are the **second cousins** of Edgar's son George, because their parents are **first cousins.** (The expression **second cousin** is also loosely used of the relationship between Tom and Betty: his aunt is married to her uncle; or of that between Edgar and Penny, who are really **first cousins once removed,** one GENERATION apart.)

PATRICK's father Paul has been married twice. His second wife, Anne, **is** the **stepmother** of PATRICK, James and Christine, his children by his first marriage. PATRICK is Anne's **stepson** and Christine is her **stepdaughter.** Robert is PATRICK's **half-brother,** and Alison is his **half-sister;** they share one parent.

Anne has also been married twice. Her second husband, Paul, is the **stepfather** of Douglas, her son by her first marriage. PATRICK is Douglas's **stepbrother,** and Christine is his **stepsister;** they do not share either parent.

(Note: first names are used in direct address, unless some other form is given.)

Table of military ranks

ROYAL NAVY	US NAVY	RAF	USAF
Admiral of the Fleet	Fleet Admiral	Marshal of the Royal Air Force	General of the Airforce
Admiral	Admiral	Air Chief Marshal	General
Vice-Admiral	Vice Admiral	Air Marshal	Lieutenant General
Rear-Admiral	Rear Admiral	Air Vice Marshal	Major General
Commodore	Commodore	Air Commodore	Brigadier General
Captain	Captain	Group Captain	Colonel
Commander	Commander	Wing Commander	Lieutenant Colonel
Lieutenant-Commander	Lieutenant Commander	Squadron Leader	Major
Lieutenant	Lieutenant	Flight Lieutenant	Captain
Sub-Lieutenant	Lieutenant Junior Grade	Flying Officer	First Lieutenant
Acting Sub-Lieutenant	Ensign	Pilot Officer	Second Lieutenant
	Chief Warrant Officer		Chief Warrant Officer
Fleet Chief Petty Officer	Warrant Officer	Warrant Officer	Chief Master Sergeant
	Master Chief Petty Officer		Senior Master Sergeant
		Flight Sergeant	Master Sergeant
	Senior Chief Petty Officer	Chief Technician	Technical Sergeant
Chief Petty Officer	Chief Petty Officer	Sergeant	Staff Sergeant
Petty Officer	Petty Officer 1st Class	Corporal	Airman First Class
	Petty Officer 2nd Class	Junior Technician	—
Leading Seaman	Petty Officer 3rd Class	Senior Aircraftman	Airman Second Class
Able Seaman	Seaman	Leading Aircraftman	Airman Third Class
Ordinary Seaman	Seaman Apprentice	Aircraftman	Airman Basic
Junior Seaman	Seaman Recruit		

ARMY	US ARMY	ROYAL MARINES	US MARINE CORPS
Field Marshal	General of the Army	General	General
General	General	Lieutenant-General	Lieutenant General
Lieutenant-General	Lieutenant General	Major-General	Major General
Major-General	Major General	Brigadier	Brigadier General
Brigadier	Brigadier General	Colonel	Colonel
Colonel	Colonel	Lieutenant-Colonel	Lieutenant Colonel
Lieutenant-Colonel	Lieutenant Colonel	Major	Major
Major	Major	Captain	Captain
Captain	Captain	Lieutenant	1st Lieutenant
Lieutenant	1st Lieutenant	2nd Lieutenant	2nd Lieutenant
2nd Lieutenant	2nd Lieutenant		Chief Warrant Officer
	Chief Warrant Officer		
Warrant Officer 1st Class	Warrant Officer	Warrant Officer 1st Class	Warrant Officer
Warrant Officer 2nd Class		Warrant Officer 2nd Class	
Staff Sergeant	Sergeant Major	Colour Sergeant	Sergeant Major
	Specialist 9		Master Gunnery Sergeant
Sergeant	1st Sergeant		
	Master Sergeant	Sergeant	First Sergeant
	Specialist 8		Master Sergeant
	Sergeant First Class		Gunnery Sergeant
	Specialist 7		Staff Sergeant
	Staff Sergeant		Sergeant
	Specialist 6	Corporal	Corporal
	Sergeant	Lance Corporal	Lance Corporal
	Specialist 5		
Corporal	Corporal	Marine	Private First Class
	Specialist 4	—	Private
Lance Corporal	Private 1st Class		
Private	Private		

Nationality and money table

Country	Adjective	Language	Money
Afghanistan	Afghan	Pashto, Dari Persian	Afghani
[person *sing.* = Afghanistani; people = Afghans]			
Albania	Albanian	Albanian	Lek
Algeria	Algerian	Arabic, French	Algerian Dinar
Andorra	Andorran	Catalan	French Franc, Spanish Peseta
Angola	Angolan	Portuguese	Angolan Escudo
Argentina	Argentinian	Spanish	New Peso
Australia	Australian	English	Australian Dollar
Austria	Austrian	German	Schilling
Bahamas	Bahamian	English	Bahamian Dollar
Bahrain	Bahraini	Arabic	Bahrain Dinar
Bangladesh	Bangladesh	Bengali	Taka
[person *sing.* = Bangladeshi]			
Barbados	Barbadian	English	Barbadian Dollar
Barbuda	Barbudan	English	E. Caribbean Dollar
Belgium	Belgian	Flemish, Dutch, French	Belgian Franc
Belize	Belizean	English	Dollar
Bermuda	Bermudan	English	Dollar
Bhutan	Bhutani	Dzongkha Butanese	Indian Rupee
Bolivia	Bolivian	Spanish	Peso Bolivano
Botswana	Botswanan	Setswana, English	Pula
[person *sing.* = Motswana, Batswana; *pl.* Batswana: people = Batswana]			
Brazil	Brazilian	Portuguese	Cruzeiro
Brunei	Bruneian	Malay	Brunei Dollar
Bulgaria	Bulgarian	Bulgarian	Lev, Leva
Burma	Burmese	Burmese	Kyat
Burundi	Burundian	French	Burundi Franc
Cameroon	Cameroonian	English, French	CFA Franc
Canada	Canadian	English, French	Canadian Dollar
Cape Verde Islands	Cape Verdean	Portuguese	Escudo
Cayman Islands	Cayman Island	English	Cayman Island Dollar
[person *sing.* = Cayman Islander]			
Central African Republic	see USAGE	French Sango	CFA Franc
Chad	Chadian	French	CFA Franc
Chile	Chilean	Spanish	Peso
China	Chinese	Mandarin Chinese	Yuan, Yuan
Colombia	Colombian	Spanish	Peso
(Brazzaville) Congo	Congolese	French	CFA Franc
Costa Rica	Costa Rican	Spanish	Colón, colones
Cuba	Cuban	Spanish	Peso
Cyprus	Cypriot	Greek, Turkish	Cyprus Pound
[person *sing.* = Cypriot]			

Country	Adjective	Language	Money
Czechoslovakia	Czech	Czech, Slovak	Koruna, Koruny
[person *sing.* = Czech or Czechoslovak]			
Dahomey	Dahomeyan	French	CFA Franc
Denmark	Danish	Danish	Krone, Kroner
[person *sing.* = Dane]			
Dominica	Dominican	English	E. Caribbean Dollar
Dominican Republic	Dominican	Spanish	Peso
Ecuador	Ecuadorian	Spanish	Sucre
Egypt	Egyptian	Arabic	Egyptian Pound
El Salvador	Salvadorian	Spanish	Colón, colones
Equatorial Guinea	Equatorial Guinean	Spanish	Peseta Guineana
[person *sing.* = Bantu: people = Bantu]			
Ethiopia	Ethiopian	Amharic	Birr
Falkland Islands	Falkland Island	English	Falkland Island Pound
[person *sing.* = Falkland Islander]			
Fiji	Fijian	English	Fiji Dollar
Finland	Finnish	Finnish, Swedish	Markka, Markkaa
[person *sing.* = Finn]			
France	French	French	French Franc
[person *sing.* = Frenchman (*fem.* = -woman); *pl.* Frenchmen: people = French]			
Gabon	Gabonese	French	CFA Franc
Gambia	Gambian	English	Dalasi
Germany: Federal Republic	West German	German	Mark, Deutschmark
Germany: Democratic Republic	East German	German	Ostmark, Mark
Ghana	Ghanaian	English	New Cedi
Gibraltar	Gibraltarian	English	Gib. Pound
Greece	Greek	Greek	Drachma
Grenada	Grenadian	English	East Caribbean Dollar
Guatemala	Guatemalan	Spanish	Quetzal, Quetzales
Guiana	Guianan	French	French Franc
Guinea	Guinean	French	Suli
Guyana	Guyanese	English	Guyana Dollar
Haiti	Haitian	French	Gourde
Honduras	Honduran	Spanish	Lempira
Hong Kong	see USAGE	English	Hong Kong Dollar
Hungary	Hungarian	Magyar	Forint
Iceland	Icelandic	Icelandic	Króna, krónur
[person *sing.* = Icelander]			
India	Indian	Hindi, English	Rupee
Indonesia	Indonesian	Bahasa Indonesian	Rupiah. Rupiah
Iran	Iranian	Farsi Persian	Rial

Country	Adjective	Language	Money
Iraq	Iraqi	Arabic	Iraqi Dinar
Irish Republic	Irish	Irish & English	Púnt
[person *sing.* = Irishman (*fem.* -woman); *pl.* Irishmen: people = Irish]			
Israel	Israeli	Hebrew & Arabic	Shekel
Italy	Italian	Italian	Lira, lire
Ivory Coast	Ivorian	French	CFA Franc
Jamaica	Jamaican	English	Jamaican Dollar
Japan	Japanese	Japanese	Yen, yen
Jordan	Jordanian	Arabic	Jordanian Dinar
Kenya	Kenyan	English, Swahili	Kenyan Shilling
Kampuchea	Kampuchean, Cambodian	Khmer	Riel
Korea N.	N. Korean	Korean	Won
Korea S.	S. Korean	Korean	Won
Kuwait	Kuwaiti	Arabic	Kuwait Dinar
Laos	Laotian	Lao	Kip, kip
Lebanon	Lebanese	Arabic	Lebanese Pound
Lesotho	Sesotho	Sesotho, English	S. Afr. Rand, Maluti
[person *sing.* Mosotho; *pl.* Basotho: people = Basotho]			
Liberia	Liberian	English	Liberian Dollar
Libya	Libyan	Arabic	Libyan Dinar
Liechtenstein	Liechtenstein	German	Swiss Franc
[person *sing.* = Liechtensteiner]			
Luxemburg	Luxemburg	French, German	Belgian or Luxemburg Franc
[person *sing.* = Luxemberger]			
Madagascar	see USAGE	French	Malagasy Franc
[person *sing.* = Malagasy citizen]			
Malawi	Malawian	English	Malawi Kwacha
Malaysia	Malaysian	Malay	Ringgit
Maldive Islands	Maldivian	Divchi	Maldivian Rupee
Mali	Malian	French	Mali Franc
Malta	Maltese	Maltese	Maltese Pound
Mauritania	Mauritanian	Arabic, French,	CFA Franc
Mauritius	Mauritian	English	Rupee
Mexico	Mexican	Spanish	Peso
Monaco	Monegasque	French	French Franc
Mongolia	Mongolian	Khalka Mongolian	Tugrik
[person *sing.* = Mongolian or Mongol: people = Mongolians or Mongols]			
Montserrat	Montserra-tian	English	E. Carib. Dollar
Morocco	Moroccan	Arabic	Dirham
Mozambique	Mozambi-quean	Portuguese	Escudo
Namibia	Namibian	Afrikaans, English	S. A. Rand
Nauru	Nauruan	Nauruan	Austr. Dollar
Nepal	Nepalese	Nepali	Rupee
The Nether-lands	Dutch	Dutch	Guilder
[person *sing.* = Dutchman (*fem.* -woman); *pl.* Dutchmen: people = Dutch]			

Country	Adjective	Language	Money
New Zealand	New Zealand, Maori	English	New Zealand Dollar
[person *sing.* = New Zealander]			
Nicaragua	Nicaraguan	Spanish	Cordoba
Niger	Nigerien	French	CFA Franc
Nigeria	Nigerian	English	Naira
Norway	Norwegian	Norwegian	Krone, Kroner
Oman	Omani	Arabic	Omani Rial
Pakistan	Pakistani	Bengali, Urdu, English	Rupee
Palestine	Palestinian	Arabic	—
Panama	Panamanian	Spanish	Balboa
Papua New Guinea	Papuan	Papuan, English	Kina
Paraguay	Paraguayan	Spanish	Guarani
Peru	Peruvian	Spanish	Sol, soles
Philippines	Philippine	Pilipino, English	Philippine Peso
[person *sing.* = Filipino; *pl.* Filipinos]			
Poland	Polish	Polish	Zloty, zlotys
Portugal	Portuguese	Portuguese	Escudo
Puerto Rico	Puerto Rican	Spanish, English	US Dollar
Qatar	Qatari	Arabic	Qatar Riyal
Romania	Romanian	Romanian	Leu, lei
Rwanda	Rwandan	Kinya-rwanda, French	Rwanda Franc
San Marino	San Marinese	Italian	Lira, lire
Saudi Arabia	Saudi Arabian	Arabic	Riyal
[person *sing.* = Saudi or Saudi Arabian]			
Senegal	Senegalese	French	CFA Franc
Seychelles	Seychellois	English, French, Creole	Seychelles Rupee
Sierra Leone	Sierra Leonean	English	Leone
Singapore	Singaporean	Malay, Chinese, Tamil, English	Singapore Dollar
Somalia	Somali	Somali	Somali Shilling
South Africa	S. African	Afrikaans, English	S. Afr. Rand
Soviet Union	Soviet or Russian	Russian	Rouble
Spain	Spanish	Spanish	Peseta
[person *sing.* = Spaniard]			
Sri Lanka	Sri Lankan	Sinhala, Tamil	Sri Lankan Rupee
Sudan	Sudanese	Arabic	Sudanese Pound
Surinam	Surinamese	Dutch	Surinam Florin
Swaziland	Swazi	siSwati, English	Lilangeni, Emalangeni, S. Afr. Rand
Sweden	Swedish	Swedish	Krona, Kronor
Switzerland	Swiss	German, French, Italian	Swiss Franc
Syria	Syrian	Arabic	Syrian Pound
Tahiti	Tahitian	English	Dollar
Taiwan	Taiwanese	Chinese	New Taiwan Dollar
Tanzania	Tanzanian	Swahili, English	Tanzanian Shilling

Country	Adjective	Language	Money
Thailand	Thai	Thai	Baht
E. Timor	Timorese	Portuguese	Escudo
Togo	Togolese	French	CFA Franc
Tonga	Tongan	Tongan	Pa'anga
Trinidad & Tobago	Trinidadian, Tobagan	English	T & T Dollar
Tunisia	Tunisian	Arabic	Tunisian Dinar
Turkey	Turkish	Turkish	Turkish Lire, Lira
[person *sing.* = Turk]			
Uganda	Ugandan	Swahili, English	Ugandan Shilling
United Kingdom of Great Britain and Northern Ireland	British		Pound Sterling or Pounds
[person *sing.* = *rare* Briton, *AmE* Britisher: people = British]			
England	English	English	
[person *sing.* = Englishman (*fem.* -woman); *pl.* Englishmen: people = English]			
Scotland	Scottish or Scots	English	
[person *sing.* = Scot or Scotsman (*fem.* -woman); *pl.* Scotsmen: people = Scots]			
Wales	Welsh	English, Welsh	
[person *sing.* = Welshman (*fem.* -woman); *pl.* Welshmen: people = Welsh]			

Country	Adjective	Language	Money
United States of America	American	English	Dollar
Upper Volta	Voltaic	French	CFA Franc
[person *sing.* = Voltain]			
Uruguay	Uruguayan	Spanish	Peso
Vatican City	Vatican	Italian	Italian Lira
[person *sing.* = Vatican citizen: people = citizens of the Vatican]			
Venezuela	Venezuelan	Spanish	Bolivar, Bolivares
Vietnam	Vietnamese	Vietnamese	Dong, dong
West Samoa	Samoan	English, Samoan	Tala
Yemen (Sana)	Yemeni	Arabic	Riyal
Yemen P.D.R. (ADEN)	Yemeni	Arabic	Yemen Dinar
Yugoslavia	Yugoslavian	Serbo-Croat, Slovenian, Macedonian	Dinar
[person *sing.* Yugoslav]			
Zaire	Zairean	French	Zaire
Zambia	Zambian	English	Kwacha
Zimbabwe	Zimbabwean	English	Zimbabwean Dollar

USAGE Unless specially shown in the table, the noun for a person from a country is always the same as the adjective: *He was* **German.** | *He was* **a German.** Unless shown in the table, the plural of the noun for a person is the adjective + *s*, except when the adjective (and noun) ends in *-ese*, in which case the plural is the same as the singular: *She is* **Japanese.** | *We met* **a Japanese.** | *We met many* **Japanese** *on our holiday*. The plural of a noun shown separately in the table is formed by adding *-s* to the singular. The word for the people of a country is the same as the plural noun, except when shown on the table. This word is used in the pattern [the + P]: **the Dutch** | **the Poles** *work hard.* Adjectives ending in *-ish* can also be used in this pattern: *the British like football.*

The adjectives are used in phrs. like *a* **Welsh** *farm* | *The aircraft was* **Ugandan.** We can say: *A* **Bulgarian**/ *2* **Frenchmen** *are coming to dinner*, and some of these words have a fem. form: *He married a* **Frenchwoman.** The names of languages are used, without *the* and with a sing. verb, in phrs. like: *to speak* **Spanish** | **Arabic** *is a difficult language*. Sometimes there is no English word for one of these patterns, and then one must express the idea in another way: *3 girls from* **Hong Kong** | *the citizens of* **the Vatican.**

Table of Codes

Table of Codes	*n* or *adj* used before a noun **A**	ordinary *adj* **B**	count noun **C**	ditransitive *v* with 2 different objects **D**	*adj, adv*, or *n* used after a noun **E**	*adj* or *adv* used after a verb **F**	group countable *n* **GC**	group uncountable *n* (or *adj*) **GU**	*adv* used with preposition and other adverbs **H**	intransitive *v* with no object **I**	linking *v* with complement **L**
nouns with no letter are [C], adjectives with no letter [B]	[A] *the* **main** *difficulty* | **General** *Smith*	[B] *a* **happy** *man* | *The man is* **happy**. | *She made him* **happy**	[C] *a/one* **dog** | *4* **boxes**		[E] *the president* **elect** | *3 years* **ago** | *Saadi* **Pasha**	[F] *She was* **asleep.** | *The meeting was* **yesterday**	[GC] *the* **committee** *is/are* | *the* **committees** *are*	[GU] *the* **Admiralty** *is/are* | *the* **accused** *is/are*	[H] **right** *through* | **splash** *into the water*		
Ø need not be followed by anything										[IØ] *We* **paused**	
followed by one or more nouns or pronouns **1**				[D1] **Give** *the boy a book.* | **Buy** *him a book*							[L1] *She* **became** *Queen.* | *It* **cost** *£6*
followed by the infinitive without *to* **2**										[I2] *I* **can** *fly*	
followed by the infinitive with *to* **3**		[B3] *an* **easy** *person to please*	[C3] *an* **attempt** *to climb the mountain*			[F3] *John is* **eager** *to please*				[I3] *He* **lived** *to be 90*	[L3] *The difficulty* **is** *to know what to do*
followed by the *-ing* form **4**										[I4] *She* **came** *running*	[L4] *She* **ended up** *dancing on the table*
followed by a *that*-clause **5**			[C5] *a* **desire** *that she (should) go*	[D5] *He* **warned** *her (that) he would come*		[F5] *He was* **sure** *(that) she knew*				[I5] *It* **appears** *(that) she will win*	[L5] *The trouble* **is** *that you know too much*
followed by a *wh*-word **6**			[C6] *the* **reason** *why he came*	[D6] **Tell** *me who should go/where to go*		[F6] *I'm not* **sure** *where to go/ where I should go*				[I6] *It* **appears** *as if she will win*	[L6] *It's as if we'd never even started*
followed by an adjective **7**											[L7] *She* **became** *famous*
followed by a past participle **8**										[I8] *Smoking* **is** *not permitted*	[L8] *He* **got** *trapped*
needs a descriptive word or phrase **9**		[B9] *politically* **aware**	[C9] *a film/tennis* **buff**			[F9] **located** *in Florida*		[GU9] *his* **posterity**			[L9] *She* **lives** *here*

N *vocative n used in direct address*	P *plural n*	R *n that is a name or namelike*	S *singular n*	T *transitive v with one object*	U *uncountable n*	V *v with one object + verb form*	Wa *adjective and adverb*	Wn *noun*	Wp *pronoun*	Wv *verb*	X *v with one object + something else*
[N] *Good-bye* **doctor**!	[P] *The* **police** *are here.* | *Do the* **dead** *return*?	[R] **God** | *the* **Earth**	[S] *a* **think** | *a* **babble** *of voices*		[U] **sugar** *is sweet*						
							Note: the numbers in the codes in this box have a different meaning				
				[T1] *She* **kicked** *the boy.* | *She* **blew up** *the bridge*			[Wa1] takes *-er, -est*: **nice, nicer, nicest**	[Wn1] plural sometimes like sing.: *several* **lions (lion)**	[Wp1] personal PRONOUNS; see table	[Wv1] the verb *be*; see table	[X1] *They* **considered** *him their enemy*
				[T2] *I* **helped** *clean the windows*		[V2] *I* **saw** *the man leave*	[Wa2] sometimes takes *-er, -est*: **secure** (+**r**/+**st**) or **more/most secure**	[Wn2] plural usu. like sing.: *several* **quail (quails)**	[Wp2] other PRONOUNS; see table	[Wv2] AUXILIARY verbs; see table	
	[P3] **qualifications** *to do the job*		[S3] *a* **yen** *to be alone*	[T3] *I* **want** *to go*	[U3] *There is some* **reason** *to believe it*	[V3] *I* **want** *him to go*	[Wa3] no /ə/ before an ending: **simply** /ˈsɪmpli/	[Wn3] plural same as sing.: *several* **grouse**		[Wv3] no /ə/ before *-ing*, *-er* ending: **coupling** /ˈkʌpliŋ/	
				[T4] *I* **enjoyed** *singing/their singing*		[V4] *He* **watched** *mother cooking the dinner*	[Wa4] *-ally* pronounced /li/: **historically** /hɪˈstɒrɪkli/			[Wv4] used in *-ing* form as *adj*: **flying** *feet*	
			[S5] *a* **feeling** *that he'll come*	[T5] *I* **know** *that he'll come*	[U5] *Is there* **proof** *that he is here*?		[Wa5] no COMPARATIVE or SUPERLATIVE: **atomic** *bomb*			[Wv5] used in *-ed* form as *adj*: **plaited** *hair*	
				[T6] *He* **decided** *where to go/who should go*						[Wv6] not used in *-ing* form: *He* **sees** *me now*	
											[X7] *They* **considered** *him dead*
						[V8] *to* **have** *a house built*					
	[P9] **powers** *of memory*	[R9] *the third* **International**	[S9] *a fine* **intelligence**		[U9] **jurisdiction** *over us all*						[X9] **Put** *it in the box*

For further information see Grammar in the Dictionary (page xxviii)